PRODIGY

Knowledge

practical, reliable, evidence-based guidance

Published by TSO (The Stationery Office) and available from:

Online
www.tsoshop.co.uk

Mail, Telephone, Fax & E-mail
TSO
PO Box 29, Norwich, NR3 1GN
Telephone orders/General enquiries: 0870 600 5522
Fax orders: 0870 600 5533
E-mail: book.orders@tso.co.uk
Textphone 0870 240 3701

TSO Shops
123 Kingsway, London, WC2B 6PQ
020 7242 6393 Fax 020 7242 6394
68-69 Bull Street, Birmingham B4 6AD
0121 236 9696 Fax 0121 236 9699
9-21 Princess Street, Manchester M60 8AS
0161 834 7201 Fax 0161 833 0634
16 Arthur Street, Belfast BT1 4GD
028 9023 8451 Fax 028 9023 5401
18-19 High Street, Cardiff CF10 1PT
029 2039 5548 Fax 029 2038 4347
71 Lothian Road, Edinburgh EH3 9AZ
0870 606 5566 Fax 0870 606 5588

TSO Accredited Agents
(see Yellow Pages)

and through good booksellers

Disclaimer
PRODIGY guidance is advisory and has been developed to assist healthcare professionals, together with patients, make decisions about the management of the patient's health. It is intended to support discussion and shared decision-making and is not a substitute for sound clinical judgement.

Drug prices in PRODIGY guidance
The Drug Tariff cost, and an estimated over-the-count sales price where appropriate, are included for the prescriptions offered in PRODIGY guidance. They giv a relative indication of the cost of drugs and devices, and are correct at the time of guidance development revision. They are not, however, updated with each price change. For up-to-date prices please refer to th Drug Tariff or MIMS.

How to cite this book
This book should be cited as: PRODIGY (2005) *PRODIGY Knowledge*. 2nd edn. London: The Stationery Office and Department of Health. An individual topic should be cited as: PRODIGY (2005) Topic title. In: PRODIGY Knowledge. 2nd edn. London: The Statione Office and Department of Health.

First edition published 2002
Second edition published 2005

ISBN 0 11 703549 1

Printed in the United Kingdom by The Stationery Offi

This book is dedicated to Sally Maloney, née Fraser

21 May 1974 – 15 February 2005

ntents

nabetical list of guidance ii

eam vi

ontact details vi

cknowledgements vii

bout PRODIGY Knowledge viii

- What is PRODIGY Knowledge? viii
- Who is PRODIGY Knowledge for? viii
- How can PRODIGY Knowledge be accessed? ix
  - PRODIGY website ix
  - Primary care computer systems ix
  - PRODIGY Knowledge book x
- How can PRODIGY Knowledge help patients? x
  - Patient Information Leaflets x
  - Shared screens x
  - Advice notes x
- How is PRODIGY Knowledge developed? xi
- How is PRODIGY Knowledge kept up-to-date? xv

guide to using this book xvii

- In the consultation xvii
- As a learning resource xvii

RODIGY guidance 1

ndex 1865

Alphabetical list of guidance

A

Acne vulgaris
Adverse drug reactions
Alcohol – problem drinking
Allergic rhinitis
Amenorrhoea
Anaemia – iron deficiency
Anaemia – macrocytic
Anal fissure
Angina
Ankylosing spondylitis
Aphthous ulcer
Asthma
Atrial fibrillation

B

Back pain – lower
Bacterial vaginosis
Balanitis
Bites – human and animal
Blepharitis . . . 22
Boils, carbuncles, furunculosis and staphylococcal whitlow . . . 235
Breast cancer – managing women with a family history . . . 245
Burns and scalds . . . 256

C

Candida – female genital . . . 263
Candida – oral . . . 278
Candida – skin and nails . . . 282
Chest infections . . . 288
Chickenpox . . . 309
Chlamydia – genital . . . 319
Chronic obstructive pulmonary disease . . . 329
Colic – infantile . . . 350
Common cold . . . 356
Conjunctivitis – allergic . . . 362
Conjunctivitis – infective . . . 368
Constipation . . . 374
Contraception . . . 388
Contraception – emergency . . . 435
Corneal superficial injury . . . 446
Coronary heart disease risk – identification and management . . . 452

D

Deep vein thrombosis . . . 468
Dental abscess . . . 477
Depression . . . 481
Dermatitis – contact . . . 505

Contents

Alphabetical list of guidance ii

Team vi

Contact details vi

Acknowledgements vii

About PRODIGY Knowledge viii

What is PRODIGY Knowledge? viii

Who is PRODIGY Knowledge for? viii

How can PRODIGY Knowledge be accessed? ix

PRODIGY website ix

Primary care computer systems ix

PRODIGY Knowledge book x

How can PRODIGY Knowledge help patients? x

Patient Information Leaflets x

Shared screens x

Advice notes x

How is PRODIGY Knowledge developed? xi

How is PRODIGY Knowledge kept up-to-date? xv

A guide to using this book xvii

In the consultation xvii

As a learning resource xvii

PRODIGY guidance 1

Index 1865

Alphabetical list of guidance

A

Acne vulgaris

Adverse drug reactions 1

Alcohol – problem drinking 2

Allergic rhinitis 3

Amenorrhoea 5

Anaemia – iron deficiency 6

Anaemia – macrocytic 7

Anal fissure 7

Angina 8

Ankylosing spondylitis 10

Aphthous ulcer 12

Asthma 13

Atrial fibrillation 16

B

Back pain – lower 18

Bacterial vaginosis 20

Balanitis 21

Bites – human and animal 21

Blepharitis 22

Boils, carbuncles, paronychia and staphylococcal whitlow 23

Breast cancer – managing women with a family history 24

Burns and scalds 25

C

Candida – female genital 26

Candida – oral 27

Candida – skin and nails 28

Chest infections 28

Chickenpox 30

Chlamydia – genital 31

Chronic obstructive pulmonary disease 32

Colic – infantile 35

Common cold 35

Conjunctivitis – allergic 36

Conjunctivitis – infective 36

Constipation 37

Contraception 38

Contraception – emergency 43

Corneal superficial injury 44

Coronary heart disease risk – identification and management 45

D

Deep vein thrombosis 46

Dental abscess 47

Depression 48

Dermatitis – contact 50

Diabetes Type 1 and 2 – foot disease ... 523
Diabetes Type 1 and 2 – hypertension ... 531
Diabetes Type 2 – blood glucose management ... 555
Diabetes Type 2 – lipid management ... 574
Diabetes Type 2 – renal disease ... 594
Diabetes Type 2 – retinopathy ... 601
Diverticular disease and diverticulitis ... 606
Dry eye syndrome ... 614
Dysmenorrhoea ... 619
Dyspepsia – pregnancy-associated ... 628
Dyspepsia – proven DU, GU, or NSAID-associated ulcer ... 631
Dyspepsia – proven gastro-oesophageal reflux disease ... 650
Dyspepsia – proven non-ulcer dyspepsia ... 664
Dyspepsia – symptoms (uninvestigated by endoscopy) ... 678

E

Earwax ... 701
Eating disorders ... 704
Eczema – atopic ... 712
Endometriosis ... 736
Enuresis – nocturnal ... 747
Epilepsy ... 756

F

Febrile convulsion ... 784
Fungal (dermatophyte) infections – skin and nails ... 791

G

Gastroenteritis ... 802
Gingivitis and periodontitis – plaque-associated ... 828
Glaucoma ... 836
Glue ear ... 840
Gout ... 845

H

Haemorrhoids ... 871
Head lice ... 878
Headache ... 885
Heart failure ... 895
Herpes simplex – genital ... 915
Herpes simplex – ocular ... 925
Herpes simplex – oral ... 929
Hiccups ... 935
Hyperlipidaemia ... 938
Hypertension ... 962
Hypertension in pregnancy ... 1001
Hyperthyroidism ... 1007
Hypnotic or anxiolytic dependence ... 1013
Hypothyroidism ... 1022

I

Immunizations – childhood vaccination programme ... 1028
Immunizations – pneumococcal vaccine ... 1047
Immunizations – travel vaccinations ... 1053

Impetigo 107
Infertility 107
Influenza 108
Insect bites and stings 109
Insomnia 110
Irritable bowel syndrome 112

L

Lacerations 113
Leg cramps – unknown cause 114
Leg ulcer – venous 115

M

Malaria prophylaxis 116
Meniere's disease 117
Menopause 118
Menorrhagia 121
Migraine 123
Molluscum contagiosum 125
Monitoring people on disease-modifying drugs (DMARDs) 125

N

Nappy rash 126
Nausea and vomiting in pregnancy 127
Neck pain 128
Nonsteroidal anti-inflammatory drugs (NSAIDs) 130

O

Obesity 131
Opioid dependence 132
Osteoarthritis 135
Osteoporosis – treatment 137
Otitis externa 139
Otitis media – acute 140

P

Palliative care – cough 141
Palliative care – dyspnoea 143
Palliative care – malodorous malignant ulcer of the skin 144
Palliative care – nausea/vomiting/malignant bowel obstruction 144
Palliative care – oral problems 146
Palliative care – pain 147
Palliative care – respiratory secretions at the end of life 149
Parkinson's disease 150
Pelvic inflammatory disease 151
Poisoning 152
Polymyalgia rheumatica 152
Preconceptual counselling 153
Prior myocardial infarction – prophylactic treatments 155
Prostate – benign hyperplasia 156
Prostatitis 157
Pruritus ani 158
Pruritus vulvae 159

Pubic lice 1599
Pyelonephritis – acute 1603

R

Raynaud's phenomenon 1607
Renal colic – acute 1612
Rheumatoid arthritis 1617
Rosacea 1644
Roundworm 1654

S

Scabies 1657
Schizophrenia 1666
Seborrhoeic dermatitis 1684
Shingles and postherpetic neuralgia 1693
Sinusitis 1713
Smoking cessation 1724
Sore throat – acute 1735
Sprains and strains 1742
Supraventricular tachycardia – paroxysmal 1755

T

Threadworm 1758
Thrombophlebitis 1762
Transient ischaemic attack – not in atrial fibrillation 1767
Trichomoniasis 1774
Trigeminal neuralgia 1779

U

Urethritis – male 1785
Urinary tract infection (lower) – men 1795
Urinary tract infection (lower) – women 1810
Urinary tract infection – children 1831
Urticaria and angio-oedema 1844

W

Warts and verrucae 1856

Team

Executive editor: Ian Purves

Editor: Sharon Smart

Clinical editor: David Finnigan

Medical practitioner informaticians: Michael Power, Margaret Sherratt, Catherine Lewis

Nurse specialist in prescribing: Gina Robinson

Medicines information specialists: Hannah Jones, Guy Jepson, Jude Misson, Iain Willits, Terry Easton, Jennifer Whitehall

Information specialists: Richard Bowley, Pauline Neison, Jennifer Forth, Naomi Shaw

Technology support team: Richard Hall, Ben Wilson, Dmytro Andriychenko, Michael Garrod

Communications co-ordinator: Rachael Parslow

Team administration support: Sunshine Stewart

Project support: Scott Hayward, Vivienne Horseman

Marketing: Marc Walker

Previous staff who have contributed to this edition: David Graham (medical practitioner informatician), Dor Wilson (information specialist), Mark Crick (medical practitioner informatician), Nikki Shiell (GP registrar), Paul Fieldhouse (medicines information specialist), Joanna Lloyd (medicines information specialist), Lucy McWhor (GP registrar), Zoë Keddie (information specialist), Helen Raison (medical practitioner informatician), Martin Duerden (medical practitioner informatician).

Contact details

For further information about PRODIGY visit www.prodigy.nhs.uk or prodigy-enquiries@schin.co.uk

From the website you can subscribe to PRODIGY Announce – an e-mail bulletin to keep you informed of PRODIGY guidance updates and developments

Acknowledgements

he PRODIGY Knowledge Authoring Team would like to thank Sir Muir ray for all the support and encouragement that he has provided. We would lso like to thank all the experts, organisations and PRODIGY Knowledge sers that have provided advice and feedback on PRODIGY guidance. We are articularly grateful for the support and efforts of the Validation Committee – eter Clappison (previous chair), Ross Taylor (RCGP), Simon Thomas (RCP), hn Grenville (GPC), and Vinaya Sharma (RPSGB).

inally we would like to acknowledge all those individuals who have worked t SCHIN and contributed to PRODIGY Knowledge over the last 10 years.

About PRODIGY Knowledge

What is PRODIGY Knowledge?

PRODIGY Knowledge is an up-to-date source of clinical knowledge that can help healthcare professionals, and patients, in managing the common conditions generally seen in primary and first-contact care. This knowledge is available in a variety of formats including 'full' guidance, quick reference guides, and patient information leaflets that cover acute and chronic illnesses and disease prevention. Around 200 topics are covered, including many of the conditions that can be managed by independent nurse prescribers and supplementary prescribers.

A key feature is that the knowledge can be accessed in an appropriate format where and when it is needed – concise information for use in a consultation, and more detailed information for use as a learning resource.

Who is PRODIGY Knowledge for?

PRODIGY Knowledge has principally been designed to be used by healthcare professionals and patients, including:

- General practitioners, GP registrars
- Nurses
- Pharmaceutical advisers, community and hospital pharmacists

Feedback has highlighted that it is also a useful resource for:

- Accident and emergency departments
- Walk-in centre staff
- Medical, nursing and pharmacy students
- Emergency care practitioners and other allied healthcare professionals
- Educational institutions
- Those involved in the development of care pathways, protocols, patient group directions and clinical management plans

In particular PRODIGY Knowledge is evolving to support Extended Formulary Nurse Prescribers and other professions who develop their role to become non-medical prescribers.

How can PRODIGY Knowledge be accessed?

PRODIGY guidance can be accessed in a variety of ways:

- From the PRODIGY website – www.prodigy.nhs.uk
- Through primary care computer systems
- In the PRODIGY Knowledge book
- Through the National Library for Health (www.library.nhs.uk)

PRODIGY website

The website is a useful resource providing healthcare professionals and patients with free access to PRODIGY Knowledge in five different formats:

- **'Full' guidance** can be accessed, with links to relevant Patient Information Leaflets (PILs) and to full text electronic journals. The guidance is suitable for downloading and printing.
- **Quick reference guides** summarise the recommendations within the full guidance with concise supporting information, and can be easily printed and laminated for desk reference. Quick reference guides are currently available from the website for only a number of topics. It is the intention that most guidance topics will be supported by a quick reference guide.
- **The Guidance Browser** simulates the way in which PRODIGY is integrated with the clinical system and how it interacts with the electronic patient record, allowing advice and prescriptions to be age and sex specific.
- **Patient Information Leaflets** (PILs) can be accessed through the website or through the browser and can be printed for patients or carers.
- **PRODIGY Drugs** provides drug and prescription information from the current set of PRODIGY guidance. PRODIGY Drugs supports the development of a local formulary that is evidence-based and consistent with PRODIGY guidance.

Primary care computer systems

PRODIGY Knowledge is available as a decision support system that is fully integrated into primary care computer systems that attained Requirements for Accreditation (RFA) 99. The clinical knowledge is developed and maintained by the PRODIGY Knowledge Authoring Team and is identical to that available through the website. However, the development and maintenance of the software that implements this clinical knowledge is the responsibility of each clinical system supplier, and there is no standard user interface. We are working with the suppliers that are developing new computer systems to ensure that healthcare professionals will continue to be able to access PRODIGY Knowledge in this way in the future.

PRODIGY Knowledge book

PRODIGY Knowledge first became available in a book at the end of 2002. Following very positive feedback and continued requests for further editions we are pleased to have worked with TSO (The Stationery Office) to publish this second edition.

How can PRODIGY Knowledge help patients?

Involving people in decision-making and providing them with information about their illnesses is now regarded as an important aspect of high-quality clinical practice. PRODIGY Knowledge supports this aspect of practice by providing through the primary care computer systems:

- Patient Information Leaflets
- Shared screens
- Advice notes

Patient Information Leaflets

One or more Patient Information Leaflets (PILs) can be printed out from the website or primary care computer system for every PRODIGY guidance. The PILs aim to complement the consultation and to be easily read by most adults. They are designed to:

- Inform people about the nature and cause of their condition
- Advise people on what they can do to help themselves
- Provide information on the options for treatment
- Provide sources of further help and advice

Shared screens

Shared computer screens display a short summary of the treatment options. They help to involve people in decision-making by providing a focus for discussion, and can also act as an aide-memoire to the healthcare professional.

Advice notes

For certain conditions, concise self-management advice for patients can be printed out on the right-hand side of a prescription. These advice notes may complement a prescription for a drug. In other circumstances they have been designed to be used when a prescription for a drug is not necessary.

low is PRODIGY Knowledge developed?

RODIGY Knowledge is developed by a multidisciplinary team based at the owerby Centre for Health Informatics at Newcastle. It is based on the best vailable evidence collated from a structured literature review, clinical xperience, and expert opinion and is developed to be in line with national olicies and guidelines. Notably, PRODIGY guidance draws together the redible sources of knowledge that are commonly used in primary care into ne readily accessible and reliable source.

'he PRODIGY literature searching protocol follows a detailed, structured rocess that has been designed to optimise the balance between sensitivity and pecificity for retrieving the relevant literature. Whenever an existing guidance opic is revised, or when a new topic is developed, search strategies are planned y an information specialist following discussion with a medicines information pecialist and a clinician. The searches identify existing clinical guidelines ompleted to an approved methodology (e.g. National Institute for Health nd Clinical Excellence [NICE] and Scottish Intercollegiate Guidelines letwork [SIGN]), systematic reviews (e.g. from the Cochrane Library), andomised controlled trials, other clinical trials, evidence summaries and vidence-based reviews (e.g. Bandolier, Drugs & Therapeutics Bulletin [DTB], linical Evidence), and national policy documents. Bibliographic databases uch as Medline and Embase are searched using validated methodological lters developed by credible sources such as:

- The Centre for Evidence-Based Medicine (www.cebm.net/searching.asp#filters)
- NHS Centre for Reviews and Dissemination (www.york.ac.uk/inst/crd/search.htm)
- McMaster University (Haynes, R.B. et al. (1994) Developing optimal search strategies for detecting clinically sound studies in Medline. *J Am Med Inform Assoc* **1**(6), 447-458)

'he literature searching is dynamic throughout the entire process of guidance levelopment or revision, allowing further sources of information to be found hrough hand searching of reference lists, or when new websites or other esources are discovered. Additionally our protocol for literature searching is onstantly under review and is continually being adapted and improved.

Core literature search sources	Url
Horizons database (in house)[1]	www.topalbertadoctors.org/guidelines/guides.as
Alberta Medical Association	www.topalbertadoctors.org/guidelines/guides.as
Clinical Evidence	www.clinicalevidence.com
British Columbia Guidelines	www.hlth.gov.bc.ca/msp/protoguides/
Dutch College of General Practitioners	http://nhg.artsennet.nl/
Canadian Medical Association	http://mdm.ca/cpgsnew/cpgs/index.asp
Institute for Clinical Systems Improvement	www.icsi.org
National Guideline Clearing House	www.guideline.gov
New Zealand Guidelines Group	www.nzgg.org.nz
NHMRC (Australia)	www.health.gov.au/nhmrc/publications/titles.htm
NICE (National Institute for Health and Clinical Excellence)	www.nice.org.uk
SIGN (Scottish Intercollegiate Guidelines Network)	www.sign.ac.uk
The Cochrane Library	www.nelh.nhs.uk/cochrane.asp
UCSF (primary care clinical practice guidelines)	http://medicine.ucsf.edu/resources/guidelines
Registered Nurses Association of Ontario	www.rnao.org/bestpractices
University of Michigan guidelines	http://cme.med.umich.edu/iCME/default.asp
Royal College of Nursing Guidelines	www.rcn.org.uk/resources/guidelines.php
Singapore Ministry of Health Guidelines	www.moh.gov.sg/corp/publications
Veterans Health (USA) Guidelines	www.oqp.med.va.gov/cpg/cpg.htm
Bandolier	www.jr2.ox.ac.uk/bandolier
DTB (Drug & Therapeutics Bulletin)	www.nelh.nhs.uk/idtb/default.asp
MeReC	www.npc.co.uk/merec_index.htm
NELH (National Electronic Library for Health)	www.nelh.nhs.uk
Trip database	www.tripdatabase.com
Best Bets	www.bestbets.org
Guidelines International Network	www.g-i-n.net
Department of Health Policy	www.dh.gov.uk/PolicyAndGuidance/fs/en

[1] Includes continuous searching of the *BMJ*, *Lancet*, *JAMA*, *NEJM* & other journals, guideline groups and other sources f new information

Bibliographic Databases

Medline	AMED
Embase	Psyc info
Cinahl	Brit Nursing Index
DARE	DH data
CENTRAL	Kings Fund

Appraisal of the literature is a vital part of the process of developing and reviewing PRODIGY guidance. Evidence used to generate key recommendations within PRODIGY guidance is independently appraised for methodological quality and appropriateness by both a clinician and a medicines information specialist. If disagreement occurs over interpretation of the evidence, this is discussed further with the Clinical Editor. If consensus still cannot be reached, the evidence is discussed in one of the critical appraisal sessions that are held every week. These critical appraisal meetings are attended by all members of the team and ensure that critical appraisal skills are maintained, and allow a cascade of skills to all members of the team from knowledge gained when an individual attends a course, in addition to allowing a forum for debate and discussion.

For some conditions, the PRODIGY literature search identifies existing national guidelines that are suitable for use within UK primary care. When implementing such guidelines through PRODIGY we are aware of the importance of correctly interpreting recommendations within the guideline and understanding the evidence upon which these recommendations are based. A clinician and a medicines information specialist read the guideline independently of each other. The clinician and medicines information specialist may take responsibility for developing different sections of the PRODIGY guidance, but each section is reviewed by both to ensure agreement that these properly represent the source guideline. If there are any uncertainties, then the authors of the source guideline are contacted for clarification.

The drugs and devices that are included in PRODIGY guidance are selected using defined criteria, principally:

- Appropriateness
- Efficacy and evidence of effectiveness
- Safety – taking into account warnings and advice from the Committee on Safety of Medicines and the length of safety record
- Adverse effect profile – balancing the risk of clinically significant and minor adverse effects against the severity of the condition

The drug selection is often made after considering these four criteria only. If this is not possible then other additional factors are taken into consideration, namely

- Product licence – indications and availability
- Concordance issues or acceptability to the patient – including the number of times to be taken daily, types of formulation available, suitability for age, and taste
- Interactions – with other drugs, food or drink
- Usage – Prescribing Analysis and CosT (PACT) data, familiarity of prescriber with the drug, and consistency with other relevant PRODIGY guidance
- Cost – including an estimate of the cost of follow-up, tests, and duration of use

Each draft guidance is reviewed internally, to check that the content is unambiguous, consistent with national standards of good practice, and practical for the primary care setting.

Draft guidance then undergoes an extensive consultation process, being reviewed by *professional organisations* and experts primarily to ensure that the texts (and in particular the recommendations) are accurate and correct, by other *primary care knowledge* providers primarily to ensure consistency for healthcare professionals and patients, by users of PRODIGY Knowledge primarily to ensure that the guidance is user-friendly and practical, by patient groups, and by the *pharmaceutical industry*.

Before being issued, all the comments received from external reviewers together with our proposed responses are presented to a committee of people nominated for their personal expertise from the Royal College of General Practitioners, the Royal College of Physicians, the General Practitioners Committee, the Royal Pharmaceutical Society of Great Britain, and chaired by Sir Muir Gray, Director of Knowledge, Process and Safety, Connecting for Health. This committee is tasked with ensuring that the recommendations contained in the guidance are consistent with national policy and appropriate to the resources available in primary care, arbitrating when external experts do not reach consensus, and finally endorsing the guidance.

How is PRODIGY Knowledge kept up-to-date?

ach guidance is given a review date (maximum of 3 years) after it has been eveloped or revised. 'Time-expired' guidance are revised following the rocess described above.

ı addition, a process to identify information that will trigger an update of a uidance has been developed and involves:

- Scanning a core set of journals
- Monitoring of key websites
- E-mail lists
- Collaboration with other organisations
- Feedback from users of PRODIGY guidance

he importance of this information is carefully considered and any revision to ıe guidance is prioritised and scheduled.

he website is updated with revised guidance every 3 months.

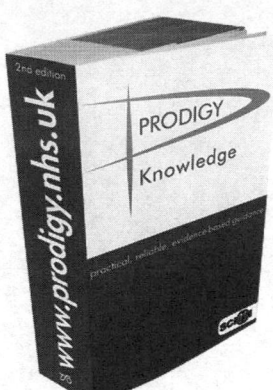

A guide to using this book

n the consultation

RODIGY knowledge that is intended to be used during the consultation is epresented in scenarios that describe realistic, distinct clinical situations. Each cenario provides succinct and easy to read specific advice on:

Recommended management options – *Which therapy?*
Whether, when, and how to review a patient – *Follow-up*
When, and how urgently to refer a patient to a specialist – *Refer and investigate?*
What investigations may be appropriate in the primary care setting – *Refer and investigate?*
Points to discuss with your patient – *Shared decision making.*
Drugs or devices to prescribe, including sufficient detail to enable you to write a prescription – *Prescriptions.*
Why prescriptions have or have not been included – *Drug rationale.*

As a learning resource

A summary of the evidence, clinical experience and expert opinion is presented n the Extended information section; this is too detailed to be read during the onsultation and has been designed to be used as a learning resource.

The Background information section describes:

- A definition of the condition
- Causes and pathophysiology
- Epidemiology
- Symptoms and signs
- Investigations
- Differential diagnosis
- Complications
- Prognosis

The Management issues section describes:

- Issues relating to the management of the condition in the primary care setting
- Practical information about using the drugs or devices that are recommende
(often under the heading of Medicines management)
- The evidence that supports the recommendations made

The References section lists the references cited in the guidance. When using the PRODIGY website, by clicking on [Full text] NHS staff in England can access the full text article free of charge.

The Evidence grading section describes the grading schemes and hierarchy of evidence used in the guidance. Recommendations in PRODIGY guidance are graded when clinical guidelines completed to an approved methodology (e.g. NICE, SIGN) are implemented through PRODIGY, and the grading scheme used in the source guideline is used.

PRODIGY GUIDANCE

Acne vulgaris

Last revised in February 2003
www.prodigy.nhs.uk/guidance.asp?gt=Acne vulgaris

Applies to people over the age of 12 years

This guidance covers the management of the commonest type of acne — acne vulgaris.

This guidance does not cover rosacea, chemically induced acne, or acneiform lesions associated with corticosteroids.

Goals

To reduce or clear skin lesions
To prevent scarring

Contents

Scenarios
- Mild acne p.1
- Moderate acne p.3
- Severe acne p.6
- Hormonal therapy — women only p.8

Extended Information, p. 10

Which scenario?

Mild acne: covers the management of people with open and closed comedones with or without sparse inflammatory lesions.
Moderate acne: covers the management of people with more widespread non-inflammatory lesions and numerous papules and pustules.
Severe acne: covers the management of people with more extensive inflammatory lesions, which may include nodules, pitting, and scarring.
Hormonal therapy — women only: covers the management of women presenting with acne having characteristics that suggest a significant hormonal influence.

Mild acne

Which therapy?

Dispel common myths about acne. It is ***not*** caused by bad hygiene, poor diet, or lack of exercise, and it is not infectious.
Assess previous treatments used, including over-the-counter preparations, and their effects, patient expectations, and psychological disability.
Assess acne type to guide treatment choice. For example, differentiate between inflammatory and non-inflammatory acne.
Treat predominantly inflammatory acne with benzoyl peroxide, azelaic acid, or topical antibiotics.
- Topical antibiotics are effective for inflammatory lesions of acne, but they do not clear comedones.

Treat predominantly non-inflammatory acne with topical retinoids, benzoyl peroxide, or azelaic acid.
- Topical retinoids are particularly effective for comedonal acne, but not so effective for inflammation.

Combining topical treatments may be useful if response to treatment is poor with individual drugs, or if both inflammatory and non-inflammatory acne are present.
Treatment needs to be used for 2 months before assuming treatment failure.

- **Choice of vehicle is largely determined by skin type and the person's preference.** Gels may be preferable for people with oily skin; creams may be preferable for people with dry skin; lotions, although drying, are useful for application to large areas of skin.

Practical prescribing points

For further information, please see the *Medicines Compendium* (www.medicines.org.uk) or the *British National Formulary* (www.bnf.org).
- **Warn people to avoid** application to the eyes, mouth, and mucous membranes.
- **Benzoyl peroxide may bleach** hair, clothing, towels, and bed linen.
- **Topical tetracycline may leave a faint yellow colour on the skin,** which could result in the staining of clothing and bed linen.
- **Topical retinoids may increase sensitivity to UV light** and should be used only at night and then washed off in the morning. People should be advised to avoid excessive exposure to sunlight.
- **Pregnancy and breastfeeding:**
  - Topical retinoids should be avoided during pregnancy and lactation.
  - The safety of azelaic acid in pregnancy and lactation has not been established. The manufacturers advise avoiding the product during pregnancy and lactation unless it is essential and no suitable alternative treatment is available.
  - The safety of topical clindamycin or topical tetracycline in pregnancy and lactation has not been established.

Should I refer or investigate?

Refer?

- Referral is rarely necessary for mild acne. It may be considered if there is severe psychological distress.

Investigate?

- Investigation is rarely necessary in mild acne.

Patient information leaflets

The following PILs are available at www.prodigy.nhs.uk
- Acne
- Acne - Antibiotic Treatments
- Acne - Rub-On Treatments
- Acne Support Group (acne or rosacea)
- Stop Spots (acne information)

Shared decision making

- **Treatments for acne take up to 2 months for any improvement,** and about 6 months for a significant reduction in spots.

- **Topical treatments** should be put onto to all of the affected area, not just onto the spots. There are several types...
- **Benzoyl peroxide** reduces inflammation and helps to reduce blackheads and whiteheads.
  - **It works best if you wash** with a mild soap or cleansing agent and water before using it.
  - **It may bleach** hair, bed linen, or clothes.
  - **It commonly causes mild irritation.** If you have particularly sensitive skin, you can reduce this irritation by:
    - Starting with the lowest strength. Increase the strength over time.
    - Applying it once a day at first, aiming to apply it twice a day when you get used to it.
- **Azelaic acid** is an alternative. It may cause less irritation than benzoyl peroxide. However, you should not use it for more than 6 months.
- **Retinoids** such as tretinoin, isotretinoin, or adapalene help clear blackheads and whiteheads. When using a retinoid:
  - The spots sometimes get a little worse before improving.
  - Your skin may be more sensitive to sunlight.
  - Women must use contraception (there is a slight risk of harm to unborn babies).
- **Topical antibiotics** reduce skin inflammation, but do not clear blackheads and whiteheads.
- **Sometimes topical treatments are combined** to improve the effect.

Drug rationale

Drugs not included

- **Abrasive agents** are not beneficial in acne [BNF 43, 2002]. Abrasive cleansers and vigorous scrubbing should be avoided, as they can aggravate acne by promoting the development of inflammatory lesions [Leyden, 1997; MeReC, 1999].
- **Peeling agents such as sulphur-containing preparations and salicylic acid** are generally considered inferior to the more modern topical treatments for acne [BNF 43, 2002]. Salicylic acid may be an option for someone with comedonal acne who cannot tolerate retinoids.
- **Nicotinamide** has potent anti-inflammatory activity *in vitro*, but there is little data to support its efficacy in acne vulgaris [Brown and Shalita, 1998].
- **Tazarotene** is a topical retinoid that is effective in the management of acne, but it is not licensed for this use in the UK. Other topical retinoids are offered.

Drugs included

- **Benzoyl peroxide** is effective in the treatment of mild-to-moderate acne. Where more than one size of the same strength and formulation is available, the most cost-effective option is offered.
- **Azelaic acid** in clinical trials exhibits similar efficacy to 5% benzoyl peroxide in the treatment of both inflamed and non-inflamed lesions. It is less likely to cause local irritation than are benzoyl peroxide and topical retinoids [Gibson, 1997].
- **Topical retinoids** are effective against comedonal acne. Tretinoin, isotretinoin, and adapalene are included.
- **Topical antibiotics erythromycin, clindamycin, and tetracycline** are included because they are effective against mild-to-moderate inflammatory acne. Where more than one size of the same strength and formulation is available, the most cost-effective option is offered.
- **The combination of erythromycin 3% with benzoyl peroxide 5%** is included, as it has been shown to be more effective against inflamed lesions than either drug alone, and shows efficacy comparable to that of erythromycin and benzoyl peroxide given as separate constituents once a day. The combination is more expensive than offering the two constituents separately.
- **The combination of erythromycin 4% with zinc acetate** is included. This combination is less efficacious than erythromycin combined with benzoyl peroxide, and we found no therapeutic trials that compared the combination of erythromycin with zinc against the individual components. The combination is more expensive than erythromycin prescribed alone.
- **The combination of isotretinoin with erythromycin** is included. In trials it has shown slightly improved efficacy over either of the individual components given alone.

Prescriptions

Antibacterial-comedolytic gels

Benzoyl peroxide 2.5% aqueous gel: once or twice a day
- Age from 12 years onwards
- Benzoyl peroxide 2.5% aq. gel. Apply to the affected area(s) once or twice a day, after washing; supply 40 grams; NHS Cost £1.76; OTC Cost £3.10.

Benzoyl peroxide 5% aqueous gel: once or twice a day
- Age from 12 years onwards
- Benzoyl peroxide 5% aq. gel. Apply to the affected area(s) once or twice a day, after washing; supply 40 grams; NHS Cost £1.92; OTC Cost £3.38.

Benzoyl peroxide 10% aqueous gel: once or twice a day
- Age from 12 years onwards
- Benzoyl peroxide 10% aq. gel. Apply to the affected area(s) once or twice a day, after washing; supply 40 grams; NHS Cost £2.07; OTC Cost £3.65.

Benzoyl peroxide 5% alcoholic gel: once or twice a day
- Age from 12 years onwards
- Benzoyl peroxide 5% gel. Apply to the affected area(s) once or twice a day, after washing; supply 40 grams; NHS Cost £1.51; OTC Cost £2.66.

Benzoyl peroxide 10% alcoholic gel: once or twice a day
- Age from 12 years onwards
- Benzoyl peroxide 10% gel. Apply to the affected area(s) once or twice a day, after washing; supply 40 grams; NHS Cost £1.69; OTC Cost £2.98.

Benzoyl peroxide 5% + erythromycin gel 3% gel: twice a day
- Age from 12 years onwards
- Erythromycin + benzoyl peroxide. Apply to the affected area(s) twice a day, after washing; supply 46 grams; NHS Cost £15.27.

Antibacterial-comedolytic creams, lotions & washes

Benzoyl peroxide 4% cream: once or twice a day
- Age from 12 years onwards
- Benzoyl peroxide 4% cream. Apply to the affected area(s) once or twice a day, after washing; supply 40 grams; NHS Cost £3.30; OTC Cost £5.82.

Benzoyl peroxide 5% cream: once or twice a day
- Age from 12 years onwards
- Benzoyl peroxide 5% cream. Apply to the affected area(s) once or twice a day, after washing; supply 40 grams; NHS Cost £1.51; OTC Cost £2.66.

Benzoyl peroxide 5% lotion: once a day
- Age from 12 years onwards
- Benzoyl peroxide 5% lotion. Apply to the affected area(s) once a day, after washing; supply 30 ml; NHS Cost £1.45; OTC Cost £2.56.

Benzoyl peroxide 10% lotion: once a day
- Age from 12 years onwards
- Benzoyl peroxide 10% lotion. Apply to the affected area(s) once a day, after washing; supply 30 ml; NHS Cost £1.45; OTC Cost £2.56.

Benzoyl peroxide 10% wash: once a day
- Age from 12 years onwards
- Benzoyl peroxide 10% wash. Apply to the affected area(s) once a day, after washing; supply 150 ml; NHS Cost £4.00; OTC Cost £7.05.

Azelaic acid 20% cream: twice a day
- Age from 12 years onwards
- Azelaic acid 20% cream. Apply to the affected area(s) twice a day, after washing; supply 30 grams; NHS Cost £4.00.

Topical retinoids

Adapalene 0.1% cream: at night
- Age from 12 years onwards
- Adapalene 0.1% cream. Apply thinly to the affected area(s) at night; supply 30 grams; NHS Cost £8.00.

Adapalene 0.1% gel: at night
- Age from 12 years onwards
- Adapalene 0.1% gel. Apply thinly to the affected area(s) at night; supply 30 grams; NHS Cost £8.00.

Tretinoin 0.01% gel: at night
- Age from 12 years onwards
- Tretinoin 0.01% gel. Apply thinly to the affected area(s) at night; supply 60 grams; NHS Cost £6.03.

Tretinoin 0.025% cream: at night
- Age from 12 years onwards
- Tretinoin 0.025% cream. Apply thinly to the affected area(s) at night; supply 60 grams; NHS Cost £6.03.

Tretinoin 0.025% gel: at night
- Age from 12 years onwards
- Tretinoin 0.025% gel. Apply thinly to the affected area(s) at night; supply 60 grams; NHS Cost £6.03.

Tretinoin 0.025% lotion: at night
- Age from 12 years onwards
- Tretinoin 0.025% lotion. Apply thinly to the affected area(s) at night; supply 100 ml; NHS Cost £6.94.

Isotretinoin 0.05% gel: at night
- Age from 12 years onwards
- Isotretinoin 0.05% gel. Apply thinly to the affected area(s) at night; supply 30 grams; NHS Cost £6.65.

Isotretinoin 0.05% + erythromycin 2% gel: up to twice a day
- Age from 12 years onwards
- Isotretinoin with erythromycin. Apply thinly to the affected area(s) once or twice a day; supply 30 grams; NHS Cost £8.00.

Topical antibiotics

Erythromycin 4% alcoholic gel: twice a day
- Age from 12 years onwards
- Erythromycin 4% alcoholic gel. Apply thinly to the affected area(s) twice a day, after washing; supply 30 grams; NHS Cost £4.97.

Erythromycin 2% alcoholic solution: twice a day
- Age from 12 years onwards
- Erythromycin 2% solution. Apply thinly to the affected area(s) twice a day, after washing; supply 50 ml; NHS Cost £8.60.

Clindamycin 1% alcoholic solution: twice a day
- Age from 12 years onwards
- Clindamycin 1% alc. solution. Apply thinly to the affected area(s) twice a day; supply 50 ml; NHS Cost £7.23.

Clindamycin 1% aqueous lotion: twice a day
- Age from 12 years onwards
- Clindamycin 1% aqueous lotion. Apply thinly to the affected area(s) twice a day; supply 50 ml; NHS Cost £8.47.

Clindamycin 1% gel: once a day
- Age from 12 years onwards
- Clindamycin 1% gel. Apply thinly to the affected area(s) at night; supply 30 grams; NHS Cost £8.66.

Tetracycline 0.22% solution: twice a day
- Age from 12 years onwards
- Tetracycline 2.2mg/ml solution. Apply to the affected area(s) twice a day; supply 70 ml; NHS Cost £6.15.

Erythromycin 4% + zinc acetate 1.2% solution
- Age from 12 years onwards
- Erythromycin with zinc acetate. Apply to the affected area(s) twice a day; supply 30 ml; NHS Cost £7.09.

Moderate acne

Which therapy?

- **Dispel the common myths about acne.** It is ***not*** caused by bad hygiene, poor diet, or lack of exercise, and it is not infectious.
- **Assess previous treatments used,** including over-the-counter preparations, and their effects, patient expectations, and psychological disability.
- **Consider topical treatments first:**
  - Treat predominantly inflammatory acne with benzoyl peroxide, azelaic acid, or topical antibiotics.
  - Treat non-inflammatory acne with topical retinoids, benzoyl peroxide, or azelaic acid.
- **Consider oral antibiotics** for moderate inflammatory acne when:
  - Topical therapy for mild-to-moderate acne has failed.
  - There is involvement of the shoulders, back or chest (where there may be difficulty applying topical treatment).
  - There is a high potential for scarring or pigmentary changes.
  - Topical therapies are inappropriate.
- **Oral oxytetracycline and tetracycline** are effective and inexpensive as first-line systemic antibiotics in the treatment of moderate acne.
- **Oral doxycycline and lymecycline,** once a day, are alternative tetracyclines to oxytetracycline and tetracycline, and may be considered for someone who may not be able to take a twice-daily regimen.
- **Oral erythromycin** is an alternative first-line systemic antibiotic to the tetracyclines. Its use is limited owing to increasing bacterial resistance.
- **It may help if oral antibiotics are combined with topical therapy.** Oral and topical antibiotics should not be combined.
- **Treatments need to be used for 2 months** before it can be assumed that treatment has failed.

Practical prescribing points

For further information, see the *Medicines Compendium* (www.medicines.org.uk) or the *British National Formulary* (www.bnf.org).

- **Benzoyl peroxide may bleach** hair, clothing, towels, and bed linen.
- **Topical retinoids** may increase sensitivity to UV light and should be used only at night and then washed off in the morning. Advise people to avoid excessive exposure to sunlight.

A

- **Topical tetracycline may leave a faint yellow colour on the skin,** which could result in the staining of clothing and bed linen.
- **Women prescribed an oral antibiotic should be advised** that it may cause oral contraceptive failure during the first few weeks of therapy.
- **Tetracycline tablets/capsules should be swallowed whole** with plenty of fluid whilst sitting or standing.
- **Pregnancy and breastfeeding:**
  - Topical retinoids should be avoided during pregnancy and lactation.
  - The safety of azelaic acid in pregnancy and lactation has not been established. The manufacturers advise avoiding the product during pregnancy and lactation unless it is essential and no suitable alternative treatment is available
  - The safety of topical clindamycin or topical tetracycline in pregnancy and lactation has not been established.
  - All oral tetracyclines are contraindicated during pregnancy and breastfeeding.

Should I refer or investigate?

Refer?

- **Referral is not usually necessary to refer people with moderate acne.** Reasons for referral include:
  - **Moderate acne that has failed to respond to treatment** with several courses of both topical and systemic therapy, over a period of at least 6 months. The person with acne is probably in the best position to judge whether treatment has failed.
  - Moderate acne where scarring is evident.
  - Severe psychological distress.

Investigate?

- Investigation is rarely necessary in moderate acne.

Patient information leaflets

The following PILs are available at www.prodigy.nhs.uk

- Acne
- Acne - Rub-On Treatments
- Acne Support Group (acne or rosacea)
- Stop Spots (acne information)

Shared decision making

- **Treatments for acne take up to 2 months for any improvement,** and about 6 months for a significant reduction in spots.
- **Antibiotic tablets** are an option for acne with skin inflammation. There are various types...
- **Oxytetracycline** and **tetracycline** are the most commonly used.
  - Food and milk affects the absorption of these antibiotics. So, take the tablets on an 'empty stomach', between meals, with a glass of water.
  - Do not take them if you are under 12, pregnant, breastfeeding, or intend to become pregnant.
  - Women taking 'the pill' should use extra precautions (such as condoms) during the first few weeks of taking these antibiotics.
- **Doxycycline, lymecycline,** and **erythromycin** are alternatives. They tend to be used if one of the above has not worked well, or is unsuitable.
- **Possible side effects** are listed in the leaflet in the packet of tablets.
- **Antibiotic tablets are not good at clearing blackheads and whiteheads.** So, a rub-on treatment may be advised instead of, as well as, antibiotic tablets.

Drug rationale

Drugs not included

- **Minocycline** should not be considered as a first-line antibiotic in the treatment of moderate to severe acne, owing to its potential for serious adverse effects, and its increased cost.
- **Anti-androgen treatment** in women is included in a separate scenario (see scenario *Hormonal acne — women*).

Drugs included

- **Benzoyl peroxide** is effective in the treatment of mild-to moderate acne. Where more than one size of the same strength and formulation is available, the most cost-effective option is offered.
- **Azelaic acid** is as efficacious as 5% benzoyl peroxide in the treatment of both inflamed and non-inflamed lesions in clinical trials. It may be less likely to cause local irritation than are benzoyl peroxide and tretinoin [Gibson, 1997].
- **Topical retinoids** are effective against comedonal acne. Tretinoin, isotretinoin, and adapalene are included.
- **Topical antibiotics erythromycin, clindamycin, and tetracycline** are included, as they have been shown to be effective against mild-to-moderate inflammatory acne. Where more than one size of the same strength and formulation is available, the most cost-effective option is offered.
- **The combination of erythromycin 3% with benzoyl peroxide 5%** is included, as it has been shown to be more effective against inflamed lesions than either drug alone, and shows efficacy comparable to that of erythromycin and benzoyl peroxide given as separate constituents once a day. The combination is more expensive than the two constituents separately.
- **The combination of erythromycin 4% with zinc acetate** is included. This combination is less efficacious than erythromycin combined with benzoyl peroxide, and we found no therapeutic trials that compared the combination of erythromycin with zinc against the individual components. The combination is more expensive than erythromycin prescribed alone.
- **The combination of isotretinoin with erythromycin** is included. In trials it has shown slightly improved efficacy over either of the individual components.
- **Oral oxytetracycline and tetracycline** are effective and inexpensive as first-line systemic antibiotics in the treatment of moderate acne, and are included here.
- **Oral doxycycline and lymecycline,** once a day, are alternative tetracyclines to oxytetracycline and tetracycline, and may be considered in someone who may not be able to take a twice-daily regimen.
- **Oral erythromycin** is an alternative first-line systemic antibiotic to the tetracyclines. It can be used in women who are pregnant or breastfeeding.

Prescriptions

Antibacterial-comedolytic gels

Benzoyl peroxide 2.5% aqueous gel: once or twice a day

- Age from 12 years onwards
- Benzoyl peroxide 2.5% aq. gel. Apply to the affected area(s) once or twice a day, after washing; supply 40 grams; NHS Cost £1.76; OTC Cost £3.10.

enzoyl peroxide 5% aqueous gel: once or twice a day
- Age from 12 years onwards
- Benzoyl peroxide 5% aq. gel. Apply to the affected area(s) once or twice a day, after washing; supply 40 grams; NHS Cost £1.92; OTC Cost £3.38.

enzoyl peroxide 10% aqueous gel: once or twice a day
- Age from 12 years onwards
- Benzoyl peroxide 10% aq. gel. Apply to the affected area(s) once or twice a day, after washing; supply 40 grams; NHS Cost £2.07; OTC Cost £3.65.

enzoyl peroxide 5% alcoholic gel: once or twice a day
- Age from 12 years onwards
- Benzoyl peroxide 5% gel. Apply to the affected area(s) once or twice a day, after washing; supply 40 gram; NHS Cost £1.51; OTC Cost £2.66.

enzoyl peroxide 10% alcoholic gel: once or twice a day
- Age from 12 years onwards
- Benzoyl peroxide 10% gel. Apply to the affected area(s) once or twice a day, after washing; supply 40 grams; NHS Cost £1.69; OTC Cost £2.98.

Benzoyl peroxide 5% + erythromycin 3% gel: twice a day
- Age from 12 years onwards
- Erythromycin + benzoyl peroxide. Apply to the affected area(s) twice a day, after washing; supply 46 grams; NHS Cost £15.27.

Antibacterial-comedolytic creams, lotions & washes

Benzoyl peroxide 4% cream: once or twice a day
- Age from 12 years onwards
- Benzoyl peroxide 4% cream. Apply to the affected area(s) once or twice a day, after washing; supply 40 grams; NHS Cost £3.30; OTC Cost £5.82.

Benzoyl peroxide 5% cream: once or twice a day
- Age from 12 years onwards
- Benzoyl peroxide 5% cream. Apply to the affected area(s) once or twice a day, after washing; supply 40 grams; NHS Cost £1.51; OTC Cost £2.66.

Benzoyl peroxide 5% lotion: once a day
- Age from 12 years onwards
- Benzoyl peroxide 5% lotion. Apply to the affected area(s) once a day, after washing; supply 30 ml; NHS Cost £1.45; OTC Cost £2.56.

Benzoyl peroxide 10% lotion: once a day
- Age from 12 years onwards
- Benzoyl peroxide 10% lotion. Apply to the affected area(s) once a day, after washing; supply 30 ml; NHS Cost £1.45; OTC Cost £2.56.

Benzoyl peroxide 10% wash: once a day
- Age from 12 years onwards
- Benzoyl peroxide 10% wash. Apply to the affected area(s) once a day; supply 150 ml; NHS Cost £4.00; OTC Cost £7.05.

Azelaic acid 20% cream: twice a day
- Age from 12 years onwards
- Azelaic acid 20% cream. Apply to the affected area(s) twice a day, after washing; supply 30 grams; NHS Cost £4.00.

Topical retinoids

Adapalene 0.1% gel: at night
- Age from 12 years onwards
- Adapalene 0.1% gel. Apply thinly to the affected area(s) at night; supply 30 grams; NHS Cost £8.00.

Adapalene 0.1% cream: at night
- Age from 12 years onwards
- Adapalene 0.1% cream. Apply thinly to the affected area(s) at night; supply 30 grams; NHS Cost £8.00.

Tretinoin 0.01% gel: at night
- Age from 12 years onwards
- Tretinoin 0.01% gel. Apply thinly to the affected area(s) at night; supply 60 grams; NHS Cost £6.03.

Tretinoin 0.025% gel: at night
- Age from 12 years onwards
- Tretinoin 0.025% gel. Apply thinly to the affected area(s) at night; supply 60 grams; NHS Cost £6.03.

Tretinoin 0.025% cream: at night
- Age from 12 years onwards
- Tretinoin 0.025% cream. Apply thinly to the affected area(s) at night; supply 60 grams; NHS Cost £6.03.

Tretinoin 0.025% lotion: at night
- Age from 12 years onwards
- Tretinoin 0.025% lotion. Apply thinly to the affected area(s) at night; supply 100 ml; NHS Cost £6.94.

Isotretinoin 0.05% gel: at night
- Age from 12 years onwards
- Isotretinoin 0.05% gel. Apply thinly to the affected area(s) at night; supply 30 grams; NHS Cost £6.65.

Isotretinoin 0.05% + erythromycin 2% gel: up to twice a day
- Age from 12 years onwards
- Isotretinoin with erythromycin. Apply to the affected area(s) once or twice a day; supply 30 grams; NHS Cost £8.00.

Topical antibiotics

Erythromycin 4% alcoholic gel: twice a day
- Age from 12 years onwards
- Erythromycin 4% alcoholic gel. Apply thinly to the affected area(s) twice a day, after washing; supply 30 grams; NHS Cost £4.97.

Erythromycin 2% alcoholic solution: twice a day
- Age from 12 years onwards
- Erythromycin 2% solution. Apply thinly to the affected area(s) twice a day, after washing; supply 50 ml; NHS Cost £8.60.

Clindamycin 1% alcoholic solution: twice a day
- Age from 12 years onwards
- Clindamycin 1% alc. solution. Apply thinly to the affected area(s) twice a day; supply 50 ml; NHS Cost £7.23.

Clindamycin 1% aqueous lotion: twice a day
- Age from 12 years onwards
- Clindamycin 1% aqueous lotion. Apply thinly to the affected area(s) twice a day; supply 50 ml; NHS Cost £8.47.

Clindamycin 1% gel: once a day
- Age from 12 years onwards
- Clindamycin 1% gel. Apply thinly to the affected area(s) at night; supply 30 grams; NHS Cost £8.66.

Tetracycline 0.22% solution: twice a day
- Age from 12 years onwards
- Tetracycline 2.2mg/ml solution. Apply to the affected area(s) twice a day; supply 70 ml; NHS Cost £6.15.

Erythromycin 4% + zinc acetate 1.2% solution: twice a day
- Age from 12 years onwards
- Erythromycin with zinc acetate. Apply to the affected area(s) twice a day; supply 30 ml; NHS Cost £7.09.

Oral antibiotics

Tetracycline tablets: 500mg twice a day
- Age from 12 years onwards
- Tetracycline 250mg tablets. Take two tablets twice a day; supply 112 tablets; NHS Cost £4.16.

A

Oxytetracycline tablets: 500mg twice a day
- Age from 12 years onwards
- Oxytetracycline 250mg tablets. Take two tablets twice a day; supply 112 tablets; NHS Cost £3.24.

Erythromycin e/c tablets: 500mg twice a day
- Age from 12 years onwards
- Erythromycin 250mg e/c tablets. Take two tablets twice a day; supply 112 tablets; NHS Cost £12.32.

Doxycycline capsules: 50mg once a day
- Age from 12 years onwards
- Doxycycline hyclate 50mg caps. Take one capsule once a day; supply 28 capsules; NHS Cost £5.82.

Lymecycline capsules: 408mg once a day
- Age from 12 years onwards
- Lymecycline 408mg capsules. Take one capsule once a day; supply 28 capsules; NHS Cost £5.00.

Severe acne

Which therapy?

- **First-line oral antibiotics:**
  - **Oral oxytetracycline and tetracycline** are effective and inexpensive as first-line systemic antibiotics in the treatment of moderate acne.
  - **Oral doxycycline and lymecycline,** once a day, are alternative tetracyclines to oxytetracycline and tetracycline, and may be considered in someone who may not be able to take a twice-daily regimen.
  - **Oral erythromycin** is an alternative first-line systemic antibiotic to the tetracyclines. Its use is limited, owing to increasing bacterial resistance.
- **If people fail to respond to a first-line oral antibiotic,** second-line treatments (e.g. minocycline) can be tried.
- **Topical non-antibiotic therapies** should usually be continued if effective.
- **In women, co-cyprindiol (Dianette®)** may also be an option (see scenario: *Hormonal acne — women*).
- **If acne remains severe and unresponsive, refer the person to a specialist.** In this case oral isotretinoin may be appropriate, but it should be prescribed only by a dermatologist.

Practical prescribing points

For further information, see the *Medicines Compendium* (www.medicines.org.uk) or the *British National Formulary* (www.bnf.org).

- **Benzoyl peroxide may bleach** hair, clothing, towels, and bed linen.
- **Topical retinoids** may increase sensitivity to UV light and should be used only at night and then washed off in the morning. Advise people to avoid excessive exposure to sunlight.
- **Women prescribed an oral antibiotic should be advised** that it may cause oral contraceptive failure during the first few weeks of therapy.
- **All tetracycline tablets/capsules should be swallowed whole** with plenty of fluid whilst sitting or standing.
- **If treatment with minocycline is continued for longer than 6 months,** monitor every 3 months for hepatotoxicity, pigmentation, and for systemic lupus erythematosus — discontinue if these develop.
- **Pregnancy and breastfeeding:**
  - Topical retinoids should be avoided during pregnancy and lactation.
  - The safety of azelaic acid in pregnancy and lactation has not been established. The manufacturers advise avoiding the product during pregnancy and lactation, unless it is essential and no suitable alternative treatment is available
  - All oral tetracyclines are contraindicated during pregnancy and breastfeeding.

Should I refer or investigate?

Refer?

- **Refer to a specialist service** someone with severe acne who:
  - Has a very severe variant of acne with systemic symptoms (acne fulminans) — urgent appointment, ideally within 2 weeks
  - Has severe acne or painful, deep nodules or cysts (nodulocystic acne) and who could benefit from oral isotretinoin — routine appointment
  - Is at risk of, or is developing, scarring despite primary care therapies — routine appointment
- **While they are waiting for an appointment,** people should be treated with oral antibiotics.

Investigate?

- Investigation is rarely necessary in severe acne.
- **GPs may be asked to monitor liver function tests and blood lipid levels** for people on isotretinoin. Monitoring will normally be carried out by the specialist dermatologist as the prescriber, rather than by the GP. These tests are required before starting, again at one month, and subsequently at three-monthly intervals. (It may be necessary to discontinue therapy if there are raised transaminases or triglycerides — seek expert advice).

Patient information leaflets

The following PILs are available at www.prodigy.nhs.uk
- Acne
- Acne - Antibiotic Treatments
- Acne - Rub-On Treatments
- Acne Support Group (acne or rosacea)
- Stop Spots (acne information)

Shared decision making

- Your acne is severe.
- **Antibiotic tablets** are an option for acne with skin inflammation. There are various types...
- **Oxytetracycline** and **tetracycline** are the most commonly used.
  - Food and milk affects the absorption of these antibiotics. So, take the tablets on an 'empty stomach', between meals, with a glass of water.
  - Do not take these if you are under 12, pregnant, breastfeeding, or intend to become pregnant.
  - Women taking 'the pill' should use extra precautions (such as condoms) during the first few weeks of taking these antibiotics.
- **Doxycycline, lymecycline** and **erythromycin** are alternatives. They tend to be used if one of the above has not worked well, or is unsuitable.
- **Minocycline** is an antibiotic that may help when other treatments have failed.
- **Referral to a specialist** is an option, with a view to using **isotretinoin.** This is a powerful treatment and usually works well. However, it is used under the supervision of a specialist because it is possible that there may be serious side-effects.
- **You can also use some topical treatments** in addition to any of the above.

)rug rationale

rugs not included

Oral isotretinoin is not included, as it should only be prescribed by, or under the supervision of, a consultant dermatologist [BNF 43, 2002], owing to the possibility of serious adverse effects.

Anti-androgen treatment is included in a separate scenario *Hormonal therapy — women only*.

Topical antibiotics are not included, as they should not be prescribed with oral antibiotics.

rugs included

Benzoyl peroxide is effective in the treatment of acne. Where more than one size of the same strength and formulation is available, the most cost-effective option is offered.

Azelaic acid is as effective as 5% benzoyl peroxide in the treatment of both inflamed and non-inflamed lesions in clinical trials. It may be less likely to cause local irritation than are benzoyl peroxide and tretinoin [Gibson, 1997].

Topical retinoids are effective against comedonal acne. Tretinoin, isotretinoin, and adapalene are included.

Oral oxytetracycline and tetracycline are effective and inexpensive as first-line systemic antibiotics in the treatment of moderate acne, and are included here.

Oral doxycycline and lymecycline, once a day, are alternative tetracyclines to oxytetracycline and tetracycline, and may be considered for someone who may not be able to take a twice-daily regimen.

Oral erythromycin is an alternative first-line systemic antibiotic to the tetracyclines. Women who are pregnant or breastfeeding can use it.

Minocycline is included as a second-line antibiotic. Modified-release minocycline is not included, as there is no evidence that it increases efficacy over standard-release minocycline.

'rescriptions

Antibacterial-comedolytic gels

enzoyl peroxide 2.5% aqueous gel: once or twice a day

- Age from 12 years onwards
- Benzoyl peroxide 2.5% aq. gel. Apply to the affected area(s) once or twice a day, after washing; supply 40 grams; NHS Cost £1.76; OTC Cost £3.10.

enzoyl peroxide 5% aqueous gel: once or twice a day

- Age from 12 years onwards
- Benzoyl peroxide 5% aq. gel. Apply to the affected area(s) once or twice a day, after washing; supply 40 grams; NHS Cost £1.92; OTC Cost £3.38.

enzoyl peroxide 10% aqueous gel: once or twice a day

- Age from 12 years onwards
- Benzoyl peroxide 10% aq. gel. Apply to the affected area(s) once or twice a day, after washing; supply 40 grams; NHS Cost £2.07; OTC Cost £3.65.

enzoyl peroxide 5% alcoholic gel: once or twice a day

- Age from 12 years onwards
- Benzoyl peroxide 5% gel. Apply to the affected area(s) once or twice a day, after washing; supply 40 grams; NHS Cost £1.51; OTC Cost £2.66.

enzoyl peroxide 10% alcoholic gel: once or twice a day

- Age from 12 years onwards
- Benzoyl peroxide 10% gel. Apply to the affected area(s) once or twice a day, after washing; supply 40 grams; NHS Cost £1.69; OTC Cost £2.98.

Antibacterial-comedolytic creams, lotions and washes

Benzoyl peroxide 4% cream: once or twice a day

- Age from 12 years onwards
- Benzoyl peroxide 4% cream. Apply to the affected area(s) once or twice a day, after washing; supply 40 grams; NHS Cost £3.30; OTC Cost £5.82.

Benzoyl peroxide 5% cream: once or twice a day

- Age from 12 years onwards
- Benzoyl peroxide 5% cream. Apply to the affected area(s) once or twice a day, after washing; supply 40 grams; NHS Cost £1.51; OTC Cost £2.66.

Benzoyl peroxide 5% lotion: once a day

- Age from 12 years onwards
- Benzoyl peroxide 5% lotion. Apply to the affected area(s) once a day, after washing; supply 30 ml; NHS Cost £1.45; OTC Cost £2.56.

Benzoyl peroxide 10% lotion: once a day

- Age from 12 years onwards
- Benzoyl peroxide 10% lotion. Apply to the affected area(s) once a day, after washing; supply 30 ml; NHS Cost £1.45; OTC Cost £2.56.

Benzoyl peroxide 10% wash: once a day

- Age from 12 years onwards
- Benzoyl peroxide 10% wash. Apply to the affected area(s) once a day; supply 150 ml; NHS Cost £4.00; OTC Cost £7.05.

Azelaic acid 20% cream: twice a day

- Age from 12 years onwards
- Azelaic acid 20% cream. Apply to the affected area(s) twice a day, after washing; supply 30 grams; NHS Cost £4.00.

Topical retinoids

Adapalene 0.1% gel: at night

- Age from 12 years onwards
- Adapalene 0.1% gel. Apply thinly to the affected area(s) at night; supply 30 grams; NHS Cost £8.00.

Adapalene 0.1% cream: at night

- Age from 12 years onwards
- Adapalene 0.1% cream. Apply thinly to the affected area(s) at night; supply 30 grams; NHS Cost £8.00.

Tretinoin 0.01% gel: at night

- Age from 12 years onwards
- Tretinoin 0.01% gel. Apply thinly to the affected area(s) at night; supply 60 grams; NHS Cost £6.03.

Tretinoin 0.025% gel: at night

- Age from 12 years onwards
- Tretinoin 0.025% gel. Apply thinly to the affected area(s) at night; supply 60 grams; NHS Cost £6.03.

Tretinoin 0.025% cream: at night

- Age from 12 years onwards
- Tretinoin 0.025% cream. Apply thinly to the affected area(s) at night; supply 60 grams; NHS Cost £6.03.

Tretinoin 0.025% lotion: at night

- Age from 12 years onwards
- Tretinoin 0.025% lotion. Apply thinly to the affected area(s) at night; supply 100 ml; NHS Cost £6.94.

Isotretinoin 0.05% gel: at night

- Age from 12 years onwards
- Isotretinoin 0.05% gel. Apply thinly to the affected area(s) at night; supply 30 grams; NHS Cost £6.65.

1st-line antibiotics

Tetracycline tablets: 500mg twice a day

- Age from 12 years onwards
- Tetracycline 250mg tablets. Take two tablets twice a day; supply 112 tablets; NHS Cost £4.16.

Oxytetracycline tablets: 500mg twice a day
- Age from 12 years onwards
- Oxytetracycline 250mg tablets. Take two tablets twice a day; supply 112 tablets; NHS Cost £3.24.

Erythromycin e/c tablets: 500mg twice a day
- Age from 12 years onwards
- Erythromycin 250mg e/c tablets. Take two tablets twice a day; supply 112 tablets; NHS Cost £12.32.

Doxycycline capsules: 50mg once a day
- Age from 12 years onwards
- Doxycycline hyclate 50mg caps. Take one capsule once a day; supply 28 capsules; NHS Cost £5.82.

Lymecycline capsules: 408mg once a day
- Age from 12 years onwards
- Lymecycline 408mg capsules. Take one capsule once a day; supply 28 capsules; NHS Cost £5.00.

2nd-line antibiotics

Minocycline tablets: 50mg twice a day
- Age from 12 years onwards
- Minocycline 50mg tablets. Take one tablet twice a day; supply 56 tablets; NHS Cost £15.30.

Hormonal therapy — women only

Which therapy?

- **Co-cyprindiol** may be useful in women with characteristics that suggest a significant hormonal influence to their acne, such as:
  - Inadequate response to other treatments
  - Acne that began or worsened in adulthood
  - Premenstrual flares of acne
  - Excessive facial oiliness
  - Inflammatory acne limited to the area of male beard distribution
  - Acne accompanied by mild-to-moderate hirsutism
- **Co-cyprindiol (Dianette®) is licensed for the treatment of women with severe acne** refractory to prolonged oral antibacterial therapy (and for moderately severe hirsutism).
- **Co-cyprindiol** is *not* authorised for the sole purpose of oral contraception and should be discontinued 3–4 menstrual cycles after the woman's acne has resolved.
- **The use of a combined oral contraceptive (COC) carries an increased risk for venous thromboembolism.** There is some epidemiological evidence that the incidence of VTE in users of co-cyprindiol is higher than in users of low-dose oestrogen COCs. In addition women with androgen-related conditions may have an inherently increased cardiovascular risk.
- **Hormonal therapy** can be used in combination with other acne therapies in women.

Practical prescribing points

For further information, see the *Medicines Compendium* (www.medicines.org.uk) or the *British National Formulary* (www.bnf.org).

- **Co-cyprindiol:** where this is being used solely for the treatment of acne, a prescription charge will be made. Where it is being used as an oral contraceptive, the GP must endorse the prescription with the female symbol, otherwise a prescription charge will be made. It is not indicated for use solely as an oral contraceptive.
- **Dianette® is contraindicated** in women with a personal or close family history of confirmed, idiopathic venous thromboembolism and in those with a known current venous thrombotic or embolic disorder.
- **Dianette® has a composition similar to that of a combined oral contraceptive (COC).** The World Health Organization has published medical eligibility criteria f combined oral contraceptive use. For a full list of the World Health Organization (WHO) medical eligibility criteria, see http://www.who.int/reproductive-health/publications/mec/3_cocs.pdf.
- **Conditions where COCs are either an unacceptable (category 4) health risk or where the risks usually outweigh the advantages (category 3)** are detailed in Table 1.
- Recommend alternative contraceptive methods and explain the potential risk of COCs to women with any these conditions, and careful follow-up will be required
- A woman with conditions where the advantages of COCs generally outweigh the theoretical or proven risk (WHO category 2) requires careful follow-up, especiall if two or more of these problems coexist.
- Many women will have no factors (WHO category 1) in their medical history that give concern about any increased individual risks for them with COCs. For any individual woman, the balance of clinical risks and benefits of COCs must be considered together with her situation, motivation, and concerns about her choice of method.

Should I refer or investigate?

Refer?

- **Refer to a specialist service** a woman with severe acne who:
  - Has a very severe variant of acne with systemic symptoms (acne fulminans) — immediate referral to be seen on the same day.
  - Has severe acne or painful, deep nodules or cysts (nodulocystic acne) and could benefit from oral isotretinoin — urgent appointment, ideally within 2 weeks.
  - Is at risk of, or is developing, scarring despite primary care therapies — routine appointment.
  - Has underlying endocrine problems, e.g. polycystic ovary syndrome (PCO).

Investigate?

- Investigation is rarely necessary in acne.

Patient information leaflets

The following PILs are available at www.prodigy.nhs.uk
- Acne
- Acne Support Group (acne or rosacea)
- Stop Spots (acne information)

Shared decision making

- **Co-cyprindiol** (Dianette®) is a treatment option for women with acne. It tends to be used if other treatments have not worked so well.
- **It is also a contraceptive pill,** so may particularly suit if you also want contraception.
- It contains oestrogen and an 'anti-androgen', which is the active part against acne.
- **As with other contraceptive pills, there is a slight risk of having serious side-effects** such as a blood clot.
- **It may take between 2 and 6 months before you see an improvement.**

able 1: Clinical conditions where COCs are considered either unacceptable (category 4), or where the risks usually itweigh the advantages (category 3) for use in contraception. Note: combined contraceptive patches have been assigned e same category ratings as COCs.

ndition	Category	Comment
weeks postpartum	4	There is some theoretical concern that the neonate may be at risk because of exposure to steroid hormones during the first 6 weeks postpartum. There is also some theoretical concern regarding the association between COC use up to 3 weeks postpartum and risk of thrombosis in the mother.
6 weeks to <6 months stpartum (primarily eastfeeding)	3	In the first 6 months postpartum, use of COCs during breastfeeding diminishes the quantity of breast milk, decreases the duration of lactation, and may thereby adversely affect the growth of the infant.
stpartum <21 days	3	Blood coagulation and fibrinolysis are essentially normalized by 3 weeks postpartum.
ged >=35 years and smoking <15 garettes a day	3	COC users who smoked were at increased risk of cardiovascular diseases, especially myocardial infarction (MI), compared with those who did not smoke. Studies have also showed an increased risk of MI with increasing number of cigarettes smoked per day.
ged >=35 years and smoking >15 garettes a day	4	
ardiovascular disease — multiple k factors for arterial rdiovascular disease	3/4	If a woman has multiple major risk factors, any of which alone would substantially increase the risk of cardiovascular disease, use of COCs may increase her risk to an unacceptable level. However, simple addition of categories for multiple risk factors is not intended; e.g. a combination of two risk factors assigned a category 2 may not necessarily warrant a higher category.
istory of hypertension, where ood pressure (BP) *cannot* be aluated (including hypertension iring pregnancy)	3	Hypertension — classifications assume that no other risk factors for cardiovascular disease exist. Risk of cardiovascular disease may increase substantially when multiple risk factors exist. Evaluation of BP level and cause is recommended, as soon as feasible. Women who did not have a BP check before COC use have been found to have an increased risk of acute MI and stroke.
dequately controlled pertension, where BP CAN be aluated	3	Women adequately treated for hypertension are at reduced risk of acute myocardial infarction (MI) and stroke as compared with untreated women. Although there are no data, COC users with adequately controlled and monitored hypertension should be at reduced risk of acute MI and stroke compared with untreated hypertensive COC users.
evated blood pressure levels roperly taken measurements) *stolic 140–159 or diastolic)–99*	3	Among women with hypertension, COC users are at increased risk of stroke and MI compared with non-users. The risk increases with incremental rises in BP. A single BP reading of 140–159/90–99 is not sufficient to classify a woman as hypertensive.
stolic >=160 or diastolic >=100	4	—
ascular disease	4	Increased risk of arterial thrombosis associated with COC use should be avoided in women with underlying vascular disease.
enous thromboembolism (VTE) - current or past history lajor surgery with prolonged nmobilization	4	The increased risk of VTE associated with COCs should have little impact on healthy women, but may have substantial impact on women with a history of thromboembolism.
nown thrombogenic mutations .g. Factor V Leiden; othrombin mutation; Protein S, rotein C and Antithrombin ficiencies)	4	Routine screening is not appropriate because of the rarity of the conditions and the high cost of screening. Among women with thrombogenic mutations, COC users have been found to have a two to twenty-fold higher risk of thrombosis than non-users.
urrent ischaemic heart disease	4	Among women with underlying vascular disease, the increased risk associated with COC use should be avoided.
roke	4	Among women with underlying vascular disease, the increased risk associated with COC use should be avoided.
nown hyperlipidaemias	3/2	Routine screening is not appropriate because of the rarity of the conditions and the high cost of screening. While some types are risk factors for vascular disease, the category should be assessed according to the type, its severity and the presence of other cardiovascular risk factors.
omplicated valvular heart disease	4	Among women with valvular heart disease, COC use may further increase the risk of arterial thrombosis; women with complicated valvular heart disease are at greatest risk.
ligraine with focal neurological mptoms at any age	4	Classification depends on accurate diagnosis of those severe headaches that are migrainous and those that are not. Any new headaches or marked changes in headaches should be evaluated. Classification is for women without any other risk factors for stroke. Risk of stroke increases with age, hypertension, and smoking.
ligraine without focal eurological symptoms <35 where ontinuous use	3	
ligraine without focal symptoms 1 women >=35 years, firstly in itiation and secondly with ontinuation	3 4	
urrent breast disease	4	Breast cancer is a hormonally sensitive tumour, and the prognosis of women with current or recent breast cancer may worsen with COC use.
ast history of breast cancer and o evidence of recurrence for 5 ears	3	
lephropathy/retinopathy/ europathy	3/4	The category should be assessed according to the severity of the condition.

A

Condition	Category	Comment
Other vascular disease or diabetes of >20 years' duration	3/4	The category should be assessed according to the severity of the condition.
Gallbladder disease — symptomatic medically treated or current	3	COCs may cause a small increased risk of gall-bladder disease. There is also concern that COC may worsen existing gall-bladder disease.
History of cholestasis — past COC-related	3	History of COC-related cholestasis predicts an increased risk with subsequent COC use.
Viral hepatitis — active	4	COCs are metabolized by the liver, and their use may adversely affect women whose liver function is already compromised.
Cirrhosis — mild compensated	3	COCs are metabolized by the liver, and their use may adversely affect women whose liver function is already compromised.
Cirrhosis — severe decompensated	4	
Liver tumours — benign and malignant	4	COCs are metabolized by the liver, and their use may adversely affect women whose liver function is compromised. In addition, COC use may enhance the growth of tumours.
Liver enzyme-inducing drugs	3	Although the interaction between commonly used liver enzyme-inducers and COCs is not harmful to women, it is likely to reduce the efficacy of COCs. Use of other contraceptives (e.g. progestogen-only injection) should be encouraged for women who are long-term users of any o these drugs. Whether increasing the hormone dose of COCs is of benefit remains unclear.

Category 4 — a condition that represents an unacceptable health risk if a COC is used.
Category 3 — a condition where the theoretical or proven risks usually outweigh the advantages of using a COC.

Drug rationale

Drugs not included

- **Drugs other than anti-androgens** are not included in this scenario, as they are offered in other scenarios for both men and women.
- **Anti-androgens other than co-cyprindiol** (e.g. bromocriptine, spironolactone) are not offered, as there is only limited evidence from randomised controlled trials to support their use. They are off-licence for this indication.

Drugs included

- **Co-cyprindiol** (cyproterone 2 mg / ethinylestradiol 35 micrograms) is effective in treating moderate acne in women. It may be particularly useful in women requiring hormonal contraception or period regulation.

Prescriptions

Cyproterone acetate 2mg + ethinylestradiol 35micrograms

Cyproterone acetate 2mg + ethinylestradiol 35micrograms

- Age from 14 years onwards
- Cyproterone + ethinylestradiol. Take one tablet once a day for 21 days. Start the next packet after a 7-day break. See package insert for full instructions; supply 63 tablets; NHS Cost £11.10.

Extended Information

Background information

- What is it? p.10
- How common is it? p.10
- How do I know my patient has it? p.10
- What else might it be? p.11
- Complications and prognosis p.11

What is it?

- **Acne is a disease of the pilosebaceous follicle,** affecting mainly the skin on the face, back, and chest.
- **Microcomedones, the precursors to all acne lesions,** are formed by the combined effect of increased sebum production (typical around puberty) and cornified material blocking the follicular duct.
- **A microcomedone can develop into a non-inflammatory lesion called a comedone,** which can be open (a blackhead) or closed (a whitehead); or into an inflammatory lesion.
- **Excess sebum encourages proliferation of bacteria,** in particular *Propionibacterium acnes,* which gives rise to inflammation and the formation of inflammatory lesion papules, pustules, nodules, or, rarely, granulomatous lesions.
- **Secondary causes of acne include excessive androgen production** (e.g. in polycystic ovary syndrome); drugs (e.g. levonorgestrel, norethisterone, corticosteroids); an chemicals (e.g. chloracne).
- **Oral contraceptives containing levonorgestrel or norethisterone may aggravate acne;** those containing desogestrel or gestodene do not, and may be considered as an alternative if acne is associated with oral contraceptive use.

[Sharpe, 1995; Medicines Resource, 1997; MeReC, 1999]

How common is it?

- **Acne is common among adolescents and young adults,** affecting approximately 80% of those aged 11–30 years at some time [Leyden, 1997].
- **Peak incidence** is seen in females aged 14–17 years and males aged 16–19 years [Sharpe, 1995].
- **Acne can occur later in life.** Approximately 5% of women and 1% of men aged 25–40 years either continu to get acne lesions or develop acne after adolescence [Layton, 2000].

How do I know my patient has it?

- **The skin may have an oily texture and appearance.**
- **Acne causes characteristic open comedones (blackheads and closed comedones (whiteheads)** on parts of the body where sebaceous glands are most abundant, i.e. the face, neck, chest, upper back, and upper arms.
- **If inflammation is present,** the comedones will be seen with papules, pustules, and nodules in this distribution.
- **Nodules are large, deep-seated abscesses** that may be fluctuant when palpated.
- **In very severe acne** these destructive lesions predominate and often run together (acne conglobata), sometimes with draining sinuses, which leave scarring on resolution
- **Scarring may be seen when nodules resolve.** This can be atrophic, with pitting or 'ice-pick' scars, or occasionally hypertrophic or keloidal, with raised, lumpy scars.

Occasionally hyperpigmentation occurs, usually in people with darker skin.
rown and Shalita, 1998]
Diagnosis of acne may be helped by illustrations. These can be found in the dermatology online atlas at: www.dermis.net/index_e.htm.

'hat else might it be?

Rosacea is most commonly seen in people over the age of 30 years and is associated with telangiectasia and flushing.
Folliculitis and boils. Swabs usually yield *Staphylococcus aureus*.
Sycosis barbae is persistent folliculitis of the beard area.
Milia are small keratin cysts, most commonly around the eyes. They do not have a central punctum.
Peri-oral dermatitis presents as erythema and small papules around the mouth, nasolabial folds, and sometimes the lower eyelids.
.ayton, 2000; Thiboutot, 2000]

omplications and prognosis

In the absence of effective treatment, acne persists for an average of 8–12 years in most people [Garner et al, 2002].
Acne of all grades can cause significant permanent scarring.
Acne can cause psychological distress and depression; it affects quality of life and self-esteem.
Suicide has been reported in people presenting with dermatological problems, including acne [Dudley and Poyner, 1998].
Thiboutot, 2000]

Management issues

General issues p.11
Treatment options p.12

ieneral issues

Assessing people with acne

The clinical signs of acne (non-inflammatory comedones, inflammatory papules, pustules, nodules, and scarring) should be noted.
The classification into mild, moderate, or severe acne relies heavily on a subjective assessment. In research, counts of lesions are used to assess severity. This is not practical in general clinical practice, but describing this approach may help to judge severity:

- **Mild:** fewer than 20 comedones, or fewer than 15 inflammatory lesions, or total lesion count fewer than 30
- **Moderate:** 20–100 comedones, or 15–50 inflammatory lesions, or total lesion count 30–125
- **Severe:** more than five cysts, or total comedone count greater than 100, or total inflammatory count greater than 50, or total lesion count greater than 125

Agency for Health Care Research and Quality, 2001]

- **Assessment should include an examination of the face, back, and chest.** Some people present with moderate acne on the face but severe acne on the back and chest.
- **Assessment should include a detailed history** covering the duration of the acne, previous treatments used and their effects, patient expectations, and psychological effects.
  - Many people with acne will have tried over-the-counter medications; assess the use of these and their relative success or failure.
  - Consider drugs or chemicals that may cause acne, including oral contraceptives, exposure to tars, polyvinyl chloride, corticosteroids, and androgens (sometimes used illegally by body-builders) [Thiboutot, 2000].
  - Acne can be associated with significant psychological distress, even if the acne appears relatively insignificant to an objective observer.
  - Psychological upset can be helped by dispelling the common myths about acne. It is not caused by bad hygiene, poor diet, or lack of exercise, and it is not infectious.

[MeReC, 1999; Layton, 2000; Webster, 2002]

Topical therapy

- **Topical therapy is indicated for people with mild-to-moderate non-inflammatory and inflammatory acne.**
- **In mild-to-moderate non-inflammatory acne,** topical retinoids, adapalene, or benzoyl peroxide are the treatments of choice, because of their anti-comedogenic properties.
- **In mild-to-moderate inflammatory acne,** benzoyl peroxide, azelaic acid, or topical antibiotics are the treatments of choice.
- **The choice of formulation** is largely determined by skin type and the person's preference:
  - **Gels and solutions** are non-greasy and have a drying effect, which may be preferable for someone with oily skin.
  - **Creams** are moisturising, and may be preferable for someone with dry skin.
  - **Lotions** are useful for application to large areas of skin.
- **Topical treatments should be applied to the entire affected area,** not just to current lesions.
- **Some topical treatments cause dry skin.** An oil-free or non-comodogenic moisturiser may help.

[Brown and Shalita, 1998; MeReC, 1999; Webster, 2002]

Oral antibiotics

- **Oral antibiotics are effective in inflammatory acne.** They will not work for purely comedonal acne.
- **Oral antibiotics improve inflammatory acne** both by inhibiting the growth of *Propionibacterium acnes* and by having an intrinsic anti-inflammatory effect.
- **Oral antibiotics are usually reserved for more severe inflammatory acne,** because of concerns about antibiotic resistance, and because they have the potential to cause troublesome systemic adverse effects.
- **Oral antibiotics may also be considered in the following cases:**
  - When topical therapy for mild-to-moderate acne has failed.
  - For someone having involvement of the shoulders, back, or chest (where it may be difficult to apply topical treatment).
  - For someone with mild-to-moderate acne with a high potential for scarring or pigmentary changes.
  - When topical therapies are unacceptable.

[Brown and Shalita, 1998]

Antibiotic resistance

- **Resistance to antibiotics is increasing worldwide.** In the UK the overall incidence of *P acnes* resistance had risen from 20% in 1988 to 62% in 1996 [Cooper, 1998].
- **Resistance to erythromycin is most common,** and most of these strains are also resistant to clindamycin. Resistance to tetracycline is less common, but when present these strains tend to be cross-resistant to doxycycline.

- ***P acnes* susceptibility to antibiotics is largely determined *in vitro***, and it is difficult to quantify the extent to which this affects clinical response. There is limited evidence that treatment failure is more common when resistant strains are present. Propionibacterial susceptibility to antibiotics resistance is not routinely tested.
- **A large multicentred trial** investigated the prevalence of resistant propionibacterial strains when one of the following regimens was used:
  - Topical erythromycin with benzoyl peroxide (administered separately once a day, or in a combined proprietary formulation twice a day)
  - Benzoyl peroxide alone
  - Oral oxytetracycline
  - Oral minocycline
- None of the regimens promoted an overall increase in the prevalence of antibiotic-resistant strains [Ozolins et al, 2002].
- **The same study also investigated whether pre-existing antibacterial resistance results in reduced efficacy.** The two topical erythromycin-containing regimens produced the largest reductions in cutaneous propionibacteria, including antibiotic-resistant variants, and these were equally effective in people with and without erythromycin-resistant propionibacteria. The clinical efficacy of both oral oxytetracycline and minocycline was compromised in a minority of people colonized with tetracycline-resistant bacteria.
- **Lack of improvement after 2 months or a worsening of acne** may indicate emergence of bacterial resistance or (rarely) the development of Gram-negative folliculitis, because of overgrowth of *Proteus*, *Enterobacter*, *Pseudomonas*, *Klebsiella* or other Gram-negative bacteria.

[MeReC, 1999]]

Duration of treatment

- **The largest reductions in acne severity appear in the first 6 weeks of treatment with topical and oral antimicrobials.** Extending treatment beyond 12 weeks increases benefit only slightly. Residual acne is likely to be present after 18 weeks [Ozolins et al, 2002].
- **As a general rule,** treatments need to be used for 2 months before one can assume that treatment has failed.
- **It is unclear how long a treatment that appears to be working should be continued.** Historically it has been recommended that oral antibiotics should be continued for at least 6 months if the response to treatment is adequate. Topical non-antibiotic treatment may need to be continued for several years.
- **Some dermatologists are now using oral antibiotics in bursts of around 6 months** (or less) until a maximum response is achieved, followed by a switch to an alternative maintenance treatment, such as topical benzoyl peroxide or topical retinoids. This is thought to decrease any resistant strains that might have developed during oral antibiotic treatment. A topical retinoid will also help to prevent the formation of comedones, the precursors of inflammatory lesions. Further research is needed to determine the best options for treatments and length of treatment.

Referral

In December 2001 the National Institute for Clinical Excellence (NICE) issued consensus guidelines on when to refer someone with acne for specialist services. The guidelines state that most people with acne can be managed in primary care. However, someone with acne should be referred to a specialist service if any of the circumstances shown in Table 2 apply, with the referral timings shown.

Table 2: Referral advice for people with acne.

Referral timing	Reason for referral **Refer to a specialist if the person with acne:**
***	Has a severe variant of acne such as acne fulminans or Gram-negative folliculitis
**	Has severe or nodulocystic acne and could benefit from o
**	Has severe social or psychological problems, such as a morbid fear of deformity (dysmorphophobia)
*	Is at risk of, or is developing, scarring despite primary-car therapies
*	Has moderate acne that has failed to respond to treatmen that included two courses of oral antibiotics, each lasting months. The person with acne is probably in the best position to assess whether or not the treatment has failed
*	Is suspected of having an underlying endocrinological cau for the acne (such as polycystic ovary syndrome) that nee assessment
^	Has, or develops, features that make the diagnosis uncertain

Key to referral timings: Arrangements should be made so that the person:
*** Is seen urgently (maximum waiting time of 2 weeks recommended, but to be agreed locally)
** Is seen soon (maximum waiting time to be agreed locally)
* Has a routine appointment (maximum waiting time to be agreed locally)
^ Is seen at your discretion, which will depend on clinical circumstances

- NICE advises that treatment should be started if someone waiting for a hospital appointment has painful deep nodules or cysts (nodulocystic acne), as there is a high risk of scarring.

[NICE, 2001]

Treatment options

- **Management of acne vulgaris** should be aimed at the specific type of lesion (whether inflammatory or non-inflammatory) and the severity of the disease (see *Assessing people with acne*).
- **Individual response to treatment varies,** but to an extent may be predicted by the type of acne and knowledge of how the treatments work.
- **Clear guidance** regarding correct usage, possible adverse effects, and realistic expectations of response can help the person keep to the treatment regime.

Benzoyl peroxide

- **Benzoyl peroxide** is an oxidising agent that has both antibacterial and anti-comedogenic properties. It is effective for treating both inflammatory and non-inflammatory acne.
- **The main benefit of treatment with benzoyl peroxide is a reduction in inflammation** related to its antibacterial activity, which is achieved at low strengths. Gel formulations of 2.5%, 5%, and 10% benzoyl peroxide are equally effective against inflammatory lesions in someone with mild-to-moderate acne.
- **Benzoyl peroxide has comparatively low anti-comedogenic activity,** which is greatest at higher strengths.
- **Washing** with mild soap or a cleansing agent and water before application helps to remove excess sebum.
- **The main adverse effects** experienced with benzoyl peroxide are skin irritation, erythema, and dry skin.
- **Irritation is common** but is usually mild. To minimize irritation, treatment should be started at low concentrations and the concentration gradually increased if required.
- **In someone with especially sensitive skin,** benzoyl peroxide can initially be applied once a day, aiming for twice a day as tolerance develops.
- **Contact dermatitis occurs rarely** and disappears when treatment is withdrawn.

Advise that using benzoyl peroxide may cause bleaching of hair, clothing, towels, and bed linen.
hiboutot, 2000; BNF 43, 2002]

zelaic acid

Azelaic acid has both antimicrobial and anti-comedogenic properties.
In clinical trials, azelaic acid is broadly comparable in efficacy to 0.05% tretinoin, 5% benzoyl peroxide, and 2% erythromycin in people with comedonal or mild-to-moderate inflammatory acne. However, feedback from expert reviewers suggests that in practice this degree of efficacy is not always experienced.
The rate of local adverse effects is lower than that observed with tretinoin or benzoyl peroxide.
Azelaic acid is only licensed in the UK for a maximum period of 6 months' use [BNF 43, 2002]. However, in practice it is often continued for longer.
/ledicines Resource, 1997; Thiboutot, 2000]

Topical retinoids

The topical retinoids available in the UK are tretinoin, isotretinoin, and the naphthoid acid derivative, adapalene, which has retinoid-like activity.
Topical retinoids act primarily to loosen and decrease retention of cornified material in the follicular canal, reducing the formation of comedones.
Topical retinoids are effective against comedonal acne, and have some anti-inflammatory effect. Where inflammation is also present, combination with benzoyl peroxide or topical antibiotics may be appropriate.
Improvements may take 6–12 weeks and people should be warned that their acne may get worse at first.
The most common adverse effects are local irritation, dryness, burning, peeling, and erythema (similar to mild sunburn).
To minimise these adverse effects, especially in people with very sensitive skin, topical retinoids can be used initially every 2–3 nights, increasing to once nightly as tolerated.
Retinoids may increase sensitivity to the sun. Give advice on sunscreen use and on avoiding too much exposure to sunlight.
Retinoids are teratogenic and are contraindicated during pregnancy [NTIS, Personal Communication, 2002]. Although systemic absorption of topical retinoids is generally thought to be negligible, they are best avoided in women who are pregnant or who are considering pregnancy. Give advice on the use of effective contraception to women of childbearing age.
Brown and Shalita, 1998; Thiboutot, 2000; BNF 43, 2002]

Topical antibiotics

- **Topical antibiotics are useful in mild-to-moderate inflammatory acne** but have little effect on non-inflammatory comedones.
- **Topical antibiotics available for acne treatment in the UK** are erythromycin, clindamycin, and tetracycline.
- **The three antibiotics appear to have similar efficacy,** with choice of treatment being largely determined by the development of resistance and by whether the person with acne finds them acceptable. Erythromycin and clindamycin are the most commonly used topical antibiotics. Topical tetracycline can stain the skin and clothing yellow.
- **Topical antibiotics can produce mild irritation,** and on rare occasions cause sensitization.
- **In a large, multicentred study of people with mild-to-moderate facial acne, the best response rates** were seen with topical erythromycin plus benzoyl peroxide (administered separately once a day, or in a combined proprietary formulation twice a day) compared with benzoyl peroxide alone, oral oxytetracycline, or oral minocycline, although treatment differences were small [Ozolins et al, 2002]. Topical retinoids were not included in this study.

[Brown and Shalita, 1998]

Other topical agents

- **Abrasive agents are not beneficial in acne** [BNF 43, 2002]. Abrasive cleansers and vigorous scrubbing should be avoided, as they can aggravate acne by promoting the development of inflammatory lesions [Leyden, 1997; MeReC, 1999].
- **Peeling agents such as sulphur-containing preparations and salicylic acid** are generally considered inferior to the more modern topical treatments for acne [Sykes and Webster, 1994; BNF 43, 2002]. Salicyclic acid may be an option for someone with comedonal acne who cannot tolerate retinoids.

Oral antibiotics

Tetracyclines

- **Oxytetracycline and tetracycline (500 mg twice a day) are first-line oral antibiotics,** as they are effective and inexpensive. However, the need to take them on an empty stomach may limit compliance.
- **Doxycycline, lymecycline, and minocycline are better absorbed than tetracycline** and can be taken with food, which reduces gastrointestinal intolerance and potentially improves compliance.
- **There is a lack of comparative data on the commonly prescribed acne treatments.** A Cochrane review for minocycline in acne concluded that the efficacy of minocycline relative to other acne therapies could not be determined owing to the poor methodological quality of trials. The reviewers found no evidence to justify its first-line use, given its increased cost and concerns over safety [Garner et al, 2002].
- **A recent large, multicentre trial** did not find any evidence that oral oxytetracycline or oral minocycline were any more effective than topical antimicrobial preparations for people with mild to moderate facial acne [Ozolins et al, 2002].
- **The tetracyclines should not be used in pregnancy, during breastfeeding, or in children under 12 years of age,** as they are deposited in the teeth and bones of the unborn or developing child. Women of childbearing age should use effective contraception (note that tetracyclines may cause oral contraceptives to fail during the first few weeks of treatment).
- **With the exception of doxycycline and minocycline, the tetracyclines may exacerbate renal failure** and should not be given to anyone with renal disease.
- **Benign intracranial hypertension** is a rare but important adverse effect of tetracycline therapy. Tell people taking tetracyclines to report headache and visual disturbances.
- **Photosensitivity** manifested by an exaggerated sunburn reaction has been observed in some individuals taking tetracyclines. Someone likely to be exposed to direct sunlight or ultraviolet light should be advised that this reaction can occur with tetracycline drugs, and treatment should be discontinued at the first evidence of skin erythema.
- **Adverse effects specifically associated with minocycline** include:
  - Reversible vestibular disturbances (e.g. dizziness, vertigo, ataxia).
  - Blue-grey discolouration of the skin, particularly in inflamed areas.

- Hepatitis resembling serum sickness and lupus-like reactions (rare) [Gough et al, 1996].
- **If treatment with minocycline is continued for longer than 6 months,** monitor every 3 months for hepatotoxicity, pigmentation, and for systemic lupus erythematosus — discontinue if these develop [BNF 43, 2002].

[Brown and Shalita, 1998; Lawrenson et al, 2000; BNF 43, 2002]

Erythromycin

- **Erythromycin is usually given at a dose of 500 mg twice a day** for the treatment of acne.
- ***P acnes* resistance to erythromycin is now common in the UK,** and skin colonisation by erythromycin-resistant propionibacteria has been strongly correlated with a poor response to orally administered erythromycin.
- **Erythromycin is used less often than other treatments,** such as tetracyclines, because it is feared that resistant strains of *P acnes* will emerge, and because it can cause gastrointestinal adverse effects.

Trimethoprim

- **Trimethoprim is occasionally used to treat acne.** Evidence of its effectiveness is limited, and its use for the treatment of acne is off-licence.
- **Current advice from the manufacturer is to monitor full blood counts in long-term use,** because of the risk of blood dyscrasias. It is recommended that users be advised to report symptoms of blood disorders.
- **Co-trimoxazole, the combination of trimethoprim with sulfamethoxazole, has also been used to treat acne.** The Committee on Safety of Medicines advises against its use for acne because of the potential for serious adverse effects, including hypersensitivity reactions and bone-marrow suppression; this risk is attributed to the sulphonamide component. Use for the treatment of acne is off-licence.

[BNF 43, 2002]

Other oral antibiotics

- **Oral clindamycin** improves inflammatory acne, but it is rarely used in this setting because of its association with pseudomembranous colitis.

Anti-androgens

- **Anti-androgen treatment may be useful in women with acne** having characteristics that suggest a significant hormonal influence:
  - Inadequate response to other treatments
  - Acne that began or worsened in adulthood
  - Premenstrual flares of acne
  - Excessive facial oiliness
  - Inflammatory acne limited to the area of male beard distribution
  - Acne accompanied by hirsutism

[Brown and Shalita, 1998]

- **Anti-androgen therapy is also useful in women with acne** when oral contraception or period regulation is required.
- **Cyproterone acetate is a potent androgen-receptor blocker.** It is available for the treatment of acne in combination with ethinylestradiol (co-cyprindiol).
- **Co-cyprindiol (Dianette®) is licensed** for the treatment of severe acne in women refractory to prolonged oral antibacterial therapy, and for moderately severe hirsutism [ABPI Medicines Compendium, 2002].
- **Co-cyprindiol is effective in treating moderate acne in women,** but may take 2–6 months to produce an improvement in acne [Healy and Simpson, 1994; Medicines Resource, 1997].
- **Co-cyprindiol is not authorised** for the sole purpose of oral contraception and should be discontinued 3–4 menstrual cycles after the woman's acne has resolved [CSM, 2002].
- **The use of a combined oral contraceptive (COC) carries an increased risk for venous thromboembolism (VTE).** There is some epidemiological evidence that the incidence of VTE in users of co-cyprindiol is higher than in users of low-dose oestrogen COCs. In addition women with androgen-related conditions may have an inherently increased cardiovascular risk [CSM, 2002].
- **The dose of cyproterone is relatively low,** but consequences of long-term use are unclear.
- **Spironolactone has been used to treat acne.** It blocks androgen receptors and inhibits androgen synthesis. Its value in clinical practice is not clear from currently available evidence [Farquhar et al, 2002]. The potential metabolites of spironolactone have been associated with liver cancer in animal studies, and the Committee on Safety of Medicines urges caution in its use. It may occasionally be prescribed off-licence by dermatologists for acne.
- **The new combined contraceptive pill, Yasmin,** which contains the progestogen drospirenone, is claimed to have a positive effect on skin conditions, such as acne. Whether it produces greater improvements in acne than do other combined oral contraceptives is unknown [DTB, 2002].

Combination therapy

Combinations of different therapies that affect different areas of pathophysiology can be useful.

Benzoyl peroxide in combination with topical antibiotics

- **Benzoyl peroxide is thought to counteract the emergence of bacterial resistance** when used with topical or oral antibiotics.
- **In people with mild-to-moderate facial acne, better response rates were achieved** with a combination of benzoyl peroxide and erythromycin (administered separately once a day, or in a combined proprietary formulation twice a day) compared with benzoyl peroxide alone, oral oxytetracycline, or oral minocycline. These differences were not statistically significant [Ozolins et al, 2002].
- **In terms of efficacy or local irritation** there is little difference between the erythromycin with benzoyl peroxide administered separately and the combined proprietary formulation [Ozolins et al, 2002].
- **The combination of clindamycin with benzoyl peroxide** has demonstrated similar efficacy to erythromycin with benzoyl peroxide, and is an effective alternative.
- **Benzoyl peroxide should not be used concomitantly with alcoholic formulations of antibiotics** because of increased skin irritation, but it can be used with the aqueous formulation of clindamycin. *When a combination of benzoyl peroxide with a topical antibiotic is used in the form of separate constituents,* they should be administered 12 hours apart.

Zinc in combination with topical antibiotics

- **Zinc has been suggested to enhance drug delivery** through the stratum corneum, potentiating the effect of the topical antibiotic.
- **The combination of topical erythromycin and zinc,** *in vitro* at appropriate concentrations, inhibits both erythromycin-sensitive and -resistant *P acnes*. It is not clear how this affects treatment success *in vivo*.
- **In clinical trials, the combination of erythromycin with zinc** has shown similar efficacy to oral tetracyclines and topical clindamycin, and less efficacy than erythromycin combined with benzoyl peroxide [Chu et al, 1997]. We found no therapeutic trials that compared the combination of erythromycin and zinc with the individual components.

Topical retinoids in combination with topical antibiotics

- **The efficacy of other topically applied agents** may be increased by concurrent therapy with retinoids, because of increased cutaneous penetration.
- **It is reasonable to introduce a topical retinoid (or retinoid like drug, such as adapalene) early on** and continue it throughout much of the treatment programme, as the microcomedo is a precursor of many acne lesions.
- **A topical retinoid alternated 12-hourly with a topical antibiotic** is a useful combination in people who have both inflammatory and non-inflammatory lesions.

Topical retinoids in combination with benzoyl peroxide

- **The concurrent use of benzoyl peroxide with a topical retinoid may be a useful treatment option.**
- **Both of these agents are irritants and, applied simultaneously, may inactivate each other.** Common clinical practice is to apply the benzoyl peroxide in the morning and the retinoid at night.

Topical therapies in combination with oral antibiotics

- **Topical therapies (benzoyl peroxide, azelaic acid, retinoids) may be used in combination with systemic therapy in moderate-to-severe acne.**
- **Topical antibiotics should not be used concurrently with oral antibiotics.**
- **Mild acne can be treated first with topical retinoids** and then by adding a topical antibiotic or benzoyl peroxide if there are inflammatory lesions. As inflammation becomes more widespread, topical retinoids and oral antibiotics may be more appropriate.
- **Combination therapies including topical retinoids and oral antibiotics** have a role to play in the treatment of moderate and severe inflammatory acne. In practice, the oral tetracyclines are used in combination with topical retinoids to treat such cases.

[Brown and Shalita, 1998; BNF 43, 2002; Webster, 2002]

Oral isotretinoin

- **Potential for teratogenicity and other severe adverse effects** mean that oral isotretinoin is restricted to prescription by consultant dermatologists, or under their supervision.
- **Referral for consideration of oral isotretinoin should be considered** in severe acne, where there is nodulocystic and conglobate acne, or where scarring is evident. It may also be used where acne is not responding to adequate courses of oral antibiotics, or where acne is associated with significant psychological problems. There may be a place for its use in women who have developed acne later in life (30s and 40s), as this is frequently unresponsive to antibiotics [BNF 43, 2002].
- **Oral isotretinoin works by dramatically reducing sebum excretion,** with reduction in comedones, inflammation, and *P acnes* count. It can significantly reduce progression to scarring.
- **Oral isotretinoin is usually given for 12–16 weeks,** at which point 80% of people have clearance of acne and have sustained response after stopping therapy [Brown and Shalita, 1998]. Repeat courses or long-term therapy are not normally given, although repeat courses are sometimes considered by dermatologists.
- **Oral isotretinoin is a teratogen** and pregnancy *must* be carefully excluded prior to treatment and avoided during treatment and for at least 1 month after treatment.
- **A full list of adverse effects experienced with isotretinoin** can be found in the *British National Formulary* or the Summary of Product Characteristics.
- **While isotretinoin is being taken, liver function and lipid levels must be monitored** [BNF 43, 2002]. The specialist responsible for treatment will usually do this.
- **Oral isotretinoin has been implicated in depression and suicide risk** in people with very severe acne, but it is difficult to tell if this is directly due to the drug or to the psychological distress caused by the disfiguring skin condition [Jick et al, 2000].

A

References

NHS staff in England can link, free of charge, from references to full text journals by clicking on [Full text] on the PRODIGY website.

1. ABPI Medicines Compendium (2002) *Summary of product characteristics for Dianette.* Electronic Medicines Compendium. Datapharm Communications Ltd. www.emc.medicines.org.uk [Accessed: 15/08/2002].
2. Agency for Health Care Research and Quality (2001) *Management of acne.* Evidence Report/Technology Assessment No. 17. Agency for Health Care Research and Quality. www.ahrq.gov [Accessed: 10/08/2002].
3. BNF 43 (2002) *British National Formulary.* 43rd edn. London: British Medical Association and Royal Pharmaceutical Society of Great Britain.
4. Brown, S.K. and Shalita, A.R. (1998) Acne vulgaris. *Lancet* **351**(9119), 1871–1876. [Full text]
5. Chu, A., Huber, F.J. and Plott, R.T. (1997) The comparative efficacy of benzoyl peroxide 5%/ erythromycin 3% gel and erythromycin 4%/zinc 1.2% solution in the treatment of acne vulgaris. *British Journal of Dermatology* **136**(2), 235–238.
6. Cooper, A.J. (1998) Systematic review of *Propionibacterium acnes* resistance to systemic antibiotics. *Medical Journal of Australia* **169**(5), 259–261.
7. CSM (2002) Cyproterone acetate (Dianette): risk of venous thromboembolism (VTE). *Current Problems in Pharmacovigilance* **28**(Oct), 9–10.
8. DTB (2002) Is Yasmin a "truly different" pill? *Drug & Therapeutics Bulletin* **40**(8), 57–59.
9. Dudley, A. and Poyner, T. (1998) Key issues in acne management. *Prescriber* **9**(Suppl), 1–12.
10. Farquhar, C., Lee, O., Toomath, R. and Jepson, R. (2002) *Spironolactone versus placebo or in combination with steroids for hirsutism and/or acne (Cochrane Review).* The Cochrane Library. Issue 3. Oxford: Update Software.
11. Garner, S.E., Eady, E.A., Popescu, C. et al (2002) *Minocycline for acne vulgaris: efficacy and safety (Cochrane Review).* The Cochrane Library. Issue 3. Oxford: Update Software.
12. Gibson, J.R. (1997) Azelaic acid 20% cream (AZELEX) and the medical management of acne vulgaris. *Dermatology Nursing* **9**(5), 339–344.
13. Gough, A., Chapman, S., Wagstaff, K. et al (1996) Minocycline induced autoimmune hepatitis and systemic lupus erythematosus-like syndrome. *British Medical Journal* **312**(7024), 169–172. [Full text]
14. Healy, E. and Simpson, N. (1994) Acne vulgaris. *British Medical Journal* **308**(6932), 831–833. [Full text]
15. Jick, S.S., Kremers, H.M. and Vasilakis-Scaramozza, C. (2000) Isotretinoin use and risk of depression, psychotic symptoms, suicide, and attempted suicide. *Archives of Dermatology* **136**(10), 1231–1236. [Full text]
16. Lawrenson, R.A., Seaman, H.E., Sundstrom, A. et al (2000) Liver damage associated with minocycline use in acne: a systematic review of the published literature and pharmacovigilance data. *Drug Safety* **23**(4), 333–349.

17. Layton, A.M. (2000) Acne vulgaris and similar eruptions. *Medicine* **28**(12), 46–50.
18. Leyden, J.J. (1997) Therapy for acne vulgaris. *New England Journal of Medicine* **336**(16), 1156–1162. [Full text]
19. Medicines Resource (1997) Management of acne vulgaris. *Medicines Resource* **37**(Feb), 143–146.
20. MeReC (1999) The treatment of acne vulgaris: an update. *MeReC Bulletin* **10**(8), 29–32.
21. NICE (2001) *Referral advice – a guide to appropriate referral from general to specialist services.* National Institute for Clinical Excellence. www.nice.org.uk [Accessed: 11/08/2002].
22. NTIS (2002) *Personal communication.* National Teratology Information Service: Wolfson Unit, Claremont Place, Newcastle upon Tyne.
23. Ozolins, M., Eady, E.A., Avery, A. et al (2002) *A randomised controlled multiple treatment compariso to provide a cost-effective rationale for the selection antimicrobial therapy in acne.* Report for NHS study 94/48.
24. Sharpe, G.R. (1995) Prescribing for acne vulgaris. *Prescribers' Journal* **35**(2), 53–58.
25. Sykes, N.L. and Webster, G.F. (1994) Acne: a review optimum treatment. *Drugs* **48**(1), 59–70.
26. Thiboutot, D. (2000) New treatments and therapeuti strategies for acne. *Archives of Family Medicine* **9**(2), 179–187. [Full text]
27. Webster, G.F. (2002) Acne vulgaris. *British Medical Journal* **325**(7362), 475–479. [Full text]

PRODIGY GUIDANCE

Adverse drug reactions

Last revised in June 2004
www.prodigy.nhs.uk/guidance.asp?gt=Adverse drug reactions

Applies to people of all ages

This guidance covers the mechanism for reporting adverse drug reactions, what to report, which drugs to report, and reporting of defective medicines.

There is separate PRODIGY guidance for *Poisoning*.

Goals

To report adverse drug reactions and defective medicines as appropriate

Extended Information

Background information

What is it? p.17
What should alert me to the possibility of an adverse drug reaction? p.17
How common is it? p.17
How do I establish causality? p.17
Complications and prognosis p.18

What is it?

An adverse drug reaction is any unwanted or harmful reaction experienced following the administration of a drug or combination of drugs under normal conditions of use and suspected to be related to the drug. Adverse drug reactions can be divided into two types:

- **Type A** (augmented) reactions result from an exaggeration of a drug's normal pharmacological actions when given at the usual therapeutic dose and are normally dose-dependent (e.g. low blood pressure with antihypertensives, low blood sugar with insulin). They also include reactions that are not directly related to the desired clinical action of the drug (e.g. dry mouth associated with tricyclic antidepressants).
- **Type B** (bizarre) reactions represent a novel response not expected from the known pharmacological actions of the drug (e.g. anaphylaxis with penicillin, angioedema with angiotensin-converting enzyme inhibiting drugs). They are not normally dependent on the dose.

The terms adverse drug reaction and adverse event are often used interchangeably but this is not always correct.

- **Adverse events** relate to any undesirable event experienced by a patient whilst taking a medicine, regardless of whether the drug is suspected of being related to the event.
- **Adverse reactions** are a subset of adverse events including those that are suspected of being related to the drug.

[MCA and CSM, 2002; BNF 47, 2004]

What should alert me to the possibility of an adverse drug reaction?

An adverse drug reaction may be identified in a number of ways:

- **Patients may spontaneously report symptoms** they have experienced since taking a new medicine.
- **Often it is the vigilance of the healthcare professional** in linking a sign or symptom to either current drug therapy or previous therapy (including over-the-counter drugs and unlicensed herbal remedies). Such signs may include:
  - Abnormal clinical measurements
  - Abnormal haematological or biochemical results
  - Initiation of new drug therapy to treat the symptoms of an adverse drug reaction

[MCA and CSM, 2002; BNF 47, 2004]

How common is it?

- Approximately 7% of medical inpatients are affected by adverse drug reactions (ADRs) and about 50% of these occur before hospital admission [Ferner, 2003].
- Up to 40% of patients in the community are thought to experience ADRs [Martys, 1979].
- Between 1964 and December 2000, there were 331 deaths in children (median age 5 years) due to suspected ADRs. The most frequently implicated drugs were anticonvulsants, cytotoxics and antibiotics. The most common suspected adverse drug reaction was hepatic failure [Clarkson et al, 2002].
- One study found that in people aged over 65 years the admission rate due to a suspected ADR was 16% compared with 4% in younger people [Beijer and de Blaey, 2002].

How do I establish causality?

- Even if it is not possible to establish with absolute certainty whether the drug has caused a reaction, the event should be reported to the Committee on Safety of Medicines.
- Some factors to consider when assessing causality include:
  - **Nature of the reaction:** some clinical reactions are commonly caused by drugs, for example acute dystonias, blood dyscrasias, and skin reactions.
  - **Timing:** the time elapsing between the administration of a drug and the reaction occurring may be characteristic of the reaction. For example, anaphylaxis usually develops within minutes of a parenteral drug administration (and usually after prior sensitization). Alternatively, some reactions may be related to the cumulative effect of the drug over months, years or even an effect on the next generation (e.g. diethylstilboestrol given to women for luteal support was found to increase the risk of female children developing vaginal cancer). The majority of adverse drug reactions occur in the first few weeks or months after a drug is started.
  - **Dose relationship:** adverse reactions are often dose-related and can often be minimized by reducing the dose. If symptoms improve when the dose is reduced this often (but not always) suggests the symptoms are drug-related.
  - **Other possible causes:** these should be excluded as far as possible. The symptoms may be manifestations of the person's underlying illness, or of another disease.

Over-the-counter and herbal medicines used for self-medication should also be considered.

[MCA and CSM, 2002; BNF 47, 2004]

Complications and prognosis

- **Complications can cover a whole spectrum** of events, from very mild to life-threatening reactions that require hospitalization; these events may be disabling, incapacitating, or produce congenital abnormalities in later generations.
- **When the reaction is a type A reaction,** dose reduction or stopping the drug will generally lead to resolution of the symptoms. A few, mainly type B reactions, if not identified early can have prolonged, permanent, or even fatal consequences.

Management issues

- Who can report? p.18
- How to make a report p.18
- What should be reported? p.18
- Special problems p.19
- What about defective medicines? p.19
- What happens to the information? p.19
- Preventing adverse reactions p.19
- Additional reporting p.20

Who can report?

- **Doctors, dentists, coroners, pharmacists, and registered nurses (including health visitors and midwives)** can report adverse drug reactions.
- **Other members of the healthcare team** should alert the general practitioner, or other recognized reporter, on encountering suspected adverse drug reactions.

[MCA and CSM, 2002; BNF 47, 2004]

How to make a report

- **The Committee on Safety of Medicines (CSM)** collects reports of possible or suspected adverse reactions through the Yellow Card scheme.
- Suspected adverse drug reactions should be reported by filling in a Yellow Card and sending it to your regional CSM centre if listed, or to the national centre. Although not obligatory, it would be good practice to tell the patient that a Yellow Card is being submitted.
- **Yellow Cards (postage paid)** can be found in the back of the British National Formulary (BNF), the Nurse Prescribers' Formulary (NPF), Dental Practitioners' Formulary (DPF), the Monthly Index of Medical Specialities (MIMS), and the ABPI Medicines Compendium, or can be obtained from the regional and national centres. Completed cards should be sent to the appropriate regional monitoring centre (see below for addresses). Yellow Cards are also accessible via:
  - Some GP systems such as EMIS.
  - The Internet, where online reporting is available on yellowcard.gov.uk.
- **Regional centres:**
  - CSM Mersey, Freepost, Liverpool L3 3AB (telephone 0151 794 8206)
  - CSM Wales, Freepost, Cardiff CF4 1ZZ (telephone 029 2074 4181)
  - CSM Northern and Yorkshire, Freepost 1085, Newcastle upon Tyne, NE1 1BR (telephone 0191 232 1525)
  - CSM West Midlands, Freepost SW2991, Birmingham B18 7BR (telephone 0121 507 5672)
  - CSM Scotland, Cards, Freepost NAT3271, Edinburgh, EH3 0BR (telephone 0131 249 2919)
- **National centre:**
  - Medicines and Healthcare products Regulatory Agency (MHRA), CSM, Freepost, London SW8 5B or
  - A 24-hour Freefone service is available to all parts o the UK for advice and information on suspected adverse drug reactions. Contact the National Yellov Card Information Service at the MHRA on 0800 73 6789. Outside office hours a telephone-answering service will take messages.
- **Pharmaceutical industry:** the report can also be made directly to the relevant pharmaceutical company. The company has a statutory duty to report these to the CS within 15 days.

[MCA and CSM, 2002; BNF 47, 2004]

What should be reported?

- Suspected adverse reactions to drugs (self-medicated as well as prescribed drugs), blood products, vaccines, X-ray contrast media, and herbal products should be reported. Only serious reactions to more established drugs are sought.
- Suspected adverse reactions to medical devices, includi dental or surgical devices, intra-uterine devices, and contact lens fluids, should also be reported. Informatio for reporting these can be found at http://devices.mhra.gov.uk.
- A note of the report should also be made in the patient' records.

Newer products

- **Report all suspected adverse reactions** to drugs with th black triangle symbol (in the British National Formula the Nurse Prescribers' Formulary, on product literature and advertising).
- **The black triangle symbol** identifies licensed medicines that are being monitored intensively by the Medicines and Healthcare products Regulatory Agency/Committe on Safety of Medicines (MHRA/CSM). A black triangl will be assigned to a product if the drug is a new active substance; if it is a new combination of active substances; if it is a new route of administration or dru delivery system; or for significant new indications that may alter the established risks and benefits of that drug There is no standard time for which products retain a black triangle; safety data are usually reviewed after 2 years. However, some products have retained the bla triangle for more than 3 years.
- **Only limited information is available from clinical trial on the safety of new medicines.** This is because they are tested in a small, often highly selected population in which it can be difficult to detect rare adverse effects. Further understanding about the safety of medicines depends on the availability of information from routine clinical practice.
- **Spontaneous reporting** is particularly valuable for recognizing possible new hazards rapidly.
  - For medicines showing the black triangle symbol, the MHRA/CSM asks that all suspected reactions be reported through the Yellow Card scheme (including those reactions not considered to be serious). An adverse reaction should be reported even if it is not certain that the drug has caused it, or if the reaction is well recognized, or if other drugs have been given at the same time.
- **More detailed information** and a list of all those products currently undergoing intensive monitoring can be found at http://medicines.mhra.gov.uk.

Established products

- **All suspected reactions that are considered to be serious** including those that are fatal, life-threatening, disabling, incapacitating, or which result in or prolong hospitalization, or are medically significant. Congenital abnormalities are also considered to be serious. Serious suspected reactions should be reported even if the effect is well recognized.

Examples include anaphylaxis, blood disorders, endocrine disturbances, effects on fertility, haemorrhage from any site, renal impairment, jaundice, ophthalmic disorders, severe central nervous system effects, severe skin reactions, reactions in pregnant women, reactions due to overdose, withdrawal reactions, and drug interactions.

Reports of serious adverse reactions are required to enable comparison with other drugs of a similar class. You do not need to report well-known, relatively minor adverse effects, such as dry mouth with tricyclic antidepressants, constipation with opioids, or nausea with digoxin.

[MCA and CSM, 2002; BNF 47, 2004]

Special problems

Delayed drug effects: some reactions (e.g. cancers, chloroquine retinopathy, and retroperitoneal fibrosis) may become manifest months or years after exposure. Any suspicion of such an association should be reported.

Elderly people: particular vigilance is required to identify adverse reactions in elderly individuals. They may metabolize medicines less efficiently and be more sensitive to their effects, therefore being more susceptible to adverse reactions. Elderly people often take a number of medicines, making them more likely to encounter drug interactions.

Congenital abnormalities: when an infant is born with a congenital abnormality or there is a malformed aborted fetus, doctors are asked to consider whether this might be an adverse reaction to a drug and to report all drugs (including self-medication) taken during pregnancy.

Children: all suspected adverse drug reactions in children should be reported even if the black triangle symbol has been removed. This is because experience in children may still be limited:

- In general, children are not exposed to medicines in clinical trials, therefore very little is known about the safe use of medicines in this age group.
- Many drugs that are routinely used are not licensed for use in children.
- The action of the drug and its distribution in children (especially in the very young) may be different from that in adults.
- Suitable formulations may not be available to allow precise dosing in children.
- The nature and course of illness and adverse drug reactions may differ between adults and children.

Herbal remedies: although some herbal medicines are licensed for use, there are many herbal remedies on general sale, or supplied by herbal practitioners, that are not licensed. It is important that all suspected adverse reactions to herbal remedies are reported so their safety can be monitored.

- When reporting please include the following information:
  - The ingredients, source, or supplier if known and what it was being used for
  - If the remedy supplied by a herbal practitioner, the name and address of that practitioner
- If the reaction is severe, retain a sample if possible, in case the MHRA/CSM needs to investigate further.

[MCA and CSM, 2002; BNF 47, 2004]

What about defective medicines?

- During the manufacture or distribution of a medicine an error or accident may occur whereby the finished product does not conform to its specification. Such errors are relatively rare and recalls are often a precautionary measure (during 2002, 20 reports were filed).
- Such an accident should not be confused with an adverse drug reaction where the product conforms to its specification.
- **Reports on suspected defective medicinal products** should include the brand or the non-proprietary name, the name of the manufacturer or supplier, the strength and dosage form of the product, the product licence number, the batch number or numbers of the product, the nature of the defect, and an account of any action already taken in consequence.
- **The Defective Medicines Report Centre operates a 24-hour service and can be contacted at:**
  - The Defective Medicines Report Centre, Medicines and Healthcare products Regulatory Agency, Room 1801, Market Towers, 1 Nine Elms Lane, London, SW8 5NQ. Telephone 020 7273 0574 (weekdays 9.00 am–5.00 pm) or 020 7210 3000 or 5371 (any other time).
  - Further information on products regarding which defects have been notified or which have already been recalled or both, together with a defect reporting form, can be obtained from mhra.gov.uk.
- Suspected defective medicines should also be reported to the pharmaceutical company.

[MCA and CSM, 2002; BNF 47, 2004]

What happens to the information?

- **When Yellow Cards are received by the CSM** an acknowledgement letter is sent which quotes a unique identification number (Adverse Drug Reactions On-line Information Tracking [ADROIT] database). This number should be quoted in any future correspondence.
- **A copy of the report** is sent back for inclusion in the patient's medical records unless the Yellow Card was submitted electronically.
- **The information is entered onto the CSM's ADROIT database** and assessed for the likely causal relationship between the drug and reported reactions. There is continuing surveillance of the situation.
- **The risk of a newly identified hazard** is considered in the context of the overall adverse drug reaction profile for the drug in comparison with relevant therapeutic alternatives. Where necessary, decisions are made on whether changes need to be made to minimize risks and maximize benefits. These may include restrictions in use, reduction in dose, special warnings and precautions.
- **Occasionally a drug may be withdrawn** from the market if the risks are considered to outweigh the benefits.

[MCA and CSM, 2002; BNF 47, 2004]

Preventing adverse reactions

- Never use any drug unless there is a good indication. If the person is pregnant do not use a drug unless the need is imperative.
- Allergy and idiosyncrasy are important causes of adverse reactions. Ask if the person had previous reactions. There may also be a family history of adverse reactions to drugs that share a common characteristic indicative of a inherited disorder (e.g. glucose-6-phosphate dehydrogenase [G6PD] deficiency).
- Ask if the person is already taking other drugs including self-medication drugs; interactions may occur.

- Age and hepatic or renal impairment may alter the metabolism or excretion of drugs, so that much smaller doses may be needed. Genetic factors may also be responsible for variations in metabolism.
- Prescribe as few drugs as possible and give clear instructions to elderly patients or any patient likely to misunderstand complicated instructions.
- Wherever possible use a familiar drug. With a new drug be particularly alert for adverse reactions or unexpected events.
- If serious adverse events are liable to occur warn the patient.

[MCA and CSM, 2002; BNF 47, 2004]

Additional reporting

- The Drug Safety Research Unit is an independent scheme that identifies patients who have been prescribed selected new medicines. The effect of these drugs is monitored by collating data on clinical events in these patients. The data are submitted on a voluntary basis by general practitioners on green forms. More information on the scheme and access to the Unit's educational material is available from dsru.org.

References

NHS staff in England can link, free of charge, from references to full text journals by clicking on [Full text] on the PRODIGY website.

1. Beijer, H.J. and de Blaey, C.J. (2002) Hospitalisations caused by adverse drug reactions (ADR): a meta-analysis of observational studies. *Pharmacy World & Science* 24(2), 46–54. [Full text]
2. BNF 47 (2004) *British National Formulary*. 47th edn. London: British Medical Association and Royal Pharmaceutical Society of Great Britain.
3. Clarkson, A., Choonara, I. and Marcovitch, H. (2002) Surveillance for fatal suspected adverse drug reactions in the UK. *Archives of Disease in Childhood* 87(6), 462–467. [Full text]
4. Ferner, R.E. (2003) Adverse drug reactions. *Medicine* 31(8), 20–24.
5. Martys, C.R. (1979) Adverse reactions to drugs in general practice. *British Medical Journal* 2(6199), 1194–1197.
6. MCA and CSM (2002) *Suspected adverse drug reactions (ADR) reporting and the yellow card scheme.* mhra.gov.uk [Accessed: 17/11/2003].

PRODIGY GUIDANCE

Alcohol — problem drinking

Last revised in June 2004
www.prodigy.nhs.uk/guidance.asp?gt=Alcohol - problem drinking

Applies to people over the age of 16 years

This guidance is based on the Scottish Intercollegiate Guidelines Network (SIGN) Guideline *The management of harmful drinking and alcohol dependence in primary care* (September 2003).

This guidance covers the identification and management of hazardous and harmful drinking, with or without alcohol dependence. It also covers alcohol detoxification in primary care and the maintenance of abstinence following detoxification.

This guidance does not cover in detail problem drinking in pregnancy, the management of acute alcohol intoxication, and the management of alcohol-related disabilities (physical or social).

There is separate PRODIGY guidance for *Depression, Hypnotic or anxiolytic dependence,* and *Opioid dependence.*

Goals

Reduction or cessation of drinking so that harm is prevented or risk of harm reduced
Where appropriate, safe and effective detoxification in primary care
Maintenance of abstinence where possible

Contents

Scenarios

- Detoxification — moderate/severe dependence p.21
- Hazardous drinker, minimal intervention p.23
- Maintaining abstinence p.24

Extended Information, p. 25

Which scenario?

Detoxification — moderate/severe dependence: covers the management of detoxification of people with moderate or severe dependence on alcohol.
Hazardous drinker, minimal intervention: covers the management of hazardous drinkers, i.e. those drinkers whose level or pattern of alcohol consumption is likely to result in harm if present drinking habits persist. Men regularly drinking more than 5 units per day and women regularly drinking more than 3 units per day can be regarded as hazardous drinkers.
Maintaining abstinence: covers the maintenance of abstinence following successful detoxification.

Detoxification — moderate/ severe dependence

Which therapy?

- **Confirm dependence,** as detoxification only needs to be considered for dependent drinkers. Mild dependence in some people can be managed without pharmacological detoxification.
- **Benzodiazepines are the drugs of choice in the treatment of acute alcohol withdrawal** if pharmacological detoxification is considered appropriate.
  - Chlordiazepoxide is recommended.
  - **Reduce the dosage of chlordiazepoxide over 5–7 days.** The initial dose and length of treatment will depend on the severity of alcohol dependence and on individual patient factors (e.g. weight, gender, liver function).
  - Dispense detoxification medication daily.
- **Prescribe thiamine throughout the detoxification** at a daily dosage of 200–300 mg in divided doses.
- **Management should also include reassurance, hydration, nutrition, and monitoring of the signs and symptoms of withdrawal.**
- **Involve family and friends** wherever possible.

Practical prescribing points

For further information see the *Medicines Compendium* (www.medicines.org.uk) or the *British National Formulary* (www.bnf.org).

Benzodiazepines

- **Elderly people:** increased risk of ataxia and confusion, leading to falls. Use half the normal dose in elderly or debilitated people.
- **Respiratory disease:** increased risk of respiratory depression. Monitor closely for signs of respiratory depression.
- **Severe hepatic impairment:** use a benzodiazepine that is not hepatically metabolized, such as oxazepam or lorazepam (chlordiazepoxide 15 mg = oxazepam 15 mg = lorazepam 500 micrograms). Specialist advice is recommended in this situation.

Follow-up advice

- **Daily review throughout the detoxification is recommended,** if possible, and again after detoxification has finished. This allows the early detection of complications and encouragement for the person to continue. Confirm abstinence by checking for alcohol on the breath, or using a breathalyser.
- **See the scenario *Maintaining abstinence* for management following detoxification.**
- **Abnormal laboratory findings** should be monitored.

Should I refer or investigate?

Refer?

- Community psychiatric nurse (CPN) support may be useful.
- **Inpatient detoxification should be considered for people with:**
  - Confusion or hallucinations
  - A history of previously complicated withdrawal (e.g. withdrawal seizures or delirium tremens)
  - Epilepsy or a history of seizures
  - Malnourishment

  - Severe vomiting or diarrhoea
  - Increased risk of suicide
  - Severe dependence coupled with unwillingness to be seen daily
  - A previously failed detoxification at home
  - Uncontrollable withdrawal symptoms
  - An acute physical or psychiatric illness
  - Multiple substance misuse
  - A home environment unsupportive of abstinence
- **Severe deficiency states such as Wernicke's encephalopathy and Korsakoff's psychosis** require hospital admission [Haines and Wiseman, 1992].
- **Delirium tremens is associated with significant mortality and urgent hospital admission should be considered.**

Investigate?

- **Full blood count** (FBC) **and liver function tests** (LFTs). FBC with a raised mean corpuscular volume (MCV), and LFTs with raised transaminases, alkaline phosphatase, or bilirubin, can be useful for:
  - **Diagnosis** of liver disease in individuals drinking at harmful levels. Raised alkaline phosphatase and bilirubin are indicative of serious liver damage.
  - **Monitoring progress** — following cessation of drinking, gamma-glutamyl transferase (GGT) levels return to normal after several weeks, unless there is significant liver damage. MCV will remain elevated for months, reflecting the 120-day lifespan of red blood cells.

Patient information leaflets

The following PILs are available at www.prodigy.nhs.uk

- Al-Anon (for families and friends of alcoholics)
- Alcohol and Sensible Drinking
- Alcohol - A Summary
- Alcohol Concern
- Alcoholics Anonymous
- Alcoholism and Problem Drinking
- Blood Test - Blood Count and Smear
- Blood Test - General
- Blood Test - Liver Function Tests
- Drinkline
- National Association for Children of Alcoholics
- Scoring of the Alcohol Use Disorders Identification Test - AUDIT

Shared decision making

- **'Detoxification'** is advised for your problem drinking.
- **Chlordiazepoxide** will ease withdrawal symptoms.
  - The dose is high to start with.
  - It is gradually reduced over 5–7 days and then stopped.
- **Vitamin B_1 tablets** (thiamine) are also advised as some people with alcohol problems have a low level of this vitamin.
- During detox:
  - You must not drink any alcohol.
  - A breathalyser may be used to confirm that you are not drinking.
  - Your GP or practice nurse will usually see you quite often.
  - Support from family or friends can be of great help.

Drug rationale

Drugs not included

- **Benzodiazepines other than chlordiazepoxide:** although all benzodiazepines appear equally efficacious in reducing the signs and symptoms of withdrawal, the shorter-acting agents (e.g. oxazepam, lorazepam) may not provide a smooth withdrawal, and those with a rapid onset of action (e.g. diazepam) have a higher potential for abuse [Mayo-Smith, 1997; Holbrook et al, 1999b]. The use of clomethiazole is not recommended as it induces dependence, and in overdose or in combination with alcohol may cause respiratory failure and coma [DH et al, 1999].
- **Anticonvulsants other than benzodiazepines** have limited evidence for a role in treating delirium, or preventing seizures in some patients [Mayo-Smith, 1997].
- **Beta-blockers** reduce the autonomic manifestations of withdrawal, but may increase the incidence of delirium [Mayo-Smith, 1997].
- **Neuroleptics** are not recommended for routine use or prophylaxis during detoxification because of a lack of evidence of efficacy, and they may lower the seizure threshold [Holbrook et al, 1999a].
- **Other agents such as alpha-agonists, clonidine, lithium, or serotonergic drugs** show little or no evidence of benefit [Mayo-Smith, 1997; Swift, 1999].
- **Intravenous vitamin B** preparations are not included, as their use is restricted to patients in whom parenteral treatment is essential, and facilities for treating anaphylaxis should be available when these preparations are administered [CSM, 1989].
- **Acamprosate and disulfiram** are licensed for the maintenance of abstinence. If used, they should be initiated after a patient has undergone detoxification.

Drugs included

- **Chlordiazepoxide** is recommended for acute alcohol detoxification [SIGN, 2003]. A tapering dose is recommended, with a maximum duration of 7 days. The regimen used should be based on the severity of alcohol dependence and on individual patient factors. The 7-day regimen, adapted from the Department of Health recommendations [DH et al, 1999], is offered as an example. Local protocols may be available.
- **Thiamine** preparations. There appears to be no consensus over the most effective dose or preparation [Hardman et al, 1996; Ashworth and Gerada, 1997; Speight and Holford, 1997; DH et al, 1999; Holbrook et al, 1999a]. As detoxification may precipitate Wernicke's encephalopathy, high-dose thiamine (200–300 mg a day in divided doses) seems appropriate for people undergoing detoxification.

Prescriptions

Chlordiazepoxide detoxification regimen (over 7 days)

Day 1 or 2: chlordiazepoxide 20mg four times a day

- Age from 16 years onwards
- Chlordiazepoxide 10mg capsules. Take two capsules four times a day; supply 8 capsules; NHS Cost £0.46.

Day 3 or 4: chlordiazepoxide 15mg four times a day

- Age from 16 years onwards
- Chlordiazepoxide 5mg capsules. Take three capsules four times a day; supply 12 capsules; NHS Cost £0.48.

Day 5: chlordiazepoxide 10mg four times a day

- Age from 16 years onwards
- Chlordiazepoxide 10mg capsules. Take one capsule four times a day; supply 4 capsules; NHS Cost £0.23.

Day 6: chlordiazepoxide 10mg twice a day

- Age from 16 years onwards
- Chlordiazepoxide 10mg capsules. Take one capsule twice a day; supply 2 capsules; NHS Cost £0.11.

ay 7: chlordiazepoxide 10mg at night
Age from 16 years onwards
Chlordiazepoxide 10mg capsules. Take one capsule at night; supply 1 capsules; NHS Cost £0.06.

hiamine: high dose (7-day supply)

iamine 100mg twice a day
Age from 16 years onwards
Thiamine 100mg tablets. Take one tablet twice a day; supply 14 tablets; NHS Cost £0.86.

iamine 100mg three times a day
Age from 16 years onwards
Thiamine 100mg tablets. Take one tablet three times a day; supply 21 tablets; NHS Cost £1.29.

Hazardous drinker, minimal intervention

Which therapy?

Hazardous and harmful drinkers can be identified using the Alcohol Use Disorders Identification Test (AUDIT) questionnaire; this is available as a *Patient information leaflet*.

Minimal interventions are effective in the management of hazardous drinking, i.e. for patients whose level or pattern of alcohol consumption is likely to result in harm if present drinking habits persist. Men regularly drinking more than 5 units per day and women regularly drinking more than 3 units per day can be regarded as hazardous drinkers.

Minimal interventions usually include:

- Assessment of alcohol intake.
- Explanation of sensible/low risk drinking.
- **Explanation of the type of harm which can arise from excessive drinking,** e.g. hypertension, liver disease, cancer, accidents, poor work performance, financial worries.
- **Positive reasons for drinking less,** e.g. lower risk of accidents, reduction of blood pressure if raised, fewer hangovers, more money available.
- Giving advice on reducing alcohol consumption to safe limits.
- **Keeping a regular drinking diary** as a way of measuring progress and adherence to low risk drinking.
- Giving a patient information leaflet.

People with chronic alcohol dependence are likely to be deficient in vitamins, especially thiamine. Consider prescribing thiamine for people who have long-standing dependence or who appear malnourished.

Practical prescribing points

For further information please see the *Medicines Compendium* (www.medicines.org) **or the** *British National Formulary* (www.bnf.org).

Should I refer or investigate?

Refer?

- **Hazardous drinking can be managed in primary care or other community settings.**
- **Consider referral for those patients with:**
  - Harmful drinking (damage has been caused to the physical or mental health of the drinker)
  - Alcohol dependence
  - Psychiatric comorbidity
- **Delirium tremens** is associated with a significant mortality and urgent hospital admission must be considered.
- **People who show substantial psychiatric comorbidity should be referred to specialist mental health services.**

Investigate?

- **Full blood count (FBC) and liver function tests (LFTs).** FBC with a raised mean corpuscular volume (MCV), and LFTs with raised transaminases, alkaline phosphatase, or bilirubin, can be useful for:
  - **Diagnosis** of liver disease in individuals drinking at harmful levels. Raised alkaline phosphatase and bilirubin are indicative of serious liver damage.
  - **Monitoring progress** — following cessation of drinking, gamma-glutamyl transferase (GGT) levels return to normal after several weeks, unless there is significant liver damage. MCV will remain elevated for months, reflecting the 120-day lifespan of red blood cells.

Patient information leaflets

The following PILs are available at www.prodigy.nhs.uk

- Al-Anon (for families and friends of alcoholics)
- Alcohol and Sensible Drinking
- Alcohol - A Summary
- Alcohol Concern
- Alcoholics Anonymous
- Alcoholism and Problem Drinking
- Biopsy - Liver
- Blood Test - Blood Count and Smear
- Blood Test - General
- Blood Test - Liver Function Tests
- Cognitive Behaviour Therapy (CBT)
- Drinkline
- National Association for Children of Alcoholics
- Scoring of the Alcohol Use Disorders Identification Test - AUDIT

Drug rationale

Drugs not included

- **Multivitamin preparations and vitamin B compound preparations** are not offered as the amount of thiamine available in these preparations is small.

Drugs included

- **Thiamine (vitamin B_1)** supplementation is recommended indefinitely for people who have a chronic alcohol problem, as their diet may be deficient [SIGN, 2003].

Prescriptions

Advice note

Advice only: reducing alcohol intake

- Age from 16 years onwards
- Your doctor has advised you that you are drinking at a level which could cause you problems. Your health or other parts of your life may suffer because of your drinking. For men, the recommended safe limits for drinking are: no more than 3 units per day, and no more than 21 units per week. For women, the recommended safe limits for drinking are: no more than 2 units per day, and no more than 14 units per week. A 'unit' is equivalent to: half a pint of ordinary strength beer, lager or cider, or 1 small glass of wine, or 1 single measure of spirits, or 1 small glass of sherry.

Thiamine: low dose

Thiamine 50mg twice a day
- Age from 16 years onwards
- Thiamine 50mg tablets. Take one tablet twice a day; supply 56 tablets; NHS Cost £2.23.

A

Maintaining abstinence

Which therapy?

- **Abstinence** is recommended if alcohol dependence is established or if there is marked physical damage.
- **Relapse** is not uncommon. Further attempts at alcohol withdrawal may be successful.
- **Psychosocial treatments and acamprosate are effective at preventing relapse.**
- **Psychosocial treatments are usually delivered by specialist workers** in alcohol specialist agencies, but may be offered in primary care by those with an interest, sometimes on a shared-care basis. Psychosocial treatments include:
  - Behavioural self-control training
  - Coping/social skills training
  - Marital/family therapy
  - Motivational enhancement therapy
- **Offer acamprosate to people who are newly detoxified, as an adjunct to psychosocial interventions.**
  - Initiate acamprosate immediately after successful detoxification, and continue treatment for up to 1 year.
  - Review treatment regularly. Do not stop treatment if the person relapses; however, if there is not a major reduction in drinking, consider withdrawal.

Practical prescribing points

For further information see the *Medicines Compendium* (www.medicines.org.uk) or the *British National Formulary* (www.bnf.org).

Follow-up advice

- Primary care teams should maintain contact over the long term with people previously treated by specialist services for alcohol dependence. Maintaining contact with someone with alcohol dependence is an important factor in maintaining abstinence. Contact need only be brief and may be maintained, for example, by telephone or brief appointment.
- Acamprosate is not effective in all people, so its efficacy should be assessed at regular appointments and the drug withdrawn if there has not been a major reduction in drinking.

Should I refer or investigate?

Refer?

- **Referral to secondary care may be necessary for psychosocial treatments** if these are unavailable in primary care. They include:
  - Behavioural self-control training
  - Coping/social skills training
  - Marital/family therapy
  - Motivational enhancement therapy
- **Patients who show substantial psychiatric comorbidity should be referred to specialist mental health services.**

Investigate?

- Blood tests can be useful for monitoring progress. Following cessation of drinking, gamma-glutamyl transferase (GGT) levels return to normal after several weeks, unless there is significant liver damage. Mean ce volume (MCV) will remain elevated for months, reflecting the 120-day lifespan of red blood cells.

Patient information leaflets

The following PILs are available at www.prodigy.nhs.uk
- Blood Test - Blood Count and Smear
- Blood Test - General
- Blood Test - Liver Function Tests
- Cognitive Behaviour Therapy (CBT)

Shared decision making

- **Acamprosate** is a medicine which helps to ease alcohol cravings. It is often prescribed to people after alcohol detox.
- Other support, counselling, or 'talking' treatments may also help you to keep stay off alcohol.
- Self-help groups such as Alcoholics Anonymous have also helped many people to stay off alcohol.

Drug rationale

Drugs not included

- **Supervised oral disulfiram** may be used to prevent relapse. However, it should only be initiated in a hospit or specialized clinic, and by physicians experienced in it use.
- **Naltrexone** increases the rates of abstinence, and decreases relapse rates in alcohol-dependent people wh have undergone detoxification. However, naltrexone is not licensed for the treatment of alcohol dependence, and should not be initiated for this purpose in primary care [SIGN, 2003].

Drugs included

- **Acamprosate** is recommended as an 'anti-craving agent' in newly detoxified dependent people as an adjunct to psychosocial interventions. It is licensed for use for up t 1 year. Acamprosate will usually be initiated by a specialist service within a few days of successful detoxification. However, if a specialist service is not available, the GP should offer acamprosate and monito its efficacy [SIGN, 2003].
- Prescriptions are offered for 2 and 4 weeks depending o the frequency of follow-up appointments.

Prescriptions

Advice note

Advice only: maintaining abstinence
- Age from 16 years onwards
- You have stopped drinking, which is good. To help you to stay off alcohol your doctor may recommend you to a specialist for support, counselling, or 'talking' treatments. In addition to this your doctor may start yo on acamprosate, a medicine that helps to ease alcohol cravings. Self-help groups such as Alcoholics Anonymous have also helped many people to stay off alcohol.

Acamprosate (2-week supply)

Acamprosate (person weighs less than 60kg)
Age from 18 to 65 years
Acamprosate 333mg e/c tablets. Take two tablets in the morning; take one tablet at midday; and take one tablet at night; supply 56 tablets; NHS Cost £9.64.

Acamprosate (person weighs 60kg or more)
Age from 18 to 65 years
Acamprosate 333mg e/c tablets. Take two tablets three times a day; supply 84 tablets; NHS Cost £14.46.

Acamprosate (4-week supply)

Acamprosate (person weighs less than 60kg)
Age from 18 to 65 years
Acamprosate 333mg e/c tablets. Take two tablets in the morning; take one tablet at midday; and take one tablet at night; supply 112 tablets; NHS Cost £19.28.

Acamprosate (person weighs 60kg or more)
Age from 18 to 65 years
Acamprosate 333mg e/c tablets. Take two tablets three times a day; supply 168 tablets; NHS Cost £28.92.

Extended Information

Background information

What is it? p.25
How common is it? p.25
How do I know my patient has a drink problem? p.26
Clinical presentations where the role of alcohol should be considered p.27
Complications and prognosis p.27

What is it?

There are many different terminologies describing both safe and excessive drinking; the following highlights those in common use.

Unit of alcohol

One unit of alcohol in the United Kingdom is defined as a drink containing 8 g of ethanol. This is equivalent to:

- Half a pint of average strength beer, lager, or cider (3–4% alcohol by volume)
- Small pub measure (25 ml) of spirits (40% alcohol by volume)
- Standard pub measure (50 ml) of fortified wine, e.g. sherry, port (20% alcohol by volume)

A small glass (125 ml) of average strength wine (12% alcohol by volume) contains 1.5 units of alcohol.
A standard pub measure (35 ml) of spirits (40% alcohol by volume) contains 1.5 units of alcohol.

Sensible drinking

Sensible drinking limits were defined in the Government White Paper *The health of the nation* (1992) as a weekly alcohol consumption of less than 21 units for men and 14 units for women.
A joint review of safe limits by the Royal Colleges of Psychiatrists, Physicians, and General Practitioners concluded that the defined limit of a weekly alcohol intake of 21 units for men and 14 units for women should remain unchanged [Royal College of Physicians et al, 1995].
A further report, *Sensible drinking* [DH, 1995] states that:

- A regular consumption of 3–4 units a day by men and 2–3 units a day by women will not cause any significant health risk. Consistent drinking of 4 or more units a day by men and 3 or more units a day by women is not advised, as this carries a progressive health risk.
- Binge drinking and intoxication should be avoided. If such episodes do occur, it is advisable to then refrain from drinking for 48 hours.
- The report also advises that men over 40 and postmenopausal women may reduce the risk of coronary heart disease by drinking 1–2 units of alcohol per day [DH, 1995].

Sensible drinking during pregnancy

- The Royal College of Obstetricians and Gynaecologists (RCOG) recommends that pregnant women should drink no more than 1 unit/day, whereas advice from the Health Education Authority states that women trying to become pregnant or at any stage of pregnancy should avoid intoxication and drink no more than 1–2 units/week. Others believe abstention is prudent [Guerri et al, 1999; RCOG, 1999].

Hazardous drinking

- **Hazardous drinking is defined** as the regular consumption of:
  - More than 5 units of alcohol daily for men
  - More than 3 units of alcohol daily for women
- Hazardous drinking on average doubles a man's risk for liver disease, raised blood pressure, some cancers, and violent death.
- Hazardous drinking increases a woman's risk for liver disease and breast cancer.

[SIGN, 2003]

Harmful drinking

- **Harmful drinking is defined** in the International Classification of Diseases (ICD-10) as a pattern of drinking that causes damage to physical or mental health secondary to heavy consumption of alcohol.
- A diagnosis of harmful drinking requires that actual damage has been caused to the physical or mental health of the drinker.

[WHO, 1992; SIGN, 2003]

Alcohol dependence

- **Alcohol dependence is defined** in the ICD-10 as a cluster of physiological, behavioural, and cognitive phenomena in which the use of alcohol takes on a much higher priority for a given individual than other behaviours that previously had greater value [WHO, 1992].
- A central characteristic is the desire (often strong, sometimes overpowering) to drink alcohol.
- A return to drinking after a period of abstinence is often associated with a rapid reappearance of the features of the syndrome (priming).

[SIGN, 2003]

Binge drinking

- **Binge drinking is defined** as drinking over half the recommended number of units of alcohol per week in one session, i.e. over 10 units for men or 7 units for women [Health Education Authority, 1997; Raistrick et al, 1999].

How common is it?

- The most up-to-date information on alcohol use in England is from the General Household Survey taken in 2001, and shows that:
  - Seventy-four per cent of men and 60% of women had drunk alcohol on at least 1 day during the previous week.

- Thirty-eight per cent of men had drunk more than 4 units of alcohol on at least 1 day during the previous week. Twenty-one per cent of men had drunk more than 8 units of alcohol on at least 1 day during the previous week.
- Twenty-two per cent of women had drunk more than 3 units of alcohol on at least 1 day during the previous week. Nine per cent of women had drunk more than 6 units of alcohol on at least 1 day during the previous week.
- Average weekly alcohol consumption was 16.9 units for men and 7.5 units for women.
- Twenty-seven per cent of men and 15% of women drank more than 21 and 14 units a week respectively. Drinking at these levels has remained stable for men since 1992; for women it has risen from 12% to 15% over the same period.

[DH, 2003]

- The most up-to-date information on alcohol use in young people in England is from 2001 and shows that:
  - Twenty-six per cent of pupils aged 11–15 years had drunk alcohol in the previous week.
  - Boys were more likely than girls to have had a drink, with 28% of boys and 25% of girls having had a drink in the previous week.
  - The number drinking rises sharply with age — 6% of those aged 11 years, compared with 52% of those aged 15 years, had drunk alcohol in the previous week.

[DH, 2002]

How do I know my patient has a drink problem?

Presentation

- **Opportunistic detection** of problem drinking or alcohol dependence when an individual presents with an unrelated condition or for a health check, e.g. new patient medical examination.
- **An active request for help** with problem drinking or alcohol dependence, from either the patient themselves, or friends or relatives.
- **Presentation with medical, psychiatric, or social problems/complications** related to problem drinking or dependence (see *Complications* section).
- **Suspicion of alcohol problems may be raised** when a person frequently requests sick notes, or presents with conditions that could be related to heavy drinking (e.g. gastritis and hypertension).
- **Certain physical signs** have been linked to heavy drinking:
  - Injuries (including those in the elderly)
  - Tremor of the hands and tongue
  - Excessive capillarization of the facial skin and conjunctivae
- **Abnormal blood test results** may be suggestive of excessive alcohol consumption:
  - Raised gamma-glutamyl transferase (GGT)
  - Raised mean corpuscular volume (MCV)
  - Raised fasting triglycerides
- **Dependency on other drugs of misuse:** alcohol and drug misuse are commonly associated in young drug misusers.
- **Symptoms of withdrawal:** these may occur on sudden cessation of use, vary in severity, and include tremor, nausea, vomiting, sweating. Generalized convulsions may also occur. Onset is 3–6 hours after the last drink, and symptoms usually last 5–7 days.
- **Delirium tremens:** this occurs in approximately 5% of those suffering from alcohol withdrawal. Delirium tremens is associated with appreciable mortality and urgent hospital admission is recommended. Symptoms such as agitation, confusion, paranoia, and visual and auditory hallucinations occur 48–72 hours after the las[t] drink. Complications include seizures, hyperthermia, dehydration, electrolyte imbalance, shock, and chest infection.

The Alcohol Use Disorders Identification Test

- **The Alcohol Use Disorders Identification Test (the AUDIT questionnaire)** has been developed by the Wor[ld] Health Organization as a screening instrument for hazardous and harmful alcohol consumption. It is designed to be administered by primary health care workers. A copy can be printed using this guidance; see *Patient information leaflets* section.
- **The 10-item questionnaire takes about 2 minutes to complete** and covers alcohol consumption, drinking behaviour, and alcohol-related problems.
  - A score of 8 or more in men and 7 or more in women indicates a strong likelihood of hazardous or harmful alcohol consumption.
  - A score of 13 or more is indicative of significant alcohol-related harm/dependence and further assessment is advisable.
- **Sensitivity is 92%** (higher in men), i.e. a negative result from the AUDIT questionnaire (or a score lower than 7 in women, 8 in men) effectively rules out a diagnosis of harmful or hazardous alcohol consumption.
- **Specificity is 93%** (higher in women), i.e. a positive resu[lt] from the AUDIT questionnaire (or a score of 8 or more in men, 7 or more in women) effectively rules in a diagnosis of harmful or hazardous alcohol consumptior[n]

[Saunders et al, 1993; Anderson, 1996; Bradley et al, 1998]

How do I know if there is dependence on alcohol?

- **There is a high index of suspicion for dependence** in me[n] drinking more than 50 units per week and in women drinking more than 35 units per week.
- **The diagnosis of alcohol dependence can be made using the ICD-10 criteria.** According to these criteria, dependence is diagnosed if three or more of the following have been present together during the previou[s] year:
  - A strong desire or sense of compulsion to drink alcohol.
  - Difficulty in controlling drinking in terms of its onset, termination, or level of use.
  - A physiological withdrawal state (e.g. tremor, sweating, rapid heart rate, anxiety, insomnia, or, less commonly, seizures, disorientation, hallucinations) when drinking has ceased or reduced; or drinking to relieve or avoid such a withdrawal state.
  - Evidence of tolerance, such that increased doses of alcohol are required in order to achieve effects originally produced by lower doses.
  - Progressive neglect of alternative pleasures or interests because of drinking; and increased amounts of time necessary to obtain or take alcohol, or to recover from its effects.
  - Persisting with alcohol use despite awareness of overtly harmful consequences.

[WHO, 1992; SIGN, 2003]

How do I assess the degree of alcohol dependence?

- **It is important to determine the degree of alcohol dependence,** as this dictates management strategy. This strategy may involve minimal interventions, brief treatments, intensive interventions in specialist settings, or pharmacological detoxification.
- **Indicators of a high degree of dependence include:**
  - Regular morning drinking

- Increased tolerance to alcohol
- Withdrawal symptoms (see above)
- Relief drinking to avoid withdrawal symptoms
- Less ability to choose when to drink and when to abstain (stereotypical drinking)
- Structuring of life around alcohol
- Blackouts (episodes of memory loss)
- Previous withdrawal

Measurement of the degree of alcohol dependence is possible by questionnaire, e.g. the Severity of Alcohol Dependence Questionnaire (SADQ) [Stockwell et al, 1979]. This is not routine in primary care.

Further evaluation

Assessment of:
- Physical health
- Mental health
- Vocational, social, and interpersonal or relationship factors
- Legal status and criminal activity
- Poly-drug use, and HIV or hepatitis risk-taking where relevant

[Abdulrahim et al, 1999]

Blood tests can be useful for diagnosis of liver disease in people drinking at harmful levels. Liver function tests may show raised transaminases, alkaline phosphatase, or bilirubin; with raised alkaline phosphatase and bilirubin being indicative of serious liver damage.

Monitoring progress: following reduction/cessation of drinking, gamma-glutamyl transferase (GGT) levels return to normal after several weeks unless there is significant liver damage. Mean corpuscular volume (MCV) will remain elevated for months, reflecting the 120-day lifespan of red blood cells.

[Edwards et al, 1997]

Clinical presentations where the role of alcohol should be considered

Social

- Marital disharmony and domestic violence
- Neglect of children
- Criminal behaviour (e.g. driving offences, breach of the peace, shoplifting)
- Unsafe sex
- Financial problems

Occupational

- Repeated absenteeism, especially around weekends
- Impaired work performance and accidents
- Poor employment record

Psychiatric

- Amnesia, memory disorders, and dementia
- Anxiety and panic disorders
- Depression
- Hallucinations
- Treatment resistance, and a cause of relapse, in other psychiatric illness
- Self harm

Physical

- Multiple presentations to accident and emergency with trauma and head injury
- Dyspepsia, gastritis, and haematemesis
- Diarrhoea and malabsorption
- Pancreatitis
- Liver abnormalities: deranged liver function tests, hepatitis, fatty liver, and cirrhosis
- Arrhythmias
- Hypertension and stroke
- Cardiomyopathy
- Peripheral neuropathy and cerebellar ataxia
- Impotence and problems with libido
- Withdrawal seizures starting in middle age
- Falls and collapses in the elderly
- Blood dyscrasias (e.g. low platelet count, low neutrophil count)
- Acne rosacea, discoid eczema, psoriasis, multiple bruising
- Cancers of the mouth, pharynx, larynx, oesophagus, breast, and colon
- Acute and chronic myopathies
- Unexplained infertility
- Gout

[SIGN, 2003]

Complications and prognosis

Complications

- **Alcohol-related mortality:** estimates of alcohol-related deaths for England and Wales range from 5,000 to 40,000 per year, and 25% of these deaths result from accidents [Health Education Authority, 1997].
- **Cancer:** alcohol causes an increased risk of squamous carcinoma of the oropharynx, larynx, and oesophagus (linear dose–response relationship). Heavy alcohol consumption is associated with carcinoma of the liver, stomach, colon, rectum, lung, pancreas, and breast [Health Education Authority, 1997].
- **Cardiovascular disease:** excessive alcohol consumption increases the risk of raised blood pressure (binge drinking may be particularly implicated), haemorrhagic stroke, coronary heart disease, cardiomyopathy, and arrhythmias. Alcohol consumption of 1–2 units per day is believed to have a cardioprotective effect in men over 40 years and postmenopausal women, and to protect against ischaemic stroke [Health Education Authority, 1997].
- **Liver damage:** in people who drink excessive amounts of alcohol, liver damage is common. Fatty liver, present in 90% of persistently heavy drinkers, is usually asymptomatic. Alcoholic hepatitis occurs in about 40% of heavy drinkers and is often the precursor to cirrhosis. Between 8% and 30% of long-term heavy drinkers develop cirrhosis. It is thought that 20 units of alcohol daily for 5 years, in men, is probably the minimum intake associated with significant liver damage [Health Education Authority, 1997; Raistrick et al, 1999].
- **Risk to the fetus:** maternal consumption of 15 units per week or more has been associated with a reduction in birth weight. Consumption in excess of 20 units per week is associated with intellectual impairment in children. Fetal alcohol syndrome (brain damage, prenatal and postnatal growth retardation, and facial malformations) is relatively uncommon even among heavily drinking pregnant women. It occurs in approximately a third of children born to women who drink about 18 units per day [RCOG, 1999].
- **Psychiatric morbidity:** this is common in heavy drinkers (excess of 10 units per day) and includes depression; suicide and attempted suicide; personality deterioration; sexual problems; hallucinations (auditory and visual, usually during withdrawal, but sometimes occurring without the other features of delirium tremens; and also, more rarely, distressing auditory hallucinations occurring in clear consciousness); amnesia; intellectual impairment; and delirium tremens [Ashworth and Gerada, 1997; Health Education Authority, 1997].
- **Social consequences:** it has been estimated that 30% of divorces, 40% of domestic violence, and 20% of child

A

abuse cases are associated with excessive alcohol consumption. Heavy drinking is also associated with workplace absenteeism, financial problems and homelessness [Health Education Authority, 1997].
- **Delirium tremens** can be complicated by seizures, hyperthermia, dehydration, electrolyte imbalance, shock, and chest infection. It is associated with appreciable mortality and urgent hospital admission must be considered [Ashworth and Gerada, 1997].
- **Other serious medical complications** include gastrointestinal haemorrhage, pancreatitis, and neurological problems such as seizures, neuropathy, acute confusional states, subdural haematoma, Wernicke's encephalopathy, and Korsakoff's psychosis.

Prognosis

- Many people with alcohol-related problems overcome them without any formal treatment. A rough estimate is that a third will improve naturally.
- People treated for alcohol-related problems achieve outcomes that lie on a continuum. About two-thirds will show some improvement after treatment.

[Anderson, 1996; Raistrick et al, 1999]

Management issues

- General issues p.28
- Driving licence implications p.28
- Reducing alcohol intake p.28
- Detoxification p.29
- Maintaining abstinence p.31
- Medicines management p.31

General issues

- **Opportunistic interventions in hazardous drinkers are recommended,** to reduce alcohol consumption to low risk levels before serious problems or dependence develop.
- **A spectrum of interventions has been suggested,** as there is a spectrum of alcohol consumption and alcohol-related problems.
  - People who drink excessively, with few or no alcohol-related problems and a low or no degree of dependence, are suitable for minimal interventions in generalist settings (e.g. primary care, accident and emergency).
  - People with definite alcohol-related problems but only a moderate degree of dependence are suitable for brief treatments in generalist or specialist settings.
  - People with definite alcohol-related problems and a severe degree of dependence are suitable for intensive treatments, usually in specialist settings.
- **Involvement of family and friends** is important in the management of problem drinking.
- **Self-help groups** may be useful for some problem drinkers (e.g. Alcoholics Anonymous (AA), Women for Sobriety, Secular Organisations for Sobriety). Al-Anon helps relatives, friends, and colleagues of problem drinkers; and Al-Teen helps young people who have a parent, relative, or friend with an alcohol problem.
- **Abstinence** (long-term) is usually recommended if alcohol dependence is established or if there is marked physical damage.
- **Relapse** back to heavy drinking after detoxification is common. Dealing with, and learning from, relapse is often a part of recovery. Further attempts at alcohol withdrawal may be successful.
- **Treatment of psychiatric comorbidities:** evidence shows that treatment with antidepressants or buspirone relieves depression or anxiety, but does not show any positive effects on alcohol dependence in alcoholics with psychiatric comorbidity [Berglund et al, 2003].

Driving licence implications

- **Persistent alcohol misuse,** confirmed by medical enquiry or by evidence of otherwise unexplained abnormal blood markers or both, requires licence revocation or refusal for a minimum of 6 months (1 year for vocational licence), during which time abstinence or controlled drinking should be attained with normalization of blood parameters.
- **Alcohol dependence** indicators may include a history of detoxification or alcohol-related seizures or both. Alcohol dependence, confirmed by medical enquiry, requires a recommended 1-year period of revocation or refusal of the driving licence. During this period, abstinence or controlled drinking only should be attained, with normalization of blood parameters if relevant. Vocational licensing will not be granted where there is a history of alcohol dependency within the past 3 years.

[Haines and Wiseman, 1992; Edwards et al, 1997; DH et al, 1999; DVLA, 2003]

Reducing alcohol intake

In the past the terms 'minimal intervention' and 'brief treatment' have been used interchangeably, whereas they should be clearly distinguished [Alcohol Concern, 1997].

Minimal interventions

- **The aim of minimal intervention is to alert people who are drinking too much and get them to cut down** before they come to any significant harm.
- **An assessment of alcohol intake is followed by a few minutes of information** on sensible or low-risk alcohol consumption, and on harmful and hazardous drinking, with advice and encouragement.
- Patient information leaflets may also be given. They are most appropriately directed at excessive drinkers who are not complaining about, or seeking help for, an alcohol problem and therefore must be identified opportunistically.
- **The Alcohol Use Disorders Identification Test (AUDIT) questionnaire** was specifically designed to detect harmful and hazardous drinkers in primary care. A copy can be printed using this guidance; see *Patient information leaflets* section.
- A World Health Organization trial found that 20 minutes of assessment followed by 5 minutes of advice and an information booklet was effective in reducing alcohol intake in adults who drank excessively but showed no signs of dependence. Overall, men in the intervention group reduced their alcohol consumption by 25% compared with the assessment-only group. Women showed a 10% reduction in the intervention group compared with the assessment-only group. However, among women, there were considerable reductions in both intervention and assessment-only groups, possibly reflecting an effect from the assessment itself.
- **Self-help manuals** are another form of minimal intervention. They can be utilized as an adjunct to counselling, a form of continued intervention after counselling or as an alternative to counselling. They should clearly state that they are not aimed at those with serious problems.

[Babor and Grant, 1992; Anderson, 1996; Abdulrahim et al, 1999; Raistrick, 1999]

Brief treatments

- **Brief treatments** are a collection of planned and structured interventions. The most popular form of brief treatment currently available is motivational interviewing.

Brief treatments take longer and are more intensive than minimal interventions. They typically involve a total of 3–4 hours of detailed assessment and counselling.

Brief treatments are usually delivered by specialist workers in secondary care, but may be offered in primary care by those with an interest, sometimes on a shared-care basis.

Motivational interviewing aims to encourage people to change their behaviour using their own self-help resources. It is based on the fact that ambivalence about changing behaviour is common, and helping individuals to explore the conflict between the advantages and disadvantages of heavy drinking can encourage change.

Brief treatments are most appropriate for individuals with definite alcohol-related problems but only a moderate degree of dependence. They are not a complete response for people who have other social and mental health problems. People with severe dependence are usually offered more intensive treatment. Brief treatments, however, may be considered for those who refuse to comply with intensive regimes, or need a stepped-care programme in which a low-intensity treatment is provided as a first step, or as a preparation for more intensive treatment if motivation is an important issue.

Intensive treatments

Intensive treatments are usually undertaken by specialists and are appropriate for people with definite alcohol-related problems and a severe degree of dependence.

[O'Connor and Schottenfeld, 1998; Abdulrahim et al, 1999; Raistrick, 1999; Raistrick et al, 1999]

Detoxification

- **Detoxification** refers to the planned withdrawal of alcohol. Alcohol withdrawal carries risks (e.g. seizures, delirium tremens) and requires careful clinical management.

Community compared with inpatient detoxification

- **For most people inpatient detoxification is not routinely required.** Outpatient or home detoxification is often appropriate, and is an effective and safe option in people with mild or moderate alcohol withdrawal symptoms. A comparison between community and inpatient detoxification of alcohol-dependent people found no difference in the number of people who remained abstinent 6 months later.
- **Inpatient detoxification should be considered for people with:**
  - Confusion or hallucinations
  - A history of previously complicated withdrawal (e.g. withdrawal seizures or delirium tremens)
  - Epilepsy or a history of seizures
  - Malnourishment
  - Severe vomiting or diarrhoea
  - Increased risk of suicide
  - Severe dependence coupled with unwillingness to be seen daily
  - A previously failed detoxification at home
  - Uncontrollable withdrawal symptoms
  - An acute physical or psychiatric illness
  - Multiple substance misuse
  - A home environment unsupportive of abstinence

[DH et al, 1999; SIGN, 2003]

- **If admission to hospital is unavailable or the person refuses,** specialist opinion should be sought to aid risk assessment (**GPP**) [DH et al, 1999; SIGN, 2003].
- Before starting home detoxification it is essential to ensure that there will be a responsible person at home to provide support and encouragement, supervise medication, and obtain medical help should it be needed. Additional support (e.g. from a community psychiatric nurse) is often useful.
- During detoxification the person should be seen at regular intervals (preferably daily).

Practical issues

- Where community detoxification is offered it should be delivered using protocols specifying daily monitoring of breath alcohol level and withdrawal symptoms, and dosage adjustment (**GPP**) [DH et al, 1999; SIGN, 2003].
- Every GP practice (and out-of-hours service) would benefit from access to a breathalyser for use in the acute situation and for follow-up (**GPP**) [DH et al, 1999; SIGN, 2003].
- Intoxicated people presenting to GP practices, accident and emergency departments, and out-of-hours services requesting detoxification should be advised to make a primary care appointment and be given written information about available community agents (**GPP**) [DH et al, 1999; SIGN, 2003].
- Personnel involved may include GPs, community psychiatric nurses, primary care nurses, and community pharmacists. There are also resource implications, including the cost of a breathalyser.

Supportive care

- Regardless of severity, management of acute alcohol withdrawal should include reassurance, hydration, nutrition, and monitoring of the signs and symptoms of withdrawal. Family and friends should be involved wherever possible.

Pharmacological detoxification

When is pharmacological detoxification appropriate?

- **Abrupt cessation of alcohol can lead to withdrawal symptoms,** and many people with alcohol dependence require controlled pharmacological detoxification to avoid discomfort, and to prevent the occurrence of seizures or delirium tremens [SIGN, 2003].
- **In milder degrees of dependence,** stopping drinking is unlikely to be complicated, and pharmacological detoxification may not be necessary if:
  - The person has no recent withdrawal symptoms, has not recently needed to drink to prevent withdrawal symptoms, and reported consumption of alcohol is <15 units per day (men) or <10 units/day (women).
  - The person has no alcohol on breath test, and no signs or symptoms of withdrawal.
- **Binge drinkers** whose bouts last less than a week and people who are sober at interview, without withdrawal symptoms, seldom need medication unless drinking is extremely heavy (>20 units/day).
- **Most regular heavy drinkers** will require controlled detoxification with pharmacological intervention.
- When medication to manage withdrawal is not needed, the person should be informed that at the start of detoxification they may feel nervous or anxious for several days, with difficulty in going to sleep for several nights (**D**).

[DTB, 2000; SIGN, 2003]

What should I prescribe for pharmacological detoxification?

- **Benzodiazepines should be used in primary care to manage withdrawal symptoms in alcohol detoxification,** but for a maximum period of 7 days (**A**) [DH et al, 1999; SIGN, 2003]. There is evidence from randomized, controlled trials to show that benzodiazepines reduce the signs and symptoms of alcohol withdrawal and the risk

A

of seizures or delirium tremens, and they are currently considered the drugs of choice in the treatment of acute alcohol detoxification [Mayo-Smith, 1997; Williams and McBride, 1998; Holbrook et al, 1999b].

- **Chlordiazepoxide is the preferred benzodiazepine** for people managed in the community (D).
  - Chlordiazepoxide has a slower onset of action than diazepam or lorazepam, and has less potential for abuse [Mayo-Smith, 1997].
  - Diazepam has similar efficacy to chlordiazepoxide but has a greater potential for abuse as it has a faster onset of action.
  - If diazepam is used in the community for acute alcohol detoxification, its use requires careful supervision [SIGN, 2003].
- **Clomethiazole (chlormethiazole) should not be used in alcohol detoxification in primary care** (D). Although clomethiazole is an effective treatment for alcohol detoxification, it should only be used under close supervision due to the risk of respiratory depression in combination with alcohol, and the danger of dependence [SIGN, 2003].
- **Antiepileptic drugs should not be used as the sole medication for alcohol detoxification in primary care** (B). People with a history of alcohol-related seizures should be referred to specialist services (**GPP**).
- **Antipsychotic drugs should not be used as first-line treatment for alcohol detoxification** (B). Although antipsychotic drugs have been shown to prevent delirium, they increase the incidence of seizures [Mayo-Smith, 1997]. Delusions and hallucinations due to alcohol withdrawal should be managed by specialist services (**GPP**).

What is the recommended regimen for detoxification with chlordiazepoxide?

- **A tapered fixed-dose regimen of a benzodiazepine is recommended** for primary care alcohol detoxification, with daily monitoring wherever possible (**GPP**).
- **Symptom-triggered therapy** (when the person is monitored by means of a structured assessment scale and given medication only when symptoms cross a threshold of severity) results in the administration of significantly less medication and a significantly shorter duration of treatment; however, it requires a high degree of supervision and is not generally practical in the primary care setting.
- **Dispensing should be daily** or should involve the support of family members to prevent any risk of misuse or overdose.
  - Confirm abstinence by checking for alcohol on the breath, or by using a breathalyser [DH et al, 1999].
  - Benzodiazepines should be stopped once detoxification has been accomplished, or if the person relapses during detoxification.
- The dose of chlordiazepoxide should be reduced over 5–7 days. The initial dose level and length of treatment will depend on the severity of alcohol dependence and on individual patient factors (e.g. weight, gender, liver function).
- The Department of Health recommends reducing the dose over 7 days (see Table 1).

[DH et al, 1999]

When should I recommend vitamin B supplements?

Vitamin B supplements in chronic deficiency

- **People with chronic alcohol dependence** are frequently malnourished and deficient in vitamins, especially thiamine, largely because of reduced absorption [Cook and Thomson, 1997].
- The SIGN guideline recommends that people who have chronic alcohol problem and whose diet may be deficient should be given oral thiamine indefinitely (**GPP**) [DH et al, 1999; SIGN, 2003].
- There is limited evidence for recommending a dosage of thiamine in the treatment of alcohol dependence [Berglund et al, 2003]. The BNF recommended dose is:
  - Severe deficiency: 200–300 mg per day. This should be given in divided doses to maximize absorption.
  - Mild chronic deficiency: 10–25 mg per day.

[BNF 46, 2003]

Vitamin B supplements during detoxification

- **Detoxification** may precipitate Wernicke's encephalopathy, which must be treated urgently with parenteral thiamine. Signs of possible Wernicke-Korsakoff syndrome (which may progress to encephalopathy) in someone undergoing detoxification include:
  - Confusion
  - Ataxia
  - Ophthalmoplegia
  - Nystagmus
  - Memory disturbance
  - Hypothermia and hypotension
  - Coma
- Anyone who presents with unexplained neurological signs or symptoms should be referred for specialist assessment.

[SIGN, 2003]

- **Anyone undergoing alcohol detoxification at home** should be given oral thiamine (200 mg daily) for 5–7 days [DTB, 2000].
- **People who are severely malnourished or have long-standing dependence** are at highest risk of developing clinical manifestations of thiamine deficiency during alcohol withdrawal. There is a strong argument for admitting such at-risk people to hospital during detoxification for parenteral administration of vitamin supplements (Pabrinex®).

[DTB, 2000; SIGN, 2003]

Table 1: Reducing dose of chlordiazepoxide over 7 days.

	First thing	12 noon	6 pm	Bedtime
Day 1	20–30 mg	20–30 mg	20–30 mg	20–30 mg
Day 2	20–30 mg	20–30 mg	20–30 mg	20–30 mg
Day 3	15 mg	15 mg	15 mg	15 mg
Day 4	15 mg	15 mg	15 mg	15 mg
Day 5	10 mg	10 mg	10 mg	10 mg
Day 6	10 mg	–	–	10 mg
Day 7	–	–	–	10 mg

Maintaining abstinence

Maintaining contact

Primary care teams should maintain contact over the long term with people previously treated by specialist services for alcohol dependence (B). Maintaining contact with someone with alcohol dependence is an important factor in maintaining abstinence.

- Low-intensity monitoring over 1–3 years has been shown to reduce the severity of relapses (possibly through earlier referral to specialist services when needed).
- Contact need only be brief and may be maintained, for example, by telephone or brief appointment.

[SIGN, 2003]

Psychosocial interventions

The following treatments have been shown to be effective at preventing relapse:

- Behavioural self-control training
- Coping/social skills training
- Marital/family therapy
- Motivational enhancement therapy

The treatments are usually delivered by specialist workers in alcohol specialist agencies, but may be offered in primary care by those with an interest, sometimes on a shared-care basis.

Minimal interventions, such as assessing alcohol intake, and providing information, advice, and encouragement, have not been shown to be effective at preventing relapse.

[SIGN, 2003; Slattery et al, 2003]

Pharmacological interventions

- Consider pharmacological interventions in the prevention of relapse in alcohol dependence in addition to (not as an alternative to) psychosocial interventions.
- Meta-analyses of the efficacy and cost-effectiveness of medications for relapse prevention have found evidence for the efficacy of acamprosate and disulfiram (the latter only if supervised).

[Slattery et al, 2003]

Acamprosate

- **Acamprosate** (calcium acetylhomotaurinate) has a chemical structure similar to that of amino acid neuromediators, such as taurine or gamma-aminobutyric acid (GABA). Although its mechanism of action is not fully known, it is thought to reduce cravings for alcohol by stimulating GABAergic inhibitory neurotransmission and antagonizing excitatory amino acids, particularly glutamate [DTB, 1997].
- **Acamprosate is recommended in newly detoxified dependent people as an adjunct to psychosocial interventions** (B) [SIGN, 2003]. Evidence from randomized, placebo-controlled trials suggests that, in association with a range of psychosocial interventions, acamprosate is significantly more effective than placebo at preventing or delaying relapse after acute detoxification, and at increasing the number of days on which no alcohol is drunk [Berglund et al, 2003; Mason, 2003; Overman et al, 2003; Slattery et al, 2003].
- The Health Technology Board for Scotland performed a meta-analysis on data from 17 studies (n = 4529 patients; including two unpublished studies). The rates of abstinence for controlled drinking compared with control at the trial end (3 months to 1 year) were 26% compared with 18% (OR 1.73, 95% CI 1.36 to 2.20) [Slattery et al, 2003].
- **Acamprosate is licensed for use for up to 1 year.** After this time, it can be stopped abruptly without any need for gradual withdrawal. Two 1-year studies have followed people for a further year after stopping treatment and found that the treatment effect persisted into the second year without any indication of sudden relapse on stopping the drug [Sass et al, 1996; Whitworth et al, 1996].
- Acamprosate will usually be initiated by a specialist service within a few days of successful detoxification. If a specialist service is not available, the GP should offer acamprosate, monitor its efficacy, and provide links to local support organizations (GPP) [SIGN, 2003].

Disulfiram

- **Disulfiram is indicated as an adjuvant in the treatment of chronic alcohol dependence.** It is recommended that it should be initiated only in a hospital or specialized clinic, and by physicians experienced in its use [ABPI Medicines Compendium, 2004].
- **If disulfiram is taken regularly there is an unpleasant reaction (including tachycardia, headache, flushing, nausea, and vomiting) when alcohol is consumed,** thus deterring the person from drinking alcohol.
- **Supervised oral disulfiram may be used to prevent relapse,** but people must be informed that this is a treatment requiring complete abstinence, and be clear about the dangers of taking alcohol with it (C) [SIGN, 2003]. When taken with large amounts of alcohol, arrhythmias, hypotension, and collapse may occur [BNF 46, 2003].
- There is some evidence to support the supervised use of disulfiram, but none for its unsupervised use [SIGN, 2003]. Disulfiram seems to have some efficacy in reducing the number of drinking days and the amounts drunk in people who are compliant, even if they continue to drink. Evidence that disulfiram increases the proportion of people who maintain total abstinence is surprisingly lacking [Hughes and Cook, 1997].
- Disulfiram supervision may be undertaken by the partner, health care or support worker, or the workplace representative if appropriate (GPP) [SIGN, 2003].

Naltrexone

- Naltrexone, an opioid antagonist, increases the rates of abstinence, and decreases relapse rates in alcohol-dependent people who are in abstinence-orientated programmes [Schaffer and Naranjo, 1998; Garbutt et al, 1999].
- Although there is evidence to support its efficacy, and it is used in some specialist centres, naltrexone is not licensed for the treatment of alcohol dependence and should not be initiated for this purpose in primary care [SIGN, 2003].

Other interventions

- **Other interventions** that have been suggested include alpha-agonists, beta-blockers, anticonvulsants, drugs that augment serotonin levels, clonidine, neuroleptics, acupuncture, transcendental meditation, and neuroelectric therapy, although evidence of benefit with these is limited and none are currently recommended as monotherapy [Brewer, 1995; Mayo-Smith, 1997; Garbutt et al, 1999; Swift, 1999; SIGN, 2003].

Medicines management

Acamprosate

When should acamprosate be started?

- Acamprosate will usually be initiated by a specialist service, which will regularly review treatment (often under a shared-care agreement).
- Treatment with acamprosate should be initiated immediately following detoxification.

A

How long should I continue treatment for?

- **The efficacy of acamprosate should be assessed at regular intervals.**
  - If the person relapses immediately to dependence drinking, acamprosate should be withdrawn.
  - If there is relapse but the overall drinking pattern is less, and the person is still willing to continue with treatment, acamprosate should be continued.
- Where it appears to be effective, acamprosate should be continued for up to 12 months.

[SIGN, 2003]

Benzodiazepines

How should I prescribe benzodiazepines in the elderly?

- Elderly people requiring pharmacological detoxification should be managed in a similar way to younger people, although the risk of accumulation in elderly people must be considered [SIGN, 2003]. There is an increased risk of ataxia and confusion in elderly people receiving benzodiazepines and the dose should be reduced by half [BNF 46, 2003].

How should I prescribe benzodiazepines in people with hepatic impairment?

- **People with liver disease have impaired metabolism of diazepam and chlordiazepoxide.** It may be necessary to consider a benzodiazepine that is not metabolized in the liver, such as oxazepam or lorazepam. Referral to specialist services is advised.

Parenteral thiamine (Pabrinex®)

- There is a small risk of serious allergic (anaphylactic) reactions occurring during or shortly after the administration of parenteral thiamine. The Committee on Safety of Medicines (CSM) recommends that:
  - Use is restricted to people in whom parenteral treatment is essential.
  - Intravenous injections are given slowly, over 10 minutes.
  - Facilities for treating anaphylaxis should be available when it is administered.

[CSM, 1989]

References

NHS staff in England can link, free of charge, from references to full text journals by clicking on [Full text] on the PRODIGY website.

1. Abdulrahim, D., Lavoie, D. and Hasan, S. (1999) *Commissioning standards for drug and alcohol treatment and care.* London: Health Advisory Service 2000.
2. Alcohol Concern (1997) *Brief interventions guidelines: information briefing for purchasers of alcohol services.* London: Alcohol Concern.
3. Anderson, P. (1996) *Alcohol and primary health care.* WHO Regional Publications: European Series 64. Copenhagen: World Health Organization.
4. Ashworth, M. and Gerada, C. (1997) Addiction and dependance – II: alcohol. *British Medical Journal* **315**(7104), 358–360. [Full text]
5. Babor, T.F. and Grant, M.G. (1992) *Programme on substance abuse: project on identification and management of alcohol related problems. Report on Phase II: a randomized clinical trial of brief interventions in primary health care.* Geneva: World Health Organization.
6. Berglund, M., Thelander, S., Salaspuro, M. et al (2003) Treatment of alcohol abuse: an evidence-based review. *Alcoholism: Clinical & Experimental Research* **27**(10), 1645–1656.
7. BNF 46 (2003) *British National Formulary.* 46th edn London: British Medical Association and Royal Pharmaceutical Society of Great Britain.
8. Bradley, K.A., Boyd-Wickizer, J., Powell, S.H. and Burman, M.L. (1998) Alcohol screening questionnair in women. *Journal of the American Medical Association* **280**(2), 166–171. [Full text]
9. Brewer, C. (1995) Second-line and alternative treatments for alcohol withdrawal; alpha-agonists, beta-blockers, anticonvulsants, acupuncture and neur electric therapy. *Alcohol & Alcoholism* **30**(6), 799–803.
10. Cook, C.C. and Thomson, A.D. (1997) B-complex vitamins in the prophylaxis and treatment of Wernick Korsakoff syndrome. *British Journal of Hospital Medicine* **57**(9), 461–465.
11. CSM (1989) Parentrovite & allergic reactions. *Curren Problems in Pharmacovigilance* **24**(Jan), 1.
12. DH (1995) *Sensible drinking.* London: Department of Health.
13. DH (2002) *Drug use, smoking and drinking among young people in England in 2001. Summary of key findings.* Department of Health. www.dh.gov.uk [Accessed: 28/04/2004]. [Full text]
14. DH (2003) *Statistics on alcohol: England, 2003.* Statistical Bulletin 2003/20. Department of Health. www.dh.gov.uk [Accessed: 28/04/2004]. [Full text]
15. DH, Scottish Office DH, Welsh Office and DH and Social Services of NI (1999) *Drug misuse and dependence – guidelines on clinical management.* Department of Health. www.dh.gov.uk [Accessed: 27/04/2004]. [Full text]
16. DTB (1997) Acamprosate for alcohol dependence? *Drug & Therapeutics Bulletin* **35**(9), 70–72.
17. DTB (2000) Managing the heavy drinker in primary care. *Drug & Therapeutics Bulletin* **38**(8), 60–64.
18. DVLA (2003) *At a glance guide to current medical standards of fitness to drive. Drug and alcohol misuse and dependency.* Drivers Medical Group, Driver and Vehicle Licensing Authority. www.dvla.gov.uk [Accessed: 29/01/2004].
19. Edwards, G., Marshall, E.J. and Cook, C.C.H. (Eds.) (1997) *The treatment of drinking problems: a guide fo helping the professions.* 3rd edn. Cambridge: Cambridge University Press.
20. Garbutt, J.C., West, S.L., Carey, T.S. et al (1999) Pharmacological treatment of alcohol dependence: a review of the evidence. *Journal of the American Medical Association* **281**(14), 1318–1325. [Full text]
21. Guerri, C., Riley, E. and Stromland, K. (1999) Commentary on the recommendations of the Royal College of Obstetricians and Gynaecologists concerning alcohol consumption in pregnancy. *Alcoho & Alcoholism* **34**(4), 497–501. [Full text]
22. Haines, A. and Wiseman, S. (1992) Management of heavy drinkers. In: Haines, A. and Hurwitz, B. (Eds.) *Clinical Guidelines: report of a local initiative. Occasional paper 58.* London: Royal College of General Practitioners. 39–43.
23. Hardman, J.G., Limbird, L.E., Molinoff, P.B. and Ruddon, R.W. (1996) *Goodman & Gilman's the pharmacological basis of therapeutics.* 9th edn. New York: McGraw-Hill.
24. Health Education Authority (1997) *Health update: alcohol.* London: Health Education Authority.
25. Holbrook, A.M., Crowther, R., Lotter, A. et al (1999a) Diagnosis and management of acute alcohol withdrawal. *Canadian Medical Association Journal* **160**(5), 675–680. [Full text]
26. Holbrook, A.M., Crowther, R., Lotter, A. et al (1999b) Meta-analysis of benzodiazepine use in the treatment

of acute alcohol withdrawal. *Canadian Medical Association Journal* **160**(5), 649–655. [Full text]

. Mason, B.J. (2003) Acamprosate and naltrexone treatment for alcohol dependence: an evidence-based risk-benefits assessment. *European Neuropsychopharmacology* **13**(6), 469–475.

. Mayo-Smith, M.F. (1997) Pharmacological management of alcohol withdrawal: a meta-analysis and evidence-based practice guideline. *Journal of the American Medical Association* **278**(2), 144–151. [Full text]

. O'Connor, P.G. and Schottenfeld, R.S. (1998) Patients with alcohol problems. *New England Journal of Medicine* **338**(9), 592–602. [Full text]

. Overman, G.P., Teter, C.J. and Guthrie, S.K. (2003) Acamprosate for the adjunctive treatment of alcohol dependence. *Annals of Pharmacotherapy* **37**(7–8), 1090–1099.

. Raistrick, D. (1999) *Review of the effectiveness of treatment for alcohol problems*. Alcoholis. Volume 17(6). Medical Council on Alcohol. www.medicouncilalcol.demon.co.uk/articles_1998.htm [Accessed: 26/01/2004].

. Raistrick, D., Hodgson, R. and Ritson, B. (1999) *Tackling alcohol together*. London: Free Association Books.

3. RCOG (1999) *Alcohol consumption in pregnancy*. No. 9. Royal College of Obstetricians and Gynaecologists. www.rcog.org.uk [Accessed: 06/11/2003].

4. Royal College of Physicians, Royal College of Psychiatrists and Royal College of General Practitioners (1995) *Alcohol and the heart in perspective: sensible limits reaffirmed*. London: Royal College of Physicians, Royal College of Psychiatrists and Royal College of General Practitioners.

5. Sass, H., Soyka, M., Mann, K. and Zieglgansberger, W. (1996) Relapse prevention by acamprosate. Results from a placebo-controlled study on alcohol dependence. *Archives of General Psychiatry* **53**(8), 673–680. [erratum appears in: Arch Gen Psychiatry (1996) 53(12), 1097].

6. Saunders, J.B., Aasland, O.G., Babor, T.F. et al (1993) Development of the alcohol use disorders identification test (AUDIT): WHO collaborative project on early detection of persons with harmful alcohol consumption – II. *Addiction* **88**(6), 791–804.

7. Schaffer, A. and Naranjo, C.A. (1998) Recommended drug treatment strategies for the alcoholic patient. *Drugs* **56**(4), 571–585.

8. SIGN (2003) *The management of harmful drinking and alcohol dependence in primary care*. Report no. 74. Scottish Intercollegiate Guidelines Network. www.sign.ac.uk [Accessed: 29/10/2003].

9. Slattery, J., Chick, J., Cochrane, M. et al (2003) *Prevention of relapse in alcohol dependence*. Health Technology Assessment Report 3. Health Technology Board for Scotland. www.htbs.co.uk [Accessed: 26/01/2004].

40. Speight, T.M. and Holford, N.H.G. (1997) *Avery's drug treatment*. 4th edn. Chester: Adis International.

41. Stockwell, T., Hodgson, R., Edwards, G. et al (1979) The development of a questionnaire to measure severity of alcohol dependence. *British Journal of Addiction to Alcohol & Other Drugs* **74**(1), 79–87.

42. Swift, R.M. (1999) Drug therapy for alcohol dependence. *New England Journal of Medicine* **340**(19), 1482–1490. [Full text]

43. Whitworth, A.B., Fischer, F., Lesch, O.M. et al (1996) Comparison of acamprosate and placebo in long-term treatment of alcohol dependence. *Lancet* **347**(9013), 1438–1442. [Full text]

44. WHO (Ed.) (1992) *The ICD-10 classification of mental and behavioural disorders. Clinical descriptions and diagnostic guidelines*. Geneva: World Health Organization.

45. Williams, D. and McBride, A.J. (1998) The drug treatment of alcohol withdrawal symptoms: a systematic review. *Alcohol & Alcoholism* **33**(2), 103–115.

Evidence grading

Evidence grading is from the Scottish Intercollegiate Guidelines Network (SIGN) Guideline *The management of harmful drinking and alcohol dependence in primary care*, September 2003. The definitions of grades of recommendation used in this guideline are as follows:

A	At least one meta-analysis, systematic review, or randomized controlled trial (RCT) rated as 1++ and directly applicable to the target population or A systematic review of RCTs or a body of evidence consisting principally of studies rated as 1+ directly applicable to the target population and demonstrating overall consistency of results
B	A body of evidence including studies rated as 2++ directly applicable to the target population and demonstrating overall consistency of results or Extrapolated evidence from studies rated as 1++ or 1+
C	A body of evidence including studies rated as 2+ directly applicable to the target population and demonstrating overall consistency of results or Extrapolated evidence from studies rated as 2++
D	Evidence level 3 or 4 or Extrapolated evidence from studies rated as 2+
GPP	Good practice point: recommended best practice based on the clinical experience of the guideline development group

PRODIGY GUIDANCE

Allergic rhinitis

Last revised in July 2005
www.prodigy.nhs.uk/guidance.asp?gt=Allergic rhinitis

Applies to people over the age of 1 month

This guidance covers the management of seasonal and perennial allergic rhinitis.

This guidance does not cover the management of allergic conjunctivitis in detail, although advice and prescriptions for associated allergic conjunctivitis (rhinoconjunctivitis) are offered.

There is separate PRODIGY guidance for *Asthma, Atopic eczema, Conjunctivitis — allergic, and Sinusitis.*

Goals

- To advise on allergen avoidance
- To alleviate symptoms
- To advise on the use of systemic corticosteroids for severe symptoms

Contents

Scenarios
- Mild intermittent allergic rhinitis p.34
- Mild persistent or moderate-severe intermittent p.36
- Moderate-severe persistent allergic rhinitis p.39
- Allergic rhinitis with eye symptoms p.42
- Failure to respond to standard treatment p.44
- Allergic rhinitis in pregnancy p.45

Extended Information, p. 48

Which scenario?

- **Mild intermittent allergic rhinitis:** covers the management of mild intermittent symptoms only.
- **Mild persistent or moderate-severe intermittent:** covers the management of moderate or severe symptoms that are intermittent, *or* mild symptoms that are persistent.
- **Moderate-severe persistent allergic rhinitis:** covers the management of symptoms which are moderate or severe *and* persistent.
- **Allergic rhinitis with eye symptoms:** covers the management of coexisting ocular symptoms. This scenario is covered in more detail in PRODIGY guidance *Conjunctivitis — allergic.*
- **Failure to respond to standard treatment:** covers the management of people with severe symptoms despite the use of maximal doses of standard treatments.
- **Allergic rhinitis in pregnancy:** covers the management of all severities of allergic rhinitis in pregnancy.

Mild intermittent allergic rhinitis

Which therapy?

- **Advise allergen avoidance** (see PRODIGY *Patient Information Leaflets*).
- **Use an antihistamine as required.** Individual preference and response to previous treatments should direct choices:
  - Intranasal antihistamines have a faster onset of action than oral preparations, but require more frequent administration.
  - If using an oral antihistamine, non-sedating oral antihistamines are preferred. Cetirizine is probably the most sedating and fexofenadine the least.
- **Consider an intranasal decongestant** for a maximum o seven days use if blockage is a problem.

Practical prescribing points

For further information see the *Medicines Compendium* (www.medicines.org.uk) or the *British National Formula* (www.bnf.org).

- **'Non-sedating' oral antihistamines:** people receiving an antihistamine should be advised that treatment can aff driving and other skilled tasks, and enhance the effects alcohol [DTB, 2002].
- **Mizolastine** has the potential to prolong the QT interv in some people and is contraindicated in people with significant cardiac disease, symptomatic arrhythmias, o those taking anti-arrhythmic drugs [BNF 48, 2004].
- **Intranasal decongestants** can cause severe rebound effects, and should not be used for more than 7 days continuously [BNF 48, 2004].

Follow-up advice

- Review if symptoms are not relieved or become persistent.

Should I refer or investigate?

Refer?

ENT referral is recommended for:

- Unilateral nasal problems
- Nasal perforations, ulceration, or collapse
- Serosanguinous discharge
- Crusting high in the nasal cavity
- Recurrent infection
- Periorbital cellulitis (urgent admission)

Patient information leaflets

The following PILs are available at www.prodigy.nhs.uk

- Allergy UK
- Hay Fever
- House Dust Mite and Pet Allergy
- Nose Drops - How To Use
- Nose Sprays (Steroid)

Shared decision making

- **An antihistamine medicine** taken 'as required' eases mos of the symptoms of allergic rhinitis (including eye symptoms if you have hay fever). It works within an hour or so, but may not totally clear a blocked nose.
- **An antihistamine nasal spray** is an alternative to use 'as required'. It usually eases nose symptoms within 15 minutes or so, but does not ease eye symptoms. The

effect wears off quicker than with antihistamine medicines.

A decongestant nasal spray works quickly to clear a blocked nose. However, it should not be used for more than 5–7 days as otherwise a worse 'rebound' congestion may occur.

Reducing exposure to pollen may help if hay fever is the cause of your symptoms.

- Stay indoors as much as possible, and keep windows and doors shut.
- Avoid cutting grass, large grassy places, and camping.
- Shower and wash your hair after being outdoors; especially after going to the countryside.
- Wear wrap-around sunglasses when out.
- Bring in washing, and close windows before the evening.
- Keep car windows closed.

Drug rationale

Drugs not included

'Sedating' antihistamines are not recommended. They cause significantly more sedation than the newer 'non-sedating' antihistamines, which may considerably impair normal daytime activity [Shamsi and Hindmarch, 2000; Casale et al, 2003].

Acrivastine and terfenadine are not recommended. Acrivastine requires three doses per day [BNF 48, 2004], whilst terfenadine has the potential to cause serious heart arrhythmias [DTB, 2002].

Intranasal corticosteroids are not usually necessary in people who only have mild intermittent symptoms [ARIA, 2001].

Intranasal sodium cromoglicate is only recommended as an add-on treatment in people with more severe or persistent symptoms. However, it is a good choice for pregnant or breastfeeding women with mild intermittent symptoms [ARIA, 2001].

Intranasal ipratropium bromide is only effective against profuse, watery discharge, which is not usually seen in people with mild intermittent symptoms [ARIA, 2001].

Oral decongestants are not as effective as intranasal decongestants, can cause systemic adverse effects, and may interact with other medications [ARIA, 2001; BNF 48, 2004].

Ephedrine 1% nose drops are not recommended as they may cause more systemic adverse effects than the 0.5% formulation.

Leukotriene antagonists are not usually necessary for mild intermittent symptoms and are not specifically licensed for this condition [BNF 48, 2004].

Drugs included

'Non-sedating' oral antihistamines are recommended as the first-line treatment for people with mild, intermittent symptoms of allergic rhinitis. They are effective in treating itching, sneezing, and runny nose as well as related eye symptoms [MeReC, 2004]. Six drugs are currently available which are considered safe and taken once a day [DTB, 2002]:

- **Cetirizine and loratadine** are well established agents with a good efficacy and safety profile. They are taken once a day and are suitable for young children.
- **Fexofenadine and mizolastine** are alternative once-daily regimens suitable for older children and adults.
- **Desloratadine (a metabolite of loratadine) and levocetirizine (an isomer of cetirizine)** are more recently marketed products that are still under close post-marketing surveillance (black triangle).

- **Intranasal antihistamines** are an equally effective alternative for people without eye symptoms. They relieve nasal symptoms, are quick acting but have a short duration, and are safe [MeReC, 2004]. Two products are available:
  - **Azelastine** is available as a nasal spray administered twice a day.
  - **Levocabastine** is available as a nasal spray administered twice a day, increasing up to four times a day if necessary.
- **Intranasal decongestants** are effective in relieving nasal congestion in the short term. They should not be used for more than a week due to the risk of rebound congestion cessation of treatment [ARIA, 2001]. Ephedrine and xylometazoline are the sympathomimetic drugs most commonly used.

Prescriptions

Oral antihistamines: non-sedating

Cetirizine s/f solution: 5mg once a day

- Age from 2 to 5 years
- Cetirizine 5mg/5ml s/f sol. Take one 5ml spoonful once a day; supply 200 ml; NHS Cost £9.77; OTC Cost £17.22.

Cetirizine s/f solution: 10mg once a day

- Age from 6 to 11 years
- Cetirizine 5mg/5ml s/f sol. Take two 5ml spoonfuls once a day; supply 300 ml; NHS Cost £14.66; OTC Cost £25.83.

Cetirizine tablets: 10mg once a day

- Age from 12 years onwards
- Cetirizine 10mg tablets. Take one tablet once a day; supply 30 tablets; NHS Cost £5.64; OTC Cost £9.94.

Loratadine syrup: 5mg once a day

- Age from 2 to 5 years
- Loratadine 5mg/5ml syrup. Take one 5ml spoonful once a day; supply 200 ml; NHS Cost £10.86; OTC Cost £19.14.

Loratadine syrup: 10mg once a day

- Age from 6 to 11 years
- Loratadine 5mg/5ml syrup. Take two 5ml spoonfuls once a day; supply 300 ml; NHS Cost £16.29; OTC Cost £28.71.

Loratadine tablets: 10mg once a day

- Age from 12 years onwards
- Loratadine 10mg tablets. Take one tablet once a day; supply 30 tablets; NHS Cost £4.09; OTC Cost £7.21.

Fexofenadine tablets: 30mg twice a day

- Age from 6 to 11 years
- Fexofenadine 30mg tablets. Take one tablet twice a day; supply 60 tablets; NHS Cost £6.11.

Fexofenadine tablets: 120mg once a day

- Age from 12 years onwards
- Fexofenadine 120mg tablets. Take one tablet once a day; supply 30 tablets; NHS Cost £8.14.

Mizolastine tablets: 10mg once a day

- Age from 12 years onwards
- Mizolastine 10mg tablets. Take one tablet once a day; supply 30 tablets; NHS Cost £5.77.

Levocetirizine tablets: 5mg once a day

- Age from 6 years onwards
- Levocetirizine 5mg tablets. Take one tablet once a day; supply 30 tablets; NHS Cost £7.45.

Desloratadine syrup: 1.25mg once a day

- Age from 12 months to 5 years
- Desloratadine 2.5mg/5ml syrup. Take 2.5ml once a day; supply 100 ml; NHS Cost £7.04.

Desloratadine syrup: 2.5mg once a day
- Age from 6 to 11 years
- Desloratadine 2.5mg/5ml syrup. Take one 5ml spoonful once a day; supply 200 ml; NHS Cost £14.08.

Desloratadine tablets: 5mg once a day
- Age from 12 years onwards
- Desloratadine 5mg tablets. Take one tablet once a day; supply 30 tablets; NHS Cost £7.04.

Intranasal antihistamines

Azelastine 140microgram (0.1%) nasal spray
- Age from 5 years onwards
- Azelastine 0.1% nasal spray. Spray once into each nostril twice a day when required; supply 1 spray; NHS Cost £11.92.

Levocabastine 500microgram (0.05%) nasal spray
- Age from 9 years onwards
- Levocabastine 0.05% nasal spray. Spray twice into each nostril twice a day when required; supply 1 spray; NHS Cost £9.74.

Intranasal decongestants – for nasal blockage (short term)

Ephedrine 0.5% nose drops
- Age from 3 months onwards
- Ephedrine 0.5% nose drops. Put one to two drops into each nostril up to four times a day when required for nasal blockage. Do not use for more than 7 days; supply 10 ml; NHS Cost £1.27.

Xylometazoline 0.05% nose drops
- Age from 3 months to 11 years
- Xylometazoline paed nose drops. Put one to two drops into each nostril once or twice a day when required for nasal blockage. Do not use for more than 7 days; supply 10 ml; NHS Cost £1.59.

Xylometazoline 0.1% nose drops
- Age from 12 years onwards
- Xylometazoline 0.1% nose drops. Put two to three drops into each nostril 2 to 3 times a day when required for nasal blockage. Do not use for more than 7 days; supply 10 ml; NHS Cost £1.91.

Mild persistent or moderate-severe intermittent

Which therapy?

- **Advise allergen avoidance** (See PRODIGY *Patient Information Leaflets*).
- **Use either an antihistamine or an intranasal corticosteroid.** Individual preference and response to previous treatments should direct choice. If nasal blockage is a problem intranasal corticosteroids are preferred.
  - **Intranasal corticosteroid preparations are equally effective,** but drops are more likely than sprays to be administered incorrectly, resulting in systemic absorption.
  - **Intranasal antihistamines** have a faster onset of action than oral preparations but require more frequent administration.
  - **Oral antihistamines:** non-sedating antihistamines are preferred. Cetirizine is probably the most sedating and fexofenadine the least.
- **Intranasal decongestants** may be used *in the short term* to relieve congestion and allow penetration of an intranasal corticosteroid.
- **Intranasal sodium cromoglicate** is suitable as an alternative treatment if other drugs are contraindicated or as an add-on drug if symptoms are troublesome despite other treatments.

Practical prescribing points

For further information see the *Medicines Compendium* (www.medicines.org.uk) or the *British National Formulc* (www.bnf.org).

- **'Non-sedating' oral antihistamines:** people receiving ar antihistamine should be advised that treatment can aff driving and other skilled tasks, and enhance the effects alcohol [DTB, 2002].
- **Mizolastine** has the potential to prolong the QT interv in some people and is contraindicated in people with significant cardiac disease, symptomatic arrhythmias, c those taking anti-arrhythmic drugs [BNF 48, 2004].
- **Intranasal corticosteroids:** occasionally, local adverse effects can occur (e.g. crusting, dryness, minor nosebleed) that may require treatment to stop for a while. The CSM advises that the height of children receiving prolonged treatment with intranasal corticosteroids should be regularly monitored.
- **Intranasal decongestants** can cause severe rebound effects, and should not be used for more than 7 days continuously [BNF 48, 2004].

Follow-up advice

- **Reassess** how effective treatment was after 2–4 weeks:
  - If the person is symptom free or the symptoms are le then continue the current treatment.
  - Continue the treatment long-term if the symptoms ar perennial.
  - If the person has persistent mild symptoms and is using antihistamines or sodium cromoglicate, consid changing to intranasal corticosteroids.
- **If the person is taking intranasal corticosteroids:**
  - The dose of intranasal corticosteroid should be titrat to the lowest dose that controls symptoms.
  - The height of children receiving prolonged treatment with intranasal corticosteroids should be regularly monitored. If growth is slowed, treatment should be reviewed with the aim of reducing the dose of corticosteroid to the lowest dose that maintains symptom control, and paediatric referral should be considered.

Should I refer or investigate?

Refer?

- **Paediatric referral should be considered in children receiving prolonged treatment with intranasal corticosteroids who have evidence of slowed growth** (particularly if this persists when the dose of corticosteroid is reduced to the lowest dose that maintains symptom control).
- **Refer all people with persistent rhinitis** as it recommended that they have a nasal examination. Anterior rhinoscopy only gives limited information and nasal endoscopy is recommended.
- **ENT referral is also recommended for:**
  - Unilateral nasal problems
  - Nasal perforations, ulceration, or collapse
  - Serosanguinous discharge
  - Crusting high in the nasal cavity
  - Recurrent infection
  - Periorbital cellulitis (urgent admission)

ıtient information leaflets

e following PILs are available at www.prodigy.nhs.uk
Allergy UK
Hay Fever
House Dust Mite and Pet Allergy
Nose Drops - How To Use
Nose Sprays (Steroid)
Rhinitis (Persistent)

ıared decision making

A steroid nasal spray (or steroid nasal drops) usually works well to ease most of the symptoms of allergic rhinitis (including eye symptoms).
- It takes a few days to build up and work fully.
- Then needs to be taken regularly to keep symptoms away.

An antihistamine medicine is an alternative. It eases most symptoms (runny nose, sneezing, etc.) but may not totally clear a blocked nose. It can be used in addition to a steroid nasal spray if symptoms are not eased by either alone.
An antihistamine nasal spray is another alternative, but you need to use it quite frequently.
Sodium cromoglicate nasal spray is an option if you cannot use any of the above, or as an add-on treatment if symptoms remain troublesome despite other treatments.
A decongestant nasal spray works quickly to clear a blocked nose. However, it should not be used for more than 5–7 days as otherwise a worse 'rebound' congestion may occur.
If you know the cause of the allergy, avoiding it may ease symptoms. For example:
- Hay fever: reduce your exposure to pollen. Keep windows closed, do not cut grass, stay indoors as much as possible, use wrap-around sunglasses, etc.
- House-dust mite: numbers may be reduced by regular cleaning and vacuuming of carpets and bedding. A leaflet explains this further.
- Pets: keep them out of living areas if you cannot give them up.

Drug rationale

rugs not included

'Sedating' antihistamines are not recommended. They cause significantly more sedation than the newer 'non-sedating' antihistamines, which may considerably impair normal daytime activity [Shamsi and Hindmarch, 2000; Casale et al, 2003].
Acrivastine and terfenadine are not recommended. Acrivastine requires three doses per day [BNF 48, 2004], whilst terfenadine has the potential to cause serious heart arrhythmias [DTB, 2002].
Intranasal dexamethasone is only available combined with tramazoline, which is not recommended for long-term use [BNF 48, 2004].
Intranasal ipratropium bromide is only effective against profuse, watery discharge, which is usually only seen in people with moderate to severe persistent symptoms [ARIA, 2001].
Oral decongestants are not as effective as intranasal decongestants, can cause systemic adverse effects, and may interact with other medications [ARIA, 2001; BNF 48, 2004].
Ephedrine 1% nose drops are not recommended as they may cause more systemic adverse effects than the 0.5% formulation.

- **Leukotriene antagonists** are usually only considered for moderate to severe persistent symptoms, and are not specifically licensed for this condition [BNF 48, 2004].

Drugs included

- **'Non-sedating' oral antihistamines** are recommended for people with moderate to severe intermittent or mild persistent allergic rhinitis. They are effective in treating itching, sneezing, and runny nose as well as related eye symptoms [MeReC, 2004]. Six drugs are currently available that are considered safe and taken once a day [DTB, 2002]:
  - **Cetirizine and loratadine** are well-established agents with a good efficacy and safety profile. They are taken once a day and are suitable for young children.
  - **Fexofenadine and mizolastine** are alternative once-daily regimens suitable for older children and adults.
  - **Desloratadine (a metabolite of loratadine) and levocetirizine (an isomer of cetirizine)** are more recently marketed products that are still under close post-marketing surveillance (black triangle).
- **Intranasal antihistamines** are as effective as oral antihistamines for people without eye symptoms. They relieve nasal symptoms, are quick acting (but have a short duration), and are safe [MeReC, 2004]. Two products are available:
  - **Azelastine** is available as a nasal spray administered twice a day.
  - **Levocabastine** is available as a nasal spray administered twice a day, increasing up to four times a day if necessary.
- **Intranasal corticosteroids are a good alternative to antihistamines.** They are more effective than oral antihistamines at relieving most nasal symptoms, including nasal congestion, and are equally as effective for relieving eye symptoms [Weiner et al, 1998]. Intranasal corticosteroids should be regarded as preventative rather than relieving treatment; they take time to work and ideally should be applied one week before exposure to allergens (e.g. pollen in hay fever):
  - **There are no known differences in efficacy between individual intranasal corticosteroids** [Waddell et al, 2003]: use of beclometasone, betamethasone, budesonide, flunisolide, fluticasone, mometasone, and triamcinolone should be selected according to patient preference.
  - **Drops or sprays are both offered:** however drops may have an increased risk of systemic effects [BNF 48, 2004].
- **Intranasal sodium cromoglicate** is useful as an alternative treatment if antihistamines and intranasal corticosteroids are contraindicated, or as an add-on therapy if treatment with these is not fully effective. It is safe [ARIA, 2001], but requires frequent dosing. The stronger 4% spray is recommended over the 2% spray as it requires less frequent dosing [BNF 48, 2004].
- **Intranasal decongestants** are effective in relieving nasal congestion in the short term. They should not be used for more than a week due to the risk of rebound congestion following cessation of treatment [ARIA, 2001]. Ephedrine and xylometazoline are the sympathomimetic drugs most commonly used.

A

Prescriptions

Oral antihistamines: non-sedating

Cetirizine s/f solution: 5mg once a day
- Age from 2 to 5 years
- Cetirizine 5mg/5ml s/f sol. Take one 5ml spoonful once a day; supply 200 ml; NHS Cost £9.77; OTC Cost £17.22.

Cetirizine s/f solution: 10mg once a day
- Age from 6 to 11 years
- Cetirizine 5mg/5ml s/f sol. Take two 5ml spoonfuls once a day; supply 300 ml; NHS Cost £14.66; OTC Cost £25.83.

Cetirizine tablets: 10mg once a day
- Age from 12 years onwards
- Cetirizine 10mg tablets. Take one tablet once a day; supply 30 tablets; NHS Cost £5.64; OTC Cost £9.94.

Loratadine syrup: 5mg once a day
- Age from 2 to 5 years
- Loratadine 5mg/5ml syrup. Take one 5ml spoonful once a day; supply 200 ml; NHS Cost £10.86; OTC Cost £19.14.

Loratadine syrup: 10mg once a day
- Age from 6 to 11 years
- Loratadine 5mg/5ml syrup. Take two 5ml spoonfuls once a day; supply 300 ml; NHS Cost £16.29; OTC Cost £28.71.

Loratadine tablets: 10mg once a day
- Age from 12 years onwards
- Loratadine 10mg tablets. Take one tablet once a day; supply 30 tablets; NHS Cost £4.09; OTC Cost £7.21.

Fexofenadine tablets: 30mg twice a day
- Age from 6 to 11 years
- Fexofenadine 30mg tablets. Take one tablet twice a day; supply 60 tablets; NHS Cost £6.11.

Fexofenadine tablets: 120mg once a day
- Age from 12 years onwards
- Fexofenadine 120mg tablets. Take one tablet once a day; supply 30 tablets; NHS Cost £8.14.

Mizolastine tablets: 10mg once a day
- Age from 12 years onwards
- Mizolastine 10mg tablets. Take one tablet once a day; supply 30 tablets; NHS Cost £5.77.

Levocetirizine tablets: 5mg once a day
- Age from 6 years onwards
- Levocetirizine 5mg tablets. Take one tablet once a day; supply 30 tablets; NHS Cost £7.45.

Desloratadine syrup: 1.25mg once a day
- Age from 12 months to 5 years
- Desloratadine 2.5mg/5ml syrup. Take 2.5ml once a day; supply 100 ml; NHS Cost £7.04.

Desloratadine syrup: 2.5mg once a day
- Age from 6 to 11 years
- Desloratadine 2.5mg/5ml syrup. Take one 5ml spoonful once a day; supply 200 ml; NHS Cost £14.08.

Desloratadine tablets: 5mg once a day
- Age from 12 years onwards
- Desloratadine 5mg tablets. Take one tablet once a day; supply 30 tablets; NHS Cost £7.04.

Intranasal antihistamines

Azelastine 140microgram (0.1%) nasal spray
- Age from 5 years onwards
- Azelastine 0.1% nasal spray. Spray once into each nostril twice a day when required; supply 1 spray; NHS Cost £11.92.

Levocabastine 500microgram (0.05%) nasal spray
- Age from 9 years onwards
- Levocabastine 0.05% nasal spray. Spray twice into ea nostril twice a day when required; supply 1 spray; NHS Cost £9.74.

Intranasal corticosteroids

Beclometasone 50microgram nasal spray
- Age from 6 years onwards
- Beclometasone nasal spray. Spray twice into each nos twice a day; supply 1 spray; NHS Cost £3.38.

Betamethasone 0.1% nose drops
- Age from 12 months onwards
- Betamethasone 0.1% nose drops. Put two drops into each nostril twice a day; supply 10 ml; NHS Cost £2.3

Budesonide 64microgram nasal spray
- Age from 12 years onwards
- Budesonide 64mcg nasal spray. Spray once into each nostril twice a day; supply 1 spray; NHS Cost £4.49.

Flunisolide 25microgram nasal spray
- Age from 5 to 13 years
- Flunisolide 25mcg nasal spray. Spray once into each nostril up to three times a day; supply 1 spray; NHS Cost £5.05.

Flunisolide 25microgram nasal spray
- Age from 14 years onwards
- Flunisolide 25mcg nasal spray. Spray twice into each nostril twice a day; supply 1 spray; NHS Cost £5.05.

Fluticasone 50microgram nasal spray
- Age from 4 to 11 years
- Fluticasone 50mcg nasal spray. Spray once into each nostril each morning; supply 1 spray; NHS Cost £11.6

Fluticasone 50microgram nasal spray
- Age from 12 years onwards
- Fluticasone 50mcg nasal spray. Spray twice into each nostril each morning; supply 1 spray; NHS Cost £11.6

Mometasone 50microgram nasal spray
- Age from 6 to 11 years
- Mometasone 50mcg nasal spray. Spray once into each nostril once a day; supply 1 spray; NHS Cost £7.83.

Mometasone 50microgram nasal spray
- Age from 12 years onwards
- Mometasone 50mcg nasal spray. Spray twice into each nostril once a day; supply 1 spray; NHS Cost £7.83.

Triamcinolone 55microgram nasal spray
- Age from 6 to 11 years
- Triamcinolone 55mcg nasal spray. Spray once into eac nostril once a day; supply 1 spray; NHS Cost £7.39.

Triamcinolone 55microgram nasal spray
- Age from 12 years onwards
- Triamcinolone 55mcg nasal spray. Spray twice into eac nostril once a day; supply 1 spray; NHS Cost £7.39.

Alternative/add on: sodium cromoglicate

Sodium cromoglicate 4% nasal spray
- Age from 1 month onwards
- Sod cromoglicate 4% nasal spray. Spray once into each nostril 2 to 4 times a day; supply 1 spray; NHS Cost £18.09.

Intranasal decongestants – for nasal blockage (short term)

Ephedrine 0.5% nose drops
- Age from 3 months onwards
- Ephedrine 0.5% nose drops. Put one to two drops into each nostril up to four times a day when required for nasal blockage. Do not use for more than 7 days; supply 10 ml; NHS Cost £1.27.

ometazoline 0.05% nose drops
Age from 3 months to 11 years
Xylometazoline paed nose drops. Put one to two drops into each nostril once or twice a day when required for nasal blockage. Do not use for more than 7 days; supply 10 ml; NHS Cost £1.59.

ometazoline 0.1% nose drops
Age from 12 years onwards
Xylometazoline 0.1% nose drops. Put two to three drops into each nostril 2 to 3 times a day when required for nasal blockage. Do not use for more than 7 days; supply 10 ml; NHS Cost £1.91.

Moderate-severe persistent allergic rhinitis

Which therapy?

- **Advise on avoiding allergens** (See PRODIGY *Patient Information Leaflets*).
- **Use an intranasal corticosteroid** as treatment.
- **Consider using an intranasal decongestant** in the short term to relieve congestion and allow penetration of the intranasal corticosteroid.
- **If alternative or add-on treatment is required consider:**
  - **An antihistamine** (oral or intranasal). Intranasal antihistamines have a faster onset of action than oral preparations, but require more frequent administration. If using an oral antihistamine, non-sedating oral antihistamines are preferred. Cetirizine is probably the most sedating and fexofenadine the least.
  - **Intranasal sodium cromoglicate** has no reported adverse effects.
  - **Intranasal ipratropium bromide** in people with persistent watery effusion.
  - **Leukotriene antagonists** may have a role in people with coexisting asthma.

Practical prescribing points

For further information see the *Medicines Compendium* (www.medicines.org.uk) or the *British National Formulary* (www.bnf.org).

- **'Non-sedating' oral antihistamines:** people receiving any antihistamine should be advised that treatment can affect driving and other skilled tasks, and enhance the effects of alcohol [DTB, 2002].
- **Mizolastine** has the potential to prolong the QT interval in some people and is contraindicated in people with significant cardiac disease, symptomatic arrhythmias, or those taking anti-arrhythmic drugs [BNF 48, 2004].
- **Intranasal corticosteroids:** occasionally, local adverse effects can occur (e.g. crusting, dryness, minor nosebleed) that may require treatment to stop for a while. The CSM advises that the height of children receiving prolonged treatment with intranasal corticosteroids should be regularly monitored.
- **Intranasal decongestants** can cause severe rebound effects, and should not be used for more than 7 days continuously [BNF 48, 2004].
- **Leukotriene antagonists are not licensed for the treatment of allergic rhinitis** [BNF 48, 2004].

Follow-up advice

If the person improves on intranasal corticosteroids, a step-down approach should be used.

- The dose of intranasal corticosteroid should be titrated to the lowest dose that controls symptoms.
- **Consider coexistent infection if there is failure to respond to treatment.**
- **If symptoms continue to be poorly controlled,** consider a short course of oral corticosteroid (see scenario *Failure to respond to standard treatment*).
- **The height of children receiving prolonged treatment with intranasal corticosteroids should be regularly monitored.** If growth is slowed, treatment should be reviewed with the aim of reducing the dose of corticosteroid to the lowest dose that maintains symptom control, and paediatric referral should be considered.

Should I refer or investigate?

Refer?

- **Specialist referral is recommended for people who do not respond to maximal management by their general practitioner.** This is to confirm the diagnosis, optimize treatment, and consider the need for immunotherapy or surgery.
- **Paediatric referral should be considered in children receiving prolonged treatment with intranasal corticosteroids who have evidence of slowed growth** (particularly if this persists when the dose of corticosteroid is reduced to the lowest dose that maintains symptom control).
- **Refer all people with persistent rhinitis** as it recommended that they have a nasal examination. Anterior rhinoscopy only gives limited information and a nasal endoscopy is recommended.
- **ENT referral is also recommended for:**
  - Unilateral nasal problems
  - Nasal perforations, ulceration, or collapse
  - Serosanguinous discharge
  - Crusting high in the nasal cavity
  - Recurrent infection
  - Periorbital cellulitis (urgent admission)

Patient information leaflets

The following PILs are available at www.prodigy.nhs.uk

- Allergy UK
- Hay Fever
- House Dust Mite and Pet Allergy
- Nose Drops - How To Use
- Nose Sprays (Steroid)
- Rhinitis (Persistent)

Shared decision making

- **A steroid nasal spray (or steroid nasal drops)** usually works well to ease most of the symptoms of allergic rhinitis.
  - It takes a few days to build up and work fully.
  - Then needs to be taken regularly to keep symptoms away.
- **An antihistamine medicine** is an alternative. It eases most symptoms (runny nose, sneezing, etc) but may not totally clear a blocked nose. It can be used in addition to a steroid nose spray if symptoms are not eased by either alone.
- **An antihistamine nasal spray** is another alternative, but you need to use it quite frequently.
- **A decongestant spray** works quickly to clear a blocked nose.
  - It may be helpful to take for a few days whilst starting with a steroid spray. It allows the steroid to get to the lining of the nose to work.

A

  - However, it should not be used for more than 5–7 days as otherwise a worse 'rebound' congestion may occur.
- **Sodium cromoglicate nasal spray** is an option if you cannot use any of the above, or as an add-on treatment if symptoms remain troublesome despite other treatments.
- **Ipratropium spray** is an alternative or add-on treatment when a watery nose is the main symptom. It does not help sneezing, itch, or a blocked nose.
- **A leukotriene antagonist medicine** may help if you also have asthma.
- **If you know the cause of the allergy,** avoiding it may ease symptoms. For example:
  - House-dust mite: numbers may be reduced by regular cleaning and vacuuming of carpets and bedding. A leaflet explains this further.
  - Pets: keep them out of living areas if you cannot give them up.

Drug rationale

Drugs not included

- **'Sedating' antihistamines** are not recommended. They cause significantly more sedation than the newer 'non-sedating' antihistamines, which may considerably impair normal daytime activity [Shamsi and Hindmarch, 2000; Casale et al, 2003].
- **Acrivastine and terfenadine** are not recommended. Acrivastine requires three doses per day [BNF 48, 2004], whilst terfenadine has the potential to cause serious heart arrhythmias [DTB, 2002].
- **Intranasal dexamethasone** is only available combined with tramazoline, which is not recommended for long-term use [BNF 48, 2004].
- **Oral decongestants** are not as effective as intranasal decongestants, can cause systemic adverse effects, and may interact with other medications [ARIA, 2001; BNF 48, 2004].
- **Ephedrine 1% nose drops** are not recommended as they may cause more systemic adverse effects than the 0.5% formulation.
- **Systemic corticosteroids** (oral prednisolone) should only be used in severe case of allergic rhinitis that is unresponsive to all other treatment options (see scenario *Failure to respond to standard treatment*).

Drugs included

- **Intranasal corticosteroids are the first-line treatment** in people with moderate or severe symptoms of allergic rhinitis that are persistent. They are more effective than oral antihistamines at relieving most nasal symptoms, including nasal congestion, and are equally as effective for relieving eye symptoms [Weiner et al, 1998]. Intranasal corticosteroids should be regarded as preventative rather than relieving treatment; they take time to work and ideally should be applied one week before exposure to allergens (e.g. pollen in hay fever):
  - **There are no known differences in efficacy between individual intranasal corticosteroids** [Waddell et al, 2003]: use of beclometasone, betamethasone, budesonide, flunisolide, fluticasone, mometasone, and triamcinolone should be selected according to patient preference.
  - **Drops or sprays are both offered:** however drops may have an increased risk of systemic effects [BNF 48, 2004].
- **'Non-sedating' oral antihistamines** can be used as an additional treatment (or alternative if intranasal corticosteroids are contraindicated). They are effective in treating itching, sneezing, and runny nose as well as related eye symptoms [MeReC, 2004]. Six drugs are currently available which are considered safe and take once a day [DTB, 2002]:
  - **Cetirizine and loratadine** are well-established agents with a good efficacy and safety profile. They are tak once a day and are suitable for young children.
  - **Fexofenadine and mizolastine** are alternative once-daily regimens suitable for older children and adults
  - **Desloratadine (a metabolite of loratadine) and levocetirizine (an isomer of cetirizine)** are more recently marketed products that are still under close post-marketing surveillance (black triangle).
- **Intranasal antihistamines** are as effective as oral antihistamines for people without eye symptoms. They relieve nasal symptoms, are quick acting (but have a short duration), and safe [MeReC, 2004]. Two produ are available:
  - **Azelastine** is available as a nasal spray administered twice a day.
  - **Levocabastine** is available as a nasal spray administered twice a day, increasing up to four time day if necessary.
- **Intranasal sodium cromoglicate** is useful as an alternative treatment if antihistamines and intranasal corticosteroids are contraindicated, or as an add-on therapy if treatment with these is not fully effective. It safe [ARIA, 2001], but requires frequent dosing. The stronger 4% spray is recommended over the 2% spray it requires less frequent dosing [BNF 48, 2004].
- **Intranasal ipratropium bromide** is useful if there is persistent, profuse, watery discharge present [ARIA, 2001].
- **Leukotriene antagonists** should be considered in peopl who have persistent moderate or severe symptoms and have accompanying asthma. They are not licensed for use in allergic rhinitis alone. Montelukast is taken once at night; zafirlukast is taken twice a day [BNF 48, 200
- **Intranasal decongestants** are effective in relieving nasal congestion in the short term. They should not be used more than a week due to the risk of rebound congestion following cessation of treatment [ARIA, 2001]. Ephedrine and xylometazoline are the sympathomimet drugs most commonly used.

Prescriptions

1st line: intranasal corticosteroids

Beclometasone 50microgram nasal spray
- Age from 6 years onwards
- Beclometasone nasal spray. Spray twice into each nostr twice a day; supply 1 spray; NHS Cost £3.38.

Betamethasone 0.1% nose drops
- Age from 12 months onwards
- Betamethasone 0.1% nose drops. Put two drops into each nostril twice a day; supply 10 ml; NHS Cost £2.3

Budesonide 64microgram nasal spray
- Age from 12 years onwards
- Budesonide 64mcg nasal spray. Spray once into each nostril twice a day; supply 1 spray; NHS Cost £4.49.

Flunisolide 25microgram nasal spray
- Age from 5 to 13 years
- Flunisolide 25mcg nasal spray. Spray once into each nostril up to three times a day; supply 1 spray; NHS Cost £5.05.

Flunisolide 25microgram nasal spray
- Age from 14 years onwards
- Flunisolide 25mcg nasal spray. Spray twice into each nostril twice a day; supply 1 spray; NHS Cost £5.05.

ticasone 50microgram nasal spray
- Age from 4 to 11 years
- Fluticasone 50mcg nasal spray. Spray once into each nostril each morning; supply 1 spray; NHS Cost £11.69.

ticasone 50microgram nasal spray
- Age from 12 years onwards
- Fluticasone 50mcg nasal spray. Spray twice into each nostril each morning; supply 1 spray; NHS Cost £11.69.

metasone 50microgram nasal spray
- Age from 6 to 11 years
- Mometasone 50mcg nasal spray. Spray once into each nostril once a day; supply 1 spray; NHS Cost £7.83.

metasone 50microgram nasal spray
- Age from 12 years onwards
- Mometasone 50mcg nasal spray. Spray twice into each nostril once a day; supply 1 spray; NHS Cost £7.83.

iamcinolone 55microgram nasal spray
- Age from 6 to 11 years
- Triamcinolone 55mcg nasal spray. Spray once into each nostril once a day; supply 1 spray; NHS Cost £7.39.

iamcinolone 55microgram nasal spray
- Age from 12 years onwards
- Triamcinolone 55mcg nasal spray. Spray twice into each nostril once a day; supply 1 spray; NHS Cost £7.39.

lternative/add-on: oral antihistamines (non-sedating)

etirizine s/f solution: 5mg once a day
- Age from 2 to 5 years
- Cetirizine 5mg/5ml s/f sol. Take one 5ml spoonful once a day; supply 200 ml; NHS Cost £9.77; OTC Cost £17.22.

etirizine s/f solution: 10mg once a day
- Age from 6 to 11 years
- Cetirizine 5mg/5ml s/f sol. Take two 5ml spoonfuls once a day; supply 300 ml; NHS Cost £14.66; OTC Cost £25.83.

etirizine tablets: 10mg once a day
- Age from 12 years onwards
- Cetirizine 10mg tablets. Take one tablet once a day; supply 30 tablets; NHS Cost £5.64; OTC Cost £9.94.

oratadine syrup: 5mg once a day
- Age from 2 to 5 years
- Loratadine 5mg/5ml syrup. Take one 5ml spoonful once a day; supply 200 ml; NHS Cost £10.86; OTC Cost £19.14.

oratadine syrup: 10mg once a day
- Age from 6 to 11 years
- Loratadine 5mg/5ml syrup. Take two 5ml spoonfuls once a day; supply 300 ml; NHS Cost £16.29; OTC Cost £28.71.

oratadine tablets: 10mg once a day
- Age from 12 years onwards
- Loratadine 10mg tablets. Take one tablet once a day; supply 30 tablets; NHS Cost £4.09; OTC Cost £7.21.

exofenadine tablets: 30mg twice a day
- Age from 6 to 11 years
- Fexofenadine 30mg tablets. Take one tablet twice a day; supply 60 tablets; NHS Cost £6.11.

exofenadine tablets: 120mg once a day
- Age from 12 years onwards
- Fexofenadine 120mg tablets. Take one tablet once a day; supply 30 tablets; NHS Cost £8.14.

izolastine tablets: 10mg once a day
- Age from 12 years onwards
- Mizolastine 10mg tablets. Take one tablet once a day; supply 30 tablets; NHS Cost £5.77.

Levocetirizine tablets: 5mg once a day
- Age from 6 years onwards
- Levocetirizine 5mg tablets. Take one tablet once a day; supply 30 tablets; NHS Cost £7.45.

Desloratadine syrup: 1.25mg once a day
- Age from 12 months to 5 years
- Desloratadine 2.5mg/5ml syrup. Take 2.5ml once a day; supply 100 ml; NHS Cost £7.04.

Desloratadine syrup: 2.5mg once a day
- Age from 6 to 11 years
- Desloratadine 2.5mg/5ml syrup. Take one 5ml spoonful once a day; supply 200 ml; NHS Cost £14.08.

Desloratadine tablets: 5mg once a day
- Age from 12 years onwards
- Desloratadine 5mg tablets. Take one tablet once a day; supply 30 tablets; NHS Cost £7.04.

Alternative/add-on: intranasal preparations

Azelastine 140microgram (0.1%) nasal spray
- Age from 5 years onwards
- Azelastine 0.1% nasal spray. Spray once into each nostril twice a day when required; supply 1 spray; NHS Cost £11.92.

Levocabastine 500microgram (0.05%) nasal spray
- Age from 9 years onwards
- Levocabastine 0.05% nasal spray. Spray twice into each nostril twice a day when required; supply 1 spray; NHS Cost £9.74.

Sodium cromoglicate 4% nasal spray
- Age from 1 month onwards
- Sod cromoglicate 4% nasal spray. Spray once into each nostril 2 to 4 times a day; supply 1 spray; NHS Cost £18.09.

Ipratropium 0.03% (21mcg) nasal spray for watery rhinorrhoea
- Age from 12 years onwards
- Ipratropium 21mcg nasal spray. Spray twice into each nostril 2 to 3 times a day; supply 1 spray; NHS Cost £4.55.

Alternative/add-on: leukotriene receptor antagonists

Montelukast chewable tablets: 4mg at night
- Age from 2 to 5 years
- Montelukast sodium 4mg chewable. Chew one tablet at night; supply 28 tablet; NHS Cost £25.69.

Montelukast chewable tablets: 5mg at night
- Age from 6 to 13 years
- Montelukast sodium 5mg chewable. Chew one tablet at night; supply 28 tablet; NHS Cost £25.69.

Montelukast 10mg at night
- Age from 14 years onwards
- Montelukast 10mg tablets. Take one tablet at night; supply 28 tablets; NHS Cost £25.69.

Zafirlukast 20mg twice a day
- Age from 12 years onwards
- Zafirlukast 20mg tablets. Take one tablet twice a day; supply 56 tablets; NHS Cost £25.69.

Intranasal decongestants – for nasal blockage (short term)

Ephedrine 0.5% nose drops
- Age from 3 months onwards
- Ephedrine 0.5% nose drops. Put one to two drops into each nostril up to four times a day when required for nasal blockage. Do not use for more than 7 days; supply 10 ml; NHS Cost £1.27.

A

Xylometazoline 0.05% nose drops

- Age from 3 months to 11 years
- Xylometazoline paed nose drops. Put one to two drops into each nostril once or twice a day when required for nasal blockage. Do not use for more than 7 days; supply 10 ml; NHS Cost £1.59.

Xylometazoline 0.1% nose drops

- Age from 12 years onwards
- Xylometazoline 0.1% nose drops. Put two to three drops into each nostril 2 to 3 times a day when required for nasal blockage. Do not use for more than 7 days; supply 10 ml; NHS Cost £1.91.

Allergic rhinitis with eye symptoms

Which therapy?

- **Exclude the possibility of a more serious cause of red eye.**
- **Treat with a drug that reduces both eye and nasal symptoms:**
  - **'Non-sedating' oral antihistamines** are a good choice for mild intermittent allergic symptoms. Cetirizine is probably the most sedating and fexofenadine the least.
  - **Intranasal corticosteroids** are as effective as oral antihistamines, and are preferred when there are more persistent symptoms.
- **Eye drops:** if oral antihistamines and intranasal corticosteroids are not appropriate, or do not adequately control eye symptoms, consider using an additional topical ocular drug:
  - **Antihistamines:** azelastine, emedastine, and levocabastine provide rapid relief.
  - **Mast-cell stabilizers:** sodium cromoglicate, lodoxamide and nedocromil are effective but take longer to act than antihistamines.
  - **Olopatadine and ketotifen** are newer drugs with combined actions.

Practical prescribing points

For further information please see the *Medicines Compendium* (www.medicines.org.uk) or the *British National Formulary* (www.bnf.org).

- **Contact lenses** should generally not be worn during treatment with eye drops. However:
  - **Hard lenses:** use eye drops 30 minutes before inserting lenses.
  - **Soft lenses:** eye drops containing preservatives should not be used with soft lenses. (Some preservatives, particularly benzalkonium chloride, accumulate in soft contact lenses and cause irritation.)
- **'Non-sedating' oral antihistamines:** people receiving any antihistamine should be advised that treatment can affect driving and other skilled tasks, and enhance the effects of alcohol [DTB, 2002].
- **Mizolastine** has the potential to prolong the QT interval in some people and is contraindicated in people with significant cardiac disease, symptomatic arrhythmias, or those taking anti-arrhythmic drugs [BNF 48, 2004].
- **Intranasal corticosteroids:** occasionally, local adverse effects can occur (e.g. crusting, dryness, minor nosebleed) that may require treatment to stop for a while. The CSM advises that the height of children receiving prolonged treatment with intranasal corticosteroids should be regularly monitored.

Follow-up advice

- **Reassess** how effective treatment was after 2–4 week.
  - If the person is symptom free or the symptoms are le then continue the current treatment.
  - Continue the treatment long-term if the symptoms a perennial.
  - If the person has persistent mild symptoms and is using antihistamines or sodium cromoglicate, consid changing to intranasal corticosteroids.
- **If the person is taking intranasal corticosteroids:**
  - If the person improves on intranasal corticosteroids, step-down approach should be used. The dose of intranasal corticosteroid should be titrated to the lowest dose that controls symptoms.
  - The height of children receiving prolonged treatmen with intranasal corticosteroids should be regularly monitored. If growth is slowed, treatment should be reviewed with the aim of reducing the dose of corticosteroid to the lowest dose that maintains symptom control, and paediatric referral should be considered.
- **If symptoms continue to be poorly controlled,** consider short course of oral corticosteroid (see scenario *Failure to respond to standard treatment*).

Should I refer or investigate?

- **Refer all people for same-day assessment** if they have a of the following features that could indicate iritis, keratitis or acute glaucoma:
  - Moderate to severe eye pain
  - Marked eye redness
  - Ciliary injection
  - Loss of visual acuity
- **Refer all babies if they have any signs of conjunctivitis within the first 28 days of life** (this must be distinguishe from a simple sticky eye when there are no signs of inflammation of the conjunctiva).
- **Refer people with symptoms that persist despite treatment** particularly if there are features of atopic keratoconjunctivitis, vernal keratoconjunctivitis or allergic contact allergic dermatitis with conjunctivitis o when these conditions are associated with corneal involvment.
- **Refer all people with persistent rhinitis** as it recommended that they have a nasal examination. Anterior rhinoscopy only gives limited information and nasal endoscopy is recommended.
- **Paediatric referral should be considered in children receiving prolonged treatment with intranasal corticosteroids who have evidence of slowed growth** (particularly if this persists when the dose of corticosteroid is reduced to the lowest dose that maintains symptom control).
- **ENT referral is also recommended for:**
  - Unilateral nasal problems
  - Nasal perforations, ulceration, or collapse
  - Serosanguinous discharge
  - Crusting high in the nasal cavity
  - Recurrent infection
  - Periorbital cellulitis (urgent admission)
  - Non-response to treatment
  - Poor response to maximal therapy

Patient information leaflets

The following PILs are available at www.prodigy.nhs.uk

- Allergy UK
- Conjunctivitis - Allergic
- Eye Drops - (How to Use)
- Hay Fever

House Dust Mite and Pet Allergy Rhinitis (Persistent)

hared decision making

A steroid nasal spray (or steroid nasal drops) usually works well to ease most of the symptoms of allergic rhinitis including eye symptoms.

- It may take a few days to build up and work fully.
- Then need to be taken regularly to keep symptoms away.

An antihistamine medicine is an alternative, and can also be used in addition to nose sprays if symptoms are not cleared by either alone.

Eye drops are an option if you cannot use any of the above, or as an add-on treatment if symptoms remain troublesome despite other treatments.

- **Antihistamine eye drops** work quickly. You can use them regularly or 'as required' to ease a flare up of symptoms.
- **Mast-cell stabilisers** stop the release of histamine from cells called mast cells. You need to use them regularly to prevent symptoms.
- **Some** drops have both actions–antihistamine and mast-cell stabiliser.

Reducing your exposure to pollen may help if hay fever is the cause of your symptoms.

- Stay indoors as much as possible, and keep windows and doors shut.
- Avoid cutting grass, large grassy places, and camping.
- Shower and wash your hair after being outdoors. Especially after going to the countryside.
- Wear wrap-around sunglasses when out.
- Bring in washing, and close windows before the evening.
- Keep car windows closed.

)rug rationale

rugs not included

'Sedating' antihistamines are not recommended. They cause significantly more sedation than the newer 'non-sedating' antihistamines, which may considerably impair normal daytime activity [Shamsi and Hindmarch, 2000; Casale et al, 2003].

Acrivastine and terfenadine are not recommended. Acrivastine requires three doses per day [BNF 48, 2004], whilst terfenadine has the potential to cause serious heart arrhythmias [DTB, 2002].

Otrivine-Antistin® eye drops contain antazoline (antihistamine) and xylometazoline (vasoconstrictor). Although this is an established product that may be used for short-term relief, systemic effects are possible and it should not be used for long periods of time [BNF 48, 2004].

Topical ocular corticosteroids should not be initiated in primary care for this condition [BNF 48, 2004]. Problems with their use include steroid-induced glaucoma and inadvertent treatment of an eye infected with herpes simplex virus (dendritic ulcer).

)rugs included

'Non-sedating' oral antihistamines are effective in treating eye symptoms as well as nasal itching, sneezing, and runny nose [MeReC, 2004]. Six drugs are currently available which are considered safe and taken once a day [DTB, 2002]:

- **Cetirizine and loratadine** are well-established agents with a good efficacy and safety profile. They are taken once a day and are suitable for young children.
- **Fexofenadine and mizolastine** are alternative once-daily regimens suitable for older children and adults.
- **Desloratadine (a metabolite of loratadine) and levocetirizine (an isomer of cetirizine)** are more recently marketed products that are still under close post-marketing surveillance (black triangle).

- **Intranasal corticosteroids are** equally as effective for relieving eye symptoms as oral antihistamines, and more effective at relieving most nasal symptoms, including nasal congestion [Weiner et al, 1998]. Intranasal corticosteroids should be regarded as preventative rather than relieving treatment; they take time to work and ideally should be applied one week before exposure to allergens (e.g. pollen in hay fever):
  - **There are no known differences in efficacy between individual intranasal corticosteroids** [Waddell et al, 2003]: use of beclometasone, betamethasone, budesonide, flunisolide, fluticasone, mometasone, and triamcinolone should be selected according to patient preference.
  - **Drops or sprays are both offered:** however drops may have an increased risk of systemic effects [BNF 48, 2004].
- **Azelastine, emedastine, and levocabastine** are single-agent topical antihistamines that give quick relief of allergic conjunctivitis. They are well tolerated, have few adverse effects, and have a rapid onset of action [Owen et al, 2004].
- **Topical mast-cell stabilizers** are safe and effective both in relieving, and preventing, allergic conjunctivitis [Owen et al, 2004]. Three products are available in the United Kingdom [BNF 48, 2004]:
  - **Sodium cromoglicate** is the preferred first-line choice. It is inexpensive and suitable for use in young children.
  - **Lodoxamide and nedocromil** are newer, more expensive topical agents available as alternatives to sodium cromoglicate.
- **Olopatadine and ketotifen** are newer topical antihistamines that have mast cell stabilizer activity. They currently have black triangle status and are recommended for use when standard topical treatment has been poorly tolerated or is ineffective [DTB, 2002].

Prescriptions

Oral antihistamines: non-sedating

Cetirizine s/f solution: 5mg once a day

- Age from 2 to 5 years
- Cetirizine 5mg/5ml s/f sol. Take one 5ml spoonful once a day; supply 200 ml; NHS Cost £9.77; OTC Cost £17.22.

Cetirizine s/f solution: 10mg once a day

- Age from 6 to 11 years
- Cetirizine 5mg/5ml s/f sol. Take two 5ml spoonfuls once a day; supply 300 ml; NHS Cost £14.66; OTC Cost £25.83.

Cetirizine tablets: 10mg once a day

- Age from 12 years onwards
- Cetirizine 10mg tablets. Take one tablet once a day; supply 30 tablets; NHS Cost £5.64; OTC Cost £9.94.

Loratadine syrup: 5mg once a day

- Age from 2 to 5 years
- Loratadine 5mg/5ml syrup. Take one 5ml spoonful once a day; supply 200 ml; NHS Cost £10.86; OTC Cost £19.14.

Loratadine syrup: 10mg once a day

- Age from 6 to 11 years
- Loratadine 5mg/5ml syrup. Take two 5ml spoonfuls once a day; supply 300 ml; NHS Cost £16.29; OTC Cost £28.71.

Loratadine tablets: 10mg once a day
- Age from 12 years onwards
- Loratadine 10mg tablets. Take one tablet once a day; supply 30 tablets; NHS Cost £4.09; OTC Cost £7.21.

Fexofenadine tablets: 30mg twice a day
- Age from 6 to 11 years
- Fexofenadine 30mg tablets. Take one tablet twice a day; supply 60 tablets; NHS Cost £6.11.

Fexofenadine tablets: 120mg once a day
- Age from 12 years onwards
- Fexofenadine 120mg tablets. Take one tablet once a day; supply 30 tablets; NHS Cost £8.14.

Mizolastine tablets: 10mg once a day
- Age from 12 years onwards
- Mizolastine 10mg tablets. Take one tablet once a day; supply 30 tablets; NHS Cost £5.77.

Levocetirizine tablets: 5mg once a day
- Age from 6 years onwards
- Levocetirizine 5mg tablets. Take one tablet once a day; supply 30 tablets; NHS Cost £7.45.

Desloratadine syrup: 1.25mg once a day
- Age from 12 months to 5 years
- Desloratadine 2.5mg/5ml syrup. Take 2.5ml once a day; supply 100 ml; NHS Cost £7.00.

Desloratadine syrup: 2.5mg once a day
- Age from 6 to 11 years
- Desloratadine 2.5mg/5ml syrup. Take one 5ml spoonful once a day; supply 200 ml; NHS Cost £14.08.

Desloratadine tablets: 5mg once a day
- Age from 12 years onwards
- Desloratadine 5mg tablets. Take one tablet once a day; supply 30 tablets; NHS Cost £7.04.

Intranasal corticosteroids

Beclometasone 50microgram nasal spray
- Age from 6 years onwards
- Beclometasone nasal spray. Spray twice into each nostril twice a day; supply 1 spray; NHS Cost £3.38.

Betamethasone 0.1% nose drops
- Age from 12 months onwards
- Betamethasone 0.1% nose drops. Put two drops into each nostril twice a day; supply 10 ml; NHS Cost £2.32.

Budesonide 64microgram nasal spray
- Age from 12 years onwards
- Budesonide 64mcg nasal spray. Spray once into each nostril twice a day; supply 1 spray; NHS Cost £4.49.

Flunisolide 25microgram nasal spray
- Age from 5 to 13 years
- Flunisolide 25mcg nasal spray. Spray once into each nostril up to three times a day; supply 1 spray; NHS Cost £5.05.

Flunisolide 25microgram nasal spray
- Age from 14 years onwards
- Flunisolide 25mcg nasal spray. Spray twice into each nostril twice a day; supply 1 spray; NHS Cost £5.05.

Fluticasone 50microgram nasal spray
- Age from 4 to 11 years
- Fluticasone 50mcg nasal spray. Spray once into each nostril each morning; supply 1 spray; NHS Cost £11.69.

Fluticasone 50microgram nasal spray
- Age from 12 years onwards
- Fluticasone 50mcg nasal spray. Spray twice into each nostril each morning; supply 1 spray; NHS Cost £11.69.

Mometasone 50microgram nasal spray
- Age from 6 to 11 years
- Mometasone 50mcg nasal spray. Spray once into each nostril once a day; supply 1 spray; NHS Cost £7.83.

Mometasone 50microgram nasal spray
- Age from 12 years onwards
- Mometasone 50mcg nasal spray. Spray twice into each nostril once a day; supply 1 spray; NHS Cost £7.83.

Triamcinolone 55microgram nasal spray
- Age from 6 to 11 years
- Triamcinolone 55mcg nasal spray. Spray once into eac nostril once a day; supply 1 spray; NHS Cost £7.39.

Triamcinolone 55microgram nasal spray
- Age from 12 years onwards
- Triamcinolone 55mcg nasal spray. Spray twice into eac nostril once a day; supply 1 spray; NHS Cost £7.39.

Antihistamine eye drops for rapid relief

Azelastine 0.05% eye drops
- Age from 4 years onwards
- Azelastine 0.05% eye drops. Put one drop into each ey twice a day. Increase to four times a day if required; supply 8 ml; NHS Cost £6.88.

Emedastine 0.05% eye drops
- Age from 3 years onwards
- Emedastine 0.05% eye drops. Put one drop into each e twice a day; supply 5 ml; NHS Cost £7.69.

Levocabastine 0.05% eye drops
- Age from 12 years onwards
- Levocabastine 0.05% eye drops. Put one drop into eacl eye twice a day. Increase to 3 to 4 times a day if require Stop if there is no improvement within 3 days; supply 3 ml; NHS Cost £3.28; OTC Cost £5.75.

Mast cell stabilizer eye drops for prophylaxis

Sodium cromoglicate 2% eye drops
- Age from 1 month onwards
- Sodium cromoglicate 2% eyedrops. Put one drop into each eye four times a day; supply 14 ml; NHS Cost £1.96; OTC Cost £3.45.

Lodoxamide 0.1% eye drops
- Age from 4 years onwards
- Lodoxamide 0.1% eye drops. Put one drop into each ey four times a day; supply 10 ml; NHS Cost £5.48.

Nedocromil 2% eye drops
- Age from 6 years onwards
- Nedocromil 2% eye drops. Put one drop into each eye twice a day. Increase to four times a day if required; supply 5 ml; NHS Cost £9.31.

Olopatadine and ketotifen (2nd line combined action drugs)

Olopatadine 1mg/ml eye drops
- Age from 3 years onwards
- Olopatadine 1mg/ml eye drops. Put one drop into each eye twice a day; supply 5 ml; NHS Cost £8.77.

Ketotifen 250micrograms/ml eye drops
- Age from 3 years onwards
- Ketotifen 250mcg/ml eye drops. Put one drop into each eye twice a day; supply 5 ml; NHS Cost £9.75.

Failure to respond to standard treatment

Which therapy?

- **Advise on avoiding allergens** (see PRODIGY *Patient Information Leaflets*).
- **Ensure that intranasal corticosteroids, antihistamines, and any add-on therapy are being taken optimally.**
- **Consider coexistent infection.**
- **Consider a short course of oral corticosteroids:**

- To reduce congestion and allow penetration of intranasal preparations.
- To cover examinations and important occasions.

Practical prescribing points

For further information, see the *Medicines Compendium* (www.medicines.org.uk) or the *British National Formulary* (www.bnf.org).

Oral corticosteroids

Document history of chickenpox (risk of potentially fatal disseminated chickenpox if non-immune). Advise people taking systemic corticosteroids to avoid close contact with people who have chickenpox or shingles, and to seek urgent medical advice if they are exposed.
Systemic corticosteroids may worsen diabetic control or heart failure.

Follow-up advice

Review within one week if symptoms have not settled.

Should I refer or investigate?

Refer?

- **Specialist referral is recommended for people** unresponsive to maximal management by their general practitioner. This is to confirm the diagnosis, optimize treatment, and consider the need for immunotherapy or surgery.
- **All people with persistent rhinitis should be referred** as it recommended that they have a nasal examination. Anterior rhinoscopy only gives limited information and a nasal endoscopy is recommended.
- **Paediatric referral should be considered in children receiving prolonged treatment with intranasal corticosteroids who have evidence of slowed growth** (particularly if this persists when the dose of corticosteroid is reduced to the lowest dose that maintains symptom control).
- **ENT referral is also recommended for:**
  - Unilateral nasal problems
  - Nasal perforations, ulceration, or collapse
  - Serosanguinous discharge
  - Crusting high in the nasal cavity
  - Recurrent infection
  - Periorbital cellulitis (urgent admission)

Patient information leaflets

The following PILs are available at www.prodigy.nhs.uk

- Allergy UK
- Eye Drops - (How to Use)
- Hay Fever
- House Dust Mite and Pet Allergy
- Nose Drops - How To Use
- Nose Sprays (Steroid)
- Rhinitis (Persistent)

Shared decision making

- **Steroid tablets** usually clear symptoms of allergic rhinitis (nose inflammation due to allergy such as hay fever).
- Steroid tablets are usually only used when symptoms are severe and are not helped much by other treatments.
- A 5-day course will usually work well. Occasionally, a longer course is needed.
- Side-effects are unlikely to occur with a short course of steroids.
- Continue with your other treatments for rhinitis such as a steroid nasal spray, antihistamines, or eye drops.

Drug rationale

Drugs not included

- **Intramuscular depot corticosteroid injections** are not offered. Depot corticosteroids result in prolonged corticosteroid effect, and any adverse effects are difficult to reverse [Dykewicz et al, 1998; MeReC, 1998; DTB, 1999; BSACI, 2000; Van Cauwenburge et al, 2000; ARIA, 2001].

Drugs included

- **Oral corticosteroids:** a short course of oral corticosteroid is rapidly effective at treating all the symptoms of allergic rhinitis [ARIA, 2001]:
  - They are particularly useful for people with severe symptoms to cover exam times or other special or important occasions.
  - They may also be used to reduce severe nasal inflammation and congestion, to allow penetration of a topical corticosteroid.
  - Typically course should not exceed one week in duration.

Prescriptions

Short course of oral prednisolone for severe symptoms

Plain prednisolone: 30mg each morning for 5 days
- Age from 14 years onwards
- Prednisolone 5mg tablets. Take six tablets each morning (as a single dose) for 5 days; supply 30 tablets; NHS Cost £0.73.

Plain prednisolone: 30mg each morning for 7 days
- Age from 14 years onwards
- Prednisolone 5mg tablets. Take six tablets each morning (as a single dose) for 7 days; supply 42 tablets; NHS Cost £1.02.

E/C prednisolone: 30mg each morning for 5 days
- Age from 14 years onwards
- Prednisolone 5mg e/c tablets. Take six tablets each morning (as a single dose) for 5 days; supply 30 tablets; NHS Cost £0.51.

E/C prednisolone: 30mg each morning for 7 days
- Age from 14 years onwards
- Prednisolone 5mg e/c tablets. Take six tablets each morning (as a single dose) for 7 days; supply 42 tablets; NHS Cost £0.71.

Allergic rhinitis in pregnancy

Which therapy?

- **Advise on avoiding allergens** (see PRODIGY *Patient Information Leaflets*). If possible avoid drug treatment, especially in the first trimester.
- **If symptoms persist despite avoidance of allergen, then drug treatment is indicated.** The chance of harm to the unborn child is remote for some drugs, and the benefit to the mother is considerable.
- **Always get informed consent** before treatment commences, and give the woman reassurance about the safety of the drug. In general, avoid the use of oral drugs. Treat with the following topical drugs that are all considered safe in pregnancy:

- **Mild intermittent:** use intranasal antihistamines or intranasal sodium cromoglicate as required.
- **Moderate-severe intermittent or mild persistent:** use intranasal antihistamines or corticosteroids, depending on patient preference. Sodium cromoglicate is a useful alternative or add-on drug.
- **Moderate-severe persistent:** use intranasal corticosteroids as first-line treatment. Intranasal antihistamines and intranasal sodium cromoglicate are useful as an add-on treatment.
- **Sodium cromoglicate eye drops** are safe to use if there are significant eye symptoms.

Practical prescribing points

For further information, see the *Medicines Compendium* (www.medicines.org.uk) or the *British National Formulary* (www.bnf.org).

- **Intranasal corticosteroids:** occasionally, local adverse effects can occur (e.g. crusting, dryness, minor nosebleed) that may require treatment to stop for a while.
- **Sodium cromoglicate eye drops: contact lenses** should generally not be worn during treatment. However:
  - **Hard lenses:** use eye drops 30 minutes before inserting lenses.
  - **Soft lenses:** eye drops containing preservatives should not be used with soft lenses. (Some preservatives, particularly benzalkonium chloride, accumulate in soft contact lenses and cause irritation.)

Follow-up advice

- **Reassess** how effective treatment was after 2–4 weeks or earlier if symptoms are severe.
  - If the person is symptom free or the symptoms are less then continue the current treatment.
  - Continue the treatment long-term if the symptoms are perennial.
- **If the woman improves on intranasal corticosteroids,** a step-down approach should be used.
  - The dose of intranasal corticosteroid should be titrated to the lowest dose that controls symptoms.
- **If eye symptoms are unresolved** with intranasal corticosteroids, consider using a topical ocular drug. See scenario *Allergic rhinitis with eye symptoms*.
- **If symptoms remain very severe,** and there is a serious allergic comorbidity such as severe asthma present, consider a short course of oral corticosteroid (see scenario *Failure to respond to standard treatment*). Use the lowest effective dose and consider referral in this instance.

Should I refer or investigate?

Refer?

- **Refer all people with persistent rhinitis** as it recommended that they have a nasal examination. Anterior rhinoscopy only gives limited information and a nasal endoscopy is recommended.
- **Specialist referral is recommended for people who do not respond to maximal management by their general practitioner.** This is to confirm the diagnosis, optimize treatment, and consider the need for immunotherapy or surgery.
- **ENT referral is also recommended for:**
  - Unilateral nasal problems
  - Nasal perforations, ulceration, or collapse
  - Serosanguinous discharge
  - Crusting high in the nasal cavity
  - Recurrent infection
  - Periorbital cellulitis (urgent admission)
- **Refer all people for same-day assessment** if they have any of the following features that could indicate iritis, keratitis or acute glaucoma:
  - Moderate to severe eye pain
  - Marked eye redness
  - Ciliary injection
  - Loss of visual acuity
- **Refer people with symptoms that persist despite treatment** particularly if there are features of atopic keratoconjunctivitis, vernal keratoconjunctivitis or allergic contact allergic dermatitis with conjunctivitis or when these conditions are associated with corneal involvment.

Patient information leaflets

The following PILs are available at www.prodigy.nhs.uk

- Allergy UK
- Hay Fever
- House Dust Mite and Pet Allergy
- Nose Drops - How To Use
- Nose Sprays (Steroid)
- Rhinitis (Persistent)

Shared decision making

- When you are pregnant, the following nasal sprays are preferred to medicines to treat allergic rhinitis as they are considered safe to take when pregnant.
- **An antihistamine nasal spray can be taken** 'as required' for mild symptoms that come and go, or taken regularly for persistent symptoms. It usually eases nose symptoms within 15 minutes (but has no effect on eye symptoms).
- **A steroid nasal spray (or steroid nasal drops)** usually works well to ease most of the symptoms of allergic rhinitis including eye symptoms.
  - It takes a few days to build up and work fully.
  - Then, each day, use the lowest dose that keeps symptoms away.
- **Sodium cromoglicate spray** is an option if you cannot use the above, or as an add-on treatment if symptoms remain troublesome despite using one of the above. Sodium cromoglicate eye drops can also be used if you have troublesome eye symptoms.
- **If you know the cause of the allergy,** avoiding it may ease symptoms. For example:
  - Hay fever: reduce your exposure to pollen. Keep windows closed, do not cut grass, stay indoors as much as possible, use wrap-around sunglasses, etc.
  - House-dust mite: numbers may be reduced by regular cleaning and vacuuming of carpets and bedding. A leaflet explains this further.
  - Pets: keep them out of living areas if you cannot give them up.

Drug rationale

Drugs not included

- **Oral antihistamines** are not usually recommended, as there have been few studies that confirm their safety in pregnancy and there are alternative safer topical treatments available:
  - **Older 'sedating' antihistamines,** such as chlorphenamine, are usually recommended if oral antihistamines are considered essential, as there is more conclusive evidence of their safety owing to the longer period they have been marketed [Mazzotta et al, 1999]. However, their sedative effects should be taken into account (especially if the woman is driving).

- **Limited evidence suggests that cetirizine and loratadine are safe** if a 'non-sedating' antihistamine is considered essential [Curran et al, 2004].

Decongestants are not suitable in pregnancy:

- **Most oral decongestants are contraindicated** as they have been found to be teratogenic in animal studies [Mazzotta et al, 1999].
- **Intranasal decongestants should be avoided throughout pregnancy,** mainly based on theoretical concerns [Curran et al, 2004].

Intranasal dexamethasone is only available combined with tramazoline, which is not recommended in pregnancy [BNF 48, 2004].

- **Intranasal ipratropium bromide should be avoided,** especially during the first trimester [Curran et al, 2004].
- **Topical eye drops (for eye symptoms) are not recommended,** with the exception of sodium cromoglicate. Topical azelastine, emedastine, levocabastine, lodoxamide, epinastine, nedocromil, olopatadine, and ketotifen are unlikely to be harmful in pregnancy, but have not been adequately studied to verify this.
- **Oral prednisolone should only be used in exceptional circumstances** when there is an accompanying severe morbidity (e.g. asthma). Corticosteroids have been found to be teratogenic in animal studies, and a meta-analysis has found there was an increased risk of cleft lip in the children of women who had taken systemic corticosteroids in the first trimester of pregnancy [Park-Wyllie et al, 2000].

Drugs included

- **Intranasal antihistamines are probably safe,** and are suitable for use as a single agent when intermittent or mild symptoms are present, or as an add-on drug when allergic rhinitis is moderate-severe and persistent. They are preferred to oral antihistamines due to their minimal systemic absorption, although there have been no studies in humans to confirm their absolute safety.
- **Intranasal sodium cromoglicate is a safe choice for pregnant women** and is recommended if there are worries about other drugs [ARIA, 2001]. It can be used regularly as a single agent or combined with other intranasal formulations as an add-on agent. The stronger 4% spray is recommended over the 2% spray as it requires less frequent dosing [BNF 48, 2004].
- **Sodium cromoglicate eye drops** are a safe option for pregnant women with troublesome eye symptoms, either alone or as 'add-on' [BNF 48, 2004].
- **Intranasal corticosteroids are the preferred choice in pregnant women with moderate-severe persistent allergic rhinitis:**
  - Intranasal corticosteroids are the most potent standard drugs available for allergic rhinitis. Absorption of the corticosteroid is low and consequently systemic effects are rare.
  - Although there are few studies on intranasal corticosteroids in pregnant women, data from pregnant women with asthma taking inhaled corticosteroids have not shown any adverse effects on the new born [Curran et al, 2004].
  - The lowest effective dose for the least time should be used.

Prescriptions

Intranasal antihistamines

Azelastine 140microgram (0.1%) nasal spray

- Age from 12 to 60 years
- Azelastine 0.1% nasal spray. Spray once into each nostril twice a day when required; supply 1 spray; NHS Cost £11.92.

Levocabastine 500microgram (0.05%) nasal spray

- Age from 12 to 60 years
- Levocabastine 0.05% nasal spray. Spray twice into each nostril twice a day when required; supply 1 spray; NHS Cost £9.74.

Intranasal sodium cromoglicate

Sodium cromoglicate 4% nasal spray

- Age from 12 to 60 years
- Sod cromoglicate 4% nasal spray. Spray once into each nostril 2 to 4 times a day; supply 1 spray; NHS Cost £18.09.

Intranasal corticosteroids

Beclometasone 50microgram nasal spray

- Age from 12 to 60 years
- Beclometasone nasal spray. Spray twice into each nostril twice a day; supply 1 spray; NHS Cost £3.38.

Betamethasone 0.1% nose drops

- Age from 12 to 60 years
- Betamethasone 0.1% nose drops. Put two drops into each nostril twice a day; supply 10 ml; NHS Cost £2.32.

Budesonide 64microgram nasal spray

- Age from 12 to 60 years
- Budesonide 64mcg nasal spray. Spray once into each nostril twice a day; supply 1 spray; NHS Cost £4.49.

Flunisolide 25microgram nasal spray

- Age from 12 to 13 years
- Flunisolide 25mcg nasal spray. Spray once into each nostril up to three times a day; supply 1 spray; NHS Cost £5.05.

Flunisolide 25microgram nasal spray

- Age from 14 to 60 years
- Flunisolide 25mcg nasal spray. Spray twice into each nostril twice a day; supply 1 spray; NHS Cost £5.05.

Fluticasone 50microgram nasal spray

- Age from 12 to 60 years
- Fluticasone 50mcg nasal spray. Spray twice into each nostril each morning; supply 1 spray; NHS Cost £11.69.

Mometasone 50microgram nasal spray

- Age from 12 to 60 years
- Mometasone 50mcg nasal spray. Spray twice into each nostril once a day; supply 1 spray; NHS Cost £7.83.

Triamcinolone 55microgram nasal spray

- Age from 12 to 60 years
- Triamcinolone 55mcg nasal spray. Spray twice into each nostril once a day; supply 1 spray; NHS Cost £7.39.

Sodium cromoglicate eye drops

Sodium cromoglicate 2% eye drops

- Age from 12 to 60 years
- Sodium cromoglicate 2% eyedrops. Put one drop into each eye four times a day; supply 14 ml; NHS Cost £1.96; OTC Cost £3.45.

Extended Information

A

Background information

- What is it? p.48
- How is it classified? p.48
- What are the triggers? p.48
- How common is it? p.48
- How do I know my patient has it? p.48
- What else might it be? p.49
- Complications and prognosis p.49

What is it?

- **Allergic rhinitis is defined as a symptomatic disorder of the nose** caused by immunoglobulin-E-mediated (IgE-mediated) inflammation after the membranes of the nose have been exposed to allergens. There are two distinct phases:
  - **The acute-phase response:** following exposure to an allergen, histamine and other inflammatory mediators are released from mast cells in the nasal mucosa. These act on cells, nerve endings, and blood vessels to produce the acute symptoms of allergic rhinitis. Inflammatory cells then migrate to the nasal mucosa, in a process known as priming, resulting in sneezing, nasal congestion and/or secretion.
  - **The late-phase response:** symptoms usually peak about 6–12 hours after the initial exposure to allergens, and tend to manifest as nasal obstruction, although runny nose and sneezing may still be present.

[ARIA, 2001]

How is it classified?

- A new international classification for allergic rhinitis has been proposed [ARIA, 2001]. Previously, allergic rhinitis was described as seasonal, perennial, or occupational.
- The new classification is based on the frequency and duration of symptoms (intermittent or persistent), and the severity of symptoms and effect on quality of life (mild or moderate-severe).
- See Table 1 for the definitions of each classification.
- People are then grouped according to a combination of the severity, frequency, and duration of their symptoms:
  - Mild intermittent
  - Mild persistent
  - Moderate-severe intermittent
  - Moderate-severe persistent

What are the triggers?

- **Intermittent allergic rhinitis** (seasonal allergic rhinitis or hay fever) is most commonly due to hypersensitivity to pollens (tree pollen in springtime, grass and weed pollen during the summer) and occasionally mould spores (during the late summer and autumn months).
- **Persistent allergic rhinitis** is most commonly due to hypersensitivity to house-dust mite and domestic pets.
- There is increasing evidence that rhinitis is exacerbated by pollutants, in particular tobacco smoke and car emissions.

[BSACI, 2000; Van Cauwenburge et al, 2000; ARIA, 2001]

How common is it?

- **There is a high prevalence of allergic disease in the United Kingdom.** Studies have consistently shown that allergic rhinitis and related diseases such as atopic eczema and asthma in the United Kingdom are among the highest in the world [The International Study of Asthma and Allergies in Childhood Steering Committee. 1998].
- **The true prevalence and incidence of allergic rhinitis is difficult to assess accurately,** with surveys of the general population invariably showing a much higher prevalence than surveys confined to general practice:
  - Many people self diagnose and treat themselves, as there is a product in each drug class available over the counter [Mason, 2003].
  - It is possible that people who have mild symptoms may not perceive their symptoms to be serious enough to seek a consultation [Ross and Fleming, 2004].
  - A recent telephone survey of adults has estimated that the lifetime prevalence of allergic rhinitis is at least 20%, but probably over 30% [Bauchau and Durham, 2004].
- **The incidence of the type and severity of allergic rhinitis is related to age** [ARIA, 2001]:
  - **Children of school age and adolescents** are most commonly affected by seasonal allergic rhinitis.
  - **Adults** are more likely than children or adolescents to suffer from persistent allergic rhinitis.

Table 1: Classification of allergic rhinitis, according to frequency and duration of symptoms, and their impact on quality of life [ARIA, 2001].

Classification	Definition
Intermittent	Occur 4 days or less per week *or* for less than 4 weeks
Persistent	Occur more than 4 days per week *and* for more than 4 weeks
Mild	All of the following: normal sleep; normal daily activities, sport, leisure; normal work and school; symptoms not troublesome
Moderate-severe	One or more of the following: abnormal sleep; impairment of daily activities, sport, leisure; problems caused at work or school; troublesome symptoms

How do I know my patient has it?

History

- **A diagnosis of allergic rhinitis is mainly based on the history.**
- **The most common symptoms are sneezing, nasal blockage, runny nose, and an itchy nose.** They are usually bilateral and more intense in the morning in 70% of sufferers. Other symptoms include itching of eyes and throat, impaired sense of smell, headache, and facial pains. The most common pattern of symptoms in intermittent (seasonal) and persistent (perennial) allergic rhinitis is outlined in Table 2.

[Van Cauwenburge et al, 2000]

Table 2: Pattern of symptoms in intermittent and persistent allergic rhinitis.

Characteristic	Intermittent	Persistent
Obstruction	Variable	Always, predominant
Secretion	Watery, common	Seromucous, postnasal drip, variable
Sneezing	Always	Variable
Smell disturbance	Variable	Common
Eye symptoms	Common	Rare
Asthma	Variable	Common
Chronic sinusitis	Occasional	Frequent

Allergic rhinitis is often associated with:
- **Allergic conjunctivitis:** symptoms include sudden onset of itching, burning sensation and minimal photophobia.
- **Asthma and eczema:** a history of atopy (personal or family) increases the likelihood that nasal symptoms are due to allergic rhinitis [ARIA, 2001].

xamination

Nasal examination can be carried out using a nasal speculum, or, alternatively, an auriscope can provide a good view (ask the person to breathe through the mouth in order to avoid misting the lens) [BSACI, 2000].
Examination may show:
- Mucosal oedema and blockage
- Nasal polyps
- Septal deviation
- Pale, engorged nasal mucous membranes with a clear watery secretion

Eye examination: signs of allergic conjunctivitis include bilateral 'red eye', clear watery discharge, oedema, papillae, and lid swelling.

nvestigations

The main role of allergy testing is to direct allergen avoidance and enable allergen identification if desensitisation is being carried out.
Specialist investigation may include skin-prick testing for reaction to a specific allergen or the measurement of allergen-specific immunoglobulin-E in serum (a radioallergosorbent test — RAST) in some individuals. A positive result does not necessarily mean that the allergen is causing clinical disease, and the results should be interpreted cautiously in the light of the clinical history.
Nasal endoscopy can detect nasal and sinus pathology that is not detectable with a nasal speculum. Referral for nasal endoscopy is indicated when symptoms persist despite treatment. It is also indicated for the assessment of nasal polyps, crusting high in the nasal cavity, serosanguinous discharge, acute and chronic rhinosinusitis, and nasal perforations and ulceration.
Plain radiographs of sinuses are not discriminating. Other specialist investigations may include computerized tomography and magnetic resonance imaging, but they are rarely indicated.
molensky et al, 1995; ARIA, 2001]

Vhat else might it be?

Infectious rhinitis (acute or chronic): acute infectious rhinitis is usually due to viral infection. Symptoms of chronic infectious rhinosinusitis include purulent nasal discharge, facial pain and pressure, and postnasal drip with cough (see separate PRODIGY guidance *Sinusitis* and *Common Cold*).
Non-allergic perennial rhinitis (also called idiopathic or vasomotor rhinitis): affected individuals have chronic nasal symptoms that are not due to allergy or infection. Most develop rhinitis in response to environmental conditions, such as cold air, high humidity, strong odours, and inhaled irritants.
Non-allergic rhinitis with eosinophilia syndrome (NARES): affected individuals have persistent symptoms of sneezing paroxysms, profuse watery runny nose, nasal pruritus, and occasional loss of smell. It is characterized by the presence of nasal eosinophilia despite the lack of evidence of an allergic cause as determined by skin testing or serum immunoglobulin-E (IgE) levels. Its prevalence in the general population is unknown.
Occupational rhinitis: this may be due to an allergic or non-allergic reaction to airborne substances in the workplace (e.g. laboratory animal antigens, wood dusts, and chemicals). It should be suspected in individuals with nasal symptoms that are related to exposure at work and that improve away from the workplace.
- **Hormonal rhinitis:** pregnancy, puberty, the use of oral contraceptives or conjugated oestrogens, and hypothyroidism may all be associated with nasal obstruction and discharge.
- **Drug-induced rhinitis** may be caused by several drugs, including angiotensin-converting enzyme inhibitors, beta-blockers, and oral contraceptives. Aspirin and nonsteroidal anti-inflammatory drugs may cause rhinitis by inhibition of intracellular cyclo-oxygenase enzymes. Use of intranasal decongestants for more than 5–7 days may cause rebound nasal congestion on withdrawal. This encourages continued use, which may lead to hypertrophy of the nasal mucosa (rhinitis medicamentosa).
- **A condition that mimics the symptoms of rhinitis:** structural or mechanical factors include deviated nasal septum, nasal polyps, hypertrophic turbinates, adenoidal hypertrophy, foreign bodies, and (rarely) nasal tumours. Systemic conditions include primary defects in mucus (e.g. cystic fibrosis), primary ciliary dyskinesia (Kartagener's syndrome), immunological conditions (e.g. rheumatoid arthritis, systemic lupus erythematosis), and granulomatous disease (e.g. Wegener's granulomatosis, sarcoidosis).
- **Obstruction alternating from side to side** indicates a generalized rhinitis that has made the normal 'nasal cycle' more apparent [BSACI, 2000]. (The nasal cycle occurs as a result of alternating vasodilation and vasoconstriction of the inferior turbinates, resulting in one side of the nose staying 'open' while the other side 'rests'. This cycle occurs about every 4 hours.)

[Dykewicz et al, 1998; BSACI, 2000]

Complications and prognosis

Complications

- **Allergic rhinitis is underestimated as a cause of suffering and impaired quality of life.**
  - A survey of adults with allergic rhinitis found that symptoms adversely affected work, home, and social life in over 30% of people [Scadding et al, 2000].
  - In children, poorly controlled symptoms may contribute to learning problems and sleep disturbance [Van Cauwenburge et al, 2000; ARIA, 2001].

Prognosis

- **The symptoms of many people with seasonal allergic rhinitis will improve over time.** Studies have reported spontaneous 'cure' rates of 10–20% and improvement rates of 40–65% over 5–23 years of follow-up [Greisner et al, 1998].

Management issues

- Overview of management of allergic rhinitis p.50
- Allergen avoidance p.50
- What drug treatments should I use first-line? p.50
- What alternative or add-on drugs are useful? p.52
- When should I use oral corticosteroids? p.53
- When is surgery of benefit? p.53
- When should immunotherapy (desensitization) be used? p.53
- How should I manage allergic rhinitis in pregnancy? p.53
- How should I manage related eye symptoms? p.53
- Are complementary therapies effective? p.54
- Medicines management p.54

Overview of management of allergic rhinitis

- **Advise the person on allergen avoidance,** and how best to achieve this, although make it clear that drug treatment is also usually necessary.
- **Ask about previous treatments,** including those bought over the counter, and ensure compliance was not a problem.
- **Assess the type and severity of the allergic rhinitis** (see *Classification*):
  - Is it intermittent or persistent?
  - Is it mild, moderate, or severe?
- **Ask about related allergic conditions.** Some treatments for allergic rhinitis may also improve coexisting allergic conjunctivitis or asthma.
- **Treat** according to the type and severity of allergic rhinitis, related conditions, and personal preference. See Table 3 for treatment options.
- **If symptoms persist despite** maximum safe dose of intranasal corticosteroids and add-on drugs as required, consider the following:
  - **Check compliance** as failure to respond to previous treatments is often due to poor technique when using sprays or drops, or failure to use treatments regularly or for the required duration [Walker, 2003].
  - **Consider using an oral corticosteroid in the short-term.**
  - **Consider referral to an Ear Nose and Throat, or allergy clinic.** Options available in secondary care include surgery and immunotherapy (desensitization).

Allergen avoidance

Allergen avoidance is recommended for all people with a confirmed allergic cause of rhinitis. However, there are practical difficulties in avoiding many allergens, and presently there are few good quality studies to support this approach.

Is allergen avoidance effective?

- **There is little robust evidence that allergen avoidance is effective in treating allergic rhinitis.** Most controlled studies have examined the effect of house-dust mite avoidance in people with asthma, but results have generally been disappointing [ARIA, 2001; Woodcock et al, 2003].
- **A systematic review and meta-analysis** identified four studies (totalling 122 subjects) that examined the effect of house-dust-mite avoidance in people with persistent allergic rhinitis [Sheikh and Hurwitz, 2003]:
  - The trials included were small and judged to be of poor quality.
  - The load of house-dust mite allergy was reduced significantly by physical and chemical means compared to controls.
  - There was little evidence that the achieved allergen-load reduction related to clinically significant improvements in allergic rhinitis.

What practical advice can be given on allergen avoidance?

Note: before recommending allergen avoidance, it is necessary to make an accurate diagnosis of an allergic cause through patient history, examination, and investigations (see *How do I know my patient has it?*).

- **It is not usually possible to avoid allergens completely.** However, reducing exposure may lessen the severity of symptoms and minimize the need for drug treatment [Dykewicz et al, 1998].
- **There are a variety of techniques available to reduce exposure to allergens:**
  - **Persistent allergic rhinitis** is often caused by house-d[ust] mites and animal dander, which can be reduced by cleaning techniques, using special covers, etc.
  - **Intermittent allergic rhinitis** is often caused by pollen (hay fever), which is difficult to avoid. However, dail[y] pollen counts are forecast and can be used to predict when hay fever is likely to be worst. The person can then prepare for this eventuality by adjusting their daily activity (e.g. avoiding outdoor work), or taking drug prophylactically (e.g. an oral antihistamine).
- **PRODIGY** ***Patient Information Leaflets*** (PILs) are available that give detailed advice on these matters.

[BSACI, 2000; Van Cauwenburge et al, 2000]

What drug treatments should I use first-line?

Antihistamines and intranasal corticosteroids are the first line treatments for allergic rhinitis. Sodium cromoglicate, ipratropium bromide, decongestants, or leukotriene antagonists are alternative or add-on treatments.

- **Drug treatment should be selected according to the severity, frequency and duration of symptoms** (see *Classification*):
  - **Mild intermittent:** use an oral or intranasal antihistamine as required. Consider using an intranasal decongestant in the short term (7 days maximum) if blockage is a problem.
  - **Mild persistent or moderate-severe intermittent:** use a oral or intranasal antihistamine, or an intranasal corticosteroid. Intranasal decongestants and sodium cromoglicate are useful add-on drugs.
  - **Moderate-severe persistent:** intranasal corticosteroids are the drug of choice. Antihistamines, intranasal decongestants, and sodium cromoglicate are alternatives if steroids are contraindicated, or can be used as add-on drugs. Ipratropium bromide is useful for people with persistent watery effusion. Leukotrien[e] antagonists may have a role in people with coexisting asthma.

Table 3: Treatment options for allergic rhinitis adapted from ARIA, 2001.

Type of allergic rhinitis	First-line treatments	Alternative or add-on treatments*	Comment
Mild intermittent	Oral antihistamines, intranasal antihistamines	Intranasal decongestants	Allergen avoidance may eliminate need for drugs.
Mild persistent or moderate-severe intermittent	Oral antihistamines, intranasal corticosteroids, intranasal antihistamines	Intranasal decongestants, sodium cromoglicate	Sodium cromoglicate is a useful alternative to antihistamines and corticosteroids, especially in children.
Moderate-severe persistent	Intranasal corticosteroids	Oral antihistamines, intranasal antihistamines, sodium cromoglicate, ipratropium bromide, leukotriene antagonists†	Ipratropium bromide is useful for persistent runny nose. Leukotriene antagonists may be useful if there is coexisting asthma.

* These drugs should usually be used if initial treatment alone has proved ineffective, although they may be used first if standard first-line drugs are unsuitable or contraindicated.
† Not licensed for use in allergic rhinitis.

[ARIA, 2001]

- The drugs recommended for treating each group are listed in Table 3.

Drug treatment should be tailored to the person's individual needs, as well as the severity, frequency, and duration of their condition. The suitability of each drug for an individual is also dependent on its efficacy for individual symptoms, its onset and length of action, its formulation, and its adverse-effects profile (see *Practical issues of drug treatment*).

Oral antihistamines

What is the evidence for oral antihistamines?

- **Oral antihistamines are effective in the treatment of allergic rhinitis.** The newer, 'non-sedating' (sometimes called 'second generation') oral antihistamines have been found to be more effective than placebo in relieving the symptoms of allergic rhinitis in randomized controlled trials (RCTs) [Sheikh et al, 2004].
- **Itching, sneezing, and watery runny nose** are relieved by oral antihistamines. They are less effective at clearing nasal blockage, but are widely believed to relieve ocular symptoms [MeReC, 2004], despite a lack of trial evidence to substantiate this.

When should I use oral antihistamines?

- **Oral antihistamines** should be considered in the following instances [ARIA, 2001]:
  - **Mild intermittent allergic rhinitis:** use as first-line treatment in equal preference to intranasal antihistamines. Although they are more effective when taken regularly, occasional use can be justified when contact with an allergen can be forecast (e.g. predicted high pollen counts or coming into contact with an animal).
  - **Moderate-severe intermittent or mild persistent allergic rhinitis:** use first-line in equal preference to intranasal antihistamines and intranasal corticosteroids, according to patient preference. Oral antihistamines may be preferred when symptoms are not persistent.
  - **Moderate-severe allergic rhinitis:** use secondary to intranasal corticosteroids, possibly as an add-on treatment.
- Oral antihistamines should usually be avoided in pregnancy and in people where sedation is particularly undesirable.

Which oral antihistamine should I use?

- **Newer, 'non-sedating' antihistamines are preferred** to the older, sedating antihistamines. There are few RCTs to support the effectiveness of the older drugs compared to placebo, and no evidence to suggest they are more effective than 'non-sedating' antihistamines [DTB, 2002]. However, there is now substantial evidence that suggests sedating antihistamines do cause increased sedation compared to their newer counterparts [Shamsi and Hindmarch, 2000; Casale et al, 2003].
- **The 'non-sedating' antihistamines are probably equally effective,** and there have been few RCTs comparing individual drug efficacy and safety with one another [DTB, 2002]. However, there are some differences between drugs that may guide choice:
  - **Cetirizine** is an established 'non-sedating' antihistamine available as a once-daily regimen, and is available over the counter. It may have a sedative effect in some people.
  - **Loratadine** is established as a once-daily preparation and is available over the counter. It may have a small sedative effect, but this is probably less pronounced than cetirizine [Mann et al, 2000; Mason, 2003].
  - **Fexofenadine,** a metabolite of terfenadine, is taken once a day (in adults) and is only available on prescription. It probably causes less sedation than other antihistamines, as shown in a direct RCT comparison with cetirizine [Hampel et al, 2003]. Fexofenadine may be useful for people who work in safety-critical occupations [Mann et al, 2000; Mohler et al, 2002].
  - **Mizolastine** is a newer 'non-sedating' antihistamine available on prescription as a once-daily regimen. It should not be used in people with a prolonged QT interval [BNF 48, 2004].

  [Shamsi and Hindmarch, 2000; DTB, 2002]
- **More recent 'non-sedating' antihistamines,** desloratadine and levocetirizine, are available as once-daily regimens on prescription, and are currently undergoing post-marketing surveillance (black triangle):
  - **Desloratadine** is a metabolite of loratadine. It has been reported to relieve symptoms of nasal congestion in one RCT [Berger et al, 2002], although it is unlikely to have any significant advantage over other 'non-sedating' antihistamines [Knockler, 2003].
  - **Levocetirizine** is an isomer of cetirizine. It is at least as effective as other 'non-sedating' antihistamines, but, as with desloratadine, large comparative RCTs are needed to show superior effectiveness compared to older 'non-sedating' antihistamines [DTB, 2002].
- **Acrivastine and terfenadine are not recommended.** Acrivastine requires three doses per day [BNF 48, 2004], and terfenadine has the potential to cause serious heart arrhythmias [DTB, 2002].

Intranasal antihistamines

What is the evidence for intranasal antihistamines?

- **Intranasal antihistamines are effective in treating the symptoms of allergic rhinitis.** Although presently there are no systematic reviews to verify the effectiveness of intranasal antihistamines, several randomized controlled trials have shown that they are more effective than placebo and equally effective as oral antihistamines in the treatment of seasonal allergic rhinitis [Sheikh et al, 2004].

When should I use intranasal antihistamines?

- **Intranasal antihistamines relieve itching, sneezing, and runny nose.** They are useful for people who have intermittent allergic rhinitis, or who have persistent disease and require additional therapy on an 'as required' basis:
  - **They act rapidly, but are relatively short-acting.** Typically symptoms are relieved within 15 minutes, but they need to be taken up to four times a day.
  - **They relieve nasal symptoms only.** They have little effect on nasal congestion, and there is little evidence that they have any effect on related ocular symptoms.
  - **They have few adverse effects,** and do not cause noticeable sedation.

[Van Cauwenburge et al, 2000; MeReC, 2004]

Which intranasal antihistamine should I use?

- **Azelastine and levocabastine** are licensed for the treatment of allergic rhinitis in the United Kingdom [BNF 48, 2004]:
  - **Azelastine** is available as a nasal spray administered twice a day. It is also available over the counter as non-aerosol aqueous formulations, including Allereze®.
  - **Levocabastine** is available as a nasal spray administered twice a day, increasing up to four times a day if necessary. It is available from pharmacies as Livostin® Direct Nasal Spray.

Intranasal corticosteroids

What is the evidence for intranasal corticosteroids?

- **Intranasal corticosteroids are the most effective standard treatment available** for allergic rhinitis. They have been shown to have greater efficacy in treating symptoms than antihistamines:

- **Oral antihistamines:** a systematic review and meta-analysis of 2267 subjects concluded that intranasal corticosteroids were more effective that oral antihistamines in relieving most nasal symptoms of allergic rhinitis. They were both equally effective in relieving eye symptoms [Weiner et al, 1998].
- **Intranasal antihistamines:** a systematic review and meta-analysis of 648 people found that intranasal corticosteroids were more effective than intranasal antihistamines in treating nasal symptoms of allergic rhinitis [Yanez and Rodrigo, 2002].
- **Intranasal corticosteroids are effective in reducing nasal congestion,** unlike most topical or oral antihistamines. They are also more effective in relieving itching, sneezing and runny nose [Nielsen et al, 2001].

When should I use intranasal corticosteroids?

- **Intranasal corticosteroids need to be taken regularly to be effective.** They have a relatively slow onset of action (12 hours), and maximum efficacy develops over days or weeks [ARIA, 2001]. The slower, longer-lasting nature of these drugs makes them more suitable for long-term prevention of allergic rhinitis:
  - Intranasal corticosteroids are not necessary in people with intermittent allergic rhinitis unless it is severe and symptoms are affecting quality of life, despite regular treatment with antihistamines.
  - Treatment should be started at least a week before the anticipated start of the pollen season in people with severe seasonal allergic rhinitis.

  [Van Cauwenburge et al, 2000]
- **Intranasal corticosteroids are safe** and have few adverse effects. They are not contraindicated in any group, although they should be used with added caution in children.

Which intranasal corticosteroid should I use?

- **Individual intranasal corticosteroids are likely to be equally effective as each other.** No randomized controlled trials have consistently identified any particular product as having superior efficacy or improved safety over another [Nielsen et al, 2001; Waddell et al, 2003]. In addition, it should not be assumed that more potent corticosteroids have greater efficacy [CSM, 1998].
- **There are a variety of intranasal corticosteroids available.** Individual drugs include beclometasone, betamethasone, budesonide, flunisolide, fluticasone, mometasone, and triamcinolone. As all are equally effective, patient preference and cost should inform drug selection:
  - **Sprays or drops** should be selected according to individual preference. However, drops are more commonly administered incorrectly and systemic effects are more likely [BNF 48, 2004].
  - **Self medication:** beclometasone, budesonide, fluticasone and triamcinolone are available over the counter in a range of proprietary products [BNF 48, 2004].

What alternative or add-on drugs are useful?

Intranasal sodium cromoglicate

- **Intranasal sodium cromoglicate is a useful treatment in relieving and preventing symptoms of allergic rhinitis.** Although useful in treating symptoms such as runny nose, itching and sneezing (but less useful in nasal blockage), it is probably not as effective as other treatments. Evidence from randomized controlled trials suggests that intranasal sodium cromoglicate is:
  - More effective than placebo
  - Not as effective as antihistamines (although some trials have shown equivalence)
  - Not as effective as intranasal corticosteroids

  [ARIA, 2001; Conner, 2002]
- **Intranasal sodium cromoglicate is suitable as an alternative treatment** if other drugs are contraindicated or as an additional drug if symptoms are troublesome despite other treatments:
  - **It has virtually no adverse effects** making it especially suitable for children or pregnant women [ARIA, 2001].
  - **A significant disadvantage** is that it requires frequent administration to be effective (up to 6 times daily) [BNF 48, 2004].
  - **Self medication:** sodium cromoglicate is available over the counter combined with xylometazoline (a sympathomimetic decongestant) as Rynacrom Allergy® [BNF 48, 2004]. However, prolonged use of this product (more than 5–7 days) is not recommended because of the risk of rebound effects due to the decongestant component.

Intranasal ipratropium bromide

- **Intranasal ipratropium bromide is effective in treating watery nasal discharge** associated with allergic rhinitis. It has no effect on nasal blockage or other nasal symptoms [ARIA, 2001].
- **Intranasal ipratropium should be considered as additional treatment** in people who have moderate or severe allergic conjunctivitis where runny nose is a problematic symptom:
  - **Adverse effects are uncommon.** If present, they are usually localized and not severe (e.g. nasal dryness, irritation and stuffy nose) [Van Cauwenburge et al, 2000].
  - Ipratropium bromide is taken two or three times daily and is available on prescription only [BNF 48, 2004].

Intranasal decongestants

- **Intranasal decongestants are effective in relieving nasal obstruction in the short-term** [ARIA, 2001]. Long-term use is associated with rebound nasal congestion upon withdrawal, which in turn encourages further use that can result in hypertrophy of the nasal mucosa (rhinitis medicamentosa). Therefore use should be limited to a maximum of 5–7 days:
  - **Intranasal decongestants** may prove useful in the initial treatment of nasal blockage as they can 'open up' nasal airways to allow penetration of other drugs.
  - **Ephedrine and xylometazoline** (sympathomimetic drugs) are most commonly used. They are available over the counter in a variety of formulations, some of which are not available on the NHS [BNF 48, 2004].

Oral decongestants

- **Oral decongestants are not generally recommended** as they have doubtful clinical value and have adverse effects [Van Cauwenburge et al, 2000; ARIA, 2001]:
  - **They are not as effective as intranasal decongestants,** although they do not cause rebound effects [Van Cauwenburge et al, 2000].
  - **They can cause systemic sympathomimetic effects** such as tachycardia and hypertension. They should not be used in infants, pregnant women, or people with cardiovascular disease [ARIA, 2001].
  - **They can cause significant and dangerous interactions with other drugs,** such as monoamine-oxidase inhibitors [BNF 48, 2004].
- **Pseudoephedrine is preferred** if an oral decongestant is to be used, as it has fewer sympathomimetic-related adverse

effects compared to other drugs in this class. It is available in a wide variety of products over the counter.

.eukotriene antagonists

Leukotriene antagonists are effective treatments for allergic rhinitis, either used as single agents or combined with an oral antihistamine.

- A systematic review of five randomized controlled trials (RCTs) showed that montelukast was superior to placebo in four of the trials.
- A systematic review of three RCTs were unanimous that montelukast and loratadine combined were more effective than placebo, but not more effective than either drug given separately.
- There was no adverse effects reported for either drug alone or combined.

heikh et al, 2004; Wilson et al, 2004]

Leukotriene antagonists are presently *not* licensed for the treatment of allergic rhinitis. However, they should be considered for people who have moderate-severe persistent allergic rhinitis with accompanying asthma (they are licensed for prophylaxis of asthma):

- **Montelukast** is taken once a day at night time.
- **Zafirlukast** is taken twice a day.

3NF 48, 2004]

/hen should I use oral corticosteroids?

A short course of oral corticosteroids should be used in primary care as a last resort. Although there is no trial evidence to support their use in allergic rhinitis, they are highly effective. Systemic absorption allows penetration to all structures of the nose and the paranasal sinuses. They are especially useful in clearing nasal blockage [ARIA, 2001].

Oral corticosteroids are preferred to depot injections [ARIA, 2001]. Oral treatment can be tailored to the severity of symptoms and adjusted according to the level of the pollen count. Morning dosing with an oral corticosteroid may be less likely to cause adrenal suppression than continuous release of corticosteroid from a depot injection. Depot corticosteroids result in prolonged corticosteroid effect and any adverse effects are difficult to reverse.

Oral corticosteroids should be avoided in young children and pregnant women. To reduce the risk of severe adverse effects, short courses should be used (maximum 2 weeks) and not repeated more than once every 3 months [ARIA, 2001].

Vhen is surgery of benefit?

Surgical treatments are rarely indicated in the treatment of allergic rhinitis.

There have been no randomized controlled trials of surgical treatment of allergic rhinitis. However, surgery may be beneficial in people with coexisting conditions causing airflow obstruction, such as nasal polyps or septal deviation. Inferior turbinectomy may be considered if the inferior turbinates are enlarged [ARIA, 2001].

Vhen should immunotherapy desensitization) be used?

Treatment usually requires specialist referral. There is a small risk of anaphylaxis, and treatment should be given only where facilities for resuscitation are available. Anaphylaxis is particularly likely in people who also have chronic asthma [CSM, 1986; Bousquet et al, 1998; BSACI, 2000].

Immunotherapy (desensitisation) should be considered in people whose symptoms are insufficiently controlled despite adequate antigen avoidance and pharmacotherapy, or who have adverse effects, or do not want to take treatment long-term [ARIA, 2001].

- **Immunotherapy is only indicated in people who have been shown to have immunoglobulin-E (IgE) mediated disease** (either by positive skin tests and /or by serum-specific IgE) and who also have symptoms demonstrated to be caused by a particular allergen. There is no evidence that immunotherapy for any allergen is effective in the absence of specific IgE antibodies [Li et al, 2003].
- **Controlled studies have suggested that subcutaneous immunotherapy is an effective prophylactic treatment for allergic rhinitis** [Bousquet et al, 1998; BSACI, 2000; ARIA, 2001]. It is suitable for house-dust mite, pollen and cat allergy.
- **Sublingually immunotherapy** (SLIT) is effective in reducing rhinitis symptom scores and anti-allergic medication requirements compared to placebo. There is insufficient evidence comparing it to injection immunotherapy to quantify the treatment effect. The studies in a recent Cochrane review did not report any clinically important adverse effects [Wilson et al, 2003]. It is suitable for people with mite or pollen allergies who have had a systemic reaction to injection immunotherapy or who do not wish to have an injection [ARIA, 2001]. It is currently only available privately or in research centres in the United Kingdom.

How should I manage allergic rhinitis in pregnancy?

- **Pregnancy can cause or exacerbate rhinitis.** However, not all drugs are suitable for use in pregnant women, so extra care should be taken when prescribing [Demoly et al, 2003].
- **Allergen avoidance is the first treatment option,** although it should be realized that this is not always practical or effective. If symptoms persist despite avoidance of allergen, then drug treatment is indicated. The chances of harm to the unborn child is remote for some drugs, and the benefits to the mother are considerable [Demoly et al, 2003].
- **Always get informed consent** before treatment commences, and give the woman reassurance about the safety of the drug [Mazzotta et al, 1999]. Treat with the following topical drugs, which are all considered safe in pregnancy:
  - **Mild intermittent:** use intranasal antihistamines or sodium cromoglicate as required.
  - **Moderate-severe intermittent or mild persistent:** use intranasal antihistamines or corticosteroids, depending on patient preference. Sodium cromoglicate is a useful alternative or add-on drug.
  - **Moderate-severe persistent:** use intranasal corticosteroids as first-line treatment. Intranasal antihistamines and sodium cromoglicate are useful as add-on therapy.
  - **Sodium cromoglicate eye drops** are safe to use if there are significant eye symptoms.
- In general, all oral drugs, topical ipratropium bromide, and decongestants should be avoided in pregnancy (see *Drug treatment in pregnant women*).

How should I manage related eye symptoms?

Treatment of allergic conjunctivitis is covered in detail in the PRODIGY guidance *Conjunctivitis — allergic.*

- **Oral antihistamines** reduce the symptoms of allergic conjunctivitis and rhinitis, and are convenient to take.
- **Topical ocular antihistamines** act quickly and are suitable for people with infrequent eye symptoms.

Azelastine, emedastine, and levocabastine give rapid relief of allergic conjunctivitis. They are well tolerated, have few adverse effects, and have a rapid onset of action.

- **Intranasal corticosteroids** are effective in reducing ocular symptoms as well as nasal symptoms. The mechanism of action is unclear: it may partly be due to a systemic effect resulting from local absorption, although systemically related adverse effects are uncommon.
- **Topical mast-cell stabilizers** are best used for prophylaxis of allergic eye symptoms. Sodium cromoglicate is effective in most people. Lodoxamide and nedocromil are more expensive, but may be worth trying in people with inadequate response to sodium cromoglicate.
- **Olopatadine and ketotifen are newer topical products** that have both antihistamine and mast-cell stabilizing properties, and are a useful alternative if other topical products have been ineffective.
- **Topical ocular corticosteroids should *not* be used, unless under specialist supervision,** when they are occasionally used for severe allergic conjunctivitis. Problems include steroid-induced glaucoma and inadvertent treatment of an eye infected with herpes simplex virus (dendritic ulcer).

Are complementary therapies effective?

- **There is little information on the value of complementary treatments** [ARIA, 2001]. People considering complementary treatments should be advised of the lack of evidence regarding their effectiveness, in contrast to the considerable amount of evidence for the effectiveness and safety of standard medical treatments.
- **Homeopathic treatment has been studied in randomized controlled trials but only compared to placebo.** Although current data suggest that homeopathy may be of some benefit in the treatment of allergic rhinitis, further large high-quality controlled trials are needed [Taylor et al, 2000; Ernst, 2001a]. Until there is more convincing evidence of effectiveness, homeopathic treatment is not generally recommended.
- **Butterbur (*Petasites hybridus*)** is a herbal treatment that is not recommended for allergic rhinitis because of a lack of data on safety and effectiveness. A randomized double-blind trial found it to be as effective as cetirizine for the treatment of pollen-related allergic rhinitis over a 2-week period [Schapowal, 2002]. Although no safety concerns were identified in the trial, a standardised extract of butterbur was used from which hepatotoxic alkaloids had been removed.
- **Other therapies:** acupuncture, hypnotherapy, diet modification (prevention by avoiding certain foodstuffs), and diet supplementation (fish oils) are not recommended as they have either not shown significant efficacy in the treatment or prevention of allergic rhinitis, or require more rigorous methodology to substantiate claims of benefit [Ernst, 2001b].

Medicines management

Practical issues of drug treatment

- Treatment of allergic rhinitis is mainly based on the severity, frequency and duration of the illness. Howeve other factors that may guide drug choice include the following:
  - The effectiveness of the drug in relieving particular symptoms
  - Whether symptom relief or prevention is primarily desired:
    - The time taken until onset of drug action
    - The duration of drug action
    - The frequency of drug dosing
  - Personal preference for the formulation and route of administration
  - Adverse effects, which may be more significant in some individuals (e.g. intranasal corticosteroid use in children, sedation in adults who wish to avoid drowsiness)
  - The availability of drugs over the counter
  - The cost of drugs, both to the NHS and to the patient if they are using self medication
- A comparison of the effectiveness of each drug on particular symptoms, and the time taken until onset of action, and the duration of action, are given in Table 4. [Van Cauwenburge et al, 2000]

Significant adverse effects of drug treatment

Oral antihistamines

- **Unwanted sedation** is the most significant adverse effec of the oral antihistamines [DTB, 2002]:
  - Oral antihistamines are usually categorized as being either sedating or 'non-sedating'. However it is important to note that these terms are misleading, an *both* categories of drugs can cause sedation to varyin degrees.
  - People receiving any antihistamine should be advised that treatment can affect driving and other skilled tasks, and enhance the effects of alcohol [DTB, 2002]
  - Fexofenadine causes the least sedation of the 'non-sedating antihistamines', but the degree of sedation caused by other drugs is less clear; although all 'non-sedating' antihistamines cause less sedation than sedating antihistamines [Shamsi and Hindmarch, 2000].
- **Cardiotoxicity:** the risk of arrhythmia is very low with cetirizine, loratadine, fexofenadine, levocetirizine, and desloratadine. There is a small risk with mizolastine in people who are predisposed to having a prolonged QT interval [BNF 48, 2004].

Table 4: Comparison of standard drugs used in allergic rhinitis.

	Oral antihist.	Nasal antihist.	Nasal steroids	Nasal decong.	Nasal ipratropium	Nasal cromoglicate
Runny nose	++	++	+++	0	++	+
Sneezing	++	++	+++	0	0	+
Itching	++	++	+++	0	0	+
Blockage	+	+	+++	++++	0	+
Eye symptoms	++	0	++	0	0	+
Onset of action	1 h	15 min	12 h	5–15 min	15–30 min	Variable
Duration	12–24 h	6–12 h	12–48 h	3–6 h	4–12 h	Variable

\+ Marginal effect
++++ Substantial effect (under natural exposure conditions)

Intranasal corticosteroids

Intranasal corticosteroids are safe if used correctly. Adverse effects are usually localized and include dryness, irritation, and nose bleed (which may require stopping treatment for a period). Rarely, ulceration and nasal septal perforation (usually after nose surgery) can occur. Headaches, smell and taste disturbances, and hypersensitivity reactions have been reported [BNF 48, 2004].

Systemic effects caused by intranasal corticosteroids are rare. The MHRA (Medicines and Healthcare products Regulatory Agency) has noted that although the risks of systemic corticosteroids is low if used within licensed doses, the following precautions should be used:

- **Systemic effects are possible** in some people using high doses over a prolonged period. Adrenal suppression and associated adverse effects should be monitored in people who are at particular risk. Additional systemic corticosteroid cover should also be considered in individuals during periods of stress or elective surgery.
- **The lowest dose** that gives effective control should be used.
- **The height of children** receiving high doses over extended periods should be frequently monitored, and treatment reviewed if any effect is observed.

[CSM, 1998]

Drops or sprays: the risk of systemic effects is thought to be more likely with drops than sprays, as these are more likely to be administered incorrectly [BNF 48, 2004].

Concomitant use of other corticosteroids: when prescribing intranasal corticosteroids, it is necessary to take into account the use of other systemic and topical corticosteroids (e.g. creams, ointments and inhalers). There is likely to be an additive effect of these drugs, which requires close monitoring.

Decongestants

Intranasal decongestants can cause severe rebound effects, and should not be used for more than 7 days continuously [BNF 48, 2004].

Oral decongestants can cause sympathomimetic effects, such as hypertension. They can also interact with other prescription drugs (e.g. monoamine oxidase inhibitors) [BNF 48, 2004].

Oral corticosteroids

Oral corticosteroids cause a large number of adverse effects, but when taken in short courses are relatively safe.

Following concerns about severe chickenpox, the Committee on Safety of Medicines has advised that *anyone* prescribed a systemic corticosteroid should receive the patient information leaflet produced by the manufacturer. Patients should be encouraged to read this which gives details of likely short-term adverse effects, such as euphoria, mood swings, and insomnia.

Drug treatment in children

In general, treatment of allergic rhinitis is the same in children as it is in adults. Some drugs are not suitable for younger children:

- **Antihistamines:** oral desloratadine is licensed in children from the age of 12 months; oral cetirizine and loratadine can be used in children from the age of 2 years. Some topical products can be used from the age of 5 years.
- **Intranasal corticosteroids:** some products (such as betamethasone drops) are licensed for use in infants, but the development of adverse effects should be closely monitored in children.
- **Intranasal sodium cromoglicate** is safe in children.
- **Intranasal ipratropium bromide** is not licensed for children under the age of 12 years.
- **Decongestants:** there are intranasal products available specifically for children aged over 3 months. Oral decongestants should be avoided in very young children [ARIA, 2001].
- **Leukotriene antagonists:** montelukast can be used in children from 6 months with asthma; zafirlukast is not recommended in children under 12 years.

[BNF 48, 2004]

Drug treatment in pregnant women

- **In general, systemic drugs for allergic rhinitis are not recommended during pregnancy.** Most are probably safe, but they have the potential for harm as prospective studies are limited, and many cross the placental barrier (including 'non-sedating' antihistamines). There are safer topical alternatives that are just as effective.

Oral drugs

- **Oral antihistamines are not usually recommended, but can be used if necessary:**
  - **Older sedating antihistamines, such as chlorphenamine, are usually recommended** as there is more conclusive evidence of their safety owing to the longer period they have been marketed [Mazzotta et al, 1999]. However, their sedative effects should be taken into account (especially if the woman is driving).
  - **Limited evidence suggests that cetirizine and loratadine are safe** if a 'non-sedating' antihistamine is considered essential [Demoly et al, 2003].
- **Most oral decongestants are contraindicated** as they have been found to be teratogenic in animal studies [Mazzotta et al, 1999].
- **Oral prednisolone should only be used in exceptional circumstances** when there is an accompanying severe morbidity (e.g. asthma). Corticosteroids have been found to be teratogenic in animal studies, and a meta-analysis has found there was an increased risk of cleft lip in the children of women who had taken systemic corticosteroids in the first trimester of pregnancy [Park-Wyllie et al, 2000].

Topical drugs

- **Intranasal corticosteroids are the preferred choice in pregnant women with moderate-severe persistent allergic rhinitis:**
  - Intranasal corticosteroids are the most potent standard drugs available for allergic rhinitis. Absorption of the corticosteroid is low and consequently systemic effects are rare.
  - Although there are few studies on intranasal corticosteroids in pregnant women, data from pregnant women with asthma taking inhaled corticosteroids have not shown any adverse effects on the new born [Curran et al, 2004].
  - The lowest effective dose for the least time should be used.
- **Other topical drugs:** in general there is a lack of good quality studies of the effect of these drugs on pregnant women and the unborn child. Most recommendations are based on expert opinion:
  - **Intranasal antihistamines are probably safe,** and may be preferred to oral antihistamines due to their minimal systemic absorption, although there have been no studies to confirm this.
  - **Intranasal sodium cromoglicate is a safe choice for pregnant women** and is recommended if there are worries about other drugs [ARIA, 2001].
  - **Intranasal ipratropium bromide should probably be avoided,** especially during the first trimester [Curran et al, 2004].
  - **Intranasal decongestants should be avoided throughout pregnancy,** mainly based on theoretical concerns [Curran et al, 2004].

- **Sodium cromoglicate eye drops** are safe to use if there are significant eye symptoms.

References

A

NHS staff in England can link, free of charge, from references to full text journals by clicking on [Full text] on the PRODIGY website.

1. ARIA (2001) *Allergic rhinitis and its impact on asthma.* Allergic Rhinitis and its Impact on Asthma Initiative. www.whiar.com [Accessed: 04/10/2004].
2. Bauchau, V. and Durham, S.R. (2004) Prevalence and rate of diagnosis of allergic rhinitis in Europe. *European Respiratory Journal* **24**(5), 758–764.
3. Berger, W.E., Schenkel, E.J., Mansfield, L.E. and Desloratadine Study Group (2002) Safety and efficacy of desloratadine 5 mg in asthma patients with seasonal allergic rhinitis and nasal congestion. *Annals of Allergy, Asthma, & Immunology* **89**(5), 485–491. [Full text]
4. BNF 48 (2004) *British National Formulary.* 48th edn. London: British Medical Association and Royal Pharmaceutical Society of Great Britain.
5. Bousquet, J., Lockey, R. and Malling, H.J. (1998) Allergen immunotherapy: therapeutic vaccines for allergic diseases. A WHO position paper. *Journal of Allergy & Clinical Immunology* **102**(4 Pt 1), 558–562.
6. BSACI (2000) *Rhinitis management guidelines.* London: British Society for Allergy and Clinical Immunology ENT Sub-Committee.
7. Casale, T.B., Blaiss, M.S., Gelfand, E. et al (2003) First do no harm: managing antihistamine impairment in patients with allergic rhinitis. *Journal of Allergy & Clinical Immunology* **111**(5), S835-S842.
8. Conner, S.J. (2002) Evaluation and treatment of the patient with allergic rhinitis. *Journal of Family Practice* **51**(10), 883–890.
9. CSM (1986) Desensitising vaccines. Committee on Safety of Medicines. *British Medical Journal* **293**(6555), 948–948.
10. CSM (1998) The safety of inhaled and nasal corticosteroids. Committee on Safety of Medicines. *Current Problems in Pharmacovigilance* **24**(May), 8–9.
11. Curran, M.P., Scott, L.J. and Perry, C.M. (2004) Cetirizine: a review of its use in allergic disorders. *Drugs* **64**(5), 523–561.
12. Demoly, P., Piette, V. and Daures, J.P. (2003) Treatment of allergic rhinitis during pregnancy. *Drugs* **63**(17), 1813–1820.
13. DTB (1999) Any place for depot triamcinolone in hay fever? *Drug & Therapeutics Bulletin* **37**(3), 17–18. [Full text]
14. DTB (2002) Oral antihistamines for allergic disorders. *Drug & Therapeutics Bulletin* **40**(8), 59–62. [Full text]
15. Dykewicz, M.S., Fineman, S., Skoner, D.P. et al (1998) Diagnosis and management of rhinitis: complete guidelines of the Joint Task Force on Practice Parameters in Allergy, Asthma and Immunology. American Academy of Allergy, Asthma, and Immunology. *Annals of Allergy, Asthma, & Immunology* **81**(5 Pt 2), 478–518. [Full text]
16. Ernst, E. (2001a) *Homeopathy.* Desktop guide to complementary and alternative medicine. London: Mosby.
17. Ernst, E. (2001b) *Hay fever.* Desktop guide to complementary and alternative medicine. London: Mosby.
18. Greisner, W.A., Settipane, R.J. and Settipane, G.A. (1998) Natural history of hay fever: a 23-year follow-up of college students. *Allergy & Asthma Proceedings* **19**(5), 271–275.
19. Hampel, F., Ratner, P., Mansfield, L. et al (2003) Fexofenadine hydrochloride, 180 mg, exhibits equivalent efficacy to cetirizine, 10 mg, with less drowsiness in patients with moderate-to-severe seasonal allergic rhinitis. *Annals of Allergy, Asthma, & Immunology* **91**(4), 354–361. [Full text]
20. Knockler, L.L. (2003) Desloratadine: a nonsedating antihistamine. *Annals of Pharmacotherapy* **37**(2), 237–246.
21. Li, J.T., Lockley, R.F., Bernstein, I.L. et al (2003) Allergen immunotherapy: a practice parameter. *Annals of Allergy, Asthma, & Immunology* **90**(Suppl 1), 1–4[illegible] [Full text]
22. Mann, R.D., Pearce, G.L., Dunn, N. and Shakir, S. (2000) Sedation with "non-sedating" antihistamines: four prescription-event monitoring studies in general practice. *British Medical Journal* **320**(7243), 1184–1187. [Full text]
23. Mason, P. (2003) Management of hayfever in the pharmacy. *Pharmaceutical Journal* **270**(7242), 443–445.
24. Mazzotta, P., Loebstein, R. and Koren, G. (1999) Treating allergic rhinitis in pregnancy. Safety considerations. *Drug Safety* **20**(4), 361–375.
25. MeReC (1998) Treatment of seasonal allergic rhinitis (hay fever). *MeReC Bulletin* **9**(3), 1–2. [Full text]
26. MeReC (2004) Common questions about hayfever. *MeReC Bulletin* **14**(5), 17–20. [Full text]
27. Mohler, S.R., Nicholson, A., Harvey, P. et al (2002) The use of antihistamines in safety-critical jobs: a meeting report. *Current Medical Research & Opinion* **18**(6), 332–337. [Full text]
28. Nielsen, L.P., Mygind, N. and Dahl, R. (2001) Intranasal corticosteroids for allergic rhinitis. Superior relief? *Drugs* **61**(11), 1563–1579.
29. Owen, C.G., Shah, A., Henshaw, K. et al (2004) Topical treatments for seasonal allergic conjunctivitis: systematic review and meta-analysis of efficacy and effectiveness. *British Journal of General Practice* **54**(503), 451–456.
30. Park-Wyllie, L., Mazzotta, P., Pastuszak, A. et al (2000) Birth defects after maternal exposure to corticosteroids: prospective cohort study and meta-analysis of epidemiological studies. *Teratology* **62**(6), 385–392.
31. Ross, A. and Fleming, A. (2004) Hayfever: practical management issues. *British Journal of General Practice* **54**(503), 412–414.
32. Scadding, G.K., Richards, D.H. and Price, M.J. (2000) Patient and physician perspectives on the impact and management of perennial and seasonal allergic rhinitis. *Clinical Otolaryngology & Allied Sciences* **25**(6), 551–557.
33. Schapowal, A. (2002) Randomised controlled trial of butterbur and cetirizine for treating seasonal allergic rhinitis. *British Medical Journal* **324**(7330), 144–146. [Full text]
34. Shamsi, Z. and Hindmarch, I. (2000) Sedation and antihistamines: a review of inter-drug differences using proportional impairment ratios. *Human Psychopharmacology* **15**(Suppl 1), S3-S30.
35. Sheikh, A. and Hurwitz, B. (2003) House dust mite avoidance measures for perennial allergic rhinitis: a systematic review of efficacy. *British Journal of General Practice* **53**(589), 318–322.
36. Sheikh, A., Singh-Panesar, S. and Dhami, S. (2004) *Seasonal allergic rhinitis.* Clinical Evidence. Volume 11. www.clinicalevidence.com [Accessed: 22/04/2005]
37. Smolensky, M.H., Reinberg, A. and Labrecque, G. (1995) Twenty-four hour pattern in symptom intensity of viral and allergic rhinitis: treatment implications.

Journal of Allergy & Clinical Immunology **95**(5 Pt 2), 1084–1096.

38. Taylor, M.A., Reilly, D., Llewellyn-Jones, R.H. et al (2000) Randomised controlled trial of homoeopathy versus placebo in perennial allergic rhinitis with overview of four trial series. *British Medical Journal* **321**(7259), 471–476. [Full text]
39. The International Study of Asthma and Allergies in Childhood Steering Committee. (1998) Worldwide variations in the prevalence of asthma, allergic rhinoconjunctivitis, and atopic eczema: ISAAC the International Study of Asthma and Allergies in Childhood (ISAAC). *Lancet* **351**(9111), 1225–1232. [Full text]
40. Van Cauwenburge, P., Bachert, C., Passalacqua, G. et al (2000) Consensus statement on the treatment of allergic rhinitis. European Academy of Allergology and Clinical Immunology. *Allergy* **55**(2), 116–134.
41. Waddell, A.N., Patel, S.K., Toma, A.G. and Maw, A.R. (2003) Intranasal steroid sprays in the treatment of rhinitis: is one better than another? *Journal of Laryngology & Otology* **117**(11), 843–845. [Full text]
42. Walker, S. (2003) Management of allergic rhinitis. *Nursing Times* **99**(23), 60–61.
43. Weiner, J.M., Abramson, M.J. and Puy, R.M. (1998) Intranasal corticosteroids versus oral H1 receptor antagonists in allergic rhinitis: systematic review of randomised controlled trials. *British Medical Journal* **317**(7173), 1624–1629. [Full text]
44. Wilson, D.R., Torres Lima, M. and Durham, S.R. (2003) *Sublingual immunotherapy for allergic rhinitis (Cochrane Review)*. The Cochrane Library. Issue 2. Chichester, UK: John Wiley & Sons, Ltd. www.nelh.nhs.uk/cochrane.asp [Accessed: 22/04/2005]. [Full text]
45. Wilson, A.M., O'Byrne, P.M. and Parameswaran, K. (2004) Leukotriene receptor antagonists for allergic rhinitis: a systematic review and meta-analysis. *American Journal of Medicine* **116**(5), 338–344.
46. Woodcock, A., Forster, L., Matthews, E. et al (2003) Control of exposure to mite allergen and allergen impermeable bed covers for adults with asthma. *New England Journal of Medicine* **349**(3), 225–236. [Full text]
47. Yanez, A. and Rodrigo, G.J. (2002) Intranasal corticosteroids versus topical H1 receptor antagonists for the treatment of allergic rhinitis: a systematic review with meta-analysis. *Annals of Allergy, Asthma & Immunology* **89**(5), 479–484. [Full text]

A

PRODIGY GUIDANCE

Amenorrhoea

A

Last revised in February 2005
www.prodigy.nhs.uk/guidance.asp?gt=Amenorrhoea

Applies to women over the age of 10 years

This guidance covers the causes, initial assessment, and investigation of amenorrhoea.

This guidance does not cover in detail the management of the specific causes of amenorrhoea.

There is separate PRODIGY guidance for *Infertility, Menopause*, and *Osteoporosis treatment.*

Goals

- To establish a diagnosis of the cause of the amenorrhoea
- To refer to secondary care appropriately
- To prevent the development of osteoporosis in amenorrhoeic women who are oestrogen-deficient

Contents

Scenarios
- Primary amenorrhoea – initial assessment p.58
- Secondary amenorrhoea – initial assessment p.58

Extended Information, p. 59

Which scenario?

- **Primary amenorrhoea — initial assessment:** covers the relevant features in the history and examination of a girl presenting with primary amenorrhoea.
- **Secondary amenorrhoea — initial assessment:** covers the relevant features in the history and examination of a woman with secondary amenorrhoea with some investigations that may be appropriately performed in primary care.

Primary amenorrhoea — initial assessment

Which therapy?

- In general, consider amenorrhoea to be abnormal:
  - In girls aged 14 years who have not started menstruating and have no secondary sexual characteristics
  - In girls with normal secondary sexual characteristics who have not started menstruating by the age of 16 years
- Enquire about age at menarche of mother and sisters, family history of genetic anomalies, presence of cyclical abdominal pain, presence of chronic illness, emotional upsets, weight loss, level of exercise, medication, and previous chemotherapy.
- Note the presence or absence of secondary sexual characteristics.
- Measure height and weight. Calculate body mass index if appropriate.
- Examine for galactorrhoea, hirsutism, features of Turner's syndrome, signs of thyroid disease, clitoromegaly, and other abnormalities of the external genitalia.
- Pelvic examination is inappropriate in young girls who are not sexually active.
- Consider and exclude pregnancy if appropriate.
- Refer together with any findings. Investigations are usually carried out by specialists.

Should I refer or investigate?

Refer?

- **In general refer for specialist investigation:**
  - Girls aged 14 years who have not started menstruating and have no secondary sexual characteristics
  - Girls with normal secondary sexual characteristics who have not started menstruating by the age of 16 years
- **Earlier referral** is appropriate if there are symptoms and signs of androgen excess or thyroid disease; if there is galactorrhoea or growth retardation; or if genital tract malformation, intracranial tumour, chromosomal anomaly, or other pathology is suspected.

Patient information leaflets

The following PILs are available at www.prodigy.nhs.uk

- Blood Test - General
- Medicines - Name Changes of Medicines
- Women's Health
- Women's Health Concern

Shared decision making

- Your periods have not started.
- Girls usually start their periods before the age of 16 years.
- Periods are just one sign of a girl developing into a woman (puberty).
- The first signs of puberty (such as the start of breasts growing) are usual by the age of 14.
- There are many different reasons why periods and puberty may not start.
- Referral to a specialist is usual to find out why.

Drug rationale

- There are no prescriptions offered.

Secondary amenorrhoea — initial assessment

Which therapy?

- **Exclude pregnancy.**
- In general investigate when amenorrhoea has persisted for 6 months.
- Enquire about previous menstrual, obstetric and surgical history, hot flushes and vaginal dryness, galactorrhoea, hirsutism, symptoms of thyroid disease, weight loss, emotional upsets, exercise level, medication, chemotherapy, and family history.
- Examine for galactorrhoea, hirsutism, acanthosis nigricans, signs of thyroid disease, and clitoromegaly.

Pelvic examination may indicate enlarged ovaries. Measure height and weight. Calculate body mass index if appropriate. Encourage weight loss if overweight. Management depends on the underlying cause and should be based on the woman's oestrogen status, desire for fertility, or contraceptive needs.

Should I refer or investigate?

Refer?

Refer women to an endocrinologist/gynaecologist:
- If you are unable to establish an underlying cause for the amenorrhoea
- If you are uncertain about management of the underlying cause
- If they have suspected polycystic ovary syndrome (PCOS)
- If they have hyperprolactinaemia
- If they have mildly raised testosterone levels but not PCOS
- If they have testosterone levels in the normal male range

Refer women with premature ovarian failure for screening for auto-immune disease, e.g. Addison's disease, when this is clinically indicated. Chromosomal analysis may also be considered for those younger than 30 years.

Refer women with low gonadotrophin levels that cannot be explained by stress, exercise, or weight loss.

Women who wish to conceive should be referred to a gynaecologist or infertility specialist.

Women with anorexia nervosa should be referred to a psychiatrist or psychologist.

Refer to a dietician:
- **Obese women with PCOS,** for weight loss or dietary advice for dyslipidaemia and diabetes
- Underweight women

Investigate?

Pregnancy test — if appropriate.

Take blood for follicle-stimulating hormone, luteinizing hormone and prolactin levels, thyroid function tests, and possibly estradiol level (but this can be unreliable). Breast examination prior to prolactin estimation may elevate prolactin levels.

Testosterone/androgen level if there is hirsutism or if there are signs of virilization, e.g. clitoromegaly or deep voice.

Pelvic ultrasound may confirm a diagnosis of PCOS, although the existence of polycystic ovaries is not necessary for diagnosis.

Patient information leaflets

The following PILs are available at www.prodigy.nhs.uk

Blood Test - General
Medicines - Name Changes of Medicines
Women's Health
Women's Health Concern

Shared decision making

- Your periods have stopped.
- There are many different reasons for periods to stop. The commonest ones are:
  - Pregnancy
  - Low bodyweight
  - Polycystic ovary syndrome
  - Hormone problems, such as high levels of prolactin or an underactive thyroid
  - Early menopause
- Having no periods does not necessarily mean you are infertile. Contraception may still be needed.
- Various tests are usual to find the cause.
- Treatment depends on the cause.

Drug rationale

- There are no prescriptions offered.

Extended Information

Background information

- What is it? p.59
- What can cause primary amenorrhoea? p.59
- What can cause secondary amenorrhoea? p.60
- How common is it? p.60
- What are the more common causes seen in general practice? p.60
- How do I assess my patient with primary amenorrhoea? p.61
- How do I assess my patient with secondary amenorrhoea? p.62
- How do I interpret the laboratory findings? p.62
- Complications and prognosis p.62

What is it?

Definitions

- **Amenorrhoea is the absence of menstruation.** It may be physiological (i.e. prior to puberty or due to pregnancy, lactation, or the menopause), or secondary to a gynaecological disorder or systemic disease.
- **Primary amenorrhoea** is the failure to establish menstruation. Such a failure is generally regarded as abnormal by the age of 14 years in girls without other signs of secondary sexual development or by the age of 16 in girls with normal secondary sexual characteristics.
- **Secondary amenorrhoea** is defined as the absence of menstruation for six consecutive months in a woman who has previously had regular periods.

[McIver et al, 1997; Balen, 1999b; Edmonds, 1999]

What can cause primary amenorrhoea?

Causes of primary amenorrhoea are best classified according to the presence or absence of secondary sexual characteristics.

- **Secondary sexual characteristics present**
  - Constitutional delay
  - Genito-urinary malformation, e.g. imperforate hymen, transverse vaginal septum, absent vagina with or without a functioning uterus
  - Androgen insensitivity: XY female or testicular feminization
  - Resistant ovary syndrome
  - Pregnancy
- **Secondary sexual characteristics absent**
  - Hypothalamic dysfunction, e.g. chronic illness, anorexia, weight loss, 'stress'
  - Gonadotrophin deficiency, e.g. Kallman's syndrome, isolated gonadotrophin-releasing hormone deficiency
  - Hydrocephalus
  - Tumours of the hypothalamus or pituitary
  - Hypopituitarism
  - Hyperprolactinaemia
  - Gonadal failure, e.g. ovarian dysgenesis/agenesis, premature ovarian failure
  - Hypothyroidism

- **Ambiguous external genitalia**
  - Congenital adrenal hyperplasia
  - Androgen-secreting tumour
  - 5-Alpha-reductase deficiency

Most of the causes of secondary amenorrhoea can also cause primary amenorrhoea if they occur before the menarche.
[Edmonds, 1999]

What can cause secondary amenorrhoea?

Secondary amenorrhoea is best classified according to the presence or absence of androgen excess.

- **No features of androgen excess present**
  - **Physiological,** e.g. pregnancy, lactation, menopause
  - **Iatrogenic,** e.g. depot medroxyprogesterone acetate contraceptive injection, radiotherapy, chemotherapy
  - **Systemic disease,** e.g. chronic illness, hypo- or hyperthyroidism
  - **Uterine causes,** e.g. cervical stenosis, Asherman's syndrome (intra-uterine adhesions)
  - **Ovarian causes,** e.g. premature ovarian failure, resistant ovary syndrome
  - **Hypothalamic causes,** e.g. weight loss, exercise, psychological distress, chronic illness, idiopathic
  - **Pituitary causes,** e.g. hyperprolactinaemia, hypopituitarism, Sheehan's syndrome
  - **Causes of hypothalamic/pituitary damage,** e.g. tumours, cranial irradiation, head injuries, sarcoidosis, tuberculosis
- **Features of androgen excess present**
  - Polycystic ovary syndrome
  - Cushing's syndrome
  - Late-onset congenital adrenal hyperplasia
  - Adrenal or ovarian androgen-producing tumour

[McIver et al, 1997; Balen, 1999a; Scholes et al, 1999; Warren and Stiehl, 1999]

How common is it?

- **Secondary amenorrhoea (prevalence about 3%) is much more common than primary amenorrhoea (prevalence about 0.3%)** [Kiningham et al, 1996].
- **Between 10 and 20% of women complaining of infertility have amenorrhoea** [Franks, 1987].
- Up to 50% of competitive runners (training 80 miles per week) and up to 44% of ballet dancers have amenorrhoea [Balen, 1999a].
- **Primary amenorrhoea**
  - The most common cause of primary amenorrhoea associated with normal secondary sexual characteristics is an anatomical abnormality of the genital tract, e.g. absent vagina and uterus [Garden, 1998; Edmonds, 1999].
  - Common causes of primary amenorrhoea with associated delayed puberty are Turner's syndrome, gonadotrophin deficiency, and constitutional delay [Garden, 1998; Edmonds, 1999].
- **Secondary amenorrhoea**
  - The commonest cause is pregnancy.
  - **Polycystic ovary syndrome** (PCOS) is present in 30% of women with amenorrhoea. It is estimated that the prevalence of PCOS is between 5% and 10% of women of reproductive age [Hopkinson et al, 1998].
  - **Hyperprolactinaemia** accounts for 20% of cases of amenorrhoea [McIver et al, 1997].
  - **Premature ovarian failure and weight-related amenorrhoea** are other common causes [Balen, 1999a].

What are the more common causes seen in general practice?

Common causes of primary amenorrhoea

Turner's syndrome

- Turner's syndrome is caused by either a complete absence or a partial abnormality of one of the two X chromosomes. About 50% have mosaic forms such as 45X/46XX or 45X/46XY.
- Features of Turner's syndrome are variable, and include short stature, web neck, lymphoedema, shield chest with widely spaced nipples, scoliosis, wide carrying angle, coarctation of the aorta, and streak ovaries.
- It may be diagnosed at birth in girls with classic signs; however, presentation in late childhood because of short stature, delayed puberty, or both, is common.
- The ovaries are unable to produce oestrogen as a result of a failure to develop properly *in utero* and an accelerated loss of oocytes (atresia).

[Garden, 1998; Edmonds, 1999]

Constitutional delay

- **In this condition there is no anatomical abnormality and endocrine investigations show normal results.**
- It is caused by immature pulsatile release of gonadotrophin-releasing hormone; maturation eventually occurs spontaneously.

[Edmonds, 1999]

Common causes of secondary amenorrhoea

Polycystic ovary syndrome

- **This condition is characterized by hirsutism, acne, alopecia, infertility, obesity, and menstrual abnormalities (amenorrhoea in 19% of cases).** It is a complex disorder of unknown aetiology. Considerable variability of symptoms and signs is seen among women with polycystic ovary syndrome (PCOS) [Balen, 1999b].
- **An accepted definition includes oligomenorrhoea, hyperandrogenism (clinical or laboratory evidence), and the absence of other endocrine disorders. It does not include the presence of polycystic ovaries** [Harborne et al, 2003].
- **Ultrasound examination** of the ovaries typically shows multiple, small peripheral cysts. On its own polycystic ovaries are not diagnostic of the syndrome, as up to a third of women in the general population have polycystic ovaries on ultrasound examination [DTB, 2001].
- **Endocrine abnormalities** include increased serum concentrations of testosterone, prolactin, luteinizing hormone (LH) (with normal follicle-stimulating hormone [FSH] levels), and insulin resistance with compensatory hyperinsulinaemia [Balen, 1999a; Balen, 1999b].
- **There is a high risk of impaired glucose tolerance and Type 2 diabetes** and studies have found that 31–35% of women had impaired glucose tolerance and 7.5–10% had Type 2 diabetes [Ehrmann et al, 1999; Legro et al, 1999].
- **The majority of women with PCOS who have glucose intolerance have normal fasting glucose levels.** Thus fasting glucose levels are a poor predictor of diabetes in women with PCOS [Legro et al, 1999]. An oral glucose tolerance test should be done.
- Women with PCOS are more likely to have risk factors for cardiovascular disease than other women of the same age. In particular they may have obesity, central body fat distribution, hypertriglyceridaemia, reduced high-density lipoprotein cholesterol levels, and hypertension [DTB, 2001].

[Kiningham et al, 1996; Balen, 1999a; Balen, 1999b]

Premature ovarian failure

- **Menopause/ovarian failure occurring before the age of 40 years** is considered premature.
- **Auto-immune disease is the most common cause;** auto-antibodies to ovarian cells, gonadotrophin receptors, and oocytes have been reported in 80% of cases. (These assays are not routinely available.) Other causes include infection (e.g. mumps oophoritis), previous surgery, radiotherapy, and chemotherapy. The toxic pollutants from tobacco smoke may account for the earlier menopause seen in smokers.
- It is associated with other auto-immune disorders such as hypothyroidism, Addison's disease, and diabetes mellitus.
- **Before puberty or in adolescents,** ovarian failure is usually due to a chromosomal abnormality, e.g. Turner mosaic, or previous radiotherapy, or chemotherapy.

[Jacobs, 1996; Balen, 1999a]

Hyperprolactinaemia

- **A prolactinoma is the commonest cause of hyperprolactinaemia** (60% of cases). Other causes include non-functioning pituitary adenoma that compresses the pituitary stalk/hypothalamus (disrupting the inhibitory influence of dopamine on prolactin secretion); dopaminergic antagonist drugs (e.g. phenothiazines, haloperidol, clozapine, metoclopramide, domperidone, methyldopa, cimetidine); primary hypothyroidism (thyrotrophin-releasing hormone stimulates the secretion of prolactin), or it may be idiopathic.
- **Prolactin acts directly on the hypothalamus** to reduce the amplitude and frequency of pulses of gonadotrophin-releasing hormone.

[Baird, 1997; McIver et al, 1997]

Weight-related amenorrhoea

- **A regular menstrual cycle is unlikely to occur if the body mass index (BMI) is less than 19** (normal range 20–25).
- **Weight loss is usually 10–15% or more of the woman's normal weight for height** when it causes amenorrhoea.
- **Weight loss may be due to illness, exercise, or eating disorders,** among which anorexia nervosa lies at the extreme end of the spectrum.
- The neuroendocrine mechanism causing this is uncertain, but the result is impaired gonadotrophin secretion, particularly luteinizing hormone, and subsequently low oestrogen levels.

[Franks, 1987; Balen, 1999a]

Exercise-associated amenorrhoea

- Exercise-associated amenorrhoea is thought to be associated with a number of factors, including bodyweight and body fat; type, intensity, and frequency of exercise; nutritional status and calorific restriction; and emotional stress.
- **It is particularly common in athletes involved in endurance events** (e.g. distance runners) and in women who participate in sports where appearance is considered important (e.g. gymnasts, ballet dancers).
- **Eating disorders have a higher prevalence in female athletes than in non-athletes.**
- **It is a hypothalamic disorder** caused by abnormal gonadotrophin-releasing hormone pulsatility, resulting in impaired gonadotrophin levels, particularly luteinizing hormone, and subsequently low oestrogen levels. This can result in delayed puberty or secondary amenorrhoea.

[Fogel, 1997; Balen, 1999a; Furia, 1999; Warren and Stiehl, 1999]

'Post-pill' amenorrhoea

- This is defined as absence of menstruation for 6 months following cessation of the combined oral contraceptive pill.
- It probably results from an underlying hormonal problem that has been masked by the induced regular bleeds that occur whilst the combined oral contraceptive pill is being taken. A transient inhibition of gonadotrophin-releasing hormone may also occur [Fogel, 1997].

Progestogen-associated amenorrhoea

- **Depot medroxyprogesterone acetate** inhibits the secretion of gonadotrophins and thus suppresses ovulation.
  - After 1 year of use, 80% of women have amenorrhoea or very scanty, infrequent vaginal bleeding.
  - It may take 12 months (or occasionally longer) for fertility and normal periods to return after they have stopped taking the drug.
  - **There is partial oestrogen deficiency** in women who use depot medroxyprogesterone acetate.
- **The progestogen-only pill** leads to reversible long-term amenorrhoea in a minority of women, due to complete suppression of ovulation.
- **The levonorgestrel-releasing intra-uterine device** commonly results in amenorrhoea after a few months. This is thought to be mainly a local effect, but suppression of ovulation can occur in some women (in some cycles).

[Glasier, 1999; BNF 46, 2003]

How do I assess my patient with primary amenorrhoea?

History

Note in particular:

- **Age at menarche of older sisters and mother:** constitutional delay of puberty is frequently familial.
- **Family history of genetic anomalies**
- **Associated symptoms,** e.g. cyclical lower abdominal pain (which may suggest haematocolpos), symptoms of hypothyroidism, absent sense of smell (which may be associated with gonadotrophin deficiency).
- **Presence of chronic illness,** e.g. diabetes, coeliac disease, chronic renal or cardiac disease
- **Recent emotional upsets**
- **Recent change in bodyweight and height**
- **Level of exercise**
- **Drug history,** e.g. chemotherapy

Examination

This is done with particular reference to the following:

- **Development of secondary sexual characteristics:** these characteristics are classified by specialists according to the staging system developed by Tanner.
- **Height and weight:** calculation of body mass index if appropriate.
- **Features of Turner's syndrome,** i.e. short stature, web neck, shield chest with widely spaced nipples, wide carrying angle, and scoliosis.
- **Signs of excess androgens,** e.g. hirsutism, acne.
- **Signs of thyroid disease.**
- **Galactorrhoea:** it is important not to examine the breasts prior to prolactin estimation as the level may then be falsely elevated.
- **Appearance of the external genitalia,** looking for clitoromegaly (indicating virilization) or signs of haematocolpos.
- **Pelvic examination is inappropriate** in young girls who are not sexually active.

Investigations

These are usually done following specialist referral (apart from pregnancy testing if this is appropriate).

- **Consider performing a pregnancy test.**
- **Pelvic ultrasound** will determine the presence or absence of a uterus and any outflow tract obstruction. It may indicate the presence of polycystic ovaries.
- **Karyotyping** will detect Turner's syndrome (45X0) and testicular feminization (46XY).
- **Raised follicle-stimulating hormone and luteinizing hormone levels** suggest gonadal dysgenesis, e.g. Turner's syndrome or testicular feminization. Hypothalamic dysfunction, due for example to stress, exercise, or weight loss, may result in low/normal levels; gonadotrophin deficiency causes low levels.
- **Thyroid function tests** will detect hypo- or hyperthyroidism.
- **Prolactin level** testing will detect hyperprolactinaemia.
- **Raised testosterone levels** with an absent uterus suggest testicular feminization. Slightly raised levels occur with polycystic ovary syndrome.

[McIver et al, 1997; Thomas and Rebar, 1997; Edmonds, 1999]

How do I assess my patient with secondary amenorrhoea?

History

Note in particular:

- **Risk of pregnancy**
- **Associated symptoms,** e.g. galactorrhoea, hirsutism, hot flushes, dry vagina, symptoms of thyroid disease
- **Recent change in bodyweight**
- **Recent emotional upsets**
- **Level of exercise**
- **Previous menstrual and obstetric history**
- **Previous surgery,** e.g. endometrial curettage, oophorectomy
- **Previous abdominal, pelvic, or cranial radiotherapy**
- **Family history,** e.g. of early menopause (premature ovarian failure can be familial)
- **Drug history,** e.g. progestogens, combined oral contraceptive, chemotherapy

Examination

This is done with particular reference to the following:

- **Height and weight:** calculate body mass index if appropriate.
- **Signs of excess androgens,** e.g. hirsutism, acne.
- **Signs of virilization,** e.g. deep voice, clitoromegaly in addition to hirsutism, and acne.
- **Signs of thyroid disease.**
- **Acanthosis nigricans:** this hyperpigmented thickening of the skin folds of the axilla and neck is a sign of profound insulin resistance. It is associated with polycystic ovary syndrome (PCOS) and obesity.
- **Breast examination for galactorrhoea.** It is important not to examine the breasts prior to prolactin estimation as the level may then be falsely elevated.
- **Fundoscopy** and assessment of visual fields if there is suspicion of pituitary tumour.
- **Pelvic examination should be avoided in young girls who have never been sexually active.** In other women, enlarged polycystic ovaries may be identified.

Investigations

- **Pregnancy testing** should be considered in all women who present with secondary amenorrhoea.
- **Follicle-stimulating hormone (FSH), luteinizing hormone (LH), and prolactin levels and thyroid function should be measured in all cases.**
  - **Gonadotrophin levels (FSH and LH)** are raised when there is ovarian failure and abnormally low when there is hypothalamic or pituitary failure. Elevation of LH alone is suggestive of PCOS.
  - **Prolactin levels** may be moderately and transiently elevated in response to stress, breast examination, and venepuncture — in these circumstances prolactin should return to usual levels within 48 hours. Prolactin levels may be moderately and more permanently elevated as a result of PCOS or pronounced hypothyroidism (thyrotrophin-releasing hormone stimulates the secretion of prolactin). A prolactin level (on two occasions) above 1000 mIU/l warrants further investigation, such as computed tomography or a magnetic resonance imaging scan of the pituitary fossa. A prolactin level above 1000 mIU/l suggests a microadenoma, and greater than 5000 mIU/l is usually associated with a macroadenoma.
  - **Thyroid function tests** will indicate the presence of hypo- or hyperthyroidism.
- **Testosterone/androgen levels should be measured in women with hirsutism.** They may be mildly elevated in PCOS. Levels above 4.8 mmol/l are suggestive of congenital adrenal hyperplasia, Cushing's syndrome, or an adrenal or ovarian tumour. Specialist advice should be sought [DTB, 2001].
- **Sex hormone-binding globulin** can be measured in people with PCOS. If this is low it can indicate insulin resistance [Jayagopal et al, 2003].
- **Estradiol levels are of limited usefulness,** as they vary considerably even in a woman with amenorrhoea.
- **Pelvic ultrasound** may show the classic picture of polycystic ovaries, i.e. enlarged ovaries with increased stroma and multiple, small, peripherally situated follicles.
- **Other investigations** include MRI and CT scans; measurement of visual field defects (for suspected hypothalamic or pituitary tumours); 17-hydroxyprogesterone measurement (for congenital adrenal hyperplasia); hysteroscopy (for Asherman's syndrome); the dexamethasone suppression test (for Cushing's syndrome); and karyotyping (in women under 30 years with ovarian failure).

[Aloi, 1995; Kiningham et al, 1996; Baird, 1997; McIver et al, 1997; Rees, 1997; Balen, 1999a]

How do I interpret the laboratory findings?

On the basis of investigations, women with amenorrhoea tend to fall into five main groups:

- **Raised testosterone/androgen level.** This group includes women with polycystic ovary syndrome (mildly raised level), and women with androgen-secreting tumours of the ovary or adrenal gland, late-onset congenital adrenal hyperplasia, or Cushing's syndrome.
- **Raised gonadotrophins (follicle-stimulating hormone [FSH] and luteinizing hormone [LH]) with a low estradiol level.** This group includes women with premature ovarian failure and resistant ovary syndrome.
- **Hyperprolactinaemia.** This group includes women with prolactinomas and hypothyroidism.
- **Low gonadotrophins (FSH and LH) with a low estradiol level.** This group includes women with amenorrhoea secondary to exercise, low weight, and stress.
- **Normal or mildly raised gonadotrophin levels with normal estradiol levels.** This group includes women with polycystic ovary syndrome (PCOS) or other mild disorders of gonadotrophin regulation or action.

[Crosignani and Vegetti, 1996; Warren, 1996; Baird, 1997; Rees, 1997]

Complications and prognosis

- **Osteoporosis:** women with amenorrhoea associated with oestrogen deficiency are at significant risk of developing

able 1: Laboratory findings in common causes of secondary amenorrhoea.

	FSH	LH	Prolactin	Testosterone	Oestrogen status
yperprolactinaemia	Normal or low	Normal or low	High	Normal	Low
:OS	Normal	Slightly raised in 40%	Normal/moderate rise in 5–30%	Slightly raised	Normal
emature menopause	Very high	High	Normal	Normal	Low
Iypothalamic' e.g. associated with weight loss, exercise, :ess	Low or normal	Low or normal	Normal	Normal	Low or normal

osteoporosis. This increased risk persists even if normal menses are resumed. Oestrogen deficiency is of particular concern in younger women as a desirable peak bone mass may not be attained. Poor nutrition in women with eating disorders may also contribute to the increased risk of osteoporosis [Committee on Sports Medicine, 1989; Fogel, 1997; Warren and Stiehl, 1999].

Cardiovascular disease

- Young women with amenorrhoea associated with oestrogen deficiency may be at increased risk of cardiovascular disease; although this has not been studied specifically, the increased risk associated with a low oestrogen state in postmenopausal women is well documented [Kiningham et al, 1996; Fogel, 1997; McIver et al, 1997].
- Women with polycystic ovary syndrome have an increased risk of developing cardiovascular disease, hypertension, and Type 2 diabetes [Hopkinson et al, 1998].

Endometrial hyperplasia: women with amenorrhoea but no associated oestrogen deficiency are at increased risk of endometrial hyperplasia and endometrial carcinoma [Kiningham et al, 1996; Balen, 1999a; Wild et al, 2000].

Infertility: women with amenorrhoea generally do not ovulate, but pregnancy can be achieved in many either by treating the underlying disorder or by specialized infertility treatment [Baird, 1997; McIver et al, 1997]. (See *Management issues* for more details.)

Psychological distress: amenorrhoea often causes considerable anxiety, altered self-image, and loss of self-esteem. Many women have concerns about loss of fertility, loss of femininity, or worry about an unwanted pregnancy. The diagnosis of Turner's syndrome, testicular feminization, or developmental anomaly can be traumatic for both girls and their parents [Fogel, 1997; Rees, 1997].

Management issues

- General p.63
- Management of infertility p.63
- Prevention of osteoporosis p.64
- Prevention of cardiovascular disease p.64
- Prevention of endometrial hyperplasia p.64
- Management of amenorrhoea secondary to use of depot medroxyprogesterone acetate p.64
- Management of 'post-pill' amenorrhoea p.64

General

- **The commonest cause of secondary amenorrhoea is pregnancy and this should always be excluded before further investigations are undertaken** [Baird, 1997].
- **The usual criteria for investigation are:**
  - The absence of menstruation for 6 consecutive months in a woman who previously had regular periods [Balen, 1999a].
  - The failure to establish menstruation by the age of 16 years in the presence of normal secondary sexual development [Edmonds, 1999].
  - The failure to develop any secondary sexual characteristics by the age of 14 years [Edmonds, 1999].
- **Establishing a firm diagnosis is important** to determine treatment, to minimize complications, to give an accurate prognosis regarding fertility, and to restore fertility where this is possible.
- **Treat any underlying causes of amenorrhoea, where possible.**
  - Hypothyroidism is easily treatable with levothyroxine (thyroxine).
  - Hyperprolactinaemia often responds well to bromocriptine (specialist supervision required).
  - Prolactinomas will commonly shrink with medical therapy, but large tumours that affect vision may need surgical treatment. Other tumours of the pituitary, hypothalamus, ovary, and adrenal glands usually require surgery.
  - Polycystic ovary syndrome (PCOS) may respond to weight loss, and recently there has been interest in the use of insulin-sensitizing agents, e.g. metformin.
  - Exercise-associated amenorrhoea will respond to modification of the exercise programme along with attention to diet and weight.
  - Weight-related amenorrhoea should be managed by weight gain and may require the assistance of psychologists or psychiatrists.
  - Some genital tract malformations are amenable to surgery, e.g. haematocolpos [McIver et al, 1997].
- **General lifestyle advice** on smoking, alcohol consumption, exercise, weight, and diet (including calcium intake) may minimize the adverse effects of amenorrhoea [Fogel, 1997]. This is particularly true of women with PCOS [Harborne et al, 2003].
- **Patients with amenorrhoea of hormonal aetiology should be warned that they are not necessarily infertile** and could conceive should a sporadic ovulation occur [Fogel, 1997; Rees, 1997].

Management of infertility

- Treatment of the underlying cause of the amenorrhoea (when this is reversible) is often all that is required to restore fertility. The onset of regular menstruation can take months and is likely to be accompanied by the resumption of fertility. Specialist referral is recommended if infertility treatment is required.
- One small study found that obese and infertile women who lose weight through a lifestyle programme of diet and exercise are more likely to ovulate spontaneously, irrespective of the cause of their infertility [Clark et al, 1998].
- **Premature ovarian failure:** restoration of fertility is not possible. However, pregnancy may be achieved with *in vitro* fertilization techniques using ovum donation.

- **Polycystic ovary syndrome (PCOS):** metformin (an insulin-sensitizing agent) has been successful for the treatment of the hyperinsulinaemia (contributes directly to excessive testosterone production) which occurs in PCOS. The rationale for metformin is that it reduces insulin resistance and may break the chain of events that lead to the signs and symptoms of the syndrome. Most trials to date have been small and open-label, and preliminary evidence suggests that metformin (1500–1700 mg per day) reduces testosterone levels and may improve menstrual regularity and fertility.
  - Metformin is not licensed for the treatment of PCOS and it should be reserved for specialist use.
  - Administration of gonadotrophins may be effective in inducing ovulation, although this is associated with a high risk of multiple pregnancy.
- **Hypothalamic amenorrhoea:** treatment with pulsatile gonadotrophin-releasing hormone by means of a portable pump is highly successful and associated with a low rate of multiple pregnancy. For those who are underweight, treatment should be deferred until a near-normal weight has been achieved, because of concern that if conception occurs, growth of the fetus may be compromised.
- **Hyperprolactinaemia:** treatment with bromocriptine or other dopamine antagonists is effective. Women with prolactinomas should be advised to defer conception for a few months after starting therapy. Pregnancy is associated with enlargement of the anterior pituitary; therefore prior shrinkage of the tumour by drug treatment is sensible.
- **Amenorrhoea secondary to pituitary disease (excluding prolactinomas):** treatment is with gonadotrophins, and this is associated with a high multiple pregnancy rate.
- For more information see the PRODIGY guidance on *Infertility*.

[Baird, 1997; McIver et al, 1997; De Sloover Koch and Ernst, 2001; DTB, 2001]

Prevention of osteoporosis

- **Women with amenorrhoea due to causes associated with low oestrogen levels have an increased risk of developing osteoporosis.** This includes women with amenorrhoea due to premature ovarian failure, weight loss, hyperprolactinaemia, and exercise.
- **All women with low oestrogen levels should be considered for oestrogen replacement** if amenorrhoea persists for longer than 6 months. An adequate intake of calcium (1500 mg/day) and vitamin D (400 IU/day) is also advisable. Referral to a specialist is advised.
- **Oestrogen replacement must be accompanied by a progestogen in women with a uterus to prevent endometrial hyperplasia.**

[Kiningham et al, 1996; Fogel, 1997; McIver et al, 1997]

Prevention of cardiovascular disease

- **Currently no studies have evaluated the risk of cardiovascular disease in young, oestrogen-deficient women.** There is concern that these women are at more risk of cardiovascular disease than older (postmenopausal) women who are oestrogen-deficient [Kiningham et al, 1996; Fogel, 1997].
- **For women with polycystic ovary syndrome (PCOS):** weight loss and treatment of hypertension, diabetes or dyslipidaemia (if present) are advised to reduce risk factors for cardiovascular disease [McIver et al, 1997].
- The long-term safety record with metformin is well established and it is generally well tolerated by women with PCOS. However, larger, long-term trials are still needed to determine whether metformin has a beneficial effect on the increased cardiovascular morbidity and mortality in PCOS.

Prevention of endometrial hyperplasia

- **Women with amenorrhoea due to causes associated with normal oestrogen levels including polycystic ovary syndrome (PCOS) are at risk of endometrial hyperplasia and should have an induced regular withdrawal bleed.**
- Women at risk of endometrial hyperplasia should be offered treatment with a low-dose oral contraceptive or cyclical progestogen. A combination of cyproterone acetate with ethinylestradiol may be used to prevent endometrial hyperplasia in those women with PCOS who suffer from acne, hirsutism, or both, but may make glucose intolerance worse [McIver et al, 1997; Morin-Papunen et al, 2000].

Management of amenorrhoea secondary to use of depot medroxyprogesterone acetate

- **Reduction in bone mineral density** (BMD) has been reported in women who use depot medroxyprogesterone acetate (DMPA) but the risk of osteoporosis and fractures in later life remains unclear.
- There is some evidence that BMD starts to recover when DMPA is discontinued; the extent of recovery is probably related to the duration of exposure.
  - One study has found that after 30 months women who discontinued DMPA had a bone density similar to that of non-users [Scholes et al, 2002].
- The effect of BMD reduction may be more important in adolescents in whom the usual process of bone mineral accretion may be reversed.
- The Committee on Safety of Medicines (CSM) therefore advises that:
  - In adolescents, DMPA may be used as first-line contraception but *only* after other methods have been discussed and considered to be unsuitable or unacceptable.
  - In women of all ages, careful re-evaluation of the risks and benefits of treatment should be carried out in women who wish to continue use for more than 2 years.
  - In women with significant lifestyle and/or medical risk factors for osteoporosis, other methods of contraception should be considered.
- For all users of DMPA, a calcium-rich diet and regular weight-bearing exercise are recommended in order to reduce any increased risk of fracture, and no smoking is recommended.

[CSM, 2004]

Management of 'post-pill' amenorrhoea

- Amenorrhoea lasting more than 6 months after use of the oral combined contraceptive pill has been stopped should be regarded as coincidental rather than resulting from the use of the pill, and should be investigated as outlined in the section *How do I assess my patient with secondary amenorrhoea?*

References

NHS staff in England can link, free of charge, from references to full text journals by clicking on [Full text] on the PRODIGY website.

1. Aloi, J.A. (1995) Evaluation of amenorrhea. *Comprehensive Therapy* **21**(10), 575–578.
2. Baird, D.T. (1997) Amenorrhoea. *Lancet* **350**(9073), 275–279. [Full text]

Balen, A. (1999a) Pathogenesis of polycystic ovary syndrome – the enigma unravels? *Lancet* **354**(9183), 966–967. [Full text]

Balen, A.H. (1999b) Secondary amenorrhea. In: Edmonds, D.K. (Ed.) *Dewhurst's textbook of obstetrics & gynaecology for postgraduates.* 6th edn. London: Blackwell Science. 42–61.

BNF 46 (2003) *British National Formulary.* 46th edn. London: British Medical Association and Royal Pharmaceutical Society of Great Britain.

Clark, A.M., Thornley, B., Tomlinson, L. et al (1998) Weight loss in obese infertile women results in improvement in reproductive outcome for all forms of fertility treatment. *Human Reproduction* **13**(6), 1502–1505.

Committee on Sports Medicine (1989) American Academy of Pediatrics: amenorrhea in adolescent athletes. *Pediatrics* **84**(2), 394–395.

Crosignani, P.G. and Vegetti, W. (1996) A practical guide to the diagnosis and management of amenorrhoea. *Drugs* **52**(5), 671–681.

CSM (2004) *Updated prescribing advice on the effect of depo-provera contraception on bones.* Committee on Safety of Medicines. http://medicines.mhra.gov.uk [Accessed: 14/02/2005].

0. De Sloover Koch, S. and Ernst, M.E. (2001) Use of metformin in polycystic ovary syndrome. *Annals of Pharmacotherapy* **35**(12), 1644–1647.

1. DTB (2001) Tackling polycystic ovary syndrome. *Drug & Therapeutics Bulletin* **39**(1), 1–5.

2. Edmonds, D.K. (1999) Primary amenorrhea. In: Edmonds, D.K. (Ed.) *Dewhurst's textbook of obstetrics & gynaecology for postgraduates.* 6th edn. London: Blackwell Science. 34–42.

3. Ehrmann, D.A., Barnes, R.B., Rosenfield, R.L. et al (1999) Prevalence of impaired glucose tolerance and diabetes in women with polycystic ovary syndrome. *Diabetes Care* **22**(1), 141–146. [Full text]

4. Fogel, C.I. (1997) Endocrine causes of amenorrhea. *Lippincotts Primary Care Practice* **1**(5), 507–518.

5. Franks, S. (1987) Primary and secondary amenorrhoea. *British Medical Journal* **294**(6575), 815–819.

6. Furia, J. (1999) The female athlete triad. *Medscape Orthopaedics & Sports Medicine eJournal* **3**(1),

7. Garden, A.S. (1998) Problems with menstruation. In: Garden, A.S. (Ed.) *Paediatric & adolescent gynaecology.* London: Arnold. 127–146.

8. Glasier, A. (1999) Contraception. In: Edmonds, D.K. (Ed.) *Dewhurst's textbook of obstetrics & gynaecology for postgraduates.* 6th edn. London: Blackwell Science. 373–386.

9. Harborne, L., Fleming, R., Lyall, H. et al (2003) Descriptive review of the evidence for the use of metformin in polycystic ovary syndrome. *Lancet* **361**(9372), 1894–1901. [Full text]

20. Hopkinson, Z.E., Sattar, N., Fleming, R. and Greer, I.A. (1998) Polycystic ovarian syndrome: the metabolic syndrome comes to gynaecology. *British Medical Journal* **317**(7154), 329–332. [Full text]

21. Jacobs, H.S. (1996) Amenorrhoea. In: Weatherall, D.J., Ledingham, J.G.G., Warrell, D.A. et al (Eds.) *Oxford textbook of medicine.* 3rd edn. Oxford: Oxford University Press.

22. Jayagopal, V., Kilpatrick, E.S., Jennings, P.E. et al (2003) The biological variation of testosterone and sex hormone-binding globulin (SHBG) in polycystic ovarian syndrome: implications for SHBG as a surrogate marker of insulin resistance. *Journal of Clinical Endocrinology & Metabolism* **88**(4), 1528–1533.

23. Kiningham, R.B., Apgar, B.S. and Schwenk, T.L. (1996) Evaluation of amenorrhea. *American Family Physician* **53**(4), 1185–1194.

24. Legro, R.S., Kunselman, A.R., Dodson, W.C. and Dunaif, A. (1999) Prevalence and predictors of risk for type 2 diabetes mellitus and impaired glucose tolerance in polycystic ovary syndrome: a prospective, controlled study in 254 affected women. *Journal of Clinical Endocrinology & Metabolism* **84**(1), 165–169.

25. McIver, B., Romanski, S.A. and Nippoldt, T.B. (1997) Evaluation and management of amenorrhea. *Mayo Clinic Proceedings* **72**(12), 1161–1169. [Full text]

26. Morin-Papunen, L.C., Vauhkonen, I., Koivunen, R.M. et al (2000) Endocrine and metabolic effects of metformin versus ethinyl estradiol-cyproterone acetate in obese women with polycystic ovary syndrome: a randomized study. *Journal of Clinical Endocrinology & Metabolism* **85**(9), 3161–3168.

27. Rees, M.C.P. (1997) Menstrual problems: amenorrhoea. In: McPherson, A. and Waller, D. (Eds.) *Women's health: Oxford general practice series 39.* 4th edn. Oxford: Oxford University Press. 303–342.

28. Scholes, D., Lacroix, A.Z., Ott, S.M. et al (1999) Bone mineral density in women using depot-medroxyprogesterone acetate for contraception. *Obstetrics & Gynecology* **93**(2), 233–238.

29. Scholes, D., Lacroix, A.Z., Ichikawa, L.E. et al (2002) Injectable hormone contraception and bone density: results from a prospective study. *Epidemiology* **13**(5), 581–587.

30. Thomas, M.A. and Rebar, R.W. (1997) Delayed puberty in girls and primary amenorrhea. *Current Therapy in Endocrinology & Metabolism* **6**, 223–226.

31. Warren, M.P. (1996) Clinical review 77: evaluation of secondary amenorrhea. *Journal of Clinical Endocrinology & Metabolism* **81**(2), 437–442.

32. Warren, M.P. and Stiehl, A.L. (1999) Exercise and female adolescents: effects on the reproductive and skeletal systems. *Journal of the American Medical Womens Association* **54**(3), 115–120.

33. Wild, S., Pierpoint, T., McKeigue, P. and Jacobs, H. (2000) Cardiovascular disease in women with polycystic ovary syndrome at long-term follow-up: a retrospective cohort study. *Clinical Endocrinology* **52**(5), 595–600.

A

PRODIGY GUIDANCE

Anaemia — iron deficiency

A

Last revised in July 2005
www.prodigy.nhs.uk/guidance.asp?gt=Anaemia - iron deficiency

Applies to people over the age of 12 years

This guidance covers the management of iron deficiency anaemia from the age of 12 years.

This guidance does not cover the management of other anaemias.

There is separate PRODIGY guidance for *Anaemia — macrocytic*.

Goals

- To establish the diagnosis
- To treat effectively
- To investigate the cause

Contents

Scenarios

- Iron deficiency anaemia excluding pregnancy p.66
- Iron deficiency anaemia during pregnancy p.67

Extended Information, p. 68

Which scenario?

- **Iron deficiency anaemia excluding pregnancy:** covers the investigation and management of iron deficiency anaemia in someone who is not pregnant.
- **Iron deficiency anaemia during pregnancy:** covers the investigation and management of iron deficiency anaemia in a woman who is pregnant.

Iron deficiency anaemia excluding pregnancy

Which therapy?

- **A reason for iron deficiency should always be sought.**
- **Consider** gastrointestinal blood loss, excessive menstrual loss, malabsorption, or nutritional deficiency.
- **Dietary deficiency,** by itself, is rarely a cause of iron deficiency anaemia in developed countries unless there are increased physiological demands for iron (e.g. during adolescence, pregnancy, lactation, and in menstruating women).
- **Give oral iron** (e.g. ferrous sulphate 200 mg three times a day) to anyone with iron deficiency anaemia. Continue treatment for 3 months once the haemoglobin has normalized.

Practical prescribing points

For further information, please see the *Medicines Compendium* (www.medicines.org.uk) or the *British National Formulary* (www.bnf.org).

- **Oral iron** is usually well tolerated.
- **If gastrointestinal adverse effects are troublesome** (e.g. nausea, abdominal pain, diarrhoea, or constipation) reduce the frequency to once or twice daily, or take iron tablets with food.

Follow-up advice

- Recheck full blood count in 2–4 weeks (earlier if symptoms are severe) in order to assess response to treatment.
- Iron replacement should be continued for 3 months onc the haemoglobin has normalized, in order to replenish iron stores.

Should I refer or investigate?

Refer?

- **Referral should always be considered** for investigation c the upper and lower bowel to exclude a source of gastrointestinal blood loss (unless you are confident tha iron deficiency is secondary to another cause, such as menorrhagia).
- **Referral guidelines for suspected cancer** recommend tha
  - Men of any age with unexplained iron deficiency anaemia and a haemoglobin of 11 g/100 ml or below, or women (non-menstruating) with unexplained iron deficiency anaemia and a haemoglobin of 10 g/100 m or below are referred urgently to a team specialising i the management of lower gastrointestinal cancer, depending upon local arrangements.
  - People of any age with iron deficiency anaemia and dyspepsia are referred urgently for endoscopy or to a team specialising in the management of upper gastrointestinal cancer, depending upon local arrangements.

Investigate?

Confirm iron deficiency anaemia by:

- **Full blood count and blood film:** low haemoglobin (Hb) mean cell volume (MCV), mean cell Hb (MCH), mean cell Hb concentration (MCHC), and microcytic hypochromic red cells on the blood film.
- **Serum ferritin level:** low (an indicator of reduced body iron stores). However, as ferritin is an acute-phase protein, levels may be normal or elevated in infective, inflammatory or malignant disease despite iron deficiency. Ferritin may also be elevated by excessive alcohol consumption.
- **Erythrocyte protoporphyrin:** increased with iron deficiency, and correlates well with a reduced ferritin level. However, levels can also be increased by infection, inflammation, lead poisoning, and haemolytic anaemia. Not usually necessary if ferritin is available.
- **Serum iron and transferrin (total iron binding capacity [TIBC]):** reduced serum iron and increased transferrin, with a consequent reduction in transferrin saturation. However, there is a marked diurnal variation, and a considerable overlap between iron deficient and normal people. Not usually necessary if ferritin is available.

Patient information leaflets

The following PILs are available at www.prodigy.nhs.uk

- Anaemia
- Anaemia Due to Iron Deficiency
- Barium Enema
- Barium Swallow / Meal / Follow Through
- Biopsy
- Blood Test - Blood Count and Smear
- Blood Test - General
- Faecal Occult Blood Test

Shared decision-making

- **Iron tablets** are the treatment for iron deficiency anaemia.
- You should take the tablets until the blood level is back to normal — and then for a further 3 months to build up the iron stores.
- Most people do not get side effects. If they do occur (such as nausea, abdominal pain, diarrhoea, or constipation) then options are: to reduce the dose, or take the iron tablets with food.
- Your stools (faeces) may be black when taking iron.
- Tests are usually needed if the cause of the anaemia is not clear.

Drug rationale

Drugs not included

- **Iron salts other than ferrous sulphate** are not included. Adverse effects are directly related to the amount of iron in the gut lumen [Cox, 2003]. When equivalent amounts of elemental iron are compared, the incidence of adverse effects is no greater with ferrous sulphate than with other iron salts.
- **Modified-release iron preparations** are not included because they release most of their iron in the lower small intestine, where it cannot be effectively absorbed [Frewin et al, 1997].
- **Compound iron and folic acid preparations** are not included. They are not routinely used to *treat* iron deficiency anaemia in the UK.
- **Compound iron and ascorbic acid preparations** are not included. They offer only a minimal therapeutic advantage and are not available on NHS prescriptions.
- **Parenteral iron preparations** are not included. They are only needed in exceptional circumstances, and are usually reserved as a secondary care treatment.

Drugs included

- **Ferrous sulphate tablets** are widely used to treat iron deficiency anaemia in the UK. They have a high content of elemental iron per tablet (200 mg dried ferrous sulphate contains 65 mg elemental iron).

Prescriptions

1st choice: ferrous sulphate three times a day

Ferrous sulphate 200mg three times a day

- Age from 12 years onwards
- Ferrous sulphate 200mg tablets. Take one tablet three times a day; supply 84 tablets; NHS Cost £2.70; OTC Cost £4.76.

Lower-dose ferrous sulphate (if adverse effects troublesome)

Ferrous sulphate 200mg twice a day

- Age from 12 years onwards
- Ferrous sulphate 200mg tablets. Take one tablet twice a day; supply 56 tablets; NHS Cost £1.80; OTC Cost £3.20.

Ferrous sulphate 200mg once a day

- Age from 12 years onwards
- Ferrous sulphate 200mg tablets. Take one tablet once a day; supply 28 tablets; NHS Cost £0.90; OTC Cost £1.60.

A

Iron deficiency anaemia during pregnancy

Which therapy?

- **Anaemia in pregnancy is defined** by the World Health Organization defines anaemia as a haemoglobin level of less than 11 g/dl.
- **Give oral iron** (e.g. ferrous sulphate 200 mg three times a day) to anyone with iron deficiency anaemia. Continue treatment for 3 months once the haemoglobin has normalized.

Practical prescribing points

For further information, please see the *Medicines Compendium* (www.medicines.org.uk) or the *British National Formulary* (www.bnf.org).

- **Oral iron** is usually well tolerated.
- **If gastrointestinal adverse effects are troublesome** (e.g. nausea, abdominal pain, diarrhoea, or constipation) reduce the frequency to once or twice daily, or take iron tablets with food.

Follow-up advice

- Recheck full blood count in 2–4 weeks (earlier if symptoms are severe) in order to assess response to treatment.
- Iron replacement should be continued for 3 months once the haemoglobin has normalized, in order to replenish iron stores.

Should I refer or investigate?

Refer?

- It is difficult to state a level of haemoglobin below which referral should always be considered. However, the risk of maternal heart failure is increased at levels below 7 g/dl, and discussion with an Obstetric unit is strongly recommended if the level is this low.

Investigate?

Confirm iron deficiency anaemia by:

- **Full blood count and blood film:** low haemoglobin (Hb), mean cell volume (MCV), mean cell Hb (MCH), mean cell Hb concentration (MCHC), and microcytic hypochromic red cells on the blood film. Note that MCV increases by approximately 4 femtolitres in pregnancy (whether iron deficient or not).
- **Serum ferritin level:** low. Considered a reliable indicator of iron deficiency in the first trimester (in the absence of infection, inflammation or excessive alcohol consumption); however serum ferritin level falls in the second and third trimesters independent of iron stores.

A

- **Erythrocyte protoporphyin:** increased. This fluctuates less than ferritin throughout pregnancy, and may be more useful than ferritin in the second and third trimesters. However, levels can also be increased by infection, inflammation, lead poisoning, and haemolytic anaemia.

Patient information leaflets

The following PILs are available at www.prodigy.nhs.uk

- Anaemia
- Anaemia Due to Iron Deficiency
- Biopsy
- Blood Test - Blood Count and Smear
- Blood Test - General
- Faecal Occult Blood Test

Shared decision-making

- Pregnant women commonly develop iron deficiency anaemia.
- **Iron tablets** are the treatment.
- You should take the tablets until the blood level of iron is back to normal — and then for a further 3 months to build up the iron stores.
- Most people do not get side effects. If they do occur (such as nausea, abdominal pain, diarrhoea, or constipation) then options are: to reduce the dose, or take the iron tablets with food.
- Your stools (faeces) may be black when taking iron.

Drug rationale

Drugs not included

- **Iron salts other than ferrous sulphate** are not included. Adverse effects are directly related to the amount of iron in the gut lumen [Cox, 2003]. When equivalent amounts of elemental iron are compared, the incidence of adverse effects is no greater with ferrous sulphate than with other iron salts.
- **Modified-release iron preparations** are not included because they release most of their iron in the lower small intestine, where it cannot be effectively absorbed [Frewin et al, 1997].
- **Compound iron and folic acid preparations** are not included. They are not routinely used to *treat* iron deficiency anaemia in the UK.
- **Compound iron and ascorbic acid preparations** are not included. They offer only a minimal therapeutic advantage and are not available on NHS prescriptions.
- **Parenteral iron preparations** are not included. They are only needed in exceptional circumstances, and are usually reserved as a secondary care treatment.

Drugs included

- **Ferrous sulphate tablets** are widely used to treat iron deficiency anaemia in the UK. They have a high content of elemental iron per tablet (200 mg dried ferrous sulphate contains 65 mg elemental iron).

Prescriptions

1st choice: ferrous sulphate three times a day

Ferrous sulphate 200mg three times a day

- Age from 12 years onwards
- Ferrous sulphate 200mg tablets. Take one tablet three times a day; supply 84 tablets; NHS Cost £2.70; OTC Cost £4.75.

Lower-dose ferrous sulphate (if adverse effects troublesome)

Ferrous sulphate 200mg twice a day

- Age from 12 years onwards
- Ferrous sulphate 200mg tablets. Take one tablet twice a day; supply 56 tablets; NHS Cost £1.80; OTC Cost £3.20.

Ferrous sulphate 200mg once a day

- Age from 12 years onwards
- Ferrous sulphate 200mg tablets. Take one tablet once a day; supply 28 tablets; NHS Cost £0.90; OTC Cost £1.60.

Extended Information

Background information

- What is it? p.68
- How common is it? p.68
- How do I know my patient has it? p.69
- What else might it be? p.69
- Complications and prognosis p.69

What is it?

- **Iron deficiency** is defined as a condition in which there are no mobilizable iron stores, causing a compromised supply of iron to tissues (including the red blood cell). The more severe stages of iron deficiency cause anaemia. Iron deficiency is estimated as being 2–5 times more common than iron deficiency anaemia.
- **Iron deficiency anaemia** is the main cause of microcytic hypochromic anaemia, in which mean cell volume (MCV), mean cell haemoglobin (MCH) and mean cell haemoglobin concentration (MCHC) are all reduced, and the blood film shows microcytic hypochromic red cells. Haemoglobin is more than 2 standard deviations below the mean for a population of healthy people of the same age and sex. This represents a level of less than 13 g/dl for men and less than 12 g/dl for women (less than 11 g/dl in pregnancy).
- **In developed countries it is most commonly due to blood loss:**
  - Menorrhagia in premenopausal women
  - Gastrointestinal bleeding in men and postmenopausal women
  - Other causes are iron-deficient diet and malabsorption (e.g. coeliac disease)
- **In developing countries several factors may combine:**
  - Poor diet
  - Increased requirements (e.g. frequent pregnancy)
  - Blood loss due to menorrhagia and gastrointestinal bleeding (e.g. hookworm, trichuriasis, amoebiasis and schistosomiasis)
  - Haemolysis due to malaria or haemoglobinopathies

[Frewin et al, 1997; WHO et al, 2001; Cox, 2003]

How common is it?

- Iron deficiency anaemia is the most common type of anaemia in all countries. It affects up to 30% of the world's population, with prevalence in developed countries of about 8%. The most common cause in developing countries is hookworm infestation; it is estimated that a billion people are infected worldwide [Stoltzfus and Dreyfuss, 1997].
- It occurs in up to 14% of premenopausal women in developed countries [Hercberg et al, 2001].

It occurs during pregnancy in 23% of pregnant women in developed countries, and 52% of pregnant women in developing countries [WHO et al, 2001].
[Frewin et al, 1997; Cox, 2003]

How do I know my patient has it?

Which symptoms may be present?

Symptoms may be few if the anaemia develops gradually, but are typically:

- Fatigue
- Breathlessness
- Palpitations
- Headache
- Tinnitus
- Unusual dietary cravings (pica)

Which signs may be present?

- Pallor of eyelids, tongue, nail beds and palms
- Atrophic glossitis and angular cheilosis (also signs of megaloblastic anaemia and riboflavin deficiency, respectively)
- Brittle, longitudinally-ridged, flaking nails and koilonychia (spoon-shaped nails) in chronic cases
- Dysphagia (due to an oesophageal web — Plummer-Vinson syndrome)
- Hair loss
- Splenomegaly
- Tachycardia, murmurs, cardiac enlargement, and heart failure (if severe anaemia)

Which investigations are useful in the diagnosis of iron deficiency anaemia?

- **Full blood count:**
  - Low haemoglobin (Hb) concentration, less than 13 g/dl for men and less than 12 g/dl for women
  - Low MCV, MCH, and MCHC (mean cell volume, mean cell Hb, mean cell Hb concentration)
  - Reticulocyte count low for the degree of anaemia
  - There may be a mild thrombocytosis (raised platelet concentration)
- **Blood film:** microcytic hypochromic red cells, with occasional target cells and pencil-shaped poikilocytes.
- **Serum ferritin level:** low (an indicator of reduced body-iron stores). However, as ferritin is an acute-phase protein, levels may be normal or elevated in infective, inflammatory or malignant disease despite iron deficiency. Serum ferritin level is also increased by excessive alcohol consumption.
- **Erythrocyte protoporphyrin:** increased with iron deficiency, and correlates well with a reduced ferritin level. However, levels can also be increased by infection, inflammation, lead poisoning, and haemolytic anaemia.
- **Serum iron and transferrin (total iron-binding capacity [TIBC]):** reduced serum iron and increased transferrin, with a consequent reduction in transferrin saturation. However, there is a marked diurnal variation, and a considerable overlap between iron-deficient and normal people.
- **Serum transferrin receptors:** a relatively new test that is not widely available. Raised in iron deficiency. Its major advantage is that it is not affected by infection or inflammation, and does not vary with age, sex or pregnancy. It is, however, elevated by increased red-cell production or turnover (e.g. haemolytic anaemia). There is a lack of standardization of the different methods available.
- **Bone-marrow aspiration:** rarely needed, but will show absent bone-marrow iron stores.

How are these investigations affected by pregnancy?

- **Full blood count:** in pregnancy a physiological reduction in Hb concentration occurs, which does not represent anaemia. There is an increase in red-cell mass and plasma volume; the plasma volume increases more than the red-cell mass, causing the Hb reduction.
- **There is a lack of agreement on the Hb level for the diagnosis of anaemia during pregnancy:**
  - The World Health Organization (WHO) defines anaemia as an Hb level less than 11 g/dl throughout pregnancy (this is the most widely used definition worldwide).
  - The American Centers for Disease Control and Prevention modified this by trimester of pregnancy:
    - First-trimester Hb level less than 11 g/dl
    - Second-trimester Hb level less than 10.5 g/dl
    - Third-trimester Hb level less than 11 g/dl
- **MCV:** increases by approximately 4 femtolitres in pregnancy (whether iron deficient or not).
- **Serum ferritin level:** considered a reliable indicator of iron deficiency in the first trimester (in the absence of infection, inflammation or excessive alcohol consumption); however serum ferritin level falls in the second and third trimester independent of iron stores.
- **Erythrocyte protoporphyin:** this fluctuates less than ferritin throughout pregnancy, and may be more useful than ferritin in the second and third trimester.
- **Serum iron and transferrin (total iron-binding capacity [TIBC]):** these tests have a low sensitivity for the diagnosis of iron deficiency during pregnancy; in addition, normal ranges for pregnancy have not been firmly established.
- **Serum transferrin receptors:** this test has potential use as it not affected by pregnancy; however it is not yet widely available.

[Institute of Medicine, 1990; US Preventive Services Task force, 1993; Frewin et al, 1997; Haram et al, 2001; Hoffbrand et al, 2001; WHO et al, 2001; Cox, 2003; Mungen, 2003]

What else might it be?

Other anaemias that may be mistaken for iron deficiency anaemia:

- **Anaemia of chronic disorders:** inhibition of release of iron from macrophages to red-cell precursors results in a normocytic or mildly microcytic anaemia (serum iron and total iron-binding capacity [TIBC] both reduced, serum ferritin normal or raised). It does not respond to iron therapy.
- **Other causes of impaired haemoglobin synthesis and microcytic anaemia:**
  - Sideroblastic anaemia — a refractory hypochromic anaemia, with ring sideroblasts and increased iron in the bone marrow.
  - Thalassaemia trait (alpha or beta) — a hypochromic microcytic anaemia, the mean cell volume tends to be particularly low for the degree of anaemia.

[Hoffbrand et al, 2001; Weatherall, 2003]

Complications and prognosis

Complications

- Increased morbidity from infectious disease, due to adverse effects on the immune system
- Heart failure
- Angina

Complications specific to pregnancy

- Increased maternal mortality
- Increased prenatal and perinatal infant mortality
- Increased prematurity

- Infants born to iron deficient mothers require more iron than is supplied by breast milk, and at an earlier stage, to avoid iron deficiency in the infant

[WHO et al, 2001]

A

Management issues

- How do I diagnose the cause of iron deficiency anaemia? p.70
- How do I treat iron deficiency anaemia? p.70
- How do I treat iron deficiency anaemia during pregnancy? p.70
- Medicines management p.71

How do I diagnose the cause of iron deficiency anaemia?

- **Difficulties in diagnosis may occur when more than one type of anaemia is present.** A dimorphic blood picture may be present, and additional investigations such as vitamin B_{12} and folate levels may help diagnose the different causes of anaemia.
- **A reason for iron deficiency should always be sought.** History-taking should attempt to determine whether gastrointestinal (GI) blood loss, menstrual loss, malabsorption, or nutritional deficiency is likely. Drug history of nonsteroidal anti-inflammatory use is particularly important, as this might point to possible GI bleeding. In developed countries dietary deficiency, by itself, is rarely a cause of iron deficiency anaemia unless there are increased physiological demands for iron (e.g. during infancy, adolescence, pregnancy, lactation, and in menstruating women).
- **Both upper and lower GI investigations should be considered,** because of the high incidence of pathology (except possibly in premenopausal women with heavy periods).
  - A study of people with iron deficiency anaemia and no obvious cause from history found that 84% had a GI cause of blood loss: 28% due to upper GI pathology alone, 27% due to lower GI pathology alone, and 29% due to dual pathology [Hardwick and Armstrong, 1997].
  - Another study of people presenting to their GP with iron deficiency anaemia found that 11% had GI carcinoma, 35% had other GI pathology, 5% had non-GI carcinoma, 10% had other non-GI pathology, and 39% had no diagnosis [Yates et al, 2004].
- **Referral guidelines for suspected cancer** published by the National Institute for Health and Clinical Excellence (NICE) [NICE, 2005] recommend that:
  - Men of any age with unexplained iron deficiency anaemia and a haemoglobin of 11 g/100 ml or below, or women (non-menstruating) with unexplained iron deficiency anaemia and a haemoglobin of 10 g/100 ml or below are referred urgently to a team specialising in the management of lower gastrointestinal cancer, depending upon local arrangements.
  - People of any age with iron deficiency anaemia and dyspepsia are referred urgently for endoscopy or to a team specialising in the management of upper gastrointestinal cancer, depending upon local arrangements.
- **Faecal occult blood (FOB) testing should not be used.** In the investigation of iron deficiency anaemia FOB has very poor sensitivity (50–55%), with positive predictive values of 17–43% and 16–26% for upper and lower GI lesions respectively. Positive tests discriminate poorly between upper and lower GI lesions. Upper and lower GI investigations would be necessary regardless of FOB results, which therefore merely delay more appropriate tests.
- **Coeliac disease** has been found to be the cause in 2–3% of people presenting with iron deficiency anaemia.
  - The definitive test for coeliac disease is a small-bowel biopsy; these should therefore be taken during upper GI endoscopy [Goddard et al, 2000].
  - Serological testing for antiendomysial antibodies has a sensitivity and specificity of 90–95% for the diagnosis of coeliac disease, and has the advantage of being less invasive than small-bowel biopsy.
- **Haematuria is an uncommon cause of iron deficiency anaemia** and is usually clinically obvious.
- **Stool examination** should be considered in people with a history of travel to the tropics, in order to exclude hookworm infestation, which is the commonest cause of iron deficiency anaemia worldwide.

[Hoffbrand et al, 2001; Cox, 2003]

How do I treat iron deficiency anaemia?

- **Management involves treatment of the underlying cause and oral iron-replacement therapy** (e.g. with ferrous sulphate 200 mg three times a day). Haemoglobin (Hb) should rise by about 0.1–0.2 g/dl per day (about 2 g/dl every 3 weeks).
- **Iron replacement should be continued for 3 months once the Hb has normalized,** in order to replenish iron stores.
- **Failure to respond to treatment is usually due to poor compliance.** It can also be due to continuing excessive blood loss, associated inflammatory disease, malabsorption, a combined deficiency state, or another cause of hypochromic anaemia such as sideroblastic anaemia or thalassaemia trait.
- **Intramuscular or intravenous iron-replacement therapy** might be considered if the person is completely unable to tolerate oral iron, or if losses exceed the amount that can be absorbed orally. However, this therapy should rarely be used outside a specialist setting. The rise in Hb is no faster than with effective oral therapy. Injections are painful, and there is a risk of anaphylaxis.
- **Blood transfusion should usually be avoided.** Someone with profound anaemia who has severe symptoms (e.g. severe heart failure) may require transfusion. This should be done with extreme caution, under diuretic cover, owing to the risk of precipitating or worsening heart failure.

[Frewin et al, 1997; Hoffbrand et al, 2001; WHO et al, 2001; Cox, 2003]

How do I treat iron deficiency anaemia during pregnancy?

- **The daily absorption of iron outside pregnancy is 1 mg.** The total requirement throughout pregnancy is estimated at 500–1400 mg [Haram et al, 2001]. The requirement is very small in the first trimester, increasing throughout the second and third trimester. The increased demands of pregnancy can therefore result in iron deficiency anaemia; as pregnancy proceeds many women show haematological changes suggesting iron deficiency.
- **Prophylactic iron supplementation for all pregnant women is not recommended in the UK.** Likewise it is not recommended in Australia, Canada, and New Zealand; it is however recommended in France and the USA [Makrides et al, 2003]. In some countries, iron supplementation is routinely given with folic acid during the second half of pregnancy [WHO et al, 2001].
- **Treatment with oral iron-replacement therapy in pregnancy** is recommended when iron deficiency anaemia is detected. There is inconclusive evidence upon which to base this recommendation due to the shortage of good quality trials [Cuervo and Mahomed, 2004;

Rasmussen, 2001]. This recommendation is, however, widely accepted, and is common practice.

The risk of maternal heart failure is increased at haemoglobin levels less than 7 g/dl, and discussion with an Obstetric unit is strongly recommended if the level is this low.

[Institute of Medicine, 1990; WHO et al, 2001]

Medicines management

Adverse effects of oral iron are a common cause of non-compliance. They include epigastric discomfort, nausea, diarrhoea, constipation, or black faeces.

Taking iron with meals reduces adverse effects, but absorption is also reduced by about 40%. Although vitamin C (e.g. in citrus fruits and fruit juices) has been shown to increase oral iron absorption, high-dose vitamin C supplements should not be given with iron as the combination frequently causes epigastric pain.

Alternatively, a lower daily dosage can be given, e.g. ferrous sulphate 200 mg once or twice a day — one tablet taken consistently is better than total rejection of a higher dose because of unacceptable adverse effects.

Oral iron reduces the absorption of tetracyclines, quinolones, bisphosphonates, and zinc.

The absorption of oral iron is reduced by zinc, magnesium salts (e.g. in antacids), calcium (e.g. in milk and dairy products), tannins (e.g. in tea, coffee, and cocoa), and phytates (present in cereal grains, legumes, nuts, and seeds).

[WHO et al, 2001]

References

NHS staff in England can link, free of charge, from references to full text journals by clicking on [Full text] on the PRODIGY website.

1. Cox, T.M. (2003) Iron metabolism and its disorders. In: Warrell, D.A., Cox, T.M., Firth, J.D. and Benz, E.J.Jr (Eds.) *Oxford textbook of medicine*. 4th edn. Oxford: Oxford University Press. Section 22.5.4.
2. Cuervo, L.G. and Mahomed, K. (2004) *Treatments for iron deficiency anaemia in pregnancy (Cochrane Review)*. The Cochrane Library. Issue 3. Chichester, UK: John Wiley & Sons, Ltd.
3. Frewin, R., Henson, A. and Provan, D. (1997) ABC of clinical haematology: iron deficiency anaemia. *British Medical Journal* 314(7077), 360–363. [Full text]
4. Haram, K., Nilsen, S.T. and Ulvik, R.J. (2001) Iron supplementation in pregnancy – evidence and controversies. *Acta Obstetricia et Gynecologica Scandinavica* 80(8), 683–688.
5. Hercberg, S., Preziosi, P. and Galan, P. (2001) Iron deficiency in Europe. *Public Health Nutrition* 4(2B), 537–545.
6. Hoffbrand, A.V., Pettit, J.E. and Moss, P.A.H. (2001) *Essential haematology*. 4th edn. Oxford: Blackwell Science.
7. Institute of Medicine (1990) *Iron nutrition during pregnancy*. The National Academy of Sciences. www.iom.edu/report.asp?id=18257[Accessed: 22/07/2004]. [Full text]
8. Makrides, M., Crowther, C.A., Gibson, R.A. et al (2003) Efficacy and tolerability of low-dose iron supplements during pregnancy: a randomized controlled trial. *American Journal of Clinical Nutrition* 78(1), 145–153.
9. Mungen, E. (2003) Iron supplementation in pregnancy. *Journal of Perinatal Medicine* 31(5), 420–426.
10. Rasmussen, K. (2001) Is there a causal relationship between iron deficiency or iron-deficiency anemia and weight at birth, length of gestation and perinatal mortality? *Journal of Nutrition* 131(2S-2), 590S-601S. [Full text]
11. Stoltzfus, R.J. and Dreyfuss, M.L. (1997) *Guidelines for the use of iron supplements to prevent and treat iron deficiency anemia*. Washington: International Life Sciences Institute Press.
12. US Preventive Services Task force (1993) Routine iron supplementation during pregnancy. *Journal of the American Medical Association* 270(23), 2848–2854. [Full text]
13. Weatherall, D.J. (2003) Disorders of the synthesis or function of haemoglobin. In: Warrell, D.A., Cox, T.M., Firth, J.D. and Benz, E.J.Jr (Eds.) *Oxford textbook of medicine*. 4th edn. Oxford: Oxford University Press. Section 22.5.7.
14. WHO, UN Children's Fund and UN University (2001) *Iron deficiency anaemia: assessment, prevention, and control. A guide for programme managers.* WHO/NHD/01.3. World Health Organization. www.who.int [Accessed: 08/07/2004].

PRODIGY GUIDANCE

Anaemia — macrocytic

A

Last revised in July 2005
www.prodigy.nhs.uk/guidance.asp?gt=Anaemia - macrocytic

Applies to people over the age of 16 years

This guidance covers the management of the most common causes of macrocytic anaemias — namely, vitamin B_{12} deficiency anaemia and folate deficiency anaemia.

This guidance does not cover the management of other causes of macrocytic anaemia, or of other types of anaemia.

There is separate PRODIGY guidance for *Anaemia — iron deficiency.*

Goals

- To establish the diagnosis
- To treat effectively

Contents

Scenarios
- Macrocytic anaemia p.72

Extended Information, p. 74

Macrocytic anaemia

Which therapy?

Treatment of established vitamin B_{12} deficiency anaemia

Pernicious anaemia, or history of total gastrectomy or ileal resection

- **Initial treatment:** hydroxocobalamin 1 mg intramuscularly every 2–4 days for six doses.
- **Maintenance treatment:** hydroxocobalamin 1 mg intramuscularly every 3 months for life.

Poor diet (rare)

- **Initial treatment:** as above.
- **Maintenance treatment** is not usually necessary if diet improved. Vegans should be advised to take oral vitamin B_{12} supplements following acute treatment, although a twice-yearly injection is an alternative.

Treatment of established folate deficiency anaemia

- **Folic acid** 5 mg daily continued for 4 months.
- **Maintenance treatment is rarely necessary** if poor diet is corrected, or if coeliac disease is effectively treated with a gluten-free diet.
- **Check vitamin B_{12} levels before starting treatment for folate deficiency** because of the risk of neuropathy in coexisting vitamin B_{12} deficiency.

Indications for iron supplements

- **Coexisting iron deficiency:** see the PRODIGY guidance *Anaemia — iron deficiency.*
- **Severe anaemia** (i.e. haemoglobin less than 8 g/dl): iron deficiency may develop following treatment, and iron supplements in the first few weeks should be considered.

Practical prescribing points

For further information, please see the *Medicines Compendium* (www.medicines.org.uk) or the *British National Formulary* (www.bnf.org).

Iron supplements

- **Oral iron** is usually well tolerated.
- **If gastrointestinal adverse effects are troublesome** (e.g. nausea, abdominal pain, diarrhoea, or constipation) reduce the frequency to once or twice daily, or take iron tablets with food.

Follow-up advice

- Recheck full blood count in 2 weeks to assess response to treatment (earlier if symptoms are severe).
- Annual full blood count is not recommended if the person is well.

Should I refer or investigate?

Refer?

- **Lack of response to prescribed treatment** (bone marrow examination is necessary).
- **In folate deficiency** to exclude coeliac disease (upper gastrointestinal endoscopy with duodenal or jejunal biopsy).
- **Dyspepsia in association with pernicious anaemia for urgent assessment,** either as an outpatient or by direct referral for endoscopy.

Investigate?

If vitamin B_{12} deficiency is diagnosed

- **Check intrinsic factor (IF) antibody** (if positive, this is virtually diagnostic of pernicious anaemia).
- **Consider a Schilling test** if IF antibody is negative.
- **In elderly people** with a low vitamin B_{12} level who are IF negative, if further investigation by Schilling test is felt to be inappropriate then response to vitamin B_{12} injections may be adequate to confirm a diagnosis of vitamin B_{12} deficiency anaemia.
- **Consider upper gastrointestinal (GI) endoscopy,** to confirm atrophic gastritis and to exclude gastric carcinoma or gastric polyps (2–3 times more common in pernicious anaemia).

If folate deficiency is diagnosed

- **Consider coeliac disease** as a cause of the folate deficiency:
  - The definitive test for coeliac disease is a small-bowel biopsy; these should therefore be taken during upper GI endoscopy.

- Serological testing for antiendomysial antibodies has a sensitivity and specificity of 90–95% for the diagnosis of coeliac disease, and has the advantage of being less invasive than small-bowel biopsy.

Patient information leaflets

The following PILs are available at www.prodigy.nhs.uk

Anaemia
Anaemia Due to Folic Acid Deficiency
Anaemia (Pernicious) and Vitamin B12 Deficiency
Biopsy
Blood Test - Blood Count and Smear
Blood Test - General
Medicines - Name Changes of Medicines

Shared decision-making

For anaemia due to vitamin B_{12} deficiency:

- **Vitamin B_{12} injections are the treatment.**
- At first about six injections are needed over a few weeks.
- Then one every 3 months for the rest of your life.
- There are usually no side effects from treatment.
- An annual blood test is usual, once the anaemia is corrected.

For anaemia due to folic acid deficiency:

- **Folic acid tablets** are the treatment.
- A poor diet is the most common cause of folic acid deficiency.
  - You should take the tablets for about 4 months.
  - This corrects the anaemia and builds up the body's store of folic acid.
  - There is no need to continue after four months if your diet improves.
- Treatment may be long term if there is another cause such as a blood problem.

Drug rationale

Drugs not included

Folic acid 400 micrograms is not included. It does not contain enough folic acid for replacement therapy in folate deficiency.

Folinic acid (available as calcium folinate) is not included. It is effective for treating folate deficiency, but is markedly more expensive than folic acid.

Iron salts other than ferrous sulphate are not included. Adverse effects are directly related to the amount of iron in the gut lumen [Hoffbrand, 2003]. When equivalent amounts of elemental iron are compared, the incidence of adverse effects is no greater with ferrous sulphate than with other iron salts.

Modified-release iron preparations are not included. They release most of their iron in the lower small intestine, where it cannot be absorbed effectively [Frewin et al, 1997].

Compound iron and folic acid preparations are not included. They do not contain enough folic acid to *treat* folate deficiency.

Compound iron and ascorbic acid preparations are not included. They offer only a minimal therapeutic advantage and are not available on NHS prescriptions.

Multivitamins containing vitamin B_{12} or folic acid are not included. There is no justification for their use in macrocytic anaemias.

Parenteral iron preparations are not included. They are only needed in exceptional circumstances, and are usually reserved as a secondary care treatment.

Drugs included

- **Hydroxocobalamin** is the treatment of choice for vitamin B_{12} deficiency.
- **Oral vitamin B_{12} (cyanocobalamin)** is included. It is suitable only for the very small minority of people with proven dietary deficiency of vitamin B_{12} (most vitamin B_{12} deficiency is due to malabsorption). It is available on an NHS prescription only for this indication, and the prescription must be endorsed 'SLS'.
- **Folic acid, 5 mg per dose,** is the standard replacement dose for folate deficiency.
- **Ferrous sulphate tablets** are offered for someone at risk of, or who develops, iron deficiency anaemia in the first few weeks of therapy. Ferrous sulphate tablets are widely used in the UK and have a high content of elemental iron (200 mg dried ferrous sulphate contains 65 mg of elemental iron).

[Hoffbrand, 2003]

Prescriptions

Vitamin B_{12} deficiency: start hydroxocobalamin

Hydroxocobalamin 1mg IM injection every 2-4 days for 6 doses

- Age from 16 years onwards
- Hydroxocobalamin 1mg/ml inj. FOR INTRAMUSCULAR INJECTION. Inject the contents of one ampoule (1mg) every 2 to 4 days for six doses, then every 3 months thereafter; supply 6 1ml ampoules; NHS Cost £11.77.

Vitamin B_{12}deficiency: hydroxocobalamin maintenance therapy

Hydroxocobalamin 1mg IM injection every 3 months

- Age from 16 years onwards
- Hydroxocobalamin 1mg/ml inj. FOR INTRAMUSCULAR INJECTION. Inject the contents of one ampoule (1mg) every 3 months; supply 1 1ml ampoules; NHS Cost £2.46.

Vegans/proven dietary deficiency only: cyanocobalamin (SLS)

- Age from 16 years onwards
- Cyanocobalamin 50mcg tablets. Take two tablets once a day, between meals; supply 56 tablets; NHS Cost £3.40.

Folate deficiency

Folic acid 5mg once a day

- Age from 16 years onwards
- Folic acid 5mg tablets. Take one tablet once a day; supply 28 tablets; NHS Cost £0.44.

Treat or prevent iron deficiency

Ferrous sulphate 200mg three times a day

- Age from 16 years onwards
- Ferrous sulphate 200mg tablets. Take one tablet three times a day; supply 84 tablets; NHS Cost £2.70; OTC Cost £4.75.

Ferrous sulphate 200mg twice a day

- Age from 16 years onwards
- Ferrous sulphate 200mg tablets. Take one tablet twice a day; supply 56 tablets; NHS Cost £1.80; OTC Cost £3.20.

Ferrous sulphate 200mg once a day

- Age from 16 years onwards
- Ferrous sulphate 200mg tablets. Take one tablet once a day; supply 28 tablets; NHS Cost £0.90; OTC Cost £1.60.

Extended Information

Background information

A

- What is it? p.74
- How common is it? p.74
- How do I know my patient has it? p.74
- What else might it be? p.75
- Complications and prognosis p.75

What is it?

- **Macrocytic anaemia** is defined as anaemia with a raised mean cell volume (MCV) and macrocytes on the blood film. Haemoglobin is more than 2 standard deviations below the mean for a population of healthy people of the same age and sex. This represents a level of less than 13 g/dl for men and less than 12 g/dl for women.
- **Macrocytic anaemia can be divided into megaloblastic and non-megaloblastic causes.** The term megaloblastic refers to a characteristic abnormality of the erythroblasts in the bone marrow — the maturation of the nucleus is delayed relative to the cytoplasm.
- **Megaloblastic anaemias are the most common cause of macrocytic anaemia.** These occur when defective DNA synthesis occurs in the bone marrow, leading to the development of megaloblasts in the bone marrow, and the release of macrocytes into the blood stream.
- **Vitamin B_{12} or folate deficiency account for the vast majority of cases of megaloblastic anaemias.** Deficiency of either produces similar clinical and haematological effects.
- **Vitamin B_{12} deficiency owing to pernicious anaemia** accounts for 80% of megaloblastic anaemias.
  - Pernicious anaemia is caused by an autoimmune gastritis resulting in reduced or absent acid production and absent intrinsic factor, which is necessary for the absorption of vitamin B_{12}.
  - **Other causes of vitamin B_{12} deficiency are rare in the UK,** but include strict vegan diets, gastrectomy or gastric bypass surgery, other causes of intestinal malabsorption such as ileal resection and Crohn's disease, and HIV infection.
  - **Vitamin B_{12} deficiency takes about 4 years to develop** if supplies are totally cut off by malabsorption. There is enterohepatic circulation of vitamin B_{12}, which may account for the ability of vegans to maintain low body stores without progressing to severe deficiency.
- **Folate deficiency** may occur because of one or a combination of the following:
  - Inadequate dietary intake (body stores are sufficient for only about 4 months)
  - Malabsorption, e.g. coeliac disease, Crohn's disease
  - Increased demands, e.g. pregnancy, infancy, rapid cell turnover (such as occurs with haemolysis or leukaemia)
  - Increased urinary excretion, e.g. heart failure, acute hepatitis, dialysis
  - Drug-induced, e.g. alcohol, antiepileptics, methotrexate, sulfasalazine, trimethoprim (if high-dose and prolonged course)
- Non-megaloblastic anaemias are described in the section *What else might it be?*

[Hoffbrand and Provan, 1997; Donnelly, 2001; Hoffbrand et al, 2001; Hoffbrand, 2003]

How common is it?

Vitamin B_{12} deficiency

- **Pernicious anaemia** (PA) occurs in all races, but is most common in northern Europe. The incidence in Caucasians is 127:100,000.
- **The peak incidence of PA** occurs at 60 years of age. There is a female: male ratio of 1.6:1.
- **A positive family history occurs in** 30% of cases of PA. [...] is often associated with other autoimmune conditions, especially hypothyroidism, hyperthyroidism, Addison's disease, and vitiligo.

Folate deficiency

- **During pregnancy** there is an increase in folic acid requirements. As a result, 30% of women in late pregnancy who do not take folate supplements have reduced folate levels. However, only a minority develop megaloblastic anaemia [Mahomed, 2004].

[Hoffbrand and Provan, 1997; Hoffbrand et al, 2001; Hoffbrand, 2003]

How do I know my patient has it?

Which symptoms may be present?

- Fatigue
- Breathlessness
- Anorexia and weight loss
- Indigestion or episodic diarrhoea or both
- Reversible sterility
- Neuropathy:
  - Subacute combined degeneration of the cord — a symmetrical neuropathy affecting the legs more than the arms; it causes paraesthesiae and numbness (especially in the feet), unsteadiness, ataxia, and difficulty in walking (with a tendency to fall in the dark).
  - Visual disturbance.
  - Psychiatric disturbances — mild neurosis, depression, dementia.
  - It was thought that these occurred only with vitamin B_{12} deficiency, but it is now known that they can also occur with folate deficiency [Green and Miller, 1999]. They may occur even in the absence of anaemia.

Which signs may be present?

- Pallor
- Mild jaundice (lemon-yellow tint)
- Atrophic glossitis and angular cheilosis (both may also occur with iron deficiency anaemia)
- Hepatomegaly
- Mild pyrexia
- Neuropathy (subacute combined degeneration of the cord), ataxia, mental disturbance, or optic atrophy
- Tachycardia, murmurs, cardiac enlargement, and heart failure (if severe anaemia)

Which investigations are useful in the diagnosis of vitamin B_{12} deficiency and folate deficiency anaemia?

- **Full blood count:**
  - Low haemoglobin (Hb) and increased mean cell volume (MCV) — although macrocytosis can precede the development of anaemia.
  - Pancytopenia in severe cases.
  - Reticulocyte count low for the degree of anaemia (1–3% only).
  - MCV may be normal if there is associated iron deficiency. There is the possibility that coexistent

pathology could be missed. There will be a dimorphic blood film. The ferritin level should be checked.

- **Blood film:** macrocytic red cells, neutrophils with hypersegmented nuclei, and Howell Jolly bodies
- **Biochemistry:** increased plasma unconjugated bilirubin (increased destruction of red-cell precursors in the marrow)
- **Serum vitamin B_{12} and serum or red-cell folate levels:**
  - Folate deficiency will result in reduced levels of serum and red-cell folate. Red-cell folate is a better guide to body folate stores than is serum folate.
  - Vitamin B_{12} deficiency will result in reduced serum vitamin B_{12} levels. It may also result in increased serum folate and reduced red-cell folate levels, because of the effect on intracellular folate metabolism. Combined deficiency usually results in both reduced serum vitamin B_{12} and serum folate levels.
  - False-positive vitamin B_{12} levels (low levels in the absence of deficiency) may occur in folate deficiency, pregnancy, multiple myeloma, and excessive vitamin C intake.
  - False-negative vitamin B_{12} levels (normal levels in the presence of deficiency) may occur in true deficiency, liver disease, lymphoma, autoimmune disease, and myeloproliferative disorders.
- **Autoantibody screen:**
  - Intrinsic factor (IF) antibodies are virtually diagnostic of pernicious anaemia (PA). However, absence of IF antibodies does not exclude the diagnosis, as they are present in only 50% of people with PA (i.e. it has high specificity but low sensitivity).
  - Gastric parietal-cell antibodies are present in 85% of people with PA, but are also found in 3–10% of people who do not have PA (i.e. it has high sensitivity but low specificity).
- **Schilling test (radioactive vitamin B_{12} absorption study):** to determine if malabsorption of vitamin B_{12} is occurring and whether it is due to PA or due to an intestinal lesion. People with PA show impaired absorption of vitamin B_{12}, which can be corrected by giving IF. People with malabsorption because of an intestinal lesion do not respond to IF.
  - The Schilling test has many limitations, and the result often does not alter clinical management.
  - In elderly people with a low vitamin B_{12} level and a negative IF, if further investigation by Schilling test is felt to be inappropriate, then a response to vitamin B_{12} injections may be adequate to confirm a diagnosis of vitamin B_{12} deficiency anaemia:
    - The person feels better in 1–2 days, with an improvement in general well-being
    - Reticulocyte count increases in 2–3 days, and peaks in 5–8 days
    - Red blood cell count increases within 1 week, and normalizes in 4–8 weeks
    - MCV increases for 3–4 days (due to the increased reticulocyte count), then decreases, reaching the normal range in 25–78 days
    - Haemoglobin level increases by 2–3 g/dl every 2 weeks
    - White blood cell and platelet counts normalize in 7–10 days
- **Bone-marrow aspiration:** megaloblasts and giant metamyelocytes (early granulocyte precursors) are seen in both vitamin B_{12} and folate deficiency anaemia.

[Hoffbrand and Provan, 1997; Snow, 1999; Dharmarajan and Norkus, 2001; Hoffbrand et al, 2001; Hoffbrand, 2003]

What else might it be?

- **Alcohol excess:** the most common cause of macrocytosis in the UK. This is a direct effect of alcohol, although there is often coexistent folate deficiency in spirit drinkers because of poor diet (beer drinkers are relatively protected against folate deficiency, owing to the high folate content of beer).
- **Liver disease** can also cause macrocytosis.
- **Severe hypothyroidism** can result in a mild macrocytosis.
- **Reticulocytosis** causes a macrocytosis (e.g. haemolytic anaemia or post acute blood loss).
- **Other blood disorders causing a macrocytosis,** e.g. aplastic anaemia, red-cell aplasia, myelodysplastic syndromes, myeloid leukaemia.
- **Changes in plasma proteins** (e.g. increased paraprotein because of multiple myeloma) may cause a spurious rise in mean cell volume without macrocytes being present in the blood film.
- **Drugs that affect DNA synthesis** (e.g. hydroxycarbamide [hydroxyurea], azathioprine).

[Hoffbrand and Provan, 1997; Hoffbrand et al, 2001]

Complications and prognosis

Complications

- Heart failure
- Angina
- Neuropathy — subacute combined degeneration of the cord, optic atrophy, mild neurosis, depression, or dementia
- Gastric carcinoma occurs in 4% of people with pernicious anaemia (a threefold-increased risk)
- Neural tube defect in the fetus if the mother is deficient in vitamin B_{12} or folate
- Sterility

Prognosis

- Macrocytic anaemia due to deficiency of vitamin B_{12} or folate responds rapidly to replacement therapy.
- Associated neuropathy does not always respond, and may be irreversible.

[Hoffbrand and Provan, 1997; Hoffbrand et al, 2001; Hoffbrand, 2003]

Management issues

- General issues p.75
- How do I treat vitamin B_{12} deficiency? p.76
- How do I treat folate deficiency? p.76
- Which issues of folate deficiency are particular to pregnancy? p.76

General issues

- **Excess alcohol consumption** is the most common cause of a macrocytosis in the UK.
- **Hypothyroidism or liver disease** can result in a mild macrocytosis and should be considered in all cases.
- **Iron deficiency may develop** following treatment of megaloblastic anaemia, and giving iron supplements in the first few weeks should be considered, especially in more severe degrees of anaemia.
- **Refractory macrocytic anaemia requires bone marrow analysis** to exclude another underlying problem such as myelodysplasia. Coexisting iron deficiency should also be considered.
- **Blood transfusion should usually be avoided.** Someone with profound anaemia who has severe symptoms (e.g. severe heart failure) may require transfusion. This should be done with extreme caution, under diuretic cover,

owing to the risk of precipitating or worsening heart failure.

[Hoffbrand and Provan, 1997; Hoffbrand et al, 2001; Hoffbrand, 2003]

A

How do I treat vitamin B_{12} deficiency?

- **Vitamin B_{12} replacement requires intramuscular injection,** as the usual cause is malabsorption. Initial treatment is with six injections of hydroxocobalamin 1 mg at intervals of between 2–4 days, followed by injections every 3 months for life.
- **Symptoms usually improve rapidly,** but residual neuropathy may persist.
- **Vegans can absorb vitamin B_{12} normally,** and after acute treatment should be given oral vitamin B_{12} supplements, although a twice-yearly injection is an alternative.
- **Someone who has undergone total gastrectomy or ileal resection** is unable to absorb vitamin B_{12}, and long-term treatment with intramuscular hydroxocobalamin is necessary.
- **Gastric carcinoma and gastric polyps** are 2–3 times more common in pernicious anaemia. Endoscopy should be performed urgently if other features of these conditions (e.g. iron deficiency, dyspepsia) develop [NICE, 2005].

[Hoffbrand and Provan, 1997; Hoffbrand et al, 2001]

How do I treat folate deficiency?

- **It is important to assess dietary intake and consider alcohol excess.**
- **Treatment with oral folic acid,** 5 mg daily, usually results in a rapid improvement in symptoms.
- **Treatment is continued for 4 months** to replenish stores, and should persist only if the underlying cause cannot be corrected.
- **Vitamin B_{12} deficiency must be excluded in all people starting treatment for folate deficiency.** If vitamin B_{12} deficiency is present, treatment with folate alone may improve the anaemia and cause the raised mean cell volume to fall, but may result in development of neurological complications. The process by which vitamin B_{12} deficiency causes anaemia is mediated via its effect on folate metabolism, while the process by which it causes neuropathy is separate from this [Drazkowski et al, 2002].
- **Chronic haemolytic anaemias,** such as sickle cell anaemia, thalassaemia major, and hereditory spherocytosis, result in increased folate demands because of the high turnover of red cells. Prophylactic folic acid is usually given.
- **Coeliac disease** should be considered in folate deficiency.
  - The definitive test for coeliac disease is a small-bowel biopsy; these should therefore be taken during upper GI endoscopy.
  - Serological testing for antiendomysial antibodies has a sensitivity and specificity of 90–95% for the diagnosis of coeliac disease, and has the advantage of being less invasive than small-bowel biopsy.

[Hoffbrand and Provan, 1997; Hoffbrand et al, 2001]

Which issues of folate deficiency are particular to pregnancy?

- **Probably the most common cause of megaloblastic anaemia worldwide** is folate deficiency in pregnancy when associated with poor nutrition.
- **Folate requirements in pregnancy are increased to abo[ut] twice those of normal.** Serum and red-cell folate levels tend to fall as pregnancy progresses, and in the UK 30 of women in late pregnancy who do not take folate supplements have reduced folic acid levels. However, only a minority develop megaloblastic anaemia [Mahomed, 2004].
- **Folic acid 400 micrograms daily is now recommended for all pregnant women,** starting prior to conception a[nd] continuing for at least the first 12 weeks of pregnancy. This treatment has been shown to reduce the risk of neural tube defect in the developing fetus. A woman should take 5 mg of folic acid daily for the first 12 wee[ks] of pregnancy if any of the following is true:
  - She is taking antiepileptic drugs
  - She is taking proguanil or maloprim
  - She has previously had a baby with a neural tube defect
- There is no consensus on whether folic acid supplemen[ts] should be continued beyond the first 12 weeks of pregnancy. Although studies show a reduced incidence of low folate levels, there is no convincing evidence of either benefit or harm to the mother or fetus.

[Hoffbrand et al, 2001; Mahomed, 2004]

References

NHS staff in England can link, free of charge, from references to full text journals by clicking on [Full text] o[n] the PRODIGY website.

1. Donnelly, J.G. (2001) Folic acid. *Critical Reviews in Clinical Laboratory Sciences* **38**(3), 183–223.
2. Drazkowski, J., Sirven, J. and Blum, D. (2002) Symptoms of B12 deficiency can occur in women of child bearing age supplemented with folate. *Neurolog[y]* **58**(10), 1572–1573.
3. Frewin, R., Henson, A. and Provan, D. (1997) ABC of clinical haematology: iron deficiency anaemia. *British Medical Journal* **314**(7077), 360–363. [Full text]
4. Green, R. and Miller, J.W. (1999) Folate deficiency beyond megaloblastic anemia: hyperhomocysteinemia and other manifestations of dysfunctional folate status. *Seminars in Hematology* **36**(1), 47–64.
5. Hoffbrand, A.V. (2003) Megaloblastic anaemia and miscellaneous deficiency anaemias. In: Warrell, D.A., Cox, T.M., Firth, J.D. and Benz, E.J.Jr (Eds.) *Oxford textbook of medicine*. 4th edn. Oxford: Oxford University Press. Section 22.5.6.
6. Hoffbrand, V. and Provan, D. (1997) ABC of clinical haematology: macrocytic anaemias. *British Medical Journal* **314**(7078), 430–433. [Full text]
7. Hoffbrand, A.V., Pettit, J.E. and Moss, P.A.H. (2001) *Essential haematology*. 4th edn. Oxford: Blackwell Science.
8. Mahomed, K. (2004) *Folate supplementation in pregnancy (Cochrane Review)*. The Cochrane Library. Issue 3. Chichester, UK: John Wiley & Sons, Ltd.
9. NICE (2005) *Referral guidelines for suspected cancer – quick reference guide*. Clinical guideline 27. National Institute for Health and Clinical Excellence. www.nice.org.uk [Accessed: 01/07/2005].

RODIGY GUIDANCE

Anal fissure

ast revised in July 2005
ww.prodigy.nhs.uk/guidance.asp?gt=Anal fissure

pplies to people over the age of 1 month

his guidance covers the management of acute and chronic uncomplicated anal fissures in primary care, in both hildren and adults.

his guidance does not cover the treatment of atypical anal fissures associated with underlying disease.

here is separate PRODIGY guidance for *Constipation, Haemorrhoids,* and *Pruritus ani.*

oals

o relieve the pain of an anal fissure
o promote healing of an anal fissure

ontents

cenarios
- Acute anal fissure p.77
- Chronic anal fissure p.79

xtended Information, p. 81

Vhich scenario?

Acute anal fissure: covers the management of anal issures that have been present for less than 6 weeks.
Chronic anal fissure: covers the management of anal issures that have been present for 6 weeks or more.

Acute anal fissure

Vhich therapy?

Treat or prevent constipation from developing.
- **Advise a high-fibre diet and an adequate fluid intake.**
- **Bulk-forming laxatives (methylcellulose, ispaghula, or sterculia) are recommended if there is constipation.**
- Lactulose is recommended:
  - In older children and adults if bulk forming laxatives are ineffective or not tolerated
  - As a first-line treatment for constipation in young children, who would find taking bulk-forming laxatives difficult

Provide symptomatic relief.
- **Advise warm or sitz baths (hip baths in hot water for 2–5 minutes followed by cold water for 1 minute).**
- Consider lidocaine (lignocaine) 1% or 2% gel, or 5% ointment. The optimum strength for pain relief is not known and may vary from person to person. Note: this should not be used long-term.
- Consider hydrocortisone ointment (but avoid if there is local infection).
- Advise applying lubricants (e.g. petroleum jelly) prior to bowel movements.

Practical prescribing points

or further information, please see the *Medicines ompendium* (www.medicines.org.uk) or the *British ational Formulary* (www.bnf.org).

Bulk-forming laxatives

Advise that bulk-forming laxatives will take 2–3 days to relieve constipation.

- Advise an adequate fluid intake for people taking bulk-forming laxatives. Powder and granule forms should be mixed in at least 250 ml of fluid and taken immediately. An additional 250 ml of fluid is recommended to increase efficacy and prevent intestinal obstruction — ensure there is adequate supervision of fluid intake in frail elderly or immobile people.
- Advise people not to take bulk-forming laxatives before going to bed.

Follow-up advice

- Follow-up should continue until the fissure has healed.

Should I refer or investigate?

Refer?

Routine referral

- **Anal fissures that are multiple, off the midline, large, or irregular** (atypical fissures) should be referred, as these may be the manifestation of underlying disease (e.g. Crohn's disease, ulcerative colitis, anal herpes, syphilis, chlamydia, gonorrhoea, AIDS, tuberculosis, or neoplasm).

Urgent referral

- Referral guidelines for suspected cancer published by the National Institute for Health and Clinical Excellence (NICE) [NICE, 2005] recommend that people who present with symptoms and signs suggestive of colorectal or anal cancer (see Table 1) are urgently referred to a team specialising in the management of lower gastrointestinal cancer (depending on local arrangements).

Patient information leaflets

The following PILs are available at www.prodigy.nhs.uk
- Anal Fissure
- Medicines - Name Changes of Medicines

Shared decision making

- **Simple anal fissures usually heal** if there is no constipation or straining on the toilet.
- **A high-fibre diet with plenty of fluids** is the important part of treatment and prevention. This means eating more fruit, vegetables, cereals, wholemeal bread etc and drinking at least 8 glasses (12 cups) of fluid a day.
- **Fibre supplements** (ispaghula etc) are options if a high-fibre diet does not help with constipation
- **Bulk-forming laxatives** such as methylcellulose may help treat constipation if you cannot achieve a high-fibre diet.
- Lactulose may be preferred in children.

A

Table 1: Guidelines for urgent referral of suspected lower gastrointestinal cancer.

Person	Symptoms and signs
Aged 40 years and older	Rectal bleeding with a change in bowel habit towards looser stools and/or increased stool frequency persisting 6 weeks or more.
Aged 60 years and older	Rectal bleeding persisting for 6 weeks or more without a change in bowel habit and without anal symptoms. A change in bowel habit to looser stools and/or more frequent stools persisting for 6 weeks or more without re bleeding.
Of any age	A right abdominal mass consistent with involvement of the large bowel. A palpable rectal mass (intraluminal and not pelvic; a pelvic mass outside the bowel would warrant an urgent referral to a urologist or gynaecologist).
Woman (not menstruating)	Unexplained iron deficiency anaemia and a haemoglobin 10 g/100 ml or below.*
Man of any age	Unexplained iron deficiency anaemia and a haemoglobin 11 g/100 ml or below.*

*Anaemia considered on the basis of history and examination in primary care not to be related to other sources of blood loss (e.g. ingestions of NSAIDs) or blood dyscra

- **Warm or sitz baths** have a soothing effect and may help healing.
- **Anaesthetic creams or ointments** help ease pain, but do not use them for more than 5–7 days. They may irritate the skin around the anus.
- **Hydrocortisone** may help reduce inflammation around the fissure and ease pain. In general, try not to use it for more than 7 days. Hydrocortisone is available at pharmacies.
- **Lubricants,** such as petroleum jelly, may help ease the pain associated with the bowel movement, when used beforehand.
- **Good toilet hygiene.** Keep the anal area clean and dry. If you are cleaning a child with anal fissure, use a moistened cloth or soft material and not toilet tissue, as this may be too harsh. When treating infants, ensure the nappy is changed regularly.
- **Painkillers** such as paracetamol can be taken if they help you with the pain.

Drug rationale

Drugs not included

- **Stimulant laxatives** are not recommended for the treatment of constipation associated with anal fissure, as the aim is to produce large, soft stools that gently dilate the anal sphincter.
- **Bran supplements** are not included, as they are no longer commercially available.

Drugs included

- **Bulk-forming laxatives** (ispaghula husk, sterculia, and methylcellulose) are recommended for the treatment of constipation associated with anal fissure in adults and older children.
  - Ispaghula and sterculia are the bulk-forming laxatives of choice.
    - To encourage people to adhere to treatment, only products available in convenient sachets are included.
    - Ispaghula sachets are available in a variety of flavours — a generic prescription is included so that the person can choose the flavour at the time of dispensing.
  - Methylcellulose is less preferred because the large number of tablets that need to be taken may reduce compliance.
- **Lactulose** is recommended for the treatment of constipation in young children, as bulk-forming laxatives are difficult to give to this age group. Additionally, methylcellulose is not specifically licensed for use in children and is available only as a tablet. Ispaghula and sterculia are not licensed in children younger than 6 years. Lactulose is licensed in all age groups.
- **Lidocaine (lignocaine)** is the only topical anaesthetic available that is not combined with soothing agents an or corticosteroids in a compound preparation. It may ease symptoms.
  - It is offered as 1% or 2% gel, or 5% ointment: the optimum strength for pain relief is not known and may vary from person to person.
  - Continuous use of lignocaine should be limited to 5- days. It is absorbed through mucosal surfaces; hence skin sensitization and systemic allergic reaction are more likely.
- **Hydrocortisone 1% ointment** is included, as it may reduce inflammation and ease symptoms.

Prescriptions

Non-drug management

Advice only: high fibre diet and fluid intake
- Age from 1 month onwards
- Causes of constipation include: a low fibre diet, a low fluid intake, some medical problems, medication side effects, regular stimulant laxatives, poor mobility. In most people there is no obvious cause. Eat more fibre – fruit, vegetables, cereals, wholemeal bread, etc. Try to drink at least 12 cups (8 glasses or mugs) of liquid a da Avoid drinks with a high caffeine content as these may make constipation worse. Exercise regularly – keeping the body active helps to keep the bowels active.

Bulk-forming agents (if high-fibre diet fails)

Ispaghula 3.5g s/f sachets (Fybogel or Ispagel Orange)
- Age from 6 to 11 years
- Ispaghula husk 3.5g s/f granules. Take half to one level 5ml spoonful (mixed in a glass of water) each morning and evening; supply 30 sachets; NHS Cost £2.12; OTC Cost £4.65.

Ispaghula 3.5g s/f sachets (Fybogel or Ispagel Orange)
- Age from 12 years onwards
- Ispaghula husk 3.5g s/f granules. Take the contents of one sachet (dissolved in water) each morning and evening; supply 60 sachets; NHS Cost £4.24; OTC Cost £7.74.

Ispaghula 3.4g s/f sachets (Regulan)
- Age from 6 to 11 years
- Ispaghula husk 3.4g s/f powder. Take half to one level 5ml spoonful (mixed in a glass of water) each morning and evening; supply 30 sachets; NHS Cost £1.97; OTC Cost £3.47.

Ispaghula 3.4g s/f sachets (Regulan)
- Age from 12 years onwards
- Ispaghula husk 3.4g s/f powder. Take the contents of o sachet (mixed in a glass of water) 1 to 3 times a day; supply 60 sachets; NHS Cost £3.94; OTC Cost £6.94.

rculia 62% sachets (Normacol)
ge from 6 to 11 years
terculia 62% granules. Take half to one sachet (added
food) once or twice a day after meals. Wash down
ith plenty of water without chewing; supply 30 sachets;
HS Cost £2.59; OTC Cost £4.57.

rculia 62% sachets (Normacol)
ge from 12 years onwards
terculia 62% granules. Take the contents of one to two
achets, once or twice a day after meals. Wash down
ith plenty of water without chewing; supply 60 sachets;
HS Cost £5.19; OTC Cost £9.15.

rculia 62% and frangula 8% sachets (Normacol Plus)
ge from 16 years onwards
terculia62%+frangula8% granules. Take the contents
f one to two sachets, once or twice a day after meals.
Vash down with plenty of water without chewing;
upply 60 sachets; NHS Cost £5.56; OTC Cost £9.80.

thylcellulose 500mg tablets
ge from 16 years onwards
Methylcellulose 500mg tablets. Take three to six tablets
with two glasses of water) each morning and evening;
upply 224 tablets; NHS Cost £5.38; OTC Cost £9.50.

smotic laxative: lactulose

ctulose solution
Age from 1 month to 11 months
Lactulose 3.35g/5ml solution. Take 2.5ml twice a day;
upply 50 ml; NHS Cost £0.25; OTC Cost £3.50.

ctulose solution
Age from 12 months to 4 years
Lactulose 3.35g/5ml solution. Take one 5ml spoonful
wice a day; supply 100 ml; NHS Cost £0.50;
OTC Cost £3.50.

ctulose solution
Age from 5 to 9 years
Lactulose 3.35g/5ml solution. Take two 5ml spoonfuls
wice a day; supply 150 ml; NHS Cost £0.75;
OTC Cost £3.50.

ctulose solution
Age from 10 years onwards
Lactulose 3.35g/5ml solution. Take three 5ml spoonfuls
twice a day; supply 200 ml; NHS Cost £1.00;
OTC Cost £3.50.

opical preparations for symptomatic relief

docaine (lignocaine) 1% gel
Age from 1 month onwards
Lidocaine 1% gel. Apply a small amount to the anal rim when required for pain relief, and a few minutes before each bowel movement; supply 7 tubes; NHS Cost £9.10; OTC Cost £16.03.

docaine (lignocaine) 2% gel
Age from 1 month onwards
Lidocaine 2% gel. Apply a small amount to the anal rim when required for pain relief, and a few minutes before each bowel movement; supply 7 tubes; NHS Cost £9.10; OTC Cost £16.03.

docaine (lignocaine) 5% ointment
Age from 1 month onwards
Lidocaine 5% ointment. Apply a small amount to the anal rim when required for pain relief, and a few minutes before each bowel movement; supply 15 grams; NHS Cost £0.88; OTC Cost £1.55.

ydrocortisone 1% ointment
Age from 1 month onwards
Hydrocortisone 1% ointment (30g). Apply a small amount to the anal rim once or twice a day; supply 30 grams; NHS Cost £0.37; OTC Cost £0.65.

Chronic anal fissure

Which therapy

- **In adults prescribe glyceryl trinitrate (GTN) ointment** (0.2%) for at least 6 weeks, unless earlier healing is confirmed.
  - Advise that GTN often relieves pain before healing is complete, so should be continued until a healthcare professional recommends stopping.
- In children consider prescribing GTN ointment or seeking specialist advice.
- **Continue to treat or prevent constipation from developing.**
  - Advise a high-fibre diet and an adequate fluid intake.
  - Bulk-forming laxatives (methylcellulose, ispaghula, or sterculia) are recommended if there is constipation.
  - Lactulose is recommended:
    - In older children and adults if bulk-forming laxatives are ineffective or not tolerated
    - As a preferred treatment for constipation in young children, who would find taking bulk-forming laxatives difficult
- **Provide symptomatic relief.**
  - Advise warm or sitz baths (hip baths in hot water for 2–5 minutes followed by cold water for 1 minute).
  - Advise applying lubricants (e.g. petroleum jelly) before bowel movements.
- **Refer if the fissure has not healed after 8 weeks of topical GTN treatment.**

Practical prescribing points

For further information, please see the *Medicines Compendium* (www.medicines.org.uk) or the *British National Formulary* (www.bnf.org).

Bulk-forming laxatives

- Advise the person that bulk-forming laxatives will take 2–3 days to relieve constipation.
- Advise an adequate fluid intake for people taking bulk-forming laxatives. Powder and granule forms should be mixed in at least 250 ml of fluid and taken immediately. An additional 250 ml of fluid is recommended to increase efficacy and prevent intestinal obstruction — ensure there is adequate supervision of fluid intake in frail elderly or immobile people.
- Advise people not to take bulk-forming agents before going to bed.

Glyceryl trinitrate ointment

- GTN ointment 0.2% is not licensed for the treatment of anal fissure, but is available in the UK through special manufacturers. Some formulations expire 4 weeks from manufacture.
- GTN ointment can cause headaches, which are usually mild, are easily tolerated, or respond to paracetamol, and diminish if treatment is continued [Nelson, 2004]. However, in some people the headaches are severe enough to stop treatment.

Follow-up advice

- Follow-up should continue until the fissure has healed.

Should I refer or investigate?

Refer?

Routine referral

Referral is recommended for:

- **Anal fissures that are multiple, off the midline, large, or irregular** (atypical fissures), as these may be the manifestation of underlying disease (e.g. Crohn's disease, ulcerative colitis, anal herpes, syphilis, chlamydia, gonorrhoea, AIDS, tuberculosis, or neoplasm).
- **Chronic fissures that have not healed after 8 weeks of treatment with topical GTN.**
- **People with chronic fissures who are unable to tolerate topical GTN.**

Urgent Referral

- Referral guidelines for suspected cancer published by the National Institute for Health and Clinical Excellence (NICE) [NICE, 2005] recommend that people who present with symptoms and signs suggestive of colorectal or anal cancer (see Table 2) are urgently referred to a team specialising in the management of lower gastrointestinal cancer (depending on local arrangements).

Patient information leaflets

The following PILs are available at www.prodigy.nhs.uk

- Anal Fissure (Chronic)

Shared decision making

- **A high-fibre diet with plenty of fluids** is the important part of treatment and prevention. This means eating more fruit, vegetables, cereals, wholemeal bread etc and drinking at least 8 glasses (12 cups) of fluid a day.
- **Fibre supplements** (ispaghula etc) are options if a high-fibre diet does not help with constipation.
- **Bulk-forming agents** such as methylcellulose may help treat constipation if you are unable to achieve a high-fibre diet.
- **Osmotic laxatives** such as lactulose may be preferred in children.
- **Warm baths** have a soothing effect and may help healing (particularly if used with other treatments).

Table 2: Guidelines for urgent referral of suspected lower gastrointestinal cancer.

Person	Symptoms and signs
Aged 40 years and older	Rectal bleeding with a change in bowel habit towards looser stools and/or increased stool frequency persisting 6 weeks or more.
Aged 60 years and older	Rectal bleeding persisting for 6 weeks or more without a change in bowel habit and without anal symptoms. A change in bowel habit to looser stools and/or more frequent stools persisting for 6 weeks or more without rectal bleeding.
Of any age	A right abdominal mass consistent with involvement of the large bowel. A palpable rectal mass (intraluminal and not pelvic; a pelvic mass outside the bowel would warrant an urgent referral to a urologist or gynaecologist).
Woman (not menstruating)	Unexplained iron deficiency anaemia and a haemoglobin 10 g/100 ml or below.*
Man of any age	Unexplained iron deficiency anaemia and a haemoglobin 11 g/100 ml or below.*

*Anaemia considered on the basis of history and examination in primary care not to be related to other sources of blood loss (e.g. ingestions of NSAIDs) or blood dyscrasia.

- **Good toilet hygiene.** Keep the anal area clean and dry you are cleaning a child with anal fissure, use a moistened cloth or soft material and not toilet tissue, this may be too harsh. When treating infants, ensure t nappy is changed regularly.
- **Painkillers** such as paracetamol can be taken if they h you with the pain.
- **Glyceryl trinitrate ointment** helps healing if you have an anal fissure for some weeks. The pain often gets be before healing is complete, but it is very important tha you continue the course of treatment. It is rubbed ont the anus twice a day for 6 weeks. Headaches are common and often get better with continued use of th ointment. If the headaches are troublesome, this may be the right treatment for you.
- **Referral to a surgeon** may be needed if the fissure doe not heal with these treatments.

Drug rationale

Drugs not included

- **Stimulant laxatives** are not recommended for the treatment of constipation associated with anal fissure, the aim is to produce large, soft stools that gently dila the anal sphincter.
- **Topical anaesthetics** are not recommended for the treatment of chronic anal fissure, as prolonged use ma lead to skin sensitization.
- **Topical corticosteroids** are not offered, as their use fo more than 7 days is not recommended.
- **Bran supplements** are not included, as they are no lon commercially available.
- **Botulinum toxin** is not included. There is still insuffici evidence for its effectiveness, and its role in the management of chronic anal fissure is not clear [Nelso 2003b]. It is expensive, and injection into the internal anal sphincter requires a high degree of competence.
- **Diltiazem** and **nifedipine** have been proposed as alternatives to topical GTN ointment, as they have fe adverse effects [Kocher et al, 2002; Bielecki and Kolodziejczak, 2003]. They are not licensed for the treatment of anal fissure, and there is still insufficient evidence to recommend their use for the treatment of anal fissure in primary care.

Drugs included

- **Glyceryl trinitrate (GTN) 0.2% ointment** is recommended as a preferred treatment for chronic ana fissure. The evidence for the effectiveness of GTN in healing chronic anal fissures is not conclusive. Howeve topical GTN is safe to use, without any apparent long-term adverse effects, and may avoid the need for surge and the associated risk of incontinence.
- **Bulk-forming laxatives** (ispaghula husk, sterculia, and methylcellulose) are recommended for the treatment o constipation associated with anal fissure in adults and older children.
  - Ispaghula and sterculia are the bulk-forming laxativ of choice.
    - To encourage people to adhere to treatment, only products available in convenient sachets are included.
    - Ispaghula sachets are available in a variety of flavours — a generic prescription is included so tha the person can choose the flavour at the time of dispensing.
  - Methylcellulose is less preferred because the large number of tablets that need to be taken may reduce compliance.

actulose is recommended for the treatment of onstipation in young children, as bulk-forming laxatives re difficult to give to this age group. Additionally, ethylcellulose is not specifically licensed for use in hildren and is available only as a tablet. Ispaghula and terculia are not licensed in children younger than 6 ears. Lactulose is licensed in all age groups.

escriptions

pical glyceryl trinitrate

ceryl trinitrate 0.2% ointment
- ge from 12 years onwards
- lyceryl trinitrate 0.2% ointment. Apply a pea-sized mount to the anal rim twice a day for at least 6 weeks; upply 20 grams; NHS Cost £25.00.

on-drug management

vice only: high fibre diet and fluid intake
- ge from 1 month onwards
- auses of constipation include: a low fibre diet, a low luid intake, some medical problems, medication side ffects, regular stimulant laxatives, poor mobility. In most people there is no obvious cause. Eat more fibre – ruit, vegetables, cereals, wholemeal bread, etc. Try to drink at least 12 cups (8 glasses or mugs) of liquid a day. Avoid drinks with a high caffeine content as these may make constipation worse. Exercise regularly – keeping he body active helps to keep the bowels active.

ulk-forming agents (if high-fibre diet fails)

aghula 3.5g s/f sachets (Fybogel or Ispagel Orange)
- Age from 6 to 11 years
- spaghula husk 3.5g s/f granules. Take half to one level 5ml spoonful (mixed in a glass of water) each morning and evening; supply 30 sachets; NHS Cost £2.12; OTC Cost £4.65.

aghula 3.5g s/f sachets (Fybogel or Ispagel Orange)
- Age from 12 years onwards
- spaghula husk 3.5g s/f granules. Take the contents of one sachet (dissolved in water) each morning and evening; supply 60 sachets; NHS Cost £4.24; OTC Cost £7.74.

aghula 3.4g s/f sachets (Regulan)
- Age from 6 to 11 years
- Ispaghula husk 3.4g s/f powder. Take half to one level 5ml spoonful (mixed in a glass of water) each morning and evening; supply 30 sachets; NHS Cost £1.97; OTC Cost £3.47.

aghula 3.4g s/f sachets (Regulan)
- Age from 12 years onwards
- Ispaghula husk 3.4g s/f powder. Take the contents of one sachet (mixed in a glass of water) 1 to 3 times a day; supply 60 sachets; NHS Cost £3.94; OTC Cost £6.94.

erculia 62% sachets (Normacol)
- Age from 6 to 11 years
- Sterculia 62% granules. Take half to one sachet (added to food) once or twice a day after meals. Wash down with plenty of water without chewing; supply 30 sachets; NHS Cost £2.59; OTC Cost £4.57.

erculia 62% sachets (Normacol)
- Age from 12 years onwards
- Sterculia 62% granules. Take the contents of one to two sachets, once or twice a day after meals. Wash down with plenty of water without chewing; supply 60 sachets; NHS Cost £5.19; OTC Cost £9.15.

Sterculia 62% and frangula 8% sachets (Normacol Plus)
- Age from 16 years onwards
- Sterculia 62% + frangula 8% granules. Take the contents of one to two sachets, once or twice a day after meals. Wash down with plenty of water without chewing; supply 60 sachets; NHS Cost £5.56; OTC Cost £9.80.

Methylcellulose 500mg tablets
- Age from 16 years onwards
- Methylcellulose 500mg tablets. Take three to six tablets (with two glasses of water) each morning and evening; supply 224 tablets; NHS Cost £5.38; OTC Cost £9.50.

Osmotic laxative: lactulose

Lactulose solution
- Age from 1 month to 11 months
- Lactulose 3.35g/5ml solution. Take 2.5ml twice a day; supply 50 ml; NHS Cost £0.25; OTC Cost £3.50.

Lactulose solution
- Age from 12 months to 4 years
- Lactulose 3.35g/5ml solution. Take one 5ml spoonful twice a day; supply 100 ml; NHS Cost £0.50; OTC Cost £3.50.

Lactulose solution
- Age from 5 to 9 years
- Lactulose 3.35g/5ml solution. Take two 5ml spoonfuls twice a day; supply 150 ml; NHS Cost £0.75; OTC Cost £3.50.

Lactulose solution
- Age from 10 years onwards
- Lactulose 3.35g/5ml solution. Take three 5ml spoonfuls twice a day; supply 200 ml; NHS Cost £1.00; OTC Cost £3.50.

Extended Information

Background information

- What is it? p.81
- What causes it? p.81
- How common is it? p.82
- How do I know my patient has it? p.82
- What else might it be? p.82
- Complications and prognosis p.82

What is it?

- **An anal fissure is a longitudinal or elliptical tear/ulcer of the squamous lining of the distal anal canal,** immediately within the anal verge.
- **Fissures are defined as acute if present for less than 6 weeks, and chronic if present for more than 6 weeks.**
- **Ninety per cent of fissures occur in the posterior midline;** the second most common site is the anterior midline.
- **Atypical fissures — multiple, off the midline, large or irregular, may be the manifestation of underlying disease** (e.g. Crohn's disease, ulcerative colitis, anal herpes, syphilis, chlamydia, gonorrhoea, AIDS, tuberculosis, or neoplasm).

[Jonas and Scholefield, 2001; Utzig et al, 2003; Castillo and Margolin, 2004]

What causes it?

- **The cause of typical or uncomplicated anal fissures is uncertain.**
- **Trauma is thought to cause the anal fissure initially.**
  - **Hard stools** may cause a laceration in the anal mucosa, either by local trauma as the hard stool is passed or by straining. However, constipation is only

reported in 25% of people with anal fissure, and diarrhoea precedes the occurrence of anal fissures in 4% to 7% of cases.
  - **Childbirth** may cause an anal fissure, commonly in the anterior midline. The risk is increased with traumatic deliveries. Women with postpartum fissures tend not to display the raised anal canal pressures generally associated with chronic fissures.
  - Anal injury may also result from anal intercourse, rectal examination, and habitual use of laxatives.
- **People with anal fissures (particularly chronic fissures) often have a raised anal canal pressure caused by spasm of the internal anal sphincter.** It is unclear if the increased pressure results from, or predisposes to, the development of anal fissures. The raised anal canal pressure causes local ischaemia, resulting in pain and failure of the fissure to heal.

[Jonas and Scholefield, 2001; American Gastroenterology Association, 2003; Utzig et al, 2003; Castillo and Margolin, 2004]

How common is it?

- **Anal fissure is a common condition** that can affect people of all ages.
- **Overall, anal fissures affect men and women equally,** but anterior fissures are more common in women (25%) than in men (8%) [American Gastroenterology Association, 2003].
- **Most people (87%) with a chronic anal fissure are between 20 and 60 years old.**
- **About 10% of chronic anal fissures are caused by childbirth** [Jonas and Scholefield, 2001; Castillo and Margolin, 2004].

How do I know my patient has it?

Symptoms

- **Pain** is sharp, searing, or burning and is often severe. It is usually associated with defecation, and may last from a few minutes to several hours.
- **Bleeding** (bright red, often on toilet paper) is common, but is usually modest and separate from the stool.
- **Discharge and pruritis** (because of the discharge) can also occur.

Signs

- **Spasm of the anus** is very suggestive of an anal fissure and may prevent visualization.
- **A linear or pear-shaped split in the posterior midline of the anal mucosa** may be seen as the buttocks are gently parted and the perianum is carefully everted with steady traction. If a fissure cannot be seen, gentle pressure on the anal verge posteriorly will produce tenderness.
- **Acute fissures** are superficial with sharply demarcated edges.
- **Chronic fissures** are usually deeper and may have secondary features, including induration of the edge of the fissure, a sentinel skin tag, hypertrophied anal papillae, associated anal stenosis secondary to spasm, or a fibrotic anal sphincter.
- **There may be signs of underlying disease** (e.g. Crohn's disease, ulcerative colitis, anal herpes, syphilis, chlamydia, gonorrhoea, AIDS, tuberculosis, or neoplasm), particularly with atypical fissures (multiple, off the midline, large or irregular).

[Jonas and Scholefield, 2001; Castillo and Margolin, 2004]

What else might it be?

- **Anal fissures may be the manifestation of an underlying disease:**
  - **Crohn's disease.** About 4% of people with Crohn's disease present with atypical anal fissures (multiple, irregular, and broad-based) and almost half of peo[ple] with Crohn's disease will develop anal ulceration at some time [Castillo and Margolin, 2004].
  - **Infection** (e.g. anal herpes, chlamydia, gonorrhoea [or] syphilis, AIDS, or tuberculosis) should be considere[d] particularly if there are atypical anal fissures in the absence of Crohn's disease [Castillo and Margolin, 2004].
  - **Anal carcinoma** is rarely confused with anal fissure [Castillo and Margolin, 2004].
- **Thrombosed haemorrhoids** may cause similar symptoms.

Complications and prognosis

Complications

- **Constipation or faecal impaction may occur.** The pain [of] anal fissure can be so severe that it discourages people[,] especially children, from defecating.
- **The diagnosis of serious underlying pathology may be missed,** especially if rectal bleeding is a presenting feature. Most anal fissures produce only minor bleedi[ng].

Prognosis

- **About half of all anal fissures will heal with conservat[ive] measures** (e.g. laxatives and sitz baths) [Shub et al, 19[78;] Hananel and Gordon, 1997].
- **Relief of symptoms and healing will be seen in up to 90% of acute anal fissures** with conservative treatmen[t] [Jensen, 1986].
- **Fissures that have healed with conservative measures may reoccur** in up to 27% of people [Shub et al, 1978; Hananel and Gordon, 1997].

See *Management issues* for healing and recurrence rates [of] chronic anal fissures treated with topical glyceryl trinitra[te,] botulinum toxin, or surgery.

Management issues

- Management overview p.82
- How should I manage acute anal fissures in adults? p.8[2]
- How do I manage chronic anal fissures in adults? p.83
- How do I manage recurrent anal fissures? p.84
- How do I manage children with anal fissure in primary care? p.84
- What treatments are available in secondary care? p.84
- What new drug treatments may be effective for the treatment of chronic anal fissures? p.85

Management overview

- **Acute fissures — manage conservatively by:**
  - Treating or preventing constipation
  - Providing pain relief using topical treatments and warm baths
- **Chronic fissures — manage by:**
  - Prescribing topical glyceryl trinitrate
  - Continuing conservative measures
  - Referring to secondary care if the fissure fails to hea[l]

How should I manage acute anal fissures i[n] adults?

- **Conservative treatment with simple measures** (dietary advice, laxatives, and baths) is recommended, as most acute uncomplicated fissures heal spontaneously.

Constipation should be treated or prevented from developing.

- **A high-fibre diet with an increased intake of water is recommended.** Ensure there is an adequate amount of fruit and vegetables in the diet, and advise against processed and fatty foods.
- **Bulk-forming laxatives** (e.g. methylcellulose, ispaghula, or sterculia) are recommended if constipation is present. The aim is to produce soft, bulky stools to ease defecation and physiologically dilate the internal anal sphincter.

Symptomatic relief can be provided with:

- **Warm or sitz baths.** Hip baths in hot water for 2–5 minutes followed by cold water for 1 minute (sitz bath) have a soothing effect, particularly after bowel movements. They help to promote good anal hygiene, and are believed to decrease anal sphincter spasm and improve blood flow to the anal mucosa.
  - One randomized controlled trial (RCT) with 103 people showed that warm sitz baths and dietary bran healed 87% of acute anal fissures and provided more rapid relief of symptoms than topical lignocaine or hydrocortisone [Jensen, 1986].
- **Lubricants** (e.g. petroleum jelly). The pain associated with bowel movements may be relieved by using a lubricant beforehand.
- **Topical anaesthetics.**
  - Topical lidocaine (lignocaine) may relieve the pain of acute anal fissure, but it is no more effective than placebo and considerably less effective than topical glyceryl trinitrate, bran, and hydrocortisone at healing fissures [Nelson, 2003b].
  - Further, one RCT (103 people) showed that lignocaine was statistically significantly less effective at relieving symptoms than were warm sitz baths and dietary bran [Jensen, 1986].
  - The optimum strength for pain relief is not known and may vary from person to person. Strengths of up to 5% lidocaine may be needed.
  - Continuous use of topical anaesthetics may lead to skin sensitization, and their long-term use is not recommended.
- **Topical steroids** may reduce associated inflammation but probably are of little benefit. They should not be used if there is local infection.
  - One RCT (103 people) showed that hydrocortisone 2% ointment was statistically significantly less effective than warm sitz baths and dietary bran at relieving symptoms and no more effective at healing acute anal fissures [Jensen, 1986]. One person in this study developed extensive local spread of a previously undiagnosed anal herpes with topical hydrocortisone.

How do I manage chronic anal fissures in adults?

Most chronic anal fissures require intervention to heal. Treatment is directed at reducing internal sphincter spasm and anal canal pressure, thereby improving blood flow to the anal mucosa and healing of the fissure.

Simple measures (i.e. high-fibre diet, laxatives if required, and warm baths) should be continued.

Topical glyceryl trinitrate (GTN) is recommended first-line for the treatment of chronic anal fissure. GTN is a nitric-oxide donor that causes vasodilatation and reverses anal sphincter spasm by reducing sphincter tone. The evidence for the effectiveness of GTN in healing chronic anal fissures is not conclusive. However, topical GTN is safe to use, without any apparent long-term adverse effects, and may avoid the need for surgery and the associated risk of incontinence.

- Topical 0.2% GTN ointment (about 0.5 g, a pea-sized amount) should be applied to the anal margin twice a day and continued until full epithelialization of the anal mucosa has occurred.
- Relief of pain can be considerable and may occur many days or weeks before complete healing. Follow-up is therefore important.
- Topical GTN is not currently licensed for anal fissure. It has to be made up by diluting commercially available 2% ointment, and is available from a specialist manufacturer.
- Headaches occur in about a third of people who use topical GTN [Nelson, 2003b]. They are usually mild, easily tolerated, or respond to paracetamol, and diminish if treatment is continued [Jonas and Scholefield, 2001]. In some people the headaches are severe enough to stop treatment.

- Consider referring to secondary care for surgery or botulinum toxin if healing has not occurred after using topical GTN for 8 weeks or if GTN is not tolerated.

[Jonas and Scholefield, 2001; Castillo and Margolin, 2004]

What is the evidence for the use of glyceryl trinitrate in adults?

- **A Cochrane systematic review concluded that glyceryl trinitrate (GTN) is far less effective than surgery, and marginally better than placebo, in curing chronic anal fissure** [Nelson, 2003b].
  - Seven RCTs (694 people) comparing topical GTN to placebo in adults were identified.
    - Inclusion of all seven trials in the analysis showed that the use of topical GTN was significantly more likely to result in healing when compared with placebo (OR 1.79, 95% CI 1.35 to 2.44).
    - When two studies were excluded from the analysis because of concerns about their methodological quality, GTN was not significantly better than placebo in curing anal fissure (OR 1.37, 95% CI 0.93 to 2.00).
    - However, when an additional study that may have included people with acute anal fissure was also excluded from the analysis, the use of topical GTN was significantly more effective than placebo in healing anal fissures (OR 1.56, 95% CI 1.09 to 2.27).
  - Analysis of three RCTs (132 people) showed GTN to be significantly more effective than lidocaine (lignocaine) at healing anal fissures (OR 5.88, 95% CI 2.63 to 12.5).
  - Analysis of four RCTs (249 people) found that GTN was significantly less effective than internal anal sphincterotomy at healing anal fissures (OR 0.11, 95% CI 0.06 to 0.21).
  - Analysis of two RCTs (107 people) found no significant difference between GTN and botulinum toxin in healing anal fissures (OR 2.08, 95% CI 0.91 to 4.76).
- A subsequent RCT (200 people) compared the healing rates of chronic anal fissures after 8 weeks of treatment with 0.1%, 0.2%, and 0.4% GTN ointment with placebo [Scholefield et al, 2003]. No significant difference in healing between all the GTN treatments and placebo was found. The healing rate in the placebo group was 38% (95% CI 24 to 53), in the 0.1% GTN group was 47% (95% CI 33 to 63), in the 0.2% GTN group was 40% (95% CI 26 to 56), and in the 0.4% GTN group was 54% (95% CI 37 to 71). The authors of this study considered that the placebo response rate was high, and postulated that some of the fissures were more typically acute than chronic, and therefore could be expected to heal spontaneously. However, a Cochrane

A

systematic review found the healing rate in the placebo group to be 35%, and this was fairly uniform across most of the studies [Nelson, 2003a; Nelson, 2003b].

- Another RCT (64 people) compared the healing rate of 0.2% GTN ointment with placebo (Vaseline), 5% lidocaine, and a proprietary ointment, Proctosedyl (containing hydrocortisone acetate, heparin, framycetin sulphate, eculoside, ethoform, butoform) for chronic anal fissure [Maan et al, 2004]. At 6 weeks, healing of the anal fissure occurred significantly ($p < 0.0001$) more often in people receiving GTN (15/16) than in those receiving placebo (4/16). Healing also occurred in 11/16 people in the lignocaine group and 12/16 people in the Proctosedyl group.
- **Recurrence rates of anal fissure after treatment with topical GTN of up to 40%** have been reported [American Gastroenterology Association, 2003]. However, only a few trials have followed-up people long-term, and the risk of recurrence is uncertain.

How do I manage recurrent anal fissures?

- **The incidence of recurrence of anal fissure can be reduced** if additional dietary fibre is taken.
  - One randomized controlled trial showed significantly fewer recurrences in people taking 15 g of bran daily (recurrence rate 16%, 95% CI 4.54 to 36.08) compared with 7.5 g bran daily (recurrence rate 60%, 95% CI 38.67 to 78.87) and placebo (recurrence rate 68%, 95% CI 46.50 to 85.05) [Jensen, 1987].
- **Topical glyceryl trinitrate (GTN) is an option,** and may be considered for someone who has previously responded to GTN. A follow-up questionnaire given to 41 people, who in a previous study had been randomized to GTN treatment for their chronic anal fissure, found that 8/11 who had a symptomatic relapse healed with a second course of GTN [Jonas and Scholefield, 2001].
- **Referral for surgery may be needed.** For someone who has previously had surgery, a further operation may be necessary.

How do I manage children with anal fissure in primary care?

It is not known whether spasm of the internal anal sphincter and ischaemia cause persistence of anal fissures in children. Until recently, standard treatment has been laxatives and lubricants. Surgical treatment is rarely recommended [Nelson, 2004].

- **As in adults, treat constipation or prevent it from developing, and provide symptomatic relief.**
- **Older children may need to limit their intake of milk,** as drinking too much milk and not enough solid food can cause constipation [Andiran et al, 2003].
- **Osmotic laxatives (e.g. lactulose) are recommended for the management of constipation in young children,** because bulk-forming laxatives may be difficult to give to this age group. Additionally, methylcellulose is not specifically licensed for use in children and is only available as a tablet. Ispaghula and sterculia are not licensed in children younger than 6 years. Lactulose is licensed in all age groups.
- **Topical GTN should be considered if conservative measures have failed to heal the anal fissure.** The evidence supporting the use of glyceryl trinitrate in children is inconclusive, and further studies are needed. However, it is a safe treatment and may prevent the need for surgery. The optimum dose of topical GTN in children is not clear, but 0.2% GTN ointment has been studied the most.

What is the evidence for the use of glyceryl trinitrate in children?

- **A Cochrane review concluded that glyceryl trinitrate (GTN) was marginally better than placebo in curing a fissure in children** [Nelson, 2003b]. Four RCTs (165 children) comparing topical 0.2% GTN ointment with placebo in children were identified.
  - Inclusion of all four trials in the analysis showed that the use of topical GTN was significantly more likely to result in healing when compared with placebo (OR 1.92, 95% CI 1.06 to 3.45).
  - When two studies were excluded from the analysis because of concerns about their methodological quality, GTN was not significantly better than placebo in curing anal fissure (OR 1.04, 95% CI 0.52 to 2.0
- One RCT (15 children) compared the effectiveness and adverse effects of 0.1% and 0.05% GTN ointment [Simpson et al, 2003]. At 8 weeks all the fissures in the 0.05% GTN group (7 children) had healed and the fissures in 5 children in the 0.1% GTN group (8 children) had healed. Two of the three anal fissures that failed to respond in the 0.1% group healed during a second 8-week course. In the first few days of treatment two children (one from each group) experienced a short-lived headache that settled spontaneously.

What treatments are available in secondary care?

Surgical treatments

- Surgical techniques that have been used to treat anal fissure include anal stretch, lateral internal sphincterotomy (LIS), and posterior midline sphincterotomy. By disrupting the muscle complex they reduce internal sphincter tone and anal canal pressure, thereby improving blood flow and healing of the fissure.
- **LIS is the standard surgical treatment for chronic anal fissure.**
  - **Most anal fissures heal after LIS.** Healing rates of 93–100% are consistently reported [American Gastroenterology Association, 2003].
  - **Recurrence rates are generally low.** Studies report rates between 0% and 25% [American Gastroenterology Association, 2003].
  - **Overall, the risk of incontinence is about 10%** [Nelson, 2001; Nelson, 2003a]. There is considerable variability in post-operative incontinence rates across studies, probably reflecting the nature of the follow-up [American Gastroenterology Association, 2003]. Incontinence is usually to flatus, and it is not clear from studies to date whether this is permanent or transitory [Nelson, 2003a].
- **LIS is far more effective than available medical treatments at healing chronic anal fissure.**
  - **Glyceryl trinitrate (GTN).** A Cochrane systematic review (four randomized controlled trials [RCTs], 22 people) showed that sphincterotomy was significantly more effective than GTN at healing anal fissure (OR 11.15, 95% CI 5.90 to 21.05) [Nelson, 2003b].
  - **Botulinum toxin.** A Cochrane systematic review (one RCT, 111 people) showed that sphincterotomy was significantly more effective than botulinum toxin at healing anal fissure (OR 17.95, 95% CI 4.90 to 65.7 [Nelson, 2003b].
- **Anal dilatation** is rarely used, as it is difficult to standardize, occasionally causes uncontrolled tearing of the sphincter, and may cause severe incontinence [Utzig et al, 2003]. It is not recommended by a recent Cochrane review [Nelson, 2003b].

otulinum toxin

Botulinum toxin is a potent neurotoxin that inhibits the release of acetylcholine at the neuromuscular junction and reduces spasm when injected into the internal anal sphincter.

Evidence of the effectiveness of botulinum toxin for the treatment of chronic anal fissure is inconclusive, and its role in the management of chronic anal fissure is unclear.

- Some published studies have indicated a healing rate of up to 89% after a single injection of 15 or 20 units of botulinum toxin. A second injection has been reported to increase healing rates up to 96% [Maria et al, 2002]. In contrast, some studies have found botulinum to be ineffective.
- A Cochrane systematic review (one randomized controlled trial [RCT], 55 people) found no significant difference between botulinum A toxin (20 units of Botox) and placebo (OR 1.33, 95% CI 0.56 to 3.13) [Nelson, 2003b]. A subsequent RCT (44 people) also found no significant difference between botulinum A toxin (100 units of Dysport) and placebo for the treatment of chronic anal fissure [Siproudhis et al, 2003].
- A Cochrane systematic review (two RCTs, 107 people) found no significant difference between glyceryl trinitrate and botulinum toxin in healing anal fissures (OR 2.08, 95% CI 0.91 to 4.76) [Nelson, 2003b].
- Two RCTs (200 people) found no significant difference between different doses of botulinum toxin in the healing of chronic anal fissures. One study compared 20 units of Botox (plus retreatment with 30 units if the fissure persisted after one month) with 30 units of Botox (plus retreatment with 50 units if the fissure persisted after one month) [Brisinda et al, 2002]. The other study compared 20 units of Dysport with 40 units of Dysport [Jost and Schrank, 1999].

Transitory incontinence of flatus has been reported in up to 12% of people, and of faeces in 7% of people. Perianal haematoma and infection may also occur [Jonas and Scholefield, 2001; Utzig et al, 2003]. The Cochrane systematic review (one RCT, 55 people) found no significant difference in adverse effects between botulinum toxin and placebo [Nelson, 2003b].

Recurrence rates are unclear, and vary in published studies between 0% and 52% [Maria et al, 2002].

What new drug treatments may be effective for the treatment of chronic anal fissures?

Treatments, other than topical GTN, that reduce internal anal sphincter spasm may be effective in treating chronic anal fissure. They are not currently recommended for use in primary care, as most have only been studied in a small number of people and have limited evidence of effectiveness. Furthermore, the topical preparations are not commercially available in the UK.

Calcium-channel blockers

In the limited evidence currently available, topical calcium-channel blockers seem to be as effective as topical GTN, with fewer adverse effects.

Diltiazem

- One randomized control trial (RCT) (50 people) found that there was no significant difference between oral diltiazem 60 mg twice a day and topical 2% diltiazem in the healing of chronic anal fissures. However, there was a statistically significant increase in adverse effects with oral diltiazem compared with topical diltiazem [Jonas and Scholefield, 2001].
- One RCT (60 people) compared GTN 0.2% ointment to diltiazem 2% cream [Kocher et al, 2002] and another RCT (43 people) compared GTN 0.5% ointment to diltiazem 2% ointment in the healing of anal fissure [Bielecki and Kolodziejczak, 2003]. Both studies found no statistically significant difference between topical GTN and topical diltiazem. However, there were significantly more adverse effects, including headache, with GTN compared with diltiazem [Bielecki and Kolodziejczak, 2003].

- **Topical nifedipine**
  - One RCT (52 people) found that nifedipine 0.2% gel was significantly more effective than GTN 0.2% ointment for the healing of chronic anal fissure [Ezri and Susmallian, 2003].
  - One RCT (110 people) found that topical 0.3% nifedipine and 1.5% lidocaine (lignocaine) ointment was significantly more effective than 1.5% lidocaine ointment and 1% hydrocortisone ointment in healing chronic anal fissures [Perrotti et al, 2002].
- **Oral lacidipine**
  - An open trial using oral lacidipine reported healing in 19 people by 28 days (90.4%), and a reduction in pain after 14 days [Ansaloni et al, 2002]. Blood pressure was not altered, and 7 people had adverse effects.

Topical nitrates other than GTN

- Topical preparations of isosorbide mononitrate and isosorbide dinitrate have shown a trend towards greater healing when compared with placebo in two small studies: 8/10 people and 17/20 people respectively [Werre et al, 2001; Tankova et al, 2002].
- One RCT (54 people) showed that sphincterotomy was more effective at healing chronic anal fissures when compared with 0.2% isosorbide dinitrate ointment at 5 weeks (healing rate 96%, compared with 67%) and at 10 weeks (healing rate 100%, compared with 89%) [Parellada, 2004].

Muscarinic agonists

- Topical bethanechol 0.1% gel was found to heal 9/15 (60%) of chronic anal fissures without adverse effects in one small study [Carapeti et al, 2000].

Alpha-adrenoreceptor blockers

- Oral indoramin 20 mg twice daily was not found to be significantly more effective than placebo for the treatment of chronic anal fissure in one small RCT (13 people) [Pitt et al, 2001].

References

NHS staff in England can link, free of charge, from references to full text journals by clicking on [Full text] on the PRODIGY website.

1. American Gastroenterology Association (2003) AGA technical review on the diagnosis and care of patients with anal fissure. *Gastroenterology* **124**(1), 235–245. [Full text]
2. Andiran, F., Dayi, S. and Mete, E. (2003) Cows milk consumption in constipation and anal fissure in infants and young children. *Journal of Paediatric Child Health* 39(5), 329–331.
3. Ansaloni, L., Bernabe, A., Ghetti, R. et al (2002) Oral lacidipine in the treatment of anal fissure. *Techniques in Coloproctology* 6(2), 79–82.
4. Bielecki, K. and Kolodziejczak, M. (2003) A prospective randomized trial of diltiazem and glyceryltrinitrate ointment in the treatment of chronic anal fissure. *Colorectal Disease* 5(3), 256–257.

5. Brisinda, G., Maria, G., Sganga, G. et al (2002) Effectiveness of higher doses of botulinum toxin to induce healing in patients with chronic anal fissures. *Surgery* **131**(2), 179–184.
6. Carapeti, E.A., Kamm, M.A. and Phillips, R.K. (2000) Topical diltiazem and bethanechol decrease anal sphincter pressure and heal anal fissures without side effects. *Diseases of the Colon & Rectum* **43**(10), 1359–1362.
7. Castillo, E. and Margolin, D.A. (2004) Anal fissures: diagnosis and management. *Techniques in Gastrointestinal Endoscopy* **6**(1), 12–16.
8. Ezri, T. and Susmallian, S. (2003) Topical nifedipine vs. topical glyceryl trinitrate for treatment of chronic anal fissure. *Diseases of the Colon & Rectum* **46**(6), 805–808.
9. Hananel, N. and Gordon, P.H. (1997) Re-examination of clinical manifestations and response to therapy of fissure-in-ano. *Diseases of the Colon & Rectum* **40**(2), 229–233.
10. Jensen, S.L. (1986) Treatment of first episodes of acute anal fissure: prospective randomised study of lignocaine ointment versus hydrocortisone ointment or warm sitz baths plus bran. *British Medical Journal* **292**(6529), 1167–1169.
11. Jensen, S.L. (1987) Maintenance therapy with unprocessed bran in the prevention of acute anal fissure recurrence. *Journal of the Royal Society of Medicine* **80**(5), 296–298.
12. Jonas, M. and Scholefield, J.H. (2001) Anal fissure. *Gastroenterology Clinics of North America* **30**(1), 167–181.
13. Jost, W.H. and Schrank, B. (1999) Chronic anal fissures treated with botulinum toxin injections: a dose-finding study with Dysport®. *Colorectal Disease* **1**(1), 26–28.
14. Kocher, H.M., Steward, M., Leather, A.J. and Cullen, P.T. (2002) Randomized clinical trial assessing the side-effects of glyceryl trinitrate and diltiazem hydrochloride in the treatment of chronic anal fissure. *British Journal of Surgery* **89**(4), 413–417.
15. Maan, M.S., Mishra, R., Thomas, S. and Hadke, N.S. (2004) Randomized, double-blind trial comparing topical nitroglycerine with xylocaine and Proctosedyl in idiopathic chronic anal fissure. *Indian Journal of Gastroenterology* **23**(3), 91–93.
16. Maria, G., Sganga, G., Civello, I.M. and Brisinda, G. (2002) Botulinum neurotoxin and other treatments for fissure-in-ano and pelvic floor disorders. *British Journal of Surgery* **89**(8), 950–961.
17. Nelson, R. (2001) *Operative procedures for fissure in ano (Cochrane Review).* The Cochrane Library. Issue 2. Chichester, UK: John Wiley & Sons, Ltd. www.nelh.nhs.uk/cochrane.asp [Accessed: 19/04/2005]. [Full text]
18. Nelson, R.L. (2003a) Treatment of anal fissure. *British Medical Journal* **327**(7411), 354–355. [Full text]
19. Nelson, R. (2003b) *Non surgical therapy for anal fissure (Cochrane Review).* The Cochrane Library. Issue 4. Chichester, UK: John Wiley & Sons, Ltd. www.nelh.nhs.uk/cochrane.asp [Accessed: 20/04/2005]. [Full text]
20. Nelson, R. (2004) A systematic review of medical therapy for anal fissure. *Diseases of the Colon & Rectum* **47**(4), 422–431.
21. NICE (2005) *Referral guidelines for suspected cance quick reference guide.* Clinical guideline 27. Nationa Institute for Health and Clinical Excellence. www.nice.org.uk [Accessed: 01/07/2005].
22. Parellada, C. (2004) Randomized, prospective trial comparing 0.2 percent isosorbide dinitrate ointment with sphincterotomy in treatment of chronic anal fissure: a two-year follow-up. *Diseases of the Colon Rectum* **47**(4), 437–443.
23. Perrotti, P., Bove, A., Antropoli, C. et al (2002) Topi nifedipine with lidocaine ointment vs. active control treatment of chronic anal fissure: results of a prospective, randomized, double-blind study. *Diseas of the Colon & Rectum* **45**(11), 1468–1475. [Full tex
24. Pitt, J., Dawson, P.M., Hallan, R.I. and Boulos, P.B. (2001) A double-blind randomized placebo-controlle trial of oral indoramin to treat chronic anal fissure. *Colorectal Disease* **3**(3), 165–168.
25. Scholefield, J.H., Bock, J.U., Marla, B. et al (2003) A dose finding study with 0.1%, 0.2%, and 0.4% glyceryl trinitrate ointment in patients with chronic anal fissures. *Gut* **52**(2), 264–269. [Full text]
26. Shub, H.A., Salvati, E.P. and Rubin, R.J. (1978) Conservative treatment of anal fissure: an unselected, retrospective and continuous study. *Diseases of the Colon & Rectum* **21**(8), 582–583.
27. Simpson, J., Lund, J.N., Thompson, R.J. et al (2003) The use of glyceryl trinitrate (GTN) in the treatment chronic anal fissure in children. *Medical Science Monitor* **9**(10), PI123-PI126.
28. Siproudhis, L., Sebille, V., Pigot, F. et al (2003) Lack effficacy of botulinum toxin in chronic anal fissure. *Alimentary Pharmacology & Therapeutics* **18**(5), 515–524.
29. Tankova, L., Yoncheva, K., Muhtarov, M. et al (200 Topical mononitrate treatment in patients with anal fissure. *Alimentary Pharmacology & Therapeutics* **16**(1), 101–103.
30. Utzig, M.J., Kroesen, A.J. and Buhr, H.J. (2003) Concepts in pathogenesis and treatment of chronic an fissure – a review of the literature. *American Journal Gastroenterology* **98**(5), 968–974.
31. Werre, A.J., Palamba, H.W., Bilgen, E.J. and Eggink, W.F. (2001) Isosorbide dinitrate in the treatment of anal fissure: a randomised, prospective, double blind, placebo-controlled trial. *European Journal of Surgery* **167**(5), 382–385.

PRODIGY GUIDANCE

Angina

Last revised in April 2003

At the time of print this topic was being updated. The newly revised guidance will be issued on to the website in 2006.

www.prodigy.nhs.uk/guidance.asp?gt=Angina

Applies to people over the age of 16 years

This guidance covers the primary care management of people with stable angina.

This guidance does not cover Prinzmetal's angina, unstable angina, crescendo angina, angina at rest, acute coronary insufficiency, or angina occurring early after initially successful coronary artery bypass grafting (CABG), or percutaneous transluminal coronary angioplasty (PTCA). This guidance does not specifically cover the management of people recently discharged from hospital after a myocardial infarction (MI), although many of the therapeutic interventions are the same as for chronic stable angina.

There is separate PRODIGY guidance for *Atrial fibrillation, Hyperlipidaemia, Hypertension*, and *Prior myocardial infarction — prophylactic treatments.*

Goals

To prevent symptoms of angina
To increase exercise tolerance
To prevent myocardial infarction and associated mortality
To manage cardiovascular risk factors

Contents

Scenarios

- Initial management p.87
- Managing beta-blocker therapy (1st choice) p.91
- Managing rate-limiting calcium-channel blockers p.93
- Managing dihydropyridine calcium-channel blocker therapy p.95
- Managing nitrate or nicorandil therapy p.97
- Poor control on monotherapy p.99
- Advice if poor control on dual therapy p.102

Extended Information, p. 102

Which scenario?

Initial management: covers the initial management of a person presenting with angina, including prescribing of aspirin and glyceryl trinitrate (GTN). Monotherapy for long-term symptom control is recommended. Advice on the choice of agent is given. The starting doses of therapies for long-term symptom control are also included (i.e. beta-blockers, calcium-channel blockers, nitrates, or potassium-channel activators).

Managing beta-blocker therapy (1st choice): prescriptions for continuing beta-blocker therapy, and advice on managing common adverse effects.

Managing rate-limiting calcium-channel blockers: prescriptions for continuing verapamil and diltiazem, and advice on managing common adverse effects.

Managing dihydropyridine calcium-channel blocker therapy: prescriptions for continuing dihydropyridine therapy, and advice on managing common adverse effects.

Managing nitrate or nicorandil therapy: prescriptions for continuing nitrate or nicorandil therapy, and advice on managing common adverse effects.

Poor control on monotherapy: prescribing options for people not controlled on *maximum tolerated* monotherapy (e.g. initiating dual therapies).

- **Advice if poor control on dual therapy:** information on the management of people not controlled on maximum doses of dual therapy (*referral advised and prescriptions not offered*).

Initial management

Which therapy?

- **Start aspirin** (unless contraindicated). Aspirin reduces the risk of myocardial infarction (MI), stroke, or vascular deaths by about 30%.
- **Clopidogrel** is an alternative for someone hypersensitive to aspirin (i.e. for whom aspirin induces angio-oedema or bronchospasm). Dyspepsia is common with both aspirin and clopidogrel.
- **Prescribe sublingual glyceryl trinitrate (GTN).** Advise people how to use their GTN to abort attacks, or to provide a short period of prophylaxis while doing activities likely to precipitate angina.
- **Start regular treatment for long-term symptom control:**
  - **A beta-blocker is the preferred treatment** (unless contraindicated).
  - **There is no clear choice of treatment when a beta-blocker cannot be taken.** Options include a rate-limiting calcium-channel blocker (verapamil or diltiazem); a long-acting dihydropyridine calcium-channel blocker (e.g. modified-release nifedipine); a nitrate; or a potassium-channel activator.
- **The usual starting doses for long-term symptom control are offered in this scenario.** Someone who is already on one of these drugs for another indication may already be on a higher dose, or require a step up to a higher dose than is offered in this scenario. Higher-dose prescriptions can be found in the *Managing therapy* scenarios.
- **Hormone replacement therapy (HRT) should not be started for prevention of coronary heart disease (CHD).** If the woman is already taking HRT, consider stopping it.
- **Manage cardiovascular risk factors:** offer personalized advice on Mediterranean diet, weight management, regular exercise, smoking cessation, and moderate alcohol intake. See the separate PRODIGY guidance for *Obesity* and *Smoking cessation.*
- **Manage coexisting hypertension, hyperlipidaemia, and diabetes.** See the separate PRODIGY guidance for *Hypertension* and *Hyperlipidaemia.*
- **A person's occupation may be affected by angina.** Holders of Large Goods Vehicle (LGV) and Passenger

A

Carrying Vehicle (PCV) licences should notify the DVLA and stop driving their vehicle. Holders of an ordinary driving licence may still drive providing that symptoms are controlled, but must inform their motor vehicle insurance company. People who operate heavy machinery may also be affected.
- **Give heart-attack education.** This includes recognition of symptoms and instruction to seek help rapidly by phoning '999'.

Factors affecting the choice of long-term treatments

- **Driving:** people taking nicorandil should not drive until it is established that their performance is unimpaired.
- **Asthma or a history of bronchospasm:** do not use beta-blockers (Committee on Safety of Medicines warning).
- **Severe peripheral vascular disease:** avoid beta-blockers.
- **Diabetes:** if using a beta-blocker, use atenolol or metoprolol (cardioselective). Avoid beta-blockers in people who experience frequent hypoglycaemia. Advise people that beta-blockers may slightly raise their blood glucose levels, and their response to hypoglycaemia may be delayed or symptoms of hypoglycaemia may not occur in the usual way.
- **Heart failure:** do not use verapamil. Avoid using diltiazem. Beta-blockers may be used in heart failure, but the licensed drugs and doses are different in the case of angina. See the separate PRODIGY guidance for *Heart failure* guidance or *Prior myocardial infarction — prophylactic treatments*.
- **Closed-angle glaucoma:** do not use nitrates.

Practical prescribing points

For further information please see the *Medicines Compendium* (www.medicines.org.uk) or the *British National Formulary* (www.bnf.org).

Glyceryl trinitrate (GTN)

- GTN spray is particularly useful for people who do not use nitrates often, as, unlike tablets, it does not need to be discarded 8 weeks after opening.

Low-dose aspirin

- **Concurrent nonsteroidal anti-inflammatory drugs (NSAIDs):** the risk of serious gastrointestinal complications doubles in people who regularly take low-dose aspirin and another NSAID. If possible, stop the second NSAID.
- **If a second NSAID must be continued, avoid ibuprofen** — it may reduce the cardiovascular protective effect of low-dose aspirin. Consider using diclofenac if a second NSAID must be used.
- **Asthma:** aspirin can induce bronchospasm in someone hypersensitive to aspirin, but this is rare.

Beta-blockers

- There is no significant increased risk of depressive symptoms while on beta-blockers, and only a small increase in the risk of fatigue or sexual dysfunction.

Verapamil

- **Constipation is common.** Give advice on high-fibre diet with adequate fluid intake.

Follow-up advice

- Review within 1–4 weeks, depending on severity of symptoms and outstanding investigations.

Should I refer or investigate?

Refer?

Refer for a stress test (usually an exercise electrocardiogram)

- **Use rapid access chest pain clinics, open access exercis[e] testing, or cardiology outpatient services** (depending o[n] local availability).
- **An exercise electrocardiogram (ECG)** gives valuable *prognostic* information in people with a high likeliho[od] of angina, and helps to identify people who warrant further investigation by angiography.
- **Refer all people with clinically certain angina.**
  - People referred to assess prognosis should have the t[est] while taking their normal medication.
- **People should not be referred for an exercise ECG if:**
  - They are on maximal medical treatment and still ha[ve] symptoms
  - The diagnosis of coronary heart disease is unlikely
  - They are physically incapable of taking the test
  - They may have aortic stenosis or cardiomyopathy
  - The results of an exercise ECG would not affect management
- Consider referring to a cardiologist someone who can[not] have an exercise ECG.

Referral to a cardiologist

- **It is important *not* to delay treatment while awaiting referral.**
- Note: not all people need to be referred, and some may not wish to be referred.

Factors that should prompt early referral to a cardiologis[t]
- **People who have had a previous myocardial infarction (MI), coronary artery bypass grafting, or** percutaneous transluminal coronary angioplasty and develop angina
- **People who seem to have ECG evidence of a previous MI,** or other significant abnormality.
- **People who fail to respond to medical treatment.**
- **People who have an ejection systolic murmur** suggestin[g] aortic stenosis.

People with the following symptoms should be consider[ed] for urgent referral:
- **Pain on minimal exertion**
- **Pain at rest** (which may occur at night)
- **Angina that seems to be progressing rapidly** despite increasing medical treatment

Further reasons to refer people to a cardiologist include:
- **To confirm or refute a diagnosis** with uncertain or atypical symptoms.
- **To advise on the management of an individual,** particularly where the person has not responded to treatment or risk factor modification.
- **The presence of several risk factors** or a strong family history.
- **The person's preference** for referral.
- **Problems with employment,** life insurance, or unacceptable interference with lifestyle.
- **Significant comorbidity** (e.g. diabetes).

Investigate?

- Check blood pressure.
- Record resting pulse.
- Check fasting full lipid profile.
- Check haemoglobin and fasting blood glucose.
- Only check thyroid function tests if there is clinical suspicion of thyroid disease.

. resting 12-lead ECG should be recorded in all people vith suspected angina. A normal ECG does not exclude ngina.

'he 'diagnosis' of angina implies coronary artery lisease, and so all people with *confirmed* angina are onsidered to have a cardiovascular risk of more than 0% over 10 years. There is, therefore, no need to use a isk calculator to estimate cardiovascular risk in these eople.

atient information leaflets

e following PILs are available at www.prodigy.nhs.uk

Angina
Aspirin to Prevent Blood Clots
British Cardiac Patients Association
British Heart Foundation
Cholesterol
Coronary Angiography
Coronary Angioplasty
Eat More Fruit and Vegetables
Exercise for Health
Healthy Eating
Healthy Eating - A Summary
Healthy Lifestyle - Five Choices
Heart Disease - Prevention
Heart UK
How the Heart Works
Smoking - Help to Stop with Bupropion
Smoking - Nicotine Replacement Therapy
Smoking - The Facts
Smoking - Tips on Stopping

hared decision making

You can help to prevent angina from becoming worse if you:

- Stop smoking if you are a smoker
- Exercise regularly
- Eat a low-fat 'Mediterranean' diet
- Lose weight if you are overweight
- Do not drink too much alcohol

Aspirin reduces the risk of a blood clot forming that may cause a heart attack.

- It is uncommon to have side effects with low dose aspirin. Tell your doctor if you develop any stomach symptoms.

Glyceryl trinitrate (GTN) relieves angina pains when they occur.

- GTN is absorbed quickly from inside the mouth.
- It works by 'opening wide' the blood vessels.
- You can also take a dose before exercise to prevent an angina pain (e.g. before walking up a hill).
- Some people get a headache after taking GTN.
- GTN tablets 'go off' 8 weeks after a bottle is opened. So the prescription needs renewing every 8 weeks or so.
- GTN sprays have a longer 'shelf life'.

Regular medication with a beta-blocker or other medicines can prevent angina pains.

Call an ambulance if you develop a severe chest pain that lasts longer than usual, and is not eased by GTN.

Drug rationale

Drugs not included

Enteric-coated aspirin: enteric-coating is not offered, as there is no convincing evidence that this reduces toxicity at a dose of 75 mg [DTB, 1997].

- **Buccal glyceryl trinitrate** (GTN) **tablets** are effective but much more expensive than sublingual tablets or sprays. They may be useful in unstable or crescendo angina.
- **Beta-blockers other than atenolol, metoprolol, and propranolol:** despite the large number of beta-blocker drugs listed in the *British National Formulary*, there is little to choose between them. People should be treated with the cheapest preparation that they can tolerate and comply with, and that controls their symptoms. Atenolol, metoprolol, and propranolol are inexpensive and meet nearly all clinical needs; other beta-blockers are, therefore, not offered. Modified-release preparations are expensive, so have not been included [DTB, 1996; North of England Guideline Development Group, 1999].
- **Modified-release preparations: verapamil** modified-release preparations should be used at maximum dose for angina (240 mg twice a day). This is a markedly higher dose than when using standard tablets, and is more expensive.
- **Dihydropyridine calcium-channel blockers other than nifedipine, felodipine, and amlodipine:** dihydropyridine calcium-channel blockers that are not licensed for use in angina, or less widely used, have not been included.
- **Nifedipine immediate-release capsules** are not recommended because their use is associated with large variations in blood pressure and reflex tachycardia [BNF 44, 2002].
- **Isosorbide dinitrate** is metabolised to isosorbide mononitrate (ISMN), and it is likely that its action depends on production of this metabolite. It requires more frequent dosing than ISMN [SIGN, 2001; BNF 44, 2002].
- **Modified-release nitrate preparations:** these are more expensive than standard tablets. However, they may be useful for someone who finds it difficult to comply with an asymmetric dosing regimen. They must be taken as a once-daily dose to maintain a nitrate-low period, and thus avoid tolerance [BNF 44, 2002].
- **Nitrate patches:** these are considerably more expensive than other nitrate formulations. High-dose patches are more effective than low-dose patches, but *must* be used with a patch-free interval. Continuous therapy is ineffective [BNF 44, 2002].

Drugs included

- **Aspirin dispersible tablets:** aspirin 75 mg daily is included because studies have shown that low-dose aspirin reduces the risk of subsequent myocardial infarction or sudden death in people with angina. Higher doses have not been offered. Soluble aspirin produces less occult bleeding than ordinary tablets.
- **Clopidogrel:** this is included for people who are hypersensitive to aspirin (i.e. aspirin induces angio-oedema or bronchospasm). People who experience dyspepsia with aspirin should be co-prescribed an acid-suppressing drug. See the separate PRODIGY guidance *Dyspepsia — symptoms (uninvestigated by endoscopy)*.
- **Glyceryl trinitrate (GTN):** sublingual GTN usually relieves acute symptoms within a few minutes, and can be used as prophylaxis prior to activities likely to cause angina pain [SIGN, 2001].
- **Standard preparations of three inexpensive beta-blockers** (the non-selective propranolol and the beta-1-selective atenolol and metoprolol) seem to meet nearly all clinical needs and have been included [DTB, 1996; North of England Guideline Development Group, 1999].
- **Rate-limiting calcium-channel blockers:**
    - **Standard tablets:** verapamil and diltiazem are included.
    - **Modified-release preparations:** diltiazem is included by brand name at higher dosages because of potential

problems caused by switching brands [BNF 44, 2002]. Both once a day and twice a day preparations are included, but are more expensive than standard tablets. The cheapest formulations in the BNF offering a range of strengths and dosages for use in angina are offered.

- **Dihydropyridine calcium-channel blockers**
  - **Nifedipine, felodipine, and amlodipine** have been included because they have been shown to provide symptom relief in angina, and are widely used in the UK [Heidenreich et al, 1999].
  - **Modified-release preparations: nifedipine** is included by brand name because of potential problems caused by switching brands [BNF 44, 2002]. Both once a day and twice a day preparations are included. The cheapest formulations in the BNF offering a range of strengths and dosages for use in angina are offered.
- **Standard isosorbide mononitrate(ISMN) tablets** have been shown to control symptoms when used as an asymmetrically dosed twice-daily preparation (e.g. 8 am and 3 pm). This provides protection during the day, and a nitrate-low period overnight when symptoms are generally less frequent [SIGN, 2001].
- **Nicorandil** is a further alternative for symptom control when beta-blockers are contraindicated. As with nitrates, headache is a common adverse effect.

Prescriptions

Start antiplatelet (unless contraindicated) and GTN

Aspirin 75mg dispersible once a day
- Age from 16 years onwards
- Aspirin 75mg dispersible tabs. Take one tablet once a day; supply 28 tablets; NHS Cost £0.13; OTC Cost £1.00.

Clopidogrel 75mg once a day – only if intolerant of aspirin
- Age from 16 years onwards
- Clopidogrel 75mg tablets. Take one tablet once a day; supply 28 tablets; NHS Cost £35.31.

GTN 400mcg spray: spray once under the tongue when required
- Age from 16 years onwards
- Glyceryl Trinitrate 400mcg spray. Spray one puff under the tongue when required for chest pain; supply 1 200-dose pump spray; NHS Cost £3.13; OTC Cost £5.78.

GTN 500mcg tabs: place 1 tab under the tongue when required
- Age from 16 years onwards
- Glyceryl Trinit 500mcg sl tabs. Place one tablet under the tongue when required for chest pain; supply 100 tablets; NHS Cost £1.06; OTC Cost £1.50.

1st choice: start beta-blocker

Atenolol 50mg once a day
- Age from 16 years onwards
- Atenolol 50mg tablets. Take one tablet once a day; supply 28 tablets; NHS Cost £0.85.

Atenolol 100mg once a day
- Age from 16 years onwards
- Atenolol 100mg tablets. Take one tablet once a day; supply 28 tablets; NHS Cost £0.98.

Atenolol 50mg twice a day
- Age from 16 years onwards
- Atenolol 50mg tablets. Take one tablet twice a day; supply 56 tablets; NHS Cost £1.70.

Metoprolol 50mg twice a day
- Age from 16 years onwards
- Metoprolol 50mg tablets. Take one tablet twice a day; supply 56 tablets; NHS Cost £2.35.

Metoprolol 50mg three times a day
- Age from 16 years onwards
- Metoprolol 50mg tablets. Take one tablet three times day; supply 84 tablets; NHS Cost £3.52.

Propranolol 40mg twice a day
- Age from 16 years onwards
- Propranolol 40mg tablets. Take one tablet twice a day supply 56 tablets; NHS Cost £1.30.

Propranolol 40mg three times a day
- Age from 16 years onwards
- Propranolol 40mg tablets. Take one tablet three times day; supply 84 tablets; NHS Cost £1.95.

Alternative option: start verapamil or diltiazem

Verapamil 40mg three times a day
- Age from 16 years onwards
- Verapamil 40mg tablets. Take one tablet three times a day; supply 84 tablets; NHS Cost £1.61.

Verapamil 80mg three times a day
- Age from 16 years onwards
- Verapamil 80mg tablets. Take one tablet three times a day; supply 84 tablets; NHS Cost £2.10.

Diltiazem standard tablets 60mg twice a day (if elderly)
- Age from 60 years onwards
- Diltiazem HCl 60mg m/r tablets. Take one tablet twice day; supply 56 tablets; NHS Cost £3.84.

Diltiazem standard tablets 60mg three times a day
- Age from 16 years onwards
- Diltiazem HCl 60mg m/r tablets. Take one tablet three times a day; supply 84 tablets; NHS Cost £5.76.

Diltiazem: Slozem 120mg once a day
- Age from 60 years onwards
- Slozem 120mg m/r capsules. Take one capsule once a day; supply 28 capsules; NHS Cost £7.00.

Diltiazem: Slozem 180mg once a day
- Age from 16 years onwards
- Slozem 180mg m/r capsules. Take one capsule once a day; supply 28 capsules; NHS Cost £7.80.

Diltiazem: Slozem 240mg once a day
- Age from 16 years onwards
- Slozem 240mg m/r capsules. Take one capsule once a day; supply 28 capsules; NHS Cost £8.20.

Diltiazem: Angitil SR 90mg twice a day
- Age from 16 years onwards
- Angitil SR 90mg capsules. Take one capsule twice a da supply 56 capsules; NHS Cost £8.45.

Alternative choice: start dihydropyridine CCB

Nifedipine: Coracten XL 30mg each morning
- Age from 16 years onwards
- Coracten XL 30mg m/r capsules. Take one capsule each morning; supply 28 capsules; NHS Cost £6.73.

Nifedipine: Cardilate MR 10mg twice a day
- Age from 16 years onwards
- Cardilate MR 10mg m/r tablets. Take one tablet twice day; supply 56 tablets; NHS Cost £4.97.

Felodipine 5mg m/r each morning
- Age from 16 years onwards
- Felodipine 5mg m/r tablets. Take one tablet each morning; supply 28 tablets; NHS Cost £8.12.

Amlodipine 5mg once a day
- Age from 16 years onwards
- Amlodipine 5mg tablets. Take one tablet once a day; supply 28 tablets; NHS Cost £11.85.

ernative choice: start nitrate or nicorandil

orbide mononitrate 10mg twice a day (if nitrate-naive)
ge from 16 years onwards
osorbide mononitrate10mg tab. Take one tablet at
am and another at 3pm; supply 56 tablets;
HS Cost £1.13.

orbide mononitrate 20mg twice a day
ge from 16 years onwards
osorbide mononitrate20mg tab. Take one tablet at
am and another at 3pm; supply 56 tablets;
HS Cost £2.10.

orandil 5mg twice a day (if nitrate-headache a
blem)
ge from 16 years onwards
icorandil 10mg tablets. Take half a tablet twice a day;
pply 60 tablets; NHS Cost £8.00.

orandil 10mg twice a day
ge from 16 years onwards
icorandil 10mg tablets. Take one tablet twice a day;
upply 60 tablets; NHS Cost £8.00.

lanaging beta-blocker therapy st choice)

hich therapy?

- **beta-blocker is the preferred treatment for long-term ymptom control,** unless contraindicated or not olerated.
- **tep up the dose until symptoms are controlled,** or the aximum tolerated dose is reached.
- **still poorly controlled at maximum tolerated dose of eta-blocker,** add another drug:
  - 1st **choice:** *add* a long-acting dihydropyridine (e.g. nifedipine). Diltiazem can be considered but should be used with caution, owing to the risk of bradycardia.
  - 2nd **choice:** *add* isosorbide mononitrate (ISMN).
- **o not use verapamil with a beta-blocker** (it may recipitate heart failure).
- **void stopping beta-blockers suddenly** if possible (may xacerbate angina).
- **ontinue regular aspirin** (or clopidogrel) and 'as equired' glyceryl trinitrate (GTN).
- **yspepsia is common with aspirin and clopidogrel.** ersistent dyspepsia can be managed with acid-uppressing medication; see the separate PRODIGY uidance for *Dyspepsia — symptoms* for further nformation.
- **Manage cardiovascular risk factors** (e.g. smoking, blood ressure, and cholesterol).
- **onsider stopping hormone replacement therapy** (if applicable).

ractical prescribing points

r further information please see the *Medicines mpendium* (www.medicines.org.uk) or the *British tional Formulary* (www.bnf.org).

anaging adverse effects

- **Bronchospasm:** withdraw beta-blocker therapy.
- **Bradycardia:** reduce dose or withdraw beta-blocker (and/or diltiazem), depending on severity.
- **Sleep disturbance or nightmares:** less likely with atenolol than with metoprolol or propranolol.
- **Fatigue or sexual dysfunction:** less likely with atenolol or metoprolol than with propranolol.
- **Cold extremities:** assess objective signs of peripheral vascular disease.

Starting a beta-blocker

- **Asthma or a history of bronchospasm:** do not use beta-blockers (Committee on Safety of Medicines warning).
- **Severe peripheral vascular disease:** avoid beta-blockers.
- **Diabetes:** if using a beta-blocker, use atenolol or metoprolol (cardioselective). Avoid beta blockers in people who experience frequent hypoglycaemia. Advise people that beta-blockers may slightly raise their blood glucose levels, and their response to hypoglycaemia may be delayed or symptoms of hypoglycaemia may not occur in the usual way.
- **Heart failure:** beta-blockers may be used in heart failure, but the licensed drugs and doses are different in the case of angina. See the separate PRODIGY guidance for *Heart failure* or *Prior myocardial infarction — prophylactic treatments.*

Follow-up advice

- Review within 1–4 weeks, depending on severity of symptoms and outstanding investigations.

Should I refer or investigate?

Refer?

Referral for a stress test, usually an exercise electrocardiogram (ECG) — if not already done

- **Use rapid access chest pain clinics, open access exercise testing, or cardiology outpatient services** (depending on local availability).
- **An exercise ECG** gives valuable *prognostic* information in people with a high likelihood of angina, and helps to identify people who warrant further investigation by angiography.
- **Refer all people with clinically certain angina.**
  - People referred to assess prognosis should have the test while taking their normal medication.
- **People should not be referred for an exercise ECG if:**
  - They are on maximal medical treatment and still have symptoms.
  - The diagnosis of coronary heart disease is unlikely.
  - They are physically incapable of taking the test.
  - They may have aortic stenosis or cardiomyopathy.
  - The results of an exercise ECG would not affect management.
- **Consider referring to a cardiologist someone who cannot have an exercise ECG.**

Referral to a cardiologist

- **It is important *not* to delay treatment while awaiting referral.**
- Note: not all people need to be referred, and some may not wish to be referred.

Factors that should prompt early referral to a cardiologist:

- **People who have had a previous myocardial infarction (MI),** coronary artery bypass grafting, **or** percutaneous transluminal coronary angioplasty and develop angina.
- **People who seem to have ECG evidence of a previous MI,** or other significant abnormality.
- **People who fail to respond to medical treatment.**
- **People who have an ejection systolic murmur** suggesting aortic stenosis.

People with the following symptoms should be considered for urgent referral:

- **Pain on minimal exertion**
- **Pain at rest** (which may occur at night)
- **Angina that seems to be progressing rapidly** despite increasing medical treatment

Further reasons to refer people to a cardiologist include:

- **To confirm or refute a diagnosis** with uncertain or atypical symptoms.
- **To advise on the management of an individual,** particularly where the person has not responded to treatment or risk factor modification.
- **The presence of several risk factors** or a strong family history.
- **The person's preference** for referral.
- **Problems with employment,** life insurance, or unacceptable interference with lifestyle.
- **Significant comorbidity** (e.g. diabetes).

Investigate?

- Ensure monitoring of cholesterol level is up-to-date.
- A resting 12-lead electrocardiogram (ECG) should be recorded in all people with suspected angina. A normal ECG does not exclude angina.

Patient information leaflets

The following PILs are available at www.prodigy.nhs.uk

- Angina
- Aspirin to Prevent Blood Clots
- British Cardiac Patients Association
- British Heart Foundation
- Cholesterol
- Coronary Angiography
- Coronary Angioplasty
- Eat More Fruit and Vegetables
- Exercise for Health
- Healthy Eating
- Healthy Eating - A Summary
- Healthy Lifestyle - Five Choices
- Heart Disease - Prevention
- Heart UK
- How the Heart Works
- Smoking - Help to Stop with Bupropion
- Smoking - Nicotine Replacement Therapy
- Smoking - The Facts
- Smoking - Tips on Stopping

Shared decision making

- **A beta-blocker medicine** is commonly prescribed to reduce the number and severity of angina pains. They work by 'relaxing' the heart muscle.
- Beta-blocker medicines include **atenolol, metoprolol,** and **propranolol.**
- **Some people develop side effects.** These include
  - Cool hands and feet
  - Poor sleep
  - Tiredness
  - Impotence
- **If you have asthma** you should not take beta-blockers, as they can bring on wheeze.
- If side effects occur, a different beta-blocker, or a different anti-angina medicine, may suit better. But:
- Do not suddenly stop taking a beta-blocker medicine.
- Most people with angina also take a daily dose of aspirin, and carry some glyceryl trinitrate (GTN), which can be taken if an angina pain occurs.

Drug rationale

Drugs included

- **Beta-blockers:** despite the large number of beta-blocker drugs listed in the *British National Formulary*, there is little to choose between them. People should be treated with the cheapest preparation that they can tolerate and comply with, and that controls their symptoms. Standard preparations of three inexpensive beta-bloc (the non-selective propranolol, the beta-1-selective atenolol, and metoprolol) seem to meet nearly all clin needs and have been included. Modified-release preparations are expensive, so have not been include [DTB, 1996; North of England Guideline Developme Group, 1999].
- **Aspirin, clopidogrel, and sublingual glyceryl trinitrat** (GTN) are available for repeat prescriptions in this scenario.

Prescriptions

Atenolol

Atenolol 25mg once a day

- Age from 16 years onwards
- Atenolol 25mg tablets. Take one tablet once a day; supply 28 tablets; NHS Cost £2.07.

Atenolol 50mg once a day

- Age from 16 years onwards
- Atenolol 50mg tablets. Take one tablet once a day; supply 28 tablets; NHS Cost £0.85.

Atenolol 100mg once a day

- Age from 16 years onwards
- Atenolol 100mg tablets. Take one tablet once a day; supply 28 tablets; NHS Cost £1.91.

Atenolol 50mg twice a day

- Age from 16 years onwards
- Atenolol 50mg tablets. Take one tablet twice a day; supply 56 tablets; NHS Cost £1.70.

Metoprolol

Metoprolol 50mg twice a day

- Age from 16 years onwards
- Metoprolol 50mg tablets. Take one tablet twice a day supply 56 tablets; NHS Cost £2.07.

Metoprolol 50mg three times a day

- Age from 16 years onwards
- Metoprolol 50mg tablets. Take one tablet three times day; supply 84 tablets; NHS Cost £3.11.

Metoprolol 100mg twice a day

- Age from 16 years onwards
- Metoprolol 100mg tablets. Take one tablet twice a da supply 56 tablets; NHS Cost £3.89.

Metoprolol 100mg three times a day

- Age from 16 years onwards
- Metoprolol 100mg tablets. Take one tablet three time day; supply 84 tablets; NHS Cost £5.84.

Propranolol

Propranolol 40mg twice a day

- Age from 16 years onwards
- Propranolol 40mg tablets. Take one tablet twice a day supply 56 tablets; NHS Cost £1.48.

Propranolol 40mg three times a day

- Age from 16 years onwards
- Propranolol 40mg tablets. Take one tablet three times day; supply 84 tablets; NHS Cost £2.22.

Propranolol 80mg twice a day

- Age from 16 years onwards
- Propranolol 80mg tablets. Take one tablet twice a day supply 56 tablets; NHS Cost £2.23.

Propranolol 80mg three times a day

- Age from 16 years onwards
- Propranolol 80mg tablets. Take one tablet three times day; supply 84 tablets; NHS Cost £3.34.

ntiplatelet (unless contraindicated) and GTN

pirin 75mg dispersible once a day
Age from 16 years onwards
Aspirin 75mg dispersible tabs. Take one tablet once a day; supply 28 tablets; NHS Cost £0.18; OTC Cost £1.00.

opidogrel 75mg once a day – only if intolerant of aspirin
Age from 16 years onwards
Clopidogrel 75mg tablets. Take one tablet once a day; supply 28 tablets; NHS Cost £35.31.

TN 400mcg spray: spray once under the tongue when quired
Age from 16 years onwards
Glyceryl Trinitrate 400mcg spray. Spray one puff under the tongue when required for chest pain; supply 1 200-dose pump spray; NHS Cost £3.13; OTC Cost £5.78.

TN 500mcg tabs: place 1 tab under the tongue when quired
Age from 16 years onwards
Glyceryl Trinit 500mcg sl tabs. Place one tablet under the tongue when required for chest pain; supply 100 tablets; NHS Cost £1.06; OTC Cost £1.50.

Managing rate-limiting calcium-channel blockers

Which therapy?

A rate-limiting calcium-channel blocker (verapamil or diltiazem) is an appropriate choice if a beta-blocker is not tolerated or contraindicated.
Step up the dose until symptoms are controlled, or the maximum tolerated dose is reached.
If still poorly controlled at maximum tolerated dose, add another drug:
- **1st choice:** *add* isosorbide mononitrate (ISMN).
- **2nd choice:** *add* nicorandil.

Do not co-prescribe verapamil with a beta-blocker (may precipitate heart failure).
Do not co-prescribe another calcium-channel blocker with either verapamil or diltiazem.
A beta-blocker could be added to diltiazem therapy (if not contraindicated) but this combination can cause bradycardia, so should only be used cautiously.
Avoid stopping calcium-channel blockers suddenly if possible (may exacerbate angina).
Continue regular aspirin (or clopidogrel) and 'as required' glyceryl trinitrate (GTN).
Dyspepsia is common with aspirin and clopidogrel. Persistent dyspepsia can be managed with acid-suppressing medication, see the separate PRODIGY guidance for *Dyspepsia — symptoms (uninvestigated by endoscopy)* for further information.
Manage cardiovascular risk factors (e.g. smoking, blood pressure, and cholesterol).

Practical prescribing points

For further information please see the *Medicines Compendium* (www.medicines.org.uk) or the *British National Formulary* (www.bnf.org).

Managing adverse effects

Bradycardia: reduce dose or withdraw verapamil/diltiazem, depending on severity.
Constipation: common with verapamil. Give advice on high-fibre diet with adequate fluid intake.
Dizziness or facial flushing: generally become less severe after a few days.
- **Ankle oedema:** often persistent. Do not prescribe diuretics (they only partially reduce ankle oedema caused by calcium-channel blockers).
- **Postural hypotension:** reduce dose of calcium-channel blocker.

Starting verapamil or diltiazem

- **Heart failure:** do not use verapamil. Avoid using diltiazem if possible.

Follow-up advice

- Review within 1–4 weeks, depending on severity of symptoms and outstanding investigations.

Should I refer or investigate?

Refer?

Referral for a stress test, usually an exercise electrocardiogram (ECG) — if not already done

- **Use rapid access chest pain clinics, open access exercise testing, or cardiology outpatient services** (depending on local availability).
- **An exercise ECG** gives valuable *prognostic* information in people with a high likelihood of angina, and helps to identify people who warrant further investigation by angiography.
- **Refer all people with clinically certain angina.**
  - People referred to assess prognosis should have the test while taking their normal medication.
- **People should not be referred for an exercise ECG if:**
  - They are on maximal medical treatment and still have symptoms.
  - The diagnosis of coronary heart disease is unlikely.
  - They are physically incapable of taking the test.
  - They may have aortic stenosis or cardiomyopathy.
  - The results of an exercise ECG would not affect management.
- **Consider referring to a cardiologist someone who cannot have an exercise ECG.**

Referral to a cardiologist

- **It is important *not* to delay treatment while awaiting referral.**
- Note: not all people need to be referred, and some may not wish to be referred.

Factors that should prompt early referral to a cardiologist:
- **People who have had a previous myocardial infarction (MI), coronary artery bypass grafting, or percutaneous transluminal coronary angioplasty and develop angina.**
- **People who seem to have ECG evidence of a previous MI,** or other significant abnormality.
- **People who fail to respond to medical treatment.**
- **People who have an ejection systolic murmur** suggesting aortic stenosis.

People with the following symptoms should be considered for urgent referral:
- **Pain on minimal exertion**
- **Pain at rest** (which may occur at night)
- **Angina that seems to be progressing rapidly** despite increasing medical treatment

Further reasons to refer people to a cardiologist include:
- **To confirm or refute a diagnosis** with uncertain or atypical symptoms.
- **To advise on the management of an individual,** particularly where the person has not responded to treatment or risk factor modification.

A

- **The presence of several risk factors** or a strong family history.
- **The person's preference** for referral.
- **Problems with employment,** life insurance, or unacceptable interference with lifestyle.
- **Significant comorbidity** (e.g. diabetes).

Investigate?

- Ensure monitoring of cholesterol level is up-to-date.
- A resting 12-lead electrocardiogram (ECG) should be recorded in all people with suspected angina. A normal ECG does not exclude angina.

Patient information leaflets

The following PILs are available at www.prodigy.nhs.uk

- Angina
- Aspirin to Prevent Blood Clots
- British Cardiac Patients Association
- British Heart Foundation
- Cholesterol
- Coronary Angiography
- Coronary Angioplasty
- Eat More Fruit and Vegetables
- Exercise for Health
- Healthy Eating
- Healthy Eating - A Summary
- Healthy Lifestyle - Five Choices
- Heart Disease - Prevention
- Heart UK
- How the Heart Works
- Smoking - Help to Stop with Bupropion
- Smoking - Nicotine Replacement Therapy
- Smoking - The Facts
- Smoking - Tips on Stopping

Shared decision making

- **Verapamil or diltiazem** are commonly prescribed to reduce the number and severity of angina pains.
  - These medicines are called 'calcium-channel blockers'.
  - They work by 'relaxing' the heart muscle.
- **The dose may be increased** if the initial dose does not control your pains.
- **Some people develop side effects.** These include constipation, feeling sick, flushing, headaches, dizziness, ankle swelling, and tiredness.
- **If side effects occur,** a different anti-angina medicine may suit better. But:
- ***Do not suddenly stop taking an anti-anginal medicine.***
- Most people with angina also take a daily dose of aspirin, and carry some glyceryl trinitrate (GTN), which can be taken if an angina pain occurs.

Drug rationale

Drugs not included

- **Modified-release preparations: verapamil** modified-release preparations should be used at maximum dose for angina (240 mg twice a day). This is a markedly higher dose than when using standard tablets, and is more expensive.

Drugs included

- **Aspirin, clopidogrel, and sublingual glyceryl trinitrate** (GTN) are available for repeat prescriptions in this scenario.
- **Standard tablets: verapamil and diltiazem** are included.
- **Modified-release preparations: diltiazem** is included by brand name at higher dosages because of potential problems caused by switching brands [BNF 44, 2002]. Both once a day and twice a day preparations are included, but are more expensive than standard tablet[s]. The cheapest formulations in the BNF offering a rang[e of] strengths and dosages for use in angina are offered.

Prescriptions

Verapamil

Verapamil 40mg three times a day

- Age from 16 years onwards
- Verapamil 40mg tablets. Take one tablet three times a day; supply 84 tablets; NHS Cost £1.61.

Verapamil 80mg three times a day

- Age from 16 years onwards
- Verapamil 80mg tablets. Take one tablet three times a day; supply 84 tablets; NHS Cost £1.54.

Verapamil 120mg three times a day

- Age from 16 years onwards
- Verapamil 120mg tablets. Take one tablet three times a day; supply 84 tablets; NHS Cost £3.93.

Diltiazem (three times a day)

Diltiazem standard tablets 60mg three times a day

- Age from 16 years onwards
- Diltiazem HCl 60mg m/r tablets. Take one tablet three times a day; supply 84 tablets; NHS Cost £5.76.

Diltiazem (once a day)

Slozem 120mg once a day

- Age from 60 years onwards
- Slozem 120mg m/r capsules. Take one capsule once a day; supply 28 capsules; NHS Cost £7.00.

Slozem 180mg once a day

- Age from 16 years onwards
- Slozem 180mg m/r capsules. Take one capsule once a day; supply 28 capsules; NHS Cost £7.80.

Slozem 240mg once a day

- Age from 16 years onwards
- Slozem 240mg m/r capsules. Take one capsule once a day; supply 28 capsules; NHS Cost £8.20.

Slozem 360mg once a day

- Age from 16 years onwards
- Slozem 180mg m/r capsules. Take two capsules once a day; supply 56 capsules; NHS Cost £15.60.

Diltiazem (twice a day)

Diltiazem standard tablets 60mg twice a day (if elderly)

- Age from 60 years onwards
- Diltiazem HCl 60mg m/r tablets. Take one tablet twice day; supply 56 tablets; NHS Cost £3.84.

Angitil SR 90mg twice a day

- Age from 16 years onwards
- Angitil SR 90mg capsules. Take one capsule twice a day; supply 56 capsules; NHS Cost £8.45.

Angitil SR 120mg twice a day

- Age from 16 years onwards
- Angitil SR 120mg capsules. Take one capsule twice a day; supply 56 capsules; NHS Cost £9.00.

Angitil SR 180mg twice a day

- Age from 16 years onwards
- Angitil SR 180mg capsules. Take one capsule twice a day; supply 56 capsules; NHS Cost £14.08.

ntiplatelet (unless contraindicated) and GTN

pirin 75mg dispersible once a day
Age from 16 years onwards
Aspirin 75mg dispersible tabs. Take one tablet once a day; supply 28 tablets; NHS Cost £0.18; OTC Cost £1.00.

opidogrel 75mg once a day – only if intolerant of aspirin
Age from 16 years onwards
Clopidogrel 75mg tablets. Take one tablet once a day; supply 28 tablets; NHS Cost £35.31.

TN 400mcg spray: spray once under the tongue when quired
Age from 16 years onwards
Glyceryl Trinitrate 400mcg spray. Spray one puff under the tongue when required for chest pain; supply 1 200-dose pump spray; NHS Cost £3.13; OTC Cost £5.78.

TN 500mcg tabs: place 1 tab under the tongue when quired
Age from 16 years onwards
Glyceryl Trinit 500mcg sl tabs. Place one tablet under the tongue when required for chest pain; supply 100 tablets; NHS Cost £1.06; OTC Cost £1.50.

Managing dihydropyridine calcium-channel blocker therapy

Which therapy?

A long-acting dihydropyridine calcium-channel blocker (e.g. nifedipine, felodipine, or amlodipine) is an option if the person is intolerant of beta-blockers, or if they are contraindicated.
Step up the dose until symptoms are controlled, or the maximum tolerated dose is reached.
If still poorly controlled at maximum tolerated dose, add another drug:
- **1st choice:** ideally a beta-blocker should be added, if not contraindicated.
- **2nd choice:** if a beta-blocker is contraindicated, *add* isosorbide mononitrate (ISMN) or nicorandil.

Do not co-prescribe another calcium-channel blocker.
Avoid stopping calcium channel blockers suddenly if possible (may exacerbate angina).
Continue regular aspirin (or clopidogrel) and 'as required' glyceryl trinitrate (GTN).
Dyspepsia is common with aspirin and clopidogrel. Persistent dyspepsia can be managed with acid-suppressing medication; see the separate PRODIGY guidance for *Dyspepsia — symptoms (uninvestigated by endoscopy)* for further information.
Manage cardiovascular risk factors (e.g. smoking, blood pressure, and cholesterol).

Practical prescribing points

or further information please see the *Medicines Compendium* (www.medicines.org.uk) or the *British National Formulary* (www.bnf.org).

Managing adverse effects

Dizziness or facial flushing: generally become less severe after a few days.
Ankle oedema: often persistent. Do not prescribe diuretics (they only partially reduce ankle oedema caused by calcium-channel blockers).
Postural hypotension: reduce dose of calcium-channel blocker.

Follow-up advice

- Review within 1–4 weeks, depending on severity of symptoms and outstanding investigations.

Should I refer or investigate?

Refer?

Referral for a stress test, usually an exercise electrocardiogram (ECG) — if not already done

- **Use rapid access chest pain clinics, open access exercise testing, or cardiology outpatient services** (depending on local availability).
- **An exercise ECG** gives valuable *prognostic* information in people with a high likelihood of angina, and helps to identify people who warrant further investigation by angiography.
- **Refer all people with clinically certain angina.**
  - People referred to assess prognosis should have the test while taking their normal medication.
- **People should not be referred for an exercise ECG if:**
  - They are on maximal medical treatment and still have symptoms.
  - The diagnosis of coronary heart disease is unlikely.
  - They are physically incapable of taking the test.
  - They may have aortic stenosis or cardiomyopathy.
  - The results of an exercise ECG would not affect management.
- **Consider referring to a cardiologist someone who cannot have an exercise ECG.**

Referral to a cardiologist

- **It is important *not* to delay treatment while awaiting referral.**
- Note: not all people need to be referred, and some may not wish to be referred.

Factors that should prompt early referral to a cardiologist:
- **People who have had a previous myocardial infarction (MI), coronary artery bypass grafting, or percutaneous transluminal coronary angioplasty** and develop angina.
- **People who seem to have ECG evidence of a previous MI,** or other significant abnormality.
- **People who fail to respond to medical treatment.**
- **People who have an ejection systolic murmur** suggesting aortic stenosis.

People with the following symptoms should be considered for urgent referral:
- **Pain on minimal exertion**
- **Pain at rest** (which may occur at night)
- **Angina that seems to be progressing rapidly** despite increasing medical treatment

Further reasons to refer people to a cardiologist include:
- **To confirm or refute a diagnosis** with uncertain or atypical symptoms.
- **To advise on the management of an individual,** particularly where the person has not responded to treatment or risk factor modification.
- **The presence of several risk factors** or a strong family history.
- **The person's preference** for referral.
- **Problems with employment,** life insurance, or unacceptable interference with lifestyle.
- **Significant comorbidity,** for example diabetes.

Investigate?

- Ensure monitoring of cholesterol level is up-to-date.
- A resting 12-lead electrocardiogram (ECG) should be recorded in all people with suspected angina. A normal ECG does not exclude angina.

Patient information leaflets

The following PILs are available at www.prodigy.nhs.uk

- Angina
- Aspirin to Prevent Blood Clots
- British Cardiac Patients Association
- British Heart Foundation
- Cholesterol
- Coronary Angiography
- Coronary Angioplasty
- Eat More Fruit and Vegetables
- Exercise for Health
- Healthy Eating
- Healthy Eating - A Summary
- Healthy Lifestyle - Five Choices
- Heart Disease - Prevention
- Heart UK
- How the Heart Works
- Smoking - Help to Stop with Bupropion
- Smoking - Nicotine Replacement Therapy
- Smoking - The Facts
- Smoking - Tips on Stopping

Shared decision making

- **A calcium-channel blocker medicine** is commonly prescribed to reduce the number and severity of angina pains. It works by 'relaxing' the heart muscle and blood vessels.
- Calcium-channel blockers include **nifedipine, felodipine** and **amlodipine.**
- **The dose may be increased** if the initial dose does not control your pains.
- **Some people develop side effects.** These include constipation, feeling sick, flushing, headaches, dizziness, ankle swelling, and tiredness.
- **If side effects occur,** a different anti-angina medicine may suit you better. But:
- ***Do not suddenly stop taking an anti-anginal medicine.***
- Most people with angina also take a daily dose of aspirin, and carry some glyceryl trinitrate (GTN) that can be taken if an angina pain occurs.

Drug rationale

Drugs not included

- **Dihydropyridine calcium-channel blockers other than nifedipine, felodipine and amlodipine:** dihydropyridine calcium-channel blockers that are not licensed for use in angina, or are less widely used, have not been included.
- **Nifedipine immediate-release capsules** are not recommended because their use is associated with large variations in blood pressure and reflex tachycardia [BNF 44, 2002].

Drugs included

- **Aspirin, clopidogrel, and sublingual glyceryl trinitrate** (GTN) are available for repeat prescriptions in this scenario.
- **Nifedipine, felodipine, and amlodipine** have been included because they have been shown to provide symptom relief in angina [Heidenreich et al, 1999], and are widely used in the UK.
- **Modified-release preparations: nifedipine** is included by brand name because of potential problems caused by switching brands [BNF 44, 2002]. Both once a day and twice a day preparations are included. The cheapest formulations in the BNF offering a range of strengths and dosages for use in angina are offered.

Prescriptions

Nifedipine (once a day)

Coracten XL 30mg each morning
- Age from 16 years onwards
- Coracten XL 30mg m/r capsules. Take one capsule eac morning; supply 28 capsules; NHS Cost £6.73.

Coracten XL 60mg each morning
- Age from 16 years onwards
- Coracten XL 60mg m/r capsules. Take one capsule eac morning; supply 28 capsules; NHS Cost £10.01.

Nifedipine (twice a day)

Cardilate MR 10mg twice a day
- Age from 16 years onwards
- Cardilate MR 10mg m/r tablets. Take one tablet twice day; supply 56 tablets; NHS Cost £4.97.

Cardilate MR 20mg twice a day
- Age from 16 years onwards
- Cardilate MR 20mg m/r tablets. Take one tablet twice day; supply 56 tablets; NHS Cost £6.20.

Cardilate MR 40mg twice a day
- Age from 16 years onwards
- Cardilate MR 20mg m/r tablets. Take two tablets twic day; supply 56 tablets; NHS Cost £12.40.

Felodipine (once a day)

Felodipine 5mg m/r each morning
- Age from 16 years onwards
- Felodipine 5mg m/r tablets. Take one tablet each morning; supply 28 tablets; NHS Cost £8.12.

Felodipine 10mg m/r each morning
- Age from 16 years onwards
- Felodipine 10mg m/r tablets. Take one tablet each morning; supply 28 tablets; NHS Cost £10.92.

Amlodipine (once a day)

Amlodipine 5mg once a day
- Age from 16 years onwards
- Amlodipine 5mg tablets. Take one tablet once a day; supply 28 tablets; NHS Cost £11.85.

Amlodipine 10mg once a day
- Age from 16 years onwards
- Amlodipine 10mg tablets. Take one tablet once a day; supply 28 tablets; NHS Cost £17.70.

Antiplatelet (unless contraindicated) and GTN

Aspirin 75mg dispersible once a day
- Age from 16 years onwards
- Aspirin 75mg dispersible tabs. Take one tablet once a day; supply 28 tablets; NHS Cost £0.18; OTC Cost £1.00.

Clopidogrel 75mg once a day – only if intolerant of aspiri
- Age from 16 years onwards
- Clopidogrel 75mg tablets. Take one tablet once a day; supply 28 tablets; NHS Cost £35.31.

GTN 400mcg spray: spray once under the tongue when required
- Age from 16 years onwards
- Glyceryl Trinitrate 400mcg spray. Spray one puff unde the tongue when required for chest pain; supply 1 200-dose pump spray; NHS Cost £3.13; OTC Cost £5.78.

GTN 500mcg tabs: place 1 tab under the tongue when required
- Age from 16 years onwards
- Glyceryl Trinit 500mcg sl tabs. Place one tablet under the tongue when required for chest pain; supply 100 tablets; NHS Cost £1.06; OTC Cost £1.50.

·anaging nitrate or nicorandil erapy

·hich therapy?

·long-acting nitrate or a potassium-channel activator is · appropriate choice if a person is intolerant of beta-·ockers, or if they are contraindicated.
·nitrate must be given as an asymmetric regimen to ·oid nitrate tolerance (e.g. at 8 am and 3 pm). Consider ·anging dosing times to 4 pm and 10 pm if symptoms ·e most severe early in the morning.
·ep up the dose until symptoms are controlled, or the ·aximum tolerated dose is reached.
·still poorly controlled at maximum tolerated dose, add ·other drug:
- 1st choice: ideally a beta-blocker should be added, if not contraindicated.
- 2nd choice: if a beta-blocker is contraindicated, *add* a long-acting dihydropyridine calcium-channel blocker.

·ontinue regular aspirin (or clopidogrel) and 'as ·quired' glyceryl trinitrate (GTN).
·yspepsia is common with aspirin and clopidogrel. ·rsistent dyspepsia can be managed with acid-·ppressing medication; see the separate PRODIGY ·idance for *Dyspepsia — symptoms (uninvestigated by ·doscopy)* for further information.
·anage cardiovascular risk factors (e.g. smoking, blood ·essure, and cholesterol).

·actical prescribing points

· further information please see the *Medicines ·mpendium* (www.medicines.org.uk) or the *British ·ional Formulary* (www.bnf.org).

·naging adverse effects

·eadache, flushing, or dizziness: generally become less ·vere after a few days. Increasing the dose slowly ·duces their occurrence.
·ostural hypotension or tachycardia: reduce dose of ·trate or nicorandil.

·arting nitrates or nicorandil

·losed-angle glaucoma: do not use nitrates.
·riving: people taking nicorandil should not drive until · is established that their performance is unimpaired.

·llow-up advice

·eview within 1–4 weeks, depending on severity of ·ymptoms and outstanding investigations.

·ould I refer or investigate?

·fer?

·eferral for a stress test, usually an exercise ·ectrocardiogram (ECG) — if not already done

·Jse rapid access chest pain clinics, open access exercise ·esting, or cardiology outpatient services (depending on ·ocal availability).
·An exercise ECG gives valuable *prognostic* information ·n people with a high likelihood of angina, and helps to ·dentify people who warrant further investigation by ·ngiography.
·Refer all people with clinically certain angina.
People referred to assess prognosis should have the test while taking their normal medication.

- **People should not be referred for an exercise ECG if:**
  - They are on maximal medical treatment and still have symptoms.
  - The diagnosis of coronary heart disease is unlikely.
  - They are physically incapable of taking the test.
  - They may have aortic stenosis or cardiomyopathy.
  - The results of an exercise ECG would not affect management.
- **Consider referring to a cardiologist someone who cannot have an exercise ECG.**

Referral to a cardiologist

- **It is important *not* to delay treatment while awaiting referral.**
- Note: not all people need to be referred, and some may not wish to be referred.

Factors that should prompt early referral to a cardiologist:
- **People who have had a previous myocardial infarction (MI), coronary artery bypass grafting, or percutaneous transluminal coronary angioplasty** and develop angina.
- **People who seem to have ECG evidence of a previous MI,** or other significant abnormality.
- **People who fail to respond to medical treatment.**
- **People who have an ejection systolic murmur suggesting aortic stenosis.**

People with the following symptoms should be considered for urgent referral:
- **Pain on minimal exertion**
- **Pain at rest** (which may occur at night)
- **Angina that seems to be progressing rapidly** despite increasing medical treatment

Further reasons to refer people to a cardiologist include:
- **To confirm or refute a diagnosis** with uncertain or atypical symptoms.
- **To advise on the management of an individual,** particularly where the person has not responded to treatment or risk factor modification.
- **The presence of several risk factors** or a strong family history.
- **The person's preference** for referral.
- **Problems with employment,** life insurance, or unacceptable interference with lifestyle.
- **Significant comorbidity** (e.g. diabetes).

Investigate?

- Ensure monitoring of cholesterol level is up-to-date.
- A resting 12-lead electrocardiogram (ECG) should be recorded in all people with suspected angina. A normal ECG does not exclude angina.

Patient information leaflets

The following PILs are available at www.prodigy.nhs.uk
- Angina
- Aspirin to Prevent Blood Clots
- British Cardiac Patients Association
- British Heart Foundation
- Cholesterol
- Coronary Angiography
- Coronary Angioplasty
- Eat More Fruit and Vegetables
- Exercise for Health
- Healthy Eating
- Healthy Eating - A Summary
- Healthy Lifestyle - Five Choices
- Heart Disease - Prevention
- Heart UK
- How the Heart Works
- Smoking - Help to Stop with Bupropion
- Smoking - Nicotine Replacement Therapy

- Smoking - The Facts
- Smoking - Tips on Stopping

Shared decision making

- **A nitrate medicine such as isosorbide mononitrate (ISMN)** is commonly prescribed to reduce the number and severity of angina pains.
  - Nitrates work by 'opening up' blood vessels, which ease the pressure on the heart.
  - One is commonly used in addition to other anti-angina medicines such as a beta-blocker or a calcium-channel blocker.
  - The dose may be increased if the initial dose does not control the angina pains.
  - You may get a headache when you first start a nitrate. This usually eases if you continue taking it.
  - The dose timings aim to allow a few hours each day when your body is free of nitrate (usually in the night) to prevent 'tolerance'.
- **If side effects occur,** different medication may be tried.
- **Nicorandil** is another alternative anti-anginal medicine.
- Most people with angina also take a daily dose of aspirin, and carry some glyceryl trinitrate (GTN), which can be taken if an angina pain occurs.

Drug rationale

Drugs not included

- **Isosorbide dinitrate** is metabolised to isosorbide mononitrate (ISMN), and it is likely that its action depends on production of this metabolite. It requires more frequent dosing than does ISMN.
- **Modified-release nitrate preparations:** these are more expensive than standard tablets. However, they may be useful for people who find it difficult to comply with an asymmetric dosing regimen. They must be taken as a once-daily dose to maintain a nitrate-low period, and thus avoid tolerance.
- **Nitrate patches:** these are considerably more expensive than other nitrate formulations. High-dose patches are more effective than low-dose patches, but *must* be used with a patch-free interval. Continuous therapy is ineffective.

[BNF 44, 2002]

Drugs included

- **Aspirin, clopidogrel, and sublingual glyceryl trinitrate** (GTN) are available for repeat prescriptions in this scenario.
- **Nitrates: standard isosorbide mononitrate (ISMN) tablets** have been shown to control symptoms when used as an asymmetrically dosed twice-daily preparation, e.g. 8 am and 3 pm. This provides protection during the day, and a nitrate-low period overnight when symptoms are generally less frequent.
- **Potassium-channel activators: nicorandil** is a further alternative for symptom control when beta-blockers are contraindicated. As with nitrates, headache is a common adverse effect.

[BNF 44, 2002]

Prescriptions

Isosorbide mononitrate

Isosorbide mononitrate 10mg twice a day

- Age from 16 years onwards
- Isosorbide mononitrate10mg tab. Take one tablet at 8am and another at 3pm; supply 56 tablets; NHS Cost £1.13.

Isosorbide mononitrate 20mg twice a day

- Age from 16 years onwards
- Isosorbide mononitrate20mg tab. Take one tablet at 8am and another at 3pm; supply 56 tablets; NHS Cost £2.10.

Isosorbide mononitrate 30mg twice a day

- Age from 16 years onwards
- Isosorbide mononitrate10mg tab. Take three tablets 8am, and another three tablets at 3pm; supply 168 tablets; NHS Cost £3.39.

Isosorbide mononitrate 40mg twice a day

- Age from 16 years onwards
- Isosorbide mononitrate40mg tab. Take one tablet at 8am and another at 3pm; supply 56 tablets; NHS Cost £3.56.

Nicorandil

Nicorandil 5mg twice a day (if nitrate-headache a problem)

- Age from 16 years onwards
- Nicorandil 10mg tablets. Take half a tablet twice a d supply 60 tablets; NHS Cost £8.00.

Nicorandil 10mg twice a day

- Age from 16 years onwards
- Nicorandil 10mg tablets. Take one tablet twice a day supply 60 tablets; NHS Cost £8.00.

Nicorandil 20mg twice a day

- Age from 16 years onwards
- Nicorandil 20mg tablets. Take one tablet twice a day supply 60 tablets; NHS Cost £15.54.

Nicorandil 30mg twice a day

- Age from 16 years onwards
- Nicorandil 10mg tablets. Take three tablets twice a d supply 180 tablets; NHS Cost £24.54.

Antiplatelet (unless contraindicated) and GTN

Aspirin 75mg dispersible once a day

- Age from 16 years onwards
- Aspirin 75mg dispersible tabs. Take one tablet once a day; supply 28 tablets; NHS Cost £0.18; OTC Cost £1.00.

Clopidogrel 75mg once a day – only if intolerant of aspi

- Age from 16 years onwards
- Clopidogrel 75mg tablets. Take one tablet once a day supply 28 tablets; NHS Cost £35.31.

GTN 400mcg spray: spray once under the tongue whe required

- Age from 16 years onwards
- Glyceryl Trinitrate 400mcg spray. Spray one puff und the tongue when required for chest pain; supply 1 200 dose pump spray; NHS Cost £3.13; OTC Cost £5.78.

GTN 500mcg tabs: place 1 tab under the tongue when required

- Age from 16 years onwards
- Glyceryl Trinit 500mcg sl tabs. Place one tablet under the tongue when required for chest pain; supply 100 tablets; NHS Cost £1.06; OTC Cost £1.50.

Poor control on monotherapy

Which therapy?

- **Maximum tolerated doses of monotherapy should be tried before adding another drug.**
- **People taking beta-blockers:** *add* any calcium-channel blocker *except* verapamil. Only use diltiazem with caution (owing to the increased risk of bradycardia). If the person is intolerant of calcium-channel blockers, add a nitrate.
- **If the person is not on a beta-blocker** and there are no contraindications to this, prescribe a beta-blocker in preference to any other therapy.
  - Do not use verapamil with a beta-blocker (may precipitate heart failure).
  - Diltiazem can be considered but should be used with caution, owing to the risk of bradycardia.
- **People taking verapamil or diltiazem:** *add* a nitrate or nicorandil.
- **People taking nifedipine, felodipine, or amlodipine:** *add* a beta-blocker (unless this is contraindicated), *or* a nitrate, *or* nicorandil.
- **People taking a nitrate or nicorandil:** *add* a beta-blocker (unless this is contraindicated), *or* any calcium-channel blocker.
- The usual start doses for angina symptom control are offered in this scenario. Someone who is on one of these drugs for another indication may already be on a higher dose, or require a step up to a higher dose than is offered in this scenario. Higher-dose prescriptions can be found in the *Managing therapy* scenarios.
- **Continue regular aspirin** (or clopidogrel) and 'as required' glyceryl trinitrate (GTN).
- **Dyspepsia is common with aspirin and clopidogrel.** Persistent dyspepsia can be managed with acid-suppressing medication; see the separate PRODIGY guidance for *Dyspepsia — symptoms (uninvestigated by endoscopy)* for further information.
- **Manage cardiovascular risk factors** (e.g. smoking, blood pressure, and cholesterol).
- **Consider stopping hormone replacement therapy** (if applicable).

Factors affecting the choice of long-term treatments

- **Driving:** people taking nicorandil should not drive until it is established that their performance is unimpaired.
- **Asthma or a history of bronchospasm:** do not use beta-blockers (Committee on Safety of Medicines warning).
- **Severe peripheral vascular disease:** avoid beta-blockers.
- **Diabetes:** if using a beta-blocker, use atenolol or metoprolol (cardioselective). Avoid beta-blockers in people who experience frequent hypoglycaemia. Advise people that beta-blockers may slightly raise their blood glucose levels, and their response to hypoglycaemia may be delayed or symptoms of hypoglycaemia may not occur in the usual way.
- **Heart failure:** do not use verapamil. Avoid using diltiazem. Beta-blockers may be used in heart failure, but the licensed drugs and doses are different in the case of angina. See the separate PRODIGY guidance for *Heart failure* or *Prior myocardial infarction — prophylactic treatments.*
- **Closed-angle glaucoma:** do not use nitrates.

Practical prescribing points

For further information, please see the *Medicines Compendium* (www.medicines.org.uk) or the *British National Formulary* (www.bnf.org).

Beta-blockers

- **There is no significant increased risk of depressive symptoms** while on beta-blockers, and only a small increase in the risk of fatigue or sexual dysfunction.

Verapamil

- **Constipation is common.** Give advice on high-fibre diet with adequate fluid intake.

Follow-up advice

- Review within 1–4 weeks, depending on severity of symptoms and outstanding investigations.

Should I refer or investigate?

Refer?

Referral for a stress test, usually an exercise electrocardiogram (ECG) — if not already done

- **Use rapid access chest pain clinics, open access exercise testing, or cardiology outpatient services** (depending on local availability).
- **An exercise ECG** gives valuable *prognostic* information in people with a high likelihood of angina, and helps to identify people who warrant further investigation by angiography.
- **Refer all people with clinically certain angina.**
  - People referred to assess prognosis should have the test while taking their normal medication.
- **People should not be referred for an exercise ECG if:**
  - They are on maximal medical treatment and still have symptoms.
  - The diagnosis of coronary heart disease is unlikely.
  - They are physically incapable of taking the test.
  - They may have aortic stenosis or cardiomyopathy.
  - The results of an exercise ECG would not affect management.
- **Consider referring to a cardiologist someone who cannot have an exercise ECG.**

Referral to a cardiologist

- **It is important *not* to delay treatment while awaiting referral.**
- Note: not all people need to be referred, and some may not wish to be referred.

Factors that should prompt early referral to a cardiologist:

- **People who have had a previous myocardial infarction (MI), coronary artery bypass grafting, or percutaneous transluminal coronary angioplasty** and develop angina.
- **People who seem to have ECG evidence of a previous MI,** or other significant abnormality.
- **People who fail to respond to medical treatment.**
- **People who have an ejection systolic murmur** suggesting aortic stenosis.

People with the following symptoms should be considered for urgent referral:

- **Pain on minimal exertion**
- **Pain at rest** (which may occur at night)
- **Angina that seems to be progressing rapidly** despite increasing medical treatment

Further reasons to refer people to a cardiologist include:

- **To confirm or refute a diagnosis** with uncertain or atypical symptoms.
- **To advise on the management of an individual,** particularly where the person has not responded to treatment or risk factor modification.

- **The presence of several risk factors** or a strong family history.
- **The person's preference** for referral.
- **Problems with employment,** life insurance, or unacceptable interference with lifestyle.
- **Significant comorbidity** (e.g. diabetes).

Investigate?

- Ensure monitoring of cholesterol level is up-to-date.
- A resting 12-lead electrocardiogram (ECG) should be recorded in all people with suspected angina. A normal ECG does not exclude angina.

Patient information leaflets

The following PILs are available at www.prodigy.nhs.uk

- Angina
- Aspirin to Prevent Blood Clots
- British Cardiac Patients Association
- British Heart Foundation
- Cholesterol
- Coronary Angiography
- Coronary Angioplasty
- Eat More Fruit and Vegetables
- Exercise for Health
- Healthy Eating
- Healthy Eating - A Summary
- Healthy Lifestyle - Five Choices
- Heart Disease - Prevention
- Heart UK
- How the Heart Works
- Smoking - Help to Stop with Bupropion
- Smoking - Nicotine Replacement Therapy
- Smoking - The Facts
- Smoking - Tips on Stopping

Shared decision making

- Four groups of medicines are used to treat angina: **beta-blockers, calcium-channel blockers, nitrates, and potassium-channel activators.**
- If angina pains are not well controlled with one medicine, another from a different group can be added. This 'combination therapy' is often used.
- Some medicines suit some people better than others. So, different people end up with different combinations.
- **If you develop any side effects, don't suddenly stop the treatment** — see your doctor. Some side effects from each group include the following:
  - **Beta-blockers:** cool hands and feet, bad dreams, tiredness (and rarely, impotence)
  - **Calcium-channel blockers:** flushing, headaches, palpitations, and swelling around the ankles
  - **Nitrates:** headache when first started, but this usually eases if the medicine is continued
  - Potassium-channel activators: headache
- Most people with angina also take a daily dose of **aspirin,** and carry some **glyceryl trinitrate (GTN),** which can be taken if an angina pain occurs.

Drug rationale

Drugs not included

- **Enteric-coated aspirin:** enteric-coating is not offered, as there is no convincing evidence that this reduces toxicity at a dose of 75 mg [DTB, 1997].
- **Buccal glyceryl trinitrate (GTN) tablets** are effective, but much more expensive than sublingual tablets or sprays. They may be useful in unstable or crescendo angina.
- **Beta-blockers other than atenolol, metoprolol, and propranolol:** despite the large numbers of beta-blocker drugs listed in the *British National Formulary*, there is little to choose between them. People should be treated with the cheapest preparation that they can tolerate and comply with, and that controls their symptoms. Atenolol, metoprolol, and propranolol are inexpensive and meet nearly all clinical needs; other beta-blockers are therefore not offered. Modified-release preparations are expensive, so have not been included [DTB, 1996; North of England Guideline Development Group, 199
- **Modified-release preparations: verapamil** modified-release preparations should be used at maximum dose for angina (240 mg twice a day). This is a markedly higher dose than when using standard tablets, and is more expensive.
- **Dihydropyridine calcium-channel blockers other than nifedipine, felodipine, and amlodipine:** dihydropyridine calcium-channel blockers that are not licensed for use i angina, or less widely used, have not been included.
- **Nifedipine immediate-release capsules** are not recommended because their use is associated with large variations in blood pressure and reflex tachycardia [BN 44, 2002].
- **Isosorbide dinitrate** is metabolised to isosorbide mononitrate (ISMN), and it is likely that its action depends on production of this metabolite. It requires more frequent dosing than does ISMN [SIGN, 2001; BNF 44, 2002].
- **Modified-release nitrate preparations:** these are more expensive than standard tablets. However, they may be useful for someone who finds it difficult to comply with an asymmetric dosing regimen. They must be taken as once-daily dose to maintain a nitrate-low period, and thus avoid tolerance [BNF 44, 2002].
- **Nitrate patches:** these are considerably more expensive than other nitrate formulations. High-dose patches are more effective than low-dose patches, but *must* be used with a patch-free interval. Continuous therapy is ineffective [BNF 44, 2002].

Drugs included

- **Aspirin, clopidogrel, and sublingual glyceryl trinitrate (GTN)** are available for repeat prescriptions in this scenario.
- **Standard preparations of three inexpensive beta-blocke** (the non-selective propranolol, the beta-1-selective atenolol, and metoprolol) seem to meet nearly all clinic needs and have been included [DTB, 1996; North of England Guideline Development Group, 1999].
- **Rate-limiting calcium-channel blockers (standard tablets): verapamil and diltiazem** are included.
- **Modified-release preparations of rate-limiting calcium-channel blockers: diltiazem** is included by brand name a higher dosages because of potential problems caused by switching brands [BNF 44, 2002]. Both once a day and twice a day preparations are included, but are more expensive than standard tablets. The cheapest formulations in the BNF offering a range of strengths and dosages for use in angina are offered.
- **Dihydropyridine calcium-channel blockers — nifedipin felodipine, and amlodipine** have been included because they have been shown to provide symptom relief in angina, and are widely used in the UK [Heidenreich et a 1999].
- **Modified-release preparations of dihydropyridine calcium-channel blockers: nifedipine** is included by brand name because of potential problems caused by switching brands [BNF 44, 2002]. Both once a day and twice a day preparations are included. The cheapest

rmulations in the BNF offering a range of strengths ɪd dosages for use in angina are offered.

andard isosorbide mononitrate (ISMN) tablets have en shown to control symptoms when used as an ymmetrically dosed twice-daily preparation (e.g. 8 am ɪd 3 pm). This provides protection during the day, and nitrate-low period overnight when symptoms are nerally less frequent [SIGN, 2001].

icorandil is a further alternative for symptom control hen beta-blockers are contraindicated. Like nitrates, adache is a common adverse effect.

escriptions

tiplatelet (unless contraindicated) and GTN

irin 75mg dispersible once a day
- ge from 16 years onwards
- spirin 75mg dispersible tabs. Take one tablet once a ay; supply 28 tablets; NHS Cost £0.18; TC Cost £1.00.

oidogrel 75mg once a day – only if intolerant of aspirin
- ge from 16 years onwards
- lopidogrel 75mg tablets. Take one tablet once a day; ipply 28 tablets; NHS Cost £35.31.

N 400mcg spray: spray once under the tongue when ɪired
- ge from 16 years onwards
- lyceryl Trinitrate 400mcg spray. Spray one puff under e tongue when required for chest pain; supply 1 200-ose pump spray; NHS Cost £3.13; OTC Cost £5.78.

N 500mcg tabs: place 1 tab under the tongue when ɪired
- ge from 16 years onwards
- lyceryl Trinit 500mcg sl tabs. Place one tablet under e tongue when required for chest pain; supply 100 blets; NHS Cost £1.06; OTC Cost £1.50.

t choice: start beta-blocker

nolol 50mg once a day
- ge from 16 years onwards
- tenolol 50mg tablets. Take one tablet once a day; ipply 28 tablets; NHS Cost £0.85.

nolol 100mg once a day
- ge from 16 years onwards
- tenolol 100mg tablets. Take one tablet once a day; ipply 28 tablets; NHS Cost £0.98.

nolol 50mg twice a day
- ge from 16 years onwards
- tenolol 50mg tablets. Take one tablet twice a day; ipply 56 tablets; NHS Cost £1.70.

toprolol 50mg twice a day
- ge from 16 years onwards
- Metoprolol 50mg tablets. Take one tablet twice a day; ipply 56 tablets; NHS Cost £2.35.

toprolol 50mg three times a day
- ge from 16 years onwards
- Metoprolol 50mg tablets. Take one tablet three times a lay; supply 84 tablets; NHS Cost £3.52.

opranolol 40mg twice a day
- ge from 16 years onwards
- Propranolol 40mg tablets. Take one tablet twice a day; ipply 56 tablets; NHS Cost £1.30.

opranolol 40mg three times a day
- ge from 16 years onwards
- Propranolol 40mg tablets. Take one tablet three times a lay; supply 84 tablets; NHS Cost £1.95.

Alternative option: start verapamil or diltiazem

Verapamil 40mg three times a day
- Age from 16 years onwards
- Verapamil 40mg tablets. Take one tablet three times a day; supply 84 tablets; NHS Cost £1.61.

Verapamil 80mg three times a day
- Age from 16 years onwards
- Verapamil 80mg tablets. Take one tablet three times a day; supply 84 tablets; NHS Cost £2.10.

Diltiazem standard tablets 60mg twice a day (if elderly)
- Age from 60 years onwards
- Diltiazem HCl 60mg m/r tablets. Take one tablet twice a day; supply 56 tablets; NHS Cost £3.84.

Diltiazem standard tablets 60mg three times a day
- Age from 16 years onwards
- Diltiazem HCl 60mg m/r tablets. Take one tablet three times a day; supply 84 tablets; NHS Cost £5.76.

Diltiazem: Slozem 120mg once a day
- Age from 60 years onwards
- Slozem 120mg m/r capsules. Take one capsule once a day; supply 28 capsules; NHS Cost £7.00.

Diltiazem: Slozem 180mg once a day
- Age from 16 years onwards
- Slozem 180mg m/r capsules. Take one capsule once a day; supply 28 capsules; NHS Cost £7.80.

Diltiazem: Slozem 240mg once a day
- Age from 16 years onwards
- Slozem 240mg m/r capsules. Take one capsule once a day; supply 28 capsules; NHS Cost £8.20.

Diltiazem: Angitil SR 90mg twice a day
- Age from 16 years onwards
- Angitil SR 90mg capsules. Take one capsule twice a day; supply 56 capsules; NHS Cost £8.45.

Alternative choice: start dihydropyridine CCB

Nifedipine: Coracten XL 30mg each morning
- Age from 16 years onwards
- Coracten XL 30mg m/r capsules. Take one capsule each morning; supply 28 capsules; NHS Cost £6.73.

Nifedipine: Cardilate MR 10mg twice a day
- Age from 16 years onwards
- Cardilate MR 10mg m/r tablets. Take one tablet twice a day; supply 56 tablets; NHS Cost £4.97.

Felodipine 5mg m/r each morning
- Age from 16 years onwards
- Felodipine 5mg m/r tablets. Take one tablet each morning; supply 28 tablets; NHS Cost £8.12.

Amlodipine 5mg once a day
- Age from 16 years onwards
- Amlodipine 5mg tablets. Take one tablet once a day; supply 28 tablets; NHS Cost £11.85.

Alternative choice: start nitrate or nicorandil

Isosorbide mononitrate 10mg twice a day (if nitrate-naive)
- Age from 16 years onwards
- Isosorbide mononitrate10mg tab. Take one tablet at 8am and another at 3pm; supply 56 tablets; NHS Cost £1.13.

Isosorbide mononitrate 20mg twice a day
- Age from 16 years onwards
- Isosorbide mononitrate20mg tab. Take one tablet at 8am and another at 3pm; supply 56 tablets; NHS Cost £2.10.

Nicorandil 5mg twice a day (if nitrate-headache a problem)
- Age from 16 years onwards
- Nicorandil 10mg tablets. Take half a tablet twice a day; supply 60 tablets; NHS Cost £8.00.

Nicorandil 10mg twice a day
- Age from 16 years onwards
- Nicorandil 10mg tablets. Take one tablet twice a day; supply 60 tablets; NHS Cost £8.00.

Advice if poor control on dual therapy

Which therapy?

- **Maximum tolerated doses of the two anti-anginal medications should be tried** (*for prescriptions, refer to relevant drug-group scenarios*).
- **There is no evidence that addition of a third drug improves symptom control.**
- Someone whose symptoms are uncontrolled on maximal medical therapy should be referred to a cardiologist (for angiography).
- If a third drug is introduced, for instance while awaiting an outpatient appointment, its effects should be monitored, and if it has no effect it should be stopped.

Practical prescribing points

For further information, please see the *Medicines Compendium* (www.medicines.org.uk) or the *British National Formulary* (www.bnf.org).

Should I refer or investigate?

Refer?

Refer someone whose symptoms are uncontrolled on maximum medical therapy to a cardiologist (usually at maximum tolerated doses of two drugs).

Several other factors should prompt early referral to a cardiologist:

- **People who have had a previous myocardial infarction (MI), coronary artery bypass grafting, or percutaneous transluminal coronary angioplasty and develop angina.**
- **People who seem to have electrocardiogram (ECG) evidence of a previous MI,** or other significant abnormality.
- **People who have an ejection systolic murmur** suggesting aortic stenosis.
- **People identified as having poor prognosis on exercise tolerance testing:** angiography is usually indicated.

People with the following symptoms should be considered for urgent referral:

- **Pain on minimal exertion**
- **Pain at rest** (which may occur at night)
- **Angina that seems to be progressing rapidly** despite increasing medical treatment

Patient information leaflets

The following PILs are available at www.prodigy.nhs.uk

- Angina
- Aspirin to Prevent Blood Clots
- British Cardiac Patients Association
- British Heart Foundation
- Cardiac Catheterisation
- Cholesterol
- Coronary Angiography
- Coronary Angioplasty
- Eat More Fruit and Vegetables
- Exercise for Health
- Healthy Eating
- Healthy Eating - A Summary
- Healthy Lifestyle - Five Choices
- Heart Disease - Prevention
- Heart UK
- How the Heart Works
- Smoking - Help to Stop with Bupropion
- Smoking - Nicotine Replacement Therapy
- Smoking - The Facts
- Smoking - Tips on Stopping

Shared decision making

- **Some people still have regular angina pains despite taking the full dose of medication.**
- **You may need further investigation** by a heart special
- **Angiography** may be advised. This involves injecting dye into the blood vessels of the heart. Special X-ray pictures are then taken, which show where the arterie are narrowed.
- Possible options for further treatment include the following.
  - **Percutaneous transluminal coronary angioplasty (PTCA)** involves a tiny balloon being blown up ins a narrowed part of an artery. This opens it wide ag Only certain people may benefit, as only arteries wi small sections that are narrowed can be treated this way.
  - **Coronary artery bypass graft** (CABG) involves an operation to bypass narrow arteries with segments healthy blood vessels taken from other parts of the body. Not everyone with angina is suitable for this, it depends on where the narrowed arteries are.
- **Both of these treatments have a small risk of serious problems.**

Drug rationale

- There are no prescriptions offered in this scenario.

Extended Information

Background information

- What is it? p.102
- How common is it? p.102
- How do I know my patient has it? p.103
- What else might it be? p.103
- Complications and prognosis p.103

What is it?

Angina is a *symptom*, not a diagnosis.

- **Angina pectoris describes the classic symptom of ches pain,** and is due to transient myocardial ischaemia. Episodes of angina are typically caused by exertion or emotion, and are relieved by rest.
- **Coronary artery disease** is the main cause. Rarely, angina is caused by valve disease (e.g. aortic stenosis), hypertrophic obstructive cardiomyopathy, hypertensi heart disease, hypoperfusion from arrhythmias, arteri or anaemia.

[SIGN, 2001]

How common is it?

- **About 1.2 million people** in the UK have angina.
- **The incidence of angina is higher in men** than in wom and increases with age. Studies suggest that about 9% men and 5% of women aged 55–64, and about 14% c men and 8% of women aged 65–74, have or have had angina.

ɔr each 1000 people, a practice can expect to have ɔout 17 consulting with coronary heart disease (CHD) ·r year; 12 of these will have angina.

HD is the most common cause of death in the UK: in ɔ01, 120,000 people died from CHD in England and 'ales. This accounts for about one in four deaths in .en, and one in six deaths in women.

HD is the most common cause of *premature* death in .e UK: of the 120,000 deaths from CHD in 2001, 3,000 occurred in people aged less than 75 years. These :counted for 23% of premature deaths in men, and 4% of premature deaths in women.

outh Asian people living in the UK have higher remature death rates from CHD than do the general opulation. The rate is 46% higher for men, and 51% igher for women.

mong Black Caribbean people, by contrast, CHD eath rates are about 25–50% lower than in the general opulation.

he premature death rate from CHD is also different etween social groups: it is 58% higher for male manual orkers, such as builders and cleaners, than it is for non-ıanual workers, such as doctors and lawyers. The remature death rate from CHD is twice as high for omen who are manual workers than for women who re not manual workers.

H, 2000; Primatesta and Brookes, 2001; British Heart :ndation, 2003]

w do I know my patient has it?

ngina is a symptom, not a diagnosis. It is characterized y heaviness in the centre of the chest induced by effort r emotion.

People often describe angina as a great weight on their chest or as squeezing, crushing, gripping, or a vice-like grip. The pain is only rarely localized — this is usually muscular chest-wall pain.

It is typically a central and symmetrical pain, which may be described as 'discomfort'. However, it can affect the neck and jaw, or down the arms.

Exertional breathlessness may also characterize angina. Sometimes this is the only symptom and there is no pain.

Chest pain is more likely to be due to coronary heart disease (CHD) in people with two or more existing risk actors for CHD, e.g. smoker, obese, family history of ɔremature CHD, hyperlipidaemia, hypertension, or liabetes.

There are also many non-cardiac causes of chest pain, uch as gastro-oesophageal reflux, musculoskeletal pain, ɔr anxiety.

The 'diagnosis' of CHD is based on the clinical mpression from a careful history and examination.

f a diagnosis of CHD is uncertain (e.g. pain occurs at est; pain tends to last longer than 5 minutes; or exertion ıas a variable effect on chest pain), it is important to ıvoid giving people the impression that they have CHD ıntil this is confirmed by further investigations. It can be lifficult to persuade people with proven non-cardiac :hest pain that they do not have CHD in this situation Bass and Mayou, 2002].

istory

Precipitants of anginal attacks should be identified and liscussed so that the person can use short-acting nitrates ıppropriately to prevent anginal pain (GPP).

Precipitants include exertion, particularly climbing stairs ɔr an incline; emotion, especially anger, anxiety, or :xcitement; reduced exercise tolerance after a large meal, ıs cardiac output rises by 20%; or cold, windy weather.

- **Assessment of the intensity and length of physical activity** that precipitates angina
- **Stability** of symptoms
- **Smoking** history
- **Basic dietary** assessment
- **Alcohol** intake
- **Drug** history
- **Family** history

Note: family history of premature CHD has several 'operational' definitions. For example:

- The Joint British Recommendations use 'CHD, or other atherosclerotic disease, in a male first-degree relative before the age of 55 years, or in a female first-degree relative before the age of 65 years' [Wood et al, 1998].
- The Simon Broome Register uses 'family history of myocardial infarction under 60 years old in a first-degree relative or under 50 years old in a second-degree relative' [Simon Broome Register Group, 1999].

Examination

- **Weight and height** (to allow calculation of body mass index [BMI]), or waist-to-hip ratio
- **Blood pressure**
- **Pulse** rate and rhythm
- **Presence of murmurs,** especially aortic stenosis (although *very severe* aortic stenosis may not cause a murmur)
- **Evidence of hyperlipidaemia,** e.g. xanthelasma, tendon xanthomata
- **Evidence of vascular disease**
- **Evidence of anaemia**

A resting 12-lead electrocardiogram (ECG) should be recorded in all people with suspected angina.

[British Heart Foundation, 2000; SIGN, 2001]

What else might it be?

Cardiac causes of chest pain

- Myocardial infarction
- Prinzmetal's angina
- An arrhythmia
- Pericardial pain

Non-cardiac causes of chest pain

- Oesophageal disorders (e.g. gastro-oesophageal reflux, oesophageal dysmotility)
- Musculoskeletal pain
- Referred pain from thoracic spine
- Psychological (e.g. anxiety, panic attacks, depression)
- Acute cholecystitis
- Pleural pain

Note: someone with proven cardiac chest pain can also experience non-cardiac chest pain, and often interprets the non-cardiac pains as symptoms of heart disease. It is important to distinguish between the two causes early on in order to reduce levels of distress, and avoid inappropriate use of medical treatments.

[DH, 2000; SIGN, 2001; Bass and Mayou, 2002]

Complications and prognosis

Complications

- Unstable angina
- Myocardial infarction
- Sudden death from arrhythmias

Prognosis

- **Few studies have followed-up angina cases** arising in the population.
- **The British Regional Heart Study** found that of 157 men aged 42–65 who were diagnosed with angina between

1978 and 1985 and had no history of heart attack, 89% were alive 5 years after the diagnosis, and 73% were alive at 10 years. Of men of the same age without any evidence of coronary heart disease (CHD), 96% survived for 5 years and 91% for 10 years [British Heart Foundation, 2003].

Management issues

- How might angina affect the person's lifestyle? p.104
- Diagnosis and investigations p.104
- Referral to a cardiologist p.104
- Managing risk factors p.105
- Immediate relief of symptoms p.106
- Long-term prevention of symptoms p.106
- Medicines management p.106
- The place of hormone replacement therapy (HRT) in the management of angina p.107
- Surgical treatment p.107

How might angina affect the person's lifestyle?

- **Driving:** holders of an ordinary driving licence who are diagnosed as suffering from angina may still drive, provided that their symptoms are controlled. There is no need to notify the Driver and Vehicle Licensing Agency (DVLA). Motor insurance companies must be notified — otherwise the insurance policy may be invalid.
- **Occupation:** a person's occupation may be affected by angina. People who operate heavy machinery may need to alter their work practices or change their occupation. Holders of Large Goods Vehicle (LGV) and Passenger Carrying Vehicle (PCV) licences should be advised to notify the DVLA and to cease driving their vehicles. Re-licensing may be permitted when they have been free from angina for at least 6 weeks, provided that the DVLA requirements for exercise testing can be met, and that there is no other disqualifying condition. For further information, see the DVLA website at www.dvla.gov.uk/at_a_glance/content.htm.
- **Sex:** most people can continue to enjoy sex. People who can briskly climb up and down two flights of stairs without any angina symptoms do not usually find that sex precipitates angina. (Someone taking nitrates or nicorandil should not take sildenafil [Viagra], because of additive hypotensive effects.)
- **Travel:** in general, those with stable angina who can climb 12 stairs and walk 50 metres on the level without severe breathlessness and without developing angina are fit to fly as passengers.

[DH, 2001; British Heart Foundation, 2002a; DVLA, 2003]

Diagnosis and investigations

- **Check fasting full lipid profile (C).**
- **Check blood pressure (B).**
- **Check haemoglobin and fasting blood glucose** to exclude anaemia and diabetes **(GPP).**
- **Check thyroid function tests.**
- **A resting 12-lead electrocardiogram (ECG)** should be recorded in anyone with suspected angina **(B).**
  - **A normal ECG does not exclude angina.** A review of 109 people with recent onset chest pain who had normal ECGs found that 39% continued to experience cardiac pain, and 90% of those who underwent angiography showed significant coronary artery disease [Norell et al, 1992].
  - **An abnormal ECG supports a diagnosis of angina** and identifies someone who may have a worse prognosis. Consider the person for urgent referral to a cardiologist.
- **Therapeutic response to sublingual glyceryl trinitrate (GTN)** can be used to *assist* in the 'diagnosis' of angi[na]. However, it does also relieve oesophageal pain.

Estimation of cardiovascular risk

- **The 'diagnosis' of angina implies coronary artery disease,** and so all people with *confirmed* angina are considered to have a cardiovascular risk of more tha[n] 30% over 10 years. There is, therefore, no need to us[e a] risk calculator to estimate cardiovascular risk for the[m].
- **People with diabetes or hyperlipidaemia** are at increa[sed] risk.
- **An exercise ECG** gives valuable *prognostic* informati[on] in someone with a high likelihood of angina, and hel[ps] to identify a person who warrants further investigati[on] by angiography.
  - People with angina should be referred for exercise testing for risk stratification **(B).**
  - People referred to assess prognosis should have the[ir test] while taking their normal medication **(B).**
- **The risks of serious complications from an exercise E[CG]** (ventricular fibrillation, myocardial infarction [MI]) i[n a] population known to have ischaemic heart disease ar[e of] the order of 2–4 per 1000 tests; deaths occur at a rat[e of] 1–5 per 10,000 tests.
- **Explain exercise testing and its implications** so that th[e] person has the opportunity of declining the test **(GPP)**.
- **People should not be referred for an exercise ECG if (GPP):**
  - They are on maximal medical treatment and still ha[ve] symptoms.
  - The diagnosis of coronary heart disease (CHD) is unlikely.
  - They are physically incapable of taking the test.
  - They may have aortic stenosis or cardiomyopathy.
  - The results of the exercise ECG would not affect management.
- **Consider referring to a cardiologist** someone who can[not] have an exercise ECG.

[DH, 2000; SIGN, 2001]

Referral to a cardiologist

- **It is important *not* to delay treatment** while awaiting referral **(GPP).**
- **Not all people need to be referred,** and some may not wish to be referred.
- Factors that should prompt early referral to a cardiologist:
  - **The person has had a previous MI,** coronary artery bypass graft (CABG), or percutaneous transluminal coronary angioplasty (PTCA), and has developed angina.
  - **The person seems to have ECG evidence of a previo[us] MI,** or other significant abnormality.
  - **The person fails to respond to medical treatment.**
  - **The person has an ejection systolic murmur** suggest[ing] aortic stenosis.
- People with the following symptoms should be considered for urgent referral:
  - **Pain on minimal exertion**
  - **Pain at rest** (which may occur at night)
  - **Angina that seems to be progressing rapidly** despite increasing medical treatment
- Further reasons to refer people to a cardiologist inclu[de]:
  - **To confirm or refute a diagnosis** with uncertain or atypical symptoms.
  - **To advise on the management of an individual,** particularly where the person has not responded to treatment or to modification of the risk factors.

- The presence of several risk factors or a strong family history.
- The person's preference for referral.
- Problems with employment, life insurance, or unacceptable interference with lifestyle.
- Significant comorbidity (e.g. diabetes).

[DH, 2000; SIGN, 2001]

Managing risk factors

Lifestyle interventions

Lifestyle interventions are covered briefly below. For further information see the separate PRODIGY guidance *Cardiovascular risk — identification and management*.

- **Lifestyle measures** should continue beyond three months, even if pharmacological treatment is also required (**GPP**).
- **Smoking:** anyone with angina who smokes should be advised to stop (**B**). Smokers have a higher incidence of ischaemic heart disease, and a greater risk of dying from it. The greater the number of cigarettes smoked, the greater the risk. Nicotine replacement therapy is recommended as part of a smoking cessation programme in people with angina (**B**). See the separate PRODIGY guidance *Smoking cessation* for further information.
- **Physical activity, diet management, weight, and alcohol consumption:** personalized advice and information should be given about how to alter these modifiable risk factors.
- **People with angina should modify their diet** in line with healthy eating advice (**B**).
  - Increase fruit and vegetable consumption to five portions per day.
  - Increase fish consumption, including at least one portion of oily fish per week.
  - Decrease total fat consumption, increasing the proportion of monounsaturated and non-hydrogenated polyunsaturated fat.
  - Increase starch food intake and reduce sugary food intake.
- **Encourage all obese and overweight people to lose weight** towards a body mass index (BMI) less than 25 (**C**). See the separate PRODIGY guidance *Obesity* for more information.
- **Encourage all people with angina to increase their aerobic exercise levels** within the limits set by their symptoms (**B**). Actively involve people in decisions about their exercise levels in order to improve perseverance (**B**).
- **Encourage people to limit their alcohol consumption** to three units per day for men, and two units per day for women (**B**).
- **Give education about heart attacks,** and, should one develop, instructions to seek help rapidly by phoning '999' (**C**).
- **Primary-care teams should take account of people's ethnicity** when giving advice:
  - South Asian men living in the UK have a 46% *higher* premature death rate from CHD than in the general population. The rate is 51% higher for South Asian women.
  - By contrast, CHD death rates are about 25–50% *lower* among Black Caribbean people than in the general population.

Therapeutic interventions

- **Give low-dose aspirin (75 mg daily)** unless contraindicated (**A**). Aspirin reduces the risk of MI, stroke, or vascular deaths by about 30%.
- **Clopidogrel** is an alternative for someone hypersensitive to aspirin (i.e. for whom aspirin induces angio-oedema or bronchospasm) (**A**). This is an off-licence use of clopidogrel.
- **Begin cholesterol reduction for someone with a baseline serum total cholesterol of more than 5 mmol/l,** or a serum low-density lipoprotein (LDL) cholesterol of more than 3 mmol/l (**A**). Recommend dietary measures, and start a statin if required. Re-check non-fasting total cholesterol after 6–12 weeks (**C**). Aim to lower serum total cholesterol below 5 mmol/l or by 20–25% of baseline, whichever would result in the lower level. Aim to lower serum LDL cholesterol below 3 mmol/l or by 30% of baseline, whichever would result in the lower level. See the separate PRODIGY guidance *Hyperlipidaemia* for more information.
- **There is a case for lowering lipid levels in people with established CHD,** whatever their baseline lipid level. The Heart Protection Study recently found that lowering lipid levels from 4 mmol/l to 3 mmol/l reduced the risk of CHD by about 25% [Heart Protection Study Collaborative Group, 2002]. This is close to the 30% reduction in cardiovascular risk achieved by previous studies, all of which had higher baseline cholesterol levels (generally between 5.5 mmol/l and 7 mmol/l) [LaRosa et al, 1999].
- The findings of the Heart Protection Study are not reflected in the NSF for CHD and NICE guidance on prior myocardial infarction. There are significant financial implications of implementing this policy. Consider seeking local primary care trust (PCT) advice.
- **Prescribe an ACE inhibitor for someone with left ventricular dysfunction** (as assessed by echocardiography). See the separate PRODIGY guidance for *Heart failure*.
- **Give beta-blockers and ACE inhibitors to people who have had a MI.** See the separate PRODIGY guidance for *Prior myocardial infarction — prophylactic treatments*.
- **Prescribe warfarin (or aspirin) for someone over 60 years old who also has atrial fibrillation.** Note: the final choice will depend on the individual's overall risk of stroke. See the separate PRODIGY guidance for *Atrial fibrillation* for further advice about deciding on antithrombotic treatment in atrial fibrillation.

Management of coexisting disease

- **Diabetes:** aim for tight control of blood glucose (**B**), and rigorous control of blood pressure (see Table 1).
- **Hypertension:** all people with angina should have their blood pressure assessed and managed (**B**). Aim to achieve the British Hypertension Society target for blood pressure — 140/85, except for people with diabetes, whose target is 140/80. For details see the separate PRODIGY guidance for *Hypertension* and Table 1.

[DH, 2000]

Table 1: British Hypertension Society targets for blood pressure.

	Clinic BP		Mean daytime ABPM or home BP	
	No diabetes	Diabetes	No diabetes	Diabetes
Optimal BP	<140/85	<140/80	<130/80	<130/75
Audit standard	<150/90	<140/85	<140/85	<140/80

BP = blood pressure. ABPM = ambulatory blood pressure monitoring

Immediate relief of symptoms

- **Sublingual GTN** can be used to abort attacks or to provide a short period of prophylaxis while undertaking activities likely to precipitate an angina attack. People should be advised to seek urgent medical help if the pain persists after three doses over 15 minutes (**GPP**).
- **Response to GTN does not automatically confirm that the person has angina** — some people with non-cardiac chest pain will have a placebo response to GTN.

Long-term prevention of symptoms

- **A beta-blocker is the preferred treatment** when regular symptom control is required (unless contraindicated) (B).
- **People receiving beta-blockers (either singly or in combination therapy) benefited equally or significantly more** in terms of anginal relief than did people on alternative monotherapies [Heidenreich et al, 1999].
- **Warn the person not to stop beta-blockers suddenly or to allow them to run out** (B). Acute withdrawal of beta-blockers has been associated with an increase in coronary events in the months after stopping treatment in hypertensive people.
- **There is no clear choice of treatment when a beta-blocker cannot be taken. Options include** a rate-limiting calcium-channel blocker (verapamil or diltiazem); a long-acting dihydropyridine calcium-channel blocker (e.g. modified-release nifedipine); a nitrate; or a potassium-channel activator (C).
- **Short-acting dihydropyridines** can cause tachycardia in some people, and should be avoided.

Dual therapy

- **If symptom control is poor when the person is receiving maximum tolerated monotherapy, try dual therapy.**
- **For someone taking a beta-blocker,** the recommended choices of combination therapy (provided that maximal tolerated monotherapy does not control symptoms) are:
  - *Add* a long-acting dihydropyridine (e.g. modified-release nifedipine). Diltiazem can be considered for use with a beta-blocker, but should be used with caution owing to the increased risk of bradycardia. Do not use verapamil with a beta-blocker — as well as risking bradycardia, it may also precipitate heart failure.
  - *Add* isosorbide mononitrate (ISMN) or a potassium-channel activator. These combinations are recommended when the person is intolerant of long-acting dihydropyridines or diltiazem.
- **For someone not on a beta-blocker** and for whom there is no contraindication to this, prescribe a beta-blocker in preference to any other therapy.
- **When a beta-blocker is contraindicated or not tolerated,** the recommended options for combination therapy (provided that maximal tolerated monotherapy does not control symptoms) are different.
  - For someone taking verapamil or another calcium-channel blocker: *add* ISMN or a potassium-channel activator.
  - For someone taking a nitrate: *add* a calcium-channel blocker or a potassium-channel activator.
- **There is no evidence that addition of a third drug improves symptom control.**

[North of England Guideline Development Group, 1999; DH, 2000; SIGN, 2001]

Supporting evidence

- **Beta-blockers:** short-term studies of beta-blocker therapy have found that, in terms of anginal relief, they provided equal or significantly more benefit when compared with alternative monotherapies [Freemantle et al, 1999; Heidenreich et al, 1999].
- **There are no long-term studies** examining the effect of beta-blockers (or calcium-channel blockers, or nitrates on mortality and morbidity in stable angina. However there is supporting evidence from post-MI trials that beta-blockers are of benefit. They have also been show to reduce cardiovascular mortality and morbidity in high-risk people [SIGN, 2001]. Beta-blockers are therefore the preferred initial treatment for long-term symptom control (unless they are contraindicated).
- **Calcium-channel blockers:** a meta-analysis of calcium-channel blockers and beta-blockers found outcomes similar to those for beta-blockers, but a similar or raise level of adverse events [Heidenreich et al, 1999].
- **Short-acting dihydropyridine calcium-channel blocker** (e.g. immediate-release nifedipine capsules) can cause reflex tachycardia in some people [SIGN, 2001]. Verapamil and diltiazem are rate limiting and do not cause this effect. They are often considered to be a 'saf alternative for this reason.
- **Nitrates:** there are too few short-term trials comparing nitrates with calcium-channel blockers or beta-blocker to draw firm conclusions about their relative efficacy [Heidenreich et al, 1999]. Oral nitrates can be used as monotherapy, provided they are used in a way that avoids nitrate tolerance (e.g. in an eccentric dosage) (A
- **Potassium-channel activators: nicorandil** is a further alternative for symptom control when beta-blockers ar contraindicated.
- **The IONA study examined the use of nicorandil as ad on therapy** compared to placebo. The primary end-poi (CHD death, non-fatal MI, or unplanned hospital admission for cardiac chest pain) was statistically significant, but the main benefit was from a reduction i unplanned hospital admission. There was no difference in the secondary composite end-point of CHD death ar non-fatal MI [IONA Study Group, 2002; MeReC, 2002].

Medicines management

Antiplatelet drugs

- **Aspirin** often causes dyspepsia. Increasing doses of aspirin are associated with greater risks of gastrointestinal toxicity (e.g. ulceration, bleeding, and perforation). People who experience dyspepsia with aspirin should be co-prescribed an acid-suppressing drug. See *Dyspepsia – symptoms (uninvestigated by endoscopy)* guidance. Presence of dyspepsia is not a go guide to severity of adverse effects: many people who experience perforations do not have prior aspirin-induced dyspepsia.
- **There is also no robust evidence that different formulations are associated with alterations in risk** [CSM, 2002b]. Enteric-coated preparations are also more expensive than standard preparations of aspirin.
- A recent retrospective study found that people with cardiovascular disease who took ibuprofen as well as low-dose aspirin had a higher risk of all-cause mortality than those who only took low-dose aspirin (adjusted hazard ratio 1.93, 95% CI 1.3-2.87) [MacDonald and Wei, 2003]. There was no difference in mortality for people taking diclofenac plus low-dose aspirin, or another nonsteroidal anti-inflammatory drug (NSAID) plus low-dose aspirin. (Note: cyclo-oxygenase (COX)-2 selective NSAIDs selective NSAIDs were not included i this study.)
- The results of this study should be viewed with caution as it was not able to control for confounding factors, ar only small numbers of people were taking ibuprofen or diclofenac (303). However, until more evidence becom available, it would seem prudent to follow the advice o

the British Heart Foundation and avoid ibuprofen in people taking low-dose aspirin [British Heart Foundation, 2002b]. Diclofenac is probably a better option if an NSAID is required.

Clopidogrel is an alternative for someone hypersensitive to aspirin (i.e. for whom aspirin induces angio-oedema or bronchospasm). This is an off-licence use of clopidogrel. Dyspepsia is also a common adverse effect of clopidogrel.

Beta-blockers

Compared with calcium-channel blockers, beta-blockers are probably better tolerated and associated with fewer adverse effects [Heidenreich et al, 1999].

Beta-blockers can precipitate bronchospasm that is unresponsive to beta-2 agonists in someone with asthma, or with chronic obstructive pulmonary disease that has an asthmatic component. Beta-blockers should be avoided in such a case.

Advise someone with diabetes that beta-blockers may slightly raise blood glucose levels. This may delay a response to hypoglycaemia, or symptoms of hypoglycaemia may not occur in the usual way. Cardioselective beta-blockers (e.g. atenolol or metoprolol) may be preferable. Avoid beta-blockers for someone who experiences frequent hypoglycaemia [BNF 44, 2002].

Sleep disturbance or nightmares are less likely with a water-soluble beta-blocker such as atenolol, as it is less likely to cross the blood-brain barrier [BNF 44, 2002].

A recent meta-analysis highlighted that there is no significant increased risk of depressive symptoms while taking beta-blockers, and only a small increase in the risk of fatigue or sexual dysfunction [Ko et al, 2002].

Assess objective signs of peripheral vascular disease in someone who experiences cold extremities with beta-blockers.

Calcium-channel blockers

Dizziness, facial flushing, ankle oedema, and postural hypotension are common adverse effects [BNF 44, 2002] that generally reduce in severity on continued treatment. Ankle oedema is often persistent. Diuretics should not be prescribed, as they only partially reduce ankle oedema caused by calcium-channel blockers.

Verapamil commonly causes constipation. Advise the person to eat more fibre (fruit, vegetables, cereals, wholemeal bread, etc); to try to drink at least 12 cups (8 glasses or mugs) of liquid a day; but to avoid drinks with a high caffeine-content as these may make constipation worse.

Both verapamil and diltiazem can cause bradycardia. Verapamil should not be used with a beta-blocker owing to the risk of reduced cardiac output and heart failure. Diltiazem has a smaller negative inotropic effect than verapamil. It may be used with a beta-blocker, provided that they do not cause bradycardia.

Nifedipine is generally safe to use in heart failure, as any negative inotropic effect is offset by a reduction in left ventricular work. Amlodipine and felodipine do not produce clinical deterioration in heart failure [BNF 44, 2002].

Nitrates

- **The most common adverse effects** are a throbbing headache, flushing, dizziness, and postural hypotension. Headache and flushing usually reduce in severity after a few days [BNF 44, 2002].
- **Nitrate tolerance:** if nitrates are given continuously over 24 hours, their anti-anginal effects are quickly lost. An asymmetric regimen that allows nitrate levels to fall to low concentrations for several hours overnight usually avoids tolerance.
- **Standard tablets of ISMN** have been shown to reduce tolerance when given twice a day using an asymmetric dosing interval (e.g. at 8 am and 3 pm). This allows a nitrate-low period of 6–8 hours. Isosorbide dinitrate requires more frequent dosing than does ISMN, making it more challenging to take as an asymmetric dosing regimen.
- **A modified-release preparation** may be useful for someone who finds it difficult to comply with an asymmetric dosing regimen. It must be taken as a once-daily dose to maintain a nitrate-low period, and thus avoid tolerance [BNF 44, 2002].
- **Patches:** high-dose patches are more effective than low-dose patches, but *must* be used with a patch-free interval. Continuous therapy is ineffective [BNF 44, 2002].

Potassium-channel activators

- **As with nitrates, headache, flushing, and dizziness are common adverse effects.** Gastrointestinal adverse effects are also common. People taking nicorandil should not drive until it is established that their performance is unimpaired. People taking nitrates or nicorandil should not take sildenafil (Viagra) because of additive hypotensive effects.

The place of hormone replacement therapy (HRT) in the management of angina

- **HRT has *not* been shown to be beneficial in preventing CHD** in women both with and without CHD. In fact, studies have shown a slight tendency to *increased rates* of CHD in the 1–2 years of treatment with HRT.
- **HRT should not be initiated for prevention of CHD,** and consideration should be given to stopping HRT after any cardiovascular disease event.

[CSM, 2002a]

Surgical treatment

- **A person identified as having poor prognosis** on exercise tolerance testing or with poorly controlled symptoms when receiving maximal medical treatment should be assessed for surgical treatment.
- **Coronary artery bypass grafting** (CABG) can provide relief from angina in 60–90% of people after 1 year. However, it is a major operation.
- **Percutaneous transluminal coronary angioplasty** (PTCA), or balloon angioplasty, is a technique in which a balloon is inflated in the lumen of the narrowed artery. This cracks the atheromatous plaque responsible for the narrowing. When the balloon is removed, the plaque retracts where it has split, leaving a wider lumen in the artery. Unfortunately, restenosis occurs within 6 months in about 20% of people, requiring re-intervention.
- **Coronary artery stents are now used routinely.** The stent is a metal mesh that is placed in the artery after PTCA to keep the lumen open. Stents reduce the need for repeat vascularization after PTCA. When people are eligible for both PTCA and CABG, PTCA with a stent is preferred, as it does not require an operation and recovery time is quicker.
- **Note: the term percutaneous coronary intervention (PCI) is now often used** to refer to both PTCAs alone, and PTCAs with a stent.
- **CABG is still the treatment of choice** in someone with disease of the left main coronary artery; multi-vessel disease involving the proximal left anterior descending artery; or three-vessel disease (especially if there is impaired left ventricular systolic function), as survival is improved.

[Meads et al, 2000; NICE, 2002]

References

NHS staff in England can link, free of charge, from references to full text journals by clicking on [Full text] on the PRODIGY website.

1. Bass, C. and Mayou, R. (2002) ABC of psychological medicine: chest pain. *British Medical Journal* **325**(7364), 588–591. [Full text]
2. BNF 44 (2002) *British National Formulary*. 44th edn. London: British Medical Association and Royal Pharmaceutical Society of Great Britain.
3. British Heart Foundation (2000) *Chest pain – is it angina?* Factfile 5/2000. British Heart Foundation. www.bhf.org.uk [Accessed: 11/11/2002].
4. British Heart Foundation (2002a) *Angina: information for people with angina, and for their family and friends*. Heart Information Series Number 6. British Heart Foundation. www.bhf.org.uk [Accessed: 12/12/2002].
5. British Heart Foundation (2002b) *Aspirin and ibuprofen*. Factfile 11/2002. British Heart Foundation. www.bhf.org.uk [Accessed: 01/12/2002].
6. British Heart Foundation (2003) *Coronary heart disease statistics 2003*. British Heart Foundation. www.heartstats.org//datapage.asp?id=1652 [Accessed: 07/02/2003].
7. CSM (2002a) New product information for hormone replacement therapy. *Current Problems in Pharmacovigilance* **28**(April), 1–2.
8. CSM (2002b) Non-steroidal anti-inflammatory drugs (NSAIDs) and gastrointestinal (GI) safety. *Current Problems in Pharmacovigilance* **28**(Apr), 5.
9. DH (2000) *National service framework for coronary heart disease*. Department of Health. www.dh.gov.uk [Accessed: 15/07/2005]. [Full text]
10. DH (2001) *Health information for overseas travel*. Department of Health. www.dh.gov.uk [Accessed: 03/06/2004]. [Full text]
11. DTB (1996) Too many beta-blockers. *Drug & Therapeutics Bulletin* **34**(7), 49–52.
12. DTB (1997) Which prophylactic aspirin? *Drug & Therapeutics Bulletin* **35**(1), 7–8. [Full text]
13. DVLA (2003) *At a glance guide to current medical standards of fitness to drive*. Drivers Medical Group, Driver and Vehicle Licensing Authority. www.dvla.gov.uk [Accessed: 08/07/2005].
14. Freemantle, N., Cleland, J., Young, P. et al (1999) Beta-blockade after myocardial infarction: systematic review and meta regression analysis. *British Medical Journal* **318**(7200), 1730–1737. [Full text]
15. Heart Protection Study Collaborative Group (2002) MRC/BHF heart protection study of cholesterol lowering with simvastatin in 20536 high-risk individuals: a randomised placebo-controlled trial. *Lancet* **360**(9326), 7–22. [Full text]
16. Heidenreich, P.A., McDonald, K.M., Hastie, T. et al (1999) Meta-analysis of trials comparing beta-blockers, calcium antagonists and nitrates for stable angina. *Journal of the American Medical Association* **281**(20), 1927–1936. [Full text]
17. IONA Study Group (2002) Effect of nicorandil on coronary events in patients with stable angina: the impact of nicorandil in angina (IONA) randomised trial. *Lancet* **359**(9314), 1269–1275. [Full text]
18. Ko, D.T., Hebert, P.R., Coffey, C.S. et al (2002) Beta-blocker therapy and symptoms of depression, fatigue and sexual dysfunction. *Journal of the American Medical Association* **288**(3), 351–352. [Full text]
19. LaRosa, J.C., Jiang, H.E. and Vupputuri, S. (1999) Effect of statins on risk of coronary disease. *Journal o the American Medical Association* **282**(24), 2340–2346. [Full text]
20. MacDonald, T.M. and Wei, L. (2003) Effect of ibuprofen on cardioprotective effect of aspirin. *Lance* **361**(9357), 573–574. [Full text]
21. Meads, C., Cummins, C., Jolly, K. et al (2000) Coronary artery stents in the treatment of ischaemic heart disease: a rapid and systematic review. *Health Technology Assessment* **4**(23), 1–153.
22. MeReC (2002) Lifestyle measures to reduce cardiovascular risk. *MeReC Briefing* **19**(July), 1–8.
23. NICE (2002) *Guidance on coronary artery stents in th treatment of ischaemic heart disease*. National Institu for Clinical Excellence. www.nice.org.uk [Accessed: 04/12/2002].
24. Norell, M., Lythall, D., Coghlan, G. et al (1992) Limited value of the resting electrocardiogram in assessing patients with recent onset chest pain: lessons from a chest pain clinic. *British Heart Journal* **67**(1), 53–56.
25. North of England Guideline Development Group (1999) *The primary care management of stable angin* Newcastle-upon-Tyne: University of Newcastle, Centr for Health Services Research.
26. Primatesta, P. and Brookes, M. (2001) Cardiovascula disease: prevalence and risk factors. In: Erens, B., Primatesta, P., Prior, G. et al (Eds.) *Health survey for England – the health of minority ethnic groups '99*. London: The Stationery Office.
27. SIGN (2001) *Management of stable angina*. Report no 51. Scottish Intercollegiate Guidelines Network. www.sign.ac.uk [Accessed: 24/10/2002].
28. Simon Broome Register Group (1999) Mortality in treated heterozygous familial hypercholesterolaemia: implications for clinical management. *Atherosclerosis* **142**(1), 105–112.
29. Wood, D., Durrington, D., Poulter, N. et al (1998) Joint British recommendations on prevention of coronary heart disease in clinical practice. *Heart* **80**(Suppl 2), S1-S29. [Full text]

Evidence grading

This guidance is based mainly on the National Service Framework for Coronary Heart Disease (especially Chapter 4: *Angina*) and the Scottish Intercollegiate Network Guidelines (SIGN) guideline *Management of Stable Angina*, 2001.

The definitions of the SIGN grades of recommendations are:

A Requires at least one randomized controlled trial as part of a body of literature of overall good quality and consistency addressing the specific recommendation.

B Requires the availability of well-conducted clinical studies but no randomized clinical trials on the topic of recommendation.

C Requires evidence obtained from expert committee reports or opinions and/or clinical experiences of respected authorities. Indicates an absence of directly applicable clinical studies of good quality.

GPP Good practice points (GPP) are recommended best practice based on the clinical experience of the guideline development group.

PRODIGY GUIDANCE

Ankylosing spondylitis

Last revised in July 2005
www.prodigy.nhs.uk/guidance.asp?gt=Ankylosing spondylitis

Applies to people over the age of 16 years

This guidance covers the management of people with ankylosing spondylitis in primary care.

This guidance does not cover the treatment of complications of ankylosing spondylitis such as uveitis, or give details of the use of disease-modifying anti-rheumatic drugs as these would usually be started in secondary care.

There is separate PRODIGY guidance for *Back pain — lower*, *Nonsteroidal anti-inflammatory drugs (NSAIDs)*, the treatment and prevention of NSAID-induced ulcer: *Dyspepsia — symptoms* and *Dyspepsia — proven DU or GU*, and on *Monitoring people on DMARDs*.

Goals

To diagnose early and accurately
To control symptoms, i.e. pain, stiffness, and fatigue
To maintain posture and flexibility
To detect and manage complications and associated conditions as soon as possible
To minimize and manage disabilities

Contents

Scenarios

- Newly diagnosed ankylosing spondylitis p.109
- Exacerbations of established ankylosing spondylitis p.112
- Peripheral joint problems p.115
- Systemic problems p.119

Extended Information, p. 119

Which scenario?

- **Newly diagnosed ankylosing spondylitis:** covers investigation and management of newly diagnosed ankylosing spondylitis.
- **Exacerbations of established ankylosing spondylitis:** covers the management of acute and chronic exacerbations of ankylosing spondylitis.
- **Peripheral joint problems:** covers the management of peripheral joint involvement in ankylosing spondylitis.
- **Systemic problems:** provides brief advice on the diagnosis and management of systemic involvement in ankylosing spondylitis.

Newly diagnosed ankylosing spondylitis

Which therapy?

- **Refer promptly** for confirmation of diagnosis and access to specialist care.
- **Control pain and stiffness with a nonsteroidal anti-inflammatory drug** (NSAID)
  - **Naproxen** has a longer duration of action than diclofenac and ibuprofen, and thus may help to reduce morning stiffness.
  - **Paracetamol or paracetamol plus codeine** may be used to control pain if NSAIDs are not tolerated or are contraindicated.
- **Physical therapy** is key to managing ankylosing spondylitis. The focus is on (i) *deportment* to maintain posture and (ii) *exercise and stretching* to maintain spinal and joint mobility.
- **Advise on lifestyle and health maintenance** (see *Shared decision making*).

Practical prescribing points

For further information, please see the *Medicines Compendium* (www.medicines.org.uk) or the *British National Formulary* (www.bnf.org).

NSAIDs

- **Only one NSAID should be prescribed at a time.**
- **NSAIDs may worsen asthma, hypertension, renal impairment, or heart failure.**
- Do not give ibuprofen, diclofenac, indometacin, or naproxen without gastroprotection if there is a history of peptic ulceration.
- Do not give meloxicam if there is active peptic ulceration, or a history or recurrent ulceration.
- **Pregnancy and breastfeeding:** use paracetamol if possible. If an NSAID is essential, ibuprofen may be used during breastfeeding and before 30 weeks of pregnancy.
- **People with cardiovascular disease:** ibuprofen may reduce the cardiovascular protective effect of low-dose aspirin.
- **In people with risk factors for gastrointestinal NSAID complications:**
  - Use paracetamol (with or without codeine) instead of a NSAID if possible.
  - Or, use gastroprotection (a PPI or full-dose misoprostol) combined with a standard NSAID
  - Or, consider switching to meloxicam alone (COX-2 selective).
- **Risk factors for gastrointestinal NSAID complications include:**
  - Age of 65 years and over.
  - Previous history of gastroduodenal ulcer, gastrointestinal (GI) bleeding, or gastroduodenal perforation.
  - Concomitant use of medications that are known to increase the likelihood of upper-GI adverse events, e.g. anticoagulants, aspirin (even a low dose), and corticosteroids.
  - Presence of serious comorbidity, such as cardiovascular disease, renal or hepatic impairment, diabetes, or hypertension.
  - Requirement for prolonged duration of NSAID use.
  - Use of maximum recommended doses of NSAIDs.

Codeine

- Codeine may cause nausea, vomiting, constipation, and drowsiness. A regular laxative is often needed when it is used long-term.

A

Misoprostol

- Diarrhoea and abdominal pain are common. Advise women of childbearing age to use adequate contraception, since misoprostol increases the risk of miscarriage.

Follow-up advice

- **Follow up to assess disease activity and response to treatment:**
  - **Symptoms** (length of morning stiffness, pain, fatigue, arising at night to relieve back pain)
  - **Disability** (disease impact): interference with activities of daily life
  - **Objective measures** (record every 6–12 months):
    - **Occiput-to-wall distance** (standing as erect as possible with heels against the wall)
    - **Fingertip-to-floor distance** (bending from the hip with knees as straight as possible)
  - **Compliance** with physical and drug therapies
- Failure to respond to a drug after 3–4 weeks should lead to a change in drug or an increase in dose or frequency.

Should I refer or investigate?

Refer?

- **To rheumatology:**
  - **All new or suspected cases of ankylosing spondylitis**
- **To physiotherapy and/or occupational therapy:**
  - For development of a home exercise programme
  - For assessment
  - To obtain aids for the activities of daily living
- **To ophthalmology** (urgently) if acute uveitis is suspected

Investigate?

- **Erythrocyte sedimentation rate or C-reactive protein:** may provide evidence to support a diagnosis of chronic inflammation.
- **Full blood count:** a normochromic, normocytic anaemia would support a diagnosis of chronic inflammation.
- **Rheumatoid factor and anti-nuclear antibody tests:** negative in ankylosing spondylitis.
- **Plain radiology of spine and sacroiliac joints:**
  - May be useful to rule out other conditions.
  - Plain X-rays of the spine and sacroiliac joints are often normal in newly diagnosed ankylosing spondylitis.
- **Human leukocyte antigen B27:** seldom done in primary care because of its low predictive values.

Patient information leaflets

The following PILs are available at www.prodigy.nhs.uk

- Ankylosing Spondylitis
- Antibody and Antigen Tests
- Anti-inflammatory Painkillers
- Arthritis Research Campaign - ARC
- Blood Test - Detecting Inflammation
- Blood Test - General
- National Ankylosing Spondylitis Society

Shared decision making

- **Exercise** is a mainstay of treatment for ankylosing spondylitis.
  - A physiotherapist can advise on the correct exercises.
  - A daily exercise routine aims to keep the full range of spinal movement and to prevent your spine from stiffening up.
  - Aim to do 2–4 hours exercise per week.
  - Swimming is an excellent additional exercise.
- **A good posture** counteracts the tendency to become bent forward.
  - Always sit upright, and move your neck and back often.
  - Each day lie face down for 20 minutes before getting out of bed and again before going to sleep.
  - Sleep on a firm bed.
- **Painkillers** ease pain and stiffness and allow regular exercise. They are needed only when symptoms are troublesome.
  - **An anti-inflammatory painkiller** is usually used when symptoms flare up. There are several brands. If one does not suit, try another. Side-effects sometimes occur:
    - Bleeding from the stomach is the most serious possible side-effect. Stop the medicine and see a doctor if you develop stomach symptoms.
    - Some people with asthma, high blood pressure, kidney failure, or heart failure may not be able to take anti-inflammatories.
  - **Paracetamol** may be fine if symptoms are mild. Codeine may be added for a short while if paracetamol alone is not sufficient.
- If you want to drive and you find it difficult to turn your head, you should have wide rear-view mirrors and a proper head support fitted to your car.
- It is important to keep to a healthy lifestyle.
  - If you smoke you should quit.
  - You should get the flu immunization every year.
  - It is important to avoid physical injury and falls.
- If you have physical difficulties at work it is usually possible to have changes made to the workplace to make things easier.
- Although sometimes it might seem worthwhile trying a splint, brace, or corset, these are not helpful and should be avoided.

Drug rationale

Drugs not included

- **Analgesics other than paracetamol and codeine taken separately** are not recommended:
  - **Strong opioids** (e.g. morphine, pethidine) should be avoided because of the risk of dependence if they are used inappropriately.
  - **Weak opioids, other than codeine,** have either not been shown to be more effective than codeine (when used in combination with paracetamol), or are more expensive.
  - **Low-dose weak opioids with paracetamol** (combination products), e.g. co-codamol 8/500 mg: There is no evidence that these offer any clinical benefit over paracetamol alone and they are likely to lead to opioid adverse effects [MeReC, 1993; De Craen et al, 1996; Moore and McQuay, 1997].
  - **High-dose weak opioids with paracetamol** (combination products), e.g. co-codamol 30/500 mg: These do not allow titration to the most effective and safe analgesic dose to match individual requirements.
  - **Co-proxamol** (dextropropoxyphene 32.5 mg/ paracetamol 325 mg) has been withdrawn by the Committee on Safety of Medicines due to its unfavourable risk/benefit ratio; it is associated with an unacceptable risk of overdose [CSM, 2005a].
- **Nonsteroidal anti-inflammatory drugs (NSAIDs), other than ibuprofen, diclofenac, naproxen, indometacin, and meloxicam** are not generally recommended, as they are not specifically licensed for ankylosing spondylitis, or they have a worse balance between their general efficacy

and adverse effect profile than the recommended drugs [CSM, 1994; Hernández-Diaz et al, 2000; BNF 49, 2005].

Modified-release NSAIDs may be useful in some people, but they are more expensive [BNF 49, 2005]. If a longer-acting NSAID is required (e.g. to reduce early morning stiffness), naproxen is a suitable choice.

Strong opioids (e.g. morphine, pethidine) should be avoided, owing to the risk of dependence if they are used inappropriately. They are usually reserved for moderate to severe pain of a visceral origin [BNF 49, 2005].

Gastroprotective agents are sometimes needed, but not all are recommended:

- **H_2-receptor antagonists (H_2RAs):** at standard doses, H_2RAs reduce the risk of duodenal ulceration, and there is some evidence that double doses reduce the risk of gastric ulceration [Rostom et al, 2002]. However, no H_2RAs are currently licensed for the prevention of gastric ulceration induced by NSAIDs [BNF 49, 2005], which is more common than duodenal ulceration.
- **Rabeprazole** is not included as it is not specifically licensed for the prevention of NSAID-induced gastrointestinal ulcers [BNF 49, 2005].
- **Fixed-dose combinations of standard NSAIDs with misoprostol:** the optimum dose of misoprostol (i.e. 800 micrograms daily) cannot be reached using these preparations. In particular, only 400 micrograms daily of misoprostol is given with the higher doses of NSAID in these preparations.

Disease-modifying anti-rheumatic drugs (DMARDs) should only be initiated with specialist advice. Information on monitoring people taking methotrexate, sulfasalazine, and other DMARDs is detailed in separate PRODIGY guidance *Monitoring people on DMARDs.*

Drugs included

Nonsteroidal anti-inflammatory drugs

Standard NSAIDs: ibuprofen, diclofenac, and naproxen have a good balance of efficacy against adverse effect profile [CSM, 1994; Henry et al, 1996; Hernández-Diaz and Rodriguez, 2000]. Naproxen has a longer duration of action than ibuprofen and diclofenac, and thus may be more suitable for nocturnal pain and early morning stiffness. Standard doses are offered as these are generally accepted to be sufficient for anti-inflammatory prophylaxis, although data is lacking.

Indometacin has been traditionally used for the treatment of ankylosing spondylitis [Calin and Elswood, 1989]. However, it has a greater risk of adverse gastrointestinal effects than ibuprofen, diclofenac, or naproxen, and is therefore only recommended when these other NSAIDs do not provide adequate control.

Meloxicam is a selective cyclo-oxygenase 2 (COX-2) inhibitor, and is the only NSAID specifically licensed for ankylosing spondylitis. It can be considered when there is a high risk of NSAID-induced gastrointestinal toxicity.

Gastroprotective agents

- **Proton pump inhibitors (PPIs): lansoprazole, omeprazole, esomeprazole, and pantoprazole** are licensed for the prevention of gastroduodenal ulceration induced by NSAIDs [BNF 49, 2005]. PPIs reduce the risk of endoscopically proven ulcers, but there are no data on prevention of ulcer complications [Rostom et al, 2002]. However, PPIs are generally considered to be the first-line treatment for gastroprotection, as they are better tolerated than misoprostol.
- **Misoprostol** is licensed for the prevention of gastroduodenal ulceration induced by NSAIDs [BNF 49, 2005]. It reduces the risk of endoscopically proven ulcers and has also been shown to reduce the risk of ulcer complications [Rostom et al, 2002]. It is less well tolerated than PPIs owing to gastrointestinal (GI) adverse effects, particularly diarrhoea.

Standard analgesics

- **Paracetamol** is an option for pain relief, and is not associated with GI toxicity [SIGN, 2000]. It may be used when NSAIDs are contraindicated or pain is mild.
- **Codeine (in combination with paracetamol):** higher-dose codeine is included for use with regular paracetamol for additional pain relief. Codeine 60 mg plus paracetamol has been shown to provide more pain relief than either codeine 60 mg alone or paracetamol 1000 mg alone [Moore et al, 1997]. Codeine should be prescribed separately to paracetamol to allow flexibility of dosing and titration of analgesic effect.

Prescriptions

Analgesia

Paracetamol tablets: 1g up to four times a day

- Age from 16 years onwards
- Paracetamol 500mg tablets. Take two tablets every 4 to 6 hours when required for pain relief. Maximum of 8 tablets in 24 hours; supply 200 tablets; NHS Cost £2.12; OTC Cost £3.75.

Add on if required: codeine 30-60mg up to four times a day

- Age from 16 years onwards
- Codeine 30mg tablets. Take one to two tablets every 4 to 6 hours when required for pain relief. Maximum of 8 tablets in 24 hours; supply 60 tablets; NHS Cost £4.58.

Paracetamol 500mg tablets + codeine 30mg tablets

- Age from 16 years onwards
- Paracetamol 500mg tablets. Take two tablets every 4 to 6 hours when required for pain relief. Maximum of 8 tablets in 24 hours; supply 200 tablets; NHS Cost £2.12; OTC Cost £3.75.
- Codeine 30mg tablets. Take one to two tablets every 4 to 6 hours when required for pain relief. Maximum of 8 tablets in 24 hours; supply 60 tablets; NHS Cost £4.58.

Standard NSAIDs: ibuprofen, naproxen and diclofenac

Ibuprofen tablets: 400mg three times a day

- Age from 16 years onwards
- Ibuprofen 400mg tablets. Take one tablet three times a day; supply 84 tablets; NHS Cost £2.74; OTC Cost £4.83.

Ibuprofen tablets: 400mg four times a day

- Age from 16 years onwards
- Ibuprofen 400mg tablets. Take one tablet four times a day; supply 112 tablets; NHS Cost £3.65; OTC Cost £6.44.

Ibuprofen tablets: 600mg three times a day

- Age from 16 years onwards
- Ibuprofen 600mg tablets. Take one tablet three times a day; supply 84 tablets; NHS Cost £2.81.

Ibuprofen tablets: 800mg three times a day

- Age from 16 years onwards
- Ibuprofen 400mg tablets. Take two tablets three times a day; supply 168 tablets; NHS Cost £4.58.

Diclofenac sodium e/c tablets: 25mg three times a day

- Age from 16 years onwards
- Diclofenac 25mg e/c tablets. Take one tablet three times a day; supply 84 tablets; NHS Cost £1.72.

Diclofenac sodium e/c tablets: 50mg three times a day
- Age from 16 years onwards
- Diclofenac 50mg e/c tablets. Take one tablet three times a day; supply 84 tablets; NHS Cost £1.45.

Naproxen tablets: 250mg twice a day
- Age from 16 years onwards
- Naproxen 250mg tablets. Take one tablet twice a day; supply 56 tablets; NHS Cost £2.68.

Naproxen tablets: 500mg twice a day
- Age from 16 years onwards
- Naproxen 500mg tablets. Take one tablet twice a day; supply 56 tablets; NHS Cost £4.90.

Indometacin (2nd-line NSAID)

Indometacin capsules: 25mg three times a day
- Age from 16 years onwards
- Indometacin 25mg capsules. Take one capsule three times a day; supply 84 capsules; NHS Cost £6.63.

Indometacin capsules: 50mg three times a day
- Age from 16 years onwards
- Indometacin 50mg capsules. Take one capsule three times a day; supply 84 capsules; NHS Cost £5.97.

COX-2 selective NSAID: if HIGH RISK of NSAID-induced ulcer

Meloxicam tablets: 7.5mg once a day
- Age from 16 years onwards
- Meloxicam 7.5mg tablets. Take one tablet once a day; supply 30 tablets; NHS Cost £9.70.

Meloxicam tablets: 15mg once a day
- Age from 16 to 65 years
- Meloxicam 15mg tablets. Take one tablet once a day; supply 30 tablets; NHS Cost £13.48.

GI protection: use ONLY with a standard NSAID

Omeprazole capsules: 20mg once a day
- Age from 16 years onwards
- Omeprazole 20mg capsules. Take one capsule once a day; supply 28 capsules; NHS Cost £12.75.

Omeprazole tablets: 20mg once a day
- Age from 16 years onwards
- Omeprazole 20mg tablets. Take one tablet once a day; supply 28 tablets; NHS Cost £12.75.

Lansoprazole capsules: 15mg each morning
- Age from 16 years onwards
- Lansoprazole 15mg capsules. Take one capsule each morning (on an empty stomach); supply 28 capsules; NHS Cost £12.92.

Lansoprazole capsules: 30mg each morning
- Age from 16 years onwards
- Lansoprazole 30mg capsules. Take one capsule each morning (on an empty stomach); supply 28 capsules; NHS Cost £23.63.

Pantoprazole e/c tablets: 20mg once a day
- Age from 16 years onwards
- Pantoprazole 20mg e/c tablets. Take one tablet once a day; supply 28 tablets; NHS Cost £12.31.

Esomeprazole tablets: 20mg once a day
- Age from 16 years onwards
- Esomeprazole 20mg tablets. Take one tablet once a day; supply 28 tablets; NHS Cost £18.50.

Lansoprazole orodispersible tablets: 15mg each morning
- Age from 16 years onwards
- Lansoprazole 15mg orodisp tabs. Take one tablet each morning (on an empty stomach); supply 28 tablets; NHS Cost £10.86.

Lansoprazole orodispersible tablets: 30mg each morning
- Age from 16 years onwards
- Lansoprazole 30mg orodisp tabs. Take one tablet each morning (on an empty stomach); supply 28 tablets; NHS Cost £21.38.

Misoprostol tablets: 200micrograms four times a day
- Age from 16 years onwards
- Misoprostol 200microgram tabs. Take one tablet four times a day; supply 120 tablets; NHS Cost £18.72.

Exacerbations of established ankylosing spondylitis

Which therapy?

- Consider referral back to rheumatology service for rapid access review.
- **NSAIDs**
  - If the person is not already taking a nonsteroidal anti-inflammatory drug (NSAID), consider starting one:
    - NSAIDs are frequently effective in reducing pain and particularly stiffness.
    - **Naproxen** has a longer duration of action than diclofenac and ibuprofen, and thus may help to reduce morning stiffness.
  - If the person is already taking an NSAID:
    - Review compliance, dose, and frequency.
    - Consider changing to another NSAID if the current NSAID is poorly tolerated, or is ineffective despite being taken at an adequate dosage.
- **DMARDs**
  - If the person is taking a disease-modifying drug (DMARD), continue with the current regimen and check adherence to prescription.
- **Exercise**
  - It is vital to maintain an exercise programme through periods of exacerbation. Avoid bed rest. Consider referral back to physiotherapy.

Practical prescribing points

For further information, please see the *Medicines Compendium* (www.medicines.org.uk) or the *British National Formulary* (www.bnf.org).

NSAIDs

- **Only one NSAID should be prescribed at a time.**
- **NSAIDs may worsen asthma, hypertension, renal impairment, or heart failure.**
- Do not give ibuprofen, diclofenac, indometacin, or naproxen without gastroprotection if there is a history of peptic ulceration.
- Do not give meloxicam if there is active peptic ulceration, or a history or recurrent ulceration.
- **Pregnancy and breastfeeding:** use paracetamol if possible. If an NSAID is essential, ibuprofen may be used during breastfeeding and before 30 weeks of pregnancy.
- **People with cardiovascular disease:** ibuprofen may reduce the cardiovascular protective effect of low-dose aspirin.
- **In people with risk factors for gastrointestinal NSAID complications:**
  - Use paracetamol (with or without codeine) instead of a NSAID if possible.
  - Or, use gastroprotection (a PPI or full-dose misoprostol) combined with a standard NSAID.
  - Or, consider switching to meloxicam alone (COX-2 selective).
- **Risk factors for gastrointestinal NSAID complications include:**

- Age of 65 years and over.
- Previous history of gastroduodenal ulcer, gastrointestinal (GI) bleeding, or gastroduodenal perforation.
- Concomitant use of medications that are known to increase the likelihood of upper-GI adverse events, e.g. anticoagulants, aspirin (even a low dose), and corticosteroids.
- Presence of serious comorbidity, such as cardiovascular disease, renal or hepatic impairment, diabetes, or hypertension.
- Requirement for prolonged duration of NSAID use.
- Use of maximum recommended doses of NSAIDs.

Codeine

Codeine may cause nausea, vomiting, constipation, and drowsiness. A regular laxative is often needed when it is used long-term.

Misoprostol

Diarrhoea and abdominal pain are common. Advise women of childbearing age to use adequate contraception, since misoprostol increases the risk of miscarriage.

Follow-up advice

Follow up in 1–4 weeks, depending on the severity of the flare-up.

On follow-up assess disease activity and response to treatment:

- **Symptoms** (length of morning stiffness, pain, fatigue, arising at night to relieve back pain)
- **Disability** (disease impact): interference with activities of daily life
- **Objective measures** (record every 6–12 months):
  - **Occiput-to-wall distance** (standing as erect as possible with heels against the wall)
  - **Fingertip-to-floor distance** (bending from the hip with knees as straight as possible)
- **Compliance** with physical and drug therapies

Should I refer or investigate?

Refer?

- **Active disease** that has not responded to treatment within a week.
- **Uncertain diagnosis.**
- **Systemic involvement:** e.g. acute uveitis requires urgent ophthalmology assessment; inflammatory bowel disease requires a gastroenterology review.
- **Physiotherapy** and advice on home exercise programme.
- **Peripheral joints** that require intra-articular injections of steroids, using techniques beyond local competence.

Investigate?

- **Erythrocyte sedimentation rate or C-reactive protein:** may provide evidence of active inflammation.
- **Full blood count:** a normochromic, normocytic anaemia would support a diagnosis of chronic inflammation.
- **Monitoring people on DMARDs**
  - People on disease-modifying anti-rheumatic drugs (DMARDs) need regular monitoring. Monitoring details vary with each DMARD, and should be guided by specialist advice and local shared-care arrangements.
  - There is separate PRODIGY guidance on *Monitoring people on DMARDs*.

Patient information leaflets

The following PILs are available at www.prodigy.nhs.uk

- Ankylosing Spondylitis
- Antibody and Antigen Tests
- Anti-inflammatory Painkillers
- Arthritis Research Campaign - ARC
- Blood Test - Detecting Inflammation
- Blood Test - General
- National Ankylosing Spondylitis Society

Shared decision making

- Ankylosing spondylitis symptoms may flare up from time to time.
- **Exercise is the main treatment.** Even during a flare-up, continue with your exercises as much as possible.
  - A physiotherapist can advise on the correct exercises.
  - A daily exercise routine aims to keep the full range of spinal movement and to prevent your spine from stiffening up.
  - Aim to do 2–4 hours exercise per week.
  - Swimming is an excellent additional exercise.
- **A good posture** counteracts the tendency to become bent forward.
  - Always sit upright, and move your neck and back often.
  - Each day lie face down for 20 minutes before getting out of bed and again before going to sleep.
  - Sleep on a firm bed.
- **An anti-inflammatory painkiller** is usually used when symptoms flare up. There are several brands. If one does not suit, try another. Side-effects sometimes occur:
  - Bleeding from the stomach is the most serious possible side-effect. Stop the medicine and see a doctor if you develop stomach symptoms.
  - Some people with asthma, high blood pressure, kidney failure, or heart failure may not be able to take anti-inflammatories.

Drug rationale

Drugs not included

- **Analgesics other than paracetamol and codeine taken separately,** are not recommended:
  - **Strong opioids** (e.g. morphine, pethidine) should be avoided because of the risk of dependence if they are used inappropriately.
  - **Weak opioids, other than codeine,** have either not been shown to be more effective than codeine (when used in combination with paracetamol), or are more expensive.
  - **Low-dose weak opioids with paracetamol** (combination products), e.g. co-codamol 8/500 mg: There is no evidence that these offer any clinical benefit over paracetamol alone and they are likely to lead to opioid adverse effects [MeReC, 1993; De Craen et al, 1996; Moore and McQuay, 1997].
  - **High-dose weak opioids with paracetamol** (combination products), e.g. co-codamol 30/500 mg: These do not allow titration to the most effective and safe analgesic dose to match individual requirements.
  - **Co-proxamol** (dextropropoxyphene 32.5 mg/ paracetamol 325 mg) has been withdrawn by the Committee on Safety of Medicines due to its unfavourable risk/benefit ratio; it is associated with an unacceptable risk of overdose [CSM, 2005a].
- **Nonsteroidal anti-inflammatory drugs (NSAIDs), other than ibuprofen, diclofenac, naproxen, indometacin, and meloxicam** are not generally recommended, as they are not specifically licensed for ankylosing spondylitis, or

they have a worse balance between their efficacy and adverse effect profile than the recommended drugs [CSM, 1994; Hernández-Diaz et al, 2000; BNF 49, 2005].

- **Modified-release NSAIDs** may be useful in some people, but they are more expensive [BNF 49, 2005]. If a longer-acting NSAID is required (e.g. to reduce early morning stiffness), naproxen is a suitable choice.
- **Strong opioids** (e.g. morphine, pethidine) should be avoided, owing to the risk of dependence if they are used inappropriately. They are usually reserved for moderate to severe pain of a visceral origin [BNF 49, 2005].
- **Gastroprotective agents** are sometimes needed, but not all are recommended:
  - **H_2-receptor antagonists (H_2RAs):** at standard doses, H_2RAs reduce the risk of duodenal ulceration, and there is some evidence that double doses reduce the risk of gastric ulceration [Rostom et al, 2002]. However, no H_2RAs are currently licensed for the prevention of gastric ulceration induced by NSAIDs [BNF 49, 2005], which is more common than duodenal ulceration.
  - **Rabeprazole** is not included as it is not specifically licensed for the prevention of NSAID-induced gastrointestinal ulcers [BNF 49, 2005].
  - **Fixed-dose combinations of standard NSAIDs with misoprostol:** the optimum dose of misoprostol (i.e. 800 micrograms daily) cannot be reached using these preparations. In particular, only 400 micrograms daily of misoprostol is given with the higher doses of NSAID in these preparations.
- **Disease-modifying anti-rheumatic drugs** (DMARDs) should only be initiated with specialist advice. Information on monitoring people taking methotrexate, sulfasalazine, and other DMARDs is detailed in separate PRODIGY guidance *Monitoring people on DMARDs.*

Drugs included

Nonsteroidal anti-inflammatory drugs

- **Standard nonsteroidal anti-inflammatory drugs (NSAIDs): ibuprofen, diclofenac, and naproxen** have a good balance of efficacy against adverse effect profile [CSM, 1994; Henry et al, 1996; Hernández-Diaz and Rodriguez, 2000]. Naproxen has a longer duration of action than ibuprofen and diclofenac, and thus may be more suitable for nocturnal pain and early morning stiffness. Standard doses are offered as these are generally accepted to be sufficient for anti-inflammatory prophylaxis, although data are lacking.
- **Indometacin** has traditionally been used for the treatment of ankylosing spondylitis [Calin and Elswood, 1989]. However, it has a greater risk of adverse gastrointestinal (GI) effects than ibuprofen, diclofenac, or naproxen, and is therefore only recommended when these other NSAIDs do not provide adequate control.
- **Meloxicam** is a selective cyclo-oxygenase 2 (COX-2) inhibitor, and is the only NSAID specifically licensed for ankylosing spondylitis. It can be considered when there is a high risk of NSAID-induced GI toxicity.

Gastroprotective agents

- **Proton pump inhibitors (PPIs): lansoprazole, omeprazole, esomeprazole and pantoprazole** are licensed for the prevention of gastroduodenal ulceration induced by NSAIDs [BNF 49, 2005]. PPIs reduce the risk of endoscopically proven ulcers, but there are no data on prevention of ulcer complications [Rostom et al, 2002]. However, PPIs are generally considered to be the preferred choice for gastroprotection, as they are better tolerated than misoprostol.
- **Misoprostol** is licensed for the prevention of gastroduodenal ulceration induced by NSAIDs [BNF 4 2005]. It reduces the risk of endoscopically proven ulce and has also been shown to reduce the risk of ulcer complications [Rostom et al, 2002]. It is less well tolerated than PPIs owing to GI adverse effects, particularly diarrhoea.

Standard analgesics

- **Paracetamol** is an option for pain relief and is not associated with GI toxicity [SIGN, 2000]. It may be use when NSAIDs are contraindicated or pain is mild.
- **Codeine (in combination with paracetamol):** higher-do codeine is included for use with regular paracetamol fo additional pain relief. Codeine 60 mg plus paracetamol has been shown to provide more pain relief than either codeine 60 mg alone or paracetamol 1000 mg alone [Moore et al, 1997]. Codeine should be prescribed separately to paracetamol to allow flexibility of dosing and titration of analgesic effect.

Prescriptions

Analgesia

Paracetamol tablets: 1g up to four times a day

- Age from 16 years onwards
- Paracetamol 500mg tablets. Take two tablets every 4 to 6 hours when required for pain relief. Maximum of 8 tablets in 24 hours; supply 200 tablets; NHS Cost £2.1 OTC Cost £3.75.

Add on if required: codeine 30-60mg up to four times a day

- Age from 16 years onwards
- Codeine 30mg tablets. Take one to two tablets every 4 t 6 hours when required for pain relief. Maximum of 8 tablets in 24 hours; supply 60 tablets; NHS Cost £4.58.

Paracetamol 500mg tablets + codeine 30mg tablets

- Age from 16 years onwards
- Paracetamol 500mg tablets. Take two tablets every 4 to 6 hours when required for pain relief. Maximum of 8 tablets in 24 hours; supply 200 tablets; NHS Cost £2.1 OTC Cost £3.75.
- Codeine 30mg tablets. Take one to two tablets every 4 6 hours when required for pain relief. Maximum of 8 tablets in 24 hours; supply 60 tablets; NHS Cost £4.58.

Standard NSAIDs: ibuprofen, naproxen and diclofenac

Ibuprofen tablets: 400mg three times a day

- Age from 16 years onwards
- Ibuprofen 400mg tablets. Take one tablet three times a day; supply 84 tablets; NHS Cost £2.74; OTC Cost £4.83.

Ibuprofen tablets: 400mg four times a day

- Age from 16 years onwards
- Ibuprofen 400mg tablets. Take one tablet four times a day; supply 112 tablets; NHS Cost £3.65; OTC Cost £6.44.

Ibuprofen tablets: 600mg three times a day

- Age from 16 years onwards
- Ibuprofen 600mg tablets. Take one tablet three times a day; supply 84 tablets; NHS Cost £2.81.

Ibuprofen tablets: 800mg three times a day

- Age from 16 years onwards
- Ibuprofen 400mg tablets. Take two tablets three times a day; supply 168 tablets; NHS Cost £4.58.

iclofenac sodium e/c tablets: 25mg three times a day
- Age from 16 years onwards
- Diclofenac 25mg e/c tablets. Take one tablet three times a day; supply 84 tablets; NHS Cost £1.72.

iclofenac sodium e/c tablets: 50mg three times a day
- Age from 16 years onwards
- Diclofenac 50mg e/c tablets. Take one tablet three times a day; supply 84 tablets; NHS Cost £1.45.

aproxen tablets: 250mg twice a day
- Age from 16 years onwards
- Naproxen 250mg tablets. Take one tablet twice a day; supply 56 tablets; NHS Cost £2.68.

aproxen tablets: 500mg twice a day
- Age from 16 years onwards
- Naproxen 500mg tablets. Take one tablet twice a day; supply 56 tablets; NHS Cost £4.90.

Indometacin (2nd-line NSAID)

ndometacin capsules: 25mg three times a day
- Age from 16 years onwards
- Indometacin 25mg capsules. Take one capsule three times a day; supply 84 capsules; NHS Cost £6.63.

ndometacin capsules: 50mg three times a day
- Age from 16 years onwards
- Indometacin 50mg capsules. Take one capsule three times a day; supply 84 capsules; NHS Cost £5.97.

COX-2 selective NSAID: if HIGH RISK of NSAID-induced ulcer

Meloxicam tablets: 7.5mg once a day
- Age from 16 years onwards
- Meloxicam 7.5mg tablets. Take one tablet once a day; supply 30 tablets; NHS Cost £9.70.

Meloxicam tablets: 15mg once a day
- Age from 16 to 65 years
- Meloxicam 15mg tablets. Take one tablet once a day; supply 30 tablets; NHS Cost £13.48.

GI protection: use ONLY with a standard NSAID

Omeprazole capsules: 20mg once a day
- Age from 16 years onwards
- Omeprazole 20mg capsules. Take one capsule once a day; supply 28 capsules; NHS Cost £12.75.

Omeprazole tablets: 20mg once a day
- Age from 16 years onwards
- Omeprazole 20mg tablets. Take one tablet once a day; supply 28 tablets; NHS Cost £12.75.

Lansoprazole capsules: 15mg each morning
- Age from 16 years onwards
- Lansoprazole 15mg capsules. Take one capsule each morning (on an empty stomach); supply 28 capsules; NHS Cost £12.92.

Lansoprazole capsules: 30mg each morning
- Age from 16 years onwards
- Lansoprazole 30mg capsules. Take one capsule each morning (on an empty stomach); supply 28 capsules; NHS Cost £23.63.

Pantoprazole e/c tablets: 20mg once a day
- Age from 16 years onwards
- Pantoprazole 20mg e/c tablets. Take one tablet once a day; supply 28 tablets; NHS Cost £12.31.

Esomeprazole tablets: 20mg once a day
- Age from 16 years onwards
- Esomeprazole 20mg tablets. Take one tablet once a day; supply 28 tablets; NHS Cost £18.50.

Lansoprazole orodispersible tablets: 15mg each morning
- Age from 16 years onwards
- Lansoprazole 15mg orodisp tabs. Take one tablet each morning (on an empty stomach); supply 28 tablets; NHS Cost £10.86.

Lansoprazole orodispersible tablets: 30mg each morning
- Age from 16 years onwards
- Lansoprazole 30mg orodisp tabs. Take one tablet each morning (on an empty stomach); supply 28 tablets; NHS Cost £21.38.

Misoprostol tablets: 200micrograms four times a day
- Age from 16 years onwards
- Misoprostol 200microgram tabs. Take one tablet four times a day; supply 120 tablets; NHS Cost £18.72.

A

Peripheral joint problems

Which therapy?

- **Intra-articular long-acting corticosteroid**
  - If the flare-up involves a peripheral joint (or a few peripheral joints), consider injection with a long-acting corticosteroid — if expertise is available locally.
- **NSAIDs**
  - If the person is not already taking a nonsteroidal anti-inflammatory drug (NSAID), consider starting one.
    - NSAIDs are frequently effective in reducing pain and particularly stiffness.
    - **Naproxen** has a longer duration of action than diclofenac and ibuprofen, and thus may help to reduce morning stiffness.
  - If the person is already taking an NSAID:
    - Review compliance, dose, and frequency.
    - Consider changing to another NSAID if the current NSAID is poorly tolerated, or is ineffective despite being taken at an adequate dose.
- **DMARDs**
  - If the person is taking a disease-modifying drug (DMARD), continue with the current regimen, and check adherence to prescription.
- **Exercise**
  - It is vital to maintain an exercise programme through periods of exacerbation. Avoid bed rest. Consider referral back to physiotherapy.

Practical prescribing points

For further information, please see the *Medicines Compendium* (www.medicines.org.uk) or the *British National Formulary* (www.bnf.org).

NSAIDs

- **Only one NSAID should be prescribed at a time.**
- **NSAIDs may worsen asthma, hypertension, renal impairment, or heart failure.**
- Do not give ibuprofen, diclofenac, indometacin, or naproxen without gastroprotection if there is a history of peptic ulceration.
- Do not give meloxicam if there is active peptic ulceration, or a history or recurrent ulceration.
- **Pregnancy and breastfeeding:** use paracetamol if possible. If an NSAID is essential, ibuprofen may be used during breastfeeding and before 30 weeks of pregnancy.
- **People with cardiovascular disease:** ibuprofen may reduce the cardiovascular protective effect of low-dose aspirin.
- **In people with risk factors for gastrointestinal NSAID complications:**
  - Use paracetamol (with or without codeine) instead of a NSAID if possible.

- Or, use gastroprotection (a PPI or full-dose misoprostol) combined with a standard NSAID.
- Or, consider switching to meloxicam alone (COX-2 selective).

A

- **Risk factors for gastrointestinal NSAID complications include:**
  - Age of 65 years and over.
  - Previous history of gastroduodenal ulcer, gastrointestinal (GI) bleeding, or gastroduodenal perforation.
  - Concomitant use of medications that are known to increase the likelihood of upper-GI adverse events, e.g. anticoagulants, aspirin (even a low dose), and corticosteroids.
  - Presence of serious comorbidity, such as cardiovascular disease, renal or hepatic impairment, diabetes, or hypertension.
  - Requirement for prolonged duration of NSAID use.
  - Use of maximum recommended doses of NSAIDs.

Intra-articular corticosteroids

- **Atrophy of subcutaneous tissues and local skin depigmentation** may occur from peri-articular leakage of corticosteroid. The risk is greatest if large or repeated doses of a long-acting, potent corticosteroid are given. In general, hydrocortisone or prednisolone is recommended for injection of small joints (e.g. hand), and triamcinolone or methylprednisolone for injection of large joints (e.g. knee).
- **Injection of corticosteroids adjacent to a tendon** may be followed by rupture of the tendon.
- **A joint into which a steroid has been injected may become acutely painful for a day or two.**
- **A joint which has been injected with corticosteroid should be rested** as much as possible for the following 24 hours.

Codeine

- Codeine may cause nausea, vomiting, constipation, and drowsiness. A regular laxative is often needed when it is used long-term.

Misoprostol

- Diarrhoea and abdominal pain are common. Advise women of childbearing age to use adequate contraception, since misoprostol increases the risk of miscarriage.

Follow-up advice

- **Follow up in 1–12 weeks,**
  - Shorter follow-up would be indicated with more severe disease.
  - Longer follow-up would be indicated if an intra-articular injection was made and was expected to provide relief lasting for several months.
- **On follow-up assess disease activity and response to treatment:**
  - **Symptoms** (length of morning stiffness, pain, fatigue, arising at night to relieve back pain)
  - **Disability** (disease impact): interference with activities of daily life
  - **Objective measures** (record every 6–12 months):
    - **Occiput-to-wall distance** (standing as erect as possible with heels against the wall)
    - **Fingertip-to-floor distance** (bending from the hip with knees as straight as possible)
  - **Compliance** with physical and drug therapies

Should I refer or investigate?

Refer?

- **Active disease** that has not responded to treatment within a week.
- **Uncertain diagnosis** e.g. possible septic arthritis.
- **Physiotherapy** and advice on home exercise programme
- **Peripheral joints** that require intra-articular injections o steroids, using techniques beyond local competence.
- **Systemic involvement:** e.g. acute uveitis requires urgent ophthalmology assessment; inflammatory bowel disease requires a gastroenterology review.

Investigate?

- **Erythrocyte sedimentation rate or C-reactive protein:** may provide evidence to support a diagnosis of chronic inflammation.
- **Full blood count:** a normochromic, normocytic anaemia would support a diagnosis of chronic inflammation.
- **Plain radiology** of joints: helpful to assess disease progression, or if orthopaedic surgery is planned.
- **Monitoring people taking DMARDs**
  - People taking disease-modifying anti-rheumatic drugs (DMARDs) need regular monitoring. Monitoring details vary with each DMARD, and should be guided by specialist advice and local shared-care arrangements.
  - There is separate PRODIGY guidance on *Monitoring people on DMARDs.*

Patient information leaflets

The following PILs are available at www.prodigy.nhs.uk

- Ankylosing Spondylitis
- Antibody and Antigen Tests
- Anti-inflammatory Painkillers
- Arthritis Research Campaign - ARC
- Blood Test - Detecting Inflammation
- Blood Test - General
- Medicines - Name Changes of Medicines
- National Ankylosing Spondylitis Society

Shared decision making

- Ankylosing spondylitis symptoms may flare up from time to time.
- **Exercise is the main treatment.** Even during a flare-up, continue with your exercises as much as possible.
  - A physiotherapist can advise on the correct exercises.
  - A daily exercise routine aims to keep the full range of spinal movement and to prevent your spine from stiffening up.
  - Aim to do 2–4 hours exercise per week.
  - Swimming is an excellent additional exercise.
- **A good posture** counteracts the tendency to become bent forward:
  - Always sit upright, and move your neck and back often.
  - Each day lie face down for 20 minutes before getting out of bed; repeat again before going to sleep.
  - Sleep on a firm bed.
- **An anti-inflammatory painkiller** is usually used when symptoms flare up. There are several brands. If one does not suit, try another. Side-effects sometimes occur:
  - Bleeding from the stomach is the most serious possible side-effect. Stop the medicine and see a doctor if you develop stomach symptoms.
  - Some people with asthma, high blood pressure, kidney failure, or heart failure may not be able to take anti-inflammatories.

A **steroid injection into a joint** is an option if it is badly inflamed.

A **disease-modifying medicine** is an option if symptoms are not helped by the above. This is usually prescribed after advice from a specialist.

Drug rationale

Drugs not included

Analgesics other than paracetamol and codeine taken separately, are not recommended:

- **Strong opioids** (e.g. morphine, pethidine) should be avoided because of the risk of dependence if they are used inappropriately.
- **Weak opioids,** other than codeine, have either not been shown to be more effective than codeine (when used in combination with paracetamol), or are more expensive.
- **Low-dose weak opioids with paracetamol** (combination products), e.g. co-codamol 8/500 mg: There is no evidence that these offer any clinical benefit over paracetamol alone and they are likely to lead to opioid adverse effects [MeReC, 1993; De Craen et al, 1996; Moore and McQuay, 1997].
- **High-dose weak opioids with paracetamol** (combination products), e.g. co-codamol 30/500 mg: These do not allow titration to the most effective and safe analgesic dose to match individual requirements.
- **Co-proxamol** (dextropropoxyphene 32.5 mg/ paracetamol 325 mg) has been withdrawn by the Committee on Safety of Medicines due to its unfavourable risk/benefit ratio; it is associated with an unacceptable risk of overdose [BNF 49, 2005].

Nonsteroidal anti-inflammatory drugs (NSAIDs) other than ibuprofen, diclofenac, naproxen, indometacin, and meloxicam are not generally recommended, as they are not specifically licensed for ankylosing spondylitis, or they have a worse balance between their efficacy and adverse effect profile than the recommended drugs [CSM, 1994; Hernández-Diaz et al, 2000; BNF 49, 2005].

Modified-release NSAIDs may be useful in some people, but they are more expensive [BNF 49, 2005]. If a longer-acting NSAID is required (e.g. to reduce early morning stiffness), naproxen is a suitable choice.

Strong opioids (e.g. morphine, pethidine) should be avoided, owing to the risk of dependence if they are used inappropriately. They are usually reserved for moderate to severe pain of a visceral origin [BNF 49, 2005].

Gastroprotective agents are sometimes needed, but not all are recommended:

- **H_2-receptor antagonists (H_2RAs):** at standard doses, H_2RAs reduce the risk of duodenal ulceration, and there is some evidence that double doses reduce the risk of gastric ulceration [Rostom et al, 2002]. However, no H_2RAs are currently licensed for the prevention of gastric ulceration induced by NSAIDs [BNF 49, 2005], which is more common than duodenal ulceration.
- **Rabeprazole** is not included as it is not specifically licensed for the prevention of NSAID-induced gastrointestinal ulcers [BNF 49, 2005].
- **Fixed-dose combinations of standard NSAIDs with misoprostol:** the optimum dose of misoprostol (i.e. 800 micrograms daily) cannot be reached using these preparations. In particular, only 400 micrograms daily of misoprostol is given with the higher doses of NSAID in these preparations.

Disease-modifying anti-rheumatic drugs (DMARDs) should only be initiated with specialist advice.

Information on monitoring people taking methotrexate, sulfasalazine, and other DMARDs is detailed in separate PRODIGY guidance *Monitoring people on DMARDs.*

Drugs included

Nonsteroidal anti-inflammatory drugs

- **Standard nonsteroidal anti-inflammatory drugs (NSAIDs): ibuprofen, diclofenac, and naproxen** have a good balance of efficacy against adverse effect profile [CSM, 1994; Henry et al, 1996; Hernández-Diaz and Rodriguez, 2000]. Naproxen has a longer duration of action than ibuprofen and diclofenac, and thus may be more suitable for nocturnal pain and early morning stiffness. Standard doses are offered as these are generally accepted to be sufficient for anti-inflammatory prophylaxis, although data are lacking.
- **Indometacin** has traditionally been used for the treatment of ankylosing spondylitis [Calin and Elswood, 1989]. However, it has a greater risk of adverse gastrointestinal (GI) effects than ibuprofen, diclofenac, or naproxen, and is therefore only recommended when these other NSAIDs do not provide adequate control.
- **Meloxicam** is a selective cyclo-oxygenase 2 (COX-2) inhibitor, and is the only NSAID specifically licensed for ankylosing spondylitis. It can be considered when there is a high risk of NSAID-induced GI toxicity.

Gastroprotective agents

- **Proton pump inhibitors (PPIs): lansoprazole, omeprazole, esomeprazole, and pantoprazole** are licensed for the prevention of gastroduodenal ulceration induced by NSAIDs [BNF 49, 2005]. PPIs reduce the risk of endoscopic ulcers, but there are no data on prevention of ulcer complications [Rostom et al, 2002]. However, PPIs are generally considered to be the preferred choice for gastroprotection, as they are better tolerated than misoprostol.
- **Misoprostol** is licensed for the prevention of gastroduodenal ulceration induced by NSAIDs [BNF 49, 2005]. It reduces the risk of endoscopically proven ulcers and has also been shown to reduce the risk of ulcer complications [Rostom et al, 2002]. It is less well tolerated than PPIs owing to GI adverse effects, particularly diarrhoea.

Standard analgesics

- **Paracetamol:** is an option for pain relief, and is not associated with GI toxicity [SIGN, 2000]. It may be used when NSAIDs are contraindicated or pain is mild.
- **Codeine (in combination with paracetamol):** higher-dose codeine is included for use with regular paracetamol for additional pain relief. Codeine 60 mg plus paracetamol has been shown to provide more pain relief than either codeine 60 mg alone or paracetamol 1000 mg alone [Moore et al, 1997]. Codeine should be prescribed separately to paracetamol to allow flexibility of dosing and titration of analgesic effect.

Intra-articular corticosteroids

- Intra-articular corticosteroids vary in their potency and duration of effect. They often give rapid relief of severe symptoms when injected by an appropriately skilled person. Lidocaine (lignocaine) is available for local anaesthesia:
  - **Triamcinolone acetonide and methylprednisolone** are suitable for injection of large joints.
  - **Hydrocortisone acetate, dexamethasone sodium phosphate, and prednisolone acetate** are recommended for injection of small joints.

Prescriptions

Intra-articular corticosteroids

Large joint: triamcinolone acetonide 40mg/ml + lidocaine 1%
- Age from 16 years onwards
- Triamcinolone acet 40mg/ml inj. Inject into large joint: 0.25ml (10mg) to 1ml (40mg), according to joint size; supply 1 1ml vial; NHS Cost £1.70.
- Lidocaine 1% injection (2ml). For local anaesthetic injection; supply 1 2ml ampoule; NHS Cost £0.28.

Large joint: methylprednisolone 80mg/2ml + lidocaine 1%
- Age from 16 years onwards
- Depo-Medrone+lidocaine 80/20mg. Inject into large joint: 0.5ml (20mg) to 2ml (80mg), according to joint size; supply 1 2ml vial; NHS Cost £5.88.

Medium joint: methylprednisolone 40mg/ml + lidocaine 1%
- Age from 16 years onwards
- Depo-Medrone+lidocaine 40/10mg. Inject into medium joint: 0.25ml (10mg) to 1ml (40mg), according to joint size; supply 1 1ml vial; NHS Cost £3.28.

Small joint: dexamethasone sod phos 5mg/ml + lidocaine 1%
- Age from 16 years onwards
- Dexamethasone sod phos 5mg/ml. Inject into small joint: 0.16ml (0.8mg) to 0.2ml (1mg), according to joint size; supply 1 1ml ampoule; NHS Cost £0.83.
- Lidocaine 1% injection (2ml). For local anaesthetic injection; supply 1 2ml ampoule; NHS Cost £0.28.

Small joint: hydrocortisone acetate 25mg/ml + lidocaine 1%
- Age from 16 years onwards
- Hydrocortisone 25mg/ml inj. Inject into small joint: 0.2ml (5mg) to 0.5ml (12.5mg), according to joint size; supply 1 1ml vial; NHS Cost £4.77.
- Lidocaine 1% injection (2ml). For local anaesthetic injection; supply 1 2ml ampoule; NHS Cost £0.28.

Small joint: prednisolone acetate 25mg/ml + lidocaine 1%
- Age from 16 years onwards
- Prednisolone acet 25mg/ml inj. Inject into small joint: 0.2ml (5mg) to 0.4ml (10mg), according to joint size; supply 1 1ml ampoule; NHS Cost £4.77.
- Lidocaine 1% injection (2ml). For local anaesthetic injection; supply 1 2ml ampoule; NHS Cost £0.28.

Standard NSAIDs: ibuprofen, naproxen and diclofenac

Ibuprofen tablets: 400mg three times a day
- Age from 16 years onwards
- Ibuprofen 400mg tablets. Take one tablet three times a day; supply 84 tablets; NHS Cost £2.74; OTC Cost £4.83.

Ibuprofen tablets: 400mg four times a day
- Age from 16 years onwards
- Ibuprofen 400mg tablets. Take one tablet four times a day; supply 112 tablets; NHS Cost £3.65; OTC Cost £6.44.

Ibuprofen tablets: 600mg three times a day
- Age from 16 years onwards
- Ibuprofen 600mg tablets. Take one tablet three times a day; supply 84 tablets; NHS Cost £2.81.

Ibuprofen tablets: 800mg three times a day
- Age from 16 years onwards
- Ibuprofen 400mg tablets. Take two tablets three times a day; supply 168 tablets; NHS Cost £4.58.

Diclofenac sodium e/c tablets: 25mg three times a day
- Age from 16 years onwards
- Diclofenac 25mg e/c tablets. Take one tablet three time a day; supply 84 tablets; NHS Cost £1.72.

Diclofenac sodium e/c tablets: 50mg three times a day
- Age from 16 years onwards
- Diclofenac 50mg e/c tablets. Take one tablet three time a day; supply 84 tablets; NHS Cost £1.45.

Naproxen tablets: 250mg twice a day
- Age from 16 years onwards
- Naproxen 250mg tablets. Take one tablet twice a day; supply 56 tablets; NHS Cost £2.68.

Naproxen tablets: 500mg twice a day
- Age from 16 years onwards
- Naproxen 500mg tablets. Take one tablet twice a day; supply 56 tablets; NHS Cost £4.90.

Analgesia

Paracetamol tablets: 1g up to four times a day
- Age from 16 years onwards
- Paracetamol 500mg tablets. Take two tablets every 4 t 6 hours when required for pain relief. Maximum of 8 tablets in 24 hours; supply 200 tablets; NHS Cost £2.1 OTC Cost £3.75.

Add on if required: codeine 30-60mg up to four times a day
- Age from 16 years onwards
- Codeine 30mg tablets. Take one to two tablets every 4 6 hours when required for pain relief. Maximum of 8 tablets in 24 hours; supply 60 tablets; NHS Cost £4.58

Paracetamol 500mg tablets + codeine 30mg tablets
- Age from 16 years onwards
- Paracetamol 500mg tablets. Take two tablets every 4 t 6 hours when required for pain relief. Maximum of 8 tablets in 24 hours; supply 200 tablets; NHS Cost £2.1 OTC Cost £3.75.
- Codeine 30mg tablets. Take one to two tablets every 4 6 hours when required for pain relief. Maximum of 8 tablets in 24 hours; supply 60 tablets; NHS Cost £4.58

Alternative NSAIDs: indometacin and meloxicam

Indometacin capsules: 25mg three times a day
- Age from 16 years onwards
- Indometacin 25mg capsules. Take one capsule three times a day; supply 84 capsules; NHS Cost £6.63.

Indometacin capsules: 50mg three times a day
- Age from 16 years onwards
- Indometacin 50mg capsules. Take one capsule three times a day; supply 84 capsules; NHS Cost £5.97.

Meloxicam tablets: 7.5mg once a day (COX-2 selective)
- Age from 16 years onwards
- Meloxicam 7.5mg tablets. Take one tablet once a day; supply 30 tablets; NHS Cost £9.70.

Meloxicam tablets: 15mg once a day (COX-2 selective)
- Age from 16 to 65 years
- Meloxicam 15mg tablets. Take one tablet once a day; supply 30 tablets; NHS Cost £13.48.

GI protection: use ONLY with a standard NSAID

Omeprazole capsules: 20mg once a day
- Age from 16 years onwards
- Omeprazole 20mg capsules. Take one capsule once a day; supply 28 capsules; NHS Cost £12.75.

Omeprazole tablets: 20mg once a day
- Age from 16 years onwards
- Omeprazole 20mg tablets. Take one tablet once a day; supply 28 tablets; NHS Cost £12.75.

nsoprazole capsules: 15mg each morning
- Age from 16 years onwards
- Lansoprazole 15mg capsules. Take one capsule each morning (on an empty stomach); supply 28 capsules; NHS Cost £12.92.

nsoprazole capsules: 30mg each morning
- Age from 16 years onwards
- Lansoprazole 30mg capsules. Take one capsule each morning (on an empty stomach); supply 28 capsules; NHS Cost £23.63.

ntoprazole e/c tablets: 20mg once a day
- Age from 16 years onwards
- Pantoprazole 20mg e/c tablets. Take one tablet once a day; supply 28 tablets; NHS Cost £12.31.

omeprazole tablets: 20mg once a day
- Age from 16 years onwards
- Esomeprazole 20mg tablets. Take one tablet once a day; supply 28 tablets; NHS Cost £18.50.

nsoprazole orodispersible tablets: 15mg each morning
- Age from 16 years onwards
- Lansoprazole 15mg orodisp tabs. Take one tablet each morning (on an empty stomach); supply 28 tablets; NHS Cost £10.86.

nsoprazole orodispersible tablets: 30mg each morning
- Age from 16 years onwards
- Lansoprazole 30mg orodisp tabs. Take one tablet each morning (on an empty stomach); supply 28 tablets; NHS Cost £21.38.

soprostol tablets: 200micrograms four times a day
- Age from 16 years onwards
- Misoprostol 200microgram tabs. Take one tablet four times a day; supply 120 tablets; NHS Cost £18.72.

ystemic problems

Vhich therapy?

Acute uveitis (iritis)

- This is the most common systemic complication associated with ankylosing spondylitis.
- Refer immediately for ophthalmology assessment and treatment.

Cardiac complications

- Cardiac complications include conduction defects and aortic valve problems, and occur rarely. They are normally complications of late disease.
- Refer for specialist cardiology management.

Chest complications

- Chest complications include upper-lobe pulmonary fibrosis, and limited respiratory reserve owing to rigidity of the chest wall. These tend to be complications of late severe disease.
- Refer for specialist respiratory management.

Anaemia of chronic disease

- Anaemia of chronic disease may occur, particularly in patients with elevated markers of inflammation (i.e. erythrocyte sedimentation rate, C-reactive protein, and platelet count).
- Refer for specialist management, e.g. treatment with a disease-modifying drug.

Acute back pain

- People with ankylosing spondylitis are at increased risk of suffering acute vertebral fractures. Refer without delay.
- People with ankylosing spondylitis may also get acute disc prolapse with sciatica. Manage accordingly. See separate PRODIGY guidance on *Back pain — lower*.

Should I refer or investigate?

Refer?

- Refer patients with new or deteriorating systemic problems to the appropriate specialist.

Patient information leaflets

The following PILs are available at www.prodigy.nhs.uk

- Ankylosing Spondylitis
- Antibody and Antigen Tests
- Arthritis Research Campaign - ARC
- Blood Test - Detecting Inflammation
- Blood Test - General
- National Ankylosing Spondylitis Society

Drug rationale

- There are no drugs offered in this scenario.

Prescriptions

Non-drug management

Advice only: regular exercise
- Age from 16 years onwards
- It is important to keep to a regular exercise program to maintain range of movement in your spine and joints.

Extended Information

Background information

- What is it? p.119
- How common is it? p.120
- How do I know my patient has it? p.120
- What else might it be? p.121
- Complications and prognosis p.121

What is it?

Ankylosing spondylitis is an inflammatory disease of unknown cause and is in the group of diseases known as the sero-negative spondylarthropathies. 'Sero-negative' implies that tests for rheumatoid factor and anti-nuclear antibody are negative. The principal features are:

- **Insidious onset** (at least 3 months, often several years).
- **Low back pain,** which typically radiates to the buttocks, sometimes to the thighs, and never below the knee.
- **Stiffness and fatigue** that are relieved by exercise.
- **Inflammation of the spinal ligaments,** intervertebral discs, facet joints, and costovertebral joints leading to ankylosis (i.e. fusion from fibrosis and calcification).
- **Inflammation of the sacroiliac joints.**
- **Enthesitis:** inflammation of the sites of insertions of tendons and ligaments into bone (e.g. patella, tibial tuberosity, heel [tendo Achilles and plantar fascia], ischial tuberosity, iliac crest, or greater trochanter).
- **Anterior uveitis** (acute, painful inflammation of the anterior structures of the eye).
- **Arthritis of peripheral joints:** usually asymmetric and usually involving large joints of the lower limbs. In older men, hips, shoulders, costovertebral, and sternomanubrial joints tend to be the most troublesome.
- **Association with human leukocyte antigen B27,** inflammatory bowel diseases, psoriasis, uveitis, or Reiter's syndrome.

[Sieper et al, 2002]

A

How common is it?

- **The spectrum of severity** ranges from mild (common) to severe and crippling (rare). Each year about 2% of people in a general practice will present with back pain, and up to 5% of these will show features of ankylosing spondylitis [Underwood and Dawes, 1995].
- **Ankylosing spondylitis mainly presents in young people before the age of 30 years** [Moll et al, 1974]. In many cases symptoms start in the mid-teens.
- **Prevalence estimated from hospital surveys is about 1 in 1000.** Population studies suggest the prevalence is higher, with more undiagnosed cases than diagnosed cases [Boyer et al, 1997].
- **Ankylosing spondylitis is more common in men than in women,** in a ratio of about 3 to 1 [Sieper et al, 2002].
- **The disease is more common in Northern European populations** [Kaipiainen-Seppanen et al, 1997] and less common in Afro-Caribbean populations. This reflects the prevalence of human leukocyte antigen B27 (HLA-B27) in differing populations.
- **About 95% of people with ankylosing spondylitis have the HLA-B27 histocompatibility group** [Brewerton et al, 1973; Schlosstein et al, 1973]. HLA-B27 is present in about 8% of the UK population, but most people with HLA-B27 do not have the disease.
- Ankylosing spondylitis shows a strong familial tendency. The risk for spondyloarthropathies among HLA-B27–positive persons who have a first-degree relative with ankylosing spondylitis is increased threefold [Khan, 2002].

How do I know my patient has it?

Clinical features of ankylosing spondylitis

- **The typical presentation** is a young man with gradual onset of stiffness and pain in the low back, buttocks, or upper posterior aspect of thighs. The back pain is worse at night. Stiffness is worst on waking and lasts for more than 30 minutes. Pain and stiffness are relieved by exercise. Early diagnosis is difficult before typical signs have appeared.
- **Fatigue.** Some people have significant systemic symptoms and signs, including fatigue, loss of weight, depression, and anaemia of chronic disease [Jones et al, 1996a].
- **Low back pain.** In about 90% of people with ankylosing spondylitis, the initial complaint is back pain in the lumbar region and sacroiliac joints. However, occasionally someone presents with pain in the thoracic or cervical area. The pain has an insidious onset, developing over several months. Pain is persistent, with periods of exacerbation and remission, but is diffuse and the site may be poorly localized. There is a sensation of deep ache in the buttocks or hips, radiating down the back of the thigh. Symptoms may be exacerbated by coughing or straining. The pain, which is relieved by mild physical activity, tends to be worse in the morning and lessens later in the day (in contrast to mechanical back pain). The person may need to get up from bed during the night to relieve the back pain.
- **Response to NSAIDs.** Back pain usually improves substantially within 48 hours of starting NSAIDs (and relapses rapidly on discontinuing NSAIDs), and this can be a helpful in diagnosis — the sensitivity was 77% and specificity 85% in one study [Dougados et al, 2002].
- **Stiffness.** A characteristic symptom of someone with ankylosing spondylitis is morning stiffness that may last from minutes to several hours. The stiffness is relieved by exercise.
- **Spinal movements.** There may be limited flexibility of spine in all three planes of motion, loss of lumbar lordosis, increased fingertip-to-floor distance, and reduced chest expansion.
- **Sacroiliitis, ankylosis, and spondylosis:** Bilateral sacroiliac inflammation, ankylosis, and spondylosis ar the hallmarks of the condition.
- **Arthritis of the appendicular skeleton.** Peripheral joint are eventually inflamed in about 40% of people with t disease, but at presentation the proportion with peripheral arthritis is only about 10%. Ankylosing spondylitis occasionally presents in women and childre with arthritis of peripheral joints. Peripheral-joint arthritis in ankylosing spondylitis tends to be asymmetrical (in contrast to the symmetrical pattern ir rheumatoid arthritis) and mostly affects large joints. Inflammatory activity in joints tends to mirror spinal inflammation.
- **Enthesitis.** Inflammation at areas of insertion of ligaments or tendons into bones may be a presenting feature. Common sites for enthesitis are the heel (Achilles tendon behind the calcaneum, and the planta fascia in the heel pad), tibial tuberosity, patella, greater trochanter, ischial tuberosity, and iliac crest.
- **Chest pain.** Anterior chest pain is described as non-anginal and mechanical, typically a sharp, stabbing pa encircling the hemithorax and precipitated by coughin and laughing. It can be an island of pain or may co-exi with pain in the dorsal spine.
- **Acute anterior uveitis** (iritis). This occurs in about a thi of patients and may precede the onset of ankylosing spondylitis. Many patients experience recurrent episodes. The main symptom is pain in the eye.

Investigations

- **Laboratory tests:**
  - Ankylosing spondylitis is a clinical diagnosis since nc laboratory tests are diagnostic. In the initial presentation special investigations may be more usef to exclude other conditions than to help diagnose ankylosing spondylitis.
  - Erythrocyte sedimentation rate (ESR) and C-reactive protein (CRP) tests may be helpful, although results are often within normal limits or mildly elevated.
  - Full blood count. There may be a mild normochrom normocytic anaemia.
  - Rheumatoid factor and anti-nuclear antibody tests a negative and are not indicated.
  - Liver function tests are not routinely done. Mild elevations of liver enzymes (e.g. alkaline phosphatas and gamma-glutamyl transferase) are not uncommo
  - HLA-B27 testing would usually be done in secondar care.
    - Its sensitivity and specificity are about 90% [Siepe and Rudwaleit, 2005].
    - Testing unaffected or asymptomatic relatives for HLA-B27 status is not justified as there no preventive or curative therapy [Khan, 2002].
- **Radiology.**
  - At first presentation there is often no radiographic abnormality. In established cases, radiographs of the sacroiliac joints and spine are diagnostic: extensive sclerosis and erosions in the sacroiliac joints; bony bridging between vertebrae; ligamentous calcificatior joining posterior spinous processes; and erosions and sclerosis in the vertebrae.

odified New York criteria for diagnosing nkylosing spondylitis

e British Society for Rheumatology recommends that the odified New York criteria' be used to diagnose kylosing spondylitis (AS):

Clinical criteria

- Low back pain, for more than 3 months; improved by exercise, not relieved by rest
- Limitation of lumbar spine motion in both the sagittal and the frontal planes
- Limitation of chest expansion relative to normal values for age and sex

Radiological criterion

- Sacroiliitis

Diagnose:

- **Definite AS** if the radiological criterion is present plus at least 1 clinical criterion
- **Probable AS** if: 3 clinical criteria are present, *or* if the radiological criterion is present, but no clinical criteria are present

an der Linden et al, 1984; BSR, 2004]

hat else might it be?

Mechanical back pain (e.g. prolapsed disc, spondylolisthesis, sciatica)

Other inflammatory conditions (e.g. psoriatic arthritis, reactive arthritis)

Infections (e.g. sepsis; tuberculous, fungal, or viral infection; infectious spondylitis)

Neoplastic diseases (e.g. metastatic, primary)

Referred pain

Other rare conditions (e.g. diffuse idiopathic skeletal hyperostosis [DISH] syndrome)

omplications and prognosis

ommon complications

Late diagnosis or misdiagnosis leading to failure to exercise, with resultant poor posture and rigidity.

Progressive involvement of the lumbar, thoracic, and cervical spine can lead to loss of movement of the spine (poker spine), but seldom leads to grave disabilities unless there is also severe arthritis of the hips.

Damage to peripheral joints.

Anterior uveitis (including iritis).

Association with psoriasis, inflammatory bowel disease, or Reiter's syndrome.

ess common complications

Vertebral osteoporosis with increased risk of wedge fracture

Fracture of spine — most serious complication

Heart: aortic regurgitation, mitral regurgitation, atrioventricular block, fibrosis with decreased left ventricular compliance

Lung: apical fibrosis

Cauda equina syndrome: altered bladder and bowel function; saddle anaesthesia; widespread or progressive motor weakness in the legs or a gait disturbance

Amyloidosis

Osteoarthritis

Secondary osteoporosis: usually at the large joints, e.g. hips, shoulders and knees

Blindness from uveitis

rognosis

Most people with the disease do well, although progression of the disease varies widely between different individuals. After an initial period of inflammation, the disease tends to settle down, and 90% of those affected remain fully independent or minimally disabled in the long term. This is despite severe restriction of spinal flexibility in 40% of those affected.

- **Most people have mainly spinal symptoms,** with occasional episodes of peripheral joint arthritis or iritis. A minority have recurrent extraspinal problems as well as spinal symptoms.
- **Women** tend to have milder spinal disease than men, but more symptoms in knees, wrists, ankles, hips, and/or pelvis.
- **Men** tend to have more severe disease than women, with involvement of the spine, pelvis, chest wall, hips, shoulders and/or feet.
- **Early onset of peripheral arthritis or intractable iritis** is associated with severe spinal restriction.
- **Fusion of vertebral bodies and costovertebral joints** may lead to a frozen thorax; usually this causes little respiratory impairment.
- **Rarely, fusion of the spine can lead to severe deformities and disability,** especially if the hips are also involved. Replacement of affected hip joints will not only relieve pain in the hips and improve mobility, but will also allow flexion of the lower limb to compensate for restricted movement of the spine.
- **Traumatic accidents** pose a high risk of vertebral fractures to people with ankylosing spondylitis: the spine is made brittle by rigidity and weak by osteoporosis [Will et al, 1989].
- **Radiotherapy** has not been used to treat ankylosing spondylitis for many years, but those who have been irradiated are at increased risk of developing leukaemia in the early post-radiation stage or carcinomas in the irradiation field at later stages.
- **Uveitis** may lead to blindness if not treated.
- **Heredity.**
  - If the parent has ankylosing spondylitis and is HLA-B27–positive, the chance of a child developing ankylosing spondylitis is less than 1 in 5
  - If the parent has ankylosing spondylitis and is HLA-B27–negative, the chance of a child developing ankylosing spondylitis is less than 1 in 10

[van der Linden et al, 1984; Sieper et al, 2002; NASS, 2004a]

Quality of life

The quality of life can be severely impacted by ankylosing spondylitis. Concerns of people with ankylosing spondylitis include:

- Stiffness (90%)
- Pain (83%)
- Fatigue (62%)
- Poor sleep (54%)
- Appearance (51%)
- Worries abut the future (50%)
- Medication adverse effects (41%)

[Ward, 1998; Doward et al, 2003; BSR, 2004]

Socio-economic impact

- Sick leave, work disability, and withdrawal from work are increased in people with ankylosing spondylitis when compared with the general population.
- Little research has been done on the socio-economic impact of ankylosing spondylitis, and many of the studies that have been made suffer from methodological weaknesses, such as not adjusting for age and sex, and not providing comparative data from a reference population.
- One Dutch study of people with ankylosing spondylitis found that, after adjusting for age and sex, employment was 11% less, and work disability 15% higher than expected in the general population.

- Work disability rates vary significantly between countries, probably because of different social security systems and economic development.
- A cost of illness (COI) study in the USA estimated the average total COI per person with ankylosing spondylitis to be US$6,720 per year [Ward, 2002]. A similar study in Europe estimated the COI to be 8862 euros in the Netherlands, 3188 euros in France, and 3609 euros in Belgium [Boonen et al, 2002]. About 70–75% of the COI in the European and in the US studies was due to lost productivity [Boonen, 2002].

[Sieper et al, 2002]

Management issues

- Overview of management of ankylosing spondylitis p.122
- How do I manage ankylosing spondylitis? p.122
- Medicines management p.123

Overview of management of ankylosing spondylitis

When ankylosing spondylitis is first recognized and/or suspected:

- Check inflammatory markers and X-ray the pelvis to check for the presence of sacroiliitis.
- Start treatment with an NSAID (or paracetamol) — symptoms should be alleviated within 1 or 2 days.
- Refer for confirmation of diagnosis and possible further treatment.
- Advise the person about the nature of ankylosing spondylitis and treatment options.
- Ensure that a programme of exercise and stretching will be arranged.

On follow-up:

- Follow up and monitor according to local shared care arrangements.
  - When reviewing, include assessments of disability, possible uveitis, response to treatment, and adverse effects of drugs.
- If NSAIDs have proved ineffective, refer for assessment for further treatment, such as a TNF-alpha blocking agent.
- If one or a few peripheral joints are inflamed, consider intra-articular injection with a long-acting corticosteroid.
- If there are features of complications such as uveitis, or cardiac or pulmonary problems, refer for specialist management.

How do I manage ankylosing spondylitis?

Early recognition of ankylosing spondylitis is important, but is difficult when, as is usual, the onset is insidious. [Khan, 2002]

- Refer promptly for confirmation of diagnosis and access to specialist care.

Non-drug management

- Advise the person about the nature of ankylosing spondylitis and treatment options [Khan, 2002].
  - Most cases will be mild and progress slowly, if at all.
  - Drug treatment and exercise can provide effective relief of most symptoms; however, some people will have painful enthesitis (inflammation where a tendon, ligament, or joint capsule joins bone) that responds poorly to treatment.
  - People with substantially limited range of motion of the neck should use wide rear-view mirrors, seat belt and proper head support while driving.
  - A healthy lifestyle should be maintained. Smoking cessation may be especially important in people with ankylosing spondylitis. People with a stiff spine or st joints should take care to avoid physical injury and falls. People receiving immunosuppressive therapy should be immunized yearly against influenza.
  - Modifications to the workplace may be useful and ar sometimes necessary.
  - Splints, braces, corsets, and bed rest are not helpful and should be avoided.
  - The National Ankylosing Spondylitis Society (NASS provides information and support for people with ankylosing spondylitis (www.nass.co.uk).
  - The Arthritis Research Campaign publishes a useful booklet on ankylosing spondylitis (www.arc.org.uk/about_arth/booklets/6001/6001.htm).
- Ensure that a programme of exercise and stretching has been arranged and is being followed. Effective management of ankylosing spondylitis depends on a combination of exercise and drugs.
  - A systematic review of physiotherapy interventions f ankylosing spondylitis (search date February 2004, 6 trials, 561 participants) found evidence to suggest th
    - A home exercise programme is better than no intervention.
    - Supervised group physiotherapy is better than hom exercises.
    - Inpatient spa-exercise therapy followed by supervised outpatient weekly group physiotherapy better than weekly group physiotherapy alone [Dagfinrud et al, 2004].
  - A trial of a home-based exercise intervention packag significantly improved self-reported levels of exercise and showed a trend towards improving function ove 6 months [Sweeney et al, 2002].
  - NASS has a network of over 100 centres in the UK that provide weekly exercise sessions supervised by a physiotherapist. NASS also publishes and sells an audio cassette and a home exercise video (www.nass.co.uk).

Drug treatment

Nonsteroidal anti-inflammatory drugs

- Treat with a nonsteroidal anti-inflammatory drug (NSAID). Alternatively, if symptoms are mild or NSAII are contraindicated or poorly tolerated, treat with a standard analgesic (paracetamol with or without codeine).
  - NSAIDs were shown to reduce radiographic progression of ankylosing spondylitis in a randomize controlled trial which followed 215 people for 2 year [Wanders et al, 2005].
  - NSAIDs have been shown to relieve pain effectively i the short term.
  - The various NSAIDs, including cyclo-oxygenase 2 specific inhibitors, have similar effectiveness in relieving the symptoms of ankylosing spondylitis (wit some clinically unimportant exceptions).
  - Different people may respond differently to individua NSAIDs, hence the recommendation to try another NSAID if a particular drug is ineffective in a particula person.
  - There is little robust evidence to guide the choice of dose, or duration of treatment, or whether to treat intermittently or continuously.
  - The effectiveness of paracetamol in ankylosing spondylitis has not been tested in any randomized controlled trial — we searched the Cochrane central

register of controlled trials (CENTRAL), Medline, and Embase on 31 March 2005.

[Dougados et al, 2002]

Which nonsteroidal anti-inflammatory drug should I use?

Start treatment with ibuprofen, diclofenac, or naproxen. There is no good evidence that any one NSAID is more effective than another in the treatment of ankylosing spondylitis. Ibuprofen, diclofenac, and naproxen are recommended for initial treatment as their general efficacy and adverse effect profiles are more favourable than the profiles of other NSAIDs [CSM, 1994; Hernández-Diaz et al, 2000; BNF 49, 2005].

Ibuprofen is probably the least toxic NSAID and should be used first. Doses of up to 2.4 g per day may be necessary.

Diclofenac is an alternative to ibuprofen with greater potency but more risk of adverse effects. The standard dosage is 50 mg taken three times a day.

Naproxen has similar potency and risk of adverse effects to diclofenac. Naproxen has a longer duration of action than ibuprofen and diclofenac, and thus may be more suitable for early morning stiffness. Up to 1 g a day in two divided doses can be prescribed if necessary.

Change to indometacin if lower risk NSAIDs do not provide adequate control.

Indometacin has been traditionally used for the treatment of ankylosing spondylitis [Calin and Elswood, 1989]. However, the risk of gastrointestinal (GI) adverse effects is higher than with ibuprofen, diclofenac, or naproxen. Indometacin is therefore only recommended when treatment with lower-risk NSAIDs provides inadequate control.

Consider adding gastroprotection with a proton pump inhibitor (PPI) if dyspepsia is troublesome or GI toxicity is a major concern — see separate PRODIGY guidance on *Dyspepsia — symptoms (uninvestigated by endoscopy)* and *Nonsteroidal anti-inflammatory drugs (NSAIDs)*.

Meloxicam is an alternative if GI toxicity is a major concern:

- Meloxicam is a selective cyclo-oxygenase 2 (COX-2) inhibitor, and is the only NSAID specifically licensed for ankylosing spondylitis. It may be an option when there is a high risk of NSAID-induced GI toxicity, although there are insufficient data of medium to long-term duration to support claims that it has a better adverse effect profile than standard NSAIDs.

Coxibs (e.g. celecoxib and etoricoxib) are not recommended. After the withdrawal of rofecoxib and suspension of valdecoxib, there have been growing concerns that COX-2 selective inhibitors may cause serious cardiovascular events. Following a European-wide review of the data, the Committee on Safety of Medicines (CSM) has recently advised that [CSM, 2005b]:

- The evidence suggests that coxibs, as a class, may cause an increased risk of thrombotic events (e.g. myocardial infarction and stroke) compared with placebo and some NSAIDs.

The risk may increase with dose and duration of exposure.

TNF-alpha blocking agents

If NSAIDs are ineffective, refer for assessment for further treatment, such as a TNF-alpha blocking agent.

- NICE plan to publish in December 2006 a technology appraisal on the use of TNF-alpha blocking agents (adalimumab, etanercept, and infliximab) for the treatment of ankylosing spondylitis.
- The evidence for TNF-alpha blockers has been recently reviewed [DTB, 2005].
- In July 2004 the British Society for Rheumatology (BSR) published a guidelines on prescribing TNF-alpha blockers licensed in the UK for treating ankylosing spondylitis: etanercept and infliximab. According to the BSR guidelines, treatment with TNF blocking agents may be appropriate if:
  - The person's disease satisfies the modified New York criteria for diagnosing ankylosing spondylitis (detailed in *Background issues* above.
  - Ankylosing spondylitis is active (and formally quantified).
  - Conventional treatment with NSAIDs has failed — at least two NSAIDs should have been taken separately for at least 4 weeks at maximum tolerated/recommended doses.
  - No exclusion criteria present (e.g. pregnancy, breastfeeding, significant infection, severe heart failure, demyelinating disease).
- Information on monitoring people taking TNF-alpha blocking agents is detailed in separate PRODIGY guidance *Monitoring people on DMARDs*.

Methotrexate and sulfasalazine

- Methotrexate and sulfasalazine have been widely used to treat ankylosing spondylitis, but the body of evidence from a number of trials suggests that any benefits are slight and limited to peripheral arthritis.
- Information on monitoring people taking methotrexate, sulfasalazine, and other DMARDs is detailed in separate PRODIGY guidance *Monitoring people on DMARDs*.

[Dougados et al, 2002; Maksymowych et al, 2002; Chen and Liu, 2005]

Long-acting corticosteroids for injection

- Long-acting corticosteroids injected into a large joint can provide rapid relief lasting for many months [Dougados et al, 2002].
- The large joint most commonly affected in ankylosing spondylitis is the sacroiliac joint, but, because of its anatomy, injection has to be done with the aid of radiographic imaging and is rarely done.

[Dougados et al, 2002]

Surgery

- A small proportion of people will eventually require surgery. Ankylosis of the spine can lead to severe deformities and disability, especially if the hips are also involved. Replacing the affected hip joints will not only relieve pain in the hips and improve mobility, but will also allow hip flexion to compensate for restricted spinal movement. Hip arthroplasty is the most common surgical intervention, being required by 5% of people with ankylosing spondylitis [Calin and Elswood, 1989]. One concern with relatively young people needing joint replacement is the likely future need for revision surgery.
- Rarely, severe spinal deformities are corrected surgically.

New and specialized treatments

- Bisphosphonates have shown promising results in preliminary trials, but further trials are required to determine their place in the treatment of ankylosing spondylitis [Dougados et al, 2002].
- Pulse therapy with intravenous corticosteroids has been shown in two small trials to improve disease activity in ankylosing spondylitis [Richter et al, 1983; Peters and Ejstrup, 1992].

Medicines management

Nonsteroidal anti-inflammatory drugs

A full discussion on the contraindications, adverse effects, monitoring issues, and interactions of NSAIDs is beyond the scope of this guidance. For further information, see the

A

separate PRODIGY guidance on *Nonsteroidal anti-inflammatory drugs (NSAIDs)*.

- Consider comorbidity when prescribing nonsteroidal anti-inflammatory drugs (NSAIDs).
- NSAIDs commonly cause gastrointestinal adverse effects, and can worsen asthma, hypertension, renal impairment, and heart failure.
- For people with ankylosing spondylitis who are at high risk of gastrointestinal adverse events, we recommend the following options:
  - Use paracetamol (with or without codeine) instead of a NSAID if possible, or
  - Use a gastroprotective agent with a standard NSAID [NICE, 2001], or
  - Use a cyclo-oxygenase 2 (COX-2) selective NSAID alone [NICE, 2001].
- For advice on the management of dyspepsia due to NSAIDs, see the separate PRODIGY guidance on *Dyspepsia — symptoms (uninvestigated by endoscopy)* and *Dyspepsia — proven DU, GU, or NSAID-associated ulcer*.

Analgesia

Paracetamol

- Paracetamol is safe and effective for the treatment of mild to moderate pain when used correctly, and is well tolerated at the recommended daily dose.
- It is more likely to be effective for ankylosing spondylitis when used regularly rather than 'as required'.

Codeine

- Codeine may be added to paracetamol if more pain relief is required.
- Paracetamol and codeine should be prescribed separately so they can be individually titrated; combination products such as co-codamol are not recommended.
- Codeine may cause nausea, vomiting, constipation, and drowsiness. A regular laxative is often needed when it is used long-term.

Intra-articular corticosteroids

How should intra-articular corticosteroids be administered?

- Intra-articular corticosteroids can be used to treat peripheral joints (the number depending on the person's ability to tolerate the injections).
- They should only be administered by health-care professionals with experience of giving intra-articular injections [DTB, 1995].

Which injectable corticosteroid should I use?

- Intra-articular corticosteroids are not specifically licensed in the treatment of ankylosing spondylitis.
- **Specific corticosteroids are recommended for different joints according to their size.** Atrophy of subcutaneous tissues and local skin depigmentation may occur from periarticular leakage of corticosteroid. The risk is greatest if large or repeated doses of a long-acting, potent corticosteroid are given:
  - **Smaller joints:** hydrocortisone, dexamethasone, or prednisolone are recommended.
  - **Larger joints:** triamcinolone or methylprednisolone are recommended.

When should I avoid injecting a joint?

- **Avoid injecting:**
  - Prosthetic joints
  - When there is any possibility of sepsis
  - Joints within 3 months of a previous injection
- **Inject with caution if the person is taking anti-coagulants.**

References

NHS staff in England can link, free of charge, from references to full text journals by clicking on [Full text] • the PRODIGY website.

1. BNF 49 (2005) *British National Formulary*. 49th ed London: British Medical Association and Royal Pharmaceutical Society of Great Britain.
2. Boonen, A. (2002) Socioeconomic consequences of ankylosing spondylitis. *Clinical & Experimental Rheumatology* **20**(Suppl 28), S23-S26.
3. Boonen, A., van der, Heijde D., Landewe, R. et al (2002) Work status and productivity costs due to ankylosing spondylitis: comparison of three Europe countries. *Annals of the Rheumatic Diseases* **61**(5), 429–437. [Full text]
4. Boyer, G.S., Templin, D.W., Bowler, A. et al (1997) comparison of patients with spondyloarthropathy se in speciality clinic with those identified in a community-wide epidemiological study. Has the clas case misled us? *Archives of Internal Medicine* **157**(1 2111–2117. [Full text]
5. Brewerton, D.A., Hart, F.D., Nicholls, A. et al (1973 Ankylosing spondylitis and HL-A 27. *Lancet* **1**(7809 904–907.
6. BSR (2004) *BSR guideline for prescribing TNF alph blockers in adults with ankylosing spondylitis*. Britis Society for Rheumatology. www.rheumatology.org. [Accessed: 07/03/2005].
7. Calin, A. and Elswood, J. (1989) The outcome of 13 total hip replacements and 12 revisions in ankylosin spondylitis: high success rate after a mean follow-up 7.5 years. *Journal of Rheumatology* **16**(7), 955–958.
8. Calin, A., Garrett, S., Whitelock, H. et al (1994) A n approach to defining functional ability in ankylosing spondylitis: the development of the Bath Ankylosing Spondylitis Functional Index. *Journal of Rheumatolo* **21**(12), 2281–2285.
9. Chen, J. and Liu, C. (2005) *Sulfasalazine for ankylosing spondylitis (Cochrane Review)*. The Cochrane Library. Issue 2. Chichester, UK: John Wil & Sons, Ltd. www.nelh.nhs.uk/cochrane.asp [Accessed: 03/06/2005]. [Full text]
10. CSM (1994) Relative safety of oral non-aspirin NSAIDs. *Current Problems in Pharmacovigilance* **20**(Aug), 9–11.
11. CSM (2005a) *Withdrawal of co-proxamol products and interim updated prescribing information*. Committee on Safety of Medicines. www.mca.gov.u [Accessed: 24/03/2005].
12. CSM (2005b) *Updated advice on the safety of selecti cox-2 inhibitors*. Committee on Safety of Medicines. http://medicines.mhra.gov.uk [Accessed: 30/03/2005
13. Dagfinrud, H., Hagen, K.B. and Kvien, T.K. (2004) *Physiotherapy interventions for ankylosing spondyli (Cochrane Review)*. The Cochrane Library. Issue 4. Chichester, UK: John Wiley & Sons, Ltd. www.nelh.nhs.uk/cochrane.asp [Accessed: 07/03/ 2005]. [Full text]
14. De Craen, A.J., Di Giulio, G., Lampe-Schoenmaecke J.E. et al (1996) Analgesic efficacy and safety of paracetamol-codeine combinations versus paracetam alone: a systematic review. *British Medical Journal* **313**(7053), 321–325. [Full text]
15. Dougados, M., Dijkmans, B., Khan, M. et al (2002) Conventional treatments for ankylosing spondylitis. *Annals of the Rheumatic Diseases* **61**(Suppl 3), iii40-iii50. [Full text]
16. Doward, L.C., Spoorenberg, A., Cook, S.A. et al (2003) Development of the ASQoL: a quality of life

instrument specific to ankylosing spondylitis. *Annals of the Rheumatic Diseases* **62**(1), 20–26. [Full text]

DTB (1995) Articular and periarticular corticosteroid injections. *Drug & Therapeutics Bulletin* **33**(9), 67–70. [Full text]

DTB (2005) TNF antagonists for ankylosing spondylitis. *Drug & Therapeutics Bulletin* **43**(3), 19–22.

Garrett, S., Jenkinson, T., Kennedy, L.G. et al (1994) A new approach to defining disease status in ankylosing spondylitis: the Bath Ankylosing Spondylitis Disease Activity Index. *Journal of Rheumatology* **21**(12), 2286–2291.

Henry, D., Lim, L.L., Garcia-Rodriguez, L.A. et al (1996) Variability in risk of gastrointestinal complications with individual non-steroidal anti-inflammatory drugs: results of a collaborative meta-analysis. *British Medical Journal* **312**(7046), 1563–1566. [Full text]

Hernández-Diaz, S. and Rodriguez, L.A. (2000) Association between nonsteroidal anti-inflammatory drugs and upper gastrointestinal tract bleeding/perforation: an overview of epidemiologic studies published in the 1990s. *Archives of Internal Medicine* **160**(14), 2093–2099. [Full text]

Hernández-Diaz, S., Werler, M.M., Walker, A.M. and Mitchell, A.A. (2000) Folic acid antagonists during pregnancy and the risk of birth defects. *New England Journal of Medicine* **343**(22), 1608–1614. [Full text]

Jenkinson, T.R., Mallorie, P.A., Whitelock, H.C. et al (1994) Defining spinal mobility in ankylosing spondylitis (AS). The Bath AS Metrology Index. *Journal of Rheumatology* **21**(9), 1694–1698.

Jones, S.D., Koh, W.H., Steiner, A. et al (1996a) Fatigue in ankylosing spondylitis: its prevalence and relationship to disease activity, sleep and other factors. *Journal of Rheumatology* **23**(3), 487–490.

Jones, S.D., Steiner, A., Garrett, S.L. and Calin, A. (1996b) The Bath Ankylosing Spondylitis Patient Global Score (BAS-G). *British Journal of Rheumatology* **35**(1), 66–71. [Full text]

Kaipiainen-Seppanen, O., Aho, K. and Heliovaara, M. (1997) Incidence and prevalence of ankylosing spondylitis in Finland. *Journal of Rheumatology* **24**(3), 496–499.

7. Khan, M.A. (2002) Update on spondyloarthropathies. *Annals of Internal Medicine* **136**(12), 896–907.

Maksymowych, W.P., Breban, M. and Braun, J. (2002) Ankylosing spondylitis and current disease-controlling agents: do they work? *Best Practice & Research Clinical Rheumatology* **16**(4), 619–630.

MeReC (1993) Combination analgesics. *MeReC Bulletin* **4**(12), 45–48.

Moll, J.H., Haslock, I., Macrae, I.F. and Wright, V. (1974) Associations between ankylosing spondylitis, psoriatic arthritis, Reiter's disease, the intestinal arthropathies and Behcet's syndrome. *Medicine* **53**(5), 343–364.

1. Moore, R.A. and McQuay, H.J. (1997) Single-patient data meta-analysis of 3453 postoperative patients: oral tramadol versus placebo, codeine and combination analgesics. *Pain* **69**(3), 287–294.

2. Moore, A., Collins, S., Carroll, D. and McQuay, H. (1997) Paracetamol with and without codeine in acute pain: a quantitative systematic review. *Pain* **70**(2–3), 193–201.

3. NASS (2004a) *Guidebook for patients. A positive response to ankylosing spondylitis.* National Ankylosing Spondylitis Society. www.nass.co.uk [Accessed: 09/03/2005].

4. NASS (2004b) *The Bath indices. Outcome measures for use with ankylosing spondylitis patients.* National Ankylosing Spondylitis Society. www.nass.co.uk/bath_indices.htm [Accessed: 09/03/2005].

35. NICE (2001) *Guidance on the use of cyclo-oxygenase (Cox) II selective inhibitors, celecoxib, rofecoxib, meloxicam and etodolac for osteoarthritis and rheumatoid arthritis.* Technology appraisal no. 27. National Institute for Health and Clinical Excellence. www.nice.org.uk [Accessed: 16/10/2003].

36. Peters, N.D. and Ejstrup, L. (1992) Intravenous methylprednisolone pulse therapy in ankylosing spondylitis. *Scandinavian Journal of Rheumatology* **21**(3), 134–138.

37. Richter, M.B., Woo, P., Panayi, G.S. et al (1983) The effects of intravenous pulse methylprednisolone on immunological and inflammatory processes in ankylosing spondylitis. *Clinical & Experimental Immunology* **53**(1), 51–59.

38. Rostom, A., Wells, G., Tugwell, P. et al (2002) *Prevention of NSAID-induced gastroduodenal ulcers (Cochrane Review).* The Cochrane Library. Issue 4. Chichester, UK: John Wiley & Sons, Ltd. www.nelh.nhs.uk/cochrane.asp [Accessed: 04/04/2005]. [Full text]

39. Schlosstein, L., Terasaki, P.I., Bluestone, R. and Pearson, C.M. (1973) High association of an HL-A antigen, W27, with ankylosing spondylitis. *New England Journal of Medicine* **288**(14), 704–706.

40. Sieper, J. and Rudwaleit, M. (2005) Early referral recommendations for ankylosing spondylitis (including pre-radiographic and radiographic forms) in primary care. *Annals of the Rheumatic Diseases* **64**(5), 659–663.

41. Sieper, J., Braun, J., Rudwaleit, M. et al (2002) Ankylosing spondylitis: an overview. *Annals of the Rheumatic Diseases* **61**(Suppl 3), iii8-iii18. [Full text]

42. SIGN (2000) *Management of early rheumatoid arthritis.* Report no. 48. Scottish Intercollegiate Guidelines Network. www.sign.ac.uk [Accessed: 01/04/2002].

43. Spoorenberg, A., Van Tubergen, A., Landewe, R. et al (2005) Measuring disease activity in ankylosing spondylitis: patient and physician have different perspectives. *Rheumatology* **44**(6), 789–795.

44. Sweeney, S., Taylor, G. and Calin, A. (2002) The effect of a home based exercise intervention package on outcome in ankylosing spondylitis: a randomized controlled trial. *Journal of Rheumatology* **29**(4), 763–766.

45. Underwood, M.R. and Dawes, P. (1995) Inflammatory back pain in primary care. *British Journal of Rheumatology* **34**(11), 1074–1077. [Full text]

46. van der Heijde, D., Braun, J., McGonagle, D. and Siegel, J. (2002) Treatment trials in ankylosing spondylitis: current and future considerations. *Annals of the Rheumatic Diseases* **61**(Suppl 3), iii24-iii32. [Full text]

47. van der Linden, S., Valkenburg, H.A. and Cats, A. (1984) Evaluation of diagnostic criteria for ankylosing spondylitis. A proposal for modification of the New York criteria. *Arthritis & Rheumatism* **27**(4), 361–368.

48. Wanders, A., Heijde, D.V., Landewe, R. et al (2005) Nonsteroidal antiinflammatory drugs reduce radiographic progression in patients with ankylosing spondylitis: a randomized clinical trial. *Arthritis & Rheumatism* **52**(6), 1756–1765.

49. Ward, M.M. (1998) Quality of life in patients with ankylosing spondylitis. *Rheumatic Diseases Clinics of North America* **24**(4), 815–827.

50. Ward, M.M. (2002) Functional disability predicts total costs in patients with ankylosing spondylitis. *Arthritis & Rheumatism* **46**(1), 223–231.

51. Will, R., Palmer, R., Bhalla, A.K. et al (1989) Osteoporosis in early ankylosing spondylitis: a primary pathological event? *Lancet* **2**(8678–8679), 1483–1485.

PRODIGY GUIDANCE

Aphthous ulcer

A

Last revised in July 2005
www.prodigy.nhs.uk/guidance.asp?gt=Aphthous ulcer

Applies to people over the age of 5 years

This guidance covers the management of aphthous ulcers. These are also known as aphthous stomatitis, aphthae, or canker sores.

This guidance does not cover the management of ulceration due to infection with herpes simplex, or ulcers from other causes.

There is separate PRODIGY guidance for *Herpes simplex — oral* (which includes cold sores) and *Palliative care — oral problems*.

Goals

- To ease symptoms and speed healing

Contents

Scenarios

- Treating aphthous ulcers p.126

Extended Information, p. 128

Treating aphthous ulcers

Which therapy?

- **For ulcers that recur only a few times a year:** medication may not be needed. If the patient already uses an over-the-counter remedy that suits them, encourage them to continue using it.
- **For frequently recurring ulcers:**
  - Identify and avoid any precipitating factors (e.g. local trauma, stress).
  - Consider underlying systemic disease; iron, folate, or vitamin B_{12} deficiency; gluten allergy; or adverse drug reactions.
- **To aid healing of frequently recurring, or very painful ulcers:**
  - **Give a short course of topical corticosteroids.** These should be applied as soon as symptoms start.
  - **Chlorhexidine mouthwash** can also be used to aid healing and prevent secondary bacterial infection.
- **If local analgesia is needed, consider:**
  - Choline salicylate gel for mildly painful aphthae.
  - Benzydamine mouthwash or spray for more painful aphthae.
  - Lidocaine (lignocaine) ointment or spray for extremely painful apthae.

All the products discussed are available as over-the-counter remedies.

Practical prescribing points

For further information please see the *Medicines Compendium* (www.medicines.org.uk) or the *British National Formulary* (www.bnf.org).

- **Benzydamine mouthwash or spray:** numbness and stinging are sometimes a problem. Diluting the mouthwash in an equal volume of water before use reduces stinging.
- **Chlorhexidine mouthwash:** this can stain teeth brown when used regularly. The stain is not usually permanent, and can be reduced by avoiding drinks that contain tannin (e.g. tea, coffee, or red wine), and by brushing teeth before use. Note: rinse the mouth well after brushing as chlorhexidine can be inactivated by some ingredients in toothpaste.)
- **Choline salicylate dental gel:** excessive use can cause ulceration, particularly in denture wearers.
- **Lidocaine (lignocaine) ointment or spray:** avoid using before meals. Lidocaine can numb the pharynx, leadin to aspiration or choking.

Should I refer or investigate?

Refer?

- **Refer where there is evidence of a contributing systemi disease** suggested by history, examination, or results o investigations.
- **Refer when ulceration is particularly painful and disabling or if recurrences are frequent and severe.**
- **Referral guidelines for suspected cancer** published by t National Institute for Health and Clinical Excellence (NICE) [NICE, 2005] recommend referral or follow-u for people with persistent symptoms or signs related to the oral cavity in whom a definitive diagnosis of a beni lesion cannot be made. If the symptoms and signs have not disappeared after 6 weeks refer urgently.
- **NICE recommends urgent referral for people with:**
  - Unexplained ulceration of the oral mucosa or mass persisting for more than 3 weeks
  - Unexplained red and white patches (included suspected lichen planus) of the oral mucosa that *are* painful or swollen or bleeding
- NICE recommends non-urgent referral for people with unexplained red and white patches (included suspected lichen planus) of the oral mucosa that are *not* painful o swollen or bleeding.

Investigate?

Screen for vitamin deficiency where appropriate (e.g. 6-month history of recurrent aphthous ulcers or immediatel if systemic disease, malabsorption, or nutritional deficien is suspected) — full blood count, serum and red cell folat serum B_{12}, and serum ferritin.

- Further investigation may be guided by blood test resul (for example, investigation of suspected malabsorption
- Biopsy of the lesion may occasionally be needed, but is conducted by specialists.

Patient information leaflets

The following PILs are available at www.prodigy.nhs.uk

- Medicines - Name Changes of Medicines
- Mouth Ulcers (Minor Aphthous Type)

ared decision making

Aphthous mouth ulcers typically recur. Their cause is not known.

General measures which may help when you have an ulcer include:

- Avoid spicy and salty foods and acidic fruit drinks.
- Use a straw to drink cool (not hot) drinks to by-pass painful ulcers.
- Use a very soft toothbrush.

teroid lozenges or paste may also reduce the pain and elp ulcers to heal more quickly. These work best the ooner they are started once an ulcer erupts.

hlorhexidine mouthwash may reduce the pain and help ılcers to heal more quickly. It also helps to prevent ılcers from becoming infected.

A painkilling oral rinse, gel, or mouth spray may help to ase pain: for example, benzydamine spray, choline alicylate gel, or lidocaine ointment. The effect of each lose does not last long.

You can buy all the above from pharmacies without a prescription.

f you use *oral* nicotine replacement therapy such as gum, consider changing to patches or nasal spray if you hink that the ulcers started after you started using the nicotine gum.

rug rationale

ugs not included

Betamethasone soluble tablets or beclometasone spray are not licensed for the treatment of oral lesions. They should be reserved for use in extensive ulceration, or for ulcers in areas that are difficult to reach, possibly under specialist supervision.

Carbenoxolone or carmellose provide mechanical protection over the ulcer site. They are probably most helpful for episodes of minor apthous ulceration that only recur a few times a year.

Oral chlorhexidine preparations other than 0.2% mouthwash: chlorhexidine 1% dental gel is more difficult to apply evenly to all areas of the mouth than a mouthwash. We found no evidence that chlorhexidine 0.12% mouthwash or 0.2% spray have been evaluated for treating aphthous ulcers.

Povidone-iodine mouthwash: we have found no evidence that povidone-iodine mouthwash has been evaluated for treating aphthous ulcers, and it should be avoided in view of possible iodine sensitivity.

Tetracycline mouthwash may reduce the duration and severity of ulcers, but can cause oral candidiasis and a burning-like sensation of the pharynx [Porter et al, 2000]. Tetracycline capsules are no longer available in the UK, so doxycycline capsules are generally substituted instead; the contents of a 100-mg capsule are dispersed in water and rinsed around the mouth for 2–3 minutes, four times a day.

rugs included

Topical corticosteroids: triamcinolone oral paste or hydrocortisone lozenges are probably most useful when applied in the prodromal period, before the ulcer develops. Concerns have been raised that long-term or repeated application could cause adrenal suppression. However, there is little evidence that even some of the more potent steroids (such as fluocinonide or betamethasone) can cause any significant problem in this respect [Scully et al, 2002]. Note: triamcinolone oral paste may be difficult to apply to some parts of the mouth.

- **Chlorhexidine gluconate 0.2% mouthwash** is used for aphthous ulcers. There is some evidence that it reduces duration and severity of ulceration. Recurrence of ulceration is not prevented but it may help to prevent secondary bacterial infection [Porter and Scully, 2004]. It can also provide oral hygiene when people are unable to brush their teeth. However, regular use causes tooth staining, which may not be acceptable to some people.
- **Choline salicylate dental gel** (Bonjela or Dinnefords Teejel) may provide analgesia for some people, but excessive application can cause further ulceration.
- **Benzydamine mouthwash or spray** may be considered for some people. Although they have not been shown to affect the course of an ulcerative episode, they may be useful when analgesia is required [Scully et al, 2003]. The spray is more convenient to carry for frequent applications. The mouthwash is not licensed for use in children aged 12 years and under.
- **Lidocaine (lignocaine) 5% ointment or 10% spray** should be reserved for severe pain (e.g. chemotherapy- or radiotherapy-induced mucositis). Again, the duration of action is relatively short, so it will not provide continuous analgesia throughout the day. Care should also be taken not to anaesthetize the pharynx before meals as this might lead to aspiration or choking.

Prescriptions

Advice note

Advice only: over-the-counter purchase

- Age from 1 month onwards
- Mouth (aphthous) ulcers are common. They typically recur. Their cause is not known. You can buy some remedies from a pharmacy: **Steroid gel or pellets** reduce inflammation. They are placed next to an ulcer, and dissolve. They may reduce pain and the length of time the ulcer lasts if they are used early. **Chlorhexidine** is an antiseptic mouthwash that helps to heal mouth ulcers and prevents them becoming infected. **A painkilling gel, mouthwash, or spray** is occasionally used for very painful ulcers, but their effect is short lived.

Topical corticosteroids

Triamcinolone 0.1% oral paste: apply 2 to 4 times a day

- Age from 5 years onwards
- Triamcinolone 0.1% oral paste. Apply a thin layer to the affected area(s) 2 to 4 times a day. Do not rub in; supply 10 grams; NHS Cost £1.27; OTC Cost £7.90.

Hydrocortisone 2.5mg lozenges: use four times a day

- Age from 7 years onwards
- Hydrocortisone 2.5mg lozenges. Place one lozenge over the affected area and allow it to dissolve slowly, four times a day; supply 20 lozenges; NHS Cost £2.73; OTC Cost £3.50.

Chlorhexidine mouthwash

Chlorhexidine 0.2% mouthwash: rinse with 10ml twice a day

- Age from 7 years onwards
- Chlorhexidine 0.2% mouthwash. Rinse the mouth with 10ml for about 1 minute twice a day; supply 300 ml; NHS Cost £1.82; OTC Cost £3.14.

Topical analgesia: use when required

Choline salicylate: use 1/4 inch of gel up to 6 times a day

- Age from 5 to 11 years
- Choline salicylate oral gel. Gently massage 1/4 inch of gel onto the affected area when required for pain relief.

Maximum of 6 applications in 24 hours; supply 15 grams; NHS Cost £1.70; OTC Cost £2.65.

Choline salicylate: use 1/2 inch of gel up to 6 times a day

- Age from 12 years onwards
- Choline salicylate oral gel. Gently massage 1/2 inch of gel onto the affected area when required for pain relief. Maximum of 6 applications in 24 hours; supply 15 grams; NHS Cost £1.70; OTC Cost £2.65.

Benzydamine 0.15% mouthwash: rinse with 15ml every 3 hours

- Age from 13 years onwards
- Benzydamine 0.15% mouthwash. Rinse the mouth with 15ml every 3 hours when required for pain relief. Increase to every one and a half hours if required; supply 300 ml; NHS Cost £3.92; OTC Cost £6.91.

Benzydamine 0.15% spray: use 4 sprays every 3 hours

- Age from 6 to 12 years
- Benzydamine 0.15% spray. Spray four times onto the affected area every 3 hours when required for pain relief. Increase to every one and a half hours if required; supply 30 ml; NHS Cost £3.41; OTC Cost £5.99.

Benzydamine 0.15% spray: use 4 to 8 sprays every 3 hours

- Age from 13 years onwards
- Benzydamine 0.15% spray. Spray 4 to 8 times onto the affected area every 3 hours when required for pain relief. Increase to every one and a half hours if required; supply 30 ml; NHS Cost £3.41; OTC Cost £5.99.

Lidocaine 5% ointment: use when required

- Age from 12 years onwards
- Lidocaine 5% ointment. Apply a small amount of ointment to the affected area when required for pain relief; supply 15 grams; NHS Cost £0.85.

Lidocaine 10% spray: use when required

- Age from 12 years onwards
- Lidocaine 10% spray. Spray one puff into the mouth when required for pain relief; supply 1 50ml spray; NHS Cost £3.13.

Extended Information

Background information

- What is it? p.128
- What causes it? p.128
- How common is it? p.128
- How do I know my patient has it? p.128
- What else might it be? p.128
- Complications and prognosis p.129

What is it?

- **Aphthous ulcers are painful, clearly defined, rounded, shallow, oral ulcers.**
- They often recur at intervals of a few days to a few months.

[Scully et al, 2003]

What causes it?

- The cause of recurrent aphthous ulceration is unclear.
- There may be a genetic predisposition to aphthous ulceration; about 40% of people with recurrent aphthous ulcers have a family history of oral ulceration.
- In a minority of people, precipitating factors can be identified, including:
  - Local trauma (e.g. excessive tooth brushing, chewing sharp or hard foods)
  - Stress
  - Food sensitivity (e.g. foods containing some preservatives and flavouring agents such as benzoic acid or cinnamaldehyde)
  - Hormone imbalance (there are a few women whose aphthae remit during pregnancy)
  - Stopping smoking (the reason for this is unclear)

[Scully et al, 2002; Scully et al, 2003]

How common is it?

- **Recurrent aphthous ulceration** affects about 20% of th UK population [Scully and Shotts, 2000].
- It is most common in young adults, and about 60% gi a history of aphthous ulceration [Porter and Scully, 2004].
- Symptoms normally begin in childhood or adolescenc However, the frequency and severity of attacks genera decreases with increasing age.

How do I know my patient has it?

- **Aphthous ulcers present as** one or more rounded ulcer with a clearly defined margin, a floor of yellowish-grey slough, and an erythematous periphery. There is usual a history of recurrence.
- **They generally occur on non-keratinized surfaces such** the labial and buccal mucosae and the floor of the mouth. They never occur on the hard palate.
- **Some people experience a prodrome** of localized burni or pain for 24–48 hours before the ulcers appear.
- **There are three main clinical types:**
  - **Minor aphthous ulcers** (about 80% of aphthae) are 5–8 mm in diameter and heal in 10–14 days without scarring.
  - **Major aphthous ulcers** (about 10% of aphthae) are larger and have an irregular border. They heal slowl over weeks or months and may lead to scarring.
  - **Herpetiform ulcers** are rare (about 5% of aphthae) and are multiple, pinpoint ulcers. They tend to fuse t form much larger ulcers lasting 10–14 days. (These ulcers are called 'herpetiform' because the clinical appearance suggests a viral cause. However, they are not caused by viral infection.)
- Aphthous-like ulcers are seen in many systemic disorders. (See *What else might it be?*) These should particularly be considered if there are ulcers affecting other sites, or other features suggestive of a systemic disorder.

[Scully et al, 2002; Scully et al, 2003]

What else might it be?

- Oral herpes simplex — often causes fever, malaise, and cervical lymphadenopathy. Lesions more likely to be o keratinized mucosa, especially the gingivae.
- Chickenpox
- Hand, foot, and mouth disease — lesions may also be seen on hands or feet; positive Cocksackie virus culture from lesions or stool
- Oral malignancy — signs include:
  - Ulceration of the oral mucosa persisting for more tha 3 weeks.
  - Oral swellings persisting for more than 3 weeks.
  - Red or red and white patches of the oral mucosa, particularly if they are painful or swollen or bleeding
  - The level of suspicion is further increased if the patie is a heavy smoker or heavy alcohol drinker and is ag over 45 years and male; other forms of tobacco use and chewing betel, gutkha, or pan also raise suspicio
- Adverse drug reaction (e.g. nonsteroidal anti-inflammatory drugs)
- Systemic conditions that present with aphthous-like ulcers, include:
  - Vitamin B_{12}, folate, or iron deficiency

Coeliac disease; occasionally Crohn's disease, ulcerative colitis, or other malabsorption syndromes
Behçet's syndrome
Reiter's syndrome
Immunodeficiency, e.g. neutropaenia, HIV infection
·es and Binnie, 1996; NICE, 2005]

›mplications and prognosis

›mplications

›econdary bacterial infection is a potential, but ıncommon, complication.

·ognosis

Лany people have infrequent recurrences (two to four ımes a year).
›ome have almost continuous disease activity, or have ıphthous-like ulcers associated with systemic disease.

Лanagement issues

Ꞁeneral issues p.129
Which factors might precipitate aphthous ulcers? p.129
How should I treat aphthous ulcers? p.129
›pecialist treatments p.130

·eneral issues

n the majority of cases, aphthous ulcers are managed ·ymptomatically.
For those with frequently recurring aphthous ulceration, ·onditions that can mimic classic aphthae should also be onsidered:

- **Many systemic disorders** cause severe and frequent apthous-like ulcers. (See *What else might it be?*) These should particularly be considered if there are other features suggestive of a systemic disorder.
- **Iron, vitamin B_{12}, or folate deficiency** is present in up to 20% of people with recurrent aphthous ulcers, and correcting these deficiencies can sometimes reduce recurrence. Note: it is important that any underlying *cause* of deficiency is also identified and treated.
- Although zinc deficiency has been proposed as an underlying cause of recurrent aphthous ulceration, zinc sulphate therapy has not been shown to be effective in randomized, controlled studies.
- **Gluten allergy** (coeliac disease) is a causative factor in less than 5% of people.
- **Drug reactions** are an infrequent cause of aphthous-like ulcers. Nicorandil, nonsteroidal anti-inflammatory drugs, sodium lauryl sulphate (in toothpastes), and oral nicotine replacement therapy have been reported to induce ulceration in some people.

'hich factors might precipitate aphthous ·cers?

Identifying and avoiding precipitating factors can be useful for some people.
Local trauma can cause ulcers in susceptible people and is usually easily corrected, e.g. use a softer toothbrush, avoid eating sharp or hard foods.
Stress is a precipitating factor in some people but the mechanism is unclear. Some people may find relaxation techniques or exercise helpful to reduce general stress levels.
Stopping smoking sometimes precipitates or aggravates aphthae.
If there is an *obvious* relationship to certain foods, these should be avoided.
·cully et al, 2002; Scully et al, 2003]

How should I treat aphthous ulcers?

- **There are few robust data to guide treatment recommendations.**
- **If a precipitating factor can be identified, discuss ways to avoid it with the individual** [Scully et al, 2002; Scully et al, 2003].
- **A short course of topical corticosteroids can be used** [Scully et al, 2002; Scully et al, 2003; Natah et al, 2004]. Although they do not prevent recurrence, topical corticosteroids may help to reduce the duration of ulcers and hasten pain relief [Porter and Scully, 2004].
  - Encourage individuals with prodromal symptoms to apply corticosteroids at this stage. Otherwise, corticosteroids should be applied as soon as the ulcers appear.
  - Triamcinolone in an adhesive paste (Adcortyl in Orabase) and hydrocortisone 2.5 mg lozenges are licensed for use in aphthous ulcers.
  - Concerns have been raised that long-term or repeated application could cause adrenal suppression. However, there is little evidence that even some of the more potent steroids (such as fluocinonide or betamethasone) can cause any significant problem in this respect [Scully et al, 2002].
- **Chlorhexidine aqueous mouthwash can be used to prevent secondary bacterial infection** (particularly if it is too painful to brush teeth) [Scully et al, 2002; Scully et al, 2003; Natah et al, 2004]. There is also some evidence that chlorhexidine reduces the duration and severity of ulceration, although it does not prevent recurrence [Porter and Scully, 2004].
  - Chlorhexidine can stain teeth brown when used regularly.
  - The stain is not usually permanent, and can be reduced by avoiding drinks that contain tannin (e.g. tea, coffee, or red wine), and by brushing teeth before use. However, the mouth should be rinsed well after tooth brushing as some ingredients in toothpaste can inactivate chlorhexidine.
- **Local analgesics can be useful if ulcers are very painful,** although their duration of action is short [Scully et al, 2002; Scully et al, 2003].
  - **Choline salicylate gel** is often sufficient for mildly painful apthae.
  - **Benzydamine mouthwash or spray** can provide short term pain relief but numbness and stinging are sometimes a problem. Diluting the mouthwash in an equal volume of water before use reduces stinging. The spray is useful for ulcers in difficult-to-reach areas.
  - **Topical lidocaine** (lignocaine) ointment or spray is sometimes used for severely painful ulceration, although it only has a short duration of action. Care should be taken not to anaesthetize the pharynx before meals as this might lead to aspiration or choking.
- **Treatment choices should be guided by disease severity (pain), the frequency of flare-ups,** and the tolerability of medication. The following advice reflects common practice and expert consensus [Scully et al, 2002; Scully et al, 2003]:
  - **Aphthous ulcers that recur a few times a year: medication may not be indicated.** Pain is often tolerated as aphthae tend to only last a few days in this situation. If the individual already uses a product that suits them, then it is reasonable to encourage them to continue to use it.
  - **Aphthous ulcers that recur monthly:** these aphthae tend to be painful and last longer (3–10 days). Some individuals may have changed their diet or oral hygiene habits because of the pain. Topical corticosteroids and chlorhexidine mouthwash are often required each month to reduce the severity of

bouts. Referral to a specialist in oral medicine may be needed if these therapies do not control aphthae sufficiently.

- **Continuous aphthous ulceration:** these individuals suffer painful, chronic courses of recurrent aphthous ulceration in which by the time one ulcer heals, another develops. Referral to a specialist in oral medicine is indicated as more potent corticosteroids or immunosuppressants are needed to control symptoms.

Specialist treatments

- **Potent topical corticosteroids** (beclometasone spray applied locally, or betamethasone soluble tablets used as a mouthwash) are often used. They may be particularly useful if ulceration is extensive, or at a difficult-to-reach site. They have increased risk of oral candidiasis, and a potential increased risk of adrenal suppression if used long-term.
- **Short-term systemic corticosteroid therapy** is occasionally used for severe recurrent ulcers.
- **Tetracycline mouthwash** has been used for severe recurrent aphthous ulceration. Although it may reduce the duration and severity of ulcers, it can cause oral candidiasis and a burning-like sensation of the pharynx [Porter et al, 2000]. Tetracycline capsules are no longer available in the UK so doxycycline is usually substituted instead; the contents of a doxycycline 100 mg capsule are dispersed in water and rinsed around the mouth four times a day.
- **Other immunosuppressants** (e.g. thalidomide, colchicine, levamisole, dapsone, pentoxifylline, and topical sodium cromoglicate) are sometimes used by specialists, but it is unusual for general practitioners to use these.

[Scully et al, 2002; Scully et al, 2003; Natah et al, 2004]

References

NHS staff in England can link, free of charge, from references to full text journals by clicking on [Full text] the PRODIGY website.

1. Natah, S.S., Konttinen, Y.T., Enattah, N.S. et al (200 Recurrent aphthous ulcers today: a review of the growing knowledge. *International Journal of Oral & Maxillofacial Surgery* 33(3), 221–234.
2. NICE (2005) *Referral guidelines for suspected cancer quick reference guide.* Clinical guideline 27. National Institute for Health and Clinical Excellence. www.nice.org.uk [Accessed: 01/07/2005].
3. Porter, S. and Scully, C. (2004) *Aphthous ulcers (recurrent).* Clinical Evidence. Volume 11. www.clinicalevidence.com [Accessed: 01/06/2004].
4. Porter, S.R., Hegarty, A., Kaliakatsou, F. et al (2000) Recurrent aphthous stomatitis. *Clinics in Dermatolog* **18**(5), 569–578.
5. Rees, T.D. and Binnie, W.H. (1996) Recurrent aphth stomatitis. *Dermatologic Clinics* **14**(2), 243–256.
6. Scully, C. and Shotts, R. (2000) ABC of oral health: mouth ulcers and other causes of orofacial soreness a pain. *British Medical Journal* **321**(7254), 162–165. [F text]
7. Scully, C., Gorsky, M. and Lozada-Nur, F. (2002) Aphthous ulcerations. *Dermatologic Therapy* **15**(3), 185–205.
8. Scully, C., Gorsky, M. and Lozada-Nur, F. (2003) Th diagnosis and management of recurrent aphthous stomatitis: a consensus approach. *Journal of the American Dental Association* **134**(2), 200–207.

PRODIGY GUIDANCE

Asthma

Last revised in October 2005
At the time of print this topic was being updated. The newly revised guidance will be issued on to the website in late 2005.
www.prodigy.nhs.uk/guidance.asp?gt=Asthma

Applies to people over the age of 1 month

This guidance is based on the Scottish Intercollegiate Guidelines Network/British Thoracic Society *British guideline on the management of asthma* (2004 update).

This guidance covers the primary care management of acute and chronic asthma in adults and children.

There is separate PRODIGY guidance for *Chest infections, Chronic obstructive pulmonary disease, Osteoporosis,* and *Smoking cessation.*

Goals

The following goals for treatment are set in the Scottish Intercollegiate Guidelines Network/British Thoracic Society guideline on asthma:

- Minimal symptoms during day and night
- Minimal need for reliever medication
- No exacerbations
- No limitation of physical activity
- 'Normal' lung function, i.e. forced expiratory volume in 1 second (FEV_1) or peak expiratory flow (PEF), or both, greater than 80% predicted (or best)

Note that goals must be individualized. It is not appropriate to define general goals with fixed levels of lung function or symptom control because individuals will want to balance the ideal of perfect control against the inconvenience and adverse effects of treatment.
[SIGN and BTS, 2004]

Contents

Scenarios

- New presentation: as required short-acting beta$_2$-agonist p.131
- Poor control: add inhaled corticosteroids (standard doses) p.134
- Poor control: add LABA and/or increase ICS (standard doses) p.137
- Poor control: increase inhaled corticosteroid (higher doses) p.140
- Poor control: add on therapy p.143
- Using alternative delivery systems p.145
- Occupational asthma p.147
- Exercise induced asthma p.149
- Acute exacerbation of asthma p.150

Extended Information, p. 152

Which scenario?

- **New presentation: as-required short-acting beta$_2$-agonist:** covers the initial management of people diagnosed with asthma and the prescription of as-required short-acting bronchodilator.
- **Poor control: add inhaled corticosteroid (standard doses):** covers the management of people who use an inhaled short-acting beta$_2$-agonist three times a week or more, or more than two canisters a month, but who are not using regular prophylactic inhaled corticosteroids.
- **Poor control: add LABA and/or increase ICS (standard doses):** covers the management of people who have poorly controlled asthma and are taking 400–800 micrograms of beclometasone daily, or equivalent inhaled corticosteroid (ICS), in addition to as required short-acting beta$_2$-agonist (SABA).
- **Poor control: increase inhaled corticosteroid (higher doses):** covers the management of people who have poorly controlled asthma and are taking 800 micrograms of beclometasone daily, or equivalent ICS, plus long-acting beta$_2$-agonist (LABA) or other add-on therapy.
- **Poor control: add-on therapy:** covers the addition of leukotriene antagonists, modified-release theophylline, long-acting, modified-release oral beta$_2$-agonists or cromones.
- **Using alternative delivery systems:** covers alternative options to a pressurized metered-dose inhaler (pMDI) or pMDI plus spacer device in those unable or unwilling to use pMDI with or without a spacer device.
- **Occupational asthma:** covers the management of people with occupational asthma.
- **Exercise induced asthma:** covers the management of people with exercise-induced asthma.
- **Acute exacerbation of asthma:** covers the management of people who present with an acute exacerbation of asthma, or who require a rescue course of oral corticosteroids.

New presentation: as required short-acting beta$_2$-agonist

Which therapy?

- **Offer advice and education** regarding the causes, possible triggers or allergens, the effects of smoking and passive exposure to tobacco smoke, and treatment options for asthma.
- **Advise on smoking cessation,** where appropriate.
- **Offer specific advice about what to do in an emergency.**
- **Provide a written action plan.**
- **Start a short-acting inhaled beta$_2$-agonist,** to be used as required.
- **Metered-dose inhalers (MDIs)** are as effective as other types of delivery system and are first choice for as-required bronchodilator therapy.
- **Consider a spacer with an MDI** in children under 15 years and in people who cannot co-ordinate the actuation of an MDI with inhalation. In children less than 5 years use a facemask with the spacer.
- **A dry powder device or a breath-actuated MDI may be considered as an alternative delivery system** in people who are unable or unwilling to use an MDI with a spacer. These are not offered here but are offered in the scenario *Using alternative delivery systems.*
- **Ensure that inhaler technique is adequate.**

A

- **Ensure that children with asthma keep a short acting inhaled beta$_2$-agonist and spacer at school.**
- Consider prescribing a peak flow meter (especially if asthma is severe) to be used as part of the written action plan and for assessing responses to treatment.

Practical prescribing points

For further information please see the *Medicines Compendium* (www.medicines.org.uk) or the *British National Formulary* (www.bnf.org).

Beta$_2$-agonists

- Hypokalaemia may occur with regular high doses, or when taken together with other drugs that also predispose to hypokalaemia (such as theophylline and its derivatives, and diuretics).

Follow-up advice

- **Review in one month** to establish response to treatment, assess how much short-acting beta$_2$-agonist is being used, and to confirm diagnosis of asthma.
- **If asthma is stable with good control,** and the short-acting beta$_2$-agonist is being used less than three times a week, continue treatment and review in 3–6 months (depending on the individual).
- If the short-acting beta$_2$-agonist is being used three times a week or more, or more than two canisters a month, add ICS (see scenario *Poor control: add inhaled corticosteroid (standard doses)*.

Should I refer or investigate?

Refer?

Indications for referral of older children and adults with possible asthma

- Diagnosis unclear or in doubt
- Unexpected clinical findings e.g. crackles, clubbing, cyanosis, heart failure
- Spirometry or peak expiratory flow (PEF) measurements do not fit the clinical picture
- Suspected occupational asthma
- Persistent shortness of breath (not episodic; not with associated wheeze)
- Unilateral or fixed wheeze
- Stridor
- Persistent chest pain or atypical features
- Weight loss
- Persistent cough and/or sputum production
- Non-resolving pneumonia
- Inadequate response to maximum guideline treatment

Indications for referral of younger children with possible asthma

- Diagnosis unclear or in doubt; the younger the child, the more difficult it is to be sure that wheezing is due to asthma
- Symptoms present from birth, or perinatal lung problem
- Excessive vomiting
- Severe upper respiratory tract infection
- Persistent wet cough
- Family history of unusual chest disease
- Failure to thrive
- Unexpected clinical findings, e.g. abnormal voice, focal chest signs, dysphagia, inspiratory wheeze, stridor

Investigate

- A chest X-ray may be considered where there is diagnostic doubt, particularly in smokers, if chest infection or malignancy are possible.
- **Objective measurements that can be used to confirm a diagnosis of asthma include:**
  - More than 20% diurnal variation on at least 3 days in a week for 2 weeks on a peak expiratory flow (PEF) diary, or
  - More than 15% (and 200-ml) increase in forced expiratory volume in 1 second (FEV$_1$) after short-acting beta$_2$-agonist (bronchodilator response test), or
  - More than 15% (and 200-ml) increase in FEV$_1$ after trial of oral corticosteroids, or
  - More than 15% decrease in FEV$_1$ after 6 minutes of running, or
  - Histamine or methacholine challenge in difficult cases (usually requires referral)
- Spirometry (e.g. in smokers) may be useful to characterize the lung disorder as obstructive, restrictive, or mixed.

Patient information leaflets

The following PILs are available at www.prodigy.nhs.uk

- Asthma
- Asthma - Action Plan
- Asthma - Inhalers
- Asthma - Peak Flow Diary
- Asthma - Peak Flow Meter
- Asthma - Picture Summary
- Asthma UK
- Asthma UK (Scotland)
- Spirometry

Shared decision making

- The symptoms of asthma are due to narrowing of the airways.
- Smoking, passive smoking, and other 'triggers' can make symptoms worse.
- A 'reliever' inhaler eases symptoms quickly. Take two puffs whenever symptoms develop. Always ensure that you carry your 'reliever inhaler' with you.
- If exercise, sport, or other things trigger symptoms, use the inhaler beforehand.
- To make inhalers easier to use, some people attach them to a 'spacer' chamber.
- See a doctor or nurse if you need a reliever inhaler once a day or more.

Drug rationale

Drugs not included

- **Oral short-acting beta$_2$-agonists** are not included. The inhaled route is preferred for initial management with short-acting beta$_2$-agonists, to minimize adverse effects by providing direct local application of the drug.
- **Inhaled salbutamol in a chlorofluorocarbon** (CFC) - **containing formulation** is not included because of the current transition to hydrofluoroalkane (HFA) - containing products. There are now a number of branded and generic alternatives available. There are also spacer devices licensed for use with branded inhalers.
- **Long-acting beta$_2$-agonists (LABAs) (formoterol [eformoterol] and salmeterol)** are not recommended for the immediate relief of acute attacks.
- **Ephedrine and the partially selective inhaled beta agonist, orciprenaline,** are less suitable and less safe than

selective $beta_2$-agonists and are more likely to cause arrhythmias and other adverse effects [NICE, 2000; BNF 45, 2003].

Inhaled antimuscarinics (ipratropium and oxitropium) are regarded as being more effective in relieving bronchoconstriction associated with chronic obstructive pulmonary disease (COPD) than in relieving asthma [BNF 45, 2003].

Inhalers other than pressurized metered-dose inhalers (pMDIs) are not offered. A meta-analysis found there was no evidence that alternative inhaler devices are more effective for the delivery of inhaled $beta_2$-agonists than pMDIs [Brocklebank et al, 2001]. If an alternative device is considered necessary, a selection is offered in the scenario *Using alternative delivery systems.*

Drugs included

Inhaled short-acting $beta_2$-agonists (salbutamol and terbutaline) are effective bronchodilators. They should be used 'when required', unless benefit is shown from regular use [SIGN and BTS, 2004].

Chlorofluorocarbon (CFC) -free preparations of salbutamol are offered in this scenario in line with the current UK transition to CFC-free propellants [CMO, 2003]. Terbutaline is not currently available as a CFC-free metered-dose inhaler (MDI).

Spacer devices are offered for children and people who cannot coordinate actuation with inhalation. The choice of spacer device for the chosen MDI is guided by the Summary of Product Characteristics:

- Airomir and Salbulin inhalers — Aerochamber
- Bricanyl inhaler — Nebuhaler
- Salamol and Ventolin inhalers — Volumatic

Note: switching between different inhaler or spacer types, or both, can affect the deposition characteristics of the inhaled drug, which may alter the clinical response to a drug. To maintain good asthma control, it is important that people are not switched back and forth between inhalers and spacer devices.

Peak flow meters are also included in this scenario to be used as part of a personalized asthma action plan.

Prescriptions

Short-acting $beta_2$-agonist when required

Salbutamol 100mcg MDI: 1 to 2 puffs up to four times a day
- Age from 5 years onwards
- Salbutamol 100mcg CFC-free inhaler. Inhale one to two puffs as required for shortness of breath, up to four times a day; supply 1 200 dose inhaler; NHS Cost £1.90.

Airomir 100mcg MDI: 1 to 2 puffs up to four times a day
- Age from 1 month to 4 years
- Airomir 100mcg CFC-free inhaler. Inhale one to two puffs as required for shortness of breath, up to four times a day; supply 1 200 dose inhaler; NHS Cost £1.97.

Airomir 100mcg MDI: 1 to 2 puffs up to four times a day
- Age from 5 years onwards
- Airomir 100mcg CFC-free inhaler. Inhale one to two puffs as required for shortness of breath, up to four times a day; supply 1 200 dose inhaler; NHS Cost £1.97.

Salamol 100mcg MDI: 1 to 2 puffs up to four times a day
- Age from 1 month to 4 years
- Salamol 100mcg CFC-free inhaler. Inhale one to two puffs as required for shortness of breath, up to four times a day; supply 1 200 dose inhaler; NHS Cost £1.95.

Salamol 100mcg MDI: 1 to 2 puffs up to four times a day
- Age from 5 years onwards
- Salamol 100mcg CFC-free inhaler. Inhale one to two puffs as required for shortness of breath, up to four times a day; supply 1 200 dose inhaler; NHS Cost £1.95.

Ventolin 100mcg MDI: 1 to 2 puffs up to four times a day
- Age from 1 month to 4 years
- Ventolin 100mcg CFC-free inhaler. Inhale one to two puffs as required for shortness of breath, up to four times a day; supply 1 200 dose inhaler; NHS Cost £2.30.

Ventolin 100mcg MDI: 1 to 2 puffs up to four times a day
- Age from 5 years onwards
- Ventolin 100mcg CFC-free inhaler. Inhale one to two puffs as required for shortness of breath, up to four times a day; supply 1 200 dose inhaler; NHS Cost £2.30.

Terbutaline 250mcg MDI: 1 to 2 puffs up to four times a day
- Age from 1 month to 4 years
- Terbutaline 250mcg inhaler. Inhale one to two puffs as required for shortness of breath, up to four times a day; supply 1 400 dose inhaler; NHS Cost £5.31.

Terbutaline 250mcg MDI: 1 to 2 puffs up to four times a day
- Age from 5 years onwards
- Terbutaline 250mcg inhaler. Inhale one to two puffs as required for shortness of breath, up to four times a day; supply 1 400 dose inhaler; NHS Cost £5.31.

Short-acting $beta_2$-agonist when required + spacer

Airomir 100mcg MDI + Infant Aerochamber: use when required
- Age from 1 month to 23 months
- Airomir 100mcg CFC-free inhaler. Inhale one to two puffs up to four times a day using the spacer, when required to relieve breathlessness; supply 1 200 dose inhaler; NHS Cost £1.97.
- Aerochamber (infant) + mask. Use to aid inhalation; supply 1 spacer; NHS Cost £7.14.

Airomir 100mcg MDI + Child Aerochamber: use when required
- Age from 2 to 3 years
- Airomir 100mcg CFC-free inhaler. Inhale one to two puffs up to four times a day using the spacer, when required to relieve breathlessness; supply 1 200 dose inhaler; NHS Cost £1.97.
- Aerochamber (child) + mask. Use to aid inhalation; supply 1 spacer; NHS Cost £7.14.

Airomir MDI + Aerochamber: use when required
- Age from 4 years onwards
- Airomir 100mcg CFC-free inhaler. Inhale one to two puffs up to four times a day using the spacer, when required to relieve breathlessness; supply 1 200 dose inhaler; NHS Cost £1.97.
- AeroChamber Plus spacer device. Use to aid inhalation; supply 1 spacer; NHS Cost £4.28.

Salamol 100mcg MDI + Volumatic + mask : use when required
- Age from 1 month to 23 months
- Salamol 100mcg CFC-free inhaler. Inhale one to two puffs up to four times a day using the spacer, when required to relieve breathlessness; supply 1 200 dose inhaler; NHS Cost £1.95.
- Volumatic spacer device+mask. Use to aid inhalation; supply 1 spacer; NHS Cost £2.75.

Salamol 100mcg MDI + Volumatic: use when required
- Age from 4 years onwards
- Salamol 100mcg CFC-free inhaler. Inhale one to two puffs up to four times a day using the spacer, when required to relieve breathlessness; supply 1 200 dose inhaler; NHS Cost £1.95.

- Volumatic spacer device. Use to aid inhalation; supply 1 spacer; NHS Cost £2.75.

Ventolin 100mcg MDI + Volumatic+mask: use when required
- Age from 1 month to 2 years
- Ventolin 100mcg CFC-free inhaler. Inhale one to two puffs up to four times a day using the spacer, when required to relieve breathlessness; supply 1 200 dose inhaler; NHS Cost £2.30.
- Volumatic spacer device+mask. Use to aid inhalation; supply 1 spacer; NHS Cost £2.75.

Ventolin 100mcg MDI + Volumatic: use when required
- Age from 3 years onwards
- Ventolin 100mcg CFC-free inhaler. Inhale one to two puffs up to four times a day using the spacer, when required to relieve breathlessness; supply 1 inhaler; NHS Cost £2.30.
- Volumatic spacer device. Use to aid inhalation; supply 1 spacer; NHS Cost £2.75.

Terbutaline 250mcg MDI + Nebuhaler+mask: use when required
- Age from 1 month to 2 years
- Terbutaline 250mcg inhaler. Inhale one to two puffs up to four times a day using the spacer, when required to relieve breathlessness; supply 1 400 dose inhaler; NHS Cost £5.31.
- Nebuhaler spacer device + mask. Use to aid inhalation; supply 1 spacer; NHS Cost £4.28.

Terbutaline 250mcg MDI + Nebuhaler: use when required
- Age from 3 years onwards
- Terbutaline 250mcg inhaler. Inhale one to two puffs up to four times a day using the spacer, when required to relieve breathlessness; supply 1 400 dose inhaler; NHS Cost £5.31.
- Nebuhaler spacer device. Use to aid inhalation; supply 1 spacer; NHS Cost £4.28.

Peak flow meters: low range

Peak flow meter: Pocketpeak (Ferraris)
- Age from 1 month onwards
- Ferraris Pocketpeak 209 p.f.m. Use as directed; supply 1 meter; NHS Cost £6.53.

Peak flow meter: Mini-Wright (Clement Clarke)
- Age from 1 month onwards
- Mini-Wright low range p.f.m. Use as directed; supply 1 meter; NHS Cost £6.97.

Peak flow meter: Vitalograph (Vitalograph)
- Age from 1 month onwards
- Vitalograph low range p.f.m. Use as directed; supply 1 meter; NHS Cost £5.95.

Peak flow meters: standard range

Peak flow meter: Pocketpeak (Ferraris)
- Age from 5 years onwards
- Pocketpeak standard p.f.m. Use as directed; supply 1 meter; NHS Cost £6.53.

Peak flow meter: Mini-Wright (Clement Clarke)
- Age from 5 years onwards
- Mini-Wright standard p.f.m. Use as directed; supply 1 meter; NHS Cost £6.92.

Peak flow meter: Vitalograph (Vitalograph)
- Age from 5 years onwards
- Vitalograph standard p.f.m. Use as directed; supply 1 meter; NHS Cost £5.95.

Peak flow meter: MicroPeak (Micro Medical)
- Age from 5 years onwards
- MicroPeak standard pfm. Use as directed; supply 1 meter; NHS Cost £6.86.

Peak flow meter: Vitalograph Child (Vitalograph)
- Age from 5 years onwards
- Vitalograph Child standard pfm. Use as directed; supply 1 meter; NHS Cost £5.95.

Spacers

Infant Aerochamber + facemask: for use with Airomir
- Age from 1 month to 23 months
- Aerochamber (infant) + mask. Use to aid inhalation; supply 1 spacer; NHS Cost £7.14.

Child Aerochamber + facemask: for use with Airomir
- Age from 2 to 3 years
- Aerochamber (child) + mask. Use to aid inhalation; supply 1 spacer; NHS Cost £7.14.

Aerochamber: for use with Airomir
- Age from 4 years onwards
- AeroChamber Plus spacer device. Use to aid inhalation; supply 1 spacer; NHS Cost £4.28.

Nebuhaler + facemask: for use with terbutaline
- Age from 1 month to 2 years
- Nebuhaler spacer device + mask. Use to aid inhalation; supply 1 spacer; NHS Cost £4.28.

Nebuhaler: for use with terbutaline
- Age from 3 years onwards
- Nebuhaler spacer device. Use to aid inhalation; supply 1 spacer; NHS Cost £4.28.

Volumatic + facemask: for use with Salamol/Ventolin
- Age from 1 month to 2 years
- Volumatic spacer device+mask. Use to aid inhalation; supply 1 spacer; NHS Cost £2.75.

Volumatic: for use with Salamol/Ventolin
- Age from 3 years onwards
- Volumatic spacer device. Use to aid inhalation; supply 1 spacer; NHS Cost £2.75.

Poor control: add inhaled corticosteroids (standard doses)

Which therapy?

- **Before initiating a new drug therapy,** re-check compliance and inhaler technique, and eliminate trigger factors.
- **Consider prescribing inhaled corticosteroids (ICS) for people:**
  - Who have had exacerbations of asthma in the last 2 years
  - Are using inhaled beta$_2$-agonists three times a week or more
  - Who are symptomatic three times a week or more, waking one night a week
- Usual starting doses for beclometasone (as MDI) are:
  - Older than 12 years: beclometasone 200 micrograms twice a day
  - 5–12 years old: beclometasone 100 micrograms twice a day
  - Less than 5 years old: beclometasone 100 micrograms twice a day (higher doses may be required to ensure adequate drug delivery)
- **Advise on smoking cessation, where appropriate.**

Which inhaled corticosteroid and delivery system?

- Treat people with asthma with the cheapest inhaled corticosteroid (ICS) and delivery system that suits their needs and which controls their symptoms.
  - **Metered-dose inhalers (MDIs)** are as effective as other types of inhaler and are first choice for delivery of ICS.

- **Use a spacer with an MDI to deliver ICS** for all children under 15 years and in people who cannot coordinate the actuation of a MDI with inhalation. For children under 5 years, use a facemask where necessary.
- **Consider a spacer device in all people using ICS:** a large volume spacer will reduce deposition of steroid in the oropharynx (which is associated with oral candidiasis).
- **A dry powder device or a breath-actuated MDI may be considered as an alternative delivery system** in people who are unable or unwilling to use an MDI with a spacer. These are not offered here but are offered in the scenario *Using alternative delivery systems*.

If there are concerns about adverse effects from the ICS consider a trial of another class of preventer agent. Prescriptions are available for these in the *Poor control: add-on therapy* scenario, but not in this scenario.

'ractical prescribing points

ɔr further information please see the *Medicines ompendium* (www.medicines.org.uk) or the *British 'ational Formulary* (www.bnf.org).

ɜeta$_2$-agonists

Hypokalaemia may occur with regular high doses, or when taken together with other drugs that also predispose to hypokalaemia (such as theophylline and its derivatives, and diuretics).

ɿhaled corticosteroids

Oral candidiasis and sore mouth are common. Use a large volume spacer with a metered-dose inhaler (MDI), and rinse the mouth with water after inhaled corticosteroid (ICS) use.

Do not exceed the licensed dose of ICS when prescribing for children.

For people on prolonged treatment with ICS:

- Check height of children regularly. If growth slows, reduce the dose if possible and/or refer to a specialist.
- Give lifestyle advice to prevent osteoporosis: exercise, dietary calcium, and smoking.
- There is a small increased risk of glaucoma and cataracts with prolonged high doses.

Consider the possibility of adrenal insufficiency if someone using ICS presents with decreased consciousness. Check blood glucose levels and consider the need for intramuscular hydrocortisone.

'ollow-up advice

Review in 1 month to establish response to treatment and assess how much short-acting beta$_2$-agonist is being used.

If asthma is stable and control is good, and the short-acting beta$_2$-agonist is being used less than three times a week, continue treatment and review in 3–6 months.

Use the lowest dose inhaled corticosteroid (ICS) at which effective control of asthma is maintained. Consider the possibility of stepping down the dose of ICS in people whose asthma is well controlled.

If asthma control is poor and/or if the short-acting beta$_2$-agonist is being used three times a week or more (or more than two canisters a month), add a long-acting beta$_2$-agonist (LABA) (see scenario *Poor control: add LABA and/or increase ICS*).

Should I refer or investigate?

Refer?

- Refer if the diagnosis is unclear or in doubt.
- Note that in the case of a wheezing child, the younger they are, the more difficult it is to be sure that the cause is asthma, and the lower the threshold is for referral.

Investigate?

- Monitor height in growing children, at least once a year.
- Check blood glucose levels in any child (or adult) who presents with a decreased level of consciousness and is maintained on inhaled corticosteroids.

Patient information leaflets

The following PILs are available at www.prodigy.nhs.uk

- Asthma
- Asthma - Action Plan
- Asthma - Inhalers
- Asthma - Peak Flow Diary
- Asthma - Peak Flow Meter
- Asthma - Picture Summary
- Asthma UK
- Asthma UK (Scotland)

Shared decision making

- **A steroid inhaler** prevents asthma symptoms from developing.
  - Steroids reduce inflammation in the airways, which causes the symptoms.
  - Use the inhaler twice a day, every day.
  - To make inhalers easier to use, and to reduce side-effects, many people attach them to a 'spacer' chamber.
  - The most common side-effect is a thrush infection in the mouth. To help prevent this, rinse your mouth with water after using the inhaler.
  - Other side-effects are rare, as little steroid is absorbed into the body.
- **Continue to use your 'reliever' inhaler when needed,** but you should need it much less often.

Drug rationale

Drugs not included

- **Oral corticosteroids and oral short-acting beta$_2$-agonists** are not included. The inhaled route is preferred for initial management, to minimize adverse effects by providing direct local application of the drug. Short courses of prednisolone may be used to gain control of symptoms, and prescriptions for prednisolone are offered in the scenario *Acute exacerbation of asthma*.
- **Long-acting beta$_2$-agonists (LABA) (formoterol [eformoterol] and salmeterol)** are not recommended unless the person remains symptomatic despite use of inhaled corticosteroids (ICS) (see scenario *Poor control: add LABA and/or increase ICS (standard dose)*.
- **Ephedrine and the partially selective inhaled beta agonist, orciprenaline,** are less suitable and less safe than selective beta$_2$-agonists and are more likely to cause arrhythmias and other adverse effects [NICE, 2000; BNF 45, 2003].
- **Mometasone** is not offered as an alternative inhaled corticosteroid (ICS) because it is a black triangle drug, and post-marketing data are needed to confirm its safety. It is currently only available as a dry powder inhaler.

A

- **Inhaled antimuscarinics (ipratropium and oxitropium)** are regarded as being more effective in relieving bronchoconstriction associated with chronic obstructive pulmonary disease than in relieving asthma [BNF 45, 2003].
- **Inhalers other than metered-dose inhalers (MDIs)** are not offered. A meta-analysis found there was no evidence that alternative inhaler devices are more effective for the delivery of inhaled beta$_2$-agonists and ICS than MDIs [Brocklebank et al, 2001; Ram et al, 2001]. If an alternative device is considered necessary, a selection is offered in the scenario *Using alternative delivery systems.*
- **Other regular inhaled and oral preventer therapies** are not included (e.g. sodium cromoglicate, leukotriene receptor antagonists, theophyllines). The first choice of preventer therapy is regular inhaled corticosteroid, and other preventer drugs may only be rarely needed, for example when the person is unable to tolerate corticosteroids. See scenario *Poor control: add-on therapy* for prescriptions.

Drugs included

- **Beclometasone and budesonide** are offered in a range of doses up to 800 micrograms daily.
- **Beclometasone chlorofluorocarbon** (CFC) **-free metered-dose inhaler (MDI)** (Qvar) is offered should this option be required. The total daily dose of beclometasone from a CFC-free inhaler is approximately half that of the CFC-containing product. The Summary of Product Characteristics for the product should be followed carefully for both initiating CFC-free beclometasone and, in particular, transferring someone from CFC-containing to CFC-free products.
- **Fluticasone** is offered in doses up to 400 micrograms daily. All fluticasone inhalers are now CFC-free.
- **Spacer devices** are offered separately from the inhalers in this scenario. The choice of spacer device for the chosen MDI should be guided by the Summary of Product Characteristics:
  - Qvar inhaler — Aerochamber.
  - Becotide and Flixotide inhalers — Volumatic.
  - Pulmicort inhalers — Nebuhaler.
- Note: switching between different inhaler or spacer types, or both, can affect the deposition characteristics of the inhaled drug, which may alter the clinical response to a drug. To maintain good asthma control, it is important that people are not switched back and forth between inhalers and spacer devices.

Prescriptions

Beclometasone (standard dose)

Beclometasone MDI: 200mcg daily (100mcg twice a day)
- Age from 12 years onwards
- Beclometasone 50mcg inhaler. Inhale two puffs twice a day; supply 1 200 dose inhaler; NHS Cost £4.29.

Beclometasone MDI: 400mcg daily (200mcg twice a day)
- Age from 12 years onwards
- Beclometasone 100mcg inhaler. Inhale two puffs twice a day; supply 1 200 dose inhaler; NHS Cost £8.24.

Beclometasone MDI: 800mcg daily (400mcg twice a day)
- Age from 12 years onwards
- Beclometasone 200mcg inhaler. Inhale two puffs twice a day; supply 1 200 dose inhaler; NHS Cost £19.61.

Becotide MDI: 100mcg daily (50mcg twice a day)
- Age from 1 month to 11 years
- Becotide-50 50mcg inhaler. Inhale one puff twice a day using the spacer; supply 1 200 dose inhaler; NHS Cost £5.43.

Becotide MDI: 200mcg daily (100mcg twice a day)
- Age from 1 month to 11 years
- Becotide-50 50mcg inhaler. Inhale two puffs twice a da using the spacer; supply 1 200 dose inhaler; NHS Cost £5.43.

Becotide MDI: 400mcg daily (200mcg twice a day)
- Age from 1 month to 11 years
- Becotide-100 100mcg inhaler. Inhale two puffs twice a day using the spacer; supply 1 200 dose inhaler; NHS Cost £10.32.

Becotide MDI: 200mcg daily (100mcg twice a day)
- Age from 12 years onwards
- Becotide-100 100mcg inhaler. Inhale one puff twice a day; supply 1 200 dose inhaler; NHS Cost £10.32.

Becotide MDI: 400mcg daily (200mcg twice a day)
- Age from 12 years onwards
- Becotide-200 200mcg inhaler. Inhale one puff twice a day; supply 1 200 dose inhaler; NHS Cost £19.61.

Becotide MDI: 800mcg daily (400mcg twice a day)
- Age from 12 years onwards
- Becotide-200 200mcg inhaler. Inhale two puffs twice a day; supply 1 200 dose inhaler; NHS Cost £19.61.

Qvar (beclometasone CFC-free)

Qvar CFC-free MDI: 100mcg daily (50mcg twice a day)
- Age from 12 years onwards
- Qvar 50mcg CFC-free inhaler. Inhale one puff twice a day; supply 1 200 dose inhaler; NHS Cost £7.87.

Qvar CFC-free MDI: 200mcg daily (100mcg twice a day)
- Age from 12 years onwards
- Qvar 50mcg CFC-free inhaler. Inhale two puffs twice a day; supply 1 200 dose inhaler; NHS Cost £7.87.

Qvar CFC-free MDI: 400mcg daily (200mcg twice a day)
- Age from 12 years onwards
- Qvar 100mcg CFC-free inhaler. Inhale two puffs twice day; supply 1 200 dose inhaler; NHS Cost £17.21.

Fluticasone / Budesonide

Fluticasone CFC-free MDI: 100mcg daily (50mcg twice a day)
- Age from 4 to 15 years
- Fluticasone 50mcg CFC-free inhaler. Inhale one puff twice a day using the spacer; supply 1 120 dose inhaler; NHS Cost £5.85.

Fluticasone CFC-free MDI: 200mcg daily (100mcg twice day)
- Age from 4 to 15 years
- Fluticasone 50mcg CFC-free inhaler. Inhale two puffs twice a day using the spacer; supply 1 120 dose inhaler; NHS Cost £5.85.

Fluticasone CFC-free MDI: 100mcg daily (50mcg twice a day)
- Age from 16 years onwards
- Fluticasone 50mcg CFC-free inhaler. Inhale one puff twice a day; supply 1 120 dose inhaler; NHS Cost £5.8

Fluticasone CFC-free MDI: 200mcg daily (100mcg twice day)
- Age from 16 years onwards
- Fluticasone 50mcg CFC-free inhaler. Inhale two puffs twice a day; supply 1 120 dose inhaler; NHS Cost £5.8

Fluticasone CFC-free MDI: 400mcg daily (200mcg twice day)
- Age from 16 years onwards
- Fluticasone 50mcg CFC-free inhaler. Inhale four puffs twice a day; supply 2 120 dose inhaler; NHS Cost £11.70.

udesonide MDI: 100mcg daily (50mcg twice a day)
- Age from 1 month to 11 years
- Budesonide 50mcg inhaler. Inhale one puff twice a day using the spacer; supply 1 200 dose inhaler; NHS Cost £6.66.

udesonide MDI: 200mcg daily (100mcg twice a day)
- Age from 1 month to 11 years
- Budesonide 50mcg inhaler. Inhale two puffs twice a day using the spacer; supply 1 200 dose inhaler; NHS Cost £6.66.

udesonide MDI: 400mcg daily (200mcg twice a day)
- Age from 1 month to 11 years
- Budesonide 200mcg inhaler. Inhale one puff twice a day using the spacer; supply 1 200 dose inhaler; NHS Cost £19.00.

udesonide MDI: 200mcg daily (100mcg twice a day)
- Age from 12 years onwards
- Budesonide 50mcg inhaler. Inhale two puffs twice a day; supply 1 200 dose inhaler; NHS Cost £6.66.

udesonide MDI: 400mcg daily (200mcg twice a day)
- Age from 12 years onwards
- Budesonide 200mcg inhaler. Inhale one puff twice a day; supply 1 200 dose inhaler; NHS Cost £19.00.

udesonide MDI: 800mcg daily (400mcg twice a day)
- Age from 12 years onwards
- Budesonide 200mcg inhaler. Inhale two puffs twice a day; supply 1 200 dose inhaler; NHS Cost £19.00.

Short-acting beta$_2$-agonist when required

albutamol 100mcg MDI: 1 to 2 puffs up to four times a ay
- Age from 5 years onwards
- Salbutamol 100mcg CFC-free inhaler. Inhale one to two puffs up to four times a day, when required to relieve breathlessness; supply 1 200 dose inhaler; NHS Cost £1.90.

iromir 100mcg MDI: 1 to 2 puffs up to four times a day
- Age from 1 month to 4 years
- Airomir 100mcg CFC-free inhaler. Inhale one to two puffs up to four times a day using the spacer, when required to relieve breathlessness; supply 1 200 dose inhaler; NHS Cost £1.97.

iromir 100mcg MDI: 1 to 2 puffs up to four times a day
- Age from 5 years onwards
- Airomir 100mcg CFC-free inhaler. Inhale one to two puffs up to four times a day, when required to relieve breathlessness; supply 1 200 dose inhaler; NHS Cost £1.97.

alamol 100mcg MDI: 1 to 2 puffs up to four times a day
- Age from 1 month to 4 years
- Salamol 100mcg CFC-free inhaler. Inhale one to two puffs up to four times a day using the spacer, when required to relieve breathlessness; supply 1 200 dose inhaler; NHS Cost £1.95.

alamol 100mcg MDI: 1 to 2 puffs up to four times a day
- Age from 5 years onwards
- Salamol 100mcg CFC-free inhaler. Inhale one to two puffs up to four times a day, when required to relieve breathlessness; supply 1 200 dose inhaler; NHS Cost £1.97.

entolin 100mcg MDI: 1 to 2 puffs up to four times a day
- Age from 1 month to 4 years
- Ventolin 100mcg CFC-free inhaler. Inhale one to two puffs up to four times a day using the spacer, when required to relieve breathlessness; supply 1 200 dose inhaler; NHS Cost £2.30.

Ventolin 100mcg MDI: 1 to 2 puffs up to four times a day
- Age from 5 years onwards
- Ventolin 100mcg CFC-free inhaler. Inhale one to two puffs up to four times a day, when required to relieve breathlessness; supply 1 200 dose inhaler; NHS Cost £2.30.

Terbutaline 250mcg MDI: 1 to 2 puffs up to four times a day
- Age from 1 month to 4 years
- Terbutaline 250mcg inhaler. Inhale one to two puffs up to four times a day using the spacer, when required to relieve breathlessness; supply 1 400 dose inhaler; NHS Cost £5.31.

Terbutaline 250mcg MDI: 1 to 2 puffs up to four times a day
- Age from 5 years onwards
- Terbutaline 250mcg inhaler. Inhale one to two puffs up to four times a day, when required to relieve breathlessness; supply 1 400 dose inhaler; NHS Cost £5.31.

Spacers

Infant Aerochamber+facemask: for use with Airomir
- Age from 1 month to 23 months
- Aerochamber (infant) + mask. Use to aid inhalation; supply 1 spacer; NHS Cost £7.14.

Child Aerochamber + facemask: for use with Airomir
- Age from 2 to 3 years
- Aerochamber (child) + mask. Use to aid inhalation; supply 1 spacer; NHS Cost £7.14.

Aerochamber: for use with Airomir
- Age from 4 to 11 years
- AeroChamber Plus spacer device. Use to aid inhalation; supply 1 spacer; NHS Cost £4.28.

Aerochamber: for use with Qvar/Airomir
- Age from 12 years onwards
- AeroChamber Plus spacer device. Use to aid inhalation; supply 1 spacer; NHS Cost £4.28.

Nebuhaler + facemask: for use with budesonide/terbutaline
- Age from 1 month to 2 years
- Nebuhaler spacer device + mask. Use to aid inhalation; supply 1 spacer; NHS Cost £4.28.

Nebuhaler: for use with budesonide/terbutaline
- Age from 3 years onwards
- Nebuhaler spacer device. Use to aid inhalation; supply 1 spacer; NHS Cost £4.28.

Volumatic+facemask: for use with Becotide/Flixotide/Ventolin
- Age from 1 month to 2 years
- Volumatic spacer device+mask. Use to aid inhalation; supply 1 spacer; NHS Cost £2.75.

Volumatic: for use with Becotide/Flixotide/Ventolin/Salamol
- Age from 3 years onwards
- Volumatic spacer device. Use to aid inhalation; supply 1 spacer; NHS Cost £2.75.

Poor control: add LABA and/or increase ICS (standard doses)

Which therapy?

Before initiating a new drug therapy, re-check compliance and inhaler technique, and eliminate trigger factors.

For children aged less than 2 years

- Consider referring to a respiratory paediatrician.

A

For children aged 2–5 years

- Add a leukotriene receptor antagonist (see scenario *Poor control: add-on therapy*).

For people above the age of 5 years

- **Add in an inhaled long-acting beta$_2$-agonist (LABA):**
  - Salmeterol 50 micrograms twice a day.
  - Formoterol (eformoterol) 6–12 micrograms twice a day.
- **If there is good response to the inhaled long-acting beta$_2$-agonist and good control, continue the long-acting beta$_2$-agonist plus inhaled corticosteroids (ICS).**
- **If there is benefit from the inhaled long-acting beta$_2$-agonist but control is still inadequate:**
  - Continue the long-acting beta$_2$-agonist.
  - Increase ICS to 800 micrograms per day (adults) or 400 micrograms per day (children).
- **If there is no response to the inhaled long-acting beta$_2$-agonist:**
  - Stop the long-acting beta$_2$-agonist.
  - Increase ICS to 800 micrograms per day (adults) or 400 micrograms per day (children).
  - If control still inadequate, try another add-on therapy. See scenario *Poor control: add-on therapy*.
- **Continue the inhaled short-acting beta$_2$-agonist on an 'as required' basis.**
- **Advise on smoking cessation, where appropriate.**

Which inhaled corticosteroid and delivery system?

- Treat people with asthma with the cheapest inhaled corticosteroid (ICS) and delivery system that suits their needs and which controls their symptoms.
  - **Metered-dose inhalers (MDIs)** are as effective as other types of inhaler and are first choice for delivery of ICS and bronchodilators.
  - **Use a spacer with an ICS MDI** for all children under 15 years and in people who cannot coordinate the actuation of a MDI with inhalation. For children under 5 years, use a facemask where necessary.
  - **Consider a spacer device in all people using ICS:** a large volume spacer will reduce deposition of steroid in the oropharynx (which is associated with oral candidiasis).
  - **A dry powder device or a breath-actuated MDI may be considered as an alternative delivery system** in people who are unable or unwilling to use an MDI with a spacer. These are not offered here but are offered in the scenario ***Using alternative devices***.

Practical prescribing points

For further information please see the *Medicines Compendium* (www.medicines.org.uk) or the *British National Formulary* (www.bnf.org).

Inhaled corticosteroids

- **Oral candidiasis and sore mouth are common.** Use a large volume spacer with a pressurized metered-dose inhaler (pMDI), and rinse the mouth with water after inhaled corticosteroid (ICS) use.
- **Do not exceed the licensed dose** of ICS when prescribing for children.
- **For people on prolonged treatment with ICS:**
  - Check height of children regularly. If growth slows, reduce the dose or refer to a specialist, or both.
  - Give lifestyle advice to prevent osteoporosis: exercise, dietary calcium, and smoking.
  - There is a small increased risk of glaucoma and cataracts with prolonged high doses.
- Consider the possibility of adrenal insufficiency if someone using ICS presents with decreased consciousness. Check blood glucose levels and consider the need for intramuscular hydrocortisone.

Beta$_2$-agonists

- Hypokalaemia may occur with regular high doses, or when taken together with other drugs that also predispose to hypokalaemia (such as theophylline and its derivatives, and diuretics).
- Paradoxical bronchospasm has been noted to occur with beta$_2$-agonists. This appears to be more common with salmeterol (incidence approx 1%) [DTB, 1997].

Follow-up advice

- Review in 1 month to establish response to treatment and assess how much short-acting beta$_2$-agonist is being used.
- If there is good response to the inhaled long-acting beta$_2$-agonist and good control, continue the long-acting beta$_2$-agonist plus inhaled corticosteroids (ICS) and review in 3–6 months.
- If there is benefit from the inhaled long-acting beta$_2$-agonist but control is still inadequate:
  - Continue the long-acting beta$_2$-agonist.
  - Increase ICS to 800 micrograms per day (adults) or 400 micrograms per day (children).
- If there is no response to the inhaled long-acting beta$_2$-agonist:
  - Stop the long-acting beta$_2$-agonist.
  - Increase ICS to 800 micrograms per day (adults) or 400 micrograms per day (children).

Should I refer or investigate?

Refer?

- Refer if the diagnosis is unclear or in doubt.
- Consider referring children less than 2 years old to a respiratory paediatrician. Note that in the case of a wheezing child, the younger they are, the more difficult it is to be sure that the cause is asthma, and the lower the threshold is for referral.

Investigate?

- Monitor height in growing children, at least annually.
- Check blood glucose levels in any child (or adult) who presents with a decreased level of consciousness and is maintained on inhaled corticosteroids.

Patient information leaflets

The following PILs are available at www.prodigy.nhs.uk

- Asthma
- Asthma - Action Plan
- Asthma - Inhalers
- Asthma - Peak Flow Diary
- Asthma - Peak Flow Meter
- Asthma - Picture Summary
- Asthma UK
- Asthma UK (Scotland)

Shared decision making

- Your asthma symptoms are not well controlled.
- **One option** is to add in another inhaler such as **salmeterol** or **formoterol** (eformoterol).

These relax the muscles in the airways for up to 12 hours (which is longer than the commonly used 'reliever' inhalers).

An alternative is to increase the dose of your **steroid inhaler:**

The most common side-effect is a thrush infection in the mouth. To help prevent this, rinse your mouth with water after using the inhaler.

Other side-effects are rare, as little steroid is absorbed into the body.

A high dose of inhaled steroid over a long time may be a 'risk factor' for osteoporosis. You can help to prevent this by regular exercise, not smoking, and taking a diet with enough calcium.

Children taking high dose inhaled steroids should have their growth monitored.

To make inhalers easier to use, and to enhance the effect, many people attach them to a 'spacer' chamber.

Continue to use your 'reliever' inhaler when needed, but you should need it much less often.

Drug rationale

Drugs not included

Oral corticosteroids and long-acting beta$_2$-agonists (LABAs) are not included. The inhaled route is preferred for initial management, to minimize adverse effects by providing direct local application of the drug. Short courses of oral prednisolone may be used to gain control of symptoms, and prescriptions for prednisolone are offered in the scenario *Acute exacerbation of asthma.*

'Reliever' therapy: there are no prescriptions for short-acting beta2-agonists in this scenario although they should still be used on a 'when required' basis. See scenario *New presentation* for prescriptions.

Mometasone is not offered as an alternative inhaled corticosteroid because it is a black triangle drug, and post-marketing data are needed to confirm its safety. It is currently only available as a dry powder inhaler.

Inhaled antimuscarinics (ipratropium and oxitropium) are regarded as being more effective in relieving bronchoconstriction associated with chronic obstructive pulmonary disease than in relieving asthma, and thus are not included [BNF 45, 2003].

Inhalers other than metered-dose inhalers (MDIs) are not included for inhaled corticosteroids (ICS) and salmeterol. A meta-analysis found there was no evidence that alternative inhaler devices were more effective for the delivery of inhaled beta$_2$-agonists and ICS than MDIs [Brocklebank et al, 2001; Ram et al, 2001]. If an alternative device is necessary, a selection is offered in the scenario *Using alternative delivery systems.*

Combination products are not offered as this scenario is aimed at achieving control of the person's asthma. They may be an option for someone whose symptoms are well controlled on stable doses and where a trial of stepping down inhaled corticosteroids is not appropriate.

Other regular inhaled or oral preventer therapy is not included (e.g. sodium cromoglicate, leukotriene receptor antagonists, theophyllines). The first choice of preventer therapy is regular ICS, and other preventer drugs may be needed only rarely, for example when the person is unable to tolerate corticosteroids. See scenario *Poor control: add-on therapy* for prescriptions.

Drugs included

The long-acting beta$_2$-agonists (LABAs) (formoterol [eformoterol] and salmeterol) are included. Salmeterol and formoterol have an equivalent bronchodilator effect over 12 hours but formoterol has a faster onset of action [van Noord et al, 1996]. Only salmeterol is available as a metered-dose inhaler MDI; formoterol is available as a choice of two dry powder inhalers.

- **Budesonide and beclometasone** are offered in a range of doses up to 800 micrograms daily
- **Beclometasone chlorofluorocarbon (CFC) -free metered dose inhaler** (Qvar) is offered, should this option be required. The total daily dose of beclometasone from a CFC-free inhaler is approximately half that of the CFC-containing product. The Summary of Product Characteristics for the product should be followed carefully, for both initiating CFC-free beclometasone and for transferring someone from CFC-containing to CFC-free products.
- **Fluticasone** is offered in doses up to 400 micrograms daily. All fluticasone inhalers are now CFC-free.
- **Spacer devices** for the chosen metered-dose inhaler (MDI) should be guided by the Summary of Product Characteristics:
  - Becotide, Flixotide, and Serevent inhalers — Volumatic.
  - Qvar inhaler — Aerochamber.
  - Pulmicort inhaler — Nebuhaler.
- Note: switching between different inhaler and/or spacer types can affect the deposition characteristics of the inhaled drug, which may alter the clinical response to a drug. To maintain good asthma control, it is important that people are not switched back and forth between inhalers and spacer devices.

Prescriptions

Long-acting beta$_2$-agonists

Salmeterol MDI: 50mcg twice a day

- Age from 5 years onwards
- Salmeterol 25microgram inhaler. Inhale two puffs twice a day; supply 1 120 dose inhaler; NHS Cost £28.60.

Formoterol (eformoterol) Turbohaler: 12mcg once/twice a day

- Age from 6 to 12 years
- Formoterol 6mcg Turbohaler. Inhale two puffs once or twice a day; supply 1 60 dose inhaler; NHS Cost £24.80.

Formoterol (eformoterol) Turbohaler:6-12mcg once/twice a day

- Age from 13 years onwards
- Formoterol 6mcg Turbohaler. Inhale one to two puffs once or twice a day. ; supply 1 60 dose inhaler; NHS Cost £24.80.

Formoterol (eformoterol) Turbohaler: 12mcg once/twice a day

- Age from 6 years onwards
- Formoterol 12mcg Turbohaler. Inhale one puff once or twice a day. ; supply 1 60 dose inhaler; NHS Cost £24.80.

Formoterol (eformoterol) capsule dry-powder inhaler

- Age from 5 years onwards
- Formoterol 12mcg DPI inhaler. Inhale the contents of one capsule twice a day; supply 1 56 dose inhaler; NHS Cost £24.80.

Beclometasone (standard dose)

Beclometasone MDI: 200mcg daily (100mcg twice a day)

- Age from 12 years onwards
- Beclometasone 50mcg inhaler. Inhale two puffs twice a day; supply 1 200 dose inhaler; NHS Cost £4.27.

Beclometasone MDI: 400mcg daily (200mcg twice a day)

- Age from 12 years onwards
- Beclometasone 100mcg inhaler. Inhale two puffs twice a day; supply 1 200 dose inhaler; NHS Cost £8.24.

Beclometasone MDI: 800mcg daily (400mcg twice a day)
- Age from 12 years onwards
- Beclometasone 200mcg inhaler. Inhale two puffs twice a day; supply 1 200 dose inhaler; NHS Cost £19.61.

Becotide MDI: 100mcg daily (50mcg twice a day)
- Age from 1 month to 11 years
- Becotide-50 50mcg inhaler. Inhale one puff twice a day using the spacer; supply 1 200 dose inhaler; NHS Cost £5.43.

Becotide MDI: 200mcg daily (100mcg twice a day)
- Age from 1 month to 11 years
- Becotide-50 50mcg inhaler. Inhale two puffs twice a day using the spacer; supply 1 200 dose inhaler; NHS Cost £5.43.

Becotide MDI: 400mcg daily (200mcg twice a day)
- Age from 1 month to 11 years
- Becotide-100 100mcg inhaler. Inhale two puffs twice a day using the spacer; supply 1 200 dose inhaler; NHS Cost £10.32.

Becotide MDI: 200mcg daily (100mcg twice a day)
- Age from 12 years onwards
- Becotide-100 100mcg inhaler. Inhale one puff twice a day; supply 1 200 dose inhaler; NHS Cost £10.32.

Becotide MDI: 400mcg daily (200mcg twice a day)
- Age from 12 years onwards
- Becotide-200 200mcg inhaler. Inhale one puff twice a day; supply 1 200 dose inhaler; NHS Cost £19.61.

Becotide MDI: 800mcg daily (400mcg twice a day)
- Age from 12 years onwards
- Becotide-200 200mcg inhaler. Inhale two puffs twice a day; supply 1 200 dose inhaler; NHS Cost £19.61.

Qvar (beclometasone CFC-free)

Qvar CFC-free MDI: 100mcg daily (50mcg twice a day)
- Age from 12 years onwards
- Qvar 50mcg CFC-free inhaler. Inhale one puff twice a day; supply 1 200 dose inhaler; NHS Cost £7.87.

Qvar CFC-free MDI: 200mcg daily (100mcg twice a day)
- Age from 12 years onwards
- Qvar 50mcg CFC-free inhaler. Inhale two puffs twice a day; supply 1 200 dose inhaler; NHS Cost £7.87.

Qvar CFC-free MDI: 400mcg daily (200mcg twice a day)
- Age from 12 years onwards
- Qvar 100mcg CFC-free inhaler. Inhale two puffs twice a day; supply 1 200 dose inhaler; NHS Cost £17.21.

Fluticasone / Budesonide

Fluticasone CFC-free MDI: 100mcg daily (50mcg twice a day)
- Age from 5 to 15 years
- Fluticasone 50mcg CFC-free inhaler. Inhale one puff twice a day using the spacer; supply 1 120 dose inhaler; NHS Cost £5.85.

Fluticasone CFC-free MDI: 200mcg daily (100mcg twice a day)
- Age from 5 to 15 years
- Fluticasone 50mcg CFC-free inhaler. Inhale two puffs twice a day using the spacer; supply 1 120 dose inhaler; NHS Cost £5.85.

Fluticasone CFC-free MDI: 100mcg daily (50mcg twice a day)
- Age from 16 years onwards
- Fluticasone 50mcg CFC-free inhaler. Inhale one puff twice a day; supply 1 120 dose inhaler; NHS Cost £5.85.

Fluticasone CFC-free MDI: 200mcg daily (100mcg twice a day)
- Age from 16 years onwards
- Fluticasone 50mcg CFC-free inhaler. Inhale two puffs twice a day; supply 1 120 dose inhaler; NHS Cost £5.85.

Fluticasone CFC-free MDI: 400mcg daily (200mcg twic day)
- Age from 16 years onwards
- Fluticasone 50mcg CFC-free inhaler. Inhale four puffs twice a day; supply 2 120 dose inhaler; NHS Cost £11.70.

Budesonide MDI: 100mcg daily (50mcg twice a day)
- Age from 5 to 11 years
- Budesonide 50mcg inhaler. Inhale one puff twice a da using the spacer; supply 1 200 dose inhaler; NHS Cost £6.66.

Budesonide MDI: 200mcg daily (100mcg twice a day)
- Age from 5 to 11 years
- Budesonide 50mcg inhaler. Inhale two puffs twice a d using the spacer; supply 1 200 dose inhaler; NHS Cost £6.66.

Budesonide MDI: 400mcg daily (200mcg twice a day)
- Age from 5 to 11 years
- Budesonide 200mcg inhaler. Inhale one puff twice a d using the spacer; supply 1 200 dose inhaler; NHS Cost £19.00.

Budesonide MDI: 200mcg daily (100mcg twice a day)
- Age from 12 years onwards
- Budesonide 50mcg inhaler. Inhale two puffs twice a d supply 1 200 dose inhaler; NHS Cost £6.00.

Budesonide MDI: 400mcg daily (200mcg twice a day)
- Age from 12 years onwards
- Budesonide 200mcg inhaler. Inhale one puff twice a d supply 1 200 dose inhaler; NHS Cost £19.00.

Budesonide MDI: 800mcg daily (400mcg twice a day)
- Age from 12 years onwards
- Budesonide 200mcg inhaler. Inhale two puffs twice a day; supply 1 200 dose inhaler; NHS Cost £19.00.

Spacers

Aerochamber: for use with Qvar/Airomir
- Age from 5 years onwards
- AeroChamber Plus spacer device. Use to aid inhalation supply 1 spacer; NHS Cost £4.28.

Nebuhaler: for use with budesonide/terbutaline
- Age from 5 years onwards
- Nebuhaler spacer device. Use to aid inhalation; supply spacer; NHS Cost £4.28.

Volumatic: for use with Serevent/Becotide/Flixotide/ Ventolin
- Age from 5 years onwards
- Volumatic spacer device. Use to aid inhalation; supply spacer; NHS Cost £2.75.

Poor control: increase inhaled corticosteroid (higher doses)

Which therapy?

- **Before increasing the dose of inhaled corticosteroid (ICS),** re-check compliance and inhaler technique, and eliminate trigger factors.
- Refer children under the age of 5 years to a respiratory paediatrician.
- For people over the age of 5 years consider referral to a specialist if asthma remains inadequately controlled — especially children.
- For adults and children above the age of 5 years consid a trial of increasing inhaled corticosteroids to the maximum recommended daily dose; for beclometasone this is:
  - 2000 micrograms for adults and children over 12 years of age

800 micrograms for children under 12 (Note: not licensed at this dose)
Jse the lowest dose at which effective control of asthma s maintained, i.e. step down the dose of inhaled orticosteroids in people whose asthma is well ontrolled.
Advise on smoking cessation, where appropriate.
Jse a spacer with an inhaled corticosteroid (ICS) netered-dose inhaler (MDI) in all children under 5 years and in people who cannot coordinate the ctuation of an MDI with inhalation.
Consider a spacer device in all people using high-dose CS: a large volume spacer may improve delivery and educe adverse effects due to deposition of steroid in the ropharynx.
A dry powder device or a breath-actuated MDI may be considered as an alternative delivery system in people who are unable or unwilling to use an MDI with a spacer. These are not offered here but are offered in the scenario ***Using alternative delivery systems.***

ractical prescribing points

r further information please see the *Medicines mpendium* (www.medicines.org.uk) or the *British tional Formulary* (www.bnf.org).

eta$_2$-agonists

Hypokalaemia may occur with regular high doses, or when taken together with other drugs that also predispose to hypokalaemia (such as theophylline and its derivatives, and diuretics).

haled corticosteroids

Oral candidiasis and sore mouth are common. Use a large volume spacer with a metered-dose inhaler (MDI), and rinse the mouth with water after inhaled corticosteroid (ICS) use.
Do not exceed the licensed dose of ICS when prescribing for children.
For people on prolonged treatment with ICS:

- Check height of children regularly. If growth slows, reduce the dose, or refer to a specialist, or both.
- Give lifestyle advice to prevent osteoporosis: exercise, dietary calcium, and smoking.
- There is a small increased risk of glaucoma and cataracts with prolonged high doses.

Consider the possibility of adrenal insufficiency if someone using ICS presents with decreased consciousness. Check blood glucose levels and consider the need for intramuscular hydrocortisone.

ollow-up advice

Review in 1 month to establish response to treatment and assess how much short-acting beta$_2$-agonist is being used.
If asthma is stable and control is good, continue treatment and review in 3–6 months.
Use the lowest dose inhaled corticosteroid (ICS) at which effective control of asthma is maintained. Consider the possibility of stepping down the dose of ICS in people whose asthma is well controlled.

hould I refer or investigate?

efer?

Refer children under the age of 5 years to a respiratory paediatrician.

- For people over the age of 5 years consider referral to a specialist if asthma remains inadequately controlled — especially children.

Investigate?

- Monitor height in growing children, at least once a year.
- Check blood glucose levels in any child (or adult) who presents with a decreased level of consciousness and is maintained on inhaled corticosteroids.

Patient information leaflets

The following PILs are available at www.prodigy.nhs.uk

- Asthma
- Asthma - Action Plan
- Asthma - Inhalers
- Asthma - Peak Flow Diary
- Asthma - Peak Flow Meter
- Asthma - Picture Summary
- Asthma UK
- Asthma UK (Scotland)
- Medicines - Name Changes of Medicines

Shared decision making

- Your asthma symptoms are not well controlled.
- An option is to increase the dose of your **steroid inhaler:**
  - The most common side-effect is a thrush infection in the mouth. To help prevent this, rinse your mouth with water after using the inhaler.
  - Other side-effects are rare, as little steroid is absorbed into the body.
  - A high dose of inhaled steroid over a long time may be a 'risk factor' for osteoporosis. You can help to prevent this by regular exercise, not smoking, and a diet with enough calcium.
  - Children taking high dose inhaled steroids should have their growth monitored.
- To make inhalers easier to use, and to enhance the effect, many people attach them to a 'spacer' chamber.
- **Continue to use your 'reliever' inhaler when needed,** but you should need it much less often.

Drug rationale

Drugs not included

- Prescriptions are not offered for children under the age of 5 years as they should be referred to a respiratory paediatrician.
- **Oral corticosteroids** are not included. The inhaled route is preferred for initial management with corticosteroids, to minimize adverse effects by providing direct local application of the drug. Short courses of prednisolone may be used to gain control of symptoms, and prescriptions for oral prednisolone are offered in the scenario *Acute exacerbation of asthma.*
- **Mometasone** is not offered as an alternative inhaled corticosteroid (ICS) because it is a black triangle drug, and post-marketing data are needed to confirm its safety. It is currently only available as a dry powder inhaler.
- **Combination products** are not offered as this scenario is aimed at achieving control of the person's asthma. They may be an option for someone whose symptoms are well controlled on stable doses that can be provided by available strengths of combination products, and where a trial of stepping down inhaled corticosteroids is not appropriate.
- **Other regular inhaled and oral preventer therapy** are not included (e.g. sodium cromoglicate, leukotriene receptor antagonists, theophyllines). If the trial of ICS shows that

increasing the corticosteroid dose is not effective, return to the original dose and consider sequential trials of add-on therapy See scenario *Poor control: add-on therapy*.

- **Inhalers other than metered-dose inhalers (MDIs)** are not offered. Meta-analyses found there was no evidence that alternative inhaler devices were more effective for the delivery of inhaled beta$_2$-agonists and ICS than MDIs [Brocklebank et al, 2001; Ram et al, 2001]. If an alternative device is necessary, a selection is offered in the scenario *Using alternative delivery systems*.

Drugs included

- **Beclometasone** is offered in a range of doses up to 2000 micrograms daily.
- **Budesonide** is offered in a range of doses up to 1600 micrograms daily.
- **Fluticasone** is offered in doses up to 1000 micrograms daily. The Committee on Safety of Medicines advise that doses higher than 500 micrograms twice daily should be supervised by a specialist (who might be primary care- or hospital-based) because of the potential for systemic effects [CSM, 2001]. All fluticasone inhalers are now chlorofluorocarbon (CFC) -free.
- **Spacer devices** are offered separately to the inhalers in this scenario. The choice of spacer device for the chosen metered-dose inhaler (MDI) should be guided by the Summary of Product Characteristics:
  - Qvar inhaler — Aerochamber.
  - Becloforte, Becotide and Flixotide inhalers — Volumatic.
  - Pulmicort inhalers — Nebuhaler.
- Note: switching between different inhaler or spacer types, or both, can affect the deposition characteristics of the inhaled drug, which may alter the clinical response to a drug. To maintain good asthma control, it is important that people are not switched back and forth between inhalers and spacer devices.

Prescriptions

Beclometasone (higher doses)

Beclometasone MDI: 800mcg daily (400mcg twice a day)
- Age from 5 to 11 years
- Beclometasone 200mcg inhaler. Inhale two puffs twice a day; supply 1 200 dose inhaler; NHS Cost £19.00.

Beclometasone MDI: 1000mcg daily (500mcg twice a day)
- Age from 12 years onwards
- Beclometasone 250mcg inhaler. Inhale two puffs twice a day; supply 1 200 dose inhaler; NHS Cost £17.80.

Beclometasone MDI: 1200mcg daily (600mcg twice a day)
- Age from 12 years onwards
- Beclometasone 200mcg inhaler. Inhale three puffs twice a day; supply 1 200 dose inhaler; NHS Cost £19.61.

Beclometasone MDI: 1500mcg daily (750mcg twice a day)
- Age from 12 years onwards
- Beclometasone 250mcg inhaler. Inhale three puffs twice a day; supply 1 200 dose inhaler; NHS Cost £17.80.

Beclometasone MDI: 1600mcg daily (800mcg twice a day)
- Age from 12 years onwards
- Beclometasone 200mcg inhaler. Inhale four puffs twice a day; supply 2 200 dose inhaler; NHS Cost £39.22.

Beclometasone MDI: 2000mcg daily (1000mcg twice a day)
- Age from 12 years onwards
- Beclometasone 250mcg inhaler. Inhale four puffs twic day; supply 2 200 dose inhaler; NHS Cost £35.60.

Qvar (beclometasone CFC-free)

Qvar CFC-free MDI: 600mcg daily (300mcg twice a day
- Age from 12 years onwards
- Qvar 100mcg CFC-free inhaler. Inhale three puffs twi a day; supply 1 200 dose inhaler; NHS Cost £17.21.

Qvar CFC-free MDI: 800mcg daily (400mcg twice a day
- Age from 12 years onwards
- Qvar 100mcg CFC-free inhaler. Inhale four puffs twic day; supply 1 200 dose inhaler; NHS Cost £17.21.

Becotide / Becloforte (higher doses)

Becotide MDI: 800mcg daily (400mcg twice a day)
- Age from 5 to 11 years
- Becotide-200 200mcg inhaler. Inhale two puffs twice a day using the spacer; supply 1 200 dose inhaler; NHS Cost £19.61.

Becloforte MDI: 1000mcg daily (500mcg twice a day)
- Age from 12 years onwards
- Becloforte 250mcg inhaler. Inhale two puffs twice a da supply 1 200 dose inhaler; NHS Cost £23.10.

Becotide MDI: 1200mcg daily (600mcg twice a day)
- Age from 12 years onwards
- Becotide-200 200mcg inhaler. Inhale three puffs twice day; supply 1 200 dose inhaler; NHS Cost £19.61.

Becloforte MDI: 1500mcg daily (750mcg twice a day)
- Age from 12 years onwards
- Becloforte 250mcg inhaler. Inhale three puffs twice a day; supply 1 200 dose inhaler; NHS Cost £23.10.

Becotide MDI: 1600mcg daily (800mcg twice a day)
- Age from 12 years onwards
- Becotide-200 200mcg inhaler. Inhale four puffs twice a day; supply 2 200 dose inhaler; NHS Cost £39.22.

Becloforte MDI: 2000mcg daily (1000mcg twice a day)
- Age from 12 years onwards
- Becloforte 250mcg inhaler. Inhale four puffs twice a da supply 2 200 dose inhaler; NHS Cost £46.20.

Fluticasone CFC-free / budesonide (higher doses)

Fluticasone CFC-free MDI: 400mcg daily (200mcg twice day)
- Age from 5 to 15 years
- Fluticasone 50mcg CFC-free inhaler. Inhale four puffs twice a day using the spacer; supply 2 120 dose inhaler NHS Cost £11.70.

Fluticasone CFC-free MDI: 500mcg daily (250mcg twice day)
- Age from 16 years onwards
- Fluticasone 250mcgCFC-free inhaler. Inhale one puff twice a day; supply 1 120 dose inhaler; NHS Cost £38.86.

Fluticasone CFC-free MDI: 750mcg daily (375mcg twice day)
- Age from 16 years onwards
- Fluticasone 125mcgCFC-free inhaler. Inhale three puffs twice a day; supply 2 120 dose inhaler; NHS Cost £45.72.

Fluticasone CFC-free MDI: 1000mcg daily (500mcg twic a day)
- Age from 16 years onwards
- Fluticasone 250mcgCFC-free inhaler. Inhale two puffs twice a day; supply 1 120 dose inhaler; NHS Cost £38.86.

lesonide MDI: 800mcg daily (400mcg twice a day)
ge from 5 to 11 years
udesonide 200mcg inhaler. Inhale two puffs twice a day sing the spacer; supply 1 200 dose inhaler; IHS Cost £19.00.

lesonide MDI: 1200mcg daily (600mcg twice a day)
ge from 12 years onwards
udesonide 200mcg inhaler. Inhale three puffs twice a ay; supply 1 200 dose inhaler; NHS Cost £19.00.

lesonide MDI: 1600mcg daily (800mcg twice a day)
ge from 12 years onwards
udesonide 200mcg inhaler. Inhale four puffs twice a ay; supply 2 200 dose inhaler; NHS Cost £38.00.

acers

ochamber: for use with Qvar
Age from 5 years onwards
AeroChamber Plus spacer device. Use to aid inhalation; upply 1 spacer; NHS Cost £2.75.

ouhaler: for use with budesonide
Age from 5 years onwards
Nebuhaler spacer device. Use to aid inhalation; supply 1 pacer; NHS Cost £4.28.

umatic: for use with Becotide/Becloforte/Flixotide
Age from 5 years onwards
Volumatic spacer device. Use to aid inhalation; supply 1 pacer; NHS Cost £2.75.

oor control: add on therapy

hich therapy?

f trials of inhaled long-acting beta$_2$-agonist (LABA) and higher doses of inhaled corticosteroids (ICS) have not produced adequate control, consider sequential trials of one 'add-on' therapy, i.e. a leukotriene receptor antagonist, oral modified-release theophylline; a cromone, or an oral long-acting or modified-release beta$_2$-agonist.

n children over 5 years and adults, sequential trials of one add-on therapy should be considered when:

- There are concerns about adverse effects such as growth retardation in children taking an ICS.
- Control of asthma is inadequate after a trial of a long-acting beta$_2$-agonist and standard-dose ICS.
  - **Stop the long-acting beta$_2$-agonist** before starting an alternative add-on therapy.
- Control of asthma is inadequate after a trial of high dose ICS shows that increasing the corticosteroid dose is not effective. Return to the original dose of ICS if high dose is not effective.

In children aged between 2 and 5 years, consider a trial of a leukotriene receptor antagonist. (For this age group, the only licensed leukotriene receptor antagonist is montelukast.)

'Add-on' therapy is unlikely to be 'steroid-sparing'.

'Add-on' therapy should not be used to treat acute exacerbations of asthma.

Advise on smoking cessation, where appropriate.

ractical prescribing points

r further information please see the *Medicines ompendium* (www.medicines.org.uk) or the *British ational Formulary* (www.bnf.org).

heophylline

Theophylline has a narrow therapeutic window: aim for a plasma level between 10 and 20 mg/litre.

- Prescribe theophylline by brand. (Bioavailability varies between brands.)
- Blood levels may be raised by drugs that inhibit hepatic enzymes (e.g. cimetidine, ciprofloxacin, erythromycin).
- Blood levels may be lowered by smoking, chronic alcoholism, and by drugs that induce hepatic enzymes (e.g. phenytoin, carbamazepine, rifampicin).

Leukotriene receptor antagonists

- **Zafirlukast:** hepatic disorders may occur and people should be advised to seek medical attention in the event of persistent nausea, vomiting, malaise or jaundice.

Follow-up advice

- **Review after 1 month** (or sooner if appropriate).
- **The trigger to changing treatment is** if the short-acting beta$_2$-agonist is being used three times a week or more, or if symptom control is not good. The British Thoracic Society defines good control as minimal chronic symptoms, ideally none; minimal exacerbations; minimal need for relieving bronchodilators; no limitation on activities.
- A 3-month period of stability (depending on the individual person with asthma) should be shown before slow stepping down of medication is considered.
- If theophylline is prescribed, monitor blood levels.

Should I refer or investigate?

Refer?

- Consider referral if:
  - There is diagnostic doubt.
  - There are problems in management, or if the person is failing to respond to treatment. This may be particularly indicated when considering 'add-on' therapy.
  - Long-term oral corticosteroids or home use of a nebulizer are being considered.

Investigate?

- Monitor height in growing children, at least annually.
- Check blood glucose levels in any child (or adult) who presents with a decreased level of consciousness and is maintained on inhaled corticosteroids.

Patient information leaflets

The following PILs are available at www.prodigy.nhs.uk

- Asthma
- Asthma - Action Plan
- Asthma - Inhalers
- Asthma - Peak Flow Diary
- Asthma - Peak Flow Meter
- Asthma - Picture Summary
- Asthma UK
- Asthma UK (Scotland)

Shared decision making

- If asthma symptoms remain poorly controlled there are various options that you can use in addition to your regular steroid inhaler.
- **Sodium cromoglicate** or **nedocromil inhalers.** They need to be taken three or four times a day.
- **Salbutamol** or **terbutaline tablets.**
  - These are the same medicines that are in the common 'reliever' inhalers, and work by opening up the airways.

A

- The dose is higher than in inhalers, so side-effects are more common. These include tremor, palpitations, headaches, and muscle cramps.
- **Theophylline tablets** are an alternative that open up the airways.
  - Possible side-effects include palpitations, feeling sick, headaches, poor sleep.
  - You will need blood tests to monitor the dose as too high a dose may lead to serious side-effects.
- **Montelukast** or **zafirlukast** tablets are also sometimes used.
- **Continue to use your 'reliever' inhaler when needed.**

Drug rationale

Drugs not included

- **Short-acting beta$_2$-agonists, long-acting beta$_2$-agonists (LABA), and inhaled corticosteroids:** there are no prescriptions for short-acting and long-acting beta$_2$-agonists and inhaled corticosteroids (ICS) in this scenario although they should continued as appropriate. See scenarios *New presentation, Poor control: add inhaled corticosteroids, and Poor control: add LABA and/or increase ICS* for prescriptions.
- **Inhaled antimuscarinics (ipratropium and oxitropium)** are regarded as being more effective in relieving bronchoconstriction associated with chronic obstructive pulmonary disease than in relieving asthma and are thus not included [BNF 45, 2003].

Drugs included

- **Oral long-acting and modified-release beta$_2$-agonists** are included at standard doses.
- **Inhaled sodium cromoglicate and nedocromil sodium,** as metered-dose inhalers (MDIs) are included for second-line add-on therapy or if the person is intolerant of or unwilling to use corticosteroids. Nedocromil is an option for children between 5 and 12 years. Sodium cromoglicate is an alternative for children older than 12 years and adults.
- **Modified-release preparations of theophylline** are included as branded products. It is important to keep the person stabilized on one brand of theophylline. Each brand has a narrow therapeutic window and fluctuations can occur by switching between brands. The dose should be adjusted according to response.
- **Oral leukotriene receptor antagonists:** montelukast is licensed for add-on therapy in mild-to-moderate asthma, which is not adequately controlled with inhaled corticosteroid and an inhaled short-acting beta$_2$-agonist taken as required. It may also be used in preventing exercise-induced bronchospasm. Zafirlukast is licensed for treatment of asthma.

Prescriptions

Oral long-acting/modified-release beta$_2$-agonists

Salbutamol s/f syrup: 1-2mg three to four times a day
- Age from 5 to 5 years
- Salbutamol 2mg/5ml s/f syrup. Take 2.5ml to 5ml three to four times a day; supply 600 ml; NHS Cost £2.88.

Salbutamol s/f syrup: 2mg three to four times a day
- Age from 6 to 11 years
- Salbutamol 2mg/5ml s/f syrup. Take one 5ml spoonful 3 to 4 times a day; supply 600 ml; NHS Cost £2.88.

Salbutamol m/r tablets: 4mg twice a day
- Age from 5 to 11 years
- Salbutamol 4mg m/r tablets. Take one tablet twice a d supply 56 tablets; NHS Cost £10.55.

Salbutamol m/r tablets: 8mg twice a day
- Age from 12 years onwards
- Salbutamol 8mg m/r tablets. Take one tablet twice a d supply 56 tablets; NHS Cost £12.66.

Salbutamol m/r capsules: 4mg twice a day
- Age from 5 to 11 years
- Salbutamol 4mg m/r capsules. Take one capsule twice day; supply 56 capsules; NHS Cost £8.57.

Salbutamol m/r capsules: 8mg twice a day
- Age from 12 years onwards
- Salbutamol 8mg m/r capsules. Take one capsule twice day; supply 56 capsules; NHS Cost £10.28.

Terbutaline s/f syrup: 2.4mg two to three times a day
- Age from 7 to 14 years
- Terbutaline 1.5mg/5ml sf syrup. Take 8ml two to thre times a day; supply 300 ml; NHS Cost £2.36.

Terbutaline tablets: 2.5mg twice a day
- Age from 7 to 14 years
- Terbutaline 5mg tablets. Take half a tablet twice a day supply 28 tablets; NHS Cost £1.04.

Terbutaline tablets: 5mg three times a day
- Age from 15 years onwards
- Terbutaline 5mg tablets. Take half a tablet three times day for 2 weeks, then take one tablet three times a day supply 63 tablets; NHS Cost £2.33.

Terbutaline m/r tablets: 7.5mg twice a day
- Age from 16 years onwards
- Terbutaline 7.5mg m/r tablets. Take one tablet twice a day; supply 60 tablets; NHS Cost £4.65.

Bambuterol tablets: 10mg at bedtime
- Age from 12 years onwards
- Bambuterol 10mg tablets. Take one tablet at bedtime; supply 28 tablet; NHS Cost £10.95.

Bambuterol tablets: 20mg at bedtime
- Age from 12 years onwards
- Bambuterol 20mg tablets. Take one tablet at bedtime; supply 28 tablet; NHS Cost £13.14.

Inhaled nedocromil and cromoglicate MDIs

Nedocromil MDI: 4mg four times a day
- Age from 6 to 11 years
- Nedocromil 2mg inhaler. Inhale two puffs four times a day; supply 2 56 dose inhaler; NHS Cost £42.98.

Nedocromil MDI + spacer: 4mg four times a day
- Age from 6 to 11 years
- Nedocromil 2mg inhaler + spacer. Inhale two puffs fou times a day; supply 2 112 dose inhaler + spacer; NHS Cost £85.95.

Sodium cromoglicate MDI: 10mg four times a day
- Age from 12 years onwards
- Sodium cromoglicate 5mg inhaler. Inhale two puffs fou times a day; supply 2 112 dose inhaler; NHS Cost £30.60.

Sodium cromoglicate MDI + spacer: 10mg four times a day
- Age from 12 years onwards
- Sod cromoglicate inhaler + spacer. Inhale two puffs fou times a day; supply 2 112 dose inhaler + spacer; NHS Cost £44.12.

Theophylline: Nuelin + Slo-Phyllin

Nuelin SA m/r tabs: 125mg twice a day
- Age from 6 to 11 years
- Nuelin SA-250 250mg m/r tabs. Take half a tablet twic a day; supply 60 tablets; NHS Cost £4.80.

lin SA m/r tablets: 175mg twice a day
- ge from 6 to 11 years
- uelin SA 175mg m/r tablets. Take one tablet twice a ay; supply 60 tablets; NHS Cost £3.43; TC Cost £6.05.

lin SA m/r tablets: 250mg twice a day
- ge from 6 years onwards
- uelin SA-250 250mg m/r tabs. Take one tablet twice a ay; supply 60 tablets; NHS Cost £4.80; TC Cost £8.46.

lin SA m/r tablets: 350mg twice a day
- ge from 12 years onwards
- uelin SA 175mg m/r tablets. Take two tablets twice a ay; supply 120 tablets; NHS Cost £6.86; TC Cost £12.10.

lin SA m/r tablets: 500mg twice a day
- ge from 12 years onwards
- uelin SA-250 250mg m/r tabs. Take two tablets twice a ay; supply 120 tablets; NHS Cost £9.60; TC Cost £16.92.

-Phyllin m/r capsules: 60mg twice a day
- ge from 5 to 6 years
- lo-Phyllin 60mg m/r capsules. Take one capsule twice a ay; supply 56 capsules; NHS Cost £1.92.

-Phyllin m/r capsules: 120mg twice a day
- ge from 5 to 6 years
- lo-Phyllin 60mg m/r capsules. Take two capsules twice day; supply 112 capsules; NHS Cost £3.84.

-Phyllin m/r capsules: 125mg twice a day
- ge from 7 to 11 years
- lo-Phyllin 125mg m/r capsules. Take one capsule twice day; supply 56 capsules; NHS Cost £2.42.

-Phyllin m/r capsules: 250mg twice a day
- ge from 7 years onwards
- lo-Phyllin 250mg m/r capsules. Take one capsule twice day; supply 56 capsules; NHS Cost £3.02; TC Cost £5.32.

-Phyllin m/r capsules: 500mcg twice a day
- ge from 12 years onwards
- lo-Phyllin 250mg m/r capsules. Take two capsules twice day; supply 112 capsules; NHS Cost £6.04; TC Cost £10.64.

eophylline: Uniphyllin Continus

iphyllin Continus: 200mg twice a day
- Age from 12 years onwards
- Jniphyllin Cont 200mg m/r tabs. Take one tablet twice a lay; supply 56 tablets; NHS Cost £4.12; OTC Cost £7.21.

iphyllin Continus: 300mg twice a day
- Age from 12 years onwards
- Jniphyllin Cont 300mg m/r tabs. Take one tablet twice a lay; supply 56 tablets; NHS Cost £6.27; OTC Cost £11.05.

iphyllin Continus: 400mg twice a day
- Age from 12 years onwards
- Jniphyllin Cont 400mg m/r tabs. Take one tablet twice a lay; supply 56 tablets; NHS Cost £7.44; OTC Cost £13.11.

eukotriene receptor antagonists: montelukast + afirlukast

ontelukast chewable tablets: 4mg at night
- Age from 2 to 5 years
- Montelukast sodium 4mg chewable. Chew one tablet at night; supply 28 tablet; NHS Cost £25.69.

Montelukast chewable tablets: 5mg at night
- Age from 6 to 13 years
- Montelukast sodium 5mg chewable. Chew one tablet at night; supply 28 tablet; NHS Cost £25.69.

Montelukast 10mg at night
- Age from 14 years onwards
- Montelukast 10mg tablets. Take one tablet at night; supply 28 tablets; NHS Cost £25.69.

Zafirlukast 20mg twice a day
- Age from 12 years onwards
- Zafirlukast 20mg tablets. Take one tablet twice a day; supply 56 tablets; NHS Cost £25.69.

Using alternative delivery systems

Which therapy

- **Metered-dose inhalers (MDIs) or MDIs plus a spacer are just as effective as alternative devices** and are considerably cheaper. These should be recommended for most people who can use them correctly and comply with prescribed regimens.
- **Breath-actuated metered-dose inhalers and dry powder inhalers (DPI)** offer alternative systems for those who have problems using, or are unwilling to use, an MDI or an MDI plus spacer.
- **Inspiratory flow considerations.** Breath-actuated inhalers and dry powder-inhalers require an adequate inspiratory flow rate to work. Some frail people and younger children may be unable to consistently achieve this and an MDI with spacer is likely to be more effective for them.
- **Preferred delivery is by MDI plus spacer in people on higher doses of inhaled corticosteroid** (i.e. daily dose more than: 800 micrograms beclometasone, 800 micrograms budesonide, or 500 micrograms fluticasone) as this minimizes oropharyngeal deposition and reduces the risk of systemic and local side-effects.
- **Familiarity.** There are many types of devices. It is recommended that prescribers familiarize themselves with a selection of the devices so they can confidently inform, supervise and assist patients.
- **Control should initially be monitored,** using a symptom diary and possibly a peak flow diary.

Practical prescribing points

For further information please see the *Medicines Compendium* (www.medicines.org) **or the** *British National Formulary* (www.bnf.org).

Beta$_2$-agonists

- Hypokalaemia may occur with regular high doses, or when taken together with other drugs that also predispose to hypokalaemia (such as theophylline and its derivatives, and diuretics).

Inhaled corticosteroids

- **Oral candidiasis and sore mouth are common.** Use a large volume spacer with a pMDI, and rinse the mouth with water after inhaled corticosteroid (ICS) use.
- **Do not exceed the licensed dose of ICS when prescribing for children.**
- **For people on prolonged treatment with ICS:**
  - Check height of children regularly. If growth slows, reduce the dose and/or refer to a specialist.
  - Give lifestyle advice to prevent osteoporosis: exercise, dietary calcium, and smoking.

- There is a small increased risk of glaucoma and cataracts with prolonged high doses.
- Consider the possibility of adrenal insufficiency if someone using ICS presents with decreased consciousness. Check blood glucose levels and consider the need for intramuscular hydrocortisone.

Follow-up advice

- **Review after a month** (or sooner, if necessary), to establish that the new therapy is being used appropriately and that symptoms are well controlled.

Refer or investigate

Refer?

- Consider referral if:
  - There is diagnostic doubt.
  - There is possible occupational asthma: for confirmation of diagnosis, the management of sensitizer avoidance, and the management of other workers in the workplace.
  - There are problems in management; for example, failure to respond to appropriate treatment.
  - Long-term oral corticosteroids or home use of a nebulizer are being considered.

Investigate?

- Monitor height in growing children, at least annually.

Patient information leaflets

The following PILs are available at www.prodigy.nhs.uk

- Asthma
- Asthma - Action Plan
- Asthma - Inhalers
- Asthma - Peak Flow Diary
- Asthma - Peak Flow Meter
- Asthma - Picture Summary
- Asthma UK
- Asthma UK (Scotland)

Shared decision making

- Preventer and reliever medicines come in various inhaler devices.
- **The MDI (Metered Dose Inhaler) is the most commonly used inhaler.**
  - It is quick to use, small, and convenient to carry.
  - You need some co-ordination to use it properly.
- **A 'spacer' chamber is often used with an MDI.**
  - The chamber holds the medicine like a reservoir until you breathe in through the valve.
  - So, you don't need to have good co-ordination to use these.
  - Children commonly use 'spacers', but many adults do too.
- **Breath-activated MDIs are an alternative.**
  - You trigger a dose by breathing in at the mouthpiece.
  - So, you need less co-ordination than with the standard MDI.
- **Dry powder inhalers are another alternative.**
  - Each dose is in a powder that you suck in.
  - Different companies make various devices. Each has a different method of releasing the correct amount of powder for each dose.
  - You need to breathe in fairly hard to get the powder into your lungs.
  - They are not usually suitable for younger children.
- **It is important that you know how to use your inhale correctly.**

Drug rationale

Drugs not included

- **Metered-dose inhaler preparations** of short-acting an long-acting beta$_2$-agonists (LABAs), and corticostero are not included. These are offered as first choices in other scenarios.
- **Formoterol (eformoterol)** is only available as a dry-powder inhaler; prescriptions for this are offered in th scenario *Poor control: add LABA and/or increase IC (standard doses)*.

Drugs included

- **Salbutamol, terbutaline, salmeterol, beclometasone, budesonide and fluticasone** are offered as both aeroso breath-actuated and dry powder inhalers for people w are unable or unwilling to use metered-dose inhalers (MDIs). Although they do not involve such a high deg of coordination between actuation and inhalation, th still require considerable manual dexterity and rely on the person's inspiratory effort to disperse the drug in lungs.
- **Only initial doses of beta2-agonists** are included beca patients are most likely to be started on these product when they are newly diagnosed. Standard recommen doses of inhaled corticosteroids are offered for adults and children.

Prescriptions

Beta$_2$-agonist: breath-actuated inhalers

Airomir CFC-free Autohaler: 1-2 puffs up to 4 times a d

- Age from 5 years onwards
- Airomir 100 CFC-free Autohaler. Inhale one to two puffs up to four times a day, when required to relieve breathlessness; supply 1 200 dose inhaler; NHS Cost £6.02.

Salamol CFC-free Easi-Breathe: 1-2 puffs up to 4 times day

- Age from 5 years onwards
- Salamol 100mcg Easi-Breathe. Inhale one to two puffs up to four times a day, when required to relieve breathlessness; supply 1 200 dose inhaler; NHS Cost £6.30.

Beta$_2$-agonist: dry-powder inhalers

Salbutamol Diskhaler: 200mcg up to four times a day

- Age from 5 years onwards
- Salbutamol 200mcg Diskhaler. Inhale the contents of one blister up to four times a day, when required to relieve breathlessness; supply 1 120 dose inhaler; NHS Cost £7.50.

Salbutamol Accuhaler: 200mcg up to four times a day

- Age from 5 years onwards
- Salbutamol 200mcg Accuhaler. Inhale one puff up to four times a day, when required to relieve breathlessn supply 1 60 dose inhaler; NHS Cost £5.00.

Pulvinal salbutamol: 200mcg up to four times a day

- Age from 5 years onwards
- Pulvinal salbutamol 200mcg. Inhale one puff up to fou times a day, when required to relieve breathlessness; supply 1 100 dose inhaler; NHS Cost £5.05.

Salbutamol Cyclocaps: 200mcg up to four times a day
- Age from 5 years onwards
- Salbutamol 200micrograms capsule. Inhale the contents of one capsule up to four times a day via the cyclohaler, when required to relieve breathlessness; supply 120 capsules for inhalation; NHS Cost £5.00.

Terbutaline Turbohaler: 500mcg up to four times a day
- Age from 5 years onwards
- Terbutaline 500mcg Turbohaler. Inhale one puff up to four times a day, when required to relieve breathlessness; supply 1 100 dose inhaler; NHS Cost £6.30.

Asmasal Clickhaler: 1 to 2 puffs up to four times a day
- Age from 5 years onwards
- Asmasal 95microgram Clickhaler. Inhale one to two puffs up to four times a day, when required to relieve breathlessness; supply 1 200 dose inhaler; NHS Cost £6.32.

Long-acting beta$_2$-agonist: dry-powder inhalers

Salmeterol Accuhaler: 50mcg twice a day
- Age from 5 years onwards
- Salmeterol 50mcg Accuhaler. Inhale one puff twice a day; supply 1 60 dose inhaler; NHS Cost £28.60.

Salmeterol Diskhaler: 50mcg twice a day
- Age from 5 years onwards
- Salmeterol 50mcg Diskhaler. Inhale the contents of one blister twice a day; supply 1 60 dose inhaler; NHS Cost £35.28.

Steroid: breath-actuated inhalers

AeroBec Autohaler: 100mcg daily (50mcg twice a day)
- Age from 5 to 11 years
- AeroBec Autohaler 50mcg/inhaler. Inhale one puff twice a day; supply 1 inhaler; NHS Cost £10.51.

AeroBec Autohaler: 200mcg daily (100mcg twice a day)
- Age from 5 years onwards
- AeroBec 100mcg Autohaler. Inhale one puff twice a day; supply 1 200 dose inhaler; NHS Cost £12.89.

AeroBec Autohaler: 400mcg daily (200mcg twice a day)
- Age from 12 years onwards
- AeroBec 100mcg Autohaler. Inhale two puffs twice a day; supply 1 200 dose inhaler; NHS Cost £12.89.

Beclazone Easi-Breathe: 100mcg (50mcg twice a day)
- Age from 5 to 11 years
- Beclazone 50 Easi-Breathe inhaler. Inhale one puff twice a day; supply 1 inhaler; NHS Cost £4.34.

Beclazone Easi-Breathe: 200mcg daily (100mcg twice a day)
- Age from 5 years onwards
- Beclazone 100mcg Easi-Breathe. Inhale one puff twice a day; supply 1 200 dose inhaler; NHS Cost £8.24.

Beclazone Easi-Breathe: 400mcg daily (200mcg twice a day)
- Age from 12 years onwards
- Beclazone 100mcg Easi-Breathe. Inhale two puffs twice a day; supply 1 200 dose inhaler; NHS Cost £8.24.

Qvar CFC-free Autohaler: 100mcg daily (50mcg twice a day)
- Age from 12 years onwards
- Qvar 50mcg CFC-free Autohaler. Inhale one puff twice a day; supply 1 200 dose inhaler; NHS Cost £7.87.

Qvar CFC-free Autohaler 200mcg daily (100mcg twice a day)
- Age from 12 years onwards
- Qvar 100mcg CFC-free Autohaler. Inhale one puff twice a day; supply 1 200 dose inhaler; NHS Cost £17.21.

Steroid: dry-powder inhalers

Asmabec Clickhaler: 200mcg daily (100mcg twice a day)
- Age from 5 to 11 years
- Asmabec 100mcg Clickhaler. Inhale one puff twice a day; supply 1 200 dose inhaler; NHS Cost £10.55.

Asmabec Clickhaler: 400mcg daily (200mcg twice a day)
- Age from 12 years onwards
- Asmabec 100mcg Clickhaler. Inhale two puffs twice a day; supply 1 200 dose inhaler; NHS Cost £10.55.

Beclometasone Diskhaler: 200mcg daily (100mcg twice a day)
- Age from 5 to 11 years
- Beclometasone 100mcg Diskhaler. Inhale the contents of one blister twice a day; supply 1 120 dose inhaler; NHS Cost £12.90.

Beclometasone Diskhaler: 400mcg daily (200mcg twice a day)
- Age from 12 years onwards
- Beclometasone 200mcg Diskhaler. Inhale the contents of one blister twice a day; supply 1 120 dose inhaler; NHS Cost £24.59.

Pulvinal beclometasone: 200mcg daily (100mcg twice a day)
- Age from 5 to 11 years
- Pulvinal beclometasone 100mcg. Inhale one puff twice a day; supply 1 100 dose inhaler; NHS Cost £5.58.

Pulvinal beclometasone: 400mcg daily (200mcg twice a day)
- Age from 12 years onwards
- Pulvinal beclometasone 200mcg. Inhale one puff twice a day; supply 1 100 dose inhaler; NHS Cost £10.29.

Budesonide Turbohaler: 200mcg daily (100mcg twice a day)
- Age from 5 to 11 years
- Budesonide 100mcg Turbohaler. Inhale one puff twice a day; supply 1 200 dose inhaler; NHS Cost £18.50.

Budesonide Turbohaler: 400mcg daily (200mcg twice a day)
- Age from 12 years onwards
- Budesonide 200mcg Turbohaler. Inhale one puff twice a day; supply 1 100 dose inhaler; NHS Cost £18.50.

Fluticasone Diskhaler: 100mcg daily (50mcg twice a day)
- Age from 5 to 11 years
- Fluticasone 50mcg Diskhaler. Inhale the contents of one blister twice a day; supply 1 60 dose inhaler; NHS Cost £8.78.

Fluticasone Diskhaler: 200mcg daily (100mcg twice a day)
- Age from 12 years onwards
- Fluticasone 100mcg Diskhaler. Inhale the contents of one blister twice a day; supply 1 120 dose inhaler; NHS Cost £13.67.

Fluticasone Accuhaler: 100mcg daily (50mcg twice a day)
- Age from 5 to 11 years
- Fluticasone 50mcg Accuhaler. Inhale one puff twice a day; supply 1 60 dose inhaler; NHS Cost £6.86.

Fluticasone Accuhaler: 200mcg daily (100mcg twice a day)
- Age from 12 years onwards
- Fluticasone 100mcg Accuhaler. Inhale one puff twice a day; supply 1 60 dose inhaler; NHS Cost £9.60.

Occupational asthma

Which therapy?

- Use standard objective criteria to confirm the diagnosis of asthma and the relationship between work and symptoms before recommending relocation or retirement on the grounds of work-related asthma.

- Confirm and document a causal relationship between work and asthma by:
  - Recording serial measurements of peak expiratory flow (PEF) at home and at work, every 2 hours while awake, for 4 weeks, keeping treatment constant and recording times at work. There should be at least 3 series of consecutive days at work with 3 periods away from work; at least 4 evenly spaced readings per day; and at least 3 days in each consecutive work period. More details, information for patients, and a computer tool for analysing the data are available from www.occupationalasthma.com.
  - Referring for specific bronchial challenges to identify the cause. These tests should only be conducted in specialized units.
  - Ruling out exercise-induced asthma if the person is more active at work than at home.
- Advise relocation away from exposure within 12 months of the first work-related symptoms of asthma.
- Delay assessment of long-term impairment for at least 2 years following relocation away from exposure.
- Pharmacological management of asthma symptoms follows the stepwise approach.
- Tailor treatment plans to the needs and preferences of the individual.

Practical prescribing points

For further information please see the *Medicines Compendium* (www.medicines.org.uk) or the *British National Formulary* (www.bnf.org).

Beta$_2$-agonists

- Hypokalaemia may occur with regular high doses, or when taken together with other drugs that also predispose to hypokalaemia (such as theophylline and its derivatives, and diuretics).

Follow-up advice

- **Review after a month** (or sooner, if necessary), to establish that treatment is being used appropriately and that symptoms are improving or well controlled.
- **Review with results of any investigations** to confirm the diagnosis of asthma and the relationship with work.

Should I refer or investigate?

Refer?

- Consider referral to the occupational health service at the workplace.
- Refer for specific bronchial challenges to identify the cause. These tests should only be conducted in specialized units.

Investigate?

- **Tests to confirm the diagnosis of asthma (and exclude other conditions) include:**
  - Reversibility tests: increased peak expiratory flow (PEF) after an inhaled short-acting beta$_2$-agonist, or after a 2-week course of oral corticosteroids; decreased PEF after 6 minutes of running.
  - Serial peak flow measurements: variability of 20% or more in serial peak flow measurements is highly suggestive of asthma.
  - Dynamic lung function tests/spirometry to differentiate obstructive, restrictive, and mixed lung function disorders.
  - Transfer factor: consider this in heavy smokers to exclude emphysema.
- **Confirm and document the relationship between work and asthma.**
  - Serial measurements of peak expiratory flow (PEF) at home and at work, every 2 hours while awake, for 4 weeks, keeping treatment constant and recording times at work. More details, information for patients and a computer tool for analysing the data are available from www.occupationalasthma.com.
  - Specific bronchial challenges should only be conducted in specialized units familiar with the performance and interpretation of such tests.

Patient information leaflets

The following PILs are available at www.prodigy.nhs.uk

- Asthma
- Asthma - Inhalers
- Asthma - Peak Flow Diary
- Asthma - Peak Flow Meter
- Asthma - Picture Summary
- Asthma UK
- Asthma UK (Scotland)
- Spirometry

Shared decision making

- Asthma is sometimes caused by chemicals, fumes, etc at work. This is called occupational asthma.
- To confirm that your asthma is work-related you may need to keep a diary of symptoms, and peak flow meter readings, noting when you are at home or at work.
- Special lung tests may be needed to confirm which substance is causing your symptoms.
- Treatment is similar to that of other people with asthma but avoiding the cause may cure you.
- So, sometimes a change of job is the best option.

Drug rationale

Drugs not included

- **Drugs other than inhaled short-acting beta$_2$-agonists** are not offered in this scenario. They should be prescribed as part of a stepwise approach to management.

Drugs included

- **Inhaled short-acting beta$_2$-agonists (salbutamol and terbutaline)** are effective bronchodilators. They should be used 'when required', unless benefit is shown from regular use [SIGN and BTS, 2004].
- **Peak flow meters** are included in this scenario to enable people to record their peak expiratory flow at home and at work.

Prescriptions

Short-acting beta$_2$-agonist when required

Salbutamol 100mcg MDI: 1 to 2 puffs up to four times a day

- Age from 16 years onwards
- Salbutamol 100mcg CFC-free inhaler. Inhale one to two puffs as required for shortness of breath, up to four times a day; supply 1 200 dose inhaler; NHS Cost £1.94.

Airomir 100mcg MDI: 1 to 2 puffs up to four times a day

- Age from 16 years onwards
- Airomir 100mcg CFC-free inhaler. Inhale one to two puffs as required for shortness of breath, up to four times a day; supply 1 200 dose inhaler; NHS Cost £1.97.

alamol 100mcg MDI: 1 to 2 puffs up to four times a day
Age from 16 years onwards
Salamol 100mcg CFC-free inhaler. Inhale one to two puffs as required for shortness of breath, up to four times a day; supply 1 200 dose inhaler; NHS Cost £1.97.

entolin 100mcg MDI: 1 to 2 puffs up to four times a day
Age from 16 years onwards
Ventolin 100mcg CFC-free inhaler. Inhale one to two puffs as required for shortness of breath, up to four times a day; supply 1 200 dose inhaler; NHS Cost £2.30.

erbutaline 250mcg MDI: 1 to 2 puffs up to four times a ay
Age from 16 years onwards
Terbutaline 250mcg inhaler. Inhale one to two puffs as required for shortness of breath, up to four times a day; supply 1 400 dose inhaler; NHS Cost £5.31.

Peak flow meter: standard range

eak flow meter: Ferraris (Pocketpeak)
Age from 16 years onwards
Pocketpeak standard p.f.m. Use as directed; supply 1 meter; NHS Cost £6.53.

eak flow meter: Mini-Wright (Clement Clarke)
Age from 16 years onwards
Mini-Wright standard p.f.m. Use as directed; supply 1 meter; NHS Cost £6.90.

eak flow meter: Asmaplan (Vitalograph)
Age from 16 years onwards
Vitalograph standard p.f.m. Use as directed; supply 1 meter; NHS Cost £6.65.

Exercise induced asthma

Which therapy?

Optimise the control of asthma: exercise-induced asthma is often an indication of poorly controlled asthma.
If asthma is otherwise well controlled, prescribe an inhaled short-acting beta$_2$-agonist to be used shortly before exercise and as required during exercise.
If control is not adequate with an inhaled short-acting beta$_2$-agonist, consider adding:

- Inhaled corticosteroids (ICS).
- Inhaled long-acting beta$_2$-agonist (LABA); however, a degree of tolerance tends to develop.
- Oral beta$_2$-agonist.
- Leukotriene receptor antagonist.
- Nedocromil in children aged 5 to 12 years. Cromoglicate in older children and adults.
- Modified-release theophylline.

Advise elite athletes to consult the controlling body of their sport for specific advice on what drugs are banned and what procedures need to be followed to obtain permission to use drugs that require prior registration.

- Details for individual drugs and individual controlling bodies may be found at www.uksport.gov.uk/did/.
- Asthma Victoria publishes a useful summary of International Olympic Committee (IOC) regulations for asthma drugs at www.asthma.org.au.

Practical prescribing points

For further information please see the *Medicines Compendium* (www.medicines.org.uk) or the *British National Formulary* (www.bnf.org).

Beta$_2$-agonists

- Hypokalaemia may occur with regular high doses, or when taken together with other drugs that also predispose to hypokalaemia (such as theophylline and its derivatives, and diuretics).

Follow-up advice

- **Review after a month** (or sooner, if necessary), to establish that treatment is being used appropriately and that symptoms are well controlled.

Should I refer or investigate?

Refer?

- Refer if the diagnosis is unclear or in doubt.

Patient information leaflets

The following PILs are available at www.prodigy.nhs.uk

- Asthma
- Asthma - Inhalers
- Asthma - Peak Flow Diary
- Asthma - Peak Flow Meter
- Asthma - Picture Summary
- Asthma UK
- Asthma UK (Scotland)

Shared decision making

- Exercise can trigger symptoms of asthma.
- Do you have symptoms at other times? It may be that your overall control of asthma is not good. You may need to start using a preventer, or increase the dose of your preventer inhaler.
- **A dose of a reliever inhaler** (bronchodilator) just before exercise will usually prevent exercise-induced symptoms.
- If you need more than a reliever inhaler, there are several additional options to choose from.

Drug rationale

Drugs not included

- **Prescriptions for inhaled corticosteroids (ICS)** are available in the scenario *Poor control: add inhaled corticosteroid (standard doses)*.
- **Prescriptions for inhaled long-acting beta$_2$-agonist (LABA), oral beta$_2$-agonist, leukotriene receptor antagonist, cromones, and theophylline** are available in the scenarios *Poor control: add LABA and/or increase ICS (standard doses)* and *Poor control: add-on therapy*.

Drugs included

- **Short-acting beta$_2$-agonists** (**salbutamol and terbutaline**) are effective bronchodilators. They should be used 'when required', shortly before exercise, and when required during exercise [SIGN and BTS, 2004]

Prescriptions

Short-acting beta$_2$-agonist when required

Salbutamol 100mcg MDI: 1 to 2 puffs up to four times a day

- Age from 5 years onwards
- Salbutamol 100mcg CFC-free inhaler. Inhale one to two puffs up to four times a day, when required to relieve breathlessness; supply 1 200 dose inhaler; NHS Cost £1.94.

Airomir 100mcg MDI: 1 to 2 puffs up to four times a day

- Age from 5 years onwards
- Airomir 100mcg CFC-free inhaler. Inhale one to two puffs up to four times a day, when required to relieve breathlessness; supply 1 200 dose inhaler; NHS Cost £1.97.

Salamol 100mcg MDI: 1 to 2 puffs up to four times a day

- Age from 5 years onwards
- Salamol 100mcg CFC-free inhaler. Inhale one to two puffs up to four times a day, when required to relieve breathlessness; supply 1 200 dose inhaler; NHS Cost £1.97.

Ventolin 100mcg MDI: 1 to 2 puffs up to four times a day

- Age from 5 years onwards
- Ventolin 100mcg CFC-free inhaler. Inhale one to two puffs up to four times a day, when required to relieve breathlessness; supply 1 200 dose inhaler; NHS Cost £2.30.

Terbutaline 250mcg MDI: 1 to 2 puffs up to four times a day

- Age from 5 years onwards
- Terbutaline 250mcg inhaler. Inhale one to two puffs up to four times a day, when required to relieve breathlessness; supply 1 400 dose inhaler; NHS Cost £5.31.

Acute exacerbation of asthma

Which therapy?

- **Assessment of severity and response to treatment**
  - Assess severity on presentation (detailed in Table 5 in *Management issues*).
  - **Reassess severity and response** as often as is appropriate for the level of severity, e.g. about every 15 minutes for acute severe exacerbation of asthma.
  - **Adjust treatment according to severity and response.**
  - Be aware of the increased risk of death in people with severe asthma and adverse psychosocial factors such as psychiatric illness, substance abuse, denial, and unemployment.
- **Oxygen**
  - Give high flow oxygen (6 litres/minute, 40–60%) if acute severe, or life-threatening asthma.
  - Use a tight-fitting facemask or a nasal cannula for young children.
  - Oxygen saturation should exceed 92% when breathing air and measured by pulse oximetry.
- **High dose inhaled short-acting beta$_2$-agonist**
  - **Life-threatening asthma:** deliver by nebulizer, oxygen-driven if available.
  - **Acute severe asthma:** deliver by pressurised metered dose inhaler (pMDI) and a large volume spacer for adults and older children; for children under the age of 12 years use a nebulizer (oxygen-driven if available).
  - **Moderate asthma:** use a pMDI and a large volume spacer for adults and children.
  - When using a spacer and pMDI each puff should be inhaled separately. With:
    - **Adult or older child:** give 4–6 puffs according to severity
    - **Child between 2 and 12 years old:** give 2–10 puffs according to severity
  - Repeat/continue bronchodilator therapy according to severity and response.
- **Ipratropium bromide**
  - If symptoms are severe, or life-threatening, or are failing to improve give nebulized ipratropium in combination with a short-acting beta$_2$-agonist.
  - Repeat the combined nebulization if response is poor.
- **Corticosteroids.** Give oral prednisolone if:
  - Peak expiratory flow (PEF) remains below about 75% of previous best (or predicted) PEF
  - Symptoms and PEF rate get progressively worse, day by day, and response to inhaled bronchodilator diminishes
  - Emergency treatment has been given recently
  - Note: if the person vomits after prednisone has been given, repeat the dose, or consider giving intravenous hydrocortisone.
- **Criteria for admission to hospital**
  - **Life-threatening asthma:** start emergency treatment, then arrange admission.
  - **Acute severe asthma:** reassess about 15–20 minutes after administration of high-dose bronchodilator and if response is poor arrange admission.
- **When admitting someone to hospital**
  - Stay with the patient and continue emergency treatment until the ambulance arrives.
  - Send written assessment and referral details to hospital.
  - During transport in the ambulance give high-dose bronchodilator via oxygen-driven nebulizer.

Practical prescribing points

For further information please see the *Medicines Compendium* (www.medicines.org.uk) or the *British National Formulary* (www.bnf.org).

Corticosteroids

- **Oral corticosteroids** cause a large number of adverse effects, but when taken in short courses are relatively safe. Following concern about severe chickenpox, the Committee on Safety of Medicines has advised that anyone prescribed a systemic corticosteroid should receive the patient information leaflet produced by the manufacturer.
- **Oral corticosteroids** can be stopped abruptly if the course length has been 21 days or less. If taken for more than 21 days or if the patient has had repeated courses of corticosteroids, or has adrenocortical insufficiency, it is necessary to taper the dose gradually.
- **Intravenous hydrocortisone** is an alternative to oral prednisolone in people who vomit or who have life-threatening asthma.

Follow-up advice

- Review within 48 hours after emergency treatment for an acute exacerbation of asthma.
- Monitor symptoms and peak expiratory flow.
- Check inhaler technique.
- Provide a written asthma action plan.
- Consider whether current treatment needs to be stepped up.
- Assess potentially preventable contributors to admission.

Should I refer or investigate?

Refer?

Admit to hospital if any:

- Life-threatening features
- Features of acute severe asthma
- Previous near-fatal asthma

Lower threshold for admission if:

- Young child
- Pregnant
- Afternoon or evening attack
- Recent nocturnal symptoms

Hospital admission
Previous severe attacks
Patient unable to assess their own condition
Concern over social circumstances

admitting the patient to hospital:

Stay with the patient and continue emergency treatment until the ambulance arrives
Send written assessment and referral details to hospital
Give high dose bronchodilator via oxygen-driven nebulizer during transport in the ambulance

ıvestigate?

Chest X-ray is not routinely recommended, but is indicated when there is:

- Suspected pneumomediastinum or pneumothorax
- Suspected consolidation
- Life-threatening asthma
- Failure to respond to treatment satisfactorily
- Requirement for ventilation

ᵃatient information leaflets

ıe following PILs are available at www.prodigy.nhs.uk

Asthma
Asthma - Action Plan
Asthma - Inhalers
Asthma - Peak Flow Diary
Asthma - Peak Flow Meter
Asthma - Picture Summary
Asthma UK
Asthma UK (Scotland)

›hared decision making

Your asthma symptoms are bad at present.

A high dose of reliever inhaler will often improve symptoms quickly.

A course of oral steroids will continue to ease the symptoms. Oral steroids:

- Work by reducing inflammation in the airways.
- Take 12–24 hours to work.
- Rarely cause side-effects if you take them for 2 weeks or less.

Continue to use your inhalers. Use your reliever inhaler regularly until symptoms settle.

It is often best to use your inhalers with a spacer. This allows more of the medicine to get into your lungs, and less on your mouth and throat.

)rug rationale

)rugs not included

Orally administered drugs other than prednisolone are not included. Orally administered drugs act more slowly than the inhaled route and are not appropriate in an acute situation.

Oral corticosteroids, other than prednisolone, are not routinely used in the treatment of asthma.

Inhaled corticosteroids are not included. They will not provide any additional benefit to the oral treatment in an acute situation, but should be continued or initiated as part of ongoing treatment.

The long-acting beta$_2$-agonists (LABAs) (formoterol [eformoterol] and salmeterol) are not included as they are not appropriate for the relief of acute attacks [ABPI Medicines Compendium, 2002; BNF 45, 2003]

Parenteral beta$_2$-agonists are not included. These should be reserved for people in whom inhaled therapy cannot be used, or in emergency treatment of acute severe or life-threatening asthma where response to inhaled therapy has been poor.

- **Parenterally administered aminophylline** should ideally only be administered under specialist medical supervision. It is usually only used in emergency treatment of acute severe or life-threatening asthma where response to treatment has been poor.

Drugs included

- **Prednisolone** should be given at dose of 40 to 50 mg daily for at least 5 days for acute exacerbations of asthma in adults. Up to 3 days is usually sufficient for children. Duration should be tailored to clinical need.
- **The short-acting beta$_2$-agonists salbutamol and terbutaline** are included both as metered-dose inhalers plus large volume spacer devices and as solutions for nebulization.

Prescriptions

Prednisolone tablets

Prednisolone soluble tablets: 20mg each morning for 3 days

- Age from 2 to 5 years
- Prednisolone 5mg sol tablets. Take four tablets each morning (as a single dose) for 3 days; supply 12 tablets; NHS Cost £0.88.

Soluble prednisolone: 30mg each morning for 3 days

- Age from 6 to 11 years
- Prednisolone 5mg sol tablets. Take six tablets each morning (as a single dose) for 3 days; supply 18 tablets; NHS Cost £1.32.

Soluble prednisolone: 40mg each morning for 3 days

- Age from 6 to 11 years
- Prednisolone 5mg sol tablets. Take eight tablets each morning (as a single dose) for 3 days; supply 24 tablets; NHS Cost £1.76.

Plain prednisolone: 40mg each morning for 5 days

- Age from 12 years onwards
- Prednisolone 5mg tablets. Take eight tablets each morning (as a single dose) for 5 days; supply 40 tablets; NHS Cost £0.96.

Plain prednisolone: 50mg each morning for 5 days

- Age from 12 years onwards
- Prednisolone 5mg tablets. Take ten tablets each morning (as a single dose) for 5 days; supply 50 tablets; NHS Cost £1.20.

E/C prednisolone: 40mg each morning for 5 days

- Age from 12 years onwards
- Prednisolone 5mg e/c tablets. Take eight tablets each morning (as a single dose) for 5 days; supply 40 tablets; NHS Cost £0.57.

E/C prednisolone: 50mg each morning for 5 days

- Age from 12 years onwards
- Prednisolone 5mg e/c tablets. Take ten tablets each morning (as a single dose) for 5 days; supply 50 tablets; NHS Cost £0.71.

Short-acting beta$_2$-agonist + spacer (emergency use)

Airomir CFC-free MDI + Child Aerochamber: emergency use

- Age from 2 to 4 years
- Airomir 100mcg CFC-free inhaler. Inhale two to ten puffs using the spacer. Repeat after 20-30 minutes if symptoms have not completely resolved; supply 1 200 dose inhaler; NHS Cost £1.97.
- Aerochamber (child) + mask. Use to aid inhalation; supply 1 spacer; NHS Cost £7.14.

Airomir CFC-free MDI + Aerochamber: emergency use
- Age from 5 to 11 years
- Airomir 100mcg CFC-free inhaler. Inhale two to ten puffs using the spacer. Repeat after 20-30 minutes if symptoms have not completely resolved; supply 1 200 dose inhaler; NHS Cost £1.97.
- AeroChamber Plus spacer device. Use to aid inhalation; supply 1 spacer; NHS Cost £4.28.

Airomir CFC-free MDI + Aerochamber: emergency use
- Age from 12 years onwards
- AeroChamber Plus spacer device. Use to aid inhalation; supply 1 spacer; NHS Cost £2.75.
- Airomir 100mcg CFC-free inhaler. Inhale four to six puffs using the spacer. Repeat after 10-20 minutes if symptoms have not completely resolved; supply 1 200 dose inhaler; NHS Cost £1.97.

Salamol CFC-free MDI + Volumatic + mask: emergency use
- Age from 2 to 4 years
- Salamol 100mcg CFC-free inhaler. Inhale two to ten puffs using the spacer. Repeat after 20-30 minutes if symptoms have not completely resolved; supply 1 200 dose inhaler; NHS Cost £1.95.
- Volumatic spacer device+mask. Use to aid inhalation; supply 1 spacer; NHS Cost £2.00.

Salamol CFC-free MDI + Volumatic: emergency use
- Age from 5 to 11 years
- Salamol 100mcg CFC-free inhaler. Inhale two to ten puffs using the spacer. Repeat after 20-30 minutes if symptoms have not completely resolved; supply 1 200 dose inhaler; NHS Cost £1.95.
- Volumatic spacer device. Use to aid inhalation; supply 1 spacer; NHS Cost £2.00.

Salamol CFC-free MDI + Volumatic: emergency use
- Age from 12 years onwards
- Volumatic spacer device. Use to aid inhalation; supply 1 spacer; NHS Cost £2.75.
- Salamol 100mcg CFC-free inhaler. Inhale four to six puffs using the spacer. Repeat after 10-20 minutes if symptoms have not completely resolved; supply 1 200 dose inhaler; NHS Cost £1.95.

Ventolin CFC-free MDI + Volumatic + mask: emergency use
- Age from 2 to 4 years
- Volumatic spacer device+mask. Use to aid inhalation; supply 1 spacer; NHS Cost £2.75.
- Ventolin 100mcg CFC-free inhaler. Inhale two to ten puffs using the spacer. Repeat after 20-30 minutes if symptoms have not completely resolved; supply 1 200 dose inhaler; NHS Cost £2.30.

Ventolin CFC-free MDI + Volumatic: emergency use
- Age from 5 to 11 years
- Volumatic spacer device. Use to aid inhalation; supply 1 spacer; NHS Cost £2.75.
- Ventolin 100mcg CFC-free inhaler. Inhale two to ten puffs using the spacer. Repeat after 20-30 minutes if symptoms have not completely resolved; supply 1 200 dose inhaler; NHS Cost £2.30.

Ventolin CFC-free MDI + Volumatic: emergency use
- Age from 12 years onwards
- Ventolin 100mcg CFC-free inhaler. Inhale four to six puffs using the spacer. Repeat after 10-20 minutes if symptoms have not completely resolved; supply 1 200 dose inhaler; NHS Cost £2.30.
- Volumatic spacer device. Use to aid inhalation; supply 1 spacer; NHS Cost £2.75.

Terbutaline MDI + Nebuhaler + mask: emergency use
- Age from 2 to 4 years
- Terbutaline 250mcg inhaler. Inhale two to ten puffs using the spacer. Repeat after 20-30 minutes if symptoms have not completely resolved; supply 1 400 dose inhaler; NHS Cost £5.31.
- Nebuhaler spacer device + mask. Use to aid inhalation supply 1 spacer; NHS Cost £4.28.

Terbutaline MDI + Nebuhaler: emergency use
- Age from 5 to 11 years
- Terbutaline 250mcg inhaler. Inhale two to ten puffs using the spacer. Repeat after 20-30 minutes if symptoms have not completely resolved; supply 1 400 dose inhaler; NHS Cost £5.31.
- Nebuhaler spacer device. Use to aid inhalation; supply spacer; NHS Cost £4.28.

Terbutaline MDI + Nebuhaler: emergency use
- Age from 12 years onwards
- Nebuhaler spacer device. Use to aid inhalation; supply spacer; NHS Cost £4.28.
- Terbutaline 250mcg inhaler. Inhale four to six puffs using the spacer. Repeat after 10-20 minutes if symptoms have not completely resolved; supply 1 400 dose inhaler; NHS Cost £5.31.

Nebulized beta$_2$-agonist

Salbutamol 2.5mg nebules
- Age from 2 years onwards
- Salbutamol 2.5mg/2.5ml nebules. Inhale the contents o one nebule (2.5mg) every 3 to 4 hours using nebuliser, as directed by your doctor; supply 20 2.5ml nebules; NHS Cost £3.38.

Terbutaline 5mg respules
- Age from 2 years onwards
- Terbutaline 5mg/2ml respule. Inhale the contents of on respule (5mg) every 3 to 4 hours using the nebuliser, or as directed by your doctor; supply 20 2ml respules; NHS Cost £3.00.

Salbutamol 5mg nebules
- Age from 6 years onwards
- Salbutamol 5mg/2.5ml nebule. Inhale the contents of o nebule (5mg) every 3 to 4 hours using the nebuliser, or directed by your doctor; supply 20 2.5ml nebules; NHS Cost £5.00.

Terbutaline 5mg respules
- Age from 6 years onwards
- Terbutaline 5mg/2ml respule. Inhale the contents of on (5mg) to two (10mg) respules every 3 to 4 hours using the nebuliser, or as directed by your doctor; supply 40 2ml respules; NHS Cost £7.34.

Extended Information

Background information

- What is asthma? p.152
- How common is asthma? p.153
- How do I know my patient has asthma? p.153
- What else might it be? p.153
- Complications and prognosis p.154

What is asthma?

- **Asthma is a chronic inflammatory condition of the airways,** the cause of which is not completely understood. The airways are hyper-responsive and constrict easily in response to a wide range of stimuli. This may result in coughing, wheezing, chest tightness, and shortness of breath.
- **Narrowing of the airways is usually reversible** (either spontaneously or with medication), but in some people with chronic asthma the inflammation may lead to irreversible airflow obstruction.

Work-aggravated asthma is pre-existing asthma that is aggravated non-specifically by dust and fumes at work.
Occupational asthma is asthma due to exposure to specific substances at work.
Exercise-induced asthma is, for most people, an expression of poorly controlled asthma.
[Roth et al, 2002; SIGN and BTS, 2004]

How common is asthma?

The best estimate of asthma 12-month prevalence in adults is approximately 4%, but it may be up to 10% [SIGN, 1998; Eccles et al, 2001].
In 1996, about 6.6% of males and 6.8% of females were receiving treatment for asthma. Treatment rates for asthma were highest in children aged 5 to 15 years, and adults aged 65 years and over [Office for National Statistics, 1999].
Each year a GP with a list size of 2000 patients will see about 85 people with asthma, and each of these will consult three times on average [McCormick et al, 1995].
About 2% of adults consult their GP annually with asthma [McCormick et al, 1995].
In a national survey, wheezing was reported in the previous 12 months in 21% of all adults [DH, 1996].
A third of 12–14-year-old children in Great Britain reported 'wheezing' in the previous 12 months in another study [Kaur et al, 1998].
Occupational asthma accounts for about 10% of adult-onset asthma [Meredith and Nordman, 1996].

How do I know my patient has asthma?

Asthma is diagnosed on clinical grounds. Tests and investigations are used to corroborate (not to make) the diagnosis.
Symptoms: episodic shortness of breath, wheeze, cough, and chest tightness. Symptoms are often worse during the night and with exercise. The severity and duration of symptoms tend to be highly variable and unpredictable.
Signs: prolonged expiration and wheezes (generalized, bilateral, predominantly expiratory, polyphonic) are usually found. The absence of wheeze does not rule out a diagnosis of asthma. There may sometimes be crackles if there is another associated disease, such as chest infection or heart failure. In severe cases, there may be reduced chest wall movement on both sides and wheezes may not be audible.
Possible triggers include: inhaled allergens, viral and bacterial infections, cold air, irritant dusts, vapours and fumes, emotion, exercise, pollens, dust, occupational sensitizers such as isocyanates, atmospheric pollution, cigarette smoke, certain foods, animals, or drugs (e.g. nonsteroidal anti-inflammatory drugs [NSAIDs], beta-blockers).
Helpful additional information when taking the history.

- Personal or family history of asthma, atopy (e.g. eczema, allergic rhinitis), or both
- History of worsening after use of aspirin, NSAID, or beta-blocker (including eye drops)
- Recognized triggers
- Patterns and severity of symptoms and exacerbations

Objective measurements that can be used to confirm a diagnosis of asthma.

- More than 20% diurnal variation on at least 3 days in a week for 2 weeks on a peak expiratory flow (PEF) diary, or
- More than 15% (and 200-ml) increase in forced expiratory volume in 1 second (FEV_1) after short-acting $beta_2$-agonist, or
- More than 15% (and 200-ml) increase in FEV_1 after trial of oral corticosteroids, or
- More than 15% decrease in FEV_1 after 6 minutes of running, or
- Histamine or methacholine challenge in difficult cases (usually requires referral)

- **Occupational asthma is diagnosed** when all the following are true:
  - The diagnosis of asthma is confirmed.
  - A relationship between asthma and work exposures is confirmed, e.g. by:
    - Serial measurements of PEF at home and at work (at least three series of consecutive days at work with three periods away from work; at least four evenly spaced readings per day; at least 3 days in each consecutive work period).
    - Specific and non-specific bronchial provocation tests (which would usually require referral to secondary care).
  - A specific cause is identified.
- **Diagnosing asthma in young children (under 5 years of age).**
  - Diagnosing asthma in young children is difficult, although at all ages the principles described above apply. The reasons include:
    - Bronchodilators are often ineffective in young children. A negative bronchodilator response test may not rule out asthma.
    - Objective lung measurements, such as PEF, are not possible in young children.
    - Viral respiratory infections are common and often cause wheezing.
  - Because diagnosis is difficult, it is likely that many children are not treated adequately.
  - Asthma is more probable (or is more likely to develop) if the child has allergies such as eczema, allergic rhinitis, or allergic conjunctivitis, or if there is a family history of asthma or allergy, or if the child has been exposed perinatally to tobacco smoke.
  - Children with recurrent wheezing or chronic cough should be closely followed to enable early diagnosis of asthma and prompt introduction of treatment.

[National Heart Lung and Blood Institute, 1997; SIGN and BTS, 2004]

What else might it be?

Differential diagnosis of asthma in older children and adults

- Chest infection
- Chronic obstructive pulmonary disease, emphysema
- Left ventricular failure ('cardiac asthma')
- Foreign body
- Cancer (laryngeal, tracheal, lung)
- Rarely: bronchiectasis, bronchiolitis, cystic fibrosis, Churg–Strauss syndrome (allergic angiitis and granulomatosis; often coexisting severe upper airways disease and systemic symptoms [D'Cruz et al, 1999]), post-tracheostomy stenosis, vocal cord dysfunction with wheeze, pulmonary emboli, aspiration
- Gastro-oesophageal reflux
- Psychological dyspnoea, for example panic attacks or anxiety states
- Dysfunctional breathing: 'hyperventilation syndrome'

Note: asthma can coexist with the above conditions.
[SIGN and BTS, 2004]

Differential diagnosis of asthma in younger children and infants

- Inhaled foreign body
- Bronchiolitis, pneumonia, croup, bronchiectasis, tuberculosis, histoplasmosis, post-infection syndrome

(bronchiolitis obliterans), bronchitis, sinusitis, pertussis, post-nasal drip
- Allergic bronchopulmonary aspergillosis, Churg–Strauss syndrome, allergic alveolitis, hypersensitivity pneumonitis, polyarteritis nodosa
- Cystic fibrosis, chronic lung disease, ciliary dyskinesia, developmental anomaly (vascular ring), bronchopulmonary dysplasia
- Laryngeal disorder, laryngotracheomalacia, tracheo-oesophageal fistula
- Gastro-oesophageal reflux with/without aspiration, swallowing problems with aspiration
- Congestive heart failure, pulmonary thromboembolism, psychogenic cough, sarcoidosis
- Tumour, lymphoma, neuromuscular disorder, immune deficiency

Note: asthma can coexist with the above conditions.
[SIGN and BTS, 2004]

Complications and prognosis

Complications

- Reduced quality of life may result from suboptimal control of asthma (which can cause tiredness, underperformance at school or work, and time off school or work).
- Psychological problems associated with social stigma, or development of the 'sick role'.
- Growth and final stature may be reduced in children with asthma.
- Approximately 1500 deaths per year in the UK are directly attributed to asthma [British Thoracic Society, 1997].

[SIGN and BTS, 2004]

Management issues

- What are the principles of managing asthma? p.154
- How can asthma be prevented? p.154
- What interventions other than drugs are used in managing asthma? p.154
- What is the role of patient education and self-management? p.155
- What drugs should be used to manage chronic asthma? p.155
- What else do I need to know about managing asthma? p.158
- How should I review and monitor someone with asthma? p.158
- When should I refer someone with asthma? p.159
- How do I manage exercise-induced asthma? p.159
- How do I manage occupational asthma? p.159
- How do I manage asthma during pregnancy and breastfeeding? p.160
- How do I manage someone with an acute exacerbation of asthma? p.160
- What delivery system should I recommend for inhaled drugs? p.162
- Medicines management p.163

What are the principles of managing asthma?

- The aim of treatment is to achieve early control and to maintain control by stepping up treatment as necessary and stepping down when control is good.
- Start treatment at the step most appropriate to the initial level of severity of the asthma.
- Treatment plans should be tailored to the needs and preferences of the individual.
- Before starting a new drug therapy, check that:
  - Current treatment and advice are being followed correctly
  - Inhaler technique is effective
  - Trigger factors have been eliminated
- Advise on smoking cessation and, for parents of children with asthma, advise on avoiding exposure of their children to tobacco smoke.
- Offer self-management education, including written asthma action plans focusing on individual needs, to all people with asthma, particularly those admitted to hospital.

[SIGN and BTS, 2004]

How can asthma be prevented?

- **Smoking:** parents and parents-to-be who smoke should be advised on the many adverse effects of smoking on their children, including increased wheezing in infancy. They should be offered appropriate support to stop smoking.
- **Breastfeeding:** breastfeeding should be encouraged. Its benefits include a protective effect in relation to wheezing in early life.
- **Allergen avoidance and modified infant milk formulae:** trials of allergen avoidance and modified infant milk formulae have shown inconsistent effects in relation to asthma.
- **Non-sedating antihistamines:** these have been shown in three small trials to reduce the development of asthma in infants, but this is insufficient evidence to support a general recommendation for their use.

[SIGN and BTS, 2004]

What interventions other than drugs are used in managing asthma?

Does allergen avoidance help?

- Evidence that reducing allergen exposure can reduce morbidity and mortality from asthma is tenuous.
- **House dust mite allergens:** measures to control these do not appear to be a cost-effective method of treating asthma [Woodcock et al, 2003]. In committed families who wish to try mite avoidance, the following are recommended when there is evidence of house dust mite allergy in a family member:
  - Complete barrier bed-covering systems
  - Removal of carpets
  - Removal of soft toys from beds
  - High temperature washing of bed linen
  - Application of acaricides to soft furnishings
  - Dehumidification
- **Animal allergens,** particularly cat and dog allergens, are potent inducers of asthma symptoms. Observational studies have not found that removing a pet from the home improves asthma symptoms. Nevertheless, many experts would still recommend the removal of pets from the home of an allergic individual with asthma.

[SIGN and BTS, 2004]

Is it advisable to stop smoking?

Key Scottish Intercollegiate Guidelines Network/British Thoracic Society recommendations

- Smoking cessation should be encouraged as it is good for general health and may decrease asthma severity.
- Parents who smoke should be advised about the dangers for themselves and their children, and offered appropriate support to stop smoking.
- The current smoking status of all people with asthma should be recorded, thus enabling ready identification of smokers to target interventions.

[SIGN and BTS, 2004]

hat is the supporting evidence?

- There is a direct causal relationship between parental smoking and lower respiratory tract illness in children up to 3 years of age [Strachan and Cook, 1997].
- Infants whose mothers smoke are four times more likely to develop wheezing illnesses in the first year of life [Dezateux et al, 1999].
- Exposure to tobacco smoke in the home contributes to the severity of childhood asthma [IOM, 2000].
- One small study suggests that, by stopping smoking, parents can decrease the severity of asthma in their children [Murray and Morrison, 1993].
- Teenagers who smoke experience more asthma than non-smokers [Henningfield, 1995].

ow do I help people to stop smoking?

- **Advice should be clear, strong, and personalized.** For example: 'As your doctor I need you to know that the most important thing you can do to protect your health now and in the future is to stop smoking' [Anderson et al, 2002]. It is important to consider the patient's views and their reactions to advice, in order to avoid damaging the doctor–patient relationship.
- **Advice about how to stop smoking should include the use of nicotine replacement therapy (NRT) or bupropion.**
- NRT or bupropion should normally only be prescribed when the person has made a commitment to stop smoking on or before a particular date (target stop date). Ideally, the initial prescription should only be sufficient to last until 2 weeks after the target stop date. Normally, this will be after 2 weeks of NRT therapy, and 3–4 weeks for bupropion. Further prescriptions should be given only to people who demonstrate that they are continuing their attempts to quit [NICE, 2002b].
- **Relapse** is a normal part of the quitting process and occurs on average 3–4 times. If a smoker has made repeated attempts to stop and failed, or has experienced severe withdrawal, or has requested more intensive help, then referral to a specialist smoking cessation service should be considered.
- For further information, see the separate PRODIGY guidance on *Smoking cessation.*

/hat is the role of patient education and elf-management?

(ey Scottish Intercollegiate Guidelines Network/ British Thoracic Society recommendations

- Offer self-management education, including written asthma action plans focusing on individual needs, to all people with asthma, particularly those admitted to hospital.
- Introduce asthma action plans as part of a structured educational discussion.

IGN and BTS, 2004]

/hat is the supporting evidence?

- Written personalized action plans as part of self-management education have been shown to improve health outcomes for people with asthma [Ignacio-Garcia and Gonzalez-Santos, 1995; Lahdensuo et al, 1996; Madge et al, 1997; Ghosh et al, 1998; Gallefoss et al, 1999; Cote et al, 2000; Gallefoss and Bakke, 2000; Moudgil et al, 2000; Cote et al, 2001; Gibson, 2001; Guevara et al, 2003].
- The evidence is particularly good for the management of asthma in secondary care and for those who have had recent exacerbations [Yoon et al, 1993; Osman et al, 1994].
- There is a relative paucity of evidence of benefit in primary care and in very young children [Haby et al, 2001; Wolf et al, 2002].
- Recent systematic reviews and conclusions from a new randomized controlled trial, however, are more doubtful about the evidence for additional benefit from written action plans compared with standard treatment [Lefevre et al, 2002; Thoonen BP et al, 2003; Toelle and Ram, 2004]. However, another recent systematic review concluded that educational interventions for the self-management of asthma in children and adolescents can reduce symptoms, school absenteeism, and visits to emergency treatment services [Guevara et al, 2003].

[SIGN and BTS, 2004]

How do I set up a structured asthma programme and offer an asthma action plan?

Successful patient education programmes have used a wide range of approaches. Drawing on these programmes, the Scottish Intercollegiate Guidelines Network/British Thoracic Society guideline on the management of asthma has the following suggestions [SIGN and BTS, 2004]:

- Checklist for setting up a structured asthma programme:
  - Investigate the availability of resources.
    - **Patient Information Leaflets (PILs) and proforma written asthma action plans** are available from PRODIGY and the National Asthma Campaign (www.asthma.org.uk).
  - Seek consensus opinion to ensure that all members of the team are giving consistent advice.
  - Discuss practical aspects of implementation. Points to consider will include which patients to target, and whether education is to be integrated into routine care and delivered in one-to-one consultations, or whether it should be delivered in groups.
  - Tailor the education and advice to the individual needs of the patient, respecting different ambitions, wishes for autonomy, and age.
- Checklist for an educational programme/discussion:
  - Nature of the disease
  - Nature of the treatment
  - Identifying areas where the individual most wants treatment to have effect
  - How to use the treatment
  - Development of self-monitoring/self-assessment skills
  - Negotiation of the asthma action plan in the light of identified goals
  - Recognition and management of acute exacerbations
  - Appropriate allergen or trigger avoidance
- Self-management plans may be particularly helpful in some people with a history of:
  - Insidious deterioration of asthma
  - Poor perception of deteriorating breathing
  - Poor adherence to medication
- Examples of asthma action plans are available online from the National Asthma Campaign (www.asthma.org.uk) and as a PRODIGY PIL.

What drugs should be used to manage chronic asthma?

In general, the level of evidence to support recommendations for the management of asthma tends to be higher for adults and older children than it is for children between 5 and 12 years old, because more studies have been conducted in adults. Few trials have been undertaken in children who are under the age of 5 years and have asthma.

A

What is the stepwise approach to the management of chronic asthma?

Tables 1 and 2 below summarize the stepwise approach to the long-term management of asthma.

Step 1: as-required reliever therapy

- Prescribe inhaled short-acting beta$_2$-agonists for use 'as required' (unless the individual has been shown to benefit from regular use).
- Choose an effective delivery mechanism on the basis of convenience and cost. For full details see the section *What delivery system should I recommend for inhaled drugs?*
- Review asthma management (and check inhaler technique) in people using two or more canisters of short-acting beta$_2$-agonist per month, or taking more than 10–12 puffs per day as their asthma may be chronically poorly controlled or they may be experiencing an acute exacerbation.

[SIGN and BTS, 2004]

Step 2: introduction of regular preventer therapy

- Before initiating a new drug therapy, re-check adheren[ce,] inhaler technique, and eliminate trigger factors.
- Consider prescribing inhaled corticosteroids (ICS) for people:
  - Who have had exacerbations of asthma in the last 2 years
  - Are using inhaled beta$_2$-agonists three times a week [or] more
  - Who are symptomatic three times a week or more, waking one night a week

Table 1: Summary of the stepwise approach to management of chronic asthma in adults and children 5 years or older [SIGN and BTS, 2004]. Further details for each step are given in the appropriate sections below.

Step	Therapy added if control is inadequate; the therapy for previous steps is continued
1	**As required reliever therapy:** short-acting beta$_2$-agonist as required
2	**Regular preventer therapy:** inhaled corticosteroids twice a day For beclometasone* the appropriate dose to start with is often: 400 micrograms† per day in adults and children over the age of 12 years 200 micrograms† per day in children up to the age of 12 years *Or*, one of the less effective preventer agents listed in step 4 'add-on' drugs
3a	**Add-on therapy:** inhaled long-acting beta$_2$-agonist (LABA)
3b	**Add-on therapy:** increase dose of inhaled corticosteroids For beclometasone* increase the dose up to: 800 micrograms† per day in adults and children over the age of 12 years 400 micrograms† per day in children up to the age of 12 years Stop inhaled long-acting beta$_2$-agonist if it has not helped at all.
3c	**Add-on therapy:** sequential trials of adding other 'add-on' drugs Stop inhaled long-acting beta$_2$-agonist and start ***one*** of: Leukotriene receptor antagonist Modified-release theophylline Oral modified-release/long-acting beta-agonist Cromone (cromoglicate in adults; nedocromil in children)
4	**Trials of:** **Maximum recommended dose of inhaled corticosteroids;** for beclometasone* this is: 2000 micrograms† per day in adults and children over the age of 12 years 800 micrograms† per day in children up to the age of 12 years (off-label use) Return to previous dose if no benefit is evident **Dual treatment with add-on drugs (only recommended for adults and children over the age of 12 years)** Trials of two of: Inhaled long-acting beta$_2$-agonist (usually first selection) Leukotriene receptor antagonist Modified-release theophylline Cromone (cromoglicate in adults; nedocromil in children) Oral modified-release/long-acting beta$_2$-agonist (*Note: prescribe with caution the combination of inhaled and oral long-acting/modified-release beta$_2$-agonists.*)
5	**Continuous daily oral corticosteroids** (at lowest effective dose) Maintain maximum licensed dose of inhaled corticosteroids Refer children to a respiratory paediatrician Consider referring adults for possible immunosuppression

* Beclometasone is beclometasone delivered by chlorofluorocarbon (CFC) pressurized metered dose inhaler.
† See Table 3 for equivalent doses of other inhaled corticosteroids.

Table 2: Stepwise approach to management of chronic asthma in children aged less than 5 years [SIGN and BTS, 2004]. Further details for each step are given in the appropriate sections below.

Step	Therapy added if control is inadequate; the therapy for previous steps is continued
1	**As required reliever therapy:** short-acting beta$_2$-agonist
2	**Regular preventer therapy:** inhaled corticosteroids For beclometasone* the appropriate dose to start with is often 200 micrograms† per day in children under 5 years of age *Or*, if inhaled corticosteroids cannot be used, a leukotriene receptor antagonist
3	**Children aged 2–5 years:** trial of a leukotriene receptor antagonist **Children aged <2 years:** refer to respiratory paediatrician
4	**Refer to respiratory paediatrician**

* Beclometasone is beclometasone delivered by chlorofluorocarbon (CFC) pressurized metered dose inhaler.
† See Table 3 for equivalent doses of other inhaled corticosteroids.

ICS should initially be used twice a day at a dose appropriate to the severity of symptoms (use the lowest dose at which effective control of asthma is maintained). Comparable total daily doses for ICS are given in Table 3. Suitable starting doses for beclometasone taken twice a day often are:
- *Older than 12 years*: beclometasone 200 micrograms twice a day.
- *5–12 years old*: beclometasone 100 micrograms twice a day.
- *Less than 5 years old*: beclometasone 100 micrograms twice a day; higher doses may be required to ensure adequate drug delivery.

If good control is established consider decreasing frequency of ICS to once a day at the same total daily dose, although the evidence from studies in children is inconsistent [Radzik and Pavanello, 2002].
Use the lowest dose at which effective control of asthma is maintained; i.e. reduce the dose of ICS in people whose asthma is well controlled.
If control of asthma is inadequate, carry out trials of add-on treatments before increasing the dose of ICS above the usual starting dose — see Step 3.
ICS are more effective than other agents used for long-term prevention of asthma. Sometimes, however, there are concerns about adverse effects, such as growth retardation in children. In these cases consider a trial of another preventer agent, i.e. leukotriene receptor antagonist, nedocromil (5–12-year-olds only), sodium cromoglicate (adults only), inhaled long-acting beta$_2$-agonist, or modified-release theophylline.
IGN and BTS, 2004]

tep 3: add-on therapy

Before initiating a new drug therapy, re-check compliance, inhaler technique, and eliminate trigger factors.
The duration of a trial of add-on therapy depends on the desired outcome. For example to prevent nocturnal awakening requires a relatively short trial (days or weeks), while to prevent exacerbations of asthma or to reduce use of oral corticosteroids requires a longer trial, e.g. weeks or months.

- **For children aged less than 2 years whose asthma is inadequately controlled** on level 2 treatment: consider referral to a respiratory paediatrician.
- **For children between the age of 2 and 5 years whose asthma is inadequately controlled** on level 2 treatment: add a leukotriene receptor antagonist.
- For people above the age of 5 years whose asthma is inadequately controlled on level 2 treatment:
  - **Step 3a:** add an inhaled long-acting beta$_2$-agonist (LABA)
  - Carry out a trial of a long-acting beta$_2$-agonist before increasing the ICS
  - **Step 3b:** increase ICS to the appropriate 'higher' dose in Table 3 (if not already at this level); for beclometasone this is:
    - 800 micrograms per day in adults and children over the age of 12
    - 400 micrograms per day in children up to 12 years
    - If there has been no response to the long acting beta$_2$-agonist, stop it at the same time as increasing the ICS.
  - **Step 3c:** sequential trials of one additional add-on therapy. If control is still inadequate: offer sequential trials of single add-on therapy; i.e. stop inhaled long-acting beta$_2$-agonist and start one of:
    - Leukotriene receptor antagonist
    - Modified-release theophylline
    - Oral modified-release/long-acting beta$_2$-agonist
    - Cromone (i.e. cromoglicate in adults; nedocromil in children aged 5 to 12 years)

[SIGN and BTS, 2004]

Step 4: trials of dual treatment with add-on drugs or maximum licensed dose of inhaled corticosteroid or both

- Before initiating a new drug therapy, re-check compliance, inhaler technique, and eliminate trigger factors.
- Refer children who are less than 5 years old to a respiratory paediatrician.
- If asthma remains inadequately controlled, especially in children, consider referral to specialist care.
- For adults and children above the age of 5 years consider a trial of increasing inhaled corticosteroids (ICS) to the

able 3: Recommended daily doses of inhaled corticosteroids (ICS) delivered by pressurized metered dose inhaler (pMDI). osage adjustment may be necessary for alternative devices.

:S MDI delivery	Age years	Dose (total daily) of ICS, in micrograms			
		Lower	Intermediate	Higher	Maximum
:clometasone*	>12	200 mcg	400 mcg	800 mcg	2000 mcg
	5–12	100 mcg	200 mcg	400 mcg	800 mcg
	0.5–5	100 mcg	200 mcg	400 mcg	800 mcg
eclometasone FC-free† (Qvar)	>12	100 mcg	200 mcg	400 mcg	800 mcg
	5–12	UNLICENSED			
	<5	(§ RCPCH *Medicines for children* suggests: 'use lower doses than for adults')			
udesonide ower doses)	>12	200 mcg	400 mcg	800 mcg	1600 mcg
	5–12	100 mcg	200 mcg	400 mcg	800 mcg
	<5	100 mcg	200 mcg	400 mcg	800 mcg
'uticasone‡	>16	100 mcg	200 mcg	500 mcg	1000 mcg
	4–16	50 mcg	100 mcg	200 mcg	400 mcg
	<4	UNLICENSED			

Start ICS with a dose appropriate to disease severity. It is often appropriate to start with the dose in the 'Intermediate' column.
In children under 5 years of age it may be necessary to prescribe higher doses to achieve adequate delivery.
Give ICS initially twice a day. Consider once-a-day ICS at the same total daily dose if good control is established.
Use the lowest dose at which effective control of asthma is maintained.
ICS should be used with appropriate spacer devices.
The maximum licensed daily dose of inhaled beclometasone for children is 400 micrograms.
When converting to chlorofluorocarbon (CFC) -free beclometasone dipropionate, double the dose in the table if control of asthma is poor.
The maximum licensed daily dose of fluticasone for adults is 2000 micrograms. The Committee on Safety of Medicines (CSM) has advised that doses of fluticasone above 000 micrograms a day should only be prescribed for adults with severe asthma, and should only be initiated by a physician with a special interest in asthma [CSM, 2001].
Medicines for Children, Royal College of Paediatrics and Child Health, 1999

A

maximum recommended daily dose; for beclometasone this is:
- 2000 micrograms for adults and children over 12 years of age
- 800 micrograms for children under 12 years (Note: exceeds maximum licensed dose)

- If the trial shows that increasing the corticosteroid dose is not effective, return to the original dose.
- For adults and children above the age of 12 years consider sequential trials of adding two of the following:
  - Inhaled long-acting beta$_2$-agonist (LABA) (usually the first selection)
  - Leukotriene receptor antagonist
  - Modified-release theophylline
  - Cromone (cromoglicate in adults; nedocromil in children aged 5 to 12 years)
  - Oral modified-release/long-acting beta$_2$-agonist.
  - Note: use caution when co-prescribing an inhaled long-acting beta$_2$-agonist with an oral modified-release/long-acting beta$_2$-agonist.
- If the trial shows that an add-on therapy is ineffective, stop the drug.

[SIGN and BTS, 2004]

Step 5: continuous or frequent courses of daily oral corticosteroids

'Frequent use' of oral corticosteroids is considered to be more than two or three courses per year.

- Use daily oral corticosteroids in the lowest dose giving adequate control.
- Maintain inhaled corticosteroids at the maximum recommended daily dose; for beclometasone this is:
  - 2000 micrograms for adults and children aged 12 or more years.
  - 800 micrograms for children under the age of 12 (NB: exceeds maximum licensed dose).
- Aim to prevent, or minimize, or detect as soon as possible adverse effects from corticosteroids.
- General and lifestyle recommendations to minimize the adverse effects of corticosteroids are to:
  - Reduce the dose of glucocorticoids to a minimum.
  - Use inhaled corticosteroids in preference to oral corticosteroids if possible.
  - Encourage adequate levels of dietary calcium intake and good nutrition.
  - Maintain normal bodyweight where possible.
  - Advise on smoking cessation.
  - Advise on moderate alcohol consumption.
  - Encourage physical exercise within the limits imposed by the underlying disease.
  - Perform falls risk assessment and advise those at increased risk of fractures from falling.
- Monitor, prevent and treat the systemic adverse effects of continuous or frequent courses of oral corticosteroids:
  - Blood pressure: monitor regularly and treat if necessary.
  - Diabetes mellitus: screen regularly and treat if necessary.
  - Osteoporosis: see PRODIGY *Osteoporosis* guidance and Royal College of Physicians guideline *Glucocorticoid-induced osteoporosis* [Royal College of Physicians of London, 2002].
  - Growth retardation: record height of children regularly.
  - Cataracts: screen children periodically.
- Refer children who are on continuous oral corticosteroids to a respiratory paediatrician. Consider referring children who are on frequent courses of oral corticosteroids or on prolonged high dose inhaled corticosteroids.
- Consider referring adults for specialist assessment and consideration of other therapies.

[SIGN and BTS, 2004]

What else do I need to know about managing asthma?

Interventions which may be beneficial in specific circumstances

- **Influenza vaccination** is recommended for all over the age of 6 months who have required hospital admission for an exacerbation of asthma, or who need continuou[s] or frequently repeated use of inhaled or oral corticosteroids [CMO, 2002].
- **Weight reduction** to improve asthma control is recommended in obese people with asthma [SIGN and BTS, 2004].
- **Family therapy** may have a role in difficult childhood asthma as an adjunct to pharmacotherapy [Panton and Barley, 2005].

Interventions for which asthma alone is not an indication

- **Allergic rhinitis** is common in people with asthma. This is most effectively treated with intranasal corticosteroi[ds]. Treatment of allergic rhinitis has not been shown to improve asthma [SIGN and BTS, 2004].
- **Gastro-oesophageal reflux** should be treated if present, but this will generally have no effect on asthma control [Gibson et al, 2003b; Gibson et al, 2003a].
- **Pneumococcal vaccination:** asthma is *not* an indication unless so severe as to require continuous or frequently repeated use of *systemic* corticosteroids, i.e. at a dose equivalent to prednisolone 20 mg or more per day (any age) or, for children under 20 kg, a dose of 1 mg or mo[re] per kilogram bodyweight per day, for more than a month [CMO, 2005].

Complementary and alternative medicine

- There is insufficient evidence to recommend herbal and traditional Chinese medicine; acupuncture; Alexander technique; homeopathy; hypnosis; manual therapy, including massage and spinal manipulation; physical exercise training; breathing exercises, including yoga ar[nd] buteyko; dietary supplementation with vitamins, minerals, or omega n-3 fatty acids; high altitude and speleotherapy; or immunotherapy with hypo-sensitization or desensitization [Dennis, 2000; Cates, 2001; Hondras et al, 2005].
- There is no evidence of benefit, and some evidence of adverse effects, from the use of air ionizers.
- People with asthma should not be treated solely with an[y] of the above therapies.

[SIGN and BTS, 2004]

How should I review and monitor someone with asthma?

Is there a standard way to structure and record the clinical review?

- The SIGN guideline recommends that clinical review should be structured and should use a standard recording system, such as the Royal College of Physicians (RCP) 'three questions', the Tayside Asthma stamp, and modified Jones Morbidity Index. These and other tools are available on the British Thoracic Society web site www.brit-thoracic.org.uk/sign/management_tools.html, and are conveniently formatte[d] for printing on sticky labels.

The three questions recommended by the RCP are listed n Table 4. Responses can be recorded easily and can orm the basis of a symptom diary. arson and Bucknall.C.E., 1999; SIGN and BTS, 2004]

hould I prescribe a peak flow meter to be used at ome?

e SIGN guideline recommends that many people with hma, and all those with severe asthma, should have their n peak flow meter. Individual peak flow meters should used to reduce the risk of cross infection.

Home charting of peak flows is useful:

- At diagnosis and initial assessment
- In assessing response to changes in treatment
- When monitoring response during exacerbations
- As part of an asthma action plan

However, a recent Cochrane systematic review concluded that 'individualised written action plans based on peak expiratory flow are equivalent to action plans based on symptoms' [Powell et al, 2002].

There is little evidence of value in using a peak flow meter at home for long-term regular monitoring. GN and BTS, 2004]

hen should I refer someone with asthma?

lications for admission of a person having an acute acerbation of asthma are given in the section *How do I nage someone with an acute exacerbation of asthma?*. e indications for referral of someone who has, or may ve, asthma are listed below.

dications for referral of older children and adults ith possible asthma

- Diagnosis unclear or in doubt
- Unexpected clinical findings, e.g. crackles, clubbing, cyanosis, heart failure
- Spirometry or peak expiratory flow (PEF) measurements do not fit the clinical picture
- Suspected occupational asthma
- Persistent shortness of breath (not episodic; not with associated wheeze)
- Unilateral or fixed wheeze
- Stridor
- Persistent chest pain or atypical features
- Weight loss
- Persistent cough and/or sputum production
- Non-resolving pneumonia
- Inadequate response to maximum guideline treatment
- Parental anxiety

IGN and BTS, 2004]

able 4: Royal College of Physicians 'three questions' for sessing asthma control.

	Yes	No
the last week/month:		
ave you had difficulty sleeping because of your asthma mptoms (including cough)?	1	0
ave you had your usual asthma symptoms during the y (e.g. cough, wheeze, chest tightness, or eathlessness)?	1	0
as your asthma interfered with your usual activities g. housework, work, school, etc)?	1	0
3 questions score (0–3)		

e RCP three questions score should be used only:
For people who are at least 16 years old
After the diagnosis of asthma has been established

Indications for referral of younger children with possible asthma

- Diagnosis unclear or in doubt; the younger the child, the more difficult it is to be sure that wheezing is due to asthma
- Symptoms present from birth, or perinatal lung problem
- Excessive vomiting or posseting
- Severe upper respiratory tract infection
- Persistent productive cough
- Family history of unusual chest disease
- Failure to thrive
- Unexpected clinical findings, e.g. abnormal voice, focal chest signs, dysphagia, inspiratory wheeze, stridor
- Inadequate response to maximum guideline treatment, particularly if oral corticosteroids are needed frequently, or on maximum licensed dose of inhaled corticosteroids (which for beclometasone is 800 micrograms per day)
- Parental anxiety

[SIGN and BTS, 2004]

How do I manage exercise-induced asthma?

- Exercise-induced asthma (EIA) is often an indication of poorly controlled asthma. If control of asthma is improved, the symptoms of EIA usually cease. People who are on preventative treatment for asthma but find EIA problematic should have their current medication reviewed to ensure that treatment advice is being followed, inhaler technique is correct, and doses are adequate.
- The symptoms of exercise-induced asthma can usually be prevented by using an inhaled short-acting beta$_2$-agonist shortly before the start of exercise. Sometimes during prolonged exercise it is necessary to repeat use of the inhaled short-acting beta$_2$-agonist.
- A few people may require medication in addition to, or instead of, an inhaled short-acting beta$_2$-agonist and an inhaled corticosteroid. In these people consider prescribing one of:
  - Inhaled long-acting beta$_2$-agonist (LABA). However, a degree of tolerance, especially with respect to duration of action, tends to develop.
  - Oral beta$_2$-agonist.
  - Leukotriene receptor antagonist.
  - Nedocromil in children aged 5 to 12 years. Cromoglicate in older children and adults.
  - Theophylline.

[SIGN and BTS, 2004]

How do I manage occupational asthma?

- Maintain a high level of suspicion for occupational asthma in all adults, especially those who developed asthma in adulthood.
- Ask adults with airflow obstruction:
  - Are you better on days away from work?
  - Are you better on holiday?
- Investigate those with positive answers for possible occupational asthma, asthma due to exposure to agents at home, and exercise-induced asthma if work entails much more physical activity than home.
- Use standard objective criteria to confirm the diagnosis of asthma and the relationship between work and symptoms before recommending relocation or retirement on the grounds of work-related asthma.
- Tests to confirm the diagnosis of asthma (and exclude other conditions) include:
  - Reversibility tests: increased peak expiratory flow (PEF) after an inhaled short-acting beta$_2$-agonist, or after a 2-week course of oral corticosteroids; decreased peak expiratory flow (PEF) after 6 minutes of running.

A

- Serial peak flow measurements: variability of 20% or more in serial peak flow measurements is highly suggestive of asthma.
- Dynamic lung function tests/spirometry to differentiate obstructive, restrictive, and mixed lung function disorders.
- Transfer factor: consider this in heavy smokers to exclude emphysema.

- Confirm and document the relationship between work and asthma.
  - Serial measurements of PEF at home and at work, every 2 hours while awake, for 4 weeks, keeping treatment constant and recording times at work. More details, information for patients, and a computer tool for analysing the data are available from www.occupationalasthma.com.
  - Specific bronchial challenges should only be conducted in specialized units familiar with the performance and interpretation of such tests.
- Relocation away from exposure should occur within 12 months of the first work-related symptoms of asthma.
- Delay assessment of long-term impairment for at least 2 years following relocation away from exposure.
- Consider referral to the occupational health service at the workplace.

[SIGN and BTS, 2004]

How do I manage asthma during pregnancy and breastfeeding?

- The risks from uncontrolled asthma are much greater than the risks from conventional asthma treatments during pregnancy. Use beta$_2$-agonists, inhaled/oral corticosteroids, and theophylline as normal in pregnancy. Leukotriene receptor antagonists should not be started during pregnancy. The Scottish Intercollegiate Guidelines Network (SIGN) suggests that they may be continued during pregnancy if they have produced a good response. Since there are limited data regarding their safety in pregnant or nursing women, leukotriene receptor antagonists should not be used during pregnancy or in nursing mothers unless it is considered to be clearly essential.
- Offer pre-pregnancy counselling to women with asthma. Good control of asthma should be maintained by continuing current treatment.
- Monitor pregnant women closely so that treatment can be adjusted according to changes in the severity of asthma.
- Advise women who smoke about the dangers that smoking poses to themselves and their children. Give appropriate support for smoking cessation.
- Encourage women with asthma to breastfeed their babies.
- Use asthma medications as normal during lactation, in line with the manufacturer's recommendations.

[SIGN and BTS, 2004]

How do I manage someone with an acute exacerbation of asthma?

- **The principles of managing an acute exacerbation of asthma are to:**
  - Ensure that patients and/or their carers are able to assess severity, initiate treatment, and seek help without delay when required.
  - Recognise people with risk factors for death from asthma and ensure that they receive prompt treatment.
  - Assess and record severity with objective measurements, e.g. peak expiratory flow (PEF), oxygen saturation, vital signs. Similarly, record response to treatment.
  - Individualize treatment and frequency of reassessme[nt] according to severity and response to treatment.
  - Treat with oxygen, inhaled bronchodilator and oral corticosteroids.
  - Admit people with any feature of a life-threatening attack, or severe attack persisting after initial treatment, or previous near-fatal attack.
  - Follow up in primary care within 48 hours of treatment in primary care or discharge from hospita[l].

[SIGN and BTS, 2004]

- **Ensure that people with asthma or their carers, or bot[h] are able to assess severity and seek help without delay when required.**
  - Offer self-management education, including written asthma action plans focusing on individual needs, to all people with asthma, particularly those previously admitted to hospital. For details see the section *Pati[ent] education and self-management* in *Management issues*.
- **Recognise people with risk factors for death from asthma and ensure that they seek and receive prompt treatment when they experience an acute attack of asthma.** The important risk factors for death from asthma are:
  - Previous near-fatal episode of asthma (i.e. ventilatio[n] or respiratory acidosis).
  - Previous hospital admission for asthma, especially if within the last year.
  - Requiring three or more classes of asthma medicatio[n]
  - Heavy use of beta$_2$-agonists.
  - Repeated attendance at accident and emergency (A&E) unit for asthma, especially in the last year.
  - 'Brittle' asthma (defined in Table 5).
  - **Adverse behavioural or psychosocial features:**
    - Non-compliance with treatment or monitoring
    - Failure to attend appointments
    - Self-discharge from hospital
    - Psychosis, depression, other psychiatric illness, deliberate self-harm
    - Current or recent major tranquilliser use
    - Denial
    - Alcohol or drug abuse
    - Obesity
    - Learning difficulties
    - Employment problems
    - Income problems
    - Social isolation
    - Child abuse
    - Severe domestic, marital or legal stress
- **Assess and record severity with objective measurement**
  - Assess and record symptoms and response to treatment.
  - Make a rapid initial assessment with the peak expiratory flow (PEF), if the person is old enough to cooperate. Use the best of three consecutive measurements of PEF. Severity according to PEF, percentage of best or predicted:
    - Moderate: 50–75%
    - Acute severe: 33–50%
    - Life-threatening: <33%
  - Grade and record the severity of asthma exacerbatio[n] using the criteria in Table 5 and, if available, pulse oximetry to measure oxygen saturation in room air.

[SIGN and BTS, 2004]

- **Start treatment immediately according to the severity o[f] the attack.**
  - Until severity has been objectively assessed (as in Tab[le] 5 above), manage as for acute severe asthma.
  - Individualise management according severity and response.
  - Give oxygen, inhaled bronchodilator, and corticosteroid.

ıle 5: Levels of severity of acute asthma exacerbations.

·l	Criteria	
r-fatal	Respiratory acidosis (raised arterial carbon dioxide) and/or requiring mechanical ventilation with raised inflation pressures	
- ıtening	Any one of the following in someone with severe asthma:	
	Peak expiratory flow rate less than 33% of best or predicted Oxygen saturation less than 92% Silent chest Cyanosis Feeble respiratory effort	Bradycardia Dysrhythmia Hypotension Exhaustion Confusion Coma
te severe	Any one of: Peak expiratory flow rate 33–50% of best or predicted Tachypnoea: **2–5 years old** 50 breaths per minute **5–12 years old** 30 breaths per minute **>12 years old** 25 breaths per minute Tachycardia: **2–5 years old** 130 beats per minute **5–12 years old** 120 beats per minute **>12 years old** 110 beats per minute Inability to complete sentences in one breath Use of accessory neck muscles (in children)	
derate ıma cerbation	Increasing symptoms Peak expiratory flow rate greater than 50–70% of best or predicted No features of acute severe asthma	
tle ıma	**Type 1:** wide peak expiratory flow rate variability despite intense therapy (i.e. more than 40% diurnal variation for more than 50% of the time over a period greater than 150 days) **Type 2:** sudden severe attacks on a background of apparently well-controlled asthma	

ıtion: people with severe or life-threatening attacks sometimes do appear to be distressed and may not have all the features listed. ard the occurrence of any feature as an alert for the presence of ere or life-threatening asthma.

Reassess as frequently as required by severity and response.

ievere or life-threatening attack of asthma:

- **High-flow oxygen** (6 l/min, 40–60%); young children require a tightly fitting face mask or nasal cannula.
  - Aim to exceed 92% saturation when breathing room air and measured by pulse oximetry while breathing air.
- **High dose inhaled short-acting beta$_2$-agonist**
  - Deliver by high-flow oxygen-driven nebulizer. If unavailable, deliver by air-driven nebulizer, or, if nebulization is unavailable, by pMDI and large volume spacer.
  - Continuous nebulization is preferred as it is at least as effective as intermittent bolus nebulization in relieving acute asthma. (Continuous nebulization requires a large volume nebulizer or one incorporating a constant infusion device. Dosing for a continuous nebulizer is not equivalent to continuously repeated conventional nebulizer doses.)
  - Doses for nebulized salbutamol and terbutaline are given in Table 6 below.
- **Ipratropium bromide**
  - Nebulize ipratropium bromide combined with the beta$_2$-agonist.
  - Repeat combined nebulization if response is poor, up to 6 times a day.
  - Doses for nebulized ipratropium bromide are given in Table 6 below.
- **Corticosteroids**
  - Give orally, unless unable to swallow, in which case give intravenously.
  - Repeat dose or give intravenously if vomiting.
  - Aim to stop corticosteroids when they are no longer required. For adults oral corticosteroids should be given for at least 5 days or until recovery; for children up to 3 days is usually sufficient but the length of course should be tailored to the number of days necessary to bring about recovery.
  - A short course (up to three weeks) of oral corticosteroids can be stopped without tapering the dose, unless the person is on maintenance oral corticosteroid treatment.
  - Doses for oral prednisolone and intravenous hydrocortisone are given in Table 7.
- **Hospital admission**
  - **If life-threatening attack of asthma,** start emergency treatment and then arrange urgent admission to hospital.
  - **If severe exacerbation of asthma,** and after about 20 minutes there is poor response to the initial treatment with high-dose inhaled bronchodilator, arrange admission to hospital.

- **Moderate exacerbation of asthma:**
  - **High dose of a short-acting inhaled beta$_2$-agonist**
    - Deliver by nebulizer, or alternatively, deliver by pMDI and large volume spacer device — a facemask might be needed for young children. If multiple puffs are needed, they should be given as single actuations into the spacer, and inhaled with minimum delay after each, repeating until the prescribed number of puffs has been given.
    - For an adult give 4–6 puffs rapidly in a set. Repeat every 10–20 minutes according to clinical response.
    - For a child give between 2 and 10 puffs rapidly in a set (2–4 puffs may be sufficient to relieve a mild attack, up to 10 puffs may be needed for more severe asthma). Repeat every 20–30 minutes according to clinical response.
    - Adjust the number of puffs in a set and the intervals between repeating sets according to severity and response.
    - Doses of nebulized bronchodilators are given in Table 6.
  - **Corticosteroids**
    - Give orally unless unable to swallow, in which case give intravenously.
    - Doses are given in Table 7 below.
- **Reassess frequently, according to severity,** e.g. every 15–30 minutes for severe–moderate cases, and adjust treatment accordingly.
  - **Good response** (peak expiratory flow [PEF] greater than 50% predicted/best, symptoms improved, respiration and pulse rate settling):
    - Manage at home.
    - Continue frequent (at least every 4 hours) high dose inhaled beta$_2$-agonist as long as necessary.
    - Refer children under 13 to hospital if the symptoms are not controlled.
    - Continue prednisolone for up to 3 days.
  - **Poor response:**
    - Continue with high dose inhaled beta$_2$-agonist and oxygen.
    - If severe symptoms fail to improve, consider using combined nebulization of ipratropium and beta$_2$-agonists (see above).
    - Admit to hospital if any features of life-threatening or acute severe asthma still present, or if previous near-fatal asthma attack, or if a child has not responded after 10 puffs of beta$_2$-agonist. The urgency of admission should be appropriate for the severity of the attack.
    - Lower the threshold for admission if afternoon or evening attack, recent nocturnal symptoms or

A

hospital admission, previous severe attacks, patient/carer unable to reliably assess severity, or concern about social circumstances.
- **If admitting to hospital:**
  - Continue with high dose inhaled bronchodilator and oxygen.
  - Stay with the patient until the ambulance arrives.
  - Send written referral and assessment details to hospital.
  - In the ambulance give high dose bronchodilator via oxygen-driven nebulizer.
- **Follow up after treatment in primary care and after discharge from hospital:**
  - GP review within 48 hours.
  - Monitor symptoms and peak expiratory flow (PEF).
  - Check inhaler technique.
  - Give written asthma action plan.
  - Consider stepping up treatment of chronic asthma.
  - Address potentially preventable contributors to admission.

Table 6: Doses of nebulized bronchodilators used in acute severe exacerbation of asthma. When using intermittent nebulization repeat beta$_2$-agonists every 15–30 minutes. Repeat ipratropium bromide up to 6 times a day. When using a continuous nebulizer give the tabulated doses over 30–60 minutes.

Drug	2–5 years old	6–12 years old	>12 years old
Salbutamol	2.5 mg	2.5–5 mg (higher dose for more severe)	5 mg
Terbutaline	5 mg	5–10 mg	10 mg
Ipratropium (every 4–6 hours)	250 micrograms	250 micrograms	500 micrograms

Table 7: Doses of glucocorticoids used in acute severe exacerbation of asthma.

Drug	2–5 years old	6–12 years old	>12 years old
Prednisolone tablets (once a day)			
Not taking regular oral corticosteroid	20 mg	30–40 mg	40–50 mg
Taking regular oral corticosteroid	2 mg/kg (max 60 mg)	2 mg/kg (max 60 mg)	2 mg/kg (max 60 mg)
Intravenous hydrocortisone	4 mg/kg (every 4 hours)	4 mg/kg (every 4 hours)	100 mg (every 6 hours)

[SIGN and BTS, 2004]

What delivery system should I recommend for inhaled drugs?

A wide variety of devices, masks and spacers are used to deliver inhaled drugs, including
- Pressurized metered-dose inhalers (pMDI)
- Breath-actuated metered dose inhalers
- Dry powder inhalers
- Nebulizers, driven by air or oxygen
- Spacer devices with a variety of different volumes
- Face masks with a variety of designs

To ensure that an appropriate system is prescribed for someone with asthma it is necessary to consider the options suitable for the age, abilities and preferences of the patient.

What factors influence the choice of inhaler device?

- In addition to therapeutic need (including chosen drug and dose), the following factors should be taken into account when choosing inhaler devices for people wit asthma:
  - The ability of the person to develop and maintain a effective technique with the specific device — devic suitable for adults and children are discussed below
  - The suitability of the device for the person's (and carer's) lifestyles, considering factors such as portability and convenience.
  - The person's preference for and willingness to use a particular device.
- The device with the lowest overall cost (taking into account daily required dose and product price per dos should be chosen.
- Good technique is essential in ensuring the correct use inhaler devices. Only prescribe inhalers after the pers using them (or their carer) has received training in the use of the device, and has demonstrated acceptable technique.
- Check inhaler technique regularly (at least once a yea as part of structured clinical review in all people to av deterioration in technique.

[MeReC, 2002; SIGN and BTS, 2004]

What inhaler devices are suitable for adults?
- A pressurized metered-dose inhaler with or without a spacer is recommended as first-line choice for the delivery of both inhaled corticosteroids and bronchodilators.
- For inhaled corticosteroids and bronchodilators, Heal Technology Assessment systematic reviews have foun no evidence that alternative inhaler devices are more effective than pressurized metered-dose inhalers [Brocklebank et al, 2001; Ram et al, 2001].
- Consider patient preference and ability to use the devi adequately.

[MeReC, 2002]

What inhaler devices are suitable for children aged 5–15 years?
- A pressurized metered-dose inhaler with a suitable spacer device is recommended as the first-line choice f the delivery of inhaled corticosteroids.
- If the child's use of the pressurized metered-dose inha plus spacer is likely to be so poor as to undermine effective asthma control, consider alternative devices (dry powder inhaler or breath-actuated metered-dose inhaler), bearing in mind the need to minimize the adverse effects of corticosteroids.
- For bronchodilators, a wider range of devices may be considered, to take account of the more frequent spontaneous use, the greater need for portability, and clear feedback that symptom response provides.

[NICE, 2002a]

What inhaler devices are suitable for children under 5 years?
- Both inhaled corticosteroid and bronchodilator therap should be delivered by a pressurized metered-dose inhaler plus suitable spacer device, with a facemask where necessary.
- Where this combination is not clinically effective for th child, consider nebulized therapy. Few children under age of 5 years will be able use a dry powder inhaler adequately.

[NICE, 2002a]

What spacer device for pressurized metered-dose inhalers, and when?

- Standard pressurized metered-dose inhalers (pMDIs), with or without a spacer, are at least as effective as dry powder devices and autohalers if used correctly, and current recommendations are that people should initia be treated with a pMDI [Brocklebank et al, 2001; Ran et al, 2001; SIGN and BTS, 2004].

large volume spacer is recommended for the dministration of inhaled corticosteroids (ICS) in hildren and for giving high doses of ICS (more than 00 micrograms daily of beclometasone or equivalent) in dults. Spacer devices reduce oropharyngeal deposition f the drug by filtering out larger particles, thus lowering ne incidence of local adverse effects of inhaled orticosteroids, such as oral candidiasis, and reducing he amount of drug absorbed from the gastrointestinal ract [DTB, 2000a].

arge volume spacer devices should be used for people vho have difficulty coordinating actuation of a pMDI vith inhalation [DTB, 2000a].

ortability may be an important issue with large volume pacer devices. This is less of a problem with ICS as they re generally only used twice a day.

n acute exacerbations of asthma, large volume spacer evices are an effective alternative to nebulizers for elivering high-dose bronchodilators [EBM, 2001; Cates t al, 2002].

able 8 shows which large volume spacer devices are ompatible with which pMDIs.

pacer devices should be washed according to the nanufacturer's instructions, and should be replaced very 6–12 months.

rugs should be administered as single actuations into he spacer, and inhaled with minimum delay after each uff, repeating until the prescribed number of puffs has een given. Multiple actuations of the metered-dose nhaler into the spacer before inhalation may reduce the roportion of the drug inhaled [DTB, 2000a].

hen should a breath-actuated device be commended?

eople who are unable or unwilling to use a standard ressurized metered-dose inhaler (pMDI) plus large olume spacer may find a dry powder inhaler or a reath-actuated metered-dose inhaler acceptable.

ecause large volume spacer devices are not easily ortable, a dry powder inhaler or a breath-actuated netered-dose inhaler may be appropriate for ronchodilator (reliever) use during the day or when ravelling.

ry powder devices and breath-actuated metered dose nhalers require an inspiratory flow of at least 30 litres/ ninute to activate the device. Some frail people and ounger children are unable to consistently achieve the equired minimum inspiratory flow rate [NICE, 2002a].

ropharyngeal deposition with dry powder inhalers and utohalers is high.

- Advise people to rinse their mouth with water after inhaling; this minimizes the risks of oral candidiasis.
- In autohalers, oropharyngeal deposition can be minimized by use of a short 'open tube' spacer, which comes with some brands of inhaled corticosteroid autohalers.

ble 8: Compatibilities of pressurized metered-dose alers (pMDIs) and large volume spacer devices.

nchodilator	Large volume spacer	Inhaled corticosteroid
omir/Salbulin lbutamol)	Aerochamber	Qvar (chlorofluorocarbon-free beclometasone)
canyl rbutaline)	Nebuhaler	Pulmicort (budesonide)
ntolin Evohaler lbutamol) event lmeterol)	Volumatic	Becotide/Becloforte (beclometasone) Flixotide/Flixotide Evohaler (fluticasone)

te: inhalers should be used with the spacers recommended in the Summary of duct Characteristics for each inhaler.

- There are many types of breath-actuated devices and dry powder devices. Prescribers should familiarize themselves with a selection of these devices so they can inform, supervise, and assist patients appropriately.

[DTB, 2000a]

When is a nebulizer recommended?

- A nebulizer converts a solution of drug into an aerosol for inhalation by means of an electrical compressor or compressed gas. The aerosol is then delivered via a mouthpiece or a facemask.
- The use of nebulizers in the community is declining. The main indication for their use is to deliver a bronchodilator in the treatment of acute, severe asthma in adults and children too ill to use a pressurized metered-dose inhaler (pMDI) plus spacer.
  - Continuous nebulization of beta$_2$-agonists is at least as effective as bolus nebulization in relieving acute asthma, however
- Nebulizers may also be used for regular delivery of higher doses of drug than is usual with standard hand-held inhalers.
- A recent Cochrane review of randomized controlled trials comparing pMDI plus spacer to nebulizer for the delivery of beta$_2$-agonists for mild and moderate exacerbations of asthma found that pMDIs plus spacer were at least as effective as nebulizers [Cates et al, 2002].
- Nebulizers are not prescribable on the NHS.
- When a nebulizer is used by multiple people (e.g. in a clinic), the risk of cross infection should be considered. Manufacturers guidelines about the use/reuse of nebulizer masks should be adhered to.

Medicines management

Stepping down

- Stepping down treatment once asthma is controlled is therefore an important part of therapy to ensure maximum benefit with minimum adverse effects.
- When deciding whether to step down treatment, which drug to step down first and at what rate, take into account the following factors:
  - Seasonal variations in asthma
  - Severity of asthma
  - Adverse effects (both those experienced and potential adverse effects)
  - The beneficial effect of the treatment
  - The person's preference
- Regularly review asthma control as treatment is stepped down, to ensure that good control is maintained.
- People should be maintained on the lowest dose of inhaled corticosteroid (ICS) at which effective control can be maintained. There is little evidence regarding the most appropriate way to step down treatment. Reduction in ICS dose should be undertaken slowly as control deteriorates at different rates. The Scottish Intercollegiate Guidelines Network/British Thoracic Society (SIGN/BTS) guidelines recommend considering reductions every 3 months, reducing the dose by approximately 25–50% each time.

[SIGN and BTS, 2004]

Inhaled corticosteroids: safety issues

- The safety of inhaled corticosteroids (ICS) is of crucial importance and a balance between benefits and risks for each individual needs to be assessed. Take account of the use of other systemic or topical corticosteroid therapy when assessing risk.

A

- **Oral candidiasis and sore mouth** are commonly recognized problems with ICS use. They can be minimized by using a pressurized metered-dose inhaler with a large volume spacer device (which reduces oropharyngeal deposition by filtering out larger particles), and by rinsing the mouth with water after ICS use.
- **Hoarseness and dysphonia** are seen in many people taking ICS. Use of a spacer device does not appear to alleviate this.
- **Cataracts, glaucoma, and skin thinning** are associated with prolonged ICS use.

[DTB, 2000b; MeReC, 2002]

ICS in adults

- **Osteoporosis:** the effect of ICS on bone mineral density (BMD) and osteoporosis is currently unclear. Epidemiological studies examining the relationship between ICS and BMD give conflicting results and are difficult to interpret due to confounding factors. However, they tend to show that with long-term use of ICS at high doses (above 800 micrograms per day of beclometasone or equivalent) there may be a decrease in BMD [Cave et al, 1999; DTB, 2000b; Royal College of Physicians of London, 2002; SIGN and BTS, 2004]. The clinical significance of these changes in BMD is not known, as there is a lack of long-term studies.
- In people who require high doses of ICS for prolonged periods of time, general measures to counteract osteoporosis (such as regular exercise, smoking cessation, adequate dietary calcium) are prudent.
- **Adrenal suppression:** a recent systematic review provides evidence that at high doses of ICS (equivalent to 1.5 mg/day chlorofluorocarbon [CFC] -containing beclometasone), significant adrenal suppression occurs [EBM, 1999]. The Committee on Safety of Medicines (CSM) has advised that adrenal suppression is a dose-related class effect of inhaled corticosteroids and that, because of its greater potency, fluticasone should be used at half the dose of budesonide or CFC-containing beclometasone [CSM, 2001].

ICS in children

- **Childhood growth:** there may be some initial slowing of growth in children who have used ICS, but final adult height does not appear to be affected [The Childhood Asthma Management Program Research Group., 2000; MeReC, 2002].
  - **All children receiving prolonged treatment with ICS should have their height regularly monitored** [CSM, 1998]. Any slowing of growth should prompt a reduction in dose if possible, and referral to a specialist, or both.
- There is evidence that poorly controlled asthma, particularly in association with social deprivation, is likely to affect height [McCowan et al, 1998].
- **Bone mineral density:** one long-term study in children with chronic asthma treated with ICS suggests no adverse effect of inhaled corticosteroids on bone mineral density [Agertoft and Pedersen, 2000]. Further long-term studies are needed to confirm this.
- **Acute adrenal crisis:** a recent survey suggests that acute adrenal crisis associated with inhaled corticosteroids might be more frequent in children than has previously been supposed [Todd et al, 2002].
  - Presenting symptoms of adrenal crisis are non-specific, and include anorexia, abdominal pain, weight loss, tiredness, headache, nausea, vomiting, decreased level of consciousness, hypoglycaemia and seizures.
  - Acute adrenal crisis may be precipitated by infection, trauma, surgery, or rapid reduction in corticosteroid dosage.
  - Consider the possibility of adrenal insufficiency in a child maintained on ICS presenting with a decreased level of consciousness–blood glucose levels should be checked urgently. Consider whether intramuscular hydrocortisone is required.
- **The Committee on Safety of Medicines** has 'strongly advised that the paediatric licensed doses of all inhaled corticosteroids should not be exceeded' [CSM, 2002]. Use the lowest dose of ICS that will maintain disease control. If adequate control is not achieved, consider using add-on agents.

Theophylline

- Theophylline has a narrow margin between the therapeutic and toxic dose. In most people, plasma concentrations between 10 and 20 mg/litre are usually required for satisfactory bronchodilation, although a lower concentration may be effective.
- Adverse effects can occur within the range 10–20 mg/litre. Both the frequency and severity of adverse effect increase above concentrations of 20 mg/litre.
- The half-life of theophylline is increased (i.e. increased levels of theophylline) in people with heart failure or hepatic impairment, in elderly people, and by drugs th inhibit hepatic enzymes (e.g. cimetidine, ciprofloxacin, erythromycin).
  - If people who are stabilized on theophylline begin to take one of these drugs, a reduction of the theophyll dose is recommended.
- The half-life of theophylline is decreased (i.e. decrease levels of theophylline) in people who smoke, in chroni alcoholism, and by drugs that induce hepatic enzymes (e.g. phenytoin, carbamazepine, rifampicin).
  - If people who are stabilized on theophylline begin to take one of those drugs, the theophylline dosage ma need to be increased.
  - If people who are stabilized on theophylline stop smoking, plasma levels of theophylline may increase and a reduction in dosage may be necessary.
- Due to bioavailability differences between brands, people should be maintained on the same brand of theophylline. To assist this the brand should be specifi on the prescription.

[Stockley, 2002; BNF 45, 2003]

Leukotriene receptor antagonists

- Hepatic disorders may occur with zafirlukast. Advise people to seek medical advice in the event of persistent nausea, vomiting, malaise, or jaundice [BNF 45, 2003]

Chlorofluorocarbon-free inhaler devices

- The Montreal Protocol has mandated that chlorofluorocarbon (CFC) propellant should be phased out, and in the UK the transition to CFC-free propellants, usually hydrofluoroalkane, (HFA), is currently underway [NHS Executive, 1998].
- This change is due to environmental requirements and not because of any safety or clinical reasons.

Which pressurized metered-dose inhalers are available as HFA products?

- The transition for salbutamol is now well underway ar as the availability of CFC-containing salbutamol pressurized metered-dose inhalers (pMDIs) is decreasin the Department of Health has advised that all people currently using them should be transferred to a CFC-fr product [CMO, 2003].
- The only currently available HFA beclometasone pMD is Qvar. Until more than one CFC-free brand is license and licensed for all ages, CFC-containing brands will s be in use.

uticasone pMDI is available as a HFA pMDI (Flixotide vohaler) in strengths.

ll dry powder devices are CFC-free.

v do I transfer someone from CFC pMDI to HFA DI?

'hen transferring from a CFC pMDI to a HFA pMDI, eople will need reassurance that the new inhalers are qually safe and effective despite any differences in taste, mperature and impact that they may notice.

albutamol: most people will be able to transfer directly a HFA salbutamol pMDI. HFA salbutamol is as fective as CFC salbutamol at standard therapeutic oses [Hughes et al, 1999; CMO, 2003] and should be ıbstituted for CFC salbutamol at 1:1 dosing.

eclometasone: the only currently available CFC-free eclometasone pMDI is Qvar.

If the asthma is well controlled, substitute Qvar for CFC beclometasone pMDI at 1:2 dosing. Monitor the person closely to ensure that adequate control is maintained. This 1:2 ratio may not apply to future reformulated CFC-free beclometasone pMDIs.

If asthma is poorly controlled, substitute Qvar for CFC beclometasone at 1:1 dosing [BNF 45, 2003].

the Summary of Product Characteristics for Qvar for her details.

GN and BTS, 2004]

porting adverse reactions to HFA pMDIs

he Committee on Safety of Medicines (CSM) has equested that adverse reactions to the new HFA devices e reported. Any such report should include the brand ame of the inhaler.

sthma medication issues for elite athletes

ach controlling body for competitive sport has its own egulations for the use of drugs that may be taken to nhance performance. Details for individual drugs and ndividual controlling bodies may be found at www.uksport.gov.uk/did/.

Many sports follow the regulations of the International Olympic Committee (IOC), which classes most asthma rugs as either banned or requiring prior registration. Asthma Victoria publishes a useful summary of IOC egulations for asthma drugs at www.asthma.org.au.

Elite athletes should be advised to consult the controlling ody of their sport for specific advice on what drugs are anned and what procedures need to be followed to btain permission to use drugs that require prior egistration.

eferences

IS staff in England can link, free of charge, from erences to full text journals by clicking on [Full text] on PRODIGY website.

ations in this document primarily refer to the **Scottish ercollegiate Guidelines Network (SIGN) /British oracic Society (BTS)** *British guideline on the nagement of asthma* [SIGN and BTS, 2004].

casionally this is supplemented by other citations, which ovide additional information or newer evidence, since SIGN/BTS guideline is based on a search of the rature up to September 2001. These are listed below.

ABPI Medicines Compendium (2002) *Summary of product characteristics for Foradil.* Electronic Medicines Compendium. Datapharm Communications Ltd. www.emc.medicines.org.uk [Accessed: 10/04/2002].

Agertoft, L. and Pedersen, S. (2000) Effect of long-term treatment with inhaled budesonide on adult height in children with asthma. *New England Journal of Medicine* 343(15), 1064–1069. [Full text]

3. Anderson, J.E., Jorenby, D.E., Scott, W.J. and Fiore, M.C. (2002) Treating tobacco use and dependence: an evidence-based clinical practice guideline for tobacco cessation. *Chest* **121**(3), 932–941. [Full text]
4. BNF 45 (2003) *British National Formulary.* 45th edn. London: British Medical Association and Royal Pharmaceutical Society of Great Britain.
5. British Thoracic Society (1997) The British guidelines on asthma management: 1995 review and position statement. *Thorax* **52**(Suppl 1), S1-S20. [Full text]
6. Brocklebank, D., Wright, J. and Cates, C. (2001) Systematic review of clinical effectiveness of pressurised metered dose inhalers versus other hand held inhaler devices for delivering corticosteroids in asthma. *British Medical Journal* **323**(7318), 896–900. [Full text]
7. Cates, C. (2001) An alternative for air-driven nebulisers in acute asthma in the community. *British Medical Journal* **323**(7304), 98–100.
8. Cates, C.J., Rowe, B.H. and Bara, A. (2002) *Holding chambers versus nebulisers for beta-agonist treatment of acute asthma (Cochrane Review).* The Cochrane Library. Issue 2. Chichester, UK: John Wiley & Sons Ltd. www.nelh.nhs.uk [Accessed: 19/07/2005]. [Full text]
9. Cave, A., Arlett, P. and Lee, E. (1999) Inhaled and nasal corticosteroids: factors affecting the risks of systemic adverse effects. *Pharmacology & Therapeutics* **83**(3), 153–179.
10. CMO (2002) *Update on immunisation issues.* PL/CMO/2002/4. Department of Health. www.dh.gov.uk [Accessed: 27/04/2004]. [Full text]
11. CMO (2003) *CFC-containing salbutamol metered dose inhalers.* CEM/CMO/2003/9. Department of Health. www.dh.gov.uk [Accessed: 27/04/2004]. [Full text]
12. CMO (2005) *The pneumococcal immunisation programme for older people and risk groups.* Department of Health. www.dh.gov.uk [Accessed: 04/10/2005]
13. Cote, J., Cartier, A., Robichaud, P. et al (2000) Influence of asthma education on asthma severity, quality of life and environmental control. *Canadian Respiratory Journal* **7**(5), 395–400.
14. Cote, J., Bowie, D.M., Robichaud, P. et al (2001) Evaluation of two different educational interventions for adult patients consulting with an acute asthma exacerbation. *American Journal of Respiratory & Critical Care Medicine* **163**(6), 1415–1419.
15. CSM (1998) Focus on corticosteroids. *Current Problems in Pharmacovigilance* **24**(May), 5–10.
16. CSM (2001) Reminder: Fluticasone propionate (Flixotide): use of high doses (>500 micrograms/twice daily). *Current Problems in Pharmacovigilance* **27**(Aug), 10.
17. CSM (2002) Inhaled corticosteroids and adrenal suppression in children. *Current Problems in Pharmacovigilance* **28**(Oct), 7.
18. D'Cruz, D.P., Barnes, N.C. and Lockwood, C. (1999) Difficult asthma or Churg-Strauss syndrome? *British Medical Journal* **318**(7182), 475–476. [Full text]
19. Dennis, J. (2000) *Alexander technique for chronic asthma (Cochrane Review).* The Cochrane Library. Issue 2. Chichester, UK: John Wiley & Sons Ltd.
20. Dezateux, C., Stocks, J., Dundas, I. and Fletcher, M.E. (1999) Impaired airway function and wheezing in infancy: the influence of maternal smoking and a genetic predisposition to asthma. *American Journal of Respiratory & Critical Care Medicine* **159**(2), 403–410.
21. DH (1996) *Health survey for England 1996.* Department of Health. www.dh.gov.uk [Accessed: 01/09/2005]. [Full text]

A

22. DTB (1997) Using b_2-stimulants in asthma. *Drug & Therapeutics Bulletin* 35(1), 1–4.
23. DTB (2000a) Inhaler devices for asthma. *Drug & Therapeutics Bulletin* 38(2), 9–14.
24. DTB (2000b) The use of inhaled corticosteroids in adults with asthma. *Drug & Therapeutics Bulletin* 38(1), 5–8.
25. EBM (1999) High-dose inhaled corticosteroids increase the risk for some systemic adverse effects in asthma. *Evidence Based Medicine* 4(6), 191.
26. EBM (2001) Spacers were better and less expensive than nebulisers for giving albuterol to children with moderate to severe acute asthma. *Evidence Based Medicine* 6(1), 31.
27. Eccles, M., Rousseau, N., Higgins, B. and Thomas, L. (2001) Evidence-based guideline on the primary care management of asthma. *Family Practice* 18(2), 223–229. [Full text]
28. Gallefoss, F. and Bakke, P.S. (2000) Impact of patient education and self-management on morbidity in asthmatics and patients with chronic obstructive pulmonary disease. *Respiratory Medicine* 94(3), 279–287.
29. Gallefoss, F., Bakke, P.S. and Rsgaard, P.K. (1999) Quality of life assessment after patient education in a randomized controlled study on asthma and chronic obstructive pulmonary disease. *American Journal of Respiratory & Critical Care Medicine* 159(3), 812–817.
30. Ghosh, C.S., Ravindran, P., Joshi, M. and Stearns, S.C. (1998) Reductions in hospital use from self management training for chronic asthmatics. *Social Science & Medicine* 46(8), 1087–1093.
31. Gibson, P.G. (2001) *Limited (information only) patient education programs for adults with asthma.* The Cochrane Library. Issue 4. Oxford: Update Software.
32. Gibson, P.G., Powell, H., Coughlan, J. et al (2003a) *Self-management education and regular practitioner review for adults with asthma (Cochrane Review).* The Cochrane Library. Issue 3. Chichester, UK: John Wiley & Sons Ltd. www.nelh.nhs.uk/cochrane.asp [Accessed: 18/07/2005]. [Full text]
33. Gibson, P.G., Coughlan, J.L. and Henry, R.L. (2003b) *Gastro-oesophageal reflux treatment for asthma in adults and children (Cochrane Review).* The Cochrane Library. Issue 1. Chichester, UK: John Wiley & Sons Ltd. www.nelh.nhs.uk/cochrane.asp [Accessed: 19/07/2005].
34. Guevara, J.P., Wolf, F.M., Grum, C.M. and Clark, N.M. (2003) Effects of educational interventions for self management of asthma in children and adolescents: systematic review and meta-analysis. *British Medical Journal* 326(7402), 1308–1309. [Full text]
35. Haby, M.M., Waters, E., Robertson, C.F. et al (2001) *Interventions for educating children who have attended the emergency room for asthma (Cochrane Review).* The Cochrane Library. Issue 1. Oxford: Update Software. www.nelh.nhs.uk/cochrane.asp [Accessed: 19/07/2005]. [Full text]
36. Henningfield, J.E. (1995) Nicotine medications for smoking cessation. *New England Journal of Medicine* 333(18), 1196–1203.
37. Hondras, M.A., Linde, K. and Jones, A.P. (2005) *Manual therapy for asthma (Cochrane Review).* The Cochrane Library. Issue 2. Chichester, UK: John Wiley & Sons Ltd. www.nelh.nhs.uk/cochrane.asp [Accessed: 18/07/2005]. [Full text]
38. Hughes, D.A., Woodcock, A. and Walley, T. (1999) Review of therapeutically equivalent alternatives to short acting [beta]$_2$ adrenoreceptor agonists delivered via chlorofluorocarbon-containing inhalers. *Thorax* 54(12), 1087–1092. [Full text]
39. Ignacio-Garcia, J.M. and Gonzalez-Santos, P. (199 Asthma self-management education program by ho monitoring of peak expiratory flow. *American Jour of Respiratory & Critical Care Medicine* 151(2 Pt 1 353–359.
40. IOM (2000) Exposure to environmental tobacco smoke. In: Institute of Medicine (Ed.) *Clearing the asthma and indoor exposures.* Washington DC: National Academic Press. 263–297.
41. Kaur, B., Anderson, H.R., Austin, A. et al (1998) Prevalence of asthma symptoms, diagnosis, and treatment in 12–14 year old children across Great Britain (International Study of Asthma and Allergie Childhood, ISAAC UK). *British Medical Journal* 316(7125), 118–124.
42. Lahdensuo, A., Haahtela, T., Herrala, J. et al (1996 Randomised comparison of guided self managemen and traditional treatment of asthma over one year. *British Medical Journal* 312(7033), 748–752. [Full text]
43. Lefevre, F., Piper, M., Weiss, K. et al (2002) Do wri action plans improve patient outcomes in asthma? evidence-based analysis. *Journal of Family Practice* 51(10), 842–848.
44. Madge, P., McColl, J. and Paton, J. (1997) Impact o nurse-led home management training programme in children admitted to hospital with acute asthma: a randomised controlled study. *Thorax* 52(3), 223–2 [Full text]
45. McCormick, A., Fleming, D. and Charlton, J. (199 *Morbidity statistics from general practice. Fourth national study 1991–1992.* Office of Population Censuses and Surveys. www.statistics.gov.uk [Accessed: 03/05/2005].
46. McCowan, C., Neville, R.G., Thomas, G.E. et al (1998) Effect of asthma and its treatment on growth four year follow up of cohort of children from gener practices in Tayside, Scotland. *British Medical Jour* 316(7132), 668–672. [Full text]
47. MeReC (2002) Chronic asthma. *MeReC Briefing* 18(Jun), 1–5.
48. Meredith, S. and Nordman, H. (1996) Occupationa asthma: measures of frequency from four countries. *Thorax* 51(4), 435–440.
49. Moudgil, H., Marshall, T. and Honeybourne, D. (2000) Asthma education and quality of life in the community: a randomised controlled study to evalu the impact on white European and Indian subcontin ethnic groups from socioeconomically deprived area in Birmingham, UK. *Thorax* 55(3), 177–183. [Full text]
50. Murray, A.B. and Morrison, B.J. (1993) The decreas in severity of asthma in children of parents who smo since the parents have been exposing them to less cigarette smoke. *Journal of Allergy & Clinical Immunology* 91(1 Pt 1), 102–110.
51. National Heart Lung and Blood Institute (1997) *Guidelines for the diagnosis and management of asthma.* Expert Panel Report 2 97–4051, . National Institutes of Health. www.nhlbi.nih.gov [Accessed: 1 10/2003].
52. NHS Executive (1998) *Phase out of CFC containing metered dose inhalers for the treatment of asthma ar COPD.* HSC 1998/180. London: Department of Health.
53. NICE (2000) *Guidance on the use of inhaler systems (devices) in children under the age of 5 years with chronic asthma.* Technology appraisal no. 10. Natio Institute for Clinical Excellence.
54. NICE (2002a) *Inhaler devices for routine treatment chronic asthma in older children (aged 5 – 15 years).* Technology appraisal guidance no. 38. National

Institute for Clinical Excellence. www.nice.org.uk [Accessed: 19/07/2003].

NICE (2002b) *Guidance on the use of nicotine replacement therapy (NRT) and bupropion for smoking cessation.* Technology appraisal no. 39. National Institute for Clinical Excellence. www.nice.org.uk [Accessed: 18/07/2005]

Office for National Statistics (1999) Prescribing for patients with asthma by general practitioners in England and Wales 1994–1996. *Health Statistics Quarterly* 1(Spring), 16–20.

Osman, L.M., Abdalla, M.I., Beattie, J.A. et al (1994) Reducing hospital admission through computer supported education for asthma patients. Grampian Asthma Study of Integrated Care (GRASSIC). *British Medical Journal* 308(6928), 568–571. [Full text]

Panton, J. and Barley, E.A. (2005) *Family therapy for asthma in children (Cochrane Review).* The Cochrane Library. Issue 2. Chichester, UK: John Wiley & Sons Ltd. www.nelh.nhs.uk/cochrane.asp [Accessed: 19/07/2005].

Pearson, M.G. and Bucknall.C.E. (Eds.) (1999) *Measuring clinical outcome in asthma.* London: The Royal College of Physicians.

Powell, C.V., McNamara, P., Solis, A. and Shaw, N.J. (2002) A parent completed questionnaire to describe the patterns of wheezing and other respiratory symptoms in infants and preschool children. *Archives of Disease in Childhood* 87(5), 376–379. [Full text]

Radzik, D. and Pavanello, L. (2002) Inhaled steroids in the treatment of mild to moderate persistent asthma in children: once or twice daily administration? *Archives of Disease in Childhood* 87(5), 415–416. [Full text]

Ram, F.S., Wright, J., Brocklebank, D. and White, J.E. (2001) Systematic review of clinical effectiveness of pressurised metered dose inhalers versus other hand held inhaler devices for delivering [beta]2 agonists bronchodilators in asthma. *British Medical Journal* 323(7318), 901–905. [Full text]

Roth, M., Johnson, P.R., Rudiger, J.J. et al (2002) Interaction between glucocorticoids and beta2 agonists on bronchial airway smooth muscle cells through synchronised cellular signalling. *Lancet* 360(9342), 1293–1299. [Full text]

Royal College of Physicians of London (2002) *Glucocorticoid-induced osteoporosis.* Royal College of Physicians. www.rcplondon.ac.uk [Accessed: 22/04/2003].

SIGN (1998) *Primary care management of asthma.* Report no. 33. Scottish Intercollegiate Guidelines Network. www.sign.ac.uk [Accessed: 23/04/2002].

66. SIGN and BTS (2004) *2004 update to the British guideline on the management of asthma.* Report no. 63. Scottish Intercollegiate Guidelines Network and The British Thoracic Society. www.sign.ac.uk [Accessed: 04/08/2004].
67. Stockley, I.H. (Ed.) (2002) *Drug interactions.* 6th edn. London: The Pharmaceutical Press.
68. Strachan, D.P. and Cook, D.G. (1997) Health effects of passive smoking – 1. Parental smoking and lower respiratory illness in infancy and early childhood. *Thorax* **52**(10), 905–914. [Full text]
69. The Childhood Asthma Management Program Research Group. (2000) Long-term effects of budesonide or nedocromil in children with asthma. *New England Journal of Medicine* **343**(15), 1054–1063. [Full text]
70. Thoonen BP, Schermer TR, Van Den Boom G et al (2003) Self-management of asthma in general practice, asthma control and quality of life: a randomised controlled trial. *Thorax* 58(1), 30–36. [Full text]
71. Todd, G.R., Acerini, C.L., Ross-Russell, R. et al (2002) Survey of adrenal crisis associated with inhaled corticosteroids in the United Kingdom. *Archives of Disease in Childhood* 87(6), 457–461. [Full text]
72. Toelle, B.G. and Ram, F.S.F. (2004) *Written individualised management plans for asthma in children and adults.* The Cochrane Library. Issue 1. Chichester, UK: John Wiley & Sons Ltd. www.nelh.nhs.uk/cochrane.asp [Accessed: 19/07/2005].
73. van Noord, J.A., Smeets, J.J., Raaijmakers, J.A. et al (1996) Salmeterol versus formoterol in patients with moderately severe asthma: onset and duration of action. *European Respiratory Journal* 9(8), 1684–1688.
74. Wolf, F.M., Guevara, J.P., Grum, C.M. et al (2002) *Educational interventions for asthma in children.* The Cochrane Library. Issue 4. Chichester, UK: John Wiley & Sons Ltd. www.nelh.nhs.uk/cochrane.asp [Accessed: 19/07/2005].
75. Woodcock, A., Forster, L., Matthews, E. et al (2003) Control of exposure to mite allergen and allergen impermeable bed covers for adults with asthma. *New England Journal of Medicine* 349(3), 225–236. [Full text]
76. Yoon, R., McKenzie, D.K., Bauman, A. and Miles, D.A. (1993) Controlled trial evaluation of an asthma education programme for adults. *Thorax* 48(11), 1110–1116.

PRODIGY GUIDANCE

Atrial fibrillation

A

Last revised in April 2003
At the time of print this topic was being updated. The newly revised guidance will be issued on to the website in 2006.
www.prodigy.nhs.uk/guidance.asp?gt=Atrial fibrillation

Applies to people over the age of 16 years

This guidance covers the management of people with atrial fibrillation, including people with paroxysmal atrial fibrillation. It includes advice on control of ventricular rate, indications for cardioversion, and need for antithrombot treatment.

This guidance does not cover the management of atrial fibrillation in children.

There is separate PRODIGY guidance for the management of *SVT — paroxysmal.*

Goals

- To establish the diagnosis
- To control ventricular rate
- To identify those people suitable for attempted cardioversion
- To identify those people suitable for antithrombotic medication to reduce the risk of stroke

Contents

Scenarios

- New presentation of atrial fibrillation p.168
- Paroxysmal atrial fibrillation p.170
- Deciding on antithrombotic treatment p.171
- Managing rate-control drugs p.173
- Managing antithrombotic therapy p.175
- Rate uncontrolled on monotherapy p.177
- Rate uncontrolled on dual therapy p.179

Extended Information, p. 180

Which scenario?

- **New presentation of atrial fibrillation:** covers advice and prescriptions for starting rate-control drugs (beta-blockers, verapamil, or digoxin).
- **Paroxysmal atrial fibrillation:** covers the management of paroxysmal AF.
- **Deciding on antithrombotic treatment:** covers starting antithrombotic treatment in people with AF.
- **Managing rate-control drugs:** covers the maintenance/ dose adjustment of rate-control drugs, and advice on management of adverse effects.
- **Managing antithrombotic therapy:** covers advice on monitoring international normalized ratio (INR) and managing adverse effects of aspirin and warfarin.
- **Rate uncontrolled on monotherapy:** covers management when heart rate is uncontrolled on maximal tolerated monotherapy.
- **Rate uncontrolled on dual therapy:** covers management when heart rate is uncontrolled on dual therapy.

New presentation of atrial fibrillation

Which therapy?

- **Confirm the diagnosis by ECG.**
- **Treat any precipitating cause** (e.g. thyrotoxicosis, chest infection).
- **Refer, if appropriate, for attempted cardioversion** (se *Refer?* section).
- **Decide whether warfarin or aspirin is needed** (see scenario *Deciding antithrombotic treatment*).
- **Start rate-control treatment** to control ventricular rat and to relieve symptoms.
- Aim for a ventricular rate of less than 90/minute at re and 180/minute on exercise.
  - **1st line:** *consider a beta-blocker or verapamil,* particularly if there is coexisting hypertension or angina.
  - **2nd line:** *digoxin is preferred if the person has coexisting heart failure.* However, it is less effective than other agents at controlling heart rate during exercise. Beta-blockers may also be used in heart failure, but the starting doses are low, and can be increased only slowly.
- Step up the dose until the ventricular rate is controlle or the maximum tolerated dose is reached.
- **If rate control is not achieved at the maximal tolerate dose of monotherapy,** then consider combining digox with a beta-blocker or verapamil, or consider referral
  - **Do not use verapamil with a beta-blocker** (it may precipitate heart failure).
  - **If verapamil is added to digoxin,** reduce the digoxi dose by 30–50%, and then adjust according to plas levels. Maximal effect on digoxin levels occurs wit 14 days.

Factors affecting choice of treatment

- **Asthma or a history of bronchospasm:** do not use bet blockers (CSM warning).
- **Severe peripheral vascular disease:** avoid beta-blocke
- **Diabetes:** if using a beta-blocker, use atenolol or metoprolol (cardioselective). Avoid beta-blockers in someone who experiences frequent hypoglycaemia.
- **Heart failure:** use digoxin. Beta-blockers may be used heart failure, but the licensed drugs and doses are different for AF. (See PRODIGY *Heart Failure* guidanc Do not use verapamil.

Practical prescribing points

For further information please see the *Medicines Compendium* (www.medicines.org.uk) or the *British National Formulary* (www.bnf.org).

Beta-blockers

- There is no significant increased risk of depressive symptoms while on beta-blockers, and only a very sm increase in the risk of fatigue or sexual dysfunction.

rapamil

'onstipation is common. Give advice on high-fibre diet ·ith adequate fluid intake.

ɟoxin

·igoxin levels do not need to be routinely monitored, ·ecause ventricular rate is usually a good guide to ·ierapeutic effect.

. loading dosage of 500 micrograms daily for 3 days is ɪggested.

he maintenance dosage usually ranges from 125 to 50 micrograms daily.

ower loading and maintenance dosages should be used ı the elderly or in renal impairment (e.g. use 250 ·ıicrograms daily for 3 days, followed by a maintenance ·ose of 62.5 to 125 micrograms daily).

·llow-up advice

ₗeview within 1–2 weeks, depending on severity of ·ymptoms and outstanding investigations.

ɟoxin

;heck serum electrolytes and creatinine annually if ·aking digoxin.

)igoxin levels do not need to be routinely monitored, ·ecause ventricular rate is usually a good guide to ·herapeutic effect.

)nly check digoxin levels to assess possible toxicity or ·dherence to treatment. Plasma levels must be measured ·t least 6 hours after the last dosage.

.evels less than 1.5 micrograms/litre, in the absence of ·ypokalaemia, indicate that digoxin toxicity is unlikely.

.evels greater than 3.0 micrograms/litre indicate that ·oxicity is likely.

Vith levels between 1.5 and 3.0 micrograms/litre, ·igoxin toxicity should be considered a possibility.

·ould I refer or investigate?

·fer?

'eople who are very symptomatic and in need of urgent ·ate control (emergency admission).

'eople with acute atrial fibrillation (AF) and severe ·ypotension, acute heart failure, or unstable angina, who ·o not respond promptly to medical management, may ·equire immediate cardioversion.

'eople suitable for cardioversion are those with:

- **Recent-onset AF:** the time of onset is not always easy to determine, and there is a case for referring anyone with newly diagnosed AF for at least one attempt at cardioversion. Someone with acute-onset AF should ideally see a specialist within 48 hours in order to decide whether to cardiovert. The success rates for cardioversion diminish the longer a person is in AF, and anticoagulation prior to and after cardioversion is necessary if the person has been in AF for longer than 2 days.
- **No structural heart disease** (e.g. the person has no mitral valve disease; or the person has good left ventricular function, and an undilated left atrium).
- Successful treatment of any precipitating cause (e.g. thyrotoxicosis, chest infection).
- **Young age** (although age should not be an automatic barrier).

f there is inadequate control despite maximal primary ·are treatment.

Further assessment is needed (e.g. suspected valvular ·isease, moderate to severe heart failure).

- **Syncopal attacks.**
- **Suspected Wolff–Parkinson–White (WPW) syndrome.**

Investigate?

- **Electrocardiogram to confirm the diagnosis.**
- **Base-line blood tests:** full blood count, electrolytes, creatinine, thyroid function tests (plus coagulation screen and liver function tests if anticoagulation is being considered).
- **The routine use of echocardiography continues to be debated.** It may provide useful information on the presence of associated valvular disease and ventricular failure, and a recent consensus statement recommends that it should be part of the optimal assessment of people with AF. However, for most people it is unlikely to affect the decision on whether to recommend anticoagulation or not. Local guidelines may be available regarding the use of this.
- **Consider chest X-ray** (which can give information on the size of the heart and whether heart failure is present).

Patient information leaflets

The following PILs are available at www.prodigy.nhs.uk

- Atrial Fibrillation
- Atrial Fibrillation and Warfarin
- Blood Test - General
- British Heart Foundation
- How the Heart Works

Shared decision making

- Treatment of atrial fibrillation (AF) aims to reduce your heart rate to 90 beats per minute or less when you are resting.
- Medicines commonly used to control the heart rate include:
  - **Beta-blockers** such as atenolol, metoprolol, and propranolol
  - **Verapamil**
  - **Digoxin**
- **The one chosen may depend on whether you have other conditions,** such as some heart conditions, peripheral vascular disease, diabetes, asthma, or other diseases of the airways.
- **You may need a combination of medicines** if one alone does not control your heart rate.
- **Side effects are not common.** Tell your doctor if they occur. They include:
  - **Beta-blockers:** cool hands and feet, poor sleep, tiredness, impotence
  - **Verapamil:** constipation
  - **Digoxin:** feeling sick, vomiting, diarrhoea, mental confusion, blurred vision

Drug rationale

Drugs not included

- **Amiodarone** requires specialist initiation. It may be useful for rate control in refractory cases, but has a high incidence of adverse effects.
- **Digitoxin** is not commonly used in the UK and is more expensive than digoxin. It may be considered if there is an absolute requirement for a cardiac glycoside and the person has severe renal impairment.
- **Dihydropyridine calcium-channel blockers** (e.g. nifedipine) are not rate-limiting, and therefore have no place in the treatment of atrial fibrillation (AF).
- **Diltiazem** is not licensed for the treatment of arrhythmias. In addition, it is difficult to recommend

dosing (trials have been small and dosing has varied enormously).
- **Other anti-arrhythmic drugs** require specialist initiation and are used for maintenance of sinus rhythm after cardioversion, or for pharmacological cardioversion, rather than purely for ventricular rate control.
- **Sotalol** requires specialist initiation and is licensed only for paroxysmal AF.

Drugs included

- **Beta-blockers** reduce the ventricular rate at rest and during exercise. Beta-blockers should be considered as first-line therapy, especially in someone with coexisting hypertension or angina [Royal College of Physicians of Edinburgh, 1999]. **Atenolol, metoprolol, and propranolol** are included because they are licensed for the treatment of arrhythmias and are less expensive than other beta-blockers.
- **Digoxin** reduces the ventricular rate at rest, but is less effective at controlling the heart rate during exercise. Digoxin is the preferred choice if the person has coexisting heart failure. It can be used in combination with a beta-blocker or a rate-limiting calcium-channel blocker if rate control is not achieved with adequate monotherapy [Royal College of Physicians of Edinburgh, 1999].
- **Verapamil** is licensed for use in arrhythmias. In atrial fibrillation, verapamil reduces the ventricular rate at rest and during exercise. Verapamil should also be considered as first-line therapy, especially in someone with coexisting hypertension or angina [Royal College of Physicians of Edinburgh, 1999]. Standard doses of verapamil are included, as modified-release verapamil is not licensed for the treatment of arrhythmias.

Prescriptions

1st line: start beta-blocker (unless contraindicated)

Atenolol 50mg once a day
- Age from 16 years onwards
- Atenolol 50mg tablets. Take one tablet once a day; supply 28 tablets; NHS Cost £0.85.

Atenolol 100mg once a day
- Age from 16 years onwards
- Atenolol 100mg tablets. Take one tablet once a day; supply 28 tablets; NHS Cost £0.98.

Atenolol 50mg twice a day
- Age from 16 years onwards
- Atenolol 50mg tablets. Take one tablet twice a day; supply 56 tablets; NHS Cost £1.70.

Metoprolol 50mg twice a day
- Age from 16 years onwards
- Metoprolol 50mg tablets. Take one tablet twice a day; supply 56 tablets; NHS Cost £2.35.

Metoprolol 50mg three times a day
- Age from 16 years onwards
- Metoprolol 50mg tablets. Take one tablet three times a day; supply 84 tablets; NHS Cost £3.52.

Propranolol 10mg three times a day
- Age from 16 years onwards
- Propranolol 10mg tablets. Take one tablet three times a day; supply 84 tablets; NHS Cost £1.77.

Propranolol 40mg three times a day
- Age from 16 years onwards
- Propranolol 40mg tablets. Take one tablet three times a day; supply 84 tablets; NHS Cost £1.95.

Alternative: start verapamil (unless contraindicate

Verapamil 40mg three times a day
- Age from 16 years onwards
- Verapamil 40mg tablets. Take one tablet three times a day; supply 84 tablets; NHS Cost £1.61.

Verapamil 80mg three times a day
- Age from 16 years onwards
- Verapamil 80mg tablets. Take one tablet three times a day; supply 84 tablets; NHS Cost £3.93.

Heart failure: start digoxin

Digoxin 500mcg daily for 3 days, then 250mcg daily
- Age from 16 years onwards
- Digoxin 250microgram tablets. Take two tablets once day for 3 days, then take one tablet once a day; supply 28 tablets; NHS Cost £0.59.

Digoxin 500mcg daily for 3 days, then 125mcg daily
- Age from 16 years onwards
- Digoxin 125microgram tablets. Take four tablets onc day for 3 days, then take one tablet once a day; supply 28 tablets; NHS Cost £0.59.

Digoxin 250mcg daily for 3 days, then 125mcg daily
- Age from 16 years onwards
- Digoxin 125microgram tablets. Take two tablets once day for 3 days, then take one tablet once a day; supply 28 tablets; NHS Cost £0.59.

Digoxin 250mcg daily for 3 days, then 62.5mcg daily
- Age from 16 years onwards
- Digoxin 62.5microgram tablets. Take four tablets onc day for 3 days, then take one tablet once a day; supply 28 tablets; NHS Cost £0.77.

Paroxysmal atrial fibrillation

Which therapy?

- **Suspect in a person with recurring episodes of fast irregular palpitations,** who may otherwise be asymptomatic or complain of associated dyspnoea, giddiness, or chest pains.
- **If possible, confirm diagnosis by ECG** (the person may need to present when symptomatic in order to for the arrhythmia to be caught).
- **Anti-arrhythmic treatment for paroxysmal AF should initiated only under specialist supervision,** as this can b a difficult diagnosis to make.
  - It aims to reduce the frequency and severity of attac and possibly prevent progression to persistent AF.
  - It may not be necessary if symptomatic episodes are mild, infrequent, and short-lasting. The benefits of treatment have to be balanced against the risks of long-term anti-arrhythmic medication.
- **Decide whether warfarin or aspirin is needed:** thromboembolic risk is similar to that of persistent AF (see scenario *Deciding antithrombotic treatment*).
- **Co-administration of drugs that control rate** (verapam diltiazem, or beta-blockers) with anti-arrhythmic drug may reduce symptoms during attacks.
- **Digoxin is not generally recommended,** as it does not reduce the frequency of paroxysms and may worsen ra control during paroxysms.

Practical prescribing points

For further information please see the *Medicines Compendium* (www.medicines.org.uk) or the *British National Formulary* (www.bnf.org).

hould I refer or investigate ?

efer?

People who are very symptomatic and in need of urgent rate control (emergency admission).
If there is doubt about the diagnosis.
If symptoms are severe enough to warrant assessment for anti-arrhythmic therapy.
People with acute AF and severe hypotension, acute heart failure, or unstable angina, and who do not respond promptly to medical management, may require immediate cardioversion.
If further assessment is needed (e.g. suspected valvular disease, moderate to severe heart failure).
Syncopal attacks.
Suspected Wolff-Parkinson-White (WPW) syndrome.

ıvestigate?

Confirm the diagnosis by electrocardiogram if possible (the person may need to present when symptomatic in order for the arrhythmia to be caught).
Base-line blood tests: full blood count, electrolytes, creatinine, thyroid function tests (plus coagulation screen and liver function tests if anticoagulation being considered).
The routine use of echocardiography continues to be debated. It may provide useful information on the presence of associated valvular disease and ventricular failure, and a recent consensus statement recommends that it should be part of the optimal assessment of people with atrial fibrillation. However, for the majority of people it is unlikely to affect the decision on whether to recommend anticoagulation or not. Local guidelines may be available regarding the use of this.
Consider a chest X-ray (which can give information on the size of the heart and whether heart failure is present).

'atient information leaflets

he following PILs are available at www.prodigy.nhs.uk
Atrial Fibrillation
Atrial Fibrillation and Warfarin
Blood Test - General
British Heart Foundation
How the Heart Works

hared decision making

Paroxysmal atrial fibrillation means that you develop a fast, irregular heart beat from time to time.
Each episode usually lasts a short time then reverts back to normal.
You may feel palpitations, and feel dizzy, during each episode.
The length and frequency of episodes varies.
Some people have wrong ideas that their 'heart will stop', or they will have a 'heart attack', when an episode occurs. This is not so, and you should not stop your usual activities.
You may not need treatment if the episodes are short and infrequent.
You may be prescribed medication by a heart specialist to reduce the frequency and severity of episodes.
Several medicines can stabilise the electrical activity of the heart. If one does not work or suit you at first, you may need to change to another.

Drug rationale

- **Anti-arrhythmic treatment should be initiated only under specialist supervision, and therefore no prescriptions are offered.**
- Amiodarone, disopyramide, flecainide, propafenone, quinidine, or sotalol can be used to treat paroxysmal atrial fibrillation (AF). Since they all require specialist initiation, they are not offered in this scenario.
- Co-administration of verapamil, diltiazem, or a beta-blocker can be used to reduce symptoms during attacks. Co-administration of these drugs with anti-arrhythmic drugs should only be initiated on specialist advice.
- Digoxin is not effective in paroxysmal AF; it does not reduce the ventricular rate in paroxysmal AF and may be associated with longer attacks.

[Royal College of Physicians of Edinburgh, 1999; Fuster et al, 2001]

A

Deciding on antithrombotic treatment

Which therapy?

- **Confirm diagnosis by ECG.**
- **Treat any precipitating cause** (e.g. thyrotoxicosis or chest infection).
- **Refer, if appropriate, for attempted cardioversion** (see *Refer?* section).
- Control heart rate if appropriate (see scenarios *New presentation of AF* or *Uncontrolled on monotherapy*).
- **Offer treatment with warfarin to someone at moderate or high risk of stroke (if not contraindicated):**
  - Mitral valve disease
  - Previous thromboembolic stroke, transient ischaemic attack (TIA), or other arterial thromboembolism
  - Person aged 65 years or more
  - Person less than 65 years of age with hypertension, diabetes, heart failure, or left ventricular dysfunction
- **Consider echocardiography if none of the above conditions exists,** and treat with warfarin if echocardiography reveals:
  - Left atrial enlargement
  - Left ventricular dysfunction
  - Mitral valve disease
- **Treat with aspirin** if the person fulfils the criteria for anticoagulation but warfarin is contraindicated or declined.
- No treatment is usually recommended for people with 'lone AF' under age 65 years, unless aspirin is given for other indications.
- **Asymptomatic AF:** the decision to start antithrombotic treatment is less clear, but it should still be based on a person's risk of stroke, compared with their risk of bleeding and their personal preference.
- **Remember to reassess the need for warfarin or aspirin regularly;** a person's risk of stroke and the risk of bleeding will change over time.
- **Do not use warfarin or aspirin in someone who:**
  - Has uncorrected major bleeding
  - Has an uncorrected major bleeding disorder (e.g. thrombocytopenia, haemophilias, liver failure, renal failure)
  - Has uncontrolled severe hypertension (e.g. systolic greater than 200 mmHg or diastolic greater than 120 mmHg)
  - Has a potential bleeding disorder (e.g. active peptic ulcer; oesophageal varices; aneurysm; proliferative retinopathy; recent organ biopsy; recent trauma or surgery to head, orbit, spine; recent stroke; confirmed intracranial or intraspinal bleed)

- Is pregnant (owing to the risk of teratogenicity of warfarin)

Practical prescribing points

For further information please see the *Medicines Compendium* (www.medicines.org.uk) or the *British National Formulary* (www.bnf.org).

Other considerations

- **Uncooperative or unreliable person:** concordance and follow-up may be difficult. Consider using aspirin in preference to warfarin.
- **Someone with unstable gait or who falls frequently:** such a person is at increased risk of injury and head trauma. The risks of warfarin or aspirin therapy may outweigh the benefits.
- **Concurrent NSAIDs:** the risk of serious GI complications increases in someone who regularly takes warfarin or low-dose aspirin, and an NSAID. If possible, stop the second NSAID.
- **If a second NSAID must be continued with low-dose aspirin, avoid ibuprofen** — it may reduce the cardiovascular protective effect of low-dose aspirin. Consider using diclofenac if a second NSAID must be used.
- **Asthma:** aspirin can induce bronchospasm in aspirin-hypersensitive individuals, but this is rare.
- **Protein C deficiency:** skin necrosis may occur after initiation of warfarin.

Warfarin loading dose

- A large loading dose is not required if there is no need to achieve anticoagulation rapidly.
- **International normalized ratio (INR) target is 2.5** (range 2–3).
- **An INR of 2.0 can usually be reached by giving warfarin 5 mg for 4–5 days.**
- A lower starting dose is more suitable for elderly people and people at high risk of bleeding.
- **INR monitoring should usually be managed by local anticoagulant clinics.**
- If this is not available, check INR daily until the result has stayed in the therapeutic range for at least 2 consecutive days. Then check INR 2–3 times a week for 1–2 weeks, and then less often, depending on the stability of the results.

Drug interactions with warfarin

- **Where possible, prescribe drugs that do not interact with warfarin.**
- **If an interacting drug will be used for less than 5 days,** then often no dosage change is necessary. A minor dosage reduction or omission of one full warfarin dosage may be prudent with known potentiating drugs (see BNF).
- **If an interacting drug will be used for more than 5 days,** check the INR 1 week after starting therapy and adjust the warfarin dose accordingly. The INR should also be monitored when an interacting drug is stopped.
- **Amiodarone:** reduce the dose of warfarin by one- to two-thirds, and check the INR every week until it is stable (this monitoring period must include the entire amiodarone loading schedule). This interaction persists for a month or more after amiodarone is withdrawn.

Follow-up advice

- **A person on warfarin needs regular monitoring of international normalized ratio (INR).** Ideally this should take place in the setting of an organized anticoagulant clinic.
- **If no clinic is available,** monitor INR daily until the result has stayed in the therapeutic range for at least 2 consecutive days. Then check INR 2–3 times a week fo 1–2 weeks, and then less often, depending on the stability of the results.
- **INR target is 2.5** (range 2–3).
- Aim for a target INR at the lower end of this range for people over age 75 years, because of their increased risk of cerebral haemorrhage.
- **Advise people on warfarin** to check with their pharmacist that any new medicine they are prescribed c buy is OK to take with warfarin.

Should I refer or investigate?

Refer?

- **People who are very symptomatic and in need of urgent rate control** (emergency admission).
- People with acute atrial fibrillation (AF) and severe hypotension, acute heart failure, or unstable angina, wh do not respond promptly to medical management, may require immediate cardioversion.
- **People suitable for cardioversion are those with:**
  - **Recent-onset AF:** the time of onset is not always easy to determine, and there is a case for referring anyone with newly diagnosed AF for at least one attempt at cardioversion. Someone with acute-onset AF should ideally see a specialist within 48 hours in order to decide whether to cardiovert. Success rates for cardioversion diminish the longer the person is in AF, and anticoagulation prior to and after cardioversion i necessary if the person has been in AF for longer than 2 days.
  - **No structural heart disease** (e.g. the person has no mitral valve disease; or the person has good left ventricular function, and an undilated left atrium).
  - Successful treatment of any precipitating cause (e.g. thyrotoxicosis, chest infection).
  - **Young age** (although age should not be an automatic barrier).
- **If there is inadequate control** despite maximal primary care treatment.
- **If further assessment is needed** (e.g. suspected valvular disease, moderate to severe heart failure)
- **Syncopal attacks.**
- **Suspected Wolff–Parkinson–White (WPW) syndrome.**

Investigate?

- **Electrocardiogram to confirm the diagnosis.**
- **Base-line blood tests:** full blood count, electrolytes, creatinine, thyroid function tests (plus coagulation scree and liver function tests if anticoagulation being considered).
- **The routine use of echocardiography continues to be debated.** It may provide useful information on the presence of associated valvular disease and ventricular failure, and a recent consensus statement recommends that it should be part of the optimal assessment of peopl with AF. However, for the majority of people it is unlikely to affect the decision on whether to recommend anticoagulation or not. Local guidelines may be availab regarding the use of this.
- **Consider a chest X-ray** (which can give information on the size of the heart and whether heart failure is present)

'atient information leaflets

he following PILs are available at www.prodigy.nhs.uk

Atrial Fibrillation
Atrial Fibrillation and Warfarin
Blood Test - General
British Heart Foundation
How the Heart Works

hared decision making

Atrial fibrillation (AF) can cause a turbulent flow of blood through the heart. This sometimes causes a small blood clot to form, which may travel in the blood vessels to the brain and cause a stroke.

The risk of stroke with AF is higher if you are over 65, or if you have certain other heart problems.

Warfarin is advised if your risk of stroke is high. If you take warfarin, you are less likely to form blood clots. For every 1000 people with AF who take warfarin, about 30 strokes per year will be prevented.

There is a slight risk with treatment. For every 1000 people taking warfarin, about 3 will have a serious bleeding complication.

You will need regular blood tests to check that the blood is 'thinned' by just the right amount. This reduces the risk of bleeding complications.

Aspirin is an alternative, but is not as effective as warfarin. It is an option if you have other conditions where warfarin is not advised.

)rug rationale

)rugs not included

Oral anticoagulants other than warfarin: nicoumalone and phenindione are rarely used in the UK.

Antiplatelet agents other than aspirin: the role of clopidogrel, dipyridamole, and ticlopidine is not certain at the present time. An ongoing Cochrane systematic review will address this issue [Segal, 2000].

Enteric-coated and modified-release preparations of aspirin are not offered, as they are more expensive than soluble aspirin. It was hoped that these formulations would reduce the toxicity of aspirin, but this has not been shown to be the case [DTB, 1997].

)rugs included

Warfarin reduces the risk of stroke in someone with atrial fibrillation (AF) by nearly two-thirds. It is the antithrombotic of choice where treatment is required, provided that there are no contraindications to its use.

- **We recommend that people be given a supply of 1-mg tablets on initiation of warfarin,** to reduce possible confusion about changing doses. Once a person has been *stabilized* on warfarin, a combination of tablet strengths may be used to achieve the required dose with the least number of tablets.

Aspirin reduces the risk of stroke in people with atrial fibrillation by about a fifth. Aspirin should be used where antithrombotic treatment is required but warfarin is contraindicated or declined.

- Recommended dosages of aspirin range from 75 to 300 mg daily. Local guidelines on aspirin dosage should be followed where available.
- In the absence of local guidelines, we recommend a dose of 75 mg per day. This is a widely used dose in the UK, and tends to cause less dyspepsia and other gastrointestinal adverse effects than a dose of 300 mg per day.

[Royal College of Physicians of Edinburgh, 1999; SIGN, 1999; Benavente et al, 2000; Fuster et al, 2001]

Prescriptions

Start warfarin

Warfarin 1mg tablets

- Age from 16 years onwards
- Warfarin 1mg tablets. Take as directed in your yellow anticoagulant booklet; supply 56 tablets; NHS Cost £2.76.

Alternative: start aspirin

Aspirin 75mg dispersible once a day

- Age from 16 years onwards
- Aspirin 75mg dispersible tabs. Take one tablet once a day; supply 28 tablets; NHS Cost £0.37; OTC Cost £1.13.

Managing rate-control drugs

Which therapy

- **Rate-control treatment is given to relieve symptoms.**
- **Aim for a ventricular rate of less than 90/minute at rest and 180/minute on exercise.**
- **A beta-blocker or verapamil is recommended as a first-line treatment,** particularly if there is coexisting hypertension or angina.
- **Digoxin is preferred if the person has coexisting heart failure.** However, it is less effective than other agents at controlling heart rate during exercise. Beta-blockers may also be used in heart failure, but the starting doses are low, and can be increased only slowly.
- **Step up the dose until the ventricular rate is controlled,** or the maximum tolerated dose is reached.
- **If rate control is not achieved at maximal tolerated dose of monotherapy,** then consider combining digoxin with a beta-blocker or verapamil, or consider referral.
  - **Do not use verapamil with a beta-blocker** (it may precipitate heart failure).
  - **If verapamil is added to digoxin,** reduce the digoxin dose by 30–50%, and then adjust according to plasma levels. Maximal effect on digoxin levels occurs within 14 days.
- **Refer, if appropriate, for attempted cardioversion** (see *Refer?* section).
- **Remember to reassess the need for warfarin and aspirin regularly;** a person's risk of stroke and their risk of bleeding will change over time. See *Deciding antithrombotic treatment* scenario.

Practical prescribing points

For further information please see the *Medicines Compendium* (www.medicines.org.uk) or the *British National Formulary* (www.bnf.org).

Managing adverse effects

Beta-blockers

- **Bronchospasm:** withdraw beta-blocker therapy.
- **Bradycardia:** reduce dose.
- **Sleep disturbance or nightmares:** less likely with atenolol than with metoprolol or propranolol.
- **Fatigue or sexual dysfunction:** less likely with atenolol or metoprolol than with propranolol.
- **Cold extremities:** assess objective signs of peripheral vascular disease.

Verapamil

- **Bradycardia:** reduce dose.
- **Constipation:** give advice on high-fibre diet with adequate fluid intake.
- **Dizziness or facial flushing:** generally become less severe after a few days.
- **Ankle oedema:** often persistent. Do not prescribe diuretics (they only partially reduce ankle oedema caused by calcium-channel blockers).
- **Postural hypotension:** reduce dose if possible.

Digoxin

- Toxicity may be precipitated by:
  - **Metabolic disturbances** (e.g. hypokalaemia, hypercalcaemia, hypoxia and acidosis, renal impairment, dehydration, and hypothyroidism)
  - **Drugs that increase digoxin levels** (e.g. verapamil, amiodarone, and quinidine)
- **Suspect toxicity if** there is anorexia, nausea, vomiting, diarrhoea, mental confusion, or blurred vision.
- **Toxicity may cause a variety of arrhythmias,** and apparent return of sinus rhythm may be due to digoxin toxicity. At toxic levels, digoxin may cause or worsen heart failure.
- **Digoxin levels do not need to be routinely monitored,** because ventricular rate is usually a good guide to therapeutic effect.
- **Only check levels to assess possible toxicity** or adherence to treatment. Plasma levels must be measured at least 6 hours after the last dosage.

Follow-up advice

- Review within 1–2 weeks of dose titration or management of adverse effects, depending on severity of symptoms and outstanding investigations.

Digoxin

- Check serum electrolytes and creatinine annually if taking digoxin.
- **Digoxin levels do not need to be routinely monitored,** because ventricular rate is usually a good guide to therapeutic effect.
- **Only check digoxin levels to assess possible toxicity** or adherence to treatment. Plasma levels must be measured at least 6 hours after the last dosage.
- **Levels less than 1.5 micrograms/litre,** in the absence of hypokalaemia, indicate that digoxin toxicity is unlikely.
- **Levels greater than 3.0 micrograms/litre** indicate that toxicity is likely.
- **With levels between 1.5 and 3.0 micrograms/litre,** digoxin toxicity should be considered a possibility.

Should I refer or investigate?

Refer?

- **People who are very symptomatic and in need of urgent rate control** (emergency admission).
- People with acute atrial fibrillation (AF) and severe hypotension, acute heart failure, or unstable angina, who do not respond promptly to medical management, may require immediate cardioversion.
- **People suitable for cardioversion include those with:**
  - **Recent-onset AF:** the time of onset is not always easy to determine, and there is a case for referring anyone with newly diagnosed AF for at least one attempt at cardioversion. Someone with acute onset AF should ideally see a specialist within 48 hours in order to decide whether to cardiovert. Success rates for cardioversion diminish the longer the person is in AF, and anticoagulation prior to and after cardioversion is necessary if the person has been in AF for longer than 2 days.
  - **No structural heart disease** (e.g. the person has no mitral valve disease; or the person has good left ventricular function, and an undilated left atrium).
  - Successful treatment of any precipitating cause (e.g. thyrotoxicosis, chest infection).
  - **Young age** (although age should not be an automatic barrier).
- **If there is inadequate control** despite maximal primary care treatment.
- **If further assessment is needed** (e.g. suspected valvular disease, moderate to severe heart failure).
- **Syncopal attacks.**
- **Suspected Wolff–Parkinson–White (WPW) syndrome.**

Investigate?

- **Electrocardiogram to confirm the diagnosis.**
- **Base-line blood tests:** full blood count, electrolytes, creatinine, thyroid function tests (plus coagulation screen and liver function tests if anticoagulation is being considered).
- **The routine use of echocardiography continues to be debated.** It may provide useful information on the presence of associated valvular disease and ventricular failure, and a recent consensus statement recommends that it should be part of the optimal assessment of people with AF. However, for most people it is unlikely to affect the decision on whether to recommend anticoagulation or not. Local guidelines may be available regarding the use of this.
- **Consider a chest X-ray** (which can give information on the size of the heart and whether heart failure is present).

Patient information leaflets

The following PILs are available at www.prodigy.nhs.uk

- Atrial Fibrillation
- Atrial Fibrillation and Warfarin
- Blood Test - General
- British Heart Foundation
- How the Heart Works

Shared decision making

- Treatment of atrial fibrillation (AF) aims to reduce your heart rate to 90 beats per minute or less when you are resting.
- Medicines commonly used to control the heart rate include:
  - **Beta-blockers** such as atenolol, metoprolol, and propranolol
  - **Verapamil**
  - **Digoxin**
- **The one chosen may depend on whether you have other conditions** such as some heart conditions, peripheral vascular disease, diabetes, asthma, or other diseases of the airways.
- **You may need a combination of medicines** if one alone does not control your heart rate.
- **Side effects are not common.** Tell your doctor if they occur. They include:
  - **Beta-blockers:** cool hands and feet, poor sleep, tiredness, impotence
  - **Verapamil:** constipation
  - **Digoxin:** feeling sick, vomiting, diarrhoea, mental confusion, blurred vision

Drug rationale

Maintenance doses/dose adjustments for atenolol, metoprolol, propranolol, verapamil, and digoxin (i.e. those rate-control drugs that have initiation prescriptions offered in the scenario *New presentation of atrial fibrillation*) are included.

Prescriptions

Atenolol

Atenolol 25mg once a day
- Age from 16 years onwards
- Atenolol 25mg tablets. Take one tablet once a day; supply 28 tablets; NHS Cost £2.07.

Atenolol 50mg once a day
- Age from 16 years onwards
- Atenolol 50mg tablets. Take one tablet once a day; supply 28 tablets; NHS Cost £0.85.

Atenolol 100mg once a day
- Age from 16 years onwards
- Atenolol 100mg tablets. Take one tablet once a day; supply 28 tablets; NHS Cost £0.98.

Atenolol 50mg twice a day
- Age from 16 years onwards
- Atenolol 50mg tablets. Take one tablet twice a day; supply 56 tablets; NHS Cost £1.70.

Metoprolol

Metoprolol 50mg twice a day
- Age from 16 years onwards
- Metoprolol 50mg tablets. Take one tablet twice a day; supply 56 tablets; NHS Cost £2.35.

Metoprolol 50mg three times a day
- Age from 16 years onwards
- Metoprolol 50mg tablets. Take one tablet three times a day; supply 84 tablets; NHS Cost £3.52.

Metoprolol 100mg twice a day
- Age from 16 years onwards
- Metoprolol 100mg tablets. Take one tablet twice a day; supply 84 tablets; NHS Cost £3.52.

Metoprolol 100mg three times a day
- Age from 16 years onwards
- Metoprolol 100mg tablets. Take one tablet three times a day; supply 84 tablets; NHS Cost £5.84.

Propranolol

Propranolol 10mg three times a day
- Age from 16 years onwards
- Propranolol 10mg tablets. Take one tablet three times a day; supply 84 tablets; NHS Cost £1.77.

Propranolol 40mg three times a day
- Age from 16 years onwards
- Propranolol 40mg tablets. Take one tablet three times a day; supply 84 tablets; NHS Cost £1.95.

Propranolol 80mg three times a day
- Age from 16 years onwards
- Propranolol 80mg tablets. Take one tablet three times a day; supply 84 tablets; NHS Cost £1.44.

Verapamil

Verapamil 40mg three times a day
- Age from 16 years onwards
- Verapamil 40mg tablets. Take one tablet three times a day; supply 84 tablets; NHS Cost £1.61.

Verapamil 80mg three times a day
- Age from 16 years onwards
- Verapamil 80mg tablets. Take one tablet three times a day; supply 84 tablets; NHS Cost £2.10.

Verapamil 120mg three times a day
- Age from 16 years onwards
- Verapamil 120mg tablets. Take one tablet three times a day; supply 84 tablets; NHS Cost £3.93.

Digoxin

Digoxin 62.5mcg once a day
- Age from 16 years onwards
- Digoxin 62.5microgram tablets. Take one tablet once a day; supply 28 tablets; NHS Cost £0.77.

Digoxin 125micrograms once a day
- Age from 16 years onwards
- Digoxin 125microgram tablets. Take one tablet once a day; supply 28 tablets; NHS Cost £0.59.

Digoxin 250micrograms once a day
- Age from 16 years onwards
- Digoxin 250microgram tablets. Take one tablet once a day; supply 28 tablets; NHS Cost £0.59.

Digoxin 187.5 micrograms once a day
- Age from 16 years onwards
- Digoxin 62.5microgram tablets. Take three tablets once a day; supply 84 tablets; NHS Cost £2.31.

Digoxin 375micrograms once a day
- Age from 16 years onwards
- Digoxin 125microgram tablets. Take three tablets once a day; supply 84 tablets; NHS Cost £1.77.

Digoxin 500micrograms once a day
- Age from 16 years onwards
- Digoxin 250microgram tablets. Take two tablets once a day; supply 56 tablets; NHS Cost £1.18.

Managing antithrombotic therapy

Which therapy

- **Antithrombotic therapy is given to reduce the risk of stroke.**
- **Remember to reassess the need for warfarin or aspirin regularly;** a person's risk of stroke and the risk of bleeding will change over time. See *Deciding antithrombotic treatment* scenario.
- **People on warfarin need regular monitoring** of international normalized ratio (INR). (See *Prescribing points* below.)
- **INR target is 2.5** (range 2–3).
- Aim for a target INR at the lower end of this range for people over age 75 years, because of their increased risk of cerebral haemorrhage.
- **Advise people on warfarin** to check with their pharmacist that any new medicine they are prescribed or buy is OK to take with warfarin.
- **The risk of bleeding increases considerably above an INR of 4.**
- Refer, if appropriate, for attempted cardioversion (see *Refer?* section).
- Control heart rate if appropriate (see *New presentation of AF* or *Uncontrolled on monotherapy* scenario).

Practical prescribing points

For further information please see the *Medicines Compendium* (www.medicines.org.uk) or the *British National Formulary* (www.bnf.org).

A

Monitoring warfarin

- **INR monitoring should usually be managed by local anticoagulant clinics.**
- **If this is not available, check INR daily** until the result has stayed in the therapeutic range for at least 2 consecutive days. Then check INR 2–3 times a week for 1–2 weeks, and then less often, depending on the stability of the results.

Drug interactions with warfarin

- Where possible, prescribe drugs that do not interact with warfarin.
- **If an interacting drug will be used for less than 5 days,** then often no dosage change is necessary. A minor dosage reduction or omission of one full warfarin dosage may be prudent with known potentiating drugs (see BNF).
- **If an interacting drug will be used for more than 5 days,** check the INR 1 week after starting therapy and adjust the warfarin dose accordingly. The INR should also be monitored when an interacting drug is stopped.
- **Amiodarone:** reduce the dose of warfarin by one- to two-thirds, and check the INR every week until it is stable (this monitoring period must include the entire amiodarone loading schedule). This interaction persists for a month or more after amiodarone is withdrawn.

Managing adverse effects

Warfarin

The major adverse effect of warfarin is bleeding. Strategies for reversing the effect of warfarin (adapted from SIGN, 1999) are outlined in Table 1.

Aspirin

- **Dyspepsia is common with aspirin.** Persistent dyspepsia can be managed with acid-suppressing medication, see PRODIGY guidance on *Dyspepsia — symptoms (uninvestigated by endoscopy)* for further information.
- **Concurrent nonsteroidal anti-inflammatory drugs (NSAIDs):** the risk of serious gastrointestinal complications doubles in people who regularly take low-dose aspirin and another NSAID. If possible, stop the second NSAID.
- **If a second NSAID must be continued, avoid ibuprofen** — it may reduce the cardiovascular protective effect of low-dose aspirin. Consider using diclofenac if a second NSAID must be used.

Follow-up advice

- **A person on warfarin needs regular monitoring** of international normalized ratio (INR). Ideally this should take place in the setting of an organized anticoagulant clinic.
- **If no clinic is available,** monitor INR daily until the result has stayed in the therapeutic range for at least 2 consecutive days. Then check INR 2–3 times a week for 1–2 weeks, and then less often, depending on the stability of the results.
- **INR target is 2.5** (range 2–3).
- Aim for a target INR at the lower end of this range for people over age 75 years, due to their increased risk of cerebral haemorrhage.
- **The risk of bleeding increases considerably above an INR of 4.**
- **Advise people on warfarin** to check with their pharmacist that any new medicine they are prescribed or buy is OK to take with warfarin.

Table 1: Strategies for reversing the effect of warfarin.

Life threatening bleeding (e.g. intracranial or major gastrointestinal bleed)
Admit urgently
Less severe bleeding (e.g. haematuria, epistaxis)
Stop warfarin for 1–2 days
Give vitamin K: 0.5–2 mg intravenously, or 5–10 mg orally
High INR but no bleeding
Stop warfarin, monitor INR, restart warfarin when INR <5.0
Consider giving vitamin K (0.5 mg intravenously or 5 mg orally) if: INR >8.0 Other risk factors for bleeding are present

Should I refer or investigate?

Refer?

- **People who are very symptomatic and in need of urgent rate control** (emergency admission).
- **People with acute atrial fibrillation (AF) and severe hypotension, acute heart failure, or unstable angina,** who do not respond promptly to medical management, may require immediate cardioversion.
- **People suitable for cardioversion include those with:**
  - **Recent-onset AF:** the time of onset is not always easy to determine, and there is a case for referring anyone with newly diagnosed AF for at least one attempt at cardioversion. Someone with acute onset AF should ideally see a specialist within 48 hours in order to decide whether to cardiovert (success rates for cardioversion reduce the longer the person is in AF, and anticoagulation prior to and after cardioversion is necessary if the person has been in AF for longer than 2 days).
  - **No structural heart disease** (e.g. the person has no mitral valve disease; or the person has good left ventricular function, and an undilated left atrium).
  - **Successful treatment of any precipitating cause** (e.g. thyrotoxicosis, chest infection).
  - **Young age** (although age should not be an automatic barrier).
- **If there is inadequate control** despite maximal primary care treatment.
- **If further assessment is needed** (e.g. suspected valvular disease, moderate to severe heart failure).
- **Syncopal attacks.**
- **Suspected Wolff–Parkinson–White (WPW) syndrome.**

Investigate?

- **Electrocardiogram to confirm the diagnosis.**
- **Base-line blood tests:** full blood count, electrolytes, creatinine, thyroid function tests (plus coagulation screen and liver function tests if anticoagulation being considered).
- **The routine use of echocardiography continues to be debated.** It may provide useful information on the presence of associated valvular disease and ventricular failure, and a recent consensus statement recommends that it should be part of the optimal assessment of people with AF. However, for the majority of people it is unlikely to affect the decision on whether to recommend anticoagulation or not. Local guidelines may be available regarding the use of this.
- **Consider a chest X-ray** (which can give information on the size of the heart and whether heart failure is present)

A

Patient information leaflets

The following PILs are available at www.prodigy.nhs.uk
- Atrial Fibrillation
- Atrial Fibrillation and Warfarin
- Blood Test - Clotting Tests
- Blood Test - General
- British Heart Foundation
- How the Heart Works

Shared decision making

Atrial fibrillation (AF) can cause a turbulent flow of blood through the heart. This sometimes causes a small blood clot to form, which may travel in the blood vessels to the brain and cause a stroke.
The risk of stroke with AF is higher if you are over 65, or if you have certain other heart problems.
Warfarin is advised if your risk of stroke is high. If you take warfarin, you are less likely to form blood clots. For every 1000 people with AF who take warfarin, about 30 strokes per year will be prevented.
There is a slight risk with treatment. For every 1000 people taking warfarin, about 3 will have a serious bleeding complication.
You will need regular blood tests to check that the blood is 'thinned' by just the right amount. This reduces the risk of bleeding complications.
Aspirin is an alternative, but is not as effective as warfarin. It is an option if you have other conditions where warfarin is not advised.

Drug rationale

A variety of maintenance doses/dose adjustments warfarin are offered.
Aspirin 75 mg is included.

Prescriptions

Warfarin

Warfarin 1mg tablets
- Age from 16 years onwards
- Warfarin 1mg tablets. Take as directed in your yellow anticoagulant booklet; supply 56 tablets; NHS Cost £2.76.

Warfarin 3mg tablets
- Age from 16 years onwards
- Warfarin 3mg tablets. Take as directed in your yellow anticoagulant booklet; supply 56 tablets; NHS Cost £3.12.

Warfarin 5mg tablets
- Age from 16 years onwards
- Warfarin 5mg tablets. Take as directed in your yellow anticoagulant booklet; supply 28 tablets; NHS Cost £1.70.

Warfarin 1mg tablets + 3mg tablets
- Age from 16 years onwards
- Warfarin 1mg tablets. Take as directed in your yellow anticoagulant booklet; supply 28 tablets; NHS Cost £1.38.
- Warfarin 3mg tablets. Take as directed in your yellow anticoagulant booklet; supply 56 tablets; NHS Cost £3.12.

Warfarin 1mg tablets + 5mg tablets
- Age from 16 years onwards
- Warfarin 1mg tablets. Take as directed in your yellow anticoagulant booklet; supply 28 tablets; NHS Cost £1.38.
- Warfarin 5mg tablets. Take as directed in your yellow anticoagulant booklet; supply 28 tablets; NHS Cost £1.70.

Warfarin 3mg tablets + 5mg tablets
- Age from 16 years onwards
- Warfarin 3mg tablets. Take as directed in your yellow anticoagulant booklet; supply 28 tablets; NHS Cost £1.56.
- Warfarin 5mg tablets. Take as directed in your yellow anticoagulant booklet; supply 28 tablets; NHS Cost £1.70.

Warfarin 1mg tablets + 3mg tablets + 5mg tablets
- Age from 16 years onwards
- Warfarin 1mg tablets. Take as directed in your yellow anticoagulant booklet; supply 28 tablets; NHS Cost £1.38.
- Warfarin 3mg tablets. Take as directed in your yellow anticoagulant booklet; supply 28 tablets; NHS Cost £1.56.
- Warfarin 5mg tablets. Take as directed in your yellow anticoagulant booklet; supply 28 tablets; NHS Cost £1.70.

Aspirin

Aspirin 75mg dispersible once a day
- Age from 16 years onwards
- Aspirin 75mg dispersible tabs. Take one tablet once a day; supply 28 tablets; NHS Cost £0.37; OTC Cost £1.13.

Rate uncontrolled on monotherapy

Which therapy

- **Maximum tolerated doses of monotherapy should be tried before adding another drug.**
- **If rate control is still not achieved,** then consider combining digoxin with a beta-blocker or verapamil, or consider referral.
- **Do not use verapamil with a beta-blocker** (it may precipitate heart failure).
- **If verapamil is added to digoxin,** reduce the digoxin dose by 30–50%, and then adjust according to plasma levels. Maximal effect on digoxin levels occurs within 14 days.
- **Aim for a ventricular rate of less than 90/minute at rest and 180/minute on exercise.**
- **Remember to reassess the need for warfarin or aspirin regularly;** a person's risk of stroke and the risk of bleeding will change over time. See *Deciding antithrombotic treatment* scenario.

Factors affecting choice of treatment

- **Asthma or a history of bronchospasm:** do not use beta-blockers (CSM warning).
- **Severe peripheral vascular disease:** avoid beta-blockers.
- **Diabetes:** if using a beta-blocker, use atenolol or metoprolol (cardioselective). Avoid beta-blockers in someone who experiences frequent hypoglycaemia.
- **Heart failure:** use digoxin. Beta-blockers may be used in heart failure, but the licensed drugs and doses are different for AF. (See PRODIGY guidance on *Heart Failure.*) Do not use verapamil.

Practical prescribing points

For further information please see the *Medicines Compendium* (www.medicines.org.uk) or the *British National Formulary* (www.bnf.org).

Beta-blockers

- **There is no significant increased risk of depressive symptoms** while on beta-blockers, and only a very small increase in the risk of fatigue or sexual dysfunction.

Verapamil

- **Constipation is common.** Give advice on high-fibre diet with adequate fluid intake.

Digoxin

- **Digoxin levels do not need to be routinely monitored,** because ventricular rate is usually a good guide to therapeutic effect.
- **A loading dosage** of 500 micrograms daily for 3 days is suggested.
- **The maintenance dosage** usually ranges from 125 to 250 micrograms daily.
- **Lower loading and maintenance dosages** should be used in the elderly or in renal impairment (e.g. use 250 micrograms daily for 3 days, followed by a maintenance dose of 62.5 to 125 micrograms daily).

Follow-up advice

- **Review within 1–2 weeks,** depending on severity of symptoms and outstanding investigations.

Digoxin

- **Check serum electrolytes and creatinine annually** if taking digoxin.
- **Digoxin levels do not need to be routinely monitored,** because ventricular rate is usually a good guide to therapeutic effect.
- **Only check digoxin levels to assess possible toxicity** or adherence to treatment. Plasma levels must be measured at least 6 hours after the last dosage.
- **Levels less than 1.5 micrograms/litre,** in the absence of hypokalaemia, indicate that digoxin toxicity is unlikely.
- **Levels greater than 3.0 micrograms/litre indicate that toxicity is likely.**
- **With levels between 1.5 and 3.0 micrograms/litre,** digoxin toxicity should be considered a possibility.

Should I refer or investigate?

Refer?

- **People who are very symptomatic and in need of urgent rate control** (emergency admission).
- People with acute atrial fibrillation (AF) and severe hypotension, acute heart failure, or unstable angina, who do not respond promptly to medical management, may require immediate cardioversion.
- **People suitable for cardioversion include those with:**
  - **Recent-onset AF:** the time of onset is not always easy to determine, and there is a case for referring anyone with newly diagnosed AF for at least one attempt at cardioversion. Someone with acute onset AF should ideally see a specialist within 48 hours in order to decide whether to cardiovert. Success rates for cardioversion diminish the longer the person is in AF, and anticoagulation prior to and after cardioversion is necessary if the person has been in AF for longer than 2 days).
  - **No structural heart disease** (e.g. the person has no mitral valve disease, or the person has good left ventricular function, and an undilated left atrium).
  - **Successful treatment of any precipitating cause** (e.g. thyrotoxicosis, chest infection).
  - **Young age** (although age should not be an automatic barrier).
- **If there is inadequate control** despite maximal primary care treatment.
- **If further assessment is needed** (e.g. suspected valvular disease, moderate to severe heart failure).
- **Syncopal attacks.**
- **Suspected Wolff–Parkinson–White (WPW) syndrome.**

Investigate?

- **Electrocardiogram to confirm the diagnosis.**
- **Base-line blood tests:** full blood count, electrolytes, creatinine, thyroid function tests (plus coagulation scre and liver function tests if anticoagulation is being considered).
- **The routine use of echocardiography continues to be debated.** It may provide useful information on the presence of associated valvular disease and ventricular failure, and a recent consensus statement recommends that it should be part of the optimal assessment of peop with AF. However, for most people it is unlikely to affe the decision on whether to recommend anticoagulation or not. Local guidelines may be available regarding the use of this.
- **Consider a chest X-ray** (which can give information on the size of the heart and whether heart failure is present

Patient information leaflets

The following PILs are available at www.prodigy.nhs.uk

- Atrial Fibrillation
- Atrial Fibrillation and Warfarin
- Blood Test - General
- British Heart Foundation
- How the Heart Works

Shared decision making

- **Treatment of atrial fibrillation (AF)** aims to reduce your heart rate to 90 beats per minute or less when you are resting.
- Medicines commonly used to control the heart rate include:
  - **Beta-blockers** such as atenolol, metoprolol, and propranolol
  - **Verapamil**
  - **Digoxin**
- **If your heart rate is not well controlled with one medicine, another one can be added.** This 'combination therapy' is often used.
- **Some medicines suit some people better than others.** So, different people end up with different combinations.
- If you develop any side effects, don't suddenly stop the treatment, but see your doctor. Some side-effects from each group include the following:
  - **Beta-blockers:** cool hands and feet, bad dreams, tiredness (and rarely, impotence)
  - **Verapamil:** constipation
  - **Digoxin:** feeling sick, vomiting, diarrhoea, mental confusion, blurred vision

Drug rationale

Drugs not included

- **Amiodarone** requires specialist initiation. It may be useful for rate control in refractory cases, but has a high incidence of adverse effects.
- **Digitoxin** is not commonly used in the UK and is more expensive than digoxin. It may be considered if there is

an absolute requirement for a cardiac glycoside and the person has severe renal impairment.

Dihydropyridine calcium-channel blockers (e.g. nifedipine) are not rate-limiting, and therefore have no place in the treatment of atrial fibrillation (AF).

Diltiazem is not licensed for the treatment of arrhythmias. In addition, it is difficult to recommend dosing (trials have been small and dosing has varied enormously).

Other anti-arrhythmic drugs require specialist initiation, and are used for maintenance of sinus rhythm after cardioversion, or pharmacological cardioversion, rather than purely for ventricular rate control.

Sotalol requires specialist initiation and is only licensed for paroxysmal AF.

Drugs included

Beta-blockers reduce the ventricular rate at rest and during exercise. Beta-blockers should be considered as first-line therapy, especially in people with coexisting hypertension or angina [Royal College of Physicians of Edinburgh, 1999]. **Atenolol, metoprolol, and propranolol** are included because they are licensed for the treatment of arrhythmias and are less expensive than other beta-blockers.

Digoxin reduces the ventricular rate at rest, but is less effective at controlling the heart rate during exercise. Digoxin is the preferred choice if the person has coexisting heart failure. It can be used in combination with a beta-blocker or a rate-limiting calcium-channel blocker if rate control is not achieved with adequate monotherapy [Royal College of Physicians of Edinburgh, 1999].

Verapamil is licensed for use in arrhythmias. In AF, verapamil reduces the ventricular rate at rest and during exercise. Verapamil should also be considered as first-line therapy, especially in someone with coexisting hypertension or angina [Royal College of Physicians of Edinburgh, 1999]. Standard doses of verapamil are included, as modified-release verapamil is not licensed for the treatment of arrhythmias.

Prescriptions

1st line: start beta-blocker (unless contraindicated)

Atenolol 50mg once a day
- Age from 16 years onwards
- Atenolol 50mg tablets. Take one tablet once a day; supply 28 tablets; NHS Cost £0.85.

Atenolol 100mg once a day
- Age from 16 years onwards
- Atenolol 100mg tablets. Take one tablet once a day; supply 28 tablets; NHS Cost £0.98.

Metoprolol 50mg twice a day
- Age from 16 years onwards
- Metoprolol 50mg tablets. Take one tablet twice a day; supply 56 tablets; NHS Cost £2.35.

Metoprolol 50mg three times a day
- Age from 16 years onwards
- Metoprolol 50mg tablets. Take one tablet three times a day; supply 84 tablets; NHS Cost £3.52.

Propranolol 10mg three times a day
- Age from 16 years onwards
- Propranolol 10mg tablets. Take one tablet three times a day; supply 84 tablets; NHS Cost £1.77.

Propranolol 40mg three times a day
- Age from 16 years onwards
- Propranolol 40mg tablets. Take one tablet three times a day; supply 84 tablets; NHS Cost £1.95.

Alternative: start verapamil (unless contraindicated)

Verapamil 40mg three times a day
- Age from 16 years onwards
- Verapamil 40mg tablets. Take one tablet three times a day; supply 84 tablets; NHS Cost £1.61.

Verapamil 80mg three times a day
- Age from 16 years onwards
- Verapamil 80mg tablets. Take one tablet three times a day; supply 84 tablets; NHS Cost £3.93.

Heart failure: start digoxin

Digoxin 500mcg daily for 3 days, then 250mcg daily
- Age from 16 years onwards
- Digoxin 250microgram tablets. Take two tablets once a day for 3 days, then take one tablet once a day; supply 28 tablets; NHS Cost £0.59.

Digoxin 500mcg daily for 3 days, then 125mcg daily
- Age from 16 years onwards
- Digoxin 125microgram tablets. Take four tablets once a day for 3 days, then take one tablet once a day; supply 28 tablets; NHS Cost £0.59.

Digoxin 250mcg daily for 3 days, then 125mcg daily
- Age from 16 years onwards
- Digoxin 125microgram tablets. Take two tablets once a day for 3 days, then take one tablet once a day; supply 28 tablets; NHS Cost £0.59.

Digoxin 250mcg daily for 3 days, then 62.5mcg daily
- Age from 16 years onwards
- Digoxin 62.5microgram tablets. Take four tablets once a day for 3 days, then take one tablet once a day; supply 28 tablets; NHS Cost £0.77.

Rate uncontrolled on dual therapy

Which therapy

- **Maximum tolerated doses of the two rate-control medications should be tried** (for prescriptions, see the *Managing rate-control drugs* scenario).
- **Someone whose ventricular rate is still uncontrolled on maximal medical therapy should be referred urgently to a cardiologist.**

Practical prescribing points

For further information please see the *Medicines Compendium* (www.medicines.org.uk) or the *British National Formulary* (www.bnf.org).

Should I refer or investigate?

Refer?

- **people who are very symptomatic and in need of urgent rate control** (emergency admission).
- **People with acute atrial fibrillation (AF) and severe hypotension, acute heart failure, or unstable anginas, who do not respond promptly to medical management, may require immediate cardioversion.**
- **People suitable for cardioversion include those with:**
  - **Recent-onset AF:** the time of onset is not always easy to determine, and there is a case for referring anyone with newly diagnosed AF for at least one attempt at cardioversion. Someone with acute onset AF should ideally see a specialist within 48 hours in order to decide whether to cardiovert. Success rates for cardioversion diminish the longer the person is in AF,

A

and anticoagulation prior to and after cardioversion is necessary if the person has been in AF for longer than 2 days).
  - **No structural heart disease** (e.g. the person has no mitral valve disease; or the person has good left ventricular function, and an undilated left atrium).
  - **Successful treatment of any precipitating cause** (e.g. thyrotoxicosis, chest infection).
  - **Young age** (although age should not be an automatic barrier).
- **If there is inadequate control** despite maximal primary care treatment.
- **If further assessment is needed** (e.g. suspected valvular disease, moderate to severe heart failure).
- **Syncopal attacks.**
- **Suspected Wolff–Parkinson–White (WPW) syndrome.**

Patient information leaflets

The following PILs are available at www.prodigy.nhs.uk

- Atrial Fibrillation
- Atrial Fibrillation and Warfarin
- Blood Test - General
- British Heart Foundation
- How the Heart Works

Shared decision making

- Some people still have a fast heart rate with atrial fibrillation (AF), despite taking full dose medication.
- You may need further investigation by a heart specialist.
- **Cardioversion** may be an option. This means reverting the erratic heart beat back to a normal regular rhythm. It is done either by using an 'electric shock', or by taking certain medicines.
- Cardioversion is not advisable in all cases. It is most commonly tried in certain situations which include:
  - If you have developed AF recently. (Cardioversion is less likely to work the longer you have AF.)
  - If you have an otherwise normal heart.
  - If your AF was caused by a non-heart disease which is now treated. For example, an overactive thyroid, chest infection.
  - If your AF is not well controlled by medication.

Drug rationale

- There are no prescriptions offered in this scenario.

Extended Information

Background information

- What is it? p.180
- What causes atrial fibrillation? p.180
- How common is it? p.180
- How do I know my patient has it? p.180
- What else might it be? p.180
- Complications and prognosis p.180

What is it?

- **Atrial fibrillation (AF) is an arrhythmia in which electrical activity in the atria is disorganized.** The atrioventricular (AV) node receives more electrical impulses than it can conduct, and most are blocked, resulting in an irregular ventricular rhythm. The ventricular rate can vary from 50 to 200 per minute, depending on the degree of AV conduction.
- **Atrial fibrillation is classified according to the pattern of episodes:**
  - **Paroxysmal AF** is intermittent and recurrent, but terminates spontaneously.
  - **Persistent AF** requires cardioversion to return to sinus rhythm.
  - **Permanent AF** cannot be terminated by cardioversion. It is also the term used for long-standing AF (present for more than one year) in which cardioversion has not been attempted.

[Fuster et al, 2001; Peters et al, 2002]

What causes atrial fibrillation?

- **Hypertension, ischaemic heart disease, heart failure, cardiomyopathy, and mitral valve disease** underlie many cases of permanent atrial fibrillation (AF).
- **Prior myocardial infarction** increases the risk of AF by 40% in men, but not in women.
- **Hypertension** is responsible for more cases of AF (14%) than any other risk factor is, because of its high prevalence within the population.
- **Alcohol excess, pulmonary embolism, and hyperthyroidism** can also precipitate AF. It may also occur with acute systemic infection, hypoxia, and post-cardiac surgery.
- **Rheumatic heart disease** is now an uncommon cause in developed countries.
- **About 15% of patients have 'lone AF'** — a structurally normal heart and no significant comorbid disease.

[Fuster et al, 2001; Peters et al, 2002]

How common is it?

- Atrial fibrillation (AF) is the commonest sustained cardiac arrhythmia.
- The incidence of permanent AF in the UK has been estimated to be 1.7 per 1000 person-years. In people older than 60 years, it was 3 per 1000 person-years.
- About 1 in 20 people aged over 65 years have AF (i.e. about 5%).
- The prevalence increases with age: among those aged 75 years and older, the prevalence in men is 10% and in women is 5.6%.
- Paroxysmal AF accounts for 35–66% of all cases of AF, with prevalence peaking at age 50–69 years.
- AF is found in 15% of all stroke patients and in 2–8% of people with transient ischaemic attack.

[Sudlow et al, 1998b; Royal College of Physicians of Edinburgh, 1999; Bandolier, 2002; Peters et al, 2002]

How do I know my patient has it?

- The person may be asymptomatic, or may complain of palpitations, chest pain, breathlessness, or giddiness.
- **The pulse is irregular** and can range from 50 to 200 beats per minute.
- **The diagnosis is confirmed by electrocardiography,** which shows no P waves, a chaotic baseline, and an irregular ventricular rate. The ventricular complexes look normal unless there is a ventricular conduction defect.

What else might it be?

- An irregular pulse may be due to multiple atrial or ventricular ectopic beats, or variable atrioventricular block.

Complications and prognosis

Complications

- **Cardiac performance can be impaired** by the loss of synchronized atrial contractions and the irregular and often rapid ventricular rate, leading to myocardial ischaemia, hypotension, heart failure, and tachycardia-induced cardiomyopathy. People with pre-existing cardiac disease are particularly vulnerable.

Atrial fibrillation (AF) increases the risk of thromboembolic stroke (see *Risk of stroke* below).

isk of stroke

There is an 18-fold increase in the risk of thromboembolism in people with AF and rheumatic mitral stenosis.

AF increases the risk of thromboembolism by a factor of about six even in the absence of rheumatic heart disease.

The overall incidence of stroke is about 5% per year in people with AF. However, there is a wide variation in risk, depending on a person's age and on the presence or absence of co-existing cardiovascular disease (e.g. hypertension, heart failure, diabetes, previous transient ischaemic attack [TIA], or stroke).

Table 2 (adapted from SIGN, 1999) illustrates the variation in stroke risk for people with AF.

The relative risk of stroke is thought to be similar for paroxysmal AF.

People who have had a previous stroke or TIA, and are taking aspirin, still have a rate of subsequent stroke of 10–12% per year.

SIGN, 1999]

Prognosis

Mortality in people with AF is twice that of the general population.

It is linked with the severity of underlying heart disease (e.g. heart failure, cardiomyopathy, or myocardial ischaemia). Note: heart disease can be the cause of atrial fibrillation, as well be induced by atrial fibrillation

Mortality in people with AF and heart failure is as likely to be due to heart failure as to thromboembolism.

Fuster et al, 2001]

Management issues

Role of the GP in managing atrial fibrillation p.181
Diagnosis and investigation p.181
Rate control p.181
Rhythm control p.182
Rate control or rhythm control? p.183
Cardioversion p.183
Paroxysmal atrial fibrillation p.183
Antithrombotic treatment p.184

Role of the GP in managing atrial fibrillation

Although the initial assessment and treatment *may* be carried out in secondary care, GPs have an important role in managing atrial fibrillation (AF). Specific areas include:

- **Diagnosing AF,** particularly asymptomatic AF
- **Monitoring** treatment
- **Identifying people for referral** (see *Indications for attempted cardioversion*)
- **Minimising the risk of toxicity** from treatment (e.g. digoxin toxicity)
- **Anticipating clinically relevant drug interactions** (e.g. warfarin and amiodarone)

[MeReC, 2002]

Table 2: Variation in stroke risk for people with AF.

Risk group	Risk of stroke if untreated
Very high Previous ischaemic stroke or TIA	12%
High Age over 65 and with one other risk factor from: hypertension, diabetes, heart failure, left ventricular dysfunction	5–8%
Moderate Age over 65, with no other risk factors Age under 65, with other risk factors	3–5%
Low Age under 65, with no other risk factors	1–2%

Diagnosis and investigation

- **Screening** by detection of an irregular pulse misses few cases of atrial fibrillation (AF), but only 8–23% of patients are subsequently found to have AF on electrocardiogram (ECG) [Sudlow et al, 1998a].
- **Always confirm the presence of AF by ECG** (i.e. no P waves, a baseline that appears to be irregular and undulating, and an irregular ventricular rate). The ventricular complexes look normal unless there is a ventricular conduction defect.
- **An ECG may also indicate a possible underlying cause** (e.g. signs of ischaemia, an old myocardial infarction, left ventricular hypertrophy, or a pre-excitation syndrome).
- **Arrange baseline blood tests:** full blood count to identify anaemia; serum electrolytes and creatinine, in case digoxin is needed, and to identify impaired renal function; and thyroid function tests to identify thyrotoxicosis. If anticoagulation is planned, additional investigations are a coagulation screen and liver function tests [British Society for Haematology, 1998; SIGN, 1999].
- **Echocardiography is often needed for further assessment.** The routine use of echocardiography continues to be debated. It may provide useful information on the presence of associated valvular disease and ventricular failure, and a recent consensus statement recommends that it should be part of the optimal assessment of people with AF [Royal College of Physicians of Edinburgh, 1999]. However, for most people it is unlikely to affect the decision on whether to recommend anticoagulation or not [Sudlow et al, 1998b; Cantley et al, 2000].
- **A chest X-ray** can also be used to detect whether heart failure is present, but is less useful than echocardiography for this purpose. It is more useful for detecting intrinsic pulmonary pathology, and for evaluating the pulmonary vasculature [Fuster et al, 2001].
- **Ambulatory ECG monitoring, event recorders, and exercise-tolerance testing** may be of value in selected people [Fuster et al, 2001].

Rate control

- **Inappropriate ventricular rate is one of the main causes of symptoms** in people with atrial fibrillation (AF).
- **The goal of treatment** is usually to keep the ventricular rate less than 90/minute at rest and 180/minute on exercise [Royal College of Physicians of Edinburgh, 1999].
- **Beta-blockers** control resting heart rate and heart rate on exercise. However there is some suggestion that they may cause a transient decrease in exercise tolerance [Segal et al, 2000b].
- **Rate-limiting calcium-channel blockers** (verapamil or diltiazem) have also been shown to control heart rate at rest and on exercise, without a decrease in exercise tolerance [Segal et al, 2000b].
- **Digoxin** may control the ventricular rate in a resting person, but is less effective at controlling heart rate during exercise [Segal et al, 2000b].
- **Beta-blockers or a rate-limiting calcium-channel blocker should be considered for first-line use (C),** particularly in people with hypertension or angina [Fuster et al, 2001]. Note: verapamil is the only rate-limiting calcium-channel

blocker licensed for the treatment of arrhythmias in the UK. Although several trials studied diltiazem, it is difficult to recommend specific dosing schedules, as the trials were small and dosages varied enormously.

- **If rate control is not achieved despite adequate monotherapy,** then consider combining digoxin with a beta-blocker or verapamil (C), or consider referral. Verapamil must not be combined with a beta-blocker, owing to the risk of bradycardia and reduced cardiac output.
  - If digoxin therapy is started, we suggest using a loading dosage of 500 micrograms daily for 3 days. The maintenance dosage usually ranges from 125 to 250 micrograms daily. The slowing of the ventricular rate is usually a good guide to the therapeutic effect.
  - Lower loading and maintenance dosages should be used in the elderly or in renal impairment (e.g. 250 micrograms daily for 3 days, followed by 62.5 to 125 micrograms daily).
- **Combining digoxin with a beta-blocker or verapamil may be particularly useful in exercise-induced tachycardia** and may avoid the need for higher dosages of either medication [Royal College of Physicians of Edinburgh, 1999; Segal et al, 2000b].
- **Amiodarone** may be effective in refractory cases when other drugs have failed. However, this has a high incidence of adverse effects and should only be initiated under specialist supervision.
- **Radiofrequency ablation of the atrioventricular (AV) node and pacemaker implantation** should be considered for people in whom medical treatment is ineffective or not tolerated. Although there is a lack of good-quality data from studies of AV-blocking drugs, recent studies of AV-node ablation and pacing show significant improvements in symptoms and exercise tolerance [Royal College of Physicians of Edinburgh, 1999; Fuster et al, 2001]. There are currently no large randomized controlled trials comparing AV-node ablation and pacing against medical management.

Medicines management: drugs used for rate control

Beta-blockers

- **People with diabetes** should be advised that beta-blockers may slightly raise their blood glucose levels, and that their response to hypoglycaemia may be delayed or symptoms of hypoglycaemia may not occur in the usual way. Cardioselective beta-blockers (e.g. atenolol or metoprolol) may be preferable. Avoid beta-blockers for someone who experiences frequent hypoglycaemia [BNF 44, 2002].
- **Beta-blockers can precipitate bronchospasm** that is unresponsive to beta-2 agonists in people with asthma, or in people with chronic obstructive pulmonary disease that has an asthmatic component. Beta-blockers should be avoided in these people.
- **Sleep disturbance or nightmares** are less likely with a water-soluble beta-blocker such as atenolol, as it is less likely to cross the blood-brain barrier [BNF 44, 2002].
- **A recent meta-analysis highlighted that there is no significant increased risk of depressive symptoms** while on beta-blockers, and only a small increase in the risk of fatigue or sexual dysfunction [Ko et al, 2002].
- Assess objective signs of peripheral vascular disease in someone who experiences cold extremities with beta-blockers.

Verapamil

- **Constipation is common.** Advise patients to eat more fibre (fruit, vegetables, cereals, wholemeal bread, etc); to try to drink at least 12 cups (8 glasses or mugs) of liquid a day; but to avoid drinks with a high caffeine content, as these may make constipation worse.
- **Dizziness, facial flushing, ankle oedema, and postural hypotension** are also common adverse effects [BNF 44, 2002]. They generally reduce in severity on continued treatment. Ankle oedema is often persistent. Diuretics should not be prescribed, as they only partially reduce ankle oedema caused by calcium-channel blockers.
- **Verapamil should not be used with beta-blockers,** owing to the risk of reduced cardiac output and heart failure. Diltiazem has a smaller negative inotropic effect than does verapamil. It may be used with beta-blockers provided that they do not cause bradycardia. Similarly, digoxin may be used with verapamil, provided that they do not cause bradycardia.

Digoxin

- **Digoxin toxicity** is the most serious, and avoidable, adverse effect of digoxin therapy. Digoxin has a narrow therapeutic window. The usual therapeutic plasma concentration ranges from 1 to 2 micrograms/litre [BNF 44, 2002]. Toxicity may be precipitated by:
  - **Metabolic disturbances** (e.g. hypokalaemia, hypercalcaemia, hypoxia and acidosis, renal impairment, dehydration, and hypothyroidism)
  - **Drugs that increase digoxin levels** (e.g. verapamil, amiodarone, and quinidine)
- **It is important to check serum electrolytes and creatinine at least annually** in people taking digoxin, to assess renal function and potassium levels. This is particularly important if they are also taking diuretics.
- **Suspect digoxin toxicity if** there is anorexia, nausea, vomiting, diarrhoea, mental confusion, or blurred vision.
- **Toxicity may cause a variety of arrhythmias,** and apparent return of sinus rhythm may be due to digoxin toxicity (e.g. atrial tachycardia with atrioventricular [AV] block, junctional tachycardia, or atrial fibrillation [AF] with complete AV block). At toxic levels, digoxin may cause or worsen heart failure.
- **Digoxin levels do not need to be routinely monitored in** AF, because ventricular rate is usually a good guide to therapeutic effect.
- **Check levels only to assess possible toxicity, or adherence to treatment.** Plasma levels must be measured at least 6 hours after the last dose [BNF 44, 2002].
  - Levels less than 1.5 micrograms/litre, in the absence of hypokalaemia, indicate that digoxin toxicity is unlikely.
  - Levels greater than 3.0 micrograms/litre indicate that toxicity is likely.
  - With levels between 1.5 and 3.0 micrograms/litre, digoxin toxicity should be considered a possibility.

Rhythm control

- **Anti-arrhythmic drugs** are often prescribed in those with troublesome symptoms from paroxysmal atrial fibrillation (AF), and to maintain sinus rhythm in people with recurrences of AF after cardioversion. Anti-arrhythmic drugs can also be used for pharmacological cardioversion of AF [Fuster et al, 2001].
- **Treatment should be initiated only under specialist supervision.**
- **A variety of anti-arrhythmics can be used:** flecainide, propafenone, disopyramide, and quinidine (class I); beta blockers, including sotalol (class II/III); and amiodarone (class III). The choice often depends on the adverse effect profile of the drug (B), and the presence of underlying factors precipitating AF [Fuster et al, 2001].
- **The use of anti-arrhythmic drugs after cardioversion** to attempt to maintain sinus rhythm is controversial, and is not without risk. A recent large, but unblinded, randomized controlled trial found that over a 16-month period 35% of people taking amiodarone had a

recurrence of AF, compared with 63% of people taking sotalol or propafenone [Roy et al, 2000].

Medicines management: amiodarone

Amiodarone is commonly used in the UK, and is considered to be the safest agent in heart failure. It provides both rhythm and rate control in AF, but it can cause serious non-cardiac adverse effects. These include corneal microdeposits, grey/blue skin discoloration, photosensitivity, hypothyroidism or hyperthyroidism, peripheral neuropathy, liver damage, and pulmonary toxicity. Anyone taking amiodarone should have their liver function and their thyroid function checked every 6 months, and their eyes checked annually (by slit examination). They should also be advised to limit sunlight exposure and to use a sunscreen [MeReC, 2002].

Rate control or rhythm control?

Rate control (using drugs that block the atrioventricular node) controls the symptoms of atrial fibrillation (AF). **Rhythm control** (i.e. restoration of sinus rhythm) also controls symptoms. Other potential benefits were thought to be: better exercise tolerance; a lower risk of stroke; a reduced risk of thromboembolism; better quality of life; and better survival if sinus rhythm is maintained.

The recently published Atrial Fibrillation Follow-up Investigation of Rhythm Management (AFFIRM) study found that, in people with atrial fibrillation at moderate to high risk of stroke:

- Survival rates were similar for rate control or rhythm control
- Most ischaemic strokes occurred in people who had stopped taking warfarin, or whose international normalized ratio (INR) was subtherapeutic at the time of the stroke
- People taking drugs for rhythm control experienced more adverse effects than those taking rate-control drugs

People presenting with a first episode of AF should be carefully assessed, and given rate-control treatment to control symptoms.

An attempt to restore sinus rhythm will still be appropriate for many people, particularly if electrical cardioversion is used (i.e. anti-arrhythmic drugs are not used).

If symptoms persist despite rate control, repeated cardioversion with the addition of anti-arrhythmic drugs should be considered.

Note: many people still experience symptoms despite attempts to control the ventricular rate (e.g. young people with paroxysmal AF but no structural heart disease). Rhythm control will often need to be attempted in these people.

Whether rate control or rhythm control is used, antithrombotic treatment is paramount to increasing survival.

[AFFIRM, 2002; Falk, 2002]

Cardioversion

This is a secondary-care intervention.

Cardioversion is often performed electively to restore sinus rhythm in people with persistent atrial fibrillation (AF). It can be achieved using electrical shocks or drugs:

- **Electrical cardioversion** (using direct-current [DC] shocks) is currently the preferred method, and has an initial success rate of 70–90% in selected people. Success is more likely in recent-onset AF and in younger people. Failure is more likely in people with underlying heart disease (see Indications for attempted cardioversion below).
- **Pharmacological cardioversion** has less initial success, but does not require sedation or anaesthesia. The quality of clinical trials is generally poor, but evidence best supports the use of flecainide, with cardioversion rates of 60–90%. Quinidine, disopyramide, propafenone, and amiodarone can also be used. Digoxin, beta-blockers, and verapamil have no effect on helping to restore sinus rhythm.

- **Cardioversion is most likely to be successful and maintained when the duration of AF is short.**
- **Cardioversion is associated with an increased risk of thromboembolism in people who have been in AF for more than 2 days.** Such a person should be treated with warfarin for 3 weeks prior to cardioversion, and for at least 4 weeks after this (B) [British Society for Haematology, 1998; SIGN, 1999; Fuster et al, 2001].
- **Relapse rate following successful electrical cardioversion is high:** only about 20% of people will still be in sinus rhythm 1 year after electrical cardioversion. More people can be maintained in sinus rhythm if anti-arrhythmic drugs are given after cardioversion. However these drugs have substantial adverse effects, and are often reserved for use after a second successful cardioversion.

[Royal College of Physicians of Edinburgh, 1999; Houghton et al, 2000; Fuster et al, 2001]

Indications for attempted cardioversion

- **Recent-onset AF** — however, it is not always easy to know the time of onset, and there is a case for referring anyone with newly diagnosed AF for at least one attempt at cardioversion (C) [Fuster et al, 2001].
- **No structural heart disease** (e.g. the person has no mitral valve disease; or the person has good left ventricular function and an undilated left atrium).
- **Successful treatment of any precipitating cause** of AF (e.g. thyrotoxicosis, chest infection).
- **Young age,** although age should not be an automatic barrier.
- **People with acute AF and severe hypotension, acute heart failure, acute MI, or unstable angina,** who do not respond promptly to medical management, require immediate cardioversion (C) [Fuster et al, 2001].

Paroxysmal atrial fibrillation

- **Paroxysmal atrial fibrillation (AF) is defined as** intermittent episodes of AF with sinus rhythm in between. There is no accepted threshold for the time between episodes.
- **Psychological morbidity may be significant.** Many patients avoid activities for fear of precipitating an episode. People may believe that their 'heart will stop' or that they will have a 'heart attack', and such fears should be addressed [Royal College of Physicians of Edinburgh, 1999].
- **The risk of thromboembolism is probably the same as that for permanent AF,** and the same criteria for antithrombotic treatment apply (A). See *Antithrombotic treatment*.
- **Anti-arrhythmic treatment** aims to reduce the frequency and severity of attacks, and possibly prevent progression to persistent AF [Royal College of Physicians of Edinburgh, 1999; Fuster et al, 2001].
- **Treatment may not be necessary if symptomatic episodes are mild, infrequent, and short.** The benefits of treatment have to be balanced against the risks of long-term anti-arrhythmic medication.
- **Anti-arrhythmic treatment should be initiated only under specialist supervision.**

- **A large number of drugs have been shown to reduce the frequency of episodes.** Flecainide, propafenone, and sotalol have been most studied, and are generally well tolerated. Disopyramide and quinidine are effective, but are more likely to cause adverse effects. Recent trial data suggest that amiodarone may be particularly effective [Roy et al, 2000].
- **Co-administration** of atrioventricular blocking drugs (verapamil, diltiazem, and beta-blockers) with anti-arrhythmic drugs may reduce symptoms during attacks, and may reduce the risk of dangerous one-to-one conduction of atrial flutter [Royal College of Physicians of Edinburgh, 1999].
- **Digoxin is not generally recommended,** as it does not reduce the ventricular rate in paroxysmal AF and may be associated with longer attacks [Royal College of Physicians of Edinburgh, 1999; Fuster et al, 2001].

Antithrombotic treatment

- **There is an 18-fold increase in the risk of thromboembolism** in people with atrial fibrillation (AF) and rheumatic mitral stenosis. Despite the few randomized trials carried out, it is accepted that such people should be treated with warfarin (C).
- **AF increases the risk of thromboembolism by a factor of about six** even in the absence of mitral valve disease (i.e. non-valvular AF). Warfarin, and also aspirin, have been shown to reduce the risk of stroke in these people, although the reduction is larger and more consistent with warfarin.
- **Warfarin reduces the risk of stroke by nearly two-thirds,** while aspirin reduces the risk by about a fifth.
  - Note: the overall incidence of stroke is about 5% per year in people with non-valvular AF. However, there is a wide variation in risk, depending on a person's age, and the presence of any additional risk factors (e.g. hypertension, heart failure, diabetes, previous stroke, or previous transient ischaemic attack [TIA]).
  - The decision to use warfarin or aspirin should ultimately be based on the balance of an individual's overall risk of stroke compared with the risk of adverse effects.

Who should receive antithrombotic prophylaxis?

- **The overall risk of stroke should be assessed for each individual with AF.** It should also be reassessed regularly, as a person's risk of stroke will change over time (A).
- The individual's attitude to anticoagulation will strongly influence the cost/benefit of treatment, and should always be taken into account.
- **The decision to use warfarin or aspirin should ultimately be based on the balance of an individual's overall risk of stroke compared with the risk of adverse effects (A), and their personal preference:**
  - For people with AF who are at high risk of stroke (e.g people with a previous stroke or TIA), about 90 even (mostly strokes) will be prevented each year, for ever 1000 people treated with warfarin.
  - For people with AF who are at moderate risk of strok (e.g. people aged over 65 years with no other risk factors for stroke), about 25 strokes will be prevente each year, for every 1000 people treated with warfarin.
  - Treating 1000 people with AF (whatever their risk of stroke) for 1 year with warfarin rather than aspirin would prevent 23 ischaemic strokes, while causing 9 major bleeds.
- **There are many different risk stratification schemes available.** The guidelines for antithrombotic prophylaxi outlined below are taken from the ACC/AHA/ESC guidelines [Fuster et al, 2001] for the management of patients with atrial fibrillation:
  - **Warfarin is preferred in people at high risk of stroke** (untreated stroke risk more than 6% per year), as the benefits usually outweigh the risks. This includes people with a previous ischaemic stroke or TIA, or people aged over 65 years with one other risk factor for stroke (see Table 2 below) (A).
  - **People at moderate risk of stroke** (untreated stroke risk of 3–5%) require antithrombotic therapy, but th decision to use warfarin or aspirin is less clear. Many would still choose warfarin in this situation. The decision to use warfarin or aspirin should ultimately be based on the balance of an individual's overall risk of stroke compared with the risk of bleeding, and the individual's personal preference (A).
  - **People aged under 65 years with no other risk factors for stroke are at low risk,** and should not be given antithrombotic prophylaxis unless aspirin is given for other indications (A).
- **If it is a person's first presentation with atrial fibrillatio** it is difficult to know whether it is the person's first *episode* of AF, particularly if symptoms are minimal or absent. The decision to anticoagulate should still be based on their risk of stroke, and can be reviewed when the pattern of AF becomes apparent (e.g. a single self-terminating episode, persistent, etc).
- **Table 3 highlights those people who are likely to have a significantly increased risk of stroke,** and the degree of benefit from treatment with either warfarin or aspirin [SIGN, 1999]. The numbers needed to treat (NNT) wit warfarin instead of aspirin for 1 year to prevent one stroke are also shown.
- **If an acute cerebral ischaemic event has occurred,** anticoagulant treatment should be delayed until most o the deficit has resolved or, in the case of more severe strokes, more than 2 weeks has elapsed.

[SIGN, 1999; Benavente et al, 2000; Koudstaal, 2000]

Table 3: Risk of stroke if taking antithrombotic therapy.

Risk group	Risk of stroke if untreated	Risk of stroke if on aspirin	Risk of stroke if on warfarin	NN
Very high Previous ischaemic stroke or TIA	12%	10%	5%	13
High Age over 65 and one other risk factor, from: hypertension, diabetes, heart failure, left ventricular dysfunction	5–8%	4–6%	2–3%	22–
Moderate Age over 65, with no other risk factors Age under 65, with other risk factors	3–5%	2–4%	1–2%	47–
Low Age under 65, with no other risk factors	1–2%	1%	0.5%	200

upporting evidence for stroke prevention

A meta-analysis of five *primary prevention* studies showed that warfarin reduced the incidence of stroke by 68% (95% CI 50% to 79%), with an absolute annual risk reduction of 3.1% [Atrial Fibrillation Investigators, 1994]. Recent meta-analyses come to virtually identical conclusions [Benavente et al, 2000; Segal et al, 2000a].

The annual risk of stroke is higher in people who have had a previous stroke or transient ischaemic attack (TIA): about 12% per year. A meta-analysis of two *secondary prevention* studies showed that warfarin reduced the incidence of stroke by 64% (95% CI 42% to 78%), with an absolute annual risk reduction of 7% [Koudstaal, 2000].

A Cochrane systematic review that combined data from all placebo-controlled randomized trials of aspirin in atrial fibrillation found that aspirin reduced the risk of stroke by about 20% [Benavente et al, 2000]. The effect of aspirin on stroke in these trials was less consistent than that of oral anticoagulation. Aspirin reduced the relative risk of stroke by 33% in primary prevention studies (in which the stroke rate with placebo averaged 5% per year) compared with 11% for secondary prevention trials (in which the stroke rate with placebo averaged 14% per year).

A recent meta-analysis that combined data from all randomised studies of aspirin compared with warfarin showed that people who took warfarin were significantly less likely to experience a stroke. Warfarin reduced the risk of stroke by 45% compared with aspirin (95% CI 29% to 57%). However, people taking warfarin were more likely to experience major bleeding [van Walraven et al, 2002].

A small primary care study found that there was no difference between aspirin and warfarin in preventing stroke in people at *low risk* of stroke [Hellemons et al, 1999]. Other conclusions from this study are limited because of methodological problems, in particular small sample size, and further primary care-based studies are needed.

The combination of low-dose warfarin (INR less than 1.5) with aspirin 325 mg gives little additional protection against stroke compared with aspirin alone in people with lone AF [SPAF-III, 1998]. The incidence of primary events (ischaemic stroke and systemic embolism) was higher in people given combination therapy than with people given adjusted-dose warfarin.

isk of major bleeding with warfarin

The annual rate of proven cerebral haemorrhage and other bleeding complications has been low in all the trials. It is not known whether such low bleeding risks can be routinely achieved in normal clinical practice. However, data from a large prospective community cohort study shows that similar low rates are achievable [Palareti et al, 1996].

Major haemorrhage occurred in 1.3% of warfarin-treated people and 1.0% of controls [Atrial Fibrillation Investigators, 1994] in the primary prevention studies. The corresponding rates for intracranial haemorrhage were 0.3% and 0.1%.

Risk of bleeding is greatest during the first 3 months of anticoagulation and increases with age, intensity of anticoagulation, prior gastrointestinal bleed, prior stroke, and severe comorbid disease [Palareti et al, 1996].

isk of major adverse effects with aspirin

The risk of major bleeding is lower with aspirin than with warfarin. A meta-analysis of data from all studies of aspirin compared with warfarin illustrated this: the hazard ratio for major bleeding for warfarin compared with aspirin was 1.71 (95% CI 1.21 to 2.41).

- Although the risk of bleeding is considerably lower with aspirin, there is still a small absolute increase in risk of intracranial haemorrhage of 12 events per 10,000 people treated with aspirin [He et al, 1998].
- **Aspirin can also cause serious gastrointestinal adverse effects** such as ulceration, bleeding, and perforation. People who experience dyspepsia with aspirin should be co-prescribed an acid-suppressing drug. See PRODIGY guidance on *Dyspepsia — symptoms*. Presence of dyspepsia is not a good guide to severity of adverse effects: many people who experience perforations do not have prior aspirin-induced dyspepsia. There is no robust evidence that different formulations are associated with alterations in risk [CSM, 2002]. Enteric-coated preparations are also more expensive than standard preparations of aspirin.

A

Other antiplatelet agents

- **The role of other antiplatelet agents is uncertain at the present time.** An ongoing Cochrane systematic review will address this issue [Segal, 2000]. Although clopidogrel has been shown to have a slight benefit over aspirin in preventing ischaemic stroke, myocardial infarction, and vascular death in people with atherosclerotic disease [CAPRIE Steering Committee, 1996], we have found no evidence that it has been specifically studied in people with atrial fibrillation.
- It may be an option if warfarin is contraindicated and the individual is also hypersensitive to aspirin (i.e. aspirin induces angio-oedema or bronchospasm). This is an off-licence use of clopidogrel.

Medicines management: antithrombotic treatment

- **The risk of bleeding** is the major risk of antithrombotic treatment.
- **Suggested contraindications and cautions** to minimize this risk (adapted from SIGN, 1999) are given in Table 4.

Warfarin

- **The consensus is to aim for a target international normalized ratio (INR) of 2.5** (range 2.0–3.0) (**A**).
- **For people older than 75 years,** it may be safer to aim for a target INR at the lower end of this range, owing to

Table 4: Suggested contraindications and cautions concerning antithrombotic therapy.

Contraindications/cautions	Comments
Uncorrected major bleeding	-
Uncorrected major bleeding disorder	For example, thrombocytopenia, haemophilias, liver failure, renal failure
Uncontrolled severe hypertension	For example, systolic greater than 200 mmHg or diastolic greater than 120 mmHg
Potential bleeding lesions	For example, active peptic ulcer; oesophageal varices; aneurysm; proliferative retinopathy; recent organ biopsy; recent trauma or surgery to head, orbit, or spine; recent stroke; confirmed intracranial or intraspinal bleed
Pregnancy	Risk of teratogenicity with warfarin
Uncooperative/unreliable person	Concordance and follow-up issues
Repeated falls or unstable gait	Increased chance of injury and head trauma
Concomitant use of nonsteroidal anti-inflammatory drugs (NSAIDs)	Increased risk of gastrointestinal bleeding
Protein C deficiency	Risk of skin necrosis on initiation of warfarin, so caution needed

A

their increased risk of cerebral haemorrhage. Alternatively, aspirin may be a safer option in some people (**A**).

- **A large loading dose is often unnecessary when starting warfarin** for persistent atrial fibrillation, as there is no need to achieve anticoagulation rapidly.
- **An INR of 2.0 can usually be reached by giving warfarin 5 mg for 4–5 days.**
- A lower starting dose is often more suitable for elderly people and people at high risk of bleeding.
- **People on warfarin need regular monitoring of INR.** Ideally this should take place in the setting of an organized anticoagulant clinic.
- **If no clinic is available,** monitor INR daily until the result has stayed in the therapeutic range for at least 2 consecutive days. Then check INR 2–3 times a week for 1–2 weeks, and then less often, depending on the stability of the results.
- **The risk of bleeding increases considerably above an INR of 4.**
- **Less severe bleeding is the most common adverse effect of warfarin.** Strategies for reversing the effect of warfarin (adapted from SIGN, 1999) are outlined in Table 5 below.
- **Drugs that interact with warfarin** can also increase the risk of bleeding. Where possible, prescribe drugs that do not interact with warfarin.
- **If an interacting drug will be used for less than 5 days,** then often no dosage change is necessary. A minor dosage reduction or omission of one full warfarin dosage may be prudent with known potentiating drugs (see BNF).
- **If an interacting drug will be used for more than 5 days,** check the INR 1 week after starting therapy and adjust the warfarin dose accordingly. The INR should also be monitored when an interacting drug is stopped.
- **Amiodarone markedly increases the effect of warfarin.** Reduce the dose of warfarin by one- to two-thirds, and check the INR every week until it is stable (this monitoring period must include the entire amiodarone loading schedule). This interaction persists for a month or more after amiodarone is withdrawn.

[British Society for Haematology, 1998; SIGN, 1999; Ansell et al, 2001; Fuster et al, 2001; Peters et al, 2002]

Aspirin

- **Aspirin should be considered for people who fulfil the criteria for anticoagulation but where warfarin is contraindicated or declined (A).** It may also be more suitable for people who are likely to have difficulty following dosing instructions for warfarin.
- **Treatment with aspirin is not usually recommended for people under age 65 with 'lone AF',** unless aspirin is given for other indications [SIGN, 1999; Fuster et al, 2001].

Table 5: Strategies for reversing the effect of warfarin.

Life-threatening bleeding (e.g. intracranial or major gastrointestinal bleed)
Admit urgently
Less severe bleeding (e.g. haematuria, epistaxis)
Stop warfarin for 1–2 days
Give vitamin K: 0.5–2 mg intravenously, or 5–10 mg orally
High INR but no bleeding
Stop warfarin, monitor INR, restart warfarin when INR <5.0
Consider giving vitamin K (0.5 mg intravenously or 5 mg orally) if: INR >8.0 Other risk factors for bleeding are present

- **Recommended dosages range between 75 mg and 300 mg daily** [Royal College of Physicians of Edinburgh 1999; SIGN, 1999; Fuster et al, 2001].
- **Most studies have used a dose of 325 mg per day.** The only study to use aspirin 75 mg per day [Petersen et al, 1989] found a non-significant 18% reduction in stroke rate.
- **Local guidelines on aspirin dose should be followed where available. Otherwise, we recommend a dose of 75 mg per day.**
- A recent retrospective study found that people with cardiovascular disease who took ibuprofen as well as low-dose aspirin had a higher risk of all-cause mortality than those who only took low-dose aspirin (adjusted hazard ratio 1.93, 95% CI 1.3-2.87) [MacDonald and Wei, 2003]. There was no difference in mortality for people taking diclofenac plus low-dose aspirin, or another nonsteroidal anti-inflammatory drug (NSAID) plus low-dose aspirin. (Note: cyclo-oxygenase (COX)-2 selective NSAIDs selective NSAIDs were not included in this study.)
- The results of this study should be viewed with caution as it was not able to control for confounding factors, and only small numbers of people were taking ibuprofen or diclofenac (303). However, until more evidence becomes available, it would seem prudent to follow the advice of the British Heart Foundation and avoid ibuprofen in people taking low-dose aspirin [British Heart Foundation, 2002]. Diclofenac is probably a better option if an NSAID is required.

References

NHS staff in England can link, free of charge, from references to full text journals by clicking on [Full text] on the PRODIGY website.

1. AFFIRM (2002) A comparison of rate control and rhythm control in patients with atrial fibrillation. *New England Journal of Medicine* **347**(23), 1825–1833. [Full text]
2. Ansell, J., Hirsh, J., Dalen, J. et al (2001) Managing oral anticoagulant therapy. *Chest* **119**(1), 22S-38S. [Full text]
3. Atrial Fibrillation Investigators (1994) Risk factors for stroke and efficacy of antithrombotic therapy in atrial fibrillation. Analysis of pooled data from five randomized controlled trials on behalf of the Atrial Fibrillation Investigators. *Archives of Internal Medicine* **154**(13), 1449–1457.
4. Bandolier (2002) *Atrial fibrillation.* Bandolier. www.jr2.ox.ac.uk/bandolier/booth/booths/AF.html [Accessed: 19/12/2002].
5. Benavente, O., Hart, R., Koudstaal, P. et al (2000) *Oral anticoagulants for preventing stroke in patients with non valvular atrial fibrillation and no previous history of stroke or transient ischemic attacks (Cochrane Review).* The Cochrane Library. Issue 4. Oxford: Update Software.
6. BNF 44 (2002) *British National Formulary.* 44th edn. London: British Medical Association and Royal Pharmaceutical Society of Great Britain.
7. British Heart Foundation (2002) *Aspirin and ibuprofen.* Factfile 11/2002. British Heart Foundation www.bhf.org.uk [Accessed: 01/12/2002].
8. British Society for Haematology (1998) Guidelines on oral anticoagulation: third edition. *British Journal of Haematology* **101**(2), 374–387.
9. Cantley, P., McKinstry, B., Macaulay, D. et al (2000) Atrial fibrillation in general practice: how useful is echocardiography in selection of suitable patients for

anticoagulation? *British Journal of General Practice* 49(440), 219–220.

10. CAPRIE Steering Committee (1996) A randomised, blinded, trial of clopidogrel versus aspirin in patients at risk of ischaemic events (CAPRIE). *Lancet* 348(9038), 1329–1339. [Full text]
11. CSM (2002) Non-steroidal anti-inflammatory drugs (NSAIDs) and gastrointestinal (GI) safety. *Current Problems in Pharmacovigilance* 28(Apr), 5.
12. DTB (1997) Which prophylactic aspirin? *Drug & Therapeutics Bulletin* 35(1), 7–8. [Full text]
13. Falk, R.H. (2002) Management of atrial fibrillation – radical reform or modest modification? *New England Journal of Medicine* 347(23), 1883–1884. [Full text]
14. Fuster, V., Ryden, L.E., Asinger, R.W. et al (2001) ACC/AHA/ESC guidelines for the management of patients with atrial fibrillation. *Journal of the American College of Cardiology* 38(4), 1231–1266.
15. He, J., Whelton, P.K., Vu, B. and Klag, M.J. (1998) Aspirin and risk of hemorrhagic stroke: a meta-analysis of randomized controlled trials. *Journal of the American Medical Association* 280(22), 1930–1935. [Full text]
16. Hellemons, B.S.P., Langenberg, M., Lodder, J. et al (1999) Primary prevention of arterial thromboembolism in non-rheumatic atrial fibrillation in primary care: randomised controlled trial comparing two intensities of coumarin with aspirin. *British Medical Journal* 319(7215), 958–964. [Full text]
17. Houghton, A.R., Sharman, A. and Pohl, J.E.F. (2000) Determinants of successful direct current cardioversion for atrial fibrillation and flutter: the importance of rapid referral. *British Journal of General Practice* 50(458), 710–711.
18. Ko, D.T., Hebert, P.R., Coffey, C.S. et al (2002) Beta-blocker therapy and symptoms of depression, fatigue and sexual dysfunction. *Journal of the American Medical Association* 288(3), 351–352. [Full text]
19. Koudstaal, P. (2000) *Anticoagulants for preventing stroke in patients with nonrheumatic atrial fibrillation and a history of stroke or transient ischaemic attack (Cochrane Review)*. The Cochrane Library. Issue 4. Oxford: Update Software.
20. MacDonald, T.M. and Wei, L. (2003) Effect of ibuprofen on cardioprotective effect of aspirin. *Lancet* 361(9357), 573–574. [Full text]
21. MeReC (2002) Primary care management of atrial fibrillation. *MeReC Bulletin* 12(5), 17–20.
22. Palareti, G., Leali, N., Coccheri, S. et al (1996) Bleeding complications of oral anticoagulant treatment: an inception-cohort, prospective collaborative study (ISCOAT). Italian Study on Complications of Oral Anticoagulant Therapy. *Lancet* 348(9025), 423–428.
23. Petersen, P., Boysen, G., Godtfredsen, J. et al (1989) Placebo-controlled, randomised trial of warfarin and aspirin for prevention of thromboembolic complications in chronic atrial fibrillation. The Copenhagen AFASAK Study. *Lancet* 1(8631), 175–179.
24. Peters, N.S., Schilling, R.J., Kanagaratnam, P. and Markides, V. (2002) Atrial fibrillation: strategies to control, combat, and cure. *Lancet* 359(9306), 593–603. [Full text]
25. Royal College of Physicians of Edinburgh (1999) The Sir James MacKenzie Consensus Conference: atrial fibrillation in hospital and general practice. *Proceedings of the Royal College of Physicians of Edinburgh* 29(Suppl 6), 1–34.
26. Roy, D., Talajic, M., Dorian, P. et al (2000) Amiodarone to prevent recurrence of atrial fibrillation. *New England Journal of Medicine* 342(13), 913–920. [Full text]
27. Segal, J. (2000) *Anticoagulants versus antiplatelet drugs for preventing thromboembolism in atrial fibrillation (Protocol for a Cochrane Review)*. The Cochrane Library. Issue 4. Oxford:Update Software.
28. Segal, J.B., McNamara, R.L., Miller, M.R. et al (2000a) Prevention of thromboembolism in atrial fibrillation. A meta-analysis of trials of anticoagulants and antiplatelet drugs. *Journal of General Internal Medicine* 15(1), 56–67.
29. Segal, J.B., McNamara, R.L., Miller, M.R. et al (2000b) The evidence regarding the drugs used for ventricular rate control. *Journal of Family Practice* 49(1), 47–59.
30. SIGN (1999) *Antithrombotic therapy*. Report no. 36. Scottish Intercollegiate Guidelines Network. www.sign.ac.uk [Accessed: 19/12/2002].
31. SPAF-III (1998) Patients with nonvalvular atrial fibrillation at low risk of stroke during treatment with aspirin: Stroke Prevention in Atrial Fibrillation III study. The SPAF III. Writing committee for the stroke prevention in atrial fibrillation investigators. *Journal of the American Medical Association* 279(16), 1273–1277. [Full text]
32. Sudlow, M., Thomson, R., Thwaites, B. et al (1998a) Prevalence of atrial fibrillation and eligibility for anticoagulants in the community. *Lancet* 352(9135), 1167–1171. [Full text]
33. Sudlow, M., Rodgers, H., Kenny, R.A. and Thomson, R. (1998b) Identification of patients with atrial fibrillation in general practice: a study of screening methods. *British Medical Journal* 317(7154), 327–328. [Full text]
34. van Walraven, C., Hart, R.G., Singer, D.E. et al (2002) Oral anticoagulants vs aspirin in nonvalvular atrial fibrillation: an individual patient meta-analysis. *Journal of the American Medical Association* 288(19), 2441–2448. [Full text]

Evidence grading

This PRODIGY guidance is mainly based on the *ACC/AHA/ESC guidelines for the management of patients with atrial fibrillation* [Fuster et al, 2001].

The definitions of the grades of recommendations used in this guideline are as follows:

A Highest weight of evidence: data were derived from multiple randomized clinical trials.

B Intermediate weight of evidence: data were obtained from a limited number of randomized trials, non-randomized studies, or observational registries.

C Lowest weight of evidence: the primary basis for the recommendation was expert consensus.

PRODIGY GUIDANCE

Back pain — lower

Last revised in July 2005
www.prodigy.nhs.uk/guidance.asp?gt=Back pain - lower

B

Applies to people over the age of 10 years

This guidance takes account of the 2004 European Guidelines for the management of (i) acute simple low back pain in primary care, (ii) chronic simple low back pain, (iii) the prevention of low back pain, and (iv) the diagnosis and treatment of pelvic girdle pain [Airaksinen et al, 2004; Burton et al, 2004; van Tulder et al, 2004; Vleeming et al, 2004].

This guidance covers the symptomatic management of simple low back pain. It includes acute, sub-acute, and chronic low back pain in children, adolescents and adults, and it includes low back pain with and without pain due to nerve root compression.

This guidance does not cover the management of back pain with a specific cause such as osteoarthritis, osteoporosis, ankylosing spondylitis, polymyalgia rheumatica, and pregnancy. This guidance does not cover the management of low back pain when this requires specialist care, for example the occupational health management of low back pain, complications such as cauda equina syndrome, and low back pain persisting after surgery or other invasive treatments.

There is separate PRODIGY guidance for *Ankylosing spondylitis*, *Neck pain*, *Osteoarthritis*, *Osteoporosis — treatment*, *Rheumatoid arthritis*, and *Polymyalgia rheumatica*.

Goals

- To recognize possible serious specific causes of pain in the lower back — 'red flags'
- To recognize psycho-social barriers to recovery — 'yellow flags'
- To recognize disability from simple low back pain [Waddell, 2004]
- To relieve pain [van Tulder et al, 2004]
- To improve ability to function and alleviate disability [van Tulder et al, 2004]
- To prevent recurrence and the development of chronicity [van Tulder et al, 2004]

Contents

Scenarios

- Acute simple low back pain p.188
- Simple low back pain — follow-up and reassessment p.191
- Low back pain — red flags for serious pathology present p.195

Extended Information, p. 196

Which scenario?

- **Acute simple low back pain:** covers the management of acute simple low back pain, initial, recurrent, or exacerbation, and with or without nerve root pain.
- **Simple low back pain — follow-up and reassessment:** covers the continued management of simple low back pain, with or without nerve root pain. The focus is on managing both pain and the long consequences of pain in the sub-acute phase.
- **Low back pain — red flags for serious pathology present:** covers the management of someone who has red flags, indicating the possible presence of a serious condition.

Acute simple low back pain

Which therapy?

- **Assessment**
  - Exclude serious pathology, or act appropriately to the presence of any 'red flag'.
  - Assess psycho-social risk factors ('yellow flags').
  - Assess distress, disability, and loss of work.
  - Assess presence of nerve root pain.
- **Management**
  - Provide educational advice, including the absence of serious pathology, good prognosis, no need for X-ray best to remain active, and substantial risk of recurrence.
  - Provide adequate symptom control. Use paracetamol or a nonsteroidal anti-inflammatory (NSAID) alone, or, if pain is not fully controlled, use paracetamol anc codeine combined, an NSAID and paracetamol combined, or an NSAID combined with codeine.
  - Consider using a short-term muscle relaxant (diazepam) if spasm is present.
  - Recommend rapid return to usual activities including work.
  - If symptoms require rest for a few days, ensure as much mobility as possible is continued.
  - Consider referral for physical methods given with a psycho-social approach by musculoskeletal physiotherapists or osteopaths, or chiropractors.
  - Address any psychosocial risk factors. Common issue such as fear avoidance and unhelpful beliefs and thoughts about back pain may be addressed through education. If more than a brief GP intervention is required, refer to physiotherapy or other spinal specialist.

Practical prescribing points

For further information please see the *Medicines Compendium* (www.medicines.org.uk) or the *British National Formulary* (www.bnf.org).

NSAIDs

- **Only one NSAID should be prescribed at a time.**
- **NSAIDs may worsen asthma, hypertension, renal impairment, or heart failure.**
- Do not give ibuprofen, diclofenac, or naproxen without gastroprotection if there is a history of peptic ulceration
- **Pregnancy and breastfeeding:** use paracetamol if possible. If an NSAID is essential, ibuprofen may be use during breastfeeding and before 30 weeks of pregnancy.
- **People with cardiovascular disease:** ibuprofen may reduce the cardiovascular protective effect of low-dose aspirin.

In people with risk factors for gastrointestinal NSAID complications:

- Use paracetamol (with or without codeine) instead of a NSAID if possible.
- Or, use gastroprotection (a PPI or full-dose misoprostol) combined with a standard NSAID.

Risk factors for gastrointestinal NSAID complications include:

- Age of 65 years and over.
- Previous history of gastroduodenal ulcer, gastrointestinal (GI) bleeding, or gastroduodenal perforation.
- Concomitant use of medications that are known to increase the likelihood of upper-GI adverse events, e.g. anticoagulants, aspirin (even a low dose), and corticosteroids.
- Presence of serious comorbidity, such as cardiovascular disease, renal or hepatic impairment, diabetes, or hypertension.
- Requirement for prolonged duration of NSAID use.
- Use of maximum recommended doses of NSAIDs.

Codeine

Codeine may cause nausea, vomiting, constipation, and drowsiness. A regular laxative is often needed when it is used long-term.

Diazepam

Diazepam has strong sedative effects. People should be warned not to drive while taking the drug or for a full day after stopping drug treatment. In addition, people should be warned that the effects of alcohol may be exaggerated whilst taking this medication.

Diazepam has a high potential for tolerance and dependence: only courses of 3–7 days should be used in people with significant spasm.

Avoid use in pregnancy and breastfeeding.

Misoprostol

Diarrhoea and abdominal pain are common. Advise women of childbearing age to use adequate contraception, since misoprostol increases the risk of miscarriage.

Follow-up advice

Assess response to treatment in about 4 weeks.

Should I refer or investigate?

Refer?

Refer immediately for emergency treatment if cauda equina syndrome or rapidly progressing neurological deficit.

Refer if serious pathology still suspected after basic investigations have been done.

Referral advice from the National Institute for Clinical Excellence

Referral advice: a guide to appropriate referral from general to specialist services [NICE, 2001b] contains the following advice for people with acute low back pain. The referral advice is meant to encourage local health communities to discuss referral issues and enable local referral guidelines and protocols to be produced (for further information see www.nice.org.uk). Almost all people with acute low back pain can be managed in primary care. Table 1 outlines when referral to a specialist service is advised.

Table 1: Referral to a specialist service is advised if:

****	The person has neurological features of cauda equina syndrome, e.g. sphincter disturbance, progressive motor weakness, perineal anaesthesia, or evidence of bilateral nerve root involvement.
***	Serious spinal pathology is suspected (preferably seen within 1 week).
***	The person develops progressive neurological deficit, e.g. weakness, anaesthesia (preferably seen within 1 week).
***	The person has nerve root pain that is not resolving after 6 weeks (preferably seen within 3 weeks).
**	An underlying inflammatory disorder such as ankylosing spondylitis is suspected.
**	The person has simple back pain and has not resumed normal activities in 3 months. The effects of pain will vary and could include reduced quality of life, functional capacity, independence, or psychological well-being. Where possible, referral should be to a multidisciplinary back pain team.

Key to referral timings

Arrangements should be made so that the person:

**** is seen immediately (within a day)

*** is seen urgently (maximum wait of 2 weeks recommended, but to be agreed locally)

** is seen soon (maximum waiting time to be agreed locally)

* has a routine appointment (maximum waiting time to be agreed locally)

^ is seen within an appropriate time depending on his or her clinical circumstances (discretionary)

Investigate?

- **First-line investigations if red flags are present include:**
  - Plain X-ray of lumbosacral spine if red flags for spinal fracture, cancer, or infection — note that a negative X-ray does not on its own rule out serious disease.
  - X-ray of thoracic spine if thoracic pain is also present.
  - Full blood count if red flags for cancer or infection.
  - Erythrocyte sedimentation rate if red flags for cancer or infection.
  - Urine analysis if red flags for cancer or infection.
- **Second-line investigations include:**
  - Computed tomographic or magnetic resonance imaging.
  - Bone scan.

Patient information leaflets

The following PILs are available at www.prodigy.nhs.uk

- Anti-inflammatory Painkillers
- BackCare (National Back Pain Association)
- Back Pain
- Back Pain - A Summary

Shared decision making

- Most bouts of back pain ease within a few weeks or so. As far as possible, keep on with normal activities. You are less likely to develop persistent back pain if you keep active rather than rest a lot.
- **Paracetamol** is commonly used for pain. The normal adult dosage is two 500 mg tablets, four times a day.
- **An anti-inflammatory painkiller** may be an option.
  - Bleeding from the stomach is the most serious possible side-effect. Stop the medicine and see a doctor if you develop stomach symptoms.
  - Some people with asthma, high blood pressure, kidney failure, or heart failure may not be able to take anti-inflammatories.
- **Codeine** is a painkiller that is stronger than paracetamol. It may be used in combination with paracetamol or an anti-inflammatory. Possible side-effects include constipation and drowsiness.
- **A muscle relaxant** such as diazepam is sometimes used for a few days if the back muscles are tense and make the pain worse. Possible side-effects include drowsiness.

- To prevent further bouts of back pain, good posture, lifting correctly, a good mattress, and losing excess weight may help.

Drug rationale

B

Drugs not included

- **Analgesics other than paracetamol and codeine taken separately** are not recommended:
  - **Strong opioids** (e.g. morphine, pethidine) should be avoided because of the risk of dependence if they are used inappropriately.
  - **Weak opioids, other than codeine,** have either not been shown to be more effective than codeine (when used in combination with paracetamol), or are more expensive.
  - **Low-dose weak opioids with paracetamol** (combination products), e.g. co-codamol 8/500 mg: There is no evidence that these offer any clinical benefit over paracetamol alone and they are likely to lead to opioid adverse effects [MeReC, 1993; De Craen et al, 1996; Moore and McQuay, 1997].
  - **High-dose weak opioids with paracetamol** (combination products), e.g. co-codamol 30/500 mg: These do not allow titration to the most effective and safe analgesic dose to match individual requirements.
  - **Co-proxamol** (dextropropoxyphene 32.5 mg/ paracetamol 325 mg) has been withdrawn by the Committee on Safety of Medicines due to its unfavourable risk/benefit ratio; it is associated with an unacceptable risk of overdose [CSM, 2005a].
- **Standard nonsteroidal anti-inflammatory drugs (NSAIDs), other than ibuprofen, diclofenac, and naproxen,** are not generally recommended, as they have a worse balance between their efficacy and adverse effect profile than these three recommended drugs [CSM, 1994; Hernández-Diaz et al, 2000; BNF 49, 2005].
- **Cyclo-oxygenase 2 (COX-2) selective inhibitors** are not recommended. After the withdrawal of rofecoxib from the market (the only selective inhibitor licensed for acute pain), there are growing concerns that COX-2 selective inhibitors may cause serious cardiovascular events. Following a European-wide review of the data, the Committee on Safety of Medicines (CSM) has recently advised that [CSM, 2005b]:
  - The evidence suggests that coxibs, as a class, may cause an increased risk of thrombotic events (e.g. myocardial infarction and stroke) compared with placebo and some NSAIDs.
  - The risk may increase with dose and duration of exposure.
- **Strong opioids** (e.g. morphine, pethidine) should be avoided, owing to the risk of dependence if they are used inappropriately. They are usually reserved for moderate to severe pain of a visceral origin [BNF 49, 2005].
- **Gastroprotective agents** are sometimes needed, but not all are recommended:
  - **H_2-receptor antagonists (H_2RAs):** at standard doses, H_2RAs reduce the risk of duodenal ulceration, and there is some evidence that double doses reduce the risk of gastric ulceration [Rostom et al, 2002]. However, no H_2RAs are currently licensed for the prevention of gastric ulceration induced by NSAIDs [BNF 49, 2005], which is more common than duodenal ulceration.
  - **Rabeprazole** is not included as it is not specifically licensed for the prevention of NSAID-induced gastrointestinal ulcers [BNF 49, 2005].
  - **Fixed-dose combinations of standard NSAIDs with misoprostol:** the optimum dose of misoprostol (i.e. 800 micrograms daily) cannot be reached using these preparations. In particular, only 400 micrograms dail of misoprostol is given with the higher doses of NSAID in these preparations.

Drugs included

Standard analgesics and NSAIDs

- **Paracetamol:** this is a good first-line choice for pain relief, and is not associated with gastrointestinal toxicit [SIGN, 2000].
- **Codeine (in combination with paracetamol):** higher-dos codeine is included for use with regular paracetamol for additional pain relief. Codeine 60 mg plus paracetamol has been shown to provide more pain relief than either codeine 60 mg alone or paracetamol 1000 mg alone [Moore and McQuay, 1997]. Codeine should be prescribed separately to paracetamol to allow flexibility of dosing and titration of analgesic effect.
  - Note: codeine can also be combined with an NSAID, or paracetamol can be combined with an NSAID, but there is less evidence to support this.
- **Standard NSAIDs: ibuprofen, diclofenac, and naproxen** have a good balance of efficacy against adverse effect profile [CSM, 1994; Henry et al, 1996; Hernández-Dia and Rodriguez, 2000]. Standard doses are offered as these are generally accepted to be sufficient for anti-inflammatory prophylaxis, although data are lacking.

Muscle relaxants

- **Diazepam** is recommended as a muscle relaxant, as it ha been shown to reduce acute low back pain effectively. However, adverse effects are common, and there is a ris of dependency even after one week of treatment. Course of 3–7 days should be used only in people with significant spasm [Clinical Standards Advisory Group, 1994; Waddell et al, 1999].

Gastroprotective agents

- **Proton pump inhibitors (PPIs): lansoprazole, omeprazole, esomeprazole, and pantoprazole** are licensed for the prevention of gastroduodenal ulceration induced by NSAIDs [BNF 49, 2005]. PPIs reduce the ris of endoscopically proven ulcers, but there are no data o prevention of ulcer complications [Rostom et al, 2002]. However, PPIs are generally considered to be the first-line choice for gastroprotection, as they are better tolerated than misoprostol.
- **Misoprostol** is licensed for the prevention of gastroduodenal ulceration induced by NSAIDs [BNF 49 2005]. It reduces the risk of endoscopically proven ulcer and has also been shown to reduce the risk of ulcer complications [Rostom et al, 2002]. It is less well tolerated than PPIs owing to gastrointestinal adverse effects, particularly diarrhoea.

Prescriptions

Paracetamol or codeine

Paracetamol tablets: 1g up to four times a day

- Age from 16 years onwards
- Paracetamol 500mg tablets. Take two tablets every 4 to 6 hours when required for pain relief. Maximum of 8 tablets in 24 hours; supply 200 tablets; NHS Cost £2.12 OTC Cost £3.75.

odeine tablets: 30mg to 60mg up to four times a day
- Age from 16 years onwards
- Codeine 30mg tablets. Take one to two tablets every 4 to 6 hours when required for pain relief. Maximum of 8 tablets in 24 hours; supply 60 tablets; NHS Cost £4.58.

aracetamol 500mg tablets + codeine 30mg tablets
- Age from 16 years onwards
- Paracetamol 500mg tablets. Take two tablets every 4 to 6 hours when required for pain relief. Maximum of 8 tablets in 24 hours; supply 200 tablets; NHS Cost £2.12; OTC Cost £3.75.
- Codeine 30mg tablets. Take one to two tablets every 4 to 6 hours when required for pain relief. Maximum of 8 tablets in 24 hours; supply 60 tablets; NHS Cost £4.58.

Standard NSAIDs: ibuprofen, naproxen and diclofenac

uprofen tablets: 400mg three times a day
- Age from 16 years onwards
- Ibuprofen 400mg tablets. Take one tablet three times a day; supply 84 tablets; NHS Cost £2.74; OTC Cost £4.83.

uprofen tablets: 400mg four times a day
- Age from 16 years onwards
- Ibuprofen 400mg tablets. Take one tablet four times a day; supply 112 tablets; NHS Cost £3.65; OTC Cost £6.44.

uprofen tablets: 600mg three times a day
- Age from 16 years onwards
- Ibuprofen 600mg tablets. Take one tablet three times a day; supply 84 tablets; NHS Cost £2.81.

uprofen tablets: 800mg three times a day
- Age from 16 years onwards
- Ibuprofen 400mg tablets. Take two tablets three times a day; supply 168 tablets; NHS Cost £5.48.

iclofenac sodium e/c tablets: 25mg three times a day
- Age from 16 years onwards
- Diclofenac 25mg e/c tablets. Take one tablet three times a day; supply 84 tablets; NHS Cost £1.72.

iclofenac sodium e/c tablets: 50mg three times a day
- Age from 16 years onwards
- Diclofenac 50mg e/c tablets. Take one tablet three times a day; supply 84 tablets; NHS Cost £1.45.

aproxen tablets: 250mg twice a day
- Age from 16 years onwards
- Naproxen 250mg tablets. Take one tablet twice a day; supply 56 tablets; NHS Cost £2.68.

aproxen tablets: 500mg twice a day
- Age from 16 years onwards
- Naproxen 500mg tablets. Take one tablet twice a day; supply 56 tablets; NHS Cost £4.90.

GI protection: use ONLY with a standard NSAID

meprazole capsules: 20mg once a day
- Age from 16 years onwards
- Omeprazole 20mg capsules. Take one capsule once a day; supply 28 capsules; NHS Cost £12.75.

meprazole tablets: 20mg once a day
- Age from 16 years onwards
- Omeprazole 20mg tablets. Take one tablet once a day; supply 28 tablets; NHS Cost £12.75.

ansoprazole capsules: 15mg each morning
- Age from 16 years onwards
- Lansoprazole 15mg capsules. Take one capsule each morning (on an empty stomach); supply 28 capsules; NHS Cost £12.92.

Lansoprazole capsules: 30mg each morning
- Age from 16 years onwards
- Lansoprazole 30mg capsules. Take one capsule each morning (on an empty stomach); supply 28 capsules; NHS Cost £23.63.

Pantoprazole e/c tablets: 20mg once a day
- Age from 16 years onwards
- Pantoprazole 20mg e/c tablets. Take one tablet once a day; supply 28 tablets; NHS Cost £12.31.

Esomeprazole tablets: 20mg once a day
- Age from 16 years onwards
- Esomeprazole 20mg tablets. Take one tablet once a day; supply 28 tablets; NHS Cost £18.50.

Lansoprazole orodispersible tablets: 15mg each morning
- Age from 16 years onwards
- Lansoprazole 15mg orodisp tabs. Take one tablet each morning (on an empty stomach); supply 28 tablets; NHS Cost £10.86.

Lansoprazole orodispersible tablets: 30mg each morning
- Age from 16 years onwards
- Lansoprazole 30mg orodisp tabs. Take one tablet each morning (on an empty stomach); supply 28 tablets; NHS Cost £21.38.

Misoprostol tablets: 200micrograms four times a day
- Age from 16 years onwards
- Misoprostol 200microgram tabs. Take one tablet four times a day; supply 120 tablets; NHS Cost £18.72.

Muscle relaxant (diazepam): 1-week supply

Diazepam tablets: 2mg to 4mg three times a day
- Age from 16 years onwards
- Diazepam 2mg tablets. Take one to two tablets three times a day; supply 28 tablets; NHS Cost £1.14.

Simple low back pain — follow-up and reassessment

Which therapy

Assessment

- Formally assess risk factors for continued chronic low back pain ('yellow flags').
- Reassess distress, disability, and loss of work.
- Reassess risk factors for serious pathology ('red flags').
- Reassess presence of nerve root pain.

Management

- Provide 'brief educational advice' on chronic low back pain.
- Adjust analgesia to control pain as far as possible.
  - Use paracetamol or a nonsteroidal anti-inflammatory (NSAID) alone, or, if pain is not fully controlled, use paracetamol and codeine combined, an NSAID and paracetamol combined, or an NSAID combined with codeine.
  - Other options to consider if these are not suitable include:
    - An antidepressant (e.g. amitriptyline)
    - A short-term muscle relaxant (e.g. diazepam)
    - Topical capsaicin
    - Gabapentin
    - Strong opioids (usually only prescribed on specialist advice)
- If radicular pain has not responded to non-invasive treatment, consider referral for surgery.
- If yellow flags are present, consider referral for cognitive behavioural therapy or multi-disciplinary (bio-psycho-social) assessment and treatment.

- Consider referral for one or more of the following interventions, if they are available locally, given with a psycho-social approach, and if the patient would like to try them:
  - Spinal manipulation or mobilization, as a short course
  - Exercise therapy
  - Back school

B

Practical prescribing points

For further information please see the *Medicines Compendium* (www.medicines.org.uk) or the *British National Formulary* (www.bnf.org).

NSAIDs

- **Only one NSAID should be prescribed at a time.**
- **NSAIDs may worsen asthma, hypertension, renal impairment, or heart failure.**
- Do not give ibuprofen, diclofenac, or naproxen without gastroprotection if there is a history of peptic ulceration.
- **Pregnancy and breastfeeding:** use paracetamol if possible. If an NSAID is essential, ibuprofen may be used during breastfeeding and before 30 weeks of pregnancy.
- **People with cardiovascular disease:** ibuprofen may reduce the cardiovascular protective effect of low-dose aspirin.
- **In people with risk factors for gastrointestinal NSAID complications:**
  - Use paracetamol (with or without codeine) instead of a NSAID if possible.
  - Or, use gastroprotection (a PPI or full-dose misoprostol) combined with a standard NSAID.
- **Risk factors for gastrointestinal NSAID complications include:**
  - Age of 65 years and over.
  - Previous history of gastroduodenal ulcer, gastrointestinal (GI) bleeding, or gastroduodenal perforation.
  - Concomitant use of medications that are known to increase the likelihood of upper-GI adverse events, e.g. anticoagulants, aspirin (even a low dose), and corticosteroids.
  - Presence of serious comorbidity, such as cardiovascular disease, renal or hepatic impairment, diabetes, or hypertension.
  - Requirement for prolonged duration of NSAID use.
  - Use of maximum recommended doses of NSAIDs.

Codeine

- Codeine may cause nausea, vomiting, constipation, and drowsiness. A regular laxative is often needed when it is used long-term.

Diazepam

- Diazepam has strong sedative effects. People should be warned not to drive while taking the drug or for a full day after stopping drug treatment. In addition, people should be warned that the effects of alcohol may be exaggerated whilst taking this medication.
- Diazepam has a high potential for tolerance and dependence: only courses of 3–7 days should be used in people with significant spasm.
- Avoid use in pregnancy and breastfeeding.

Amitriptyline

- Amitriptyline may cause drowsiness: if this occurs advise the patient to avoid driving or performing skilled tasks where there is the potential for harm.
- Abrupt withdrawal may be a problem with tricyclic antidepressants.
- Avoid use in people with who have had a myocardial infarction, people with arrhythmias, or women in the third trimester of pregnancy.

Gabapentin

- Sudden withdrawal of gabapentin may cause anxiety, insomnia, nausea, pain, and sweating: it should be tapered off over the course of at least one week.
- Reduce the dose of gabapentin in renal impairment. See the *Medicines Compendium* (www.medicines.org.uk) fo dosage information.

Misoprostol

- Diarrhoea and abdominal pain are common. Advise women of childbearing age to use adequate contraception, since misoprostol increases the risk of miscarriage.

Follow-up advice

- Assess response to treatment in about 4 weeks, or as clinically indicated.

Should I refer or investigate?

Refer?

- Almost all people with acute low back pain can be managed in primary care.
- Refer immediately for emergency treatment if cauda equina syndrome or rapidly progressing neurological deficit is present.
- Refer if serious pathology is still suspected after basic investigations have been done.

Referral advice from the National Institute for Clinical Excellence

Referral advice: a guide to appropriate referral from general to specialist services [NICE, 2001b] Table 2 contains the following advice for people with acute low back pain. The referral advice is meant to encourage local health communities to discuss referral issues and enable local referral guidelines and protocols to be produced (for further information see www.nice.org.uk).

Investigate?

- **First-line investigations if red flags are present include:**
  - Plain X-ray of lumbosacral spine if red flags for spinal fracture, cancer, or infection — note that a negative X ray does not on its own rule out serious disease.
  - X-ray of thoracic spine if thoracic pain is also present.
  - Full blood count if red flags for cancer or infection.
  - Erythrocyte sedimentation rate if red flags for cancer or infection.
  - Urine analysis if red flags for cancer or infection.
- **Second-line investigations include:**
  - Computed tomographic or magnetic resonance imaging.
  - Bone scan.

Patient information leaflets

The following PILs are available at www.prodigy.nhs.uk

- Anti-inflammatory Painkillers
- BackCare (National Back Pain Association)
- Back Pain
- Back Pain - A Summary

able 2: Referral to a specialist service is advised if:

**	The person has neurological features of cauda equina syndrome, e.g. sphincter disturbance, progressive motor weakness, perineal anaesthesia, or evidence of bilateral nerve root involvement.
**	Serious spinal pathology is suspected (preferably seen within 1 week).
**	The person develops progressive neurological deficit, e.g. weakness, anaesthesia (preferably seen within 1 week).
**	The person has nerve root pain that is not resolving after 6 weeks (preferably seen within 3 weeks).
*	An underlying inflammatory disorder such as ankylosing spondylitis is suspected.
*	The person has simple back pain and has not resumed normal activities in 3 months. The effects of pain will vary and could include reduced quality of life, functional capacity, independence, or psychological well-being. Where possible, referral should be to a multidisciplinary back pain team.

y to referral timings

rangements should be made so that the person:

*** is seen immediately (within a day)

** is seen urgently (maximum wait of 2 weeks recommended, but to be agreed locally)

* is seen soon (maximum waiting time to be agreed locally)

* has a routine appointment (maximum waiting time to be agreed locally)

^ is seen within an appropriate time depending on his or her clinical circumstances (discretionary)

hared decision making

The outlook for back pain is good. Most people with a recent bout of low back pain are:

- Back at work, housework, school within a few days or weeks.
- Pain free, or nearly pain free, within 3-6 weeks.

But low back pain frequently fluctuates in intensity, or recurs.

People with low back pain are often helped by information about their problem. For example, from BackCare (The National Back Pain Association) www.backcare.org.uk.

Recovery is helped by keeping active as much as possible, getting back to work as soon as possible, and restoring normal fitness.

Various pain-relieving treatments may be options. For example:

- Painkillers
- A short course of a muscle relaxant
- Physical treatments such as spinal manipulation
- Anti-depressants or anti-convulsants used for their pain-relieving effects
- Exercise therapy
- Back school

)rug rationale

)rugs not included

Analgesics other than paracetamol and codeine taken separately are not recommended:

- **Strong opioids** (e.g. morphine, pethidine) should be avoided because of the risk of dependence if they are used inappropriately.
- **Weak opioids, other than codeine,** have either not been shown to be more effective than codeine (when used in combination with paracetamol), or are more expensive.
- **Low-dose weak opioids with paracetamol** (combination products), e.g. co-codamol 8/500 mg: there is no evidence that these offer any clinical benefit over paracetamol alone and they are likely to lead to opioid adverse effects [MeReC, 1993; De Craen et al, 1996; Moore and McQuay, 1997].
- **High-dose weak opioids with paracetamol** (combination products), e.g. co-codamol 30/500 mg: these do not allow titration to the most effective and safe analgesic dose to match individual requirements.
- **Co-proxamol** (dextropropoxyphene 32.5 mg/ paracetamol 325 mg) has been withdrawn by the Committee on Safety of Medicines due to its unfavourable risk/benefit ratio; it is associated with an unacceptable risk of overdose [CSM, 2005a].

B

- **Standard nonsteroidal anti-inflammatory drugs (NSAIDs), other than ibuprofen, diclofenac, and naproxen,** are not generally recommended, as they have a worse balance between their efficacy and adverse effect profile than these three recommended drugs [CSM, 1994; Hernández-Diaz et al, 2000; BNF 49, 2005].
- **Cyclo-oxygenase 2 (COX-2) selective inhibitors** are not recommended. After the withdrawal of rofecoxib from the market (the only selective inhibitor licensed for acute pain), there are growing concerns that COX-2 selective inhibitors may cause serious cardiovascular events. Following a European-wide review of the data, the Committee on Safety of Medicines (CSM) has recently advised that [CSM, 2005b]:
  - The evidence suggests that coxibs, as a class, may cause an increased risk of thrombotic events (e.g. myocardial infarction and stroke) compared with placebo and some NSAIDs.
  - The risk may increase with dose and duration of exposure.
- **Strong opioids** (e.g. morphine, pethidine) should be avoided, owing to the risk of dependence if they are used inappropriately. They are usually reserved for moderate to severe pain of a visceral origin [BNF 49, 2005].
- **Gastroprotective agents** are sometimes needed, but not all are recommended:
  - **H_2-receptor antagonists (H_2RAs):** at standard doses, H_2RAs reduce the risk of duodenal ulceration, and there is some evidence that double doses reduce the risk of gastric ulceration [Rostom et al, 2002]. However, no H_2RAs are currently licensed for the prevention of gastric ulceration induced by NSAIDs [BNF 49, 2005], which is more common than duodenal ulceration.
  - **Rabeprazole** is not included as it is not specifically licensed for the prevention of NSAID-induced gastrointestinal ulcers [BNF 49, 2005].
  - **Fixed-dose combinations of standard NSAIDs with misoprostol:** the optimum dose of misoprostol (i.e. 800 micrograms daily) cannot be reached using these preparations. In particular, only 400 micrograms daily of misoprostol is given with the higher doses of NSAID in these preparations.
- **Diazepam:** there is no good-quality evidence to support its use as a muscle relaxant in chronic low back pain.
- **Pregabalin** has a similar mechanism of action to gabapentin, and is licensed for the treatment of neuropathic pain [BNF 49, 2005]. However, it is currently undergoing post-marketing surveillance (black triangle), and should reserved for use under specialist supervision.

Drugs included

Standard analgesics and NSAIDs

- **Paracetamol:** this is a good first-line choice for pain relief, and is not associated with gastrointestinal toxicity [SIGN, 2000].
- **Codeine (in combination with paracetamol):** higher-dose codeine is included for use with regular paracetamol for additional pain relief. Codeine 60 mg plus paracetamol has been shown to provide more pain relief than either

codeine 60 mg alone or paracetamol 1000 mg alone [Moore and McQuay, 1997]. Codeine should be prescribed separately to paracetamol to allow flexibility of dosing and titration of analgesic effect.
  - Note: codeine can also be combined with an NSAID, or paracetamol can be combined with an NSAID, but there is less evidence to support this.
- **Standard NSAIDs: ibuprofen, diclofenac, and naproxen** have a good balance of efficacy against adverse effect profile [CSM, 1994; Henry et al, 1996; Hernández-Diaz and Rodriguez, 2000]. Standard doses are offered as these are generally accepted to be sufficient for anti-inflammatory prophylaxis, although data are lacking.

Gastroprotective agents

- **Proton pump inhibitors (PPIs): lansoprazole, omeprazole, esomeprazole, and pantoprazole** are licensed for the prevention of gastroduodenal ulceration induced by NSAIDs [BNF 49, 2005]. PPIs reduce the risk of endoscopically proven ulcers, but there are no data on prevention of ulcer complications [Rostom et al, 2002]. However, PPIs are generally considered to be the first-line choice for gastroprotection, as they are better tolerated than misoprostol.
- **Misoprostol** is licensed for the prevention of gastroduodenal ulceration induced by NSAIDs [BNF 49, 2005]. It reduces the risk of endoscopically proven ulcers and has also been shown to reduce the risk of ulcer complications [Rostom et al, 2002]. It is less well tolerated than PPIs owing to gastrointestinal adverse effects, particularly diarrhoea.

Drugs for chronic pain

Note: although commonly used, amitriptyline and gabapentin are not licensed for the treatment of chronic pain.

- **Amitriptyline** is a tricyclic antidepressant widely used for chronic pain of various causes [McQuay and Moore, 1997]. At present there is uncertain benefit of tricyclic antidepressants in chronic low back pain, but an initial one-month trial of therapy may be worth considering in people in whom standard analgesia and/or NSAIDs have proved ineffective.
- **Gabapentin** can be considered if amitriptyline has proved ineffective or is contraindicated, although there is little trial evidence at present to verify its efficacy. The exact dose of gabapentin that is required to alleviate chronic lower back pain is not known, but the full 'antiepileptic dose' is probably necessary.

Prescriptions

Paracetamol or codeine

Paracetamol tablets: 1g up to four times a day
- Age from 16 years onwards
- Paracetamol 500mg tablets. Take two tablets every 4 to 6 hours when required for pain relief. Maximum of 8 tablets in 24 hours; supply 200 tablets; NHS Cost £2.12; OTC Cost £3.75.

Codeine tablets: 30mg to 60mg up to four times a day
- Age from 16 years onwards
- Codeine 30mg tablets. Take one to two tablets every 4 to 6 hours when required for pain relief. Maximum of 8 tablets in 24 hours; supply 60 tablets; NHS Cost £4.58.

Paracetamol 500mg tablets + codeine 30mg tablets
- Age from 16 years onwards
- Paracetamol 500mg tablets. Take two tablets every 4 to 6 hours when required for pain relief. Maximum of 8 tablets in 24 hours; supply 200 tablets; NHS Cost £2.12; OTC Cost £3.75.
- Codeine 30mg tablets. Take one to two tablets every 4 to 6 hours when required for pain relief. Maximum of 8 tablets in 24 hours; supply 60 tablets; NHS Cost £4.58

Standard NSAIDs: ibuprofen, naproxen and diclofenac

Ibuprofen tablets: 400mg three times a day
- Age from 16 years onwards
- Ibuprofen 400mg tablets. Take one tablet three times a day; supply 84 tablets; NHS Cost £2.74; OTC Cost £4.83.

Ibuprofen tablets: 400mg four times a day
- Age from 16 years onwards
- Ibuprofen 400mg tablets. Take one tablet four times a day; supply 112 tablets; NHS Cost £3.65; OTC Cost £6.44.

Ibuprofen tablets: 600mg three times a day
- Age from 16 years onwards
- Ibuprofen 600mg tablets. Take one tablet three times a day; supply 84 tablets; NHS Cost £2.81.

Ibuprofen tablets: 800mg three times a day
- Age from 16 years onwards
- Ibuprofen 400mg tablets. Take two tablets three times a day; supply 168 tablets; NHS Cost £5.48.

Diclofenac sodium e/c tablets: 25mg three times a day
- Age from 16 years onwards
- Diclofenac 25mg e/c tablets. Take one tablet three time a day; supply 84 tablets; NHS Cost £1.72.

Diclofenac sodium e/c tablets: 50mg three times a day
- Age from 16 years onwards
- Diclofenac 50mg e/c tablets. Take one tablet three time a day; supply 84 tablets; NHS Cost £1.45.

Naproxen tablets: 250mg twice a day
- Age from 16 years onwards
- Naproxen 250mg tablets. Take one tablet twice a day; supply 56 tablets; NHS Cost £2.68.

Naproxen tablets: 500mg twice a day
- Age from 16 years onwards
- Naproxen 500mg tablets. Take one tablet twice a day; supply 56 tablets; NHS Cost £4.90.

GI protection: use ONLY with a standard NSAID

Omeprazole capsules: 20mg once a day
- Age from 16 years onwards
- Omeprazole 20mg capsules. Take one capsule once a day; supply 28 capsules; NHS Cost £12.75.

Omeprazole tablets: 20mg once a day
- Age from 16 years onwards
- Omeprazole 20mg tablets. Take one tablet once a day; supply 28 tablets; NHS Cost £12.75.

Lansoprazole capsules: 15mg each morning
- Age from 16 years onwards
- Lansoprazole 15mg capsules. Take one capsule each morning (on an empty stomach); supply 28 capsules; NHS Cost £12.92.

Lansoprazole capsules: 30mg each morning
- Age from 16 years onwards
- Lansoprazole 30mg capsules. Take one capsule each morning (on an empty stomach); supply 28 capsules; NHS Cost £23.63.

Pantoprazole e/c tablets: 20mg once a day
- Age from 16 years onwards
- Pantoprazole 20mg e/c tablets. Take one tablet once a day; supply 28 tablets; NHS Cost £12.31.

Esomeprazole tablets: 20mg once a day
- Age from 16 years onwards
- Esomeprazole 20mg tablets. Take one tablet once a day supply 28 tablets; NHS Cost £18.50.

ansoprazole orodispersible tablets: 15mg each morning
Age from 16 years onwards
Lansoprazole 15mg orodisp tabs. Take one tablet each morning (on an empty stomach); supply 28 tablets; NHS Cost £10.86.

ansoprazole orodispersible tablets: 30mg each morning
Age from 16 years onwards
Lansoprazole 30mg orodisp tabs. Take one tablet each morning (on an empty stomach); supply 28 tablets; NHS Cost £21.38.

isoprostol tablets: 200micrograms four times a day
Age from 16 years onwards
Misoprostol 200microgram tabs. Take one tablet four times a day; supply 120 tablets; NHS Cost £18.72.

Amitriptyline: 1-month trial

mitriptyline tablets: 10mg at night
Age from 16 years onwards
Amitriptyline 10mg tablets. Take one tablet at night; supply 28 tablets; NHS Cost £1.00.

mitriptyline tablets: 25mg at night
Age from 16 years onwards
Amitriptyline 25mg tablets. Take one tablet at night; supply 28 tablets; NHS Cost £1.71.

Gabapentin: 1-month trial

abapentin: titrate up to 300mg three times a day
Age from 18 years onwards
Gabapentin 100mg capsules. Take one capsule three times a day for 3 days, then take two capsules three times a day for 3 days, then start taking the gabapentin 300mg capsules; supply 27 capsules; NHS Cost £6.92.
Gabapentin 300mg capsules. Start, once the course of gabapentin 100mg capsules is complete. Take one capsule three times a day; supply 84 capsules; NHS Cost £48.20.

Low back pain — red flags for serious pathology present

Which therapy

Red flags for spine fracture

Flags from medical history
- Major trauma such as vehicle accident or fall from a height.
- Minor trauma, or even just strenuous lifting, in people who may have osteoporosis.

Management
- Plain X-ray of lumbosacral spine.
- Refer if fracture detected, else follow up in about 10 days.
- On follow-up, if fracture still suspected, or multiple sites of pain, consider bone scan and referral.

Red flags for cancer or infection

Flags from medical history
- Age over 50 years and new low back pain, or age under 20 years
- History of cancer
- Constitutional symptoms, e.g. fever, chills, unexplained weight loss
- Recent bacterial infection (e.g. urinary tract infection)
- Intravenous drug abuse
- Immune suppression
- Pain that worsens when supine; severe night-time pain

Management
- Check full blood count, erythrocyte sedimentation rate, urine analysis.
- If still concerned, consider referral, or seek further clinical evidence with bone scan, X-ray, or other laboratory tests.
- Note that a negative X-ray alone does not rule out disease.

Red flags for cauda equina syndrome or rapidly progressing neurological deficit

- **Flags from medical history**
  - Saddle anaesthesia
  - Recent onset of bladder dysfunction (e.g. urine retention, increased frequency, overflow incontinence)
- **Flags from physical examination**
  - Severe or progressive neurological deficit in the lower extremities
  - Unexpected laxity of the anal sphincter
  - Perianal/perineal sensory loss
  - Major motor weakness: knee extension, ankle plantar eversion, foot dorsiflexion
- **Management**
  - Refer immediately for emergency studies and definitive care.

Follow-up advice

- If follow-up of test results does not allay suspicion of possible serious pathology, refer for definitive workup.

Should I refer or investigate?

Refer?

- Refer immediately if cauda equina syndrome or rapidly progressing neurological deficit is present.
- Refer if serious pathology is still suspected after basic investigations have been done.

Investigate?

First-line investigations include:
- Plain X-ray of lumbosacral spine if red flags for spinal fracture, cancer, or infection — note that a negative X-ray does not on its own rule out serious disease.
- X-ray of thoracic spine if thoracic pain is also present.
- Full blood count if red flags for cancer or infection.
- Erythrocyte sedimentation rate if red flags for cancer or infection.
- Urine analysis if red flags for cancer or infection.

Second-line investigations include:
- Computed tomographic or magnetic resonance imaging
- Bone scan, if available

Patient information leaflets

The following PILs are available at www.prodigy.nhs.uk
- Anti-inflammatory Painkillers
- BackCare (National Back Pain Association)
- Back Pain
- Back Pain - A Summary

Shared decision making

- You have a symptom or sign that requires some tests.
- These tests are to find out if you have ordinary back pain, or if there is another cause for your back pain.

Drug rationale

- There are no drugs included in this scenario.

B

Extended Information

Background information

- What is simple low back pain? p.196
- What are the origins of low back pain? p.196
- What are the risk factors for low back pain? p.196
- How common is low back pain? p.197
- How do I know my patient has simple low back pain? p.197
- What else might it be? p.198
- Complications and prognosis p.198

What is simple low back pain?

Low back pain: definitions and classifications

- **Low back pain** is pain between the bottom of the ribs at the back and the top of the legs — the anatomical location is illustrated in the review by Jensen [Jensen, 2004].
- **Simple low back pain** is low back pain in which the cause of the pain cannot be attributed to any specific pathology — it is also commonly called non-specific, or uncomplicated, low back pain.
- **Simple back pain is mechanical** in the sense that it varies with posture or activity, and it varies over time in response to altered activities or treatment [Waddell, 2004].
- **Nerve root pain (or radicular pain)** is pain due to nerve root irritation. Simple low back pain can occur with or without radicular pain.
- **'Sciatica'** is a lay term for pain and sensations of tingling that travel into the buttocks, back of the thigh, and into the calf and heel. These symptoms are caused by irritation of the sciatic nerve. Additionally, non-specific pain from the lumbar area can be referred in the distribution of the sciatic nerve.
- Low back pain is classified as:
  - **Acute** if it has lasted less than 6 weeks
  - **Sub-acute** if it has lasted 6–12 weeks
  - **Chronic** if it has lasted more than 12 weeks
- The classification of low back pain into acute, sub-acute, and chronic is necessary for scientific studies and useful in clinical practice, but it is a substantial simplification of reality, and may be misleading [Waddell, 2004].
  - Low back pain tends to follow a course that fluctuates over days, weeks, and months. It is thus not always possible to distinguish between a new acute event and an exacerbation of a chronic process.
  - Chronic pain and disability often seem to become dissociated from the original physical problem.

[van Tulder et al, 2004]

Disability: definition and distinction from pain

- Disability is limitation of activity.
- Although pain and disability go hand in hand with each other, they are not the same, and failure to distinguish them has a major impact on management.
- Pain is a symptom, whereas disability is perceived restriction of function.

[Waddell, 2004]

What are the origins of low back pain?

It is seldom possible or useful (with the exception of nerve root pain) to identify the precise source or sources of pain in a particular individual with simple low back pain. The pain could arise from any combination of muscle, nerve root, fascia, ligament, bone, joint, or disc in the back. In practice, for almost all people with acute simple low back pain, the initial treatment (and often the chronic management) does not target a specific anatomic source c pain. Further research is needed to identify strategies that can effectively identify and target specific sources of low back pain.

[van Tulder et al, 2004; Waddell, 2004]

What are the risk factors for low back pain?

Risk factors for acute simple low back pain in adult

Risk factors for acute simple low back pain are poorly understood. Age, sex, height, weight, and genetics have little material influence on simple low back pain. The mos frequently reported risk factors relate to physical aspects work:

- Heavy physical work
- Lifting and handling of loads
- Awkward postures and movements (for example: bending; twisting; static postures)
- Whole body vibration (for example truck driving)

[European Agency for Safety and Health at Work, 2000; van Tulder et al, 2004; Waddell, 2004; Health and Safety Executive, 2005]

Risk factors for acute simple low back pain in children

Many factors have been put forward as likely risks for acute low back pain in children. A number observational studies have been made, and these provide some evidence of absence of effect and no good evidence of effect. Thus, no evidence-based recommendations can be made for any measures to prevent acute simple low back pain in children.

- Jones and Macfarlane Summarize the evidence from a structured review of risk factors for low back pain in children [Jones and Macfarlane, 2005]:
  - **Weight, height, body mass index, growth, and maturation**
    - There is no good evidence to relate the onset of low back pain to height, growth, weight, or body mass index (BMI).
    - Hypermobility was associated with severe low back pain in one cross-sectional study.
  - **Lifestyle factors**
    - Although cross-sectional studies have consistently found correlations between level of activity and low back pain, evidence for a causal link has not been found by the few prospective studies that have been carried out.
  - **Mechanical load**
    - Despite widespread claims that carrying heavy school bags causes low back pain, this is not supported by the evidence.
  - **Psychological factors and the social environment**
    - There is good evidence that children with low back pain are more likely to have negative psychosocial experiences such as emotional and conduct problems, and they are more likely to have other somatic symptoms and musculoskeletal pain.
    - There is some evidence to support the hypothesis that such negative experiences predict those at high risk of back pain in the future.
- **Flexed posture** was significantly associated with low back pain in a more recent cross-sectional study of 66 schoolchildren aged 11–16 years [Murphy et al, 2004].

Risk factors for developing chronic low back pain

Yellow flags

Risk factors for developing and/or persisting chronic pain and long-term disability are called 'yellow flags'. Yellow flags are psycho-social barriers to recovery. They include:

- Belief that pain and activity are harmful
- Sickness behaviours such as extended rest
- Social withdrawal
- Emotional problems such as low or negative mood, depression, anxiety, stress
- Problems and/or dissatisfaction at work
- Problems with claims or compensation or time off work
- Overprotective family; lack of support
- Inappropriate expectations of treatment, e.g. low expectations of active participation in treatment

ie New Zealand screening questionnaire for psycho-cial barriers to recovery may be the most commonly used rmal tool for assessing yellow flags. It is available online www.nzgg.org.nz.

ie European guideline for the management of acute low ck pain recommends the urgent development and lidation of instruments to assess psycho-social risk ctors and identify groups of people at high risk of ronicity.

IZGG, 2004; Pecukonis, 2004; van Tulder et al, 2004]

ow common is low back pain?

w back pain is a common problem in adults and ildren.

owever, it is difficult to obtain precise and consistent antitative answers to the question 'How common is low ck pain?' There are a number of reasons for this fficulty, including:

- Studies of the epidemiology of low back pain have used various case definitions of low back pain.
- The natural history of low back pain, with fluctuations and recurrences, is not accurately reflected in the classification of low back pain into acute, sub-acute, and chronic back pain.
- Cross-sectional studies and questionnaires relying on self-reporting may be subject to systematic bias.

Vaddell, 2004]

low often does low back pain occur?

ccurrence of low back pain in adults

- Most people have low back pain sometime; the lifetime prevalence of low back pain is over 60–80% in industrialized countries [Clinical Standards Advisory Group, 1994].
- Men and women are equally affected.
- It occurs most often between ages 30 and 50.

ccurrence of low back pain in children

- A structured review of the evidence indexed in Medline [Jones and Macfarlane, 2005] found that:
  - Low back pain in children is common, but surveys of incidence and prevalence provide widely varying estimates. For example, as many as 5% of children may be experiencing low back pain at any one time.
- A more recent questionnaire survey [Jones et al, 2004] of 500 schoolchildren aged between 10 and 16 years in north-west England found:
  - The lifetime prevalence of low back pain was 40%.
  - 13% of the children experienced recurrent low back pain

How common is disability due to simple low back pain?

ecause disability has been assessed in a variety of ways, ata on the prevalence and natural history of disability due simple low back pain provide imprecise evidence Waddell, 2004]. Nevertheless, the available evidence hows that disability due to simple low back pain has a rge impact on individuals and the economy.

Disability due to low back pain in adults

- Low back pain accounts for about 52 million lost working days each year in Britain [Bandolier, 1995].

Disability due to low back pain in children

There is inconsistent evidence on how frequently children are disabled by low back pain.

- A structured review of the evidence indexed in Medline [Jones and Macfarlane, 2005] found that 'few children' report low back pain severe enough to prevent them from participating in sport or attending school.
- In contrast, a more recent questionnaire survey of 500 schoolchildren in north-west England aged between 10 and 16 years found that 26% had been absent from school because of low back pain [Jones et al, 2004].

B

What is the impact of low back pain on the health services?

Low back pain in adults

Low back pain has a large impact on health services.

- Low back pain accounts for about 4% of GP consultations [Jones et al, 2004].
- The NHS was estimated in 1994 to be spending about £480 million on services used by people with back pain, including about 14 million GP consultations, 7 million physical therapy sessions, and 800,000 in-patient bed-days [Clinical Standards Advisory Group, 1994].
- The direct health care costs of back pain in the UK were estimated in 1998 to be £1632 million [Directorate of Information and Clinical Effectiveness, 2001].

Low back pain in children

Evidence on how frequently children consult about low back pain is conflicting.

- A structured review of the evidence indexed in Medline found that consultations for low back pain in children are 'uncommon' [Jones and Macfarlane, 2005].
- A more recent questionnaire survey of 500 schoolchildren in north-west England found that 23% of the children had consulted a medical practitioner about low back pain [Jones et al, 2004].

How common are serious causes of low back pain?

- Less than 5% of people with low back pain have true nerve root pain (and only a small proportion of these will require an operation).
- Less than 1% of people with low back pain have serious disease such as spinal tumour or infection.
- Less than 1% of people with low back pain have inflammatory disease such as ankylosing spondylitis.

[Waddell, 2004]

How do I know my patient has simple low back pain?

A simple diagnostic triage should be used to decide if someone with back pain is suffering from simple low back pain, or nerve root pain from the low back, or possible serious pathology.

- Take a thorough history, complemented by a brief clinical examination. This will be sufficient for most people with acute simple low back pain [van Tulder et al, 2004; Waddell, 2004].
- Confirm that the pain *is* in the low back [Australasian Faculty of Musculoskeletal Medicine, 2002].
  - For example people sometimes complain of pain in the hips but show the location of pain to be in the low back [Jensen, 2004].
- Establish whether the pain is acute, sub-acute, or chronic; and whether it is the first episode, a recurrence, or an exacerbation.
- Ask about psycho-social risk factors (*Yellow flags*) [van Tulder et al, 2004].

B

- If there are recurrent episodes or failure to respond to treatment, consider using an explicit screen of psychosocial factors such as the New Zealand screening questionnaire [van Tulder et al, 2004].
- Distinguish referred pain from nerve root pain.
  - About 70% of people with simple low back pain have pain referred to the buttocks and thighs. Referred pain is usually a dull, poorly localized pain, and can affect both legs.
  - In contrast, nerve root pain is sharp and well localized, following a dermatome quite closely. People with nerve root pain often have a sensation of numbness, or tingling.
  - Nerve root pain at the common L5 and S1 levels usually extends to the foot or toes.
  - When nerve root pain is present it is usually the chief complaint.
  - The passive straight leg raise test (PSLT) is widely used to help diagnose nerve root pain. The PSLT is also known as the test of Lasegue. It has high sensitivity (about 90%) but low specificity (about 20%) for diagnosing nerve root pain due to herniated discs [Devillè et al, 2000].
    - With the person lying flat on their back with both legs straight, raise one leg until limited by pain and/or tight hamstrings. Slightly lower the leg to provide relief.
    - In this position, increase tension on the sciatic nerve by dorsiflexion of the foot (or flexion of the neck or compression of the nerve in the popliteal fossa). This will aggravate or elicit pain radiating down the raised leg if there is nerve root irritation. The pain should be relieved by flexion of the knee.
  - The PSLT can also be performed in the sitting position. A discrepancy with the supine PSLT suggests that the symptoms could be factitious.
- Rule out serious pathology — see *Red flags* below.
- Consider diagnostic imaging only if there are indications of serious pathology [van Tulder et al, 2004].
  - Radiography of the lumbar spine is not useful in simple low back pain, and may even increase the workload of general practitioners with no improvement in clinical outcomes (other than patient satisfaction) [Kendrick et al, 2001].
  - Magnetic resonance imaging is the best procedure for use in diagnosing nerve root compression, discitis, and neoplasms [van Tulder et al, 2004].

What else might it be?

Pain from an adjacent structure

- Thoracic pain
- Loin pain: in the renal angle, i.e. in the lower back and side between the lowest rib and the pelvic girdle
- Hip pain: alteration or reduction of hip rotation is an early sign of pain in the hip
- Abdominal pain
- Pelvic girdle pain

Low back pain with a specific cause:

- **Referred pain from:**
  - **Abdomen:** aortic aneurysm
  - **Kidney:** pyelonephritis, hydronephrosis, calculi, tumour, perinephric abscess
  - **Ovary:** cysts, cancer
  - **Pelvis:** endometriosis, period pain, pelvic inflammatory disease
  - **Bladder:** infections
- **Degenerative and structural changes**
  - **Spondylosis** (spinal osteoarthritis with bony overgrowths — osteophytes — at the margins of the vertebra and degenerative spinal facet and disc damage; results in narrowing of spinal canal and nerve root impingement)
  - **Spondylolisthesis** (forward displacement of one vertebra on its lower neighbour, often with a stress fracture in the pars interarticularis)
  - **Gross scoliosis and/or kyphosis**
- **Inflammatory conditions**
  - Ankylosing spondylitis
  - Polymyalgia rheumatica
  - Rheumatoid arthritis (rarely a cause of back pain)
  - Coccydynia
- **Infections**
  - Shingles before the rash has developed, or post-herpetic neuralgia
  - Discitis
  - Osteomyelitis, bacterial or tuberculous
  - Epidural abscess
- **Neoplasms**
  - Secondary deposits in bone
  - Myeloma or other (more rare) primary cancer
- **Metabolic bone disease**
  - Osteoporosis with vertebral collapse
  - Osteomalacia
  - Paget's disease

Complications and prognosis

Complications of low back pain

- Development of chronicity and depression
- Disability and loss of employment
- Cauda equina syndrome: when disc material is pushed into the spinal canal and compresses the bundle of lumbar and sacral nerve roots. Permanent neurological damage may result if this is not treated as an emergency

Prognosis for acute low back pain

The prognosis for acute low back pain is described in detail in a systematic review [Pengel et al, 2003].

- Pain and disability usually decrease rapidly within 1 month, and continue to decrease, albeit more slowly, until about 12 months. For example:
  - Mean pain levels on a 100 point scale were about:
    - 65 initially
    - 22 at 1 month
    - 15 between 3 and 12 months
- About 75% of people initially off work are able to return to work within 4 weeks.
- The risk of recurrence is about 25% within 3 months and about 75% with 12 months.

Prognosis for chronic disability due to low back pain

Data on the development of chronic pain and disability are discussed in several narrative reviews [Frank et al, 1996; Frank et al, 1998; Waddell, 2004].

- The longer people are off work because of low back pain, the less likely it is that they will ever return to work.
  - During the acute phase the proportion of people off work falls rapidly to about 50%
  - During the sub-acute phase the proportion of people off work falls steadily to about 25%
  - During the chronic phase the proportion of people off work decreases ever more slowly, and the prognosis for return to work steadily worsens

Management issues

How do I manage acute low back pain? p.199
What do I do if significant low back pain remains after 4–6 weeks? p.200
Occupational health issues — work and back pain p.201
Interventions not recommended for the treatment of low back pain p.202
How can low back pain be prevented? p.202
Medicines management p.202
Supporting evidence for drug therapies p.203
Additional supporting evidence p.203

How do I manage acute low back pain?

The rationale for the recommendations in this section, and systematic reviews of the evidence supporting these recommendations can be found in the European guidelines on low back pain and the book by Waddell [van Tulder et al, 2004; Waddell, 2004].

Relevant new information published later than these sources is reviewed in the section *Additional supporting evidence*.

Overview

Assessment

- Exclude serious pathology, or act appropriately to the presence of any 'Red flag'.
- Assess psycho-social risk factors ('Yellow flags').
- Assess distress, disability, and loss of work.
- Assess presence of nerve root pain.

Treatment and support

- Provide educational advice, including the absence of serious pathology, good prognosis, no need for X-rays, best to remain active, and substantial risk of recurrence.
- Provide adequate symptom control, e.g. with paracetamol or an NSAID, or combination of analgesics. Use a short term muscle relaxant if there is spasm present.
- Recommend rapid return to usual activities including work.
- If symptoms require rest for a few days, ensure as much mobility as possible is continued.
- Consider referral for physical methods given with a psycho-social approach by musculoskeletal physiotherapists or osteopaths, or chiropractors.
- Address any psycho-social risk factors. Common issues such as fear avoidance and unhelpful beliefs and thoughts about back pain may be addressed through education. If more than a brief GP intervention is required, refer to physiotherapy or other spinal specialist.
- Assess response to treatment after about 4 weeks.

Red flags

- Rule out serious pathology by assessing the presence or absence of 'red flags'.
- Red flags are indicators of increased risk of serious pathology — but they do not always indicate a specific condition.
- Further investigation and referral are indicated if one or more red flags are present.

Red flags for spine fracture

- **Flags from medical history**
  - Major trauma such as vehicle accident or fall from a height
  - Minor trauma, or even just strenuous lifting, in people with osteoporosis
- **Management to consider if one or more flags are present**
  - Plain X-ray of lumbosacral spine.
  - Refer if fracture detected, otherwise follow up in about 10 days.
  - On follow-up, if fracture still suspected, or multiple sites of pain, consider bone scan and referral.

Red flags for cancer or infection

- **Flags from medical history**
  - Age over 50 years and new back pain, or age under 20 years
  - History of cancer
  - Constitutional symptoms, e.g. fever, chills, unexplained weight loss
  - Recent bacterial infection (e.g. urinary tract infection)
  - Intravenous drug abuse
  - Immune suppression
  - Pain that worsens when supine; severe night-time pain; thoracic pain
- **Flags from physical examination**
  - Structural deformity
- **Management to consider if one or more flags are present**
  - Check full blood count, erythrocyte sedimentation rate, urine analysis.
  - If still concerned, consider referral, or seek further clinical evidence with bone scan, X-ray, or other laboratory tests.
  - Note that a negative X-ray alone does not rule out disease.

Red flags for cauda equina syndrome or rapidly progressing neurological deficit

- **Flags from medical history**
  - Saddle anaesthesia
  - Recent onset of bladder dysfunction (e.g. urine retention, increased frequency, overflow incontinence)
  - Recent onset of faecal incontinence
- **Flags from physical examination**
  - Severe or progressive neurological deficit in the lower extremities
  - Unexpected laxity of the anal sphincter
  - Perianal/perineal sensory loss
  - Major motor weakness: knee extension, ankle plantar eversion, foot dorsiflexion
- **Management to consider if one or more flags are present**
  - Refer immediately for emergency investigations and definitive care

Psycho-social risk factors ('yellow flags')

- Ask about psycho-social risk factors including mood and emotions, problems at work, and fears and beliefs about low back pain and its treatment — see *Yellow flags* above.

Disability and work loss

- Assess loss of work, housework, or school attendance.
- Assess restrictions in activities of daily living.

Table 3 lists a set of questions to ask about the activities of daily living. These question have been simplified for use in clinical practice, and may be as reliable as the disability questionnaires used in research [Waddell and Main, 1984].

Educational advice

Educational advice should include the following:

- Back pain is a physical, not a psychological problem.
- Back pain is a mechanical problem; a disturbance of function rather than structural damage.
- Back pain is an everyday bodily symptom. It is not a disease, or a signal of serious disease.
- The outlook is good. Most people with acute low back pain are:
  - Back at work, housework, or school within a few days or weeks
  - Pain-free, or nearly pain-free, within about 3 weeks

B

Table 3: Questions for disability assessment.

Does back pain limit you in:	Standard limits
Bending and lifting?	Lift 15–20 kg, heavy suitcase, 3- to 4-year-old child
Sitting?	Sit in an ordinary chair: less than 30 minutes
Standing?	Stand in one place: less than 30 minutes
Walking?	Walk less than 30 minutes or 1–2 miles
Travelling by car or bus?	Travel less than 30 minutes
Socializing?	Socialize: miss or curtail social activities (excluding sport)
Sleeping?	Sleep disturbed by pain at least twice a week
Sex life?	Sexual activity reduced or curtailed
Dressing?	Dress: help required with footwear

- *But* low back pain frequently fluctuates in intensity, and it tends to recur.
- People with low back pain usually want (and are helped by) information about their problem.
  - An enormous amount on low back pain is published on the Internet, and in books. However, much patient-orientated information is advertising for remedies and treatments which have not been shown to be effective [Waddell, 2004].
- Pain control is routinely provided, but the aim is relief, not cure.
- The person with back pain must accept that responsibility for dealing with the back pain is shared between patient and healthcare professional.
- Recovery depends on getting moving again, getting back to work as soon as possible, and restoring normal function and fitness.
- Positive attitudes are important. 'Copers' suffer less at the time, get better quicker, and have less trouble in the long term.

Drug treatment

- Paracetamol is preferred as the first choice for analgesia because it is effective and the risk of adverse effects is low.
- Other options (to be considered if paracetamol is unsuitable or ineffective) include:
  - A nonsteroidal anti-inflammatory drug (NSAID), if suitable
  - A combination of two analgesics: e.g. paracetamol, an NSAID, or codeine
- If analgesics fail to provide adequate relief, consider a short course of a muscle relaxant, on its own or together with an NSAID.
  - Several muscle relaxants have been studied in relation to lower back pain. Diazepam is usually the first-line choice.
  - Due to the risk of the development of benzodiazepine dependency, diazepam is recommended only for short courses.

Rapid return to usual activities

- Recommend rapid return to usual activities, including work if possible. More information is given in the section *Occupational health issues — work and back pain.*
- As a consequence of their pain some patients may need to remain in bed for a few days, but this should not be regarded as treatment, and as much movement as possible should be continued.
- There is good evidence that bed rest does not promote recovery from acute simple low back pain, with or without sciatica.

Physical methods for comfort and to control symptoms

- If available locally and in accordance with the patient's preferences, consider recommending or referring for active physical methods.
  - Physical interventions may provide some short-term comfort, but there is little evidence of long-term benefit.
  - An active approach to management, which may include manipulation, and is cognisant of the psycho-social approach, should be taken. This approach can adequately be given by all physiotherapists, in musculoskeletal services, or by osteopaths or chiropractors.
- Local heat or cold applied by the person at home may provide some comfort. This can be used as desired. Give appropriate safety advice to take care not to use excessive heat or cold.

Follow up and reassess

- There is no international consensus on an appropriate time interval for follow-up to assess response to treatment of acute low back pain. Use clinical judgement and follow local guidelines.

What do I do if significant low back pain remains after 4–6 weeks?

The rationale for the recommendations in this section and systematic reviews of the evidence supporting these recommendations can be found in the European guideline on low back pain and the book by Waddell [Airaksinen et al, 2004; van Tulder et al, 2004; Waddell, 2004]. Relevant new information published after these sources is reviewed in the section *Additional supporting evidence*.

Overview

Assessment

- Formally assess risk factors for continued chronic low back pain ('Yellow flags').
- Reassess distress, disability, and loss of work.
- Reassess risk factors for serious pathology ('Red flags').
- Reassess presence of nerve root pain.

Management

- Provide 'brief educational advice' on chronic low back pain.
- Address any problems relating to return to work.
- Adjust analgesia to control pain as far as possible.
  - Paracetamol and NSAIDs are the usual first- and second-line options.
  - Other options to consider if these are not suitable include:
    - An antidepressant
    - A weak opioid
    - Short-term muscle relaxant
    - Gabapentin
    - Strong opioids (usually only prescribed on specialist advice)
- If radicular pain has not responded to non-invasive treatment, consider referral for orthopaedic assessment.
- If yellow flags are present, consider referral for cognitive behavioural therapy or multi-disciplinary (bio-psycho-social) assessment and treatment.
- Consider referral for one or more of the following interventions, if they are available locally, given with a psycho-social approach, and if the patient would like to try them:
  - Spinal manipulation or mobilization, as a short course
  - Exercise therapy
  - Back school

Assessment of the clinical problems

- Reassess the presence or absence of 'red flags' indicating possible serious pathology.
  - Further investigation and/or referral are likely to be indicated if 1 or more red flags indicating possible serious pathology are present.
- Reassess psycho-social risk factors (*'yellow flags'*)
  - Consider using an explicit screen of psychosocial factors such as the New Zealand screening questionnaire.
- **Reassess distress, disability, and loss of work due to low back pain.**
- **Reassess the presence of nerve root pain.**

Educational advice

Re-enforce the advice given for acute low back pain. If more than a brief session with the GP is required, consider referring to a physiotherapist.

Return to work

Address any problems relating to return to work. More information is given in the section *Occupational health issues — work and back pain.*

Pain management

Adjust analgesia to control pain as far as possible

- Paracetamol and NSAIDs are the usual first-line options.
- Combinations of two analgesics (paracetamol, an NSAID and codeine) are the usual second-line options.
- Other options to consider if first- and second-line options are unsuitable or ineffective include:
  - Amitriptyline. Consider prescribing amitriptyline if there is chronic lower back pain (after 4–6 weeks), despite the use of standard analgesia or NSAIDs, or if the pain is neuropathic in origin.
  - Short-term muscle relaxant.
  - Gabapentin. Consider prescribing gabapentin if amitriptyline has proved ineffective or is contraindicated.
- Strong opioids would usually only be prescribed with the advice of a pain clinic.
- There is no evidence to suggest how long treatment with analgesics should be continued. The European Back Pain guidelines recommend that NSAIDs be prescribed for a short course, i.e. up to 3 months.

If adequate pain control is not achieved with analgesia, consider referral for one or more of the following, if they are available locally, given with a psycho-social approach, and if the patient would like to try them:

- Multi-disciplinary (bio-psycho-social) assessment
- Cognitive behavioural therapy
- Spinal manipulation or mobilization, as a short course
- Exercise therapy
- Back school

The European Back Pain guidelines also recommend consideration of percutaneous electrical nerve stimulation (PENS) and neuroreflexotherapy, but these are unlikely to be available in the UK [van Tulder et al, 2004].

Management of persistent radicular pain

If radicular pain has not responded to non-invasive treatment after 4–6 weeks, consider referral for assessment for surgery or other invasive interventions.

Management of distress and disability and psychosocial risk factors

If significant distress or disability is present:

- Ask if factors other than pain could be involved in the continuing disability.
- Consider a formal assessment of *Yellow flags* such as the New Zealand screening questionnaire.
- Continue to encourage progressively increasing activity and exercise.
- Address specific barriers to recovery or consider arranging psycho-social and vocational evaluation.
- Consider referral for second opinion to specialist physiotherapist, or GP with special interest, or secondary care.
- If available, consider referral for
  - Cognitive behavioural therapy, or
  - Multi-disciplinary (bio-psycho-social) assessment and treatment

- The European guidelines for the management of acute and chronic low back pain are enthusiastic about the potential for cognitive behavioural therapy, but recognize that there are significant barriers to its implementation in primary care [Airaksinen et al, 2004; van Tulder et al, 2004]. These barriers are being addressed in a large randomized controlled trial that is due to reports its results in 2007 [DH, 2005].

Occupational health issues — work and back pain

- Back pain is common in adults of working age, and, although it may be precipitated by factors at work, only a small proportion of cases are actually *caused by* work.
- Most people continue working most of the time despite their back pain.
- Remaining at work or returning to work early leads to faster recovery and less trouble in the long term.
- It will be appropriate to refer some people with occupation-related back pain to occupational health services, but it is likely that many people, if not most, will be managed in primary care.
- Key steps in primary care that can help ensure a rapid return to work are:
  - Routinely ask people about their job and any difficulties.
  - Consider the yellow flags for risk of chronicity.
  - Ensure the person understands the myths about occupational back pain — see PRODIGY patient information leaflet *Low back pain: common myths*.
  - Avoid diagnostic labels, especially those that link symptoms to work.
  - Explain that continuing to work will speed recovery and reduce recurrences.
  - Remind the person that you are there to help and support.
  - Advise that corsets and belts are not recommended.
  - Do not recommend work modifications too readily.
  - Offer to discuss any problems, the benefits of work retention, and, if appropriate, possible modification of duties with the employer or occupational health department.
  - Do not suggest sick leave (except in the rare instances where there is a strong clinical reason).
  - If sick leave is unavoidable, make it short-term, and review progress regularly; advise the employer of the benefits of regular positive and sympathetic contact during sick leave.
  - If early return to work proves difficult:
    - Make sure that the person (and the employer) appreciates all the disadvantages of long-term absence.
    - Refer to an occupational health professional who can review job demands more closely and advise on suitable temporary modifications.
    - Reassess and address psycho-social obstacles to work return.

B

- If these steps are failing, try to refer the person to an active rehabilitation programme, preferably linked to the workplace.

[Waddell, 2004]

Interventions not recommended for the treatment of low back pain

A number of interventions are not recommended for the treatment of low back pain due to lack of evidence of effectiveness [Airaksinen et al, 2004]. These include:

- Traction
- Electrotherapy
- Ultrasound
- Interferential therapy
- Laser treatments
- Transcutaneous electrical nerve stimulation (TENS — not to be confused with PENS)

How can low back pain be prevented?

The rationale for the recommendations in this section, and systematic reviews of the evidence supporting these recommendations can be found in [Burton et al, 2004].

Methodological issues

- The possibility of primary prevention of low back pain is limited.
- In principle there is considerable scope for prevention of the consequences of low back pain, which include recurrence, care seeking, disability, and loss of work.
- The evidence supporting preventative interventions for low back pain is generally limited, or the size of the effect is modest.
- Prevention in low back pain is both a societal and an individual concern. No single intervention is likely to be effective.

Assessments of interventions

- **Promising interventions** for the prevention of low back pain include:
  - For the general population
    - Physical exercise.
    - Information and education about low back pain problems, provided that it is based on bio-psycho-social principles. For example, 'back schools' with an educational/skills programme and exercises, but not traditional back schools that only provide biomedical/biomechanical information.
  - For workers (in addition to the above interventions for the general population)
    - Temporarily modified work, and ergonomic workplace adaptations
- **Interventions with insufficient evidence** to recommend for or against their use include:
  - For the general population
    - Specific chairs
    - Specific mattresses — although a medium–firm mattress may be preferable to a hard mattress
  - For school-age children
    - Education about the prevention of low back pain
  - For workers (in addition to the above interventions for the general population)
    - Soft shoes, soft flooring, anti-fatigue mats
    - Organizational interventions
- **Interventions that are not recommended** for the prevention of low back pain include:
  - Lumbar supports, back belts
  - Spinal manipulation
  - Shoe insoles; correction of leg length discrepancy

Medicines management

Paracetamol

- Paracetamol is safe and effective for the treatment of mild to moderate pain when used correctly, and is well tolerated at the recommended daily dose.
- It is more likely to be effective for back pain when used regularly rather than 'as required'.

Codeine

- Codeine may be added to paracetamol or an NSAID if more pain relief is required.
- Paracetamol and codeine should be prescribed separate so they can be individually titrated; combination products such as co-codamol are not recommended.
- Codeine may cause nausea, vomiting, constipation, an drowsiness. A regular laxative is often needed when it i used long-term.

Nonsteroidal anti-inflammatory drugs

A full discussion on the contraindications, adverse effects monitoring issues, and interactions of nonsteroidal anti-inflammatory drugs (NSAIDs) is beyond the scope of this guidance. For further information, see the separate PRODIGY guidance on *Nonsteroidal anti-inflammatory drugs (NSAIDs)*.

- None of the NSAIDs is specifically licensed for lower back pain.
- Long-term use of NSAIDs is not required and is not appropriate for lower back pain.
- Consider patient comorbidity when prescribing NSAID they commonly cause gastrointestinal adverse effects, and can worsen asthma, hypertension, renal impairmen and heart failure.
- For people with back pain who are at high risk of gastrointestinal adverse events, we recommend the following options:
  - Use paracetamol (with or without codeine) instead o an NSAID if possible, or
  - Use a gastroprotective agent with a standard NSAID [NICE, 2001a].
- For advice on the management of dyspepsia due to NSAIDs, see the separate PRODIGY guidance on *Dyspepsia — symptoms (uninvestigated by endoscopy)* and *Dyspepsia — proven DU, GU, or NSAID-associated ulcer*.

Muscle relaxants

What dose of diazepam should I use?

- Suggested treatment regimens are 2–4 mg three times a day for 3–7 days.

What are the adverse effects of diazepam?

- Diazepam has strong sedative effects. People should be warned not to drive while taking the drug or for a full day after stopping drug treatment. In addition, people should be warned that the effects of alcohol may be exaggerated whilst taking this medication.
- Diazepam, like all the benzodiazepines, has a high potential for tolerance and dependence. In addition to avoiding extended use of the drug, it should be avoided in people with a history of drug or alcohol abuse, and i pregnant or breastfeeding women.

Amitriptyline

What dose of amitriptyline should I use?

- Reassure the person that the drug is not for psychiatric purposes, and prescribe low-dose amitriptyline on the basis of a one month trial. Reassess drug efficacy and adverse effects after this period [BNF 49, 2005]:

- An initial dose of 10 or 25 mg at night should be used.
- After reassessment, the dose can be titrated up (in weekly increments) to 75 mg per day; higher doses should only be initiated by a specialist. For many people, however, the effective dose is between 25 mg and 75 mg at night.

hat are the adverse effects of amitriptyline?

Most of the adverse effects of amitriptyline are dose-related and are less likely to present a significant problem at lower doses:

- Antimuscarinic adverse effects such as dry mouth, sedation, blurred vision, constipation, and urinary retention are most common.
- Postural hypotension (especially in the elderly), arrhythmias or weight gain may also occur.

People should be warned about the risk of sedation and warned not to drive if they are affected [BNF 49, 2005].

'ho should avoid taking amitriptyline?

Amitriptyline should be avoided in people who have had a recent myocardial infarction or have existing cardiac arrhythmias.

Amitriptyline is very dangerous in overdose and should not be prescribed to people who are considered at risk of suicide.

;abapentin

'hat dose of gabapentin should I use?

There is little evidence on what dose of gabapentin is required to alleviate chronic lower back pain, but the full 'antiepileptic dose' is probably necessary:

- Titrate slowly (e.g. over 7 days) from 100 mg three times a day to 300 mg three times a day. (Note: this is slower than suggested in the summary of product characteristics.)
- If pain is inadequately controlled, slowly increase the dose until adequate relief is obtained, or the maximum licensed dose is reached. The minimum effective dose usually lies between 900 mg per day and 1800 mg per day (licensed maximum).
- Specialist advice should be sought if higher doses are required.

'hat are the adverse effects of gabapentin?

Common adverse effects of gabapentin include drowsiness, dizziness, ataxia, and fatigue.

Sudden withdrawal of gabapentin may cause anxiety, insomnia, nausea, pain, and sweating: it should be tapered off over the course of at least one week [BNF 49, 2005].

The clearance of gabapentin is markedly reduced in renal impairment. The total daily dose should not exceed 1200 mg in those with mild renal impairment (common in the elderly). For further information on dosing in renal impairment, see the summary of product characteristics (www.medicines.org.uk).

;upporting evidence for drug therapies

What is the supporting evidence for analgesia?

Codeine in combination with regular paracetamol is more effective than either paracetamol or codeine used alone for acute pain [Moore et al, 1997]. Note: the use of codeine combined with a nonsteroidal anti-inflammatory drug (NSAID) has not been formally studied, but most health care professionals agree that this is a practical option.

- **Paracetamol may also be combined with an NSAID** if either drug alone does not provide adequate pain relief.
- **Combining an NSAID with codeine phosphate** may be a further option worth considering. However, the greatest body of evidence is for codeine combined with paracetamol.

Which nonsteroidal anti-inflammatory drug should I use?

- **There is a lack of good evidence to support the use of one NSAID over another in the treatment of lower back pain.** Consequently ibuprofen, diclofenac, and naproxen are recommended on the basis of the balances between their general efficacy and adverse effect profile, which are more favourable than for other NSAIDs [CSM, 1994; Hernández-Diaz et al, 2000; BNF 49, 2005]:
  - **Ibuprofen** is probably the least toxic NSAID and should be used first-line. Doses of up to 2.4 g per day may be necessary for acute pain.
  - **Diclofenac** is an alternative to ibuprofen with greater general efficacy but more risk of adverse effects. The standard dosage for acute pain relief is 50 mg taken three times a day.
  - **Naproxen** has similar efficacy and risk of adverse effects as diclofenac. Up to 1 g a day in two divided doses can be prescribed if necessary.
- **Cyclo-oxygenase 2 (COX-2) selective inhibitors are not recommended.** Following the withdrawal of rofecoxib and suspension of valdecoxib, there have been growing concerns that COX-2 selective inhibitors may cause serious cardiovascular events. Following a European-wide review of the data, the Committee on Safety of Medicines (CSM) has recently advised that [CSM, 2005b]:
  - The evidence suggests that coxibs, as a class, may cause an increased risk of thrombotic events (e.g. myocardial infarction and stroke) compared with placebo and some NSAIDs.
  - The risk may increase with dose and duration of exposure.

Drugs for management of chronic pain

- Various antidepressant and anticonvulsant drugs have been suggested for use in people with chronic back pain.
- In practice, amitriptyline (tricyclic antidepressant) and gabapentin (anticonvulsant) are most commonly used, although there is limited evidence to support the use of these drugs in chronic low back pain, and neither is specifically licensed for it.

Additional supporting evidence

This section reviews relevant studies that were published after the main sources of evidence for this guidance, the European guidelines on low back pain, and the book by Waddell [Waddell, 2004].

What is the evidence for physiotherapy?

- A multi-centre randomized controlled trial of 402 people with low back pain of less than 12 weeks' duration concluded that brief pain management techniques were as effective as manual therapy [Hay et al, 2005].
  - The brief pain management programme was provided by physiotherapists and was designed to identify and address psycho-social risk factors for persistent and recurrent disability related to back pain. Management included general fitness, exercise, explanation about pain mechanisms, advice on positive strategies for coping with distress and overcoming fear of hurt, and a graded return to usual activities.
  - The package of manual physiotherapy was designed to be consistent with current best practice in the UK.
  - The primary outcome was change in the Roland–Morris disability questionnaire at 3 and 12 months. There was no significant difference between the two interventions.

- A multi-centre randomized controlled trial concluded that routine physiotherapy was no more effective for chronic low back pain than one session of assessment and advice from a physiotherapist [Frost et al, 2004].
  - **Participants** had had low back pain (with or without leg pain or neurological signs) for at least 6 weeks. About 75% of the 286 initial participants provided information at the 12 month follow-up.
  - **Interventions.** All participants were assessed by a physiotherapist and given a booklet and advice to remain active. Half the participants were given in addition up to five sessions of physiotherapy as routinely provided in the English NHS, which could include any combination of joint mobilization and manipulation; soft tissue techniques, including stretching; spinal mobility and strengthening exercises; heat or cold treatment; and advice.
  - **Results at the 12 month follow-up.** The difference in the change in the Oswestry Disability Index was –1.04 (95% confidence interval –3.7 to +1.59), which is neither statistically nor clinically significant.

What is the evidence for exercise? What is the evidence for spinal manipulation therapy?

Exercise and spinal manipulation therapy (SMT) provide at best only modest clinical benefits.

- A systematic review of exercise therapies for chronic low back pain, search date to October 2004, found 43 trials of 72 exercise treatments [Hayden et al, 2005b].
  - The reviewers found that studies were limited by inconsistent and poor reporting, publication bias and the use of heterogenous outcome measures.
  - The reviewers concluded that individually designed programmes of exercise therapy including stretching or strengthening and delivered under supervision may improve pain and function in chronic low back pain. Exercise performed over more than 20 hours seemed to be more effective than exercise over shorter periods.
- A meta-analysis of exercise therapies for non-specific low back pain, search date to October 2004, found 11 trials of acute low back pain, 6 trials for sub-acute low back pain, and 43 trials for chronic low back pain [Hayden et al, 2005a].
  - The reviewers found that studies were limited by inconsistent and poor reporting, possible publication bias and the use of heterogenous outcome measures.
  - The reviewers concluded that exercise therapy seems slightly effective at decreasing pain and improving function in adults with chronic low back pain. In people with subacute low back pain there is some evidence to suggest that graded exercise programmes may improve absenteeism; evidence to support other types of exercise is unclear. In acute low back pain exercise is as effective as no treatment or other conservative treatments.
- A randomized controlled trial of 93 people with low back pain of at least 4 months' duration found that a programme of exercise combined with motivation was clinically and statistically significantly more effective than a programme of exercise alone [Friedrich et al, 2005].
  - Although regression analysis was not performed the results presented graphically show that mean pain intensity scores steadily decreased from about 50 on entry to about 15 at 5 years in the group with the combined exercise and motivation programme. In the group with exercise alone, mean pain scores changed from about 55 on entry to about 45 at 5 years. The pain scores were significantly different at 5 years.
  - Similar results were found for working ability and disability.
- The UK BEAM trial evaluated the additional benefit provided to 'best practice care provided by general practitioners' by exercise and/or spinal manipulation therapy provided by physiotherapists, osteopaths, and manipulators [UK BEAM Trial Team, 2004a; UK BEA Trial Team, 2004b].
  - **Participants** were 1334 people aged between 18 and 65 years who had simple low back pain of at least on month's duration.
  - **Treatments** studied were:
    - **GP:** 'Best care' in general practice as defined by UK National guidelines for acute back pain (continue normal activities, avoid rest, analgesics)
    - **Exercise:** a class-based exercise programme ('back fitness'): 1–8 sessions of 1 hour over 4–8 weeks, pl refresher class 12 weeks after randomisation
    - **SMT:** a package of treatment by a spinal manipulator (chiropractor, osteopath, or physiotherapist) given in private or NHS premises; up to 8 sessions of 20 minutes over 12 weeks, included at least one high velocity thrust on most patients
  - **Interventions** were compared in 6 groups:
    - GP
    - GP + exercise
    - GP + SMT (private)
    - GP + SMT (NHS)
    - GP + SMT (private) + exercise
    - GP + SMT (NHS) + exercise
  - **Results.** The main results for changes in the Roland Disability Score (RDI) are shown in Table 4 below. Possible scores in the RDI range from best = 0 to wor = 24. A clinically meaningful difference was taken to be 2.5 in the trial, but others have suggested that it should be 3 or 4 [Stratford et al, 1996; Ostelo et al, 2004].

Table 4: Roland Disability Index scores in the UK BEAM trial. Results shown are mean and (95% confidence interval).

		Net benefit at	
Intervention	**Baseline**	**3 months**	**12 months**
Exercise	6.83	1.36 (0.63 to 2.10)	0.39 (–0.41 to +1.1
SMT	6.66	1.57 (0.82 to 2.32)	1.01 (0.22 to 1.81
Exercise+SMT	6.71	1.87 (1.15 to 2.60)	1.30 (0.54 to 2.07

What is the evidence for acupuncture?

- A meta-analysis of 33 randomized controlled trials [Manheimer et al, 2005] that compared acupuncture with other active treatment or no treatment found evidence that acupuncture is more effective than sham c no treatment for chronic low back pain. Evidence about acupuncture's effectiveness compared with other active treatments (or for people with acute back pain) is inconclusive.

References

NHS staff in England can link, free of charge, from references to full text journals by clicking on [Full text] on the PRODIGY website.

1. Airaksinen, O., Brox, J.I., Cedraschi, C. et al (2004) *European guidelines for the management of chronic non-specific low back pain.* European Commission, Research Directorate General. www.backpaineurope.org [Accessed: 03/02/2005].
2. Australasian Faculty of Musculoskeletal Medicine (2002) *Acute low back pain guide: chapter 2.* Australasian Faculty of Musculoskeletal Medicine. www.emia.com.au/MedicalProviders/

EvidenceBasedMedicine/index.html [Accessed: 29/03/2005].

Bandolier (1995) *Back pain*. Bandolier. www.jr2.ox.ac.uk/bandolier/band19/b19-1.html [Accessed: 29/03/2005].

BNF 49 (2005) *British National Formulary*. 49th edn. London: British Medical Association and Royal Pharmaceutical Society of Great Britain.

Burton, A.K., Balagu, F., Cardon, G. et al (2004) *European guidelines for prevention in low back pain*. European Commission, Research Directorate General. www.backpaineurope.org [Accessed: 03/02/2005].

Clinical Standards Advisory Group (1994) *Report on back pain*. London: HMSO.

CSM (1994) Relative safety of oral non-aspirin NSAIDs. *Current Problems in Pharmacovigilance* **20**(Aug), 9–11.

CSM (2005a) *Withdrawal of co-proxamol products and interim updated prescribing information*. Committee on Safety of Medicines. www.mca.gov.uk [Accessed: 24/03/2005].

CSM (2005b) *Updated advice on the safety of selective cox-2 inhibitors*. Committee on Safety of Medicines. http://medicines.mhra.gov.uk [Accessed: 30/03/2005].

. De Craen, A.J., Di Giulio, G., Lampe-Schoenmaeckers, J.E. et al (1996) Analgesic efficacy and safety of paracetamol-codeine combinations versus paracetamol alone: a systematic review. *British Medical Journal* **313**(7053), 321–325. [Full text]

1. Devillè, W.L., van der Windt, D.A., Dzaferagic, A. et al (2000) The test of Lasegue: systematic review of the accuracy in diagnosing herniated discs. *Spine* **25**(9), 1140–1147.

2. DH (2005) *UK-Best Project Description. A multi-centred randomised controlled trial of a primary-care based cognitive behavioural programme for low back pain (UK-Best)*. Department of Health. www.hta.nhsweb.nhs.uk/projectdata/1_project_record_notpublished.asp?PjtId=1358 [Accessed: 29/03/2005].

3. Directorate of Information and Clinical Effectiveness (2001) *Topic of the month: acute and chronic low back pain*. Directorate of Information and Clinical Effectiveness. www.show.scot.nhs.uk [Accessed: 29/03/2005].

4. European Agency for Safety and Health at Work (2000) *Work-related low back disorders*. European Agency for Safety and Health at Work. http://agency.osha.eu.int/ [Accessed: 30/03/2005].

5. Frank, J.W., Brooker, A.S., DeMaio, S.E. et al (1996) Disability resulting from occupational low back pain. Part II: What do we know about secondary prevention? A review of the scientific evidence on prevention after disability begins. *Spine* **21**(24), 2918–2929.

6. Frank, J., Sinclair, S., Hogg-Johnson, S. et al (1998) Preventing disability from work-related low-back pain. New evidence gives new hope – if we can just get all the players onside. *Canadian Medical Association Journal* **158**(12), 1625–1631. [Full text]

7. Friedrich, M., Gittler, G., Arendasy, M. and Friedrich, K. (2005) Long-term effect of a combined exercise and motivational program on the level of disability of patients with chronic low back pain. *Spine* **30**(9), 995–1000.

8. Frost, H., Lamb, S.E., Doll, H.A. et al (2004) Randomised controlled trial of physiotherapy compared with advice for low back pain. *British Medical Journal* **329**(7468), 708.

9. Hayden, J.A., van Tulder, M.W., Malmivaara, A.V. and Koes, B.W. (2005a) Meta-analysis: exercise therapy for nonspecific low back pain. *Annals of Internal Medicine* **142**(9), 765–775. [Full text]

20. Hayden, J.A., van Tulder, M.W. and Tomlinson, G. (2005b) Systematic review: strategies for using exercise therapy to improve outcomes in chronic low back pain. *Annals of Internal Medicine* **142**(9), 776–785. [Full text]

21. Hay, E.M., Mullis, R., Lewis, M. et al (2005) Comparison of physical treatments versus a brief pain-management programme for back pain in primary care: a randomised clinical trial in physiotherapy practice. *Lancet* **365**(9476), 2024–2030. [Full text]

22. Health and Safety Executive (2005) *Back pain in the workplace: prevention and management*. Health and Safety Executive. www.hse.gov.uk/msd/backpain/index.htm [Accessed: 30/03/2005].

23. Henry, D., Lim, L.L., Garcia-Rodriguez, L.A. et al (1996) Variability in risk of gastrointestinal complications with individual non-steroidal anti-inflammatory drugs: results of a collaborative meta-analysis. *British Medical Journal* **312**(7046), 1563–1566. [Full text]

24. Hernández-Diaz, S. and Rodriguez, L.A. (2000) Association between nonsteroidal anti-inflammatory drugs and upper gastrointestinal tract bleeding/perforation: an overview of epidemiologic studies published in the 1990s. *Archives of Internal Medicine* **160**(14), 2093–2099. [Full text]

25. Hernández-Diaz, S., Werler, M.M., Walker, A.M. and Mitchell, A.A. (2000) Folic acid antagonists during pregnancy and the risk of birth defects. *New England Journal of Medicine* **343**(22), 1608–1614. [Full text]

26. Jensen, S. (2004) Back pain – clinical assessment. *Australian Family Physician* **33**(6), 393–401.

27. Jones, G.T. and Macfarlane, G.J. (2005) Epidemiology of low back pain in children and adolescents. *Archives of Disease in Childhood* **90**(3), 312–316.

28. Jones, M.A., Stratton, G., Reilly, T. and Unnithan, V.B. (2004) A school-based survey of recurrent non-specific low-back pain prevalence and consequences in children. *Health Education Research* **19**(3), 284–289. [Full text]

29. Kendrick, D., Fielding, K., Bentley, A. et al (2001) The role of radiography in primary care patients with low back pain of at least 6 weeks duration: a randomised (unblinded) controlled trial. *Health Technology Assessment* **5489**(30), 1–69.

30. Manheimer, E., White, A., Berman, B. et al (2005) Meta-analysis: acupuncture for low back pain. *Annals of Internal Medicine* **142**(8), 651–663. [Full text]

31. McQuay, H.J. and Moore, R.A. (1997) Antidepressants and chronic pain. *British Medical Journal* **314**(7083), 763–764. [Full text]

32. MeReC (1993) Combination analgesics. *MeReC Bulletin* **4**(12), 45–48.

33. Moore, R.A. and McQuay, H.J. (1997) Single-patient data meta-analysis of 3453 postoperative patients: oral tramadol versus placebo, codeine and combination analgesics. *Pain* **69**(3), 287–294.

34. Moore, A., Collins, S., Carroll, D. and McQuay, H. (1997) Paracetamol with and without codeine in acute pain: a quantitative systematic review. *Pain* **70**(2–3), 193–201.

35. Murphy, S., Buckle, P. and Stubbs, D. (2004) Classroom posture and self-reported back and neck pain in schoolchildren. *Applied Ergonomics* **35**(2), 113–120.

36. Myles, P.S., Troedel, S., Boquest, M. and Reeves, M. (1999) The pain visual analog scale: is it linear or nonlinear? *Anesthesia & Analgesia* **89**(6), 1517–1520.

37. NICE (2001a) *Guidance on the use of cyclo-oxygenase (Cox) II selective inhibitors, celecoxib, rofecoxib, meloxicam and etodolac for osteoarthritis and rheumatoid arthritis*. Technology appraisal no. 27.

B

B

National Institute for Health and Clinical Excellence. www.nice.org.uk [Accessed: 16/10/2003].
38. NICE (2001b) *Referral advice – a guide to appropriate referral from general to specialist services.* National Institute for Clinical Excellence. www.nice.org.uk [Accessed: 11/08/2002].
39. NZGG (2004) *New Zealand acute low back pain guide.* New Zealand Guidelines Group. www.nzgg.org.nz [Accessed: 30/03/2005].
40. Ostelo, R.W.J.G., de Vet, H.C.W., Knol, D.L. and van den Brandt, P.A. (2004) 24-item Roland-Morris Disability Questionnaire was preferred out of six functional status questionnaires for post-lumbar disc surgery. *Journal of Clinical Epidemiology* 57(3), 268–276.
41. Pecukonis, E.V. (2004) Female children of alcoholics and chronic back pain. *Pain Medicine* 5(2), 196–201.
42. Pengel, L.H.M., Herbert, R.D., Maher, C.G. and Refshauge, K.M. (2003) Acute low back pain: systematic review of its prognosis. *British Medical Journal* 327(7410), 323–327. [Full text]
43. Roland, M. and Fairbank, J. (2000) The Roland-Morris Disability Questionnaire and the Oswestry Disability Questionnaire. *Spine* 25(24), 3115–3124.
44. Rostom, A., Wells, G., Tugwell, P. et al (2002) *Prevention of NSAID-induced gastroduodenal ulcers (Cochrane Review).* The Cochrane Library. Issue 4. Chichester, UK: John Wiley & Sons, Ltd. www.nelh.nhs.uk/cochrane.asp [Accessed: 04/04/2005]. [Full text]
45. SIGN (2000) *Management of early rheumatoid arthritis.* Report no. 48. Scottish Intercollegiate Guidelines Network. www.sign.ac.uk [Accessed: 01/04/2002].
46. Stratford, P.W., Binkley, J., Solomon, P. et al (1996) Defining the minimum level of detectable change for the Roland-Morris Questionnaire. *Physical Therapy* 76(4), 359–368.
47. UK BEAM Trial Team (2004a) United Kingdom back pain exercise and manipulation (UK BEAM) randomised trial: effectiveness of physical treatments for back pain in primary care. *British Medical Journal* 329(7479), 1377.
48. UK BEAM Trial Team (2004b) United Kingdom back pain exercise and manipulation (UK BEAM) randomised trial: cost effectiveness of physical treatments for back pain in primary care. *British Medical Journal* 329(7479), 1381.
49. van Tulder, M., Becker, A., Bekkering, T. et al (2004) *European guidelines for the management of acute nonspecific low back pain in primary care.* European Commission, Research Directorate General. www.backpaineurope.org [Accessed: 03/02/2005].
50. Vleeming, A., Albert, H.A., Östgaar, H.C; et al (2004) *European guidelines on the diagnosis and treatment of pelvic girdle pain.* European Commission, Research Directorate General. www.backpaineurope.org [Accessed: 03/02/2005].
51. Waddell, G. (2004) *The back pain revolution.* 2nd edn. London: Churchill Livingstone.
52. Waddell, G. and Main, C.J. (1984) Assessment of severity in low-back disorders. *Spine* 9(2), 204–208.
53. Waddell, G., McIntosh, A., Hutchinson, A. et al (1999) *Low back pain evidence review.* London: Royal College of General Practitioners.

B

RODIGY GUIDANCE

3acterial vaginosis

Last revised in March 2004
www.prodigy.nhs.uk/guidance.asp?gt=Bacterial vaginosis

Applies to women over the age of 12 years

This guidance covers the management of bacterial vaginosis.

There is separate PRODIGY guidance for *Candida — female genital*, *Chlamydia — genital*, *Pelvic inflammatory disease*, *Pruritus vulvae*, and *Trichomoniasis*.

;oals

To cure infection
To reduce risk of complications, such as preterm delivery in infected pregnant women

;ontents

;cenarios

- Bacterial vaginosis p.207

;xtended Information, p. 208

3acterial vaginosis

Vhich therapy?

'ho to treat

In women who are not pregnant, treatment is indicated if they have symptoms.

In women who are pregnant, treatment is indicated if:

- They have symptoms, or
- They have a history of 'idiopathic' preterm birth or second trimester loss (even if they do not have symptoms)

ow to treat

Oral metronidazole, intravaginal metronidazole, and intravaginal clindamycin are equally effective at curing bacterial vaginosis.

In women who are not pregnant, choice of treatment is based on patient preference.

In women who are pregnant, avoid single high-dose metronidazole or topical treatments (there is no evidence that topical treatments reduce the risk of complications during pregnancy).

In women who are breastfeeding, topical treatments may be preferred (to minimize the amount of drug delivered to the infant via breast milk). Avoid single high-dose metronidazole.

'ractical prescribing points

or further information see the *Medicines Compendium* (www.medicines.org.uk) or the *British National Formulary* (www.bnf.org).

- **Metronidazole and pregnancy:** there is no evidence of teratogenicity from the use of metronidazole in women during the first trimester of pregnancy. However, single large doses should be avoided.
- **Metronidazole and breastfeeding:** women should be encouraged to continue breastfeeding while taking metronidazole. Small amounts of metronidazole may enter breast milk and affect its taste, but feeding problems are unusual. Topical intravaginal treatment may be preferable, to minimize the amount of drug in breast milk. The single 2-gram oral dose of metronidazole should be avoided during breastfeeding.
- **Metronidazole and alcohol:** it is recommended that alcohol be avoided while taking oral metronidazole (manufacturer's SPC).

Follow-up advice

- If symptoms resolve, repeat testing is not necessary.
- If treatment is prescribed during pregnancy to reduce the risk of preterm birth, a repeat test should be carried out after a month and further treatment offered if the bacterial vaginosis has recurred.

Should I refer or investigate?

Refer?

- Non-medical prescribers should seek advice from the person's GP if uncertain regarding management.
- If necessary, specialist advice on management in pregnancy may be obtained from the local obstetric or genito urinary medicine department. Alternatively, contact the National Teratology Information Service for latest information regarding safety of metronidazole during pregnancy (telephone 0191 232 1525).

Investigate?

- **The diagnostic 'gold standard' is based on Amsel's criteria.** At least three of the following four criteria must be present:
  - Thin, white, homogenous discharge
  - Clue cells on microscopy (vaginal epithelial cells heavily coated with bacilli)
  - Vaginal fluid pH greater than 4.5
  - Release of a fishy odour on adding alkali (10% potassium hydroxide)
- **In practice, the diagnosis is usually made on the basis of** symptoms and a positive vaginal swab showing an excess of anaerobic organisms and few lactobacilli.
- Laboratories may report the Hay/Ison criteria or the Nugent criteria.
- **The Hay/Ison criteria** are defined as:
  - Grade 1 (Normal): *Lactobacillus* morphotypes predominate
  - Grade 2 (Intermediate): mixed flora with some lactobacilli present, but or *Mobiliuncus* morphotypes are also present
  - Grade 3 (BV): predominantly *Gardnerella* and/or *Mobiluncus* morphotypes, few or absent lactobacilli.
- **The Nugent score** is derived from estimating the relative proportions of bacterial morphotypes to give a score between 0 and 10. A score of less than 4 is normal, 4–6 is intermediate, and greater than 6 is BV.

- **Other infections should be screened for at the same time,** as co-infection with chlamydia, gonorrhoea, and trichomoniasis is common.

Patient information leaflets

The following PILs are available at www.prodigy.nhs.uk

- Bacterial Vaginosis
- Women's Health
- Women's Health Concern

Shared decision making

- Bacterial vaginosis is due to an overgrowth of bacteria that can be found in low numbers in the normal vagina. Why this overgrowth occurs is not clear. It is not a sexually transmitted infection.
- No treatment may be an option as the normal balance of bacteria may correct itself.
- Metronidazole (or similar antibiotic) will usually clear the discharge.
- Tell your doctor if you are pregnant, as treatment may be different.
- Recurrences are common. Treatment can be repeated as necessary.
- The use of condoms will not aggravate the condition.

Drug rationale

Drugs not included

- Oral antibiotics other than metronidazole (e.g. ampicillin or doxycycline) or sulphonamide vaginal creams have not been shown to be as effective as the treatments included.
- **Oral tinidazole** has been poorly studied in the treatment of bacterial vaginosis (BV) — we were unable to find any published randomized controlled trials.
- **Oral clindamycin** effectively treats BV. However, clindamycin is only licensed for serious anaerobic infections and Gram-positive infections, and there is less data on efficacy than for metronidazole [DTB, 1998; BNF 43, 2002].

Drugs included

- **Oral metronidazole** effectively treats BV [CEG, 2001]. It is the preferred treatment in all stages of pregnancy. The recommended regimen is 400 mg twice daily for 7 days. An alternative in women who are not pregnant or breastfeeding is a single dose of 2 grams, which may improve compliance but may be slightly less effective.
- **Topical treatments (metronidazole or clindamycin)** are as effective as oral treatments [CEG, 2001]. They are not recommended for use in pregnancy, as there is no evidence that they reduce the risk of complications.

Prescriptions

Pregnant or breastfeeding: oral metronidazole for 7 days

Metronidazole tablets: 400mg twice a day for 7 days

- Age from 12 years onwards
- Metronidazole 400mg tablets. Take one tablet twice a day for 7 days; supply 14 tablets; NHS Cost £1.54.

Oral metronidazole

Metronidazole tablets: 400mg twice a day for 7 days

- Age from 12 years onwards
- Metronidazole 400mg tablets. Take one tablet twice a day for 7 days; supply 14 tablets; NHS Cost £1.03.

Metronidazole tablets: 2g single dose

- Age from 12 years onwards
- Metronidazole 400mg tablets. Take five tablets togethe as one dose; supply 5 tablets; NHS Cost £0.37.

Topical treatment: metronidazole or clindamycin

Metronidazole 0.75% vaginal gel: use at night for 5 nigh

- Age from 12 years onwards
- Metronidazole 0.75% vaginal gel. Insert one 5g applicatorful into the vagina each night for 5 nights; supply 40 grams; NHS Cost £4.85.

Clindamycin 2% vaginal cream: use at night for 7 nights

- Age from 12 years onwards
- Clindamycin 2% vaginal cream. Insert one 5g applicatorful into the vagina each night for 7 nights; supply 40 grams; NHS Cost £9.05.

Extended Information

Background information

- What is it? p.208
- How common is it? p.208
- How do I know my patient has it? p.208
- What else might it be? p.209
- Complications and prognosis p.209

What is it?

- **Bacterial vaginosis (BV)** is a common cause of abnorm vaginal discharge. In women of childbearing age, lactobacilli are normally the predominant bacteria in th vagina. BV is characterized by an overgrowth of anaerobic organisms, leading to replacement of lactobacilli and an increase in vaginal pH from less tha 4.5 to as high as 7.0.
- ***Gardnerella vaginalis* is one of the main bacteria foun in BV;** however, this can also be found on culture in approximately 50% of healthy women. Other organism commonly associated with BV are *Provotella* species, *Mycoplasma hominis*, and *Mobiluncus* species.
- **The aetiology of BV is unknown.** It is not thought to be sexually transmitted — it can arise and remit spontaneously in sexually active and non-sexually activ women, and treatment of male partners does not reduc recurrence rates. However, it is associated with early ag at first intercourse and higher number of lifetime sexual partners.

[DTB, 1998; CEG, 2001; Joesoef and Schmid, 2001]

How common is it?

- **Bacterial vaginosis (BV)** is the commonest cause of abnormal vaginal discharge in women of childbearing age. It is twice as common as vaginal candidiasis [Joeso and Schmid, 2001].
- **The prevalence** of BV has varied from 5% in asymptomatic college students, 12% in pregnant women, and 30% in women undergoing termination of pregnancy [CEG, 2001].
- **The incidence** of BV is uncertain — one study found th over a 2-year period, 50% of women using an intra-uterine device had at least one episode, as did 20% of women using oral contraceptives [Joesoef and Schmid, 2001].

How do I know my patient has it?

Symptoms

- Symptomatic women usually complain of an offensive, fishy-smelling vaginal discharge.

- The discharge is not associated with soreness, itching, or irritation.
- Many women (about 50%) have no symptoms, but may be found to have bacterial vaginosis (BV) when vaginal swabs are taken for other indications.

Signs

- On examination, the usual finding is a thin, white, homogenous discharge coating the walls of the vagina.

Investigations

- **The diagnostic 'gold standard' is based on Amsel's criteria.** At least three of the following four criteria must be present:
  - Thin, white, homogenous discharge
  - Clue cells on microscopy (vaginal epithelial cells heavily coated with bacilli)
  - Vaginal fluid pH greater than 4.5
  - Release of a fishy odour on adding alkali (10% potassium hydroxide)
- **In practice, the diagnosis is usually made on the basis of** symptoms and a positive swab showing an excess of anaerobic organisms and few lactobacilli.
- Laboratories may report the Hay/Ison criteria or the Nugent criteria.
- **The Hay/Ison criteria** are defined as:
  - Grade 1 (Normal): *Lactobacillus* morphotypes predominate
  - Grade 2 (Intermediate): mixed flora with some lactobacilli present, but *Gardnerella* or *Mobililuncus* morphotypes are also present
  - Grade 3 (BV): predominantly *Gardnerella* and/or *Mobiluncus* morphotypes, few or absent lactobacilli.
- **The Nugent score** is derived from estimating the relative proportions of bacterial morphotypes to give a score between 0 and 10. A score of less than 4 is normal, 4–6 is intermediate, and greater than 6 is BV.
- **Isolation of *Gardnerella vaginalis* cannot be used to diagnose BV,** because *Gardnerella* can be cultured from the vagina of more than 50% of normal women.
- **Other infections should be screened for at the same time,** as co-infection with *Chlamydia trachomatis*, *Neisseria gonorrhoeae* and *Trichomonas vaginalis* is common.

[DTB, 1998; CEG, 2001]

What else might it be?

Other infections that may result in vaginal discharge include:

- Candida
- Trichomonas
- Chlamydia
- Gonococci
- Herpes virus

Irritants that may result in vaginal discharge include:

- Spermicides, perfumed soaps and washing powders; frequent douching; tight non-absorbent underwear.
- There is little evidence to know to what extent these irritants cause discharge.

Other causes of discharge include:

- **Normal physiological variation in discharge** throughout the menstrual cycle.
- **Discharge secondary to tumours** of the vulva, vagina, cervix, or uterine lining.
- **Normal physiological increases in discharge during pregnancy,** although there should be no irritation, pruritis, or malodour.
- **Postmenopausal vaginal discharge** due to atrophic vaginitis (but consider neoplasia in this group).
- **Vaginal discharge following surgery** of the vagina or uterus — may last up to 6 weeks.
- **Foreign body.**
- **Cervical ectropion.**

[Plummer and Walters, 1993]

Complications and prognosis

Complications

- **Following termination of pregnancy,** bacterial vaginosis (BV) is associated with the development of endometritis and pelvic inflammatory disease [CEG, 2001].
- **Following vaginal hysterectomy,** BV has been associated with an increased incidence of vaginal cuff cellulitis and abscess formation. It is uncertain whether this is a problem in UK practice where many units routinely administer perioperative antibiotics [CEG, 2001].
- **In pregnancy,** BV is associated with late miscarriage, preterm birth, premature rupture of membranes, low birth weight, and postpartum endometritis [CEG, 2001; Joesoef and Schmid, 2001]. Women who have had a previous premature delivery are especially at risk of complications in pregnancy.
- BV may increase the risk of acquiring and transmitting HIV.

Prognosis

- **Without treatment,** symptoms may resolve [Joesoef and Schmid, 2001].
- **Following antibiotic treatment,** cure rates vary from 70–80% after 4 weeks [CEG, 2001]. Relapse rates reach around 60% within 3 months, despite successful treatment [DTB, 1998].

Management issues

- General issues p.209
- Non-drug treatments p.209
- Drug treatments p.209
- Pregnancy p.210
- Breastfeeding p.210
- Termination of pregnancy p.210

General issues

- **Routine screening and treatment of male partners** of women with bacterial vaginosis (BV) is not indicated. No reduction in relapse rate has been reported following treatment of male partners [CEG, 2001; Joesoef and Schmid, 2001].

Non-drug treatments

- **Current UK guidelines recommend that** vaginal douching, use of shower gel, and use of antiseptic agents or shampoo in the bath should be avoided [DTB, 1998; CEG, 2001]. The effectiveness of these measures is uncertain.
- **Studies of live yoghurt** or *Lactobacillus acidophilus* have not found benefit [Bandolier, 1999; CEG, 2001].

Drug treatments

- **Treatment is indicated for** symptomatic women, women undergoing some surgical procedures, and some pregnant women (see below) [CEG, 2001].
- **Women who do not volunteer symptoms may elect to take treatment if offered.** They may report a beneficial change in their discharge following treatment [CEG, 2001].

B

- **Oral metronidazole, intravaginal metronidazole, and intravaginal clindamycin** achieve cure rates of 70–80% after 4 weeks in controlled trials [CEG, 2001]. Choice of treatment should be based on patient preference. The recommended regimen for oral metronidazole is 400 mg twice daily for 7 days [PHLS, 2002]. An alternative is a single oral dose of 2 grams, which may improve compliance but may be less effective at 4-week follow-up [DTB, 1998; CEG, 2001; Joesoef and Schmid, 2001; PHLS, 2002].

Pregnancy

- **There is conflicting evidence over the value of screening for and treating BV during pregnancy** [CEG, 2001]. Studies are difficult to interpret due to differences between the populations studied and the use of differing treatment regimens. In three randomized controlled trials, oral antibiotic treatment reduced the incidence of preterm birth in pregnant women with BV who had a history of preterm birth or second trimester loss. However, a large randomized controlled trial found no benefit from oral antibiotic treatment, even in those women with a prior preterm birth.
- **Current UK guidelines recommend:**
  - Pregnant women with symptomatic BV should receive treatment.
  - Asymptomatic pregnant women with a history of 'idiopathic' preterm birth or second trimester loss may be screened and treated.
  - Current evidence does not support routine screening for BV [CEG, 2001].
- **The recommended treatment is oral metronidazole** 400 mg twice daily for 7 days. Meta-analyses have concluded that there is no evidence of teratogenicity from the use of metronidazole in women during the first trimester of pregnancy [National Teratology Information Service, 1999; CEG, 2001]. Although topical treatments effectively treat BV, it is uncertain whether they reduce the risk of preterm delivery.

Breastfeeding

- **Intravaginal treatments may be preferred,** to minimize the amount of drug excreted into breast milk [CEG, 2001].
- **Breastfeeding can continue if a mother is given oral metronidazole.** It is estimated that less than 10% of the recommended daily therapeutic infant dose is delivered via breast milk [Passmore et al, 1988]. However, single large doses should be avoided if possible, as there are theoretical safety concerns.
- **Metronidazole in breast milk may taste unpleasant bu[t] feeding problems are unusual.** It is important that breastfeeding is not discouraged if oral metronidazole [is] prescribed, as the benefits of breastfeeding are likely t[o] outweigh any problems.

Termination of pregnancy

- **Screening women for BV prior to termination of pregnancy (TOP) should be considered.** There is trial evidence that treatment with oral metronidazole or topical clindamycin reduces the risk of post-TOP endometritis and pelvic inflammatory disease [CEG, 2001; Joesoef and Schmid, 2001].

References

1. Bandolier (1999) *Yoghurt and vaginal infections.* Bandolier. www.jr2.ox.ac.uk/bandolier/band60/b60 3.html [Accessed: 12/02/2002].
2. BNF 43 (2002) *British National Formulary.* 43rd ed[i] London: British Medical Association and Royal Pharmaceutical Society of Great Britain.
3. CEG (2001) *National guideline for the management [of] bacterial vaginosis.* Clinical Effectiveness Group (Association for Genitourinary Medicine and the Medical Society for the Study of Venereal Diseases). www.bashh.org/guidelines/2002/bv_0601.pdf [Accessed: 22/04/2005].
4. DTB (1998) Management of bacterial vaginosis. *Dru[g] & Therapeutics Bulletin* 36(5), 33–35.
5. Joesoef, M. and Schmid, G. (2001) *Bacterial vaginos[is].* Clinical Evidence. Volume 6. www.clinicalevidence.com [Accessed: 05/03/2004].
6. National Teratology Information Service (1999) *Metronidazole in pregnancy.* NHS Northern and Yorkshire: Regional Drug and Therapeutics Centre.
7. Passmore, C.M., McElnay, J.C., Rainey, E.A. and D'Arcy, P.F. (1988) Metronidazole excretion in hum[an] milk and its effect on the suckling neonate. *British Journal of Clinical Pharmacology* 26(1), 45–51.
8. PHLS (2002) *Management of infection guidance for primary care: draft for consultation & local adaptation.* Public Health Laboratory Service. www.hpa.org.uk [Accessed: 01/04/2002].
9. Plummer, D.C. and Walters, W.A. (1993) Female genital tract discharge. *Baillieres Clinical Obstetrics [&] Gynaecology* 7(1), 139–159.

RODIGY GUIDANCE

3alanitis

.ast revised in February 2004
vww.prodigy.nhs.uk/guidance.asp?gt=Balanitis

\pplies to men of all ages

This guidance covers the diagnosis and management of the infectious causes of balanitis.

This guidance does not cover in detail the diagnosis and management of the non-infectious causes of balanitis.

There is separate PRODIGY guidance for *Herpes simplex — genital* and *Urethritis — male.*

B

;oals

Rapid resolution of symptoms.

;ontents

cenarios
- Balanitis p.211

xtended Information, p. 213

3alanitis

Vhich therapy?

Regular bathing with saline may provide short-term relief while specific treatment takes effect.

The following treatments are effective for *Candida albicans* balanitis:

- **First-line treatment** is with a topical imidazole (clotrimazole, econazole, ketoconazole, miconazole, or sulconazole).
- **Second-line treatment** is with a topical imidazole combined with 0.5% or 1% hydrocortisone.
- **Alternative topical treatments** are nystatin and terbinafine. These treatments are options if resistance to, or adverse effects from, the imidazole is suspected. If inflammation is marked, they can be combined with hydrocortisone.
- **Oral fluconazole** is an option if the candidal infection has not responded to topical treatment.
- Note: there is no need to treat the sexual partner unless she has symptoms suggestive of vaginal thrush.

If the balanitis does not respond to anticandidal treatment, take a swab and treat according to the result, or refer to the genito-urinary medicine clinic.

If at presentation the diagnosis is thought to be infective, but not to be candidal balanitis, take a swab and treat according to the result, or refer to the genito-urinary medicine clinic.

If at presentation the diagnosis is thought to be non-infective, management should be directed to the likely cause, including referral to a specialist if appropriate.

'ractical prescribing points

or further information please see the *Medicines ompendium* (www.medicines.org.uk) or the *British ational Formulary* (www.bnf.org).

Topical preparations containing hydrocortisone should be applied sparingly to avoid skin atrophy on thin skin areas. If no improvement is seen, the diagnosis should be reassessed and, if appropriate, another preparation considered.

Topical nystatin can stain clothes yellow, which may affect compliance.

- **Oral fluconazole may enhance the anticoagulant effect of warfarin.**
- **Occasional hypersensitivity reactions** are listed for many of the topical products. Such a reaction should be suspected if the rash is getting worse or failing to heal.
- **Flucloxacillin:** the Committee on Safety of Medicines has advised that cholestatic jaundice may occur up to several weeks after treatment with flucloxacillin has been stopped. Administration for more than two weeks is a risk factor.
- **Erythromycin:** use with caution in children with hepatic and renal impairment, and prolongation of the QT interval. Erythromycin may increase the level of certain drugs (e.g. theophylline, carbamazepine).

Should I refer or investigate?

Refer?

- **If the diagnosis is infective, but not candidal balanitis,** consider referring the person to the genito-urinary medicine clinic.
- **If the diagnosis is non-infective,** consider referring the person to the appropriate specialist.

Investigate?

- **In adults, if the diagnosis is candidal balanitis,** consider investigating for diabetes mellitus.
- **In adults, if treatment for candidal balanitis has failed,** investigate for other causes (e.g. *Gardnerella vaginalis, Staphylococcus aureus, Trichomonas vaginalis,* anaerobes, chlamydia, herpes simplex, streptococci, syphilis). The investigation may be done in primary care if expertise allows, or may require referral to the local genito-urinary medicine clinic.

Patient information leaflets

The following PILs are available at www.prodigy.nhs.uk

- Antifungal Medicines
- Balanitis

Shared decision making

- **Balanitis is common in boys and men.** There are various causes.
- **Salt baths** are soothing whilst treatment takes effect.
- **An anti-yeast cream or a course of anti-yeast tablets** is the most common treatment, as most cases are due to infection with *Candida.*
- **A mild steroid cream** can reduce inflammation caused by allergies or irritants. Sometimes it is used in addition to anti-yeast medication to reduce inflammation caused by infection.
- **Antibiotics** will clear infection caused by bacteria.
- **Referral** may be needed if a sexually transmitted disease is suspected, or if the cause is not clear.

B

- **Tips which may help to prevent some cases of balanitis** include:
  - Wash the glans each day with just water, or water and a bland soap.
  - If symptoms are related to condom use, use ones designed for sensitive skin.
  - Wash underwear with non-biological detergents and rinse well.
  - Wash your hands before going to the toilet if you work with chemicals that can irritate delicate skin.

Drug rationale

Drugs not included

- **Emollients** are not recommended. They help relieve pruritus but do not treat the candidal infection.
- **Salicylic acid and undecenoate preparations** are considered less suitable for prescribing in fungal skin infections.
- **Products containing a corticosteroid alone** are not recommended. An undiagnosed fungal or secondary bacterial infection may be present, which could be exacerbated by their use.
- **Topical antibacterial products** that do not contain an anticandidal component are not recommended, as they are not effective in treating candidal infections.
- **Oral antifungals other than fluconazole** are not recommended. Itraconazole and ketoconazole are not licensed for the treatment of candidal balanitis, and they tend to be used in immunocompromised people and where more severe or resistant candidal infection is present. Oral terbinafine is not appropriate for use where candidal infection has not responded to topical treatment, and is therefore not recommended.

Drugs included

- **Topical imidazole preparations (clotrimazole, econazole, ketoconazole, miconazole, and sulconazole)** are recommended, as they are effective against *Candida albicans*. There is little evidence of difference between these preparations, and they are all licensed to treat candidal skin infections in people of all ages. Product selection will depend on prescriber/user preference.
- **Topical nystatin preparations** are also effective against *C albicans*. They are licensed for use in all ages.
- **Topical combination products containing hydrocortisone 0.5% or 1% plus an anticandial** (an imidazole or nystatin) are recommended as an option to reduce accompanying inflammation. They should not be used for more than a week unless otherwise directed, in order to try to avoid any adverse effects.
- **Topical terbinafine cream** is licensed for treating cutaneous candidiasis for up to 2 weeks in adults, but it is notably more expensive than other anticandidal creams.
- **Ointment *and* cream formulations of active anticandidals** are included. Creams are emulsions of oil and water; they tend to be well absorbed into the skin. Ointments are greasy preparations that are insoluble in water, are more occlusive than creams and, unlike creams, do not contain preservatives. There is no evidence to support the use of one preparation over another, and the patient's preference will often govern choice.
- **Oral fluconazole** is an option if the candidal infection has not responded to topical treatment. Fluconazole is well absorbed after oral administration, and is licensed as a single-dose treatment for candidal balanitis in men over 16 years. Note: fluconazole is available to buy as an over-the-counter preparation for this indication in tho[se] aged from 16 to 60 years old.
- **Flucloxacillin** is offered as it is effective against the mo[st] likely bacterial causes of balanitis.
- **Erythromycin** is offered for people allergic to penicilli[n]

Prescriptions

Non-drug management

Advice only: washing
- All ages
- You should keep the area as clean as possible. Good toilet hygiene, including hand washing, is strongly recommended. Regular cleaning of the area using a we[ak] salt solution can be soothing and help relieve discomf[ort]. A weak salt solution can be made up by adding rough[ly] a teaspoonful of salt to half a litre (500 ml) of warm water.

Anticandidal-only preparations

Clotrimazole 1% cream
- All ages
- Clotrimazole 1% cream. Apply to the affected area 2 t[o] 3 times a day. Continue for at least 2 weeks after the affected area has healed; supply 20 grams; NHS Cost £1.77; OTC Cost £2.14.

Econazole 1% cream
- All ages
- Econazole 1% cream. Apply to the affected area twice day. Continue for at least 2 weeks the affected area ha[s] healed; supply 30 grams; NHS Cost £2.75; OTC Cost £4.85.

Ketoconazole 2% cream
- All ages
- Ketoconazole 2% cream. Apply to the affected area twice a day. Continue for at least 2 weeks the affected area has healed; supply 30 grams; NHS Cost £3.81.

Miconazole 2% cream
- All ages
- Miconazole 2% cream. Apply to the affected area twic[e] a day. Continue for 10 days after the affected area has healed; supply 30 grams; NHS Cost £2.07; OTC Cost £3.65.

Sulconazole 1% cream
- All ages
- Sulconazole 1% cream. Apply to the affected area twic[e] a day. Continue for at least 2 weeks the affected area h[as] healed; supply 30 grams; NHS Cost £3.00; OTC Cost £5.29.

Terbinafine 1% cream
- Age from 12 years onwards
- Terbinafine 1% 30g. Apply to the affected area once o[r] twice a day. Continue for 2 weeks after the affected are[a] has healed; supply 30 grams; NHS Cost £8.76.

Nystatin 100,000units/g cream
- All ages
- Nystatin 100,000units/g cream. Apply to the affected area 2 to 4 times a day. Continue for 7 days after the affected area has healed; supply 30 grams; NHS Cost £2.18.

Nystatin 100,000units/g ointment
- All ages
- Nystatin 100,000units/g ointment. Apply to the affecte[d] area 2 to 4 times a day. Continue for 7 days after the affected area has healed; supply 30 grams; NHS Cost £1.75.

ıticandidal + hydrocortisone preparations

›trimazole 1% + hydrocortisone 1% cream
- ıll ages
- Iydrocortisone+clotrimaz cream. Apply thinly to the ffected area once or twice a day. Use for a maximum of ' days unless otherwise directed; supply 30 grams; NHS Cost £2.38.

conazole 2% + hydrocortisone 1% cream
- ıll ages
- Iydrocortisone+miconazole cream. Apply thinly to the ffected area once or twice a day. Use for a maximum of ' days unless otherwise directed; supply 30 grams; NHS Cost £2.24.

conazole 2% + hydrocortisone 1% ointment
- ıll ages
- Iydrocortisone+miconazole ointment. Apply thinly to he affected area once or twice a day. Use for a naximum of 7 days unless otherwise directed; supply 30 ;rams; NHS Cost £2.25.

onazole 1% + hydrocortisone 1% cream
- Age under 11 years
- Iydrocortisone+econazole cream. Apply thinly to the ıffected area twice a day. Use for a maximum of 5 days ınless otherwise directed; supply 30 grams; NHS Cost £2.25.

onazole 1% + hydrocortisone 1% cream
- Age from 12 years onwards
- Iydrocortisone+econazole cream. Apply thinly to the ıffected area twice a day. Use for a maximum of 7 days ınless otherwise directed; supply 30 grams; NHS Cost £2.25.

statin + chlorhexidine + hydrocortisone 0.5% cream
- All ages
- Nystaform-HC 0.5% cream. Apply thinly to the affected ırea twice a day. Use for a maximum of 7 days unless otherwise directed; supply 30 grams; NHS Cost £2.66.

statin + chlorhexidine + hydrocortisone 1% ointment
- All ages
- Nystaform-HC 1% ointment. Apply thinly to the ıffected area twice a day. Use for a maximum of 7 days ınless otherwise directed; supply 30 grams; NHS Cost £2.66.

nodine cream (contains nystatin + hydrocortisone 5%)
- All ages
- Timodine cream. Apply thinly to the affected area twice a day. Use for a maximum of 7 days unless otherwise directed; supply 30 grams; NHS Cost £2.38.

luconazole: single dose

uconazole 150mg as a single dose
- Age from 16 years onwards
- Fluconazole 150mg capsules. Take the capsule as a single dose; supply 1 capsule; NHS Cost £6.49; OTC Cost £12.50.

ntibiotic (if indicated by sensitivities) for 5 days

ucloxacillin syrup: 62.5mg four times a day
- Age from 1 month to 23 months
- Flucloxacillin 125mg/5ml syrup. Take 2.5ml four times a day for 5 days; supply 100 ml; NHS Cost £3.23.

ucloxacillin syrup: 125mg four times a day
- Age from 2 to 4 years
- Flucloxacillin 125mg/5ml syrup. Take one 5ml spoonful four times a day for 5 days; supply 100 ml; NHS Cost £3.23.

Flucloxacillin syrup: 250mg four times a day
- Age from 5 to 11 years
- Flucloxacillin 250mg/5ml syrup. Take one 5ml spoonful four times a day for 5 days; supply 100 ml; NHS Cost £6.97.

Flucloxacillin capsules: 250mg four times a day
- Age from 12 years onwards
- Flucloxacillin 250mg capsules. Take one capsule four times a day for 5 days; supply 20 capsules; NHS Cost £2.09.

Flucloxacillin capsules: 500mg four times a day
- Age from 12 years onwards
- Flucloxacillin 500mg capsules. Take one capsule four times a day for 5 days; supply 20 capsules; NHS Cost £3.38.

Erythromycin s/f suspension: 125mg four times a day
- Age from 1 month to 23 months
- Erythromycin 125mg/5ml sf susp. Take one 5ml spoonful four times a day for 5 days; supply 100 ml; NHS Cost £1.14.

Erythromycin s/f suspension: 250mg four times a day
- Age from 2 to 11 years
- Erythromycin 250mg/5ml sf susp. Take one 5ml spoonful four times a day for 5 days; supply 100 ml; NHS Cost £1.97.

Erythromycin s/f suspension: 500mg four times a day
- Age from 9 to 11 years
- Erythromycin 500mg/5ml sf susp. Take one 5ml spoonful four times a day for 5 days; supply 100 ml; NHS Cost £3.38.

Erythromycin e/c tablets: 250mg four times a day
- Age from 12 years onwards
- Erythromycin 250mg e/c tablets. Take one tablet four times a day for 5 days; supply 20 tablets; NHS Cost £2.20.

Erythromycin e/c tablets: 500mg four times a day
- Age from 12 years onwards
- Erythromycin 250mg e/c tablets. Take two tablets four times a day for 5 days; supply 40 tablets; NHS Cost £4.40.

Extended Information

Background information

- What is it? p.213
- How common is it? p.214
- How do I know my patient has it? p.214
- What else might it be? p.214
- Complications and prognosis p.214

What is it?

- **Balanitis is defined as inflammation of the glans penis.** Unless the person is circumcised, the inflammation usually involves the foreskin; the term balanoposthitis is therefore more correct, but is rarely used.
- **Balanitis has many causes, which can be divided into infectious, dermatological, and miscellaneous.** Most cases are due to infection.
- **Infectious causes include:**
  - *Candida albicans* — the most common cause, especially after treatment with antibiotics, or in people with diabetes mellitus
  - Anaerobes — predominantly *Bacteroides*
  - *Chlamydia*
  - *Entamoeba histolytica*
  - *Gardnerella vaginalis*
  - Herpes simplex

- Human papillomavirus
- Mycobacteria
- *Staphylococcus aureus*
- Streptococci
- Syphilis
- *Trichomonas vaginalis*

- **Most cases of balanitis, irrespective of the age of the individual, are due to *C albicans*.** Candidal balanitis typically presents as generalized erythema of the glans and/or foreskin (which may have a dry glazed appearance), with eroded white papules and a white discharge.
- **The diagnosis of candidal balanitis is often made on clinical grounds.**

[Edwards, 1996; CEG, 1999]

How common is it?

- **Balanitis is a relatively common condition,** affecting 11% of men attending a genito-urinary clinic [CEG, 1999].
- **Balanitis is less common in boys,** affecting 4%. Most such boys are of pre-school age, but the condition is rare before they are toilet-trained [Escala and Rickwood, 1989].
- Candidal balanitis is more common after oral antibiotics, and in men with diabetes mellitus.

How do I know my patient has it?

- **Symptoms** include penile soreness, itch, odour, inability to retract the foreskin (phimosis), and discharge from the glans or from under the foreskin.
- **Signs** include erythema, scaling, ulceration, fissuring, crusting, exudate, oedema, leucoplakia, sclerosis, purpura, and phimosis.

[CEG, 1999]

What else might it be?

- **Dermatological causes include:**
  - Circinate balanitis — due to sexually acquired Reiter's syndrome
  - Lichen *sclerosus et atrophicus* (balanitis *xerotica obliterans*) — may cause phimosis
  - Zoon's balanitis — orange-red lesions with pinpoint redder spots
  - Erythroplasia of Queyrat — carcinoma *in situ*, red velvety appearance
  - Bowen's disease — carcinoma *in situ*, scaly erythematous plaque
  - Psoriasis
  - Seborrhoeic dermatitis
  - Pemphigus
  - Lichen planus
- **Miscellaneous causes include:**
  - Trauma
  - Irritants
  - Poor hygiene
  - Contact dermatitis
  - Fixed drug eruption — a predilection for the glans penis, especially tetracyclines and sulphonamides
  - Stevens-Johnson syndrome

[Edwards, 1996; CEG, 1999]

Complications and prognosis

Prognosis

- Infectious balanitis responds promptly to appropriate treatment.
- The likelihood of any complication is low.

Management issues

- General issues p.214
- Treatment issues p.214
- Circumcision p.214

General issues

- **If at presentation the diagnosis is thought to be candid balanitis,** a pragmatic approach is to treat with appropriate therapy without taking a swab, and to ask the individual to return if the balanitis does not impro over the next few days. If the balanitis has not improv a swab should then be taken (treatment being directed the results), or the person should be referred to the genito-urinary medicine clinic.
- **If at presentation the diagnosis is thought to be infecti but not to be candidal balanitis,** either a swab should b taken (treatment being directed by the results), or the person should be referred to the genito-urinary medici clinic.
- **If at presentation the diagnosis is thought to be non-infective,** management should be directed to the likely cause, including referral to a specialist if appropriate.

[Edwards, 1996; CEG, 1999]

Treatment issues

- **Regular bathing with saline is soothing** for any cause c balanitis, and will provide short-term relief while speci treatment takes effect.
- **The following treatments are effective for *Candida albicans* balanitis:**
  - **First-line treatment** is with a topical imidazole (clotrimazole, econazole, ketoconazole, miconazole, sulconazole). There is no evidence of any difference efficacy between the imidazoles.
  - **Second-line treatment** is with a combination produc containing a topical imidazole plus 0.5% or 1% hydrocortisone. These preparations are particularly effective if there is inflammation associated with an infection, as the corticosteroid component will help relieve itching.
  - **Alternative topical treatments** are nystatin and terbinafine. These treatments are options if resistanc to, or adverse effects from, the imidazole is suspecte If inflammation is marked, they can be combined wi 0.5% or 1% hydrocortisone.
  - **Oral fluconazole** is an option if the candidal infectio has not responded to topical treatment.
- **Although sexual partners** of men with candidal balanit may be colonized by *C albicans* themselves, there is no evidence that their treatment reduces the risk of recurrent balanitis.
- **If the cause is not *C albicans*,** treatment should be directed by the swab result or by the clinical diagnosis.

[Edwards, 1996; CEG, 1999; Au and Yeung, 2003]

Circumcision

- Balanitis is less common in those who have been circumcised.
- There are no trial data on circumcision as a treatment for recurrent balanitis. Consensus, however, is that circumcision may benefit individuals with recurrent infective balanitis.

[Escala and Rickwood, 1989; Edwards, 1996]

References

NHS staff in England can link, free of charge, from references to full text journals by clicking on [Full text] o the PRODIGY website.

Au, T.S. and Yeung, K.H. (2003) *Balanitis, bacterial vaginosis and other genital conditions*. Hong Kong Medical Association. www.hkmj.org.hk/skin/balaniti.htm [Accessed: 02/09/2003].

CEG (1999) National guideline for the management of balanitis. *Sexually Transmitted Infections* 75(Suppl 1), S85-S88. [Full text]

3. Edwards, S. (1996) Balanitis and balanoposthitis: a review. *Genitourinary Medicine* 72(3), 155–159.
4. Escala, J.M. and Rickwood, A.M. (1989) Balanitis. *British Journal of Urology* 63(2), 196–197.

B

B

PRODIGY GUIDANCE

Bites — human and animal

Last revised in September 2004
www.prodigy.nhs.uk/guidance.asp?gt=Bites - human and animal

Applies to people of all ages

This guidance covers the management of human and animal bites (dog and cat).

There is separate PRODIGY guidance for *Insect bites and stings* and *Lacerations*.

Goals

- To offer immediate first aid
- To reduce the risk of infection
- To treat any established infection
- To achieve satisfactory wound healing with good cosmetic outcome
- To prevent tetanus
- To refer appropriately anyone at risk of contracting hepatitis or HIV for specialist advice

Contents

Scenarios

- Human/dog/cat bite p.216

Extended Information, p. 219

Human/dog/cat bite

Which therapy?

General measures

- **Apply pressure** to control bleeding.
- **Examine for damage** to the arteries, nerves, muscles, and tendons. Note: puncture injuries may be more extensive than they appear.
- **Irrigate thoroughly** with sodium chloride 0.9%.
- **Do not close** non-facial wounds that are clinically infected, deep punctures (particularly likely with cat bites), bites to the hand, or wounds that are more than 6 hours old. Seek advice or consider delayed closure after 3–5 days.
- **Cover with a sterile, non-adhesive dressing** to protect the wound.
- **Facial bites (unless very minor), more serious injuries, and/or more serious infections** should be seen in accident and emergency/plastic surgery — see section *Should I refer or investigate?*

Antibiotics

- **Antibiotic treatment is indicated** if the wound is clinically infected.
- **Antibiotic prophylaxis** is generally recommended for human bite wounds where there has been clear penetration of the skin; hand, foot, or facial animal bite wounds; puncture wounds; wounds involving joints, tendons, ligaments, or suspected fractures; wounds that are primarily closed; or where the person is diabetic, cirrhotic, asplenic, or immunosuppressed.
- **Antibiotics are not generally needed** if the wound is more than 2 days old and there is no sign of local or systemic infection.
- **If an antibiotic is indicated,** co-amoxiclav is first choice for bites managed in primary care.
- **If the person is allergic to penicillin:**
  - **Dog or cat bite:** oxytetracycline or doxycycline plus metronidazole (not for children under 12 years, pregnant women, or breastfeeding women).
  - **Human bite:** erythromycin plus metronidazole.
  - If a tetracycline cannot be used for a dog or cat bite (see above) seek advice from local microbiologist.

Tetanus, rabies, hepatitis, and HIV risk

- **Check tetanus immunization status** and give vaccine where appropriate (see section *Tetanus prophylaxis*).
- **Consider rabies if the person was bitten whilst abroad** (discuss management with local microbiologist).
- **Consider hepatitis B/C and HIV risk in any person wi a human bite.** If there is any suggestion of risk or genu uncertainty then seek urgent advice from the local pub health department regarding further management.

Practical prescribing points

For further information please see the *Medicines Compendium* (www.medicines.org.uk) or the *British National Formulary* (www.bnf.org).

- **Ibuprofen:** may cause gastrointestinal irritation and occasionally gastrointestinal haemorrhage. Avoid if th is a history of peptic ulceration. May worsen asthma, hypertension, renal impairment, or cardiac failure.
- **Tetracyclines:** may cause photosensitivity reactions (advise the person to avoid exposure to sunlight or sur lamps) and should not be taken within 2–3 hours of food, iron, calcium, zinc, or antacids.
- The Blood Transfusion Service distributes tetanus immunoglobulin to general practitioners on demand.

Follow-up advice

- **If the wound is not infected,** advise the person regardi signs of infection and the need for urgent review if ther is evidence of this.
- **If the wound is infected,** review at 24 and 48 hours to ensure the infection is responding to treatment, and advise that if signs of infection worsen or if the person feeling increasingly unwell, urgent review is needed.

Should I refer or investigate?

Refer?

Referral to accident and emergency/plastic surgery shoul be considered for:

- Bites involving arteries, nerves, muscles, tendons, or bones
- Penetrating bites to the hands or feet
- Facial wounds (excluding very minor wounds)
- Bites where there is a possibility of a foreign body (e.g. tooth) in the wound
- Wounds which might benefit from closure
- Devitalized wounds where debridement is required
- Bites where the severity of the injury is difficult to asses

- People with infected wounds who are systemically unwell
- People presenting with severe cellulitis
- Asplenic individuals, especially if not taking prophylactic penicillin
- People with diabetes or cirrhosis or who are immunosuppressed, as there is increased risk of infection

...vestigate?

- If the wound is clinically infected, take a swab for culture and sensitivity. Therapy should be reviewed on the basis of the results.
- Swabs should also be sent for culture and sensitivity if there is no response to first-line therapy.

...atient information leaflets

...e following PILs are available at www.prodigy.nhs.uk

- Bites (Human)
- Dog and Cat Bites
- Tetanus Immunisation

...hared decision making

- How did this bite happen? Did it happen abroad? Can any changes be made to prevent this happening again?
- **Bite wounds must be cleaned thoroughly.**
- If stitches are needed, keep the wound dry until the stitches are removed.
- **Paracetamol** or **ibuprofen** will help to ease pain.
- **Are you up-to-date with tetanus immunizations?**
- **Antibiotics** to prevent infection may be advised in certain situations.
- See a doctor promptly if:
  - The wound area becomes more tender, painful, swollen, or red.
  - You develop fever or other worrying symptoms within a week or so.
- For human bites: is there any concern that the person who bit you has hepatitis or HIV?

...rug rationale

...rugs not included

- **Penicillins (except co-amoxiclav)** are not included. They are less active against Pasteurella species and/or less active against beta-lactamase-producing anaerobes than co-amoxiclav [DTB, 1996; Smith et al, 2000].
- **Oral cephalosporins** are not included since they cannot achieve high enough tissue concentrations to eradicate *Pasteurella multocida*.
- **Quinolones** are not included as they should be reserved for treatment of infections when sensitivities are known [DH and SMAC, 1998].
- **Topical antibiotics** are not effective in the treatment of wounds [DTB, 1991].

...rugs included

- **Co-amoxiclav** is a broad-spectrum antibiotic, recommended as first-line empirical treatment for animal and human bites [Monteiro, 1995; DTB, 1996; Moore, 1997; Smith et al, 2000; Talan et al, 2003; BNF 47, 2004].
- **For penicillin-allergic people with dog/cat bites:**
  - Doxycycline/oxytetracycline plus metronidazole is recommended. Doxycycline and oxytetracycline have good activity against *Pasteurella* species (the most common pathogen), staphylococci, and streptococci [Smith et al, 2000; Talan et al, 2003]. Metronidazole is included to cover beta-lactamase-producing anaerobes.
  - If a tetracycline cannot be used for a dog or cat bite (e.g. for children under 12 years, pregnant women, or breastfeeding women), specialist advice should be sought from a local microbiologist. Erythromycin plus metronidazole may be considered, but erythromycin is far less active against *Pasteurella* species and treatment failures have occurred.
- **For penicillin-allergic people with human bites:**
  - Erythromycin plus metronidazole is recommended. Erythromycin has good activity against staphylococci and streptococci (the most common pathogens).
  - Metronidazole (in addition to tetracyclines or erythromycin) covers beta-lactamase-producing anaerobes.
- **Paracetamol** is included for simple analgesia.
- **Ibuprofen** is included as an alternative to paracetamol for analgesia.
- **When tetanus vaccination is indicated** (see section *Tetanus prophylaxis*) [DH, 2004]:
  - Children aged under 10 years: DTaP/IPV/Hib (combined diphtheria, tetanus, acellular pertussis, inactivated poliomyelitis, and *Haemophilus influenzae* type b vaccine) is recommended for primary immunization. dTaP/IPV (combined low-dose diphtheria, tetanus, acellular pertussis, and inactivated poliomyelitis vaccine) is recommended for booster doses.
  - People aged 10 years or over: Td/IPV (combined low-dose diphtheria, tetanus, and inactivated poliomyelitis vaccine) is recommended for both primary immunization and booster doses.

Prescriptions

Analgesia: use when required

Paracetamol s/f susp: 60mg to 120mg up to four times a day

- Age from 3 to 11 months
- Paracetamol 120mg/5ml s/f susp. Take 2.5ml to 5ml every 4 to 6 hours when required for pain relief. Maximum of 4 doses in 24 hours; supply 150 ml; NHS Cost £0.65; OTC Cost £1.14.

Paracetamol s/f susp: 120mg to 240mg up to four times a day

- Age from 12 months to 5 years
- Paracetamol 120mg/5ml s/f susp. Take one to two 5ml spoonfuls every 4 to 6 hours when required for pain relief. Maximum of 4 doses in 24 hours; supply 300 ml; NHS Cost £1.30; OTC Cost £2.28.

Paracetamol s/f susp: 250mg to 500mg up to four times a day

- Age from 6 to 11 years
- Paracetamol 250mg/5ml s/f susp. Take one to two 5ml spoonfuls every 4 to 6 hours when required for pain relief. Maximum of 4 doses in 24 hours; supply 300 ml; NHS Cost £1.70; OTC Cost £2.99.

Paracetamol tablets: 500mg to 1g up to four times a day

- Age from 12 to 15 years
- Paracetamol 500mg tablets. Take one to two tablets every 4 to 6 hours when required for pain relief. Maximum of 8 tablets in 24 hours; supply 100 tablets; NHS Cost £0.75; OTC Cost £1.32.

Paracetamol tablets: 1g up to four times a day

- Age from 16 years onwards
- Paracetamol 500mg tablets. Take two tablets every 4 to 6 hours when required for pain relief. Maximum of 8 tablets in 24 hours; supply 100 tablets; NHS Cost £0.75; OTC Cost £1.32.

Ibuprofen s/f susp: 50mg three to four times a day
- Age from 12 months to 2 years
- Ibuprofen 100mg/5ml s/f susp. Take 2.5ml three to four times a day when required for pain relief. Do not exceed the stated dose; supply 100 ml; NHS Cost £1.82; OTC Cost £3.21.

B

Ibuprofen s/f susp: 100mg three to four times a day
- Age from 3 to 7 years
- Ibuprofen 100mg/5ml s/f susp. Take one 5ml spoonful 3 to 4 times a day when required for pain relief. Do not exceed the stated dose; supply 150 ml; NHS Cost £2.73; OTC Cost £4.81.

Ibuprofen s/f susp: 200mg three to four times a day
- Age from 8 to 11 years
- Ibuprofen 100mg/5ml s/f susp. Take two 5ml spoonfuls 3 to 4 times a day when required for pain relief. Do not exceed the stated dose; supply 300 ml; NHS Cost £5.46; OTC Cost £9.62.

Ibuprofen tablets: 400mg three times a day
- Age from 12 years onwards
- Ibuprofen 400mg tablets. Take one tablet three times a day when required for pain relief. Do not exceed the stated dose; supply 24 tablets; NHS Cost £0.70; OTC Cost £1.23.

1st-line antibiotic (IF indicated): co-amoxiclav for 7 days

Co-amoxiclav 125/31mg/5ml susp: 0.25ml/kg three times a day
- Age from 1 month to 11 months
- Co-amoxiclav 125/31mg/5ml susp. *WEIGHT REQUIRED* Take 0.25ml per kg bodyweight THREE times a day for 7 days; supply 100 ml; NHS Cost £4.57.

Co-amoxiclav s/f suspension: 125/31mg three times a day
- Age from 12 months to 6 years
- Co-amoxiclav 125/31mg/5ml susp. Take one 5ml spoonful three times a day for 7 days; supply 100 ml; NHS Cost £4.57.

Co-amoxiclav s/f suspension: 250/62mg three times a day
- Age from 7 to 11 years
- Co-amoxiclav 250/62mg/5ml susp. Take one 5ml spoonful three times a day for 7 days; supply 100 ml; NHS Cost £6.42.

Co-amoxiclav tablets: 250/125mg three times a day
- Age from 12 years onwards
- Co-amoxiclav 375mg tablets. Take one tablet three times a day for 7 days; supply 21 tablets; NHS Cost £9.70.

Co-amoxiclav tablets: 500/125mg three times a day
- Age from 12 years onwards
- Co-amoxiclav 625mg tablets. Take one tablet three times a day for 7 days; supply 21 tablets; NHS Cost £15.72.

Penicillin allergy: human bite

Erythromycin 125mg/5ml + metronidazole 200mg/5ml suspension
- Age from 1 month to 23 months
- Erythromycin 125mg/5ml sf susp. Take one 5ml spoonful four times a day for 7 days; supply 200 ml; NHS Cost £2.24.
- Metronidazole 200mg/5ml susp. *WEIGHT REQUIRED* Take 7.5mg per kg bodyweight THREE times a day for 7 days. (Max 400mg per dose.); supply 100 ml; NHS Cost £7.70.

Erythromycin 250mg/5ml + metronidazole 200mg/5ml suspension
- Age from 2 to 11 years
- Erythromycin 250mg/5ml sf susp. Take one 5ml spoonful four times a day for 7 days; supply 200 ml; NHS Cost £3.68.
- Metronidazole 200mg/5ml susp. *WEIGHT REQUIRED* Take 7.5mg per kg bodyweight THREE times a day for 7 days. (Max 400mg per dose.); supply 200 ml; NHS Cost £15.34.

Erythromycin 500mg/5ml + metronidazole 200mg/5ml suspension
- Age from 9 to 11 years
- Erythromycin 500mg/5ml sf susp. Take one 5ml spoonful four times a day for 7 days; supply 200 ml; NHS Cost £6.54.
- Metronidazole 200mg/5ml susp. *WEIGHT REQUIRED* Take 7.5mg per kg bodyweight THREE times a day for 7 days. (Max 400mg per dose.); supply 200 ml; NHS Cost £15.34.

Erythromycin 250mg e/c + metronidazole 400mg tablets
- Age from 12 years onwards
- Erythromycin 250mg e/c tablets. Take one tablet four times a day for 7 days; supply 28 tablets; NHS Cost £3.08.
- Metronidazole 400mg tablets. Take one tablet three times a day for 7 days; supply 21 tablets; NHS Cost £1.54.

Erythromycin 500mg e/c + metronidazole 400mg tablets
- Age from 12 years onwards
- Erythromycin 250mg e/c tablets. Take two tablets four times a day for 7 days; supply 56 tablets; NHS Cost £6.16.
- Metronidazole 400mg tablets. Take one tablet three times a day for 7 days; supply 21 tablets; NHS Cost £1.54.

Penicillin allergy: dog/cat bite (NOT if pregnant)

Doxycycline 100mg capsules + metronidazole 400mg tablets
- Age from 12 years onwards
- Doxycycline 100mg capsules. Take TWO capsules now and then take ONE capsule once a day for the next 6 days; supply 8 capsules; NHS Cost £2.47.
- Metronidazole 400mg tablets. Take one tablet three times a day for 7 days; supply 21 tablets; NHS Cost £1.54.

Oxytetracycline 250mg + metronidazole 400mg tablets
- Age from 12 years onwards
- Oxytetracycline 250mg tablets. Take one tablet four times a day for 7 days; supply 28 tablets; NHS Cost £0.81.
- Metronidazole 400mg tablets. Take one tablet three times a day for 7 days; supply 21 tablets; NHS Cost £1.54.

Oxytetracycline 500mg + metronidazole 400mg tablets
- Age from 12 years onwards
- Oxytetracycline 250mg tablets. Take two tablets four times a day for 7 days; supply 56 tablets; NHS Cost £1.62.
- Metronidazole 400mg tablets. Take one tablet three times a day for 7 days; supply 21 tablets; NHS Cost £1.54.

Tetanus prophylaxis and dressings

Primary course: diphtheria+tetanus+pertussis+polio+Hib
- Age from 2 months to 9 years
- Pediacel injection. Give 0.5ml by intramuscular injection. For primary immunization, give three doses at intervals of 1 month between doses; supply 1 0.5ml vial

ster: low-dose diphtheria+tetanus+pertussis+polio
ge from 3 to 9 years
epevax injection. Give 0.5ml by intramuscular
jection; supply 1 0.5ml prefilled syringe.

nary course: low-dose diphtheria+tetanus+polio
ge from 10 years onwards
evaxis injection. Give 0.5ml by intramuscular injection. or primary immunization, give three doses at intervals f 1 month between doses; supply 1 0.5ml prefilled yringe.

ster: low-dose diphtheria+tetanus+polio
ge from 10 years onwards
evaxis injection. Give 0.5ml by intramuscular injection; upply 1 0.5ml prefilled syringe.

n x 5cm Absorbent perforated plastic film faced ssing
All ages
erforated FA 5x5cm dressing. Apply to the affected rea as directed; supply 5 single dressings; NHS Cost £0.45; OTC Cost £0.80.

cm x 10cm Absorbent perforated plastic film faced ssing
All ages
erforated FA 10x10cm dressing. Apply to the affected rea as directed; supply 5 single dressings; NHS Cost £0.75; OTC Cost £1.32.

cm x 10cm Absorbent perforated plastic film faced ssing
All ages
erforated FA 10x20cm dressing. Apply to the affected rea as directed; supply 5 single dressings; NHS Cost £1.60; OTC Cost £2.82.

rmeable non-woven synthetic adhesive tape
All ages
Perm non-wvn tape 1.25cmx5m. Apply as required; supply 1 5metre roll; NHS Cost £0.39; OTC Cost £0.69.

xtended Information

ackground information

What is it? p.219
How common is it? p.219
What else might it be? p.219
Complications and prognosis p.219

hat is it?

- **Dogs** have large teeth that can cause tearing and crushing of tissue: lacerations occur in 30–45% of cases, puncture wounds in 13–34%, and superficial abrasions in 30–43% of cases [Dire, 1992].
- **Cats** have fine, sharp teeth and, despite having a weaker bite than dogs, are capable of penetrating bone and joint capsules [Smith et al, 2000]. Puncture wounds occur in 57–86% of cases, lacerations in 5–17%, and superficial abrasions in 9–25% of cases [Dire, 1992].
- **Most adult human bites** (60–75%) occur on the hand. Human bites are either occlusal injuries (inflicted by actual biting) or clenched-fist injuries (sustained when a clenched fist hits a person's teeth, often during a fight). Clenched-fist injury is particularly prone to infection [Monteiro, 1995; Smith et al, 2000].

ow common is it?

The incidence of mammalian bites is difficult to determine because many people who receive such bites do not seek medical attention.

- Dog bites are the most common mammalian bite, with about 200,000 cases being reported each year in the UK. It has been estimated that dog bites account for 60–90% of bites; cat bites for 5–18%, and human bites for 4–23% [Dire, 1992; Monteiro, 1995].
- Animal bites often involve children (commonly bitten by a household pet). The mean age of dog-bite victims is 13 years, and 75% of patients are less than 20 years old [Brogan et al, 1995].

B

What else might it be?

- Non-accidental injury.

Complications and prognosis

Complications

- **Wound infection** is the most common complication, occurring in 2–30% of dog bites, 15–50% of cat bites, and 9–50% of human bites [Baker and Moore, 1987; Dire, 1992; Cummings, 1994; Monteiro, 1995]. This compares with 1–12% of non-bite wounds managed in accident and emergency [Cummings, 1994].
- **Risk of infection is particularly high in:** puncture wounds; hand injuries; full-thickness wounds; wounds requiring surgical debridement; and wounds involving joints, tendons, ligaments, or fractures. Diabetic, asplenic, cirrhotic, and immunosuppressed patients are also at increased risk of wound infection [Dire, 1992; Monteiro, 1995; Smith et al, 2000].
- **Less frequent complications include** tetanus, rabies, septicaemia, septic arthritis, tenosynovitis, tendonitis, fractures, osteomyelitis, peritonitis, endocarditis, endophthalmitis, meningitis, and disfiguring wounds from severe mauling [Monteiro, 1995; Smith et al, 2000].
- **Cat-scratch disease** is caused by *Bartonella henselae* and can follow a bite or scratch from a cat or dog. Cat-scratch disease presents with a primary erythematous papule 3–10 days following the injury, followed by lymphadenopathy and fever. Cat-scratch disease is generally self-limiting and resolves in less than 2 months [Smith et al, 2000; Bower, 2001].
- ***Capnocytophaga canimorsus*** (part of the normal canine oral flora but also occasionally isolated from cat bite wounds) has been associated with severe infections in immunocompromised patients, which may result in meningitis, endocarditis, renal failure, and septicaemia [Smith et al, 2000].

Management issues

- Initial management p.219
- Wound closure p.220
- Antibiotic prophylaxis p.220
- Treatment of established infection p.220
- Tetanus prophylaxis p.221
- Rabies prophylaxis p.221
- Hepatitis B, hepatitis C, and HIV p.221

Initial management

- **Apply pressure to control bleeding.** Animal bites seldom result in major bleeding, but if blood loss is heavy or does not stop, maintain pressure and refer urgently to accident and emergency [Lewis, 2001].
- **Irrigate the wound thoroughly to remove dirt and bacteria,** minimizing the risk of infection.
- Irrigation should be with sodium chloride 0.9% using a syringe.
  - High-pressure irrigation is more effective than low-pressure irrigation at reducing bacterial wound counts

and wound infection rates. However, sustained high-pressure irrigation may be associated with increased tissue damage and should be used with caution, especially in highly vascularized areas.
- Adequate high pressure can be achieved using a 30–60 ml syringe and 16–19 gauge needle. Note: there is a high risk of spray back onto the clinician with this method; this can be minimized by cupping a gloved hand around the wound, or using a cup-like device or shield to prevent spray back. Protective goggles should be worn.
- More gentle irrigation can be achieved using a saline aerosol, Steripod, or a syringe without a needle.

[Singer et al, 1997; Hollander and Singer, 1999; Capellan and Hollander, 2003; Cole, 2003]

- **Antiseptic cleansers are not usually necessary** and there is some concern that they damage tissue and delay wound healing [Hollander and Singer, 1999].
- **If debridement is required** to remove devitalized tissue, a local anaesthetic (e.g. lidocaine) should be used. Puncture wounds should not generally be debrided [Smith et al, 2000].
- **Assessment should include** documenting the number, location, and type of injury/injuries and when the wound(s) occurred.
  - If adult bites have been inflicted on a child, consider child protection issues.
  - If an animal has bitten a child, consider the possibility of poor parenting and supervision.
  - Follow local policies for referral of children considered at risk.
- **Injuries may be more extensive than they appear, due to the high incidence of puncture wounds.** If pain is out of proportion to the apparent extent of the wound, especially with a cat bite on the hand, it is likely that a joint or tendon may have perforated [Lewis, 2001].
- **Signs of infection** should be noted (redness, tenderness, swelling, heat, discharge), especially if presentation is late.
- **Consider referral to accident and emergency/plastic surgery for:**
  - Bites involving arteries, nerves, muscles, tendons, or bones.
  - Penetrating bites to the hands or feet.
  - Facial wounds (excluding very minor wounds).
  - Bites where there is the possibility of a foreign body (e.g. a tooth) in the wound.
  - Wounds which might benefit from closure.
  - Devitalized wounds where extensive debridement is required.
  - Bites where the severity of the injury is difficult to assess.
  - People with infected wounds who are systemically unwell.
  - People presenting with severe cellulitis.
  - Asplenic individuals, especially if not taking prophylactic penicillin.
  - People with diabetes, cirrhosis, or who are immunosuppressed, as there is an increased risk of infection.

[Monteiro, 1995; Smith et al, 2000]

Wound closure

- **Primary closure with sutures is not generally recommended for non-facial bite wounds,** especially deep punctures, bites to the hand, and clinically infected wounds. Anecdotal data suggest an increased risk of infection after closure of these wounds. Sterile skin closure strips or delayed closure may be appropriate [Smith et al, 2000]. Delayed closure is usually more appropriate and should also be considered for wound more than 6 hours old [Dire, 1992].
- **Facial wounds and larger lacerations may require sutu** (or sterile skin closure strips) to prevent scarring and improve cosmetic outcome [Smith et al, 2000]. There uncertainty about the risks of this, but in most cases it safe providing the person has presented early and the wound has been adequately cleaned [Dire, 1992; Monteiro, 1995].
- **Delayed primary closure** (after 3–5 days) is advisable bites to the hand, bites with extensive crush injury, wounds needing a considerable amount of debrideme and wounds more than 6 hours old [Dire, 1992].
- **Consider referral to accident and emergency/plastic surgery** for wounds that may require sutures or delaye primary closure.
- **Cover** with a sterile, non-adhesive dressing to protect wound.

Antibiotic prophylaxis

- **There are only limited data available on the effect of antibiotic prophylaxis for preventing complications of mammalian bite wounds.** A Cochrane systematic revie found evidence that:
  - Antibiotic prophylaxis significantly reduced the incidence of infection after a dog, cat, or human bite to the hand. Four people need to be given antibiotic prophylaxis to prevent one infection developing afte any bite to the hand.
  - There are insufficient data to determine whether prophylactic antibiotics are effective for dog or cat bites (only one study with 11 patients analysed cat bites).
  - The only trial to analyse human bites found that the infection rate in the antibiotic group was significant lower than in the control group (0/33 compared wit 7/15, $p < 0.05$). This result should be interpreted wit caution due to the small sample size (OR 0.02, 95% CI 0 to 0.33).

[Medeiros, 2004]

- **Antibiotic prophylaxis is generally recommended for:**
  - **Human bites** where there has been clear penetration the skin.
  - **People with high-risk animal bite wounds,** i.e. hand, foot, and facial injuries; puncture wounds (particula likely with cat bites); wounds requiring surgical debridement; wounds involving joints, tendons, ligaments, or suspected fractures [Dire, 1992; Cummings, 1994].
  - Wounds that have undergone primary closure.
  - **People who are at risk of serious wound infection complications,** e.g. those who are diabetic, cirrhotic, asplenic, or immunosuppressed [Monteiro, 1995].
  - **People with a prosthetic valve** or who have suffered bite proximal to prosthetic joints.
- **Antibiotics are not generally needed if** the wound is mo than 2 days old and there is no sign of local or systemi infection [Smith et al, 2000].
- **The choice of antibiotic** is the same as for treatment of established mild-to-moderate infection (see below).

Treatment of established infection

- **Clinically infected bite wounds should be treated with systemic antibiotics.**
- Most infections resulting from bites are polymicrobial, often including anaerobes.
- **Infected dog bites** often contain multiple species of bacteria, including *Pasteurella canis*, *Pasteurella multocida*, *Staphylococcus aureus*, other staphylococci streptococci, and anaerobic bacteria.

ıfected cat bites are usually due to *P multocida*. *taphylococcus* species, *Streptococcus* species, and naerobes are also important pathogens.

ıfected human bites usually contain *Streptococcus* pecies, *S aureus*, *Eikenella corrodens*, and anaerobic acteria.

ɔok, 2003; Merriam et al, 2003; Talan et al, 2003]

Co-amoxiclav is recommended as first-line treatment for ıild to moderate infections following a dog, cat, or uman bite managed in primary care.

f the person is allergic to penicillin, first-line treatment is ased on the type of wound and the likely infecting rganisms:

- **Dog or cat bite: oxytetracycline/doxycycline plus metronidazole.** If a tetracycline cannot be used for a dog or cat bite (e.g. in children under 12 years, pregnant women, or breastfeeding women), seek advice from the local microbiologist.
- **Human bite: erythromycin plus metronidazole.** There is increasing resistance to erythromycin, therefore arrange to review the person at 24 and 48 hours to ensure that the infection is responding to treatment.

People presenting with severe infections or who are ystemically unwell should be referred to accident and mergency, as intravenous antibiotics may be required.

iggins et al, 1994; Monteiro, 1995; DTB, 1996; Moore,)7; Smith et al, 2000; Brook, 2003; Talan et al, 2003]

ɛtanus prophylaxis

Check tetanus immunization status for all bite wounds.

A total of five doses of vaccine, administered at the ppropriate intervals, is considered to give lifelong mmunity (see Table 1).

Note: existing stocks of Td (adsorbed diphtheria [low-dose] and tetanus vaccine) can be used for administration at the time of a tetanus-prone wound if appropriate. However, if the polio, or polio, and liphtheria vaccination needs to be updated at the same ime then Td/IPV should be used.

Following a bite, tetanus prophylaxis should be given as ollows:

- **Person fully immunized, i.e. has received five doses of vaccine at appropriate intervals:** tetanus booster not needed. Consider giving human tetanus immunoglobulin for tetanus-prone wounds where the risk of infection is especially high, e.g. those contaminated with manure or extensive devitalized tissue.
- **Primary immunization complete, boosters incomplete but up-to-date:** tetanus booster not needed but may be given if booster is due and it is convenient to give now. Consider giving human tetanus immunoglobulin for tetanus-prone wounds where the risk of infection is especially high, e.g. those contaminated with manure or extensive devitalized tissue.
- **Primary immunization incomplete, or boosters not up-to-date:** give tetanus booster and further doses as needed to complete the recommended schedule (note: if the primary course is interrupted it should be resumed but not repeated). Add human tetanus immunoglobulin if it is a tetanus-prone wound (defined as: a puncture wound; a significant degree of devitalized tissue; contaminated with soil or manure; containing foreign bodies; compound fractures; clinical signs of sepsis; wounds or burns sustained more than 6 hours before surgical treatment). *Note:* inject tetanus vaccine and immunoglobulin at different sites.
- **Not immunized or immunization status uncertain:** give an immediate dose of vaccine. Add human tetanus immunoglobulin if it is a tetanus-prone wound (see above). Arrange further doses of tetanus vaccine as needed to complete the recommended five-dose schedule.

[DH, 2004]

ıble 1: Immunization schedule for tetanus.

ıedule	Children	Adults and children over 10 years
mary ırse	3 doses of vaccine (usually as DTaP/IPV/Hib) at 2, 3, and 4 months of age	3 doses of vaccine (as Td/IPV), each one month apart
ırth se	At least 3 years after the last dose of the primary course, usually pre-school entry (as dTaP/IPV)	5–10 years after the last dose of the primary course (as Td/IPV)
th se	Aged 13–18 years or before leaving school (as Td/IPV)	10 years after fourth dose (as Td/IPV)

aP/IPV/Hib = Diphtheria, tetanus, acellular pertussis, inactivated poliomyelitis, l *Haemophilus influenzae* type b vaccine
aP/IPV = Low-dose diphtheria, tetanus, acellular pertussis, and inactivated iomyelitis vaccine
/IPV = Low-dose diphtheria, tetanus, and inactivated poliomyelitis vaccine for ılts and children over 10 years of age

Rabies prophylaxis

- Consider the risk of rabies in anyone who has sustained a bite or scratch from a dog or cat whilst abroad [de Medeiros and Saconato, 2003; HPA, 2003].
- **Discuss the need for post-exposure prophylaxis urgently** with the local consultant in communicable diseases at the Health Protection Agency. The combination of human rabies immunoglobulin and rabies vaccine is recommended for bite exposure regardless of the interval between exposure and initiation of treatment [HPA, 2003].

Hepatitis B, hepatitis C, and HIV

- All human bite injuries should be taken seriously, and enquiry made into the risk status of the perpetrator. Blood-borne viruses are potentially transmissible by a human bite if the skin is broken — this risk is greater if there is blood in the perpetrator's saliva [Expert Advisory Group on AIDS and the Advisory Group on Hepatitis., 1998].
- The risk from needle-stick injury for hepatitis B ranges from 6% to 30%, and that for HIV ranges from 0.3% to 0.5%. The risk from a bite is thought to be considerably less than this [Richman and Rickman, 1993].
- There are some cases reported where hepatitis C has been transmitted through bites [Dusheiko et al, 1990; Figueiredo et al, 1994]. Although there is no prophylaxis available, serological testing should be performed where necessary.
- Several studies have followed up people bitten by HIV-infected individuals; no one in these studies has seroconverted [Richman and Rickman, 1993]. Only four cases have been published in which HIV transmission through bites may have occurred [Richman and Rickman, 1993; Vidmar et al, 1996; Khajotia and Lee, 1997].
- **If there is any suggestion of risk or genuine uncertainty** then discuss urgently with the local public health department regarding further management (this may involve post-exposure prophylaxis with hepatitis B immunoglobulin [HBIG] and hepatitis B vaccine, and the use of antiretroviral drugs following exposure to HIV infection).
    - If post-exposure prophylaxis for hepatitis B with HBIG is considered necessary it should be started preferably within 12 hours, and not later than 1 week after exposure.

B

- If post-exposure prophylaxis for HIV is considered necessary it should be started as soon as possible, i.e. within hours. Animal studies suggest that post-exposure prophylaxis is not effective later than 24–36 hours after exposure; however, in humans the time interval after which it is not effective is not known and treatment may be started after 36 hours [Bottiger et al, 1997; MMWR, 1998; Tsai et al, 1998].

B

References

NHS staff in England can link, free of charge, from references to full text journals by clicking on [Full text] on the PRODIGY website.

1. Baker, M.D. and Moore, S.E. (1987) Human bites in children. A six-year experience. *American Journal of Diseases in Children* **141**(12), 1285–1290.
2. BNF 47 (2004) *British National Formulary*. 47th edn. London: British Medical Association and Royal Pharmaceutical Society of Great Britain.
3. Bottiger, D., Johansson, N.G., Samuelsson, B. et al (1997) Prevention of simian immunodeficiency virus, SIVsm, or HIV-2 infection in cynomolgus monkeys by pre- and postexposure administration of BEA-005. *AIDS* **11**(2), 157–162.
4. Bower, M.G. (2001) Managing dog, cat, and human bite wounds. *Nurse Practitioner* **26**(4), 36–38. [Full text]
5. Brogan, T.V., Bratton, S.L., Dowd, M.D. and Hegenbarth, M.A. (1995) Severe dog bites in children. *Pediatrics* **96**(5), 947–950.
6. Brook, I. (2003) Microbiology and management of human and animal bite wound infections. *Primary Care; Clinics in Office Practice* **30**(1), 25–39.
7. Capellan, O. and Hollander, J.E. (2003) Management of lacerations in the emergency department. *Emergency Medicine Clinics of North America* **21**(1), 205–231.
8. Cole, E. (2003) Wound management in the A&E department. *Nursing Standard* **17**(46), 45–52. [Full text]
9. Cummings, P. (1994) Antibiotics to prevent infection in patients with dog bite wounds: a meta-analysis of randomized trials. *Annals of Emergency Medicine* **23**(3), 535–540.
10. de Medeiros, I.M. and Saconato, H (2003) Bites (mammalian). *Clinical Evidence* **10**(Dec), 2219–2224.
11. DH (2004) *New (August 2004) chapter 30 – tetanus*. Immunisation against infectious disease. Department of Health. www.dh.gov.uk [Accessed: 22/06/2005]. [Full text]
12. DH and SMAC (1998) *The path of least resistance*. Department of Health. www.dh.gov.uk [Accessed: 27/04/2004]. [Full text]
13. Dire, D.J. (1992) Emergency management of dog and cat bite wounds. *Emergency Medicine Clinics of North America* **10**(4), 719–736.
14. DTB (1991) Local applications to wounds: II – dressings for wounds and ulcers. *Drug & Therapeutics Bulletin* **29**(25), 97–99.
15. DTB (1996) Augmentin reconsidered. *Drug & Therapeutics Bulletin* **34**(10), 76–78.
16. Dusheiko, G.M., Smith, M. and Scheuer, P.J. (1990) Hepatitis C virus transmitted by human bite. *Lancet* **336**(8713), 503–504. [Full text]
17. Expert Advisory Group on AIDS and the Advisory Group on Hepatitis. (1998) *Guidance for clinical health care workers: protection against infection wi[th] blood borne viruses*. Department of Health. www.dh.gov.uk [Accessed: 24/02/2004]. [Full text]
18. Figueiredo, J.F., Borges, A.S., Martinez, R. et al (19[94]) Transmission of hepatitis C virus but not human immunodeficiency virus type 1 by a human bite. *Clinical Infectious Diseases* **19**(3), 546–547.
19. Hollander, J.E. and Singer, A.J. (1999) Laceration management. *Annals of Emergency Medicine* **34**(3), 356–367.
20. HPA (2003) *Joint protocol for rabies queries*. Healt[h] Protection Agency. www.hpa.org.uk [Accessed: 24/(2004].
21. Khajotia, R.R. and Lee, E. (1997) Transmission of human immunodeficiency virus through saliva after lip bite. *Archives of Internal Medicine* **157**(16), 190[1] [Full text]
22. Lewis, L. (2001) Office management of animal bites. *Patient Care* **35**(13), 66–76.
23. Medeiros, I. (2004) *Antibiotic prophylaxis for mammalian bites (Cochrane Review)*. The Cochrane Library. Issue 1. Chichester, UK: John Wiley & Sons Ltd..
24. Merriam, C.V., Fernandez, H.T., Citron, D.M. et al (2003) Bacteriology of human bite wound infections *Anaerobe* **9**(2), 83–86.
25. MMWR (1998) Public health service guidelines for t[he] management of health-care worker exposures to HI[V] and recommendations for postexposure prophylaxis *Morbidity & Mortality Weekly Report* **47**(RR-7), 1–28.
26. Monteiro, J.A. (1995) Human and animal bite woun[d] infections. *European Journal of Internal Medicine* **6**(209–215.
27. Moore, F. (1997) "I've just been bitten by a dog". *British Medical Journal* **314**(7074), 88–90. [Full text]
28. Richman, K.M. and Rickman, L.S. (1993) The potential for transmission of human immunodeficien[cy] virus through human bites. *Journal of Acquired Immune Deficiency Syndromes* **6**(4), 402–406.
29. Singer, A.J., Hollander, J.E. and Quinn, J.V. (1997) Evaluation and management of traumatic lacerations *New England Journal of Medicine* **337**(16), 1142–1148. [Full text]
30. Smith, P.F., Meadowcroft, A.M. and May, D.B. (200[0]) Treating mammalian bite wounds. *Journal of Clinica[l] Pharmacy & Therapeutics* **25**(2), 85–99.
31. Talan, D.A., Abrahamian, F.M., Moran, G.J. et al (2003) Clinical presentation and bacteriologic analys[is] of infected human bites in patients presenting to emergency departments. *Clinical Infectious Diseases* **37**(11), 1481–1489.
32. Tsai, C.C., Emau, P., Follis, K.E. et al (1998) Effectiveness of postinoculation (R)-9-(2-phosphonylmethoxypropyl) adenine treatment for prevention of persistent simian immunodeficiency vir[us] SIVmne infection depends critically on timing of initiation and duration of treatment. *Journal of Virology* **72**(5), 4265–4273.
33. Vidmar, L., Poljak, M., Tomazic, J. et al (1996) Transmission of HIV-1 by human bite. *Lancet* **347**(9017), 1762–1763. [Full text]
34. Wiggins, M.E., Akelman, E. and Weiss, A.P. (1994) The management of dog bites and dog bite infections [to] the hand. *Orthopedics* **17**(7), 617–623.

RODIGY GUIDANCE

3lepharitis

ast revised in April 2005
'ww.prodigy.nhs.uk/guidance.asp?gt=Blepharitis

pplies to people over the age of 1 month

his guidance covers the management of blepharitis of the anterior and posterior aspects of the eyelid.

his guidance does not cover blepharitis caused by herpes simplex or *Candida*, and does not cover the management of :borrhoeic dermatitis or rosacea.

'here is separate PRODIGY guidance on *Conjunctivitis — infective, Conjunctivitis — allergic, Dry eye syndrome, czema — atopic, Glaucoma, Herpes simplex — ocular, and Seborrhoeic dermatitis.*

oals

'o improve patient comfort
'o preserve vision
'o prevent or minimize structural damage to the ocular urface and eyelids
nerican Academy of Ophthalmology, 2003]

ontents

cenarios

- Initial presentation or mild disease — no marked infection p.223
- Blepharitis with marked infection p.225
- Persistent blepharitis — no marked infection p.228

xtended Information, p. 230

'hich scenario?

nitial presentation/mild disease — no marked infection: :overs the first-line management of both anterior and posterior blepharitis when infection is not marked.

3lepharitis with marked infection: covers management when there is marked eyelid infection.

'ersistent blepharitis — no marked infection: covers the nanagement of people with persistent and troublesome ymptoms when infection is not marked.

nitial presentation or mild isease — no marked infection

'hich therapy?

'nform the person that blepharitis is a chronic disease :hat cannot always be cured, but that symptoms can be :ontrolled.

Advise eyelid hygiene, twice daily until symptoms resolve and then once daily for an indefinite period. This is vital, both in the initial treatment of an acute episode and as a long-term factor in reducing likelihood of recurrence.

Advise:

- Warm compresses to the eyelid and lid margin.
- Massage and expression of meibomian gland contents when there is posterior blepharitis.
- **Cleansing of lid margins** — traditionally baby shampoo diluted with warm water (50:50 mixture) is applied with fingertips or a cotton bud and rubbed along the lid margin. Commercial lid scrubs (not available on FP10) are an alternative.

Treat underlying or associated disorders (e.g. atopic eczema, seborrhoeic dermatitis, or rosacea).

Artificial tears are recommended for symptom relief in people with dry eyes or an abnormal tear film.

Practical prescribing points

For further information please see the *Medicines Compendium* (www.medicines.org.uk) or the *British National Formulary* (www.bnf.org).

- **Use preservative-free preparations if** more than 6 applications per day are necessary: the more frequently drops containing benzalkonium chloride are used, the greater the risk of ocular irritation.
- **Contact lenses** should generally not be worn during treatment with eye drops. However:
  - **Hard lenses:** use eye drops 30 minutes before inserting lenses.
  - **Soft lenses:** eye drops containing preservatives should not be used with soft lenses. (Some preservatives, particularly benzalkonium chloride, accumulate in soft contact lenses and cause irritation.) Preservative-free drops should be used instead.
  - **Preservative-free eye drops:** generally, lenses can be put in 5–10 minutes after using preservative-free eye drops, that is, once the drop has dispersed. Contact lenses should not be put in for 30 minutes after using Viscotears single-use eye drops, because of their viscosity.
  - **Eye ointments:** eye ointments should not be used when contact lenses are worn.
- **Drops should be used in preference to ointment if other eye drops are being used** (e.g. for glaucoma).

Follow-up advice

- Review if eyelid hygiene is not effective.

Should I refer or investigate?

Refer?

- **Admit urgently if orbital cellulitis is suspected** (person is unwell, tender sinuses, restriction of eye movements).
- **Refer** in the following instances:
  - To exclude malignancy if there is:
    - Persistent localized disease or resistance to treatment
    - Marked eyelid asymmetry
  - If there is evidence of corneal disease
  - If vision deteriorates
  - If there is moderate or severe pain
  - If the diagnosis is uncertain
  - Associated disease, for example Sjögren's syndrome or eyelid deformities, that requires specialist management.

Patient information leaflets

The following PILs are available at www.prodigy.nhs.uk
- Blepharitis
- Dry Eyes

Shared decision making

B

- **Eyelid hygiene** is the main treatment for blepharitis. Do this twice a day until the inflammation settles. You may then to do this once a day indefinitely to reduce the chance of a further flare-up.
  - Bathe and gently press on the eyelids with a cloth soaked in very warm water for 5-10 minutes. This softens the skin and any crusts.
  - Then, massage the eyelids – gently roll your first finger on the eyelids. This helps to push out any of the oily fluid from the tiny eyelid glands.
  - Then, clean the eyelids with a cotton wool bud dipped in a mixture of baby shampoo and water (50/50). In particular, try to clean off any crusts.
  - Then, wash off the shampoo with a cloth.
- **Artificial tears** may be useful in people who also have dry eyes.
- Sometimes the eyelids become infected. See your doctor if they become worse or sticky.

Drug rationale

Drugs not included

- **Hypromellose artificial tear drops other than the 0.3% strength** are not included in this scenario. There is little data to support the use of other strengths of hypromellose drops over the 0.3% strength which is overwhelmingly the most commonly used artificial tear solution from national Prescribing Analysis and Cost data.
- **Acetylcysteine eye drops** are mucolytic, and can be useful for people with sticky, viscous mucus on the eye (filamentary keratitis). However, they often sting and are expensive [BNF 47, 2004]. Prescriptions can be found in the PRODIGY *Dry eye syndrome* guidance.
- **Zinc sulphate drops** are a traditional astringent that is now little used [BNF 47, 2004].
- **Lid Care solution,** a commercially available eyelid cleanser, is not available for prescribing on the NHS.

Drugs included

- **Artificial tears** are indicated if the blepharitis is accompanied by dry eye:
  - Hypromellose 0.3% is overwhelmingly the most commonly used artificial tear solution from national Prescribing Analysis and Cost data. It is effective, and remains the cheapest option.
  - Polyvinyl alcohol is another commonly used artificial tear preparation and can be useful when ocular surface mucin is reduced.
  - Carbomer eye drops can cling to the eye surface, which may help to reduce the frequency of application to four times a day.
- **Preservative-free, single-dose artificial tears** are recommended for users of soft contact lens, and those people unable to tolerate preservatives [Harman et al, 1990]. Preservative-free products licensed for the relief of dry eyes include hypromellose, hydroxyethycellulose, carbomer 980, polyvinyl alcohol, and povidone.
- **Carmellose sodium** is a relatively new product and therefore remains under the surveillance of the Committee on Safety of Medicines. It is used 'as required'.
- **Paraffin eye ointments: simple eye ointment, Lacri-Lu and Lubri-Tears** provide prolonged lubrication. They cause temporary blurred vision, and so are best used before bedtime [Khaw and Elkington, 1999; BNF 47, 2004]. They are all preservative-free.

Prescriptions

Advice note

Advice only: cleansing eyelids
- All ages
- You have blepharitis (inflammation of the eyelid). Thi can be recurring. Bathe and clean the eyelids at least twice a day. Soak a flannel in hot water and press it o the eyelids to bathe them for 5-10 minutes. Then clea the eyelids with cotton wool buds, or a cloth, dipped i mixture of baby shampoo and water (half shampoo a half water). Wash off the shampoo. Keep bathing and cleaning the eyelids once a day after the inflammation has settled. This will reduce the chance of a further fla up.

Artificial tears: hypromellose

Hypromellose 0.3% eye drops
- Age from 1 month onwards
- Hypromellose 0.3% eye drops. Put one drop into the affected eye(s) when required; supply 10 ml; NHS Cost £0.75; OTC Cost £1.32.

Artificial tears: polyvinyl alcohol or carbomer

Liquifilm Tears (polyvinyl alcohol 1.4%) eye drops
- Age from 1 month onwards
- Liquifilm Tears 1.4% eye drops. Put one drop into the affected eye(s) when required; supply 15 ml; NHS Cost £1.61; OTC Cost £2.85.

Sno Tears (polyvinyl alcohol) eye drops
- Age from 1 month onwards
- Sno Tears 1.4% eye drops. Put one drop into the affected eye(s) when required; supply 10 ml; NHS Cost £1.06; OTC Cost £1.90.

GelTears (carbomer 980) eye drops
- Age from 1 month onwards
- GelTears 0.2% eye drop gel. Put one drop into the affected eye(s) when required; supply 10 grams; NHS Cost £2.80; OTC Cost £4.94.

Viscotears (carbomer 980) eye drops
- Age from 12 years onwards
- Viscotears 0.2% eye drop gel. Put one drop into the affected eye(s) when required; supply 10 grams; NHS Cost £3.12; OTC Cost £4.62.

Liposic (carbomer 980) eye drops
- Age from 12 years onwards
- Liposic 0.2% eye drop gel. Put one drop into the affect eye(s) when required; supply 10 grams; NHS Cost £2.96; OTC Cost £4.44.

Liquivisc (carbomer 980) eye drops
- Age from 12 years onwards
- Liquivisc 0.25% eye drop gel. Put one drop into the affected eye(s) when required; supply 10 grams; NHS Cost £3.96; OTC Cost £6.98.

Paraffin eye ointment (use at bedtime)

Simple eye ointment
- Age from 1 month onwards
- Simple 10% eye ointment. Put a small amount into the affected eye(s) at bedtime; supply 4 grams; NHS Cost £2.68; OTC Cost £4.74.

ri-Lube eye ointment
ge from 1 month onwards
acri-Lube eye ointment. Put a small amount into the fected eye(s) at bedtime; supply 5 grams;
HS Cost £2.47; OTC Cost £4.35.

ri-Tears eye ointment
ge from 1 month onwards
ubri-Tears eye ointment. Put a small amount into the fected eye(s) at bedtime; supply 5 grams;
HS Cost £2.29; OTC Cost £4.03.

tificial tears: preservative-free

lroxyethylcellulose preservative-free drops (single-)
ge from 12 years onwards
linims artificial tears. Put one drop into the affected ye(s) when required; supply 60 single doses;
HS Cost £17.25; OTC Cost £30.39.

romellose 0.32% preservative-free drops (single-use)
ge from 1 month onwards
ypromellose 0.32% single-use. Put one drop into the ffected eye(s) when required; supply 60 single doses;
HS Cost £23.76; OTC Cost £32.50.

bomer 980 preservative-free drops (single-use)
ge from 12 years onwards
iscotears single-use eye gel. Put one drop into the ffected eye(s) when required; supply 60 single doses;
HS Cost £11.50; OTC Cost £20.27.

yvinyl alcohol 1.4% preservative-free drops (single-)
ge from 1 month onwards
iquifilm Tears single-use. Put one drop into the affected ye(s) when required; supply 60 single doses;
HS Cost £10.70; OTC Cost £18.86.

idone 5% preservative-free drops (single-use)
ge from 12 years onwards
)culotect unit dose eye drops. Put one drop into the ffected eye(s) when required; supply 60 single doses;
HS Cost £10.20; OTC Cost £17.98.

rmellose 1% preservative-free drops (single-use)
ge from 1 month onwards
armellose 1% single-use drops. Put one drop into the ffected eye(s) when required; supply 60 single doses;
HS Cost £11.50; OTC Cost £20.27.

lepharitis with marked nfection

hich therapy?

onsider the possibility of orbital cellulitis. Admit rgently if this is suspected (person unwell, tender inuses, restriction of eye movements).

nform the person that blepharitis is a chronic disease hat cannot always be cured, but that symptoms can be ontrolled.

Advise eyelid hygiene, twice daily until symptoms resolve nd then once daily for an indefinite period. This is mportant, both in the initial treatment of an acute pisode and as a long-term factor in reducing likelihood f recurrence. Advise:

- Warm compresses to the eyelid and lid margin.
- Massage and express meibomian gland contents when there is posterior blepharitis.
- Cleanse lid margins — traditionally baby shampoo diluted with warm water (50:50 mixture) is applied with fingertips or a cotton bud and rubbed along the lid margin. Commercial lid scrubs (not available on FP10) are an alternative.

- **Prescribe a topical antibiotic in most situations:**
  - **Chloramphenicol ointment** applied to the lid margins with a finger tip or cotton bud, after attending to eyelid hygiene or at night, is recommended.
  - **Fusidic acid eye drops** are an alternative.
  - **Continue for 1 month after the inflammation has settled.**
- **Prescribe an oral antibiotic** for recalcitrant staphylococcal blepharitis, severe secondary infection of the meibomian glands, and local cellulitis.
  - Flucloxacillin is recommended first-line.
  - Erythromycin or azithromycin is recommended if a penicillin is contraindicated.
- **Treat any associated conditions (e.g. atopic eczema, seborrhoeic dermatitis or rosacea).**
- **Artificial tears** are recommended for symptom relief in people with dry eyes or an abnormal tear film.

Practical prescribing points

For further information please see the *Medicines Compendium* (www.medicines.org.uk) or the *British National Formulary* (www.bnf.org).

Topical antibiotics

- **Chloramphenicol:** concerns over aplastic anaemia associated with ocular chloramphenicol have largely been discounted.
  - Do not use concurrently with other myelotoxic drugs
  - Do not use in the last trimester of pregnancy
  - Avoid prolonged treatment periods
- **Contact lenses are contraindicated** during treatment with topical antibiotics, or if untreated infection is present. They should be avoided until at least 24 hours after treatment has finished.

Oral antibiotics

- **Erythromycin** may increase the level of certain drugs (e.g. theophylline, carbamazepine, statins), or potentiate warfarin.

Artificial tears for dry eyes

- **Use preservative-free preparations if** more than 6 applications per day are necessary: the more frequently drops containing benzalkonium chloride are used, the greater the risk of ocular irritation.
- **Contact lenses** should generally not be worn during treatment with eye drops. However:
  - **Hard lenses:** use eye drops 30 minutes before inserting lenses.
  - **Soft lenses:** eye drops containing preservatives should not be used with soft lenses. (Some preservatives, particularly benzalkonium chloride, accumulate in soft contact lenses and cause irritation.) Preservative-free drops should be used instead.
  - **Preservative-free eye drops:** generally, lenses can be put in 5–10 minutes after using preservative-free eye drops, that is, once the drop has dispersed. Contact lenses should not be put in for 30 minutes after using Viscotears single-use eye drops, because of their viscosity.
  - **Eye ointments:** eye ointments should not be used when contact lenses are worn.
- **Drops should be used in preference to ointment if other eye drops are being used** (e.g. for glaucoma).

Follow-up advice

- Review after 5 days or sooner if clinically indicated.

Should I refer or investigate?

Refer?

- **Admit urgently if orbital cellulitis is suspected** (person is systemically unwell, tender sinuses, restriction of eye movements).
- **Refer** in the following instances:
  - To exclude malignancy if there is:
    - Persistent localized disease or resistance to treatment
    - Marked eyelid asymmetry
  - If there is evidence of corneal disease
  - If vision deteriorates
  - If there is moderate or severe pain
  - If the diagnosis is uncertain
  - Associated disease, for example Sjögren's syndrome or eyelid deformities, that requires specialist management.

Investigate?

- **Microbial culture and sensitivity tests** are not routine in clinical practice. Specific indications for testing include:
  - Recurrent anterior blepharitis with severe inflammation
  - No response to treatment (discontinue antibiotic treatment for 48 hours before swabbing)

Patient information leaflets

The following PILs are available at www.prodigy.nhs.uk

- Blepharitis
- Dry Eyes

Shared decision making

- **Eyelid hygiene** is the main treatment for blepharitis. Do this twice a day until the inflammation settles. You may then to do this once a day indefinitely to reduce the chance of a further flare-up.
  - Bathe and gently press on the eyelids with a cloth soaked in very warm water for 5-10 minutes. This softens the skin and any crusts.
  - Then, massage the eyelids – gently roll your first finger on the eyelids. This helps to push out any of the oily fluid from the tiny eyelid glands.
  - Then, clean the eyelids with a cotton wool bud dipped in a mixture of baby shampoo and water (50/50). In particular, try to clean off any crusts.
  - Then, wash off the shampoo with a cloth.
- **An antibiotic ointment** is also used if the eyelids are infected. A course of up to a month or so is often needed.
- **An antibiotic eye drop** is an alternative — particularly if you are pregnant.
- Do not wear contact lenses if the eyelids are infected or while using antibiotic ointment or drops.
- **Artificial tears** may be useful in people who also have dry eyes.

Drug rationale

Drugs not included

- **Topical antibiotic eye preparations other than chloramphenicol ointment and fusidic acid drops** are not included to combat emerging resistance. Other eye preparations (e.g. aminoglycosides, fluoroquinolones) should be reserved for more serious ocular infections and as second-line treatments when the sensitivity is known [Robert and Adenis, 2001; BNF 47, 2004].
- **Oral antibiotics other than flucloxacillin, erythromycin and azithromycin** are not included. These antibiotics are considered to be the most suitable where topical penetration is unlikely to be adequate [Dart, Persona Communication, 2004] when there is recalcitrant staphylococcal blepharitis, severe secondary infection the meibomian glands, or local cellulites.
- **Lid Care solution,** a commercially available eyelid cleanser, is not available for prescribing on the NHS.
- **Corticosteroid eye drops:** although topical corticosteroids can be useful for severe inflammation, they are not recommended for general use owing to t significant complications associated with their chroni use (e.g. glaucoma, cataracts, severe opportunistic infections) [Smith and Flowers, 1995; McCulley and Shine, 2000].
- **Hypromellose artificial tear drops other than the 0.3% strength** are not included in this scenario. There is litt data to support the use of other strengths of hypromellose drops over the 0.3% strength which is overwhelmingly the most commonly used artificial te solution from national Prescribing Analysis and Cost data.
- **Acetylcysteine eye drops** are mucolytic, and can be us for people with sticky, viscous mucus on the eye (filamentary keratitis). However, they often sting and expensive [BNF 47, 2004]. Prescriptions can be found the PRODIGY *Dry eye syndrome* guidance.
- **Zinc sulphate drops** are a traditional astringent that is now little used [BNF 47, 2004].

Drugs included

- **Topical chloramphenicol** is the antibiotic of choice in UK. It has a relatively broad spectrum of action again most gram-positive and gram-negative bacteria [Robe and Adenis, 2001]. Concerns about the systemic toxic of topical chloramphenicol, in particular aplastic anaemia, have been discounted [Lancaster et al, 1998; Walker et al, 1998; Field et al, 1999].
- **Topical fusidic acid** is an alternative to chlorampheni Fusidic acid is most effective against *Staphylococcus aureus*. However studies have shown that it is as effective as chloramphenicol against other pathogens to the high ocular concentrations achieved [Hvidberg, 1987; Horven, 1993; Boberg-Ans and Nissen, 1998; Carr, 1998; Leeming, 1999].
- **Oral antiobiotics** are usually unnecessary for treating anterior blepharitis but are recommended when there recalcitrant staphylococcal blepharitis, severe seconda infection of the meibomian glands, or local cellulitis:
  - **Flucloxacillin** is recommended as the first-line antibiotic for 5 day treatment of *S aureus infection.*
  - **Erythromycin or azithromycin** is recommended if a penicillin is contraindicated. Erythromycin is recommended for 5 days and azithromycin for 3 da
- **Artificial tears** are indicated if the blepharitis is accompanied by dry eye:
  - Hypromellose 0.3% is overwhelmingly the most commonly used artificial tear solution from nationa Prescribing Analysis and Cost data. It is effective, ar remains the cheapest option.
  - Polyvinyl alcohol is another commonly used artifici tear preparation and can be useful when ocular surf mucin is reduced.
  - Carbomer eye drops can cling to the eye surface, which may help to reduce the frequency of applicati to four times a day.
- **Preservative-free, single-dose artificial tears** are recommended for users of soft contact lens, and those people unable to tolerate preservatives [Harman et al, 1990]. Preservative-free products licensed for the relie dry eyes include hypromellose, hydroxyethycellulose, carbomer 980, polyvinyl alcohol, and povidone.

:armellose sodium is a relatively new product and ıerefore remains under the surveillance of the :ommittee on Safety of Medicines. It is used 'as equired'.

araffin eye ointments: simple eye ointment, Lacri-Lube, nd Lubri-Tears provide prolonged lubrication. They ause temporary blurred vision, and so are best used efore bedtime [Khaw and Elkington, 1999; BNF 47, 004]. They are all preservative-free.

·escriptions

·pical antibiotics

'oramphenicol 1% eye ointment
- ıge from 1 month onwards
- :hloramphenicol 1% eye ointment. Apply to the eyelid nargins twice a day; supply 4 grams; NHS Cost £1.04.

ısidic acid 1% eye drops
- ıge from 1 month onwards
- 'usidic acid 1% eye drops. Apply to the eyelid margins wice a day; supply 5 grams; NHS Cost £2.09.

ral antibiotics

ıcloxacillin syrup: 62.5mg four times a day for 5 days
- ıge from 1 month to 23 months
- 'lucloxacillin 125mg/5ml syrup. Take 2.5ml four times a lay for 5 days; supply 100 ml; NHS Cost £3.23.

ıcloxacillin syrup: 125mg four times a day for 5 days
- ıge from 2 to 4 years
- 'lucloxacillin 125mg/5ml syrup. Take one 5ml spoonful 'our times a day for 5 days; supply 100 ml; NHS Cost £3.23.

ıcloxacillin syrup: 250mg four times a day for 5 days
- ıge from 5 to 11 years
- 'lucloxacillin 250mg/5ml syrup. Take one 5ml spoonful 'our times a day for 5 days; supply 100 ml; NHS Cost £6.97.

ıcloxacillin capsules: 250mg four times a day for 5 days
- Age from 12 years onwards
- Flucloxacillin 250mg capsules. Take one capsule four times a day for 5 days; supply 20 capsules; NHS Cost £2.09.

ıcloxacillin capsules: 500mg four times a day for 5 days
- Age from 12 years onwards
- Flucloxacillin 500mg capsules. Take one capsule four times a day for 5 days; supply 20 capsules; NHS Cost £3.38.

ythromycin s/f suspension: 125mg four times a day (5 ys)
- Age from 1 month to 23 months
- Erythromycin 125mg/5ml sf susp. Take one 5ml spoonful four times a day for 5 days; supply 100 ml; NHS Cost £1.11.

ythromycin s/f suspension: 250mg four times a day (5 ys)
- Age from 2 to 11 years
- Erythromycin 250mg/5ml sf susp. Take one 5ml spoonful four times a day for 5 days; supply 100 ml; NHS Cost £1.90.

ythromycin s/f suspension: 500mg four times a day (5 ıys)
- Age from 9 to 11 years
- Erythromycin 500mg/5ml sf susp. Take one 5ml spoonful four times a day for 5 days; supply 100 ml; NHS Cost £3.23.

Erythromycin e/c tablets: 250mg four times a day for 5 days
- Age from 12 years onwards
- Erythromycin 250mg e/c tablets. Take one tablet four times a day for 5 days; supply 20 tablets; NHS Cost £2.20.

Erythromycin e/c tablets: 500mg four times a day for 5 days
- Age from 12 years onwards
- Erythromycin 250mg e/c tablets. Take two tablets four times a day for 5 days; supply 40 tablets; NHS Cost £4.40.

Azithromycin suspension: 10mg/kg once a day for 3 days
- Age from 6 months to 2 years
- Azithromycin 200mg/5ml susp. *WEIGHT REQUIRED* Take 10mg per kg bodyweight ONCE a day for 3 days; supply 15 ml; NHS Cost £5.08.

Azithromycin suspension: 200mg once a day for 3 days
- Age from 3 to 7 years
- Azithromycin 200mg/5ml susp. Take one 5ml spoonful once a day for 3 days; supply 15 ml; NHS Cost £5.08.

Azithromycin suspension: 300mg once a day for 3 days
- Age from 8 to 11 years
- Azithromycin 200mg/5ml sf susp. Take 7.5ml once a day for 3 days; supply 1 22.5 ml bottle; NHS Cost £7.62.

Azithromycin suspension: 400mg once a day for 3 days
- Age from 12 to 13 years
- Azithromycin 200mg/5ml susp. Take two 5ml spoonfuls once a day for 3 days; supply 30 ml; NHS Cost £13.80.

Azithromycin capsules: 500mg once a day for 3 days
- Age from 14 years onwards
- Azithromycin 250mg capsules. Take two capsules once a day for 3 days; supply 6 capsules; NHS Cost £13.43.

Artificial tears: polyvinyl alcohol / carbomer / hypromellos

Hypromellose 0.3% eye drops
- Age from 1 month onwards
- Hypromellose 0.3% eye drops. Put one drop into the affected eye(s) when required; supply 10 ml; NHS Cost £0.75; OTC Cost £1.32.

Liquifilm Tears (polyvinyl alcohol 1.4%) eye drops
- Age from 1 month onwards
- Liquifilm Tears 1.4% eye drops. Put one drop into the affected eye(s) when required; supply 15 ml; NHS Cost £1.61; OTC Cost £2.85.

Sno Tears (polyvinyl alcohol) eye drops
- Age from 1 month onwards
- Sno Tears 1.4% eye drops. Put one drop into the affected eye(s) when required; supply 10 ml; NHS Cost £1.06; OTC Cost £1.90.

GelTears (carbomer 980) eye drops
- Age from 1 month onwards
- GelTears 0.2% eye drop gel. Put one drop into the affected eye(s) when required; supply 10 grams; NHS Cost £2.80; OTC Cost £4.94.

Viscotears (carbomer 980) eye drops
- Age from 12 years onwards
- Viscotears 0.2% eye drop gel. Put one drop into the affected eye(s) when required; supply 10 grams; NHS Cost £3.12; OTC Cost £4.62.

Liposic (carbomer 980) eye drops
- Age from 12 years onwards
- Liposic 0.2% eye drop gel. Put one drop into the affected eye(s) when required; supply 10 grams; NHS Cost £2.96; OTC Cost £4.44.

Liquivisc (carbomer 980) eye drops
- Age from 12 years onwards
- Liquivisc 0.25% eye drop gel. Put one drop into the affected eye(s) when required; supply 10 grams; NHS Cost £3.96; OTC Cost £6.98.

Paraffin eye ointment (use at bedtime)

Simple eye ointment
- Age from 1 month onwards
- Simple 10% eye ointment. Put a small amount into the affected eye(s) at bedtime; supply 4 grams; NHS Cost £2.68; OTC Cost £4.74.

Lacri-Lube eye ointment
- Age from 1 month onwards
- Lacri-Lube eye ointment. Put a small amount into the affected eye(s) at bedtime; supply 5 grams; NHS Cost £2.47; OTC Cost £4.35.

Lubri-Tears eye ointment
- Age from 1 month onwards
- Lubri-Tears eye ointment. Put a small amount into the affected eye(s) at bedtime; supply 5 grams; NHS Cost £2.29; OTC Cost £4.03.

Artificial tears: preservative-free

Hydroxyethylcellulose preservative-free drops (single-use)
- Age from 12 years onwards
- Minims artificial tears. Put one drop into the affected eye(s) when required to lubricate the eye(s); supply 60 single doses; NHS Cost £17.25; OTC Cost £30.40.

Hypromellose 0.32% preservative-free drops (single-use)
- Age from 1 month onwards
- Hypromellose 0.32% single-use. Put one drop into the affected eye(s) when required to lubricate the eye(s); supply 60 single doses; NHS Cost £23.76; OTC Cost £32.50.

Carbomer 980 preservative-free drops (single-use)
- Age from 12 years onwards
- Viscotears single-use eye gel. Put one drop into the affected eye(s) when required to lubricate the eye(s); supply 60 single doses; NHS Cost £11.50; OTC Cost £20.27.

Polyvinyl alcohol 1.4% preservative-free drops (single-use)
- Age from 1 month onwards
- Liquifilm Tears single-use. Put one drop into the affected eye(s) when required to lubricate the eye(s); supply 60 single doses; NHS Cost £10.70; OTC Cost £18.86.

Povidone 5% preservative-free drops (single-use)
- Age from 12 years onwards
- Oculotect unit dose eye drops. Put one drop into the affected eye(s) when required to lubricate the eye(s); supply 60 single doses; NHS Cost £10.20; OTC Cost £17.98.

Carmellose 1% preservative-free drops (single-use)
- Age from 1 month onwards
- Carmellose 1% single-use drops. Put one drop into the affected eye(s) when required to lubricate the eye(s); supply 60 single doses; NHS Cost £11.50; OTC Cost £20.27.

Persistent blepharitis — no marked infection

Which therapy?

- **Check compliance with previous advice or treatment.**
  - Twice daily (minimum) eyelid hygiene is important.
  - Lids should be kept clean by using cotton buds or a cloth dipped in baby shampoo diluted with warm water (50:50 mixture).
  - People should be advised to continue cleaning their eyelids once daily in this way even after symptoms have completely gone, in order to minimize recurre[nce].
- **Treat underlying or associated disorders,** such as atop[ic] eczema, seborrhoeic dermatitis or rosacea.
- **In adults, consider oxytetracycline (twice a day), tetracycline (twice a day), or doxycycline (once a day)** when there is posterior blepharitis which is severe, or unresponsive to eyelid hygiene, or associated with rosacea.
  - **Continue for a minimum of 6 weeks.**
  - **Stop after 3 months** — a prolonged period of improvement is usual.
  - **Repeat courses are often required intermittently.**
- **Artificial tears** are recommended for symptom relief in people with co-existing dry eyes or an abnormal tear film.

Practical prescribing points

For further information please see the *Medicines Compendium* (www.medicines.org.uk) or the *British National Formulary* (www.bnf.org).

Tetracyclines

- Tetracyclines are contraindicated in pregnancy, breastfeeding and children less than 12 years of age.
- Benign intracranial hypertension is a rare but importa[nt] adverse effect of tetracycline therapy. If a person takin[g] tetracycline develops headache and visual disturbance stop the tetracycline.
- Doxycycline is the tetracycline of choice in people wit[h] hepatic and renal impairment.
- Photosensitivity has been reported with doxycycline. Advise people to avoid exposure to direct sunlight or ultraviolet light.

Artificial tears for dry eyes

- **Use preservative-free preparations if** more than 6 applications per day are necessary: the more frequentl[y] drops containing benzalkonium chloride are used, the greater the risk of ocular irritation.
- **Contact lenses** should generally not be worn during treatment with eye drops. However:
  - **Hard lenses:** use eye drops 30 minutes before inserti[ng] lenses.
  - **Soft lenses:** eye drops containing preservatives shoul[d] not be used with soft lenses. (Some preservatives, particularly benzalkonium chloride, accumulate in s[oft] contact lenses and cause irritation.) Preservative-free drops should be used instead.
  - **Preservative-free eye drops:** generally, lenses can be put in 5–10 minutes after using preservative-free eye drops, that is, once the drop has dispersed. Contact lenses should not be put in for 30 minutes after using Viscotears single-use eye drops, because of their viscosity.
  - **Eye ointments:** eye ointments should not be used wh[en] contact lenses are worn.
- **Drops should be used in preference to ointment if othe[r] eye drops are being used** (e.g. for glaucoma).

Follow-up advice

- Review according to clinical judgement.
- Review after 6 weeks treatment with oral tetracyclines

ould I refer or investigate?

fer?

- dmit urgently if orbital cellulitis is suspected (person is stemically unwell, tender sinuses, restriction of eye ovements).
- efer in the following instances:
  - To exclude malignancy if there is:
    - Persistent localized disease or resistance to treatment
    - Marked eyelid asymmetry
  - If there is evidence of corneal disease
  - If vision deteriorates
  - If there is moderate or severe pain
  - If the diagnosis is uncertain
  - Associated disease, for example Sjögren's syndrome or eyelid deformities, that requires specialist management.

estigate?

- ndications for microbial culture and sensitivity tests clude:
  - Recurrent anterior blepharitis with severe inflammation
  - No response to treatment (discontinue antibiotic treatment for 48 hours before swabbing)

tient information leaflets

: following PILs are available at www.prodigy.nhs.uk

- lepharitis
- Dry Eyes

ared decision making

- yelid hygiene is the main treatment for blepharitis. Do is twice a day until the inflammation settles. You may en need to do this once a day indefinitely to reduce the hance of a further flare-up.
  - Bathe and gently press on the eyelids with a cloth soaked in very warm water for 5-10 minutes. This softens the skin and any crusts.
  - Then, massage the eyelids – gently roll your first finger on the eyelids. This helps to push out any of the oily fluid from the tiny eyelid glands.
  - Then, clean the eyelids with a cotton wool bud dipped in a mixture of baby shampoo and water (50/50). In particular, try to clean off any crusts.
  - Then, wash off the shampoo with a cloth.
- **An oral antibiotic** may be helpful in some situations e.g. f you also have rosacea.
- **Artificial tears** may be useful in people who also have dry yes.

rug rationale

ugs not included

- **Topical antibiotic eye preparations are not ecommended for the treatment of persistent blepharitis nless there is marked eyelid infection** [Robert and Adenis, 2001; BNF 47, 2004].
- **id Care solution,** a commercially available eyelid leanser, is not available for prescribing on the NHS.
- **Corticosteroid eye drops:** although topical orticosteroids can be useful for severe inflammation, hey are not recommended for general use owing to the ignificant complications associated with their chronic se (e.g. glaucoma, cataracts, severe opportunistic nfections) [Smith and Flowers, 1995; McCulley and hine, 2000].
- **Hypromellose artificial tear drops other than the 0.3% strength** are not included in this scenario. There is little data to support the use of other strengths of hypromellose drops over the 0.3% strength which is overwhelmingly the most commonly used artificial tear solution from national Prescribing Analysis and Cost data.
- **Acetylcysteine eye drops** are mucolytic, and can be useful for people with sticky, viscous mucus on the eye (filamentary keratitis). However, they often sting and are expensive [BNF 47, 2004]. Prescriptions can be found in the PRODIGY *Dry eye syndrome* guidance.
- **Zinc sulphate drops** are a traditional astringent that is now little used [BNF 47, 2004].

Drugs included

- **Oxytetracycline** is recommended for people with persistent blepharitis due to meibomian dysfunction or ocular rosacea [Dougherty J.M. et al, 1991; Seal et al, 1995a].
- **Tetracycline** is an alternative option for people with persistent blepharitis due to meibomian dysfunction or ocular rosacea.
- **Doxycycline** is a further alternative [Frucht-Pery J. et al, 1993; Johnson et al, 1997]. It is more expensive but needs to be taken only once a day. It is better absorbed than oxytetracycline or tetracycline and can be taken with food which reduces gastrointestinal intolerance and potentially improves compliance.
- Note: lower doses of oral antibiotics are offered than those recommended in the BNF. This reflects the doses used in trials and minimizes the risk of adverse effects.

Prescriptions

Advice note

Advice only: cleansing eyelids

- All ages
- You have blepharitis (inflammation of the eyelid). This can be recurring. Bathe and clean the eyelids at least twice a day. Soak a flannel in hot water and press it on the eyelids to bathe them for 5-10 minutes. Then clean the eyelids with cotton wool buds, or a cloth, dipped in a mixture of baby shampoo and water (half shampoo and half water). Wash off the shampoo. Keep bathing and cleaning the eyelids once a day after the inflammation has settled. This will reduce the chance of a further flare up.

Oral antibiotics

Oxytetracycline tablets: 250mg twice a day (6 weeks supply)

- Age from 12 years onwards
- Oxytetracycline 250mg tablets. Take one tablet twice a day; supply 84 tablets; NHS Cost £5.82.

Tetracycline tablets: 250mg twice a day (6 weeks supply)

- Age from 12 years onwards
- Tetracycline 250mg tablets. Take one tablet twice a day; supply 84 tablets; NHS Cost £6.51.

Doxycycline capsules: 50mg once a day (6 weeks supply)

- Age from 12 years onwards
- Doxycycline hyclate 50mg caps. Take one capsule once a day; supply 42 capsules; NHS Cost £6.21.

B

Artificial tears: polyvinyl alcohol / carbomer / hypromellos

Hypromellose 0.3% eye drops
- Age from 1 month onwards
- Hypromellose 0.3% eye drops. Put one drop into the affected eye(s) when required; supply 10 ml; NHS Cost £0.75; OTC Cost £1.32.

B

Liquifilm Tears (polyvinyl alcohol 1.4%) eye drops
- Age from 1 month onwards
- Liquifilm Tears 1.4% eye drops. Put one drop into the affected eye(s) when required; supply 15 ml; NHS Cost £1.61; OTC Cost £2.85.

Sno Tears (polyvinyl alcohol) eye drops
- Age from 1 month onwards
- Sno Tears 1.4% eye drops. Put one drop into the affected eye(s) when required; supply 10 ml; NHS Cost £1.06; OTC Cost £1.90.

GelTears (carbomer 980) eye drops
- Age from 1 month onwards
- GelTears 0.2% eye drop gel. Put one drop into the affected eye(s) when required; supply 10 grams; NHS Cost £2.80; OTC Cost £4.94.

Viscotears (carbomer 980) eye drops
- Age from 12 years onwards
- Viscotears 0.2% eye drop gel. Put one drop into the affected eye(s) when required; supply 10 grams; NHS Cost £3.12; OTC Cost £4.62.

Liposic (carbomer 980) eye drops
- Age from 12 years onwards
- Liposic 0.2% eye drop gel. Put one drop into the affected eye(s) when required; supply 10 grams; NHS Cost £2.96; OTC Cost £4.44.

Liquivisc (carbomer 980) eye drops
- Age from 12 years onwards
- Liquivisc 0.25% eye drop gel. Put one drop into the affected eye(s) when required; supply 10 grams; NHS Cost £3.96; OTC Cost £6.98.

Paraffin eye ointment (use at bedtime)

Simple eye ointment
- Age from 1 month onwards
- Simple 10% eye ointment. Put a small amount into the affected eye(s) at bedtime; supply 4 grams; NHS Cost £2.68; OTC Cost £4.74.

Lacri-Lube eye ointment
- Age from 1 month onwards
- Lacri-Lube eye ointment. Put a small amount into the affected eye(s) at bedtime; supply 5 grams; NHS Cost £2.47; OTC Cost £4.35.

Lubri-Tears eye ointment
- Age from 1 month onwards
- Lubri-Tears eye ointment. Put a small amount into the affected eye(s) at bedtime; supply 5 grams; NHS Cost £2.29; OTC Cost £4.03.

Artificial tears: preservative-free

Hydroxyethylcellulose preservative-free drops (single-use)
- Age from 12 years onwards
- Minims artificial tears. Put one drop into the affected eye(s) when required to lubricate the eye(s); supply 60 single doses; NHS Cost £17.25; OTC Cost £30.40.

Hypromellose 0.32% preservative-free drops (single-use)
- Age from 1 month onwards
- Hypromellose 0.32% single-use. Put one drop into the affected eye(s) when required to lubricate the eye(s); supply 60 single doses; NHS Cost £23.76; OTC Cost £32.50.

Carbomer 980 preservative-free drops (single-use)
- Age from 12 years onwards
- Viscotears single-use eye gel. Put one drop into the affected eye(s) when required to lubricate the eye(s); supply 60 single doses; NHS Cost £11.50; OTC Cost £20.27.

Polyvinyl alcohol 1.4% preservative-free drops (single-use)
- Age from 1 month onwards
- Liquifilm Tears single-use. Put one drop into the affec eye(s) when required to lubricate the eye(s); supply 6C single doses; NHS Cost £10.70; OTC Cost £18.86.

Povidone 5% preservative-free drops (single-use)
- Age from 12 years onwards
- Oculotect unit dose eye drops. Put one drop into the affected eye(s) when required to lubricate the eye(s); supply 60 single doses; NHS Cost £10.20; OTC Cost £17.98.

Carmellose 1% preservative-free drops (single-use)
- Age from 1 month onwards
- Carmellose 1% single-use drops. Put one drop into th affected eye(s) when required to lubricate the eye(s); supply 60 single doses; NHS Cost £11.50; OTC Cost £20.27.

Extended Information

Background information

- What is it? p.230
- How common is it? p.231
- How do I know my patient has it? p.231
- How do I determine the cause of blepharitis? p.231
- Complications and prognosis p.231
- What else might it be? p.232

What is it?

- **Blepharitis is inflammation of the margin of the eyelid is usually a chronic condition** that is typically bilateral is a complex condition with several causes, which are characterized by overlapping symptoms and signs.
- **Classification:** blepharitis can be classified anatomicall into disorders that affect the base of the lashes (anteric blepharitis) and disorders that primarily affect the meibomian glands (posterior blepharitis). Blepharitis may also be classified according to clinical symptoms and signs into staphylococcal; seborrhoeic; mixed seborrhoeic and staphylococcal; and meibomian gland dysfunction.
  - **Staphylococcal blepharitis** affects the anterior eyelid margin and is characterized by lash collarettes and crusting, lid ulceration, and folliculitis in association with a positive culture for staphylococci.
  - **Seborrhoeic blepharitis** is also a disease of the anteri eyelid margin and is caused by excessive sebum. It is frequently associated with seborrhoeic dermatitis involving other areas of the body.
  - **Meibomian gland dysfunction** causes disease of the posterior eyelid margin and is often associated with seborrhoeic dermatitis and/or rosacea. Meibomian glands are modified sebaceous glands that run along the lid margin posterior to the lid lashes and open or to the posterior lid margin. Their lipid secretion have an important role in preventing evaporation of tears from the eye.
- **The role of bacteria in the pathophysiology of blephar is not clear.** *Staphylococcus epidermidis* (96%), *Propionibacterium acnes* (93%), and *Cornyebacterium* species (77%) are isolated more often from people wit

lepharitis when compared with controls. *S. aureus* is ot found significantly more often in people with lepharitis, and it is not cultured in significantly greater umbers compared with controls, except when 'clinical' aphylococcal blepharitis is present, either alone or ixed with seborrhoea. Three possible mechanisms by hich staphylococci cause anterior blepharitis have been iggested:

Direct infection of the lid

Reaction to staphylococcal exotoxin

Allergic response to staphylococcal antigen

osterior blepharitis is not thought to be directly due to ifection. Lipases produced by bacterial flora may break own the lipids produced by the meibomian glands into ee fatty acids, which are irritant to the ocular surface nd destabilize the tear film.

here is a complex relationship between dry eye yndrome (keratoconjunctivitis sicca) and blepharitis — ry eye is associated with, a complication of, and may be xacerbated by chronic blepharitis. Low levels of tear lm phospholipids may result in increased tear film vaporation and dry eyes. It is also possible that low evels of local lysozyme and immunoglobulin levels ssociated with tear deficiency may predispose to the evelopment of staphylococcal blepharitis. Dry eye has een reported to be present in:

50% of people with staphylococcal blepharitis

25–40% people with seborrhoeic blepharitis

52% of people with ocular rosacea

skin et al, 1992; Seal et al, 1995b; Smith and Flowers,)5; Driver and Lemp, 1996; Mills, 1998; Seal et al, 98; McCulley and Shine, 2000; Pray and Pray, 2002]

ow common is it?

lepharitis accounts for 4.5% of all ophthalmological roblems presenting in primary care. About 2–5% of GP onsultations are related to eye problems [Manners, 997].

ases of new or recurrent (i.e. new episode of) lepharitis are reported as 1.8 per 1000 population per ear [Manners, 1997].

osterior blepharitis is strongly associated with ncreasing age [Driver and Lemp, 1996].

ow do I know my patient has it?

ymptoms

nptoms are often intermittent and are usually bilateral.

ore eyelids are the most common symptom.

yes may feel 'gritty'.

ymptoms of dry eye include blurred vision and contact ens intolerance.

yelids sticking together, particularly in the morning, uggest infection.

igns

wollen eyelids are the defining sign of staphylococcal lepharitis and meibomitis, but are unusual in the less evere types of blepharitis.

nflamed lid margins are usually present.

ltered eyelash appearances include misdirection, rusting, and eyelash loss.

Eyelid surfaces may be scaly, oily or greasy. Ulceration of the anterior lid indicates infection.

tyes and chalazions are much more common in people with blepharitis.

nflamed conjunctiva are a common complication of lepharitis.

Investigations

- **Visual acuity** should be normal, although dry eyes may cause some intermittent blurring.
- **Examination with a slit lamp and fluorescein staining** may reveal corneal defects (see Table 1).
- **Microbial culture and sensitivity tests are not required for diagnosis. Specific indications for testing include:**
  - Recurrent anterior blepharitis with severe inflammation
  - No response to treatment (discontinue antibiotic treatment for 48 hours before swabbing)

[American Academy of Ophthalmology, 2003]

How do I determine the cause of blepharitis?

- The cause of blepharitis can usually be determined by the appearance of the condition.
- Inflammation of the anterior margin is usually associated with staphylococcus or is seborrhoeic in nature.
- Inflammation of the posterior margin is typically caused by meibomian gland dysfunction, which is not usually infected.
- Infected meibomian glands are extremely uncommon. The diagnosis should be made if there is severe inflammation in the lid and generalised eyelid swelling together with purulent material coming from the meibomian gland orifice [Dart, Personal Communication, 2004].
- Table 1 lists the principle features of staphylococcal and seborrhoeic blepharitis and meibomian gland dysfunction.

[Frith et al, 2001]

Complications and prognosis

Complications

- **Conjunctivitis** results from infiltration of the conjunctiva with bacterial debris from the eyelid.
- **Conjunctival cysts and concretions may occur, but do not usually present significant problems.**
- **Meibomian cyst formation:** symptoms (other than cosmetic concerns) are uncommon. Occasionally an upper lid meibomian cyst can press on the cornea and cause astigmatism.
- **Meibomian abscess** can arise from acute infection of a meibomian gland (internal hordeoleum).
- **Corneal inflammation and ulceration:** marginal keratitis typically affects middle-aged and elderly people with blepharitis, and is thought to represent a local hypersensitivity reaction to infection of the lid margin or conjunctiva, typically by *Staphylococcus*. Recurrence is frequent. Punctate keratitis is also thought to be due to hypersensitivity to staphylococcal exotoxins.
- **Trichiasis** can result from distortion of the lid margin causing the lashes to turn inwards to the eye surface.
- **Scarring** may occur if blepharitis becomes chronic. It may cause complete closure or deformity of the meibomian gland, sparsity of eye lashes, and thickened, irregular lid margins.
- **Contact lens intolerance** is commonly seen in people with blepharitis.
- **Dry eye (keratoconjunctivitis sicca):** blepharitis can cause or exacerbate dry eye syndrome.

Prognosis

- Permanent cure is unlikely but symptoms can usually be controlled.
- Vision is rarely affected.

[Raskin et al, 1992; Smith and Flowers, 1995; Driver and Lemp, 1996; Seal and Bron, 1997b; Mills, 1998; McCulley and Shine, 2000; American Academy of Ophthalmology, 2003]

B

Table 1: Features associated with the different causes of blepharitis.

Feature	Anterior eyelid margin (Staphylococcal)	Anterior eyelid margin (Seborrhoeic)	Posterior eyelid margin meibomian gland dysfunction
Eyelash loss	Frequent	Rare	Loss is unusual
Eyelash misdirection	Frequent	Rare	May occur with longstanding disease
Eyelid deposits	Matted, hard scales	Oily or greasy	Excess lipids that may be foamy
Eyelid ulceration*	With occasional severe exacerbations	—	—
Eyelid scarring	May occur	—	Common with longstanding disease
Chalazion (tarsal or meibomian cyst)	Rare	Rare	Occasional to frequent, sometimes multiple. White exudate on pressure suggests infectio
Stye	May occur	—	—
Conjunctiva	Mild to moderate injection, phlyctenules may occur	Mild injection	Mild to moderate injection, papillary reactic tarsal conjunctiva
Aqueous tear deficiency*	Frequent	Frequent	Frequent
Cornea*	Inferior punctuate epithelial erosions, peripheral marginal infiltrates, scarring, neovascularization and pannus†, thinning, phlyctenules+	Corneal defects are not usually present.	Inferior punctate epithelial erosions, periphe marginal infiltrates, scarring, neovasculariza and pannus, ulceration
Dermatologic disease	Atopic eczema (uncommon)	Seborrhoeic dermatitis	Rosacea

* Detection of some of these features may require the use of a slit lamp.
† Panuus is fibrovascular connective tissue that proliferates in the anterior layers of the peripheral cornea in inflammatory corneal disease
+ Phlyctenules are crops of small yellow-grey nodules at the limbus of the cornea

What else might it be?

- **Orbital cellulitis: symptoms include** systemic upset, tender sinuses, and restricted eye movement.
- **Squamous cell, basal cell, or sebaceous cell carcinoma** of the eyelid margin may be mistaken for thickening due to chronic blepharitis.
- **Viral or bacterial conjunctivitis.**
- **Dry eye syndrome:** often there is overlap between these two conditions.
- **Chalazion (tarsal or Meibomian cyst).**
- **Allergy:** for example, to cosmetics.
- **Ocular herpes simplex:** typically presents as a painful red eye, with dendritic ulcer seen on staining with fluorescein.
- **Herpes zoster ophthalmicus:** conjunctival or corneal inflammation with associated vesicular rash in the distribution of the fifth cranial nerve.
- **Molluscum contagiosum** of the eyelids can present as blepharitis.
- **Crab lice: infestation with *Phthirus pubis*.**

[Frith et al, 2001]

Management issues

- Overview of management p.232
- What information should I give people with blepharitis? p.232
- How should eyelid hygiene be performed? p.233
- How should infection be treated? p.233
- When should tear replacement be used? p.233
- When should topical corticosteroids be used? p.233
- How should I treat meibomian gland dysfunction that is not adequately managed with eyelid hygiene? p.233
- When should I refer? p.234

Overview of management

- **Examine** both eyes to determine the cause of the blepharitis, and to rule out other diagnoses.
- **Inform** the individual about the likely course of the illness and address their expectations of treatment.
- **Eyelid hygiene** is the first line of treatment regardless o the cause of blepharitis. Advise the individual on practical techniques on keeping the eyelid clean.
- **Treat marked infection** with topical chloramphenicol fusidic acid.
- **Treat underlying conditions** that may be causing or exacerbating the blepharitis:
  - **Rosacea** (meibomian gland dysfunction)
  - **Seborrhoeic dermatitis** (seborrhoeic blepharitis)
  - **Atopic eczema** (staphylococcal blepharitis)
  - **Dry eye** (all causes)

What information should I give people with blepharitis?

- **People with blepharitis should be informed about the following:**
  - Blepharitis is a chronic condition.
  - Symptoms can frequently be improved, but the condition may not be cured permanently.
  - Compliance with the recommended treatment is important, particularly lid hygiene.
  - Sight is rarely affected.
  - Contact lenses should not be worn during any eye infection.
- **Understanding of the disease and expectations of the outcome of therapy should be periodically reassessed, and education reinforced.**

Frith et al, 2001; American Academy of Ophthalmology 2003

w should eyelid hygiene be performed?

- **his is the priority in management;** eyelid hygiene alone often adequate treatment for uncomplicated :borrhoeic blepharitis.
- **/arm compresses to the eyelids and eyelid margins** >osen the collarettes and crusts, making cleaning more ffective and comfortable. Cloths warmed with hot 'ater are applied to the closed eyelids for 5–10 minutes.
- **id massage** expresses the contents of the meibomian lands and is important in the management of posterior lepharitis. The meibomian glands are compressed by ıeans of a rotary action of the fingers at the lid margin.
- **:leansing of the eyelids** can be carried out using a ariety of agents (e.g. sodium bicarbonate: a teaspoonful ı a cup of boiled water; baby shampoo diluted with 'arm water — 50:50 mixture, and commercial eyelid :rubs — note these are not available on FP10].
  - Traditionally, diluted baby shampoo is applied with a clean cloth or cotton bud and rubbed along the lid margins.
  - Boiled water or preserved water (for contact lens wearers) is probably as effective as sodium bicarbonate or diluted baby shampoo [Dart, Personal Communication, 2004]. There is a lack of trial data to recommend any particular regimen.
- **:leansing of the eyelids should be done twice daily ıitially.** Once symptoms have improved this can be educed to once daily. Daily cleansing should be ontinued indefinitely in order to reduce the likelihood of ecurrence.
- **:ye make-up, especially eye-liner, may contribute to lepharitis.** Advise avoidance, or use of an eye-liner that vashes off easily.

ıskin et al, 1992; Smith and Flowers, 1995; Denton et 1999; Frith et al, 2001; Pray and Pray, 2002; American ıdemy of Ophthalmology, 2003]

w should infection be treated?

- **opical antibiotics should usually be used if there is ıarked eyelid infection** (based on clinical features).
  - They should be rubbed into the lid margin using a finger tip or cotton bud. This is carried out after attending to eyelid hygiene, or just at night [Raskin et al, 1992; Smith and Flowers, 1995; Denton et al, 1999; Frith et al, 2001].
  - Experts recommend treating for one month after the inflammation has subsided although there is no evidence from clinical trials to guide the length of treatment.
  - Topical antibiotics are not recommended for long-term use.
- **)intments are usually preferred to solutions** because hey are in contact with the eyelid margin for longer.)intments affect tear film stability and should be used paringly, with care to minimize ointment getting onto he eye itself.
- **Topical chloramphenicol** remains the drug of choice for ıll superficial eye infections because it is effective, 'eliable, and inexpensive.
  - Concern about the systemic toxicity of topical chloramphenicol, in particular aplastic anaemia, is not well founded [Rayner and Buckley, 1996; Lancaster et al, 1998; Walker et al, 1998; Field et al, 1999; Robert and Adenis, 2001; BNF 47, 2004].
  - Due to the potential risk of systemic absorption, chloramphenicol is not recommended for prolonged treatment periods or when treatment is combined with other myelotoxic drugs [Walker et al, 1998].
  - In the third trimester of pregnancy: there is a theoretical risk of grey baby syndrome (chloramphenicol toxicity in newborns resulting from the lack of liver enzymes necessary to metabolize the drug) and alternative treatment strategies should be considered [Lancaster et al, 1998; Walker et al, 1998; Field et al, 1999; Robert and Adenis, 2001; BNF 47, 2004].
- **Topical fusidic acid is an alternative to chloramphenicol.** It is active against gram-positive organisms, especially staphylococcal species [Robert and Adenis, 2001]. Despite its narrow spectrum of activity, several studies have shown that topical fusidic acid is as effective as topical chloramphenicol owing to the high ocular concentrations achieved [Hvidberg, 1987; Horven, 1993; Carr, 1998; Boberg-Ans and Nissen, 1998].
- **Systemic antibiotics are recommended for recalcitrant staphylococcal blepharitis, severe secondary infection of the meibomian glands, and local cellulitis** [Denton et al, 1999]. A short course of flucloxacillin, erythromycin or azithromycin is generally recommended.

When should tear replacement be used?

- Blepharitis is often associated with a poor quality tear film and dry eye syndrome.
- Artificial tears can provide symptom relief. See PRODIGY guidance *Dry eye syndrome* for more details on treating this condition.

[Denton et al, 1999; Frith et al, 2001]

When should topical corticosteroids be used?

- **Topical corticosteroids should never be given for an undiagnosed red eye, or when visual acuity is impaired, or if there is a history of ocular herpes simplex infection** [Watson and Coroneo, 2001]. They can transform a simple herpetic dendritic ulcer into an extensive amoeboid ulcer involving all layers of the cornea, with resultant corneal scarring and visual loss [Seal and Bron, 1997a; Frith et al, 2001].
- **Primary healthcare professionals are advised against starting corticosteroids for ophthalmic conditions** unless they have access to a slit lamp and the necessary expertise. Treatment should not be repeated without slit lamp review and intraocular pressure measurement [Watson and Coroneo, 2001].
- **Topical corticosteroid therapy in the management of blepharitis should be reserved for severe cases** and for complications such as marginal keratitis [Denton et al, 1999].
- **Long-term use of a corticosteroid should be avoided** as it can result in cataract, glaucoma and severe bacterial or fungal infections involving the eyelid, conjunctiva, and cornea [Denton et al, 1999; American Academy of Ophthalmology, 2003].

How should I treat meibomian gland dysfunction that is not adequately managed with eyelid hygiene?

- **Oral tetracyclines are useful in managing meibomian gland dysfunction.**
  - They should be prescribed for at least 6 weeks.
  - A 3 month course will usually provide a prolonged effect [Dart, Personal Communication, 2004].
  - Repeat courses are often required intermittently.
- The mechanism of action of systemic tetracycline may in part be due to the inhibition of bacterial lipases and subsequent reduction in free fatty acid production. Inhibition of keratinization and antimicrobial activity may also be important.

[Smith and Flowers, 1995; Denton et al, 1999; Frith et al, 2001; American Academy of Ophthalmology, 2003]

When should I refer?

- **Admit urgently if orbital cellulitis is suspected** (person is systemically unwell, tender sinuses, restriction of eye movements).
- **Refer** in the following instances:
  - To exclude malignancy if there is:
    - Persistent localized disease or resistance to treatment
    - Marked eyelid asymmetry
  - If there is evidence of corneal disease
  - If vision deteriorates
  - If there is moderate or severe pain
  - If the diagnosis is uncertain
  - Associated disease, for example Sjögren's syndrome or eyelid deformities, requires specialist management.

References

NHS staff in England can link, free of charge, from references to full text journals by clicking on [Full text] on the PRODIGY website.

1. American Academy of Ophthalmology (2003) *Blepharitis*. American Academy of Ophthalmology. www.aao.org [Accessed: 07/07/2004].
2. BNF 47 (2004) *British National Formulary*. 47th edn. London: British Medical Association and Royal Pharmaceutical Society of Great Britain.
3. Boberg-Ans, G. and Nissen, K.R. (1998) Comparison of Fucithalmic® viscous eye drops and Chloramphenicol eye ointment as a single treatment in corneal abrasion. *Acta Ophthalmologica Scandinavica* **76**(1), 108–111.
4. Carr, W.D. (1998) Comparison of fucithalmic (fusidic acid viscous eye drops 1%) and chloromycetin redidrops (chloramphenicol eye drops 0.5%) in the treatment of acute bacterial conjunctivitis. *Journal of Drug Assessment* **1**(4), 615–623.
5. Dart, J.K.D. (2004) *Personal communication. Use of systemic antibiotics to treat infected blepharitis.* Deputy Director of Research, Moorfields Eye Hospital: London.
6. Denton, P., Barequet, I.S. and O'Brien, T.P. (1999) Therapy of infectious blepharitis. *Ophthalmology Clinics of North America* **12**(1), 9–14.
7. Dougherty J.M., McCulley J.P., Silvany R.E. and Meyer D.R (1991) The role of tetracycline in chronic blepharitis. Inhibition of lipase production in staphylococci. *Investigative Ophthalmology and Visual Science* **32**(11), 2970–2975.
8. Driver, P.J. and Lemp, M.A. (1996) Meibomian gland dysfunction. *Survey of Ophthalmology* **40**(5), 343–367.
9. Field, D., Martin, D. and Witchell, L. (1999) Ophthalmic chloramphenicol: a review of the literature. *Accident & Emergency Nursing* **7**(1), 13–17.
10. Frith, P., Gray, R., MacLennan, A.H. and Ambler, P. (Eds.) (2001) *The eye in clinical practice*. 2nd edn. London: Blackwell Science.
11. Frucht-Pery J., Sagi, E., Hemo, I. and Ever-Hadani, P. (1993) Efficacy of doxycycline and tetracycline in ocular rosacea. *American Journal of Ophthalmology* **116**(1), 88–92.
12. Harman, R.J., Neathercoat, G.C. and Gotecha, P. (Eds.) (1990) *Handbook of pharmacy health care: diseases and patient advice.* London: Pharmaceutical Press.
13. Horven, I. (1993) Acute conjunctivitis: a comparison of fusidic acid viscous eye drops and chloramphenicol. *Acta Ophthalmologica Scandinavica* **71**(2), 165–168.
14. Hvidberg, J (1987) Fusidic acid in acute conjunctivi single-blind, randomized comparison of fusidic and chloramphenicol viscous eye drops. *Acta Ophthalmologica* **65**(1), 43–47.
15. Johnson, D.W., Abele, D.C., Lesher, J.L.Jr. et al (19 Ocular Rosacea. Signs, symptoms and tear studies before and after treatment with doxycycline. *Archiv of Dermatology* **133**(1), 49–54.
16. Khaw, P.T. and Elkington, A.R. (Eds.) (1999) *ABC eyes*. 3rd edn. London: BMJ Publishing Group.
17. Lancaster, T., Swart, A.M. and Jick, H. (1998) Risk serious haematological toxicity with use of chloramphenicol eye drops in a British general pract database. *British Medical Journal* **316**(7132), 667. [Full text]
18. Leeming, J.P. (1999) Treatment of ocular infections with topical antibacterials. *Clinical Pharmacokineti* **37**(5), 351–360.
19. Manners, T. (1997) Managing eye conditions in general practice. *British Medical Journal* **315**(7111), 816–817. [Full text]
20. McCulley, J.P. and Shine, W.E. (2000) Changing concepts in the diagnosis and management of blepharitis. *Cornea* **19**(5), 650–658.
21. Mills, R. (1998) Posterior blepharitis caused by meibomain gland dysfunction. *Modern Medicine of Australia* **41**(6), 133–135.
22. Pray, J.J. and Pray, W.S. (2002) *Blepharitis and prop eyelid hygiene*. Medscape. www.medscape.com [Accessed: 08/07/2004].
23. Raskin, E.M., Speaker, M.G. and Laibson, P.R. (19 Blepharitis. *Infectious Disease Clinics of North America* **6**(4), 777–787.
24. Rayner, S.A. and Buckley, R.J. (1996) Ocular chloramphenicol and aplastic anaemia. Is there a lin *Drug Safety* **14**(5), 273–276.
25. Robert, P.Y. and Adenis, J.P. (2001) Comparative review of topical ophthalmic antibacterial preparations. *Drugs* **61**(2), 175–185.
26. Seal, D.V. and Bron, A.J. (1997a) Infections of the ey Herpes simplex virus eye disease. In: O'Grady, F., Finch, R., Lambert, H.P. and Greenwood, D. (Eds.) *Antibiotic and chemotherapy: Anti-infective agents a their use in therapy*. 7th edn. Edinburgh: Churchill Livingstone. 780–782.
27. Seal, D.V. and Bron, A.J. (1997b) Infections of the ey Blepharitis. In: O'Grady, F., Lambert, H.P., Finch, R and Greenwood, D. (Eds.) *Antibiotic and chemotherapy. Anti-infective agents and their use in therapy*. 7th edn. Edinburgh: Churchill Livingstone. 769–772.
28. Seal, D.V., Wright, P., Ficker, L. et al (1995a) Placeb controlled trial of fusidic acid gel and oxytetracyclin for recurrent blepharitis and rosacea. *British Journal Ophthalmology* **79**(1), 42–45.
29. Seal, D.V., Ficker, L.A. and Wright, P. (1995b) Staphylococcal blepharitis. In: Pepose, J.S. and Holland, G.N. (Eds.) *Infectious ocular diseases*. London: Mosby. 788–798.
30. Seal, D.V., Bron, A.J. and Hay, J. (1998) *Ocular infection. Investigation and treatment in practice.* London: Martin Dunitz Ltd.
31. Smith, R.E. and Flowers, C.W.Jr. (1995) Chronic blepharitis: a review. *CLAO Journal* **21**(3), 200–207
32. Walker, S., Diaper, C.J., Bowman, R. et al (1998) La of evidence for systemic toxicity following topical chloramphenicol use. *Eye* **12**(5), 875–879.
33. Watson, S. and Coroneo, M. (2001) Steroids and the eye. *Medicine Today* **2**(3), 79–85.

PRODIGY GUIDANCE

Boils, carbuncles, paronychia, & staphylococcal whitlow

Last revised in February 2004
www.prodigy.nhs.uk/guidance.asp?gt=Boils and paronychia

Applies to people over the age of 1 month

This guidance covers the management of folliculitis, boils and carbuncles, acute paronychia, and staphylococcal whitlow.

This guidance does not cover the management of cellulitis or chronic paronychia.

There is separate PRODIGY guidance for *Acne vulgaris; Candida — skin and nails; Fungal (dermatophyte) infections — skin and nails;* and *Impetigo.*

Goals

To alleviate symptoms
To limit the duration of infection
To minimize the risks of complications

Contents

Scenarios

- Boils and carbuncles p.235
- Recurrent furunculosis p.237
- Acute paronychia and staphylococcal whitlow p.239

Extended Information, p. 241

Which scenario?

Boils and carbuncles: covers the management of boils and carbuncles.
Recurrent furunculosis: covers the management of chronic furunculosis, including the elimination of staphylococcal carriage.
Acute paronychia and staphylococcal whitlow: covers the initial management of acute paronychia and staphylococcal whitlow, and when to refer people for incision and drainage.

Boils and carbuncles

Which therapy?

Small non-fluctuant lesions: apply moist heat to relieve discomfort and localize the infection.
If associated fever or surrounding cellulitis: treat with flucloxacillin. If the person is penicillin-allergic, give erythromycin. Give antibiotics for at least 7 days.
Large but localized painful and fluctuant lesions:

- Incise and drain.
- After adequate drainage (spontaneous or surgical), cover with a sterile dressing to prevent autoinnoculation.
- Treat with antibiotics until inflammation resolves.

Practical prescribing points

For further information please see the *Medicines Compendium* (www.medicines.org.uk) or the *British National Formulary* (www.bnf.org).

- **Ibuprofen:** as with other nonsteroidal anti-inflammatory drugs, ibuprofen may worsen or precipitate gastrointestinal haemorrhage, asthma, hypertension, renal impairment, or cardiac failure. Avoid if there is a history of peptic ulcers and in pregnant women.
- **Flucloxacillin:** the Committee on Safety of Medicines has advised that cholestatic jaundice may occur up to several weeks after treatment with flucloxacillin has been stopped. Administration for more than two weeks and increasing age are risk factors.
- **Erythromycin:** use with caution in people with hepatic and renal impairment, prolongation of the QT interval, and those who are breastfeeding. Erythromycin may increase the level of certain drugs (e.g. theophylline, carbamazepine, statins), or potentiate warfarin.

Follow-up advice

- Arrange for dressing changes with the practice or district nurse.

Should I refer or investigate?

Refer?

- **Refer** if facilities for incision and drainage are not available in the practice.
- **Admit urgently** if there are symptoms or signs of metastatic infection, e.g. cavernous sinus thrombosis, osteomyelitis, acute endocarditis, or brain abscess.
- **Consider admission** if the person is systemically unwell or if there is severe infection, particularly in an area where complications are high.

Investigate?

- Identify the causative organism by culture if infection is severe, or if the person is immunocompromised, has diabetes, or appears to be in a toxic state.
- Check fasting blood glucose to eliminate diabetes in someone who develops a carbuncle.

Patient information leaflets

The following PILs are available at www.prodigy.nhs.uk

- Boils, Carbuncles and Furunculosis
- Folliculitis

Shared decision making

- Small boils may subside and go without any treatment.
- You can ease pain by covering the boil with a flannel soaked in hot water. Do this for 30 minutes, 3–4 times a day.
- Larger boils should have the pus let out by a small cut.
- A course of antibiotics may also be needed.

B

Drug rationale

Drugs not included

- **Oral antibiotics other than flucloxacillin and macrolides** are not included. Other antibiotics are generally either less active against staphylococcal infections or more expensive, or both.
- **Topical antibiotics** are not included. Resistance to topical antibiotics such as fusidic acid is increasing and widespread use may increase this problem.

Drugs included

- **Paracetamol** is usually effective for pain relief associated with boils and carbuncles.
- **Ibuprofen** is offered as alternative pain relief for people with no contraindications.
- **Oral flucloxacillin or erythromycin** are usually effective against *Staphylococcus aureus* infections. Optimal treatment length is not evident from the literature, but 7 days' treatment is generally recommended.
- **Clarithromycin and azithromycin** are alternative macrolides when erythromycin is not tolerated. Azithromycin is a useful choice where there are potential drug interactions, e.g. with statins.
- **Non-adherent dressings** are offered to protect the lesion after drainage and to prevent autoinnoculation.

Prescriptions

Analgesia: use when required

Paracetamol s/f susp: 60mg to 120mg up to four times a day
- Age from 3 to 11 months
- Paracetamol 120mg/5ml s/f susp. Take 2.5ml to 5ml every 4 to 6 hours when required for pain relief. Maximum of 4 doses in 24 hours; supply 150 ml; NHS Cost £0.65; OTC Cost £1.14.

Paracetamol s/f susp: 120mg to 240mg up to four times a day
- Age from 12 months to 5 years
- Paracetamol 120mg/5ml s/f susp. Take one to two 5ml spoonfuls every 4 to 6 hours when required for pain relief. Maximum of 4 doses in 24 hours; supply 300 ml; NHS Cost £1.30; OTC Cost £2.28.

Paracetamol s/f susp: 250mg to 500mg up to four times a day
- Age from 6 to 11 years
- Paracetamol 250mg/5ml s/f susp. Take one to two 5ml spoonfuls every 4 to 6 hours when required for pain relief. Maximum of 4 doses in 24 hours; supply 300 ml; NHS Cost £1.59; OTC Cost £2.80.

Paracetamol tablets: 500mg to 1g up to four times a day
- Age from 12 to 15 years
- Paracetamol 500mg tablets. Take one to two tablets every 4 to 6 hours when required for pain relief. Maximum of 8 tablets in 24 hours; supply 100 tablets; NHS Cost £0.75; OTC Cost £1.32.

Paracetamol tablets: 1g up to four times a day
- Age from 16 years onwards
- Paracetamol 500mg tablets. Take two tablets every 4 to 6 hours when required for pain relief. Maximum of 8 tablets in 24 hours; supply 100 tablets; NHS Cost £0.75; OTC Cost £1.32.

Ibuprofen s/f susp: 50mg three to four times a day
- Age from 12 months to 2 years
- Ibuprofen 100mg/5ml s/f susp. Take 2.5ml three to four times a day when required for pain relief. Do not exceed the stated dose; supply 100 ml; NHS Cost £2.00; OTC Cost £3.52.

Ibuprofen s/f susp: 100mg three to four times a day
- Age from 3 to 7 years
- Ibuprofen 100mg/5ml s/f susp. Take one 5ml spoonful 3 to 4 times a day when required for pain relief. Do not exceed the stated dose; supply 150 ml; NHS Cost £2.73; OTC Cost £4.81.

Ibuprofen s/f susp: 200mg three to four times a day
- Age from 8 to 11 years
- Ibuprofen 100mg/5ml s/f susp. Take two 5ml spoonfuls 3 to 4 times a day when required for pain relief. Do not exceed the stated dose; supply 300 ml; NHS Cost £5.46; OTC Cost £9.62.

Ibuprofen tablets: 400mg three times a day
- Age from 12 years onwards
- Ibuprofen 400mg tablets. Take one tablet three times a day when required for pain relief. Do not exceed the stated dose; supply 24 tablets; NHS Cost £0.70; OTC Cost £1.23.

1st-line antibiotic: flucloxacillin for 7 days

Flucloxacillin syrup: 62.5mg four times a day
- Age from 1 month to 23 months
- Flucloxacillin 125mg/5ml syrup. Take 2.5ml four times day for 7 days; supply 100 ml; NHS Cost £3.23.

Flucloxacillin syrup: 125mg four times a day
- Age from 2 to 4 years
- Flucloxacillin 125mg/5ml syrup. Take one 5ml spoonful four times a day for 7 days; supply 200 ml; NHS Cost £6.46.

Flucloxacillin syrup: 250mg four times a day
- Age from 5 to 11 years
- Flucloxacillin 250mg/5ml syrup. Take one 5ml spoonful four times a day for 7 days; supply 200 ml; NHS Cost £13.94.

Flucloxacillin capsules: 250mg four times a day
- Age from 12 years onwards
- Flucloxacillin 250mg capsules. Take one capsule four times a day for 7 days; supply 28 capsules; NHS Cost £2.93.

Flucloxacillin capsules: 500mg four times a day
- Age from 12 years onwards
- Flucloxacillin 500mg capsules. Take one capsule four times a day for 7 days; supply 28 capsules; NHS Cost £4.73.

1st-line in penicillin allergy: erythromycin for 7 days

Erythromycin s/f suspension: 125mg four times a day
- Age from 1 month to 23 months
- Erythromycin 125mg/5ml sf susp. Take one 5ml spoonful four times a day for 7 days; supply 140 ml; NHS Cost £2.32.

Erythromycin s/f suspension: 250mg four times a day
- Age from 2 to 11 years
- Erythromycin 250mg/5ml sf susp. Take one 5ml spoonful four times a day for 7 days; supply 140 ml; NHS Cost £3.90.

Erythromycin s/f suspension: 500mg four times a day
- Age from 9 to 11 years
- Erythromycin 500mg/5ml sf susp. Take one 5ml spoonful four times a day for 7 days; supply 140 ml; NHS Cost £6.70.

Erythromycin e/c tablets: 250mg four times a day
- Age from 12 years onwards
- Erythromycin 250mg e/c tablets. Take one tablet four times a day for 7 days; supply 28 tablets; NHS Cost £3.08.

rythromycin e/c tablets: 500mg four times a day
Age from 12 years onwards
Erythromycin 250mg e/c tablets. Take two tablets four times a day for 7 days; supply 56 tablets; NHS Cost £6.16.

2nd-line in penicillin allergy: azithromycin/ clarithromycin

larithromycin suspension: 62.5mg twice a day
Age from 12 months to 2 years
Clarithromycin 125mg/5ml susp. Take 2.5ml twice a day for 7 days; supply 70 ml; NHS Cost £6.00.

larithromycin suspension: 125mg twice a day
Age from 3 to 6 years
Clarithromycin 125mg/5ml susp. Take one 5ml spoonful twice a day for 7 days; supply 70 ml; NHS Cost £6.00.

larithromycin suspension: 187.5mg twice a day
Age from 7 to 9 years
Clarithromycin 125mg/5ml susp. Take 7.5ml twice a day for 7 days; supply 140 ml; NHS Cost £12.00.

larithromycin suspension: 250mg twice a day
Age from 10 to 11 years
Clarithromycin 250mg/5ml susp. Take one 5ml spoonful twice a day for 7 days; supply 70 ml; NHS Cost £12.00.

larithromycin tablets: 250mg twice a day
Age from 12 years onwards
Clarithromycin 250mg tablets. Take one tablet twice a day for 7 days; supply 14 tablets; NHS Cost £11.76.

zithromycin suspension: 10mg/kg once a day
Age from 6 months to 2 years
Azithromycin 200mg/5ml susp. *WEIGHT REQUIRED* Take 10mg per kg bodyweight ONCE a day for 3 days; supply 15 ml; NHS Cost £5.08.

zithromycin suspension: 200mg once a day
Age from 3 to 7 years
Azithromycin 200mg/5ml susp. Take one 5ml spoonful once a day for 3 days; supply 15 ml; NHS Cost £5.08.

zithromycin suspension: 300mg once a day
Age from 8 to 11 years
Azithromycin 200mg/5ml susp. Take 7.5ml once a day for 3 days; supply 22 ml; NHS Cost £7.62.

zithromycin suspension: 400mg once a day
Age from 12 to 13 years
Azithromycin 200mg/5ml susp. Take two 5ml spoonfuls once a day for 3 days; supply 30 ml; NHS Cost £13.80.

zithromycin capsules: 500mg once a day
Age from 14 years onwards
Azithromycin 250mg capsules. Take two capsules once a day for 3 days; supply 6 capsules; NHS Cost £13.42.

Dressings

'cm x 8cm Absorbent perforated dressing with adhesive border
Age from 1 month onwards
Absorb perf 7x8cm dressing. Apply to the affected area as directed; supply 7 single dressings; NHS Cost £0.63; OTC Cost £1.11.

0cm x 11cm Absorbent perf. dressing with adhesive border
Age from 1 month onwards
Absorb perf 10x11cm dressing. Apply to the affected area as directed; supply 7 Single dressings; NHS Cost £1.26; OTC Cost £2.22.

1cm x 15cm Absorbent perf. dressing with adhesive border
Age from 1 month onwards
Absorb perf 10x15cm dressing. Apply to the affected area as directed; supply 7 single dressings; NHS Cost £2.17; OTC Cost £3.82.

Recurrent furunculosis

Which therapy

- **Look for potential underlying causes of recurrence:**
  - Systemic, e.g. immunocompromised, diabetes
  - Skin disease, e.g. scabies, pediculosis, eczema
  - Localized predisposing factors, e.g. industrial exposure to chemicals and oils, hyperhidrosis, ingrown hairs, pressure from tight clothing or belts
- **Treat with oral antibiotics:**
  - Choice of antibiotic in chronic furunculosis should be guided by sensitivities. Flucloxacillin is recommended for blind treatment (or erythromycin for people with a penicillin allergy).
  - Treat for two weeks initially. Some people will need a longer course, e.g. 6–8 weeks.
- **If persistent or recurrent infection is present,** swabs should be taken from the person's nose, throat, umbilicus, axillae, and perineum.
- **If furunculosis persists** after screening and treating the person, consider eliminating potential sources of infection in the family and close contacts.
- **If found, eliminate nasal and skin carriage of *Staphylococcus aureus*:**
  - Use chlorhexidine/neomycin (Naseptin) nasal cream applied to the nostrils four times a day for 10 days to eliminate nasal carriage of *S aureus*.
  - Mupirocin nasal ointment is also effective at eliminating nasal staphylococci, but should be reserved for resistant cases.
  - Use an antiseptic soap solution, e.g. triclosan or chlorhexidine, to reduce staphylococcal skin colonization. If the person suffers from dry or inflamed skin, an antiseptic emollient should be used (Dermol 500, Oilatum Plus, Emulsiderm, or Dermol 600).
  - Advise on washing sheets and underwear on a hot wash cycle (above 55°C).
  - Advise on using own towel and flannel, and washing the flannel in hot water before use.
  - Change dressings frequently if purulent discharge collects.

Practical prescribing points

For further information please see the *Medicines Compendium* (www.medicines.org.uk) or the *British National Formulary* (www.bnf.org).

- **Chlorhexidine/neomycin (Naseptin) nasal cream** contains pharmaceutical grade arachis (peanut) oil. This is highly refined and therefore the peanut protein should have been removed. As a precaution, however the Committee on Safety of Medicines (CSM) advises that people with a known allergy to peanuts or soya (possible cross-sensitivity) should not use medicines containing peanut oil.
- **Flucloxacillin:** the CSM has advised that cholestatic jaundice may occur up to several weeks after treatment with flucloxacillin has been stopped. Administration for more than two weeks and increasing age are risk factors.
- **Erythromycin:** use with caution in people with hepatic and renal impairment, prolongation of the QT interval, and those who are breastfeeding. Erythromycin may increase the level of certain drugs (e.g. theophylline, carbamazepine, statins), or potentiate warfarin.

Follow-up advice

- Arrange for dressing changes with practice or district nurse.

Should I refer or investigate?

Refer?

- Refer to a dermatologist if the diagnosis is in doubt or if it is impossible to prevent recurrence.

B

Investigate?

- Full blood count
- Fasting blood glucose
- Swabs from lesions, and carrier sites of the person and their immediate family

Patient information leaflets

The following PILs are available at www.prodigy.nhs.uk

- Boils, Carbuncles and Furunculosis
- Folliculitis

Shared decision making

- Small boils may subside and go without any treatment.
- You can ease pain by covering the boil with a flannel soaked in hot water. Do this for 30 minutes, 3–4 times a day.
- Larger boils should have the pus let out by a small cut.
- A course of antibiotics may also be needed.
- If you have recurring boils:
  - Swabs of your nose, throat, and parts of your skin will show if you are a 'carrier' of the *Staphylococcus aureus* bacterium.
  - Sometimes swabs of family members are also advised.
  - If you are found to be a carrier, then getting rid of these bacteria from your body may prevent recurring boils. This may involve:
    - Antibiotic nasal cream or ointment
    - A course of antibiotic tablets
    - Using an antibiotic soap solution
    - Cleaning underwear, sheets, etc., in a hot wash cycle
    - A thorough clean of your bedroom

Drug rationale

Drugs not included

- **Oral antibiotics other than flucloxacillin and erythromycin** are not included. Other antibiotics are generally either less active against staphylococcal infections or more expensive, or both.
- **Topical antibiotics** are not included. Resistance to topical antibiotics such as fusidic acid is increasing and widespread use may increase this problem.

Drugs included

- **Choice of antibiotic in chronic furunculosis should be guided by sensitivities.** Flucloxacillin is recommended for blind treatment (or erythromycin for people with a penicillin allergy).
- **Treat for 2 weeks initially.** Some people will need longer courses, e.g. 6–8 weeks.
- **Non-adherent dressings** are offered to protect the lesions after drainage and to prevent autoinnoculation.
- **Chlorhexidine/neomycin nasal cream** is recommended for the elimination of nasal carriage.
- **Mupirocin nasal ointment** should be reserved for resistant cases.

Prescriptions

If no sensitivities available: flucloxacillin for 2 weeks

Flucloxacillin syrup: 62.5mg four times a day

- Age from 1 month to 23 months
- Flucloxacillin 125mg/5ml syrup. Take 2.5ml four times day for 14 days; supply 200 ml; NHS Cost £6.98.

Flucloxacillin syrup: 125mg four times a day

- Age from 2 to 4 years
- Flucloxacillin 125mg/5ml syrup. Take one 5ml spoonful four times a day for 14 days; supply 300 ml; NHS Cost £10.47.

Flucloxacillin syrup: 250mg four times a day

- Age from 5 to 11 years
- Flucloxacillin 250mg/5ml syrup. Take one 5ml spoonful four times a day for 14 days; supply 300 ml; NHS Cost £20.91.

Flucloxacillin capsules: 250mg four times a day

- Age from 12 years onwards
- Flucloxacillin 250mg capsules. Take one capsule four times a day for 14 days; supply 56 capsules; NHS Cost £5.86.

Flucloxacillin capsules: 500mg four times a day

- Age from 12 years onwards
- Flucloxacillin 500mg capsules. Take one capsule four times a day for 14 days; supply 56 capsules; NHS Cost £9.46.

If no sensitivities available: erythromycin for 2 weeks

Erythromycin s/f suspension: 125mg four times a day

- Age from 1 month to 23 months
- Erythromycin 125mg/5ml sf susp. Take one 5ml spoonful four times a day for 14 days; supply 280 ml; NHS Cost £4.64.

Erythromycin s/f suspension: 250mg four times a day

- Age from 2 to 11 years
- Erythromycin 250mg/5ml sf susp. Take one 5ml spoonful four times a day for 14 days; supply 280 ml; NHS Cost £7.80.

Erythromycin s/f suspension: 500mg four times a day

- Age from 9 to 11 years
- Erythromycin 500mg/5ml sf susp. Take one 5ml spoonful four times a day for 14 days; supply 280 ml; NHS Cost £13.40.

Erythromycin e/c tablets: 250mg four times a day

- Age from 12 years onwards
- Erythromycin 250mg e/c tablets. Take one tablet four times a day for 14 days; supply 56 tablets; NHS Cost £6.16.

Erythromycin e/c tablets: 500mg four times a day

- Age from 12 years onwards
- Erythromycin 250mg e/c tablets. Take two tablets four times a day for 14 days; supply 112 tablets; NHS Cost £12.32.

Elimination of nasal carriage of *Staphylococcus aureus*

Chlorhexidine 0.1% + neomycin 3250units/g cream (Naseptin)

- Age from 1 month onwards
- Naseptin cream. Apply a small amount of cream to the inside of each nostril four times a day for 10 days; supply 15 grams; NHS Cost £1.48.

upirocin 2% nasal ointment (Bactroban Nasal)
Age from 1 month onwards
Mupirocin 2% w/v nasal ointment. Apply a small amount of ointment to the inside of each nostril three times a day for 5 days; supply 3 grams; NHS Cost £6.24.

Dressings

cm x 8cm Absorbent perforated dressing with adhesive order
Age from 1 month onwards
Absorb perf 7x8cm dressing. Apply to the affected area as directed; supply 7 single dressings; NHS Cost £0.63; OTC Cost £1.11.

0cm x 11cm Absorbent perf. dressing with adhesive order
Age from 1 month onwards
Absorb perf 10x11cm dressing. Apply to the affected area as directed; supply 7 single dressings; NHS Cost £1.26; OTC Cost £2.22.

1cm x 15cm Absorbent perf. dressing with adhesive order
Age from 1 month onwards
Absorb perf 10x15cm dressing. Apply to the affected area as directed; supply 7 single dressings; NHS Cost £2.17; OTC Cost £3.82.

Acute paronychia and staphylococcal whitlow

Which therapy

Paronychia

Treat with oral flucloxacillin. If the person is penicillin-allergic, give erythromycin. Give antibiotics for at least 7 days.
Mild paronychia: treat with warm soaks 3–4 times a day.
If fluctuant, incise and drain:
- Superficial lesions may point close to the nail: drain by incision without anaesthesia.
- Deeper lesions should be incised under local anaesthesia if there is no improvement after 2 days of antibiotic treatment.

Proximal red streaking or lymphadenopathy— consider the possibility of a mixed infection with *Streptococcus* and treat with both penicillin and flucloxacillin.

Staphlyococcal whitlow

Initial phase of cellulitis and inflammation (rarely encountered): treat with elevation, oral antibiotics, and soaks.
If there is abscess formation and fluctuation of the pulp space (more common): refer urgently for drainage of loculated abscesses within the tissue and oral or intravenous antibiotic therapy.

Practical prescribing points

For further information please see the *Medicines Compendium* (www.medicines.org.uk) or the *British National Formulary* (www.bnf.org).
Ibuprofen: as with other nonsteroidal anti-inflammatory drugs, ibuprofen may worsen or precipitate gastrointestinal haemorrhage, asthma, hypertension, renal impairment, or cardiac failure. Avoid if there is a history of peptic ulcers and in pregnant women.
Flucloxacillin: the Committee on Safety of Medicines has advised that cholestatic jaundice may occur up to several weeks after treatment with flucloxacillin has been stopped. Administration for more than 2 weeks and increasing age are risk factors.
- **Erythromycin:** use with caution in people with hepatic and renal impairment, prolongation of the QT interval, and those who are breastfeeding. Erythromycin may increase the level of certain drugs (e.g. theophylline, carbamazepine, statins), or potentiate warfarin.

B

Follow-up advice

- Advise the person to:
  - Return if infection persists or if the lesion becomes fluctuant.
  - Attend for dressings with practice or district nurse.

Should I refer or investigate?

Refer?

- Refer staphylococcal paronychia if necessary for incision and drainage if appropriate facilities and expertise are not available in the practice.
- Refer staphylococcal whitlow for incision and drainage and intravenous antibiotics.

Patient information leaflets

The following PILs are available at www.prodigy.nhs.uk
- Paronychia

Shared decision making

- A mild infection next to the nail may subside and go without any treatment. It may be helped to go by soaking the finger in warm water. Do this for 20–30 minutes, 3–4 times a day.
- A course of antibiotics may be needed if the infection is more severe.
- If pus collects next to the nail, it needs to be let out by a small cut.

Drug rationale

Drugs not included

- **Oral antibiotics other than flucloxacillin, penicillin V, and macrolides** are not included. Other antibiotics are generally either less active against staphylococcal/streptococcal infections or more expensive, or both.

Drugs included

- **Paracetamol** is usually effective for pain relief.
- **Ibuprofen** is offered as alternative pain relief for people with no contraindications.
- **Oral flucloxacillin or macrolides** are usually effective against *Staphylococcus aureus* infections. Optimal treatment length is not evident from the literature, but 7 days' treatment is generally recommended.
- **Clarithromycin and azithromycin** are alternative macrolides. Azithromycin is a useful choice where there are potential drug interactions, e.g. with statins.
- **Oral penicillin V** should be added to flucloxacillin if infection appears to be spreading and *Streptococcus* is suspected.

B

Prescriptions

Analgesia: use when required

Paracetamol s/f susp: 60mg to 120mg up to four times a day
- Age from 3 to 11 months
- Paracetamol 120mg/5ml s/f susp. Take 2.5ml to 5ml every 4 to 6 hours when required for pain relief. Maximum of 4 doses in 24 hours; supply 150 ml; NHS Cost £0.65; OTC Cost £1.14.

Paracetamol s/f susp: 120mg to 240mg up to four times a day
- Age from 12 months to 5 years
- Paracetamol 120mg/5ml s/f susp. Take one to two 5ml spoonfuls every 4 to 6 hours when required for pain relief. Maximum of 4 doses in 24 hours; supply 300 ml; NHS Cost £1.30; OTC Cost £2.28.

Paracetamol s/f susp: 250mg to 500mg up to four times a day
- Age from 6 to 11 years
- Paracetamol 250mg/5ml s/f susp. Take one to two 5ml spoonfuls every 4 to 6 hours when required for pain relief. Maximum of 4 doses in 24 hours; supply 300 ml; NHS Cost £1.59; OTC Cost £2.80.

Paracetamol tablets: 500mg to 1g up to four times a day
- Age from 12 to 15 years
- Paracetamol 500mg tablets. Take one to two tablets every 4 to 6 hours when required for pain relief. Maximum of 8 tablets in 24 hours; supply 100 tablets; NHS Cost £0.75; OTC Cost £1.32.

Paracetamol tablets: 1g up to four times a day
- Age from 16 years onwards
- Paracetamol 500mg tablets. Take two tablets every 4 to 6 hours when required for pain relief. Maximum of 8 tablets in 24 hours; supply 100 tablets; NHS Cost £0.75; OTC Cost £1.32.

Ibuprofen s/f susp: 50mg three to four times a day
- Age from 12 months to 2 years
- Ibuprofen 100mg/5ml s/f susp. Take 2.5ml three to four times a day when required for pain relief. Do not exceed the stated dose; supply 100 ml; NHS Cost £2.00; OTC Cost £3.52.

Ibuprofen s/f susp: 100mg three to four times a day
- Age from 3 to 7 years
- Ibuprofen 100mg/5ml s/f susp. Take one 5ml spoonful 3 to 4 times a day when required for pain relief. Do not exceed the stated dose; supply 150 ml; NHS Cost £2.73; OTC Cost £4.81.

Ibuprofen s/f susp: 200mg three to four times a day
- Age from 8 to 11 years
- Ibuprofen 100mg/5ml s/f susp. Take two 5ml spoonfuls 3 to 4 times a day when required for pain relief. Do not exceed the stated dose; supply 300 ml; NHS Cost £5.46; OTC Cost £9.62.

Ibuprofen tablets: 400mg three times a day
- Age from 12 years onwards
- Ibuprofen 400mg tablets. Take one tablet three times a day when required for pain relief. Do not exceed the stated dose; supply 24 tablets; NHS Cost £0.70; OTC Cost £1.23.

1st-line antibiotic: flucloxacillin for 7 days

Flucloxacillin syrup: 62.5mg four times a day
- Age from 1 month to 23 months
- Flucloxacillin 125mg/5ml syrup. Take 2.5ml four times a day for 7 days; supply 100 ml; NHS Cost £3.23.

Flucloxacillin syrup: 125mg four times a day
- Age from 2 to 4 years
- Flucloxacillin 125mg/5ml syrup. Take one 5ml spoonfu four times a day for 7 days; supply 200 ml; NHS Cost £6.46.

Flucloxacillin syrup: 250mg four times a day
- Age from 5 to 11 years
- Flucloxacillin 250mg/5ml syrup. Take one 5ml spoonfu four times a day for 7 days; supply 200 ml; NHS Cost £13.94.

Flucloxacillin capsules: 250mg four times a day
- Age from 12 years onwards
- Flucloxacillin 250mg capsules. Take one capsule four times a day for 7 days; supply 28 capsules; NHS Cost £2.93.

Flucloxacillin capsules: 500mg four times a day
- Age from 12 years onwards
- Flucloxacillin 500mg capsules. Take one capsule four times a day for 7 days; supply 28 capsules; NHS Cost £4.73.

1st-line in penicillin allergy: erythromycin for 7 days

Erythromycin s/f suspension: 125mg four times a day
- Age from 1 month to 23 months
- Erythromycin 125mg/5ml sf susp. Take one 5ml spoonful four times a day for 7 days; supply 140 ml; NHS Cost £2.32.

Erythromycin s/f suspension: 250mg four times a day
- Age from 2 to 11 years
- Erythromycin 250mg/5ml sf susp. Take one 5ml spoonful four times a day for 7 days; supply 140 ml; NHS Cost £3.90.

Erythromycin s/f suspension: 500mg four times a day
- Age from 9 to 11 years
- Erythromycin 500mg/5ml sf susp. Take one 5ml spoonful four times a day for 7 days; supply 140 ml; NHS Cost £6.70.

Erythromycin e/c tablets: 250mg four times a day
- Age from 12 years onwards
- Erythromycin 250mg e/c tablets. Take one tablet four times a day for 7 days; supply 28 tablets; NHS Cost £3.08.

Erythromycin e/c tablets: 500mg four times a day
- Age from 12 years onwards
- Erythromycin 250mg e/c tablets. Take two tablets four times a day for 7 days; supply 56 tablets; NHS Cost £6.16.

2nd-line in penicillin allergy: azithromycin/ clarithromycin

Clarithromycin suspension: 62.5mg twice a day
- Age from 12 months to 2 years
- Clarithromycin 125mg/5ml susp. Take 2.5ml twice a da for 7 days; supply 70 ml; NHS Cost £6.00.

Clarithromycin suspension: 125mg twice a day
- Age from 3 to 6 years
- Clarithromycin 125mg/5ml susp. Take one 5ml spoonfu twice a day for 7 days; supply 70 ml; NHS Cost £6.00.

Clarithromycin suspension: 187.5mg twice a day
- Age from 7 to 9 years
- Clarithromycin 125mg/5ml susp. Take 7.5ml twice a da for 7 days; supply 140 ml; NHS Cost £12.00.

Clarithromycin suspension: 250mg twice a day
- Age from 10 to 11 years
- Clarithromycin 250mg/5ml susp. Take one 5ml spoonfu twice a day for 7 days; supply 70 ml; NHS Cost £12.00.

larithromycin tablets: 250mg twice a day
Age from 12 years onwards
Clarithromycin 250mg tablets. Take one tablet twice a day for 7 days, supply 14 tablets; NHS Cost £11.76.

zithromycin suspension: 10mg/kg once a day
Age from 6 months to 2 years
Azithromycin 200mg/5ml susp. *WEIGHT REQUIRED* Take 10mg per kg bodyweight ONCE a day for 3 days; supply 15 ml; NHS Cost £5.08.

zithromycin suspension: 200mg once a day
Age from 3 to 7 years
Azithromycin 200mg/5ml susp. Take one 5ml spoonful once a day for 3 days; supply 15 ml; NHS Cost £5.08.

zithromycin suspension: 300mg once a day
Age from 8 to 11 years
Azithromycin 200mg/5ml susp. Take 7.5ml once a day for 3 days; supply 22 ml; NHS Cost £7.62.

zithromycin suspension: 400mg once a day
Age from 12 to 13 years
Azithromycin 200mg/5ml susp. Take two 5ml spoonfuls once a day for 3 days; supply 30 ml; NHS Cost £13.80.

zithromycin capsules: 500mg once a day
Age from 14 years onwards
Azithromycin 250mg capsules. Take two capsules once a day for 3 days; supply 6 capsules; NHS Cost £13.42.

Streptococcus suspected: penicillin V + flucloxacillin

enicillin V 62.5mg/2.5ml sol + flucloxacillin 62.5mg/2.5ml
Age from 1 month to 23 months
Penicillin V 125mg/5ml sol. Take 2.5ml four times a day for 7 days; supply 100 ml; NHS Cost £1.66.
Flucloxacillin 125mg/5ml syrup. Take 2.5ml four times a day for 7 days; supply 100 ml; NHS Cost £3.23.

enicillin V 125mg/5mg sol + flucloxacillin 125mg/5ml yrup
Age from 2 to 5 years
Penicillin V 125mg/5ml sol. Take one 5ml spoonful four times a day for 7 days; supply 200 ml; NHS Cost £3.32.
Flucloxacillin 125mg/5ml syrup. Take one 5ml spoonful four times a day for 7 days; supply 200 ml; NHS Cost £6.97.

enicillin V 250mg/5ml sol + flucloxacillin 250mg/ml syrup
Age from 6 to 11 years
Penicillin V 250mg/5ml sol. Take one 5ml spoonful four times a day for 7 days; supply 200 ml; NHS Cost £4.58.
Flucloxacillin 250mg/5ml syrup. Take one 5ml spoonful four times a day for 7 days; supply 200 ml; NHS Cost £13.94.

enicillin V 250mg tablets + flucloxacillin 250mg capsules
Age from 12 years onwards
Penicillin V 250mg tablets. Take one tablet four times a day for 7 days; supply 28 tablets; NHS Cost £1.78.
Flucloxacillin 250mg capsules. Take one capsule four times a day for 7 days; supply 28 capsules; NHS Cost £2.93.

enicillin V 500mg tablets + flucloxacillin 500mg capsules
Age from 12 years onwards
Penicillin V 250mg tablets. Take two tablets four times a day for 7 days; supply 56 tablets; NHS Cost £3.56.
Flucloxacillin 500mg capsules. Take one capsule four times a day for 7 days; supply 28 capsules; NHS Cost £4.73.

Extended Information

Background information

- What is it? p.241
- How common is it? p.241
- How do I know my patient has it? p.242
- Risk factors and predisposing conditions p.242
- What else might it be? p.242
- Complications and prognosis p.242

B

What is it?

Definition

- **A boil (furuncle)** is an acute infection of a hair follicle, usually with *Staphylococcus aureus* [Hunter et al, 2002].
- **Chronic furunculosis** is the term used to describe multiple crops of boils that occur over a period of time, either continuously or intermittently [Hay and Adriaans, 1998].
- **A carbuncle** is a swollen, painful area discharging pus from several points. It occurs when a group of adjacent hair follicles become deeply infected, usually with *S aureus* [Hunter et al, 2002]. Intense inflammatory changes occur in the surrounding and underlying connective tissue including the subcutaneous fat [Hay and Adriaans, 1998].
- **Folliculitis** is an inflammation of the hair follicles caused by infection (usually *Staphylococcus*), physical injury, or chemical irritation. It is classified as superficial or deep folliculitis by the depth of involvement of the hair follicle [Cyr, 2001; Stulberg et al, 2002].
- **Acute paronychia** is an infection of the skin and soft tissue of the proximal and lateral nail fold, most commonly caused by *S aureus*. It often originates from a break in the skin or cuticle as a result of minor trauma, e.g. nail biting, finger sucking, aggressive manicuring, a hangnail, or a penetrating trauma [Rockwell, 2001; Lee et al, 2003].
- **Staphylococcal whitlow (felon)** is a purulent infection or abscess involving the bulbous distal pulp of the finger. It can either follow trauma or it can be an extension from an acute paronychia [Jebson, 1998; Hunter et al, 2002; Lee et al, 2003].

Causative organisms

- ***Staphylococcus aureus*** is almost always the cause of furuncles and carbuncles [Lee et al, 2003]. An infecting reservoir of *Staphylococcus* is usually present in the nose or the perineum and it is thought that the infection is disseminated by the fingers and by clothing [Hay and Adriaans, 1998].
- ***S aureus*** is the most common causative organism of acute paronychia and superficial and deep folliculitis.
- **If acute paronychia occurs secondary to chronic paronychia** then other organisms may be involved, e.g. *Pseudomonas aeruginosa, Proteus vulgaris,* streptococci, or coliform organisms [Dawber et al, 1998].

How common is it?

- **The incidence and prevalence of boils, carbuncles, acute paronychia, and staphylococcal whitlow is uncertain.**
- **Boils are rare in children** except in those who have atopic eczema. However they are common in adolescents and in early adult life, especially in boys, and the peak incidence is the same as that of acne vulgaris [Hay and Adriaans, 1998].

B

How do I know my patient has it?

Boil

- **A boil starts as a hard, tender, red nodule** surrounding a hair follicle that enlarges and becomes fluctuant after several days (i.e. it undergoes abscess formation). Later it may discharge pus and its central 'core' before healing and may leave a scar [Hunter et al, 2002; Lee et al, 2003].
- **Boils arise in hair-bearing sites,** particularly where there is friction, occlusion, and perspiration, e.g. the neck, face, axillae, arms, wrists, fingers, buttocks, and anogenital region [Hay and Adriaans, 1998; Lee et al, 2003].
- Boils may be either solitary lesions or multiple lesions (in sites such as the buttocks) [Lee et al, 2003].
- Occasionally there may be mild constitutional symptoms, such as fever and malaise [Hay and Adriaans, 1998].

Carbuncle

- **A carbuncle is initially a smooth, dome-shaped, acutely tender, painful lesion** that often occurs at the nape of the neck, the back, or thighs, and develops into a swollen, painful area discharging pus from several sites [Hunter et al, 2002; Lee et al, 2003].
- **Constitutional symptoms, such as fever and malaise,** may accompany or even precede the development of the carbuncle [Hay and Adriaans, 1998].

Staphylococcal folliculitis

- **Superficial folliculitis** consists of several small, fragile dome-shaped pustules that occur in crops at the opening of hair follicles, usually at sites where hair follicles are damaged by friction from clothing, blockage of the follicle, or shaving. It often occurs on the scalp or limbs in children, and in the beard area, axillae, extremities, and buttocks of adults. Superficial folliculitis is often painless but may cause mild discomfort or pruritus.
- **Deep folliculitis** includes inflammation around the follicle and often occurs in the bearded areas of the face and upper lip (e.g. sycosis barbae). Deep folliculitis tends to be more painful and scarring may occur.

[Hay and Adriaans, 1998]

Acute paronychia

- **The skin and soft tissue of the proximal and lateral nail fold are red, hot, and tender.** The nail may appear discoloured and even distorted [Rockwell, 2001; Lee et al, 2003].

Staphylococcal whitlow

- **The finger bulb is red, hot, oedematous, and usually exquisitely tender.** The onset of pain is rapid and there is swelling of the entire finger pulp [Jebson, 1998; Lee et al, 2003].
- An obvious portal of entry is usually apparent.

Risk factors and predisposing conditions

- **A predisposing cause is usually absent,** although boils may complicate atopic dermatitis, excoriations, abrasions, scabies, or pediculosis.
- **Diabetes is widely believed to predispose people to furunculosis,** although evidence is conflicting. When furunculosis does occur in people with diabetes, it is often more extensive.
- **Other conditions associated with furunculosis include** infection with HIV, obesity, blood dyscrasias, and treatment with immunosuppressive drugs.
- **Carbuncles** are associated with malnutrition, cardiac failure, drug addiction, severe generalized dermatosis, and prolonged steroid therapy. Evidence is conflicting regarding their association with diabetes [Pozzilli et al, 1997].
- **In adults the use of topical steroids** is associated with th[e] development of folliculitis.

[Hay and Adriaans, 1998; Lee et al, 2003]

What else might it be?

- **Cystic acne** — associated with papules and comedones and usually confined to the face and trunk.
- **Hidradenitis suppurativa** — bacterial infection of the apocrine glands which should be considered if only the groin and the axillae are involved.
- **Ruptured epidermal inclusion cyst.**
- **Dental abscess** (face).
- **Underlying osteomyelitis.**
- **Orf** — starts as a small, firm red or reddish blue lump that enlarges to form a flat-topped, blood-tinged pustul[e] or blister that is usually 2–3 cm in diameter but may be as large as 5 cm [Duffill, 2002].
- **Anthrax** — can resemble a carbuncle but has a distinctive haemorrhagic crust and vesicular margin.
- **Herpetic whitlow** — in contrast to staphylococcal whitlow, there is usually a history of prior lesions at the same site. Lesions present with a group of haemorrhagi[c] vesicles that may become confluent and form a single bulla.

[Dawber et al, 1998; Lee et al, 2003]

Complications and prognosis

Complications

Boils and carbuncles

- **Scarring** may result from boils and carbuncles.
- **Surrounding cellulitis or bacteraemia may develop** if furunculosis or carbuncles extend.
- **Cavernous sinus thrombosis** is an unusual complication of boils or carbuncles on the upper lip and cheek.
- **Metastatic infection,** e.g. osteomyelitis, acute endocarditis, or brain abscess, rarely occurs from boils or carbuncles.
- **Septicaemia** is a very rare complication of both furuncle[s] and carbuncles [Hunter et al, 2002].

[Hay and Adriaans, 1998; Lee et al, 2003]

Paronychia

- **If left untreated,** the infection may extend to the opposi[te] lateral nail fold (runaround infection). A collection of pus may develop as an abscess around the perionychium. Fluctuance and local purulence at the nail margin may occur and infection may extend beneath the nail margin to involve the nail bed, producing elevation of the nail plate [Jebson, 1998; Rockwell, 2001].
- Bone infection or chronic paronychia with or without permanent damage to the nail plate may result from acute paronychia [Wollina, 2001].

Staphylococcal whitlow

- **Local vascular impairment and congestion** from the increased pressure within the non-compliant pulp space may cause tissue necrosis.
- **The abscess may spread** to involve the distal phalanx, o[r] the flexor tendon sheath, or it may spontaneously decompress out of the skin through a sinus tract.
- **Rarely osteomyelitis, suppurative flexor tenosynovitis, o[r] septic arthritis** of the distal interphalangeal joint may occur.

[Jebson, 1998]

Prognosis

Boils and carbuncles

Over a period of 2 days to 3 weeks the boil becomes necrotic and develops into an abscess. Rupture occurs with discharge of pus and often a core of necrotic material. Pain surrounding the lesion then subsides, and the redness and oedema diminish over several days to several weeks.

In people who have HIV, boils may coalesce into violaceous plaques.

A carbuncle increases in size for a few days to reach a diameter of 3–10 cm, occasionally more. After 5–7 days, suppuration occurs and multiple pustules soon appear on the surface, draining externally around multiple hair follicles.

- A yellow-grey irregular crater develops at the centre. In some cases, the necrosis develops more acutely without a follicular discharge and the entire central core is shed to leave a deep ulcer with a purulent floor.
- Healing takes place slowly by granulation and the area may remain deeply violaceous for a prolonged period of time.

Death may occur in the frail and ill from toxaemia or from metastatic infection.

[Hay and Adriaans, 1998; Lee et al, 2003]

Staphylococcal superficial folliculitis

- The lesions may heal spontaneously within 7–10 days, or may become chronic [Hay and Adriaans, 1998].

Staphylococcal deep folliculitis

- If untreated, the lesions may become more deeply seated and chronic and cause scarring [Stulberg et al, 2002; Lee et al, 2003].

Management issues

- Folliculitis p.243
- Furunculosis and carbuncles p.243
- Staphylococcal paronychia p.243
- Staphylococcal whitlow p.243
- Recurrent furunculosis p.243
- Which antibiotic should I prescribe, and for how long? p.244

Folliculitis

- Superficial folliculitis is often self-limiting if the predisposing factors are removed. Cleansing with antibacterial washes/antiseptics (e.g. triclosan, chlorhexidine) may help to prevent or control mild cases.
- If folliculitis is more extensive or severe, oral antibiotics may be needed.
- If folliculitis is persistent or recurrent then search for sites of staphylococcal carriage in the person and his or her contacts (see *Who should I swab for carriage of Staphylococcus aureus?*) [Hay and Adriaans, 1998; Lee et al, 2003].

Furunculosis and carbuncles

- **For lesions that are non-fluctuant** apply moist heat to relieve discomfort, help localise the infection, and promote drainage.
- **If there is associated fever or surrounding cellulitis** treat with oral antibiotics.
- **For lesions that are large, but localised, painful, and fluctuant:**
  - Incise and drain.
  - Treat with oral antibiotics until inflammation resolves. Oral flucloxacillin is usually effective against *Staphylococcus aureus*, erythromycin is an alternative if the person is allergic to penicillin.
  - After adequate drainage (spontaneous or surgical), cover with a sterile dressing to prevent autoinoculation.
- **Start antibiotic treatment promptly if there is infection in an area where complications can be dangerous** (e.g. the face). Monitor the person closely checking for signs of systemic upset. Most cases can be treated in primary care. The decision of whether to admit the person will depend on clinical judgement, taking into account the rapidity and degree of spread and whether or not the person (or carer) is able to follow instructions reliably regarding monitoring of complications.

[Lee et al, 2003]

Staphylococcal paronychia

- **Treat acute paronychia with oral antibiotics** [Rockwell, 2001]. Oral flucloxacillin is usually effective against *S aureus*, erythromycin is an alternative if the person is allergic to penicillin.
- **In mild paronychia** warm soaks 3–4 times a day may help if an abscess has not formed [Rockwell, 2001].
- **Fluctuance suggests moderate or severe paronychia,** which should be drained [Scott, 2002].
  - If superficial it may point close to the nail and can be easily drained by incision without anaesthesia [Dawber et al, 1998].
  - Deeper lesions should be incised under local anaesthesia if there is no improvement after 2 days of antibiotics [Dawber et al, 1998; Rockwell, 2001].
- **If there is proximal red streaking or lymphadenopathy** then the possibility of a mixed infection with *Streptococcus* should be considered [Keyser et al, 1990]. Consider treating for both staphylococcal and streptococcal infection, or be guided by swab results.

Staphylococcal whitlow

- **Initial cellulitis and inflammation** (rarely encountered) may respond to elevation, oral antibiotics, and warm soaks.
- **Abscess formation and fluctuation of the pulp space** (more common) requires urgent referral for drainage of loculated abscesses within the tissue, and oral or intravenous antibiotic therapy.

[Jebson, 1998; Lee et al, 2003]

Recurrent furunculosis

Exclude underlying causes:

- **Underlying systemic disorders,** e.g. the person is immunocompromised.
- **Underlying skin disease,** e.g. scabies, pediculosis, eczema.
- **Localized predisposing factors,** e.g. industrial exposure to chemicals, oils, poor hygiene.
- **Sources of staphylococcal contact,** e.g. autoinnoculation, pyogenic infections in family members, contact sports.

[Hay and Adriaans, 1998; Lee et al, 2003]

Who should I swab for carriage of *Staphylococcus aureus*?

- *S aureus* is a persistent member of the microbial flora in 10–20% of the population, and approximately 30–50% of healthy adults harbour *S aureus* at some site at any given time [Lee et al, 2003].
- **In persistent or recurrent infection,** swabs should be taken from the person's nose, throat, umbilicus, axillae, and perineum.
- **If furunculosis persists** after screening and treating the person, consider eliminating potential sources of infection in the family and close contacts. Actual

B

infections are a more likely source of infection than asymptomatic carriage, but consider screening household members if they are willing to co-operate with an eradication strategy.

How do I minimize staphylococcal carriage?

- **Elimination of nasal staphylococci** in nasal carriers can be achieved using a cream containing chlorhexidine plus neomycin (Naseptin) applied to the nostrils four times a day for 10 days. Re-colonization frequently occurs. Mupirocin nasal ointment is also effective at eliminating nasal staphylococci, but should be reserved for resistant cases.
- **If sites other than the nose are involved** then oral treatment with antibiotics may be necessary, the choice of antibiotic being guided by sensitivities.
- **Antiseptic preparations should be used** to reduce staphylococcal skin colonization. Washing the skin (preferably including hair) and daily bathing in an antiseptic solution of chlorhexidine or triclosan in a detergent vehicle is recommended. If the person suffers from dry or inflamed skin then an antiseptic emollient should be used (Dermol 500, Oilatum Plus, Emulsiderm, or Dermol 600).
- **The person should also be advised to:**
  - Wash his or her sheets and underwear regularly on a hot wash cycle (above 55°C). The clothes should be turned inside out and the machine not overloaded so that the water can penetrate.
  - Thoroughly clean the bedroom at the same time as treatment is started.
  - Use his or her own towel and flannel, and rinse the flannel in hot water before use.

[HPA, Personal Communication, 2003]

- **Dressings should be changed frequently** if purulent discharge collects [Lee et al, 2003].

Which antibiotic should I prescribe, and for how long?

- **Oral flucloxacillin or erythromycin** are usually effective against *Staphylococcus aureus* infections. Optimal treatment length is not evident from the literature, but 7 days' treatment is generally recommended.
- In chronic furunculosis the choice of antibiotic should be guided by sensitivities. Flucloxacillin is recommended for blind treatment (or erythromycin for people with a penicillin allergy). Treat for two weeks initially. Some people will need a longer course, e.g. 6–8 weeks.

References

NHS staff in England can link, free of charge, from references to full text journals by clicking on [Full text] on the PRODIGY website.

1. Cyr, P.R. (2001) *Folliculitis*. eMedicine.com, Inc. www.emedicine.com [Accessed: 06/10/2003].
2. Dawber, R.P.R, Baran, R. and De Berker, D. (1998) Disorders of nails. In: Champion, R.H., Burton, J.L., Breathnach, S.M. and Burns, D.A. (Eds.) *Textbook of dermatology*. 6th edn. Oxford: Blackwell Science. 2835–2837.
3. Duffill, M. (2002) *Orf*. New Zealand Dermatological Society. www.dermnetnz.org/dna.orf/orf.html [Accessed: 07/10/2003].
4. Hay, R.M. and Adriaans, B.M. (1998) Bacterial infections. In: Champion, R.H., Burton, J.L., Breathnach, S.M. and Burns, D.A. (Eds.) *Textbook of dermatology*. 6th edn. Oxford: Blackwell Science. 1116–1121.
5. HPA (2003) *Personal communication*. Health Protection Agency: London.
6. Hunter, J.A.A, Savin, J.A. and Dahl, M.V. (Eds.) (2002) *Clinical dermatology*. 3rd edn. Oxford: Blackwell Science.
7. Jebson, P.J. (1998) Infections of the fingertip. Paronychias and felons. *Hand Clinics* **14**(4), 547–555.
8. Keyser, J.J., Littler, J.W. and Eaton, R.G. (1990) Surgical treatment of infections and lesions of the perionychium. *Hand Clinics* **6**(1), 137–153.
9. Lee, P.K., Weinberg, A.N., Swartz, M.N. and Johnson A.R. (2003) Pyodermas: *Staphylococcus aureus*, steptococcus, and other gram-positive bacteria. In: Freedberg, I.M., Eisen, A.Z., Wolff, K. et al (Eds.) *Fitzpatrick's dermatology in general medicine*. London McGraw-Hill. 2182–2207.
10. Pozzilli, P., Signore, A. and Leslie, R.D.G. (1997) Infections, immunity and diabetes. In: Alberti, K.G.M.N., Zimmet, P, Delfrons, R.A. et al (Eds.) *International textbook of diabetes mellitus*. 2nd edn. Chichester: Wiley.
11. Rockwell, P.G. (2001) Acute and chronic paronychia. *American Family Physician* **63**(6), 1113–1116. [Full text]
12. Scott, P.M. (2002) Procedures in family practice. Drainage for an acute paronychia. *Journal of the American Academy of Physician Assistants* **15**(11), 57–58.
13. Stulberg, D.L., Penrod, M.A. and Blatny, R.A. (2002) Common bacterial skin infections. *American Family Physician* **66**(1), 119–124. [Full text]
14. Wollina, U. (2001) Acute paronychia: comparative treatment with topical antibiotic alone or in combination with corticosteroid. *Journal of the European Academy of Dermatology & Venereology* **15**(1), 82–84.

PRODIGY GUIDANCE

Breast cancer — managing women with a family history

Last revised in February 2005
www.prodigy.nhs.uk/guidance.asp?gt=Breast cancer - managing FH

Applies to women over the age of 16 years

This guidance is based on the National Institute for Clinical Excellence (NICE) guideline and quick reference guide, *Familial breast cancer: The classification and care of women at risk of familial breast cancer in primary, secondary and tertiary care* (May 2004). It also takes into account the full guideline document, *The classification and care of women at risk of familial breast cancer in primary, secondary and tertiary care* produced by the School of Health and Related Research (ScHARR), University of Sheffield.

This guidance covers the primary-care management of women presenting with concerns about developing breast cancer because of a family history.

This guidance does not cover secondary- and tertiary-care management of women with concerns about breast cancer, but outlines the advice/monitoring and treatment that is offered.

There is separate PRODIGY guidance for *Breast cancer — suspected* and *Gynaecological cancer — suspected.*

Goals

To help primary health care professionals advise women with a family history of breast cancer about their risk of developing breast cancer and how this should be managed

Contents

Scenarios

- Aged <30 years with family history of breast cancer p.245
- Aged 30–39 years with a family history of breast cancer p.246
- Aged 40–49 years with a family history of breast cancer p.247
- Aged 50 yrs and over with a family history of breast cancer p.248

Extended Information, p. 249

Which scenario?

Aged <30 years with family history of breast cancer: covers the advice and management of a woman aged under thirty years with a family history of breast cancer and concerned about her risk of developing breast cancer.
Aged 30–39 years with a family history of breast cancer: covers the advice and management of a woman aged 30–39 years with a family history of breast cancer and concerned about her risk of developing breast cancer.
Aged 40–49 years with a family history of breast cancer: covers the advice and management of a woman aged 40–49 years with a family history of breast cancer and concerned about her risk of developing breast cancer.
Aged 50 yrs and over with a family history of breast cancer: covers the advice and management of a woman aged 50 years or over with a family history of breast cancer and concerned about her risk of developing breast cancer.

Aged <30 years with family history of breast cancer

Which therapy?

Follow local protocols where available.
Note: women under 30 years estimated to be at moderate risk of developing breast cancer will not usually be offered any intervention, but referral will allow an accurate assessment.
For definitions of first-, second-, and third-degree relatives, see *How is family defined?* (in *Management issues*).

Manage in primary care women with:
- No first- or second-degree maternal or paternal family history with breast cancer.

Usually manage in primary care a woman with:
- Only one first-degree relative with breast cancer diagnosed at any age. Consider specialist advice if the relative was diagnosed at younger than age 40 years and the family is small.
- One second-degree relative with breast cancer diagnosed at any age. Consider specialist advice if the relative was diagnosed at younger than age 40 years and the family is small.
- Women with two second-degree relatives with breast cancer of whom at least one was diagnosed over age 50 years.
- One first-degree *and* one second-degree relative with breast cancer diagnosed after an average age of 50 years.
- Two first-degree relatives diagnosed with breast cancer after an average age of 50 years.

But seek advice from secondary care if there is:
- Paternal history of breast cancer
- Jewish ancestry
- Any unusual cancers in the family:
  - Bilateral breast cancer
  - Male breast cancer
  - Ovarian cancer
  - Sarcoma at younger than age 45 years
  - Glioma or childhood adrenal cortical carcinoma
  - Complicated patterns of multiple cancers at a young age

Consider referral to secondary care for a woman with:
- One first-degree relative and one second-degree relative diagnosed with breast cancer before an average age of 50 years.

- Two first-degree relatives with breast cancer diagnosed before an average age of 50 years.
- Two second-degree relatives with breast cancer diagnosed before the age of 50 years.
- Three or more first- or second-degree relatives with breast cancer diagnosed at any age.
- One first-degree male relative diagnosed with breast cancer at any age.
- One first-degree relative with *bilateral* breast cancer, where the first primary was diagnosed before age 50 years.
- One first- or second-degree relative with *ovarian* cancer at any age *plus* one first- or second-degree relative with breast cancer at any age (one should be a first-degree relative).
- A first- or second-degree relative with breast cancer, where the woman does not fall into any of the above categories but:
  - Would like counselling or advice on risk management.
  - Would like to be considered for inclusion in a prevention trial.

Offer referral to a specialist genetics service if:
- A faulty gene has been identified in the family.

Advise
- About risks (See *What advice can I give reg*arding risk?) and follow-up.

Follow-up advice

- Inform the woman that her risk may change with changes in her family history, and that she should then return to have her risk reassessed.
- Advise the woman to return for reassessment when she reaches the age of 40 years. She will be need to be referred to secondary care when she reaches the age of 40 years because she may be eligible for annual mammographic surveillance if she has:
  - One first-degree relative diagnosed with breast cancer under the age of 40 years.
  - One first-degree and one second-degree relative diagnosed with breast cancer after an average age of 50 years.
  - Two first-degree relatives diagnosed with breast cancer after an average age of 50 years.
  - Two second-degree relatives diagnosed at any age.

Patient information leaflets

The following PILs are available at www.prodigy.nhs.uk
- Breast Cancer Care
- Cancer of the Breast
- Cancer of the Breast - Hereditary Factors

Shared decision making

- Breast cancer develops more commonly than average in some families.
- It is important to remember that most women with a family history of breast cancer are not at a substantially increased risk of breast cancer.
- A family history can assess your risk of breast cancer.
- Most women have a near-normal risk (about a 1 in 9 chance of developing breast cancer at some stage in life — most commonly after the age of 50).
- Women with an increased risk are referred for specialist advice.
- You may wish to consider these other risk factors for breast cancer:
  - Regular exercise reduces the risk.
  - If you drink a lot of alcohol, the risk is increased.
  - There is a slightly increased risk if you use the combined oral contraceptive pill.
  - Women who breast-feed have a reduced risk of developing breast cancer compared with those who bottle-feed.
- See your GP if there is a change in your family history that may alter your risk assessment.

Drug rationale

- No prescription is offered.

Aged 30–39 years with a family history of breast cancer

Which therapy

Follow local protocols where available.
For definitions of first-, second-, and third-degree relatives see *How is family defined?* (in *Management issues*).

Manage in primary care a woman with:
- No first- or second-degree maternal or paternal family history of breast cancer.

Usually manage in primary care a woman with:
- One first-degree relative with breast cancer diagnosed at any age. Consider specialist advice if the relative was diagnosed at younger than age 40 years and the family is small.
- One second-degree relative with breast cancer diagnosed at any age. Consider specialist advice if the relative was diagnosed at younger than age 40 years and the family is small.
- Two second-degree relatives with breast cancer of whom at least one was diagnosed over age 50 years.
- One first-degree and one second-degree relative with breast cancer diagnosed after an average age of 50 years.
- Two first-degree relatives with breast cancer diagnosed after an average age of 50 years.

But seek advice from secondary care if there is a:
- Paternal history of breast cancer
- Jewish ancestry
- Any unusual cancers in the family:
  - Bilateral breast cancer
  - Male breast cancer
  - Ovarian cancer
  - Sarcoma at younger than age 45 years
  - Glioma or childhood adrenal cortical carcinoma
  - Complicated patterns of multiple cancers at a young age.

Consider referral to secondary care for a woman with:
- One first-degree relative *and* one second-degree relative diagnosed with breast cancer before an average age of 50 years.
- Two first-degree relatives diagnosed with breast cancer before an average age of 50 years.
- Two second-degree relatives diagnosed with breast cancer before an average age of 50 years.
- Three or more first- or second-degree relatives diagnosed with breast cancer at any age.
- One first-degree male relative diagnosed with breast cancer at any age.
- One first-degree relative with *bilateral* breast cancer, where the first primary was diagnosed before age 50 years.
- One first- or second-degree relative with *ovarian* cancer at any age *plus* one first- or second-degree relative with breast cancer at any age (one should be a first-degree relative).
- A first- or second-degree relative with breast cancer, where the woman does not fall into any of the above categories but:
  - Would like counselling or advice on risk management

- Would like to be considered for inclusion in a prevention trial.

fer referral to a specialist genetics service if:

A faulty gene has been identified in the family.

lvise:

About risks (See *What advice can I give regarding risk?*) and follow-up.

ollow-up advice

Inform the woman that her risk may change with changes in her family history, and that she should then return to have her risk reassessed.

Advise her to return for reassessment when she reaches the age of 40 years. She will be need to be referred to secondary care when she reaches the age of 40 years because she may be eligible for annual mammographic surveillance if she has:

- One first-degree relative diagnosed <40 years.
- One first-degree and one second-degree relative diagnosed after an average age 50 years.
- Two first-degree relatives diagnosed after an average age 50 years.
- Two second-degree relatives diagnosed at any age.

'atient information leaflets

ıe following PILs are available at www.prodigy.nhs.uk

Breast Cancer Care

Cancer of the Breast

Cancer of the Breast - Hereditary Factors

hared decision making

Breast cancer develops more commonly than average in some families.

It is important to remember that most women with a family history of breast cancer are not at a substantially increased risk of breast cancer.

A family history can assess your risk of breast cancer. Most women have a near-normal risk (about a 1 in 9 chance of developing breast cancer at some stage in life — most commonly after the age of 50).

Women with an increased risk are referred for specialist advice.

You may wish to consider these other risk factors for breast cancer:

- Regular exercise reduces the risk.
- If you drink a lot of alcohol, the risk is increased.
- There is a slightly increased risk if you use the combined oral contraceptive pill.
- Women who breast-feed have a reduced risk of developing breast cancer compared with those who bottle-feed.

See your GP if there is a change in your family history that may alter your risk assessment.

)rug rationale

No prescription is offered.

Aged 40–49 years with a family history of breast cancer

Vhich therapy

ollow local protocols where available.

or definitions of first-, second-, and third-degree relatives, e *How is family defined?* (in *Management issues*).

lanage in primary care a woman with:

- No first- or second-degree maternal or paternal family history of breast cancer.

Usually manage in primary care a woman with:

- Only one first-degree relative with breast cancer over 40 years. Consider specialist advice if the family is small.
- One second-degree relative with breast cancer diagnosed at any age. Consider specialist advice if the relative was diagnosed at younger than age 40 years and the family is small.

But seek advice from secondary care if there is:

- Paternal history of breast cancer
- Jewish ancestry
- Any unusual cancers in the family:
  - Bilateral breast cancer
  - Male breast cancer
  - Ovarian cancer
  - Sarcoma at younger than age 45 years
  - Glioma or childhood adrenal cortical carcinoma
  - Complicated patterns of multiple cancers at a young age

Consider referral to secondary care for a woman with:

- One first-degree relative with breast cancer diagnosed *under* 40 years.
- One first-degree male relative with breast cancer diagnosed at any age.
- One first-degree relative with *bilateral* breast cancer where the first primary was diagnosed before age 50 years.
- One first- or second-degree relative with *ovarian* cancer at any age *plus* one first- or second-degree relative with breast cancer at any age (one should be a first-degree relative).
- Two first-degree relatives with breast cancer diagnosed at any age.
- One first-degree relative *and* one second-degree relative with breast cancer diagnosed at any age.
- Two second-degree relatives with breast cancer diagnosed at any age.
- Three or more first- or second-degree relatives with breast cancer diagnosed at any age.
- A first- or second-degree relative with breast cancer, where the woman does not fall into any of the above categories but:
  - Would like counselling or advice on risk management.
  - Would like to be considered for inclusion in a prevention trial.

Offer referral to a specialist genetics service if:

- A faulty gene has been identified in the family.

Advise:

- About risks (See *What advice can I give regarding risk?*) and follow-up.

Follow-up advice

- Inform the woman that her risk may change with changes in her family history, and that she should then return to have her risk reassessed.

Patient information leaflets

The following PILs are available at www.prodigy.nhs.uk

- Breast Cancer Care
- Cancer of the Breast
- Cancer of the Breast - Hereditary Factors

Shared decision making

- Breast cancer develops more commonly than average in some families.
- It is important to remember that most women with a family history of breast cancer are not at a substantially increased risk of breast cancer.

B

- A family history can assess your risk of breast cancer.
- Most women have a near-normal risk (about a 1 in 9 chance of developing breast cancer at some stage in life — most commonly after the age of 50).
- Women with an increased risk are referred for specialist advice.
- You may wish to consider these other risk factors for breast cancer:
  - Regular exercise reduces the risk.
  - If you drink a lot of alcohol, the risk is increased.
  - There is a slightly increased risk if you use the combined oral contraceptive pill or HRT.
  - Women who breast-feed have a reduced risk of developing breast cancer compared with those who bottle-feed.
  - If you are overweight, losing some weight will reduce your risk of postmenopausal breast cancer.
- See your GP if there is a change in your family history that may alter your risk assessment.

Drug rationale

- No prescription is offered.

Aged 50 yrs and over with a family history of breast cancer

Which therapy

Follow local protocols where available.

For definitions of first-, second-, and third-degree relatives, see *How is family defined?* (in *Management issues).*

Manage in primary care a woman with:

- No first- or second-degree maternal or paternal family history of breast cancer.

Usually manage in primary care a woman with:

- Only one first-degree relative with breast cancer diagnosed at any age. Consider specialist advice if the relative was diagnosed at younger than age 40 years and the family is small.
- One second-degree relative with breast cancer diagnosed at any age. Consider specialist advice if the relative was diagnosed at younger than age 40 years and the family is small.
- Two second-degree relatives with breast cancer of whom at least one was diagnosed over age 50 years.
- One first-degree and one second-degree relative diagnosed with breast cancer after an average age of 50 years.
- Two first-degree relatives with breast cancer diagnosed after an average age of 50 years.

But seek advice from secondary care if:

- Paternal history of breast cancer
- Jewish ancestry
- Any unusual cancers in the family:
  - Bilateral breast cancer
  - Male breast cancer
  - Ovarian cancer
  - Sarcoma at younger than age 45 years
  - Glioma or childhood adrenal cortical carcinoma
  - Complicated patterns of multiple cancers at a young age

Consider referral to secondary care for a woman with:

- One first-degree relative and one second-degree relative with breast cancer diagnosed before an average age of 50 years.
- Two first-degree relatives with breast cancer diagnosed before an average age of 50 years.
- Two second-degree relatives with breast cancer diagnosed before the age of 50 years.
- Three or more first- or second-degree relatives with breast cancer diagnosed at any age.
- One first-degree male relative with breast cancer diagnosed at any age.
- One first-degree relative with *bilateral* breast cancer where the first primary was diagnosed before age 50 years.
- One first- or second-degree relative with *ovarian* cance at any age *plus* one first- or second-degree relative with breast cancer at any age (one should be a first-degree relative).
- A first- or second-degree relative with breast cancer, where the woman does not fall into any of the above categories but:
  - Would like counselling or advice on risk managemen
  - Would like to be considered for inclusion in a prevention trial.

Note: a woman over 50 years estimated to be at moderat risk (e.g. having only one relative with breast cancer) will already be eligible for mammographic surveillance and w not usually receive any additional intervention if referred.

Offer referral to a specialist genetics service if:

- A faulty gene has been identified in the family

Advise:

- About risks (See *What advice can I give regarding risk?* and follow-up.

Follow-up advice

- Inform the woman that her risk may change with changes in her family history, and that she should then return to have her risk reassessed.

Should I refer or investigate?

Patient information leaflets

The following PILs are available at www.prodigy.nhs.uk

- Breast Cancer Care
- Cancer of the Breast
- Cancer of the Breast - Hereditary Factors

Shared decision making

- Breast cancer develops more commonly than average in some families.
- It is important to remember that most women with a family history of breast cancer are not at a substantially increased risk of breast cancer.
- A family history can assess your risk of breast cancer.
- Most women have a near-normal risk (about a 1 in 9 chance of developing breast cancer at some stage in life — most commonly after the age of 50.)
- Women with an increased risk are referred for specialis advice.
- You may wish to consider these other risk factors for breast cancer:
  - Regular exercise reduces the risk.
  - If you drink a lot of alcohol, the risk is increased.
  - There is a slightly increased risk if you use HRT.
  - If you are overweight, losing some weight will reduce your risk of postmenopausal breast cancer.
- See your GP if there is a change in your family history that may alter your risk assessment.

Drug rationale

- No prescription is offered.

Extended Information

Background information

How common is breast cancer? p.249
What is known about the genetic risk factors? p.249
How does family history affect the risk of developing breast cancer? p.249
What are the risk categories? p.249

How common is breast cancer?

Breast cancer is the most common cancer in women in the UK, accounting for nearly 30% of cancers in women. It is also the commonest cancer in women worldwide, accounting for 18–25% of all female malignancies [McPherson et al, 2000; Office for National Statistics, 2001; McIntosh et al, 2004].

The lifetime risk of developing breast cancer (to 85 years of age) in the UK is 11% (one in nine women) [Office for National Statistics, 2001; McIntosh et al, 2004].

The overall incidence in the UK is 114 per 100,000 of the female population. The incidence increases with age. Four in five new cases are in women over 50 years: because of screening, there is a peak in distribution of new cases in women aged 50–54 years [Office for National Statistics, 2001; McIntosh et al, 2004].

Only 3–5% of women are likely to carry a particular gene that would confer a high risk (over 50%) of developing breast cancer [Claus et al, 1994; Ford et al, 1998].

What is known about the genetic risk factors?

Early onset, a high incidence of bilateral disease and an association with other malignancies [Hill et al, 1997] usually characterize familial cancer.

Several genes have been identified:

- BRCA1 mutation on chromosome 17: lifetime risk of breast cancer is 65–85% [McIntosh et al, 2004].
- BRCA2 mutation on chromosome 13: lifetime risk of breast cancer is 40–85% [McIntosh et al, 2004]. There is also an increased risk of prostate cancer within these families.
- TP53 mutation on chromosome 17: Li-Fraumeni syndrome associated with a high risk; most women are affected before the age of 50 years. TP53 is also associated with sarcomas of childhood, leukaemias, adrenocortical carcinomas and brain tumours [Emery et al, 2001; McIntosh et al, 2004].
- PTEN gene: Cowden's syndrome, which predisposes to early-onset breast cancer, thyroid cancer, ovarian cancer and hamartomatous lesions of the skin [Emery et al, 2001].
- ATM gene and CHEK2 gene: moderate risk of breast cancer [McIntosh et al, 2004].

Most women who have a family history do not have a mutation of BRCA1, BRCA2 or TP53 genes. Some such histories will be due to lower-penetrance genes not yet discovered [McIntosh et al, 2004].

Certain populations, notably the Ashkenazi Jewish community, have different rates of genetic mutations. There are founder mutations in several populations, e.g. Norwegian, Dutch and Icelandic people [McIntosh et al, 2004]. (A founder mutation describes the initial mutation in a family or population.)

The largest proportions of hereditary ovarian cancer cases are in families with definite histories of either breast or ovarian cancer or both, most being due to mutations in BRCA1 [McIntosh et al, 2004].

How does family history affect the risk of developing breast cancer?

- It is important to remember that most women with a family history of breast cancer are not at a substantially increased risk of breast cancer [McIntosh et al, 2004]. As one in nine women will develop breast cancer during their lifetime, most people have a relative with breast cancer.
- **Between 6% and 19% of women with breast cancer will have a family history of the disease.** This clustering may be due to chance, shared environmental or lifestyle risk factors, or increased genetic susceptibility [Hill et al, 1997; DH, 2000].
- **Most cases of breast cancer arise in women with no family history of the disease** McIntosh et al, 2004. Breast cancer is a multifactorial disease, which may involve lifestyle, environmental, reproductive, and genetic factors as well as other unknown factors. If a relative of a woman has breast cancer, this may be due to chance rather than to genetic or shared lifestyle factors. [McIntosh et al, 2004]. Other risk factors include the use of hormonal contraceptives and hormonal replacement therapy, early menarche, and nulliparity.
- **A history of breast cancer in a relative is one of the strongest risk factors** identified for the development of breast cancer [Emery et al, 2001].
- **The probability that a woman in a developed country will develop breast cancer increases according to the number of affected relatives** [Collaborative Group on Hormonal Factors in Breast Cancer, 2001].
- **The risk of developing breast cancer is greater the younger the relative was when she developed the disease** [Claus et al, 1994].

What are the risk categories?

- **Whether a woman is managed in primary care or referred to secondary or tertiary care is related to the level of risk,** which the NICE guideline group has divided into three categories of risk: near-population, medium, and high (see Table 2).
- The risk categories and cut-off points, decided by the NICE guideline group, are based on three datasets from:
  - The Office of National Statistics [Office for National Statistics, 2001]
  - The Cancer and Steroid Hormone study, a population-based, case-control study conducted by the Centers for Disease Control [Claus et al, 1994]
  - The Collaborative Group on Hormonal Factors in Breast Cancer [Collaborative Group on Hormonal Factors in Breast Cancer, 2001]
- The lifetime risks of breast cancer were calculated from these three datasets and are shown in Table 1.
- In many situations, the breast-cancer risk to a woman with a family history of breast cancer can be estimated

Table 1: Lifetime risks of breast cancer

Age in years	Office of National Statistics Population — 10-year risk	Claus — risk in the next 10 years if sister or mother had breast cancer aged 30–39 years	Collaborative Group — risk in the next 10 years if sister or mother had breast cancer aged 30–39 years
20	0.1%	0.5%	0.4%
30	0.4%	1.2%	2.2%
40	1.5%	2.7%	4.1%
50	2.8%	4.2%	5.1%
60	2.8%	4.4%	3.8%
70	3.1%	3.5%	4.2%

straightforwardly from epidemiological studies (e.g. a woman with one affected first-degree relative has about twice the normal risk). With more complex situations, risks can be estimated by applying risk algorithms, although these models can give inconsistent results and have not been thoroughly evaluated [McIntosh et al, 2004].

- Different risks apply to women who are carriers of mutations in the known high-risk genes.
- Risks associated with family history are modified by other breast-cancer risk factors, including age of menopause, parity, and breastfeeding.
- It is not expected that precise risks will be calculated in primary care or secondary care, but that health workers will use the family history to estimate the risk of breast cancer developing, so that the woman can be placed into a risk category. The risk category determines where care is most likely to be delivered (See Table 2*)*.

[McIntosh et al, 2004]

Management issues

- General issues p.250
- When and how do I make an initial assessment? p.250
- How is family defined? p.250
- When should I refer to secondary care or to a specialist genetic service? p.251
- What advice can I give regarding risk? p.252
- What should I do with those I don't refer? p.253
- What is likely to happen in secondary care? p.253
- What is likely to happen in tertiary care? p.254
- How is genetic testing carried out? p.254
- Who should have mammographic surveillance? p.254
- Risk-reducing surgery p.254

General issues

- **NICE has recommended that local protocols should be developed, with clear referral mechanisms between primary, secondary, and tertiary care.**
- **Service provision in secondary care** may be undertaken by breast-care teams, family-history clinics, or breast clinics, depending on locality.
- **Tertiary-care provision** is undertaken by a specialist genetics clinic.
- Local referral pathways may differ from those suggested by NICE. For instance, some tertiary-care centres with strong links to secondary care may prefer that primary health care professionals refer women at high risk directly to them: the NICE guidelines recommend that women at high risk are initially referred to secondary care unless a gene mutation predisposing to high risk has been identified in a family member.

Table 2: Place where care is most likely to be delivered, depending on risk estimate.

Where care is most likely to be delivered	Risk category	10-year risk of developing breast cancer aged 40–50 years	Lifetime risk of developing breast cancer
Primary care	Near-population	<3%	<17%
Secondary care	Moderate risk	3–8%	17% and greater but <30%
Tertiary care	High risk	>8%	>=30%, or a >=20% chance of a BRCA1, BRCA2, or TP53 mutation being harboured in the family

- **Consider referring to secondary or tertiary care someo who is particularly concerned about her risk of developing breast cancer but in whom it is impossible t assess risk accurately:**
  - A woman with a small family (e.g. no sisters or aunts
  - Women whose mothers were adopted and in whom there was a diagnosis of breast cancer at a young age i.e. 40 years or less.
- Seek advice if the woman herself is adopted and has a family history of breast cancer in her biological family.
- **Seek advice for a woman who has a third-degree relati with breast cancer** if she also has any of these risk factors:
  - Paternal history of breast cancer.
  - Jewish ancestry.
  - Any unusual cancers in the family.
  - Bilateral breast cancer.
  - A family history of male breast cancer.
  - Ovarian cancer.
  - Sarcoma at younger than age 45 years.
  - Glioma or childhood adrenal cortical carcinoma.
  - Complicated patterns of multiple cancers at a young age.

When and how do I make an initial assessment?

- **A family history of breast cancer should be taken in primary care** to assess risk when a woman presents wit a concern about a family history of breast cancer.
- **It may be clinically relevant to take a family history in other circumstances** (e.g. in a woman older than 35 yea who is using combined oral contraception, or who is being considered for long-term use of hormone replacement therapy).
- **A family history allows a classification of risk to be ma** that will direct further management decisions. It should be noted that third-degree relatives are not relevant to primary-care assessment.
- **Try to gather as accurate information as possible on:**
  - Age at which any relative was diagnosed with cancer
  - Certainty of the diagnosis
  - Site of the tumour (e.g. ovarian, sarcoma, glioma, or adrenal cortical cancer)
  - Complicated pattern of multiple cancers at any age
  - Bilateral breast cancer; each breast cancer has the same count-value for risk as one relative
  - Jewish ancestry

How is family defined?

- **To be considered relevant, all affected relatives must be on the same side of the family and be blood relatives of the woman and of each other.** Ask about paternal as we as maternal relatives. See Table 3.
- **Paternal history is considered relevant** if there are two c more relatives diagnosed with breast cancer on the woman's father's side of the family.

[McIntosh et al, 2004]

Table 3: Family history.

Degree of relative	Relative
First-degree relative	Mother, father, daughter, son, sister, brother
Second-degree relative	Grandparents, grandchildren, aunt, uncle, niece, nephe half-sister, half-brother
Third-degree relative	Great-grandparents, great-grandchildren, great aunt, great uncle, first cousin, grand nephew, grand niece

When should I refer to secondary care or to specialist genetic service?

All women concerned about developing breast cancer should be advised about the risk factors, whether or not referral is recommended. Please see the section *What advice can I give regarding risk?*

All women concerned about developing breast cancer should be advised that their risk may change with age and with changes in their family history. Please see the section *What should I do with those I don't refer?*

Some women will not fit into a particular category because of doubt over the diagnosis of breast cancer in their relative (s) or over the age at which the cancer occurred. Consider discussing with a specialist in these circumstances to decide the most appropriate management.

Women up to the age of 39 years

Primary-care management appropriate

- Women concerned about their risk of developing breast cancer who have no first- or second-degree maternal or paternal family history should be managed in primary care.

Primary-care management usually appropriate

The following women can usually be managed in primary care:

- Women with only one first-degree relative with breast cancer diagnosed at any age. Consider specialist advice if the relative was diagnosed at younger than age 40 years and the family is small.
- Women who have one second-degree relative with breast cancer diagnosed at any age. Consider specialist advice if the relative was diagnosed at younger than age 40 years and the family is small.
- Women with two second-degree relatives with breast cancer of whom at least one was diagnosed over age 50 years.
- Women with one first-degree *and* one second-degree relative with breast cancer diagnosed after an average age of 50 years.
- Women with two first-degree relatives with breast cancer diagnosed after an average age of 50 years.

However, if they have any of the following in their history, seek advice from secondary care about their level of risk and appropriateness of referral:

- Paternal history of breast cancer
- Jewish ancestry
- Any unusual cancers in the family:
  - Bilateral breast cancer
  - Male breast cancer
  - Ovarian cancer
  - Sarcoma at younger than age 45 years
  - Glioma or childhood adrenal cortical carcinoma
  - Complicated patterns of multiple cancers at a young age

Consider referral to secondary care

It should be noted that a woman under 30 years of age estimated to be at moderate risk will not in practice be offered any intervention. Offer referral to determine if she should be entered into an early screening programme or intervention.

- **Offer referral to a woman with:**
  - One first-degree relative *and* one second-degree relative with breast cancer diagnosed before an average age of 50 years.
  - Two first-degree relatives with breast cancer diagnosed before an average age of 50 years.
  - Two second-degree relatives with breast cancer diagnosed before the age of 50 years.
  - Three or more first- or second-degree relatives with breast cancer diagnosed at any age.
  - One first-degree male relative with breast cancer diagnosed at any age.
  - *Bilateral* breast cancer in one first-degree relative where the first primary was diagnosed before age 50 years.
  - One first- or second-degree relative with *ovarian* cancer at any age *plus* one first- or second-degree relative with breast cancer at any age (one should be a first-degree relative).
- **Consider referral** for women with a first- or second-degree relative with breast cancer who do not fall into the above categories and:
  - Who would like counselling or advice on risk management.
  - Who would like to be considered for inclusion in a prevention trial.

Offer referral to a specialist genetics service

- Refer the woman to a geneticist if a faulty gene has been identified in the family.

[NICE, 2004]

Women aged 40–49 years

Primary-care management appropriate

- Women concerned about their risk of developing breast cancer but who have no first- or second-degree maternal or paternal family history should be managed in primary care.

Primary care management usually appropriate

The following women aged 40–49 years can usually be managed in primary care:

- Women with only one first-degree relative diagnosed with breast cancer *over* 40 years. Consider specialist advice if the family is small.
- Women who have one second-degree relative with breast cancer diagnosed at any age. Consider specialist advice if the relative was diagnosed at younger than age 40 years and the family is small.

However, if they have any of the following in their history, seek advice from secondary care about the level of risk and appropriateness of referral:

- Paternal history of breast cancer
- Jewish ancestry
- Any unusual cancers in the family:
  - Bilateral breast cancer
  - Male breast cancer
  - Ovarian cancer
  - Sarcoma at younger than age 45 years
  - Glioma or childhood adrenal cortical carcinoma
  - Complicated patterns of multiple cancers at a young age

Consider referral to secondary care

- **Offer referral to women with:**
  - One first-degree relative with breast cancer diagnosed *under* 40 years.
  - One first-degree male relative with breast cancer diagnosed at any age.
  - One first-degree relative with *bilateral* breast cancer where the first primary was diagnosed before age 50 years.
  - One first- or second-degree relative with *ovarian* cancer at any age *plus* one first- or second-degree relative with breast cancer at any age (one should be a first-degree relative).
  - Two first-degree relatives with breast cancer diagnosed at any age.
  - One first-degree relative *and* one second-degree relative with breast cancer diagnosed at any age.
  - Two second-degree relatives with breast cancer diagnosed at any age

- Three or more first- or second-degree relatives with breast cancer diagnosed at any age.
- **Consider referral** for women with a first- or second-degree relative with breast cancer who do not fall into the above categories and:
  - Who would like counselling or advice on risk management.
  - Who would like to be considered for inclusion in a prevention trial.

Offer referral to a specialist genetics service

- Refer the woman to a geneticist if a faulty gene has been identified in the family.

[NICE, 2004]

Women aged 50 years and over

It should be noted that women aged over 50 years are eligible for mammographic screening. Women in this age group at moderate risk are unlikely to receive any additional intervention.

Primary-care management appropriate

- Women concerned about their risk of developing breast cancer but who have no first- or second-degree maternal or paternal family history should be managed in primary care.

Primary care management is usually appropriate

The following women can usually be managed in primary care:

- Women with only one first-degree relative with breast cancer diagnosed at any age. Consider specialist advice if the relative was diagnosed at younger than age 40 years and the family is small.
- Women who have one second-degree relative with breast cancer diagnosed at any age. Consider specialist advice if the relative was diagnosed at younger than age 40 years and the family is small.
- Women with two second-degree relatives with breast cancer of whom at least one was diagnosed over age 50 years.
- Women with one first-degree *and* one second-degree relative with breast cancer diagnosed after an average age of 50 years.
- Women with two first-degree relatives diagnosed after an average age of 50 years.

However, if they have any of the following in their history, advice should be sought from secondary care about the level of risk and appropriateness of referral:

- Paternal history of breast cancer
- Jewish ancestry
- Any unusual cancers in the family:
  - Bilateral breast cancer
  - Male breast cancer
  - Ovarian cancer
  - Sarcoma at younger than age 45 years
  - Glioma or childhood adrenal cortical carcinoma
  - Complicated patterns of multiple at a young age cancers at a young age

Consider referral to secondary care

- **Offer referral to women with:**
  - One first-degree relative *and* one second-degree relative with breast cancer diagnosed before an average age of 50 years.
  - Two first-degree relatives with breast cancer diagnosed before an average age of 50 years.
  - Two second-degree relatives with breast cancer diagnosed before the age of 50 years.
  - Three or more first- or second-degree relatives with breast cancer diagnosed at any age.
  - One first-degree male relative with breast cancer diagnosed at any age.
  - One first-degree relative with *bilateral* breast cancer where the first primary was diagnosed before age 50 years.
  - One first- or second-degree relative with *ovarian* cancer at any age *plus* one first- or second-degree relative with breast cancer at any age (one should be a first-degree relative).
- **Consider referral** for women with a first- or second-degree relative with breast cancer who do not fall into the above categories and:
  - Who would like counselling or advice on risk management.
  - Who would like to be considered for inclusion in a prevention trial.

Offer referral to a specialist genetics service

- Refer the woman to a geneticist if a faulty gene has been identified in the family.

[NICE, 2004]

What advice can I give regarding risk?

Reassurance

- **Most women who have a relative with breast cancer are not at a substantially increased risk of breast cancer themselves.**
- **Most women do not develop breast cancer,** and of those who do, most will not have a known family history of the disease.
- **Most women with a family history of breast cancer do not develop breast cancer** and are not in a high-risk category.

[McIntosh et al, 2004]

Alcohol consumption

- **Alcohol consumption increases the risk of breast cancer slightly (III).**
- **There is an increase of 1.071 in relative risk for each additional 10 g per day intake of alcohol (III).**
- There is no good evidence to suggest that the risk is any different for women with a family history compared with women as a whole (III).

Breastfeeding

- **Breastfeeding confers a small protective effect on the risk of breast cancer (III).**
- **The reduction in breast-cancer risk** is related to the total duration of breastfeeding. Each 12 months of breastfeeding confers a reduction of about 4% (III). The protection is in addition to the protective effect of pregnancy alone (III). The risk reduction is similar for women with a family history of breast cancer (III).
- **Advise women to breastfeed if possible,** because this is likely to reduce their risk of breast cancer and is in accordance with general health advice (C).

Hormonal contraceptives

- **The use of combined oral contraceptives (COCs) slightly increases the risk of breast cancer (III).**
- **The increase in risk seems to be confined to current and recent use** (within 5–10 years, relative risk 1.24 for current users).
- **In women with a positive family history, the relative risk of developing breast cancer is the same as that found in the general population (III).** Women under 35 years should be given general health advice on the use of the pill. Women over 35 years should be informed that their absolute risk increases with age.
- **BRCA1 mutation.** For women who are known to carry the BRCA mutation, taking the COC may increase the risk of breast cancer further. Evidence is from one case-control study only, and should be balanced against the

lifetime protection against ovarian-cancer risk from taking the COC (C).

Progestogen-only pill. There is no evidence regarding the risk associated with family history (III).

(For further information, see PRODIGY guidance on *Contraception*.)

Hormone replacement therapy

Hormone replacement therapy (HRT) is associated with an increase in breast cancer risk (III). The risk seems to be two-fold for women taking combined HRT for 10 years or more, but is small for short-duration use (up to 2 years) (III).

The risk associated with HRT disappears 5 years after stopping treatment (III).

Family history of breast cancer:

- Inform women who are considering taking or already taking HRT of the increase in breast-cancer risk with the type and duration of treatment (C). The relative risk is the same as that found in the general population (III).
- Keep the dose as low as possible for as short a time as possible. Prescribe oestrogen-only HRT where possible (D).

Early menopause (natural or artificial): inform women of the risks and benefits of HRT. Generally, HRT usage should be confined to women younger than age 50 years if they are at moderate or high risk (D).

(For further information, see PRODIGY guidance on *Menopause*.)

[McIntosh et al, 2004]

Physical activity

Moderate physical exercise is associated with a decreased risk in breast cancer in the general population (III). Advise women that there are potential benefits of this (C).

Reproductive factors

Early menarche (under 12 years) and older age at first birth are associated with an increased risk of breast cancer (III).

Increased parity is usually associated with an decreased risk of breast cancer (38% decrease in risk in women with five or more live births, and 32% decreased risk in women who reported three or more births compared with women who reported one birth) (III).

A family history of breast cancer does not alter these risks (III).

[McIntosh et al, 2004]

Smoking

There is no good evidence for an association between smoking and breast cancer (1V). Women should be advised not to smoke, in line with current health advice (D).

Weight

A high Body Mass Index is associated with a clinically significant increase in postmenopausal breast cancer risk in the general population (III). Advise women that being overweight probably increases the postmenopausal risk of breast cancer (C).

What should I do with those I don't refer?

Risk reduction

- **Give advice and reassurance on risk and risk-reduction** (See *What advice can I give regarding risk?*).
- **Recommend breast-awareness and self-examination** to all women, particularly those considered to be at high to moderate risk.
- **Encourage attendance at the local breast-screening programme** for those aged 50 years and over.

Follow-up

- Inform the woman that her risk may change with changes in her family history, and that she should then return to have her risk reassessed.
- Refer a woman aged 40 years and under when she reaches the age of 40 years if she has:
  - One first-degree relative diagnosed under 40 years
  - One first-degree and one second-degree relative diagnosed after an average age of 50 years
  - Two first-degree relatives diagnosed after an average age of 50 years

[McIntosh et al, 2004]

What is likely to happen in secondary care?

- A more detailed family history, including a history of breast cancer in third-degree relatives, should be taken where appropriate and possible.
- Tools such as family-history questionnaires and computer packages that can aid the accurate collection of family-history information and risk assessment may be used.
- All women satisfying referral criteria to secondary care (i.e. who have a moderate to high risk of developing breast cancer) will be offered mammographic surveillance from age 40 years.

Women who should be referred to a specialist genetics service for a formal risk assessment

It is recommended that women satisfying referral criteria for tertiary care (i.e. regarded as at high risk of developing breast cancer) should be referred to genetic services. These criteria will include the following:

- If the woman has at least the following female breast cancers in the family:
  - Two first- or second-degree relatives diagnosed at younger than an average age of 50 years (at least one must be a first-degree relative), or
  - Three first- or second-degree relatives diagnosed before an average age of 60 years (at least one must be a first-degree relative), or
  - Four relatives diagnosed at any age (at least one must be a first-degree relative)
- Families containing one relative diagnosed with ovarian cancer at any age and on the same side of the family if there is:
  - One first-degree relative (including the relative with ovarian cancer) or one second-degree relative diagnosed with breast cancer at younger than age 50 years, or
  - Two first-degree or second-degree relatives diagnosed with breast cancer at younger than an average age of 60 years, or
  - Another ovarian cancer at any age
- Families containing bilateral breast cancer (each breast's cancer has the same risk-count as one relative):
  - One first-degree relative with cancer diagnosed in both breasts at younger than an average age 50 years, or
  - One first- or second-degree relative diagnosed with bilateral breast cancer *plus* one first- or second-degree relative diagnosed with breast cancer before an average age of 60 years
  - Families containing male breast cancer at any age with, on the same side of the family, at least:
    - One first- or second-degree relative diagnosed with breast cancer at younger than age 50 years, or

  - Two first- or second-degree relatives diagnosed with breast cancer at younger than an average age of 60 years
- **A formal risk assessment has given risk estimates of:**
  - A 20% or greater chance of a gene mutation being harboured in the family, or
  - A greater than 8% risk of developing breast cancer in the next 10 years, or
  - A 30% or greater lifetime risk of developing breast cancer

Women classified as moderate risk who have any of the following may also need referral to tertiary care, and advice should be sought:

- Jewish ancestry
- A strong paternal history of breast cancer (four relatives diagnosed at younger than 60 years of age on the father's side of the family)
- Any unusual cancers in the family:
  - Bilateral breast cancer
  - Male breast cancer
  - Ovarian cancer
  - Sarcoma in a relative younger than age 45 years
  - Glioma or childhood adrenal cortical carcinoma
  - Complicated patterns of multiple cancers at a young age

[NICE, 2004]

What is likely to happen in tertiary care?

- A woman at high risk of breast cancer (i.e. meeting the criteria for a referral to tertiary care) should be offered genetic counselling.
- She should be forewarned that referral to a genetics service may involve the investigation of other relatives with breast cancer, including the histological diagnosis.
- She should receive standardised information beforehand detailing the process of genetic counselling, and brief educational material about familial breast cancer and genetic testing.
- She will be offered an estimate of her personal risk of developing breast cancer. She will, however, be informed about the uncertainties of the estimation regarding the risk of inheriting a predisposing gene, of penetrance, and hence of developing cancer [NICE, 2004].
- After discussion of risks and benefits, she may be offered the following:
  - Mammographic surveillance.
  - Genetic testing. If there is greater than a 20% risk of BRCA1, BRCA2, or TP53 mutation in the family and there is an affected relative available, then genetic testing should be offered after two sessions of pre-test counselling. (The affected relative is always screened initially.)
  - Risk-reducing surgery (prophylactic bilateral mastectomy and/or oophorectomy).

How is genetic testing carried out?

- Genetic testing is appropriate only for a small number of women from high-risk families and is possible only if there is a living relative with the disease who is willing to be tested.
- Genetic testing is a two-stage process and begins with testing a relative with cancer for BRCA1, BRCA2, and TP53.
- If positive, a predictive test (mutation test) is made available to all female blood relatives.
- If negative:
  - The woman who has been tested should be reassured that there is no risk of transmitting the gene fault to her children.
  - The woman who initially presented should be informed that genetic testing on her or any other unaffected family member is likely to be uninformativ and is not recommended.
- The preliminary test in a relative should take no more than 8 weeks. It determines how likely that person is to carry a gene mutation [DH, 2000]. Further investigations are targeted accordingly, and determining the exact nature of a mutation can take up to one year.
- Predictive testing is much quicker (e.g. 1 month [Douglas, Personal Communication, 2004]).

Who should have mammographic surveillance?

- Women aged under 30 years should not have mammographic surveillance.
- Women aged 30–39 years should have mammography a part of an individualised strategy only if they are from families with BRCA1, BRCA2, or TP53 mutations or have an equivalent high risk of breast cancer.
- Women aged 40 years and over who are at moderate ris or greater should have annual surveillance.
- Women aged 50 years and over should have screening every 3 years as part of the NHS breast-screening programme unless they are from families with BRCA1, BRCA2, or TP53 mutations or have an equivalent high risk of cancer, in which case an individualised strategy should be developed.

Efficacy and risks

- Mammographic surveillance for women aged 50–69 years has been shown to reduce mortality for breast cancer in this group (III) [McIntosh et al, 2004].
- Surveillance is less sensitive in younger women, in women with a family history of breast cancer, and in carriers of the BRCA1/2 mutation (III) [Kerlikowske et al, 1996; Kerlikowske et al, 2000; Goffin et al, 2001]. There is no evidence that breast screening reduces mortality in this group of women [McIntosh et al, 2004]
- The risk of radiation-induced breast cancer is small compared with the benefits of breast-cancer detection, and the margin of benefit over risk is sufficient in wome with a family history of breast cancer down to the age o 40 years [Law and Faulkner, 2001; Law, 1997].

Risk-reducing surgery

- Mastectomy and/or oophorectomy reduce the risk of breast cancer in women with a family history of breast cancer or with BRCA1 and BRCA2 mutations, but they are appropriate for only a small proportion of women who are from high-risk families.
- Risk-reducing total mastectomy is associated with fairly high levels of satisfaction and a reduction in both anxiet and psychological morbidity. It will not prevent the development of all breast cancers. There is inconsistent evidence about psychosocial outcomes after oophorectomy [McIntosh et al, 2004].
- Any woman considering risk-reducing surgery should have access to a support group and be able to discuss reconstruction options, the effects and management of early menopause (if she is having an oophorectomy), an possible psychosocial and sexual consequences of surgery.
- If risk-reducing surgery is being considered and no mutation has been identified, then seek confirmation of family history through medical records, cancer registry, or death certificates. When it is impossible to verify the family history, seek agreement from a multidisciplinary before proceeding.

[McIntosh et al, 2004]

References

HS staff in England can link, free of charge, from eferences to full text journals by clicking on [Full text] on e PRODIGY website.

. Claus, E.B., Risch, N. and Thompson, W.D. (1994) Autosomal dominant inheritance of early-onset breast cancer. Implications for risk prediction. *Cancer* 73(3), 643–651.

. Collaborative Group on Hormonal Factors in Breast Cancer (2001) Familial breast cancer: collaborative reanalysis of individual data from 52 epidemiological studies including 58209 women with breast cancer and 101986 women without the disease. *Lancet* **358**(9291), 1389–1399. [Full text]

. DH (2000) *Interim advice to GPs on familial breast cancer.* Department of Health. www.dh.gov.uk [Accessed: 15/07/2004]. [Full text]

. Douglas, F. (2004) *Personal communication. How is genetic testing carried out?* Honorary Lecturer, Institute of Human Genetics, University of Newcastle upon Tyne: Newcastle upon Tyne.

. Emery, J., Lucassen, A. and Murphy, M. (2001) Common hereditary cancers and implications for primary care. *Lancet* **358**(9275), 56–63. [Full text]

. Ford, D., Easton, D.F., Stratton, M. et al (1998) Genetic heterogeneity and penetrance analysis of the BRCA1 and BRCA2 genes in breast cancer families. *American Journal of Human Genetics* **62**(3), 676–689.

. Goffin, J., Chappuis, P.O., Wong, N. and Foulkes, W.D. (2001) Magnetic resonance imaging and mammography in women with a hereditary risk of breast cancer. *Journal of the National Cancer Institute* **93**(22), 1754–1755. [Full text]

. Hill, A.D., Doyle, J.M., McDermott, E.W. and O'Higgins, N.J. (1997) Hereditary breast cancer. *British Journal of Surgery* **84**(10), 1334–1339.

. Kerlikowske, K., Grady, D., Barclay, J. et al (1996) Effect of age, breast density, and family history on the sensitivity of first screening mammography. *Journal of the American Medical Association* **276**(1), 33–38. [Full text]

0. Kerlikowske, K., Carney, P.A.P., Geller, B. et al (2000) Performance of screening mammography among women with and without a first-degree relative with breast cancer. *Annals of Internal Medicine* **133**(11), 855–863.

1. Law, J. (1997) Cancers detected and induced in mammographic screening: new screening schedules and younger women with family history. *British Journal of Radiology* **70**(829), 62–69.

2. Law, J. and Faulkner, K. (2001) Cancers detected and induced, and associated risk and benefit, in a breast screening programme. *British Journal of Radiology* **74**(888), 1121–1127.

13. McIntosh, A., Shaw, C., Evans, G. et al (2004) *Clinical guidelines and evidence review for the classification and care of women at risk of familial breast cancer.* National Collaborating Centre for Primary Care, University of Sheffield. www.nice.org.uk [Accessed: 18/08/2004].

14. McPherson, K., Steel, C.M. and Dixon, J.M. (2000) ABC of breast diseases: breast cancer – epidemiology, risk factors, and genetics. *British Medical Journal* **321**(7261), 624–628. [Full text]

15. NICE (2004) *Familial breast cancer. The classification and care of women at risk of familial breast cancer in primary, secondary and tertiary care.* Clinical guideline 14. National Institute for Clinical Excellence. www.nice.org.uk [Accessed: 18/08/2004]. [Full text]

16. Office for National Statistics (2001) *Cancer trends in England and Wales 1950–1999: studies on medical and population studies no. 66.* The Stationery Office. www.statistics.gov.uk [Accessed: 15/07/2004].

Evidence grading

Evidence grading is from the NICE Guideline *Familial breast cancer: The classification and care of women at risk of familial breast cancer in primary, secondary and tertiary care* [NICE, 2004]. The grades of recommendation used in that guideline are defined as follows:

Recommendation grade	Evidence
A	Directly based on category-I evidence
B	Directly based on: Category-II evidence, or Extrapolated recommendation from category-I evidence
C	Directly based on: Category-III evidence, or Extrapolated recommendation from category-I or -II evidence
D	Directly based on: Category-IV evidence, or Extrapolated recommendation from category-I, -II, or -III evidence

Evidence category	Source
I	Evidence from: Meta-analysis of randomised controlled trials, or At least one randomised controlled trial
II	Evidence from: At least one controlled study without randomisation, or At least one other type of quasi-experimental study
III	Evidence from non-experimental descriptive studies, such as comparative studies, correlation studies, or case–control studies
IV	Evidence from expert committee reports or opinions and/or clinical experience of respected authorities

PRODIGY GUIDANCE

Burns and scalds

Last revised in September 2004
www.prodigy.nhs.uk/guidance.asp?gt=Burns and scalds

Applies to people of all ages

This guidance covers the management of minor heat burns (including sunburn) and scalds.

This guidance does not cover in any detail the management of chemical or electrical burns.

Goals

- To relieve symptoms
- To prevent complications (e.g. infection, scarring)
- To prevent tetanus
- To identify potential cases of non-accidental injury

Contents

Scenarios
- Minor burns and scalds p.256

Extended Information, p. 259

Minor burns and scalds

Which therapy?

- **Minor burns can usually be safely managed in primary care.** If in doubt refer for expert assessment.
- **Minor burns are commonly defined as:**
  - Simple erythema or superficial burns on any part of the body
  - Total body surface area of less than 5% superficial partial thickness in a fit individual aged between 5 and 60 years
- **Non-accidental injury** should always be considered.
- **Wound management:** clean the burn with 0.9% sodium chloride or tap water and give advice on keeping the burn clean.
- **Cover the wound with a dressing;** if the wound is heavily exuding, reinforce the primary dressing with several layers of absorbent, lint-free dressing to prevent 'strike-through' of exudate.
- **Blisters:** there is controversy over whether to leave blisters intact. Small thick-walled blisters are often left intact; large confluent or thin-walled blisters are usually drained and de-roofed.
- **Pain relief:** paracetamol or ibuprofen is usually adequate. Codeine may occasionally be required for more severe pain.
- **Preventing infection:** prophylactic antibiotics are not indicated for superficial burns. If the burn is clinically infected, give oral antibiotics according to cultures.
- **Check tetanus immunization status** and give tetanus vaccination or immunoglobulin as appropriate (see section *Tetanus prophylaxis*).

Practical prescribing points

For further information please see the *Medicines Compendium* (www.medicines.org.uk) or the *British National Formulary* (www.bnf.org).

- **Ibuprofen:** may cause gastrointestinal irritation and occasionally gastrointestinal haemorrhage. Avoid if there is a history of peptic ulceration. May worsen asthma, hypertension, renal impairment, or cardiac failure.

Follow-up advice

- **Review at 24–48 hours,** to reassess the condition of the burn and advise whether any further wound management is necessary (this may best be done by the practice or district nurse).
- **As the burn heals** the use of an emollient may soothe and ease itching.

Should I refer or investigate?

Refer?

Local facilities may differ and local guidelines should be consulted.

- **Immediate referral to local burn centre or burn unit** is recommended for people with:
  - Burns (with dermal or full-thickness loss) covering more than 5% TBSA (children) or 10% TBSA (adults)
  - Burns (with dermal or full-thickness loss) to the face, hands, feet, perineum, or any flexure (particularly the neck or axilla).
  - Circumferential dermal or full-thickness burns of the limbs, torso, or neck.
  - Any significant infection, septic episode, or suggestion of toxic-shock-like illness.
  - Any significant inhalation injury.
  - Any electrical burn injury.
  - Chemical burn injury (>5% TBSA).
  - Suspicion of non-accidental injury (see section *Non-accidental injury*).
- In addition to the above the following are more likely to be associated with a complex clinical course and referral should be considered seriously:
  - Children under 5 years or adults over 60 years.
  - People who have coexisting medical problems, e.g. cardiac, respiratory, or hepatic disease or diabetes, or people who are immunosuppressed or who are pregnant.
  - Burns associated with other injuries, e.g. crush injuries, fractures, head injury, penetrating injury.
- **Non-acute referral to a local plastic surgery unit** should be considered for:
  - Any wound that has not healed 14 days after injury
  - Any healed wound where scarring suggests there may be:
    - A significant aesthetic impact and/or psychological disturbance
    - The need to consider skin camouflage
    - Functional limitation
    - The need to consider pressure therapy, scar modification, or surgical reconstruction
- **If in doubt** it is always best to refer for expert assessment.

Patient information leaflets

The following PILs are available at www.prodigy.nhs.uk
- Burns and Scalds
- Tetanus Immunisation

Shared decision making

Most small burns will heal by themselves. Small burns can be left uncovered, but if it will be difficult to keep clean, a dressing may be best.
How did this burn happen? Can any changes be made to prevent this from happening again?
Painkillers such as paracetamol or ibuprofen will usually relieve pain. Codeine can be added if needed.
Are you up-to-date with tetanus immunizations?
For future burns:
- Cool the burn immediately with cool running water for 20 minutes.
- Remove rings, bracelets, watches, etc, from the affected area.
- Before going to hospital or to a doctor's surgery, cover the burn with cling film or a clean plastic bag. Apply cling film in layers rather than round like a bandage.

Drug rationale

Drugs not included

Oral and topical antibacterials are not offered. Prophylactic antibiotics are not necessary for minor burns [Mertens et al, 1997].
Paraffin gauze dressing may stick to the burn, and the paraffin can reduce the absorbency of the dressing [BNF 47, 2004].

Drugs included

Paracetamol is included for simple analgesia.
Ibuprofen is included as an alternative to paracetamol.
Codeine is included for the treatment of more severe pain.
Vapour-permeable adhesive films are suitable for wounds with a light exudate [DTB, 1991]. They are transparent, so the wound can be inspected without removing the dressing. A range of sizes is offered.
Simple low-adherent dressings, such as absorbent perforated plastic film-faced dressings, are suitable for dry wounds or wounds with a light exudate [DTB, 1991].
Gauze and cotton tissue BP should be used as an absorbent, protective pad on top of the low-adherent layer to prevent 'strike-through' of exudate if the wound is exuding heavily.
When tetanus vaccination is indicated (see section *Tetanus prophylaxis*) [DH, 2004]:
- Children aged under 10 years: DTaP/IPV/Hib (combined diphtheria, tetanus, acellular pertussis, inactivated poliomyelitis, and *Haemophilus influenzae* type b vaccine) is recommended for primary immunization. dTaP/IPV (combined low-dose diphtheria, tetanus, acellular pertussis, and inactivated poliomyelitis vaccine) is recommended for booster doses.
- People aged 10 years or over: Td/IPV (combined low-dose diphtheria, tetanus, and inactivated poliomyelitis vaccine) is recommended for both primary immunizations and booster doses.

Prescriptions

Analgesia: use when required

Paracetamol s/f susp: 60mg to 120mg up to four times a day
- Age from 3 to 11 months
- Paracetamol 120mg/5ml s/f susp. Take 2.5ml to 5ml every 4 to 6 hours when required for pain relief. Maximum of 4 doses in 24 hours; supply 150 ml; NHS Cost £0.65; OTC Cost £1.14.

Paracetamol s/f susp: 120mg to 240mg up to four times a day
- Age from 12 months to 5 years
- Paracetamol 120mg/5ml s/f susp. Take one to two 5ml spoonfuls every 4 to 6 hours when required for pain relief. Maximum of 4 doses in 24 hours; supply 300 ml; NHS Cost £1.30; OTC Cost £2.28.

Paracetamol s/f susp: 250mg to 500mg up to four times a day
- Age from 6 to 11 years
- Paracetamol 250mg/5ml s/f susp. Take one to two 5ml spoonfuls every 4 to 6 hours when required for pain relief. Maximum of 4 doses in 24 hours; supply 300 ml; NHS Cost £1.70; OTC Cost £2.99.

Paracetamol tablets: 500mg to 1g up to four times a day
- Age from 12 to 15 years
- Paracetamol 500mg tablets. Take one to two tablets every 4 to 6 hours when required for pain relief. Maximum of 8 tablets in 24 hours; supply 100 tablets; NHS Cost £0.75; OTC Cost £1.32.

Paracetamol tablets: 1g up to four times a day
- Age from 16 years onwards
- Paracetamol 500mg tablets. Take two tablets every 4 to 6 hours when required for pain relief. Maximum of 8 tablets in 24 hours; supply 100 tablets; NHS Cost £0.75; OTC Cost £1.32.

Ibuprofen s/f susp: 50mg three to four times a day
- Age from 12 months to 2 years
- Ibuprofen 100mg/5ml s/f susp. Take 2.5ml three to four times a day when required for pain relief. Do not exceed the stated dose; supply 100 ml; NHS Cost £1.82; OTC Cost £3.21.

Ibuprofen s/f susp: 100mg three to four times a day
- Age from 3 to 7 years
- Ibuprofen 100mg/5ml s/f susp. Take one 5ml spoonful 3 to 4 times a day when required for pain relief. Do not exceed the stated dose; supply 150 ml; NHS Cost £2.73; OTC Cost £4.81.

Ibuprofen s/f susp: 200mg three to four times a day
- Age from 8 to 11 years
- Ibuprofen 100mg/5ml s/f susp. Take two 5ml spoonfuls 3 to 4 times a day when required for pain relief. Do not exceed the stated dose; supply 300 ml; NHS Cost £5.46; OTC Cost £9.62.

Ibuprofen tablets: 400mg three times a day
- Age from 12 years onwards
- Ibuprofen 400mg tablets. Take one tablet three times a day when required for pain relief. Do not exceed the stated dose; supply 24 tablets; NHS Cost £0.70; OTC Cost £1.23.

Codeine 30mg tablets: add on to paracetamol if required
- Age from 16 years onwards
- Codeine 30mg tablets. Take one to two tablets every 4 to 6 hours when required for pain relief. Maximum of 8 tablets in 24 hours; supply 56 tablets; NHS Cost £2.90.

Paracetamol 500mg tablets + codeine 30mg tablets
- Age from 16 years onwards
- Paracetamol 500mg tablets. Take two tablets every 4 to 6 hours when required for pain relief. Maximum of 8 tablets in 24 hours; supply 100 tablets; NHS Cost £0.75; OTC Cost £1.32.
- Codeine 30mg tablets. Take one to two tablets every 4 to 6 hours when required for pain relief. Maximum of 8 tablets in 24 hours; supply 56 tablets; NHS Cost £2.90.

Vapour permeable dressings (small)

5cm x 8cm Blisterfilm dressing
- All ages
- Blisterfilm 5cm x 8cm dressing. Apply to the affected area as directed; supply 5 single dressings; NHS Cost £2.00; OTC Cost £3.53.

6cm x 7cm C-view dressing
- All ages
- C-view 6cm x 7cm dressing. Apply to the affected area as directed; supply 5 single dressings; NHS Cost £1.85; OTC Cost £3.26.

6cm x 9cm Hydrofilm dressing
- All ages
- Hydrofilm 6cm x 9cm dressing. Apply to the affected area as directed; supply 5 single dressings; NHS Cost £2.45; OTC Cost £4.32.

6cm x 7cm Mefilm dressing
- All ages
- Mefilm 6cm x 7cm dressing. Apply to the affected area as directed; supply 5 single dressings; NHS Cost £2.00; OTC Cost £3.53.

6cm x 7cm OpSite Flexigrid dressing
- All ages
- OpSite Flexigrid 6cm x 7cm. Apply to the affected area as directed; supply 5 single dressings; NHS Cost £1.70; OTC Cost £3.00.

5cm x 7cm Polyskin II dressing
- All ages
- Polyskin II 5cm x 7cm dressing. Apply to the affected area as directed; supply 5 single dressings; NHS Cost £1.90; OTC Cost £3.35.

5cm x 7cm Polyskin MR dressing
- All ages
- Polyskin MR 5cm x 7cm dressing. Apply to the affected area as directed; supply 5 single dressings; NHS Cost £2.00; OTC Cost £3.53.

6cm x 7cm Tegaderm dressing
- All ages
- Tegaderm HP 9534 6cmx7cm dressing. Apply to the affected area as directed; supply 5 single dressings; NHS Cost £1.90; OTC Cost £3.35.

Vapour permeable dressings (medium)

10.2cm x 12.7cm Bioclusive dressings
- All ages
- Bioclusive 10.2cm x 12.7cm. Apply to the affected area as directed; supply 5 single dressings; NHS Cost £7.15; OTC Cost £12.60.

10cm x 13cm Blisterfilm dressing
- All ages
- Blisterfilm 10cm x 13cm dressing. Apply to the affected area as directed; supply 5 single dressings; NHS Cost £4.50; OTC Cost £7.93.

10cm x 12cm C-view dressing
- All ages
- C-view 10cm x 12cm dressing. Apply to the affected area as directed; supply 5 single dressings; NHS Cost £5.10; OTC Cost £8.99.

10cm x 15cm Hydrofilm dressing
- All ages
- Hydrofilm 10cm x 15cm dressing. Apply to the affected area as directed; supply 5 single dressings; NHS Cost £6.45; OTC Cost £11.37.

10cm x 12cm Mefilm dressing
- All ages
- Mefilm 10cm x 12cm dressing. Apply to the affected area as directed; supply 5 single dressings; NHS Cost £5.30; OTC Cost £9.34.

12cm x 12cm Opsite Flexigrid dressing
- All ages
- OpSite Flexigrid 12cm x 12cm. Apply to the affected area as directed; supply 5 single dressings; NHS Cost £4.80; OTC Cost £8.46.

10cm x 12cm Polyskin II dressing
- All ages
- Polyskin II 10cm x 12cm dressing. Apply to the affected area as directed; supply 5 single dressings; NHS Cost £4.95; OTC Cost £8.72.

10cm x 12cm Polyskin MR dressing
- All ages
- Polyskin MR 10cm x 12cm dressing. Apply to the affected area as directed; supply 5 single dressings; NHS Cost £5.40; OTC Cost £9.52.

12cm x 12cm Tegaderm dressing
- All ages
- Tegaderm 12cm x 12cm dressing. Apply to the affected area as directed; supply 5 single dressings; NHS Cost £6.15; OTC Cost £10.85.

Low adherence dressings (all sizes) + tape

5cm x 5cm Absorbent perforated plastic film faced dressing
- All ages
- Perforated FA 5x5cm dressing. Apply to the affected area as directed; supply 5 single dressings; NHS Cost £0.45; OTC Cost £0.80.

10cm x 10cm Absorbent perforated plastic film faced dressing
- All ages
- Perforated FA 10x10cm dressing. Apply to the affected area as directed; supply 5 single dressings; NHS Cost £0.75; OTC Cost £1.32.

20cm x 10cm Absorbent perforated plastic film faced dressing
- All ages
- Perforated FA 10x20cm dressing. Apply to the affected area as directed; supply 5 single dressings; NHS Cost £1.60; OTC Cost £2.82.

5cm x 7cm Mepitel silicone dressing
- All ages
- Mepitel 5cm x 7cm dressing. Apply to the affected area as directed; supply 2 single dressings; NHS Cost £3.08; OTC Cost £5.42.

8cm x 10cm Mepitel silicone dressing
- All ages
- Mepitel 8cm x 10cm dressing. Apply to the affected are as directed; supply 2 single dressings; NHS Cost £5.40; OTC Cost £9.51.

Gauze and cotton tissue BP 500g (secondary dressing)
- All ages
- Gauze & cotton tissue BP 500g. Apply several layers over the primary dressing to prevent strike through of exudate; supply 1 500g; NHS Cost £6.24.

Permeable non-woven synthetic adhesive tape
- All ages
- Perm non-wvn tape 1.25cmx5m. Apply as required; supply 1 5metre roll; NHS Cost £0.39; OTC Cost £0.6

Tetanus prophylaxis

Primary course: diphtheria+tetanus+pertussis+polio+Hib
- Age from 2 months to 9 years
- Pediacel injection. Give 0.5ml by intramuscular injection. For primary immunization, give three doses at intervals of 1 month between doses; supply 1 0.5ml vial.

Booster: low-dose diphtheria+tetanus+pertussis+polio
- Age from 3 to 9 years
- Repevax injection. Give 0.5ml by intramuscular injection; supply 1 0.5ml prefilled syringe.

Primary course: low-dose diphtheria+tetanus+polio
- Age from 10 years onwards
- Revaxis injection. Give 0.5ml by intramuscular injection. For primary immunization, give three doses at intervals of 1 month between doses; supply 1 0.5ml prefilled syringe.

Booster: low-dose diphtheria+tetanus+polio
- Age from 10 years onwards
- Revaxis injection. Give 0.5ml by intramuscular injection; supply 1 0.5ml prefilled syringe.

Extended Information

Background information

- What is it? p.259
- How common is it? p.259
- What else might it be? p.259
- Complications and prognosis p.259

What is it?

- **A burn** is usually a heat injury to the skin.
  - Burns are most commonly caused by exposure to flames, hot objects, chemicals, or radiation (e.g. sunburn) [Mertens et al, 1997].
  - Electrical burns are less common, but are potentially more serious, as the depth of the burn is usually greater than is apparent, and cardiac damage may occur [Atkinson, 1998].
- **A scald** is a heat injury caused by hot liquid or steam.

How common is it?

- **Burns are common;** most are minor and will be treated at home, without the need for medical intervention.
- In the UK it is estimated that about 250,000 people each year present to primary care teams with burn injuries.
- A further 175,000 people are estimated to visit accident and emergency departments each year as a result of burns or scalds. Of these around 13,000 are admitted to hospital or specialized burns units. Each year over 200 people die as a result of these injuries.
- **Children under 5 years old account for nearly 45%** of all severe burns and scalds. About 50% of these accidents happen in the kitchen, with scalds from hot liquids being the most frequent type of burn injury seen in children.
- **Hot drinks** are involved in about 1265 severe burns a year requiring admission to hospital, of which 1100 occur in children less than 5 years of age. Most involve the child reaching up and pulling a mug or cup of hot drink onto himself or herself.
- **Hot baths** are involved in over 570 severe burns a year. Most involve an unsupervised child falling or climbing into a bath of very hot water.
- **Other common causes** of severe burns and scalds include kettles, teapots and coffee-pots, jugs of hot water, saucepans, irons, cookers, fires and heaters, chip pans, and deep fat fryers.

[DTI, 1999; National Burn Care Review Committee, 2001]

What else might it be?

- **Non-accidental injury**
- **Blistering skin disease,** e.g. Stevens-Johnson syndrome
- **Skin infection,** e.g. cellulitis
- **Skin necrosis,** e.g. caused by pressure

Complications and prognosis

B

Complications

- **Respiratory distress** from smoke inhalation or a circumferential chest burn. Smoke inhalation can cause bronchospasm and pulmonary and laryngeal oedema. A seemingly well patient may deteriorate later. Suspect airway problems due to thermal or chemical damage if the person has singed nasal hairs, a sore throat, a hoarse voice, stridor, or wheeze.
- **Fluid loss.**
- **Infection and possible septicaemia.**
- **Vascular insufficiency and distal ischaemia** from a circumferential burn of limb or digit.
- **Muscle damage** from an electrical burn may be severe even with minimal skin injury, and rhabdomyolysis may cause renal failure.
- **Poisoning from inhalation of noxious gases** released by burning (e.g. cyanide poisoning due to smouldering plastics) may cause dizziness, headaches, and seizures.
- **Scarring** and possible psychosocial consequences.
- **Death** may result from severe extensive burns or electric shock.

[Vale et al, 1996; Harrington and Jordan, 1997; Saffle, 1998; Simon et al, 2002]

Management issues

- First aid for burns and scalds p.259
- How do I assess a burn? p.260
- Who should I refer? p.260
- Management of minor burns and scalds p.260
- Tetanus prophylaxis p.261
- Non-accidental injury p.261

First aid for burns and scalds

- The following first-aid measures are advised immediately following a burn or scald:
  - **Remove the person from the source of heat** (turn off the electricity in the case of an electrical burn).
  - **Immediately apply cool (preferably running) water for at least 20 minutes,** taking care not to induce hypothermia. Note: very cold water or ice should not be used as it may cause local vasoconstriction, deepening tissue injury, and it also increases the risk of hypothermia [McCormack et al, 2003].
  - **Do not attempt to neutralize chemical burns** as this can exacerbate the injury by producing heat [Simon et al, 2002].
  - **Do not attempt to remove clothing** if it is stuck or if burns are extensive.
  - **Wrap the area in cling film or a clean plastic bag** and leave it on until the person is either seen at the hospital or in general practice. This helps minimize pain from exposure to air, prevents excess evaporation, and keeps the wound clean. Cling film should be applied in layers rather than circumferentially like a bandage, to prevent any tourniquet effect if tissue oedema develops [Flanagan et al, 1994; Fowler, 1998; Khot and Polmear, 2003].

[Mertens et al, 1997; Dowsett, 2002]

How do I assess a burn?

- **Establish the cause of the burn and how it occurred.** The cause of the burn (e.g. scald or electrical) may indicate the likely severity. A description of how the burn occurred may indicate ways to avoid future injury, identify unrecognized illness (e.g. the burn may have occurred because of a faint, a seizure, or alcohol intoxication), or alert to the possibility of non-accidental injury.
- **Assessing the extent and depth of the burn** provides important information on the severity, the potential risk of complications, the rate of healing, the amount of scarring that can be expected, and the need for specialist care. Note: a burn is rarely uniform; a mixed pattern of burn is usually found.

Extent of burn

- **The extent of the burn** is usually expressed as a percentage of total body surface area (TBSA), which is calculated and documented on specific charts.
- **In adults, the 'Rule of Nines' is commonly used** (areas of slight redness or simple erythema should be ignored): 9% of TBSA for the head, 9% for each arm, 18% for each leg, 18% for either the back or the front of the trunk, and 1% for the genitalia and perineal area. This method should not be used when assessing children less than 16 years.
- **The Lund and Browder chart,** if available, is a more reliable method of assessing the extent of the burn in children as it takes into account the different relative body proportions of children. This method can also be used in adults.
- A cruder method is to use the palmar surface of the person's extended hand, with fingers closed, as approximately 1% of TBSA. This is useful to estimate the extent of small or patchy burns over multiple surfaces, or in early assessment at the scene of an accident.

[Mertens et al, 1997; Fowler, 1998; Taylor, 2001; Dowsett, 2002]

Depth of burn

- **Assessment of the depth of the burn** can often be made clinically, although this may be difficult, especially for burns of intermediate depth. Classification of burn depth is based on observation and examination of the person, cause of the burn, history of the burn, and first-aid treatment used [Dowsett, 2002].
- **Epidermal (superficial) burns** (e.g. sunburn or minor scalds) involve only the epidermis. The skin is dry and intact, usually erythematous, painful, and does not blister. Epidermal burns heal well within a few days with no scarring.
- **Superficial dermal (partial-thickness) burns** involve the epidermis and the superficial part of the dermis. They present as painful, red, blistered areas, which become moist as the blisters burst. They heal within 10–21 days if there is no infection, pressure, or trauma within or on the wound.
- **Deep dermal (partial-thickness) burns** involve deeper layers of the dermis. They present as pale or red areas, which may be painful or relatively anaesthetic. There is usually less blistering than with superficial partial-thickness burns. Healing takes 3–6 weeks, and occurs with variable degrees of scarring, depending on the depth of the burn.
- **Subdermal (full-thickness) burns** destroy the entire dermis. They result in a painless, dry, leathery, white or charred wound, which heals by contraction and scarring usually requiring skin grafting.

[Ward and Saffle, 1995; Phipps, 1998]

Who should I refer?

- **Minor burns and scalds can usually be managed safely in primary care.** Minor burns are commonly defined as:
  - Simple erythema or superficial burns on any part of the body.
  - Superficial partial-thickness burns in a fit individual aged between 5 and 60 years where the TBSA is less than 5%.
- **Social circumstances** should always be taken into account in a decision to treat at home.
- **More severe burns** require assessment in the local accident and emergency department or local burns facility (see below).

[Fowler, 1998]

The following guidelines have been produced by the National Burn Care Review Committee. Local facilities may differ and local guidelines should be consulted.

- **Immediate referral to local burn centre or burn unit** is recommended for people with complex burn injuries (i.e. a burn injury associated with any of the following criteria):
  - Burns (with dermal or full-thickness loss) covering more than 5% TBSA (children) or 10% TBSA (adults) (Note: burns covering more than 10% TBSA in children and 15% TBSA in adults will require immediate fluid replacement.)
  - Burns (with dermal or full-thickness loss) to the face, hands, feet, perineum, or any flexure (particularly the neck or axilla).
  - Circumferential dermal or full-thickness burns of the limbs, torso, or neck.
  - Any significant infection, septic episode, or suggestion of toxic-shock-like illness.
  - Any significant inhalation injury.
  - Any electrical burn injury.
  - Chemical burn injury (>5% TBSA).
  - Suspicion of non-accidental injury (see section on *Non-accidental injury*).
- In addition to the above the following are more likely to be associated with a complex clinical course and referral should be considered seriously:
  - Children under 5 years or adults over 60 years.
  - People who have coexisting medical problems, e.g. cardiac, respiratory, or hepatic disease or diabetes, or people who are immunosuppressed or who are pregnant.
  - Burns associated with other injuries, e.g. crush injuries, fractures, head injury, penetrating injury.
- **Non-acute referral to a local plastic surgery unit** should be considered for:
  - Any wound that has not healed 14 days after injury
  - Any healed wound where scarring suggests there may be:
    - A significant aesthetic impact and/or psychological disturbance
    - The need to consider skin camouflage
    - Functional limitation
    - The need to consider pressure therapy, scar modification, or surgical reconstruction

[National Burn Care Review Committee, 2001]

Management of minor burns and scalds

- **Cleaning the burn** (and keeping it clean) is probably the most important aspect of wound care and can be done simply by washing with sterile saline, sterile water, or tap water and patting (rather than rubbing) dry, or allowing the wound to air dry [Mertens et al, 1997; Staley and Richard, 1997; Atkinson, 1998].

There is controversy over whether to leave blisters intact or not [Staley and Richard, 1997; Pearson and Wolford, 2000]. There is some evidence that burn blister fluid may impair wound healing. However, there is also some evidence that draining or de-roofing blisters may increase the likelihood of the burn becoming infected [Pearson and Wolford, 2000]. In practice, small or thick-walled blisters are often left intact, whereas large confluent or thin-walled blisters are usually drained.

Prophylactic systemic or topical antimicrobials (e.g. Flamazine) are not indicated for minor burns [Mertens et al, 1997]. Antimicrobials should only be used in minor burns if infection is clinically present.

Cover with a dressing. This helps to keep the wound clean and creates a humid environment to promote healing [Mertens et al, 1997]. The choice of dressing will depend on the depth of the burn, the tissue type (e.g. necrotic), the amount of exudate, and the location of the wound [Dowsett, 2002].

- For heavily exuding wounds, the primary dressing (contact) layer may need to be reinforced with several layers of absorbent, lint-free dressing (e.g. gauze and cotton tissue) to prevent 'strike-through' of exudate with increased risk of infection.
- Dressings need to be securely fixed with a bandage or permeable adhesive tape, to prevent exposure of raw areas with increased risk of infection and delayed wound healing.

Pain relief with paracetamol or ibuprofen is usually adequate [Mertens et al, 1997]. The addition of a weak opioid, such as codeine, may be useful for more severe pain.

Review the person at 24–48 hours, to reassess the condition of the burn and advise whether any further wound management is necessary (this may best be done by the practice or district nurse) [Fowler, 1998].

As the burn heals the use of an emollient may soothe and ease itching [Mertens et al, 1997].

Management of sunburn

There is little evidence regarding best practice for managing sunburn. The following symptomatic measures are often recommended:

- A cool bath or shower
- Moisturizing cream if the skin is not blistered
- Simple analgesia with paracetamol or ibuprofen

Tetanus prophylaxis

Check tetanus immunization status for all burn wounds. A total of five doses of vaccine, administered at the appropriate intervals, is considered to give lifelong immunity (see Table 1).

Note: existing stocks of Td (adsorbed diphtheria [low-dose] and tetanus vaccine) can be used for administration at the time of a tetanus-prone wound if appropriate. However, if the polio, or polio, and diphtheria vaccination needs to be updated at the same time then Td/IPV should be used.

Following a burn, tetanus prophylaxis should be given as follows:

- **Person fully immunized, i.e. has received five doses of vaccine at appropriate intervals:** tetanus booster not needed. Consider giving human tetanus immunoglobulin for tetanus-prone wounds where the risk of infection is especially high, e.g. those contaminated with manure or extensive devitalized tissue.
- **Primary immunization complete, boosters incomplete but up-to-date:** tetanus booster not needed but may be given if booster is due and it is convenient to give now. Consider giving human tetanus immunoglobulin for tetanus-prone wounds where the risk of infection is especially high, e.g. those contaminated with manure or extensive devitalized tissue.
- **Primary immunization incomplete, or boosters not up-to-date:** give tetanus booster and further doses as needed to complete the recommended schedule (note: if the primary course is interrupted it should be resumed but not repeated). Add human tetanus immunoglobulin if it is a tetanus-prone wound (defined as: a puncture wound; a significant degree of devitalized tissue; contaminated with soil or manure; containing foreign bodies; compound fractures; clinical signs of sepsis; wounds or burns sustained more than 6 hours before surgical treatment). *Note:* inject tetanus vaccine and immunoglobulin at different sites.
- **Not immunized or immunization status uncertain:** give an immediate dose of vaccine. Add human tetanus immunoglobulin if it is a tetanus-prone wound (see above). Arrange further doses of tetanus vaccine as needed to complete the recommended five-dose schedule.

[DH, 2004]

Table 1: Immunization schedule for tetanus.

Schedule	Children	Adults and children over 10 years
Primary course	3 doses of vaccine (usually as DTaP/IPV/Hib) at 2, 3, and 4 months of age	3 doses of vaccine (as Td/IPV), each one month apart
Fourth dose	At least 3 years after the last dose of the primary course, usually pre-school entry (as dTaP/IPV)	5–10 years after the last dose of the primary course (as Td/IPV)
Fifth dose	Aged 13–18 years or before leaving school (as Td/IPV)	10 years after fourth dose (as Td/IPV)

DTaP/IPV/Hib = Diphtheria, tetanus, acellular pertussis, inactivated poliomyelitis, and *Haemophilus influenzae* type b vaccine
dTaP/IPV = Low-dose diphtheria, tetanus, acellular pertussis, and inactivated poliomyelitis vaccine
Td/IPV = Low-dose diphtheria, tetanus, and inactivated poliomyelitis vaccine for adults and children over 10 years of age

Non-accidental injury

- **Suspected non-accidental injury in a child or an adult always requires urgent referral.** Consider admission and/or referral to the local social services department according to local policy.
- **Indicators of possible non-accidental injury include:**
  - Child brought for treatment by an unrelated adult
  - Unexplained delay in seeking medical attention
  - History of injury inconsistent with developmental capacity of the child
  - History of injury inconsistent with injury
  - Historical accounts of injury that differ over time
  - Prior history of injury or accidents to child or siblings
  - Scalds with clear-cut immersion lines
  - Scalds with no splash marks
  - Scalds involving perineum, genitalia, and buttocks
  - Mirror image injury of extremities
  - Other physical signs of abuse (e.g. bruises, welts, or fractures)

[Mertens et al, 1997; Dowsett, 2002]

References

NHS staff in England can link, free of charge, from references to full text journals by clicking on [Full text] on the PRODIGY website.

1. Atkinson, A. (1998) Treating minor burns. *Journal of Community Nursing* 12(1), 18–25.
2. BNF 47 (2004) *British National Formulary*. 47th edn. London: British Medical Association and Royal Pharmaceutical Society of Great Britain.
3. DH (2004) *New (August 2004) chapter 30 – tetanus.* Immunisation against infectious disease. Department of Health. www.dh.gov.uk [Accessed: 22/06/2005]. [Full text]
4. Dowsett, C. (2002) The assessment and management of burns. *British Journal of Community Nursing* 7(5), 230–239.
5. DTB (1991) Local applications to wounds – I: cleansers, antibacterials, debriders. *Drug & Therapeutics Bulletin* 29(24), 93–95.
6. DTI (1999) *Home safety: report summary. Burns and scalds accidents in the home.* Department of Trade and Industry. www.dti.gov.uk/homesafetynetwork/bs_rhome.htm [Accessed: 16/03/2004].
7. Flanagan, M., Fletcher, J. and Hollinworth, J. (1994) Cling film as a temporary dressing. *Journal of Wound Care* 3(7), 339.
8. Fowler, A. (1998) Nursing management of minor burn injuries. *Emergency Nurse* 6(6), 31–37.
9. Harrington, D.T. and Jordan, B.S. (1997) Management of the burn wound. *Nursing Clinics of North America* 32(2), 252–273.
10. Khot, A. and Polmear, A. (Eds.) (2003) Surgical problems. In: *Practical general practice: guidelines for effective clinical management.* 4th edn. Edinburgh: Butterworth-Heinemann.
11. McCormack, R.A., La Hei, E.R. and Martin, H.C. (2003) First-aid management of minor burns in children: a prospective study of children presenting to the Children's Hospital at Westmead, Sydney. *Medica Journal of Australia* 178(1), 31–33.
12. Mertens, D.M., Jenkins, M.E. and Warden, G.D. (1997) Outpatient burn management. *Nursing Clinics of North America* 32(2), 343–364.
13. National Burn Care Review Committee (2001) *National burn care review.* British Association of Plastic Surgeons. www.baps.co.uk [Accessed: 23/02/2004].
14. Pearson, A.S. and Wolford, R.W. (2000) Managemen of skin trauma. *Primary Care; Clinics in Office Practice* 27(2), 475–492.
15. Phipps, A. (1998) Evidence based management of patients with burns. *Journal of Wound Care* 7(6), 299–302.
16. Saffle, J.R. (1998) Predicting outcomes of burns. *New England Journal of Medicine* 338(6), 387–388. [Full text]
17. Simon, C., Everitt, H, Birtwistle, J. and Stevenson, B. (Eds.) (2002) Scalds and burns. In: *Oxford handbook of general practice.* Oxford: Oxford University Press.
18. Staley, M. and Richard, R. (1997) Management of the acute burn wound: an overview. *Advances in Wound Care* 10(2), 39–44.
19. Taylor, K. (2001) The management of minor burns an scalds in children. *Nursing Standard* 16(11), 45–51. [Full text]
20. Vale, A.J., Proudfoot, A.T. and Meredith, T.J. (1996) Poisoning by inhalational agents. In: Weatherall, D.J., Ledingham, J.G.G., Warrell, D.A. et al (Eds.) *Oxford textbook of medicine.* 3rd edn. Oxford: Oxford University Press. 1101–1102.
21. Ward, R.S. and Saffle, J.R. (1995) Topical agents in burn and wound care. *Physical Therapy* 75(6), 526–3

PRODIGY GUIDANCE

Candida — female genital

Last revised in July 2004
www.prodigy.nhs.uk/guidance.asp?gt=Candida - female genital

Applies to women over the age of 10 years

This guidance covers the management of genital thrush (vulvovaginal candidiasis) in women.

This guidance does not cover other causes of vaginal discharge and itching.

There is separate PRODIGY guidance for *Pruritus vulvae, Bacterial vaginosis, Chlamydia — genital, Trichomoniasis, Candida — skin and nails*, and *Candida — oral*.

Goals

To cure the symptoms of an isolated event of vulvovaginal candidiasis within 7 days
To cure the symptoms of recurrent vulvovaginal candidiasis, and to prevent or reduce recurrence

Contents

Scenarios

- Uncomplicated vulvovaginal candidiasis p.263
- Treatment failure p.265
- Recurrent vulvovaginal candidiasis (4+ episodes in a year) p.267
- Pregnancy p.268
- Severe vulvovaginal candidiasis p.269

Extended Information, p. 271

Which scenario?

Uncomplicated vulvovaginal candidiasis: covers the management of women presenting with an uncomplicated isolated episode of thrush.
Treatment failure: covers the management of women woman returning with the same isolated episode, as first-line treatment did not work.
Recurrent vulvovaginal candidiasis (4+ episodes in a year): covers the management of women woman suffering from four or more episodes of symptomatic thrush in one year.
Pregnancy: covers the management of women who are pregnant.
Severe vulvovaginal candidiasis: covers the management of women presenting with severe symptoms of vulvovaginal candidiasis, which often does not respond adequately to standard treatment.

Uncomplicated vulvovaginal candidiasis

Which therapy?

Examination is generally recommended at the first presentation but usually unnecessary if a previous episode with similar symptoms was successfully treated. Consider whether investigation to confirm *Candida* infection is appropriate (see *Should I refer or investigate?*).

Treat according to patient preference, as topical and oral products are equally effective:

- **Clotrimazole, econazole, or miconazole** are available as intravaginal creams and pessaries, and are taken as short courses (1–3 days).
- **Fluconazole or itraconazole** are taken as one or two single doses.
- **Topical creams applied to the vulva** should be considered in addition to intravaginal or oral treatment.

Practical prescribing points

For further information see the *Medicines Compendium* (www.medicines.org.uk) or the *British National Formulary* (www.bnf.org).

- Fluconazole and itraconazole are contraindicated in pregnant or breastfeeding women.
- Women who are prescribed a cream in addition to a pessary or oral preparation may be subject to an additional prescription charge.
- Products containing topical imidazoles may damage latex condoms and diaphragms.
- There is anecdotal evidence that oral fluconazole and itraconazole may cause oral contraceptive failure.

Follow-up advice

- Advise the woman to return for follow-up if symptoms have not completely resolved 7–14 days after the start of treatment.

Should I refer or investigate?

Refer?

- Consider referral to a genito-urinary medicine clinic if there is suspicion of a sexually transmitted infection.

Investigate?

- A high vaginal swab to collect discharge from the anterior fornix or lateral wall of the vagina is recommended when:
  - The woman requests diagnostic conformation.
  - Symptoms and/or signs are not typical.
  - Infection is recurrent (defined as four episodes or more in one year).
  - Infection is severe.
  - The woman is pregnant.
  - The woman is immunocompromised, or has uncontrolled diabetes mellitus, or is debilitated.
  - Note: a high vaginal swab is not necessary on a first visit if typical symptoms are present but consider if an examination is undertaken.
- If a sexually transmitted infection is possible, investigations should also include tests for chlamydia and gonorrhoea (but consider referral to a genito-urinary medicine clinic).

C

Patient information leaflets

The following PILs are available at www.prodigy.nhs.uk

- Antifungal Medicines
- Thrush - Vaginal

Shared decision making

- The main treatment options for thrush are:
  - **Pessaries** or **vaginal cream** which you put inside the vagina with an applicator, or
  - **Tablets** taken by mouth. These are just as effective. You only need one or two doses. You should not take these if you are pregnant or breastfeeding.
- **Anti-thrush cream** to rub onto the vulval skin may also help ease itch.
- You can get all these treatments on prescription, or you can buy them.
- Come back if symptoms do not go within 1-2 weeks of starting treatment.

Drug rationale

Drugs not included

- **Nystatin** is not recommended for the treatment of uncomplicated vulvovaginal candidiasis. Trials have shown intravaginal nystatin to be more effective than placebo and as effective as topical imidazoles in the treatment of vulvovaginal thrush [Spence, 2003]. However, it is only available as a 14-day regimen and it stains clothing yellow, making it unsuitable for most women [Working Group of the British Society for Medical Mycology, 1995].
- **Oral ketoconazole** is not indicated in the treatment of uncomplicated vulvovaginal candidiasis. It can rarely cause fulminant hepatitis and is therefore reserved for recurrent vulvovaginal candidiasis unresponsive to other therapies [Spence, 2003; BNF 47, 2004].
- **Povidone-iodine** is an antiseptic available in topical intravaginal formulations (gel and pessaries). It is licensed for the treatment of candidal, trichomonal, non-specific, or mixed infections of the vagina [BNF 47, 2004]. However, there is little published evidence to support its use.

Drugs included

- **Topical intravaginal imidazoles** are effective drugs in the treatment of uncomplicated vulvovaginal candidiasis. Three are currently licensed in the United Kingdom for this indication: clotrimazole, econazole, and miconazole. There are a variety of formulations and regimens licensed which are all equally effective:
  - Intravaginal pessaries, ovules, and creams (used with an applicator) are available.
  - External creams in combination with pessaries are available.
  - Courses vary from a single dose to once a night for 6 days.

[CEG, 2002; BNF 47, 2004]

- **Fluconazole and itraconazole** (oral triazoles) are as effective in the treatment of vulvovaginal candidiasis as topical imidazoles. They are convenient to use (taken as one or two doses), which may improve compliance, but are associated with an increased frequency of systemic adverse effects (usually mild and transient in nature). They are more expensive than topical products [BNF 47, 2004; MeReC, 2004].
- **Creams for external use** (clotrimazole, econazole, and miconazole) are offered as additional treatments to intravaginal or oral therapy. They are especially useful in cases of extensive vulvovaginal candidiasis. Some women find they have a soothing effect, and external application may speed up resolution of symptoms [BNF 47, 2004; MeReC, 2004].

Prescriptions

Oral treatment

Fluconazole 150mg x1 day

- Age from 16 years onwards
- Fluconazole 150mg capsules. Take the capsule as a single dose; supply 1 capsule; NHS Cost £5.60; OTC Cost £9.99.

Itraconazole 400mg x1 day

- Age from 16 to 60 years
- Itraconazole 100mg capsules. Take two capsules twice a day for 1 day only; supply 4 capsules; NHS Cost £4.19.

Pessary

Clotrimazole 500mg pessary x1 night

- Age from 12 years onwards
- Clotrimazole 500mg pessaries. Insert one pessary into the vagina at night; supply 1 pessary; NHS Cost £3.43; OTC Cost £7.49.

Econazole 150mg pessary x1 night

- Age from 12 years onwards
- Ecostatin-1 150mg pessaries. Insert one pessary into the vagina at night; supply 1 pessary; NHS Cost £3.35.

Miconazole 1.2g vaginal ovule x1 night

- Age from 12 years onwards
- Miconazole 1.2g vaginal ovule. Insert one ovule into the vagina at night; supply 1 vaginal ovule; NHS Cost £3.35.

Clotrimazole 200mg pessaries x3 nights

- Age from 12 years onwards
- Clotrimazole 200mg pessaries. Insert one pessary into the vagina each night for 3 nights; supply 3 pessaries; NHS Cost £3.89; OTC Cost £6.35.

Econazole 150mg pessaries x3 nights

- Age from 12 years onwards
- Econazole 150mg pessaries. Insert one pessary into the vagina each night for 3 nights; supply 3 pessaries; NHS Cost £3.17; OTC Cost £5.59.

Intravaginal cream

Clotrimazole 10% vaginal cream x1 night

- Age from 12 years onwards
- Clotrimazole 10% cream. Insert one 5g applicatorful into the vagina at night as a single dose; supply 5 grams; NHS Cost £4.50; OTC Cost £8.99.

Pessary and external cream

Clotrimazole 500mg pessary (x1 night) + 2% cream

- Age from 12 years onwards
- Clotrimazole 500mg pessary+2% cream. Insert one pessary into the vagina at night for 1 night, and apply cream to the outer affected area 2 to 3 times a day for up to 7 days; supply 1 combi-pack; NHS Cost £4.95; OTC Cost £9.99.

Econazole 150mg pessary (x1 night) + 1% cream

- Age from 12 years onwards
- Gyno-Pevaryl-1 CP pack. Insert one pessary into the vagina at night for 1 night, and apply cream to the outer affected area once a day for 14 days; supply 1 CP pack; NHS Cost £4.35; OTC Cost £7.67.

conazole 150mg pessaries (x3 nights) + 1% cream
Age from 12 years onwards
Gyno-Pevaryl Combi-pack. Insert one pessary into the vagina each night for 3 nights, and apply cream to the outer affected area each night for 14 nights; supply 1 combi-pack; NHS Cost £4.35; OTC Cost £7.67.

xternal cream (additional treatment)

otrimazole 1% cream
Age from 10 years onwards
Clotrimazole 1% cream. Apply to the affected area 2 to 3 times a day for at least 14 days; supply 20 grams; NHS Cost £1.76; OTC Cost £4.15.

conazole 1% cream
Age from 10 years onwards
Econazole 1% cream. Apply to the affected area 2 to 3 times a day until symptoms have fully resolved, and for several days after; supply 1 15 gram tube; NHS Cost £1.49; OTC Cost £2.63.

Treatment failure

Which therapy?

Consider the reason for treatment failure: poor compliance, severe infection, resistant pathogen or mixed infection present, misdiagnosis, or an underlying cause.
If concordance with a topical product was a problem, consider a single dose of oral fluconazole or two doses of itraconazole in one day.
If there have been four or more episodes in a one-year period, see *Recurrent infection* scenario.
Otherwise, investigate to confirm the diagnosis and identify potentially resistant species.
Consider treating empirically using a longer course of antifungal drugs, according to patient preference:
- Intravaginal clotrimazole, econazole, or miconazole for 6–14 days (possible off-licence use)
- Oral fluconazole or itraconazole for 7 days (off-licence use)
- Topical intravaginal nystatin for 14 days

Topical creams applied to the vulva should be considered in addition to intravaginal or oral treatment.

Practical prescribing points

For further information see the *Medicines Compendium* (www.medicines.org.uk) or the *British National Formulary* (www.bnf.org).
Fluconazole and itraconazole are contraindicated in pregnant or breastfeeding women.
Women who are prescribed a cream in addition to a pessary or oral preparation may be subject to an additional prescription charge.
Products containing topical imidazoles may damage latex condoms and diaphragms.
There is anecdotal evidence that oral fluconazole and itraconazole may cause oral contraceptive failure.

Follow-up advice

Advise the woman to return for follow-up if symptoms have not completely resolved 7–14 days after the start of treatment.

Should I refer or investigate?

Refer?

- Consider referral to a genito-urinary medicine clinic if there is suspicion of a sexually transmitted infection.
- Referral to a specialist is advised if the infection is caused by a resistant species such as *Candida glabrata*.

Investigate?

- **Investigation is recommended** in treatment failure.
- **A high vaginal swab** should be used to collect discharge from the anterior fornix or lateral wall of the vagina and sent to the laboratory for microscopy and/or culture.
- **If diabetes mellitus** is suspected as an underlying cause, consider urinalysis or testing for abnormal blood glucose concentrations.
- **If the woman is suspected of being immunocompromised,** investigate or refer as appropriate.

Patient information leaflets

The following PILs are available at www.prodigy.nhs.uk
- Antifungal Medicines
- Thrush - Vaginal

Shared decision making

- Reasons why treatment for thrush may have failed include:
  - The symptoms may not be due to thrush.
  - Some cases are caused by strains of *Candida* which are resistant to usual treatments.
  - You may not have used the treatment correctly.
  - You may have had a quick recurrence of a new thrush infection.
- You may need a vaginal swab to clarify the cause of your symptoms.
- If thrush is confirmed then treatment options include:
  - **Pessaries** or **vaginal cream** which you put inside the vagina with an applicator, or
  - **Tablets** taken by mouth. These are just as effective. You should not take these if you are pregnant or breastfeeding.
- A longer course of treatment is usual (6-14 days) if the original treatment did not work.
- **Anti-thrush cream** to rub onto the vulval skin may also help ease itch.
- Come back if symptoms do not go within 1-2 weeks of starting treatment.

Drug rationale

Drugs not included

- **Oral ketoconazole** is not indicated in the treatment of vulvovaginal candidiasis. It can rarely cause fulminant hepatitis and is therefore reserved for recurrent vulvovaginal candidiasis unresponsive to other therapies [Spence, 2003; BNF 47, 2004].
- **Povidone-iodine** is an antiseptic available in topical intravaginal formulations (gel and pessaries). It is licensed for the treatment of candidal, trichomonal, non-specific, or mixed infections of the vagina [BNF 47, 2004]. However, there is little published evidence to support its use.

Drugs included

- **Fluconazole and itraconazole** (oral triazoles) are effective in the treatment of vulvovaginal candidiasis. Most

women find them more convenient to use than topical imidazoles:
  - Single doses of fluconazole, or two doses of itraconazole (in one day), are offered if a previous regimen of topical imidazole failed.
  - Longer courses of fluconazole or itraconazole (one week) are offered if compliance was not originally a problem. This is not a licensed indication.

[BNF 47, 2004]

C

- **Longer courses of topical intravaginal imidazoles** are offered in the treatment of vulvovaginal candidiasis in the event of unexplained treatment failure (6–14 days). The consensus of expert opinion is that longer courses of antifungal drugs may be beneficial following treatment failure [Working Group of the British Society for Medical Mycology, 1995].

[CEG, 2002; BNF 47, 2004]

- **Nystatin** is recommended in the treatment of uncomplicated vulvovaginal candidiasis. Trials have shown intravaginal nystatin to be more effective than placebo and as effective as topical imidazoles in the treatment of vulvovaginal candidiasis [Spence, 2003]. It may have more activity than topical or oral azoles against certain species of *Candida* [Working Group of the British Society for Medical Mycology, 1995].
- **Creams for external use** (clotrimazole, econazole, and miconazole) are recommended as additional treatments to intravaginal or oral therapy. They are especially useful in cases of extensive vulvovaginal candidiasis. Some women find they have a soothing effect and external application may speed up resolution of symptoms [BNF 47, 2004; MeReC, 2004].

Prescriptions

Oral Treatment

Fluconazole 150mg x1 day
- Age from 16 years onwards
- Fluconazole 150mg capsules. Take the capsule as a single dose; supply 1 capsule; NHS Cost £5.80; OTC Cost £10.68.

Itraconazole 400mg x1 day
- Age from 16 to 60 years
- Itraconazole 100mg capsules. Take two capsules twice a day for 1 day only; supply 4 capsules; NHS Cost £4.19.

Fluconazole 100mg x7 days
- Age from 16 years onwards
- Fluconazole 50mg capsules. Take two capsules once a day for 7 days; supply 14 capsules; NHS Cost £22.42.

Itraconazole 200mg x7 days
- Age from 16 to 60 years
- Itraconazole 100mg capsules. Take two capsules once a day for 7 days; supply 14 capsules; NHS Cost £29.33.

Pessary (6-14 nights)

Clotrimazole 200mg pessaries x6 nights
- Age from 12 years onwards
- Clotrimazole 200mg pessaries. Insert one pessary into the vagina each night for 6 nights; supply 6 pessaries; NHS Cost £7.78.

Econazole 150mg pessaries x6 nights
- Age from 12 years onwards
- Econazole 150mg pessaries. Insert one pessary into the vagina each night for 6 nights; supply 6 pessaries; NHS Cost £6.70.

Miconazole 100mg pessaries x7 days
- Age from 12 years onwards
- Miconazole 100mg pessaries. Insert one pessary into the vagina twice a day for 7 days; supply 14 pessaries; NHS Cost £3.17.

Clotrimazole 100mg pessaries x12 nights
- Age from 12 years onwards
- Clotrimazole 100mg pessaries. Insert one pessary into the vagina each night for 12 nights; supply 12 pessaries; NHS Cost £14.70.

Miconazole 100mg pessaries x14 nights
- Age from 12 years onwards
- Miconazole 100mg pessaries. Insert one pessary into the vagina each night for 14 nights; supply 14 pessaries; NHS Cost £3.17.

Nystatin 100,000 units pessaries x14 nights
- Age from 12 years onwards
- Nystatin 100,000units pessary. Insert one to two pessaries into the vagina each night for 14 nights; supply 28 pessaries; NHS Cost £1.96.

Intravaginal cream (7-14 nights)

Miconazole 2% vaginal cream x7 days
- Age from 12 years onwards
- Miconazole 2% vaginal cream. Insert one 5g applicatorful into the vagina twice a day for 7 days, and apply cream to the outer affected area twice a day for 7 days; supply 78 grams; NHS Cost £4.95.

Miconazole 2% vaginal cream x14 nights
- Age from 12 years onwards
- Miconazole 2% vaginal cream. Insert one 5g applicatorful into the vagina each night for 14 nights, and apply cream to the outer affected area twice a day for 14 days; supply 78 grams; NHS Cost £4.95.

Nystatin 100,000units/4g vaginal cream x14 nights
- Age from 12 years onwards
- Nystatin 100,000u/4g vag cream. Insert one to two applicatorfuls into the vagina each night for 14 nights; supply 60 grams; NHS Cost £2.77.

Pessary (7-14 nights) and external cream

Miconazole 100mg pessaries (x7 days) + 2% cream
- Age from 12 years onwards
- Miconazole pessaries+cream. Insert one pessary into the vagina twice a day for 7 days, and apply cream to the outer affected area twice a day for 7 days; supply 1 combi-pack; NHS Cost £4.35.

Miconazole 100mg pessaries (x14 nights) + 2% cream
- Age from 12 years onwards
- Miconazole pessaries+cream. Insert one pessary into the vagina each night for 14 nights, and apply cream to the outer affected area twice a day for 14 days; supply 1 combi-pack; NHS Cost £4.35.

External cream (additional treatment)

Clotrimazole 1% cream
- Age from 10 years onwards
- Clotrimazole 1% cream. Apply to the affected area 2 to 3 times a day for at least 14 days; supply 50 grams; NHS Cost £3.80; OTC Cost £7.99.

Econazole 1% cream
- Age from 10 years onwards
- Econazole 1% cream. Apply to the affected area 2 to 3 times a day until symptoms have fully resolved, and for several days after; supply 1 30 gram tube; NHS Cost £2.75; OTC Cost £4.85.

₹ecurrent vulvovaginal andidiasis (4+ episodes in a ear)

/hich therapy?

:current vulvovaginal candidiasis is defined as four more isodes in one year — it is otherwise often distinguishable from acute infection.

Manage the woman sympathetically and be aware of possible accompanying depression or psychosexual problems.

Assess whether there are any underlying causes, for example the woman being immunocompromised or having diabetes mellitus.

Investigate using culture to confirm the diagnosis and identify potentially resistant species.

Treat confirmed cases using long-term oral or intravaginal preparations according to patient preference (this is an off-licence use):

- **Induction:** 6–14 days of daily treatment
- **Maintenance:** 6 months of weekly or monthly treatment

After the maintenance period is complete, test for persisting infection and stop treatment if there has been a microbiological cure.

ractical prescribing points

›r further information see the *Medicines Compendium* ·ww.medicines.org.uk) or the *British National Formulary* ·ww.bnf.org).

Fluconazole and itraconazole are contraindicated in pregnant or breastfeeding women.

The long-term use of topical and oral azoles for recurrent vulvovaginal candidiasis is off-licence.

Products containing topical imidazoles may damage latex condoms and diaphragms.

There is anecdotal evidence that oral fluconazole and itraconazole may cause oral contraceptive failure.

ollow-up advice

Advise the woman to return to her healthcare professional if there is an episode of vulvovaginal candidiasis during maintenance, as this may be indicative of azole resistance occurring.

A follow-up appointment should be arranged after 6 months (after completion of maintenance therapy).

hould I refer or investigate?

efer?

Refer to a specialist when:

- A non-albicans species has been identified by culture.
- The induction period fails to resolve symptoms.
- There is an episode of vulvovaginal candidiasis during the maintenance period.

Seek specialist advice if vulvovaginal candidiasis reoccurs after cessation of maintenance therapy.

ıvestigate?

Culture is essential to identify the species of *Candida* involved in recurrent vulvovaginal candidiasis. Use a high vaginal swab to collect discharge from the anterior fornix or lateral wall of the vagina and send to the laboratory for culture.

- **If diabetes mellitus** is suspected as an underlying cause, consider urinalysis or testing for abnormal blood glucose concentrations.
- **If the woman is suspected of being immunocompromised,** investigate or refer as appropriate.

Patient information leaflets

The following PILs are available at www.prodigy.nhs.uk

- Antifungal Medicines
- Thrush - Recurring Vaginal Thrush
- Thrush - Vaginal

Shared decision making

- The main treatment options for thrush are:
  - **Pessaries** or **vaginal cream** which you put inside the vagina with an applicator, or
  - **Fluconazole** or **itraconazole** tablets taken by mouth. These are just as effective. You should not take these if you are pregnant or breastfeeding.
- To prevent recurring thrush, an option is:
  - Use one of the above treatments every day for 7-14 days, then
    - Use a **pessary** or **vaginal cream** or take a **fluconazole** tablet once per week, or
    - Take a dose of **itraconazole** once a month.
  - Continue for 6 months and then come back for review.
  - Come back sooner if you get thrush whilst on this treatment.

Drug rationale

Drugs not included

- **Econazole and miconazole** are not recommended as there are no guidelines citing their use in induction and maintenance treatment for recurrent thrush. This is possibly because they exhibit less favourable pharmacokinetics for weekly maintenance than clotrimazole [Sobel, 2003].
- **Nystatin** is not recommended because there is a lack of evidence of its efficacy in the treatment of recurrent vulvovaginal candidiasis, and it is impractical for longer-term use as it stains clothes yellow [BNF 47, 2004]. However, it is sometimes used under specialist supervision during the maintenance period of women with non-albicans thrush [Scharbo-DeHaan and Anderson, 2003].
- **Oral ketoconazole** is not indicated in the treatment of recurrent vulvovaginal candidiasis. It can rarely cause fulminant hepatitis and is therefore reserved for recurrent vulvovaginal candidiasis unresponsive to other therapies [Spence, 2003; BNF 47, 2004].
- **Povidone-iodine** is an antiseptic available in topical intravaginal formulations (gel and pessaries). It is licensed for the treatment of candidal, trichomonal, non-specific, or mixed infections of the vagina [BNF 47, 2004]. However, there is little published evidence to support its use.

Drugs included

- **Oral fluconazole** is included. It is commonly used in recurrent vulvovaginal candidiasis, although it is not licensed for long-term use for this indication:
  - **Induction:** fluconazole 100 mg once a day, for one week
  - **Maintenance:** fluconazole 100 mg once a week, for 6 months

C

[CEG, 2002; Scharbo-DeHaan and Anderson, 2003; BNF 47, 2004]

- **Oral itraconazole** is offered for both the induction and maintenance therapy of vulvovaginal candidiasis, although it is not licensed for this purpose. It has favourable pharmacokinetics that allow for once-monthly dosing during the maintenance stage:
  - **Induction:** itraconazole 200 mg taken once a day, for one week
  - **Maintenance:** itraconazole 200 mg taken twice in a single day once a month, for 6 months

[Ringdahl, 2000; CEG, 2002; Scharbo-DeHaan and Anderson, 2003; BNF 47, 2004]

- **Topical intravaginal clotrimazole** has been successfully used for recurrent vulvovaginal candidiasis. Typically regimens consist of daily doses for 6–14 days, followed by weekly doses for 6 months. This is an off-licence use of clotrimazole [CEG, 2002; Scharbo-DeHaan and Anderson, 2003; BNF 47, 2004].

Prescriptions

Induction

Clotrimazole pessaries: 200mg at night for 6 nights
- Age from 12 years onwards
- Clotrimazole 200mg pessaries. Insert one pessary into the vagina each night for 6 nights; supply 6 pessaries; NHS Cost £7.78.

Clotrimazole pessaries: 200mg at night for 12 nights
- Age from 12 years onwards
- Clotrimazole 200mg pessaries. Insert one pessary into the vagina each night for 12 nights; supply 12 pessaries; NHS Cost £15.56.

Fluconazole capsules: 100mg once a day for 7 days
- Age from 16 years onwards
- Fluconazole 50mg capsules. Take two capsules once a day for 7 days; supply 14 capsules; NHS Cost £24.06.

Itraconazole capsules: 200mg once a day for 7 days
- Age from 16 to 60 years
- Itraconazole 100mg capsules. Take two capsules once a day for 7 days; supply 14 capsules; NHS Cost £14.67.

Maintenance (2-month supply)

Clotrimazole pessary: 500mg once a WEEK
- Age from 12 years onwards
- Clotrimazole 500mg pessaries. Insert one pessary into the vagina at night once a WEEK; supply 8 pessaries; NHS Cost £27.44.

Fluconazole capsules: 100mg once a WEEK
- Age from 16 years onwards
- Fluconazole 50mg capsules. Take two capsules in one day once a WEEK; supply 16 capsules; NHS Cost £24.73.

Itraconazole capsules: 200mg twice in one day once a MONTH
- Age from 16 to 60 years
- Itraconazole 100mg capsules. Take two capsules twice in one day once a MONTH; supply 8 capsules; NHS Cost £8.38.

Pregnancy

Which therapy?

- **Examine and investigation is generally recommended** at the first presentation.
- **Treat with intavaginal clotrimazole, econazole, or miconazole.** Courses lasting for around a week or more are recommended.
- **Topical creams applied to the vulva** should be considered in addition to intravaginal treatment.
- **Oral treatment should NOT be used in pregnancy or breastfeeding.**

Practical prescribing points

For further information please see the *Medicines Compendium* (www.medicines.org.uk) or the *British National Formulary* (www.bnf.org).

- Care should be taken when using an applicator during pregnancy to avoid physical damage to the cervix. Some women prefer to insert pessaries by hand when pregnant.

Follow-up advice

- Advise the woman to return for follow-up if symptoms have not completely resolved 7–14 days after the start of treatment.

Should I refer or investigate?

Refer?

- Consider referral to a genito-urinary medicine clinic if there is suspicion of a sexually transmitted infection.

Investigate?

- A high vaginal swab to collect discharge from the anterior fornix or lateral wall of the vagina is generally recommended at first presentation. Candidiasis is often diagnosed on the basis of clinical features alone and as many as half of these women may have other conditions e.g. bacterial vaginosis.
- If a sexually transmitted infection is possible investigations should also include tests for chlamydia and gonorrhoea (but consider referral to a genito-urinary medicine clinic).

Patient information leaflets

The following PILs are available at www.prodigy.nhs.uk
- Antifungal Medicines
- Thrush - Vaginal

Shared decision making

- Thrush will not harm your pregnancy, but is unpleasant and can be treated.
- **Pessaries** or **vaginal cream** which you put inside the vagina with an applicator are usually used to treat thrush when pregnant.
- A dose each day for a week is often needed to clear thrush during pregnancy.
- **Anti-thrush cream** to rub onto the vulval skin may also help ease itch.
- Come back if symptoms do not go within 1-2 weeks of starting treatment.
- Note: anti-thrush tablets taken by mouth should not be used if you are pregnant or breastfeeding.

Drug rationale

Drugs not included

- **Oral triazoles are contraindicated in pregnant women** [CEG, 2002]. Animal studies have shown that high doses of itraconazole cause fetal abnormalities, and there are concerns that fluconazole may have caused congenital defects in human babies. Ketoconazole may affect implantation and maintenance of embryos early in pregnancy [Weiner and Buhimschi, 2004]. The manufacturers advise that these drugs should not be used in pregnancy or breastfeeding, and that women of childbearing age should use adequate contraception. **Nystatin** is not recommended in the treatment of uncomplicated vulvovaginal candidiasis in pregnancy. Trials have shown intravaginal nystatin to be more effective than placebo and as effective as topical imidazoles in the treatment of vulvovaginal thrush [Spence, 2003]. However, it is only available as a 14-day regimen and it stains clothing yellow, making it unsuitable for most women [Working Group of the British Society for Medical Mycology, 1995]. **Povidone-iodine** is an antiseptic available in topical intravaginal formulations (gel and pessaries). It is licensed for the treatment of candidal, trichomonal, non-specific, or mixed infections of the vagina [BNF 47, 2004]. However, there is little published evidence to support its use.

rugs included

Topical intravaginal imidazoles are safe and effective drugs in the treatment of vulvovaginal candidiasis in pregnancy. Clotrimazole, econazole, and miconazole are most commonly used in expectant mothers. There are a variety of formulations and regimens licensed which are all equally effective:

- Intravaginal pessaries, ovules, and creams (used with an applicator) are available
- External creams in combination with pessaries are available
- Courses in pregnancy should last around a week or more

charbo-DeHaan and Anderson, 2003; Young and Jewell, 04; BNF 47, 2004]

Creams for external use (clotrimazole, econazole, and miconazole) are offered as additional treatments to intravaginal or oral therapy. They are especially useful in cases of extensive vulvovaginal candidiasis. Some women find they have a soothing effect and external application may speed up resolution of symptoms [BNF 47, 2004; MeReC, 2004].

rescriptions

essary (6-14 nights)

otrimazole 100mg pessaries x6 nights

- Age from 12 years onwards
- Clotrimazole 100mg pessaries. Insert one pessary into the vagina each night for 6 nights; supply 6 pessaries; NHS Cost £3.62; OTC Cost £6.35.

otrimazole 200mg pessaries x6 nights

- Age from 12 years onwards
- Clotrimazole 200mg pessaries. Insert one pessary into the vagina each night for 6 nights; supply 6 pessaries; NHS Cost £7.78.

conazole 150mg pessaries x6 nights

- Age from 12 years onwards
- Econazole 150mg pessaries. Insert one pessary into the vagina each night for 6 nights; supply 6 pessaries; NHS Cost £6.70.

iconazole 100mg pessaries x7 days

- Age from 12 years onwards
- Miconazole 100mg pessaries. Insert one pessary into the vagina twice a day for 7 days; supply 14 pessaries; NHS Cost £3.17.

Clotrimazole 100mg pessaries x12 nights

- Age from 12 years onwards
- Clotrimazole 100mg pessaries. Insert one pessary into the vagina each night for 12 nights; supply 12 pessaries; NHS Cost £14.70.

Miconazole 100mg pessaries x14 nights

- Age from 12 years onwards
- Miconazole 100mg pessaries. Insert one pessary into the vagina each night for 14 nights; supply 14 pessaries; NHS Cost £3.35.

Intravaginal cream (7-14 nights)

Miconazole 2% vaginal cream x7 days

- Age from 12 years onwards
- Miconazole 2% vaginal cream. Insert one 5g applicatorful into the vagina twice a day for 7 days, and apply cream to the outer affected area twice a day for 7 days; supply 78 grams; NHS Cost £4.95.

Miconazole 2% vaginal cream x14 nights

- Age from 12 years onwards
- Miconazole 2% vaginal cream. Insert one 5g applicatorful into the vagina each night for 14 nights, and apply cream to the outer affected area twice a day for 14 days; supply 78 grams; NHS Cost £4.95.

Pessary (7-14 nights) and external cream

Miconazole 100mg pessaries (7 days) + 2% cream

- Age from 12 years onwards
- Miconazole pessaries+cream. Insert one pessary into the vagina twice a day for 7 days, and apply cream to the outer affected area twice a day for 7 days; supply 1 combi-pack; NHS Cost £4.35.

Miconazole 100mg pessaries (14 nights) + 2% cream

- Age from 12 years onwards
- Miconazole pessaries+cream. Insert one pessary into the vagina each night for 14 nights, and apply cream to the outer affected area twice a day for 14 days; supply 1 combi-pack; NHS Cost £8.70.

External cream (additional treatment)

Clotrimazole 1% cream

- Age from 12 years onwards
- Clotrimazole 1% cream. Apply to the affected area 2 to 3 times a day for at least 14 days; supply 50 grams; NHS Cost £3.80; OTC Cost £7.99.

Econazole 1% cream

- Age from 12 years onwards
- Econazole 1% cream. Apply to the affected area 2 to 3 times a day until symptoms have fully resolved, and for several days after; supply 1 30 gram tube; NHS Cost £2.75; OTC Cost £4.85.

Severe vulvovaginal candidiasis

Which therapy?

- **Examination and investigation is recommended** to assess the extent of infection and confirm the diagnosis.
- **Treat according to the woman's preference** (these are off-licence uses):
  - **Intravaginal clotrimazole, econazole, or miconazole** should be used for 7–14 days
  - **Fluconazole** 150 mg, repeated after 72 hours
- **Topical imidazole creams applied to the vulva** should be considered in addition to intravaginal treatment, as they may have a soothing action and hasten resolution of symptoms.

Practical prescribing points

For further information please see the *Medicines Compendium* (www.medicines.org.uk) or the *British National Formulary* (www.bnf.org).

- Fluconazole and itraconazole are contraindicated in pregnant or breastfeeding women.
- The use of two doses of fluconazole in a 72-hour period for vulvovaginal candidiasis is off-licence.
- Women who are prescribed a cream in addition to a pessary or oral preparation may be subject to an additional prescription charge.
- Products containing topical imidazoles may damage latex condoms and diaphragms.
- There is anecdotal evidence that oral fluconazole may cause oral contraceptive failure.

Follow-up advice

- Advise the woman to return for follow-up if symptoms have not completely resolved 7–14 days after the start of treatment.

Should I refer or investigate?

Refer?

- Consider referral to a genito-urinary medicine clinic if there is suspicion of a sexually transmitted infection.

Investigate?

- **A high vaginal swab** to collect discharge from the anterior fornix or lateral wall of the vagina is recommended to confirm the diagnosis.
- **If diabetes mellitus** is suspected as an underlying cause, urinalysis or testing for abnormal blood glucose concentrations is recommended.
- **If the woman is suspected of being immunocompromised,** investigate or refer as appropriate.

Patient information leaflets

The following PILs are available at www.prodigy.nhs.uk

- Antifungal Medicines
- Thrush - Vaginal

Shared decision making

- The main treatment options for severe thrush are:
  - **Pessaries** or **vaginal cream** which you put inside the vagina with an applicator for 7-14 days, or
  - **Fluconazole tablets,** two doses taken 72 hours apart. This is just as effective. (You should not take this if you are pregnant or breastfeeding.)
- **Anti-thrush cream** to rub onto the vulval skin may also help ease itch.
- You can get all these treatments on prescription, or you can buy them.
- Come back if symptoms do not go within 1-2 weeks of starting treatment.

Drug rationale

Drugs not included

- **Nystatin** is not recommended for the treatment of severe vulvovaginal candidiasis. Trials have shown intravaginal nystatin to be more effective than placebo and as effective as topical imidazoles in the treatment of vulvovaginal thrush [Spence, 2003]. However, it is only available as a 14-day regimen and stains clothing yello making it unsuitable for most women [Working Grou of the British Society for Medical Mycology, 1995].
- **Oral ketoconazole** is not usually indicated in the treatment of vulvovaginal candidiasis. It can rarely cau fulminant hepatitis and is therefore reserved for recurrent vulvovaginal candidiasis unresponsive to oth therapies [Spence, 2003; BNF 47, 2004].
- **Povidone-iodine** is an antiseptic available in topical intravaginal formulations (gel and pessaries). It is licensed for the treatment of candidal, trichomonal, nc specific, or mixed infections of the vagina [BNF 47, 2004]. However, there is little published evidence to support its use.
- **Itraconazole** is not recommended for the treatment of severe vulvovaginal candidiasis, as it has not been specifically studied in this condition, and has a slightly worse safety profile than fluconazole [BNF 47, 2004].

Drugs included

- **Fluconazole** is effective in the treatment of vulvovagina candidiasis. It is offered as two doses of 150 mg, taken sequentially 72 hours apart, which is more effective in the treatment of severe infection than the standard sing dose. This regimen is off-licence [Sobel et al, 2001].
- **Topical intravaginal imidazoles** (clotrimazole, econazo and miconazole) are recommended, as they are effectiv in the treatment of vulvovaginal candidiasis. Severe infection necessitates longer courses lasting 7–14 days [Scharbo-DeHaan and Anderson, 2003].
- **Creams for external use** (clotrimazole, econazole, and miconazole) are recommended as additional treatment to intravaginal or oral therapy. They are especially use in cases of extensive vulvovaginal candidiasis. Some women find they have a soothing effect and external application may speed up resolution of symptoms [BN 47, 2004; MeReC, 2004].

Prescriptions

Oral treatment

Fluconazole 150mg (twice in 72 hours)

- Age from 16 years onwards
- Fluconazole 150mg capsules. Take one capsule, then repeat after 72 hours; supply 2 capsule; NHS Cost £11.20.

Pessary (6-14 nights)

Clotrimazole 200mg pessaries x6 nights

- Age from 12 years onwards
- Clotrimazole 200mg pessaries. Insert one pessary into the vagina each night for 6 nights; supply 6 pessaries; NHS Cost £7.78.

Econazole 150mg pessaries x6 nights

- Age from 12 years onwards
- Econazole 150mg pessaries. Insert one pessary into the vagina each night for 6 nights; supply 6 pessaries; NHS Cost £6.70.

Miconazole 100mg pessaries x7 days

- Age from 12 years onwards
- Miconazole 100mg pessaries. Insert one pessary into th vagina twice a day for 7 days; supply 14 pessaries; NHS Cost £3.17.

Clotrimazole 100mg pessaries x12 nights

- Age from 12 years onwards
- Clotrimazole 100mg pessaries. Insert one pessary into the vagina each night for 12 nights; supply 12 pessaries NHS Cost £7.24.

:onazole 100mg pessaries x14 nights
\ge from 12 years onwards
Miconazole 100mg pessaries. Insert one pessary into the ,agina each night for 14 nights; supply 14 pessaries; NHS Cost £3.17.

travaginal cream (7-14 nights)

:onazole 2% vaginal cream x7 days
\ge from 12 years onwards
Miconazole 2% vaginal cream. Insert one 5g applicatorful into the vagina twice a day for 7 days, and apply cream to the outer affected area twice a day for 7 days; supply 78 grams; NHS Cost £4.95.

:onazole 2% vaginal cream x14 nights
\ge from 12 years onwards
Miconazole 2% vaginal cream. Insert one 5g applicatorful into the vagina each night for 14 nights, and apply cream to the outer affected area twice a day for 14 days; supply 78 grams; NHS Cost £4.95.

essary (7-14 nights) and external cream

:onazole 100mg pessaries (7 days) + 2% cream
Age from 12 years onwards
Miconazole pessaries+cream. Insert one pessary into the vagina twice a day for 7 days, and apply cream to the outer affected area twice a day for 7 days; supply 1 combi-pack; NHS Cost £4.35.

:onazole 100mg pessaries (14 nights) + 2% cream
Age from 12 years onwards
Miconazole pessaries+cream. Insert one pessary into the vagina each night for 14 nights, and apply cream to the outer affected area twice a day for 14 days; supply 1 combi-pack; NHS Cost £4.35.

xternal cream (additional treatment)

otrimazole 1% cream
Age from 10 years onwards
Clotrimazole 1% cream. Apply to the affected area 2 to 3 times a day for at least 14 days; supply 50 grams; NHS Cost £3.80; OTC Cost £7.99.

onazole 1% cream
Age from 10 years onwards
Econazole 1% cream. Apply to the affected area 2 to 3 times a day until symptoms have fully resolved, and for several days after; supply 1 30 gram tube; NHS Cost £2.75; OTC Cost £4.85.

:xtended Information

ackground information

What is it? p.271
How common is it? p.271
What are the precipitating factors? p.272
How do I know my patient has it? p.272
What else might it be? p.272
Complications and prognosis p.273

'hat is it?

licrobiological cause of thrush

Vulvovaginal candidiasis (thrush of the vagina) is caused by abnormal colonization of the vagina by yeast cells:

- *Candida albicans* accounts for 80–95% of infections, and *C glabrata* is responsible for a further 5%.
- Other yeast infections are less common, with fewer than 5% of cases being caused by *Candida tropicalis, C parapsilosis, C krusei, C kefyr, C guilliermondii*, or *Saccharomyces cerevisiae*. These infections may be harder to treat.

[Working Group of the British Society for Medical Mycology, 1995; Bingham, 1999]

- ***Candida* is often present in women with no symptoms,** and is probably part of the normal vaginal flora. A change in the vaginal environment is necessary before the yeast exerts a pathological action. The precise conditions required for pathogenesis are unknown at present [Working Group of the British Society for Medical Mycology, 1995; MeReC, 2004].
- **Recurrent vulvovaginal candidiasis** has the same clinical manifestations as acute infection, and often has a similar microbiological profile, with only a modest increase in the involvement of non-albicans infection. The cause of recurrent infection is complex and poorly understood [Sobel, 2003].

Classification of thrush

- **Acute vulvovaginal candidiasis** refers to simple infections typically caused by *Candida albicans* [CEG, 2002]. It accounts for 80–90% of cases of genital candidiasis and usually responds well to short courses of treatment. Acute vulvovaginal candidiasis is often referred to as *uncomplicated* vulvovaginal candidiasis by American guidelines [Nyirjesy and Sobel, 2003; Scharbo-DeHaan and Anderson, 2003].
- **Recurrent vulvovaginal candidiasis** is defined as four or more episodes of candidiasis in a one-year period [CEG, 2002].
- **Complicated vulvovaginal candidiasis** includes the following:
  - **Recurrent infection,** defined as four episodes or more in one year.
  - **Severe infection,** which has additional complications and often responds poorly to short courses of treatment.
  - **Non-albicans infection,** which may respond poorly to treatment.
  - **Infection in pregnant women,** who may require different treatment.
  - **Other forms of complicated vulvovaginal candidiasis,** such as infection in immunocompromised women, infection in women with uncontrolled diabetes mellitus, and infection in women who are debilitated.

[Nyirjesy and Sobel, 2003; Scharbo-DeHaan and Anderson, 2003]

How common is it?

- **Vulvovaginal candidiasis is the second most common cause of vaginitis and vaginal discharge** after bacterial vaginosis:
  - **The lifetime incidence** of vulvovaginal candidiasis is estimated at 50–75%.
  - **The prevalence** of vulvovaginal candidiasis is not known, but the disease is diagnosed in 5–15% of women who attend sexually transmitted disease and family planning clinics.
  - **Recurrent vulvovaginal candidiasis** is present in less than 5% in women of childbearing age.
  - ***Candida albicans*** is found in 10–20% of women of reproductive age in the absence of symptoms. These women do not require treatment.
- **Women of childbearing age** are most likely to develop vulvovaginal candidiasis, as *C albicans* proliferates in an oestrogen-rich environment:
  - The incidence of thrush rises rapidly after the menarche, and peaks in the third and fourth decade of life.
  - Vulvovaginal candidiasis is more common during pregnancy.

   - Vulvovaginal candidiasis is much less common in prepubertal girls and postmenopausal women.
- **Diabetes mellitus** increases the incidence of vulvovaginal candidiasis, possibly because a high-glucose environment encourages the proliferation of *Candida*.

[Working Group of the British Society for Medical Mycology, 1995; Sobel et al, 1998; CEG, 2002; Nyirjesy and Sobel, 2003; Spence, 2003]

What are the precipitating factors?

A variety of factors have been implicated in triggering episodes of vulvovaginal candidiasis. Often the evidence to substantiate these claims is poor and based mainly on anecdote. However, avoidance of these factors may be beneficial in some individuals.

- **Contraception:** there is some controversy whether certain forms of contraception are associated with vulvovaginal candidiasis or not:
   - **Oral contraceptives:** evidence that the contraceptive pill is causally associated with vulvovaginal candidiasis is contradictory.
   - **Barrier contraceptives:** condoms probably do not cause vulvovaginal candidiasis *per se*, but there is some evidence that spermicides (such as nonoxynol-9) increase the incidence of vaginal thrush by harming the natural vaginal flora.
   - **Intra-uterine devices** probably increase the incidence of vulvovaginal candidiasis.
- **Sexual practice:** vulvovaginal candidiasis is not a sexually transmitted infection, but there is limited evidence that women receiving oral sex may be at greater risk of contracting the condition [CEG, 2002; Mardh et al, 2002].
- **Diet:** a high intake of glucose probably does not increase the likelihood of an episode of vulvovaginal candidiasis occurring, but poor diabetic control is a known underlying causal factor of the condition [de Leon et al, 2002].
- **Tight-fitting clothing,** particularly underwear, is reputed to result in more episodes of vulvovaginal candidiasis, but the evidence for this is conflicting. In any case, many women who suffer from this condition prefer to wear loose-fitting cotton underwear, as it is more comfortable.
- **Female hygiene and sanitation** may have some influence on the incidence of vulvovaginal candidiasis:
   - **Tampons:** there is no evidence that tampons cause vulvovaginal candidiasis.
   - **Sanitary towels:** there is limited evidence that sanitary towels may cause episodes of thrush, although sufferers often prefer their use.
   - **Vaginal douching:** there is no evidence this practice increases the likelihood of vulvovaginal candidiasis.
- **Broad-spectrum antibiotics** are a known precipitant of vulvovaginal candidiasis.

[Mardh et al, 2002]

How do I know my patient has it?

No symptoms or signs, either alone or combined, are specific for the diagnosis of vulvovaginal candidiasis. Other infections, particularly bacterial vaginosis (which is more common), can present in a similar way, and it is not always possible to distinguish between these infections on the basis of history and examination alone [Sobel et al, 1998].

Symptoms

Symptoms of vulvovaginal candidiasis tend to occur rapidly, often about a week before menstruation:

- **Vulval itching** is often the defining symptom, or soreness may be present.
- **Vaginal discharge** is usually present.
- **Dyspareunia** (pain or discomfort during intercourse).
- **Dysuria** (pain or discomfort during urination).

[Working Group of the British Society for Medical Mycology, 1995; CEG, 2002]

Signs

- **Erythema,** which is usually localized to the vagina and vulva, but may extend to the labia majora and perineu
- **Fissuring of the vagina,** and oedema, may be present.
- **Vaginal discharge,** which is often described as white a 'cheese-like', but may be watery or purulent. It is usua odourless.
- **Satellite lesions** may be present.

[Working Group of the British Society for Medical Mycology, 1995; CEG, 2002]

Investigations

Investigation is not always necessary on the first presentation if the signs and symptoms are consistent wi uncomplicated vulvovaginal candidiasis.

- **pH test:** vaginal fluid in the normal pH range of 4.0–4 is indicative of vulvovaginal candidiasis. A higher pH (more than 5.0) is suggestive of bacterial vaginosis or trichomoniasis [CEG, 2002]. Although useful in theor there is little evidence to support the use of pH testing, and it is seldom used in practice.
- **A high vaginal swab** should be used to collect discharg from the anterior fornix or lateral wall of the vagina a sent to the laboratory for microscopy and/or culture.
   - Microscopy looking for spores and/or pseudohypha may detect up to 70% of cases
   - Culture is useful for identification of resistant specie as well as other infections.

[Sherrard, 2001; CEG, 2002]

What else might it be?

Infections

- **Bacterial vaginosis** is the most common infection that causes abnormal vaginal discharge. Itch is not usually prominent, and discharge is usually white, homogeneous, and malodorous.
- **Trichomoniasis** is associated with itch and vaginal discharge, which is usually profuse, frothy, grey-greenish, and malodorous.
- **Chlamydia** can cause vaginal discharge and dysuria, b does not usually present with itch.
- **Gonorrhoea** rarely presents with itch, but is associated with pain, fever, and a purulent cervical discharge.
- **Genital herpes** may present with redness, although itch and discharge are uncommon, and pain is often the defining symptom.
- **Simultaneous infection:** it is possible for two or more infections to coexist, although this is not particularly common with *Candida albicans*.

[Plummer and Walters, 1993; Seller, 1996]

Non-infective causes

- **Normal physiological discharge** may be mistaken for thrush, although there should be no irritation, itch, or pain, and it should not be profuse:
   - Physiological discharge increases suddenly in menarchal girls, and varies throughout the menstrua cycle.
   - Pregnancy often causes physiological discharge.
- **Irritants** may result in vaginal discharge, although ther is little evidence concerning the possible extent of their contribution to the problem. Potential irritants include spermicides, perfumed soap or washing powders, frequent douching, or wearing tight, non-absorbent underwear (such as nylon).

:czema or psoriasis may cause itch similar to that caused ·y vulvovaginal candidiasis.
Malignancies of the vulva, vagina, cervix, or uterine ıning are rare but serious causes of vaginal discharge.
Atrophic vaginitis may cause vaginal discharge in postmenopausal women, although possible malignancy should also be considered.
A foreign body, such as a tampon, may result in vaginal lischarge.
[Summer and Walters, 1993; Seller, 1996]

omplications and prognosis

omplications

Treatment failure may occur in up to 20% of women eceiving antifungal treatment for uncomplicated 'ulvovaginal candidiasis. Treatment failure may be onsidered to have occurred if symptoms do not resolve within 7–14 days [Sobel et al, 1998; Watson et al, 2002].
Recurrent vulvovaginal candidiasis occurs in up to 50% of women who have uncomplicated vulvovaginal andidiasis at some point in their lifetimes. It is defined as four or more episodes in a one-year period [CEG, 2002].
Depression and psychosexual problems may affect women who suffer from recurrent candidiasis [Working Group of the British Society for Medical Mycology, 1995].
Vulvovaginal candidiasis can be more difficult to cure in pregnant women. However, there is no evidence that this ondition is harmful to the fetus [Lee et al, 2000].
Balanitis may rarely occur in male partners of women with vulvovaginal candidiasis [Spence, 2003].

rognosis

The natural progression of vulvovaginal candidiasis has not been extensively studied. Untreated women are likely o have persisting discomfort, with possible pain during ntercourse or urination [Spence, 2003].
Treatment cures vulvovaginal candidiasis in about 80% of women, in both the short term and the longer term [Watson et al, 2002].

Management issues

General issues p.273
Drug treatments p.273
Management of uncomplicated infection p.274
Management of complicated infection p.274
Self management p.276
Prophylactic measures p.276

eneral issues

Women with vulvovaginal candidiasis should be managed sympathetically. Vulvovaginal candidiasis can be a distressing and embarrassing condition, and recurrent infection can lead to depression and psychosexual problems (see *Recurrent vulvovaginal candidiasis*) [MeReC, 2004].
Preventative measures should be discussed with the woman, such as avoidance of irritants and synthetic underwear, where appropriate (see *What are the precipitating factors?*) [CEG, 2002].
Physical examination: women presenting for the first time with symptoms suggestive of vulvovaginal candidiasis should be examined as:

- Differential diagnosis based on history alone is less accurate than that based on history *and* examination. There are numerous conditions with similar symptoms to vulvovaginal candidiasis (see *What else might it be?*).
- Self-diagnosis of thrush is common practice, but follow-up microbiological studies have shown it to be accurate in less than half of cases [Ferris et al, 2002].
- Sexually transmitted infections, which may have serious long-term effects, should be ruled out by examination and investigation (e.g. endocervical swabs), as appropriate.

- Women presenting with symptoms of vulvovaginal candidiasis for a second time may be managed without examination if the initial treatment was successful [Sobel et al, 1998].
- **Investigation** is not usually warranted on the first visit if classical symptoms are present. However, suspected vulvovaginal candidiasis should be investigated under the following circumstances:
  - The woman wants further diagnostic investigation.
  - Symptoms persist despite empirical antifungal treatment.
  - There is suspicion it is a complicated infection.
  - There is suspicion it may be a sexually transmitted infection.

[Working Group of the British Society for Medical Mycology, 1995; CEG, 2002]

- **Treatment with antifungal drugs** can be administered if vulvovaginal candidiasis is suspected and symptoms are problematic, while waiting for test results [MeReC, 2004].
- **There is no evidence that treatment of asymptomatic male partners is beneficial** [Spence, 2003; Mardh et al, 2002], and this practice should not be carried out [CEG, 2002].

Drug treatments

Clotrimazole, econazole, and miconazole are topical imidazoles commonly used in the treatment of vulvovaginal candidiasis. Fluconazole and itraconazole are part of the triazole drug group and are taken orally. Other drugs are less commonly used.

Topical imidazoles

- **Topical imidazoles (clotrimazole, econazole or miconazole) are an effective cure for uncomplicated vulvovaginal candidiasis.** A systematic review found that for every three women treated with topical imidazoles, one extra had resolution of symptoms compared to placebo in the short term (NNT = 3). No particular topical imidazole was found to be superior to any other [Spence, 2003].
- **The efficacy of topical imidazoles is not dependent on the length of the course of treatment,** but is related to the total dose of drug received. A single high dose is as effective as a lower divided dose over several days [Marrazzo, 2002; Sobel, 2003].
- **To be effective, intravaginal application is required.** However, women should apply cream to the vulva as well as inserting a pessary or intravaginal cream where possible, as this area is also commonly affected. Application of topical treatment can be painful in some instances where there is particularly bad inflammation [MeReC, 2004].

Oral triazoles

- **Fluconazole and itraconazole** are available as oral formulations for the treatment of vulvovaginal candidiasis. Both drugs have been shown to be effective in treating vulvovaginal candidiasis in randomized controlled trials (RCTs):
  - Oral itraconazole is more effective than placebo in reducing symptoms after one week.

- Oral fluconazole is as effective as oral ketoconazole or itraconazole.
- Oral fluconazole and itraconazole are as effective as topical imidazoles. A systematic review of 17 RCTs found no significant difference in effectiveness between the two treatment types [Watson et al, 2002].

[Marrazzo, 2002; Spence, 2003]

Other drug treatments

C

- **Topical nystatin** is more effective against certain resistant strains of yeast such as *Candida glabrata*. It is not normally recommended for uncomplicated vulvovaginal candidiasis as it is taken as a 14-day intravaginal regimen and may stain clothes yellow, but it may be useful in treatment failure [Hainsworth, 2002].
- **Oral ketoconazole** is not usually indicated in the treatment of vulvovaginal candidiasis. It can rarely cause fulminant hepatitis and is therefore reserved for recurrent vulvovaginal candidiasis unresponsive to other therapies [Spence, 2003; BNF 47, 2004].
- **Povidone-iodine** is an antiseptic available in topical intravaginal formulations (gel and pessaries). It is licensed for the treatment of candidal, trichomonal, non-specific, or mixed infections of the vagina [BNF 47, 2004]. However, there is little published evidence to support its use.

Management of uncomplicated infection

- Antifungal treatment with either topical imidazoles (clotrimazole, econazole, and miconazole) or oral triazoles (fluconazole and itraconazole) is the mainstay of treatment for uncomplicated vulvovaginal candidiasis. These drugs are usually fast and effective and have few adverse effects.
- As topical and oral preparations are equally effective, the choice of treatment of uncomplicated vulvovaginal candidiasis should be based on individual preference. Factors that may influence the decision on which preparation to use are listed in Table 1.

[CEG, 2002; Spence, 2003; MeReC, 2004]

Treatment failure

- **Treatment failure in uncomplicated vulvovaginal candidiasis is unusual.** However, if symptoms have not cleared up after 7–14 days, treatment failure may have occurred and the woman should return to her healthcare professional for further advice and treatment [MeReC, 2004].
- **Possible reasons** for treatment failure should be considered, and further treatment or investigation should be carried out accordingly:
  - **Poor compliance** with the initial course of treatmen (although this is unlikely in single-dose preparation Consider using fluconazole or itraconazole.
  - **There is continued presence of an irritant,** such as perfumed products or nylon clothing. Advise avoidance of the irritant.
  - **The condition was originally misdiagnosed** (see *Wh else might it be?*). Use relevant investigations or refe to a genito-urinary medicine clinic.
  - **There is a resistant organism present,** such as *Cand glabrata*. Consider culture for identification of the organism involved and treat accordingly. Topical nystatin may be an option.
  - **There is a mixed infection,** such as candidiasis and bacterial vaginosis (up to 10% of infections are mixed). Use appropriate investigations (especially f bacterial vaginosis and trichomoniasis), and treat accordingly. Povidone-iodine is licensed in this even but not recommended.
  - **There is recurrent infection,** defined as four or more episodes in one year (see *Recurrent vulvovaginal candidiasis*).
  - **There is an underlying cause,** such as diabetes melli immunosuppression, or the woman is taking broad- spectrum antibiotics. Treat accordingly (consider longer term treatment), or refer for appropriate treatment or investigation.

[CEG, 2002; MeReC, 2004]

Management of complicated infection

'Complicated thrush' covers recurrent vulvovaginal candidiasis, vulvovaginal candidiasis in pregnancy, non-albicans infections, and infection with an underlying cau factor such as coexisting diabetes mellitus or an immunological problem (see *Classification of thrush*). Treatment for these conditions tends to be longer term a less effective.

Recurrent vulvovaginal candidiasis

- **The diagnosis of recurrent vulvovaginal candidiasis should be confirmed by culture.** If resistant non-albica species of yeast are present, the woman should be referred for treatment by a specialist (see *Non-albican thrush*) [Sobel, 2003].
- **Underlying or predisposing factors** for recurrent vulvovaginal candidiasis should be removed or controlled wherever possible (See *Other complicated thrush infections*) [Nyirjesy, 2001].
- **Treatment of recurrent infection** with *Candida albica* should consist of an initial induction period, when symptoms are treated, followed by a longer maintenan

Table 1: Factors that may influence the decision to use topical or oral treatment in uncomplicated vulvovaginal candidia

Factor	Topical imidazoles	Oral triazoles
Preference and compliance issues	Some women prefer not to use pessaries or products delivered with an intravaginal applicator, which can be painful if there is particularly bad inflammation. Some women find topical cream soothing, however.	Simple and painless to use. Available as one or two dose no compliance issues.
Time until effect	Antifungal cream (applied externally) may relieve symptoms sooner than an intravaginal or oral preparation alone.	Oral treatment alone may tak slightly longer to take effect.
Adverse effects	Vulval inflammation and discharge most commonly reported.	More systemic effects such as nausea, headache, and abdominal pain.
Pregnancy	Suitable during pregnancy and breastfeeding.	Contraindicated during pregnancy and breastfeeding.
Contraception	Products containing topical imidazoles may damage latex condoms and diaphragms.	Anecdotal evidence that oral triazoles may cause oral contraceptive failure.
Cost to NHS*	Relatively inexpensive	Relatively expensive

* If a women is prescribed a cream in addition to a pessary or oral preparation, she may have to pay two prescription charges.

period, when the pathogen is prevented from regrowing and possibly eliminated:

- **Induction period:** consists of 6–12 days of daily treatment with a topical imidazole (clotrimazole, econazole or miconazole) or oral triazole (itraconazole, fluconazole). Topical clotrimazole and oral fluconazole or itraconazole are the usual drugs used.
- **Maintenance period:** consists of weekly treatment with a topical imidazole (typically clotrimazole), or weekly treatment with oral fluconazole, or monthly treatment with oral itraconazole. Maintenance is usually continued for 6 months.
- **Patient preference** should partly decide which regimen is used. Most women prefer the use of oral products to intravaginal creams or pessaries, especially over the longer term.
- **Licence status:** the use of antifungal drugs in maintenance therapy is not licensed.

[MacNeill and Carey, 2001; Nyirjesy, 2001; CEG, 2002; Scharbo-DeHaan and Anderson, 2003; Sobel, 2003; BNF [illegible], 2004]

The evidence for the treatment of recurrent vulvovaginal candidiasis is relatively poor. Most regimens are based on empirical data, expert opinion, extrapolation and theory rather than randomized controlled trials (RCTs). Consequently specific drug regimens are not often stated in guidelines [CEG, 2002].

The strongest evidence for the maintenance period comes from a recent RCT of 387 women with recurrent vulvovaginal candidiasis, who received either weekly fluconazole or placebo, for 6 months, after clinical and microbiological remission had been achieved following the induction period [Sobel et al, 2004]. They found:

- Most women receiving fluconazole remained disease-free during the maintenance period (91% compared to 36% in the placebo group, $p < 0.001$).
- A significantly greater proportion of women who had received fluconazole were disease-free 6 months after the maintenance period had finished (43% compared with 22% in the placebo group, $p < 0.001$).
- However, it was noted that the majority of women who had received maintenance treatment had suffered relapse within the space of one year (see below).

After the maintenance period is complete, treatment can be stopped once eradication is confirmed by culture. Nonthelesss, about half of women relapse 1–2 months after treatment cessation, even if they have been shown to be microbiologically cured. In these women, induction and maintenance therapy has to be repeated, possibly for a longer period (e.g. 12 months). A small number of women may require maintenance therapy for several years [Nyirjesy, 2001; Scharbo-DeHaan and Anderson, 2003; Sobel, 2003].

Depression and psychosexual problems (such as feeling 'unclean' or not wanting sex) can affect women with recurrent vulvovaginal candidiasis. These women should be treated sympathetically and given reassurance or counselling if necessary [Working Group of the British Society for Medical Mycology, 1995].

Severe vulvovaginal candidiasis

Severe vulvovaginal candidiasis can be a distressing and painful condition. It is characterized by extensive vulvar redness, oedema, excoriation, and fissure formation [Scharbo-DeHaan and Anderson, 2003].

Women with severe vulvovaginal candidiasis tend to have poorer responses to standard treatment than those with uncomplicated infection, and may require longer courses. A randomized controlled trial of women with severe vulvovaginal candidiasis found that treatment with two doses of fluconazole was more effective in curing symptoms of infection than standard one-dose treatment [Sobel et al, 2001].

- **Longer courses of treatment are recommended** in women with severe vulvovaginal candidiasis (although this use is unlicensed):
  - **Topical imidazoles** (e.g. clotrimazole) for 7–14 days
  - **Oral fluconazole** taken as two sequential doses, 72 hours apart

[Nyirjesy and Sobel, 2003]

Vulvovaginal candidiasis in pregnancy

- **Vulvovaginal candidiasis is more common in pregnant women,** with a higher prevalence of both asymptomatic colonization with *Candida albicans* and symptomatic candidiasis throughout pregnancy [CEG, 2002].
- **Oral triazoles (fluconazole and itraconazole) are contraindicated in pregnant women** [CEG, 2002]. Animal studies have shown that high doses of itraconazole cause fetal abnormalities, and there are concerns that fluconazole may have caused congenital defects in human babies [Weiner and Buhimschi, 2004]. The manufacturers advise that the drug should not be used in pregnancy or breastfeeding and that women of childbearing age should use adequate contraception. For further information contact the National Teratology Information Service (telephone 0191 232 1525).
- **Topical imidazoles (clotrimazole, econazole or miconazole) are safe to use in pregnant women.** Studies have shown that systemic absorption of these drugs is minimal and there have been no reported cases of fetal abnormalities using these preparations. Clotrimazole, miconazole, and econazole have been most extensively studied and are safe in pregnancy [Reef et al, 1995].
- **A recent Cochrane review** of ten trials concluded that topical imidazoles are more effective than topical nystatin in the treatment of pregnant women, and that longer courses of treatment may be necessary [Young and Jewell, 2004]. Typically guidelines recommend the use of topical imidazoles for 7 days [Scharbo-DeHaan and Anderson, 2003].

Non-albicans infections

- **Women who have vulvovaginal candidiasis caused by a species other than *Candida albicans*** are often more difficult to treat as there may be resistance to azoles. Referral to a specialist is recommended in this instance [Working Group of the British Society for Medical Mycology, 1995].
- **Treatment options** include maintenance with nystatin, topical boric acid, and flucytosine, and are generally reserved for secondary care [Scharbo-DeHaan and Anderson, 2003].

Other complicated infections

- **Diabetes mellitus** increases the likelihood of both colonization with *Candida* and the occurrence of symptomatic disease. It has been suggested that improving glucose control in these women may reduce the risk of vulvovaginal candidiasis [de Leon et al, 2002].
- **Immunocompromised or immunosuppressed** women are more likely to suffer from vulvovaginal candidiasis:
  - **HIV predisposes women to recurrent infection,** although the presence of recurrent thrush should not be taken as a reason to test for the virus.
  - **Long-term corticosteroid therapy** (or treatment with other immunosuppressive drugs) can cause thrush — these drugs should be avoided if possible.
- **Longer regimens of imidazoles (clotrimazole, econazole or miconazole)** are generally recommended in women who have vulvovaginal candidiasis in combination with

diabetes mellitus or who are immunosuppressed. Typically treatment should be prolonged to 7–14 days rather than a 3-day course or single dose.

Self management

- **Self diagnosis is unreliable** and use of over-the-counter (OTC) products should not be encouraged over the longer term. Studies have shown that up to two-thirds of women who have self-diagnosed uncomplicated thrush do not actually have the condition [Ferris et al, 2002].
- **Once an initial diagnosis of vulvovaginal candidiasis has been made,** women can be advised to consider using OTC products if a subsequent episode occurs. However, a consultation with a GP should always be sought in the following instances if the woman:
  - Is under 16, or over 60, years of age
  - May be pregnant or is breastfeeding
  - Has symptoms that are not entirely consistent with a previous episode (e.g. discharge is coloured or malodorous, there are ulcers or blisters)
  - Has systemic symptoms
  - Has had two episodes in 6 months, and has not consulted her GP about the condition for more than a year
  - Has had a previous sexually transmitted infection (or her partner has)
  - Has had abnormal menstrual bleeding or lower abdominal pain
  - Has suffered previous adverse reactions to antifungal drugs or they have proved ineffective
  - Does not experience complete resolution of symptoms after 7 days of treatment

[Watson and Bond, 2003]

- **All products are available at pharmacies only,** and consist of vaginal pessaries or creams (imidazoles), and oral fluconazole. Topical products are significantly less expensive than fluconazole.

Prophylactic measures

- **Depletion of lactobacilli** has been implicated in the pathogenesis of vulvovaginal candidiasis, which has led to research into replacement therapy, using live cultures of lactobacilli by either the oral or intravaginal route. However, at present these preparations are not recommended:
  - **Lactobacillus products** available often do not contain the correct hydrogen peroxide producing species usually present in healthy vaginal flora.
  - **There is presently no regulatory authority** regarding the contents of these products.
  - **Overall there is a lack of evidence** based on high quality randomized controlled clinical trials regarding the efficacy of these products.

[Mardh et al, 2002; Jeavons, 2003]

- **The ingestion of yoghurt** containing live lactobacilli for the prevention of vulvovaginal candidiasis is controversial. Whilst some studies have shown beneficial effects, at least one study suggested that yoghurt may actually increase the reoccurrence of vulvovaginal candidiasis, and so it is not recommended at present [Mardh et al, 2002].
- **Other products** sometimes used in the prevention of vulvovaginal candidiasis include pH reducing agents and oils, but there is no documented evidence to support their use. Tampons impregnated with tea tree oil are used by some women, but there is no information on their efficacy. In addition, it should be remembered that these products can provoke allergic reactions [Mardh et al, 2002].

References

NHS staff in England can link, free of charge, from references to full text journals by clicking on [Full text] c the PRODIGY website.

1. Bingham, J.S. (1999) What to do with the patient wi recurrent vulvovaginal candidiasis. *Sexually Transmitted Infections* 75(4), 225–227. [Full text]
2. BNF 47 (2004) *British National Formulary*. 47th ed London: British Medical Association and Royal Pharmaceutical Society of Great Britain.
3. CEG (2002) *National guideline on the management vulvovaginal candidiasis*. Clinical Effectiveness Grou www.bashh.org/guidelines/ceguidelines.htm [Access 16/03/2004].
4. de Leon, E.M., Jacober, S.J., Sobel, J.D. and Foxman B. (2002) Prevalence and risk factors for vaginal Candida colonization in women with type 1 and typ diabetes. *BMC Infectious Diseases* 2(1), 1.
5. Ferris, D.G., Nyirjesy, P., Sobel, J.D. et al (2002) Ov the-counter antifungal drug misuse associated with patient-diagnosed vulvovaginal candidiasis. *Obstetri & Gynecology* 99(3), 419–425.
6. Hainsworth, T. (2002) Diagnosis and management c candidiasis vaginitis. *Nursing Times* 98(49), 30–32.
7. Jeavons, H.S. (2003) Prevention and treatment of vulvovaginal candidiasis using exogenous Lactobacillus. *Journal of Obstetric, Gynecologic, & Neonatal Nursing* 32(3), 287–296.
8. Lee, A., Inch, S. and Finnigan, D. (Eds.) (2000) *Therapeutics in pregnancy and lactation*. Abingdon: Radcliffe Medical Press Ltd.
9. MacNeill, C. and Carey, J.C. (2001) Recurrent vulvovaginal candidiasis. *Current Women's Health Reports* 1(1), 31–35.
10. Mardh, P.A., Rodrigues, A.G., Genc, M. et al (2002) Facts and myths on recurrent vulvovaginal candidosi a review on epidemiology, clinical manifestations, diagnosis, pathogenesis and therapy. *International Journal of STD & AIDS* 13(8), 522–539. [Full text]
11. Marrazzo, J. (2002) Vulvovaginal candidiasis. *Britis Medical Journal* 325(7364), 586–587. [Full text]
12. MeReC (2004) An update on vulvovaginal candidias (thrush). *MeReC Bulletin* 14(4), 13–16.
13. Nyirjesy, P. (2001) Chronic vulvovaginal candidiasis *American Family Physician* 63(4), 697–702. [Full tex
14. Nyirjesy, P. and Sobel, J.D. (2003) Vulvovaginal candidiasis. *Obstetrics & Gynecology Clinics of Nor America* 30(4), 671–684.
15. Plummer, D.C. and Walters, W.A. (1993) Female genital tract discharge. *Baillieres Clinical Obstetrics Gynaecology* 7(1), 139–159.
16. Reef, S.E., Levine, W.C., McNeil, M.M. et al (1995) Treatment options for vulvovaginal candidiasis: 199 *Clinical Infectious Dieseases* 20(Suppl 1), S80-S90.
17. Ringdahl, E.N. (2000) Treatment of recurrent vulvovaginal candidiasis. *American Family Physician* 61(11), 3306–3312.
18. Scharbo-DeHaan, M. and Anderson, D.G. (2003) Th CDC 2002 guidelines for the treatment of sexually transmitted diseases: implications for women's healt care. *Journal of Midwifery & Women's Health* 48(2) 96–104.
19. Seller, R.H. (1996) Vaginal discharge with itching. In Seller, R.H. (Ed.) *Differential diagnosis of common complaints*. 3rd edn. London: W.B. Saunders Company. 353–361.
20. Sherrard, J. (2001) European guideline for the management of vaginal discharge. *International Journal of STD & AIDS* 12(Suppl 3), 73–77. [Full te

Sobel, J.D. (2003) Management of patients with recurrent vulvovaginal candidiasis. *Drugs* **63**(11), 1059–1066.
Sobel, J.D., Faro, S., Force, R.W. et al (1998) Vulvovaginal candidiasis: epidemiologic, diagnostic, and therapeutic considerations. *American Journal of Obstetrics and Gynecology* **178**(2), 203–211.
Sobel, J.D., Kapernick, P.S., Zervos, M. et al (2001) Treatment of complicated Candida vaginitis: comparison of single and sequential doses of fluconazole. *American Journal of Obstetrics & Gynecology* **185**(2), 363–369.
Sobel, J.D., Wiesenfeld, H.C., Martens, M. et al (2004) Maintenance fluconazole therapy for recurrent vulvovaginal candidiasis. *New England Journal of Medicine* **351**(9), 876–883.
Spence, D. (2003) Candidiasis (vulvovaginal). *Clinical Evidence* **10**(Dec), 2044–2057.
Watson, M.C. and Bond, C.M. (2003) Evidence-based guidelines for non-prescription treatment of vulvovaginal candidiasis (VVC). *Pharmacy World & Science* **25**(4), 129–134.

27. Watson, M.C., Grimshaw, J.M., Bond, C.M. et al (2002) Oral versus intra-vaginal imidazole and triazole anti-fungal agents for the treatment of uncomplicated vulvovaginal candidiasis (thrush): a systematic review. *BJOG: an International Journal of Obstetrics & Gynaecology* **109**(1), 85–95.
28. Weiner, C.P. and Buhimschi, C. (Eds.) (2004) *Drugs for pregnant and lactating women*. Philadelphia: Churchill Livingstone.
29. Working Group of the British Society for Medical Mycology (1995) Management of genital candidiasis. *British Medical Journal* **310**(6989), 1241–1244.
30. Young, G.L. and Jewell, D. (2004) *Topical treatment for vaginal candidiasis (thrush) in pregnancy (Cochrane Review)*. The Cochrane Library. Issue 1. Chichester, UK: John Wiley & Sons, Ltd.

PRODIGY GUIDANCE

Candida — oral

Last revised in February 2004
www.prodigy.nhs.uk/guidance.asp?gt=Candida - oral

Applies to people of all ages

This guidance covers the management of oral thrush in immunocompetent people.

This guidance does not cover the management of oral thrush in people with HIV infection, or in people receiving chemotherapy. It does not cover prophylaxis against oral thrush.

There is separate PRODIGY guidance for *Aphthous ulcer, Candida — female genital, Candida — skin and nails, Herpes simplex — oral,* and *Sore throat — acute.*

C

Goals

- The speedy resolution of symptoms

Contents

Scenarios
- Candida — oral p.278

Extended Information, p. 279

Candida — oral

Which therapy?

General issues

- **Treat any predisposing factor in conjunction with specific anticandidal therapy:**
  - Diabetes mellitus control should be optimized.
  - Review corticosteroid therapy (oral, inhaled, and topical).
  - Review oral antibiotic therapy.
  - Review medication that causes a dry mouth (e.g. antidepressants, antipsychotics).
  - Denture hygiene should be optimized.
  - Iron and folate deficiency should be treated if present.

Anticandidal therapy

- **First-line therapy is with topical anticandidal treatment,** consisting of amphotericin, miconazole, or nystatin. Prescribing habits and the person's preference will govern choice.
- **Second-line therapy is with systemic anticandidal treatment,** consisting of fluconazole or itraconazole.
- **Immunocompetent children should only receive topical anticandidal treatment.**

Practical prescribing points

For further information please see the *Medicines Compendium* (www.medicines.org.uk) or the *British National Formulary* (www.bnf.org).

- **Retain topical anticandidal treatment in contact with the lesions for as long as possible.** When deciding on the most appropriate choice of formulation, note that topically applied products may be easier to use (e.g. a gel may be better suited to an infant than a suspension that may be immediately swallowed).
- **Nystatin and amphotericin suspensions and miconazole gel** are not licensed in babies less than a month old. However, the risk benefit should be assessed on an individual basis.
- **Oral candidiasis and sore mouth** are commonly recognized problems with inhaled corticosteroid (ICS) use. They can be minimized by using a pressurized metered-dose inhaler with a large-volume spacer devic (which reduces oropharyngeal deposition by filtering o larger particles), and by rinsing the mouth with water after ICS use.
- **Itraconazole should not be prescribed to anyone with high risk of heart failure. The Committee on Safety of Medicines advises that those at risk include** people receiving high doses and longer treatment courses, old patients and those with cardiac disease, and patients receiving treatment with negatively inotropic drugs.
- **Fluconazole or itraconazole should not be used by pregnant or breastfeeding women.**
- **The anticoagulant effect of warfarin may be enhanced** by oral itraconazole and fluconazole, and also by the systemic absorption of miconazole oral gel.

Follow-up advice

- Follow-up is rarely necessary, but is advised if there is doubt about the diagnosis (e.g. if leukoplakia is the differential diagnosis).

Should I refer or investigate?

Refer?

- Refer if there is doubt about the diagnosis (e.g. leukoplakia).

Investigate?

- Consider investigations for diabetes mellitus, iron deficiency, folate deficiency, or immune status (e.g. HI if clinically appropriate.

Patient information leaflets

The following PILs are available at www.prodigy.nhs.uk

- Antifungal Medicines
- Thrush - Oral
- Thrush - Oral in Babies

Shared decision making

- **Topical nystatin, amphotericin,** or **miconazole** will usually clear oral thrush.
  - With drops, use a dropper to put the liquid onto affected areas.
  - With lozenges, suck them as they dissolve in the mouth.
  - With gel, smear it onto the affected areas (and onto dentures if appropriate).

Anti-thrush tablets such as **fluconazole** and **itraconazole** tend to be used only in more serious cases.

Some bouts of oral thrush can be prevented:

- If you have diabetes — is your blood sugar well controlled?
- If you use steroid inhalers — do you use a spacer? Also, gargle and rinse your mouth after using the inhaler.
- If you wear dentures — remove and soak them overnight in cleansing solution, and use an antiseptic mouthwash.
- If you take medication that causes a dry mouth — take frequent sips of water.
- Babies — make sure dummies and feeding equipment are sterilized.

Drug rationale

Drugs not included

Oral anticandidal treatment other than preparations containing fluconazole and itraconazole are either not licensed for oral candidiasis, or are licensed only for the treatment of serious resistant cases.

Drugs included

Nystatin and amphotericin (polyene anticandidals) are offered. There is no evidence of a difference in efficacy between them. Nystatin and amphotericin are not absorbed systemically. Adverse effects include hypersensitivity and gastrointestinal reactions. Both are applied topically to the mucosal membrane and are available as suspension and lozenges/pastilles. Nystatin pastilles contain sugar. Nystatin and amphotericin are both available as sugar-free suspensions, and amphotericin is available as a sugar-free lozenge.
Miconazole is the only imidazole anticandidal drug available that can be applied topically. However, although it is locally applied, it is absorbed sufficiently for consideration of adverse effects and drug interactions to be needed. Miconazole is available as a sugar-free gel.
Fluconazole and itraconazole are offered. They are the only oral imidazoles licensed for the treatment of acute, uncomplicated oral mucosal candidiasis. Fluconazole is offered at two doses — the higher dose of 100 mg daily is for more severe infections.
[BNF 46, 2003]

Prescriptions

Topical liquids

Nystatin 100,000units/ml s/f susp: use 1ml four times a day

- Age from 1 month onwards
- Nystatin 100,000u/ml s/f susp. Using the oral dispenser provided, place 1 ml in the mouth and hold near the affected area(s) four times a day; supply 30 ml; NHS Cost £1.96.

Amphotericin 100mg/ml s/f susp: use 1ml four times a day

- Age from 1 month onwards
- Amphotericin 100mg/ml susp. Using the oral dispenser provided, place 1 ml in the mouth and hold near the affected area(s) four times a day; supply 12 ml; NHS Cost £2.31.

Topical lozenges/gels

Miconazole oral gel: use 2.5ml twice a day

- Age from 1 month to 23 months
- Miconazole 24mg/ml oral gel. Place 2.5ml in the mouth and hold near the affected area(s) twice a day; supply 15 grams; NHS Cost £2.37.

Miconazole oral gel: use 5ml twice a day

- Age from 2 to 5 years
- Miconazole 24mg/ml oral gel. Place 5ml in the mouth and hold near the affected area(s) twice a day; supply 15 grams; NHS Cost £2.37.

Miconazole oral gel: use 5ml four times a day

- Age from 6 to 11 years
- Miconazole 24mg/ml oral gel. Place 5ml in the mouth and hold near the affected area(s) four times a day; supply 80 grams; NHS Cost £5.00.

Miconazole oral gel: use 5ml to10ml four times a day

- Age from 12 years onwards
- Miconazole 24mg/ml oral gel. Place 5ml to 10ml in the mouth and hold near the affected area(s) four times a day; supply 80 grams; NHS Cost £5.00.

Nystatin pastilles: use one pastille four times day

- Age from 12 years onwards
- Nystatin 100,000unit pastilles. Suck one pastille slowly four times a day; supply 28 pastilles; NHS Cost £3.00.

Amphotericin 10mg lozenges: use one lozenge four times a day

- Age from 12 years onwards
- Amphotericin 10mg lozenges. Allow one lozenge to dissolve slowly in the mouth four times a day; supply 60 lozenge; NHS Cost £3.00.

Systemic treatment

Fluconazole 50mg once a day for 7 days

- Age from 16 years onwards
- Fluconazole 50mg capsules. Take one capsule once a day for 7 days; supply 7 capsules; NHS Cost £14.51.

Fluconazole 50mg once a day for 14 days

- Age from 16 years onwards
- Fluconazole 50mg capsules. Take one capsule once a day for 14 days; supply 14 capsules; NHS Cost £29.02.

Itraconazole 100mg once a day for 15 days

- Age from 16 years onwards
- Itraconazole 100mg capsules. Take one capsule once a day for 15 days; supply 15 capsules; NHS Cost £15.72.

Systemic treatment (severe infection)

Fluconazole 100mg once a day for 7 days

- Age from 16 years onwards
- Fluconazole 50mg capsules. Take two capsules once a day for 7 days; supply 14 capsules; NHS Cost £29.02.

Fluconazole 100mg once a day for 14 days

- Age from 16 years onwards
- Fluconazole 50mg capsules. Take two capsules once a day for 14 days; supply 28 capsules; NHS Cost £58.04.

Extended Information

Background information

- What is it? p.280
- How common is it? p.280
- How do I know my patient has it? p.280
- What else might it be? p.280
- Complications and prognosis p.280

What is it?

- **Oral thrush is infection of the oral cavity by *Candida* species.** The infection is usually due to *Candida albicans*, although many other species of *Candida* have been implicated in people who are immunocompromised.
- ***C albicans* is a common commensal in the oral cavity.** Reports of carriage rates vary, from 18% in healthy adults to 50% in infants [Lynch, 1994].
- **The oral cavity is sterile at birth, but may become colonized by *C albicans*** during vaginal delivery, during breastfeeding or bottle-feeding, by kissing, or by dummies. Oral thrush is rare during the first week of life, and is most common in the fourth week.
- **The development of oral thrush from asymptomatic carriage requires the presence of one or more of the following risk factors:**
  - **Infancy** — this is presumed to be due to immaturities in the immune system.
  - **Old age** — ageing by itself is considered a risk factor. In addition, many elderly people have a cluster of the risk factors given below.
  - **Dentures** — especially if they do not fit well.
  - **Oral antibiotic therapy** — particularly after broad-spectrum antibiotics.
  - **Corticosteroids** (oral, topical, or inhaled).
  - **Excessive use of antibacterial mouthwash.**
  - **Dry mouth** — medication-induced (e.g. antidepressants, antipsychotics, chemotherapy), after radiotherapy to the head or neck, or in Sjögren's syndrome.
  - **Trauma** to the oral cavity — including surgery.
  - **Diabetes mellitus.**
  - **Iron deficiency.**
  - **Folate deficiency.**
  - **Immunodeficiency** — including HIV infection, chemotherapy, and malignancy.

[Scully et al, 1994; Hoppe, 1997; Marsh and Martin, 1999]

How common is it?

- **In infants,** oral thrush is rare in the first week of life, is most common in the fourth week of life affecting 14%, and decreases to 4% by the tenth week [Hoppe, 1997].
- Studies of other age groups use only subjects at high risk of oral thrush, and we were not able to obtain reliable data for the general population.

How do I know my patient has it?

Symptoms

- Oral thrush may be asymptomatic.
- Symptoms include pain, a burning sensation, and hypersensitivity to stimuli (hot, cold, salt, or spices).

Signs

- **Oral thrush typically presents as white plaques on the mucosal surfaces.** These are most commonly seen on the buccal mucosa, tongue, and gums; they may also occur on the palate, fauces, uvula, and tonsils. The plaques may coalesce, and may even cover the entire oral cavity. They may become yellow or grey. They can be wiped off to reveal a raw, erythematous base that may bleed.
- **Oral thrush may present as an atrophic form.** There are no plaques, but there are erythematous areas on the tongue, palate, or buccal mucosa. This form may follow therapy with oral antibiotics or corticosteroids.
- **Denture wearers** may develop an area of chronic erythema and oedema under the upper dentures. The mucosal surface under lower dentures is rarely affected.
- **Angular stomatitis may occur,** particularly in denture wearers, or in someone deficient in vitamin B_{12} or iron [Lynch, 1994; Scully et al, 1994; Hoppe, 1997; Marsh and Martin, 1999]

What else might it be?

- **Leukoplakia** is a premalignant condition that can usually be distinguished from oral thrush because the plaque of leukoplakia cannot be wiped off. A plaque of oral thrush can be wiped off to reveal a raw, erythematous base that may bleed.

Complications and prognosis

- **Feeding problems may occur in infants.** Complications are otherwise rare.
- **Oral thrush usually responds promptly** to appropriate management.

Management issues

- General issues p.280
- Anticandidal therapy p.280

General issues

- **It is important to treat any predisposing factor in conjunction with specific anticandidal therapy:**
  - **Diabetes mellitus** control should be optimized.
  - **Corticosteroid therapy (oral, inhaled, and topical)** should be reviewed. Gargling and rinsing the mouth should be performed immediately after the use of inhaled corticosteroids.
  - **Oral antibiotic therapy** should be reviewed.
  - **Medication that causes a dry mouth** (e.g. antidepressants, antipsychotics) should be reviewed.
  - **Denture hygiene** should be optimized, including removing dentures at night, soaking them overnight in cleansing solution, and using antiseptic mouthwash.
  - **Iron and folate deficiency** should be treated if present.

Anticandidal therapy

- **First-line therapy is with topical anticandidal treatment,** which consists of amphotericin, miconazole, and nystatin. Trials comparing these treatments have small sample sizes and are methodologically flawed. We are therefore not able to offer guidance on the choice of topical anticandidal treatment. It is likely that prescribing habits and the person's preference will govern the choice. Although it is a topical treatment, miconazole is absorbed to such an extent that possible interaction may need to be considered.
- **Second-line therapy is with systemic anticandidal treatment.** Drugs indicated for treatment of immunocompetent people are fluconazole and itraconazole. Most trials of these treatments are in immunocompromised people (mainly those with HIV infection, or those receiving chemotherapy). There are few trials comparing these treatments with each other or with topical treatments in immunocompetent people; those trials that have been undertaken are of small size. We are therefore not able to offer guidance on the choice of systemic anticandidal treatment, other than to point out that systemic anticandidal treatment is much more expensive than is topical. It is likely that personal preference and prescribing habits will govern choice.
- **Immunocompetent children should only receive topical anticandidal treatment.** Results of trials with topical treatments are such that there is no justification to

rescribe systemic anticandidal treatment for mmunocompetent children [Hoppe, 1997].
arsh and Martin, 1999; Scully, 2002; Pankhurst, 2003]

eferences

BNF 46 (2003) *British National Formulary*. 46th edn. London: British Medical Association and Royal Pharmaceutical Society of Great Britain.
Hoppe, J.E. (1997) Treatment of oropharyngeal candidiasis and candidal diaper dermatitis in neonates and infants: review and reappraisal. *Pediatric Infectious Disease Journal* 16(9), 885–894.

3. Lynch, D.P. (1994) Oral candidiasis. History, classification, and clinical presentation. *Oral Surgery, Oral Medicine, Oral Pathology* 78(2), 189–193.
4. Marsh, P. and Martin, M.V. (Eds.) (1999) Oral fungal infections. In: *Oral microbiology*. 4th edn. Oxford: Wright. 153–162.
5. Pankhurst, C. (2003) Candidiasis (oropharyngeal). *Clinical Evidence* 10(Dec), 1623–1639.
6. Scully, C. (2002) *Candidiasis, mucosal*. eMedicine.com, Inc. www.emedicine.com [Accessed: 02/09/2003].
7. Scully, C., el Kabir, M. and Samaranayake, L.P. (1994) Candida and oral candidosis: a review. *Critical Reviews in Oral Biology & Medicine* 5(2), 125–157.

PRODIGY GUIDANCE

Candida — skin and nails

Last revised in December 2002
www.guidance.prodigy.nhs.uk/Candida - skin and nails

Applies to people of all ages

This guidance covers the management of people with *Candida* infection of the skin and nail folds (paronychia), with o without nail involvement.

This guidance does not cover the management of oral or systemic candidiasis, angular cheilitis, nappy rash, other fungal infections (dermatophyte or 'tinea'), erythrasma, bacterial skin infections, or candidal balanitis.

There is separate PRODIGY guidance for the treatment of vulvovaginal thrush (*Candida — female genital*).

Goals

- Eradication of candidal infection
- Prevention of recurrence

Contents

Scenarios

- Candida of skin p.282
- Candidal paronychia and associated nail infection p.284

Extended Information, p. 285

Which scenario?

- **Candida of skin:** covers the treatment of cutaneous candidiasis (most commonly intertriginous).
- **Candidal paronychia and associated nail infection:** covers the treatment of paronychia and associated nail infection caused by *Candida*.

Candida of skin

Which therapy?

- **Offer general advice** regarding hygiene, keeping the skin dry, and avoiding skin occlusion. Simply keeping the area dry may be sufficient treatment.
- **Topical nystatin** is effective against *Candida,* but not against tinea.
- **Topical imidazoles** (clotrimazole, econazole, ketoconazole, miconazole, and sulconazole) are effective against both *Candida* and tinea, and may be preferred if diagnostic doubt exists.
- **A combination product containing an imidazole/nystatin plus 0.5% or 1% hydrocortisone** may be considered if there is marked inflammation and the person is very uncomfortable, or underlying eczema is present.
- **Systemic treatment** is only indicated in severe, extensive skin infection; and/or systemic infection (e.g. in immunosuppressed people); or in the rare person unresponsive to topical treatment. Specialist assessment should usually be considered in such cases.

Practical prescribing points

For further information see the *Medicines Compendium* (www.medicines.org.uk) or the *British National Formulary* (www.bnf.org).

- **Topical preparations containing hydrocortisone** should be applied sparingly to avoid skin atrophy on thin skin areas. If no improvement is seen, the diagnosis should be reassessed and, if appropriate, another preparation considered.
- **Topical nystatin** can stain clothes yellow, which may affect compliance.

Should I refer or investigate?

Refer?

- **Consider referring:**
  - People not responding to appropriate treatment of adequate duration
  - Widespread severe infection (possibility of immunosuppression)
- Appropriate mycological samples should be taken bef referral.
- **Admit any person with suspected systemic candidiasis** (e.g. individual with immunosuppression).

Investigate?

- **Skin swab or scrapings** for microscopic examination a culture may be useful if the diagnosis is uncertain, or t person is not responding to treatment. (Note that such investigation is likely to lead to false negative results if skin swabs or scrapings are taken within 2 weeks of applying topical preparations.)
- **Blood glucose,** if the condition is a recurrent problem, order to exclude diabetes mellitus.

Patient information leaflets

The following PILs are available at www.prodigy.nhs.uk

- Antifungal Medicines
- Candidal Skin Infection

Shared decision making

- You have an infection of the skin with a bug called *Candida*.
- **Antifungal cream** is the usual treatment. It may be needed for several weeks before the infection goes completely.
- **An antifungal cream with a mild steroid** is sometimes used to reduce inflammation caused by the infection.

Drug rationale

Drugs not included

- **Oral (systemic) treatment** is only indicated in: severe, extensive skin infection; systemic infection (e.g. in immunosuppressed people); or in the rare person unresponsive to topical treatment. Specialist assessmen should usually be considered in such cases.
- **Topical terbinafine** not licensed for use in children.

Salicylic acid and undecenoate preparations are considered less suitable for prescribing in fungal skin infections.

Products containing a corticosteroid alone are not recommended. An undiagnosed fungal or secondary bacterial infection may be present, which could be exacerbated by their use.

Topical antibacterial products that do not contain an anticandial component are not recommended, as they are not effective in treating candidal infections.

rugs included

Topical nystatin is effective against *Candida* (but not dermatophyte infections, thus requiring a definite diagnosis).

Topical imidazoles (clotrimazole, econazole, ketoconazole, miconazole, and sulconazole) are effective against *Candida* (and also against dermatophytes). There is little evidence of difference between these preparations. Product selection will depend on prescriber/user preference.

Topical combination products containing hydrocortisone 0.5% or 1% plus an anticandial (an imidazole or nystatin) are included for the management of infection with uncomfortable marked inflammation, or if underlying eczema is present. They should not be used for more than a week unless otherwise directed, in order to try to avoid any adverse effects.

Ointment and cream formulations of active anticandidals are included. Creams are emulsions of oil and water; they tend to be well absorbed into the skin. Ointments are greasy preparations that are insoluble in water, are more occlusive than creams and, unlike creams, do not contain preservatives. There is no evidence to support the use of one preparation over another, and the patient's preference will often govern choice.

/IcKay, 1988; American Academy of Dermatology, 1996; NF 44, 2002]

rescriptions

nticandidal-only preparations

/statin 100,000units/g cream
- All ages
- Nystatin 100,000units/g cream. Apply to the affected area 2 to 4 times a day. Continue for 7 days after the affected area has healed; supply 30 grams; NHS Cost £2.18.

/statin 100,000units/g ointment
- All ages
- Nystatin 100,000units/g ointment. Apply to the affected area 2 to 4 times a day. Continue for 7 days after the affected area has healed; supply 30 grams; NHS Cost £1.75.

otrimazole 1% cream
- All ages
- Clotrimazole 1% cream. Apply to the affected area 2 to 3 times a day. Continue for at least 2 weeks after the affected area has healed; supply 20 grams; NHS Cost £1.77; OTC Cost £2.14.

otrimazole 1% solution (for application to hairy areas)
- All ages
- Clotrimazole 1% solution. Apply to the affected area twice a day. Continue for at least 2 weeks the affected area has healed; supply 20 ml; NHS Cost £2.43; OTC Cost £4.25.

Econazole 1% cream
- All ages
- Econazole 1% cream. Apply to the affected area twice a day. Continue for at least 2 weeks the affected area has healed; supply 30 grams; NHS Cost £2.75; OTC Cost £4.85.

Ketoconazole 2% cream
- All ages
- Ketoconazole 2% cream. Apply to the affected area twice a day. Continue for at least 2 weeks the affected area has healed; supply 30 grams; NHS Cost £3.81.

Miconazole 2% cream
- All ages
- Miconazole 2% cream. Apply to the affected area twice a day. Continue for 10 days after the affected area has healed; supply 30 grams; NHS Cost £2.07; OTC Cost £3.65.

Sulconazole 1% cream
- All ages
- Sulconazole 1% cream. Apply to the affected area twice a day. Continue for at least 2 weeks the affected area has healed; supply 30 grams; NHS Cost £3.00; OTC Cost £5.29.

Anticandidal + hydrocortisone preparations

Clotrimazole 1% + hydrocortisone 1% cream
- All ages
- Hydrocortisone+clotrimaz cream. Apply thinly to the affected area once or twice a day. Use for a maximum of 7 days unless otherwise directed; supply 30 grams; NHS Cost £2.38.

Miconazole 2% + hydrocortisone 1% cream
- All ages
- Hydrocortisone+miconazole cream. Apply thinly to the affected area once or twice a day. Use for a maximum of 7 days unless otherwise directed; supply 30 grams; NHS Cost £2.24.

Miconazole 2% + hydrocortisone 1% ointment
- All ages
- Hydrocortisone+miconazole ointment. Apply thinly to the affected area once or twice a day. Use for a maximum of 7 days unless otherwise directed; supply 30 grams; NHS Cost £2.25.

Econazole 1% + hydrocortisone 1% cream
- Age under 11 years
- Hydrocortisone+econazole cream. Apply thinly to the affected area twice a day. Use for a maximum of 5 days unless otherwise directed; supply 30 grams; NHS Cost £2.25.

Econazole 1% + hydrocortisone 1% cream
- Age from 12 years onwards
- Hydrocortisone+econazole cream. Apply thinly to the affected area twice a day. Use for a maximum of 7 days unless otherwise directed; supply 30 grams; NHS Cost £2.25.

Nystatin + chlorhexidine + hydrocortisone 0.5% cream
- All ages
- Nystaform-HC 0.5% cream. Apply thinly to the affected area twice a day. Use for a maximum of 7 days unless otherwise directed; supply 30 grams; NHS Cost £2.66.

Nystatin + chlorhexidine + hydrocortisone 1% ointment
- All ages
- Nystaform-HC 1% ointment. Apply thinly to the affected area twice a day. Use for a maximum of 7 days unless otherwise directed; supply 30 grams; NHS Cost £2.66.

Timodine cream (contains nystatin + hydrocortisone 0.5%)

- All ages
- Timodine cream. Apply thinly to the affected area twice a day. Use for a maximum of 7 days unless otherwise directed; supply 30 grams; NHS Cost £2.38.

Candidal paronychia and associated nail infection

Which therapy?

- **Offer general advice** regarding hygiene, keeping the skin dry, and avoiding skin occlusion.
- Topical nystatin or an imidazole (clotrimazole, econazole, ketoconazole, miconazole, or sulconazole) is usually effective for candidal paronychia and associated nail infection.
- **Treatment for 3–6 months may be necessary,** until a new cuticle has formed.
- **A combination product containing an imidazole/nystatin plus 0.5% or 1% hydrocortisone** may be considered if there is marked inflammation and the person is very uncomfortable, or underlying eczema is present.
- **Advise people with *Candida* infection of the proximal nail plate** to apply treatment to the paronychia and proximal nail plate.
- **Resistant cases or distal nail involvement** require treatment with tioconazole or amorolfine nail paint, usually for at least 6 months for fingernails and 12 months for toenails.
  - **Tioconazole nail paint** is applied twice daily and can be used in children.
  - **Amorolfine nail lacquer** is applied to the affected nail once weekly, but is not licensed for use in children.
- **Systemic treatment is rarely necessary,** except in the context of immunosuppression. It is usually best to seek specialist advice in such cases.

Practical prescribing points

For further information please see the *Medicines Compendium* (www.medicines.org.uk) or the *British National Formulary* (www.bnf.org).

- **Topical preparations containing hydrocortisone** should be applied sparingly to avoid skin atrophy on thin skin areas. If no improvement is seen, the diagnosis should be reassessed and, if appropriate, another preparation considered.
- **Topical nystatin** can stain clothes yellow, which may affect compliance.

Should I refer or investigate?

Refer?

- **Consider referring:**
  - People with resistant nail disease (either to clarify diagnosis or to assist in treatment)
  - Widespread nail disease or severe, chronic candidal paronychia (possible immunosuppression)
- Appropriate mycological samples should be investigated before referral.
- **Admit any person with suspected systemic candidiasis** (e.g. individual with immunosuppression).

Investigate?

- **Swab or scrapings** of paronychial area for microscopic examination and culture may be useful if the diagnosis is uncertain or the person is not responding to treatment. (Note that such investigation is likely to lead to false negative results if skin swabs or scrapings are taken within 2 weeks of applying topical preparations.)
- **Take nail clippings** for microscopic examination and culture to confirm candidal nail infection prior to treating and to exclude tinea infection.
- **Blood glucose,** if the condition is a recurrent problem, order to exclude diabetes mellitus.

Patient information leaflets

The following PILs are available at www.prodigy.nhs.uk

- Antifungal Medicines
- Paronychia

Shared decision making

- You have an infection of the nail fold with a germ calle *Candida.*
- **Slight damage to the nail fold,** such as biting nails, allo in infection. Infection is also common in people who work with their hands in water a lot.
- **Antifungal cream or paint** is the usual treatment. It ma be needed for several months before the infection goes completely.
- To help prevent a recurrence:
  - Do not bite your nails.
  - Keep your hands and feet dry as much as possible. D well after washing.
  - Wear rubber gloves (preferably cotton lined) if working a lot with water.
  - Do not wear gloves or artificial nails for long periods

Drug rationale

Drugs not included

- **Oral (systemic) therapy** is indicated in severe or extensi candidal paronychia or onychomycosis, especially as such cases are often associated with an immune deficiency state [Denning et al, 1995]. Specialist assessment should usually be considered before commencing treatment.
- **Salicylic acid or undecenoate preparations:** there is littl published evidence of efficacy in fungal nail infections.
- **Products containing a corticosteroid alone** are not recommended. An undiagnosed fungal or secondary bacterial infection may be present, which could be exacerbated by their use.
- **Topical antibacterial products** that do not contain an anticandial component are not recommended, as they are not effective in treating candidal infections.

Drugs included

- **Topical nystatin** is usually effective for candidal paronychia and proximal nail involvement. Treatment lasting 3–6 months is usually necessary [Denning et al, 1995].
- **A topical imidazole (clotrimazole, econazole, ketoconazole, miconazole, or sulconazole)** is also effective for candidal paronychia and proximal nail involvement. Treatment lasting 3–6 months is usually necessary [Denning et al, 1995]. There is little evidence of difference between these preparations. Product selection will depend on prescriber/user preference.
- **Topical combination products containing hydrocortisone 0.5% or 1% plus an anticandial** (an imidazole or nystatin) are included for the management of infection with uncomfortable marked inflammation, or if underlying eczema is present. They should not be

used for more than a week unless otherwise directed, in order to try to avoid any adverse effects.

Tioconazole or amorolfine nail paint can be used for resistant cases or distal nail involvement, usually for at least 6 months for fingernails and 12 months for toenails [Denning et al, 1995]. Note: amorolfine nail lacquer is not licensed for use in children.

Prescriptions

Anticandidal-only preparations

Nystatin 100,000units/g cream
- All ages
- Nystatin 100,000units/g cream. Apply to the affected area 2 to 4 times a day. Continue for 7 days after the affected area has healed; supply 30 grams; NHS Cost £2.18.

Nystatin 100,000units/g ointment
- All ages
- Nystatin 100,000units/g ointment. Apply to the affected area 2 to 4 times a day. Continue for 7 days after the affected area has healed; supply 30 grams; NHS Cost £1.75.

Clotrimazole 1% cream
- All ages
- Clotrimazole 1% cream. Apply to the affected area 2 to 3 times a day. Continue for at least 2 weeks after the affected area has healed; supply 20 grams; NHS Cost £1.77; OTC Cost £2.14.

Econazole 1% cream
- All ages
- Econazole 1% cream. Apply to the affected area twice a day. Continue for at least 2 weeks the affected area has healed; supply 30 grams; NHS Cost £2.75; OTC Cost £4.85.

Ketoconazole 2% cream
- All ages
- Ketoconazole 2% cream. Apply to the affected area twice a day. Continue for at least 2 weeks the affected area has healed; supply 30 grams; NHS Cost £3.81.

Miconazole 2% cream
- All ages
- Miconazole 2% cream. Apply to the affected area twice a day. Continue for 10 days after the affected area has healed; supply 30 grams; NHS Cost £2.07; OTC Cost £3.65.

Sulconazole 1% cream
- All ages
- Sulconazole 1% cream. Apply to the affected area twice a day. Continue for at least 2 weeks the affected area has healed; supply 30 grams; NHS Cost £3.00; OTC Cost £5.29.

Anticandidal + hydrocortisone preparations

Clotrimazole 1% + hydrocortisone 1% cream
- All ages
- Hydrocortisone+clotrimaz cream. Apply thinly to the affected area once or twice a day. Use for a maximum of 7 days unless otherwise directed; supply 30 grams; NHS Cost £2.38.

Miconazole 2% + hydrocortisone 1% cream
- All ages
- Hydrocortisone+miconazole cream. Apply thinly to the affected area once or twice a day. Use for a maximum of 7 days unless otherwise directed; supply 30 grams; NHS Cost £2.24.

Miconazole 2% + hydrocortisone 1% ointment
- All ages
- Hydrocortisone+miconazole ointment. Apply thinly to the affected area once or twice a day. Use for a maximum of 7 days unless otherwise directed; supply 30 grams; NHS Cost £2.25.

Econazole 1% + hydrocortisone 1% cream
- Age under 11 years
- Hydrocortisone+econazole cream. Apply thinly to the affected area twice a day. Use for a maximum of 5 days unless otherwise directed; supply 30 grams; NHS Cost £2.25.

Econazole 1% + hydrocortisone 1% cream
- Age from 12 years onwards
- Hydrocortisone+econazole cream. Apply thinly to the affected area twice a day. Use for a maximum of 7 days unless otherwise directed; supply 30 grams; NHS Cost £2.25.

Nystatin + chlorhexidine + hydrocortisone 0.5% cream
- All ages
- Nystaform-HC 0.5% cream. Apply thinly to the affected area twice a day. Use for a maximum of 7 days unless otherwise directed; supply 30 grams; NHS Cost £2.66.

Nystatin + chlorhexidine + hydrocortisone 1% ointment
- All ages
- Nystaform-HC 1% ointment. Apply thinly to the affected area twice a day. Use for a maximum of 7 days unless otherwise directed; supply 30 grams; NHS Cost £2.66.

Timodine cream (contains nystatin + hydrocortisone 0.5%)
- All ages
- Timodine cream. Apply thinly to the affected area twice a day. Use for a maximum of 7 days unless otherwise directed; supply 30 grams; NHS Cost £2.38.

Nail paint (for resistant cases or distal nail involvement)

Tioconazole 28% nail solution
- All ages
- Tioconazole 28% solution. Apply to the affected nail(s) and surrounding skin twice a day. Treatment should continue for up to six months; supply 12 ml; NHS Cost £27.38.

Amorolfine 5% nail lacquer
- Age from 12 years onwards
- Amorolfine lacquer. Apply to the affected nail(s) once or twice a week; supply 1 5ml pack; NHS Cost £25.00.

Extended Information

Background information

- What is it? p.285
- How common is it? p.286
- How do I know my patient has it? p.286
- What are the risk factors? p.286
- What else might it be? p.286
- Complications and prognosis p.286

What is it?

- *Candida* **yeasts** are part of the normal flora of the skin, mouth, intestinal tract, and vagina.
- **Cutaneous candidiasis results from an overgrowth of the** *Candida* **yeast**, a type of fungus, usually caused by *Candida albicans*, although other *Candida* species are occasionally involved.

- This overgrowth most commonly occurs as a consequence of occlusion, maceration, and altered barrier function of the skin.
- **Candidiasis may also affect** the proximal nail fold (cuticle) resulting in paronychia, and occasionally involves the nail itself.

[McKay, 1988; Hymes and Duvic, 1993; Denning et al, 1995; American Academy of Dermatology, 1996]

How common is it?

- **Cutaneous candidiasis** is a common condition. It occurs particularly in immunosuppressed people, in whom it may be a feature of systemic infection [Pariser, 1990].
- **Paronychia:** *Candida* nail fold infection is relatively common and is usually seen in people with occupations requiring prolonged immersion of hands or feet in water. Micro-organisms, both *Candida* species and bacteria, invade the area under the nail fold. This is identified by swelling, inflammation, and sometimes discharge of pus. The cuticle is lost and the nail plate surface develops irregular ridges and deformity. There may be some lifting of the nail (onycholysis), which allows further access to micro-organisms and ongoing deformity [British Association of Dermatologists, 2000].
- **Onychomycosis:** *Candida* is a relatively uncommon cause of onychomycosis, which is much more likely to be due to dermatophyte (ringworm) fungi. Note that yeasts and dermatophytes are both a type of fungus but each requires a different therapeutic approach. Onychomycosis does not typically cause paronychia, although both may be present if the infection is due to *Candida*; the surface of the nail plate is generally smooth but there is marked hyperkeratosis under the nail.
- Candidal onychomycosis is uncommon — isolation of *Candida* from nails is most likely when there is peripheral vascular disease (such as Raynaud's phenomenon) or when there is a previously damaged nail due to other causes [British Association of Dermatologists, 2000].

How do I know my patient has it?

Cutaneous candidiasis

- **Site:** usually located in intertriginous areas (skin folds), e.g. groin, axillae, and under the breasts. It can also occur in the interdigital web spaces and at the corners of the mouth (angular cheilitis).
- **Symptoms:** pain or burning, itching.
- **Signs:** red inflamed skin, often with satellite lesions (pustules and papules) and skin erosions. The flexures are typically involved. Candidal folliculitis (inflammation of the hair follicle) can occur and may be confused with bacterial folliculitis.
- **Investigations:** skin swabs or scrapings for microscopic examination and culture of the organism may be helpful if the diagnosis is uncertain.

Candidal paronychia

- **Site:** usually affects fingernails rather than toenails.
- **Signs:** erythema, oedema, and usually a small amount of purulent discharge with loss of cuticle and deformity of the surface of the nail plate.
- **Symptoms:** often uncomfortable, tends to be chronic.
- **Investigations:** swabs or scrapings of the nail fold for microscopic examination and culture may be helpful if the diagnosis is uncertain.

Candidal onychomycosis

- **Site:** usually affects fingernails rather than toenails.
- **Signs:** onycholysis, hyperkeratosis, and discolouration. Affected nails are discoloured white, green, or occasionally black (although green or black discolouration usually suggests secondary bacterial infection rather than *Candida*).
- **Symptoms:** candidal onychomycosis is generally not symptomatic, apart from pressure effects of a thickene[d] nail.
- **Investigations:** nail clippings are necessary to make a diagnosis of candidal onychomycosis where there is no associated paronychia, particularly if distal.

What are the risk factors?

The presence of risk factors for candidiasis should height[en] suspicion:

- Risk factors for cutaneous candidiasis:
  - Diabetes mellitus
  - Obesity
  - Dermatosis at flexures (e.g. psoriasis, eczema)
  - Vascular insufficiency
  - Occlusion (e.g. dressings, casts)
  - Use of systemic corticosteroids or antibiotic therapy
  - Immunosuppression (e.g. neutropaenia, HIV infectio[n])
  - Tropical environment
- Risk factors for candidal paronychia/onychomycosis:
  - Prolonged exposure to water (e.g. in dish washers, bartenders, beauticians)
  - Occlusion (e.g. artificial nails, prolonged use of glove[s])
  - Trauma to nail folds and cuticles (e.g. nail biting, manicure, occupational)
  - Immunosuppression

[McKay, 1988; Pariser, 1990; Vartivarian and Smith, 1993; Denning et al, 1995; MeReC, 1997]

What else might it be?

Cutaneous candidiasis

- Dermatophyte (tinea) infection (no satellite lesions, sparing of scrotum)
- Erythrasma
- Bacterial skin infection
- Eczema (atopic or contact)

Candidal paronychia/onychomycosis

- Bacterial paronychia (often acute, very inflamed, purulent, and painful)
- Herpetic whitlow
- Dermatophyte (tinea) infection of nail (usually toes)
- Other fungal nail infection
- Non-fungal condition associated with nail dystrophy (e.g. onychogryphosis, psoriasis, eczema). The presence of nail surface pitting and of psoriasis at other sites supports a diagnosis of psoriasis rather than fungal nail infection; however, the two can only be reliably distinguished, particularly in toenails, by mycological examination of nail clippings.
- Very rarely, nail bed tumour such as squamous cell carcinoma
- *Candida* infection of the nails may be secondary to oth[er] nail dystrophy.

[Denning et al, 1995; American Academy of Dermatolog[y], 1996; MeReC, 1997]

Complications and prognosis

- Bacterial superinfection can occur.
- Disfiguring and uncomfortable nail dystrophy can occu[r].

Management issues

- General measures p.287
- Cutaneous candidiasis p.287
- Candidal paronychia p.287

Candidal nail infection p.287

General measures

- **Offer general advice** regarding hygiene, keeping the skin dry, and avoiding occlusion in order to aid healing and prevent recurrence.
- **Identify risk factors** for *Candida* infection and treat where appropriate.
- **Exclude diabetes mellitus** if infection is recurrent.
- Inappropriate use of antibiotic or topical corticosteroids may aggravate the condition.

Cutaneous candidiasis

- **Topical antifungals** should be prescribed in most cases — nystatin and the imidazoles (clotrimazole, econazole, ketoconazole, miconazole, and sulconazole) are all effective.
- **Topical hydrocortisone 0.5% or 1% in combination with a topical antifungal** is not usually necessary, but may be appropriate if there is marked inflammation.
- **Systemic treatment** is only indicated: in severe, extensive skin infection; if there is associated systemic infection (e.g. in immunosuppressed people); or in the rare person unresponsive to topical treatment. Ideally, skin scrapings should be examined to confirm the diagnosis before commencing systemic treatment.

Candidal paronychia

- **A topical antifungal** is usually effective. Treatment with nystatin or an imidazole (clotrimazole, econazole, ketoconazole, miconazole, and sulconazole) lasting 3–6 months may be required, until a new cuticle has formed [Denning et al, 1995].
- **Combined topical preparations** of an antifungal with a corticosteroid may be considered for infection with uncomfortable marked inflammation, or if underlying eczema is present.
- **Systemic treatment is only indicated in the rare person unresponsive to topical treatment.** Ideally, a swab or scrapings should be examined to confirm the diagnosis before commencing systemic treatment.
- **Severe chronic candidal paronychia** may occur in immunosuppressed people, when systemic treatment is usually necessary.
- **Antiseptics** may be necessary to treat associated bacterial infection of the nail fold.

Candidal nail infection

- **Resistant cases or distal nail involvement** require treatment with tioconazole or amorolfine nail paint, usually for at least 6 months for fingernails and 12 months for toenails. A 40–50% cure rate is possible.
- **Tioconazole nail paint** is applied to the affected nail twice daily and can be used in children.
- **Amorolfine nail lacquer** is applied to the affected nail once weekly, but is not licensed for use in children.
- **Severe or widespread candidal onychomycosis** is likely to require systemic treatment, especially since such cases are often associated with an immune deficiency state.
- **We have not offered systemic therapies for candidal nail infections in this guidance,** as this is rarely necessary, except in the context of immunosuppression, where treatment is usually supervised by a specialist. However, the following should be noted:
  - **Oral itraconazole** is active against most *Candida* species and dermatophytes, with cure rates of about 80% for dermatophyte nail infection. It can be given either as continuous treatment or as pulsed treatment, with treatment duration of at least 3 months. Itraconazole is not licensed for use in children, but a working party set up by the British Society for Medical Mycology suggests that older children, weighing over 20 kg, may be prescribed half the adult dosage [Denning et al, 1995].
  - **Oral terbinafine** has only been shown in clinical trials to be effective against dermatophyte nail infections. It has fungistatic activity against *Candida albicans*.
  - **Fluconazole** is not licensed for nail disease, but is used for severe infection in immunosuppressed people.
  - **Griseofulvin** is not effective against *Candida*.

[Pariser, 1990; Bodey, 1993; Denning et al, 1995; American Academy of Dermatology, 1996; Hay and Mackenzie, 1996; MeReC, 1997]

References

NHS staff in England can link, free of charge, from references to full text journals by clicking on [Full text] on the PRODIGY website.

1. American Academy of Dermatology (1996) *Guidelines of care for superficial mycotic infections of the skin: mucocutaneous candidiasis.* www.aadassociation.org/Guidelines [Accessed: 22/10/2002].
2. BNF 44 (2002) *British National Formulary.* 44th edn. London: British Medical Association and Royal Pharmaceutical Society of Great Britain.
3. Bodey, G.P. (1993) Antifungal agents. In: Bodey, G.P. (Ed.) *Candidiasis: pathogenesis, diagnosis, and treatment.* 2nd edn. New York: Raven Press. 371–406.
4. British Association of Dermatologists (2000) *Treatment guidelines: onychomycosis.* London: British Association of Dermatologists.
5. Denning, D.W., Evans, E.G.V., Kibbler, C.C. et al (1995) Fortnightly review: fungal nail disease: a guide to good practice (report of a Working Group of the British Society for Medical Mycology). *British Medical Journal* **311**(7015), 1277–1281. [Full text]
6. Hay, R.J. and Mackenzie, D.W.R. (1996) Superficial candidosis (candidiasis). In: Weatherall, D.J., Ledingham, J.G.G., and Warrell, D.A. (Ed.) *Oxford textbook of medicine.* 3rd edn. Oxford: Oxford University Press and Electronic Publishing BV.
7. Hymes, S.R. and Duvic, M. (1993) Cutaneous candidiasis. In: Bodey, G.P. (Ed.) *Candidiasis: pathogenesis, diagnosis, and treatment.* 2nd edn. New York: Raven Press. 159–166.
8. McKay, M. (1988) Cutaneous manifestations of candidiasis. *American Journal of Obstetrics and Gynecology* **158**(4), 991–993.
9. MeReC (1997) Fungal nail infections (onychomycosis). *MeReC Bulletin* 8(12), 45–48.
10. Pariser, D.M. (1990) Cutaneous candidiasis: a practical guide for primary care physicians. *Postgraduate Medicine* 87(6), 101–108.
11. Vartivarian, S. and Smith, C.B. (1993) Pathogenesis, host resistance and predisposing factors. In: Bodey, G.P. (Ed.) *Candidiasis: pathogenesis, diagnosis, and treatment.* 2nd edn. New York: Raven Press. 59–84.

PRODIGY GUIDANCE

Chest infections

Last revised in July 2005
www.prodigy.nhs.uk/guidance.asp?gt=Chest infections

Applies to people of all ages

This guidance covers the management of acute bronchitis, exacerbation of chronic obstructive pulmonary disease, community-acquired pneumonia, and chest infection due to a known organism.
The guidance does not cover upper respiratory tract infections, bronchiolitis, hospital-acquired or rare forms of pneumonia, or infections in people who are immunocompromised.

There is separate PRODIGY guidance on *Common cold, Influenza, Asthma,* and *Chronic obstructive pulmonary disease* (in which the management of exacerbations is also covered).

Goals

- To alleviate symptoms
- To prescribe antibiotics appropriately

Contents

Scenarios

- Acute Bronchitis p.288
- Exacerbation of COPD p.291
- Community—acquired pneumonia p.295
- Chest infection with known organism p.298

Extended Information, p. 302

Which scenario?

- **Acute bronchitis:** covers the empirical treatment of people with simple acute bronchitis.
- **Exacerbation of COPD:** covers the empirical treatment of people with an infective exacerbation of chronic obstructive pulmonary disease (COPD).
- **Community — acquired pneumonia:** covers the empirical treatment of people with suspected community-acquired pneumonia.
- **Chest infection with known organism:** covers the specific treatment when a pathogen has been identified.

Acute Bronchitis

Which therapy?

- **Antibiotics are not indicated for previously healthy people with acute bronchitis.**
- **Explanation and reassurance is usually all that is needed.** Advice should cover the fact that the condition is self-limiting, that cough mixtures and antibiotics are of limited value, and that cough may persist for 4 weeks irrespective of whether or not antibiotics are given. A Patient Information Leaflet will reinforce these points.
- **Encourage a smoker to stop.**
- **Consider antibiotics if there is significant comorbidity, or if the person is deteriorating clinically.**
  - First-line antibiotics are amoxicillin, erythromycin, oxytetracycline, or doxycycline.
  - If the infection is not responding to the initial antibiotic choice, a tetracycline (if this has not already been tried), co-amoxiclav, clarithromycin, or azithromycin is a suitable choice.
  - Follow local antibiotic guidelines if available.

Practical prescribing points

For further information, please see the *Medicines Compendium* (www.medicines.org.uk) or the *British National Formulary* (www.bnf.org).

- **Ibuprofen:** increased risk of gastrointestinal haemorrhage. Avoid in pregnancy and if there is a history of peptic ulcers. May worsen asthma, hypertension, renal impairment, or cardiac failure.
- **Women taking combined hormonal contraceptives:**
  - Erythromycin is not thought to interact with combir hormonal contraceptives.
  - Non-enzyme-inducing broad-spectrum antibiotics — use additional contraception during the short course and for 7 days afterwards. Miss out the pill-free interval if the 7 days run beyond the end of the pack and the inactive tablets in the case of an every-day preparation.
- **Pregnant women:** amoxicillin and erythromycin are nc known to be harmful, and may be preferred options. Tetracyclines are contraindicated in pregnancy and should never be used.
- **Breastfeeding:** amoxicillin, erythromycin, and co-amoxiclav may be used. Tetracyclines are best avoided
- **Renal impairment:** doxycycline may be the preferred option, as no dosage adjustment or monitoring is required. Oxytetracycline is contraindicated in people with kidney disease. All other recommended antibiotic need to be carefully monitored.
- **Liver impairment:** amoxicillin may be the preferred option. Other agents should be avoided or need carefu monitoring.
- **Erythromycin:** avoid in people with a predisposition to cardiac arrhythmias. Erythromycin may increase the level of certain drugs (e.g. theophylline, carbamazepine or potentiate warfarin.
- **Clarithromycin and azithromycin:** these are less likely to cause gastrointestinal adverse effects than is erythromycin. Similar drug interactions apply as for erythromycin, and clarithromycin should also be avoid in people with a predisposition to cardiac arrhythmias.
- **Tetracyclines:** these are contraindicated in porphyria, and in children aged under 12 years. They may cause photosensitivity reactions (avoid exposure to sunlight c sun lamps).
- **Co-amoxiclav:** the Committee on Safety of Medicines has advised that the incidence of cholestatic jaundice (usually self-limiting) is about six times greater than wi amoxicillin alone, and people at greatest risk include men and those over 65 years old. Do not prescribe co-amoxiclav to people with a history of co-amoxiclav-associated or penicillin-associated jaundice or hepatic dysfunction [BNF 47, 2004].

llow-up advice

outine follow-up of people with acute bronchitis is nnecessary.

ould I refer or investigate?

fer?

erral guidelines for suspected lung cancer [NICE, 2005] ommend:

Jrgent referral for chest X-ray (the report should be eturned within 5 days) for people with any of the ollowing:**

Haemoptysis

Unexplained or persistent (more than 3 weeks):

- Chest and/or shoulder pain
- Dyspnoea
- Weight loss
- Chest signs
- Hoarseness
- Finger clubbing
- Cervical or supraclavicular lymphadenopathy
- Cough
- Features suggestive of metastasis from a lung cancer (e.g. brain, bone, liver, or skin)

Underlying chronic respiratory problems with unexplained changes in existing symptoms

Jrgent referral* for people with:

Persistent haemoptysis in smokers/ex-smokers aged 40 years of age and older

A chest X-ray suggestive/suspicious of lung cancer (including pleural effusion and slowly resolving consolidation)

A normal chest X-ray where there is a high suspicion of lung cancer

A history of asbestos exposure and recent onset chest pain, shortness of breath or unexplained systemic symptoms where a chest X-ray indicates pleural effusion, pleural mass or any suspicious lung pathology

mmediate referral* for people with:

Signs of superior vena caval obstruction (swelling of face/neck with fixed elevation of jugular venous pressure)

Stridor

o a team specialising in the management of lung cancer, pending upon local arrangements.

tient information leaflets

e following PILs are available at www.prodigy.nhs.uk

Bronchitis (Acute)

Quit (help to stop smoking)

Smoking - The Facts

Smoking - Tips on Stopping

ared decision making

For chest colds or acute bronchitis:

- **Paracetamol, ibuprofen,** or **aspirin** will reduce fever and ease any pains. (Children under 16 should not take aspirin.)
- Have lots to drink.
- There is no 'quick fix' for the cough, which may persist for 2–4 weeks. There is little evidence that cough medicines help.

Antibiotics are not usually advised if you are normally healthy.

- Antibiotics do not kill viruses.
- Even for a bacterial bronchitis, antibiotics usually do little to speed recovery.
- Antibiotics may cause side-effects.
- **Antibiotics may be advised in some cases** — for example, if you have a condition that increases your risk of developing a severe chest infection.
- **If you smoke, you should try to stop for good.**

Drug rationale

The choice of antibiotic is based on recommendations for the empirical treatment for acute bronchitis by the Health Protection Agency (HPA) and by the BNF (Table 1, Chapter 5: Infections) [BNF 47, 2004]. These also reflect the recommendations made by the Standing Medical Advisory Committee [DH and SMAC, 1998].

C

Drugs not included

- **Ampicillin** has a spectrum of activity similar to that of amoxicillin, but it is poorly absorbed (less than 50% of the dose is absorbed when food is in the stomach). Ampicillin has a higher incidence of diarrhoea than amoxicillin does, and requires more frequent dosing [Finch et al, 2003].
- **Phenoxymethylpenicillin** is active against *Streptococcus pneumoniae*, but has poor activity against *Haemophilus influenzae* and *Moraxella catarrhalis* [Finch et al, 2003]. Phenoxymethylpenicillin is therefore not included for empirical treatment.
- **Flucloxacillin** has not been specifically offered as a prescription in this scenario, but it is recommended if a staphylococcal infection is suspected (e.g. secondary infection after influenza or measles) [DTB, 1996b; BNF 47, 2004].
- **Oral cephalosporins** are not included for empirical treatment, since they are less active than amoxicillin against pneumococci, particularly against strains with intermediate-level penicillin resistance [DTB, 1999a].
- **Quinolones** are not included because the established agents have only moderate activity against *S pneumoniae* and should be reserved for use when sensitivities are known [DH and SMAC, 1998]. Levofloxacin may have better activity against *S pneumoniae* than ciprofloxacin and ofloxacin do; however, in view of concerns that resistance may develop, it should also be reserved for use when sensitivities are known [MeReC, 1998].
- **Tetracyclines other than oxytetracycline and doxycycline** are not included. The spectrum of activity of the tetracyclines is similar [Finch et al, 2003], and these two seem to be most commonly recommended.
- **Trimethoprim** is reserved for use when sensitivities are known. Trimethoprim generally has poor activity against *S pneumoniae* and *M catarrhalis* [McNulty, Personal Communication, 2004].
- **Beta$_2$-agonists** are not included, as a Cochrane review found no evidence to support their use in children and only limited evidence to support their use in adults [Smucny et al, 2004b].
- **Aspirin** is not included, as the Committee on Safety of Medicines has advised that aspirin is unsuitable for children under 16 years old because of its association with Reye's syndrome [CSM, 2002]. Also, hypersensitivity-type reactions may be worse at the higher doses needed for an analgesic and antipyretic effect.

Drugs included

- **Paracetamol** is an effective and safe analgesic and antipyretic agent for most people.
- **Ibuprofen** is an effective alternative to paracetamol if there are no contraindications.

C

- **For all antimicrobials, a 5-day course is given in line with recommendations by the Health Protection Agency (HPA).**
- **Amoxicillin** is included for empirical treatment, as it is active against most *Streptococcus pneumoniae* and several *Haemophilus influenzae* strains (two of the most common respiratory pathogens [Finch et al, 2003]). Clinical trial data comparing amoxicillin with other antibiotic agents has found amoxicillin to be at least as good in terms of clinical improvement or cure [Wark, 2003]
- **Erythromycin** is included for empirical treatment, as it is particularly active against *S pneumoniae* and *Moraxella catarrhalis*, although it has low activity against *H influenza* [DTB, 1998; Finch et al, 2003]. Erythromycin is also an option for people with penicillin allergy.
- **Doxycycline** is included for empirical treatment. Doxycycline has a broad spectrum of activity against respiratory pathogens (it covers most typical and atypical pathogens) and is given once a day [Finch et al, 2003]. Doxycycline is also an option for people with penicillin allergy.
- **Oxytetracycline** has a spectrum of activity similar to that of doxycycline, but must be taken four times a day [Finch et al, 2003; BNF 47, 2004]. Oxytetracycline is also an option for people with penicillin allergy.
- **Co-amoxiclav** is included as an option for second-line treatment when there is no response to the initial antibiotic (to prevent unnecessary build-up of resistance) [DTB, 1998]. Many bacterial beta-lactamases are inhibited by clavulanic acid, and a mixture of this with amoxicillin results in the antibiotic being effective against most penicillinase-producing organisms.
- **Azithromycin and clarithromycin** may be useful for people who experience unwanted gastrointestinal effects with erythromycin, and they have more acceptable dosage regimens. They are included when there is no response to the initial antibiotic — as an option for second-line treatment (to prevent unnecessary build-up of resistance) [DTB, 1998; Zhanel et al, 2001]. They are also alternative options for people with penicillin allergy. Modified-release clarithromycin is also included, as the once-daily dose may offer benefits in terms of compliance and it is no more costly than the standard-release formulation [Allin et al, 2001].

Prescriptions

Analgesia/antipyretics: use when required

Paracetamol s/f susp: 60mg to 120mg up to four times a day
- Age from 3 to 11 months
- Paracetamol 120mg/5ml s/f susp. Take 2.5ml to 5ml every 4 to 6 hours when required for relief of pain or high temperature. Maximum of 4 doses in 24 hours; supply 150 ml; NHS Cost £0.65; OTC Cost £1.14.

Paracetamol s/f susp: 120mg to 240mg up to four times a day
- Age from 12 months to 5 years
- Paracetamol 120mg/5ml s/f susp. Take one to two 5ml spoonfuls every 4 to 6 hours when required for relief of pain or high temperature. Maximum of 4 doses in 24 hours; supply 300 ml; NHS Cost £1.30; OTC Cost £2.28.

Paracetamol s/f susp: 250mg to 500mg up to four times a day
- Age from 6 to 11 years
- Paracetamol 250mg/5ml s/f susp. Take one to two 5ml spoonfuls every 4 to 6 hours when required for relief of pain or high temperature. Maximum of 4 doses in 24 hours; supply 300 ml; NHS Cost £1.70; OTC Cost £2.99.

Paracetamol tablets: 500mg to 1g up to four times a da
- Age from 12 to 15 years
- Paracetamol 500mg tablets. Take one to two tablets every 4 to 6 hours when required for relief of pain or high temperature. Maximum of 8 tablets in 24 hours; supply 100 tablets; NHS Cost £0.75; OTC Cost £1.3

Paracetamol tablets: 1g up to four times a day
- Age from 16 years onwards
- Paracetamol 500mg tablets. Take two tablets every 4 6 hours when required for relief of pain or high temperature. Maximum of 8 tablets in 24 hours; supply 100 tablets; NHS Cost £0.75; OTC Cost £1.3

Ibuprofen s/f susp: 50mg three to four times a day
- Age from 12 months to 2 years
- Ibuprofen 100mg/5ml s/f susp. Take 2.5ml three to fo times a day when required for relief of pain or high temperature. Do not exceed the stated dose; supply 1 ml; NHS Cost £1.82; OTC Cost £3.21.

Ibuprofen s/f susp: 100mg three to four times a day
- Age from 3 to 7 years
- Ibuprofen 100mg/5ml s/f susp. Take one 5ml spoonfu to 4 times a day when required for relief of pain or hi temperature. Do not exceed the stated dose; supply 1 ml; NHS Cost £2.73; OTC Cost £4.81.

Ibuprofen s/f susp: 200mg three to four times a day
- Age from 8 to 11 years
- Ibuprofen 100mg/5ml s/f susp. Take two 5ml spoonfu 3 to 4 times a day when required for relief of pain or high temperature. Do not exceed the stated dose; supply 300 ml; NHS Cost £5.46; OTC Cost £9.62.

Ibuprofen tablets: 400mg three times a day
- Age from 12 years onwards
- Ibuprofen 400mg tablets. Take one tablet three times day when required for relief of pain or high temperatu Do not exceed the stated dose; supply 24 tablets; NHS Cost £0.70; OTC Cost £1.23.

1st-line antibiotic for 5 days (not usually indicated

Amoxicillin s/f suspension: 125mg three times a day
- Age from 1 month to 23 months
- Amoxicillin 125mg/5ml s/f susp. Take one 5ml spoon three times a day for 5 days; supply 100 ml; NHS Cost £1.30.

Amoxicillin s/f suspension: 250mg three times a day
- Age from 2 to 9 years
- Amoxicillin 250mg/5ml s/f susp. Take one 5ml spoon three times a day for 5 days; supply 100 ml; NHS Cost £2.25.

Amoxicillin s/f suspension: 500mg three times a day
- Age from 10 to 11 years
- Amoxicillin 250mg/5ml s/f susp. Take two 5ml spoonfuls three times a day for 5 days; supply 200 ml; NHS Cost £4.50.

Amoxicillin capsules: 500mg three times a day
- Age from 12 years onwards
- Amoxicillin 500mg capsules. Take one capsule three times a day for 5 days; supply 15 capsules; NHS Cost £1.85.

Erythromycin s/f suspension: 125mg four times a day
- Age from 1 month to 23 months
- Erythromycin 125mg/5ml sf susp. Take one 5ml spoonful four times a day for 5 days; supply 100 ml; NHS Cost £1.12.

ythromycin s/f suspension: 250mg four times a day
- Age from 2 to 8 years
- Erythromycin 250mg/5ml sf susp. Take one 5ml spoonful four times a day for 5 days; supply 100 ml; NHS Cost £1.93.

ythromycin s/f suspension: 500mg four times a day
- Age from 9 to 11 years
- Erythromycin 500mg/5ml sf susp. Take one 5ml spoonful four times a day for 5 days; supply 100 ml; NHS Cost £3.27.

ythromycin e/c tablets: 500mg four times a day
- Age from 12 years onwards
- Erythromycin 250mg e/c tablets. Take two tablets four times a day for 5 days; supply 40 tablets; NHS Cost £4.40.

xycycline 100mg once a day
- Age from 12 years onwards
- Doxycycline 100mg capsules. Take TWO capsules now and then take ONE capsule once a day for the next 4 days; supply 6 capsules; NHS Cost £1.24.

ytetracycline 250mg four times a day
- Age from 12 years onwards
- Oxytetracycline 250mg tablets. Take one tablet four times a day for 5 days; supply 20 tablets; NHS Cost £0.57.

ytetracycline 500mg four times a day
- Age from 12 years onwards
- Oxytetracycline 250mg tablets. Take two tablets four times a day for 5 days; supply 40 tablets; NHS Cost £1.16.

nd-line antibiotic for 3 or 5 days

xycycline 100mg once a day-IF not already tried
- Age from 12 years onwards
- Doxycycline 100mg capsules. Take TWO capsules now and then take ONE capsule once a day for the next 4 days; supply 6 capsules; NHS Cost £1.24.

ytetracycline 250mg four times a day-IF not already ed
- Age from 12 years onwards
- Oxytetracycline 250mg tablets. Take one tablet four times a day for 5 days; supply 20 tablets; NHS Cost £0.57.

ytetracycline 500mg four times a day-IF not already ed
- Age from 12 years onwards
- Oxytetracycline 250mg tablets. Take two tablets four times a day for 5 days; supply 40 tablets; NHS Cost £1.16.

-amoxiclav 125/31mg/5ml susp: 0.25ml/kg three times day
- Age from 1 month to 11 months
- Co-amoxiclav 125/31mg/5ml susp. *WEIGHT REQUIRED* Take 0.25ml per kg bodyweight THREE times a day for 5 days; supply 100 ml; NHS Cost £4.57.

-amoxiclav s/f suspension: 125/31mg three times a day
- Age from 12 months to 6 years
- Co-amoxiclav 125/31mg/5ml susp. Take one 5ml spoonful three times a day for 5 days; supply 100 ml; NHS Cost £4.57.

-amoxiclav s/f suspension: 250/62mg three times a day
- Age from 7 to 11 years
- Co-amoxiclav 250/62mg/5ml susp. Take one 5ml spoonful three times a day for 5 days; supply 100 ml; NHS Cost £6.42.

Co-amoxiclav tablets: 500/125mg three times a day
- Age from 12 years onwards
- Co-amoxiclav 625mg tablets. Take one tablet three times a day for 5 days; supply 15 tablets; NHS Cost £11.24.

Clarithromycin suspension: 62.5mg twice a day
- Age from 12 months to 2 years
- Clarithromycin 125mg/5ml susp. Take 2.5ml twice a day for 5 days; supply 70 ml; NHS Cost £6.00.

Clarithromycin suspension: 125mg twice a day
- Age from 3 to 6 years
- Clarithromycin 125mg/5ml susp. Take one 5ml spoonful twice a day for 5 days; supply 70 ml; NHS Cost £6.00.

Clarithromycin suspension: 187.5mg twice a day
- Age from 7 to 9 years
- Clarithromycin 125mg/5ml susp. Take 7.5ml twice a day for 5 days; supply 100 ml; NHS Cost £10.32.

Clarithromycin suspension: 250mg twice a day
- Age from 10 to 11 years
- Clarithromycin 125mg/5ml susp. Take two 5ml spoonfuls twice a day for 5 days; supply 100 ml; NHS Cost £10.32.

Clarithromycin tablets: 250mg twice a day
- Age from 12 years onwards
- Clarithromycin 250mg tablets. Take one tablet twice a day for 5 days; supply 10 tablets; NHS Cost £8.40.

Clarithromycin tablets: 500mg twice a day
- Age from 12 years onwards
- Clarithromycin 500mg tablets. Take one tablet twice a day for 5 days; supply 10 tablets; NHS Cost £16.82.

Azithromycin suspension: 10mg/kg once a day for 3 days
- Age from 6 months to 2 years
- Azithromycin 200mg/5ml susp. *WEIGHT REQUIRED* Take 10mg per kg bodyweight ONCE a day for 3 days; supply 15 ml; NHS Cost £5.08.

Azithromycin suspension: 200mg once a day for 3 days
- Age from 3 to 7 years
- Azithromycin 200mg/5ml susp. Take one 5ml spoonful once a day for 3 days; supply 15 ml; NHS Cost £5.08.

Azithromycin suspension: 300mg once a day for 3 days
- Age from 8 to 11 years
- Azithromycin 200mg/5ml susp. Take 7.5ml once a day for 3 days; supply 23 ml; NHS Cost £7.62.

Azithromycin suspension: 400mg once a day for 3 days
- Age from 12 to 13 years
- Azithromycin 200mg/5ml susp. Take two 5ml spoonfuls once a day for 3 days; supply 30 ml; NHS Cost £13.80.

Azithromycin capsules: 500mg once a day for 3 days
- Age from 14 years onwards
- Azithromycin 250mg capsules. Take two capsules once a day for 3 days; supply 6 capsules; NHS Cost £13.43.

Exacerbation of COPD

Which therapy?

Bronchodilators

- Add or increase bronchodilators.
- These may need to be taken more frequently and in higher doses.

Oral corticosteroids

- **Consider oral corticosteroids if an exacerbation significantly increases breathlessness that interferes with daily activities.**
- Prescribe prednisolone 30 mg for 7–14 days.

- Start prednisolone as soon as possible to achieve optimum benefit. In selected people, consider provision of a treatment course at home as part of an agreed management programme.

Antibiotics

- Prescribe an antibiotic if the sputum is more purulent than usual.
- **If the sputum is not more purulent than usual,** prescribe an antibiotic only if there are clinical signs of pneumonia.
- **First-line antibiotics** are amoxicillin, oxytetracycline, or doxycycline.
- **If the infection does not respond to the initial antibiotic choice,** a tetracycline (if this has not already been tried) or co-amoxiclav is a suitable choice.
- Follow local antibiotic guidelines, if available.

Other issues

- Encourage a smoker to stop.
- Ensure influenza and pneumococcal vaccinations have been given.

Practical prescribing points

For further information, please see the *Medicines Compendium* (www.medicines.org.uk) or the *British National Formulary* (www.bnf.org).

Beta$_2$-agonists

- **Regularly reinforce inhaler technique.** Where the technique is poor, its effects may be mistaken for a lack of response to the drug.
- People may experience varying degrees of sensation in the mouth and throat with different inhaler products. These may depend on the actuation and the drug inhaled.
- **Where a chlorofluorocarbon (CFC)-free inhaler is intended,** it is recommended that this term be specified on the prescription. Beta$_2$-agonists can cause tremor, palpitations, headache, and muscle cramps.
- **Hypokalaemia** — high doses can reduce plasma potassium concentration (which therefore needs monitoring) and the Committee on Safety of Medicines has advised that this may be potentially serious. Hypokalaemia may be potentiated by concomitant treatment with theophylline and its derivatives, corticosteroids, and diuretics, and by hypoxia.

Oral corticosteroids

- After concern about severe chickenpox, the Committee on Safety of Medicines has advised that anyone prescribed a systemic corticosteroid should receive the Patient Information Leaflet produced by the manufacturer.
- **Osteoporosis prophylaxis** should be considered in people requiring frequent courses of oral corticosteroids.

Spacer devices

- **Clean spacers no more than once a month** (more frequent cleaning will build up static, affecting their performance). Wash in mild detergent, rinse, and then allow to air-dry.

Antibiotics

- **Women taking combined hormonal contraceptives:** non-enzyme-inducing broad-spectrum antibiotics — use additional contraception during the short course and for 7 days afterwards. Miss out the pill-free interval if the 7 days runs beyond the end of the packet, and the inactive tablets in the case of an every-day (ED) preparation.
  - **Pregnant women:** amoxicillin is not known to be harmful, and may be the preferred option. Tetracyclines are contraindicated in pregnancy and should never be used.
  - **Breastfeeding:** amoxicillin and co-amoxiclav may b the preferred options. Tetracyclines are best avoide
- **Renal impairment:** doxycycline may be the preferred option, as no dosage adjustment or monitoring is required. Oxytetracycline is contraindicated in people with kidney disease. All other recommended antibioti need to be carefully monitored.
- **Liver impairment:** amoxicillin may be the preferred option. Other agents should be avoided or need carefu monitoring.
- **Tetracyclines:** contraindicated also in porphyria and children aged under12 years. Tetracyclines may cause photosensitivity reactions (avoid exposure to sunlight sun lamps).
- **Co-amoxiclav:** the Committee on Safety of Medicines has advised that the incidence of cholestatic jaundice (usually self-limiting) is about six times greater than w amoxicillin alone and people at greatest risk include m and those over 65 years old. Do not prescribe co-amoxiclav to people with a history of co-amoxiclav-associated or penicillin-associated jaundice or hepatic dysfunction [BNF 47, 2004]. Co-amoxiclav should be considered when resistant beta-lactamase-producing strains are known or might be present.

Follow-up advice

- Depending on the severity of the illness, consider reviewing the person within 24 hours, either by telephone or in person, to assess response to treatmen
- If the person fails to respond or has frequent exacerbations, sputum culture may be useful to determine if resistant organisms are present.

Should I refer or investigate?

Refer?

Admit

Suggested criteria for admission are:

- Severe breathlessness
- Confusion
- Cyanosis
- Worsening peripheral oedema
- Impaired consciousness
- The person is unable to cope at home
- General condition is poor or is deteriorating
- Activity level is poor, or the person is confined to bed
- The person lives alone
- The person is on long-term oxygen therapy
- The exacerbation was of rapid onset
- Significant comorbidity is present

Urgently refer

Referral guidelines for suspected lung cancer [NICE, 200 **recommend:**

- **Urgent referral for chest X-ray (the report should be returned within 5 days) for people with any of the following:**
  - Haemoptysis
  - Unexplained or persistent (more than 3 weeks):
    - Chest and/or shoulder pain
    - Dyspnoea
    - Weight loss

- Chest signs
- Hoarseness
- Finger clubbing
- Cervical or supraclavicular lymphadenopathy
- Cough
- Features suggestive of metastasis from a lung cancer (e.g. brain, bone, liver, or skin)

Underlying chronic respiratory problems with unexplained changes in existing symptoms

rgent referral* for people with:

Persistent haemoptysis in smokers/ex-smokers aged 40 years of age and older

A chest X-ray suggestive/suspicious of lung cancer (including pleural effusion and slowly resolving consolidation)

A normal chest X-ray where there is a high suspicion of lung cancer

A history of asbestos exposure and recent onset chest pain, shortness of breath or unexplained systemic symptoms where a chest X-ray indicates pleural effusion, pleural mass or any suspicious lung pathology

nmediate referral* for people with:

Signs of superior vena caval obstruction (swelling of face/neck with fixed elevation of jugular venous pressure)

Stridor

) a team specialising in the management of lung cancer, ending upon local arrangements.

atient information leaflets

: following PILs are available at www.prodigy.nhs.uk
:OPD (Chronic Obs. Pulmonary Disease)
)uit (help to stop smoking)
moking - The Facts
moking - Tips on Stopping

ıared decision making

'or a flare-up of COPD:

- **Inhalers** — increase the dose and frequency of your bronchodilator inhaler.
- **A short course of steroid tablets** may be prescribed if you are more breathless than usual.
- **Antibiotics** may be needed, especially if your sputum is more yellow or green than usual.

ee a doctor if your symptoms get worse or do not mprove.

Iave you been immunized against 'flu and neumococcal infection?

f you are still smoking, would you like advice or help to top?

rug rationale

e choice of antibiotic is based on recommendations for empirical treatment for acute bronchitis by the Health tection Agency (HPA) and by the BNF (Table 1, apter 5: Infections) [BNF 47, 2004]. These also reflect recommendations made by the Standing Medical visory Committee [DH and SMAC, 1998].

rugs not included

- **Macrolides** are not recommended for treating xacerbations. Erythromycin has only weak activity gainst *Haemophilus influenzae* (one of the most ommon pathogens implicated in exacerbations of COPD) and there are growing concerns about the build-ıp of resistance to clarithromycin and azithromycin McNulty, Personal Communication, 2004]. Also, all macrolides concentrate intracellularly and *H influenzae* is an extracellular pathogen.
- **Ampicillin** has a spectrum of activity similar to that of amoxicillin, but it is poorly absorbed (less than 50% of the dose is absorbed when food is in the stomach); it has a higher incidence of diarrhoea than amoxicillin; and it requires more frequent dosing.
- **Phenoxymethylpenicillin** has poor activity against *H influenzae* [Finch et al, 2003] and *Moraxella catarrhalis*. Phenoxymethylpenicillin is therefore not included for empirical treatment.
- **Flucloxacillin** has not been specifically offered as a prescription in this scenario, but it is recommended if a staphylococcal infection is suspected (e.g. secondary infection after influenza or measles) [BNF 47, 2004].
- **Oral cephalosporins** are not included for empirical treatment. They should be reserved for use specifically when sensitivity is known and (depending upon local policy) to prevent resistance developing [DH and SMAC, 1998].
- **Quinolones** are not included. Trials have found that they showed no clinical superiority over other antibiotics, and they should be reserved for use when sensitivities are known [DH and SMAC, 1998; MeReC, 1998; SIGN, 2002].
- **Tetracyclines** other than oxytetracycline and doxycycline are not included. The spectrum of activity of the tetracyclines is similar [Finch et al, 2003] and these two seem to be most commonly recommended.
- **Trimethoprim** is reserved for use when sensitivities are known. Trimethoprim generally has poor activity against *Streptococcus pneumoniae* and *M catarrhalis* [McNulty, Personal Communication, 2004].
- **Dry-powder inhalers are not included.** They should be reserved for people who are unable to use pressurized metered-dose inhalers effectively after receiving appropriate instruction.
- **Long-acting bronchodilators** are not included, as they are not licensed for the relief of acute bronchospasm.
- **Oral corticosteroids other than prednisolone** are not routinely used in the treatment of exacerbations of chronic obstructive airway disease [National Collaborating Centre for Chronic Conditions, 2004].
- **Inhaled corticosteroids** are not included, as their use in the short term has not been found to be beneficial. Whether their use for 6 months or longer offers clinical benefits remains inconclusive; however, they may predispose to adverse effects, including osteoporosis, skin bruising, and oral candidiasis [Kerstjens and Postma, 2003].

Drugs included

- **Short-acting beta$_2$-agonists: salbutamol and terbutaline** CFC-free pressurized metered dose inhalers (pMDIs) are included, as well as salbutamol breath-actuated pMDIs and terbutaline turbohaler. Short-acting beta$_2$-agonists may offer some relief, as they are fast-acting [McCrory and Brown, 2004], and prescriptions are included for either initiation or repeat purposes.
- **Short-acting anticholinergic: ipratropium** is included. Ipratropium is also a fast-acting bronchodilator and has been found to provide some clinical benefit in exacerbations of COPD [McCrory and Brown, 2004].
- **Spacer devices** are included for use with bronchodilators:
  - Aerochamber® is compatible with Airomir® and Salbulin® CFC-free MDIs.
  - Volumatic® is compatible with Ventolin® CFC-free MDI.
  - Nebuhaler® is compatible with Terbutaine® MDI.
- Note: switching between different spacer types can affect the deposition characteristics of the inhaled drug. The

same may apply if there is a change in the inhaler device used, but no change in spacer. This change of device may alter clinical response to the inhaled drug [NHS Executive, 1998].

- **Oral corticosteroid: prednisolone** has predominately glucocortocoid activity and is the corticosteroid most commonly used orally for exacerbations of COPD. A dose of 30 mg daily for 7–14 days is recommended [National Collaborating Centre for Chronic Conditions, 2004].
- **Amoxicillin** is included for empirical treatment, as it is active against *Streptococcus pneumoniae* and *Haemophilus influenzae* (two of the most common respiratory pathogens) [Finch et al, 2003].
- **Doxycycline** is included for empirical treatment, as it has a broad spectrum of activity against respiratory pathogen (it covers most typical and atypical pathogens) and can be given once a day [Finch et al, 2003]. Doxycycline is also an option for people with penicillin allergy.
- **Oxytetracycline** has a spectrum of activity similar to that of doxycycline, but must be taken four times a day [Finch et al, 2003]. They are also alternative options for people with penicillin allergy.
- **Co-amoxiclav** is included as an option for second-line treatment when there is no response to the initial antibiotic [DTB, 1998]. Many bacterial beta-lactamases are inhibited by clavulanic acid, and a mixture of this with amoxicillin results in the antibiotic being effective against most penicillinase-producing organisms.

Prescriptions

Bronchodilators and spacer devices

Salbutamol 100mcg MDI: 1 to 2 puffs up to four times a day

- Age from 16 years onwards
- Salbutamol 100mcg CFC-free inhaler. Inhale one to two puffs up to four times a day, when required to relieve breathlessness; supply 1 200 dose inhaler; NHS Cost £1.86.

Airomir 100mcg MDI: 1 to 2 puffs up to four times a day

- Age from 16 years onwards
- Airomir 100mcg CFC-free inhaler. Inhale one to two puffs up to four times a day, when required to relieve breathlessness; supply 1 200 dose inhaler; NHS Cost £1.97.

Salamol 100mcg MDI: 1 to 2 puffs up to four times a day

- Age from 16 years onwards
- Salamol 100mcg CFC-free inhaler. Inhale one to two puffs up to four times a day, when required to relieve breathlessness; supply 1 200 dose inhaler; NHS Cost £1.75.

Ventolin 100mcg MDI: 1 to 2 puffs up to four times a day

- Age from 16 years onwards
- Ventolin 100mcg CFC-free inhaler. Inhale one to two puffs up to four times a day, when required to relieve breathlessness; supply 1 200 dose inhaler; NHS Cost £2.30.

Terbutaline 250mcg MDI: 1 to 2 puffs up to four times a day

- Age from 16 years onwards
- Terbutaline 250mcg inhaler. Inhale one to two puffs up to four times a day, when required to relieve breathlessness; supply 1 400 dose inhaler; NHS Cost £5.84.

Ipratropium 20mcg MDI: 1 to 2 puffs up to four times a

- Age from 16 years onwards
- Ipratropium 20mcg inhaler. Inhale one to two puffs u to four times a day, when required to relieve breathlessness; supply 1 200 dose inhaler; NHS Cost £4.21.

AeroChamber Plus spacer: for use with Airomir/Atrove

- Age from 16 years onwards
- AeroChamber Plus spacer device. Use to aid inhalatio supply 1 spacer; NHS Cost £4.36.

Nebuhaler spacer: for use with Bricanyl

- Age from 16 years onwards
- Nebuhaler spacer device. Use to aid inhalation; suppl spacer; NHS Cost £4.28.

Volumatic spacer: for use with Salamol/Ventolin

- Age from 16 years onwards
- Volumatic spacer device. Use to aid inhalation; supply spacer; NHS Cost £2.75.

1st-line antibiotic for 7 days

Amoxicillin 500mg three times a day

- Age from 16 years onwards
- Amoxicillin 500mg capsules. Take one capsule three times a day for 7 days; supply 21 capsules; NHS Cost £1.25.

Doxycycline 100mg once a day

- Age from 16 years onwards
- Doxycycline 100mg capsules. Take TWO capsules no and then take ONE capsule once a day for the next 6 days; supply 8 capsules; NHS Cost £2.47.

Oxytetracycline 250mg four times a day

- Age from 16 years onwards
- Oxytetracycline 250mg tablets. Take one tablet four times a day for 7 days; supply 28 tablets; NHS Cost £0.81.

Oxytetracycline 500mg four times a day

- Age from 16 years onwards
- Oxytetracycline 250mg tablets. Take two tablets four times a day for 7 days; supply 56 tablets; NHS Cost £1.62.

2nd-line antibiotic for 7 days

Doxycycline 100mg once a day-IF not already tried

- Age from 16 years onwards
- Doxycycline 100mg capsules. Take TWO capsules no and then take ONE capsule once a day for the next 6 days; supply 8 capsules; NHS Cost £2.49.

Oxytetracycline 250mg four times a day-IF not already tried

- Age from 16 years onwards
- Oxytetracycline 250mg tablets. Take one tablet four times a day for 7 days; supply 28 tablets; NHS Cost £0.81.

Oxytetracycline 500mg four times a day

- Age from 16 years onwards
- Oxytetracycline 250mg tablets. Take two tablets four times a day for 7 days; supply 56 tablets; NHS Cost £1.62.

Co-amoxiclav 500/125mg three times a day

- Age from 16 years onwards
- Co-amoxiclav 625mg tablets. Take one tablet three times a day for 7 days; supply 21 tablets; NHS Cost £15.72.

ednisolone tablets

: prednisolone: 30mg each morning for 7 days
ge from 16 years onwards
rednisolone 5mg e/c tablets. Take six tablets each
orning (as a single dose) for 7 days; supply 42 tablets;
IHS Cost £0.71.

: prednisolone: 30mg each morning for 10 days
ge from 16 years onwards
rednisolone 5mg e/c tablets. Take six tablets each
orning (as a single dose) for 10 days; supply 60 tablets;
IHS Cost £1.02.

: prednisolone: 30mg each morning for 14 days
ge from 16 years onwards
rednisolone 5mg e/c tablets. Take six tablets each
orning (as a single dose) for 14 days; supply 84 tablets;
IHS Cost £1.42.

in prednisolone: 30mg each morning for 7 days
ge from 16 years onwards
rednisolone 5mg tablets. Take six tablets each morning
s a single dose) for 7 days; supply 42 tablets;
IHS Cost £1.02.

in prednisolone: 30mg each morning for 10 days
ge from 16 years onwards
rednisolone 5mg tablets. Take six tablets each morning
s a single dose) for 10 days; supply 60 tablets;
IHS Cost £1.46.

in prednisolone: 30mg each morning for 14 days
ge from 16 years onwards
rednisolone 5mg tablets. Take six tablets each morning
s a single dose) for 14 days; supply 84 tablets;
IHS Cost £2.04.

ommunity-acquired pneumonia

hich therapy?

onsider admission in all cases.
ntibiotics should be started as soon as possible.
reatment for 7 days is recommended, except where aphylococcal infections are suspected, when treatment or 14 days is recommended.
irst-line antibiotics are amoxicillin, or erythromycin if ypersensitive to penicillin.
the infection does not respond to treatment within 48 ours, then (depending on the condition of the person) ither add erythromycin or a tetracycline, or admit.
ollow local antibiotic guidelines, if available.
admitting the person to hospital, administer antibiotics mmediately if the pneumonia is life-threatening, or if here will be delays of more than 2 hours in admission.
uggested treatments (adult doses) are:

- Benzylpenicillin 1.2 grams by intramuscular or intravenous injection
- Amoxicillin 1 grams orally
- Erythromycin (if penicillin hypersensitivity) 500 mg orally

ractical prescribing points

 further information, please see the *Medicines mpendium* (www.medicines.org.uk) or the *British tional Formulary* (www.bnf.org).
he Committee on Safety of Medicines has advised that holestatic jaundice (usually self-limiting) may occur with use of either co-amoxiclav or flucloxacillin. People t greatest risk include men and those over 65 years old.
Vomen taking combined hormonal contraceptives:

- Erythromycin is not thought to interact with combined hormonal contraceptives.
- Non-enzyme-inducing broad-spectrum antibiotics — use additional contraception during the short course and for 7 days afterwards. Miss out the pill-free interval if the 7 days runs beyond the end of the packet, and the inactive tablets in the case of an ED (every-day) preparation.

- **Pregnant women:** amoxicillin and erythromycin are not known to be harmful and may be preferred options. Tetracyclines are contraindicated in pregnancy and should never be used.
- **Breastfeeding:** amoxicillin or erythromycin may be used. Tetracyclines are best avoided.
- **Renal impairment:** doxycycline may be the preferred option, as no dosage adjustment or monitoring is required. Oxytetracycline is contraindicated in people with kidney disease. All other recommended antibiotics need to be carefully monitored.
- **Liver impairment:** amoxicillin may be the preferred option. Other agents should be avoided or need careful monitoring.
- **Erythromycin:** should be avoided in people with a predisposition to cardiac arrhythmias. Erythromycin may increase the level of certain drugs (e.g. theophylline, carbamazepine), or potentiate warfarin.
- **Clarithromycin and azithromycin:** these are less likely to cause gastrointestinal adverse effects than erythromycin is. Similar drug interactions apply as for erythromycin, and clarithromycin should also be avoided in people with a predisposition to cardiac arrhythmias.
- **Tetracyclines:** contraindicated also in porphyria and children aged under 12 years. They may cause photosensitivity reactions (avoid exposure to sunlight or sun lamps).
- **Co-amoxiclav:** never prescribe in people with a history of co-amoxiclav-associated or penicillin-associated jaundice or hepatic dysfunction.
- **Flucloxacillin:** use with caution in renal impairment and avoid in porphyria.
- **Ibuprofen:** increased risk of gastrointestinal haemorrhage. Avoid in pregnancy or if there is a history of peptic ulcers. May worsen asthma, hypertension, renal impairment, or cardiac failure.

Follow-up advice

- **Ideally, follow up within 24 hours,** either by telephone or in person, to assess response to treatment.
- **A follow-up chest X-ray** is advisable for people who present with focal chest signs, as a proportion will have an underlying malignancy. The Royal College of Radiologists recommends a follow-up chest X-ray 6 weeks after recovery from pneumonia for all adults who have persistent symptoms or signs, or who are at higher risk of underlying malignancy (smokers and people aged over 50 years). Follow-up chest X-ray in children is only recommended if there are persisting clinical signs or symptoms.

Should I refer or investigate?

Refer?

Admit

There should be a low threshold for hospital admission. Treatment at home is usually safe if none of the following features is present:

- Age >50 years
- Comorbid disease: cancer, cerebrovascular disease, heart failure, liver disease, or renal disease
- New confusion

- Low or high temperature (<35°C or >=40°C)
- Raised respiratory rate (>30/minute)
- Tachycardia (>125/minute)
- Low blood pressure (systolic <90 mmHg or diastolic <60 mmHg)

Urgently refer

Referral guidelines for suspected lung cancer [NICE, 2005] recommend:

- **Urgent referral for chest X-ray (the report should be returned within 5 days) for people with any of the following:**
  - Haemoptysis
  - Unexplained or persistent (more than 3 weeks):
    - Chest and/or shoulder pain
    - Dyspnoea
    - Weight loss
    - Chest signs
    - Hoarseness
    - Finger clubbing
    - Cervical or supraclavicular lymphadenopathy
    - Cough
    - Features suggestive of metastasis from a lung cancer (e.g. brain, bone, liver, or skin)
  - Underlying chronic respiratory problems with unexplained changes in existing symptoms
- **Urgent referral* for people with:**
  - Persistent haemoptysis in smokers/ex-smokers aged 40 years of age and older
  - A chest X-ray suggestive/suspicious of lung cancer (including pleural effusion and slowly resolving consolidation)
  - A normal chest X-ray where there is a high suspicion of lung cancer
  - A history of asbestos exposure and recent onset chest pain, shortness of breath or unexplained systemic symptoms where a chest X-ray indicates pleural effusion, pleural mass or any suspicious lung pathology
- **Immediate referral* for people with:**
  - Signs of superior vena caval obstruction (swelling of face/neck with fixed elevation of jugular venous pressure)
  - Stridor

*To a team specialising in the management of lung cancer, depending upon local arrangements.

Patient information leaflets

The following PILs are available at www.prodigy.nhs.uk

- Pneumonia
- Quit (help to stop smoking)
- Smoking - The Facts
- Smoking - Tips on Stopping

Shared decision making

- **You should take antibiotics,** as you have pneumonia (a severe chest infection).
- Tell your doctor if you are allergic to any antibiotics.
- **If symptoms are not settling within two days, tell your doctor.**
  - A switch to another antibiotic may be needed.
  - You may need to be admitted to hospital.
- **Paracetamol, ibuprofen, or aspirin** will reduce fever and ease any pains. (Children under 16 should not take aspirin.)
- Have lots to drink.

Drug rationale

The choice of antibiotic is based on recommendations f the empirical treatment for acute bronchitis, by the Hea Protection Agency (HPA), the BNF (Table 1, Chapter 5 Infections) [HPA, 2003; BNF 47, 2004] and the British Thoracic Society [British Thoracic Society, 2002; Britis Thoracic Society, 2004]. These also reflect the recommendations made by the Standing Medical Advis Committee [DH and SMAC, 1998].

Drugs not included

- **Ampicillin** has a spectrum of activity similar to that o amoxicillin, but it is poorly absorbed (less than 50% the dose is absorbed when food is in the stomach); it a higher incidence of diarrhoea than amoxicillin does and it requires more frequent dosing [Finch et al, 200
- **Phenoxymethylpenicillin** is active against *Streptococc pneumoniae*, but has poor activity against *Haemophi influenzae* and *Moraxella catarrhalis* [Finch et al, 200 Phenoxymethylpenicillin is therefore not included for empirical treatment.
- **Co-amoxiclav** should be reserved for bacterial infecti likely or known to be caused by amoxicillin-resistant lactamase-producing strains [DTB, 1998]. Co-amoxic may also be useful during influenza epidemics, as an alternative to erythromycin plus flucloxacillin.
- **Oral cephalosporins** are not included for empirical treatment, because they are less active than amoxicill against pneumococci, particularly against strains with intermediate-level penicillin resistance [DTB, 1999a].
- **Quinolones** are not recommended for empirical thera Levofloxacin and moxifloxacin are the only two quinolones licensed for community-acquired pneumo and they may have better activity against *S pneumoni* than other quinolones do. However, in view of conce that resistance may be developing [Davidson et al, 20 they should be used only where first-line agents have been ineffective [Regional Drug and Therapeutics Centre, 2003] and when sensitivities are known [DH SMAC, 1998].
- **Tetracyclines other than oxytetracycline and doxycyc** are not included. The spectrum of activity of the tetracyclines is similar [Finch et al, 2003], and these t seem to be commonly recommended.
- **Trimethoprim** is reserved for use when sensitivities ar known. Trimethoprim generally has poor activity aga *S pneumoniae* and *M catarrhalis* [McNulty, Personal Communication, 2004].
- **Aspirin** is not included, as the Committee on Safety o Medicines has advised that aspirin is unsuitable for children under 16 years old because of its association with Reye's syndrome [CSM, 2002]. Also, hypersensitivity-type reactions may be worse at the higher doses needed for an analgesic and antipyretic effect.

Drugs included

- **Paracetamol** is an effective and safe analgesic and antipyretic agent for most people.
- **Ibuprofen** is an effective alternative to paracetamol if there are no contraindications.
- **Amoxicillin** is included for empirical treatment and should be used as first-line treatment, as it is active against *Streptococcus pneumoniae* and *Haemophilus influenzae* (two of the most common respiratory pathogens) [Finch et al, 2003].
- **Erythromycin** is included for empirical treatment as a alternative to amoxicillin in people with penicillin alle or for the treatment of suspected atypical pneumonia. Erythromycin provides adequate coverage for the mos

f the commonly presenting pathogens: *S pneumoniae*, *Ìycoplasma pneumoniae*, *Chlamydia pneumoniae*. ›rythromycin has only weak activity against *Iaemophilus influenzae* [Finch et al, 2003].

›zithromycin and clarithromycin may be useful for eople who experience unwanted gastrointestinal effects vith erythromycin, and they have more acceptable osage regimens. They are included as an option for econd-line treatment when there is no response to the iitial antibiotic [DTB, 1998; Zhanel et al, 2001]. They re also alternative options for people with penicillin llergy. Modified-release clarithromycin is also included, s the once-daily dose may offer benefits in terms of ompliance and it is no more costly than the standard-elease formulation [Allin et al, 2001].

)oxycycline is included for empirical treatment, as it has broad spectrum of activity against respiratory athogens (it covers most typical and atypical athogens) and can be given once a day [Finch et al, 003]. Doxycycline has less reliable activity against *S neumoniae* than macrolides do.

)xytetracycline has a spectrum of activity similar to that f doxycycline, but must be taken four times a day Finch et al, 2003].

'lucloxacillin should be used in addition to standard herapy with amoxicillin or erythromycin if a taphylococcal infection is suspected (e.g. secondary nfection after influenza or measles) [DTB, 1996b; BNF 7, 2004].

·escriptions

›mmunity acquired pneumonia: antibiotics for 7 ›ys

oxicillin s/f susp: 125mg three times a day
- Age from 1 month to 23 months
- Amoxicillin 125mg/5ml s/f susp. Take one 5ml spoonful three times a day for 7 days; supply 200 ml; NHS Cost £2.58.

oxicillin s/f susp: 250mg three times a day
- Age from 2 to 9 years
- Amoxicillin 250mg/5ml s/f susp. Take one 5ml spoonful three times a day for 7 days; supply 200 ml; NHS Cost £4.50.

oxicillin s/f susp: 500mg three times a day
- Age from 10 to 11 years
- Amoxicillin 250mg/5ml s/f susp. Take two 5ml spoonfuls three times a day for 7 days; supply 200 ml; NHS Cost £4.50.

oxicillin capsules: 500mg three times a day
- Age from 12 years onwards
- Amoxicillin 500mg capsules. Take one capsule three times a day for 7 days; supply 21 capsules; NHS Cost £2.62.

·thromycin s/f suspension: 125mg four times a day
- Age from 1 month to 23 months
- Erythromycin 125mg/5ml sf susp. Take one 5ml spoonful four times a day for 7 days; supply 200 ml; NHS Cost £2.24.

·thromycin s/f suspension: 250mg four times a day
- Age from 2 to 11 years
- Erythromycin 250mg/5ml sf susp. Take one 5ml spoonful four times a day for 7 days; supply 200 ml; NHS Cost £3.68.

·thromycin s/f suspension: 500mg four times a day
- Age from 9 to 11 years
- Erythromycin 500mg/5ml sf susp. Take one 5ml spoonful four times a day for 7 days; supply 200 ml; NHS Cost £5.72.

Erythromycin e/c tablets: 500mg four times a day
- Age from 12 years onwards
- Erythromycin 250mg e/c tablets. Take two tablets four times a day for 7 days; supply 56 tablets; NHS Cost £6.16.

Add-on antibiotics for 7 days (if no response by 48 hours)

Erythromycin s/f suspension: 125mg four times a day
- Age from 1 month to 23 months
- Erythromycin 125mg/5ml sf susp. Take one 5ml spoonful four times a day for 7 days; supply 200 ml; NHS Cost £2.24.

Erythromycin s/f suspension: 250mg four times a day
- Age from 2 to 11 years
- Erythromycin 250mg/5ml sf susp. Take one 5ml spoonful four times a day for 7 days; supply 200 ml; NHS Cost £3.68.

Erythromycin s/f suspension: 500mg four times a day
- Age from 9 to 11 years
- Erythromycin 500mg/5ml sf susp. Take one 5ml spoonful four times a day for 7 days; supply 200 ml; NHS Cost £5.72.

Erythromycin tablets: 500mg four times a day
- Age from 12 years onwards
- Erythromycin 250mg e/c tablets. Take two tablets four times a day for 7 days; supply 80 tablets; NHS Cost £8.80.

Doxycycline capsules: 100mg once a day
- Age from 12 years onwards
- Doxycycline 100mg capsules. Take TWO capsules now and then take ONE capsule once a day for the next 6 days; supply 8 capsules; NHS Cost £2.27.

Oxytetracycline tablets: 500mg four times a day
- Age from 12 years onwards
- Oxytetracycline 250mg tablets. Take two tablets four times a day for 7 days; supply 56 tablets; NHS Cost £2.31.

Suspected atypical pneumonia: antibiotics for 7 days

Erythromycin s/f suspension: 125mg four times a day
- Age from 1 month to 23 months
- Erythromycin 125mg/5ml sf susp. Take one 5ml spoonful four times a day for 7 days; supply 200 ml; NHS Cost £2.10.

Erythromycin s/f suspension: 250mg four times a day
- Age from 2 to 11 years
- Erythromycin 250mg/5ml sf susp. Take one 5ml spoonful four times a day for 7 days; supply 200 ml; NHS Cost £3.68.

Erythromycin s/f suspension: 500mg four times a day
- Age from 9 to 11 years
- Erythromycin 500mg/5ml sf susp. Take one 5ml spoonful four times a day for 7 days; supply 200 ml; NHS Cost £5.72.

Erythromycin e/c tablets: 500mg four times a day
- Age from 12 years onwards
- Erythromycin 250mg e/c tablets. Take two tablets four times a day for 7 days; supply 56 tablets; NHS Cost £10.85.

Doxycycline capsules: 100mg once a day – NOT legionella
- Age from 12 years onwards
- Doxycycline 100mg capsules. Take TWO capsules now and then take ONE capsule once a day for the next 6 days; supply 8 capsules; NHS Cost £2.27.

C

Oxytetracycline tab: 500mg four times a day – NOT legionella
- Age from 12 years onwards
- Oxytetracycline 250mg tablets. Take two tablets four times a day for 7 days; supply 56 tablets; NHS Cost £2.31.

Staph suspected: add on flucloxacillin for 14 days

Flucloxacillin syrup: 62.5mg four times a day
- Age from 1 month to 11 months
- Flucloxacillin 125mg/5ml syrup. Take 2.5ml four times a day for 14 days; supply 200 ml; NHS Cost £6.98.

Flucloxacillin syrup: 125mg four times a day
- Age from 12 months to 4 years
- Flucloxacillin 125mg/5ml syrup. Take one 5ml spoonful four times a day for 14 days; supply 300 ml; NHS Cost £10.47.

Flucloxacillin syrup: 250mg four times a day
- Age from 5 to 11 years
- Flucloxacillin 250mg/5ml syrup. Take one 5ml spoonful four times a day for 14 days; supply 200 ml; NHS Cost £20.91.

Flucloxacillin capsules: 500mg four times a day
- Age from 12 years onwards
- Flucloxacillin 500mg capsules. Take one capsule four times a day for 14 days; supply 56 capsules; NHS Cost £9.46.

Analgesia/antipyretics: use when required

Paracetamol s/f susp: 60mg to 120mg up to four times a day
- Age from 3 to 11 months
- Paracetamol 120mg/5ml s/f susp. Take 2.5ml to 5ml every 4 to 6 hours when required for relief of pain or high temperature. Maximum of 4 doses in 24 hours; supply 150 ml; NHS Cost £0.65; OTC Cost £1.16.

Paracetamol s/f susp: 120mg to 240mg up to four times a day
- Age from 12 months to 5 years
- Paracetamol 120mg/5ml s/f susp. Take one to two 5ml spoonfuls every 4 to 6 hours when required for relief of pain or high temperature. Maximum of 4 doses in 24 hours; supply 300 ml; NHS Cost £1.30; OTC Cost £2.28.

Paracetamol s/f susp: 250mg to 500mg up to four times a day
- Age from 6 to 11 years
- Paracetamol 250mg/5ml s/f susp. Take one to two 5ml spoonfuls every 4 to 6 hours when required for relief of pain or high temperature. Maximum of 4 doses in 24 hours; supply 300 ml; NHS Cost £1.70; OTC Cost £2.99.

Paracetamol tablets: 500mg to 1g up to four times a day
- Age from 12 to 15 years
- Paracetamol 500mg tablets. Take one to two tablets every 4 to 6 hours when required for relief of pain or high temperature. Maximum of 8 tablets in 24 hours; supply 100 tablets; NHS Cost £0.75; OTC Cost £1.32.

Paracetamol tablets: 1g up to four times a day
- Age from 16 years onwards
- Paracetamol 500mg tablets. Take two tablets every 4 to 6 hours when required for relief of pain or high temperature. Maximum of 8 tablets in 24 hours; supply 100 tablets; NHS Cost £0.75; OTC Cost £1.32.

Ibuprofen s/f susp: 50mg three to four times a day
- Age from 12 months to 2 years
- Ibuprofen 100mg/5ml s/f susp. Take 2.5ml three to four times a day when required for relief of pain or high temperature. Do not exceed the stated dose; supply 1(ml; NHS Cost £2.00; OTC Cost £3.52.

Ibuprofen s/f susp: 100mg three to four times a day
- Age from 3 to 7 years
- Ibuprofen 100mg/5ml s/f susp. Take one 5ml spoonfu to 4 times a day when required for relief of pain or hig temperature. Do not exceed the stated dose; supply 1 ml; NHS Cost £2.73; OTC Cost £4.81.

Ibuprofen s/f susp: 200mg three to four times a day
- Age from 8 to 11 years
- Ibuprofen 100mg/5ml s/f susp. Take two 5ml spoonfu 3 to 4 times a day when required for relief of pain or high temperature. Do not exceed the stated dose; supply 300 ml; NHS Cost £5.46; OTC Cost £9.62.

Ibuprofen tablets: 400mg three times a day
- Age from 12 years onwards
- Ibuprofen 400mg tablets. Take one tablet three times day when required for relief of pain or high temperatu Do not exceed the stated dose; supply 24 tablets; NHS Cost £0.70; OTC Cost £1.23.

Chest infection with known organism

Which therapy?

- Choose an antibiotic to which the organism is reporte to be sensitive.
- **Treatment duration:** 5 days for acute bronchitis, 5–10 days for exacerbations of chronic obstructive pulmonary disease, and 7 days for pneumonia.
- Local antibiotic prescribing policies should be considered.

Practical prescribing points

For further information, please see the *Medicines Compendium* (www.medicines.org.uk) or the *British National Formulary* (www.bnf.org).

- **The Committee on Safety of Medicines** has advised th cholestatic jaundice (usually self-limiting) may occur with use of either co-amoxiclav or flucloxacillin. Peop at greatest risk include men and those over 65 years o
- **Women taking combined hormonal contraceptives:**
  - Erythromycin is not thought to interact with combi hormonal contraceptives.
  - Non-enzyme-inducing broad-spectrum antibiotics – use additional contraception during the short course and for 7 days afterwards. Miss out the pill-free interval if the 7 days runs beyond the end of the packet, and the inactive tablets in the case of an eve day (ED) preparation.
- **Pregnant women:** amoxicillin and erythromycin are nc known to be harmful, and may be preferred options. Quinolones and tetracyclines are contraindicated in pregnancy and should never be used.
- **Breastfeeding:** amoxicillin or erythromycin may be use Quinolones and tetracyclines should be avoided.
- **Renal impairment:** doxycycline may be the preferred option, as no dosage adjustment or monitoring is required. Oxytetracycline is contraindicated in people with kidney disease, and trimethoprim is best avoided. All other recommended antibiotics need to be carefully monitored.
- **Liver impairment:** amoxicillin may be the preferred option. Other agents should be avoided or need carefu monitoring.
- **Erythromycin:** should be avoided in people with a predisposition to cardiac arrhythmias. Erythromycin

may increase the level of certain drugs (e.g. theophylline, carbamazepine), or potentiate warfarin.
Clarithromycin and azithromycin: are less likely to cause gastrointestinal adverse effects than erythromycin is. Similar drug interactions apply as for erythromycin, and clarithromycin should also be avoided in people with a predisposition to cardiac arrhythmias.
Tetracyclines: contraindicated also in porphyria and children aged under 12 years. They may cause photosensitivity reactions (avoid exposure to sunlight or sun lamps).
Quinolones:

- The Committee on Safety of Medicines (CSM) advises that quinolones can cause tendon damage, and that treatment should be stopped if pain or inflammation of a tendon occurs.
- Use with caution in people with epilepsy or who are predisposed to seizures (because of other conditions or medicines they are taking).
- May affect the performance of driving, and concurrent use of alcohol may potentiate any sedative effects.
- Are contraindicated (except nalidixic acid) in children under 16 years, owing to possible arthropathy defects.

Cephalosporins: penicillin-allergic people may be cross-sensitive to cephalosporins [DTB, 1996a].
Trimethoprim is a folate antagonist and should be avoided in women with known folate deficiency (as well as in pregnant women or women of child-bearing age), or who are on another folate antagonist (e.g. antiepileptics or proguanil), unless they are taking folate supplementation. Trimethoprim can be used to treat acute infections during pregnancy and breastfeeding. For further information, telephone the National Teratology Information Service (0191 2321525).

ollow-up advice

Depending on the severity of the illness, consider reviewing the patient within 24 hours, either by telephone or in person, to assess response to treatment.
After pneumonia, a follow-up chest X-ray is advisable for people who present with focal chest signs, as a proportion will have an underlying malignancy. The Royal College of Radiologists recommends a follow-up chest X-ray 6 weeks after recovery from pneumonia for all adults who have persistent symptoms or signs, or who are at higher risk of underlying malignancy (smokers and people aged over 50 years). Follow-up chest X-ray in children is recommended only if there are persisting clinical signs or symptoms.

hould I refer or investigate?

efer?

dmit

pneumonia, there should be a low threshold for hospital mission. Treatment at home is usually safe if none of the llowing features is present:

- Age >50 years
- Comorbid disease: cancer, cerebrovascular disease, heart failure, liver disease, or renal disease
- New confusion
- Low or high temperature (<35°C or >=40°C)
- Raised respiratory rate (>30/minute)
- Tachycardia (>125/minute)
- Low blood pressure (systolic <90 mmHg or diastolic <60 mmHg)

exacerbation of COPD, suggested criteria for admission e:

- Severe breathlessness
- Confusion
- Cyanosis
- Worsening peripheral oedema
- Impaired consciousness
- The person is unable to cope at home
- General condition is poor or is deteriorating
- Activity level is poor, or the person is confined to bed
- The person lives alone
- The person is on long-term oxygen therapy
- The exacerbation was of rapid onset
- Significant comorbidity is present

Urgently refer

Referral guidelines for suspected lung cancer [NICE, 2005] **recommend:**

- **Urgent referral for chest X-ray (the report should be returned within 5 days) for people with any of the following:**
  - Haemoptysis
  - Unexplained or persistent (more than 3 weeks):
    - Chest and/or shoulder pain
    - Dyspnoea
    - Weight loss
    - Chest signs
    - Hoarseness
    - Finger clubbing
    - Cervical or supraclavicular lymphadenopathy
    - Cough
    - Features suggestive of metastasis from a lung cancer (e.g. brain, bone, liver, or skin)
  - Underlying chronic respiratory problems with unexplained changes in existing symptoms
- **Urgent referral* for people with:**
  - Persistent haemoptysis in smokers/ex-smokers aged 40 years of age and older
  - A chest X-ray suggestive/suspicious of lung cancer (including pleural effusion and slowly resolving consolidation)
  - A normal chest X-ray where there is a high suspicion of lung cancer
  - A history of asbestos exposure and recent onset chest pain, shortness of breath or unexplained systemic symptoms where a chest X-ray indicates pleural effusion, pleural mass or any suspicious lung pathology
- **Immediate referral* for people with:**
  - Signs of superior vena caval obstruction (swelling of face/neck with fixed elevation of jugular venous pressure)
  - Stridor

*To a team specialising in the management of lung cancer, depending upon local arrangements.

Patient information leaflets

The following PILs are available at www.prodigy.nhs.uk

- Bronchitis (Acute)
- COPD (Chronic Obs. Pulmonary Disease)
- Pneumonia
- Quit (help to stop smoking)
- Smoking - The Facts
- Smoking - Tips on Stopping
- Upper Respiratory Tract Infection (URTI)

Shared decision making

- **You should take antibiotics,** as you have a chest infection caused by a bacterium.
- Tell your doctor if you are allergic to any antibiotics.
- **If symptoms are not settling within two days, tell your doctor.**

- **Paracetamol, ibuprofen, or aspirin** will reduce fever and ease any pains. (Children under 16 should not take aspirin.)
- Have lots to drink.

Drug rationale

Drugs not included

C

- **Ampicillin** has a spectrum of activity similar to that of amoxicillin, but it is poorly absorbed (less than 50% of the dose is absorbed when food is in the stomach); it has a higher incidence of diarrhoea than amoxicillin does; and it requires more frequent dosing [Finch et al, 2003].
- **Quinolones other than ciprofloxacin, ofloxacin, and levofloxacin** have not been included. Moxifloxacin is licensed for community-acquired pneumonia and exacerbations of chronic bronchitis, but trial data have shown that it offers a similar clinical benefit to that of levofloxacin. Its use should be reserved for when sensitivities are known, in order to minimize the development of bacterial resistance [Regional Drug and Therapeutics Centre, 2003]. Other quinolones are not licensed for treatment of respiratory tract infections.
- **Cephalosporins other than cefalexin, cefaclor, cefuroxime, and cefixime** are not included, since other orally active cephalosporins have a similar broad spectrum of activity [Finch et al, 2003] and probably provide little advantage over those offered.
- **Tetracyclines other than oxytetracycline and doxycycline** are not included. The spectrum of activity of the tetracyclines is similar [Finch et al, 2003], and these two seem to be most commonly recommended.

Drugs included

A selection of antibiotics is offered for use when sensitivities are known:

- **Amoxicillin** is active against *Streptococcus pneumoniae* and *Haemophilus influenzae* (two of the most common respiratory pathogens) [Finch et al, 2003].
- **Co-amoxiclav** can be useful for bacterial infections caused by amoxicillin-resistant beta-lactamase-producing strains. Co-amoxiclav may also be useful during influenza epidemics, as an alternative to erythromycin plus flucloxacillin.
- **Flucloxacillin** may be useful where the infection is due to *Staphylococcus aureus* (e.g. secondary infection after influenza or measles) [DTB, 1998; BNF 47, 2004].
- **Phenoxymethylpenicillin** is active against *S pneumoniae*, but has poor activity against *H influenzae* and *Moraxella catarrhalis* [Finch et al, 2003].
- **Erythromycin** is included for empirical treatment, as it is particularly active against *S pneumoniae* and *M catarrhalis*, although it has low activity against *H influenza* [DTB, 1998; Finch et al, 2003]. Erythromycin is also an option for people with penicillin allergy.
- **Azithromycin and clarithromycin** may be useful for someone who experiences unwanted gastrointestinal effects with erythromycin [HPA, 2003]. Modified-release clarithromycin is also included, as the once-daily dose may offer benefits in terms of compliance, and it is no more costly than the standard-release formulation [Allin et al, 2001].
- **Doxycycline** is included. Doxycycline has a broad spectrum of activity against respiratory pathogens (it covers most typical and atypical pathogens) and is given once a day [Finch et al, 2003]. Doxycycline is also an option for people with penicillin allergy.
- **Oxytetracycline** has a spectrum of activity similar to that of doxycycline, but must be given four times a day [Finch et al, 2003; BNF 47, 2004]. Oxytetracycline is also an option for people with penicillin allergy.
- **Ciprofloxacin, ofloxacin and levofloxacin** are included for use when sensitivities are known [DH and SMAC, 1998].
- **Cefalexin, cefaclor, cefuroxime, and cefixime** are included for use when sensitivities are known. Cefuroxime must be taken with food to increase its absorption. Cefaclor generally causes fewer gastrointestinal adverse effects than do cefuroxime or cefixime. Cefalexin has little activity against *H influenz* [MeReC, 1992; Thompson and Jacobs, 1993].
- **Trimethoprim** is reserved for use when sensitivities are known. Trimethoprim generally has poor activity agai *S pneumoniae* and *M catarrhalis* [McNulty, Personal Communication, 2004].

Prescriptions

Penicillins for 5 days

Amoxicillin s/f suspension: 125mg three times a day

- Age from 1 month to 23 months
- Amoxicillin 125mg/5ml s/f susp. Take one 5ml spoonf three times a day for 5 days; supply 100 ml; NHS Cost £1.30.

Amoxicillin s/f suspension: 250mg three times a day

- Age from 2 to 9 years
- Amoxicillin 250mg/5ml s/f susp. Take one 5ml spoonf three times a day for 5 days; supply 100 ml; NHS Cost £2.25.

Amoxicillin s/f suspension: 500mg three times a day

- Age from 10 to 11 years
- Amoxicillin 250mg/5ml s/f susp. Take two 5ml spoonfuls three times a day for 5 days; supply 200 ml; NHS Cost £4.50.

Amoxicillin capsules: 500mg three times a day

- Age from 12 years onwards
- Amoxicillin 500mg capsules. Take one capsule three times a day for 5 days; supply 15 capsules; NHS Cost £1.32.

Co-amoxiclav 125/31mg/5ml susp: 0.25ml/kg three time a day

- Age from 1 month to 11 months
- Co-amoxiclav 125/31mg/5ml susp. *WEIGHT REQUIRED* Take 0.25ml per kg bodyweight THREE times a day for 5 days; supply 100 ml; NHS Cost £4.5

Co-amoxiclav s/f suspension: 125/31mg three times a d

- Age from 12 months to 6 years
- Co-amoxiclav 125/31mg/5ml susp. Take one 5ml spoonful three times a day for 5 days; supply 100 ml; NHS Cost £4.57.

Co-amoxiclav s/f suspension: 250/62mg three times a d

- Age from 7 to 11 years
- Co-amoxiclav 250/62mg/5ml susp. Take one 5ml spoonful three times a day for 5 days; supply 100 ml; NHS Cost £6.42.

Co-amoxiclav tablets: 500/125mg three times a day

- Age from 12 years onwards
- Co-amoxiclav 625mg tablets. Take one tablet three times a day for 5 days; supply 15 tablets; NHS Cost £11.24.

Flucloxacillin syrup: 62.5mg four times a day

- Age from 1 month to 11 months
- Flucloxacillin 125mg/5ml syrup. Take 2.5ml four times day for 5 days; supply 100 ml; NHS Cost £3.49.

ucloxacillin syrup: 125mg four times a day
Age from 12 months to 4 years
Flucloxacillin 125mg/5ml syrup. Take one 5ml spoonful four times a day for 5 days; supply 100 ml; NHS Cost £3.49.

ucloxacillin syrup: 250mg four times a day
Age from 5 to 11 years
Flucloxacillin 250mg/5ml syrup. Take one 5ml spoonful four times a day for 5 days; supply 100 ml; NHS Cost £6.97.

ucloxacillin capsules: 500mg four times a day
Age from 12 years onwards
Flucloxacillin 500mg capsules. Take one capsule four times a day for 5 days; supply 20 capsules; NHS Cost £3.38.

enicillin V solution: 62.5mg four times a day
Age from 1 month to 11 months
Penicillin V 125mg/5ml sol. Take 2.5ml four times a day for 5 days; supply 100 ml; NHS Cost £1.66.

enicillin V solution: 125mg four times a day
Age from 12 months to 5 years
Penicillin V 125mg/5ml sol. Take one 5ml spoonful four times a day for 5 days; supply 100 ml; NHS Cost £1.66.

enicillin V solution: 250mg four times a day
Age from 6 to 11 years
Penicillin V 250mg/5ml sol. Take one 5ml spoonful four times a day for 5 days; supply 100 ml; NHS Cost £2.28.

enicillin V tablets: 500mg four times a day
Age from 12 years onwards
Penicillin V 250mg tablets. Take two tablets four times a day for 5 days; supply 40 tablets; NHS Cost £2.54.

Macrolides for 3 or 5 days

rythromycin s/f suspension: 125mg four times a day x 5 ays
Age from 1 month to 23 months
Erythromycin 125mg/5ml sf susp. Take one 5ml spoonful four times a day for 5 days; supply 100 ml; NHS Cost £1.05.

rythromycin s/f suspension: 250mg four times a day x 5 ays
Age from 2 to 11 years
Erythromycin 250mg/5ml sf susp. Take one 5ml spoonful four times a day for 5 days; supply 100 ml; NHS Cost £1.84.

rythromycin s/f suspension: 500mg four times a day x 5 ays
Age from 9 to 11 years
Erythromycin 500mg/5ml sf susp. Take one 5ml spoonful four times a day for 5 days; supply 100 ml; NHS Cost £2.86.

rythromycin e/c tablets: 250mg four times a day for 5 ays
Age from 12 years onwards
Erythromycin 250mg e/c tablets. Take one tablet four times a day for 5 days; supply 20 tablets; NHS Cost £2.72.

rythromycin e/c tablets: 500mg four times a day for 5 ays
Age from 12 years onwards
Erythromycin 250mg e/c tablets. Take two tablets four times a day for 5 days; supply 40 tablets; NHS Cost £5.44.

larithromycin suspension: 62.5mg twice a day for 5 days
Age from 12 months to 2 years
Clarithromycin 125mg/5ml susp. Take 2.5ml twice a day for 5 days; supply 70 ml; NHS Cost £6.00.

Clarithromycin suspension: 125mg twice a day for 5 days
- Age from 3 to 6 years
- Clarithromycin 125mg/5ml susp. Take one 5ml spoonful twice a day for 5 days; supply 70 ml; NHS Cost £6.00.

Clarithromycin suspension: 187.5mg twice a day for 5 days
- Age from 7 to 9 years
- Clarithromycin 125mg/5ml susp. Take 7.5ml twice a day for 5 days; supply 100 ml; NHS Cost £10.32.

Clarithromycin suspension: 250mg twice a day for 5 days
- Age from 10 to 11 years
- Clarithromycin 125mg/5ml susp. Take two 5ml spoonfuls twice a day for 5 days; supply 100 ml; NHS Cost £10.32.

Clarithromycin tablets: 250mg twice a day for 5 days
- Age from 12 years onwards
- Clarithromycin 250mg tablets. Take one tablet twice a day for 5 days; supply 10 tablets; NHS Cost £8.40.

Clarithromycin tablets: 500mg twice a day for 5 days
- Age from 12 years onwards
- Clarithromycin 500mg tablets. Take one tablet twice a day for 5 days; supply 10 tablets; NHS Cost £16.82.

Azithromycin suspension: 10mg/kg once a day for 3 days
- Age from 6 months to 2 years
- Azithromycin 200mg/5ml susp. *WEIGHT REQUIRED* Take 10mg per kg bodyweight ONCE a day for 3 days; supply 15 ml; NHS Cost £5.08.

Azithromycin suspension: 200mg once a day for 3 days
- Age from 3 to 7 years
- Azithromycin 200mg/5ml susp. Take one 5ml spoonful once a day for 3 days; supply 15 ml; NHS Cost £5.08.

Azithromycin suspension: 300mg once a day for 3 days
- Age from 8 to 11 years
- Azithromycin 200mg/5ml susp. Take 7.5ml once a day for 3 days; supply 23 ml; NHS Cost £7.62.

Azithromycin suspension: 400mg once a day for 3 days
- Age from 12 to 13 years
- Azithromycin 200mg/5ml susp. Take two 5ml spoonfuls once a day for 3 days; supply 30 ml; NHS Cost £13.80.

Azithromycin capsules: 500mg once a day for 3 days
- Age from 14 years onwards
- Azithromycin 250mg capsules. Take two capsules once a day for 3 days; supply 6 capsules; NHS Cost £13.42.

Tetracyclines for 5 days

Doxycycline 100mg once a day
- Age from 12 years onwards
- Doxycycline 100mg capsules. Take TWO capsules now and then take ONE capsule once a day for the next 4 days; supply 6 capsules; NHS Cost £1.24.

Oxytetracycline 250mg four times a day
- Age from 12 years onwards
- Oxytetracycline 250mg tablets. Take one tablet four times a day for 5 days; supply 20 tablets; NHS Cost £0.57.

Oxytetracycline 500mg four times a day
- Age from 12 years onwards
- Oxytetracycline 250mg tablets. Take two tablets four times a day for 5 days; supply 40 tablets; NHS Cost £1.16.

Cephalosporins for 5 days

Cefalexin suspension: 125mg twice a day
- Age from 1 month to 11 months
- Cefalexin 125mg/5ml mixture. Take one 5ml spoonful twice a day for 5 days; supply 100 ml; NHS Cost £1.28.

C

Cefalexin suspension: 125mg three times a day
- Age from 12 months to 5 years
- Cefalexin 125mg/5ml mixture. Take one 5ml spoonful three times a day for 5 days; supply 100 ml; NHS Cost £1.28.

Cefalexin suspension: 250mg three times a day
- Age from 6 to 11 years
- Cefalexin 250mg/5ml mixture. Take one 5ml spoonful three times a day for 5 days; supply 100 ml; NHS Cost £2.19.

Cefalexin capsules: 500mg three times a day
- Age from 12 years onwards
- Cefalexin 500mg capsules. Take one capsule three times a day for 5 days; supply 15 capsules; NHS Cost £2.47.

Cefaclor s/f suspension: 62.5mg three times a day
- Age from 1 month to 11 months
- Cefaclor 125mg/5ml s/f susp. Take 2.5ml three times a day for 5 days; supply 100 ml; NHS Cost £4.91.

Cefaclor s/f suspension: 125mg three times a day
- Age from 12 months to 4 years
- Cefaclor 125mg/5ml s/f susp. Take one 5ml spoonful three times a day for 5 days; supply 100 ml; NHS Cost £4.91.

Cefaclor s/f suspension: 250mg three times a day
- Age from 5 to 11 years
- Cefaclor 250mg/5ml s/f susp. Take one 5ml spoonful three times a day for 5 days; supply 100 ml; NHS Cost £9.80.

Cefaclor capsules: 500mg three times a day
- Age from 12 years onwards
- Cefaclor 500mg capsules. Take one capsule three times a day for 5 days; supply 15 capsules; NHS Cost £7.51.

Cefuroxime suspension: 125mg twice a day
- Age from 3 to 23 months
- Cefuroxime 125mg/5ml susp. Take one 5ml spoonful twice a day for 5 days; supply 70 ml; NHS Cost £5.94.

Cefuroxime suspension: 250mg twice a day
- Age from 2 to 11 years
- Cefuroxime 125mg/5ml susp. Take two 5ml spoonfuls twice a day for 5 days; supply 140 ml; NHS Cost £11.88.

Cefuroxime tablets: 250mg twice a day
- Age from 12 years onwards
- Cefuroxime 250mg tablets. Take one tablet twice a day for 5 days; supply 10 tablets; NHS Cost £7.43.

Cefixime suspension: 75mg once a day
- Age from 6 to 11 months
- Cefixime 100mg/5ml suspension. Take 3.75ml once a day for 5 days; supply 38 ml; NHS Cost £7.90.

Cefixime suspension: 100mg once a day
- Age from 12 months to 4 years
- Cefixime 100mg/5ml suspension. Take one 5ml spoonful once a day for 5 days; supply 38 ml; NHS Cost £7.90.

Cefixime suspension: 200mg once a day
- Age from 5 to 11 years
- Cefixime 100mg/5ml suspension. Take two 5ml spoonfuls once a day for 5 days; supply 75 ml; NHS Cost £14.18.

Cefixime tablets: 200mg once a day
- Age from 12 years onwards
- Cefixime 200mg tablets. Take one tablet once a day for 5 days; supply 5 tablets; NHS Cost £8.59.

Cefixime tablets: 400mg once a day
- Age from 12 years onwards
- Cefixime 200mg tablets. Take two tablets once a day for 5 days; supply 10 tablets; NHS Cost £17.19.

Quinolones or trimethoprim for 5 days

Ciprofloxacin 250mg twice a day
- Age from 16 years onwards
- Ciprofloxacin 250mg tablets. Take one tablet twice a day for 5 days; supply 10 tablets; NHS Cost £6.05.

Ciprofloxacin 500mg twice a day
- Age from 16 years onwards
- Ciprofloxacin 500mg tablets. Take one tablet twice a day for 5 days; supply 10 tablets; NHS Cost £11.66.

Ciprofloxacin 750mg twice a day
- Age from 16 years onwards
- Ciprofloxacin 750mg tablets. Take one tablet twice a day for 5 days; supply 10 tablets; NHS Cost £17.45.

Ofloxacin 400mg once a day
- Age from 16 years onwards
- Ofloxacin 400mg tablets. Take one tablet once a day fo 5 days; supply 5 tablets; NHS Cost £10.74.

Ofloxacin 400mg twice a day
- Age from 16 years onwards
- Ofloxacin 400mg tablets. Take one tablet twice a day f 5 days; supply 10 tablets; NHS Cost £21.80.

Levofloxacin 500mg once a day
- Age from 16 years onwards
- Levofloxacin 500mg f/c tablets. Take one tablet once a day for 5 days; supply 5 tablets; NHS Cost £13.90.

Levofloxacin 500mg twice a day
- Age from 16 years onwards
- Levofloxacin 500mg f/c tablets. Take one tablet twice a day for 5 days; supply 10 tablets; NHS Cost £27.80.

Trimethoprim 50mg/5ml s/f suspension: 4mg/kg twice a day
- Age from 1 month to 11 years
- Trimethoprim 50mg/5ml s/f susp. *WEIGHT REQUIRED* Take 4mg per kg bodyweight TWICE a day for 5 days. (Max 200mg per dose); supply 100 ml; NHS Cost £1.77.

Trimethoprim tablets: 200mg twice a day
- Age from 12 years onwards
- Trimethoprim 200mg tablets. Take one tablet twice a day for 5 days; supply 10 tablets; NHS Cost £0.47.

Extended Information

Background information

- What is it? p.302
- What are the usual pathogens? p.303
- How common is it? p.303
- How do I know my patient has it? p.303
- What else might it be? p.304
- Complications and prognosis p.304

What is it?

- 'Chest infection' is a term that covers a wide variety of different clinical situations, ranging from a mild, self-limiting illness to a severe life-threatening condition. Chest infections can be broadly split into three main groups: acute bronchitis, exacerbation of chronic obstructive pulmonary disease (COPD), and communit acquired pneumonia. There is no widely agreed definition of these terms, and for the purposes of this PRODIGY guidance they are described as follows.
- **The term 'acute bronchitis'** implies that there is transien inflammation of the trachea and major bronchi because of infection. The diagnosis is made if a previously well person presents with cough, with or without sputum production, in the absence of focal chest signs or severe

systemic upset. Dyspnoea and wheeze may be present [Wark, 2003].

COPD is a chronic, slowly progressive disease characterized by airflow obstruction that does not change markedly over several months. For more information, see the PRODIGY guidance on *Chronic obstructive pulmonary disease (COPD)*. A person with an exacerbation of COPD usually presents with worsening breathlessness, a worsening cough, increased sputum volume, and change in sputum colour [NICE, 2004].

Community-acquired pneumonia is contracted in the community rather than in hospital. Most cases of pneumonia developing within the first 48 hours of hospitalization also involve community-acquired infection. Infection of the lung parenchyma results in a cough, purulent sputum (which may be bloodstained or rusty coloured), breathlessness, pleuritic chest pain, fever (>38°C), and systemic upset. Focal chest signs (e.g. dullness to percussion, bronchial breathing, crepitations, and pleural rub) may be present [British Thoracic Society, 2004].

'hat are the usual pathogens?

udies investigating the cause of chest infection report ixed findings. Such variety is probably due to seasonal ıriation, different patient mix, different definitions of ıest infection, and different diagnostic techniques.

ʌcute bronchitis

Virus infections probably account for most cases of acute bronchitis. A study of people presenting between October 1997 and March 1998 found that viruses accounted for 19% of infections [Macfarlane et al, 2001]. No organism was identified in 45% of cases, but it is likely that many of these cases will have been virus infections. Other organisms identified were *Streptococcus pneumoniae* (17%), *Chlamydia pneumoniae* (17%), *Haemophilus influenzae* (9%), *Mycoplasma pneumoniae* (7%), and *Moraxella catarrhalis* (2%). An earlier study of people presenting between November 1990 and December 1991 found that *S pneumoniae* accounted for 30% of infections [Macfarlane et al, 1993; Macfarlane, 1999]. This study also found that *M pneumoniae* accounted for only 0.5% of infections. However, *M pneumoniae* occurs in epidemics with a 4 year cycle, and an epidemic coincided with the time the 1997/1998 study was carried out. The 1990/1991 study found that *C pneumoniae* accounted for only 0.5% of infections. The 1997/1998 study used more sensitive tests for *C pneumoniae*. As well as identifying more cases, this may have resulted in several false positives.

Exacerbation of COPD

There is ongoing uncertainty about the exact role of infection in exacerbations of COPD. Studies are difficult to interpret, owing to high rates of bacterial colonization of the sputum of people with COPD [Bach et al, 2001]. The usual pathogens isolated are *Haemophilus influenzae* (22%), *Pseudomonas aeruginosa* (15%), *Streptococcus pneumoniae* (10%), and *Moraxella catarrhalis* (9%). Non-pathogenic bacteria account for up to a third of isolates. *Mycoplasma pneumoniae* or *Chlamydia pneumoniae* may precipitate 1–10% of exacerbations. There is increasing evidence that viruses may account for a large number of exacerbations [Bach et al, 2001].

Non-infectious agents are responsible for some exacerbations (e.g. nitrogen dioxide, particulates, sulphur dioxide, ozone).

- The cause of the exacerbation may be unidentifiable in up to 30% of exacerbations.

[National Collaborating Centre for Chronic Conditions, 2004]

Community-acquired pneumonia

- ***Streptococcus pneumoniae* is the most common identified cause** [Bartlett et al, 2000; Lim et al, 2001]. A study of people admitted to hospital with pneumonia found that *S pneumoniae* accounted for 48% of infections. Other identified pathogens were *Chlamydia pneumoniae* (13%), *Haemophilus influenzae* (7%), *Mycoplasma pneumoniae* (3%), *Legionella pneumophila* (3%), *Moraxella catarrhalis* (2%), and *Staphylococcus aureus* (1.5%) [Lim et al, 2001]. Viruses accounted for 23% of infections, most commonly influenza A virus (19%). No pathogen was identified in 25% of cases.
- A single pathogen is identified in 85% of people where a cause is found; however, the true frequency of polymicrobial community-acquired pneumonia is not known.
- **Staphylococcal pneumonia** is usually secondary to influenza. In the above study of people admitted to hospital with pneumonia, *S aureus* was isolated from two out of 267 people [Lim et al, 2001]. Both of these also had influenza A infection, and required treatment in the intensive care unit.
- **Legionella pneumonia** is unusual. Hospital admission is usually necessary because of the severity of the pneumonia. In the above study, however, out of the nine people diagnosed as having *L pneumophila* infection, only two had severe pneumonia [Lim et al, 2001]. The infection is more common in younger people.
- ***Mycoplasma* infection occurs in epidemics with a 4 year cycle.** The infection is more common in younger people [Macfarlane, 1999].
- The likely agent causing community acquired pneumonia cannot be accurately predicted from clinical features.

[British Thoracic Society, 2004]

How common is it?

- **Acute respiratory infections commonly present in general practice,** accounting for 17% of all acute consultations [DTB, 1998].
- **The annual incidence of acute bronchitis is 44 per 1000 adult population.** Most episodes occur during autumn or winter [Wark, 2003].
- **The annual incidence of community-acquired pneumonia is 5–11 per 1000 adult population** [British Thoracic Society, 2004]. The illness results in about 83 000 hospital admissions each year, and is the fifth leading cause of death in the UK [Guest and Morris, 1997]. Most episodes occur during autumn or winter [Loeb, 2003]. Pneumonia is likely to be present in no more than 5% of people presenting with acute respiratory symptoms [Metlay et al, 1997; DTB, 1998; Macfarlane et al, 2001].
- People with COPD suffer on average 1–3 exacerbations per year [Sethi et al, 2002].

How do I know my patient has it?

General issues

- **In general practice, the diagnosis of chest infection will nearly always be made on clinical grounds alone** [DTB, 1998].
- **No combination of symptoms or signs clearly diagnoses chest infection.** In addition, there is poor agreement between doctors on the presence or absence of abnormal

C

chest signs in people with respiratory symptoms [Metlay et al, 1997].
- **Cough is the most common symptom.** Other symptoms include sputum production, breathlessness, wheeze, chest pain, fever, sore throat, and coryza.

Acute bronchitis

- **Acute bronchitis** is usually diagnosed if a person presents with acute cough in the absence of focal chest signs or severe systemic upset, when a simple upper respiratory tract infection is not thought to be the cause. Sputum, dyspnoea, and wheeze may be present.

C

Exacerbation of COPD

- **Exacerbation of chronic obstructive pulmonary disease (COPD)** is usually diagnosed when a person with COPD presents with worsening cough, increased breathlessness, increased sputum volume, and change in sputum colour.

Community-acquired pneumonia

- **Pneumonia** should be suspected if a person presents with cough, purulent sputum (which may be bloodstained or rusty-coloured), breathlessness, pleuritic chest pain, fever (>38°C), and systemic upset. Focal chest signs (e.g. dullness to percussion, bronchial breathing, crepitations, and pleural rub) may be heard on auscultation.
- The accurate diagnosis of pneumonia requires a chest X-ray. No individual clinical finding or combination of findings is clearly predictive of the diagnosis of pneumonia. In particular, the presence or absence of crepitations is not sufficient to rule in or rule out the diagnosis [Metlay et al, 1997].
- However, pneumonia is unlikely if there are no focal chest signs and no abnormal vital signs:
  - Dullness to percussion
  - Bronchial breathing
  - Crepitations
  - Pleural rub
  - Heart rate >100 beats/minute
  - Respiratory rate >24 breaths/minute
  - Temperature >38°C [Metlay et al, 1997]
- **The elderly may present with few chest symptoms,** but may present with confusion, general malaise, fatigue, anorexia, and myalgia.
- **Young children may present with non-specific symptoms or abdominal pain** [Ruuskanen and Mertsola, 1999].

[British Thoracic Society, 2004]

Investigations in primary care

- **Sputum culture is not routinely indicated:** results are not usually back in time to guide immediate management and treatment is usually empirical. Sputum culture may guide the choice of treatment in those with persistent symptoms or who do not respond to initial antibiotic treatment [Macfarlane, 1999]. However, sputum culture results may be extremely difficult to interpret in these situations (e.g. due to alteration in the normal sputum flora owing to previous antibiotic treatment). Sputum culture for *Mycobacterium tuberculosis* should be considered for people with a persistent productive cough, especially if other features (e.g. malaise, weight loss, night sweats) or risk factors (e.g. ethnic origin, immunosuppression, old age) are present.
- **Blood tests, such as full blood count, or serology for viruses or atypical organisms, are not routinely indicated.** They rarely affect immediate management, but may be useful in those with persistent symptoms or poor response to treatment.
- **Chest X-ray is not routinely indicated for people well enough to be treated in the community.** Chest X-ray should be considered for people who are slow to recover or who have recurrent chest infections, particularly if they smoke [DTB, 1998].
- **A follow-up chest X-ray** is advisable for people who present with focal chest signs, as a proportion will have an underlying malignancy [Macfarlane, 1999]. The Royal College of Radiologists recommends a follow-up chest X-ray 6 weeks after recovery from pneumonia for all adults who have persistent symptoms or signs, or wh[o] are at higher risk of underlying malignancy (smokers ar[e] people aged over 50 years). It is important to wait for 6 weeks, as resolution of X-ray changes can be slow (especially in the elderly). Follow-up chest X-ray in children is recommended only if there are persisting clinical signs or symptoms [Royal College of Radiologists, 2003].

[British Thoracic Society, 2004; NICE, 2004]

What else might it be?

- Asthma
- Chest infection with underlying malignancy
- Heart failure
- Influenza
- Pulmonary embolism
- Subdiaphragmatic pathology (e.g. cholecystitis, pancreatitis, perforated duodenal ulcer, subphrenic/hepatic abscess)
- Whooping cough

Complications and prognosis

Acute bronchitis

- **Acute bronchitis is usually a mild, self-limiting illness.** The cough usually lasts 7–10 days, but can persist for 3 weeks [Alberta Medical Association, 2001; SIGN, 2002].

Exacerbation of COPD

- **Exacerbations requiring hospital admission are associated with an inpatient mortality rate of 3–4%,** which increases to 11–24% for those who require treatment in an intensive care unit [Bach et al, 2001].
- Of people admitted to hospital with an exacerbation, 34% were readmitted and 14% died within 3 months [National Collaborating Centre for Chronic Conditions, 2004].

Community-acquired pneumonia

- **The mortality of adults admitted to hospital in the UK i[s] 6–12%.** For those people requiring admission to an intensive care unit, the mortality is >50% [British Thoracic Society, 2004].
- **The mortality of adults managed in the community is <1%** [British Thoracic Society, 2004].
- Factors associated with a poor outcome are:
  - Cause of the pneumonia (highest with *Pseudomonas aeruginosa*, intermediate with *Streptococcus pneumoniae*, and lowest with *Mycoplasma pneumoniae* and *Chlamydia psittaci*)
  - Increasing age
  - Male sex
  - Pleuritic chest pain
  - Tachypnoea
  - Hypotension
  - Neurological disease
  - Malignancy
  - Low white-cell count
  - Bacteraemia
  - Multi-lobar X-ray opacities

Management issues

Patient advice p.305
Symptom relief p.305
Should I use an antibiotic? p.305
Antibiotic resistance p.305
Which antibiotic? p.306
Non-antibiotic treatments? p.306
Treat at home or admit? p.306

Patient advice

- **In acute bronchitis, explanation and reassurance is often all that is needed.** Explanation should cover the self-limiting nature of the cough and other symptoms, and the ineffectiveness of treatments, such as antibiotics or cough mixtures. Explain that the cough may last for 3 weeks. The use of a Patient Information Leaflet will reinforce these points [Macfarlane et al, 2002; SIGN, 2002].
  - When explaining the condition, the term 'chest cold' instead of 'bronchitis' is less likely to imply that antibiotics are needed [Gonzales et al, 2000].
- **Smokers should be strongly advised to stop smoking.** The presentation of a smoker with a chest infection is an ideal opportunity to introduce smoking cessation measures. See the separate PRODIGY guidance on *Smoking cessation*.

Symptom relief

- Analgesia and antipyretics should be used as appropriate (e.g. paracetamol or ibuprofen).
- **Cough mixtures are either ineffective or are little better than placebo.** They often contain a variety of different agents, including antihistamines, anticholinergics, cough suppressants, stimulant decongestants, expectorants, mucolytics, and analgesics [DTB, 1999b; SIGN, 2002; Wark, 2003]. Many people will already have tried over-the-counter preparations prior to consulting.

Should I use an antibiotic?

General issues about antibiotics

- Antibiotics are of limited value in previously healthy people presenting with acute respiratory symptoms (unless pneumonia is suspected). Antibiotics may cause adverse effects, and use of antibiotics may increase the likelihood of re-attendance for future episodes of respiratory illness [Butler et al, 1998].
- Indiscriminate prescribing of antibiotics may increase bacterial resistance in the community (see the section *Antibiotic resistance*).
- Most penicillin resistance is low-level and may be overcome by use of higher antibiotic doses [McNulty, Personal Communication, 2004].

Acute bronchitis

- **Antibiotics are not indicated for previously healthy people with acute bronchitis.** A systematic review of antibiotics for acute cough in adults found no evidence of benefit [Fahey et al, 1998]. Two systematic reviews of antibiotics for acute bronchitis found that antibiotics offer only slight benefit, possibly reducing the duration of illness by about half a day [Bent et al, 1999; Smucny et al, 2004a]. This minimal benefit has to be balanced against the possible adverse effects of antibiotics [Wark, 2003].
- **Sputum purulence alone is not an indication for antibiotics** in previously healthy people with acute bronchitis [SIGN, 2002].

Exacerbation of COPD

- **Antibiotics benefit some people with exacerbation of COPD.** People with severe exacerbations are most likely to benefit [Bach et al, 2001]. The National Institute for Clinical Excellence (NICE) recommends that:
  - Antibiotics should be used to treat exacerbations if the sputum is more purulent than usual.
  - Exacerbations in which the sputum is not more purulent than usual should only be treated with an antibiotic if there are clinical signs of pneumonia [NICE, 2004].

Community-acquired pneumonia

- **Antibiotics are indicated in all people with suspected pneumonia** [DTB, 1998; Bjerre et al, 2004]. Mortality from pneumonia before the antibiotic era was extremely high compared with current mortality figures, emphasizing the appropriateness of antibiotic treatment.
- **Antibiotics should be started as soon as possible.** Studies have shown that delay in commencing antibiotic therapy is associated with increased mortality.
- A systematic review that evaluated different oral antibiotics in outpatient settings has found clinical cure or improvement in over 90% of people regardless of the antibiotic taken [Pomilla and Brown, 1994].
- A more recent systematic review found that (compared with other macrolides, cephalosporins, or penicillins) azithromycin significantly reduced clinical failures over 6–21 days. However, most of the trials were not blinded, so this has to be interpreted with caution [Contopoulos-Ioannidis et al, 2001]. Treatment withdrawal was reduced with azithromycin because of its better adverse effect profile.
- **For people admitted to hospital with community-acquired pneumonia,** general practitioners should administer antibiotics immediately if the illness is life threatening, or if there are likely to be delays of more than 2 hours in admission. Suggested treatments (adult doses) are:
  - Benzylpenicillin 1.2 grams by intramuscular or intravenous injection
  - Amoxicillin 1 grams orally
  - Erythromycin (if penicillin allergy) 500 mg orally

[British Thoracic Society, 2004]

Antibiotic resistance

- ***Streptococcus pneumoniae.*** Data from all *S pneumoniae* isolated by Public Health Laboratories in England and Wales over a 2-week period in 1990 and 1995 found that resistance to penicillin had increased from 1.5% to 3.9% [DH and SMAC, 1998]. Resistance to erythromycin had increased from 2.8% to 8.6%. There was no change in resistance to tetracycline (5% to 5.1%). In recent surveys, prevalence of penicillin-resistant *S pneumoniae* has varied in the range 5–10% and resistance to erythromycin in the range 10–15% [Felmingham et al, 1998; Henwood et al, 2000; Reacher et al, 2000]. There is less recent published information on tetracycline resistance, but a study in 1997 found that 99% of isolates of *S pneumoniae* were sensitive to doxycycline [Felmingham and Gruneberg, 2000].
- ***Haemophilus influenzae.*** A study during the winter of 1995–1996 found that 84% of isolates were sensitive to amoxicillin, 96% to clarithromycin, and 99% to co-amoxiclav [Felmingham et al, 1998]. A study in 1997 found no resistance to doxycycline [Felmingham and Gruneberg, 2000]. Erythromycin has weak activity against *H influenzae*, unlike clarithromycin and azithromycin [DTB, 1998]; only 1% of isolates are sensitive to erythromycin, with 5% resistant and 94%

having intermediate resistance [McNulty, Personal Communication, 2004].

- ***Moraxella catarrhalis.*** Only 6% of isolates tested during the winter of 1995–1996 were sensitive to amoxicillin [Felmingham et al, 1998]. No resistance to macrolides or co-amoxiclav was found.
- **Atypical infections.** *Mycoplasma pneumoniae*, *Legionella pneumophila*, and *Chlamydia pneumoniae* are all thought to be sensitive to macrolides or tetracyclines.

Which antibiotic?

- **In general practice, the choice of antibiotic for treating chest infection is nearly always empirical** [DTB, 1998].
- Local resistance patterns and prescribing policies should be taken into account.

Acute bronchitis

- Antibiotics are not indicated for previously healthy people with acute bronchitis.
- If antibiotics are prescribed for acute bronchitis (e.g. in someone with significant comorbidity), amoxicillin, erythromycin, oxytetracycline, or doxycycline is recommended for first-line treatment [HPA, 2003].
- If a person with acute bronchitis is not responding to the initial antibiotic, suitable alternative choices are: co-amoxiclav; a tetracycline (if this has not already been tried); or clarithromycin or azithromycin (provided that treatment has not already failed with erythromycin, as *Streptococcus pneumoniae* has considerable cross-resistance to these agents) [HPA, 2003].

Exacerbation of COPD

- **In exacerbations of COPD,** amoxicillin or a tetracycline are recommended [McNulty, Personal Communication, 2004].
- **Macrolides are not recommended for treating exacerbations.** Erythromycin has only weak activity against *Haemophilus influenzae* (one of the most common pathogens implicated in exacerbations of COPD) and there are growing concerns about the build-up of resistance to clarithromycin and azithromycin [McNulty, Personal Communication, 2004]. Also, all macrolides concentrate intracellularly and *H influenzae* is an extracellular pathogen.
- **If a person with an exacerbation of COPD is not responding to the initial antibiotic,** then suitable alternative choices are: co-amoxiclav; tetracycline (if this has not already been tried); or clarithromycin or azithromycin (provided that treatment has not already failed with erythromycin, as *Streptococcus pneumoniae* has considerable cross-resistance to these agents) [McNulty, Personal Communication, 2004].

Community-acquired pneumonia

- **In community-acquired pneumonia, amoxicillin** (or erythromycin if the person is hypersensitive to penicillin) is recommended. The recommended dose of amoxicillin has increased to 500–1000 mg three times daily, because of the increasing prevalence of *Streptococcus pneumoniae* species with reduced susceptibility to penicillin. The recommended dose of erythromycin remains at 500 mg four times daily. Azithromycin or clarithromycin may be substituted for erythromycin for people with gastrointestinal intolerance to erythromycin. Treatment for 7 days is recommended.
- If there is no response to treatment within 48 hours, then either erythromycin or a tetracycline should be added, or the person should be admitted to hospital.

[British Thoracic Society, 2004]

Non-antibiotic treatments?

Acute bronchitis

- **Beta$_2$-agonists should not be used routinely.** A Cochra systematic review looked at the evidence for the use of beta$_2$-agonists in previously well people with acute bronchitis. Limited evidence of benefit was found only for those with evidence of airflow obstruction, such as wheezing.
- A Cochrane systematic review has concluded that ther is no evidence to support the use of beta$_2$-agonists in children with acute cough who do not have evidence o airflow obstruction. There is also little evidence that th use of beta$_2$-agonists for adults with acute cough is helpful [Smucny et al, 2004b].

Exacerbation of COPD

- Bronchodilator use should be increased during an exacerbation of COPD.
- **Combination of a beta$_2$-agonist with an anticholinergi** has not been found to increase the effect on FEV$_1$ more than either used alone [McCrory and Brown, 2004], b it may be worth trying once the maximum dose of eith agent has been reached.
- **Oral corticosteroids may benefit some people with an exacerbation of COPD.** They improve FEV$_1$ and reduc treatment failures, although no effect on survival has been shown [Thompson et al, 1996; Barnes, 1998; Bac et al, 2001]. Maximum benefits occur if treatment wit oral corticosteroids is started early; in selected people, consider the provision of a course of treatment at hom so that the individual can commence this as part of an agreed management programme.
- Current recommendations for oral corticosteroids duri an exacerbation are:
  - Consider oral corticosteroids if an exacerbation significantly increases breathlessness that interferes with daily activities.
  - Prescribe prednisolone 30 mg for 7–14 days.
  - Do not treat for more than 14 days, as this offers no benefit.
  - Refer to the BNF for guidance on stopping oral corticosteroid therapy.
  - Consider osteoporosis prophylaxis for people requiring frequent courses of oral corticosteroids. Se the separate PRODIGY guidance on *Osteoporosis*.

[National Collaborating Centre for Chronic Conditions, 2004]

Treat at home or admit?

- **Most people with a chest infection do not require hospital admission.** One study found that 9% of peopl diagnosed as having chest infection were admitted to hospital. The decision to admit was mainly influenced clinical signs of more severe infection, or a suspected diagnosis of pneumonia [Schaberg et al, 1996].
- **Many people with an exacerbation of COPD can be treated at home.** Admission to hospital is recommende if any of the following factors is present [NICE, 2004]:
  - Severe breathlessness
  - Confusion
  - Cyanosis
  - Worsening peripheral oedema
  - Impaired consciousness
  - The person is unable to cope at home
  - General condition is poor or is deteriorating
  - Activity level is poor, or the person is confined to be
  - The person lives alone
  - The person is on long-term oxygen therapy
  - The exacerbation was of rapid onset

- Significant comorbidity is present
- **Community-acquired pneumonia is a potentially fatal condition, and there should be a low threshold for hospital admission.** However, treatment at home is usually safe in younger people (i.e. under 50 years of age) if none of the following features is present:
  - Comorbid disease: cancer, cerebrovascular disease, heart failure, liver disease, or renal disease
  - New confusion
  - Low or high temperature (<35°C or >=40°C)
  - Raised respiratory rate (>30/minute)
  - Tachycardia (>125/minute)
  - Low blood pressure (systolic <90 mmHg or diastolic <60 mmHg)

Fine et al, 1997; Macfarlane, 1999; Bartlett et al, 2000]

References

NHS staff in England can link, free of charge, from references to full text journals by clicking on [Full text] on the PRODIGY website.

1. Alberta Medical Association (2001) *Guideline for the management of acute bronchitis.* Alberta Clinical Practice Guidelines. Alberta Medical Association. www.albertadoctors.org [Accessed: 29/01/2004].
2. Allin, D., James, I., Zachariah, J. et al (2001) Comparison of once- and twice-daily clarithromycin in the treatment of adults with severe acute lower respiratory tract infections. *Clinical Therapeutics* **23**(12), 1958–1968.
3. Bach, P.B., Brown, C., Gelfand, S.E. and McCrory, D.C. (2001) Management of acute exacerbations of chronic obstructive pulmonary disease: a summary and appraisal of published evidence. *Annals of Internal Medicine* **134**(7), 600–620.
4. Barnes, N.C. (1998) Inhaled steroids in COPD. *Lancet* **351**(9105), 766–767. [Full text]
5. Bartlett, J.G., Dowell, S.F., Mandell, L.A. et al (2000) Practice guidelines for the management of community-acquired pneumonia in adults. *Clinical Infectious Diseases* **31**(2), 347–382.
6. Bent, S., Saint, S., Vittinghoff, E. and Grady, D. (1999) Antibiotics in acute bronchitis: a meta-analysis. *American Journal of Medicine* **107**(1), 62–67.
7. Bjerre, L.M., Verheij, T.J.M. and Kochen, M.M. (2004) *Antibiotics for community acquired pneumonia in adult outpatients (Cochrane Review).* The Cochrane Library. Issue 2. Chichester, UK: John Wiley & Sons, Ltd.
8. BNF 47 (2004) *British National Formulary.* 47th edn. London: British Medical Association and Royal Pharmaceutical Society of Great Britain.
9. British Thoracic Society (2002) *BTS guidelines for the management of community acquired pneumonia in children.* British Thoracic Society. www.brit-thoracic.org.uk [Accessed: 01/05/2002].
10. British Thoracic Society (2004) *BTS guidelines for the management of community acquired pneumonia in adults: 2004 update.* British Thoracic Society. www.brit-thoracic.org.uk [Accessed: 12/05/2004].
11. Butler, C.C., Rollnick, S., Kinnersley, P. et al (1998) Reducing antibiotics for respiratory tract symptoms in primary care: consolidating 'why' and considering 'how'. *British Journal of General Practice* **48**(437), 1865–1871.
12. Contopoulos-Ioannidis, D.G., Ioannidis, J.P.A., Chew, P. and Lau, J. (2001) Meta-analysis of randomized controlled trials on the comparative efficacy and safety of azithromycin against other antibiotics for lower respiratory tract infections. *Journal of Antimicrobial Chemotherapy* **48**(5), 691–703. [Full text]
13. CSM (2002) Aspirin and Reye's syndrome in children up to and including 15 years of age. *Current Problems in Pharmacovigilance* **28**(Apr), 4.
14. Davidson, R., Cavalcanti, R., Brunton, J.L. et al (2002) Resistance to levofloxacin and failure of treatment of pneumococcal pneumonia. *New England Journal of Medicine* **346**(10), 747–750. [Full text]
15. DH and SMAC (1998) *The path of least resistance.* Department of Health. www.dh.gov.uk [Accessed: 27/04/2004]. [Full text]
16. DTB (1996a) Penicillin allergy. *Drug & Therapeutics Bulletin* **34**(11), 87–88.
17. DTB (1996b) Augmentin reconsidered. *Drug & Therapeutics Bulletin* **34**(10), 76–78.
18. DTB (1998) Antibiotic treatment of adults with chest infection in general practice. *Drug & Therapeutics Bulletin* **36**(9), 68–72.
19. DTB (1999a) Tackling antimicrobial resistance. *Drug & Therapeutics Bulletin* **37**(2), 9–16.
20. DTB (1999b) Cough medications in children. *Drug & Therapeutics Bulletin* **37**(3), 19–21.
21. Fahey, T., Stocks, N. and Thomas, T. (1998) Quantitative systematic review of randomised controlled trials comparing antibiotic with placebo for acute cough in adults. *British Medical Journal* **316**(7135), 906–910. [Full text]
22. Felmingham, D. and Gruneberg, R.N. (2000) The Alexander Project 1996–1997: latest susceptibility data from this international study of bacterial pathogens from community-acquired lower respiratory tract infections. *Journal of Antimicrobial Chemotherapy* **45**(2), 191–203. [Full text]
23. Felmingham, D., Robbins, M.J., Tesfaslasie, Y. et al (1998) Antimicrobial susceptibility of community-acquired lower respiratory tract bacterial pathogens isolated in the UK during the 1995–1996 cold season. *Journal of Antimicrobial Chemotherapy* **41**(3), 411–415.
24. Finch, R.G, Greenwood, D, Norrby, S.R. and Whitley, R.J. (2003) *Antibiotic and chemotherapy: anti-infective agents and their use in therapy.* 8th edn. London: Churchill Livingstone.
25. Fine, M.J., Auble, T.E., Yealy, D.M. et al (1997) A prediction rule to identify low risk patients with community acquired pneumonia. *New England Journal of Medicine* **336**(4), 243–250. [Full text]
26. Gonzales, R., Wilson, A., Crane, L.A. and Barrett, P.H.Jr. (2000) What's in a name? Public knowledge, attitudes, and experiences with antibiotic use for acute bronchitis. *American Journal of Medicine* **108**(1), 83–85.
27. Guest, J.F. and Morris, A. (1997) Community-acquired pneumonia: the annual cost to the National Health Service in the UK. *European Respiratory Journal* **10**(7), 1530–1534.
28. Henwood, C.J., Livermore, D.M., Johnson, A.P. et al (2000) Susceptibility of Gram-positive cocci from 25 UK hospitals to antimicrobial agents including linezolid. *Journal of Antimicrobial Chemotherapy* **46**(6), 931–940. [Full text]
29. HPA (2003) *Management of infection guidance for primary care: for consultation and local adaptation.* Health Protection Agency. www.hpa.org.uk [Accessed: 26/02/2004]. [Full text]
30. Kerstjens, H. and Postma, D. (2003) Chronic obstructive pulmonary disease. *Clinical Evidence* **10**(Dec), 1786–1803.
31. Lim, W.S., Macfarlane, J.T., Boswell, T.C.J. et al (2001) Study of community acquired pneumonia aetiology (SCAPA) in adults admitted to hospital: implications for management guidelines. *Thorax* **56**(4), 296–301. [Full text]

C

32. Loeb, M. (2003) Community acquired pneumonia. *Clinical Evidence* **10**(Dec), 1724–1737.
33. Macfarlane, J. (1999) Lower respiratory tract infection and pneumonia in the community. *Seminars in Respiratory Infections* **14**(2), 151–162.
34. Macfarlane, J.T., Colville, A., Guion, A. et al (1993) Prospective study of aetiology and outcome of adult lower-respiratory-tract infections in the community. *Lancet* **341**(8844), 511–514. [Full text]
35. Macfarlane, J., Holmes, W., Gard, P. et al (2001) Prospective study of the incidence, aetiology and outcome of adult lower respiratory tract illness in the community. *Thorax* **56**(2), 109–114. [Full text]
36. Macfarlane, J., Holmes, W., Gard, P. et al (2002) Reducing antibiotic use for acute bronchitis in primary care: blinded, randomised controlled trial of patient information leaflet. *British Medical Journal* **324**(7329), 91–96. [Full text]
37. McCrory, D.C. and Brown, C.D. (2004) *Anticholinergic bronchodilators versus beta2-sympathomimetic agents for acute exacerbations of chronic obstructive pulmonary disease (Cochrane Review)*. The Cochrane Library. Issue 2. Chichester, UK: John Wiley & Sons, Ltd. www.nelh.nhs.uk/cochrane.asp [Accessed: 25/01/2004].
38. McNulty, C. (2004) *Personal communication.* Medical Microbiologist, HPA Primary Care Unit: Gloucestershire Royal Hospital, Gloucester.
39. MeReC (1992) Newer oral cephalosporins. *MeReC Bulletin* **3**(4), 13–15.
40. MeReC (1998) Levofloxacin and grepafloxacin- two new quinolone antibiotics. *MeReC Bulletin* **9**(8), 29–32.
41. Metlay, J.P., Kapoor, W.N. and Fine, M.J. (1997) Does this patient have community-acquired pneumonia? Diagnosing pneumonia by history and physical examination. *Journal of the American Medical Association* **278**(17), 1440–1445. [Full text]
42. National Collaborating Centre for Chronic Conditions (2004) Chronic obstructive pulmonary disease: national clinical guideline on management of chronic obstructive pulmonary disease in adults in primary and secondary care. *Thorax* **59**(Suppl 1), 1–232.
43. NHS Executive (1998) *Phase out of CFC containing metered dose inhalers for the treatment of asthma and COPD*. HSC 1998/180. London: Department of Health.
44. NICE (2004) *Chronic obstructive pulmonary disease*. Clinical guideline 12. National Institute for Clinical Excellence. www.nice.org.uk [Accessed: 25/02/2004].
45. NICE (2005) *Referral guidelines for suspected cancer – quick reference guide.* Clinical guideline 27. National Institute for Health and Clinical Excellence. www.nice.org.uk [Accessed: 01/07/2005].
46. Pomilla, P.V. and Brown, R.B. (1994) Outpatient treatment of community-acquired pneumonia in adults. *Archives of Internal Medicine* **154**(16), 1793–1802.
47. Reacher, M.H., Shah, A., Livermore, D.M. et al (2000) Bacteraemia and antibiotic resistance of its pathogens reported in England and Wales between 1990 and 1998: trend analysis. *British Medical Journal* **320**(7229), 213–216. [Full text]
48. Regional Drug and Therapeutics Centre (2003) Moxifloxacin. *New Drug Evaluation* **62**(Sep), 1–2.
49. Royal College of Radiologists (2003) *Making the best use of a department of clinical radiology*. 5th edn. London: Royal College of Radiologists.
50. Ruuskanen, O. and Mertsola, J. (1999) Childhood community-acquired pneumonia. *Seminars in Respiratory Infections* **14**(2), 163–172.
51. Schaberg, T., Gialdroni-Grassi, G., Huchon, G. et al (1996) An analysis of decisions by European general practitioners to admit to hospital patients with lower respiratory tract infections. *Thorax* **51**(10), 1017–1022.
52. Sethi, S., Evans, N., Grant, B.J.B. and Murphy, T.F. (2002) New strains of bacteria and exacerbations of chronic obstructive pulmonary disease. *New England Journal of Medicine* **347**(7), 465–471. [Full text]
53. SIGN (2002) *Community management of lower respiratory tract infection in adults*. Report no. 59. Scottish Intercollegiate Guidelines Network. www.sign.ac.uk [Accessed: 21/01/2004].
54. Smucny, J., Fahey, T., Becker, L. and Glazier, R. (2004a) *Antibiotics for acute bronchitis (Cochrane Review)*. The Cochrane Library. Issue 2. Chichester, UK: John Wiley & Sons, Ltd.
55. Smucny, J., Flynn, C., Becker, L. and Glazier, R. (2004b) *Beta2-agonists for acute bronchitis (Cochrane Review)*. The Cochrane Library. Issue 1. Chichester, UK: John Wiley & Sons, Ltd.
56. Thompson, J.W and Jacobs, R.F (1993) Adverse effects of newer cephalosporins. *Drug Safety* **9**(2), 132–142.
57. Thompson, W.H., Nielson, C.P., Carvalho, P. et al (1996) Controlled trial of oral prednisone in outpatients with acute COPD exacerbation. *American Journal of Respiratory & Critical Care Medicine* **154**(2 Pt 1), 407–412.
58. Wark, P. (2003) Acute bronchitis. *Clinical Evidence* **10**(Dec), 1716–1723.
59. Zhanel, G.G., Dueck, M, Hoban, D.J. et al (2001) Review of macrolides and ketolides: focus on respiratory tract infections. *Drugs* **61**(4), 443–498.

PRODIGY GUIDANCE

Chickenpox

Last revised in November 2004
www.prodigy.nhs.uk/guidance.asp?gt=Chickenpox

Applies to people of all ages

This guidance covers the management of chickenpox in healthy children and adults, during pregnancy, and in people who are immunocompromised. It also offers advice on the management of pregnant women and immunocompromised individuals following exposure to a person with chickenpox. Advice on vaccination of non-immune health care workers is also included.

There is separate PRODIGY guidance on *Shingles and postherpetic neuralgia.*

C

Goals

To advise on self-care and infection control
To minimize the severity and duration of symptoms
To reduce the likelihood of complications

Contents

Scenarios
- Healthy adults and children p.309
- Pregnancy and neonates p.311
- Immunocompromised p.312

Extended Information, p. 313

Which scenario?

Healthy adults and children: covers the management of chickenpox in healthy adults and children.
Pregnancy and neonates: covers the management of chickenpox in pregnant women. The management of exposure to chickenpox for neonates and during pregnancy is also discussed.
Immunocompromised: covers the management of chickenpox in people who are immunocompromised. The management of exposure to chickenpox is also discussed.

Healthy adults and children

Which therapy?

Paracetamol or ibuprofen will ease systemic symptoms and also help to reduce fever.
Advise on disease transmission, infectivity, and the importance of hygiene in preventing secondary bacterial infection (keep the skin clean). Exclusion from school or work is not necessary after 6 days from the onset of the rash.
Topical crotamiton cream or lotion may help to relieve itch.
Chlorphenamine (chlorpheniramine) or hydroxyzine (sedating antihistamines) may relieve itch and reduce sleeplessness.

Factors affecting choice of treatment
Asthma: NSAIDs can worsen asthma in some people.
Epilepsy: avoid antihistamines (they may lower the seizure threshold).
Peptic ulceration: do not use ibuprofen.
Pregnancy: management and drug choices are different. See the scenario *Pregnancy and neonates.*

Practical prescribing points

For further information see the *Medicines Compendium* (www.medicines.org.uk) or the *British National Formulary* (www.bnf.org).

- **Advise people that sedative antihistamines** cause drowsiness that may persist the next day. People should not drive or operate machinery if affected.
- **Advise people to avoid** applying crotamiton cream or lotion to broken or excoriated skin.

Should I refer or investigate?

Refer?

- **Hospital admission is indicated if serious complications develop,** such as pneumonia (i.e. chest symptoms) or encephalitis (neurological symptoms).
- **Seek specialist advice if the adult or child is immunocompromised.**
- **Seek specialist advice if the woman is pregnant.**

Patient information leaflets

The following PILs are available at www.prodigy.nhs.uk

- Chickenpox in Adults
- Chickenpox in Children
- Medicines - Name Changes of Medicines
- Paracetamol
- Temperatures (Fevers) in Children

Shared decision making

- Chickenpox is usually not serious, but it can be unpleasant (particularly in adults).
- **Paracetamol or ibuprofen** will ease fever or pains.
- **Crotamiton lotion or cream** is soothing.
- **Antihistamine tablets or liquid medicine** at bedtime may help sleeping if itch is a problem. You can buy these at pharmacies or get them on prescription.
- Try not to scratch because it may cause scarring. Keeping fingernails cut short helps to stop deep scratching, which may cause scars.
- Chickenpox is very infectious from 2 days before until 5–6 days after the rash starts. During the infectious time:
  - Keep children off school. Adults with chickenpox should keep off work.
  - Avoid contact with pregnant women who have not had chickenpox.
  - Avoid contact with people with serious illness (e.g. on chemotherapy, with immune problems, taking steroids, etc).
  - Healthy people who have not had chickenpox may want to keep away too.

C

Drug rationale

Drugs not included

- **Antiviral medication** is not recommended for use in healthy children or adults with uncomplicated chickenpox. There is evidence of minor benefit if it is started within 24 hours of the onset of the rash, with time to last new lesions or time to cessation of fever reduced by about 1 day [Swingler, 2003]. There is no available evidence on whether complication rates are reduced.
- **Aspirin** is associated with Reye's syndrome in children aged less than 16 years, and has an extensive adverse effect profile.
- **Calamine lotion** does not offer significant benefit in most people and is not recommended.
- **Non-sedating antihistamines** have not been demonstrated to be effective in relieving pruritus [Klein and Clark, 1999].
- **Long-acting sedating antihistamines** are more likely to have a greater 'hangover effect'. They are therefore not included.

Drugs included

- **Paracetamol or ibuprofen** is effective for fever, headaches, and myalgia.
- **Crotamiton** cream or lotion has soothing qualities and may help to relieve the itch caused by chickenpox, although there is no objective proof of its anti-pruritic activity.
- **Chlorphenamine** (chlorpheniramine) is specifically licensed for pruritus in chickenpox, and is an inexpensive and widely used sedating antihistamine. It is licensed for use in adults and children over the age of 1 year.
- **Hydroxyzine** is specifically licensed for pruritus and is sedating; it is licensed for use in adults and in children over the age of 6 months. It is offered as a night-time dose for temporary help with sleeping to help break the itch–scratch cycle.

Prescriptions

Analgesia/antipyretics: use when required

Paracetamol s/f susp: 60mg to 120mg up to four times a day
- Age from 3 to 11 months
- Paracetamol 120mg/5ml s/f susp. Take 2.5ml to 5ml every 4 to 6 hours when required for relief of pain or high temperature. Maximum of 4 doses in 24 hours; supply 150 ml; NHS Cost £0.65; OTC Cost £1.14.

Paracetamol s/f susp: 120mg to 240mg up to four times a day
- Age from 12 months to 5 years
- Paracetamol 120mg/5ml s/f susp. Take one to two 5ml spoonfuls every 4 to 6 hours when required for relief of pain or high temperature. Maximum of 4 doses in 24 hours; supply 300 ml; NHS Cost £1.30; OTC Cost £2.28.

Paracetamol s/f susp: 250mg to 500mg up to four times a day
- Age from 6 to 11 years
- Paracetamol 250mg/5ml s/f susp. Take one to two 5ml spoonfuls every 4 to 6 hours when required for relief of pain or high temperature. Maximum of 4 doses in 24 hours; supply 300 ml; NHS Cost £1.70; OTC Cost £2.99.

Paracetamol tablets: 500mg to 1g up to four times a day
- Age from 11 to 16 years
- Paracetamol 500mg tablets. Take one to two tablets every 4 to 6 hours when required for relief of pain or high temperature. Maximum of 8 tablets in 24 hours; supply 100 tablets; NHS Cost £0.75; OTC Cost £1.32.

Paracetamol tablets: 1g up to four times a day
- Age from 16 years onwards
- Paracetamol 500mg tablets. Take two tablets every 4 to 6 hours when required for relief of pain or high temperature. Maximum of 8 tablets in 24 hours; supply 100 tablets; NHS Cost £0.75; OTC Cost £1.32.

Ibuprofen s/f susp: 50mg three to four times a day
- Age from 12 months to 2 years
- Ibuprofen 100mg/5ml s/f susp. Take 2.5ml three to four times a day when required for relief of pain or high temperature. Do not exceed the stated dose; supply 100 ml; NHS Cost £1.82; OTC Cost £3.21.

Ibuprofen s/f susp: 100mg three to four times a day
- Age from 3 to 7 years
- Ibuprofen 100mg/5ml s/f susp. Take one 5ml spoonful 3 to 4 times a day when required for relief of pain or high temperature. Do not exceed the stated dose; supply 150 ml; NHS Cost £2.73; OTC Cost £4.81.

Ibuprofen s/f susp: 200mg three to four times a day
- Age from 8 to 11 years
- Ibuprofen 100mg/5ml s/f susp. Take two 5ml spoonfuls 3 to 4 times a day when required for relief of pain or high temperature. Do not exceed the stated dose; supply 300 ml; NHS Cost £5.46; OTC Cost £9.62.

Ibuprofen tablets: 400mg three times a day
- Age from 12 years onwards
- Ibuprofen 400mg tablets. Take one tablet three times a day when required for relief of pain or high temperature. Do not exceed the stated dose; supply 24 tablets; NHS Cost £0.70; OTC Cost £1.23.

Topical antipruritic

Crotamiton 10% cream: apply 2 to 3 times a day
- Age from 1 month onwards
- Crotamiton 10% cream. Apply to the affected area 2 to 3 times a day when required for relief of itching; supply 30 grams; NHS Cost £2.27; OTC Cost £3.55.

Crotamiton 10% lotion: apply 2 to 3 times a day
- Age from 1 month onwards
- Crotamiton 10% lotion. Apply to the affected area 2 to 3 times a day when required for relief of itching; supply 100 ml; NHS Cost £2.99; OTC Cost £4.69.

Sedating antihistamine (for sleep disturbance)

Chlorphenamine (chlorpheniramine) syrup: 1mg at night prn
- Age from 12 to 23 months
- Chlorphenamine 2mg/5ml syrup. Take 2.5ml at night when required for relief of itching; supply 50 ml; NHS Cost £0.72; OTC Cost £1.26.

Chlorphenamine (chlorpheniramine) syrup: 1-2mg at night prn
- Age from 2 to 5 years
- Chlorphenamine 2mg/5ml syrup. Take 2.5ml to 5ml at night when required for relief of itching; supply 100 ml; NHS Cost £1.43; OTC Cost £2.53.

Chlorphenamine (chlorpheniramine) syrup: 2-4mg at night prn
- Age from 6 to 11 years
- Chlorphenamine 2mg/5ml syrup. Take one to two 5ml spoonfuls at night when required for relief of itching; supply 100 ml; NHS Cost £1.43; OTC Cost £2.53.

hlorphenamine (chlorpheniramine) tablets: 4mg at night
n
Age from 12 years onwards
Chlorphenamine 4mg tablets. Take one tablet at night when required for relief of itching; supply 14 tablets, NHS Cost £0.22; OTC Cost £1.40.

ydroxyzine syrup: 5mg to 15mg at night when required
Age from 6 months to 6 years
Hydroxyzine 10mg/5ml syrup. Take 2.5ml to 7.5ml at night when required for relief of itching; supply 100 ml; NHS Cost £0.96.

ydroxyzine syrup: 15mg to 25mg at night when required
Age from 7 to 11 years
Hydroxyzine 10mg/5ml syrup. Take 7.5ml to 12.5ml at night when required for relief of itching; supply 200 ml; NHS Cost £1.91.

ydroxyzine tablets: 25mg at night when required
Age from 12 years onwards
Hydroxyzine 25mg tablets. Take one tablet at night when required for relief of itching; supply 14 tablets; NHS Cost £0.51.

Advice note

dvice only: chickenpox
Age from 1 month onwards
Chickenpox is not usually serious in children but it can be unpleasant. It can be more unpleasant in adults. Keep fingernails cut short to stop deep scratching which may scar. It is very infectious from 2 days before, until 5 days after the rash starts. Whilst it is infectious: Keep children off school. Adults with chickenpox should stay away from work. Avoid pregnant women who have not had chickenpox. Avoid people with serious illness (eg on chemotherapy, with immune problems, taking steroids, etc). Healthy people who have not had chickenpox may want to keep away too.

Pregnancy and neonates

Which therapy?

ALWAYS SEEK SPECIALIST ADVICE (from the local public health, obstetric, or paediatric department, depending on local expertise).

Treatment of the pregnant woman

Offer symptomatic treatment:

- **Paracetamol** eases systemic symptoms and reduces fever.
- Calamine lotion may relieve itch.

Oral aciclovir is recommended for pregnant women who are at more than 20 weeks' gestation and who present within 24 hours of the onset of the rash. Aciclovir is not licensed for use in pregnancy; however, no adverse fetal or neonatal effects have been reported. It is important to obtain informed consent prior to starting treatment. **Varicella-zoster immunoglobulin (VZIG) is of no benefit once chickenpox has developed.**

Post-exposure prophylaxis for pregnant women

VZIG is recommended for varicella-zoster (VZ) *antibody-negative* women who are exposed to chickenpox at any stage of pregnancy, providing VZIG can be given within 10 days of contact. However, when supplies of VZIG are short, issue may be restricted to those exposed during the first 20 weeks of pregnancy or near term (within 21 days of the estimated date of delivery).

- **Pregnant women who have previously had chickenpox do not require VZIG.**
- **Those without a history of chickenpox must be tested for VZ antibody before VZIG is given.** The outcome is not adversely affected if administration of VZIG is delayed for up to 10 days after initial contact while an antibody test is done.
- **Women who have been exposed to chickenpox should seek medical advice if a rash develops,** regardless of whether or not they have received VZIG.

Post-exposure prophylaxis for the neonate

- **If the mother develops chickenpox 7 days before to 7 days after delivery,** VZIG is recommended for the infant.
- **If the mother develops chickenpox 4 days before to 2 days after delivery,** the infant should also be considered for early treatment with intravenous aciclovir, due to the higher risk of a fatal outcome despite VZIG prophylaxis.

Significant exposure is likely if *all* of the following apply:

- Contact with chickenpox, disseminated zoster, exposed shingles (e.g. ophthalmic shingles), or contact with an immunosuppressed individual with shingles on any part of the body (in whom viral shedding may be greater);
- *Plus* exposure to chickenpox between 48 hours before onset of the rash until cropping has ceased and all lesions have crusted; for localized shingles, exposure between the onset of the rash until crusting has occurred;
- *Plus* contact in the same room for 15 minutes or more, or face-to-face contact (e.g. while having a conversation).

Practical prescribing points

For further information see the *Medicines Compendium* (www.medicines.org.uk) or the *British National Formulary* (www.bnf.org).

Follow-up advice

- Pregnant women who have been exposed to chickenpox should seek medical advice if a rash develops, regardless of whether or not they received varicella-zoster immunoglobulin.

Should I refer or investigate?

Refer?

- **ALWAYS SEEK SPECIALIST ADVICE** (from the local public health, obstetric, or paediatric department, depending on local expertise).
    - **Treatment of chickenpox: oral aciclovir** is recommended for pregnant women who are at more than 20 weeks' gestation and who present within 24 hours of the onset of the rash (off-licence use).
    - **Post-exposure prophylaxis:** varicella-zoster immunoglobulin (VZIG) may be indicated.
- **Indications for hospital admission include** the development of chest symptoms, neurological symptoms, haemorrhagic rash or bleeding, a dense rash with or without mucosal lesions, and significant immunosuppression.
- **Hospital assessment should be considered,** even in the absence of complications, if the woman smokes, has chronic lung disease, is taking corticosteroids, or is in the latter half of pregnancy.

Investigate?

- If significant exposure to varicella has occurred (see *Which therapy?*) and there is no past history of chickenpox, check for the presence of varicella-zoster antibodies. Seronegative individuals require prophylaxis with varicella-zoster immunoglobulin (VZIG).

Patient information leaflets

C

The following PILs are available at www.prodigy.nhs.uk

- Chickenpox Contact and Pregnancy

Shared decision making

- Most pregnant women with chickenpox make a full recovery. However, it can be a nasty infection and some women and babies develop complications.
- If you are pregnant and have come into contact with chickenpox or shingles:
  - If you have had chickenpox in the past, you are immune and are not at risk.
  - If you have not had chickenpox, or are not sure, a blood test can check to see if you are immune.
  - **An antiserum** can be given if you are not immune. This may stop you getting chickenpox. It is best given within 7 days but may still work up to 10 days after contact with the virus.
- If you are pregnant and have chickenpox:
  - **Paracetamol** will ease fever or pains.
  - Calamine lotion or cream is soothing.
  - **Antiviral medicine** is recommended if you are more than 20 weeks pregnant. It helps to reduce the severity of the illness. It needs to be started within 24 hours of the rash appearing.

Drug rationale

Drugs not included

- **Intravenous aciclovir** is not offered because it is not appropriate for use in primary care and is indicated only in women with severe or complicated chickenpox.
- **Varicella-zoster immunoglobulin** (**VZIG**) is not offered because this is obtained from the local public health laboratory. It is of no value in the treatment of pregnant women with chickenpox, but is indicated for non-immune women exposed to chickenpox during pregnancy, and for neonates born to mothers who develop chickenpox 7 days before to 7 days after delivery (see *Which therapy?*).
- **Ibuprofen** is an alternative to paracetamol, but should be avoided after 30 weeks' gestation owing to its association with premature closure of the ductus arteriosus.
- **Crotamiton** should be avoided because there is no experience with using it during pregnancy.
- **Sedating antihistamines** are not included. If an antihistamine is considered necessary to help break the itch–scratch cycle and aid sleep, there is most clinical experience with chlorphenamine (chlorpheniramine) [DTB, 2002].

Drugs included

- **Paracetamol** is effective for fever, headaches, and myalgia. It is the analgesic of choice during pregnancy.
- **Calamine lotion** generally soothes itch, although the residue (when dried) can exacerbate itch in some people.
- **Oral aciclovir is offered (but should usually be prescribed only following specialist advice).** It is recommended if chickenpox develops in a woman who is more than 20 weeks pregnant and if treatment can be started within 24 hours of the onset of the rash. Aciclov is not licensed for use in pregnancy. No adverse fetal or neonatal effects have been reported, although there is a theoretical risk of teratogenesis if taken in the first trimester [RCOG, 2001].

Prescriptions

Analgesia/antipyretics: use when required

Paracetamol 500mg to 1g up to four times a day

- Age from 12 to 15 years
- Paracetamol 500mg tablets. Take one to two tablets every 4 to 6 hours when required for relief of pain or high temperature. Maximum of 8 tablets in 24 hours; supply 100 tablets; NHS Cost £0.75; OTC Cost £1.32.

Paracetamol 1g up to four times a day

- Age from 16 to 60 years
- Paracetamol 500mg tablets. Take two tablets every 4 to 6 hours when required for relief of pain or high temperature. Maximum of 8 tablets in 24 hours; supply 100 tablets; NHS Cost £0.75; OTC Cost £1.32.

Calamine lotion

Calamine lotion: apply when required to relieve itching

- Age from 12 to 60 years
- Calamine lotion. Apply to the affected area(s) when required to relieve itching; supply 200 ml; NHS Cost £0.64; OTC Cost £1.13.

Advice note

Advice only: chickenpox in pregnancy

- Age from 12 to 60 years
- Most pregnant women with chickenpox make a full recovery. However, it can be a nasty infection and some women and babies develop complications. If you have had chickenpox in the past, you are immune and are not at risk. If you have not had chickenpox, or are not sure, a blood test can check to see if you are immune. An antiserum can be given if you are not immune. This may stop you getting chickenpox. It is best given within 7 days but may still work up to 10 days after contact with the virus. Antiviral medicine is an option if you are more than 20 weeks pregnant. It helps to reduce the severity of the illness. It needs to be started within 24 hours of the rash appearing.

Aciclovir (on specialist advice only)

Aciclovir tablets: 800mg five times a day for 7 days

- Age from 12 to 60 years
- Aciclovir 800mg disp tablets. Take one tablet five times day for 7 days; supply 35 tablets; NHS Cost £21.57.

Immunocompromised

Which therapy?

ALWAYS SEEK SPECIALIST ADVICE because immunocompromised individuals are at high risk of severe chickenpox and complications.

- The Health Protection Agency (HPA) recommendations regarding the likelihood of a person being immunocompromised are outlined at the end of this section. If still in doubt, seek advice.

Treatment of chickenpox

- **Antiviral medication is indicated in all people who are immunocompromised.**

Intravenous aciclovir is the preferred treatment in most immunocompromised individuals.
Oral antiviral treatment may be appropriate for people who are considered to be only mildly immunocompromised (e.g. people taking continuous or intermittent high-dose corticosteroids, and those taking low-dose daily cytotoxic chemotherapy).

Post-exposure prophylaxis

Varicella-zoster immunoglobulin (VZIG) is recommended if significant exposure has occurred (see definition below) and the person has no antibodies to varicella-zoster (VZ) virus. Whenever possible, contacts with a positive history of chickenpox should be tested to confirm the presence of VZ antibody. Those with a positive history in whom VZ antibody is not detected should be given VZIG.
VZIG should ideally be given within 7 days of exposure, although current UK guidelines recommend that it may be given up to 10 days after exposure.

Significant exposure is likely if *all* of the following apply:

Contact with chickenpox, disseminated zoster, exposed shingles (e.g. ophthalmic shingles), or contact with an immunocompromised individual with shingles on any part of the body (in whom viral shedding may be greater);
Plus exposure to chickenpox between 48 hours before onset of the rash until cropping has ceased and all lesions have crusted; for localized shingles, exposure between the onset of the rash until crusting has occurred;
Plus contact in the same room for 15 minutes or more, or face-to-face contact (e.g. while having a conversation).

The HPA states that people who are likely to be significantly immunocompromised include:

People being treated with chemotherapy or generalized radiotherapy, or who have received this within the past 6 months.
People who have received an organ transplant and are currently on immunosuppressive treatment.
People who have received a bone marrow transplant and who are still considered to be immunosuppressed, including those with graft versus host disease.
Children who have taken systemic corticosteroids within the past 3 months, equivalent to prednisolone 2 mg/kg per day for at least 1 week, or 1 mg/kg per day for 1 month; for adults, an equivalent dose is harder to define, but immunosuppression should be considered in those who within the past 3 months have taken around 40 mg/day of prednisolone for more than 1 week in the previous 3 months.
People on lower doses of corticosteroids given in combination with cytotoxic drugs.
People with impaired cell immunity (e.g. severe combined immune deficiency syndromes, DiGeorge syndrome).
People with symptomatic HIV infection or asymptomatic people with low CD4 counts. (Prophylaxis is not indicated for people with asymptomatic HIV infection and normal CD4 counts because there is no evidence of an increased risk of severe chickenpox in such individuals.)

Should I refer or investigate?

Refer?

- **ALWAYS SEEK SPECIALIST ADVICE** because immunocompromised individuals are at high risk of severe chickenpox and complications. Admission for treatment with intravenous aciclovir may be recommended.

Investigate?

- If significant exposure to varicella has occurred (see *Which therapy?*) check for the presence of varicella antibodies. (Whenever possible, immunocompromised contacts with a positive history of chickenpox should be tested to confirm the presence of antibody.) Seronegative individuals require prophylaxis with varicella-zoster immunoglobulin.

Patient information leaflets

The following PILs are available at www.prodigy.nhs.uk
- Chickenpox Contact and Pregnancy
- Chickenpox in Adults
- Chickenpox in Children
- Paracetamol

Shared decision making

- Chickenpox can be a severe infection if you have a poor immune system.
- If you have come into contact with chicken pox or shingles:
  - A blood test can check to see if you are immune.
  - **An antiserum** can be given if you are not immune. This may stop you getting chickenpox. It is best given within 4 days but may still work up to 10 days after contact with the virus.
- Contact a doctor urgently if you develop chickenpox. Referral to hospital is advised. Antiviral medicine is usually given to reduce the severity of the illness. It needs to be commenced within 24 hours of the rash starting.

Drug rationale

- No prescriptions are offered. Specialist advice should be sought for immunocompromised individuals with symptomatic chickenpox and those who have had significant exposure to chickenpox.

Extended Information

Background information

- What is it? p.313
- How common is it? p.314
- How do I know my patient has it? p.314
- What else might it be? p.314
- Complications and prognosis p.314

What is it?

- **Chickenpox is due to primary infection with varicella-zoster virus (VZV).** It is usually a mild self-limiting illness, characterized by low-grade fever, malaise, and a generalized, itchy vesicular rash [Swingler, 2003]. Some individuals are at high risk of severe illness and complications, particularly pregnant women, neonates, and immunocompromised individuals.

C

- **Chickenpox is very infectious;** about 90% of susceptible household contacts become infected [HPA, 2004b]. It is transmitted by airborne respiratory droplets, by direct personal contact with vesicle fluid, and through contact with infected articles such as clothing or bedding.
- **The incubation period is 10–21 days** (i.e. the time from becoming infected until symptoms appear).
- **Individuals are infectious from about 48 hours before until 5–6 days after the appearance of the rash.** However, transmission can occur as early as 4 days before the appearance of the rash [HPA, 2003]. Traditionally, children have been excluded from school until all lesions have crusted; however, transmission has never been reported beyond the 5th day of the rash.
- **After recovery from primary infection, VZV is not eliminated from the body,** but lies dormant in the sensory nervous system. Latent infection may reactivate, resulting in shingles (see separate PRODIGY guidance *Shingles and postherpetic neuralgia*).

How common is it?

- **Chickenpox is predominantly a childhood illness.** More than 90% of people have had chickenpox by the age of 15 years [International Herpes Management Forum, 2002]. In the period 1995–1997, 81% of consultations for chickenpox were for children aged 14 years or younger [Rawson et al, 2001].
- However, 25–40% of adults in tropical countries are susceptible to chickenpox [International Herpes Management Forum, 2002]; this is particularly important in those areas in the UK where significant proportions of the population are originally from tropical countries.
- **Peak incidence** is in 5 to 9 year-olds (50% of all cases).
- **Chickenpox is estimated to occur in up to 3/1000 pregnancies** [RCOG, 2001].

How do I know my patient has it?

Prodrome

- Systemic symptoms sometimes precede the rash by up to 6 days. Symptoms include fever, headache, backache, sore throat, and general malaise [Australian Herpes Management Forum, 2002].

Rash

- The rash typically begins on the face and scalp, and spreads to the trunk and limbs.
- The characteristic lesions are vesicles with surrounding erythema, which develop into pustules and then crust over prior to healing. The spots are usually intensely itchy. They appear in successive crops over 3–4 days, so that at the peak of the illness there are lesions at all stages of development, from new vesicles through to crusts.
- The rash may involve mucous membranes, forming multiple aphthous-like ulcers.
- Total healing time is usually about 16 days.

What else might it be?

- Herpes simplex
- Herpes zoster (shingles)
- Impetigo
- Urticaria
- Scabies
- Coxsackie virus (e.g. hand, foot, and mouth disease)
- Drug rash
- Smallpox (officially declared eradicated in 1977 by the World Health Organization, but there are recent concerns that it may be used in bioterrorism)

Complications and prognosis

In children

- Chickenpox is usually a mild self-limiting illness.
- Bacterial skin infection is the most common complication.
- Acute cerebellar ataxia may occur, particularly in older children.
- Serious complications, such as pneumonia or encephalitis, are rare in otherwise healthy children.
- Mortality from chickenpox is reported to be about 1.4/100,000 [Swingler, 2003].

In adults

- The disease is more severe, and complications are more common than in children.
- Scarring of the skin is particularly likely in older childre and adults. These are round, deep, punched-out lesions, which are commonly called 'pock marks'.
- Varicella pneumonia is the most common serious complication [Swingler, 2003]. Other complications include hepatitis and encephalitis.
- Mortality from chickenpox is reported to be about 31/100,000 [Swingler, 2003]. Chickenpox accounts for about 25 deaths annually in England and Wales [Rawson et al, 2001].

In pregnancy

- There is some evidence that chickenpox may be more severe if it is contracted during pregnancy [Nathwani et al, 1998]. Pneumonia occurs in up to 10% of pregnant women with chickenpox, and the severity of this complication seems to be increased in later gestation [RCOG, 2001]. Prior to the introduction of antiviral drugs, mortality from varicella pneumonia was reportec to be as high as 25%. However, in the period 1985–1996 there were only nine deaths reported in the UK, suggesting a mortality of less than 1% [RCOG, 2001].
- **If maternal chickenpox occurs in the first half of pregnancy,** there is a 1–2% risk of fetal abnormality [Enders et al, 1994]. The most common abnormalities are dermatomal skin scarring, eye defects (microphthalmia, chorioretinitis, cataracts), limb hypoplasia, and neurological abnormalities (microcephaly, mental handicap, bowel and bladder sphincter dysfunction). Congenital abnormalities have not been reported following maternal chickenpox after 20 weeks' gestation [RCOG, 2001].
- **If maternal chickenpox occurs in the second half of pregnancy,** the main danger to the fetus is from acquiring symptomatic varicella infection. This becomes increasingly likely as gestation progresses. If maternal chickenpox occurs 1–4 weeks before delivery, a third of newborn infants develop clinical infection despite the protection of passively acquired maternal antibody [RCOG, 2001]. Neonatal infection is particularly severe if maternal chickenpox occurs 4 days before delivery an up to 2 days postpartum, owing to the lack of maternal antibody [HPA, 2004a].

In neonates

- Risk to the neonate includes severe disseminated chickenpox, pneumonia, and fulminant hepatitis. Prophylactic varicella-zoster immunoglobulin (VZIG) is given to neonates at high risk of contracting chickenpox Observational data show that mortality is now substantially lower than the 30% previously reported without VZIG. However, some of the improvement in outcome may also reflect developments in neonatal care ınd the use of aciclovir in neonates who develop :hickenpox.

ı Immunocompromised people

Immunocompromised people (e.g. HIV-infected ndividuals, children with leukaemia, transplant ·ecipients, people receiving chemotherapy) are at high ·isk of severe disseminated chickenpox, pneumonia, and ıepatitis. In particular, they have a 20–40% risk of leveloping a severe progressive form of varicella, which :an be fatal [International Herpes Management Forum, 2002].

Ianagement issues

Iealthy adults and children p.315
ʔregnant women p.315
Neonates p.316
Breastfeeding p.316
mmunocompromised individuals p.316
Medicines management p.317

ealthy adults and children

ow should I treat chickenpox in healthy adults and hildren?

Symptomatic treatment is all that is usually required in immunocompetent people. Although there are few data on which to base recommendations, the following are commonly used and seem to be beneficial in some people:

- **Antipyretics** (e.g. paracetamol or ibuprofen) help to reduce fever and also ease systemic symptoms.
- **Crotamiton cream or lotion** has soothing qualities and may help to relieve itching, although there is no objective proof of its anti pruritic activity.
- **Sedating antihistamines** such as chlorphenamine (chlorpheniramine) are of little help in treating pruritus [Klein and Clark, 1999; DTB, 2002]. However a short course of a sedative antihistamine at night may be useful to break the itch–scratch cycle and help with sleep.

Antiviral medication is not recommended for use in healthy adults and children with uncomplicated chickenpox. There is evidence of minor benefit if it is started within 24 hours of the onset of the rash; time to last new lesions or time to cessation of fever is reduced by about 1 day. The available evidence showed no important difference between aciclovir and placebo with respect to complications associated with chickenpox [Klassen et al, 2004]. We found no studies that assess the efficacy of famciclovir or valaciclovir for the treatment of chickenpox.

:an chickenpox be prevented in healthy adults and :hildren?

Live attenuated varicella vaccine is only recommended for [DH, 2003]:

- Non-immune health care workers (in primary or secondary care) who have direct patient contact (to protect vulnerable patients from acquiring chickenpox from an infected member of staff).
- Non-immune close contacts of immunocompromised patients, where continuing close contact is unavoidable, e.g. siblings of a child with leukaemia.

Health care workers with a definite history of chickenpox or herpes zoster can be considered protected. Those with a negative or uncertain history should be serologically tested, and vaccine only offered to those without varicella-zoster antibody.

- Antibody-negative health care workers should receive two doses of live attenuated varicella vaccine 4–8 weeks apart. A booster dose is not currently recommended.
- There are few data on the efficacy of varicella vaccine in adults. However, it has been estimated to be 65–70% effective following household exposure to chickenpox [International Herpes Management Forum, 2002].
- **About 10% of adults experience a rash** up to a month after vaccination. This can be local around the injection site or more generalized.
- **Advise health care workers to report rash** to their occupational health department for assessment. If the rash is generalized, they should avoid patient contact until all the lesions have crusted. However, if the rash is localized and can be covered with a bandage and/or clothing, they should usually be able to continue working, unless they are in contact with high-risk patients (e.g. immunocompromised, neonates, or pregnant women).
- **Varicella vaccine is not currently recommended for routine use in children** in the UK [DH, 2003].

Pregnant women

General issues

- **Women with no history of chickenpox should be advised to avoid contact with people with chickenpox or shingles during pregnancy** and to seek medical advice immediately if they think they have been exposed [Morgan-Capner and Crowcroft, 2000]. If their immune status is uncertain, then serum can be checked for the presence of varicella-zoster antibody.

How should I treat chickenpox in pregnant women?

- **Symptomatic treatment should be offered.** Paracetamol is effective for fever, headaches, and myalgia. It is the analgesic of choice during pregnancy. Ibuprofen is an alternative, but should be avoided after 30 weeks' gestation owing to its association with premature closure of the ductus arteriosus.
- There are no data on using crotamiton cream or lotion during pregnancy, so it is best avoided. Calamine lotion generally soothes itch, although the residue (when dried) can exacerbate itch in some people. If an antihistamine is considered necessary to help break the itch–scratch cycle and aid sleep, there is most clinical experience with chlorphenamine (chlorpheniramine) [DTB, 2002].
- **The Royal College of Obstetricians and Gynaecologists recommend oral aciclovir for women who are more than 20 weeks pregnant and who present within 24 hours of the onset of the rash** (off-licence use) [RCOG, 2001]. No adverse fetal or neonatal effects have been reported, although there is a theoretical risk of teratogenesis if taken in the first trimester [RCOG, 2001]. It is important to obtain informed consent from the pregnant woman prior to starting treatment.
- **Varicella-zoster immunoglobulin is of no benefit once chickenpox has developed** [RCOG, 2001; HPA, 2004a].
- **Indications for hospital admission include** the development of chest symptoms, neurological symptoms, haemorrhagic rash or bleeding, a dense rash with or without mucosal lesions, and significant immunosuppression [RCOG, 2001]. If the woman smokes, has chronic lung disease, is taking corticosteroids, or is in the latter half of pregnancy, hospital assessment should be considered, even in the absence of complications [RCOG, 2001].

C

Which pregnant women need post-exposure prophylaxis?

- **Varicella-zoster immunoglobulin (VZIG) is recommended for varicella-zoster (VZ) *antibody-negative* women who become exposed to chickenpox at any stage of pregnancy,** providing VZIG can be given within 10 days of contact [HPA, 2004a]. However, when supplies of VZIG are short, issues may be restricted to those who have had a significant exposure to infection during the first 20 weeks of pregnancy or are near term (within 21 days of the estimated date of delivery).
- **Significant exposure** to chickenpox or shingles is likely if *all* of the following apply:
  - Contact with chickenpox, disseminated zoster, exposed shingles (e.g. ophthalmic shingles), or contact with an immunosuppressed individual with shingles on any part of the body (in whom viral shedding may be greater);
  - *Plus* exposure to chickenpox or disseminated zoster between 48 hours before onset of the rash until cropping has ceased and all lesions have crusted; for localized shingles, exposure between the onset of the rash until crusting has occurred;
  - *Plus* contact in the same room for 15 minutes or more, or face-to-face contact (e.g. while having a conversation) [HPA, 2004a].
- **Pregnant women who have previously had chickenpox do not require VZIG.** Those with a negative history must be tested for VZ antibody before VZIG is given. The outcome is not adversely affected if administration of VZIG is delayed for up to 10 days after initial contact while an antibody test is done [HPA, 2004a].
- **Pregnant women who have had exposure to chickenpox should seek medical advice if a rash develops,** regardless of whether or not they have received VZIG.

Neonates

- General practitioners are unlikely to be in a position where they need to decide whether prophylactic treatment is indicated in a neonate, because most will be in hospital. However, it is important to be aware of current recommendations because some women choose a home birth and increasing numbers of women are being discharged from hospital within 24 hours of delivery.
- **Varicella-zoster immunoglobulin (VZIG) is recommended for infants whose mothers develop chickenpox in the period 7 days before to 7 days after delivery** [HPA, 2004a]. Antibody testing of the infant is not needed in this situation.
- VZIG is also recommended for varicella-zoster (VZ) antibody-negative infants who are exposed to chickenpox or shingles (other than in the mother) in the first 7 days of life, or infants of any age who are exposed while still requiring special care nursing. (Note: an infant blood sample should be tested to determine VZ antibody status).
- **Early treatment with intravenous aciclovir should also be considered in** infants whose mothers develop chickenpox 4 days before to 2 days after delivery, because these babies are at highest risk of a fatal outcome despite VZIG prophylaxis [DH, 2003].

Breastfeeding

- Mothers with chickenpox should be allowed to breastfeed. If they have lesions close to the nipple, they should express milk from the affected breast until the lesions have crusted. This expressed milk can be used if the infant is covered by varicella-zoster immunoglobulin and/or aciclovir [Morgan-Capner and Crowcroft, 2000].
- Paracetamol is safe to use during breastfeeding. (Ibuprofen in an alternative.) Calamine lotion should be safe to use, although it is sensible to advise mothers to avoid applying it to the nipples. There are no data on the safety of crotamiton, chlorphenamine (chlorpheniramine), or hydroxyzine during breastfeeding.

Immunocompromised individuals

People who are likely to be significantly immunocompromised are defined as [HPA, 2004a]:

- People being treated with chemotherapy or generalized radiotherapy, or who have received this within the past months.
- People who have received an organ transplant and are currently on immunosuppressive treatment.
- People who have received a bone marrow transplant and who are still considered to be immunosuppressed, including those with graft versus host disease.
- Children who have taken systemic corticosteroids within the past 3 months, equivalent to prednisolone 2 mg/kg per day for at least 1 week, or 1 mg/kg per day for 1 month; for adults, an equivalent dose is harder to define, but immunosuppression should be considered in those who have taken around 40 mg/day of prednisolone for more than 1 week in the previous 3 months.
- People receiving lower doses of corticosteroids given in combination with cytotoxic drugs.
- People with impaired cell immunity (e.g. severe combined immune deficiency syndromes, DiGeorge syndrome).
- People with symptomatic HIV infection or asymptomatic people with low CD4 counts. (Prophylaxis is not indicated for people with asymptomatic HIV infection and normal CD4 counts because there is no evidence of an increased risk of severe chickenpox in such individuals.)

How should I treat chickenpox in immunocompromised people?

- **Antiviral treatment is indicated in people who are immunocompromised** (see earlier definition). The risk of severe disease and complications is much greater in this group.
- **Specialist advice should be sought;** hospital admission for intravenous aciclovir is often indicated:
  - Intravenous aciclovir is the preferred treatment in most immunocompromised individuals [Ogilvie, 1998].
  - Oral antiviral treatment may be appropriate for people who are considered to be only mildly immunocompromised (e.g. people taking continuous or intermittent high-dose corticosteroids, and those taking low-dose daily cytotoxic chemotherapy) [International Herpes Management Forum, 2002].
- Generally, varicella-zoster immunoglobulin has no place in the *treatment* of severe chickenpox [DH, 2003]. However, in immunosuppressed individuals, the Health Protection Agency (HPA) suggests that, because antibody production may be delayed such people, intravenous commercial preparations of human normal immunoglobulin may be used to provide an immediate source of antibody [HPA, 2004a].

Supporting evidence for antiviral treatment in immunocompromised people

- **In immunocompromised people,** studies using antiviral treatment have only been undertaken in children with cancer. We found no randomized, controlled trials in immunocompromised adults.
- Antiviral treatment has been shown to reduce the severity of chickenpox and the likelihood of clinical

deterioration in children receiving chemotherapy [Swingler, 2003]. The largest trial was in 50 children, of whom 60% had a rash of more than 24 hours' duration prior to starting antiviral treatment. The children receiving aciclovir were less likely to deteriorate, 4% aciclovir group compared with 48% placebo group; RR 0.08, 95% CI 0.01 to 0.59; for every three children given aciclovir, one extra child was less likely to deteriorate compared with those taking placebo (NNT = 3). We found no studies that assess the efficacy of famciclovir or valaciclovir for the treatment of chickenpox in immunocompromised people.

Which immunocompromised people need post-exposure prophylaxis?

Varicella-zoster immunoglobulin (VZIG) given shortly after exposure will not prevent infection, but can lessen the severity of disease [Ogilvie, 1998]. There are no placebo-controlled studies in people who are immunocompromised, but clinical experience and comparison with historical controls shows that VZIG is effective in this population [International Herpes Management Forum, 2002].

VZIG prophylaxis is recommended for individuals who fulfil all of the following criteria:

- A clinical condition that increases the risk of severe chickenpox. This includes people who are immunocompromised (see earlier definition), neonates, and pregnant women;
- *Plus* no antibodies to varicella-zoster virus — whenever possible, immunocompromised contacts with a positive history of chickenpox should be tested to confirm the presence of antibody;
- *Plus* significant exposure to chickenpox or shingles (see earlier definition) [HPA, 2004a].

VZIG should ideally be given within 7 days of exposure, although current UK guidelines recommend that it may be given up to 10 days after exposure [HPA, 2004a]. A second dose should be given if further exposure occurs and 3 weeks have elapsed since the first dose.

If VZIG is not indicated, the Health Protection Agency (HPA) suggests that antiviral treatment may be used for individuals in whom attenuation of an attack of chickenpox would be desirable, such as those with cystic fibrosis [HPA, 2004a]. The recommended regimen is oral aciclovir 40 mg/kg per day in four divided doses given from days 7 to 14 after exposure.

Can chickenpox be prevented in immunocompromised people?

Live varicella vaccine is contraindicated in immunocompromised patients [DH, 2003]. However, prophylactic vaccination is occasionally considered in selected groups (e.g. people with leukaemia in remission, or people undergoing bone marrow transplant) [International Herpes Management Forum, 2002]. Seek specialist advice if immunization is being considered in these groups. Although there is some evidence that varicella vaccine is effective in immunocompromised children, there are few data on its use in immunocompromised adults. Note: some studies used an inactivated varicella vaccine, but only live varicella vaccines are currently available.

There is only limited evidence of the effectiveness of antiviral medication in preventing chickenpox. A systematic review found that high-dose aciclovir (at least 3200 mg/day) taken for up to 22 months reduced the risk of clinical chickenpox in people with HIV infection; for every 23 people with HIV infection who received aciclovir for up to 22 months, one extra person had a reduced risk of developing clinical chicken pox compared with those taking placebo (NNT = 23) [Swingler, 2003]. However, it does not seem to have been studied in other forms of immunocompromise.

Medicines management

Aciclovir

- Oral aciclovir is generally well tolerated. Gastrointestinal adverse effects (e.g. nausea, vomiting, diarrhoea, and abdominal pain) and skin rashes (including photosensitivity and urticaria) are the most common adverse effects.

Ibuprofen

- The Committee on Safety of Medicines (CSM) advises that all nonsteroidal anti-inflammatory drugs (NSAIDs) are associated with serious gastrointestinal toxicity. The risk is greatest in the elderly. All non-selective NSAIDs (such as ibuprofen) are contraindicated in people with a history of peptic ulceration.
- The CSM also warns that any degree of worsening of asthma may be related to the ingestion of NSAIDs either prescribed or bought over the counter.

Sedating antihistamines

- Antimuscarinic adverse effects (sedation, dry mouth, urinary retention, blurred vision) are common. Sedating antihistamines should therefore be avoided in someone with prostatic hypertrophy, urinary retention, or glaucoma. Advise people that drowsiness may persist the next day, and that they should not drive or operate machinery if affected. Antihistamines may also reduce the seizure threshold, and so should be avoided in someone with epilepsy.

C

References

NHS staff in England can link, free of charge, from references to full text journals by clicking on [Full text] on the PRODIGY website.

1. Australian Herpes Management Forum (2002) *Chickenpox: an overview*. Australian Herpes Management Forum. www.ahmf.com.au [Accessed: 18/05/2004].
2. DH (2003) *Chickenpox (varicella) immunisation for health care workers*. PL/CMO/2003/8. Department of Health. www.dh.gov.uk [Accessed: 18/05/2004]. [Full text]
3. DTB (2002) Oral antihistamines for allergic disorders. *Drug & Therapeutics Bulletin* **40**(8), 59–62. [Full text]
4. Enders, G., Miller, E., Cradock-Watson, J. et al (1994) Consequences of varicella and herpes zoster in pregnancy: prospective study of 1739 cases. *Lancet* **343**(8912), 1548–1551.
5. HPA (2003) *Guidelines on the management of communicable disease in schools and nurseries: chickenpox*. Health Protection Agency. www.hpa.org.uk [Accessed: 27/09/2004]. [Full text]
6. HPA (2004a) *Immunoglobulin handbook: indications and dosage for normal and specific immunoglobulin preparations issued by the HPA*. Health Protection Agency. www.hpa.org.uk [Accessed: 27/09/2004]. [Full text]
7. HPA (2004b) *Chickenpox – varicella zoster*. Health Protection Agency. www.hpa.org.uk [Accessed: 27/09/2004]. [Full text]
8. International Herpes Management Forum (2002) *Improving the management of varicella, herpes zoster and zoster-associated pain*. International Herpes

Management Forum. www.ihmf.org/guidelines/summary11.asp [Accessed: 18/05/2004].
9. Klassen, T.P., Belseck, E.M., Wiebe, N. and Hartling, L. (2004) *Acyclovir for treating varicella in otherwise healthy children and adolescents (Cochrane Review)*. The Cochrane Library. Issue 2. Chichester, UK: John Wiley & Sons, Ltd.
10. Klein, P.A. and Clark, R.A. (1999) An evidence-based review of the efficacy of antihistamines in relieving pruritus in atopic dermatitis. *Archives of Dermatology* 135(12), 1522–1525. [Full text]
11. Morgan-Capner, P. and Crowcroft, N. (2000) *Guidance on the management of, and exposure to, rash illness in pregnancy (including consideration of relevant antibody screening programmes in pregnancy). Report of a PHLS Working Group*. Health Protection Agency. www.hpa.org.uk [Accessed: 27/09/2004].
12. Nathwani, D., Maclean, A., Conway, S. and Carrington, D. (1998) Varicella infections in pregnancy and the newborn: a review prepared for the UK Advisory Group on chickenpox on behalf of the British Society for the Study of Infection. *Journal of Infection* 36(Suppl 1), 59–71.
13. Ogilvie, M.M. (1998) Antiviral prophylaxis and treatment in chickenpox: a review prepared for the UK Advisory Group on chickenpox on behalf of the British Society for the Study of Infection. *Journal of Infection* 36(Suppl 1), 31–38.
14. Rawson, H., Crampin, A. and Noah, N. (2001) Deaths from chickenpox in England and Wales 1995–7: analysis of routine mortality data. *British Medical Journal* 323(7321), 1091–1093. [Full text]
15. RCOG (2001) *Chickenpox in pregnancy*. Royal College of Obstetricians & Gynaecologists. www.rcog.org.uk [Accessed: 27/09/2004]. [Full text]
16. Swingler, G. (2003) Chickenpox. *Clinical Evidence* 1‍1 951–958.

RODIGY GUIDANCE

hlamydia — genital

Last revised in December 2002
www.prodigy.nhs.uk/guidance.asp?gt=Chlamydia - genital

Applies to women over the age of 14 years

This guidance covers the management of urogenital infection in women caused by *Chlamydia trachomatis* types D–K, referred to as chlamydia in the rest of the text.

This guidance does not cover the management of pharyngitis, proctitis, conjunctivitis, and pneumonitis caused by C *trachomatis*. It also does not cover the management of infections caused by *Chlamydophila psittica*, *Chlamydophila pneumoniae*, or *C trachomatis* type L (causative organism of lymphogranuloma venereum) and types A–C (cause of the blinding disease trachoma).

There is separate PRODIGY guidance on *Pelvic inflammatory disease*, *Urethritis — male*, *Bacterial vaginosis*, *Trichomoniasis*, and *Candida — female genital*.

C

ioals

To alleviate symptoms
To prevent complications of pelvic inflammatory disease (PID) (e.g. infertility, ectopic pregnancy, chronic pelvic pain)
To prevent transmission to sexual partners or neonate
To prevent reinfection

ontents

icenarios

- Uncomplicated genital chlamydial infection p.319
- Genital chlamydial infection — pregnant/ breastfeeding p.320
- Pelvic inflammatory disease — tests positive for chlamydia p.322

xtended Information, p. 324

Vhich scenario?

Uncomplicated genital chlamydial infection: covers the management of genital chlamydial infection in women where there is no clinical evidence of pelvic inflammatory disease (PID) (i.e. abdominal pain, fever, adnexal tenderness and/or cervical excitation).
Genital chlamydial infection — pregnant/breastfeeding: covers the management of genital chlamydial infection in pregnant and breastfeeding women where there is no clinical evidence of PID (i.e. abdominal pain, fever, adnexal tenderness and/or cervical excitation).
Pelvic inflammatory disease — tests positive for chlamydia: covers the management of PID where chlamydial organisms have been identified. (There is separate PRODIGY guidance on *Pelvic inflammatory disease*, which covers the management of clinically suspected PID without a microbiological diagnosis.)

Uncomplicated genital chlamydial infection

Vhich therapy?

possible, refer to a genito-urinary medicine (GUM) clinic or screening for other sexually transmitted infections, ollow-up, and partner notification.
Doxycycline for 7 days or single-dose azithromycin are recommended first-choice treatments. Azithromycin is more expensive than doxycycline, but useful when poor compliance is anticipated.

- **Ofloxacin is an alternative treatment** (200 mg twice a day or 400 mg once a day for 7 days). It has similar efficacy to doxycycline and azithromycin, but is more expensive.
- **Advise sexual abstinence until** the infected woman and her partner(s) have both completed the course of treatment. If treatment with single-dose azithromycin is given, then sexual abstinence for the following 7 days is advised.
- **Screen for other sexually transmitted infections** (obtain informed consent). Ideally, this should be carried out by a GUM clinic.
- **Partner notification is best carried out by a GUM clinic.** All sexual partners within the previous 6 months (or the most recent sexual partner if there have been no sexual contacts within the previous 6 months) should be notified, offered screening for sexually transmitted infections, and treated for chlamydial infection (even if they have a negative chlamydial screen).
- **Guidance on how to treat the male partner** is covered in the separate PRODIGY guidance *Urethritis — male*.

Practical prescribing points

For further information please see the *Medicines Compendium* (www.medicines.org.uk) or the *British National Formulary* (www.bnf.org).

- **Doxycycline** can cause oesophageal irritation and, rarely, photosensitivity.
- **Ofloxacin:** the Committee on Safety of Medicines (CSM) advises that quinolones can cause tendon damage, and that treatment should be stopped if pain or inflammation of a tendon occurs. Use with caution in people with epilepsy or who are predisposed to seizures (because of other conditions or medicines they are taking).

Follow-up advice

Follow-up is advisable in 3–4 weeks, in order to:

- **Confirm partner notification.**
- **Repeat tests for chlamydial infection in women with** continuing symptoms or where reinfection is suspected. (If still infected, consider referring to a genito-urinary medicine [GUM] clinic to ensure adequate treatment of the woman and her partner.)
- **Advise on prevention of reinfection** (e.g. use of condoms).

C

Should I refer or investigate?

Refer?

- **Referral to a genito-urinary medicine (GUM) clinic is generally advised** for screening for other sexually transmitted infections, follow-up, and partner notification.
- **Management in primary care is appropriate providing that** screening for other sexually transmitted infections and partner notification is possible. Primary care management will be necessary for people who refuse referral to a GUM clinic.

Investigate?

- **Screen for other sexually transmitted infections** (obtain informed consent). Referral to a GUM clinic is generally advised for this.
- **It is not necessary to confirm eradication of infection unless** symptoms persist or reinfection is suspected.

Patient information leaflets

The following PILs are available at www.prodigy.nhs.uk

- Chlamydia in Women
- Women's Health

Shared decision making

- **Chlamydial infection** is caught by having sex with an infected person.
- **Many infected people** have no symptoms but can still pass on the infection.
- **You are also advised** to be tested for other sexually transmitted infections.
- **Treatment is advised, even if you have no symptoms,** to prevent possible complications such as pelvic inflammatory disease (PID), chronic pelvic pain, ectopic pregnancy, and infertility.
- **Doxycycline or azithromycin** are antibiotics which are commonly used to clear chlamydia.
- **Side effects** are uncommon with these antibiotics. A switch to another antibiotic may be advised if side effects do occur, or if you are pregnant.
- **Any sexual partner in the last 6 months** (or if no sexual partner within this time, the last sexual partner) should also have treatment.
- **Do not have sex until** you and your sexual partner have finished treatment. (If treated with the single dose of azithromycin, avoid sex for 7 days.)
- **Condoms** help to protect against sexually transmitted infections.

Drug rationale

Drugs not included

- **Penicillins (other than amoxicillin in pregnancy) and cephalosporins** have no role in the treatment of genital chlamydial infection.
- **Erythromycin** is an alternative treatment but it is less effective than doxycycline or azithromycin, and a test of cure is recommended 3 weeks after completing the course.
- **Clarithromycin** has not been as well studied as erythromycin or azithromycin [CEG, 2001b]. It is not licensed for the treatment of genital chlamydial infection.
- **Tetracyclines other than doxycycline** are also effective [SIGN, 2000; CEG, 2001b; Low and Cowan, 2001] but are not offered for the following reasons:
  - **Tetracycline and oxytetracycline** need to be taken fou times a day and compliance may be a problem [CEG, 2001b].
  - **Deteclo** is taken twice a day and is probably as effective as doxycycline, but contains demeclocycline which is more likely to cause photosensitivity than doxycycline [BNF 43, 2002].
  - **Lymecycline and minocycline** require a longer course of treatment. Minocycline has more adverse effects than other tetracyclines [BNF 43, 2002].
- **Quinolones,** other than ofloxacin, are either not as effective or have not been as extensively studied in the treatment of chlamydia [SIGN, 2000; CEG, 2001b].
- **Clindamycin** has been studied in a small number of tria and seems to be effective. It is not offered, as there is les data on its effectiveness compared with established treatments, and it is only licensed for serious anaerobic infections and Gram-positive infections [BNF 43, 2002]

Drugs included

- **Doxycycline** is an effective and established treatment fo genital chlamydial infection. It is taken at a dosage of 100 mg twice a day for 7 days [SIGN, 2000; CEG, 2001b; Low and Cowan, 2001].
- **Azithromycin** as a single 1-gram dose is an effective and established treatment for chlamydia. It is more expensiv than doxycycline, but the single-dose regimen may improve compliance [SIGN, 2000; CEG, 2001b].
- **Ofloxacin** has similar efficacy to azithromycin or doxycycline, but is more expensive. It is an alternative i doxycycline or azithromycin cannot be taken. Ofloxaci is taken as either a single dose of 400 mg once a day, or divided dosage of 200 mg twice a day, for 7 days. Both regimens appear to be equally effective [CEG, 2001b]. Ofloxacin is not offered for those aged under 16 years, as it is contraindicated in growing adolescents (quinolones are associated with the development of arthropathy in weight-bearing joints in young animals).

Prescriptions

1st-choice treatment

Doxycycline 100mg twice a day for 7 days

- Age from 14 years onwards
- Doxycycline 100mg capsules. Take one capsule twice a day for 7 days; supply 14 capsules; NHS Cost £2.91.

Azithromycin 1g single dose

- Age from 14 years onwards
- Azithromycin 250mg capsules. Take four capsules as a single dose; supply 4 capsules; NHS Cost £8.95.

Alternative treatment

Ofloxacin 200mg twice a day for 7 days

- Age from 16 years onwards
- Ofloxacin 200mg tablets. Take one tablet twice a day fo 7 days; supply 14 tablets; NHS Cost £15.11.

Ofloxacin 400mg once a day for 7 days

- Age from 16 years onwards
- Ofloxacin 400mg tablets. Take one tablet once a day fo 7 days; supply 7 tablets; NHS Cost £15.01.

Genital chlamydial infection — pregnant/breastfeeding

Which therapy?

Note: this scenario does not cover pelvic inflammatory disease (PID) (upper genital tract infection).

Pregnant women with uncomplicated (lower genital tract) infection may be safely treated in primary care. However, prior to initiating treatment, discussion with the local obstetric unit or genito-urinary medicine (GUM) clinic is advisable. As with the non-pregnant woman, referral to a GUM clinic is recommended, for partner notification and screening for co-existing sexually transmitted infections.
Erythromycin or amoxicillin are recommended treatments.
- **Erythromycin** is effective taken in a dosage of 500 mg twice a day for 14 days. It may also be taken four times a day for 7 days (this regimen is not specifically licensed for the treatment of genital chlamydial infection and may be less well tolerated).
- **Amoxicillin** 500 mg three times a day for 7 days (unlicensed indication) is better tolerated than erythromycin.

Advise sexual abstinence until the infected woman and her partner(s) have both completed the course of treatment.
Screen for other sexually transmitted infections (obtain informed consent). Ideally, this should be carried out by a GUM clinic.
Partner notification is best carried out by a GUM clinic. All sexual partners within the previous 6 months (or the most recent sexual partner if there have been no sexual contacts within the previous 6 months) should be notified, offered screening for sexually transmitted infections, and treated for chlamydial infection (even if they have a negative chlamydial screen).
Guidance on how to treat the male partner is covered in the separate PRODIGY guidance *Urethritis — male*.

ractical prescribing points

or further information please see the *Medicines ompendium* (www.medicines.org.uk) or the *British ational Formulary* (www.bnf.org).

ollow-up advice

ollow-up is advisable in 3–4 weeks, in order to:
Confirm partner notification.
Repeat tests for chlamydial infection 3 weeks after finishing the course of treatment (this is advised for women treated with erythromycin or amoxicillin, as they are not as effective as treatments that can be taken by non-pregnant women). If still infected, seek further advice from the obstetric unit or genito-urinary medicine (GUM) clinic.
Advise on prevention of reinfection (e.g. use of condoms).

hould I refer or investigate?

efer?

his scenario does not cover pelvic inflammatory disease ID) (upper genital tract infection). If PID is suspected, dmission for intravenous antibiotics is recommended.
Discussion with the local obstetric unit or genito-urinary medicine (GUM) clinic is advisable prior to initiating treatment (particularly if the pregnancy is near term).
Referral to a GUM clinic is generally advised for screening for other sexually transmitted infections, follow-up, and partner notification.

nvestigate?

Screen for other sexually transmitted infections (obtain informed consent). Referral to a GUM clinic is generally advised for this.

- **Retest 3 weeks after completing treatment** to confirm eradication of infection (as erythromycin and amoxicillin are less effective than treatments that can be taken by non-pregnant women).

Patient information leaflets

The following PILs are available at www.prodigy.nhs.uk
- Chlamydia in Women
- Women's Health

Shared decision making

- **Chlamydial infection** is caught by having sex with an infected person.
- **Many infected people** have no symptoms but can still pass on the infection.
- **You are also advised** to be tested for other sexually transmitted infections.
- **Treatment is advised even if you have no symptoms.** This is to try and prevent:
  - Pelvic inflammatory disease (PID)
  - Ectopic pregnancy in future pregnancies
  - Future infertility
  - Eye or lung infection passed to your baby during childbirth
  - Possible complications of pregnancy such as miscarriage, premature birth, and stillbirth, which are more common if you have untreated chlamydia
- **Erythromycin or amoxicillin** are antibiotics that are commonly used to clear chlamydia if you are pregnant or breastfeeding.
- **Erythromycin** makes some people feel sick. Both antibiotics may cause some diarrhoea. A switch to another antibiotic may be advised if side effects become troublesome.
- **Any sexual partner in the last 6 months** (or if no sexual partner within this time, the last sexual partner) should also have treatment.
- **Do not have sex until** you and your sexual partner have finished treatment. You should have a swab test 3 weeks after finishing treatment to check the infection has cleared.
- **Condoms** help to protect against sexually transmitted infections.

Drug rationale

Drugs not included

- **Macrolides other than erythromycin are not offered.** There is a lack of information on the safety of azithromycin and clarithromycin during pregnancy and breastfeeding [CEG, 2001b]. In addition, clarithromycin has not been as well studied as erythromycin or azithromycin in the treatment of genital chlamydial infection, and it is not licensed for this purpose [BNF 43, 2002].
- **Penicillins (with the exception of amoxicillin) and cephalosporins** have no role in the management of chlamydia.
- **Quinolones**, including ofloxacin, are contraindicated in pregnancy, as they are associated with the development of arthropathy in weight-bearing joints in young animals. They are also excreted into breast milk and therefore should be avoided during breastfeeding [BNF 43, 2002].
- **Tetracyclines** are contraindicated in pregnancy, as they are deposited in growing bone and teeth. They should also be avoided during breastfeeding.
- **Clindamycin** is not offered, as its safety in pregnancy has not been established. In addition, it is only licensed for

C

serious anaerobic infections and Gram-positive infections [BNF 43, 2002].

Drugs included

- **Erythromycin** is effective in the treatment of genital chlamydial infection, and is known to be safe in pregnancy. However, it is not as effective as treatments that can be taken by non-pregnant women, and a test of cure is recommended 3 weeks after finishing the course of treatment [CEG, 2001b]. The licensed dosage is 500 mg twice a day for 14 days [BNF 43, 2002]. Erythromycin is also effective given at a dosage of 500 mg four times daily for 7 days, although this regimen is not specifically licensed for the treatment of genital chlamydial infection [SIGN, 2000; CEG, 2001b]. It may be less well tolerated than the twice-daily dosage regimen [DTB, 1995].
- **Amoxicillin** seems to be as effective as erythromycin and is better tolerated [CEG, 2001b; Brocklehurst and Rooney, 2002]. It is known to be safe in pregnancy. However, it is not licensed for the treatment of genital chlamydial infection. As with erythromycin, a test of cure is recommended 3 weeks after finishing the course of treatment.

Prescriptions

Antibiotic treatment

Erythromycin 500mg twice a day for 14 days

- Age from 14 years onwards
- Erythromycin 250mg e/c tablets. Take two tablets twice a day for 14 days; supply 56 tablets; NHS Cost £6.16.

Erythromycin 500mg four times a day for 7 days

- Age from 14 years onwards
- Erythromycin 250mg e/c tablets. Take two tablets four times a day for 7 days; supply 56 tablets; NHS Cost £6.16.

Amoxicillin 500mg three times a day for 7 days

- Age from 14 years onwards
- Amoxicillin 500mg capsules. Take one capsule three times a day for 7 days; supply 21 capsules; NHS Cost £1.85.

Pelvic inflammatory disease — tests positive for chlamydia

Which therapy?

- **Pregnant women with suspected pelvic inflammatory disease (PID) should be admitted for intravenous antibiotics.** In addition, the antibiotic regimens recommended for the treatment of PID in primary care are not suitable for use during pregnancy.
- **Treatment should not be delayed** while waiting for the results of tests if PID is clinically suspected. It is likely that delaying treatment increases the risk of long-term complications.
- **Broad-spectrum antibiotic treatment** to cover *Neisseria gonorrhoeae*, *Chlamydia trachomatis*, and anaerobic infection is recommended, even if only chlamydial infection is identified. The incidence of gonorrhoea is increasing, and the absence of gonorrhoea on an endocervical swab does not exclude gonococcal PID.
- **Recommended regimens** are:
  - Ofloxacin and metronidazole for 14 days
  - Initial intramuscular dose of ceftriaxone followed by oral doxycycline and metronidazole for 14 days (less convenient for use in primary care, but an option if a quinolone is contraindicated)
- **If neither of these regimens is suitable,** seek advice from local microbiologist or genito-urinary medicine (GUM) clinic.
- **Advise sexual abstinence until** the infected woman and her partner(s) have been treated.
- **Screen for other sexually transmitted infections** (obtain informed consent). Ideally, this should be carried out by a GUM clinic.
- **Partner notification is best carried out by a GUM clinic.** All sexual partners within the previous 6 months (or the most recent sexual partner if there have been no sexual contacts within the previous 6 months) should be notified, offered screening for sexually transmitted infections, and treated for chlamydial infection (even if they have a negative chlamydial screen).

Practical prescribing points

For further information please see the *Medicines Compendium* (www.medicines.org.uk) or the *British National Formulary* (www.bnf.org).

- **Ofloxacin:** the Committee on Safety of Medicines (CSM) advises that quinolones can cause tendon damage, and that treatment should be stopped if pain or inflammation of a tendon occurs. Use with caution in people with epilepsy or who are predisposed to seizures (because of other conditions or medicines they are taking).
- **Doxycycline:** can cause oesophageal irritation and, rarely, photosensitivity. Avoid during pregnancy and breastfeeding.
- **Metronidazole:** advise avoidance of alcohol for the duration of treatment and for at least 48 hours afterwards, because of the possibility of a disulfiram-like (Antabuse) reaction.
- **Ibuprofen:** causes an increased risk of gastrointestinal haemorrhage. Avoid if there is a history of peptic ulceration. May worsen asthma, hypertension, renal impairment, and cardiac failure.

Follow-up advice

- **Review within 3 days to ensure clinical improvement,** particularly for women with a moderately severe presentation (women with severe symptoms and signs should be admitted). Admit if there is no substantial improvement.
- **Follow-up at 3–4 weeks** is also advisable in order to:
  - **Confirm partner notification.**
  - **Repeat tests for chlamydial infection in women with** continuing symptoms or where reinfection is suspected. (If still infected, consider referring to a genito-urinary medicine [GUM] clinic to ensure adequate treatment of the woman and her partner.)
  - Advise on prevention of reinfection (e.g. use of condoms).

Should I refer or investigate?

Refer?

- **Admit pregnant women with suspected pelvic inflammatory disease (PID)** for intravenous antibiotics. In addition, the antibiotic regimens recommended for the treatment of PID in primary care are not suitable for use during pregnancy.
- **Also consider admission** in the following situations:
  - Severe symptoms or signs
  - Immunodeficiency (e.g. HIV infection, taking immunosuppressive therapy)
  - Clinical failure with oral therapy (i.e. failure to show substantial improvement within 3 days)

- Inability to tolerate an oral regimen (e.g. due to nausea and vomiting)
- Presence of a tubo-ovarian abscess
- Diagnostic uncertainty (e.g. where appendicitis or an ectopic pregnancy cannot be excluded)
- **Referral to a genito-urinary medicine (GUM) clinic is generally advised for** screening for other sexually transmitted infections, follow-up, and partner notification.

nvestigate?

- **Screen for other sexually transmitted infections** (obtain informed consent). Referral to a GUM clinic is generally advised for this.
- **It is not necessary to confirm eradication of infection unless** symptoms persist or reinfection is suspected.

Patient information leaflets

The following PILs are available at www.prodigy.nhs.uk
- Chlamydia in Women
- Women's Health

Shared decision making

- **You have an infection of the uterus and fallopian tubes** (pelvic inflammatory disease [PID]).
- **Infection with chlamydia** is the commonest cause. It is caught by having sex with an infected person. (Many people infected with chlamydia do not have any symptoms.)
- **You are advised** to be tested for other sexually transmitted infections.
- **Ofloxacin plus metronidazole** for 14 days will usually clear the infection. Two antibiotics are needed because other bacteria may be present in addition to chlamydia.
- **Don't drink alcohol whilst** you are taking metronidazole, and for a further 48 hours after finishing treatment. Metronidazole may also cause a metallic taste.
- **A switch to another antibiotic** may be advised if side effects occur.
- **Painkillers** may be needed too.
- **Any sexual partner in the last 6 months** (or if no sexual partner within this time, the last sexual partner) should also have treatment.
- **Do not have sex until** you and your sexual partner have finished treatment.
- **Condoms** help to protect against sexually transmitted infections.

Drug rationale

Drugs not included

- **Regimens that require intravenous administration** are unsuitable for use in primary care and are not offered.
- **Oral doxycycline and metronidazole** is not offered as cure rates are less than with other regimens used in the treatment of pelvic inflammatory disease (PID) [Ross, 2001]. In addition, it does not adequately cover *Neisseria gonorrhoeae*. Recommendations from the Association for Genitourinary Medicine and the Medical Society for the Study of Venereal Diseases [CEG, 2001a] recommend that treatment of PID should cover *N gonorrhoeae* for the following reasons:
  - Although much of the evidence supporting the use of antibiotics active against *N gonorrhoeae* is from the US, and anecdotally *N gonorrhoeae* is a less common cause of PID in the UK, the only recent British study found gonococcal infection in 14% of women with PID. There is evidence that the incidence of gonorrhoea is increasing in the UK. In England, Wales and Northern Ireland between 1995 and 2000, diagnoses of gonorrhoea made by genito-urinary medicine (GUM) clinics more than doubled (10,204 to 20,663) [PHLS et al, 2001].
  - The absence of endocervical gonorrhoea does not exclude gonococcal PID.
  - Although PID presenting in primary care may be less severe than in other settings, there is no published evidence to support the use of less intensive regimens.

C

Drugs included

Antibiotic treatment

- **Broad-spectrum antibiotic treatment** to cover *N gonorrhoeae*, *Chlamydia trachomatis*, and anaerobic infection is recommended in guidelines produced by the Association for Genitourinary Medicine and the Medical Society for the Study of Venereal Diseases [CEG, 2001a]. The recommended regimens that are suitable for use in primary care are:
  - Oral ofloxacin 400 mg twice a day plus oral metronidazole 400 mg twice a day, both for 14 days
  - Intramuscular ceftriaxone 250 mg immediately, followed by oral doxycycline 100 mg twice a day plus oral metronidazole 400 mg twice a day, both for 14 days (this may be less convenient for use in primary care owing to the need for the initial intramuscular injection)
- **The regimen containing ofloxacin is not offered for those aged under 16 years,** as quinolones are contraindicated in growing adolescents (they are associated with the development of arthropathy in weight-bearing joints in young animals).

Analgesia

- **Paracetamol** is a safe, effective analgesic and antipyretic suitable for most people.
- **Ibuprofen** is also effective at relieving symptoms. It has less adverse effects than other nonsteroidal anti-inflammatory drugs (NSAIDs) [CSM, 1994; DTB, 1994; Henry et al, 1996; Bandolier, 1998; Hernández-Diaz and Rodriguez, 2000].
- **Codeine (in combination with paracetamol):** higher-dose codeine is included for use with regular paracetamol for additional pain relief. Codeine 60 mg plus paracetamol has been shown to provide more pain relief than either codeine 60 mg alone or paracetamol alone [De Craen et al, 1996; Moore et al, 1997; MeReC, 2000].

Prescriptions

Antibiotic treatment for 14 days

Ofloxacin + metronidazole
- Age from 16 years onwards
- Ofloxacin 400mg tablets. Take one tablet twice a day for 14 days; supply 28 tablets; NHS Cost £62.88.
- Metronidazole 400mg tablets. Take one tablet twice a day for 14 days; supply 28 tablets; NHS Cost £1.16.

Ceftriaxone im (stat) + doxycycline + metronidazole
- Age from 14 years onwards
- Ceftriaxone 250mg injection. For intramuscular injection; supply 1 250mg vial; NHS Cost £2.74.
- Doxycycline 100mg capsules. Take one capsule twice a day for 14 days; supply 28 capsules; NHS Cost £5.82.
- Metronidazole 400mg tablets. Take one tablet twice a day for 14 days; supply 28 tablets; NHS Cost £1.16.

Analgesia

Paracetamol 500mg to 1g up to four times a day

- Age from 14 to 15 years
- Paracetamol 500mg tablets. Take one to two tablets every 4 to 6 hours when required for relief of pain or high temperature. Maximum of 8 tablets in 24 hours; supply 32 tablets; NHS Cost £0.43; OTC Cost £0.75.

Paracetamol 1g up to four times a day

- Age from 16 years onwards
- Paracetamol 500mg tablets. Take two tablets every 4 to 6 hours when required for pain relief. Maximum of 8 tablets in 24 hours; supply 56 tablets; NHS Cost £0.42; OTC Cost £1.10.

Ibuprofen 400mg three to four times a day

- Age from 14 years onwards
- Ibuprofen 400mg tablets. Take one tablet 3 to 4 times a day when required for pain relief; supply 28 tablets; NHS Cost £0.82; OTC Cost £2.30.

Add on if required: codeine 30-60mg up to four times a day

- Age from 14 years onwards
- Codeine 30mg tablets. Take one to two tablets every 4 to 6 hours when required for pain relief. Maximum of 8 tablets in 24 hours; supply 56 tablets; NHS Cost £2.69.

Extended Information

Background information

- What is it? p.324
- How common is it? p.324
- How do I know my patient has it? p.324
- What else might it be? p.325
- Complications and prognosis p.325

What is it?

- **Genital chlamydial infection is a sexually transmitted infection** caused by the obligate intracellular bacterium *Chlamydia trachomatis*.
- **It is asymptomatic in up to 80% of infected women** [CEG, 2001b].
- **It is the commonest cause of pelvic inflammatory disease (PID)** (endometritis, salpingitis, and pelvic peritonitis), which may result in ectopic pregnancy, infertility, and chronic pelvic pain. It is estimated that 50% of cases of PID and 43% of ectopic pregnancies are caused by genital chlamydial infection.
- **Little is known of the natural history of untreated genital chlamydial infection** [Golden et al, 2000]. Evidence from one small cohort study of female college students suggests that untreated chlamydial infection may persist for at least 15 months [McCormack et al, 1979].
- **Genital chlamydial infection** is associated with the following:
  - Age less than 25 years
  - Women undergoing termination of pregnancy
  - New sexual partner or more than one sexual partner in the recent past
  - Lack of barrier contraception
  - Use of oral contraception
  - Other sexually transmitted infection
  - Nulliparity [Low and Cowan, 2001]

How common is it?

- **Chlamydia is the commonest sexually transmitted bacterial infection in the UK.**
- **It is estimated that 3–5% of sexually active women attending UK general practice are infected.** However, the chlamydia opportunistic screening pilot studies in Portsmouth and the Wirral, involving women aged less than 25 years, report a higher prevalence of approximately 10% [CEG, 2001b].
- Prevalence has varied in previous surveys, depending on the population studied (see Table 1) [DH, 1998a].
- **The incidence of genital chlamydial infection is increasing.** In 1995, 30,877 cases were reported by GUM clinics in England, Wales and Northern Ireland. By 2000, this had increased to 64,000 cases (36,298 females and 27,702 males) — a 107% increase [PHLS, 2002c]. The incidence in 2000 was highest in females 16–19 years old, with almost 1% of the UK female population in this age group diagnosed with chlamydia in a GUM clinic [PHLS, 2002b]. The number of genital chlamydial infections diagnosed in GUM clinics is likely to represent only a small proportion of the number in the general population.

Table 1: Prevalence of genital chlamydial infection in females.

Survey population	Median prevalence (%)	Rang
General Practice attendees	4.5	1–1
Antenatal clinic or obstetric unit attendees	4.6	2–7
Gynaecology clinic attendees	4.8	3–6
Family planning clinic attendees	5.1	3–7
Women seeking terminations	8.0	7–1
Genito-urinary medicine (GUM) clinic attendees	16.4	7–2

How do I know my patient has it?

- **Microbiological diagnosis is essential,** as symptoms and signs are non-specific, and most infected women are asymptomatic.
- **Always consider doing a chlamydia swab when examining the cervix or when taking any other genital samples,** especially in women under the age of 25 years and those with a new sexual partner in the last 6 months [PHLS, 2002d]. Remember to obtain informed consent.

Symptoms

- **Symptoms are not present in up to 80% of women** with genital chlamydial infection.
- **The commonest symptoms include:**
  - Abnormal vaginal discharge
  - Postcoital or intermenstrual bleeding — intermenstrual bleeding in women previously well regulated taking the combined oral contraceptive pill is a marker for chlamydial infection
  - Lower abdominal pain (if PID)
  - Dyspareunia
  - Dysuria (due to urethritis) — consider chlamydial infection in women with sterile pyuria
- Chlamydial infection can cause right upper quadrant pain due to perihepatitis. Right iliac fossa pain may occur due to periappendicitis.

Signs

- **Abnormal findings on vaginal examination are often absent.**
- **The commonest findings are:**
  - Purulent vaginal discharge
  - Mucopurulent cervicitis and/or contact bleeding (40% of cases of mucopurulent cervicitis are due to chlamydial infection)
- **PID is suggested by abdominal tenderness, pyrexia, and cervical excitation and adnexal tenderness** on pelvic examination.

Investigations

Diagnosis is confirmed by laboratory test. Individual GPs should confirm with their local laboratory the testing methods available, required samples, and how soon these should reach the laboratory.
Specificity and sensitivity vary depending on the test used and the site sampled, i.e. urine, urethral swab, vaginal swab, or endocervical swab (see Table 2).
Adequate sample collection is important. Chlamydia are intracellular organisms, therefore samples for diagnostic tests must contain cellular material. When carrying out a cervical swab, the swab should be inserted inside the cervical os and firmly rotated against the endocervix. Swabbing a collection of discharge will result in an inadequate specimen (it is generally recommended that excess cervical secretions be cleaned away prior to taking the swab).
Serology is not useful in diagnosing lower genital tract infection. A high-titre positive antibody test is associated with upper genital tract infection but will not distinguish between a previous and a current infection.
[SIGN, 2000; CEG, 2001b]

What else might it be?

Other causes of vaginal discharge, such as:
- Cervical ectropion
- Foreign body
- Infection (e.g. candidiasis, trichomoniasis, bacterial vaginosis, gonorrhoea)
- Irritants (e.g. perfumed soaps)
- Physiological discharge
- Tumours (e.g. cervical carcinoma)

Other causes of postcoital or intermenstrual bleeding, such as:
- Breakthrough bleeding while taking the combined oral contraceptive pill
- Cervical polyp
- Cervical carcinoma

Other causes of abdominal pain, such as:
- Appendicitis
- Cholecystitis
- Ectopic pregnancy
- Endometriosis
- Irritable bowel syndrome
- Torsion or rupture of an ovarian cyst
- Urinary tract infection

Other causes of mucopurulent cervicitis, such as:
- Gonorrhoea
- Non-specific cervicitis (no organism can be isolated)

Other causes of dysuria, such as urinary tract infection

Table 2: Tests used for diagnosing chlamydia.

Test	Comments
Enzyme immunoassays	Endocervical swab preferred specimen High specificity, variable sensitivity, relatively inexpensive 10–20% additional positives detected by assaying a urethral specimen as well (but urethral swabbing is painful and poorly tolerated)
Direct fluorescent antibody testing	Endocervical swab preferred specimen High sensitivity in experienced hands, labour intensive and expensive, can be used to confirm positive result with other assays
Nucleic acid amplification techniques	Endocervical swabs, vulvovaginal swabs, and first void urine sample are all suitable specimens High sensitivity and specificity, expensive compared with enzyme immunoassays
Cell culture	Endocervical swab required High specificity (100%) but variable sensitivity, expensive, and expertise needed

Complications and prognosis

Complications

- **Pelvic inflammatory disease (PID):** chlamydia is responsible for up to 50% of cases of PID [PHLS, 2002a]. Between 10% and 30% of women with genital chlamydial infection develop PID [PHLS et al, 2001].
- **Infertility:** about 20% of women treated for PID will become infertile due to tubal damage. Serological studies indicate that over half of cases of tubal infertility are due to chlamydia — many of these women do not have a history of PID [DH, 1998a].
- **Ectopic pregnancy:** genital chlamydial infection is responsible for about 40% of ectopic pregnancies [DH, 1998a; PHLS, 2002a]. Ectopic pregnancy occurs in about 1% of pregnancies; it is the commonest cause of maternal death in the first trimester, and accounts for 9% of maternal deaths in the UK [DH, 1998b].
- **Chronic pelvic pain:** about 20% of women treated for PID will develop chronic pelvic pain, probably due to the development of adhesions [DH, 1998a; CEG, 2001b].
- **Perihepatitis (Fitz–Hugh–Curtis syndrome):** this is a rare disorder that may complicate PID. It is characterized by adhesions between the liver and the peritoneum, causing right upper quadrant pain.
- **Reactive arthritis (Reiter's syndrome):** this is an inflammatory polyarthropathy that is triggered by exposure to a number to different infections, most commonly genital chlamydial infection. It occurs more commonly in men [Jones, 1995; CEG, 2001b].
- **Adult conjunctivitis:** this most commonly results from transfer of infected genital discharge to the eye. It usually presents as a unilateral red eye with mucopurulent discharge. People with confirmed chlamydial conjunctivitis should usually be referred and treated with systemic antibiotics. Most cases resolve without complication but scarring can occur if untreated [Jones, 1995; CEG, 2001b].
- **Complications of pregnancy:** there is some evidence that genital chlamydial infection may contribute to miscarriage, premature rupture of membranes, preterm birth, stillbirth and low birth weight [Jones, 1995]. It is uncertain whether microbiological cure of maternal chlamydia infection results in reduced complications. Postpartum endometritis has also been associated with chlamydial infection, although the risk of this occurring in women infected at the time of delivery is unknown [Brocklehurst and Rooney, 2002].
- **Transmission to neonate:** this may result in conjunctivitis (ophthalmia neonatorum) or pneumonitis. Conjunctivitis develops in 15–25% of babies born to mothers with genital chlamydia infection, usually 5–12 days after delivery. Pneumonitis develops in 5–15% of babies, usually 4–17 days after delivery [Jones, 1995; Brocklehurst and Rooney, 2002]. It is uncertain whether microbiological cure of maternal chlamydia infection reduces the risk of neonatal transmission.

Prognosis

- **Reinfection following successful treatment of genital chlamydial infection seems to be common.** Most of the data comes from the US, with reported reinfection rates of between 13% and 36% over a 3-year period [Richey et al, 1999; Whittington et al, 2001; Rietmeijer et al, 2002]. It is difficult to extrapolate this data to the UK, as most of the women in the US studies were young black women attending GUM clinics. A UK retrospective study of 540 women diagnosed with genital chlamydial infection, attending GUM clinics either at Leicestershire Royal Infirmary or Derbyshire Royal Infirmary, found

C

reinfection rates of 9% and 17% at the two sites respectively [Herieka et al, 2001]. The average period for presentation with reinfection was about 10 months.

- A large UK study on reinfection rates is currently underway, which will provide information on what screening interval should be used in the national chlamydia screening programme currently being rolled out.
- A consistent finding in all the studies is that reinfection is strongly associated with having sex with untreated partners. This emphasizes the importance of partner notification and treatment.

C

Management issues

- Screening p.326
- General issues on the management of confirmed infection p.326
- Treatment of uncomplicated (lower genital tract) infection p.326
- Treatment of pelvic inflammatory disease with tests positive for chlamydia p.327
- Pregnancy and breastfeeding p.327

Screening

- **A national screening programme for genital chlamydial infection is to be rolled out from 2002** [DH, 2001]. Initially, the screening programme will be introduced in ten sites, building on successful pilots in Portsmouth and the Wirral. This will be an opportunistic screening programme, which will mainly target women who access services such as family planning clinics [DH, 2002]. The design of the programme, in particular screening intervals, will be informed by a study currently underway looking at rates of reinfection with chlamydia.
- **The decision to consider a national screening programme followed recommendations made by** the Chief Medical Officer's (CMO's) Expert Advisory Group on *Chlamydia trachomatis* [DH, 1998a]. The conclusions of this group are outlined in Table 3.
- **The Expert Advisory Group also recommended that women undergoing instrumentation of the uterus should be considered for screening.** Limited evidence suggests that screening before intra-uterine device (IUD) insertion reduces the risk of pelvic inflammatory disease (PID). However the prevalence of chlamydia in women receiving IUDs is likely to be low, as most are multiparous and over 25 years. The Royal College of Obstetricians and Gynaecologists recommends that women under 35 years should be screened prior to IUD insertion [Rowe, 1996]. The Family Planning Association states that it is good practice to screen for infection in all women before IUD insertion [Belfield, 1999].

Table 3: CMO's Expert Advisory Group recommendations on who should be offered screening and why.

Opportunistic screening for genital chlamydial infection	
Genito-urinary medicine (GUM) clinic attendees	Evidence of consistently high prevalence rates
Women seeking termination of pregnancy	Evidence of high prevalence rates, and termination procedure increases the risk of infection ascending to cause pelvic infection
Sexually active women aged under 25 years, especially teenagers or Women aged over 25 years with a new sexual partner or who have had two or more partners in the last 12 months	A study based on UK general practice found that if this strategy were used in their study population of women aged 18–35 years, 49% of women would be tested but 87% of genital chlamydial infections would be detected [Grun et al, 1997]

General issues on the management of confirmed infection

- **Sexual abstinence is recommended until** both the infected woman and her partner(s) have completed the course of treatment [CEG, 2001b]. If treatment with single-dose azithromycin is given, then sexual abstinence for the following 7 days is advised. Safe sexual practices should be explained.
- **Screening for co-existing sexually transmitted infections is recommended** [CEG, 2001b]. Informed consent prior to screening should be obtained.
- **Referral to a GUM clinic is recommended,** for screening for other sexually transmitted infections and for partner notification [CEG, 2001b]. However, not all women will be willing to attend a GUM clinic, and management in primary care may be necessary.
- **Contact tracing of all sexual partners in the previous 6 months is recommended.** If there have been no sexual contacts within the previous 6 months, the most recent sexual partner should be notified [CEG, 2001b]. Partner should be offered screening for sexually transmitted infections, treated for chlamydial infection even if this is not identified on testing, and offered advice on safe sexual practices.
- **Retesting for chlamydial infection after completion of treatment is not usually required** (as treatment is highly effective). Retesting is recommended in women treated with erythromycin or amoxicillin (see section *Pregnancy and breastfeeding*), in women with persistent symptoms, or if reinfection is suspected [CEG, 2001b]. Retesting should be no earlier than 3 weeks after the end of treatment, as early testing will miss late failures and may detect non-viable organisms.

Treatment of uncomplicated (lower genital tract) infection

- **Preferred treatments are doxycycline 100 mg twice a day for 7 days or azithromycin 1 g as a single dose** [CEG, 2001b]. In clinical trials, these are equally effective. Azithromycin is more expensive than doxycycline, but the single-dose regimen may improve compliance — therefore, it may be particularly useful in people with erratic health-care seeking behaviour.
- **An alternative treatment is ofloxacin** (200 mg twice a day or 400 mg once a day for 7 days). It has similar efficacy to doxycycline and azithromycin but is more expensive [CEG, 2001b]. Other quinolones are either not as effective (ciprofloxacin, norfloxacin) or have not been evaluated [SIGN, 2000].
- **Other tetracyclines** are also effective [SIGN, 2000; CEG 2001b; Low and Cowan, 2001]. Tetracycline and oxytetracycline need to be taken four times a day and compliance may be a problem. Deteclo is taken twice a day and is probably as effective as doxycycline, but is more likely to cause photosensitivity. Lymecycline and minocycline require a longer course of treatment. Minocycline has more adverse effects than other tetracyclines [BNF 43, 2002].
- **Erythromycin** is less effective than doxycycline or azithromycin, and therefore is not recommended [CEG, 2001b]. It does have a role in treating pregnant women (see section *Pregnancy and breastfeeding*). Clarithromycin has not been as well studied as erythromycin or azithromycin [CEG, 2001b].

Penicillins are not recommended for the treatment of chlamydia. The exception is amoxicillin, which has a role in treating infection during pregnancy (see section *Pregnancy and breastfeeding*) [Brocklehurst and Rooney, 2002].

Treatment of pelvic inflammatory disease with tests positive for chlamydia

For a fuller discussion of pelvic inflammatory disease (PID) see separate PRODIGY guidance *Pelvic inflammatory disease*.

Broad-spectrum antibiotic treatment to cover *Neisseria gonorrhoeae*, *C trachomatis*, and anaerobic infection is recommended in guidelines produced by the Association for Genitourinary Medicine and the Medical Society for the Study of Venereal Diseases [CEG, 2001a].

The reasons for this are:

- Although much of the evidence supporting the use of antibiotics active against *N gonorrhoeae* is from the US, and anecdotally *N gonorrhoeae* is a less common cause of PID in the UK, the only recent British study found gonococcal infection in 14% of women with PID. There is evidence that the incidence of gonorrhoea is increasing in the UK. In England, Wales and Northern Ireland between 1995 and 2000, diagnoses of gonorrhoea made by GUM clinics more than doubled (10,204 to 20,663) [PHLS et al, 2001].
- The absence of endocervical gonorrhoea does not exclude gonococcal PID.
- Although PID presenting in primary care may be less severe than in other settings, there is no published evidence to support the use of less intensive regimens.

Treatment should not be delayed while waiting for the results of tests if PID is clinically suspected. It is likely that delaying treatment increases the risk of long-term complications, such as ectopic pregnancy, infertility, and pelvic pain [CEG, 2001a].

Antibiotic regimens suitable for use in primary care are outlined in Table 4.

If neither of these regimens is suitable, seek advice from a local microbiologist or GUM specialist.

Pain relief may be required. Simple analgesics and nonsteroidal anti-inflammatory drugs (NSAIDs) are both appropriate.

Pregnancy and breastfeeding

Uncomplicated (lower genital tract) infection

Pregnant women with uncomplicated (lower genital tract) chlamydial infection may be safely treated in primary care. However, prior to initiating treatment, discussion with the local obstetric unit or GUM clinic is advisable. As with the non-pregnant woman, referral to a GUM clinic is recommended, for partner notification and screening for co-existing sexually transmitted infections.

- **Erythromycin or amoxicillin are recommended** [CEG, 2001b]. Doxycycline and ofloxacin are contraindicated in pregnancy and during breastfeeding. Tetracyclines are deposited in growing bone and teeth, and quinolones are associated with the development of arthropathy in weight-bearing joints in young animals. There is a lack of information on the safety of azithromycin in pregnancy and during breastfeeding. In breastfeeding women, if erythromycin or amoxicillin are unsuitable, a single 1-gram dose of azithromycin may be given, but the mother must be advised to express and discard the breast milk for 48 hours after this [Leicester Drug Information Service, Personal Communication, 2002].
- **Retesting 3 weeks after completing treatment with erythromycin or amoxicillin is recommended,** to confirm eradication of infection (as they are less effective than treatments that can be taken by non-pregnant women) [CEG, 2001b].
- Contact Leicester Drug Information service (telephone 0116 255 5779) for advice on drugs in breastfeeding, and the National Teratology Information Service (NTIS) (telephone 0191 232 1525) for advice on drugs in pregnancy.

Pelvic inflammatory disease

- Admission for parenteral antibiotics is recommended for pregnant women with suspected pelvic inflammatory disease [CEG, 2001b].

References

NHS staff in England can link, free of charge, from references to full text journals by clicking on [Full text] on the PRODIGY website.

1. Bandolier (1998) *The 4th Bandolier Conference: chlamydia*. Bandolier. www.jr2.ox.ac.uk/bandolier/bandopubs/bandocon4/chlamyd.html [Accessed: 01/07/2002].
2. Belfield, T. (Ed.) (1999) *FPA contraceptive handbook: a guide for family planning and other health professionals*. 3rd edn. London: Family Planning Association.
3. BNF 43 (2002) *British National Formulary*. 43rd edn. London: British Medical Association and Royal Pharmaceutical Society of Great Britain.
4. Brocklehurst, P. and Rooney, G. (2002) *Interventions for treating genital Chlamydia trachomatis infection in pregnancy (Cochrane Review)*. The Cochrane Library. Issue 2. Oxford: Update Software.
5. CEG (2001a) *Guidelines for the management of pelvic infection and perihepatitis*. Clinical Effectiveness Group (Association for Genitourinary Medicine and the Medical Society for the Study of Venereal Diseases). www.bashh.org/guidelines/ceguidelines.htm [Accessed: 07/05/2002].
6. CEG (2001b) *Clinical effectiveness guideline for the management of Chlamydia trachomatis genital tract*

Table 4: Antibiotic regimens suitable for the primary care treatment of PID.

Antibiotic regimen	Comments
Oral ofloxacin 400 mg twice a day plus oral metronidazole 400 mg twice a day, both for 14 days	Ofloxacin is not recommended as monotherapy; although it is effective against *C trachomatis* and *N gonorrhoeae* it does not cover anaerobic infections [CEG, 2001a]. Ofloxacin monotherapy may have a place in people who are unable to tolerate metronidazole. Two randomized controlled trials compared oral ofloxacin with parenteral cefoxitin and doxycycline and found no difference in cure rates (clinical cure rates about 95% for all treatments) [Ross, 2001].
Intramuscular ceftriaxone 250 mg immediately followed by oral doxycycline 100 mg twice a day plus oral metronidazole 400 mg twice a day both for 14 days	Less convenient for use in primary care, but an option if a quinolone is contraindicated. Oral cephalosporins have not been evaluated sufficiently to recommend their use [CEG, 2001a].

C

infection. Clinical Effectiveness Group (Association for Genitourinary Medicine and the Medical Society for the Study of Venereal Diseases). www.bashh.org/guidelines/ceguidelines.htm [Accessed: 07/05/2002].

7. CSM (1994) Relative safety of oral non-aspirin NSAIDs. *Current Problems in Pharmacovigilance* 20(Aug), 9–11.
8. De Craen, A.J., Di Giulio, G., Lampe-Schoenmaeckers, J.E. et al (1996) Analgesic efficacy and safety of paracetamol-codeine combinations versus paracetamol alone: a systematic review. *British Medical Journal* 313(7053), 321–325. [Full text]
9. DH (1998a) *Summary and conclusions of CMO's Expert Advisory Group Report on chlamydia trachomatis.* Department of Health. www.dh.gov.uk [Accessed: 26/04/2004]. [Full text]
10. DH (1998b) *Why mothers die: report on confidential enquiries into maternal deaths in the United Kingdom 1994–1996.* Department of Health. [Accessed: 24/05/2002]. [Full text]
11. DH (2001) *The national strategy for sexual health and HIV.* Department of Health. www.dh.gov.uk [Accessed: 27/04/2004]. [Full text]
12. DH (2002) *The national strategy for sexual health and HIV: implementation action plan.* Department of Health. www.dh.gov.uk [Accessed: 27/04/2004]. [Full text]
13. DTB (1994) Management of genital Chlamydia trachomatis infections. *Drug & Therapeutics Bulletin* 32(11), 87–88.
14. DTB (1995) Giving erythromycin by mouth. *Drug & Therapeutics Bulletin* 33(10), 77–79.
15. Golden, M.R., Schillinger, J.A., Markowitz, L. and St Louis, M.E. (2000) Duration of untreated genital infections with Chlamydia trachomatis: a review of the literature. *Sexually Transmitted Diseases* 27(6), 329–337.
16. Grun, L., Tassano-Smith, J., Carder, C. et al (1997) Comparison of two methods of screening for genital chlamydial infection in women attending in general practice: cross sectional survey. *British Medical Journal* 315(7102), 226–230. [Full text]
17. Henry, D., Lim, L.L., Garcia-Rodriguez, L.A. et al (1996) Variability in risk of gastrointestinal complications with individual non-steroidal anti-inflammatory drugs: results of a collaborative meta-analysis. *British Medical Journal* 312(7046), 1563–1566. [Full text]
18. Herieka, E., Schober, P. and Dhar, J. (2001) Chlamydia trachomatis reinfection rate: a forgotten aspect of female genital chlamydia management. *Sexually Transmitted Infections* 77(3), 223. [Full text]
19. Hernández-Diaz, S. and Rodriguez, L.A. (2000) Association between nonsteroidal anti-inflammatory drugs and upper gastrointestinal tract bleeding/perforation: an overview of epidemiologic studies published in the 1990s. *Archives of Internal Medicine* 160(14), 2093–2099. [Full text]
20. Jones, R.B. (1995) Chlamydia trachomatis (trachoma, perinatal infections, lymphogranuloma venereum, and other genital infections). In: Mandell, G.L., Dolin, R., Bennet, J.E. et al (Eds.) *Principles and practice of infectious diseases.* 4th edn. London: Churchill Livingstone. 1679–1693.
21. Leicester Drug Information Service (2002) *Personal communication.* Leicester Drug Information Service: Leicester.
22. Low, N. and Cowan, F. (2001) Genital chlamydial infection. *Clinical Evidence* 6(Dec), 1216–1222.
23. McCormack, W.M., Alpert, S., McComb, D.E. et al (1979) Fifteen-month follow-up study of women infected with Chlamydia trachomatis. *New England Journal of Medicine* 300(3), 123–125.
24. MeReC (2000) The use of oral analgesics in primary care. *MeReC Bulletin* 11(1), 1–4.
25. Moore, A., Collins, S., Carroll, D. and McQuay, H. (1997) Paracetamol with and without codeine in acute pain: a quantitative systematic review. *Pain* 70(2–3), 193–201.
26. PHLS (2002a) *Genital Chlamydia trachomatis infection.* Public Health Laboratory Service. www.hpa.org.uk [Accessed: 07/05/2002].
27. PHLS (2002b) Sexually transmitted infections quarterly report: genital chlamydial infection in the United Kingdom. *CDR Weekly* 12(5), 13–17.
28. PHLS (2002c) *New episodes of selected diagnoses by age and sex: England, Wales and Northern Ireland 1995–2000: genital chlamydia (uncomplicated).* Public Health Laboratory Service. www.hpa.org.uk [Accessed: 01/07/2002].
29. PHLS (2002d) *Diagnosis of chlamydia: quick reference guide.* Public Health Laboratory Services. www.hpa.org.uk [Accessed: 01/07/2002].
30. PHLS, DHSS & PS and Scottish ISD(D)5 Collaborative Group (2001) *Sexually transmitted infections in the UK: new episodes seen at genitourinary medicine clinics, 1995 to 2000.* London: Public Health Laboratory Service.
31. Richey, C.M., Macaluso, M. and Hook, E.W. (1999) Determinants of reinfection with Chlamydia trachomatis. *Sexually Transmitted Diseases* 26(1), 4–11.
32. Rietmeijer, C.A., Van Bemmelen, R., Judson, F.N. and Douglas, J.M. (2002) Incidence and repeat infection rates of Chlamydia trachomatis among male and female patients in an STD clinic: implications for screening and rescreening. *Sexually Transmitted Diseases* 29(2), 65–72.
33. Ross, J. (2001) Pelvic inflammatory disease. *Clinical Evidence* 6(Dec), 1256–1260.
34. Rowe, P.J. (1996) Sequelae of pelvic infection. In: Templeton, A. (Ed.) *The prevention of pelvic infection* London: Royal College of Obstetricians and Gynaecologists. 14–32.
35. SIGN (2000) *Management of genital chlamydia trachomatis infection.* Report no. 42. Scottish Intercollegiate Guidelines Network. www.sign.ac.uk [Accessed: 08/05/2002].
36. Whittington, W.L., Kent, C., Kissinger, P. et al (2001) Determinants of persistent and recurrent Chlamydia trachomatis infection in young women: results of a multicenter cohort study. *Sexually Transmitted Diseases* 28(2), 117–123.

PRODIGY GUIDANCE

Chronic obstructive pulmonary disease

Last revised in July 2005
www.prodigy.nhs.uk/guidance.asp?gt=COPD

Applies to people over the age of 16 years

This guidance covers the management of people with chronic obstructive pulmonary disease (COPD).

This guidance does not cover the management of asthma.

There is separate PRODIGY guidance for *Asthma* and *Smoking cessation.*

Contents

Scenarios

- Establishing a diagnosis p.329
- Stable COPD p.330
- Exacerbation of COPD p.334
- Oxygen therapy p.337

Extended Information, p. 339

Which scenario?

Establishing a diagnosis: offers guidance on making a diagnosis of COPD.
Stable COPD: covers the management of people with stable COPD.
Exacerbation of COPD: covers the management of an exacerbation of COPD.
Oxygen therapy: offers guidance on the procedure for initiating oxygen therapy, how to decide who to refer for assessment and initiation of therapy, and how to deal with people with COPD who are on oxygen in the community.

Establishing a diagnosis

Which therapy?

History

Early in the disease, there may be minimal or no symptoms. As COPD progresses, symptoms vary between different people. Breathlessness is the most important symptom in most people with COPD.
A diagnosis of COPD should be considered in smokers who present with one or more of the following symptoms:

- Exertional breathlessness
- Chronic cough
- Regular sputum production
- Frequent 'winter bronchitis'
- Wheeze

Other symptoms which may be present include:

- Weight loss
- Effort intolerance
- Waking at night
- Ankle swelling
- Fatigue

Examination

In some people with COPD, examination may be normal.
There is no individual sign that is diagnostic of COPD.
The following signs may be present:

- Breathlessness
- Cachexia
- Cyanosis
- Hyperinflated chest
- Nicotine staining of fingers
- Paradoxical movement of lower ribs
- Peripheral oedema
- Prolonged expiration
- Purse lip breathing
- Raised jugular venous pulse (JVP)
- Reduced crico-sternal distance
- Use of accessory muscles of respiration
- Reduced cardiac dullness on percussion
- Wheeze or quiet breath sounds

Spirometry

- **Demonstration of the presence of airflow obstruction by spirometry is vital for the correct diagnosis of COPD.**
  - Airflow obstruction is defined as a reduced FEV_1 and a reduced FEV_1/FVC ratio; such that FEV_1 is less than 80% predicted, and FEV_1/FVC is less than 0.7.
  - Predicted normal values of FEV_1 and FVC depend on the person's age, height, and sex. A calculator to compare spirometry with normal values can be found at www.jhucct.com/CCT/calculate.htm.

Should I refer or investigate?

Refer?

Consider referral to a respiratory specialist in any of the following situations:

- Diagnostic uncertainty
- Suspected severe COPD
- Cor pulmonale
- A rapid decline in FEV_1
- Assessment for oxygen therapy
- Assessment for long-term nebulizer therapy
- Assessment for oral corticosteroid therapy
- Assessment for pulmonary rehabilitation
- Age under 40 years, or a family history of $alpha_1$-antitrypsin deficiency

Investigate?

- **Spirometry** to confirm diagnosis (see *Which therapy*).
- **Chest X-ray** to exclude other pathology.
- **Full blood count** to check for anaemia or polycythaemia (the latter indicative of chronic hypoxia).
- **Body mass index (BMI)** should be calculated.
- **Serum $alpha_1$-antitrypsin** level should be considered in the following cases:
  - COPD in a non-smoker
  - Early onset of COPD
  - Family history of $alpha_1$-antitrypsin deficiency or of early-onset COPD.

Patient information leaflets

The following PILs are available at www.prodigy.nhs.uk

- British Lung Foundation
- COPD (Chronic Obs. Pulmonary Disease)
- Smoking - Help to Stop with Bupropion
- Smoking - Nicotine Replacement Therapy
- Smoking - The Facts
- Smoking - Tips on Stopping
- Spirometry

C

Shared decision making

- Your symptoms are likely to be due to COPD (chronic obstructive pulmonary disease).
- Spirometry is a breathing test that helps to confirm the diagnosis.
- A chest X-ray and a blood test may help to rule out other problems.
- **Smoking is the main cause of COPD.**
    - If you stop smoking, the symptoms will not usually become much worse.
    - If you have COPD and continue to smoke, symptoms such as cough, wheeze, breathlessness, and repeated chest infections usually become worse.

Drug rationale

- No prescriptions are offered.

Stable COPD

Which therapy?

- **Smoking cessation is vital** (see PRODIGY *Smoking cessation* guidance).
- **For people troubled by breathlessness and exercise limitation, the following therapy steps are recommended:**
    - Use a short-acting bronchodilator (beta$_2$-agonist or anticholinergic) as required.
    - If still symptomatic, use one of the following 2 options:
        - Combined therapy with a short-acting beta$_2$-agonist and a short-acting anticholinergic.
        - A long-acting bronchodilator (beta$_2$-agonist or anticholinergic).
    - In moderate or severe COPD if still symptomatic, consider a trial of combination of a long-acting beta$_2$-agonist and inhaled corticosteroid. Discontinue if no benefit after 4 weeks.
    - If still symptomatic, consider adding theophylline.
- **For people troubled by frequent exacerbations, the following therapy steps are recommended:**
    - Optimize bronchodilator therapy with one or more long-acting bronchodilator (beta$_2$-agonist or anticholinergic).
    - If still troubled by frequent exacerbations, add inhaled corticosteroids if FEV$_1$ <50% and two or more exacerbations are experienced in a 12-month period.
- Mucolytic therapy should be considered in people with a chronic cough productive of sputum, and continued if there is a symptomatic improvement. People who experience frequent exacerbations are most likely to benefit from mucolytics.
- For all of these steps, stop the therapy if it is ineffective.

Practical prescribing points

For further information please see the *Medicines Compendium* (www.medicines.org.uk) or the *British National Formulary* (www.bnf.org).

- **Regularly reinforce inhaler technique** — where this is poor, it may be mistaken for a lack of response to the drug.
- People may experience varying degrees of sensation in the mouth and throat with different inhaler products. These may depend on the actuation and the drug inhaled.
- **Where a chlorofluorocarbon (CFC)-free inhaler is intended,** it is recommended that this term be specified on the prescription.

Beta$_2$-agonists

- **Hypokalaemia:** high doses can reduce plasma potassium concentration (therefore this needs monitoring), and the Committee on Safety of Medicines has advised that this may be potentially serious. Hypokalaemia may be potentiated by concomitant treatment with theophylline and its derivatives, corticosteroids, and diuretics, and by hypoxia.

Anticholinergics

- **Use of nebulized ipratropium:** the eyes need to be protected as acute angle-closure glaucoma has been reported. This is also a problem when given with nebulized beta$_2$-agonists.

Inhaled corticosteroids

- Oral candidiasis and sore mouth are common. Use a large-volume spacer with a metered-dose inhaler (MDI), and rinse the mouth with water after inhaled corticosteroid (ICS) use.
- **For people on prolonged treatment with ICS:** give lifestyle advice to prevent osteoporosis: exercise, dietary calcium, and smoking.
- **Abrupt withdrawal of ICS in stable COPD** may increase the risk of exacerbation, so careful monitoring is required if withdrawal is attempted.

Oral corticosteroids

- Following concern about severe chickenpox, the Committee on Safety of Medicines has advised that anyone prescribed a systemic corticosteroid should receive the patient information leaflet produced by the manufacturer.

Theophylline

- Theophylline has a narrow therapeutic window — aim for a plasma level between 10 and 20 mg/litre.
- Prescribe theophylline by brand as the bioavailability varies between brands.
- Blood levels may be raised by drugs that inhibit hepatic enzymes (e.g. cimetidine, ciprofloxacin, erythromycin).
- Blood levels may be lowered by smoking, chronic alcoholism, and by drugs that induce hepatic enzymes (e.g. phenytoin, carbamazepine, rifampicin).
- **Hypokalaemia** may be potentiated by concomitant treatment with beta$_2$-agonists. The Committee on Safety of Medicines has advised that this may potentially be serious.

Spacer devices

- **Clean spacers no more than once a month** (more frequent cleaning will build up static affecting their performance) — wash in mild detergent, rinse, and then allow to air dry.

Follow-up advice

- Follow-up should be tailored to the individual.

ıould I refer or investigate?

ɘfer?

ɒnsider referral to a respiratory specialist in any of the ˈlowing situations:

- Diagnostic uncertainty
- Suspected severe COPD
- Cor pulmonale
- A rapid decline in FEV_1
- Assessment for oxygen therapy
- Assessment for long-term nebulizer therapy
- Assessment for oral corticosteroid therapy
- Assessment for pulmonary rehabilitation
- Age under 40 years, or a family history of $alpha_1$-antitrypsin deficiency

vestigate?

- **Spirometry** to confirm diagnosis (see *Establishing a diagnosis* scenario).
- **Chest X-ray** to exclude other pathology.
- **Full blood count** to check for anaemia or polycythaemia (the latter indicative of chronic hypoxia).
- **Body mass index (BMI)** should be calculated.
- **Serum $alpha_1$-antitrypsin** level should be considered in the following cases:
  - COPD in a non-smoker
  - Early onset of COPD
  - Family history of $alpha_1$-antitrypsin deficiency, or of early onset COPD.

atient information leaflets

ıe following PILs are available at www.prodigy.nhs.uk

- British Lung Foundation
- COPD (Chronic Obs. Pulmonary Disease)
- Medicines - Name Changes of Medicines
- Quit (help to stop smoking)
- Smoking - The Facts
- Smoking - Tips on Stopping

hared decision making

- **If you do not smoke** the symptoms of COPD will not usually become much worse.
- No other treatment may be needed if symptoms remain mild.
- **Short-acting bronchodilator inhalers** are often used for COPD to open the airways as wide as possible.
  - **Salbutamol** or **terbutaline** relax the muscles in the airways. They can be taken regularly or 'as required'.
  - **Ipratropium** is an alternative that works in a different way. Each dose takes slightly longer to work than the above inhalers, but the effect of each dose lasts longer.
  - Some people take both types of inhaler.
- **A long-acting bronchodilator inhaler** such as **formoterol, salmeterol,** or **tiotropium** is an option if symptoms remain troublesome. Each dose lasts at least 12 hours.
- **A steroid inhaler** may be advised if you have more severe COPD. It may not have much effect on your 'usual' symptoms, but may help to prevent flare-ups.
- **Theophylline** tablets may be advised if you are unable to use inhalers. They may also be added in to the above treatments in severe cases.
- **A mucolytic medicine** such as **carbocisteine** or **mecysteine** may be advised in more severe cases. It makes sputum less thick and easier to cough up.
- **You should be immunized** against pneumococcal infection, and against flu each autumn.

Drug rationale

Drugs not included

- **Dry-powder inhalers are not included.** They should be reserved for people who are unable to use pMDIs effectively after receiving appropriate instruction.
- **Oral $beta_2$-agonists** are not recommended in the routine management of COPD [MeReC, 1998b].
- **Inhaled cromoglicate or nedocromil** are not recommended for the routine management of COPD [MeReC, 1998b].
- **Inhaled corticosteroid: mometasone furoate** is not included. It is a black triangle drug under the surveillance of the Committee of Safety on Medicines, there are limited trial data of its use, and it is very costly.
- **Maintenance oral corticosteroid treatment** in COPD is not normally recommended and therefore prescriptions are not included. Some patients with advanced COPD may require maintenance oral corticosteroids when these cannot be withdrawn following an exacerbation.
- **Theophylline preparations other than Nuelin SA®, Slo-Phyllin® and Uniphyllin®** are not included. Due to the potential for toxicity and significant drug interaction, they are less commonly used.
- **Mucolytic** drug prescriptions are not included but they should be considered in people with a chronic cough productive of sputum, and continued if there is a symptomatic improvement.

Drugs included

- **Inhaled agents are preferred** to oral because of the reduction in systemic adverse effects.
- **Short-acting bronchodilators,** as necessary should be the initial empirical treatment for the relief of breathlessness and exercise limitation (**B**) [National Collaborating Centre for Chronic Conditions, 2004].
  - **Short-acting $beta_2$-agonists: salbutamol and terbutaline** CFC-free pressurized metered dose inhalers (pMDIs) are included as well as salbutamol breath-actuated pMDIs and terbutaline turbohaler. Daily breathlessness scores have been found to be reduced with their use and they improve FEV_1 [Sestini et al, 2004]. Use on an as-needed basis appears to be as effective as regular use [Cook et al, 2001].
  - **Short-acting anticholinergic: ipratropium** (CFC)-**free pMDI** is included. It has been shown to be as effective as $beta_2$-agonists in people with COPD and may provide a greater and longer bronchodilator response [National Collaborating Centre for Chronic Conditions, 2004]. There is no spacer device specifically designed to fit the MDI inhaler, but an Aerochamber, Volumatic or Nebuhaler can all be tried.
- **Long-acting bronchodilators** are an option in people who remain symptomatic despite the use of a short-acting bronchodilator (**A**) [National Collaborating Centre for Chronic Conditions, 2004]. Long-acting bronchodilators appear to have additional benefits over combinations of short-acting drugs (**A**). They should be used in people who have two or more exacerbations per year (**D**).
  - **Long-acting $beta_2$-agonists: formoterol** (eformoterol) and salmeterol are included. They have similar effects to the short-acting agents but their duration of action is around 12 hours. Trial data are inconsistent as to their benefit in COPD, but some people appear to show improvement from their use [Kerstjens and Postma, 2003].
  - **Long-acting anticholinergic: tiotropium** is licensed for maintenance treatment of COPD and can be used once

C

a day, which may help compliance. There are trial data to support its efficacy, but more data are needed to identify whether it has any clinical advantages over other products [DTB, 2003]. Tiotropium is a black triangle drug under the surveillance of the Committee on Safety of Medicines, it should be reserved for people who remain symptomatic with alternative therapy and where there is a good response following a therapeutic trial.

C

- **Modified-release theophylline** preparations are included as branded products. These formulations are preferred as they provide more stable blood levels of theophylline. They should only be used after a trial of short-acting and long-acting bronchodilators or in people who are unable to use inhaled therapy. Their usefulness is limited by the need to monitor plasma levels and their potential for drug interactions (D) [National Collaborating Centre for Chronic Conditions, 2004].
- **Inhaled corticosteroids: beclometasone, budesonide, and fluticasone** are included. They should be prescribed for people with an FEV_1 =<50% predicted who are having two or more exacerbations requiring treatment with antibiotics or oral corticosteroids in a 12-month period. The primary aim of treatment is to reduce exacerbation rates and slow the decline in health status (B) [National Collaborating Centre for Chronic Conditions, 2004], but they have been found to show no reduction in the decline in lung function. There is insufficient evidence to establish the minimum dose of inhaled corticosteroid required to achieve the proven benefits [National Collaborating Centre for Chronic Conditions, 2004].
- **Beclometasone chlorofluorocarbon (CFC)-free metered-dose inhaler (MDI)** (Qvar®) is also offered should this option be required. The true potency ratio for Qvar® in COPD is unclear; however, it seems logical to apply the recommendations currently available with asthma management, and therefore the Summary of Product Characteristics for the product should be followed carefully both for initiating CFC-free beclometasone and, in particular, transferring someone from CFC-containing to CFC-free products.
- **Fixed-dose combination inhaler preparations Seretide® and Symbicort®** are included. Both preparations are licensed for the symptomatic treatment of patients with severe COPD and a history of repeated exacerbations who have significant symptoms despite regular bronchodilator therapy. They may improve adherence to therapy where people with COPD are stabilized on both an inhaled corticosteroid and long-acting beta$_2$-agonist [DTB, 2004].
- **Spacer devices** that fit the inhaler devices offered where possible are included. Switching between different spacer types can affect the deposition characteristics of the inhaled drug. The same may apply if there is a change in the inhaler device used, but no change in spacer. This change of device may alter clinical response to the inhaled drug [NHS Executive, 1998].
- **Note: switching between different inhaler or spacer types, or both,** can affect the deposition characteristics of the inhaled drug, which may alter the clinical response to a drug. To maintain good control, it is important that people are not switched back and forth between inhalers and spacer devices.
- **Oral corticosteroid: prednisolone** can be used in the short-term (in the absence of contraindications) to improve lung function, but no randomized controlled trial data of long-term treatment effect on lung function is available.
- **Nebulizer solutions** are included as they may be of benefit to people with distressing or disabling breathlessness despite maximal therapy using inhalers. They should only be repeatedly prescribed after it has been assessed and confirmed that the patient has clinically benefited [National Collaborating Centre for Chronic Conditions, 2004].

Prescriptions

Salbutamol preparations +/- spacer device

Salbutamol 100mcg MDI: 1 to 2 puffs up to 4 times a day

- Age from 16 years onwards
- Salbutamol 100mcg CFC-free inhaler. Inhale one to two puffs up to four times a day, when required to relieve breathlessness; supply 1 200 dose inhaler; NHS Cost £1.86.

Airomir 100mcg MDI + AeroChamber Plus

- Age from 16 years onwards
- Airomir 100mcg CFC-free inhaler. Inhale one to two puffs up to four times a day using the spacer, when required to relieve breathlessness; supply 1 200 dose inhaler; NHS Cost £1.97.
- AeroChamber Plus spacer device. Use to aid inhalation; supply 1 spacer; NHS Cost £4.36.

Salamol 100mcg MDI + Volumatic

- Age from 16 years onwards
- Salamol 100mcg CFC-free inhaler. Inhale one to two puffs up to four times a day using the spacer, when required to relieve breathlessness; supply 1 200 dose inhaler; NHS Cost £1.95.
- Volumatic spacer device. Use to aid inhalation; supply spacer; NHS Cost £2.00.

Ventolin 100mcg MDI + Volumatic

- Age from 16 years onwards
- Ventolin 100mcg CFC-free inhaler. Inhale one to two puffs up to four times a day using the spacer, when required to relieve breathlessness; supply 1 200 dose inhaler; NHS Cost £2.30.
- Volumatic spacer device. Use to aid inhalation; supply spacer; NHS Cost £2.75.

Airomir 100mcg Autohaler: 1 to 2 puffs up to 4 times a day

- Age from 16 years onwards
- Airomir 100 CFC-free Autohaler. Inhale one to two puffs up to four times a day, when required to relieve breathlessness; supply 1 200 dose inhaler; NHS Cost £6.02.

Salamol 100mcg Easi-Breathe: 1-2 puffs up to 4 times a day

- Age from 16 years onwards
- Salamol 100mcg Easi-Breathe. Inhale one to two puffs up to four times a day, when required to relieve breathlessness; supply 1 200 dose inhaler; NHS Cost £6.30.

Salbutamol nebules: 2.5mg up to four times a day

- Age from 16 years onwards
- Salbutamol 2.5mg/2.5ml nebules. Inhale the contents of one nebule (2.5mg) using nebuliser up to four times a day, or as directed by your doctor; supply 20 2.5ml nebules; NHS Cost £2.74.

Salbutamol nebules: 5mg up to four times a day

- Age from 16 years onwards
- Salbutamol 5mg/2.5ml unit dose. Inhale the contents of one nebule (5mg) using nebuliser up to four times a day or as directed by your doctor; supply 20 2.5ml nebules; NHS Cost £5.47.

Terbutaline preparations +/- spacer device

Terbutaline 250mcg MDI: 1 to 2 puffs up to 4 times a day

- Age from 16 years onwards
- Terbutaline 250mcg inhaler. Inhale one to two puffs up to four times a day, when required to relieve

breathlessness; supply 1 400 dose inhaler; NHS Cost £5.84.

rbutaline MDI + Nebuhaler
- Age from 16 years onwards
- Terbutaline 250mcg inhaler. Inhale one to two puffs up to four times a day, when required to relieve breathlessness; supply 1 400 dose inhaler; NHS Cost £5.84.
- Nebuhaler spacer device. Use to aid inhalation; supply 1 spacer; NHS Cost £4.28.

rbutaline 500mcg Turbohaler: 1 puff up to 4 times a day
- Age from 16 years onwards
- Terbutaline 500mcg Turbohaler. Inhale one puff up to four times a day, when required to relieve breathlessness; supply 1 100 dose inhaler; NHS Cost £6.92.

rbutaline respules: 5mg to 10mg up to four times a day
- Age from 16 years onwards
- Terbutaline 5mg/2ml respule. Inhale the contents of one (5mg) or two (2 x 5mg) respule(s) using the nebuliser up to four times a day, or as directed by your doctor; supply 40 2ml respules; NHS Cost £8.08.

nticholinergic and long-acting beta$_2$-agonist reparations

ratropium 20mcg MDI: 1 to 2 puffs up to 4 times a day
- Age from 16 years onwards
- Ipratropium 20mcg inhaler. Inhale one to two puffs up to four times a day, when required to relieve breathlessness; supply 1 200 dose inhaler; NHS Cost £4.00.

ratropium nebules: 250mcg up to four times a day
- Age from 16 years onwards
- Ipratropium 250mcg/1ml neb.sol. Inhale the contents of one vial (250micrograms) using nebuliser up to four times a day; supply 20 1ml vial; NHS Cost £6.98.

ratropium nebules: 500mcg up to four times a day
- Age from 16 years onwards
- Ipratropium 500mcg/2ml neb.sol. Inhale the contents of one vial (500micrograms) using nebuliser up to four times a day; supply 20 2ml vials; NHS Cost £7.60.

otropium Combopack: 18micrograms once a day
- Age from 18 years onwards
- Tiotropium18mcg cap+HandiHaler. Inhale the contents of one capsule once a day, when required to relieve breathlessness; supply 1 Combopack; NHS Cost £37.62.

otropium capsules refill pack: 18micrograms once a day
- Age from 18 years onwards
- Tiotropium 18mcg capsules. Inhale the contents of one capsule once a day, when required to relieve breathlessness; supply 30 capsules; NHS Cost £36.60.

almeterol MDI: up to 100mcg twice a day
- Age from 16 years onwards
- Salmeterol 25microgram inhaler. Inhale up to four puffs twice a day, when required to relieve breathlessness; supply 1 120 dose inhaler; NHS Cost £31.46.

ormoterol (eformoterol) Turbohaler: 12mcg-24mcg twice day
- Age from 16 years onwards
- Formoterol 12mcg Turbohaler. Inhale one to two puffs twice a day, when required to relieve breathlessness; supply 1 60 dose inhaler; NHS Cost £24.80.

eroChamber Plus spacer: for use with Atrovent inhaler
- Age from 16 years onwards
- AeroChamber Plus spacer device. Use to aid inhalation; supply 1 spacer; NHS Cost £4.36.

olumatic spacer: for use with Serevent inhaler
- Age from 16 years onwards
- Volumatic spacer device. Use to aid inhalation; supply 1 spacer; NHS Cost £2.75.

Inhaled corticosteroids +/- long-acting beta$_2$-agonist

Beclometasone MDI: 400mcg twice a day
- Age from 16 years onwards
- Beclometasone 200mcg inhaler. Inhale two puffs twice a day; supply 1 200 dose inhaler; NHS Cost £19.61.

Beclometasone MDI: 500mcg to 1000mcg twice a day
- Age from 16 years onwards
- Beclometasone 250mcg inhaler. Inhale two to four puffs twice a day; supply 2 200 dose inhaler; NHS Cost £46.20.

Beclometasone CFC-free MDI: 200mcg to 400mcg twice a day
- Age from 16 years onwards
- Qvar 100mcg CFC-free inhaler. Inhale two to four puffs twice a day; supply 1 200 dose inhaler; NHS Cost £17.21.

Beclometasone CFC-free MDI+ AeroChamber Plus
- Age from 16 years onwards
- Qvar 100mcg CFC-free inhaler. Inhale two puffs twice a day; supply 1 200 dose inhaler; NHS Cost £17.00.
- AeroChamber Plus spacer device. Use to aid inhalation; supply 1 spacer; NHS Cost £4.00.

Budesonide MDI + Nebuhaler
- Age from 16 years onwards
- Budesonide 200mcg inhaler. Inhale two puffs twice a day; supply 1 200 dose inhaler; NHS Cost £20.90.
- Nebuhaler spacer device. Use to aid inhalation; supply 1 spacer; NHS Cost £4.28.

Fluticasone CFC-free MDI: 250-1000mcg twice a day
- Age from 16 years onwards
- Fluticasone 250mcg CFC-free inhaler. Inhale one to four puffs twice a day; supply 1 120 dose inhaler; NHS Cost £38.86.

Volumatic spacer: for use with Becotide/Becloforte/Flixotide
- Age from 16 years onwards
- Volumatic spacer device. Use to aid inhalation; supply 1 spacer; NHS Cost £2.75.

Symbicort 400/12 Turbohaler: one puff twice a day
- Age from 16 years onwards
- Symbicort 400 + 12 micrograms. Inhale one puff twice a day; supply 1 60 dose inhaler; NHS Cost £38.00.

Seretide 500 Accuhaler: one puff twice a day
- Age from 16 years onwards
- Seretide 500 accuhaler. Inhale the contents of one blister twice a day; supply 1 60 dose inhaler; NHS Cost £44.00.

Theophylline preparations

Nuelin SA m/r tablets: 175mg twice a day
- Age from 16 years onwards
- Nuelin SA 175mg m/r tablets. Take one tablet twice a day; supply 60 tablets; NHS Cost £3.43; OTC Cost £6.05.

Nuelin SA m/r tablets: 350mg twice a day
- Age from 16 years onwards
- Nuelin SA 175mg m/r tablets. Take two tablets twice a day; supply 120 tablets; NHS Cost £6.86; OTC Cost £12.10.

Nuelin SA m/r tablets: 500mg twice a day
- Age from 16 years onwards
- Nuelin SA-250 250mg m/r tabs. Take two tablets twice a day; supply 120 tablets; NHS Cost £9.60; OTC Cost £16.92.

Slo-Phyllin m/r capsules: 250mg twice a day
- Age from 16 years onwards
- Slo-Phyllin 250mg m/r capsules. Take one capsule twice a day; supply 56 capsules; NHS Cost £3.62; OTC Cost £6.38.

Slo-Phyllin m/r capsules: 500mg twice a day

- Age from 16 years onwards
- Slo-Phyllin 250mg m/r capsules. Take two capsules twice a day; supply 112 capsules; NHS Cost £7.24; OTC Cost £12.72.

Uniphyllin Continus m/r tablets: 200mg twice a day

- Age from 16 years onwards
- Uniphyllin Cont 200mg m/r tabs. Take one tablet twice a day; supply 56 tablets; NHS Cost £4.12; OTC Cost £7.26.

Uniphyllin Continus m/r tablets: 300mg twice a day

- Age from 16 years onwards
- Uniphyllin Cont 300mg m/r tabs. Take one tablet twice a day; supply 56 tablets; NHS Cost £6.27; OTC Cost £11.05.

Uniphyllin Continus m/r tablets: 400mg twice a day

- Age from 16 years onwards
- Uniphyllin Cont 400mg m/r tabs. Take one tablet twice a day; supply 56 tablets; NHS Cost £7.44; OTC Cost £13.11.

Exacerbation of COPD

Which therapy?

Bronchodilators

- Add or increase bronchodilators.
- These may need to be taken more frequently and in higher doses.

Oral corticosteroids

- **Consider oral corticosteroids if an exacerbation significantly increases breathlessness, which interferes with daily activities.**
- Prescribe prednisolone 30 mg for 7–14 days.
- Start prednisolone as soon as possible to achieve optimum benefit; in selected people consider provision of a treatment course at home as part of an agreed management programme.

Antibiotics

- Prescribe an antibiotic if the sputum is more purulent than usual.
- **If the sputum is not more purulent than usual,** only prescribe an antibiotic if there are clinical signs of pneumonia.
- **First-line antibiotics** are amoxicillin, oxytetracycline, or doxycycline.
- **If the infection does not respond to the initial antibiotic choice,** a tetracycline (if this has not already been tried) or co-amoxiclav is a suitable choice.
- Follow local antibiotic guidelines, if available.

Other issues

- Encourage a smoker to stop.
- Ensure influenza and pneumococcal vaccinations have been given.

Practical prescribing points

For further information, please see the *Medicines Compendium* (www.medicines.org.uk) or the *British National Formulary* (www.bnf.org).

Beta$_2$-agonists

- **Regularly reinforce inhaler technique:** where this is poor, it may be mistaken for a lack of response to the drug.
- People may experience varying degrees of sensation in the mouth and throat with different inhaler products. These may depend on the actuation and the drug inhaled.
- **Where a chlorofluorocarbon (CFC)-free inhaler is intended,** it is recommended that this term be specified on the prescription.
- **Beta$_2$-agonists** can cause tremor, palpitations, headache and muscle cramps.
- **Hypokalaemia:** high doses can reduce plasma potassium concentration (therefore this needs monitoring), and the Committee on Safety of Medicines has advised that this may be potentially serious. Hypokalaemia may be potentiated by concomitant treatment with theophylline and its derivatives, corticosteroids, and diuretics, and by hypoxia.

Oral corticosteroids

- Following concern about severe chickenpox, the Committee on Safety of Medicines has advised that anyone prescribed a systemic corticosteroid should receive the patient information leaflet produced by the manufacturer.
- **Osteoporosis prophylaxis** should be considered in people requiring frequent courses of oral corticosteroids.

Spacer devices

- **Clean spacers no more than once a month** (more frequent cleaning will build up static affecting their performance) — wash in mild detergent, rinse, and then allow to air dry.

Antibiotics

- **Women taking combined hormonal contraceptives:** non-enzyme-inducing broad-spectrum antibiotics — use additional contraception during the short course and for 7 days afterwards. Miss out the pill-free interval if the 7 days runs beyond the end of the packet, and the inactive tablets in the case of an every-day (ED) preparation.
  - **Pregnant women:** amoxicillin is not known to be harmful and may be the preferred option. Tetracyclines are contraindicated in pregnancy and should never be used.
  - **Breastfeeding:** amoxicillin and co-amoxiclav may be the preferred options. Tetracyclines are best avoided.
- **Renal impairment:** doxycycline may be the preferred option as no dosage adjustment or monitoring is required. Oxytetracycline is contraindicated in people with kidney disease. All other recommended antibiotics need to be carefully monitored.
- **Liver impairment:** amoxicillin may be the preferred option. Other agents should be avoided or need careful monitoring.
- **Tetracyclines:** contraindicated also in porphyria and children aged under 12 years. They may cause photosensitivity reactions (avoid exposure to sunlight or sun lamps).
- **Co-amoxiclav:** the Committee on Safety of Medicines has advised that the incidence of cholestatic jaundice (usually self-limiting) is about six times greater than with amoxicillin alone, and people at greatest risk include those over 65 years old and men. Do not prescribe co-amoxiclav to people with a history of co-amoxiclav-associated or penicillin-associated jaundice or hepatic dysfunction [BNF 47, 2004]. Co-amoxiclav should be considered when resistant beta-lactamase-producing strains are known or might be present.

ollow-up advice

Depending on the severity of the illness, consider reviewing the person within 24 hours, either by telephone or in person, to assess response to treatment. If the person fails to respond or has frequent exacerbations, sputum culture may be useful to determine whether resistant organisms are present.

hould I refer or investigate?

efer?

dmit

ggested criteria for admission are:

Severe breathlessness
Confusion
Cyanosis
Worsening peripheral oedema
Impaired consciousness
The person is unable to cope at home
General condition is poor or is deteriorating
Activity level is poor, or the person is confined to bed
The person lives alone
The person is on long-term oxygen therapy
The exacerbation was of rapid onset
Significant comorbidity is present

rgently refer

eferral guidelines for suspected lung cancer [NICE, 2005] **commend:**

Urgent referral for chest X-ray (the report should be returned within 5 days) for people with any of the following:

- Haemoptysis
- Unexplained or persistent (more than 3 weeks):
  - Chest and/or shoulder pain
  - Dyspnoea
  - Weight loss
  - Chest signs
  - Hoarseness
  - Finger clubbing
  - Cervical or supraclavicular lymphadenopathy
  - Cough
  - Features suggestive of metastasis from a lung cancer (e.g. brain, bone, liver, or skin)
- Underlying chronic respiratory problems with unexplained changes in existing symptoms

Urgent referral* for people with:

- Persistent haemoptysis in smokers/ex-smokers aged 40 years of age and older
- A chest X-ray suggestive/suspicious of lung cancer (including pleural effusion and slowly resolving consolidation)
- A normal chest X-ray where there is a high suspicion of lung cancer
- A history of asbestos exposure and recent onset chest pain, shortness of breath or unexplained systemic symptoms where a chest X-ray indicates pleural effusion, pleural mass or any suspicious lung pathology

Immediate referral* for people with:

- Signs of superior vena caval obstruction (swelling of face/neck with fixed elevation of jugular venous pressure)
- Stridor

To a team specialising in the management of lung cancer, epending upon local arrangements.

Patient information leaflets

The following PILs are available at www.prodigy.nhs.uk

- British Lung Foundation
- COPD (Chronic Obs. Pulmonary Disease)
- Medicines - Name Changes of Medicines
- Quit (help to stop smoking)
- Smoking - The Facts
- Smoking - Tips on Stopping

Shared decision making

- For a flare-up of COPD:
  - **Inhalers:** increase the dose and frequency of your bronchodilator inhaler.
  - **A short course of steroid tablets** may be prescribed if you are more breathless than usual.
  - **Antibiotics** may be needed, especially if your sputum is more yellow or green than usual.
- See a doctor if your symptoms get worse or do not improve.
- Have you been immunized against 'flu and pneumococcal infection?
- If you are still smoking, would you like advice or help to stop?

Drug rationale

The choice of antibiotic is based on recommendations for the empirical treatment for acute bronchitis by the Health Protection Agency (HPA) and by the BNF (Table 1, Chapter 5: Infections) [HPA, 2003; BNF 47, 2004]. These also reflect the recommendations made by the Standing Medical Advisory Committee [DH and SMAC, 1998].

Drugs not included

- **Macrolides** are not recommended for treating exacerbations. Erythromycin has only weak activity against *Haemophilus influenzae* (one of the most common pathogens implicated in exacerbations of COPD) and there are growing concerns about the build-up of resistance to clarithromycin and azithromycin [McNulty, Personal Communication, 2004]. Also, all macrolides concentrate intracellularly and *H influenzae* is an extracellular pathogen.
- **Ampicillin** has a spectrum of activity similar to that of amoxicillin, but it is poorly absorbed (less than 50% of the dose is absorbed when food is in the stomach), has a higher incidence of associated diarrhoea than amoxicillin, and requires more frequent dosing.
- **Phenoxymethylpenicillin** has poor activity against *H influenzae* [Finch et al, 2003] and *Moraxella catarrhalis*. It is therefore not included for empirical treatment.
- **Flucloxacillin** has not been specifically offered as a prescription in this scenario, but it is recommended if a staphylococcal infection is suspected (e.g. secondary infection after influenza or measles) [BNF 47, 2004].
- **Oral cephalosporins** are not included for empirical treatment. They should be reserved for use specifically when sensitivity is known and (depending upon local policy) to prevent resistance developing [DH and SMAC, 1998].
- **Quinolones** are not included; trials have found that they demonstrate no clinical superiority over other antibiotics, and they should be reserved for use when sensitivities are known [DH and SMAC, 1998; MeReC, 1998a; SIGN, 2002].
- **Tetracyclines** other than oxytetracycline and doxycycline are not included. The spectrum of activity of the tetracyclines is very similar [Finch et al, 2003], and these two appear to be most commonly recommended.

- **Trimethoprim** is reserved for use when sensitivities are known. It generally has poor activity against *Streptococcus pneumoniae* and *M catarrhalis* [McNulty, Personal Communication, 2004].
- **Dry-powder inhalers are not included.** They should be reserved for people who are unable to use pMDIs effectively after receiving appropriate instruction.
- **Long-acting bronchodilators** are not included as they are not licensed for the relief of acute bronchospasm.
- **Oral corticosteroids** other than prednisolone are not routinely used in the treatment of exacerbations of COPD [National Collaborating Centre for Chronic Conditions, 2004].
- **Inhaled corticosteroids** are not included as their use in the short term has not been found to be beneficial. Whether their use for 6 months or longer offers clinical benefits remains inconclusive; however, they may predispose to adverse effects including osteoporosis, skin bruising, and oral candidiasis [Kerstjens and Postma, 2003].

Drugs included

- **Short-acting beta$_2$-agonists: salbutamol and terbutaline** CFC-free pressurized metered dose inhalers (pMDIs) are included as well as salbutamol breath-actuated pMDIs and terbutaline turbohaler. Short-acting beta$_2$-agonists may offer some relief as they are fast-acting [McCrory and Brown, 2004], and prescriptions are included for either initiation or repeat purposes.
- **Short-acting anticholinergic: ipratropium (CFC)-free pMDI** is included. Ipratropium is also a fast-acting bronchodilator and has also been found to provide some clinical benefit in exacerbations of COPD [McCrory and Brown, 2004].
- **Spacer devices** are included for use with bronchodilators:
  - AeroChamber® Plus is compatible with Airomir® and Salbulin® CFC-free MDIs
  - Volumatic® is compatible with Ventolin® CFC-free MDI
  - Nebuhaler® is compatible with Terbutaine® MDI
- Note: switching between different spacer types can affect the deposition characteristics of the inhaled drug. The same may apply if there is a change in the inhaler device used, but no change in spacer. This change of device may alter clinical response to the inhaled drug [NHS Executive, 1998].
- **Oral corticosteroid: prednisolone** has predominately glucocortocoid activity and is the corticosteroid most commonly used orally for exacerbations of COPD. A dose of 30 mg daily for 7–14 days is recommended [National Collaborating Centre for Chronic Conditions, 2004].
- **Amoxicillin** is included for empirical treatment, as it is active against *Streptococcus pneumoniae* and *Haemophilus influenzae* (two of the most common respiratory pathogens) [Finch et al, 2003].
- **Doxycycline** is included for empirical treatment, as it has a broad spectrum of activity against respiratory pathogens (it covers most typical and atypical pathogens) and can be given once a day [Finch et al, 2003]. It is also an option for people with penicillin allergy.
- **Oxytetracycline** has a spectrum of activity similar to that of doxycycline, but must be taken four times a day [Finch et al, 2003]. Oxytetracycline is also an alternative option for people with penicillin allergy.
- **Co-amoxiclav** is included as an option for second-line treatment when there is no response to the initial antibiotic [DTB, 1998]. Many bacterial beta-lactamases are inhibited by clavulanic acid, and a mixture of this with amoxicillin results in the antibiotic's being effecti against most penicillinase-producing organisms.

Prescriptions

Bronchodilator inhalers +/- spacer devices

Salbutamol 100mcg MDI: 1 to 2 puffs up to 4 times a da

- Age from 16 years onwards
- Salbutamol 100mcg CFC-free inhaler. Inhale one to tw puffs up to four times a day, when required to relieve breathlessness; supply 1 200 dose inhaler; NHS Cost £1.86.

Airomir 100mcg MDI: 1 to 2 puffs up to 4 times a day

- Age from 16 years onwards
- Airomir 100mcg CFC-free inhaler. Inhale one to two puffs up to four times a day, when required to relieve breathlessness; supply 1 200 dose inhaler; NHS Cost £1.97.

Salamol 100mcg MDI: 1 to 2 puffs up to 4 times a day

- Age from 16 years onwards
- Salamol 100mcg CFC-free inhaler. Inhale one to two puffs up to four times a day using the spacer, when required to relieve breathlessness; supply 1 200 dose inhaler; NHS Cost £1.00.

Ventolin 100mcg MDI: 1 to 2 puffs up to 4 times a day

- Age from 16 years onwards
- Ventolin 100mcg CFC-free inhaler. Inhale one to two puffs up to four times a day, when required to relieve breathlessness; supply 1 200 dose inhaler; NHS Cost £2.30.

Terbutaline 250mcg MDI: 1 to 2 puffs up to 4 times a da

- Age from 16 years onwards
- Terbutaline 250mcg inhaler. Inhale one to two puffs u to four times a day, when required to relieve breathlessness; supply 1 400 dose inhaler; NHS Cost £5.84.

Ipratropium 20mcg MDI: 1 to 2 puffs up to 4 times a day

- Age from 16 years onwards
- Ipratropium 20mcg inhaler. Inhale one to two puffs up to four times a day, when required to relieve breathlessness; supply 1 200 dose inhaler; NHS Cost £4.21.

AeroChamber Plus spacer: for use with Airomir/Atroven

- Age from 16 years onwards
- AeroChamber Plus spacer device. Use to aid inhalation supply 1 spacer; NHS Cost £4.36.

Nebuhaler spacer: for use with Bricanyl

- Age from 16 years onwards
- Nebuhaler spacer device. Use to aid inhalation; supply spacer; NHS Cost £4.28.

Volumatic spacer: for use with Salamol/Ventolin

- Age from 16 years onwards
- Volumatic spacer device. Use to aid inhalation; supply spacer; NHS Cost £2.75.

1st-line antibiotic for 7 days

Amoxicillin 500mg three times a day

- Age from 16 years onwards
- Amoxicillin 500mg capsules. Take one capsule three times a day for 7 days; supply 21 capsules; NHS Cost £1.85.

Doxycycline 100mg once a day

- Age from 16 years onwards
- Doxycycline 100mg capsules. Take TWO capsules now and then take ONE capsule once a day for the next 6 days; supply 8 capsules; NHS Cost £2.47.

ytetracycline 250mg four times a day
Age from 16 years onwards
Oxytetracycline 250mg tablets. Take one tablet four times a day for 7 days; supply 28 tablets;
NHS Cost £0.81.

nd-line antibiotic for 7 days

xycycline 100mg once a day – IF not already tried
Age from 16 years onwards
Doxycycline 100mg capsules. Take TWO capsules now and then take ONE capsule once a day for the next 6 days; supply 8 capsules; NHS Cost £2.47.

ytetracycline 250mg four times a day -IF not already ed
Age from 16 years onwards
Oxytetracycline 250mg tablets. Take one tablet four times a day for 7 days; supply 28 tablets;
NHS Cost £0.81.

ytetracycline 500mg four times a day -IF not already ed
Age from 16 years onwards
Oxytetracycline 250mg tablets. Take two tablets four times a day for 7 days; supply 56 tablets;
NHS Cost £1.62.

-amoxiclav 500/125mg three times a day
Age from 16 years onwards
Co-amoxiclav 625mg tablets. Take one tablet three times a day for 7 days; supply 21 tablets;
NHS Cost £15.72.

rednisolone tablets

C prednisolone: 30mg each morning for 7 days
Age from 16 years onwards
Prednisolone 5mg e/c tablets. Take six tablets each morning (as a single dose) for 7 days; supply 42 tablets;
NHS Cost £0.71.

C prednisolone: 30mg each morning for 10 days
Age from 16 years onwards
Prednisolone 5mg e/c tablets. Take six tablets each morning (as a single dose) for 10 days; supply 60 tablets;
NHS Cost £1.02.

C prednisolone: 30mg each morning for 14 days
Age from 16 years onwards
Prednisolone 5mg e/c tablets. Take six tablets each morning (as a single dose) for 14 days; supply 84 tablets;
NHS Cost £1.42.

ain prednisolone: 30mg each morning for 7 days
Age from 16 years onwards
Prednisolone 5mg tablets. Take six tablets each morning (as a single dose) for 7 days; supply 42 tablets;
NHS Cost £0.45.

ain prednisolone: 30mg each morning for 10 days
Age from 16 years onwards
Prednisolone 5mg tablets. Take six tablets each morning (as a single dose) for 10 days; supply 60 tablets;
NHS Cost £1.46.

ain prednisolone: 30mg each morning for 14 days
Age from 16 years onwards
Prednisolone 5mg tablets. Take six tablets each morning (as a single dose) for 14 days; supply 84 tablets;
NHS Cost £1.02.

Oxygen therapy

Which therapy?

Inappropriate oxygen therapy in people with COPD may cause respiratory depression.

- **Oxygen therapy should only be prescribed after specialist assessment.**
- **The following people should be referred to a specialist for consideration of long-term oxygen therapy (LTOT):**
  - All people with severe airflow obstruction (FEV_1 <30% predicted)
  - People with cyanosis
  - People with polycythaemia
  - People with peripheral oedema
  - People with a raised jugular venous pressure (JVP)
  - People with oxygen saturation =<92% breathing air
  - In addition, consider referral of people with moderate airflow obstruction (FEV_1 30–49% predicted).
- **LTOT is not recommended for people unwilling to stop smoking.** There is a substantial fire hazard, and someone who smokes while taking LTOT may develop severe facial burns.
- Oxygen concentrators should be used to supply the fixed supply of oxygen for LTOT.
- **Ambulatory oxygen therapy,** for use during exercise or when outdoors, may benefit some people but should be prescribed only after specialist assessment. Ambulatory oxygen therapy is mainly indicated for the following:
  - Someone on LTOT who is mobile and wishes to continue oxygen therapy outside the house.
  - Someone who has exercise desaturation, and has been shown to have an improvement in exercise capacity or dyspnoea with oxygen.
  - Someone with severe hypoxaemia who is taking LTOT for up to 24 hours daily and is mainly housebound, but who may need occasional supplemental oxygen in order to leave the house.

Prescribing domiciliary oxygen

- **Cylinders are supplied by pharmacy contractors;** health authorities have lists of such pharmacies.
- **Concentrators are available direct from suppliers.**
- **In general, someone requiring oxygen intermittently will use a cylinder, and someone requiring LTOT will use a concentrator.** It is more cost-effective to provide a concentrator for someone who is using the equivalent of 21 cylinders or more per month (i.e. 8 hours per day).
- **Cylinders and masks are still charged to GPs** via the prescription and Prescription Pricing Authority. The cost of cylinder rental, purchase of sets, and delivery fees is handled by local agreement between the health authority and the local pharmaceutical committee.

Prescribing oxygen cylinders and apparatus

- **Oxygen cylinders** are prescribed as a cylinder with a set.
- **Only 1360-litre cylinders may be prescribed,** usually in multiples of three. If support is not available at home to change the head, single-cylinder prescriptions may be needed.
- **Oxygen flow can be adjusted,** as the cylinders are equipped with an oxygen flow meter with medium (2 litres/minute) and high (4 litres/minute) settings.
- **Constant-performance masks** provide a nearly constant supply of oxygen irrespective of the person's breathing pattern.
- **A nasal cannula** for use with an oxygen cylinder cannot be obtained via a prescription.
- **The oxygen flow rate should be set at the most appropriate level tailored to the patient's requirements.** The most economical oxygen flow rate is 2 litres/minute (the medium setting on the control head).
- **Portable oxygen cylinder:** local arrangements differ, and information can be obtained from health authority advisors and pharmacy contractors.

Prescribing arrangements for concentrators

- Prescribe on an FP10 with any accessories (face mask or nasal cannula).
- Specify amount of oxygen required (hours per day) and flow rate.
- A back-up oxygen set and cylinder should be prescribed at the same time for new patients. People transferring from the cylinder system will have to return all the cylinders and equipment to their pharmacy contractor when the concentrator company takes over their supply.
- Inform supplier by telephone (see telephone numbers below by your NHS region).
- Inform the patient that the supplier will be in contact to make arrangements and that the prescription form is to be given to the person who installs the concentrator.
- At present, concentrators and associated items are funded by health authorities.

Telephone numbers for concentrators

- **Eastern, North Western, London North, North Wales, West Midlands:** De Vilbiss Medquip Ltd. To order, telephone 0800 020202.
- **London South (includes Kent, Surrey, and Sussex), South Western:** BOC Gases. To order, telephone 0800 136603.
- **Central and South Wales, Northern, Yorkshire (South and West) and Humberside:** Oxygen Therapy Co. Ltd. To order, telephone 0800 373580.
- **Scotland:** refer the person for assessment by a respiratory consultant. If the need for a concentrator is confirmed, the consultant will arrange for the concentrator to be provided through the Common Services Agency.

Practical prescribing points

For further information, please see the *Medicines Compendium* (www.medicines.org.uk) or the *British National Formulary* (www.bnf.org).

Follow-up advice

- Follow-up should be tailored to the individual.

Should I refer or investigate?

Refer?

- Specialist assessment is required before making a decision to initiate oxygen therapy.
- The following people should be referred to a specialist for consideration of long-term oxygen therapy (LTOT):
  - All people with severe airflow obstruction (FEV_1 <30% predicted)
  - People with cyanosis
  - People with polycythaemia
  - People with peripheral oedema
  - People with a raised jugular venous pressure (JVP)
  - People with oxygen saturation =<92% breathing air
  - In addition, consider referral of people with moderate airflow obstruction (FEV_1 30–49% predicted)

Patient information leaflets

The following PILs are available at www.prodigy.nhs.uk

- British Lung Foundation
- COPD (Chronic Obs. Pulmonary Disease)
- Quit (help to stop smoking)
- Smoking - The Facts
- Smoking - Tips on Stopping

Shared decision making

- **Oxygen** helps some people who have COPD (chronic obstructive pulmonary disease).
- Oxygen is only prescribed after assessment by a specialist.
- If you require long-term oxygen therapy, you should u oxygen for at least 15 hours a day, including at night. You are likely to get most benefit if you use it for 20 hours per day.
- Oxygen comes in cylinders or concentrators. These wi be delivered to your home.
- You must not smoke if you use oxygen therapy. Smok next to oxygen is very dangerous.

Drug rationale

Drugs not included

- **Humidifiers** have not been included because there is n evidence that humidification is necessary when oxygen given by nasal cannulae at flows less than 5.0 litres/mi [American Thoracic Society, 1995].
- **Masks other than constant-performance types** providi 28% oxygen are not offered, since their availability through FP10 is variable and needs to be checked with the local health authority.

Drugs included

- **Domiciliary oxygen** is provided by either cylinders or concentrators, chosen according to usage.
- You may need to edit the prescriptions locally.
- **Only constant-flow masks** are included in these prescriptions.

Prescriptions

New patient – Oxygen cylinder with oxygen mask

New patient – 1 oxygen cylinder + set + mask

- Age from 16 years onwards
- Oxygen BP 1360litres cylinder. Use as directed by you doctor; supply 1 cylinders; NHS Cost £7.77.
- Intersurgical 28%/010 oxy.mask. Use as directed by your doctor; supply 1 mask; NHS Cost £0.97.
- Oxygen giving set. Use as directed by your doctor; supply 1 giving set.

New patient – 3 oxygen cylinders + set + mask

- Age from 16 years onwards
- Oxygen BP 1360litres cylinder. Use as directed by you doctor; supply 3 cylinders; NHS Cost £23.31.
- Intersurgical 28%/010 oxy.mask. Use as directed by your doctor; supply 1 mask; NHS Cost £0.97.
- Oxygen giving set. Use as directed by your doctor; supply 1 giving set.

New patient – 6 oxygen cylinders + set + mask

- Age from 16 years onwards
- Oxygen BP 1360litres cylinder. Use as directed by you doctor; supply 6 cylinders; NHS Cost £46.62.
- Intersurgical 28%/010 oxy.mask. Use as directed by your doctor; supply 1 mask; NHS Cost £0.97.
- Oxygen giving set. Use as directed by your doctor; supply 1 giving set.

New patient – 12 oxygen cylinders + set + mask

- Age from 16 years onwards
- Oxygen BP 1360litres cylinder. Use as directed by you doctor; supply 12 cylinders; NHS Cost £93.24.
- Intersurgical 28%/010 oxy.mask. Use as directed by your doctor; supply 1 mask; NHS Cost £0.97.

Oxygen giving set. Use as directed by your doctor; supply 1 giving set.

Oxygen concentrator with accessories

Concentrator with nasal cannula + oxygen cylinder + set

Age from 20 years onwards

Oxygen Concentrator 1. Oxygen required for ______hours per day at flow rate ______litres per minute. Supply with nasal cannula; supply 1 concentrator.

Oxygen BP 1360litres cylinder. Use as directed by your doctor; supply 1 cylinders; NHS Cost £7.77.

Oxygen giving set. Use as directed by your doctor; supply 1 giving set.

Oxygen nasal cannula. Use as directed by your doctor; supply nasal cannula.

Concentrator with mask + oxygen cylinder + set

Age from 20 years onwards

Oxygen Concentrator 1. Oxygen required for ______ hours per day at flow rate ______litres per minute; supply 1 concentrator.

Oxygen BP 1360litres cylinder. Use as directed by your doctor; supply 1 cylinders; NHS Cost £7.77.

Oxygen giving set. Use as directed by your doctor; supply 1 giving set.

Intersurgical 28%/010 oxy.mask. Use as directed by your doctor; supply 1 mask; NHS Cost £0.97.

Concentrator with nasal cannula

Age from 20 years onwards

Oxygen Concentrator 1. Oxygen required for ______hours per day at flow rate ______litres per minute. Supply with nasal cannula; supply 1 concentrator.

Oxygen nasal cannula. Use as directed by your doctor; supply 1 nasal cannula.

Concentrator with mask

Age from 20 years onwards

Oxygen Concentrator 1. Oxygen required for ______ hours per day at flow rate ______litres per minute; supply 1 concentrator.

Intersurgical 28%/010 oxy.mask. Use as directed by your doctor; supply 1 mask; NHS Cost £0.97.

Replacement oxygen cylinder or mask

oxygen cylinder

Age from 20 years onwards

Oxygen BP 1360litres cylinder. Use as directed by your doctor; supply 1 cylinders; NHS Cost £7.77.

3 oxygen cylinders

Age from 20 years onwards

Oxygen BP 1360litres cylinder. Use as directed by your doctor; supply 3 cylinders; NHS Cost £23.31.

6 oxygen cylinders

Age from 20 years onwards

Oxygen BP 1360litres cylinder. Use as directed by your doctor; supply 6 cylinders; NHS Cost £46.62.

12 oxygen cylinders

Age from 20 years onwards

Oxygen BP 1360litres cylinder. Use as directed by your doctor; supply 12 cylinders; NHS Cost £93.24.

Mask

Age from 20 years onwards

Intersurgical 28%/010 oxy.mask. Use as directed by your doctor; supply 1 mask; NHS Cost £0.97.

Extended Information

Background information

- What is it? p.339
- How common is it? p.339
- How do I know my patient has it? p.339
- What else might it be? p.340
- Complications and prognosis p.340

C

What is it?

- **Chronic obstructive pulmonary disease (COPD) is characterized by airflow obstruction.** The airflow obstruction is usually progressive, not fully reversible, and does not change markedly over several months.
  - Airflow obstruction is defined as a reduced FEV_1 and a reduced FEV_1/FVC ratio; such that FEV_1 is less than 80% predicted, and FEV_1/FVC is less than 0.7.
  - The airflow obstruction is due to a combination of airway and parenchymal damage.
  - The damage is the result of chronic inflammation that differs from that seen in asthma, and which is usually the result of smoking.
  - Significant airflow obstruction may be present before the person is aware of it.
  - COPD produces symptoms and disability and impairs quality of life in ways that may respond to treatments that have little or no impact on the degree of airflow obstruction.
  - COPD is the preferred term for chronic bronchitis, emphysema, or chronic obstructive airways disease.
- **Smoking is the major risk factor for the development of COPD.** About 15% of one-pack-per-day and 25% of two-pack-per-day cigarette smokers go on to develop COPD if they continue their habit [Kanner, 1996]. Considerable variability in risk from smoking suggests that additional environmental factors, genetic factors, and occupational exposures contribute to the impact of smoking on the development of airflow obstruction [Fletcher and Peto, 1977; Canadian Thoracic Society Workshop Group, 1992; Silverman and Speizer, 1996].
- The only other risk factor of comparable importance for the individual is homozygous $alpha_1$-antitrypsin deficiency, but this accounts for less than 1% of COPD cases [American Thoracic Society, 1995].
- **Exacerbation of COPD** is usually diagnosed when a person with COPD presents with worsening cough, increased breathlessness, increased sputum volume, and change in sputum colour.
- **Cor pulmonale** is right heart failure secondary to lung disease. It is characterized by fluid retention, peripheral oedema, and raised venous pressure in people with COPD who have no other cause for the ventricular dysfunction.

[NICE, 2004]

How common is it?

- In the United Kingdom nearly 900,000 people have been diagnosed as having COPD. It is thought that half as many again have COPD without its having been diagnosed.

[National Collaborating Centre for Chronic Conditions, 2004]

How do I know my patient has it?

The diagnosis of COPD depends initially on considering it in a person with breathlessness or cough. There is no single diagnostic test for COPD — the diagnosis is made by clinical judgement based on a combination of history, examination, and confirmation of the presence of airflow obstruction using spirometry.

History

- Early in the disease, there may be minimal or no symptoms. As COPD progresses, symptoms vary between different people; individuals may make limitations to their lifestyle, making symptoms less apparent. Breathlessness is the most important symptom in most people with COPD.
- A diagnosis of COPD should be considered in smokers who present with one or more of the following symptoms: (D)
  - Exertional breathlessness
  - Chronic cough
  - Regular sputum production
  - Frequent 'winter bronchitis'
  - Wheeze
- Other symptoms which may be present include: (D)
  - Weight loss
  - Effort intolerance
  - Waking at night
  - Ankle swelling
  - Fatigue
- The following symptoms are uncommon in COPD; their presence should lead to reconsideration of the diagnosis or the presence of coexisting pathology: (D)
  - Chest pain
  - Haemoptysis
- An occupational history should be taken.

Examination

- In some people with COPD, examination may be normal.
- There is no individual sign that is diagnostic of COPD.
- The following signs may be present:
  - Breathlessness
  - Cachexia
  - Cyanosis
  - Hyperinflated chest
  - Tar staining of fingers
  - Paradoxical movement of lower ribs
  - Peripheral oedema
  - Prolonged expiration
  - Purse lip breathing
  - Raised jugular venous pulse (JVP)
  - Reduced crico-sternal distance
  - Use of accessory muscles of respiration
  - Reduced cardiac dullness on percussion
  - Wheeze or quiet breath sounds

Investigations

Spirometry

- **Demonstration of the presence of airflow obstruction by spirometry is vital for the correct diagnosis of COPD.**
  - Airflow obstruction is defined as a reduced FEV_1 and a reduced FEV_1/FVC ratio; such that FEV_1 is less than 80% of the predicted value, and FEV_1/FVC is less than 0.7.
  - Predicted normal values of FEV_1 and FVC depend on the person's age, height, and sex. These normal values, however, have not been validated in the elderly, or in black and Asian people; this may lead to under-diagnosis in these populations. A calculator to compare spirometry with normal values can be found at www.jhucct.com/CCT/calculate.htm.
- **The severity of airflow limitation in COPD can be graded as follows: (D)**
  - Mild: FEV_1 50–80% of predicted value
  - Moderate: FEV_1 30–49% of predicted value
  - Severe: FEV_1 <30% of predicted value
- Spirometry should be performed at the time of diagnosi It should also be performed to reconsider the diagnosis a person responds exceptionally well to treatment (D).
- Spirometry contributes to the assessment of the severity of COPD, and predicts prognosis; however, it poorly predicts disability and quality of life in people with COPD.
- **Peak expiratory flow (PEF) is not recommended for the diagnosis or assessment of people with COPD,** as it may significantly underestimate the degree of airflow obstruction.

Radiology

- At diagnosis, all people should undergo chest X-ray (D) This may show hyperinflation, flat hemidiaphragms, reduced peripheral vascular markings, and bullae. Chest X-ray also helps to exclude other serious lung patholog such as lung cancer, which may have precipitated the presentation [British Thoracic Society, 1997].

Full blood count

- To check for anaemia or polycythaemia, the latter indicative of chronic hypoxia (D).

Body mass index

- Body mass index (BMI) should be calculated (D).

Serum alpha$_1$-antitrypsin

- Alpha$_1$-antitrypsin deficiency should be considered in the following cases:
  - COPD in a non-smoker
  - Early onset of COPD
  - Family history of alpha$_1$-antitrypsin deficiency, or of early-onset COPD

[National Collaborating Centre for Chronic Conditions, 2004; NICE, 2004]

What else might it be?

It is important to realise that whilst these conditions may mimic COPD, they may also coexist in someone with COPD.

- Anaemia
- Asbestosis
- Asthma
- Bronchiectasis
- Bronchopulmonary dysplasia
- Congestive cardiac failure
- Fibrosing alveolitis
- Lung carcinoma
- Obliterative bronchiolitis
- Pneumoconiosis

[National Collaborating Centre for Chronic Conditions, 2004]

Complications and prognosis

- **Morbidity from COPD is high:**
  - Up to one in eight hospital admissions may be due to COPD. Admissions are more common in the winter. The mean length of inpatient stay in England in 2001–2 was 9.1 days.
  - In primary care, consultation rates for COPD are at least twice as high as for angina. An average GP's list will contain 200 people with COPD (some of these will be undiagnosed).
- **Exacerbations of COPD requiring hospital admission are associated with an inpatient mortality rate of 3–4%,** which increases to 11–24% for those who require treatment in an intensive care unit [Bach et al, 2001].
- Of people admitted to hospital with an exacerbation, 34% were readmitted and 14% died within 3 months [National Collaborating Centre for Chronic Conditions 2004].
- **The true mortality rate due to COPD is difficult to quantify,** as many people with COPD die with the

disease rather than because of it. In 1999 there were approximately 30,000 deaths due to COPD in the UK (5.9% of all male deaths, and 4.3% of all female deaths). Mortality rates in men have fallen over the last 30 years; in women they have increased slightly over the last 20 years.

Predictors of mortality in people with COPD are:

- Advancing age
- Severity of airflow obstruction
- Severity of hypoxaemia
- Presence of hypercapnia [Burrows and Earle, 1969; British Thoracic Society, 1997; DTB, 1997]

Five-year survival from diagnosis is 78% in men and 72% in women with mild disease. This falls to 30% in men and 24% in women with severe disease.

In the UK, the mean age of death of people with severe COPD is 74.2 years; for people with mild COPD it is 77.2 years; and for people without COPD it is 78.3 years.

[National Collaborating Centre for Chronic Conditions, 2004]

Management issues

Prevention p.341
Compliance p.341
Spirometry and reversibility testing p.341
Delivery systems for inhaled treatment p.341
Stable COPD p.342
Exacerbation of COPD p.344
Pulmonary rehabilitation p.345
Bronchopulmonary hygiene therapy p.345
Immunization p.345
Mucolytic therapy p.345
Therapy not recommended p.345
Medicines management p.345

Prevention

Stopping smoking is a priority for all people with COPD, regardless of their age, and has been shown to reduce the rate of decline of FEV_1 in people with COPD to that of non-smokers [Fletcher and Peto, 1977; Kanner, 1996; British Thoracic Society, 1997]. For more detailed information, see the PRODIGY guidance on *Smoking cessation*.

Compliance

Poor compliance with medication is common in people with COPD, with about half underusing their maintenance medication, and a similar proportion overusing their medication at times of exacerbation (particularly serious if the person is on theophylline) [Canadian Thoracic Society Workshop Group, 1992].

Spirometry and reversibility testing

Routine reversibility testing is no longer recommended (D). It is the spirometric response to bronchodilators or corticosteroids. It has been advocated in the past both as a diagnostic test for COPD and also to assess the response to treatment. This is now considered unnecessary, and may even be misleading:

- Repeated spirometry can show small spontaneous fluctuations (B).
- Reversibility testing performed on different occasions can be inconsistent, and is not reproducible (B).
- The response to long-term therapy is not predicted by acute reversibility testing (A).

Reversibility testing was previously considered a useful test to diagnose between asthma and COPD. This is no longer recommended; the two diseases can usually be distinguished on the basis of history and examination (D). If diagnostic doubt remains, or both COPD and asthma are present, the following findings on reversibility testing should be used to help identify asthma: (D)

- A large (>400 ml) response to bronchodilators.
- A large (>400 ml) response to 30 mg oral prednisolone daily for 2 weeks.

- The place of spirometry in the management of diagnosed COPD is in the reconsideration of the diagnosis if an individual reports a marked improvement in symptoms in response to inhaled treatment. In this situation, a return of spirometry to normal (or a marked improvement) with treatment effectively excludes a diagnosis of COPD.

C

Delivery systems for inhaled treatment

- Most people with COPD, regardless of their age, can be taught adequate inhaler technique. A small number of people, however, with significant cognitive impairment, cannot use any form of inhaler device.
- For most people, an individual assessment will enable the choice of the most suitable delivery system to be made. This assessment may best be carried out by a member of the primary health care team with particular skills and experience in the management of COPD.
- Reassessment of the person's use of the delivery system is of utmost importance. Many people who acquired satisfactory technique initially have been shown a month later to have unsatisfactory technique. This is particularly true in the elderly.

Inhalers

- For most people with COPD, bronchodilator or corticosteroid therapy is best administered using a hand-held inhaler, including a spacer if appropriate (D).
- If the person is unable to use a particular inhaler, an alternative should be found (D).
- Inhalers should only be prescribed after the individual has been taught how to use it and has been shown to have satisfactory technique (D).
- Inhaler technique should be reassessed regularly. If technique has become unsatisfactory, further instruction is necessary (D).

Spacers

- A standard metered dose inhaler (MDI) is rarely appropriate for elderly people when used without a large-volume spacer. The spacer improves acquisition and retention of technique; it also allows carers to help people with cognitive impairment or with physical problems affecting their hands (and thus impairing use of MDIs).
- Use of a large-volume spacer with an MDI requires less inspiratory co-ordination, improves lung deposition of the active drug, and reduces oropharyngeal deposition [MeReC, 1995; McEvoy and Niewoehner, 1997].
- Large-volume spacers have been shown to reduce systemic absorption of inhaled corticosteroids.
- The spacer must be compatible with the person's MDI (D). Note: more than one spacer may be required to cope with different inhalers.
- Recommendations for spacer use are: (D)
  - Administer the drug by repeated single actuations of the MDI into the spacer, each actuation followed by inhalation.
  - There should be minimal delay between actuation and inhalation.
  - Tidal breathing can be used as it is as effective as single breaths.

- Spacers should be cleaned no more than monthly, as more frequent cleaning affects performance due to build up of static. They should be cleaned with water and washing-up liquid and allowed to dry in air. The mouthpiece should be wiped clean of detergent before use (D).

Nebulizers

- Nebulizers are not an answer for those people unable to acquire or retain satisfactory inhaler technique — loading and operating the nebulizer requires physical and cognitive skills. A healthcare professional should assess the likelihood of whether a person unable to use an inhaler would be able to use a nebulizer. Like spacers, however, nebulizers have the advantage that carers can assist in their use.
- Nebulizers should be considered for people with distressing or disabling breathlessness despite maximal inhaled therapy (D).
- Nebulizers should only be continued if one or more of the following occurs: (D)
  - A reduction in symptoms
  - An increase in the ability to undertake activities of daily living
  - An increase in exercise capacity
  - An improvement in lung function
- Nebulizers can use a facemask or a mouthpiece; however, anticholinergics require the use of a mouthpiece (D).
- The performance of nebulizers and compressors varies considerably. It is important to ensure that the nebulizer used complies with European standards EN 13544-1:2001. Complementary equipment including tubing and connectors also needs to comply with European standards; for more details see the following website: www.cenorm.be/cenorm/index.htm.

[National Collaborating Centre for Chronic Conditions, 2004; NICE, 2004]

Stable COPD

Currently recommended therapy steps

- **For people troubled by breathlessness and exercise limitation, the following therapy steps are recommended:**
  - Use a short-acting bronchodilator (beta$_2$-agonist or anticholinergic) as required.
  - If still symptomatic, use one of the following 2 options:
    - Combined therapy with a short-acting beta$_2$-agonist and a short-acting anticholinergic.
    - A long-acting bronchodilator (beta$_2$-agonist or anticholinergic).
  - In moderate or severe COPD, if still symptomatic, consider a trial of combination of a long-acting bronchodilator and inhaled corticosteroid. Discontinue if no benefit after 4 weeks.
  - If still symptomatic, consider adding theophylline.
- **For people troubled by frequent exacerbations, the following therapy steps are recommended:**
  - Optimize bronchodilator therapy with one or more long-acting bronchodilator (beta$_2$-agonist or anticholinergic).
  - If still troubled by frequent exacerbations, add inhaled corticosteroids if FEV$_1$ <50% and two or more exacerbations in a 12-month period.
- **The effectiveness of all of these therapy steps should not be assessed by spirometry alone, but should include:**
  - Improvement in symptoms
  - Improvement in activities of daily living
  - Improvement in exercise capacity
  - Rapidity of symptom relief
- **For all of these steps, stop the therapy if it is ineffective.**

Short-acting beta$_2$-agonists

- Short-acting beta$_2$-agonists act directly on bronchial smooth muscle to cause bronchodilation. They also appear to work by reducing hyperinflation (this probab explains why some people may benefit from them without an improvement in spirometry).
- Their time to peak response is slower than in asthma, and their effects last for up to 4 hours. They can be use on a regular or an as-required basis.
- They have been found to increase FEV$_1$.
- They have been found to reduce daily breathlessness scores, dyspnoea, and fatigue.
- There is no evidence to suggest that regular use of short acting beta$_2$-agonists adversely affects survival of peopl with COPD [American Thoracic Society, 1995; British Thoracic Society, 1997].
- The optimal dose is uncertain. The dose–response curve in COPD is almost flat, and the ratio of adverse effects benefits is such that there is little benefit in giving more than 1 mg of salbutamol per single dose via an MDI in stable COPD. It is likely that daily inhaled salbutamol doses of 200–600 micrograms are needed in stable COPD, depending on the severity of the disease [Kesten and Rebuck, 1989; Ferguson and Cherniack, 1993; Ku et al, 1994].

Short-acting anticholinergics

- Short-acting anticholinergics block cholinergic nerves, which are the main neural bronchoconstrictor pathway in the airways; the resting tone in bronchial smooth muscle is increased in COPD, and anticholinergics caus bronchodilation by blocking this bronchoconstrictor effect. Anticholinergics block muscarinic receptors, and therefore also reduce mucus secretion. They also appea to work by reducing hyperinflation (this probably explains why some people may benefit from them without an improvement in spirometry).
- They have been found to increase FEV$_1$.
- Studies of dyspnoea, walking distance, quality of life, and the need for rescue medication have found conflicting results when short-acting anticholinergics have been compared with placebo.
- Short-acting anticholinergics have a slower onset and longer action than short-acting beta$_2$-agonists, and are less suitable for as-required use. They maintain their effectiveness over years of regular continuous use but, like short-acting beta$_2$-agonists, they have not been shown to reduce the rate of progression of COPD [Chapman, 1991; Kanner, 1996].
- The optimal dose in stable COPD is uncertain. It is likel that daily inhaled ipratropium doses of 40–240 micrograms via an MDI are needed in stable COPD, depending on the severity of the disease [Ferguson and Cherniack, 1993; Ikeda et al, 1996].

Long-acting beta$_2$-agonists

- Long-acting beta$_2$-agonists act directly on bronchial smooth muscle to cause bronchodilation. They also appear to work by reducing hyperinflation (this probabl explains why some people may benefit from them without an improvement in spirometry).
- Their bronchodilator effects are similar to the short-acting beta$_2$-agonists, but their duration of action is around 12 hours.
- They have been found to reduce dyspnoea and sympton scores for COPD when compared with placebo.

In some studies, they have been found to reduce exacerbations; in others, there has been no effect on exacerbation frequency compared with placebo.

Long-acting anticholinergics

Long-acting anticholinergics block cholinergic nerves, which are the main neural bronchoconstrictor pathway in the airways; the resting tone in bronchial smooth muscle is increased in COPD, and anticholinergics cause bronchodilation by blocking this bronchoconstrictor effect. Anticholinergics block muscarinic receptors, and therefore also reduce mucus secretion. They also appear to work by reducing hyperinflation (this probably explains why some people may benefit from them without an improvement in spirometry).

They have been found to increase FEV_1 and FVC compared with placebo and with short-acting anticholinergics.

They have been found to improve dyspnoea compared with placebo and with short-acting anticholinergics.

They have been found to reduce the need for rescue medication compared with placebo and with short-acting anticholinergics.

They have been found to reduce exacerbation frequency compared with placebo and with short-acting anticholinergics.

They have been found to improve wheezing compared with placebo.

They have been found to increase FEV_1 compared with long-acting $beta_2$-agonists; however, there was no difference in dyspnoea, need for rescue medication, or exacerbation frequency when compared with long-acting $beta_2$-agonists.

Theophylline

The mechanism of action of theophylline is unknown, but it is assumed to relax airway smooth muscle. It may also increase diaphragmatic strength and improve mucociliary clearance in COPD. It also improves cardiac output, which may be beneficial in some people with COPD.

There is potential for toxicity and significant drug interaction; theophylline therefore no longer has a place as first-line therapy. Plasma levels of theophylline must be monitored to ensure they remain in the therapeutic range.

Theophylline has been found to increase FEV_1 and FVC compared with placebo.

There was no difference found in wheeze, dyspnoea, walking distance, use of rescue medication, or exacerbation frequency in comparison with placebo.

Inhaled corticosteroids

Inhaled steroids are unlicensed for use in COPD, except in combination products with a long-acting $beta_2$-agonist.

There is little evidence that inhaled corticosteroids have any effects on the inflammatory cells present in COPD — neutrophils, unlike the eosinophils found in asthma, are relatively insensitive to the effects of corticosteroids. In spite of this, up to 70% of people with COPD are prescribed inhaled corticosteroids.

The response to inhaled corticosteroids cannot be predicted by the response to a short course of oral corticosteroids.

Concerning exacerbation frequency:

- They have been found to have no effect on exacerbation rates in mild COPD.
- They have been found to reduce exacerbation rates in more severe COPD (FEV_1 <50%).
- It is therefore recommended that they are prescribed for people with FEV_1 <50% who have two or more exacerbations in a 12-month period.
- Note: the beneficial effects seen in trials may be less than would be seen in clinical practice as trials used carefully selected populations.

- They have been found to have no effect on the rate of decline of FEV_1.
- They have been found to have no effect on symptom scores.
- Large-volume spacers have been shown to reduce systemic absorption of inhaled corticosteroids.
- They have been found to increase the rates of oropharyngeal candidiasis and skin bruising, but not to increase the rates of cataract or fractures.
- Studies looking at bone mineral density have found conflicting results. Certain groups of patients including people over 50 years old as well as peri- or postmenopausal women would need to be assessed for risk of osteoporosis when prescribed high-dose inhaled corticosteroids and be given osteoporosis prophylaxis [DTB, 2000].
- If a trial off inhaled steroids is considered, it is uncertain how best to do this. A recent observational study suggests that rapid withdrawal of inhaled corticosteroids may increase the risk of early exacerbation [Jarad et al, 1999]. People should therefore be carefully monitored when they withdraw from inhaled corticosteroids.

Oral corticosteroids

- There are no long-term studies of the use of oral corticosteroids in COPD.
- Maintenance use of oral corticosteroids is not normally recommended. Some people with severe COPD may require maintenance oral corticosteroids when these cannot be withdrawn following an exacerbation. In these cases, the dosage should be as low as possible.
- People on long-term oral corticosteroids should be monitored for the development of osteoporosis and given appropriate prophylaxis; for further details see the PRODIGY guidance on *Osteoporosis*.

Combination therapy

- As $beta_2$ agonists, anticholinergics, and theophylline affect airway calibre and lung function through different mechanisms, there is a logical argument for combining therapies in people with COPD who are uncontrolled on monotherapy. Combination also gives the potential to reduce adverse effects by avoiding the need to use individual drugs near the top of their dose–response curves.
- The following combinations have been found to be effective in COPD: (**A**)
  - $Beta_2$-agonist and anticholinergic
  - $Beta_2$-agonist and theophylline
  - Anticholinergic and theophylline
  - Long-acting $beta_2$-agonist and inhaled corticosteroid
- The effectiveness of combination therapy should not be assessed by spirometry alone, but should include: (**D**)
  - Improvement in symptoms
  - Improvement in activities of daily living
  - Improvement in exercise capacity
- Combination therapy should be discontinued if there is no benefit after 4 weeks (**D**).

Oxygen therapy

- **Inappropriate oxygen therapy in people with COPD may cause respiratory depression (C).**
- **Oxygen therapy should only be prescribed after specialist assessment.**

- **The following people should be referred to a specialist for consideration of long-term oxygen therapy (LTOT): (D)**
  - All people with severe airflow obstruction (FEV_1 <30% predicted)
  - People with cyanosis
  - People with polycythaemia
  - People with peripheral oedema
  - People with a raised jugular venous pressure
  - People with oxygen saturation =<92% breathing air
  - In addition, consider referral of people with moderate airflow obstruction (FEV_1 30–49% predicted).
- LTOT refers to daily treatment at home with supplemental oxygen for chronic hypoxaemia (PaO_2 <7.3 kPa) sufficient to raise the waking oxygen tension above 8 kPa. LTOT improves survival in people with severe COPD and chronic hypoxaemia. No beneficial effect on quality of life has been shown, although small improvements in sleep quality and mental functioning may occur.
- LTOT is usually given for at least 15 hours per day, including at night, because of the possibility of worsening hypoxaemia during sleep. Greater benefits are seen if it is given for 20 hours per day [Nocturnal Oxygen Therapy Trial Group, 1980; British Thoracic Society, 1997; Royal College of Physicians, 1999].
- **LTOT is not recommended for people unwilling to stop smoking.** There is a substantial fire hazard, and someone who smokes while taking LTOT may develop severe facial burns. Beneficial effects of LTOT, such as a reduction in secondary polycythaemia, may be lessened by the effect of smoking [British Thoracic Society, 1997; Royal College of Physicians, 1999].
- Oxygen concentrators should be used to supply the fixed supply of oxygen for LTOT; they are more economical than cylinders for people requiring LTOT. They are cost-effective for people requiring oxygen for more than 8 hours each day (or 21 cylinders each month) [BNF 47, 2004]. There is no evidence that humidification is necessary when oxygen is given by nasal cannula. Note: it is up to an individual primary care trust to recommend when to switch people to an oxygen concentrator.
- **Ambulatory oxygen therapy,** for use during exercise or when outdoors, may benefit some people but should be prescribed only after specialist assessment. Ambulatory oxygen therapy is mainly indicated for the following:
  - Someone on LTOT who is mobile and wishes to continue oxygen therapy outside the house **(D)**.
  - Someone who has exercise desaturation, and has been shown to have an improvement in exercise capacity or dyspnoea with oxygen **(D)**.
  - Someone with severe hypoxaemia who is taking LTOT for up to 24 hours daily and is mainly housebound, but who may need occasional supplemental oxygen in order to leave the house [Royal College of Physicians, 1999].
- **Short-burst oxygen therapy** should only be considered for episodes of severe breathlessness not relieved by other treatments **(C)**. It should only continue to be prescribed if it improves breathlessness **(D)**.

[National Collaborating Centre for Chronic Conditions, 2004; NICE, 2004]

Exacerbation of COPD

- **There is ongoing uncertainty about the exact role of infection in exacerbations of COPD.** Studies are difficult to interpret, owing to high rates of bacterial colonization of the sputum of people with COPD [Bach et al, 2001]. The usual pathogens isolated are *Haemophilus influenzae* (22%), *Pseudomonas aeruginosa* (15%), *Streptococcus pneumoniae* (10%), and *Moraxella catarrhalis* (9%). Non-pathogenic bacteria account for up to a third of isolates. *Mycoplasma pneumoniae* or *Chlamydia pneumoniae* may precipitate 1–10% of exacerbations. There is increasing evidence that viruses may account for a large number of exacerbations [Bach et al, 2001].
- Non-infectious agents are responsible for some exacerbations, e.g. nitrogen dioxide, particulates, sulphur dioxide, ozone.
- The cause of the exacerbation may be unidentifiable in up to 30% of exacerbations.

[National Collaborating Centre for Chronic Conditions, 2004]

Antibiotics

- **Antibiotics benefit some people with exacerbation of COPD.** People with severe exacerbations are most likel to benefit [Bach et al, 2001]. The National Institute for Clinical Excellence (NICE) recommends that:
  - **Antibiotics** should be used to treat exacerbations if tl sputum is more purulent than usual **(A)**.
  - Exacerbations in which the sputum is not more purulent than usual should only be treated with an antibiotic if there are clinical signs of pneumonia **(B)** [NICE, 2004].
- **In exacerbations of COPD,** amoxicillin or a tetracyclin are recommended [McNulty, Personal Communication 2004]. Sensitivity patterns may be available from local microbiology laboratories.
- **Macrolides are not recommended for treating exacerbations.** Erythromycin has only weak activity against *Haemophilus influenzae* (one of the most common pathogens implicated in exacerbations of COPD) and there are growing concerns about the build up of resistance to clarithromycin and azithromycin [McNulty, Personal Communication, 2004]. Also, all macrolides concentrate intracellularly and *H influenzae* is an extracellular pathogen.
- **If a person with an exacerbation of COPD is not responding to the initial antibiotic,** then suitable alternative choices are: co-amoxiclav; tetracycline (if th has not already been tried); or clarithromycin or azithromycin (providing treatment has not already faile with erythromycin, as *Streptococcus pneumoniae* has considerable cross-resistance to these agents) [McNulty Personal Communication, 2004].

Non-antibiotic treatments

- **Bronchodilator use should be increased during an exacerbation of COPD.** Combination of regular or as-required use of a $beta_2$-agonist with an anticholinergic may be beneficial once the maximum dose of either age has been reached.
- **Oral corticosteroids may benefit some people with an exacerbation of COPD.** They improve FEV_1 and reduce treatment failures, although no effect on survival has been shown [Thompson et al, 1996; Barnes, 1998; Bac et al, 2001]. Maximum benefits occur if treatment with oral corticosteroids is started early; in selected patients consider the provision of a course of treatment at home so the individual can commence this as part of an agree management programme.
- Current recommendations for oral corticosteroids duri an exacerbation are:
  - Consider oral corticosteroids if an exacerbation significantly increases breathlessness, which interfere with daily activities **(B)**.
  - Prescribe prednisolone 30 mg for 7–14 days **(D)**.
  - Do not treat for more than 14 days, as this offers no benefit **(A)**.

- Refer to the *British National Formulary* for guidance on stopping oral corticosteroid therapy (D).
- Consider osteoporosis prophylaxis for people requiring frequent courses of oral corticosteroids (D). See the separate PRODIGY guidance on *Osteoporosis*.

[National Collaborating Centre for Chronic Conditions, 2004]

Treat at home or admit?

Many people with an exacerbation of COPD can be treated at home. Admission to hospital is recommended if any of the following factors is present:

- Severe breathlessness
- Confusion
- Cyanosis
- Worsening peripheral oedema
- Impaired consciousness
- The person is unable to cope at home
- General condition is poor or is deteriorating
- Activity level is poor, or the person is confined to bed
- The person lives alone
- The person is on long-term oxygen therapy
- The exacerbation was of rapid onset
- Significant comorbidity is present

[National Collaborating Centre for Chronic Conditions, 2004; NICE, 2004]

Pulmonary rehabilitation

Pulmonary rehabilitation is a multidisciplinary programme which is individually tailored to a person with COPD. Programmes include ventilatory muscle training, exercise programmes, and psychosocial, behavioural, and educational components. Most are based in secondary care settings.

Pulmonary rehabilitation is effective for people with moderate to severe COPD.

It should be offered to all people with COPD who consider themselves functionally disabled. It is not suitable for people unable to walk, who have unstable angina, or who have had a recent myocardial infarction (D).

[National Collaborating Centre for Chronic Conditions, 2004]

Bronchopulmonary hygiene therapy

Bronchopulmonary hygiene physical therapy (postural drainage) is of uncertain value in COPD and is not recommended as a standard treatment. The data available suggests that it may help clear sputum, but there is no evidence that it improves lung function [Jones and Rowe, 2004].

Immunization

Annual influenza vaccination is strongly recommended. Revaccination is not routinely recommended. For further details see the PRODIGY guidance on *Influenza* and *Pneumococcal vaccination*.

Mucolytic therapy

Mucolytics increase sputum expectoration by reducing its viscosity.

Three systematic reviews have addressed the effect of mucolytics [Grandjean et al, 2000; Stey et al, 2000; Poole and Black, 2004]. The two smaller reviews only considered N-acetylcysteine (not prescribable in the UK) [Grandjean et al, 2000; Stey et al, 2000].

The systematic reviews suggest that mucolytics:

- Reduce the number of exacerbations compared with placebo.
- Are cost-effective compared with placebo as they reduce the need for hospitalization.
- Do not seem to have any significant adverse effects.
- Do not improve lung function.

- **However the findings of these systematic reviews should be adopted cautiously as:**
  - All but two trials were in people labelled with chronic bronchitis rather than COPD.
  - Significant heterogeneity was found between the trials and many confounding factors were not consistently accounted for (e.g. mucolytic drug dosage).
  - The largest review included trials of ten different mucolytics but it is not known whether a class effect exists or if there are differences between these drugs.
  - Most of the studies were done in winter when more exacerbations will occur, so there will be a tendency to overestimate the annual reduced exacerbation rates.
  - Some trials reported high drop out rates and the consequences of this were unknown.
  - Most trials were short-term.
- On the available evidence, people who experience frequent exacerbations of COPD are most likely to benefit.
- NICE have recommended that mucolytic therapy should be considered in people with a chronic cough productive of sputum (B), and continued if there is a symptomatic improvement (D) [National Collaborating Centre for Chronic Conditions, 2004; NICE, 2004].

Therapy not recommended

- The following therapies are not recommended for people with COPD:
  - Prophylactic antibiotics (D)
  - Antitussives (D)
  - Anti-oxidants, e.g. alpha-tocopherol, beta-carotene (A)

[NICE, 2004]

Medicines management

Counselling and compliance issues

- **Inhaler training** — inhalers should only be prescribed after patients have received training in the use of the device and have demonstrated satisfactory technique (D) [National Collaborating Centre for Chronic Conditions, 2004].
- **Regularly reinforce inhaler technique** — where this is poor, it may be mistaken for a lack of response to the drug.
- There has been found to be no difference in clinical efficacy between standard pressurized metered-dose inhalers and other inhaler devices so long as people have been adequately educated [Brocklebank et al, 2001].
- People may experience varying degrees of sensation in the mouth and throat with different inhaler products. These may depend on the actuation and the drug inhaled.
- **Where a chlorofluorocarbon (CFC)-free inhaler is intended,** it is recommended that this term be specified on the prescription.
- **Paradoxical bronchospasm** — all inhaled therapy has the potential for this. Where this occurs, a change in therapy is required.

Beta$_2$-agonists: short- and long-acting

- **The risk of adverse events may be higher** in people with a predisposition to arrhythmias as well as in people with pre-existing cardiovascular disease, including those with hypertension; therefore, prescribe with caution.
- **Also use with caution** in people with hyperthyroidism and in those with diabetes (monitor blood glucose

C

because of the risk of ketoacidosis, especially after administering $beta_2$-agonist intravenously).

- **Fine tremor is the most common adverse effect;** it occurs particularly in the hands and is usually worse in the first few days of treatment [Cook et al, 2001].
- **Hypokalaemia** — high doses can reduce plasma potassium concentration (therefore this needs monitoring), and the Committee on Safety of Medicines has advised that this may be potentially serious. Hypokalaemia may be potentiated by concomitant treatment with theophylline and its derivatives, corticosteroids, and diuretics, and by hypoxia.

C

Anticholinergics: short- and long-acting

- **Use with caution** in men with prostatic hyperplasia and bladder outflow obstruction as urinary retention has been reported in elderly men.
- **Dry mouth is the most common minor adverse effect;** it has been more frequently reported with tiotropium use in trials that have compared tiotropium with ipratropium [Vincken et al, 2002].
- **Use of nebulized ipratropium** — the eyes need to be protected as acute angle-closure glaucoma has been reported. This is also a problem when given with nebulized $beta_2$-agonists.

Inhaled corticosteroids

- **In people treated with high-dose inhaled corticosteroids** (ICS), clinicians should be aware of the potential risk of developing osteoporosis and other adverse effects (especially in the presence of other risk factors), and should discuss the risk with patients **(D)** [National Collaborating Centre for Chronic Conditions, 2004].
- Take account of the use of other systemic or topical corticosteroid therapy when assessing risk. Elderly people may be particularly susceptible to their adverse effects.
- **Oral candidiasis and sore mouth** commonly occur. They can be minimized by using a pressurized metered-dose inhaler with a large-volume spacer device (which filters out larger particles, reducing oropharyngeal deposition), and by rinsing the mouth with water after use.
- **Many people taking ICS experience hoarseness and dysphonia.** Use of a spacer device does not appear to alleviate this.
- **Cataracts, glaucoma, skin thinning, and bruising** are also associated with prolonged use.
- **Osteoporosis:** the effect of ICS on bone mineral density (BMD) and osteoporosis is currently unclear as studies examining the relationship between ICS and BMD give conflicting results and are difficult to interpret due to confounding factors [Alsaeedi et al, 2002]. With long-term use of ICS at high doses (above 800 micrograms per day of beclometasone or equivalent) there may be a trend towards a decrease in BMD, but the long-term clinical significance of this is not known [DTB, 2000; Royal College of Physicians of London, 2002; SIGN and BTS, 2003]. Repeated courses of oral corticosteroids should prompt consideration of measurement of BMD or measures to improve bone strength.
- **General measures to counteract osteoporosis** (such as regular exercise, smoking cessation, and adequate calcium intake) are advisable if high doses of ICS are required for prolonged periods.
- **Adrenal suppression:** a recent systematic review provides evidence that at high doses of ICS (equivalent to 1.5 mg/day chlorofluorocarbon [CFC]-containing beclometasone), significant adrenal suppression occurs [Lipworth, 1999]. The Committee on Safety of Medicines (CSM) has advised that adrenal suppression is a dose-related class effect of ICS and that, because of its greater potency, fluticasone should be used at half the dose of budesonide or CFC-containing beclometasone [CSM, 2001].
- **Abrupt withdrawal of ICS in stable COPD** may increase the risk of exacerbation, so careful monitoring is required if withdrawal is attempted [Jarad et al, 1999].

Oral corticosteroids

- **To reduce the disturbance to circadian cortisol secretion** oral corticosteroids are best taken as a single dose in the morning.
- **Use with caution** in people with a history of peptic ulceration.
- **Oral corticosteroids cause a large number of adverse effects, but when taken in short courses are relatively safe.** Following concern about severe chickenpox, the Committee on Safety of Medicines has advised that anyone prescribed a systemic corticosteroid should receive the patient information leaflet produced by the manufacturer.
- **Oral corticosteroids can be stopped abruptly if the course length has been 21 days or less.** If they have been taken for more than 21 days, or if the patient has had repeated courses of corticosteroids or has adrenocortical insufficiency, it is necessary to taper the dose gradually.
- **In people treated with long-term oral corticosteroids,** therapy should be monitored for the development of osteoporosis and appropriate prophylaxis given. Patients over the age of 65 should be started on prophylactic treatment, without monitoring **(D)** [National Collaborating Centre for Chronic Conditions, 2004].
- **Long-term systemic corticosteroids** are associated with other serious adverse effects including the induction of diabetes [McEvoy and Niewoehner, 1997], adrenal suppression, and increased susceptibility to infections and severity of infections.

Theophyllines

- **Particular caution needs to be observed with the use of theophylline in elderly people** because of differences in pharmacokinetics, increased likelihood of comorbidities and the use of other medications **(D)** [National Collaborating Centre for Chronic Conditions, 2004].
- **Check for use of over-the-counter** cough and decongestant preparations containing theophylline such as Do-Do Chesteze, Franol, and Franol Plus.
- **Hypokalaemia** may be potentiated by concomitant treatment with $beta_2$-agonists. The Committee on Safety of Medicines has advised that this may be potentially serious.
- In most people, plasma concentrations between 10 and 20 mg/litre are usually required for satisfactory bronchodilation, although a lower concentration may be effective.
- **Adverse effects** include nausea (most common), vomiting, tremor, palpitations, and arrhythmias [Barr et al, 2004]. They can occur within the range of 10–20 mg/litre. Both the frequency and severity of adverse effects increase when concentrations are above 20 mg/litre.
- **Theophylline plasma levels are raised** in elderly people or those with heart failure or liver impairment, and by liver enzyme inhibitors (e.g. cimetidine, ciprofloxacin, and erythromycin).
- **Reduce the dose of theophylline** prescribed at the time of an exacerbation if drugs known to interact such as macrolide or quinolone antibiotics are prescribed **(D)** [National Collaborating Centre for Chronic Conditions, 2004].
- **Theophylline plasma levels are lowered** in people who smoke, in chronic alcoholism, and by liver enzyme-

nducing drugs (e.g. phenytoin, carbamazepine, and rifampicin). If people who are stabilized on theophylline:

- Begin to take one of those drugs, the theophylline dosage may need to be increased.
- Stop smoking, a dosage reduction may be necessary.

Also use with caution in people with cardiovascular disease, hyperthyroidism, and peptic ulcer disease.

Due to bioavailability differences between brands, people should be maintained on the same brand of theophylline. To assist this, the brand should be specified on the prescription.

ockley, 2002]

ixed-dose combination inhalers

Combining therapies from different drug classes is recommended if patients remain symptomatic on monotherapy (**A**). See section on *Combination therapy* for more information.

Of the combination strategies recommended, the only fixed-dose combination inhaler preparations available on prescription contain a long-acting beta$_2$-agonist and inhaled corticosteroid. The two options are:

- Fluticasone and salmeterol — Seretide® Accuhaler
- Budesonide and formoterol — Symbicort® Turbohaler

Both Seretide and Symbicort are licensed for the symptomatic treatment of patients with severe COPD and a history of repeated exacerbations who have significant symptoms despite regular bronchodilator therapy.

There is trial data to support their use but neither combination product has been compared in published trials with its individual components taken concomitantly via separate inhalers [DTB, 2004].

Seretide and Symbicort may have a role in improving adherence to therapy where people with COPD are stabilized on both an inhaled corticosteroid and long-acting beta$_2$-agonist.

lebulizer solutions

The dose of a bronchodilator given by nebulization is usually much higher than that from an aerosol inhaler. Nebulizers should only be prescribed for use at home in a very few cases, e.g. those requiring large doses of inhaled bronchodilators, and only after assessment by a respiratory specialist.

pacer devices

It is important to prescribe a spacer device that is compatible with the metered dose inhaler (**D**) [National Collaborating Centre for Chronic Conditions, 2004].

Are particularly useful for people:

- With poor inhalation technique
- Requiring higher doses
- Prone to oral candidiasis with inhaled corticosteroids

It is recommended that spacers are used in the following way (**D**) [National Collaborating Centre for Chronic Conditions, 2004]:

- Administer the drug by single dose actuations from the metered-dose inhaler into the spacer with each followed by inhalation.
- There should be minimal delay between inhaler actuation and inhalation as the drug aerosol is very short-lived.
- Tidal breathing can be used as it is as effective as single breaths.

Clean spacers no more than once a month (more frequent cleaning will build up static affecting their performance) — wash in mild detergent, rinse, and then allow to air dry (**D**) [National Collaborating Centre for Chronic Conditions, 2004]. Spacer devices should be replaced every 6–12 months.

Chlorofluorocarbon-free inhaler devices

- The Montreal Protocol has mandated that chlorofluorocarbon (CFC) propellant should be phased out, and in the UK the transition to CFC-free propellants, usually hydrofluoroalkane, (HFA), is currently underway [NHS Executive, 1998].
- This change is due to environmental requirements and not because of any safety or clinical reasons.

Which pressurized metered-dose inhalers are available as HFA products?

- The transition for salbutamol is now well underway and, as the availability of CFC-containing salbutamol pressurized metered-dose inhalers (pMDIs) is decreasing, the Department of Health has advised that all people currently using them should be transferred to a CFC-free product [CMO, 2003].
- The only currently available HFA beclometasone pMDI is Qvar®. Until more than one CFC-free brand is licensed, and licensed for all ages, CFC-containing brands will still be in use.
- Fluticasone pMDI is available as an HFA pMDI (Flixotide Evohaler) in strengths above 25 micrograms per actuation.
- All dry-powder devices are CFC-free.

How do I transfer someone from CFC pMDI to HFA pMDI?

- When transferring from a CFC pMDI to an HFA pMDI, people will need reassurance that the new inhalers are equally safe and effective despite any differences in taste, temperature, and impact that they may notice.
- **Salbutamol:** most people will be able to transfer directly to an HFA salbutamol pMDI. HFA salbutamol is as effective as CFC salbutamol at standard therapeutic doses [Hughes et al, 1999; CMO, 2003] and should be substituted for CFC salbutamol at 1:1 dosing.
- **Beclometasone:** the only currently available CFC-free beclometasone pMDI is Qvar®. Inhaled corticosteroids are not licensed for use in COPD and the true potency ratio for Qvar® in COPD is unclear; however, it seems logical to apply the recommendations currently available with asthma management.
  - **If well controlled,** substitute Qvar® for CFC beclometasone pMDI at 1:2 dosing. Monitor the person closely to ensure that adequate control is maintained. This 1:2 ratio may not apply to future reformulated CFC-free beclometasone pMDIs.
  - **If poorly controlled,** substitute Qvar® for CFC beclometasone at 1:1 dosing [BNF 47, 2004].
  - See the Summary of Product Characteristics for Qvar® for further details.

[SIGN and BTS, 2003]

References

NHS staff in England can link, free of charge, from references to full text journals by clicking on [Full text] on the PRODIGY website.

1. Alsaeedi, A., Sin, D.D. and McAlister, F.A. (2002) The effects of inhaled corticosteroids in chronic obstructive pulmonary disease: a systematic review of randomized placebo-controlled trials. *American Journal of Medicine* **113**(1), 59–65.
2. American Thoracic Society (1995) Standards for the diagnosis and care of patients with chronic obstructive pulmonary disease. *American Journal of Respiratory & Critical Care Medicine* **152**(5 Pt 2), S77-S121.
3. Bach, P.B., Brown, C., Gelfand, S.E. and McCrory, D.C. (2001) Management of acute exacerbations of

chronic obstructive pulmonary disease: a summary and appraisal of published evidence. *Annals of Internal Medicine* **134**(7), 600–620.

4. Barnes, N.C. (1998) Inhaled steroids in COPD. *Lancet* **351**(9105), 766–767. [Full text]
5. Barr, R.G., Rowe, B.H. and Camargo, C.A., Jr. (2004) *Methylxanthines for exacerbations of chronic obstructive pulmonary disease (Cochrane Review)*. The Cochrane Library. Issue 1. Chichester, UK: John Wiley & Sons, Ltd. www.nelh.nhs.uk/cochrane.asp [Accessed: 26/02/2004].
6. BNF 47 (2004) *British National Formulary*. 47th edn. London: British Medical Association and Royal Pharmaceutical Society of Great Britain.
7. British Thoracic Society (1997) BTS guidelines for the management of chronic obstructive pulmonary disease. *Thorax* **52**(Suppl 5), S1-S28. [Full text]
8. Brocklebank, D., Ram, F., Wright, J. et al (2001) Comparison of the effectiveness of inhaler devices in asthma and chronic obstructive airways disease: a systematic review of the literature. *Health Technology Assessment* **5**(26), 1–155.
9. Burrows, B. and Earle, R. (1969) Course and prognosis of chronic obstructive lung disease: a prospective study of 200 patients. *New England Journal of Medicine* **280**(8), 397–404.
10. Canadian Thoracic Society Workshop Group (1992) Guidelines for the assessment and management of chronic obstructive pulmonary disease. *Canadian Medical Association Journal* **147**(4), 420–428.
11. Chapman, K. (1991) Therapeutic algorithm for chronic obstructive pulmonary disease. *American Journal of Medicine* **91**(Suppl 4A), 17S-23S.
12. CMO (2003) *CFC-containing salbutamol metered dose inhalers*. CEM/CMO/2003/9. Department of Health. www.dh.gov.uk [Accessed: 27/04/2004]. [Full text]
13. Cook, D., Guyatt, G., Wong, E. et al (2001) Regular versus as-needed short-acting inhaled β-agonist therapy for chronic obstructive pulmonary disease. *American Journal of Respiratory and Critical Care Medicine* **163**(1), 85–90.
14. CSM (2001) Reminder: Fluticasone propionate (Flixotide): use of high doses (>500 micrograms/twice daily). *Current Problems in Pharmacovigilance* **27**(Aug), 10.
15. DH and SMAC (1998) *The path of least resistance*. Department of Health. www.dh.gov.uk [Accessed: 27/04/2004]. [Full text]
16. DTB (1997) Peak flow meters and spirometers in general practice. *Drug & Therapeutics Bulletin* **35**(7), 52–55.
17. DTB (1998) Antibiotic treatment of adults with chest infection in general practice. *Drug & Therapeutics Bulletin* **36**(9), 68–72.
18. DTB (2000) The use of inhaled corticosteroids in adults with asthma. *Drug & Therapeutics Bulletin* **38**(1), 5–8.
19. DTB (2003) Tiotropium for chronic obstructive pulmonary disease. *Drug & Therapeutics Bulletin* **41**(2), 15–16.
20. DTB (2004) Are Seretide and Symbicort useful in COPD? *Drug & Therapeutics Bulletin* **42**(3), 18–21.
21. Ferguson, G. and Cherniack, R. (1993) Management of chronic obstructive pulmonary disease. *New England Journal of Medicine* **328**(4), 1017–1022.
22. Finch, R.G, Greenwood, D, Norrby, S.R. and Whitley, R.J. (2003) *Antibiotic and chemotherapy: anti-infective agents and their use in therapy*. 8th edn. London: Churchill Livingstone.
23. Fletcher, C. and Peto, R. (1977) The natural history of chronic airflow obstruction. *British Medical Journal* **1**(6077), 1645–1648.
24. Grandjean, E.M., Berther, P.H., Ruffman, R. and Leunberger, P.H. (2000) Cost-effectiveness analysis o oral N-acetylcysteine as a preventive treatment in chronic bronchitis. *Pharmacological Research* **42**(1), 39–50.
25. HPA (2003) *Management of infection guidance for primary care: for consultation and local adaptation.* Health Protection Agency. www.hpa.org.uk [Accesse 26/02/2004]. [Full text]
26. Hughes, D.A., Woodcock, A. and Walley, T. (1999) Review of therapeutically equivalent alternatives to short acting [beta]$_2$ adrenoreceptor agonists deliverec via chlorofluorocarbon-containing inhalers. *Thorax* **54**(12), 1087–1092. [Full text]
27. Ikeda, A., Nishmura, K., Koyama, H. et al (1996) Do response study of ipratropium bromide aerosol on maximum exercise performance in stable patients wi chronic obstructive pulmonary disease. *Thorax* **51**(1 48–53.
28. Jarad, N.A., Wedzicha, J.A., Burge, P. and Calverley, P.M.A. (1999) An observational study of inhaled corticosteroid withdrawal in stable chronic obstructi pulmonary disease. *Respiratory Medicine* **93**(3), 161–166.
29. Jones, A.P. and Rowe, B.H. (2004) *Bronchopulmona hygiene physical therapy for chronic obstructive pulmonary disease and bronchiectasis (Cochrane Review)*. The Cochrane Library. Issue 2. Chichester, UK: John Wiley & Sons, Ltd. www.nelh.nhs.uk/ cochrane.asp [Accessed: 26/02/2004].
30. Kanner, R. (1996) Early intervention in chronic obstructive pulmonary disease: a review of the Lung Health Study results. *Medical Clinics of North Ameri* **80**(3), 523–547.
31. Kerstjens, H. and Postma, D. (2003) Chronic obstructive pulmonary disease. *Clinical Evidence* **10**(Dec), 1786–1803.
32. Kesten, S. and Rebuck, A.S. (1989) Management of chronic obstructive pulmonary disease. *Drugs* **38**(1), 160–174.
33. Kuhl, D.A., Agiri, O.A. and Mauro, L.S. (1994) Beta-agonists in the treatment of acute exacerbation of chronic obstructive pulmonary disease. *Annals of Pharmacotherapy* **28**(12), 1379–1388.
34. Lipworth, B.J. (1999) Systemic adverse effects of inhaled corticosteroid therapy: a systematic review ar meta-analysis. *Archives of Internal Medicine* **159**(9), 941–955. [Full text]
35. McCrory, D.C. and Brown, C.D. (2004) *Anticholinergic bronchodilators versus beta2-sympathomimetic agents for acute exacerbations of chronic obstructive pulmonary disease (Cochrane Review)*. The Cochrane Library. Issue 2. Chichester, UK: John Wiley & Sons, Ltd. www.nelh.nhs.uk/ cochrane.asp [Accessed: 25/01/2004].
36. McEvoy, C.E. and Niewoehner, D.E. (1997) Adverse effects of corticosteroid therapy for COPD. A critical review. *Chest* **111**(3), 732–743. [Full text]
37. McNulty, C. (2004) *Personal communication*. Medic Microbiologist, HPA Primary Care Unit: Gloucestershire Royal Hospital, Gloucester.
38. MeReC (1995) Inhaler devices: an update. *MeReC Bulletin* **6**(9), 1–4.
39. MeReC (1998a) Levofloxacin and grepafloxacin- two new quinolone antibiotics. *MeReC Bulletin* **9**(8), 29–32.
40. MeReC (1998b) The management of chronic obstructive pulmonary disease. *MeReC Bulletin* **9**(10 1–9.
41. National Collaborating Centre for Chronic Conditior (2004) Chronic obstructive pulmonary disease: national clinical guideline on management of chronic

obstructive pulmonary disease in adults in primary and secondary care. *Thorax* 59(Suppl 1), 1–232.

. NHS Executive (1998) *Phase out of CFC containing metered dose inhalers for the treatment of asthma and COPD.* HSC 1998/180. London: Department of Health.

. NICE (2004) *Chronic obstructive pulmonary disease.* Clinical guideline 12. National Institute for Clinical Excellence. www.nice.org.uk [Accessed: 25/02/2004].

. NICE (2005) *Referral guidelines for suspected cancer – quick reference guide.* Clinical guideline 27. National Institute for Health and Clinical Excellence. www.nice.org.uk [Accessed: 01/07/2005].

. Nocturnal Oxygen Therapy Trial Group (1980) Continuous or nocturnal oxygen therapy in hypoxemic chronic obstructive lung disease: a clinical trial. *Annals of Internal Medicine* 93(3), 391–398.

. Poole, P.J. and Black, P.N. (2004) *Mucolytic agents for chronic bronchitis or chronic obstructive pulmonary disease (Cochrane Review).* The Cochrane Library. Issue 1. Chichester, UK: John Wiley & Sons, Ltd. www.nelh.nhs.uk/cochrane.asp [Accessed: 26/02/2004].

. Royal College of Physicians (1999) *Domiciliary oxygen therapy services: clinical guidelines and advice for prescribers.* London: Royal College of Physicians.

. Royal College of Physicians of London (2002) *Glucocorticoid-induced osteoporosis.* Royal College of Physicians. www.rcplondon.ac.uk [Accessed: 22/04/2003].

. Sestini, P., Renzoni, E., Robinson, S. et al (2004) *Short-acting beta 2 agonists for stable chronic obstructive pulmonary disease (Cochrane Review).* The Cochrane Library. Issue 2. Chichester, UK: John Wiley & Sons, Ltd. www.nelh.nhs.uk/cochrane.asp [Accessed: 26/02/2004].

. SIGN (2002) *Community management of lower respiratory tract infection in adults.* Report no. 59. Scottish Intercollegiate Guidelines Network. www.sign.ac.uk [Accessed: 21/01/2004].

. SIGN and BTS (2003) *British guideline on the management of asthma.* Report no. 63. Scottish Intercollegiate Guidelines Network and The British Thoracic Society. www.sign.ac.uk [Accessed: 30/01/2003].

52. Silverman, E.K. and Speizer, F.E. (1996) Risk factors for the development of chronic obstructive pulmonary disease. *Medical Clinics of North America* 80(3), 501–522.

53. Stey, C., Steurer, J., Bachmann, S. et al (2000) The effect of oral N-acetylcysteine in chronic bronchitis: a quantitative systematic review. *European Respiratory Journal* 16(2), 253–262.

54. Stockley, I.H. (Ed.) (2002) *Drug interactions.* 6th edn. London: The Pharmaceutical Press.

55. Thompson, W.H., Nielson, C.P., Carvalho, P. et al (1996) Controlled trial of oral prednisone in outpatients with acute COPD exacerbation. *American Journal of Respiratory & Critical Care Medicine* 154(2 Pt 1), 407–412.

56. Vincken, W., van Noord, J.A., Greefhorst, A.P. et al (2002) Improved health outcomes in patients with COPD during 1 yr's treatment with tiotropium. *European Respiratory Journal* 19(2), 209–216.

Evidence grading

Evidence grading is from the National Institute of Clinical Excellence guideline, *Chronic obstructive pulmonary disease,* February 2004. The definitions of grades of recommendation used in this guideline are as follows:

A Directly based on category I evidence (systematic review of randomized controlled trials or at least one randomized controlled trial)

B Directly based on category II evidence (at least one controlled study without randomization or one other type of quasi-experimental study) or extrapolated recommendation from category I evidence

C Directly based on category III evidence (non-experimental descriptive studies) or extrapolated recommendation from category I or II evidence

D Directly based on category IV evidence (expert committee reports, opinions, or clinical experience of respected authorities) or extrapolated recommendation from category I, II, or III evidence

PRODIGY GUIDANCE

Colic — infantile

Last revised in November 2004
www.prodigy.nhs.uk/guidance.asp?gt=Colic - infantile

Applies to children under the age of 6 months

This guidance covers the management of infantile colic.

This guidance does not cover the management of other forms of colic.

C

Goals

- To reduce parental anxiety and stress
- To relieve the baby's symptoms

Contents

Scenarios

- Infantile colic p.350

Extended Information, p. 352

Infantile colic

Which therapy?

- **Exclude common causes** of excessive crying such as hunger, cold, discomfort, or itch.
- **Reassure parents that infantile colic:**
  - Is a condition that usually resolves within 3–4 months.
  - Is not due to them doing something wrong.
  - Does no physical harm even if there is a poor response to treatment (as is often the case).
- **Advise the parents:**
  - Simple strategies may help them cope: e.g. checking the baby is not hungry, checking the nappy, establishing a routine to the day, avoiding carrying and holding the baby excessively, and not intervening immediately when the baby cries.
  - They should schedule 'time out', and should share caring for the baby.
  - Herbal products are not recommended. Some (e.g. star anise) have poisoned babies. None have been shown to be safe.
  - Many alternative therapies are promoted, but none have been shown to be effective, and they may be expensive.
- **Consider the following factors before prescribing any trial of therapy:**
  - **Level of distress of the parents** — and their response to advice and reassurance
  - **Ability of the parents to cope** — assess coping abilities on follow-up
  - **Levels of evidence supporting therapeutic interventions** — this is limited
- Consider sequential trials of eliminating lactose then cows' milk protein or a trial of simeticone (activated dimeticone).

Sequential trials of eliminating lactose then cows' milk protein, or a trial of simeticone

- **Eliminate lactose with lactase, or low-lactose milk formula;** reassess after about a week.
- **Sustained response to lactose elimination:**
  - Continue until about 12 weeks of age.
  - Wean on to usual milk over 1 week.
- **No sustained response to lactose elimination:**
  - **Eliminate cows' milk protein;** reassess after about a week.
    - **Breastfed infants:** mother eliminates all dairy products from her diet.
    - **Formula fed infants:** hypoallergenic milk formula.
- **Response to hypoallergenic diet:**
  - Refer for specialist advice.
  - Continue until weaned on to solids.
- **No response to hypoallergenic diet:**
  - Consider possibility of rare conditions.
  - Refer if concerned.
- **Simeticone (activated dimeticone)** could be considered for a trial. Take personal preferences into account whe[n] deciding whether to try simeticone before or after trials of dietary modification.

Practical prescribing points

For further information please see the *Medicines Compendium* (www.medicines.org.uk) or the *British National Formulary* (www.bnf.org).

Should I refer or investigate?

Refer?

- **Refer to the health visitor** if the parents/carers are struggling to cope on their own.
- **Refer to dietician** if cows' milk allergy is strongly suspected.
- **Refer to paediatrician** or paediatric gastroenterologist a[s] appropriate if a serious medical condition is suspected i[n] the baby.
- **Refer** as appropriate if a serious psychosocial disorder i[s] suspected in parents.

Patient information leaflets

The following PILs are available at www.prodigy.nhs.uk

- Colic
- CRY-SIS Helpline (for crying & sleepless children)
- Medicines - Name Changes of Medicines

Shared decision making

- **The cause of colic is not known.** Colic has usually gone by 3–4 months of age.
- **Tips which may help include:**
  - If possible, arrange to have 'time out'. For example, b[y] having a 'rota' of colic times with other family members.
  - A trip out in a pram or car.
  - 'White noise' such as a washing machine or vacuum cleaner.
- **Medicines do not usually help.**
- **Lactose intolerance** may be a factor in some cases.
  - Adding lactase to the usual milk (breast or formula) may help.
  - An alternative is to use a low-lactose milk formula.

Eliminating cows' milk may be worth a try.

- For breastfed babies, this means that the mother stops eating all dairy produce for the trial period.
- For bottle-fed babies, it means switching to a special 'hypoallergenic' milk formula for the trial period.

Soya milk is usually not recommended.

Let your health visitor know if things become difficult to cope with.

rug rationale

ugs not included

Antimuscarinic drugs are not recommended. There is limited evidence that **dicycloverine** (dicyclomine) reduces crying compared with placebo. However, serious adverse effects can occur, including breathing difficulties, seizures, syncope, asphyxia, apnoea, muscular hypotonia, and coma [Kilgour and Wade, 2003]. Dicycloverine is contraindicated in infants under the age of 6 months. Antimuscarinic drugs are used for colic causing abdominal pain in adults and older children. However, they have no place in the treatment of infantile colic.

Soya formula milk: the Chief Medical Officer has advised that soya-based infant formulas should not be used as first choice in the management of infants with proven cows' milk sensitivity, lactose intolerance, galactose deficiency or galactosaemia [CMO, 2004]. This follows a report from the Committee on Toxicity advising that soya-based formulations have a high phytoestrogen content which could pose a risk to the long-term reproductive health of infants [Committee on Toxicity, 2003].

ugs included

Lactase added to usual milk for a minimum of 3 days. There is limited evidence that the symptoms of infantile colic can be relieved if parents use lactase to eliminate lactose from infant formula and expressed breast milk. Lactase 50,000 units/gram drops are available on NHS prescription when endorsed ACBS by the prescriber.

Low-lactose formula milk. There is an absence of evidence for the efficacy of low-lactose infant milk formulas. However, if parents find benefit from using lactase to eliminate lactose from infant formula, it would seem reasonable to expect that similar success would be obtained if they used an infant milk formula with no lactose. Low-lactose infant milk formulas available on NHS prescription (when endorsed ACBS by the prescriber) are SMA LF® and Enfamil Lactofree®.

Hypoallergenic milk formula. There is weak evidence of efficacy for hypoallergenic milk formula derived from either casein or whey hydrolysate. Hypoallergenic infant milk formulas available on NHS prescription (when endorsed ACBS by the prescriber) are:

- **Casein hydrolysate milk formula:** Nutramigen 1® and Pregestimil®
- **Whey hydrolysate milk formula:** Pepti-Junior®

Simeticone (activated dimeticone). There is no convincing evidence of benefit but it is widely used, cheap and safe. A low-sodium, sugar-free formulation is included.

Prescriptions

Advice note

Advice only: symptom management

- Age under 6 months
- Colic is common. The cause is not known. In most babies it has gone by 3-4 months. There is little evidence that the available medicines are effective but they may be worth a try. Try not to over handle the baby or become anxious – colic does not harm the baby. If possible have 'time out', for example by arranging a 'rota' of colic times with other family members. Stopping cows' milk from the diet may help in some babies. It may be worth a try for a week if colic is severe. For breastfed babies, this means the mother stops eating all dairy produce. For bottle fed babies it means switching to a special type of baby feed. Let your health visitor know if things become difficult to cope with.

1-week trial of eliminating lactose

Breastfed or bottle-fed infants: lactase drops

- Age under 6 months
- Lactase drops 50,000 units/g. Add to the prepared feed (or expressed breast milk) as directed in the instructions to patient. ; supply 7 ml; NHS Cost £7.00; OTC Cost £9.00.

Bottle-fed infants: SMA LF low-lactose infant milk formula

- Age under 6 months
- SMA LF powder. Use as baby milk. Follow directions on the side of the container; supply 430 grams; NHS Cost £3.99; OTC Cost £4.99.

Bottle-fed infants: Enfamil Lactofree infant milk formula

- Age under 6 months
- Enfamil Lactofree powder. Use as baby milk. Follow directions on the side of the container; supply 400 grams; NHS Cost £3.51; OTC Cost £4.50.

1-week trial of eliminating cows milk protein

Breast-fed infants: advice note

- Age under 6 months
- Some babies cry less if cows milk is stopped, but this does not occur in most babies. However, if colic is severe, it may be worth Mum trying without cows milk for one week. This means not having any dairy products as part of the cows milk can get into breast milk. If there is an improvement, continue without cows milk until the baby is three months old. Colic is not a 'true' allergy though, and after the colic has settled the baby will be able to take cows milk again. If there is no improvement after one week, there is no point in continuing without cows milk, and you should resume normal feeds.

Bottle-fed infants: Nutramigen 1 milk formula (casein-based)

- Age under 6 months
- Nutramigen 1 powder. Use as baby milk. Follow directions on the side of the container; supply 425 grams; NHS Cost £7.81; OTC Cost £11.51.

Bottle-fed infants: Pregestimil milk formula (casein-based)

- Age under 6 months
- Pregestimil powder. Use as baby milk. Follow directions on the side of the container; supply 450 grams; NHS Cost £8.91; OTC Cost £13.00.

Bottle-fed infants: Pepti-Junior milk formula (whey-based)

- Age under 6 months
- Pepti-junior powder. Use as baby milk. Follow directions on the side of the container; supply 450 grams; NHS Cost £8.80; OTC Cost £13.00.

C

1-week trial of simeticone drops

Simeticone (activated dimeticone) drops
- Age under 6 months
- Simeticone 40mg/ml drops. Give one dropperful (0.5ml) before each feed. Increase to two dropperfuls (1ml) if required; supply 50 ml; NHS Cost £1.97; OTC Cost £3.29.

Extended Information

Background information

- What is it? p.352
- How common is it? p.352
- How do I know my patient has it? p.352
- What else might it be? p.352
- Complications and prognosis p.352

What is it?

- **Infantile colic** causes repeated episodes of excessive and inconsolable crying in an infant that otherwise appears to be healthy and thriving.
- **For research purposes infantile colic is defined** as crying for at least 3 hours a day, at least 3 days a week, and for at least 3 weeks' duration [Garrison and Christakis, 2000].
- **The underlying cause of infantile colic is unknown** and may be due to multiple factors. Theories include transient intolerance to lactose and/or cows' milk protein, and psychosocial factors (e.g. emotional and behavioural problems in the mother) [Gupta, 2002].

How common is it?

- **Estimates of prevalence** range from 5–20% of infants [Lucassen et al, 2001].
- **Maternal smoking** may be associated with infantile colic [Reijneveld et al, 2000].
- A large community survey found that colic was more likely to be reported with breastfeeding [Crowcroft and Strachan, 1997]. However, this result may be biased by methodological problems in the study [Lucassen et al, 2001].

How do I know my patient has it?

- **Colic starts in the first weeks of life** and usually resolves by the age of 3–4 months.
- **Crying** typically occurs in the late afternoon or evening.
- **Frequently noted features are** high-pitched, inconsolable crying, flushing of the face, drawing up of the legs, passing of wind, and difficulty in passing stools. However, these are not specific to infantile colic [Lucassen et al, 1998; Reust and Blake, 2000].
- **History and examination** reveal no abnormality other than inconsolable crying.

What else might it be?

- **Discomfort** e.g. poor feeding technique, hunger, pain, cold, heat, or itch.
- **Parental psychosocial problems** e.g. excessive concern, inability to interact normally with the baby.
- **Gastrointestinal conditions:**
  - **Gastro-oesophageal reflux disease** (GORD) can present with excessive crying. But this is less intense than in infantile colic and is usually accompanied by visible regurgitation and sometimes by respiratory symptoms due to aspiration. These babies may have difficulty feeding and sucking, and discomfort associated with feeding. [Miller-Loncar et al, 2004]
  - **Acute intestinal conditions** such as intussusception, volvulus, and strangulated hernia may need to be excluded if symptoms started suddenly and recently.
- **Metabolic conditions** e.g. lactose intolerance, cows' mi intolerance.
- **Cognitive deficit**
  - A prospective cohort study found that, at the age of five years, children who had had prolonged crying (defined as symptoms of infantile colic reported at th ages of 6 weeks and 13 weeks) had an adjusted mea IQ 9 points lower than children who had not had co [Rao et al, 2004].

Referral for specialist advice may be required if, on follow up, the history and examination cannot confirm that the parents are coping and that the child is otherwise well an thriving.
[Gupta, 2002]

Complications and prognosis

- **Babies usually 'grow out' of infantile colic** by 3–4 months of age.
- **The child suffers no harm** in the short term, although some doubts have been raised about long-term outcomes:
  - Some studies have suggested an association with late psychosocial problems in the child and family [Gupt 2002].
  - There is conflicting evidence for an association with the later development of allergies [Gupta, 2002].
- A prospective cohort study found that, at the age of fiv years, children who had had infantile colic that had resolved by the age of 13 weeks had no detectable cognitive deficit [Rao et al, 2004].
- **Infantile colic causes significant suffering:**
  - Parents are distressed and sleep deprived.
  - Stress on the parents may affect their relationships with the child.
  - Breastfeeding might be stopped earlier and weaning to solid foods begun sooner than otherwise would have happened.

Management issues

- How do I manage infantile colic? p.352
- What is the supporting evidence? p.353
- What resources can support parents of babies with infantile colic? p.354
- What infant milk formulas are available on NHS prescription? And, how do they differ? p.354
- Managing treatments with lactase and infant milk formulas p.354

How do I manage infantile colic?

- **Exclude common causes** of excessive crying such as hunger and discomfort from pain, cold, heat, and itch.
- **Reassure the parents.** This alone may suffice. Reassure them that:
  - Although most babies do not respond to treatment, n physical harm is done by colic.
  - Most infants are free of symptoms by the age of 3–4 months.
  - Parents are in no way at fault.
- **Advise the parents:**
  - They may need to 'take time out', and they should share caring for the baby.
  - Interventions such as increased carrying, early/delaye response to crying, soothing motion, or 'white noise' (e.g. from a vacuum cleaner) have not been shown to be effective, but they may be worth trying as they are safe, inexpensive, and involve the parents.

- Some herbal products (e.g. star anise) have poisoned babies, and these are not recommended.
- Many alternative therapies are promoted, but none have been shown to be effective, and they may be expensive.

Consider therapeutic intervention after weighing up the following factors:

- The level of distress of the parents.
- The ability of the parents to cope — on follow-up assess the level of confidence that reassurance and explanation have given them.
- The evidence to support therapeutic interventions — the evidence is limited and the interventions may be costly for prolonged treatment.

Consider sequential trials of eliminating lactose then cows' milk protein, or a trial of simeticone (activated dimeticone).

equential trials of eliminating lactose then cows' ilk protein, or a trial of simeticone

Begin a trial of lactase added to the usual milk or, alternatively, a trial of low-lactose milk formula, and reassess in about a week.

- **Breastfed infants:**
  - Lactase is advised to avoid having to change to an infant milk formula
- **Formula-fed infants:**
  - Some mothers might prefer lactase to avoid having to change infant milk formulas if the infant is fussy about their milk.
  - Other mothers might find a low-lactose infant milk formula more convenient than lactase.

Sustained response to lactose elimination:

- Continue lactose elimination until about 12 weeks of age.
- Then, over about 1 week, wean to usual milk. Suddenly changing to the usual milk is not recommended because it is theoretically possible that temporary lactose intolerance might have been induced by the extended period over which the gut has lacked the stimulation by lactose to produce lactase.

No sustained response to lactose elimination:

- Consider a trial eliminating cows' milk allergens for several days.
  - **Breastfed infants:** mother eliminates all dairy products from her diet.
  - **Formula-fed infants:** give a hypoallergenic milk formula.

Sustained response to elimination of cows' milk antigens:

- Refer for specialist advice.
- Continue elimination diet until weaned on to solids.

No sustained response to elimination of cows' milk antigens:

- Consider the possibility of rare but serious conditions that would usually present with features such as failure to thrive.
- Refer if concerned:
  - Health visitors can support parents.
  - Specialists can help with the diagnosis and management of rare conditions.

Simeticone (activated dimeticone) could be considered for a trial. As supporting evidence of efficacy is limited, the decision to try simeticone before or after trying dietary alterations depends largely on personal preferences and cost.

hat is the supporting evidence?

ere is limited evidence to support the above protocol, t the underlying theory is plausible, no better treatments e available, it is safe and relatively inexpensive, and a similar approach is advocated by the 'Expert Working Group' [Marks et al, 2003].

Using lactase to reduce the levels of lactose in milk formula or breast milk

- Lactase added to milk formula or, for breastfed babies, the expressed foremilk, has been studied in four small randomized controlled trials. Methodological weaknesses in the trials make it difficult to place much weight on the claims of benefit [Kilgour and Wade, 2003].

Using low-lactose infant milk formulas to reduce the levels of lactose in the diet

- Low-lactose formula milks containing cows' milk proteins have not been studied as a treatment for infantile colic [Kilgour and Wade, 2003].

Using hypoallergenic infant milk formulas to eliminate cows' milk proteins from the baby's diet

- **Whey hydrolysate** formula milk, in one study of 43 infants, reduced crying by 63 minutes a day, but the 95% confidence interval was very wide (from 1 to 127 minutes crying/day) and the blinding may have been unmasked [Lucassen et al, 2000; Kilgour and Wade, 2003].
- **Casein hydrolysate** formula milk has limited evidence of benefit: there have been two small randomized controlled trials and both have methodological weaknesses [Forsyth, 1989; Hill et al, 1995; Kilgour and Wade, 2003].
- **Soya-based infant feeds** were found to reduce the duration of crying compared with standard cows' milk formula in one randomized controlled trial of 19 infants [Campbell, 1989; Kilgour and Wade, 2003]. The Chief Medical Officer recommends that soya infant milk formulas should not be the first choice of treatment for cows' milk sensitivity or lactose intolerance [CMO, 2004]. This is because they have a high phytoestrogen content, and this may pose a risk to future fertility and sexual development [Committee on Toxicity, 2003].

Excluding dairy products from the diet of breastfeeding mothers

- For breastfed infants intolerant of cows' milk protein, a trial of continuing breastfeeding while excluding dairy products from the mother's diet might be effective, because breast milk contains intact cows' milk proteins. But, there are no randomized controlled trials to test this hypothesis [DTB, 1992; Lucassen et al, 1998].

Drug treatments

- **Dicycloverine (dicyclomine)**, an antimuscarinic antispasmodic, is effective, and historically has been widely used. However, dicycloverine is not safe: serious adverse effects include breathing difficulties, seizures, syncope, asphyxia, apnoea, muscular hypotonia, and coma [Kilgour and Wade, 2003].
  - **Antimuscarinics** are used for colic and abdominal pain in adults and older children. However, they have no place in the treatment of infantile colic.
- **Simeticone (activated dimeticone)** has been commonly used to treat infantile colic. Two trials in a total of 110 babies showed no significant difference, while a third trial in 26 babies had methodological limitations and found a small improvement in the number of crying attacks on days 4–7 of treatment [Lucassen et al, 1998; Garrison and Christakis, 2000; Kilgour and Wade, 2003].

C

Behavioural interventions

- Evidence for the efficacy of behavioural interventions comes from studies with methodological weaknesses [Garrison and Christakis, 2000].
- Other strategies, such as increased carrying, early response to crying, soothing motion, car-ride simulators, white noise, etc., have not been shown to be of benefit [Garrison and Christakis, 2000].

Miscellaneous treatments

- **Herbal teas and infusions:**
  - **Japanese star anise** is neurotoxic and has been reported to have poisoned babies, possibly by contaminating Chinese star anise, which has been advertised as a remedy for infant colic [Minodier et al, 2003].
  - One trial of an infusion with five different herbs showed a marked decrease in crying, but there were methodological problems with the study, and the safety of the infusion has not been established [Garrison and Christakis, 2000].
  - **Fennel seed oil emulsion,** in a randomized placebo-controlled trial of 125 infants with colic, eliminated symptoms in 65% of the treatment group and 24% of the placebo group, $p < 0.01$, but its safety has not been established [Alexandrovich et al, 2003].
- **Sucrose:** sucrose seems to have a pacifying effect, but the benefit is so short-lived that it is not a practical treatment [Garrison and Christakis, 2000].
- **Chiropractic spinal manipulation:** one randomized, blinded trial showed no difference from placebo [Olafsdottir et al, 2001]. An earlier trial of spinal manipulation reported improvement with respect to simeticone (activated dimeticone) [Wiberg et al, 1999], but interpretation of the results is marred by methodological weaknesses.
- **Cranial osteopathy:** no randomized controlled trials were found [Kilgour and Wade, 2003]. One randomized controlled trial of 25 infants with colic compared treatment with infant massage with treatment with a crib vibrator and found no statistically significant difference [Kilgour and Wade, 2003].

What resources can support parents of babies with infantile colic?

CRY-SIS is a support group for families with excessively crying, sleepless, and demanding children. Their helpline is available every day from 9 am to 10 pm. Tel: 020 7404 5011.
The CRY-SIS website is at: www.cry-sis.com/index.asp.

What infant milk formulas are available on NHS prescription? And, how do they differ?

Low-lactose and lactose-free infant milk formulas

- Low-lactose infant formulas are prepared by removing almost all lactose from cows' milk, and the resultant product is 'clinically lactose free'. Completely lactose-free milks are prepared from non-milk sources of protein, fat, carbohydrate, and micro-nutrients.
- Available, clinically lactose-free infant milk formulas (with cows' milk protein) are:
  - Enfamil Lactofree® and SMA LF®.

Hypoallergenic infant milk formulas

- Hypoallergenic infant milk formulas are made from hydrolyzed cows' milk protein (casein or whey) or other sources of protein such as soya.
- Hypoallergenic infant milk formulas are also low in, c free of, lactose.
- Available infant milk formulas are:
  - Casein hydrolysate — Nutramigen 1® and Pregestimil®
  - Whey hydrolysate — Pepti-Junior®
- The Chief Medical Officer recommends that soya infa milk formulas should not be the first choice of treatme for cows' milk sensitivity or lactose intolerance [CMC 2004]. This is because they have a high phytoestrogen content, and this may pose a risk to future fertility anc sexual development [Committee on Toxicity, 2003].

Managing treatments with lactase and infa milk formulas

Lactase

- **Formula feeding:** add two drops of lactase to the feed; shake gently; refrigerate for about 4 hours before warming and feeding.
- **Breastfeeding:** express the foremilk into a sterile container; add four drops of lactase; breastfeed as usu and give foremilk with lactase at the end of the feed.
- **Stopping treatment:** stop treatment after about 1 week there has been no response. If there has been a respons wean off the lactase over about 1 week after the age o 3 months.

Low-lactose, lactose-free, and hypoallergenic infa milk formulas

- Feeding is the same as with usual infant milk formulas Preparation is similar; full instructions are with the packaging.
- Continue a trial of treatment until the product is finished, unless it is poorly tolerated.

References

NHS staff in England can link, free of charge, from references to full text journals by clicking on [Full text] c the PRODIGY website.

1. Alexandrovich, I., Rakovitskaya, O., Kolmo, E. et al (2003) The effect of fennel *(Foeniculum vulgare)* see oil emulsion in infantile colic: a randomized, placebc controlled study. *Alternative Therapies in Health an Medicine* 9(4), 58–61. [Full text]
2. Campbell, J.P. (1989) Dietary treatment of infant co a double-blind study. *Journal of the Royal College o General Practitioners* 39(318), 11–14.
3. CMO (2004) *Advice issued on soya-based infant formulas*. CMO Update 37. Department of Health. www.dh.gov.uk [Accessed: 18/05/2004]. [Full text]
4. Committee on Toxicity (2003) *Phytoestrogens and health*. Food Standards Agency. www.food.gov.uk [Accessed: 20/09/2004].
5. Crowcroft, N.S. and Strachan, D.P. (1997) The socia origins of infantile colic: questionnaire study coverin 76747 infants. *British Medical Journal* **314**(7090), 1325–1328. [Full text]
6. DTB (1992) Management of infantile colic. *Drug & Therapeutics Bulletin* **30**(4), 15–16.
7. Forsyth, B.W. (1989) Colic and the effect of changin formulas: a double-blind, multiple-crossover study. *Journal of Pediatrics* **115**(4), 521–526.
8. Garrison, M.M. and Christakis, D.A. (2000) A systematic review of treatments for infant colic. *Pediatrics* **106**(1 Pt 2), 184–190.
9. Gupta, S.K. (2002) Is colic a gastrointestinal disorde *Current Opinion in Pediatrics* **14**(5), 588–592.

10. Hill, D.J., Hudson, I.L., Sheffield, L.J. et al (1995) A low allergen diet is a significant intervention in infantile colic: results of a community-based study. *Journal of Allergy and Clinical Immunology* **96**(6 Pt 1), 886–892.
11. Kilgour, T and Wade, S. (2003) Infantile colic. *Clinical Evidence* **10**, 406–417.
12. Lucassen, P.L., Assendelft, W.J., Gubbels, J.W. et al (1998) Effectiveness of treatments for infantile colic: systematic review. *British Medical Journal* **316**(7144), 1563–1569. [Full text]
13. Lucassen, P.L., Assendelft, W.J., Gubbels, J.W. et al (2000) Infantile colic: crying time reduction with a whey hydrolysate: a double-blind, randomized, placebo-controlled trial. *Pediatrics* **106**(6), 1349–1354. [Full text]
14. Lucassen, P.L., Assendelft, W.J., Gubbels, J.W. and van Geldrop, W.J. (2001) Systematic review of the occurrence of infantile colic in the community. *Archives of Disease in Childhood* **84**(5), 398–403. [Full text]
15. Marks, V., Archbold, P., Augstburger, N. et al (2003) *A systematic approach to the differential diagnosis and management of infant colic*. eGuidelines. Medendium Group Publishing Ltd. www.eguidelines.co.uk [Accessed: 15/06/2004].
16. Miller-Loncar, C., Bigsby, R., High, P. et al (2004) Infant colic and feeding difficulties. *Archives of Disease in Childhood* **89**(10), 908–912.
17. Minodier, P., Pommier, P., Moulene, E. et al (2003) Star anise poisoning in infants. *Archives de Pediatrie* **10**(7), 619–621.
18. Olafsdottir, E., Forshei, S., Fluge, G. and Markestad, T. (2001) Randomised controlled trial of infantile colic treated with chiropractic spinal manipulation. *Archives of Disease in Childhood* **84**(2), 138–141. [Full text]
19. Rao, M.R., Brenner, R.A., Schisterman, E.F. et al (2004) Long term cognitive development in children with prolonged crying. *Archives of Disease in Childhood* **89**(11), 989–992.
20. Reijneveld, S.A., Brugman, E. and Hirasing, R.A. (2000) Infantile colic: maternal smoking as potential risk factor. *Archives of Disease in Childhood* **83**(4), 302–303. [Full text]
21. Reust, C.E. and Blake, R.L., Jr. (2000) Diagnostic workup before diagnosing colic. *Archives of Family Medicine* **9**(3), 282–283. [Full text]
22. Wiberg, J.M., Nordsteen, J. and Nilsson, N. (1999) The short-term effect of spinal manipulation in the treatment of infantile colic: a randomized controlled clinical trial with a blinded observer. *Journal of Manipulative & Physiological Therapeutics* **22**(8), 517–522.

PRODIGY GUIDANCE

Common cold

Last revised in June 2004
www.prodigy.nhs.uk/guidance.asp?gt=Common cold

Applies to people of all ages

This guidance covers management of the common cold.

C

This guidance does not cover influenza, sore throat, or management of the complications of the common cold.

There is separate PRODIGY guidance for *Allergic rhinitis, Chest infections, Febrile convulsion, Influenza, Otitis media — acute, Sinusitis*, and *Sore throat — acute.*

Goals

- Symptomatic management, avoiding over-treatment
- Patient education

Contents

Scenarios
- Treating the common cold in adults p.356
- Treating the common cold in infants and children p.357

Extended Information, p. 358

Which scenario?

- **Treating the common cold in adults:** covers the management of the uncomplicated common cold in adults.
- **Treating the common cold in infants and children:** covers the management of the uncomplicated common cold in infants and children.

Treating the common cold in adults

Which therapy?

- **Reassure** that the common cold is a mild self-limiting illness.
- **Explain** the likely course of the illness, address any underlying concerns, and advise on self-treatment of future episodes of the common cold.
- **Recommend symptomatic treatment** only.
  - Ensure adequate fluid intake.
  - Use paracetamol or ibuprofen as first-choice analgesics/antipyretics.
  - Paracetamol (and increasingly, ibuprofen) are present in many over-the-counter cold remedies. People who are also self-medicating must take care to avoid accidental overdosage.
- **There is no evidence to support the use of the wide variety of other products marketed for the management of the common cold.** Although generally harmless, some contain drugs that may interact with other drugs or exacerbate underlying medical conditions (e.g. decongestants should be avoided in people with hypertension or ischaemic heart disease).
- **A large number of other treatments,** such as steam inhalation and saline nasal drops, are commonly advocated for the relief of symptoms of the common cold. There is little or no evidence to support their use, and clinicians will need to make their own judgement on whether to advise them or not.

Practical prescribing points

For further information please see the *Medicines Compendium* (www.medicines.org.uk) or the *British National Formulary* (www.bnf.org).

- **Paracetamol (and increasingly, ibuprofen)** are present in many over-the-counter cold remedies. People who are also self-medicating must take care to avoid accidental overdosage.
- The Committee on Safety of Medicines (CSM) advises that all nonsteroidal anti-inflammatory drugs (NSAIDs) are associated with serious gastrointestinal toxicity. The risk is greatest in the elderly. All non-selective NSAIDs (such as ibuprofen) are contraindicated in people with a history of peptic ulceration.
- The CSM also warns that any degree of worsening of asthma may be related to the ingestion of NSAIDs either prescribed or bought over the counter.

Patient information leaflets

The following PILs are available at www.prodigy.nhs.uk

- Antibiotics - Why No Antibiotic?
- Common Cold - Adults and Older Children
- Paracetamol

Shared decision making

- **Paracetamol, aspirin,** or **ibuprofen** will ease fever, sore throat, aches, and pains, which may occur with a cold.
- **Have lots to drink.**
- **'Cold remedies'** often contain a mixture of ingredients. There is little evidence that they do much good. However:
  - Some may make you drowsy (possibly helpful at bedtime).
  - Some contain paracetamol, so be careful not to exceed the maximum dose of paracetamol.
  - Antibiotics are not usually advised for a cold as it is caused by a virus.

Drug rationale

Drugs not included

- **Aspirin and nonsteroidal anti-inflammatory drugs,** other than ibuprofen, are excluded because of their extensive adverse effect profiles [Henry et al, 1996; Hernández-Diaz and Rodriguez, 2000; CSM, 2002].
- **Oral decongestants (pseudoephedrine, phenylpropanolamine) are not included** because there is no evidence to support their regular use [Taverner et al, 2003]. They also have potential to cause unwanted sympathomimetic effects, and they should be used with caution in people with diabetes, hypertension, hyperthyroidism, raised intraocular pressure, prostatic

hypertrophy, hepatic or renal impairment, and ischaemic heart disease. People taking monoamine oxidase inhibitors should avoid oral decongestants due to the risk of precipitating a hypertensive crisis [BNF 46, 2003]
Topically administered nasal decongestants (ephedrine, oxymetazoline, xylometazoline) are not included. Prolonged regular use may cause rebound congestion on withdrawal (rhinitis medicamentosa). This may result in the further use of decongestant setting up a vicious circle of over-use.
There are also many other products marketed for sale over the counter to treat the common cold, comprising various combinations of decongestants, demulcents, expectorants, antitussives, and antihistamines. There is no good evidence for or against their use. Many contain illogical combinations and produce a spectrum of adverse effects.

rugs included

Paracetamol is an effective analgesic and antipyretic in most people. It is generally well tolerated and safe. Paracetamol is present in many over-the-counter cold remedies, so people who are self-medicating must take care to avoid accidental overdosage.
Ibuprofen is offered as an alternative analgesic. It is has the most favourable risk–benefit profile of all the nonsteroidal anti-inflammatory drugs [CSM, 2002].

rescriptions

aracetamol preparations

aracetamol tablets: 1g up to four times a day
Age from 16 years onwards
Paracetamol 500mg tablets. Take two tablets every 4 to 6 hours when required for relief of pain or high temperature. Maximum of 8 tablets in 24 hours; supply 56 tablets; NHS Cost £0.42; OTC Cost £0.67.

buprofen preparations

uprofen tablets: 400mg three times a day
Age from 16 years onwards
Ibuprofen 400mg tablets. Take one tablet three times a day when required for relief of pain or high temperature. Do not exceed the stated dose; supply 21 tablets; NHS Cost £0.62; OTC Cost £1.75.

Treating the common cold in nfants and children

Which therapy

Reassure the parents that the common cold is a mild self-limiting illness and that there is no specific curative treatment.
Explain the likely course of the illness, address any underlying concerns, and advise the parents on self-treating future episodes of the common cold.
Recommend symptomatic treatment only.
- Ensure adequate fluid intake.
- Use paracetamol or ibuprofen as first-choice analgesics/antipyretics.
- Paracetamol (and, increasingly, ibuprofen) are present in many over-the-counter cold remedies. Parents who are administering over-the-counter medicines must take care to avoid accidental overdosage.

Saline nasal drops are commonly advocated for the relief of symptoms of the common cold in infants. There is little or no evidence to support their use, and clinicians will need to make their own judgement on whether to advise them or not.
- **In infants there may be irritability, snuffles with difficulty feeding, and diarrhoea.** Diagnosis may be difficult and fever can be the main symptom during the early part of the illness. Septicaemia, meningitis, and pneumonia can also be present and it is important to consider these possibilities.

Practical prescribing points

For further information please see the *Medicines Compendium* (www.medicines.org.uk) or the *British National Formulary* (www.bnf.org).
- **Paracetamol (and, increasingly, ibuprofen)** are present in many over-the-counter cold remedies. Parents who are administering over-the-counter medicines must take care to avoid accidental overdosage.
- The Committee on Safety of Medicines (CSM) advises that all nonsteroidal anti-inflammatory drugs (NSAIDs) are associated with serious gastrointestinal toxicity. All non-selective NSAIDs (such as ibuprofen) are contraindicated in people with a history of peptic ulceration.
- The CSM also warns that any degree of worsening of asthma may be related to the ingestion of NSAIDs either prescribed or bought over the counter.

Patient information leaflets

The following PILs are available at www.prodigy.nhs.uk
- Antibiotics - Why No Antibiotic?
- Coughs and Colds in Children
- Paracetamol
- Temperatures (Fevers) in Children

Shared decision making

- Your child has a cold.
- **Paracetamol** or **ibuprofen** will ease fever, sore throat, aches, and pains.
- **Children under 16 years should not be given aspirin.**
- **Give the child lots to drink.**
- **'Cold remedies'** often contain a mixture of ingredients. There is little evidence that they do much good. However:
  - Some may make a child drowsy (possibly helpful at bedtime).
  - Some contain paracetamol, so be careful not to exceed the maximum dose of paracetamol.
  - Antibiotics are not usually advised for a cold as it is caused by a virus.

Drug rationale

Drugs not included

- **Aspirin is not licensed for use in children under the age of 16 years** because of the risk of Reye's syndrome [CSM, 2002].
- **Nonsteroidal anti-inflammatory drugs,** other than ibuprofen, are not licensed to treat pyrexia in children.
- **Oral/topical decongestants:** there is no evidence to support the use of oral or topical decongestants in children less than 12 years old with the common cold [Taverner et al, 2003].
- **There are also many other products marketed** for sale over the counter to treat the common cold, comprising various combinations of decongestants, demulcents, expectorants, antitussives, and antihistamines. There is no good evidence for or against their use. Many contain illogical combinations and produce a spectrum of

adverse effects. Antitussives containing codeine or opioid derivatives are not recommended in children and should be avoided altogether in children under the age of 1 year [BNF 46, 2003].

Drugs included

- **Paracetamol** is an effective first-choice analgesic and antipyretic in most children. It is generally well tolerated and safe. Paracetamol is present in many over-the-counter cold remedies, so parents using over-the-counter medication must take care to avoid accidental overdosage.
- **Ibuprofen** is offered as an alternative analgesic and antipyretic. It is has the most favourable risk–benefit profile of all the nonsteroidal anti-inflammatory drugs [CSM, 2002].

Prescriptions

Paracetamol preparations

Paracetamol s/f susp: 10-15 mg/kg up to four times a day

- Age from 1 month to 2 months
- Paracetamol 120mg/5ml s/f susp. *WEIGHT REQUIRED* Give 10-15 mg per kg bodyweight every 4 to 6 hours. Max of 4 doses (or 60mg per kg) in 24 hours; supply 100 ml; NHS Cost £0.43; OTC Cost £1.95.

Paracetamol s/f susp: 60mg to 120mg up to four times a day

- Age from 3 to 11 months
- Paracetamol 120mg/5ml s/f susp. Take 2.5ml to 5ml every 4 to 6 hours when required for relief of pain or high temperature. Maximum of 4 doses in 24 hours; supply 150 ml; NHS Cost £0.65; OTC Cost £3.49.

Paracetamol s/f susp: 120mg to 240mg up to four times a day

- Age from 12 months to 5 years
- Paracetamol 120mg/5ml s/f susp. Take one to two 5ml spoonfuls every 4 to 6 hours when required for relief of pain or high temperature. Maximum of 4 doses in 24 hours; supply 300 ml; NHS Cost £1.26; OTC Cost £6.98.

Paracetamol s/f susp: 250mg to 500mg up to four times a day

- Age from 6 to 11 years
- Paracetamol 250mg/5ml s/f susp. Take one to two 5ml spoonfuls every 4 to 6 hours when required for relief of pain or high temperature. Maximum of 4 doses in 24 hours; supply 300 ml; NHS Cost £1.70; OTC Cost £10.17.

Paracetamol tablets: 500mg to 1g up to four times a day

- Age from 12 to 15 years
- Paracetamol 500mg tablets. Take one to two tablets every 4 to 6 hours when required for relief of pain or high temperature. Maximum of 8 tablets in 24 hours; supply 56 tablets; NHS Cost £0.42; OTC Cost £0.67.

Ibuprofen preparations

Ibuprofen s/f susp: 5mg/kg three to four times a day

- Age from 1 month to 11 months
- Ibuprofen 100mg/5ml s/f susp. *WEIGHT REQUIRED* Take 5mg per kg bodyweight 3 to 4 times a day when required for relief of pain or high temperature; supply 100 ml; NHS Cost £1.82; OTC Cost £3.53.

Ibuprofen s/f susp: 50mg three to four times a day

- Age from 12 months to 2 years
- Ibuprofen 100mg/5ml s/f susp. Take 2.5ml three to four times a day when required for relief of pain or high temperature. Do not exceed the stated dose; supply 100 ml; NHS Cost £1.82; OTC Cost £3.53.

Ibuprofen s/f susp: 100mg three to four times a day

- Age from 3 to 7 years
- Ibuprofen 100mg/5ml s/f susp. Take one 5ml spoonful to 4 times a day when required for relief of pain or hig temperature. Do not exceed the stated dose; supply 15 ml; NHS Cost £2.73; OTC Cost £4.81.

Ibuprofen s/f susp: 200mg three to four times a day

- Age from 8 to 11 years
- Ibuprofen 100mg/5ml s/f susp. Take two 5ml spoonful 3 to 4 times a day when required for relief of pain or high temperature. Do not exceed the stated dose; supply 300 ml; NHS Cost £5.46; OTC Cost £9.62.

Ibuprofen tablets: 200mg three times a day

- Age from 12 to 16 years
- Ibuprofen 200mg tablets. Take one tablet three times a day when required for relief of pain or high temperatu Do not exceed the stated dose; supply 21 tablets; NHS Cost £0.42; OTC Cost £0.49.

Ibuprofen tablets: 400mg three times a day

- Age from 12 to 16 years
- Ibuprofen 400mg tablets. Take one tablet three times a day when required for relief of pain or high temperatu Do not exceed the stated dose; supply 21 tablets; NHS Cost £0.62; OTC Cost £1.75.

Extended Information

Background information

- What is it? p.358
- How common is it? p.358
- How do I know my patient has it? p.359
- What else might it be? p.359
- Complications and prognosis p.359

What is it?

- **The common cold** is an acute, mild, self-limiting catarrhal syndrome [Gwaltney, 1995a].
- It is an infection usually caused by members of five families of viruses — myxovirus, paramyxovirus (parainfluenza, respiratory syncytial virus), adenovirus picornavirus (rhinovirus), and coronavirus groups. Rhinoviruses (40% of colds) and coronaviruses (10% colds) are the most common causes [Gwaltney, 1995a; Durand and Joseph, 2001].
- **Influenza viruses and adenoviruses** also produce a spectrum of disease that overlaps with the common col [Gwaltney, 1995a].
- **The incubation period** varies from 24–72 hours depending on the infecting virus [Gwaltney, 1995a].
- **Transmission of the infection:**
  - Is caused by inhalation of airborne respiratory droplets from people infected with the virus [Dolin, 2001]
  - Possibly also occurs by direct contact with infectious secretions. Some viruses may be spread by hand contact [Gwaltney, 1995a].
  - Is not associated with exposure to cold temperatures, fatigue, or sleep deprivation [Dolin, 2001].
  - Transmission most commonly occurs in the home, school, and day-care centres. The main reservoir of viruses is in young children [Gwaltney, 1995a].

How common is it?

- **Adults** have an average of between two and four colds year [Gwaltney, 1995a].
- **Children** have up to 12 colds a year [Helms and Henderson, 2003]. Young children in nursery schools

may average up to nine colds during the winter months [Gwaltney, 1995a].

Boys have slightly more colds than girls up to adolescence, but the incidence is then slightly higher in women [Gwaltney, 1995a].

Adults with children at home have more colds than people without children [Gwaltney, 1995a].

Annual epidemics occur within the colder months in temperate climates and during the rainy season in the tropics [Gwaltney, 1995a].

In the UK, the incidence of the common cold is highest in the cold months, peaking during December and January [Royal College of General Practitioners, 2003]. One of the causes for this is believed to be the bringing together of children at school and the increased crowding of the population indoors during the winter months [Gwaltney, 1995a].

How do I know my patient has it?

The most frequent symptoms are nasal discharge, nasal obstruction, sore or 'scratchy' throat, headache, and cough. Hoarseness, loss of taste and smell, mild burning of the eyes, and a feeling of pressure in the ears or sinuses due to obstruction and/or mucosal swelling may also occur [Gwaltney, 1995a].

Cough is associated with 30% of colds and tends to become the most bothersome symptom. It generally starts on about the 4th or 5th day when nasal symptoms decrease [Turner, 1998].

There may be a mild increase in body temperature, although this is rarely above 1°C in adults. Infants and young children are more likely to develop higher temperatures [Gwaltney, 1995a].

In infants there may be irritability, snuffles resulting in difficulty feeding, and diarrhoea [Helms and Henderson, 2003]. Diagnosis may be difficult and fever can be the main symptom during the early part of the illness [Heikkinen and Jarvinen, 2003].

Most people will reliably self-diagnose themselves within 16 hours of the onset of symptoms [Arruda et al, 1997]. Otherwise, the diagnosis will be evident from the clinical history and examination [Anzueto and Niederman, 2003].

What else might it be?

Adults

Allergic rhinitis is characterized by nasal itching, sneezing, watery rhinorrhoea, and nasal obstruction. It is also often accompanied by itchy, watery eyes. It can be perennial, seasonal, or due to occupational exposure.

Non-allergic rhinitis includes non-allergenic perennial rhinitis and also rhinitis due to occupational, hormonal, and environmental factors. People present with chronic nasal symptoms.

Pharyngitis: acute pharyngitis is caused by a variety of organisms including the adenoviruses and *Streptococcus pyogenes*. This pharyngitis is often more severe than the mild-to-moderate pharyngeal discomfort in the common cold.

Influenza initially presents with systemic symptoms, including fever, rigors, headaches, myalgia, malaise, and anorexia.

Children

In addition to the above list consider:

Foreign body in nose: the discharge is unilateral, purulent, foul-smelling, and bloodstained.

Infants

In infants who are feeding poorly, consider the possibility of a more serious condition:

- Meningitis
- Septicaemia
- Pneumonia

[Betts, 1995; Gwaltney, 1995a; Gwaltney, 1995b; Weinberger, 1995; Van Cauwenburge et al, 2000; Helms and Henderson, 2003]

Complications and prognosis

Complications

- **Young children may develop** bronchiolitis, viral pneumonia, and croup [Gwaltney, 1995a; Dolin, 2001].
- **Infants less than 3 months of age** are particularly susceptible to developing secondary bacterial lower respiratory infections [Helms and Henderson, 2003].
- **Approximately 65% of people over 60 years** who live in the community and develop a rhinovirus infection can be expected to develop a lower respiratory tract illness. If there is a coexisting chronic medical condition or the person smokes then this risk is increased [Nicholson et al, 1996].
- **Acute otitis media** (AOM) occurs in 2% of people with a cold [Gwaltney, 1995a]. The incidence of AOM positively correlates with the incidence of the common cold in children each year [Royal College of General Practitioners, 2003].
- **Bacterial infection of the paranasal sinuses** occurs in 0.5% of people with a cold [Gwaltney, 1995a].
- **People with chronic obstructive pulmonary disease** who have a rhinovirus infection are more likely to have a longer duration of illness, a more severe illness, and to cough for longer afterwards than those without lung disease [Wald et al, 1995].
- The common cold is a major cause of absenteeism from work and school [Gwaltney, 1995a].

Prognosis

- The median duration of a common cold is a week [Gwaltney, 1995a].
- Approximately 25% of colds will last up to 2 weeks, and in smokers with a rhinovirus infection the cough is more likely to be troublesome and prolonged [Gwaltney, 1995a; Turner, 1998]. Cigarette smokers are likely to have a more severe illness than non-smokers but do not have higher incidence of colds [Gwaltney, 1995a; Greenberg et al, 2000].

Management issues

- General p.359
- Supportive (non-pharmacological) management p.360
- Recommended pharmacological management p.360
- Other common symptomatic treatments, not recommended by PRODIGY p.360

General

- There are no drugs of proven benefit for the prophylaxis or treatment of the common cold. Therefore, medical management is centred around providing symptomatic relief.
- Some studies have been performed under laboratory conditions on people with experimentally induced colds, making extrapolation to the clinical situation difficult.

Supportive (non-pharmacological) management

- **Reassure** that the common cold is a mild self-limiting illness.
- **Give a full explanation** of the likely course of the illness.
- **Recommend** symptomatic treatment only.
- **Ensure adequate fluid intake.**
- **Educate the person** about self-treatment in the future, addressing any underlying concerns. Taking the time to educate people that colds are self-limiting and have no specific curative treatment may reduce anxiety and prevent unnecessary visits to the doctor in the future [Lissauer and Clayden, 2001].

Recommended pharmacological management

- **Paracetamol** is an effective first-choice analgesic and antipyretic in most people [MeReC, 2000]. It is generally well tolerated and safe. Paracetamol is present in many over-the-counter cold remedies, so people who are self-medicating must take care to avoid accidental overdosage.
- **Aspirin (in adults) and ibuprofen (in children)** are the only nonsteroidal anti-inflammatory drugs licensed to treat pyrexia. Aspirin has a higher incidence of adverse effects than does ibuprofen [Henry et al, 1996; Hernández-Diaz and Rodriguez, 2000; CSM, 2002].
- **There is no evidence to support the use of the wide variety of other products marketed for the management of the common cold.**

Other common symptomatic treatments, not recommended by PRODIGY

- **A large number of different treatments** have been advocated for the relief of symptoms of the common cold. There is little or no evidence to support their use, and clinicians will need to make their own judgement on whether to advise them or not. The treatments most commonly advised are discussed below.
- **Saline nose drops** (0.9%) administered immediately before feeding in infants may ease nasal stuffiness [BNF 46, 2003]. There is no evidence to support their use.
- **Steam inhalation** has been used for the symptomatic relief of the common cold for decades. Although there does not appear to be any clear evidence of benefit (e.g. objective evidence of decreased viral shedding), neither is there a worsening of clinical symptom scores [Singh, 2003].
- **Vitamin C** in large daily doses (more than 1 g daily) may provide a modest benefit in terms of reducing the duration of cold symptoms. However, long-term supplementation does not appear to prevent colds [Douglas et al, 2003].
- **Oral decongestants (e.g. pseudoephedrine, phenylpropanolamine) or topically administered nasal decongestants (e.g. ephedrine, oxymetazoline, xylometazoline):** there is no evidence to support regular use of any of these. Topical nasal decongestants have an immediate beneficial effect on reducing nasal stuffiness, but prolonged regular use may cause rebound congestion on withdrawal (rhinitis medicamentosa), resulting in continued inappropriate use. Although oral preparations are not as immediately effective as topical preparations, they do not cause rebound congestion on withdrawal. Adverse effects of systemic decongestants result from unwanted sympathomimetic effects, and they should be used with caution in people with diabetes, hypertension, hyperthyroidism, raised intraocular pressure, prostatic hypertrophy, hepatic or renal impairment, or ischaemic heart disease. Avoid in people taking monoamine oxidase inhibitors due to the possibility of hypertensiv crisis [BNF 46, 2003]. There is no evidence to support the use of oral or topical decongestants in children less than 12 years old with the common cold [Taverner et a 2003].
- **Demulcents, expectorants, antitussives, and antihistamines:** there is no good evidence for or agains the use of over-the-counter remedies in the treatment o acute cough [Schroeder and Fahey, 2003]. Many conta illogical combinations and produce a spectrum of adverse effects. Antitussives containing codeine or opic derivatives are not recommended in children and shou be avoided altogether in children under the age of 1 ye [BNF 46, 2003].
- **Antibiotics:** a Cochrane review did not find enough evidence to warrant their routine use in either children adults, and there is a significant increase in adverse effects associated with their use in adults [Aroll and Kenealy, 2003]. *They do not influence either the cours of the illness or the likelihood of complications in children* [Fahey et al, 1998]. In people with chronic obstructive pulmonary disease, antibiotics have been shown to be effective only if the person has at least twc out of the following three features: increased breathlessness, increased sputum volume, and development of purulent sputum [British Thoracic Society, 1997].
- **Alternative remedies**
  - **Echinacea:** recent randomized controlled trials have shown no benefit in either adults or children. Its increased use in recent years has highlighted concern regarding possible adverse effects [Barrett et al, 200 UK Medicines Information, 2002; Melchart et al, 2003; Taylor et al, 2003].
  - **Zinc lozenges:** there is no strong evidence of efficacy There are doubts about the bioavailability of differe formulations, and most formulations produce advers effects (nausea, taste disturbances, and irritation of t oral mucosa) [Jackson et al, 1997; Marshall, 2003].
  - **Complementary therapies:** there is a lack of compelling evidence for relieving symptoms of uppe respiratory infections [Ernst, 2001].

References

NHS staff in England can link, free of charge, from references to full text journals by clicking on [Full text] o the PRODIGY website.

1. Anzueto, A. and Niederman, M.S. (2003) Diagnosis and treatment of rhinovirus respiratory infections. *Chest* **123**(5), 1664–1672. [Full text]
2. Arruda, E., Pitkaranta, A., Witek, T.J., Jr. et al (1997 Frequency and natural history of rhinovirus infection in adults during autumn. *Journal of Clinical Microbiology* **35**(11), 2864–2868.
3. Betts, R.F. (1995) Influenza virus. In: Mandell, G.L., Bennett, J.E., Dolin, R. et al (Eds.) *Principles and practice of infectious diseases: volume* 2. 4th edn. London: Churchill Livingstone. 1546–1567.
4. BNF 46 (2003) *British National Formulary*. 46th edn London: British Medical Association and Royal Pharmaceutical Society of Great Britain.
5. CSM (2002) Non-steroidal anti-inflammatory drugs (NSAIDs) and gastrointestinal (GI) safety. *Current Problems in Pharmacovigilance* **28**(Apr), 5.
6. Dolin, R. (2001) Common viral respiratory infection In: Braunwald, E., Fauci, A.S., Kasper, D.L. et al (Ed *Harrison's principles of internal medicine*. 15th edn. New York: McGraw-Hill. 1120–1125.

Durand, M. and Joseph, M. (2001) Infections of the upper respiratory tract. In: Braunwald, E., Fauci, A.S., Kasper, D.L. et al (Eds.) *Harrison's principles of internal medicine*. 15th edn. New York: McGraw-Hill. 187–193.

Greenberg, S.B., Allen, M., Wilson, J. and Atmar, R.L. (2000) Respiratory viral infections in adults with and without chronic obstructive pulmonary disease. *American Journal of Respiratory & Critical Care Medicine* **162**(1), 167–173.

Gwaltney, J.M., Jr (1995a) The common cold. In: Mandell, G.L., Bennett, J.E., Dolin, R. et al (Eds.) *Principles and practice of infectious diseases: volume 1*. 4th edn. London: Churchill Livingstone. 561–566.

Gwaltney, J.M., Jr (1995b) Pharyngitis. In: Mandell, G.L., Bennett, J.E., Dolin, R. et al (Eds.) *Principles and practice of infectious diseases: volume 1*. 4th edn. London: Churchill Livingstone. 566–572.

Heikkinen, T. and Jarvinen, A. (2003) The common cold. *Lancet* **361**(9351), 51–59. [Full text]

Helms, P.J. and Henderson, J. (2003) Respiratory disorders. In: McIntosh, N., Helms, P.J., Smyth, R.L. et al (Eds.) *Textbook of pediatrics*. 6th edn. London: Churchill Livingstone. 774–775.

Henry, D., Lim, L.L., Garcia-Rodriguez, L.A. et al (1996) Variability in risk of gastrointestinal complications with individual non-steroidal anti-inflammatory drugs: results of a collaborative meta-analysis. *British Medical Journal* **312**(7046), 1563–1566. [Full text]

Hernández-Diaz, S. and Rodriguez, L.A. (2000) Association between nonsteroidal anti-inflammatory drugs and upper gastrointestinal tract bleeding/perforation: an overview of epidemiologic studies published in the 1990s. *Archives of Internal Medicine* **160**(14), 2093–2099. [Full text]

15. Lissauer, T. and Clayden, G. (Eds.) (2001) Respiratory disorders. In: *Illustrated textbook of pediatrics*. 2nd edn. London: Mosby. 216–217.
16. MeReC (2000) The use of oral analgesics in primary care. *MeReC Bulletin* **11**(1), 1–4.
17. Nicholson, K.G., Kent, J., Hammersley, V. and Cancio, E. (1996) Risk factors for lower respiratory complications of rhinovirus infections in elderly people living in the community: prospective cohort study. *British Medical Journal* **313**(7065), 1119–1123. [Full text]
18. Royal College of General Practitioners (2003) Reporting respiratory illness in the weekly returns service. *CDR Weekly* **13**(4), 13–15.
19. Taverner, D., Bickford, L. and Draper, M. (2003) *Nasal decongestants for the common cold (Cochrane Review)*. The Cochrane Library. Issue 4. Oxford: Update Software.
20. Turner, R.B. (1998) The common cold. *Pediatric Annals* **27**(12), 790–795. [Full text]
21. Van Cauwenburge, P., Bachert, C., Passalacqua, G. et al (2000) Consensus statement on the treatment of allergic rhinitis. European Academy of Allergology and Clinical Immunology. *Allergy* **55**(2), 116–134.
22. Wald, T.G., Shult, P., Krause, P. et al (1995) A rhinovirus outbreak among residents of a long-term care facility. *Annals of Internal Medicine* **123**(8), 588–593.
23. Weinberger, S.E. (1995) Bronchiectasis. In: Braunwald, E., Fauci, A.S., Kasper, D.L. et al (Eds.) *Harrison's principles of internal medicine*. 15th edn. New York: McGraw-Hill. 1485–1487.

C

PRODIGY GUIDANCE

Conjunctivitis — allergic

Last revised in February 2005
www.prodigy.nhs.uk/guidance.asp?gt=Conjunctivitis - allergic

Applies to people over the age of 1 month

This guidance covers the management of seasonal allergic conjunctivitis and perennial allergic conjunctivitis.

This guidance does not cover the management of atopic keratoconjunctivitis, vernal keratoconjunctivitis, or giant papillary conjunctivitis.

There is separate PRODIGY guidance for *Conjunctivitis — infective*, *Blepharitis*, *Dry eye syndrome*, and *Allergic rhinitis*.

C

Goals

- To relieve symptoms
- To reduce the incidence and severity of symptoms

Contents

Scenarios
- Allergic conjunctivitis p.362

Extended Information, p. 364

Allergic conjunctivitis

Which therapy?

Assess the cause of the red eye

- Exclude the serious causes of a red eye.
- Distinguish infective from allergic causes of conjunctivitis.
- Distinguish the type of allergic conjunctivitis.

Treating seasonal and perennial conjunctivitis

- **Prescribe a topical antihistamine for rapid relief if symptomatic at presentation;** azelastine, emedastine, levocabastine, ketotifen, and olopatadine are alternatives.
- **Prescribe a mast cell stabilizer for prophylaxis.** Sodium cromoglicate eye drops are effective and may also provide symptom relief. Lodoxamide and nedocromil are alternatives.
- **Consider oral antihistamines** if there are associated nasal symptoms e.g. rhinorrhoea.
- Cold compresses can be suggested for soothing the eyes.

Managing giant papillary conjunctivitis

- **Consider discontinuing the wearing of contact lenses** to allow the inflammation to settle, if they are causing irritation.
- Contact lenses can be re-commenced with new lenses, once the major symptoms of inflammation have settled.
- **Advice the patient to seek advice from their optician** regarding hygiene measures, more frequent contact lens changing, and a possible change of contact lens type, if the problem recurs. Topical sodium cromoglicate (2%) can be used to relieve symptoms while hygiene measures take effect.

Managing allergic contact dermatitis with conjunctivitis

- Identify and avoid the causative allergen, usually eye drops, cosmetics, or industrial chemicals.

Practical prescribing points

For further information please see the *Medicines Compendium* (www.medicines.org.uk) or the *British National Formulary* (www.bnf.org).

- **Contact lenses** should generally not be worn during treatment with eye drops. However:
  - **Hard lenses:** use eye drops 30 minutes before insertin[g] lenses.
  - **Soft lenses:** eye drops containing preservatives should not be used with soft lenses. (Some preservatives, particularly benzalkonium chloride, accumulate in so[ft] contact lenses and cause irritation.)
- **Non-sedating oral antihistamines:** although drowsiness [is] rare, people should be advised that it can occur and tha[t] these agents may affect the performance of skilled tasks such as driving.

Should I refer or investigate?

- Refer all people for same-day assessment if they have a[ny] of the following features that could indicate iritis, keratitis, or acute glaucoma:
  - Moderate to severe eye pain
  - Marked eye redness
  - Ciliary injection
  - Loss of visual acuity
- Refer all babies if they have any signs of conjunctivitis within the first 28 days of life (this must be distinguishe[d] from a simple sticky eye when there are no signs of inflammation of the conjunctiva).
- Refer people with symptoms that persist despite treatment, particularly if there are features of atopic keratoconjunctivitis, vernal keratoconjunctivitis, or allergic contact dermatitis with conjunctivitis, or when these conditions are associated with corneal involvement.

Patient information leaflets

The following PILs are available at www.prodigy.nhs.uk

- Conjunctivitis - Allergic
- Eye Drops - (How to Use)
- Hay Fever

Shared decision making

- Allergic conjunctivitis is usually due to pollen and occu[rs] in the hay fever season. Allergies to other things are sometimes the cause.

Do not wear contact lenses if you have conjunctivitis, if you are using anti-allergy eye drops, or if you have used anti-allergy eye drops in the previous 24 hours. If symptoms are mild, contact lenses can be applied 5–10 minutes after eye drop application, however.
Try to ensure low exposure to pollen when hay fever symptoms are expected. For example, keep windows closed, do not cut grass, stay indoors as much as possible, etc.
A cold compress with a flannel and cold water are soothing.
Sodium cromoglicate eye drops are effective and safe. For the best effect, you should use them regularly throughout the season when symptoms are expected.
Antihistamine eye drops are an alternative. They have a quick action and can be used 'as required' for short periods if symptoms are not too bad but flare up from time to time.
Antihistamine tablets or medicine are alternatives if other symptoms of hay fever are also present (such as a runny nose).

Drug rationale

Drugs not included

Otrivine-Antistin® eye drops contain antazoline (antihistamine) and xylometazoline (vasoconstrictor). Although this is an established product that may be used for short-term relief, systemic effects are possible and it should not be used for long periods of time [BNF 47, 2004].
Sedating oral antihistamines are not recommended because they are no more effective than non-sedating antihistamines, but have more adverse effects and generally require more than once-a-day dosing.
Non-sedating oral antihistamines: acrivastine requires more than once-a-day dosing, and there are safety concerns associated with terfenadine [BNF 47, 2004].
Topical ocular corticosteroids should not be initiated in primary care for this condition [BNF 47, 2004].

Drugs included

Topical mast cell stabilizers are safe and effective both in relieving, and preventing, allergic conjunctivitis. Three products are available in the United Kingdom:
- **Sodium cromoglicate** is the preferred first-line choice. It is inexpensive and suitable for use in young children.
- **Lodoxamide and nedocromil** are newer, more expensive topical agents available as alternatives to sodium cromoglicate.

[BNF 47, 2004; Owen et al, 2004]
Azelastine, emedastine, and levocabastine are single-agent topical antihistamines which give quick relief of allergic conjunctivitis. They are well tolerated, have few adverse effects, and have a rapid onset of action [Owen et al, 2004].
Olopatadine and ketotifen are newer topical antihistamines that have mast cell stabilizer activity. They currently have black triangle status and are recommended for use when standard topical treatment has been poorly tolerated or is ineffective.
Non-sedating antihistamines are recommended when there is coexisting allergic rhinitis:
- **Cetirizine and loratadine** are well established agents with a good efficacy and safety profile. They are taken once a day and are suitable for young children.
- **Fexofenadine and mizolastine** are alternative once-daily regimens suitable for older children and adults.
- **Desloratadine (a metabolite of loratadine) and levocetirizine (an isomer of cetirizine)** are more recently marketed products that are still under close post-marketing surveillance (black triangle).

[DTB, 2002]

Prescriptions

Antihistamine eye drops for rapid relief

Otrivine-Antistin eye drops
- Age from 5 years onwards
- Otrivine-Antistin eye drops. Put one drop into each eye 2 to 3 times a day; supply 10 ml; NHS Cost £2.35; OTC Cost £4.39.

Azelastine 0.05% eye drops
- Age from 4 years onwards
- Azelastine 0.05% eye drops. Put one drop into each eye twice a day. Increase to four times a day if required; supply 8 ml; NHS Cost £6.88.

Emedastine 0.05% eye drops
- Age from 3 years onwards
- Emedastine 0.05% eye drops. Put one drop into each eye twice a day; supply 5 ml; NHS Cost £7.69.

Levocabastine 0.05% eye drops.
- Age from 9 years onwards
- Levocabastine 0.05% eye drops. Put one drop into each eye twice a day. Increase to 3 to 4 times a day if required. Stop if there is no improvement within 3 days; supply 4 ml; NHS Cost £8.49.

Levocabastine 0.05% eye drops
- Age from 12 years onwards
- Levocabastine 0.05% eye drops. Put one drop into each eye twice a day. Increase to 3 to 4 times a day if required. Stop if there is no improvement within 3 days; supply 3 ml; NHS Cost £3.28; OTC Cost £5.75.

Mast cell stabiliser eye drops for prophylaxis

Sodium cromoglicate 2% eye drops
- Age from 1 month onwards
- Sodium cromoglicate 2% eyedrops. Put one drop into each eye four times a day; supply 14 ml; NHS Cost £1.96; OTC Cost £3.45.

Nedocromil 2% eye drops
- Age from 6 years onwards
- Nedocromil 2% eye drops. Put one drop into each eye twice a day. Increase to four times a day if required; supply 5 ml; NHS Cost £9.31.

Lodoxamide 0.1% eye drops
- Age from 4 years onwards
- Lodoxamide 0.1% eye drops. Put one drop into each eye four times a day; supply 10 ml; NHS Cost £5.48.

Olopatadine and ketotifen (2nd line combined action drugs)

Olopatadine 1mg/ml eye drops
- Age from 3 years onwards
- Olopatadine 1mg/ml eye drops. Put one drop into each eye twice a day; supply 5 ml; NHS Cost £8.77.

Ketotifen 250micrograms/ml eye drops
- Age from 3 years onwards
- Ketotifen 250mcg/ml eye drops. Put one drop into each eye twice a day; supply 5 ml; NHS Cost £9.75.

Oral antihistamines: non-sedating

Cetirizine s/f solution: 5mg once a day
- Age from 2 to 5 years
- Cetirizine 5mg/5ml s/f sol. Take one 5ml spoonful once a day; supply 200 ml; NHS Cost £9.77; OTC Cost £17.22.

C

Cetirizine s/f solution: 10mg once a day
- Age from 6 to 11 years
- Cetirizine 5mg/5ml s/f sol. Take two 5ml spoonfuls once a day; supply 300 ml; NHS Cost £14.66; OTC Cost £25.83.

Cetirizine tablets: 10mg once a day
- Age from 12 years onwards
- Cetirizine 10mg tablets. Take one tablet once a day; supply 30 tablets; NHS Cost £5.64; OTC Cost £9.94.

Loratadine syrup: 5mg once a day
- Age from 2 to 5 years
- Loratadine 5mg/5ml syrup. Take one 5ml spoonful once a day; supply 200 ml; NHS Cost £10.86; OTC Cost £19.14.

Loratadine syrup: 10mg once a day
- Age from 6 to 11 years
- Loratadine 5mg/5ml syrup. Take two 5ml spoonfuls once a day; supply 300 ml; NHS Cost £16.29; OTC Cost £28.71.

Loratadine tablets: 10mg once a day
- Age from 12 years onwards
- Loratadine 10mg tablets. Take one tablet once a day; supply 30 tablets; NHS Cost £4.09; OTC Cost £7.21.

Fexofenadine tablets: 30mg twice a day
- Age from 6 to 11 years
- Fexofenadine 30mg tablets. Take one tablet twice a day; supply 60 tablets; NHS Cost £6.11.

Fexofenadine tablets: 120mg once a day
- Age from 12 years onwards
- Fexofenadine 120mg tablets. Take one tablet once a day; supply 30 tablets; NHS Cost £8.14.

Mizolastine tablets: 10mg once a day
- Age from 12 years onwards
- Mizolastine 10mg tablets. Take one tablet once a day; supply 30 tablets; NHS Cost £5.77.

Levocetirizine tablets: 5mg once a day
- Age from 6 years onwards
- Levocetirizine 5mg tablets. Take one tablet once a day; supply 30 tablets; NHS Cost £7.45.

Desloratadine syrup: 1.25mg once a day
- Age from 2 to 5 years
- Desloratadine 2.5mg/5ml syrup. Take 2.5ml once a day; supply 100 ml; NHS Cost £7.00.

Desloratadine syrup: 2.5mg once a day
- Age from 6 to 11 years
- Desloratadine 2.5mg/5ml syrup. Take one 5ml spoonful once a day; supply 200 ml; NHS Cost £14.08.

Desloratadine tablets: 5mg once a day
- Age from 12 years onwards
- Desloratadine 5mg tablets. Take one tablet once a day; supply 30 tablets; NHS Cost £7.04.

Extended Information

Background information

- What is it? p.364
- How common is it? p.364
- How do I know my patient has it? p.364
- What else might it be? p.365
- Complications and prognosis p.365

What is it?

- **Allergic conjunctivitis is inflammation of the conjunctiva** that occurs due to hypersensitivity reactions following sensitization and re-exposure to an allergen. The conjunctiva is a thin protective membrane that covers the surface of the eye and the inside surface of the eyelids.
- **Type I hypersensitivity** reactions occur immediately following contact with the allergen, causing mast cells to degranulate, leading to conjunctivitis.
- **Type IV hypersensitivity** reactions develop 24–48 hours after contact with an allergen and lead to inflammation without degranulation of mast cells.
- **Mast cells degranulate, releasing histamine** and other inflammatory mediators. These mediators cause:
  - Conjunctival blood vessels to dilate and the eye to appear red
  - Increased permeability of blood vessels resulting in oedema
  - Itch and pain
- **Pure Type I hypersensitivity reactions** are frequently associated with allergic rhinitis/hay fever; they are caused by airborne allergen and rarely involve the cornea.
  - **Seasonal allergic conjunctivitis** is caused mostly by pollens, which occur seasonally.
  - **Perennial allergic conjunctivitis** is caused by allergens that are present in the environment year-round, primarily house dust mites.
- **Pure Type IV hypersensitivity reactions occur with contact allergic dermatitis with conjunctivitis,** most commonly caused by eye drops, cosmetics, and industrial chemicals, and may involve the cornea.
- **Mixed Type IV and Type I reactions occur with giant papillary conjunctivitis,** a syndrome of inflammation of the conjunctiva lining the upper eyelid occurring in the presence of an ocular foreign body (primarily soft contact lenses, but also hard lenses and sutures following surgery to the eye).

[Freissler et al, 1997]

How common is it?

- **Allergic conjunctivitis** is the cause of around 15% of all eye problems presenting in general practice [Manners, 1997], accounting for 4–5 cases per 1000 population per year [Royal College of General Practitioners and Royal College of Ophthalmologists, 2001]; 2–5% of all general practice consultations are eye-related [Manners, 1997].
- **Seasonal allergic conjunctivitis** accounts for half of all cases of allergic conjunctivitis [Freissler et al, 1997].
- **Contact allergic dermatitis with conjunctivitis** is the most common form of allergic reaction seen by the ophthalmologist [Rubenstein and Jick, 2004].
- **Giant papillary conjunctivitis:** estimates of prevalence vary from 1–5% of people using soft lenses, to 1% of people using hard lenses [Rubenstein and Jick, 2004].

How do I know my patient has it?

Seasonal and perennial allergic conjunctivitis (atopic conjunctivitis)

Symptoms
- **Sudden onset of itching** is the main symptom.
- **A burning sensation** may be reported.
- **Minimal photophobia** may occur.

Signs
- **Bilateral 'red eye'** caused by engorgement of the conjunctival blood vessels may be minimal to severe.
- **Clear watery discharge** may be present.
- **Oedema** may be seen collecting between the conjunctiva and the eye, forming a boggy sac filled with clear fluid below the coloured part of the eye (chemosis).
- **Papillae** (oedema in round swellings with an appearance like cobblestones) may be seen on the inside of the eyelids when inflammation is chronic.
- **Lid swelling** may occur.

Contact allergic dermatitis with conjunctivitis

- Symptoms and signs are as for allergic conjunctivitis but onset is gradual following contact of the eye with allergen.
- Contact dermatitis of the eyelids is also seen.
- Punctate epithelial keratitis and erosions may be seen with fluorescein staining.
- Commonly presents in individuals who are not atopic who are using eye drops.
- May be distinguished from other allergic conjunctivitis by complete lack of response to treatment with antihistamines or mast cell stabilizers.

Giant papillary conjunctivitis

Giant papillary conjunctivitis should be considered in people with conjunctivitis who wear contact lenses or who have had surgery to the eye. Symptoms develop slowly and precede signs.

Symptoms

- Itching after removal of contact lenses.
- Increased awareness of contact lenses, proceeding to discomfort and intolerance of contact lenses.

Examination

- Giant papillae develop on inside of upper eyelid.
- White dots may be seen on lenses.

What else might it be?

The three main serious causes of a red eye

All patients with features of a serious cause of a red eye must be referred for same-day assessment by a specialist.

- **Acute glaucoma** causes markedly raised intraocular pressure presenting with pain in the eye, headache, and blurring of vision. Signs include:
  - Ciliary injection
  - Markedly diminished vision
  - Hazy cornea
  - Fixed and dilated pupil
  - Eye is rock hard and tender
  - Headache and vomiting
- **Keratitis** presents with a unilateral, painful, photophobic, injected eye. Signs include:
  - Ciliary injection.
  - Corneal ulceration is demonstrated with fluorescein. The ulcer is dendritic when caused by herpes simplex.
  - Vision may be affected depending on the site of the ulcer.
- **Iritis** (uveitis) typically presents with pain and watering of the eye.
  - Ciliary injection may be the only sign.
  - The pupil may be fixed and mid-dilated or distorted from previous attacks.
  - Less commonly, vision may be diminished.
  - Headache.

Infective conjunctivitis

- **Features of infective conjunctivitis include:**
  - History of close contact with another affected person.
  - Eyes glued together by discharge after sleep.
  - Symptoms of upper respiratory tract infection may be present.
  - Mucopurulent discharge.
  - Enlarged lymph nodes in front of the ear.
- **Blepharitis** may present with similar symptoms to allergic conjunctivitis, but itching is usually lacking.

Irritant conjunctivitis

- Irritant conjunctivitis may have a mechanical or chemical cause.
  - **Common mechanical causes** of conjunctivitis include eyelashes rubbing against the surface of the eye, such as occurs with entropion or a foreign body. A foreign body usually becomes lodged beneath the upper eyelid. If a penetrating injury of the eye from high speed sharp particles may have occurred, refer for same-day assessment by a specialist.
  - **Chemical causes** such as getting shampoo in the eye, or chlorine in a swimming pool, are usually obvious and settle when the underlying cause is removed.

Rare types of allergic conjunctivitis

- Vernal keratoconjunctivitis and atopic keratoconjunctivitis occur with a mixed Type IV and Type I hypersensitivity reaction and as such may not respond fully to treatment with antihistamine and mast cell stabilizers.
- They should be suspected if an atopic person has a chronic allergic conjunctivitis that responds poorly to treatment. There may be signs of corneal involvement with fluorescein staining.

Complications and prognosis

Complications

- Seasonal and perennial allergic conjunctivitis rarely lead to involvement of the cornea, but this may occur with allergic contact dermatitis with conjunctivitis. When it does, corneal involvement may be seen as:
  - Punctate epithelial keratitis
  - Keratitis

Management issues

- Assessment p.365
- Seasonal and perennial conjunctivitis p.366
- Allergic dermatitis with conjunctivitis p.366
- Giant papillary conjunctivitis p.367

Assessment

- **Exclude the serious causes of a red eye.** If any of the following features are present a full examination (including fluorescein staining) must be carried out. All patients with features of a serious cause of a red eye must be referred for same-day assessment by a specialist.
  - **Moderate to severe eye pain:** if there is moderate to severe pain or moderate to severe photophobia, a secondary cause for the conjunctivitis must be excluded.
  - **Marked redness of the eye:** the greater the redness the more likely that there is a serious secondary cause. Ciliary injection, which is not always obvious, occurs with inflammation of deeper structures due to a secondary cause. It is indicated by redness and dilated blood vessels seen between the white of the eye and the coloured part of the eye.
  - **Reduced visual acuity:** any loss of visual acuity, measured with a Snellen chart, may indicate a serious secondary cause of conjunctivitis. Blurring of vision may occur with infective conjunctivitis, but this clears with blinking.
- **Distinguish infective from allergic** conjunctivitis
- **Distinguish the type of allergic conjunctivitis.**
  - **Seasonal conjunctivitis** is most likely in an atopic individual who has recurrent allergic conjunctivitis at the same time each year, particularly if associated with symptoms of allergic rhinitis.
  - **Perennial conjunctivitis** is most likely in an atopic individual who has daily symptoms of conjunctivitis,

particularly if associated with allergic rhinitis on waking each morning.
- **Allergic contact dermatitis with conjunctivitis** should be suspected in all patients who present with conjunctivitis associated with dermatitis of the eyelids, particularly if they are not atopic and are using eye drops. It distinguished from other types of allergic conjunctivitis by a complete lack of response to antihistamines and mast cell stabilizers.
- **Giant papillary conjunctivitis** should be suspected in all patients who wear contact lenses, particularly if they are not atopic.

C

Seasonal and perennial conjunctivitis

What general measures might be useful?

- **Cold compresses** may be soothing.
- **Contact lenses should not be worn** if conjunctivitis is present or during a course of topical therapy. Soft lenses should not be worn within 5–10 minutes of instilling eye drops containing the preservative benzalkonium chloride.

What topical treatments are available?

Topical antihistamines and mast cell stabilizers are the mainstay of treatment if conservative measures are not effective.

Topical antihistamines

- **Topical antihistamines directly block the action of histamine** in the conjunctiva, and have a rapid onset of action. Several randomized controlled trials (RCTs) have demonstrated that topical antihistamines are more effective than placebo at reducing the signs and symptoms of allergic conjunctivitis [Owen et al, 2004].
- **Azelastine, emadastine, and levocabastine** are single-agent topical antihistamines which give rapid relief of allergic conjunctivitis. They are well tolerated, have few adverse effects, and have a rapid onset of action.
- **Otrivine-Antistin®**, a combination of antazoline and xylometazoline, a vasoconstrictor, is an established preparation. It has the potential for systemic effects, and is not recommended for long-term use [BNF 47, 2004].
- **Olopatadine** has both antihistamine and mast cell stabilizing properties. Preliminary RCTs have found olopatadine to be safe and effective:
  - Olopatadine is more effective than placebo [Abelson and Turner, 2003].
  - Olopatadine is at least as effective as sodium cromoglicate [Katelaris et al, 2002].
- **Ketotifen** is primarily an antihistamine, but is thought to have some mast cell stabilizing properties. It has been found to be safe and effective in RCTs:
  - Ketotifen is safe and well tolerated, and more effective than placebo [Abelson et al, 2002; Abelson et al, 2003].
  - Ketotifen is at least as effective as levocabastine, sodium cromoglicate, nedocromil, and olopatadine [Greiner et al, 2002; Ganz et al, 2003; Greiner and Minno, 2003; Kidd et al, 2003].

Topical mast cell stabilizers

- **Topical mast cell stabilizers prevent the release of histamine** and other inflammatory mediators from mast cells. They have been proven to be more effective than placebo in several RCTs [Owen et al, 2004]. Mast cell stabilizers may take up to 14 days to relieve symptoms if used alone.
- **There have been no RCTs directly comparing one topical mast cell stabilizer with another.** Currently, three products are available in the United Kingdom [BNF 47, 2004]:
  - **Sodium cromoglicate** has been used extensively and is safe, effective, and well tolerated. It is suitable for use in children [BNF 47, 2004].
  - **Lodoxamide and nedocromil** are newer, more expensive topical agents available as alternatives to sodium cromoglicate.

Topical corticosteroids (not recommended)

- **Topical corticosteroids should never be given for an undiagnosed red eye.** They can transform a simple herpetic dendritic ulcer into an extensive amoeboid ulcer involving all layers of the cornea, with resultant corneal scarring and visual loss.
- **GPs are advised against starting corticosteroids for ophthalmic conditions** unless they have access to a slit lamp and the necessary expertise. Treatment should not be repeated without slit lamp review and intraocular pressure measurement. Long-term use should be avoided because this can result in adverse effects such as cataract, glaucoma, and severe bacterial or fungal infections involving the eyelid, conjunctiva, and cornea.

Should I prescribe a topical antihistamine or mast cell stabilizer?

- **A recent systematic review and meta-analysis** did not find sufficient evidence to recommend the use of either class of drug, or any specific drug, over another. However, it did find limited evidence that topical antihistamines are quicker to act than mast cell stabilizers. None of the drugs was associated with any significant safety concerns [Owen et al, 2004].
- **The choice of topical treatment** should be made according to the needs and preference of the patient:
  - **If a rapid response is required,** particularly if contact with allergens is intermittent, a topical antihistamine may be preferred.
  - **If prevention of allergy over a longer period is required,** topical mast cell stabilizers may be the first treatment choice.
  - **Individual products** should be selected on the basis of their convenience of use and cost.

What systemic treatments may be useful?

- **Oral antihistamines are commonly used** in the treatment of allergic conjunctivitis, despite there being little trial evidence to support their use. They have a role in suppressing Type I immunoglobulin E-mediated associated hypersensitivity, and are especially useful when there is coexisting allergic rhinitis.
- **Non-sedating antihistamines** are preferred to the older, first-generation antihistamines, which frequently cause drowsiness:
  - **Cetirizine and loratadine** are well established agents with a good efficacy and safety profile. They are taken once a day and are suitable for young children.
  - **Fexofenadine and mizolastine** are alternative once-daily regimens suitable for older children and adults.
  - **Desloratadine (a metabolite of loratadine) and levocetirizine (an isomer of cetirizine)** are more recently marketed products that are still under close post-marketing surveillance (black triangle).

Allergic dermatitis with conjunctivitis

- Management requires identification and avoidance of the causative allergen, which is usually eye drops, cosmetics or industrial chemicals.
- If inflammation is severe, or there are signs of corneal involvement, topical corticosteroids may be required to settle the inflammation quickly. In these circumstances refer the patient for specialist assessment and management.

Giant papillary conjunctivitis

- Consider discontinuing the wearing of contact lenses to allow inflammation to settle, if they are causing irritation.
- Wearing contact lenses can be re-commenced with new lenses, once the major symptoms of inflammation have settled.
- Advice the patient to seek advice from their optician regarding hygiene measures, more frequent contact lens changing, and a possible change of contact lens type, if the problem recurs. Topical sodium cromoglicate (2%) can be used to relieve symptoms while hygiene measures take effect.

References

NHS staff in England can link, free of charge, from references to full text journals by clicking on [Full text] on the PRODIGY website.

1. Abelson, M.B. and Turner, D. (2003) A randomized, double-blind, parallel-group comparison of olopatadine 0.1% ophthalmic solution versus placebo for controlling the signs and symptoms of seasonal allergic conjunctivitis and rhinoconjunctivitis. *Clinical Therapeutics* **25**(3), 931–947.
2. Abelson, M.B., Chapin, M.J., Kapik, B.M. and Shams, N.B. (2002) Ocular tolerability and safety of ketotifen fumarate ophthalmic solution. *Advances in Therapy* **19**(4), 161–169.
3. Abelson, M.B., Chapin, M.J., Kapik, B.M. and Shams, N.B. (2003) Efficacy of ketotifen fumarate 0.025% ophthalmic solution compared with placebo in the conjunctival allergen challenge model. *Archives of Ophthalmology* **121**(5), 626–630. [Full text]
4. BNF 47 (2004) *British National Formulary*. 47th edn. London: British Medical Association and Royal Pharmaceutical Society of Great Britain.
5. DTB (2002) Oral antihistamines for allergic disorders. *Drug & Therapeutics Bulletin* **40**(8), 59–62. [Full text]
6. Freissler, K., Lang, G.E. and Lang, G.K. (1997) Allergic diseases of the lids, conjunctiva and cornea. *Current Opinion in Ophthalmology* **8**(4), 25–30.
7. Ganz, M., Koll, E., Gausche, J. et al (2003) Ketotifen fumarate and olopatadine hydrochloride in the treatment of allergic conjunctivitis: a real-world comparison of efficacy and ocular comfort. *Advances in Therapy* **20**(2), 79–91.
8. Greiner, J.V. and Minno, G. (2003) A placebo-controlled comparison of ketotifen fumarate and nedocromil sodium ophthalmic solutions for the prevention of ocular itching with the conjunctival allergen challenge model. *Clinical Therapeutics* **25**(7), 1988–2005.
9. Greiner, J.V., Michaelson, C., McWhirter, C.L. and Shams, N.B. (2002) Single dose of ketotifen fumarate .025% vs 2 weeks of cromolyn sodium 4% for allergic conjunctivitis. *Advances in Therapy* **19**(4), 185–193.
10. Katelaris, C.H., Ciprandi, G., Missotten, L. et al (2002) A comparison of the efficacy and tolerability of olopatadine hydrochloride 0.1% ophthalmic solution and cromolyn sodium 2% ophthalmic solution in seasonal allergic conjunctivitis. *Clinical Therapeutics* **24**(10), 1561–1575.
11. Kidd, M., McKenzie, S., Steven, I. et al (2003) Efficacy and safety of ketotifen eye drops in the treatment of seasonal allergic conjunctivitis. *British Journal of Ophthalmology* **87**(10), 1206–1211. [Full text]
12. Manners, T. (1997) Managing eye conditions in general practice. *British Medical Journal* **315**(7111), 816–817. [Full text]
13. Owen, C.G., Shah, A., Henshaw, K. et al (2004) Topical treatments for seasonal allergic conjunctivitis: systematic review and meta-analysis of efficacy and effectiveness. *British Journal of General Practice* **54**(503), 451–456.
14. Royal College of General Practitioners and Royal College of Ophthalmologists (2001) *Ophthalmology for general practice trainees*. London: Medical Protection Society.
15. Rubenstein, J.B. and Jick, S.L. (2004) Disorders of the conjunctiva and limbus. In: Yanoff, M. and Duker, J.S. (Eds.) *Ophthalmology*. 2nd edn. St Louis, MO: Mosby. 397–412.

PRODIGY GUIDANCE

Conjunctivitis — infective

Last revised in February 2005
www.prodigy.nhs.uk/guidance.asp?gt=Conjunctivitis - infective

Applies to people of all ages

This guidance covers bacterial conjunctivitis and adenoviral conjunctivitis.

This guidance does not cover the management of allergic conjunctivitis, ocular herpes simplex, or herpes zoster ophthalmicus.

There is separate PRODIGY guidance for *Blepharitis, Conjunctivitis — allergic, Dry eye syndrome*, and *Herpes simplex — ocular*.

Goals

- To control the symptoms
- To eradicate the infection
- To prevent complications

Contents

Scenarios

- Acute infective conjunctivitis p.368

Extended Information, p. 369

Acute infective conjunctivitis

Which therapy?

Assess the cause of the red eye

- Exclude the serious causes of a red eye.
- Distinguish infective from allergic causes of conjunctivitis.
- If possible, differentiate between a viral and bacterial cause on the basis of clinical features.

Managing uncomplicated infective conjunctivitis

- **Advise on measures to reduce the spread of infection:**
  - Wash hands regularly, particularly after touching infected secretions.
  - Avoid sharing towels, pillows, or utensils.
  - Time off work or school until conjunctivitis settles may be necessary, when the risk of transmission is high.
- **Contact lenses should not be worn** until all symptoms and signs have completely settled and any treatment has been completed for 24 hours.

Topical antibiotics

- Most doctors treat all uncomplicated infective conjunctivitis with topical antibiotics without delay. Alternative strategies to reduce the number of people receiving treatment with no benefit include:
  - Delay treatment for 5 days and treat if there are no signs of improvement.
  - Treat people who have clinical features that make bacterial conjunctivitis the most likely cause.
- **Chloramphenicol** is recommended as first-choice treatment.
- **Fusidic acid** is recommended as an alternative treatment.

Practical prescribing points

For further information please see the *Medicines Compendium* (www.medicines.org.uk) or the *British National Formulary* (www.bnf.org).

- **Contact lenses** should not be worn during a course of topical antibacterial therapy and for 24 hours after administration of preparations containing benzalkonium chloride preservative (benzalkonium chloride accumulates in soft contact lenses and causes irritation).
- **Chloramphenicol:** concerns over aplastic anaemia associated with ocular chloramphenicol have largely been discounted.
  - Do not use concurrently with other myelotoxic drugs.
  - Do not use in the last trimester of pregnancy.

Follow-up advice

- Swab the eye for culture and sensitivity if the infective conjunctivitis is not resolving after 7 days of treatment. Await results before prescribing further treatment.
- Swab all people who are sexually active who have a conjunctivitis that persists for 14 days despite a course of treatment.

Should I refer or investigate?

Refer?

- Refer all people for same-day assessment if they have any of the following features that could indicate iritis, keratitis, or acute glaucoma:
  - Moderate to severe eye pain
  - Marked eye redness
  - Ciliary injection
  - Loss of visual acuity
- Refer all newborn babies (less than 28 days) where there are severe symptoms such as profuse mucopurulent discharge or eyelid cellulitis, or where there are symptoms that do not respond to antibiotics.
- Refer all patients for contact tracing and systemic therapy who have a positive *Chlamydia* swab.

Patient information leaflets

The following PILs are available at www.prodigy.nhs.uk

- Conjunctivitis - Infective
- Eye Drops - (How to Use)

Shared decision making

- Infective conjunctivitis is an infection of the front 'skin' of the eye.
- **Not treating is an option** for mild cases as it often goes without any treatment.

Antibiotic eye drops or ointments are commonly advised if it is more than just a mild infection, or if it is not settling after a few days.
Do not wear contact lenses until symptoms have completely gone, and for 24 hours after the last dose of any eye drop or ointment.
Conjunctivitis is contagious, so:

- Wash your hands regularly, particularly after touching your eyes.
- Do not share towels, pillows, or utensils.

Drug rationale

Drugs not included

Aminoglycosides should be reserved for treatment once the sensitivity of the infecting organism is known. Incomplete coverage of *Streptococcus* and *Staphylococcus* species rules out aminoglycosides as first-line therapy. A relatively higher incidence of toxicity to corneal epithelium has been recorded with prolonged use [Robert and Adenis, 2001; BNF 47, 2004].
Fluoroquinolones such as ciprofloxacin, lomefloxacin, and ofloxacin should be reserved for serious ocular infections to limit the development of bacterial resistance. Cases of keratitis with methicillin-resistant *S aureus* have been reported. The fluoroquinolones have poor coverage of *Streptococcus* species [Robert and Adenis, 2001; BNF 47, 2004].

Drugs included

Chloramphenicol is regarded as the first-line antibiotic. It has a relatively broad spectrum of action against most gram-positive and gram-negative bacteria [Robert and Adenis, 2001]. Concerns about the systemic toxicity of topical chloramphenicol, in particular aplastic anaemia, have been discounted [Doona and Walsh, 1995; Rayner and Buckley, 1996; Lancaster et al, 1998; Walker et al, 1998; Field et al, 1999; Robert and Adenis, 2001; BNF 47, 2004].
Fusidic acid is an alternative antibacterial to chloramphenicol. Fusidic acid is most effective against *Staphylococcus aureus*. However, studies have shown that it is as effective as chloramphenicol against other pathogens due to the high ocular concentrations achieved [Hvidberg, 1987; Horven, 1993; Boberg-Ans and Nissen, 1998; Carr, 1998].

Prescriptions

Chloramphenicol eye drops or ointment

Chloramphenicol 0.5% eye drops
Age from 1 month onwards
Chloramphenicol 0.5% eye drops. Put one drop into the affected eye(s) every 2 hours for 2 days, and then every 4 hours for 5 days. You only need to use the drops while you are awake; supply 10 ml; NHS Cost £1.23; OTC Cost £2.17.

Chloramphenicol 1% eye ointment
Age from 1 month onwards
Chloramphenicol 1% eye ointment. Put a small amount into the affected eye(s) four times a day for 2 days, and then twice a day for 5 days; supply 4 grams; NHS Cost £1.04.

Chloramphenicol 0.5% eye drops + 1% eye ointment
Age from 1 month onwards
Chloramphenicol 0.5% eye drops. Put one drop into the affected eye(s) every 2 hours for 2 days, and then every 4 hours for 5 days. You only need to use the drops while you are awake; supply 10 ml; NHS Cost £1.23; OTC Cost £2.17.

Fusidic acid eye drops

Fusidic acid 1% eye drops

- Age from 1 month onwards
- Fusidic acid 1% eye drops. Put one drop into the affected eye(s) twice a day for 7 days; supply 5 grams; NHS Cost £2.09.

C

Extended Information

Background information

- What is it? p.369
- How common is it? p.369
- How do I know my patient has infective conjunctivitis? p.370
- What else might it be? p.370
- Complications and prognosis p.370

What is it?

- **The conjunctiva** is a thin protective membrane that covers the surface of the eye and the inside surface of the eyelids.
- **Conjunctivitis is inflammation of the conjunctiva** causing the conjunctival blood vessels to dilate and the eye to appear red. Inflammation may be limited to the conjunctiva, when it is classified as primary conjunctivitis, or may occur secondary to more serious pathology affecting other parts of the eye, such as iritis.

What are the infective causes of primary conjunctivitis?

- **Bacterial conjunctivitis:** the most common pathogens include Staphylococcus species, *Streptococcus pneumoniae, Haemophilus influenzae,* and *Moraxella catarrhalis* [Seal et al, 1982; Miller et al, 1992; Weiss et al, 1993].
- **Viral conjunctivitis** is commonly associated with upper respiratory tract infections, and is usually caused by adenovirus.
- **Chlamydia** presents with a chronic conjunctivitis in newborns and people who are sexually active.
- **Infective conjunctivitis of the newborn** (previously called ophthalmia neonatorum) is most commonly caused by chlamydia. Occasionally a profusely purulent conjunctivitis in newborns occurs, usually caused by gonorrhoea.

Conjunctivitis of the newborn (ophthalmia neonatorum)

- **Conjunctivitis in the first 28 days of life** is a serious condition that requires urgent intervention and must be distinguished from a simple sticky eye, which is not associated with any signs of conjunctivitis.
- **Gonorrhoea** is an uncommon but serious cause of conjunctivitis in the newborn causing a profuse purulent discharge usually in the first 7 days of life.
- **Chlamydia** presents with a chronic conjunctivitis usually around 14 days after birth.

How common is it?

- In general practice 2—5% of all consultations concern the eye [Manners, 1997].
- Infective conjunctivitis accounts for around 35% of all eye problems presenting in general practice, with 13–14 cases per 1000 population per year [Royal College of

General Practitioners and Royal College of Ophthalmologists, 2001].
- About 50% of cases of infective conjunctivitis are bacterial and 50% viral [Rietveld et al, 2004].
- Children and the elderly have an increased incidence of infective conjunctivitis [Scott and Dhillon, 1998].

How do I know my patient has infective conjunctivitis?

Before diagnosing infective conjunctivitis it is essential to exclude serious causes of a red eye that can lead to permanent impairment of vision and to distinguish it from allergic and irritant causes — see *What else might it be?*

What are the clinical features of infective conjunctivitis?

Symptoms:
- **Eye discomfort,** usually described as burning or gritty, or minimal pain may be present.
- **Minimal photophobia** is occasionally present.
- **Eyes may be stuck together** by discharge after sleep.
- **Blurring of vision** due to discharge may occur, but this clears with blinking.
- **History of close contact** with another affected person increases the likelihood of an infective cause.

Examination
- **'Red eye'** caused by engorgement of the conjunctival blood vessels is usually mild.
- **Discharge** may be mucopurulent or watery.
- **Enlarged lymph nodes** in front of the ears (particularly associated with chlamydial and adenoviral conjunctivitis).

Investigations
- **Microbiological investigations** are generally not undertaken in primary care to make the diagnosis, but are used when infective conjunctivitis diagnosed clinically fails to respond to treatment.

How do I distinguish bacterial from viral conjunctivitis?

- **Determining the cause of infective conjunctivitis** on clinical features alone is associated with a significant degree of diagnostic uncertainty. Bacterial conjunctivitis is more likely when:
  - The eyes are glued by discharge, particularly when both eyes are affected.
  - There is an absence of itching.
  - There is no history of previous episodes of conjunctivitis.

[Rietveld et al, 2004]

What else might it be?

Excluding the serious causes of a red eye

If any of the following features are present, a full examination (including fluorescein staining) must be carried out.
- **Moderate to severe eye pain:** if there is moderate to severe pain, a secondary cause for the conjunctivitis must be excluded.
- **Marked redness of the eye:** the greater the redness, the more likely it is that there is a serious secondary cause. Ciliary injection, which is not always obvious, occurs with inflammation of deeper structures due to a secondary cause. It is indicated by redness and dilated blood vessels seen between the white of the eye and the coloured part of the eye.
- **Reduced visual acuity:** any loss of visual acuity, measured with a Snellen chart, may indicate a serious secondary cause of conjunctivitis.

The main three serious causes of a red eye

All patients with features of a serious cause of a red eye must be referred for same-day assessment by a specialist.
- **Acute glaucoma** causes markedly raised intraocular pressure presenting with pain in the eye, headache, and blurring of vision. Signs include:
  - Ciliary injection
  - Markedly diminished vision
  - Hazy cornea
  - Fixed and dilated pupil
  - Eye is rock hard and tender
- **Keratitis** presents with a unilateral, painful, photophobic, injected eye. Signs include:
  - Ciliary injection.
  - Corneal ulceration is demonstrated with fluorescein. The ulcer is dendritic when caused by herpes simplex
  - Vision may be affected, depending on the site of the ulcer.
- **Iritis** (uveitis) typically presents with pain and watering of the eye.
  - Ciliary injection may be the only sign.
  - The pupil may be fixed and mid-dilated or distorted from previous attacks.
  - Less commonly, vision may be diminished.
  - Headache may be present.

Allergic conjunctivitis

- **Features that make an allergic cause more likely include**
  - Bilateral itchy eyes.
  - Oedema, producing a cobblestone appearance on the deep surface of the upper eyelids.
  - An individual who also has eczema, allergic rhinitis, o asthma.
- **Features that make an allergic cause less likely include:**
  - History of close contact with another affected person
  - Eyes glued together by discharge after sleep.
  - Symptoms of upper respiratory tract infection.
  - Mucopurulent discharge.
  - Enlarged lymph nodes in front of the ear.

Irritant conjunctivitis

- Irritant conjunctivitis may have a mechanical or chemical cause.
  - **Common mechanical causes** of conjunctivitis include eyelashes rubbing against the surface of the eye such a occurs with entropion or a foreign body. A foreign body usually becomes lodged beneath the upper eyeli If a penetrating injury of the eye from high speed shar particles may have occurred, refer for same-day assessment by a specialist.
  - **Chemical causes** such as getting shampoo in the eye, or chlorine in a swimming pool, are usually obvious and the conjunctivitis settles when the underlying cause is removed.

Complications and prognosis

Complications

- **Significant complications are rare** following bacterial conjunctivitis [Sheikh and Hurwitz, 2001].
- **Pneumonia** occurs in 10–20% of infants following chlamydial conjunctivitis.
- **Any bacterial conjunctivitis,** particularly in the premature infant, can cause secondary meningitis, cellulitis, or septicaemia, particularly if the conjunctiviti is caused by *Escherichia coli*, *Staphylococcus aureus*, or *Haemophilus influenzae*.
- **Corneal penetration** can occur within 2 days of untreated conjunctivitis caused by gonorrhoea in the newborn [Silverman and Bessman, 2003].

Otitis media may develop in 25% of children with *H influenzae* conjunctivitis.
Punctate epithelial keratitis (small multiple erosions of the conjunctiva seen with fluorescein staining) may occur following infective conjunctivitis. It presents with ongoing discomfort following resolution of the infection and may persist for several weeks before resolving spontaneously.

Prognosis

Primary infective conjunctivitis is usually a self-limiting disease that does not cause any serious harm and resolves spontaneously. A recent meta-analysis has shown clinical remission by days 2–5 in 64% of people receiving placebo [Sheikh and Hurwitz, 2001].
Topical antibiotics improve the clinical remission rate of bacterial conjunctivitis at days 2–5 by 30% [Everitt and Little, 2002].

Management issues

Managing uncomplicated infective conjunctivitis p.371
What should I do if infective conjunctivitis fails to respond to treatment? p.372
Conjunctivitis of the newborn (ophthalmia neonatorum) p.372

Managing uncomplicated infective conjunctivitis

Conjunctivitis will usually remit spontaneously and clinical trials have shown evidence that offering no treatment has a similar outcome to treatment with topical antibiotics; the incidence of complications due to untreated infection appears to be rare [Sheikh et al, 2004].

General measures

Infective conjunctivitis is contagious. Advice should be given to wash hands regularly, particularly after touching infected secretions, and to avoid sharing pillows, towels, and utensils [Donahue et al, 1996]:

- **Time off school or work may be necessary,** depending on individual circumstances.
- **Adenovirus is extremely infectious,** and confirmed infection necessitates at least 2 weeks off work or school [Dart, Personal Communication, 2004].

Contact lenses should not be worn until all symptoms and signs of infection have completely resolved and any treatment has been completed for 24 hours. Keratitis may complicate conjunctivitis if contact lenses continue to be used.

Should I prescribe a topical antibiotic?

The benefit of antibiotic treatment remains controversial. A recently updated Cochrane review and meta-analysis found three randomized controlled trials (RCTs), totalling 527 participants with bacterial conjunctivitis, who received various topical antibiotics [Sheikh et al, 2004]. It found that:

- **Bacterial conjunctivitis is usually a self-limiting condition.** Most people (64%) receiving placebo experienced clinical remission after 2–5 days.
- **Treatment with antibiotics was associated with a significantly better outcome in the short term,** although the benefits were modest (relative risk after 2–5 days was 1.31, CI 1.11 to 1.74). There were no adverse effects associated with treatment.
- **The subjects included in the meta-analysis may not be typical of those seen in primary care,** as they had microbiologically proven or clinically 'diagnosed' *bacterial* conjunctivitis. The real benefit of topical antibiotics may be considerably less. In addition, the study had been previously criticized for grouping together very heterogeneous RCTs [Fleetcroft, 2001].
- **Antibiotics are routinely prescribed for acute infective conjunctivitis.** A recent survey found that 95% of GPs usually prescribe antibiotics for the condition, regardless of the cause of the infection [Everitt and Little, 2002].
- **Different approaches to treatment have been suggested,** such as treating all cases, offering a delayed prescribing strategy, or selectively treating cases that are most likely to have a bacterial cause. The most suitable method depends on individual clinical circumstances, and should be done with the knowledge and consent of the patient (shared decision making).
  - **Immediate treatment of all cases of infective conjunctivitis:** advantages of this approach include:
    - Increased rate of resolution of bacterial infection reduces the risk of transmission. Earlier resolution allows an earlier return to work or school.
    - Prevention of secondary bacterial infection with viral conjunctivitis.
    - It may reduce the (slight) risk of complications.
  - **Delayed prescribing strategy:** treat if the condition has not resolved spontaneously after 5 days. Benefits include:
    - Reduction in unnecessary treatment of infective conjunctivitis (viral and early spontaneous resolution of bacterial conjunctivitis).
    - Reduction in the number of people having adverse effects from treatment.
    - Reduction in the cost of managing infective conjunctivitis for the NHS and for the individual.
  - **Immediate treatment only when the cause is likely to be bacterial:** patients who are untreated should be treated if they deteriorate or if they show no signs of improvement within 5 days. This:
    - Targets people who are likely to get benefit from treatment.
    - Reduces the number of people having adverse effects from treatment.
    - Reduces the cost of managing infective conjunctivitis for the NHS and for the individual.

Which topical antibiotic should I prescribe?

- **Chloramphenicol is regarded as the first line antibiotic.** It has a relatively broad spectrum of action against most Gram-positive and Gram-negative bacteria, and there is little evidence of bacterial resistance to chloramphenicol.
  - **Concern about the systemic toxicity of topical chloramphenicol,** in particular aplastic anaemia, is not well founded [Rayner and Buckley, 1996; Lancaster et al, 1998; Walker et al, 1998; Field et al, 1999; Robert and Adenis, 2001; BNF 47, 2004].
  - **Due to the potential risk of systemic absorption,** chloramphenicol is not recommended for prolonged treatment periods or when treatment is combined with other myelotoxic drugs [Walker et al, 1998].
  - **In the third trimester of pregnancy:** there is a theoretical risk of grey baby syndrome (chloramphenicol toxicity in newborns resulting from the lack of liver enzymes necessary to metabolize the drug) and alternative treatment strategies should be considered [Walker et al, 1998].
- **Fusidic acid is an alternative antibiotic to chloramphenicol.**
  - Several comparative trials have shown that topical fusidic acid is equally as effective as topical chloramphenicol [Hvidberg, 1987; Horven, 1993; Boberg-Ans and Nissen, 1998; Carr, 1998].
  - Fusidic acid is bacteriostatic and is active against Gram-positive bacteria, especially *Staphylococcus*

species, and achieves good anterior chamber penetration. Acquired resistance within Gram-positive species is low [Robert and Adenis, 2001].

Should I prescribe ointment or drops?

- Drops may be more practical for daytime use as ointments may smear, causing blurred vision.
- Viscous drops may be more convenient for elderly people and children who need assistance to apply eye drops.

C

What should I do if infective conjunctivitis fails to respond to treatment?

- Failure to respond to treatment for infective conjunctivitis occurs when:
  - There is a viral cause.
  - There is a chlamydial cause.
  - The bacteria is not sensitive to the prescribed antibiotic.
- Take swabs for bacterial culture (and sensitivity), viruses, and *Chlamydia* (in the sexually active) if conjunctivitis persists, and await results before commencing any further treatment.
  - If tests are negative, and warning signs of a serious cause of a red eye have not developed, the most likely cause is viral and the conjunctivitis should settle without further treatment.
  - If signs of a severe conjunctivitis continue, this may indicate the presence of adenoviral conjunctivitis.
- Adult chlamydial conjunctivitis requires referral for contact testing of sexual contacts and systemic therapy.
- If swabs demonstrate bacteria that are not sensitive to the prescribed antibiotic, the antibiotic can be changed according to the sensitivities.

Conjunctivitis of the newborn (ophthalmia neonatorum)

It important to distinguish between a simple sticky eye, which is common and not associated with conjunctivitis, and conjunctivitis of the newborn, which should be treated urgently.

- **Conjunctivitis of the newborn caused by gonorrhoea** (and occasionally other bacteria) can cause corneal penetration within 48 hours of its onset. If this is suspected, immediate admission is required for further investigation and treatment.
- **Conjunctivitis of the newborn caused by *Chlamydia*** requires systemic therapy to eliminate it from other sites and to prevent pneumonia developing. Refer for confirmation of the diagnosis and for treatment.

References

NHS staff in England can link, free of charge, from references to full text journals by clicking on [Full text] on the PRODIGY website.

1. BNF 47 (2004) *British National Formulary*. 47th edn. London: British Medical Association and Royal Pharmaceutical Society of Great Britain.
2. Boberg-Ans, G. and Nissen, K.R. (1998) Comparison of Fucithalmic® viscous eye drops and Chloramphenicol eye ointment as a single treatment in corneal abrasion. *Acta Ophthalmologica Scandinavica* 76(1), 108–111.
3. Carr, W.D. (1998) Comparison of fucithalmic (fusidic acid viscous eye drops 1%) and chloromycetin redidrops (chloramphenicol eye drops 0.5%) in the treatment of acute bacterial conjunctivitis. *Journal of Drug Assessment* 1(4), 615–623.
4. Dart, J.K.G. (2004) *Personal communication.* Consultant Eye Specialist, Moorfields Eye Hospital: London.
5. Donahue, S.P., Khoury, J.M. and Kowalski, R.P. (1996) Common ocular infections. A prescriber's guide. *Drugs* **52**(4), 526–540.
6. Doona, M. and Walsh, J.B. (1995) Use of chloramphenicol as topical eye medication: time to cry halt? *British Medical Journal* **310**(6989), 1217–1218. [Full text]
7. Everitt, H. and Little, P. (2002) How do GP's diagnose and manage acute infective conjunctivitis? A GP survey. *Family Practice* **19**(6), 658–660. [Full text]
8. Field, D., Martin, D. and Witchell, L. (1999) Ophthalmic chloramphenicol: a review of the literature. *Accident & Emergency Nursing* **7**(1), 13–1
9. Fleetcroft, R. (2001) Topical antibiotics for acute bacterial conjunctivitis. *British Journal of General Practice* **51**(469), 673–674.
10. Horven, I. (1993) Acute conjunctivitis: a comparison of fusidic acid viscous eye drops and chloramphenicol. *Acta Ophthalmologica Scandinavica* **71**(2), 165–168.
11. Hvidberg, J (1987) Fusidic acid in acute conjunctivitis single-blind, randomized comparison of fusidic and chloramphenicol viscous eye drops. *Acta Ophthalmologica* **65**(1), 43–47.
12. Lancaster, T., Swart, A.M. and Jick, H. (1998) Risk of serious haematological toxicity with use of chloramphenicol eye drops in a British general practice database. *British Medical Journal* **316**(7132), 667. [Full text]
13. Manners, T. (1997) Managing eye conditions in general practice. *British Medical Journal* **315**(7111), 816–817. [Full text]
14. Miller, I., Wittreich, J., Cook, T. and Vogel, R. (1992) The safety and efficacy of topical norfloxacin compared with chloramphenicol for the treatment of external ocular bacterial infections. *Eye* **6**(Pt 1), 111–114.
15. Rayner, S.A. and Buckley, R.J. (1996) Ocular chloramphenicol and aplastic anaemia. Is there a link? *Drug Safety* **14**(5), 273–276.
16. Rietveld, R.P., ter Riet, G., Bindels, P.J.E. et al (2004) Predicting bacterial cause in infectious conjunctivitis: cohort study on informativeness of combination of signs and symptoms. *British Medical Journal* **329**(7459), 206–210.
17. Robert, P.Y. and Adenis, J.P. (2001) Comparative review of topical ophthalmic antibacterial preparations. *Drugs* **61**(2), 175–185.
18. Royal College of General Practitioners and Royal College of Ophthalmologists (2001) *Ophthalmology for general practice trainees.* London: Medical Protection Society.
19. Scott, C. and Dhillon, B. (1998) Conjunctivitis. *Practitioner* **242**(1585), 305. [Full text]
20. Seal, D.V., Barrett, S.P. and McGill, J.I. (1982) Aetiology and treatment of acute bacterial infection of the external eye. *British Journal of Ophthalmology* **66**(6), 357–360.
21. Sheikh, A. and Hurwitz, B. (2001) Topical antibiotics for acute bacterial conjunctivitis: a systematic review. *British Journal of General Practice* **51**(467), 473–477.
22. Sheikh, A., Hurwitz, B. and Cave, J. (2004) *Antibiotics versus placebo for acute bacterial conjunctivitis (Cochrane Review).* The Cochrane Library. Issue 2. Chichester, UK: John Wiley & Sons, Ltd.
23. Silverman, M.A. and Bessman, E. (2003) *Conjunctivitis.* emedicine.com, Inc. www.emedicine.com [Accessed: 15/07/2004].

24. Walker, S., Diaper, C.J., Bowman, R. et al (1998) Lack of evidence for systemic toxicity following topical chloramphenicol use. *Eye* 12(5), 875–879.

25. Weiss, A., Brinser, J.H. and Nazar-Stewart, N. (1993) Acute conjunctivitis in childhood. *Journal of Paediatrics* 122(1), 10–15.

C

PRODIGY GUIDANCE

Constipation

Last revised in July 2002
At the time of print this topic was being updated. The newly revised guidance will be issued on to the website in late 2005.
www.prodigy.nhs.uk/guidance.asp?gt=Constipation

C

Applies to people of all ages

This guidance covers the management of constipation.

This guidance does not cover in detail bowel preparation prior to investigation or surgery, or the management of chronic laxative abuse.

There is separate PRODIGY guidance for *Anal fissure, Diverticular disease, Haemorrhoids, Irritable bowel syndrome,* and *Pruritis ani.*

Goals

- To establish regular, comfortable defecation, using the least number of drug therapies (ideally none) for the shortest possible time
- To establish what the normal frequency of defecation is for the individual
- To prevent laxative dependence
- To relieve the discomfort associated with constipation

Contents

Scenarios

- Adults and fit elderly people p.374
- Frail elderly or immobile younger adults p.376
- Children p.378
- Pregnancy p.380
- Terminal Care p.381

Extended Information, p. 383

Which scenario?

- **Adults and fit elderly people:** covers the management of adults with constipation who are mobile and active.
- **Frail elderly and immobile younger adults:** covers the management of adults with constipation who are frail and inactive, for example the housebound, and those who are wheelchair-bound.
- **Children:** covers the management of constipation in children.
- **Pregnancy:** covers the management of constipation in pregnant women.
- **Terminal care:** covers the management of constipation in those who are terminally ill.

Adults and fit elderly people

Which therapy?

- **Treat active, fit elderly as younger adults.**
- **Consider underlying causes and stop or reduce any causative drugs.**
- **Advice on a high-fibre diet with adequate fluid intake and exercise** is first-line treatment.
- **If laxatives are used,** give the smallest effective dose, and reduce once symptoms resolve.
- **Bulk-forming laxatives** (plus increased fluid intake) should be tried if increasing dietary fibre and fluid intake is ineffective, particularly if medium or long-term use is anticipated (chronic constipation). Maximum effect is seen at 2–3 days.
- **Stimulant laxatives** should be considered if fibre or bulk forming laxatives are not effective or tolerated. These a after 8–12 hours. In general they should be reserved for short-term or intermittent use; however, in the elderly long-term use may be appropriate.
- **Stimulant suppositories** provide more rapid relief (20–6 minutes) than oral preparations (8–12 hours). Do not use for more than 7 days.
- **Stool softeners** should only be used short-term.
- **Osmotic laxatives** (e.g. lactulose) should be reserved fo second-line use when other laxatives have failed to produce an effect. In addition to being expensive, they commonly cause flatulence, bloating, and cramping, an some people find them unpalatable.

Practical prescribing points

For further information please see the *Medicines Compendium* (www.medicines.org.uk) or the *British National Formulary* (www.bnf.org).

- **Rectal preparations** may be uncomfortable if the persor has haemorrhoids or an anal fissure. Rectal docusate should not be used in these people.
- **Stimulant laxatives** often cause abdominal cramp; avoi if intestinal obstruction is a possibility.
- **Bulk-forming laxatives** may cause flatulence and distension. There is a risk of intestinal or oesophageal obstruction and faecal impaction, especially when swallowed dry.

Should I refer or investigate?

Refer?

- **If constipation does not respond to treatment,** consider admission for manual evacuation, according to facilitie available in the surgery (often this can be done by the district nurse).
- **Consider referral to a dietitian** as appropriate.

Investigate?

- **Long standing constipation** which responds to treatmer may not require investigation (a digital rectal examination should be performed).
- **Consider investigation** (barium enema, sigmoidoscopy, colonoscopy) if:
  - **A change in bowel habit in the middle-aged and elderly,** or those at high risk of neoplasia
  - **Rectal bleeding** at any age
  - **Symptoms are severe, new, and unresponsive to treatment**
  - **Symptoms are of sudden onset**
  - Weight loss

Depending on facilities and expertise within the practice, this may necessitate referral to secondary care.

'atient information leaflets

ıe following PILs are available at www.prodigy.nhs.uk
Constipation in Adults
Eat More Fruit and Vegetables
Faecal Occult Blood Test
Fibre in the Diet

hared decision making

A low fibre diet is the most common cause of constipation.
Eat more fibre — fruit, vegetables, cereals, wholemeal bread, etc.
Have lots to drink — at least 8–10 cups of fluid per day. But, don't have too much tea or coffee, which may make constipation worse.
Exercise regularly — keeping your body active helps to keep your bowels active.
Fibre supplements — bulk-forming agents such as **ispaghula** usually work if the measures above do not help.
Laxatives — other than fibre supplements, should only be used as a temporary remedy if constipation is severe. There are different types.

- *Stimulant laxatives* — such as **bisacodyl** and **senna** make the bowel work harder. They may cause stomach cramps.
- *Stool softeners* — such as **docusate**, make the stools easier to pass.
- *Suppositories* — are sometimes used as an alternative.

)rug rationale

›rugs not included

;timulants

Co-danthramer (a combination of dantron and poloxamer) and co-danthrusate (a combination of dantron and docusate) are indicated only in people who are terminally ill because of accumulating evidence confirming that dantron is genotoxic [CSM, 2000].
Oxyphenisatin (which is available only as an enema) is more appropriately used for bowel evacuation procedures in hospital.
Sodium picosulfate is relatively expensive, and tends to be reserved for bowel clearance.

3ulk-forming agents

Methylcellulose is excluded on grounds of compliance (the dose has to be titrated up to six tablets twice a day).
Bran supplements are no longer included as the only commercially available medicinal product containing bran (Trifyba) has been discontinued.

)smotic laxatives

Prolonged use of osmotic laxatives should be avoided [Bateman, 1990].
Lactulose and lactitol are not suitable for rapid relief of constipation. They have a tendency to cause bloating and colic, and can take 2–3 days to have an effect [Fallon and O'Neill, 1997]. Many people find the taste of lactulose sickly [Medicines Resource, 1996]. In older people lactulose has been shown to be less cost-effective than senna plus fibre [Petticrew et al, 1997].

- **Macrogol** (polyethylene glycol) is expensive. The products available are indicated for chronic constipation or bowel clearance [BNF 43, 2002].
- **Magnesium salts** produce watery stool with urgency and sometimes incontinence, which limits their acceptability [Spiller, 1990].
- **Rectal phosphates** are not appropriate in this scenario, and they have a risk of phosphate absorption with routine use [Bateman, 1990].
- **Sodium salts** (sodium citrate) may cause sodium and water retention in susceptible people. Sodium citrate should only be administered rectally and occasionally [Medicines Resource, 1996; BNF 43, 2002].

C

Faecal softeners

- **Rectal arachis oil** is only available as a large volume enema. It has a limited role for softening of impacted faeces [MeReC, 1994; Fallon and O'Neill, 1997]. There is no consensus at the present time about the risk of peanut allergy linked to refined arachis oil.
- **Liquid paraffin** can cause anal seepage and irritation, lipoid pneumonia and malabsorption of lipid-soluble vitamins. It is not recommended [Gattuso and Kamm, 1994; Medicines Resource, 1996].

Drugs included

Bulk-forming agents

- **Bulk-forming agents including ispaghula, and sterculia** are included. They are a good choice if prolonged treatment is required. Clinically there is little to choose between the different agents [MeReC, 1999]. Since palatability and convenience of use are very important if people are to adhere to long-term treatment, only products available in sachets and in a variety of flavours are offered. Sugar-free products are offered where available.

Stimulant laxatives

- **Stimulant bisacodyl and senna** are well tolerated by most people. They have been in use for many years and their adverse effects and contraindications are well known. In general they should be used on a short-term or intermittent basis; however, in the elderly long-term use may be appropriate. Senna is included only as tablets on cost grounds.
- **Glycerol suppositories** have been in use for many years. They have a rapid action.

Faecal softeners

- **Docusate** is a wetting agent that softens stool and is a weak stimulant. The suppositories act particularly quickly.

[Bateman, 1990; DTB, 1992; MeReC, 1994; Medicines Resource, 1996; Fallon and O'Neill, 1997; BNF 43, 2002]

Prescriptions

Non-drug management

Advice only: high fibre diet and fluid intake

- Age from 16 years onwards
- Causes of constipation include: a low fibre diet, a low fluid intake, some medical problems, medication side effects, regular stimulant laxatives, poor mobility. In most people there is no obvious cause. Eat more fibre – fruit, vegetables, cereals, wholemeal bread, etc. Try to drink at least 12 cups (8 glasses or mugs) of liquid a day. Avoid drinks with a high caffeine content as these may make constipation worse. Exercise regularly – keeping the body active helps to keep the bowels active.

C

Bulk-forming agents

Ispaghula 3.5g s/f sachets (Fybogel or Ispagel Orange)
- Age from 16 years onwards
- Ispaghula husk 3.5g s/f granules. Take the contents of one sachet (mixed in a glass of water) each morning and evening; supply 60 sachets; NHS Cost £4.24; OTC Cost £9.30.

Ispaghula 3.4g s/f sachets (Regulan)
- Age from 16 years onwards
- Ispaghula husk 3.4g s/f powder. Take the contents of one sachet (mixed in a glass of water) 1 to 3 times a day; supply 60 sachets; NHS Cost £3.14; OTC Cost £5.54.

Sterculia 62% sachets (Normacol)
- Age from 16 years onwards
- Sterculia 62% granules. Take the contents of one to two sachets, once or twice a day after meals. Wash down with plenty of water without chewing; supply 60 sachets; NHS Cost £5.11; OTC Cost £9.01.

Sterculia 62% and frangula 8% sachets (Normacol Plus)
- Age from 16 years onwards
- Sterculia62%+frangula8% granules. Take the contents of one to two sachets, once or twice a day after meals. Wash down with plenty of water without chewing; supply 60 sachets; NHS Cost £5.45; OTC Cost £9.61.

Oral stimulant laxatives

Senna 7.5mg tablets
- Age from 16 years onwards
- Senna 7.5mg tablets. Take two tablets at night to relieve constipation. Increase to four tablets at night if required; supply 20 tablets; NHS Cost £0.29; OTC Cost £1.75.

Bisacodyl 5mg tablets
- Age from 16 years onwards
- Bisacodyl 5mg tablets. Take one tablet at night to relieve constipation. Increase to two tablets at night if required; supply 10 tablets; NHS Cost £0.30; OTC Cost £1.05.

Faecal softener/weak stimulant

Docusate 100mg capsules
- Age from 16 years onwards
- Docusate 100mg capsules. Take one capsule three times a day to relieve constipation. Increase to a maximum of 5 capsules in 24 hours if required; supply 30 capsules; NHS Cost £1.75; OTC Cost £3.08.

Suppositories or enema for rapid effect

Glycerol 4g suppositories
- Age from 16 years onwards
- Glycerol 4g suppositories. Insert one suppository into the rectum when required to relieve constipation; supply 7 suppositories; NHS Cost £0.34; OTC Cost £1.00.

Docusate 120mg micro-enema (Norgalax)
- Age from 16 years onwards
- Norgalax 10g micro-enema. Use one enema when required to relieve constipation; supply 6 enemas; NHS Cost £3.85; OTC Cost £6.00.

Bisacodyl 10mg suppositories
- Age from 16 years onwards
- Bisacodyl 10mg suppositories. Insert one suppository into the rectum in the morning when required to relieve constipation; supply 7 suppositories; NHS Cost £0.34; OTC Cost £2.55.

Frail elderly or immobile younger adults

Which therapy?

- **Consider underlying causes. If appropriate, stop or reduce causative drugs.**
- **If appropriate, advise high fibre diet with adequate fluid intake and exercise.**
- **If diet is ineffective:**
  - **Consider stimulant laxatives.** These act after 8–12 hours. In general they should be reserved for short-term or intermittent use; however, in the elderly long term use may be appropriate.
  - **Stimulant suppositories** provide more rapid relief (20–60 minutes) than oral preparations (8–12 hours). Do not use for more than 7 days.
  - **Stool softeners** such as liquid paraffin should not be used. Docusate is a wetting agent that softens stool and can be used short-term.
- **If faecal impaction is present consider a phosphate enema.** Then use a stimulant to clear the colon completely, with consideration of regular bulk-forming agents or stimulant laxatives to prevent recurrence, depending on the reason for constipation.

Practical prescribing points

For further information please see the *Medicines Compendium* (www.medicines.org.uk) or the *British National Formulary* (www.bnf.org).

- **Rectal preparations** may be uncomfortable if the person has haemorrhoids or an anal fissure. Rectal docusate should not be used in these people.
- **Stimulant laxatives** often cause abdominal cramp; avoid if intestinal obstruction is a possibility.
- **Osmotic laxatives — sodium salts (sodium citrate)** may cause sodium and water retention in susceptible people. Sodium citrate should only be administered rectally and occasionally [Medicines Resource, 1996; BNF 43, 2002].

Should I refer or investigate?

Refer?

- **If constipation does not respond to treatment,** consider admission for manual evacuation, according to facilities available in the surgery (often this can be done by the district nurse).
- **Consider referral to a dietician** as appropriate.

Investigate?

- **Long standing constipation** which responds to treatment may not require investigation (a digital rectal examination should be performed).
- **Consider investigation** (barium enema, sigmoidoscopy, colonoscopy) if:
  - **A change in bowel habit in the middle-aged and elderly,** or those at high risk of neoplasia
  - **Rectal bleeding at any age**
  - **Symptoms are severe, new and unresponsive to treatment**
  - **Symptoms are of sudden onset**
  - Weight loss
- **Depending on facilities and expertise within the practice this may necessitate referral to secondary care.**

'atient information leaflets

ıe following PILs are available at www.prodigy.nhs.uk

Constipation in Adults
Eat More Fruit and Vegetables
Faecal Occult Blood Test
Fibre in the Diet

hared decision making

A low fibre diet is the most common cause of constipation. Poor mobility can also cause constipation, or make it worse.

Eat more fibre — fruit, vegetables, cereals, wholemeal bread, etc.

Have lots to drink — at least 8–10 cups of fluid per day. But, don't have too much tea or coffee, which may make constipation worse.

Exercise regularly — if possible. Keeping your body active helps to keep your bowels active.

Fibre supplements — bulk-forming agents such as **ispaghula** usually work if the measures above do not help.

Laxatives — other than fibre supplements, should only be used as a temporary remedy if constipation is severe. There are different types.

- *Stimulant laxatives* — such as **bisacodyl** and **senna** make the bowel work harder. They may cause stomach cramps.
- *Stool softeners* — such as **docusate**, make the stools easier to pass.
- *Suppositories* — are sometimes used as an alternative.
- *An enema* or a powerful laxative is sometimes required if other treatments do not work.

)rug rationale

'rugs not included

3ulk-forming agents

Bulk-forming laxatives are not appropriate, they should only be used in more active people who are also able to drink sufficient fluids.

3timulants

Co-danthramer (a combination of dantron and poloxamer) and co-danthrusate (a combination of dantron and docusate) are indicated only in people who are terminally ill because of accumulating evidence confirming that dantron is genotoxic [CSM, 2000].

Oxyphenisatin (which is available only as an enema) is more appropriately used for bowel evacuation procedures in hospital.

Sodium picosulfate is relatively expensive, and tends to be reserved for bowel clearance.

)smotic laxatives

Lactitol is more expensive than lactulose.

Macrogol (polyethylene glycol) is expensive. The products available are indicated for chronic constipation or bowel clearance [BNF 43, 2002].

Magnesium salts produce watery stool with urgency and sometimes incontinence which limits their acceptability [Spiller, 1990].

Sodium salts (sodium citrate) may cause sodium and water retention in susceptible people. Sodium citrate should only be administered rectally and occasionally [Medicines Resource, 1996; BNF 43, 2002].

Faecal softeners

- **Rectal arachis oil** is only available as a large volume enema. It has a limited role for softening of impacted faeces [MeReC, 1994; Fallon and O'Neill, 1997]. There is no consensus at the present time about the risk of peanut allergy linked to refined arachis oil.
- **Liquid paraffin** can cause anal seepage and irritation, lipoid pneumonia and malabsorption of lipid-soluble vitamins. It is not recommended [Gattuso and Kamm, 1994; Medicines Resource, 1996].

C

Drugs included

Stimulants

- **Bisacodyl and senna** are well tolerated by most people. They have been in use for many years and their adverse effects and contraindications are well known. In general they should be used on a short-term or intermittent basis; however, in the elderly long-term use may be appropriate. Either bisacodyl or senna can be given concurrently with docusate to allow each component to be titrated to individual requirements.
- **Glycerol suppositories** have been in use for many years. They have a rapid action.

Faecal softeners

- **Docusate** is effective and well tolerated.

Osmotic laxatives

- **Phosphate enemas** are effective in severe constipation (that may lead to faecal impaction), which is more common in elderly than younger people.
- **Lactulose** may sometimes be of benefit, but it may cause adverse effects, has a sickly taste, and can take 2–3 days to have an effect. It should be reserved for use when other laxatives have failed to produce an effect.

[Bateman, 1990; DTB, 1992; MeReC, 1994; Medicines Resource, 1996; Fallon and O'Neill, 1997; BNF 43, 2002]

Prescriptions

Oral stimulant laxatives

Senna 7.5mg tablets

- Age from 16 years onwards
- Senna 7.5mg tablets. Take two tablets at night to relieve constipation. Increase to four tablets at night if required; supply 20 tablets; NHS Cost £0.29; OTC Cost £1.75.

Senna 7.5mg/5ml syrup

- Age from 16 years onwards
- Senna 7.5mg/5ml syrup. Take two 5ml spoonfuls at night to relieve constipation. Increase to four 5ml spoonfuls at night if required; supply 100 ml; NHS Cost £1.98; OTC Cost £3.05.

Bisacodyl 5mg tablets

- Age from 16 years onwards
- Bisacodyl 5mg tablets. Take one tablet at night to relieve constipation. Increase to two tablets at night if required; supply 10 tablets; NHS Cost £0.30; OTC Cost £1.05.

Non-drug management

Advice only: high fibre diet and fluid intake

- Age from 16 years onwards
- Causes of constipation include: a low fibre diet, a low fluid intake, some medical problems, medication side effects, regular stimulant laxatives, poor mobility. In most people there is no obvious cause. Eat more fibre – fruit, vegetables, cereals, wholemeal bread, etc. Try to drink at least 12 cups (8 glasses or mugs) of liquid a day.

Avoid drinks with a high caffeine content as these may make constipation worse. Try to keep as active as possible – keeping the body active helps to keep the bowels active. Laxatives are best used as a temporary remedy only if constipation becomes severe.

Stimulant suppositories for rapid effect

Glycerol 4g suppositories
- Age from 16 years onwards
- Glycerol 4g suppositories. Insert one suppository into the rectum when required to relieve constipation; supply 7 suppositories; NHS Cost £0.34; OTC Cost £1.00.

Bisacodyl 10mg suppositories
- Age from 16 years onwards
- Bisacodyl 10mg suppositories. Insert one suppository into the rectum in the morning when required to relieve constipation; supply 7 suppositories; NHS Cost £0.34; OTC Cost £2.55.

Stool softeners

Docusate 100mg capsules (also weak stimulant)
- Age from 16 years onwards
- Docusate 100mg capsules. Take one capsule three times a day to relieve constipation. Increase to a maximum of 5 capsules in 24 hours if required; supply 30 capsules; NHS Cost £1.75; OTC Cost £3.08.

Docusate 50mg/5ml solution (also weak stimulant)
- Age from 16 years onwards
- Docusate 50mg/5ml solution. Take two 5ml spoonfuls up to three times a day to relieve constipation. Increase to a maximum of ten 5ml spoonfuls in 24 hours if required; supply 300 ml; NHS Cost £2.48; OTC Cost £3.08.

Lactulose solution
- Age from 16 years onwards
- Lactulose 3.35g/5ml solution. Take three 5ml spoonfuls twice a day; supply 200 ml; NHS Cost £1.00; OTC Cost £3.50.

Faecal impaction: phosphate enema

Phosphate enema – long tube
- Age from 16 years onwards
- Phosphates B long tube enema. Use one enema when required to relieve constipation; supply 1 128ml enema; NHS Cost £0.64.

Phosphate enema – standard tube
- Age from 16 years onwards
- Phosphates formula B (128ml). Use one enema when required to relieve constipation; supply 1 128ml enema; NHS Cost £0.46.

Fleet enema
- Age from 16 years onwards
- Fleet enema. Use one enema when required to relieve constipation; supply 1 118ml enema; NHS Cost £0.46.

Children

Which therapy?

Acute constipation

- **High dietary fibre** with plenty of fluid should always be tried first, with a *reduction in excessive milk drinking* in toddlers. It may be prudent to warn parents that drinks which are acidic or have a high sugar content are known to be a causative factor in dental caries, and that children should not be encouraged to drink to the extent that they reduce their intake of necessary nutrients.
- **Encourage the use of the toilet or potty** after meals, wit positive reinforcement (e.g. with star charts).
- **If no response** to dietary and behavioural treatments:
  - **Bulk laxatives, stool softeners, or stimulant laxatives** often combined with a softener should be tried.

Chronic constipation

- **If constipation is chronic it is essential to achieve coloni evacuation prior to initiating maintenance laxative therapy.**
- **A faecal softener usually with a stimulant laxative** is prescribed for maintenance therapy. Parents should be encouraged to give them regularly for several months; intermittent use may provoke a series of relapses. After several months, assuming treatment is successful, the dose can be gradually reduced; the reduction itself should take several months to avoid a relapse.
- **Oral laxative therapy is preferred.** Suppositories and enemas are used as a last resort.

Practical prescribing points

For further information please see the *Medicines Compendium* (www.medicines.org.uk) or the *British National Formulary* (www.bnf.org).

- **Stimulant laxatives** may cause abdominal cramp; avoid if intestinal obstruction is a possibility. In the presence rectal faecal impaction, stimulant laxatives may increas faecal overflow.

Follow-up advice

- Regular review should include a reinforcement of how ensure a high fibre diet, in order to improve complianc

Should I refer or investigate?

Refer?

- **Referral to a paediatrician is indicated if:**
  - Severe, intractable constipation
  - Suspicion of Hirschsprung's disease or intestinal pseudo-obstruction:
    - History of delayed passage of meconium
    - Problems date from new born
    - Family history of Hirschsprung's disease
  - Minimal soiling
  - Marked abdominal distension
  - Failure to thrive
  - Episodes of severe diarrhoea
  - Persistent vomiting
  - Severe family distress
  - Blood in the stool and/or bottom pain not resolving after 6 weeks of treatment
  - Constipation fails to resolve after 3 months of treatment

[BSPGHAN, 1998; Gallagher et al, 1998]

- **Referral to a child psychiatrist for behavioural therapy or biofeedback** is sometimes recommended, depending on the individual child's circumstances, e.g. if there is major psychological disturbance. This aims to teach the child to be aware of the presence of stool, and to relax the pelvic muscles and evacuate the stool [Kamm, 1994
- **Consider referral to a dietitian** as appropriate.

Investigate?

- **Avoid invasive investigations** where possible, as these can be distressing for the child. Where examination is felt necessary it is important to obtain verbal consent, give a full explanation, and exercise sensitivity [Beach, 1996].

Patient information leaflets

The following PILs are available at www.prodigy.nhs.uk
Constipation in Children
Eat More Fruit and Vegetables
Fibre in the Diet

Shared decision making

Constipation is common in children, and is usually temporary. Not eating enough fibre is the usually cause.
Give foods with more fibre — fruit, vegetables, cereals, wholemeal bread, etc.
Give lots to drink — to soften the stools. Water is best. Too much milk can make constipation worse in toddlers and older children.
Fibre supplements — such as bulk-forming agents usually work if the measures above do not help.
Constipation becomes severe in some children. A combination of laxatives may then be needed for several months. For example:

- *A stimulant laxative* — to make the bowel work harder.
- *A stool softener* — to make the stools softer and easier to pass.

Referral for specialist advice is sometimes needed if constipation persists.

Drug rationale

Drugs not included

Products not available in a liquid formulation or suitable for sprinkling onto food.
Products without easy to use paediatric dosage instructions.
Products not licensed for use in children.
Suppositories and enemas are not appropriate for use in children at home in most circumstances.

Faecal softeners

Liquid paraffin can cause anal seepage and irritation, lipoid pneumonia, and malabsorption of lipid-soluble vitamins. It is contraindicated in children under 3 years of age and the CSM has advised against its long-term use [Gattuso and Kamm, 1994; Medicines Resource, 1996; BNF 43, 2002].

Bulk-forming agents

Bran supplements are no longer included as the only commercially available medicinal product containing bran (Trifyba) has been discontinued.

Drugs included

Stimulant laxatives

Senna has been in use for many years, its adverse effects and contraindications are well known [Gallagher et al, 1998].

Faecal softeners

Docusate has been in use for many years, its adverse effects and contraindications are well known.

Bulk-forming agents

Bulk-forming agents containing ispaghula are included. Clinically there is little to choose between the different agents [MeReC, 1999]. They are a good choice if prolonged treatment is required. Since palatability and convenience of use are very important if children are to adhere to long-term treatment, only products available in sachets and in a variety of flavours are offered. Sugar-free products are offered where available. The ispaghula preparation with the simplest children's dosing measurement is included on compliance grounds.
[Bateman, 1990; DTB, 1992; MeReC, 1994; Medicines Resource, 1996; Fallon and O'Neill, 1997; BNF 43, 2002]

Osmotic laxatives

- **Lactulose** may sometimes be of benefit, but it may cause adverse effects, has a sickly taste, and can take 2–3 days to have an effect [Bateman, 1990; Medicines Resource, 1996; Fallon and O'Neill, 1997]. It may be used in combination with a stimulant laxative if individual drugs fail [DTB, 2000].

Prescriptions

Non-drug management

Advice only: high fibre diet and fluid intake
- Age under 16 years
- Constipation is common in children. A low fibre diet or a low fluid intake tend to make constipation worse. Give foods with more fibre – fruit, vegetables, cereals, wholemeal bread, etc. Give lots to drink to soften the motions. Water and fruit juices are best. Milk is not so good and too much milk drinking by toddlers is best cut down. If constipation persists, return to see the doctor.

Bulk-forming agents – not in faecal impaction

Ispaghula 3.5g s/f sachets (Fybogel or Ispagel Orange)
- Age from 1 month to 5 years
- Ispaghula husk 3.5g s/f granules. Take half a 5ml spoonful (dissolved in water) each morning and evening when required to relieve constipation; supply 30 sachets; NHS Cost £2.12; OTC Cost £4.65.

Ispaghula 3.5g s/f sachets (Fybogel or Ispagel Orange)
- Age from 6 to 11 years
- Ispaghula husk 3.5g s/f granules. Take half to one level 5ml spoonful (dissolved in water) each morning and evening when required to relieve constipation; supply 56 sachets; NHS Cost £4.24; OTC Cost £9.30.

Ispaghula 3.5g s/f sachets (Fybogel or Ispagel Orange)
- Age from 12 to 15 years
- Ispaghula husk 3.5g s/f granules. Take the contents of one sachet (dissolved in water) each morning and evening; supply 60 sachets; NHS Cost £4.24; OTC Cost £9.30.

Ispaghula 3.4g s/f sachets (Regulan)
- Age from 6 to 11 years
- Ispaghula husk 3.4g s/f powder. Take half to one level 5ml spoonful (mixed in water) 1 to 3 times a day; supply 56 sachets; NHS Cost £4.24; OTC Cost £9.30.

Ispaghula 3.4g s/f sachets (Regulan)
- Age from 12 to 15 years
- Ispaghula husk 3.4g s/f powder. Take the contents of one sachet (mixed in a glass of water) 1 to 3 times a day; supply 60 sachets; NHS Cost £3.14; OTC Cost £7.50.

Stimulant: senna

Senna 7.5mg/5ml syrup
- Age from 2 to 5 years
- Senna 7.5mg/5ml syrup. Take 2.5ml to 5ml each morning; supply 50 ml; NHS Cost £0.99; OTC Cost £3.05.

Senna 7.5mg/5ml syrup
- Age from 6 to 11 years
- Senna 7.5mg/5ml syrup. Take one to two 5ml spoonfuls each morning; supply 100 ml; NHS Cost £1.98; OTC Cost £3.05.

C

Senna 7.5mg tablets
- Age from 12 to 15 years
- Senna 7.5mg tablets. Take two tablets at night to relieve constipation. Increase to four tablets at night if required; supply 20 tablets; NHS Cost £0.29; OTC Cost £1.75.

Softener and weak stimulant: docusate

Docusate 12.5mg/5ml solution
- Age from 6 to 23 months
- Docusate 12.5mg/5ml sol. Take one 5ml spoonful three times a day; supply 100 ml; NHS Cost £0.54; OTC Cost £2.87.

Docusate 12.5mg/5ml solution
- Age from 2 to 11 years
- Docusate 12.5mg/5ml sol. Take one to two 5ml spoonfuls three times a day; supply 300 ml; NHS Cost £1.63; OTC Cost £2.87.

Docusate 100mg capsules
- Age from 12 to 15 years
- Docusate 100mg capsules. Take one capsule three times a day to relieve constipation. Increase to a maximum of 5 capsules in 24 hours if required; supply 30 capsules; NHS Cost £1.75; OTC Cost £3.08.

Osmotic laxative: lactulose

Lactulose solution
- Age under 11 months
- Lactulose 3.35g/5ml solution. Take 2.5ml twice a day; supply 50 ml; NHS Cost £0.25; OTC Cost £3.50.

Lactulose solution
- Age from 12 months to 4 years
- Lactulose 3.35g/5ml solution. Take one 5ml spoonful twice a day; supply 100 ml; NHS Cost £0.50; OTC Cost £3.50.

Lactulose solution
- Age from 5 to 9 years
- Lactulose 3.35g/5ml solution. Take two 5ml spoonfuls twice a day; supply 150 ml; NHS Cost £0.75; OTC Cost £3.50.

Lactulose solution
- Age from 10 to 15 years
- Lactulose 3.35g/5ml solution. Take three 5ml spoonfuls twice a day; supply 200 ml; NHS Cost £1.00; OTC Cost £3.50.

Pregnancy

Which therapy?

- **Increased dietary fibre, fluid intake, and exercise are effective in most cases.**
- **Use drugs with caution for short periods only.**
- **If diet, fluid, and exercise fail, try bulk-forming laxatives,** which are thought to be safer.
- Stimulant laxatives may be more helpful in some women.

Practical prescribing points

For further information please see the *Medicines Compendium* (www.medicines.org.uk) or the *British National Formulary* (www.bnf.org).

- **In pregnancy any drug should be used with caution.** In particular, caution should be taken with senna if near term or if pregnancy is unstable (i.e. if there are risk factors for premature delivery).
- Contact the National Teratology Information Service for further information (0191 232 1525).

Should I refer or investigate?

Refer?

- **If constipation is severe or there is faecal impaction, admit for specialist review.**
- **Referral to, or discussion with, an obstetrician** may be appropriate if investigations (barium enema, sigmoidoscopy, colonoscopy) are being considered due to:
  - Rectal bleeding
  - Symptoms which are severe, new, and unresponsive t[o] treatment
  - Symptoms which are of sudden onset
- **Consider referral to a dietitian** as appropriate.

Patient information leaflets

The following PILs are available at www.prodigy.nhs.uk
- Constipation in Adults
- Eat More Fruit and Vegetables
- Fibre in the Diet

Shared decision making

- Constipation is common in pregnancy.
- **Eat more fibre** — fruit, vegetables, cereals, wholemeal bread, etc.
- **Have lots to drink** — at least 8–10 cups of fluid per day But, don't have too much tea or coffee, which may mak[e] constipation worse.
- **Exercise regularly** — keeping your body active helps to keep your bowels active.
- **Fibre supplements** — bulk-forming agents such as **ispaghula** usually work if the measures above do not help.
- **Laxatives** other than fibre supplements are best used on as a temporary remedy if constipation becomes severe.

Drug rationale

Drugs not included

- Any preparations without a long safety track record of use in pregnancy.

Faecal softners

- **Docusate** has not been shown to cause fetal toxicity, bu[t] there is insufficient evidence of its safety to recommend its routine use [Lee and Schofield, 1994].

Bulk-forming

- **Methylcellulose** is excluded on grounds of compliance (the dose has to be titrated up to six tablets twice a day)
- **Bran supplements** are no longer included as the only commercially available medicinal product containing bran (Trifyba) has been discontinued.

Drugs included

Bulk-forming agents

- **Ispaghula, and sterculia** are safe to use in pregnancy, although they may not be as effective as stimulant laxatives [MeReC, 1994; Medicines Resource, 1996; Jewell and Young, 2001;].

Stimulants

- **Senna** has not been shown to be teratogenic in animal studies, and there are no reports of human teratogenicit[y] or fetal toxicity [MeReC, 1994]. Senna is included only as tablets on cost grounds. It may cause uterine contractions and should be used with caution if near term or if pregnancy is unstable (i.e. if there are risk factors for premature delivery).

Osmotic laxatives

Lactulose has been used during pregnancy without evidence of adverse effect, but it has a tendency to cause bloating and colic, and can take 2–3 days to have an effect. Many people find the taste of lactulose sickly [Gattuso and Kamm, 1994; Lee and Schofield, 1994; Medicines Resource, 1996; Petticrew et al, 1997].

Prescriptions

Non-drug management

Advice only: high fibre diet and fluid intake
Age from 12 to 60 years
Constipation is common in pregnancy. Eat more fibre – fruit, vegetables, cereals, wholemeal bread, etc. Try to drink at least 12 cups (8 glasses or mugs) of liquid a day. Avoid drinks with a high caffeine content as these may make constipation worse. Exercise regularly- keeping the body active helps to keep the bowels active.

Bulk-forming agents

Ispaghula 3.5g s/f sachets (Fybogel or Ispagel Orange)
Age from 12 to 60 years
Ispaghula husk 3.5g s/f granules. Take the contents of one sachet (dissolved in water) each morning and evening; supply 60 sachets; NHS Cost £4.24; OTC Cost £9.30.

Ispaghula 3.4g s/f sachets (Regulan)
Age from 12 to 60 years
Ispaghula husk 3.4g s/f powder. Take the contents of one sachet (mixed in a glass of water) 1 to 3 times a day; supply 60 sachets; NHS Cost £3.14; OTC Cost £7.50.

Sterculia 62% sachets (Normacol)
Age from 12 to 60 years
Sterculia 62% granules. Take the contents of one to two sachets, once or twice a day after meals. Wash down with plenty of water without chewing; supply 60 sachets; NHS Cost £4.65; OTC Cost £8.20.

Senna (NOT 3rd trimester)

Senna 7.5mg tablets
Age from 12 to 60 years
Senna 7.5mg tablets. Take two tablets at night to relieve constipation. Increase to four tablets at night if required; supply 20 tablets; NHS Cost £0.29; OTC Cost £1.75.

Osmotic laxative

Lactulose solution
Age from 12 to 60 years
Lactulose 3.35g/5ml solution. Take three 5ml spoonfuls twice a day; supply 200 ml; NHS Cost £1.00; OTC Cost £3.50.

Terminal Care

Which therapy?

- **In terminal care, prevent constipation wherever possible.**
- **Consider all causes of constipation** and treat appropriately.
- **Start regular laxatives as soon as weak or strong opioids are prescribed,** increasing the laxative as the dose of the opioid is increased.
- **If the rectum is full:**
  - And hard faeces — hydrate orally and start co-danthramer, co-danthrusate, or docusate. Glycerin suppositories may help.
  - And soft faeces — try stimulant laxatives such as senna or bisacodyl.
  - If unsuccessful, consider enemas or manual evacuation.
- **If the colon is full:**
  - And colic is present — try docusate (a wetting agent and mild stimulant).
  - And colic is absent — try co-danthramer or co-danthrusate.
- **If the rectum is empty:**
  - Try high lubrication (arachis oil) and rectal stimulant laxative.

Practical prescribing points

For further information please see the *Medicines Compendium* (www.medicines.org.uk) or the *British National Formulary* (www.bnf.org).

- Stimulant laxatives can cause abdominal cramp — avoid if intestinal obstruction is a possibility.
- Rectal docusate should not be given to people who have haemorrhoids or an anal fissure.

Should I refer or investigate?

Refer?

- If poor response to treatment, or uncertain regarding cause of constipation, consider referral to, or seek advice from, a palliative medicine specialist or hospice.

Patient information leaflets

The following PILs are available at www.prodigy.nhs.uk

- Constipation in Adults
- Eat More Fruit and Vegetables
- Fibre in the Diet

Shared decision making

- Constipation often occurs when someone is seriously ill.
- Strong painkillers often cause constipation too.
- Try and have plenty to drink to soften the stools.
- Regular laxatives are commonly needed. Various laxatives are available, and one can usually be found to ease constipation.

Drug rationale

Drugs not included

- **Oxyphenisatin** (which is available only as an enema) is more appropriately used for bowel evacuation procedures in hospital.
- **Sodium picosulfate** is relatively expensive, and tends to be reserved for bowel clearance.
- **Liquid paraffin** can cause anal seepage and irritation, lipoid pneumonia, and malabsorption of lipid-soluble vitamins. It is not recommended [Medicines Resource, 1996].
- **Bulk-forming laxatives** are not usually sufficiently effective in terminal care. There is a risk of intestinal or oesophageal obstruction. Faecal impaction, flatulence, and distension may occur.
- **Osmotic laxatives:**
  - **Lactulose and lactitol** have a tendency to cause bloating and colic, and can take 2–3 days to have an effect [Fallon and O'Neill, 1997]. Many people find the taste of lactulose sickly [Medicines Resource,

1996; Regnard and Tempest, 1998]. It is an alternative to docusate if colic is a problem, although its use is limited by possible postural hypotension due to fluid shift to the bowel.
- **Macrogol** (polyethylene glycol) is expensive. The products available are indicated for chronic constipation or bowel clearance [BNF 43, 2002].
- **Magnesium salts** produce watery stool with urgency and sometimes incontinence which limits acceptability. They may upset electrolyte balance [Spiller, 1990].
- **Rectal phosphates** have a risk of phosphate absorption [Bateman, 1990].
- **Rectal sodium citrate** may cause sodium and water retention in some people if used regularly [BNF 43, 2002].

C

Drugs included

Oral

- **Bisacodyl and senna** are recommended if faeces are soft and the rectum is full. Senna is included only as tablets on cost grounds.
- **Docusate** is a wetting agent that softens stool and is a weak stimulant. It is recommended if the colon is full, and colic is present.
- **Co-danthramer** (a combination of dantron and poloxamer) is effective and recommended if faeces are hard and the rectum is full. It is also a good choice if colic is absent and the colon is full.
- **Co-danthrusate** (a combination of dantron and docusate) is useful on grounds of convenience, when both are needed, and the dose of the combined product suits individual needs.

[Regnard and Tempest, 1998]

Rectal

- **Glycerol suppositories** are effective if faeces are hard and the rectum is full. They have a rapid action.
- **Arachis oil large volume enema** is effective if the rectum is empty and a full colon is accompanied by colic.
- **Docusate enema** is recommended, as an alternative to glycerol suppositories, if the faeces are hard and the rectum is full.

[Regnard and Tempest, 1998]

Prescriptions

If faeces are hard and rectum is full

Co-danthramer 25/200mg/5ml suspension
- Age from 16 years onwards
- Co-danthramer 25/200mg/5ml susp. Take one to two 5ml spoonfuls at night; supply 100 ml; NHS Cost £3.78.

Co-danthramer 25/200mg capsules
- Age from 16 years onwards
- Co-danthramer 25/200mg caps. Take one to two capsules at night; supply 14 capsules; NHS Cost £3.00.

Glycerol 4g suppositories
- Age from 16 years onwards
- Glycerol 4g suppositories. Insert one suppository into the rectum when required to relieve constipation; supply 7 suppositories; NHS Cost £0.34; OTC Cost £1.00.

Docusate 120mg micro-enema (Norgalax)
- Age from 16 years onwards
- Norgalax 10g micro-enema. Use one enema when required to relieve constipation; supply 6 enemas; NHS Cost £3.85; OTC Cost £6.00.

Co-danthrusate 50/60mg capsules
- Age from 16 years onwards
- Co-danthrusate 50/60mg caps. Take one to three capsules at night; supply 21 capsules; NHS Cost £4.49.

Co-danthrusate 50/60mg/5ml suspension
- Age from 16 years onwards
- Co-danthrusate 50/60mg susp. Take one to three 5ml spoonfuls at night; supply 200 ml; NHS Cost £6.40.

If faeces are soft and the rectum is full

Senna 7.5mg tablets
- Age from 16 years onwards
- Senna 7.5mg tablets. Take two tablets at night to relieve constipation. Increase to four tablets at night if required; supply 20 tablets; NHS Cost £0.29; OTC Cost £1.75.

Bisacodyl 5mg tablets
- Age from 16 years onwards
- Bisacodyl 5mg tablets. Take one tablet at night to relieve constipation. Increase to two tablets at night if required; supply 10 tablets; NHS Cost £0.30; OTC Cost £1.05.

Senna 7.5mg/5ml syrup
- Age from 16 years onwards
- Senna 7.5mg/5ml syrup. Take two 5ml spoonfuls at night to relieve constipation. Increase to four 5ml spoonfuls at night if required; supply 100 ml; NHS Cost £1.98; OTC Cost £3.05.

If the colon is full and colic is present

Docusate 100mg capsules
- Age from 16 years onwards
- Docusate 100mg capsules. Take one capsule three times a day to relieve constipation. Increase to a maximum of 5 capsules in 24 hours if required; supply 30 capsules; NHS Cost £1.75; OTC Cost £3.08.

Docusate 50mg/5ml solution
- Age from 16 years onwards
- Docusate 50mg/5ml solution. Take two 5ml spoonfuls up to three times a day to relieve constipation. Increase to a maximum of ten 5ml spoonfuls in 24 hours if required; supply 300 ml; NHS Cost £2.48; OTC Cost £3.08.

Arachis oil (peanut) large volume enema
- Age from 16 years onwards
- Arachis oil enema. Use one enema when required to relieve constipation; supply 1 130 ml enema; NHS Cost £1.07; OTC Cost £2.00.

If colon is full and colic is absent

Co-danthramer 25/200mg capsules
- Age from 16 years onwards
- Co-danthramer 25/200mg caps. Take one to two capsules at night; supply 14 capsules; NHS Cost £3.00.

Co-danthramer 25/200mg/5ml suspension
- Age from 16 years onwards
- Co-danthramer 25/200mg/5ml susp. Take one to two 5ml spoonfuls at night; supply 100 ml; NHS Cost £3.78

Co-danthramer strong 37.5/500mg capsules
- Age from 16 years onwards
- Co-danthramer strong caps. Take one to two capsules a night; supply 14 capsules; NHS Cost £3.63.

Co-danthramer strong 75/1000mg/5ml suspension
- Age from 16 years onwards
- Co-danthramer strong susp. Take one 5ml spoonful at night; supply 100 ml; NHS Cost £10.11.

Co-danthrusate 50/60mg capsules
- Age from 16 years onwards
- Co-danthrusate 50/60mg caps. Take one to three capsules at night; supply 21 capsules; NHS Cost £4.49.

Co-danthrusate 50/60mg/5ml suspension
Age from 16 years onwards
Co-danthrusate 50/60mg susp. Take one to three 5ml spoonfuls at night; supply 200 ml; NHS Cost £6.40.

Extended Information

Background information

What is it? p.383
How common is it? p.383
How do I know my patient has it? p.383
What else might it be? p.383
Complications and prognosis p.383

What is it?

- **The exact definition of constipation is not clear.** Most definitions include infrequent bowel actions of twice a week or less, which often require straining to pass hard faeces. Sensations of pain and incomplete evacuation are sometimes associated.
- **The perception of normal bowel function varies;** what is constipation to one person may be normal bowel activity to another [MeReC, 1994].
- **Normal bowel function** in 90% of people in Western populations is defecation between 3 times a day and once every 3 days [Bandolier, 1997].
- **Likely causes include:** lack of dietary fibre, low fluid intake, immobility, slimming diets, and adverse drug effects [MeReC, 1994]. In children, battles over potty training may cause constipation [Beach, 1996].
- **Pathophysiology:** constipation can be due to small, hard stools with normal colonic muscle tone; or alternatively, normal stool with lack of muscle tone and failure to respond to the stimulus of faecal bulk.
- **In palliative care:** reduced stool frequency (quantity) is normal in the last months and weeks of life. Consequently the comfort (quality) of stool is a deciding factor. For example, a comfortable stool twice weekly may be normal, whereas a hard painful stool daily indicates constipation.

How common is it?

- **In 2001 over 12 million prescriptions for laxatives were written in England** in general practice [DH, 2001].
- **Constipation is more common in the elderly:**
  - 20% of elderly people (often associated with immobility and poor diet; also perineal muscle tone is lower)
  - 8% of middle-aged people
  - 2.9% of young people seek medical advice for constipation [Kamm, 1989; Medicines Resource, 1996; Petticrew et al, 1997]
- **Women are thought to have a higher prevalence of constipation than men** [Petticrew et al, 1997], although whether this reflects the greater likelihood of women to seek medical advice is not clear.
- **Constipation is common in late pregnancy,** as a result of reduced gastrointestinal motility, and delayed bowel emptying due to the pressure of the uterus [Medicines Resource, 1996].
- **51% of people with cancer** experience constipation [Regnard and Tempest, 1998].
- **5–10% of children** are thought to have constipation [Leung et al, 1996].

How do I know my patient has it?

History

- **May reveal longstanding symptoms or a recent change in bowel frequency,** with or without change in consistency of stool, which is perceived as abnormal by the person.
- **One standard set of criteria for the diagnosis of constipation is the Rome II Criteria,** which requires two or more of the following symptoms to be present for at least 12 weeks out of the preceding 12 months:
  - Straining at defecation for at least a quarter of the time
  - Lumpy and or hard stools for at least a quarter of the time
  - A sensation of incomplete evacuation for at least a quarter of the time
  - 3 or fewer bowel movements per week

[Thompson et al, 1999]

- **Severe constipation may paradoxically present with overflow diarrhoea and faecal incontinence.**
- **The diagnosis of constipation in young children is often difficult,** since it depends on the parents' view as to whether or not their child's bowel habit is normal [Staiano and Tozzi, 1998].

Examination

- **May be normal.**
- **There may be palpable faeces** predominantly in the left upper and lower quadrants of the abdomen ('loaded colon').
- **A digital rectal examination should be performed.** Note:
  - The presence of faeces compared with an empty rectum
  - Whether there is rectal impaction of faeces
  - The consistency of faeces
  - Any non-faecal masses (tumour, haemorrhoids)
  - The presence of blood (fresh, melaena)

What else might it be?

It is important to consider underlying conditions which may present with symptoms of constipation. Examples include:

- Dehydration
- Irritable bowel syndrome
- Intestinal obstruction (e.g. gastrointestinal carcinoma, ileus, ovarian or uterine tumours, benign stricture)
- Painful anal conditions (e.g. anal fissure, haemorrhoids)
- Metabolic conditions (e.g. hypothyroidism, hypercalcaemia, hypokalaemia)
- Neurological conditions (e.g. spinal or pelvic nerve injury, Parkinson's disease, autonomic neuropathy — most commonly due to diabetes mellitus)
- Psychiatric conditions (e.g. depression)
- Adverse effects of drugs (see *Management issues/General issues/Drugs which commonly cause constipation*).

[Kamm, 1994; MeReC, 1994; Medicines Resource, 1996]

In childhood constipation it is important to consider social and psychological problems and rare anatomical, neurological (e.g. Hirschsprung's disease), endocrine and metabolic causes. Most cases are, however, idiopathic [Medicines Resource, 1996].

Complications and prognosis

- **Haemorrhoids** may develop if persistent constipation is inadequately treated.
- **An atonic and non-functioning colon** may result from persistent constipation or from laxative abuse [MeReC, 1994].
- **Long-term constipation** may also, depending on the severity and duration, result in:
  - Faecal impaction

C

- Intestinal obstruction or perforation
- Faecal and urinary incontinence
- Urinary tract infection
- Rectal bleeding
- Generalised weakness and psychological disorders [McCormack, 1996; Petticrew et al, 1997]
- **Straining** to defecate causes an increase in intrathoracic pressure. This can lead to:
  - A reduction in coronary, cerebral, and peripheral circulation
  - The development of hernias
  - Worsening of gastro-oespophageal reflux
  - Transient ischaemic attacks and syncope in elderly people [McCormack, 1996].
- **Most children with idiopathic constipation** improve with time and respond to a combination of non-drug, drug, and behavioural therapies. A small proportion retain their symptoms into adult life [Kamm, 1994].
- **An association between chronic constipation and carcinoma of the colon** is suggested in some of the literature. Although the evidence for this is not conclusive, it is prudent to recommend a high fibre, low-red meat diet, and regular exercise — in itself this helps to reduce the risk of colonic carcinoma [Le Marchand, 1998].

Management issues

- General issues p.384
- Non-drug treatments p.384
- Drug treatments p.384
- Specific situations p.385

General issues

- **A stepped-care approach** to management should be followed where possible [Petticrew et al, 1997]:
  - The first step (after excluding underlying conditions) being advice about dietary improvement.
  - The second step being drug treatment.
- **Education and lifestyle advice** (diet and exercise) is the mainstay of therapy for uncomplicated constipation, and this alone may adequately control symptoms in many cases [MeReC, 1994; Medicines Resource, 1996].
- **Reassurance** — that the person does not have cancer, that different people defecate at different frequencies, and that mild constipation is not usually harmful — may be helpful.
- **Drugs which commonly cause constipation** include [Bateman, 1990; Medicines Resource, 1996]:
  - Antacids containing aluminium hydroxide or calcium carbonate
  - Amiodarone
  - Anticholinergics (e.g. tricyclic antidepressants, antihistamines, antipsychotics)
  - Antidiarrhoeal agents
  - Antiparkinsonian agents
  - Calcium-channel blockers
  - Calcium supplements
  - Clonidine
  - Disopyramide
  - Diuretics
  - Iron preparations
  - Lithium
  - Nonsteroidal anti-inflammatory drugs
  - Opioid analgesics and cough suppressants
- If possible these drugs should be stopped, or the dose reduced, or prophylactic laxatives used, according to the individual situation.

Non-drug treatments

- **Fibre** — high dietary fibre is effective in increasing stool weight, and increases faecal transit time. A high-fibre diet — about 30 g per day — (e.g. high in fruit, vegetables, wholemeal bread, cereals, and grain foods) should be tried for at least one month before its effects on constipation are determined, although most people will notice an effect within 3–5 days [Medicines Resource, 1996]. Two litres of water each day is also recommended for people on a high-fibre diet [MeReC, 1994]. If adequate fluid intake is not possible, avoid increasing dietary fibre.
- **Adverse effects of a high-fibre diet** include flatulence, bloating and distension, and an unpalatable taste. These are likely to wear off after several months once the bowel has adjusted. Drinking 2 litres of water daily may also be difficult. Some people may find these a disincentive to following the diet.
- **High fibre is not recommended in certain groups of people:**
  - Those with megacolon or hypotonic colon or rectum will not respond to bulk in the colon.
  - Those taking opioids as increasing bulk may lead to obstruction [MeReC, 1994].
- **Caffeine has diuretic properties,** therefore caffeine-containing drinks may make constipation worse [NGC, 1998].

Drug treatments

- **Indications for laxative use are:**
  - No response to adequate non-drug treatment (e.g. After 1 month)
  - Faecal impaction
  - Constipation or painful defecation associated with illness, surgery, or pregnancy
  - Elderly people with a poor diet
  - Drug-induced constipation
  - Medical conditions in which bowel strain is undesirable
  - preparation for an operation or investigation [McCormack, 1996; Medicines Resource, 1996]
- **Excessive use of laxatives** can lead to severe adverse effects, such as hypokalaemia and atonic colon. Excessive use is more common in people with coexisting psychiatric disorders such as depression, anorexia nervosa, or a personality disorder [Medicines Resource, 1996].
- **Data on comparative efficacy** between different laxative groups, and between different individual preparations within each group, are lacking. From the evidence available it is likely that bulk-forming agents are as effective as the other groups for adults with chronic idiopathic constipation [Tramonte et al, 1997].
- **Therefore drugs should be chosen on the basis of suitability for the individual.**
- **The smallest effective dose of a laxative should be used,** and this dose reduced once symptoms resolve [Moriarty and Irving, 1992]. The treatment of children is an exception to this as the laxative should continue for several months to avoid a relapse (see *Children* below).

Bulk-forming agents (e.g. ispaghula):

- **These are only required if dietary fibre cannot be sufficiently increased** [Medicines Resource, 1996].
- **Their action** is by retention of fluid and increase in faecal mass, leading to stimulation of peristalsis. Their effect is within 12–24 hours [Medicines Resource, 1996]. Bulk laxatives also have stool-softening properties.
- **Adequate amounts of fluid are essential** to avoid obstruction [MeReC, 1994].

Bulk-forming agents can be safely used long-term, and adverse effects are few, although flatulence and distension may occur [DTB, 1988; Medicines Resource, 1996].

They are probably less effective in the acute situation than stimulant laxatives due to their delayed onset of action, although comparative data are lacking.

Stimulant laxatives (e.g. senna, bisacodyl):

Their action is by direct stimulation of colonic nerves to cause movement of faecal mass, resulting in passage of stool. Their effect is within 8–12 hours, therefore bedtime dosing is recommended. Suppositories act more quickly (within 20–60 minutes).

Adverse effects — abdominal cramp is the most common immediate adverse effect. Electrolyte disturbances and atonic colon may result from chronic use, which is therefore not usually recommended. In the elderly, however, atonic colon is of less concern and prolonged use of stimulant laxatives may be appropriate in some cases [Passmore et al, 1993; MeReC, 1994; Medicines Resource, 1996].

The Committee on Safety of Medicines has advised that the indications for dantron be restricted to constipation in terminally ill people of all ages. People who are currently taking dantron, and are not terminally ill, should be transferred to other treatments. This is because of accumulating evidence confirming genotoxicity [CSM, 2000].

Osmotic laxatives (e.g. lactulose, phosphate enemas):

Their action is by retaining fluid in the bowel by osmosis or changing water distribution in faeces. Therefore a good fluid intake should be encouraged.

Rectal preparations of phosphates and sodium citrate (used occasionally to avoid sodium and water retention) and oral magnesium salts are useful when quick relief is desirable. Phosphate enemas are used most often for bowel clearance prior to surgery or bowel investigations.

Lactulose increases faecal weight, volume, and bowel movements. It must be taken regularly and takes 2 days (or more) to have an effect; therefore *it is not suitable for rapid relief of constipation.* Adverse effects include abdominal pain and bowel distension. Some people find lactulose unpalatable. Studies have shown it to be considerably more expensive, but no more effective, than fibre or senna. Lactulose should not be regarded as first-choice therapy in the management of constipation. Similar products include lactitol.

There is limited evidence from several recent studies that polyethylene glycol is a safe and effective alternative in the management of chronic constipation [Attar et al, 1999; Corazziari et al, 2000].

[Medicines Resource, 1996]

Faecal softeners / emollient laxatives (e.g. docusate):

Their action is by softening the faeces by decreasing surface tension and increasing the penetration of intestinal fluids into the faecal mass.

They are particularly useful administered orally in the management of conditions for which rectal administration would be painful, e.g. haemorrhoids and anal fissure. Docusate sodium is a wetting agent that softens stool, but also has weak stimulant properties.

Rectal docusate may be useful for rapid relief, although it should not be used for haemorrhoids or anal fissure.

Bulk laxatives also have stool-softening properties.

Liquid paraffin is a stool softener/lubricant. It can cause anal seepage and irritation, lipoid pneumonia (rarely, on aspiration), and malabsorption of lipid-soluble vitamins. It is not recommended.

[McCormack, 1996; Medicines Resource, 1996]

Specific situations

The elderly

- **Fit and active elderly people** should be treated as younger adults (e.g. try fibre first).
- **More frail elderly people** may have different needs.
- **There is no conclusive evidence that one form of laxative is more effective than another in the elderly,** therefore the appropriate drug should be chosen according to the individual person's circumstances [Petticrew et al, 1997; Petticrew et al, 1999]. One study suggested that senna-fibre combinations are significantly more effective than lactulose [Passmore et al, 1993].
- **Immobility** leads to difficulty in propelling the faecal mass, therefore bulk-forming agents may be less effective and may even worsen the problem [Petticrew et al, 1997]. Instead, stimulant laxatives should be considered, but generally for short-term use only. In addition, difficulty in getting to the toilet may exacerbate the problem.
- **Polypharmacy** can cause constipation. It is important, therefore, to reduce or if possible to stop potentially constipating drugs [Kamm, 1994].
- **Severe constipation,** leading to faecal impaction, is more common in the elderly than younger people — phosphate enemas are effective in this situation [Medicines Resource, 1996].

Children

- **Avoid invasive treatments and investigations** where possible, as these can be distressing for the child [Beach, 1996]. Where examination is felt necessary it is important to obtain verbal consent, give a full explanation, and exercise sensitivity.
- **High dietary fibre** (e.g. prunes, bran cereal, fruits and vegetables) **with plenty of fluid** should always be tried first, with a **reduction in excessive milk drinking** in toddlers [MeReC, 1994; Leung et al, 1996; Gallagher et al, 1998]. Ongoing dietary counselling may be needed to ensure compliance [McClung et al, 1995]. It may be prudent to warn parents that drinks which are acidic or have a high sugar content are known to be a causative factor in dental caries, and that children should not be encouraged to drink to the extent that they reduce their intake of necessary nutrients.
- **Use of the toilet or potty** after meals should be encouraged, and positive reinforcement (e.g. with star charts) may be helpful [MeReC, 1994; Leung et al, 1996; Gallagher et al, 1998].
- **There is insufficient evidence to decide which is the most appropriate laxative for use in childhood.**
- **Laxatives** such as bulk-forming agents, stool softeners, or a combination of a stimulant laxative and a softener should be tried if increasing fibre and fluids fails.
- **Adequate early treatment of childhood constipation is recommended** as chronic constipation can result in megarectum, faecal impaction and overflow, leading to soiling.
- **It is essential to achieve colonic evacuation prior to maintenance laxative therapy.**
- **To prevent recurrence of constipation or faecal impaction,** long-term use of a faecal softener combined with a stimulant laxative is often prescribed. Parents should be encouraged to give them regularly for several months; intermittent use may provoke a relapse. After several months, assuming treatment is successful, the dose can be gradually reduced; the reduction itself

should take several months to avoid a relapse [DTB, 2000].

- **Oral laxative therapy is preferable** to the use of suppositories and enemas, which should be used as a last resort.
- **Behavioural therapy or biofeedback** is sometimes recommended, depending on the individual child's circumstances. This aims to teach the child to be aware of the presence of stool, and to relax the pelvic muscles and evacuate the stool [Kamm, 1994; Leung et al, 1996].

[Royal College of Paediatrics and Child Health, 1999; BNF 43, 2002]

C

Pregnancy

- **In pregnancy, use increased dietary fibre, fluid intake and exercise wherever possible.** This is effective in most cases [Jewell and Young, 2001].
- **Bulk-forming agents, including ispaghula and sterculia** should be tried first. They are effective in most cases and raise no serious concerns about adverse effects to mother or fetus [Jewell and Young, 2001].
- **If these are ineffective, senna or lactulose may be tried.**
- **The main concern in pregnancy is the safety of any drugs used** and whether or not there are potentially harmful effects on the fetus. All drugs should be used with caution for short periods only.
- **Bulk-forming agents** are thought to be safer in pregnancy, although stimulant laxatives may be more appropriate because constipation in pregnancy is partly due to the relaxant effects of progesterone on gut smooth muscle [MeReC, 1994].
- **Senna** is thought to be safe if used occasionally in normal doses, although caution should be used if senna is used near term, or if pregnancy is unstable (i.e. if there are risk factors for premature delivery). In theory, it may cause uterine contractions if used in the third trimester.
- **Lactulose** is not known to be harmful during pregnancy, but some sources do not recommend its use.
- **Evidence for which laxative is best when breastfeeding is lacking.** Bulk-forming agents and lactulose are considered to be safe as they are not absorbed. Senna in large doses, although not toxic, may cause colic and diarrhoea in infants as it enters breast milk.

[Medicines Resource, 1996; Lee et al, 2000; BNF 43, 2002]

Terminally-ill people

- **Prevention of constipation is of great importance in the terminally ill.**
- **Constipation is likely** in all people on constipating drugs, those who are immobile, who have reduced fluid intake and nutrition, or who are taking low-fibre diets. Rehydration and use of prophylactic laxatives is therefore recommended in these people [Regnard and Tempest, 1998].
- **More specific causes** in the terminally-ill include local gastrointestinal obstruction due to tumour, hypercalcaemia, depression, and neurological symptoms such as spinal cord compression [Fallon and O'Neill, 1997].
- **Constipation can mimic some of the features of advanced cancer** (e.g. pain, abdominal masses, anorexia), particularly where opioids, anticholinergics, anti-emetics, and NSAIDs are used [Medicines Resource, 1996; Fallon and O'Neill, 1997; Regnard and Tempest, 1998].
- **Even anorexic people with cancer need bowel movements** to remove faeces formed from normal renewal of bowel mucosa [Medicines Resource, 1996].
- **If faeces are hard, and the rectum is full,** an increase in fluid intake with co-danthramer, glycerin suppositories, or docusate are recommended. If faeces are soft, stimulant laxatives such as senna or bisacodyl are recommended. If unsuccessful, manual evacuation should be considered [Regnard and Tempest, 1998].
- **If the colon is full and colic is present,** a stool softener/mild stimulant such as docusate is recommended. If col is absent, co-danthramer is recommended. An alternati to docusate in colic is lactulose, although its use is limited by abdominal bloating, and possible postural hypotension due to fluid shift to the bowel [Regnard an Tempest, 1998].

Diabetics

- **Bulk-forming laxatives are generally safe** and may be useful for those people who are unable or unwilling to increase dietary fibre. People with diabetes mellitus should avoid lactulose and sorbitol since their metabolites (fructose and lactose) are absorbed and ma alter blood glucose levels, particularly in a person with brittle Type 1 diabetes [Haines, 1995].

References

NHS staff in England can link, free of charge, from references to full text journals by clicking on [Full text] or the PRODIGY website.

1. Attar, A., Lemann, M., Ferguson, A. et al (1999) Comparison of a low dose polyethylene glycol electrolyte solution with lactulose for treatment of chronic constipation. *Gut* **44**(2), 226–230. [Full text]
2. Bandolier (1997) *Constipation.* Bandolier 46. www.jr2.ox.ac.uk/Bandolier/band46/b46-3.html [Accessed: 04/03/2002].
3. Bateman, N. (1990) Management of constipation. *Prescriber* **31**, 7–15.
4. Beach, R.C. (1996) Management of childhood constipation. *Lancet* **348**(9030), 766–767. [Full text]
5. BNF 43 (2002) *British National Formulary.* 43rd edn London: British Medical Association and Royal Pharmaceutical Society of Great Britain.
6. BSPGHAN (1998) *A guide for purchasers of paediatr gastroenterology, hepatology and nutrition services.* British Society for Paediatric Gastroenterology, Hepatology and Nutrition. http://bspghan.org.uk/guides.htm [Accessed: 05/03/2002].
7. Corazziari, E., Badiali, D., Bazzocchi, G. et al (2000) Long term efficacy, safety, and tolerability of low dail doses of isosmotic polyethylene glycol electrolyte balanced solution (PMF-100) in the treatment of functional chronic constipation. *Gut* **46**(4), 522–526. [Full text]
8. CSM (2000) Danthron restricted to constipation in th terminally ill. *Current Problems in Pharmacovigilanc* **26**(May), 4.
9. DH (2001) *Prescription cost analysis.* London: Department of Health.
10. DTB (1988) Laxatives: replacing danthron. *Drug & Therapeutics Bulletin* **26**(14), 53–55.
11. DTB (1992) Trifba: an improved bulk laxative. *Drug & Therapeutics Bulletin* **30**(16), 63–64.
12. DTB (2000) Managing constipation in children. *Drug & Therapeutics Bulletin* **38**(8), 57–60.
13. Fallon, M. and O'Neill, B. (1997) ABC of palliative care: constipation and diarrhoea. *British Medical Journal* **315**(7118), 1293–1296. [Full text]
14. Gallagher, B., West, D., Puntis, J.W. and Stringer, M.D. (1998) Characteristics of children under 5 referred to hospital with constipation: a one-year prospective study. *International Journal of Clinical Practice* **52**(3), 165–167.

15. Gattuso, J.M. and Kamm, M.A. (1994) Adverse effects of drugs used in the management of constipation and diarrhoea. *Drug Safety* **10**(1), 47–65.
16. Haines, S.T. (1995) Treating constipation in the patient with diabetes. *Diabetes Educator* **21**(3), 223–232.
17. Jewell, D.J. and Young, G. (2001) *Interventions for treating constipation in pregnancy (Cochrane Review)*. The Cochrane Library. Issue 2. Oxford: Update Software. www.nelh.nhs.uk/cochrane.asp [Accessed: 25/04/2005]. [Full text]
18. Kamm, M.A. (1989) Constipation. *British Journal of Hospital Medicine* **41**(3), 244–250.
19. Kamm, M.A. (1994) Constipation. *Medicine International* **22**(8), 305–308.
20. Lee, A. and Schofield, S. (1994) Drug use in pregnancy: general principles. *Pharmaceutical Journal* **253**, 27–30.
21. Lee, A., Inch, S. and Finnigan, D. (Eds.) (2000) *Therapeutics in pregnancy and lactation*. Abingdon: Radcliffe Medical Press Ltd.
22. Le Marchand, L. (1998) Constipation and colon cancer. *Epidemiology* **9**(4), 371–372.
23. Leung, A.K., Chan, P.Y. and Cho, H.Y. (1996) Constipation in children. *American Family Physician* **54**(2), 611–618.
24. McClung, H.J., Boyne, L. and Heitlinger, L. (1995) Constipation and dietary fiber intake in children. *Pediatrics* **96**(5 Pt 2), 999–1000.
25. McCormack, J. (1996) Gastrointestinal diseases: drug therapy for constipation. In: McCormack, J. (Ed.) *Drug Therapy: decision making guide*. London: W.B.Saunders & Co. 60–64.
26. Medicines Resource (1996) Constipation. *Medicines Resource* **29**(Apr), 111–114.
27. MeReC (1994) The treatment of constipation. *MeReC Bulletin* **5**(6), 21–24.
28. MeReC (1999) The management of constipation. *MeReC Bulletin* **10**(9), 33–36.
29. Moriarty, K.J. and Irving, M.H. (1992) ABC of colorectal disease: constipation. *British Medical Journal* **304**(6836), 1237–1240.
30. NGC (1998) *University of Iowa: gerontological nursing interventions research centre. Management of constipation*. Rockville, MD: National Guideline Clearinghouse.
31. Passmore, A.P., Wilson-Davies, K., Stoker, C. and Scott, M.E. (1993) Chronic constipation in long stay elderly patients: a comparison of lactulose and a senna-fibre combination. *British Medical Journal* **307**(6907), 769–771.
32. Petticrew, M., Watt, I. and Sheldon, T. (1997) *Systematic review of the effectiveness of laxatives in the elderly*. NHS R&D Health Technology Appraisal Programme. www.ncchta.org/ProjectData/3_project_record_published.asp?PjtId=969 [Accessed: 05/03/2002].
33. Petticrew, M., Watt, I. and Brand, M. (1999) What's the 'best buy' for treatment of constipation? Results of a systematic review of the efficacy and comparative efficacy of laxatives in the elderly. *British Journal of General Practice* **49**(442), 387–393.
34. Regnard, C. and Tempest, S. (Eds.) (1998) *A guide to symptom relief in advanced disease*. 4th edn. Hale: Hochland & Hochland Ltd.
35. Royal College of Paediatrics and Child Health (Ed.) (1999) *Medicines for children*. London: RCPCH Publications.
36. Spiller, R. (1990) When fibre fails. *British Medical Journal* **300**(6731), 1064–1065.
37. Staiano, A. and Tozzi, A. (1998) Diagnosis and treatment of constipation in children. *Current Opinion in Pediatrics* **10**(5), 512–515.
38. Thompson, W.G., Longstretch, G.F., Drossman, D.A. et al (1999) Functional bowel disorders and functional abdominal pain. *Gut* **45**(Supp. II), 1143–1147. [Full text]
39. Tramonte, S.M., Brand, M.B., Mulrow, C.D. et al (1997) The treatment of chronic constipation in adults: a systematic review. *Journal of General Internal Medicine* **12**(1), 15–24.

PRODIGY GUIDANCE

Contraception

Last revised in February 2005
www.prodigy.nhs.uk/guidance.asp?gt=Contraception

Applies to women from the age of 12 to 60 years

This guidance covers contraceptive methods currently available and incorporates the recommendations of the Faculty of Family Planning and Reproductive Health Care (FFPRHC) guidance, *First Prescription of Combined Oral Contraception* (October 2003); and the FFPRHC guidance, *The Copper Intra-uterine Device as Long-term Contraception* (January 2004).

This guidance does not cover how to fit intra-uterine devices, the levonorgestrel-releasing intra-uterine system, diaphragms, or caps; how to insert contraceptive implants; or how to teach natural family planning methods. Specific training is required for each of these activities. This guidance also does not cover the management of women requesting emergency contraception.

There is separate PRODIGY guidance for *Contraception — emergency, Amenorrhoea, Endometriosis, Menorrhagia, Chlamydia — genital, Preconceptual counselling*, and *Infertility*.

Goals

- To provide effective and acceptable contraception for women who wish to avoid pregnancy

Contents

Scenarios

- Which contraceptive method is suitable? p.388
- Combined oral contraceptive pill — first choice p.390
- Progestogen-only pill p.392
- Barrier methods/spermicides p.393
- Long-acting progestogens p.395
- Intra-uterine devices and system p.397
- Combined contraceptive pill or patch – alternative choice p.399
- Breastfeeding and after childbirth p.401
- Taking a liver enzyme-inducing drug p.404

Extended Information, p. 406

Which scenario?

- **Which contraceptive method is suitable?** outlines contraceptive options for healthy women, women with hypertension, diabetes, menorrhagia, or past history of ectopic pregnancy, and women who smoke.
- **Combined oral contraceptive pill — first choice:** offers information and prescriptions for combined oral contraceptive pills that are recommended as first choice.
- **Progestogen-only pill:** offers information and prescriptions for progestogen-only pills.
- **Barrier methods/spermicides:** offers information and prescriptions for diaphragms, caps, and spermicides, and information on male and female condoms.
- **Long-acting progestogens:** offers information and prescriptions for injectable contraceptives and the etonogestrel implant. See *Intra-uterine device and system* scenario for information and prescriptions for the levonorgestrel-releasing intra-uterine system.
- **Intra-uterine devices and system:** offers information and prescriptions for copper IUDs (with a surface area of more than 300 mm² of copper) and the levonorgestrel-releasing intra-uterine system.
- **Combined contraceptive pill or patch — alternative choice:** offers information and prescriptions for combined oral contraceptive pills and the combined contraceptive patch, when an alternative combined contraceptive preparation is required.
- **Breastfeeding and after childbirth:** offers information and prescriptions that are suitable for women who require contraception after the birth of a child, and for women who are breastfeeding. Prescriptions for the combined oral contraceptive pill are not included. If they are required, the *Combined oral contraceptive — first choice* or the *Combined contraceptive — alternative choice* scenario should be used.
- **Taking a liver enzyme-inducing drug:** covers the management of women who are taking, or wish to use, hormonal contraception while taking a liver enzyme-inducing drug (concurrently or within 28 days). Liver enzyme-inducing drugs include rifampicin, rifabutin, barbiturates, bosentan, carbamazepine, oxcarbazepine, phenytoin, ritonavir (and possibly other antivirals), griseofulvin, topiramate, and St John's wort.

Which contraceptive method is suitable?

Which therapy?

- Women should be able to access information on the full range of contraceptive methods available so that they can make a fully informed decision.
- The benefits and risks of contraception, plans for future pregnancies, presence and treatment of certain medical conditions, and client preferences should all be considered and discussed.
- **If a hormonal method is preferred,** consider whether oestrogen is suitable or acceptable.
  - If appropriate, consider a combined oral contraceptive (COC) pill; an alternative option is the transdermal combined contraceptive patch.
  - If inappropriate, consider the progestogen-only pill (POP), injectable contraceptives, the etonogestrel implant, or the levonorgestrel-releasing intra-uterine system (LNG-IUS).
- **The choice of progestogen-only method** will depend upon the woman's requirement for either long- or short-term contraception, and whether a delay in return to fertility is acceptable.
- **If a hormonal method is not suitable or acceptable, consider barrier methods** (male and female condoms, and diaphragms or caps with spermicide), an intra-uterine device (IUD), natural family planning methods, or sterilization.
- **For women with migraine with aura, avoid combined contraceptives (oral pills or transdermal patch).** Barrier

methods, the POP, injectable contraceptives, the etonogestrel implant, IUDs, or the LNG-IUS are all suitable alternatives. Women with migraine without aura may consider combined contraceptives if there are no other risk factors.

- **For women with sustained hypertension** >140 mmHg systolic and/or 90 mmHg diastolic, IUDs and barrier methods are options. Progestogen-only contraception may be suitable, but careful consideration is required in the presence of heart disease, and it is contraindicated with severe arterial disease.
- **For women with diabetes mellitus** that is well controlled and free of complications, and who have no other cardiovascular risk factors, all contraceptive methods are options. Diabetes with vascular complications, including hypertension, contraindicates COC or transdermal patch use.
- **For women with idiopathic menorrhagia,** the LNG-IUS will reduce menstrual blood loss. Women may report less bleeding with COC use, but there is insufficient evidence to confirm this clinically. Women could also consider using medroxyprogesterone acetate injections, as most will become amenorrhoeic after initially experiencing some irregular bleeding.
- **For women with a past history of ectopic pregnancy,** methods of contraception that inhibit ovulation (i.e. the combined contraceptives, injectable contraceptives, and the etonogestrel implant) are particularly suitable, as they reduce ectopic pregnancy to a greater degree than other methods. However, compared with using no contraception, the overall risk of ectopic pregnancy is still reduced with the POP, the LNG-IUS, and copper IUDs.
- **If over 35 years and smoking at least 15 cigarettes a day,** COC or patch use is contraindicated.
- **If over 35 years and smoking less than 15 cigarettes a day,** COC or patch use should be avoided.
- **If under 35 years, smoking, and with additional risk factors** where the benefits of COC use would normally outweigh the risks, COC use should be avoided. These additional risk factors include superficial thrombophlebitis, uncomplicated valvular heart disease, migraine without focal symptoms, and diabetes without vascular complications.

Should I refer or investigate?

Refer?

- If further advice is required, consider contacting a local family planning clinic or: the Family Planning Association — Helpline and Information Service.
  - fpa (Family Planning Association) 0845 310 1334
  - www.fpa.org.uk
  - Brook Helpline: 0800 0185023
  - www.brook.org.uk
  - www.ruthinking.co.uk — specifically tailored to suit young people

Investigate?

- Routinely test for chlamydia and other sexually transmitted infections (STI) in women with a high-risk of acquiring an STI:
  - Sexually active women under the age of 25 years.
  - Women over 25 years with a new partner or who have had two or more partners in the previous 12 months.

Patient information leaflets

The following PILs are available at www.prodigy.nhs.uk

- Blood Test - Clotting Tests
- Blood Test - General
- FPA (sexual health & contraception)
- Laparoscopy and Laparoscopic Surgery

Shared decision making

- **Choosing a method of contraception** involves a balance between:
  - Effectiveness
  - Risks
  - Possible side effects
  - Plans for future pregnancies
  - Personal preference
  - If you have a medical condition that needs to be considered
- **Combined pill** contains two hormones — oestrogen and progestogen.
  - Some pros — very effective, side effects uncommon.
  - Some cons — tiny risk of serious problems such as a blood clot (thrombosis) in a vein.
- **Progestogen-only pill** — commonly taken if the combined pill is not suitable, for example, breastfeeding women, smokers over the age of 35 years, and some women with migraine.
  - Some pros — less risk of serious problems than the combined pill has.
  - Some cons — irregular bleeding may occur. Not quite as effective as the combined pill
- **Barrier methods** — condoms, diaphragms and caps.
  - Some pros — no serious medical risks or side effects. Helps protect from infection.
  - Some cons — not quite as reliable as other methods.
- **Contraceptive injections** — need an injection every 8–12 weeks.
  - Some pros — very effective, don't have to remember to take pills.
  - Some cons — irregular bleeding may occur, especially in the first months of use. Return to previous fertility after stopping may be delayed.
- **Contraceptive implants** — last 3 years.
  - Some pros — very effective, don't have to remember to take pills.
  - Some cons — irregular bleeding may occur, especially in the first months of use.
- **Transdermal contraceptive patch:** once-weekly application.
  - Some pros — very effective when used correctly.
  - Some cons — reports of breast tenderness, and patch may become detached and cause skin irritation.
- **Intra-uterine device (IUD)** — most last 5 years.
  - Some pros — very effective, don't have to remember to take pills.
  - Some cons — periods may get heavy. Small risk of pelvic infection.
- **Hormone-releasing intra-uterine system (IUS)** — also used to treat heavy periods.
  - Some pros — very effective, don't have to remember to take pills. Periods light.
  - Some cons — some bleeding between periods is common for the first few months.
- **Sterilization** — (vasectomy or tubal tie) is a choice if you do not want any more children.
  - Some pros — very effective, don't have to think further about contraception.
  - Some cons — extremely difficult to reverse.
- **Natural methods** — fertility awareness or breastfeeding after childbirth.
  - Some pros — no side effects or medical risks.
  - Some cons — require motivation and commitment of both partners, and teaching.

Drug rationale

- No prescriptions are offered.

Combined oral contraceptive pill — first choice

Which therapy?

C

General

- **Enquire about** the medical, sexual (to assess risk of sexually transmitted infection), family, and drug (including non-prescription) history, as well as details of reproductive and previous contraceptive use.
- **Record blood pressure.**
- Measure height and weight, and calculate body mass index if obesity is a concern.
- Breast or pelvic examination is unnecessary unless clinically indicated by symptoms.
- **A combined oral contraceptive (COC) containing 30–35 micrograms of oestrogen plus a low dose of either levonorgestrel or norethisterone is a suitable first choice of pill.**
- **Women should be advised:**
  - To take the pill daily within 12 hours of the same time, and to establish a daily routine.
  - To take the pill for 21 days followed by a 7-day pill-free interval (except for Every Day [ED] COCs) — advise that contraception is still provided in the pill-free interval.
  - What to do if a pill is missed or taken more than 12 hours late (see *Management issues*/advice on right-hand side of prescription).
  - What to do if vomiting occurs within 2 hours of taking the COC, or if there is very severe diarrhoea (see *Management issues*/advice on right-hand side of prescription).

Starting the pill

- **Preferably start from day 1 of the menstrual cycle,** but a COC can be started up to and including day 5 of the cycle without the need for additional contraception. If started outside this time period, exclude pregnancy and advise additional contraception for 7 days.
- **After childbirth (if not breastfeeding),** start from 21 days post-partum. If started later than 3 weeks post-partum, additional contraceptive precautions should be used for 7 days.
- **After a termination of pregnancy,** a COC should be started immediately, but can be started within 7 days to provide immediate contraceptive protection.
- **After major surgery and all surgery to the legs,** start on day 1 of the first period that occurs at least 2 weeks after full mobilization.

Practical prescribing points

For further information please see the *Medicines Compendium* (www.medicines.org.uk) or the *British National Formulary* (www.bnf.org).

- **Combined oral contraceptives (COCs) do not protect against sexually transmitted infections (STI) or human immunodeficiency virus (HIV).** If there is a risk of STI/HIV, the correct and ongoing use of condoms is recommended, either alone or with another method of contraception. Male latex condoms are proven to protect against STI/HIV.
- **The World Health Organization (WHO) has published medical eligibility criteria** for COC use. See Table 3 in the *Management issues* section for details of unacceptable (category 4) health risk or where the risks usually outweigh the advantages (category 3). For a full list of the WHO criteria, see www.who.int/reproductive-health/publications/mec/3_cocs.pdf.
- **Category 2: women with any of these medical problems** require careful follow-up. If two or more of these problems coexist, the risk/benefit balance moves towards category 3.
- **Category 1: often there will be no factor that gives** concern about increased individual risks for COC use. For any woman, the balance of clinical risks and benefits of COCs must be considered together with her situation, motivation, and concerns about her preferred method.

Non-life-threatening adverse effects include:

- Breakthrough bleeding
- Breast tenderness
- Acne
- Mood changes

Risks

There is a small increased absolute risk of:

- Venous thromboembolism
- Myocardial infarction (in smokers only)
- Stroke
- Breast cancer
- Cervical cancer
- Primary liver cancer

Follow-up advice

- **First follow-up appointment** is usually offered 10–12 weeks after the initial visit to check blood pressure and to enquire about adverse effects. Also check correct and consistent pill use, and knowledge of what to do if a pill is missed.
- **Where there are medical or non-medical concerns,** follow-up after 6 weeks is usual.
- **For established users of combined oral contraceptive (COC) pills,** 6-monthly checks are accepted UK practice. Blood pressure, clinical history, and adverse effects should be checked, together with correct and consistent pill use, and knowledge of what to do if a pill is missed.
- **In the absence of special problems,** women may be given up to 12 months' supply of a COC at the first visit and encouraged to return at any time if problems arise.

Should I refer or investigate?

Refer?

- If further advice is required, consider contacting a local family planning clinic or the Family Planning Association — Helpline and Information Service.
  - fpa UK 0845 310 1334
  - www.fpa.org.uk
  - Brook Helpline: 0207-284-6040
  - www.brook.org.uk
  - www.ruthinking.co.uk

Investigate?

Before commencing the combined oral contraceptive pill

Lipid screening

- **There is little evidence to support screening as part of a strategy to improve combined oral contraceptive (COC) safety.**

Routine fasting lipid profiles are only recommended for women less than 45 years if there is a family history of dyslipidaemia, or the woman has other cardiovascular risk factors.

Thrombophilia screening

It is not appropriate to screen all women for thrombophilia before COC use.

If a woman with a family history of venous thromboembolism in a first-degree relative under 45 years of age still wishes to use a COC despite having considered other methods, a thrombophilia screen should be performed.

Breast and pelvic examination

In asymptomatic women, breast and pelvic examinations are unnecessary before first prescriptions of a COC pill.

Breakthrough bleeding

Routinely test for chlamydia and other sexually transmitted infections (STIs) in women with a high risk of acquiring an STI:

- Sexually active women under the age of 25 years.
- Women over 25 years with a new partner or who have had two or more partners in the previous 12 months.

Other causes of breakthrough bleeding include missed pills, interacting drugs, cervical cancer, pregnancy, and severe diarrhoea or vomiting.

Patient information leaflets

The following PILs are available at www.prodigy.nhs.uk

- Blood Test - Clotting Tests
- Blood Test - General
- FPA (sexual health & contraception)

Shared decision making

- **The combined pill** is very effective if taken correctly.
- Start the first pack on the first day of your next period — it is fully effective from then on.
- Take one pill a day for 21 days. The pills are then stopped for 7 days, during which it is usual to have a period. After 7 pill-free days, the next packet of pills is started.
- Some pill packets (known as Every Day or ED preparations) contain seven inactive pills, which are taken instead of having a 7-day pill-free break.
- Read and keep the information leaflet that comes in the packet. It will remind you about how to take the pill, possible side effects, risks, what to do if you miss a pill, vomit or take other medication whilst taking the pill, etc.

Very briefly...

- Take the pill at about the same time each day.
- If you are more than 12 hours late in taking a pill — you will need to take steps to reduce the risk of pregnancy. Refer to the leaflet for advice on what to do.
- If you are prescribed antibiotics or other medication — tell the prescribing doctor, nurse, or dentist that you take a combined pill.
- Side effects can occur, and include — headache, nausea, breast tenderness, and mood changes. These are usually temporary.
- Breakthrough bleeding ('spotting' or a light blood loss from time to time) can be a side effect. Do not stop taking the pill. This bleeding usually settles within the first 3 months, but tell a doctor or the practice nurse if it persists for longer than this.
- Risks and complications are rare — though they are more common in smokers. They include a slightly increased chance of developing a serious blood clot that can block a vein in the leg (deep vein thrombosis) or block an artery and cause a heart attack or stroke.

Drug rationale

Drugs not included

- **The choice of which product to prescribe as a first pill is not well supported by good comparative data** [FFPRHC Clinical Effectiveness Unit, 2003a].
- **Careful consideration should be made of** safety, freedom from adverse effects, individual preference, and cost. Potential drug interactions should also be considered [FFPRHC Clinical Effectiveness Unit, 2003a].
- **Preparations containing desogestrel or gestodene** are probably associated with an increased risk of venous thromboembolism compared with preparations containing levonorgestrel. Therefore, combined oral contraceptives (COCs) containing desogestrel or gestodene are usually less preferred first-line.
- **COCs with higher doses of levonorgestrel or norethisterone** are not included, as there is no evidence that they offer any advantages over COCs with lower doses of these progestogens.
- **COCs containing 20 micrograms oestrogen** do not seem to offer any advantage over those containing 30–35 micrograms oestrogen, and some women may have poorer cycle control.
- **Biphasic and triphasic preparations** are not offered. A recent Cochrane review has found a lack of evidence to support their use in preference to monophasic preparations [Van Vliet et al, 2003]. They are also notably more expensive than monophasic COCs.
- **Every Day preparations** are not routinely used in the UK, but can be useful to help women who have difficulty starting the next packet at the correct time.
- **Dianette®** (cyproterone acetate and ethinylestradiol) is not licensed solely for use as a contraceptive. It should be reserved for selected women requiring treatment for severe acne or refractory to prolonged antibiotic therapy, or with moderately severe hirsutism [ABPI Medicines Compendium, 2002a].
- **Yasmin®** (drospirenone and ethinylestradiol) is a black-triangle drug (currently under the surveillance of the Committee on Safety of Medicines) and is expensive compared with other COCs. There is limited evidence to support its use as a first-line agent, and because of the unknown risk of venous thromboembolism its use is best avoided in women with a BMI ≥30. It may be an option where there has been progestogenic intolerance with at least two other COCs.

Drugs included

- **The choice of which product to prescribe as a first pill is not well supported by good comparative data** [FFPRHC Clinical Effectiveness Unit, 2003a].
- **Careful consideration should be made of** safety, freedom from adverse effects, individual preference and cost. Potential drug interactions should also be considered [FFPRHC Clinical Effectiveness Unit, 2003a].
- **Monophasic** combined oral contraceptives (COCs) containing 30–35 micrograms ethinylestradiol and low-dose progestogen (levonorgestrel 150 micrograms or norethisterone 500 micrograms) are therefore included.
- Note: both Microgynon 30 and Ovranette contain ethinylestradiol 30 micrograms plus levonorgestrel 150 micrograms. Both Brevinor and Ovysmen contain ethinylestradiol 35 micrograms plus norethisterone 500 micrograms.

C

Prescriptions

COC containing levonorgestrel or norethisterone

Microgynon 30 (levonorgestrel 150micrograms)
- Age from 12 to 60 years
- Microgynon 30 tablets. Take one tablet once a day for 21 days. Start the next packet after a 7-day break. See package insert for full instructions; supply 63 tablets; NHS Cost £2.82.

C

Ovranette (levonorgestrel 150micrograms)
- Age from 12 to 60 years
- Ovranette tablets. Take one tablet once a day for 21 days. Start the next packet after a 7-day break. See package insert for full instructions; supply 63 tablets; NHS Cost £2.46.

Brevinor (norethisterone 500micrograms)
- Age from 12 to 60 years
- Brevinor tablets. Take one tablet once a day for 21 days. Start the next packet after a 7-day break. See package insert for full instructions; supply 63 tablets; NHS Cost £1.99.

Ovysmen (norethisterone 500micrograms)
- Age from 12 to 60 years
- Ovysmen tablets. Take one tablet once a day for 21 days. Start the next packet after a 7-day break. See package insert for full instructions; supply 63 tablets; NHS Cost £1.70.

Progestogen-only pill

Which therapy?

General

- **Enquire about** the medical, sexual (to assess risk of sexually transmitted infection), family and drug (including non-prescription) history, as well as details of reproductive and previous contraceptive use.
- **Progestogen-only pills (POPs) are an alternative** for women who want oral contraception, but who do not choose to use oestrogen or where oestrogen is contraindicated (e.g. women who are breastfeeding, smokers over the age of 35 years, and women with migraine with aura).
- **The choice of which POP to prescribe is not supported by evidence.**
- **Women should be advised:**
  - To take the pill at the same time each day.
  - What to do if a pill is missed or taken more than 3 hours late (see *Management issues*/advice on right-hand side of the prescription).
  - What to do if vomiting occurs within 3 hours of taking the POP or if there is very severe diarrhoea (see *Management issues*/advice on right-hand side of prescription).
  - About the high incidence of menstrual irregularities.

Starting the progestogen-only pill

- **Usually start on the first day of the period** and then take continuously.
- **After childbirth,** the POP can be started from day 21 and no additional contraception is required. Use before this increases the risk of breakthrough bleeding and is unnecessary, as contraception is not required before day 21 post-partum.
  - UK practice is to start POPs on day 21 post-partum in women who are breastfeeding.
  - However, advice from the World Health Organization recommends waiting until 6 weeks post-partum, in which case alternative methods of contraception should be used from day 21 until 7 days after the POP is started.
- **After termination of pregnancy,** the POP can be taken immediately and is effective immediately.
- **Changing from a combined oral contraceptive (COC):** start the POP at the end of the packet of COC pills, omitting the pill-free interval. In the case of Every Day (ED) preparations, the POP should be commenced after the last active tablet, omitting the inactive tablets.

Practical prescribing points

For further information please see the *Medicines Compendium* (www.medicines.org.uk) or the *British National Formulary* (www.bnf.org).

- **Progestogen-only pills (POPs) do not protect against sexually transmitted infections (STI) or human deficiency virus (HIV).** If there is a risk of STI/HIV, the correct and consistent use of condoms is recommended, either alone or with another contraceptive method. Male latex condoms are proven to protect against STI/HIV.
- **The World Health Organization (WHO) has published medical eligibility criteria** for progestogen-only contraceptives. See Table 5 in the *Management issues* section for details of unacceptable (category 4) health risk or where the risks usually outweigh the advantages (category 3). For a full list of the WHO criteria, see www.who.int/reproductive-health/publications/mec/5_pocs.pdf.
- **Category 2:** women with any of these medical problems require careful follow-up. If two or more of these problems coexist, the risk/benefit balance moves towards category 3.
- **Category 1:** many women will have no factor in their medical history that gives concern about any increased individual risks for them with progestogen-only pills.
- Note: If progestogen-only pills are accidentally used during pregnancy, there is no known harm to the woman, the course of her pregnancy, or the fetus.

Non-life-threatening adverse effects include:

- Amenorrhoea
- Breakthrough bleeding
- Breast tenderness
- Acne
- Mood changes

Risks

- There is a small increased absolute risk of ovarian cysts.
- There is a trend towards a possible increased risk of breast cancer.

Follow-up advice

- **First follow-up appointment** is usually offered 10–12 weeks after the initial visit to enquire about adverse effects. Check correct and consistent pill use, and knowledge of what to do if a pill is missed.
- For established users of progestogen-only pills, 6-monthly checks are accepted UK practice.

Should I refer or investigate?

Refer?

- If further advice is required, consider contacting a local family planning clinic or the Family Planning Association — Helpline and Information Service.
  - fpa UK 0845 310 1334
  - www.fpa.org.uk

- Brook Helpline: 0207-284-6040
- www.brook.org.uk
- www.ruthinking.co.uk

Patient information leaflets

The following PILs are available at www.prodigy.nhs.uk

- FPA (sexual health & contraception)

Shared decision making

- **The progestogen-only pill** is very effective if taken correctly (but not quite as effective as the combined pill).
- Start the first pack on the first day of your next period — it is fully effective from then on.
- Read and keep the information leaflet that comes in the packet. It will remind you about how to take the pill, possible side effects, risks, what to do if you miss a pill, vomit or take other medication whilst taking the pill, etc.

Very briefly...

- Take the pill at the same time each day — this is very important.
- If you are more than 3 hours late in taking a pill, then you need to take steps to decrease the risk of pregnancy. Refer to the leaflet for advice on what to do.
- Irregular periods are the most common side effect. Your periods may stop altogether or be irregular, light, or more frequent. This is not harmful, but a change to another brand may help if it is troublesome
- Sometimes other side effects occur, such as breast tenderness or acne. These are usually temporary and go away after a few months.
- Risks and complications are rare, but include a small increased risk of ectopic pregnancy (but less than if not using contraception).

Drug rationale

Drugs included

- **All progestogen-only pills (POPs) except Cerazette® are** recommended as first-line options where a POP is the contraceptive method of choice.
- **Cerazette® (desogestrel-only pill) is included** as a second-line POP option, as it is a black-triangle drug (currently under the surveillance of the Committee on Safety of Medicines) and there is no evidence to support its use as a first-line agent. Bleeding patterns are unlikely to be any better with Cerazette® compared with other POPs, and it is notably more expensive. Cerazette® may have a role in carefully selected women [DTB, 2003b].

Prescriptions

1st-line progestogen-only pill

Femulen (etynodiol diacetate 500micrograms)

- Age from 12 to 60 years
- Femulen tablets. Take one tablet once a day. See package insert for full instructions; supply 84 tablets; NHS Cost £3.31.

Microval (levonorgestrel 30micrograms)

- Age from 12 to 60 years
- Microval tablets. Take one tablet once a day. See package insert for full instructions; supply 105 tablets; NHS Cost £2.70.

Norgeston (levonorgestrel 30micrograms)

- Age from 12 to 60 years
- Norgeston tablets. Take one tablet once a day. See package insert for full instructions; supply 105 tablets; NHS Cost £2.94.

Micronor (norethisterone 350micrograms)

- Age from 12 to 60 years
- Micronor tablets. Take one tablet once a day. See package insert for full instructions; supply 84 tablets; NHS Cost £1.89.

Noriday (norethisterone 350micrograms)

- Age from 12 to 60 years
- Noriday tablets. Take one tablet once a day. See package insert for full instructions; supply 84 tablets; NHS Cost £2.10.

2nd-line progestogen-only pill

Cerazette (desogestrel 75micrograms)

- Age from 12 to 60 years
- Cerazette tablets. Take one tablet once a day. See package insert for full instructions; supply 84 tablets; NHS Cost £8.85.

Barrier methods/spermicides

Which therapy?

Barrier methods (male and female condoms, diaphragms and caps plus spermicide) are suitable for many women. They provide an alternative for those who do not wish to use, are unable to reliably use, or have contraindications to using hormonal methods of contraception (e.g. women taking liver enzyme-inducing drugs).

Diaphragms and caps

- **Diaphragms and caps need to be fitted by trained personnel.**
- **They should be used in conjunction with a spermicide.**
- **There are three types of diaphragm:**
  - *Flat spring* — suitable for women with normal vaginal muscular support.
  - *Coil spring* — more flexible and can be more comfortable.
  - *Arcing spring* — useful for women with poor vaginal muscular support or where the length or position of the cervix makes fitting of the other types difficult.
- **Caps are a useful alternative for women who are unable to use a diaphragm,** but have a higher failure rate particularly for parous women.
- **Advise women to:**
  - **Insert anytime before intercourse.** If it is inserted more than 3 hours before intercourse, or intercourse occurs more than once, additional spermicide should be used without removing the diaphragm or cap.
  - **Leave in place for at least 6 hours after intercourse,** but no longer than 30 hours.
  - **Avoid oil-based products,** including vaginal and rectal preparations, as they cause rapid deterioration of rubber.

Spermicides

- **Spermicides are available as aerosol foams, jellies, creams, films, sponges, or pessaries.** Applicators for some creams, jellies, and foams are available.
- They should be used in conjunction with barrier methods.

Male condoms

- Male condoms are not available on prescription. They are available free of charge from family planning clinics and from some primary healthcare teams.
- Condoms that carry the British Standards Institute (BSI) Kitemark (BS EN 600) and the European CE mark are recommended.

C

- Non-spermicidal lubricated condoms are recommended. It is no longer recommended to use condoms with spermicides, as they are neither necessary for contraceptive efficacy of condoms nor useful for infection protection.
- Additional spermicide products can be used, but there is no evidence of additional benefit.
- Advise the woman or her partner:
  - To use the condom before any genital contact.
  - To avoid the use of all oil-based products with latex condoms.
- Latex condoms are consistently highly effective at protecting against pregnancy, but non-latex condoms still provide an acceptable alternative for those with allergies, sensitivities, or preferences that might prevent the consistent use of latex condoms.

Female condoms

- Female condoms are not available on prescription. They are available free of charge from family planning clinics.
- They can be used with additional spermicides and any lubricant (unlike latex male condoms).

Practical prescribing points

For further information please see the *Medicines Compendium* (www.medicines.org.uk) or the *British National Formulary* (www.bnf.org).
The World Health Organization (WHO) has published medical eligibility criteria for barrier methods of contraception see www.who.int/reproductive-health/publications/mec/9_bar.pdf.

Contraindications to diaphragms and caps

- Lax muscle tone may be a contraindication for the diaphragm.
- Women with a shallow pubic ledge (diaphragm only).
- Abnormality of the vagina.
- Women who are unable or unwilling for physical, psychological, or cultural reasons to touch their genital area.
- Any irritation, sensitivity, or allergy to latex or spermicides.
- A current vaginal, cervical, or pelvic infection, or recurrent urinary tract infection.
- Past toxic shock syndrome.
- Lack of privacy for insertion, removal, or care of the diaphragm or cap.

Adverse effects of diaphragms or caps

- There are few adverse effects, but occasionally some women may experience:
  - Irritation or allergy.
  - Urinary tract infection.
  - Toxic shock syndrome — very rare, and associated with wearing the diaphragm for more than 30 hours.
- **CSM advice** states that products such as petroleum jelly (Vaseline), baby oil, and oil-based vaginal and rectal preparations are likely to damage condoms and contraceptive diaphragms made from latex rubber, and may render them less effective as a barrier method of contraception and as a protection from sexually transmitted diseases (including HIV).

Adverse effects of spermicides

- If sensitivity or irritation occurs, another brand should be tried.
- Pre-existing vaginal infection can be exacerbated by spermicide use.
- Allergy is rare.

Follow-up advice

Diaphragms and caps should be:

- Replaced immediately if there are any holes or puckering of the rubber.
- Replaced annually and a check for size and fitting carried out.
- Checked for size and fitting after childbirth, abortion, or miscarriage, or if the woman gains or loses 3 kg or more in weight.

Should I refer or investigate?

Refer?

- If further advice is required, consider contacting a local family planning clinic or the Family Planning Association — Helpline and Information Service.
  - fpa UK 0845 310 1334
  - www.fpa.org.uk
  - Brook Helpline: 0207-284-6040
  - www.brook.org.uk
  - www.ruthinking.co.uk

Patient information leaflets

The following PILs are available at www.prodigy.nhs.uk

- FPA (sexual health & contraception)

Shared decision making

- **Barrier methods of contraception** are effective if used properly. However, they are not as reliable as the contraceptive pill or the intra-uterine device.
- **Spermicides** are used with diaphragms and caps to increase their effectiveness. They are available as aerosol foams, jellies, creams, films, sponges, or pessaries.
- **Diaphragms or caps:**
  - Need to be fitted by a doctor or nurse.
  - Are best used with a spermicide.
  - Can be inserted anytime before sex — if it is inserted more than 3 hours before sex, or sex occurs more than once, extra spermicide should be used without removing the diaphragm or cap.
  - Must be left in place for at least 6 hours after sex — but no longer than 30 hours.
  - Should not be used with oil-based lubricants, which can affect the rubber.
  - Should be replaced immediately if there are any holes or puckering of the rubber.
  - Should be replaced annually and a check for size and fitting carried out.
  - Should be checked for size and fitting after childbirth, abortion, or miscarriage, or if you gain or lose 3 kg or more in weight.
- **Male condoms**
  - Use those with a BSI (BS EN 600) Kitemark and a European CE mark.
  - Put on the condom before any genital contact.
  - Oil-based lubricants should not be used with latex-based condoms, as they can affect the rubber.
- **Female condoms**
  - You can put the condom into the vagina any time before sex. Always put it in before the penis touches the vagina or genital area.
  - Additional spermicides and any lubricant can be used (unlike latex male condoms).

rug rationale

ugs not included

Male condoms and female condoms are not available on prescription in the UK and are therefore not included. They are available free of charge from all Family Planning Clinics, sexual health clinics, and some GP surgeries.

rugs included

All caps, diaphragms, and spermicides currently available on prescription in the UK are included in this scenario.

rescriptions

permicides (use with a cap or diaphragm method)

ragel
- Age from 12 to 60 years
- Duragel 2% w/v gel. Follow the instructions given inside this pack; supply 100 grams; NHS Cost £3.45; OTC Cost £6.09.

nol II jelly
- Age from 12 to 60 years
- Gynol II 2% jelly. Follow the instructions given inside this pack; supply 81 grams; NHS Cost £2.61; OTC Cost £4.61.
- Gynol II applicator. Use for vaginal application of jelly; supply 1 applicator; NHS Cost £0.75; OTC Cost £1.32.

tho-Creme
- Age from 12 to 60 years
- Ortho-Creme 2% cream. Follow the instructions given inside this pack; supply 70 grams; NHS Cost £2.44; OTC Cost £4.30.
- Ortho vaginal applicator. Use for vaginal application of cream; supply 1 applicator; NHS Cost £0.75; OTC Cost £1.32.

thoforms pessaries
- Age from 12 to 60 years
- Orthoforms 5% w/w pessaries. Follow the instructions given inside this pack; supply 15 pessaries; NHS Cost £2.40; OTC Cost £4.23.

ubber caps

mas vault cap
- Age from 18 to 60 years
- Type A cap Size__mm. Follow the instructions given inside this pack; supply 1 cap; NHS Cost £7.03.

entif cavity rim cervical cap
- Age from 18 to 60 years
- Type B cap Size__mm. Follow the instructions given inside this pack; supply 1 cap; NHS Cost £8.20.

mule cap
- Age from 18 to 60 years
- Type C cap Size__mm. Follow the instructions given inside this pack; supply 1 cap; NHS Cost £7.03.

ilicone caps

mCap 22mm
- Age from 18 to 60 years
- FemCap Size: 22mm. Follow the instructions given inside this pack; supply 1 cap; NHS Cost £14.75.

mCap 26mm
- Age from 18 to 60 years
- FemCap Size: 26mm. Follow the instructions given inside this pack; supply 1 cap; NHS Cost £14.75.

FemCap 30mm
- Age from 18 to 60 years
- FemCap Size: 30mm. Follow the instructions given inside this pack; supply 1 cap; NHS Cost £14.75.

Diaphragms

Reflexions diaphragm
- Age from 18 to 60 years
- Type A diaphragm Size__mm. Follow the instructions given inside this pack; supply 1 diaphragm; NHS Cost £5.59.

Ortho diaphragm
- Age from 18 to 60 years
- Type B diaphragm Size__mm. Follow the instructions given inside this pack; supply 1 diaphragm; NHS Cost £6.14.

All-Flex diaphragm
- Age from 18 to 60 years
- Type C diaphragm Size__mm. Follow the instructions given inside this pack; supply 1 diaphragm; NHS Cost £6.98.

Long-acting progestogens

Which therapy?

Injectable or implant?

- Injectable contraceptives and the etonogestrel implant (Implanon) are alternative ways of delivering progestogens. They can provide long-acting but reversible contraception for women who choose not to take oestrogen, or in whom oestrogen is contraindicated.
- **Use of depot medroxyprogesterone acetate is associated with a delay in return to baseline fertility of a year or more in some women.**
- There is a rapid return of fertility after removal of the etonogestrel implant.
- Injectables are effective for 8–12 weeks (depending on type used), and the only currently available implant remains effective for 3 years.

Injectable contraceptives

- **Medroxyprogesterone acetate** is licensed for long-term use and is the preferred injectable.
- **Norethisterone enantate** is licensed only for short-term use (two injections only) for women whose partners have undergone vasectomy and are waiting for this to be effective, and for women immunized against rubella.
- **Women should be advised:**
  - Of the high incidence of menstrual irregularities.
  - That there may be a long delay in the return of fertility. This can be a year or more with depot medroxyprogesterone acetate, but there is no evidence of permanent infertility.
  - That medroxyprogesterone acetate causes a reduction in bone mineral density in many women that use it but it is unclear whether there is an increased risk of osteoporosis and fractures in later life.

Starting injectable contraceptives

- **The contraceptive is usually given within the first 5 days of the cycle,** and no additional precautions are then required.
- **If given after day 5 of the cycle,** exclude the risk of pregnancy since the last period, and advise that an additional method of contraception should be used for 7 days.

- **After childbirth,** the first dose is best delayed until 6 weeks post-partum. However, if the woman is not breastfeeding, the injection may be given within 5 days post-partum if she is counselled regarding the risk of heavy and prolonged bleeding.
- **After termination of pregnancy,** injectable progestogens can be started immediately and are effective immediately.

Etonogestrel contraceptive implant

- **The implant should be inserted and removed only by appropriately trained personnel.**
- **Blood pressure** should be checked before insertion.
- Women should be advised of the high incidence of menstrual irregularities.

Timing of insertion of etonogestrel implant

- **Insert during the first 5 days of the cycle;** no additional contraception will then be required. If inserted after this, additional contraception is required for the first 7 days.
- **After childbirth and second-trimester abortion:** insert 21 days after delivery or abortion. If inserted after this, additional contraception is required for the first 7 days.
- **After a miscarriage or abortion in the first trimester:** if inserted immediately, no additional contraception will be required.

Practical prescribing points

For further information please see the *Medicines Compendium* (www.medicines.org.uk) or the *British National Formulary* (www.bnf.org).

- **Progestogen-only contraceptives do not protect against sexually transmitted infections (STIs) or human immunodeficiency virus (HIV).** If there is a risk of STI/HIV, the correct and consistent use of condoms is recommended, either alone or with another contraceptive method. Male latex condoms are proven to protect against STI/HIV.
- **The World Health Organization (WHO) has published medical eligibility criteria** for use of progestogen-only contraceptives. See Table 6 in the *Management issues* section for details of unacceptable (category 4) health risk or where the risks usually outweigh the advantages (category 3) for progestogen-only contraceptive injections.
- **For a full list of the WHO criteria for progestogen-only contraceptives,** see www.who.int/reproductive-health/publications/mec/5_pocs.pdf.
- **Category 2:** women with any of these medical problems require careful follow-up. If two or more of these problems coexist, the risk/benefit balance moves towards category 3.
- **Category 1:** many women will have no factor in their medical history that gives concern about any increased individual risks for them with progestogen-only pills.
- Note: if progestogen-only contraceptives are accidentally used during pregnancy, there is no known harm to the woman, the course of her pregnancy, or the fetus.
- **Depot medroxyprogesterone acetate** may reduce bone mineral density in women who use it:
  - In adolescents: only use DMPA after other methods have been discussed and considered unsuitable or unacceptable.
  - In women of all ages: evaluate the risks and benefits of treatment for more than 2 years.
  - In women with significant lifestyle and/or medical risk factors for osteoporosis: consider other methods of contraception [CSM, 2004].

Follow-up advice

Injectable contraceptives

- Follow up at 12 weeks for repeat injection of medroxyprogesterone acetate.
- Follow up at 8 weeks for repeat injection of norethisterone enantate (licensed for two injections only).

Etonogestrel implant

- Follow up at 3 months to check blood pressure and to enquire about adverse effects.
- The frequency of further checks should be guided by clinical judgement.
- Removal of the implant after 3 years (or sooner if ther are unacceptable adverse effects, or the woman wishes conceive) should be performed only by appropriately trained personnel.

Should I refer or investigate?

Refer?

- If further advice is required, consider contacting a loca family planning clinic or the Family Planning Associati — Helpline and Information Service.
  - fpa UK 0845 310 1334
  - www.fpa.org.uk
  - Brook Helpline: 0207-284-6040
  - www.brook.org.uk
  - www.ruthinking.co.uk

Patient information leaflets

The following PILs are available at www.prodigy.nhs.uk

- FPA (sexual health & contraception)

Shared decision making

- **The progestogen injection** is a very effective form of contraception.
- There are two types of progestogen injection. One protects you against pregnancy for 12 weeks. The othe injection protects you for 8 weeks.
- The injection is usually first given within 5 days of starting a period. It is fully effective from then on. Repeat injections are then every 8–12 weeks (dependin upon the type).
- **Your periods will probably change.** They may become irregular, light, or more frequent, or they may stop all together. This may be a nuisance but is not harmful.
- **Other side effects** that can occur include — weight gair headaches, some fluid retention or bloating, changes in mood, tender breasts, and acne.
- Your periods, and previous fertility, will usually take a few months to return after stopping the injection. Sometimes it can take a year or more.
- **The progestogen implant** is a very effective form of contraception.
- It protects you from pregnancy for 3 years.
- It is given within 5 days of starting a period. It is fully effective from then on.
- **Your periods will probably change.** They may become irregular, light, or more frequent, or they may stop all together. This may be a nuisance but is not harmful.
- **Other possible side effects** include — weight gain, bruising or itching at the insertion site, headache, acne, breast discomfort, and bloating.
- It can be taken out at any time and periods and fertility quickly returns to normal.

rug rationale

rugs included

All injectable progestogens and progestogen implants that are currently available are included in this scenario.

rescriptions

rogestogen depot injections

edroxyprogesterone acetate 150mg injection

Age from 12 to 60 years

Medroxyprogest. ac. 150mg/ml. Give 150mg (1ml) by deep intramuscular injection; supply 1 1ml prefilled syringe; NHS Cost £5.01.

orethisterone enantate 200mg injection

Age from 12 to 60 years

Norethisterone 200mg/ml injection. Give 200mg (1ml) by deep intramuscular injection into gluteal muscle; supply 1 1ml ampoule; NHS Cost £3.59.

rogestogen implant

onogestrel 68mg implant

Age from 12 to 60 years

Etonogestrel 68mg implant. For subdermal implantation; supply 1 implant; NHS Cost £90.00.

ntra-uterine devices and system

Vhich therapy?

opper intra-uterine devices

Intra-uterine devices (IUDs) are particularly suitable for women who want effective long-term contraception, provided that they are at low risk of sexually transmitted infection and do not have menorrhagia.

IUDs should be fitted only by professionals who have been appropriately trained. Different devices have different insertion techniques.

Devices with a large surface area of copper (greater than 300 mm²) are more effective and are recommended.

A frameless device, GyneFix, is available. The insertion technique is different from that for a framed IUD, and requires specific training.

IUDs are effective for a minimum of 5 years, but IUDs inserted after the age of 40 years can be left in until the menopause.

iming of insertion of copper IUDs

IUDs are usually inserted at the end of a period, but can be inserted at any time if there has been no risk of conception since the last period.

After childbirth: for women who are fully or nearly fully breastfeeding, amenorrhoeic, and less than 6 months postpartum (including Caesarian section), an IUD can be fitted within 48 hours of birth. If later than this, it should be inserted safely 4 or more weeks postpartum. The risk of uterine perforation is increased if an IUD is inserted between 49 hours and up to 4 weeks postpartum.

After a first-trimester abortion or miscarriage, IUDs can be inserted immediately. If not inserted immediately, it can be fitted 2–4 weeks later.

As a postcoital contraceptive, within 5 days of unprotected intercourse, or in good faith up to 5 days after the calculation of earliest likely ovulation (see PRODIGY *Emergency Contraception* guidance).

Levonorgestrel-releasing intra-uterine system

- **The levonorgestrel-releasing intra-uterine system (LNG-IUS) is suitable for** women who require effective long-term contraception, and particularly for those who have menorrhagia. It is also licensed to prevent endometrial hyperplasia in women taking oestrogen replacement therapy.
- **The LNG-IUS should be fitted only by professionals trained to do so.** Insertion may require local anaesthesia and dilatation of the cervical canal, particularly in nulliparous or perimenopausal women.
- The LNG-IUS is effective for 5 years.

Timing of insertion of the LNG-IUS

- **Ideally the IUS should be fitted within the first 7 days** of a period, and is then effective immediately. If fitted after this, any risk of pregnancy since the last period should be excluded, and an additional method of contraception should be used for 7 days.
- **After childbirth:** the IUS can be fitted 6 weeks after a vaginal delivery or a Caesarian section in women who are not breastfeeding.
- **After a first-trimester abortion or miscarriage,** the IUS can be fitted immediately and is effective immediately.

Practical prescribing points

For further information please see the *Medicines Compendium* (www.medicines.org.uk) or the *British National Formulary* (www.bnf.org).

- **IUDs and the LNG-IUS do not protect against sexually transmitted infections (STI) or human immunodeficiency virus (HIV).** If there is a risk of STI/HIV, the correct and consistent use of condoms is recommended, either alone or with another contraceptive method. Male latex condoms are proven to protect against STI/HIV.
- Prophylactic antibiotics are not recommended for routine insertion of an IUD or LNG-IUS. However, women with previous endocarditis, or with a prosthetic heart valve, require intravenous antibiotic prophylaxis to protect against bacterial endocarditis during insertion or removal of an IUD or LNG-IUS.
- **The World Health Organization (WHO) has published medical eligibility criteria** for IUD use. See Table 7 in the *Management issues* section for details of unacceptable (category 4) health risk or where the risks usually outweigh the advantages (category 3). For a full list of the WHO criteria, see www.who.int/reproductive-health/publications/mec/7_iud.pdf.
- **Category 2:** women with any of these medical problems require careful follow-up. If two or more of these problems coexist, the risk/benefit balance moves towards category 3.
- **Category 1:** many women will have no factor in their medical history that gives concern about any increased individual risks for them with progestogen-only pills.

Adverse effects of intra-uterine devices

- Irregular bleeding, menorrhagia, dysmenorrhoea.
- Uterine or cervical perforation (rare).
- Displacement or expulsion.
- There is a small increase in risk of pelvic infection in the 20 days after IUD insertion, but the risk is the same as that for the non-IUD-using population thereafter.

Adverse effects of the LNG-IUS

- Irregular bleeding (generally in the first 3 months, but normally improves)

- Breast tenderness, headaches and acne (usually transient)
- Uterine or cervical perforation (rare)
- Displacement or expulsion

Follow-up advice

- **Women should be examined 4–6 weeks after the intra-uterine device (IUD) or levonorgestrel-releasing intra-uterine system (LNG-IUS) was inserted, or alternatively after the first period after insertion.** Thereafter it is usual practice to offer a check annually.
- **Women should be taught to feel for the threads, and thus check that the IUD or LNG-IUS is in place, after the end of each period.** If the strings cannot be felt, or if the plastic end of the IUD or LNG-IUS can be felt, the woman should seek medical advice and use an alternative method of contraception in the meantime.
- IUDs (with more than a 300 mm^2 surface area of copper) and the LNG-IUS may be left in place for 5 years.
- IUDs inserted in women after the age of 40 years can be left until after the menopause.

Should I refer or investigate?

Refer?

- **Missing threads** should be investigated by an appropriately trained practitioner.
- If further advice is required, consider contacting a local family planning clinic or the Family Planning Association — Helpline and Information Service.
  - fpa UK 0845 310 1334
  - www.fpa.org.uk
  - Brook Helpline: 0207-284-6040
  - www.brook.org.uk
  - www.ruthinking.co.uk

Investigate?

Screening:

- **Consider or offer screening for sexually transmitted infections before IUD insertion.**

Investigate:

- **Any suspected pregnancy immediately.** Urgently refer women with suspected ectopic pregnancy.
- **Any suspected pelvic inflammatory disease** (see PRODIGY *Pelvic Inflammatory Disease* guidance).
- **Actinomyces-like organisms (ALOs) in cervical smears:**
  - **In a symptomatic woman,** limited evidence suggests that the IUD should be removed and appropriate treatment provided (usually a penicillin, tetracycline, or erythromycin for at least 2 weeks), as well as referral to a genito-urinary Medicine (GUM) clinic or a gynaecologist.
  - **In an asymptomatic woman,** there is no evidence to support either the routine removal of an IUD or periodic ALO screening.

Patient information leaflets

The following PILs are available at www.prodigy.nhs.uk
- FPA (sexual health & contraception)

Shared decision making

- **Intra-uterine devices (IUDs)** are effective for a minimum of 5 years. Modern IUDs inserted after you are 40 can be left in until after the menopause.
- It is usually inserted at the end of a period and is then effective immediately.
- **Possible side effects** include heavier, longer, or more painful periods. These may improve after a few month
- Risks and complications are rare, but include ectopic pregnancy, infection, or damage (perforation) of the uterus.
- **Seek medical help urgently if you think you may be pregnant** (but pregnancy is rare if you use an IUD).
- **Check that the IUD is in place at the end of each perio** (you will be shown how). It may rarely fall out withou you realising.
- **The levonorgestrel-releasing IUD** is a special type of IU that slowly releases a progestogen. This provides contraception and is a treatment for **heavy periods.**
- The progestogen can cause some women to get breast tenderness, headaches, and acne.

Drug rationale

Drugs not included

- IUDs that contain less than 300 mm^2 copper, or are no available on prescription in the UK, have not been included.

Drugs included

- All IUDs containing more than 300 mm^2 copper that a available on prescription in the UK, and the levonorgestrel-releasing intra-uterine system, are included.

Prescriptions

Framed intrauterine devices

Flexi T-300 intra-uterine device
- Age from 12 to 60 years
- Flexi T-300 IUD. For insertion into the uterine cavity; supply 1 IUD; NHS Cost £8.65.

Multiload Cu-375 intra-uterine device
- Age from 12 to 60 years
- Multiload Cu-375 IUD. For insertion into the uterine cavity; supply 1 IUD; NHS Cost £9.24.

Nova-T 380 intra-uterine device
- Age from 12 to 60 years
- Nova-T 380 IUD. For insertion into the uterine cavity; supply 1 IUD; NHS Cost £13.50.

T-Safe 380A intra-uterine device
- Age from 12 to 60 years
- T-Safe 380A IUD. For insertion into the uterine cavity; supply 1 IUD; NHS Cost £9.40.

Frameless intra-uterine device

GyneFix intra-uterine device
- Age from 12 to 60 years
- GyneFixIN IUD. For insertion into the uterine cavity; supply 1 IUD; NHS Cost £24.75.

Progestogen-releasing intra-uterine system

Levonorgestrel 20mcg/24hours intra-uterine system
- Age from 18 to 60 years
- Levonorgestrel 20mcg/24hrs IUS. For insertion into the uterine cavity; supply 1 device; NHS Cost £98.18.

Combined contraceptive pill or patch — alternative choice

Which therapy?

General

- Finding the most suitable combined oral contraceptive (COC) formulation for an individual woman can only be done empirically. Anecdotal advice exists, but there is a lack of evidence on which to guide practice.
- Changing COC pills is an appropriate strategy to cope with 'minor' adverse effects.
- Women should be encouraged to persist with a particular preparation for 3 months.
- Consider changing:
  - To a pill with either a higher or lower dose of the same progestogen.
  - To a pill with a different second-generation progestogen (either norethisterone, norgestimate, or levonorgestrel), starting with the lowest available dose.
  - To a pill with a third-generation progestogen (either gestodene or desogestrel).
  - To a phased preparation.
  - To the combined contraceptive patch if there are compliance problems with COCs.
  - From a combined contraceptive preparation to a progestogen-only pill.
- **Note: different brands of COC pill may contain identical doses and types of progestogen.**

Changing to a different pill

- When changing from a higher-dose preparation to a lower-dose preparation, or from a combined pill to a progestogen pill, or vice versa, the current packet should be finished and the new brand started the next day, avoiding any pill-free interval.
- **For Every Day preparations (ED)**, the new brand should be started the next day after the last active tablet in the current packet. The inactive tablets should be omitted.

Practical prescribing points

For further information please see the *Medicines Compendium* (www.medicines.org.uk) or the *British National Formulary* (www.bnf.org).

- **Combined oral contraceptives (COCs) do not protect against sexually transmitted infections (STI) or human immunodeficiency virus (HIV).** If there is a risk of STI/HIV, the correct and ongoing use of condoms is recommended, either alone or with another method of contraception. Male latex condoms are proven to protect against STI/HIV.
- **The World Health Organization (WHO) has published medical eligibility criteria** for COC use. See Table 3 in the *Management issues* section for details of unacceptable (category 4) health risk or where the risks usually outweigh the advantages (category 3). For a full list of the WHO criteria, see www.who.int/reproductive-health/publications/mec/3_cocs.pdf (for low dose combined oral contraceptives) and www.who.int/reproductive-health/publications/mec/4_cics.pdf (for the combined contraceptive patch).
- **Category 3 and 4:** alternative contraceptive methods should be recommended and the potential risk of COCs should be explained to women with any of these conditions. COC should be the last method of choice for these women, and careful follow-up will be required.
- **Category 2:** women with any of these medical problems require careful follow-up. If two or more of these problems coexist, the risk/benefit balance moves towards category 3.
- **Category 1:** often there will be no factor that gives concern about increased individual risks for COC use. For any woman, the balance of clinical risks and benefits of COCs must be considered together with her situation, motivation, and concerns about her preferred method.

Non-life-threatening adverse effects include:

- Breakthrough bleeding
- Breast tenderness
- Acne
- Mood changes

Risks

- There is a small increased absolute risk of:
  - Venous thromboembolism
  - Myocardial infarction
  - Stroke
  - Breast cancer
  - Cervical cancer
  - Primary liver cancer

Follow-up advice

- **First follow-up appointment after changing the brand of pill** is usually offered 10–12 weeks after the initial visit, to check blood pressure and to enquire about adverse effects. Also, check correct and consistent pill use, and knowledge of what to do if a pill is missed.
- **Where there are medical or non-medical concerns,** follow-up after 6 weeks is usual.
- **For established users of combined oral contraceptive (COC) pills,** 6-monthly checks are accepted UK practice. Blood pressure, clinical history, and adverse effects should be checked, together with correct and consistent pill use, and knowledge of what to do if a pill is missed.
- **In the absence of special problems,** women may be given up to 12 months' supply of a COC at the first visit, and encouraged to return at any time if problems arise.

Should I refer or investigate?

Refer?

- If further advice is required, consider contacting a local family planning clinic or the Family Planning Association — Helpline and Information Service.
  - fpa UK 0845 310 1334
  - www.fpa.org.uk
  - Brook Helpline: 0207-284-6040
  - www.brook.org.uk
  - www.ruthinking.co.uk

Investigate?

Breakthrough bleeding

- Routinely test for chlamydia and other sexually transmitted infections (STI) in women with a high-risk of acquiring an STI:
  - Sexually active women under the age of 25 years.
  - Women over 25 years with a new partner or who have had two or more partners in the previous 12 months.
- Other causes of breakthrough bleeding include missed pills, interacting drugs, cervical cancer, pregnancy, and severe diarrhoea and vomiting.

Patient information leaflets

The following PILs are available at www.prodigy.nhs.uk

- Blood Test - Clotting Tests

- Blood Test - General
- FPA (sexual health & contraception)

Shared decision making

- Different brands of contraceptive pill have different hormone types and doses.
- A change to a different brand may suit if you have side effects or problems with one.
- Your doctor or nurse will advise how and when to switch to a new brand.
- Read and keep the information leaflet that comes in the new packet. It will remind you about how to take the pill, possible side effects, risks, and what to do if you miss a pill, vomit, or take other medication whilst taking the pill.

C

Drug rationale

Drugs not included

- **Dianette®** (cyproterone acetate and ethinylestradiol) is not licensed solely for use as a contraceptive. It should be reserved for selected women requiring treatment for severe acne or refractory to prolonged antibiotic therapy, or with moderately severe hirsutism [ABPI Medicines Compendium, 2002a].
- **Norinyl-1 is not included as it contains high-dose oestrogen. Norinyl-1 contains** mestranol 50 micrograms, which is extensively metabolised to ethinyloestradiol as mestraol is a prodrug.

Drugs included

All combined oral contraceptive (COC) preparations currently available in the UK (except those containing high-dose oestrogen) are included in this scenario.

- **The choice of which product to prescribe as a second pill is not well supported by good comparative data.**
- COCs are listed in alphabetical order according to progestogen, and in ascending order of strength.
- **Preparations containing desogestrel or gestodene** are probably associated with an increased risk of venous thromboembolism compared with preparations containing levonorgestrel. Therefore, COCs containing desogestrel or gestodene are usually less preferred first-line.
- **COCs containing 20 micrograms oestrogen** do not seem to offer any advantage over those containing 30–35 micrograms oestrogen, and some women may have poorer cycle control.
- **Every Day preparations** may be useful for women who find it easier to take a pill every day.
- **Biphasic or triphasic preparations** are alternatives to monophasic preparations. A recent Cochrane review has found a lack of evidence to support their use in preference to monophasic preparations [Van Vliet et al, 2003]. They are also notably more expensive than monophasic COCs.
- **Yasmin®** (drospirenone and ethinylestradiol) is a black-triangle drug (currently under the surveillance of the Committee on Safety of Medicines) and is expensive compared with other COCs. There is limited evidence to support its use as a first-line agent, and because of the unknown risk of venous thromboembolism its use is best avoided in women with a BMI >=30. It may be an option where there has been progestogenic intolerance with at least two other COCs.
- **Note that many COCs contain the same amount of active drug:**
  - Microgynon 30 and Ovranette — ethinylestradiol 30 micrograms plus levonorgestrel 150 micrograms.
  - Brevinor and Ovysmen — ethinylestradiol 35 micrograms plus norethisterone 500 micrograms
  - Logynon and Trinordiol — the same phased doses o ethinylestradiol and levonorgestrel.
  - Femodene and Minulet — ethinylestradiol 30 micrograms and gestodene 75 micrograms.
  - Triadene and Tri-Minulet — the same phased doses ethinylestradiol and gestodene.

Prescriptions

COCs containing low-dose levonorgestrel or norethisterone

Microgynon 30 (levonorgestrel 150micrograms)
- Age from 12 to 60 years
- Microgynon 30 tablets. Take one tablet once a day for 21 days. Start the next packet after a 7-day break. See package insert for full instructions; supply 63 tablets; NHS Cost £2.82.

Ovranette (levonorgestrel 150micrograms)
- Age from 12 to 60 years
- Ovranette tablets. Take one tablet once a day for 21 days. Start the next packet after a 7-day break. See package insert for full instructions; supply 63 tablets; NHS Cost £2.46.

Microgynon 30 Every Day (levonorgestrel 150micrograms)
- Age from 12 to 60 years
- Microgynon 30 ED tablets. Take one tablet once a day See package insert for full instructions; supply 84 table NHS Cost £2.56.

Brevinor (norethisterone 500micrograms)
- Age from 12 to 60 years
- Brevinor tablets. Take one tablet once a day for 21 day Start the next packet after a 7-day break. See package insert for full instructions; supply 63 tablets; NHS Cost £1.99.

Ovysmen (norethisterone 500micrograms)
- Age from 12 to 60 years
- Ovysmen tablets. Take one tablet once a day for 21 days. Start the next packet after a 7-day break. See package insert for full instructions; supply 63 tablets; NHS Cost £1.70.

COCs containing higher-dose levonorgestrel or norethisterone

Eugynon 30 (levonorgestrel 250micrograms)
- Age from 12 to 60 years
- Eugynon 30 tablets. Take one tablet once a day for 21 days. Start the next packet after a 7-day break. See package insert for full instructions; supply 63 tablets; NHS Cost £2.48.

Norimin (norethisterone 1mg)
- Age from 12 to 60 years
- Norimin tablets. Take one tablet once a day for 21 day Start the next packet after a 7-day break. See package insert for full instructions; supply 63 tablets; NHS Cost £2.28.

Loestrin 30 (norethisterone 1.5mg)
- Age from 12 to 60 years
- Loestrin 30 tablets. Take one tablet once a day for 21 days. Start the next packet after a 7-day break. See package insert for full instructions; supply 63 tablets; NHS Cost £3.93.

ewer COCs (explain extra risks)

st – explain unknown risks (norgestimate micrograms)
- ge from 12 to 60 years
- ilest tablets. Take one tablet once a day for 21 days. tart the next packet after a 7-day break. See package nsert for full instructions; supply 63 tablets; HS Cost £6.42.

velon – explain extra risks (desogestrel micrograms)
- ge from 12 to 60 years
- larvelon tablets. Take one tablet once a day for 21 ays. Start the next packet after a 7-day break. See ackage insert for full instructions; supply 63 tablets; HS Cost £6.70.

nodene – explain extra risks (gestodene nicrograms)
- ge from 12 to 60 years
- emodene tablets. Take one tablet once a day for 21 ays. Start the next packet after a 7-day break. See ackage insert for full instructions; supply 63 tablets; HS Cost £6.84.

ulet – explain extra risks (gestodene 75micrograms)
- ge from 12 to 60 years
- Ainulet tablets. Take one tablet once a day for 21 days. tart the next packet after a 7-day break. See package nsert for full instructions; supply 63 tablets; HS Cost £6.84.

nodene Every Day – explain extra risks (gestodene ncg)
- ge from 12 to 60 years
- emodene ED tablets. Take one tablet once a day. See ackage insert for full instructions; supply 84 tablets; HS Cost £6.84.

min – explain unknown risks (drospirenone 3mg)
- ge from 12 to 60 years
- asmin tablets. Take one tablet once a day for 21 days. tart the next packet after a 7-day break. See package nsert for full instructions; supply 63 tablets; HS Cost £14.70.

w-dose (20micrograms) oestrogen combined pill patch

strin 20 (norethisterone 1mg)
- ge from 12 to 60 years
- oestrin 20 tablets. Take one tablet once a day for 21 ays. Start the next packet after a 7-day break. See ackage insert for full instructions; supply 63 tablets; HS Cost £2.73.

rcilon tablets – explain extra risks (desogestrel mcg)
- ge from 12 to 60 years
- Aercilon tablets. Take one tablet once a day for 21 days. tart the next packet after a 7-day break. See package nsert for full instructions; supply 63 tablets; HS Cost £8.57.

nodette – explain extra risks (gestodene 75mcg)
- ge from 12 to 60 years
- emodette tablets. Take one tablet once a day for 21 ays. Start the next packet after a 7-day break. See ackage insert for full instructions; supply 63 tablets; HS Cost £8.25.

a patches – unknown risks (norelgestromin 150mcg/ rs)
- ge from 12 to 60 years
- vra patches. Apply one patch once a week for 3 weeks, ollowed by a 7-day patch free interval and then repeat he course. ; supply 9 patches; NHS Cost £23.23.

Biphasic or triphasic COCs

Logynon (contains levonorgestrel)
- Age from 12 to 60 years
- Logynon tablets. Take one tablet once a day for 21 days. Start the next packet after a 7-day break. See package insert for full instructions; supply 63 tablets; NHS Cost £3.92.

Trinordiol (contains levonorgestrel)
- Age from 12 to 60 years
- Trinordiol tablets. Take one tablet once a day for 21 days. Start the next packet after a 7-day break. See package insert for full instructions; supply 63 tablets; NHS Cost £4.34.

Logynon Every Day (contains levonorgestrel)
- Age from 12 to 60 years
- Logynon-ED tablets. Take one tablet once a day. See package insert for full instructions; supply 84 tablets; NHS Cost £3.92.

BiNovum (contains norethisterone)
- Age from 12 to 60 years
- BiNovum tablets. Take one tablet once a day for 21 days. Start the next packet after a 7-day break. See package insert for full instructions; supply 63 tablets; NHS Cost £2.24.

Synphase (contains norethisterone)
- Age from 12 to 60 years
- Synphase tablets. Take one tablet once a day for 21 days. Start the next packet after a 7-day break. See package insert for full instructions; supply 63 tablets; NHS Cost £3.60.

TriNovum (contains norethisterone)
- Age from 12 to 60 years
- TriNovum tablets. Take one tablet once a day for 21 days. Start the next packet after a 7-day break. See package insert for full instructions; supply 63 tablets; NHS Cost £3.11.

Triadene (contains gestodene – explain extra risks)
- Age from 12 to 60 years
- Triadene tablets. Take one tablet once a day for 21 days. Start the next packet after a 7-day break. See package insert for full instructions; supply 63 tablets; NHS Cost £9.54.

Tri-Minulet (contains gestodene – explain extra risks)
- Age from 12 to 60 years
- Tri-Minulet tablets. Take one tablet once a day for 21 days. Start the next packet after a 7-day break. See package insert for full instructions; supply 63 tablets; NHS Cost £9.54.

Breastfeeding and after childbirth

Which therapy?

General

- **Contraception is not necessary in the 21 days after childbirth.**
- **Methods that are suitable choices for breastfeeding women** include barrier methods; intra-uterine devices (IUD) or the levonorgestrel-releasing intra-uterine system (LNG-IUS); the progestogen-only pill (POP); injectable contraceptives; the etonogestrel implant; the lactational amenorrhoea method (LAM); and sterilization. The combined oral contraceptive (COC) pill is not recommended, as it interferes with lactation.
- **Methods that are suitable choices for women who are not breastfeeding after childbirth** include COCs, barrier

C

methods, IUDs, LNG-IUS, the POP, injectable contraceptives, the etonogestrel implant, and sterilization.

Timing

- **A COC,** if the woman is not breastfeeding, can be started 21 days after childbirth. If started later than this, additional contraception should be used for 7 days.
- **A POP** can be started 21 days after delivery. Note: UK practice is to start a POP on day 21 post-partum in women who are breastfeeding. However, advice from the World Health Organization recommends waiting until 6 weeks post-partum, in which case alternative methods of contraception should be used from day 21 until the POP is started.
- **Injectable contraceptives** should normally be deferred until 6 weeks after childbirth. They can be administered during the first 5 days after delivery in women who are not breastfeeding, as long as the woman accepts the risk of heavy and prolonged bleeding.
- **The etonogestrel implant** can be inserted 21 days after childbirth. If inserted later than this, additional contraceptive precautions should be used for 7 days.
- **IUDs and LNG-IUS** can be inserted:
  - After vaginal delivery — IUDs are usually inserted 4 weeks after childbirth. The IUS can be fitted 6 weeks after a vaginal delivery in women who are not breastfeeding.
  - After Caesarian section — it is usual practice to defer insertion for at least 6 weeks after a Caesarian section.
  - If menstruation has returned, then IUDs are usually inserted at the end of a period and within 5 days after the calculated time of ovulation. They can be fitted at any time if there is no risk of conception since the last period.
- **The diaphragm or cap** can be used 6 weeks after delivery, and should always be checked for size and fit.

Lactational amenorrhoea method

- Lactational amenorrhoea method can be a very effective method of contraception when the following conditions are met:
  - **A woman is fully or almost fully breastfeeding** — feeding with no substitutes and at regular periods on demand, day and night.
  - **The baby is less than 6 months old.**
  - Menstruation has not returned.

See *Management issues* and other scenarios for more information on each contraceptive method.

Practical prescribing points

For further information please see the *Medicines Compendium* (www.medicines.org.uk) or the *British National Formulary* (www.bnf.org).

- See the relevant scenarios for *Prescribing points* for progestogen-only pills, IUDs, the LNG-IUS, diaphragms, caps, spermicides, and long-acting progestogens.

Follow-up advice

Progestogen-only pills

- **First follow-up appointment** is usually offered 10–12 weeks after the initial visit, to enquire about adverse effects. Check correct and consistent pill use, and knowledge of what to do if a pill is missed.
- For established users of progestogen-only pills, 6-monthly checks are accepted UK practice.

Injectable contraceptives

- Follow up at 12 weeks for repeat injection of medroxyprogesterone acetate.
- Follow up at 8 weeks for repeat injection of norethisterone enantate (licensed for two injections only).

Etonogestrel implant

- Follow up at 3 months to check blood pressure and tc enquire about adverse effects.
- The frequency of further checks should be guided by clinical judgement.
- Removal of the implant after 3 years (or sooner if the are unacceptable adverse effects, or the woman wishe conceive) should be performed only by appropriately trained personnel.

Diaphragms and caps should be:

- Replaced immediately if there are any holes or pucker of the rubber.
- Replaced annually and a check for size and fitting car out.
- Checked for size and fitting after childbirth, abortion, miscarriage, or if the woman gains or loses 3 kg or m in weight.

Intra-uterine devices and the levonorgestr releasing intra-uterine system

- **Women should be examined 4–6 weeks after the intra uterine device (IUD) or levonorgestrel-releasing intra-uterine system (LNG-IUS) was inserted, or alternative after the first period after insertion.** Thereafter it is us practice to offer a check annually and to encourage th woman to return at any time if there are problems wi unusual bleeding or pain.
- **Women should be taught to feel for the threads, and t check that the IUD or LNG-IUS is in place, after the e of each period.** If the strings or the plastic end of the I or LNG-IUS can be felt, the woman should seek medi advice and use an alternative method of contraceptio the meantime. Note: progestogen-only emergency contraception may be indicated.
- IUDs (with over 300 mm^2 surface area of copper) and the LNG-IUS may be used for 5 years.
- IUDs inserted in women after the age of 40 years can left until after the menopause.

Combined oral contraceptives

- **First follow-up appointment** is usually offered 10–12 weeks after the initial visit, to check blood pressure ar to enquire about adverse effects. Also, check correct a consistent pill use, and knowledge of what to do if a p is missed.
- **Where there are medical or non-medical concerns,** follow-up after 6 weeks is usual.
- **For established users of combined oral contraceptive (COC) pills,** 6-monthly checks are accepted UK practi Blood pressure, clinical history, and adverse effects should be checked together with correct and consister pill use, and knowledge of what to do if a pill is misse
- **In the absence of special problems,** women may be giv up to 12 months' supply of a COC at the first visit an encouraged to return at any time if problems arise.

Should I refer or investigate?

Refer?

If further advice is required, consider contacting a local family planning clinic or the Family Planning Association — Helpline and Information Service.

- fpa UK 0845 310 1334
- www.fpa.org.uk
- Brook Helpline: 0207-284-6040
- www.brook.org.uk
- www.ruthinking.co.uk

Patient information leaflets

The following PILs are available at www.prodigy.nhs.uk
FPA (sexual health & contraception)

Shared decision making

Contraception is not needed for the first 21 days after childbirth.

Most methods of contraception can be used after childbirth *apart from* the combined contraceptive pill if you *breastfeed*, as it interferes with milk production.

Condoms can be used at any time after childbirth.

Contraceptive pills can be started 21 days after childbirth.

The contraceptive injection is normally deferred until 6 weeks after childbirth.

The contraceptive implant can be inserted 21 days after childbirth.

An intra-uterine device (IUD) can be fitted within 48 hours of birth in women who are fully or nearly fully breastfeeding, amenorrhoeic, and less than 6 months after childbirth (including Caesarian section). If later than this, it should be inserted 4 or more weeks after childbirth but not between 49 hours and up to 4 weeks postpartum.

The levonorgestrel-releasing IUD is a special type of IUD that slowly releases a progestogen. This provides contraception and is also a treatment for **heavy periods.** The IUS can be fitted 6 weeks after a vaginal delivery in women who are not breastfeeding.

The diaphragm or cap can be used 6 weeks after childbirth. It should be checked for size and fit *after* childbirth.

Sterilization is an option to consider if you do not wish to have any more children and you are aware of all the other methods of contraception.

Breastfeeding itself can be an effective method of contraception for 6 months after childbirth. You may wish to discuss this further as a 'natural' method. You must be *fully* breastfeeding (feeding with no substitutes and at regular periods, on demand, day and night) and your periods must not have returned.

Drug rationale

Drugs not included

- **Combined oral contraceptives** (COCs) are not recommended for women who are breastfeeding. Prescriptions for all currently available low-strength COCs can be found in the COC *or patch — other choice* scenario.
- IUDs that contain less than 300 mm² copper, or are not available on prescription in the UK, have not been included.

Drugs included

- All prescribable progestogen-only contraceptives, intra-uterine devices containing more than 300 mm² copper, caps, diaphragms, spermicides, and the levonorgestrel-releasing intra-uterine system are offered in this scenario.

Prescriptions

Progestogen-only pills

Femulen (etynodiol diacetate 500micrograms)
- Age from 12 to 60 years
- Femulen tablets. Take one tablet once a day. See package insert for full instructions; supply 84 tablets; NHS Cost £3.31.

Microval (levonorgestrel 30micrograms)
- Age from 12 to 60 years
- Microval tablets. Take one tablet once a day. See package insert for full instructions; supply 105 tablets; NHS Cost £2.70.

Norgeston (levonorgestrel 30micrograms)
- Age from 12 to 60 years
- Norgeston tablets. Take one tablet once a day. See package insert for full instructions; supply 105 tablets; NHS Cost £2.94.

Micronor (norethisterone 350micrograms)
- Age from 12 to 60 years
- Micronor tablets. Take one tablet once a day. See package insert for full instructions; supply 84 tablets; NHS Cost £1.89.

Noriday (norethisterone 350micrograms)
- Age from 12 to 60 years
- Noriday tablets. Take one tablet once a day. See package insert for full instructions; supply 84 tablets; NHS Cost £2.10.

Cerazette (desogestrel 75micrograms)
- Age from 12 to 60 years
- Cerazette tablets. Take one tablet once a day. See package insert for full instructions; supply 84 tablets; NHS Cost £8.85.

Progestogen depot injections or implants

Medroxyprogesterone acetate 150mg injection
- Age from 12 to 60 years
- Medroxyprogest. ac. 150mg/ml. Give 150mg (1ml) by deep intramuscular injection; supply 1 1ml prefilled syringe; NHS Cost £5.01.

Norethisterone enantate 200mg injection
- Age from 12 to 60 years
- Norethisterone 200mg/ml injection. Give 200mg (1ml) by deep intramuscular injection into gluteal muscle; supply 1 1ml ampoule; NHS Cost £3.59.

Etonogestrel 68mg implant
- Age from 12 to 60 years
- Etonogestrel 68mg implant. For subdermal implantation; supply 1 implant; NHS Cost £90.00.

Intrauterine device or system

Flexi T-300 framed intra-uterine device
- Age from 12 to 60 years
- Flexi T-300 IUD. For insertion into the uterine cavity; supply 1 IUD; NHS Cost £8.65.

Multiload Cu-375 framed intrauterine device
- Age from 12 to 60 years
- Multiload Cu-375 IUD. For insertion into the uterine cavity; supply 1 IUD; NHS Cost £9.24.

Nova-T 380 framed intra-uterine device

- Age from 12 to 60 years
- Nova-T 380 IUD. For insertion into the uterine cavity; supply 1 IUD; NHS Cost £13.50.

T-Safe Cu-380A framed intra-uterine device

- Age from 12 to 60 years
- T-Safe 380A IUD. For insertion into the uterine cavity; supply 1 IUD; NHS Cost £9.40.

GyneFix frameless intra-uterine device

- Age from 12 to 60 years
- GyneFixIN IUD. For insertion into the uterine cavity; supply 1 IUD; NHS Cost £24.75.

Levonorgestrel 20mcg/24hrs intra-uterine system

- Age from 12 to 60 years
- Levonorgestrel 20mcg/24hrs IUS. For insertion into the uterine cavity; supply 1 device; NHS Cost £98.18.

Caps and diaphragms

Dumas vault cap

- Age from 18 to 60 years
- Type A cap Size__mm. Follow the instructions given inside this pack; supply 1 cap; NHS Cost £7.03.

Prentif cavity rim cervical cap

- Age from 18 to 60 years
- Type B cap Size__mm. Follow the instructions given inside this pack; supply 1 cap; NHS Cost £8.20.

Vimule cap

- Age from 18 to 60 years
- Type C cap Size__mm. Follow the instructions given inside this pack; supply 1 cap; NHS Cost £7.03.

FemCap 22mm

- Age from 18 to 60 years
- FemCap Size: 22mm. Follow the instructions given inside this pack; supply 1 cap; NHS Cost £14.75.

FemCap 26mm

- Age from 18 to 60 years
- FemCap Size: 26mm. Follow the instructions given inside this pack; supply 1 cap; NHS Cost £14.75.

FemCap 30mm

- Age from 18 to 60 years
- FemCap Size: 30mm. Follow the instructions given inside this pack; supply 1 cap; NHS Cost £14.75.

Reflexions diaphragm

- Age from 18 to 60 years
- Type A diaphragm Size__mm. Follow the instructions given inside this pack; supply 1 diaphragm; NHS Cost £5.59.

Ortho diaphragm

- Age from 18 to 60 years
- Type B diaphragm Size__mm. Follow the instructions given inside this pack; supply 1 diaphragm; NHS Cost £6.14.

All-flex diaphragm

- Age from 18 to 60 years
- Type C diaphragm Size__mm. Follow the instructions given inside this pack; supply 1 diaphragm; NHS Cost £6.98.

Spermicides (use with a cap or diaphragm method)

Duragel

- Age from 12 to 60 years
- Duragel 2% w/v gel. Follow the instructions given inside this pack; supply 100 grams; NHS Cost £3.45; OTC Cost £6.09.

Gynol II jelly

- Age from 12 to 60 years
- Gynol II 2% jelly. Follow the instructions given inside this pack; supply 81 grams; NHS Cost £2.61; OTC Cost £4.61.
- Gynol II applicator. Use for vaginal application of jelly; supply 1 applicator; NHS Cost £0.75; OTC Cost £1.32

Ortho-Creme

- Age from 12 to 60 years
- Ortho-Creme 2% cream. Follow the instructions given inside this pack; supply 70 grams; NHS Cost £2.44; OTC Cost £4.30.
- Ortho vaginal applicator. Use for vaginal application of cream; supply 1 applicator; NHS Cost £0.75; OTC Cost £1.32.

Orthoforms pessaries

- Age from 12 to 60 years
- Orthoforms 5% w/w pessaries. Follow the instructions given inside this pack; supply 15 pessaries; NHS Cost £2.40; OTC Cost £4.23.

Taking a liver enzyme-inducing drug

Which therapy?

- **The effectiveness of combined oral contraceptives (COCs) and progestogen-only pills (POPs)** can be reduced by drugs that induce liver enzymes.
- **Users of COCs or the POP who require a short course** (7 days or less) of a rifamycin (rifampicin or rifabutin) should be advised to:
  - Continue taking their oral contraceptive.
  - Omit any pill-free interval that occurs whilst taking the rifamycin or within 7 days after the last dose of it. For Every Day (ED) preparations, discard the inactive tablets.
  - Use additional contraceptive precautions whilst taking the rifamycin and for 4 weeks after the last dose.
- **Women who require long-term use of a rifamycin** should always be advised to use an alternative method of contraception to oral contraceptives (e.g. an intra-uterine device).
- **Women requiring contraception whilst taking certain antiepileptics (AEDs)**, i.e. phenobarbital, phenytoin, primidone, carbamazepine, oxcarbazepine, or topiramate, should be advised to use alternative method of contraception to oral contraceptives.
- **Where a COC is still the preferred method** either Norinyl-1 (containing mestranol 50 micrograms, a prodrug of EE) or two low-dose COCs providing a total daily dose of 50–60 micrograms EE is recommended, but there remains an enhanced risk of pregnancy. Should the long-term liver-enzyme inducer be stopped, additional barrier methods are advised until 4 weeks after cessation.
- **If breakthrough bleeding occurs with 50 micrograms oestrogen,** increase the dose to 80 or 100 micrograms and consider tricycling (taking three packets without a break, followed by a tablet-free interval of 4 days) of the COC. Note: this represents an off-licence use of a COC.
- **AEDs that do not induce liver enzymes do not interfere with the efficacy of COCs.**
- **Short courses of broad-spectrum antibiotics may reduce the efficacy of COCs.** Additional contraceptive precautions should be used whilst taking the short course of the antibiotic and for 7 days after. If the pill-free interval was due whilst taking the antibiotic, or within 7 days after the last dose of the antibiotic, the pill-free interval should be omitted. For Every Day preparations, the inactive tablets should be discarded.
- **Erythromycin, co-trimoxazole, and sulphonamides** are not thought to interact with COCs.
- **Additional contraceptive precautions are recommended for women on the COC pill for the first 3 weeks after starting a course of a long-term broad-spectrum**

antibiotic. No additional precautions are required if a woman starts the COC having been on a course of antibiotic for more than 3 weeks.

St John's wort also induces liver enzymes, reducing the effectiveness of COCs and POPs.

ractical prescribing points

›r further information please see the *Medicines ›mpendium* (www.medicines.org.uk) or the *British ıtional Formulary* (www.bnf.org).

See the relevant scenarios for *Prescribing points* for IUDs, the LNG-IUS, diaphragms, caps, spermicides, and long-acting progestogens.

hould I refer or investigate?

efer?

If further advice is required, consider contacting a local family planning clinic or the Family Planning Association — Helpline and Information Service.

- fpa UK 0845 310 1334
- www.fpa.org.uk
- Brook Helpline: 0207-284-6040
- www.brook.org.uk
- www.ruthinking.co.uk

'atient information leaflets

ıe following PILs are available at www.prodigy.nhs.uk FPA (sexual health & contraception)

hared decision making

Antibiotics — short courses of antibiotics may interfere with the combined pill.

- Carry on taking the pill, AND:
- Use other methods of contraception (such as condoms) whilst taking antibiotics.
- Continue to use other methods of contraception for a further 7 days after the last dose.
- If there are less than seven pills in the packet when you finish the antibiotic, omit the next pill-free gap and go straight into the next pack. If you take an Every Day pill, miss out the inactive tablets.

Antibiotics — for courses lasting 3 weeks or more:

- Carry on taking the pill, BUT:
- Use other methods of contraception (such as condoms) for the first three weeks of the antibiotic course.

Rifamycin (rifampicin or rifabutin) may interfere with the combined pill or the progestogen-only pill. Other methods of contraception are best if long courses are needed. For a short course (a week or less):

- Carry on taking your pill, AND:
- Use other methods of contraception (such as condoms) whilst taking rifamycin.
- Continue to use other methods of contraception for a further 4 weeks after the last dose.
- Omit the next pill-free gap and go straight into the next pack. If you take an Every Day pill, miss out the inactive tablets.

Medication for epilepsy:

- Ethosuximide, diazepam, clonazepam, sodium valproate, vigabatrin, lamotrigine, tiagabine, levetiractem, and gabapentin DO NOT affect the contraceptive pill.
- Phenobarbital, phenytoin, primidone, carbamazepine, oxcarbazepine, and topiramate DO interfere with contraceptive pills. Alternative methods of contraception are usually recommended.

Drug rationale

Drugs not included

- **Progestogen-only pills** are not offered, since their efficacy is reduced by liver enzyme-inducing drugs, and no regimens for this situation are clearly highlighted in the literature.
- **The etonogestrel implant** is not included, since its efficacy is likely to be reduced by liver enzyme-inducing drugs [ABPI Medicines Compendium, 2003a].
- **Combined oral contraceptives except for Norinyl-1** are not included, since their efficacy may be reduced.
- **IUDs that contain less than 300 mm² copper,** or are not available on prescription in the UK, have not been included.

Drugs included

- **Intra-uterine devices** (containing more than 300 mm² copper) are offered, since these will not be affected by liver enzyme-inducing drugs.
- **The levonorgestrel-releasing intra-uterine system** is unlikely to be affected by liver enzyme-inducing drugs or broad-spectrum antibiotics, since the action of the levonorgestrel is mainly local on the endometrium [Belfield, 1999; BNF 47, 2004].
- **Medroxyprogesterone acetate depot injection:** it is unlikely that liver enzyme-inducing drugs will significantly affect the metabolism of medroxyprogesterone acetate, and therefore no dose adjustment is recommended for women receiving such drugs [ABPI Medicines Compendium, 2002b]. However, it is often recommended that the interval between injections is reduced from 12 to 10 weeks for women taking enzyme-inducing drugs [SIGN, 2003].
- **Diaphragms, caps, and spermicides** are offered, since these will not be affected by drug interactions.
- **A regimen containing approximately 50 micrograms ethinylestradiol (EE) is recommended** where COCs remain the preferred contraceptive method when using a liver enzyme-inducer [FFPRHC Clinical Effectiveness Unit, 2003a]. Both the following options are included (additional barrier contraception is also advised until 4 weeks after cessation of the liver enzyme-inducer):
  - Norinyl-1 (containing mestranol 50 micrograms, a prodrug of EE).
  - Two low-dose COCs providing a total daily dose of 50–60 micrograms EE.

Prescriptions

Intrauterine device or system

Flexi T-300 framed intra-uterine device

- Age from 12 to 60 years
- Flexi T-300 IUD. For insertion into the uterine cavity; supply 1 IUD; NHS Cost £8.65.

Multiload Cu-375 framed intra-uterine device

- Age from 12 to 60 years
- Multiload Cu-375 IUD. For insertion into the uterine cavity; supply 1 IUD; NHS Cost £9.24.

Nova-T 380 framed intra-uterine device

- Age from 12 to 60 years
- Nova-T 380 IUD. For insertion into the uterine cavity; supply 1 IUD; NHS Cost £13.50.

T-Safe Cu-380A framed intra-uterine device

- Age from 12 to 60 years
- T-Safe 380A IUD. For insertion into the uterine cavity; supply 1 IUD; NHS Cost £9.40.

C

GyneFix frameless intra-uterine device
- Age from 12 to 60 years
- GyneFixIN IUD. For insertion into the uterine cavity; supply 1 IUD; NHS Cost £24.75.

Levonorgestrel 20mcg/24hrs intra-uterine system
- Age from 12 to 60 years
- Levonorgestrel 20mcg/24hrs IUS. For insertion into the uterine cavity; supply 1 device; NHS Cost £98.18.

Caps and diaphragms

Dumas vault cap
- Age from 18 to 60 years
- Type A cap Size__mm. Follow the instructions given inside this pack; supply 1 cap; NHS Cost £7.03.

Prentif cavity rim cervical cap
- Age from 18 to 60 years
- Type B cap Size__mm. Follow the instructions given inside this pack; supply 1 cap; NHS Cost £8.20.

Vimule cap
- Age from 18 to 60 years
- Type C cap Size__mm. Follow the instructions given inside this pack; supply 1 cap; NHS Cost £7.03.

FemCap 22mm
- Age from 18 to 60 years
- FemCap Size: 22mm. Follow the instructions given inside this pack; supply 1 cap; NHS Cost £14.75.

FemCap 26mm
- Age from 18 to 60 years
- FemCap Size: 26mm. Follow the instructions given inside this pack; supply 1 cap; NHS Cost £14.75.

FemCap 30mm
- Age from 18 to 60 years
- FemCap Size: 30mm. Follow the instructions given inside this pack; supply 1 cap; NHS Cost £14.75.

Reflexions diaphragm
- Age from 18 to 60 years
- Type A diaphragm Size__mm. Follow the instructions given inside this pack; supply 1 diaphragm; NHS Cost £5.59.

Ortho diaphragm
- Age from 18 to 60 years
- Type B diaphragm Size__mm. Follow the instructions given inside this pack; supply 1 diaphragm; NHS Cost £5.84.

All-flex diaphragm
- Age from 18 to 60 years
- Type C diaphragm Size__mm. Follow the instructions given inside this pack; supply 1 diaphragm; NHS Cost £6.64.

Spermicides (use with a cap or diaphragm method)

Duragel
- Age from 12 to 60 years
- Duragel 2% w/v gel. Follow the instructions given inside this pack; supply 100 grams; NHS Cost £3.45; OTC Cost £6.09.

Gynol II jelly
- Age from 12 to 60 years
- Gynol II 2% jelly. Follow the instructions given inside this pack; supply 81 grams; NHS Cost £2.61; OTC Cost £4.61.
- Gynol II applicator. Use for vaginal application of jelly; supply 1 applicator; NHS Cost £0.75; OTC Cost £1.32.

Ortho-Creme
- Age from 12 to 60 years
- Ortho-Creme 2% cream. Follow the instructions given inside this pack; supply 70 grams; NHS Cost £2.44; OTC Cost £4.30.
- Ortho vaginal applicator. Use for vaginal application c cream; supply 1 applicator; NHS Cost £0.75; OTC Cost £1.32.

Orthoforms pessaries
- Age from 12 to 60 years
- Orthoforms 5% w/w pessaries. Follow the instructions given inside this pack; supply 15 pessaries; NHS Cost £2.40; OTC Cost £4.23.

Progestogen depot injection

Medroxyprogesterone acetate 150mg depot injection
- Age from 12 to 60 years
- Medroxyprogest. ac. 150mg/ml. Give 150mg (1ml) by deep intramuscular injection; supply 1 1ml prefilled syringe; NHS Cost £5.01.

Combined oral contraceptives: less preferred

Norinyl-1 (norethisterone 1mg)
- Age from 12 to 60 years
- Norinyl-1 50mcg + 1mg tablets. Take one tablet once a day for 21 days. Start the next packet after a 7-day break. See package insert for full instructions; supply 6 tablets; NHS Cost £2.19.

Microgynon 30 (levonorgestrel 150micrograms)
- Age from 12 to 60 years
- Microgynon 30 tablets. Take two tablets once a day whilst on the interacting drug. Use a barrier method during this time and for 28 days after stopping the interacting drug; supply 21 tablets; NHS Cost £0.94.

Ovranette (levonorgestrel 150micrograms)
- Age from 12 to 60 years
- Ovranette tablets. Take two tablets once a day whilst c the interacting drug. Use a barrier method during this time and for 28 days after stopping the interacting dru supply 63 tablets; NHS Cost £2.46.

Eugynon 30 (levonorgestrel 250micrograms)
- Age from 12 to 60 years
- Eugynon 30 tablets. Take two tablets once a day whils on the interacting drug. Use a barrier method during th time and for 28 days after stopping the interacting dru supply 63 tablets; NHS Cost £2.48.

Loestrin 30 (norethisterone 1.5mg)
- Age from 12 to 60 years
- Loestrin 30 tablets. Take two tablets once a day whilst on the interacting drug. Use a barrier method during th time and for 28 days after stopping the interacting dru supply 63 tablets; NHS Cost £3.93.

Extended Information

Background information

- Methods available p.406
- Current use of contraception p.407
- Efficacy of contraceptive methods p.407

Methods available

Currently in the UK the following methods of contraception are available, and are provided principally by GPs, nurses, and family planning and sexual health clinics:

- Combined oral contraceptive pill
- Progestogen-only pill
- Injectable contraceptives
- Etonogestrel implant
- Combination transdermal contraceptive patch
- Levonorgestrel-releasing intra-uterine system
- Intra-uterine device (IUD)

Female barrier methods — diaphragm or cap and spermicide, and female condoms
Spermicides
Male condoms
Natural family planning or fertility awareness
Male and female sterilization
Emergency contraception — progestogen-only pill and IUD method; for more information see the separate PRODIGY guidance on *Contraception — emergency*

urrent use of contraception

Almost three-quarters (74%) of women aged 16–49 use at least one form of contraception.

The most commonly used methods for avoiding pregnancy are:

- Contraceptive pill (25% of women)
- Sterilization of either the woman or her partner (23%)
- Male condoms (20%)

Jational Statistics, 2003]

fficacy of contraceptive methods

There are two types of contraceptive failure — user failure and method failure.

- **User failure** relates to pregnancy having occurred owing to the incorrect use, or non-use, of a method of contraception.
- **Method failure** relates to pregnancy having occurred despite the method of contraception being used correctly (or fitted correctly in the case of implants, intra-uterine devices and the intra-uterine system) and consistently.

Contraceptive failure rates are higher in day-to-day practice than in clinical trials, because of user failure. For user-dependent methods of contraception (e.g. barrier methods, contraceptive pills, contraceptive patch, or natural family planning) failure rates are highest in the first 12 months.

The efficacy of different contraceptive methods available is summarized in Table 1.

`russell, 2004]

Table 1: Summary of the efficacy of different contraceptive methods available in the UK.

	Percentage of women experiencing an unintended pregnancy within the first year of use	
	Typical use (user failure)	***Perfect use (method failure)***
Combined oral contraceptive pill	5%	0.1%
Progestogen-only contraceptive pill	5%	0.5%
Injectable contraception	0.3%	0.3%
Levonorgestrel implant*	0.05%	0.05%
Etonogestrel implant	0.06%†	0.01%†
Combination transdermal contraceptive patch	8%	0.3%
Intra-uterine device	Less than 1%, depending on the type of device	Less than 1%, depending on the type of device
Levonorgestrel-releasing intra-uterine system	0.1%	0.1%
Diaphragm plus spermicide	16%	6%
Cervical cap plus spermicide: Parous women Nulliparous women	- 32% 16%	- 20% 9%
Female condom (without spermicide)	21%	5%
Male condom (without spermicide)	15%	2%
Withdrawal	27%	4%
Female sterilization	0.5% 1 in 200 lifetime-failure rate	0.5% 1 in 200 lifetime-failure rate
Male sterilization	0.15% 1 in 700 lifetime-failure rate	0.10% 1 in 1000 lifetime-failure rate

* Discontinued, but some women may have in place till 2004
† [Organon Laboratories Medical Information, Personal Communication, 2004]

Management issues

Combined oral contraceptive pill p.407
Progestogen-only pills p.414
Progestogen-only contraceptive injection p.417
Subdermal progestogen-only contraceptive implant p.419
Transdermal combination contraceptive patch p.420
Copper intra-uterine devices p.421
Progestogen-only intra-uterine system p.423
Diaphragms and caps p.425
Female condom p.426
Spermicides p.426
Male condoms p.426
Natural family planning p.427
Specific contraceptive information p.427
Legal issues with young women p.430

ombined oral contraceptive pill

General information

There are many combined oral contraceptive (COC) pill formulations available. Each product contains a synthetic oestrogen (usually ethinylestradiol) plus a progestogen.

- Levonorgestrel, norethisterone, and norgestimate (metabolized to levonorgestrel) are otherwise known as second-generation progestogens.
- Desogestrel and gestodene are known as third-generation progestogens.
- Drospirenone (a derivative of spironolactone) has been more recently developed. It has anti-androgenic properties and anti-mineralocorticoid activity (unlike most other progestogens).

- **Low-dose COCs containing 20–35 micrograms of oestrogen in combination with a progestogen** have generally replaced older COCs containing 50 micrograms oestrogen or more. Low-dose COCs are preferred because of a lower risk of thromboembolism [CSM, 1999]; see the section on *Venous thromboembolism* for more information. Higher doses may be appropriate where women are taking liver enzyme-inducers.
- **There is currently no robust evidence** regarding the comparative non-life-threatening adverse effects and non-contraceptive benefits of each COC.

Mode of action

- **COCs work by inhibition of ovulation** — follicle-stimulating hormone [FSH] and luteinising hormone [LH] release are suppressed (B).
- Cervical mucus is thickened, preventing sperm penetration.

- Endometrial receptiveness is reduced.

[FFPRHC Clinical Effectiveness Unit, 2003a]

Efficacy

- Advise women that COCs can be over 99% effective at preventing pregnancy, if used consistently and correctly (B). For more information, see Table 1.

Risk-benefit profile

- Before deciding on whether a prescription for a COC is acceptable, the risks and benefits of COCs should be considered by both the clinician and woman — see Table 2. See also sections on *Advantages* and *Disadvantages* for more information.

[FFPRHC Clinical Effectiveness Unit, 2000]

Advantages

- **Highly effective, reversible** method of contraception.
- **Convenient** — not intercourse-related.
- **Women may be advised that menstrual pain and blood loss may be reduced with COC use: (C)**
  - A reduction in menstrual blood loss has been found [Iyer et al, 2003].
  - A recent small double-blind, placebo-controlled, randomized controlled trial showed a significant reduction in cramps with use of desogestrel-containing COCs [Hendrix and Alexander, 2002]. However, a Cochrane review found insufficient evidence to determine whether COCs reduce dysmenorrhoea [Proctor et al, 2003].
  - A Cochrane review looking at the efficacy of COCs for reducing the pain of endometriosis found only one study that satisfied the inclusion criteria — this showed benefit [Moore et al, 2003].
- **Possible protection against pelvic inflammatory disease (PID).** Barrier methods of contraception, however, will offer more protection against PID and against tubal infertility [Cramer et al, 1987; Panser and Phipps, 1991].
- **Possible protection against osteoporosis.** There are limited data to support the suggestion that low-dose formulations (30–35 micrograms oestrogen) may have a favourable effect on bone mineral density [Berenson et al, 2001]; others, however, have found no association between COCs and changes in bone mineral density [Wanichsetakul et al, 2002].

[FFPRHC Clinical Effectiveness Unit, 2003a]

Ovarian Cancer

- Women may be advised of a reduction in risk of ovaria cancer and ovarian cysts with COC use (B).
- **The risk of ovarian cancer** is reduced by about 50% in women who have used COCs containing greater than 35 micrograms of ethinylestradiol for 5 years [IARC, 1999].
  - There does not seem to be an additional benefit after 6 years of use.
  - This protective effect lasts for up to 15 years after stopping COCs.
- **Mortality from ovarian cancer** is reduced with increasi duration of COC use [Vessey et al, 2003].
- **COCs containing less than 35 micrograms of ethinylestradiol** have also been found to have a protective effect in a recent retrospective case-control study [FFPRHC Clinical Effectiveness Unit, 2003a].

Endometrial cancer

- Women may be advised of a reduction in the risk of endometrial cancer with COC use (C).
- **The risk of endometrial cancer** is reduced by 50% if th COC is used for more than 1 year, and the effect has been found to persist for about 15 years after stopping. There are little data available on the lower-dose formulations [IARC, 1999; Tuckey, 2000].
- **Mortality** from endometrial cancer is also reduced wit COC use [Vessey et al, 2003].

Colorectal cancer

- **The risk of colorectal cancer** may be reduced, accordin to the result of a meta-analysis that identified an overal relative risk of 0.82 (95% CI 0.74 to 0.92) [Fernandez al, 2001]. However, it has not been established if this protective effect occurs with low-dose COCs.

[FFPRHC Clinical Effectiveness Unit, 2003a]

Disadvantages

- **Adverse effects include** breakthrough bleeding, breast tenderness, acne, and mood changes.
- **Weight gain** — a recent Cochrane review investigated the association between COC use and weight change. (three placebo-controlled randomized trials identified, two examined COCs [Gallo et al, 2003c]. Although many clinicians and women believe that an association exists, no large effect seems evident, but more data are needed to determine a precise effect on weight.

Table 2: Risk–benefit profiles for COCs to consider before first COC prescription.

Disease	Rates per 100,000 women	Relative risk with COC use
Risks		
Coronary artery disease*	1500	No increase
Stroke*	100	Two-fold increase in ischaemic stroke. No increase in haemorrhagic stroke.
Venous thromboembolism (VTE)	5	Three-fold increase with levonorgestrel and norethisterone COCs. Five-fold increase with desogest and gestodene COCs.
Breast cancer**	1 in 9 women sometime in their lives (estimated risk is 1 in 1900 up to 30 years, 1 in 200 up to 40 years, and 1 in 50 up to 50 years).	Any increased risk likely to be small; no increased risk 10 years after stopping (Note: data is particularly complex here).
Cervical cancer	11	Small increase after 5 years and a two-fold increase aft 10 years.
Benefits		
Ovarian cancer	22	Halving of risk lasting for 10 years or more.
Endometrial cancer	15	Halving of risk lasting for 10 years or more.

* Prevalence of treated coronary heart disease and stroke recorded in general practice in England and Wales for women aged up to 54 years [Collaborative Group on Hormonal Factors in Breast Cancer, 1996].

** NHS Screening Programme: www.cancerscreening.nhs.uk

Use of a COC offers no protection against sexually transmitted infections.

Contraindications

Conditions where COCs are either an unacceptable (category 4) health risk or where the risks usually outweigh the advantages (category 3) are detailed in Table 3.

Alternative contraceptive methods should be recommended and the potential risk of COCs should be explained to women with any of these conditions.

For a full list of the World Health Organization (WHO) medical eligibility criteria, see www.who.int/reproductive-health/publications/mec/3_cocs.pdf.

[WHO, 2004]

Venous thromboembolism

Advise women that although the relative risk of venous thromboembolism (VTE) with COC use can increase up to five-fold (compared with non-users), in absolute terms the risk is still low, and still considerably lower than the risk of VTE in pregnancy (**B**). The risk of VTE is greatest in the first year of COC use.

The incidence of VTE [CSM, 1999] is reported as varying in different populations:

- Healthy non-pregnant women — about 5–10 cases per 100,000 per year
- Second-generation pill users — about 15 per 100,000 per year
- Third-generation pill users — about 25 per 100,000 per year
- Pregnancy — estimated to be about 60 per 100,000 per year

The incidence of VTE in women taking Dianette® (cyproterone acetate/ethinylestradiol) has been found to be at least twice as high as two times higher than that in women using second-generation COCs [Seaman et al, 2003]. For more information, see the section on *Women with acne*.

There is evidence that the risk of VTE is reduced in COCs containing lower doses of the oestrogen [Hannaford, 2000; Lidegaard et al, 2002].

Obese women have an increased risk of VTE, and the risk increases with increasing body body mass index (BMI). However there is inconsistent advice regarding the BMI cut-off point at which the benefit of COCs may outweigh the risks [FFPRHC Clinical Effectiveness Unit, 2003a]. For more information, see section on *Women who are overweight or obese*.

- One recommendation is that women with a BMI of more than 39 should not use a COC [BNF 47, 2004].
- The World Health Organization (WHO) recommends that the benefits of COC use in women with a BMI of more than 30 outweigh the risks.

Women who have inherited clotting-factor defects (e.g. factor V Leiden mutation, protein C or S deficiencies, or antithrombin III defect) have a substantially increased risk of VTE with acquired risk factors, including COC use [Hannaford, 2000].

If a woman has a family history of VTE (in a first-degree relative under the age of 45 years), and has considered other contraceptive methods, but still wishes to use a COC, a thrombophilia screen should be performed.

A family history of VTE may alert clinicians to women at higher risk, but there is ongoing debate about the value of screening, and whether the presence of a family history adequately identifies women who are carriers of thrombophilia mutations with any degree of sensitivity [Cosmi et al, 2003].

To minimize the risk of VTE before pelvic surgery or procedures that may require extensive immobilization, COCs should be stopped 2–4 weeks before the procedure, and should not be resumed until 2 weeks after achieving complete mobilization [Weisberg, 2002].

- **People with established risk factors for VTE,** may be more at risk of developing travel related deep vein thrombosis/pulmonary embolism, as immobilization can occur during long-haul flights. For more information, see PRODIGY guidance on *Deep vein thrombosis*.

Myocardial infarction

- **Healthy non-smokers** can be advised that they have no increased risk of myocardial infarction (MI) with COC use (**B**).
- **COC users with hypertension** have a three-fold increased risk of MI compared with COC users without hypertension.
- **In COC users who are heavy smokers** (more than 15 cigarettes per day) the relative risk of MI may be up to 10 times that of smokers who do not use COCs [WHO, 1998; Dunn et al, 1999].
- **Studies analysing the risk of MI in different 'generation' COCs** have found inconsistent results. The Myocardial infarction and oral contraceptives (MICA) study found no difference in risk between second- and third-generation COCs [Dunn et al, 1999]. Interpretation of an earlier study that did find differences is limited by its study size [Lewis et al, 1997; DTB, 2000].
- **Current oral contraceptive use is the key risk factor for MI,** whereas the risk from being a past user is not significantly different from that of never having been a user, according to the findings of a recent meta-analysis [Khader et al, 2003].

Stroke

- Advise women of a very small increase in the absolute risk of ischaemic stroke with COC use (**B**).
- **Ischaemic stroke:** a case-control study showed that COC use by healthy non-smokers increases the risk two-fold [WHO, 1996a].
  - In smokers (smoking at least 10 cigarettes a day), the risk of ischaemic stroke is further increased with COC use (OR 7.2, 95% CI 3.23 to 16.1).
  - Women with hypertension who use COCs have a three-fold increased risk of ischaemic stroke (compared with users without hypertension).
- **Haemorrhagic stroke:** current COC users under the age of 35 years who do not smoke and do not have hypertension have no increased risk [FFPRHC Clinical Effectiveness Unit, 2003a].
  - Women with hypertension who use COCs however, may have a ten-fold increased risk of haemorrhagic stroke (compared with non-users without hypertension) [WHO, 1996b].
  - The risk of haemorrhagic stroke in smokers who are current users of COCs is three times more than in non-smokers.
- **Mortality** from haemorrhagic and ischaemic stroke is not increased with COC use [Vessey et al, 2003].

[WHO, 1998; Hannaford, 2000]

Breast cancer

- Women with and without a family history of breast cancer may be advised that any increased risk of breast cancer with COC use is likely to be small (**B**). Most breast cancers are not due to genetic mutations.
- One in nine women will develop breast cancer at some time in their lives. The estimated risk of developing breast cancer up to age 30 years is 1 in 1900, up to age 40 years is 1 in 200, and up to age 50 years is 1 in 50. For more information, see www.cancerscreening.nhs.uk.
- Any slight increased risk of breast cancer in COC users decreases throughout the 10 years after cessation of use [Collaborative Group on Hormonal Factors in Breast Cancer, 1996].

Table 3: Clinical conditions where COCs are considered either unacceptable, or where the risks usually outweigh the advantages for use in contraception. Note: combined contraceptive patches have been assigned the same category ratings as COCs.

Condition	Category	Comment
<6 weeks postpartum	4	There is some theoretical concern that the neonate may be at risk because of exposure to steroi hormones during the first 6 weeks postpartum. There is also some theoretical concern regardin the association between COC use up to 3 weeks postpartum and risk of thrombosis in the mother.
>=6 weeks to <6 months postpartum (primarily breastfeeding)	3	In the first 6 months postpartum, use of COCs during breastfeeding diminishes the quantity of breast milk, decreases the duration of lactation, and may thereby adversely affect the growth of the infant.
Postpartum <21 days	3	Blood coagulation and fibrinolysis are essentially normalized by 3 weeks postpartum.
Aged >=35 years and smoking <15 cigarettes a day	3	COC users who smoked were at increased risk of cardiovascular diseases, especially myocardia infarction (MI), compared with those who did not smoke. Studies have also showed an increase risk of MI with increasing number of cigarettes smoked per day.
Aged >=35 years and smoking >15 cigarettes a day	4	
Cardiovascular disease — multiple risk factors for arterial cardiovascular disease	3/4	If a woman has multiple major risk factors, any of which alone would substantially increase the risk of cardiovascular disease, use of COCs may increase her risk to an unacceptable level. However, simple addition of categories for multiple risk factors is not intended; e.g. a combination of two risk factors assigned a category 2 may not necessarily warrant a higher category.
History of hypertension, where blood pressure (BP) *cannot* be evaluated (including hypertension during pregnancy)	3	Hypertension — classifications assume that no other risk factors for cardiovascular disease exis Risk of cardiovascular disease may increase substantially when multiple risk factors exist. Evaluation of BP level and cause is recommended, as soon as feasible. Women who did not hav a BP check before COC use have been found to have an increased risk of acute MI and stroke.
Adequately controlled hypertension, where BP *can* be evaluated	3	Women adequately treated for hypertension are at reduced risk of acute myocardial infarction (MI) and stroke as compared with untreated women. Although there are no data, COC users with adequately controlled and monitored hypertension should be at reduced risk of acute MI and stroke compared with untreated hypertensive COC users.
Elevated blood pressure levels (properly taken measurements) *systolic 140–159 or diastolic 90–99*	3	Among women with hypertension, COC users are at increased risk of stroke and MI compared with non-users. The risk increases with incremental rises in BP. A single BP reading of 140–159, 90–99 is not sufficient to classify a woman as hypertensive.
Systolic >=160 or diastolic >=100	4	—
Vascular disease	4	Increased risk of arterial thrombosis associated with COC use should be avoided in women wit underlying vascular disease.
Venous thromboembolism (VTE) — current or past history Major surgery with prolonged immobilization	4	The increased risk of VTE associated with COCs should have little impact on healthy women, but may have substantial impact on women with a history of thromboembolism.
Known thrombogenic mutations (e.g. Factor V Leiden; Prothrombin mutation; Protein S, Protein C and Antithrombin deficiencies)	4	Routine screening is not appropriate because of the rarity of the conditions and the high cost of screening. Among women with thrombogenic mutations, COC users have been found to have a two to twenty-fold higher risk of thrombosis than non-users.
Current ischaemic heart disease	4	Among women with underlying vascular disease, the increased risk associated with COC use should be avoided.
Stroke	4	Among women with underlying vascular disease, the increased risk associated with COC use should be avoided.
Known hyperlipidaemias	3/2	Routine screening is not appropriate because of the rarity of the conditions and the high cost of screening. While some types are risk factors for vascular disease, the category should be assesse according to the type, its severity and the presence of other cardiovascular risk factors.
Complicated valvular heart disease	4	Among women with valvular heart disease, COC use may further increase the risk of arterial thrombosis; women with complicated valvular heart disease are at greatest risk
Migraine with focal neurological symptoms at any age	4	Classification depends on accurate diagnosis of those severe headaches that are migrainous and those that are not. Any new headaches or marked changes in headaches should be evaluated. Classification is for women without any other risk factors for stroke. Risk of stroke increases with age, hypertension, and smoking.
Migraine without focal neurological symptoms <35 where continuous use	3	
Migraine without focal symptoms in women >=35 years, firstly in initiation and secondly with continuation	3 4	
Current breast disease	4	Breast cancer is a hormonally sensitive tumour, and the prognosis of women with current or recent breast cancer may worsen with COC use.
Past history of breast cancer and no evidence of recurrence for 5 years	3	
Nephropathy/retinopathy/ neuropathy	3/4	The category should be assessed according to the severity of the condition.

ondition	Category	Comment
ther vascular disease or diabetes >20 years' duration	3/4	The category should be assessed according to the severity of the condition.
allbladder disease — mptomatic medically treated or urrent	3	COCs may cause a small increased risk of gall-bladder disease. There is also concern that COCs may worsen existing gall-bladder disease.
istory of cholestasis — past OC-related	3	History of COC-related cholestasis predicts an increased risk with subsequent COC use.
iral hepatitis — active	4	COCs are metabolized by the liver, and their use may adversely affect women whose liver function is already compromised.
irrhosis — mild compensated	3	COCs are metabolized by the liver, and their use may adversely affect women whose liver function is already compromised.
irrhosis — severe decompensated	4	
iver tumours — benign and alignant	4	COCs are metabolized by the liver, and their use may adversely affect women whose liver function is compromised. In addition, COC use may enhance the growth of tumours.
iver enzyme-inducing drugs	3	Although the interaction between commonly used liver enzyme-inducers and COCs is not harmful to women, it is likely to reduce the efficacy of COCs. Use of other contraceptives (e.g. progestogen-only injection) should be encouraged for women who are long-term users of any of these drugs. Whether increasing the hormone dose of COCs is of benefit remains unclear.

ategory 4 — a condition that represents an unacceptable health risk if a COC is used.
ategory 3 — a condition where the theoretical or proven risks usually outweigh the advantages of using a COC.

After 10 years since last use, the incidence of breast cancer is the same as in women who have never used COCs.

Mortality from breast cancer was not increased with any duration of COC use [Vessey et al, 2003].

ervical cancer

Advise women that use of oral contraceptives for less than 5 years does not increase the risk of cervical cancer, but the risk increases with more than 5 years' use (**B**).

The crude rate of cervical cancer per 100,000 women in the UK is 11. For more information, see www.statistics.gov.uk [Office for National Statistics, 1997].

A recent systematic review compared the risk of cervical cancer or neoplasia over time in users of oral contraceptives compared with non-users [Smith et al, 2003]. Oral contraceptive use for:

- Less than 5 years increased the risk by 10% (RR 1.1, 95% CI 1.1 to 1.2).
- 10 years or more doubled the risk (RR 2.2, 95% CI 1.9 to 2.4).

After taking into account confounding factors such as human papilloma virus infection, sexual partners, barrier contraception, and cervical screening, results still did not differ.

Cervical screening — women should be encouraged to participate in the NHS programme to reduce their risk of cervical cancer.

iver cancer

An increased risk of primary liver cancer has been associated with long-term use of COCs containing 50 micrograms of oestrogen [IARC, 1999]. Preparations containing less than 50 micrograms of oestrogen do not seem to be associated with an increased risk of serious illness [Hannaford and Kay, 1998].

Primary liver cancer is rare in developed countries, and although COC use increases the risk depending on duration of use, the absolute risk is very small [Tuckey, 2000; FFPRHC Clinical Effectiveness Unit, 2003a].

Mortality

Mortality related to the use of COCs can be reduced but not eliminated by careful selection and follow-up of women for treatment (paying particular attention to establishing if there are any pre-existing risks for cardiovascular disease, hepatic system disease, or migraine with focal neurological symptoms). The estimated excess annual risk of death [WHO, 1998] for women taking COC with no risk factors is age-dependent:

- 20–24 years of age it is 2 per million users.
- 30–34 years of age it is 2–5 per million users.
- 40–44 years of age it is 20–25 per million users.
- Ten or more years after stopping the COC, mortality in past users is similar to that in women who have never used COCs [Beral et al, 1999].

Amenorrhoea

- Amenorrhoea lasting more than 6 months after use of the COC pill has been stopped should be regarded as coincidental rather than resulting from the use of the pill, and should be investigated. For more information, see PRODIGY guidance on *Amenorrhoea*.

Screening before starting a combined oral contraceptive

- **Women with a blood pressure** (**BP**) consistently over 140 mmHg systolic or 90 mmHg diastolic should be advised against use of COCs (**C**).
  - Hypertension is a risk factor for cardiovascular disease, and in users of COCs is associated with further increased risk of MI and ischaemic or haemorrhagic stroke.
- **A thrombophilia screen** is not recommended routinely before prescribing a COC (**C**).
  - **If a woman has a family history of VTE** in a first-degree relative under the age of 45 years, has considered other contraceptive methods, and still wishes to use a COC, a thrombophilia screen should be performed (**C**).
  - Note: a past or current history of deep vein thrombosis (DVT) or pulmonary embolus (PE) contraindicates the use of COCs [WHO, 2004].
  - **Factor V Leiden mutation** is the most common genetic risk factor for DVT and is present in 5% of the Caucasian population. Although the presence of the mutation increases the risk of developing DVT and PE, most women will not experience either.
- **Ideally, the risk of sexually transmitted infection** (**STI**) **should be assessed,** and opportunistic Chlamydia testing offered when appropriate; but this is not essential for safe use (**C**).
  - Consider testing for STI (particularly for *Chlamydia trachomatis*) in women with a high-risk of acquiring an STI:
    - Sexually active women under the age of 25 years.
    - Women over 25 years with a new partner, or who have had two or more partners in the previous 12 months.
  - If results are positive — follow up appropriately.

- See PRODIGY guidance on *Chlamydia — genital* for more information.

[FFPRHC Clinical Effectiveness Unit, 2003a]

Starting the combined oral contraceptive pill

- **Advise women that they may use a COC from menarche to the menopause** unless there are medical or other contraindications (C).
- **Initially a COC should be started on day 1 of the menstrual cycle,** but women may be advised that a COC can be started up to and including day 5 of the cycle without the need for additional contraception (C).
- **If started outside this time period,** exclude pregnancy and advise additional contraception for 7 days.
- **Advise women that a COC can be started at any other time in the cycle if there has been no risk of pregnancy,** but additional contraception is required for the first 7 days (C).
- **Advise women that COCs should be taken within 12 hours of the same time every day for 21 consecutive days** (C).
- Advise women that contraceptive cover is still provided during the seven hormone-free days, provided that the previous packet of pills has been taken correctly and the new packet is started on time (B).
- In the absence of special problems, women can be given up to 12 months' supply of a COC at the first visit, and encouraged to return at any time if problems arise (C).
- Appropriate written information should be provided to all women prescribed COC (B).

[FFPRHC Clinical Effectiveness Unit, 2003a]

Starting the combined oral contraceptive pill in special circumstances

- **After childbirth,** women who are not breastfeeding should be advised to start a COC 21 days postpartum (C).
  - Contraception is not needed in the first 3 weeks, and there is an increased risk of VTE.
  - If started later than 3 weeks post-partum, additional contraception is required for 7 days [BNF 47, 2004].
- **After termination of pregnancy,** advise women that, ideally, a COC should be started on the day of the termination [RCOG, 2002a] but can be started within 7 days to provide immediate contraceptive protection (C).
- **Changing from a different COC pill or progestogen-only pill:**
  - When changing from a higher-dose to a lower-dose preparation, or from a COC pill to a progestogen-only pill or vice versa, the current packet should be finished and the new brand started the next day, avoiding any pill-free interval [Belfield, 1999].
  - For Every Day (ED) preparations, the new brand should be started the next day after the last active tablet in the current packet. The inactive tablets should be omitted [BNF 47, 2004].

[FFPRHC Clinical Effectiveness Unit, 2003a]

First choice of pill

- **A monophasic COC** containing 30–35 micrograms of ethinylestradiol with a low dose of either norethisterone or levonorgestrel is a suitable first-line option (C).
- The choice of which product to prescribe as a first pill is not well supported by good comparative data [FFPRHC Clinical Effectiveness Unit, 2003a].
- **Careful consideration should be made of safety, freedom from adverse effects, and cost.** Potential drug interactions should also be considered [FFPRHC Clinical Effectiveness Unit, 2003a].
- **VTE risk** — preparations containing desogestrel and gestodene may be less preferred as first-line options, as they are associated with a slightly increased risk of VTE compared with those containing levonorgestrel and norethisterone. There is no evidence that COCs with higher doses of norethisterone and levonorgestrel offer any advantages over other preparations.
- **Formulations containing 20 micrograms of oestrogen** offer limited advantages over preparations containing 30–35 micrograms of oestrogen, and some women may experience breakthrough bleeding more frequently.
- **Generally, monophasic preparations containing levonorgestrel and norethisterone are less expensive** tha biphasic or triphasic preparations [BNF 47, 2004].
- **A Cochrane review found a lack of evidence supporting biphasic and triphasic COCs,** and suggested that the choice of progestogen may be more important than the phasic regimen [Van Vliet et al, 2003].

Second choice/alternative pill

- **The effectiveness of COCs depends upon their correct and consistent use.** There are no robust data to guide practice regarding which formulations to prescribe for women experiencing either poor cycle control or other adverse effects with their current COC. The following can be tried empirically:
  - Changing to a pill with either a higher or lower dose of the same progestogen.
  - Changing to a pill with a different second-generation progestogen and starting with the lowest available dose.
  - Changing to a pill with a third-generation progestogen (either gestodene or desogestrel).
- **Note: different brands of COC pill may contain identical doses and types of progestogen.**
- **A Cochrane review** compared the efficacy, adverse effects, cycle control, and continuity rates of monophasic and biphasic COCs. The data showed that biphasic preparations offer no advantage over monophasic preparations [Van Vliet et al, 2001].
- **A more recent Cochrane review** compared the clinical characteristics of biphasic and triphasic COCs. There were limited trial data available, and what evidence there was suggested that the choice of progestogen may be more important than the phasic regimen [Van Vliet et al, 2003].

Yasmin®

- Yasmin® (ethinylestradiol 30 micrograms/drospirenone 3 mg) is the most recent COC to be licensed in the UK. Drospirenone combines anti-androgenic properties, and unlike other progestogens it also has mild anti-mineralocorticoid activity — giving it a pharmacological profile similar to progesterone.
- Randomised controlled trial (RCT) data over 1- and 2-year periods [DTB, 2002b] comparing clinical characteristics of Yasmin® with Marvelon® (desogestrel/ethinylestradiol) found:
  - Acne and seborrhoea — similar improvement.
  - Discontinuation rates — similar.
  - Intermenstrual bleeding occurrence — no significant difference.
  - Premenstrual symptoms — similar reporting.
  - Weight loss — slightly more with Yasmin®, but interpretation of this is limited, as there was no treatment-blinding.
- **Acne** — a recent randomized controlled trial has suggested that Yasmin® is as effective as Dianette® (cyproterone acetate 2 mg/ethinylestradiol 35 micrograms) in women with mild-to-moderate facial acne. More data are needed to establish whether this effect is different from that of other COCs [DTB, 2002b].

Venous thromboembolism (VTE) — there have been reports of VTE among women taking Yasmin® [van Grootheest and Vrieling, 2003]. At present there are insufficient data to assess the risk of VTE with Yasmin® use compared with second- and third-generation COCs.

Missed pills

A COC pill is regarded as missed if it is taken more than 12 hours late. Ideally, COCs should be taken at approximately the same time each day.
If the pill is remembered within the 12 hours, contraceptive protection is maintained.
If the pill is taken more than 12 hours late, contraceptive protection is lost — the missed pill should be taken as soon as it is remembered and subsequent pills taken at the usual time.
Current UK recommendations regarding the necessary action required in different circumstances of missed pills are summarized in Table 4.
[FFPRHC Clinical Effectiveness Unit, 2003a; FFPRHC Clinical Effectiveness Unit, 2003b]

Diarrhoea and vomiting

Vomiting within 2 hours of taking the COC pill, or very severe diarrhoea, can affect absorption of the pill.
The general advice for women using oral contraceptives who have vomiting or severe diarrhoea for more than 24 hours is to follow the instructions for missed pills. For more information, see the section on *Missed pills*.
Advise women to return for a pregnancy test if there is a very light or no withdrawal bleed after missed or late pills, vomiting or severe diarrhoea, or use of any new drug (C).
[WHO, 2002; FFPRHC Clinical Effectiveness Unit, 2003a]

Key drug interactions

- Women using liver enzyme-inducing drugs should be counselled regarding the risks of reduced efficacy of the COC (C).
- **Rifamycins (i.e. rifampicin and rifabutin)** can *profoundly* induce liver enzymes, and concurrent use may severely compromise the efficacy of oral contraception.
- **Antiepileptic liver enzyme-inducers include:** carbamazepine, oxcarbazepine, phenobarbital, phenytoin, primidone, and topiramate. These drugs will reduce the plasma concentrations of both oestrogen and progestogen sufficiently to risk pregnancy [MeReC, 1995; Feely, 1999]. For more information, see section on *Women with epilepsy*.
- **Other liver enzyme-inducing drugs include:** griseofulvin, modafinil, nelfinavir, nevirapine, ritonavir and St John's wort. Advice on the possibility of interaction with newer antiretroviral drugs should be sought from HIV specialists.
- **St John's wort** (*Hypericum perforatum*) is an unlicensed herbal remedy for depression that can induce liver enzymes including cytochrome P450, and should be avoided by women taking oral contraceptives. It is available without prescription, and therefore women should always be asked about self-medication [CSM, 2000] or complementary therapies.

Table 4: Recommendations on the use of emergency contraception (EC) after missed pills.

Circumstances in which pill is missed	Instruction for COC use	Indications for EC
One active pill missed (days 1–21)	Take missed pill as soon as possible and the next pill at the usual time. Continue taking the pill as usual. No additional contraception required.	No EC required as long as the pills from days 15–21 in the previous pack were taken correctly.
Starting a pill pack two or more days late	Start the new pack that day and continue to take pills as usual. Abstain from sex or use additional barrier contraception for the next 7 days.	EC is indicated if the woman has had unprotected sex either in the pill-free week or in the first 7 days of the pack.
Missed any two or more of the seven active pills (days 1–7)	Take the missed pill as soon as possible and the next pill at the usual time. Continue taking pills as usual. Abstain from sex or use additional barrier contraception for the next 7 days.	EC is indicated if the woman has had unprotected sex either in the pill-free week or in the first 7 days of the pack.
Missed three or fewer of the seven active pills (days 8–14)	Take the missed pill as soon as possible and take the next pill at the usual time. Continue taking the pill as usual. Additional barrier contraception not required.	No EC is required as long as the pills from days 15–21 in the previous pack were taken correctly.
Missed three or fewer of the seven active pills (days 15–21)	Taking the missed pill as soon as possible and take the next pill at the usual time. Continue taking the pill as usual, and after finishing the current packet go straight on to the new packet. (Note: if pack has 7 inactive pills, discard these.) Additional barrier contraception not required. Women who are 'tricycling' and require emergency contraception in the 7 days before the pill-free interval may be advised to continue the COC to the end of the pack, start the next pack without a pill-free interval, and delay the pill-free interval until that pack is completed.	No EC required as long as the next pack is started without a pill-free interval (and as long as the pills from days 15–21 in the previous pack were taken correctly).
Missed four or more pills in a row in any week (days 1–21)	Take the missed pill as soon as possible and the next pill at the usual time. Continue taking the pills as usual and go straight onto the next packet. Abstain from sex or use additional barrier contraception for 7 days.	EC indicated if unprotected sex has occurred in the 7 days since missing the third pill.
Missed one or more inactive pills in everyday packaging	Discard the missed inactive pills. Continue taking pill as usual. Start a new packet as usual. Additional contraceptive cover not required.	EC is not required.

C

- **Women using liver enzyme-inducers who, having considered other methods, still choose to use COCs** should be prescribed a regimen containing 50 micrograms of ethinylestradiol (EE) (C). Note: there remains an enhanced risk of pregnancy in this scenario.
  - Options include using either Norinyl-1 (containing mestranol 50 micrograms, a prodrug of EE) or two low-dose COCs providing a total daily dose of 50–60 micrograms EE.
  - Women should be warned that the efficacy of the COC is reduced, and additional barrier contraception should be advised until 4 weeks after cessation of the liver enzyme-inducer.
- **If breakthrough bleeding occurs with 50 micrograms of oestrogen,** the dose should be increased to 80 or 100 micrograms and tricycling of the COC should be considered, although data are limited here. Tricycling means taking three packs of the high-dose COC without a break, followed by a reduced pill-free interval of 4 days after the final pack [BNF 47, 2004]. Note: taking COCs in this way represents off-licence use.
- **Women using a COC who require a short course (7 days or less) of a rifamycin (for meningococcal prophylaxis)** should be advised to continue taking the COC and omit any pill-free interval that would have occurred whilst taking the rifamycin or during the 7 days after the last dose of it. Further contraceptive precautions are required whilst taking the rifamycin and for 4 weeks after the last dose (C).
- **Women who require long-term use of a rifamycin** should be advised to use an alternative non-hormonal contraceptive method where possible (e.g. a copper intra-uterine device).
- **Women who have been taking non-enzyme-inducing antibiotics** do not require additional contraceptive protection when starting the COC (C).
- **Women using short courses (less than 3 weeks) of non-enzyme-inducing, broad-spectrum antibiotics** should be advised to use additional contraception during the course and for 7 days afterwards (C). Miss out the pill-free interval if the 7 days runs beyond the end of the packet, and the inactive tablets in the case of an Every Day preparation [BNF 47, 2004].
- Erythromycin, co-trimoxazole, and sulphonamides are not thought to interact with COCs.
- **Long-term antibiotics** are less likely to affect hormone levels, as resistant gut flora rapidly emerge [Weaver and Glasier, 1999].

[FFPRHC Clinical Effectiveness Unit, 2003a]

Breakthrough bleeding

- **Advise women that breakthrough bleeding** can occur with COC use, especially in the first few months, but, in the absence of missed or late pills, vomiting or drug interactions, has not been shown to be a measure of reduced efficacy (B).
- Whilst a woman is taking the COC pill, spotting or bleeding at times other than the expected withdrawal bleed is a common problem [The Consensus Committee of the Society of Obstetricians and Gynaecologists of Canada, 1998]. A change of pill is recommended if breakthrough bleeding persists for more than 3 months.
- There are limited data to suggest that breakthrough bleeding may be more common with use of preparations containing ethinylestradiol 20 micrograms than with 30 micrograms.
- **Consider** the possibility of infection (especially with *Chlamydia trachomatis*), missed pills, interacting drugs, cervical neoplasia, pregnancy, and severe diarrhoea and vomiting.

Surgery

- For a woman using a COC who is due to have a major elective operation or leg surgery, management needs to balance the increased risk of VTE (if the COC is continued), the possibility of an unwanted pregnancy (if the pill were stopped without adequate alternative contraception), and the preferences of the woman herself.
- **One strategy for women for whom major *elective* surgery is planned is to:**
  - Continue the COC and administer thromboprophylaxis (subcutaneous low-molecular-weight heparin and graduated elastic compression stockings) in the peri-operative period [DTB, 2000].
- **An alternative strategy is to:**
  - Discontinue the COC 4 weeks before elective major surgery and all surgery to the legs.
  - Restart the COC on the first day of the period that occurs at least 2 weeks after mobilization.
  - Discuss effective alternative contraceptive arrangements and provide as appropriate.
  - Use a depot injection of a progestogen-only contraceptive, and restart the COC before the next injection is due.
- **Women on the COC undergoing *emergency* surgery should be given thromboprophylaxis** (subcutaneous low-molecular-weight heparin and graduated elastic compression stockings).

[DTB, 1999; Guillebaud, 1999; Weisberg, 2002; BNF 47, 2004]

Progestogen-only pills

General information

- **Progestogen-only pills (POPs) contain low doses of the following progestogens** — norethisterone, etynodiol diacetate (converts to norethisterone), levonorgestrel, or desogestrel.
- **A POP may be a suitable alternative for women who:**
  - Want hormonal contraception but who cannot or do not wish to take oestrogen.
  - Have risk factors for cardiovascular complications with COCs, or women who are breastfeeding or suffer from migraine with aura.
- However, there remain few data on the cardiovascular effects of progestogen-only pills [DTB, 2000].

Mode of action

- **Ovulation is inhibited is prevented** in about 60% of cycles [McCann and Potter, 1994]. However, a randomized double-blind trial has shown that the desogestrel-only pill (Cerazette®) inhibited ovulation in 97% of cycles [Rice et al, 1999].
- **Ovum transport is delayed.**
- **Cervical mucus is thickened,** preventing sperm penetration.
- **Uterine receptivity is reduced** by endometrial changes.

[DTB, 2003b]

Efficacy

- **POPs are a very effective method of contraception** if taken consistently and correctly, with perfect-use failure rates of less than 1% [Trussell et al, 1990].
- In typical use, the pregnancy rate in the first year of use is 5% [Trussell et al, 1990].
- **There is no good evidence that the efficacy of POPs is reduced in women weighing over 70 kg** [Vessey et al, 1990; Vessey and Painter, 2001].

Advantages

Reliable, reversible method of contraception without the oestrogen-dependent cardiovascular risks.
Convenient — not related to intercourse.
Can be used by women who are breastfeeding and many women with cautions or contraindications to oestrogen, including:
- Older women (35 years and over)
- Heavy smokers (15 or more cigarettes a day)
- Hypertension
- Valvular heart disease
- Diabetes mellitus
- Migraine with aura
- Major surgery, as well as surgery affecting the legs

[BNF 47, 2004]

Disadvantages

Menstrual irregularities, including amenorrhoea and breakthrough bleeding, may cause discontinuation of the pill. The POP leads to reversible long-term amenorrhoea in a minority of women, owing to complete suppression of ovulation.
Pills must be taken at the same time each day (at least, within 3 hours) for contraceptive cover to be maintained.
Functional ovarian cysts develop in some women. POP use is associated with roughly a 30% higher risk of developing spontaneously reversible ovarian retention cysts [Robinson and Kubba, 1997].
The risk of breast cancer may be increased in POP users. A re-evaluation of worldwide cohort and case-control studies showed a similar trend to that of COCs. The results were not statistically significant, possibly owing to small study sample sizes [Collaborative Group on Hormonal Factors in Breast Cancer, 1996].
- **The Committee on Safety of Medicines** has advised that the possible small increase in the risk of breast cancer should be weighed against the benefits.
- **The most important risk factor** seems to be the age at which the POP is stopped — the risk disappears gradually during the 10 years after stopping, and there is no excess risk by 10 years [Collaborative Group on Hormonal Factors in Breast Cancer, 1996].

Offers no protection against sexually transmitted infections.

Contraindications

Conditions where POPs are an unacceptable (category 4) health risk or where the risks usually outweigh the advantages (category 3) are detailed in Table 5.
Alternative contraceptive methods should be recommended and the potential risk of POPs should be explained to women with any of these conditions.
For a full list of the WHO medical eligibility criteria, see www.who.int/reproductive-health/publications/mec/5_pocs.pdf.
[WHO, 2004]

Starting the progestogen-only pill

Usually started on the first day of the period and then taken continuously.

Starting the progestogen-only pill in special circumstances

After childbirth, POPs can be started from day 21, and no additional contraception is required. Use before this increases the risk of breakthrough bleeding, and is unnecessary, as contraception is not required before day 21 post-partum.
- UK practice is to start POPs from day 21 post-partum.
- However, advice from the World Health Organization recommends waiting until 6 weeks post-partum, in which case alternative methods of contraception should be used from day 21 until 7 days after the POP is started [WHO, 2002; WHO, 2004].

- **After termination of pregnancy,** the POP can be taken immediately after any trimester abortion and is effective immediately.
- **Changing from a COC to a POP** — start the POP at the end of the packet of COC pills, omitting the pill-free interval. In the case of Every Day (ED) preparations, the POP should be commenced after the last active tablet, omitting the inactive tablets.

Missed pills

- **A POP is regarded as missed if it was taken more than 3 hours late, except for Cerazette®.**
- **If the pill is more than 3 hours late,** contraceptive protection will be reduced. The missed pill should be taken immediately, and subsequent pills taken at the usual time. Additional contraceptive precautions should be taken for 2 days [WHO, 2002; FFPRHC Clinical Effectiveness Unit, 2003a].
- **Emergency contraception** is recommended when one or more POPs have been missed or taken more than 3 hours late, and unprotected sex has occurred within 2 days after missed or late pills [FFPRHC Clinical Effectiveness Unit, 2003b]. The POP should be continued with additional barrier contraception until pills have been taken correctly on two consecutive days.

Diarrhoea and vomiting

- Vomiting within 2 hours of taking the POP, or very severe diarrhoea, can affect absorption of the pill.
- An additional contraceptive method should be used for any intercourse during the period of symptoms, and for 7 days after recovery.

Management of menstrual irregularities

- **Menstrual irregularities including irregular bleeding and amenorrhoea** are common but can resolve with time. A change to a different formulation of pill may be helpful.

Drug interactions

- **Rifamycins (i.e. rifampicin and rifabutin)** can *profoundly* induce liver enzymes, and concurrent use may severely compromise the efficacy of oral contraception.
- **Women using a POP who require a short course** (one **week or less) of a rifamycin** should be advised to continue taking the POP. Further contraceptive precautions are required whilst taking the rifamycin and for 4 weeks after the last dose.
- **Women who require long-term use of a rifamycin** should always be advised to use an alternative non-hormonal contraceptive method where possible (e.g. an intra-uterine device).
- **Anti-epileptics:** carbamazepine, oxcarbazepine, phenobarbital, phenytoin, primidone, and topiramate induce liver enzymes and will reduce the plasma concentrations of progestogen sufficiently to risk pregnancy [MeReC, 1995; Feely, 1999]. POPs are therefore not generally recommended for women taking any of these drugs.
- **Other liver enzyme-inducing drugs include** griseofulvin, modafinil, nelfinavir, nevirapine, and ritonavir. Advice on the possibility of interaction with newer antiretroviral drugs should be sought from HIV specialists.
- **St John's wort** (*Hypericum perforatum*) is an unlicensed herbal remedy for depression that can induce liver enzymes including cytochrome P450, and should be avoided by women taking oral contraceptives. It is

C

Table 5: Clinical conditions where POPs are considered by the WHO to be unacceptable, or where the risks usually outweigh the advantages for use in contraception.

Condition	Category	Comment
Breastfeeding <6 weeks postpartum	3	There is concern that the neonate may be at risk of exposure to steroid hormones during the first 6 weeks postpartum. However, in many of these settings, pregnancy morbidity and mortality risks are high, and access t services is limited. POPs may be one of the few types of methods widely available and accessible to breastfeedin women immediately postpartum.
Venous thromboembolism — current deep vein thrombosis or pulmonary embolism	3	Theoretically, POPs may increase the risk of thrombosis, although this increase is substantially less than with COCs.
Current ischaemic heart disease	3*	There is concern regarding the hypo-oestrogenic effect and reduced high-density lipoprotein (HDL) levels.
Stroke	3*	There is concern regarding reduced HDL levels. Some POPs may increase the risk of arterial thrombosis, although this increase is substantially less than with COCs.
Migraine headaches with focal neurological symptoms at any age	3*	Classification depends on accurate diagnosis of those severe headaches that are migrainous and those that are not. Any new headaches or marked changes in headaches should be evaluated. Classification is for women without any other risk factors for stroke. Risk of stroke increases with age, hypertension, and smoking.
Current breast cancer	4	Breast cancer is a hormonally sensitive tumour, and the prognosis of women with current or recent breast cance may worsen with POP use.
Past history of breast cancer and no evidence of recurrence for 5 years	3	
Viral hepatitis — active	3	There is concern about the hormonal load associated with POP use in active liver disease, but it is less than for COCs.
Cirrhosis — severe decompensated	3	There is concern about the hormonal load associated with POP use in active liver disease, but it is less than for COCs.
Liver tumours — benign and malignant	3	POPs are metabolized by the liver, and their use may adversely affect women whose liver function is compromised. In addition, POP use may enhance the growth of tumours. This concern is similar to, but less tha that with COCs.
Liver enzyme-inducing drugs	3	Commonly used liver enzyme-inducers are likely to reduce the efficacy of POPs. Use of other contraceptives should be encouraged for women who are using any of these drugs long-term. Whether increasing the hormone dose of POPs alleviates this concern remains unclear.

Category 4 — a condition that represents an unacceptable health risk if a POP is used.
Category 3 — a condition where the theoretical or proven risks usually outweigh the advantages of using a POP.
* For continuation of POP

available without prescription, and therefore women should always be asked about self-medication [CSM, 2000] or complementary therapies.

- **Broad-spectrum antibiotics do not affect the effectiveness of POPs.**

[BNF 47, 2004]

Cerazette®

- Cerazette® (desogestrel 75 micrograms) contains a selective progestogen that is metabolized to the active metabolite etonogestrel.
- A double-blind randomized controlled trial (RCT), primarily designed to assess vaginal bleeding patterns after taking desogestrel 75 micrograms or levonorgestrel 30 micrograms over 13 cycles [Collaborative Study Group on the Desogestrel-containing Progestogen-only Pill, 1998], also reported as follows:
  - Desogestrel — overall pregnancy rate 0.41 per 100 woman-years (95% CI 0.085 to 1.200).
  - Levonorgestrel — overall pregnancy rate 1.55 per 100 woman-years (95% CI 0.422 to 3.963).
  - The confidence intervals overlapped because the trial was too small to detect differences in pregnancy rates.
- **Bleeding** was initially less common in desogestrel-users, and by 11 months amenorrhoea or infrequent bleeding occurred in 50% of desogestrel users, compared with 10% of levonorgestrel users.
- **Effect on ovulation** — in a double-blind RCT over 13 cycles, ovulation was judged to have occurred in 1 out c 59 studied cycles with desogestrel compared with 16 ou of 57 cycles with levonorgestrel. However, it is not clea whether there is any improved contraceptive effect over existing POPs, and for ovulation there is no available published comparison with a COC [Rice et al, 1999].
- There is no evidence to indicate how desogestrel compares with other POPs (norethisterone and etynodiol) or with COCs.
- **Missed doses** — the missed-Pill window for Cerazette® is four times longer than the standard three-hour window for conventional POPs.
  - Contraceptive protection may be reduced if more tha 36 hours have elapsed between two tablets.
  - **If the user is less than 12 hours late in taking any tablet,** the missed tablet should be taken as soon as it remembered and the next tablet should be taken at th usual time.
  - **If the user is more than 12 hours late,** she should use an additional method of contraception for the next 7 days.
  - If tablets were missed in the first week and intercours took place in the week before the tablets were missed, the possibility of a pregnancy should be considered.
  - If vomiting occurs within 3-4 hours after tablet-takin the same advice is applicable as for a missed tablet.

Adverse effects were no different from those with the levonorgestrel-only pill due to the low affinity of desogestrel for androgen receptors, despite relatively greater concentrations being used. No extra barrier method is required.
[DTB, 2003b; FFPRHC Clinical Effectiveness Unit, 2003c]

Progestogen-only contraceptive injection

General information

There are two injectable methods of contraception currently available in the UK:

- **Medroxyprogesterone acetate** (Depo-Provera), a long-acting progestogen given by intramuscular injection, which provides contraception for 12 weeks.
- **Norethisterone enantate** (Noristerat), a long-acting progestogen given by intramuscular injection, which provides contraception for 8 weeks.

Medroxyprogesterone acetate (DMPA) is licensed as a first line contraceptive, and for long-term use, in women who have been counselled concerning the likelihood of menstrual disturbance and the potential for a delay in return to full fertility.

Norethisterone enantate is licensed for short-term use (two injections only) for women whose partners have undergone vasectomy and are waiting for this to be effective, and for women who have just been immunized against rubella.

Mode of action

Prevention of ovulation.

Cervical mucus is thickened, preventing sperm penetration.

Uterine receptivity is reduced by endometrial changes.

Efficacy

Highly effective method of contraception, with failure rates of around 0.3%. It is therefore similar to combined oral preparations when comparing 'method' failure rates [Trussell et al, 1990].

Advantages

Very effective, reversible method of contraception.

Convenient — not related to intercourse. Each injection lasts 8 or 12 weeks, depending on the type used.

Can be used by women who are breastfeeding.

Protect against ectopic pregnancy and functional ovarian cysts, as the injection reliably inhibits ovulation.

DMPA may be used as a short-term or long-term contraceptive for women who have been counselled about the likelihood of menstrual disturbance and the potential for a delay in return to full fertility.
[BNF 47, 2004]

Disadvantages

Administration issues — to avoid risking failure, the injection must be given as a deep intramuscular injection and administered at the recommended intervals, and the appropriate technique must be adopted to avoid depositing the contents of the injection in tissues superficial to the muscles [ADRAC, 2003].

Once administered, it cannot be withdrawn.

For information on menstrual irregularities, see section on *Management of menstrual irregularities secondary to medroxyprogesterone acetate.*

Weight gain: more than 70% of women gain weight with DMPA, and the mean weight gain after one year is 2 kg [Bigrigg et al, 1999].

There may be delay in the return of fertility, and irregular cycles (may be more than 1 year with medroxyprogesterone acetate), but there is no evidence of permanent infertility. About 60% of women conceive within 12 months of discontinuing DMPA injections, and 85% within 24 months [DTB, 1996].

- **Reduction in bone mineral density** (BMD) has been reported in women who use DMPA but the risk of osteoporosis and fractures in later life remains unclear.
  - There is some evidence that BMD starts to recover when DMPA is discontinued; the extent of recovery is probably related to the duration of exposure.
    - One study has found that after 30 months women who discontinued DMPA had a bone density similar to that of non-users [Scholes et al, 2002].
  - The effect of BMD reduction may be more important in adolescents in whom the usual process of bone mineral accretion may be reversed.
  - **The Committee on Safety of Medicines (CSM) therefore advises** that:
    - In adolescents, DMPA may be used as first-line contraception but *only* after other methods have been discussed and considered to be unsuitable or unacceptable.
    - In women of all ages, careful re-evaluation of the risks and benefits of treatment should be carried out in women who wish to continue use for more than 2 years.
    - In women with significant lifestyle and/or medical risk factors for osteoporosis, other methods of contraception should be considered.
  - For all users of DMPA, a calcium-rich diet and regular weight-bearing exercise are recommended in order to reduce any increased risk of fracture, and no smoking is recommended.

[CSM, 2004]

- Offers no protection against sexually transmitted infections.
- **The risk of breast cancer** may be increased in progestogen-only contraceptive users. A re-evaluation of worldwide cohort and case-control studies showed a trend similar to that of COCs. The results were not statistically significant, possibly owing to small study sample sizes [Collaborative Group on Hormonal Factors in Breast Cancer, 1996].

Contraindications

- Conditions where progestogen-only contraceptive injections are an unacceptable (category 4) health risk or where the risks usually outweigh the advantages (category 3) are detailed in Table 6.
- Alternative contraceptive methods should be recommended and the potential risk of progestogen-only contraceptive injections should be explained to women with any of these conditions.
- For a full list of the WHO medical eligibility criteria, see www.who.int/reproductive-health/publications/mec/5_pocs.pdf.

[WHO, 2004]

When to start

- **Injectable contraceptives are usually administered within 5 days of onset of menstruation** and are effective immediately.
- **If given after day 5 of the cycle,** exclude the risk of pregnancy since the last period before giving the injection, and advise that an additional method of contraception should be used for 7 days [WHO, 2002].

Starting the progestogen-only contraceptive injection in special circumstances

- **After childbirth,** the first dose is best delayed until 6 weeks post-partum, as heavy bleeding has been reported when it was given to women in the immediate puerperium. However, if the woman is not

C

Table 6: Clinical conditions where progestogen-only contraceptive injections are considered unacceptable, or where the risks usually outweigh the advantages for use in contraception.

Condition	Category	Comment
Breastfeeding <6 weeks postpartum	3	There is concern that the neonate may be at risk of exposure to steroid hormones during the first 6 weeks postpartum. However, in many of these settings, pregnancy morbidity a mortality risks are high, and access to services is limited.
Multiple risk factors for arterial cardiovascular disease (e.g. older age, smoking, diabetes, hypertension)	3	When multiple major risk factors exist, risk of cardiovascular disease may increase substantially. The effects of progestogen-only contraceptive injections may persist for so time after discontinuation.
Hypertension with systolic >=160 or diastolic >=100 mmHg	3	Limited evidence suggests that, among women with hypertension, those who use progestogen-only contraceptive injections may have an increased risk of cardiovascular events compared with women who do not use these methods.
Vascular disease	3	There is concern about progestogen-only contraceptive injections with regard to the potential hypo-oestrogenic effect and decreasing HDL levels. The effect of progestogen-only contraceptive injections may persist for some time after discontinuation.
Venous thromboembolism — current deep vein thrombosis or pulmonary embolism	3	Theoretically, progestogen-only contraceptive injections may increase the risk of thrombosis, although this increase is substantially less than with COCs.
Current ischaemic heart disease	3*	There is concern regarding the hypo-oestrogenic effect and reduced high-density lipoprotein (HDL) levels, particularly among users of progestogen-only contraceptive injections. The effects of progestogen-only contraceptive injections may persist for some time after discontinuation.
Stroke	3*	There is concern regarding reduced HDL levels. The effects of progestogen-only contraceptive injections may persist for some time after discontinuation.
Migraine headaches with focal neurological symptoms at any age is an issue with continuation of progestogen-only contraceptive injections	3	Classification depends on accurate diagnosis of those severe headaches that are migraino and those that are not. Any new headaches or marked changes in headaches should be evaluated. Classification is for women without any other risk factors for stroke. Risk of stroke increases with age, hypertension, and smoking. There is concern that severe headaches may increase in frequency with use of progestoge only contraceptive injections, whose effects persist for some time after discontinuation.
Unexplained vaginal bleeding	3	Progestogen-only contraceptives may cause irregular bleeding patterns that may mask symptoms of underlying pathology. The effects of progestogen-only contraceptive injections may persist for some time after discontinuation.
Current breast cancer	4	Breast cancer is a hormonally sensitive tumour, and the prognosis of women with curren or recent breast cancer may worsen with POP use.
Past history of breast cancer and no evidence of recurrence for 5 years	3	
Nephropathy/retinopathy/neuropathy	3	There is concern about the possible negative effect of progestogen-only contraceptive injections on lipid metabolism, possibly affecting progression of nephropathy, retinopath or other vascular disease. There is concern regarding the potential hypo-oestrogenic effect and decreasing HDL levels. Theoretically, progestogen-only contraceptive injections may increase the risk of thrombosis although this increase is substantially less than with COCs. The effects of progestogen-only contraceptive injections may persist for some time after discontinuatio
Other vascular disease, or diabetes of >20 years duration	3	
Viral hepatitis — active	3	There is concern about the hormonal load associated with progestogen-only contracepti injection use in active liver disease, but it is less than for COCs.
Cirrhosis — severe decompensated	3	There is concern about the hormonal load associated with progestogen-only contracepti injection use in active liver disease, but it is less than for COCs.
Liver tumours — benign and malignant	3	Progestogen-only contraceptive injections are metabolized by the liver and their use may adversely affect women whose liver function is compromised. In addition, progestogen-only contraceptive injection use may enhance the growth of tumours. This concern is similar to, but less than, that with COCs.

Category 4 — a condition that represents an unacceptable health risk if a progestogen-only contraceptive injection is used
Category 3 — a condition where the theoretical or proven risks usually outweigh the advantages of using a progestogen-only injection
* For continuation of progestogen-only contraceptive injection

breastfeeding, the injection may be given within 5 days post-partum if she is informed of the risk of heavy and prolonged bleeding [ABPI Medicines Compendium, 2002b].

- **After a first or second trimester abortion or miscarriage,** injectable progestogens can be started immediately and are effective immediately.

Management of menstrual irregularities secondary to medroxyprogesterone acetate

- **Menstrual irregularities are common.** Women should be appropriately counselled, and other contraceptive methods should be considered if menstrual irregularities are found to be unacceptable.
- **Heavy or prolonged bleeding** is common in the first injection cycle.
- **Amenorrhoea** is reported by a significant proportion of users after 12 months. Irregular spotting and bleeding i less common, and only rarely (1–2% of women) does heavy prolonged bleeding occur [DTB, 1996; RCOG, 1998]. It may take 12 months (or occasionally longer) for fertility and normal periods to return after stopping the drug.
- **Gynaecological problems** should be excluded, treated, o referred to a specialist as necessary in women with persistent spotting or bleeding, or in women with bleeding after a period of amenorrhoea.

There is no long-term effective treatment for excessive or irregular bleeding with injectable contraceptives. The current recommendation is to give additional oestrogen treatment, usually in the form of a low-dose combined pill as a short-term measure [RCOG, 2002b]. Early administration of the next injection is not routinely recommended, as there is a lack of data regarding the effectiveness of this practice.
[WHO, 2002]

Drug interactions

Interactions between injectable progestogens and other medicinal products, including liver enzyme-inducing antiepileptic drugs, have been reported rarely [ABPI Medicines Compendium, 2002b], but to date there are no case reports of unintentional pregnancy.
Depot injections of medroxyprogesterone acetate may be used with liver enzyme-inducing antiepileptic drugs, but for long-term contraception should be given every 10 weeks [SIGN, 2003]. The Summary of Product Characteristics, however, recommends that injections should be repeated every 12 weeks for long-term contraception, and does not discuss this specific scenario [ABPI Medicines Compendium, 2002b]. The risk of interaction seems to be just a theoretical one, and may be related to the potency of the enzyme-inducer.

Subdermal progestogen-only contraceptive implant

General Information

The etonogestrel implant (Implanon) is a progestogen-only contraceptive subdermal implant. It is the only subdermal implantable contraceptive currently available in the UK, after the discontinuation of Norplant. Note: Norplant implants were licensed for 5 years, and 2004 should be the last year of their use [BNF 47, 2004].
The etonogestrel implant is a single matchstick-sized rod (40 mm by 2 mm) containing 68 mg of etonogestrel. Serum concentrations of etonogestrel high enough to inhibit ovulation are reached within 1 day of inserting the etonogestrel implant. Release of etonogestrel from the implant declines over time.
Insertion and removal should be undertaken only by trained professionals, who should also provide adequate counselling to women. The rod is inserted into the inner aspect of the upper arm, using a preloaded single-use applicator.
It is effective for 3 years. Regarding the duration of Implanon use in women with a bodyweight of 75 kg or more, the manufacturers state that clinicians may wish to consider earlier replacement of the implant [ABPI Medicines Compendium, 2003a]. However, there is no evidence to back up this statement.
The contraceptive effects reverse rapidly on removal of the implant, and there is a rapid return of the normal menstrual cycle.

Mode of action

Prevents ovulation.
Thickens cervical mucus, and therefore prevents sperm penetration.
Suppresses the endometrium, making implantation of the fertilized egg less likely.

Efficacy

Advise women that etonogestrel implants can be nearly 100% effective at preventing a pregnancy [Organon Laboratories Medical Information, Personal Communication, 2004].

- However, only limited trial data have been published in peer-reviewed journals on the efficacy of the etonogestrel implant, and there are no data on direct comparisons with other contraceptive methods currently available.
- Two non-comparative studies of 191 women who used the etonogestrel implant for 3 years found that no pregnancies occurred [DTB, 2001].

Advantages

- Very effective, long-lasting, reversible method of contraception.
- No action required at the time of intercourse.
- No daily action required.

Disadvantages

- **Irregular menstrual bleeding** may occur, especially in the first year of use. This is occasionally unacceptable to the woman, and may require implant removal [ADRAC, 2003]. After removal of the implant, menses return to the previous pattern within 3 months in 80% of women. The following patterns were reported for the etonogestrel implant [Edwards and Moore, 1999]:
  - Amenorrhoea in 30–40%.
  - Infrequent bleeding in 30%.
  - Prolonged bleeding in 10–20%.
  - Frequent bleeding in <10%
- **For the management of light or heavy bleeding,** it is currently recommended to give additional oestrogen treatment, usually in the form of a low-dose combined pill as a short-term measure [RCOG, 2002b].
- **Weight gain may occur.** Studies have shown that 20% of women will have an increase in body mass index of 10% or more. It is not known whether the weight increase observed with the etonogestrel implant is any different from that expected with other hormonal contraceptives [Edwards and Moore, 1999].
- **Reduction in bone mineral density** with levonorgestrel implants has been reported in short-term current users, but after discontinuation it was found to reverse [The Contraception Report, 2003]; data, however, are limited.
- **Other adverse effects include** acne, breast pain, and headache.
- Insertion and removal require a minor operation (under local anaesthesia), and local reactions such as bruising and itching may occur at the insertion site.
- Offers no protection against sexually transmitted infections.

Contraindications

- For a full list of the World Health Organization (WHO) medical eligibility criteria, see www.who.int/reproductive-health/publications/mec/5_pocs.pdf.

Time of insertion

- **The etonogestrel implant can be inserted during the first 5 days of the cycle,** and no additional contraception is required. If inserted after this, additional contraception is required for the first 7 days.

Starting the subdermal progestogen-only contraceptive implant in special circumstances

- **Changing from the combined oral contraceptive (COC) pill** — insert preferably on the day after the last (active) tablet of the COC; but at the latest on the day after the pill-free interval or last placebo tablet.
- **After a miscarriage or abortion in the first trimester,** the implant can be inserted immediately, and no additional contraception will be required.
- **After childbirth or second trimester abortion,** insert on day 21 to 28 after delivery or abortion. If inserted after

28 days, additional contraception is required for the first 7 days.
[DTB, 2001; ABPI Medicines Compendium, 2003a]

Drug interactions

- No specific interaction studies have been performed with the etonogestrel implant.
- **Progestogen implants may not be suitable** for women taking liver enzyme-inducing antiepileptic drugs (carbamazepine, oxcarbazepine, phenobarbital, phenytoin, primidone, and topiramate) (**D**), as they are potentially less effective when these drugs are used.
- **The effectiveness of the etonogestrel implant may be reduced by liver enzyme-inducing drugs.** On the basis of interactions reported with other hormonal contraceptives, it is therefore recommended that additional or alternative contraceptive methods be used by women concurrently taking liver enzyme-inducing drugs [BNF 47, 2004]. For more information, see the *Progestogen-only pill drug interactions* section.

[Glasier, 1999; Elliman, 2000; BNF 47, 2004; Organon Laboratories Medical Information, Personal Communication, 2004]

Transdermal combination contraceptive patch

General information

- The patch is three-layered, measuring around 20 cm^2 (4.5 cm by 4.5 cm).
- The patch contains 600 micrograms ethinylestradiol and 6 mg norelgestromin, and releases:
  - Ethinylestradiol: approximately 20 micrograms every 24 hours.
  - Norelgestromin: approximately 150 micrograms every 24 hours.
- Apply the patch to clean, dry, hair-free skin on the buttock, abdomen, upper outer arm, or upper torso. Avoid irritated or broken skin, breasts, or skin in contact with tight clothing or cosmetics. Changing the position of each new patch will help reduce skin irritation.
- **Patch disposal:** to minimize possible environmental water pollution, patches should be sealed with the disposal label provided, and discarded according to local requirements, or returned to a pharmacy after use.
- **Risk of venous thromboembolism:** the risk with transdermal patches is not yet known.
- **Other risks:** there is insufficient data to quantify the degree of risk associated with its use but the likelihood is that the patch has a comparable safety and pharmacokinetic profile to COCs.

[DTB, 2003a]

Mode of action

- **The contraceptive patch works by inhibition of ovulation** (follicle-stimulating hormone [FSH] and luteinising hormone [LH] release is suppressed).
- Cervical mucus is also thickened, preventing sperm penetration.
- Endometrial receptiveness is reduced.

[ABPI Medicines Compendium, 2003b]

Efficacy

- When used correctly, it can be over 99% effective.

[FFPRHC Clinical Effectiveness Unit, 2004b]

Advantages

- Very effective when used correctly.
- Once-weekly application.
- Easy to use.
- Does not interfere with sex.
- Hormone absorption is not affected by vomiting or diarrhoea.
- If the patch change is delayed by up to 48 hours in the middle of the cycle, there is no need for additional contraception.
- With a once-weekly application, there are fewer problems for error.

Disadvantages

- May cause local reactions (skin irritation) at the application site.
- Other unwanted effects are similar to those of COCs: s *Disadvantages*. Temporary adverse effects may be experienced in the first few months of first starting the patch, including:
  - Breast tenderness in particular
  - Headaches
  - Nausea
  - Mood changes
  - Weight gain or loss
- Withdrawal bleeding with the patch has been found to start, on average, a day later than with a COC; to last 5–6 days; and then to extend into the next cycle of patc use.
- It is not recommended for women weighing 90 kg or more [ABPI Medicines Compendium, 2003b]. It has been reported that of 15 pregnancies that occurred in 3319 patch users, five of these occurred in women over 90 kg [Zieman et al, 2001].
- Patches may become fully or partially detached — in o study, around 5% of patches needed to be replaced [Audet et al, 2001].
- The patch may be visible.
- Offers no protection (as with COCs) against sexually transmitted infections.
- Potential for some drug interactions.

[DTB, 2003a]

Contraindications

- Conditions where the contraceptive patch is either an unacceptable (category 4) health risk or where the risks usually outweigh the advantages (category 3) are detailed in Table 3.
- Alternative contraceptive methods should be recommended and the potential risk of the contracepti patch should be explained to women with any of these conditions.
- For a full list of the World Health Organization (WHO medical eligibility criteria, see www.who.int/reproductive-health/publications/mec/4_cics.pdf.

Starting the transdermal combination contraceptive patch

- A new patch is applied every week for 3 weeks. Ideally, the first patch is applied on the first day of the menstrua cycle (day 1); no additional contraception is needed if started on the first day of bleeding. Otherwise, a non-hormonal contraceptive method must be used concurrently for the first 7 days of the new cycle.
- After 7 days the patch is removed (at any time of the day), and immediately replaced with a new one. These change days will be days 8 and 15 of the cycle.
- The fourth week is patch-free, starting on day 22, durin which a period should occur.
- A new cycle starts after 7 patch-free days, whether bleeding has stopped or not even started.
- If it is decided to postpone a menstrual period for one cycle, a patch must be applied in what would have been the patch-free interval. After 6 consecutive weeks of

patch wear, there should be a patch-free interval of 7 days.

arting the transdermal contraceptive patch in special cumstances

Changing from the COC: the patch should be applied on the first day of withdrawal bleeding.

- If there is no withdrawal bleeding within 5 days of the last 'active' pill, pregnancy must be ruled out before starting the patch.
- If the patch is applied after the first day of withdrawal bleeding, a non-hormonal contraceptive must be used concurrently for 7 days.
- If more than 7 days have passed since taking the last active COC pill, then before starting the patch confirm whether sex has occurred in the extended pill-free period, and if so consider the possibility of pregnancy. Emergency contraception may be indicated.

After abortion or miscarriage:

- If either occurs before 20 weeks' gestation, the patch may be started immediately. No back-up contraceptive is needed if the patch is started immediately. Note: ovulation may occur within 10 days of an abortion or miscarriage.
- If either occurs at or after 20 weeks' gestation, the patch may be started either on day 21 post-abortion, or on the first day of the first spontaneous period, whichever comes first.

After delivery:

- Users who choose not to breastfeed should start contraceptive therapy with the patch no sooner than 4 weeks after childbirth [ABPI Medicines Compendium, 2003b].
- When starting later, women should be advised to use a barrier method as well for the first 7 days. If sex has already occurred, pregnancy should be excluded before starting the patch, or the woman must wait for her first menstrual period.

BPI Medicines Compendium, 2003b]

ompliance issues

There are limited data available to indicate whether compliance may be better with a contraceptive patch than with an oral contraceptive [Audet et al, 2001]. Diary records of contraceptive use were recorded in one large randomized controlled trial comparing use of the patch with a triphasic COC. Perfect compliance was calculated as being higher with the patch than with the COC (88% compared with 78%, $p < 0.001$). Study limitations included that the trial:

- Was not assessing compliance as a primary end-point.
- Was not blinded, and the data were based on self-reported information.
- Did not consider discontinuation rates, which were higher with the patch.

Women seem to be twice as likely to discontinue the patch because of unwanted effects as they are with a COC.

TB, 2003a]

hat to do if the patch either fully or partly etaches

In the first week of use, if the patch has been off for more than 24 hours then a new cycle of patches should be started immediately, and an additional non-hormonal contraceptive method is needed for the next 7 days. Emergency contraception should also be considered if appropriate.

In the second and third week, if the patch has been off for:

- Up to 48 hours — the woman should apply a new patch immediately and a new patch on the next scheduled change day. No additional contraceptive cover is required if the patch was worn correctly for the 7 days before the first non-compliant day.
- 48 hours or more — emergency contraception should be considered, as there may be no protection from pregnancy. The user should stop the current contraceptive cycle and start a new 4-week cycle immediately by putting on a new patch. Concurrent non-hormonal contraception should be used for the first 7 days of the new cycle.

[ABPI Medicines Compendium, 2003b]

Drug interactions

- These are likely to be the same as for the combined oral contraceptive. For more information, see the section *Key drug interactions.*
- **Liver enzyme-inducing drugs including St John's Wort** — a barrier contraceptive method should be used while on the enzyme-inducing drug, and for 28 days after stopping it. For women on long-term enzyme-inducing drugs, consider another method of contraception.
- **Antibiotics (except for tetracycline)** — women should also use a barrier method of contraception until 7 days after stopping antibiotic therapy. If these 7 days run into the patch-free week, start using the next patch immediately. If concomitant medical product administration runs beyond the 3 weeks of patch application, a new cycle should be started immediately without having the usual patch-free interval.

[ABPI Medicines Compendium, 2003b]

Copper intra-uterine devices

General information

- **Intra-uterine devices (IUDs) available in the UK are small polyethylene and copper devices.** Some also have a central silver core.
- **Clinicians who insert IUDs** are responsible for being appropriately trained and maintaining their clinical competence (C).
- **Clinicians involved in IUD insertions** should attend regular updates in dealing with likely emergencies (C). Different IUDs require different techniques.
- **Six framed IUDs** are available on prescription — each varies in size, shape, and surface area of copper.
- GyneFix is the only frameless IUD available. It consists of six copper sleeves on a surgical nylon thread that is anchored to the uterine fundus. Insertion or removal of the device (which is different from that of other IUDs) requires training and competence in the technique.
- A recent Cochrane review of framed and frameless devices was unable to identify whether frameless devices were less likely to cause pain in nulliparous women, because only parous women were included in the randomized trials reviewed [O'Brien and Marfleet, 2003].
- **Prophylactic antibiotics are not recommended for routine IUD insertion** (A). However, women with previous endocarditis, or with a prosthetic heart valve, require intravenous antibiotic prophylaxis to protect against bacterial endocarditis during IUD insertion or removal (C).
- **All devices have monofilament threads** to allow for checking that the device is still in place and for removal.
- **IUDs with the longest licensed duration of use** should be used to minimize the established risks associated with reinsertion (C).
- Modern copper IUDs, with a surface area of copper of greater than 300 mm^2, can be left *in situ* for 5 years. IUDs inserted after the age of 40 years can be left until at

C

least one year after the last menstrual period in the absence of any problems.
[FFPRHC Clinical Effectiveness Unit, 2004a]

Mode of action

- Women should be informed that the primary mode of action of an IUD is prevention of fertilization (B).
- Additionally, the copper ions alter the biochemical processes and enzymes involved in implantation.

[FFPRHC Clinical Effectiveness Unit, 2004a]

Efficacy

- Women should be advised of the low failure rate of IUDs, which is around 1% (C).
- IUDs with a surface area of at least 300 mm^2 copper should be used, as they have the lowest failure rates (A).

[FFPRHC Clinical Effectiveness Unit, 2004a]

Advantages

- Highly effective and reversible method of contraception.
- Effective immediately after fitting.
- No action required at the time of intercourse.
- No daily action required.
- There are no drugs that are known to affect IUD use and efficacy (C).

[FFPRHC Clinical Effectiveness Unit, 2004a]

Disadvantages or adverse effects

- Women should be informed that menstrual abnormalities (including spotting, light bleeding, and heavy or longer menstrual periods) are common in the first 3–6 months of IUD use (C).
- Women should be informed that unacceptable bleeding is one of the most common reasons for requesting IUD removal (B).
- Women should be informed that dysmenorrhoea is a common reason for requesting IUD removal (B).
- Women should be advised that a small increase in risk of pelvic infection occurs in the 20 days after IUD insertion, but the risk is the same as that for the non-IUD-using population thereafter (A).
- **IUD expulsion** — women should be advised that this is the most likely cause of IUD failure. The risk of this happening is around 1 in 20, and is most common in the first year of use, particularly within 3 months of insertion (B).
- **Uterine perforation** — women may be informed that this occurs in less than 1 in 1000 insertions (B).
  - A Cochrane review included a total experience of over 23,000 women-years. No perforations were reported in two trials that represented around 5,000 insertions [O'Brien and Marfleet, 2003].
- **Ectopic pregnancy** — women should be informed that the overall risk of ectopic pregnancy is reduced with IUD use when compared with using no contraception (B).
  - Alternative contraceptive methods that inhibit ovulation will, however, reduce the risk of ectopic pregnancy to a greater degree.

[FFPRHC Clinical Effectiveness Unit, 2004a]

Testing for sexually transmitted infection before IUD insertion

- **Sexually transmitted infection (STI) risk assessment** (history and examination) should be performed for all women considering an IUD (C).
- **Women assessed to have a higher risk of STI** should be offered testing for *Chlamydia trachomatis* (as a minimum) before IUD insertion (C). Higher risk groups include:
  - Sexually active women under the age of 25 years.
  - Women over 25 years with a new partner, or who have had two or more partners in the previous 12 months.
- **If results are positive,** follow up appropriately.
- Women assessed to have a higher risk of STI may also offered testing for *Neisseria gonorrhoeae* before IUD insertion, depending on its local prevalence.
- There is no indication to test for other lower-genital-tract organisms in asymptomatic women attending for IUD insertion.
- Ideally, for women assessed as being at a higher risk of STI, the results of tests should be available and appropriate treatment provided before IUD insertion.
- For women assessed as being at a higher risk of STI, if results are not available and IUD insertion cannot be delayed, the use of prophylactic antibiotics may be considered.

[FFPRHC Clinical Effectiveness Unit, 2004a]

Timing of insertion

- An IUD can be inserted at any time in the menstrual cycle if it is reasonably certain the woman is not pregnant (C). Pregnancy is unlikely if there are no sign as well as:
  - No intercourse having occurred since last normal menses.
  - There having been correct and consistent use of a reliable method of contraception.
  - Insertion having been within 7 days of the start of normal menses.
  - Insertion having been within 4 weeks postpartum (fo non-lactating women).
  - Insertion having been within the first 7 days post-abortion or miscarriage.
  - The woman being fully or nearly fully breastfeeding, amenorrhoeic, and less than 6 months postpartum.
  - The woman being within 5 days of the earliest expected date of ovulation.
- **After childbirth:** for women who are fully or nearly ful breastfeeding, amenorrhoeic, and less than 6 months postpartum (including Caesarian section), an IUD can fitted within 48 hours of birth. If later than this, it shou be inserted safely 4 or more weeks postpartum (C). Th risk of uterine perforation is increased if an IUD is inserted between 49 hours and up to 4 weeks postpartum.
- An IUD may be inserted safely immediately after a first or second-trimester termination of pregnancy (C). Expulsion rates may be higher after the latter.
- **Emergency contraception** — a copper-containing IUD may be inserted within 5 days (120 hours) of unprotected intercourse, or up to 5 days after the earlie likely day of ovulation. For more information, see PRODIGY guidance *Contraception — emergency*.

[FFPRHC Clinical Effectiveness Unit, 2004a]

Missing threads

- **Women should be offered instruction on how to check for the IUD and its threads,** and advised that if they are unable to feel them it may be that the device has been expelled.
- If threads are not present, women should be advised to use condoms until a clinician is able to determine that the IUD is intra-uterine. Progestogen-only emergency contraception may be indicated; for more information, see PRODIGY guidance *Contraception — emergency*.

[FFPRHC Clinical Effectiveness Unit, 2004a]

Pregnancy with an intra-uterine device in place

- **Investigate any suspected pregnancy immediately.**
- Most pregnancies occurring in women using an IUD will be intra-uterine, but ectopic pregnancy must be excluded (C). Urgently refer women with suspected ectopic pregnancy.
- Women who become pregnant whilst using an IUD should be informed of the increased risks of second-trimester miscarriage, preterm delivery, and infection, if the IUD is left *in situ* (B).
- Women who are pregnant with an IUD *in situ*, and who wish to continue with the pregnancy, should be informed that, when possible, IUD removal would reduce adverse outcomes. However, removal itself carries a small risk of miscarriage (C).
- If IUD threads are visible on speculum examination, or can easily be retrieved from the endocervical canal, the IUD should be removed by gently pulling on the threads. Traditionally, IUD removal is done in the first 12 weeks, if the threads are clearly visible and there is no resistance to removal.
- If threads cannot be easily retrieved, an ultrasound scan should be arranged to assess the location of the IUD.
- Whether or not the IUD is removed, a pregnant woman should be advised to seek medical care if she develops heavy bleeding, cramping pain, abnormal vaginal discharge, or fever (C).
- If there is no evidence that the IUD was expelled before pregnancy, it should be sought at delivery or termination of pregnancy and, if not identified, a plain abdominal X-ray should be arranged to determine if the IUD is extrauterine.

[FFPRHC Clinical Effectiveness Unit, 2004a]

Actinomyces-like organisms in cervical smears of IUD users

- *Actinomyces* are bacteria that may colonize the vagina and are a rare cause of pelvic inflammatory disease (PID). Identification of actinomyces-like organisms (ALOs) on cervical smear is more common in women with an IUD; however, detection of ALOs by smear or culture is not diagnostic or predictive of any disease.
- **In an asymptomatic woman with ALOs,** there is no evidence to support either the routine removal of an IUD or periodic ALO screening. A 2-year follow-up of asymptomatic women with untreated ALOs who retained their IUDs did not identify PID in any women. There is little evidence to support routine follow-up unless symptoms occur.
- **Asymptomatic IUD users** with (ALOs) detected on a cervical smear should be advised there is no reason to remove the IUD unless signs or symptoms of infection occur (B).
- **In a symptomatic woman,** limited evidence suggests that the IUD should be removed and appropriate treatment provided (usually a penicillin, tetracycline, or erythromycin for at least 2 weeks), as well as referral to a genito-urinary Medicine (GUM) clinic or a gynaecologist.

[FFPRHC Clinical Effectiveness Unit, 2004a]

Contraindications

- The World Health Organization (WHO) considers that the same eligibility criteria apply to the insertion of a copper-containing IUD in normal circumstances as for post-coital use.
- Conditions where copper-containing IUDs are an unacceptable (category 4) health risk or where the risks usually outweigh the advantages (category 3) are detailed in Table 7 [FFPRHC Clinical Effectiveness Unit, 2004a].
- For a full list of the medical eligibility criteria and other category classification for IUD (emergency) contraceptive use, please see www.who.int/reproductive-health/publications/mec/7_iud.pdf.

[FFPRHC Clinical Effectiveness Unit, 2004a; WHO, 2004]

Progestogen-only intra-uterine system

General information

- **The intra-uterine system (IUS) is a levonorgestrel- (LNG-) releasing T-shaped intra-uterine device.**
- The only LNG-IUS currently available in the UK is Mirena.
- It contains 52 mg of levonorgestrel, and releases 20 micrograms of levonorgestrel every 24 hours.
- **Prophylactic antibiotics are not recommended for routine insertion of the LNG-IUS.** However, women with previous endocarditis, or with a prosthetic heart valve, require intravenous antibiotic prophylaxis to protect against bacterial endocarditis during insertion or removal of the LNG-IUS.
- It is licensed for use for 5 years.

[BNF 47, 2004]

- **Note: it is ineffective as a method of emergency contraception** [FFPRHC Clinical Effectiveness Unit, 2000].
- **The levonorgestrel-releasing intra-uterine system** is not licensed for the treatment of dysmenorrhoea, but has been shown to be of benefit. It might be considered for a woman who needs long-term contraception, especially if menorrhagia is also a problem [Smith, 1993; Luukkainen and Toivonen, 1995].

Mode of action

- **Suppression of the endometrium** and prevention of implantation.
- **Thickening of the cervical mucus,** preventing sperm penetration.
- **Impairment of sperm migration** by alteration of cervical and uterine environment.
- Suppression of ovulation in some women, in some cycles.

[BNF 47, 2004]

Efficacy

- The LNG-IUS is highly effective, with failure rates of less than 1% [Andersson et al, 1994].

Advantages

- Highly effective, with a rapid return of fertility after removal [Andersson et al, 1992].
- Reduces menstrual loss (see below).
- Reduces dysmenorrhoea [Sturridge and Guillebaud, 1997].
- Convenient: independent of intercourse, and long-lasting.
- Possible reduction in pelvic inflammatory disease compared with the use of copper IUDs [Andersson et al, 1994; Sturridge and Guillebaud, 1997], by thickening cervico-utero mucus.
- No significant interaction with liver enzyme-inducing drugs, as the action of the progestogen is mainly local [ABPI Medicines Compendium, 2002b].
- The LNG-IUS commonly results in amenorrhoea after a few months. This is thought to be mainly a local effect, but suppression of ovulation can occur in some women (in some cycles).

Disadvantages

- There is a high incidence of menstrual irregularities in the first few months of use (see below).

C

Table 7: Clinical conditions where IUDs are considered unacceptable, or where the risks usually outweigh the advantage for use in contraception and emergency contraception.

Condition	Category		Comment
	Insertion	Continuation	
Pregnancy	4	4	The IUD should not be used because of the risk of serio pelvic infection and septic spontaneous abortion.
Postpartum (breastfeeding or non-breastfeeding, including post-Caesarian section) between 48 hours and 4 weeks after delivery	3	3	There is an increased risk of perforation for IUD insertic done between 48 hours and 4 weeks postpartum.
Postpartum (breastfeeding or non-breastfeeding, including post-Caesarian section) — puerpal sepsis	4	4	Insertion of an IUD may substantially worsen the condition.
Post-abortion — immediate post-septic abortion	4	4	Insertion of an IUD may substantially worsen the condition.
Anatomical abnormalities — distorted uterine cavity (any congenital or acquired uterine abnormality distorting the uterine cavity in a manner that is incompatible with IUD insertion)	4	4	In the presence of an anatomic abnormality that distorts the uterine cavity, proper IUD placement may not be possible.
Unexplained vaginal bleeding (suspicion for serious condition) — before evaluation	4	(2)	If pregnancy or an underlying pathological condition (s as pelvic malignancy) is suspected, it must be evaluated and the category adjusted after evaluation. There is no need to remove the IUD before evaluation.
Benign gestational trophoblastic disease	3	3	—
Malignant gestational trophoblastic disease	4	4	There is an increased risk of perforation, since the treatment for the condition may require multiple uterine curettages.
Cervical cancer (awaiting treatment)	4	(2)	There is concern about the increased risk of infection an bleeding at insertion; this may make the condition wors
Endometrial cancer	4	(2)	There is concern about the increased risk of infection, perforation, and bleeding at insertion; this may make th condition worse.
Ovarian cancer	3	(2)	IUD will probably need removal at the time of treatmen but until then the woman is at risk of pregnancy.
Uterine fibroids — with distortion of the uterine cavity	4	4	Pre-existing uterine fibroids that distort the uterine cavit may be incompatible with IUD insertion.
Pelvic inflammatory disease (PID) — now/within last 3 months	4	(2)	The FFPRHC recommends that, after considering other contraceptive methods, a woman may use an IUD withi 3 months of treated pelvic infection, provided she has n signs and symptoms.
Sexually transmitted infections (STIs) — current or within 3 months (including purulent cervicitis)	4	4	The FFPRHC recommends that, after considering other contraceptive methods, women who are at high risk of STIs, or who have had treatment for a STI within the las months, may use an IUD, provided there are no signs an symptoms of infection. Safer sex and condom use in addition should be promoted.
Sexually transmitted infections (STIs) — increased risk of STIs (e.g. multiple partners, or partner who has multiple partners)	2/3	(2)	—
AIDS	3	(2)	Clarification for continuation: IUD users with AIDS should be closely monitored for pelvic infection.
Tuberculosis — known pelvic	4	3	Insertion of an IUD may substantially worsen the condition.
Antiretroviral (ARV) therapy	2/3	(2)	Although there is no known drug interaction between ARV therapy and IUD use women, category 2 applies where women are clinically well on ARV therapy.

Category 4 — a condition that represents an unacceptable health risk if an IUD is used.
Category 3 — a condition where the theoretical or proven risks usually outweigh the advantages of using an IUD.
Category 2 — a condition where the advantage of using an IUD generally outweighs the theoretical or proven risks

- Progestogenic adverse effects occur in a small number of women (e.g. breast tenderness, depression, and acne) [Andersson et al, 1994].
- Functional ovarian cysts may occur, although these usually resolve spontaneously. One study showed an incidence, diagnosed by scan, of 12%. However, another study looked at the clinically diagnosed incidence and this was 1.2 per 100 woman-years, compared with 0.4 per 100 woman-years in women using copper IUDs [Sturridge and Guillebaud, 1997].
- It has to be fitted. Additionally, the device has a larger insertion diameter than some copper IUDs, and may require local anaesthesia and dilatation of the cervical canal in nulliparous or perimenopausal women.
- Offers no protection against sexually transmitted infections.
- It may become expelled or displaced [BNF 47, 2004].

Contraindications

- For a full list of the World Health Organization (WHO medical eligibility criteria, see www.who.int/reproductive-health/publications/mec/7_iud.pdf.

iming of insertion

Ideally the IUS should be fitted within the first 7 days of a period and is then effective immediately. If fitted after this, the risk of a pregnancy since the last period should be excluded before insertion, and an additional method of contraception should be used for 7 days.

After childbirth: the LNG-IUS can be fitted 6 weeks after a vaginal or Caesarian delivery.

After a first-trimester abortion or miscarriage, the LNG-IUS can be fitted immediately and is effective immediately.

lenstrual effects

The total number of bleeding days (menstrual bleeding plus intermenstrual bleeding/spotting) increases in most women during the first few months of LNG-IUS use [DTB, 1996].

After 3 months the number of bleeding days settles, and the menstrual blood loss falls by more than 75% [DTB, 1996].

By 12 months most women bleed lightly for 1 day each month, and 15% are amenorrhoeic [DTB, 1996].

In women with menorrhagia treated with LNG-IUS, case studies have shown reductions of up to 97% in menstrual blood loss. Treatment with LNG-IUS results in a smaller mean reduction in menstrual blood loss than does transcervical resection of the endometrium, and women are less likely to become amenorrhoeic; but there is no difference in the rate of satisfaction with the treatment. There are no data from randomized controlled trials comparing the LNG-IUS to either placebo or other commonly used medical therapies for menorrhagia [RCOG, 1998; Lethaby et al, 2000].

See the section on *Copper intra-uterine devices* for management of missed threads and actinomyces-like organisms (ALOs) in cervical smears.

iaphragms and caps

ieneral information

Diaphragms are thin, soft, latex rubber, dome-shaped devices with a flexible circular ring covered by rubber. There are three types:

- Flat spring: suitable for women with normal vaginal muscular support.
- Coil spring: more flexible and can be more comfortable.
- Arcing spring: useful for women with poor vaginal muscular support or those with a retroverted uterus.

There are different sizes, ranging from 55 mm to 100 mm.

They cover the cervix, fitting in the vagina between the posterior fornix and behind the pubic bone.

Caps are smaller than diaphragms. They fit directly over the cervix and are held in place by suction.

More recently, caps have become available that are made of silicone, whereas established caps are made of rubber.

Diaphragms and caps should always be used with spermicide.

ielfield, 1999]

lode of action

Diaphragms and caps are barrier methods of contraception and therefore prevent fertilization. They cover the cervix, acting as a barrier blocking the cervix as well as providing a reservoir for spermicide.

fficacy

When used correctly with spermicide:

- Diaphragms have a first-year failure rate of 4–8%.
- Caps a first-year failure rate of 9–26%.

- **The probability of failure with consistent and correct use is significantly higher among women who use the cap who have given birth.** Parity has no effect on the probability of failure of the diaphragm [Trussell et al, 1990; Trussell et al, 1993; Bounds, 1994].
- **A Cochrane review** compared the efficacy of the cervical cap with that of the diaphragm [Gallo et al, 2003b]. Trial data were only available comparing two types of cervical caps against a diaphragm. The Prentif cap was as effective as the Ortho diaphragm in preventing pregnancy, but the FemCap was not as effective as the All-Flex diaphragm. Both the Prentif cap and the FemCap seem to be medically safe.

Advantages

- Can be inserted before intercourse so that spontaneity can be maintained.
- May protect against cervical cancer, sexually transmitted bacterial infections, and pelvic inflammatory disease.
- Can be used whilst a woman is menstruating.
- No systemic adverse effects.

[Belfield, 1999]

Disadvantages

- Degree of effectiveness is low in comparison to other methods [Belfield, 1999].
- Requires motivation and careful use to be effective [Belfield, 1999].
- Must be used with spermicide. This may cause irritation or allergy.
- There may be allergy to the material from which the diaphragm is made.
- There may be an increased incidence of urinary tract infection in some women who use diaphragms — this often relates to the fit and size of the diaphragm causing pressure on the urethra.
- They offer no protection against sexually transmitted infections including HIV.

Contraindications

- For a full list of the World Health Organization (WHO) medical eligibility criteria, see www.who.int/reproductive-health/publications/mec/9_bar.pdf.

Use of diaphragms and caps

- **Diaphragms and caps should be initially fitted by a trained healthcare professional.** They should be replaced annually (or immediately if there are any holes or puckering) and a check for size and fitting carried out. They should also be checked after childbirth, abortion, or miscarriage, or if the woman gains or loses 3 kg or more in weight.
- **They can be inserted at any time before intercourse.** If one is inserted more than 3 hours before intercourse, additional spermicide should be used without removing the diaphragm or cap.
- **Latex varieties must be left in place for at least 6 hours after intercourse** — but no longer than 30 hours because of a very small risk of toxic shock syndrome.
- **Silicone varieties vary:** OvesCap can be used for a 48-hour period and FemCap for 3 days (this includes leaving it in for 6 hours after last intercourse).
- **Oil-based products should not be used,** as they cause rapid deterioration of rubber. Common oil-based topical preparations that may be applied to the vaginal and rectal areas include:
  - Clotrimazole, econazole and miconazole formulations
  - Corticosteroid formulations
  - Combination corticosteroid plus antifungal formulations

C

- Oestrogen creams and pessaries
- Emulsifying ointment
- Vaseline
- Baby oil
- Massage oils

[Belfield, 1999]

Female condom

General information

C

- Currently Femidom is the only female condom available.
- Femidom is designed to line the vagina. It is made of soft, pliable polyurethane and is pre-lubricated with dimeticone — an odourless, non-spermicidal lubricant. It is 17 cm long with two (labial and apical) flexible rings [DTB, 1993].
- It is available in only one size, and does not require fitting by a health professional.
- Female condoms are available free from a few family planning clinics, and for sale from pharmacies and by mail order. They are individually packaged within a pack of three. They are not available on prescription.

Mode of action

- Female condoms are a barrier method of contraception, and therefore prevent fertilization.

Efficacy

- Femidom has a failure rate of 5–21% [Trussell et al, 1990].

Advantages

- No known adverse effects.
- Reduces the risk of sexually transmitted diseases, including HIV. It may protect against cervical cancer.
- Spermicide not required.
- Can be used with oil-based products.
- Polyurethane is less likely to tear than latex.
- Can be inserted anytime before sex.

[DTB, 1993; Belfield, 1999]

Disadvantages

- Requires careful insertion to be effective.
- The device can be pushed into the vagina, or the penis can be inserted between the vaginal wall and the Femidom.
- The outer or inner ring may cause discomfort.

[Belfield, 1999]

Contraindications

- For a full list of the World Health Organization (WHO) medical eligibility criteria, see www.who.int/reproductive-health/publications/mec/9_bar.pdf.

Spermicides

General information

- **Spermicides are composed of a spermicidal agent in a carrier** that allows dispersion and retention of the agent in the vagina.
- **Nonoxinol-9 is the most commonly used spermicidal agent,** and is the active component in the prescribable spermicidal agents available in the UK.
- Spermicides are available as aerosol foams, jellies, creams, films, sponges, or pessaries.
- **It is no longer recommended to use condoms with spermicides, as they are neither necessary for contraceptive efficacy of condoms nor useful for infection protection.**
    - Two recent large randomized controlled trials in developing countries compared whether or not protection was provided against gonorrhoea, chlamydial infection, and HIV-1 infection with gel formulations containing nonoxinol-9 [Roddy et al, 2002; Van Damme et al, 2002].
    - The studies found that the spermicidal agent offered no clinical benefit; and so currently the extent to which protection may be provided by use of spermicidal agents is inconclusive.
- **Avoid spermicides in men and women who might be at high risk of infection,** as multiple use of spermicide may cause irritation to the vagina and rectum, increasing the chance of infection.
- **Spermicides should be used by women at low risk of infection** who wish to use a barrier method (except condoms).

Mode of action

- Alteration of the integrity of the sperm cell membrane.
- Alteration of the vaginal pH, causing a hostile environment for sperm.

Advantages

- Provides lubrication.
- Spermicides are thought to increase the effectiveness of the diaphragm, and it remains common practice to use spermicide with a diaphragm. However, a recent Cochrane review only found one (under-powered) study that indicated a trend towards lower pregnancy rates with this strategy [Cook et al, 2003].

Disadvantages

- May cause irritation and rarely allergy [Belfield, 1999].
- May be perceived as messy or having unpleasant odour or taste [The Consensus Committee of the Society of Obstetricians and Gynaecologists of Canada, 1998; Belfield, 1999].

Contraindications

- For a full list of the World Health Organization (WHO) medical eligibility criteria, see www.who.int/reproductive-health/publications/mec/9_bar.pdf.

Male condoms

General information

- Male condoms are made from latex or polyurethane.
- They are available from family planning clinics, sexual health clinics, and many other sources. Although not available on prescription, they are becoming increasingly available from family doctors free of charge (as part of health initiatives to reduce teenage pregnancy and promote safer sex).
- Non-spermicidal lubricated condoms are recommended.
- It is no longer recommended to use condoms with spermicides, as they are neither necessary for contraceptive efficacy of condoms nor useful for infection protection. See section on *Spermicides* for more information.
- Latex condoms are also available unlubricated, in different sizes, shapes, colours, textures, and flavours.

[Belfield, 1999]

- A recent Cochrane review has compared non-latex condoms with latex condoms in terms of efficacy, breakage, slippage, safety, and user preference [Gallo et al, 2003a].
    - Latex condoms were found to be consistently highly effective at protecting against pregnancy, whereas non-latex condoms varied more from brand to brand

although efficacy was still within the expected range for barrier methods.
- Latex condoms had lower rates of clinical breakage and slippage.
- In almost all the comparisons, substantial proportions of participants preferred the non-latex condom.
- Non-latex condoms still provide an acceptable alternative for those with allergies, sensitivities, or preferences that might prevent the consistent use of latex condoms.

Mode of action

Provide a physical barrier against the deposition of semen into the vagina during sex.

Efficacy

Male condoms have a failure rate of 3–14% [Trussell et al, 1990].

Advantages

Adverse effects are rare. Sensitivity to latex and spermicide can occur.
Significant protection against sexually transmitted infection including HIV.
May protect against cervical cancer.
Easy to obtain and use.
[The Consensus Committee of the Society of Obstetricians and Gynaecologists of Canada, 1998; Belfield, 1999]

Disadvantages

Requires forward planning and may interrupt sex.
Requires the participation and commitment of both partners.
Possible loss of sensitivity during intercourse.
Can break or slip off.
Needs careful disposal.
Latex condoms should not be used in contact with topical oil-based products, including:
- Clotrimazole, econazole, and miconazole formulations
- Corticosteroid formulations
- Combination corticosteroid plus antifungal formulations
- Oestrogen creams and pessaries
- Emulsifying ointment
- Massage oils

Contraindications

For a full list of the World Health Organization (WHO) medical eligibility criteria, see www.who.int/reproductive-health/publications/mec/9_bar.pdf.

Natural family planning

General information

Natural family planning methods, when used well, identify the fertile and infertile phases of the menstrual cycle by recognising symptoms and signs of ovulation. To avoid pregnancy, the couple must then abstain from intercourse during the fertile period.
Identification of ovulation can be by means of a calendar (cycle length); waking temperature (immediately after ovulation the basal body temperature drops slightly, and then rises by about 0.2–0.4°C until just before the next period); cervical mucus; palpating the cervix; and a combination of these.
Education provided by specially trained natural family planning teachers is required (to obtain a list of these, phone the Family Planning Association helpline, 0845-310-1334).

- Persona is a computerized device that identifies the fertile phase from measurements of urinary estrone 3-glucuronide and luteinising hormone, and does not require teaching from specially trained individuals. There are also several other menstrual-cycle monitors that have been developed and are available, but they vary in their efficacy and cost [Freundl et al, 2003].
- Women with conditions which make pregnancy an unacceptable risk (i.e. WHO category 4) should be advised that this method may not be appropriate for them because of its relatively higher typical use failure rates [WHO, 2004].

[Pyper, 1997; Belfield, 1999]

Efficacy

- Efficacy is increased by using a combination of the fertility indicators, and ranges from 80–98% [Trussell et al, 1990; Freundl, 1999].

Advantages

- No drug-related adverse effects.

Disadvantages

- Requires the participation and commitment of both partners.
- If a woman has irregular cycles, it is not a reliable time to start learning to use the natural family planning method at this time.

[The Consensus Committee of the Society of Obstetricians and Gynaecologists of Canada, 1998]

Specific contraceptive information

Women over 35 years old

- **Pregnancy in women over 40 years old** is associated with increased maternal morbidity and mortality, increased perinatal mortality, and chromosomal abnormalities — particularly Down's syndrome.

General information
- **It is generally accepted that:**
  - Contraception should be continued for *1 year* after the last menstrual period, *for women over 50 years.*
  - Contraception should be continued for *2 years* after the last menstrual period, *for women under the age of 50 years.*
  - Fertility declines with increasing age.
- User failure rates of all methods of contraception reduce after the age of 35 years.
- Most women (93%) aged 40–55 years with regular cycles seem to ovulate each cycle. Ovulation can occur up to the menopause.

[DTB, 1991; Loudon et al, 1995; Pitkin, 2000]

Suitability of methods
- **Combined oral contraceptive (COC) pills**
  - **Women aged over 35 years old who smoke** should be advised that the risks of COC use outweigh the benefits (B).
  - **The presence of cardiovascular risk factors** needs to be investigated before COC pills are prescribed to any women over 35 years old who smoke.
  - **COC is suitable for women over the age of 35 years who do not smoke,** who do not have a family history of ischaemic heart disease in a first-degree relative, nor a history of hyperlipidaemia, diabetes, or hypertension, and are not overweight.
  - Advantages to older women may include better perimenopausal bleeding control and relief of perimenopausal symptoms [DTB, 1991; Loudon et al, 1995].

C

- There is an increased relative risk of breast cancer in all current users of COCs, and the effect will become most numerically significant in women over 40 years. For more information, see the section on *Breast cancer*.
- **Routine fasting lipid profiles are recommended for women younger than 45 only if there is a family history of dyslipidaemia,** or the woman has other cardiovascular risk factors [Seibert et al, 2003].
- **Progestogen-only contraception**
  - **Progestogen-only pills,** if taken correctly, are as effective as COCs in the over-forties [DTB, 1991].
  - **It is unlikely that the progestogen-only contraceptive pill will relieve menopausal symptoms,** and it may contribute to them if pituitary suppression and amenorrhoea occur [DTB, 1991; Pitkin, 2000].
  - **The development of amenorrhoea cannot be assumed to be due to the menopause,** as a significant number of women develop amenorrhoea using progestogen-only contraception. In this situation, two raised follicle-stimulating hormone (FSH) levels, with values over 30 iu/l, taken 4–8 weeks apart, can confirm the diagnosis. The woman should continue with contraception as indicated above [Pitkin, 2000]. Alternatively, the progestogen-only contraception can be discontinued, and alternative contraception provided until the diagnosis is established [DTB, 1991].
- **Intra-uterine device (IUD)/levonorgestrel-releasing intra-uterine system (LNG-IUS)**
  - Any copper IUD currently licensed in the UK and that is fitted in a woman over the age of 40 years may remain in the uterus until the menopause.
  - **IUDs should be removed from postmenopausal women** once contraception is no longer indicated [Loudon et al, 1995].
  - **The LNG-IUS** has potential advantages in older women. It can provide contraception and control or eliminate menorrhagia (which is present in 1 in 20 women aged 30–49 years) [Lethaby et al, 2000]. Currently Mirena is licensed in the UK for use as a contraceptive and for the treatment of menorrhagia.
- **Barrier methods of contraception** are also suitable for older women.
- **Spermicides** are generally used with barrier methods of contraception, but can be used alone by women during the menopause when fertility is low [BNF 47, 2004]. However, it must be appreciated that an unplanned pregnancy in this age group may have greater implications. The additional lubrication provided by the spermicide can be advantageous in the presence of vaginal dryness.
- **Natural family planning methods** can be more difficult to initiate when cycles are irregular or anovulatory. However, established users will note longer infertile phases.

Hormone replacement therapy (HRT) and contraception

- **HRT preparations do not suppress ovulation and do not provide contraceptive cover.** Barrier methods of contraception, an intra-uterine device, or the levonorgestrel-releasing intra-uterine system can provide contraceptive protection.
- **There are no data to support prescribing the progestogen-only pill simultaneously with a standard cyclical combined oestrogen–progestogen HRT preparation.** There are theoretical concerns that the oestrogen may interfere with the action of the progestogen-only pill on the cervical mucus [Pitkin, 2000]. However, this is widely done in practice, and any theoretical concerns are not apparent [Mansour, Personal Communication, 2004].
- **Many women commence HRT before the menopause,** and it is therefore difficult to know when the menopause has occurred, and for how long contraception is necessary.
- **It is possible to discontinue the HRT and measure the FSH level after 6–8 weeks.** A value over 30 iu/l is indicative of the menopause, but should be repeated 4–8 weeks later to confirm this. Even if the FSH levels are in the postmenopausal range, contraception should be continued, the length of time being dependent on the woman's age [Pitkin, 2000].
- **For women on the oral contraceptive pill who wish to change to HRT at the appropriate time,** it is possible to change to the progestogen-only pill or a barrier method of contraception and measure the FSH level to determine if the menopause has been reached. Contraception should be continued after the menopause, the length of time being dependent on the woman's age.

Women who are breastfeeding

Note: the combined oral contraceptive is not recommended, as it adversely affects lactation.

- **Lactational amenorrhoea method (LAM)**
  - Breastfeeding is associated with suppression of ovarian activity, and therefore a variable period of amenorrhoea and infertility [WHO Task Force on Methods for the Natural Regulation of Fertility, 1999].
  - A consensus conference held in Bellagio, Italy, in 1988 postulated that *full or nearly full* breastfeeding (feeding with no substitutes and at regular periods on demand, day and night) causing lactational amenorrhoea confers 98% protection against pregnancy in the first 6 months after childbirth [Kennedy et al, 1989]. This is similar to the protection provided by many contraceptive methods in clinical practice.
  - Results from other studies uphold the 'Bellagio Consensus'. A prospective, longitudinal study involving 4,118 women from both developing and developed countries found that the cumulative 6-month pregnancy rate during lactational amenorrhoea was between 0.8% (95% CI 0.1 to 1.4%) and 1.2% (95% CI 0 to 2.4%). This study concluded that lactational amenorrhoea is a viable approach to post-partum contraception [WHO Task Force on Methods for the Natural Regulation of Fertility, 1999].
  - The LAM method does not protect against the risk of sexually transmitted infection (STI) including HIV [WHO, 2004]. If there is a risk of STI (including during pregnancy or postpartum), condom use is recommended. Note: latex condoms are preferable unless contraindicted.
  - Women with conditions which make pregnancy an unacceptable risk (WHO category 4) should be advised that the LAM method may not be appropriate for them because of its relatively higher typical use failure rates [WHO, 2004].
  - For breastfeeding to be sufficient to be used for family planning, the following should apply:
    - Breastfeeding should constitute the overwhelming majority of the baby's diet.
    - Breastfeeding frequency should be high, and not affected by additional feedings.
    - Additional feedings should not act as replacements for breastfeeding.

[Kennedy et al, 1989]

The effectiveness of many other 'complementary' methods of contraception is increased because of the suppression of

ovarian activity. Suitable methods for women who are breastfeeding include the following:**

- **Condoms** can be used immediately after childbirth and have no effect on breastfeeding.
- **The diaphragm or cap** can be used 6 weeks after delivery when vaginal tone is restored. If the woman used the diaphragm or cap method before pregnancy, the size must be checked after childbirth [Belfield, 1999].
- **Spermicides** may pass into breast milk in very small amounts, but no adverse effects on the infant have been reported [Loudon et al, 1995].
- **Intra-uterine devices** have no effect on breastfeeding. For women who are fully or nearly fully breastfeeding, amenorrhoeic, and less than 6 months postpartum (including Caesarian section), an IUD can be inserted within 48 hours of delivery or 4 or more weeks postpartum (C). The risk of uterine perforation is increased if an IUD is inserted between 49 hours and up to 4 weeks postpartum.
- **Progestogen-only contraceptives** (oral, injectable, or implants) do not affect lactation.
  - The progestogen present in breast milk after use of injectable medroxyprogesterone acetate and progestogen-only pills has not been shown to have any adverse effects on the infant. Long-term effects relating to the use of the etonogestrel implant in breastfeeding mothers are not known, but it is presumed to have no adverse effect on infant growth or development.
  - Progestogen-only pills (POPs): two options are available. UK practice is to start from day 21 post-partum in women who are breastfeeding, as use before this is unnecessary and can cause an increase in irregular bleeding. Alternatively, the World Health Organization recommends waiting until 6 weeks post-partum; therefore alternative methods of contraception should be used from day 21 until 7 days after the POP is started [WHO, 2002].
  - Injectable progestogens should not be given until 6 weeks after childbirth, because of the risk of heavy and prolonged bleeding.
  - The etonogestrel implant can be inserted 21 days after childbirth. If inserted after this, additional contraceptive precautions should be used for 7 days.
  - The levonorgestrel-releasing intra-uterine system should be delayed until 6 weeks after delivery. The daily dose and the plasma concentrations of levonorgestrel are lower than with any other hormonal contraceptive method. Concentrations of levonorgestrel have been detected in the breast milk of lactating women, but the long-term effects on the nursing infant are unknown [ABPI Medicines Compendium, 2001].

Women who are overweight or obese

- **Women with a body mass index (BMI) greater than 30 should be counselled regarding an increased risk of venous thromboembolism, and consider contraceptive methods other than the COC (B).**
- **Women can be advised that there is no evidence of weight gain with COC use (A).**

[FFPRHC Clinical Effectiveness Unit, 2003a]

- A recent Cochrane review investigated the association between COC use and weight change. Of three placebo-controlled randomized controlled trials identified, two examined COCs [Gallo et al, 2003c]. Although many clinicians and women believe that an association exists, no large effect seems evident; but more data are needed to determine a precise effect on weight.
- The effect on BMI and weight on the risk of pregnancy while using oral contraceptives (ethinylestradiol 35 micrograms or less, multiphasic COC, and progestogen-only) has been investigated in a recently published case-control study [Holt et al, 2005].
  - The absolute risk of pregnancy was found to increase in women having a BMI greater than 27.3 suggesting a possible reduction in efficacy of hormonal contraception.
  - However the evidence available is not strong enough to support a change in current practice. Note: the option to explore using additional or alternative contraceptive methods should be discussed with overweight women.

Women who smoke

- **Women aged over 35 years who smoke should be advised that the risks of COC use outweigh the benefits** [FFPRHC Clinical Effectiveness Unit, 2003a].
- Combined oral contraception (COC):
  - Smoking has also been found to be associated with a two-fold increase in the risk of stroke compared with non-smokers [WHO, 1996a].
  - In heavy smokers, the risk of MI is further increased with COC use (RR 20.8, 95% CI 5.2 to 83.1), as is the risk of ischaemic stroke (OR 7.2, 95% CI 3.23 to 16.1).
  - Smoking increases the risk of haemorrhagic stroke in current users of COC three-fold. Current users of COC who smoke and have hypertension have substantially increased risk of haemorrhagic stroke (up to 10-fold) [WHO, 1998; Hannaford, 2000].
  - Smokers under the age of 35 years can use COC, but should be given advice, information, and support to aid smoking cessation. For more information, see the PRODIGY guidance on *Smoking cessation*.
- Suitable contraceptive methods for women over 35 years who smoke include progestogen-only contraception, barrier methods of contraception, natural family planning methods, and intra-uterine devices or the levonorgestrel-releasing intra-uterine system.

Women with acne

- **Dianette® (cyproterone acetate/ethinylestradiol) should be used only for severe acne** when oral antibiotics have failed, or for moderately severe hirsutism. It should be discontinued 3–4 months after the condition treated has resolved (C).
- **Dianette® is useful in women who also require contraception, but it is not indicated for use solely as an oral contraceptive.** If prescribed as a contraceptive, this should be marked on the prescription form (a female symbol will suffice) to avoid the women being charged for the prescription.
- **The use of Dianette® has been found to be associated with an increased risk of venous thromboembolism (VTE).**
  - Some investigators have considered that this represents a four-fold increase compared with the use of second-generation COCs [Vasilakis-Scaramozza and Jick, 2001].
  - Other research has taken into account the underlying cardiovascular risks of the patient groups studied, and has concluded that Dianette® use represents a two-fold increase in the risk of VTE when compared with conventional COCs [Seaman et al, 2003].
- It is possible that women with androgen-related conditions (e.g. acne or hirsutism) may have an inherently increased cardiovascular risk [CSM, 2002].
- Dianette® is contraindicated in a variety of circumstances. These include women with a personal or close family history of confirmed idiopathic VTE, and in those with a known current venous thrombotic or embolic disorder.

- **Acne is reduced by all COC pills regardless of the progestogen component.** There are few studies comparing the benefits of specific COCs for treating acne, and more data are needed to establish how COCs differ in their effect on skin.

[CSM, 2002]

Women with epilepsy

- **Liver enzyme induction** occurs with carbamazepine, oxcarbazepine, phenobarbital, phenytoin, primidone, and topiramate, which therefore interact with a large number of drugs, particularly hormonal contraceptive products [MeReC, 1995; Feely, 1999].
- **If a woman with epilepsy is taking the combined oral contraceptive (COC), an antiepileptic drug (AED) that does not induce liver enzymes is preferable** (e.g. sodium valproate, lamotrigine, or ethosuximide). These AEDs do not alter the efficacy of the COC.
- **Women using liver enzyme-inducers who, having considered other methods, still choose to use COCs** should be prescribed a regimen containing 50 micrograms of ethinylestradiol (EE) (C). Note: there remains an enhanced risk of pregnancy in this scenario.
  - Options include using either Norinyl-1 (containing mestranol 50 micrograms, a prodrug of EE) or two low-dose COCs providing a total daily dose of 50–60 micrograms EE.
  - Women should be warned that the efficacy of the COC is reduced, and additional barrier contraception should be advised until 4 weeks after cessation of the liver enzyme-inducer.
- **If breakthrough bleeding occurs with 50 micrograms of oestrogen,** the dose should be increased to 80 or 100 micrograms and tricycling of the COC should be considered [SIGN, 2003]. 'Tricycling' means taking three packs of the high-dose COC without interruption, followed by a reduced pill-free interval of 4 days after the final pack. Note: use of COCs in this way represents off-licence use.
- **The oral progestogen-only contraceptive pill is not recommended for women taking enzyme-inducing AEDs** [SIGN, 2003], as these increase the metabolism of progestogen.
- **Depot injections of progesterone-only contraceptives: medroxyprogesterone (Depo-Provera)** may be used with liver enzyme-inducing AEDs, but for long-term contraception should be given every 10 weeks [SIGN, 2003]. The Summary of Product Characteristics, however, recommends that injections should be repeated every 12 weeks for long-term contraception, and does not discuss this specific scenario. The risk of interaction seems to be just a theoretical one, and may be related to the potency of the enzyme-inducer.
- **Note: depot norethisterone (Noristerat) injection** is licensed only for short-term use (two injections) in the UK, and so no formal recommendations are available.
- **Progestogen implants are not suitable** for women taking enzyme-inducing AEDs [SIGN, 2003], as they are less effective when these AEDs are used.
- **For emergency contraception,** women using liver enzyme-inducing drugs should take two tablets of levonorgestrel (1.5 mg) as a single dose as soon as possible after unprotected sex, followed by one tablet (750 micrograms) 12 hours later [FFPRHC Clinical Effectiveness Unit, 2003b]. Note: levonorgestrel taken in this way is an off-licence use and dose.
- **In view of the difficulties with oral contraception,** alternative forms of contraception should be considered in women taking enzyme-inducing AEDs.

Women with migraine

- **Migraine is classified** [Bates et al, 1994] as:
  - **Migraine with aura** (focal or classical migraine)
  - **Migraine without aura** (simple or common migraine)
- **About 30% of migraine attacks are migraines with aura.** The aura comprises focal neurological symptoms (e.g. visual disturbance, olfactory symptoms, focal numbness or paraesthesiae) that usually precede and resolve before the onset of the migraine and associated symptoms [MacGregor, 2001].
- **Women of any age complaining of migraine with focal aura should be advised that the risks of COC use outweigh the benefits (B).**
- **Migraine is associated with increased risk of ischaemic but not haemorrhagic stroke.** Migraine with aura poses higher risk than does migraine without aura [MacGregor, 2001].
- Several studies have shown an increased risk of ischaemic stroke in women with a history of migraine with aura [Lidegaard, 1995; Tzourio et al, 1995].
- **A case-control study confirmed that a personal history of migraine with aura was associated with a more than three-fold risk of ischaemic stroke.** Coexistence of risk factors for stroke (e.g. COC use, high blood pressure, or smoking) had more than multiplicative effects on the odds ratio for ischaemic stroke associated with migraine. However, a change in frequency or type of migraine on using oral contraceptives did not seem to predict future stroke [Chang et al, 1999].
- **Contraindications for the use of COCs in women with migraine are based on limited evidence and expert opinion.** These recommendations are intended to enable most women with migraine to use COCs safely with minimal risk of ischaemic stroke, while protecting those at risk. The contraindications apply whether the conditions are present before starting COCs or arise during COC use, and are as follows:
  - Migraine with aura in which there are focal neurological symptoms preceding the headache onset.
  - Migraine without aura in a woman who has a history of more than one additional risk factor for stroke (i.e. age 35 years or over, diabetes mellitus, close family history of arterial disease under 45 years, hyperlipidaemia, hypertension, obesity [body mass index greater than 30], or smoking).
  - Severe migraine — attacks of migraine that are unusually severe, lasting longer than 72 hours despite treatment.
  - Migraine treated with ergot derivatives.

[MacGregor, 2001]

- **Women without an aura with only one additional risk factor for ischaemic stroke** can be given a COC containing a low-dose oestrogen (30 micrograms). There is no evidence available on which to base any recommendation regarding the most suitable progestogen for women with a history of migraine who wish to use the COC pill [DTB, 2000].
- Suitable alternative methods of contraception for women with a history of migraine with aura include progestogen-only contraceptives, intra-uterine devices or systems, and barrier methods.

Legal issues with young women

- **COCs can be prescribed, without parental consent, to a woman aged less than 16 years if she is assessed to be competent to make an informed choice (C).**
- Health professionals dealing with young people should be aware of local procedures for dealing with issues relating to child protection, confidentiality, and disclosure (C).

When young people present for the first consultation, it is sensible to explain that asking about personal or family medical history is needed to help choose an appropriate method of contraception [DTB, 2002a].

Young people should be encouraged to always use a condom regardless of whether other contraception is also used. Condoms offer the best protection against sexually transmitted infections, including HIV.

In the UK, people under the age of 16 years can consent to medical treatment if they have sufficient maturity and judgement to enable them fully to understand what is proposed.

In England and Wales, it is lawful to provide contraceptive advice and treatment without parental consent, provided that the practitioner is satisfied that the following Fraser Guideline criteria [Teenage Pregnancy Unit, 2001] are met:

- The young person understands the practitioner's advice.
- The young person cannot be persuaded to inform his or her parents or allow the practitioner to inform the parents that contraceptive advice has been sought.
- The young person is very likely to begin or continue having intercourse with or without contraceptive treatment.
- Unless he or she receives contraceptive advice or treatment, the young person's physical or mental health, or both, are likely to suffer.
- The young person's best interest requires the prescriber to give contraceptive advice, treatment, or both, without parental consent.

In Scotland, statutory provision by way of The Age of Legal Capacity Act 1991 applies similar criteria. The Act actually seems to assign more legal rights to children under 16 years, in that parental responsibility cannot authorize procedures a competent child has refused [Fernie, Personal Communication, 2003].

Note: child protection issues (which relate to young people under 18 years) should be taken into account — it is important to be satisfied that sex has been consensual and is not occurring in an incestuous relationship. If it is suspected that force has been used or that any sexual abuse has occurred, healthcare professionals have a duty to follow national and local child protection procedures. FFPRHC Clinical Effectiveness Unit, 2003a]

References

NHS staff in England can link, free of charge, from references to full text journals by clicking on [Full text] on the PRODIGY website.

1. ABPI Medicines Compendium (2001) *Summary of product characteristics for Mirena*. Electronic Medicines Compendium. Datapharm Communications Ltd. www.emc.medicines.org.uk [Accessed: 19/04/2004].
2. ABPI Medicines Compendium (2002a) *Summary of product characteristics for Dianette*. Electronic Medicines Compendium. Datapharm Communications Ltd. www.emc.medicines.org.uk [Accessed: 15/08/2002].
3. ABPI Medicines Compendium (2002b) *Summary of product characteristics for Depo-Provera*. Electronic Medicines Compendium. Datapharm Communications Ltd. www.emc.medicines.org.uk [Accessed: 22/07/2003].
4. ABPI Medicines Compendium (2003a) *Summary of product characteristics for Implanon*. Electronic Medicines Compendium. Datapharm Communications Ltd. www.emc.medicines.org.uk [Accessed: 28/04/2004].
5. ABPI Medicines Compendium (2003b) *Summary of product characteristics for EVRA transdermal patch*. Electronic Medicines Compendium. Datapharm Communications Ltd. www.emc.medicines.org.uk [Accessed: 05/02/2004].
6. ADRAC (2003) Implanon and vaginal bleeding. *Australian Adverse Drug Reactions Bulletin* **22**(3), 11–12.
7. Andersson, K., Batar, I. and Rybo, G. (1992) Return to fertility after removal of a Levonorgestrel-releasing intrauterine device and Nova-T. *Contraception* **46**(6), 575–584.
8. Andersson, K., Odlind, V. and Rybo, G. (1994) Levonorgestrel-releasing and copper releasing (Nova T) IUDs during five years of use: a randomized comparative trial. *Contraception* **49**(1), 56–72.
9. Audet, M.C., Moreau, M., Koltun, W.D. et al (2001) Evaluation of contraceptive efficacy and cycle control of a transdermal contraceptive patch vs an oral contraceptive: a randomized controlled trial. *Journal of the American Medical Association* **285**(18), 2347–2354. [Full text]
10. Bates, D., Ashford, E., Dawson, R. et al (1994) Subcutaneous sumatriptan during the migraine aura. Sumatriptan Aura Study Group. *Neurology* **44**(9), 1587–1592.
11. Belfield, T. (Ed.) (1999) *FPA contraceptive handbook: a guide for family planning and other health professionals*. 3rd edn. London: Family Planning Association.
12. Beral, V., Hermon, C., Kay, C. et al (1999) Mortality associated with oral contraceptive use: 25 year follow up of cohort of 46000 women from Royal College of General Practitioners' oral contraception study. *British Medical Journal* **318**(7176), 96–100. [Full text]
13. Berenson, A.B., Radecki, C.M., Grady, J.J. et al (2001) A prospective, controlled study of the effects of hormonal contraception on bone mineral density. *Obstetrics & Gynecology* **98**(4), 576–582.
14. Bigrigg, A., Evans, A., Gbolade, B. et al (1999) Depo provera. Position paper on clinical use, effectiveness and side effects. *British Journal of Family Planning* **25**(2), 69–76.
15. BNF 47 (2004) *British National Formulary*. 47th edn. London: British Medical Association and Royal Pharmaceutical Society of Great Britain.
16. Bounds, W. (1994) Contraceptive efficacy of the diaphragm and cervical caps used in conjunction with a spermicide – a fresh look at the evidence. *British Journal of Family Planning* **20**(3), 84–87.
17. Chang, C.L., Donaghy, M. and Poulter, N. (1999) Migraine and stroke in young women: case-control study. *British Medical Journal* **318**(7175), 13–18. [Full text]
18. Collaborative Group on Hormonal Factors in Breast Cancer (1996) Breast cancer and hormonal contraceptives: collaborative reanalysis of individual data on 53297 women with breast cancer and 100239 women without breast cancer from 54 epidemiological studies. *Lancet* **347**(9017), 1713–1727. [Full text]
19. Collaborative Study Group on the Desogestrel-containing Progestogen-only Pill (1998) A double-blind study comparing the contraceptive efficacy, acceptability and safety of two progestogen-only pills containing desogestrel 75 micrograms/day or levonorgestrel 30 micrograms/day. *European Journal of Contraception & Reproductive Health Care* **3**(4), 169–178.
20. Cook, L., Nanda, K. and Grimes, D. (2003) *Diaphragm versus diaphragm with spermicides for*

C

contraception (Cochrane Review). The Cochrane Library. Issue 4. Oxford: Update Software. [Accessed: 13/01/2004].
21. Cosmi, B., Legnani, C., Bernardi, F. et al (2003) Role of family history in identifying women with thrombophilia and higher risk of venous thromboembolism during oral contraception. *Archives of Internal Medicine* **163**(9), 1105–1109. [Full text]
22. Cramer, D.W., Goldman, M.B., Schiff, I. et al (1987) The relationship of tubal infertility to barrier method and oral contraceptive use. *Journal of the American Medical Association* **257**(18), 2446–2450.
23. CSM (1999) Combined oral contraceptives containing desogestrel or gestodene and the risk of venous thromboembolism. *Current Problems in Pharmacovigilance* **25**(Jun), 12
24. CSM (2000) Reminder: St John's wort (hypericum perforatum) interactions. *Current Problems in Pharmacovigilance* **26**(May), 6–7.
25. CSM (2002) Cyproterone acetate (Dianette): risk of venous thromboembolism (VTE). *Current Problems in Pharmacovigilance* **28**(Oct), 9–10.
26. CSM (2004) *Updated prescribing advice on the effect of depo-provera contraception on bones*. Committee on Safety of Medicines. http://medicines.mhra.gov.uk [Accessed: 14/02/2005].
27. DTB (1991) Helping patients to make the best use of medicines. *Drug & Therapeutics Bulletin* **29**(1), 1–4.
28. DTB (1993) Femidom – a condom for women. *Drug & Therapeutics Bulletin* **31**(4), 15–16.
29. DTB (1996) Long-acting progestogen-only contraception. *Drug & Therapeutics Bulletin* **34**(12), 93–96.
30. DTB (1999) Drugs in the peri-operative period: 3 – hormonal contraceptives and hormone replacement therapy. *Drug & Therapeutics Bulletin* **37**(10), 78–79.
31. DTB (2000) Oral contraceptives and cardiovascular risk. *Drug & Therapeutics Bulletin* **38**(1), 1–5. [Full text]
32. DTB (2001) Etonogestrel implant (Implanon) for contraception. *Drug & Therapeutics Bulletin* **39**(8), 57–59.
33. DTB (2002a) Contraception in teenagers. *Drug & Therapeutics Bulletin* **40**(12), 92–95.
34. DTB (2002b) Is Yasmin a "truly different" pill? *Drug & Therapeutics Bulletin* **40**(8), 57–59.
35. DTB (2003a) Evra – a patch on oral contraception? *Drug & Therapeutics Bulletin* **41**(12), 89–91.
36. DTB (2003b) Is Cerazette the minipill of choice? *Drug & Therapeutics Bulletin* **41**(9), 68–69.
37. Dunn, N., Thorogood, M. and Faragher, B. (1999) Oral contraceptives and myocardial infarction: results of the NICA case-control study. *British Medical Journal* **318**(7198), 1579–1583.
38. Edwards, J.E. and Moore, A. (1999) Implanon: a review of clinical studies. *British Journal of Family Planning* **24**(4), 3–16.
39. Elliman, A. (2000) Interactions with hormonal contraception. *Journal of Family Planning & Reproductive Health Care* **26**(2), 109–111.
40. Feely, M. (1999) Fortnightly review: drug treatment of epilepsy. *British Medical Journal* **318**(7176), 106–109. [Full text]
41. Fernandez, E., La Vecchia, C., Balducci, A. et al (2001) Oral contraceptives and colorectal cancer risk: a meta-analysis. *British Journal of Cancer* **84**(5), 722–727.
42. Fernie, C.G.M (2003) *Personal communication*. Medical Adviser, Medical and Dental Defense Union of Scotland: Glasgow.
43. FFPRHC Clinical Effectiveness Unit (2000) First prescription of combined oral contraception: recommendations for clinical practice. *British Journal of Family Planning* **26**(1), 27–38.
44. FFPRHC Clinical Effectiveness Unit (2003a) FFPRHC guidance: first prescription of combined oral contraception. *Journal of Family Planning and Reproductive Health Care* **29**(4), 209–223.
45. FFPRHC Clinical Effectiveness Unit (2003b) FFPRHC guidance: emergency contraception. *Journal of Family Planning and Reproductive Health Care* **29**(2), 9–15.
46. FFPRHC Clinical Effectiveness Unit (2003c) *New product review: Desogestrel-only pill (Cerazette)*. Faculty of Family Planning and Reproductive Health Care. www.ffprhc.org.uk [Accessed: 16/01/2004].
47. FFPRHC Clinical Effectiveness Unit (2004a) FFPRHC guidance: the copper intrauterine device as long-term contraception. *Journal of Family Planning and Reproductive Health Care* **30**(1), 29–42.
48. FFPRHC Clinical Effectiveness Unit (2004b) New Product Review (September 2003): Norelgestromin/ethinyl oestradiol transdermal contraceptive system (Evra). *Journal of Family Planning & Reproductive Health Care* **30**(1), 43–45.
49. Freundl, G. (1999) European multicentre study of natural family planning (1989–1995): efficacy and drop-out. *Advances in Contraception* **15**(1), 69–82.
50. Freundl, G., Godehardt, E., Kern, P.A. et al (2003) Estimated maximum failure rates of cycle monitors using daily conception probabilities in the menstrual cycle. *Human Reproduction* **18**(12), 2628–2633.
51. Gallo, M.F., Grimes, D.A. and Schulz, K.F. (2003a) Nonlatex vs. latex male condoms for contraception: a systematic review of randomized controlled trials. *Contraception* **68**(5), 319–326.
52. Gallo, M.F., Grimes, D.A. and Schulz, K.F. (2003b) *Cervical cap versus diaphragm for contraception (Cochrane Review)*. The Cochrane Library. Issue 4. Oxford: Update Software.
53. Gallo, M.F., Grimes, D.A., Schulz, K.F. and Helmerhorst, F.M. (2003c) *Combination contraceptives: effects on weight (Cochrane Review)*. The Cochrane Library. Issue 4. Oxford: Update Software. [Full text]
54. Glasier, A. (1999) Contraception. In: Edmonds, D.K. (Ed.) *Dewhurst's textbook of obstetrics & gynaecology for postgraduates*. 6th edn. London: Blackwell Science. 373–386.
55. Guillebaud, J. (Ed.) (1999) *Contraception: your questions answered*. 3rd edn. Edinburgh: Churchill Livingstone.
56. Hannaford, P. (2000) Cardiovascular events associated with different combined oral contraceptives: a review of current data. *Drug Safety* **22**(5), 361–371.
57. Hannaford, P.C. and Kay, P.C. (1998) The risk of serious illness among oral contraceptive users: evidence from the RCGP's oral contraceptive study. *British Journal of General Practice* **48**(435), 1657–1662.
58. Hendrix, S.L. and Alexander, N.J. (2002) Primary dysmenorrhea treatment with a desogestrel-containing low-dose oral contraceptive. *Contraception* **66**(6), 393–399.
59. Holt, V.L., Scholes, D., Wicklund, K.G. et al (2005) Body mass index, weight, and oral contraceptive failure risk. *Obstetrics & Gynecology* **105**(1), 46–52.
60. IARC (Ed.) (1999) *Hormonal contraception and post menopausal hormonal therapy*. Lyons: World Health Organisation.

1. Iyer, V., Farquhar, C. and Jepson, R. (2003) *Oral contraceptive pills for heavy menstrual bleeding (Cochrane Review)*. The Cochrane Library. Issue 4. Oxford: Update Software.
2. Kennedy, K.I., Rivera, R. and McNeilly, A.S. (1989) Consensus statement on the use of breastfeeding as a family planning method. *Contraception* **39**(5), 477–496.
3. Khader, Y.S., Rice, J., John, L. and Abueita, O. (2003) Oral contraceptives use and the risk of myocardial infarction: a meta-analysis. *Contraception* **68**(1), 11–17.
4. Lethaby, A.E., Cooke, I. and Rees, M. (2000) *Progesterone/progestogen releasing intrauterine systems versus either placebo or any other medication for heavy menstrual bleeding (Cochrane Review)*. The Cochrane Library. Issue 4. Oxford: Update Software.
5. Lewis, M.A., Heinemann, L.A., Spitzer, W.O. et al (1997) The use of oral contraceptives and the occurrence of acute myocardial infarction in young women. Results from the Transnational Study on Oral Contraceptives and the Health of Young Women. *Contraception* **56**(3), 129–140.
6. Lidegaard, O. (1995) Oral contraceptives, pregnancy and the risk of cerebral thromboembolism: the influence of diabetes, hypertension, migraine and previous thrombotic disease. *British Journal of Obstetrics & Gynaecology* **102**(2), 153–159.
7. Lidegaard, O., Edstrom, B. and Kreiner, S. (2002) Oral contraceptives and venous thromboembolism: a five-year national case-control study. *Contraception* **65**(3), 187–196.
8. Loudon, N., Glasier, A. and Gebbie, A. (Eds.) (1995) *Handbook of family planning and reproductive health care*. 3rd edn. Edinburgh: Churchill Livingstone.
9. Luukkainen, T. and Toivonen, J. (1995) Levonorgestrel-releasing IUD as a method of contraception with therapeutic properties. *Contraception* **52**(5), 269–276.
0. MacGregor, E.A. (2001) Hormonal contraception and migraine. *Journal of Family Planning & Reproductive Health Care* **27**(1), 49–52.
1. Mansour, D. (2004) *Personal communication. Coming off HRT*. Consultant in Community Gynaecology and Reproductive Health Care, Newcastle upon Tyne.
2. McCann, M.F. and Potter, L.S. (1994) Progestin-only oral contraception: a comprehensive review. *Contraception* **50**(6 Suppl 1), 1–195.
3. MeReC (1995) The treatment of epilepsy (part 1). *MeReC Bulletin* **6**(5), 17–20.
4. Moore, J., Kennedy, S. and Prentice, A. (2003) *Modern combined oral contraceptives for pain associated with endometriosis (Cochrane Review)*. The Cochrane Library. Issue 4. Oxford: Update Software.
5. National Statistics (2003) *Contraception and sexual health, 2002*. Office for National Statistics. www.statistics.gov.uk [Accessed: 07/01/2004].
6. O'Brien, P.A. and Marfleet, C. (2003) *Frameless versus classical intrauterine device for contraception (Cochrane Review)*. The Cochrane Library. Issue 4. Oxford: Update Software.
7. Office for National Statistics (1997) *Incidence of Health of the Nation cancers by social class*. Population Trends 90. Office for National Statistics. www.statistics.gov.uk [Accessed: 03/02/2004].
8. Organon Laboratories Medical Information (2004) *Personal communication*. Organon Laboratories Medical Information: Cambridge.
79. Panser, L.A. and Phipps, W.R. (1991) Type of oral contraceptive in relation to acute, initial episodes of pelvic inflammatory disease. *Contraception* **43**(1), 91–99.
80. Pitkin, J. (2000) Contraception and the menopause. *Maturitas* **34**(Suppl 1), S29-S36.
81. Proctor, M.L., Roberts, H. and Farquhar, C.M. (2003) *Combined oral contraceptive pill (OCP) as treatment for primary dysmenorrhoea (Cochrane Review)*. The Cochrane Library. Issue 4. Oxford: Update Software.
82. Pyper, C.M.M. (1997) Fertility awareness and natural family planning. *European Journal of Contraception & Reproductive Health Care* **2**(2), 131–146.
83. RCOG (1998) *The initial management of menorrhagia. Evidence-based clinical guidelines no. 1*. London: Royal College of Obstetricians & Gynaecologists.
84. RCOG (2002a) *The care of women requesting induced abortion*. Royal College of Obstetricians. www.rcog.org.uk [Accessed: 13/12/2002]. [Full text]
85. RCOG (2002b) *Key points from the faculty of family planning and reproductive healthcare expert consensus meeting 2002*. Royal College of Obstetricians & Gynaecologists. www.ffprhc.org.uk [Accessed: 17/12/2003].
86. Rice, C.F., Killick, S.R., Dieben, T. and Coelingh Bennink, H. (1999) A comparison of the inhibition of ovulation achieved by desogestrel 75 ug and levonorgestrel 30 ug daily. *Human Reproduction* **14**(4), 982–985. [Full text]
87. Robinson, C. and Kubba, A.A. (1997) Medical problems and oral contraceptives. *Current Obstetrics & Gynaecology* **7**(3), 173–179.
88. Roddy, R.E., Zekeng, L., Ryan, K.A. et al (2002) Effect of nonoxynol-9 gel on urogenital gonorrhea and chlamydial infection: a randomized controlled trial. *Journal of the American Medical Association* **287**(9), 1117–1122. [Full text]
89. Scholes, D., Lacroix, A.Z., Ichikawa, L.E. et al (2002) Injectable hormone contraception and bone density: results from a prospective study. *Epidemiology* **13**(5), 581–587.
90. Seaman, H.E., de Vries, C.S. and Farmer, R.D.T. (2003) The risk of venous thromboembolism in women prescribed cyproterone acetate in combination with ethinyl estradiol: a nested cohort analysis and case-control study. *Human Reproduction* **18**(3), 522–526.
91. Seibert, C., Barbouche, E., Fagan, J. et al (2003) Prescribing oral contraceptives for women older than 35 years of age. *Annals of Internal Medicine* **138**(1), 54–64. [Full text]
92. SIGN (2003) *Diagnosis and management of epilepsy in adults*. Report no. 70. Scottish Intercollegiate Guidelines Network. www.sign.ac.uk [Accessed: 30/05/2003].
93. Smith, R.P. (1993) Cyclic pelvic pain and dysmenorrhea. *Obstetrics & Gynecology Clinics of North America* **20**(4), 753–764.
94. Smith, J.S., Green, J., Berrington de Gonzalez, A. et al (2003) Cervical cancer and use of hormonal contraceptives: a systematic review. *Lancet* **361**(9364), 1159–1167. [Full text]
95. Sturridge, F. and Guillebaud, J. (1997) Gynaecological aspects of the levonorgestrel-releasing intrauterine system. *British Journal of Obstetrics & Gynaecology* **104**(3), 285–289.
96. Teenage Pregnancy Unit (2001) *Guidance for the field social workers, residential social workers and foster carers providing information and referring young people to contraception and sexual health services*.

Department of Health. www.dh.gov.uk [Accessed: 29/04/2004]. [Full text]
97. The Consensus Committee of the Society of Obstetricians and Gynaecologists of Canada (1998) The Canadian consensus conference on contraception. *Journal SOGC* **20**(8), 1–75.
98. The Contraception Report (2003) Hormonal contraception and bone density. *The Contraception Report* **14**(2), 4–9.
99. Trussell, J. (2004) Contraceptive efficacy. In: Hatcher, R.A., Trussell, J., Stewart, F. et al (Eds.) *Contraceptive technology*. 18th edn. New York: Ardent Media.
100. Trussell, J., Hatcher, R.A., Cates, W. et al (1990) Contraceptive failure in the United States: an update. *British Journal of Family Planning* **21**(1), 51–63.
101. Trussell, J., Strickler, J. and Vaughan, B. (1993) Contraceptive efficacy of the diaphragm, the sponge and the cervical cap. *Family Planning Perspectives* **25**(3), 100–135.
102. Tuckey, J. (2000) Combined oral contraception and cancer. *British Journal of Family Planning* **26**(4), 237–240.
103. Tzourio, C., Tehindrazanarivelo, A., Iglésias, S. et al (1995) Case-control study of migraine and risk of ischaemic stroke in young women. *British Medical Journal* **310**(6983), 830–833. [Full text]
104. Van Damme, L., Ramjee, G., Alary, M. et al (2002) Effectiveness of COL-1492, a nonoxynol-9 vaginal gel, on HIV-1 transmission in female sex workers: a randomised controlled trial. *Lancet* **360**(9338), 971–977. [Full text]
105. van Grootheest, K. and Vrieling, T. (2003) Drug points: thromboembolism associated with the new contraceptive Yasmin. *British Medical Journal* **326**(7383), 257. [Full text]
106. Van Vliet, H.A.A.M., Grimes, D.A., Helmerhorst, F.M. and Schulz, K.F. (2001) *Biphasic versus monophasic oral contraceptives for contraception (Cochrane Review)*. The Cochrane Library. Issue 2. Oxford: Update Software.
107. Van Vliet, H.A.A.M., Grimes, D.A., Helmerhorst, F.M. and Schulz, K.F. (2003) *Biphasic versus triphasic oral contraceptives for contraception (Cochrane Review)*. The Cochrane Library. Issue 4. Oxford: Update Software.
108. Vasilakis-Scaramozza, C. and Jick, H. (2001) Risk of venous thromboembolism with cyproterone or levonorgestrel contraceptives. *Lancet* **358**(9291), 1427–1429. [Full text]
109. Vessey, M. and Painter, R. (2001) Oral contraceptive failures and body weight: findings in a large cohort study. *Journal of Family Planning and Reproductive Health Care* **27**(2), 90–91.
110. Vessey, M., Villard-Mackintosh, L. and Yeates, D. (1990) Effectiveness of progestogen-only oral contraceptives. *British Journal of Family Planning* **16**(2), 79.
111. Vessey, M., Painter, R. and Yeates, D. (2003) Mortality in relation to oral contraceptive use and cigarette smoking. *Lancet* **362**(9379), 185–191. [Ful text]
112. Wanichsetakul, P., Kamudhamas, A., Watanaruangkovit, P. et al (2002) Bone mineral density at various anatomic bone sites in women receiving combined oral contraceptives and depot-medroxyprogesterone acetate for contraception. *Contraception* **65**(6), 407–410.
113. Weaver, K. and Glasier, A. (1999) Interaction between broad-spectrum antibiotics and the combined oral contraceptive pill. *Contraception* **59**(2), 71–78.
114. Weisberg, E. (2002) Contraception, hormone replacement therapy and thrombosis. *Australian Prescriber* **25**(3), 57–59.
115. WHO (1996a) Ischaemic stroke and combined oral contraceptives: results of an international, multicentre, case-control study. *Lancet* **348**(9026), 498–505. [Full text]
116. WHO (1996b) Haemorrhagic stroke, overall stroke risk, and combined oral contraceptives: results of an international, multicentre, case-control study. *Lance* **348**(9026), 505–510. [Full text]
117. WHO (1998) *Cardiovascular disease and steroid hormone contraception*. WHO Technical Report Series 877. Geneva: World Health Organisation.
118. WHO (2002) *Selected practice recommendations for contraceptive use*. World Health Organisation. www.who.int/reproductive-health/publications/rhr_02_7/index.htm [Accessed: 15/08/2003].
119. WHO (2004) *Medical eligibility criteria for contraceptive use (third edition)*. World Health Organisation. www.who.int/reproductive-health/publications/mec [Accessed: 30/09/2004].
120. WHO Task Force on Methods for the Natural Regulation of Fertility (1999) The World Health Organization multinational study of breast-feeding and lactational amenorrhea III. Pregnancy during breast-feeding. *Fertility & Sterility* **72**(3), 431–440.
121. Zieman, M., Guillebaud, J., Weisberg, E. et al (2001) Integrated summary of contraceptive efficacy with th ORTHO EVRA(TM)/EVRA(TM) transdermal system. *Fertility and Sterility* **76**(3 Suppl 1), S19.

Evidence grading

The evidence grading used in this guidance represents that used by the Faculty of Family Planning and Reproductive Health Care Clinical Effectiveness Unit. The definitions of grades of recommendation are as follows:

A Evidence is based on randomized, controlled trials

B Evidence is based on other robust experimental or observational studies

C Evidence is limited, but the advice relies on expert opinion and has the endorsement of respected authorities

PRODIGY GUIDANCE

Contraception — emergency

Last revised in September 2004
www.prodigy.nhs.uk/guidance.asp?gt=Contraception - emergency

Applies to women from the age of 12 to 60 years

This guidance is based on the Faculty of Family Planning and Reproductive Health Care guidance, Emergency Contraception (June 2003).

This guidance covers the management of women who wish to avoid a pregnancy after unprotected sexual intercourse or potential contraceptive failure.

This guidance does not cover the management of women requesting regular contraception.

There is separate PRODIGY guidance on *Contraception* (covering regular contraception).

C

Goals

- Avoidance of unintended pregnancies after unprotected intercourse or potential contraceptive failure

Contents

Scenarios

- Oral progestogen-only emergency contraception p.435
- Intra-uterine device p.436
- Taking a liver enzyme-inducing drug p.438

Extended Information, p. 440

Which scenario?

- **Oral progestogen-only emergency contraception:** covers the management of women requesting the oral hormonal emergency contraceptive Levonelle-2®.
- **Intra-uterine device:** covers the management of women requesting an intra-uterine device for emergency contraception.
- **Taking a liver enzyme-inducing drug:** covers the management of women who request emergency contraception and are taking a liver enzyme-inducing drug (concurrently or within 28 days). Liver enzyme-inducing drugs include: rifampicin, rifabutin, barbiturates, bosentan, carbamazepine, oxcarbazepine, phenytoin, ritonavir (and possibly other antivirals) griseofulvin, topiramate and St John's Wort.

Oral progestogen-only emergency contraception

Which therapy?

See *When is emergency contraception indicated?* in *Management issues*.

- **Discuss the options and failure rates of copper-containing intra-uterine devices (IUDs) and progestogen-only emergency contraception** to allow the woman to make an informed choice. The copper-containing IUD is more effective and may be the method of choice when maximum efficacy is the woman's priority.
- **Progestogen-only emergency contraception should be taken as a single dose of 1.5 mg of levonorgestrel as soon as possible and within 72 hours (3 days)** of unprotected sex or potential contraceptive failure.
- **The risk of vomiting is low; but if it occurs within 2 hours,** either repeat the dose, or alternatively consider an IUD. Domperidone can also be used to reduce nausea and vomiting.
- **Advise the use of barrier methods or abstinence from sex for the rest of the cycle** (or until the combined oral contraceptive pill has been resumed for 7 consecutive days or the progestogen-only pill has been resumed for 2 consecutive days).
- **Advise a woman who takes oral emergency contraception because of missed pills:**
  - To resume her hormonal contraception at the usual time as long as it is within 12 hours of taking the oral emergency contraception.
  - To omit the pill-free period or inactive pills (combined oral contraceptives) if the missed pills were from the last 7 pills in the packet.
- **Advise the woman to return if her next period is more than 7 days late** or if it is unusually short or light.
- **Discuss future contraception.**

Practical prescribing points

For further information please see the *Medicines Compendium* (www.medicines.org.uk) or the *British National Formulary* (www.bnf.org).

Contraindications to progestogen-only emergency contraception

- **Established pregnancy is a contraindication to use.**
- The World Health Organization (WHO) considers that there are no other absolute medical contraindications to the use of emergency contraceptive pills, on currently available evidence.
- **Caution should be used in women with** acute active porphyria, severe liver disease, or severe malabsorption syndromes [ABPI Medicines Compendium, 2003; FFPRHC Clinical Effectiveness Unit, 2003].
- For a full list of the WHO medical eligibility criteria and other category classifications for progestogen-only emergency contraceptive use, see www.who.int/reproductive-health/publications/mec/6_ecps_july.pdf.

Follow-up advice

- **Explain the need to return promptly** if the next period is delayed more than 7 days or if the period is shorter or lighter than usual. Consider the possibility of an ectopic pregnancy, particularly in someone with a previous history of ectopic pregnancy, fallopian tube surgery, or pelvic inflammatory disease.
- Offer an appointment or explain arrangements in case of any problems with the treatment (e.g. vomiting).
- Offer an appointment or explain arrangements for future contraceptive information or supply.

- Offer an appointment or make arrangements for communication of infection screen results.

Should I refer or investigate?

Refer?

- **If a sexually transmitted infection is suspected,** test as appropriate and/or refer to the genito-urinary medicine clinic for follow-up and partner notification.
- **If further advice is required,** consider contacting a local family planning clinic or the Family Planning Association Helpline and Information Service:
  - fpa UK 0845-310-1334
  - www.fpa.org.uk

Investigate?

- **Routinely test for chlamydia and other sexually transmitted infections (STI) in women with a high-risk of acquiring an STI:**
  - Sexually active women under the age of 25 years.
  - Women over 25 years with a new partner or who have had two or more partners in the previous 12 months.

Patient information leaflets

The following PILs are available at www.prodigy.nhs.uk

- FPA (sexual health & contraception)

Shared decision making

- Emergency contraception can prevent pregnancy if you have had sex without using contraception, or if you had a mistake with a contraceptive method.
- **Emergency contraceptive pills** prevent at least three out of four pregnancies that would have occurred without emergency contraception.
- **An alternative is to insert an intra-uterine device (IUD).** The IUD needs to be fitted within 5 days of your having unprotected sex, or within 5 days of the earliest time you could have ovulated. The IUD has the advantage of providing ongoing contraception, and is more effective (almost 100%).
- **If you take the emergency contraceptive pills:**
  - Take it as a single dose as soon as possible, and no later than 72 hours after the episode of unprotected sex.
  - If you vomit within two hours of taking it, then contact a healthcare professional as soon as possible for advice.
- **Emergency contraceptive pills do not provide cover for the rest of the cycle,** so it is important to discuss ongoing contraception with a doctor or nurse.
- **If your period is more than seven days late,** you should see a doctor or a nurse.

Drug rationale

Drugs not included

- **Combined oral contraceptive pills** are not licensed for emergency contraception in the UK and are not recommended.
- **Anti-emetics other than domperidone** are not recommended: metoclopramide and phenothiazines can cause extrapyramidal adverse effects, particularly in young women. Anti-emetics that can cause drowsiness are also not recommended.
- **Levonelle One Step®** is an alternative preparation of levonorgestrel. It contains levonorgestrel 1.5 mg in a single tablet, but it is over twice as expensive as Levonelle-2®.

Drugs included

- **Levonelle-2®** contains two levonorgestrel 750 microgram tablets which are taken together as a single dose. Data from one large randomized controlled trial has found no differences in pregnancy rates between single and divided doses within 120 hours of unprotected intercourse [von Hertzen et al, 2002].
- **Domperidone is the anti-emetic** recommended for women who vomit after taking oral emergency contraception or for women have previously vomited after taking it [FFPRHC Clinical Effectiveness Unit, 2003].

Prescriptions

Levonelle-2

Levonelle-2 tablets

- Age from 12 to 60 years
- Levonelle-2 750microgram tabs. Take two tablets together as soon as possible after unprotected intercourse; supply 2 tablets; NHS Cost £5.50; OTC Cost £24.00.

Levonelle-2 and domperidone

Levonelle-2 tablets + domperidone 10mg tablets

- Age from 12 to 60 years
- Levonelle-2 750microgram tabs. Take two tablets together as soon as possible after unprotected intercourse; supply 2 tablets; NHS Cost £5.50; OTC Cost £24.00.
- Domperidone 10mg tablets. Take one tablet at the same time or just before you take Levonelle-2 to prevent nausea and vomiting; supply 1 tablets; NHS Cost £0.08.

Intra-uterine device

Which therapy?

See *When is emergency contraception indicated?* in *Management issues.*

- **An intra-uterine device (IUD) containing COPPER is the most effective method of emergency contraception.**
- **At any time in the cycle, insert up to 120 hours (5 days)** after unprotected intercourse or potential contraceptive failure.
- **The IUD can also be fitted up to 5 days after the estimated earliest day of ovulation** (i.e. up to day 19 of a 28-day cycle).
- **If it is not possible to fit an IUD immediately, consider prescribing progestogen-only emergency contraception** as preliminary cover if within 72 hours of unprotected sexual intercourse or potential contraceptive failure.
- **A sexual history should be taken** to assess the risk of a sexually transmitted infection (STI). A woman at high-risk of infection should be routinely tested for an STI, particularly *Chlamydia trachomatis*.
- **Consider prophylactic antibiotics in a woman at high risk of sexually transmitted infection.** Note: *routine* antibiotic use prior to IUD insertion is not recommended.
- **Discuss future contraception needs.**

Practical prescribing points

For further information please see the *Medicines Compendium* (www.medicines.org.uk) or the *British National Formulary* (www.bnf.org).

Contraindications to intra-uterine device insertion

The World Health Organization (WHO) considers that the same eligibility criteria that apply to the insertion of a copper-containing intra-uterine device (IUD) in normal circumstances should be applied for post-coital insertion. For a full list of the WHO medical eligibility criteria and other category classifications for the copper IUD for emergency contraceptive, see www.who.int/reproductive-health/publications/mec/8_e_iud.pdf.

The Faculty of Family Planning and Reproductive Health Care Clinical Effectiveness Unit recommends that:

- A woman at higher risk of sexually transmitted infections (STIs) may still choose to use an IUD after counselling about other contraceptive methods.
- A woman with pelvic inflammatory disease within the last 3 months may use an IUD after considering other contraceptive methods, provided there are no signs and symptoms of infection.
- A woman who is HIV-positive may be offered an IUD after testing for bacterial STIs.

Follow-up advice

Explain the need to return promptly if the next period is delayed more than 7 days or if the period is shorter or lighter than usual.

If an intra-uterine device (IUD) is to be used for ongoing contraception, a follow-up visit is recommended 3–6 weeks after insertion (provided the woman has had a normal period).

Offer an appointment or make arrangements for communication of infection screen results.

- Offer an appointment after the next period for the IUD to be removed if it is not required for ongoing contraception.

Should I refer or investigate?

Refer?

- **If a sexually transmitted infection is suspected,** consider testing and/or refer to the genito-urinary medicine clinic for follow-up and partner notification.
- **If further advice is required,** consider contacting a local family planning clinic or the Family Planning Association Helpline and Information Service:
  - fpa 0845-310-1334
  - www.fpa.org.uk

Investigate?

- Prior to emergency insertion of an intra-uterine device, routinely test for chlamydia and other sexually transmitted infections (STIs) in women with a high-risk of acquiring an STI:
  - Sexually active women under the age of 25 years.
  - Women over 25 years with a new partner or who have had two or more partners in the previous 12 months.

Patient information leaflets

The following PILs are available at www.prodigy.nhs.uk

- FPA (sexual health & contraception)

Shared decision making

- **An intra-uterine device (IUD)** is effective (almost 100%) at preventing pregnancy after unprotected sex.
- **The IUD needs to be fitted within 5 days** of your having unprotected sex, or within 5 days of the earliest time you could have ovulated.
- The IUD provides long-term contraception, or can be removed with your next period.
- **If you are at risk of getting a sexually transmitted infection,** you could develop a pelvic infection when an IUD is inserted.
- **You should have a check-up** a few weeks after the IUD has been inserted.

C

Drug rationale

Drugs not included

- **Intra-uterine devices containing a surface area of less than 300 mm² of copper have not been included;** for ongoing contraception, they are less effective than devices with a large surface area of copper (greater than 300 mm²).

Drugs included

- **Intra-uterine devices (IUDs) containing a surface area of 300 mm² of copper or more** (Flexi-T 300, Multiload Cu375, Nova-T 380, and T-Safe Cu 380) are recommended for emergency contraception, and can also be used if the IUD is required for ongoing contraception. Training is required before inserting or removing any IUD.
- **Gynefix, a frameless IUD,** is another option, particularly for a woman unable to use framed IUDs. The healthcare professional inserting or removing the device requires training and competence in the technique (which is different from that used with other IUDs).

Prescriptions

Framed intra-uterine devices

Flexi T-300 intra-uterine device

- Age from 12 to 60 years
- Flexi T-300 IUD. For insertion into the uterine cavity; supply 1 IUD; NHS Cost £8.65.

Multiload Cu-375 intra-uterine device

- Age from 12 to 60 years
- Multiload Cu-375 IUD. For insertion into the uterine cavity; supply 1 IUD; NHS Cost £9.24.

Nova-T 380 intra-uterine device

- Age from 12 to 60 years
- Nova-T 380 IUD. For insertion into the uterine cavity; supply 1 IUD; NHS Cost £13.50.

T-Safe 380A intra-uterine device

- Age from 12 to 60 years
- T-Safe 380A IUD. For insertion into the uterine cavity; supply 1 IUD; NHS Cost £9.40.

Frameless intra-uterine device

GyneFix intra-uterine device

- Age from 12 to 60 years
- GyneFixIN IUD. For insertion into the uterine cavity; supply 1 IUD; NHS Cost £24.75.

C

Taking a liver enzyme-inducing drug

Which therapy?

See *When is emergency contraception indicated?* in *Management issues.*

General points

- **An intra-uterine device (IUD) containing copper is recommended** for emergency contraception in a woman taking liver enzyme-inducing drugs (concurrently or within 28 days). Liver enzyme-inducing drugs include rifampicin, rifabutin, barbiturates, bosentan, carbamazepine, oxcarbazepine, phenytoin, ritonavir (and possibly other antivirals) griseofulvin, topiramate and St John's Wort.
- **Progestogen-only emergency contraception at a 50% increased dose is an alternative.** Note: this option is not recommended for a woman taking a potent inducer of liver enzymes (i.e. rifampicin or rifabutin).
- **Advise the woman to return if her next period is more than 7 days late** or if it is unusually short or light.
- **Discuss future contraception needs.**

Copper-containing IUD

- **An IUD with a surface area of COPPER of 300 mm^2 is recommended.**
- **At any time in the cycle, insert up to 120 hours (5 days)** after unprotected intercourse or potential contraceptive failure.
- **The IUD can also be fitted up to 5 days after the estimated earliest day of ovulation** (i.e. up to day 19 of a 28-day cycle).
- **If it is not possible to fit an IUD immediately, consider prescribing progestogen-only emergency contraception** as preliminary cover if within 72 hours of unprotected sexual intercourse or potential contraceptive failure.
- **A sexual history should be taken** to assess the risk of a sexually transmitted (STI) and a woman at high risk of infection should be routinely tested for an STI, particularly *Chlamydia trachomatis.*
- **Consider prophylactic antibiotics in a woman at high risk of sexually transmitted infection.** Note: *routine* antibiotic use prior to IUD insertion is not recommended.

Progestogen-only emergency contraception

- **An increased dose of Levonelle-2® is recommended:** prescribe 1.5 mg of levonorgestrel (2 tablets) to be taken as soon as possible and not later than 72 hours after the first episode of unprotected sex in that cycle. These tablets should be followed by 750 micrograms of levonorgestrel (1 tablet) 12 hours after the first dose. Note: this use is off-licence and there is no evidence of its potential efficacy.
- **If vomiting occurs within 2 hours of taking either dose,** either repeat the dose, or alternatively consider an IUD. Domperidone can be used to reduce nausea and vomiting.
- **Advise women who take progestogen-only emergency contraception because of missed pills to resume their hormonal contraception at the usual time,** as long as it is within 12 hours of taking the oral emergency contraception.
- **Advise the use of barrier methods or abstinence from sex for the rest of the cycle** (or until the combined oral contraceptive pill has been resumed for 7 consecutive days).
- Women who are 'tricycling' and require emergency contraception in the 7 days before the pill-free interval may be advised to continue the combined oral contraceptive pill to the end of the pack, start the next pack without a pill-free interval, and delay the pill-free interval until that pack is completed.

Practical prescribing points

For further information please see the *Medicines Compendium* (www.medicines.org.uk) or the *British National Formulary* (www.bnf.org).

Contraindications to insertion of an intra-uterine device

- The World Health Organization (WHO) considers that the same eligibility criteria that apply to the insertion of a copper-containing intra-uterine device (IUD) in norma[l] circumstances should be applied for post-coital insertion.
- For a full list of the WHO medical eligibility criteria and other category classifications for the copper IUD for emergency contraceptive, see www.who.int/reproductive-health/publications/mec/8_e_iud.pdf.

Contraindications to progestogen-only emergency contraception

- **Established pregnancy is a contraindication to use.**
- The WHO considers that there are no other absolute medical contraindications to the use of emergency contraceptive pills.
- Caution should be used in women with acute active porphyria, severe liver disease, or severe malabsorption syndromes [ABPI Medicines Compendium, 2003; FFPRHC Clinical Effectiveness Unit, 2003].

Follow-up advice

- **Explain the need to return promptly if the next period is delayed more than 7 days or if the period is shorter or lighter than usual.** If progestogen-only emergency contraception fails, consider the possibility of an ectopic pregnancy, particularly in a woman with a previous history of ectopic pregnancy, fallopian tube surgery, or pelvic inflammatory disease.
- Offer an appointment or explain arrangements for futur[e] contraceptive information or supply.
- Offer an appointment or make arrangements for communication of infection screen results.
- If an IUD is to be used for ongoing contraception, a follow-up visit is recommended 3–6 weeks after insertio[n] (provided the woman has had a normal period).
- Offer an appointment after the next period for the intra-uterine device (IUD) to be removed if it is not required for ongoing contraception.

Should I refer or investigate?

Refer?

- **If a sexually transmitted infection is suspected,** test as appropriate and/or refer to the genito-urinary medicine clinic for follow-up and partner notification.
- **If further advice is required,** consider contacting a local family planning clinic or the Family Planning Associatio[n] Helpline and Information Service:
  - fpa UK 0845-310-1334
  - www.fpa.org.uk

Investigate?

- Routinely test (prior to insertion, if an emergency intra-uterine device is to be used) for chlamydia and other sexually transmitted infections (STIs) in women with a high risk of acquiring an STI:

- Sexually active women under the age of 25 years.
- Women over 25 years with a new partner or who have had two or more partners in the previous 12 months.

Patient information leaflets

The following PILs are available at www.prodigy.nhs.uk
FPA (sexual health & contraception)

Shared decision making

Emergency contraception with an intra-uterine device (IUD) or with hormone pills can prevent pregnancy if you have had sex without using contraception, or if you had a mistake with a contraceptive method.

If you take 'enzyme inducing' medicines, they may reduce the effect of the hormone pills. In that case, experts advise taking a higher than usual dose of the pills.

Inserting an IUD is effective (almost 100%) at preventing pregnancy after unprotected sex.

- The IUD needs to be fitted within 5 days of your having unprotected sex, or within 5 days of the earliest time you could have ovulated.
- The IUD provides long-term contraception, or can be removed with your next period.
- If you are at risk of getting a sexually transmitted infection, you could develop a pelvic infection when an IUD is inserted.
- You should have a check-up a few weeks after the IUD has been fitted.

If you take emergency contraceptive pills whilst on an 'enzyme inducing' medicine:

- Take two pills together as soon as possible, and no later than 72 hours after the episode of unprotected sex.
- This action should be followed by one pill 12 hours after the first dose.
- If you vomit within 2 hours of taking either dose, then contact your GP or practice nurse as soon as possible for advice.

Emergency contraceptive pills do not provide cover for the rest of the cycle, so it is important to discuss ongoing contraception with a doctor or nurse.

If your period is more than seven days late, you should see a doctor or a nurse.

Drug rationale

Drugs not included

- **Intra-uterine devices (IUDs) containing a surface area of less than 300 mm² of copper have not been included;** for ongoing contraception, they are less effective than devices with a large surface area of copper (greater than 300 mm²).
- **Combined oral contraceptive pills** are not licensed for emergency contraception and are not recommended.
- **Anti-emetics other than domperidone** are not recommended: metoclopramide and phenothiazines can cause extrapyramidal adverse effects, particularly in young women. Anti-emetics that can cause drowsiness are also not recommended.

Drugs included

- **IUDs containing a surface area of 300 mm² of copper or more** (Flexi-T 300, Multiload Cu375, Nova-T 380, and T-Safe Cu 380) are recommended for emergency contraception, and can also be used if the IUD is required for ongoing contraception. Training is required before inserting or removing any IUD.
- **Gynefix, a frameless IUD,** is another option, particularly for a woman unable to use framed IUDs. The healthcare professional inserting or removing the device requires training and competence in the technique (which is different from that used for other IUDs).
- **Levonelle-2®** is the only licensed oral progestogen-only emergency contraception preparation available. A prescription is recommended for Levonelle-2® as a 1.5 mg immediate dose followed by 750 micrograms 12 hours later. Note: this use is off-licence and there is no evidence of its potential efficacy.
- **Domperidone is the anti-emetic** recommended for women who have previously vomited with progestogen-only emergency contraception or for those who have vomited after their first or second dose of levonorgestrel [FFPRHC Clinical Effectiveness Unit, 2003].

Prescriptions

Framed intra-uterine devices

Flexi T-300 intra-uterine device

- Age from 12 to 60 years
- Flexi T-300 IUD. For insertion into the uterine cavity; supply 1 IUD; NHS Cost £8.65.

Multiload Cu-375 intra-uterine device

- Age from 12 to 60 years
- Multiload Cu-375 IUD. For insertion into the uterine cavity; supply 1 IUD; NHS Cost £9.24.

Nova-T 380 intra-uterine device

- Age from 12 to 60 years
- Nova-T 380 IUD. For insertion into the uterine cavity; supply 1 IUD; NHS Cost £13.50.

T-Safe 380A intra-uterine device

- Age from 12 to 60 years
- T-Safe 380A IUD. For insertion into the uterine cavity; supply 1 IUD; NHS Cost £9.40.

Frameless intra-uterine device

GyneFix intra-uterine device

- Age from 12 to 60 years
- GyneFixIN IUD. For insertion into the uterine cavity; supply 1 IUD; NHS Cost £24.75.

Levonelle-2: if an IUD is not suitable

Levonelle-2 tablets

- Age from 12 to 60 years
- Levonelle-2 750microgram tabs. Take two tablets together as soon as possible after unprotected intercourse. Take a further tablet after 12 hours (and no later than 16 hours); supply 3 tablets; NHS Cost £11.00.

Levonelle-2 and domperidone: if an IUD is not suitable

Levonelle-2 tablets + domperidone 10mg tablets

- Age from 12 to 60 years
- Levonelle-2 750microgram tabs. Take two tablets together as soon as possible after unprotected intercourse. Take a further tablet after 12 hours (and no later than 16 hours); supply 3 tablets; NHS Cost £11.00.
- Domperidone 10mg tablets. Take one tablet at the same time or just before you take Levonelle-2 to prevent nausea and vomiting; supply 2 tablets; NHS Cost £0.16.

Extended Information

Background information

- What is it? p.440
- How often is it used? p.440
- How does it work? p.440

What is it?

- **Emergency contraception is a method of preventing pregnancy after unprotected sexual intercourse or potential contraceptive failure.**
- Two methods of emergency contraception are currently available in the UK:
  - Oral progestogen-only emergency contraceptive pills.
  - Post-coital insertion of a copper-containing intra-uterine device.

How often is it used?

- **In 1998, emergency contraception was prescribed on about 0.8 million occasions:**
  - Emergency contraception pills were prescribed in most cases.
  - Post-coital insertion of a copper-containing intra-uterine device was used in only 2–3% of cases.
- **In 2001, emergency contraceptives were prescribed on about 0.63 million occasions.** This slight fall may reflect the availability of Levonelle® without prescription from pharmacies.

[Office for National Statistics, 2003]

How does it work?

The established legal and medical view is that emergency contraception is not a method of abortion, as pregnancy is not legally recognized to exist until implantation is complete [DH, 2002]. *This view should be emphasized when counselling people.*

Mode of action of progestogen-only emergency contraception pills

- The precise mode of action is unknown [Croxatto, 2003].
- Ovulation is inhibited in up to 80% of women if progestogen-only emergency contraception is taken before the luteinizing hormone surge [Durand et al, 2001].
- An anti-implantation effect has been hypothesized, but there is limited evidence to support this [Durand et al, 2001; Marions et al, 2002].

Mode of action of post-coital copper-containing intra-uterine device (IUD)

- An intra-uterine device inhibits fertilization by reducing sperm numbers in the fallopian tube.
- Additionally, the copper ions alter the biochemical processes and enzymes involved in implantation.

[FFPRHC Clinical Effectiveness Unit, 2003; WHO, 2004]

Management issues

- When is emergency contraception indicated? p.440
- Emergency contraceptive products p.440
- Oral progestogen-only emergency contraception p.440
- Intra-uterine device p.443
- Legal issues relating to providing emergency contraception to girls under 16 years p.443

When is emergency contraception indicated?

- **The overall risk of pregnancy after a single act of unprotected sex on any day of the cycle is 2–4%** [Wilco et al, 1995] and is highest (20–30%) in the days before and just after ovulation (i.e. days 10–17 of a normal 28-day cycle). There is no day of the menstrual cycle when there can be *certainty* that unprotected sex would not result in pregnancy, although the probability is negligibl in the first 3 days of the cycle [Wilcox et al, 2001].
- **Emergency contraception is indicated when there is a risk of unintended pregnancy after:**
  - **Unprotected sex**, including situations where no contraceptive method was used, after rape or sexual assault (unless the woman is using regular contraception or has been sterilized), when withdraw methods have been used, or after ejaculation onto the external genitalia.
  - Potential method failures, summarized in Table 1.

[FFPRHC Clinical Effectiveness Unit, 2003]

Emergency contraceptive products

- **Progestogen-only emergency contraception (POEC)** — available as Levonelle-2® (prescription-only product) an Levonelle® and Levonelle One Step® (for sale as a pharmacy-only medicine to women aged 16 years or over). The packs of Levonelle-2 and Levonelle contain two levonorgestrel 750 microgram tablets. Levonelle One Step contains one levonorgestrel 1.5 mg tablet.
- **Copper-containing intra-uterine device (IUD)** — seven licensed products are currently available. These have different dimensions to fit a range of uterine lengths, and different surface areas of copper that are related to their recommended duration of use. The levonorgestrel-releasing intra-uterine system (LNG-IUS) should not be used for emergency contraception (C), as there is a lack of evidence of its effectiveness and it is not licensed for this indication.
- **Mifepristone** is a progesterone antagonist that has been shown to be an effective emergency contraceptive agent. However, it is not licensed for this indication in the UK and is not available for routine use in primary care.

[FFPRHC Clinical Effectiveness Unit, 2003]

Oral progestogen-only emergency contraception

Recommended regimens

- **Progestogen-only emergency contraception (POEC) should be taken as a single dose of 1.5 mg of levonorgestrel.** The tablets should be taken as soon as possible and within 72 hours (3 days) of unprotected sex or potential contraceptive failure [ABPI Medicines Compendium, 2003]. Previously it was recommended that progestogen-only emergency contraception should be taken as one 750 microgram tablet of levonorgestrel, repeated 12 hours later.
- The change to the dosage directions is supported by data from one large World Health Organization (WHO) multicentre, multinational randomized controlled trial (RCT) involving 4136 healthy women [von Hertzen et al, 2002]. The study found no difference in pregnancy rates between single and divided doses of levonorgestrel taken within 120 hours of unprotected sexual intercourse.
- **POEC use beyond 72 hours cannot currently be recommended.** There are limited trial data to support its effectiveness up to 120 hours; but because of the small sample sizes and wide confidence intervals, accurate

'able 1: Recommendations on the use of emergency contraception after potential contraceptive failure.

ontraception ethod	Emergency contraception indicated	Emergency contraception not indicated	Comment
ombined ral ontraceptive COC) pills	2 or more pills missed from the first 7 pills in a pack	1 of the first 7 pills missed from a pack, as long as the pills from days 15–21 in the previous pack were taken correctly	Whether emergency contraception is indicated or not, continue the COC and also use a barrier method until 7 consecutive pills taken
	4 or more pills are missed in a row from pack days 8–14	3 or fewer pills have been missed from pack days 8–14, as long as the first 7 pills were taken correctly	Continue the COC to end of pack and use a barrier method for 7 days ,whether emergency contraception indicated or not
	4 or more pills are missed in a row from pack days 15–21	3 or fewer pills missed from pack days 15–21, as long as the next pack is started without a pill-free interval (Note: if pack has 7 inactive pills, discard these)	Continue the COC and also use a barrier method until 7 consecutive active pills have been taken, whether emergency contraception is indicated or not. Women who are 'tricycling' and require emergency contraception in the 7 days before the pill-free interval may be advised to continue the COC to the end of the pack, start the next pack without a pill-free interval, and delay the pill-free interval until that pack is completed.
ransdermal ombination ontraceptive atch	Patch off for *longer* than 24 hours	Patch off for *less* than 24 hours	If the patch has been off for *longer* than 24 hours — immediately apply a new patch and start a new cycle. Use a barrier method for the first 7 days of the new cycle. If the patch has been off for less than 24 hours — immediately reapply the patch if still sticky, or apply a new patch.
rogestogen-nly pill 'OP)	1 or more pills missed or taken more than 3 hours late, and unprotected sex occurred within 2 days after missed or late pills	Pill taken less than 3 hours late	Where emergency contraception is indicated, continue the POP and use a barrier method until pills have been taken correctly for 2 consecutive days
ledroxy-rogesterone cetate Depo-rovera)	Injection is *more* than 2 weeks overdue† (i.e. more than 14 weeks from the last injection) and the first episode of unprotected sex has occurred within the previous 72 hours	Injection is *up to* 2 weeks overdue† (i.e. 12–14 weeks from the last injection)	Where emergency contraception is *not* indicated, Depo-Provera can be given and no additional barrier method is required.
rogestogen-nly implants	Unprotected sex within 28 days after the use of liver enzyme-inducers unless additional barrier method has been used	—	—
ntra-uterine evice (IUD) r intra-terine system US)	Complete or partial expulsion	—	Replace IUD up to 5 days after sex or up to day 5 after the expected date of ovulation, or progestogen-only emergency contraception (POEC) can be used up to 72 hours after sex.
	Mid-cycle removal is necessary	—	Offer POEC if sex has occurred within the previous 72 hours.
ondoms — ale and emale	Rupture or dislodgement during intercourse	—	—
iaphragm nd cap	Inserted incorrectly, torn/dislodged during sex, removed too early	—	—

This advice is from the WHO, covering use in developing countries [WHO, 2002a]. The Summary of Product Characteristics more cautiously states that emergency ontraception is indicated where an injection is 5 days or more late (i.e. more than 12 weeks and 5 days after the last injection). Health care professionals should therefore se their clinical discretion.

details of efficacy are unknown [Rodrigues et al, 2001; von Hertzen et al, 2002; Ellertson et al, 2003].

Where there is concomitant use of liver enzyme-inducing drugs, levonorgestrel may be prescribed at a 50% higher dose. This is an off-licence dose. See the *Drug interactions* section for more details.

Overall effectiveness

A WHO trial, involving 1998 women from 21 centres worldwide, showed that POEC, taken within 72 hours of unprotected intercourse, prevented about 85% of expected pregnancies (estimated from the coital and menstrual histories) [WHO, 1998].

POEC is not as effective as conventional regular use of hormonal contraceptives and is suitable only as an emergency measure [United Nations Development Programme et al, 2000].

Factors influencing effectiveness

Timing of treatment

- **Oral POEC is more effective the sooner it is taken after unprotected sex** (Table 2). The Chief Medical Officer has advised that women should be encouraged to seek treatment as early as possible.
- **For every 12 hours that treatment is delayed, the risk of treatment failure is increased by 50%** [Piaggio et al, 1999].

[WHO, 1998; von Hertzen et al, 2002; DH, 2003]

Table 2: Efficacy of progestogen-only emergency contraception after unprotected sex.

Time contraception taken after intercourse	Proportion of pregnancies prevented
24 hours or less	95%
25–48 hours	85%
49–72 hours	58%

C

Timing and frequency of unprotected sex

- **The effectiveness of emergency contraception depends on the pregnancy rate without treatment,** which varies throughout the menstrual cycle. As the risk of pregnancy after unprotected sex is highest around the time of ovulation (20–30%), the residual risk of pregnancy after POEC is used at this stage of the cycle is greater than the residual risk when POEC is used at a time in the cycle when the risk of pregnancy is low (2-4%). When the risk of pregnancy is low, POEC reduces the risk to less than 1%; and when the risk of pregnancy is high, it reduces the risk to around 5%.
- The residual risk of pregnancy risk after POEC may therefore remain unacceptably high for some women and an intra-uterine device (IUD) may be a better option.
- The risk of pregnancy may also therefore be influenced by recall of the date of the last menstrual period and whether the woman experiences regular-length cycles or not.

[FFPRHC Clinical Effectiveness Unit, 2003]

Drug interactions

- **Liver enzyme-inducing drugs can accelerate the metabolism and reduce the efficacy of hormonal contraceptives:**
  - **Rifamycins** (i.e. rifampicin and rifabutin) can *profoundly* induce liver enzymes.
  - Barbiturates, bosentan, carbamazepine, oxcarbazepine, phenytoin, ritonavir (and possibly other antivirals), griseofulvin, topiramate and St John's Wort are liver enzyme-inducing drugs.
- **An IUD is recommended for emergency contraception for women taking liver enzyme-inducing drugs,** particularly the rifamycins, concurrently or in the last 28 days. Consider referral to a family-planning clinic if the resources and facilities to fit an IUD are not available.
- **If an IUD is contraindicated or unacceptable,** there are no trial data to guide practice on the use of POEC, but some experts advise increasing the dose by 50%. Women using liver enzyme-inducing drugs should take two tablets of levonorgestrel (1.5 mg) as a single dose as soon as possible after unprotected sex, followed by one tablet (750 micrograms) 12 hours later (C) [FFPRHC Clinical Effectiveness Unit, 2003]. Note: levonorgestrel taken in this way is an off-licence use and dose.
- **Where non-enzyme-inducing antibiotics are being taken,** the normal POEC regimen should be followed (C) [FFPRHC Clinical Effectiveness Unit, 2003].
- **Other drug interactions that may be potentially hazardous include:**
  - **Warfarin** — a reduced anticoagulant effect is usual, but an increased effect has also been reported.
  - **Ciclosporin** — metabolism may be inhibited resulting in an increased plasma-ciclosporin concentration.

Testing for sexually transmitted infections

- An Edinburgh study based in primary care identified prevalence rates of chlamydia of between 5.3% and 7.6% in women attending for emergency contraception [Kettle et al, 2002].
- **A sexual history should be taken from anyone attending for emergency contraception,** to assess the risk of sexually transmitted infection (STI) and other sexual health issues (C) [FFPRHC Clinical Effectiveness Unit, 2003].
- Consider testing for STI (particularly for *Chlamydia trachomatis*) in women with a high risk of acquiring an STI:
  - Sexually active women under the age of 25 years.
  - Women over 25 years with a new partner or who have had two or more partners in the previous 12 months.
- If results are positive, follow up appropriately.

Timing of next period

- **The next period after taking emergency contraceptive pills may be early, on time, or delayed.** Most women will start their next period within 3 days of the expected date [WHO, 1998].
- Women should be advised that menstrual irregularity can occur within the cycle after POEC use (A) [FFPRHC Clinical Effectiveness Unit, 2003].

Follow-up

- Women should be advised to return for a pregnancy test if their expected period is more than 7 days late, or is lighter than usual (B) [FFPRHC Clinical Effectiveness Unit, 2003].
- **The possibility of an ectopic pregnancy should be considered** after failure of POEC, particularly in women with a previous ectopic pregnancy, fallopian tube surgery, or pelvic inflammatory disease. Twelve ectopic pregnancies (out of a total of 201 unintended pregnancies) have been reported to the Committee on Safety of Medicines (CSM) after failure of POEC [DH, 2003]. However, it is important to note that:
  - The proportion of ectopic pregnancies is consistent with the reported national rate of 12.4 per 1000 pregnancies in England and Wales [Rajkhowa et al, 2000].
  - It is possible that the CSM does not receive all reports of emergency contraception failures where the pregnancy is normal.
  - POEC reduces a woman's absolute risk of ectopic pregnancy, as it is so effective at preventing pregnancy.

Subsequent contraception

- **POEC does not provide contraceptive cover for the remainder of the cycle,** and effective contraception or abstinence must be advised (B) [FFPRHC Clinical Effectiveness Unit, 2003].
- **After missed pills,** women should be advised to resume their hormonal contraception at the usual time as long as it is within 12 hours of taking POEC. Additional barrier contraception or abstinence is advised until the combined oral contraceptive pill has been resumed for 7 consecutive days or the progestogen-only pill has been resumed for 2 consecutive days [FFPRHC Clinical Effectiveness Unit, 2003]. For further information, see Table 1.
- **Use of POEC more than once in a cycle** is not recommended, but should be considered on an individual basis [FFPRHC Clinical Effectiveness Unit, 2003].
- **Future contraception should also be discussed** if appropriate, and should preferably be arranged for the next cycle.

Adverse effects

- **About a quarter of women experience nausea, but only 5% of women actually vomit** [WHO, 1998].
- Other adverse effects include:
  - Lower abdominal pain (18%)
  - Headaches (17%)
  - Fatigue (17%)

- Dizziness (11%)
- Breast tenderness (11%)

If vomiting occurs within 2 hours of taking either dose of POEC, consider advising either a further dose with or without an anti-emetic, or an IUD (C) [WHO, 2002a; FFPRHC Clinical Effectiveness Unit, 2003].

Domperidone is a suitable anti-emetic for women with previous vomiting after POEC or persistent vomiting during current use (C) [FFPRHC Clinical Effectiveness Unit, 2003]. Domperidone does not readily cross the blood–brain barrier and is therefore less likely than other anti-emetics to cause extrapyramidal adverse effects. Domperidone should be taken at the same time as, or just before, the POEC.

Contraindications

Established pregnancy is a contraindication to use of POEC [WHO, 2004].

The World Health Organization considers that there are no other absolute medical contraindications to the use of POEC on currently available evidence. The dosage of hormones is relatively small and the pills are used for only a short time; therefore the contraindications associated with the regular use of progestogen-only oral contraceptive pills are not applicable to emergency hormonal contraception [WHO, 2004].

Caution should be used in women with acute active porphyria, severe liver disease, or severe malabsorption syndromes [ABPI Medicines Compendium, 2003; FFPRHC Clinical Effectiveness Unit, 2003].

Intra-uterine device

Effectiveness

Copper-containing intra-uterine devices (IUDs) are the most effective method of emergency contraception. They prevent 98% of expected pregnancies and are the first choice where efficacy is a priority.

An IUD containing more than 300 mm^2 copper should be used (B), especially if it is intended that the IUD will be used for ongoing contraception.

[FFPRHC Clinical Effectiveness Unit, 2003]

Timing of post-coital IUD insertion

A copper-containing IUD can be inserted in the usual way within 5 days (120 hours) of unprotected sex at any time during the menstrual cycle (C).

However, when the time of ovulation can be estimated, the IUD can be inserted beyond 5 days after intercourse if necessary, as long as the insertion does not occur more than 5 days after ovulation (C).

An IUD is therefore the emergency contraceptive method of choice more that 72 hours after unprotected sex, as use of progestogen-only emergency contraception (POEC) is not currently recommended after this time.

Refer the woman to a family planning clinic if the resources and facilities are not available to immediately fit an IUD at the GP practice.

If it is not possible to fit an IUD immediately, consider prescribing POEC as preliminary cover if there have been less than 72 hours since unprotected sexual intercourse or potential contraceptive failure.

[FFPRHC Clinical Effectiveness Unit, 2003]

Testing for sexually transmitted infections

A sexual history should be taken from all those attending for emergency contraception to assess the risk of sexually transmitted infection (STI) and other sexual health issues (C).

- **Prior to emergency IUD insertion, testing for STI, particularly *Chlamydia trachomatis*, is recommended in women with a high risk of acquiring an STI:**
  - Sexually active women under the age of 25 years.
  - Women over 25 years with a new partner or who have had two or more partners in the previous 12 months.
- **If results are positive,** follow up appropriately.
- **The routine use of prophylactic antibiotics** prior to emergency IUD insertion is not recommended, but their use may be considered in women with a high risk of acquiring an STI (C).
- Pending test results, consider prescribing azithromycin 1 gm as a single dose, or doxycycline 100 mg twice a day for 7 days, and advising abstinence for women at high risk of an STI and undergoing emergency IUD insertion (C).

[FFPRHC Clinical Effectiveness Unit, 2003]

Follow-up and IUD removal

- **Women should be advised to return for a pregnancy test** if their expected period is more than 7 days late, or is lighter than usual (B) [FFPRHC Clinical Effectiveness Unit, 2003].
- **If a woman wishes to continue to use the IUD for ongoing contraception,** a follow-up visit is recommended 3–6 weeks after insertion (provided she has a normal period) [WHO, 2002a].
- **An IUD can be removed** any time after the next period if no unprotected sex has occurred since menses, or if hormonal contraception has been started within the first 5 days of the next cycle (C) [FFPRHC Clinical Effectiveness Unit, 2003]. Before removal, ensure no unprotected sex has occurred since the start of the last period (unless additional contraception has been used), otherwise there is a risk of pregnancy.

Adverse effects

- **Irregular bleeding or heavier and longer periods,** especially in the first few months.
- **Pelvic inflammatory disease (PID),** although it is the exposure to an STI rather than IUD use that is responsible for any increased risk of PID. The woman should be counselled regarding a six-fold increase in the risk of pelvic infection in the 21 days after insertion of an IUD. She should be told how to recognise symptoms and when to seek medical advice (B) [FFPRHC Clinical Effectiveness Unit, 2003].
- **Uterine or cervical perforation.**
- **Displacement or expulsion.**

[WHO, 2002a; FFPRHC Clinical Effectiveness Unit, 2004]

Contraindications

- The WHO also considers that the same eligibility criteria that apply to the insertion of a copper-containing IUD in normal circumstances should be applied for post-coital insertion.
- Conditions where copper-containing IUDs are an unacceptable (category 4) health risk or where the risks usually outweigh the advantages (category 3) are detailed in Table 3 [WHO, 2002b].
- For a full list of the medical eligibility criteria and other category classifications for the copper IUD emergency contraceptive, see www.who.int/reproductive-health/publications/mec/8_e_iud.pdf.

[FFPRHC Clinical Effectiveness Unit, 2004; WHO, 2004]

Legal issues relating to providing emergency contraception to girls under 16 years

- **In the UK, people under the age of 16 years can consent to medical treatment if they have sufficient maturity and**

C

C

Table 3: Clinical conditions where IUDs are considered unacceptable, or where the risks usually outweigh the advantage for use in contraception and emergency contraception.

Condition	Category		Comment
	Insertion	Continuation	
Pregnancy	4	4	The IUD should not be used because of the risk of seriou pelvic infection and septic spontaneous abortion.
Postpartum (breastfeeding or non-breastfeeding, including post-Caesarian section) between 48 hours and 4 weeks after delivery	3	3	There is an increased risk of perforation for IUD insertic done between 48 hours and 4 weeks postpartum.
Postpartum (breastfeeding or non-breastfeeding, including post-Caesarian section) — puerpal sepsis	4	4	Insertion of an IUD may substantially worsen the condition.
Post-abortion — immediate post-septic abortion	4	4	Insertion of an IUD may substantially worsen the condition.
Anatomical abnormalities — distorted uterine cavity (any congenital or acquired uterine abnormality distorting the uterine cavity in a manner that is incompatible with IUD insertion)	4	4	In the presence of an anatomic abnormality that distorts the uterine cavity, proper IUD placement may not be possible.
Unexplained vaginal bleeding (suspicion for serious condition) — before evaluation	4	(2)	If pregnancy or an underlying pathological condition (su as pelvic malignancy) is suspected, it must be evaluated and the category adjusted after evaluation. There is no need to remove the IUD before evaluation.
Benign gestational trophoblastic disease	3	3	—
Malignant gestational trophoblastic disease	4	4	There is an increased risk of perforation, since the treatment for the condition may require multiple uterine curettages.
Cervical cancer (awaiting treatment)	4	(2)	There is concern about the increased risk of infection an bleeding at insertion; this may make the condition worse
Endometrial cancer	4	(2)	There is concern about the increased risk of infection, perforation, and bleeding at insertion; this may make th condition worse.
Ovarian cancer	3	(2)	IUD will probably need removal at the time of treatmen but until then the woman is at risk of pregnancy.
Uterine fibroids — with distortion of the uterine cavity	4	4	Pre-existing uterine fibroids that distort the uterine cavit may be incompatible with IUD insertion.
Pelvic inflammatory disease (PID) — now/within last 3 months	4	(2)	The FFPRHC recommends that, after considering other contraceptive methods, a woman may use an IUD withir 3 months of treated pelvic infection, provided she has nc signs and symptoms.
Sexually transmitted infections (STIs) — current or within 3 months (including purulent cervicitis)	4	4	The FFPRHC recommends that, after considering other contraceptive methods, women who are at high risk of STIs, or who have had treatment for a STI within the las months, may use an IUD, provided there are no signs an symptoms of infection. Safer sex and condom use in addition should be promoted.
Sexually transmitted infections (STIs) — increased risk of STIs (e.g. multiple partners, or partner who has multiple partners)	2/3	(2)	—
Rape — high risk of STI	3	—	—
AIDS	3	(2)	Clarification for continuation: IUD users with AIDS should be closely monitored for pelvic infection.
Tuberculosis — known pelvic	4	3	Insertion of an IUD may substantially worsen the condition.
Antiretroviral (ARV) therapy	2/3	(2)	Although there is no known drug interaction between ARV therapy and IUD use women, category 2 applies where women are clinically well on ARV therapy.

Category 4 — a condition that represents an unacceptable health risk if an IUD is used.
Category 3 — a condition where the theoretical or proven risks usually outweigh the advantages of using an IUD.
Category 2 — a condition where the advantage of using an IUD generally outweighs the theoretical or proven risks

judgement to enable them to fully understand what is proposed.

- **In England and Wales,** it is lawful to provide contraceptive advice and treatment without parental consent, provided that the practitioner is satisfied that the following Fraser Guideline criteria [Teenage Pregnancy Unit, 2001] are met:
  - The young person understands the practitioner's advice.
  - The young person cannot be persuaded to inform his or her parents or allow the practitioner to inform the parents that contraceptive advice has been sought.
  - The young person is likely to begin or to continue having intercourse with or without contraceptive treatment.
  - Unless he or she receives contraceptive advice or treatment, the young person's physical or mental health or both are likely to suffer.
  - The young person's best interest requires the practitioner to give contraceptive advice, treatment, c both without parental consent.
- **In Scotland,** statutory provision by way of The Age of Legal Capacity Act 1991 applies similar criteria. The A actually appears to assign more legal rights to children

under 16 years, in that parental responsibility cannot authorise procedures a competent child has refused [Fernie, Personal Communication, 2003].

Note: child protection issues should be taken into account — it is important to be satisfied that sex has been consensual and is not occurring in an incestuous relationship. If it is suspected that force has been used or that any sexual abuse has occurred, health care professionals have a duty to follow national and local child protection procedures.

References

NHS staff in England can link, free of charge, from references to full text journals by clicking on [Full text] on the PRODIGY website.

1. ABPI Medicines Compendium (2003) *Summary of product characteristics for Levonelle® – 2*. Electronic Medicines Compendium. Datapharm Communications Ltd. www.emc.medicines.org.uk [Accessed: 17/12/2003].
2. Croxatto, H.B. (2003) Emergency contraception pills: how do they work? *IPPF Medical Bulletin* **36**(6), 1–2.
3. DH (2002) *Judicial review of emergency contraception*. Department of Health. www.dh.gov.uk [Accessed: 29/04/2004]. [Full text]
4. DH (2003) *Levonelle/Levonelle-2 emergency contraception: new advice*. CMO Update 35. Department of Health. www.doh.gov.uk [Accessed: 03/02/2003]. [Full text]
5. Durand, M., del Carmen Cravioto, M., Raymond, E.G. et al (2001) On the mechanisms of action of short-term levonorgestrel administration in emergency contraception. *Contraception* **64**(4), 227–234.
6. Ellertson, C., Evans, M., Ferden, S. et al (2003) Extending the time limit for starting the Yuzpe regimen of emergency contraception to 120 hours. *Obstetrics & Gynecology* **101**(6), 1168–1171.
7. Fernie, C.G.M (2003) *Personal communication*. Medical Adviser, Medical and Dental Defense Union of Scotland: Glasgow.
8. FFPRHC Clinical Effectiveness Unit (2003) FFPRHC guidance: emergency contraception. *Journal of Family Planning and Reproductive Health Care* **29**(2), 9–15.
9. FFPRHC Clinical Effectiveness Unit (2004) FFPRHC guidance: the copper intrauterine device as long-term contraception. *Journal of Family Planning and Reproductive Health Care* **30**(1), 29–42.
10. Kettle, H., Cay, S., Brown, A. and Glasier, A. (2002) Screening for Chlamydia trachomatis infection is indicated for women under 30 using emergency contraception. *Contraception* **66**(4), 251–253.
11. Marions, L., Hultenby, K., Lindell, I. et al (2002) Emergency contraception with mifepristone and levonorgestrel: mechanism of action. *Obstetrics & Gynecology* **100**(1), 65–71.
12. Office for National Statistics (2003) *Number of emergency contraceptives prescribed, 1990 to 2000: social trends 33*. Office for National Statistics. www.statistics.gov.uk [Accessed: 11/08/2003].
13. Piaggio, G., von Hertzen, H., Grimes, D.A. and van Look, P.F.A. (1999) Timing of emergency contraception with levonorgesterel or the Yuzpe regimen. *Lancet* **353**(9154), 721.
14. Rajkhowa, M., Glass, M.R., Rutherford, A.J. et al (2000) Trends in the incidence of ectopic pregnancy in England and Wales from 1966 to 1996. *British Journal of Obstetrics & Gynaecology* **107**(3), 369–374.
15. Rodrigues, I., Grou, F. and Joly, J. (2001) Effectiveness of emergency contraceptive pills between 72 and 120 hours after unprotected sexual intercourse. *American Journal of Obstetrics & Gynecology* **184**(4), 531–537.
16. Teenage Pregnancy Unit (2001) *Guidance for the field social workers, residential social workers and foster carers providing information and referring young people to contraception and sexual health services*. Department of Health. www.dh.gov.uk [Accessed: 29/04/2004]. [Full text]
17. United Nations Development Programme, United Nations Population Fund, WHO et al (2000) Efficacy and side effects of immediate postcoital levonorgestrel used repeatedly for contraception. *Contraception* **61**(5), 303–308.
18. von Hertzen, H., Piaggio, G., Ding, J. et al (2002) Low dose mifepristone and two regimens of levonorgestrel for emergency contraception: a WHO multicentre randomised trial. *Lancet* **360**(9348), 1803–1810. [Full text]
19. WHO (1998) Randomised controlled trial of levonorgestrel versus the Yuzpe regimen of combined oral contraceptives for emergency contraception. Task force on postovulatory methods of fertility regulation. *Lancet* **352**(9126), 428–433. [Full text]
20. WHO (2002a) *Selected practice recommendations for contraceptive use*. World Health Organisation. www.who.int/reproductive-health/publications/rhr_02_7/index.htm [Accessed: 15/08/2003].
21. WHO (2002b) *Copper IUD for emergency contraception (E-IUD)*. Department of Reproductive Health and Research. www.who.int [Accessed: 01/09/2003].
22. WHO (2004) *Medical eligibility criteria for contraceptive use (third edition)*. World Health Organisation. www.who.int/reproductive-health/publications/mec [Accessed: 30/09/2004].
23. Wilcox, A.J., Weinberg, C.R. and Baird, D.D. (1995) Timing of sexual intercourse in relation to ovulation – effects on the probability of conception, survival of the pregnancy, and sex of the baby. *New England Journal of Medicine* **333**(23), 1517–1521.
24. Wilcox, A.J., Dunson, D.B., Weinberg, C.R. et al (2001) Likelihood of conception with a single act of intercourse: providing benchmark rates for assessment of post-coital contraceptives. *Contraception* **63**(4), 211–215.

Evidence grading

The evidence grading used in this guidance, represents that used by the Faculty of Family Planning and Reproductive Health Care Clinical Effectiveness Unit in development of their different guidance. The definitions of grades of recommendation are as follows:

A Evidence is based on randomized, controlled trials

B Evidence is based on other robust experimental or observational studies

C Evidence is limited, but the advice relies on expert opinion and has the endorsement of respected authorities

PRODIGY GUIDANCE

Corneal superficial injury

Last revised April 2005
www.prodigy.nhs.uk/guidance.asp?gt=Cornealsuperficial injury

Applies to people over the age of 1 month

This guidance covers the management of superficial corneal abrasions, foreign bodies, and their complications.

This guidance does not cover injuries that penetrate the Bowman's membrane of the cornea.

There is separate PRODIGY guidance on *Blepharitis, Conjunctivitis — infective, Conjunctivitis — allergic, Dry eye syndrome, Glaucoma,* and *Herpes simplex — ocular.*

C

Goals

- To provide pain relief
- To prevent secondary infection
- To promote corneal re-epithelialization

Contents

Scenarios

- Corneal superficial injury p.446

Extended Information, p. 448

Corneal superficial injury

Which therapy?

- **Seek a history of trauma** and a history of activities that may cause painless injury. Note: it is important to refer suspected penetrating injuries.
- **Measure visual acuity** with a Snellen chart.
- **Examine the cornea and anterior chamber for damage.**
  - Use fluorescein to stain abrasions bright green, and view with a cobalt-blue filter.
  - Slit-lamp examination (if available) is useful for assessing the depth of the injury.
- **Remove foreign bodies.**
  - Anaesthetize the eye and remove using a cotton-wool bud or triangle of card.
  - If unsuccessful, and if experienced, use a sterile 25-gauge needle.
- **Patch the eye for a few hours if an anaesthetic has been used,** to protect the eye from further damage while the anaesthetic wears off and the corneal reflex returns.
- **Prescribe a topical antibiotic to prevent infection.**
  - **Chloramphenicol** is the antibiotic of choice. It is available as drops or ointment. Ointment may be more useful at night.
  - **Fusidic acid** is an alternative. The drops are instilled twice a day and may be practical for children and the elderly.
- **Analgesia may be required:**
  - **Paracetamol or ibuprofen** is recommended first-line.
  - **Topical diclofenac eye drops** may be useful if paracetamol or ibuprofen is not effective. Note: they may take time to obtain from a community pharmacy.
- **Advise that contact lenses** must not be used until 24 hours after finishing treatment with antibiotic eye drops.

Practical prescribing points

For further information, please see the *Medicines Compendium* (www.medicines.org.uk) or the *British National Formulary* (www.bnf.org).

- **Chloramphenicol:** concerns over aplastic anaemia associated with ocular chloramphenicol have largely been discounted.
  - Do not use concurrently with other myelotoxic drugs.
  - Do not use in the last trimester of pregnancy.
- **Ibuprofen:** increased risk of gastrointestinal haemorrhage. Avoid if there is a history of peptic ulceration. May worsen asthma, hypertension, renal impairment, or cardiac failure.
- **Contact lenses** should generally not be worn during treatment with eye drops. However:
  - **Hard lenses:** use eye drops 30 minutes before insertin[g] lenses.
  - **Soft lenses:** eye drops containing preservatives should not be used with soft lenses. (Some preservatives, particularly benzalkonium chloride, accumulate in so[ft] contact lenses and cause irritation.) Preservative-free drops should be used instead.
  - **Eye ointments:** eye ointments should not be used whe[n] contact lenses are worn.

Follow-up advice

- Follow-up at 24 and 48 hours is recommended.
  - Check visual acuity with a Snellen chart.
  - Stain with fluorescein and assess progress with healin[g]
  - Look for rust rings.

Should I refer or investigate?

Refer?

Immediate referral to an ophthalmologist or ophthalmology outpatients is indicated for:

- **All high-velocity injuries** (e.g. while hammering, chiselling, grinding or lawn mowing). They should be treated as penetrating injuries until proved otherwise.
- **All chemical injuries.** Begin immediate and continuous irrigation of the eye with a fluid such as tap water or contact-lens saline. Copious amounts of fluid should be used.
- **All strongly adherent foreign bodies.** Those in or near the centre of the cornea increase the risk of permanent loss of vision.
- **Pain not relieved by topical local anaesthetic.** Assume that such pain is due to something more serious than a superficial corneal injury (e.g. corneal ulceration, iritis, acute glaucoma).
- **A reduction in visual acuity.**
- **Large abrasions** (more than 60% of the cornea).
- **Corneal opacities.**
- **Rust rings** that remain after removal of a metallic foreig[n] body, as these may cause permanent damage. The rust ring may be removed with a cotton-wool bud or a piece of cardboard. If this does not work, a needle or a special rotary drill can be used. If expert assistance is needed

with removal or if there is any doubt about complete removal of the rust ring, refer the person immediately.

Hyphaema (blood in the anterior chamber of the eye), as this is associated with the risk of further haemorrhage.

A distorted pupil, as this may be associated with a penetrating injury.

Suspected damage to the retina.

Deep laceration of the orbit: beware intraorbital and ocular penetration and retained foreign bodies.

Subconjunctival haemorrhage if it tracks posteriorly and there is a history consistent with a possible orbital fracture.

Marginal lacerations, as the lacrimal ducts may be damaged.

on-urgent referral is indicated for:

Recurrent abrasions. These usually occur at night when there is little secretion of tears and the epithelium may be torn off. Treatment is long-term, and a surgical procedure (e.g. epithelial debridement or corneal stroma puncture) may be needed.

'atient information leaflets

he following PILs are available at www.prodigy.nhs.uk

Corneal Injury

hared decision making

Your cornea has a minor injury. This will normally heal within a few days.

Antibiotic eye drops or **ointment** is usually advised to prevent infection.

Painkillers such as **paracetamol** or **ibuprofen** help to ease any pain in the eye.

An eye patch is not necessary (unless local anaesthetic has been used in the eye, when it should be worn for a few hours until sensation returns).

Do not wear contact lenses while the cornea is healing, or until 24 hours after the final dose of antibiotic eye drops.

Always protect your eyes with goggles if there is a risk of eye injury — for example, when drilling, hammering, etc.

)rug rationale

)rugs not included

Corticosteroid eye preparations (including combination antibiotic/corticosteroid preparations) should not be used, because they slow the healing of corneal epithelium, increase the risk of infection, and cause serious damage if a diagnosis of dendritic ulcer is missed [Shields, 2000a].

Cycloplegics: there are no controlled studies to indicate that treating superficial corneal injuries with cycloplegics reduces ocular pain and inflammation [Sabri et al, 1998; Carley and Carley, 2001].

Antibiotic eye preparations other than chloramphenicol and fusidic acid, including aminoglycosides and fluoroquinolones, should be reserved for more serious ocular infections and treatment of infection when the sensitivity is known [Robert and Adenis, 2001].

Tetanus prophylaxis is not required for non-penetrating eye injuries [Melton et al, 1991].

)rugs included

Topical chloramphenicol is the antibiotic of choice for the prevention of eye infections. It has a relatively broad spectrum of action against most Gram-positive and Gram-negative bacteria [Robert and Adenis, 2001]. Concerns about the systemic toxicity of topical chloramphenicol, in particular aplastic anaemia, have been discounted [Lancaster et al, 1998; Walker et al, 1998; Field et al, 1999].

- **Fusidic acid eye drops** are an effective alternative to chloramphenicol. Administration of the drops is required only twice-daily, which may be of benefit for young children or elderly people who require assistance in applying eye drops [Robert and Adenis, 2001].
- **Paracetamol** is an effective analgesic and is generally well tolerated and safe.
- **Ibuprofen** is offered as an alternative oral analgesic. It is has the most favourable risk–benefit profile of all the nonsteroidal anti-inflammatory drugs [CSM, 2002].
- **Diclofenac eye drops** may be used to relieve the pain and discomfort associated with corneal abrasion [Weaver and Terrell, 2003]. However, there is only limited evidence to support their use, they are more expensive compared with other analgesics, and they may take time to obtain from a community pharmacy.

C

Prescriptions

Chloramphenicol eye drops or ointment

Chloramphenicol 0.5% eye drops

- Age from 1 month onwards
- Chloramphenicol 0.5% eye drops. Put one drop into the affected eye(s) every 3 hours for 2 days, and then four times a day for 5 days; supply 10 ml; NHS Cost £1.23.

Chloramphenicol 1% eye ointment

- Age from 1 month onwards
- Chloramphenicol 1% eye ointment. Put a small amount into the affected eye(s) four times a day for 2 days, and then twice a day for 5 days; supply 4 grams; NHS Cost £2.07.

Chloramphenicol 0.5% eye drops + 1% eye ointment

- Age from 1 month onwards
- Chloramphenicol 0.5% eye drops. Put one drop into the affected eye(s) every 3 hours for 2 days, and then three times a day for 5 days. Use the ointment at bedtime; supply 10 ml; NHS Cost £1.23.
- Chloramphenicol 1% eye ointment. Put a small amount into the affected eye(s) at bedtime for 7 days; supply 4 grams; NHS Cost £2.07.

Fusidic acid eye drops

Fusidic acid 1% eye drops

- Age from 1 month onwards
- Fusidic acid 1% eye drops. Put one drop into the affected eye(s) twice a day for 7 days; supply 5 grams; NHS Cost £2.09.

1st-line analgesia: paracetamol or ibuprofen when required

Paracetamol s/f susp: 60mg to 120mg up to four times a day

- Age from 3 to 11 months
- Paracetamol 120mg/5ml s/f susp. Take 2.5ml to 5ml every 4 to 6 hours when required for pain relief. Maximum of 4 doses in 24 hours; supply 150 ml; NHS Cost £0.65; OTC Cost £1.15.

Paracetamol s/f susp: 120mg to 240mg up to four times a day

- Age from 12 months to 5 years
- Paracetamol 120mg/5ml s/f susp. Take one to two 5ml spoonfuls every 4 to 6 hours when required for pain relief. Maximum of 4 doses in 24 hours; supply 300 ml; NHS Cost £1.30; OTC Cost £2.29.

Paracetamol s/f susp: 250mg to 500mg up to four times a day
- Age from 6 to 11 years
- Paracetamol 250mg/5ml s/f susp. Take one to two 5ml spoonfuls every 4 to 6 hours when required for pain relief. Maximum of 4 doses in 24 hours; supply 300 ml; NHS Cost £1.59; OTC Cost £2.80.

Paracetamol tablets: 500mg to 1g up to four times a day
- Age from 12 to 15 years
- Paracetamol 500mg tablets. Take one to two tablets every 4 to 6 hours when required for pain relief. Maximum of 8 tablets in 24 hours; supply 50 tablets; NHS Cost £0.38; OTC Cost £0.67.

Paracetamol tablets: 1g up to four times a day
- Age from 16 years onwards
- Paracetamol 500mg tablets. Take two tablets every 4 to 6 hours when required for pain relief. Maximum of 8 tablets in 24 hours; supply 50 tablets; NHS Cost £0.38; OTC Cost £0.67.

Ibuprofen s/f susp: 50mg three to four times a day
- Age from 12 months to 2 years
- Ibuprofen 100mg/5ml s/f susp. Take 2.5ml three to four times a day when required for pain relief. Do not exceed the stated dose; supply 100 ml; NHS Cost £2.00; OTC Cost £3.53.

Ibuprofen s/f susp: 100mg three to four times a day
- Age from 3 to 7 years
- Ibuprofen 100mg/5ml s/f susp. Take one 5ml spoonful 3 to 4 times a day when required for pain relief. Do not exceed the stated dose; supply 150 ml; NHS Cost £2.73; OTC Cost £4.81.

Ibuprofen s/f susp: 200mg three to four times a day
- Age from 8 to 11 years
- Ibuprofen 100mg/5ml s/f susp. Take two 5ml spoonfuls 3 to 4 times a day when required for pain relief. Do not exceed the stated dose; supply 300 ml; NHS Cost £5.46; OTC Cost £9.62.

Ibuprofen tablets: 400mg three times a day
- Age from 12 years onwards
- Ibuprofen 400mg tablets. Take one tablet three times a day when required for pain relief. Do not exceed the stated dose; supply 24 tablets; NHS Cost £0.70; OTC Cost £1.75.

2nd-line analgesia: diclofenac eye drops

Diclofenac sodium 0.1% eye drops
- Age from 12 years onwards
- Diclofenac 0.1% multidose eye drops. Put one drop into the affected eye(s) four times a day for up to 2 days; supply 5 ml; NHS Cost £6.68.

Extended Information

Background information

- What is it? p.448
- How common is it? p.448
- How do I know my patient has it? p.448
- What else might it be? p.448
- Complications and prognosis p.448

What is it?

- **Corneal superficial abrasion is the loss of corneal *epithelial tissue* caused by trauma.**
- The cornea is made up of five layers. From the outermost to the innermost, they are:
  - Epithelium
  - Bowman's membrane
  - Stroma
  - Descemet's membrane
  - Endothelium
- **Superficial injuries** do not extend beyond Bowman's membrane.
- An injury that penetrates through Bowman's membrane into the corneal stroma is regarded as complicated, and is beyond the scope of this guidance.

How common is it?

Presenting in primary care there are:
- 3.2 cases of corneal injury per 1000 of population per year
- 2.7 cases of foreign bodies per 1000 of population per year

[Royal College of General Practitioners and Royal College of Ophthalmologists, 2001]

How do I know my patient has it?

History

- **A painful eye** is the main presenting complaint.
- **There is often a recent history of trauma** (e.g. from grit, wood chip, fingernails, hairbrush, or contact-lens problems).
- **Trauma may be unrecognised.** It is therefore important to ask about activities that may have caused a high-velocity injury (e.g. chiselling, grinding, hammering, or lawn mowing) which may cause a foreign body to enter the eye without the person realising this. The person may have photophobia, pain on extra-ocular muscle movement, watering eyes, blepharospasm, blurring of vision, or sensation of a foreign body.

On examination

- **On visual inspection, the eye may be red** because of ciliary injection (capillary dilation around the limbus) and the loosened corneal epithelium may have a translucent appearance.
- **Fluorescein will stain an abrasion bright green,** and viewing with a cobalt-blue filter enhances this appearance.
- **Corneal oedema and epithelial disruption** may be revealed by slit-lamp examination, if available.

[Eagling and Roper-Hall, 1986; Newell, 1996]

What else might it be?

- **A foreign body** may be present.
- **Contact-lens problems** (e.g. poor fit, trapped foreign body, sensitivity to solutions, infection).
- **Dendritic ulcer** caused by *Herpes simplex*.
- **Ultraviolet keratitis** (e.g. sunbed damage, welder's arc).
- **The injury may be complicated** (e.g. penetrating injury, contusion, chemical burn, eyelid injury).
- **Acute glaucoma and acute iritis** (anterior uveitis) cause a painful red eye.
- **Conjunctivitis, episcleritis, scleritis, and subconjunctival haemorrhages** are all causes of a red eye.

Complications and prognosis

Complications

- **Secondary infection** may develop.
- **In deep injuries that penetrate Bowman's membrane,** permanent scarring may occur (for a description of the five membranes of the cornea, see *What is it?*).
- **Recurrent abrasion** may occur, owing to new corneal epithelium not adhering completely to the basement membrane.

rognosis

- Healing takes 24–48 hours in superficial corneal injuries.
- Corneal injuries that penetrate through Bowman's membrane will result in scarring, as corneal translucency is based primarily on the geometric array of collagen fibres in the stroma [Goldberg, 2001].

Management issues

- How do I assess a corneal abrasion? p.449
- How do I remove any conjunctival or corneal foreign bodies? p.449
- When should I refer to a specialist? p.449
- How should I manage superficial corneal abrasions that are not referred? p.449
- Which topical antibiotic should I use? p.450
- Should I prescribe antibiotic ointment or drops? p.450
- What treatments are not recommended for a superficial corneal injury? p.450

ow do I assess a corneal abrasion?

- **It is extremely important to seek a history of trauma** and a history of activities that may cause painless injury. If there is a history of a possible high-velocity injury (e.g. from hammering, chiselling, grinding, or lawn mowing) or an injury caused by glass, knives, thorns, darts, or pencils, then a penetrating injury should be strongly suspected and referred immediately to secondary care, with no further action in primary care.
- **Test visual acuity** in both eyes with a Snellen chart. Consider anaesthetising the eye if examination is difficult.
- **Examine the cornea and anterior chamber** for damage.
  - Use fluorescein to stain abrasions bright green when viewed with a cobalt-blue light. Note the size, shape, and position of the corneal abrasion and draw it in the notes.
  - Look for blood in the anterior chamber (hyphaema).
  - Check that extra-ocular muscle movements are normal.
  - Slit-lamp examination (if available) may reveal corneal oedema, epithelial disruption, or anterior chamber penetration.

ow do I remove any conjunctival or corneal oreign bodies?

- **Anaesthetize the eye to prevent pain during the examination.** Note: if the topical anaesthetic does not remove the pain, assume that a more serious problem exists and refer to an ophthalmologist.
- **Use a cotton-wool bud or triangle of card** to remove the foreign body gently; or, if the foreign body is loose, irrigate the eye with water.
- **If unsuccessful, and only if experienced,** carefully lift the foreign body using a sterile 25-gauge needle; otherwise refer to Casualty. Complete removal of metallic foreign bodies is essential to prevent 'rust rings' on the cornea from causing permanent damage.
- **Evert the upper lid** to exclude a subtarsal foreign body, particularly if there are corneal scratches or a feeling that the foreign body is still there. This should never be done if there is any possibility of a penetrating eye injury, as the contents of the eye may prolapse.
- **If the eye has been anaesthetized, apply an eye patch** for a few hours to protect the eye until the anaesthetic wears off and the corneal reflex has returned.

When should I refer to a specialist?

Immediate referral to an ophthalmologist or to ophthalmology outpatients is indicated for:

- **All high-velocity injuries** (e.g. while hammering, chiselling, grinding, or lawn mowing). They should be treated as penetrating injuries until proved otherwise.
- **All chemical injuries.** Begin immediate and continuous irrigation of the eye with a fluid such as tap water or contact-lens saline. Copious amounts of fluid should be used.
- **All strongly adherent foreign bodies.** Those in or near the centre of the cornea increase the risk of permanent loss of vision.
- **Pain not relieved by topical local anaesthetic** should be assumed to be due to something more serious than a superficial corneal injury (e.g. corneal ulceration, iritis, acute glaucoma).
- **A reduction in visual acuity.**
- **Large abrasions** (more than 60% of the cornea).
- **Corneal opacities.**
- **Rust rings** that remain after removal of a metallic foreign body, as these may cause permanent damage. The rust ring may be removed with a cotton-wool bud or a piece of cardboard. If this does not work, a needle or a special rotary drill can be used. If expert assistance is needed with removal or if there is any doubt about complete removal of the rust ring, refer the person immediately.
- **Hyphaema** (blood in the anterior chamber of the eye), as this is associated with the risk of further haemorrhage.
- **A distorted pupil,** as this may be associated with a penetrating injury.
- **Suspected damage to the retina**
- **Deep laceration of the orbit:** beware intraorbital and ocular penetration and retained foreign bodies.
- **Subconjunctival haemorrhage** if it tracks posteriorly and there is a history consistent with a possible orbital fracture.
- **Marginal lacerations,** as the lacrimal ducts may be damaged.

Non-urgent referral is indicated for:

- **Recurrent abrasions.** These usually occur at night when there is little secretion of tears and the epithelium may be torn off. Treatment is long-term, and a surgical procedure (e.g. epithelial debridement or corneal stroma puncture) may be needed [Khaw et al, 2004].

[Eagling and Roper-Hall, 1986; McGuinness, 1998; Shields, 2000a; Shields, 2000b; Khaw et al, 2004]

How should I manage superficial corneal abrasions that are not referred?

- **Topical antibiotics** are recommended for prophylaxis against secondary infection [Melton et al, 1991; Torok and Mader, 1996; Khaw and Elkington, 1999].
- **Contact lenses** must not be worn while the corneal abrasion is healing (24–48 hours) and until 24 hours after finishing treatment with antibiotic eye drops.
- **Analgesia may be required:**
  - Oral paracetamol or ibuprofen is recommended first-line.
  - There is limited evidence to suggest that topical nonsteroidal anti-inflammatory (NSAID) eye drops may be beneficial in decreasing pain without reducing healing times [Weaver and Terrell, 2003]. The only NSAID currently licensed for pain relief of corneal abrasions in the UK is diclofenac; however, it may take time to obtain from a community pharmacy and is more expensive compared with other analgesics.

Which topical antibiotic should I use?

- **Chloramphenicol is the antibiotic of choice in the UK.** It has a relatively broad spectrum of activity against Gram-positive and Gram-negative bacteria, and some anterior chamber penetration. There is little evidence of bacterial resistance to chloramphenicol [Robert and Adenis, 2001].
  - Eye drops should be applied at least every 2 hours and continued for 48 hours after healing. Eye ointment should be applied either at night (if eye drops used during the day), otherwise 3–4 times daily.
  - Concern about the systemic toxicity of topical chloramphenicol, in particular aplastic anaemia, is not well-founded [Rayner and Buckley, 1996; Lancaster et al, 1998; Walker et al, 1998; Field et al, 1999; Robert and Adenis, 2001; BNF 47, 2004].
  - Owing to the potential risk of systemic absorption, chloramphenicol is not recommended for prolonged treatment periods or when treatment is combined with other myelotoxic drugs [Walker et al, 1998].
  - In the third trimester of pregnancy there is a theoretical risk of grey-baby syndrome (chloramphenicol toxicity in a newborn resulting from the lack of liver enzymes necessary to metabolize the drug) and alternatives should be used [Walker et al, 1998].
- **Fusidic acid is an alternative** antibiotic to chloramphenicol. It is active against Gram-positive bacteria, especially *Staphylococcus* species, and achieves good anterior chamber penetration. Acquired resistance within Gram-positive species is low [Robert and Adenis, 2001].
  - Several comparative trials have shown that topical fusidic acid is as effective as topical chloramphenicol [Hvidberg, 1987; Horven, 1993; Boberg-Ans and Nissen, 1998; Carr, 1998].
  - Fusidic acid is in the form of viscous eye drops and may be used as a preferred treatment where administration of chloramphenicol is difficult. Administration of the drops is required only twice-daily, which may be of benefit for young children or elderly people who require assistance in applying eye drops. Treatment should be continued for at least 48 hours after healing.
- Aminoglycosides and fluoroquinolones are not recommended for prophylaxis of a superficial corneal injury, and should be reserved for more serious ocular infections and treatment when the sensitivity is known [Robert and Adenis, 2001].

Should I prescribe antibiotic ointment or drops?

- **Ointment lasts longer in the eye,** and at night may help prevent the eyelid sticking to the cornea during sleep [McGuinness, 1998].
  - A single application of chloramphenicol ointment has an efficacy similar to that of 13 applications of eye-drop preparation every 15 minutes [Hanna et al, 1978; Field et al, 1999].
- **Drops may be more practical for daytime use,** as ointments may smear causing blurred vision.
- **Viscous drops may be more convenient for elderly people and children** who need assistance to apply eye drops.

What treatments are not recommended for a superficial corneal injury?

- **Tetanus immunization** is not routinely needed for non-penetrating injuries.
- **Topical anaesthetics** should not be used, except as part of the examination. They abolish the corneal reflex, which increases the risk of further corneal damage. Th slow healing and aggravate associated keratitis [Torok and Mader, 1996].
- **Cycloplegics** are claimed to reduce ocular pain and inflammation by alleviating ciliary spasm. There are no controlled studies to support this hypothesis [Sabri et a 1998; Carley and Carley, 2001].
- **Corneal patches** worn for 24–48 hours do not improve the rate of abrasion recovery or reduce pain in adults and children, and are not a useful intervention in the treatment of corneal abrasions [Flynn et al, 1998; Bandolier, 1999; Le Sage et al, 2001; Michael et al, 2002].
- **Corneal patches** are only recommended for a few hour after an anaesthetic has been instilled during examination to protect the eye from further damage un the corneal reflex returns.
- **Topical corticosteroids should not be used.** They slow corneal epithelial and stromal healing, increase the risk of infection, and cause serious scarring and visual loss i a dendritic ulcer has been missed [Shields, 2000a].
- **Soft bandage contact lenses** and **collagen shields** have both been used in the treatment of corneal abrasion, bu there are potential risks from both treatments and ther is not enough evidence for their efficacy to make a recommendation [Acheson et al, 1987; Wedge and Rootman, 1992; Sabri et al, 1998; Willoughby et al, 2002].

References

NHS staff in England can link, free of charge, from references to full text journals by clicking on [Full text] o the PRODIGY website.

1. Acheson, J.F., Joseph, J. and Spalton, D.J. (1987) Use of soft contact lenses in an eye casualty department fo the primary treatment of traumatic corneal abrasions *British Journal of Ophthalmology* **71**(4), 285–289.
2. Bandolier (1999) *Corneal abrasion treatment.* Bandolier. www.jr2.ox.ac.uk/bandolier/band63/b63-2.html [Accessed: 06/09/2004].
3. Carley, F. and Carley, S. (2001) Mydriatics in cornea abrasion. *Emergency Medicine Journal* **18**(4), 273.
4. CSM (2002) Non-steroidal anti-inflammatory drugs (NSAIDs) and gastrointestinal (GI) safety. *Current Problems in Pharmacovigilance* **28**(Apr), 5.
5. Eagling, E.M. and Roper-Hall, M.J. (Eds.) (1986) *Ey injuries: an illustrated guide.* London: Gower Medica Publishing.
6. Field, D., Martin, D. and Witchell, L. (1999) Ophthalmic chloramphenicol: a review of the literature. *Accident & Emergency Nursing* **7**(1), 13–1
7. Flynn, C.A., D'Amico, F. and Smith, G. (1998) Shoul we patch corneal abrasions? A meta-analysis. *Journal of Family Practice* **47**(4), 264–270.
8. Goldberg, S. (Ed.) (2001) *Ophthalmology made ridiculously simple.* Miami: MedMaster, Inc.
9. Hanna, C., Massey, J.Y., Hendrickson, R.O. et al (1978) Ocular penetration of topical chloramphenico in humans. *Archives of Ophthalmology* **96**(7), 1258–1261.
10. Khaw, P.T. and Elkington, A.R. (Eds.) (1999) *ABC o eyes.* 3rd edn. London: BMJ Publishing Group.
11. Khaw, P.T., Shah, P. and Elkington, A.R. (2004) Inju to the eye. *British Medical Journal* **328**(7430), 36–38.
12. Lancaster, T., Swart, A.M. and Jick, H. (1998) Risk c serious haematological toxicity with use of chloramphenicol eye drops in a British general practic

database. *British Medical Journal* **316**(7132), 667. [Full text]
13. Le Sage, N., Verreault, R. and Rochette, L. (2001) Efficacy of eye patching for traumatic corneal abrasions: a controlled clinical trial. *Annals of Emergency Medicine* **38**(2), 129–134.
14. McGuinness, R. (1998) Ocular trauma: how to treat and when to refer. *Modern Medicine of Australia* **41**(4), 82–89.
15. Melton, N.R., Maino, J.H. and thomas, R.K. (1991) Management of corneal abrasions. *Optometry Clinics* **1**(4), 119–126.
16. Michael, J.G., Hug, D. and Dowd, M.D. (2002) Management of corneal abrasion in children: a randomized clinical trial. *Annals of Emergency Medicine* **40**(1), 67–72.
17. Newell, F.W. (Ed.) (1996) *Ophthalmology: principles and concepts*. 8th edn. London: Mosby.
18. Robert, P.Y. and Adenis, J.P. (2001) Comparative review of topical ophthalmic antibacterial preparations. *Drugs* **61**(2), 175–185.
19. Royal College of General Practitioners and Royal College of Ophthalmologists (2001) *Ophthalmology for general practice trainees*. London: Medical Protection Society.
20. Sabri, K., Pandit, J.C., Thaller, V.T. et al (1998) National survey of corneal abrasion treatment. *Eye* **12**(2), 278–281.
21. Shields, S.R. (2000a) Managing eye disease in primary care. Part 2. How to recognize and treat common eye problems. *Postgraduate Medicine* **108**(5), 83–86.
22. Shields, S.R. (2000b) Managing eye disease in primary care. Part 3. When to refer for ophthalmologic care. *Postgraduate Medicine* **108**(5), 99–106.
23. Torok, P.G. and Mader, T.H. (1996) Corneal abrasions: diagnosis and management. *American Family Physician* **55**(2), 442.
24. Walker, S., Diaper, C.J., Bowman, R. et al (1998) Lack of evidence for systemic toxicity following topical chloramphenicol use. *Eye* **12**(5), 875–879.
25. Weaver, C.S. and Terrell, K.M. (2003) Evidence-based emergency medicine. Update: do ophthalmic nonsteroidal anti-inflammatory drugs reduce the pain associated with simple corneal abrasion without delaying healing? *Annals of Emergency Medicine* **41**(1), 134–140.
26. Wedge, C.I and Rootman, D.S (1992) Collagen shields: efficacy, safety and comfort in the treatment of human traumatic corneal abrasion and effect on vision on healthy eyes. *Canadian Journal of Ophthalmology* **27**(6), 295–298.
27. Willoughby, C.E., Batterbury, M. and Kaye, S.B. (2002) Collagen corneal shields. *Survey of Ophthalmology* **47**(2), 174–182.

PRODIGY GUIDANCE

Coronary heart disease risk — identification and management

Last revised in July 2003
At the time of print this topic was being updated. The newly revised guidance will be issued on to the website in 2006.
www.prodigy.nhs.uk/guidance.asp?gt=CHD risk - identify and manage

C

Applies to people over the age of 16 years

This guidance covers the priorities for screening for coronary heart disease (CHD) as given in the *National Service Framework for Coronary Heart Disease* and how to calculate CHD risk. It includes diet and lifestyle advice to reduce the risk of CHD, the use of low-dose aspirin, and the recommended treatments for both primary and secondary prevention of CHD. Advice about treatment thresholds for hyperlipidaemia and hypertension is also included.

This guidance does not cover advice about management and drug treatment of individual cardiovascular conditions.

There is separate PRODIGY guidance for *Angina, Atrial Fibrillation, Diabetes Type 2 — lipid management, Diabetes Type 1 and 2 — hypertension, Heart failure, Hyperlipidaemia, Hypertension, Obesity, Prior myocardial infarction — prophylactic treatments, and Smoking cessation.*

Goals

Organizational goals

- To identify people who have established coronary heart disease (CHD) or other occlusive arterial disease; they require secondary prevention of CHD and are the group with the highest risk
- To identify people who are at significant risk of CHD but who have not yet developed symptoms of CHD. This group requires primary prevention of CHD

Clinical goals

- To offer advice and treatment to these people in order to reduce the risk of developing CHD or other major atherosclerotic disease

[DH, 2000]

Contents

Scenarios

- Who should be screened for CHD risk? p.452
- Established CHD p.453
- Initial check: CHD risk > 30%, but no CHD p.455
- Initial check: CHD risk 15–30% p.456
- Initial check: CHD risk < 15% p.458

Extended Information, p. 459

Which scenario?

- **Who should be screened for CHD risk?** Advice on which individuals require coronary heart disease (CHD) risk assessment, and how to calculate CHD risk.
- **Established CHD:** offers advice on the recommended interventions for people with established CHD. If treatment for hypertension, hyperlipidaemia, or other cardiovascular disorders is needed, see separate PRODIGY guidance on *Angina*, *Hypertension*, *Hyperlipidaemia*, and *Prior myocardial infarction — prophylactic treatments*.
- **Initial check: CHD risk >30%, but no CHD:** offers advice on the recommended interventions for people whose 10-year risk of CHD is greater than 30%. If treatment for hypertension or hyperlipidaemia is required, see separate PRODIGY guidance on *Hypertension* and *Hyperlipidaemia*.
- **Initial check: CHD risk 15–30%:** offers advice on the recommended interventions for people whose 10-year risk of CHD is between 15% and 30%. If treatment for hypertension is required, see separate PRODIGY guidance on *Hypertension*.
- **Initial check: CHD risk <15%:** offers healthy lifestyle advice. If treatment for hypertension is required, see PRODIGY *Hypertension* guidance.

Who should be screened for CHD risk?

Which therapy?

- **Coronary heart disease (CHD) risk should be calculated for people with:**
  - Diabetes
  - Hypertension
  - A family history of severe dyslipidaemia, premature CHD, or physical signs of hypercholesterolaemia
- **CHD risk calculation is unnecessary for people who are already at high risk,** that is:
  - People with established occlusive arterial disease (i.e. established CHD)
  - People with a familial dyslipidaemia
- Use the Joint British Societies Coronary Risk Prediction chart (at the back of the *British National Formulary*) or at www.bhsoc.org/resources/prediction_chart.htmfor initial CHD risk calculation.
- **Data required for risk calculation:** sex; age (years); smoking status; presence/absence of diabetes; blood pressure (mmHg); total cholesterol (mmol/l); and high-density lipoprotein cholesterol (mmol/l).
- **Baseline CHD risk should be calculated using the averages of 2–3 measurements of blood pressure (BP) and lipids taken several weeks apart.**
- Use pretreatment BP and lipid measurements if the individual is already on treatment.
- If the individual has quit smoking within last 5 years, classify as a current smoker.
- If cholesterol results are not available, use average values for age and sex for preliminary calculation. Recalculate using the average of 2–3 measurements when results become available.

- **CHD risk assessment tools should be used to supplement clinical judgement, not replace it.**
- **Risk is underestimated in:**
  - People with a family history of premature CHD multiply the calculated risk by 1.5
  - People of south Asian descent
  - Those with the lowest incomes
  - People with raised triglyceride levels
  - Those who are not yet diabetic, but have impaired fasting glucose (6.1–6.9 mmol/l)
  - People with Type 1 diabetes
  - Women with premature menopause

Follow-up advice

- For people at low risk of coronary heart disease (CHD), re-assess in 3–5 years.
- For people whose 10-year risk of CHD is <15% and who have hypertension; diabetes; or a family history of severe dyslipidaemia, premature CHD, or physical signs of hypercholesterolaemia, reassess annually.
- If the calculated risk is >15%, recalculate risk with the averages of 2–3 measurements of blood pressure and lipids (biological variation is large), taken several weeks apart.
- For people found to be at high risk of CHD (i.e. >30% over 10 years), offer a trial of lifestyle advice and reassess after 3 months, or start treatment as appropriate, and reassess after 1 month. Once treatment is stable, reassess annually.

Should I refer or investigate?

Investigate?

Data required for coronary heart disease calculation

- 2–3 blood pressure (BP) readings, taken several weeks apart.
- 2–3 total cholesterol and HDL-C levels, also taken several weeks apart. This should include at least one fasting full lipid profile (i.e. total cholesterol, LDL-C, HDL-C, and triglyceride levels).
- Use pretreatment BP and lipid measurements for those already on treatment.

Patient information leaflets

The following PILs are available at www.prodigy.nhs.uk

- Alcohol and Sensible Drinking
- British Heart Foundation
- British Nutrition Foundation
- Cholesterol
- Eat More Fruit and Vegetables
- Exercise for Health
- Healthy Eating
- Healthy Eating - A Summary
- Healthy Lifestyle - Five Choices
- Heart Disease - Prevention
- Heart Disease Prevention - A Summary
- Smokeline
- Smoking - A Summary
- Smoking - Help to Stop with Bupropion
- Smoking - Nicotine Replacement Therapy
- Smoking - The Facts
- Smoking - Tips on Stopping
- Weight Reduction - A Summary
- Weight Reduction - How to Lose Weight

Shared decision making

- Your risk of future heart disease is based on risk factors such as smoking, high blood pressure, your cholesterol level, family history, obesity, diabetes, existing heart disease, and too little exercise.
- You can reduce your risk of future heart disease by:
  - Not smoking
  - Regular exercise
  - Losing weight if you are overweight or obese
  - Eating more vegetables, fruit, cereals, wholegrain bread, poultry, fish, rice, skimmed or semi-skimmed milk, grilled food, lean meat, pasta
  - Eating less fatty meats, fatty cheeses, full cream milk, fried food, lard
  - If you do fry food, choosing a vegetable oil such as sunflower or rapeseed
  - Using low-fat spreads
  - Adding less salt to food, and avoiding foods that are very salty
  - Drinking alcohol in moderation

Drug rationale

- No prescriptions are offered in this scenario.

C

Established CHD

Which therapy?

All people with established coronary heart disease, stroke, transient ischaemic attack, or peripheral vascular disease should receive:

- **Advice about how to stop smoking,** including advice on the use of nicotine replacement therapy or bupropion.
- **Personalized advice about lifestyle changes** (including advice about physical activity, diet, alcohol consumption, weight, and diabetes).
- **Advice and treatment to reduce blood pressure (BP)** below 140/85 mmHg (or 140/80 mmHg in people who have diabetes).
- **Low-dose aspirin** (75 mg daily), or other antiplatelet therapy for those hypersensitive to aspirin.
- **Statins and dietary advice to reduce serum total cholesterol** by 20–25%, or to lower it to below 5.0 mmol/l, whichever would result in the lower level. (Serum low-density lipoprotein cholesterol should be reduced by 30% or lowered to below 3.0 mmol/l, whichever would result in the lower level.)

Additional medication should be prescribed in certain conditions:

- **People with left ventricular dysfunction** should receive ACE inhibitors or beta-blockers.
- **People who have had a prior myocardial infarction** should be prescribed beta-blockers and ACE inhibitors.
- **People over 65 years with atrial fibrillation** should be prescribed warfarin instead of aspirin.
- **People with diabetes** require meticulous control of BP and glucose.

Practical prescribing points

For further information please see the *Medicines Compendium* (www.medicines.org.uk) or the *British National Formulary* (www.bnf.org).

Low-dose aspirin

- **Concurrent nonsteroidal anti-inflammatory drugs (NSAIDs):** the risk of serious gastrointestinal complications doubles in people who regularly take low-dose aspirin and another NSAID. If possible, stop the second NSAID.
- **If a second NSAID must be continued, avoid ibuprofen** — it may reduce the cardiovascular protective effect of

low-dose aspirin. Consider using diclofenac if a second NSAID must be used.
- **Asthma:** aspirin can induce bronchospasm in people who are hypersensitive to aspirin, but this is rare.

Follow-up advice

- People with established coronary heart disease should be followed up at least annually.

C

Should I refer or investigate?

Refer?

- **Consider referral** for people with:
  - Possible secondary hypertension
  - Unusual blood pressure variability
  - Severe hypercholesterolaemia or hypertriglyceridaemia (>10 mmol/l), or suspected familial hypercholesterolaemia
- **Consider referral for specialist assessment of treatment,** e.g. for antiarrhythmic therapy in paroxysmal atrial fibrillation (AF), or people with AF who are suitable for cardioversion.

Investigate?

Investigations to exclude diabetes or target organ damage (if not already done)

- Urine test strip for protein and blood
- Serum creatinine and electrolytes
- Blood glucose

Other investigations (if not already done)

- An electrocardiogram (ECG) should be performed in all people with suspected angina or atrial fibrillation, to confirm the diagnosis. It should also be checked in people presenting with hypertension, or a suspected transient ischaemic attack.
- People with heart failure should have an echocardiogram to confirm the diagnosis and exclude underlying causes (e.g. valvular heart disease). Alternatively an ECG and chest X-ray can be used. Full blood count, thyroid function tests, and liver function tests should be checked to exclude anaemia, hypothyroidism or hyperthyroidism, or alcohol-related cardiomyopathy respectively.

Investigations before starting drug treatment

- ACE inhibitors: check renal function (serum creatinine and electrolytes).
- Statins: check fasting lipid profile, aspartate aminotransferase (AST) or alanine aminotransferase (ALT), and creatine kinase.
- Warfarin: check liver function tests and coagulation screen.

Patient information leaflets

The following PILs are available at www.prodigy.nhs.uk

- Alcohol and Sensible Drinking
- British Heart Foundation
- British Nutrition Foundation
- Cholesterol
- Eat More Fruit and Vegetables
- Exercise for Health
- Healthy Eating
- Healthy Eating - A Summary
- Healthy Lifestyle - Five Choices
- Heart Disease - Prevention
- Heart Disease Prevention - A Summary
- Smokeline
- Smoking - A Summary
- Smoking - Help to Stop with Bupropion
- Smoking - Nicotine Replacement Therapy
- Smoking - The Facts
- Smoking - Tips on Stopping
- Weight Reduction - A Summary
- Weight Reduction - How to Lose Weight

Shared decision making

- Your risk of further heart disease is based on risk factors such as smoking, high blood pressure, your cholesterol level, family history, obesity, diabetes, existing heart disease, and too little exercise.
- **You can reduce your risk of further heart disease by:**
  - Not smoking
  - Regular exercise
  - Losing weight if you are overweight or obese
  - Eating more vegetables, fruit, cereals, wholegrain bread, poultry, fish, rice, skimmed or semi-skimmed milk, grilled food, lean meat, pasta.
  - Eating less fatty meats, fatty cheeses, full cream milk, fried food, lard.
  - If you do fry food, choosing a vegetable oil such as sunflower or rapeseed
  - Using low-fat spreads
  - Adding less salt to food, and avoiding foods that are very salty
  - Drinking alcohol in moderation

Drug rationale

Drugs not included

- **Enteric-coated aspirin:** enteric-coating is not offered, as there is no convincing evidence that this reduces toxicity at a dose of 75 mg [DTB, 1997].
- Increasing doses of aspirin are associated with greater risks of gastrointestinal toxicity, and aspirin doses of 75–150 mg per day have been found on systematic review to be at least as effective as higher daily doses [Antithrombotic Trialists' Collaboration, 2002]. Higher doses have not therefore been offered.

Drugs included

- **Aspirin 75 mg dispersible tablets:** regular low-dose aspirin reduces the risk of any serious vascular event by 25% in people with established coronary heart disease (CHD), stroke, transient ischaemic attack, or peripheral vascular disease. The risk of non-fatal myocardial infarction is reduced by a third, non-fatal stroke is reduced by a quarter, and vascular mortality is reduced by a sixth [Antithrombotic Trialists' Collaboration, 2002].
- Low-dose aspirin may also be used for primary prevention in people aged 50 years and over with a 10-year CHD risk greater than15%; or in people with diabetes; or in people with target organ damage from hypertension [Wood et al, 1998].
- **Clopidogrel** is included for people who are hypersensitive to aspirin, i.e. in whom aspirin induces angio-oedema or bronchospasm. People who experience dyspepsia with aspirin should be co-prescribed an acid-suppressing drug. See the separate PRODIGY guidance on *Dyspepsia — symptoms (uninvestigated by endoscopy)*.
- A non-drug prescription giving diet and lifestyle advice is offered.

Prescriptions

Non-drug management

Advice only: diet and lifestyle

- Age from 16 years onwards
- Lifestyle and dietary changes can help to reduce the risk of heart disease. You should aim to eat and live healthily. This means: No smoking. Regular exercise. Moderate alcohol consumption. Lose weight if you are overweight or obese. MORE vegetables, fruit, cereals, wholegrain bread, poultry, fish, rice, skimmed or semi-skimmed milk, grilled food, lean meat, pasta etc. LESS fatty meats, fatty cheeses, full cream milk, fried food, lard, etc. If you do fry, choose a vegetable oil such as sunflower or rapeseed. Use low fat spreads. Add less salt to food, and avoid foods that are very salty.

Start antiplatelet therapy

Aspirin 75mg dispersible once a day

- Age from 16 years onwards
- Aspirin 75mg dispersible tabs. Take one tablet once a day; supply 28 tablets; NHS Cost £0.36.

Clopidogrel 75mg once a day – only if intolerant of aspirin

- Age from 16 years onwards
- Clopidogrel 75mg tablets. Take one tablet once a day; supply 28 tablets; NHS Cost £35.31.

Initial check: CHD risk >30%, but no CHD

Which therapy?

All people with a calculated coronary heart disease (CHD) risk greater than 30% over 10 years (but without diagnosed CHD or other occlusive arterial disease) should receive:

- **Advice about how to stop smoking,** including advice on the use of nicotine replacement therapy or bupropion.
- **Personalized advice about lifestyle changes** (including advice about physical activity, diet, alcohol consumption, weight, and diabetes).
- **Advice and treatment to reduce blood pressure** below 140/85 mmHg (or 140/80 mmHg in people who have diabetes).
- **Statins and dietary advice to reduce serum total cholesterol** by 20–25%, or to lower it to below 5.0 mmol/l, whichever would result in the lower level. (Serum low-density lipoprotein cholesterol should be reduced by 30% or lowered to below 3.0 mmol/l, whichever would result in the lower level.)

Additional medication should be prescribed in certain conditions:

- **Give low-dose aspirin (75 mg daily)** to people over the age of 50 years with a 10-year CHD risk greater than 15%, or who have diabetes, or who have target organ damage from hypertension. Use alternative antiplatelet therapy in individuals hypersensitive to aspirin.

Practical prescribing points

For further information please see the *Medicines Compendium* (www.medicines.org.uk) or the *British National Formulary* (www.bnf.org).

Low-dose aspirin

- **Concurrent nonsteroidal anti-inflammatory drugs (NSAIDs):** the risk of serious gastrointestinal complications doubles in people who regularly take low-dose aspirin and another NSAID. If possible, stop the second NSAID.
- **If a second NSAID must be continued, avoid ibuprofen** — it may reduce the cardiovascular protective effect of low-dose aspirin. Consider using diclofenac if a second NSAID must be used.
- **Asthma:** aspirin can induce bronchospasm in people who are hypersensitive to aspirin, but this is rare.

Follow-up advice

- For those on a trial of lifestyle advice, reassess after 3 months.
- If treatment has been started, reassess after 1 month.
- Once treatment is stable, reassess annually.

Should I refer or investigate?

Refer?

- **Consider referral** for people with:
  - Possible secondary hypertension
  - Unusual blood pressure variability
  - Severe hypercholesterolaemia or hypertriglyceridaemia (>10 mmol/l), or suspected familial hypercholesterolaemia

Investigate?

Investigations to exclude diabetes or target organ damage (if not already done)

- Urine test strip for protein and blood
- Serum creatinine and electrolytes
- Blood glucose

Other investigations (if not already done)

- An electrocardiogram should be checked in people presenting with hypertension, suspected angina, or a suspected transient ischaemic attack.

Investigations before starting drug treatment

- ACE inhibitors: check renal function (serum creatinine and electrolytes).
- Statins: check fasting lipid profile, aspartate aminotransferase (AST) or alanine aminotransferase (ALT), and creatine kinase.

Patient information leaflets

The following PILs are available at www.prodigy.nhs.uk

- Alcohol and Sensible Drinking
- British Heart Foundation
- British Nutrition Foundation
- Cholesterol
- Eat More Fruit and Vegetables
- Exercise for Health
- Healthy Eating
- Healthy Eating - A Summary
- Healthy Lifestyle - Five Choices
- Heart Disease - Prevention
- Heart Disease Prevention - A Summary
- Smokeline
- Smoking - A Summary
- Smoking - Help to Stop with Bupropion
- Smoking - Nicotine Replacement Therapy
- Smoking - The Facts
- Smoking - Tips on Stopping
- Weight Reduction - A Summary
- Weight Reduction - How to Lose Weight

C

Shared decision making

- You are at higher risk of future heart disease than most people.
- Your risk of future heart disease is based on risk factors such as smoking, high blood pressure, your cholesterol level, family history, obesity, diabetes, existing heart disease, and too little exercise.
- **You can reduce your risk of future heart disease by:**
  - Not smoking
  - Regular exercise
  - Losing weight if you are overweight or obese
  - Eating more vegetables, fruit, cereals, wholegrain bread, poultry, fish, rice, skimmed or semi-skimmed milk, grilled food, lean meat, pasta
  - Eating less fatty meats, fatty cheeses, full cream milk, fried food, lard
  - If you do fry food, choosing a vegetable oil such as sunflower or rapeseed
  - Using low-fat spreads
  - Adding less salt to food, and avoiding foods that are very salty
  - Drinking alcohol in moderation

Drug rationale

Drugs not included

- **Enteric-coated aspirin:** enteric-coating is not offered, as there is no convincing evidence that this reduces toxicity at a dose of 75 mg [DTB, 1997].
- Increasing doses of aspirin are associated with greater risks of gastrointestinal toxicity, and aspirin doses of 75–150 mg per day have been found on systematic review to be at least as effective as higher daily doses [Antithrombotic Trialists' Collaboration, 2002]. Higher doses have not therefore been offered.

Drugs included

- **Aspirin 75 mg dispersible tablets:** regular low-dose aspirin reduces the risk of any serious vascular event by 25% in people with established coronary heart disease (CHD), stroke, transient ischaemic attack, or peripheral vascular disease. The risk of non-fatal myocardial infarction is reduced by a third, non-fatal stroke is reduced by a quarter, and vascular mortality is reduced by a sixth [Antithrombotic Trialists' Collaboration, 2002].
- Low-dose aspirin may also be used for primary prevention in people aged 50 years and over with a 10-year CHD risk greater than 15%; or people with diabetes; or people with target organ damage from hypertension [Wood et al, 1998].
- **Clopidogrel** is included for people who are hypersensitive to aspirin, i.e. in whom aspirin induces angio-oedema or bronchospasm. People who experience dyspepsia with aspirin should be co-prescribed an acid-suppressing drug. See the separate PRODIGY guidance on *Dyspepsia — symptoms (uninvestiagted by endoscopy).*
- A non-drug prescription giving diet and lifestyle advice is offered.

Prescriptions

Non-drug management

Advice only: diet and lifestyle

- Age from 16 years onwards
- Lifestyle and dietary changes can help to reduce the risk of heart disease. You should aim to eat and live healthily. This means: No smoking. Regular exercise. Moderate alcohol consumption. Lose weight if you are overweight or obese. MORE vegetables, fruit, cereals, wholegrain bread, poultry, fish, rice, skimmed or semi-skimmed milk, grilled food, lean meat, pasta etc. LESS fatty meats, fatty cheeses, full cream milk, fried food, lard, etc. If you do fry, choose a vegetable oil such as sunflower or rapeseed. Use low fat spreads. Add less salt to food, and avoid foods that are very salty.

Start antiplatelet therapy

Aspirin 75mg dispersible once a day

- Age from 16 years onwards
- Aspirin 75mg dispersible tabs. Take one tablet once a day; supply 28 tablets; NHS Cost £0.36.

Clopidogrel 75mg once a day – only if intolerant of aspirin

- Age from 16 years onwards
- Clopidogrel 75mg tablets. Take one tablet once a day; supply 28 tablets; NHS Cost £35.31.

Initial check: CHD risk 15–30%

Which therapy

All people with a calculated coronary heart disease (CHD) risk of 15–30% over 10 years should receive:

- **Advice about how to stop smoking,** including advice on the use of nicotine replacement therapy or bupropion.
- **Personalized advice about lifestyle changes** (including advice about physical activity, diet, alcohol consumption, weight, and diabetes).
- **Advice and treatment to reduce blood pressure** below 140/85 mmHg (or 140/80 mmHg in people who have diabetes).

Additional medication should be prescribed in certain conditions:

- **Give low-dose aspirin (75 mg daily) to** people over the age of 50 years with a 10-year CHD risk greater than 15%, or who have diabetes, or who have target organ damage from hypertension. Use alternative antiplatelet therapy in individuals hypersensitive to aspirin.
- **People with diabetes** should be offered statins and dietary advice to lower serum total cholesterol. Otherwise, offer diet and lifestyle advice, and follow-up every 3–5 years.
- **Consider using a statin if familial hypercholesterolaemia is suspected,** e.g. total cholesterol is greater than 7.5 mmol/l and physical signs of hyperlipidaemia or family history of premature CHD (refer for specialist assessment). See the separate PRODIGY guidance on *Hyperlipidaemia* for further information.
- **Meticulous control of BP and glucose is required in people who also have diabetes.**

Practical prescribing points

For further information please see the *Medicines Compendium* (www.medicines.org.uk) or the *British National Formulary* (www.bnf.org).

Low-dose aspirin

- **Concurrent nonsteroidal anti-inflammatory drugs (NSAIDs):** the risk of serious gastrointestinal complications doubles in people who regularly take low-dose aspirin and another NSAID. If possible, stop the second NSAID.
- **If a second NSAID must be continued, avoid ibuprofen** — it may reduce the cardiovascular protective effect of

low-dose aspirin. Consider using diclofenac if a second NSAID must be used.
- **Asthma:** aspirin can induce bronchospasm in people who are hypersensitive to aspirin, but this is rare.

Follow-up advice

- People who are not receiving treatment should be reassessed every 3–5 years, or earlier if required. For example, consider reassessing older people, or people with one or more risk factors for coronary heart disease annually. (Cardiovascular risk also increases with age.)
- If on a trial of lifestyle advice, reassess after 3 months.
- If treatment has been started, reassess after 1 month.
- Once treatment is stable, reassess annually.

Should I refer or investigate?

Refer?

- **Consider referral** for people with:
  - Possible secondary hypertension
  - Unusual blood pressure variability
  - Severe hypercholesterolaemia or hypertriglyceridaemia (>10 mmol/l), or suspected familial hypercholesterolaemia

Investigate?

Investigations to exclude diabetes or target organ damage (if not already done)

- Urine test strip for protein and blood
- Serum creatinine and electrolytes
- Blood glucose

Other investigations (if not already done)

- An electrocardiogram should be checked in people presenting with hypertension, suspected angina, or a suspected transient ischaemic attack.

Investigations before starting drug treatment

- ACE inhibitors: check renal function (serum creatinine and electrolytes).
- Statins: check fasting lipid profile, aspartate aminotransferase (AST) or alanine aminotransferase (ALT), and creatine kinase.

Patient information leaflets

The following PILs are available at www.prodigy.nhs.uk

- Alcohol and Sensible Drinking
- British Heart Foundation
- British Nutrition Foundation
- Cholesterol
- Eat More Fruit and Vegetables
- Exercise for Health
- Healthy Eating
- Healthy Eating - A Summary
- Healthy Lifestyle - Five Choices
- Heart Disease - Prevention
- Heart Disease Prevention - A Summary
- Smokeline
- Smoking - A Summary
- Smoking - Help to Stop with Bupropion
- Smoking - Nicotine Replacement Therapy
- Smoking - The Facts
- Smoking - Tips on Stopping
- Weight Reduction - A Summary
- Weight Reduction - How to Lose Weight

Shared decision making

- Your risk of future heart disease is based on risk factors such as smoking, high blood pressure, your cholesterol level, family history, obesity, diabetes, existing heart disease, and too little exercise.
- **You can reduce your risk of future heart disease by:**
  - Not smoking
  - Regular exercise
  - Losing weight if you are overweight or obese
  - Eating MORE vegetables, fruit, cereals, wholegrain bread, poultry, fish, rice, skimmed or semi-skimmed milk, grilled food, lean meat, pasta
  - Eating LESS fatty meats, fatty cheeses, full cream milk, fried food, lard
  - If you do fry, choosing a vegetable oil such as sunflower or rapeseed
  - Using low-fat spreads
  - Adding less salt to food, and avoiding foods that are very salty
  - Drinking alcohol in moderation

Drug rationale

Drugs not included

- **Enteric-coated aspirin:** enteric-coating is not offered, as there is no convincing evidence that this reduces toxicity at a dose of 75 mg [DTB, 1997].
- Increasing doses of aspirin are associated with greater risks of gastrointestinal toxicity, and aspirin doses of 75–150 mg per day have been found on systematic review to be at least as effective as higher daily doses [Antithrombotic Trialists' Collaboration, 2002]. Higher doses have not therefore been offered.

Drugs included

- **Aspirin 75 mg dispersible tablets:** regular low-dose aspirin reduces the risk of any serious vascular event by 25% in people with established coronary heart disease (CHD), stroke, transient ischaemic attack, or peripheral vascular disease. The risk of non-fatal myocardial infarction is reduced by a third, non-fatal stroke is reduced by a quarter, and vascular mortality is reduced by a sixth [Antithrombotic Trialists' Collaboration, 2002].
- Low-10-year CHD risk greater than15%; or people with diabetes; or people with target organ damage dose aspirin may also be used for primary prevention in people aged 50 years and over with a from hypertension [Wood et al, 1998].
- **Clopidogrel** is included for people who are hypersensitive to aspirin, i.e. in whom aspirin induces angio-oedema or bronchospasm. People who experience dyspepsia with aspirin should be co-prescribed an acid-suppressing drug. See the separate Prodigy guidance on *Dyspepsia — symptoms (uninvestigated by endoscopy).*
- A non-drug prescription giving diet and lifestyle advice is offered.

Prescriptions

Non-drug management

Advice only: diet and lifestyle

- Age from 16 years onwards
- Lifestyle and dietary changes can help to reduce the risk of heart disease. You should aim to eat and live healthily. This means: No smoking. Regular exercise. Moderate alcohol consumption. Lose weight if you are overweight or obese. MORE vegetables, fruit, cereals, wholegrain

bread, poultry, fish, rice, skimmed or semi-skimmed milk, grilled food, lean meat, pasta etc. LESS fatty meats, fatty cheeses, full cream milk, fried food, lard, etc. If you do fry, choose a vegetable oil such as sunflower or rapeseed. Use low fat spreads. Add less salt to food, and avoid foods that are very salty.

Start antiplatelet (if 50+/diabetes/target organ damage)

C

Aspirin 75mg dispersible once a day

- Age from 16 years onwards
- Aspirin 75mg dispersible tabs. Take one tablet once a day; supply 28 tablets; NHS Cost £0.36.

Clopidogrel 75mg once a day – only if intolerant of aspirin

- Age from 16 years onwards
- Clopidogrel 75mg tablets. Take one tablet once a day; supply 28 tablets; NHS Cost £35.31.

Initial check: CHD risk <15%

Which therapy?

- **Most people will not require treatment.**
- Reassure and offer diet and lifestyle advice to prevent coronary heart disease (CHD).
- **If blood pressure (BP) is above usual treatment threshold** (e.g. >160 mmHg systolic or >100 mmHg diastolic), offer advice and treatment to maintain BP below 140/85 mmHg.
- **People with familial hypercholesterolaemia should be offered treatment.** Consider this as a possibility if total cholesterol is greater than 7.5 mmol/l and there are physical signs of hyperlipidaemia or family history of premature CHD (refer for specialist assessment). See the separate PRODIGY guidance on *Hyperlipidaemia* for further information.
- **Meticulous control of BP and glucose is important in people who have diabetes,** especially if they have signs of target organ damage.

Practical prescribing points

For further information please see the *Medicines Compendium* (www.medicines.org.uk) or the *British National Formulary* (www.bnf.org).

Follow-up advice

- If treatment is not required, re-assess coronary heart disease (CHD) risk after 3–5 years.
- For people whose 10-year risk of CHD is less than 15% and who have hypertension; diabetes; or a family history of severe dyslipidaemia, premature CHD, or physical signs of hypercholesterolaemia, reassess annually.

Should I refer or investigate?

Refer?

- Consider referral for people with:
  - Possible secondary hypertension
  - Unusual blood pressure variability
  - Severe hypercholesterolaemia or hypertriglyceridaemia (>10 mmol/l), or suspected familial hypercholesterolaemia

Investigate?

Investigations to exclude diabetes or target organ damage (if not already done)

- Urine test strip for protein and blood
- Serum creatinine and electrolytes
- Blood glucose

Other investigations (if not already done)

- An electrocardiogram should be checked in people presenting with hypertension, suspected angina, or a suspected transient ischaemic attack.

Investigations before starting drug treatment

- ACE inhibitors: check renal function (serum creatinine and electrolytes).
- Statins: check fasting lipid profile, aspartate aminotransferase (AST) or alanine aminotransferase (ALT), and creatine kinase.

Patient information leaflets

The following PILs are available at www.prodigy.nhs.uk

- Alcohol and Sensible Drinking
- British Heart Foundation
- British Nutrition Foundation
- Cholesterol
- Eat More Fruit and Vegetables
- Exercise for Health
- Healthy Eating
- Healthy Eating - A Summary
- Healthy Lifestyle - Five Choices
- Heart Disease - Prevention
- Heart Disease Prevention - A Summary
- Smokeline
- Smoking - A Summary
- Smoking - Help to Stop with Bupropion
- Smoking - Nicotine Replacement Therapy
- Smoking - The Facts
- Smoking - Tips on Stopping
- Weight Reduction - A Summary
- Weight Reduction - How to Lose Weight

Shared decision making

- You are at low risk of future heart disease.
- Your risk of future heart disease is based on risk factors such as smoking, high blood pressure, your cholesterol level, family history, obesity, diabetes, existing heart disease, and too little exercise.
- **You can reduce your risk of future heart disease by:**
  - Not smoking
  - Regular exercise
  - Losing weight if you are overweight or obese
  - Eating MORE vegetables, fruit, cereals, wholegrain bread, poultry, fish, rice, skimmed or semi-skimmed milk, grilled food, lean meat, pasta
  - Eating LESS fatty meats, fatty cheeses, full cream milk, fried food, lard
  - If you do fry food, choosing a vegetable oil such as sunflower or rapeseed
  - Using low-fat spreads
  - Adding less salt to food, and avoiding foods that are very salty
  - Drinking alcohol in moderation

Drug rationale

- A non-drug prescription giving diet and lifestyle advice is offered.

rescriptions

on-drug management

vice only: diet and lifestyle
Age from 16 years onwards
Lifestyle and dietary changes can help to reduce the risk of heart disease. You should aim to eat and live healthily. This means: No smoking. Regular exercise. Moderate alcohol consumption. Lose weight if you are overweight or obese. MORE vegetables, fruit, cereals, wholegrain bread, poultry, fish, rice, skimmed or semi-skimmed milk, grilled food, lean meat, pasta etc. LESS fatty meats, fatty cheeses, full cream milk, fried food, lard, etc. If you do fry, choose a vegetable oil such as sunflower or rapeseed. Use low fat spreads. Add less salt to food, and avoid foods that are very salty.

xtended Information

ackground information

What is coronary heart disease? p.459
How common is it? p.459
How do I know my patient is at risk of CHD? p.459
Complications and prognosis p.459

hat is coronary heart disease?

Coronary heart disease (CHD) is a condition characterized by the development of atherosclerotic plaques (fibro-fatty deposits) in coronary arteries. Atherosclerotic plaques and associated blood clots obstruct blood flow through coronary arteries to the heart muscle.
The reduced supply of oxygen to the heart muscle causes coronary ischaemia. This can present as angina, myocardial infarction, unstable angina, or sudden death. Note: atherosclerotic disease in cerebrovascular arteries can lead to stroke or transient ischaemic attacks (i.e. cerebrovascular disease). Atherosclerotic plaques in the peripheral arteries can lead to peripheral vascular disease.

ow common is it?

Coronary heart disease (CHD) is a leading cause of death in the UK.
About 5% of the population currently have CHD.
The proportion of the population at risk of developing CHD is detailed in Table 1 below. The statistics are for men and women aged 30 to 74 years and exclude those with reported CHD or other atherosclerotic disease [Wood et al, 1998].
Some ethnic groups have substantially higher risks for developing CHD. In the UK, people of south Asian descent have a 40% greater risk of CHD than white people [DH, 2000].

able 1: Risk of developing CHD over 10 years.

sk of developing CHD	Percentage of people at different levels of CHD risk (aged 30 to 74 years)	
	Men	Women
% or more	3%	–
–29%	5%	2%
–24%	8%	2%
–19%	12%	5%
% or more	28%	9%

- **People of Afro-Caribbean descent have a lower risk of CHD, but a higher risk of stroke** than the white population in the UK. For West African people the rate of stroke is nearly three times higher for men and 81% higher for women. For Caribbean people it is 68% higher for men and 57% higher for women [British Heart Foundation, 2003].

How do I know my patient is at risk of CHD?

- **Selected screening of the people likely to be at highest risk of CDH is recommended.** (This also effectively targets people at high risk for cerebrovascular disease and peripheral vascular disease).
- For further information about who should be screened, see the *Management Issues* section.

Complications and prognosis

Complications of CHD

- Myocardial infarction
- Heart failure
- Atrial fibrillation, and other dysrhythmias

Complications of other occlusive arterial disease

- Stroke
- Transient ischaemic attack
- Peripheral vascular disease

Prognosis

- About half of all cardiovascular deaths are from CHD, and about a quarter are from stroke.
- CHD is a leading cause of death in the UK. It accounts for about 1 in 4 deaths in men, and 1 in 6 deaths in women.
- Although many elderly people die from CHD, it also accounts for 23% of premature deaths in men and 14% of premature deaths in women, i.e. deaths in people under the age of 75 years.
- Whilst mortality from CHD is falling rapidly, morbidity is not falling, and, in older age groups has risen by over a third in the past 10 years.

[British Heart Foundation, 2003]

Management issues

- Who should be screened for risk of coronary heart disease (CHD)? p.459
- Calculating CHD risk p.460
- Recommended interventions to reduce cardiovascular risk p.461
- Lifestyle measures to prevent CHD p.462
- Low-dose aspirin p.464
- Management of coexisting conditions p.465
- Does hormone replacement therapy prevent CHD? p.466

Who should be screened for risk of coronary heart disease (CHD)?

- **About 5% of the population have pre-existing CHD, and another 3% of people aged 35–69 years have a 30% risk of a CHD event within 10 years.**
- **Unselected screening is not recommended.** If the threshold for screening is lowered to a 15% risk of a CHD event within 10 years, about 30% of men and 10% of women would need to be screened. This is a large proportion of the population. The *National Service Framework for Coronary Heart Disease* has prioritized who should be screened for hyperlipidaemia so that those at highest risk are treated first.

- **Note: family history of premature CHD** is defined by the Joint British Recommendations as 'CHD, or other atherosclerotic disease, in a male first-degree relative before the age of 55 years, or in a female first-degree relative before the age of 65 years' [Wood et al, 1998].

[NHS CRD, 1998; Wood et al, 1998; DH, 2000]

Calculating CHD risk

- Risk assessment charts are printed at the back of the *British National Formulary*. See below, *Other risk calculators*, for some of the popular risk assessment tools to be found on the Internet.
- Different risk assessment tools require slightly different sets of data (see, e.g. Table 3).
- **CHD risk should be calculated using the averages of 2–3 measurements of blood pressure (BP) and lipids taken several weeks apart.**
- **Use baseline BP and lipid measurements** if people are already receiving antihypertensive or lipid-lowering drugs.
- **If baseline measurements are not available, assume the risk of CHD is higher** than predicted using current levels of BP or lipids in people receiving treatment [British Heart Foundation, 2002a].
- **If cholesterol results are not available,** use average total cholesterol values for age and sex (see Table 4), and assume that high-density lipoprotein cholesterol (HDL-C) is 1.0 mmol/l. If the calculated risk is greater than15%, recalculate risk with the averages of at least two (and preferably three) lipid results, once they are available.
- Antihypertensive medication should always be started if BP is persistently above 160/100 mmHg, or when target organ damage due to hypertension is present, irrespective of the calculated 10-year CHD risk [British Heart Foundation, 2002a].
- Lipid-lowering therapy should still be started (or continued) if modification of risk factors (e.g. the person has quit smoking, or has started treatment for hypertension) results in the calculated risk falling below the threshold for drug treatment.

Table 2: Priorities for screening for CHD.

Screen for CHD?	Population	Risk calculation required?	Risk of CHD
First priority	People with established CHD, stroke, transient ischaemic attacks, or peripheral vascular disease People with suspected familial dyslipidaemias	A risk calculation is not required. It can be assumed that these people have a 10-year CHD risk of >30%	High risk
Second priority	People with diabetes People with hypertension People with a family history of severe dyslipidaemia or of premature CHD, or those with physical signs of hypercholesterolaemia	Check serum lipid levels and calculate 10-year CHD risk (These people will have a minimum 10-year CHD risk of >15%, assuming their serum lipid levels are normal)	Significant risk
Not currently	People with none of the above criteria	A risk calculation is not required for people at low risk of CHD These people have a 10-year CHD risk of <15%, assuming their serum lipid levels are normal	Low risk

Table 3: Data required for the Joint British Societies Coronary Risk Prediction Chart.

Data required	Comments
Sex	-
Age (years)	-
Smoking status	The British Heart Foundation states that: 'Smoking status should reflect lifetime exposure tobacco and not simply tobacco use at the time assessment. For example, those who have given smoking within 5 years should be regarded as current smokers for the purposes of the charts.'
Presence/absence of diabetes	-
Blood pressure (mmHg)	Use an average of 2–3 measurements taken sitti in the consulting room If on antihypertensive drugs, use pretreatment values
Total cholesterol (mmol/l)	Fasting specimen not required If receiving lipid-lowering therapy, use pretreatment values
High-density lipoprotein cholesterol	Fasting specimen not required If receiving lipid-lowering therapy, use pretreatment values

- If lifestyle advice results in BP or lipid levels falling bel treatment targets, drug treatment is not needed. However, results should be re-checked annually as the are likely to alter with time.
- **Certain individuals are at higher risk than the charts/ calculators predict.** Higher risks occur in:
  - **Individuals with a family history of premature CHD**; adjust risk upwards by a factor of 1.5.
  - **People with familial dyslipidaemia,** e.g. hypercholesterolaemia, familial combined hyperlipidaemia, and other inherited dyslipidaemia.
  - **People with raised triglyceride levels.**
  - **Those who are not yet diabetic,** but have impaired fasting glucose (6.1–6.9 mmol/l).
  - **People with Type 1 diabetes.** The risk is often greate than that predicted by the cholesterol to HDL-C rati in Type 1 diabetes. It may be more accurate to ignor HDL-C and use the lipid scale for total serum cholesterol alone, but there is no direct evidence for this approach.
  - **Women with premature menopause.**
  - **Those with the lowest incomes.**
  - **Increasing age.** Risk increases exponentially with age so the risk will be closer to the next age category on the risk prediction charts for the last four years of ea decade.
  - **People of south Asian descent,** i.e. originating from t Indian subcontinent. (The risk charts have not been validated in ethnic minority populations).
- **CHD risk assessment tools should be used to supplement, not replace, clinical judgement.**

[Durrington, 1995; Wood et al, 1998; Robson et al, 200

Table 4: Median serum cholesterol levels for men and women in England [Durrington, 1995]

Age (years)	Median serum total cholesterol (mmol/	
	Men	Women
0–24	-	-
25–34	5.4	5.2
35–44	6.0	5.5
45–75	6.2	6.1
75+	5.9	6.8

ther risk calculators

Most of the CHD risk assessment tools listed in Table 5 are based on data from the Framingham Heart Study. The Framingham study population excluded people with pre-existing cardiovascular disease and included relatively few people with diabetes and hypertension. Some CHD risk calculators have been developed specifically for people with diabetes or hypertension [Robson et al, 2000].

ecommended interventions to reduce ardiovascular risk

Cardiovascular risk calculators (for primary prevention) vastly underestimate the risk of CHD in people with a family history of CHD. Adjust the calculated risk upwards by 50%, and base treatment decisions on this higher level of risk.

eople with diagnosed CHD, stroke, transient schaemic attacks, or peripheral vascular disease

ople with established occlusive arterial disease should ceive:

Advice about how to stop smoking, including advice on the use of nicotine replacement therapy, and bupropion.

Information about other modifiable risk factors and personalized advice about how they can be reduced (including advice about physical activity, diet, alcohol consumption, weight, and diabetes).

Advice and treatment to maintain blood pressure (BP) below 140/85 mmHg. People with diabetes should have their BP maintained below 140/80 mmHg, or below 135/ 75 mmHg in the presence of microalbuminuria or proteinuria.

- Low-dose aspirin (75 mg daily), or other antiplatelet therapy if hypersensitive to aspirin.
- Statins and dietary advice to lower serum total cholesterol by 20–25% or to reduce it below 5.0 mmol/l, whichever would result in the lower level. (Serum low-density lipoprotein cholesterol should be lowered by 30% or reduced to below 3.0 mmol/l, whichever would result in the lower level.)
- ACE inhibitors for people who also have left ventricular dysfunction. Note that beta-blockers and spironolactone may also be added to therapy. Angiotensin-II receptor antagonists are an alternative in people who are intolerant of ACE inhibitors.
- Beta-blockers and ACE inhibitors for people who have had a myocardial infarction.
- Warfarin or aspirin for people over 60 years old who have atrial fibrillation. Note that the final choice will depend on the individual's overall risk of stroke. See the separate PRODIGY guidance on *Atrial fibrillation* for further advice about deciding on antithrombotic treatment in atrial fibrillation.
- Meticulous control of BP and glucose in people who also have diabetes.

[Boyle, 2000; DH, 2000; NICE, 2001a]

able 5: Selected tools for assessing CHD risk and their cations on the Internet.

ID risk assessment ol	Source
int British Societies rdiac Risk Assessor ogram	Download www.bnf.org or www.bhsoc.org/resources/ prediction_chart.htm
K Prospective abetes Study Risk gine: sk in people with pe 2 diabetes	Download www.dtu.ox.ac.uk/
DANA risk lculator: sk in people with pertension	Download www.riskscore.org.uk
int British Societies ronary Risk ediction Chart	View www.bhsoc.org/Cardiovascular_ Risk_Charts_and_Calculators.htm Download www.heartuk.org.uk/
effield table for imary prevention of HD (3rd edition, rrected)	View bmj.com/content/vol320/issue7236/images/ large/wale3599.f1.jpeg
amingham function r risk estimation	Online calculator www.cvhealth.ed.ac.uk/index.html (Hint, look at the bottom of the screen and click on the numbers 1, 2, 3, 4, 5)
ew Zealand tables r absolute 5-year risk a cardiovascular ent	View www.cebm.net/prognosis.asp
suite of algorithms d risk prediction ols	www.medal.org

People with a 10-year CHD risk more than 30% but who do not have CHD

People with a calculated CHD risk greater than 30% over 10 years (but without diagnosed CHD or other occlusive arterial disease) should receive:

- Advice about how to stop smoking, including advice on the use of nicotine replacement therapy and bupropion.
- Information about other modifiable risk factors and personalized advice about how they can be reduced (including advice about physical activity, diet, alcohol consumption, weight, and diabetes).
- Advice and treatment to maintain blood pressure (BP) below 140/85 mmHg. People with diabetes should have their BP maintained below 140/80 mmHg, or below 135/ 75 mmHg in the presence of microalbuminuria or proteinuria.
- Low-dose aspirin (75 mg daily) for those aged 50 years or over with a 10-year CHD risk greater than 15%, or people with diabetes, or people with target organ damage [Ramsay et al, 1999]. Note: only use other antiplatelet therapy if the individual is hypersensitive to aspirin.
- Statins and dietary advice to lower serum total cholesterol by 20–25% or to reduce it to below 5.0 mmol/l, which ever would result in the lower level. (Serum low-density lipoprotein cholesterol should be lowered by 30% or reduced to below 3.0 mmol/l, whichever would result in the lower level.)
- Meticulous control of BP and glucose in people who also have diabetes.

[DH, 2000]

People with a 10-year CHD risk of 15–30%

People with a calculated CHD risk of 15–30% over 10 years should receive:

- Advice about how to stop smoking, including advice on the use of nicotine replacement therapy and bupropion.
- Information about other modifiable risk factors and personalized advice about how they can be reduced (including advice about physical activity, diet, alcohol consumption, weight, and diabetes).
- Advice and treatment to maintain blood pressure (BP) below 140/85 mmHg. People with diabetes should have their BP maintained below 140/80 mmHg, or below 135/

75 mmHg in the presence of microalbuminuria or proteinuria.
- Low-dose aspirin (75 mg daily) for those aged 50 years or over with a 10-year CHD risk greater than 15%, or for people with diabetes, or those with target organ damage [Ramsay et al, 1999]. Note: only use other antiplatelet therapy if the individual is hypersensitive to aspirin.
- Statins and dietary advice to lower serum total cholesterol below 5.0 mmol/l should be offered to people with diabetes, and people with a familial dyslipidaemia. Otherwise, offer diet and lifestyle advice, and follow-up every 3–5 years. (Consider the possibility of familial dyslipidaemia if total cholesterol is greater than 7.8 mmol/l. See the separate PRODIGY guidance *Hyperlipidaemia* for further information.)
- Meticulous control of BP and glucose in people who also have diabetes.

People with a 10-year CHD risk of less than 15%

- Most of these people will not require treatment. They should be reassured and offered diet and lifestyle advice to prevent coronary heart disease (CHD). Their 10-year risk of CHD should be reassessed after 3–5 years.
- Some people may wish to buy simvastatin 10 mg at night, which can now be bought over the counter by people with a 10–15% CHD risk over 10 years. This applies to:
  - All men aged 55 years and over
  - Men aged 45–55 and women aged over 55 who have a family history of CHD, are smokers, are obese, or are of south Asian descent
- Note: people with CHD or diabetes cannot buy simvastatin over the counter and will be referred back to their GP by the pharmacist. Higher doses of simvastatin cannot be bought from a pharmacy.
- Again, people with BP above the usual treatment thresholds for hypertension should be offered advice and treatment, and people with a familial dyslipidaemia should also be offered treatment.
- Meticulous control of BP and glucose is important in people who have diabetes, especially if they have signs of target organ damage.

[Wood et al, 1998]

Lifestyle measures to prevent CHD

Lifestyle measures should be regarded as long-term lifestyle changes. They should always be encouraged, even if pharmacological treatment is also required.

Smoking cessation

- Smoking is responsible for about 20% of deaths from coronary heart disease (CHD) in men and 17% of deaths from CHD in women.
- Stopping smoking has been shown in several large cohort studies to decrease associated risks. For CHD, the risk of coronary events declines in 2–3 years to that of people who have never smoked. The risk of stroke declines more slowly [Murphy et al, 2001].
- **All people who smoke should be encouraged to stop.**
- **Advice should be clear, strong, and personalized,** for example, 'As your doctor I need you to know that the most important thing you can do to protect your health now and in the future is to stop smoking' and 'You have already had one heart attack' [Anderson et al, 2002]. It is important to consider the patient's views and their reactions to advice, in order to avoid damaging the doctor–patient relationship.
- **Brief advice** (up to 5 minutes) given by a GP to smokers to encourage them to make an attempt to quit is effective in promoting smoking cessation. As a direct consequence of GP advice, about 40% of smokers will make some attempt to quit, but only 1–3% (more than controls) w stop smoking for at least 6 months.
- Although the overall efficacy of brief advice is small, if sufficient numbers of GPs offer advice, the reduction in rates of smoking in the general population could be substantial.
- **Behavioural support and advice from a clinic run by smoking cessation specialists is effective in helping smokers to quit.** In smokers motivated to quit, a programme of support involving multiple contacts for a period of 4 weeks or more, given by specialists employe and trained for the purpose, approximately doubles success rates even in smokers not using nicotine replacement therapy (NRT) or bupropion. In patients using these medications success rates are quadrupled compared with unaided quit attempts [West et al, 2000
- Advice about how to stop smoking should include discussion of NRT or bupropion.
- NRT or bupropion should normally only be prescribed when the person has made a commitment to stop smoking on or before a particular date (target stop date
- Ideally, the initial prescription should only be sufficient to last until 2 weeks after the target stop date. Normall this will be after 2 weeks of NRT, and 3–4weeks for bupropion. Second prescriptions should be given only t people who have demonstrated that their quit attempt i continuing at their next assessment [NICE, 2002a].
- Relapse is a normal part of the quitting process, and occurs on average 3–4 times. If a smoker has made repeated attempts to stop and failed, or has experience severe withdrawal, or has requested more intensive hel then referral to a specialist smoking cessation service should be considered.
- For further information, see the separate PRODIGY guidance on *Smoking cessation.*

Exercise

- **People who are moderately physically active have a 30–50% lower risk of CHD than people who are sedentary** [Murphy et al, 2001].
- Moderate-to-high physical activity also reduces the risk of stroke. It also helps control weight, BP, and diabetes, protects against osteoporosis; and increases well-being.
- Offer advice on gradually increasing exercise, if appropriate; about 60% of men and 70% of women in the UK are considered to be sedentary [DH, 2000].
- Sudden death after physical activity is rare (but when it does occur, it is more likely to happen in sedentary people). The benefits of physical exercise outweigh the risk of sudden death.
- Brisk walking for half an hour (or more) per day reduce the relative risk of CHD by about 20% [Tanasescu et al 2002].
- **Adults should do at least 30 minutes of moderate exercise on five or more days a week** [DH, 2000]. Ideall this should be done in one period, but it can be done in two bouts of 15 minutes, e.g. walking or cycling to and from work.
- Moderate exercise should leave the individual warm an slightly out of breath.
- **It is not necessary to participate in sport or weight training activities to achieve the exercise targets:** brisk walking, climbing stairs, heavy DIY, heavy gardening, and heavy housework are all moderate-intensity physica activities.
- **Strategies to promote long-term uptake of exercise include:**
  - Encouragement of routine activities such as brisk walking, walking or cycling to and from work; using stairs instead of lifts.

ıble 6: Examples of common physical activities for althy adults, by intensity of effort required.

‹tivity	Light <3 METS or <4 kcal/ min	Moderate 3–6 METS or 4–6 kcal/ min	Hard/ vigorous >6 METS or >7 kcal/min
alking	Slowly/ strolling (1–2 mph)	Briskly (3–4 mph)	Briskly uphill or with a load
cling	Stationary (<50 W)	For pleasure or transportation (<10 mph)	Fast or racing (>10 mph)
‹imming	Slow treading	Moderate effort	Fast treading or crawl
›nditioning ercise	Light stretching	General callisthenics	Stair ergometer, ski machine
cket orts	-	Table tennis	Singles tennis, squash
wling	Bowling	–	–
ating	Power boating	Leisurely canoeing (2–4 mph)	Canoeing rapidly (>4 mph)
ome care	Carpet sweeping	General cleaning	Moving furniture
owing vn	Riding mower	Power mower	Hand mower
ome repair	Carpentry	Painting	-

ble reproduced from Pate et al, 1995 [Pate et al, 1995].
ETs (working/resting metabolic rates) are multiples during physical activity of resting rate of oxygen consumption. One MET is equivalent to using 1 kcal/kg/ ır of energy.

- Telephone- or mail-supervised home-based approaches to physical activity can aid long-term exercise adherence with a minimal amount of face-to-face contact.
- GP referral schemes, in some areas, where people are referred to leisure centres.

Iealth Education Authority, 1998; Murphy et al, 2001; ŁeReC, 2002; Tanasescu et al, 2002]

Dietary management

Up to 30% of all deaths from CHD have been attributed to unhealthy diets [British Heart Foundation, 2003]. Dietary management is an important part of care to prevent CHD [DH, 2000].

People should be encouraged to adopt a healthier overall diet; the focus should not just be on reducing fat intake. At least three dietary strategies are likely to be effective in preventing CHD.

- **Replace saturated and *trans*-fats with unsaturated fats** (especially monounsaturated and non-hydrogenated polyunsaturated fat).
- **Increase consumption of omega-3 fatty acids** from fish oil or plant sources.
- **Consume a diet high in fruits, vegetables, nuts, and whole grains** and low in refined grains.

A Mediterranean diet contains many of the dietary elements that are thought to be protective in CHD.

- Replace butter with olive oil and monounsaturated margarine (e.g. rapeseed- or olive oil-based).
- Eat less red meat (replace beef, lamb, and pork with poultry). If eating red meat, use lean cuts. Remove the skin from poultry.
- Eat more fish, including at least one portion of oily fish per week, e.g. mackerel, herring, kipper, pilchard, sardine, salmon, or trout.
- Eat more bread (especially wholegrain bread).
- Eat more root vegetables and green vegetables.
- No day without fruit.
- Also encourage people to eat fewer commercial bakery and deep-fried foods (these contain high levels of *trans*-fats and sugar).
- **People should aim to eat five portions of fruit and vegetables every day.**
- Tinned and frozen fruit and vegetables are as good as fresh vegetables. Table 7 gives some examples of portions. Further details of portions can be found at www.dh.gov.uk.
- **Reduced salt intake** is recommended to reduce BP, especially in the elderly and those with higher initial BP levels. Encourage people to check the salt content of tinned and processed foods, since many have a high salt content.
- A systematic review found that reducing sodium intake in people with hypertension by 6.7g per day for 28 days reduced systolic BP by about 3.9/1.9 mmHg [Graudal et al, 1998]. A more recent systematic review concluded that without the intensive dietary interventions used in trials, comparable reductions in BP are less likely to be routinely achieved in primary care, particularly in the long term [Hooper et al, 2002].
- **Dietary supplements of antioxidants are not protective;** the Heart Protection Study found that antioxidants (e.g. beta carotene, vitamin C, vitamin E, copper, zinc, manganese, flavonoids) given as dietary supplements are of no benefit in the prevention of CHD [Heart Protection Study Collaborative Group, 2002]. Additionally, concerns have been raised about the safety of beta-carotene supplements.

[British Heart Foundation, 1999; Murphy et al, 2001; MeReC, 2002; Hu and Willett, 2002]

Weight control

- Excess weight is associated with raised BP, raised blood cholesterol, Type 2 diabetes, and low levels of physical activity, all of which increase the risk of CHD.
- The risk of CHD is 2–3 times greater in overweight women than in lean women.
- The risks are further increased when fat is concentrated mainly in the abdomen (central obesity).
- **Encourage all obese and overweight people to lose weight, aiming towards a body mass index (BMI) of less than 25.**
- Even if a BMI less than 25 cannot be achieved, a reduction in 5–10% of initial bodyweight still has significant health benefits [NICE, 2001b; NICE, 2001c].

Table 7: What counts as a portion?

Fruit or vegetable	One portion
Apple	1 medium apple
Apricot, dried	3 apricots
Banana	1 medium banana
Beans	3–4 heaped tablespoons
Broccoli	2 spears
Carrots (canned or fresh)	3 heaped tablespoons
Fruit juice	1 glass
Fruit salad (canned or fresh)	3 heaped tablespoons
Lettuce	1 cereal bowl
Orange	1 orange
Peas (fresh, frozen or canned)	3 heaped tablespoons
Raisins	1 tablespoon
Satsumas	2 small satsumas
Tomato (fresh)	1 medium tomato or 7 cherry tomatoes

- **Diet and exercise are an integral part of weight management.**
- Frequent fluctuations in weight are also associated with an increased risk of CHD. Weight-management programmes must therefore aim to maintain weight loss, not just to achieve initial weight loss.
- For further information see the separate PRODIGY guidance on *Obesity*.

Alcohol consumption

C

- **Encourage people who choose to drink to limit their alcohol consumption to 1–2 units a day.**
- Men should limit their alcohol consumption to a maximum of 21 units per week (i.e. a maximum of 3 units per day). For women, the maximum is 14 units per week (i.e. a maximum of 2 units per day).
- One unit is equivalent to:
  - About half a pint of ordinary strength beer, lager, or cider
  - One small glass of wine
  - A single 25 ml pub measure of spirits
- It is thought that moderate alcohol consumption increases high-density lipoprotein cholesterol levels, and improves other biological markers for CHD. However in many cases a positive effect on markers does not always translate into positive clinical outcomes.
- Many studies that show a protective effect of alcohol are of poor quality and may overestimate its effects [MeReC, 2002]. An analysis of the good-quality studies found that up to 2 units of alcohol per day was associated with a 20% relative risk reduction of CHD [Marmot, 2001]. However, not all studies have found a protective effect of moderate drinking.
- All types of alcohol have been associated with lowering the risk of CHD; the effect is not solely confined to red wine [MeReC, 2002].
- The pattern of drinking is also important — consumption of alcohol on at least 3–4 days per week has been found to be inversely associated with the risk of myocardial infarction in men [Mukamal et al, 2003]. Conversely binge drinking is associated with increased mortality and fatal myocardial infarction.
- Some studies have found that the risk of CHD mortality appears to be the same for non-drinkers as for heavy drinkers. This could be due to confounding factors rather than a protective effect of alcohol. For example, a large proportion of non-drinkers could be those who gave up drinking because of ill health. Some people who drink heavily may have falsely reported themselves as abstainers through embarrassment [Marmot, 2001].
- It is important to remember that heavy drinking does have adverse cardiovascular effects: it increases the risk of hypertension, arrhythmias, cardiomyopathy, and haemorrhagic stroke. There is also an increased risk of death from liver cirrhosis, injury, and upper gastrointestinal cancer.
- A major public health concern is that moderate drinking may lead to problem drinking. In the UK 26% of men already drink more than 21 units per week, and 15% of women drink more than 14 units per week.
- There is not enough information available to justify encouraging those who do not drink alcohol to start doing so. Moderate drinking is likely to have most benefits in people who are at highest risk of CHD, i.e. middle aged and elderly people. In younger people (who are at low risk of CHD) the risks of alcohol-related problems, such as accidents, may outweigh the potential benefits. There are also concerns that moderate drinking may increase the risk of breast cancer in young women (less than 50 years).

[Bovet and Paccaud, 2001; Marmot, 2001; MeReC, 200[illegible] British Heart Foundation, 2003]

Low-dose aspirin

Secondary prevention of cardiovascular disease

- Regular low-dose aspirin reduces the risk of any seriou[s] vascular event by 25% in people with established CH[D], stroke, transient ischaemic attacks (TIA), or peripheral vascular disease PVD). The risk of non-fatal myocardia[l] infarction is reduced by a third, non-fatal stroke is reduced by a quarter, and vascular mortality is reduce[d] by a sixth [Antithrombotic Trialists' Collaboration, 2002].
- The absolute benefits outweigh the absolute risks of major extracranial bleeding in these high-risk people.
- **Low-dose aspirin (75 mg daily) should be given to all people with established CHD, stroke, TIA, or PVD (unless contraindicated).**

Primary prevention of cardiovascular disease

- Thresholds for using aspirin to prevent CHD events in people *without* existing cardiovascular disease are mor[e] difficult to define; people without existing CHD are at lower risk of an event, and therefore the risk of advers[e] effects of aspirin will outweigh the benefits in many people.
- Current UK guidelines are to consider the use of low-dose aspirin for primary prevention in people aged 50 years and over with a 10-year CHD risk greater tha[n] 15%, or people with diabetes, or people with target organ damage from hypertension [Wood et al, 1998; Ramsay et al, 1999; NICE, 2002b].
- Recently published US guidelines also recommend aspirin to individuals with similar levels of CHD risk [U[S] Preventative Services Task Force, 2002].

Medicines management: aspirin

- Hypertension should be well controlled before aspirin i[s] started to minimize the risk of stroke.
- Increasing doses of aspirin are associated with greater risks of gastrointestinal toxicity, and aspirin doses of 75–150 mg per day have been found on systematic review to be at least as effective as higher daily doses [Antithrombotic Trialists' Collaboration, 2002]. There also no robust evidence that different formulations are associated with alterations in risk [CSM, 2002b]. Enteric-coated preparations are more expensive than standard preparations of aspirin.
- A recent retrospective study found that people with cardiovascular disease who took ibuprofen as well as low-dose aspirin had a higher risk of all-cause mortalit[y] than those who only took low-dose aspirin (adjusted hazard ratio 1.93, 95% CI 1.3 to 2.87) [MacDonald an[d] Wei, 2003]. There was no difference in mortality for people taking diclofenac plus low-dose aspirin, or another nonsteroidal anti-inflammatory drug (NSAID) plus low-dose aspirin. (Note: cyclo-oxygenase (COX)-2 selective NSAIDs were not included in this study.)
- The results of this study should be viewed with caution as it was not able to control for confounding factors, an[d] only small numbers of people were taking ibuprofen or diclofenac (303). However, until more evidence becom[es] available, it would seem prudent to follow the advice o[f] the British Heart Foundation and avoid ibuprofen in people taking low-dose aspirin [British Heart Foundation, 2002b]. Diclofenac is probably a better option if an NSAID is required.
- People who experience dyspepsia with aspirin should b[e] co-prescribed an acid-suppressing drug. See the separat[e]

ble 8: British Hypertension Society targets for BP.

	Clinic BP		Mean daytime ABPM or home BP	
	No diabetes	Diabetes	No diabetes	Diabetes
:imal BP	<140/85	<140/80	<130/80	<130/75
lit standard	<150/90	<140/85	<140/85	<140/80

M, ambulatory blood pressure monitoring

'RODIGY guidance on *Dyspepsia — symptoms uninvestigated by endoscopy)*.
Clopidogrel is an alternative for people who are hypersensitive to aspirin, i.e. in whom aspirin induces angio-oedema or bronchospasm.

anagement of coexisting conditions

iabetes

Type 2 diabetes increases the risk of cardiovascular disease 2–4 times in men, and 3–5 times in women British Heart Foundation, 2003]. People with Type 1 diabetes are also at increased risk. Metabolic disturbances such as hyperlipidaemia, hypertension, and obesity are common in Type 2 diabetes, and are all independent risk factors for coronary heart disease CHD).
Aim for tight control of blood glucose and rigorous control of blood pressure (BP).
Although raised blood glucose levels are known to increase the risk of cardiovascular disease, it is not certain whether keeping tight control on blood glucose levels will reduce this risk [Gerstein, 1998].

ypertension

The risk of cardiovascular events is increased 2–3 times n men and women with hypertension.
Risk of CHD is directly related to both systolic and diastolic BP levels.
t is estimated that 14% of deaths from CHD in men and 12% of deaths from CHD in women are due to a raised BP (defined as a systolic BP of 140 mmHg or over, or a diastolic BP of 90 mmHg or over) [British Heart Foundation, 2003].
Antihypertensive treatment reduces the relative risk of stroke by 38%, and produces a 16% reduction in coronary events for a 5–6 mmHg reduction in diastolic pressure [Collins and Peto, 1994]. The absolute risk reduction depends on the initial level of cardiovascular risk.
f systolic BP is 160 mmHg or more or diastolic BP is 100 mmHg or more, or both, treatment must be given.
f systolic BP is 140–159 mmHg or diastolic BP is 85–99 mmHg, or both, treat when:

- There is any complication of hypertension or target organ damage, or
- The 10-year CHD risk is 30% or more despite advice on non-pharmacological measures, or
- The 10-year CHD risk is greater than 15% and the person has diabetes

f the decision is made not to treat a person with mild hypertension (e.g. because their 10-year risk of CHD is less than 15%, and they do not have target organ damage) non-pharmacological methods to reduce BP should be advised. These include weight loss in obesity, increasing exercise, and reducing salt and alcohol intake.
BP should be monitored at least annually in people with mild hypertension (and every 6 months in people with diabetes) with recalculation of CHD risk, as this increases with age.

- For further information see the separate PRODIGY guidance on *Hypertension*.

[Ramsay et al, 1999; NICE, 2002b]

Hyperlipidaemia

- The decision to treat hyperlipidaemia depends on both the lipid profile, and the 10-year risk of CHD (see Table 9).
- CHD risk should be calculated using the averages of at least two (and preferably three) measurements of BP and lipids.
- Note: the ratio of total cholesterol to high-density lipoprotein cholesterol (HDL-C) is used for predicting an individual's 10-year CHD risk. It is no longer used on its own as a treatment threshold for hyperlipidaemia, e.g. people with a total cholesterol greater than 5 mmol (and who are at high risk of CHD) should be offered lipid lowering treatment, even if the total cholesterol to HDL-C ratio is satisfactory.
- **Dietary measures should be recommended, and if required, a statin should be started.**
- Re-check non-fasting total cholesterol after 6–12 weeks.
- **Aim to lower serum total cholesterol by 20–25% of baseline, or to reduce it to below 5 mmol/l,** whichever would result in the lower level.
- **Aim to lower serum low-density lipoprotein cholesterol to below 3.0 mmol/l or by 30% of baseline,** whichever would result in the lower level.
- There is a case for lowering lipid levels in people with established CHD, whatever their baseline lipid level. The Heart Protection Study recently found that lowering lipid levels by 1 mmol/l from 4 mmol/l to 3 mmol/l reduced the risk of CHD by about 25% [Heart Protection Study Collaborative Group, 2002]. This is close to the 30% reduction in cardiovascular risk achieved by previous studies, all of which had higher baseline cholesterol levels (generally between 5.5 mmol/l and 7 mmol/l) [LaRosa et al, 1999].

Table 9: Who should be offered treatment for hyperlipidaemia? [DH, 2000; NICE, 2002b]

10-year risk of CHD	Treat hyperlipidaemia if:
Established CHD	TC >5.0 mmol/l, LDL-C >3.0 mmol/l, or TG >2.3 mmol/l
>30% but no CHD	TC >5.0 mmol/l, LDL-C >3.0 mmol/l, or TG >2.3 mmol/l
<30%	Most people are at lower risk of CHD. Only consider treatment for hyperlipidaemia if familial hypercholesterolaemia is suspected, e.g. TC >7.5 mmol/l AND physical signs of hyperlipidaemia or family history of premature CHD (refer for specialist assessment).
15–30% and diabetes	TC >5.0 mmol/l, LDL-C >3.0 mmol/l, or TG >2.3 mmol/l
—	TG >10 mmol/l (refer for specialist assessment)

CHD = coronary heart disease
TC = total cholesterol
TG = triglycerides
LDL-C = low-density lipoprotein cholesterol

- The findings of the Heart Protection Study are not reflected in the *National Service Framework for Coronary Heart Disease* and the National Institute for Clinical Excellence (NICE) guidance on prior myocardial infarction. There are significant financial implications of implementing this policy. Consider seeking local primary care trust advice.
- For further information see the separate PRODIGY guidance on *Hyperlipidaemia*.

[Wood et al, 1998; DH, 2000]

C

Additional measures for people with established occlusive arterial disease

- ACE inhibitors for people who also have left ventricular dysfunction. Note that beta-blockers and spironolactone may also be added to therapy. Angiotensin-II receptor antagonists are an alternative in people who are intolerant of ACE inhibitors.
- Beta-blockers and ACE inhibitors for people who have had a myocardial infarction.
- Warfarin or aspirin for people over 60 years old who have atrial fibrillation. Note that the final choice will depend on the individuals overall risk of stroke. See the separate PRODIGY guidance on *Atrial fibrillation* for further advice about deciding on antithrombotic treatment in atrial fibrillation.

[DH, 2000]

Does hormone replacement therapy prevent CHD?

- Hormone replacement therapy (HRT) has *not* been shown to be beneficial in preventing CHD in women both with and without CHD. In fact, studies have shown a slight tendency to *increased rates* of CHD in the 1–2 years of treatment with HRT.
- HRT should not be initiated for prevention of CHD, and consideration should be given to stopping HRT after any cardiovascular disease event [CSM, 2002a].

References

NHS staff in England can link, free of charge, from references to full text journals by clicking on [Full text] on the PRODIGY website.

1. Anderson, J.E., Jorenby, D.E., Scott, W.J. and Fiore, M.C. (2002) Treating tobacco use and dependence: an evidence-based clinical practice guideline for tobacco cessation. *Chest* **121**(3), 932–941. [Full text]
2. Antithrombotic Trialists' Collaboration (2002) Collaborative meta-analysis of randomised trials of antiplatelet therapy for the prevention of death, myocardial infarction and death in high risk patients. *British Medical Journal* **324**(7329), 71–86. [Full text]
3. Bovet, P. and Paccaud, F. (2001) Commentary: alcohol, coronary heart disease and public health: which evidence-based policy. *International Journal of Epidemiology* **30**(4), 734–737. [Full text]
4. Boyle, R. (2000) DoH explains thinking behind national service framework for coronary heart disease. *British Medical Journal* **321**(7268), 1083. [Full text]
5. British Heart Foundation (1999) *Fish, fruit, vegetables and mediterranean diet*. Factfile 2/1999. British Heart Foundation. www.bhf.org.uk [Accessed: 12/01/2003].
6. British Heart Foundation (2002a) *How to use the coronary risk prediction charts for primary prevention.* Factfile 1/2002. British Heart Foundation. www.bhf.org.uk [Accessed: 28/01/2003].
7. British Heart Foundation (2002b) *Aspirin and ibuprofen*. Factfile 11/2002. British Heart Foundation. www.bhf.org.uk [Accessed: 01/12/2002].
8. British Heart Foundation (2003) *Coronary heart disease statistics 2003*. British Heart Foundation. www.heartstats.org//datapage.asp?id=1652 [Accesse 07/02/2003].
9. Collins, R. and Peto, R. (1994) Antihypertensive dru therapy: effects on stroke and coronary heart disease In: Swales, J.D. (Ed.) *Textbook of hypertension*. Oxford: Blackwell Scientific Publications. 1156–116
10. CSM (2002a) New product information for hormon replacement therapy. *Current Problems in Pharmacovigilance* **28**(April), 1–2.
11. CSM (2002b) Non-steroidal anti-inflammatory drug (NSAIDs) and gastrointestinal (GI) safety. *Current Problems in Pharmacovigilance* **28**(Apr), 5.
12. DH (2000) *National service framework for coronary heart disease*. Department of Health. www.dh.gov.u [Accessed: 15/07/2005]. [Full text]
13. DTB (1997) Which prophylactic aspirin? *Drug & Therapeutics Bulletin* **35**(1), 7–8. [Full text]
14. Durrington, P.N. (Ed.) (1995) *Hyperlipidaemia: diagnosis and management*. 2nd edn. Oxford: Butterworth-Heinemann.
15. Gerstein, H.C. (1998) Glucose abnormalities and cardiovascular disease: 'dysglycemia' as an emerging cardiovascular risk factor. In: Yusuf, S., Cairns, J.A., Camm, A.J. et al (Eds.) *Evidence Based Cardiology*. London: BMJ Books. 239–250.
16. Graudal, N.A., Galloe, A.M. and Garred, P. (1998) Effects of sodium restriction on blood pressure, renir aldosterone, catecholamines, cholesterols, and triglycerides. *Journal of the American Medical Association* **279**(17), 1383–1391. [Full text]
17. Health Education Authority (1998) *Moving on. International perspectives on promoting physical activity*. Health Development Agency. www.hda-online.org.uk [Accessed: 05/02/2003].
18. Heart Protection Study Collaborative Group (2002) MRC/BHF heart protection study of antioxidant vitamin supplementation in 20536 high-risk individuals: a randomised placebo-controlled trial. *Lancet* **360**(9326), 23–33. [Full text]
19. Hooper, L., Bartlett, C., Davey-Smith, G. and Ebrahi S. (2002) Systematic review of long term effects of advice to reduce dietary salt in adults. *British Medica Journal* **325**(7365), 628–632. [Full text]
20. Hu, F.B. and Willett, W.C. (2002) Optimal diets for prevention of coronary heart disease. *Journal of the American Medical Association* **288**(20), 2569–2578. [Full text]
21. MacDonald, T.M. and Wei, L. (2003) Effect of ibuprofen on cardioprotective effect of aspirin. *Lanc* **361**(9357), 573–574. [Full text]
22. Marmot, M.G. (2001) Alcohol and coronary heart disease. *International Journal of Epidemiology* **30**(4) 724–729. [Full text]
23. MeReC (2002) Lifestyle measures to reduce cardiovascular risk. *MeReC Briefing* **19**(July), 1–8.
24. Mukamal, K.J., Conigrave, K.M., Mittleman, M.A. e al (2003) Roles of drinking pattern and type of alcoh consumed in coronary heart disease in men. *New England Journal of Medicine* **348**(2), 109–118. [Full text]
25. Murphy, M., Foster, C., Sudlow, C. et al (2001) Cardiovascular disorders: primary prevention. *Clinic Evidence* **6**, 82–113.
26. NHS CRD (1998) Cholesterol and coronary heart disease: screening and treatment. *Effective Health Ca Bulletin* **4**(1), 1–16.
27. NICE (2001a) *Prophylaxis for patients who have experienced a myocardial infarction.* Inherited clinica guideline A. National Institute for Clinical Excellenc www.nice.org.uk [Accessed: 28/01/2003].

28. NICE (2001b) *Guidance on the use of orlistat for the treatment of obesity in adults.* Technology appraisal no. 22. National Institute for Clinical Excellence. www.nice.org.uk [Accessed. 3/02/24].
29. NICE (2001c) *Guidance on the use of sibutramine for the treatment of obesity in adults.* Technology appraisal no. 31. National Institute for Clinical Excellence. www.nice.org.uk [Accessed: 3/02/24].
30. NICE (2002a) *Guidance on the use of nicotine replacement therapy (NRT) and bupropion for smoking cessation.* Technology appraisal no. 39. National Institute for Clinical Excellence. www.nice.org.uk [Accessed: 18/07/2005].
31. NICE (2002b) *Management of type 2 diabetes – management of blood pressure and blood lipids.* Inherited clinical guideline H. National Institute for Clinical Excellence. www.nice.org.uk [Accessed: 28/01/2003].
32. Pate, R.R., Pratt, M., Blair, S.N. et al (1995) Physical activity and public health. A recommendation from the Centers for Disease Control and Prevention and the American College of Sports Medicine. *Journal of the American Medical Association* **273**(5), 402–407. [Full text]
33. Ramsay, L.E., Williams, B., Johnston, G. et al (1999) Guidelines for management of hypertension: report of the third working party of the British Hypertension Society. *Journal of Human Hypertension* **13**(9), 569–592.
34. Robson, J., Boomla, K., Hart, B. and Feder, G. (2000) Estimating cardiovascular risk for primary prevention: outstanding questions for primary care. *British Medical Journal* **320**(7236), 702–704. [Full text]
35. Tanasescu, M., Leitzmann, M.F., Rimm, E.B. et al (2002) Exercise type and intensity in relation to coronary heart disease in men. *Journal of the American Medical Association* **288**(16), 1994–2000. [Full text]
36. US Preventative Services Task Force (2002) Aspirin for the prevention of cardiovascular events: recommendation and rationale. *Annals of Internal Medicine* **136**(2), 157–160.
37. West, R., McNeill, A. and Raw, M. (2000) Smoking cessation guidelines for health professionals: an update. *Thorax* **55**(12), 987–999. [Full text]
38. Wood, D., Durrington, D., Poulter, N. et al (1998) Joint British recommendations on prevention of coronary heart disease in clinical practice. *Heart* **80**(Suppl 2), S1-S29. [Full text]

PRODIGY GUIDANCE

Deep vein thrombosis

Last revised in December 2002
www.prodigy.nhs.uk/guidance.asp?gt=Deep vein thrombosis

Applies to people over the age of 16 years

This guidance covers the identification and management of acute deep vein thrombosis (DVT) and subsequent maintenance treatment. This guidance also covers advice on avoiding travel-related DVT but does not cover prophylaxis of DVT, for example at the time of surgery.
The guidance does not cover people with coagulation disorders or with recurrent DVT who require long-term anticoagulation.

There is separate PRODIGY guidance on *Thrombophlebitis* and *Leg cramps*.

D

Goals

- To refer appropriately
- To provide appropriate maintenance anticoagulation
- To prevent post-thrombotic syndrome
- To prevent/reduce occurrence of travel-related deep vein thrombosis (DVT)

Contents

Scenarios

- Initial management p.468
- Maintenance therapy (anticoagulation and stockings) p.468
- Advice on risk of travel-related deep vein thrombosis p.470

Extended Information, p. 471

Which scenario?

- **Initial management:** covers the initial assessment and management of a person presenting with suspected deep vein thrombosis (DVT).
- **Maintenance therapy (anticoagulation and stockings):** covers the ongoing management of a person with DVT following discharge from hospital.
- **Advice on risk of travel-related deep vein thrombosis:** covers measures that can be taken to help reduce the risk of DVT in people considering long-distance travel.

Initial management

Which therapy?

- **All people with suspected deep vein thrombosis (DVT) need urgent hospital assessment or admission.**
- **DVT is difficult to diagnose clinically** and should be suspected in a person presenting with any of the following:
  - Swelling of the calf and/or thigh in one leg
  - Pain and tenderness in the limb
  - Increased skin temperature
  - Distension of superficial veins
  - Colour change (red or purple)
  - Low-grade pyrexia (uncommon)
- **Presence of risk factors should heighten the suspicion of possible DVT** (e.g. recent surgery, immobility, cancer, previous DVT or pulmonary embolism).

Should I refer or investigate?

Refer?

- **All people with suspected deep vein thrombosis** (DVT) need urgent hospital assessment or admission.

Patient information leaflets

The following PILs are available at www.prodigy.nhs.uk

- Blood Test - Clotting Tests
- Blood Test - General
- British Vascular Foundation
- Deep Vein Thrombosis (DVT)

Shared decision making

- **Deep vein thrombosis (DVT)** is a blood clot in a leg vein.
- **In a small number of cases** the clot becomes larger, breaks off, and travels to the lungs. This can be serious, but is usually prevented with treatment.
- **Anticoagulation** reduces the clotting ability of the blood and prevents the clot becoming larger and more serious.
  - Heparin injections are given at first for immediate effect.
  - Warfarin tablets are the usual ongoing treatment. This may continue for several months.
- **A compression stocking** may be advised if the DVT was in a thigh vein. You wear this every day. It helps to prevent swelling, discomfort and skin ulceration of the leg that sometimes occurs after a DVT.
- **A daily walk, and keeping the leg raised** as much as possible when you rest, may also help to prevent persistent calf symptoms after a DVT.

Drug rationale

- No prescriptions are offered as hospital assessment is recommended in all cases of suspected deep vein thrombosis (DVT).

Maintenance therapy (anticoagulation and stockings)

Which therapy?

- **The optimal target International Normalized Ratio (INR)** during oral anticoagulant therapy for a first episode of venous thromboembolism (VTE) is 2.5 (2.0–3.0).
- **The recommended duration of oral anticoagulant therapy** following a first episode of deep vein thrombosis (DVT) is for at least 3 months. Treatment of 6 months' duration is commonly recommended.

In people with postoperative calf vein thrombosis without persistent risk factors, 6 weeks' anticoagulation only may be recommended.
Duration of treatment is influenced by the presence of continuing risk factors. If risk factors persist, long-term anticoagulation may be necessary.
Graduated compression stockings should be worn on the affected leg following proximal DVT for at least 2 years. This reduces the incidence of severe post-thrombotic leg syndrome.
A daily walk helps reduce the risk of further DVT and improves circulation in the affected limb.
All patients should be encouraged to elevate their leg when sitting.

Practical prescribing points

For further information please see the *Medicines Compendium* (www.medicines.org.uk) or the *British National Formulary* (www.bnf.org).

Compression stockings

Adequate arterial circulation should be ensured by Doppler assessment before compression stockings are prescribed.

Issues to consider for people taking heparin

The risk of hyperkalaemia (due to inhibition of aldosterone secretion by heparin) seems to increase with duration of therapy. The CSM recommends that plasma potassium be measured in people at risk before starting heparin (e.g. people with diabetes mellitus, chronic renal failure, acidosis, those taking potassium-sparing drugs) and monitored regularly thereafter, particularly if heparin is to be continued for more than 7 days.
Heparin-induced thrombocytopenia (HIT) occurs in approximately 1–2% of people, usually within 5–10 days of starting treatment. Monitoring of platelets is necessary and HIT should be suspected if the platelet count falls to less than 30% from baseline.

Issues to consider for people taking warfarin

Cautions and contraindications to warfarin are outlined in Table 1.

Drug interactions

Consult the *British National Formulary* (BNF) for relevant drug interactions with warfarin. If a drug can interact then it should be used only if necessary. A non-interacting drug should be prescribed where possible.
If the interacting drug will be used for less than 5 days, then often no dosage change is necessary. A minor dosage reduction or omission of one full warfarin dose may be prudent with known potentiating drugs (see BNF).

- **If the interacting drug will be used for more than 5 days,** the INR should be checked a week after starting therapy and the warfarin dose adjusted accordingly. The INR should also be monitored when an interacting drug is stopped.
- Check whether the person taking warfarin has been given an anticoagulant booklet.

Follow-up advice

- **People taking warfarin need regular monitoring of International Normalized Ratio (INR)** — every 4–8 weeks if well stabilized. Any change in clinical state or medication should prompt more frequent checks.
- Ideally, monitoring should take place in a setting with adequate management, follow-up, and recall procedures.
- INR target is 2.5 (range 2.0–3.0).

Patient information leaflets

The following PILs are available at www.prodigy.nhs.uk

- Blood Test - Clotting Tests
- Blood Test - General
- British Vascular Foundation
- Deep Vein Thrombosis (DVT)

Shared decision making

- **Deep vein thrombosis** (DVT) is a blood clot in a leg vein.
- **Anticoagulation** with warfarin tablets is the usual treatment. This reduces the clotting ability of the blood and prevents the clot becoming larger and more serious.
- **You need to have regular blood tests** whilst you take warfarin to check that you are taking just the right amount.
- **A compression stocking** may be advised if the DVT was in a thigh vein. You wear this every day. It helps to prevent swelling, discomfort and skin ulceration of the leg that sometimes occurs after a DVT.
- **A daily walk, and keeping the leg raised** as much as possible when you rest, may also help to prevent persistent calf symptoms after a DVT.

Drug rationale

Drugs not included

- Oral anticoagulants other than warfarin, such as acenocoumarol (nicoumalone) or phenindione, are seldom used in the UK [MeReC, 1997; BNF 43, 2002].
- Unfractionated and low molecular weight heparins are not included, as they require administration by injection and are usually provided by hospital services.

Table 1: Contraindications and cautions for warfarin.

Contraindications/cautions	Comments
Uncorrected major bleeding	-
Uncorrected major bleeding disorder	For example thrombocytopenia, haemophilia, liver failure, renal failure
Uncontrolled severe hypertension	For example systolic >200 mmHg or diastolic >120 mmHg
Potential bleeding lesions	For example active peptic ulcer; oesophageal varices; aneurysm; proliferative retinopathy; recent organ biopsy; recent trauma or surgery to head, orbit, spine; recent stroke; confirmed intracranial or intraspinal bleed
Pregnancy	Risk of teratogenicity/fetal haemorrhage
Uncooperative/unreliable patient	Compliance and follow-up issues
Repeated falls or unstable gait	Increased chance of injury and head trauma
Lifestyle factors	People who undertake sports in which the risk of head injury is significant should be counselled accordingly
Concomitant use of nonsteroidal anti-inflammatory drugs (NSAIDs)	Increased risk of gastrointestinal bleeding

Drugs included

- **Warfarin** is the oral anticoagulant of choice [MeReC, 1997; BNF 43, 2002].
- **Knee-length graduated compression stockings** have been shown to reduce the risk of severe post-thrombotic syndrome following proximal DVT, from 23% to 11% over a 2-year period [Brandjes et al, 1997].
- **Hospital specialists often recommend full-length stockings**, at least in the first weeks after discharge, and these are also included.

D

Prescriptions

Continuing warfarin

Warfarin 1mg tablets
- Age from 16 years onwards
- Warfarin 1mg tablets. Take as directed in your yellow anticoagulant booklet; supply 56 tablets; NHS Cost £2.82.

Warfarin 3mg tablets
- Age from 16 years onwards
- Warfarin 3mg tablets. Take as directed in your yellow anticoagulant booklet; supply 56 tablets; NHS Cost £3.18.

Warfarin 5mg tablets
- Age from 16 years onwards
- Warfarin 5mg tablets. Take as directed in your yellow anticoagulant booklet; supply 56 tablets; NHS Cost £3.40.

Warfarin 1mg tablets + 3mg tablets
- Age from 16 years onwards
- Warfarin 1mg tablets. Take as directed in your yellow anticoagulant booklet; supply 56 tablets; NHS Cost £2.82.
- Warfarin 3mg tablets. Take as directed in your yellow anticoagulant booklet; supply 56 tablets; NHS Cost £3.18.

Warfarin 1mg tablets + 5mg tablets
- Age from 16 years onwards
- Warfarin 1mg tablets. Take as directed in your yellow anticoagulant booklet; supply 56 tablets; NHS Cost £2.82.
- Warfarin 5mg tablets. Take as directed in your yellow anticoagulant booklet; supply 56 tablets; NHS Cost £3.40.

Warfarin 3mg tablets + 5mg tablets
- Age from 16 years onwards
- Warfarin 3mg tablets. Take as directed in your yellow anticoagulant booklet; supply 56 tablets; NHS Cost £3.18.
- Warfarin 5mg tablets. Take as directed in your yellow anticoagulant booklet; supply 56 tablets; NHS Cost £3.40.

Warfarin 1mg tablets + 3mg tablets + 5mg tablets
- Age from 16 years onwards
- Warfarin 1mg tablets. Take as directed in your yellow anticoagulant booklet; supply 56 tablets; NHS Cost £2.82.
- Warfarin 3mg tablets. Take as directed in your yellow anticoagulant booklet; supply 56 tablets; NHS Cost £3.18.
- Warfarin 5mg tablets. Take as directed in your yellow anticoagulant booklet; supply 56 tablets; NHS Cost £3.40.

Class II compression stockings

Knee-length stockings
- Age from 16 years onwards
- Class II knee-length stocking. One pair of circular knit, knee length class II compression stockings to be measured and fitted in the pharmacy; supply 2 single stockings; NHS Cost £8.77.

Thigh-length stockings with suspender belt
- Age from 16 years onwards
- Class II thigh-length stocking. One pair of circular knit, thigh length class II compression stockings to be measured and fitted in the pharmacy; supply 2 single stockings; NHS Cost £9.76.
- Suspender belt SP13. Use as directed; supply 2 belts; NHS Cost £8.74.

Thigh-length stockings with trouser suspenders
- Age from 16 years onwards
- Class II thigh-length stocking. One pair of circular knit, thigh length class II compression stockings to be measured and fitted in the pharmacy; supply 2 single stockings; NHS Cost £9.76.
- Trouser suspenders. Use as directed; supply 4 trouser suspenders; NHS Cost £2.24.

Advice on risk of travel-related deep vein thrombosis

Which therapy?

- **Deep vein thrombosis (DVT) may be associated with an form of long-distance travel,** whether by air, car, coach or train, when seated for long periods of time. In particular, long-haul air travel (flights lasting longer than 5 hours) may be most strongly associated with an increased risk.
- **People with established risk factors for venous thromboembolism (VTE)** are likely to be more at risk of developing travel-related DVT or pulmonary embolism (PE).
- **Most air passengers on long-haul flights do not need to take medication to prevent DVT.** Available information suggests that the proportion of people who develop DVT related to air travel is small.
- **Air passengers can reduce the chance of developing DVT** by doing simple calf and foot exercises and ensuring adequate hydration (this is covered in the patient information leaflet).
- **Below-knee compression stockings** (Class 2) worn during long-haul flights may prevent the development of DVT. Although the evidence is limited, these may be advocated for those with strong risk factors for DVT.
- **There is no evidence that aspirin is effective in** preventing travel-related DVT or PE.
- **Use of low molecular weight heparin is controversial.** Some experts recommend it for those with strong risk factors for DVT.

Should I refer or investigate?

Refer?

- **Urgent referral** is necessary if a DVT is suspected.
- **Consider referral** in very high-risk people contemplating a long journey (e.g. a long-haul flight), for further advice and management.

Patient information leaflets

The following PILs are available at www.prodigy.nhs.uk
British Vascular Foundation
Deep Vein Thrombosis (DVT)

Shared decision making

The following helps to prevent a deep vein thrombosis (DVT) whilst on a long journey:

Exercise your calf and foot muscles regularly:

- Every half hour or so, bend and straighten your legs, feet and toes when you are seated.
- Press the balls of your feet down hard against the floor every so often. This helps to increase the blood flow in your legs.
- Take a walk up and down the aisle every hour or so, when the aircraft crew say it is safe to do so.
- If you are allowed, get off the plane and walk about if the plane stops for refuelling.
- Consider buying a leg exerciser for the journey.

Elastic compression stockings may be advised, particularly if you have an increased risk of DVT.
Drink plenty of water (to avoid dehydration).
Do not drink too much alcohol. (Alcohol can cause dehydration and immobility.)
Do not take sleeping tablets, which cause immobility.
Some people at high risk may also be advised to take anticoagulant medication.
After the trip, if you develop a swollen painful calf or breathing difficulties, see a doctor urgently.

Drug rationale

No prescriptions are included in this scenario.

- Aspirin is not included as there is no evidence that it is effective in preventing travel-related deep vein thrombosis (DVT).
- People may wish to purchase elastic compression stockings prior to travel. These should be equivalent to Class 2 (18–24 mmHg) and ideally be fitted by a pharmacist.

Prescriptions

Advice note

Advice note

Age from 16 years onwards
Exercise your calf and foot muscles regularly: Every half hour or so, bend and straighten your legs, feet and toes when you are seated. Press the balls of your feet down hard against the floor every so often. This helps to increase the blood flow in your legs. Take a walk up and down the aisle every hour or so, when the aircraft crew say it is safe to do so. If you are allowed, get off the plane and walk about if the plane stops for refuelling. Elastic compression stockings may be advised, particularly if you have an increased risk of DVT. Drink plenty of water (to avoid dehydration). Do not drink too much alcohol. (Alcohol can cause dehydration and immobility.) Do not take sleeping tablets, which cause immobility. After the trip, if you develop a swollen painful calf or breathing difficulties, then see a doctor urgently.

Extended Information

Background information

- What is it? p.471
- How common is it? p.471
- Risk factors p.471
- How do I know my patient has it? p.472
- What else might it be? p.472
- Complications and prognosis p.472

What is it?

- **Deep vein thrombosis (DVT)** occurs when a thrombus forms in deep veins in the lower limbs.
- **The most frequent site** is in the deep veins of the calf (distal DVT). The less common popliteal, femoral, or ileofemoral thrombi (proximal DVT) are more serious due to the much higher risk of pulmonary embolism (PE). However, a fifth of untreated newly developing calf vein thrombi extend proximally [Gorman et al, 2000].
- **The factors that promote venous thrombosis** are reduction of blood flow (stasis), alteration of blood clotting (hypercoagulability), and abnormalities in the vessel wall (loss of thromboresistance) [MeReC, 1997].

How common is it?

- Venous thromboembolism (VTE) (deep vein thrombosis [DVT] and/or pulmonary embolism [PE]) has an annual incidence of about 1 in 2000 people in the general population, ranging from less than 1 in 3000 in people under the age of 40 years up to 1 in 500 in those over 80 years [DH, 2002]. DVT is the third most common cardiovascular disease after acute coronary syndromes and stroke [Anand et al, 1998].
- **In pregnancy,** the incidence of DVT or PE is around 1 in 1000, with a further 2 in 1000 women presenting in the postnatal period [Walker, 1993].
- **Following surgery,** objective measurements (for example, venography) have shown that without antithrombotic prophylaxis 8–15% of people develop DVT after major general surgery, 36–60% after surgery for hip fracture, 47–57% after hip replacement, and 40–80% after knee replacement [Verstraete, 1997]. These figures do not represent symptomatic DVT.
- **Travel-related DVT:** immobility is a common risk factor for DVT, but information is still unclear on how common travel-related DVT really is, what the risk factors are, and how it can be prevented.

Risk factors

- **There are many risk factors for deep vein thrombosis (DVT) and pulmonary embolism (PE)** — their presence should increase the suspicion of a diagnosis of venous thromboembolism in a person with suggestive symptoms and signs.
- **The most important risk factors in general practice are:**
  - Age over 40 years
  - Obesity
  - Having a past history of DVT or PE
  - A strong family history of DVT or PE
  - Having cancer or having had treatment for cancer (particularly hormone therapy)
  - Treatment for heart failure and circulation problems
  - Recent surgery, especially on the hips or knees
  - An inherited clotting tendency (thrombophilia)
  - Hemiplegic stroke or paralysis
  - Immobility while travelling long distances
- **DVT and PE are also more common in women who:**
  - Are pregnant
  - Have recently had a baby
  - Are taking the contraceptive pill
  - Are receiving hormone replacement therapy

[Anand et al, 1998; SIGN, 1999; Gorman et al, 2000]

D

D

How do I know my patient has it?

- **Deep vein thrombosis (DVT) is difficult to diagnose clinically** — if suspected, imaging techniques are necessary to confirm or refute the diagnosis.
- **Symptoms are usually of acute or recent onset.**
- **Clinical features may be absent or include one or more of the following:**
  - Swelling of the calf or thigh in one leg
  - Pain and tenderness along the line of the deep venous system
  - Low-grade pyrexia (very uncommon)
  - Increased skin temperature
  - Distension of superficial veins
  - Colour change (red or purple)
- **Homans' sign is poorly predictive of DVT and attempts to elicit this sign are no longer recommended.** Homans' sign is pain in the calf or popliteal region on forceful and abrupt dorsiflexion of the ankle with the knee in a flexed position.
- **Secondary care investigations may include:**
  - **Compression ultrasound examination or impedance plethysmography** (reliably detect proximal vein thrombosis but less so calf vein thrombosis).
  - **D-dimer blood assay test** (highly sensitive for the presence of DVT). A negative result is reassuring if the likelihood of DVT is clinically thought to be low prior to the test, or if an ultrasound scan is negative. It is often used to decide whether a follow-up ultrasound examination is necessary in people with an initial negative scan. The D-dimer test is intended for use in otherwise healthy people presenting with suspicious symptoms and it should be used alongside a thorough clinical assessment of the likelihood of DVT.
  - **Venography** is the 'gold standard' that is used when the diagnosis is still uncertain after non-invasive testing.

[Becker et al, 1996; Anand et al, 1998; Baker, 1998; Bernardi et al, 1998; Cogo et al, 1998; Aschwanden et al, 1999; Lennox et al, 1999; Perrier et al, 1999; SIGN, 1999]

What else might it be?

- Cellulitis
- Superficial thrombophlebitis
- Ruptured Baker's cyst
- Haematoma in muscle
- Muscle tear or strain
- Dependent (stasis) oedema
- Post-thrombotic syndrome
- Lymphatic obstruction
- Arthritis
- Heart failure, cirrhosis, nephrotic syndrome
- External compression of major veins (e.g. by fetus, cancer)
- Arteriovenous fistula

[Anand et al, 1998; Gorman et al, 2000]

Complications and prognosis

- **Pulmonary embolism (PE):** there is a 10% incidence of symptomatic PE in untreated proximal deep vein thrombosis (DVT) with a mortality of 18–30% without treatment [Baker, 1998; Hull and Pineo, 1998]. Calf DVT are much less likely to embolize; however, a fifth of untreated newly developing calf vein thrombi extend proximally [Gorman et al, 2000]. PE following DVT is rare if the person is receiving anticoagulation therapy [British Society for Haematology, 1998; Douketis et al, 1998; Hutten and Prins, 2002].
- **Critical limb ischaemia:** severe DVT can result in extremely high venous pressures and impairment of arterial blood flow. This is a rare complication.
- **Recurrent DVT:** the risk of recurrent venous thromboembolism is markedly reduced while the person is receiving anticoagulation therapy [Hutten and Prins, 2002]. In the long term, however, more than 20% of DVT recur within 5 years. The risk of recurrence is higher if there are underlying risk factors, such as cancer or certain coagulation defects, and lower if risk factors are transient, such as after surgery [Prandoni et al, 1996].
- **Post-thrombotic syndrome** (chronic venous insufficiency with venous ulceration in severe cases): this complication occurs in 50–75% of people following DVT, with varying degrees of severity [Beyth et al, 1995; Prandoni et al, 1996; Brandjes et al, 1997; Gorman et al, 2000]. Proximal DVT is associated with a higher incidence and greater severity of post-thrombotic syndrome. Studies have mainly included people with proximal DVT, and it is likely that post-thrombotic syndrome is less common in people with isolated calf DVT.
  - One study found that the use of use of compression stockings for 2 years following proximal DVT reduced the incidence of severe post-thrombotic syndrome from 23% to 11% [Brandjes et al, 1997]. Some experts also recommend their use following calf DVT.

Management issues

- Screening for suspected thrombophilia (increased tendency for blood clotting) p.472
- Initial management p.472
- Anticoagulation (hospital-initiated) p.473
- Maintenance anticoagulant treatment (following hospital discharge) p.473
- Compression stockings p.473
- Other treatments (given in hospital) p.473
- Pregnancy p.474
- Risk of travel-related deep vein thrombosis p.474

Screening for suspected thrombophilia (increased tendency for blood clotting)

- **Screening for possible congenital or acquired thrombophilias** may be recommended for some people with deep vein thrombosis (DVT) — this should be done under specialist supervision. There is debate on how clinically useful testing for thrombophilia is, as in most instances it will not influence the immediate or long-term management of an individual person. The criteria for testing are not universally agreed, but it should be considered in people with a family history of venous thromboembolism (VTE) or thrombophilic abnormality or who have a VTE before the age of 45 years, or who have a history of recurrent VTE or thrombophlebitis [SIGN, 1999].
- **Factor V Leiden** is an inherited coagulation defect due to a single point mutation in the factor V gene. Factor V is coagulant factor and is usually inactivated by activated protein C. Factor V Leiden is relatively resistant to this inactivation, resulting in increased thrombotic tendency. Factor V Leiden is present in about 5% of the population, but is found in 20% of all people with DVT in 50% of people with DVT who also have a positive family history of VTE, and in 60% of women developing DVT during pregnancy [Bick and Kaplan, 1998; Bandolier, 1999].

Initial management

- **Urgent referral is necessary for all people with suspected DVT,** both to confirm the diagnosis and to urgently anticoagulate in order to reduce the risk of extension and embolization of the thrombus.

- **Diagnostic imaging should be performed expeditiously (within 24 hours if possible) in people with suspected DVT** (venography, ultrasound examination) to minimize exposure to the risks of inappropriate continued full-dosage anticoagulation in those individuals in whom VTE is not confirmed (C) [SIGN, 1999].
- **In all people with clinically suspected DVT, the diagnosis should be confirmed or excluded by diagnostic imaging:**
  - Non-invasive testing by ultrasound (compression or duplex scanning), followed by contrast venography if negative to detect calf DVT and non-occlusive proximal DVT, or
  - Contrast venography (which detects both calf and proximal DVT), or
  - Serial (repeat after 7 days) non-invasive testing by ultrasound (compression or duplex scanning) to detect proximal extension of calf DVT (B) [SIGN, 1999]
- **A single negative ultrasound examination** may be sufficient to exclude DVT in people with low clinical pretest probability and/or a normal fibrin D-dimer assay (B) [SIGN, 1999].

Anticoagulation (hospital-initiated)

- **Heparin is the initial treatment of choice,** because of its fast onset of anticoagulation and evidence of reduced risk of further thromboembolic events [SIGN, 1999]. A randomized controlled trial of intravenous heparin plus oral anticoagulants compared with oral anticoagulants alone, in people with confirmed proximal DVT, showed that heparin reduced the risk of further thromboembolism [Brandjes et al, 1992].
- **In clinically suspected DVT, heparin should be commenced (unless strongly contraindicated) until the diagnosis is excluded by diagnostic imaging** (A) [SIGN, 1999].
- **Conventional treatment is with unfractionated heparin (UFH).** This is usually given by continuous intravenous infusion; however, subcutaneous administration is an effective alternative (A) [SIGN, 1999].
- **Low molecular weight heparin (LMWH) is an effective alternative treatment to UFH** (A) [SIGN, 1999]. A recent Cochrane systematic review found that LMWH is at least as effective as UFH in preventing recurrent VTE. It also found that LMWH, compared with UFH, significantly reduces the occurrence of major bleeding during initial treatment and overall mortality at the end of follow-up [van den Belt et al, 2002]. LMWH has the advantage of simpler dosages, once-daily subcutaneous administration, no need for routine laboratory monitoring of anticoagulant effect, and cost-effectiveness compared with traditional UFH use.
- **Following initial heparinization, maintenance anticoagulation with oral anticoagulants is recommended** (unless the person is pregnant — see *Pregnancy* section) (A) [SIGN, 1999]. Warfarin markedly reduces the risk of recurrent thromboembolism [Hutten and Prins, 2002], and early institution of oral anticoagulants is recommended in most non-pregnant people (A) [SIGN, 1999]. Long-term heparin is not recommended owing to the risks of osteoporosis and thrombocytopenia.
- **When oral anticoagulant therapy is initiated for treatment of acute DVT it should be overlapped with heparin therapy** for 4–6 days and until the International Normalized Ratio (INR) is greater than 2.0 on 2 consecutive days (C) [SIGN, 1999].
- **In people without complications, LMWH is increasingly being used to allow home management of early DVT while anticoagulating with warfarin.** This has been shown to be an effective strategy in selected people [Koopman et al, 1996; Levine et al, 1996; DTB, 1998].

The type of LMWH used, the duration of treatment, and the loading dosage of warfarin will vary according to local practice.

Maintenance anticoagulant treatment (following hospital discharge)

- **The optimal target INR** during oral anticoagulant therapy for a first episode of VTE is 2.5 (2.0–3.0) (A) [SIGN, 1999].
- **The routine recommended duration of oral anticoagulant therapy** following a first episode of DVT is at least 3 months (A) [SIGN, 1999]. A treatment of 6 months is commonly recommended.
- **The British Committee for Standards in Haematology (BCSH) recommends 6 weeks of oral anticoagulation** in people with postoperative calf vein thrombosis *without* persistent risk factors [British Society for Haematology, 1998].
- **Duration of treatment** is influenced by the presence of continuing risk factors (e.g. certain coagulation defects, malignancy, chronic infection, inflammatory bowel disease, nephrotic syndrome, thromboembolic pulmonary hypertension). If risk factors persist, long-term anticoagulation may be necessary.
- **Adjusted-dosage subcutaneous UFH or subcutaneous LMWH** are effective alternatives to oral anticoagulation where there are contraindications, such as pregnancy [SIGN, 1999; van der Heijden et al, 2002]. Heparin therapy, however, may cause thrombocytopenia and osteoporosis, but LMWH is less likely to cause these than UFH [van der Heijden et al, 2002].

Compression stockings

- **Graduated elastic compression stockings should be worn on the affected leg following proximal DVT** for at least 2 years, to reduce the incidence of severe post-thrombotic leg syndrome (A) [SIGN, 1999]. Some experts also recommend their use following calf DVT. One study showed that if below-knee compression stockings were applied within 2–3 weeks of a diagnosis of proximal DVT and used for a 2-year period they reduced the risk of severe post-thrombotic syndrome (chronic venous insufficiency) from 23% to 11%. There was no effect on the rate of recurrent DVT [Brandjes et al, 1997; McCollum, 1998].
- If compression hosiery is prescribed, it is essential to check arterial circulation is not compromised. Such assessment would usually include measurement of the ankle-brachial pressure index (ABPI) by Doppler (see separate PRODIGY guidance *Leg ulcer — venous*).
  - **ABPI less than 0.5:** arterial disease is likely and compression treatment is contraindicated.
  - **ABPI between 0.5 and 0.8:** assume that the person has arterial disease. Compression in such instances may further compromise arterial blood supply, and should be generally avoided.
  - **ABPI greater than 0.8:** graduated support stockings may be applied safely.
  - **Arterial disease may develop in people with venous disease,** and health professionals should be aware that the ABPI may drop after the initial measurement [Royal College of Nursing, 2000].

Other treatments (given in hospital)

- **Thrombolytic therapy** is given rarely for DVT. It may be indicated for people with severe DVT causing critical limb ischaemia, or for those with massive pulmonary embolism (PE). Controlled trials have not been large enough to show whether or not there is clinical benefit, but there are anecdotal reports of success [Ludlam et al, 1995; SIGN, 1999].

- **Surgical intervention** (venous thrombectomy for DVT and pulmonary embolectomy for PE) is an alternative to thrombolytic therapy in the above situations. Again, there is only anecdotal evidence of effectiveness [Ludlam et al, 1995; SIGN, 1999].
- **Inferior vena cava filters** are occasionally used when anticoagulation is contraindicated or when adequate anticoagulation fails to prevent recurrent embolism [Bick and Haas, 1998; Haas, 1998; SIGN, 1999].

D

Pregnancy

- **Diagnosis of DVT may be more difficult during pregnancy.** It is difficult on ultrasound examination to differentiate between extrinsic compression of the iliac veins or inferior vena cava by the uterus and venous obstruction due to thrombus. The D-dimer test has not been validated in pregnancy — levels of fibrin degradation products rise in healthy pregnancy, therefore a positive result is more likely to occur in the absence of venous thrombosis. A negative result from a D-dimer blood test and ultrasound examination is of value in excluding venous thrombosis, but venography is the most reliable investigation [Walker, 1993].
- **Specialist guidance** is necessary for those who are pregnant and who need anticoagulant therapy.
- **Oral anticoagulants should not be used in pregnancy,** particularly because of the risk of possible teratogenicity during the first trimester and the risk of fetal intracranial haemorrhage during delivery [Walker, 1993; Bick and Haas, 1998; British Society for Haematology, 1998].
- **Heparin does not cross the placenta and is not thought to affect the fetus.** It is therefore the anticoagulant of choice for the prevention and treatment of VTE during pregnancy. UFH is probably preferable, owing to long experience with its use in pregnancy. However, interpretation of laboratory coagulation results for UFH monitoring may be difficult during pregnancy [Walker, 1993]. LMWH is thought to be as safe and may become standard therapy.
- **Long-term heparin can result in osteoporosis or thrombocytopenia;** treatment courses should therefore be kept as short as possible. Heparin-induced thrombocytopenia (HIT) occurs in approximately 1–2% of people, usually within 5–10 days of starting treatment. Monitoring of platelets is necessary and HIT should be suspected if the platelet count falls to less than 30% from baseline. HIT is of particular importance because, paradoxically, life-threatening thrombosis often accompanies the thrombocytopenia [CSM, 1990; Walker, 1993; Walenga and Bick, 1998].
- **The risk of hyperkalaemia (due to inhibition of aldosterone secretion by heparin) seems to increase with duration of therapy.** The CSM recommends that plasma potassium be measured in people at risk before starting heparin (e.g. people with diabetes mellitus, chronic renal failure, acidosis, or those taking potassium-sparing drugs) and monitored regularly thereafter, particularly if heparin is to be continued for more than 7 days.
- **After delivery,** warfarin can be started immediately [Walker, 1993]. If previously taking warfarin, people should be restarted on their maintenance dosage before pregnancy, and the dosage adjusted according to the INR. If the person is starting warfarin for the first time, the Maternal and Neonatal Haemostasis Working Party of the Haemostasis and Thrombosis Task Force recommends doses of 7 mg, 7 mg, and 5 mg respectively on the first 3 days. Heparin must be continued for at least 3 days until warfarin has become fully effective [Walker, 1993].
- **Warfarin is not secreted in any large quantities in the breast milk.** Women can therefore safely breastfeed while taking warfarin [Walker, 1993].
- **Women with a history of VTE** (with or without thrombophilia) are believed to have a higher risk of recurrence during pregnancy and for up to 6 weeks postpartum. Estimates of the rate of recurrent VTE have varied between 0% and 13% [Ginsberg et al, 2001]. Based on the results of a recent prospective study [Brill-Edwards et al, 2000], the American College of Chest Physicians (ACCP) recommends:
    - **For a single episode of prior VTE associated with a transient risk factor (and no additional current risk factors):** surveillance and postpartum anticoagulants (warfarin for 4–6 weeks with a target INR of 2.0 to 3.0, with initial UFH or LMWH until the INR is greater than 2.0).
    - **For a single episode of idiopathic VTE in women not receiving long-term anticoagulation therapy:** surveillance or heparin, plus postpartum anticoagulants (as above).
    - **For multiple episodes of VTE and/or in women receiving long-term anticoagulation therapy:** heparin followed by resumption of long-term anticoagulation therapy postpartum.

[Hirsh et al, 2001]

Risk of travel-related deep vein thrombosis

- **Immobility is a common risk factor for DVT,** and a possible link between DVT and long-haul air travel was first suggested by reports in medical journals in the 1950s.
- **It is still unclear how common travel-related DVT is,** what the risk factors are, and how it can be prevented.
- **DVT has been associated with all types of long-distance travel, whether by air, car, coach, or train.** In particular, long-haul air travel (flights lasting longer than 5 hours) where passengers remain immobile in the seated position for long periods may be most strongly associated with an increased risk.
- **Available information suggests that the proportion of people who develop DVT related to air travel is small.** It is difficult to decide whether the flight itself caused the DVT or PE, or whether these people were at risk for other reasons. This is because DVT and PE are relatively common conditions and many people now travel by air every year. It is likely that people with established risk factors for VTE are more at risk of developing travel-related DVT/PE (see *Risk factors* section).
- **Most air passengers do not need to take any medication on long-haul flights to prevent DVT.** All air passengers, even those at greatest risk, can reduce the chances of developing DVT by doing simple calf and foot exercises (this is covered in the patient information leaflet).
- **There is some evidence that compression stockings may be useful.** One study in people over 50 years of age found that below-knee compression stockings (equivalent to Class 2) reduced the incidence of asymptomatic DVT during long-haul flight from 10% to 0% [Scurr et al, 2001]. There is no information on whether the incidence of clinically significant DVT is reduced.
- **There is no evidence that aspirin is effective in preventing travel-related DVT or PE.**
- **Some experts recommend LMWH for those with strong risk factors for DVT,** although there is little evidence to support this [Geroulakos, 2001].

[The House of Lords Select Committee on Science and Technology, 2000; DH, 2002]

References

1. Anand, S.S., Wells, P.S., Hunt, D. et al (1998) Does this patient have deep vein thrombosis? *Journal of the American Medical Association* **279**(14), 1094–1099.
2. Aschwanden, M., Labs, K.H., Jeanneret, C. et al (1999) The value of rapid D-dimer testing combined with structured clinical evaluation for the diagnosis of deep vein thrombosis. *Journal of Vascular Surgery* **30**(5), 929–935.
3. Baker, W.F., Jr. (1998) Diagnosis of deep venous thrombosis and pulmonary embolism. *Medical Clinics of North America* **82**(3), 459–476.
4. Bandolier (1999) *Resistance to activated protein C due to factor V R506Q (Factor V Leiden)*. Bandolier. www.jr2.ox.ac.uk/bandolier/bandopubs/keeling.html [Accessed: 11/11/2002].
5. Becker, D.M., Philbrick, J.T., Bachhuber, T.L. and Humphries, J.E. (1996) D-dimer testing and acute venous thromboembolism. A shortcut to accurate diagnosis? *Archives of Internal Medicine* **156**(9), 939–946.
6. Bernardi, E., Prandoni, P., Lensing, A.W. et al (1998) D-dimer testing as an adjunct to ultrasonography in patients with clinically suspected deep vein thrombosis: prospective cohort study. The Multicentre Italian D-dimer Ultrasound Study Investigators Group. *British Medical Journal* **317**(7165), 1037–1040.
7. Beyth, R.J., Cohen, A.M. and Landefeld, C.S. (1995) Long-term outcomes of deep-vein thrombosis. *Archives of Internal Medicine* **155**(10), 1031–1037.
8. Bick, R.L. and Haas, S.K. (1998) International consensus recommendations. Summary statement and additional suggested guidelines. *Medical Clinics of North America* **82**(3), 613–633.
9. Bick, R.L. and Kaplan, H. (1998) Syndromes of thrombosis and hypercoagulability. Congenital and acquired causes of thrombosis. *Medical Clinics of North America* **82**(3), 409–458.
10. BNF 43 (2002) *British National Formulary*. 43rd edn. London: British Medical Association and Royal Pharmaceutical Society of Great Britain.
11. Brandjes, D.P., Heijboer, H., Buller, H.R. et al (1992) Acenocoumarol and heparin compared with acenocoumarol alone in the initial treatment of proximal-vein thrombosis. *New England Journal of Medicine* **327**(21), 1485–1489.
12. Brandjes, D.P., Buller, H.R., Heijboer, H. et al (1997) Randomised trial of effect of compression stockings in patients with symptomatic proximal-vein thrombosis. *Lancet* **349**(9054), 759–762.
13. British Society for Haematology (1998) Guidelines on oral anticoagulation: third edition. *British Journal of Haematology* **101**(2), 374–387.
14. Cogo, A., Lensing, A.W.A., Koopman, M.M.W. et al (1998) Compression ultrasonography for diagnostic management of patients with clinically suspected deep vein thrombosis prospective cohort study. *British Medical Journal* **316**, 17–20.
15. DH (2002) *Advice on travel-related deep vein thrombosis*. Department of Health. www.dh.gov.uk [Accessed: 27/04/2004].
16. Douketis, J.D., Kearon, C., Bates, S. et al (1998) Risk of fatal pulmonary embolism in patients with treated venous thromboembolism. *Journal of the American Medical Association* **279**(6), 458–462.
17. DTB (1998) Low molecular weight heparins for venous thromboembolism. *Drug & Therapeutics Bulletin* **36**(7), 25–29.
18. Geroulakos, G. (2001) The risk of venous thromboembolism from air travel. *British Medical Journal* **322**(7280), 188.
19. Gorman, W.P., Davis, K.R. and Donnelly, R. (2000) ABC of arterial and venous disease. Swollen lower limb-1: general assessment and deep vein thrombosis. *British Medical Journal* **320**(7247), 1453–1456.
20. Haas, S.K. (1998) Treatment of deep venous thrombosis and pulmonary embolism. Current recommendations. *Medical Clinics of North America* **82**(3), 495–510.
21. Hull, R.D. and Pineo, G.F. (1998) Prophylaxis of deep venous thrombosis and pulmonary embolism. Current recommendations. *Medical Clinics of North America* **82**(3), 477–493.
22. Hutten, B.A. and Prins, M.H. (2002) *Duration of oral anticoagulant treatment for symptomatic venous thromboembolism (Cochrane Review)*. The Cochrane Library. Issue 4. Oxford: Update Software.
23. Koopman, M.M., Prandoni, P., Piovella, F. et al (1996) Treatment of venous thrombosis with intravenous unfractionated heparin administered in the hospital as compared with subcutaneous low-molecular-weight heparin administered at home. The Tasman Study Group. *New England Journal of Medicine* **334**(11), 682–687. [erratum appears in *N Engl J Med* (1997) 337(17), 1251].
24. Lennox, A.F., Delis, K.T., Serunkuma, S. et al (1999) Combination of a clinical risk assessment score and rapid whole blood D-dimer testing in the diagnosis of deep vein thrombosis in symptomatic patients. *Journal of Vascular Surgery* **30**(5), 794–803.
25. Levine, M., Gent, M., Hirsh, J. et al (1996) A comparison of low-molecular-weight heparin administered primarily at home with unfractionated heparin administered in the hospital for proximal deep-vein thrombosis. *New England Journal of Medicine* **334**(11), 677–681.
26. Ludlam, C.A., Bennett, B., Fox, K.A.A. et al (1995) Guidelines for the use of thrombolytic therapy. *Blood Coagulation & Fibrinolysis* **6**(3), 273–285.
27. McCollum, C. (1998) Avoiding the consequences of deep vein thrombosis. Elevation and compression are important – and too often forgotten. *British Medical Journal* **317**(7160), 696.
28. MeReC (1997) Anticoagulant therapy. *MeReC Bulletin* **8**(1), 1–4.
29. Perrier, A., Desmarais, S., Miron, M. et al (1999) Non-invasive diagnosis of venous thromboembolism in outpatients. *Lancet* **353**(9148), 190–195.
30. Prandoni, P., Lensing, A.W., Cogo, A. et al (1996) The long-term clinical course of acute deep venous thrombosis. *Annals of Internal Medicine* **125**(1), 1–7.
31. Royal College of Nursing (2000) *The management of patients with venous leg ulcers. Audit protocol.* Royal College of Nursing. www.rcn.org.uk [Accessed: 02/04/2004].
32. Scurr, J.H., Machin, S.J., Bailey-King, S. et al (2001) Frequency and prevention of symptomless deep-vein thrombosis in long-haul flights: a randomised trial. *Lancet* **357**(9267), 1485–1489.
33. SIGN (1999) *Antithrombotic therapy*. Report no. 36. Scottish Intercollegiate Guidelines Network. www.sign.ac.uk [Accessed: 19/12/2002].
34. The House of Lords Select Committee on Science and Technology (2000) *Air travel and health: fifth report from the Science & Technology Committee*. Session 1999–2000: Fifth Report. HMSO. www.publications.parliament.uk/pa/ld199900/ldselect/ldsctech/121/12101.htm [Accessed: 12/10/2002].
35. van den Belt, A.G.M., Prins, M.H., Lensing, A.W. et al (2002) *Fixed dose subcutaneous low molecular weight*

D

heparins versus adjusted dose unfractionated heparin for venous thromboembolism. The Cochrane Library. Issue 4. Oxford: Update Software.

36. van der Heijden, J.F., Hutten, B.A., Buller, H.R. and Prins, M.H. (2002) *Vitamin K antagonists or low-molecular-weight heparin for the long term treatment of symptomatic venous thromboembolism (Cochrane Review)*. The Cochrane Library. Issue 4. Oxford: Update Software.
37. Verstraete, M. (1997) Prophylaxis of venous thromboembolism. *British Medical Journal* **314**(7074), 123–125.
38. Walker, I.D. (1993) Guidelines on the prevention, investigation and management of thrombosis associated with pregnancy. Maternal and Neonatal Haemostasis Working Party of the Haemostasis and Thrombosis Task. *Journal of Clinical Pathology* **46**(6), 489–496.

Evidence grading

Evidence grading is from the Scottish Intercollegiate Guidelines Network (SIGN) guideline *Antithrombotic Therapy*, March 1999. The definition of types of evidence and grading of recommendation is as follows:

Strength of evidence:

Ia Evidence obtained from meta-analysis of randomized controlled trials.

Ib Evidence obtained from at least one randomized controlled trial.

IIa Evidence obtained from at least one well-designed controlled study without randomization.

IIb Evidence obtained from at least one other type of well-designed quasi-experimental study.

III Evidence obtained from well-designed non-experiment descriptive studies, such as comparative studies, correlatic studies and case studies.

IV Evidence from expert committee reports or opinions and/or clinical experiences of respected authorities.

Strength of recommendation:

A Requires at least one randomized controlled trial as par of a body of literature of overall good quality and consistency addressing the specific recommendation.
(Evidence levels Ia, Ib)

B Requires the availability of well-conducted clinical studies but no randomized clinical trials on the topic of recommendation.
(Evidence levels IIa, IIb, III)

C Requires evidence obtained from expert committee reports or opinions and /or clinical experiences of respecte authorities. Indicates an absence of directly applicable clinical studies of good quality.
(Evidence level IV)

PRODIGY GUIDANCE

Dental abscess

Last revised in November 2004
www.prodigy.nhs.uk/guidance.asp?gt=Dental abscess

Applies to people over the age of 12 months

This guidance covers the management of dental abscess in primary medical care, including out of hours.

This guidance does not cover the definitive management of dental abscess by a dental practitioner.

There is separate PRODIGY guidance for *Gingivitis and periodontitis,* and *Aphthous ulcer.*

Goals

Reduction of pain
All people with dental abscess should see a dental practitioner within a week

Contents

Scenarios

- Dental abscess p.477

Extended Information, p. 479

Dental abscess

Which therapy?

If the person has access to a dental practitioner, advise that he or she contacts the dental practitioner for definitive treatment.
If the person does not have access to a dental practitioner:

- Prescribe analgesia:
  - Paracetamol with or without codeine phosphate
  - Ibuprofen is an alternative to paracetamol
  - Diclofenac is an alternative to ibuprofen
- Prescribe an antibiotic:
  - Amoxicillin (erythromycin if allergic to penicillin), or
  - Metronidazole
- Advise that the person must see a dental practitioner as soon as possible.

Practical prescribing points

For further information please see the *Medicines Compendium* (www.medicines.org.uk) or the *British National Formulary* (www.bnf.org).

Ibuprofen or diclofenac: may cause gastrointestinal irritation and occasionally gastrointestinal haemorrhage. Avoid if there is a history of peptic ulceration. Ibuprofen or diclofenac may worsen asthma, hypertension, renal impairment, or cardiac failure.

Follow-up advice

Follow-up should be provided by a dental practitioner.

Should I refer or investigate?

Refer?

Everyone with a dental abscess must see a dental practitioner as soon as possible for definitive treatment. The following should be admitted to an oral surgery or maxillofacial unit:

- People who are systemically unwell.
- People with trismus.
- People with swelling severe enough to compromise their airway, especially if it affects the floor of the mouth.

Investigate?

- No investigations are necessary in primary medical care.

Patient information leaflets

The following PILs are available at www.prodigy.nhs.uk

- Dental Abscess
- Dental Anxiety & Phobia Association
- Dental Phobia & Anxiety Website
- Dental Practice Board of England and Wales

Shared decision making

- You have a dental abscess. You should see a dentist as soon as possible.
- An antibiotic may help to prevent the abscess from getting worse. However, an antibiotic will not clear the abscess and you still need to see a dentist as soon as possible.
- You may also need painkillers.

Drug rationale

Drugs not included

- Antibiotics other than amoxicillin, erythromycin, and metronidazole are not included. The most commonly prescribed antibiotics for dental abscess are amoxicillin and metronidazole [Palmer et al, 2000; Sweeney et al, 2004].

Drugs included

- **Analgesia:**
  - **Paracetamol** is included for simple analgesia.
  - **Ibuprofen** is included as an alternative to paracetamol.
  - **Diclofenac** is included as an alternative to ibuprofen, especially if the person has tried over-the-counter ibuprofen and found it ineffective.
  - **Codeine** is included for the treatment of more severe pain.
- **Antibiotics:**
  - **Amoxicillin** is the antibiotic most commonly used for dental abscess.
  - **Erythromycin** is included for people allergic of penicillins.
  - **Metronidazole** is included as an alternative to amoxicillin.

D

Prescriptions

Analgesia: use when required

Paracetamol s/f susp: 120mg to 240mg up to four times a day
- Age from 12 months to 5 years
- Paracetamol 120mg/5ml s/f susp. Take one to two 5ml spoonfuls every 4 to 6 hours when required for pain relief. Maximum of 4 doses in 24 hours; supply 300 ml; NHS Cost £1.30; OTC Cost £2.28.

Paracetamol s/f susp: 250mg to 500mg up to four times a day
- Age from 6 to 11 years
- Paracetamol 250mg/5ml s/f susp. Take one to two 5ml spoonfuls every 4 to 6 hours when required for pain relief. Maximum of 4 doses in 24 hours; supply 300 ml; NHS Cost £1.70; OTC Cost £2.99.

Paracetamol tablets: 500mg to 1g up to four times a day
- Age from 12 to 15 years
- Paracetamol 500mg tablets. Take one to two tablets every 4 to 6 hours when required for pain relief. Maximum of 8 tablets in 24 hours; supply 100 tablets; NHS Cost £0.75; OTC Cost £1.32.

Paracetamol tablets: 1g up to four times a day
- Age from 16 years onwards
- Paracetamol 500mg tablets. Take two tablets every 4 to 6 hours when required for pain relief. Maximum of 8 tablets in 24 hours; supply 100 tablets; NHS Cost £0.75; OTC Cost £1.32.

Codeine 30mg tablets: add on to paracetamol if required
- Age from 16 years onwards
- Codeine 30mg tablets. Take one to two tablets every 4 to 6 hours when required for pain relief. Maximum of 8 tablets in 24 hours; supply 56 tablets; NHS Cost £2.90.

Paracetamol 500mg tablets + codeine 30mg tablets
- Age from 16 years onwards
- Paracetamol 500mg tablets. Take two tablets every 4 to 6 hours when required for pain relief. Maximum of 8 tablets in 24 hours; supply 100 tablets; NHS Cost £0.75; OTC Cost £1.32.
- Codeine 30mg tablets. Take one to two tablets every 4 to 6 hours when required for pain relief. Maximum of 8 tablets in 24 hours; supply 56 tablets; NHS Cost £2.90.

Ibuprofen s/f susp: 50mg three to four times a day
- Age from 12 months to 2 years
- Ibuprofen 100mg/5ml s/f susp. Take 2.5ml three to four times a day when required for pain relief. Do not exceed the stated dose; supply 100 ml; NHS Cost £1.82; OTC Cost £3.21.

Ibuprofen s/f susp: 100mg three to four times a day
- Age from 3 to 7 years
- Ibuprofen 100mg/5ml s/f susp. Take one 5ml spoonful 3 to 4 times a day when required for pain relief. Do not exceed the stated dose; supply 150 ml; NHS Cost £2.73; OTC Cost £4.81.

Ibuprofen s/f susp: 200mg three to four times a day
- Age from 8 to 11 years
- Ibuprofen 100mg/5ml s/f susp. Take two 5ml spoonfuls 3 to 4 times a day when required for pain relief. Do not exceed the stated dose; supply 300 ml; NHS Cost £5.46; OTC Cost £9.62.

Ibuprofen tablets: 400mg three times a day
- Age from 12 years onwards
- Ibuprofen 400mg tablets. Take one tablet three times a day when required for pain relief. Do not exceed the stated dose; supply 24 tablets; NHS Cost £0.70; OTC Cost £1.23.

Diclofenac sodium e/c tablets: 50mg three times a day
- Age from 16 years onwards
- Diclofenac 50mg e/c tablets. Take one tablet three times a day when required for pain relief. Do not exceed the stated dose; supply 21 tablets; NHS Cost £0.89.

Diclofenac sodium e/c tablets: 25mg three times a day
- Age from 16 years onwards
- Diclofenac 25mg e/c tablets. Take one tablet three times a day when required for pain relief. Do not exceed the stated dose; supply 21 tablets; NHS Cost £0.62.

Antibiotics: amoxicillin

Amoxicillin s/f suspension: 125mg three times a day
- Age from 12 to 23 months
- Amoxicillin 125mg/5ml s/f susp. Take one 5ml spoonful three times a day for 5 days; supply 100 ml; NHS Cost £1.30.

Amoxicillin s/f susp: 250mg three times a day
- Age from 2 to 9 years
- Amoxicillin 250mg/5ml s/f susp. Take one 5ml spoonful three times a day for 5 days; supply 100 ml; NHS Cost £2.25.

Amoxicillin s/f susp: 500mg three times a day
- Age from 10 to 11 years
- Amoxicillin 250mg/5ml s/f susp. Take two 5ml spoonfuls three times a day for 5 days; supply 200 ml; NHS Cost £4.50.

Amoxicillin capsules: 500mg three times a day
- Age from 12 years onwards
- Amoxicillin 500mg capsules. Take one capsule three times a day for 5 days; supply 15 capsules; NHS Cost £1.32.

Antibiotics (if penicillin allergy): erythromycin for 5 days

Erythromycin s/f suspension: 125mg four times a day
- Age from 12 to 23 months
- Erythromycin 125mg/5ml sf susp. Take one 5ml spoonful four times a day for 5 days; supply 100 ml; NHS Cost £1.12.

Erythromycin s/f suspension: 250mg four times a day
- Age from 2 to 8 years
- Erythromycin 250mg/5ml sf susp. Take one 5ml spoonful four times a day for 5 days; supply 100 ml; NHS Cost £1.84.

Erythromycin s/f suspension: 500mg four times a day
- Age from 9 to 11 years
- Erythromycin 500mg/5ml sf susp. Take one 5ml spoonful four times a day for 5 days; supply 100 ml; NHS Cost £2.86.

Erythromycin e/c tablets: 500mg four times a day
- Age from 12 years onwards
- Erythromycin 250mg e/c tablets. Take two tablets four times a day for 5 days; supply 40 tablets; NHS Cost £4.40.

Antibiotics: metronidazole for 5 days

Metronidazole 200mg/5ml susp: 7.5mg/kg three times a day
- Age from 12 months to 11 years
- Metronidazole 200mg/5ml susp. *WEIGHT REQUIRED* Take 7.5mg per kg bodyweight THREE times a day for 5 days. (Max 400mg per dose.); supply 200 ml; NHS Cost £6.54.

Metronidazole tablets: 400mg three times a day
- Age from 12 years onwards
- Metronidazole 400mg tablets. Take one tablet three times a day for 5 days; supply 15 tablets; NHS Cost £0.62.

Extended Information

Background information

What is it? p.479
How common is it? p.479
How do I know my patient has it? p.479
What else might it be? p.479
Complications and prognosis p.479

What is it?

A dental abscess is a localized collection of pus in the teeth, supporting structures of the teeth (periodontal ligament, alveolar bone), or gums. There are two types of dental abscess:

- **Periapical abscess** — this originates in the dental pulp, and is usually secondary to dental caries. It is the most common type in children.
- **Periodontal abscess** — this originates in the supporting structures of the teeth (periodontal ligament, alveolar bone). It is the most common type in adults [Herrera et al, 2000; Schneider and Segal, 2004].

These two forms are distinct, both anatomically and in terms of dental management. However, as this guidance is written for primary medical care, and the management therein is the same for both, they will be considered as the single entity of dental abscess throughout.

Microbiological studies usually isolate three or more organisms from a dental abscess. These are predominantly gram-negative anaerobic rods [Herrera et al, 2000; Wilson and Kornman, 2003].

How common is it?

The lifetime prevalence of dental abscess has been reported as being between 5% and 46% [Matthews et al, 2003].

How do I know my patient has it?

Any combination of the following features may be present.

- **Pain:** this is usually of sudden onset, and worsens over a few hours to a few days. It may be intense and throbbing. The tooth may be tender to percussion, or to pressure from biting.
- **Tooth:** the affected tooth may display increased mobility, and may be elevated.
- **Lymphadenopathy.**
- **Gingival swelling:** this is smooth, shiny, and erythematous. It may involve one or several teeth. It is tender to touch. It may develop into a fluctuant mass. There may be a purulent exudate.
- **Facial swelling, with or without cellulitis:** most commonly in the submandibular, sublingual, or buccal areas.
- **Heat sensitivity.**
- **Fever.**
- **Malaise.**
- In severe cases, trismus (inability to open the mouth) or dysphagia may be present.

[American Academy of Periodontology, 2000; Herrera et al, 2000; Wilson and Kornman, 2003; Schneider and Segal, 2004]

What else might it be?

- Mumps
- Localized lymphadenopathy due to other intraoral infection
- Blocked salivary gland due to stone or dehydration/dry mouth
- Intraoral neoplasm
- Salivary gland neoplasm
- Unerupted teeth
- Sinusitis
- Acute otitis media

Complications and prognosis

Complications

- If incompletely treated (i.e. the person does not undergo definitive dental treatment):
  - A chronic abscess may develop, with a sinus that may discharge intraorally or to the overlying skin.
  - A chronic dental (radicular) cyst may develop around the apex of the tooth.
- Osteomyelitis.
- Cavernous sinus thrombosis: it is estimated that 10% of cases have a dental origin.
- Ludwig's angina.
- Maxillary sinusitis.

[Schneider and Segal, 2004]

Prognosis

- The prognosis is excellent with appropriate dental care, but the tooth can rarely be saved. If the tooth is severely broken down, or if there is advanced periodontal disease, extraction of the tooth is necessary.

[Herrera et al, 2000; Schneider and Segal, 2004]

Management issues

- Where, by whom, and what form of treatment should be given? p.479
- Which analgesia should be prescribed by medical practitioners? p.479
- What is the role of antibiotics? p.480

Where, by whom, and what form of treatment should be given?

- **Definitive treatment of a dental abscess should be provided by a dental practitioner.** Access to emergency treatment by a dental practitioner is via:
  - The person's registered General Dental Practitioner, or
  - The accident and emergency department of a Dental Hospital, or
  - The accident and emergency department of a District General Hospital, or
  - The local Dental Access Centre (these are available in some areas)
- **It is recognized, however, that access to a dental practitioner is not available to every individual at all times throughout the year** [Anderson and Thomas, 2000]. A person with a dental abscess may require treatment from medical care providers, especially out of hours. This treatment may be provided by the person's GP, medical out-of-hours service, or local accident and emergency department. Such treatment will consist of:
  - Analgesia
  - Antibiotics
  - Advice to see a dental practitioner as soon as possible for definitive treatment

Which analgesia should be prescribed by medical practitioners?

- Although we could find no trials that specifically looked at analgesia in the treatment of dental abscess by medical practitioners, experts recommend standard analgesia:
  - Paracetamol with or without codeine phosphate
  - Nonsteroidal anti-inflammatory drugs

- By the time of presentation, the person may already have tried over-the-counter medication, including a combination of the above.

What is the role of antibiotics?

- Although we could find no trials that specifically looked at antibiotics in the treatment of dental abscess by medical practitioners, it is common practice to prescribe an antibiotic as an interim measure. We could find no studies comparing antibiotics in this situation. Experts recommend the use of one of:
  - Amoxicillin (or erythromycin if intolerant of penicillins), or
  - Metronidazole
- There is no consensus on the role of antibiotics when combined with definitive treatment of dental abscess by a dental practitioner. Some advise antibiotics as the only initial treatment; some recommend antibiotics in conjunction with definitive dental treatment; others only suggest antibiotics if systemic infection is present [Herrera et al, 2000; Wilson and Kornman, 2003]. A systematic review of eight papers (531 people with dental abscess) showed antibiotics to be of no additional benefit when added to definitive dental treatment [Matthews et al, 2003]. The antibiotics most commonly prescribed by dental practitioners for dental abscess are amoxicillin and metronidazole [Palmer et al, 2000; Sweeney et al, 2004].

D

References

NHS staff in England can link, free of charge, from references to full text journals by clicking on [Full text] on the PRODIGY website.

1. American Academy of Periodontology (2000) Parameters of care. *Journal of Periodontology* **71**(5 Suppl), 847–883.
2. Anderson, R. and Thomas, D.W. (2000) Out-of-hours dental services: a survey of current provision in the United Kingdom. *British Dental Journal* **188**(5), 269–274.
3. Herrera, D., Roldan, S. and Sanz, M. (2000) The periodontal abscess: a review. *Journal of Clinical Periodontology* **27**(6), 377–386.
4. Matthews, D.C., Sutherland, S. and Basrani, B. (2003) Emergency management of acute apical abscesses in the permanent dentition: a systematic review of the literature. *Journal of the Canadian Dental Association* **69**(10), 660.
5. Palmer, N.O., Martin, M.V., Pealing, R. and Ireland, R.S. (2000) An analysis of antibiotic prescriptions from general dental practitioners in England. *Journal of Antimicrobial Chemotherapy* **46**(6), 1033–1035.
6. Schneider, K. and Segal, G. (2004) *Dental abscess.* eMedicine.com, Inc. www.emedicine.com [Accessed: 1 05/2004]. [Full text]
7. Sweeney, L.C., Dave, J., Chambers, P.A. and Heritage, (2004) Antibiotic resistance in general dental practice – a cause for concern? *Journal of Antimicrobial Chemotherapy* **53**(4), 567–576. [Full text]
8. Wilson, T.G.Jr and Kornman, K.S. (Eds.) (2003) *Fundamentals of periodontics.* 2nd edn. London: Quintessence Publishing Co, Inc.

RODIGY GUIDANCE

Depression

Last revised in July 2004

At the time of print this topic was being updated. The newly revised guidance will be issued on to the website in late 2005.

www.prodigy.nhs.uk/guidance.asp?gt=Depression

Applies to people over the age of 18 years

This guidance covers the management of major depression, dysthymia, and milder depression, including postnatal depression.

This guidance does not cover the management of childhood depression, bipolar disorder, puerperal psychosis, or other psychiatric conditions.

There is separate PRODIGY guidance on *Stress — acute reaction*, *Alcohol — problem drinking*, *Obsessive compulsive disorder*, *Opiate dependence*, and *Panic disorder*.

Goals

To identify people with depression
To treat effectively (to improve mood, social and occupational functioning, and quality of life)
To reduce chance of relapse or recurrence

Contents

Scenarios

- Major depression (+ starting dosages antidepressants) p.482
- Dysthymia (+ starting dosages antidepressants) p.484
- Milder depression (+ starting dosages antidepressants) p.487
- Postnatal depression (+ starting dosages antidepressants) p.489
- Maintenance/dosage adjustment (+ advice on poor response) p.492
- Switching antidepressants p.494
- Stopping antidepressants p.495

Extended Information, p. 497

Which scenario?

Major depression (with starting dosages of antidepressants)
Dysthymia (with starting dosages of antidepressants)
Milder depression (with starting dosages of antidepressants)
Postnatal depression (with starting dosages of antidepressants)
Maintenance/dosage adjustment (with advice on poor response)
Switching antidepressants (advice only)
Stopping antidepressants

Major depression (with starting dosages of antidepressants)

This scenario is for people with major depression, diagnosed according to DSM–IV criteria (see Table 1). Starting dosages of antidepressants suitable for the initial management of depression in primary care are offered.

Table 1: DSM–IV criteria for major depression.

At least five of the following symptoms (including either the first or the second) have been present during the last 2 weeks most of the day, or nearly every day, and cause clinically significant distress or impairment in functioning. The symptoms are not due to a physical/organic factor (e.g. substance abuse) or illness and are not better explained by bereavement (although this can be complicated by major depression).
Depressed mood
Loss of interest or pleasure in almost all activities
Significant weight loss or gain, or change in appetite
Insomnia or hypersomnia
Psychomotor agitation or retardation (observable by others)
Fatigue or loss of energy
Feelings of worthlessness or excessive or inappropriate guilt
Diminished ability to think or concentrate, or indecisiveness
Recurrent thoughts of death (not just fear of dying) or suicidal thoughts/actions

Dysthymia (with starting dosages of antidepressants)

This scenario is for people with dysthymia, a chronic milder depressive disorder, with depressive symptoms for at least 2 years not meeting DSM–IV criteria for major depression. Starting dosages of antidepressants suitable for the initial management of dysthymia in primary care are offered.

Milder depression (with starting dosages of antidepressants)

- This scenario is for people who present with recent onset depressive symptoms but who do not meet the DMS–IV criteria for major depression. The depressed mood often develops following an identifiable stressor, but the degree of distress exceeds the level expected and social or occupational functioning may be impaired. Starting dosages of antidepressants suitable for the initial management of depression in primary care are offered.

Postnatal depression (with starting dosages of antidepressants)

- This scenario is for women who present with major depression, diagnosed according to DSM–IV criteria, ***of mild to moderate severity occurring during the first postnatal year.*** Starting dosages of antidepressants suitable for the initial management of depression in primary care are offered.

Maintenance/dosage adjustment (with advice on poor response)

- This scenario provides prescriptions for maintenance dosages of antidepressants and allows for adjustment of antidepressant dosage. The antidepressants offered are those that could have been started in the earlier initiation scenarios.

Switching antidepressants (advice only)

- This scenario offers advice on how best to switch between different antidepressants (e.g. a person may need to change to an alternative antidepressant because their current antidepressant is either ineffective or poorly tolerated). The switching regimens described cover those antidepressants suitable for the initial management of depression in primary care, as offered in the previous scenarios.

Stopping antidepressants

- This scenario offers advice on how to stop antidepressant medication so as to reduce the risk of discontinuation symptoms. Prescriptions are offered that gradually reduce and stop the antidepressant over a 3–4 week period. The stopping regimens offered are for those antidepressants available as prescriptions in previous scenarios. Withdrawal prescriptions for people who are receiving long-term maintenance treatment are not offered (usually needs to be withdrawn over several months).

Major depression (+ starting dosages antidepressants)

Which therapy?

- Confirm the diagnosis according to DSM–IV criteria (see section *Which scenario? above*).
- **Antidepressants are a preferred treatment, irrespective of psychosocial factors.**
- **Psychological treatments are an effective alternative to antidepressants.** The best evidence is for mild to moderate major depression. Cognitive behaviour therapy and interpersonal therapy have been most studied. Other psychological treatments that have shown benefit include behavioural therapy, problem-solving therapy, group therapy, and marital and family intervention. The value of non-directive counselling is uncertain.
- The decision whether to choose antidepressants or psychological treatments will depend on availability and preference of the individual. Drug treatment is preferable for severe major depression.
- **If medication is necessary:**
  - Tricyclic antidepressants (TCAs), trazodone, and selective serotonin re-uptake inhibitors (SSRIs) are suitable first-choice antidepressants.
  - **Choice should be determined by individual patient factors,** including likelihood of adverse effects, comorbidity, concomitant medication, and preference of the individual.
  - **Lofepramine, trazodone, or an SSRI are preferable if there is a concern about suicide risk,** as these are associated with the lowest risk of fatal poisoning. However, if suicide risk is a genuine concern admission should be strongly considered, especially if the person has poor social support.
  - **If there has been a previous good response to a particular drug it is sensible to prescribe this again.** Similarly, if a person has previously failed to respond to or could not tolerate the adverse effects of a particular drug, it is best avoided.

Practical prescribing points

For further information see the *Medicines Compendium* (www.medicines.org.uk) or the *British National Formulary* (www.bnf.org).

- **Suspected risk of overdose:** lofepramine, trazodone, or an SSRI are preferred choices.
- **Driving:** the Driver and Vehicle Licensing Agency (DVLA) recommends avoiding drugs that have antimuscarinic effects, such as TCAs. SSRIs are less likely to cause sedation, but some people have idiosyncratic responses. All people taking antidepressants should be advised not to drive if adversely affected, particularly during the first month o starting or increasing the dosage.
- **Elderly people:** TCAs (other than lofepramine) may be less suitable owing to their antimuscarinic adverse effects.
- **Pregnancy:** use amitriptyline or imipramine. If an SSRI essential, use fluoxetine. Contact the National Teratology Information Service (0191 232 1525) for further information.
- **Cardiac disease:** SSRIs may be preferred to TCAs, but use with caution.
- **Epilepsy:** SSRIs may be preferred to TCAs, but use with caution.
- **Known/suspected bipolar disorder:** caution with TCAs and SSRIs (may precipitate mania).
- **Prostatism, narrow-angle glaucoma, urinary retention:** use an SSRI or trazodone.
- **Weight gain** is more likely with TCAs than with SSRIs.
- **Sexual dysfunction** is more likely with SSRIs than with TCAs.
- **Priapism** has been reported rarely with trazodone. Trazodone should be discontinued immediately if priapism occurs.
- **Hyponatraemia** is associated with both TCAs and SSRI More common in elderly people or those taking diuretics. Consider hyponatraemia in all people who develop drowsiness, confusion, or convulsions while taking an antidepressant.

Follow-up advice

- **Follow-up should initially be every 1–2 weeks** dependir on the severity of depression (for at least the first 4–6 weeks) to monitor progress and ensure medication tolerated.
- **For a first episode of major depression,** medication should be continued at full antidepressant dosage until the person has been free of major symptoms for at least 6 months. A longer treatment course is recommended i people with residual symptoms, those with a history of depression, and in elderly people.
- Maintenance treatment reduces the risk of recurrence and is indicated in people with:
  - Three or more episodes of major depression in the pa 5 years.
  - More than five episodes altogether.
  - Fewer recurrent depressive episodes but with persistent risk factors for relapse or recurrence (e.g. continued psychosocial issues).
- Maintenance treatment should be continued at the sam dosage that was used to treat the acute episode and continued for at least 5 years and possibly indefinitely.

Should I refer or investigate?

Refer?

- **Urgently admit** people at high risk of suicide.
- **Consider admission** for people at less obvious risk of suicide but with poor social support.
- **Admission is advised** for people with psychotic features (delusions, hallucinations) or stupor.

Consider referral if the person is not responding to treatment, or if there is diagnostic uncertainty (e.g. physical symptoms or signs not consistent with a diagnosis of depression).

Patient information leaflets

The following PILs are available at www.prodigy.nhs.uk

Antidepressants - SSRIs
Antidepressants - St John's Wort
Antidepressants - Tricyclic
Anxiety Disorders
Anxiety - Generalised Anxiety Disorder
Association for Post-Natal Illness
Cognitive Behaviour Therapy (CBT)
Depression
Depression Alliance
Depression - A Summary
Depression (Post-Natal)
Fellowship of Depressives Anonymous
MAMA - Meet-A-Mum Association
Manic Depression Fellowship
Phobia - Agoraphobia
Phobia - Social Phobia
Post-Traumatic Stress Disorder
Psychosomatic Disorders
SAD Association (Seasonal Affective Disorder)
Seasonal Affective Disorder
Somatization and Somatoform Disorders

Shared decision making

Depression is common. Most people recover but treatment speeds recovery.

Talking things through with family, friends, or a counsellor is often helpful.

Antidepressants are usually effective. They take 4–6 weeks to work fully. A course for at least 6 months after symptoms improve is usual.

A tricyclic antidepressant (TCA), such as amitriptyline, imipramine, or lofepramine, is commonly prescribed.

A selective serotonin re-uptake inhibitor (SSRI) antidepressant (such as citalopram, fluoxetine, paroxetine, and sertraline) or **trazodone** is an alternative.

The choice of antidepressant may depend on your age, previous use of antidepressants, possible side effects, other medicines that you take, other medical conditions that you have, and personal preference. If one antidepressant does not suit at first, a change to a different one is an option.

Side effects are often minor or improve in time. The packet insert lists all possible side effects.

- TCAs: common side effects include slight drowsiness, a dry mouth, and blurred vision.
- SSRIs: an upset stomach is the commonest side effect.

Talking treatments such as cognitive therapy, psychotherapy, or counselling for specific problems such as relationship difficulties may be options in some cases.

See a doctor if you get worse, feel suicidal, or develop persistent troublesome side effects.

Drug rationale

The choice of antidepressant should be determined by individual patient factors, including likelihood of adverse effects, comorbidity, concomitant medication, and preference of the individual.

Drugs not included

Tricyclic antidepressants (TCAs) other than amitriptyline, imipramine, and lofepramine: other TCAs are more expensive than amitriptyline or imipramine without offering any significant advantage in terms of their adverse effect profiles (i.e. sedation compared with no sedation). The exception is lofepramine, which although more expensive causes fewer antimuscarinic adverse effects and has low toxicity in overdose.

- **Heterocyclic antidepressants other than trazodone:** maprotiline is more likely to cause seizures or rashes than TCAs [CSM, 1985]. Seizures have occurred in people with no past history of seizure disorders. Mianserin is associated with blood dyscrasias and clinical monitoring of blood counts is required during treatment [BNF 41, 2001].
- **Fluvoxamine:** a recent systematic review found that fluvoxamine was poorly tolerated compared with other selective serotonin re-uptake inhibitors (SSRIs). The overall incidence of adverse effects was similar, suggesting that poor tolerability was due to the severity rather than the frequency of adverse effects [Edwards and Anderson, 1999].
- **Newer antidepressants** (such as mirtazapine, nefazodone, reboxetine, and venlafaxine): These may have a place when first-choice drugs are poorly tolerated or ineffective. However, further experience and studies are required to confirm their precise role in primary care [MeReC, 2000].
- **Monoamine-oxidase inhibitors (MAOIs):** these have considerable dietary and drug interactions and are therefore not included as first-choice agents.
- **Reversible MAOIs:** moclobemide should be reserved as a second-line treatment [BNF 41, 2001]. Tyramine-rich foods and sympathomimetics still need to be avoided while taking moclobemide, despite its lower potential for interactions.

Drugs included

TCAs

- **Lofepramine** is a suitable choice in people at risk of suicide [Eccles et al, 1999; Mason et al, 2000]. Lofepramine is also less sedating than other TCAs, has less antimuscarinic adverse effects, and requires minimal dosage titration [Taylor et al, 2001].
- **Imipramine** is less sedating than other TCAs and is an inexpensive choice for people who require an antidepressant with little sedation [Taylor et al, 2001]. However, it should not be used in people at risk of suicide.
- **Amitriptyline** is an inexpensive choice when a sedative antidepressant is required. However, it should not be used in people at risk of suicide.

Heterocyclic antidepressants

- **Trazodone** is highly sedating. It has no antimuscarinic adverse effects and therefore may be suitable in some elderly people, particularly when sedation is required. However, there is less information available on toxicity if taken in overdose compared with lofepramine [Mason et al, 2000].

SSRIs

- **Citalopram** has less potential for drug interactions than paroxetine or fluoxetine and does not interact with alcohol [Taylor et al, 2001].
- **Fluoxetine** has a long half-life. This may be an advantage when compliance is a problem. Insomnia, agitation, weight loss, and rash may be slightly more common than with other SSRIs [Edwards and Anderson, 1999; Taylor et al, 2001]. It does not interact with alcohol.
- **Paroxetine** is commonly used in the UK. Extrapyramidal symptoms are relatively rare, but are reported to the CSM more frequently with paroxetine than with other

SSRIs. Discontinuation symptoms are also reported more frequently with paroxetine than with other SSRIs [CSM, 2000b]. However, the CSM points out that spontaneous reporting cannot provide a reliable estimate of the frequency of discontinuation problems, as many factors affect the level of recording with different drugs.

- **Sertraline** has less potential for interactions than paroxetine or fluoxetine and does not interact with alcohol [Taylor et al, 2001].

D

Prescriptions

Start amitriptyline – sedative (NOT if suicide risk)

Amitriptyline: titrate from 25mg to 100mg at night in 2weeks

- Age from 18 years onwards
- Amitriptyline 25mg tablets. Take 1 tab at night for 4 nights, then take 2 tabs at night for 4 nights, then take 3 tabs at night for 4 nights, then take 4 tabs at night; supply 32 tablets; NHS Cost £0.93.

Amitriptyline: 25mg for 7 nights, then 50mg at night

- Age from 18 years onwards
- Amitriptyline 25mg tablets. Take one tablet at night for 7 nights, then take two tablets at night for 7 nights, then increase the dose as instructed by your doctor; supply 21 tablets; NHS Cost £0.61.

Start imipramine – less sedative (NOT if suicide risk)

Imipramine: titrate from 25mg to 100mg at night in 2weeks

- Age from 18 years onwards
- Imipramine 25mg tablets. Take 1 tab at night for 4 nights, then take 2 tabs at night for 4 nights, then take 3 tabs at night for 4 nights, then take 4 tabs at night; supply 32 tablets; NHS Cost £1.15.

Imipramine: 25mg for 7 nights, then 50mg at night

- Age from 18 years onwards
- Imipramine 25mg tablets. Take one tablet at night for 7 nights, then take two tablets at night for 7 nights, then increase the dose as instructed by your doctor; supply 21 tablets; NHS Cost £0.76.

Start lofepramine (less sedative) / trazodone (sedative)

Lofepramine 70mg at night (low dose)

- Age from 65 years onwards
- Lofepramine 70mg tablets. Take one tablet at night; supply 14 tablets; NHS Cost £2.54.

Lofepramine: 70mg for 4 nights, then 140mg at night

- Age from 18 years onwards
- Lofepramine 70mg tablets. Take one tablet at night for 4 nights, then take two tablets at night; supply 24 tablets; NHS Cost £4.50.

Lofepramine: 70mg for 7 nights, then 140mg at night

- Age from 18 years onwards
- Lofepramine 70mg tablets. Take one tablet at night for 7 nights, then take two tablets at night; supply 21 tablets; NHS Cost £3.81.

Trazodone: 50mg for 7 nights, then 100mg at night

- Age from 65 years onwards
- Trazodone 50mg capsules. Take one capsule at night for 7 nights, then take two capsules at night; supply 21 capsules; NHS Cost £4.27.

Trazodone: titrate from 50mg to 150mg at night over 8 nights

- Age from 18 years onwards
- Trazodone 50mg capsules. Take one capsule at night for 4 nights, then take two capsules at night for 4 nights, then take three capsules at night; supply 30 capsules; NHS Cost £6.10.

Start SSRI

Citalopram 20mg once a day

- Age from 18 years onwards
- Citalopram 20mg tablets. Take one tablet once a day; supply 14 tablets; NHS Cost £8.02.

Fluoxetine 20mg once a day

- Age from 18 years onwards
- Fluoxetine 20mg capsules. Take one capsule once a day supply 15 capsules; NHS Cost £3.72.

Paroxetine 20mg each morning

- Age from 18 years onwards
- Paroxetine 20mg tablets. Take one tablet each morning supply 15 tablets; NHS Cost £7.58.

Sertraline 50mg once a day

- Age from 18 years onwards
- Sertraline 50mg tablets. Take one tablet once a day; supply 14 tablets; NHS Cost £8.10.

Dysthymia (+ starting dosages antidepressants)

Which therapy?

- **Dysthymia is a chronic milder depressive disorder** (at least 2 years of depressive symptoms not meeting DSM–IV criteria for major depression), which is not a consequence of a partially resolved major depression.
- **Antidepressants are a preferred treatment.**
- **Psychological treatments are of uncertain value** and are therefore not recommended for preferred use.
- Tricyclic antidepressants (TCAs), trazodone, and selective serotonin re-uptake inhibitors (SSRIs) are suitable first-choice antidepressants.
- **Choice should be determined by individual patient factors,** including likelihood of adverse effects, comorbidity, concomitant medication, and preference o the individual.
- **Lofepramine, trazodone, or an SSRI are preferable if there is a concern about suicide risk,** as these are associated with the lowest risk of fatal poisoning. However, if suicide risk is a genuine concern admission should be strongly considered, especially if the person has poor social support.
- **If there has been a previous good response to a particula drug it is sensible to prescribe this again.** Similarly, if a person has previously failed to respond to or could not tolerate the adverse effects of a particular drug, it is best avoided.

Practical prescribing points

For further information see the *Medicines Compendium* (www.medicines.org.uk) or the *British National Formular* (www.bnf.org).

- **Suspected risk of overdose:** lofepramine, trazodone, or an SSRI are preferred choices.
- **Driving:** the Driver and Vehicle Licensing Agency (DVLA) recommends avoiding drugs that have antimuscarinic effects, such as TCAs. SSRIs are less likely to cause sedation, but some people have idiosyncratic responses. All people taking antidepressants should be advised not to drive if adversely affected, particularly during the first month o starting or increasing the dosage.
- **Elderly people:** TCAs (other than lofepramine) may be less suitable owing to their antimuscarinic adverse effects.

Pregnancy: use amitriptyline or imipramine. If an SSRI is essential, use fluoxetine. Contact the National Teratology Information Service (0191 232 1525) for further information.
Cardiac disease: SSRIs may be preferred to TCAs, but use with caution.
Epilepsy: SSRIs may be preferred to TCAs, but use with caution.
Known or suspected bipolar disorder: caution with TCAs and SSRIs (may precipitate mania).
Prostatism, narrow-angle glaucoma, urinary retention: use an SSRI or trazodone.
Weight gain is more likely with TCAs than with SSRIs.
Sexual dysfunction is more likely with SSRIs than with TCAs.
Priapism has been reported rarely with trazodone. Trazodone should be discontinued immediately if priapism occurs.
Hyponatraemia is associated with both TCAs and SSRIs. More common in elderly people or those taking diuretics. Consider hyponatraemia in all people who develop drowsiness, confusion, or convulsions while taking an antidepressant.

ollow-up advice

Follow up should initially be every 1–2 weeks, at least for the first 4–6 weeks, to monitor progress and to ensure medication is being tolerated.
Duration of treatment should usually be for at least 6 months from resolution of main symptoms, but is frequently required for longer periods owing to persistent residual symptoms.

hould I refer or investigate?

efer?

Consider referral if the person is not responding to treatment, or if there is diagnostic uncertainty (e.g. physical symptoms or signs not consistent with a diagnosis of depressive disorder).

atient information leaflets

he following PILs are available at www.prodigy.nhs.uk
Antidepressants - SSRIs
Antidepressants - St John's Wort
Antidepressants - Tricyclic
Anxiety Disorders
Anxiety - Generalised Anxiety Disorder
Association for Post-Natal Illness
Cognitive Behaviour Therapy (CBT)
Depression
Depression Alliance
Depression - A Summary
Depression (Post-Natal)
Fellowship of Depressives Anonymous
MAMA - Meet-A-Mum Association
Manic Depression Fellowship
Phobia - Agoraphobia
Phobia - Social Phobia
Post-Traumatic Stress Disorder
Psychosomatic Disorders
SAD Association (Seasonal Affective Disorder)
Seasonal Affective Disorder
Somatization and Somatoform Disorders

Shared decision making

- You have an ongoing low mood that is called dysthymia.
- **Antidepressants** are often effective. They take 4–6 weeks to work fully. A course for at least 6 months after symptoms improve is usual.
- **A tricyclic antidepressant** (TCA), such as amitriptyline, imipramine, or lofepramine, is commonly prescribed.
- **A selective serotonin re-uptake inhibitor (SSRI) antidepressant** (such as citalopram, fluoxetine, paroxetine, and sertraline) or **trazodone** is an alternative.
- The choice of antidepressant may depend on your age, previous use of antidepressants, possible side effects, other medicines that you take, other medical conditions that you have, and personal preference. If one does not suit at first, a change to a different one is an option.
- Side effects are often minor or improve in time. The packet insert lists all possible side effects.
  - Tricyclics: common side effects include slight drowsiness, a dry mouth, and blurred vision.
  - SSRIs: an upset stomach is the commonest side effect.
- **Counselling** for specific problems, such as relationship difficulties, may be an option in some cases.

Drug rationale

The choice of antidepressant should be determined by individual patient factors, including likelihood of adverse effects, comorbidity, concomitant medication, and preference of the individual.

Drugs not included

- **Tricyclic antidepressants (TCAs) other than amitriptyline, imipramine, and lofepramine:** other TCAs are more expensive than amitriptyline or imipramine without offering any significant advantage in terms of their adverse effect profiles (i.e. sedation compared with no sedation). The exception is lofepramine, which although more expensive causes fewer antimuscarinic adverse effects and has low toxicity in overdose.
- **Heterocyclic antidepressants other than trazodone:** maprotiline is more likely to cause seizures or rashes than TCAs [CSM, 1985]. Seizures have occurred in people with no past history of seizure disorders. Mianserin is associated with blood dyscrasias and clinical monitoring of blood counts is required during treatment [BNF 41, 2001].
- **Fluvoxamine:** a recent systematic review found that fluvoxamine was poorly tolerated compared with other selective serotonin re uptake inhibitors (SSRIs). The overall incidence of adverse effects was similar, suggesting that poor tolerability was due to the severity rather than the frequency of adverse effects [Edwards and Anderson, 1999].
- **Newer antidepressants** (such as mirtazapine, nefazodone, reboxetine, and venlafaxine): These may have a place when first-choice drugs are poorly tolerated or ineffective. However, further experience and studies are required to confirm their precise role in primary care [MeReC, 2000].
- **Monoamine-oxidase inhibitors (MAOIs):** these have considerable dietary and drug interactions and are therefore not included as first-choice agents.
- **Reversible MAOIs:** moclobemide should be reserved as a second-line treatment [BNF 41, 2001]. Tyramine-rich foods and sympathomimetics still need to be avoided while taking moclobemide, despite its lower potential for interactions.

Drugs included

TCAs

- **Lofepramine** is a suitable choice in people at risk of suicide [Eccles et al, 1998; Eccles et al, 1999; Mason et al, 2000]. Lofepramine is also less sedating than other TCAs, has fewer antimuscarinic adverse effects, and requires minimal dosage titration [Taylor et al, 2001].
- **Imipramine** is less sedating than other TCAs and is an inexpensive choice for people who require an antidepressant with little sedation [Taylor et al, 2001]. However, it should not be used in people at risk of suicide.
- **Amitriptyline** is an inexpensive choice when a sedative antidepressant is required. However, it should not be used in people at risk of suicide.

Heterocyclic antidepressants

- **Trazodone** is highly sedating. It has no antimuscarinic adverse effects and therefore may be suitable in some elderly people, particularly when sedation is required. However, there is less information available on toxicity if taken in overdose compared with lofepramine [Mason et al, 2000].

SSRIs

- **Citalopram** has less potential for drug interactions than paroxetine or fluoxetine and does not interact with alcohol [Taylor et al, 2001].
- **Fluoxetine** has a long half-life. This may be an advantage when compliance is a problem. Insomnia, agitation, weight loss, and rash may be slightly more common than with other SSRIs [Edwards and Anderson, 1999; Taylor et al, 2001]. It does not interact with alcohol.
- **Paroxetine** is commonly used in the UK. Extrapyramidal adverse effects are relatively rare, but are reported to the CSM more frequently with paroxetine than with other SSRIs. Discontinuation symptoms are also reported more frequently with paroxetine than with other SSRIs [CSM, 2000b]. However, the CSM points out that spontaneous reporting cannot provide a reliable estimate of the frequency of discontinuation problems, as many factors affect the level of recording with different drugs.
- **Sertraline** has less potential for interactions than paroxetine or fluoxetine and does not interact with alcohol [Taylor et al, 2001].

Prescriptions

Start amitriptyline – sedative (NOT if suicide risk)

Amitriptyline: titrate from 25mg to 100mg at night in 2weeks

- Age from 18 years onwards
- Amitriptyline 25mg tablets. Take 1 tab at night for 4 nights, then take 2 tabs at night for 4 nights, then take 3 tabs at night for 4 nights, then take 4 tabs at night; supply 32 tablets; NHS Cost £0.93.

Amitriptyline: 25mg for 7 nights, then 50mg at night

- Age from 18 years onwards
- Amitriptyline 25mg tablets. Take one tablet at night for 7 nights, then take two tablets at night for 7 nights, then increase the dose as instructed by your doctor; supply 21 tablets; NHS Cost £0.61.

Start imipramine – less sedative (NOT if suicide risk)

Imipramine: titrate from 25mg to 100mg at night in 2 weeks

- Age from 18 years onwards
- Imipramine 25mg tablets. Take 1 tab at night for 4 nights, then take 2 tabs at night for 4 nights, then take tabs at night for 4 nights, then take 4 tabs at night; supply 32 tablets; NHS Cost £1.15.

Imipramine: 25mg for 7 nights, then 50mg at night

- Age from 18 years onwards
- Imipramine 25mg tablets. Take one tablet at night for 7 nights, then take two tablets at night for 7 nights, then increase the dose as instructed by your doctor; supply 2 tablets; NHS Cost £0.76.

Start lofepramine (less sedative) / trazodone (sedative)

Lofepramine 70mg at night (low dose)

- Age from 65 years onwards
- Lofepramine 70mg tablets. Take one tablet at night; supply 14 tablets; NHS Cost £2.54.

Lofepramine: 70mg for 4 nights, then 140mg at night

- Age from 18 years onwards
- Lofepramine 70mg tablets. Take one tablet at night for nights, then take two tablets at night; supply 24 tablets; NHS Cost £4.50.

Lofepramine: 70mg for 7 nights, then 140mg at night

- Age from 18 years onwards
- Lofepramine 70mg tablets. Take one tablet at night for nights, then take two tablets at night; supply 21 tablets; NHS Cost £3.81.

Trazodone: 50mg for 7 nights, then 100mg at night

- Age from 65 years onwards
- Trazodone 50mg capsules. Take one capsule at night fo 7 nights, then take two capsules at night; supply 21 capsules; NHS Cost £4.27.

Trazodone: titrate from 50mg to 150mg at night over 8 nights

- Age from 18 years onwards
- Trazodone 50mg capsules. Take one capsule at night fo 4 nights, then take two capsules at night for 4 nights, then take three capsules at night; supply 30 capsules; NHS Cost £6.10.

Start SSRI

Citalopram 20mg once a day

- Age from 18 years onwards
- Citalopram 20mg tablets. Take one tablet once a day; supply 14 tablets; NHS Cost £8.02.

Fluoxetine 20mg once a day

- Age from 18 years onwards
- Fluoxetine 20mg capsules. Take one capsule once a day supply 15 capsules; NHS Cost £3.72.

Paroxetine 20mg each morning

- Age from 18 years onwards
- Paroxetine 20mg tablets. Take one tablet each morning supply 15 tablets; NHS Cost £7.58.

Sertraline 50mg once a day

- Age from 18 years onwards
- Sertraline 50mg tablets. Take one tablet once a day; supply 14 tablets; NHS Cost £8.10.

Milder depression (+ starting dosages antidepressants)

Which therapy?

Milder depression is usually diagnosed in people with recent onset depressive symptoms that do not meet the DMS–IV criteria for major depression. The depressed mood often develops following an identifiable stressor, but the degree of distress exceeds the level expected and social or occupational functioning may be impaired.

Support and simple problem solving are often adequate. Antidepressants or specific psychological treatments are seldom indicated at initial presentation. However, if there is a history of major depression, early treatment with antidepressants should be considered.

If symptoms persist, a trial of antidepressants should be considered.

If medication is necessary:

- Tricyclic antidepressants (TCAs), trazodone, and selective serotonin re-uptake inhibitors (SSRIs) are suitable first-choice antidepressants.
- **Choice should be determined by individual patient factors,** including likelihood of adverse effects, comorbidity, concomitant medication, and preference of the individual.
- **Lofepramine, trazodone, or an SSRI are preferable if there is a concern about suicide risk,** as these are associated with the lowest risk of fatal poisoning. However, if suicide risk is a genuine concern, admission should be strongly considered, especially if the person has poor social support.
- **If there has been a previous good response to a particular drug it is sensible to prescribe this again.** Similarly, if a person has previously failed to respond to or could not tolerate the adverse effects of a particular drug, it is best avoided.

Practical prescribing points

For further information see the *Medicines Compendium* (www.medicines.org.uk) or the *British National Formulary* (www.bnf.org).

Suspected risk of overdose: lofepramine, trazodone, or an SSRI are preferred choices.

Driving: the Driver and Vehicle Licensing Agency (DVLA) recommends avoiding drugs that have antimuscarinic effects, such as TCAs. SSRIs are less likely to cause sedation, but some people have idiosyncratic responses. All people taking antidepressants should be advised not to drive if adversely affected, particularly during the first month of starting or increasing the dosage.

Elderly people: TCAs (other than lofepramine) may be less suitable owing to their antimuscarinic adverse effects.

Pregnancy: use amitriptyline or imipramine. If an SSRI is essential, use fluoxetine. Contact the National Teratology Information Service (0191 232 1525) for further information.

Cardiac disease: SSRIs may be preferred to TCAs, but use with caution.

Epilepsy: SSRIs may be preferred to TCAs, but use with caution.

Known/suspected bipolar disorder: caution with TCAs and SSRIs (may precipitate mania).

Prostatism, narrow-angle glaucoma, urinary retention: use an SSRI or trazodone.

Weight gain is more likely with TCAs than with SSRIs.

Sexual dysfunction is more likely with SSRIs than with TCAs.

- **Priapism** has been reported rarely with trazodone. Trazodone should be discontinued immediately if priapism occurs.
- **Hyponatraemia** is associated with both TCAs and SSRIs. More common in the elderly or those taking diuretics. Consider hyponatraemia in all people who develop drowsiness, confusion, or convulsions while taking an antidepressant.

Follow-up advice

- **Follow-up should initially be every 1–2 weeks,** at least for the first 4–6 weeks, to monitor progress and to ensure medication is being tolerated.
- **Duration of treatment** should usually be for at least 6 months from resolution of main symptoms.

Should I refer or investigate?

Refer?

- **Consider** referring for specific psychological treatment if not settling with support and simple problem solving or an adequate trial of medication.

Patient information leaflets

The following PILs are available at www.prodigy.nhs.uk

- Antidepressants - SSRIs
- Antidepressants - St John's Wort
- Antidepressants - Tricyclic
- Anxiety Disorders
- Anxiety - Generalised Anxiety Disorder
- Association for Post-Natal Illness
- Cognitive Behaviour Therapy (CBT)
- Depression
- Depression Alliance
- Depression - A Summary
- Depression (Post-Natal)
- Fellowship of Depressives Anonymous
- MAMA - Meet-A-Mum Association
- Manic Depression Fellowship
- Phobia - Agoraphobia
- Phobia - Social Phobia
- Post-Traumatic Stress Disorder
- Psychosomatic Disorders
- SAD Association (Seasonal Affective Disorder)
- Seasonal Affective Disorder
- Somatization and Somatoform Disorders

Shared decision making

- **Depression is common** after a stressful event and most people recover naturally.
- **Talking things through** with family, friends, or a counsellor is often helpful.
- **Antidepressants** may be needed if symptoms do not improve. See a doctor if symptoms do not ease over the next few weeks.
- **If antidepressants are needed** they take 4–6 weeks to work fully. A course for at least 6 months after symptoms improve is usual.
- **A tricyclic antidepressant** (TCA) such as amitriptyline, imipramine, or lofepramine, is commonly prescribed.
- **A selective serotonin re-uptake inhibitor (SSRI) antidepressant** (such as citalopram, fluoxetine, paroxetine, and sertraline) or **trazodone** is an alternative.
- The choice of antidepressant may depend on your age, previous use of antidepressants, possible side effects, other medicines that you take, other medical conditions that you have, and personal preference. If one

antidepressant does not suit at first, a change to a different one is an option.

- Side effects are often minor or improve in time. The packet insert lists all possible side effects.
  - Tricyclics — common side effects include slight drowsiness, a dry mouth, and blurred vision.
  - SSRIs — an upset stomach is the commonest side effect.
- **Counselling** for specific problems, such as relationship difficulties, may be an option in some cases.

Drug rationale

The choice of antidepressant should be determined by individual patient factors, including likelihood of adverse effects, comorbidity, concomitant medication, and preference of the individual.

Drugs not included

- **Tricyclic antidepressants (TCAs) other than amitriptyline, imipramine, and lofepramine:** other TCAs are more expensive than amitriptyline or imipramine without offering any significant advantage in terms of their adverse effect profiles (i.e. sedation compared with no sedation). The exception is lofepramine, which although more expensive causes fewer antimuscarinic adverse effects and has low toxicity in overdose.
- **Heterocyclic antidepressants other than trazodone: maprotiline** is more likely to cause seizures or rashes than TCAs [CSM, 1985]. Seizures have occurred in people with no past history of seizure disorders. Mianserin is associated with blood dyscrasias and clinical monitoring of blood counts is required during treatment [BNF 41, 2001].
- **Fluvoxamine:** a recent systematic review found that fluvoxamine was poorly tolerated compared with other **selective serotonin re-uptake inhibitors** (SSRIs). The overall incidence of adverse effects was similar, suggesting that poor tolerability was due to the severity rather than the frequency of adverse effects [Edwards and Anderson, 1999].
- **Newer antidepressants** (such as mirtazapine, nefazodone, reboxetine, and venlafaxine): These may have a place when first-choice drugs are poorly tolerated or ineffective. However, further experience and studies are required to confirm their precise role in primary care [MeReC, 2000].
- **Monoamine-oxidase inhibitors (MAOIs):** these have considerable dietary and drug interactions and are therefore not included as first-choice agents.
- **Reversible MAOIs:** moclobemide should be reserved as a second-line treatment [BNF 41, 2001]. Tyramine-rich foods and sympathomimetics still need to be avoided while taking moclobemide, despite its lower potential for interactions.

Drugs included

TCAs

- **Lofepramine** is a suitable choice in people at risk of suicide [Eccles et al, 1999; Mason et al, 2000]. Lofepramine is also less sedating than other TCAs, has fewer antimuscarinic adverse effects, and requires minimal dosage titration [Taylor et al, 2001].
- **Imipramine** is less sedating than other TCAs and is an inexpensive choice for people who require an antidepressant with little sedation [Taylor et al, 2001]. However, it should not be used in people at risk of suicide.
- **Amitriptyline** is an inexpensive choice when a sedative antidepressant is required. However, it should not be used in people at risk of suicide.

Heterocyclic antidepressants

- **Trazodone** is highly sedating. It has no antimuscarinic adverse effects and therefore may be suitable in some elderly people, particularly when sedation is required. However, there is less information available on toxicity if taken in overdose compared with lofepramine [Maso et al, 2000].

SSRIs

- **Citalopram** has less potential for drug interactions than paroxetine or fluoxetine and does not interact with alcohol [Taylor et al, 2001].
- **Fluoxetine** has a long half-life. This may be an advanta when compliance is a problem. Insomnia, agitation, weight loss, and rash may be slightly more common tha with other SSRIs [Edwards and Anderson, 1999; Taylo et al, 2001]. Fluoxetine does not interact with alcohol.
- **Paroxetine** is commonly used in the UK. Extrapyramida adverse effects are relatively rare, but are reported to th CSM more frequently with paroxetine than with other SSRIs. Discontinuation symptoms are also reported mo frequently with paroxetine than with other SSRIs [CSM 2000b]. However, the CSM points out that spontaneou reporting cannot provide a reliable estimate of the frequency of discontinuation problems, as many factors affect the level of recording with different drugs.
- **Sertraline** has less potential for interactions than paroxetine or fluoxetine and does not interact with alcohol [Taylor et al, 2001].

Prescriptions

Non-drug management

Advice only: antidepressants often not needed

- Age from 18 years onwards
- Mild depression is common. Most people recover naturally. It is best not to bottle things up. Talking thin through with family or friends is often helpful, particularly if a recent stressful event is the cause. Regular exercise is thought to help ease depression. Try and distract yourself by doing things that do not need much concentration, for example, watching TV or listening to the radio. Don't drink too much alcohol. This can be tempting as the immediate effect may seem to help. However alcohol is a depressor drug and will always make things worse in the long run. Sometimes a traumatic event in the past may lead to depression even years later. Tell your doctor if you feel something like this is the root cause. Counselling may be available. Antidepressants may help if symptoms do not improve. See a doctor if you do not improve over the next few weeks.

Start amitriptyline – sedative (NOT if suicide risk)

Amitriptyline: titrate from 25mg to 100mg at night in 2weeks

- Age from 18 years onwards
- Amitriptyline 25mg tablets. Take 1 tab at night for 4 nights, then take 2 tabs at night for 4 nights, then take tabs at night for 4 nights, then take 4 tabs at night; supply 32 tablets; NHS Cost £0.93.

Amitriptyline: 25mg for 7 nights, then 50mg at night

- Age from 18 years onwards
- Amitriptyline 25mg tablets. Take one tablet at night fo 7 nights, then take two tablets at night for 7 nights, the

increase the dose as instructed by your doctor; supply 21 tablets; NHS Cost £0.61.

tart imipramine – less sedative (NOT if suicide isk)

ipramine: titrate from 25mg to 100mg at night in 2 eeks

Age from 18 years onwards
Imipramine 25mg tablets. Take 1 tab at night for 4 nights, then take 2 tabs at night for 4 nights, then take 3 tabs at night for 4 nights, then take 4 tabs at night; supply 40 tablets; NHS Cost £1.44.

ipramine: 25mg for 7 nights, then 50mg at night

Age from 18 years onwards
Imipramine 25mg tablets. Take one tablet at night for 7 nights, then take two tablets at night for 7 nights, then increase the dose as instructed by your doctor; supply 21 tablets; NHS Cost £0.76.

tart lofepramine (less sedative) / trazodone sedative)

ofepramine 70mg at night (low dose)

Age from 65 years onwards
Lofepramine 70mg tablets. Take one tablet at night; supply 14 tablets; NHS Cost £2.54.

ofepramine: 70mg for 4 nights, then 140mg at night

Age from 18 years onwards
Lofepramine 70mg tablets. Take one tablet at night for 4 nights, then take two tablets at night; supply 24 tablets; NHS Cost £4.50.

ofepramine: 70mg for 7 nights, then 140mg at night

Age from 18 years onwards
Lofepramine 70mg tablets. Take one tablet at night for 7 nights, then take two tablets at night; supply 21 tablets; NHS Cost £3.81.

azodone: 50mg for 7 nights, then 100mg at night

Age from 65 years onwards
Trazodone 50mg capsules. Take one capsule at night for 7 nights, then take two capsules at night; supply 21 capsules; NHS Cost £4.27.

azodone: titrate from 50mg to 150mg at night over 8 ghts

Age from 18 years onwards
Trazodone 50mg capsules. Take one capsule at night for 4 nights, then take two capsules at night for 4 nights, then take three capsules at night; supply 30 capsules; NHS Cost £6.10.

tart SSRI

italopram 20mg once a day

Age from 18 years onwards
Citalopram 20mg tablets. Take one tablet once a day; supply 14 tablets; NHS Cost £8.02.

uoxetine 20mg once a day

Age from 18 years onwards
Fluoxetine 20mg capsules. Take one capsule once a day; supply 15 capsules; NHS Cost £3.72.

aroxetine 20mg each morning

Age from 18 years onwards
Paroxetine 20mg tablets. Take one tablet each morning; supply 15 tablets; NHS Cost £7.58.

ertraline 50mg once a day

Age from 18 years onwards
Sertraline 50mg tablets. Take one tablet once a day; supply 14 tablets; NHS Cost £8.10.

Postnatal depression (+ starting dosages antidepressants)

Which therapy?

- Manage postnatal depression in the same way as depression at any other time.
- Ensure that other relevant health professionals such as health visitors are involved.
- **Support and problem solving are often adequate for milder depression** (where the degree of distress exceeds the level expected and social or occupational functioning are impaired, but symptoms do not meet the DMS–IV criteria for major depression).
- **Psychological interventions are alternatives in women with mild to moderate depression.** Non-directive counselling (supportive listening without giving opinions or advice) may be sufficient. Some women may benefit from brief interventions using cognitive behavioural or problem-solving approaches, or interpersonal therapy.
- Antidepressants are a preferred treatment for more severe depression.
- The decision whether to choose antidepressants or psychological treatments will depend on availability and patient preference.
- If there is concern of a risk of suicide or infanticide, refer the mother to mental health services, preferably to relevant specialist teams.
- **If medication is necessary:**
  - Tricyclic antidepressants (TCAs), trazodone, and selective serotonin re-uptake inhibitors (SSRIs) are suitable first-choice antidepressants.
  - **Choice should be determined by individual patient factors,** including likelihood of adverse effects, comorbidity, concomitant medication, and preference of the individual.
  - **If there has been a previous good response to a particular drug it is sensible to prescribe this again.** Similarly, if a person has previously failed to respond to or could not tolerate the adverse effects of a particular drug, it is best avoided.
  - Imipramine is the preferred TCA and paroxetine the preferred SSRI for breastfeeding mothers.

Practical prescribing points

For further information see the *Medicines Compendium* (www.medicines.org.uk) or the *British National Formulary* (www.bnf.org).

- **Breastfeeding:** no drug is recommended by its manufacturer for use whilst breastfeeding. Limited evidence suggests no short-term toxic effects to the infant, and long-term developmental effects have not been demonstrated. Imipramine is the preferred TCA and paroxetine the preferred SSRI. Contact the West Midland Medicines Information Service (0121 311 1974) for further information.
- **Driving:** the Driver and Vehicle Licensing Agency (DVLA) recommends avoiding drugs that have antimuscarinic effects, such as TCAs. SSRIs are less likely to cause sedation, but some people have idiosyncratic responses. All people taking antidepressants should be advised not to drive if adversely affected, particularly during the first month of starting or increasing the dosage.
- **Pregnancy:** use amitriptyline or imipramine. If an SSRI is essential, use fluoxetine. Contact the National Teratology Information Service (0191 232 1525) for further information.
- **Cardiac disease:** SSRIs may be preferred to TCAs, but use with caution.

- **Epilepsy:** SSRIs may be preferred to TCAs, but use with caution.
- **Known/suspected bipolar disorder:** caution with TCAs and SSRIs (may precipitate mania).
- **Narrow-angle glaucoma, urinary retention:** use an SSRI or trazodone.
- **Weight gain** is more likely with TCAs than with SSRIs.
- **Hyponatraemia** is associated with both TCAs and SSRIs. More common in those taking diuretics. Consider hyponatraemia in all people who develop drowsiness, confusion, or convulsions while taking an antidepressant.

Follow-up advice

- **Follow-up should initially be every 1–2 weeks** depending on the severity of depression (for at least the first 4–6 weeks) to monitor progress and ensure medication is tolerated.
- **For a first episode of major depression,** medication should be continued at full antidepressant dosage until the person has been free of major symptoms for at least 6 months. A longer treatment course is recommended in people with residual symptoms, and those with a history of depression.
- Maintenance treatment reduces the risk of recurrence and is indicated in people with:
    - Three or more episodes of major depression in the past 5 years.
    - More than five episodes altogether.
    - Fewer recurrent depressive episodes but with persistent risk factors for relapse or recurrence (e.g. continued psychosocial issues).
- Maintenance treatment should be continued at the same dosage that was used to treat the acute episode and continued for at least 5 years and possibly indefinitely.

Should I refer or investigate?

Refer?

- **Urgently refer** mother to mental health services, preferably to relevant specialist teams such as mother and baby units, if there is risk of suicide or infanticide.
- **Admit** if there are psychotic features (delusions, hallucinations) or stupor.
- **Consider referral** of mother and baby at less obvious risk of suicide but with poor social support.
- **Consider referral** if the person is not responding to treatment, or if there is diagnostic uncertainty (e.g. physical symptoms or signs not consistent with a diagnosis of depression).

Patient information leaflets

The following PILs are available at www.prodigy.nhs.uk

- Antidepressants - St John's Wort
- Cognitive Behaviour Therapy (CBT)
- Depression
- Depression Alliance
- Depression - A Summary
- Depression (Post-Natal)
- MAMA - Meet-A-Mum Association

Shared decision making

- **Depression is common.** Most people recover but treatment speeds recovery.
- **Talking things through** with family, friends, or a counsellor is often helpful.
- **Antidepressants** are usually effective. They take 4–6 weeks to work fully. A course for at least 6 months after symptoms improve is usual.
- **A tricyclic antidepressant (TCA),** such as amitriptyline, imipramine, or lofepramine, is commonly prescribed.
- **A selective serotonin re-uptake inhibitor (SSRI) antidepressant** (such as citalopram, fluoxetine, paroxetine, and sertraline) is an alternative.
- The choice of antidepressant may depend on your age, previous use of antidepressants, possible side effects, other medicines that you take, other medical conditions that you have, and personal preference. If one antidepressant does not suit at first, a change to a different one is an option.
- Side effects are often minor or improve in time. The packet insert lists all possible side effects.
    - TCAs: common side effects include slight drowsiness, a dry mouth and blurred vision.
    - SSRIs: an upset stomach is the commonest side effect.
- **Talking treatments** such as cognitive therapy, psychotherapy, or counselling for specific problems such as relationship difficulties may be options in some cases.
- See a doctor if you get worse, feel suicidal, or develop persistent troublesome side effects.

Drug rationale

The choice of antidepressant should be determined by individual patient factors, including likelihood of adverse effects, comorbidity, concomitant medication, and preference of the individual.

Drugs not included

- **Tricyclic antidepressants (TCAs) other than amitriptyline, imipramine, and lofepramine:** other TCA are more expensive than amitriptyline or imipramine without offering any significant advantage in terms of their adverse effect profiles (i.e. sedation compared with no sedation). The exception is lofepramine, which although more expensive causes fewer antimuscarinic adverse effects and has low toxicity in overdose.
- **Heterocyclic antidepressants other than trazodone:** maprotiline is more likely to cause seizures or rashes than TCAs [CSM, 1985]. Seizures have occurred in people with no past history of seizure disorders. Mianserin is associated with blood dyscrasias and clinical monitoring of blood counts is required during treatment [BNF 41, 2001].
- **Fluvoxamine:** a recent systematic review found that fluvoxamine was poorly tolerated compared with other **selective serotonin re-uptake inhibitor** (SSRIs). The overall incidence of adverse effects was similar, suggesting that poor tolerability was due to the severity rather than the frequency of adverse effects [Edwards and Anderson, 1999].
- **Newer antidepressants** (such as mirtazapine, nefazodone, reboxetine, and venlafaxine): These may have a place when first-choice drugs are poorly tolerated or ineffective. However, further experience and studies are required to confirm their precise role in primary care [MeReC, 2000].
- **Monoamine-oxidase inhibitors (MAOIs):** these have considerable dietary and drug interactions and are therefore not included as first-choice agents.
- **Reversible MAOIs:** moclobemide should be reserved as second-line treatment [BNF 41, 2001]. Tyramine-rich foods and sympathomimetics still need to be avoided while taking moclobemide, despite its lower potential for interactions.

)rugs included

TCAs

Lofepramine is less sedating than other TCAs, has fewer antimuscarinic adverse effects, and requires minimal dosage titration [Taylor et al, 2001].
Imipramine is less sedating than other TCAs and is an inexpensive choice for people who require an antidepressant with little sedation [Taylor et al, 2001]. However, it should not be used in people at risk of suicide. Imipramine is the preferred TCA for mothers who breastfeed [BNF 41, 2001].
Amitriptyline is an inexpensive choice when a sedative antidepressant is required. However, it should not be used in people at risk of suicide.

Heterocyclic antidepressants

Trazodone is highly sedating. It has no antimuscarinic adverse effects and therefore may be suitable in some elderly people, particularly when sedation is required. However, there is less information available on toxicity if taken in overdose compared with lofepramine [Mason et al, 2000].

SSRIs

Paroxetine is commonly used in the UK. Extrapyramidal adverse effects are relatively rare, but are reported to the Committee on Safety of Medicines (CSM) more frequently with paroxetine than with other SSRIs. Discontinuation symptoms are also reported more frequently with paroxetine than with other SSRIs [CSM, 2000b]. However, the CSM points out that spontaneous reporting cannot provide a reliable estimate of the frequency of discontinuation problems, as many factors affect the level of recording with different drugs. Paroxetine produces low milk and infant plasma drug concentrations compared with other SSRIs.
Fluoxetine has a long half-life. This may be an advantage when compliance is a problem. Insomnia, agitation, weight loss, and rash may be slightly more common than with other SSRIs [Edwards and Anderson, 1999; Taylor et al, 2001]. It does not interact with alcohol.
Sertraline has less potential for interactions than paroxetine or fluoxetine and does not interact with alcohol [Taylor et al, 2001].
Citalopram has less potential for drug interactions than paroxetine or fluoxetine and does not interact with alcohol [Taylor et al, 2001]. There is very limited evidence on the use of citalopram whilst breastfeeding but the milk/maternal plasma ratio is relatively high.

'rescriptions

Breastfeeding: start preferred antidepressant

'aroxetine 20mg once a day
- Age from 18 years onwards
- Paroxetine 20mg tablets. Take one tablet once a day; supply 15 tablets; NHS Cost £7.58.

nipramine: titrate from 25mg to 100mg at night in 2 veeks
- Age from 18 years onwards
- Imipramine 25mg tablets. Take 1 tab at night for 4 nights, then take 2 tabs at night for 4 nights, then take 3 tabs at night for 4 nights, then take 4 tabs at night; supply 32 tablets; NHS Cost £1.15.

nipramine: 25mg for 7 nights, then 50mg at night
- Age from 18 years onwards
- Imipramine 25mg tablets. Take one tablet at night for 7 nights, then take two tablets at night for 7 nights, then increase the dose as instructed by your doctor; supply 21 tablets; NHS Cost £0.76.

Start amitriptyline – sedative (NOT if suicide risk)

Amitriptyline: titrate from 25mg to 100mg at night in 2weeks
- Age from 18 years onwards
- Amitriptyline 25mg tablets. Take 1 tab at night for 4 nights, then take 2 tabs at night for 4 nights, then take 3 tabs at night for 4 nights, then take 4 tabs at night; supply 32 tablets; NHS Cost £0.93.

Amitriptyline: 25mg for 7 nights, then 50mg at night
- Age from 18 years onwards
- Amitriptyline 25mg tablets. Take one tablet at night for 7 nights, then take two tablets at night for 7 nights, then increase the dose as instructed by your doctor; supply 21 tablets; NHS Cost £0.61.

Start imipramine – less sedative (NOT if suicide risk)

Imipramine: titrate from 25mg to 100mg at night in 2weeks
- Age from 18 years onwards
- Imipramine 25mg tablets. Take 1 tab at night for 4 nights, then take 2 tabs at night for 4 nights, then take 3 tabs at night for 4 nights, then take 4 tabs at night; supply 32 tablets; NHS Cost £1.15.

Imipramine: 25mg for 7 nights, then 50mg at night
- Age from 18 years onwards
- Imipramine 25mg tablets. Take one tablet at night for 7 nights, then take two tablets at night for 7 nights, then increase the dose as instructed by your doctor; supply 21 tablets; NHS Cost £0.76.

Start lofepramine or trazodone

Lofepramine: 70mg for 4 nights, then 140mg at night
- Age from 18 years onwards
- Lofepramine 70mg tablets. Take one tablet at night for 4 nights, then take two tablets at night; supply 24 tablets; NHS Cost £4.50.

Lofepramine: 70mg for 7 nights, then 140mg at night
- Age from 18 years onwards
- Lofepramine 70mg tablets. Take one tablet at night for 7 nights, then take two tablets at night; supply 21 tablets; NHS Cost £3.81.

Trazodone: titrate from 50mg to 150mg at night over 8 nights
- Age from 18 years onwards
- Trazodone 50mg capsules. Take one capsule at night for 4 nights, then take two capsules at night for 4 nights, then take three capsules at night; supply 30 capsules; NHS Cost £6.10.

Start SSRI

Citalopram 20mg once a day
- Age from 18 years onwards
- Citalopram 20mg tablets. Take one tablet once a day; supply 14 tablets; NHS Cost £8.02.

Fluoxetine 20mg once a day
- Age from 18 years onwards
- Fluoxetine 20mg capsules. Take one capsule once a day; supply 15 capsules; NHS Cost £3.72.

Paroxetine 20mg each morning
- Age from 18 years onwards
- Paroxetine 20mg tablets. Take one tablet each morning; supply 15 tablets; NHS Cost £7.58.

Sertraline 50mg once a day

- Age from 18 years onwards
- Sertraline 50mg tablets. Take one tablet once a day; supply 14 tablets; NHS Cost £8.10.

Maintenance/dosage adjustment (+ advice on poor response)

Which therapy?

D

The dosage of antidepressant may need increasing to reach the recommended therapeutic dosage, or because the person is not responding to the current dosage.

Recommended therapeutic dosage

- **The minimum recommended therapeutic dosage of tricyclic antidepressants (TCAs) is 125–150 mg daily.** Lower dosages may be appropriate in elderly people, as higher plasma concentrations for a given dosage are generally found.
- The starting dosage of a selective serotonin re-uptake inhibitor (SSRI) is usually the minimum recommended treatment dosage.
- **The recommended target dose of paroxetine is 20 mg daily.** Increasing the dose above this level does not seem to increase efficacy, increasing the dose soon after starting treatment may be detrimental. However, people who are already being successfully treated at higher doses should continue with the higher dose of paroxetine until the end of the planned course of treatment.
- **If a response occurs at a lower than target dosage of an antidepressant,** the dosage should still be increased to reduce the likelihood of relapse. If this is not possible, then the drug should be continued at the same dosage and the person monitored for relapse.

Non-response to treatment

- **Before deciding that a person is not responding,** treatment should be continued at an adequate dosage for at least 4 weeks, or 6 weeks in elderly people. If there is a partial response after this time, then treatment should be continued for another 2 weeks.
- **If not responding to treatment:** check adequacy of treatment, including dosage and compliance; review the diagnosis, including the possibility of additional physical or psychiatric conditions; and consider maintaining social factors.
- **If a person is failing to respond despite an adequate trial of treatment,** either increase the dosage further or switch to another antidepressant class (see separate scenario *Switching antidepressants*).
- **Psychological treatments should be considered if the person fails to respond to a second antidepressant.** Alternatively, augmentation treatment (e.g. the addition of lithium) or electroconvulsive therapy (ECT) can be considered, but requires psychiatric referral.

Practical prescribing points

For further information see the *Medicines Compendium* (www.medicines.org.uk) or the *British National Formulary* (www.bnf.org).

- **Suspected risk of overdose:** lofepramine, trazodone, or an SSRI are preferred choices.
- **Driving:** the Driver and Vehicle Licensing Agency (DVLA) recommends avoiding drugs that have antimuscarinic effects, such as TCAs. SSRIs are less likely to cause sedation, but some people have idiosyncratic responses. All people taking antidepressants should be advised not to drive if adversely affected, particularly during the first month of starting or increasing the dosage.
- **Elderly people:** TCAs (other than lofepramine) may be less suitable due to their antimuscarinic adverse effects.
- **Pregnancy:** use amitriptyline or imipramine. If an SSRI is essential, use fluoxetine. Contact the National Teratology Information Service (0191 232 1525) for further information.
- **Cardiac disease:** SSRIs may be preferred to TCAs, but use with caution.
- **Epilepsy:** SSRIs may be preferred to TCAs, but use with caution.
- **Known/suspected bipolar disorder:** caution with TCAs and SSRIs (may precipitate mania).
- **Prostatism, narrow-angle glaucoma, urinary retention:** use an SSRI or trazodone.
- **Weight gain** is more likely with TCAs than with SSRIs.
- **Sexual dysfunction** is more likely with SSRIs than with TCAs.
- **Priapism** has been reported rarely with trazodone. Trazodone should be discontinued immediately if priapism occurs.
- **Hyponatraemia** is associated with both TCAs and SSRIs. More common in the elderly or those taking diuretics. Consider hyponatraemia in all people who develop drowsiness, confusion, or convulsions while taking an antidepressant.

Follow-up advice

- **Follow-up should initially be every 1–2 weeks** depending on the severity of the depression, at least for the first 4–6 weeks, to monitor progress and to ensure medication is being tolerated.
- Treatment should be continued at full antidepressant dosage until the person has been free of the main symptoms for at least 6 months. A longer treatment course is recommended in people with residual symptoms, those with a previous history of depression, and in elderly people. People with dysthymia frequently require longer courses of treatment owing to the persistence of residual symptoms.
- In major depression, maintenance treatment reduces the risk of recurrence and is indicated in people with:
  - Three or more episodes of major depression in the last 5 years.
  - More than five episodes altogether.
  - Fewer recurrent depressive episodes but with persistent risk factors for relapse or recurrence (e.g. continued psychosocial issues).
- Maintenance treatment should be continued at the same dosage that was used to treat the acute episode and should continue for at least 5 years and possibly indefinitely.

Should I refer or investigate?

Refer?

- **Urgently admit** people at high risk of suicide.
- **Consider admission** for people at less obvious risk of suicide but with poor social support.
- **Admit people** with psychotic features (delusions, hallucinations) or stupor.
- **Consider referral** if the person is not responding to treatment, or if there is diagnostic uncertainty (e.g. physical symptoms or signs not consistent with a diagnosis of depression).

Patient information leaflets

The following PILs are available at www.prodigy.nhs.uk

- Antidepressants - SSRIs
- Antidepressants - St John's Wort
- Antidepressants - Tricyclic
- Anxiety Disorders
- Anxiety - Generalised Anxiety Disorder
- Association for Post-Natal Illness
- Cognitive Behaviour Therapy (CBT)
- Depression
- Depression Alliance
- Depression - A Summary
- Depression (Post-Natal)
- Fellowship of Depressives Anonymous
- MAMA - Meet-A-Mum Association
- Manic Depression Fellowship
- Phobia - Agoraphobia
- Phobia - Social Phobia
- Post-Traumatic Stress Disorder
- Psychosomatic Disorders
- SAD Association (Seasonal Affective Disorder)
- Seasonal Affective Disorder
- Somatization and Somatoform Disorders

Shared decision making

- **The dosage** of an antidepressant medicine is commonly increased if the initial dosage has not helped much after 4–6 weeks.
- **Antidepressant medication** usually takes 1–2 weeks to start working and 4–6 weeks to work fully. A course for at least 6 months after symptoms improve is usual.
- **A tricyclic antidepressant** (TCA), such as amitriptyline, imipramine, or lofepramine, is commonly prescribed.
- **A selective serotonin re-uptake inhibitor** (SSRI) **antidepressant** (such as citalopram, fluoxetine, paroxetine, and sertraline) or **trazodone** is an alternative.
- Side effects are often minor or improve in time. The packet insert lists all possible side effects.
  - Tricyclics: common side effects are slight drowsiness, a dry mouth, and blurred vision.
  - SSRIs: an upset stomach is the commonest side effect.
- **The type** of antidepressant may need to be changed if the one you are taking has not worked after taking the maximum dosage, or is causing persistent troublesome side effects.

Drug rationale

Drugs not included

- Antidepressants that are not included in the separate scenarios *Major depression*, *Dysthymia*, and *Milder depression* are not offered.
- **Dosages of paroxetine above 20 mg daily are not included.** The Committee on Safety of Medicines has recently advised that there is no evidence from clinical trials that increasing the dose above this level increases efficacy in the treatment of depression [CSM, 2004]. In addition, the adverse events that occur soon after starting treatment may be difficult to distinguish from depression: there is evidence that increasing the dose in this situation may be detrimental.

Drugs included

- Maintenance dosages/dosage adjustments are offered for amitriptyline, citalopram, fluoxetine, imipramine, lofepramine, paroxetine, sertraline, and trazodone (i.e. those antidepressants that have initiation prescriptions offered in the separate scenarios *Major depression*, *Dysthymia* and *Milder depression*).

Prescriptions

Amitriptyline (NOT if suicide risk)

Titrate amitriptyline:75mg for 7 nights, then 100mg at night
- Age from 18 years onwards
- Amitriptyline 25mg tablets. Take three tablets at night for 7 nights, then take four tablets at night for 7 nights, then increase the dose as instructed by your doctor; supply 49 tablets; NHS Cost £1.40.

Amitriptyline 75mg at night
- Age from 65 years onwards
- Amitriptyline 25mg tablets. Take three tablets at night; supply 84 tablets; NHS Cost £2.40.

Amitriptyline 100mg at night
- Age from 65 years onwards
- Amitriptyline 50mg tablets. Take two tablets together at night; supply 56 tablets; NHS Cost £1.40.

Amitriptyline 125mg at night
- Age from 18 years onwards
- Amitriptyline 25mg tablets. Take one tablet at night; supply 28 tablets; NHS Cost £0.80.
- Amitriptyline 50mg tablets. Take two tablets together at night; supply 56 tablets; NHS Cost £2.40.

Amitriptyline 150mg at night
- Age from 18 years onwards
- Amitriptyline 50mg tablets. Take three tablets at night; supply 84 tablets; NHS Cost £3.60.

Amitriptyline 175mg at night
- Age from 18 years onwards
- Amitriptyline 25mg tablets. Take one tablet at night; supply 28 tablets; NHS Cost £0.80.
- Amitriptyline 50mg tablets. Take three tablets at night; supply 84 tablets; NHS Cost £2.40.

Amitriptyline 200mg at night
- Age from 18 years onwards
- Amitriptyline 50mg tablets. Take four tablets at night; supply 112 tablets; NHS Cost £3.60.

Imipramine (NOT if suicide risk)

Titrate imipramine: 75mg for 7 nights, then 100mg at night
- Age from 18 years onwards
- Imipramine 25mg tablets. Take three tablets at night for 7 nights, then take four tablets at night for 7 nights, then increase the dose as instructed by your doctor; supply 49 tablets; NHS Cost £1.77.

Imipramine 75mg at night
- Age from 65 years onwards
- Imipramine 25mg tablets. Take three tablets at night; supply 84 tablets; NHS Cost £3.03.

Imipramine 100mg at night
- Age from 65 years onwards
- Imipramine 25mg tablets. Take four tablets at night; supply 112 tablets; NHS Cost £4.04.

Imipramine 125mg at night
- Age from 18 years onwards
- Imipramine 25mg tablets. Take five tablets at night; supply 140 tablets; NHS Cost £5.05.

Imipramine 150mg at night
- Age from 18 years onwards
- Imipramine 25mg tablets. Take six tablets at night; supply 168 tablets; NHS Cost £6.06.

Imipramine 175mg per day
- Age from 18 years onwards
- Imipramine 25mg tablets. Take three tablets each morning and take four tablets at night; supply 196 tablets; NHS Cost £7.07.

Imipramine 200mg per day
- Age from 18 years onwards
- Imipramine 25mg tablets. Take four tablets twice a day; supply 224 tablets; NHS Cost £8.08.

Lofepramine or trazodone

Lofepramine 70mg at night
- Age from 65 years onwards
- Lofepramine 70mg tablets. Take one tablet at night; supply 28 tablets; NHS Cost £5.08.

Lofepramine 140mg at night
- Age from 18 years onwards
- Lofepramine 70mg tablets. Take two tablets together at night; supply 56 tablets; NHS Cost £10.15.

Lofepramine 210mg at night
- Age from 18 years onwards
- Lofepramine 70mg tablets. Take three tablets at night; supply 84 tablets; NHS Cost £15.23.

Trazodone 100mg at night
- Age from 65 years onwards
- Trazodone 100mg capsules. Take one capsule at night; supply 28 capsules; NHS Cost £10.02.

Trazodone 150mg at night
- Age from 18 years onwards
- Trazodone 150mg tablets. Take one tablet at night; supply 28 tablets; NHS Cost £11.42.

Trazodone 200mg at night
- Age from 18 years onwards
- Trazodone 100mg capsules. Take two capsules at night; supply 56 capsules; NHS Cost £20.03.

Trazodone 300mg at night
- Age from 18 years onwards
- Trazodone 150mg tablets. Take two tablets together at night; supply 56 tablets; NHS Cost £22.84.

Citalopram or fluoxetine

Citalopram 20mg once a day
- Age from 18 years onwards
- Citalopram 20mg tablets. Take one tablet once a day; supply 28 tablets; NHS Cost £16.03.

Citalopram 40mg once a day
- Age from 18 years onwards
- Citalopram 40mg tablets. Take one tablet once a day; supply 28 tablets; NHS Cost £27.10.

Citalopram 60mg once a day
- Age from 18 to 65 years
- Citalopram 40mg tablets. Take one tablet once a day; supply 28 tablets; NHS Cost £27.10.
- Citalopram 20mg tablets. Take one tablet once a day; supply 28 tablets; NHS Cost £16.03.

Fluoxetine 20mg once a day
- Age from 18 years onwards
- Fluoxetine 20mg capsules. Take one capsule once a day; supply 30 capsules; NHS Cost £7.43.

Fluoxetine 40mg once a day
- Age from 18 years onwards
- Fluoxetine 20mg capsules. Take two capsules once a day; supply 60 capsules; NHS Cost £14.86.

Fluoxetine 60mg once a day
- Age from 18 years onwards
- Fluoxetine 20mg capsules. Take three capsules once a day; supply 90 capsules; NHS Cost £22.29.

Paroxetine or sertraline

Paroxetine 20mg each morning
- Age from 18 years onwards
- Paroxetine 20mg tablets. Take one tablet each morning; supply 30 tablets; NHS Cost £15.16.

Sertraline 50mg once a day
- Age from 18 years onwards
- Sertraline 50mg tablets. Take one tablet once a day; supply 28 tablets; NHS Cost £16.20.

Sertraline 100mg once a day
- Age from 18 years onwards
- Sertraline 100mg tablets. Take one tablet once a day; supply 28 tablets; NHS Cost £26.51.

Sertraline 150mg once a day
- Age from 18 years onwards
- Sertraline 50mg tablets. Take one tablet once a day; supply 28 tablets; NHS Cost £16.20.
- Sertraline 100mg tablets. Take one tablet once a day; supply 28 tablets; NHS Cost £26.51.

Sertraline 200mg once a day
- Age from 18 years onwards
- Sertraline 100mg tablets. Take two tablets once a day; supply 56 tablets; NHS Cost £53.02.

Switching antidepressants

Which therapy?

- A person may need to change to an alternative antidepressant because the current antidepressant is either ineffective or poorly tolerated.
- When switching from a tricyclic antidepressant (TCA) to a selective serotonin re-uptake inhibitor (SSRI), or vice versa, cross-tapering is recommended (i.e. the dosage of the drug to be discontinued is slowly reduced while the new drug is slowly introduced). The exceptions are clomipramine, which should not be given with an SSRI, and fluoxetine, which should be stopped before starting a TCA.
- An example of a cross-tapering regimen is shown in Table 2.
- The speed of cross-tapering is best judged by monitoring patient tolerability. No clear guidelines are available so caution is required.
- **When switching between SSRIs, the first SSRI should be withdrawn before the second SSRI is started.** After stopping fluoxetine, a different SSRI should not be started until 4–7 days later, as it has a long half-life and active metabolites.
- Switching recommendations from the Maudsley Hospital are outlined in Table 3.

Table 2: Cross-tapering regimen when switching from a TCA and SSRI, or vice versa.

		Week 1	Week 2	Week 3	Week 4
Withdrawing amitriptyline	150 mg daily	100 mg daily	50 mg daily	25 mg daily	nil
Introducing citalopram	nil	10 mg daily	10 mg daily	20 mg daily	20 mg daily

Table 3: Recommendations for switching between SSRIs.

From / To	TCA	Trazodone	Citalopram	Fluoxetine	Paroxetine	Sertraline
TCA	Cross-taper cautiously	Halve dosage and add trazodone then slow withdrawal	Halve dosage and add citalopram then slow withdrawal	Halve dosage and add fluoxetine then slow withdrawal	Halve dosage and add paroxetine then slow withdrawal	Halve dosage and add sertraline then slow withdrawal
Trazodone	Cross-taper cautiously with very low dosage of TCA	—	Withdraw then start citalopram	Withdraw then start fluoxetine	Withdraw then start paroxetine	Withdraw then start sertraline
Citalopram	Cross-taper cautiously	Withdraw then start trazodone	—	Withdraw then start fluoxetine	Withdraw then start paroxetine 10 mg/day	Withdraw then start sertraline at 25 mg/day
Fluoxetine	Stop fluoxetine. Start TCA at very low dosage and increase very slowly	Stop fluoxetine. Wait 4–7 days then start low dosage trazodone	Stop fluoxetine. Wait 4–7 days. Start citalopram 10 mg/day and increase slowly	—	Stop fluoxetine. Wait 4–7 days then start paroxetine 10 mg/day	Stop fluoxetine. Wait 4–7 days then start sertraline 25 mg/day
Paroxetine	Cross-taper cautiously with very low dosage of TCA	Withdraw then start trazodone	Withdraw then start citalopram	Withdraw then start fluoxetine	—	Withdraw then start sertraline at 25 mg/day
Sertraline	Cross-taper cautiously with very low dosage of TCA	Withdraw then start trazodone	Withdraw then start citalopram	Withdraw then start fluoxetine	Withdraw then start paroxetine	—

Practical prescribing points

For further information see the *Medicines Compendium* (www.medicines.org.uk), the *British National Formulary* (www.bnf.org), or the Maudsley Prescribing Guidelines [Taylor et al, 2001].

- **Do NOT co-administer two SSRIs.** Withdraw first SSRI before starting the next SSRI.
- **Do NOT co-administer clomipramine with SSRIs or venlafaxine.** Withdraw clomipramine before starting.
- **Co-administration of two antidepressants** may result in additive adverse effects, such as drowsiness, hypotension, and occasionally serotonin syndrome.
- **Symptoms of serotonin syndrome** (listed in increasing order of severity) are restlessness, diaphoresis, tremor, shivering, myoclonus, confusion, convulsions, and death.
- **Tricyclic plasma levels are elevated by some SSRIs** (fluoxetine, fluvoxamine, and paroxetine) therefore cross-taper very cautiously between these antidepressants.
- For switches between other types of antidepressants: see Maudsley Prescribing Guidelines [Taylor et al, 2001].

Should I refer or investigate?

Refer?

- **Urgently admit** people at high risk of suicide.
- **Consider admission** for people at less obvious risk of suicide but with poor social support.
- **Admit people** with psychotic features (delusions, hallucinations) or stupor.
- **Consider referral** if the person is not responding to treatment, or if there is diagnostic uncertainty (e.g. physical symptoms or signs not consistent with a diagnosis of depression).

Patient information leaflets

The following PILs are available at www.prodigy.nhs.uk

- Antidepressants - SSRIs
- Antidepressants - St John's Wort
- Antidepressants - Tricyclic
- Cognitive Behaviour Therapy (CBT)
- Depression
- Depression Alliance
- Depression - A Summary

Shared decision making

- The type of antidepressant that you are taking may need to be changed if the one you are taking:
  - Has not worked after taking the maximum dosage, or
  - Is causing troublesome side effects
- **When switching between certain types of antidepressant** it is common to gradually reduce the dosage of the first medicine at the same time as increasing the dosage of the new one. However, some changes of medication need special instructions — your doctor will advise you.
- **Antidepressant medication** usually takes 4–6 weeks to work fully. A course for at least 6 months after symptoms improve is usual.
  - A tricyclic antidepressant (TCA), such as amitriptyline, imipramine, or lofepramine, is commonly prescribed.
  - A selective serotonin re-uptake inhibitor (SSRI) antidepressant (such as citalopram, fluoxetine, paroxetine, and sertraline) or trazodone is an alternative.
- Side effects are often minor or improve in time. The packet insert lists all possible side effects.
  - Tricyclics: common side effects include slight drowsiness, a dry mouth, and blurred vision.
  - SSRIs: an upset stomach is the commonest side effect.

Drug rationale

- There are no prescriptions offered.

Stopping antidepressants

Which therapy?

- An antidepressant may be stopped because it is either ineffective or poorly tolerated (see the separate scenario *Switching antidepressants*) or because an adequate course of treatment has been given and the condition has resolved.
- **Discontinuation symptoms may occur on abruptly stopping all classes of antidepressants** and seem to be

more common with longer treatment courses. Discontinuation symptoms rarely occur with treatment lasting less than 5 weeks.
- **Symptoms usually appear within a few days of stopping the antidepressant.** Onset more than a week later is unusual. Most reactions are mild and rarely last more than 1–2 weeks. Symptoms include dizziness, anxiety and agitation, insomnia, 'flu-like symptoms, diarrhoea and abdominal cramps, paraesthesiae, mood swings, nausea, and low mood. There have been isolated reports of electric shock sensations, vertigo, and manic reactions on selective serotonin re-uptake inhibitor (SSRI) withdrawal.
- **If possible, taper the dosage (or frequency) of antidepressants over about 4 weeks when stopping treatment.** More rapid discontinuation may be necessary in people with severe adverse reactions to antidepressant medication.
- Taper the dosage over 6 months in people who have been receiving long-term maintenance treatment.
- Fluoxetine may be stopped abruptly if the dose is 20 mg/day, as it has a long half-life and active metabolites.
- **If a discontinuation reaction occurs,** explanation and reassurance are often all that is required. If this is not sufficient, and for more severe reactions, the antidepressant should be restarted and subsequently reduced more slowly.

Patient information leaflets

The following PILs are available at www.prodigy.nhs.uk
- Antidepressants - SSRIs
- Antidepressants - St John's Wort
- Antidepressants - Tricyclic
- Cognitive Behaviour Therapy (CBT)
- Depression
- Depression Alliance
- Depression - A Summary

Shared decision making

- It is best to gradually reduce the dosage of your antidepressant before stopping it completely.
- A reducing dosage over 4 weeks is usual.
- This is because stopping it suddenly may cause 'withdrawal' symptoms such as dizziness, anxiety and agitation, sleep disturbance, 'flu-like symptoms, diarrhoea, abdominal cramps, pins and needles, mood swings, feeling sick, and low mood.
- These symptoms are unlikely to occur if you reduce the dosage gradually.
- If symptoms do occur then they will usually last less than 2 weeks.
- Restarting the medicine and reducing the dosage even more slowly is an option if withdrawal symptoms occur when the medicine is stopped.

Drug rationale

Drugs not included

- Tapering dosages are not offered for antidepressants not included in previous scenarios.

Drugs included

- **Tapering dosages (generally over 4 weeks)** are included for amitriptyline, citalopram, fluoxetine, imipramine, lofepramine, paroxetine, sertraline, and trazodone (i.e. those antidepressants included in the separate scenarios *Major depression*, *Dysthymia*, *Milder depression*, and *Maintenance/dosage adjustment*).
- Note: the dosage should usually be tapered over 6 months in people who have been receiving long-term maintenance treatment.

Prescriptions

Amitriptyline

Stop amitriptyline 75mg at night
- Age from 65 years onwards
- Amitriptyline 25mg tablets. Reduce these tablets as instructed on the right hand side of this prescription; supply 42 tablets; NHS Cost £1.20.

Stop amitriptyline 100mg at night
- Age from 65 years onwards
- Amitriptyline 25mg tablets. Reduce these tablets as instructed on the right hand side of this prescription; supply 60 tablets; NHS Cost £1.71.

Stop amitriptyline 125mg at night
- Age from 18 years onwards
- Amitriptyline 25mg tablets. Reduce these tablets as instructed on the right hand side of this prescription; supply 70 tablets; NHS Cost £2.00.

Stop amitriptyline 150mg at night
- Age from 18 years onwards
- Amitriptyline 25mg tablets. Reduce these tablets as instructed on the right hand side of this prescription; supply 70 tablets; NHS Cost £2.00.

Stop amitriptyline 175mg at night
- Age from 18 years onwards
- Amitriptyline 25mg tablets. Reduce these tablets as instructed on the right hand side of this prescription; supply 112 tablets; NHS Cost £3.20.

Stop amitriptyline 200mg at night
- Age from 18 years onwards
- Amitriptyline 25mg tablets. Reduce these tablets as instructed on the right hand side of this prescription; supply 112 tablets; NHS Cost £3.20.

Imipramine

Stop imipramine 75mg at night
- Age from 65 years onwards
- Imipramine 25mg tablets. Reduce these tablets as instructed on the right hand side of this prescription; supply 42 tablets; NHS Cost £1.52.

Stop imipramine 100mg at night
- Age from 65 years onwards
- Imipramine 25mg tablets. Reduce these tablets as instructed on the right hand side of this prescription; supply 60 tablets; NHS Cost £2.16.

Stop imipramine 125mg at night
- Age from 18 years onwards
- Imipramine 25mg tablets. Reduce these tablets as instructed on the right hand side of this prescription; supply 70 tablets; NHS Cost £2.52.

Stop imipramine 150mg at night
- Age from 18 years onwards
- Imipramine 25mg tablets. Reduce these tablets as instructed on the right hand side of this prescription; supply 70 tablets; NHS Cost £2.52.

Stop imipramine 175mg per day
- Age from 18 years onwards
- Imipramine 25mg tablets. Reduce these tablets as instructed on the right hand side of this prescription; supply 112 tablets; NHS Cost £4.04.

Stop imipramine 200mg per day
- Age from 18 years onwards
- Imipramine 25mg tablets. Reduce these tablets as instructed on the right hand side of this prescription; supply 112 tablets; NHS Cost £4.04.

Lofepramine or trazodone

Stop lofepramine 70mg at night
- Age from 65 years onwards
- Lofepramine 70mg tablets. Reduce these tablets as instructed on the right hand side of this prescription; supply 21 tablets; NHS Cost £3.82.

Stop lofepramine 140mg at night
- Age from 18 years onwards
- Lofepramine 70mg tablets. Reduce these tablets as instructed on the right hand side of this prescription; supply 25 tablets; NHS Cost £4.55.

Stop lofepramine 210mg at night
- Age from 18 years onwards
- Lofepramine 70mg tablets. Reduce these tablets as instructed on the right hand side of this prescription; supply 32 tablets; NHS Cost £5.82.

Stop trazodone 100mg at night
- Age from 65 years onwards
- Trazodone 50mg capsules. Reduce these capsules as instructed on the right hand side of this prescription; supply 21 capsules; NHS Cost £4.27.

Stop trazodone 150mg at night
- Age from 18 years onwards
- Trazodone 50mg capsules. Reduce these capsules as instructed on the right hand side of this prescription; supply 35 capsules; NHS Cost £5.34.

Stop trazodone 200mg at night
- Age from 18 years onwards
- Trazodone 50mg capsules. Reduce these capsules as instructed on the right hand side of this prescription; supply 46 capsules; NHS Cost £9.35.

Stop trazodone 300mg at night
- Age from 18 years onwards
- Trazodone 50mg capsules. Reduce these capsules as instructed on the right hand side of this prescription; supply 74 capsules; NHS Cost £15.04.

Citalopram or fluoxetine

Stop citalopram 20mg once a day
- Age from 18 years onwards
- Citalopram 10mg tablets. Reduce these tablets as instructed on the right hand side of this prescription; supply 21 tablets; NHS Cost £7.23.

Stop citalopram 40mg once a day
- Age from 18 years onwards
- Citalopram 10mg tablets. Reduce these tablets as instructed on the right hand side of this prescription; supply 46 tablets; NHS Cost £15.84.

Stop citalopram 60mg once a day
- Age from 18 to 65 years
- Citalopram 10mg tablets. Reduce these tablets as instructed on the right hand side of this prescription; supply 53 tablets; NHS Cost £18.25.

Stop fluoxetine 20mg once a day (advice)
- Age from 18 years onwards
- You do not need to take any more fluoxetine 20mg capsules. You can just stop taking them. You do not usually need to reduce the dose more slowly. (Other antidepressants or higher doses of fluoxetine need to be reduced gradually before stopping.) Please return any unused capsules to your local pharmacy for safe disposal.

Stop fluoxetine 40mg once a day
- Age from 18 years onwards
- Fluoxetine 20mg capsules. Reduce these capsules as instructed on the right hand side of this prescription; supply 30 capsules; NHS Cost £7.58

Stop fluoxetine 60mg once a day
- Age from 18 years onwards
- Fluoxetine 20mg capsules. Reduce these capsules as instructed on the right hand side of this prescription; supply 42 capsules; NHS Cost £10.61.

Paroxetine or sertraline

Stop paroxetine 20mg once a day
- Age from 18 years onwards
- Paroxetine 20mg tablets. Reduce these tablets as instructed on the right hand side of this prescription; supply 21 tablets; NHS Cost £12.43.

Stop paroxetine 30mg once a day
- Age from 18 years onwards
- Paroxetine 20mg tablets. Reduce these tablets as instructed on the right hand side of this prescription; supply 25 tablets; NHS Cost £14.80.

Stop paroxetine 40mg once a day
- Age from 18 years onwards
- Paroxetine 20mg tablets. Reduce these tablets as instructed on the right hand side of this prescription; supply 32 tablets; NHS Cost £18.94.

Stop paroxetine 50mg once a day
- Age from 18 to 65 years
- Paroxetine 20mg tablets. Reduce these tablets as instructed on the right hand side of this prescription; supply 46 tablets; NHS Cost £27.23.

Stop sertraline 50mg once a day
- Age from 18 years onwards
- Sertraline 50mg tablets. Reduce these tablets as instructed on the right hand side of this prescription; supply 21 tablets; NHS Cost £10.42.

Stop sertraline 100mg once a day
- Age from 18 years onwards
- Sertraline 50mg tablets. Reduce these tablets as instructed on the right hand side of this prescription; supply 25 tablets; NHS Cost £12.40.

Stop sertraline 150mg once a day
- Age from 18 years onwards
- Sertraline 50mg tablets. Reduce these tablets as instructed on the right hand side of this prescription; supply 32 tablets; NHS Cost £15.88.

Stop sertraline 200mg once a day
- Age from 18 years onwards
- Sertraline 50mg tablets. Reduce these tablets as instructed on the right hand side of this prescription; supply 53 tablets; NHS Cost £26.30.

Extended Information

Background information

- What is it? p.497
- How common is it? p.498
- How do I know my patient has it? p.498
- What else might it be? p.499
- Complications and prognosis p.499

What is it?

- **Depressive states cover a spectrum between normal sadness at one end and severe illness at the other.** Most depressive states are at the mild to moderate end of the

D

D

spectrum and it is these that are mainly seen in primary care [Anderson et al, 2000].

- **Depression is usually defined by one of two main classification systems:** the 4th Revision of the American Psychiatric Association's Diagnostic and Statistics Manual (DSM–IV) or the 10th Revision of the International Classification of Diseases (ICD–10). *The DSM–IV classification is used throughout this guidance, as this is most commonly used in the UK* [Anderson et al, 2000].
- **Major depression** is defined by the presence of at least five out of nine symptoms, one of which must be depressed mood or loss of interest or pleasure. These must have been present for at least the last 2 weeks and cause clinically significant distress or impaired functioning (see section *How do I know my patient has it?*).
- **Dysthymia** is a chronic depressive state of more than 2 years' duration, which does not meet full criteria for major depression and is not the consequence of a partially resolved major depression. People with dysthymia are likely to experience episodes of major depression ('double depression').
- **Milder depression** may be diagnosed in people who do not meet the full criteria for diagnosis of major depression. People with psychological responses to life stresses (e.g. bereavement and adjustment disorders) will often fall into this category.
- **Postnatal depression** can present with a similar range of symptom severity to depression occurring at any other time of life. It is defined by DSM–IV criteria as occurring within 4 weeks postpartum. The ICD–10 allows classification of postnatal depression as depression with onset within six weeks postpartum [National Health and Medical Research Council, 2002]. For a significant number of women, depression may originate in the antenatal period.
- **The cause of depression is unknown** but seems to be a complex interaction between external and internal stresses, genetic factors, and biochemical changes in the brain. The old definitions of 'endogenous' and 'reactive' depression are no longer thought to be useful. Adverse life events commonly precede all types of major depression, irrespective of the clinical picture, and there is no clear relationship between apparent cause of depression and response to antidepressant drug treatment [Anderson et al, 2000].

How common is it?

Depressive disorders are common. The prevalence of major depression in people seen in primary care is between 5% and 10%, and two to three times as many people have depressive symptoms but do not meet the criteria for major depression [Geddes and Butler, 2001]. About two thirds of adults will at some time experience depressed mood of sufficient severity to influence their activities [NHS CRD, 1993].

Major depression

- **Between 5% and 10%** of people seen in primary care will have major depression [NHS CRD, 1993; Geddes and Butler, 2001].
- **Lifetime risk for major depression** is 15% overall: 19% for women and 10% for men [NHC, 1996].
- **Psychiatric referral rates** are about 3/1000 population or approximately 10% of those diagnosed in primary care. Only about 1/1000 are admitted to hospital [Paykel and Priest, 1992].
- Episodes peak in middle age and are strongly associated with adverse social and economic circumstances, such as unemployment, divorce or separation, inadequate housing, and lower social class [NHS CRD, 1993].

Dysthymia

- **Dysthymia increases with age** and affects about 10% of 55–64-year-olds [NHC, 1996]. Lifetime risk is 4% for women and 2% for men [AHCPR, 1993a].
- **It is estimated that 2–4% of people seen in primary care have dysthymia** [AHCPR, 1993a].

Postnatal depression

- For every 1000 live births, 100–150 women will suffer a depressive illness [SIGN, 2002].

How do I know my patient has it?

- **A high index of suspicion is necessary.** Only about half of people with major depression are identified as having this by their GP. People often present with mainly physical (somatic) symptoms. Many people have a physical illness, diverting attention away from their mental state [AHCPR, 1993a; NHS CRD, 1993; Anderson et al, 2000].
- **Depression should be particularly suspected if** there is a history of major depression, a family history of mood disorder, or a history of suicide attempt [AHCPR, 1993a].
- **Screening questions and self-report scales** for the detection of depressive disorders are reasonably sensitive but not very specific (i.e. have few false negatives but many false positives). They are therefore most useful when a depressive disorder is suspected or in high-risk populations [Anderson et al, 2000].
  - The Hospital Anxiety and Depression (HAD) Scale, when used in primary care, has 90% sensitivity at picking up depression, with 86% specificity [Anderson et al, 2000]. This is self-completed and can be given during the consultation for the person to fill in at home and bring back for discussion when they are next seen.
  - The Edinburgh Postnatal Depression Scale (EPDS) is commonly used as a screening tool in the postnatal period. There is good evidence of its effectiveness, although sensitivity and specificity are dependent on the cut-off scores chosen, and a clinical evaluation of the person is still required [SIGN, 2002]. However, the National Screening Commitee recommends that the EPDS be only used as a checklist as part of a mood assessment for postnatal mothers, used alongside professional judgement and a clinical interview. Users need to be aware of cultural difficulties for the interpretation, particularly when used with non-English speaking mothers and those from non-Western cultures [UK National Screening Committee, 2002].

Major depression

- People suspected of having depression, either clinically or from the results of screening questions or self-report scales, should be assessed for major depression according to DSM–IV criteria.
- **DSM–IV criteria for major depression:** at least five of the following symptoms (including either the first or second symptoms listed) need to have been present during the past 2 weeks most of the day, or nearly every day, and cause clinically significant distress or impairment in functioning. The symptoms are not due to a physical/organic factor (e.g. substance abuse) or illness and are not better explained by bereavement (although this can be complicated by major depression). They are:
  - Depressed mood
  - Loss of interest or pleasure in almost all activities
  - Significant weight loss or gain, or change in appetite
  - Insomnia or hypersomnia

- Psychomotor agitation or retardation (observable by others)
- Fatigue or loss of energy
- Feelings of worthlessness or excessive or inappropriate guilt
- Diminished ability to think or concentrate, or indecisiveness
- Recurrent thoughts of death (not just fear of dying) or suicidal thoughts/actions

- **Mild to moderate major depression** ranges from a threshold number (five) of symptoms with minimal functional impairment through to marked symptoms and impairment of function [Anderson et al, 2000].
- **Severe major depression** is characterized by the presence of all, or nearly all, DSM–IV depressive symptoms to a clinically severe degree, and marked functional impairment in all areas of life [Anderson et al, 2000].

Milder depression

- Milder depression is usually diagnosed in people who present with recent onset depressive symptoms not meeting DMS–IV criteria for major depression [Anderson et al, 2000]. The depressed mood often develops following an identifiable stressor, but the degree of distress exceeds the level expected and social or occupational functioning may be impaired.

Dysthymia

- Dysthymia is a chronic milder depressive disorder (at least 2 years of depressive symptoms not meeting DSM–IV criteria for depressive episode), which is not a consequence of a partially resolved major depression [Anderson et al, 2000].

Postnatal depression

- Postnatal depression occurs after childbirth and presents with a similar symptom pattern to depression occurring at any stage in life. It is often related to the stresses associated with a new infant in the family. In addition to symptoms meeting DSM–IV criteria, anxiety, obsessional phenomena, and panic may be evident. Depressive thoughts often focus on the maternal role, guilt, fears, worthlessness, or the infant [National Health and Medical Research Council, 2002; SIGN, 2002].

What else might it be?

- **Drug adverse effects** are an uncommon cause of depression. Medications that may cause depressed mood include:
  - Centrally acting antihypertensives (e.g. methyldopa)
  - Lipid soluble beta-blockers (e.g. propranolol)
  - Benzodiazepines or other central nervous system depressants
- **Substance misuse** is frequently associated with depression.
- **Other psychiatric conditions** may coexist with depression (e.g. anxiety, panic disorder, obsessive–compulsive disorder, personality disorders).
- **Dementia** may occasionally present as depression and vice versa.
- **Several mood and anxiety disorders** can occur in association with childbearing, such as postnatal anxiety disorders, maternity blues, and puerperal psychosis [National Health and Medical Research Council, 2002].

Complications and prognosis

Complications

- **Depression** is a major cause of impaired quality of life, reduced productivity, and increased mortality [MeReC, 2000]. Social difficulties are common (e.g. social stigma, loss of employment, marital break-up). People with depression are at increased risk of suicide.
- **Associated problems,** such as anxiety symptoms and substance misuse, may cause further disability.
- **Postnatal depression** may have adverse effects on the marital relationship, the partner's level of depression, and a mother's feelings towards the infant or other children.

Prognosis

- **The outlook varies** with the severity of the condition.
- **For major depression:** approximately 80% of people who have received psychiatric care for an episode will have at least one more episode in their lifetime, with a median of four episodes. The outcome for those seen in primary care also seems to be poor, with only about a third remaining well over 11 years and about 20% having a chronic course [Anderson et al, 2000].
- **For dysthymia,** the long-term outlook is poor, with only 40–50% well at 1-year follow-up [AHCPR, 1993a].
- **Postnatal depression** often persists for many months. Estimates vary between 25% to 60% remission within 3–6 months and a further 15% to 25% within 12 months [National Health and Medical Research Council, 2002]. Women who experience a first episode of major depression postpartum are more likely to experience depression with further childbirths [National Health and Medical Research Council, 2002].

D

Management issues

- Should I use psychological treatments or antidepressants? p.499
- Influence of other psychiatric disorders p.500
- Depression in elderly people p.500
- Pregnancy and breastfeeding p.500
- Bereavement p.500
- Medicines management p.500

Should I use psychological treatments or antidepressants?

- The decision on which treatment to choose will depend on the degree of depression, the preference of the patient, and local availability of psychological treatments (there is a shortage of trained therapists in the UK, so access to most psychological treatments is currently limited).
- The patient should be included in the decision-making process, as it is likely that this will improve concordance, and ultimately the clinical outcome.
- Combining psychological treatments with antidepressants is not appropriate for most people with depression, as there is little evidence of additional benefit. It should mainly be considered in people with severe major depression [Anderson et al, 2000; Geddes and Butler, 2001].

Major depression

- **Psychological treatments or antidepressants can be used.** Specific psychological treatments and antidepressants appear equally effective in mild to moderately severe major depression. There is uncertainty with regard to relative efficacy in more severely ill patients [Anderson et al, 2000].
- Cognitive behaviour therapy and interpersonal therapy are the most widely studied psychological treatments.
  - Other psychological treatments that have shown benefit include behavioural therapy, problem-solving therapy, group therapy, and marital and family interventions [DH, 2001].

- The value of non-directive counselling (supportive listening without giving opinions or advice) is uncertain.

Dysthymia

- **Antidepressants are the preferred treatment.** A meta-analysis found that 55% of people responded to an antidepressant compared with 30% receiving placebo [Anderson et al, 2000].
- There is a lack of evidence on the benefits of psychological treatments.

Milder depression

- **Support and simple problem solving are often sufficient.**
- Specific psychological treatments or antidepressants are seldom indicated at initial presentation. However, if there is a history of major depression, early treatment should be considered. Similarly, if symptoms of milder depression persist, consider a trial of treatment [Anderson et al, 2000].

Postnatal depression

- **Postnatal depression should be managed in the same way as depression at any other time,** but with the additional considerations regarding the use of antidepressants when breastfeeding and in pregnancy [SIGN, 2002].
- Health visitors and midwives may be able to help with problems associated with postnatal depression. Non-directive counselling may be helpful [SIGN, 2002].
- Some women may benefit from brief interventions using cognitive behavioural and problem-solving approaches. Interpersonal therapy focusing on the woman's past and present relationships, including her relationship with her mother, has also been shown to reduce depressive symptoms [SIGN, 2002].

Influence of other psychiatric disorders

- **Anxiety, panic disorder, and personality disorders frequently accompany depression.** Generally, depression should be treated first, followed by treatment of the other disorder. Anxiety, in particular, will often improve following treatment of depression [AHCPR, 1993a].
- **Eating disorders may accompany depression and** should be the main target of treatment [AHCPR, 1993a]. Specialist referral is advisable.
- **Substance abuse is frequently associated with depression.** Depressive symptoms may be due to the effects of alcohol, especially in women, and depressive symptoms frequently resolve following alcohol detoxification [NHC, 1996].

Depression in elderly people

- The presentation of older people with depression is similar to that of younger people.
- **It can be difficult to distinguish depression from dementia,** as some symptoms of depression (e.g. disorientation, memory loss, and distractibility) may suggest dementia and it is common for people with dementia to develop major depression [AHCPR, 1993a]. If the person seems to have a reasonable memory the problem is likely to be depression [NHC, 1996].
- Rarely an elderly person with severe major depression presents as totally disorganized and appears to have severe dementia, which resolves with treatment for depression — 'depressive pseudo-dementia' [NHC, 1996].

Pregnancy and breastfeeding

- **Some women may find themselves pregnant** while taking an antidepressant. Such women should be reassured that there is no evidence that antidepressants are likely to cause fetal abnormalities if taken during pregnancy [National Teratology Information Service, 1997].
- **A woman should always be involved** in making a fully informed decision to start antidepressant therapy during pregnancy and in the postpartum period. Any decision to start treatment should be based on a risk–benefit evaluation. If a woman intends to breastfeed it is appropriate to choose an antidepressant that is suitable both for use in pregnancy and when breastfeeding.
- **Extensive epidemiological studies have shown no evidence** that therapeutic dosages of TCAs are associated with an increased incidence of birth defects. Although there are less data on SSRIs in pregnancy, these also appear to be safe. Fluoxetine is the SSRI with the most evidence of safety in pregnancy.
- **Wherever possible** antidepressants should be tapered in the weeks before delivery.
- **There is no clinical indication** for a breastfeeding woman not to receive a TCA (other than doxepin), provided the infant is healthy and its progress monitored [Misri and Kostaras, 2002]. However, the ideal TCA for breastfeeding mothers is non-sedating with a shorter half-life, has reduced anticholinergic effects, has no active metabolites, is highly protein bound, and has been studied clinically in pregnancy and women who breastfeed. The TCA most closely meeting these criteria is imipramine [UKMI, 2003].
- **The use of SSRIs** paroxetine, fluoxetine, and sertraline has been reported in breastfeeding mothers. Paroxetine is associated with low or undetectable serum concentrations in infants and may be preferable to other SSRIs in breastfeeding mothers.
- **Doxepin should be avoided in breastfeeding mothers** owing to reports of adverse effects on the infant: respiratory depression, poor sucking, muscle hypotonia, vomiting, jaundice, and drowsiness.
- **Where possible, medication should be prescribed as a single dose** and administered before the baby's longest sleep period. Breastfeeding is best done immediately before administering the dose and should ideally be avoided during peak levels 1–3 hours after the dose. For very young infants feeding frequently, one bottle-feed may be substituted to avoid drug peak levels. Infants should be monitored for drowsiness or other behavioural changes [UKMI, 2003]. Premature infants should not be exposed to psychotropic drugs via breast milk [Misri and Kostaras, 2002; SIGN, 2002].

Bereavement

- If depressive symptoms begin within 2–3 weeks of a loved one's death, the diagnosis is uncomplicated bereavement, which should resolve spontaneously [AHCPR, 1993a].
- Uncomplicated bereavement and major depression share many symptoms; however, active suicidal thoughts, psychotic symptoms, and profound guilt are rare.
- Major depression should be diagnosed in those who meet the criteria for this 2 months after the loss [AHCPR, 1993a].

Medicines management

Choice of antidepressant

- **Tricyclic antidepressants (TCAs) and selective serotonin reuptake inhibitors (SSRIs) are both suitable first-choice antidepressants.**
- The final choice should be determined by individual patient factors, including the preference of the patient, the risk of self-harm (avoid tricyclics), the likelihood of

adverse effects, comorbidity, and concomitant medication.

Lofepramine, trazodone, or an SSRI are preferable if there is concern about suicide risk, as these are associated with the lowest risk of fatal poisoning [Eccles et al, 1999; Mason et al, 2000]. However, if suicide risk is a genuine concern admission should be strongly considered, especially if the person has poor social support.

If there has been a previous good response to a particular drug it is sensible to prescribe this again. Similarly, if a person has previously failed to respond to or could not tolerate a particular drug, it is best avoided [AHCPR, 1993b; NHC, 1996; Anderson et al, 2000].

There is ongoing debate about whether SSRIs should be routinely used in preference to TCAs [Eccles et al, 1999; Anderson et al, 2000; Barbui et al, 2001; Geddes and Butler, 2001; MeReC, 2001]. The main issues are comparative efficacy, tolerability, adverse effects, toxicity, and cost.

Efficacy

There is no clinically significant difference in effectiveness between SSRIs and TCAs [Eccles et al, 1999; Anderson et al, 2000; Geddes and Butler, 2001; Geddes et al, 2001].

Short-term studies (up to 6 weeks) have shown response rates of 50–65% for antidepressants compared with 25–30% for placebo. This means that three to four patients need to be treated with an antidepressant for one more patient to respond than on placebo [Anderson et al, 2000]. However, these trials have generally lasted no more than 6 weeks, while a standard course of antidepressants is for about 6 months.

Tolerability

SSRIs are slightly better tolerated than TCAs.

Withdrawal rates in randomized controlled trials comparing SSRIs with TCAs is an accepted method of estimating tolerability [Eccles et al, 1999; Barbui et al, 2001; Geddes and Butler, 2001]. A Cochrane systematic review found that fewer people taking SSRIs dropped out compared with those taking TCAs, with an overall difference of 3% in favour of SSRIs [Barbui et al, 2001]. This means that 27% of people taking SSRIs will drop out compared with 30% of people taking tricyclic/heterocyclic drugs. When the SSRIs were compared with heterocyclic and related antidepressants, no statistically significant difference in drop-out rates was found, although this finding was less precise owing to the smaller number and size of studies.

Adverse effects

TCAs most commonly cause antimuscarinic adverse effects (e.g. dry mouth, sedation, blurred vision, constipation, and urinary retention). Postural hypotension, arrhythmias, or weight gain may also occur. **Lofepramine** has fewer antimuscarinic effects and is much less sedating [Eccles et al, 1999; Taylor et al, 2001].

Trazodone has no antimuscarinic effect but is very sedating [Taylor et al, 2001].

SSRIs most commonly cause gastrointestinal adverse effects (nausea and diarrhoea), central nervous system effects (dizziness, agitation, insomnia, and tremor), and sexual dysfunction [Taylor et al, 2001]. Extrapyramidal symptoms are relatively rare and seem to be most common with paroxetine [CSM, 2000b]. SSRIs may also increase the risk of upper gastrointestinal bleeding, probably by altering platelet function. This risk seems to be increased in people who are also taking low-dosage aspirin or nonsteroidal anti-inflammatory drugs, who have a history of gastrointestinal bleeding, or who are elderly [De Abajo et al, 1999; van Walraven et al, 2001].

- **Hyponatraemia** is associated with all types of antidepressant [CSM, 2000b; Taylor et al, 2001]. It should be considered in any person taking antidepressants who develops drowsiness, confusion, nausea, muscle cramps, or seizures. Risk factors include a history of hyponatraemia, extreme old age, diuretics, diabetes mellitus, hypertension, reduced renal function, and chronic obstructive pulmonary disease.
- It is generally accepted that many people become tolerant to the adverse effects of antidepressants with continued use, but there is little published evidence to support this.
- Table 4 compares the incidence of some common adverse effects between SSRIs and TCAs [Geddes and Butler, 2001].

Toxicity and suicide risk

- **SSRIs are safer than TCAs in overdose** (TCAs have serious adverse cardiovascular effects when taken in overdose), but there is considerable controversy on whether this justifies routinely prescribing SSRIs in preference to TCAs.
- **A study looking at national data** for England and Wales from 1993 to 1995 found that SSRIs and TCAs were both associated with low levels of fatal poisoning, but that SSRIs were associated with lower levels than TCAs [Mason et al, 2000]. SSRIs were associated with one fatality in 411,800 treatment episodes (assuming an average treatment episode of 3 months). Equivalent figures for TCAs were 1 in 8130. Fatality associated with use of lofepramine was not significantly different from that of SSRIs. Trazodone also seemed to have low risk of fatality when taken in overdose. These figures should be interpreted with caution, as drugs may be used selectively in people with different severities of depression and other confounding factors are likely to be present.
- **It is not known what impact a policy of using SSRIs** in preference to TCAs would have, as some people will choose other methods of committing successful suicide. However, when safety is a prime concern then lofepramine, trazodone, or an SSRI would seem to be a rational choice.
- **The Committee on Safety of Medicines (CSM)** has recently reviewed the evidence on whether there is a link between SSRIs and suicidal behaviour and was unable to find any convincing evidence of this. There continue to be anecdotal case reports of suicidal behaviour associated with fluoxetine, and the CSM has stated that it will continue to monitor this issue. The CSM highlights that it is general clinical experience that the risk of suicide may increase in the early stages of treatment with any antidepressant and that people considered to be at risk should be carefully monitored [CSM, 2000b].

Table 4: Comparison of the incidence of some common adverse effects of SSRIs and TCAs

Adverse effects	SSRIs event rates (%)	TCAs event rates (%)
Dry mouth	21	55
Constipation	10	22
Dizziness	13	23
Nausea	22	12
Diarrhoea	13	5
Anxiety	13	7
Agitation	14	8
Insomnia	12	7
Nervousness	15	11
Headache	17	14

Cost

- **TCAs are generally cheaper than SSRIs.**
- **There is no convincing evidence that SSRIs are more cost-effective than TCAs.** Some pharmacoeconomic studies have suggested that in the long term SSRIs are more cost-effective than TCAs, despite higher initial acquisition costs. However, these studies have assumed that withdrawal rates with TCAs are 8–12% higher than with SSRIs, although the actual figure is likely to be nearer 3% [Barbui et al, 2001].
- **The cost differential between SSRIs and TCAs is likely to drop** as more SSRIs come off patent, as already seen with fluoxetine.

D

Dosage of antidepressant

- **The use of lower than recommended dosages of TCAs is common in primary care,** with one study finding that only 13% of people receiving long-term treatment were taking standard therapeutic dosages [Hawley et al, 1997]. This may be due to the need for titration of TCA dosage and concern about adverse effects at higher dosages. Dosage titration is less of a problem with SSRIs as starting dosages are usually treatment dosages.
- **The minimum recommended dosage of most TCAs is 125–150 mg daily.**
  - Lower dosages may be appropriate in the elderly, as higher plasma concentrations for a given dosage are generally found.
  - Although there is little evidence on what constitutes an adequate dosage of TCA in adults, it is likely that dosages below 75 mg daily are ineffective [Anderson et al, 2000].
- **The recommended target dose of paroxetine is 20 mg daily.** The Committee on Safety of Medicines has recently advised that there is no evidence from clinical trials that increasing the dose above this level increases efficacy in the treatment of depression [CSM, 2004].
  - Rapid dose escalation of paroxetine is associated with an increased risk of adverse effects. In addition, the adverse events that occur soon after starting treatment may be difficult to distinguish from depression: there is evidence that increasing the dose in this situation may be detrimental.
  - However, people who are already being successfully treated at higher doses should continue with the higher dose of paroxetine until the end of the planned course of treatment.
- **If a response occurs at a lower than target dosage of any antidepressant,** the dosage should still be increased to reduce the likelihood of relapse. If this is not possible, then the drug should be continued at the same dosage and the person monitored for relapse [Anderson et al, 2000].
- **Close monitoring in the early stages of treatment is necessary,** irrespective of which antidepressant is prescribed, to assess response, adverse effects, compliance, and suicide risk. It is advisable initially to prescribe only small quantities of antidepressants to reduce the risk if taken in overdose.
- **Compliance** with taking antidepressants is improved by counselling about depression and the benefits and adverse effects of medication, but not by information leaflets alone [Anderson et al, 2000].

Duration of treatment

- **Following a first episode of major depression,** medicatio should be continued at full antidepressant dosage until the person has been free of major symptoms for at least 6 months [AHCPR, 1993b; NHC, 1996; Angst, 1997; Anderson et al, 2000]. A longer course of treatment is recommended in people with residual symptoms, those with a history of depression, and in elderly people.
- **Maintenance treatment reduces the risk of recurrence and is indicated in people with:**
  - Three or more episodes of major depression in the last 5 years.
  - More than five episodes altogether.
  - Fewer recurrent depressive episodes but with persistent risk factors for relapse or recurrence (e.g. continued psychosocial issues) [Anderson et al, 2000].
- **Maintenance treatment should be continued at the same dosage that was used to treat the acute episode,** and continued for at least 5 years and possibly indefinitely.

Treatment failure

- **Before deciding that a person is not responding to antidepressants,** treatment should be continued at an adequate dosage for at least 4 weeks, or 6 weeks in the elderly [Anderson et al, 2000]. If there is a partial response after this time, then treatment should be continued for another 2 weeks.
- **If not responding to treatment** check adequacy of treatment, including dosage and compliance; review the diagnosis, including the possibility of additional physica or psychiatric conditions; and consider maintaining social factors [Anderson et al, 2000].
- **If a person is failing to respond despite an adequate trial of treatment,** either increase the dosage further or switch to another antidepressant class [AHCPR, 1993b; Anderson et al, 2000].
- **Psychological treatments should be considered if the person fails to respond to a second antidepressant.** Alternatively, augmentation treatment (e.g. the addition of lithium) or electroconvulsive therapy can be considered, but require psychiatric referral.

Switching antidepressants

- A person may need to change to an alternative antidepressant because the current antidepressant is either ineffective or poorly tolerated.
- **When switching from a TCA to a SSRI, or vice versa, cross-tapering is recommended** (i.e. the dosage of the drug to be discontinued is slowly reduced while the new drug is slowly introduced). The exceptions are clomipramine, which should not be given with an SSRI, and fluoxetine, which should be stopped before starting a TCA. An example of a cross-tapering regimen is shown in Table 5.
- **The speed of cross-tapering is best judged by monitoring a person's tolerability.** No clear guidelines are available, so caution is required [Taylor et al, 2001].
- **When switching between SSRIs, the first SSRI should be withdrawn before the second SSRI is started.** After stopping fluoxetine, a different SSRI should not be started until 4–7 days later, as it has a long half-life and active metabolites.

Table 5: Cross-tapering when switching from a TCA to a SSRI, or vice versa.

		Week 1	Week 2	Week 3	Week 4
Withdrawing amitriptyline	150 mg daily	100 mg daily	50 mg daily	25 mg daily	nil
Introducing citalopram	nil	10 mg daily	10 mg daily	20 mg daily	20 mg daily

Potential dangers of simultaneously administering two antidepressants include additive effects (e.g. serotonin syndrome, hypotension, drowsiness) and pharmacokinetic interactions (e.g. some SSRIs raise TCA plasma levels).

Stopping antidepressants

Discontinuation symptoms may occur on abruptly stopping all classes of antidepressants and seem to be more common with longer treatment courses. Discontinuation symptoms rarely occur with treatments lasting less than 5 weeks [Haddad, 2001].

Symptoms usually appear within a few days of stopping the antidepressant. Onset more than a week later is unusual. Most reactions are mild and rarely last more than 1–2 weeks. Symptoms include dizziness, anxiety and agitation, insomnia, 'flu-like symptoms, diarrhoea and abdominal cramps, paraesthesiae, mood swings, nausea, and low mood. There have been isolated reports of electric shock sensations, vertigo, and manic reactions on SSRI withdrawal [CSM, 2000b; Taylor et al, 2001].

If possible, taper the dosage (or frequency) of antidepressant over a minimum of 4 weeks when stopping treatment. More rapid discontinuation may be necessary in people with severe adverse reactions to treatment. Taper the dosage over 6 months in people who have been receiving longer-term maintenance treatment.

Fluoxetine may be stopped abruptly if the dose is 20 mg/day, as it has a long half-life and active metabolites [Taylor et al, 2001].

If a discontinuation reaction occurs, explanation and reassurance are often all that is required. If this is not sufficient, and for more severe reactions, the antidepressant should be restarted and subsequently reduced more slowly [Anderson et al, 2000; Haddad, 2001; Taylor et al, 2001].

Driving

Drugs that cause sedation should be used with great care in people who drive. The Driver and Vehicle Licensing Agency (DVLA) warns that doctors who fail to advise their patients of the dangers of adverse effects of medication may have serious medicolegal difficulties should an accident occur [DVLA, 2000].

The sedative effect of antidepressants is likely to be greatest in the first month of starting or increasing the dosage. The DVLA advises that it is important to cease driving during this time if adversely affected.

The DVLA recommends avoiding drugs that have antimuscarinic effects, such as TCAs, and advise caution with drugs that have antihistamine effects. Although SSRIs are less likely to cause sedation, people started on these should still be warned of this possibility.

St John's wort (*Hypericum*)

St John's wort (*Hypericum perforatum*) is an unlicensed herbal remedy for depression, available without prescription. It has various central effects, including inhibition of serotonin, dopamine, and noradrenaline uptake, stimulation of gamma aminobutyric acid (GABA)-receptors, and weak inhibition of monoamine oxidase [MeReC, 2001].

A Cochrane systematic review found that St John's wort was more effective than placebo for the short-term treatment of mild to moderate depression. However, there was inadequate evidence to establish whether it was as effective as other antidepressants [Linde and Mulrow, 2001].

Several subsequent studies have reported mixed findings. Two randomized, double blind trials compared St John's wort with imipramine and found it to be similarly effective [Phillip et al, 1999; Woelk, 2000]. A randomized, double blind, placebo-controlled trial failed to show any benefit [Shelton et al, 2001].

- **St John's wort is best avoided** in people taking warfarin, ciclosporin, oral contraceptives, anticonvulsants, digoxin, theophylline, and several anti-HIV drugs. It induces cytochrome P450 enzymes and therefore reduces the levels of these drugs. St John's wort should not be used with SSRIs or triptans (e.g. sumatriptan) because of the risk of additive serotoninergic adverse effects [CSM, 2000a].
- **Preparations can differ widely** in their content of potentially active ingredients. Different products cannot be assumed to be equally effective or to have equal effects on interacting drugs [CSM, 2000a; MeReC, 2001].
- **St John's wort should not be used during pregnancy or breastfeeding** until further evidence as to its safety in these situations is available [SIGN, 2002].

References

1. AHCPR (1993a) *Depression in primary care: volume 1. Detection and diagnosis.* Clinical Practice Guideline, No. 5. Agency for Health Care Policy and Research, US Dept. of Health and Human Services. www.mentalhealth.com/bookah/p44-d1a.html#Head2 [Accessed: 01/03/2003].
2. AHCPR (1993b) *Depression in primary care: volume 2. Treatment of major depression.* Clinical Practice Guideline, No. 5. Agency for Health Care Policy and Research, US Dept. of Health and Human Services. www.mentalhealth.com [Accessed: 01/03/2003].
3. Anderson, I.M., Nutt, D.J. and Deakin, J.F.W. (2000) Evidence-based guidelines for treating depressive disorders with antidepressants: a revision of the 1993 British association for psychopharmacology guidelines. *Journal of Psychopharmacology* **14**(1), 3–20.
4. Angst, J. (1997) A regular review of the long term follow up of depression. *British Medical Journal* **315**(7116), 1143–1146. [Full text]
5. Barbui, C., Hotopf, M., Freemantle, N. et al (2001) *Selective serotonin reuptake inhibitors versus tricyclic and heterocyclic antidepressants: comparison of drug adherence (Cochrane Review).* The Cochrane Library. Issue 1. Oxford: Update Software.
6. BNF 41 (2001) *British National Formulary.* 41st edn. London: British Medical Association and Royal Pharmaceutical Society of Great Britain.
7. CSM (1985) Dangers of newer antidepressants. *Current Problems in Pharmacovigilance* **11**(15), 1.
8. CSM (2000a) Reminder: St John's wort (hypericum perforatum) interactions. *Current Problems in Pharmacovigilance* **26**(May), 6–7.
9. CSM (2000b) Selective serotonin reuptake inhibitors (SSRI's). *Current Problems in Pharmacovigilance* **26**(Sep), 11–12.
10. CSM (2004) *Paroxetine (Seroxat): reminder to use the recommended dose.* Committee on Safety of Medicines. http://medicines.mhra.gov.uk/aboutagency/regframework/csm/csmhome.htm [Accessed: 30/04/2004].
11. De Abajo, F.J., Rodriguez, L.A.G. and Montero, D. (1999) Association between selective serotonin reuptake inhibitors and upper gastrointestinal bleeding: population based case-control study. *British Medical Journal* **319**(7217), 1106–1109.
12. DH (2001) *Treatment choice in psychological therapies and counselling: evidence based clinical practice*

guideline. Department of Health. www.dh.gov.uk [Accessed: 27/04/2004].

13. DVLA (2000) *At a glance guide to current medical standards of fitness to drive. Psychiatric disorders.* Drivers Medical Group, Driver and Vehicle Licensing Authority. www.dvla.gov.uk/at_a_glance/content.htm [Accessed: 27/04/2001].
14. Eccles, M., Freemantle, N. and Mason, J. (1998) *The choice of antidepressants for depression in primary care.* Newcastle upon Tyne: Centre for Health Services Research.
15. Eccles, M., Freemantle, N. and Mason, J. (1999) North of England evidence-based guideline development project: summary version of guidelines for the choice of antidepressants for depression in primary care. *Family Practice* **16**(2), 103–111. [Full text]
16. Edwards, J.G. and Anderson, I. (1999) Systematic review and guide to selection of selective serotonin reuptake inhibitors. *Drugs* **57**(4), 507–533.
17. Geddes, J. and Butler, R. (2001) Depressive disorders. *Clinical Evidence* **5**(Jun), 652–667.
18. Geddes, J., Freemantle, N., Mason, J. et al (2001) *SSRIs versus other antidepressants for depressive disorder (Cochrane Review).* The Cochrane Library. Issue 1. Oxford: Update Software.
19. Haddad, P.M. (2001) Antidepressant discontinuation syndromes. *Drug Safety* **24**(3), 183–197.
20. Hawley, C.J., Quick, S.J., Harding, M.J. et al (1997) A preliminary study to examine the adequacy of long term treatment of depression and the extent of recovery in general practice. *British Journal of General Practice* **47**(417), 233–234.
21. Hutchinson, A., McIntosh, A., Field, R. et al (2001) *Evidence based aspects of care and review criteria for adults with depression.* University of Sheffield: RCGP Effective Clinical Practice Unit.
22. Linde, K. and Mulrow, C.D. (2001) *St John's Wort for depression (Cochrane Review).* The Cochrane Library. Issue 2. Oxford: Update Software.
23. Mason, J., Freemantle, N. and Eccles, M. (2000) Fatal toxicity associated with antidepressant use in primary care. *British Journal of General Practice* **50**(45), 366–370.
24. MeReC (2000) The drug treatment of depression in primary care. *MeReC Bulletin* **11**(9), 33–36.
25. MeReC (2001) St John's Wort: is it effective in depression? *MeReC Extra* **1**(Jul), 1.
26. Misri, S. and Kostaras, X. (2002) Benefits and risks to mother and infant of drug treatment for postnatal depression. *Drug Safety* **25**(13), 903–911.
27. National Health and Medical Research Council (2002) *Postnatal depression. A systematic review of published scientific literature to 1999.* National Health and Medical Research Council. www.health.gov.au/nhmrc/publications/synopses/wh29syn.htm [Accessed: 2003/03/]. [Full text]
28. National Teratology Information Service (1997) *Treatments for depression in pregnancy.* NHS Northern and Yorkshire: Regional Drug and Therapeutics Centre.
29. NHC (1996) *Guidelines for the treatment and management of depression by primary healthcare professionals.* New Zealand: National Health Committee, National Advisory Committee on Health and Disability.
30. NHS CRD (1993) The treatment of depression in primary care. *Effective Health Care Bulletin* **1**(5), 1–12.
31. Paykel, E.S. and Priest, R.G. (1992) Recognition and management of depression in general practice: consensus statement. *British Medical Journal* **305**(6863), 1198–1202.
32. Phillip, M., Kohnen, R. and Hiller, K. (1999) Hypericum extract versus imipramine or placebo in patients with moderate depression: randomised multicentre study of treatment for eight weeks. *British Medical Journal* **319**(7224), 1534–1538.
33. Shelton, R.C., Keller, M.B., Gelenberg, A. et al (2001) Effectiveness of St John's wort in major depression: a randomized controlled trial. *Journal of the American Medical Association* **285**(15), 1978–1986.
34. SIGN (2002) *Postnatal depression and puerperal psychosis.* Guideline no. 60. Scottish Intercollegiate Guidelines Network. www.sign.ac.uk [Accessed: 30/05/2003].
35. Taylor, D., McConnell, H., Duncan-McConnell, D. and Kerwin, R. (Eds.) (2001) *The Bethlem & Maudsley NHS Trust: 2001 Maudsley prescribing guidelines.* 6th edn. London: Martin Dunitz.
36. UKMI (2003) *What is the optimal management of depression in a breastfeeding mother?* UKMiCentral. UK Medicines Information. www.ukmi.nhs.uk [Accessed: 03/03/2003].
37. UK National Screening Committee (2002) *Information sheet on screening for Chlamydia trachomatis infection.* Department of Health. www.nsc.nhs.uk [Accessed: 01/07/2002].
38. van Walraven, C., Mamdani, M.M., Wells, P.S. and Williams, J.I. (2001) Inhibition of serotonin reuptake by antidepressants and upper gastrointestinal bleeding in elderly patients: retrospective cohort study. *British Medical Journal* **323**(7314), 655–660.
39. Woelk, H. (2000) Comparison of St John's wort and imipramine for treating depression: randomised controlled trial. *British Medical Journal* **321**(7260), 536–539.

PRODIGY GUIDANCE

Dermatitis — contact

Last revised in February 2005
www.prodigy.nhs.uk/guidance.asp?gt=Dermatitis - contact

Applies to people over the age of 1 month

This guidance covers the management of dermatitis caused by contact with irritants and allergens.

This guidance does not cover other forms of cutaneous response after contact with irritants or allergens such as chemical burns, urticaria, or pigmentary or necrotic reactions. It also does not cover the management of phototoxic, photoallergic, or photoaggravated contact dermatitis.

There is separate PRODIGY guidance for *Eczema — atopic, Nappy rash, Seborrhoeic dermatitis,* and *Urticaria.*

D

Goals

To treat symptoms of acute dermatitis
To identify the irritant or allergen if possible
To advise on avoidance of contact with the irritant or allergen
To advise on measures to prevent or minimize recurrence of dermatitis

Contents

Scenarios

- Dry skin p.505
- Acute dermatitis p.507
- Persistent contact dermatitis p.509
- Widespread contact dermatitis — more than 25% body affected p.512
- Preventing contact dermatitis p.513

Extended Information, p. 514

Which scenario?

Dry skin: covers the management of dry skin, which may be a presenting feature of cumulative irritant dermatitis, or may accompany an acute flare-up.
Acute dermatitis: covers the management of the initial presentation of an acute flare-up of dermatitis.
Persistent contact dermatitis: covers the management of people who present with recurrent episodes of suspected contact dermatitis, and advises on when to refer for confirmation of the diagnosis or identification of the cause by patch testing.
Widespread contact dermatitis — more than 25% body affected: covers the management of contact dermatitis when it involves more than 25% of the body.
Preventing contact dermatitis: covers advice on measures to prevent or reduce further episodes of confirmed contact dermatitis.

Dry skin

Which therapy?

In the early stages of contact dermatitis, there may be only minimal inflammation, often associated with dry skin and mild itching.

Recommend frequent, liberal use of an emollient.

- **Choice of emollient** should be based on:
  - Dryness of skin
  - Area of application
  - Individual preference
- **For mildly dry skin or weeping dermatitis:** a cream is usually appropriate.
- **For moderate to severely dry skin:** an ointment may be needed to restore skin to normal.
- **Prescribe generous quantities** of the product that is most acceptable to the person.
- **Emphasize the need for regular use** of emollients and offer sufficient quantities for application at least three times a day.
- **Advise on avoiding common environmental irritants and preventing recurrence, e.g.**
  - Use an emollient soap substitute.
  - Use gloves when unable to avoid handling irritants such as detergents.
  - Avoid extremes of temperature and humidity.
  - Reapply emollients after wetting skin.

Practical prescribing points

For further information please see the *Medicines Compendium* (www.medicines.org.uk) or the *British National Formulary* (www.bnf.org).

- **Reactions to emollients are** most commonly due to preservatives, fragrances, lanolin, or arachis oil, and if such a cause is suspected the person should switch to a product with different constituents (see Table 5).
- Cutaneous reactions to aqueous cream are particularly common. Different brands of aqueous cream may contain different antimicrobials, and the person should be advised to check this at the time of dispensing.
- Ideally, prescribe small quantities of a selection of creams and ointments to find the most acceptable treatment to the person. Where prescription charges apply, it may be cheaper for the person to buy the emollients.

Follow-up advice

- If skin is dry or if mild inflammation reoccurs or does not settle, increase the intensity of treatment by all or any of the following:
  - Change to a product with a higher lipid content (lotion to cream or cream to ointment).
  - Suggest the use of ointments at night if daytime use is unacceptable.
  - Increase the frequency of application.
  - Increase the quantity of emollient applied.
- **If mild inflammation does not settle** with emollients, prescribe a topical corticosteroid of an appropriate potency. For further information, see the scenario *Acute dermatitis.*

D

Should I refer or investigate?

Refer?

- Referral is rarely necessary for an individual with dry skin without a significant dermatitis.
- Consider referral if the diagnosis is uncertain.

Investigate?

- Investigation of dry skin without significant dermatitis is not necessary.

Patient information leaflets

The following PILs are available at www.prodigy.nhs.uk

- Contact Dermatitis
- Contact Dermatitis - Patch Testing
- Eczema - Emollients (Moisturisers)
- Eczema - Triggers and Irritants
- National Eczema Society

Shared decision making

- **Emollients (moisturizers)** help to settle a mild flare-up of dermatitis (eczema).
- **Apply liberally** as often as you need. Commonly 2–3 times per day.
- Many people use a variety. For example:
  - A thick ointment as a soap substitute.
  - A cream or ointment at other times.
    - Ointments work better and longer than creams, but are messier to use.
    - Creams for mild dry skin, or for weepy eczema.
  - Lotions for hairy areas.
  - An ointment at bedtime.
- Rarely, some people become sensitized to an ingredient in an emollient. If this occurs, you can switch to a different one.

Drug rationale

Many emollients are available and there is little evidence to support the use of one particular product over another. Emollients offered have been selected on the basis of their common usage and relative cost. However, some people may find that other preparations are more suitable for their personal needs.

Drugs not included

- **Emollients containing antiseptic agents,** such as triclosan and benzalkonium chloride, have failed to demonstrate adequately that they improve clinical symptoms or reduce the load of *Staphylococcus aureus* in people with atopic eczema. We found no study comparing their efficacy to emollients alone in contact dermatitis. Additionally, they may cause allergic and irritant contact dermatitis [DTB, 1998].
- **Emollients containing urea** are not offered. Evidence for additional benefit is limited, and their use should be reserved for when standard emollients have proved ineffective. Their odour and irritation on application also make them unsuitable for general use [MeReC, 1998].
- **Emollients containing antipruritic agents,** such as lauromacrogols, are not offered. Evidence of additional benefits over standard emollients is limited [MeReC, 1998].

Drugs included

- **Ointments:** emulsifying, hydrous, liquid and soft paraffin, Epaderm®, and Hydromol® can be applied directly to skin, or used as a soap substitute.
- **Creams:** aqueous, Aveeno®, Diprobase®, E45®, Oilatum®, and Unguentum M® have lower lipid conten than ointments, but are a good alternative for people who cannot tolerate ointments, or want an emollient for regular use during the day (especially on the face and hands).

Prescriptions

Emollient ointments

Emulsifying ointment BP

- Age from 1 month onwards
- Emulsifying ointment BP. Apply to skin frequently and liberally, as often as required. Use as a soap substitute; supply 500 grams; NHS Cost £1.54; OTC Cost £3.06.

Hydrous ointment BP

- Age from 1 month onwards
- Hydrous ointment BP. Apply to skin frequently and liberally, as often as required. Use as a soap substitute; supply 500 grams; NHS Cost £1.99; OTC Cost £3.51.

Liquid and white soft paraffin ointment NPF

- Age from 1 month onwards
- Liquid+white soft paraffin. Apply to skin frequently and liberally, as often as required. Use as a soap substitute; supply 500 grams; NHS Cost £3.76; OTC Cost £6.63.

Epaderm ointment

- Age from 1 month onwards
- Epaderm ointment (500g). Apply to skin frequently and liberally, as often as required. Use as a soap substitute; supply 1 500 gram tub; NHS Cost £6.21; OTC Cost £10.94.

Hydromol ointment

- Age from 1 month onwards
- Hydromol ointment (500g). Apply to skin frequently and liberally, as often as required. Use as a soap substitute; supply 1 500 gram tub; NHS Cost £5.58; OTC Cost £9.79.

Emollient creams

Aqueous cream BP

- Age from 1 month onwards
- Aqueous cream BP. Apply to skin frequently and liberally, as often as required. Use as a soap substitute; supply 500 grams; NHS Cost £1.06; OTC Cost £1.87.

Diprobase cream

- Age from 1 month onwards
- Diprobase cream (500g). Apply to skin frequently and liberally, as often as required. Use as a soap substitute; supply 500 grams; NHS Cost £6.61; OTC Cost £11.65.

E45 cream

- Age from 1 month onwards
- E45 cream (500g). Apply to skin frequently and liberally as often as required. Use as a soap substitute; supply 500 grams; NHS Cost £6.20; OTC Cost £9.69.

Oilatum cream

- Age from 1 month onwards
- Oilatum cream (500ml). Apply to skin frequently and liberally, as often as required. Use as a soap substitute; supply 500 ml; NHS Cost £6.35; OTC Cost £9.93.

Unguentum M cream

- Age from 1 month onwards
- Unguentum M cream (500g). Apply to skin frequently and liberally, as often as required. Use as a soap substitute; supply 500 grams; NHS Cost £9.55; OTC Cost £18.70.

Acute dermatitis

Which therapy

Settle inflammation with topical corticosteroids.

For adults:

- Face, genitals, and flexures — treat with mildly potent corticosteroid.
- The eyelids — treat with mildly potent corticosteroid for a maximum of 7 days.
- The palms, soles of the feet, and scalp — treat with potent corticosteroid.
- The trunk and limbs — select the lowest potency of corticosteroid that is likely to work within 7–14 days of treatment, based on the severity of inflammation.

For children and infants:

- Treat all skin areas with mildly potent corticosteroid as a first choice.
- Moderately potent preparations on areas other than the face, genitals, or flexures may be used second-line for short periods.

Recommend frequent, liberal use of an emollient if dermatitis is associated with dry skin (see the scenario *Dry skin*).

Treat visibly infected eczema with oral antibiotics.

- **Flucloxacillin or erythromycin** (if the person is allergic to penicillin) is recommended first-line.

Advise on avoiding common environmental irritants and preventing recurrence, e.g.

- Use an emollient soap substitute.
- Use gloves when unable to avoid handling irritants such as detergents.
- Avoid extremes of temperature and humidity.
- Reapply emollients after wetting skin.

ractical prescribing points

or further information please see the *Medicines ompendium* (www.medicines.org.uk) or the *British ational Formulary* (www.bnf.org).

opical corticosteroids

Advise the person to use topical corticosteroids sparingly, and for the shortest amount of time necessary to achieve resolution of symptoms.

ollow-up advice

rrangements for follow-up will depend on the severity of e presenting dermatitis and the response to treatment. eview if there are not clear signs of improvement within -7 days of starting treatment.

nflammation not settling on trunk or limbs

Review if not showing significant signs of improvement within 7 days, and step up to a more potent steroid.

nfection not resolving on first choice ntibiotics

Swab visibly infected areas if signs of infection are not significantly improving within 3 days.

Change oral antibiotics according to the result of sensitivities.

kin remains dry on first-choice emollient

If skin is dry, increase the intensity of treatment by all or any of the following:

- Change to a product with a higher lipid content (e.g. lotion to cream or cream to ointment).
- Suggest the use of ointments at night if daytime use is unacceptable.
- Increase the frequency of application.
- Increase the quantity of emollient applied.

Should I refer or investigate?

Refer?

- **Unresponsive severe disease,** including bacterially infected dermatitis unresponsive to treatment with oral antibiotics and topical corticosteroids — arrange emergency admission or urgent referral, depending on severity.

Investigate?

- Swab visibly infected areas and change oral antibiotics according to the result of sensitivities.

Patient information leaflets

The following PILs are available at www.prodigy.nhs.uk

- Contact Dermatitis
- Contact Dermatitis - Patch Testing
- Eczema - Emollients (Moisturisers)
- Eczema - Fingertip Units for Topical Steroids
- Eczema - Topical Steroids
- Eczema - Triggers and Irritants
- National Eczema Society

Shared decision making

- **A steroid cream or ointment** reduces skin inflammation. Apply daily until the flare-up of dermatitis (eczema) has gone, and then stop it.
  - In many cases, a 7–14 day course of a mild steroid is enough.
  - Return for a stronger steroid if there is no improvement in 5–7 days.
  - Side effects are uncommon unless used long-term.
- **Also, use liberal amounts of emollients** (moisturizers) if your skin is dry.
- **An antibiotic** may be needed if the inflamed skin becomes infected.

Drug rationale

Drugs not included

- **Oral corticosteroids** may be useful as 'rescue therapy' for particularly severe and widespread dermatitis (see the scenario *Widespread contact dermatitis*). They should not be used for localized dermatitis.
- **Very potent topical corticosteroids:** clobetasol propionate, difluocortolone valerate, and halcinonide are reserved for use under specialist supervision in dermatitis that has proved resistant to other topical corticosteroids.
- **Topical corticosteroids with antimicrobial agents:** there is a lack of evidence that these products are more effective than topical corticosteroids alone, and there is a possibility that widespread use may contribute to the development of bacterial resistance.
- **Emollients** should be used in addition to a topical corticosteroid if dermatitis is associated with dry skin. Prescriptions for emollients are given in the scenario *Dry skin.*
- **Antihistamines:** allergic contact dermatitis is a Type IV hypersensitivity reaction, and is not mediated by histamine. There is no evidence that antihistamines relieve the symptoms of contact dermatitis.

Drugs included

- **Mildly potent topical corticosteroid:** hydrocortisone is suitable for use in mild eczema, inflammation of sensitive areas such as the face or neck, and dermatitis in infants.
- **Moderately potent topical corticosteroids:** aclometasone dipropionate, clobetasone butyrate, and dilute betamethasone valerate 0.025% are suitable for use in moderate to severe dermatitis.
- **Potent topical corticosteroids:** betamethasone valerate 0.1%, betamethasone dipropionate, hydrocortisone butyrate, and mometasone furoate are suitable for use in severe dermatitis, and in dermatitis on the palms, the soles of the feet, and the scalp.
- **Lotions and foams are suitable vehicles for scalp applications** and are usually easier to apply than standard creams and ointments. Topical applications of betamethasone valerate and betamethasone dipropionate are recommended for eczema of the scalp.
- **Flucloxacillin** has activity against Gram-positive organisms, including beta-lactamase-producing staphylococci and streptococci. It is licensed in the treatment of infected skin conditions.
- **Erythromycin** is suitable for people with infected eczema who have a known hypersensitivity to penicillin and related antibiotics.

Prescriptions

Mildly potent corticosteroids

Hydrocortisone 1% ointment

- Age from 1 month onwards
- Hydrocortisone 1% ointment (30g). Apply thinly to the affected area once a day until symptoms have completely resolved; supply 30 grams; NHS Cost £0.72; OTC Cost £1.27.

Hydrocortisone 1% cream

- Age from 1 month onwards
- Hydrocortisone 1% cream (30g). Apply thinly to the affected area once a day until symptoms have completely resolved; supply 30 grams; NHS Cost £0.72; OTC Cost £1.27.

Moderately potent corticosteroids

Betamethasone valerate 0.025% ointment

- Age from 2 years onwards
- Betamethasone val 0.025% ointment. Apply thinly to the affected area once a day until symptoms have completely resolved; supply 100 grams; NHS Cost £3.34.

Clobetasone butyrate 0.05% ointment

- Age from 2 years onwards
- Clobetasone butyrate 0.05% ointment. Apply thinly to the affected area once a day until symptoms have completely resolved; supply 30 grams; NHS Cost £1.97.

Alclometasone dipropionate 0.05% ointment

- Age from 2 years onwards
- Alclometasone 0.05% ointment. Apply thinly to the affected area once a day until symptoms have completely resolved; supply 50 grams; NHS Cost £2.68.

Betamethasone valerate 0.025% cream

- Age from 2 years onwards
- Betamethasone val 0.025% cream. Apply thinly to the affected area once a day until symptoms have completely resolved; supply 100 grams; NHS Cost £3.34.

Clobetasone butyrate 0.05% cream

- Age from 2 years onwards
- Clobetasone butyrate 0.05% cream. Apply thinly to th affected area once a day until symptoms have complete resolved; supply 30 grams; NHS Cost £1.97.

Alclometasone dipropionate 0.05% cream

- Age from 2 years onwards
- Alclometasone 0.05% cream. Apply thinly to the affected area once a day until symptoms have complete resolved; supply 50 grams; NHS Cost £2.68.

Potent corticosteroids

Betamethasone valerate 0.1% ointment

- Age from 12 years onwards
- Betamethasone val 0.1% ointment. Apply thinly to the affected area once a day until symptoms have complete resolved; supply 30 grams; NHS Cost £1.54.

Hydrocortisone butyrate 0.1% ointment

- Age from 12 years onwards
- Hydrocortisone butyr 0.1% ointment. Apply thinly to the affected area once a day until symptoms have completely resolved; supply 30 grams; NHS Cost £2.2

Betamethasone dipropionate 0.05% ointment

- Age from 12 years onwards
- Diprosone 0.05% ointment (30g). Apply thinly to the affected area once a day until symptoms have complete resolved; supply 30 grams; NHS Cost £2.41.

Mometasone furoate 0.1% ointment

- Age from 12 years onwards
- Mometasone 0.1% furoate ointment. Apply thinly to th affected area once a day until symptoms have complete resolved; supply 30 grams; NHS Cost £4.88.

Betamethasone valerate 0.1% cream

- Age from 12 years onwards
- Betamethasone val 0.1% cream. Apply thinly to the affected area once a day until symptoms have complete resolved; supply 30 grams; NHS Cost £1.54.

Hydrocortisone butyrate 0.1% cream

- Age from 12 years onwards
- Hydrocortisone butyr 0.1% cream. Apply thinly to the affected area once a day until symptoms have complete resolved; supply 30 grams; NHS Cost £2.29.

Betamethasone dipropionate 0.05% cream

- Age from 12 years onwards
- Diprosone 0.05% cream (30g). Apply thinly to the affected area once a day until symptoms have complete resolved; supply 30 grams; NHS Cost £2.41.

Mometasone furoate 0.1% cream 30 grams

- Age from 12 years onwards
- Mometasone 0.1% furoate cream. Apply thinly to the affected area once a day until symptoms have complete resolved; supply 30 grams; NHS Cost £4.88.

Corticosteroid scalp applications

Betamethasone valerate 0.1% scalp application

- Age from 12 years onwards
- Betamethasone val 0.1% sca app. Apply to scalp once a day, for up to 7 days; supply 100 ml; NHS Cost £5.70.

Betamethasone valerate 0.1% lotion

- Age from 12 years onwards
- Betamethasone val 0.1% lotion. Apply to scalp once a day, for up to 7 days; supply 100 ml; NHS Cost £5.23.

Betamethasone valerate 0.12% foam

- Age from 12 years onwards
- Betamethasone val 0.12% foam. Apply to scalp once a day, for up to 7 days; supply 100 grams; NHS Cost £7.50.

etamethasone dipropionate 0.05% lotion
Age from 12 years onwards
Diprosone 0.05% lotion (30ml). Apply to scalp once a day, for up to 7 days; supply 1 30ml applicator; NHS Cost £3.04.

ydrocortisone butyrate 0.1% scalp application
Age from 12 years onwards
Hydrocortisone butyr scalp lotion. Apply to scalp once a day, for up to 7 days; supply 100 ml; NHS Cost £10.49.

ometasone furoate 0.1% scalp application
Age from 12 years onwards
Mometasone 0.1% lotion. Apply to scalp once a day, for up to 7 days; supply 60 ml; NHS Cost £9.76.

uocinolone acetonide 0.025% gel
Age from 12 years onwards
Fluocinolone acet 0.025% gel. Apply to scalp once a day, for up to 7 days; supply 30 grams; NHS Cost £3.34.

Antibiotic (IF clinically infected)

ucloxacillin syrup: 62.5mg four times a day
Age from 1 month to 23 months
Flucloxacillin 125mg/5ml syrup. Take 2.5ml four times a day for 7 days; supply 100 ml; NHS Cost £3.23.

ucloxacillin syrup: 125mg four times a day
Age from 2 to 4 years
Flucloxacillin 125mg/5ml syrup. Take one 5ml spoonful four times a day for 7 days; supply 200 ml; NHS Cost £6.46.

ucloxacillin syrup: 250mg four times a day
Age from 5 to 11 years
Flucloxacillin 250mg/5ml syrup. Take one 5ml spoonful four times a day for 7 days; supply 200 ml; NHS Cost £13.94.

ucloxacillin capsules: 250mg four times a day
Age from 12 years onwards
Flucloxacillin 250mg capsules. Take one capsule four times a day for 7 days; supply 28 capsules; NHS Cost £2.93.

ucloxacillin capsules: 500mg four times a day
Age from 12 years onwards
Flucloxacillin 500mg capsules. Take one capsule four times a day for 7 days; supply 28 capsules; NHS Cost £4.73.

rythromycin s/f suspension: 125mg four times a day
Age from 1 month to 23 months
Erythromycin 125mg/5ml sf susp. Take one 5ml spoonful four times a day for 7 days; supply 200 ml; NHS Cost £2.22.

rythromycin s/f suspension: 250mg four times a day
Age from 2 to 11 years
Erythromycin 250mg/5ml sf susp. Take one 5ml spoonful four times a day for 7 days; supply 200 ml; NHS Cost £3.80.

rythromycin s/f suspension: 500mg four times a day
Age from 9 to 11 years
Erythromycin 500mg/5ml sf susp. Take one 5ml spoonful four times a day for 7 days; supply 200 ml; NHS Cost £6.46.

rythromycin e/c tablets: 250mg four times a day
Age from 12 years onwards
Erythromycin 250mg e/c tablets. Take one tablet four times a day for 7 days; supply 28 tablets; NHS Cost £3.08.

rythromycin e/c tablets: 500mg four times a day
Age from 12 years onwards
Erythromycin 250mg e/c tablets. Take two tablets four times a day for 7 days; supply 56 tablets; NHS Cost £6.16.

Persistent contact dermatitis

Which therapy

- **Advise strict measures to avoid irritants or allergens** for all likely causes, based upon knowledge of the person's occupation and lifestyle, when contact dermatitis is suspected or cannot be excluded.
  - **Suspect contact dermatitis** as a cause of any persistent or recurrent dermatitis, particularly if the rash is localized and there is a history of exposure (including occupational) to potential irritants or allergens.
- **Step up the potency of topical corticosteroid if dermatitis is on the trunk or limbs.**
- **Ensure frequent, liberal use of an emollient** if dermatitis is associated with dry skin (see the scenario *Dry skin*).
- **Consider contact allergy to topical corticosteroids** if dermatitis fails to respond, or gets worse with their use.
- **Prescribe an oral antibiotic if dermatitis is visibly infected.**
  - Flucloxacillin or erythromycin (if the person is allergic to penicillin) is recommended first-line.

Practical prescribing points

For further information please see the *Medicines Compendium* (www.medicines.org.uk) or the *British National Formulary* (www.bnf.org).

Emollients

- **Reactions to emollients are** most commonly due to preservatives, fragrances, lanolin, or arachis oil, and if they are suspected the person should switch to a product with different constituents (see Table 5).
- Cutaneous reactions to aqueous cream are particularly common. Different brands of aqueous cream may contain different antimicrobials, and the person should be advised to check this at the time of dispensing.

Topical corticosteroids

- Advise the person to use topical corticosteroids sparingly, and for the shortest amount of time necessary to achieve resolution of symptoms.

Follow-up advice

- Review if treatment of the acute dermatitis is not significantly improving with treatment.

Infection not resolving on first-choice antibiotics

- Swab visibly infected areas if signs of infection are not significantly improving within 3 days.
- Change oral antibiotics according to the result of sensitivities.

Skin remains dry on first-choice emollient

- If skin is dry, increase the intensity of treatment by all or any of the following:
  - Change to a product with a higher lipid content (lotion to cream or cream to ointment).
  - Suggest the use of ointments at night if daytime use is unacceptable.
  - Increase the frequency of application.
  - Increase the quantity of emollient applied.

Should I refer or investigate?

Refer?

- **Unresponsive severe disease,** including bacterially infected dermatitis unresponsive to treatment with oral antibiotics and topical corticosteroids — arrange emergency admission or urgent referral, depending on severity.
- **Refer for specialist assessment, including patch testing,** if episodes of dermatitis reoccur despite avoidance measures and the irritant or allergen cannot be clearly identified by exclusion.
- **Refer people with occupational dermatitis** to a dermatologist for full assessment.

Investigate?

- Swab visibly infected areas and change oral antibiotics according to the result of sensitivities.

Patient information leaflets

The following PILs are available at www.prodigy.nhs.uk

- Contact Dermatitis
- Contact Dermatitis - Patch Testing
- Eczema - Emollients (Moisturisers)
- Eczema - Fingertip Units for Topical Steroids
- Eczema - Topical Steroids
- Eczema - Triggers and Irritants
- National Eczema Society

Shared decision making

- **A steroid cream or ointment** reduces skin inflammation. Apply daily until the flare-up of eczema (dermatitis) has gone, and then stop it.
  - In many cases, a 7–14 day course of a mild steroid is enough.
  - Return for a stronger steroid if there is no improvement in 5–7 days.
  - Side effects are uncommon unless used long-term.
- **Also, use liberal amounts of emollients** (moisturizers) if your skin is dry.
- **An antibiotic** may be needed if the inflamed skin becomes infected.
- Your recurring rash may be due to a contact with an irritant or allergen.
  - Do you know what is causing the rash?
  - Can you avoid it?
  - You may need referral for patch testing if the cause is not clear.

Drug rationale

Drugs not included

- **Oral corticosteroids** may be prescribed for particularly severe and widespread dermatitis (see the scenario *Widespread contact dermatitis*).
- **Very potent topical corticosteroids:** clobetasol propionate, difluocortolone valerate, and halcinonide are reserved for use under specialist supervision in dermatitis that has proved resistant to other topical corticosteroids.
- **Topical corticosteroids with antimicrobial agents:** there is a lack of evidence that these products are more effective than topical corticosteroids alone, and there is a possibility that widespread use may contribute to the development of bacterial resistance.
- **Emollients** should be used in addition to a topical corticosteroid if dermatitis is associated with dry skin. Prescriptions for emollients are given in the scenario *Dr skin*.
- **Antihistamines:** allergic contact dermatitis is a Type IV hypersensitivity reaction, and is not mediated by histamine. There is no evidence that antihistamines relieve the symptoms of contact dermatitis.

Drugs included

- **Mildly potent topical corticosteroid:** hydrocortisone is suitable for use in mild eczema, inflammation of sensitiv areas such as the face or neck, and dermatitis in infants.
- **Moderately potent topical corticosteroids:** aclometason dipropionate, clobetasone butyrate, and dilute betamethasone valerate 0.025% are suitable for use in moderate to severe dermatitis.
- **Potent topical corticosteroids:** betamethasone valerate 0.1%, betamethasone dipropionate, hydrocortisone butyrate, and mometasone furoate are suitable for use i severe dermatitis, and dermatitis on the palms, the soles of the feet, and the scalp.
- **Lotions and foams are suitable vehicles for scalp applications** and are usually easier to apply than standard creams and ointments. Topical applications of betamethasone valerate and betamethasone dipropiona are recommended for eczema of the scalp.
- **Flucloxacillin** has activity against Gram-positive organisms, including beta-lactamase producing staphylococci and streptococci. It is licensed in the treatment of infected skin conditions.
- **Erythromycin** is suitable for people with infected eczem who have a known hypersensitivity to penicillin and related antibiotics.

Prescriptions

Mildly potent corticosteroids

Hydrocortisone 1% ointment

- Age from 1 month onwards
- Hydrocortisone 1% ointment (30g). Apply thinly to the affected area once a day until symptoms have complete resolved; supply 30 grams; NHS Cost £0.72; OTC Cost £1.27.

Hydrocortisone 1% cream

- Age from 1 month onwards
- Hydrocortisone 1% cream (30g). Apply thinly to the affected area once a day until symptoms have complete resolved; supply 30 grams; NHS Cost £0.72; OTC Cost £1.27.

Moderately potent corticosteroids

Betamethasone valerate 0.025% ointment

- Age from 2 years onwards
- Betamethasone val 0.025% ointment. Apply thinly to the affected area once a day until symptoms have completely resolved; supply 100 grams; NHS Cost £3.34.

Clobetasone butyrate 0.05% ointment

- Age from 2 years onwards
- Clobetasone butyrate 0.05% ointment. Apply thinly to the affected area once a day until symptoms have completely resolved; supply 30 grams; NHS Cost £1.97

Alclometasone dipropionate 0.05% ointment

- Age from 2 years onwards
- Alclometasone 0.05% ointment. Apply thinly to the affected area once a day until symptoms have complete resolved; supply 50 grams; NHS Cost £2.68.

etamethasone valerate 0.025% cream
- Age from 2 years onwards
- Betamethasone val 0.025% cream. Apply thinly to the affected area once a day until symptoms have completely resolved; supply 100 grams; NHS Cost £3.34.

lobetasone butyrate 0.05% cream
- Age from 2 years onwards
- Clobetasone butyrate 0.05% cream. Apply thinly to the affected area once a day until symptoms have completely resolved; supply 30 grams; NHS Cost £1.97.

lclometasone dipropionate 0.05% cream
- Age from 2 years onwards
- Alclometasone 0.05% cream. Apply thinly to the affected area once a day until symptoms have completely resolved; supply 50 grams; NHS Cost £2.68.

otent corticosteroids

etamethasone valerate 0.1% ointment
- Age from 12 years onwards
- Betamethasone val 0.1% ointment. Apply thinly to the affected area once a day until symptoms have completely resolved; supply 30 grams; NHS Cost £1.54.

ydrocortisone butyrate 0.1% ointment
- Age from 12 years onwards
- Hydrocortisone butyr 0.1% ointment. Apply thinly to the affected area once a day until symptoms have completely resolved; supply 30 grams; NHS Cost £2.29.

etamethasone dipropionate 0.05% ointment
- Age from 12 years onwards
- Diprosone 0.05% ointment (30g). Apply thinly to the affected area once a day until symptoms have completely resolved; supply 30 grams; NHS Cost £2.41.

ometasone furoate 0.1% ointment
- Age from 12 years onwards
- Mometasone 0.1% furoate ointment. Apply thinly to the affected area once a day until symptoms have completely resolved; supply 30 grams; NHS Cost £4.88.

etamethasone valerate 0.1% cream
- Age from 12 years onwards
- Betamethasone val 0.1% cream. Apply thinly to the affected area once a day until symptoms have completely resolved; supply 30 grams; NHS Cost £1.54.

ydrocortisone butyrate 0.1% cream
- Age from 12 years onwards
- Hydrocortisone butyr 0.1% cream. Apply thinly to the affected area once a day until symptoms have completely resolved; supply 30 grams; NHS Cost £2.29.

etamethasone dipropionate 0.05% cream
- Age from 12 years onwards
- Diprosone 0.05% cream (30g). Apply thinly to the affected area once a day until symptoms have completely resolved; supply 30 grams; NHS Cost £2.41.

ometasone furoate 0.1% cream 30 grams
- Age from 12 years onwards
- Mometasone 0.1% furoate cream. Apply thinly to the affected area once a day until symptoms have completely resolved; supply 30 grams; NHS Cost £4.88.

orticosteroid scalp applications

etamethasone valerate 0.1% scalp application
- Age from 12 years onwards
- Betamethasone val 0.1% sca app. Apply to scalp once a day, for up to 7 days; supply 100 ml; NHS Cost £5.70.

etamethasone valerate 0.1% lotion
- Age from 12 years onwards
- Betamethasone val 0.1% lotion. Apply to scalp once a day, for up to 7 days; supply 100 ml; NHS Cost £5.23.

Betamethasone valerate 0.12% foam
- Age from 12 years onwards
- Betamethasone val 0.12% foam. Apply to scalp once a day, for up to 7 days; supply 100 grams; NHS Cost £7.50.

Betamethasone dipropionate 0.05% lotion
- Age from 12 years onwards
- Diprosone 0.05% lotion (30ml). Apply to scalp once a day, for up to 7 days; supply 1 30ml applicator; NHS Cost £3.04.

Hydrocortisone butyrate 0.1% scalp application
- Age from 12 years onwards
- Hydrocortisone butyr scalp lotion. Apply to scalp once a day, for up to 7 days; supply 100 ml; NHS Cost £10.49.

Mometasone furoate 0.1% scalp application
- Age from 12 years onwards
- Mometasone 0.1% lotion. Apply to scalp once a day, for up to 7 days; supply 60 ml; NHS Cost £9.76.

Antibiotic (IF clinically infected)

Flucloxacillin syrup: 62.5mg four times a day
- Age from 1 month to 23 months
- Flucloxacillin 125mg/5ml syrup. Take 2.5ml four times a day for 7 days; supply 100 ml; NHS Cost £3.23.

Flucloxacillin syrup: 125mg four times a day
- Age from 2 to 4 years
- Flucloxacillin 125mg/5ml syrup. Take one 5ml spoonful four times a day for 7 days; supply 200 ml; NHS Cost £6.46.

Flucloxacillin syrup: 250mg four times a day
- Age from 5 to 11 years
- Flucloxacillin 250mg/5ml syrup. Take one 5ml spoonful four times a day for 7 days; supply 200 ml; NHS Cost £13.94.

Flucloxacillin capsules: 250mg four times a day
- Age from 12 years onwards
- Flucloxacillin 250mg capsules. Take one capsule four times a day for 7 days; supply 28 capsules; NHS Cost £2.93.

Flucloxacillin capsules: 500mg four times a day
- Age from 12 years onwards
- Flucloxacillin 500mg capsules. Take one capsule four times a day for 7 days; supply 28 capsules; NHS Cost £4.73.

Erythromycin s/f suspension: 125mg four times a day
- Age from 1 month to 23 months
- Erythromycin 125mg/5ml sf susp. Take one 5ml spoonful four times a day for 7 days; supply 200 ml; NHS Cost £2.22.

Erythromycin s/f suspension: 250mg four times a day
- Age from 2 to 11 years
- Erythromycin 250mg/5ml sf susp. Take one 5ml spoonful four times a day for 7 days; supply 200 ml; NHS Cost £3.80.

Erythromycin s/f suspension: 500mg four times a day
- Age from 9 to 11 years
- Erythromycin 500mg/5ml sf susp. Take one 5ml spoonful four times a day for 7 days; supply 200 ml; NHS Cost £6.46.

Erythromycin e/c tablets: 250mg four times a day
- Age from 12 years onwards
- Erythromycin 250mg e/c tablets. Take one tablet four times a day for 7 days; supply 28 tablets; NHS Cost £3.08.

Erythromycin e/c tablets: 500mg four times a day
- Age from 12 years onwards
- Erythromycin 250mg e/c tablets. Take two tablets four times a day for 7 days; supply 56 tablets; NHS Cost £6.16.

D

Widespread contact dermatitis — more than 25% body affected

Which therapy

Contact dermatitis is considered widespread when greater than 25% of the body is affected and the cause is known and avoidable in future.

- **Seek specialist help if:**
  - Dermatitis is severe and widespread.
  - The cause is not known.
  - Widespread dermatitis presents in a child.
- **Prescribe oral antibiotics** if there are any visible signs of infection.
  - Flucloxacillin or erythromycin (if the person is allergic to penicillin) is first-choice antibiotics.
- **In adults: consider prescribing oral prednisolone** when the cause is known and is avoidable in the future.
  - **Prednisolone 30 mg once a day** is likely to be effective in most cases. Clinical judgement should be used to determine the exact dose in an individual case.
  - **Continue treatment with oral corticosteroids for 2–3 weeks,** reducing the dose slowly.

Practical prescribing points

For further information please see the *Medicines Compendium* (www.medicines.org.uk) or the *British National Formulary* (www.bnf.org).

Follow-up advice

- Review after 7 days of treatment, or earlier if response to treatment is poor.

Should I refer or investigate?

Refer?

- Seek specialist help, either urgent referral or admission, depending on severity, if dermatitis recurs after 3 weeks of treatment or does not settle with treatment.

Investigate?

- Swab visibly infected areas and change oral antibiotics according to the result of sensitivities.

Patient information leaflets

The following PILs are available at www.prodigy.nhs.uk

- Contact Dermatitis
- Contact Dermatitis - Patch Testing
- Eczema - Triggers and Irritants
- National Eczema Society

Shared decision making

- **A course of steroid tablets** is an option to clear your dermatitis as the rash affects a large part of your skin.
- **A course of antibiotics** may also be needed if the skin is infected.
- Your rash may be due to a contact with an irritant or allergen.
  - Do you know what is causing the rash?
  - Can you avoid it?
- You may need to see a specialist if the dermatitis is severe, or the cause is not known.

Drug rationale

Drugs not included

- **Topical corticosteroids** are not included. There is little advantage in using them in addition to oral prednisolon in widespread dermatitis, and additional use may increase the risk of adverse effects.
- **Topical corticosteroids with antimicrobial agents** are nc recommended. There is a lack of evidence that these products are more effective than topical corticosteroids alone, and there are additional concerns over the possibility that they may result in bacterial resistance.

Drugs included

- **Oral corticosteroids** are recommended when dermatitis affects more than 25% of the body surface area, or whe its resolution is prolonged. Treatment should be continued for 2–3 weeks, after which the oral steroid should be stopped and response monitored.
- **Oral antibiotics** should be prescribed when there are visible signs of infection or when infection cannot be excluded from the visible appearance of the dermatitis.
  - **Flucloxacillin** is active against Gram-positive organisms including beta-lactamase-producing staphylococci and streptococci. It is licensed in the treatment of infected skin conditions.
  - **Erythromycin** is suitable for people with infected dermatitis who have a known hypersensitivity to penicillin and related antibiotics.

Prescriptions

Oral prednisolone 30mg/day for 7 days then reduce

Prednisolone tabs: 30mg each morning for 7 days then reduce

- Age from 16 years onwards
- Prednisolone 5mg tablets. Take 6 tablets each morning (as a single dose) for 7 days, then 4 tablets each mornin for 7 days, then 2 tablets each morning for 7 days then stop; supply 84 tablets; NHS Cost £2.04.

Antibiotic (IF clinically infected)

Flucloxacillin syrup: 62.5mg four times a day

- Age from 1 month to 23 months
- Flucloxacillin 125mg/5ml syrup. Take 2.5ml four times day for 7 days; supply 100 ml; NHS Cost £3.23.

Flucloxacillin syrup: 125mg four times a day

- Age from 2 to 4 years
- Flucloxacillin 125mg/5ml syrup. Take one 5ml spoonfu four times a day for 7 days; supply 200 ml; NHS Cost £6.46.

Flucloxacillin syrup: 250mg four times a day

- Age from 5 to 11 years
- Flucloxacillin 250mg/5ml syrup. Take one 5ml spoonfu four times a day for 7 days; supply 200 ml; NHS Cost £13.94.

Flucloxacillin capsules: 250mg four times a day

- Age from 12 years onwards
- Flucloxacillin 250mg capsules. Take one capsule four times a day for 7 days; supply 28 capsules; NHS Cost £2.93.

Flucloxacillin capsules: 500mg four times a day

- Age from 12 years onwards
- Flucloxacillin 500mg capsules. Take one capsule four times a day for 7 days; supply 28 capsules; NHS Cost £4.73.

ythromycin s/f suspension: 125mg four times a day
Age from 1 month to 23 months
Erythromycin 125mg/5ml sf susp. Take one 5ml spoonful four times a day for 7 days; supply 200 ml; NHS Cost £2.22.

ythromycin s/f suspension: 250mg four times a day
Age from 2 to 11 years
Erythromycin 250mg/5ml sf susp. Take one 5ml spoonful four times a day for 7 days; supply 200 ml; NHS Cost £3.80.

ythromycin s/f suspension: 500mg four times a day
Age from 9 to 11 years
Erythromycin 500mg/5ml sf susp. Take one 5ml spoonful four times a day for 7 days; supply 200 ml; NHS Cost £6.46.

ythromycin e/c tablets: 250mg four times a day
Age from 12 years onwards
Erythromycin 250mg e/c tablets. Take one tablet four times a day for 7 days; supply 28 tablets; NHS Cost £3.08.

ythromycin e/c tablets: 500mg four times a day
Age from 12 years onwards
Erythromycin 250mg e/c tablets. Take two tablets four times a day for 7 days; supply 56 tablets; NHS Cost £6.16.

ʾreventing contact dermatitis

Vhich therapy

Identify and avoid contact with potential irritants and allergens where possible.
If complete avoidance of contact is not possible, minimising contact may be sufficient. Advise on:

- Rinsing with water or washing with soap as soon as possible after contact (note: overuse of skin cleaning agents can aggravate contact dermatitis).
- The use of soap-substitutes if frequent hand-washing is essential.
- Replacing strong irritants with weaker ones.
- Reducing the duration and frequency of contact with an irritant.
- The use of protective clothing.

For irritant contact dermatitis involving the hands, advise on the use of protective gloves.

- For handling potential irritants: cotton-lined rubber or plastic gloves.
- For otherwise dry work: fabric gloves that 'breathe' (e.g. cotton).
- Different types of gloves may be needed to protect from different irritants (see Table 2).

Maintain skin hydration with frequent use of emollients and moisturizers both during and after contact.

ʾractical prescribing points

ɔr further information please see the *Medicines ompendium* (www.medicines.org.uk) or the *British ational Formulary* (www.bnf.org).

rotective gloves

Gloves should be removed frequently, as sweating may aggravate existing dermatitis.

mollients

Reactions to emollients are most commonly due to preservatives, fragrances, lanolin, or arachis oil, and if they are suspected the person should switch to a product with different constituents (see Table 5).

- Cutaneous reactions to aqueous cream are particularly common. Different brands of aqueous cream may contain different antimicrobials, and the person should be advised to check this at the time of dispensing.

Should I refer or investigate?

Refer?

- **Refer someone with occupational dermatitis that is deteriorating despite avoidance measures, even if mild,** because:
  - If appropriate measures are not taken to identify and prevent contact with the responsible irritant or allergen, the condition is likely to progress and may become persistent.
  - Occupational dermatitis may require a person to discontinue their present job.
  - Occupational dermatitis may result in compensation claims against the employer.

Patient information leaflets

The following PILs are available at www.prodigy.nhs.uk

- Contact Dermatitis
- Contact Dermatitis - Patch Testing
- Eczema - Emollients (Moisturisers)
- Eczema - Fingertip Units for Topical Steroids
- Eczema - Topical Steroids
- Eczema - Triggers and Irritants
- National Eczema Society

Shared decision making

- **To prevent contact dermatitis, if possible, avoid the cause.** This may not be possible. For example, your job may involve using irritants.
- If you cannot completely avoid irritants, try to minimize contact.
  - Following any contact with an irritant, as soon as possible rinse affected areas of skin with water, or wash with soap.
  - Use a soap-substitute if you need to wash your hands often (and dry hands properly after washing).
  - If possible or appropriate, use weaker rather than strong irritants.
  - If possible, reduce the time and frequency of contact with irritants.
  - Can you use protective clothing?
- If your hands are affected, then consider using gloves.
  - For handling potential irritants — use cotton-lined rubber or plastic gloves.
  - For otherwise dry work — use fabric gloves that 'breathe' (such as cotton).
  - Different types of gloves may be needed to protect from different irritants.
- Use lots of moisturiser cream or ointment, and apply it frequently during and after any contact with irritants.

Drug rationale

Drugs not included

- **Barrier creams:** the use of barrier creams to prevent contact with irritants or allergens is controversial, and their use as sole protection against contact with allergens or irritants is not recommended [Bourke et al, 2001]. Their effectiveness in controlled clinical studies is not supported by clinical situations. In addition, they can exacerbate both allergic and irritant contact dermatitis.

D

- **Emollients containing antiseptic agents,** such as triclosan and benzalkonium chloride, have failed to demonstrate adequately that they improve clinical symptoms or reduce the load of *Staphylococcus aureus* in people with atopic eczema. We found no study comparing their efficacy to emollients alone in contact dermatitis. Additionally, they may cause allergic and irritant contact dermatitis [DTB, 1998].
- **Emollients containing urea** are not offered. Evidence for additional benefit is limited, and their use should be reserved for when standard emollients have proved ineffective. Their odour and irritation on application also make them unsuitable for general use [MeReC, 1998].
- **Emollients containing antipruritic agents,** such as lauromacrogols, are not offered. Evidence of additional benefits over standard emollients is limited [MeReC, 1998].

Drugs included

- **Ointments:** emulsifying, hydrous, liquid and soft paraffin, Epaderm®, and Hydromol ® can be applied directly to skin, or used as a soap substitute.
- **Creams:** aqueous, Aveeno®, Diprobase®, E45®, Oilatum®, and Unguentum M® have lower lipid content than ointments, but are a good alternative for people who cannot tolerate ointments, or want an emollient for regular use during the day (especially on the face and hands).

Prescriptions

Advice note

Advice only: preventing recurrence
- Age from 1 month onwards
- To prevent dermatitis coming back, you should try to minimize contact with irritants at home and at work. For example, this can be done by; using soap substitutes if you need to wash your hands a lot; wearing proper-fitting gloves that are suitable for the purpose (cotton-lined rubber or plastic gloves are usually suitable); applying an emollient or moisturising cream regularly before, during, and after work.

Emollient ointments

Emulsifying ointment BP
- Age from 1 month onwards
- Emulsifying ointment BP. Apply to skin frequently and liberally, as often as required. Use as a soap substitute; supply 500 grams; NHS Cost £1.54; OTC Cost £3.06.

Hydrous ointment BP
- Age from 1 month onwards
- Hydrous ointment BP. Apply to skin frequently and liberally, as often as required. Use as a soap substitute; supply 500 grams; NHS Cost £1.99; OTC Cost £3.51.

Liquid and white soft paraffin ointment NPF
- Age from 1 month onwards
- Liquid+white soft paraffin. Apply to skin frequently and liberally, as often as required. Use as a bath additive by dissolving in hot water. Use as a soap substitute; supply 500 grams; NHS Cost £3.76; OTC Cost £6.63.

Epaderm ointment
- Age from 1 month onwards
- Epaderm ointment (500g). Apply to skin frequently and liberally, as often as required. Use as a bath additive by dissolving in hot water. Use as a soap substitute; supply 1 500 gram tub; NHS Cost £6.21; OTC Cost £10.94.

Hydromol ointment
- Age from 1 month onwards
- Hydromol ointment (500g). Apply to skin frequently and liberally, as often as required. Use as a bath additiv by dissolving in hot water. Use as a soap substitute; supply 1 500 gram tub; NHS Cost £5.58; OTC Cost £5.79.

Emollient creams

Aqueous cream BP
- Age from 1 month onwards
- Aqueous cream BP. Apply to skin frequently and liberally, as often as required. Use as a soap substitute; supply 500 grams; NHS Cost £1.06; OTC Cost £1.87.

Diprobase cream
- Age from 1 month onwards
- Diprobase cream (500g). Apply to skin frequently and liberally, as often as required. Use as a soap substitute; supply 500 grams; NHS Cost £6.61; OTC Cost £11.6

E45 cream
- Age from 1 month onwards
- E45 cream (500g). Apply to skin frequently and liberal as often as required. Use as a soap substitute; supply 5(grams; NHS Cost £6.20; OTC Cost £9.69.

Oilatum cream
- Age from 1 month onwards
- Oilatum cream (500ml). Apply to skin frequently and liberally, as often as required. Use as a soap substitute; supply 500 ml; NHS Cost £6.35; OTC Cost £9.93.

Unguentum M cream
- Age from 1 month onwards
- Unguentum M cream (500g). Apply to skin frequently and liberally, as often as required. Use as a soap substitute; supply 500 grams; NHS Cost £9.55; OTC Cost £18.70.

Extended Information

Background information

- What is contact dermatitis? p.514
- How does contact dermatitis develop? p.515
- What factors affect the response to allergens and irritants? p.515
- How common is it? p.515
- How do I know my patient has it? p.515
- What common allergens and irritants cause contact dermatitis? p.516
- What else might it be? p.517
- Complications and prognosis p.517

What is contact dermatitis?

- **Contact dermatitis** is a dermatitis that occurs in respon to external agents interacting with the skin. The extern agents may be irritants or allergens.
- **Subjective irritation** presents as stinging that occurs within minutes of contact, usually on the face, in the absence of visible clinical reaction.
- **Allergic contact dermatitis occurs because of a type IV hypersensitivity reaction** that occurs in predisposed individuals after sensitization with an allergen. The potential to react persists indefinitely and the dermatitis will recur if the person is re-exposed to the allergen.
- **Irritant contact dermatitis is a non-immune inflammatory response** after damage to the skin, usuall by chemicals. It may occur in any individual exposed to an irritant for sufficient duration and in sufficient concentration.

- **Acute irritant contact dermatitis** occurs as the result of a single overwhelming exposure or a few brief exposures to strong irritants.
- **Cumulative irritant contact dermatitis** occurs because of repeated exposures to weaker irritants.

[Bourke et al, 2001]

How does contact dermatitis develop?

- **Allergic contact dermatitis first requires sensitization to occur,** when chemicals penetrate into the epidermis and are endocytosed by Langerhans cells.
  - The Langerhans cells degrade the chemical and bind it to proteins, forming the allergen.
  - The Langerhans cells with the allergen expressed on their cell surface travel to regional lymph nodes, where they become apposed with T-lymphocytes.
  - This process results in proliferation of antigen-specific T-lymphocytes that distribute throughout the body, including the skin, but particularly 'home' to the site of the original exposure. This process takes 5–25 days after exposure.
- **Allergic contact dermatitis occurs with subsequent re-exposure** to the chemical, when the Langerhans cell again processes the chemical and presents it as an allergen to antigen-specific T-lymphocytes.
  - The presentation of the allergen to the T-lymphocytes initiates the inflammatory reaction 24–48 hours after re-exposure to the allergen and leads to the development of dermatitis.
  - The distribution of the antigen-specific T-lymphocytes explains why allergic reactions may occur at the site of exposure and at other sites, particularly sites of previous exposure.
- **The risk of allergic sensitization** depends on an individual's susceptibility, the sensitizing property of a particular substance, and the quantity and concentration of the allergen applied.
- **Irritant contact dermatitis can occur in any individual** when an irritant agent penetrates the stratum corneum (the outer layer of the skin consisting of dead cells) in sufficient concentration to cause damage to the underlying structures.
  - The penetration of an irritant is affected by a number of factors, including the state and thickness of the stratum corneum, the chemical nature of the irritant, its concentration, and duration of exposure to the skin.
  - This may occur with a single exposure or, more commonly, with frequent exposures when the irritant accumulates in the stratum corneum, leading to eventual penetration.

[Beltrani and Beltrani, 1997; Beck and Wilkinson, 2004]

What factors affect the response to allergens and irritants?

- **The stratum corneum is the most important barrier** to irritants and allergens. The effectiveness of this barrier is determined by its condition, its thickness, and the rate of its replacement.
  - As it is continuously replaced, the stratum corneum sheds the absorbed irritant or allergen from its upper surface, reducing the chance of exposure of the susceptible underlying epidermis.
  - The stratum corneum varies in thickness at different sites of the body. This explains why the face and back of the hands are particularly susceptible to irritants or allergens and why the soles of the feet and palms of the hands are particularly resistant.
- **The risk of irritants and allergens causing dermatitis increases with impairment of the barrier function of the skin.** The flexibility and cohesion of the stratum corneum is determined by its water content. If the water content is reduced, cracks develop and the barrier is impaired. Factors affecting the barrier function include the following:
  - **Atopic eczema** is the most common cause of an altered barrier function of the skin. It is particularly associated with an increased risk of irritant contact dermatitis, but may also allow increased penetration of allergens, worsening allergic contact dermatitis in susceptible people.
  - **Air humidity** is the single most important factor in determining the water content of the stratum corneum. Low temperatures are associated with low ambient humidity and dry skin, causing a reduced resistance to irritants.
  - **High skin temperature** increases the penetration of antigens and allergens. Sweat may macerate the skin and dissolve allergens and irritants into it, making it easier to penetrate the stratum corneum.
  - **Detergents and soaps** remove lipids from the cell wall of the stratum corneum and allow the water-holding soluble contents to be lost.
  - **Frequent wetting** of skin also leads to loss of the water-holding soluble contents, leading to drying and impairment of the skin's barrier.

[Wilkinson and Beck, 2004]

D

How common is it?

- Good-quality epidemiological studies of the prevalence of contact dermatitis in the UK could not be identified.
- In the United States almost 10% of all dermatology consultations are for contact dermatitis [Hogan, 2002].
- It is estimated that 75% of all cases of contact dermatitis and 80–90% of occupational dermatitis involve the hands [Warshaw et al, 2003; Beck and Wilkinson, 2004].
- Irritant causes of contact dermatitis are significantly more common than allergic causes. Allergic contact dermatitis is estimated to constitute about a quarter of all contact dermatitis in the United States [National Institute for Occupational Safety and Health, 1999].
- Estimates of the prevalence of contact dermatitis vary with the population studied and particularly with different occupations. Occupations most commonly associated with irritant contact dermatitis include:
  - Agriculture and fishing
  - Cleaning
  - Engineering and construction
  - Food preparation and catering
  - Hairdressing
  - Housewife/mother
  - Medical, dentistry, and veterinary
  - Printing and painting

[Cherry et al, 2000; Wilkinson and Beck, 2004]

How do I know my patient has it?

General points

- **Distinguishing irritant contact dermatitis, allergic contact dermatitis, and other types of dermatitis** on clinical features alone can be unreliable, particularly when dermatitis affects the hands and face [Bourke et al, 2001].
- **Contact dermatitis** may be distinguished clinically from other types of dermatitis by the distribution of the rash and a history of exposure to irritants or allergens. Contact dermatitis should be suspected when any dermatitis persists or recurs frequently.
- **The diagnosis is confirmed and the cause identified** by resolution of the dermatitis upon exclusion of the suspected cause.

- **Patch testing is required when the dermatitis persists** despite exclusion of the likely causes identified from detailed enquiry [Bourke et al, 2001].

Clinical features

- Contact dermatitis (like any other type of dermatitis) is an itchy rash characterized by its appearance, which may become altered by scratching if the condition persists.
  - **Acute dermatitis** varies in appearance from collections of fluid in the skin (vesicles and occasionally bullae) to areas of poorly demarcated redness, and may include other features such as crusting, scaling, cracking, and swelling of the skin.
  - **Chronic dermatitis is characterized by lesions that** become fissured and thickened (lichenification) because of repeated scratching.
- There may be a history of localized recurrent or persistent dermatitis at sites that are exposed to potential allergens and irritants.
- The dermatitis may improve with a change of environment or activity. This is most commonly seen with occupational dermatitis, where the dermatitis typically improves when the person is away from work (for example at weekends and holidays).
- Detailed enquiry may reveal likely causes, but it must be remembered that people are often unaware of their exposure to irritants or allergens [Beltrani and Beltrani, 1997].

Distinguishing features of irritant and allergic contact dermatitis

- **The rash initially develops at the site of exposure** in both cases.
  - The rash of irritant contact dermatitis is well demarcated, when exposure to the irritant is well demarcated, giving a 'branded iron' appearance.
  - The rash of allergic contact dermatitis is usually poorly demarcated.
- **With repeated exposure, the rash from allergic contact dermatitis** may develop at other sites and may reactivate at previously exposed sites. The rash from irritant contact dermatitis usually remains limited to the sites of exposure.
- **Atopic eczema increases the risk of irritant contact dermatitis developing** and is a common association. Atopic eczema is less strongly associated with allergic contact dermatitis developing.
- **Allergic contact dermatitis may develop from a single re-exposure to an allergen,** but the inflammation is delayed by 24–48 hours. In contrast, cumulative contact dermatitis develops gradually from repeated exposure to irritants. Acute irritant contact dermatitis and subjective irritancy may develop after a single exposure to an irritant, but there is little delay in the inflammation developing.

Confirming the diagnosis of contact dermatitis and identifying the cause

- **Clinical features may help to indicate the likely irritant or allergic cause.** However, ultimately the cause is confirmed only if the dermatitis settles when the person avoids the suspected cause.
- **Identification of the irritant or allergen** may be obvious. Where it is not, specialist assessment by a visit to the home or work place may be required.
- **Patch testing** is required when a trial of avoiding likely irritants and allergens has not identified the cause, and the dermatitis persists. Patch testing has a sensitivity and specificity of between 70 and 80% [Bourke et al, 2001].
  - **The relevance of a positive patch test** to the presenting dermatitis is assessed in relation to the person's likely exposure to allergens. Interpretation of results requires training and experience [Fowler, 1994]
  - **A positive patch test identifies possible allergens** and helps to establish the diagnosis of allergic contact dermatitis. However, a positive test does not exclude the possibility that irritant contact dermatitis or atopic eczema is also present.
  - **A negative patch test excludes allergic causes used in the test series,** but does not identify possible irritant causes or exclude atopic eczema.
- **Irritant contact dermatitis is suspected** when there are clinical features of contact dermatitis, allergic causes have been excluded, and likely irritants have been identified. The diagnosis is supported if the dermatitis resolves when the irritant is excluded.

What common allergens and irritants cause contact dermatitis?

The most common irritants and allergens are given in Table 1.

[Beck and Wilkinson, 2004; Cohen, 2004; Wilkinson and Beck, 2004]

What are the likely causes of dermatitis in different skin areas?

- **Hands:** hand dermatitis may be due to atopic eczema, or to irritant or allergic contact dermatitis. Atopic eczema and irritant contact dermatitis are most commonly associated with hand dermatitis. The dermatitis often begins under a ring, because detergents and soaps get trapped or there is friction from the ring. It then typically progresses to a patchy dermatitis of the dorsum of the hand and the sides and webs of the fingers.
- **Eyelids:** contact dermatitis is the most common dermatitis of the eyelids, more commonly caused by products applied to the hair, face, and fingernails than by cosmetics applied to eye area. Irritants are rarely present in such products and most reactions have an allergic cause.
- **Face:** subjective irritant contact dermatitis with the application of cosmetics and soaps to the face is common and will occur equally with 'hypoallergenic' products. Allergic causes may be due to fragrances, lanolin, or preservatives in cosmetics.
- **Scalp:** the scalp is particularly resistant to contact dermatitis. Allergens or irritants applied to the scalp commonly produce reaction on the eyelids, ears, neck,

Table 1: Common irritants and allergens

Irritants	Allergens
Water (especially hard, chalky, and heavily chlorinated water)	Metals (e.g. nickel and cobalt in jewellery, chromate in cement)
Detergents and soaps	Topical medications, including topical corticosteroids
Solvents and abrasives	Cosmetics — particularly fragrances, hair dyes, preservatives, and nail varnish resin.
Oils	Rubber, including latex
Acids and alkalis, including cement	Textiles, particularly from dyes and formaldehyde resins
Reducing agents and oxidizing agents, including sodium hypochlorite	Epoxy resin adhesives
Powders, dust, and soil	Acrylic and formaldehyde present in adhesives and plastic resins
Certain plants (e.g. ranunculus, anemone, clematis, helleborus, mustards)	Plants — chrysanthemum, daffodils, tulips, and primula are the most common

and hands, with little or no response from the scalp. Seborrhoeic dermatitis should be considered when dermatitis is limited to the scalp.
- **Neck:** dermatitis of the neck most commonly occurs because of allergy to perfume or nickel.
- **Trunk:** allergic dermatitis is commonly due to nickel allergy (under jewellery), rubber allergy (under elastic belts), or dyes and formaldehyde (in clothing).
- **Axilla:** sensitivity to deodorants involves the whole axilla; if the sensitivity is due to clothing, the apex is usually spared.
- **Perianal:** medications, including local anaesthetics and topical corticosteroids used in the treatment of haemorrhoids, and perfumed toilet paper and wet-wipes may cause allergic contact dermatitis in the perianal area.
- **Dermatitis around a wound** is usually caused by allergy to applied dressings or topical medications.

[Beltrani and Beltrani, 1997; Wilkinson and Beck, 2004]

What else might it be?

Contact dermatitis must be distinguished from psoriasis, fungal infections, and other types of dermatitis.

- **All forms of dermatitis have a similar appearance.** Their diagnosis is rarely a problem when they are well developed, present in their typical form, and alone. However, there are many occasions when a localized area of dermatitis may make the diagnosis uncertain.
- **Atopic eczema** should be considered when dermatitis persists after potential causes of irritant contact dermatitis are avoided. Atopic eczema is likely if the person has an itchy skin condition plus three or more of the following:
  - A history of itching of skin creases (e.g. bends of the elbows or behind the knees) or cheeks in young children.
  - A history of or presence of flexural eczema or eczema affecting the cheeks, forehead, or limbs in young children.
  - A tendency towards dry skin.
  - A history of asthma or hay fever, or immediate family history of atopic eczema.
  - Onset under 2 years of age.

[MeReC, 2003]

- **Seborrhoeic dermatitis** is most common between the ages of 18 and 40 years. The rash commonly has a greasy appearance. Dandruff is usually the first manifestation of seborrhoeic dermatitis, which may progress to more significant scaling and redness of the scalp. Involvement of the nasolabial folds, external ears, eyebrows and eyelashes, the presternal areas of the chest, or the back between the shoulder blades may follow.
- **Gravitational dermatitis (eczema)** occurs because of venous hypertension in the legs. The dermatitis is localized to the lower legs and is usually, although not always, associated with the presence of varicose veins.
- **Discoid eczema** differs in appearance from other forms of dermatitis in that it has a clearly demarcated edge and a circular or oval shape. The cause of discoid eczema is unknown.
- **Juvenile plantar dermatosis** presents as dermatitis of the plantar surface of the forefoot, almost exclusively in children aged 3–14 years. It is associated with wearing footwear that retains sweat (such as trainers) and friction to the skin from playing sport.
- **Photodermatitis** presents as a typical dermatitis but with well-demarcated edges where the skin is covered by clothing.

Complications and prognosis

Complications

- **Bacterial infection** with *Staphylococcus aureus* may present with typical impetigo or as worsening of the dermatitis with increased redness, oozing, and crusting.
- **Psychosocial problems** include difficulty in fulfilling personal and family responsibilities, prolonged sick leave from work or school, restraints on leisure activities, impact on social contact, and time spent having treatment. Contact dermatitis may exclude people from certain types of employment and affect their potential to earn.

[Skoet et al, 2003]

D

Prognosis

Irritant contact dermatitis

- **The avoidance of further exposure to the irritant** determines the prognosis for the individual. Many irritants are common and are difficult to avoid, particularly when exposure occurs in the work place.
- **Healing of uncomplicated irritant contact dermatitis should occur within 4 weeks** if the irritant stimulus is removed. However, as the duration of the stimulus extends, the recovery time is prolonged.
- **People with atopic eczema** are more likely to develop irritant contact dermatitis and are known to have a worse prognosis [Akhavan and Cohen, 2003; Wilkinson and Beck, 2004]. Their prognosis is probably worse because relatively minor inadvertent or unavoidable repeat exposures to irritants may cause their irritant contact dermatitis to recur.

[Wilkinson and Beck, 2004]

Allergic contact dermatitis

- The prognosis of allergic contact dermatitis depends on whether repeated or continuous exposure can be avoided.
- Once acquired, sensitivity to an allergen tends to persist [Ayala et al, 1996].
  - **The degree of sensitivity** may decline unless boosted by repeat exposure.
  - **The duration of sensitivity** to an allergen depends on the initial degree of sensitivity to that allergen. High levels of sensitivity to strong allergens will persist for years when low levels of sensitivity to weak allergens may disappear.

[Beck and Wilkinson, 2004]

Management issues

- Overview of management p.517
- How should I manage acute dermatitis? p.518
- How should I manage infected dermatitis? p.519
- How can recurrence of contact dermatitis be prevented? p.519
- How should I manage persistent contact dermatitis? p.520
- How should I manage suspected occupational contact dermatitis? p.520
- Medicines management p.520

Overview of management

- **Where possible, identify the cause of the dermatitis** (see *What else might it be?*).
- **Treat the dermatitis.**
  - Wash off strong irritants that are likely to cause acute contact dermatitis before treatment. Use water or specific neutralizing solutions if available.

- Manage dry, chapped skin associated with dermatitis with emollients.
- Treat localized inflammation with topical corticosteroids.
- If the dermatitis is widespread, consider a systemic corticosteroid.
- **Treat any secondary infection.**
  - Prescribe oral antibiotics when contact dermatitis is visibly infected (e.g. rapid worsening of dermatitis with marked erythema).
- **Offer advice on avoiding common irritants and allergens** (see *What common allergens and irritants cause contact dermatitis?*)
- **For someone with persistent dermatitis or occupational dermatitis:**
  - Where possible, identify the causative irritant or allergen (see *How do I know my patient has it?*)
  - Consider specialist referral.

D

How should I manage acute dermatitis?

- Dry, chapped skin associated with dermatitis should be managed with frequent, liberal application of hydrating emollients and soap substitutes.
- Acute, localized inflammation should be treated with topical corticosteroids.
- If the dermatitis is widespread but not severe, and the allergen or irritant is known and avoidable in future, consider prescribing a systemic corticosteroid.

Emollients

What is the supporting evidence for emollients?

- There is little evidence from randomized controlled trials regarding the efficacy of emollients in the treatment of established contact dermatitis. However, their use is widely accepted [Bourke et al, 2001].

Which emollient should I prescribe?

- **The choice of emollient** should be determined by:
  - The dryness of the skin
  - The type of skin to which the emollient is to be applied
  - Individual preference, determined by the product's tolerability and convenience of use
- **Less to moderately dry skin** is most acceptably treated with a cream.
- **Moderately dry to very dry skin** requires a higher intensity of treatment with an ointment to restore the skin to normal.
- **Weeping dermatitis** is best treated with a water-soluble cream, as ointments will tend to slough off, becoming unacceptably messy.
- **The tolerability and convenience of a product can only be determined by a trial of treatment.** When a higher intensity of treatment is required, a trial of small quantities of a number of creams and ointments is often advocated to determine the most acceptable treatment.
  - Creams are generally better tolerated, but will need to be applied more frequently and generously to have the same effect as a single application of ointment.
  - The individual will need to balance the tolerability of a product against the convenience of its use and the acceptability of symptoms.
- **More than one type of product may be required.** Different products may be preferred at different times, depending on the intensity of treatment required and the area of skin to be treated (e.g. a cream may be preferable for application to the hands).
- **Emollient soap substitutes** are useful to avoid the drying effects of soaps and should be considered for all people with dermatitis. They are particularly useful for people who are required to wash or wet their hands frequently. The use of emollients as soap substitutes has been shown to reduce the incidence and prevalence of contact dermatitis [Lauharanta et al, 1991].

Corticosteroids

What is the supporting evidence for topical corticosteroids?

- Topical corticosteroids are widely advocated as the preferred treatment for settling inflammation in dermatitis [Bourke et al, 2001].
- Good-quality studies specifically examining the effectiveness of treating contact dermatitis with topical corticosteroids could not be identified. However, randomized controlled trials of topical corticosteroids compared with placebo suggest a large treatment effect in the treatment of atopic eczema [Hoare et al, 2000].

Which topical corticosteroid should I prescribe?

- **For areas of thin skin (e.g. the face or genitals) and in flexures,** use a mildly potent topical corticosteroid. The absorption of corticosteroid is enhanced through thin skin and in flexures because of the self-occlusive effect of the skin fold.
- **The eyelids** should be treated only with a mildly potent topical corticosteroid, taking care to avoid contact of the corticosteroid with the surface of the eye.
- **The palms, soles of the feet, and scalp** require treatment with a potent corticosteroid, because the thick skin reduces the penetration and hence the effectiveness of topical treatment.
- **In children,** start treatment with a mildly potent topical corticosteroid. Moderately potent corticosteroids should be used only infrequently. Where control of flare-ups requires frequent use of a moderately potent corticosteroid, seek specialist help.
- **For treatment of the trunk and limbs in adults,** select the lowest potency of corticosteroid that is likely to work within 7–14 days of treatment, based upon:
  - The severity of inflammation
  - The response to previous treatment
- **For lichenified dermatitis** a potent topical corticosteroid will be needed, as lichenification significantly reduces penetration of topical corticosteroids. Treatment for 4–6 weeks is commonly required to restore the skin back to normal. The exact duration of treatment will depend on the response to treatment.

When should systemic corticosteroids be used?

- **In adults, consider short-term treatment with oral prednisolone** when dermatitis affects more than 25% of the body surface area (i.e. acute treatment when a topical corticosteroid may not be practical), and has an obvious cause that can be avoided in the future. This rarely occurs, but when it does it usually has an allergic cause.
- **Treatment with oral prednisolone should be continued for 2–3 weeks.**
  - The immunological recognition and response to allergens often persists for 14–21 days after exposure to an allergen. Oral corticosteroids suppress the inflammatory reaction to the recognition of the allergen but not the recognition process. Therefore, if the oral corticosteroid is stopped as soon as the dermatitis settles, the dermatitis may reoccur.
- **There is little evidence to guide dosing of oral prednisolone,** but most experts recommend starting with a high dose (e.g. prednisolone 30 mg once a day) for one week and tapering the dose over the next 2–3 weeks. Clinical judgement should be used to determine the exact dose in an individual case.
- **Consider admission** if dermatitis is particularly severe, or in a child.

How should I manage infected dermatitis?

- **The diagnosis of bacterial infection relies on clinical signs of infection** (e.g. rapid worsening of dermatitis with marked erythema) and not on microbiological examination, because patches of dermatitis are likely to be colonized by *Staphylococcus aureus*.
  - The typical appearance of impetigo (crusted lesions that may be yellow) may be difficult to distinguish from dermatitis.
  - It is common practice to have a low threshold of diagnosing infection when dermatitis is severe or unexpectedly deteriorates.
- **Treat visibly infected dermatitis with oral antibiotics.**
  - Evidence from treatment of infected atopic eczema demonstrates improved rates of resolution of the flare-up when visibly infected eczema is treated with oral antibiotics.
  - There is no randomized controlled trial evidence to support the use of antibiotics when there is no visible sign of infection.
- **Flucloxacillin or erythromycin** (if the person is allergic to penicillin) is recommended as first-line oral antibiotic treatment for impetigo [HPA, 2003].
- **Topical antimicrobial/corticosteroid combinations** have been shown to be no more effective than topical corticosteroid alone in treating either visibly infected or uninfected flare-ups [Hoare et al, 2000]. Their use is not recommended.
- If visible infection fails to respond to a first-line antibiotic, microbiological investigations to ascertain sensitivities may be useful.

How can recurrence of contact dermatitis be prevented?

Preventing recurrence of contact dermatitis relies on avoiding the causative irritant or allergen.

What general advice should I give regarding avoidance?

- **Inform the person** about potential sources of irritant or allergen, including related allergens that could cause problems in the future by cross-sensitisation.
- **Reading the labels on products** may help to avoid problems, and should be encouraged.
- **If sensitivity to the irritant or allergen is high,** complete avoidance may be necessary to prevent dermatitis. This can be achieved by:
  - Stopping use of the allergenic or irritant product.
  - Substituting allergens or irritants with other products (e.g. use of a soap substitute).
  - Considering a change of employment where appropriate.
- **Avoidance of allergens or irritants** may be unacceptably restrictive, however, particularly if the allergen or irritant is unavoidably present at work. Other measures aimed at preventing or minimizing contact with affected areas of skin may be adequate to control the dermatitis to an acceptable level. These include:
  - Rinsing with water or washing with soap as soon as possible after contact (note: overuse of skin-cleaning agents can aggravate contact dermatitis).
  - Using soap substitutes.
  - Replacing strong irritants with weaker ones.
  - Reducing the duration and frequency of contact with an irritant.
  - The use of gloves and other forms of protective clothing.

Personal protective clothing

- Most irritant contact dermatitis involves the hands, and protective gloves are the mainstay of protection.
  - **For handling potential irritants,** cotton-lined rubber or plastic gloves are usually sufficient.
  - **For otherwise dry work,** fabric gloves that 'breathe' (e.g. cotton) should be used.
  - Different types of gloves may be needed to protect from different irritants (see Table 2).
  - Gloves should be removed frequently, as sweating may aggravate existing dermatitis. There is also some evidence that occlusion by the gloves may impair the barrier function of the stratum corneum, and exacerbate irritation.

Table reproduced from Bourke et al, 2001
[Bourke et al, 2001; Wilkinson and Beck, 2004]

Barrier creams

- The effectiveness of barrier creams to prevent contact with the irritant or allergen is controversial, and their use as sole protection against contact with allergens or irritants is not recommended [Bourke et al, 2001].
- The effectiveness of barrier creams in controlled clinical studies is not supported by clinical experience.
  - Although barrier creams have been shown to reduce both allergic and irritant contact dermatitis under experimental conditions, their use in clinical situations is often disappointing.
  - One small study demonstrated no significant difference in efficacy between a barrier preparation and its vehicle in 25 hospital nurses [Berndt et al, 2000].
- **Barrier creams may facilitate the removal of oils, greases, and resins** from the skin and prevent excessive soiling, thereby reducing the need for strong cleansers and abrasives [Wilkinson and Beck, 2004].
- **Barrier creams can exacerbate both allergic and irritant contact dermatitis,** probably through irritants becoming trapped on the skin by the barrier cream [Alvarez et al, 2001].
- **Barrier creams themselves may also be a cause of allergic or irritant contact dermatitis** [Wigger-Alberti and Elsner, 1998]. This is usually due to the vehicle, which may contain fragrances, preservatives, emulsifiers, or emollients, which could cause or induce sensitization [Alvarez et al, 2001].
- **Some barrier creams (e.g. petroleum) can cause rubber and latex gloves to deteriorate,** thereby reducing their efficacy against irritants and allergens [Alvarez et al, 2001].
- **If barrier creams are used,** education about how to use barrier creams correctly is essential.
  - There is a risk that, unless adequate education is provided, people will believe that they offer better

Table 2: A guide to the types of gloves giving some degree of protection for specific types of hazard.

Irritant	Type of glove
Microorganisms	NRL, thermoplastic elastomer
Disinfectants	NRL, PVC, PE
Pharmaceuticals	NRL (permeability time very short)
Composite materials	NRL (permeability time in minutes), 4H-glove
Solvents	PE, PVC, nitrile, NRL, neoprene, butyl rubber, Viton, 4H-glove
Corrosives	NRL, PE, PVC, neoprene, butyl rubber, Viton, 4H-glove
Detergents	NRL, EMA, PE, neoprene, PVC, nitrile (if addition of organic solvents)
Machining oils	NRL, PVC, nitrile, neoprene, 4H-glove

NRL: natural rubber latex
PVC: polyvinyl chloride
PE: polyethylene
EMA: ethylene methylmethacrylate

D

protection than they actually do. This may lead to prolonged contact with the allergen or irritant.
  - Correct and repeated application is essential to ensure that the skin is protected.

[Alvarez et al, 2001]

Emollients and 'after-work creams'

- **Frequent application of emollients** will help prevent dryness and chapping of the skin, and is a widely accepted method of preventing subsequent recurrence of dermatitis, although there is little evidence to support this [Wilkinson and Beck, 2004].
- Where irritant contact dermatitis is caused by cumulative exposure to an irritant, for example at work, emollients should be applied regularly during and after work to prevent dermatitis.

D

How should I manage persistent contact dermatitis?

- **If avoidance of the identified irritant or allergen** does not result in resolution of contact dermatitis, exclude ongoing exposure to irritants or allergens.
  - **Check patient compliance** with avoidance measures.
  - **If compliance is good,** step up avoidance measures where possible.
- **Consider contact allergy to topical corticosteroids** if dermatitis fails to respond or deteriorates with their use.
  - Confirm the suspicion by applying the product on skin that is unaffected by dermatitis, and observing for a reaction.
  - Referral for patch testing is required to identify which topical corticosteroid(s) the person is sensitized to, because cross-sensitivity is common and the person may be sensitized to a number of products [English, 2000].
  - Subsequent use of oral corticosteroids may produce systemic contact dermatitis [Goh, 1998].
- **If contact dermatitis continues to reoccur frequently** despite appropriate avoidance measures, consider specialist referral for further assessment. Either ongoing dermatitis will be because of ongoing exposure to irritants or allergens that have not been identified, or there may be an additional cause of the dermatitis, such as atopic eczema.

How should I manage suspected occupational contact dermatitis?

- Occupational contact dermatitis that is mild and well controlled with occasional symptomatic treatment and preventative measures can be managed in primary care.
- Someone with occupational dermatitis that is deteriorating despite avoidance measures should be referred to a dermatologist, even if dermatitis is mild, because:
  - If appropriate measures are not taken to identify and prevent contact with the responsible irritant or allergen, the condition is likely to progress and may become persistent.
  - Occupational dermatitis may require the person to discontinue their present job.
  - Occupational dermatitis may result in a compensation claim against the employer.

Medicines management

Topical corticosteroids

How much topical corticosteroid should be applied?

- **Give specific information about the quantity of topical corticosteroid to apply.** Overuse may increase the risk of adverse effects of corticosteroid. Underuse may delay the settling of acute dermatitis, leading to the unnecessary use of a more potent preparation [Long et al, 1998].
- **Corticosteroids should be applied to the skin in a thin layer.** As a practical guide, the quantity of topical corticosteroid to apply is often expressed in terms of fingertip units (FTUs).
  - One FTU is roughly equivalent to the amount of cream or ointment that can be squeezed from a tube with a standard nozzle onto an adult index finger from the tip of the finger to the first crease.
  - FTUs should be used together with body charts that show the number of FTUs required to cover each area of a child's or an adult's body.

[MeReC, 1999]

  - As a rough guide, one FTU of topical corticosteroid is sufficient to treat a skin area approximately twice that of the flat of the hand with the fingers together.
  - A demonstration of the use of the FTU should be backed up with written information. A Patient Information Leaflet (PIL) detailing how to apply topical corticosteroids is available through PRODIGY.
- To avoid applying excess corticosteroid to the applying fingertip, advise the person either to wash the fingertip after application or to use a polythene sleeve or cotton bud to apply the corticosteroid.

What quantity of topical corticosteroid should I prescribe?

- As a rough guide, one FTU is approximately 500 mg of ointment or cream.
- Table 3 provides a guide to suitable quantities to prescribe for specific areas of an adult body. Quantities for children may be much less.

[BNF 47, 2004]

Should corticosteroids be applied once a day or twice a day?

- **The National Institute for Clinical Excellence (NICE)** has considered trial evidence, as well as expert opinion, regarding the frequency of application of topical corticosteroids in atopic eczema.
  - An Appraisal Committee concluded that 'there was no compelling evidence of a clinically significant difference between once-daily application and more frequent application of topical corticosteroids. ... It was persuaded that current clinical practice would therefore support a recommendation for the use of topical corticosteroids no more frequently than twice daily'.

[NICE, 2004]

- The evidence considered included a systematic review that identified three good-quality randomized controlled trials comparing once-a-day with twice-a-day administration of topical corticosteroid.
  - In no studies was more frequent application superior to once-daily application.
  - While the results suggested a small difference in favour of more frequent application, this did not reach statistical significance.

Table 3: Suitable quantities of corticosteroid to prescribe for adults.

Body area	Amount of corticosteroid to prescribe
Face and neck	30 g
Both hands	30 g
Scalp	30 g
Both arms	30–60 g
Both legs	100 g
Trunk	100 g
Groins and genitalia	30 g

These amounts are usually suitable for an adult for application twice a day for 1 week (or once a day for 2 weeks).

- No good-quality study could be identified that compared frequency of application with a mildly potent topical corticosteroid [Hoare et al, 2000].
- Using a once-daily application of topical corticosteroid has a number of potential advantages, including:
  - Reduced risk of adverse effects
  - Greater convenience for the person
  - Reduced cost of treatment to the NHS
- The Committee was informed that differences in the prescription of once-daily or more frequent use exist between clinicians in clinical practice. It was agreed by the experts that when a once-daily application of topical corticosteroid is not effective, clinicians would need to increase either the potency or the frequency of the topical corticosteroid if there was no improvement in the condition [NICE, 2004].

What are the adverse effects of topical corticosteroids?

- **Adverse effects of topical corticosteroids** can be divided into localized effects (e.g. skin atrophy, exacerbation of skin infection, and acne at the site of application) and systemic adverse effects (e.g. hypophyseal-pituitary-adrenal (HPA) suppression).
- The risk of adverse effects increases with the potency of the topical corticosteroid, duration of use, and area of application (e.g. thin skin on the face and flexures). Adverse effects are most likely with potent or very potent topical corticosteroids when used in large quantities for prolonged periods. Mildly and moderately potent topical corticosteroids used for short periods are rarely associated with adverse effects.
- Weekly doses of topical corticosteroids considered unlikely to cause systemic adverse effects in adults have been determined based upon potency, quantity, and duration of use (see Table 4). It is important to realize that this does not mean that local adverse effects will not occur with this level of use, but only that HPA suppression is unlikely [Clement and Du Vivier, 1987].
- **Children, and particularly infants,** are much more susceptible to systemic adverse effects from topical corticosteroids, owing to the child's relatively large surface area. Further, the effects of HPA suppression in children may lead to growth retardation. It is strongly recommended that children requiring moderately potent topical corticosteroids on a regular basis are under the care of a specialist and have their growth carefully monitored.
- **Skin atrophy** is much more likely with potent and very potent topical corticosteroids.
  - For the skin on the trunk and limbs, thinning of the skin may occur within 1–3 weeks of starting a potent or very potent topical corticosteroid, but reverses within 4 weeks if treatment is stopped.
  - There is little risk of skin thinning with mild to moderate topical corticosteroids when used for up to 4 weeks.
  - When there is a risk of progressive skin atrophy from repeated use of potent or very potent topical corticosteroids, refer the person for review by a specialist.

[MeReC, 1999; DTB, 2003]

- **Caution is required in treating the eyelids with topical corticosteroids.** The skin of the eyelids is particularly susceptible to atrophy when treated with topical corticosteroids. Cataract formation and raised intraocular pressure may also rarely occur after incautious treatment. Therefore it is recommended that:
  - Only mildly potent topical corticosteroids are used on the eyelid.
  - Use is limited to 7 days' duration.
  - Treatment is not repeated within one month.
  - Care is taken to avoid contact with the surface of the eye.
- If treatment is required for longer or more frequently than this, refer for specialist review.

Table 4: Weekly dose of corticosteroids unlikely to cause systemic adverse effects in adults.

Treatment period (months)	Mild and moderately potent	Potent	Very potent
<2 months	100 g	50 g	30 g
2–6 months	50 g	30 g	15 g
6–12 months	25 g	15 g	7.5 g

Emollients

How often should an emollient be applied?

- For dry skin with minimal inflammation, emollients should be applied at least three times a day, increasing up to every hour if necessary to maintain skin hydration.
- For dry, chapped skin caused by excessive hand-washing, an emollient should be used as a substitute for normal soap.
- Where irritant contact dermatitis is caused by cumulative exposure to an irritant, for example at work, emollients should be applied regularly during and after work to prevent dermatitis.

How should emollients be applied with topical corticosteroids?

- Between corticosteroid treatments, emollient can be applied to all areas of dry skin, including the previously corticosteroid-treated areas. At least 30 minutes should be allowed to pass before the emollient is applied over the corticosteroid.

What are the adverse effects of emollients and how are they managed?

- **Sensitivity to constituents** such as the preservatives, fragrances, and biologically derived ingredients such as lanolin and arachis oil may occur. If sensitivity is suspected, try changing to a product with a different preservative. Alternatively, prescribe an ointment if this is acceptable, since ointments usually do not contain preservatives.

Table 5: Excipients in some commonly prescribed emollients.

Excipient	Emollients that include the excipient
Arachis (peanut) oil	Hewlett's cream
Benzyl alcohol	Aveeno cream, oilatum emollient
Cetostearyl alcohol	Aqueous cream, Aveeno cream, E45 cream, emulsifying ointment, Cetraben cream, Diprobase cream, Epaderm ointment, Hydromol cream, Oilatum cream, Ultrabase cream, Unguentum M cream
Disodium edetate	Ultrabase cream
Chlorocresol	Diprobase cream
Fragrances	Hewlett's cream, Ultrabase
Isopropyl palmitate	Aveeno cream
Parabens	Cetraben cream, E45 cream, Hydromol cream, Lipobase, Ultrabase cream
Phenoxyethanol	Aqueous cream, hydrous ointment
Polysorbates	Unguentum M cream
Propylene glycol	Unguentum M cream
Sorbic acid	Unguentum M cream
Wool fat/ lanolin	Hydrous ointment, E45 cream (hypoallergenic lanolin)

- Table 5 shows the excipients found in commonly prescribed emollients.

[BNF 47, 2004]

References

NHS staff in England can link, free of charge, from references to full text journals by clicking on [Full text] on the PRODIGY website.

1. Akhavan, A. and Cohen, S.R. (2003) The relationship between atopic dermatitis and contact dermatitis. *Clinics in Dermatology* **21**(2), 158–162.
2. Alvarez, M.S., Brown, L.H. and Brancaccio, R.R. (2001) Are barrier creams actually effective? *Current Allergy & Asthma Reports* **1**(4), 337–341.
3. Ayala, F., Balato, N., Lembo, G. et al (1996) Statistical evaluation of the persistence of acquired hypersensitivity by standardized patch tests. *Contact Dermatitis* **34**(5), 354–358.
4. Beck, M.H. and Wilkinson, S.M. (2004) Contact dermatitis: allergic. In: Burns, T., Breathnach, S., Cox, N. and Griffiths, C. (Eds.) *Rook's textbook of dermatology: volume 1*. 7th edn. Oxford: Blackwell Science. 20.1
5. Beltrani, V.S. and Beltrani, V.P. (1997) Contact dermatitis. *Annals of Allergy, Asthma, & Immunology* **78**(2), 160–173. [Full text]
6. Berndt, U., Wigger-Alberti, W., Gabard, B. and Elsner, P. (2000) Efficacy of a barrier cream and its vehicle as protective measures against occupational irritant contact dermatitis. *Contact Dermatitis* **42**(2), 77–80.
7. BNF 47 (2004) *British National Formulary*. 47th edn. London: British Medical Association and Royal Pharmaceutical Society of Great Britain.
8. Bourke, J., Coulson, I. and English, J. (2001) Guidelines for care of contact dermatitis. *British Journal of Dermatology* **145**(6), 877–885.
9. Cherry, N., Meyer, J.D., Adisesh, A. et al (2000) Surveillance of occupational skin disease: EPIDERM and OPRA. *British Journal of Dermatology* **142**(6), 1128–1134.
10. Clement, M. and Du Vivier, A. (1987) *Topical steroids for skin disorders*. Oxford: Blackwell Scientific Publications.
11. Cohen, D.E. (2004) Contact dermatitis: a quarter century perspective. *Journal of the American Academy of Dermatology* **51**(Suppl 1), S60-S63.
12. DTB (1998) Antiseptic/emollient combinations. *Drug & Therapeutics Bulletin* **36**(11), 84–86.
13. DTB (2003) Topical steroids for atopic dermatitis in primary care. *Drug & Therapeutics Bulletin* **41**(1), 5–8.
14. English, J.S. (2000) Corticosteroid-induced contact dermatitis: a pragmatic approach. *Clinical & Experimental Dermatology* **25**(4), 261–264.
15. Fowler, J.F. (1994) Reading patch tests: some pitfalls of patch testing. *American Journal of Contact Dermatitis* 5(3), 170–172.
16. Goh, C.L. (1998) Nonoccupational contact dermatitis. *Clinics in Dermatology* **16**(1), 119–127.
17. Hoare, C., Li Wan Po, A. and Williams, H. (2000) Systematic review of treatments for atopic eczema. *Health Technology Assessment* 4(37), 1–191.
18. Hogan, D. (2002) *Contact dermatitis, allergic*. eMedicine.com, Inc. www.emedicine.com/derm/topic84.htm [Accessed: 16/08/2004]. [Full text]
19. HPA (2003) *Management of infection guidance for primary care: for consultation and local adaptation*. Health Protection Agency. www.hpa.org.uk [Accessed: 26/02/2004]. [Full text]
20. Lauharanta, J., Ojajarvi, J., Sarna, S. and Makela, P. (1991) Prevention of dryness and eczema of the hands of hospital staff by emulsion cleansing instead of washing with soap. *Journal of Hospital Infection* 17(3), 207–215.
21. Long, C.C., Mills, C.M. and Finlay, A.Y. (1998) A practical guide to topical therapy in children. *British Journal of Dermatology* **138**(2), 293–296.
22. MeReC (1998) The use of emollients in dry skin conditions. *MeReC Bulletin* **9**(12), 45–48.
23. MeReC (1999) Using topical corticosteroids in general practice. *MeReC Bulletin* **10**(6), 21–24.
24. MeReC (2003) Atopic eczema in primary care. *MeReC Bulletin* **14**(1), 1–4.
25. National Institute for Occupational Safety and Health (1999) *Allergic & irritant dermatitis*. National Occupational Research Agenda. Centers for Disease Control & Prevention. www.cdc.gov/niosh/nrderm.html [Accessed: 16/08/2004]. [Full text]
26. NICE (2004) *Appraisal consultation document: frequency of application of topical corticosteroids for atopic eczema*. National Institute for Clinical Excellence. www.nice.org.uk [Accessed: 03/03/2004].
27. Skoet, R., Zachariae, R. and Agner, T. (2003) Contact dermatitis and quality of life: a structured review of the literature. *British Journal of Dermatology* **149**(3), 452–456.
28. Warshaw, E., Lee, G. and Storrs, F.J. (2003) Hand dermatitis: a review of clinical features, therapeutic options, and long-term outcomes. *American Journal of Contact Dermatitis* **14**(3), 119–137.
29. Wigger-Alberti, W. and Elsner, P. (1998) Do barrier creams and gloves prevent or provoke contact dermatitis? *American Journal of Contact Dermatitis* 9(2), 100–106.
30. Wilkinson, S.M. and Beck, M.H. (2004) Contact dermatitis: irritant. In: Burns, T., Breathnach, S., Cox, N. and Griffiths, C. (Eds.) *Rook's textbook of dermatology: volume 1*. 7th edn. Oxford: Blackwell Science. 19.1–19.30.

RODIGY GUIDANCE

Diabetes Type 1 and 2 — foot disease

Last revised in May 2004
www.prodigy.nhs.uk/guidance.asp?gt=Diabetes - foot disease

Applies to people over the age of 16 years

This guidance is the PRODIGY implementation of the National Institute for Clinical Excellence (NICE) clinical guideline for *Type 2 diabetes — prevention and management of foot problems (2004)*.

This guidance covers the prevention of ulcer development in people with diabetes and the initial management and referral of diabetic foot ulcers, infection, and Charcot's foot. It also provides background information on the identification and referral of people with feet at increased risk of ulceration. In line with the NICE guideline, this guidance is written for the management of people with Type 2 diabetes; however, the recommendations in this guidance also apply to people with Type 1 diabetes.

This guidance does not cover the management of other complications of diabetes, or the management of foot disease in people who do not have diabetes.

There is separate PRODIGY guidance for *Diabetes Type 2 — blood glucose management, Diabetes Type 2 — lipid management; Diabetes Type 1 and 2 — hypertension; Diabetes Type 2 — renal disease; Diabetes Type 2 — retinopathy*; and *Leg ulcer — venous.*

Goals

Early detection of diabetic foot complications
Prevention of development of foot ulcers
Prevention of recurrence of foot ulcers
Prevention of progression to amputation

Contents

Scenarios

- Preventing complications p.523
- Managing complications p.524

Extended Information, p. 525

Which scenario?

Preventing complications: provides information on preventing the development of complications in people with increased risk.
Managing complications: covers information on the immediate management and referral for people with diabetic foot ulcers and/or infection.

Preventing complications

Which therapy?

Examine feet and lower legs for evidence of diabetic foot disease at diagnosis and as part of annual review.
Classify foot risk as:

- At low current-risk (normal sensation, palpable pulses)
- At increased risk (loss of sensation, absent pulses, or other risk factor)
- At high risk (risk factor as above plus deformity or skin changes or previous ulcer)
- Ulcerated

For people with at increased risk of foot ulcers:

- Arrange regular review (every 3–6 months) by a foot protection team
- Review foot care education
- Advise on appropriate footwear
- Assess the need for vascular referral

For people at high risk of foot ulcers:

- Arrange frequent review (every 1–3 months) from a foot protection team
- Intensify foot care education
- Review the need for specialist footwear and insoles
- Ensure access to frequent (according to need) skin and nail care
- Assess the need for vascular referral

- Optimize blood glucose control.
- Ensure good control of blood pressure.
- Offer advice on smoking cessation where appropriate.
- Consider offering low-dose aspirin treatment to all people with diabetes and manifest cardiovascular disease or coronary heart disease (CHD) risk greater than 15%.

Follow-up advice

- For people at low current risk of foot ulcers arrange annual review.

Should I refer or investigate?

Refer?

- People with risk factors for foot ulcers: refer to a foot protection team for regular review.
- People at high risk of foot ulcers: refer to a foot protection team for frequent review.
- Ulcerated or infected feet: refer to multidisciplinary foot care team within 24 hours.
- Peripheral vascular disease (reduced pulses): refer for vascular assessment.

Investigate?

- Check glycaemic control and blood pressure control.

Patient information leaflets

The following PILs are available at www.prodigy.nhs.uk

- Blood Test - General
- Blood Test - Glucose
- Diabetes, Foot Care and Foot Ulcers
- Diabetes Foot Care - A Summary
- Diabetes Insight Website
- Diabetes Research & Wellness Foundation
- Diabetes Type 1 - A Summary
- Diabetes Type 2
- Diabetes Type 2 - A Summary
- Diabetes UK
- Diabetic Foot Page
- DiabeticLife

D

Shared decision making

If you have diabetes you should take good care of your feet:

- Look at your feet each day. If you cannot do this yourself, get someone else to do it for you.
- Use a moisturizing oil or cream for dry skin to prevent cracking. Do not apply it between the toes, however.
- Cut your nails 'straight across', following the shape of the toe. Do not try to cut your nails if you cannot see properly as you may cut your skin. Get someone else to do it.
- Do not walk barefoot, even at home.
- Always wear socks with shoes or other footwear.
- Shoes, trainers, and other footwear should:
  - Fit well to take into account any odd shapes (such as bunions)
  - Have rounded or square fronts with plenty of room for toes
  - Have low heels to avoid pressure on the toes
  - Have thick shock-absorbent soles
  - Have good laces, buckles, or Velcro fastening to prevent movement and rubbing of feet within the shoes
- Feel inside shoes for rough edges, stones, etc, before you put them on.
- If your feet are an abnormal shape, or if you have bunions or other foot problems, you may need specially fitted shoes.
- Do not deal with corns, calluses, verrucas, etc, by yourself.
- See a doctor, chiropodist, or podiatrist if you develop any foot problem.

Drug rationale

- There are no prescriptions offered.

Managing complications

Which therapy?

- **Urgently refer people with ulceration, infection, or discolouration to a multidisciplinary diabetes foot care team (within 24 hours).**
- **If referral within 24 hours is not possible,** for mild, superficial infections consider antibiotic treatment to cover staphylococci, streptococci, and anaerobes.
  - Co-amoxiclav is first choice in this situation.
  - Ciprofloxacin plus clarithromycin plus metronidazole should be prescribed for people who are allergic to penicillin.
  - Check with local policy for antibiotic resistance and drug choice.
  - Ensure review by specialist team at the earliest possible opportunity.
  - Advise the person on the appropriate action to take if the symptoms or general condition become worse.
- **Consider hospital admission if any of the following are present:**
  - Pink, painful, pulseless foot (indicating critical ischaemia)
  - Cellulitis, discolouration, or crepitus
  - Systemic symptoms of infection
  - Non-superficial and/or non-healing ulcer
  - Lack of response of the infection to oral antibiotics
  - Suspicion of bone involvement
  - Immunocompromise or physiological instability of the diabetic person

Practical prescribing points

For further information please see the *Medicines Compendium* (www.medicines.org.uk) or the *British National Formulary* (www.bnf.org).

Co-amoxiclav

- The Committee on Safety of Medicines (CSM) has advised that cholestatic jaundice has been identified as adverse reaction occurring either during or shortly afte the use of co-amoxiclav. Cholestatic jaundice is more common above the age of 65 years, and in men (CSM advice). Do not prescribe co-amoxiclav to people with history of co-amoxiclav-associated or penicillin-associated jaundice or hepatic dysfunction [CSM, 199

Ciprofloxacin

- **Ciprofloxacin:** tendon damage (including rupture) has been reported rarely in people receiving quinolones. Tendon rupture may occur within 48 hours of starting treatment. The CSM has advised that:
  - Quinolones are contraindicated in people with a history of tendon disorders related to quinolone use.
  - Elderly people are more prone to tendonitis.
  - The risk of tendon rupture is increased by the concomitant use of corticosteroids.
  - If tendonitis is suspected the quinolone should be discontinued immediately.
- The CSM has warned that quinolones may induce convulsions in people with or without a history of convulsions.

[CSM, 2002]

- **Check carefully for drug interactions** before prescribin the combination of ciprofloxacin, clarithromycin, and metronidazole.

Follow-up advice

- Arrange frequent review (every 1–3 months) from specialized podiatry/foot care team for people with fee at high risk of ulceration (risk factor plus deformity or skin changes or previous ulcer).

Should I refer or investigate?

Refer?

- **Urgent referral to a multidisciplinary diabetes footcare team** (within 24 hours) should be made for people wit
  - Ulceration
  - Infection
  - Discolouration
- **Consider hospital admission if:**
  - Pink, painful, pulseless foot (indicating critical ischaemia)
  - Associated peripheral vascular disease (reduced puls
  - Cellulitis, discolouration, or crepitus
  - Systemic symptoms of infection
  - Non-healing and/or non-superficial ulcer
  - Lack of response of the infection to oral antibiotics
  - Suspicion of bone involvement
  - Immunocompromise or physiological instability of t diabetic person
- Refer for vascular assessment if there is evidence of peripheral vascular disease (reduced or absent pulses).

Investigate?

- If urgent referral is not possible, take a swab from the ulcer base where possible. Antibiotic therapy should be adjusted according to culture results and response to treatment.

atient information leaflets

ıe following PILs are available at www.prodigy.nhs.uk

Blood Test - General
Blood Test - Glucose
Diabetes, Foot Care and Foot Ulcers
Diabetes Foot Care - A Summary
Diabetes Insight Website
Diabetes Research & Wellness Foundation
Diabetes Type 1 - A Summary
Diabetes Type 2
Diabetes Type 2 - A Summary
Diabetes UK
Diabetic Foot Page
DiabeticLife

hared decision making

You have a foot problem related to your diabetes.
Referral to a specialist is usually needed.
Antibiotics are advised if there is any infection and there is a wait before you can see a specialist.
See a GP if things get worse whilst waiting to see a specialist.

rug rationale

rugs not included

People with ulcerated or infected feet should be referred to a team with specialist expertise, or for hospital admission (depending on severity). Apart from empirical antibiotic cover where urgent referral of superficial foot infections is not possible, there are no prescriptions offered in this scenario.

rugs included

There is very limited evidence to support the choice of antibiotic. Antibiotic cover is offered on the basis of potential pathogens. A Health Technology Assessment series of systematic reviews to inform a decision analysis of microbiological sampling in infected diabetic foot ulcers is currently being undertaken. This guidance will be updated when the results of this systematic review are available.

Co-amoxiclav is included as first-choice empirical treatment to cover the usual pathogens associated with superficial infection when urgent referral (within 24 hours) is not possible. Treatment may be started whilst awaiting referral.

The combination of ciprofloxacin plus clarithromycin plus metronidazole is included as empirical treatment for people who are allergic to penicillin.

rescriptions

st-line antibiotic (superficial infection only)

ɔ-amoxiclav tablets: 250/125mg three times a day for 7 ıys

- Age from 16 years onwards
- Co-amoxiclav 375mg tablets. Take one tablet three times a day for 7 days; supply 21 tablets; NHS Cost £9.85.

ɔ-amoxiclav tablets: 500/125mg three times a day for 7 ıys

- Age from 16 years onwards
- Co-amoxiclav 625mg tablets. Take one tablet three times a day for 7 days; supply 21 tablets; NHS Cost £15.72.

Penicillin allergy (superficial infection only)

Metronidazole + clarithromycin + ciprofloxacin

- Age from 16 years onwards
- Metronidazole 400mg tablets. Take one tablet three times a day for 7 days; supply 21 tablets; NHS Cost £1.02.
- Clarithromycin 500mg tablets. Take one tablet twice a day for 7 days; supply 14 tablets; NHS Cost £22.49.
- Ciprofloxacin 500mg tablets. Take one tablet twice a day for 7 days; supply 14 tablets; NHS Cost £19.88.

Extended Information

D

Background information

- What is it? p.525
- How common is it? p.525
- How do I know my patient has it? p.525
- What are the risk factors for developing diabetic foot ulcers? p.526
- What else might it be? p.526
- Complications and prognosis p.526

What is it?

- **The diabetic foot is defined as** a group of syndromes in which neuropathy, ischaemia, and infection lead to tissue breakdown, which results in morbidity and possible amputation.
- **Neuropathy and peripheral vascular disease** are the main pathologies underlying diabetic foot disorders:
  - Peripheral vascular disease leads to poor circulation and ischaemia.
  - Peripheral neuropathy of the feet leads to loss of sensation and autonomic dysfunction.
- **These pathologies can lead to ulceration, infection, gangrene, and amputation.**

[McIntosh et al, 2003]

How common is it?

- **Foot complications are common in people with diabetes.** The prevalence of neuropathy in people with diabetes is 23–42%, and that of vascular disease is 9–23% [SIGN, 2001].
- At some time in their life, 15% of people with diabetes will develop a foot ulcer associated with peripheral neuropathy or ischaemia or both [NHS CRD, 1999].

[McIntosh et al, 2003]

How do I know my patient has it?

- **Evaluate skin, soft tissue, musculoskeletal, vascular, and neurological condition at least once a year,** to detect feet that are at increased risk of ulceration.
- **Assessment should include:**
  - **History** — previous ulceration or amputation, previous education
  - **Skin/soft tissue examination** — inspection of the legs; dorsal, plantar, and posterior surfaces of the foot; and between the toes
  - **Neurological evaluation** — tingling or pain, loss of sensation, loss of perception of pressure and vibration, reflexes
  - **Vascular evaluation** — palpation of the pulses in the lower extremities, inspection of the feet and legs for evidence of ischaemic changes
  - **Musculoskeletal evaluation** — evaluation of foot and ankle range of movement, inspection for bone abnormalities, analysis of gait and stance

- **Footwear examination** — inspection of type and fit of shoe, patterns of wear of both shoe and lining, presence of foreign bodies, use of insoles or orthoses
- **Measurement of sensation** (using a 10 g [5.07 Semmes-Weinstein] monofilament) or **vibration perception** (using a biothesiometer) predicts people at increased risk of ulceration due to neuropathy:
  - Lack of sensation to a 10 g monofilament has 93% sensitivity and 86% specificity for predicting ulceration.
  - Lack of perception of vibration using a biothesiometer has 83% sensitivity and 62% specificity for predicting ulceration.
  - The 10 g monofilament is convenient and easy to use in primary care. Biothesiometers are not widely available in primary care.
  - **Assessment of ankle reflexes is of limited value in determining risk of ulceration.**
  - Assessment of neuropathic deficit using a tuning fork has not been prospectively evaluated for its ability to predict development of ulcers and cannot be recommended.
  - The 10 g monofilament deteriorates with use and should be replaced according to the manufacturer's instructions. Each monofilament should not be used to test more than 10 people in one session and should be left for at least 24 hours to recover [NICE, 2004].
  - For further information on the use of a 10 g monofilament see www.nzgg.org.nz/guidelines/0036/Diabetes_AppendixF.pdf
- **It is less easy to accurately predict feet at risk of ischaemic ulceration.** Signs and symptoms to look for include:
  - Presence of claudication or pain at rest.
  - Absence of posterior tibial and dorsalis pedis pulses on palpation.
  - If available, assessment of ankle–brachial pressure index by Doppler ultrasonography can give a useful guide to the presence of ischaemia.
- **If an ulcer is present,** distinguish between neuropathic or ischaemic origin (see Table 1.). Approximately 50% of diabetic feet presenting at dedicated foot clinics are neuropathic and 50% neuroischaemic. In a local population study of 1077 diabetic patients, 7% were found to have past or present foot ulceration, of which 39% were neuropathic, 24% were vascular, and 36% mixed [Mason et al, 1999b; McIntosh et al, 2003].
  - **Neuropathic feet,** where good circulation remains, are warm, numb, dry, usually painless, and pulses remain palpable. Neuropathic ulcers, found mainly on the soles of the feet, infections, and neuropathic (Charcot's) joints are the main complications that may result.
  - **Neuro-ischaemic feet** are cool and pulses are absent. Pain at rest or intermittent claudication, ulceration at the edges of the foot from localized pressure damage and gangrene may occur.

[SIGN, 2001; DTB, 2002; McIntosh et al, 2003]
[Donnelly et al, 2000]

- **Consider infection** whenever local (e.g. foot pain, swelling, ulceration) or systemic (e.g. poor glycaemic control, fever, malaise) problems develop. The usual signs of infection may be absent due to immunosuppression.
- **Diagnosis of Charcot's foot** should be made by clinical examination, supported where available by the use of thermography.
  - Clinical diagnosis of Charcot's foot is based on the appearance of a red, swollen, oedematous, and possibly painful foot in the absence of infection. It is associated with increased bone blood flow, osteopen and fracture or dislocation.
  - Acute Charcot's foot is associated with a skin temperature of 2–8°C higher than the contralateral foot, as measured on thermography.

[SIGN, 2001]

Table 1: Clinical features that distinguish between neuropathic and ischaemic foot ulcers.

Sign/ symptom	Neuropathic ulcer	Ischaemic ulcer
Pain	Painless	Painful, may be relieved by hanging legs down
Location	Commonly on plantar surface of foot	Commonly located at edges of foot
Skin temperature	Warm foot	Cool foot
Foot pulses	Bounding	Absent or weak
Callus formation	Often present, especially on plantar surface	Absent

What are the risk factors for developing diabetic foot ulcers?

- An ulcer is about five times more likely to occur in a person with a history of previous or current foot ulcers or with peripheral neuropathy.
- Other factors which increase the risk include:
  - Foot deformities causing pressure on the overlying skin (e.g. corns, calluses, clawed toes, hammer toes, nail deformities)
  - Increased duration of diabetes
  - Orthopaedic problems that interfere with normal foo function (e.g. arthritis of the knee, hip, or spine)
  - Other long-term complications of diabetes (e.g. renal disease or retinopathy)
  - Poor glycaemic and hypertensive control
  - Poor sight
  - Poor mobility preventing the person from caring for their own feet
  - Poorly fitting footwear
  - Social deprivation and social isolation

[SIGN, 2001; DTB, 2002; McIntosh et al, 2003]

What else might it be?

- Peripheral neuropathy due to other causes, e.g. alcohol abuse, vitamin B_{12} deficiency, malignancy.
- Ulcer due to other causes, e.g. venous leg ulcer.

Complications and prognosis

Complications

- **Foot ulcers** develop in about 15% of people with Type diabetes at some time during their life. Between 5 and 15% of these will ultimately require amputation [NHS CRD, 1999].
- **Diabetic foot ulcers are prone to infection,** often with polymicrobial invasion. Foot infections (including cellulitis, abscesses, osteomyelitis, and joint infections) are a major cause of hospital admissions among people with Type 2 diabetes, and an important cause of lower-limb amputation.
- **Gangrene and amputation.** Diabetic foot ulcers are prone to infection, which often spreads rapidly and can lead to tissue destruction. Apart from trauma, infection originating in a diabetic foot ulcer is the most common reason for amputation [NHS CRD, 1999].
- **Charcot's foot** progressive neuroarthropathic condition characterized by osteoporosis, fracture, acute inflammation, and disorganization of the bone and join

structure. It is associated with severe peripheral neuropathy. It is estimated that 0.2% of people with diabetes seen in primary care will develop Charcot's foot [Frykberg et al, 2000; Jeffcoate et al, 2000].

Prognosis

Recurrence rates for diabetic foot ulcers are 35–40% over three years, increasing to 70% over five years [NHS CRD, 1999].

The prognosis for people with cellulitis is poor. In one study, even following apparent treatment success, 66% of people had amputation affecting part of the lower limb in the following year [McIntosh et al, 2003].

Management issues

Key priorities for implementation p.527
Service arrangements for people with diabetes in respect of their foot care p.527
Prevention of ulcer development p.528
Management of ulcerated feet p.528
Management of infected feet p.529
Management of Charcot's foot p.529
Specialist referral for diabetic foot disorders p.529

Key priorities for implementation

General management approach

- Effective care involves a partnership between patients and professionals and all decision-making should be shared (D).
- Arrange recall and annual review as part of ongoing care (A).
  - As part of annual review, trained personnel should examine patients' feet to detect risk factors for ulceration.
- **Examination of patients' feet should include:** (A)
  - Testing of foot sensation using a 10 g monofilament or vibration
  - Palpation of foot pulses
  - Inspection of any foot deformity and footwear
- **Classify foot risk as:** (C)
  - At low current risk (normal sensation, palpable pulses)
  - At increased risk (neuropathy or absent pulses or other risk factor)
  - At high risk (neuropathy or absent pulses or other risk factor plus deformity or skin changes or previous ulcer)
  - Ulcerated foot

Note: risk classification is *not* static — people can deteriorate rapidly from one risk class to another.

Care of people at low current risk of foot ulcers (normal sensation, palpable pulses)

- Arrange annual review (A).
- Agree a management plan including foot care education with each person (to encourage appropriate self-care and self-monitoring) (B).

Care of people at increased risk of foot ulcers (neuropathy or absent pulses or other risk factor)

- People with risk factors should be referred to a foot protection team (D).
- Arrange regular review (every 3–6 months) by a foot protection team (D).
- At each review:
  - Inspect patient's feet (D)
  - Consider the need for vascular assessment (if absent pulses) (D)
  - Evaluate footwear (D)
  - Enhance foot care education (D)

Note: if the person has had a previous foot ulcer or deformity or skin changes, manage as high risk (see below).

Care of people at high risk of foot ulcers (neuropathy or absent pulses or other risk factor plus deformity or skin changes or previous ulcer)

- People at high risk of foot ulceration should be referred to a foot protection team (A).
- Arrange frequent review (every 1–3 months) by a foot protection team (D).
- At each review:
  - Inspect patient's feet (A)
  - Consider need for vascular assessment (e.g. if absent pulses) (D)
  - Evaluate and ensure the appropriate provision of:
    - Intensified foot care education (D)
    - Specialist footwear and insoles (D)
    - Skin and nail care (D)
- Ensure special arrangements for those people with disabilities or immobility (D).
  - There is no available evidence concerning the most appropriate process for this. Check with your primary care organization for local arrangements.

Care of people with foot emergencies or foot ulcers

- Any footcare emergency (new ulceration, swelling, cellulitis, discolouration) should be referred to a multidisciplinary foot care team within 24 hours.
- Ongoing care of a person with an ulcerated foot should be undertaken by a multidisciplinary foot care team (D).
- Expect that team, as a minimum, to:
  - Investigate and treat vascular insufficiency.
  - Initiate and supervise wound management, including:
    - Appropriate dressings and debridement as indicated.
    - Systemic antibiotic therapy for cellulitis or bone infection as indicated.
  - Ensure an effective means of distributing foot pressures, including specialist footwear, orthotics, and casts.
  - Try to achieve optimal glucose levels and control of risk factors for cardiovascular disease.

[McIntosh et al, 2003; NICE, 2004]

Service arrangements for people with diabetes in respect of their foot care

- **The National Service Framework for Diabetes** (NSF-Diabetes) has described foot care service arrangements that should be provided for people with diabetes. Actual services may vary according to locality. The NSF-Diabetes Service Models are:
  - **Foot protection programmes** for people at increased risk of developing lower limb complications. These are provided by a 'foot protection team' with the aim of reducing the risk of lower-limb complications. Typically members of the foot protection team include podiatrists, orthotists, and footcare specialists.
  - **Multidisciplinary foot care services** for people with lower-limb complications. These are provided by a 'multidisciplinary foot care team' with the aim of providing prompt effective treatment for people who develop lower-limb complications. The multidisciplinary foot care team should comprise highly trained specialist podiatrists and orthotists, nurses with training in dressing diabetic foot wounds, and diabetologists with expertise in lower limb complications.

[DH, 2001; NICE, 2004]

Prevention of ulcer development

Screening

- **Screening and referral to foot care clinics can significantly reduce the risk of major amputation** [Mason et al, 1999b].
- **All people with diabetes should be regularly reviewed and assessed for foot complications,** as outlined in *How do I know my patient has it?*.
- There is no evidence regarding how frequently foot screening should be carried out, but consensus suggests that it should be done at least once a year in people with no previous complications or risk factors, and more frequently in people with increased risk (see Table 2).

Table 2: Recommended frequency of foot examinations.

Risk category	Risk profile	Evaluation frequency
Low-current-risk	No neuropathy or ischaemia	Annually
Increased risk	Neuropathy or ischaemia	Every 3–6 months
High risk	Neuropathy, ischaemia, and/or deformity or previous ulcer or amputation	Every 1–3 months

[NICE, 2004]

Foot care education

- **Education plays a primary role in the prevention of ulcer recurrence.** This should encompass foot hygiene, need for daily foot inspection, suitable footwear, prompt treatment of new lesions, and the importance of regular podiatric visits.
- **Structured patient education should be made available to all people with diabetes** at the time of the initial diagnosis, and then as needed on an ongoing basis, based on formal, regular assessment of need [NICE, 2003].
- **Foot care education improves knowledge and behaviour towards** foot care in the short term in people with diabetes. Education may reduce foot ulceration and complications [Valk et al, 2004].
- **A person with diabetes should be offered information about the following:**
  - What they can expect in terms of foot care
  - Education on self-care and self-monitoring
  - Details of when and where to seek advice (including out of hours)
  - Possible consequences of neglecting their feet
  - How to manage symptoms (e.g. pain, odour)

[NICE, 2004]

- **Self-care and self-monitoring should cover:**
  - Daily self-examination of feet, including areas between the toes, for problems (e.g. colour change, swelling, breaks in the skin, pain, or numbness). People who cannot inspect their own feet should have them inspected by someone else.
  - Avoidance of walking barefoot in- or outdoors and of wearing shoes without socks.
  - Correct nail cutting techniques (nails should be cut straight across, following the shape of the toe). People with impaired vision should not try to cut their nails themselves.
  - Daily inspection and palpation of the inside of the shoes to check for stones, rough edges, etc.
  - Dealing with minor skin injuries.
  - Dealing with corns and calluses. Chemical agents or plasters to remove corns and calluses should not be used. Corns and calluses should not be treated by patients, but by a health care provider.
  - The importance of appropriate well-fitting footwear and hosiery. Shoes should accommodate the shape c the foot and any deformities. They should have broa rounded or square toes, adequate toe depth, low hee to avoid excessive toe pressure, thick shock-absorbe soles, and secure fastening to prevent movement of t foot within the shoe.
  - General foot hygiene including daily washing of feet with careful drying, especially between the toes. The temperature of the water should always be less than 37°C.
  - Use of moisturizing oils or creams. These should be used for dry skin, but not between the toes.
  - Importance of blood glucose control.
- The person should be advised to seek advice from a healthcare professional if:
  - Any colour change, swelling, breaks in the skin, pai or numbness is found.
  - Self-care and monitoring is difficult or not possible (e.g. because of reduced mobility).

[NHS CRD, 1999; Apelqvist et al, 2000; DTB, 2002; NICE, 2004]

Footwear

- Changes in foot posture may lead to abnormal weight bearing, often indicated by callus under the metatarsal heads. Callus formation often precedes the developme of neuropathic ulcer.
- The provision of orthoses or therapeutic shoes, or both can reduce abnormal foot pressures and thus reduce th ulcer rate in people at high risk of developing diabetic foot ulcers, compared with those who continue to wea their own shoes [NHS CRD, 1999].

Management of other risk factors

- **Ensure good blood glucose control.** For each individua a target HbA_{1c} level should be set between 6.5 and 7.5 based on the risk of macrovascular and microvascular complications. In general, the lower target HbA_{1c} level preferred for people at significant risk of vascular complications, but higher targets are necessary for tho at risk of iatrogenic hypoglycaemia [NICE, 2002]. For further information, see the PRODIGY *Diabetes Type — blood glucose management*.
- **Ensure good control of blood pressure (BP).** For furthe information, see the PRODIGY *Diabetes Type 1 and 2 — hypertension* guidance.
- Although there is no direct evidence that improved glucose or BP control will benefit people with Type 2 diabetes who are at risk of diabetic foot complications evidence from the UK Prospective Diabetes Study (UKPDS) confirms that good glycaemic and BP contro improves microvascular outcomes [Turner et al, 1998; UK Prospective Diabetes Study Group, 1998].
- **Encourage all people with diabetes who smoke to stop.** Provide appropriate advice and help with smoking cessation. For further information, see the PRODIGY *Smoking cessation* guidance.
- **Consider low-dose aspirin treatment in people with diabetes with evidence of atherosclerotic disease or coronary heart disease risk greater than 15%.**

[DTB, 2002]

Management of ulcerated feet

Treatment of the ulcerated foot should be prompt and appropriate to prevent avoidable amputation in people with diabetes.

- **Urgently arrange foot ulcer care from a multidisciplina foot care team (within 24 hours).**
- **The primary goal in the treatment of diabetic foot ulce** is to heal the ulcer as quickly as possible, reduce the

robability of infection, and reduce the likelihood of ecurrence.

When someone presents with a diabetic foot ulcer it is nportant to decide at an early stage whether the roblem is:

- Neuropathic with an intact circulation
- Ischaemic with (usually) or without neuropathy (neuroischaemic)
- Critically ischaemic needing very urgent attention

combination of ulceration and sepsis in an ischaemic oot carries a higher risk of gangrene, and early arterial ssessment and management are essential to minimize he risk of amputation [Watkins, 2003].

he traditional (although inadequately evaluated) pproach to foot ulcer management includes ebridement, appropriate wound management, and ntibiotic treatment where infection is present.

ressure reduction ('off-loading') is the main approach to lcer management. This can be achieved in a variety of ays including total contact casting (the use of plaster ast to redistribute weight over the foot).

here is limited evidence for new treatments such as the se of hyperbaric oxygen therapy, growth factors, etanserin, and cultured human dermis, and they are not urrently widely used.

or superficial or skin-deep uncomplicated neuropathic oot ulcers, there is insufficient evidence to demonstrate he efficacy of antibiotics over placebo and standard ound care [Mason et al, 1999a].

evascularization may be necessary in people with ignificant lower-extremity ischaemia.

HS CRD, 1999; SIGN, 2001; DTB, 2002; McIntosh et 2003]

nagement of infected feet

Only people who have sufficient experience and facilities vailable should treat infected diabetic feet. Unless they ave such experience, general practitioners should refer eople for urgent specialist care.

eople with non-healing or progressive ulcers with linical signs of infection (redness, pain, swelling, or ischarge) should receive intensive systemic ntimicrobial therapy.

nfection in a diabetic foot presents a threat to the limb nd should be treated promptly and aggressively.

oot infections can be classified as non-limb-threatening requiring urgent referral to a multidisciplinary foot care eam) or limb-threatening (requiring hospital admission).

t is important to remember that a non-limb-threatening nfection can become quickly limb-threatening.

lassification will also depend on the pathogenic mix nd virulence factors and on the immune and general hysiological status of the person.

on-limb-threatening infections — urgent referral to ultidisciplinary foot care team:

Urgently refer people with non-limb-threatening nfections to a multidisciplinary foot care team (or local quivalent).

Non-limb-threatening infections include those with:

- Infection of a superficial ulcer
- No bone or joint involvement
- No signs or symptoms of systemic toxicity
- No significant ischaemia

Non limb threatening infections are usually due to taphylococci, beta-haemolytic streptococci, and ometimes anaerobes.

f referral within 24 hours is not possible, consider tarting empirical antibiotic treatment whilst the person s waiting to be seen by the specialist team. Ensure that the person is assessed by the specialist team at the earliest available opportunity.

- **Cultures should be taken from the ulcer base where possible.** Antibiotic therapy should be adjusted according to culture results and response to treatment.

Limb-threatening infections — hospital admission:

- **Consider hospital admission for people with limb-threatening infections.**
- Limb-threatening infections include those with:
  - Cellulitis, discolouration, or crepitus
  - Signs of systemic infection
  - Malodourous wound
  - Presence of soft tissue necrosis
  - Suspected bone involvement (e.g. deep ulcer exposing bone)

[Frykberg et al, 2000]

Management of Charcot's foot

- **Refer people with suspected Charcot's foot immediately** to a multidisciplinary foot care team for immobilisation of the affected joint(s) and for long-term management to prevent ulceration [NICE, 2004] (D).
- **Total contact casting and pressure relief are effective treatments for Charcot's foot.**
  - Treatment of Charcot's foot with contact casting is associated with a reduction in skin temperature, as measured by thermography, and in bone activity.
- **There is insufficient evidence to recommend the routine use of bisphosphonates** in acute Charcot's foot.

[SIGN, 2001]

Specialist referral for diabetic foot disorders

- **Refer people to a multidisciplinary foot care team within 24 hours if any of the following occur:**
  - New ulceration (wound)
  - New swelling
  - New discolouration (redder, bluer, paler, blacker, over all or part of the foot)
  - People with signs or symptoms of infection (redness, pain, swelling, or discharge)
- **Consider hospital admission if any of the following are present:**
  - Pink, painful, pulseless foot (indicating critical ischaemia)
  - Associated peripheral vascular disease (reduced pulses)
  - Cellulitis, discolouration, or crepitus
  - Systemic symptoms of infection
  - Non-healing and/or non-superficial ulcer
  - Lack of response of infection to oral antibiotics
  - Suspicion of bone involvement
  - Immunocompromise or physiological instability of the diabetic person
- **Refer people with suspected Charcot's foot immediately** to a multidisciplinary foot care team.
- **Refer for vascular assessment** if there is evidence of peripheral vascular disease (reduced or absent pulses).

References

NHS staff in England can link, free of charge, from references to full text journals by clicking on [Full text] on the PRODIGY website.

1. Apelqvist, J., Bakker, K., van Houtum, W.H. et al (2000) International consensus and practical guidelines on the management and the prevention of the diabetic foot. *Diabetes/Metabolism and Research Reviews* **16**(Suppl 1), S84-S92.

2. CSM (1997) Revised indications for co-amoxiclav (Augmentin). *Current Problems in Pharmacovigilance* **23**(May), 8.
3. CSM (2002) Reminder: fluoroquinolone antibiotics and tendon disorders. *Current Problems in Pharmacovigilance* **28**(Apr), 3–4.
4. DH (2001) *National service framework for diabetes: supplementary material, intervention details and draft service models.* Department of Health. www.publications.doh.gov.uk/nsf/diabetes [Accessed: 26/08/2004]. [Full text]
5. Donnelly, R., Emslie-Smith, A.M., Gardner, I.D. and Morris, A.D. (2000) Vascular complications of diabetes. *British Medical Journal* **320**(7241), 1062–1066. [Full text]
6. DTB (2002) Managing foot ulcers in patients with diabetes. *Drug & Therapeutics Bulletin* **40**(Feb), 11–14.
7. Frykberg, R.G., Armstrong, D.G., Giurini, J. et al (2000) Diabetic foot disorders. A clinical practice guideline. *Journal of Foot & Ankle Surgery* **39**(Suppl 5), S1-S60.
8. Jeffcoate, W., Lima, J. and Nobrega, L. (2000) The charcot foot. *Diabetic Medicine* **17**(4), 253–258.
9. Mason, J., O'Keeffe, C., Hutchinson, A. et al (1999a) A systematic review of foot ulcer in patients with type 2 diabetes mellitus. II: treatment. *Diabetic Medicine* **16**(11), 889–909.
10. Mason, J., O'Keeffe, C., McIntosh, A. et al (1999b) A systematic review of foot ulcer in patients with type 2 diabetes mellitus. I: prevention. *Diabetic Medicine* **16**(10), 801–812.
11. McIntosh, A., Peters, J., Young, R. et al (2003) *Prevention and management of foot problems in type 2 diabetes: clinical guidelines and evidence.* Sheffield: University of Sheffield. www.nice.org.uk [Accessed: 13/07/2004].
12. NHS CRD (1999) Complications of diabetes: screening for retinopathy and management of foot ulcers. *Effective Health Care Bulletin* **5**(4), 1–12.
13. NICE (2002) *Management of type 2 diabetes – managing blood glucose levels.* Inherited clinical guideline G. National Institute for Clinical Excellence. www.nice.org.uk [Accessed: 02/12/2002].
14. NICE (2003) *Guidance on the use of patient-education models for diabetes.* Technology appraisal no. 60. National Institute for Clinical Excellence. www.nice.org.uk [Accessed: 26/08/2004].
15. NICE (2004) *Type 2 diabetes: prevention and management of foot problems.* Clinical guideline no 10. National Institute for Clinical Exellence. www.nice.org.uk [Accessed: 13/07/2004].
16. SIGN (2001) *Management of diabetes.* Report no. 5 Scottish Intercollegiate Guidelines Network. www.sign.ac.uk [Accessed: 20/11/2002].
17. Turner, R.C., Holman, R.R., Cull, C.A. et al (1998) Intensive blood-glucose control with sulphonylureas insulin compared with conventional treatment and r of complications in patients with type 2 diabetes (UKPDS 33). *Lancet* **352**(9131), 837–853. [Full text]
18. UK Prospective Diabetes Study Group (1998) Tight blood pressure control and risk of macrovascular an microvascular complications in type 2 diabetes (UKPDS 38). *British Medical Journal* **317**(7160), 703–713. [Full text]
19. Valk, G.D., Kriegsman, D.M. and Assendelft, W.J. (2004) *Patient education for preventing diabetic foo ulceration.* The Cochrane Library. Issue 3. Chichest UK: John Wiley & Sons, Ltd.
20. Watkins, P.J. (2003) The diabetic foot. *British Medi Journal* **326**(7396), 977–979. [Full text]

Evidence grading

Evidence grading is from the National Institute of Clinic Excellence guideline, *Type 2 diabetes: Prevention and management of foot problems,* January 2004. The definitions of grades of recommendation used in this guideline are as follows:

A Directly based on category I evidence (systematic review of randomized controlled trials or at least one randomized controlled trial)

B Directly based on category II evidence (at least one controll study without randomization or one other type of quasi-experimental study) or extrapolated recommendation from category I evidence

C Directly based on category III evidence (non-experimental descriptive studies) or extrapolated recommendation from category I or II evidence

D Directly based on category IV evidence (expert committee reports, opinions, or clinical experience of respected authorities) or extrapolated recommendation from category II, or III evidence

PRODIGY GUIDANCE

Diabetes Type 1 and 2 — hypertension

Last revised July 2003
www.prodigy.nhs.uk/guidance.asp?gt=Diabetes - hypertension

Applies to people over the age of 16 years

This guidance is the PRODIGY implementation of the National Institute for Clinical Excellence (NICE) guideline on the *Management of Type 2 diabetes: management of blood pressure and blood lipids* and the Royal College of General Practitioners (RCGP) *Clinical Guidelines for Type 2 Diabetes: Blood Pressure Management (October 2002)*. Relevant information from the British Hypertension Society (BHS) 1999 guideline on the management of hypertension, and evidence from recently published trials are also included.

This guidance covers the management of hypertension in people with either *Type 1* or *Type 2* diabetes.

This guidance does not cover the management of hypertension in children with diabetes, hypertension in pregnant women with diabetes, or malignant hypertension in people with diabetes.

There is separate PRODIGY guidance for the management of *Hypertension (for people who do not have diabetes); Hypertension in pregnancy; Diabetes Type 1 and 2 — foot disease; Diabetes Type 2 — lipid management; and Diabetes Type 2 — renal disease.*
This guidance may require calculation of cardiovascular risk, using either the Joint British Societies computer program or risk chart, or a similar risk-assessment tool. For further information, see the PRODIGY *Coronary heart disease risk — identification and management* guidance.

Goals

- To identify hypertension in people with diabetes
- To manage people with diabetes who have hypertension, in order to reduce their risk of cardiovascular morbidity and mortality
- To identify and treat other cardiovascular risk factors

Contents

Scenarios

- On no treatment: offer starting prescription? p.531
- On treatment: advice on targets and other treatments p.535
- Change to/increase/add ACE or angiotensin-II receptor antag. p.536
- Change to or add thiazide p.538
- Change to, increase, or add beta-blocker p.540
- Change to, increase, or add calcium-channel blocker p.541
- Change to, increase, or add alpha-blocker p.543
- Aspirin — who to treat? p.545

Extended Information, p. 546

Which scenario?

- **On no treatment: offer starting prescription?:** covers the assessment of coronary-event risk and offers starting prescriptions if needed. This scenario also includes advice on how to decide whether to treat with antihypertensive medication and which drug to use; initiation doses of drugs are offered.
- **On treatment: advice on targets and other treatments:** covers blood pressure targets for people with diabetes, and discusses when to consider combination therapy for people whose blood pressure is not controlled.
- **Change to/increase/add ACE or angiotensin-II receptor antag:** ACE inhibitors or AIIRAs are best combined with thiazides or calcium-channel blockers; a first-line choice in heart failure, left ventricular dysfunction. Where an ACE inhibitor is contraindicated, give an AIIRA.
- **Change to or add thiazide:** thiazides are best combined with beta-blockers or ACE inhibitors; generally the first-line monotherapy choice, particularly for people over the age of 60 years.
- **Change to, increase, or add beta-blocker:** beta-blockers are best combined with thiazides or calcium-channel blockers (never verapamil); a first-line choice if angina or a history of myocardial infarction, and may be considered in patients with heart failure, under close specialist supervision.
- **Change to, increase, or add calcium-channel blocker:** calcium-channel blockers are best combined with beta-blockers (but never verapamil) or ACE-inhibitors; dihydropyridine calcium-channel blockers are an alternative to thiazides in elderly people; rate-limiting calcium-channel blockers are an alternative to beta-blockers in patients with angina or a history of myocardial infarction.
- **Change to, increase, or add alpha-blocker:** alpha-blockers are best combined with beta-blockers, but can be added to any other major class of antihypertensive. May be especially useful if there is prostatism.
- **Aspirin — who to treat?:** covers when to consider aspirin in people with hypertension.

On no treatment: offer starting prescription?

Which therapy?

- **Initial assessment** of a person with diabetes and hypertension should include a complete medical history with special emphasis on cardiovascular risk factors and other diabetic complications.
- **Advise a hypertensive person with diabetes on lifestyle methods of reducing blood pressure (BP),** including regular exercise, weight reduction, healthy diet, and limiting salt and alcohol intake.
- **Identify and treat other cardiovascular risk factors** as appropriate, for example smoking and hyperlipidaemia (see separate PRODIGY guidance on *Smoking cessation, Diabetes Type 2 — lipid management, Coronary heart disease risk — identification and management*).
  Maximize blood glucose control — aim to maintain (HbA_{1c}) level below 6.5%.

- **If sustained BP >=140/80 mmHg, in the presence of nephropathy:**
  - An ACE inhibitor is the usual first-line agent.
  - Assess the response every 3–6 months.
- **In someone without nephropathy,** the following recommendations are made.
  - **If BP <160/100 mmHg in someone with no history of cardiovascular disease (CVD) and the 10-year coronary event risk is =<15%:**
    - Do not offer drug treatment.
    - Monitor BP at least every 6 months.
  - **If sustained BP >=140/80 mmHg and <160/100 mmHg with a history of CVD or 10-year coronary event risk >15%:**
    - ACE inhibitors, beta-blockers, thiazide diuretics, or angiotensin-II receptor antagonists (AIIRAs) (where an ACE inhibitor is contraindicated) are all first-line options.
    - Assess the response every 3–6 months.
  - **If sustained BP >160/100 mmHg irrespective of any additional cardiovascular risk, drug treatment should be offered.** ACE inhibitors, beta-blockers, thiazide diuretics, or AIIRAs (where an ACE inhibitor is not tolerated) are all first-line options.
  - **In people without nephropathy** the choice of first-line drug should be determined using the criteria for non-diabetic people with hypertension as follows:
    - **Asthma or a history of bronchospasm:** do not use beta-blockers (Committee on Safety of Medicines warning).
    - **Gout:** generally avoid using a thiazide diuretic. If a thiazide is necessary, consider prophylaxis with allopurinol (see separate PRODIGY guidance on *Gout*).
    - **People over the age of 60 years:** a thiazide is preferred.
    - **Heart failure, left ventricular dysfunction:** an ACE inhibitor is the first choice.
    - **Angina:** a beta-blocker is preferred, but either a rate-limiting or a long-acting dihydropyridine calcium-channel blocker (CCB) is an alternative option if a beta-blocker is not tolerated or contraindicated.
    - **Post myocardial infarction: a beta-blocker,** or alternatively an ACE inhibitor is preferred.
    - **Afro-Caribbean people:** a thiazide is preferred, but a CCB is an alternative option.

Practical prescribing points

For further information please see the *Medicines Compendium* (www.medicines.org.uk) or the *British National Formulary* (www.bnf.org).

ACE inhibitors or angiotensin-II receptor antagonists (AIIRAs):

- **Avoid potassium-sparing diuretics or potassium supplements** (other than in exceptional cases — e.g. low dose spironolactone for severe heart failure) because of the risk of hyperkalaemia.
- **Monitor renal function carefully with** peripheral vascular disease (risk of renovascular disease) and raised serum creatinine.
- **The risk of first-dose hypotension or renal impairment induced either by an ACE inhibitor or by an AIIRA is increased in the following high-risk groups of people:**
  - Creatinine >150 micromol/l
  - Urea >12 mmol/l
  - Sodium <130 mmol/l
  - Systolic blood pressure <100 mmHg
  - Diuretic dose > furosemide 80 mg or bumetanide 2 mg daily
  - Known or suspected renal artery stenosis (e.g. if peripheral vascular disease)
  - People aged 70 years and over or who are frail
  - Hypovolaemia
  - With unstable heart failure
  - Receiving high-dose vasodilator therapy

Beta-blockers

- **Heart failure:** different beta-blockers are licensed for this use; see separate PRODIGY guidance on *Heart failure*.
- **Depression, fatigue, and sexual dysfunction:** proven mortality benefits of beta-blockers will normally outweigh the risk of these very small associations found in clinical trial data.

Calcium-channel blockers (rate limiting)

- **Verapamil:** never use with beta-blockers.
- **Diltiazem:** caution with beta-blockers.

Concomitant use of drug formulations with a high sodium content

- Effervescent compound analgesics should be avoided where possible as they may aggravate hypertension. Note: soluble aspirin contains no sodium.

Follow-up advice

- **Reassess response to treatment after an interval of at least 4 weeks,** unless it is necessary to lower the blood pressure (BP) more urgently.
- **At each scheduled diabetes follow-up visit,** anyone with diabetes should have routine BP measurements.
- **Optimum target BP** is less than 140/80 mmHg (with an audit standard of 140/85) in someone with diabetes and a history of cardiovascular disease or a 10-year coronary event risk greater than 15%.
- **In the presence of microalbuminuria or proteinuria,** the optimum target BP is 135/75 mmHg.
- **Once stable, review every 3 to 6 months** and measure urine albumin or urinary albumin:creatinine ratio (ACR), and serum creatinine at least annually. Check serum electrolytes annually if the person is taking: a diuretic, an ACE inhibitor, or an angiotensin-II receptor antagonist (AIIRA). Antihypertensive treatment should be continued in someone over the age of 80 years who is already receiving treatment.
- **If treatment is not started,** advise non-drug methods of reducing BP (including regular exercise, weight reduction, healthy diet, and limiting salt and alcohol intake) and monitor BP at least annually. Cardiovascular risk increases with age and should be reassessed annually.
- **People on ACE inhibitors or AIIRAs** need renal function monitored (BP, renal function, serum potassium) before and during treatment — within 1 week of starting and 1 week after each dose increase to assess response to treatment and to check BP.
- **Check for adverse effects** (e.g. symptomatic hypotension, renal dysfunction, or hyperkalaemia [i.e. a rise in urea to 12 mmol/l, creatinine to 200 micromol /l, or potassium to 5.5 mmol/l]). If these occur, either stop or reduce the ACE inhibitor or AIIRA dose, and consider specialist referral.
- **Prodrugs** (e.g. enalapril and ramipril) need close monitoring in someone with poor liver function.
- **Once on a stable dose,** serum electrolytes and renal function should be checked at least once a year.

Should I refer or investigate?

Refer?

Consider referral if:

- **Possible underlying cause (secondary hypertension):**
  - Any clue in history or examination of a secondary cause
  - Hypokalaemia or increased plasma sodium (Conn's syndrome, Cushing's syndrome)
  - Elevated serum creatinine (greater than 150 micromol/l)
  - Proteinuria or haematuria (after excluding urinary tract infection)
  - Young age (any person with hypertension less than 20 years of age; any person needing treatment less than 30 years of age)
- **Unusual blood pressure variability.**
- **Possible isolated clinic hypertension** ('white-coat hypertension') unless access to ambulatory blood pressure (BP) monitoring or home monitoring and confidence in interpreting values (see *How do I confirm a raised blood pressure?*).
- **Consider hospital initiation** of an ACE inhibitor or angiotensin-II receptor antagonist (AIIRA) in high-risk groups; see *Prescribing points.*

Assess and treat urgently if:

- **Accelerated (malignant) hypertension** (papilloedema, fundal haemorrhages and exudates)
- **Severe hypertension** (greater than 220/120 mmHg)
- **Impending cardiovascular complications** (for example transient ischaemic attack [TIA], left ventricular failure)

Investigate?

Routine investigations (if not already done as part of a diabetes follow-up) include:

- Urinalysis for protein and blood
- Serum creatinine and electrolytes
- Serum total: high-density lipoprotein (HDL) cholesterol
- Electrocardiogram (ECG)

Patient information leaflets

The following PILs are available at www.prodigy.nhs.uk

- Blood Test - General
- Blood Test - Glucose
- Blood Test - Kidney Function
- Diabetes and High Blood Pressure
- Diabetes Insight Website
- Diabetes Research & Wellness Foundation
- Diabetes Type 2
- Diabetes Type 2 - A Summary
- Diabetes UK
- DiabeticLife
- Medicines - Name Changes of Medicines

Shared decision making

- **You have high blood pressure,** which increases your risk of developing complications from diabetes such as heart disease, stroke, kidney problems, etc.
- **You can lower blood pressure** by:
  - **Losing weight** if you are overweight.
  - **Reducing your alcohol intake** if it is high.
  - **Reducing the amount salt that you eat.**
  - **Regular exercise** such as swimming, cycling, jogging, dancing, brisk walking, or anything that causes mild breathlessness. At least 30 minutes exercise, at least five times a week, is best.
  - **Eating lots of fruit and vegetables** and maintaining a low-fat diet.
- **Smoking** makes your health risk much worse.
- **Regular checks** are all that you need if:
  - Your blood pressure is only mildly raised, and
  - Other risk factors are low, and
  - You do not have any complications from diabetes.
- **Medication** to lower blood pressure is advised for all other situations.
- **Various medicines can lower blood pressure.** The one chosen depends on such things as whether you have other medical problems, whether you take other medication, etc.

Drug rationale

Drugs not included

- **Fixed-dosage combinations:** may have a place for someone taking stable dosages of drugs to aid simplicity, but are not recommended for initiation.
- **Alpha-blockers:** may be useful in some patients, particularly male patients with prostatism. However, they are generally used less often than the other classes of agent and so are not included in this scenario. See scenario *Change to, increase, or add alpha-blocker* for prescriptions.
- **Angiotensin-II receptor antagonists (AIIRAs) other than losartan and irbesartan** are not currently recommended for people intolerant of an ACE inhibitor in hypertension. Although all the AIIRAs are licensed for use in hypertension and there may be a class effect, there is more evidence available to support the use of losartan and irbesartan.
- **Thiazides other than bendroflumethiazide (bendrofluazide)** do not offer any significant advantages. Bendroflumethiazide is the most commonly used and cost-effective thiazide diuretic in the UK. Metolazone and chlortalidone are more commonly used in heart failure to control oedema.
- **Beta-blockers other than atenolol** have not been included. There is little to choose among them in terms of efficacy. Cardioselective agents are preferred because they have a better safety profile.
- **ACE inhibitors other than captopril, enalapril, lisinopril, and ramipril** are not offered. There is little to distinguish between ACE inhibitors in terms of efficacy or safety, and therefore less established or more expensive agents have not been included.
- **Dihydropyridine calcium-channel blockers other than felodipine, nifedipine, and amlodipine** are not included. Short-acting and immediate-release formulations are associated with large variations in blood pressure and reflex tachycardia.
- **Verapamil modified-release formulations** are expensive and have not been included.
- **Centrally acting agents:** insufficient evidence is available to recommend the first-line routine use of methyldopa, clonidine, or moxonidine, or older vasodilators (for example hydralazine and minoxidil) [WHO, 1999].
- **Adrenergic neurone-blocking drugs** are considered less suitable for prescribing and have largely fallen from use, but may be necessary with other therapy in resistant hypertension [BNF 44, 2002].

Drugs included

- **ACE inhibitors: captopril, enalapril, lisinopril, and ramipril** have established safety records and are included.
  - ACE inhibitors have comparable efficacy. Captopril has been available for the longest period and is well established; and enalapril, lisinopril, and ramipril are alternatives if a once-daily regimen is preferred.

D

D

- All four agents are licensed for the treatment of heart failure (although starting regimens are different from those offered here).
- Captopril is licensed for the treatment of diabetic nephropathy in people with Type 1 diabetes. Lisinopril is licensed for the treatment of diabetic nephropathy in normortensive people with Type 1 diabetes and hypertensive people with Type 2 diabetes.

- **Losartan and irbesartan are the only angiotensin-II receptor antagonists (AIIRAs) currently recommended by PRODIGY** for people with diabetes and hypertension who are intolerant of an ACE inhibitor with diabetes and hypertension. Losartan has been shown to offer effective cardiovascular protection in people with hypertension and left ventricular hypertrophy (LVH) [Dahlof et al, 2002]. Both losartan and irbesartan have been shown to reduce the progression of renal disease in people with advanced diabetic neuropathy [Regional Drug and Therapeutics Centre, 2002]. Irbesartan recently received an additional licence for the treatment of renal disease in people with Type 2 diabetes and hypertension.
- **Thiazide diuretics: bendroflumethiazide (bendrofluazide)** is the thiazide of choice in the UK and is effective, safe, well tolerated, and economical. Thiazide diuretics have a flat dosage-response curve, so there is little to be gained from increasing dosages. Low dosages cause very little biochemical disturbance, whereas higher dosages cause more marked changes to glucose and lipids, and should not be used [Ramsay et al, 1999; BNF 44, 2002].
- **Beta-blockers: atenolol** is an effective, well-established, inexpensive cardioselective beta-blocker, which can be given once daily [BNF 44, 2002].
- **Calcium-channel blockers (CCB)** are generally well tolerated [Ramsay et al, 1999; WHO, 1999]. How the benefit of CCBs in diabetes compares with that of other antihypertensive drugs remains unclear; but current opinion considers that they are less superior as initial treatment and should only be considered an option in Afro-Caribbean people or where angina is present.
- **Long-acting dihydropyridine CCBs: felodipine, nifedipine, and amlodipine** are alternatives to thiazide diuretics in Afro-Caribbean people with diabetes and hypertension. There is evidence of improved outcomes, especially in those with isolated systolic hypertension [Systolic Hypertension-Europe (Syst-Eur) Trial Investigators, 1997; SIGN, 2002]. Drugs included are licensed for use in both hypertension and in angina, and offer once-daily dosage regimens.
- **Rate-limiting calcium-channel blockers: diltiazem and verapamil** are an option in Afro-Caribbean people with diabetes and hypertension or in people with angina. The diltiazem modified-release formulations offered are included by brand name because of potential problems caused by switching brands [BNF 44, 2002]. The least expensive, once-daily formulations in a range of strengths and dosages for use in hypertension are included. Do not use verapamil in combination with a beta-blocker. Diltiazem may cause bradycardia when used in combination with a beta-blocker, and careful monitoring is required [WHO, 1999; BNF 44, 2002].

Prescriptions

Start thiazide diuretic

Bendroflumethiazide (bendrofluazide) 2.5mg each morning
- Age from 16 years onwards
- Bendroflumethiazide 2.5mg tabs. Take one tablet each morning; supply 28 tablets; NHS Cost £0.74.

Start ACE inhibitor

Captopril 6.25mg twice a day
- Age from 16 years onwards
- Captopril 12.5mg tablets. Take half a tablet twice a day; supply 28 tablets; NHS Cost £1.16.

Captopril 12.5mg twice a day
- Age from 16 to 60 years
- Captopril 12.5mg tablets. Take one tablet twice a day; supply 56 tablets; NHS Cost £2.30.

Enalapril 2.5mg once a day
- Age from 16 years onwards
- Enalapril 2.5mg tablets. Take one tablet once a day; supply 28 tablets; NHS Cost £2.57.

Enalapril 5mg once a day
- Age from 16 to 60 years
- Enalapril 5mg tablets. Take one tablet once a day; supply 28 tablets; NHS Cost £3.76.

Lisinopril 2.5mg once a day
- Age from 16 years onwards
- Lisinopril 2.5mg tablets. Take one tablet once a day; supply 28 tablets; NHS Cost £6.26.

Ramipril 1.25mg once a day
- Age from 16 years onwards
- Ramipril 1.25mg tablets. Take one tablet once a day; supply 28 tablets; NHS Cost £5.30.

Start beta-blocker

Atenolol 25mg once a day
- Age from 16 years onwards
- Atenolol 25mg tablets. Take one tablet once a day; supply 28 tablets; NHS Cost £0.74.

Atenolol 50mg once a day
- Age from 16 years onwards
- Atenolol 50mg tablets. Take one tablet once a day; supply 28 tablets; NHS Cost £0.85.

Start calcium-channel blocker (dihydropyridine)

Felodipine 2.5mg m/r each morning
- Age from 60 years onwards
- Felodipine 2.5mg m/r tablets. Take one tablet each morning; supply 28 tablets; NHS Cost £6.09.

Felodipine 5mg m/r each morning
- Age from 16 years onwards
- Felodipine 5mg m/r tablets. Take one tablet each morning; supply 28 tablets; NHS Cost £8.12.

Nifedipine: Adalat LA 20mg each morning
- Age from 16 years onwards
- Adalat LA 20mg m/r tablets. Take one tablet each morning; supply 28 tablets; NHS Cost £8.15.

Nifedipine: Adalat LA 30mg each morning
- Age from 16 years onwards
- Adalat LA 30mg m/r tablets. Take one tablet each morning; supply 28 tablets; NHS Cost £9.89.

Nifedipine: Coracten XL 30mg each morning
- Age from 16 years onwards
- Coracten XL 30mg m/r capsules. Take one capsule each morning; supply 28 capsules; NHS Cost £6.73.

Amlodipine 5mg once a day
- Age from 16 years onwards
- Amlodipine 5mg tablets. Take one tablet once a day; supply 28 tablets; NHS Cost £11.85.

Start calcium-channel blocker (rate-limiting)

Diltiazem: Slozem 120mg once a day
- Age from 60 years onwards
- Slozem 120mg m/r capsules. Take one capsule once a day; supply 28 capsules; NHS Cost £7.00.

Diltiazem: Slozem 180mg once a day
- Age from 16 years onwards
- Slozem 180mg m/r capsules. Take one capsule once a day; supply 28 capsules; NHS Cost £7.80.

Diltiazem: Slozem 240mg once a day
- Age from 16 years onwards
- Slozem 240mg m/r capsules. Take one capsule once a day; supply 28 capsules; NHS Cost £8.20.

Diltiazem: Viazem XL 120mg once a day
- Age from 60 years onwards
- Viazem XL 120mg capsules. Take one capsule once a day; supply 28 capsules; NHS Cost £6.95.

Diltiazem: Viazem XL 180mg once a day
- Age from 16 years onwards
- Viazem XL 180mg capsules. Take one capsule once a day; supply 28 capsules; NHS Cost £7.75.

Diltiazem: Viazem XL 240mg once a day
- Age from 16 years onwards
- Viazem XL 240mg capsules. Take one capsule once a day; supply 28 capsules; NHS Cost £8.15.

Verapamil 120mg twice a day
- Age from 16 years onwards
- Verapamil 120mg tablets. Take one tablet twice a day; supply 56 tablets; NHS Cost £2.66.

On treatment: advice on targets and other treatments

Which therapy?

- **Assess** whether one of the following optimum target blood pressures has been reached:
  - **=<135/75 mmHg** in the presence of nephropathy
  - **<140/80 mmHg** in other people with diabetes and a history of cardiovascular disease or a 10-year coronary-event risk greater than 15%
- **Combination therapy** with drugs from different drug classes will be required to meet treatment targets in the majority of people.
- Factors affecting choice of an additional agent include the following.
  - **Asthma or a history of bronchospasm:** do not use beta-blockers (Committee on Safety of Medicines warning).
  - **Gout:** generally avoid using a thiazide diuretic. If a thiazide is necessary, consider prophylaxis with allopurinol (see separate PRODIGY guidance on *Gout*).
  - **People over the age of 60 years:** a thiazide is preferred.
  - **Heart failure, left ventricular dysfunction:** an ACE inhibitor is first choice.
  - **Angina:** a beta-blocker is preferred, but either a rate-limiting or a long-acting dihydropyridine CCB is an alternative option if a beta-blocker is not tolerated or is contraindicated.
  - **Post myocardial infarction:** consider a beta-blocker, or alternatively an ACE inhibitor is preferred.
  - **Afro-Caribbean people:** a thiazide is preferred, but a CCB is an alternative option.
- **Advise all hypertensive people with diabetes on lifestyle methods of reducing BP,** including regular exercise, weight reduction, healthy diet, and limiting salt and alcohol intake.
- **Identify and treat other cardiovascular risk factors** as appropriate — for example smoking and hyperlipidaemia (see separate PRODIGY guidance on *Smoking cessation, Diabetes Type 2 — lipid management*, and *Coronary heart disease risk — identification and management*). Maximize blood-glucose control — aim to maintain (HbA_{1c}) level below 6.5%.

Follow-up advice

- **Once stable, review every 3 to 6 months** and measure urine albumin or urinary albumin:creatinine ratio (ACR), and serum creatinine at least annually. Check serum electrolytes annually if the person is taking a diuretic, an ACE inhibitor, or an angiotensin-II receptor antagonist (AIIRA). Antihypertensive treatment should be continued in someone over the age of 80 years who is already receiving treatment.
- **Someone on an ACE inhibitor or an AIIRA** needs renal function monitored (blood pressure [BP], renal function, serum potassium) before and during treatment — within 1 week of starting and 1 week after each dose increase to assess response to treatment and to check BP.
- **Once on a stable dose,** serum electrolytes and renal function should be checked at least annually.

Should I refer or investigate?

Refer?

- **Possible underlying cause (secondary hypertension):**
  - Any clue in history or examination of a secondary cause
  - Hypokalaemia or increased plasma sodium (Conn's syndrome, Cushing's syndrome)
  - Elevated serum creatinine (greater than 150 micromol/l)
  - Proteinuria or haematuria (after excluding urinary tract infection)
  - Young age (any person with hypertension less than 20 years of age; any person needing treatment less than 30 years of age)
- **Unusual blood-pressure (BP) variability.**
- **Possible isolated clinic hypertension** ('white-coat hypertension'): unless access to ambulatory BP monitoring or home monitoring and confidence in interpreting values (see *How do I confirm a raised blood pressure?*).
- **Consider hospital initiation** of an ACE inhibitor or angiotensin-II receptor antagonist (AIIRA) in high-risk groups.

Investigate?

Assess and treat urgently if:
- **Accelerated (malignant) hypertension** (papilloedema, fundal haemorrhages and exudates)
- **Severe hypertension** (greater than 220/120 mmHg)
- **Impending cardiovascular complications** (for example transient ischaemic attack [TIA], left ventricular failure)

Routine investigations (if not already done as part of a diabetes follow-up) include:
- Urinalysis for protein and blood
- Serum creatinine and electrolytes
- Serum total: high-density lipoprotein (HDL) cholesterol
- Electrocardiogram (ECG)

Patient information leaflets

The following PILs are available at www.prodigy.nhs.uk
- Blood Test - General
- Blood Test - Glucose
- Blood Test - Kidney Function
- Diabetes and High Blood Pressure
- Diabetes Insight Website
- Diabetes Research & Wellness Foundation
- Diabetes Type 2

- Diabetes Type 2 - A Summary
- Diabetes UK
- DiabeticLife

Shared decision making

- **Medication** aims to reduce blood pressure to below 140/80 (and to less than 135/75 if you have kidney problems caused by diabetes).
  - One medicine is sufficient in about half of cases.
  - Two medicines may be needed to get to a target blood pressure.
  - In about a third of cases, three medicines or more are needed.
- **You can also lower blood pressure** by:
  - **Losing weight** if you are overweight.
  - **Reducing your alcohol intake** if it is high.
  - **Reducing the amount of salt that you eat.**
  - **Regular exercise** such as swimming, cycling, jogging, dancing, brisk walking, or anything that causes mild breathlessness. At least 30 minutes exercise, at least five times a week, is best.
  - **Eating lots of fruit and vegetables** and maintaining a low-fat diet.
- **Smoking** makes your health risk much worse.

Drug rationale

- No prescriptions are offered in this scenario, as it is intended to signpost people to further scenarios if necessary.

Change to/increase/add ACE or angiotensin-II receptor antag.

Which therapy

- **If hypertension is mild and uncomplicated** and response to an initial drug at adequate dose is small, changing to an alternative is appropriate.
- **In more severe or complicated hypertension,** it is safer to add drugs stepwise; treatment can be stepped down later if the blood pressure falls substantially below the optimal level.
- **ACE inhibitors are best combined with** thiazides or calcium-channel blockers. Consider an angiotensin-II receptor antagonist (AIIRA) if a person is truly intolerant of an ACE.
- **For third-line drug therapy,** an ACE inhibitor or AIIRA is best combined with both a diuretic and a calcium-channel blocker, although in practice other combinations of treatment may be necessary.
- **Referral for a specialist opinion** may be considered for someone unable to tolerate an ACE inhibitor. A person who develops renal impairment when receiving an ACE inhibitor is also likely to develop renal impairment when receiving an AIIRA.

Practical prescribing points

For further information please see the *Medicines Compendium* (www.medicines.org.uk) or the *British National Formulary* (www.bnf.org).

ACE inhibitors or angiotensin-II receptor antagonists (AIIRAs):

- **Avoid potassium-sparing diuretics or potassium supplements** (other than in exceptional cases — e.g. low dose spironolactone for severe heart failure) because of the risk of hyperkalaemia.
- **Monitor renal function carefully** with peripheral vascular disease (risk of renovascular disease) and raised serum creatinine.
- **The risk of first-dose hypotension or renal impairment induced either by an ACE inhibitor or by an AIIRA is increased in the following high-risk groups of people:**
  - Creatinine >150 micromol/l
  - Urea >12 mmol/l
  - Sodium <130 mmol/l
  - Systolic blood pressure <100 mmHg
  - Diuretic dose > furosemide 80 mg or bumetanide 2 mg daily
  - Known or suspected renal artery stenosis (e.g. if peripheral vascular disease)
  - People aged 70 years and over or who are frail
  - Hypovolaemia
  - With unstable heart failure
  - Receiving high-dose vasodilator therapy
- **Stop nonsteroidal anti-inflammatory drugs (NSAIDs) (if possible)**, as they increase the risk of renal impairment with ACE inhibitors or AIIRAs.

Concomitant use of drug formulations with a high sodium content

- Effervescent compound analgesics should be avoided where possible as they may aggravate hypertension. Note: soluble aspirin contains no sodium.

Follow-up advice

- **At each scheduled diabetes follow-up visit,** a person with diabetes should have routine blood pressure (BP) measurements.
- **People on an ACE inhibitor or an angiotensin-II receptor antagonist (AIIRA)** need renal function monitored (BP, renal function, serum potassium) before and during treatment — within 1 week of starting and 1 week after each dose increase to assess response to treatment and to check BP.
- **Reassess response to treatment after an interval of at least 4 weeks,** unless it is necessary to lower the BP more urgently.
- **Optimum target BP** is less than 140/80 mmHg (with an audit standard of 140/85) in someone with diabetes and a history of cardiovascular disease or a 10-year coronary event risk greater than 15%.
- **Check for adverse effects** (e.g. symptomatic hypotension, renal dysfunction, or hyperkalaemia [i.e. a rise in urea to 12 mmol/l, creatinine to 200 micromol /l, or potassium to 5.5 mmol/l]). If these occur, either stop or reduce the ACE inhibitor or AIIRA dose, and consider specialist referral.
- **Prodrugs** (e.g. enalapril and ramipril) need close monitoring in someone with poor liver function.
- **Once stable, review every 3 to 6 months** and measure urine albumin or urinary albumin:creatinine ratio (ACR), and serum creatinine at least annually. Check serum electrolytes annually if the person is taking a diuretic, an ACE inhibitor, or an AIIRA. Antihypertensive treatment should be continued in someone over the age of 80 years who is already receiving treatment.

Should I refer or investigate?

Refer?

Consider referral if:

- **Possible underlying cause (secondary hypertension):**
  - Any clue in history or examination of a secondary cause

- Hypokalaemia or increased plasma sodium (Conn's syndrome, Cushing's syndrome)
- Elevated serum creatinine (greater than 150 micromol/l)
- Proteinuria or haematuria (after excluding urinary tract infection)
- Young age (any person with hypertension less than 20 years of age; any person needing treatment less than 30 years of age)

- **Unusual blood pressure (BP) variability.**
- **Possible isolated clinic hypertension** ('white-coat hypertension'): unless access to ambulatory BP monitoring or home monitoring and confidence in interpreting values (see *How do I confirm a raised blood pressure?*).
- **Therapeutic problems** (for example treatment resistance, multiple drug intolerance, or contraindications).
- **Consider hospital initiation** of an ACE inhibitor or angiotensin-II receptor antagonist (AIIRA) in high risk groups: see *Prescribing points.*

Investigate?

Serum electrolytes should be measured within 1 week of starting or increasing the dose of an ACE inhibitor or angiotensin-II receptor antagonist (AIIRA).

Assess and treat urgently if:

- **Accelerated (malignant) hypertension** (papilloedema, fundal haemorrhages and exudates)
- **Severe hypertension** (greater than 220/120 mmHg)
- **Impending cardiovascular complications** (for example transient ischaemic attack [TIA], left ventricular failure)

Routine investigations (if not already done as part of a diabetes follow-up) include:

- Urinalysis for protein and blood
- Serum creatinine and electrolytes
- Serum total: high-density lipoprotein (HDL) cholesterol
- Electrocardiogram (ECG)

Patient information leaflets

The following PILs are available at www.prodigy.nhs.uk

- Blood Test - General
- Blood Test - Glucose
- Blood Test - Kidney Function
- Diabetes and High Blood Pressure
- Diabetes Insight Website
- Diabetes Research & Wellness Foundation
- Diabetes Type 2
- Diabetes Type 2 - A Summary
- Diabetes UK
- DiabeticLife

Shared decision making

- **An ACE inhibitor or an angiotensin-II receptor antagonist (AIIRA)** is often prescribed to lower blood pressure.
- Sometimes an ACE inhibitor or AIIRA is used alone; sometimes one is combined with another medicine if blood pressure is not well controlled with one medicine alone.
- ACE inhibitors or AIIRAs are particularly useful if you also have heart failure or diabetes.
- ACE inhibitors or AIIRAs should not be taken by people with certain types of kidney problems, people with some types of artery problems, and in pregnancy.
- You will need a blood test before starting an ACE inhibitor or an AIIRA, and within a week after starting it. After that, a yearly blood test is usual.

Drug rationale

Drugs not included

- **ACE inhibitors other than captopril, enalapril, lisinopril, and ramipril** are not offered. From randomised controlled trials in hypertensive populations, there is little to distinguish between ACE inhibitors in terms of efficacy or safety, and therefore less established agents with limited trial data are not included.
- **Angiotensin-II receptor antagonists (AIIRAs) other than losartan and irbesartan** are not currently recommended for people intolerant of an ACE inhibitor in hypertension. Although all the AIIRAs are licensed for use in hypertension and there may be a class effect, there is more evidence available to support the use of losartan and irbesartan.

Drugs included

- **ACE inhibitors — captopril, enalapril, lisinopril, and ramipril** all have long safety records and are included.
  - ACE inhibitors have comparable efficacy. Captopril has been available for the longest period and is well established; and enalapril, lisinopril, and ramipril are alternatives if a once-daily regimen is preferred.
  - All four agents are licensed for the treatment of heart failure (although starting regimens are different from those offered here).
  - Captopril is licensed for the treatment of diabetic nephropathy in people with Type 1 diabetes. Lisinopril is licensed for the treatment of diabetic nephropathy in normortensive people with Type 1 diabetes and hypertensive people with Type 2 diabetes.

[Cleland et al, 1998]

- **Losartan and irbesartan are the only AIIRAs currently recommended by PRODIGY** for people with diabetes and hypertension who are intolerant of an ACE inhibitor with diabetes and hypertension. Losartan has been shown to offer effective cardiovascular protection in people with hypertension and left ventricular hypertrophy (LVH) [Dahlof et al, 2002]. Both losartan and irbesartan have been shown to reduce the progression of renal disease in people with advanced diabetic neuropathy [Regional Drug and Therapeutics Centre, 2002]. Irbesartan has recently received an additional licence for the treatment of renal disease in people with Type 2 diabetes and hypertension.

Prescriptions

Start ACE inhibitor

Captopril 6.25mg twice a day

- Age from 16 years onwards
- Captopril 12.5mg tablets. Take half a tablet twice a day; supply 28 tablets; NHS Cost £1.16.

Captopril 12.5mg twice a day

- Age from 16 to 60 years
- Captopril 12.5mg tablets. Take one tablet twice a day; supply 56 tablets; NHS Cost £2.30.

Enalapril 2.5mg once a day

- Age from 16 years onwards
- Enalapril 2.5mg tablets. Take one tablet once a day; supply 28 tablets; NHS Cost £2.57.

Enalapril 5mg once a day

- Age from 16 to 60 years
- Enalapril 5mg tablets. Take one tablet once a day; supply 28 tablets; NHS Cost £3.76.

Lisinopril 2.5mg once a day
- Age from 16 years onwards
- Lisinopril 2.5mg tablets. Take one tablet once a day; supply 28 tablets; NHS Cost £6.26.

Ramipril 1.25mg once a day
- Age from 16 years onwards
- Ramipril 1.25mg tablets. Take one tablet once a day; supply 28 tablets; NHS Cost £5.30.

Maintenance or increase: captopril or enalapril

Captopril 12.5mg twice a day
- Age from 16 years onwards
- Captopril 12.5mg tablets. Take one tablet twice a day; supply 56 tablets; NHS Cost £2.30.

Captopril 25mg twice a day
- Age from 16 years onwards
- Captopril 25mg tablets. Take one tablet twice a day; supply 56 tablets; NHS Cost £3.21.

Captopril 50mg twice a day
- Age from 16 years onwards
- Captopril 50mg tablets. Take one tablet twice a day; supply 56 tablets; NHS Cost £4.06.

Enalapril 2.5mg once a day
- Age from 16 years onwards
- Enalapril 2.5mg tablets. Take one tablet once a day; supply 28 tablets; NHS Cost £2.57.

Enalapril 5mg once a day
- Age from 16 years onwards
- Enalapril 5mg tablets. Take one tablet once a day; supply 28 tablets; NHS Cost £3.76.

Enalapril 10mg once a day
- Age from 16 years onwards
- Enalapril 10mg tablets. Take one tablet once a day; supply 28 tablets; NHS Cost £5.20.

Enalapril 20mg once a day
- Age from 16 years onwards
- Enalapril 20mg tablets. Take one tablet once a day; supply 28 tablets; NHS Cost £6.12.

Maintenance or increase: lisinopril or ramipril

Lisinopril 2.5mg once a day
- Age from 16 years onwards
- Lisinopril 2.5mg tablets. Take one tablet once a day; supply 28 tablets; NHS Cost £6.26.

Lisinopril 5mg once a day
- Age from 16 years onwards
- Lisinopril 5mg tablets. Take one tablet once a day; supply 28 tablets; NHS Cost £7.86.

Lisinopril 10mg once a day
- Age from 16 years onwards
- Lisinopril 10mg tablets. Take one tablet once a day; supply 28 tablets; NHS Cost £9.70.

Lisinopril 20mg once a day
- Age from 16 years onwards
- Lisinopril 20mg tablets. Take one tablet once a day; supply 28 tablets; NHS Cost £10.97.

Ramipril 1.25mg once a day
- Age from 16 years onwards
- Ramipril 1.25mg tablets. Take one tablet once a day; supply 28 tablets; NHS Cost £5.30.

Ramipril 2.5mg once a day
- Age from 16 years onwards
- Ramipril 2.5mg tablets. Take one tablet once a day; supply 28 tablets; NHS Cost £7.51.

Ramipril 5mg once a day
- Age from 16 years onwards
- Ramipril 5mg tablets. Take one tablet once a day; supply 28 tablets; NHS Cost £9.55.

Start angiotensin-II receptor antagonist

Losartan 25mg once a day (low dose)
- Age from 16 years onwards
- Losartan 25mg tablets. Take one tablet once a day; supply 28 tablets; NHS Cost £17.24.

Losartan 50mg once a day
- Age from 16 years onwards
- Losartan 50mg tablets. Take one tablet once a day; supply 28 tablets; NHS Cost £17.00.

Irbesartan 75mg once a day (low dose)
- Age from 16 years onwards
- Irbesartan 75mg tablets. Take one tablet once a day; supply 28 tablets; NHS Cost £14.00.

Irbesartan 150mg once a day
- Age from 16 years onwards
- Irbesartan 150mg tablets. Take one tablet once a day; supply 28 tablets; NHS Cost £16.00.

Maintenance or increase: angiotensin-II receptor antagonist

Losartan 25mg once a day
- Age from 16 years onwards
- Losartan 25mg tablets. Take one tablet once a day; supply 28 tablets; NHS Cost £17.24.

Losartan 50mg once a day
- Age from 16 years onwards
- Losartan 50mg tablets. Take one tablet once a day; supply 28 tablets; NHS Cost £17.23.

Losartan 100mg once a day
- Age from 16 years onwards
- Losartan 100mg tablets. Take one tablet once a day; supply 28 tablets; NHS Cost £22.00.

Irbesartan 75mg once a day
- Age from 16 years onwards
- Irbesartan 75mg tablets. Take one tablet once a day; supply 28 tablets; NHS Cost £14.00.

Irbesartan 150mg once a day
- Age from 16 years onwards
- Irbesartan 150mg tablets. Take one tablet once a day; supply 28 tablets; NHS Cost £16.00.

Irbesartan 300mg once a day
- Age from 16 years onwards
- Irbesartan 300mg tablets. Take one tablet once a day; supply 28 tablets; NHS Cost £22.21.

Change to or add thiazide

Which therapy

- **If hypertension is mild and uncomplicated** and response to an initial drug is small, then changing to an alternative is appropriate.
- **In more severe or complicated hypertension,** it is safer to add drugs stepwise; treatment can be stepped down later if the blood pressure falls substantially below the optimal level.
- **In people with gout:** generally avoid using a thiazide diuretic. If a thiazide is necessary, consider prophylaxis with allopurinol (see separate PRODIGY guidance on *Gout*).
- **Thiazides are best combined with beta-blockers or angiotensin converting enzyme (ACE) inhibitors.**
- **For third-line drug therapy, common combinations are:**
  - A diuretic, an ACE inhibitor, and a calcium-channel blocker, or
  - A diuretic, a beta-blocker, and a calcium-channel blocker

Practical prescribing points

For further information please see the *Medicines Compendium* (www.medicines.org.uk) or the *British National Formulary* (www.bnf.org).

Concomitant use of drug formulations with a high sodium content

Effervescent compound analgesics should be avoided where possible as they may aggravate hypertension. Note: soluble aspirin contains no sodium.

Follow-up advice

Reassess response to treatment after an interval of at least 4 weeks, unless it is necessary to lower the blood pressure (BP) more urgently.

At each scheduled diabetes follow-up visit, anyone with diabetes should have routine BP measurements.

Optimum target BP is less than 140/80 mmHg (with an audit standard of 140/85) in someone with diabetes and a history of cardiovascular disease or a 10-year coronary event risk greater than 15%.

In the presence of microalbuminuria or proteinuria, the optimum target BP is 135/75 mmHg.

Once stable, review every 3 to 6 months and measure urine albumin or urinary albumin:creatinine ratio (ACR), and serum creatinine at least annually. Check serum electrolytes annually if the person is taking a diuretic, an ACE inhibitor, or an angiotensin-II receptor antagonist (AIIRA). Antihypertensive treatment should be continued in someone over the age of 80 years who is already receiving treatment.

Should I refer or investigate?

Refer?

Consider referral if:

Possible underlying cause (secondary hypertension):

- Any clue in history or examination of a secondary cause
- Hypokalaemia or increased plasma sodium (Conn's syndrome, Cushing's syndrome)
- Elevated serum creatinine (greater than 150 micromol/l)
- Proteinuria or haematuria (after excluding urinary tract infection)
- Young age (any person with hypertension less than 20 years of age; any person needing treatment less than 30 years of age)

Unusual blood pressure (BP) variability.

Possible isolated clinic hypertension ('white-coat hypertension'): unless access to ambulatory BP monitoring or home monitoring and confidence in interpreting values (see *How do I confirm a raised blood pressure?*).

Therapeutic problems (for example treatment resistance, multiple drug intolerance, or contraindications).

Investigate?

Assess and treat urgently if:

Accelerated (malignant) hypertension (papilloedema, fundal haemorrhages and exudates)

Severe hypertension (greater than 220/120 mmHg)

Impending cardiovascular complications (for example transient ischaemic attack [TIA], left ventricular failure)

Routine investigations (if not already done as part of a diabetes follow-up) include:

Urinalysis for protein and blood

Serum creatinine and electrolytes

- Serum total: high-density lipoprotein (HDL) cholesterol
- Electrocardiogram (ECG)

Patient information leaflets

The following PILs are available at www.prodigy.nhs.uk

- Blood Test - General
- Blood Test - Glucose
- Blood Test - Kidney Function
- Diabetes and High Blood Pressure
- Diabetes Insight Website
- Diabetes Research & Wellness Foundation
- Diabetes Type 2
- Diabetes Type 2 - A Summary
- Diabetes UK
- DiabeticLife
- Medicines - Name Changes of Medicines

Shared decision making

- **A thiazide diuretic** ('water tablet') such as bendroflumethiazide (bendrofluazide) is commonly prescribed to lower the blood pressure.
- Sometimes a thiazide is used alone; sometimes one is combined with another medicine if blood pressure is not well controlled with one medicine alone.
- The dose needed to treat high blood pressure is low. So, you will not notice much diuretic effect (passing extra urine).
- Thiazides can sometimes cause gout, or can make gout worse.

Drug rationale

Drugs not included

- **Thiazides other than bendroflumethiazide (bendrofluazide)** do not offer any significant advantages. Bendroflumethiazide is the most commonly used and cost-effective thiazide diuretic in the UK. Metolazone and chlortalidone are more commonly used in heart failure to control oedema.

[BNF 44, 2002]

Drugs included

- **Thiazide diuretics: bendroflumethiazide (bendrofluazide)** is the drug of choice in the UK and is effective, safe, well tolerated, and economical. Thiazide diuretics have a flat dosage-response curve, so there is little to be gained from increasing dosages. Low dosages cause very little biochemical disturbance, whereas higher dosages cause more marked changes to glucose and lipids, and should not be used [Ramsay et al, 1999; BNF 44, 2002].

Prescriptions

Start thiazide diuretic

Bendroflumethiazide (bendrofluazide) 2.5mg each morning

- Age from 16 years onwards
- Bendroflumethiazide 2.5mg tabs. Take one tablet each morning; supply 28 tablets; NHS Cost £0.74.

D

Change to, increase, or add beta-blocker

Which therapy

- **If hypertension is mild and uncomplicated** and response to an initial drug at adequate dosage is small, changing to an alternative is appropriate.
- **In more severe or complicated hypertension** it is safer to add drugs stepwise; treatment can be stepped down later if the blood pressure falls substantially below the optimal level.
- **In people with asthma or a history of bronchospasm,** do not use beta-blockers (Committee on Safety of Medicines [CSM] warning).
- **Beta-blockers are best combined with** thiazides or calcium-channel blockers (not verapamil, and use caution with diltiazem).
- **For third-line drug therapy,** a beta-blocker is best combined with both a diuretic and a calcium-channel blocker (not verapamil, and use caution with diltiazem), although in practice other combinations of treatment may be necessary.

Practical prescribing points

For further information please see the *Medicines Compendium* (www.medicines.org.uk) or the *British National Formulary* (www.bnf.org).

Beta-blockers

- **Heart failure:** different beta-blockers are licensed for this use; see separate PRODIGY guidance on *Heart Failure.*
- **Depression, fatigue, and sexual dysfunction:** proven mortality benefits of beta-blockers will normally outweigh the risk of these very small associations found in clinical trials data.

Concomitant use of drug formulations with a high sodium content

- Effervescent compound analgesics should be avoided where possible as they may aggravate hypertension. Note: soluble aspirin contains no sodium.

Follow-up advice

- **Reassess response to treatment after an interval of at least 4 weeks,** unless it is necessary to lower the blood pressure (BP) more urgently.
- **At each scheduled diabetes follow-up visit,** anyone with diabetes should have routine BP measurements.
- **Optimum target BP** is less than 140/80 mmHg (with an audit standard of 140/85) in someone with diabetes and a history of cardiovascular disease or a 10-year coronary event risk greater than 15%.
- **In the presence of microalbuminuria or proteinuria,** the optimum target BP is 135/75 mmHg.
- **Once stable, review every 3 to 6 months** and measure urine albumin or urinary albumin:creatinine ratio (ACR), and serum creatinine at least annually. Check serum electrolytes annually if the person is taking a diuretic, an ACE inhibitor, or an angiotensin-II receptor antagonist (AIIRA). Antihypertensive treatment should be continued in someone over the age of 80 years who is already receiving treatment.

Should I refer or investigate?

Refer?

Consider referral if:

- **Possible underlying cause (secondary hypertension):**
  - Any clue in history or examination of a secondary cause
  - Hypokalaemia or increased plasma sodium (Conn's syndrome, Cushing's syndrome)
  - Elevated serum creatinine (greater than 150 micromo l)
  - Proteinuria or haematuria (after excluding urinary tract infection)
  - Young age (any person with hypertension less than 20 years of age; any person needing treatment less than 30 years of age)
- **Unusual blood pressure (BP) variability.**
- **Possible isolated clinic hypertension** ('white-coat hypertension'): unless access to ambulatory BP monitoring or home monitoring and confidence in interpreting values (see *How do I confirm a raised blood pressure?*).
- **Therapeutic problems** (for example treatment resistance multiple drug intolerance, or contraindications).

Investigate?

Assess and treat urgently if:

- **Accelerated (malignant) hypertension** (papilloedema, fundal haemorrhages and exudates)
- **Severe hypertension** (greater than 220/120 mmHg)
- **Impending cardiovascular complications** (for example transient ischaemic attack [TIA], left ventricular failure)

Routine investigations (if not already done as part of a diabetes follow-up) include:

- Urinalysis for protein and blood
- Serum creatinine and electrolytes
- Serum total: high-density lipoprotein (HDL) cholesterol
- Electrocardiogram (ECG)

Patient information leaflets

The following PILs are available at www.prodigy.nhs.uk

- Blood Test - General
- Blood Test - Glucose
- Blood Test - Kidney Function
- Diabetes and High Blood Pressure
- Diabetes Insight Website
- Diabetes Research & Wellness Foundation
- Diabetes Type 2
- Diabetes Type 2 - A Summary
- Diabetes UK
- DiabeticLife

Shared decision making

- **A beta-blocker medicine** such as atenolol is commonly prescribed to lower the blood pressure.
- Sometimes a beta-blocker is used alone; sometimes one is combined with another medicine if blood pressure is not well controlled with one medicine alone.
- Beta-blockers are particularly useful if you also have angina.
- **You should not take a beta-blocker if** you have asthma, chronic obstructive pulmonary disease, or certain types of heart or blood vessel problem.
- **Some people develop side effects with beta-blockers.** These include:
  - Cool hands and feet
  - Poor sleep
  - Tiredness

- Impotence

If side effects occur, a different medicine may suit better.
But:
Do not suddenly stop taking a beta-blocker medicine.

Drug rationale

Drugs not included

Beta-blockers other than atenolol have not been included. There is little to choose among them in terms of efficacy. Cardioselective agents are preferred because they have a better safety profile.

- Beta-blockers can increase serum triglyceride concentrations and reduce the ratio of high-density lipoprotein (HDL):low-density lipoprotein (LDL) cholesterol. This is most marked for non-selective beta-blockers. They can also lead to a small deterioration of glucose tolerance and interfere with metabolic and autonomic responses to hypoglycaemia. A cardioselective agent would be preferred in both these situations. These metabolic changes do not appear to affect the efficacy of antihypertensive therapy in reducing cardiovascular morbidity and mortality.
- Those with intrinsic sympathomimetic activity or partial agonist properties may have theoretical advantages in some people, but these have not been convincingly demonstrated in clinical practice [Ramsay et al, 1999; BNF 44, 2002].

Drugs included

Beta-blockers: atenolol is an effective, well-established, inexpensive cardioselective beta-blocker, which can be given once daily [BNF 44, 2002].

Prescriptions

Start or increase atenolol

Atenolol 25mg once a day
Age from 16 years onwards
Atenolol 25mg tablets. Take one tablet once a day; supply 28 tablets; NHS Cost £0.74.

Atenolol 50mg once a day
Age from 16 years onwards
Atenolol 50mg tablets. Take one tablet once a day; supply 28 tablets; NHS Cost £0.85.

Change to, increase, or add calcium-channel blocker

Which therapy

- **If hypertension is mild and uncomplicated** and response to an initial drug at adequate dosage is small, changing to an alternative is appropriate.
- **In more severe or complicated hypertension,** it is safer to add drugs stepwise; treatment can be stepped down later if the blood pressure falls substantially below the optimal level.
- **Calcium-channel blockers (CCBs) are best combined with** beta-blockers (but not verapamil and caution with diltiazem) or ACE inhibitors.
- **For third-line drug therapy,** a CCB is best combined with a beta-blocker (but not verapamil, and use caution with diltiazem) and a diuretic, or an ACE inhibitor and a diuretic, although in practice other combinations of treatment may be necessary.

Practical prescribing points

For further information please see the *Medicines Compendium* (www.medicines.org.uk) or the *British National Formulary* (www.bnf.org).

Calcium-channel blockers (rate limiting):

- **Verapamil:** never use with beta-blockers.
- **Diltiazem:** caution with beta-blockers.

Concomitant use of drug formulations with a high sodium content

- Effervescent compound analgesics should be avoided where possible as they may aggravate hypertension. Note: soluble aspirin contains no sodium.

D

Follow-up advice

- **Reassess response to treatment after an interval of at least 4 weeks,** unless it is necessary to lower the blood pressure (BP) more urgently.
- **At each scheduled diabetes follow-up visit,** anyone with diabetes should have routine BP measurements.
- **Optimum target BP** is less than 140/80 mmHg (with an audit standard of 140/85) in someone with diabetes and a history of cardiovascular disease or a 10-year coronary event risk greater than 15%.
- **Once stable, review every 3 to 6 months** and measure urine albumin or urinary albumin:creatinine ratio (ACR), and serum creatinine at least annually. Check serum electrolytes annually if the person is taking a diuretic, an ACE inhibitor, or an angiotensin-II receptor antagonist (AIIRA). Antihypertensive treatment should be continued in someone over the age of 80 years who is already receiving treatment.

Should I refer or investigate?

Refer?

Consider referral if:

- **Possible underlying cause (secondary hypertension):**
  - Any clue in history or examination of a secondary cause
  - Hypokalaemia or increased plasma sodium (Conn's syndrome, Cushing's syndrome)
  - Elevated serum creatinine (greater than 150 micromol/l)
  - Proteinuria or haematuria (after excluding urinary tract infection)
  - Young age (any person with hypertension less than 20 years of age; any person needing treatment less than 30 years of age)
- **Unusual blood pressure (BP) variability.**
- **Possible isolated clinic hypertension** ('white-coat hypertension'): unless access to ambulatory BP monitoring or home monitoring and confidence in interpreting values (see *How do I confirm a raised blood pressure?*).
- **Therapeutic problems** (for example treatment resistance, multiple drug intolerance, or contraindications).

Investigate?

Assess and treat urgently if:

- **Accelerated (malignant) hypertension** (papilloedema, fundal haemorrhages and exudates)
- **Severe hypertension** (greater than 220/120 mmHg)
- **Impending cardiovascular complications** (for example transient ischaemic attack [TIA], left ventricular failure)

D

Routine investigations (if not already done as part of a diabetes follow-up) include:

- Urinalysis for protein and blood
- Serum creatinine and electrolytes
- Serum total: high-density lipoprotein (HDL) cholesterol
- Electrocardiogram (ECG)

Patient information leaflets

The following PILs are available at www.prodigy.nhs.uk

- Blood Test - General
- Blood Test - Glucose
- Blood Test - Kidney Function
- Diabetes and High Blood Pressure
- Diabetes Insight Website
- Diabetes Research & Wellness Foundation
- Diabetes Type 2
- Diabetes Type 2 - A Summary
- Diabetes UK
- DiabeticLife

Shared decision making

- **A calcium-channel blocker** is often prescribed to lower the blood pressure. There are several types and brands.
- Sometimes a calcium-channel blocker is used alone; sometimes one is combined with another medicine if blood pressure is not well controlled with one medicine alone.
- A calcium-channel blocker may be particularly useful if you also have angina.

Drug rationale

Drugs not included

- **Dihydropyridine calcium-channel blockers (CCBs) other than felodipine, nifedipine, and amlodipine** are not included. Short acting and immediate-release formulations are associated with large variations in blood pressure and reflex tachycardia.
- **Verapamil modified-release formulations** are expensive and have not been included.

Drugs included

- **Long acting dihydropyridine CCBs: felodipine, nifedipine, and amlodipine** are alternatives to thiazide diuretics in Afro-Caribbean people with diabetes and hypertension and in the elderly. There is evidence of improved outcomes, especially in those with isolated systolic hypertension [Systolic Hypertension-Europe (Syst-Eur) Trial Investigators, 1997; SIGN, 2002]. Drugs included are licensed for use in both hypertension and angina, and offer once-daily dosage regimens.
- **Rate-limiting CCBs: diltiazem and verapamil** are an option in Afro-Caribbean people with diabetes and hypertension, or in people with angina. The diltiazem modified-release formulations offered are included by brand name because of potential problems caused by switching brands [BNF 44, 2002]. The least expensive, once-daily formulations in a range of strengths and dosages for use in hypertension are included. Do not use verapamil in combination with a beta-blocker. Diltiazem may cause bradycardia when used in combination with a beta-blocker, and careful monitoring is required [WHO, 1999; BNF 44, 2002].
- Afro-Caribbean people are more responsive to CCBs (or diuretics) than to other antihypertensive therapies [Ramsay et al, 1999].

Prescriptions

Start or increase felodipine

Start felodipine 2.5mg m/r each morning

- Age from 60 years onwards
- Felodipine 2.5mg m/r tablets. Take one tablet each morning; supply 28 tablets; NHS Cost £6.09.

Start felodipine 5mg m/r each morning

- Age from 16 years onwards
- Felodipine 5mg m/r tablets. Take one tablet each morning; supply 28 tablets; NHS Cost £8.12.

Felodipine 2.5mg m/r each morning

- Age from 60 years onwards
- Felodipine 2.5mg m/r tablets. Take one tablet each morning; supply 28 tablets; NHS Cost £6.09.

Felodipine 5mg m/r each morning

- Age from 16 years onwards
- Felodipine 5mg m/r tablets. Take one tablet each morning; supply 28 tablets; NHS Cost £8.12.

Felodipine 10mg m/r each morning

- Age from 16 years onwards
- Felodipine 10mg m/r tablets. Take one tablet each morning; supply 28 tablets; NHS Cost £10.92.

Start or increase nifedipine

Start Adalat LA 20mg each morning

- Age from 16 years onwards
- Adalat LA 20mg m/r tablets. Take one tablet each morning; supply 28 tablets; NHS Cost £8.15.

Start Adalat LA 30mg each morning

- Age from 16 years onwards
- Adalat LA 30mg m/r tablets. Take one tablet each morning; supply 28 tablets; NHS Cost £9.89.

Start Coracten XL 30mg each morning

- Age from 16 years onwards
- Coracten XL 30mg m/r capsules. Take one capsule each morning; supply 28 capsules; NHS Cost £6.73.

Adalat LA 20mg each morning

- Age from 16 years onwards
- Adalat LA 20mg m/r tablets. Take one tablet each morning; supply 28 tablets; NHS Cost £8.15.

Adalat LA 30mg each morning

- Age from 16 years onwards
- Adalat LA 30mg m/r tablets. Take one tablet each morning; supply 28 tablets; NHS Cost £9.89.

Adalat LA 60mg each morning

- Age from 16 years onwards
- Adalat LA 60mg m/r tablets. Take one tablet each morning; supply 28 tablets; NHS Cost £15.40.

Coracten XL 30mg each morning

- Age from 16 years onwards
- Coracten XL 30mg m/r capsules. Take one capsule each morning; supply 28 capsules; NHS Cost £6.73.

Coracten XL 60mg each morning

- Age from 16 years onwards
- Coracten XL 60mg m/r capsules. Take one capsule each morning; supply 28 capsules; NHS Cost £10.01.

Start or increase amlodipine

Amlodipine 5mg once a day

- Age from 16 years onwards
- Amlodipine 5mg tablets. Take one tablet once a day; supply 28 tablets; NHS Cost £11.85.

Amlodipine 10mg once a day

- Age from 16 years onwards
- Amlodipine 10mg tablets. Take one tablet once a day; supply 28 tablets; NHS Cost £17.70.

Start or increase diltiazem

iazem XL 120mg once a day
Age from 60 years onwards
Viazem XL 120mg capsules. Take one capsule once a day; supply 28 capsules; NHS Cost £6.95.

iazem XL 180mg once a day
Age from 16 years onwards
Viazem XL 180mg capsules. Take one capsule once a day; supply 28 capsules; NHS Cost £7.75.

iazem XL 240mg once a day
Age from 16 years onwards
Viazem XL 240mg capsules. Take one capsule once a day; supply 28 capsules; NHS Cost £8.15.

iazem XL 300mg once a day (do not use as start dose)
Age from 16 years onwards
Viazem XL 300mg capsules. Take one capsule once a day; supply 28 capsules; NHS Cost £8.45.

lozem 120mg once a day
Age from 60 years onwards
Slozem 120mg m/r capsules. Take one capsule once a day; supply 28 capsules; NHS Cost £7.00.

lozem 180mg once a day
Age from 16 years onwards
Slozem 180mg m/r capsules. Take one capsule once a day; supply 28 capsules; NHS Cost £7.80.

lozem 240mg once a day
Age from 16 years onwards
Slozem 240mg m/r capsules. Take one capsule once a day; supply 28 capsules; NHS Cost £8.20.

lozem 360mg once a day (do not use as start dose)
Age from 16 years onwards
Slozem 180mg m/r capsules. Take two capsules once a day; supply 56 capsules; NHS Cost £15.60.

Start or increase verapamil

tart verapamil 120mg twice a day
Age from 16 years onwards
Verapamil 120mg tablets. Take one tablet twice a day; supply 56 tablets; NHS Cost £2.66.

erapamil 120mg twice a day
Age from 16 years onwards
Verapamil 120mg tablets. Take one tablet twice a day; supply 56 tablets; NHS Cost £2.66.

erapamil 160mg twice a day
Age from 16 years onwards
Verapamil 160mg tablets. Take one tablet twice a day; supply 56 tablets; NHS Cost £5.66.

erapamil 240mg twice a day
Age from 16 years onwards
Verapamil 120mg tablets. Take two tablets twice a day; supply 112 tablets; NHS Cost £5.32.

Change to, increase, or add alpha-blocker

Which therapy

If hypertension is mild and uncomplicated and response to an initial drug at adequate dosage is small, changing to an alternative is appropriate.

In more severe or complicated hypertension it is safer to add drugs stepwise; treatment can be stepped down later if the blood pressure falls substantially below the optimal level.

Alpha-blockers are best combined with beta-blockers, but may also be combined with any of the other major classes of antihypertensives.

Practical prescribing points

For further information please see the *Medicines Compendium* (www.medicines.org.uk) or the *British National Formulary* (www.bnf.org).

Alpha-blockers

- **Avoid in someone with heart failure or impaired left ventricular function,** following the decision to discontinue the doxazosin treatment arm of the Antihypertensive and Lipid-lowering Treatment to Prevent Heart Attack Trial (ALLHAT). An interim analysis showed that there was an increase in cases of new-onset heart failure in people assigned to doxazosin compared with chlortalidone [ALLHAT Officers, 2000].

Concomitant use of drug formulations with a high sodium content

- Effervescent compound analgesics should be avoided where possible as they may aggravate hypertension. Note: soluble aspirin contains no sodium.

Follow-up advice

- **Anyone with diabetes should have routine blood pressure (BP) measurements** at each scheduled diabetes follow-up visit.
- **Reassess response to treatment after an interval of at least 4 weeks,** unless it is necessary to lower the BP more urgently.
- **Optimum target BP** is less than 140/80 mmHg (with an audit standard of 140/85) in someone with diabetes and a history of cardiovascular disease or a 10-year coronary event risk greater than 15%.
- **Once stable, review every 3 to 6 months** and measure urine albumin or urinary albumin:creatinine ratio (ACR), and serum creatinine at least annually. Check serum electrolytes annually if the person is taking a diuretic, an ACE inhibitor, or an angiotensin-II receptor antagonist (AIIRA). Antihypertensive treatment should be continued in someone over the age of 80 years who is already receiving treatment.

Should I refer or investigate?

Refer?

Consider referral if:

- **Possible underlying cause (secondary hypertension):**
    - Any clue in history or examination of a secondary cause
    - Hypokalaemia or increased plasma sodium (Conn's syndrome, Cushing's syndrome)
    - Elevated serum creatinine (greater than 150 micromol/l)
    - Proteinuria or haematuria (after excluding urinary tract infection)
    - Young age (any person with hypertension less than 20 years of age; any person needing treatment less than 30 years of age)
- **Unusual blood pressure (BP) variability.**
- **Possible isolated clinic hypertension** ('white-coat hypertension'): unless access to ambulatory BP monitoring or home monitoring and confidence in interpreting values (see *How do I confirm a raised blood pressure?*).
- **Therapeutic problems** (for example treatment resistance, multiple drug intolerance, or contraindications).

D

D

Investigate?

Assess and treat urgently if:

- **Accelerated (malignant) hypertension** (papilloedema, fundal haemorrhages and exudates)
- **Severe hypertension** (greater than 220/120 mmHg)
- **Impending cardiovascular complications** (for example transient ischaemic attack [TIA], left ventricular failure)

Routine investigations (if not already done as part of a diabetes follow-up) include:

- Urinalysis for protein and blood
- Serum creatinine and electrolytes
- Serum total: high-density lipoprotein (HDL) cholesterol
- Electrocardiogram (ECG)

Patient information leaflets

The following PILs are available at www.prodigy.nhs.uk

- Blood Test - General
- Blood Test - Glucose
- Blood Test - Kidney Function
- Diabetes and High Blood Pressure
- Diabetes Insight Website
- Diabetes Research & Wellness Foundation
- Diabetes Type 2
- Diabetes Type 2 - A Summary
- Diabetes UK
- DiabeticLife

Shared decision making

- **An alpha-blocker medicine** may be prescribed to lower the blood pressure.
- Sometimes an alpha-blocker is used alone; sometimes one is combined with another medicine if blood pressure is not well controlled with one medicine alone.
- An alpha-blocker may be particularly useful for a man with high blood pressure who also has prostatism.
- Alpha-blockers should not be taken by someone with heart failure.

Drug rationale

Drugs not included

- **Alpha-blockers: Alfuzosin and tamsulosin** are not included, as they are only licensed for prostatic hyperplasia, not for hypertension.

Drugs included

- **Alpha-blockers: Standard-release doxazosin, indoramin, prazosin, and terazosin and modified-release doxazosin** are all effective at lowering blood pressure and are included.
  - All have the potential to cause postural hypotension or first-dose hypotension; initiation dosages for standard-release preparations should therefore be started low and titrated up carefully.
  - Modified-release doxazosin is an option that avoids the need for careful titration.
  - Doxazosin and terazosin can be given once daily, but indoramin and prazosin must be given in divided dosages. Once-daily preparations may be preferred for concordance reasons, but are more expensive than prazosin, which is shorter-acting.

[BNF 44, 2002]

Prescriptions

Start or increase doxazosin

Start doxazosin 1mg once a day (2-week supply)

- Age from 16 years onwards
- Doxazosin 1mg tablets. Take one tablet once a day; supply 14 tablets; NHS Cost £4.60.

Doxazosin 1mg once a day

- Age from 16 years onwards
- Doxazosin 1mg tablets. Take one tablet once a day; supply 28 tablets; NHS Cost £9.20.

Doxazosin 2mg once a day

- Age from 16 years onwards
- Doxazosin 2mg tablets. Take one tablet once a day; supply 28 tablets; NHS Cost £12.13.

Doxazosin 4mg once a day

- Age from 16 years onwards
- Doxazosin 4mg tablets. Take one tablet once a day; supply 28 tablets; NHS Cost £14.44.

Doxazosin 8mg once a day

- Age from 16 years onwards
- Doxazosin 4mg tablets. Take two tablets once a day; supply 56 tablets; NHS Cost £28.88.

Doxazosin 12mg once a day

- Age from 16 years onwards
- Doxazosin 4mg tablets. Take three tablets once a day; supply 84 tablets; NHS Cost £43.32.

Doxazosin 16mg once a day

- Age from 16 years onwards
- Doxazosin 4mg tablets. Take four tablets once a day; supply 112 tablets; NHS Cost £57.76.

Start or increase indoramin

Start indoramin 25mg twice a day (2-week supply)

- Age from 16 years onwards
- Indoramin 25mg tablets. Take one tablet twice a day; supply 28 tablets; NHS Cost £3.00.

Indoramin 25mg twice a day

- Age from 16 years onwards
- Indoramin 25mg tablets. Take one tablet twice a day; supply 56 tablets; NHS Cost £6.00.

Indoramin 50mg twice a day

- Age from 16 years onwards
- Indoramin 25mg tablets. Take two tablets twice a day; supply 112 tablets; NHS Cost £12.00.

Indoramin 100mg twice a day

- Age from 16 years onwards
- Indoramin 25mg tablets. Take four tablets twice a day; supply 224 tablets; NHS Cost £24.00.

Start or increase prazosin

Start prazosin: starter pack

- Age from 16 years onwards
- Prazosin starter pack. Follow the instructions given inside this pack; supply 40 tablets; NHS Cost £2.52.

Prazosin 1mg twice a day

- Age from 16 years onwards
- Prazosin 1mg tablets. Take one tablet twice a day; supply 56 tablets; NHS Cost £2.70.

Prazosin 2mg twice a day

- Age from 16 years onwards
- Prazosin 2mg tablets. Take one tablet twice a day; supply 56 tablets; NHS Cost £3.90.

Prazosin 4mg twice a day

- Age from 16 years onwards
- Prazosin 2mg tablets. Take two tablets twice a day; supply 112 tablets; NHS Cost £7.80.

azosin 5mg three times a day
Age from 16 years onwards
Prazosin 5mg tablets. Take one tablet three times a day; supply 84 tablets; NHS Cost £12.59.

azosin 10mg twice a day
Age from 16 years onwards
Prazosin 5mg tablets. Take two tablets twice a day; supply 112 tablets; NHS Cost £16.79.

tart or increase terazosin

art terazosin: starter pack
Age from 16 years onwards
Terazosin starter pack. Take one tablet once a day. See package insert for full instructions; supply 28 tablets; NHS Cost £13.00.

razosin 2mg once a day
Age from 16 years onwards
Terazosin 2mg tablets. Take one tablet once a day; supply 28 tablets; NHS Cost £7.95.

razosin 4mg once a day
Age from 16 years onwards
Terazosin 2mg tablets. Take two tablets once a day; supply 56 tablets; NHS Cost £15.90.

razosin 5mg once a day
Age from 16 years onwards
Terazosin 5mg tablets. Take one tablet once a day; supply 28 tablets; NHS Cost £12.91.

razosin 10mg once a day
Age from 16 years onwards
Terazosin 10mg tablets. Take one tablet once a day; supply 28 tablets; NHS Cost £26.57.

razosin 20mg once a day
Age from 16 years onwards
Terazosin 10mg tablets. Take two tablets once a day; supply 56 tablets; NHS Cost £53.14.

tart or increase doxazosin m/r

art doxazosin 4mg m/r once a day
Age from 16 years onwards
Doxazosin 4mg m/r tablets. Take one tablet once a day; supply 28 tablets; NHS Cost £14.08.

oxazosin 4mg m/r once a day
Age from 16 years onwards
Doxazosin 4mg m/r tablets. Take one tablet once a day; supply 28 tablets; NHS Cost £14.08.

oxazosin 8mg m/r once a day
Age from 16 years onwards
Doxazosin 8mg m/r tablets. Take one tablet once a day; supply 28 tablets; NHS Cost £28.00.

Aspirin — who to treat?

Which therapy

or primary prevention

The risk/benefit ratio for prescribing aspirin is most favourable in people at high risk of coronary heart disease (CHD).

Aspirin should be offered to people with a CHD risk of 15% or more over 10 years, which includes the majority of people with diabetes and hypertension (**A**).

Before starting aspirin therapy for this group of people, reduce systolic BP to 145 mmHg or below and maintain while taking aspirin for primary prevention (**B**).

For secondary prevention

- **Aspirin** is indicated if there is evidence of established cardiovascular disease (**B**), such as:
  - Angina, myocardial infarction
  - Non-haemorrhagic cerebrovascular disease
  - Peripheral vascular disease
  - Atherosclerotic renovascular disease

Practical prescribing points

For further information please see the *Medicines Compendium* (www.medicines.org.uk) or the *British National Formulary* (www.bnf.org).

D

Low-dose aspirin

- **Concurrent nonsteroidal anti-inflammatory drugs (NSAIDs):** the risk of serious gastrointestinal complications doubles in people who regularly take low-dose aspirin and another NSAID. If possible, stop the second NSAID.
- **If a second NSAID must be continued, avoid ibuprofen** — it may reduce the cardiovascular protective effect of low-dose aspirin. Consider using diclofenac if a second NSAID must be used.
- **Asthma:** aspirin can induce bronchospasm in someone hypersensitive to aspirin, but this is rare.

Concomitant use of drug formulations with a high sodium content

- Effervescent compound analgesics should be avoided where possible as they may aggravate hypertension. Note: soluble aspirin contains no sodium.

Patient information leaflets

The following PILs are available at www.prodigy.nhs.uk

- Diabetes and High Blood Pressure
- Diabetes Insight Website
- Diabetes Research & Wellness Foundation
- Diabetes Type 2
- Diabetes Type 2 - A Summary
- Diabetes UK
- DiabeticLife

Shared decision making

- **Aspirin** (low-dose) is often prescribed if you have heart disease or stroke, to:
  - Reduce the 'stickiness' of the blood, which
  - Reduces the chance of a blood clot forming, which
  - Reduces your chance of having a heart attack or stroke.
- **Aspirin is not usually advised if you do not have these sorts of problem,** as the risk of being on treatment may outweigh the benefit.
- Aspirin may not be advisable if you have asthma, or duodenal or stomach ulcers.
- **It is uncommon to have side effects with low-dosage aspirin.** It causes some bleeding in the stomach in a few people. So . . .
- **Tell a doctor if** you develop stomach pains, black faeces (motions), or notice blood in the faeces whilst taking aspirin.
- Your risk of bleeding complications is increased if you also take other anti-inflammatory medicines or anticoagulants.

Drug rationale

Drugs not included

- **Enteric-coated preparations are not offered** as there is no convincing evidence that this reduces toxicity at a dosage of 75 mg [DTB, 1997].
- **Clopidogrel** is licensed for the secondary prevention of stroke, and may be marginally more effective than aspirin, but more data is needed [Medicines Resource, 1998; Hankey et al, 2001]. It is also very expensive. Clopidogrel could be considered in someone who is intolerant of aspirin.
- **Dipyridamole** is not included because the evidence of efficacy as an antiplatelet agent is not as great as for aspirin.

Drugs included

- **Aspirin (75 mg daily)** is included because studies have shown that low-dosage aspirin reduces the risk of subsequent cardiovascular events in people with established cardiovascular disease [Hayden et al, 2002]. Higher dosages have not been offered. Soluble aspirin produces less occult bleeding. It is recommended for someone with a coronary heart disease (CHD) risk of >=30% over 10 years. It is also recommended that aspirin be considered in someone with a CHD risk of >=15% over 10 years.

Prescriptions

Aspirin

Aspirin 75mg dispersible once a day

- Age from 16 years onwards
- Aspirin 75mg dispersible tabs. Take one tablet once a day; supply 28 tablets; NHS Cost £0.15; OTC Cost £1.00.

Extended Information

Background information

- What is it? p.546
- How common is it? p.546
- How do I confirm a raised blood pressure? p.546
- What else might it be? p.547
- Complications and prognosis p.547

What is it?

- **The level at which hypertension is diagnosed has changed** over time as more evidence has become available on the risk/benefit of treatment. Systolic and diastolic blood pressures (BPs) are both continuously related to the risk of developing cardiovascular disease, with a gradient of risk that extends into the range of BP that does not require treatment.
- **A pragmatic definition of hypertension in people with diabetes** (based on the threshold at which treatment should be considered) is a sustained BP of 140/80 mmHg or more.
- **An average of three BP readings over two months** is required to determine baseline BP measurements (D) [NICE, 2002].
- **In people with Type 1 diabetes and hypertension,** hypertension develops after several years and usually reflects the development of diabetic nephropathy [Arauz-Pacheco et al, 2002].
- **For categorization of renal disease** in diabetes, see separate PRODIGY guidance on *Diabetes Type 2 — renal disease.*
  - **Microalbuminuria (incipient nephropathy)** is the firs stage of abnormal albumin excretion in the urine.
  - **Proteinuria or macroalbuminuria (or overt nephropathy)** is the next stage, corresponding to a higher level of albumin in urine [NICE, 2002].

How common is it?

- **In Type 1 diabetes,** 30% of people eventually develop hypertension [Arauz-Pacheco et al, 2002]. Hypertensio tends to develop after several years of the condition an usually reflects the development of diabetic nephropath
- **The reported prevalence of hypertension in people wit Type 2 diabetes** varies between 35% [Hypertension in Diabetes Study Group, 1993] to greater than 70% [Colhoun et al, 1999], depending on the population studied and the blood pressure (BP) levels used to class hypertension.
- **The incidence of end-stage renal disease (ESRD)** amon African-Americans is 5–6 times that of white people [Arauz-Pacheco et al, 2002]. Asian people from the Indian subcontinent also have high rates of ESRD.

How do I confirm a raised blood pressure?

- **If blood pressure (BP) is 140/80 mmHg or higher,** take two further readings over a period of 2 months, or sooner if clinical circumstances dictate (D).
- **If BP is persistently raised to 140/80 mmHg or more,** offer lifestyle advice and drug treatment as appropriate See *When is drug treatment recommended and what is the target BP goal?*
- **When measuring BP,** use a device that is properly maintained, calibrated, and officially recommended as being accurate after having been validated [Ramsay et a 1999].
- **The mercury sphygmomanometer is still the gold standard** for routine clinical practice, although non-mercury-containing devices are gradually replacing them.
- **Further information on BP devices** can be obtained fro the British Hypertension Society Information Service (telephone: 020 8725 3412, e-mail: bhsis@sghms.ac.uk website: www.bhsoc.org).
- **Technique for checking BP:**
  - The person should be seated, with arm supported at the level of the heart.
  - If arm circumference exceeds 33 cm, use a large cuff.
  - Deflate at 2 mmHg/sec and measure BP to the neares 2 mmHg.
  - Record diastolic pressure at disappearance of sounds (phase V); if this cannot be identified, use the point where muffling of sounds occurs (phase IV).
  - At least two readings should be made and the lower two readings used.
  - Usually, there is no significant difference in BPs between the arms, and using the arm that is nearest t the observer is reasonable. If there is a consistent difference between the two arms, use the arm with th higher BP for routine monitoring (*note* that a difference in BP between the two arms may indicate coarctation of the aorta).
  - Check standing BP in someone with diabetes to exclude orthostatic (postural) hypotension, as cardiovascular autonomic neuropathy can cause falsely low or high readings.

Ambulatory blood pressure monitoring

- **There remains some controversy about the role of different methods of BP monitoring in primary care** (e.g interpretation of the limited evidence currently available to support methods for BP monitoring other than using sphygmomanometers [Hamilton and Sharp, 2002; Little et al, 2002a; Little et al, 2002b].

Treatment thresholds and targets must be adjusted downwards when making decisions based on ambulatory blood pressure monitoring (ABPM). The average difference between clinic and daytime ABPM mean pressures is approximately 12/7 mmHg.

For treatment decisions, use the average daytime BP, not the 24 hour average.

Many people purchase BP monitoring devices and it is important that these are validated against the GP practice device before any treatment decisions are made.

ABPM may be useful when:

- BP shows unusual variability.
- Hypertension seems to be resistant to treatment (i.e. greater than 150/90 mmHg on a regimen of three or more antihypertensive drugs).
- 'White-coat hypertension' is suspected (hypertension in the clinic), with normal pressures outside the clinic.

Blood pressure monitoring at home

There is less evidence regarding self-measurement of BP than there is for ABPM. However, it is less expensive and more convenient for patients.

Many of the same considerations apply, in particular an upward adjustment of 12/7 mmHg for equivalence to measurements made in a clinic.

Many people purchase blood pressure (BP) monitoring devices, and it is important that these are validated against the GP practice device before any treatment management decisions are made.

What else might it be?

Rarely, hypertension is secondary to an underlying condition that is usually suspected from physical examination and the results of routine tests. Examples include the following:

Renal disorder (considered to be the commonest secondary cause)

Chronic pyelonephritis: may be a history of vesicoureteric reflex and/or recurrent urinary tract infections.

Glomerulonephritis: often indicated by microscopic haematuria.

Polycystic kidney disease: suggested by abdominal or flank mass, microscopic haematuria, family history

Obstructive uropathy: may have abdominal or flank mass.

Renal cell carcinoma.

Drug induced

For example, the combined oral contraceptive pill, nonsteroidal anti-inflammatory drugs (NSAIDs), corticosteroids, ciclosporin, erythropoietin, appetite suppressants, and sympathomimetics such as phenylpropanolamine in some over-the-counter cough and cold remedies.

Endocrine disorder

Primary aldosteronism (Conn's syndrome): may present with tetany, muscle weakness, polyuria, hypokalaemia.

Cushing's syndrome: suspect if clinical features (e.g. truncal obesity and striae).

Phaeochromocytoma: may present with intermittent high blood pressure (BP), sweating attacks, and palpitations.

Hyperparathyroidism: hypercalcaemia.

Acromegaly: clinical features.

Vascular disorder

- **Coarctation of the aorta:** may result in a difference in BP between the left and right arms. Other signs include absent or weak femoral pulses and a murmur. The narrowing of the aorta may generally cause a high BP in the upper part of the body and low BP in the legs.
- **Renal artery stenosis:** suspect if peripheral vascular disease, presence of abdominal bruit.

Miscellaneous

- **Connective tissue disorders:** scleroderma, systemic lupus erythematosus (SLE), polyarteritis nodosa.
- **Retroperitoneal fibrosis:** corticosteroids may also be prescribed to relieve symptoms.

D

Complications and prognosis

Complications

- **Cardiovascular disease (CVD) is the most prevalent and detrimental cause of morbidity and mortality in people with diabetes and hypertension** [NICE, 2002].
- **Diabetes increases the risk of coronary events** two-fold in men and four-fold in women [American Diabetes Association, 2003].
- **In observational studies of people with hypertension, someone with diabetes has twice the risk of CVD as someone without diabetes** [American Diabetes Association, 2003].
- **The UK Prospective Diabetes Study (UKPDS)** [UK Prospective Diabetes Study Group, 1998b] found that in people with Type 2 diabetes, the risk of diabetic complications was strongly associated with raised blood pressure (BP). Tight BP control in this population was associated with:
  - 37% reduction in microvascular end points (nephropathy and advanced retinopathy)
  - 32% reduction in deaths related to diabetes
  - 24% reduction in diabetes-related end points
- **Key modifiable risk factors for the development of cardiovascular disease** [MeReC, 2000] **are:**
  - Smoking
  - Hypertension
  - High cholesterol levels
  - Glycaemic control
  - Inactive lifestyle
  - Obesity
  - Increased alcohol consumption
- **Diabetic nephropathy is the leading cause of end-stage renal disease (ESRD):**
  - 20–30% of people with Type 1 diabetes will develop ESRD.
  - 10–20% of people with Type 2 diabetes will develop ESRD [Arauz-Pacheco et al, 2002].
  - The incidence of ESRD among African-Americans with diabetes is 5–6 times that of white people with diabetes [Arauz-Pacheco et al, 2002]. Asian people from the Indian sub-continent also have high rates of ESRD.

Prognosis

- The co-existence of diabetes and hypertension has been found to double the risk of cardiovascular events, cardiovascular mortality, and total mortality [Grossman et al, 2000].
- In the USA, two-thirds of people with diabetes die from cardiovascular causes [Malcolm et al, 2002].
- A large prospective cohort study in men with 5 years' follow-up found that diabetes (mainly Type 2) alone is associated with [Lotufo et al, 2001]:
  - At least a two-fold increase in risk for all-cause death.

- At least a three-fold increase in risk of death from coronary heart disease (CHD).
- A twelve-fold increase in death from CHD in people with pre-existing CHD, compared with people with neither risk factor.

- CHD is the most common cause of death among people with Type 2 diabetes [NICE, 2002].

Management issues

- General issues p.548
- What are the benefits of blood pressure reduction? p.548
- Non-drug measures p.548
- When is drug treatment recommended and what is the target blood pressure goal? p.549
- Initial antihypertensive medication p.549
- Add-on antihypertensive treatment p.549
- Evidence to support drug selection p.549
- When should aspirin be considered? p.551
- When should lipid-lowering therapy be considered? p.551
- What about hormone replacement therapy? p.551
- Medicines management p.551

General issues

- **Initial assessment** of a person with hypertension and diabetes should include a complete medical history, with special emphasis on cardiovascular risk factors and the presence of diabetic complications and other cardiovascular complications (D).
- **Many diabetic people, especially those with Type 2 diabetes, are overweight** and have several other cardiovascular risk factors. Therefore drug intervention with aspirin, statin therapy, and antihypertensive(s) should be considered, and complemented by an attempt to optimise glycaemic control as well as lifestyle advice.
- **For categorization of renal disease** in diabetes, see separate PRODIGY guidance on *Diabetes Type 2 — renal disease*.
  - **Microalbuminuria (incipient nephropathy)** is the first stage of abnormal albumin excretion.
  - **Proteinuria or macroalbuminuria (overt nephropathy)** is the next stage, corresponding to a higher abnormal level of albumin in urine [NICE, 2002].

What are the benefits of blood pressure reduction?

- **People with hypertension and diabetes experience a greater absolute benefit from antihypertensive therapy** than do non-diabetic people with hypertension.
- **The UK Prospective Diabetes Study (UKPDS)** [UK Prospective Diabetes Study Group, 1998b] found that tight blood pressure (BP) control in people with hypertension and Type 2 diabetes was associated with:
  - 37% reduction in microvascular end points (nephropathy and advanced retinopathy)
  - 32% reduction in deaths related to diabetes
  - 24% reduction in diabetes-related end points
- **Any lowering of a person's average BP reduces the risk of complications.** Each 10 mmHg decrease in mean systolic BP has been found to be associated with reductions in the risk of [Adler et al, 2002]:
  - 15% for deaths related to diabetes
  - 13% for microvascular complications
  - 12% for any complication related to diabetes
  - 11% for myocardial infarction (MI)

Non-drug measures

- **Offer lifestyle management advice to anyone with hypertension and diabetes (C).**
- **Review and discuss other modifiable risk factors for cardiovascular disease, particularly smoking (B).**
- **Changes in diet and lifestyle may lower blood pressure** (BP) as much as drug monotherapy, reduce the need for drug therapy, enhance antihypertensive effect of drugs, reduce the need for multiple drug regimens, and reduce the overall cardiovascular risk.

Measures that lower BP

The following are measures that are known to lower BP, although they have not specifically been tested in people with diabetes and hypertension in controlled clinical trials

- **Weight reduction:** anyone with hypertension and a body mass index (BMI) greater than 25 should be encouraged to lose weight and increase physical activity (A). A 10 kg weight loss in a person with an initial weight of 100 kg with comorbidities would be expected to result in 10 mmHg fall in diastolic and systolic pressures as well as other benefits (see PRODIGY guidance on *Obesity*).
- **Physical exercise:** regular, dynamic exercise (e.g. brisk walking) tailored to the individual is recommended. A meta-analysis of 1108 normotensive people found a 4 mmHg reduction in systolic BP in those assigned to aerobic exercise compared with the control group [Whelton et al, 2002b]. Similar BP reductions were achieved with low, moderate, and high intensity exercise
- **Reduced salt intake:** is recommended, especially in the elderly and those with higher initial BP [American Diabetes Association, 2003].
  - A systematic review found that reducing sodium intake in people with hypertension by 6.7 g per day fo 28 days reduced systolic BP by about 3.9/1.9 mmHg [Graudal et al, 1998].
  - A more recent systematic review concluded that, without the intensive dietary interventions used in trials, comparable reductions in BP are less likely to be routinely achieved in primary care, particularly in the long term [Hooper et al, 2002].
- **Limited alcohol consumption:** less than 21 units/week for men and 14 units/week for women is recommended. A meta-analysis of 2234 people (mixed hypertensive and normotensive) found that overall alcohol reduction was associated with a reduction in BP of 3.3/2 mmHg [Xin et al, 2001]. For further information, see separate PRODIGY guidance on *Alcohol — problem drinking*.
- **Diet:** an intake of at least five portions/day of fruit and vegetables is recommended.
  - A change to such a diet lowers BP in hypertensive people by 7/3 mmHg and by 11/6 mmHg if combined with reduced total and saturated fat in the diet [Appel et al, 1997].
  - A recent primary-care-based randomized controlled trial (RCT) of 690 healthy people found that encouragement by a nurse to increase fruit and vegetable consumption to at least five portions/day led to an increase of about 1.4 portions/day and a significant reduction in BP of about 4/1.5 mmHg [Joh et al, 2002].

Additional measures that reduce cardiovascular risk

- **Smoking cessation** (see separate PRODIGY *Smoking cessation* guidance) is vital, and advice should be offered where appropriate (C). Smoking is a major risk factor for cardiovascular disease and increases the relative risk of coronary heart disease (CHD) death by 70%. However, there is no evidence that stopping smoking decreases BP in people with hypertension [Murphy et al, 2002; Whelton et al, 2002a].

Diet: replacing saturated fat with polyunsaturated and monounsaturated fats, eating oily fish, and reducing total fat intake will reduce cardiovascular risk.
Other methods: there is limited evidence to support supplementation with potassium, fish oil, calcium, and magnesium, but their long-term benefits are unclear and none are recommended for this purpose [Jee et al, 2002]. ⁄IeReC, 2002; Murphy et al, 2002; Whelton et al, 2002a]

⁄hen is drug treatment recommended and ⁄hat is the target blood pressure goal?

The threshold level of blood pressure (BP) at which antihypertensive medication is recommended in people with diabetes varies, depending on their 10-year coronary-event risk and whether they have microalbuminuria or proteinuria. For a detailed definition of microalbuminuria and proteinuria, see separate PRODIGY guidance on *Diabetes Type 2 — renal disease*.
Current recommendations on when to initiate treatment and the target BP to aim for are outlined in Table 1. No national guidance is currently available on the management of hypertension in people with Type 1 diabetes. However, it can be assumed that the management in this population is similar to the management of people with Type 2 diabetes and hypertension.

ıitial antihypertensive medication

f the person has microalbuminuria or proteinuria

The recommended first-line treatment is an ACE inhibitor (**A**).
If an ACE inhibitor is not tolerated, then consider an angiotensin-II receptor antagonist (AIIRA) (**B**).

f the person has no microalbuminuria or ıroteinuria

Suitable first-line treatments are thiazide diuretics, beta-blockers, ACE inhibitors, or AIIRAs (**A**). Table 2 outlines the factors that should be considered when choosing between these.
Long-acting dihydropyridine and non-dihydropyridine calcium-channel blockers have an important role in treating blood pressure (BP), but on current evidence should be prescribed as second-line or as part of a combination treatment (**B**).

ıdd-on antihypertensive treatment

The National Institute for Clinical Excellence (NICE) recommends drug classes that may be used in combination if a person is taking an ACE inhibitor or angiotensin-II receptor antagonist (AIIRA). These classes include thiazide diuretics, beta-blockers, and long-acting calcium-channel blockers (CCBs) (**B**).

- Combination therapy with drugs from different drug classes will be required to meet treatment targets in most people (**C**). In the UK Prospective Diabetes Study, 60% of the people in the trial were found to require at least two drugs to lower blood pressure (BP) to the target level [UK Prospective Diabetes Study Group, 1998b].
- **Someone with diabetes and hypertension requires more intensive medication therapy** than someone without diabetes. For renoprotection, BP control is the most important factor [Ramsay et al, 1999; Berlowitz et al, 2003].

D

Evidence to support drug selection

ACE inhibitors

- **In people with Type 1 diabetes and albuminuria, with or without hypertension,** ACE inhibitors have been shown to delay the progression from microalbuminuria to proteinuria [Hutchinson et al, 2002; American Diabetes Association, 2003].
- **In people with Type 2 diabetes, hypertension, and microalbuminuria,** ACE inhibitors have been shown to delay the progression to proteinuria [American Diabetes Association, 2003].
- **A placebo-controlled trial investigated the effect of ramipril** in 3577 people with Type 2 diabetes over 4.5 years. It found that ramipril reduced the risk of cardiovascular events by 27% (NNT = 22, 95% CI 14 to 43) [Heart Outcomes Prevention Evaluation Study Investigators, 2000]. The relative cardioprotective effect was present to the same extent in people with or without microalbuminuria.
- **A systematic review** [Pahor et al, 2000b] compared the effect of antihypertensives in people with Type 2 diabetes and found that:
  - ACE inhibitors compared with calcium-channel blockers (CCBs) significantly reduced combined cardiovascular events (cardiovascular death, acute myocardial infarction (MI), congestive heart failure, stroke, pulmonary infarction, and angina).
  - Captopril compared with diuretics or beta-blockers significantly reduced MI, stroke, or death in a randomized controlled trial (RCT) [Niskanen et al, 2001]. However, in another RCT comparing captopril with atenolol, there was no significant difference in the number of cardiovascular events [UK Prospective Diabetes Study Group, 1998a].

able 1: Recommendations on when to initiate antihypertensive medication, and target blood pressure (BP) to aim for in ɜople with Type 2 diabetes.

ood ressure	10-year coronary- event risk	Concomitant microalbuminuria or proteinuria	Recommendations
-140/) mmHg ıd <160/)0 mmHg	Lower (no history of CVD, and 10-year coronary event risk =<15%)	No	Monitor BP every 6 months, or more frequently if necessary (D). If 10-year coronary event risk is subsequently found to have increased to the higher level, treat according to below (C).
≥140/80 mHg and ɩ60/)0 mmHg	Higher (history of CVD, or 10-year coronary event risk >=15%)	No	Offer drug treatment to reduce BP (B). Aim for a target BP <140/80 mmHg (B).
≥160/)0 mmHg	Higher or lower	No	Offer drug treatment to reduce BP (B). Aim for a target BP <140/80 mmHg (B).
≥140/80 mHg	Higher or lower	Yes	Offer drug treatment to achieve a target BP =<135/75 mmHg (B).

Table 2: Initial treatment recommendations in hypertensive people with no degree of nephropathy

Antihypertensive	Recommendations
ACE inhibitors	First choice in heart failure, left ventricular dysfunction and diabetes.
Angiotensin-II receptor antagonists (AIIRAs)	Alternative option for someone who cannot tolerate an ACE inhibitor.
Thiazide diuretics	A low dose of thiazide is first choice in most people, especially those over 60 years.
Beta-blockers	Cardioselective agents are preferred. First choice if angina or history of myocardial infarction. Those that are appropriately licensed may be considered in people with heart failure.
Calcium-channel blockers (dihydropyridines)	Long-acting dihydropyridines are an alternative option in elderly people, especially those with isolated systolic hypertension. Consider as an alternative option in angina if a beta-blocker is not tolerated or is contraindicated.
Calcium-channel blockers (rate-limiting)	Alternative option for someone with angina if a beta-blocker is not tolerated or is contraindicated.
Alpha-blockers	An option in someone with prostatism, and to be considered for someone with dyslipidaemia.

- **Recently published results** from the Antihypertensive and Lipid-lowering Treatment to Prevent Heart Attack Trial (ALLHAT) indicate that in people with Type 2 diabetes, lisinopril appeared to have no increased benefit for most CVD and renal outcomes when compared with chlortalidone [ALLHAT Officers, 2002].

Angiotensin-II receptor antagonists

- **Angiotensin-II receptor antagonists (AIIRAs) are currently recommended where ACE inhibitors are not tolerated.** However, there is increasing evidence to suggest that they may be just as effective as ACE inhibitors in providing cardiovascular and renal protection in people with Type 2 diabetes and albuminuria [Mogensen et al, 2000; Brenner et al, 2001; Lewis et al, 2001; Parving et al, 2001].
- **Irbesartan** has been found to be effective in protecting against the progression of nephropathy due to Type 2 diabetes. The drug's effectiveness has been found to be independent of its antihypertensive effect, and a better outcome has been demonstrated at higher doses [Lewis et al, 2001; Parving et al, 2001].
- **A double-blind placebo-controlled RCT in 1513 people with Type 2 diabetes and nephropathy compared renal and cardiovascular outcomes of losartan compared with placebo,** both taken in addition to conventional treatment [Brenner et al, 2001]. Losartan reduced the incidence of a doubling of serum creatinine concentration and end-stage renal disease, but had no effect on the death rate.
- **A further double-blind RCT compared losartan with atenolol** in 9193 people [Dahlof et al, 2002]. Subgroup analysis in the diabetic cohort of 1195 people with left ventricular hypertrophy (LVH) found that losartan was more effective than atenolol in reducing cardiovascular end points after 4 years of follow-up, and was better tolerated [Lindholm et al, 2002]. The trial's main limitation was that it involved a selected group of high-risk people (i.e. people with hypertension and LVH), and therefore the results have to be treated with caution.

Combination of ACE and angiotensin-II receptor antagonists (AIIRAs)

- **This strategy is not currently recommended,** but there is some limited evidence for dual blockade (the use of both ACE inhibitors and AIIRAs) in diabetic nephropathy.
- **The Candesartan and Lisinopril Microalbuminuria (CALM) randomized double-blind trial** compared short-term monotherapy with candesartan or lisinopril compared with combination treatment in 199 people. There were marked reductions in BP and the urinary:creatinine ratio with dual blockade, when compared with either drug alone [Mogensen et al, 2000].
- **More trial evidence with larger sample sizes and hard clinical end points are needed** before the routine use of dual blockade can be recommended.

Thiazide diuretics

- No RCTs appear to have specifically compared diuretics with ACE inhibitors in people with diabetes.
- **The effects of captopril or conventional antihypertensive (diuretics and/or beta-blockers) treatment** were compared in a subgroup analysis of the Captopril Prevention Project (CAPPP), randomised to 572 people with diabetes [Niskanen et al, 2001]. Captopril was found to be superior in preventing cardiovascular end points, in particular cardiovascular mortality.
- **The ALLHAT trial** [ALLHAT Officers, 2002] **endorses the use of thiazide diuretics** as a first-line option in most people with hypertension. The trial also suggests that results of some of the major outcomes are more favourable for chlortalidone compared with lisinopril in individuals with diabetes, but no formal subgroup analysis has yet been published.
- **Thiazides may have a modest adverse effect on metabolic (hyperglycaemic) control:** however, the reduction offered in overall cardiovascular risk outweighs this [Hutchinson et al, 2002].
- **Afro-Caribbean people with hypertension** may be more responsive to diuretics and calcium-channel blockers than to other classes of drug, but combinations with other classes are frequently needed for control [Ramsay et al, 1999].

Beta-blockers

- **Available data comparing the effect of an ACE inhibitor with a beta-blocker in people with Type 2 diabetes are limited and inconclusive** [UK Prospective Diabetes Study Group, 1998a; Niskanen et al, 2001].
- **Non-selective beta-blockers are more likely to increase the risk of hypoglycaemia** than are selective beta-blockers [Hutchinson et al, 2002].

Calcium-channel blockers (CCBs)

- **The evidence suggests that thiazide diuretics, beta-blockers, and ACE inhibitors significantly reduce cardiovascular events** in people with diabetes and are probably superior to CCBs as initial treatment for hypertension [Malcolm et al, 2002].
- **Short-acting dihydropyridines are contraindicated in the management of hypertension and should not be**

prescribed (D). Their use is associated with large variations in BP and reflex tachycardia.
Meta-analyses have not found convincing evidence that CCBs have any benefit over other antihypertensive drugs [Pahor et al, 2000a]. Moreover, [Blood Pressure Lowering Treatment Trialists Collaboration, 2000; Opie and Schall, 2002] there is some evidence that other antihypertensive drugs are more effective in preventing the progression of renal disease [Estacio et al, 1998; Tatti et al, 1998].

lpha-blockers

There are no studies on the effect of alpha-blockers on long-term complications of diabetes.
The ALLHAT trial suggested that alpha-blockers might have less benefit than diuretics and beta-blockers in people with diabetes and hypertension [ALLHAT Officers, 2000]. The alpha-blocker arm of the study was stopped because of an increase in cases of new-onset heart failure in people taking doxazosin compared with those taking other treatments.
It is recommended that alpha-blockers should therefore be reserved for use in those in whom other antihypertensive agents are ineffective, those with prostatism, or as part of combination treatment with more than two antihypertensive agents to achieve BP targets.

/hen should aspirin be considered?

rimary prevention

The risk/benefit ratio for prescribing aspirin is most favourable in people at high risk of coronary heart disease (CHD).
Aspirin should be offered to people with a CHD risk of 15% or more over 10 years, which includes the majority of people with diabetes and hypertension (**A**).
Before starting aspirin therapy for someone in this group, reduce systolic blood pressure (BP) to 145 mmHg or below and maintain while taking aspirin for primary prevention (**B**).
Table 3 shows estimated benefits and harms of aspirin based on 1000 people receiving aspirin for 5 years and a relative risk reduction of 28% for CHD events in those who received aspirin [Hayden et al, 2002].
layden et al, 2002]

econdary prevention

Aspirin 75 mg daily is indicated if there is evidence of established cardiovascular disease (myocardial infarction, angina, non-haemorrhagic cerebrovascular disease, peripheral vascular disease, or atherosclerotic renovascular disease) (**B**).

able 3: Estimated benefits and harms of aspirin for people ith various levels of risk for CHD events.

nefits and harms	Baseline risk for CHD over 5 years		
	1%	3%	5%
tal mortality	No effect	No effect	No effect
ımber of CHD events avoided (95% CIs)	3 (1–4)	8 (4–12)	14 (16–20)
ımber of haemorrhagic strokes precipitated 5% CIs)	1 (0–2)	1 (0–2)	1 (0–2)
ımber of major gastrointestinal bleeding ents precipitated (95% CIs)	3 (2–4)	3 (2–4)	3 (2–4)

When should lipid-lowering therapy be considered?

- For advice on the risk of lipids in people with diabetes, see separate PRODIGY guidance on *Diabetes Type 2 — lipid management.*

What about hormone replacement therapy?

- **Hormone replacement therapy (HRT) does not seem to be associated with an increase in blood pressure (BP),** and women with hypertension can be given HRT as long as the BP is adequately controlled.
- **HRT has not been found to be beneficial in preventing coronary heart disease (CHD)** in women both with and without CHD. In fact, studies have found a slight trend towards increased rates of CHD in the first 1–2 years of treatment with HRT.
- **HRT should not be initiated for prevention of CHD,** and consideration should be given to stopping HRT after any cardiovascular disease event.

[CSM, 2002a]

Medicines management

ACE inhibitors

- **In all people,** measure serum creatinine and electrolytes 1 week after initiating ACE therapy and 1 week after each increase in dosage.
- **Avoid ACE inhibitors in all three trimesters of pregnancy** because of the potential for defects in fetal and neonatal blood pressure (BP) control and renal function.
- **Avoid ACE inhibitors also in:**
  - Breastfeeding — traces of ACE inhibitors have been detected in breast milk.
  - Critical renovascular disease in the form of bilateral renal artery stenosis or severe renal artery stenosis supplying a single functioning kidney — due to the risk of renal impairment, which may cause severe and progressive renal failure.
  - Significant cardiac outflow tract obstruction (e.g. due to aortic stenosis or hypertrophic obstructive cardiomyopathy) — because of the risk of hypotension and syncope due to vasodilatory effects.
- **Stop NSAIDs** if possible as they increase the risk of renal impairment with ACE inhibitors.
- **Avoid potassium-sparing diuretics or potassium supplements** other than in exceptional cases (e.g. low-dose spironolactone for severe heart failure), because of the risk of hyperkalaemia. Concomitant use with spironolactone requires careful monitoring.
- **A cough may develop** in someone using an ACE inhibitor — where this persists, angiotensin-II receptor antagonists (AIIRAs) are recommended as an alternative.

Angiotensin-II receptor antagonists (AIIRAs)

- **In all people,** measure serum creatinine and electrolytes a week after initiating AIIRA therapy and a week after each increase in dosage.
- **Avoid AIIRAs in all three trimesters of pregnancy** because of the potential for defects in fetal and neonatal BP control and renal function.
- **Avoid AIIRAs also in:**
  - Critical renovascular disease in the form of bilateral renal artery stenosis or severe renal artery stenosis supplying a single functioning kidney — due to the risk of renal impairment, which may cause severe and progressive renal failure.
  - Significant cardiac outflow tract obstruction (e.g. due to aortic stenosis or hypertrophic obstructive

cardiomyopathy) — because of the risk of hypotension and syncope due to vasodilatory effects.
- **Stop NSAIDs** if possible as they increase the risk of renal impairment with AIIRAs.
- **Avoid potassium-sparing diuretics or potassium supplements** other than in exceptional cases (e.g. low-dose spironolactone for severe heart failure), because of the risk of hyperkalaemia. Concomitant use with spironolactone requires careful monitoring.

Thiazide diuretics

- Thiazide diuretics should be avoided in someone with gout, if possible. If a thiazide is deemed necessary, consider prophylaxis with allopurinol. See separate PRODIGY guidance on *Gout.*

Beta-blockers

- **Avoid beta-blockers in someone with asthma, or with chronic obstructive pulmonary disease that has an asthmatic component,** as they can precipitate bronchospasm that is unresponsive to beta$_2$-agonists.
- **People with diabetes** should be advised that beta-blockers may slightly raise their blood glucose levels, and their response to hypoglycaemia may be delayed or symptoms of hypoglycaemia may not occur in the usual way. Cardioselective beta-blockers (e.g. atenolol) may be preferable. Avoid beta-blockers in someone who experiences frequent hypoglycaemia [BNF 44, 2002].
- **Sleep disturbance or nightmares** are less likely with a water-soluble beta-blocker (e.g. atenolol), as it is less likely to cross the blood-brain barrier [BNF 44, 2002].
- **A recent meta-analysis** highlighted that there is no significant increased risk of depressive symptoms while taking beta-blockers, and only a small increase in the risk of fatigue (18 per 1000 patients, 95% CI 5 to 30) or sexual dysfunction (5 per 1000 patients, 95% CI 2 to 8) [Ko et al, 2002].
- **Assess** objective signs of peripheral vascular disease in someone who experiences cold extremities with beta-blockers.

Calcium-channel blockers (CCBs)

- **Dizziness, facial flushing, ankle oedema, and postural hypotension** are common adverse effects of CCBs [BNF 44, 2002], but generally reduce in severity on continued treatment. Ankle oedema is often persistent. Diuretics should not be prescribed for CCB-induced ankle oedema, as they only partially reduce ankle oedema caused by CCBs.
- **Verapamil commonly causes constipation.** Advise people to eat more fibre (fruit, vegetables, cereals, wholemeal bread, etc); to try to drink at least 12 cups (8 glasses or mugs) of liquid a day; but to avoid drinks with a high caffeine-content, as these may make constipation worse. Avoid concomitant ingestion of grapefruit juice, as it may affect the metabolism of verapamil, causing an increase in serum levels.
- **Never use verapamil with a beta-blocker,** because of the risk of reduced cardiac output and heart failure. Diltiazem has a smaller negative inotropic effect than verapamil has. It may be used with a beta-blocker, provided that together they do not cause bradycardia.
- **Dihydropyridines** are generally safe to use in heart failure, as any negative inotropic effect is offset by a reduction in left ventricular work [BNF 44, 2002].

Alpha-blockers

- **Alpha-blockers have a tendency to cause a rapid reduction in BP after the first dose** and should be avoided in someone with a history of orthostatic hypotension and micturition syncope. The first-dose effect may possibly be reduced with modified-release formulations.
- **Alpha-blockers should also be avoided in someone with heart failure or impaired left ventricular function,** following the decision to discontinue the doxazosin-treatment arm of the Antihypertensive and Lipid-lowering Treatment to Prevent Heart Attack Trial (ALLHAT). An interim analysis showed that there was an increase in cases of new-onset heart failure in people assigned to doxazosin compared with chlortalidone [ALLHAT Officers, 2002].

Antiplatelet drugs

- **Aspirin** may cause dyspepsia. Increasing doses of aspiri are associated with greater risks of gastrointestinal (GI) toxicity, such as ulceration, bleeding, and perforation. Someone who experiences dyspepsia with aspirin shoul be co-prescribed an acid-suppressing drug. See separate PRODIGY guidance on *Dyspepsia — symptoms (uninvestigate by endoscopy)*. Presence of dyspepsia is not a good guide to the severity of adverse effects: man people who experience perforations do not have prior aspirin-induced dyspepsia.
- **There is no robust evidence that different formulations of aspirin are associated with different degrees of risk o GI adverse effects** [CSM, 2002b]. Enteric-coated preparations are more expensive than standard preparations of aspirin.
- **A recent retrospective study found that people with cardiovascular disease who took ibuprofen as well as low-dose aspirin** had a higher risk of all-cause mortalit than those who took only low-dose aspirin (adjusted hazard ratio 1.93, 95% CI 1.3-2.87) [MacDonald and Wei, 2003]. There was no difference in mortality for people taking diclofenac plus low-dose aspirin, or another nonsteroidal anti-inflammatory drug (NSAID) plus low-dose aspirin. (Note: Cox-II selective NSAIDs were not included in this study.)
- **The results of this study should be viewed with caution** as the study was unable to control for confounding factors, and only small numbers of people (303) were taking ibuprofen or diclofenac. However, until more evidence becomes available, it would seem prudent to follow the advice of the British Heart Foundation and avoid ibuprofen in someone taking low-dose aspirin [British Heart Foundation, 2002]. Diclofenac is probab a better option if an NSAID is required.
- **Clopidogrel** is an alternative for the small number of people genuinely hypersensitive to aspirin (i.e. for who aspirin induces angio-oedema or bronchospasm). This i an off-licence use of clopidogrel. Dyspepsia is also a common adverse effect of clopidogrel.

References

NHS staff in England can link, free of charge, from references to full text journals by clicking on [Full text] or the PRODIGY website.

1. Adler, A.I., Stratton, I.M., Neil, H.A.W. et al (2002) Association of systolic blood pressure with macrovascular and microvascular complications of type 2 diabetes (UKPDS 36): prospective observationa study. *British Medical Journal* **321**(7258), 412–419. [Full text]
2. ALLHAT Officers (2000) Major cardiovascular event in hypertensive patients randomized to doxazosin vs chlorthalidone. *Journal of the American Medical Association* **283**(15), 1967–1975. [Full text]
3. ALLHAT Officers (2002) Major outcomes in high-ris hypertensive patients randomized to angiotensin-converting enzyme inhibitor or calcium channel

blocker vs diuretic. The Antihypertensive and Lipid-Lowering Treatment to Prevent Heart Attack Trial (ALLHAT). *Journal of the American Medical Association* **288**(23), 2981–2997. [Full text]

. American Diabetes Association (2003) Treatment of hypertension in adults with diabetes. *Diabetes Care* **26**(Suppl. 1), S80-S82. [Full text]

. Appel, L.J., Moore, T.J., Obarzanek, E. et al (1997) A clinical trial of the effects of dietary patterns on blood pressure. *New England Journal of Medicine* **336**(16), 1117–1124. [Full text]

. Arauz-Pacheco, C., Parrott, M.A. and Raskin, P. (2002) The treatment of hypertension in adult patients with diabetes. *Diabetes Care* **25**(1), 134–147. [Full text]

. Berlowitz, D.R., Ash, A.S., Hickey, E.C. et al (2003) Hypertension management in patients with diabetes: the need for more aggressive therapy. *Diabetes Care* **26**(2), 355–359. [Full text]

. Blood Pressure Lowering Treatment Trialists Collaboration (2000) Effects of ACE inhibitors, calcium antagonists, and other blood-pressure-lowering drugs: results of prospectively designed overviews of randomised trials. *Lancet* **356**(9246), 1955–1964. [Full text]

. BNF 44 (2002) *British National Formulary*. 44th edn. London: British Medical Association and Royal Pharmaceutical Society of Great Britain.

0. Brenner, B.M., Cooper, M.E., De Zeeuw, D. et al (2001) Effects of losartan on renal and cardiovascular outcomes in patients with type 2 diabetes and nephropathy. *New England Journal of Medicine* **345**(12), 861–869. [Full text]

1. British Heart Foundation (2002) *Aspirin and ibuprofen*. Factfile 11/2002. British Heart Foundation. www.bhf.org.uk [Accessed: 01/12/2002].

2. Cleland, J.G., Swedberg, K. and Poole-Wilson, P.A. (1998) Successes and failures of current treatment of heart failure. *Lancet* **352**(Suppl 1), S19-S28. [Full text]

3. Colhoun, H.M., Dong, W., Barakat, M.T. et al (1999) The scope for cardiovascular disease risk factor intervention among people with diabetes mellitus in England: a population-based analysis from the Health Surveys for England 1991–94. *Diabetic Medicine* **16**(1), 35–40.

4. CSM (2002a) New product information for hormone replacement therapy. *Current Problems in Pharmacovigilance* **28**(April), 1–2.

5. CSM (2002b) Non-steroidal anti-inflammatory drugs (NSAIDs) and gastrointestinal (GI) safety. *Current Problems in Pharmacovigilance* **28**(Apr), 5.

6. Dahlof, B., Devereux, R.B., Kjeldsen, S.E. et al (2002) Cardiovascular morbidity and mortality in the Losartan Intervention For Endpoint reduction in hypertension study (LIFE): a randomised trial against atenolol. *Lancet* **359**(9311), 995–1003. [Full text]

7. DTB (1997) Which prophylactic aspirin? *Drug & Therapeutics Bulletin* **35**(1), 7–8. [Full text]

8. Estacio, R.O., Jeffers, B.W., Hiatt, W.R. et al (1998) The effect of nisoldipine as compared with enalapril on cardiovascular outcomes in patients with non-insulin-dependent diabetes and hypertension. *New England Journal of Medicine* **338**(10), 645–652. [Full text]

9. Graudal, N.A., Galloe, A.M. and Garred, P. (1998) Effects of sodium restriction on blood pressure, renin, aldosterone, catecholamines, cholesterols, and triglycerides. *Journal of the American Medical Association* **279**(17), 1383–1391. [Full text]

0. Grossman, E., Messerli, F.H. and Goldbourt, U. (2000) High blood pressure and diabetes mellitus: are all antihypertensive drugs created equal? *Archives of Internal Medicine* **160**(16), 2447–2452. [Full text]

21. Hamilton, W.T. and Sharp, D. (2002) Comparison of different measures of blood pressure. *British Medical Journal* **325**(7376), 1360. [Full text]

22. Hankey, G.J., Sudlow, C.L.M. and Dunbabin, D.W. (2001) *Thienopyridine derivatives (ticlopidine, clopidogrel) versus aspirin in the secondary prevention of stroke and other important vascular events among high risk patients (Protocol for a Cochrane Review)*. The Cochrane Library. Issue 4. Oxford:Update Software.

23. Hayden, M., Pignone, M., Phillips, C. and Mulrow, C. (2002) Aspirin for the primary prevention of cardiovascular events: a summary of the evidence for the U.S. Preventive Services Task Force. *Annals of Internal Medicine* **136**(2), 161–172.

24. Heart Outcomes Prevention Evaluation Study Investigators (2000) Effects of ramipril on cardiovascular and microvascular outcomes in people with diabetes mellitus: results of the HOPE study and MICRO-HOPE substudy. *Lancet* **355**(9200), 253–259. [Full text]

25. Hooper, L., Bartlett, C., Davey-Smith, G. and Ebrahim, S. (2002) Systematic review of long term effects of advice to reduce dietary salt in adults. *British Medical Journal* **325**(7365), 628–632. [Full text]

26. Hutchinson, A., McIntosh, A., Griffiths, C.J. et al (2002) *Clinical guidelines and evidence review for type 2 diabetes. Blood pressure management*. Sheffield: ScHARR, University of Sheffield. www.shef.ac.uk/guidelines [Accessed: 20/11/2002].

27. Hypertension in Diabetes Study Group (1993) Hypertension in Diabetes Study (HDS): I. Prevalence of hypertension in newly presenting type 2 diabetic patients and the association with risk factors for cardiovascular and diabetic complications. *Journal of Hypertension* **11**(3), 309–317.

28. Jee, S.H., Miller, E.R., Guallar, E. et al (2002) The effect of magnesium supplement on blood pressure: a meta-analysis of randomized clinical trials. *American Journal of Hypertension* **15**(8), 691–696.

29. John, J.H., Ziebland, S., Yudkin, P. et al (2002) Effects of fruit and vegetable consumption on plasma antioxidant concentrations and blood pressure: a randomised controlled trial. *Lancet* **359**(9322), 1969–1974. [Full text]

30. Ko, D.T., Hebert, P.R., Coffey, C.S. et al (2002) Beta-blocker therapy and symptoms of depression, fatigue and sexual dysfunction. *Journal of the American Medical Association* **288**(3), 351–352. [Full text]

31. Lewis, E.J., Hunsicker, L.G., Clarke, W.R. et al (2001) Renoprotective effect of the angiotensin-receptor antagonist irbesartan in patients with nephropathy due to type 2 diabetes. *New England Journal of Medicine* **345**(12), 851–860. [Full text]

32. Lindholm, L.H., Ibsen, H., Dahlof, B. et al (2002) Cardiovascular morbidity and mortality in patients with diabetes in the Losartan Intervention For Endpoint reduction in hypertension study (LIFE): a randomised trial against atenolol. *Lancet* **359**(9311), 1004–1010. [Full text]

33. Little, P., Barnett, J., Barnsley, L. et al (2002a) Comparison of acceptability of and preferences for different methods of measuring methods of measuring blood pressure in primary care. *British Medical Journal* **325**(7371), 258–259. [Full text]

34. Little, P., Barnett, J., Barnsley, L. et al (2002b) Comparison of agreement between different measures of blood pressure in primary care and daytime ambulatory blood pressure. *British Medical Journal* **325**(7358), 254–260. [Full text]

35. Lotufo, P.A., Gaziano, J.M., Chae, C.U. et al (2001) Diabetes and all-cause and coronary heart disease

mortality among US male physicians. *Archives of Internal Medicine* **161**(2), 242–247. [Full text]
36. MacDonald, T.M. and Wei, L. (2003) Effect of ibuprofen on cardioprotective effect of aspirin. *Lancet* **361**(9357), 573–574. [Full text]
37. Malcolm, J., Meggison, H. and Sigal, R (2002) Cardiovascular disease in diabetes. *Clinical Evidence* **8**, 541–568.
38. Medicines Resource (1998) Stroke prevention. *Medicines Resource* **51**(Nov), 199–202.
39. MeReC (2000) Assessing cardiovascular risk (part 1). *MeReC Bulletin* **11**(7), 25–28.
40. MeReC (2002) Lifestyle measures to reduce cardiovascular risk. *MeReC Briefing* **19**(July), 1–8.
41. Mogensen, C.E., Neldam, S., Tikkanen, I. et al (2000) Randomised controlled trial of dual blockade of renin-angiotensin system in patients with hypertension, microalbuminuria, and non-insulin dependent diabetes: the candesartan and lisinopril microalbuminuria (CALM) study. *British Medical Journal* **321**(7274), 1440–1444. [Full text]
42. Murphy, M., Foster, C., Sudlow, C. et al (2002) Cardiovascular disorders. *Clinical Evidence* **7**, 91–119.
43. NICE (2002) *Management of type 2 diabetes – management of blood pressure and blood lipids.* Inherited clinical guideline H. National Institute for Clinical Excellence. www.nice.org.uk [Accessed: 28/01/2003].
44. Niskanen, L., Hedner, T., Hansson, L. et al (2001) Reduced cardiovascular morbidity and mortality in hypertensive diabetic patients on first-line therapy with an ACE inhibitor compared with a diuretic/beta-blocker-based treatment regimen: a subanalysis of the Captopril Prevention Project. *Diabetes Care* **24**(12), 2091–2096. [Full text]
45. Opie, L.H. and Schall, R. (2002) Evidence-based evaluation of calcium channel blockers for hypertension. *Journal of the American College of Cardiology* **39**(2), 315–322.
46. Pahor, M., Psaty, B.M., Alderman, M.H. et al (2000a) Health outcomes associated with calcium antagonists compared with other first-line antihypertensive therapies: a meta-analysis of randomised controlled trials. *Lancet* **356**(9246), 1949–1954. [Full text]
47. Pahor, M., Psaty, B.M., Alderman, M.H. et al (2000b) Therapeutic benefits of ACE inhibitors and other antihypertensive drugs in patients with type 2 diabetes. *Diabetes Care* **23**(7), 888–892. [Full text]
48. Parving, H.H., Lehnert, H., Brochner-Mortensen, J. et al (2001) The effect of irbesartan on the development of diabetic nephropathy in patients with type 2 diabetes. *New England Journal of Medicine* **345**(12), 870–878. [Full text]
49. Ramsay, L.E., Williams, B., Johnston, G. et al (1999) Guidelines for management of hypertension: report of the third working party of the British Hypertension Society. *Journal of Human Hypertension* **13**(9), 569–592.
50. Regional Drug and Therapeutics Centre (2002) Angiotensin II receptor antagonists in the managemen of hypertension. *Drug Update* **23**(Nov), 1–2.
51. SIGN (2002) *Hypertension in older people.* Report no 49. Scottish Intercollegiate Guidelines Network. www.sign.ac.uk [Accessed: 12/12/2002].
52. Systolic Hypertension-Europe (Syst-Eur) Trial Investigators (1997) Randomised double blind comparison of placebo and active treatment for older patients with isolated systolic hypertension. *Lancet* **350**(9080), 757–764. [Full text]
53. Tatti, P., Pahor, M., Byington, R.P. et al (1998) Outcome results of the Fosinopril Versus Amlodipine Cardiovascular Events Randomized Trial (FACET) in patients with hypertension and NIDDM. *Diabetes Care* **21**(4), 597–603. [Full text]
54. UK Prospective Diabetes Study Group (1998a) Efficac of atenolol and captopril in reducing risk of macrovascular and microvascular complications in type 2 diabetes (UKPDS 39). *British Medical Journal* **317**(7160), 713–720. [Full text]
55. UK Prospective Diabetes Study Group (1998b) Tight blood pressure control and risk of macrovascular and microvascular complications in type 2 diabetes (UKPDS 38). *British Medical Journal* **317**(7160), 703–713. [Full text]
56. Whelton, P.K., He, J., Appel, L.J. et al (2002a) Primar prevention of hypertension. *Journal of the American Medical Association* **288**(15), 1882–1888. [Full text]
57. Whelton, S.P., Chin, A., Xin, X. and He, J. (2002b) Effect of aerobic exercise on blood pressure: a meta-analysis of randomized, controlled trials. *Annals of Internal Medicine* **136**(7), 493–503.
58. WHO (1999) International Society of Hypertension guidelines for the management of hypertension. *Journal of Hypertension* **17**(2), 151–183.
59. Xin, X, He, J., Frontini, M.G. et al (2001) Effects of alcohol reduction on blood pressure: A meta-analysis of randomized controlled trials. *Hypertension* **38**(5), 1112–1117. [Full text]

Evidence grading

A Directly based on category I evidence (systematic review of randomized controlled trials or at least one randomized controlled trial)

B Directly based on category II evidence (at least one controlled study without randomization or one other type of quasi-experimental study) or extrapolated recommendation from category I evidence

C Directly based on category III evidence (non-experimental descriptive studies) or extrapolated recommendation from category I or II evidence

D Directly based on category IV evidence (expert committee reports or opinions and/or clinical experience of respected authorities) or extrapolated recommendation from category I, II, or III evidence

PRODIGY GUIDANCE

Diabetes Type 2 — blood glucose management

Last revised in October 2003
www.prodigy.nhs.uk/guidance.asp?gt=Diabetes - glycaemic control

Applies to people over the age of 16 years

This guidance is the PRODIGY implementation of the National Institute for Clinical Excellence (NICE) guideline on the *Management of Type 2 diabetes — managing blood glucose levels* and the Royal College of General Practitioners (RCGP) *Clinical Guidelines for Type 2 Diabetes: Management of blood glucose* (September 2002).

This guidance covers the management of blood glucose levels in adults with Type 2 diabetes.

This guidance does not cover the identification of undiagnosed diabetes, the management of blood glucose in people with Type 1 diabetes, or the management of the complications of Type 2 diabetes. It does not cover gestational diabetes.

There is separate PRODIGY guidance for *Diabetes Type 1 and 2 — foot disease; Diabetes Type 1 and 2 — hypertension; Diabetes Type 2 — lipid management;* and *Diabetes Type 2 — renal disease.*

D

Goals

- To maintain haemoglobin A1c (HbA1c) at or below the target set for each individual
- To reduce the acute and chronic complications associated with Type 2 diabetes
- To prevent premature diabetes-related death
- To improve quality of life
- To prevent episodes of hypoglycaemia

Contents

Scenarios
- New presentation — diet & lifestyle advice p.555
- Poor control on diet alone p.556
- Maintenance/dose adjustment on metformin &/or sulphonylurea p.558
- Poor control on maximum tolerated dose of metformin p.560
- Poor control on maximum tolerated dose of sulphonylurea p.562
- Poor control on combination therapy p.564

Extended Information, p. 566

Which scenario?

- **New presentation — diet and lifestyle advice:** covers dietary and lifestyle advice for people who have been diagnosed with Type 2 diabetes.
- **Poor control on diet alone:** provides advice on when to start treatment, and which treatment to start, in people who are no longer controlled by diet alone.
- **Maintenance/dose adjustment on metformin and/or sulphonylurea:** includes advice and prescriptions for increasing the dose of metformin or sulphonylurea, or both together.
- **Poor control on maximum tolerated dose of metformin:** covers treatment options for people whose blood glucose is no longer controlled on the maximum tolerated dose of metformin alone.
- **Poor control on maximum tolerated dose of sulphonylurea:** covers treatment options for people whose blood glucose is no longer controlled on the maximum tolerated dose of sulphonylurea alone.
- **Poor control on combination therapy:** covers treatment options for people already on a combination therapy that is not adequately controlling their blood glucose levels.

New presentation — diet and lifestyle advice

Which therapy?

- **Initial assessment** of a person with Type 2 diabetes should include a complete medical history with special emphasis on cardiovascular risk factors, nephropathy, and other diabetic complications.
- **Identify and treat other cardiovascular risk factors** as appropriate: for example, smoking, hyperlipidaemia, and hypertension (see separate PRODIGY guidance on *Coronary heart disease risk — identification and management; Diabetes Type 1 and 2 — hypertension; Diabetes Type 2 — lipid management; Diabetes Type 2 — renal disease;* and *Smoking cessation*).
- **Advise on lifestyle methods of improving diabetic control.**
  - Encourage weight loss in people who are overweight or obese (see separate PRODIGY guidance on *Obesity*).
  - Diet based on energy intake (55–60% carbohydrate, 15–20% protein, and 20–30% fat) improves diabetic control and lipid levels. The addition of dietary fibre also improves diabetic control and lipid levels.
  - Advise people to exercise regularly. Exercise can cause significant weight loss, and improve diabetic control and lipid levels.
- **Patient education** should be offered on an ongoing basis. Models of education studied and found to be equally beneficial include computer-assisted learning, telephone-delivered education, activation and involvement of the individual concerned, didactic teaching, individualized instruction, and behaviour modification.
- **Ensure that people are referred at diagnosis for dietary advice, retinal screening, and foot care.**

Follow-up advice

- **Follow up at intervals of 2–6 months;** the interval depends on the acceptability and stability of diabetic control, as assessed by the individual's target HbA1c level.

- **Set a target haemoglobin A1c (HbA1c) level between 6·5% and 7·5%,** based on the individual's risk of macrovascular and microvascular complications.

Should I refer or investigate?

Refer?

- **At diagnosis** refer to specialist diabetes service, or to dietician, podiatrist, or retinal screening service, as available.
- **Refer people who present with complications of diabetes** (e.g. nephropathy or retinopathy).
- **Refer pregnant women with diabetes, or those planning a pregnancy,** for specialist care.

Investigate?

- **Measure HbA1c at intervals of 2–6 months;** the interval depends on the acceptability and stability of diabetic control.
- **If measurement of HbA1c is not possible** because of abnormal erythrocyte turnover or haemoglobinopathy, then use blood glucose profiles, total glycated haemoglobin estimation, or both methods.
- **Other routine investigations that should be done** in people newly diagnosed with diabetes include:
  - Urine albumin or urinary albumin:creatinine ratio (ACR)
  - Serum creatinine and electrolytes
  - Thyroid function tests
  - Serum total: high-density lipoprotein (HDL) cholesterol
  - Fasting serum triglycerides

Patient information leaflets

The following PILs are available at www.prodigy.nhs.uk

- Blood Test - General
- Blood Test - Glucose
- Diabetes - Treatments for Type 2
- Diabetes Type 1 - A Summary
- Diabetes Type 2
- Diabetes Type 2 - A Summary
- Diabetes UK
- DiabeticLife

Shared decision making

- **The goals of treating diabetes** are to:
  - Keep your blood glucose level as near normal as possible.
  - Minimize your risk of complications.
  - Detect any complications as early as possible.
- **You can reduce your blood glucose level** if you:
  - Eat a healthy diet — low in fat, high in fibre, and with plenty of starchy foods, fruit, and vegetables.
  - Lose weight if you are overweight.
  - Exercise regularly. If you are able, aim to do a minimum of 30 minutes brisk walking at least 5 times a week. Anything more is even better.
- **You can reduce your risk of complications** if you:
  - Keep your blood pressure down.
  - Stop smoking if you smoke.
  - Keep your cholesterol level down.
- **You should attend a diabetes clinic regularly** for check-ups, and to detect complications early.

Drug rationale

- A non-drug prescription giving diet advice is offered.

Prescriptions

Non-drug management

Advice note: diet advice

- Age from 16 years onwards
- You may be able to control your blood sugar levels by changing your diet. Special diabetic foods are not necessary, but it is important that you eat regular meals, reduce the amount of fat and fatty foods you eat, reduce your intake of sugar and sugary foods, reduce the amount of salt in your diet, aim to eat at least five portions of fruit and vegetables every day, and keep the amount of alcohol you drink to a minimum.

Poor control on diet alone

Which therapy

- **If a person's haemoglobin A1c (HbA1c) level remains too high, or increases above their target level,** in spite of treatment with diet and lifestyle advice, start treatment with an oral hypoglycaemic agent.
- **Overweight or obese** — metformin is the first-line oral hypoglycaemic agent for people who are overweight or obese. Increase the dose slowly over several weeks to minimize gastrointestinal adverse effects.
- **Body mass index (BMI) less than 25** — either metformin or a sulphonylurea can be used first-line in people who are not overweight. It is important to remember, however, that sulphonylureas frequently cause weight gain.
- **Renal impairment** — use a sulphonylurea in people with serum creatinine greater than 130 micromol/litre.
- **Hepatic impairment** — avoid metformin in people with clinical conditions associated with poor tissue perfusion and hence tissue hypoxia (e.g. cardiac failure, hypoxia, sepsis, hepatic impairment). Metformin is contraindicated in these people due to their increased risk of lactic acidosis.
- **Manage other cardiovascular risk factors, give diet and lifestyle advice, and continue patient education.**

Practical prescribing points

For further information, please see the *Medicines Compendium* (www.medicines.org.uk) or the *British National Formulary* (www.bnf.org).

Weight gain

- **Sulphonylureas** frequently cause weight gain, and should be avoided where possible in people who are overweight or obese.

Hypoglycaemia

- **Metformin** is unlikely to produce hypoglycaemia, even in excessive doses.
- **Sulphonylureas** are known to cause hypoglycaemia, especially in older people. In order to minimize the risk of hypoglycaemia:
  - For elderly people, do not prescribe sulphonylureas with a long duration of action (e.g. chlorpropamide, glibenclamide).
  - Ensure that people are aware of the warning signs of hypoglycaemia and how to prevent it.
  - Stress the importance of regular meals, and of not missing meals.
  - Stress the importance of limiting alcohol consumption.
- The warning symptoms of a hypoglycaemic attack may be masked during concomitant treatment with a beta-

blocker. Cardioselective beta-blockers (e.g. atenolol) may be preferable.

Renal impairment

- **Metformin:** do not prescribe metformin for people with serum creatinine greater than 130 micromol/l.
- **Sulphonylureas:** there is an increased risk of hypoglycaemia in people with renal impairment. In people with mild to moderate renal impairment, use lower doses and monitor blood glucose concentration carefully. Use a sulphonylurea with a shorter duration of action (e.g. gliclazide). Avoid using sulphonylureas in severe renal impairment (serum creatinine >700 micromol/l).

Hepatic impairment

- **Metformin:** avoid in people with clinical conditions associated with poor tissue perfusion and hence tissue hypoxia (e.g. cardiac failure, hypoxia, sepsis, hepatic impairment). Metformin is contraindicated in these people due to their increased risk of lactic acidosis. Mildly elevated serum transaminase levels are not usually associated with hepatic impairment; in such people the use of metformin is unlikely to be associated with any increase in the risk of lactic acidosis.
- **Sulphonylureas:** there is an increased risk of hypoglycaemia in people with hepatic impairment. In mild to moderate hepatic impairment, use lower doses and monitor blood glucose concentration carefully. Avoid using sulphonylureas in people with severe hepatic impairment.

Follow-up advice

- **Follow up at intervals of 2–6 months;** the interval depends on the acceptability and stability of diabetic control, as assessed by the individual's target HbA1c level, and on any change in therapy.
- **Set a target HbA1c level between 6·5% and 7·5%,** based on the individual's risk of macrovascular and microvascular complications.
  - In general, the lower target HbA1c is preferred for those people at significant risk of macrovascular complications.
  - Higher targets are necessary for those at risk of iatrogenic hypoglycaemia.
  - Hypoglycaemia is unlikely with metformin therapy, but can occur with sulphonylureas.

Should I refer or investigate?

Refer?

- **Refer people with complications** (e.g. nephropathy or retinopathy).
- **Refer pregnant women with diabetes, or those planning a pregnancy,** for specialist care.

Investigate?

- **Measure HbA1c at intervals of 2–6 months;** the interval depends on the acceptability and stability of diabetic control, and on any change in therapy.
- **If measurement of HbA1c is not possible** because of abnormal erythrocyte turnover or haemoglobinopathy, then use blood glucose profiles, total glycated haemoglobin estimation, or both methods.
- **Other routine investigations should be performed annually** (unless clinically indicated more frequently), and include:
  - Urine albumin or urinary albumin:creatinine ratio (ACR)
  - Serum creatinine and electrolytes
  - Thyroid function tests
  - Serum total: high-density lipoprotein (HDL) cholesterol
  - Fasting serum triglycerides
  - Retinal screening
  - Foot care

Patient information leaflets

The following PILs are available at www.prodigy.nhs.uk

- Blood Test - General
- Blood Test - Glucose
- Diabetes - Treatments for Type 2
- Diabetes Type 1 - A Summary
- Diabetes Type 2
- Diabetes Type 2 - A Summary
- Diabetes UK
- DiabeticLife

D

Shared decision making

- **Metformin** is commonly prescribed to reduce the blood glucose level. It:
  - Is less likely to cause weight gain than some other tablets used for diabetes.
  - Is unlikely to cause hypoglycaemia.
  - May cause you to feel sick, or have mild diarrhoea, when you first start it. So, start with a low dose and build up the dose over a few weeks. Other side-effects are uncommon.
- **A sulphonylurea** such as **glibenclamide, gliclazide, glimepiride, or glipizide:**
  - Is an alternative if you are not overweight, or if you cannot take metformin.
  - May cause some weight gain. Other side-effects are uncommon.
  - May cause hypoglycaemia. This is unlikely to happen if you have regular meals, don't miss meals, and don't drink too much alcohol.
    - Symptoms of hypoglycaemia include: trembling, sweating, anxiety, blurred vision, tingling lips, paleness, mood change, vagueness, or confusion.
    - To treat hypoglycaemia: take a sugary drink or some sweets. Then eat a starchy snack, such as a sandwich.
- **You can also help to reduce your blood glucose level** if you:
  - Eat a healthy diet.
  - Lose weight if you are overweight.
  - Exercise regularly (if you are able to do so).

Drug rationale

Drugs not included

- **Chlorpropamide** is not recommended, as it has a prolonged duration of action and consequent increased risk of hypoglycaemia. It has appreciably more adverse effects than do the other sulphonylureas.
- **Tolbutamide** is not recommended; its very short half-life means that it requires frequent dosing, which may affect compliance. Its use has largely been superseded by the 'second-line' sulphonylureas, which only require a dose once or twice a day.
- **Gliquidone** is not recommended, as frequent dosing is required and it is more expensive than generically available sulphonylureas.
- **The rapid-acting insulin secretagogues, repaglinide and nateglinide,** appear no more effective than metformin or glibenclamide in terms of lowering blood glucose or HbA1c levels, but are more expensive. Repaglinide and

nateglinide are black-triangle drugs, and post-marketing data are needed to confirm their safety. There may be a limited place for their use in people with irregular mealtimes.

- **The thiazolidinediones, rosiglitazone and pioglitazone,** are not currently licensed for monotherapy and are therefore not recommended in this scenario.
- **Acarbose** is less effective than metformin or the sulphonylureas at lowering blood glucose, and is associated with a high incidence of adverse effects. It may be useful in people who are unable to tolerate any other oral treatments.

D

Drugs included

- **Metformin** is included as the first-line oral hypoglycaemic agent for overweight or obese people with Type 2 diabetes. It may also be considered as a first-line option in people who are not overweight. Prescriptions for titration of metformin dose over 3 and 6 weeks are included to minimize gastrointestinal adverse effects.
- **The sulphonylureas glibenclamide, gliclazide, glimepiride, and glipizide** have all been shown to reduce blood glucose levels and HbA1c. Prescriptions for starting doses only are included in this scenario.

Prescriptions

Start metformin (not if renal impairment)

Metformin: titrate over 3 weeks

- Age from 16 years onwards
- Metformin 500mg tablets. Take one tablet once a day for 1 week, then take one tablet twice a day for 1 week, then take one tablet three times a day; supply 63 tablets; NHS Cost £1.73.

Metformin: titrate over 6 weeks

- Age from 16 years onwards
- Metformin 500mg tablets. Take one tablet once a day for 2 weeks, then take one tablet twice a day for 2 weeks, then take one tablet three times a day; supply 84 tablets; NHS Cost £2.31.

Start sulphonylurea

Glibenclamide 5mg once a day

- Age from 16 to 65 years
- Glibenclamide 5mg tablets. Take one tablet once a day, with breakfast; supply 28 tablets; NHS Cost £1.22.

Gliclazide 40mg once a day

- Age from 16 years onwards
- Gliclazide 80mg tablets. Take half a tablet once a day, with breakfast; supply 14 tablets; NHS Cost £1.30.

Gliclazide 80mg once a day

- Age from 16 years onwards
- Gliclazide 80mg tablets. Take one tablet once a day, with breakfast; supply 28 tablets; NHS Cost £2.59.

Glimepiride 1mg once a day

- Age from 16 years onwards
- Glimepiride 1mg tablets. Take one tablet once a day; supply 30 tablets; NHS Cost £4.41.

Glipizide 2.5mg once a day

- Age from 16 years onwards
- Glipizide 2.5mg tablets. Take one tablet once a day, before breakfast; supply 28 tablets; NHS Cost £1.48.

Glipizide 5mg once a day

- Age from 16 to 65 years
- Glipizide 5mg tablets. Take one tablet once a day, before breakfast; supply 28 tablets; NHS Cost £2.00.

Maintenance/dose adjustment on metformin and/or sulphonylurea

Which therapy

- **If blood glucose control is adequate on current treatment:**
  - Continue current treatment and review every 2–6 months, according to acceptability and stability of control.
- **If haemoglobin A1c (HbA1c) level remains too high, or increases above the target level:**
  - Ensure that compliance to current treatment is optimum.
  - Increase the dose of metformin or the sulphonylurea.
- **Manage other cardiovascular risk factors, give diet and lifestyle advice, and continue patient education.**

Practical prescribing points

For further information, please see the *Medicines Compendium* (www.medicines.org.uk) or the *British National Formulary* (www.bnf.org).

Weight gain

- **Sulphonylureas** frequently cause weight gain, and should be avoided if possible in people who are overweight or obese.

Hypoglycaemia

- **Metformin** is unlikely to produce hypoglycaemia, even in excessive doses.
- **Sulphonylureas** are known to cause hypoglycaemia, especially in older people. In order to minimize the risk of hypoglycaemia:
  - For elderly people, do not prescribe sulphonylureas with a long duration of action (e.g. chlorpropamide, glibenclamide)
  - Ensure that people are aware of the warning signs of hypoglycaemia and how to prevent it
  - Stress the importance of regular meals, and of not missing meals
  - Stress the importance of limiting alcohol consumption
- **The warning symptoms of a hypoglycaemic attack may be masked during concomitant treatment with a beta-blocker.** Cardioselective beta-blockers (e.g. atenolol) may be preferable.

Renal impairment

- **Metformin:** do not prescribe metformin for people with serum creatinine greater than 130 micromol/l.
- **Sulphonylureas:** there is an increased risk of hypoglycaemia in people with renal impairment. In people with mild to moderate renal impairment, use lower doses and monitor blood glucose concentration carefully. Use a sulphonylurea with a shorter duration of action (e.g. gliclazide). Avoid using sulphonylureas in severe renal impairment (serum creatinine >700 micromol/l).

Hepatic impairment

- **Metformin:** avoid in people with clinical conditions associated with poor tissue perfusion and hence tissue hypoxia (e.g. cardiac failure, hypoxia, sepsis, hepatic impairment). Metformin is contraindicated in these people due to their increased risk of lactic acidosis. Mildly elevated serum transaminase levels are not usually associated with hepatic impairment; in such

people the use of metformin is unlikely to be associated with any increase in the risk of lactic acidosis.
- **Sulphonylureas:** there is an increased risk of hypoglycaemia in people with hepatic impairment. In mild to moderate hepatic impairment, use lower doses and monitor blood glucose concentration carefully. Avoid using sulphonylureas in people with severe hepatic impairment.

Follow-up advice

- **Follow-up should be at intervals of 2–6 months;** the interval depends on the acceptability and stability of diabetic control, as assessed by the individual's target HbA1c level, and on any change in therapy.
- **For each individual, a target HbA1c level should be set between 6·5% and 7·5%,** based on the risk of macrovascular and microvascular complications.
  - In general, the lower target HbA1c is preferred for those people at significant risk of macrovascular complications, but higher targets are necessary for those at risk of iatrogenic hypoglycaemia. Hypoglycaemia is unlikely with metformin therapy, but can occur with sulphonylureas.

Should I refer or investigate?

Refer?

- **It is unlikely to be necessary to refer people for management of the doses of their oral hypoglycaemic agents,** as this can normally be achieved in primary care. People with diabetic complications (e.g. nephropathy or retinopathy) should be referred to the appropriate specialist.
- **Pregnant women with diabetes, or those planning a pregnancy,** should be referred for specialist care.

Investigate?

- **Haemoglobin A1c (HbA1c) should be measured at 2–6-monthly intervals;** the interval depends on the acceptability and stability of diabetic control, and any change in therapy.
- **If measurement of HbA1c is not possible** because of abnormal erythrocyte turnover or haemoglobinopathy, then use blood glucose profiles, total glycated haemoglobin estimation, or both methods.
- **Other routine investigations should be performed annually** (unless clinically indicated more frequently) and include:
  - Urine albumin or urinary albumin:creatinine ratio (ACR)
  - Serum creatinine and electrolytes
  - Thyroid function tests
  - Serum total: high-density lipoprotein (HDL) cholesterol
  - Fasting serum triglycerides
  - Retinal screening

Patient information leaflets

The following PILs are available at www.prodigy.nhs.uk

- Blood Test - General
- Blood Test - Glucose
- Diabetes - Treatments for Type 2
- Diabetes Type 1 - A Summary
- Diabetes Type 2
- Diabetes Type 2 - A Summary
- Diabetes UK
- DiabeticLife

Shared decision making

- **Metformin,** or a sulphonylurea medicine such as **glibenclamide, gliclazide, glimepiride, or glipizide,** are commonly prescribed to reduce the blood glucose level.
- **The dose may need to be increased** if your blood glucose is not controlled with a lower dose.
- **Sulphonylureas may cause hypoglycaemia.** This is unlikely to happen if you have regular meals, don't miss meals, and don't drink too much alcohol.
  - Symptoms of hypoglycaemia include: trembling, sweating, anxiety, blurred vision, tingling lips, paleness, mood change, vagueness, or confusion.
  - To treat hypoglycaemia: take a sugary drink or some sweets. Then eat a starchy snack, such as a sandwich.
- **You can also help to reduce your blood glucose level** if you:
  - Eat a healthy diet.
  - Lose weight if you are overweight.
  - Exercise regularly (if you are able to do so).

Drug rationale

Drugs not included

- **Chlorpropamide** is not recommended, as it has a prolonged duration of action and consequent increased risk of hypoglycaemia. It has appreciably more adverse effects than the other sulphonylureas.
- **Tolbutamide** is not recommended; its very short half-life means that it requires frequent dosing, which may affect compliance. Its use has largely been superseded by the 'second-line' sulphonylureas, which only require a dose once or twice a day.
- **Gliquidone** is not recommended, as frequent dosing is required and it is more expensive than generically available sulphonylureas.
- **The rapid acting insulin secretagogues, repaglinide and nateglinide,** are no more effective than metformin or glibenclamide in terms of lowering blood glucose levels or HbA1c levels, but are more expensive. Repaglinide and nateglinide are black-triangle drugs, and post-marketing data are needed to confirm their safety. There may be a limited place for their use in people with irregular mealtimes.

Drugs included

- **Metformin** is offered at doses of up to 3000 mg daily. Gastrointestinal adverse effects may persist with very high doses, so metformin is not usually prescribed in doses above 2000 mg daily.
- **The sulphonylureas glibenclamide, gliclazide, glimepiride, and glipizide** are all offered at doses up to the maximum licensed dose.

Prescriptions

Metformin: maintenance and dose adjustment

Metformin 500mg three times a day
- Age from 16 years onwards
- Metformin 500mg tablets. Take one tablet three times a day; supply 84 tablets; NHS Cost £2.31.

Metformin 850mg twice a day
- Age from 16 years onwards
- Metformin 850mg tablets. Take one tablet twice a day; supply 56 tablets; NHS Cost £2.37.

Metformin 1000mg twice a day
- Age from 16 years onwards
- Metformin 500mg tablets. Take two tablets twice a day; supply 112 tablets; NHS Cost £3.08.

Metformin 850mg three times a day
- Age from 16 years onwards
- Metformin 850mg tablets. Take one tablet three times a day; supply 84 tablets; NHS Cost £3.56.

Metformin 1000mg three times a day
- Age from 16 years onwards
- Metformin 500mg tablets. Take two tablets three times a day; supply 168 tablets; NHS Cost £4.62.

Glibenclamide: maintenance and dose adjustment

Glibenclamide 5mg once a day
- Age from 16 to 65 years
- Glibenclamide 5mg tablets. Take one tablet once a day, with breakfast; supply 28 tablets; NHS Cost £1.22.

Glibenclamide 10mg once a day
- Age from 16 to 65 years
- Glibenclamide 5mg tablets. Take two tablets once a day, with breakfast; supply 56 tablets; NHS Cost £2.44.

Glibenclamide 15mg once a day
- Age from 16 to 65 years
- Glibenclamide 5mg tablets. Take three tablets once a day, with breakfast; supply 84 tablets; NHS Cost £3.66.

Gliclazide: maintenance and dose adjustment

Gliclazide 40mg once a day
- Age from 16 years onwards
- Gliclazide 80mg tablets. Take half a tablet once a day, with breakfast; supply 14 tablets; NHS Cost £1.30.

Gliclazide 80mg once a day
- Age from 16 years onwards
- Gliclazide 80mg tablets. Take one tablet once a day with breakfast; supply 28 tablets; NHS Cost £2.59.

Gliclazide 120mg once a day
- Age from 16 years onwards
- Gliclazide 80mg tablets. Take one and a half tablets once a day, with breakfast; supply 42 tablets; NHS Cost £3.90.

Gliclazide 160mg once a day
- Age from 16 years onwards
- Gliclazide 80mg tablets. Take two tablets once a day, with breakfast; supply 56 tablets; NHS Cost £5.18.

Gliclazide 80mg twice a day
- Age from 16 years onwards
- Gliclazide 80mg tablets. Take one tablet twice a day, at mealtimes; supply 56 tablets; NHS Cost £5.18.

Gliclazide 120mg twice a day
- Age from 16 years onwards
- Gliclazide 80mg tablets. Take one and a half tablets twice a day, at mealtimes; supply 84 tablets; NHS Cost £7.27.

Gliclazide 160mg twice a day
- Age from 16 years onwards
- Gliclazide 80mg tablets. Take two tablets twice a day, at mealtimes; supply 112 tablets; NHS Cost £10.36.

Glimepiride: maintenance and dose adjustment

Glimepiride 1mg once a day
- Age from 16 years onwards
- Glimepiride 1mg tablets. Take one tablet once a day; supply 30 tablets; NHS Cost £4.41.

Glimepiride 2mg once a day
- Age from 16 years onwards
- Glimepiride 2mg tablets. Take one tablet once a day; supply 30 tablets; NHS Cost £7.25.

Glimepiride 3mg once a day
- Age from 16 years onwards
- Glimepiride 3mg tablets. Take one tablet once a day; supply 30 tablets; NHS Cost £10.94.

Glimepiride 4mg once a day
- Age from 16 years onwards
- Glimepiride 4mg tablets. Take one tablet once a day; supply 30 tablets; NHS Cost £14.49.

Glipizide: maintenance and dose adjustment

Glipizide 2.5mg once a day
- Age from 16 years onwards
- Glipizide 2.5mg tablets. Take one tablet once a day, before breakfast; supply 28 tablets; NHS Cost £1.48.

Glipizide 5mg once a day
- Age from 16 years onwards
- Glipizide 5mg tablets. Take one tablet once a day, before breakfast; supply 28 tablets; NHS Cost £2.00.

Glipizide 7.5mg once a day
- Age from 16 years onwards
- Glipizide 5mg tablets. Take one tablet once a day, before breakfast; supply 28 tablets; NHS Cost £2.00.
- Glipizide 2.5mg tablets. Take one tablet once a day, before breakfast; supply 28 tablets; NHS Cost £1.48.

Glipizide 10mg once a day
- Age from 16 years onwards
- Glipizide 5mg tablets. Take two tablets once a day, before breakfast; supply 56 tablets; NHS Cost £4.58.

Glipizide 12.5mg once a day
- Age from 16 years onwards
- Glipizide 2.5mg tablets. Take one tablet once a day, before breakfast; supply 28 tablets; NHS Cost £1.48.
- Glipizide 5mg tablets. Take two tablets once a day, before breakfast; supply 56 tablets; NHS Cost £4.58.

Glipizide 15mg once a day
- Age from 16 years onwards
- Glipizide 5mg tablets. Take three tablets once a day, before breakfast; supply 84 tablets; NHS Cost £6.58.

Glipizide 10mg twice a day
- Age from 16 years onwards
- Glipizide 5mg tablets. Take two tablets twice a day; supply 112 tablets; NHS Cost £9.16.

Poor control on maximum tolerated dose of metformin

Which therapy

- **If haemoglobin A1c (HbA1c) level remains too high, or increases above the target level,** in spite of treatment with the maximum tolerated dose of metformin:
  - Ensure that compliance to current treatment is optimum.
  - If there are no contraindications to a sulphonylurea, add a sulphonylurea to metformin.
  - If a sulphonylurea is contraindicated, or not tolerated, add a glitazone to the metformin.
- **Manage other cardiovascular risk factors, give diet and lifestyle advice, and continue patient education.**

Practical prescribing points

For further information, please see the *Medicines Compendium* (www.medicines.org.uk) or the *British National Formulary* (www.bnf.org).

Weight gain

- **Sulphonylureas** frequently cause weight gain, and should be avoided where possible in people who are overweight or obese.
- **Both rosiglitazone and pioglitazone are associated with significant weight gain** (similar to that seen with the

sulphonylureas), probably because of fluid retention. This is increased in combination with a sulphonylurea.

Hypoglycaemia

- **Metformin** is unlikely to produce hypoglycaemia, even in excessive doses.
- **Hypoglycaemia may be experienced by people taking sulphonylureas or glitazones,** especially older people. In order to minimize the risk of hypoglycaemia:
  - For elderly people, do not prescribe sulphonylureas with a long duration of action (e.g. chlorpropamide, glibenclamide).
  - Ensure that people are aware of the warning signs of hypoglycaemia and how to prevent it.
  - Stress the importance of regular meals, and of not missing meals.
  - Stress the importance of limiting alcohol consumption.
- **The warning symptoms of a hypoglycaemic attack may be masked during concomitant treatment with a beta-blocker.** Cardioselective beta-blockers (e.g. atenolol) may be preferable.

Renal impairment

- **Metformin:** do not prescribe metformin for people with serum creatinine greater than 130 micromol/l.
- **Sulphonylureas:** there is an increased risk of hypoglycaemia in people with renal impairment. In people with mild to moderate renal impairment, use lower doses and monitor blood glucose concentration carefully. Use a sulphonylurea with a shorter duration of action (e.g. gliclazide). Avoid using sulphonylureas in severe renal impairment (serum creatinine >700 micromol/l).

Hepatic impairment

- **Metformin:** avoid in people with clinical conditions associated with poor tissue perfusion and hence tissue hypoxia (e.g. cardiac failure, hypoxia, sepsis, hepatic impairment). Metformin is contraindicated in these people due to their increased risk of lactic acidosis. Mildly elevated serum transaminase levels are not usually associated with hepatic impairment; in such people the use of metformin is unlikely to be associated with any increase in the risk of lactic acidosis.
- **Sulphonylureas:** there is an increased risk of hypoglycaemia in people with hepatic impairment. In mild to moderate hepatic impairment, use lower doses and monitor blood glucose concentration carefully. Avoid using sulphonylureas in people with severe hepatic impairment.
- **Assess liver function before starting treatment** with rosiglitazone or pioglitazone, every two months for the first year, and periodically thereafter [RCGP, 2002]. Do not start treatment if ALT is greater than 2.5 times the upper limit of normal.
  - Advise people to seek immediate medical attention if symptoms such as nausea, vomiting, abdominal pain fatigue, or dark urine develop. Stop the glitazone if jaundice develops.

Fluid retention and heart failure

- **Rosiglitazone and pioglitazone are contraindicated in people with cardiac failure or a history of cardiac failure** (NYHA stages I to IV).
- **Rosiglitazone and pioglitazone can cause fluid retention.** Monitor people for signs and symptoms of heart failure and stop the glitazone if any deterioration in cardiac function is seen.
- **The glitazones are contraindicated in combination with insulin,** as an increase in heart failure has been observed with this combination.

Follow-up advice

- **Follow-up at intervals of 2–6 months;** the interval depends on the acceptability and stability of diabetic control, as assessed by the individual's target HbA1c level, and on any change in therapy.
- **Set a target HbA1c level between 6·5% and 7·5%,** based on the risk of macrovascular and microvascular complications.
  - The lower target HbA1c is preferred for those people at significant risk of macrovascular complications.
  - Higher targets are necessary for those at risk of iatrogenic hypoglycaemia.

D

Should I refer or investigate?

Refer?

- **Refer people with diabetic complications** (e.g. nephropathy or retinopathy) to the appropriate specialist.
- **Refer pregnant women with diabetes, or those planning a pregnancy,** for specialist care.
- **It is not usually necessary to refer people without complications** for management of the doses of their oral hypoglycaemic agents, as this can normally be achieved in primary care.

Investigate?

- **Measure haemoglobin A1c (HbA1c) at intervals of 2–6 months;** the interval depends on the acceptability and stability of diabetic control, and on any change in therapy.
- **If measurement of HbA1c is not possible** because of abnormal erythrocyte turnover or haemoglobinopathy, then use blood glucose profiles, total glycated haemoglobin estimation, or both methods.
- **Other routine investigations should be performed annually** (unless clinically indicated more frequently) and include:
  - Urine albumin or urinary albumin:creatinine ratio (ACR)
  - Serum creatinine and electrolytes
  - Thyroid function tests
  - Serum total: high-density lipoprotein (HDL) cholesterol
  - Fasting serum triglycerides
  - Retinal screening
  - Foot care

Patient information leaflets

The following PILs are available at www.prodigy.nhs.uk

- Blood Test - General
- Blood Test - Glucose
- Diabetes - Treatments for Type 2
- Diabetes Type 1 - A Summary
- Diabetes Type 2
- Diabetes Type 2 - A Summary
- Diabetes UK
- DiabeticLife

Shared decision making

- **Your blood glucose is not well controlled** although you are taking the maximum dose of metformin.

- **Adding a second medicine will reduce your blood glucose level further.**
- **Adding a sulphonylurea** medicine such as **glibenclamide, gliclazide, glimepiride, or glipizide** is one option. Sulphonylureas:
  - May cause some weight gain, but other side-effects are uncommon.
  - May cause hypoglycaemia. This is unlikely to happen if you have regular meals, don't miss meals, and don't drink too much alcohol.
    - Symptoms of hypoglycaemia include: trembling, sweating, anxiety, blurred vision, tingling lips, paleness, mood change, vagueness, or confusion.
    - To treat hypoglycaemia: take a sugary drink or some sweets. Then eat a starchy snack, such as a sandwich.
- **Rosiglitazone** or **pioglitazone** are other options. These:
  - Have a slight risk of causing liver damage. So, you will need a blood test to check on your liver function before starting treatment, and from time to time afterwards.
  - May cause some weight gain, but other possible side-effects are uncommon.
  - May cause hypoglycaemia. This is unlikely to happen if you have regular meals, don't miss meals, and don't drink too much alcohol.
    - Symptoms of hypoglycaemia include: trembling, sweating, anxiety, blurred vision, tingling lips, paleness, mood change, vagueness, or confusion.
    - To treat hypoglycaemia: take a sugary drink or some sweets. Then eat a starchy snack, such as a sandwich.
- **You can also help to reduce your blood glucose level** if you:
  - Eat a healthy diet.
  - Lose weight if you are overweight.
  - Exercise regularly (if you are able to do so).

Drug rationale

Drugs not included

- **Chlorpropamide** is not recommended, as it has a prolonged duration of action and consequent increased risk of hypoglycaemia. It has appreciably more adverse effects than do the other sulphonylureas [BNF 45, 2003].
- **Tolbutamide** is not recommended, as its use has largely been superseded by the 'second-line' sulphonylureas.
- **Gliquidone** is not recommended, as frequent dosing is required and it is more expensive than generically available sulphonylureas.
- **The rapid-acting insulin secretagogues, repaglinide and nateglinide,** are no more effective than glibenclamide in terms of lowering blood glucose levels or HbA1c levels, but are more expensive. Repaglinide and nateglinide are black-triangle drugs, and post-marketing data are needed to confirm their safety. There may be a limited place for their use in people with irregular mealtimes.
- **Acarbose** is less effective than metformin or the sulphonylureas at lowering blood glucose, and is associated with a high incidence of adverse effects. It may be useful in people who are unable to tolerate any other oral treatments.

Drugs included

- **Sulphonylureas in combination with metformin** reduce blood glucose levels and HbA1c. Prescriptions for starting doses of glibenclamide, gliclazide, glimepiride, and glipizide are included in this scenario.
- **The glitazones, rosiglitazone and pioglitazone,** are included in this scenario as an alternative to a sulphonylurea, when a sulphonylurea is contraindicated or not tolerated. Prescriptions for starting doses are included.

Prescriptions

1st line: add sulphonylurea (starting doses)

Glibenclamide 5mg once a day
- Age from 16 to 65 years
- Glibenclamide 5mg tablets. Take one tablet once a day, with breakfast; supply 28 tablets; NHS Cost £1.22.

Gliclazide 40mg once a day
- Age from 16 years onwards
- Gliclazide 80mg tablets. Take half a tablet once a day, with breakfast; supply 14 tablets; NHS Cost £1.30.

Gliclazide 80mg once a day
- Age from 16 years onwards
- Gliclazide 80mg tablets. Take one tablet once a day, with breakfast; supply 28 tablets; NHS Cost £2.59.

Glimepiride 1mg once a day
- Age from 16 years onwards
- Glimepiride 1mg tablets. Take one tablet once a day; supply 28 tablets; NHS Cost £2.63.

Glipizide 2.5mg once a day
- Age from 16 years onwards
- Glipizide 2.5mg tablets. Take one tablet once a day, before breakfast; supply 28 tablets; NHS Cost £1.48.

Glipizide 5mg once a day
- Age from 16 to 65 years
- Glipizide 5mg tablets. Take one tablet once a day, before breakfast; supply 28 tablets; NHS Cost £1.58.

Alternative: add glitazone (starting doses)

Rosiglitazone 4mg once a day
- Age from 16 years onwards
- Rosiglitazone 4mg tablets. Take one tablet once a day; supply 28 tablet; NHS Cost £26.60.

Pioglitazone 15mg once a day
- Age from 16 years onwards
- Pioglitazone 15mg tablets. Take one tablet once a day; supply 28 tablet; NHS Cost £26.60.

Pioglitazone 30mg once a day
- Age from 16 years onwards
- Pioglitazone 30mg tablets. Take one tablet once a day; supply 28 tablet; NHS Cost £36.96.

Poor control on maximum tolerated dose of sulphonylurea

Which therapy

- **If haemoglobin A1c (HbA1c) level remains too high, or increases above the target level,** in spite of treatment with the maximum tolerated dose of the sulphonylurea:
  - Ensure that compliance to current treatment is optimum.
  - If there are no contraindications to metformin, add metformin to the sulphonylurea.
  - If metformin is contraindicated, or not tolerated, add a glitazone to the sulphonylurea.
- **Manage other cardiovascular risk factors, give diet and lifestyle advice, and continue patient education.**

Practical prescribing points

For further information, please see the *Medicines Compendium* (www.medicines.org.uk) or the *British National Formulary* (www.bnf.org).

Metformin

- **Metformin is unlikely to produce hypoglycaemia,** even in excessive doses (although there may be weight gain when it is combined with a sulphonylurea).
- **Do not prescribe metformin for people with serum creatinine greater than 130 micromol/l,** or in people with clinical conditions associated with poor tissue perfusion and hence tissue hypoxia (e.g. cardiac failure, hypoxia, sepsis, hepatic impairment). Metformin is contraindicated in these people due to their increased risk of lactic acidosis. Mildly elevated serum transaminase levels are not usually associated with hepatic impairment; in such people the use of metformin is unlikely to be associated with any increase in the risk of lactic acidosis.
- **Gastrointestinal adverse effects are common** when starting treatment with metformin. To minimize these effects, increase the dose slowly over several weeks [BNF 45, 2003].

Glitazones

- **Assess liver function before starting treatment** with rosiglitazone or pioglitazone, every two months for the first year, and periodically thereafter [RCGP, 2002]. Do not start treatment if ALT is greater than 2.5 times the upper limit of normal.
  - Advise people to seek immediate medical attention if symptoms such as nausea, vomiting, abdominal pain fatigue, or dark urine develop. Stop the glitazone if jaundice develops.
- **Rosiglitazone and pioglitazone are contraindicated in people with cardiac failure or a history of cardiac failure** (NYHA stages I to IV).
  - Rosiglitazone and pioglitazone can cause fluid retention, which may exacerbate or precipitate heart failure, especially in people with a history of heart failure, in the elderly, or in people with mild to moderate renal failure.
  - People should be monitored for signs and symptoms of heart failure, and the thiazolidinedione should be stopped if any deterioration in cardiac function is seen.
  - Concomitant prescription of a nonsteroidal anti inflammatory drug (NSAID) may increase the risk of oedema.
- **The thiazolidinediones are contraindicated in combination with insulin,** as an increase in heart failure has been observed with this combination.
- **Both rosiglitazone and pioglitazone are associated with significant weight gain** (similar to that seen with the sulphonylureas), probably because of fluid retention. This is increased in combination with a sulphonylurea.
- **Hypoglycaemia may be experienced by people taking rosiglitazone or pioglitazone.** In order to minimize the risk of hypoglycaemia:
  - Ensure that people are aware of the warning signs of hypoglycaemia, and how to prevent it.
  - Stress the importance of regular meals, and of not missing meals.
  - Stress the importance of limiting alcohol consumption.
- **The warning symptoms of a hypoglycaemic attack may be masked during concomitant treatment with a beta-blocker.** Cardioselective beta-blockers (e.g. atenolol) may be preferable.

Follow-up advice

- **Follow up at intervals of 2–6 months;** the interval depends on the acceptability and stability of diabetic control, as assessed by the individual's target HbA1c level, and on any change in therapy.
- **Set a target HbA1c level between 6·5% and 7·5%,** based on the individual's risk of macrovascular and microvascular complications.
  - The lower target HbA1c is preferred for those people at significant risk of macrovascular complications
  - Higher targets are necessary for those at risk of iatrogenic hypoglycaemia.
- **Glitazones:** monitor liver function before treatment, then every 2 months for the first year, then periodically thereafter. Stop treatment if ALT levels are 3 times upper limit of normal.

Should I refer or investigate?

D

Refer?

- **People with diabetic complications** (e.g. nephropathy or retinopathy) should be referred to the appropriate specialist.
- **Pregnant women with diabetes, or those planning a pregnancy,** should be referred for specialist care.
- **It is not usually necessary to refer people for management of the doses** of their oral hypoglycaemic agents, as this can normally be achieved in primary care.

Investigate?

- **Measure haemoglobin A1c (HbA1c) at intervals of 2–6 months;** the interval depends on the acceptability and stability of diabetic control, and on any change in therapy.
- **If measurement of HbA1c is not possible** because of abnormal erythrocyte turnover or haemoglobinopathy, then use blood glucose profiles, total glycated haemoglobin estimation, or both methods.
- **Other routine investigations should be performed annually** (unless clinically indicated more frequently) and include:
  - Urine albumin or urinary albumin:creatinine ratio (ACR)
  - Serum creatinine and electrolytes
  - Thyroid function tests
  - Serum total: high-density lipoprotein (HDL) cholesterol
  - Fasting serum triglycerides
  - Retinal screening
  - Foot care

Patient information leaflets

The following PILs are available at www.prodigy.nhs.uk

- Blood Test - General
- Blood Test - Glucose
- Diabetes - Treatments for Type 2
- Diabetes Type 1 - A Summary
- Diabetes Type 2
- Diabetes Type 2 - A Summary
- Diabetes UK
- DiabeticLife

Shared decision making

- **Your blood glucose is not well controlled** although you are taking the maximum dose of a sulphonylurea.
- **Adding a second medicine will reduce your blood glucose level further.**
- **Metformin** is one option. When you first start metformin, it:
  - May cause you to feel sick, or have mild diarrhoea. So, start with a low dose and build up the dose over a few weeks. Other side-effects are uncommon.
- **Rosiglitazone** or **pioglitazone** are other options. These:

- Have a slight risk of causing liver damage. So, you will need a blood test to check on your liver function before starting treatment, and from time to time afterwards.
- May cause some weight gain, but other possible side-effects are uncommon.
- May cause hypoglycaemia. This is unlikely to happen if you: have regular meals, don't miss meals, and don't drink too much alcohol.
  - Symptoms of hypoglycaemia include: trembling, sweating, anxiety, blurred vision, tingling lips, paleness, mood change, vagueness, or confusion.
  - To treat hypoglycaemia: take a sugary drink or some sweets. Then eat a starchy snack, such as a sandwich.

- **You can also help to reduce your blood glucose level** if you:
  - Eat a healthy diet.
  - Lose weight if you are overweight.
  - Exercise regularly (if you are able to do so).

Drug rationale

Drugs not included

- **The rapid-acting insulin secretagogues, repaglinide and nateglinide,** are no more effective than metformin or glibenclamide in terms of lowering blood glucose levels or HbA1c levels, but are more expensive. Repaglinide and nateglinide are black-triangle drugs, and post-marketing data are needed to confirm their safety. There may be a limited place for their use in people with irregular mealtimes.
- **Acarbose** is less effective than metformin or the sulphonylureas at lowering blood glucose, and is associated with a high incidence of adverse effects. It may be useful in people who are unable to tolerate any other oral treatments.

Drugs included

- **Metformin** in combination with a sulphonylurea reduces blood glucose and HbA1c. Prescriptions for titration of metformin dose over 3 and 6 weeks are included to minimize adverse gastrointestinal adverse effects.
- **Rosiglitazone and pioglitazone** are licensed for use in combination with a sulphonylurea in people who are unable to tolerate metformin with a sulphonylurea [RCGP, 2002]. Starting doses of rosiglitazone and pioglitazone are offered.

Prescriptions

1st line: add metformin (not if renal impairment)

Metformin: titrate over 3 weeks

- Age from 16 years onwards
- Metformin 500mg tablets. Take one tablet once a day for 1 week, then take one tablet twice a day for 1 week, then take one tablet three times a day; supply 63 tablets; NHS Cost £1.73.

Metformin: titrate over 6 weeks

- Age from 16 years onwards
- Metformin 500mg tablets. Take one tablet once a day for 2 weeks, then take one tablet twice a day for 2 weeks, then take one tablet three times a day; supply 84 tablets; NHS Cost £2.31.

Alternative: add glitazone (starting doses)

Rosiglitazone 4mg once a day

- Age from 16 years onwards
- Rosiglitazone 4mg tablets. Take one tablet once a day; supply 28 tablet; NHS Cost £26.60.

Pioglitazone 15mg once a day

- Age from 16 years onwards
- Pioglitazone 15mg tablets. Take one tablet once a day; supply 28 tablet; NHS Cost £26.60.

Pioglitazone 30mg once a day

- Age from 16 years onwards
- Pioglitazone 30mg tablets. Take one tablet once a day; supply 28 tablet; NHS Cost £36.96.

Poor control on combination therapy

Which therapy

- **Ensure that compliance to current treatment is optimum.**
- **If not on maximum tolerated doses of dual combination therapy with oral hypoglycaemics, adjust dose to maximum tolerated.**
- **If on maximum tolerated doses of dual combination therapy with oral hypoglycaemics,** consider starting insulin treatment. The choice of insulin preparation will depend largely on local experience and the preference of the individual.
- **Manage other cardiovascular risk factors, give diet and lifestyle advice, and continue patient education.**

Practical prescribing points

For further information, please see the *Medicines Compendium* (www.medicines.org.uk) or the *British National Formulary* (www.bnf.org).

- **Assess liver function before starting treatment with rosiglitazone or pioglitazone,** every two months for the first year, and periodically thereafter [RCGP, 2002]. Do not start treatment if ALT is greater than 2.5 times the upper limit of normal.
  - Advise people to seek immediate medical attention if symptoms such as nausea, vomiting, abdominal pain fatigue, or dark urine develop. Stop the glitazone if jaundice develops.
- **Rosiglitazone and pioglitazone can cause fluid retention,** which may exacerbate or precipitate heart failure. Monitor people for signs and symptoms of heart failure and stop the glitazone if any deterioration in cardiac function is seen.
- **The thiazolidinediones are contraindicated in combination with insulin,** as an increase in heart failure has been observed with this combination.
- **Both rosiglitazone and pioglitazone are associated with significant weight gain** (similar to that seen with the sulphonylureas), probably because of fluid retention. Weight gain is increased in combination with a sulphonylurea.
- **Hypoglycaemia may be experienced by people taking rosiglitazone or pioglitazone.** In order to minimize the risk of hypoglycaemia:
  - Ensure that people are aware of the warning signs of hypoglycaemia, and how to prevent it.
  - Stress the importance of regular meals, and of not missing meals.
  - Stress the importance of limiting alcohol consumption.
- **The warning symptoms of a hypoglycaemic attack may be masked during concomitant treatment with a beta-**

blocker. Cardioselective beta-blockers (e.g. atenolol) may be preferable.
- **If a glitazone is prescribed to replace** one glucose-lowering drug being used in combination with another, the withdrawal of one agent coupled with the slow onset of effectiveness of the licensed glitazone can result in a temporary but marked deterioration in blood glucose control.

Follow-up advice

- **If oral therapy only is continuing, follow up at intervals of 2–6 months;** the interval depends on the acceptability and stability of diabetic control, as assessed by the individual's target haemoglobin A1c (HbA1c) level, and on any change in therapy.
- **If insulin therapy is starting, tailor follow-up to the individual person.** Initially this follow-up should be daily (some of this may be by telephone) while the person is becoming accustomed to managing insulin. Once the person is able to manage insulin on a daily basis, to monitor the blood glucose level, and to adjust the insulin dose appropriately, then follow up at intervals of 2–6 months. The interval depends on the acceptability and stability of diabetic control, as assessed by the individual's target HbA1c level, and on any change in therapy.
- **Set a target HbA1c level between 6·5% and 7·5%,** based on the individual's risk of macrovascular and microvascular complications.
  - The lower target HbA1c is preferred for those people at significant risk of macrovascular complications.
  - Higher targets are necessary for those at risk of iatrogenic hypoglycaemia.
- **Glitazones:** monitor liver function before treatment, then every 2 months for the first year, then periodically thereafter. Stop treatment if ALT levels are 3 times upper limit of normal.

Should I refer or investigate?

Refer?

- **The initiation and management of insulin therapy may take place in primary care,** depending on the level of expertise in the primary care team. In some circumstances, however, the person may need to be referred to secondary care.
- **Refer people with diabetic complications** (e.g. nephropathy or retinopathy) to the appropriate specialist.
- **Refer pregnant women with diabetes, or those planning a pregnancy,** for specialist care.
- **It is not usually necessary to refer people for management** of their oral hypoglycaemic agents, as this can normally be done in primary care.

Investigate?

- **Measure HbA1c at intervals of 2–6 months;** the interval depends on the acceptability and stability of diabetic control, and on any change in therapy.
- **If measurement of HbA1c is not possible** because of abnormal erythrocyte turnover or haemoglobinopathy, then use blood glucose profiles, total glycated haemoglobin estimation, or both methods.
- **Other routine investigations should be performed annually** (unless clinically indicated more frequently) and include:
  - Urine albumin or urinary albumin:creatinine ratio (ACR)
  - Serum creatinine and electrolytes
  - Thyroid function tests
  - Serum total: high-density lipoprotein (HDL) cholesterol
  - Fasting serum triglycerides
  - Retinal screening
  - Foot care

Patient information leaflets

The following PILs are available at www.prodigy.nhs.uk

- Blood Test - General
- Blood Test - Glucose
- Diabetes - Treatments for Type 2
- Diabetes Type 1 - A Summary
- Diabetes Type 2
- Diabetes Type 2 - A Summary
- Diabetes UK
- DiabeticLife

Shared decision making

- **If needed, medicines can be combined** to control your blood glucose level.
- **Metformin:**
  - Can be taken in addition to a sulphonylurea, a glitazone, or insulin.
  - May cause you to feel sick, or have mild diarrhoea when you first start it. So, start with a low dose and build up the dose over a few weeks. Other side-effects are uncommon.
- **A sulphonylurea** such as **glibenclamide, gliclazide, glimepiride, or glipizide:**
  - Can be combined with metformin, a glitazone, or insulin.
  - May cause some weight gain, but other side-effects are uncommon.
  - May cause hypoglycaemia. This is unlikely to happen if you have regular meals, don't miss meals, and don't drink too much alcohol.
    - Symptoms of hypoglycaemia include: trembling, sweating, anxiety, blurred vision, tingling lips, paleness, mood change, vagueness, or confusion.
    - To treat hypoglycaemia: take a sugary drink or some sweets. Then eat a starchy snack, such as a sandwich.
- **A glitazone** such as **rosiglitazone** or **pioglitazone:**
  - Can be combined with metformin or with a sulphonylurea.
  - Has a slight risk of causing liver damage. So, you will need a blood test to check on your liver function before starting treatment, and from time to time afterwards.
  - May cause hypoglycaemia. This is uncommon, and not likely if you have regular meals, don't miss meals, and don't drink too much alcohol.
  - May cause some weight gain, but other possible side-effects are uncommon.
- **Insulin injections:**
  - Can be taken alone, or taken in addition to metformin or a sulphonylurea.
  - May cause some weight gain.
  - May cause hypoglycaemia.
- **You can also help to reduce your blood glucose level** if you:
  - Eat a healthy diet.
  - Lose weight if you are overweight.
  - Exercise regularly (if you are able).

D

Drug rationale

Drugs not included

- **Insulin** is not included, as insulin treatment will often be initiated in secondary care, and choice of preparation will depend largely on local experience and the person's preference.
- **Acarbose** is less effective than metformin or the sulphonylureas at lowering blood glucose, and is associated with a high incidence of adverse effects. It may be useful in people who are unable to tolerate any other oral treatments.

Drugs included

- **Rosiglitazone and pioglitazone** are recommended for use as an alternative to treatment with a combination of metformin and a sulphonylurea in people who are unable to take metformin and a sulphonylurea in combination because of intolerance or a contraindication to one of the drugs. All doses of rosiglitazone and pioglitazone are offered, but there is currently no experience with doses of rosiglitazone above 4 mg/day in combination with a sulphonylurea.

Prescriptions

Glitazone: maintenance and dose adjustment

Pioglitazone 15mg once a day
- Age from 16 years onwards
- Pioglitazone 15mg tablets. Take one tablet once a day; supply 28 tablet; NHS Cost £26.60.

Pioglitazone 30mg once a day
- Age from 16 years onwards
- Pioglitazone 30mg tablets. Take one tablet once a day; supply 28 tablet; NHS Cost £36.96.

Rosiglitazone 4mg once a day
- Age from 16 years onwards
- Rosiglitazone 4mg tablets. Take one tablet once a day; supply 28 tablet; NHS Cost £26.60.

Rosiglitazone 8mg once a day
- Age from 16 years onwards
- Rosiglitazone 8mg tablets. Take one tablet once a day; supply 28 tablet; NHS Cost £54.60.

Extended Information

Background information

- What is it? p.566
- How common is it? p.566
- How do I know my patient has it? p.566
- What are the risk factors for developing Type 2 diabetes? p.567
- Complications and prognosis p.567

What is it?

- **Type 2 diabetes** is described by the World Health Organization (WHO) Consultation as:
  - **The most common form of diabetes,** characterized by disorders of insulin action and insulin secretion, either of which may be the predominant feature. Both are usually present at the time that this form of diabetes is clinically manifest.
- **Type 2 diabetes has in the past been known as** non-insulin-dependent diabetes mellitus (NIDDM), late-onset diabetes, or adult-onset diabetes.
- **People with Type 2 diabetes have relative (rather than absolute) insulin deficiency.** They are frequently resistant to the action of insulin. At least initially, and often throughout their lifetime, these people do not need insulin treatment to survive.

[WHO, 1999]

How common is it?

- **There are just over 1 million people in England and Wales with diagnosed diabetes** (2% of the population). Of those, about 80% have Type 2 diabetes (750,000 in England and 50,000 in Wales). [DH, 2003]
- **It is estimated that another million people in England and Wales have undiagnosed Type 2 diabetes.**
- **Type 2 diabetes is being diagnosed increasingly in children and adolescents,** despite previously being considered a disease of adults [Fagot-Campagna et al, 2001].
- **The prevalence of diabetes rises sharply with age:** in the UK, 1 in 20 people over the age of 65 has diabetes, rising to 1 in 5 over the age of 85 [DH, 2003].
- **The incidence of diabetes has been estimated at 1.7 new diagnoses per 1000 population per year** (around 85,000 per year in England and 5000 per year in Wales) [NICE, 2003a].

How do I know my patient has it?

Presentations

- **Type 2 diabetes may present with characteristic symptoms of hyperglycaemia** such as thirst, polyuria, blurred vision, weight loss, recurrent infections, or tiredness. In Type 2 diabetes these symptoms are not severe and may even be absent.
- **Type 2 diabetes is frequently undiagnosed for many years,** as the level of hyperglycaemia is often not severe enough to provoke noticeable symptoms.
- **Ketoacidosis is a rare presentation** in people with Type 2 diabetes. When seen, it usually arises in association with the stress of another illness, such as infection.
- **The diagnosis may be during the investigation of a secondary complication** in a previously undiagnosed individual (see *Complications and Prognosis*).
- **The diagnosis may be as an incidental finding,** for example during a health check or as part of routine screening.

Testing for diabetes

- **Diabetes mellitus is diagnosed by:**
  - Fasting plasma glucose greater than or equal to 7.0 mmol/L, or
  - 2-hour plasma glucose (following a 75 g glucose load) greater than or equal to 11.1 mmol/L
- **Impaired glucose tolerance is diagnosed by:**
  - Fasting plasma glucose less than 7.0 mmol/L, and
  - 2-hour plasma glucose (following a 75 g glucose load) between 7.8 and 11.0 mmol/L
- People with impaired glucose tolerance are at increased risk of developing diabetes.
- **Impaired fasting glucose is diagnosed by:**
  - Fasting plasma glucose between 6.1 and 7.0 mmol/L
- Although people with impaired fasting glucose have been studied less well, they also seem to be at increased risk of developing diabetes.
- **The gold-standard test for the diagnosis of diabetes is the 75 g oral glucose tolerance test.** Some clinicians, however, may feel that this is not a feasible option for most people because of the demands and costs involved, and may find a fasting glucose level more acceptable.
- **Diabetes UK recommends the use of a fasting plasma glucose level.** This is a more feasible option than the

glucose tolerance test, with greater sensitivity and specificity than the random plasma glucose level. The cut-off levels for diagnosis are as given earlier in this section.

- **A random plasma glucose level** has the advantage of being cheap, convenient, and acceptable to people, but has poor sensitivity and specificity compared with the glucose tolerance test.
- **Once a diagnosis of diabetes is made, the consequences for the individual are considerable and lifelong.** It is therefore vital that the clinician is confident that the diagnosis is fully established.
  - **The diagnosis of diabetes in an asymptomatic person should never be based on a single abnormal plasma glucose level.** At least one additional abnormal glucose level is essential. If these additional levels are normal, it is prudent to arrange regular review of the individual.
  - The diagnosis of diabetes in a person with characteristic symptoms can be made with more confidence on the basis of a single abnormal plasma glucose level. However, it must be remembered that severe hyperglycaemia detected under conditions of acute infective, traumatic, circulatory, or other stress may be transitory, and should not be regarded as diagnostic of diabetes.

[WHO, 1999; Gerstein and Haynes, 2001]

What are the risk factors for developing Type 2 diabetes?

- **The following are risk factors** for the development of Type 2 diabetes:
  - **Increasing age**
  - **Obesity** — the majority of people with Type 2 diabetes are obese; many of those who are not obese have an increased percentage of body fat in the abdominal region
  - **Lack of physical activity**
  - **History of gestational diabetes**
  - **Impaired glucose tolerance** — a fasting plasma glucose less than 7.0 mmol/L, with a 2-hour plasma glucose between 7.8 and 11.0 mmol/L
  - **Impaired fasting glucose** — a fasting plasma glucose between 6.1 and 7.0 mmol/L
- **Type 2 diabetes is often associated with a strong familial predisposition.** However, the genetics of Type 2 diabetes are complex and not clearly defined.

[WHO, 1999]

Complications and prognosis

Complications

- People with Type 2 diabetes are at increased risk of:
  - Cardiovascular disease
  - Cerebrovascular disease
  - Neuropathy
  - Peripheral vascular disease
  - Renal disease
  - Retinopathy

Prognosis

- **Findings from the United Kingdom Prospective Diabetes Study (UKPDS) showed that the incidence of complications was significantly associated with the degree of glycaemia.** For every percentage rise in the HbA1c level there is an increase in risk of:
  - 21% for any diabetes-related endpoint (95% CI 17 to 24, p <0.0001)
  - 21% for any diabetes-related death (95% CI 15 to 27, p <0.0001)
  - 14% for myocardial infarction (95% CI 8 to 21, p <0.0001)
  - 37% for microvascular complications (95% CI 33 to 41, p <0.0001)
- **No threshold of HbA1c for any adverse outcome was observed.** Any reduction in HbA1c is likely to reduce the risk of complications, with the lowest risk being in those with HbA1c levels in the normal range (less than 6%).

[UK Prospective Diabetes Study Group, 2000]

Management issues

- Monitoring p.567
- Self-monitoring p.568
- Patient education p.568
- Lifestyle interventions p.568
- Pharmacological management of Type 2 diabetes p.568
- Medicines management p.571
- Metabolic syndrome p.572

Monitoring

Recommendations

- **People with Type 2 diabetes should have ongoing structured evaluation** of microvascular and cardiovascular risk and the development of complications (C).
- **Haemoglobin A1c (HbA1c) should be measured at intervals of 2–6 months.** The interval should depend on acceptable levels of control (D) and one or more of the following:
  - Stability of blood glucose control (D)
  - Change in levels of blood glucose (D)
  - Change in therapies (D)
- **Six-monthly measurements should be made if the blood glucose level and blood glucose therapy are stable (D).**
- **If measurement of HbA1c is not possible** because of abnormal erythrocyte turnover or haemoglobinopathy, then blood glucose profiles or total glycated haemoglobin estimation, or both, should be used (D).
- **For each individual, a target HbA1c should be set between 6·5% and 7·5%,** based on the risk of macrovascular and microvascular complications (B).
  - In general, the lower target HbA1c is preferred for those people at significant risk of macrovascular complications, but higher targets are necessary for those at risk of iatrogenic hypoglycaemia (D).

Evidence

- **Lowering the HbA1c level lowers the risk of developing macrovascular and microvascular complications.** The United Kingdom Prospective Diabetes Study (UKPDS) suggested that the lower the level of HbA1c, the better. This study showed that for every percentage rise in the HbA1c level there is an increase in risk of:
  - 21% for any diabetes-related endpoint (95% CI 17–24, p <0.0001)
  - 21% for any diabetes-related death (95% CI 15–27, p <0.0001)
  - 14% for myocardial infarction (95% CI 8–21, p <0.0001)
  - 37% for microvascular complications (95% CI 33–41, p <0.0001)
- **Any reduction in the HbA1c level is likely to reduce the risk of complications,** with the lowest risk being in those whose HbA1c level is in the normal range (less than 6%).

D

Self-monitoring

Recommendations

- **Self-monitoring should not be considered as a stand-alone intervention (D).**
- **Self-monitoring should be taught if the need or purpose is clear and agreed with the individual (D).**
- **Self-monitoring can be used in conjunction with appropriate therapy** as part of integrated self-care (D).

Evidence

- **A systematic review looked at self-monitoring in people with diabetes.** The section looking at Type 2 diabetes comprised eight randomized controlled trials, which were of poor quality and heterogeneous in nature. One included only people on oral therapy, another included only people on oral therapy or insulin, and the rest included people who were not on insulin. The review concluded:
  - **There was no evidence to show that self-monitoring of blood or urine glucose improves control.**
  - There was no evidence that blood glucose monitoring is more effective than urine glucose monitoring.
- **Self-monitoring may prove useful to people in their overall approach to self-care,** even if it does not seem to improve control. It allows people to see the impact of particular behaviours (e.g. dietary habits) on their blood glucose levels. This may be particularly helpful in people moving to insulin therapy.
- **Primary health care teams need to reconsider** the assumption held by many that self-monitoring is necessary and beneficial for all people with Type 2 diabetes.
- **Blood glucose monitoring obviously remains necessary for insulin dose adjustment.**

[Coster et al, 2000; RCGP, 2002]

Patient education

Recommendations

- **Patient education should be offered on an ongoing basis.** Many different forms of education are available. The form chosen should reflect local availability and expertise. If the first form chosen does not suit the individual, try another form.

Evidence

- Meta-analyses of studies of patient education have found the following.
  - **Knowledge, weight loss, HbA1c level, and psychological well-being can all be improved by patient education.**
  - **The type of educational intervention appears to be unimportant;** each model of intervention studied had a positive impact. Models studied included computer-assisted learning, education delivered over the telephone, patient activation and involvement, didactic teaching, individualized instruction, and behaviour modification.
- **It is not possible to draw conclusions about which professional groups are most effective in delivering the education, or to make recommendations about the frequency of delivery,** owing to the heterogeneity of the studies.

Lifestyle interventions

Recommendations

- **Weight loss and increased physical activity should be encouraged in those who are overweight or obese (B).**
- **Healthcare professionals should work with individuals to find approaches to lifestyle change** that are likely to be adhered to and that give the best chance of success (D).

Evidence

- **A meta-analysis of studies of weight loss in people with Type 2 diabetes** looked at the effects of behavioural therapies, diet, exercise, anorectic drug therapies, surgery, or combined strategies. The meta-analysis found that (except for surgery) diet alone had the largest statistically significant impact on weight loss and diabetic control.
- **Dietary interventions based on energy intake** (55–60% carbohydrate, 15–20% protein, and 20–30% fat) lead to a modest improvement in diabetic control and lipid levels. The addition of dietary fibre has also been shown to improve diabetic control and lipid levels. Neither protein restriction nor very low-calorie diets have been shown to improve diabetic control or lipid levels.
- **Studies of exercise in people with Type 2 diabetes have demonstrated significant weight loss,** and improvements in diabetic control and lipid levels.

Pharmacological management of Type 2 diabetes

General issues

- **The evidence base for drug treatment in Type 2 diabetes is incomplete.** Many of the oral hypoglycaemic drugs have been in use for many years, and the evidence supporting their use may be less strong than that for some of the newer oral hypoglycaemic drugs. However, long-term data on some of the newer drugs are not yet available.

Recommendations

- **Concordance with therapy should be discussed and monitored** where the level of glucose control is problematic (D).
- **Glucose-lowering therapies should be prescribed on a trial basis,** and the response to therapy should be monitored using HbA1c measurement (D).
- **When glucose control deteriorates to unsatisfactory levels on current therapy,** another therapy should normally be added rather than substituted (B).

Evidence

- **There is little evidence regarding concordance with therapy in people with Type 2 diabetes.** In people with Type 1 diabetes, adherence to insulin regimens is known to be poor (between 20 and 80%) [McNabb, 1997].
- **Approximately half of all people who cannot be controlled by diet alone will require more than one glucose-lowering drug at years after diagnosis,** according to results suggested by the UK Prospective Diabetes Study (UKPDS). This increases to three-quarters by 9 years [UK Prospective Diabetes Study Group, 1999a]. This phenomenon, known as secondary failure, is probably due to a progression of the severity of the disease, rather than to a reduced response to the drug.

Metformin

- **Metformin, the only biguanide available in the UK, lowers both fasting and postprandial blood glucose concentrations in people with Type 2 diabetes** (but not in people without diabetes). The drug does so predominantly by decreasing hepatic glucose production, increasing sensitivity to insulin, and increasing the peripheral utilization of glucose [BNF 45, 2003].

Recommendations

- **Metformin should normally be used as the first-line glucose-lowering therapy for someone who is overweight**

(BMI greater than 25) and whose blood glucose is inadequately controlled using lifestyle intervention alone (A).

- **For someone who is not overweight, metformin should be considered as an option** for first-line or combination therapy (A).
- **Metformin is contraindicated** in people with renal impairment (serum creatinine greater than 130 micromol/litre) or in people with clinical conditions associated with poor tissue perfusion (e.g. cardiac failure, hypoxia, sepsis, hepatic impairment) (C).

Supporting evidence for metformin — glycaemic control

- **Metformin lowers blood glucose and HbA1c in people with Type 2 diabetes.** A recent meta-analysis compared metformin with sulphonylureas as first-line therapy. The difference between metformin and placebo for blood glucose was –2 mmol/l (95% CI –2.4 to –1.7) and for HbA1c –0.9% (95% CI –1.1 to –0.7). The study found similar reductions in fasting blood glucose and HbA1c between metformin and sulphonylureas. However, there was a significant difference between treatments in bodyweight gain: there was a mean increase of 1.7 kg with a sulphonylurea and a mean decrease of 1.2 kg with metformin [Campbell and Howlett, 1995; Johansen, 1999].
- **In the UK Prospective Diabetes Study** (UKPDS 34), after a median duration of 10.7 years, mean HbA1c was 7.4% in people taking metformin compared with 8.0% in people controlled primarily with diet alone [UK Prospective Diabetes Study Group, 1998a].
- **However, the addition of another agent is frequently necessary to maintain glycaemic goals,** owing to the progressive nature of Type 2 diabetes [UK Prospective Diabetes Study Group, 1998a; Gerstein and Haynes, 2001].
- **Improved blood glucose control with metformin is associated with less weight gain** (or greater weight loss) than is the case for other glucose-lowering therapies [Campbell and Howlett, 1995; UK Prospective Diabetes Study Group, 1998a; Johansen, 1999].

Supporting evidence for metformin — long-term outcomes

- **There is some evidence that metformin may have positive effects on cardiovascular risk factors** such as obesity, dyslipidaemia, hypertension [Saenz et al, 2003]; fibrinolysis, and endothelial dysfunction [Inzucchi, 2002].
- **The UK Prospective Diabetes Study (UKPDS 34) studied the effect of intensive glucose control with metformin in 753 overweight people with no history of coronary heart disease** [UK Prospective Diabetes Study Group, 1998a]. Compared with conventional therapy (lifestyle alone), intensive treatment with metformin reduced the risk of:
  - Any diabetes-related endpoint by 32% (95% CI 13% to 47%, p = 0.002)
  - Diabetes-related death by 42% (95% CI 9% to 63%, p = 0.017)
  - All-cause mortality by 36% (95% CI 9% to 55%, p = 0.011)
- **It is not clear to what extent these results can be extrapolated to non-overweight people with Type 2 diabetes.**

Insulin secretagogues

- **Insulin secretagogues act by increasing endogenous insulin secretion.** Insulin secretagogues include the sulphonylureas and the rapid-acting insulin secretagogues, nateglinide and repaglinide.
- **Nateglinide and repaglinide have a rapid onset and a short duration of action.** Both are licensed for use in combination with metformin in people who are not adequately controlled by maximum tolerated doses of metformin. Repaglinide is also licensed for use as monotherapy.

Recommendations

- **Insulin secretagogues should be considered as an option for first-line therapy when:**
  - Metformin is not tolerated or is contraindicated (A).
  - The person is not overweight (A).
- **Insulin secretagogues should be used in combination with metformin in overweight or obese people when glucose control becomes unsatisfactory (A).**
- **A sulphonylurea drug should normally be the insulin secretagogue of choice (B).** The National Institute for Clinical Excellence (NICE) also recommends that a generic drug should be prescribed.
- **Rapid-acting insulin secretagogues may have a role in attaining tight glucose control** in people with non-routine daily patterns (B).
- **There is a risk of hypoglycaemia,** to which clinicians and those using an insulin secretagogue should be alert (A).

Supporting evidence for sulphonylureas

- **Very little evidence is available for many of the older drugs in this class** (e.g. chlorpropamide, tolbutamide) and they have largely been replaced by the newer 'second-generation' sulphonylureas (e.g. glipizide, glimepiride, gliclazide).
- **The newer sulphonylureas typically lower the HbA1c by 1–2%** compared with placebo [Simonson et al, 1997; Schade et al, 1998; UK Prospective Diabetes Study Group, 1998b], showing efficacy comparable to that of metformin.
- **Several studies comparing individual sulphonylureas with each other found little difference in glucose-lowering effect** [Dills and Schneider, 1996; Rosskamp et al, 1996; Inzucchi, 2002; RCGP, 2002].
- **The UK Prospective Diabetes Study (UKPDS 33) studied the effect of intensive glucose control with sulphonylurea or insulin compared with conventional treatment (diet)** in 4209 people with newly diagnosed Type 2 diabetes. Over 10 years, HbA1c was 0.9% lower in people in the intensive treatment group compared with conventional treatment. Compared with conventional therapy, intensive treatment reduced the risk of:
  - Any diabetes-related endpoint by 12% (95% CI 1% to 21%, p = 0.029)
  - All microvascular endpoints by 25% (95% CI 11% to 27%, p = 0.34)
- There was no significant effect on diabetes-related death or on all-cause mortality.

[UK Prospective Diabetes Study Group, 1998b]

- **Concerns have been raised that sulphonylureas may increase cardiovascular mortality** (given the epidemiological association between hyperinsulinaemia and cardiovascular disease). One early study found increased cardiovascular mortality with sulphonylureas compared with insulin; however, there is widespread criticism of the methodology used in this study [Inzucchi, 2002]. More recently, results from UKPDS did not show increased mortality in people receiving sulphonylureas [UK Prospective Diabetes Study Group, 1998b].

Supporting evidence for nateglinide and repaglinide

- **In combination with metformin, nateglinide** produced greater reductions in HbA1c and fasting plasma glucose than either drug alone [Horton et al, 2000; Marre et al, 2002].
- **In studies over 1 year, repaglinide produces improvements in glycaemic control similar to those for glibenclamide** [Marbury et al, 1999; Wolffenbuttel and Landgraf, 1999].
- **In combination with metformin, repaglinide** produced reductions in HbA1c of 1.4% and fasting plasma glucose of 2.2 mmol/l [Moses et al, 1999; Marre et al, 2002].

D

- **Treatment with nateglinide was associated with an increase in weight** of 0.9 kg over 24 weeks [Horton et al, 2000]. Treatment with repaglinide was associated with an increase in weight of 2.4 kg [Moses et al, 1999].
- **The overall incidence of hypoglycaemia is similar to that of people treated with a sulphonylurea.** However, several small studies suggest that, unlike with the sulphonylureas, people can miss or postpone a meal (provided they omit the corresponding dose of repaglinide or nateglinide), without an increased risk of hypoglycaemia [Damsbo et al, 1999].
- **Because of their ability to reduce postprandial glucose levels, it is possible that repaglinide and nateglinide may improve cardiovascular outcomes,** which are associated with increased levels of glucose after a meal. However, there are no long-term trials looking at the effects of repaglinide and nateglinide on macrovascular outcomes.

D

Thiazolidinediones (glitazones)

- **The currently available thiazolidinediones (commonly referred to as glitazones) are pioglitazone and rosiglitazone.** They are thought to reduce peripheral insulin resistance by activation of the peroxisome proliferator-activated gamma receptor (PPAR-gamma).
- **The National Institute for Clinical Excellence (NICE) have recently updated their guidance on the place of glitazones in therapy** [NICE, 2003b]. The updated recommendations are:
  - **The use of a glitazone as second-line therapy added to either metformin or a sulphonylurea — as an alternative to treatment with a combination of metformin and a sulphonylurea — is not generally recommended** for people with Type 2 diabetes. The exception to this statement concerns someone unable to take metformin and a sulphonylurea in combination because of intolerance or a contraindication to one of the drugs. In this instance, the glitazone should replace in the combination the drug that is poorly tolerated or contraindicated.
  - **The effectiveness of glitazone combination therapy should be monitored against treatment targets** for glycaemic control (usually in terms of haemoglobin A1c [HbA1c] level) and for other cardiovascular risk factors, including lipid profile. The target HbA1c level should be set between 6.5% and 7.5%, depending on other risk factors.
  - **The present UK licence** does not allow NICE to recommend the use of glitazones in triple combination therapy (with other oral antidiabetic agents), as monotherapy, or in combination with insulin. The use of a glitazone in triple combination (with other oral antidiabetic agents) is classified in the licence under 'special warnings and special precautions for use'. This precaution is because at the time the licence was issued there was no clinical experience of triple combination therapy.
- **The licences for both rosiglitazone and pioglitazone are likely to change in the near future** to include use as an alternative to sulphonylureas, where diet and exercise have failed, in people who are intolerant to metformin or in whom it is contraindicated — in particular, those who are overweight,. When this guidance is reviewed, the recommendations will take into account any extensions to the licence for the use of glitazones.

Recommendations

- **People should be offered a glitazone as combination therapy with either metformin or an insulin secretagogue (but not with both as triple therapy) if:**
  - They are unable to take metformin and insulin secretagogues as combination therapy **(A)**, or
  - The licensed glitazones are contraindicated in combination therapy with insulin **(A)**

Supporting evidence for rosiglitazone and pioglitazone

- **When given as monotherapy or in combination with metformin or sulphonylureas,** the glitazones lower fasting and postprandial blood glucose levels. In addition, they lower HbA1c by 1–2%.
- **In combination with metformin, both rosiglitazone and pioglitazone reduced the mean HbA1c by a further 0.8% compared with metformin alone.** In combination with a sulphonylurea, the mean decrease in HbA1c was 1.1–1.3% compared with a sulphonylurea alone [RCGP, 2002].
- **We found a limited number of published studies looking at the glitazones in head-to-head studies with conventional treatment** (metformin or a sulphonylurea). In an open-label study, rosiglitazone (4 mg twice a day) produced reductions comparable to those for glibenclamide (titrated to achieve optimal glycaemic control) in HbA1c after 1 year. In another double-blind study, pioglitazone (in doses of up to 45 mg a day) was comparable to metformin (in doses of up to 2550 mg a day) in improving glycaemic control [Pavo et al, 2003]. The maximum licensed dose of pioglitazone is 30 mg a day.
- **The glitazones have been shown to improve serum HDL cholesterol and triglyceride levels.** However, there are no studies yet to show that the glitazones reduce long-term microvascular and macrovascular complications of Type 2 diabetes.

Acarbose

- **Acarbose is the only alpha-glucosidase inhibitor currently licensed** for the treatment of diabetes mellitus [BNF 45, 2003].
- **Alpha-glucosidase inhibitors act by delaying the absorption of carbohydrates,** thus diminishing postprandial peaks in glucose levels.
- **Use of acarbose is greatly limited by the high incidence of gastrointestinal adverse effects** experienced by people taking it.

Recommendation

- **Acarbose may be considered as an alternative glucose-lowering therapy in people unable to use other oral drugs (A).**

Supporting evidence for acarbose

- **The UK Prospective Diabetes Study (UKPDS 44) studied the effect of acarbose compared with placebo + diet** over 3 years in 1946 people with Type 2 diabetes. At the end of the study period, only 39% of people were still taking acarbose, compared with 58% of those assigned to placebo. Intention-to-treat analysis showed that acarbose significantly decreased HbA1c by 0.2% over 3 years, with similar results for fasting and postprandial glucose. There were no data on morbidity and mortality outcomes [UK Prospective Diabetes Study Group, 1999b].
- **Several studies have compared acarbose with sulphonylureas** (glibenclamide) and found no statistically significant differences in blood glucose-lowering effect [RCGP, 2002].
- **There is some evidence that acarbose reduces levels of hypertriglyceridaemia** [Van de Laar et al, 2003].

Insulins

Recommendations

- **Insulin therapy should be offered to people with Type 2 diabetes who have inadequate blood glucose control** on optimized oral glucose-lowering drugs **(A)**.
- **Local experience, individual preference of the person with diabetes, and relative costs should inform the choic**

of insulin type and regimen, as there is little research evidence in this area (D).

- **Clinicians and people using insulin should be aware of the risk of hypoglycaemia** and be alert to it (A).
- **When transferring a person from a combination of metformin and another oral agent to insulin therapy,** continue with metformin (B).
- **When transferring a person from a combination of sulphonylurea plus another oral agent (metformin not tolerated or contraindicated) to insulin therapy,** continue the sulphonylurea (D).

Supporting evidence for insulin

- **In people with Type 2 diabetes, insulin may need to be introduced later in therapy,** when diet, exercise, weight loss, and oral agents are no longer able to achieve adequate blood glucose control. Adding insulin to oral therapy, or using it alone, can significantly improve control. In the UK Prospective Diabetes Study (UKPDS), insulin reduced vascular complications when compared with lifestyle interventions (diet) alone [UK Prospective Diabetes Study Group, 1998b].
- **Insulin therapy is associated with a risk of hypoglycaemia greater than that with oral therapy.**
- **The addition of metformin to insulin** has been studied in people with Type 2 diabetes. This combination showed a significant improvement in diabetes control, weight, and episodes of hypoglycaemia compared with insulin therapy alone, or insulin in combination with a sulphonylurea.
- **The addition of a sulphonylurea to insulin** has been studied in people with Type 2 diabetes. The evidence for an improvement in diabetes control is not as conclusive as that with the combination of metformin and insulin. Also, the combination of a sulphonylurea and insulin has been shown to cause weight gain in people with Type 2 diabetes.

Medicines management

Metformin

- **Gastrointestinal intolerance is common** when initiating therapy with metformin (reported in 5–30% of people taking metformin, but requires discontinuation in less than 5%). To minimize this effect, increase the dose slowly over several weeks [BNF 45, 2003].
- **Metformin is contraindicated** in people with renal impairment (serum creatinine greater than 130 micromol/litre), or in people with clinical conditions associated with poor tissue perfusion and hence tissue hypoxia (e.g. cardiac failure, hypoxia, sepsis, hepatic impairment). These people are at increased risk of lactic acidosis [BNF 45, 2003; RCGP, 2002]. Mildly elevated serum transaminase levels are not usually associated with hepatic impairment; in such people the use of metformin is unlikely to be associated with any increase in the risk of lactic acidosis [Lalau and Race, 2001; ICSI, 2002; Jones et al, 2003].
- **Lactic acidosis** (characterized by elevated blood lactate concentration greater than 45 mg/dl, reduced blood pH less than 7.35, electrolyte disturbances, and an increased lactate/pyruvate ratio) is a rare but potentially fatal adverse effect of metformin therapy. The estimated incidence of lactic acidosis from population studies is between 3 and 9 cases per 100,000 person-years [Brown et al, 1998; Stang et al, 1999]. Lactic acidosis is more likely in people with renal impairment, or in people with clinical conditions associated with poor tissue perfusion and hence tissue hypoxia (e.g. cardiac failure, hypoxia, sepsis, hepatic impairment) [Gerstein and Haynes, 2001; Saenz et al, 2003].
- **A recent Cochrane review of 176 comparative trials and cohort studies, however, revealed no cases of fatal or non-fatal lactic acidosis with metformin use.** It also did not reveal any difference in lactate levels for metformin compared with placebo or other non-biguanide treatments [Salpeter et al, 2003].
- **Lactic acidosis has an insidious onset with non-specific symptoms** such as malaise, myalgia, respiratory distress, increasing somnolence, and non-specific gastrointestinal symptoms. Hypothermia, hypotension, and resistant bradyarrhythmias may occur with more marked acidosis [Saenz et al, 2003].
- **Metformin should be withdrawn during periods of suspected tissue hypoxia** (e.g. due to myocardial infarction or hypoxia) [Jones et al, 2003]. People will normally be referred for hospital admission, as insulin therapy will need to be substituted.

Sulphonylureas

- **Hypoglycaemia is a recognized adverse effect of all the sulphonylureas,** and is most likely to affect the elderly, those with worsening renal function, and those with irregular meal times. Major hypoglycaemic events occur in 1–2% of people receiving sulphonylureas.
  - **Sulphonylureas with a long duration of action** (e.g. chlorpropamide, glibenclamide) are associated with a greater risk of hypoglycaemia, and should be avoided in the elderly [BNF 45, 2003].
  - **Sulphonylureas are predominantly metabolized by the liver and cleared by the kidney.** Impairment of hepatic or renal function increases the risk of hypoglycaemia, so they must be used with caution in people with hepatic or renal impairment.
- **Weight gain,** typically from 2–5 kg, is commonly associated with the sulphonylureas [UK Prospective Diabetes Study Group, 1998b; Inzucchi, 2002].

Thiazolidinediones

- **It is currently recommended that people should have liver function tests before starting treatment** with rosiglitazone or pioglitazone, every two months for the first year, and periodically thereafter [RCGP, 2002]. (The first glitazone, troglitazone, was withdrawn because of hepatotoxic adverse effects.) Treatment should be stopped if levels are 3 times the upper limit of normal. In clinical trials, there was no evidence of hepatotoxic effects with either drug. Thiazolidinediones should not be given to people with alanine aminotransferase (ALT) greater than 2.5 times the upper limit of normal.
- **Rosiglitazone and pioglitazone are contraindicated in people with cardiac failure or a history of cardiac failure** (NYHA stages I to IV).
  - Rosiglitazone and pioglitazone can cause fluid retention, which may exacerbate or precipitate heart failure, especially in people with a history of heart failure, in the elderly, or in people with mild to moderate renal failure.
  - People should be monitored for signs and symptoms of heart failure, and the thiazolidinedione should be stopped if any deterioration in cardiac function is seen.
  - Concomitant prescription of a nonsteroidal anti-inflammatory drug (NSAID) may increase the risk of oedema.
- **The thiazolidinediones are contraindicated in combination with insulin,** as an increase in heart failure has been observed with this combination [BNF 45, 2003].
- **Both rosiglitazone and pioglitazone are associated with significant weight gain** (similar to that seen with the sulphonylureas), probably because of fluid retention.

- **After initiation, there may be a delay of 6–10 weeks** before the full effect of the glitazones is seen [RCGP, 2002].

Metabolic syndrome

- **People with insulin resistance may exhibit a collection of other features,** including central obesity, dyslipidaemia, hypertension, hyperinsulinaemia, microalbuminuria, impaired fibrinolysis, endothelial dysfunction, hyperuricaemia, vascular inflammation, and premature atherosclerosis. This combination of characteristics is known as the metabolic syndrome [Inzucchi, 2002].
- **Alone, each component of this cluster conveys increased coronary heart disease risk; as a combination, they confer a considerable increase in this risk.** Management of the metabolic syndrome must focus on every feature present in the individual.

[WHO, 1999]

D

References

NHS staff in England can link, free of charge, from references to full text journals by clicking on [Full text] on the PRODIGY website.

1. BNF 45 (2003) *British National Formulary.* 45th edn. London: British Medical Association and Royal Pharmaceutical Society of Great Britain.
2. Brown, J.B., Pedula, K., Barzilay, J. et al (1998) Lactic acidosis rates in type 2 diabetes. *Diabetes Care* **21**(10), 1659–1663. [Full text]
3. Campbell, I.W. and Howlett, H.C. (1995) Worldwide experience of metformin as an effective glucose-lowering agent: a meta-analysis. *Diabetes-Metabolism Reviews* **11**(suppl 1), S57-S62.
4. Coster, S., Gulliford, M.C., Seed, P.T. et al (2000) Monitoring blood glucose control in diabetes mellitus: a systematic review. *Health Technology Assessment* **4**(12), 1–4.
5. Damsbo, P., Clauson, P., Marbury, T.C. and Windfeld, K. (1999) A double-blind randomized comparison of meal-related glycemic control by repaglinide and glyburide in well-controlled type 2 diabetic patients. *Diabetes Care* **22**(5), 789–794. [Full text]
6. DH (2003) *National service framework for diabetes.* Department of Health. www.dh.gov.uk [Accessed: 27/04/2004]. [Full text]
7. Dills, D.G. and Schneider, J. (1996) Clinical evaluation of glimepiride versus glyburide in NIDDM in a double-blind comparative study. *Hormone & Metabolic Research* **28**(9), 426–429.
8. Fagot-Campagna, A., Narayan, K.M. and Imperatore, G. (2001) Type 2 diabetes in children. *British Medical Journal* **322**(7283), 377–378. [Full text]
9. Gerstein, H.C. and Haynes, R.B. (Eds.) (2001) *Evidence-based diabetes care.* London: BC Decker.
10. Horton, E.S., Clinkingbeard, C., Gatlin, M. et al (2000) Nateglinide alone and in combination with metformin improves glycemic control by reducing mealtime glucose levels in type 2 diabetes. *Diabetes Care* **23**(11), 1660–1665. [Full text]
11. ICSI (2002) *Management of type 2 diabetes mellitus.* Bloomington (MN): Institute for Clinical Systems Improvement.
12. Inzucchi, S.E. (2002) Oral antihyperglycemic therapy for type 2 diabetes: scientific review. *Journal of the American Medical Association* **287**(3), 360–372. [Full text]
13. Johansen, K. (1999) Efficacy of metformin in the treatment of NIDDM. *Diabetes Care* **22**(1), 33–37. [Full text]
14. Jones, G.C., Macklin, J.P. and Alexander, W.D. (2003) Contraindications to the use of metformin. *British Medical Journal* **326**(7379), 4–5. [Full text]
15. Lalau, J.D. and Race, J.M. (2001) Lactic acidosis in metformin therapy: searching for a link with metformin in reports of "metformin-associated lactic acidosis". *Diabetes, Obesity & Metabolism* **3**, 195–201.
16. Marbury, T., Huang, W.C., Strange, P. and Lebovitz, H. (1999) Repaglinide versus glyburide: a one-year comparison trial. *Diabetes Research & Clinical Practice* **43**(3), 155–166.
17. Marre, M., Van Gaal, L., Usadel, K.H. et al (2002) Nateglinide improves glycaemic control when added to metformin monotherapy: results of a randomized trial with type 2 diabetes patients. *Diabetes, Obesity & Metabolism* **4**(3), 177–186.
18. McNabb, W.L. (1997) Adherence in diabetes: can we define it and can we measure it? *Diabetes Care* **20**(2), 215–218. [Full text]
19. Moses, R., Slobodniuk, R., Boyages, S. et al (1999) Effect of repaglinide addition to metformin monotherapy on glycemic control in patients with type 2 diabetes. *Diabetes Care* **22**(1), 119–124.
20. NICE (2002) *Management of type 2 diabetes – managing blood glucose levels.* Inherited clinical guideline G. National Institute for Clinical Excellence. www.nice.org.uk [Accessed: 02/12/2002].
21. NICE (2003a) *Clinical effectiveness and cost effectiveness of glitazones for the treatment of type 2 diabetes.* Final appraisal determination. National Institute for Clinical Excellence. www.nice.org.uk [Accessed: 12/06/2003].
22. NICE (2003b) *Guidance on the use of glitazones for the treatment of type 2 diabetes.* Technology appraisal no. 63. NICE. www.nice.org.uk [Accessed: 01/09/2003].
23. Pavo, I., Jermendy, G., Varkonyi, T.T. et al (2003) Effect of pioglitazone compared with metformin on glycemic control and indicators of insulin sensitivity in recently diagnosed patients with type 2 diabetes. *Journal of Clinical Endocrinology & Metabolism* **88**(4), 1637–1645.
24. RCGP (2002) *Clinical guidelines for type 2 diabetes – management of blood glucose.* The Royal College of General Practitioners. www.shef.ac.uk [Accessed: 20/11/2002].
25. Rosskamp, R., Wernicke-Panten, K. and Draeger, E. (1996) Clinical profile of the novel sulphonylurea glimepiride. *Diabetes Research & Clinical Practice* **31**(suppl), S33-S42.
26. Saenz, A., Ausejo, M., Mataix, A. et al (2003) *Metformin for type 2 diabetes mellitus (Protocol for a Cochrane Review).* The Cochrane Library. Issue 2. Oxford: Update Software.
27. Salpeter, S., Greyber, E., Pasternak, G. and Salpeter, E. (2003) *Risk of fatal and nonfatal lactic acidosis with metformin use in type 2 diabetes mellitus.* The Cochrane Library. Issue 2. Oxford: Update Software. [Accessed: 10/07/2003].
28. Schade, D.S., Jovanovic, L. and Schneider, J. (1998) A placebo-controlled, randomized study of glimepiride in patients with type 2 diabetes mellitus for whom diet therapy is unsuccessful. *Journal of Clinical Pharmacology* **38**(7), 636–641.
29. Simonson, D.C., Kourides, I.A., Feinglos, M. et al (1997) Efficacy, safety, and dose-response characteristics of glipizide gastrointestinal therapeutic system on glycemic control and insulin secretion in NIDDM. Results of two multicenter, randomized, placebo-controlled clinical trials. *Diabetes Care* **20**(4), 597–606. [Full text]

30. Stang, M., Wysowski, D.K. and Butler-Jones, D. (1999) Incidence of lactic acidosis in metformin users. *Diabetes Care* **22**(6), 925–927. [Full text]
31. UK Prospective Diabetes Study Group (1998a) Effect of intensive blood-glucose control with metformin on complications in overweight patients with type 2 diabetes (UKPDS 34). *Lancet* **352**(9131), 854–865. [Full text]
32. UK Prospective Diabetes Study Group (1998b) Intensive blood glucose control with sulphonylureas or insulin compared with conventional treatment and risk of complications in patients with type 2 diabetes (UKPDS 33). *Lancet* **352**(9131), 837–853.
33. UK Prospective Diabetes Study Group (1999a) Glycaemic control with diet, sulphonylurea, metformin and insulin therapy in patients with type 2 diabetes: progressive requirement for multiple therapies (UKPDS 49). *Journal of the American Medical Association* **281**(21), 2005–2012. [Full text]
34. UK Prospective Diabetes Study Group (1999b) A randomised, double-blind trial of acarbose in type 2 diabetes shows improved glycaemic control over three years (UKPDS 44). *Diabetes Care* **22**(6), 960–964.
35. UK Prospective Diabetes Study Group (2000) Association of glycaemia with macrovascular and microvascular complications of Type 2 diabetes: prospective observational study (UKPDS 35). *British Medical Journal* **321**(7258), 405–412. [Full text]
36. Van de Laar, F., Wang, S., Lucassen, P et al (2003) *Alpha-glucosidase inhibitors for type 2 diabetes mellitus (Protocol for a Cochrane Review) (Protocol).* The Cochrane Library. Issue 2. Oxford: Update Software.
37. WHO (1999) *Definition, diagnosis and classification of diabetes mellitus and its complications. Part 1: diagnosis and classification of diabetes mellitus provisional report of a WHO consultation.* Geneva: World Health Organization. www.idi.org.au/downloads/who_report.pdf [Accessed: 14/07/2003].
38. Wolffenbuttel, B.H. and Landgraf, R. (1999) A 1-year multicenter randomized double-blind comparison of repaglinide and glyburide for the treatment of type 2 diabetes. *Diabetes Care* **22**(3), 463–467. [Full text]

Evidence grading

Evidence grading is from the National Institute of Clinical Excellence guideline, *Management of Type 2 diabetes: management of blood glucose*, September 2002. The definitions of grades of recommendation used in this guideline are as follows:

A Directly based on category I evidence (systematic review of randomized controlled trials or at least one randomized controlled trial)

B Directly based on category II evidence (at least one controlled study without randomization or one other type of quasi-experimental study) or extrapolated recommendation from category I evidence

C Directly based on category III evidence (non-experimental descriptive studies) or extrapolated recommendation from category I or II evidence

D Directly based on category IV evidence (expert committee reports, opinions, or clinical experience of respected authorities) or extrapolated recommendation from category I, II, or III evidence

PRODIGY GUIDANCE

Diabetes Type 2 — lipid management

Last revised in July 2003
www.prodigy.nhs.uk/guidance.asp?gt=Diabetes - lipid management

Applies to people over the age of 16 years

This is the PRODIGY implementation of the National Institute for Clinical Excellence (NICE) guideline on *Management of Type 2 diabetes: management of blood pressure and blood lipids*, and the Royal College of General Practitioners (RCGP) *Clinical guideline for Type 2 diabetes: lipids management (October 2002).*

D

This guidance covers the management of blood lipids in people with Type 2 diabetes.

This guidance does not cover in detail the management of other risk factors for cardiovascular disease; the management of other complications of diabetes; or the management of dyslipidaemia in people with Type 1 diabetes, or in people who do not have diabetes.

Although this guidance is concerned specifically with lipid management in people with Type 2 diabetes, it should be seen as part of an overall approach to reducing the risk of cardiovascular disease in people with diabetes.

There is separate PRODIGY guidance for *Coronary heart disease risk — identification and management; Diabetes Type 1 and 2 — foot disease; Diabetes Type 1 and 2 — hypertension;* and *Diabetes Type 2 — renal disease.*

Throughout this guidance 'cardiovascular disease' is used to mean 'history of or symptoms of coronary heart disease, stroke, or peripheral vascular disease'.

Goals

- To reduce mortality and morbidity from cardiovascular disease.
- Following a decision to start treatment, the aim is to lower serum total cholesterol to below 5.0 mmol/l or to reduce it by 20–25%, whichever would result in the lower level. Aim to lower low-density lipoprotein cholesterol to below 3.0 mmol/l or to reduce it by 30%, whichever would result in the lower level.
- Following a decision to start treatment, the aim is to lower serum triglyceride levels to below 2.3 mmol/l.

Contents

Scenarios

- Initial cholesterol <5 (and TG <2.3) p.574
- Cholesterol >5 or TG >2.3 (but <10): on no treatment p.575
- Cholesterol <5 and TG >2.3 (but <10) p.577
- Managing statin therapy p.580
- Managing fibrate therapy p.581
- Fasting triglyceride >10: refer p.583

Extended Information, p. 585

Which scenario?

- **Initial cholesterol <5 (and TG <2.3):** covers the management of people whose initial cholesterol is less than 5 mmol/l.
- **Cholesterol >5 or TG >2.3 (but <10): on no treatment:** covers the management of people with cholesterol greater than 5 mmol/l. People with Type 2 diabetes and a 10-year coronary heart disease risk greater than 15% are eligible for treatment for hyperlipidaemia.
- **Cholesterol <5 and TG >2.3 (but <10):** covers the management of people with cholesterol less than 5mmol/l but triglyceride greater than 2.3 mmol/l. People with Type 2 diabetes and manifest cardiovascular disease are eligible for the treatment for hypertriglyceridaemia without raised cholesterol.
- **Managing statin therapy:** covers the titration of statins according to response and adverse effects.
- **Managing fibrate therapy:** covers the titration of fibrates according to response and adverse effects.
- **Fasting triglyceride >10: refer:** covers the management and referral of people who have very severe hypertriglyceridaemia, i.e. serum TG greater than 10 mmol/l.

Initial cholesterol <5 (and TG <2.3)

Which therapy

- **Drug treatment is not generally recommended** if serum total cholesterol (TC) is less than 5.0 mmol/l and triglycerides (TG) less than 2.3 mmol/l.
- People who have serum TC less than 5 mmol/l and TG less than 2.3 mmol/l should be reassured and offered diet and lifestyle advice.
- Consideration can be given to offering treatment with a statin to people with established CHD or other occlusive artery disease. There is evidence that reducing serum cholesterol has a preventive effect on CHD, whatever the baseline cholesterol level.

Follow-up advice

- **Annually** measure total cholesterol and HDL-C and (if fasting measurements are feasible) LDL-C and triglycerides and calculate CHD risk.

Patient information leaflets

The following PILs are available at www.prodigy.nhs.uk

- Blood Test - General
- Blood Test - Glucose
- Diabetes Insight Website
- Diabetes Research & Wellness Foundation
- Diabetes Type 2
- Diabetes Type 2 - A Summary
- Diabetes UK
- DiabeticLife

Shared decision making

- **Your cholesterol level is less than 5.0 mmol/l, which is good.**
- You do not need a cholesterol-lowering medicine.

- **You should continue to eat and live healthily.** This means:
  - Do not smoke.
  - Take regular exercise.
  - Lose weight if you are overweight or obese.
  - Eat *more* vegetables, fruit, cereals, wholegrain bread, poultry, fish, rice, skimmed or semi-skimmed milk, grilled food, lean meat, pasta, etc.
  - Eat *less* of fatty meats, fatty cheeses, full cream milk, fried food, lard, etc.
  - If you do fry, choose a vegetable oil such as sunflower or rapeseed.
  - Use low-fat spreads.
  - Add less salt to food, and avoid prepared foods that are very salty.
  - Keep alcohol consumption moderate.
- Be sure to follow advice for keeping your diabetes under the best possible control.

Drug rationale

- A non-drug prescription giving diet and lifestyle advice is offered.

Prescriptions

Non-drug management

Advice only: diet and lifestyle

- Age from 16 years onwards
- Your cholesterol level is less than 5 mmol/l, which is good. You do not need a cholesterol-lowering medicine. You should continue to eat and live healthily. This means: no smoking; regular exercise; moderate alcohol consumption. Lose weight if you are overweight or obese. Eat more vegetables, fruit, cereals, poultry, fish, rice, skimmed or semi-skimmed milk, grilled food, lean meat, pasta etc. and less fatty meats, fatty cheeses, full cream milk, fried food, lard, etc. If you do fry, choose a vegetable oil such as sunflower or rapeseed. Use low-fat spreads. Add less salt to food, and avoid foods that are very salty.

Cholesterol >5 or TG >2.3 (but <10): on no treatment

Which therapy

- **Confirm results with a *fasting* lipid profile:** total cholesterol, LDL-C, HDL-C, triglycerides (TG).
- **For people without manifest cardiovascular disease, calculate the 10-year CHD risk using the average of two (preferably three) lipid and blood pressure results** (see How do I calculate cardiovascular risk? for details).
- **10-year coronary event risk less than 15% and no history of cardiovascular disease:**
  - Drug treatment is not generally recommended.
  - Consider offering drug treatment if higher levels of cholesterol or TG and any of: family history of CHD; South Asian ethnicity; presence of microalbuminuria or proteinuria (D).
- **10-year coronary event risk greater than 15% or manifest cardiovascular disease:**
  - Offer a statin (B).
- **For all people:**
  - Optimize glycaemic control.
  - Ensure appropriate management of other cardiovascular risk factors.

Practical prescribing points

For further information please see the *Medicines Compendium* (www.medicines.org.uk) or the *British National Formulary* (www.bnf.org).

- **Before starting drug treatment for an abnormal lipid profile,** measure fasting levels of total cholesterol, LDL-C, HDL-C, and triglycerides as baseline.
- **Before starting drug treatment with a statin check CK and AST/ALT.**
- **Hepatotoxicity is rare,** but is thought to be dose-dependent.
- Non-specific muscle aches or joint pains, but non-significant increase in CK, are common.
- **Myopathy is rare, but the risk is increased in the presence of:**
  - Renal impairment, hypothyroidism, alcohol abuse, or underlying muscle disorders
  - Co-prescription of statins with fibrates (do not use gemfibrozil) or nicotinic acid
  - Co-prescription of drugs that increase statin levels, e.g. ciclosporin, clarithromycin, erythromycin, HIV protease inhibitors, itraconazole, and ketoconazole
- **Use a lower starting dose of statins in people at increased risk of myopathy.** (Do not start treatment if baseline CK is greater than five times the upper limit of normal.)
- **Warfarin and simvastatin:** monitor INR closely until stable — simvastatin occasionally increases INR significantly.

Stop statin treatment if:

- There is a strong suspicion of myopathy, or CK level is more than five times the upper limit of normal.
- Myalgic symptoms persist despite a normal CK level — a trial off treatment may be needed.
- AST or ALT level persists above three times the upper limit of normal.

Follow-up advice

- **If a decision is made not to start drug treatment,** monitor lipid profile and cardiovascular risk annually.

Monitoring response to treatment

- **Aim to lower total cholesterol** (TC) by 20–25%, or to below 5 mmol/l (whichever would result in the lower level) or to LDL-C by 30%, or to below 3 mmol/l (whichever would result in the lower level). Note: a fasting sample is only needed if an LDL-C or triglycerides (TG) level is required.
- **Four to eight weeks after starting, or after a dose increase** check non-fasting TC. Titrate dose until target or maximum tolerated dose is reached.
- **For people with manifest cardiovascular disease:** if target is not reached after 6 months, consider adding a fibrate (see scenario *Managing statins*).
- **Annual check:** TC.

Monitoring toxicity

- **Four to eight weeks after starting, or after a dose increase check AST or ALT.**
- **Check CK if muscle symptoms occur.**
- **Discontinue statin** if there is a strong suspicion of myopathy, if CK exceeds five times the upper limit of the normal range, or if transaminases *persist* above three times the upper limit of the normal range.
- **Annual check: AST or ALT.**

Ask about family history (if this has not already been done)

- Consider the possibility of familial combined hyperlipidaemia if: TC is 6.5–8.0 mmol/l and TG

2.3–5.0 mmol/l *and* family history of hyperlipidaemia or premature CHD.
- Consider the possibility of familial hypercholesterolaemia when the patient has serum TC greater than 7.5 mmol/l (or LDL-C greater than 4.9 mmol/l) *and* any of the following:
  - Tendon xanthomata in himself/herself or in a first- or second-degree relative
  - Family history of myocardial infarction under age 60 in a first-degree relative or under age 50 in a second-degree relative
  - Family history of TC greater than 7.5 mmol/l in a first- or second-degree relative

Should I refer or investigate?

Refer?

- **Severe hypercholesterolaemia,** i.e. total cholesterol (TC) greater than 10 mmol/l.
- **Severe hypertriglyceridaemia,** i.e. triglycerides (TG) greater than 10 mmol/l.
- Target lipid levels are not achieved despite maximum tolerated doses.
- **Suspected familial hypercholesterolaemia:** TC greater than 7.5 mmol/l (or LDL-C greater than 4.9 mmol/l) *and* at least one of the following:
  - Tendon xanthomata in himself/herself or in a first- or second-degree relative.
  - Family history of premature CHD, e.g. CHD or other atherosclerotic disease in a male first-degree relative before the age of 55 years, or in a female first-degree relative before the age of 65 years.
  - Family history of TC greater than 7.5 mmol/l in a first- or second-degree relative.
- Reasons for referral are to make a firm diagnosis, to initiate treatment if required, and to counsel and screen the family.
- Referral may be unnecessary for someone with suspected familial hyperlipidaemia if he or she qualifies for treatment according to risk assessment. Family screening and counselling, however, should not be forgotten.

Investigate?

- **Rule out secondary causes of hypercholesterolaemia,** e.g. drugs (ciclosporin), hypothyroidism, obstructive jaundice, and nephrotic syndrome.
- **Rule out secondary causes of combined hyperlipidaemia,** e.g. pregnancy, drugs (oral corticosteroids, oral contraceptives, high doses of thiazides), multiple myeloma.

Patient information leaflets

The following PILs are available at www.prodigy.nhs.uk
- Blood Test - General
- Blood Test - Glucose
- Diabetes Insight Website
- Diabetes Research & Wellness Foundation
- Diabetes Type 2
- Diabetes Type 2 - A Summary
- Diabetes UK
- DiabeticLife

Shared decision making

- **Your cholesterol level is high.**
- **A 'statin' medicine is recommended.**
- Side effects are uncommon.
  - A few people develop mild headaches, mild upset stomach, dizziness, or itching. These often go away with continued treatment.
  - A very rare, but more serious, side effect is a muscle problem. Tell a doctor if you develop muscle pains whilst taking a statin medicine.
- You will need a blood test from time to time.
- **You should still eat and live healthily.** This means:
  - Do not smoke.
  - Take regular exercise.
  - Lose weight if you are overweight or obese.
  - Eat *more* vegetables, fruit, cereals, wholegrain bread, poultry, fish, rice, skimmed or semi-skimmed milk, grilled food, lean meat, and pasta.
  - Eat *less* of fatty meats, fatty cheeses, full cream milk, fried food, and lard.
  - If you do fry, choose a vegetable oil such as sunflower or rapeseed.
  - Use low-fat spreads.
  - Add less salt to food, and avoid prepared foods that are very salty.
  - Keep alcohol consumption moderate.
- Be sure to follow advice for keeping your diabetes under the best possible control.

Drug rationale

Drugs not included

- **Lipid-lowering agents other than statins** are not included in this scenario because evidence for their benefit is not as strong as that for the statins.
- **Ezetimibe** (a novel cholesterol absorption inhibitor) is not offered as a first-line treatment for hyperlipidaemia because it is a black triangle drug, and post-marketing data are needed to confirm its safety. Its effect on clinical end-points has not yet been assessed. It may be considered as an adjunct to other lipid-lowering therapy in people unable to achieve target lipid levels on statins or fibrates alone, or for people unable to tolerate higher doses of statins. It is also an alternative for people unable to tolerate other lipid-lowering drugs.
- **Rosuvastatin** is not offered as a first-line treatment for hyperlipidaemia because it is a black triangle drug, and post-marketing data are needed to confirm its safety. Unlike other statins, its effect on clinical end-points has not yet been assessed. It is an alternative option for people unable to achieve target lipid levels with high doses of other statins.

Drugs included

- **Statins: simvastatin, pravastatin, atorvastatin, and fluvastatin** are offered. Pravastatin has been shown to reduce the overall number of CHD events in one large primary prevention study [Shepherd et al, 1995]. Atorvastatin, simvastatin, and pravastatin have been shown in large-scale secondary prevention trials to reduce deaths from all causes, the most conservative measure of clinical outcome [LaRosa et al, 1999; Athyros et al, 2002; Heart Protection Study Collaborative Group, 2002]. Fluvastatin given to people after their first percutaneous coronary intervention has been shown to reduce the risk of major adverse coronary events [Serruys et al, 2002].
- A non-drug prescription giving diet and lifestyle advice is offered.

Prescriptions

Non-drug management

Advice only: diet and lifestyle
- Age from 16 years onwards
- Your cholesterol level is high. Lifestyle and dietary changes can sometimes reduce the cholesterol level and other risk factors for heart disease. You should aim to eat and live healthily. This means: no smoking; regular exercise; moderate alcohol consumption. Lose weight if you are overweight or obese. Eat more vegetables, fruit, cereals, poultry, fish, rice, skimmed or semi-skimmed milk, grilled food, lean meat, pasta etc. and less fatty meats, fatty cheeses, full cream milk, fried food, lard, etc. If you do fry, choose a vegetable oil such as sunflower or rapeseed. Use low-fat spreads. Add less salt to food, and avoid foods that are very salty. Have your cholesterol level checked again in three months' time.

Start statin (PRODIGY start doses)

Simvastatin 20mg at night
- Age from 16 years onwards
- Simvastatin 20mg tablets. Take one tablet at night; supply 28 tablets; NHS Cost £7.80.

Atorvastatin 10mg once a day
- Age from 16 years onwards
- Atorvastatin 10mg tablets. Take one tablet once a day; supply 28 tablets; NHS Cost £18.03.

Fluvastatin 40mg at night
- Age from 16 years onwards
- Fluvastatin 40mg capsules. Take one capsule at night; supply 28 capsules; NHS Cost £12.72.

Pravastatin 40mg at night
- Age from 16 years onwards
- Pravastatin 40mg tablets. Take one tablet at night; supply 28 tablets; NHS Cost £29.69.

Start statin (high start doses)

Simvastatin 40mg at night
- Age from 16 years onwards
- Simvastatin 40mg tablets. Take one tablet at night; supply 28 tablets; NHS Cost £15.60.

Atorvastatin 20mg once a day
- Age from 16 years onwards
- Atorvastatin 20mg tablets. Take one tablet once a day; supply 28 tablets; NHS Cost £29.69.

Pravastatin 40mg at night
- Age from 16 years onwards
- Pravastatin 40mg tablets. Take one tablet at night; supply 28 tablets; NHS Cost £29.69.

Fluvastatin 80mg m/r at night
- Age from 16 years onwards
- Fluvastatin 80mg m/r tablets. Take one tablet at night; supply 28 tablets; NHS Cost £16.00.

Start statin (low start doses)

Simvastatin 10mg at night
- Age from 16 years onwards
- Simvastatin 10mg tablets. Take one tablet at night; supply 28 tablets; NHS Cost £5.78.

Atorvastatin 10mg once a day
- Age from 16 years onwards
- Atorvastatin 10mg tablets. Take one tablet once a day; supply 28 tablets; NHS Cost £18.03.

Fluvastatin 20mg at night
- Age from 16 years onwards
- Fluvastatin 20mg capsules. Take one capsule at night; supply 28 capsules; NHS Cost £12.72.

Pravastatin 10mg at night
- Age from 16 years onwards
- Pravastatin 10mg tablets. Take one tablet at night; supply 28 tablets; NHS Cost £16.18.

Pravastatin 20mg at night
- Age from 16 years onwards
- Pravastatin 20mg tablets. Take one tablet at night; supply 28 tablets; NHS Cost £29.69.

Cholesterol <5 and TG >2.3 (but <10)

D

Which therapy

- **Confirm results with a *fasting* lipid profile:** total cholesterol, LDL-C, HDL-C, triglycerides (TG).
- **For people without manifest cardiovascular disease, calculate the 10-year CHD risk using the average of two (preferably three) lipid and blood pressure results** (see How do I calculate cardiovascular risk? for details).
- **CHD risk greater than 15%, but no history of cardiovascular disease:**
  - Offer a statin (B).
- **Manifest cardiovascular disease:**
  - Offer a statin (B) or a fibrate (C).
- Fibrates can achieve greater reductions in TG levels, but statins have a greater body of evidence showing that they prevent CHD.
- **For all people with TG greater than 2.3 mmol/l:**
  - Optimize glycaemic control.
  - Aim to reduce alcohol consumption where appropriate.
  - Ensure appropriate management of other cardiovascular risk factors.
- **Consider referral for people with** very severe hypertriglyceridaemia (usually greater than 10 mmol/l).

Practical prescribing points

For further information please see the *Medicines Compendium* (www.medicines.org.uk) or the *British National Formulary* (www.bnf.org).

- Before starting any drug treatment for an abnormal lipid profile, measure fasting levels of total cholesterol, LDL-C, HDL-C, and triglycerides as baseline.
- Check CK and AST/ALT before starting drugs. Check creatinine before starting a fibrate.
- **Hepatotoxicity is rare,** but is thought to be dose-dependent.
- Non-specific muscle aches or joint pains, but non-significant increase in CK, are common.
- **Myopathy is rare, but the risk is increased in the presence of:**
  - Renal impairment, hypothyroidism, alcohol abuse, or underlying muscle disorders
  - Co-prescription of statins with fibrates (do not use gemfibrozil) or nicotinic acid
  - Co-prescription of drugs that increase statin levels, e.g. ciclosporin, clarithromycin, erythromycin, HIV protease inhibitors, itraconazole, and ketoconazole
- **Use a lower starting dose of statins people at increased risk of myopathy.** (Do not start treatment if baseline CK is greater than five times the upper limit of normal.)
- **Warfarin and simvastatin:** INR closely until stable — simvastatin occasionally increases INR significantly.
- **Warfarin and fibrates:** reduce the dose of warfarin by about a third and make further adjustments according to changes in the INR.

Stop treatment if:

- Serum creatinine increases progressively (with fibrates).
- There is a strong suspicion of myopathy, or CK level is greater than five times the upper limit of normal.
- Myalgic symptoms persist despite a normal CK level — a trial off treatment may be needed.
- AST or ALT level persists above three times the upper limit of normal.

Prescribing a fibrate in renal impairment

- **Consider specialist referral before starting treatment** with a fibrate. Titrate the dose slowly, while carefully monitoring lipid levels, CK, AST or ALT, and renal function, e.g. every 4 weeks.
- Modified-release preparations of fibrates are contraindicated in patients with renal impairment. Use standard preparations and start at low doses. Increase dose slowly, while carefully monitoring lipid levels, CK, AST or ALT and renal function (e.g. every 4 weeks.)

D

Follow-up advice

Monitoring response to treatment

- **Aim to lower total cholesterol by** 20–25%, or to below 5 mmol/l (whichever would result in the lower level) or to lower LDL-C by 30%, or to below 3 mmol/l (whichever would result in the lower level). Note: a fasting sample is only needed if an LDL-C or triglyceride (TG) level is required.
- **Aim to lower TG below 2.3 mmol/l.** (Note: fasting lipid profile is needed to give an accurate TG level.)
- **Statins:** check serum lipid profile 4–8 weeks after starting, or after a dose increase. Titrate dose until target or maximum tolerated dose is reached.
- **Fibrates:** check fasting serum lipid profile after 12 weeks. (Dose titration is not possible for most fibrates — the starting dose is the usual maintenance dose.)
- **Check fasting serum lipid profile annually.**

Monitoring toxicity

- **Check CK if muscle symptoms occur.**
- **Statins:** check AST or ALT 4–8 weeks after starting or after a dose increase, then annually.
- **Fibrates:** check AST or ALT and serum creatinine after 12 weeks, then annually. (Check every 3 months for the first year of fenofibrate therapy.)
- **Discontinue lipid-lowering therapy** if there is a strong suspicion of myopathy, or if CK exceeds five times the upper limit of the normal range, or if transaminases *persist* above three times the upper limit of the normal range.
- **Discontinue fibrate therapy** if serum creatinine continues to rise.

Should I refer or investigate?

Refer?

- **Severe hypercholesterolaemia,** i.e. total cholesterol (TC) greater than 10 mmol/l.
- **Severe hypertriglyceridaemia,** i.e. triglycerides greater than 10 mmol/l.
- **Target lipid levels are not achieved despite maximum tolerated doses.**
- **Suspected familial hypercholesterolaemia:** TC greater than 7.5 mmol/l (or LDL-C greater than 4.9 mmol/l) *and* at least one of the following:
    - Tendon xanthomata in himself/herself or in a first- or second-degree relative.
    - Family history of premature CHD, e.g. CHD or other atherosclerotic disease, in a male first-degree relative before the age of 55 years, or in a female first-degree relative before the age of 65 years.
    - Family history of TC greater than 7.5 mmol/l in a first- or second-degree relative.
- Reasons for referral are to make a firm diagnosis, to initiate treatment if required, and to counsel and screen the family.
- Referral may be unnecessary for someone with suspected familial hyperlipidaemia if he or she qualifies for treatment according to risk assessment. Family screening and counselling, however, should not be forgotten.

Investigate?

- **If secondary hypertriglyceridaemia is suspected after history and examination, tests to investigate this are indicated.** Causes of severe hypertriglyceridaemia include: hepatitis, or hepatobiliary disease; alcoholism; pregnancy (due to raised oestrogens); drugs, including oestrogens (oral contraceptives) and isotretinoin; and renal failure.

Patient information leaflets

The following PILs are available at www.prodigy.nhs.uk

- Blood Test - General
- Blood Test - Glucose
- Diabetes Insight Website
- Diabetes Research & Wellness Foundation
- Diabetes Type 2
- Diabetes Type 2 - A Summary
- Diabetes UK
- DiabeticLife

Shared decision making

- **Your triglyceride (blood fat) levels remain high.**
- **A 'statin' or a 'fibrate' medicine is recommended.**
- Side effects are uncommon.
    - A few people develop mild headaches, mild upset stomach, dizziness, or itching. These often go away with continued treatment.
    - A very rare, but serious, side effect is a muscle problem. Tell a doctor if you develop muscle pains whilst taking one of these medicines.
- You will need a blood test from time to time.
- **You should still eat and live healthily.** This means:
    - Do not smoke.
    - Take regular exercise.
    - Lose weight if you are overweight or obese.
    - East *more* vegetables, fruit, cereals, wholegrain bread, poultry, fish, rice, skimmed or semi-skimmed milk, grilled food, lean meat, and pasta.
    - Eat *less* of fatty meats, fatty cheeses, full cream milk, fried food, and lard.
    - If you do fry, choose a vegetable oil such as sunflower or rapeseed.
    - Use low-fat spreads.
    - Add less salt to food, and avoid prepared foods that are very salty.
    - Keep alcohol consumption moderate.
- Be sure to follow advice for keeping your diabetes under the best possible control.

Drug rationale

Drugs not included

- **Omega-3 polyunsaturated fatty acids** (omega-3 PUFAs) reduce serum triglyceride (TG) levels and can therefore

be a useful adjunct in the treatment of hypertriglyceridaemia. They can increase LDL-C levels, so both LDL-C and TG levels should be monitored. These drugs are usually initiated in secondary care.
- **Anion-exchange resins** can increase TG levels and their use is not recommended if TG are greater than 3 mmol/l. In addition, they are very inconvenient to take, and are therefore reserved as adjunctive therapy for people who are unable to achieve target lipid levels on the maximum tolerated dose of a statin or fibrate.
- **High doses of nicotinic acid** can produce large increases in HDL-C, as well as lowering cholesterol and TG levels. However, nicotinic acid can worsen glycaemic control and is therefore not recommended for use in Type 2 diabetes.

Drugs included

- **Statins: simvastatin, atorvastatin, and fluvastatin** are included. Triglycerides (TG) lowering is a class effect: reduction in TG levels is related to lowering of LDL-C, but significant reductions only occur in patients with high baseline TG levels [Stein et al, 1998].
- **Fibrates: bezafibrate, ciprofibrate, fenofibrate, and gemfibrozil** are included. Compared with statins, fibrates can achieve greater reductions in TG, and greater increases in HDL-C.
- Modified-release preparations of fibrates are contraindicated in patients with renal impairment. Low doses of standard-release preparations are offered for these patients. Note: bezafibrate is not offered for patients with renal impairment because it becomes contraindicated at a milder degree of renal impairment than other fibrates.

Prescriptions

Start statin (PRODIGY start doses)

Simvastatin 20mg at night
- Age from 16 years onwards
- Simvastatin 20mg tablets. Take one tablet at night; supply 28 tablets; NHS Cost £7.80.

Atorvastatin 10mg once a day
- Age from 16 years onwards
- Atorvastatin 10mg tablets. Take one tablet once a day; supply 28 tablets; NHS Cost £18.03.

Fluvastatin 40mg at night
- Age from 16 years onwards
- Fluvastatin 40mg capsules. Take one capsule at night; supply 28 capsules; NHS Cost £12.72.

Pravastatin 40mg at night
- Age from 16 years onwards
- Pravastatin 40mg tablets. Take one tablet at night; supply 28 tablets; NHS Cost £29.69.

Start statin (high start doses)

Simvastatin 40mg at night
- Age from 16 years onwards
- Simvastatin 40mg tablets. Take one tablet at night; supply 28 tablets; NHS Cost £15.60.

Atorvastatin 20mg once a day
- Age from 16 years onwards
- Atorvastatin 20mg tablets. Take one tablet once a day; supply 28 tablets; NHS Cost £29.69.

Pravastatin 40mg at night
- Age from 16 years onwards
- Pravastatin 40mg tablets. Take one tablet at night; supply 28 tablets; NHS Cost £29.69.

Fluvastatin 80mg m/r at night
- Age from 16 years onwards
- Fluvastatin 80mg m/r tablets. Take one tablet at night; supply 28 tablets; NHS Cost £16.00.

Start statin (low start doses)

Simvastatin 10mg at night
- Age from 16 years onwards
- Simvastatin 10mg tablets. Take one tablet at night; supply 28 tablets; NHS Cost £5.78.

Atorvastatin 10mg once a day
- Age from 16 years onwards
- Atorvastatin 10mg tablets. Take one tablet once a day; supply 28 tablets; NHS Cost £18.03.

Fluvastatin 20mg at night
- Age from 16 years onwards
- Fluvastatin 20mg capsules. Take one capsule at night; supply 28 capsules; NHS Cost £12.72.

Pravastatin 10mg at night
- Age from 16 years onwards
- Pravastatin 10mg tablets. Take one tablet at night; supply 28 tablets; NHS Cost £16.18.

Pravastatin 20mg at night
- Age from 16 years onwards
- Pravastatin 20mg tablets. Take one tablet at night; supply 28 tablets; NHS Cost £29.69.

Start fibrate (normal renal function)

Bezafibrate 400mg m/r once a day
- Age from 16 years onwards
- Bezafibrate 400mg m/r tablets. Take one tablet once a day; supply 30 tablets; NHS Cost £8.70.

Bezafibrate 200mg three times a day
- Age from 16 years onwards
- Bezafibrate 200mg tablets. Take one tablet three times a day; supply 84 tablets; NHS Cost £8.24.

Ciprofibrate 100mg once a day
- Age from 16 years onwards
- Ciprofibrate 100mg tablets. Take one tablet once a day; supply 28 tablets; NHS Cost £14.72.

Fenofibrate 160mg m/r once a day (equiv to 200mg std daily)
- Age from 16 years onwards
- Fenofibrate 160mg m/r tablets. Take one tablet once a day; supply 28 tablets; NHS Cost £14.75.

Fenofibrate 200mg once a day (equivalent to 160mg m/r daily)
- Age from 16 years onwards
- Fenofibrate 200mg capsules. Take one capsule once a day; supply 28 capsules; NHS Cost £17.95.

Fenofibrate 267mg once a day
- Age from 16 years onwards
- Fenofibrate 267mg capsules. Take one capsule once a day; supply 28 capsules; NHS Cost £21.75.

Gemfibrozil 600mg twice a day
- Age from 16 years onwards
- Gemfibrozil 600mg tablets. Take one tablet twice a day; supply 56 tablets; NHS Cost £19.79.

Start fibrate (mild/moderate renal impairment)

Fenofibrate 67mg once a day
- Age from 16 years onwards
- Fenofibrate 67mg capsules. Take one capsule once a day; supply 30 capsules; NHS Cost £7.77.

Gemfibrozil 300mg twice a day
- Age from 16 years onwards
- Gemfibrozil 300mg capsules. Take one capsule twice a day; supply 56 capsules; NHS Cost £12.14.

Ciprofibrate 100mg on alternate days
- Age from 16 years onwards
- Ciprofibrate 100mg tablets. Take one tablet on alternate days; supply 14 tablets; NHS Cost £7.36.

Managing statin therapy

Which therapy?

- **Aim to lower total cholesterol by** 20–25% or to below 5 mmol/l (whichever would result in the lower level), or to lower LDL-C by 30% or to below 3 mmol/l (whichever would result in the lower level). Note: a fasting sample is only needed if an LDL-C or triglyceride (TG) level is required.
- **Aim to lower TG to below 2.3 mmol/l.**
- **Review every 4–8 weeks and adjust dose until the target lipid level is reached.**
- If the target cholesterol level is not reached at maximum titration, consider: improving compliance (if poor); using an alternative statin; referral to a specialist lipid clinic; or combination therapy. Note: the risk of myopathy is increased if a statin and a fibrate are used together.
- **If combination therapy with a statin and a fibrate is offered,** avoid using gemfibrozil as this may lead to an increased risk of myopathy.
- Prescribing combination therapy is not available through PRODIGY as it is often initiated in secondary care.
- **Optimize glycaemic control.**
- Ensure appropriate management of other cardiovascular risk factors.

Stop treatment if:

- Strong suspicion of myopathy exists, or CK level is greater than 10 times the upper limit of normal.
- Myalgic symptoms persist despite a normal CK level — a trial off treatment may be needed.
- AST or ALT level persists above three times the upper limit of normal.

Practical prescribing points

For further information please see the *Medicines Compendium* (www.medicines.org.uk) or the *British National Formulary* (www.bnf.org).

- **Hepatotoxicity is rare,** and appears to be dose-dependent.
- Non-specific muscle aches or joint pains, but non-significant increase in CK, are common.
- **Myopathy is rare, but the risk is increased in the presence of:**
  - Renal impairment, hypothyroidism, alcohol abuse, or underlying muscle disorders
  - Co-prescription of statins with fibrates (do not use gemfibrozil) or nicotinic acid
  - Co-prescription of drugs that increase statin levels, e.g. ciclosporin, clarithromycin, erythromycin, HIV protease inhibitors, itraconazole, and ketoconazole
- **Use a lower starting dose of statins in people at increased risk of myopathy.** (Do not start treatment if baseline CK is greater than five times the upper limit of normal.)
- **Warfarin and simvastatin:** monitor INR closely until stable — simvastatin occasionally increases INR significantly.

Follow-up advice

Monitoring statin therapy

- **Aim to lower total cholesterol (TC) by** 20–25% or to below 5 mmol/l (whichever would result in the lower level), or to lower LDL-C by 30% or to below 3 mmol/l (whichever would result in the lower level).
- **Aim to lower triglycerides (TG) below 2.3 mmol/l.**
- **Advise patient to report any muscular pains immediately.** CK level should then be checked.
- **Discontinue statin if** there is a strong suspicion of myopathy, if CK exceeds five times the upper limit of the normal range, or if transaminases *persist* above three times the upper limit of the normal range.
- **Four to eight weeks after starting, or after a dose increase:** check non-fasting TC and AST or ALT. A fasting sample is only needed if a LDL-C or TG level is required.
- **Annual checks:** non-fasting TC, and AST or ALT.

Should I refer or investigate?

Refer?

- If the target cholesterol level is not reached at maximum tolerated titration, consider referral to a specialist lipid clinic.

Investigate?

- If not already done, monitor efficacy and tolerability of statin treatment:
  - Check non-fasting total cholesterol. A fasting sample is only needed if a LDL-C or triglyceride level is required.
  - Check ASTor ALT for signs of hepatotoxicity.

Patient information leaflets

The following PILs are available at www.prodigy.nhs.uk
- Blood Test - General
- Blood Test - Glucose
- Blood Test - Liver Function Tests
- Diabetes Insight Website
- Diabetes Research & Wellness Foundation
- Diabetes Type 2
- Diabetes Type 2 - A Summary
- Diabetes UK
- DiabeticLife

Shared decision making

- The dose of your medicine needs adjusting.
- Most people who take these medicines have no side effects. A few people may experience mild side effects. These include mild upset stomach or gut, itching, or a rash. Tell your doctor immediately if you have any muscle pains.
- Continue with the dietary advice previously given.
- Drink alcohol in moderation, exercise regularly, and do not smoke.
- Be sure to follow advice for keeping your diabetes under the best possible control.

Drug rationale

Drugs not included

- This scenario is for the management of statin therapy: other classes of lipid-lowering drugs are therefore not included.
- **Rosuvastatin** is not offered as a first-line treatment for hyperlipidaemia because it is a black triangle drug, and post-marketing data are needed to confirm its safety. Unlike other statins, its effect on clinical end-points has not yet been assessed. It is an alternative option for

people unable to achieve target lipid levels with high doses of other statins.

Drugs included

Maintenance doses/dose adjustments are offered for atorvastatin, fluvastatin, pravastatin, and simvastatin. A non-drug prescription giving diet and lifestyle advice is offered.

Prescriptions

Non-drug management

Advice only: diet and lifestyle

- Age from 16 years onwards
- Your cholesterol level is high. Lifestyle and dietary changes can sometimes reduce the cholesterol level and other risk factors for heart disease. You should aim to eat and live healthily. This means: no smoking; regular exercise; moderate alcohol consumption. Lose weight if you are overweight or obese. Eat more vegetables, fruit, cereals, poultry, fish, rice, skimmed or semi-skimmed milk, grilled food, lean meat, pasta, etc., and less of fatty meats, fatty cheeses, full cream milk, fried food, lard, etc. If you do fry, choose a vegetable oil such as sunflower or rapeseed. Use low-fat spreads. Add less salt to food, and avoid foods that are very salty. Have your cholesterol level checked again in 3 months' time.

Simvastatin

Simvastatin 10mg at night

- Age from 16 years onwards
- Simvastatin 10mg tablets. Take one tablet at night; supply 28 tablets; NHS Cost £5.78.

Simvastatin 20mg at night

- Age from 16 years onwards
- Simvastatin 20mg tablets. Take one tablet at night; supply 28 tablets; NHS Cost £7.80.

Simvastatin 40mg at night

- Age from 16 years onwards
- Simvastatin 40mg tablets. Take one tablet at night; supply 28 tablets; NHS Cost £15.60.

Simvastatin 80mg at night

- Age from 16 years onwards
- Simvastatin 80mg tablets. Take one tablet at night; supply 28 tablets; NHS Cost £28.77.

Atorvastatin

Atorvastatin 10mg once a day

- Age from 16 years onwards
- Atorvastatin 10mg tablets. Take one tablet once a day; supply 28 tablets; NHS Cost £18.03.

Atorvastatin 20mg once a day

- Age from 16 years onwards
- Atorvastatin 20mg tablets. Take one tablet once a day; supply 28 tablets; NHS Cost £29.69.

Atorvastatin 40mg once a day

- Age from 16 years onwards
- Atorvastatin 40mg tablets. Take one tablet once a day; supply 28 tablets; NHS Cost £29.69.

Atorvastatin 80mg once a day

- Age from 16 years onwards
- Atorvastatin 80mg tablets. Take one tablet once a day; supply 28 tablets; NHS Cost £29.69.

Pravastatin

Pravastatin 10mg at night

- Age from 16 years onwards
- Pravastatin 10mg tablets. Take one tablet at night; supply 28 tablets; NHS Cost £16.18.

Pravastatin 20mg at night

- Age from 16 years onwards
- Pravastatin 20mg tablets. Take one tablet at night; supply 28 tablets; NHS Cost £29.69.

Pravastatin 40mg at night

- Age from 16 years onwards
- Pravastatin 40mg tablets. Take one tablet at night; supply 28 tablets; NHS Cost £29.69.

Fluvastatin

Fluvastatin 20mg at night

- Age from 16 years onwards
- Fluvastatin 20mg capsules. Take one capsule at night; supply 28 capsules; NHS Cost £12.72.

Fluvastatin 40mg at night

- Age from 16 years onwards
- Fluvastatin 40mg capsules. Take one capsule at night; supply 28 capsules; NHS Cost £12.72.

Fluvastatin 80mg m/r at night

- Age from 16 years onwards
- Fluvastatin 80mg m/r tablets. Take one tablet at night; supply 28 tablets; NHS Cost £16.00.

Managing fibrate therapy

Which therapy?

- **Aim to lower total cholesterol by 20–25% or to below 5 mmol/l** (whichever would result in the lower level), or to lower LDL-C by 30% or to below 3 mmol/l (whichever would result in the lower level).
- **Aim to lower triglycerides below 2.3 mmol/l.**
- **Dose titration is needed only if there is impaired renal function** — the recommended starting dose is the usual maintenance dose. Note: it can take 3–4 months before maximum effects are seen.
- **If the target cholesterol level is not reached** consider: improving compliance (if poor); changing to a statin; referral to a specialist lipid clinic; or using combination therapy. Note: the risk of myopathy is increased if a statin and a fibrate are used together.
- Prescribing combination therapy is not available through PRODIGY as it is often initiated in secondary care.
- **Reinforce lifestyle advice:** mediterranean diet, weight, exercise, smoking, alcohol.
- **Optimize glycaemic control.**
- Ensure appropriate management of other cardiovascular risk factors.

Stop fibrate treatment if:

- Serum creatinine increases progressively.
- There is a strong suspicion of myopathy, or CK level is greater than five times the upper limit of the normal range.
- Myalgic symptoms persist despite a normal CK level — a trial off treatment may be needed.
- AST or ALT level persists above three times the upper limit of the normal range.

Practical prescribing points

For further information please see the *Medicines Compendium* (www.medicines.org.uk) or the *British National Formulary* (www.bnf.org).

- **Hepatotoxicity is rare,** and appears to be dose-dependent.
- Non-specific muscle aches or joint pains, but non-significant increase in creatine kinase (CK), are common.
- **Myopathy is rare, but the risk is increased in the presence of:**
  - Renal impairment, hypothyroidism, alcohol abuse, or underlying muscle disorders
  - Co-prescription of statins with fibrates (do not use gemfibrozil) or nicotinic acid
- **Warfarin and fibrates:** reduce the dose of warfarin by about a third and make further adjustments according to changes in the INR.

D

Prescribing a fibrate in renal impairment

- Consider seeking specialist advice before adjusting the dose of a fibrate in renal impairment.
- Modified-release preparations of fibrates are contraindicated in patients with renal impairment. Use standard preparations and start at low doses. Increase dose slowly, while carefully monitoring lipid levels, CK, AST or ALT, and renal function (e.g. every 4 weeks.)

Follow-up advice

Monitoring fibrate therapy

- **Aim to lower total cholesterol by 20–25% or to below 5 mmol/l** (whichever would result in the lower level), or to lower LDL-C by 30% or to below 3 mmol/l (whichever would result in the lower level).
- **Aim to lower triglycerides below 2.3 mmol/l.**
- **Advise patient to report any muscular pains immediately.** CK level should then be checked.
- **Discontinue fibrate** if strong suspicion of myopathy exists, or if CK exceeds five times the upper limit of the normal range, if transaminases *persist* above three times the upper limit of the normal range, or if serum creatinine continues to rise progressively.
- **Twelve weeks after starting:** check fasting serum lipid profile and AST or ALT. Dose titration is not possible for most fibrates — the starting dose is the usual maintenance dose.
- **Annual checks:** fasting serum lipid profile, AST or ALT, and serum creatinine.
- **If the person has renal impairment** consider specialist referral before starting treatment with a fibrate. Titrate the dose slowly, while carefully monitoring lipid levels, CK, AST or ALT, and renal function (e.g. every 4 weeks).

Should I refer or investigate?

Refer?

- If the target cholesterol or triglyceride level is not reached at maximum tolerated titration, consider referral to a specialist lipid clinic.

Investigate?

- If not already done, monitor efficacy and tolerability of statin treatment:
  - Check non-fasting total cholesterol. A fasting sample is only needed if a LDL-C or triglyceride level is required.
  - Check AST or ALT for signs of hepatotoxicity.
  - Check serum creatinine.

Patient information leaflets

The following PILs are available at www.prodigy.nhs.uk

- Blood Test - General
- Blood Test - Glucose
- Diabetes Insight Website
- Diabetes Research & Wellness Foundation
- Diabetes Type 2
- Diabetes Type 2 - A Summary
- Diabetes UK
- DiabeticLife

Shared decision making

- The dose of your medicine needs adjusting.
- Most people who take these medicines have no side effects. A few people may experience mild side effects. These include mild upset stomach or gut, itching, or a rash. Tell your doctor immediately if you have any muscle pains.
- Continue with the dietary advice previously given.
- Drink alcohol in moderation, exercise regularly, and do not smoke.
- Be sure to follow advice for keeping your diabetes under the best possible control.

Drug rationale

Drugs not included

- This scenario is for the management of fibrate therapy: other classes of lipid-lowering drugs are therefore not included.

Drugs included

- Maintenance doses/dose adjustments are offered for bezafibrate, ciprofibrate, fenofibrate, and gemfibrozil.
- A non-drug prescription giving diet and lifestyle advice i also offered.

Prescriptions

Non-drug management

Advice only: diet and lifestyle

- Age from 16 years onwards
- Your lipid levels are high. Lifestyle and dietary changes can sometimes reduce the level and other risk factors for heart disease. You should aim to eat and live healthily. This means: no smoking; regular exercise; moderate alcohol consumption. Lose weight if you are overweight or obese. Eat more vegetables, fruit, cereals, poultry, fish rice, skimmed or semi-skimmed milk, grilled food, lean meat, pasta, etc., and less of fatty meats, fatty cheeses, full cream milk, fried food, lard, etc. If you do fry, choose a vegetable oil such as sunflower or rapeseed. Us low-fat spreads. Add less salt to food, and avoid foods that are very salty. Have your cholesterol level checked again in 3 months' time.

Step-up fenofibrate (mild/moderate renal impairment)

Fenofibrate 67mg once a day

- Age from 16 years onwards
- Fenofibrate 67mg capsules. Take one capsule once a day supply 30 capsules; NHS Cost £7.77.

Fenofibrate 67mg twice a day

- Age from 16 years onwards
- Fenofibrate 67mg capsules. Take one capsule twice a day; supply 60 capsules; NHS Cost £15.53.

Fenofibrate 67mg three times a day
Age from 16 years onwards
Fenofibrate 67mg capsules. Take one capsule three times a day; supply 90 capsules; NHS Cost £23.30.

Step-up gemfibrozil (mild/moderate renal impairment)

Gemfibrozil 300mg twice a day
Age from 16 years onwards
Gemfibrozil 300mg capsules. Take one capsule twice a day; supply 56 capsules; NHS Cost £12.14.

Gemfibrozil 300mg three times a day
Age from 16 years onwards
Gemfibrozil 300mg capsules. Take one capsule three times a day; supply 84 capsules; NHS Cost £18.21.

Gemfibrozil 600mg twice a day
Age from 16 years onwards
Gemfibrozil 600mg tablets. Take one tablet twice a day; supply 56 tablets; NHS Cost £19.79.

Step-up ciprofibrate (mild/moderate renal impairment)

Ciprofibrate 100mg on alternate days
Age from 16 years onwards
Ciprofibrate 100mg tablets. Take one tablet on alternate days; supply 14 tablets; NHS Cost £7.36.

Ciprofibrate 100mg once a day
Age from 16 years onwards
Ciprofibrate 100mg tablets. Take one tablet once a day; supply 28 tablets; NHS Cost £14.72.

Fibrate maintenance doses (normal renal function)

Bezafibrate 400mg m/r once a day
Age from 16 years onwards
Bezafibrate 400mg m/r tablets. Take one tablet once a day; supply 30 tablets; NHS Cost £8.70.

Bezafibrate 200mg three times a day
Age from 16 years onwards
Bezafibrate 200mg tablets. Take one tablet three times a day; supply 84 tablets; NHS Cost £8.24.

Ciprofibrate 100mg once a day
Age from 16 years onwards
Ciprofibrate 100mg tablets. Take one tablet once a day; supply 28 tablets; NHS Cost £14.72.

Fenofibrate 160mg m/r once a day (equiv to 200mg std daily)
Age from 16 years onwards
Fenofibrate 160mg m/r tablets. Take one tablet once a day; supply 28 tablets; NHS Cost £14.75.

Fenofibrate 200mg once a day (equivalent to 160mg m/r daily)
Age from 16 years onwards
Fenofibrate 200mg capsules. Take one capsule once a day; supply 28 capsules; NHS Cost £17.95.

Fenofibrate 267mg once a day
Age from 16 years onwards
Fenofibrate 267mg capsules. Take one capsule once a day; supply 28 capsules; NHS Cost £21.75.

Gemfibrozil 600mg twice a day
Age from 16 years onwards
Gemfibrozil 600mg tablets. Take one tablet twice a day; supply 56 tablets; NHS Cost £19.79.

Fasting triglyceride >10: refer

Which therapy?

- **Referral for specialist care is usually indicated for people with hypertriglyceridaemia greater than 10 mmol/l,** as there is a significant risk of pancreatitis.
- **Start fibrate treatment while waiting for referral appointment** (provided that there is no significant abnormality in the liver function tests and no severe renal impairment).
- **If practical,** consider stopping treatment with oestrogens, corticosteroids, and thiazides while waiting for specialist assessment.
- **Ask about and manage excessive alcohol intake.**
- **Optimize glycaemic control.**
- **Ensure appropriate management of other cardiovascular risk factors.**

D

Practical prescribing points

For further information please see the *Medicines Compendium* (www.medicines.org.uk) or the *British National Formulary* (www.bnf.org).

- Check CK, AST/ALT, and serum creatinine before starting treatment.
- **Hepatotoxicity is rare,** and appears to be dose-dependent.
- Non-specific muscle aches or joint pains, but non-significant increase in CK, are common.
- **Myopathy is rare, but the risk is increased in the presence of:**
  - Renal impairment, hypothyroidism, alcohol abuse, or underlying muscle disorders
  - Co-prescription of statins with fibrates (do not use gemfibrozil) or nicotinic acid
- **Warfarin and fibrates:** reduce the dose of warfarin by about a third and make further adjustments according to changes in the INR.

Prescribing a fibrate in renal impairment

- Consider seeking specialist advice before starting treatment with a fibrate.
- Modified-release preparations of fibrates are contraindicated in patients with renal impairment. Use standard preparations and start at low doses. Increase dose slowly, while carefully monitoring lipid levels, CK, AST or ALT, and renal function (e.g. every 4 weeks).

Stop fibrate treatment if:

- Serum creatinine increases progressively.
- There is a strong suspicion of myopathy, or CK level is greater than five times the upper limit of the normal range.
- Myalgic symptoms persist despite a normal CK level — a trial off treatment may be needed.
- AST or ALT level persists above three times the upper limit of the normal range.

Follow-up advice

- People with very severe hypertriglyceridaemia will usually be followed up by, or in shared care with, specialist services.

Monitoring fibrate therapy

- **Advise patient to report any muscular pains immediately.** CK level should then be checked.
- **Discontinue fibrate** if strong suspicion of myopathy, or if CK exceeds five times the upper limit of the normal

range, if transaminases *persist* above three times the upper limit of the normal range, or if serum creatinine continues to rise progressively.
- **Twelve weeks after starting:** check fasting serum lipid profile and AST or ALT. Dose titration is not possible for most fibrates — the starting dose is the usual maintenance dose.
- **Annual checks:** fasting serum lipid profile, AST or ALT, and serum creatinine.
- **If the person has renal impairment** consider specialist referral before starting treatment with a fibrate. Titrate the dose slowly, while carefully monitoring lipid levels, CK, AST or ALT levels, and renal function (e.g. every 4 weeks).

D

Should I refer or investigate?

Refer?

- Referral for specialist care is usually indicated if hypertriglyceridaemia is greater than 10 mmol/l — if untreated, there is a significant risk of pancreatitis.
- **Start fibrate treatment while waiting for referral appointment** (provided that there is no significant abnormality in the liver function tests and no severe renal impairment).

Investigate?

- If referring, no further investigations are necessary (avoid duplication).
- **Rule out or manage secondary causes of hypertriglyceridaemia:** hepatitis or hepatobiliary disease; alcoholism; pregnancy (due to raised oestrogens); drugs, including oestrogens (oral contraceptives), isotretinoin, and tamoxifen; and renal failure.

Patient information leaflets

The following PILs are available at www.prodigy.nhs.uk
- Blood Test - General
- Blood Test - Glucose
- Diabetes Insight Website
- Diabetes Research & Wellness Foundation
- Diabetes Type 2
- Diabetes Type 2 - A Summary
- Diabetes UK
- DiabeticLife

Shared decision making

- You have a triglyceride (blood fat) level that is very high.
- Referral to a specialist may be recommended.
- In some cases, a high triglyceride level is made worse by taking other medicines for other conditions.

Drug rationale

Drugs not included

- **Statins** are not included in this scenario since fibrates produce greater reductions in triglyceride (TG) levels.
- **Omega-3 polyunsaturated fatty acids** (omega-3 PUFAs) reduce serum TG levels and can therefore be a useful adjunct in the treatment of hypertriglyceridaemia. They can increase LDL-C levels, so both LDL-C and TG levels should be monitored. These drugs are usually initiated in secondary care.
- **High doses of nicotinic acid** can produce large increases in HDL-C, as well as lowering cholesterol and TG levels. However, it is not recommended for use in people with diabetes as it can worsen glycaemic control.

Drugs included

- **Fibrates: bezafibrate, ciprofibrate, fenofibrate, or gemfibrozil** may be initiated while waiting for referral appointment.
- Modified-release preparations of fibrates are contraindicated in patients with renal impairment. Low doses of standard-release preparations are offered for these patients. Note: bezafibrate is not offered for patients with renal impairment because it becomes contraindicated at a milder degree of renal impairment than other fibrates.
- A non-drug prescription giving diet and lifestyle advice is offered.

Prescriptions

Non-drug management

Advice only: diet and lifestyle
- Age from 16 years onwards
- Your lipid levels are high. Lifestyle and dietary changes can sometimes reduce the level and other risk factors for heart disease. You should aim to eat and live healthily. This means: no smoking; regular exercise; moderate alcohol consumption. Lose weight if you are overweight or obese. Eat more vegetables, fruit, cereals, poultry, fish, rice, skimmed or semi-skimmed milk, grilled food, lean meat, pasta, etc., and less of fatty meats, fatty cheeses, full cream milk, fried food, lard, etc. If you do fry, choose a vegetable oil such as sunflower or rapeseed. Use low-fat spreads. Add less salt to food, and avoid foods that are very salty.

Start fibrate (normal renal function)

Bezafibrate 400mg m/r once a day
- Age from 16 years onwards
- Bezafibrate 400mg m/r tablets. Take one tablet once a day; supply 30 tablets; NHS Cost £8.70.

Bezafibrate 200mg three times a day
- Age from 16 years onwards
- Bezafibrate 200mg tablets. Take one tablet three times a day; supply 84 tablets; NHS Cost £8.24.

Ciprofibrate 100mg once a day
- Age from 16 years onwards
- Ciprofibrate 100mg tablets. Take one tablet once a day; supply 28 tablets; NHS Cost £14.72.

Fenofibrate 160mg m/r once a day (equiv to 200mg std daily)
- Age from 16 years onwards
- Fenofibrate 160mg m/r tablets. Take one tablet once a day; supply 28 tablets; NHS Cost £14.75.

Fenofibrate 200mg once a day (equivalent to 160mg m/r daily)
- Age from 16 years onwards
- Fenofibrate 200mg capsules. Take one capsule once a day; supply 28 capsules; NHS Cost £17.95.

Fenofibrate 267mg once a day
- Age from 16 years onwards
- Fenofibrate 267mg capsules. Take one capsule once a day; supply 28 capsules; NHS Cost £21.75.

Gemfibrozil 600mg twice a day
- Age from 16 years onwards
- Gemfibrozil 600mg tablets. Take one tablet twice a day; supply 56 tablets; NHS Cost £19.79.

Start fibrate (mild/moderate renal impairment)

Fenofibrate 67mg once a day

- Age from 16 years onwards
- Fenofibrate 67mg capsules. Take one capsule once a day; supply 30 capsules; NHS Cost £7.77.

Gemfibrozil 300mg twice a day

- Age from 16 years onwards
- Gemfibrozil 300mg capsules. Take one capsule twice a day; supply 56 capsules; NHS Cost £12.14.

Ciprofibrate 100mg on alternate days

- Age from 16 years onwards
- Ciprofibrate 100mg tablets. Take one tablet on alternate days; supply 14 tablets; NHS Cost £7.36.

Extended Information

Background information

- What is dyslipidaemia? p.585
- How common is dyslipidaemia in people with Type 2 diabetes? p.585
- How do I know my patient has abnormal lipid levels? p.585
- What else might it be? p.585
- Complications and prognosis p.585
- What are the risk factors for cardiovascular disease in people with diabetes? p.586

What is dyslipidaemia?

- People with Type 2 diabetes often have moderately elevated circulating levels of triglycerides (TG) and small, dense low-density lipoprotein cholesterol (LDL-C) particles, together with reduced levels of high-density lipoprotein cholesterol levels.
- However, they often have normal levels of total cholesterol (TC) and LDL-C if glycaemic control is adequate.

[Papadakis et al, 2001; SIGN, 2001]

- For the purpose of this guidance, dyslipidaemia is defined by the threshold at which treatment would be recommended if a person has a history of cardiovascular disease or more than a 15% 10-year coronary heart disease risk, i.e:
  - TC greater than or equal to 5 mmol/l, or
  - LDL-C greater than or equal to 3 mmol/l, or
  - TG greater than or equal to 2.3 mmol/l

How common is dyslipidaemia in people with Type 2 diabetes?

- **Dyslipidaemias are common** in people with Type 2 diabetes.
- About 84% of men and 89% of women with diabetes have low-density lipoprotein cholesterol above 2.6 mmol/l.
- Almost 50% of people with Type 2 diabetes have a triglyceride (TG) level above 1.7 mmol/l and about 25% have a TG level above 2.3 mmol/l.

[Taskinen, 2002]

How do I know my patient has abnormal lipid levels?

- **Measure total cholesterol (TC), low-density lipoprotein cholesterol (LDL-C), high-density lipoprotein cholesterol (HDL-C), and triglyceride (TG) at diagnosis (C) and at least annually thereafter (D) in all people with Type 2 diabetes.**
- TC and HDL-C can be determined from a non-fasting sample. LDL-C and TG require a fasting sample.

[McIntosh et al, 2002; NICE, 2002b]

What else might it be?

- **Secondary causes of dyslipidaemia should be excluded or identified and managed,** particularly if total serum cholesterol is greater than 6.5 mmol/l or serum triglycerides exceed 8.0 mmol/l (see Table 1 for important causes of secondary hyperlipidaemia).

[Stone, 1994; Durrington, 1995]

Complications and prognosis

Complications

- **Type 2 diabetes is a major risk factor for cardiovascular disease.** Three-quarters of deaths in people with diabetes are due to cardiovascular causes.
- **This increase in the risk of cardiovascular events in people with diabetes is due to many factors,** including the increased prevalence of dyslipidaemia. The lipid profile commonly seen in people with Type 2 diabetes, i.e. raised low-density lipoprotein cholesterol (LDL-C), low high-density lipoprotein cholesterol (HDL-C), and raised triglyceride levels, seems to be particularly atherogenic.

[Mooradian, 2003]

- **Very severe hypertriglyceridaemia (>10 mmol/l) is a risk factor for pancreatitis.** The most common associations of very severe hypertriglyceridaemia and pancreatitis are:
  - Diabetes mellitus
  - Alcohol abuse
  - Pregnancy
  - Adverse effects of drugs (see list in Table 1)

[Durrington, 1995]

Prognosis

- **Coronary heart disease has a worse prognosis in people with diabetes** than in people without diabetes.
  - In the Framingham study, the time from first to recurrent myocardial infarction (MI) or fatal event

Table 1: Important causes of secondary hyperlipidaemia.

Lipid abnormality	Causes
Hypercholesterolaemia	Hypothyroidism Obstructive jaundice Anorexia nervosa Nephrotic syndrome Drugs*: ciclosporin
Hypertriglyceridaemia	Hepatitis, hepatobiliary disease Alcohol abuse Drugs*: isotretinoin, oral contraceptives (oestrogens), high doses of beta-blockers, anion-exchange resins Pregnancy Obesity Renal failure
Combined hypertriglyceridaemia and hypercholesterolaemia	Drugs*: oral contraceptives (progestogens and oestrogens), corticosteroids, high doses of thiazides Pregnancy Multiple myeloma Conditions that predominantly cause hypertriglyceridaemia can also result in combined hyperlipidaemia in some individuals

Secondary causes should (usually) be addressed first and then the need for specific lipid-lowering therapy reassessed.
* If a drug is thought to be the cause of clinically significant hyperlipidaemia, review the indications for the drug and consider alternative treatments or reduction of dose. Consider also the addition of a lipid-lowering diet with or without lipid-lowering drug therapy.

D

was 5.3 years in men and 5.1 years in women with diabetes, compared with 7.1 years and 8.1 years in people without diabetes.

- The mortality rate of people with diabetes who have had an MI is 1.5–2 times higher than in people without diabetes.

[Papadakis et al, 2001]

What are the risk factors for cardiovascular disease in people with diabetes?

- The following risk factors for cardiovascular disease are particularly likely to be present in people with diabetes:
  - Increased blood glucose
  - Dyslipidaemia
  - Hypertension
  - Microalbuminuria or proteinuria

[UK Prospective Diabetes Study Group, 1998; NHS CRD, 2000]

- Conventional risk factors increase the risk of cardiovascular disease in people with Type 2 diabetes to about the same extent as in those without diabetes. These include:
  - Age
  - Previous history of cardiovascular disease
  - Cigarette smoking
  - Sedentary lifestyle
  - Family history of cardiovascular disease

Management issues

- How do I calculate cardiovascular risk? p.586
- General issues p.587
- When should I treat and what should I use? p.588
- What is the evidence for lipid-lowering therapy in people with Type 2 diabetes? p.588
- Medicines management p.590
- Indications for specialist referral p.592

How do I calculate cardiovascular risk?

- **Estimate coronary heart disease risk (CHD) at least annually** for *all* people with Type 2 diabetes without manifest cardiovascular disease (C).
- Calculate 10-year CHD risk using the Joint British Societies risk assessment charts for people with diabetes (printed at the back of the BNF) or use the online calculator: www.bhsoc.org/resources/prediction_chart.htm.
- The data required for the Joint British Societies Coronary Risk Prediction Chart are shown in Table 2.
- **Management decisions should be based on the average of at least two measurements** (or three if possible) because lipid levels are subject to variation. The second sample should preferably be taken after a few weeks. Total cholesterol and high-density lipoprotein cholesterol (HDL-C) can be determined from a non-fasting sample. Low-density lipoprotein cholesterol and triglycerides (TG) require a fasting specimen.
- If cholesterol results are not available, use average values for age and sex.
- **Use baseline blood pressure (BP) and lipid measurements for risk calculation if people are already taking antihypertensive or lipid-lowering drugs.**
- Note: antihypertensive drugs or lipid-lowering therapy should still be started (or continued) if modification of risk factors (e.g. the person has quit smoking, or has started treatment for hypertension) results in the calculated risk falling below the threshold for drug treatment.
- If lifestyle advice results in BP or lipid levels falling below treatment targets, drug treatment is not needed. However, results should be re-checked annually as they are likely to alter with time.
- Other CHD risk assessment tools are available. For further information see the separate PRODIGY guidance on *CHD risk — identification and management.*
- **Certain individuals are at higher risk than the risk tools predict.** Higher risk occurs in:
  - **People with a family history of premature CHD** — adjust risk upwards by a factor of 1.5.
  - **People with familial dyslipidaemia,** e.g. hypercholesterolaemia, familial combined hyperlipidaemia, and other inherited dyslipidaemias.
  - **People with raised TG levels.**
  - **Those who are not yet diabetic,** but have impaired fasting glucose concentrations (6.1–6.9 mmol/l).
  - **People with Type 1 diabetes.** The risk is often greater than that predicted by the cholesterol to HDL-C ratio in Type 1 diabetes. It may be more accurate to ignore HDL-C and use the lipid scale for total serum cholesterol alone, but there is no direct evidence for this approach.
  - **Women with premature menopause.**
  - **Those with the lowest incomes.**
  - **Increasing age.** Risk increases exponentially with age, so the risk will be closer to the next age category on the risk prediction charts for the last four years of each decade.
  - **People of south Asian descent,** i.e. originating from the Indian subcontinent. (The risk charts have not been validated in ethnic minority populations).

Table 2: Data required for the Joint British Societies Coronary Risk Prediction Chart.

Data required	Comments
Gender	-
Age (years)	-
Smoking status	The British Heart Foundation states that: 'Smoking status should reflect lifetime exposure to tobacco and not simply tobacco use at the time of assessment. For example, those who have given up smoking within 5 years should be regarded as current smokers for the purposes of the charts.'
Blood pressure (mmHg)	Use an average of two (preferably three) measurements taken sitting in the consulting room. If antihypertensive drugs are being taken, use pretreatment values.
Total cholesterol (mmol/l)	Fasting specimen not required. If lipid-lowering therapy is being given, use pretreatment values.
HDL-C	Fasting specimen not required. If no HDL-C measurements available, assume value = 1.0. If lipid-lowering therapy is being given, use pretreatment values.

HDL-C = high-density lipoprotein cholesterol

CHD risk assessment tools should be used to supplement, not replace, clinical judgement.
[Wood et al, 1998]

Classification of risk

The National institute for Clinical Excellence (NICE) defines higher and lower 10-year coronary event risk in people with Type 2 diabetes as follows:

A person at higher risk is one:

- Who has manifest cardiovascular disease (a history or symptoms of CHD, stroke, or peripheral vascular disease), or
- Whose 10-year coronary event risk is assessed as above 15%, taking into account the known limitations of the risk assessment tools, or
- Who has microalbuminuria or proteinuria — the development of microalbuminuria or proteinuria is a particularly strong indicator of CHD risk in people with Type 2 diabetes (see separate PRODIGY guidance on *Diabetes Type 2 — renal disease*).

A person at lower risk is one:

- Who does not have manifest cardiovascular disease, and
- Whose 10-year coronary event risk is 15% or below, taking into account the known limitations of the risk assessment tools.

[McIntosh et al, 2002; NICE, 2002b]

General issues

- **Identify and manage people with adverse lipid profile secondary to conditions other than Type 2 diabetes:**
  - Ask about alcohol consumption and manage accordingly.
  - Check thyroid function tests to exclude hypothyroidism.
  - Check liver function tests to exclude liver disease.
  - Check serum creatinine and urinary protein to exclude renal disease.
- **Ensure good blood glucose control.** For each individual, a target HbA_{1c} level should be set between 6.5 and 7.5%, based on the risk of macrovascular and microvascular complications. In general, the lower target HbA_{1c} is preferred for people at significant risk of vascular complications, but higher targets are necessary for those at risk of iatrogenic hypoglycaemia [NICE, 2002a].
  - Good glycaemic control alone is not usually sufficient to correct diabetic dyslipidaemia [Papadakis et al, 2001].
- **Measure blood pressure (BP) and manage hypertension** (see separate PRODIGY guidance on *Diabetes Type 1 and 2 — hypertension*).
- **Offer lifestyle management advice.**
  - Advice should be personalized and cover cardioprotective diet, weight, exercise, stopping smoking, and moderation of alcohol consumption. For further information on lifestyle advice, see separate PRODIGY guidance on *Cardiovascular risk — identification and management.*
- **Offer smoking cessation advice** where appropriate (see separate PRODIGY guidance on *Smoking cessation*).
- **For individuals who are overweight or obese, encourage weight loss and increased physical activity (A).**
  - **Reduction in excess weight** leads to an improvement in both lipid profile and glycaemic control [Papadakis et al, 2001]. The greatest benefit is on triglycerides (TG) levels, with a slight increase in high-density lipoprotein cholesterol (HDL-C) and a modest decrease in total cholesterol (TC) and low-density lipoprotein cholesterol (LDL-C) (see separate PRODIGY guidance on *Obesity*).
  - **Increasing physical activity** is likely to provide benefits for people with Type 2 diabetes as it improves insulin sensitivity, reduces TG levels, and increases HDL-C levels [Papadakis et al, 2001].

[McIntosh et al, 2002; NICE, 2002b]

Dietary management

- **As dietary management alone only results in small reductions in cholesterol levels (1–5%), it is generally most useful as an adjunct to drug treatment.**
- However, as up to 30% of all deaths from coronary heart disease (CHD) have been attributed to unhealthy diets, people should be advised to adopt a healthier overall diet; the focus should not just be on reducing fat intake.
- A mediterranean diet contains many of the dietary elements that are thought to be protective in cardiovascular disease:
  - Replace butter with olive oil and monounsaturated margarine (e.g. rapeseed- or olive-oil-based).
  - Eat less red meat (replace beef, lamb, and pork with poultry).
  - Eat more fish, including at least one portion of oily fish per week (e.g. mackerel, herring, kipper, pilchard, sardine, salmon, or trout).
  - Eat more root vegetables and green vegetables.
  - No day without fruit.
- Encourage people to eat fewer commercial bakery and deep-fried foods (these contain high levels of sugar and trans-fats).
- Encourage people to eat high-fibre foods, specifically those with a low glycaemic index.
- Fruit and vegetables are very important and many people take insufficient amounts, but it is important to remind people of the sugar content of fruit or fruit juice, and that too much may compromise their glycaemic control. Note: tinned and frozen fruit and vegetables are as good as fresh vegetables. A glass of fruit juice also counts as a portion.
- **Margarine containing sitostanol ester may help some people** reduce the cholesterol intake from their diet. It has been shown to reduce TC by about 10% when substituted for part of the daily fat intake. Adding 2 g of plant sterol to an average daily portion of margarine reduces serum LDL-C by an average of 0.54 mmol/l in people aged 50–59, 0.43 mmol/l in people aged 40–49, and 0.33 mmol/l in those aged 30–39 [Law, 2000].
- **The place of sitostanol ester in the management of patients with hypercholesterolaemia is uncertain at the present time.** There are no randomized controlled trials with clinical outcome data, and there is limited information on safety. It is an option as part of a cholesterol-lowering diet, although its cost could deter some people.

[British Heart Foundation, 1999; Murphy et al, 2001; Hu and Willett, 2002; MeReC, 2002]

Should I use a 3-month trial of dietary management before starting drug treatment?

- People with Type 2 diabetes and established cardiovascular disease or a calculated CHD risk greater than 15% whose lipid levels are above the treatment threshold should be started on lipid-lowering treatment as soon as possible. Dietary management should be used as an adjunct to therapy.

Treatment with aspirin

Secondary prevention

- For people with manifest cardiovascular disease, offer 75 mg aspirin daily (**B**).

D

Primary prevention

- For people with diabetes and a 10-year coronary risk greater than 15%, offer 75 mg aspirin daily (A).
- Before starting aspirin therapy for this group of people, reduce systolic BP to 145 mmHg or below and maintain it there while taking aspirin (B). For details of BP management in people with diabetes, see separate PRODIGY guidance on *Diabetes Type 1 and 2 — hypertension.*

[McIntosh et al, 2002; NICE, 2002b]

When should I treat and what should I use?

D

- **The decision to treat depends on both the lipid profile and the 10-year risk of coronary heart disease (CHD)** (see Table 3).
- Clinical judgement should be used when interpreting specified action thresholds, limits, and typical levels.

[McIntosh et al, 2002; NICE, 2002b]

- There is not enough evidence to make recommendations for incorporating high-density lipoprotein cholesterol (HDL-C) levels in the recommendations on therapy [McIntosh et al, 2002].

Can I offer treatment at lower lipid levels?

- **There is a case for using statins in people with established CHD and people who are at high risk of CHD, whatever their baseline lipid level.** The Heart Protection Study recently found that lowering low-density lipoprotein cholesterol (LDL-C) levels by 1 mmol/l from 4 mmol/l to 3 mmol/l reduced the risk of CHD by about 25% [Heart Protection Study Collaborative Group, 2002]. This is close to the 30% reduction in cardiovascular risk achieved by previous studies, all of which had higher baseline cholesterol levels (generally between 5.5 mmol/l and 7 mmol/l) [LaRosa et al, 1999].
- These findings are also supported by the ASCOT-LLA study, which again found that lowering LDL-C levels by 1 mmol/l from 3.4 mmol/l to 2.3 mmol/l in people at high risk of CHD reduced the risk of CHD by 36% [Sever et al, 2003].
- The findings of these studies are not reflected in the National Service Framework for Coronary Heart Disease [DH, 2000].
- The NICE guidelines on the management of Type 2 diabetes recognize that it is possible to justify initiation of statin or fibrate treatment at lower levels of total cholesterol (TC) or triglycerides (TG) [NICE, 2002b].
- There are significant financial implications of implementing a policy to offer statins with no threshold cholesterol level. Consider seeking advice from your local primary care organization.

Is there an age limit for offering treatment?

- **There is no upper age limit for offering treatment.** The Heart Protection Study provides evidence that statin drugs reduce the risk of developing CHD irrespective of age, sex, or cholesterol level [Heart Protection Study Collaborative Group, 2002].
- National guidance does not recommend age-related restrictions on the use of lipid-lowering therapy [McIntosh et al, 2002; NICE, 2002b].

Goals for lowering serum lipids

- While recent evidence may ultimately alter the threshold of treatment, the treatment goals remain the same:
  - TC — aim to lower to below 5.0 mmol/l or by 20–25%, whichever would result in the lower level.
  - LDL-C — aim to lower to below 3.0 mmol/l or by 30%, whichever would result in the lower level.
  - Benefit increases with further reduction.

[McIntosh et al, 2002; NICE, 2002b]

- The target goal for serum TG level is difficult to establish from the evidence. If serum TG level is raised, aim to lower it below 2.3 mmol/l.

How long should people be treated for?

- Benefit from statins does not become substantial until after 1–2 years of therapy.
- In the absence of studies on stopping treatment with lipid-lowering drugs, the National Service Framework for Coronary Heart Disease recommends that treatment be continued indefinitely [DH, 2000].
- Long-term (up to 8 years) treatment with statins produces sustained benefits [LIPID Study Group, 2002].

Can simvastatin be bought over the counter?

- People with diabetes or coronary heart disease cannot buy simvastatin over the counter, and will be referred back to their GP by the pharmacist.

What is the evidence for lipid-lowering therapy in people with Type 2 diabetes?

- In the general population, the use of lipid-lowering drugs appears to bring about significant risk reductions in primary end-points including coronary deaths and (for statins) total mortality in secondary prevention.
- There is less evidence for the use of lipid-lowering drugs in primary prevention. Their use should be reserved for those people at higher risk of coronary heart disease (CHD) events.
- No large-scale study has specifically investigated whether lipid lowering is beneficial in terms of cardiovascular end-points in people with Type 2 diabetes. The available evidence is therefore based on subgroup analysis of larger trials.

Secondary prevention

Statins

- Statins inhibit the enzyme HMG-CoA reductase. This limits the synthesis of cholesterol and increases the numbers of low-density lipoprotein cholesterol (LDL-C) receptors. Statins also decrease triglyceride (TG) levels, and this is in proportion to their cholesterol-lowering effect. Statins generally reduce LDL-C by 25–45%, and total cholesterol (TC) by 20–40% at *maximum* doses. TG are lowered by 10–30%. High-density lipoprotein cholesterol (HDL-C) is increased by 5–10%, but the change can be less in those with very low initial levels of HDL-C [Probstfield and Brunzell, 1998].
- Benefit from treatment with statins in secondary prevention has been reported in the subgroups of three major studies. In people with Type 2 diabetes and pre-existing cardiovascular disease, statins reduced the risk of CHD death or non-fatal myocardial infarction (MI) by 17–49%, depending on initial cholesterol level (see Table 4).

Fibrates

- Fibrates have a much smaller effect on LDL-C than statins, but a greater effect on TG and HDL-C levels. They reduce LDL-C by 7–11% and TG by 20–35%, and increase HDL-C by 10–15%. Greater reductions in TG (40–60%) may be seen in people with moderate to severe hypertriglyceridaemia [Probstfield and Brunzell, 1998].
- Fibrates have been shown to improve outcome in people with hyperlipidaemia. However, the evidence is not as strong as that from statin trials (see Table 4).
- The largest diabetic cohort in any secondary prevention study focused on the use of gemfibrozil in people with low HDL-C, not those with raised TC and LDL-C. This form of dyslipidaemia (with hypertriglyceridaemia) is

more typical of people with Type 2 diabetes. This study showed a 22% reduction in death from CHD or non-fatal MI amongst men with CHD and low HDL-C levels but without high-risk LDL-C levels [Rubins et al, 1999].
- The Bezafibrate Infarction Prevention (BIP) Study Group demonstrated an overall trend in reduction in incidence of primary end-points, a substantial increase in HDL-C, and a reduction in TG [BIP Study Group, 2000].

Combination therapy
- Where initial secondary prevention treatment with a statin does not reduce TG to target levels of less than 2.3 mmol/l, the addition of a fibrate is considered an appropriate therapeutic option [McIntosh et al, 2002].
- There is currently no evidence to support the prescribing of a combination of statin and fibrate. Ongoing trials are expected to clarify the potential benefits of fibrate use, alone or in combination with a statin, in people with diabetes.

Primary prevention

Statins
- Although people with Type 2 diabetes have been included in primary prevention studies with statins, the number of events seen was generally too small for subgroup analysis (see Table 5).
- The Heart Protection Study included people who did not have to have an abnormal lipid profile or a previous history of cardiovascular disease. This study, which included 5963 people with Type 2 diabetes, provides evidence that statin treatment is effective for primary prevention of cardiovascular disease [Heart Protection Study Collaborative Group, 2002].

Fibrates
- There are two reports of primary prevention studies with fibrates. The number of people with Type 2 diabetes in these trials is too small to recommend the use of fibrates for primary prevention [Koskinen et al, 1992; Elkeles et al, 1998].
- A further recent study in men and women with Type 2 diabetes, with and without a history of clinical coronary artery disease, demonstrated by quantitative angiography that treatment with micronized fenofibrate corrected lipid abnormalities and reduced the progression of atherosclerosis [Diabetes Atherosclerosis Intervention Study Investigators, 2001].

D

Table 3: Royal College of General Practitioners recommendations for pharmacological management of blood lipids in people with Type 2 diabetes.

Blood lipid profile at start of therapy	10-year coronary event risk	Recommendations
TC <5.0 mmol/l (or LDL-C <3.0 mmol/l) *and* TG <3.0 mmol/l	Lower or higher	Drug treatment is not currently recommended. Annually measure TC and HDL-C and, if fasting measurements are feasible, LDL-C and TG (**D**).
TC >=5.0 mmol/l (or LDL-C >=3.0 mmol/l) *or* TG >= 2.3 mmol/l but <10 mmol/l	Lower: no history of CVD *and* 10-year coronary event risk <15%	Drug treatment is not generally recommended. Consider offering drug therapy at higher levels of TC or TG (**D**). If a decision is made *not* to start drug therapy, monitor lipid profile and cardiovascular risk annually, to consider the need for therapy (**D**). If a decision is made to start drug therapy: - Offer a statin (**B**). - Assess the effect of statin therapy within three months and titrate the dose if required (**D**). - Monitor the effect of therapy annually (**D**).
TC >= 5.0 mmol/l (or LDL-C >=3.0 mmol/l) *or* TG >=2.3 mmol/l but <10 mmol/l	Higher: 10-year coronary event risk >15% *but* no history of CVD	Offer a statin (**B**). Assess the effect of statin therapy within three months and titrate the dose if required (**D**). Monitor the effects of therapy annually (**D**).
TC >=5.0 mmol/l (or LDL-C >=3.0 mmol/l) *or* TG >=2.3 mmol/l but <10 mmol/l	Higher: manifest CVD	Offer a statin (**B**). Assess the effect of statin therapy within three months and titrate the dose if required (**D**). Consider adding a fibrate after six months if TG remains >=2.3 mmol/l (**D**). Monitor the effect of therapy annually (**D**).
TC <5.0 mmol/l (and LDL-C <3.0 mmol/l) *and* TG >=2.3 mmol/l, but <10 mmol/l	Higher: manifest CVD	Offer a statin (**B**) or a fibrate (**C**). Assess the effect of therapy within three months and titrate the dose if required (**D**). Monitor the effect of therapy annually (**D**).
Fasting TG >=10 mmol/l	Higher or lower	Start fibrate therapy and refer without delay to a diabetes or lipid clinic (**D**).

TC = total cholesterol
LDL-C = low-density lipoprotein cholesterol
CVD = cardiovascular disease
TG = triglycerides
HDL-C = high-density lipoprotein cholesterol

- Several large ongoing trials are evaluating the place of fibrates in people with diabetes. Extension to the use of fibrates in people without manifest cardiovascular disease must await the publication of these trials.

Other drug treatments

Ezetimibe

- **Ezetimibe** is a novel cholesterol absorption inhibitor that prevents the absorption of dietary and biliary cholesterol without affecting the absorption of triglycerides or fat-soluble vitamins. Unlike bile-acid sequestrants, it does not affect the absorption of other drugs.
- Ezetimibe monotherapy lowers LDL-C by about 15–20%. Addition of ezetimibe to simvastatin, atorvastatin, and pravastatin therapy increased LDL-C reductions at all doses of statin used. Simvastatin 10 mg plus ezetimibe 10 mg produced a 44% reduction in LDL, similar to that of simvastatin 80 mg alone [Davidson et al, 2002]. Ezetimibe was well tolerated in clinical studies, but it is a novel compound and a black triangle drug, and so post-marketing data are needed to confirm this. Its effects on clinical end-points have not yet been assessed.
- The numbers of people with Type 2 diabetes in the published studies is low (3–9%). We found no published studies specifically investigating the efficacy of ezetimibe in people with Type 2 diabetes.

Fish oils and omega-3 fatty acids

- **Omega-3 polyunsaturated fatty acids** (omega-3 PUFAs) reduce serum TG levels in the general population and can therefore be a useful adjunct in the treatment of hypertriglyceridaemia. They can increase LDL-C levels, so both LDL-C and TG levels should be monitored.
- **In people with diabetes** there is conflicting evidence on the effects of omega-3 PUFAs on LDL-C and glycaemic control. Trials with vascular event or mortality-defined end-points are still needed in people with Type 2 diabetes [Farmer et al, 2003].
- Moderate dietary intake should be encouraged. There are many dietary sources of omega-3 PUFAs, including oily fish, canola oil, flaxseed oil, walnuts, and leafy green vegetables.

Nicotinic acid

- **High doses of nicotinic acid** can produce large increases in HDL-C, as well as lowering TC and TG levels. However, nicotinic acid is rarely used because of its adverse effects, especially vasodilation [BNF 44, 2002].
- **Nicotinic acid can worsen glycaemic control** and is therefore not recommended for use in Type 2 diabetes.

[Best and O'Neal, 2000; Papadakis et al, 2001]

Anion-exchange resins

- **Anion-exchange resins** lower LDL-C levels and may improve glycaemic control. However, they can increase TG levels and their use is not recommended if TG is greater than 3 mmol/l [Best and O'Neal, 2000].
- **Anion-exchange resins** are inconvenient to take, and are therefore reserved as adjunctive therapy for people who are unable to achieve target lipid levels on the maximum tolerated dose of a statin and/or a fibrate.

Medicines management

Which statin?

- Five statins are licensed in the UK for prevention of coronary heart disease (CHD) and/or treatment of hyperlipidaemia: atorvastatin, fluvastatin, pravastatin, rosuvastatin, and simvastatin. Simvastatin and pravastatin have the most solid body of evidence of efficacy and safety.
- A recent cross-sectional survey of 17 UK general practices found that more people were likely to achieve a total cholesterol (TC) of less than 5 mmol/l if they were taking atorvastatin or simvastatin [Hippisley-Cox et al, 2003]. Note: this study was conducted before the launch of rosuvastatin onto the UK market.

What starting dose?

The rationale for selecting the starting dose depends on the risks and benefits of several alternative strategies:

- **The 'evidence-based dose' strategy** uses the doses used in the major trials as the starting dose. The rationale is that the best evidence of efficacy is for these doses, i.e. atorvastatin 10–20 mg, fluvastatin 80 mg, pravastatin 40 mg, and simvastatin 20–40 mg. Note: for fluvastatin and pravastatin the evidence-based doses are the maximum licensed doses.
- **The 'fire and forget' strategy** aims to use only the starting doses of a statin in all individuals whose CHD risk over 10 years is more than 15%, i.e. to give lower doses to more people [PROSPER study group, 2002]. Once the statin is prescribed people are only expected to return for assessment if they have symptoms or worries. Advantages include significantly lower total costs and smaller demands on resources such as primary care clinician time. Disadvantages include the lack of trial evidence to support the safety and efficacy of the strategy; reduced monitoring may lead to increased rates of toxicity and non-adherence to treatment.
- **The 'titrate to target' strategy** uses lower starting doses to minimize the risk of toxicity (many people will not need a higher dose to achieve treatment targets for cholesterol; and doubling the dose only reduces cholesterol levels by a further 5–6%). The National Service Framework for Coronary Heart Disease (NSF for CHD) currently recommends this approach [DH, 2000; Shepherd, 2002].
- **In the absence of other specific UK guidance, we recommend the following starting doses:** atorvastatin 10 mg, fluvastatin 40 mg, pravastatin 40 mg, and simvastatin 20 mg.

Table 4: Summary of evidence from subgroup analysis of the major secondary prevention trials for the outcome 'CHD death or non-fatal MI'.

Trial	Duration	Total n	Diabetes n	CER	EER	NNT
Statins						
Scandinavian Simvastatin Survival Study (4S) [Pyorala et al, 1997]	5.4 years	4444	202	45%	23%	5
Cholesterol And Recurrent Events (CARE) [Sacks et al, 1996]	5 years	4159	586	37%	29%	12
Long-term Intervention with Pravastatin in Ischaemic Disease (LIPID) [LIPID Study Group, 1998]	6.1 years	9014	782	23%	19	28
Fibrates						
VA-HIT [Rubins et al, 1999]	5.1 years	2531	627	37%	29%	13

Table 5: Summary of evidence from subgroup analysis of the major trials of primary prevention with statins for outcome 'CHD death or non-fatal MI'.

Trial	Duration	Total n	Diabetes n	CER	EER	NNT
West of Scotland Coronary Prevention Study [Shepherd et al, 1995]	4.9 years	6595	76	NR	NR	NR
Air Force/Texas Coronary Atherosclerosis Prevention Study [AF/TexCAPS, 1998]	5.2 years	6605	155	8.5%	4.8%	27
Heart Protection Study [Heart Protection Study Collaborative Group, 2002]	5 years	20,536	2912	13.5%	9.1%	23

NR not reported

- Lower starting doses should be considered for people at increased risk of myopathy (see below).
- Higher starting doses could be considered in younger, large, otherwise healthy people with high cholesterol levels.

How long should people be treated for?

- Benefit from statins does not become substantial until after 1–2 years of therapy.
- In the absence of studies on stopping treatment with lipid-lowering drugs, the NSF for CHD recommends that treatment be continued indefinitely [DH, 2000].
- Long-term (up to 8 years) treatment with statins is safe and produces sustained benefits [LIPID Study Group, 2002].

Measuring lipid levels and monitoring toxicity

- Serum lipid measurements are subject to biological variation and ideally require at least three measurements (with a minimum of two) to assess their true mean levels.
- Levels of triglyceride (TG) are raised by fat in recent meals; therefore a fasting TG result is needed to calculate low-density lipoprotein cholesterol (LDL-C) levels accurately.
- Levels of serum TC, LDL-C, and high-density lipoprotein cholesterol (HDL-C) decrease in people with acute myocardial infarction and take about 6 weeks to return to baseline levels.

Other tests

- Assays of apolipoproteins are increasingly used for assessment and monitoring since apolipoprotein B measurement is more reliable than LDL-C measurement and does not require fasting.
- Genetic tests are used when investigating familial dyslipidaemias, but these tests are usually done in specialist clinics

Tolerability of statins and fibrates

- **Gastrointestinal adverse effects are the most common** adverse effects, but rarely require cessation of treatment.
- **Hepatotoxicity is rare**, and is thought to be dose-dependent. Progression to liver failure specifically due to statins occurs exceedingly rarely, if ever [Pasternak et al, 2002]. Reversal of transaminase elevation is frequently noted with a reduction in dose, and elevations do not often recur with either re-challenge or selection of another statin.
- **Non-specific muscle aches or joint pains are common.** Advise anyone starting treatment with a statin or fibrate that it is important to report muscle symptoms (pain, tenderness, soreness) without delay.
- **Measure creatine kinase (CK) if muscle symptoms occur.** Regular monitoring of serum CK is unnecessary. An increase in CK is not usually significant.
- **Myositis and rhabdomyolysis associated with statin and fibrate treatment is rare** (approximately one case in every 100,000 treatment years). Although the exact mechanism is unclear, it appears to be a dose-dependent effect.
- **The Committee on the Safety of Medicines advises that the risk of myopathy is increased:**
  - In the presence of underlying muscle disorders, renal impairment, hypothyroidism, or alcohol abuse.
  - If statins are co-prescribed with other lipid-lowering drugs, e.g. fibrates (particularly gemfibrozil), or nicotinic acid.
  - With the co-prescription of other drugs that increase statin levels, e.g. ciclosporin; azole antifungals (itraconazole and ketoconazole); macrolide antibiotics (erythromycin and clarithromycin); and HIV protease inhibitors.
- **Do not start treatment if** CK is more than 5 times the upper limit of normal at baseline.
- **Stop fibrate/statin treatment if:**
  - Serum creatinine increases progressively (with fibrates).
  - Strong suspicion of myopathy, or CK level greater than five times the upper limit of normal.
  - Myalgic symptoms persist despite a normal CK level — a trial off treatment may be necessary.
  - Aspartate aminotransferase (AST) or alanine aminotransferase (ALT) level persists above three times the upper limit of normal.
- Consider seeking specialist advice if symptoms and elevated CK levels do not rapidly return to normal.

[CSM, 2001; CSM, 2002; Pasternak et al, 2002]

Significant interactions

- **Warfarin and fibrates:** reduce the dose of warfarin by about a third and make further adjustments according to changes in the international normalized ratio (INR).

Table 6: Monitoring response to treatment and toxicity [Wood et al, 1998; Pasternak et al, 2002].

Time scale	Tests	
Initial screening		Non-fasting TC and HDL-C
Pretreatment	Baseline lipid profile	Fasting full lipid profile: TC, LDL-C, HDL-C, and TG
	Baseline tests for toxicity	Creatine kinase (CK) Aspartate aminotransferase (AST) or alanine aminotransferase (ALT) Creatinine (only needed if using a fibrate)
	Exclude hypothyroidism as a secondary cause	Thyroid-stimulating hormone (TSH)
8–12 weeks after the start of treatment *or* an increase in dose	Lipid levels Liver function tests	Usually non-fasting TC and HDL-C* AST or ALT
Annually	Lipid levels Liver function tests	Usually non-fasting TC and HDL-C* AST or ALT
If muscle symptoms suspected	Check CK	CK

*If LDL-C or TG levels are needed, a fasting sample must be taken.

D

- **Warfarin and simvastatin:** monitor INR closely until stable — simvastatin occasionally increases INR significantly.

[Stockley, 1999]

Indications for specialist referral

Referral is usually appropriate if:

- **Familial hypercholesterolaemia** is suspected, i.e. when the person has a total cholesterol (TC) greater than 7.5 mmol/l (or low-density lipoprotein cholesterol > 4.9 mmol/l) *and* at least one of the following:
  - Tendon xanthomata in himself/herself or in a first- or second-degree relative
  - Family history of premature coronary heart disease (CHD)
- **Family history of TC** is suspected, i.e. the individual has a mixed hyperlipidaemia and a family history of hyperlipidaemia or premature CHD.
- **Failure of therapy:** failure to meet target lipid reduction despite maximally tolerated therapy.
- **Severe hypercholesterolaemia:** initial TC greater than 10 mmol/l.
- **Very severe hypertriglyceridaemia:** triglycerides greater than 10 mmol/l.

D

References

NHS staff in England can link, free of charge, from references to full text journals by clicking on [Full text] on the PRODIGY website.

1. AF/TexCAPS (1998) Primary prevention of acute coronary events with lovastatin in men and women with average cholesterol levels: results of Air Force/ Texas Coronary Atherosclerosis Prevention Study. *Journal of the American Medical Association* **279**(20), 1615–1622. [Full text]
2. Athyros, V.G., Papageorgiou, A.A., Mercouris, B.R. et al (2002) Treatment with atorvastatin to the national cholesterol educational program goal versus 'usual' care secondary coronary heart disease prevention. The Greek atorvastatin and coronary-heart-disease evaluation (GREACE) study. *Current Medical Research & Opinion* **18**(4), 220–228. [Full text]
3. Best, J.D. and O'Neal, D.N. (2000) Diabetic dyslipidaemia: current treatment recommendations. *Drugs* **59**(5), 1101–1111.
4. BIP Study Group (2000) Secondary prevention by raising HDL cholesterol and reducing triglycerides in patients with coronary artery disease: the Bezafibrate Infarction Prevention (BIP) study. *Circulation* **102**(1), 21–27. [Full text]
5. BNF 44 (2002) *British National Formulary*. 44th edn. London: British Medical Association and Royal Pharmaceutical Society of Great Britain.
6. British Heart Foundation (1999) *Fish, fruit, vegetables and mediterranean diet*. Factfile 2/1999. British Heart Foundation. www.bhf.org.uk [Accessed: 12/01/2003].
7. CSM (2001) Cerivastatin (Lipobay) withdrawn. *Current Problems in Pharmacovigilance* **27**(Aug), 9.
8. CSM (2002) HMG CoA reductase inhibitors (statins) and myopathy. *Current Problems in Pharmacovigilance* **28**(Oct), 8.
9. Davidson, M.H., McGarry, T., Bettis, R. et al (2002) Ezetimibe coadministered with simvastatin in patients with primary hypercholesterolemia. *Journal of the American College of Cardiology* **40**(12), 2125–2134.
10. DH (2000) *National service framework for coronary heart disease*. Department of Health. www.dh.gov.uk [Accessed: 15/07/2005]. [Full text]
11. Diabetes Atherosclerosis Intervention Study Investigators (2001) Effect of fenofibrate on progression of coronary-artery disease in type 2 diabetes: the diabetes atherosclerosis intervention study, a randomised study. *Lancet* **357**(9260), 905–910. [Full text]
12. Durrington, P.N. (Ed.) (1995) *Hyperlipidaemia: diagnosis and management*. 2nd edn. Oxford: Butterworth-Heinemann.
13. Elkeles, R.S., Diamond, J.R., Poulter, C. et al (1998) Cardiovascular outcomes in type 2 diabetes. A double-blind placebo- controlled study of bezafibrate: the St. Mary's, Ealing, Northwick Park Diabetes Cardiovascular Disease Prevention (SENDCAP) Study. *Diabetes Care* **21**(4), 641–648. [Full text]
14. Farmer, A., Montori, V., Dinneen, S. and Clar, C. (2003) *Fish oil in people with type 2 diabetes mellitus (Cochrane Review)*. The Cochrane Library. Issue 1. Oxford: Update Software.
15. Heart Protection Study Collaborative Group (2002) MRC/BHF heart protection study of cholesterol lowering with simvastatin in 20536 high-risk individuals: a randomised placebo-controlled trial. *Lancet* **360**(9326), 7–22. [Full text]
16. Hippisley-Cox, J., Cater, R., Pringle, M. and Coupland, C. (2003) Cross-sectional survey of effectiveness of lipid lowering drugs in reducing serum cholesterol concentration in patients in 17 general practices. *British Medical Journal* **326**(7391), 689–693. [Full text]
17. Hu, F.B. and Willett, W.C. (2002) Optimal diets for prevention of coronary heart disease. *Journal of the American Medical Association* **288**(20), 2569–2578. [Full text]
18. Koskinen, P., Manttari, M., Manninen, V. et al (1992) Coronary heart disease incidence in NIDDM patients in the Helsinki Heart Study. *Diabetes Care* **15**(7), 820–825.
19. LaRosa, J.C., Jiang, H.E. and Vupputuri, S. (1999) Effect of statins on risk of coronary disease. *Journal of the American Medical Association* **282**(24), 2340–2346. [Full text]
20. Law, M. (2000) Plant sterol and stanol margarines and health. *British Medical Journal* **320**(7238), 861–864. [Full text]
21. LIPID Study Group (1998) Prevention of cardiovascular events and death with pravastatin in patients with coronary heart disease and a broad range of initial cholesterol levels. The long-term intervention with pravastatin in ischaemic disease. *New England Journal of Medicine* **339**(19), 1349–1357. [Full text]
22. LIPID Study Group (2002) Long-term effectiveness and safety of pravastatin in 9014 patients with coronary heart disease and average cholesterol concentrations: the LIPID trial follow-up. *Lancet* **359**(9315), 1379–1387. [Full text]
23. McIntosh, A., Hutchinson, A., Feder, G. et al (2002) *Clinical guidelines for type 2 diabetes – lipids management*. University of Sheffield: ScHARR. www.shef.ac.uk [Accessed: 20/11/2002].
24. MeReC (2002) Lifestyle measures to reduce cardiovascular risk. *MeReC Briefing* **19**(July), 1–8.
25. Mooradian, A.D. (2003) Cardiovascular disease in type 2 diabetes mellitus: current management guidelines. *Archives of Internal Medicine* **163**(1), 33–40. [Full text]
26. Murphy, M., Foster, C., Sudlow, C. et al (2001) Cardiovascular disorders: primary prevention. *Clinical Evidence* **6**, 82–113.
27. NHS CRD (2000) Complications of diabetes: renal disease and promotion of self-management. *Effective Health Care Bulletin* **6**(1), 1–12.
28. NICE (2002a) *Management of type 2 diabetes – managing blood glucose levels*. Inherited clinical

guideline G. National Institute for Clinical Excellence. www.nice.org.uk [Accessed: 02/12/2002].

9. NICE (2002b) *Management of type 2 diabetes – management of blood pressure and blood lipids.* Inherited clinical guideline H. National Institute for Clinical Excellence. www.nice.org.uk [Accessed: 28/01/2003].

0. Papadakis, J.A., Milionis, H.J., Press, M. and Mikhailidis, D.P. (2001) Treating dyslipidaemia in non-insulin-dependent diabetes mellitus – a special reference to statins. *Journal of Diabetes and its Complications* 15(4), 211–226.

1. Pasternak, S., Smith, S.C., Bairey-Merz, C.N. et al (2002) ACC/AHA/NHLBI clinical advisory on the use and safety of statins. *Journal of the American College of Cardiology* 40(3), 568–573.

2. Probstfield, J.L. and Brunzell, J.D. (1998) Use of lipid lowering agents in the prevention of cardiovascular disease. In: Yusuf, S., Cairns, J.A., Camm, A.J. et al (Eds.) *Evidence based cardiology*. London: BMJ Books. 206–225.

3. PROSPER study group (2002) Pravastatin in elderly individuals at risk of vascular disease (PROSPER): a randomised controlled trial. *Lancet* 360(9346), 1623–1630. [Full text]

4. Pyorala, K., Pedersen, T.R., Kjekshus, J. et al (1997) Cholesterol lowering with simvastatin improves prognosis of diabetic patients with coronary heart disease. A subgroup analysis of the Scandinavian Simvastatin Survival Study (4S). *Diabetes Care* 20(4), 614–620. [Full text]

5. Rubins, H.B., Robins, S.J., Collins, D. et al (1999) Gemfibrozil for the secondary prevention of coronary heart disease in men with low levels of high-density lipoprotein cholesterol. *New England Journal of Medicine* 341(6), 410–418.

6. Sacks, F.M., Pfeffer, M.A., Moye, L.A. et al (1996) The effect of pravastatin on coronary events after myocardial infarction in patients with average cholesterol levels. The Cholesterol and Recurrent Events trial investigators (CARE). *New England Journal of Medicine* 335(14), 1001–1009. [Full text]

7. Serruys, P.W., de Feyter, P., Macaya, C. et al (2002) Fluvastatin for prevention of cardiac events following successful first percutaneous coronary intervention: a randomized controlled trial. *Journal of the American Medical Association* 287(24), 3215–3222. [Full text]

8. Sever, P.S., Dahlof, B., Poulter, N.R. et al (2003) Prevention of coronary and stroke events with atorvastatin in hypertensive patients who have average or lower-than-average cholesterol concentrations, in the Anglo-Scandinavian Cardiac Outcomes Trial – Lipid Lowering Arm (ASCOT-LLA): a multicentre randomised controlled trial. *Lancet* 361(9364), 1149–1158. [Full text]

39. Shepherd, J. (2002) Resource management in prevention of coronary heart disease: optimising prescription of lipid-lowering drugs. *Lancet* 359(9325), 2271–2273. [Full text]

40. Shepherd, J., Cobbe, S.M., Ford, I. et al (1995) Prevention of coronary heart disease with pravastatin in men with hypercholesterolemia. The West of Scotland Coronary Prevention Study (WOSCOPS). *New England Journal of Medicine* 333(20), 1301–1308.

41. SIGN (2001) *Management of diabetes.* Report no. 55. Scottish Intercollegiate Guidelines Network. www.sign.ac.uk [Accessed: 20/11/2002].

42. Stein, A.A., Lane, M. and Laskarzewski, P. (1998) Comparison of statins in hypertriglyceridemia. *American Journal of Cardiology* 81(4A), 66B-69B.

43. Stockley, I.H. (Ed.) (1999) *Drug interactions.* 5th edn. London: The Pharmaceutical Press.

44. Stone, N.J. (1994) Secondary causes of hyperlipidemia. *Medical Clinics of North America* 78(1), 117–141.

45. Taskinen, M.R. (2002) Diabetic dyslipidemia. *Atherosclerosis Supplements* 3(1), 47–51.

46. UK Prospective Diabetes Study Group (1998) Risk factors for coronary artery disease in non-insulin dependent diabetes mellitus: United Kingdom Prospective Diabetes Study (UKPDS: 23). *British Medical Journal* 316(7134), 823–828. [Full text]

47. Wood, D., Durrington, D., Poulter, N. et al (1998) Joint British recommendations on prevention of coronary heart disease in clinical practice. *Heart* 80(Suppl 2), S1-S29. [Full text]

Evidence grading

Evidence grading is from the National Institute of Clinical Excellence guideline, *Management of Type 2 diabetes: management of blood pressure and blood lipids,* October 2002. The definitions of grades of recommendation used in this guideline are as follows:

A Directly based on category I evidence (systematic review of randomized controlled trials or at least one randomized controlled trial)

B Directly based on category II evidence (at least one controlled study without randomization or one other type of quasi-experimental study) or extrapolated recommendation from category I evidence

C Directly based on category III evidence (non-experimental descriptive studies) or extrapolated recommendation from category I or II evidence

D Directly based on category IV evidence (expert committee reports or opinions and/or clinical experience of respected authorities) or extrapolated recommendation from category I, II, or III evidence

PRODIGY GUIDANCE

Diabetes Type 2 — renal disease

Last revised in July 2003
www.prodigy.nhs.uk/guidance.asp?gt=Diabetes - renal disease

Applies to people over the age of 16 years

This is the PRODIGY implementation of the National Institute for Clinical Excellence (NICE) guideline on *Diabetic renal disease: prevention and early management,* and the Royal College of General Practitioners (RCGP) *Clinical guideline for Type 2 diabetes: Diabetic renal disease: prevention and early management (February 2002).*

D

This guidance covers the screening and early management of diabetic renal disease in people over 16 years with Type 2 diabetes. We recognize that Type 2 diabetes is now being seen in children, and where they are managed will depend on the expertise available locally in primary care.

This guidance does not cover the management of end-stage renal failure, renal dialysis, or renal transplantation; the management of other diabetic complications; or the management of renal disease in people with Type 1 diabetes, or people without diabetes.

There is separate PRODIGY guidance for *Diabetes Type 1 and 2 — foot disease, Diabetes Type 2 — lipid management,* and *Diabetes Type 1 and 2 — hypertension.*

Contents

Scenarios

- Prevention and management of diabetic renal disease p.594

Extended Information, p. 596

Prevention and management of diabetic renal disease

Which therapy

- **Measure urine albumin or urinary albumin:creatinine ratio (ACR), and serum creatinine at diagnosis and at least annually thereafter** (or other timescales recommended if other considerations demand it).
- **Measure urinary ACR in spot urine sample.** Whether this is done using a laboratory method or near-patient testing will depend on local facilities available.
- **Use a first morning sample where practical.**
- **If the ACR is greater than or equal to 2.5 mg/mmol (men) or 3.5 mg/mmol (women), repeat testing on two further occasions** (within 1 month where practical). Two positive tests out of three confirm the diagnosis.
- **Following measurement, classify urinary albumin excretion as *lower-risk* or *higher-risk*.**
- **Lower-risk urine albumin excretion:**
  - ACR less than 2.5 mg/mmol (men) or 3.5 mg/mmol (women), or urinary albumin concentration less than 20 mg/l
- **Higher-risk urine albumin excretion:**
  - *Microalbuminuria* — ACR greater than or equal to 2.5 mg/mmol (men) or 3.5 mg/mmol (women), or urinary albumin concentration greater than or equal to 20 mg/l, or
  - *Proteinuria* — ACR greater than or equal to 30 mg/mmol or urinary albumin concentration greater than or equal to 200 mg/l
- **For those people with higher-risk urine albumin excretion:**
  - Start treatment with an ACE inhibitor (including in those with normal blood pressure [BP]).
  - If ACE inhibitors are not tolerated, consider an angiotensin-II receptor antagonist (AIIRA) as an alternative.
  - Titrate to highest doses tolerated, within the licensed indication.
  - Maintain BP at or below 135/75 mmHg.
  - Ensure good blood glucose control (preferably HbA_{1c} below 6.5%).
  - Ask about dietary protein intake and consider referral for dietary advice if it is unusually high (e.g. body builders).
- **To achieve target BP, use combination therapy if ACE inhibitors alone are not fully effective.** Combination therapy is likely to be necessary for most people.
- **For those people with lower-risk urine albumin excretion:**
  - Maintain good BP control (at or below 140/80 mmHg).
  - Maintain good blood glucose control.
- **Measure, assess, and treat cardiovascular risk factors** in all people with Type 2 diabetes.

Practical prescribing points

For further information please see the *Medicines Compendium* (www.medicines.org.uk) or the *British National Formulary* (www.bnf.org).

- **The risk of ACE inhibitor/angiotensin-II receptor antagonist (AIIRA) induced first-dose hypotension or renal impairment is increased in people in the higher-risk groups defined by the following:**
  - Creatinine >150 micromoles/l
  - Urea >12 mmol/l
  - Sodium <130 mmol/l
  - Systolic blood pressure (BP) <100 mmHg
  - Diuretic dose > furosemide (frusemide) 80 mg or bumetanide 2 mg daily
  - Known or suspected renal artery stenosis, e.g. if peripheral vascular disease
  - Age 70 years or over or physical frailty
  - Hypovolaemia
  - Unstable heart failure
  - Treatment with high-dose vasodilator therapy
- **Avoid potassium-sparing diuretics or potassium supplements** in people on ACE inhibitors or AIIRAs (other than in exceptional cases, e.g. low-dose spironolactone for severe heart failure) due to the risk of hyperkalaemia.
- **Stop nonsteroidal anti-inflammatory drugs (if possible)** as they reduce the effectiveness of diuretics and increase the risk of renal impairment with ACE inhibitors and AIIRAs.

Avoid ACE inhibitors and AIIRAs if significant cardiac outflow tract obstruction is present (e.g. due to aortic stenosis or hypertrophic obstructive cardiomyopathy).

Liver disease

- Use drugs that are not in the form of prodrugs (e.g. captopril or lisinopril).
- ACE inhibitors that are in the form of prodrugs require close monitoring in people with impaired liver function and are best avoided.

Pregnancy and breastfeeding: avoid ACE inhibitors and AIIRAs. Potential adverse defects in pregnancy include problems with fetal and neonatal BP control and renal function.

ollow-up advice

Measure serum creatinine and electrolytes one week after:

- Initiating ACE inhibitor or angiotensin-II receptor antagonist (AIIRA) therapy.
- Each increase in dose.

hould I refer or investigate?

efer?

Refer for specialist opinion if:

- Serum creatinine is greater than 150 micromoles/l (taking age and sex into account).
- Renal function is rapidly declining at monthly examination.
- Haematuria greater than ++ is present.

vestigate?

If retinopathy is not present, investigate other non-diabetic causes of abnormal renal function.

atient information leaflets

ne following PILs are available at www.prodigy.nhs.uk

Blood Test - General
Blood Test - Glucose
Blood Test - Kidney Function
Diabetes Insight Website
Diabetes Research & Wellness Foundation
Diabetes Type 2
Diabetes Type 2 - A Summary
Diabetes UK
DiabeticLife
Medicines - Name Changes of Medicines

hared decision making

You have a raised level of protein in your urine.

If this is not treated you may be at greater risk of heart disease or kidney disease.

To stop it getting any worse you need to maintain good control of your blood glucose level and blood pressure.

You may be given some tablets which will reduce your blood pressure and help stop the progression of disease.

An ACE inhibitor (angiotensin-converting enzyme inhibitor) is the usual treatment.

When you first start an ACE inhibitor:

- *Lie or sit down* for 2–4 hours after the very first dose.
- *Start with a low dose* at first, and gradually increase the dose.
- *A blood test* is usual before, and about a week after, starting treatment with an ACE inhibitor.
- *If you take a diuretic* ('water tablet') you may be advised not to take it for a day or so before an ACE inhibitor is started.
- **Blood tests are needed from time to time.** These aim to:
  - Detect certain uncommon problems before they become serious.
  - Check that the cholesterol level has reduced to the target level.
- You may need to be prescribed more than one treatment to ensure the best control.

Drug rationale

Drugs not included

- ACE inhibitors other than captopril, enalapril, lisinopril, and ramipril, and angiotensin-II receptor antagonists other than losartan and irbesartan, are not included as their use in diabetic nephropathy is not supported by evidence from randomized, controlled trials.

Drugs included

- **ACE inhibitors.** Captopril, enalapril, lisinopril, and ramipril are included as their use in diabetic nephropathy is supported by evidence from randomized, controlled trials. Of these, only lisinopril is licensed for the treatment of diabetic nephropathy in hypertensive people with Type 2 diabetes.
- **Angiotensin-II receptor antagonists.** Losartan and irbesartan are both licensed for the treatment of diabetic nephropathy. Losartan is indicated to delay the progression of renal disease in Type 2 diabetic people with macroalbuminuria; irbesartan is indicated for the treatment of renal disease (both microalbuminuria and macroalbuminuria) in patients with hypertension and Type 2 diabetes mellitus.

Prescriptions

Start ACE inhibitor

Captopril 6.25mg twice a day

- Age from 16 years onwards
- Captopril 12.5mg tablets. Take half a tablet twice a day; supply 28 tablets; NHS Cost £1.16.

Captopril 12.5mg twice a day

- Age from 16 to 60 years
- Captopril 12.5mg tablets. Take one tablet twice a day; supply 56 tablets; NHS Cost £2.30.

Enalapril 2.5mg once a day

- Age from 16 years onwards
- Enalapril 2.5mg tablets. Take one tablet once a day; supply 28 tablets; NHS Cost £2.57.

Enalapril 5mg once a day

- Age from 16 to 60 years
- Enalapril 5mg tablets. Take one tablet once a day; supply 28 tablets; NHS Cost £3.76.

Lisinopril 2.5mg once a day

- Age from 16 years onwards
- Lisinopril 2.5mg tablets. Take one tablet once a day; supply 28 tablets; NHS Cost £6.26.

Ramipril 1.25mg once a day

- Age from 16 years onwards
- Ramipril 1.25mg tablets. Take one tablet once a day; supply 28 tablets; NHS Cost £5.30.

Maintenance doses: captopril or enalapril

Captopril 12.5mg twice a day

- Age from 16 years onwards
- Captopril 12.5mg tablets. Take one tablet twice a day; supply 56 tablets; NHS Cost £2.30.

Captopril 25mg twice a day
- Age from 16 years onwards
- Captopril 25mg tablets. Take one tablet twice a day; supply 56 tablets; NHS Cost £3.21.

Captopril 50mg twice a day
- Age from 16 years onwards
- Captopril 50mg tablets. Take one tablet twice a day; supply 56 tablets; NHS Cost £4.06.

Enalapril 2.5mg once a day
- Age from 16 years onwards
- Enalapril 2.5mg tablets. Take one tablet once a day; supply 28 tablets; NHS Cost £2.57.

Enalapril 5mg once a day
- Age from 16 years onwards
- Enalapril 5mg tablets. Take one tablet once a day; supply 28 tablets; NHS Cost £3.76.

Enalapril 10mg once a day
- Age from 16 years onwards
- Enalapril 10mg tablets. Take one tablet once a day; supply 28 tablets; NHS Cost £5.20.

Enalapril 20mg once a day
- Age from 16 years onwards
- Enalapril 20mg tablets. Take one tablet once a day; supply 28 tablets; NHS Cost £6.12.

Maintenance doses: lisinopril or ramipril

Lisinopril 2.5mg once a day
- Age from 16 years onwards
- Lisinopril 2.5mg tablets. Take one tablet once a day; supply 28 tablets; NHS Cost £6.26.

Lisinopril 5mg once a day
- Age from 16 years onwards
- Lisinopril 5mg tablets. Take one tablet once a day; supply 28 tablets; NHS Cost £7.86.

Lisinopril 10mg once a day
- Age from 16 years onwards
- Lisinopril 10mg tablets. Take one tablet once a day; supply 28 tablets; NHS Cost £9.70.

Lisinopril 20mg once a day
- Age from 16 years onwards
- Lisinopril 20mg tablets. Take one tablet once a day; supply 28 tablets; NHS Cost £10.97.

Ramipril 1.25mg once a day
- Age from 16 years onwards
- Ramipril 1.25mg tablets. Take one tablet once a day; supply 28 tablets; NHS Cost £5.30.

Ramipril 2.5mg once a day
- Age from 16 years onwards
- Ramipril 2.5mg tablets. Take one tablet once a day; supply 28 tablets; NHS Cost £7.51.

Ramipril 5mg once a day
- Age from 16 years onwards
- Ramipril 5mg tablets. Take one tablet once a day; supply 28 tablets; NHS Cost £9.55.

Start AIIRA (if ACE inhibitor not tolerated)

Losartan 25mg once a day (low dose)
- Age from 16 years onwards
- Losartan 25mg tablets. Take one tablet once a day; supply 28 tablets; NHS Cost £17.24.

Losartan 50mg once a day
- Age from 16 years onwards
- Losartan 50mg tablets. Take one tablet once a day; supply 28 tablets; NHS Cost £17.00.

Irbesartan 75mg once a day (low dose)
- Age from 16 years onwards
- Irbesartan 75mg tablets. Take one tablet once a day; supply 28 tablets; NHS Cost £14.00.

Irbesartan 150mg once a day
- Age from 16 years onwards
- Irbesartan 150mg tablets. Take one tablet once a day; supply 28 tablets; NHS Cost £16.00.

Maintenance doses: angiotensin-II receptor antagonist

Losartan 50mg once a day
- Age from 16 years onwards
- Losartan 50mg tablets. Take one tablet once a day; supply 28 tablets; NHS Cost £17.23.

Losartan 100mg once a day
- Age from 16 years onwards
- Losartan 100mg tablets. Take one tablet once a day; supply 28 tablets; NHS Cost £22.00.

Irbesartan 150mg once a day
- Age from 16 years onwards
- Irbesartan 150mg tablets. Take one tablet once a day; supply 28 tablets; NHS Cost £16.00.

Irbesartan 300mg once a day
- Age from 16 years onwards
- Irbesartan 300mg tablets. Take one tablet once a day; supply 28 tablets; NHS Cost £22.21.

Extended Information

Background information

- What is it? p.596
- How common is it? p.596
- How do I know my patient has it? p.597
- What else might it be? p.597
- Complications and prognosis p.597

What is it?

- **Diabetic renal disease** is defined as the presence of raise urine albumin levels and/or raised serum creatinine in people with Type 2 diabetes, in the absence of other renal disease.
- **Diabetic renal disease is categorized according to progressively higher levels of albumin in the urine:**
  - Microalbuminuria (incipient nephropathy) is defined by a rise in urinary albumin loss to between 30 mg/d and 300 mg/day, or urinary albumin:creatinine ratio greater than or equal to 2.5 mg/mmol (men) or 3.5 mg/mmol (women), or urinary albumin concentration greater than or equal to 20 mg/l.
  - Proteinuria or macroalbuminuria (overt nephropath is defined by a raised urinary albumin excretion greater than 300 mg/day, or urinary albumin:creatinine ratio greater than or equal to 30 mg/mmol, or urinary albumin concentration greater than or equal to 200 mg/l.

[SIGN, 2001; McIntosh et al, 2002]

How common is it?

- **Prevalence rates for microalbuminuria range from 8% 32% of people with Type 2 diabetes;** most estimates ar around 25%.
- **Prevalence rates for proteinuria range from 5% to 19% of people with Type 2 diabetes,** but most studies give rates of around 15%.
- **At the time of diagnosis of Type 2 diabetes,** figures fror the UK Prospective Diabetes Study (UKPDS) suggest th about 12% of people have microalbuminuria and 1.9% have proteinuria [Turner et al, 1998]. Other reports suggest that as many as 25% of people have

microalbuminuria at time of diagnosis of Type 2 diabetes.

n those people who have normoalbuminuria at diagnosis, microalbuminuria develops in approximately 15% and proteinuria in 5% within 5 years.

n addition to a higher prevalence of Type 2 diabetes in people of south Asian, African, or Afro-Caribbean descent, the prevalence of people with diabetes receiving renal replacement therapy for diabetic end-stage renal failure is approximately six times higher in Asian and black populations than in white populations.

HS CRD, 2000; SIGN, 2001; McIntosh et al, 2002]

ow do I know my patient has it?

Microalbuminuria is the earliest indicator of renal disease attributable to diabetes. This may progress to proteinuria and subsequent end-stage renal failure.

Microalbuminuria and proteinuria are detected by the presence of albumin in the urine.

- **Microalbuminuria** is defined by a urinary albumin:creatinine ratio greater than or equal to 2.5 mg/mmol (men) or 3.5 mg/mmol (women), or urinary albumin concentration greater than or equal to 20 mg/l.
- **Proteinuria** or **macroalbuminuria** is defined by a urinary albumin:creatinine ratio greater than or equal to 30 mg/mmol or a urinary albumin concentration greater than or equal to 200 mg/l.

Urinary albumin:creatinine ratio (ACR), preferably determined on a first-morning sample, is the accepted method of screening for microalbuminuria. This should be done at diagnosis of Type 2 diabetes and at least annually thereafter. Whether this is done using a laboratory method or near-patient testing will depend on local facilities available.

f the ACR is greater than or equal to 2.5 mg/mmol (men) or 3.5 mg/mmol (women), repeat testing on two further occasions (within 1 month where practical). Two positive tests out of three confirm the diagnosis.

f uncertainty about the diagnosis still exists, consider confirming the result with a timed collection.

See the section on *Screening for diabetic renal disease* for details of screening and diagnostic tests.

f urinary albumin levels are raised and any degree of diabetic retinopathy is present, a diagnosis of diabetic renal disease is likely. If retinopathy is not present, the possibility of a non-diabetic, alternative cause of renal disease should be investigated.

Measure serum creatinine once a year.

Occasionally serum creatinine may be raised without the detectable presence of albumin in the urine. If there is no evidence of albuminuria or microvascular disease (e.g. diabetic retinopathy), consider other causes of renal disease.

cIntosh et al, 2002]

hat else might it be?

A single positive result for albuminuria may also indicate:

- Urinary tract infection
- Other renal pathology
- Severe hyperglycaemia
- Intercurrent cardiac failure
- Contamination with blood
- Vigorous exercise

omplications and prognosis

omplications

Microalbuminuria is the earliest sign of diabetic nephropathy and predicts increased total mortality, cardiovascular morbidity and mortality, and end-stage renal failure (ESRF).

- **Overt renal disease**
  - **Among people with established diabetes and microalbuminuria,** after 10 years approximately 20% develop proteinuria, 30% revert to normoalbuminuria, and 50% remain microalbuminuric.
  - **Diabetic nephropathy is the leading cause of ESRF in the UK.** Between 15 and 25% of people entering renal transplant programmes in the UK have diabetes. Most of these have Type 2 rather than Type 1 diabetes.
- **Cardiovascular disease**
  - **Once microalbuminuria develops there is a considerable increase in the risk of cardiovascular morbidity and mortality.** Microalbuminuria, clinical proteinuria, and ESRF are progressively stronger risk factors for cardiovascular mortality in people with diabetes.
  - **Cardiovascular risk is increased** in people with Type 2 diabetes with microalbuminuria (two- to four-fold increase) and proteinuria (five- to eight-fold increase), compared to people with normoalbuminuria.

[NHS CRD, 2000; SIGN, 2001; McIntosh et al, 2002]

Prognosis

- Clinical proteinuria is a strong risk factor for ESRF. Within 10 years, 8.4% of people with baseline proteinuria develop ESRF.
- People with diabetes and ESRF have a very high mortality rate, with an expected survival of 3 years.
- However, overall the mortality rate directly due to renal disease is low in people with Type 2 diabetes (less than 5% of deaths among people with Type 2 diabetes are directly attributed to renal disease), the majority of deaths being due to cardiovascular disease.
- Cardiovascular disease is the most common cause of death among people with Type 2 diabetes.
- A large prospective cohort study in men with 5 years' follow-up found that, compared to people without diabetes or pre-existing coronary heart disease (CHD), diabetes mellitus was associated with:
  - A two-fold increase in risk for all cause death
  - A three-fold increase in risk of death from CHD in people without pre-existing CHD
  - A twelve-fold increase in death from CHD in people with pre-existing CHD [Lotufo et al, 2001]

[NHS CRD, 2000]

Management issues

- Screening for diabetic renal disease p.597
- Classification of risk p.598
- Referral p.598
- Risk factors for the development of microalbuminuria and proteinuria p.598
- Prevention of disease progression and cardiovascular outcomes p.598

Screening for diabetic renal disease

Who should I screen?

- **Measure urine albumin or urinary albumin:creatinine ratio (ACR), and serum creatinine in all people with Type 2 diabetes at diagnosis and at least annually thereafter (C).**

Which test should I use?

- **Urinary ACR is the screening test of choice.** This is performed on a single-spot urine specimen, which can approximate a 24-hour collection because creatinine excretion is constant throughout the day. Whether this is done using a laboratory method or near-patient testing will depend on local facilities available.

- **If the ACR is greater than or equal to 2.5 mg/mmol (men) or 3.5 mg/mmol (women), repeat testing on two further occasions** (within 1 month where practical). Two positive tests out of three confirm the diagnosis.
- **If access to ACR testing is not readily available,** use a near-patient test specifically for microalbuminuria. This should be followed by laboratory confirmation.
- **Of the near-patient tests available for detecting albuminuria, there is adequate data to evaluate Micral-Test II, and Albustix.** Of these, only Micral-Test II is specific for microalbuminuria. This test is not prescribable on the NHS. Micral-Test II appears to meet acceptable levels of sensitivity (>80%) and specificity (>90%). Using radioimmunoassay as a reference standard, the sensitivity of Micral-Test II is 93% and the specificity is 93% for detecting urinary albumin levels of 20 mg/l (microalbuminuria).
- **If uncertainty about the diagnosis still exists,** consider confirming the result with a timed collection.
- **The gold standard test for albuminuria** is the 24-hour albumin excretion rate (AER), assessed by radioimmunoassay. Timed overnight and 4-hour AERs are also extremely accurate.
- **A range of 30–300 mg in a 24 hour urine sample, 20–200 micrograms/min in an overnight urine collection and 15–200 micrograms/min in a shorter timed sample** are the conventional definitions of microalbuminuria, although some authorities believe that for Type 2 diabetes patients, the lower cut-off could be set at 10 micrograms/min.

[McIntosh et al, 2002]

What type of sample should I test?

- **For a single-spot test, a first morning urine sample best** reflects a timed urine collection and is preferable to a random sample. The day-to-day variability in albumin excretion, which can be as much as 40%, is less in first morning samples.
- **Optimum precision of measurement of the urine ACR is obtained using three first morning urine samples.**
- **Urine albumin concentration is stable for 7–14 days** without preservative at room temperature.

[McIntosh et al, 2002]

Classification of risk

- **Following measurement, classify albumin excretion as lower-risk or higher-risk (C).**
- **Lower-risk urine albumin excretion is defined as:**
  - Urine albumin excretion less than the threshold for defining microalbuminuria, i.e. albumin:creatinine ratio (ACR) less than 2.5 mg/mmol (men) or 3.5 mg/mmol (women), or urinary albumin concentration less than 20 mg/l
- **Higher-risk urine albumin excretion is defined as the presence of:**
  - **Microalbuminuria** — ACR greater than or equal to 2.5 mg/mmol (men) or 3.5 mg/mmol (women), or urinary albumin concentration greater than or equal to 20 mg/l, *or*
  - **Proteinuria** — ACR greater than or equal to 30 mg/mmol or urinary albumin concentration greater than or equal to 200 mg/l

[McIntosh et al, 2002; NICE, 2002]

Referral

- **Consider referral for specialist opinion if:**
  - Serum creatinine is greater than 150 micromoles/l. This will depend on the age of the person and their previous renal function, as serum creatinine increase with age.
  - Renal function is rapidly declining. If serum creatini is higher than normal for age and sex, repeat after 1 month, if renal function is declining (i.e. serum creatinine increases), consider referral.

[McIntosh et al, 2002]

  - Presence of blood in the urine (greater than ++) may indicate the presence of other causes of renal disease and requires further investigation.

Risk factors for the development of microalbuminuria and proteinuria

- Risk factors that are strongly associated with the development of microalbuminuria and proteinuria include:
  - Poor glycaemic control
  - Raised blood pressure
  - Increased baseline urinary albumin excretion rate
- Other factors include:
  - Family history of diabetic renal disease
  - Higher body mass index
  - Increasing age
  - Low high-density lipoprotein cholesterol
  - Male sex
  - Presence of retinopathy
  - Race (people of Asian or African ethnic origin are more likely to develop diabetic renal disease than white people)
  - Raised serum homocysteine
  - Raised serum total or low-density lipoprotein cholesterol and serum triglycerides
  - Smoking

[NHS CRD, 2000; SIGN, 2001; McIntosh et al, 2002]

Prevention of disease progression and cardiovascular outcomes

Blood glucose control

- **Good glycaemic control reduces the risk of developing microalbuminuria and of progression of microalbuminuria to overt nephropathy.**
- **For people with higher-risk urine albumin excretion:**
  - **Ensure good blood glucose control.** Target HbA_{1c} should be set between 6.5% and 7.5% for each individual, according to their macro- and microvascular risk (**A**). In general, a target HbA_{1c} of 6.5% is preferred for people at significant risk of vascular complications (such as those with higher-ris urine albumin excretion), but higher targets are necessary for those at risk of hypoglycaemia.
  - There is some evidence that improved glucose contr in microalbuminuric people with Type 2 diabetes reduces the risk of development of overt diabetic nephropathy. In a small randomized controlled trial = 110), reducing the HbA_{1c} from 9.4% to 7.1% resulted in an absolute risk reduction of 24% over 6 years [Ohkubo et al, 1995].
- **For people with lower-risk urine albumin excretion:**
  - **Ensure good blood glucose control.** Target HbA_{1c} should be set between 6.5% and 7.5% for each individual, according to their macro- and microvascular risk and their risk of hypoglycaemia (**A**). Lower HbA_{1c} levels are associated with a lower

risk of developing microalbuminuria, proteinuria, or renal impairment.

- In the UK Prospective Diabetes Study (UKPDS), a reduction in mean HbA_{1c} from 7.9 to 7.0% was associated with an absolute risk reduction of developing microalbuminuria of 11%, a 3.5% absolute risk reduction of developing proteinuria, and a 74% reduction in the number of people who doubled their serum creatinine value over 12 years [Turner et al, 1998].

lood pressure control

Tight blood pressure (BP) control reduces the risk of developing microalbuminuria and delays the progression of diabetic renal disease.

For those people with higher-risk urine albumin excretion:

- Maintain BP at or below 135/75 mmHg (A).
- Reduction of BP reduces the rate of progression of renal disease.

For those people with lower-risk urine albumin excretion:

- Maintain good BP control (at or below 140/80 mm/Hg) (A).
- In the UKPDS, a reduction in mean BP from 154/87 mmHg to 144/82 mmHg was associated with an absolute risk reduction for developing microalbuminuria of 8% over 6 years [UK Prospective Diabetes Study Group, 1998].

All antihypertensive agents appear to be of benefit for people with Type 2 diabetes who have renal disease, in that lowering BP seems to lead to beneficial reductions in proteinuria, which may be taken as a proxy for improved renal function.

The reduction in albumin excretion with ACE inhibitors and with angiotensin-II receptor antagonists (AIIRAs) is generally greater than with other classes of antihypertensive agents, suggesting that these two classes of drugs have antiproteinuric effects independent of their antihypertensive effect.

To achieve target BP, use combination therapy if ACE inhibitors alone are not fully effective. Combination therapy is likely to be necessary for most people (A). See separate PRODIGY guidance *Diabetes Type 1 and 2 — hypertension.*

CE inhibitors and AIIRAs

To maximize renal and cardiovascular protection, begin therapy with an ACE inhibitor in people with Type 2 diabetes and microalbuminuria or proteinuria (A).

If ACE inhibitors are poorly tolerated or cause adverse effects, consider using an AIIRA as an alternative (B).

vidence for ACE inhibitors

There is strong evidence from systematic reviews for the effectiveness of ACE inhibitors at arresting, even reducing, the albumin excretion rate and delaying the progression of diabetic renal disease compared to placebo [Kshirsagar et al, 2000; Lovell, 2003].

These effects appear to be independent of BP reduction.

A recent Cochrane review found that ACE inhibitors prevent deterioration in albumin excretion rate in people with diabetes with microalbuminuria and normal BP. A direct link with postponement of end-stage renal failure was not detected [Lovell, 2003].

ACE inhibitors are also cardioprotective in people with diabetic renal disease. In the MICRO-HOPE study, treatment with ramipril 10 mg reduced the number of cardiovascular events by 25% over 4.5 years in people with Type 2 diabetes and microalbuminuria [Heart Outcomes Prevention Evaluation Study Investigators, 2000].

Evidence for AIIRAs

- **There is increasing evidence that AIIRAs reduce the progression of diabetic renal disease.** [Brenner et al, 2001; Lewis et al, 2001; Parving et al, 2001].
- In one study of people with Type 2 diabetes and microalbuminuria, 5% of people treated with irbesartan 300 mg developed nephropathy compared with 15% in the placebo group over 2 years [Parving et al, 2001].
- In two further studies of people with Type 2 diabetes and proteinuria, treatment with an AIIRA significantly reduced both the number of people whose serum creatinine level doubled, and the number of people who progressed to end-stage renal failure during the trial period, compared with placebo [Parving et al, 2001].
- **No effect on cardiovascular mortality has yet been demonstrated.**

Combination of ACE and AIIRAs

- **There is increasing evidence to support dual blockade** (the use of both ACE inhibitors and AIIRAs) in diabetic nephropathy.
- The Candesartan and Lisinopril Microalbuminuria (CALM) study is the largest trial of dual blockade in people with Type 2 diabetes and microalbuminuria. This 12-week trial showed a significant reduction in BP with dual blockade compared with either lisinopril (20 mg) or candesartan (16 mg) alone, and greater reductions in the urinary albumin:creatinine ratio with combination treatment (50%) compared with lisinopril (39%) or candesartan (24%) [Mogensen et al, 2000].
- **The routine use of dual blockade cannot be recommended** until evidence is available from large long-term trials with clinical end-points.

Management of other cardiovascular risk factors

- **All stages of diabetic nephropathy are independent risk factors for cardiovascular disease.**
- Measure, assess, and treat cardiovascular risk factors in all people with Type 2 diabetes [McIntosh et al, 2002].

Dietary interventions

- There is some evidence to suggest that a restriction in dietary protein intake may help to slow progression to renal failure in people with Type 1 diabetes [Waugh and Robertson, 2003]. The effect of a reduction in dietary protein in people with Type 2 diabetes is unclear.
- **Ask about dietary protein intake and consider referral for dietary advice if it is unusually high (e.g. body builders).**

References

NHS staff in England can link, free of charge, from references to full text journals by clicking on [Full text] on the PRODIGY website.

1. Brenner, B.M., Cooper, M.E., De Zeeuw, D. et al (2001) Effects of losartan on renal and cardiovascular outcomes in patients with type 2 diabetes and nephropathy. *New England Journal of Medicine* 345(12), 861–869. [Full text]
2. Heart Outcomes Prevention Evaluation Study Investigators (2000) Effects of ramipril on cardiovascular and microvascular outcomes in people with diabetes mellitus: results of the HOPE study and MICRO-HOPE substudy. *Lancet* 355(9200), 253–259. [Full text]
3. Kshirsagar, A.V., Joy, M.S., Hogan, S.L. et al (2000) Effect of ACE inhibitors in diabetic and nondiabetic chronic renal disease: a systematic overview of randomized placebo-controlled trials. *American Journal of Kidney Diseases* 35(4), 695–707.

D

4. Lewis, E.J., Hunsicker, L.G., Clarke, W.R. et al (2001) Renoprotective effect of the angiotensin-receptor antagonist irbesartan in patients with nephropathy due to type 2 diabetes. *New England Journal of Medicine* **345**(12), 851–860. [Full text]
5. Lotufo, P.A., Gaziano, J.M., Chae, C.U. et al (2001) Diabetes and all-cause and coronary heart disease mortality among US male physicians. *Archives of Internal Medicine* **161**(2), 242–247. [Full text]
6. Lovell, H.G. (2003) *Angiotensin converting enzyme inhibitors in normotensive diabetic patients with microalbuminuria (Cochrane Review)*. The Cochrane Library. Issue 1. Oxford: Update Software.
7. McIntosh, A., Hutchinson, A., Marshall, S. et al (2002) *Clinical guidelines and evidence review for type 2 diabetes – diabetic renal disease: prevention and early management*. Sheffield: ScHARR, University of Sheffield. www.shef.ac.uk/guidelines [Accessed: 29/11/2002].
8. Mogensen, C.E., Neldam, S., Tikkanen, I. et al (2000) Randomised controlled trial of dual blockade of renin-angiotensin system in patients with hypertension, microalbuminuria, and non-insulin dependent diabetes: the candesartan and lisinopril microalbuminuria (CALM) study. *British Medical Journal* **321**(7274), 1440–1444. [Full text]
9. NHS CRD (2000) Complications of diabetes: renal disease and promotion of self-management. *Effective Health Care Bulletin* **6**(1), 1–12.
10. NICE (2002) *Management of type 2 diabetes – renal disease, prevention and early management*. Inherited clinical guideline F. London: National Institute for Clinical Excellence. www.nice.org.uk [Accessed: 20/11/2002].
11. Ohkubo, Y., Kishikawa, H., Araki, E. et al (1995) Intensive insulin therapy prevents the progression of diabetic microvascular complications in Japanese patients with non-insulin-dependent diabetes mellitus: a randomized prospective 6-year study. *Diabetes Research and Clinical Practice* **28**, 103–117.
12. Parving, H.H., Lehnert, H., Brochner-Mortensen, J. et al (2001) The effect of irbesartan on the development of diabetic nephropathy in patients with type 2 diabetes. *New England Journal of Medicine* **345**(12) 870–878. [Full text]
13. SIGN (2001) *Management of diabetes*. Report no. 5 Scottish Intercollegiate Guidelines Network. www.sign.ac.uk [Accessed: 20/11/2002].
14. Turner, R.C., Holman, R.R., Cull, C.A. et al (1998) Intensive blood-glucose control with sulphonylureas insulin compared with conventional treatment and ri of complications in patients with type 2 diabetes (UKPDS 33). *Lancet* **352**(9131), 837–853. [Full text]
15. UK Prospective Diabetes Study Group (1998) Tight blood pressure control and risk of macrovascular an microvascular complications in type 2 diabetes (UKPDS 38). *British Medical Journal* **317**(7160), 703–713. [Full text]
16. Waugh, N.R. and Robertson, A.M. (2003) *Protein restriction in diabetic renal disease*. The Cochrane Library. Issue 1. Oxford: Update Software.

Evidence grading

Evidence grading is from the National Institute of Clinic Excellence guideline, *Diabetic renal disease: prevention and early management, February* 2002. The definitions c grades of recommendation used in this guideline are as follows:

A	Directly based on category I evidence (systematic review of randomized controlled trials or at least one randomized controlled trial)
B	Directly based on category II evidence (at least one controlle study without randomization or one other type of quasi-experimental study) or extrapolated recommendation from category I evidence
C	Directly based on category III evidence (non-experimental descriptive studies) or extrapolated recommendation from category I or II evidence
D	Directly based on category IV evidence (expert committee reports or opinions and/or clinical experience of respected authorities) or extrapolated recommendation from category II, or III evidence

PRODIGY GUIDANCE

Diabetes Type 2 — retinopathy

Last revised in October 2003
www.prodigy.nhs.uk/guidance.asp?gt=Diabetes - retinopathy

Applies to people over the age of 16 years

This guidance covers the detection and early management of retinopathy in adults with Type 2 diabetes.
This guidance is the PRODIGY implementation of the National Institute for Clinical Excellence (NICE) clinical guideline on *Management of Type 2 diabetes: Retinopathy — screening and early management*, and the Royal College of General Practitioners (RCGP) *Clinical guideline for Type 2 diabetes: diabetic retinopathy: early management and screening*. It is supported by recommendations from the National Screening Centre's (NSC) national programme supporting implementation of high quality systematic screening programmes by Primary Care Organizations as announced in the Diabetes National Service Framework Delivery Strategy.

This guidance does not cover the management of retinopathy in people with Type 1 diabetes; the management of other diabetic complications; or other causes of visual loss in people with Type 2 diabetes. Guidance on managing retinopathy in people with Type 1 diabetes is currently being developed by NICE. PRODIGY guidance will be updated when that is available.

There is separate PRODIGY guidance for *Diabetes Type 2 — blood glucose management, Diabetes Type 1 and 2 — foot disease, Diabetes Type 1 and 2 — hypertension, Diabetes Type 2 — lipid management, and Diabetes Type 2 — renal disease.*

Goals

To identify people with sight-threatening retinopathy who may require preventive treatment
To reduce the progression of diabetic retinopathy
To reduce blindness and visual impairment resulting from diabetic retinopathy

Contents

Scenarios

- Screening and referral p.601

Extended Information, p. 602

Screening and referral

Which therapy?

Ensure examination of eyes at the time of diagnosis of diabetes and at least once a year thereafter (include people who are registered blind and partially sighted). Ideally this should be done through a formal screening programme. Opportunistic screening is an option only if formal screening is not possible. The NHS is introducing a systematic screening programme during 2003–2006 as announced in the Priorities and Planning Framework.
Check visual acuity, corrected with glasses or pinhole.
Examine for diabetic retinopathy following dilation of pupils with tropicamide (unless contraindicated) using:

- Mydriatic retinal photography as the first choice, when undertaken and when photographs or images are evaluated by trained personnel (C), *or*
- Mydriatic slit-lamp indirect ophthalmoscopy, when used by trained personnel (C).
- Direct ophthalmoscopy may be used for opportunistic screening of people who have been missed by formal screening programmes. Opportunistic screening is not an adequate substitute for participation in a formal screening programme. It is an option only if formal screening is not possible (D).

Maintain good blood glucose control (preferably HbA1c below 6.5%, according to individual's target based on their risk of macrovascular and microvascular complications).

- **Maintain good blood pressure control** (at or below 140/80 mmHg).

Practical prescribing points

For further information, please see the *Medicines Compendium* (www.medicines.org.uk) or the *British National Formulary* (www.bnf.org).

Mydriasis

- Warn people not to drive for 1–2 hours after mydriasis.
- Mydriasis may precipitate acute angle-closure glaucoma in a very few patients. Use tropicamide with caution in people with risk factors for acute angle-closure glaucoma, e.g. hypermetropia, eyes with shallow anterior chambers, increasing age (> 60 years), family history, and a previous attack in the other eye.

Follow-up advice

- **Review annually if:**
  - There is no retinopathy present.
  - There is only minimal, mild, or low-risk background retinopathy.
- **Review every 3 to 6 months if:**
  - There is occurrence or worsening of lesions since the previous examination.
  - There are scattered exudates, which are more than one disc diameter from the fovea.
  - A person is at high risk of progression (i.e. where there is poor glycaemic control or rapid improvement in blood glucose control, or the presence of hypertension or renal disease).

D

Refer or investigate?

Refer?

Table 1: Referral recommendations following screening.

Screening Assessment	Recommendation
No retinopathy (Level 0)	Annual screening
Retinopathy: background (Level 1)	Annual screening; inform diabetes care team
Retinopathy: preproliferative (Level 2)	Refer to hospital eye service*
Retinopathy: proliferative (Level 3)	Fast-track referral to hospital eye service
Maculopathy	Refer to hospital eye service (routine appointment)
Photocoagulation	New screenee: refer to hospital eye service Quiescent post treatment: annual screening
Other lesions	Refer to hospital eye service or inform primary physician
Ungradeable/ unobtainable	Media opacity hospital eye service
Unscreenable	Discharge; inform GP

* National Screening Programme recommends a routine appointment for preproliferative retinopathy; NICE recommends that the person is seen by an ophthalmology specialist within 4 weeks, to be agreed locally.

Patient information leaflets

The following PILs are available at www.prodigy.nhs.uk

- Blood Test - General
- Blood Test - Glucose
- Diabetes Insight Website
- Diabetes Research & Wellness Foundation
- Diabetes Type 2
- Diabetes Type 2 - A Summary
- Diabetes UK
- DiabeticLife
- Diabetic Retinopathy Screening
- Diabetic Retinopathy Website

Drug rationale

- There are no prescriptions offered.

Extended Information

Background information

- What is it? p.602
- How common is it? p.602
- How do I know my patient has it? p.602
- What are the risk factors for development and progression of retinopathy? p.602
- What else might it be? p.602
- Complications and prognosis p.602

What is it?

- **Diabetic retinopathy is graded** by progressive retinal changes, which arise from a combination of microvascular leakage and occlusion.
- **Diabetic retinopathy is classified** by the presence of various clinical abnormalities (see Table 1).

How common is it?

- **Retinopathy is present in 20% of people at diagnosis of** Type 2 diabetes, with about 3% having sight-threatening disease.
- **During the 20 years following diagnosis,** about two-thirds of people with Type 2 diabetes develop retinopathy.

[SIGN, 2001; Hutchinson et al, 2002]

How do I know my patient has it?

- Arrange examination of eyes at time of diagnosis of diabetes, and at least once a year thereafter (D).
- Check visual acuity, corrected with glasses or pinhole (D).
- Screening for retinopathy should be undertaken using:
  - Mydriatic retinal photography *as the first choice*, when undertaken and evaluated by trained personnel (C), or
  - Mydriatic slit-lamp indirect ophthalmoscopy, when used by trained personnel (C).
  - Direct ophthalmoscopy may be used for opportunistic screening of people who have been missed by formal screening programmes (D). Note: opportunistic screening is not an adequate substitute for participation in a formal screening programme. It is an option only if formal screening is not possible.
- Use tropicamide to achieve mydriasis, unless contraindicated (C).

[Hutchinson et al, 2002]

- Grading and features of retinopathy are shown in Table 2.

[NSC, 2003]

What are the risk factors for development and progression of retinopathy?

- Risk factors for the development and progression of diabetic retinopathy include:
  - Duration of diabetes
  - Poor glycaemic control
  - Raised blood pressure
  - Raised triglyceride levels
  - Presence of microalbuminuria and proteinuria
  - Pregnancy

[SIGN, 2001]

What else might it be?

- Other causes of visual impairment in people with diabetes include:
  - Cataracts
  - Glaucoma
  - Senile macular degeneration
  - Retinitis pigmentosa

Complications and prognosis

Complications

- **Blindness:** diabetic retinopathy is the leading cause of blindness in people over the age of 70 in industrialized countries [Donnelly et al, 2000].

[Hutchinson et al, 2002]

Prognosis

- Visual prognosis depends on baseline severity of retinopathy and duration of diabetes.
- For people with no retinopathy at baseline, the chance of developing sight-threatening retinopathy within two years is less than 1%.

able 2: Proposed grading criteria from the National Screening Programme for Sight-Threatening Retinopathy.

rade	Examination features
etinopathy: ckground evel 1)	Microaneurysm(s) Retinal haemorrhage(s) with or without any exudate
etinopathy: eproliferative evel 2)	Venous beading Venous loop or reduplication Intraretinal microvascular abnormality Multiple deep, round, or blot haemorrhages
etinopathy: oliferative evel 3)	New vessels on optic disc New vessels elsewhere on retina Pre-retinal or vitreous haemorrhage Pre-retinal fibrosis with or without tractional retinal detachment
aculopathy	Exudate within 1 disc diameter (DD) of the centre of the fovea Circinate or group of exudates within the macula Retinal thickening within 1 DD of the centre of the fovea (if stereo available) Any microaneurysm or haemorrhage within 1 DD of the centre of the fovea only if associated with a best visual acuity of less than 6/12 (if no stereo available)
otocoagulation	Focal/grid to macula Peripheral scatter
nclassifiable	Ungradeable/unobtainable

After 20–24 years, 30% of people with Type 2 diabetes will have some degree of visual impairment, and 7% will be blind.

The progression of retinopathy can be minimized by early, rigorous control of blood glucose and blood pressure.

Meltzer et al, 1998; SIGN, 2001]

Management issues

General issues p.603
Visual acuity testing p.603
How should screening be performed? p.603
Referral p.604
Risk factor modification p.604
Surgical treatment p.604

General issues

Ensure examination of both eyes at the time of diagnosis of diabetes to assess retinopathy status, and at least once a year thereafter (include people who are registered blind and partially sighted) (D).

Ideally this should be done through a formal screening programme. Opportunistic screening is an option only if formal screening is not possible. The NHS is introducing a systematic screening programme during 2003–2006 as announced in the Priorities and Planning Framework [DH, 2003].

NICE recommends early review (every 3 to 6) months if:

- There is occurrence or worsening of lesions since the previous examination (D).
- There are scattered exudates, which are more than one disc diameter from the fovea (D).
- A person is at high risk of progression (that is, where there is poor glycaemic control or rapid improvement in blood glucose control, or the presence of hypertension or renal disease) (D).

Hutchinson et al, 2002; NICE, 2002]

A recent study concluded that a 3-year screening interval could be safely adopted for diabetic patients with no retinopathy, with yearly or more frequent screening for people with higher grades of retinopathy. However, further evidence is needed that this can achieve a reduction in loss of vision at least similar to that achieved by routine annual eye examinations [Younis et al, 2003].

Visual acuity testing

- Examination of visual acuity is an essential element of the overall approach to screening for diabetic retinopathy, and an important part of clinical practice.
- Reduction of visual acuity may be an indicator of diabetic maculopathy, or may be associated with other eye conditions such as cataract and age related macular degeneration.

How should screening be performed?

- An effective system of screening for diabetic retinopathy should achieve a sensitivity of 80% and specificity of 95% with a technical failure rate of less than 5%.
- **For best results, the pupils should be dilated.** This is best achieved by the use of tropicamide.
  - Note: mydriasis may precipitate acute angle-closure glaucoma in a very few patients. Use tropicamide with caution in people with risk factors for acute angle-closure glaucoma, e.g. hypermetropia, eyes with shallow anterior chambers, increasing age (>60 years), family history, and a previous attack in the other eye [BNF 46, 2003].

[Hutchinson et al, 2002]

Retinal photography

- **Mydriatic retinal photography** provides the most sensitive screening and monitoring test for detection of sight-threatening retinopathy.
- **Retinal photography can achieve a sensitivity of greater than 80%** independent of the type of health professional performing the test. However, results from studies examining the effectiveness of retinal photography emphasise the need for training in reading the photographs or images.
- **Retinal cameras** are now being developed that use digital imaging techniques to produce an instant enlarged retinal image on a computer monitor screen. Good agreement in grading non-sight-threatening retinopathy and sight-threatening retinopathy has been demonstrated between digital images and 35 mm colour transparencies, both read by a diabetes physician. Screening using digital cameras is being introduced across England as part of the National Screening Programme for Sight-Threatening Retinopathy [NSC, 2003].

[SIGN, 2001; Hutchinson et al, 2002]

D

Ophthalmoscopy

- **Direct ophthalmoscopy should not be the method of choice** for screening and review of retinopathy.
- Overall, studies demonstrate that direct ophthalmoscopy does not meet the required standards for retinopathy screening and review.
- Direct ophthalmoscopy may be used for opportunistic screening of people who have been missed by formal screening programmes.
- There is limited evidence that health professionals using indirect ophthalmoscopy can achieve the required standards of sensitivity and specificity. Indirect ophthalmoscopy does not provide a hard copy for quality assurance purposes.

[SIGN, 2001; Hutchinson et al, 2002]

Referral

- Recommendations for referral following screening are outlined in Table 3.

[NICE, 2002]

- **NICE also recommends referral to an ophthalmology specialist if:**
  - There is sudden loss of vision — immediate referral (within a day).
  - There is evidence of retinal detachment — immediate referral (within a day).
  - Rubeosis iridis is present — urgent referral (within 1 week, to be agreed locally).
  - There is an unexplained drop in visual acuity — within 4 weeks (or according to local agreement).
  - There are unexplained retinal findings — within 4 weeks (or according to local agreement).

[Hutchinson et al, 2002; NICE, 2002]

Risk factor modification

Blood glucose

- Maintain rigorous control of blood glucose **(A)**.
- For each individual, a target Haemoglobin A1c (HbA1c) should be set between 6.5% and 7.5%, based on their risk of macrovascular and microvascular complications.
- Tight control of blood glucose reduces the risk of onset and progression of diabetic retinopathy.
  - In the UK Prospective Diabetes Study, intensive blood glucose control led to a 25% risk reduction in microvascular endpoints, including the need for retinal photocoagulation [Turner et al, 1998].
- Rapid improvement of glycaemic control can result in short-term worsening of diabetic retinal disease although the long-term outcomes remain beneficial. If present, sight-threatening retinal disease should be stabilized before rapid improvements in glycaemic control are attempted [SIGN, 2001].

Blood pressure

- Maintain rigorous control of blood pressure (at or below 140/80 mmHg) **(A)**.
- Tight blood pressure control reduces the risk of retinopathy and deterioration of visual acuity.
  - In the UK Prospective Diabetes Study tight control of blood pressure led to a 37% risk reduction in microvascular endpoints, including the need for retinal photocoagulation [UK Prospective Diabetes Study Group, 1998].
- There is currently no evidence to suggest any additional benefit from treatment with angiotensin converting enzyme (ACE) inhibitors in reducing the progression of diabetic retinopathy. There are a number of ongoing trials.

Surgical treatment

- Surgical treatments include laser photocoagulation and vitrectomy.
- Laser photocoagulation reduces visual loss in people with proliferative retinopathy or clinically significant macular oedema (when used for focal or diffuse maculopathy, but not for ischaemic maculopathy).
- The value of vitrectomy in Type 2 diabetes is uncertain. People who have severe fibrovascular proliferation with or without retinal detachment have better visual acuity after vitrectomy.
- Vitrectomy for diffuse diabetic macular oedema has been shown to result in resolution of oedema and improvement in visual acuity.

[SIGN, 2001]

Table 3: Referral recommendations following screening.

Screening Assessment	Recommendation
No retinopathy (Level 0)	Annual screening
Retinopathy: background (Level 1)	Annual screening; inform diabetes care team
Retinopathy: preproliferative (Level 2)	Refer to hospital eye service*
Retinopathy: proliferative (Level 3)	Fast-track referral to hospital eye service
Maculopathy	Refer to hospital eye service (routine appointment)
Photocoagulation	New screenee: refer to hospital eye service Quiescent post treatment: annual screening
Other lesions	Refer to hospital eye service or inform primary physician
Ungradeable/ unobtainable	Media opacity hospital eye service
Unscreenable	Discharge; inform GP

* National Screening Programme recommends a routine appointment for preproliferative retinopathy; NICE recommends that the person is seen by an ophthalmology specialist within 4 weeks, to be agreed locally.

References

NHS staff in England can link, free of charge, from references to full text journals by clicking on [Full text] on the PRODIGY website.

1. BNF 46 (2003) *British National Formulary*. 46th edn. London: British Medical Association and Royal Pharmaceutical Society of Great Britain.
2. DH (2003) *National service framework for diabetes*. Department of Health. www.dh.gov.uk [Accessed: 27/04/2004]. [Full text]
3. Donnelly, R., Emslie-Smith, A.M., Gardner, I.D. and Morris, A.D. (2000) Vascular complications of diabetes. *British Medical Journal* 320(7241), 1062–1066. [Full text]
4. Hutchinson, A., McIntosh, A., Peters, J. et al (2002) *Clinical guidelines and evidence review for type 2 diabetes – diabetic retinopathy: early management and screening*. Sheffield: ScHARR, University of Sheffield. www.shef.ac.uk/guidelines [Accessed: 02/12/2002].
5. Meltzer, S, Leiter, L., Daneman, D et al (1998) 1998 clinical practice guidelines for the management of diabetes in Canada. *Canadian Medical Association Journal* 159(suppl 8), S1-S29. [Full text]
6. NICE (2002) *Management of type 2 diabetes retinopathy – early management and screening.*

Inherited clinical guideline E. London: National Institute for Clinical Excellence. www.nice.org.uk [Accessed: 02/12/2002].

. NSC (2003) *The website of the National Screening Programme for sight-threatening diabetic retinopathy.* National Screening Committee. www.nscretinopathy.org.uk [Accessed: 01/06/2003].

. SIGN (2001) *Management of diabetes.* Report no. 55. Scottish Intercollegiate Guidelines Network. www.sign.ac.uk [Accessed: 20/11/2002].

. Turner, R.C., Holman, R.R., Cull, C.A. et al (1998) Intensive blood-glucose control with sulphonylureas or insulin compared with conventional treatment and risk of complications in patients with type 2 diabetes (UKPDS 33). *Lancet* **352**(9131), 837–853. [Full text]

0. UK Prospective Diabetes Study Group (1998) Tight blood pressure control and risk of macrovascular and microvascular complications in type 2 diabetes (UKPDS 38). *British Medical Journal* **317**(7160), 703–713. [Full text]

1. Younis, N., Broadbent, D.M., Vora, J.P. and Harding, S.P. (2003) Incidence of sight-threatening retinopathy in patients with type 2 diabetes in the Liverpool Diabetic Eye Study: a cohort study. *Lancet* **361**(9353), 195–200. [Full text]

Evidence grading

Evidence grading is from the National Institute of Clinical Excellence guideline, *Diabetic retinopathy: screening and early management*, February 2002. The definitions of grades of recommendation used in this guideline are as follows:

A Directly based on category I evidence (systematic review of randomized controlled trials or at least one randomized controlled trial)

B Directly based on category II evidence (at least one controlled study without randomization or one other type of quasi-experimental study) or extrapolated recommendation from category I evidence

C Directly based on category III evidence (non-experimental descriptive studies) or extrapolated recommendation from category I or II evidence

D Directly based on category IV evidence (expert committee reports or opinions and/or clinical experience of respected authorities) or extrapolated recommendation from category I, II, or III evidence

PRODIGY GUIDANCE

Diverticular disease and diverticulitis

Last revised in July 2005
www.prodigy.nhs.uk/guidance.asp?gt=Diverticular disease

Applies to people over the age of 16 years

This guidance covers the management of diverticular disease and diverticulitis (infected diverticula) in adults.

This guidance does not cover the management of complications including fistula, abscess, perforation, peritonitis, obstruction, or haemorrhage.

There is separate PRODIGY guidance for *Constipation, Gastrointestinal (lower) cancer — suspected* and *Irritable bowel syndrome.*

D

Goals

- To minimize symptoms of diverticular disease (e.g. abdominal pain)
- To reduce the risk of developing diverticulitis
- To ensure appropriate referral for people with diverticulitis

Contents

Scenarios
- Asymptomatic diverticula p.606
- Diverticular disease (uncomplicated) p.606
- Acute diverticulitis p.608

Extended Information, p. 610

Which scenario?

- **Asymptomatic diverticula:** covers the management of asymptomatic people who have an incidental finding of diverticula.
- **Diverticular disease (uncomplicated):** covers the management of people who have symptoms associated with the presence of diverticula e.g. lower abdominal pain and altered bowel habit.
- **Acute diverticulitis:** covers the management of infected diverticula.

Asymptomatic diverticula

Which therapy?

- **Give an explanation** of the condition and its usually benign nature, emphasising that diverticula identified incidentally in an asymptomatic person do not require further diagnostic evaluation.
- **Advise** the person that no specific treatment or follow-up is necessary.
- **Encourage a diet high in fruit and vegetables,** as limited evidence suggests that this decreases the risk of developing diverticular disease.

Follow-up advice

- No follow-up is necessary.
- Advise the person to report new symptoms.

Should I refer or investigate?

Investigate

- No investigation is necessary in people with diverticula identified incidentally.

Patient information leaflets

The following PILs are available at www.prodigy.nhs.uk
- CORE, Fighting Gut and Liver Disease
- Diverticula
- Fibre in the Diet

Shared decision making

- Diverticula cause no symptoms in most cases. Some people develop symptoms such as pain, bloating, diarrhoea, or constipation.
- Symptoms may be prevented from developing by:
  - Eating a high-fibre diet.
    - **Fruit and vegetables** are probably the best source of fibre if you have diverticula.
    - **Have lots to drink** if you have a high-fibre diet.

Drug rationale

Drugs not included

- Drug treatment is not recommended for someone with asymptomatic diverticula.

Drugs included

- An advice note is provided for increasing fibre intake.

Prescriptions

Non-drug management

Advice only: high-fibre diet and fluid
- Age from 16 years onwards
- Diverticula cause no symptoms in most cases. Some people develop symptoms such as pain, bloating, diarrhoea, or constipation. Symptoms may be prevented from developing by eating a high-fibre diet – fruit and vegetables are the best source of fibre if you have diverticula. Always drink plenty of liquid. Try to drink at least 12 cups (8 glasses or mugs) of liquid a day.

Diverticular disease (uncomplicated)

Which therapy?

- **Referral for barium enema/colonoscopy/sigmoidoscopy** is recommended to exclude other gastrointestinal disease.
- **Recommend a diet high in insoluble fibre.**
  - Advise a gradual increase in dietary fibre, especially fruit and vegetables.

- Advise the person to maintain adequate fluid intake.

Prescribe bulk-forming agents if a high-fibre diet is not sufficient or is not achievable.

- There is little to choose between the products available.

Prescribe paracetamol for pain.

'ractical prescribing points

or further information, please see the *Medicines 'ompendium* (www.medicines.org.uk) or the *British 'ational Formulary* (www.bnf.org).

ulk-forming laxatives

Advise an adequate fluid intake for people taking bulk-forming agents. Powder and granule forms should be mixed in at least 250 ml of fluid and taken immediately. An additional 250 ml of fluid is recommended to increase efficacy and prevent intestinal obstruction — ensure there is adequate supervision of fluid intake in frail elderly or immobile people.

Advise people not to take bulk-forming agents before going to bed.

hould I refer or investigate?

lefer?

Referral to secondary care for large-bowel investigations should be considered in people with recurrent or constant abdominal pain.

Referral guidelines for suspected cancer published by the National Institute for Health and Clinical Excellence (NICE) [NICE, 2005] recommend that people who present with symptoms and signs suggestive of colorectal or anal cancer (see Table 1) are urgently referred to a team specialising in the management of lower gastrointestinal cancer (depending on local arrangements).

'atient information leaflets

he following PILs are available at www.prodigy.nhs.uk

CORE, Fighting Gut and Liver Disease
Diverticula
Fibre in the Diet
Medicines - Name Changes of Medicines

hared decision making

Diverticula often cause no symptoms, but some people develop pain, bloating, diarrhoea, or constipation.

- **A high-fibre diet** may help to ease symptoms and may prevent more diverticula from developing.
  - **Fruit and vegetables** are probably the best source of fibre if you have diverticula.
  - **Fibre supplements** such as ispaghula may be needed if a high-fibre diet does not produce regular soft stools.
  - **Have lots to drink** if you have a high-fibre diet or fibre supplements.
- **Painkillers** such as paracetamol are sometimes needed.
- You may need tests to rule out other causes of the symptoms.

Drug rationale

Drugs not included

- **Antispasmodics** such as alverine, mebeverine, and peppermint oil are not included, as there is no evidence that they improve symptoms or affect disease progression in diverticular disease.
- **Stimulant laxatives** are not recommended, because there is no evidence of efficacy in diverticular disease, and they may increase intraluminal pressure and aggravate pain [Murray and Emmanuel, 2002].
- **Analgesia other than paracetamol is not recommended.**
  - **Opioid analgesics** (including tramadol) reduce gut motility, which can lead to constipation and aggravate diverticulitis. They also cause colonic spasm, which may accentuate to hypersegmentation of the colon [Ferzoco et al, 1998; Tursi, 2004].
  - **Nonsteroidal anti-inflammatory agents (NSAIDs)** are not included, because there may be an association between increased risk of bleeding from diverticula and NSAID use [Stollman and Raskin, 1999b].

Drugs included

- **Bulk-forming agents** including ispaghula husk, sterculia, and methylcellulose are included. Clinically there is little to choose between the different products.
  - Ispaghula and sterculia are the bulk-forming agents of choice.
    - Since convenience of use is important if people are to adhere to long-term treatment, only products available in sachets are included.
    - Ispaghula sachets are available in a variety of flavours — a generic prescription is included so that the person can choose the flavour at the time of dispensing.
  - Methylcellulose is less preferred because the large number of tablets that need to be taken may reduce compliance.

'able 1: Guidelines for urgent referral of suspected lower gastrointestinal cancer.

erson	Symptoms and signs
ged 40 ears and lder	Rectal bleeding with a change in bowel habit towards looser stools and/or increased stool frequency persisting 6 weeks or more.
ged 60 ears and lder	Rectal bleeding persisting for 6 weeks or more without a change in bowel habit and without anal symptoms. A change in bowel habit to looser stools and/or more frequent stools persisting for 6 weeks or more without rectal bleeding.
f any age	A right abdominal mass consistent with involvement of the large bowel. A palpable rectal mass (intraluminal and not pelvic; a pelvic mass outside the bowel would warrant an urgent referral to a urologist or gynaecologist).
'oman (not enstruating)	Unexplained iron deficiency anaemia and a haemoglobin 10 g/100 ml or below.*
lan of any ge	Unexplained iron deficiency anaemia and a haemoglobin 11 g/100 ml or below.*

Anaemia considered on the basis of history and examination in primary care not to be related to other sources of blood loss (e.g. ingestions of NSAIDs) or blood dyscrasia.

- **Paracetamol** is an effective and safe analgesic with few gastrointestinal adverse effects.

Prescriptions

Non-drug management

Advice only: high-fibre diet and fluid
- Age from 16 years onwards
- Try to eat food rich in fibre taken with plenty to drink. Every day, eat more fruit and vegetables including potatoes (with their skins on if possible). Eat more cereals, wholemeal bread and pulses (peas, beans, lentils). Build up fibre intake gradually until it is right for you. Always drink plenty of liquid. Try to drink at least 12 cups (8 glasses or mugs) of liquid a day.

Bulk-forming agents (if diet alone fails)

Ispaghula 3.5g s/f sachets (Fybogel or Ispagel Orange)
- Age from 16 years onwards
- Ispaghula husk 3.5g s/f granules. Take the contents of one sachet (mixed in a glass of water) each morning and evening; supply 60 sachets; NHS Cost £4.24; OTC Cost £7.74.

Ispaghula 3.4g s/f sachets (Regulan)
- Age from 16 years onwards
- Ispaghula husk 3.4g s/f powder. Take the contents of one sachet (mixed in a glass of water) 1 to 3 times a day; supply 60 sachets; NHS Cost £3.94; OTC Cost £6.94.

Sterculia 62% sachets (Normacol)
- Age from 16 years onwards
- Sterculia 62% granules. Take the contents of one to two sachets, once or twice a day after meals. Wash down with plenty of water without chewing; supply 60 sachets; NHS Cost £5.19; OTC Cost £9.15.

Sterculia 62% and frangula 8% sachets (Normacol Plus)
- Age from 16 years onwards
- Sterculia62%+frangula8% granules. Take the contents of one to two sachets, once or twice a day after meals. Wash down with plenty of water without chewing; supply 60 sachets; NHS Cost £5.56; OTC Cost £9.80.

Methylcellulose 500mg tablets
- Age from 16 years onwards
- Methylcellulose 500mg tablets. Take three to six tablets (with two glasses of water) each morning and evening; supply 224 tablets; NHS Cost £5.38; OTC Cost £9.50.

Analgesia: use when required

Paracetamol tablets: 1g up to four times a day
- Age from 16 years onwards
- Paracetamol 500mg tablets. Take two tablets every 4 to 6 hours when required for pain relief. Maximum of 8 tablets in 24 hours; supply 100 tablets; NHS Cost £0.75; OTC Cost £1.32.

Acute diverticulitis

Which therapy?

- **Admit if the diagnosis is unclear or if there is doubt about appropriate treatment.**
  - Generally the people who will need admitting are: those with high fever, marked leucocytosis, substantial peritoneal signs or inability to tolerate fluids; the very elderly; people with comorbid disease; and those who are immunosuppressed or taking corticosteroids.
  - Consider admitting people under 40 years of age, as they are more likely to need urgent surgery.
- **If treating in primary care, prescribe broad-spectrum antibiotics** to cover aerobic and anaerobic bacteria.
  - Co-amoxiclav is first choice.
  - A combination of metronidazole with ciprofloxacin is an alternative for those allergic to penicillin.
  - Continue antibiotics for 7–10 days.
- **Advise the person to:**
  - Call the doctor if fever or abdominal pain gets worse, or if they cannot tolerate oral fluids.
  - Maintain a high fluid intake.
  - Eat little or no food for 2 or 3 days to rest the bowel. As symptoms begin to improve, food can be built up gradually.
- **Prescribe paracetamol** for pain relief.

Practical prescribing points

For further information please see the *Medicines Compendium* (www.medicines.org.uk) or the *British National Formulary* (www.bnf.org).
- **Co-amoxiclav:** the Committee on Safety of Medicines (CSM) has advised that cholestatic jaundice can occur either during or shortly after the use of co-amoxiclav. This is more common in men, in people aged over 65 years, and with longer courses of treatment.
- **Quinolones:** the CSM has advised that quinolones can cause tendon damage, and that treatment should be stopped if pain or inflammation of a tendon occurs. Use with caution in people with epilepsy or who are predisposed to seizures (because of other conditions or medicines they are taking). Quinolones may induce convulsions in people with or without a history of convulsions.

Follow-up advice

- The person should begin to feel better in 2 or 3 days. If not, admission is recommended.
- Food can be reintroduced as the person begins to feel better.
- Once the person has recovered, manage as for *Diverticular disease (uncomplicated)*.

Should I refer or investigate?

Refer?

- **In general admit people:**
  - With a high fever, marked leucocytosis, substantial peritoneal signs or inability to tolerate fluids
  - Who are very elderly
  - With comorbid disease
  - Who are immunosuppressed or taking corticosteroids
- Consider admitting people under 40 years of age, as they are more likely to need urgent surgery.
- Referral to secondary care for large-bowel investigation should be considered in people with recurrent or constant abdominal pain.
- Referral guidelines for suspected cancer published by the National Institute for Health and Clinical Excellence (NICE) [NICE, 2005] recommend that people who present with symptoms and signs suggestive of colorectal or anal cancer (see Table 2) are urgently referred to a team specialising in the management of lower gastrointestinal cancer (depending on local arrangements).

Investigate?

- **Full blood counts** and **urinalysis** are useful in acute diverticulitis.

able 2: Guidelines for urgent referral of suspected lower gastrointestinal cancer.

rson	Symptoms and signs
ed 40 ars and der	Rectal bleeding with a change in bowel habit towards looser stools and/or increased stool frequency persisting 6 weeks or more.
ed 60 ars and der	Rectal bleeding persisting for 6 weeks or more without a change in bowel habit and without anal symptoms. A change in bowel habit to looser stools and/or more frequent stools persisting for 6 weeks or more without rectal bleeding.
any age	A right abdominal mass consistent with involvement of the large bowel. A palpable rectal mass (intraluminal and not pelvic; a pelvic mass outside the bowel would warrant an urgent referral to a urologist or gynaecologist).
oman (not enstruating)	Unexplained iron deficiency anaemia and a haemoglobin 10 g/100 ml or below.*
an of any e	Unexplained iron deficiency anaemia and a haemoglobin 11 g/100 ml or below.*

naemia considered on the basis of history and examination in primary care not to be related to other sources of blood loss (e.g. ingestions of NSAIDs) or blood dyscrasia.

Abdominal X-rays are usually taken in secondary care to exclude obstruction and perforation. Additional investigations may be performed in secondary care, including ultrasound and CT scans. Barium enemas and endoscopy are not usually performed during the acute episode.

After recovery from an acute episode, referral for large-bowel investigations such as sigmoidoscopy, colonoscopy, and barium enema should be seriously considered.

atient information leaflets

ne following PILs are available at www.prodigy.nhs.uk

CORE, Fighting Gut and Liver Disease

Diverticula

Fibre in the Diet

hared decision making

One or more diverticula on your bowel are infected (diverticulitis).

Antibiotics are the usual treatment. Pain and fever should improve with antibiotics.

Painkillers such as paracetamol will help to ease pain too.

Have plenty to drink. Eat little or no food for 2–3 days to rest the bowel. As symptoms begin to improve, start to eat again.

Contact a doctor if you get worse. Admission to hospital for high-dose antibiotics, and sometimes an operation, may be needed if symptoms become severe.

rug rationale

rugs not included

Opioid analgesics (including tramadol) reduce gut motility, which can lead to constipation and aggravate diverticulitis. They also cause colonic spasm, which may lead to hypersegmentation of the colon [Ferzoco et al, 1998].

Nonsteroidal anti-inflammatory agents (NSAIDs) are excluded, because there may be an association between increased risk of bleeding from diverticula and NSAID use [Stollman and Raskin, 1999b].

Bulk-forming laxatives are excluded, because the bowel should be rested during an acute attack.

All broad-spectrum antibiotics that are not active against the full range of commonly infecting organisms in diverticulitis, either alone or in combination with metronidazole, are excluded.

- **Quinolones other than ciprofloxacin** are not included, as their licence does not cover use in gastrointestinal infections [BNF 48, 2004].

Drugs included

- Empirical use of broad-spectrum antibiotics to cover aerobic and anaerobic bacteria is recommended for at least 7 days.
- **Co-amoxiclav** is an effective broad-spectrum antibiotic with activity against all the likely infecting organisms, and is first choice.
- **A combination of ciprofloxacin and metronidazole** is also effective against the likely aerobic and anaerobic organisms in people allergic to penicillin.
- National concerns about increased resistance to antibiotics limit the range of antibiotics offered. Other broad-spectrum antibiotics may be necessary according to local sensitivities and resistance. Consult local Public Health Laboratories for more information.
- **Paracetamol** is an effective and safe analgesic with few gastrointestinal adverse effects.

Prescriptions

1st-line antibiotics for 7 days

Co-amoxiclav 250/125mg three times a day

- Age from 16 years onwards
- Co-amoxiclav 375mg tablets. Take one tablet three times a day for 7 days; supply 21 tablets; NHS Cost £5.77.

Penicillin allergy: antibiotics for 7 days

Ciprofloxacin 500mg tablets + metronidazole 400mg tablets

- Age from 16 years onwards
- Ciprofloxacin 500mg tablets. Take one tablet twice a day for 7 days; supply 14 tablets; NHS Cost £3.33.
- Metronidazole 400mg tablets. Take one tablet three times a day for 7 days; supply 21 tablets; NHS Cost £2.01.

Analgesia: use when required

Paracetamol 1g up to four times a day

- Age from 16 years onwards
- Paracetamol 500mg tablets. Take two tablets every 4 to 6 hours when required for pain relief. Maximum of 8 tablets in 24 hours; supply 100 tablets; NHS Cost £0.75; OTC Cost £1.32.

Extended Information

Background information

- What is it? p.610
- What causes it? p.610
- How common is it? p.610
- How do I know my patient has it? p.610
- What else might it be? p.611
- Complications and prognosis p.611

D

What is it?

- **Diverticula** of the colon are small, narrow-necked pouches formed by mucosal herniations through the muscle layers in the wall of the large bowel. Other structural changes may be present, such as thickening of the taenia coli and circular muscle fibres. Diverticula are typically 5–10 mm in diameter, but can exceed 2 cm.
- **Diverticula are usually multiple,** and in Western people occur most frequently in the sigmoid colon. In Asian people they are found more commonly in the right colon or bilaterally.
- **Asymptomatic diverticula** (or diverticulosis) describes diverticula without symptoms, often found incidentally (e.g. on a barium enema or colonoscopy).
- **Diverticular disease** is used to describe diverticula with symptoms. In uncomplicated disease, these symptoms commonly include lower abdominal pain and altered bowel habit.
- **Diverticulitis** is used to describe diverticula with associated inflammation and infection of the bowel wall.

[Kohler et al, 1999; Simpson and Spiller, 2004; Stollman and Raskin, 2004]

What causes it?

- The precise mechanism of diverticulum formation is unknown, but is likely to be related to a low-fibre diet and raised intra-luminal pressures. The diverticula are thought to form at weakened areas of the colon wall, such as where blood vessels penetrate the muscle wall. A diet high in fibre, particularly insoluble fibre, decreases the risk of developing both asymptomatic and symptomatic diverticular disease [Aldoori et al, 1998; Kohler et al, 1999].
- There is some evidence of altered smooth-muscle innervation [Golder et al, 2003].
- Caffeine, smoking, and alcohol do not seem to cause diverticular disease [Aldoori et al, 1995b].
- Some hereditary diseases such as polycystic kidney disease, Marfan syndrome, and Ehlers-Danlos syndrome are associated with an increased incidence of diverticular disease, as they impair the strength of the submucosa [Kohler et al, 1999].
- Diverticulitis is caused by faecal matter obstructing the neck of a diverticulum. This leads to inflammation and provides the ideal environment for bacterial infection. Gram-negative rods and anaerobes are the usual bacteria in local infection (e.g. *Escherichia coli* and *Bacteroides fragilis*).

How common is it?

- The true prevalence of colonic diverticula is difficult to define, as most people with diverticula are asymptomatic [Jun and Stollman, 2002; Stollman and Raskin, 2004].
- The prevalence of colonic diverticula and diverticular disease seems to be increasing worldwide, probably because of increasing 'westernisation', including a diet low in fibre and high in animal products [Manousos et al, 1985; Trowell and Burkitt, 1986; Buchanan et al, 2002; Jun and Stollman, 2002].
- The prevalence of diverticular disease rises with age [Stollman and Raskin, 2004]. The prevalence of diverticula (asymptomatic or symptomatic) is about 5% in people under 40 years of age, rising to about 65% of people over 65 years of age [Jun and Stollman, 2002]. Most of these (75–80%) will remain asymptomatic.
- In elderly people, men and women are equally affected by diverticular disease [Stollman and Raskin, 1999a; Simpson and Spiller, 2004; Stollman and Raskin, 2004
- Between 10% and 25% of people with diverticulosis w go on to develop diverticulitis [Ferzoco et al, 1998; Stollman and Raskin, 2004].
- Diverticulitis is seen in 2–5% of people under the age o 40 years, and in this younger age group is more commc in men [Stollman and Raskin, 2004].

How do I know my patient has it?

Asymptomatic diverticula (diverticulosis)

- Diverticula are often an incidental finding on barium enema, at endoscopy, or during surgery.

Diverticular disease — uncomplicated

- **Most people present with lower abdominal pain,** classically in the left iliac fossa. In some people, pain is exacerbated by eating and relieved by passage of stools or flatus.
- **People may also report other symptoms such as bloatin or constipation,** although these symptoms may not be attributable to their diverticula.
- Physical examination may reveal fullness or mild tenderness in the left lower quadrant, but frank reboun or guarding should be absent.
- There is some conflict in expert opinion regarding whether bleeding is a symptom of uncomplicated diverticular disease. Where there is rectal bleeding, oth causes should be investigated as appropriate.

[Stollman and Raskin, 1999b; Stollman and Raskin, 200

Diverticulitis

- **Constant pain** almost always occurs and is often severe The pain usually begins in the hypogastrium, and localizes to the left lower quadrant. In Asian people the pain may localize to the right lower quadrant, because right-sided diverticula predominate.
- **Fever and leucocytosis** almost always occur.
- **Altered bowel habit** is almost always reported. Diarrhoea occurs more frequently than constipation.
- **Nausea and vomiting** may occur.
- **Dysuria and urinary frequency/ and urgency** may occu if the affected area lies close to the bladder.
- **Rectal bleeding** sometimes occurs. A few people may experience a sudden urge to defecate, followed by the passage of a large bloody stool. This may be repeated, but bleeding often stops spontaneously. Bleeding is due to rupture of weakened blood vessels passing through the diverticulum.
- **Signs of local or diffuse peritonitis** may be present — rebound tenderness, guarding, and rigidity (predominantly left-sided).
- **An abdominal mass** may be felt in some people.
- **Immunocompromised people** with diverticulitis may present with more subtle signs and symptoms, making diagnosis difficult.

[Jones, 1999; Stollman and Raskin, 1999b; Stollman and Raskin, 1999a; ASCRS, 2000; Stollman and Raskin, 200

ʼhat investigations should I perform?

A full blood count and urinalysis are useful if diverticulitis is suspected.

Referral for large-bowel investigations should be considered.

- **Barium enema** has been the standard investigation for years in people with symptomatic diverticular disease. Although it provides information on the number and location of colonic diverticula, inaccurate findings have been reported in nearly a third of people with diverticulosis.
- **Colonoscopy** is now considered to be a safe investigative procedure, although the diverticular colon can be difficult to examine because of spasm, luminal narrowing, and fixation [Stollman and Raskin, 2004].

ʼhat else might it be?

istinguishing diverticular disease from irritable bowel ndrome, and diverticulitis from other bowel disease, can difficult, as symptoms overlap considerably.

ʼiverticular disease

Irritable bowel syndrome (IBS) is the main differential diagnosis for uncomplicated diverticular disease.

- Similar symptoms include abdominal cramps, left lower quadrant pain, and altered bowel habit.
- There is no rectal bleeding with IBS.
- Age may be a helpful differentiating factor — it is unusual for IBS to develop in people over 60 years.

Colonic carcinoma is an important differential diagnosis that must be excluded. It should be suspected in people who have any of the following symptoms and signs *for the first time*:

- Rectal bleeding persistently without anal symptoms
- Change in bowel habit, most commonly increased frequency and/or looser stools persistent for at least 6 weeks
- A clinically significant iron deficiency anaemia (Hb less than 11 g/dl in men or 10 g/dl in women)
- Clear signs of intestinal obstruction
- A right-sided abdominal mass
- A rectal (not pelvic) mass

ɴICE, 2005]

ʼiverticulitis

ther causes of acute abdominal pain include:

Appendicitis
Inflammatory bowel disease
Colonic carcinoma
Ischaemic colitis
Pseudomembranous colitis
Complicated ulcer disease
Gynaecological disorders, including:

- Ovarian torsion
- Ovarian cysts
- Ectopic pregnancy
- Pelvic inflammatory disease

ɾoberts and Veidenheimer, 1994; Jones, 1999; Stollman ıd Raskin, 1999b; Stollman and Raskin, 1999a; ASCRS,)00]

ʼomplications and prognosis

ʼomplications

Diverticulitis occurs when diverticula become inflamed. Diverticulitis is usually confined to localized infection, but rarely may progress to:

- Perforation
- Peritonitis
- Diverticular abscess
- Fistula, most commonly to the bladder, also to the uterus or vagina in women. Fistulae to other parts of the gastrointestinal tract or the ureters are rare. Fistulae onto the skin are very rare.
- Intestinal obstruction (from fibrosis and stricture formation after inflammation).
- Haemorrhage. This is more likely to occur when diverticula are situated in the right side of the colon (more common in Asians and younger people).

[Buchanan et al, 2002; Jun and Stollman, 2002; Stollman and Raskin, 2004]

- People with right-sided diverticulitis tend to have more complications (e.g. enteroenteric fistula, haemorrhage and abdominal abscess) than those with left-sided diverticulitis [Reisman et al, 1999; Stollman and Raskin, 1999b].

Prognosis

- **Most people (75–80%) with diverticula will remain asymptomatic** throughout their lifetime.
- **Up to a third of people with diverticulitis will experience recurrent attacks.** Recurrent attacks are less likely to respond to medical treatment. Therefore elective resection is generally advised after two attacks of uncomplicated diverticulitis [Roberts et al, 1995; Kohler et al, 1999; Stollman and Raskin, 1999a].
- **After recovery from diverticulitis,** up to two-thirds of people go on to develop short-lived recurrent pain with features more in common with irritable bowel syndrome; this pain may not be associated with further inflammation and is less likely to respond to surgical resection [Simpson et al, 2003].
- **Diverticulitis is more aggressive in younger people,** with 66–88% needing urgent surgery during their initial attack [Stollman and Raskin, 2004].
- **Immunocompromised people** are less likely to benefit from medical treatment, and have a higher rate of perforation, need for surgery, and post-operative mortality [Jones, 1999; Stollman and Raskin, 1999a; Simpson and Spiller, 2004; Stollman and Raskin, 2004].

Management issues

- How should I manage asymptomatic diverticula? p.611
- How should I manage uncomplicated diverticular disease? p.612
- How should I manage diverticulitis? p.612
- What advice should I give to prevent recurrence of diverticulitis? p.612

There is limited evidence published on the treatments for diverticular disease and diverticulitis, and most advice is based on expert recommendations.

How should I manage asymptomatic diverticula?

- Asymptomatic diverticula do not require further diagnostic evaluation [Stollman and Raskin, 1999b].
- Recommend a diet high in fruit and vegetables. Evidence from an observational study suggests that in men without diagnosed diverticular disease a high-fibre diet decreases the risk of developing symptomatic diverticular disease [Aldoori et al, 1998; Stollman and Raskin, 2004].
- In the study mentioned above, vigorous physical activity (jogging and running) also reduced the risk of developing symptomatic diverticular disease [Aldoori et al, 1995a]. It is unclear whether moderate increases in physical activity will affect disease progression or symptoms.

How should I manage uncomplicated diverticular disease?

- **Referral to secondary care** for investigation of the large bowel should be strongly considered in people with altered bowel habit, recurrent abdominal pain, or rectal bleeding. Double-contrast barium enema, flexible sigmoidoscopy, or colonoscopy is usually performed [Jones, 1999].
- **A high-fibre diet is the mainstay of treatment.** Although there is conflicting evidence of its effectiveness, a high-fibre diet is widely recommended by experts to relieve symptoms and prevent complications of diverticular disease.
  - Insoluble fibre (from fruit and vegetables) may be preferable to cereal fibre [Aldoori and Ryan-Harshman, 2002].
  - Fibre intake should be gradually increased over 2 or 3 weeks. In some people, fibre supplementation may make symptoms worse, and symptoms may initially worsen before they improve [Stollman and Raskin, 2004].
  - Any increase in fibre intake should be accompanied by an increase in fluid intake.
- **Bulk-forming agents** such bran, ispaghula, sterculia, and methylcellulose may be considered to supplement a high-fibre diet, or if a high-fibre diet is not sufficient or not acceptable. Evidence to support their use is limited.
- **Antispasmodic drugs such as mebeverine, alverine, or peppermint oil** have been advocated for the relief of pain associated with diverticular disease. However, there is no good evidence that antispasmodic drugs improve symptoms of diverticular disease. In practice, diverticular disease and irritable bowel syndrome (IBS) are often difficult to differentiate, and antispasmodics may be useful in people who have symptoms that suggest IBS, such as abdominal pain related to defecation, abdominal bloating, or rectal mucus (see separate PRODIGY guidance on *Irritable bowel syndrome*).
- **Analgesia** may be required in some people.
  - **Paracetamol is recommended** for simple analgesia.
  - **Opioid analgesics are not recommended,** as they may cause colonic spasm and may accentuate hypersegmentation of the colon [Tursi, 2004].
  - **Nonsteroidal anti-inflammatory drugs (NSAIDs) are not recommended,** because there may be an association between increased risk of bleeding from diverticula and NSAID use [Stollman and Raskin, 1999b].
- **Surgery** for people with uncomplicated diverticular disease is rarely needed, but some people with intractable symptoms may benefit from colonic resection [Jones, 1999].

How should I manage diverticulitis?

- **Acute diverticulitis usually requires hospital admission.** Hospital admission should always be considered for:
  - Very elderly people
  - People with high fever and marked leucocytosis
  - People with substantial peritoneal signs
  - People who cannot tolerate oral fluids
  - People who are immunosuppressed or taking corticosteroids
- Some, but not all, research suggests that people under 40 years are more likely to need urgent surgery, possibly because they have more right-sided disease that may be mistaken for appendicitis [Reisman et al, 1999; Stollman and Raskin, 1999a; ASCRS, 2000].
- **Treatment in primary care** may be appropriate if the symptoms are mild and the diagnosis can be made with confidence. If there is any doubt about the appropriate treatment, or if the person does not improve once on treatment, the person should be admitted to hospital.
- **Empirical treatment with broad-spectrum antibiotics** should cover aerobic and anaerobic bacteria.
  - Co-amoxiclav or a combination of ciprofloxacin and metronidazole are suitable choices.
  - Treatment should last for at least 7 days.
  - Other antibiotics may be used in secondary care.

[Roberts and Veidenheimer, 1994; Stollman and Raskin, 1999b]

- **Oral fluids for rehydration and to rest the bowel are recommended** while the person recovers. Many people will require intravenous fluids, and if so should be admitted [Ferzoco et al, 1998; Jones, 1999].
- **Analgesia and rest** while the person recovers are recommended [Jones, 1999]. If analgesia with paracetamol is insufficient, consider admitting the person.
  - **Paracetamol is recommended** for simple analgesia.
  - **Opioid analgesics are not recommended,** as they may cause colonic spasm and may accentuate hypersegmentation of the colon [Tursi, 2004].
  - **Nonsteroidal anti-inflammatory drugs (NSAIDs) are not recommended,** because there may be an association between increased risk of bleeding from diverticula and NSAID use [Stollman and Raskin, 1999b].
- **Symptoms should begin to improve within 2 to 3 days,** and solid food can gradually be reintroduced for people who have been unable to tolerate solids [Eggenberger, 1999; Stollman and Raskin, 1999a].
- **Surgery** is not usually needed, but in severe cases colonic resection or transverse loop colostomy are occasionally used. Complications such as fistulae, abscesses, peritonitis, and haemorrhage are treated by appropriate medical management and surgery in secondary care.
- **After recovery, investigations of the large bowel** should be seriously considered [ASCRS, 2000]. Double-contrast barium enema, flexible sigmoidoscopy, or colonoscopy is usually performed [Jones, 1999]. Barium enemas should not be performed in people with acute diverticulitis, because of the risk of barium extravasation through a possible perforation [ASCRS, 2000].
- After recovery from diverticulitis, up to two-thirds of people go on to develop short-lived recurrent pain with features more in common with irritable bowel syndrome; this pain may not be associated with further inflammation [Simpson et al, 2003]. Consider re-admission if the pain lasts for more than 24 hours and there is clinical evidence of infection or inflammation.

What advice should I give to prevent recurrence of diverticulitis?

- Once the person has recovered, recommend a high-fibre diet (see *How should I manage uncomplicated diverticular disease?*).
- **Mesalazine,** an aminosalicylate anti-inflammatory drug, has been studied in one randomized, placebo-controlled trial to investigate its efficacy on the prevention of recurrence in people previously treated for an episode of mild to moderate acute diverticulitis. However, this study was of poor quality, and further studies are needed to determine the role of the aminosalicylates in the prevention of acute diverticulitis [Simpson and Spiller, 2004].
- **Probiotics** are increasingly being used in people with gastrointestinal disorders. However, there are no controlled studies published regarding their efficacy and safety in people with diverticular disease. The use of these unregulated foodstuffs cannot be routinely recommended until such evidence is available.

eferences

IS staff in England can link, free of charge, from erences to full text journals by clicking on [Full text] on PRODIGY website.

Aldoori, W.H., Giovannucci, E.L., Rimm, E.B. et al (1995a) Prospective study of physical activity and the risk of symptomatic diverticular disease in men. *Gut* **36**(2), 276–282.

Aldoori, W.H., Giovannucci, E.L., Rimm, E.B. et al (1995b) A prospective study of alcohol, smoking, caffeine, and the risk of symptomatic diverticular disease in men. *Annals of Epidemiology* **5**(3), 221–228.

Aldoori, W.H., Giovannucci, E.L., Rockett, H.R.H. et al (1998) A prospective study of dietary fiber types and symptomatic diverticular disease in men. *Journal of Nutrition* **128**(4), 714–719. [Full text]

ASCRS (2000) *Practice parameters for the treatment of sigmoid diverticulitis. Supporting documentation.* American Society of Colon & Rectal Surgeons. www.fascrs.org [Accessed: 18/01/2005]. [Full text]

BNF 48 (2004) *British National Formulary.* 48th edn. London: British Medical Association and Royal Pharmaceutical Society of Great Britain.

Buchanan, G.N., Kenefick, N.J. and Cohen, C.R. (2002) Diverticulitis. *Best Practice & Research in Clinical Gastroenterology* **16**(4), 635–647.

Eggenberger, J.C. (1999) Diverticular Disease. *Current Treatment Options in Gastroenterology* **2**(6), 507–516.

Ferzoco, L.B., Raptopoulos, V. and Silen, W. (1998) Acute diverticulitis. *New England Journal of Medicine* **338**(21), 1521–1526. [Full text]

Golder, M., Burleigh, D.E., Belai, A. et al (2003) Smooth muscle cholinergic denervation hypersensitivity in diverticular disease. *Lancet* **361**(9373), 1945–1951. [Full text]

. Jones, D.J. (Ed.) (1999) *ABC of colorectal diseases.* 2nd edn. London: BMJ Books.

. Jun, S. and Stollman, N. (2002) Epidemiology of diverticular disease. *Best Practice & Research in Clinical Gastroenterology* **16**(4), 529–542.

. Kohler, L, Saurland, S. and Neugebauer, E. (1999) Diagnosis and treatment of diverticular disease: results of a consensus development conference. *Surgical Endoscopy* **13**(4), 430–436.

13. Manousos, O., Day, N.E., Tzonou, A. et al (1985) Diet and other factors in the aetiology of diverticulosis: an epidemiological study in Greece. *Gut* **26**(6), 544–549.
14. Murray, C.D. and Emmanuel, A.V. (2002) Medical management of diverticular disease. *Best Practice & Research in Clinical Gastroenterology* **16**(4), 611–620.
15. NICE (2005) *Referral guidelines for suspected cancer – quick reference guide.* Clinical guideline 27. National Institute for Health and Clinical Excellence. www.nice.org.uk [Accessed: 01/07/2005].
16. Reisman, Y., Ziv, Y., Kravrovitc, D. et al (1999) Diverticulitis: the effect of age and location on the course of disease. *International Journal of Colorectal Disease* **14**(4–5), 250–254.
17. Roberts, P.L. and Veidenheimer, M.C. (1994) Current management of diverticulitis. *Advances in Surgery* **27**, 189–208.
18. Roberts, P., Abel, M., Rosen, L. et al (1995) Practice parameters for sigmoid diverticulitis. The Standards Task Force American Society of Colon and Rectal Surgeons. *Diseases of the Colon and Rectum* **38**(2), 125–132.
19. Simpson, J. and Spiller, R. (2004) *Colonic diverticular disease.* Clinical Evidence. Volume 12. www.clinicalevidence.com [Accessed: 09/03/2005]. [Full text]
20. Simpson, J., Neal, K.R., Scholefield, J.H. and Spiller, R.C. (2003) Patterns of pain in diverticular disease and the influence of acute diverticulitis. *European Journal of Gastroenterology & Hepatology* **15**(9), 1005–1010.
21. Stollman, N.H. and Raskin, J.B. (1999a) Diverticular disease of the colon. *Journal of Clinical Gastroenterology* **29**(3), 241–252.
22. Stollman, N.H. and Raskin, J.B. (1999b) Diagnosis and management of diverticular disease of the colon in adults. *American Journal of Gastroenterology* **94**(11), 3110–3121.
23. Stollman, N. and Raskin, J.B. (2004) Diverticular disease of the colon. *Lancet* **363**(9409), 631–639. [Full text]
24. Trowell, H. and Burkitt, D. (1986) Physiological role of dietary fiber: a ten-year review. *Journal of Dentistry for Children* **53**(6), 444–447.
25. Tursi, A. (2004) Acute diverticulitis of the colon: current medical therapeutic management. *Expert Opinion on Pharmacotherapy* **5**(1), 55–59.

PRODIGY GUIDANCE

Dry eye syndrome

Last revised in February 2005
www.prodigy.nhs.uk/guidance.asp?gt=Dry eye syndrome

Applies to people over the age of 10 years

This guidance covers the management of dry eyes.

This guidance does not cover the management of xerostomia (dry mouth), blepharitis, or conjunctivitis.

There is separate PRODIGY guidance for *Blepharitis*, *Conjunctivitis — allergic*, and *Conjunctivitis — infective*.

D

Goals

- To relieve the symptoms of dry eyes
- To restore, prevent, or minimize structural damage to the ocular surface

Contents

Scenarios

- Dry eye syndrome p.614

Extended Information, p. 616

Dry eye syndrome

Which therapy?

- **Explain** that dry eyes cannot be cured, but that symptoms can be controlled.
- **Symptoms may be exacerbated by** low humidity, air conditioning, windy weather, dust, and smoke. Reduced blinking may be aggravated by prolonged reading or staring at a computer screen or television. Problems may also be caused by contact lenses.
- **Treat underlying conditions,** e.g. blepharitis.
- **Consider drugs as a possible cause** and exclude them where possible (see section *What else could it be?* for a list of drugs).
- **Artificial tears** limit damage and control discomfort. Hypromellose is effective. Use preservative-free drops where severe symptoms require regular daily 30 minute interval applications. Decrease frequency with symptom control.
- **Consider also using an eye ointment** containing paraffin (with or without lanolin) at bedtime. It provides more prolonged lubrication but is not suitable for use when awake because it blurs vision.
- **For people with viscous, stringy, mucous tears** acetylcysteine eye drops are effective; however, they sting.

Practical prescribing points

For further information please see the *Medicines Compendium* (www.medicines.org.uk) or the *British National Formulary* (www.bnf.org).

- **Use preservative-free preparations if** more than 6 applications per day are necessary: the more frequently drops containing benzalkonium chloride are used, the greater the risk of ocular irritation.
- **Contact lenses** should generally not be worn during treatment with eye drops. However:
  - **Hard lenses:** use eye drops 30 minutes before inserting lenses.
  - **Soft lenses:** eye drops containing preservatives should not be used with soft lenses. (Some preservatives, particularly benzalkonium chloride, accumulate in s[oft] contact lenses and cause irritation.) Preservative-free drops should be used instead.
  - **Preservative-free eye drops:** generally, lenses can be put in 5–10 minutes after using preservative-free eye drops, that is, once the drop has dispersed. Contact lenses should not be put in for 30 minutes after using Viscotears single-use eye drops, because of their viscosity.
  - **Eye ointments:** eye ointments should not be used wh[en] contact lenses are worn.
- **Drops should be used in preference to ointment if othe[r] eye drops are being used** (e.g. for glaucoma).

Should I refer or investigate?

Refer?

Refer if:

- Symptoms remain severe despite use of artificial tears.
- Vision deteriorates.
- Ulcers occur on the cornea.
- Associated disease (for example Sjögren's syndrome or eyelid deformities) requires specialist management.

Investigate?

- Diagnosis can usually be made on the basis of history and examination alone.
- **Special tests are usually not required.** If they are neede[d] they are best performed by a specialist because interpretation may not be straightforward and several tests may be necessary to give the full picture. Commonly used tests include:
  - **Schirmer tests:** wetting of a strip of filter paper left o[n] the eye reveals reduced tear production. The test can be done with or without ocular anaesthetic or with stimulation of the nasal mucosa.
  - **Slit-lamp examination:** this shows reduced tear meniscus at the lower lid.
  - **Fluorescein/rose bengal stains:** areas of dry cornea allow penetration of the fluorescein/rose bengal stain.
  - **Screening tests for autoimmune conditions:** these include rheumatoid factor, antinuclear antibodies, a[nd] auto-antibodies to the soluble nuclear antigens Ro/SS-A and La/SS-B.
    - **However, routine screening for autoimmunity is n[ot] indicated in the general elderly population** because sicca symptoms are unlikely to have an autoimmu[ne] basis in these people.

Patient information leaflets

The following PILs are available at www.prodigy.nhs.uk

- Blepharitis
- British Sjogren's Syndrome Association
- Dry Eyes

Shared decision making

- Dry eyes are common. The problem is that either not enough tears are made to keep the front of the eye moist or the tears are of poor quality and do not lubricate the eye.
- **Artificial teardrops** such as hypromellose usually help. They are used as often as they are needed and can be used every 30 minutes at first if the eyes are very uncomfortable.
- **Eye ointment** can be used at bedtime to keep the eye moist overnight. Eye ointment is not used during the day because it blurs vision. Paraffin eye ointments should never be used with contact lenses: remove contact lenses before applying eye ointment.
- **Acetylcysteine eye drops** are an option for people with sticky eyes. However, the drops sting.

Drug rationale

Drugs not included

Zinc sulphate is a traditional astringent that is now little used in eye drops.

Drugs included

Artificial tears [BNF 47, 2004]:
- Hypromellose 0.3% is a commonly used artificial tear. It is effective, and remains the cheapest option.
- Polyvinyl alcohol is another commonly used artificial tear.
- Carbomer eye drops can cling to the eye surface, which may help reduce the frequency of application to four times a day.

Preservative-free, single-dose artificial tears are recommended for users of soft contact lens, and those people unable to tolerate preservatives [Harman et al, 1990]. Preservative-free products licensed for the relief of dry eyes include hypromellose, hydroxyethycellulose, carbomer 980, polyvinyl alcohol, and povidone.
- Carmellose sodium is an alternative option. It is a relatively new product and therefore remains under the surveillance of the Committee on Safety of Medicines. It is used 'as required'.

Paraffin eye ointments: simple eye ointment, Lacri-Lube, and Lubri-Tears provide prolonged lubrication. Since they cause temporary blurred vision, they are best used before bedtime [Khaw and Elkington, 1999; BNF 47, 2004].

Acetylcysteine eye drops are mucolytic, and are useful for people with sticky, viscous mucus on the eye (filamentary keratitis). However, they often sting and are expensive [Khaw and Elkington, 1999].

Prescriptions

Artificial tears: hypromellose

Hypromellose 0.3% eye drops
- Age from 10 years onwards
- Hypromellose 0.3% eye drops. Put one drop into the affected eye(s) when required to lubricate the eye(s); supply 10 ml; NHS Cost £0.75; OTC Cost £1.32.

Hypromellose 0.5% eye drops
- Age from 10 years onwards
- Hypromellose 0.5% eye drops. Put one drop into the affected eye(s) when required to lubricate the eye(s); supply 10 ml; NHS Cost £0.85; OTC Cost £1.50.

Hypromellose 1% eye drops
- Age from 10 years onwards
- Hypromellose 1% eye drops. Put one drop into the affected eye(s) when required to lubricate the eye(s); supply 10 ml; NHS Cost £0.99; OTC Cost £1.75.

Hypromellose 0.3% + dextran '70' 0.1% eye drops
- Age from 10 years onwards
- Tears Naturale eye drops. Put one drop into the affected eye(s) when required to lubricate the eye(s); supply 15 ml; NHS Cost £1.68; OTC Cost £2.96.

Artificial tears: polyvinyl alcohol or carbomer

Liquifilm Tears (polyvinyl alcohol 1.4%) eye drops
- Age from 10 years onwards
- Liquifilm Tears 1.4% eye drops. Put one drop into the affected eye(s) when required to lubricate the eye(s); supply 15 ml; NHS Cost £1.61; OTC Cost £2.85.

Sno Tears (polyvinyl alcohol 1.4%) eye drops
- Age from 10 years onwards
- Sno Tears 1.4% eye drops. Put one drop into the affected eye(s) when required to lubricate the eye(s); supply 10 ml; NHS Cost £1.06; OTC Cost £1.90.

GelTears (carbomer 980) eye drops
- Age from 10 years onwards
- GelTears 0.2% eye drop gel. Put one drop into the affected eye(s) when required to lubricate the eye(s); supply 10 grams; NHS Cost £2.80; OTC Cost £4.94.

Viscotears (carbomer 980) eye drops
- Age from 10 years onwards
- Viscotears 0.2% eye drop gel. Put one drop into the affected eye(s) when required to lubricate the eye(s); supply 10 grams; NHS Cost £3.12; OTC Cost £5.50.

Liposic (carbomer 980) eye drops
- Age from 10 years onwards
- Liposic 0.2% eye drop gel. Put one drop into the affected eye(s) when required to lubricate the eye(s); supply 10 grams; NHS Cost £2.96; OTC Cost £4.44.

Liquivisc (carbomer 974) eye drops
- Age from 10 years onwards
- Liquivisc 0.25% eye drop gel. Put one drop into the affected eye(s) when required to lubricate the eye(s); supply 10 grams; NHS Cost £3.96; OTC Cost £6.98.

Artificial tears: preservative-free

Hydroxyethylcellulose preservative-free drops (single-use)
- Age from 10 years onwards
- Minims artificial tears. Put one drop into the affected eye(s) when required to lubricate the eye(s); supply 60 single doses; NHS Cost £17.25; OTC Cost £30.40.

Hypromellose 0.32% preservative-free drops (single-use)
- Age from 10 years onwards
- Hypromellose 0.32% single-use. Put one drop into the affected eye(s) when required to lubricate the eye(s); supply 60 single doses; NHS Cost £23.76; OTC Cost £32.50.

Carbomer 980 preservative-free drops (single-use)
- Age from 10 years onwards
- Viscotears single-use eye gel. Put one drop into the affected eye(s) when required to lubricate the eye(s); supply 60 single doses; NHS Cost £11.50; OTC Cost £20.27.

Polyvinyl alcohol 1.4% preservative-free drops (single-use)
- Age from 10 years onwards
- Liquifilm Tears single-use. Put one drop into the affected eye(s) when required to lubricate the eye(s); supply 60 single doses; NHS Cost £10.70; OTC Cost £18.86.

Povidone 5% preservative-free drops (single-use)

- Age from 10 years onwards
- Oculotect unit dose eye drops. Put one drop into the affected eye(s) when required to lubricate the eye(s); supply 60 single doses; NHS Cost £10.20; OTC Cost £17.98.

Carmellose 1% preservative-free drops (single-use)

- Age from 10 years onwards
- Carmellose 1% single-use drops. Put one drop into the affected eye(s) when required to lubricate the eye(s); supply 60 single doses; NHS Cost £11.50; OTC Cost £20.27.

Paraffin eye ointment (use at bedtime)

Simple eye ointment

- Age from 10 years onwards
- Simple 10% eye ointment. Put a small amount into the affected eye(s) at bedtime; supply 4 grams; NHS Cost £2.68; OTC Cost £4.72.

Lacri-Lube eye ointment

- Age from 10 years onwards
- Lacri-Lube eye ointment. Put a small amount into the affected eye(s) at bedtime; supply 5 grams; NHS Cost £2.47; OTC Cost £4.35.

Lubri-Tears eye ointment

- Age from 10 years onwards
- Lubri-Tears eye ointment. Put a small amount into the affected eye(s) at bedtime; supply 5 grams; NHS Cost £2.29; OTC Cost £4.03.

Acetylcysteine eye drops-for sticky, viscous mucus

Acetylcysteine eye drops

- Age from 10 years onwards
- Ilube eye drops. Put one drop into the affected eye(s) 3 to 4 times a day; supply 10 ml; NHS Cost £4.63.

Extended Information

Background information

- What is it? p.616
- What is the pathogenesis of dry eye syndrome? p.616
- What are the exacerbating factors and predisposing conditions? p.616
- How common is it? p.617
- How do I know my patient has it? p.617
- What else might it be? p.617
- Complications and prognosis p.617

What is it?

- **Dry eye syndrome** (or keratoconjunctivitis sicca) is a disorder of the tear film due to tear deficiency or excessive evaporation that causes damage to the interpalpebral ocular surface, and is associated with symptoms of discomfort.
- **The syndrome is aggravated by** dry air, wind, dust, and smoke.

What is the pathogenesis of dry eye syndrome?

The ocular surface, tear-secreting glands, meibomian glands, and lids function as an integrated unit to secrete and clear tears. Dysfunction of any component of this functional unit results in an unstable and unrefreshed tear film that causes the set of symptoms called dry eye syndrome [American Academy of Ophthalmology, 2003].

Tear physiology

- **Tear composition**
  - **Tears are a complex mixture** of water, lipids, salts, mucins, immunoglobulins, antimicrobial proteins, a growth factors.
- **Tear structure**
  - **Inner layer** of mucins adheres to corneal epithelium
  - **Middle layer** is an aqueous/mucin phase
  - **Outer layer** of lipids
- **Tears are produced by:**
  - Lacrimal glands, ocular surface epithelium, and conjunctival goblet cells (secrete hydrated mucous g of inner and middle layers)
  - Meibomian glands (produce outer lipid layer)
- **Tear production is under nervous and hormonal contr**
  - Sympathetic and parasympathetic somatosensory reflexes from the surfaces of the eye and nasal muco control continuous production of tears.
  - The brain, as part of the response to emotion, intermittently stimulates tear production.
  - Hormones: it has been postulated that androgens promote the secretory activity of the meibomian glands. Also, in the absence of androgens (as in the menopause), lymphocytes accumulate and secrete pr inflammatory cytokines.
- **Tear distribution** is effected by blinking.
- **Tear drainage** is through lacrimal ducts.
- **Tear evaporation** is aggravated by wind, low humidity

[Tsubota, 1998; American Academy of Ophthalmology, 2003]

Causes of dry eye syndrome

- **Decreased tear production**
  - Adverse effect of drugs such as diuretics, oestrogen (e.g. contraceptives), drugs with antimuscarinic effe (e.g. antihistamines, tricyclic antidepressants, atropi derivatives), or beta-blockers
  - Sjögren's syndrome — primary, or secondary to rheumatoid arthritis, systemic lupus erythematosus, scleroderma
  - Allergy
  - Dehydration, e.g. secondary to diabetes mellitus
  - Trauma (e.g. surgery, radiation)
- **Abnormal ocular surface and disruption of the trigeminal afferent sensory nerves**
  - Herpes zoster ophthalmicus
  - Post corneal surgery
  - Post Stevens–Johnson syndrome
  - Exophthalmos
- **Decreased lipid production by meibomian glands**
  - Meibomian gland disease
  - Chronic dermatoses of eyelids: blepharitis, seborrho dermatitis, and rosacea

[Tsubota, 1998; American Academy of Ophthalmology, 2003]

What are the exacerbating factors and predisposing conditions?

- Decreased humidity, wind, air travel, prolonged visual activity associated with decreased blink activity, e.g. reading
- Smoking and smoky environments
- Medical and surgical conditions associated with dry ey syndrome:
  - Allergic conjunctivitis, atopy
  - Sjögren's syndrome, rheumatoid arthritis, systemic lupus erythematosus, or scleroderma
  - Blepharitis
  - Bell's palsy
  - Chronic ocular surface inflammation

- Menopause

Previous ocular or eyelid surgery and trauma

Topical medication people may currently be using to help alleviate symptoms that can sometimes actually exacerbate them:

- Artificial tears, ocular lubricants

Current medication(s) that can aggravate symptoms of dry eye:

- Topical preparations include antihistamines, glaucoma medications, vasoconstrictors, and corticosteroids
- Systemic preparations include antihistamines, diuretics, estrogens, androgen antagonists, antidepressants, cardiac arrhythmic drugs, isotretinoin, atropine, beta-blockers, and other drugs with antimuscarinic effects

ow common is it?

The prevalence of dry eye syndrome rises from about 7.5% of people in their 50s to about 15% of people in their 70s.

It is about 50% more common in women than in men.

Dry eye syndrome is the most common cause of eye irritation in people over 65 years old.

Moss et al, 2000]

ow do I know my patient has it?

istory

Symptoms of dry eye:

- Both eyes are usually affected.
- Sensations are of foreign body, irritation, burning, or 'gritty' eye.
- Contact lenses are poorly tolerated.
- People with dry eye syndrome may not describe their eyes as feeling 'dry'.
- Vision may be transiently blurred.
- Photophobia is occasionally present.

xamination

Signs of dry eye syndrome:

- Conjunctivae: not red (unless irritated, for example by medication or allergy).
- Tarsal conjunctivae: may be chronically hyperaemic with few papillae and no follicles.
- Filamentary keratitis (fine filaments of epithelium and mucus attached to cornea).

Predisposing conditions:

- Chronic disease of eyelashes, eyelids, or margins of eyelids, e.g. meibomian gland disease, blepharitis or other dermatitis, trichiasis, or lid malposition.
- Proptosis.
- Abnormal cranial nerves V or VII, e.g. Bell's palsy.

nvestigations

Special tests are usually not required. If they are needed, they are best performed by a specialist because interpretation may not be straightforward and several tests may be necessary. Commonly used tests include:

- **Schirmer tests:** to reveal reduced tear production. Schirmer tests can be done with or without ocular anaesthetic or with stimulation of the nasal mucosa.
- **Slit-lamp examination:** to show reduced tear meniscus at the lower lid.
- **Fluorescein/rose bengal stains:** areas of dry cornea allow penetration of the stain.
- **Tear break-up time test:** to reveal unstable tear film with normal aqueous tear production.
- **Screening tests for autoimmune conditions** include rheumatoid factor, antinuclear antibodies, and auto-antibodies to the soluble nuclear antigens Ro/SS-A and La/SS-B.
  - **Routine screening for autoimmunity is not indicated** in the general elderly population as these people are unlikely to have an autoimmune basis for their sicca symptoms.
- **Labial biopsy** to assess inflammation in minor salivary glands, which is present in Sjögren's syndrome.

[Moss et al, 2000; American Academy of Ophthalmology, 2003]

What else might it be?

- Psychogenic: sensation of dry eyes
- Viral infection

D

Complications and prognosis

Complications

- Filamentary keratitis (in which fine filaments of epithelium and mucus are attached to the cornea).
- Epithelial damage may occasionally lead to corneal ulceration.
- Eyes irritated by prolonged and frequent use of eye medication containing preservatives [Murube et al, 1998b].

Management issues

- How should I manage dry eye syndrome? p.617
- How should artificial tears and lubricants be prescribed? p.617
- What other treatment options are there for dry eye syndrome? p.618

How should I manage dry eye syndrome?

- Treat any underlying conditions (e.g. blepharitis — see separate PRODIGY *Blepharitis* guidance).
- Manage aggravating factors (e.g. dehydrating environment, adverse effect of drugs).
- Treat symptoms with artificial tears or lubricants.
- If symptoms are poorly controlled, consider referral for treatments such as topical anti-inflammatories, punctal surgery.

How should artificial tears and lubricants be prescribed?

Artificial tears

Artificial tears are the mainstay of treatment in primary care. Hypromellose 0.3% eye drops are the cheapest and most popular artificial tear formulation used in the UK. There is little evidence to choose between the different artificial tear preparations. However, certain preservatives (i.e. benzalkonium hexachloride) can irritate the eye.

- **Control symptoms and limit damage with artificial tears (drops).**
- Initially use artificial tears at up to 30-minute intervals if symptoms are severe.
- **Decrease the frequency as symptoms improve.**
- **Use preservative-free preparations if** more than 6 applications per day are necessary: the more frequently drops containing benzalkonium chloride are used, the greater the risk of ocular irritation.

[Khaw and Elkington, 1999]

Lubricants

- **An eye ointment with paraffin or paraffin plus lanolin** (e.g. simple eye ointment, Lacri-Lube, Lubri-Tears) is useful at bedtime because it provides prolonged lubrication. It blurs vision, so is not suitable for use when awake. People who wear contact lenses should remove them prior to instillation of eye ointments. Contact lenses may be replaced in the morning. Note: contact lenses are best avoided where eye ointments are administered in the daytime.

- **Other ocular lubricants** have been shown to be effective and some have been reported as having an increased contact time with the eye. However, there is no good evidence of clinical advantage of any product over hypromellose.

[Murube et al, 1998a; Murube et al, 1998b; Khaw and Elkington, 1999; American Academy of Ophthalmology, 2003]

D

What other treatment options are there for dry eye syndrome?

Options available in primary care

- **Acetylcysteine eye drops** are an effective alternative in treating people who have problems with sticky, viscous mucus on the eye (filamentary keratitis), but they may sting [Lemp, 1994; Khaw and Elkington, 1999].

Options for secondary care interventions

- **Parasympathomimetic (cholinergic) secretogogues and mucolytics:** pilocarpine [Vivino et al, 1999] and bromhexine [Prause et al, 1984] have been used to increase tear and salivary production in people with both dry eyes and dry mouth due to Sjögren's syndrome.
- **Surgical treatments for severe disease or poor compliance** include plugging of the lacrimal puncta (temporarily with collagen or permanently with silicone) or surgical occlusion of the puncta [Manthorpe and Prause, 1986; Tabbara and Wagoner, 1996; Balaram et al, 1998; Slusser and Lowther, 1998].
- **Anti-inflammatory treatments**
  - **Ciclosporin A** has been shown to be more effective than the placebo control vehicle in two small trials [Gunduz and Ozdemir, 1994; Sall et al, 2000; Stevenson et al, 2000].
  - **Topical corticosteroids** have been compared in a small randomized controlled trial with artificial tears and topical nonsteroidal anti-inflammatory drugs (NSAIDs). Symptoms of ocular irritation and objective measures such as corneal staining were significantly improved [Avunduk et al, 2003].

References

NHS staff in England can link, free of charge, from references to full text journals by clicking on [Full text] on the PRODIGY website.

1. American Academy of Ophthalmology (2003) *Dry eye syndrome.* American Academy of Ophthalmology. www.aao.org [Accessed: 01/09/2004].
2. Avunduk, A.M., Avunduk, M.C., Varnell, E.D. and Kaufman, H.E. (2003) The comparison of efficacies of topical corticosteroids and nonsteroidal anti-inflammatory drops on dry eye patients: a clinical and immunocytochemical study. *American Journal of Ophthalmology* **136**(4), 593–602.
3. Balaram, M., Schaumberg, D.A. and Dana, M.R. (1998) Efficacy and tolerability outcomes after punctal occlusion with silicone plugs in dry eye syndrome. *American Journal of Ophthalmology* **131**(1), 30–36.
4. BNF 47 (2004) *British National Formulary.* 47th edn. London: British Medical Association and Royal Pharmaceutical Society of Great Britain.
5. Gunduz, K. and Ozdemir, O. (1994) Topical cyclosporin treatment of keratoconjunctivitis sicca in secondary Sjogren's syndrome. *Acta Ophthalmologic*[a] 72(4), 438–442.
6. Harman, R.J., Neathercoat, G.C. and Gotecha, P. (Eds.) (1990) *Handbook of pharmacy health care: diseases and patient advice.* London: Pharmaceutical Press.
7. Khaw, P.T. and Elkington, A.R. (Eds.) (1999) *ABC o[f] eyes.* 3rd edn. London: BMJ Publishing Group.
8. Lemp, M.A. (1994) Management of the dry-eye patient. *International Ophthalmology Clinics* **34**(1), 101–113.
9. Manthorpe, R. and Prause, J.U. (1986) Treatment of Sjogren's syndrome: an overview. *Scandinavian Jour[nal] of Rheumatology* **61**(Supplement), 237–241.
10. Moss, S.E., Klein, R. and Klein, B.E. (2000) Prevalen[ce] of and risk factors for dry eye syndrome. *Archives of Ophthalmology* **118**(9), 1264–1268. [Full text]
11. Murube, J., Paterson.A. and Murube, E. (1998a) Classification of artificial tears. I: composition and properties. In: Sullivan, D.A. (Ed.) *Lacrimal Gland, Tear Film and Dry Eye Syndromes 2.* 2nd edn. New York: Plenum Press. 693.
12. Murube, J., Murube, A. and Zhuo, C. (1998b) Classification of artificial tears. II: additives and commercial formulas. In: Sullivan, D.A. (Ed.) *Lacrim[al] Gland, Tear Film, and Dry Eye Syndromes 2.* 2nd ed[n]. New York: Plenum Press. 705.
13. Prause, J.U., Frost-Larsen, K., Hoj, L. et al (1984) Lacrimal and salivary secretion in Sjogren's syndrom[e]: the effect of systemic treatment with bromhexine. *Ac[ta] Ophthalmologica* **62**(3), 489–497.
14. Sall, K., Stevenson, O.D., Mundorf, T.K. and Reis, B. (2000) Two multicenter, randomized studies of the efficacy and safety of cyclosporine ophthalmic emulsion in moderate to severe dry eye disease. CsA Phase 3 Study Group. *Ophthalmology* **107**(4), 631–639.
15. Slusser, T.G. and Lowther, G.E. (1998) Effects of acrimal drainage occlusion with nondissolvable intracanalicular plugs on hydrogel contact lens wear. *Optometry and Vision Science* **75**(5), 330–338.
16. Stevenson, D., Tauber, J. and Reis, B.L. (2000) Effica[cy] and safety of cyclosporin A ophthalmic emulsion in th[e] treatment of moderate-to-severe dry eye disease: a dose-ranging, randomized trial. The Cyclosporin A Phase 2 Study Group. *Ophthalmology* **107**(5), 967–974.
17. Tabbara, K.F. and Wagoner, M.D. (1996) Diagnosis and management of dry-eye syndrome. *International Ophthalmology Clinics* **36**(2), 61–75.
18. Tsubota, K. (1998) Tear dynamics and dry eye. *Progress in Retinal & Eye Research* **17**(4), 565–596.
19. Vivino, F.B., Al Hashimi, I., Khan, Z. et al (1999) Pilocarpine tablets for the treatment of dry mouth an[d] dry eye symptoms in patients with Sjogren syndrome: randomized, placebo-controlled, fixed-dose, multicenter trial. P92–01 Study Group. *Archives of Internal Medicine* **159**(2), 174–181. [Full text]

PRODIGY GUIDANCE

Dysmenorrhoea

Last revised in February 2003
www.prodigy.nhs.uk/guidance.asp?gt=Dysmenorrhoea

Applies to women over the age of 10 years

This guidance covers the management of primary dysmenorrhoea.

This guidance does not cover the management of chronic or non-cyclical pelvic pain, or premenstrual syndrome. It also does not cover in detail the management of secondary causes of dysmenorrhoea.

There is separate PRODIGY guidance for *Endometriosis* and *Pelvic inflammatory disease.*

D

Goals

To alleviate symptoms

Contents

Scenarios
- Analgesia p.619
- Combined oral contraception — first choice p.620

Extended Information, p. 623

Which scenario?

Analgesia: offers advice on the choices of nonsteroidal anti-inflammatory drugs and paracetamol for management of symptoms in dysmenorrhoea.
Combined oral contraception: provides prescribing advice when it is appropriate to combine symptom management of dysmenorrhoea with oral contraception. More detailed advice and further choices are available in the PRODIGY *Contraception* guidance.

Analgesia

Which therapy?

Many women will successfully self-medicate with over-the-counter medications.
Nonsteroidal anti-inflammatory drugs (NSAIDs) relieve symptoms by up to 70%.
Paracetamol may offer some relief in women who cannot tolerate NSAIDs, although there is less evidence for its efficacy.
Codeine phosphate can be added for extra pain relief if needed.

Practical prescribing points

For further information, please see the *Medicines Compendium* (www.medicines.org.uk) or the *British National Formulary* (www.bnf.org).

NSAIDs

NSAIDs are contraindicated in people with a history of hypersensitivity to aspirin or to other NSAIDs.
People are at increased risk from NSAID-induced adverse effects if they:
- **Have a previous history** of gastroduodenal ulcer, gastrointestinal bleeding, or gastroduodenal perforation.
- **Use other medications concomitantly** (e.g. corticosteroids and anticoagulants) that are known to increase the likelihood of upper gastrointestinal adverse events.
- **Have serious comorbidity** (e.g. cardiovascular disease, renal or hepatic impairment, diabetes, or hypertension).

- **NSAIDs may worsen asthma, hypertension, renal impairment, or cardiac failure.**

Should I refer or investigate?

Refer?

- **If there is inadequate response to treatment.**
- **If there is suspected secondary dysmenorrhoea** (e.g. associated menstrual symptoms, such as menorrhagia, intermenstrual or post-coital bleeding, dyspareunia, and/or abnormal pelvic examination).

Investigate?

- **Consider vaginal and endocervical swabs** (for chlamydia) if pelvic inflammatory disease is suspected. See PRODIGY guidance on *Pelvic inflammatory disease.*

Patient information leaflets

The following PILs are available at www.prodigy.nhs.uk
- Anti-inflammatory Painkillers
- Laparoscopy and Laparoscopic Surgery
- Period Pain (Dysmenorrhoea)
- Periods and Some Period Problems
- Women's Health
- Women's Health Concern

Shared decision making

- **About 7 in 10** women have pain during periods.
- **Anti-inflammatory painkillers** such as ibuprofen, mefenamic acid and naproxen ease the pain by up to 70%. They also reduce the amount of bleeding.
- **Start the tablets as soon as pain begins.** Take them regularly for 2–3 days.
- **Some people cannot take anti-inflammatory painkillers** — for example, people with duodenal ulcers, and some people with asthma.
- **Side effects are uncommon.** An upset stomach sometimes occurs; tell your doctor if this is a persistent problem.
- **Paracetamol** is an alternative if an anti-inflammatory is not suitable.
- **The contraceptive pill** also reduces the amount of period pain. This may be a good option if you also need contraception.
- **Heat** (e.g. a hot-water bottle) will often ease pain too.
- **A TENS** machine is an option if medication does not help.
- **Referral** to a specialist is rarely needed, as period pain is usually eased by one of the above treatments.

Drug rationale

Drugs not included

- **Nonsteroidal anti-inflammatory drugs (NSAIDs) other than ibuprofen, naproxen, and mefenamic acid** are not included. Either an excluded drug is not licensed for dysmenorrhoea, or it is associated with a higher risk of gastrointestinal (GI) adverse events, or there is insufficient data to reach clear conclusions regarding its safety [CSM, 1994; Henry et al, 1996; Hernández-Diaz and Rodriguez, 2000; BNF 43, 2002; CSM, 2002].
- **Cyclo-oxygenase (COX)-2 selective NSAIDs** are not included as we found no trial data on their effectiveness and safety in dysmenorrhoea.
- **Aspirin** is effective in the treatment of dysmenorrhoea, but is probably less effective than NSAIDs. One systematic review showed that ibuprofen seemed much more effective than aspirin (NNT = 10 for aspirin, compared with 2.4 for ibuprofen) [Bandolier, 1998; Zhang and Li Wan Po, 1998]. Aspirin is therefore not offered.
- **Antispasmodics: Alverine citrate** is licensed for the treatment of dysmenorrhoea, but we found no published evidence on its efficacy in dysmenorrhoea.

Drugs included

- **NSAIDs** reduce menstrual blood loss and relieve dysmenorrhoea. Ibuprofen, mefenamic acid, and naproxen are all effective at relieving dysmenorrhoea. Ibuprofen may be the preferred first choice because of its more favourable risk-benefit ratio [Bandolier, 1998; Zhang and Li Wan Po, 1998; BNF 43, 2002]. Ibuprofen is licensed for use in all ages; mefenamic acid tablets can be given from age 12 years; and naproxen is licensed from 16 years onwards.
- **Paracetamol:** there is limited evidence regarding its effectiveness. However, it may offer some pain relief when an NSAID is contraindicated [Zhang and Li Wan Po, 1998].
- **Codeine** can be added for extra pain relief if needed.

Prescriptions

Advice note

Advice only: OTC purchase
- Age from 10 years onwards
- You may buy medication from a pharmacy without a prescription for dysmenorrhoea. Please ask the pharmacist to help you choose the best preparation for you.

Analgesia: use when required

Ibuprofen s/f susp: 200mg three to four times a day
- Age from 10 to 11 years
- Ibuprofen 100mg/5ml s/f susp. Take two 5ml spoonfuls 3 to 4 times a day when required for pain relief. Do not exceed the stated dose; supply 300 ml; NHS Cost £5.46; OTC Cost £9.62.

Ibuprofen tablets: 200mg three to four times a day
- Age from 12 years onwards
- Ibuprofen 200mg tablets. Take one tablet 3 to 4 times a day while having period pain; supply 56 tablets; NHS Cost £1.13; OTC Cost £1.99.

Ibuprofen tablets: 400mg three to four times a day
- Age from 12 years onwards
- Ibuprofen 400mg tablets. Take one tablet 3 to 4 times a day while having period pain; supply 56 tablets; NHS Cost £1.64; OTC Cost £2.89.

Ibuprofen tablets: 600mg three times a day
- Age from 16 years onwards
- Ibuprofen 600mg tablets. Take one tablet three times a day while having period pain; supply 84 tablets; NHS Cost £3.35.

Naproxen tablets: 250mg three to four times a day
- Age from 16 years onwards
- Naproxen 250mg tablets. Take two tablets initially, then take one tablet 3 to 4 times a day while having period pain. Maximum of 5 tablets in 24 hours; supply 60 tablets; NHS Cost £2.35.

Mefenamic acid tablets: 500mg three times a day
- Age from 12 years onwards
- Mefenamic acid 500mg tablets. Take one tablet three times a day while having period pain; supply 42 tablets; NHS Cost £3.05.

Paracetamol s/f susp: 250mg to 500mg up to four times a day
- Age from 10 to 11 years
- Paracetamol 250mg/5ml s/f susp. Take one to two 5ml spoonfuls every 4 to 6 hours when required for pain relief. Maximum of 4 doses in 24 hours; supply 300 ml; NHS Cost £1.59; OTC Cost £2.80.

Paracetamol tablets: 500mg to 1g up to four times a day
- Age from 12 to 15 years
- Paracetamol 500mg tablets. Take one to two tablets every 4 to 6 hours when required for pain relief. Maximum of 8 tablets in 24 hours; supply 50 tablets; NHS Cost £0.38; OTC Cost £0.67.

Paracetamol tablets: 1g up to four times a day
- Age from 16 years onwards
- Paracetamol 500mg tablets. Take two tablets every 4 to 6 hours when required for pain relief. Maximum of 8 tablets in 24 hours; supply 50 tablets; NHS Cost £0.38; OTC Cost £0.67.

Codeine 30mg tablets: add on to paracetamol if required
- Age from 16 years onwards
- Codeine 30mg tablets. Take one to two tablets every 4 to 6 hours when required for pain relief. Maximum of 8 tablets in 24 hours; supply 56 tablets; NHS Cost £2.04.

Combined oral contraception — first choice

Which therapy?

- **Combined oral contraceptives** (COCs) provide contraception and effectively relieve dysmenorrhoea in up to 80–90% of individuals [Muse, 1990].
- Choice should be based on suitability for the individual.
  - **Preparations containing 30–35 micrograms of oestrogen plus a low dosage of either levonorgestrel or norethisterone are a suitable first choice of pill.**
  - A range of 'first-choice' COCs is offered in this scenario with others offered in the PRODIGY *Contraception* guidance.
- Before prescribing the COC pill:
  - **Enquire about** personal and family history, current conditions and medications, any contraindications, cautions (first prescription particularly), and adverse effects (repeat prescriptions).
  - **Record blood pressure.**
  - **Measure** height and weight and calculate body mass index (BMI) if obesity is a concern.
  - **Breast or pelvic examination is unnecessary** unless clinically indicated by symptoms.
- **Women should be advised on how to take the pill** and this information is detailed on the right-hand side of the prescription and in the patient information leaflet.

- **Generally start on the first day of the menstrual cycle; no additional contraception is then necessary.** If started later, exclude the risk of pregnancy since the last menstrual period and advise the woman to use additional contraceptive precautions for 7 days.

Practical prescribing points

For further information, please see the *Medicines Compendium* (www.medicines.org.uk) or the *British National Formulary* (www.bnf.org).

- **Conditions where COCs are either an unacceptable (category 4) health risk or where the risks usually outweigh the advantages (category 3)** are detailed in Table 1.
- Recommend alternative contraceptive methods and explain the potential risk of COCs to women with any of these conditions, and careful follow-up will be required.
- A woman with conditions where the advantages of COCs generally outweigh the theoretical or proven risks (WHO category 2) requires careful follow-up, especially if two or more of these problems coexist.
- Many women will have no factors (WHO category 1) in their medical history that give concern about any increased individual risks for them with COCs. For any individual woman, the balance of clinical risks and benefits of COCs must be considered together with her situation, motivation, and concerns about her choice of method.
- For a full list of the World Health Organization (WHO) medical eligibility criteria, see www.who.int/reproductive-health/publications/mec/3_cocs.pdf.

Follow-up advice

- **The first follow-up appointment** is usually offered 10–12 weeks after the initial visit, to check blood pressure and to enquire about adverse effects. Also check correct and consistent pill use, and knowledge of what to do if a pill is missed.
- **Where there are medical or non-medical concerns,** follow-up after 6 weeks is usual.
- **For established users of combined oral contraceptive pills,** 6-monthly checks are accepted UK practice. Blood pressure, clinical history, and adverse effects should be checked, together with correct and consistent pill use, and knowledge of what to do if a pill is missed.

Should I refer or investigate?

Refer?

- **If there is inadequate response to treatment.**
- **If there is suspected secondary dysmenorrhoea** (e.g. associated menstrual symptoms, such as menorrhagia, intermenstrual or post-coital bleeding, dyspareunia, and/or abnormal pelvic examination).

Investigate?

- **Vaginal and endocervical swabs** for chlamydia should be taken if pelvic inflammatory disease is suspected.
- **Before commencing the combined oral contraceptive pill:**
  - Breast and pelvic examinations are unnecessary in asymptomatic women before first prescriptions of a combined oral contraceptive pill.
  - **Lipid screening:**
    - There is little evidence to support screening for abnormal lipids as part of a strategy to improve COC safety.
    - It is appropriate to screen women who have one or more non-smoking siblings or parents who developed arterial disease prematurely, or who come from a family known to have a hereditary atherogenic disorder (if screening was not previously performed).
  - **Thrombophilia screening:**
    - It is not appropriate to screen all women for thrombophilia prior to prescribing the combined oral contraceptive pill.
    - Testing should be discussed with women who have a definite family history of thrombophilia or venous thromboembolic disease affecting first-degree relatives.

D

Patient information leaflets

The following PILs are available at www.prodigy.nhs.uk

- Laparoscopy and Laparoscopic Surgery
- Period Pain (Dysmenorrhoea)
- Periods and Some Period Problems
- Women's Health
- Women's Health Concern

Shared decision making

Some points about most combined contraceptive pills include:

- Start the first pack on the first day of your next period — it is fully effective from then on.
- Take one pill a day for 21 days, at about the same time each day. Then stop for 7 days. You should have a period. Start the next pack after 7 days.
- Read and keep the information leaflet that comes in the packet. It will remind you about how to take the pill; possible side effects; risks; and what to do if you miss a pill, vomit, take other medication, etc. Briefly:
  - If you are more than 12 hours late in taking a pill, refer to the leaflet for advice on what to do.
  - If you are prescribed antibiotics or other medication, tell the prescribing doctor, nurse, or dentist that you take the pill.
  - Possible side effects include headache, weight gain, nausea, breast tenderness, and mood changes. These are usually temporary.
  - Breakthrough bleeding (a light blood loss from time to time) is common. Do not stop taking the pill. It usually settles within 3 months, but tell a doctor or practice nurse if it persists.
  - The risk of serious problems is small, though more common in smokers. There is a slightly increased risk of a blood clot in a leg vein (deep vein thrombosis) or in an artery, which may cause a heart attack or a stroke. There is also a slightly increased risk of cancer of the breast, cervix, or liver.

Drug rationale

Drugs not included

- **Preparations containing desogestrel or gestodene** are probably associated with an increased risk of venous thromboembolism compared with preparations containing levonorgestrel. Therefore COCs containing desogestrel or gestodene are not regarded as first choice.
- **Higher doses of levonorgestrel or norethisterone** are not included, because there is no evidence that the COCs with higher doses of norethisterone and levonorgestrel offer any advantages over preparations with lower doses of these progestogens.
- **Preparations containing 20 micrograms of oestrogen** have not been shown to offer any advantage over preparations containing 30–35 micrograms of oestrogen,

Table 1: Clinical conditions where COCs are considered either unacceptable (category 4), or where the risks usually outweigh the advantages (category 3) for use in contraception. Note: combined contraceptive patches have been assigned the same category ratings as COCs.

Condition	Category	Comment
<6 weeks postpartum	4	There is some theoretical concern that the neonate may be at risk because of exposure to steroid hormones during the first 6 weeks postpartum. There is also some theoretical concern regarding the association between COC use up to 3 weeks postpartum and risk of thrombosis in the mother.
>=6 weeks to <6 months postpartum (primarily breastfeeding)	3	In the first 6 months postpartum, use of COCs during breastfeeding diminishes the quantity of breast milk, decreases the duration of lactation, and may thereby adversely affect the growth of the infant.
Postpartum <21 days	3	Blood coagulation and fibrinolysis are essentially normalized by 3 weeks postpartum.
Aged >=35 years and smoking <15 cigarettes a day	3	COC users who smoked were at increased risk of cardiovascular diseases, especially myocardial infarction (MI), compared with those who did not smoke. Studies have also showed an increased risk of MI with increasing number of cigarettes smoked per day.
Aged >=35 years and smoking >15 cigarettes a day	4	
Cardiovascular disease — multiple risk factors for arterial cardiovascular disease	3/4	If a woman has multiple major risk factors, any of which alone would substantially increase the risk of cardiovascular disease, use of COCs may increase her risk to an unacceptable level. However, simple addition of categories for multiple risk factors is not intended; e.g. a combination of two risk factors assigned a category 2 may not necessarily warrant a higher category.
History of hypertension, where blood pressure (BP) *cannot* be evaluated (including hypertension during pregnancy)	3	Hypertension — classifications assume that no other risk factors for cardiovascular disease exist. Risk of cardiovascular disease may increase substantially when multiple risk factors exist. Evaluation of BP level and cause is recommended, as soon as feasible. Women who did not have a BP check before COC use have been found to have an increased risk of acute MI and stroke.
Adequately controlled hypertension, where BP *can* be evaluated	3	Women adequately treated for hypertension are at reduced risk of acute myocardial infarction (MI) and stroke as compared with untreated women. Although there are no data, COC users with adequately controlled and monitored hypertension should be at reduced risk of acute MI and stroke compared with untreated hypertensive COC users.
Elevated blood pressure levels (properly taken measurements) *systolic 140–159 or diastolic 90–99*	3	Among women with hypertension, COC users are at increased risk of stroke and MI compared with non-users. The risk increases with incremental rises in BP. A single BP reading of 140–159/90–99 is not sufficient to classify a woman as hypertensive.
Systolic >=160 or diastolic >=100	4	—
Vascular disease	4	Increased risk of arterial thrombosis associated with COC use should be avoided in women with underlying vascular disease.
Venous thromboembolism (VTE) — current or past history Major surgery with prolonged immobilization	4	The increased risk of VTE associated with COCs should have little impact on healthy women, but may have substantial impact on women with a history of thromboembolism.
Known thrombogenic mutations (e.g. Factor V Leiden; Prothrombin mutation; Protein S, Protein C and Antithrombin deficiencies)	4	Routine screening is not appropriate because of the rarity of the conditions and the high cost of screening. Among women with thrombogenic mutations, COC users have been found to have a two to twenty-fold higher risk of thrombosis than non-users.
Current ischaemic heart disease	4	Among women with underlying vascular disease, the increased risk associated with COC use should be avoided.
Stroke	4	Among women with underlying vascular disease, the increased risk associated with COC use should be avoided.
Known hyperlipidaemias	3/2	Routine screening is not appropriate because of the rarity of the conditions and the high cost of screening. While some types are risk factors for vascular disease, the category should be assessed according to the type, its severity and the presence of other cardiovascular risk factors.
Complicated valvular heart disease	4	Among women with valvular heart disease, COC use may further increase the risk of arterial thrombosis; women with complicated valvular heart disease are at greatest risk
Migraine with focal neurological symptoms at any age	4	Classification depends on accurate diagnosis of those severe headaches that are migrainous and those that are not. Any new headaches or marked changes in headaches should be evaluated. Classification is for women without any other risk factors for stroke. Risk of stroke increases with age, hypertension, and smoking.
Migraine without focal neurological symptoms <35 where continuous use	3	
Migraine without focal symptoms in women >=35 years, firstly in initiation and secondly with continuation	3 4	
Current breast disease	4	Breast cancer is a hormonally sensitive tumour, and the prognosis of women with current or recent breast cancer may worsen with COC use.
Past history of breast cancer and no evidence of recurrence for 5 years	3	
Nephropathy/retinopathy/neuropathy	3/4	The category should be assessed according to the severity of the condition.

Condition	Category	Comment
Other vascular disease or diabetes of >20 years' duration	3/4	The category should be assessed according to the severity of the condition.
Gallbladder disease — symptomatic medically treated or current	3	COCs may cause a small increased risk of gall-bladder disease. There is also concern that COCs may worsen existing gall-bladder disease.
History of cholestasis — past COC-related	3	History of COC-related cholestasis predicts an increased risk with subsequent COC use.
Viral hepatitis — active	4	COCs are metabolized by the liver, and their use may adversely affect women whose liver function is already compromised.
Cirrhosis — mild compensated	3	COCs are metabolized by the liver, and their use may adversely affect women whose liver function is already compromised.
Cirrhosis — severe decompensated	4	
Liver tumours — benign and malignant	4	COCs are metabolized by the liver, and their use may adversely affect women whose liver function is compromised. In addition, COC use may enhance the growth of tumours.
Liver enzyme-inducing drugs	3	Although the interaction between commonly used liver enzyme-inducers and COCs is not harmful to women, it is likely to reduce the efficacy of COCs. Use of other contraceptives (e.g. progestogen-only injection) should be encouraged for women who are long-term users of any of these drugs. Whether increasing the hormone dose of COCs is of benefit remains unclear.

Category 4 — a condition that represents an unacceptable health risk if a COC is used.
Category 3 — a condition where the theoretical or proven risks usually outweigh the advantages of using a COC.

and some women may not achieve good cycle control with them.

- **Preparations containing a high dose (50 micrograms) of oestrogen** are indicated only for women concurrently taking hepatic enzyme-inducing drugs.
- **Biphasic preparations** offer no advantage to monophasic preparations [Van Vliet et al, 2001]. It is uncertain whether triphasic preparations offer any advantage.
- **Every day preparations** are not routinely used in the UK, but can be useful to help women who have difficulty starting the next packet at the correct time.
- **Dianette** (cyproterone acetate and ethinylestradiol) is not licensed solely for use as a contraceptive. It should be reserved for selected women requiring treatment for severe acne, refractory to prolonged antibiotic therapy, or with moderately severe hirsutism.

Drugs included

- **Preparations containing low-dose oestrogen (30–35 micrograms), and oestrogen plus low-dose progestogen (levonorgestrel 150 micrograms or norethisterone 500 micrograms)** are included.
- Note: both Microgynon-30 and Ovranette contain ethinylestradiol 30 micrograms plus levonorgestrel 150 micrograms. Both Brevinor and Ovysmen contain ethinylestradiol 35 micrograms plus norethisterone 500 micrograms.
- For detailed information on the choice of COC and prescribing advice, see the PRODIGY guidance on *Contraception*.

Prescriptions

Combined oral contraception pill – 1st choice

Microgynon 30 (levonorgestrel 150micrograms)
- Age from 12 to 60 years
- Microgynon 30 tablets. Take one tablet once a day for 21 days. Start the next packet after a 7-day break. See package insert for full instructions; supply 63 tablets; NHS Cost £2.34.

Ovranette (levonorgestrel 150micrograms)
- Age from 12 to 60 years
- Ovranette tablets. Take one tablet once a day for 21 days. Start the next packet after a 7-day break. See package insert for full instructions; supply 63 tablets; NHS Cost £2.26.

Brevinor (norethisterone 500micrograms)
- Age from 12 to 60 years
- Brevinor tablets. Take one tablet once a day for 21 days. Start the next packet after a 7-day break. See package insert for full instructions; supply 63 tablets; NHS Cost £1.67.

Ovysmen (norethisterone 500micrograms)
- Age from 12 to 60 years
- Ovysmen tablets. Take one tablet once a day for 21 days. Start the next packet after a 7-day break. See package insert for full instructions; supply 63 tablets; NHS Cost £1.70.

Extended Information

Background information

- What is it? p.623
- How common is it? p.624
- How do I know my patient has it? p.624
- What may cause secondary dysmenorrhoea? p.624
- Complications and prognosis p.624

What is it?

- **Dysmenorrhoea** is cyclical lower abdominal or pelvic pain, which may also radiate to the back and thighs, occurring before or during menstruation, or both.
- **Primary dysmenorrhoea** occurs in the absence of any obvious underlying disease. Pathogenesis is uncertain;

uterine hyperactivity, prostaglandins, leukotrienes, and vasopressin have all been implicated.
- **Secondary dysmenorrhoea** is due to an underlying disease, most commonly endometriosis. Other causes include possible adhesions after pelvic inflammatory disease or previous surgery.

[Smith, 1993; Lumsden and Norman, 1997; Cameron, 1999]

How common is it?

- **Dysmenorrhoea affects 40–70% of women of reproductive age,** and affects daily activities in up to 10% of women [Zhang and Li Wan Po, 1998].

D

How do I know my patient has it?

Primary dysmenorrhoea:

- **Usually dates from about the time of menarche** (typically within 6–12 months of the first period), with the onset of ovulatory cycles.
- **Lower abdominal or pelvic pain occurs** (commonly lasting 8–72 hours), which may radiate to the back and along the thighs, occurring before or during menstruation, or both. There does not tend to be excessive menstrual bleeding; maximum pain often occurs when the period is lightest.
- **Associated symptoms,** such as headache, diarrhoea, nausea, and vomiting, may be present.
- **No abnormal findings on examination.**

Secondary dysmenorrhoea:

- **Usually has a later age of onset than primary dysmenorrhoea,** and is most often seen in women aged between 30 and 45 years [Cameron, 1999].
- **Women may complain of a change in timing or intensity of pain.**
- **Other gynaecological symptoms,** such as dyspareunia, menorrhagia, intermenstrual bleeding, and postcoital bleeding, are often present in addition to any of the above.
- **There may be abnormalities on examination,** such as uterine tenderness or enlargement, although absence of abnormal findings does not exclude secondary dysmenorrhoea.

[Rees, 1993; Smith, 1993]

What may cause secondary dysmenorrhoea?

- **Secondary dysmenorrhoea is most commonly due to:**
  - Endometriosis
  - Fibroids (myomas)
  - Adenomyosis
  - Endometrial polyps
  - Pelvic inflammatory disease
  - Intra-uterine contraceptive device
  - Cervical stenosis (e.g. after uterine or cervical surgery)

Complications and prognosis

- **Psychological distress, anxiety, depression** may be present.
- **Absenteeism** from school or work. Studies have suggested that 10–45% of young women reported that they missed or reduced time at work, school, or other activities.
- **There may be complications from underlying pathology** with secondary dysmenorrhoea (e.g. infertility with endometriosis).

[Muse, 1990; Rees, 1993; Cameron, 1999; Proctor, 2002]

Management issues

- General issues p.624
- Recommended drug treatments p.624
- Other drug treatments p.625
- Non-drug treatments p.625
- Surgical treatments p.625
- Treatments not recommended p.625

General issues

- **Enquiry into the use of over-the-counter medications** is important, as many women with dysmenorrhoea self-medicate.
- **Intra-uterine devices (IUDs)** may result in dysmenorrhoea, and may require removal if adequate pain relief is not provided with analgesics. The levonorgestrel-releasing intra-uterine system reduces dysmenorrhoea and is an alternative if an IUD is still desired [Smith, 1993; Luukkainen and Toivonen, 1995].
- **Women unresponsive to standard drug treatments** should be suspected of having secondary dysmenorrhoea, and a specialist opinion should be considered.
- **Irritable bowel syndrome** is associated with dysmenorrhoea, and may result in diagnostic confusion or inappropriate treatment [Crowell et al, 1994].

Recommended drug treatments

Nonsteroidal anti-inflammatory drugs

- **Nonsteroidal anti-inflammatory drugs (NSAIDs)** are inhibitors of prostaglandin synthesis, and probably work by decreasing uterine prostaglandin levels and reducing uterine contractility. All NSAIDs are thought to be effective, relieving pain by up to 70%. One systematic review found that aspirin was significantly more effective than placebo for pain relief but not as effective as ibuprofen, naproxen, and mefenamic acid (NNT for aspirin was 10, compared with only 2 or 3 for other NSAIDs). Naproxen and ibuprofen were significantly better in terms of the need for rescue analgesia than were mefenamic acid and aspirin [Bandolier, 1998; Zhang and Li Wan Po, 1998]. Most trials have studied the use of NSAIDs at the onset of pain. One small study in 14 women compared treatment started premenstrually against treatment from onset of pain; both strategies were equally effective [Chan et al, 1981].
- **Gastrointestinal toxicity** is a particular concern with NSAIDs [Bandolier, 2000; Hernández-Diaz and Rodriguez, 2000; CSM, 2002]. When treating women with risk factors for NSAID-induced ulceration, the potential risks and benefits of using an NSAID should be considered. If an NSAID is offered in this situation, a gastroprotective agent should be prescribed.
- **Risk factors for NSAID-induced ulceration** include [NICE, 2000]:
  - **Previous clinical history** of gastroduodenal ulcer, gastrointestinal bleeding, or gastroduodenal perforation.
  - **Concomitant use of medications** that are known to increase the likelihood of upper gastrointestinal adverse events (e.g. corticosteroids and anticoagulants).
  - **Presence of serious comorbidity,** such as cardiovascular disease, renal or hepatic impairment, diabetes, or hypertension.
  - Requirement for the prolonged use of maximum recommended doses of standard NSAIDs.
- **NSAIDs act by inhibiting cyclo-oxygenase (COX) pathways.** There are at least two isoforms of cyclo-

oxygenase: COX-1 produces prostaglandins that help to maintain gastric mucosal integrity, and COX-2 produces prostaglandins that mediate pain and inflammation. It is thought that the anti-inflammatory effect of NSAIDs is due to inhibition of COX-2. NSAIDs can be classified according to their relative effects on COX-1 and COX-2. The risk of gastrointestinal adverse effects seems to be reduced with increasing COX-2 selectivity. However, other factors are involved, as some NSAIDs that are relatively COX-2 selective are known to be associated with a higher incidence of gastrointestinal adverse events [Warner et al, 1999].

COX-2 selective NSAIDS are difficult to rank on the basis of selectivity, because there is a wide variation between different assay techniques. NICE identifies celecoxib, meloxicam, and etodolac as being COX-2 selective inhibitors [NICE, 2000]. Etoricoxib has been more recently introduced.

Other analgesics

Other analgesics have been poorly studied. Paracetamol and co-proxamol (paracetamol 325 mg and dextropropoxyphene 32.5 mg) have a more variable efficacy for the treatment of dysmenorrhoea, but are still worth considering if NSAIDs are contraindicated. Paracetamol was compared with ibuprofen in one randomized controlled trial in 67 women and found to be equally effective (RR 0.86, 95% CI 0.68 to 1.10). Co-proxamol was compared with mefenamic acid in 30 women and found to be less effective at reducing dysmenorrhoea-related symptoms. Another two randomized controlled trials of 98 women found no difference in severity of pain relief between co-proxamol and naproxen, but co-proxamol produced significantly more adverse effects [Proctor and Farquar, 2003].

The combined oral contraceptive

The combined oral contraceptive (COC) works by inducing endometrial thinning and inhibiting ovulation, resulting in low levels of uterine prostaglandins [Muse, 1990]. COCs are an accepted treatment for dysmenorrhoea, despite a lack of good-quality trials. A Cochrane systematic review of the efficacy of COCs in primary dysmenorrhoea included four trials [Proctor et al, 2003]. The review excluded most trials, either because of a lack of randomization or because they used the older types of COCs with a high oestrogen content (more than 100 micrograms). A meta-analysis of the remaining trials found that COCs significantly improved pain relief when compared with placebo (OR 2.01, 95% CI 1.22 to 2.33). However, there was evidence of heterogeneity between the studies. In addition, the studies were over 25 years old, of small size, and generally of poor quality. Thus, the data cannot necessarily be extrapolated to the modern lower-dose COCs [Proctor et al, 2003]. The COC should be prescribed in line with current World Health Organization guidelines (see PRODIGY guidance on *Contraception*).

Menstrual cycle suppressants, such as progestogens, danazol, and gonadotrophin-releasing hormone analogues, are occasionally used for resistant dysmenorrhoea, but should normally be used only on specialist advice.

Other drug treatments

The levonorgestrel-releasing intra-uterine system is not licensed for the treatment of dysmenorrhoea, but has been shown to be of benefit. It might be considered for a woman who needs long-term contraception, especially if menorrhagia is also a problem [Smith, 1993; Luukkainen and Toivonen, 1995].

Non-drug treatments

- **Transcutaneous electrical nerve stimulation** (**TENS**) may be of benefit in easing the dysmenorrhoea. TENS seems to work by altering the body's ability to receive or perceive pain signals, rather than by having a direct effect on the uterine contractions [Proctor et al, 2002].
  - **High-frequency TENS** usually consists of pulses delivered at 50–120 Hz at low intensity. High-frequency TENS has been compared with placebo in seven small randomized controlled trials and found to be effective for pain relief in primary dysmenorrhoea.
  - **Low-frequency TENS** usually consists of pulses delivered at 1–4 Hz at high intensity and with long pulse width. It was more effective than placebo TENS, but there is insufficient evidence with regard to the comparative efficacy between high- and low-frequency TENS.
- **Acupuncture may be helpful.** In one small but well-designed study in 48 women, acupuncture was compared with sham acupuncture (needles positioned away from the 'real' acupuncture sites) given once a week for 3 weeks per month over a 3-month period. Women receiving 'real' acupuncture gained significant pain relief ($p < 0.001$) but further research is needed to confirm this effect [Proctor et al, 2002; Proctor and Farquar, 2003].
- **Locally applied low-level heat** may also help pain relief. Results from one study showed that the time to noticeable pain relief was significantly reduced when ibuprofen was combined with locally applied heat, as compared with ibuprofen alone [Akin et al, 2001].

Surgical treatments

- **Laparoscopic uterine nerve ablation** (LUNA) was compared with diagnostic laparoscopy in 21 women in a small randomized controlled trial, which found that LUNA significantly increased pain relief at 3-month follow-up (OR 0.7, 95% CI 0.2 to 2.7) and 12-month follow-up (OR 10.9, 95% CI 1.5 to 77).
- **Laparoscopic presacral neurectomy** (LPSN) was compared with LUNA in another trial, which found no difference in pain relief at 3 months; but at 12 months the LPSN group had significantly better pain-relief scores (OR 0.26, 95% CI 0.10 to 0.71) [Johnson et al, 2000; Proctor and Farquar, 2003]. Although there is insufficient evidence at present to make any recommendations, two larger randomized controlled trials of LUNA are under way.

Treatments not recommended

- **Anticholinergic** antispasmodics relax the uterine smooth muscle by acting on the intramural parasympathetic ganglia. Alverine citrate is licensed for the treatment of dysmenorrhoea, but there is a lack of published evidence on its efficacy for this indication [BNF 43, 2002]. It is unlikely to be as effective as nonsteroidal anti-inflammatory drugs or the combined oral contraceptive.
- **Beta-agonists** [Akerlund et al, 1976; Kullander and Svanberg, 1981] and **calcium-channel blockers** [Sandahl et al, 1979; Andersson, 1988; Childress and Katz, 1994] are reported to be of some benefit in dysmenorrhoea, but none is licensed for this indication.
- **Spinal manipulation** has not been found to be of any benefit in relieving dysmenorrhoea [Proctor et al, 2002].
- **Behavioural therapy** has been poorly studied, and a systematic review is currently in progress [Proctor, 2002; Proctor and Farquar, 2003].
- **Dietary supplements** are not recommended, because of the lack of evidence for their benefit. The following have

all been reviewed by the Cochrane Library [Proctor and Murphy, 2002].

- **Thiamine** (100 mg daily for 3 months) was found to provide pain relief in 87% of women in a large placebo-controlled trial in India. However, these women were likely to be thiamine-deficient, which is very rare in the UK [Gokhale, 1996; Proctor and Farquar, 2003].
- **Magnesium** compared with placebo has been reviewed using data from three small randomized controlled trials. Overall, magnesium was more effective than placebo for pain relief, and the need for additional pain relief was less. However, the disparity in dosing regimens means that further evaluation is needed.
- **Pyridoxine** alone (n = 22) and combined with magnesium (n = 21) showed some benefit in reducing pain, compared with placebo.
- **Daily vitamin E** showed no benefit over ibuprofen (taken during the menses) in 50 women after 1 month of treatment.
- **Fish oil** (omega-3 fatty acids) compared with placebo in 42 women showed the use of additional pain relief to be significantly lower in the treatment group ($p < 0.001$). There were significantly more adverse effects in the women treated with fish oil, but these were not serious.

D

References

NHS staff in England can link, free of charge, from references to full text journals by clicking on [Full text] on the PRODIGY website.

1. Akerlund, M., Andersson, K.E. and Ingemarsson, I. (1976) Effects of terbutaline on myometrial activity, uterine blood flow, and lower abdominal pain in women with primary dysmenorrhoea. *British Journal of Obstetrics & Gynaecology* 83(9), 673–678.
2. Akin, M.D., Weingand, K.W., Hengehold, D.A. et al (2001) Continuous low-level topical heat in the treatment of dysmenorrhea. *Obstetrics & Gynecology* 97(3), 343–349.
3. Andersson, K.E. (1988) Calcium antagonists and dysmenorrhea. *Annals of the New York Academy of Sciences* 522, 747–756.
4. Bandolier (1998) *Analgesics for dysmenorrhoea.* Bandolier. www.jr2.ox.ac.uk/bandolier/booth/painpag/Chronrev/Analges/CP066.html [Accessed: 09/08/2002].
5. Bandolier (2000) *More on NSAID adverse effects.* Bandolier. www.jr2.ox.ac.uk/bandolier/band79/b79-6.html [Accessed: 2/12/2000].
6. BNF 43 (2002) *British National Formulary.* 43rd edn. London: British Medical Association and Royal Pharmaceutical Society of Great Britain.
7. Cameron, I.T. (1999) Menstrual disorders. In: Edmonds, D.K. (Ed.) *Dewhurst's textbook of obstetrics and gynaecology for postgraduates.* 6th edn. London: Blackwell Science. 410–419.
8. Chan, W.Y., Yusoff Dawood, M. and Fuchs, F. (1981) Prostaglandins in primary dysmenorrhoea. *American Journal of Medicine* 70(3), 535–541.
9. Childress, C.H. and Katz, V.L. (1994) Nifedipine and its indications in obstetrics and gynecology. *Obstetrics & Gynecology* 83(4), 616–624.
10. Crowell, M.D., Dubin, N.H., Robinson, J.C. et al (1994) Functional bowel disorders in women with dysmenorrhea. *American Journal of Gastroenterology* 89(11), 1973–1977.
11. CSM (1994) Relative safety of oral non-aspirin NSAIDs. *Current Problems in Pharmacovigilance* 20(Aug), 9–11.
12. CSM (2002) Non-steroidal anti-inflammatory drugs (NSAIDs) and gastrointestinal (GI) safety. *Current Problems in Pharmacovigilance* 28(Apr), 5.
13. Gokhale, L.B. (1996) Curative treatment of primary (spasmodic) dysmenorrhoea. *Indian Journal of Medica Research* 103(April), 227–231.
14. Henry, D., Lim, L.L., Garcia-Rodriguez, L.A. et al (1996) Variability in risk of gastrointestinal complications with individual non-steroidal anti-inflammatory drugs: results of a collaborative meta-analysis. *British Medical Journal* 312(7046), 1563–1566. [Full text]
15. Hernández-Diaz, S. and Rodriguez, L.A. (2000) Association between nonsteroidal anti-inflammatory drugs and upper gastrointestinal tract bleeding/perforation: an overview of epidemiologic studies published in the 1990s. *Archives of Internal Medicine* 160(14), 2093–2099. [Full text]
16. Johnson, N., Wilson, M and Farquhar, C. (2000) Surgical pelvic neuroablation for chronic pelvic pain: a systematic review. *Gynaecological Endoscopy* 9, 351–361.
17. Kullander, S. and Svanberg, L. (1981) Terbutaline inhalation for alleviation of severe pain in essential dysmenorrhea. *Acta Obstetricia et Gynecologica Scandinavica* 60(4), 425–427.
18. Lumsden, M. and Norman, J. (1997) Menstruation and menstrual abnormality. In: Shaw, R.W., Soutter, W.P., Stanton, S.L. et al (Eds.) *Gynaecology*. 2nd edn. Edinburgh: Churchill Livingstone. 421–439.
19. Luukkainen, T. and Toivonen, J. (1995) Levonorgestrel-releasing IUD as a method of contraception with therapeutic properties. *Contraception* 52(5), 269–276.
20. Muse, K.N. (1990) Cyclic pelvic pain. *Obstetrics & Gynecology Clinics of North America* 17(2), 427–440.
21. NICE (2000) *Guidance on the use of proton pump inhibitors in the treatment of dyspepsia.* Technology appraisal guidance no. 7. National Institute for Clinical Excellence. www.nice.org.uk [Accessed: 16/10/2003].
22. Proctor, ML; Murphy, PA; Pattison, HM; Farquhar, CM (2002) *Behavioural interventions for primary and secondary dysmenorrhoea (Protocol for a Cochrane Review).* The Cochrane Library. Issue 3. Oxford: Update Software. [Accessed: 22/07/2002].
23. Proctor, M. and Farquar, C. (2003) Dysmenorrhoea. *Clinical Evidence* 10(Dec), 2058–2078.
24. Proctor, M.L. and Murphy, P.A. (2002) *Herbal and dietary therapies for primary and secondary dysmenorrhoea (Cochrane Review).* The Cochrane Library. Issue 3. Oxford: Update Software.
25. Proctor, M.L., Smith, C.A., Farquhar, C.M. and Stones, R.W. (2002) *Transcutaneous electrical nerve stimulation and acupuncture for primary dysmenorrhoea (Cochrane Review).* The Cochrane Library. Issue 3. Oxford: Update Software.
26. Proctor, M.L., Roberts, H. and Farquhar, C.M. (2003 *Combined oral contraceptive pill (OCP) as treatment for primary dysmenorrhoea (Cochrane Review).* The Cochrane Library. Issue 4. Oxford: Update Software.
27. Rees, M.C.P. (1993) Menstrual problems. In: McPherson, A. (Ed.) *Women's problems in general practice.* 3rd edn. Oxford: Oxford Medical Publications. 171–197.
28. Sandahl, B., Ulmsten, U. and Andersson, K.E. (1979) Trial of the calcium antagonist nifedipine in the treatment of primary dysmenorrhoea. *Archives of Gynecology* 227(2), 147–151.
29. Smith, R.P. (1993) Cyclic pelvic pain and dysmenorrhea. *Obstetrics & Gynecology Clinics of North America* 20(4), 753–764.

30. Van Vliet, H.A.A.M., Grimes, D.A., Helmerhorst, F.M. and Schulz, K.F. (2001) *Biphasic versus monophasic oral contraceptives for contraception (Cochrane Review)*. The Cochrane Library. Issue 2. Oxford: Update Software.
31. Warner, T.D., Giuliano, F., Vojnovic, I. et al (1999) Nonsteroid drug selectivities for cyclo-oxygenase-1 rather than cyclo-oxygenase-2 are associated with human gastrointestinal toxicity: a full in vitro analysis. *Proceedings of the National Academy of Sciences of the United States of America* **96**(13), 7563–7568.
32. Zhang, W.Y. and Li Wan Po, A. (1998) Efficacy of minor analgesics in primary dysmenorrhoea: a systematic review. *British Journal of Obstetrics & Gynaecology* **105**(7), 780–789.

D

PRODIGY GUIDANCE

Dyspepsia — pregnancy-associated

Last revised in July 2005
www.prodigy.nhs.uk/guidance.asp?gt=Dyspepsia-pregnancy-associated

Applies to women from the age of 10 to 60 years

This guidance covers the management of pregnancy-associated dyspepsia.

This guidance does not cover the management of dyspepsia due to other causes during pregnancy (e.g. peptic ulcer disease).

There is separate guidance for *Hypertension in pregnancy* and *Nausea and vomiting in pregnancy*.

D

Goals

- To provide effective symptomatic control of dyspeptic symptoms

Contents

Scenarios

- Pregnancy-associated dyspepsia p.628

Extended Information, p. 629

Pregnancy-associated dyspepsia

Which therapy?

- **Give lifestyle advice:**
  - Avoid precipitating factors, e.g. bending, alcohol, coffee, fatty foods.
  - Prop up the bed head, eat smaller meals, not eating within 3 hours of bedtime.
  - Eat healthily, and stop smoking.
- **If symptoms persist,** offer an antacid or alginate to control dyspepsia symptoms.
- If symptoms cannot be controlled with appropriate doses of an antacid, consider ranitidine 150 mg twice a day.
- Further information on specific drugs and their use in pregnancy is provided by the National Teratology Information Service; tel: 0191 232 1525.

Practical prescribing points

For further information please see the *Medicines Compendium* (www.medicines.org.uk) or the *British National Formulary* (www.bnf.org).

- Advise women not to take antacids at the same time as iron supplements. If possible, they should not be taken within 2 hours before or after iron supplements.
- Consider using a product with a low sodium content for women with gestational hypertension or pre-eclampsia (e.g. co-magaldrox suspension or Algicon® suspension).

Follow-up advice

- Follow up is not usually needed. Advise women to return if symptoms persist.

Should I refer or investigate?

Refer?

- If symptoms do not adequately respond to antacids, alginates, or ranitidine.
- If the woman is unable to eat sufficiently because of symptoms.
- If a disorder unrelated to pregnancy is suspected as the cause of symptoms, e.g. peptic ulcer disease, irritable bowel syndrome.
- If the woman presents with any ALARM symptoms, e.g. chronic gastrointestinal bleeding; progressive unintentional weight loss; progressive difficulty swallowing (dysphagia); persistent vomiting.

Patient information leaflets

The following PILs are available at www.prodigy.nhs.uk

- Pregnancy and Dyspepsia

Shared decision making

- **Acid-related symptoms, especially heartburn, are common during pregnancy.**
- **Some things which may help** include:
  - Not smoking, if you do smoke.
  - Cutting out foods that may irritate the gullet or gut (such as coffee, fatty foods, citrus fruits and juices, spicy foods, alcohol).
  - Raising the head of the bed when you sleep.
  - Not eating within 3 hours of bedtime.
  - Wearing looser clothes and avoiding bending forward.
  - Eating several small meals in the day rather than a few large meals.
- **Antacid medicines** are commonly used 'as required'. They are safe to take during pregnancy.
- **Ranitidine** is an acid-suppressing medicine. It can ease symptoms if the above suggestions do not help. It is thought to be safe to take during pregnancy.

Drug rationale

Drugs not included

- **H2-receptor antagonists: cimetidine, famotidine, and nizatidine** are not recommended. Studies of cimetidine in pregnant rodents showed inhibition of testicular descent and genital differentiation [Weiner and Buhimschi, 2004]. Similar effects have not been reported in limited data on human pregnancies. There is insufficient evidence to recommend the use of famotidine and nizatidine in pregnancy.
- **Proton pump inhibitors** are not recommended. There is insufficient evidence to recommend the use of these drugs in pregnancy.

Drugs included

- **An advice prescription for lifestyle modifications** is included for first-line therapy in pregnancy-associated dyspepsia.
- **Antacids containing aluminium hydroxide and/or magnesium trisilicate** have been included. They are considered to be safe in pregnancy (when used in

appropriate doses) [Weiner and Buhimschi, 2004], but they are not specifically licensed for use in pregnancy. Co-magaldrox (contains both aluminium and magnesium) has a low sodium content.
- **Alginates** are effective and safe for most women, and are particularly useful for symptoms of reflux. All alginates offered are sugar-free except Algicon® suspension, which is the only alginate preparation with a low sodium content.
- **H_2-receptor antagonists: ranitidine** is reserved for use if lifestyle modifications and antacids or alginates do not control symptoms adequately. Although there are only limited data on its safety during pregnancy, surveillance studies do not suggest that ranitidine presents a major teratogenic risk when used in recommended doses [Cappell, 2003; Weiner and Buhimschi, 2004].

Prescriptions

1st-line treatment: lifestyle advice

Advice note: lifestyle modifications
- Age from 10 to 60 years
- Acid-related symptoms and heartburn are common during pregnancy. Some things which may help include: not smoking, if you do smoke; cutting out foods that may irritate the gullet or gut (such as coffee, fatty foods, citrus fruits and juices, spicy foods, alcohol); raising the head of the bed when you sleep; not eating within 3 hours of bedtime; wearing looser clothes and avoiding bending forward; eating several small meals in the day rather than a few large meals.

2nd-line treatment: antacids

Co-magaldrox 195/220mg suspension (low sodium content)
- Age from 12 to 60 years
- Co-magald 195/220mg/5ml susp. Take two to four 5ml spoonfuls 20-60 minutes after food and at bedtime, when required to relieve dyspepsia; supply 1000 ml; NHS Cost £3.82; OTC Cost £6.74.

Aluminium hydroxide 4% suspension
- Age from 12 to 60 years
- Aluminium hydroxide 4% mixture. Take one to two 5ml spoonfuls four times a day (between meals and at bedtime) when required to relieve dyspepsia; supply 400 ml; NHS Cost £2.84; OTC Cost £3.32.

Magnesium trisilicate mixture
- Age from 12 to 60 years
- Magnesium trisilicate mixture. Take two 5ml spoonfuls (mixed in water) three times a day when required to relieve dyspepsia; supply 400 ml; NHS Cost £0.94; OTC Cost £1.10.

2nd-line treatment: alginates

Algicon suspension (low sodium content)
- Age from 12 to 60 years
- Algicon mint 500ml suspension. Take two to four 5ml spoonfuls after meals and at bedtime, when required to relieve dyspepsia; supply 1000 ml; NHS Cost £6.14; OTC Cost £10.82.

Gastrocote liquid (sugar-free)
- Age from 12 to 60 years
- Gastrocote liquid. Take one to three 5ml spoonfuls four times a day (after meals and at bedtime) when required to relieve dyspepsia; supply 1000 ml; NHS Cost £5.58; OTC Cost £9.84.

Gaviscon Advance tablets (sugar-free)
- Age from 12 to 60 years
- Gaviscon Advance tablets. Chew one to two tablets (followed by water) after meals and at bedtime, when required to relieve dyspepsia; supply 120 tablets; NHS Cost £6.48; OTC Cost £14.98.

Gaviscon Advance liquid (sugar-free)
- Age from 12 to 60 years
- Gaviscon Advance s/f susp. Take one to two 5ml spoonfuls after meals and at bedtime, when required to relieve dyspepsia; supply 500 ml; NHS Cost £5.40; OTC Cost £9.95.

Peptac liquid (sugar-free)
- Age from 12 to 60 years
- Peptac s/f liquid. Take two to four 5ml spoonfuls after meals and at bedtime, when required to relieve dyspepsia; supply 1000 ml; NHS Cost £4.32; OTC Cost £7.98.

Rennie Duo suspension (sugar-free)
- Age from 12 to 60 years
- Rennie Duo oral suspension. Take two to four 5ml spoonfuls after meals and at bedtime, when required to relieve dyspepsia; supply 1000 ml; NHS Cost £5.34; OTC Cost £10.58.

1st and 2nd line treatment failure: ranitidine

Ranitidine 150mg twice a day
- Age from 16 to 60 years
- Ranitidine 150mg tablets. Take one tablet twice a day; supply 60 tablets; NHS Cost £18.63.

Extended Information

Background information

- What is dyspepsia? p.629
- What causes dyspepsia during pregnancy? p.629
- How common is it? p.629
- How do I know my patient has it? p.630
- What else might it be? p.630
- Complications and prognosis p.630

What is dyspepsia?

- Dyspepsia is a term used to describe a group of upper gastrointestinal symptoms. It is not a diagnosis. The group of symptoms includes epigastric pain, heartburn, or acid regurgitation, with or without bloating, nausea, or vomiting.

What causes dyspepsia during pregnancy?

- Dyspepsia in pregnancy is commonly due to gastro-oesophageal reflux.
- One possible cause of reflux is transient relaxation of the lower oesophageal sphincter. The resting pressure of the lower oesophageal sphincter is known to be reduced during pregnancy, returning to normal in the postpartum period. However, it is not known whether raised progestogen or oestrogen levels are responsible for this reduction in pressure.
- Altered oesophageal motility and increased abdominal pressure may also play a role in the pathogenesis of reflux in pregnancy.

[Modigliani, 2000]

How common is it?

- Heartburn is estimated to occur in 30–50% of all pregnancies [Modigliani, 2000].

How do I know my patient has it?

- **Symptoms are variable,** but may include upper abdominal pain or discomfort, retrosternal pain, heartburn, acid reflux, anorexia, nausea, vomiting, bloating, fullness, or early satiety.
- Pain in the right or left hypochondrium does not constitute dyspepsia.
- Symptoms may begin at any time during pregnancy, but are usually more frequent or severe in the third trimester.

[Modigliani, 2000]

D

What else might it be?

Pregnancy-related disorders

- Nausea and vomiting of pregnancy
- Hyperemesis gravidarum
- Obstetric cholestasis
- Pre-eclampsia
- HELLP (haemolysis, elevated liver enzymes, and low platelets) syndrome
- Acute fatty liver of pregnancy (late in pregnancy)

Disorders unrelated to pregnancy

- Inflammatory bowel disease
- Peptic ulcer disease
- Pancreatitis
- Biliary colic
- Acute viral hepatitis

[Cappell, 2003]

Complications and prognosis

- Symptoms are usually mild and without complications.
- Symptoms improve rapidly after delivery.

Management issues

- What is first-line treatment? p.630
- What should I do if lifestyle measures fail? p.630
- When should I refer for specialist advice? p.630

What is first-line treatment?

- **Lifestyle modifications should be used first line.** For example:
  - Avoiding precipitating factors such as bending, alcohol, coffee, fatty foods.
  - Eating smaller meals more frequently.
  - Not eating before going to bed (e.g. avoiding meals within 3 hours of going to sleep).
  - Propping up the bed head (lying flat may increase reflux episodes since gravity does not then prevent acid regurgitation).
- Advice on healthy eating and smoking cessation is also important as these have clear health benefits during pregnancy.

What should I do if lifestyle measures fail?

- **Antacids or alginates** should be prescribed first if lifestyle modifications do not control symptoms adequately.
  - Antacids and alginates (used in appropriate doses) are considered to be safe in pregnancy [Weiner and Buhimschi, 2004].
  - They can impair iron absorption, so should be taken at a different time of day from iron supplements. (If possible, they should not be taken within 2 hours before or after iron supplements.)
  - It may be prudent to offer a product with a low sodium content (e.g. co-magaldrox suspension or Algicon® suspension) to women with gestational hypertension or pre-eclampsia, although there is no good evidence to support this hypothesis because of insufficient trial data [Duley, 2004].
- If symptoms are still troublesome despite antacids, consider empirical therapy with ranitidine [Lagace, 1996; Weiner and Buhimschi, 2004]. The usual dose of 150 mg twice a day is used [Schaefer, 2002].
  - Although there are only limited data on its safety during pregnancy, surveillance studies do not suggest that ranitidine presents a major teratogenic risk when used in recommended doses [Cappell, 2003; Weiner and Buhimschi, 2004].
  - Studies of cimetidine in pregnant rodents showed inhibition of testicular descent and genital differentiation [Weiner and Buhimschi, 2004]. Similar effects have not been reported in limited data on human pregnancies.
  - There are insufficient data available on the safety of famotidine or nizatidine in pregnancy.
  - Proton pump inhibitors should be avoided unless they are specifically recommended by a specialist for an individual woman. There is much less experience with the use of these drugs during pregnancy [Nikfar et al, 2002].

Further information on specific drugs and their use in pregnancy is provided by the National Teratology Information Service; tel: 0191 232 1525.

When should I refer for specialist advice?

- If symptoms do not adequately respond to antacids, alginates, or ranitidine.
- If the woman is unable to eat sufficiently because of symptoms.
- If a disorder unrelated to pregnancy is suspected as the cause of symptoms, e.g. peptic ulcer disease, irritable bowel syndrome.
- If the woman presents with any ALARM symptoms, e.g. chronic gastrointestinal bleeding; progressive unintentional weight loss; progressive difficulty swallowing (dysphagia); persistent vomiting.

References

NHS staff in England can link, free of charge, from references to full text journals by clicking on [Full text] on the PRODIGY website.

1. Cappell, M.S. (2003) Gastric and duodenal ulcers during pregnancy. *Gastroenterology Clinics of North America* **32**(1), 263–308.
2. Duley, L. (2004) *Pre-eclampsia and hypertension.* Clinical Evidence. Volume 12. www.clinicalevidence.com [Accessed: 17/06/2005].
3. Lagace, E. (1996) Safety of first trimester exposure to H2 blockers. *Journal of Family Practice* **43**(4), 342–343.
4. Modigliani, R.M. (2000) Gastrointestinal and pancreatic diseases. In: Barron, W.M. and Lindheimer, M.D (Eds.) *Medical disorders during pregnancy.* 3rd edn. London: Mosby. 316–329.
5. Nikfar, S., Abdollahi, M., Moretti, M.E. et al (2002) Use of proton pump inhibitors during pregnancy and rates of major malformations: a meta-analysis. *Digestive Diseases & Sciences* **47**(7), 1526–1529.
6. Schaefer, C. (Ed.) (2002) *Drugs during pregnancy and lactation.* Amsterdam: Elsevier Science.
7. Weiner, C.P. and Buhimschi, C. (Eds.) (2004) *Drugs for pregnant and lactating women.* Philadelphia: Churchill Livingstone.

PRODIGY GUIDANCE

Dyspepsia — proven DU, GU, or NSAID-associated ulcer

Last revised in July 2005
www.prodigy.nhs.uk/guidance.asp?gt=Dyspepsia - proven DU or GU

Applies to people over the age of 16 years

This guidance is based on the National Institute for Clinical Excellence (NICE) guideline on *Dyspepsia* (August 2004).

This guidance covers the management of people with endoscopically determined duodenal ulcer, gastric ulcer, or nonsteroidal anti-inflammatory drug-associated ulcer.
People with uninvestigated symptoms should be managed as people with uninvestigated dyspepsia. See the PRODIGY guidance *Dyspepsia — symptoms (uninvestigated by endoscopy)*.

There is separate PRODIGY guidance for uninvestigated dyspepsia (*Dyspepsia — symptoms uninvestigated by endoscopy*); proven gastro-oesophageal reflux disease (*Dyspepsia — proven GORD*); proven non-ulcer dyspepsia (*Dyspepsia — proven non-ulcer*); and pregnancy-associated dyspepsia (*Dyspepsia — pregnancy-associated*).

Goals

- To provide effective control of dyspeptic symptoms
- To promote healing of the ulcer
- To prevent relapse and complications
- To detect any serious disease, including gastric carcinoma

Contents

Scenarios

- Initial management — proven DU or GU (not NSAID-associated) p.631
- Initial management — proven NSAID-associated ulcer p.633
- *H pylori* positive — proven DU, GU, or NSAID-associated ulcer p.635
- *H pylori* negative — proven DU, GU, or NSAID-associated ulcer p.637
- Symptoms persist or return — proven DU, GU, or NSAID ulcer p.639
- Ulcer healed but continued NSAID use needed p.640

Extended Information, p. 642

Which scenario?

- **Initial management — proven DU or GU (not NSAID-associated):** covers identification of *H pylori* infection in people with an endoscopically proven duodenal (DU) or gastric ulcer (GU), and advice regarding lifestyle factors which may help improve symptoms.
- **Initial management — proven NSAID-associated ulcer:** covers identification of *H pylori* infection in people with an endoscopically proven nonsteroidal anti-inflammatory drug (NSAID)-induced ulcer, and initial management with acid suppression.
- ***H pylori* positive — proven DU, GU, or NSAID-associated ulcer:** covers the management of people with an endoscopically proven DU, GU, or NSAID-induced ulcer who have tested positive for *H pylori* infection.
- ***H pylori* negative — proven DU, GU, or NSAID-associated ulcer:** covers the management of people with an endoscopically proven DU, GU, or NSAID-induced ulcer who have tested negative for *H pylori* infection, or who remain *H pylori positive* after two attempts at eradication. (Note: NICE recommends that, if someone with a peptic ulcer remains *H pylori* positive after two attempts at eradication, they should be managed as if they are *H pylori* negative.)
- **Symptoms persist or return — proven DU, GU, or NSAID ulcer:** covers the management of people with an endoscopically proven DU, GU, or NSAID-induced ulcer whose symptoms persist despite successful *H pylori* eradication.
- **Ulcer healed but continued NSAID use needed:** covers gastroprotection for people who need to continue using an NSAID.

Initial management — proven DU or GU (not NSAID-associated)

Which therapy?

- **Address anxieties** about the significance of symptoms.
- **Review medication which may be causing ulcer** e.g. corticosteroids, bisphosphonates.
- **Test for *Helicobacter pylori* (usually done at endoscopy).**
  - **If *H pylori* test results are available:** see scenarios *H pylori positive* and *H pylori negative* for treatment choices.
  - **If there is a delay in obtaining *H pylori* test results:** offer treatment with a full-dose proton pump inhibitor (PPI) until the results are available.
- **If an *H pylori* test was not done at endoscopy:**
  - Use a carbon-urea breath test or the stool antigen test.
  - **Do not test within** 2 weeks of PPI therapy or within 4 weeks of antibiotic therapy as false-negative results may occur.
- **Give lifestyle advice:** healthy eating, weight loss, stopping smoking.

Practical prescribing points

For further information please see the *Medicines Compendium* (www.medicines.org.uk) or the *British National Formulary* (www.bnf.org).

- **Proton pump inhibitors:** differences between the proton pump inhibitors in clinical efficacy and safety are minimal.
  - Omeprazole is currently cheapest.
  - Omeprazole and esomeprazole occasionally enhance the effects of warfarin and phenytoin. Monitor

carefully if omeprazole or esomeprazole are started or stopped.

H pylori tests

- **Carbon-urea breath tests:** advise people to fast for at least 6 hours before the test and then (for all tests except diabact UBT®) ingest citric acid or orange juice just before the test to slow gastric emptying. (The diabact UBT® tablet contains citric acid.) They then provide two or three breath samples before ingestion of the carbon-13 tablet, and again 30 minutes afterwards (only 10 minutes afterwards for diabact UBT®) by blowing through a straw into a series of glass, screw-top tubes. Breath samples are sent away for analysis by mass spectrometry.
- **Stool antigen tests:** these require the patient to collect a stool sample (at least pea-sized). The sample is then sent to the laboratory for analysis.

Follow-up advice

- **Follow-up is guided by *H pylori* test results.** See scenarios *H pylori positive* and *H pylori negative*.
- **All people with a gastric ulcer** should undergo repeat endoscopy 6–8 weeks after beginning treatment (depending on the size of the lesion) to confirm healing.

Should I refer or investigate?

Refer?

Indications for repeat endoscopy

Note: proton pump inhibitors and H_2-receptor antagonists should be stopped at least 2 weeks before endoscopy. Nonsteroidal anti-inflammatory drug use should also be suspended in all people requiring referral.

- **Consider** managing previously investigated people without new ALARM symptoms according to previous endoscopic findings. However, if an additional diagnosis is suspected, or if the person has been symptom-free for several years before symptoms recur, consider referring for a repeat endoscopy to confirm the diagnosis.
- **All people with a gastric ulcer** should undergo repeat endoscopy 6–8 weeks after beginning treatment (depending on the size of the lesion) to confirm healing.
- **Immediate endoscopy** (i.e. same day) is indicated for people presenting with dyspepsia together with significant acute gastrointestinal bleeding.
- **Anyone who develops ALARM symptoms should be referred urgently for endoscopy, or to a specialist.** That is people with:
  - Chronic gastrointestinal bleeding
  - Progressive unintentional weight loss
  - Progressive difficulty swallowing (dysphagia)
  - Persistent vomiting
  - Iron deficiency anaemia
  - Epigastric mass
  - Suspicious barium meal result
- **People 55 years and over, presenting with unexplained and persistent recent onset dyspepsia** alone, should be referred for urgent endoscopy.
- **Urgent referral to a specialist should also be considered in** a person (of any age) who has unexplained worsening of their dyspepsia and:
  - Barrett's oesophagus
  - Known dysplasia, atrophic gastritis, or intestinal metaplasia
  - Peptic ulcer surgery over 20 years ago
- **If definite dysphagia or odynophagia is present** with a suspicious history or regurgitation, it is appropriate to refer for a barium swallow.

Investigate?

- When referring, consider a full blood count to assist specialist assessment. This should be carried out in accordance with local arrangements.

Patient information leaflets

The following PILs are available at www.prodigy.nhs.uk
- Barium Swallow / Meal / Follow Through
- CORE, Fighting Gut and Liver Disease
- Duodenal Ulcer
- Gastroscopy (Endoscopy)
- Helicobacter Pylori & Stomach Pain
- Stomach (Gastric) Ulcer

Shared decision making

- You have a duodenal or stomach ulcer.
- The cause in most cases is an infection of the gut with a bacterium called *H pylori*.
- You need a test to check for *H pylori*. If it is present it can be cleared with a one week course of treatment.
- Anti-inflammatory medicines such as aspirin or ibuprofen can make ulcers worse. Tell your doctor if you are taking such medicines.

Drug rationale

Drugs not included

- **Esomeprazole** is not licensed for healing benign gastric or duodenal ulcers. It is, however, licensed for healing nonsteroidal anti-inflammatory drug-associated ulcers.
- **H_2-receptor antagonists** (cimetidine, famotidine, nizatidine, and ranitidine) are licensed for healing gastric or duodenal ulcers. However, they are widely considered to be less effective than proton pump inhibitors, due to their smaller acid suppressing effect.

Drugs included

- ***H pylori* tests** are included for use if an *H pylori* test was not undertaken at endoscopy. Prescriptions for carbon-urea breath test kits and an advice note for the stool antigen test are offered.
- **Full-dose proton pump inhibitors** (omeprazole, lansoprazole, pantoprazole, and rabeprazole) are offered for treatment if *H pylori* test results are not yet available.

[NICE, 2004]

Prescriptions

Proton pump inhibitors (if waiting for H pylori test result)

Omeprazole capsules: 20mg once a day
- Age from 16 years onwards
- Omeprazole 20mg capsules. Take one capsule once a day; supply 28 capsules; NHS Cost £12.75.

Omeprazole tablets: 20mg once a day
- Age from 16 years onwards
- Omeprazole 20mg tablets. Take one tablet once a day; supply 28 tablets; NHS Cost £12.75.

Lansoprazole capsules: 30mg each morning

- Age from 16 years onwards
- Lansoprazole 30mg capsules. Take one capsule each morning (on an empty stomach); supply 28 capsules; NHS Cost £23.63.

Lansoprazole orodispersible tablets: 30mg each morning

- Age from 16 years onwards
- Lansoprazole 30mg orodisp tabs. Take one tablet each morning (on an empty stomach); supply 28 tablets; NHS Cost £19.88.

Pantoprazole e/c tablets: 40mg once a day

- Age from 16 years onwards
- Pantoprazole 40mg e/c tablets. Take one tablet once a day; supply 28 tablets; NHS Cost £21.69.

Rabeprazole e/c tablets: 20mg once a day

- Age from 16 years onwards
- Rabeprazole 20mg e/c tabs. Take one tablet once a day; supply 28 tablets; NHS Cost £21.16.

H pylori tests (if not already done during endoscopy)

Advice note: stool antigen test

- Age from 16 years onwards
- The stool antigen test is a way of testing whether you have a current infection with Helicobacter pylori. Put a pea-sized sample of your faeces (stools) into the container provided. Please return this sample to reception so that it can be sent to the laboratory for analysis. Acid suppressing medicines and antibiotics can affect the results of this test. If you have used an acid suppressing medicine within the last 2 weeks, or have taken antibiotics within the last 4 weeks, please check with your doctor before taking this test.

Carbon urea breath test: Diabact UBT H pylori test kit

- Age from 16 years onwards
- Diabact UBT tablet + kit. Follow the instructions given inside this pack; supply 1 kit; NHS Cost £12.75.

Carbon urea breath test: Helicobacter Test Hp-plus test kit

- Age from 16 years onwards
- Helicobacter Test Hp-plus. Follow the instructions given inside this pack; supply 1 kit; NHS Cost £19.75.

Carbon urea breath test: Helicobacter Test INFAI test kit

- Age from 16 years onwards
- Helicobacter test INFAI. Follow the instructions given inside this pack; supply 1 kit; NHS Cost £17.10.

Carbon urea breath test: Pylobactell H pylori test kit

- Age from 16 years onwards
- Pylobactell H pylori test kit. Follow the instructions given inside this pack; supply 1 kit; NHS Cost £20.75.

Initial management — proven NSAID-associated ulcer

Which therapy?

- **Stop the nonsteroidal anti-inflammatory drug** where possible.
- **Address anxieties** about the significance of symptoms.
- **Review other medication which may also be causing the ulcer** e.g. corticosteroids, bisphosphonates.
- **Test for *Helicobacter pylori* (usually done at endoscopy).**
- **Give a 2-month course of full-dose proton pump inhibitor** (PPI) therapy to heal the ulcer. (This should be done *before* eradication therapy is given.)

Afterwards, if the *H pylori* result was positive, eradicate it using triple therapy to reduce the risk of ulcer recurrence.

See scenario *H pylori positive — proven DU, GU, or NSAID-associated ulcer* for prescriptions.

- **Give lifestyle advice:** healthy eating, weight loss, stopping smoking.
- If an *H pylori* test was *not* done at endoscopy, test after the PPI course:
    - Use a carbon-urea breath test or the stool antigen test.
    - **Do not test within** 2 weeks of PPI therapy or within 4 weeks of antibiotic therapy as false-negative results may occur.

Practical prescribing points

For further information please see the *Medicines Compendium* (www.medicines.org.uk) or the *British National Formulary* (www.bnf.org).

- **Proton pump inhibitors:** differences between the proton pump inhibitors in clinical efficacy and safety are minimal.
    - Omeprazole is currently cheapest.
    - Omeprazole and esomeprazole occasionally enhance the effects of warfarin and phenytoin. Monitor carefully if omeprazole or esomeprazole are started or stopped.

H pylori tests

- **Carbon-urea breath tests:** advise people to fast for at least 6 hours before the test and then (for all tests except diabact UBT®) ingest citric acid or orange juice just before the test to slow gastric emptying. (The diabact UBT® tablet contains citric acid.) They then provide two or three breath samples before ingestion of the carbon-13 tablet, and again 30 minutes afterwards (only 10 minutes afterwards for diabact UBT®) by blowing through a straw into a series of glass, screw-top tubes. Breath samples are sent away for analysis by mass spectrometry.
- **Stool antigen tests:** these require the patient to collect a stool sample (at least pea-sized). The sample is then sent to the laboratory for analysis.

Follow-up advice

- **Follow-up is guided by *H pylori* test results.** See scenarios *H pylori positive* and *H pylori negative*.
- **All people with a gastric ulcer** should undergo repeat endoscopy 6–8 weeks after beginning treatment (depending on the size of the lesion) to confirm healing.

Should I refer or investigate?

Refer?

Indications for repeat endoscopy

Note: proton pump inhibitors and H_2-receptor antagonists should be stopped at least 2 weeks before endoscopy. Nonsteroidal anti-inflammatory drug use should also be suspended in all people requiring referral.

- **Consider** managing previously investigated people without new ALARM symptoms according to previous endoscopic findings. However, if an additional diagnosis is suspected, or if the person has been symptom-free for several years before symptoms recur, consider referring for a repeat endoscopy to confirm the diagnosis.
- **All people with a gastric ulcer should undergo repeat** endoscopy 6–8 weeks after beginning treatment (depending on the size of the lesion) to confirm healing.
- **Immediate endoscopy** (i.e. same day) is indicated for people presenting with dyspepsia together with significant acute gastrointestinal bleeding.

- **Anyone who develops ALARM symptoms should be referred urgently for endoscopy, or to a specialist.** That is people with:
  - Chronic gastrointestinal bleeding
  - Progressive unintentional weight loss
  - Progressive difficulty swallowing (dysphagia)
  - Persistent vomiting
  - Iron deficiency anaemia
  - Epigastric mass
  - Suspicious barium meal result
- **People 55 years and over, presenting with unexplained and persistent recent onset dyspepsia** alone, should be referred for urgent endoscopy.
- **Urgent referral to a specialist should also be considered** in a person (of any age) who has unexplained worsening of their dyspepsia and:
  - Barrett's oesophagus
  - Known dysplasia, atrophic gastritis, or intestinal metaplasia
  - Peptic ulcer surgery over 20 years ago
- **If definite dysphagia or odynophagia is present** with a suspicious history or regurgitation, it is appropriate to refer for a barium swallow.

Investigate?

- When referring, consider a full blood count to assist specialist assessment. This should be carried out in accordance with local arrangements.

Patient information leaflets

The following PILs are available at www.prodigy.nhs.uk
- Barium Swallow / Meal / Follow Through
- CORE, Fighting Gut and Liver Disease
- Duodenal Ulcer
- Gastroscopy (Endoscopy)
- Helicobacter Pylori & Stomach Pain
- Stomach (Gastric) Ulcer

Shared decision making

- You have a duodenal or stomach ulcer.
- Your anti-inflammatory medicine can cause ulcers or make them worse. If possible, this medicine should be stopped.
- You need a test for the bacterium called *H pylori* — a common cause of ulcers. If it is present it can be cleared with a one-week course of treatment.
- Take an eight-week course of an acid-suppressing medicine to heal the ulcer.
- If you are infected with *H pylori* you should have treatment to clear it after the ulcer has healed. This should help prevent a further ulcer developing.
- If you have a stomach ulcer, you will need a repeat endoscopy in about 6–8 weeks to check that it has healed.

Drug rationale

Drugs not included

- **Pantoprazole and rabeprazole** are not licensed for healing nonsteroidal anti-inflammatory drug (NSAID)-associated peptic ulcers.
- **Misoprostol** (at full dose) is an alternative to a proton pump inhibitor (PPI) to heal an NSAID-associated ulcer. However it is widely accepted that misoprostol is less well tolerated than PPIs, and it is therefore not included.
- **H_2-receptor antagonists** (cimetidine, nizatidine, and ranitidine) are licensed for healing NSAID-associated gastric or duodenal ulcers. However, they are widely considered to be less effective than PPIs, due to their smaller acid-suppressing effect. Famotidine is not licensed for this indication.

Drugs included

- ***H pylori* tests** are included for use if an *H pylori* test was not undertaken at endoscopy. Prescriptions for carbon-urea breath test kits and an advice note for the stool antigen test are offered.
- **Full-dose proton pump inhibitors** (omeprazole, lansoprazole, and esomeprazole) are included for healing nonsteroidal anti-inflammatory drug (NSAID)-associated peptic ulcers.

[NICE, 2004]

Prescriptions

Proton pump inhibitors: healing dose for 8 weeks

Omeprazole capsules: 20mg once a day
- Age from 16 years onwards
- Omeprazole 20mg capsules. Take one capsule once a day for 8 weeks; supply 56 capsules; NHS Cost £25.50.

Omeprazole tablets: 20mg once a day
- Age from 16 years onwards
- Omeprazole 20mg tablets. Take one tablet once a day for 8 weeks; supply 56 tablets; NHS Cost £25.50.

Lansoprazole capsules: 30mg each morning
- Age from 16 years onwards
- Lansoprazole 30mg capsules. Take one capsule each morning (on an empty stomach) for 8 weeks; supply 56 capsules; NHS Cost £47.26.

Lansoprazole orodispersible tablets: 30mg each morning
- Age from 16 years onwards
- Lansoprazole 30mg orodisp tabs. Take one tablet each morning (on an empty stomach) for 8 weeks; supply 56 tablets; NHS Cost £39.76.

Esomeprazole tablets: 20mg once a day
- Age from 16 years onwards
- Esomeprazole 20mg tablets. Take one tablet once a day for 8 weeks; supply 56 tablets; NHS Cost £37.00.

H pylori tests (if not already done during endoscopy)

Advice note: stool antigen test
- Age from 16 years onwards
- The stool antigen test is a way of testing whether you have a current infection with Helicobacter pylori. Put a pea-sized sample of your faeces (stools) into the container provided. Please return this sample to reception so that it can be sent to the laboratory for analysis. Acid suppressing medicines and antibiotics can affect the results of this test. If you have used an acid suppressing medicine within the last 2 weeks, or have taken antibiotics within the last 4 weeks, please check with your doctor before taking this test.

Carbon urea breath test: Diabact UBT H pylori test kit
- Age from 16 years onwards
- Diabact UBT tablet + kit. Follow the instructions given inside this pack; supply 1 kit; NHS Cost £12.75.

Carbon urea breath test: Helicobacter Test Hp-plus test kit
- Age from 16 years onwards
- Helicobacter Test Hp-plus. Follow the instructions given inside this pack; supply 1 kit; NHS Cost £19.75.

Carbon urea breath test: Helicobacter Test INFAI test kit
- Age from 16 years onwards
- Helicobacter test INFAI. Follow the instructions given inside this pack; supply 1 kit; NHS Cost £17.10.

'arbon urea breath test: Pylobactell H pylori test kit
Age from 16 years onwards
Pylobactell H pylori test kit. Follow the instructions given inside this pack; supply 1 kit; NHS Cost £20.75.

H pylori positive — proven DU, GU, or NSAID-associated ulcer

Which therapy?

Give a 1-week eradication course if the *H pylori* test is positive.
Note: NSAID-associated ulcers should be healed with a 2-month course of a proton pump inhibitor (PPI) before eradication is undertaken. See scenario *Initial management — proven NSAID-associated ulcer*.
First-line triple therapy:

- Use a PPI plus amoxicillin 1 g and clarithromycin 500 mg, all given twice a day.
- For people with penicillin hypersensitivity: use a PPI plus metronidazole 400 mg and clarithromycin 250 mg, all given twice a day.

If clarithromycin or metronidazole has previously been taken, do not use that antibiotic in the triple therapy regimen. Choose an alternative from:

- Amoxicillin, clarithromycin, metronidazole, or oxytetracycline

Treatment failure:

- **Use quadruple therapy** (a PPI twice a day, bismuth 120 mg four times a day, metronidazole 500 mg three times a day and oxytetracycline 500 mg four times a day).
- If quadruple therapy is not tolerated, consider using a triple-therapy regimen that contains antibiotics that have not been used before.

Practical prescribing points

For further information please see the *Medicines Compendium* (www.medicines.org.uk) or the *British National Formulary* (www.bnf.org).
Remind people that it is important to complete the course and warn about adverse effects.
Advise people taking metronidazole to avoid alcohol for the duration of the course and for at least 48 hours afterwards, because of the possibility of a disulfiram-like (Antabuse) reaction.
Advise people taking bismuth that this may darken the tongue and blacken the faeces.
Clarithromycin inhibits the metabolism of other drugs and can prolong the QT interval. Check drug interactions before prescribing.
Proton pump inhibitors: differences between the proton pump inhibitors in clinical efficacy and safety are minimal.

- Omeprazole is currently cheapest.
- Omeprazole and esomeprazole occasionally enhance the effects of warfarin and phenytoin. Monitor carefully if omeprazole or esomeprazole are started or stopped.

Follow-up advice

All people with a gastric ulcer:

- Should undergo repeat endoscopy 6–8 weeks after beginning treatment (depending on the size of the lesion) to confirm healing.
- Should be re-tested for *H pylori* (using a carbon-urea breath test) 6–8 weeks after eradication therapy to confirm that eradication has been successful.

- **People with a duodenal ulcer** only need to be re-tested to confirm *H pylori* eradication if there was no response to eradication therapy, or if symptoms responded but have now relapsed.
- **For people with a nonsteroidal anti-inflammatory drug (NSAID)-associated ulcer,** the need for repeat endoscopy and *H pylori* re-testing will depend on whether the NSAID induced a gastric or a duodenal ulcer.
- **After two attempts to eradicate *H pylori*, there is no need to re-test again.**
  - If symptoms respond to eradication treatment, then no further course of treatment is needed.
  - If symptoms recur following two attempts to eradicate *H pylori*, the person should be managed as if they are *H pylori* negative. See scenario *Symptoms persist or return — proven DU, GU, or NSAID ulcer*.

D

Should I refer or investigate?

Refer?

Indications for repeat endoscopy

Note: proton pump inhibitors and H_2-receptor antagonists should be stopped at least 2 weeks before endoscopy. Nonsteroidal anti-inflammatory drug use should also be suspended in all people requiring referral.

- **Consider** managing previously investigated people without new ALARM symptoms according to previous endoscopic findings. However, if an additional diagnosis is suspected, or if the person has been symptom-free for several years before symptoms recur, consider referring for a repeat endoscopy to confirm the diagnosis.
- **All people with a gastric ulcer** should undergo repeat endoscopy 6–8 weeks after beginning treatment (depending on the size of the lesion) to confirm healing.
- **Immediate endoscopy** (i.e. same day) is indicated for people presenting with dyspepsia together with significant acute gastrointestinal bleeding.
- **Anyone who develops ALARM symptoms should be referred urgently for endoscopy, or to a specialist.** That is people with:
  - Chronic gastrointestinal bleeding
  - Progressive unintentional weight loss
  - Progressive difficulty swallowing (dysphagia)
  - Persistent vomiting
  - Iron deficiency anaemia
  - Epigastric mass
  - Suspicious barium meal result
- **People 55 years and over, presenting with unexplained and persistent recent onset dyspepsia** alone, should be referred for urgent endoscopy.
- **Urgent referral to a specialist should also be considered** in a person (of any age) who has unexplained worsening of their dyspepsia and:
  - Barrett's oesophagus
  - Known dysplasia, atrophic gastritis, or intestinal metaplasia
  - Peptic ulcer surgery over 20 years ago
- **If definite dysphagia or odynophagia is present** with a suspicious history or regurgitation, it is appropriate to refer for a barium swallow.

Investigate?

- When referring, consider a full blood count to assist specialist assessment. This should be carried out in accordance with local arrangements.

Patient information leaflets

The following PILs are available at www.prodigy.nhs.uk

- Barium Swallow / Meal / Follow Through
- CORE, Fighting Gut and Liver Disease
- Duodenal Ulcer
- Gastroscopy (Endoscopy)
- Helicobacter Pylori & Stomach Pain
- Stomach (Gastric) Ulcer

Shared decision making

- You are infected with the bacteria *H pylori* — the likely cause of your ulcer.
- It can usually be cleared with a one-week course of treatment of:
  - An acid-suppressing medicine, plus
  - Two antibiotics. Tell your doctor if you are allergic to any antibiotic. Some people develop side effects with antibiotics. The most common are diarrhoea and feeling sick.
  - It is really important to take the whole course of treatment properly or it may not work.
- See a doctor if symptoms persist or return after finishing treatment.
- If you have a stomach ulcer, even if symptoms go you will need a repeat endoscopy in about 6–8 weeks to check that it has healed. You will also need a repeat test for *H pylori* to check it has gone.
- If you had a duodenal ulcer, you don't need repeat tests if symptoms go with treatment.

Drug rationale

Drugs not included

- **Dual therapies** for *Helicobacter pylori* eradication with proton pump inhibitors (PPIs) and antibiotics are not recommended [NICE, 2004].
- **Triple therapies using ranitidine bismuth citrate** are not recommended because evidence of efficacy is less strong than for PPI triple regimens [DTB, 1996; MeReC, 1997].
- **Two-week triple therapy** is no more effective than one-week triple therapy [NICE, 2004]. Longer regimens also cost more and have a longer duration of minor adverse effects.
- **Triple therapy using a PPI plus amoxicillin and metronidazole** is no longer recommended [NICE, 2004]. Pooled data from four randomized, controlled trials have demonstrated that it is less effective than either of the two triple therapies that contain clarithromycin.

Drugs included

- **Triple therapy is recommended for first-line eradication therapy.** NICE recommends the following one-week triple therapy regimens:
  - A 'PAC' regimen (a PPI plus amoxicillin 1 g and clarithromycin 500 mg, all given twice a day)
  - Or (for people with penicillin hypersensitivity) a 'PCM' regimen (a PPI plus metronidazole 400 mg and clarithromycin 250 mg, all given twice a day)
  - Pooled data for the recommended PAC and PCM regimens show no statistically significant difference in eradication rates: 82% for PAC, and 82.6% for PCM.
- Note: the dose of clarithromycin in the Helimet® packs (containing lansoprazole, metronidazole, and clarithromycin) is higher than that recommended by NICE for a PCM regimen. However, it is included since some people find the single pack presentation helpful for compliance.
- **Quadruple therapy is recommended for second-line eradication therapy** [Malfertheiner et al, 2002]. It comprises a PPI twice a day, bismuth 120 mg four times a day, metronidazole 500 mg three times a day, and oxytetracycline 500 mg four times a day. Therefore, it is also suitable for people with penicillin hypersensitivity.

Prescriptions

1-week triple therapy: PPI + amoxicillin + clarithromycin

Omeprazole + amoxicillin + clarithromycin

- Age from 16 years onwards
- Amoxicillin 500mg capsules. Take two capsules twice a day for 7 days; supply 28 capsules; NHS Cost £1.44.
- Clarithromycin 500mg tablets. Take one tablet twice a day for 7 days; supply 14 tablets; NHS Cost £21.90.
- Omeprazole 20mg capsules. Take one capsule twice a day for 7 days; supply 14 capsules; NHS Cost £6.38.

Lansoprazole + amoxicillin + clarithromycin

- Age from 16 years onwards
- Lansoprazole 30mg capsules. Take one capsule twice a day (on an empty stomach) for 7 days; supply 14 capsules; NHS Cost £11.82.
- Clarithromycin 500mg tablets. Take one tablet twice a day for 7 days; supply 14 tablets; NHS Cost £21.90.
- Amoxicillin 500mg capsules. Take two capsules twice a day for 7 days; supply 28 capsules; NHS Cost £1.44.

HeliClear triple pack

- Age from 16 years onwards
- HeliClear triple pack. Take one lansoprazole capsule, one clarithromycin tablet, and two amoxicillin capsules twice a day for 7 days; supply 1 triple pack; NHS Cost £35.01.

Pantoprazole + amoxicillin + clarithromycin

- Age from 16 years onwards
- Pantoprazole 40mg e/c tablets. Take one tablet twice a day for 7 days; supply 14 tablets; NHS Cost £10.85.
- Amoxicillin 500mg capsules. Take two capsules twice a day for 7 days; supply 28 capsules; NHS Cost £1.44.
- Clarithromycin 500mg tablets. Take one tablet twice a day for 7 days; supply 14 tablets; NHS Cost £21.90.

Rabeprazole + amoxicillin + clarithromycin

- Age from 16 years onwards
- Amoxicillin 500mg capsules. Take two capsules twice a day for 7 days; supply 28 capsules; NHS Cost £1.44.
- Clarithromycin 500mg tablets. Take one tablet twice a day for 7 days; supply 14 tablets; NHS Cost £21.90.
- Rabeprazole 20mg e/c tabs. Take one tablet twice a day for 7 days; supply 14 tablets; NHS Cost £10.58.

Esomeprazole + amoxicillin + clarithromycin

- Age from 16 years onwards
- Amoxicillin 500mg capsules. Take two capsules twice a day for 7 days; supply 28 capsules; NHS Cost £1.44.
- Clarithromycin 500mg tablets. Take one tablet twice a day for 7 days; supply 14 tablets; NHS Cost £21.90.
- Esomeprazole 20mg tablets. Take one tablet twice a day for 7 days; supply 14 tablets; NHS Cost £9.25.

1-week triple therapy: PPI + metronidazole + clarithromycin

Omeprazole + metronidazole + clarithromycin

- Age from 16 years onwards
- Omeprazole 20mg capsules. Take one capsule twice a day for 7 days; supply 14 capsules; NHS Cost £6.38.
- Metronidazole 400mg tablets. Take one tablet twice a day for 7 days; supply 14 tablets; NHS Cost £1.03.
- Clarithromycin 250mg tablets. Take one tablet twice a day for 7 days; supply 14 tablets; NHS Cost £10.94.

ansoprazole + metronidazole + clarithromycin
- Age from 16 years onwards
- Lansoprazole 30mg capsules. Take one capsule twice a day (on an empty stomach) for 7 days; supply 14 capsules; NHS Cost £11.82.
- Metronidazole 400mg tablets. Take one tablet twice a day for 7 days; supply 14 tablets; NHS Cost £1.03.
- Clarithromycin 250mg tablets. Take one tablet twice a day for 7 days; supply 14 tablets; NHS Cost £10.94.

eliMet triple pack
- Age from 16 years onwards
- HeliMet triple pack. Take one lansoprazole capsule, one clarithromycin tablet and one metronidazole tablet twice a day for 7 days; supply 1 pack; NHS Cost £35.40.

antoprazole + metronidazole + clarithromycin
- Age from 16 years onwards
- Pantoprazole 40mg e/c tablets. Take one tablet twice a day for 7 days; supply 14 tablets; NHS Cost £10.85.
- Metronidazole 400mg tablets. Take one tablet twice a day for 7 days; supply 14 tablets; NHS Cost £1.03.
- Clarithromycin 250mg tablets. Take one tablet twice a day for 7 days; supply 14 tablets; NHS Cost £10.94.

abeprazole + metronidazole + clarithromycin
- Age from 16 years onwards
- Rabeprazole 20mg e/c tabs. Take one tablet twice a day for 7 days; supply 14 tablets; NHS Cost £10.58.
- Metronidazole 400mg tablets. Take one tablet twice a day for 7 days; supply 14 tablets; NHS Cost £1.03.
- Clarithromycin 250mg tablets. Take one tablet twice a day for 7 days; supply 14 tablets; NHS Cost £10.94.

someprazole + metronidazole + clarithromycin
- Age from 16 years onwards
- Esomeprazole 20mg tablets. Take one tablet twice a day for 7 days; supply 14 tablets; NHS Cost £9.25.
- Metronidazole 400mg tablets. Take one tablet twice a day for 7 days; supply 14 tablets; NHS Cost £1.03.
- Clarithromycin 250mg tablets. Take one tablet twice a day for 7 days; supply 14 tablets; NHS Cost £10.94.

Treatment failure: 1-week quadruple therapy

meprazole + bismuth + metronidazole + oxytetracycline
- Age from 16 years onwards
- Omeprazole 20mg capsules. Take one capsule twice a day for 7 days; supply 14 capsules; NHS Cost £6.38.
- Bismuth chelate 120mg tablets. Take one tablet four times a day for 7 days. (Take one tab 30 mins before breakfast, lunch and the evening meal, and 2 hours after the evening meal.); supply 28 tablets; NHS Cost £1.82.
- Metronidazole 500mg tablets. Take one tablet three times a day for 7 days; supply 21 tablets; NHS Cost £3.50.
- Oxytetracycline 250mg tablets. Take two tablets four times a day for 7 days; supply 56 tablets; NHS Cost £1.62.

ansoprazole + bismuth + metronidazole + xytetracycline
- Age from 16 years onwards
- Lansoprazole 30mg capsules. Take one capsule twice a day for 7 days; supply 14 capsules; NHS Cost £11.82.
- Bismuth chelate 120mg tablets. Take one tablet four times a day for 7 days. (Take one tab 30 mins before breakfast, lunch and the evening meal, and 2 hours after the evening meal.); supply 28 tablets; NHS Cost £1.82.
- Metronidazole 500mg tablets. Take one tablet three times a day for 7 days; supply 21 tablets; NHS Cost £3.50.
- Oxytetracycline 250mg tablets. Take two tablets four times a day for 7 days; supply 56 tablets; NHS Cost £1.62.

Pantoprazole + bismuth + metronidazole + oxytetracycline
- Age from 16 years onwards
- Pantoprazole 40mg e/c tablets. Take one tablet twice a day for 7 days; supply 14 tablets; NHS Cost £10.85.
- Bismuth chelate 120mg tablets. Take one tablet four times a day for 7 days. (Take one tab 30 mins before breakfast, lunch and the evening meal, and 2 hours after the evening meal.); supply 28 tablets; NHS Cost £1.82.
- Metronidazole 500mg tablets. Take one tablet three times a day for 7 days; supply 21 tablets; NHS Cost £3.50.
- Oxytetracycline 250mg tablets. Take two tablets four times a day for 7 days; supply 56 tablets; NHS Cost £1.62.

Rabeprazole + bismuth + metronidazole + oxytetracycline
- Age from 16 years onwards
- Rabeprazole 20mg e/c tabs. Take one tablet twice a day for 7 days; supply 14 tablets; NHS Cost £10.58.
- Bismuth chelate 120mg tablets. Take one tablet four times a day for 7 days. (Take one tab 30 mins before breakfast, lunch and the evening meal, and 2 hours after the evening meal.); supply 28 tablets; NHS Cost £1.82.
- Metronidazole 500mg tablets. Take one tablet three times a day for 7 days; supply 21 tablets; NHS Cost £3.50.
- Oxytetracycline 250mg tablets. Take two tablets four times a day for 7 days; supply 56 tablets; NHS Cost £1.62.

Esomeprazole + bismuth + metronidazole + oxytetracycline
- Age from 16 years onwards
- Esomeprazole 20mg tablets. Take one tablet twice a day for 7 days; supply 14 tablets; NHS Cost £9.25.
- Bismuth chelate 120mg tablets. Take one tablet four times a day for 7 days. (Take one tab 30 mins before breakfast, lunch and the evening meal, and 2 hours after the evening meal.); supply 28 tablets; NHS Cost £1.82.
- Metronidazole 500mg tablets. Take one tablet three times a day for 7 days; supply 21 tablets; NHS Cost £3.50.
- Oxytetracycline 250mg tablets. Take two tablets four times a day for 7 days; supply 56 tablets; NHS Cost £1.62.

H pylori negative — proven DU, GU, or NSAID-associated ulcer

Which therapy?

- **Negative *H pylori* test at ulcer diagnosis:** offer a course of a full-dose proton pump inhibitor for 1–2 months. (Note: NSAID-associated ulcers should have 2 months treatment.)
- **Negative *H pylori* test after eradication therapy:**
  - If symptoms have responded to eradication treatment, then no further course of treatment is needed.
  - If symptoms recur but the *H pylori* re-test was negative, see scenario *Symptoms persist or return — proven DU, GU, or NSAID ulcer*.
  - Note: re-testing is required for all gastric ulcers, but only for duodenal ulcers that relapse or do not respond to eradication therapy.)

Practical prescribing points

For further information please see the *Medicines Compendium* (www.medicines.org.uk) or the *British National Formulary* (www.bnf.org).

- **Proton pump inhibitors:** differences between the proton pump inhibitors in clinical efficacy and safety are minimal.
  - Omeprazole is currently cheapest.
  - Omeprazole and esomeprazole occasionally enhance the effects of warfarin and phenytoin. Monitor carefully if omeprazole or esomeprazole are started or stopped.

Follow-up advice

- **If symptoms respond** to treatment, then no further course of treatment is needed.
- **If symptoms recur** but the *H pylori* re-test was negative, see scenario *Symptoms persist or return — proven DU, GU, or NSAID ulcer*.
- **All people with a gastric ulcer** should undergo repeat endoscopy 6–8 weeks after beginning treatment (depending on the size of the lesion) to confirm healing.

Should I refer or investigate?

Refer?

Indications for repeat endoscopy

Note: proton pump inhibitors and H_2-receptor antagonists should be stopped at least 2 weeks before endoscopy. Nonsteroidal anti-inflammatory drug use should also be suspended in all people requiring referral.

- **Consider** managing previously investigated people without new ALARM symptoms according to previous endoscopic findings. However, if an additional diagnosis is suspected, or if the person has been symptom-free for several years before symptoms recur, consider referring for a repeat endoscopy to confirm the diagnosis.
- **All people with a gastric ulcer** should undergo repeat endoscopy 6–8 weeks after beginning treatment (depending on the size of the lesion) to confirm healing.
- **Immediate endoscopy** (i.e. same day) is indicated for people presenting with dyspepsia together with significant acute gastrointestinal bleeding.
- **Anyone who develops ALARM symptoms should be referred urgently for endoscopy, or to a specialist.** That is people with:
  - Chronic gastrointestinal bleeding
  - Progressive unintentional weight loss
  - Progressive difficulty swallowing (dysphagia)
  - Persistent vomiting
  - Iron deficiency anaemia
  - Epigastric mass
  - Suspicious barium meal result
- **People 55 years and over, presenting with unexplained and persistent recent onset dyspepsia** alone, should be referred for urgent endoscopy.
- **Urgent referral to a specialist should also be considered** in a person (of any age) who has unexplained worsening of their dyspepsia and:
  - Barrett's oesophagus
  - Known dysplasia, atrophic gastritis, or intestinal metaplasia
  - Peptic ulcer surgery over 20 years ago
- **If definite dysphagia or odynophagia is present** with a suspicious history or regurgitation, it is appropriate to refer for a barium swallow.

Investigate?

- When referring, consider a full blood count to assist specialist assessment. This should be carried out in accordance with local arrangements.

Patient information leaflets

The following PILs are available at www.prodigy.nhs.uk

- Barium Swallow / Meal / Follow Through
- CORE, Fighting Gut and Liver Disease
- Duodenal Ulcer
- Gastroscopy (Endoscopy)
- Stomach (Gastric) Ulcer

Shared decision making

- You have a duodenal or stomach ulcer.
- You are not infected with *H pylori* (a common cause of ulcers).
- Treatment for the ulcer is a 1- to 2-month course of acid-suppressing medication. This will normally allow the ulcer to heal.
- See a doctor if symptoms persist or return after finishing treatment.
- If you have a stomach ulcer, even if symptoms go you will need a repeat endoscopy in about 6–8 weeks to check that it has healed.
- If you have a duodenal ulcer, you don't need repeat tests if symptoms go with treatment.

Drug rationale

Drugs not included

- **Misoprostol** (at full dose) is an alternative to a proton pump inhibitor (PPI) to heal an nonsteroidal anti-inflammatory drug (NSAID)-associated ulcer. However, it is widely accepted that misoprostol is less well tolerated than PPIs, and it is therefore not included.
- **H_2-receptor antagonists** (cimetidine, famotidine, nizatidine, and ranitidine) are licensed for healing duodenal ulcers and gastric ulcers. However, they are widely considered to be less effective than PPIs, due to their smaller acid-suppressing effect. Unlike the other H_2 receptor antagonists, famotidine is not licensed for healing NSAID-associated ulcers.

Drugs included

- **Full-dose PPIs** are included. Omeprazole, lansoprazole, pantoprazole, and rabeprazole (but not esomeprazole) are licensed for healing benign duodenal ulcers and gastric ulcers. Only omeprazole, lansoprazole, and esomeprazole are licensed for healing NSAID-associated peptic ulcers.

Prescriptions

Proton pump inhibitors: healing dose for 4 to 8 weeks

Omeprazole capsules: 20mg once a day

- Age from 16 years onwards
- Omeprazole 20mg capsules. Take one capsule once a day; supply 28 capsules; NHS Cost £12.75.

Omeprazole tablets: 20mg once a day

- Age from 16 years onwards
- Omeprazole 20mg tablets. Take one tablet once a day; supply 28 tablets; NHS Cost £12.75.

Lansoprazole capsules: 30mg each morning

- Age from 16 years onwards
- Lansoprazole 30mg capsules. Take one capsule each morning (on an empty stomach); supply 28 capsules; NHS Cost £23.63.

ansoprazole orodispersible tablets: 30mg each morning
Age from 16 years onwards
Lansoprazole 30mg orodisp tabs. Take one tablet each morning (on an empty stomach); supply 28 tablets; NHS Cost £19.88.

'antoprazole e/c tablets: 40mg once a day
Age from 16 years onwards
Pantoprazole 40mg e/c tablets. Take one tablet once a day; supply 28 tablets; NHS Cost £21.69.

Rabeprazole e/c tablets: 20mg once a day
Age from 16 years onwards
Rabeprazole 20mg e/c tabs. Take one tablet once a day; supply 28 tablets; NHS Cost £21.16.

Esomeprazole tablets: 20mg once a day
Age from 16 years onwards
Esomeprazole 20mg tablets. Take one tablet once a day; supply 28 tablets; NHS Cost £18.50.

Symptoms persist or return — proven DU, GU, or NSAID ulcer

Which therapy?

Symptoms persist

Symptoms usually resolve once *H pylori* has been eradicated and the ulcer has healed.

- **Gastric ulcer:** repeat endoscopy and re-test for *H pylori* to confirm healing and eradication.
- **Duodenal ulcer:** *H pylori* re-testing is only indicated if there was no response to eradication, or if symptoms responded but have now relapsed.
- **There is no need to re-test for *H pylori* after two attempts at eradication.**
- For situations where referral is indicated see *Should I refer or investigate?*

If symptoms still persist (e.g. *H pylori* negative or completed two attempts at eradication):

- Offer a proton pump inhibitor (PPI) with a limited number of repeat prescriptions.
- Encourage people to use the lowest dose required to control symptoms.
- Discuss using the treatment on an 'on-demand' basis (i.e. waiting for symptoms to develop before taking treatment).

Duodenal ulcer: exclude other causes if there is no response to acid suppression therapy, including:

- Non-compliance with treatment.
- Possible malignancy.
- Failure to detect *H pylori* infection due to recent PPI or antibiotic therapy.
- Inadequate testing or simple misclassification.
- Surreptitious or inadvertent nonsteroidal anti-inflammatory drug (NSAID) or aspirin use.
- Ulceration due to ingestion of other drugs (e.g. bisphosphonates, corticosteroids. Selective serotonin re-uptake inhibitors [SSRIs] have also been implicated in gastrointestinal bleeding).
- Rare causes such as Zollinger-Ellison syndrome and Crohn's disease.

- **Gastric ulcer:** if the repeat endoscopy shows that the ulcer has not healed, refer to a specialist in secondary care for further management.
- **NSAID-associated ulcer:**
  - Manage as for a duodenal ulcer or a gastric ulcer.
  - If the NSAID must be continued, see scenario *Ulcer healed but continued NSAID use needed.*

Symptoms return

- Consider managing previously investigated people without new ALARM signs according to previous endoscopic findings.
- However, if an additional diagnosis is suspected, or if the person has been symptom-free for several years before symptoms recur, consider referring for a repeat endoscopy to confirm the diagnosis.

Practical prescribing points

For further information please see the *Medicines Compendium* (www.medicines.org.uk) or the *British National Formulary* (www.bnf.org).

- **Proton pump inhibitors:** differences between the proton pump inhibitors in clinical efficacy and safety are minimal. Omeprazole capsules are currently cheapest.

Follow-up advice

- A small number of people with chronic, refractory peptic ulceration may need maintenance acid suppression.
- In some people with an inadequate response to therapy it may become appropriate to refer to a specialist for a second opinion.
- All people with dyspepsia requiring long-term treatment should have an annual review of their condition, and lifestyle advice should be reinforced.

Should I refer or investigate?

Refer?

Indications for repeat endoscopy

Note: proton pump inhibitors and H_2-receptor antagonists should be stopped at least 2 weeks before endoscopy. Nonsteroidal anti-inflammatory drug use should also be suspended in all people requiring referral.

- **Consider** managing previously investigated people without new ALARM symptoms according to previous endoscopic findings. However, if an additional diagnosis is suspected, or if the person has been symptom-free for several years before symptoms recur, consider referring for a repeat endoscopy to confirm the diagnosis.
- **Immediate endoscopy** (i.e. same day) is indicated for people presenting with dyspepsia together with significant acute gastrointestinal bleeding.
- **Anyone who develops ALARM symptoms should be referred urgently for endoscopy, or to a specialist.** That is people with:
  - Chronic gastrointestinal bleeding
  - Progressive unintentional weight loss
  - Progressive difficulty swallowing (dysphagia)
  - Persistent vomiting
  - Iron deficiency anaemia
  - Epigastric mass
  - Suspicious barium meal result
- **People 55 years and over, presenting with unexplained and persistent recent onset dyspepsia** alone, should be referred for urgent endoscopy.
- **Urgent referral to a specialist should also be considered** in a person (of any age) who has unexplained worsening of their dyspepsia and:
  - Barrett's oesophagus
  - Known dysplasia, atrophic gastritis, or intestinal metaplasia
  - Peptic ulcer surgery over 20 years ago
- **If definite dysphagia or odynophagia is present** with a suspicious history or regurgitation, it is appropriate to refer for a barium swallow.

Investigate?

- When referring, consider a full blood count to assist specialist assessment. This should be carried out in accordance with local arrangements.

Patient information leaflets

The following PILs are available at www.prodigy.nhs.uk

- Barium Swallow / Meal / Follow Through
- CORE, Fighting Gut and Liver Disease
- Duodenal Ulcer
- Gastroscopy (Endoscopy)
- Stomach (Gastric) Ulcer

D

Shared decision making

- If your symptoms return after treatment for an ulcer has finished then options to consider are:
  - A daily dose of an acid-suppressing medicine. Start at full dose. Once symptoms have eased again, gradually reduce to the lowest dose needed to control symptoms *or*
  - Short courses of an acid-suppressing medicine just when symptoms occur.
- Depending on your circumstances, type of ulcer, cause of the ulcer, and other symptoms, your doctor may also suggest further tests.

Drug rationale

Drugs not included

- **H_2-receptor antagonists** are not one of the therapies recommended by NICE for managing persistent symptoms in people with a gastric or duodenal ulcer. However, they are appropriate for people who have returned to self-care.
- **Antacids and alginates** are not one of the therapies recommended by NICE for managing persistent symptoms in people with a gastric or duodenal ulcer. However, they are appropriate for people who have returned to self-care.

Drugs included

- **Proton pump inhibitors (PPIs):** PPIs are an effective treatment for dyspepsia symptoms. The lowest effective dose of a PPI should be used as 'on-demand' therapy or as a maintenance dose. Note: when undertaking meta-analysis of dose-related effects, NICE classed esomeprazole 20 mg as a full dose equivalent to omeprazole 20 mg.

Prescriptions

Proton pump inhibitors: full dose

Omeprazole capsules: 20mg once a day

- Age from 16 years onwards
- Omeprazole 20mg capsules. Take one capsule once a day; supply 28 capsules; NHS Cost £12.75.

Omeprazole tablets: 20mg once a day

- Age from 16 years onwards
- Omeprazole 20mg tablets. Take one tablet once a day; supply 28 tablets; NHS Cost £12.75.

Lansoprazole capsules: 30mg each morning

- Age from 16 years onwards
- Lansoprazole 30mg capsules. Take one capsule each morning (on an empty stomach); supply 28 capsules; NHS Cost £23.63.

Lansoprazole orodispersible tablets: 30mg each morning

- Age from 16 years onwards
- Lansoprazole 30mg orodisp tabs. Take one tablet each morning (on an empty stomach); supply 28 tablets; NHS Cost £19.88.

Pantoprazole e/c tablets: 40mg once a day

- Age from 16 years onwards
- Pantoprazole 40mg e/c tablets. Take one tablet once a day; supply 28 tablets; NHS Cost £21.69.

Rabeprazole e/c tablets: 20mg once a day

- Age from 16 years onwards
- Rabeprazole 20mg e/c tabs. Take one tablet once a day; supply 28 tablets; NHS Cost £21.16.

Esomeprazole tablets: 20mg once a day

- Age from 16 years onwards
- Esomeprazole 20mg tablets. Take one tablet once a day; supply 28 tablets; NHS Cost £18.50.

Proton pump inhibitors: low dose or on-demand

Omeprazole capsules: 10mg once a day

- Age from 16 years onwards
- Omeprazole 10mg capsules. Take one capsule once a day. If you are able to, try to take one capsule once a day only when your symptoms recur; supply 28 capsules; NHS Cost £7.72.

Omeprazole tablets: 10mg once a day

- Age from 16 years onwards
- Omeprazole 10mg tablets. Take one tablet once a day. If you are able to, try to take one tablet once a day only when your symptoms recur; supply 28 tablets; NHS Cost £11.40.

Lansoprazole capsules: 15mg each morning

- Age from 16 years onwards
- Lansoprazole 15mg capsules. Take one capsule each morning (on an empty stomach). If you are able to, try to take one capsule each morning only when your symptoms recur; supply 28 capsules; NHS Cost £12.92.

Lansoprazole orodispersible tablets: 15mg each morning

- Age from 16 years onwards
- Lansoprazole 15mg orodisp tabs. Take one tablet each morning (on an empty stomach). If you are able to, try to take one tablet each morning only when your symptoms recur; supply 28 tablets; NHS Cost £10.86.

Pantoprazole e/c tablets: 20mg once a day

- Age from 16 years onwards
- Pantoprazole 20mg e/c tablets. Take one tablet once a day. If you are able to, try to take one tablet once a day only when your symptoms recur; supply 28 tablets; NHS Cost £12.31.

Rabeprazole e/c tablets: 10mg once a day

- Age from 16 years onwards
- Rabeprazole 10mg e/c tabs. Take one tablet once a day. If you are able to, try to take one tablet once a day only when your symptoms recur; supply 28 tablets; NHS Cost £11.56.

Esomeprazole e/c tablets: 20mg once a day

- Age from 16 years onwards
- Esomeprazole 20mg tablets. Take one tablet once a day. If you are able to, try to take one tablet once a day only when your symptoms recur; supply 28 tablets; NHS Cost £18.50.

Ulcer healed but continued NSAID use needed

Which therapy?

- **Discuss the potential harm** from nonsteroidal anti-inflammatory drugs (NSAIDs) with the patient.

Review the need for NSAID use at least 6 monthly.
Consider using strategies to reduce NSAID use:
- Offer a trial of use on a limited 'as required' basis.
- Consider dose reduction.
- Consider using paracetamol or another analgesic instead of an NSAID.
- Consider switching to low-dose ibuprofen (400 mg three times a day).

Offer gastroprotection to all people with a previous peptic ulcer who require continued use of standard NSAIDs, as these people are at high risk of recurrent ulceration.
Substitution to a COX-2 selective NSAID is an alternative to using gastroprotection plus a standard NSAID to prevent ulcer recurrence.

Practical prescribing points

For further information please see the *Medicines Compendium* (www.medicines.org.uk) or the *British National Formulary* (www.bnf.org).

Proton pump inhibitors: differences between the proton pump inhibitors in clinical efficacy and safety are minimal.
- Omeprazole is currently cheapest.
- Omeprazole and esomeprazole occasionally enhance the effects of warfarin and phenytoin. Monitor carefully if omeprazole or esomeprazole are started or stopped.

Misoprostol: diarrhoea and abdominal pain are common. Advise women of childbearing age to use adequate contraception, since misoprostol increases the risk of miscarriage.

Follow-up advice

Review the need for nonsteroidal anti-inflammatory drug (NSAID) use at least 6 monthly.
If symptoms persist despite use of gastroprotection with a standard NSAID or despite substitution to a COX-2 selective NSAID, consider:
- Stopping the NSAID.
- Referral for a repeat endoscopy to confirm healing.
- Whether other causes of duodenal ulceration have been excluded.
- Referral to a specialist for further management.

Should I refer or investigate?

Refer?

Indications for repeat endoscopy

Note: proton pump inhibitors and H_2-receptor antagonists should be stopped at least 2 weeks before endoscopy. Nonsteroidal anti-inflammatory drug should also be suspended in all people requiring referral.

Consider managing previously investigated people without new ALARM symptoms according to previous endoscopic findings. However, if an additional diagnosis is suspected, or if the person has been symptom-free for several years before symptoms recur, consider referring for a repeat endoscopy to confirm the diagnosis.
Immediate endoscopy (i.e. same day) is indicated for people presenting with dyspepsia together with significant acute gastrointestinal bleeding.
Anyone who develops ALARM symptoms should be referred urgently for endoscopy, or to a specialist. That is people with:
- Chronic gastrointestinal bleeding
- Progressive unintentional weight loss
- Progressive difficulty swallowing (dysphagia)
- Persistent vomiting
- Iron deficiency anaemia
- Epigastric mass
- Suspicious barium meal result

- **People 55 years and over, presenting with unexplained and persistent recent onset dyspepsia** alone, should be referred for urgent endoscopy.
- **Urgent referral to a specialist should also be considered in** a person (of any age) who has unexplained worsening of their dyspepsia and:
  - Barrett's oesophagus
  - Known dysplasia, atrophic gastritis, or intestinal metaplasia
  - Peptic ulcer surgery over 20 years ago
- **If definite dysphagia or odynophagia is present** with a suspicious history or regurgitation, it is appropriate to refer for a barium swallow.

Investigate?

- When referring, consider a full blood count to assist specialist assessment. This should be carried out in accordance with local arrangements.

Patient information leaflets

The following PILs are available at www.prodigy.nhs.uk
- Barium Swallow / Meal / Follow Through
- CORE, Fighting Gut and Liver Disease
- Duodenal Ulcer
- Gastroscopy (Endoscopy)
- Stomach (Gastric) Ulcer

Shared decision making

- Your ulcer was caused, or made worse, by your ant-inflammatory medication. To help prevent a further ulcer, consider:
  - Do you still require the anti-inflammatory medicine?
  - Do you need it all the time, or can you take it for short courses 'as required'?
  - Can it be replaced by an alternative treatment?
  - If not, can the dose of the medicine be reduced?
- If you still need regular anti-inflammatory medication, you should protect against the risk of developing a further ulcer by:
  - Taking an acid-suppressing medicine each day, or
  - Taking misoprostol, which can protect the stomach lining.
- See your doctor urgently if indigestion symptoms recur, or you develop any other symptoms that suggest an ulcer, such as bleeding from the gut.

Drug rationale

Drugs not included

- **Double-doses of H_2-receptor antagonists** are effective at reducing the risk of endoscopic gastric and duodenal ulcers; however, they are not licensed for this indication [Rostom et al, 2002]. Standard doses only reduce the risk of endoscopic duodenal ulcers.
- **Low doses of misoprostol** (400 micrograms twice or three times a day) are less effective than proton pump inhibitors at reducing the incidence of endoscopic lesions, and have greater adverse effects [NICE, 2004].
- **Rabeprazole** is not licensed for prophylaxis of nonsteroidal anti-inflammatory drug-associated ulcers.

Drugs included

- **Proton pump inhibitors** are generally the preferred choice for gastroprotection. They are effective and well tolerated; they reduce the risk of endoscopic gastric ulcers by 63% and the risk of duodenal ulcers by 81% [Rostom et al, 2002]. However, there is a lack of data on prevention of ulcer complications. Omeprazole, lansoprazole, pantoprazole, and esomeprazole are all licensed for prophylaxis of nonsteroidal anti-inflammatory drug-associated ulcers.
- **Full-dose misoprostol** (800 micrograms per day) has been shown to reduce the risk of endoscopic gastric and duodenal ulcers and *clinically* important ulcer complications. However, its place is limited by adverse effects such as diarrhoea and abdominal pain [Rostom et al, 2002].

Prescriptions

GI protection: proton pump inhibitors

Omeprazole capsules: 20mg once a day
- Age from 16 years onwards
- Omeprazole 20mg capsules. Take one capsule once a day; supply 28 capsules; NHS Cost £12.75.

Omeprazole tablets: 20mg once a day
- Age from 16 years onwards
- Omeprazole 20mg tablets. Take one tablet once a day; supply 28 tablets; NHS Cost £12.75.

Lansoprazole capsules: 30mg each morning
- Age from 16 years onwards
- Lansoprazole 30mg capsules. Take one capsule each morning (on an empty stomach); supply 28 capsules; NHS Cost £23.63.

Lansoprazole orodispersible tablets: 30mg each morning
- Age from 16 years onwards
- Lansoprazole 30mg orodisp tabs. Take one tablet each morning (on an empty stomach); supply 28 tablets; NHS Cost £19.88.

Pantoprazole e/c tablets: 20mg once a day
- Age from 16 years onwards
- Pantoprazole 20mg e/c tablets. Take one tablet once a day; supply 28 tablets; NHS Cost £12.31.

Esomeprazole tablets: 20mg once a day
- Age from 16 years onwards
- Esomeprazole 20mg tablets. Take one tablet once a day; supply 28 tablets; NHS Cost £18.50.

Lansoprazole capsules: 15mg each morning
- Age from 16 years onwards
- Lansoprazole 15mg capsules. Take one capsule each morning (on an empty stomach); supply 28 capsules; NHS Cost £12.92.

Lansoprazole orodispersible tablets: 15mg each morning
- Age from 16 years onwards
- Lansoprazole 15mg orodisp tabs. Take one tablet each morning (on an empty stomach); supply 28 tablets; NHS Cost £10.86.

GI protection: misoprostol

Misoprostol 200micrograms four times a day
- Age from 16 years onwards
- Misoprostol 200microgram tabs. Take one tablet four times a day; supply 112 tablets; NHS Cost £20.79.

Extended Information

Background information

- What is dyspepsia? p.642
- What is peptic ulcer disease? p.642
- What causes peptic ulcer disease? p.642
- How common is it? p.642
- How do I know my patient has peptic ulcer disease? p.642
- What else might it be? p.643
- Complications and prognosis p.643

What is dyspepsia?

- **Dyspepsia is a term used to describe a group of symptoms** that alert the clinician to consider the possibility of upper gastrointestinal tract disease. It is not a diagnosis. The group of symptoms includes epigastric pain, heartburn or acid regurgitation (with or without bloating), nausea, or vomiting.

What is peptic ulcer disease?

- **Peptic ulcer disease** is ulceration of the intestinal mucosa commonly in the stomach (gastric ulcer) or in the duodenum (duodenal ulcer). Oesophageal ulceration can also occur. Peptic ulcer disease is difficult to discriminate clinically from non-ulcer (functional) dyspepsia.
- Those ulcers related to the use of nonsteroidal anti-inflammatory drugs (NSAIDs) are called 'NSAID-associated ulcers'.

What causes peptic ulcer disease?

- *Helicobacter pylori* infection appears to be the main cause of peptic ulcer disease. About 95% of duodenal ulcers and about 80% of gastric ulcers are associated with this bacterium.
- The use of nonsteroidal anti-inflammatory drugs is implicated in most other cases.

How common is it?

- About 4% of general practice consultations are for dyspepsia, and about 10% of these lead to referral for further investigation.
- For those people investigated by endoscopy for dyspepsia, 10–15% have duodenal ulcer and 5–10% have gastric ulcer.
- A further 30% have no abnormal findings (i.e. have non-ulcer dyspepsia or endoscopy-negative reflux disease); 30% have either gastritis, duodenitis, or hiatus hernia; 10–17% have oesophagitis; and 2% have gastric cancer

[British Society of Gastroenterology, 2002]

How do I know my patient has peptic ulcer disease?

History

- **Symptoms are variable,** but may include upper abdominal pain or discomfort, retrosternal pain, heartburn, acid reflux, anorexia, nausea, vomiting, bloating, fullness, or early satiety.
- Pain in the right or left hypochondrium does not constitute dyspepsia [Hunt et al, 2002].
- **Dyspeptic symptoms are a poor predictor of disease severity or underlying pathology (C).** For example:
  - Only about 50% of individuals with 'classic' symptoms have a specific lesion identified by endoscopy [NICE, 2004].

- Many people with peptic ulcers do not identify the epigastrium as the site of pain.
- Heartburn is a major feature of gastro-oesophageal reflux disease, but one study found that duodenal ulcer was as common in people with dominant heartburn as in those with epigastric pain [Chiba et al, 2003].
- Duodenal ulcer pain can appear at night as well as in the day.
- The relationship of pain to food is not a good discriminator.

Examination

- On examination, epigastric tenderness is often the only sign, but is poorly discriminating.

Investigations

- **Peptic ulcer disease can only be diagnosed by endoscopy.** However, it is neither necessary nor practical to investigate a diagnosis in every person with dyspepsia (in the absence of ALARM symptoms) if symptoms are controlled by empirical treatment [NICE, 2004].
  - This guidance deals with the management of people with endoscopically determined gastric ulcer, duodenal ulcer, or NSAID-associated ulcer.
  - People with dyspeptic symptoms who do *not* need an endoscopy should be managed via the PRODIGY guidance *Dyspepsia — symptoms (uninvestigated by endoscopy)*.
- ***Helicobacter pylori* testing** is commonly undertaken. Eradication is recommended in people with peptic ulcer disease who test positive for *H pylori* [Malfertheiner et al, 2002].

What else might it be?

- **Cardiac or biliary disease** (C).
  - Cardiac pain may be clinically indistinguishable from dyspepsia.
  - Biliary colic occasionally presents with epigastric pain.
- **Oesophageal or gastric carcinoma.** Investigate for malignancy in the presence of any ALARM symptoms (chronic gastrointestinal bleeding; dysphagia; progressive unintentional weight loss; persistent vomiting; iron deficiency anaemia; an epigastric mass; or suspicious barium meal). Symptom severity is a poor indicator of an underlying disease.
- **Gastro-oesophageal reflux disease** (GORD). GORD is a term used to describe diseases that cause reflux of gastric contents into the oesophagus, causing symptoms that are sufficient to interfere with quality of life.
- **Non-ulcer dyspepsia** (also known as functional dyspepsia).
- **Irritable bowel syndrome** may manifest as dyspepsia with bloating, but is usually associated with abnormal bowel habits.
- **Motility disorders** may also manifest as upper abdominal discomfort with bloating and early satiety. Gastroparesis should be suspected in people with diabetes mellitus, especially when peripheral neuropathy is present.
- **Other causes of dysphagia include** peptic stricture, Schatzki ring, and (less commonly) achalasia, diffuse spasm, systemic sclerosis, bronchial carcinoma, enlarged mediastinal nodes, aortic aneurysm, post-cricoid web, or radiation stricture.

Complications and prognosis

Complications

- Haemorrhage
- Perforation of ulcer
- Anaemia
- Pyloric stenosis
- **There may be a missed diagnosis of gastric cancer.** Carcinoma at the site of 'benign' ulcer is a result of initial misdiagnosis, even if the ulcer appeared to respond to treatment.

Prognosis

- **For people with gastric or duodenal ulceration** *Helicobacter pylori* eradication markedly reduces the risk of recurrence during their lifetime:
  - Lifetime risk of recurrence for gastric ulcer is 60% if *H pylori* positive, but 5% if *H pylori* negative.
  - Lifetime risk of recurrence for duodenal ulcer is 80% if *H pylori* positive, but 5% if *H pylori* negative.

[Graham, 1997; NICE, 2004]

D

Management issues

- Overview of management p.643
- What general measures are useful? p.644
- What is first-line treatment? p.644
- Which *H pylori* test should I use? p.644
- What follow-up is needed? p.644
- What should I do if the *H pylori* re-test is positive? p.645
- What should I do if the *H pylori* re-test is negative? p.645
- What should I do if the person is *H pylori* negative but symptoms persist? p.645
- How should I manage people who still need NSAIDs? p.645
- When is repeat endoscopy indicated? p.646
- Supporting evidence for treatment strategies p.646
- Medicines management p.648

This guidance covers the management of people with endoscopically determined duodenal ulcer, gastric ulcer, or NSAID-associated ulcer.
People with uninvestigated symptoms should be managed as patients with uninvestigated dyspepsia (C) [NICE, 2004]. See the PRODIGY guidance *Dyspepsia — symptoms (uninvestigated by endoscopy)*. Consider managing previously investigated people without new ALARM symptoms according to previous endoscopic findings.

Overview of management

- Review medication that may be causing dyspepsia.
- Offer general lifestyle advice.
- Test all people with peptic ulcer disease for *Helicobacter pylori*.
- For people with a gastric ulcer or duodenal ulcer:
  - If the *H pylori* test is positive, eradicate *H pylori* using triple therapy.
  - If the *H pylori* test is negative, offer a course of a full dose proton pump inhibitor for one or two months.
- For people with an NSAID-induced ulcer:
  - Stop the NSAID where possible
  - Prescribe a 2-month course of a full-dose proton pump inhibitor (PPI)
  - Subsequently, treat according to *H pylori* test result
- All people with a gastric ulcer should undergo repeat endoscopy 6–8 weeks after beginning treatment.
- Re-test for *H pylori*:
  - All people with a gastric ulcer
  - People with a duodenal ulcer if there is no response to eradication therapy or relapse
- If re-test is positive offer second-line eradication therapy.

- If *H pylori* has been excluded or eradicated and symptoms persist:
    - For people with a duodenal ulcer: offer a PPI at the lowest dose required to control symptoms.
    - For people with a gastric ulcer:
        - If ulcer has not healed, refer.
        - If ulcer has healed, offer a PPI at the lowest dose required to control symptoms.

What general measures are useful?

D

Which medication might be causing dyspeptic symptoms?

- **Stop nonsteroidal anti-inflammatory drugs (NSAIDs) wherever possible (A).**
- **Theophylline, nitrates, and calcium-channel blockers** may reduce lower oesophageal sphincter pressure. Consider withdrawing if there are predominant reflux symptoms.
- **Bisphosphonates and corticosteroids** commonly cause gastrointestinal adverse effects.

[MeReC, 1998; NICE, 2004]

What lifestyle advice is recommended?

- **Offer simple lifestyle advice,** including healthy eating, weight reduction, and smoking cessation (**B**). Although there is no clear evidence that lifestyle factors (such as smoking, alcohol, caffeine, and diet) affect dyspepsia, there are more important general health benefits.
- **If the person has identified a precipitating factor,** then it is sensible to advise them to avoid it (e.g. bending, alcohol, coffee, chocolate, fatty foods, spicy foods) (**C**).
- **Other suggestions for people with reflux symptoms include** eating smaller meals, not eating before going to bed, and propping up the bed head. (One possible cause of reflux disease is transient relaxation of the lower oesophageal sphincter: lying flat may therefore increase reflux episodes since gravity does not then prevent acid regurgitation.)
- **Provide people with patient information** to support the care they receive (**C**).

[MeReC, 1998; NICE, 2004]

What is first-line treatment?

All people with peptic ulcer disease should be tested for *Helicobacter pylori*; often this is done at the time of endoscopy.

People with a duodenal or gastric ulcer

- **Test for *H pylori*** (**A**) [NICE, 2004]. (This is usually done at the time of endoscopy.)
    - If the *H pylori* test is positive, eradicate it using triple therapy (**A**). (For details of triple-therapy regimens see *Which H pylori eradication regimen should I use?*)
    - If the *H pylori* test is negative, offer a course of a full-dose PPI for 1 or 2 months (**A**).
- Since *H pylori* is implicated in the majority of cases of duodenal and gastric ulcer, there is also a case for testing people who have been treated for a past duodenal ulcer, if they have not previously been tested for *H pylori*.

People with an NSAID-associated ulcer

- **Stop the nonsteroidal anti-inflammatory drug (NSAID) where possible (A).**
- Test for *H pylori*. (Since *H pylori* tests are not accurate if done within 2 weeks of proton pump inhibitor (PPI) therapy, it is usually practical to test before healing is undertaken — often this is done at the time of endoscopy.)
- **Give a 2-month course of a full-dose PPI** to heal the ulcer (**A**) [NICE, 2004].
- Subsequently, if the *H pylori* result was positive, eradicate it using triple therapy (**A**) to reduce the risk of ulcer recurrence.

Which *H pylori* test should I use?

If *Helicobacter pylori* testing has not already been undertaken during endoscopy (e.g. using a CLO [Campylobacter-like organism] test) consider the following:

- **Pretreatment testing:** a carbon-13 urea breath test or a stool antigen test is recommended [NICE, 2004] (**A**).
- **Post-eradication testing:** only a carbon-13 urea breath test should be used [NICE, 2004] (**A**).
- *H pylori* testing should not be performed within 2 weeks of proton pump inhibitor (PPI) therapy or within 4 weeks of antibiotic therapy, as false-negative results may occur [DTB, 2004].
- If the person is taking long-term antibiotics: phenoxymethylpenicillin, nitrofurantoin, and trimethoprim are not active against *H pylori*, so will not affect the test results. Advice should be sought from the local microbiology laboratory on when to test and on test interpretation for people taking other long-term antibiotics [HPA Helicobacter Working Group, Personal Communication, 2005]. (Tetracyclines, macrolides, broad-spectrum penicillins [e.g. amoxicillin] cephalosporins, and anti-tuberculosis drugs are all active against *H pylori*.)

How do I use a carbon-13 urea breath test?

- Carbon urea breath tests involve a separate appointment at the practice since the manufacturers recommend that the performance of the test is supervised.
- The kits currently prescribable on the NHS for adults include diabact UBT®, Helicobacter Test Hp-Plus®, Helicobacter Test INFAI®, and Pylobactell®.
- The person should fast for at least 6 hours before the test and then (for all tests except diabact UBT®) ingest citric acid or orange juice just before the test to slow gastric emptying. (The diabact UBT® tablet contains citric acid.)
- The person then provides two or three breath samples before ingestion of the carbon-13 tablet, and again 30 minutes afterwards (only 10 minutes afterwards for diabact UBT®) by blowing through a straw into a series of glass, screw-top tubes.
- Breath samples are sent away for analysis by mass spectrometry and results are available within 24 hours of receipt.

[DTB, 2004]

How do I use a stool antigen test?

- Stool antigen tests require the patient to collect a stool sample (at least pea-sized). The sample is then sent to the laboratory for analysis.
- Stool antigen tests do not require a separate appointment at the practice and are cheaper than carbon urea breath testing.

What follow-up is needed?

- **People with a gastric ulcer** should undergo repeat endoscopy 6–8 weeks after beginning treatment (depending on the size of the lesion) to confirm healing and exclude malignancy (**C**) [NICE, 2004]. They should also be re-tested for *Helicobacter pylori* 6–8 weeks after eradication therapy to confirm that eradication has been successful [NICE, 2004].
- **People with a duodenal ulcer** only need to be re-tested for *H pylori* if there was no response to eradication

therapy, or if symptoms responded but have now relapsed [NICE, 2004].
- **For people with a nonsteroidal anti-inflammatory drug (NSAID) associated ulcer,** the need for repeat endoscopy and *H pylori* re-testing will depend on whether the NSAID induced a gastric or a duodenal ulcer.

What should I do if the *H pylori* re-test is positive?

- **Offer second-line therapy to eradicate *Helicobacter pylori*.** For treatment options for second-line therapy, see *Which H pylori regimen should I use?*
- **After two attempts to eradicate *H pylori*, there is no need to re-test again** [NICE, 2004].
  - If symptoms respond to eradication treatment, then no further courses of treatment are needed.
  - If symptoms recur following two attempts to eradicate *H pylori*, the person should be managed as if they are *H pylori* negative [NICE, 2004].
- Sensitivity testing is not routinely needed to choose second-line eradication therapy, provided that the new eradication regimen does not contain previously used antibiotics. (See the section *Antibiotic resistance* for further information).

What should I do if the *H pylori* re-test is negative?

- If symptoms have responded to eradication treatment, then no further course of treatment is needed.
- If symptoms recur but the *Helicobacter pylori* re-test was negative, see *What should I do if the person is H pylori negative but symptoms persist?*

What should I do if the person is *H pylori* negative but symptoms persist?

The treatment of peptic ulcer disease has been revolutionized by *Helicobacter pylori* eradication treatment. Once *H pylori* has been eradicated and the ulcer has healed, most people do not require further treatment and maintenance therapy. For further information on when to consider repeat endoscopy, see *When is repeat endoscopy indicated?*

People with a duodenal ulcer

- **Offer a proton pump inhibitor** (PPI) with a limited number of repeat prescriptions (B).
  - Encourage people to use the lowest dose required to control symptoms (B).
  - Discuss using the treatment on an 'on-demand' basis (i.e. waiting for symptoms to develop before taking treatment) (B).
- **If there is no response to acid suppression therapy,** exclude other causes of duodenal ulcer (B). Consider:
  - Non-compliance with treatment
  - Possible malignancy
  - Failure to detect *Helicobacter pylori* infection due to recent PPI or antibiotic therapy
  - Inadequate testing or simple misclassification
  - Surreptitious or inadvertent nonsteroidal anti-inflammatory drug (NSAID) or aspirin use
  - Ulceration due to ingestion of other drugs (e.g. bisphosphonates, corticosteroids. Selective serotonin re-uptake inhibitors [SSRIs] have also been implicated in gastrointestinal bleeding)
  - Rare causes such as Zollinger-Ellison syndrome and Crohn's disease
- A small number of people with chronic, refractory peptic ulceration may need maintenance acid suppression. In some people with an inadequate response to therapy it may become appropriate to refer to a specialist for a second opinion.

[NICE, 2004]

People with a gastric ulcer

- **If the repeat endoscopy shows that the ulcer has not healed,** refer to a specialist in secondary care for further management.
- **If the ulcer has healed but symptoms persist:**
  - Offer a proton pump inhibitor with a limited number of repeat prescriptions (B).
  - Encourage people to use the lowest dose required to control symptoms (B).
  - Discuss using the treatment on an 'on-demand' basis (i.e. waiting for symptoms to develop before taking treatment) (B).

[NICE, 2004]

People with a history of gastrointestinal bleeding or perforation

- Management will usually be specialist-led.
- These people should have continuing acid suppression treatment until *Helicobacter pylori* eradication is confirmed by breath test.
- If they are still *H pylori* positive after two courses of eradication therapy, seek specialist advice. (*H pylori* antibiotic sensitivity testing may be indicated.)

People with an NSAID-associated ulcer

- Manage as for a duodenal ulcer or a gastric ulcer.
- If the nonsteroidal anti-inflammatory drug must be continued, see *How should I manage people who still need NSAIDs?*

How should I manage people who still need NSAIDs?

- **Discuss the potential harm** from nonsteroidal anti-inflammatory drugs (NSAIDs) with the patient (B).
- **Review the need for NSAID use regularly** (at least 6-monthly) and consider using strategies to reduce NSAID use (B). For example:
  - Offer a trial of use on a limited 'as required' basis.
  - Consider dose reduction.
  - Consider switching to paracetamol.
  - Consider switching to low-dose ibuprofen (400 mg three times a day).
- **Offer gastroprotection** to all people with a previous peptic ulcer who require continued use of standard NSAIDs, as these people are at high risk of recurrent ulceration (A). See *Which agents are suitable for gastroprotection against NSAIDs?* for treatment options.
- Substitution to a COX-2 selective NSAID is an alternative to using gastroprotection plus a standard NSAID to prevent ulcer recurrence (A).
- **If symptoms persist despite use of gastroprotection with a standard NSAID or despite substitution to a COX-2 selective NSAID, consider:**
  - Stopping the NSAID
  - Referral for a repeat endoscopy to confirm healing
  - Whether other causes of duodenal ulceration have been excluded
  - Referral to a specialist for further management
- Note: healing of all gastric ulcers should be checked by repeat endoscopy 6–8 weeks after beginning treatment to confirm healing and exclude malignancy. If repeat endoscopy shows that the ulcer has not healed, refer to a specialist in secondary care for further management.

[NICE, 2004]

When is repeat endoscopy indicated?

Note: proton pump inhibitors and H_2-receptor antagonists should be stopped at least 2 weeks before endoscopy (B). Nonsteroidal anti-inflammatory drug use should also be suspended in all people requiring referral (C).

- **Consider** managing previously investigated people without new ALARM symptoms according to previous endoscopic findings (C). However, if an additional diagnosis is suspected, or if the person has been symptom-free for several years before symptoms recur, consider referring for a repeat endoscopy to confirm the diagnosis.
- **Immediate endoscopy** (i.e. same day) is indicated for people presenting with dyspepsia together with significant acute gastrointestinal bleeding.
- **Anyone who develops ALARM symptoms should be referred urgently for endoscopy, or to a specialist** (C) [NICE, 2005]. That is people with:
  - Chronic gastrointestinal bleeding
  - Progressive unintentional weight loss
  - Progressive difficulty swallowing (dysphagia)
  - Persistent vomiting
  - Iron deficiency anaemia
  - Epigastric mass
  - Suspicious barium meal result
- **People 55 years and over, presenting with unexplained and persistent recent onset dyspepsia** alone, should be referred for urgent endoscopy (C) [NICE, 2004].
  - *Unexplained* is defined as a symptom(s) and/or sign(s) that has not led to a diagnosis being made by the primary care professional after initial assessment of the history, examination and primary care investigations (if any)'. In the context of this recommendation, the primary care professional should confirm that the dyspepsia is new rather than a recurrent episode and exclude common precipitants of dyspepsia such as ingestion of NSAIDs.
  - *Persistent* refers to the continuation of specified symptoms and/or signs beyond a period that would normally be associated with self-limiting problems. The precise period will vary depending on the severity of symptoms and associated features, as assessed by the healthcare professional. In many cases, the upper limit the professional will permit symptoms and/or signs to persist before initiating referral will be 4–6 weeks.
- **Urgent referral to a specialist should also be considered in** a person (of any age) who has unexplained worsening of their dyspepsia and Barrett's oesophagus; or known dysplasia, atrophic gastritis, or intestinal metaplasia; or peptic ulcer surgery over 20 years ago (C) [NICE, 2005].
- **If dysphagia is present** (interference with the swallowing mechanism that occurs within 5 seconds of starting the swallowing process) it is appropriate to refer for a barium swallow. There is a risk of perforation if an endoscope is pushed through a stricture. Before endoscopic examination, barium swallow will delineate the stricture to see how long it is.

[NICE, 2004; NICE, 2005]

Supporting evidence for treatment strategies

Which *H pylori* test?

Initial testing (pretreatment)

- **A carbon-13 urea breath test or a stool antigen test is recommended for pretreatment testing in primary care** [NICE, 2004].
  - Carbon urea breath tests are consistently accurate with about 95% sensitivity and specificity reported in studies. Stool antigen tests seem to perform as well as carbon urea breath tests [DTB, 2004; NICE, 2004].
  - Neither type of test should be performed within 2 weeks of proton pump inhibitor therapy or within 4 weeks of antibiotic therapy, as false-negative results may occur [DTB, 2004].
- Stool antigen tests using monoclonal antibodies appear to be more accurate (sensitivity and specificity of 96% and 97% respectively) than tests using polyclonal antibodies (sensitivity and specificity of 90% and 94% respectively) [DTB, 2004].
- Laboratory-based serology is an alternative *if* it has been locally validated [NICE, 2004]. However, the sensitivity and specificity of serology varies in different populations. (The reason for this is unclear but may relate to different strains of *H pylori* or genetic differences in the population.) Since most laboratories receive samples from wide geographical areas it is likely that they will be covering populations that vary considerably in terms of age, social class, and ethnicity, making local validation difficult. In addition, serological findings only indicate exposure to *H pylori*, not necessarily active infection: antibody levels only fall slowly over several months after eradication. Use of serology leads to at least twice as many false positives as the carbon urea breath test or the stool antigen test.
- Near-patient serology kits are not recommended because they have widely varying sensitivities and specificities. Studies of the accuracy of several new rapid whole blood test kits have shown sensitivity and specificity of 82–95% and 83–94% respectively [SIGN, 2003].
- Carbon-14 urea breath tests are not appropriate for primary care as they involve a small dose of radiation.
- **If the person requires endoscopy,** then biopsies can be taken to test for *H pylori*, e.g. with the rapid urease test (the *Campylobacter*-like organism [CLO] test). This has a sensitivity of 85–90% and a specificity of 98–100% [Meurer and Bower, 2002].

Post-eradication testing

- **Only a carbon-13 urea breath test should be used** [NICE, 2004].
- Serological tests are not reliable in determining eradication, unless more than 1 year has elapsed since eradication therapy was given [Feldman et al, 1998].
- Stool antigen tests are not currently recommended by NICE for post-eradication testing. However, there is increasing evidence that they are sensitive and specific to use for post-eradication testing and they are likely to become recommended for this purpose in the future [HPA Helicobacter Working Group, Personal Communication, 2005].

H pylori eradication

- *H pylori* infection is a recognized factor in the development of duodenal and gastric ulceration; about 15% of people with *H pylori* will develop a peptic ulcer [Graham, 1997].
- The eradication of *H pylori* dramatically reduces the recurrence rate in peptic ulcer (from over 80% per year to less than 10% for duodenal ulcer, and from 48% to 7% for gastric ulcer).
- *H pylori* infection is associated with gastric B-cell lymphoma and distal gastric cancer. About 1% of people with *H pylori* will develop gastric cancer during their lifetime [Graham, 1997]. Studies have shown that gastric atrophy and intestinal metaplasia may partially regress after *H pylori* eradication, and there is some evidence that eradicating *H pylori* helps to prevent gastric cancer [Uemura et al, 2001].

Healing peptic ulcers

- Eradication therapy is recommended as first-line treatment for peptic ulcers if the person is *H pylori* positive. If the person is *H pylori* negative, acid suppression with a proton pump inhibitor is used as first-line treatment, and will also heal peptic ulcers in the majority of cases.
- *H pylori* eradication increases duodenal ulcer healing in *H pylori* positive people. A Cochrane review found that after 4–8 weeks, people receiving acid suppression therapy average 69% healing. Eradication increases this by a further 5.4%, a number needed to treat of 18 [Delaney et al, 2003b; NICE, 2004].
- *H pylori* eradication is no more effective than acid suppression at healing gastric ulcers in *H pylori* positive people [Delaney et al, 2003b; NICE, 2004].

Preventing peptic ulcer recurrence

- *H pylori* eradication reduces duodenal ulcer recurrence in *H pylori* positive people. A Cochrane review found that after 3–12 months, 39% of people receiving short-term acid suppression therapy are without an ulcer. Eradication increases this by a further 52%, a number needed to treat of 2 [Delaney et al, 2003b; NICE, 2004].
- *H pylori* eradication also reduces gastric ulcer recurrence in *H pylori* positive people. A Cochrane review found that after 3–12 months, 45% of people receiving short-term acid suppression therapy are without an ulcer. Eradication increases this by a further 32%, a number needed to treat of 3.

First-line H pylori eradication regimens

- One-week triple therapy regimens (a proton pump inhibitor [PPI] plus two antibiotics) are recommended. Two-week regimens are no more effective than one-week regimens. Dual therapy is not as effective as triple therapy. Quadruple therapy (a PPI, bismuth, tetracycline, and metronidazole) is as effective as triple therapy, but taking 17 tablets per day does not make it a practical first-line option [Delaney et al, 2003a].
- The recommended PAC regimen (a PPI plus amoxicillin 1 g and clarithromycin 500 mg, all given twice a day) and PCM regimen (a PPI plus metronidazole 400 mg and clarithromycin 250 mg, all given twice a day) are the optimum regimens on current evidence. Data pooled by NICE show that [NICE, 2004]:
  - Double-dose PPIs are more effective than single-dose PPIs in PAC regimens (eradication rate of 85.4% for double-dose PPIs and 78.5% for single-dose PPIs). The data were less clear for PCM regimens (due to much smaller patient numbers). Double-dose PPIs are therefore also recommended in PCM regimens as there is not enough data to clearly support single dose PPIs.
  - The dose of clarithromycin differs between the two regimens. Pooled data for PAC regimens show eradication rates of 79.8% with clarithromycin 250 mg compared with 89.6% with clarithromycin 500 mg. In PCM regimens, doubling the dose of clarithromycin had no statistically significant effect: eradication rates were 87.4% for clarithromycin 250 mg and 88.9% for clarithromycin 500 mg.
  - Pooled data for the recommended PAC and PCM regimens show no statistically significant difference in eradication rates: 82% for PAC, and 82.6% for PCM.
- Although triple therapy using a PPI plus amoxicillin and metronidazole has previously been recommended as a first-line therapy, pooled data from four randomized, controlled trials have shown that it is less effective than either of the two triple therapies that contain clarithromycin [NICE, 2004].

Second-line H pylori eradication regimens

- Two randomized, controlled trials comparing one-week quadruple therapy to one-week triple therapy found that both types of eradication therapy seemed equally effective [Delaney et al, 2004]. Quadruple therapy is therefore preferred as second-line therapy since it is likely to be more effective than a PAM regimen. It can also be used by people who are penicillin-hypersensitive.
- The recommendation to use an alternative triple therapy regimen if quadruple therapy is not tolerated is based on consensus [Malfertheiner et al, 2002].
- It would seem sensible to use a regimen with a different combination of antibiotics as second-line eradication therapy. The inclusion of oxytetracycline as one of these antibiotics is a pragmatic recommendation since there is no evidence to guide which second-line triple-therapy regimens should be offered to people with penicillin hypersensitivity. However, the efficacy of the suggested combinations of a PPI, metronidazole, and tetracycline, or a PPI, clarithromycin, and tetracycline, is unknown; they have not been studied in randomized, controlled trials.

Peptic ulcers due to NSAIDs

Healing peptic ulcers due to NSAIDs

- Higher rates of healing of nonsteroidal anti-inflammatory drug (NSAID)-induced ulcers have been shown with omeprazole 20 mg once a day than with ranitidine 150 mg twice a day (80% compared with 63%).
- Treatment with conventional doses of H_2-receptor antagonists (H_2RAs) for 6–12 weeks results in healing of about 75% for gastric ulcers and 87% for duodenal ulcers, despite continued use of NSAIDs. However, healing is delayed with H_2RAs, and these drugs are only recommended for healing if the NSAID has been stopped.
- Rates of healing of NSAID-induced ulcers with continuing NSAID use are similar for omeprazole 20 mg once a day and misoprostol 200 micrograms four times a day (76% compared with 71%). However, the use of misoprostol is limited by its adverse effects.
- *H pylori* eradication seems no more effective than omeprazole for healing NSAID-associated ulcers [Delaney et al, 2004]. However, eradication does seem to help to prevent NSAID-associated ulcers recurring.

[NZGG, 2004]

Preventing peptic ulcers due to NSAIDs

- *H pylori* eradication reduces the risk of peptic ulceration compared to omeprazole at 6 months in nonsteroidal anti-inflammatory drug (NSAID) users with previous peptic ulcers [Delaney et al, 2004]. However, another study found that it is less effective than omeprazole in preventing recurrence in people with previous bleeding NSAID-associated ulcers who continued to take naproxen [Delaney et al, 2004].
- Proton pump inhibitors (PPIs) are generally the preferred choice for gastroprotection. They are effective and well tolerated; they reduce the risk of endoscopic gastric ulcers by 63% and the risk of duodenal ulcers by 81% [Rostom et al, 2002]. However, there is a lack of data on prevention of ulcer complications.
- Misoprostol 800 micrograms per day has been shown to reduce the risk of endoscopic gastric and duodenal ulcers, and *clinically* important ulcer complications, but its place is limited by its adverse effects [Rostom et al, 2002]. Lower doses (e.g. 400 micrograms per day) are less effective than PPIs at reducing the incidence of endoscopic lesions, and have greater adverse effects [NICE, 2004]. (Diarrhoea and abdominal pain are common.)
- Double doses of H_2-receptor antagonists are also effective at reducing the risk of endoscopic gastric and duodenal ulcers, but this is an off-licence use [Rostom et

al, 2002]. Standard doses only reduce the risk of endoscopic duodenal ulcers [SIGN, 2003].

Medicines management

Which *H pylori* eradication regimen should I use?

- **First-line eradication therapy:** NICE recommends that one of the following one-week triple therapy regimens is used.
  - A 'PAC' regimen (a PPI plus amoxicillin 1 g and clarithromycin 500 mg, all given twice a day)
  - *Or* (for people with penicillin hypersensitivity) a 'PCM' regimen (a PPI plus metronidazole 400 mg and clarithromycin 250 mg, all given twice a day)
  - Note: an alternative antibiotic should be used in the eradication regimen, if a course of clarithromycin or metronidazole has previously been given (for any indication). (See second-line triple therapy choices.)
- **Second-line eradication therapy:** if first-line eradication therapy fails, PRODIGY recommends that one of the following one-week eradication regimens is used.
  - Quadruple therapy (a PPI twice a day, bismuth 120 mg four times a day, metronidazole 400 mg three times a day, and oxytetracycline 500 mg four times a day) [Malfertheiner et al, 2002].
  - If quadruple therapy is not tolerated, consider using a triple-therapy regimen that contains antibiotics that have not been used before.
- Second-line eradication therapy should use different antibiotics to first-line therapy. The HPA Helicobacter Working Group recommends that two antibiotics are chosen from the following options: amoxicillin, clarithromycin, metronidazole, or oxytetracycline.
- Other antibiotics can be considered, but advice should be sought from the Helicobacter Reference Laboratory (telephone 0208 327 6538).

[HPA Helicobacter Working Group, Personal Communication, 2005]

Antibiotic resistance

- Laboratory testing suggests that *Helicobacter pylori* antibiotic resistance is around 15–66% for metronidazole, and 8–30% for clarithromycin [McLoughlin et al, 2004]. (Data on *H pylori* resistance to amoxicillin have not been published.)
- Treatment failure with a clarithromycin-containing regimen is highly correlated with clarithromycin resistance. Clarithromycin is therefore best avoided if a recent course has been given.
- The association between metronidazole resistance and treatment failure is less clear cut.
  - Data pooled by NICE suggest that there is no significant difference in eradication rates between PAC and PCM regimens. NICE suggests that possible explanations are that PCM may be more effective than PAC in metronidazole-sensitive strains, or that the impact of metronidazole resistance may not be as marked as observational studies suggest [NICE, 2004].
  - Studies also suggest that metronidazole resistance has only a modest impact on quadruple therapy success [van der Hulst et al, 1998].
  - Metronidazole could therefore be considered if a recent course had been taken and there was no suitable alternative.

[HPA Helicobacter Working Group, Personal Communication, 2005]

Which PPI?

- **Differences between the proton pump inhibitors (PPIs) in clinical efficacy and safety are minimal** [WeMeReC, 2002]. On present evidence, PPIs do not have any serious contraindications for the vast majority of users, and have been in common use for over a decade.
- Omeprazole, lansoprazole, pantoprazole, and rabeprazole are currently licensed for healing gastric and duodenal ulcers. (Esomeprazole is not currently licensed for this indication.) However, only omeprazole, lansoprazole, and esomeprazole are licensed for healing and prophylaxis of nonsteroidal anti-inflammatory drug (NSAID)-associated ulcers.
- **Omeprazole is currently the least expensive PPI,** although this may change when other PPIs become available generically.
- PPIs are generally well tolerated. Adverse effects include gastrointestinal disturbances (most commonly diarrhoea), headaches, and dizziness.
- PPIs should not be offered to people with ALARM symptoms prior to endoscopy as they may mask gastric cancer. If someone already taking a PPI needs an endoscopy, the PPI should be stopped at least 2 weeks before the endoscopy.
- PPIs undergo extensive hepatic metabolism. In liver disease, do not exceed the following doses: 20 mg daily for omeprazole, pantoprazole, and esomeprazole; 30 mg daily for lansoprazole. There are no data on the use of rabeprazole in people with severe hepatic impairment so the manufacturer advises caution.
- Omeprazole and esomeprazole occasionally enhance the effects of warfarin and phenytoin. Monitor people taking these drugs carefully if omeprazole or esomeprazole are started or stopped.

Which dose?

- Recommended doses of proton pump inhibitors are outlined in Table 1.

How should I advise people to take on-demand PPIs?

- 'On-demand' therapy is where treatment is taken only when symptoms recur. Once symptoms are relieved (often after a few days) treatment is stopped again.
- The doses most commonly studied as on-demand therapy are rabeprazole 10 mg, pantoprazole 20 mg, esomeprazole 20 mg, omeprazole 20 mg, and lansoprazole 15 mg. None are licensed for on-demand treatment in people with ulcer disease, but esomeprazole

Table 1: PRODIGY-recommended proton pump inhibitor doses.

PPI	*H pylori* eradication regimen dose	Healing gastric or duodenal ulcers	Healing NSAID-associated ulcer	Prophylaxis for NSAID-associated ulcer
Omeprazole	20 mg twice a day	20 mg once a day	20 mg once a day	20 mg once a day
Lansoprazole	30 mg twice a day	30 mg once a day	30 mg once a day	15–30 mg once a day
Pantoprazole	40 mg twice a day	40 mg once a day	*	20 mg once a day
Rabeprazole	20 mg twice a day	20 mg once a day	*	*
Esomeprazole	20 mg twice a day	*	20 mg once a day	20 mg once a day

* Not licensed for this indication.

and rabeprazole are licensed for on-demand treatment in gastro-oesophageal reflux disease.
- Some people may prefer to use treatment intermittently, i.e. use a 2–4 week course of treatment when symptoms recur.

[Bardhan, 2003]

Which agents are suitable for gastroprotection against NSAIDs?

- **Proton pump inhibitors at full dose are generally the preferred choice** for gastroprotection. Omeprazole, lansoprazole, pantoprazole, and esomeprazole are all licensed for prophylaxis of nonsteroidal anti-inflammatory drug-associated ulcers. Rabeprazole is not licensed for this indication.
- **Misoprostol** is an alternative, but its place is limited by its adverse effects [Rostom et al, 2002]. The full dose (800 micrograms per day) should be used as lower doses (e.g. 400 micrograms per day) are less effective [NICE, 2004].

References

NHS staff in England can link, free of charge, from references to full text journals by clicking on [Full text] on the PRODIGY website.

1. Bardhan, K.D. (2003) Intermittent and on-demand use of proton pump inhibitors in the management of symptomatic gastroesophageal reflux disease. *American Journal of Gastroenterology* **98**(3 Suppl), S40-S48.
2. British Society of Gastroenterology (2002) *Dyspepsia management guidelines*. British Society of Gastroenterology. www.bsg.org.uk/clinical_prac/guidelines/dyspepsia.htm [Accessed: 20/08/2002].
3. Chiba, N., Thompson, A.B.R. and Barkun, A.N. (2003) The Rome II definition of dyspepsia does not exclude patients with GERD in primary care. *Gastroenterology* **124**(4 Suppl 1), A223-A224.
4. Delaney, B.C., Moayyedi, P and Forman, D (2003a) *Initial management strategies for dyspepsia (Cochrane Review)*. The Cochrane Library. Issue 2. Chichester, UK: John Wiley & Sons, Ltd. www.nelh.nhs.uk/cochrane.asp [Accessed: 06/01/2005]. [Full text]
5. Delaney, B, Ford, A., Forman, D and Mobacken, H. (2003b) *Eradication therapy for peptic ulcer disease in Helicobacter pylori positive patients (Cochrane Review)*. The Cochrane Library. Issue 4. Chichester, UK: John Wiley & Sons, Ltd. www.nelh.nhs.uk/cochrane.asp [Accessed: 06/01/2005]. [Full text]
6. Delaney, B., Moayyedi, P. and Forman, D. (2004) *Helicobacter pylori infection*. Volume 12. www.clinicalevidence.com [Accessed: 06/01/2005].
7. DTB (1996) Medical management of gastro-oesophageal reflux. *Drug & Therapeutics Bulletin* **34**(1), 1–4.
8. DTB (2004) Which test for *Helicobacter pylori* in primary care? *Drug & Therapeutics Bulletin* **42**(9), 71–72. [Full text]
9. Feldman, M., Cryer, B., Lee, E. and Peterson, W.L. (1998) Role of seroconversion in confirming cure of *Helicobacter pylori* infection. *Journal of the American Medical Association* **280**(4), 363–365. [Full text]
10. Graham, D.Y. (1997) Can therapy even be denied for *Helicobacter pylori* infection? *Gastroenterology* **113**(Suppl 6), 113–117.
11. HPA Helicobacter Working Group (2005) *Personal communication. Antibiotic resistance and second-line antibiotics for eradication therapy*. Health Protection Agency: UK.
12. Hunt, R.H., Fallone, C., Veldhuyzen Van Zanten, S. et al (2002) Etiology of dyspepsia: implications for empirical therapy. *Canadian Journal of Gastroenterology* **16**(9), 635–641.
13. Malfertheiner, P., Megraud, F., O'Morain, C. et al (2002) Current concepts in the management of *Helicobacter pylori* infection – the Maastricht 2-2000 consensus report. *Alimentary Pharmacology & Therapeutics* **16**(2), 167–180.
14. McLoughlin, R., Racz, I., Buckley, M. et al (2004) Therapy of *Helicobacter pylori*. *Helicobacter* **9**(Suppl 1), 42–48.
15. MeReC (1997) Dyspepsia, peptic ulcer and *Helicobacter pylori*. *MeReC Bulletin* **8**(2), 5–8.
16. MeReC (1998) Proton pump inhibitors: their role in dyspepsia. *MeReC Bulletin* **9**(11), 41–44.
17. Meurer, L.N. and Bower, D.J. (2002) Management of *Helicobacter pylori* infection. *American Family Physician* **65**(7), 1327–1336. [Full text]
18. NICE (2004) *Dyspepsia: management of dyspepsia in adults in primary care: NICE guideline*. Clinical guideline 17. National Institute for Clinical Excellence. www.nice.org.uk [Accessed: 27/08/2004].
19. NICE (2005) *Referral guidelines for suspected cancer – quick reference guide*. Clinical guideline 27. National Institute for Health and Clinical Excellence. www.nice.org.uk [Accessed: 01/07/2005].
20. NZGG (2004) *Management of dyspepsia and heartburn*. New Zealand Guidelines Group. www.nzgg.org.nz [Accessed: 06/01/2005].
21. Rostom, A., Wells, G., Tugwell, P. et al (2002) *Prevention of NSAID-induced gastroduodenal ulcers (Cochrane Review)*. The Cochrane Library. Issue 4. Chichester, UK: John Wiley & Sons, Ltd. www.nelh.nhs.uk/cochrane.asp [Accessed: 04/04/2005]. [Full text]
22. SIGN (2003) *Dyspepsia*. Report no. 68. Scottish Intercollegiate Guideline Network. www.sign.ac.uk [Accessed: 19/07/2003].
23. Uemura, N., Okamoto, S., Yamamoto, S. et al (2001) *Helicobacter pylori* infection and the development of gastric cancer. *New England Journal of Medicine* **345**(11), 784–789. [Full text]
24. van der Hulst, R.W., van der Ende, A., Homan, A. et al (1998) Influence of metronidazole resistance on efficacy of quadruple therapy for *Helicobacter pylori* eradication. *Gut* **42**(2), 166–169. [Full text]
25. WeMeReC (2002) Use of proton pump inhibitors in primary care. *WeMeReC Bulletin* **9**(2), 1–6.

Evidence grading

Evidence grading is from the National Institute of Clinical Excellence guideline *Dyspepsia*, August 2004. The definitions of grades of recommendation used in this guideline are as follows:

A At least one randomized controlled trial as part of a body of literature of overall good quality and consistency addressing the specific recommendation without extrapolation.

B Well-conducted clinical studies but no randomized clinical trials on the topic of recommendation, or with extrapolation from evidence obtained from randomized trials of meta-analysis.

C Expert committee reports or opinions and/or clinical experiences of respected authorities. This grading indicates that directly applicable clinical studies of good quality are absent, or with extrapolation from higher levels of evidence.

GPP Good practice point. Recommended good practice based on the clinical experience of the guideline development group.

D

PRODIGY GUIDANCE

Dyspepsia — proven gastro-oesophageal reflux disease

Last revised in July 2005
www.prodigy.nhs.uk/guidance.asp?gt=Dyspepsia - proven GORD

Applies to people over the age of 16 years

This guidance is based on the National Institute for Clinical Excellence (NICE) guideline on *Dyspepsia* (August 2004).

D

This guidance covers the management of adults with endoscopically determined gastro-oesophageal reflux disease (GORD), i.e. oesophagitis or endoscopy-negative reflux disease.
People with uninvestigated 'reflux-like' symptoms should be managed as people with uninvestigated dyspepsia. See the PRODIGY guidance *Dyspepsia — symptoms (uninvestigated by endoscopy).*

This guidance does not cover in detail the management of complications such as stricture formation, or the management of pregnancy-associated dyspepsia.

There is separate PRODIGY guidance for uninvestigated dyspepsia (*Dyspepsia — symptoms uninvestigated by endoscopy*); proven ulcers (*Dyspepsia — proven DU or GU*); proven non-ulcer dyspepsia (*Dyspepsia — proven non-ulcer*); and pregnancy-associated dyspepsia (*Dyspepsia — pregnancy-associated*).

Goals

- To provide effective control of symptoms
- To promote healing of any mucosal lesions
- To prevent relapse
- To arrest progression of complications if present
- To detect any serious diagnoses, including oesophageal or gastric carcinoma

Contents

Scenarios
- Initial endoscopy result — first-line treatment p.650
- Symptoms persist despite PPI treatment — proven GORD p.652
- Maintenance treatment — proven GORD p.654

Extended Information, p. 657

Which scenario?

- **Initial endoscopy result — first-line treatment:** covers the management of people with proven gastro-oesophageal reflux disease (GORD), i.e. people with endoscopically determined oesophagitis or endoscopy-negative reflux disease.
- **Symptoms persist despite PPI treatment — proven GORD:** covers the management of people with endoscopically determined oesophagitis or endoscopy-negative reflux disease who have had an inadequate response to a PPI after 2 months treatment.
- **Maintenance treatment — proven GORD:** covers the management advice for people with endoscopically determined oesophagitis or endoscopy-negative reflux disease who require maintenance treatment.

Initial endoscopy result — first-line treatment

Which therapy?

- **Address anxieties** about the significance of symptoms.
- **Stop nonsteroidal anti-inflammatory drugs where possible.**
- **Review other medication which may be causing dyspepsia:** corticosteroids; bisphosphonates; medication that may lower oesophageal sphincter pressure (e.g. theophylline, nitrates, and calcium-channel blockers).
- **Offer a full-dose proton pump inhibitor for 1–2 months** to people with endoscopically determined oesophagitis or endoscopy-negative reflux disease.
- Note: people with complicated oesophagitis (past strictures, ulcers, or haemorrhage) will need to remain on long-term full-dose proton pump inhibitor therapy.
- **Give lifestyle advice:**
  - Healthy eating, weight loss, stopping smoking.
  - Avoiding precipitating factors, e.g. bending, alcohol, coffee, fatty foods.
  - Propping up the bed head, eating smaller meals, not eating close to bedtime.

Practical prescribing points

For further information please see the *Medicines Compendium* (www.medicines.org.uk) or the *British National Formulary* (www.bnf.org).

- **Proton pump inhibitors:** differences between the proton pump inhibitors in clinical efficacy and safety are minimal.
  - Omeprazole is currently cheapest.
  - Omeprazole and esomeprazole occasionally enhance the effects of warfarin and phenytoin. Monitor carefully if omeprazole or esomeprazole are started or stopped.

Follow-up advice

- **If there is inadequate response to treatment,** see scenario *Symptoms persist despite PPI treatment — proven GORD.*
- **If symptoms recur (but responded to a PPI),** offer a proton pump inhibitor (PPI) with a limited number of repeat prescriptions.
  - Encourage people to step down the PPI to the lowest dose required to control symptoms.
  - Discuss using the treatment on an 'on-demand' basis (i.e. waiting for symptoms to develop before taking treatment).
  - See scenario *Maintenance treatment — proven GORD.*
- All people with dyspepsia requiring long-term treatment should have an annual review of their condition, and lifestyle advice should be reinforced.

Follow-up for people with Barrett's oesophagus, severe ulcerative disease, stricture, ulcer, or haemorrhage should be guided by a specialist.

Should I refer or investigate?

Refer?

Indications for repeat endoscopy

Note: proton pump inhibitors and H_2-receptor antagonists should be stopped at least 2 weeks before endoscopy. Nonsteroidal anti-inflammatory drug use should also be suspended in all people requiring referral.

Consider managing previously investigated people without new ALARM symptoms according to previous endoscopic findings. However, if an additional diagnosis is suspected, or if the person has been symptom-free for several years before symptoms recur, consider referring for a repeat endoscopy to confirm the diagnosis.

Immediate endoscopy (i.e. same day) is indicated for people presenting with dyspepsia together with significant acute gastrointestinal bleeding.

Anyone who develops ALARM symptoms should be referred urgently for endoscopy, or to a specialist. That is people with:

- Chronic gastrointestinal bleeding
- Progressive unintentional weight loss
- Progressive difficulty swallowing (dysphagia)
- Persistent vomiting
- Iron deficiency anaemia
- Epigastric mass
- Suspicious barium meal result

People 55 years and over, presenting with unexplained and persistent recent onset dyspepsia alone, should be referred for urgent endoscopy.

Urgent referral to a specialist should also be considered in a person (of any age) who has unexplained worsening of their dyspepsia and:

- Barrett's oesophagus
- Known dysplasia, atrophic gastritis, or intestinal metaplasia
- Peptic ulcer surgery over 20 years ago

If definite dysphagia or odynophagia is present with a suspicious history or regurgitation, it is appropriate to refer for a barium swallow.

Investigate?

When referring, consider a full blood count to assist specialist assessment. This should be carried out in accordance with local arrangements.

Patient information leaflets

The following PILs are available at www.prodigy.nhs.uk

- Acid Reflux & Oesophagitis
- Barium Swallow / Meal / Follow Through
- Barrett's Oesophagus
- Barrett's Oesophagus Foundation
- CORE, Fighting Gut and Liver Disease
- Gastroscopy (Endoscopy)
- Hiatus Hernia

Shared decision making

- Things to consider which may help to ease acid reflux symptoms include:
  - **Changes to lifestyle:**
    - Stop smoking if you are a smoker.
    - Cut down on alcohol if you drink heavily.
    - Don't eat too much fatty or spicy food.
    - Raising the head of the bed and not eating close to bedtime.
    - Avoid bending.
    - Losing weight if you are overweight.
  - **Your medication.** Some medicines can make reflux worse. For example, anti-inflammatory painkillers (aspirin, ibuprofen, etc.), theophylline, nitrates, and calcium-channel blockers such as nifedipine.
- **Treatment of reflux is usually with a proton pump inhibitor (PPI).**
  - PPIs reduce the amount of acid made in the stomach. They include: omeprazole, lansoprazole, pantoprazole, rabeprazole, or esomeprazole.
  - Take a full dose for 4 weeks. This usually clears symptoms.
- After this you may only need antacids 'as required' if mild symptoms recur.
- (Note: if you have a complication of reflux such as a stricture, you will need to continue with a PPI.)
- Come back if troublesome symptoms return. You may need further treatment with a PPI.

Drug rationale

Drugs not included

- **Antacid and alginate preparations** are not included because although they can provide symptom relief, the limited available evidence shows that they are no more effective than placebo for healing oesophagitis [NICE, 2004].
- **Bismuth chelate, sucralfate, and misoprostol** are not included because their use is limited by their adverse effects and lack of proven usefulness in gastro-oesophageal reflux disease [Galmiche et al, 1998; WeMeReC, 2002].
- **H_2-receptor antagonists** (cimetidine, famotidine, nizatidine, ranitidine) are not included for first-line treatment because a step-down strategy using proton-pump inhibitors (PPIs) is recommended [NICE, 2004]. However, they are an option for people who have an inadequate response to PPI therapy.
- **Prokinetic agents** (metoclopramide or domperidone) are not included for first-line treatment. Trials have been few, small-scale, and heterogeneous — most evidence for prokinetics is for cisapride which is no longer available. However, they may improve symptoms such as bloating or early satiety [van Pinxteren et al, 2004].

Drugs included

- **Proton pump inhibitors:** all currently available PPIs (omeprazole, lansoprazole, pantoprazole, rabeprazole, and esomeprazole) are licensed for the treatment of gastro-oesophageal reflux disease. They are more effective than H_2-receptor antagonists at healing oesophagitis and in relieving symptoms in endoscopy-negative reflux disease [NICE, 2004; van Pinxteren et al, 2004]. Note: when undertaking meta-analysis of dose-related effects, NICE classed esomeprazole 20 mg as a full dose equivalent to omeprazole 20 mg.

Prescriptions

Proton pump inhibitors for 4 to 8 weeks

Omeprazole capsules: 20mg once a day

- Age from 16 years onwards
- Omeprazole 20mg capsules. Take one capsule once a day; supply 28 capsules; NHS Cost £12.75.

Omeprazole tablets: 20mg once a day
- Age from 16 years onwards
- Omeprazole 20mg tablets. Take one tablet once a day; supply 28 tablets; NHS Cost £12.75.

Lansoprazole capsules: 30mg each morning
- Age from 16 years onwards
- Lansoprazole 30mg capsules. Take one capsule each morning (on an empty stomach); supply 28 capsules; NHS Cost £23.63.

Lansoprazole orodispersible tablets: 30mg each morning
- Age from 16 years onwards
- Lansoprazole 30mg orodisp tabs. Take one tablet each morning (on an empty stomach); supply 28 tablets; NHS Cost £19.88.

Pantoprazole e/c tablets: 40mg once a day
- Age from 16 years onwards
- Pantoprazole 40mg e/c tablets. Take one tablet once a day; supply 28 tablets; NHS Cost £21.69.

Rabeprazole e/c tablets: 20mg once a day
- Age from 16 years onwards
- Rabeprazole 20mg e/c tabs. Take one tablet once a day; supply 28 tablets; NHS Cost £21.16.

Esomeprazole tablets: 20mg once a day
- Age from 16 years onwards
- Esomeprazole 20mg tablets. Take one tablet once a day; supply 28 tablets; NHS Cost £18.50.

Symptoms persist despite PPI treatment — proven GORD

Which therapy?

- **Severe oesophagitis: if there is still inadequate response** to a proton pump inhibitor (PPI) after 2 months of full-dose treatment:
  - Offer a double-dose PPI for 1 month, and then step down to the lowest dose that controls symptoms.
- **Mild or moderate oesophagitis or endoscopy-negative reflux disease: if there is still inadequate response** to a PPI after 2 months of full-dose treatment:
  - Consider switching to an H_2-receptor antagonist (H_2RA), as some individuals may benefit.
  - Alternatively, consider switching to a prokinetic (may improve bloating and early satiety).
- **For people with nocturnal symptoms:**
  - Consider giving a full-dose PPI at bedtime, or using a low dose twice a day.
  - Consider giving a short course of an H_2RA (in addition to the regular PPI) at bedtime.

Practical prescribing points

For further information please see the *Medicines Compendium* (www.medicines.org.uk) or the *British National Formulary* (www.bnf.org).

- **Proton pump inhibitors (PPIs):** differences between the PPIs in clinical efficacy and safety are minimal.
  - Omeprazole is currently cheapest.
  - Omeprazole and esomeprazole occasionally enhance the effects of warfarin and phenytoin. Monitor carefully if omeprazole or esomeprazole are started or stopped.
- **Cimetidine: avoid in people taking** erythromycin, warfarin, amiodarone, theophylline, carbamazepine, phenytoin, and sodium valproate as cimetidine inhibits hepatic drug metabolism by binding to microsomal cytochrome P450.
- **Prokinetics: avoid long-term use** of metoclopramide or domperidone.
- **Metoclopramide: avoid in young adults,** as extrapyramidal adverse effects are more common in this age group.

Follow-up advice

- **Encourage people to step down treatment** to the lowest dose required to control symptoms.
- Discuss using the treatment on an 'on-demand' basis (i.e waiting for symptoms to develop before taking treatment).
- All people with dyspepsia requiring long-term treatment should have an annual review of their condition, and lifestyle advice should be reinforced.
- **Follow-up for people with Barrett's oesophagus, severe ulcerative disease, stricture, ulcer, or haemorrhage** should be guided by a specialist.

Should I refer or investigate?

Refer?

- Consider referral if there is still inadequate response after 1 month of double dose PPI therapy.

Indications for repeat endoscopy

Note: proton pump inhibitors and H_2-receptor antagonists should be stopped at least 2 weeks before endoscopy. Nonsteroidal anti-inflammatory drug use should also be suspended in all people requiring referral.

- **Consider** managing previously investigated people without new ALARM symptoms according to previous endoscopic findings. However, if an additional diagnosis is suspected, or if the person has been symptom-free for several years before symptoms recur, consider referring for a repeat endoscopy to confirm the diagnosis.
- **Immediate endoscopy** (i.e. same day) is indicated for people presenting with dyspepsia together with significant acute gastrointestinal bleeding.
- **Anyone who develops ALARM symptoms should be referred urgently for endoscopy, or to a specialist.** That is people with:
  - Chronic gastrointestinal bleeding
  - Progressive unintentional weight loss
  - Progressive difficulty swallowing (dysphagia)
  - Persistent vomiting
  - Iron deficiency anaemia
  - Epigastric mass
  - Suspicious barium meal result
- **People 55 years and over, presenting with unexplained and persistent recent onset dyspepsia** alone, should be referred for urgent endoscopy.
- **Urgent referral to a specialist should also be considered** in a person (of any age) who has unexplained worsening of their dyspepsia and:
  - Barrett's oesophagus
  - Known dysplasia, atrophic gastritis, or intestinal metaplasia
  - Peptic ulcer surgery over 20 years ago
- **If definite dysphagia or odynophagia is present** with a suspicious history or regurgitation, it is appropriate to refer for a barium swallow.

Investigate?

- When referring, consider a full blood count to assist specialist assessment. This should be carried out in accordance with local arrangements.

Patient information leaflets

The following PILs are available at www.prodigy.nhs.uk

- Acid Reflux & Oesophagitis
- Barium Swallow / Meal / Follow Through
- Barrett's Oesophagus
- Barrett's Oesophagus Foundation
- CORE, Fighting Gut and Liver Disease
- Gastroscopy (Endoscopy)
- Hiatus Hernia

Shared decision making

Treatment of reflux is usually with a proton pump inhibitor (PPI) such as omeprazole, lansoprazole, pantoprazole, rabeprazole, or esomeprazole.

If symptoms have not improved much after 2 months of full-dose PPI:

- If you have severe oesophagitis, double the dose of the PPI for 1 month. Then gradually reduce the dose to the lowest dose that controls symptoms.
- If you have mild or moderate oesophagitis, or endoscopy-negative reflux disease, the options are:
  - Trying an H_2-receptor antagonist (H_2RA) such as cimetidine, famotidine, nizatidine, or ranitidine instead of a PPI.
  - Trying a prokinetic medicine such as domperidone or metoclopramide.
- If you are mainly troubled by symptoms at night, options include:
  - Taking the full dose of a PPI at bedtime.
  - Using a low-dose PPI twice a day.
  - Taking a short course of an (H_2RA) at bedtime in addition to a PPI.

Drug rationale

Drugs not included

Antacid and alginate preparations are not included because, although they can provide symptom relief, the limited available evidence shows that they are no more effective than placebo for healing oesophagitis [NICE, 2004].

Bismuth chelate, sucralfate, and misoprostol are not included because their use is limited by their adverse effects and lack of proven usefulness in gastro-oesophageal reflux disease (GORD) [Galmiche et al, 1998; WeMeReC, 2002].

Drugs included

- **Proton pump inhibitors:** all currently available PPIs (omeprazole, lansoprazole, pantoprazole, rabeprazole, and esomeprazole) are licensed for the treatment of gastro-oesophageal reflux disease (GORD). They are more effective than H_2-receptor antagonists in healing oesophagitis and in relieving symptoms in endoscopy-negative reflux disease [NICE, 2004; van Pinxteren et al, 2004]. Only omeprazole and esomeprazole are licensed as double-dose therapy for severe GORD. Note: when undertaking meta-analysis of dose-related effects, NICE classed esomeprazole 20 mg as a full-dose equivalent to omeprazole 20 mg.
- **H_2-receptor antagonists** (cimetidine, famotidine, nizatidine, ranitidine) are an option for people who have an inadequate response to PPI therapy.
- **Prokinetic agents** (metoclopramide or domperidone) are another option for people who have an inadequate response to PPI therapy. However, trials have been few, small-scale, and heterogeneous — most evidence for prokinetics is for cisapride, which is no longer available [van Pinxteren et al, 2004].

Prescriptions

Severe oesophagitis: double-dose proton pump inhibitors

Omeprazole capsules: 40mg once a day for 4 weeks
- Age from 16 years onwards
- Omeprazole 40mg capsules. Take one capsule once a day for 4 weeks; supply 28 capsules; NHS Cost £10.05.

Omeprazole tablets: 40mg once a day for 4 weeks
- Age from 16 years onwards
- Omeprazole 40mg tablets. Take one tablet once a day for 4 weeks; supply 28 tablets; NHS Cost £10.05.

Lansoprazole capsules: 30mg twice a day for 4 weeks
- Age from 16 years onwards
- Lansoprazole 30mg capsules. Take one capsule twice a day (on an empty stomach) for 4 weeks; supply 56 capsules; NHS Cost £47.26.

Lansoprazole orodisp tablets: 30mg twice a day for 4 weeks
- Age from 16 years onwards
- Lansoprazole 30mg orodisp tabs. Take one tablet twice a day (on an empty stomach) for 4 weeks; supply 56 tablets; NHS Cost £39.76.

Pantoprazole e/c tablets: 40mg twice a day for 4 weeks
- Age from 16 years onwards
- Pantoprazole 40mg e/c tablets. Take one tablet twice a day for 4 weeks; supply 56 tablets; NHS Cost £43.38.

Rabeprazole e/c tablets: 20mg twice a day for 4 weeks
- Age from 16 years onwards
- Rabeprazole 20mg e/c tabs. Take one tablet twice a day for 4 weeks; supply 56 tablets; NHS Cost £42.32.

Esomeprazole tablets: 40mg once a day for 4 weeks
- Age from 16 years onwards
- Esomeprazole 40mg tablets. Take one tablet once a day for 4 weeks; supply 28 tablets; NHS Cost £25.19.

Mild/mod oesophagits or ENRD: H2RAs or prokinetics

Cimetidine tablets: 400mg twice a day
- Age from 16 years onwards
- Cimetidine 400mg tablets. Take one tablet twice a day; supply 60 tablets; NHS Cost £5.58.

Ranitidine tablets: 150mg twice a day
- Age from 16 years onwards
- Ranitidine 150mg tablets. Take one tablet twice a day; supply 60 tablets; NHS Cost £7.21.

Nizatidine capsules: 150mg twice a day
- Age from 16 years onwards
- Nizatidine 150mg capsules. Take one capsule twice a day; supply 60 capsules; NHS Cost £12.26.

Famotidine tablets: 20mg twice a day
- Age from 16 years onwards
- Famotidine 20mg tablets. Take one tablet twice a day; supply 56 tablets; NHS Cost £23.28.

Metoclopramide tablets: 10mg three times a day (short term)
- Age from 20 years onwards
- Metoclopramide 10mg tablets. Take one tablet three times a day. If you are able to, try to take one tablet three times a day only when your symptoms recur; supply 84 tablets; NHS Cost £2.61.

Domperidone tablets: 10-20mg four times a day (short term)
- Age from 16 years onwards
- Domperidone 10mg tablets. Take one to two tablets four times a day (before meals and at bedtime). If you are able to, try to take these tablets only when your symptoms recur; supply 200 tablets; NHS Cost £16.62.

Nocturnal symptoms: full-dose PPI at night

Omeprazole capsules: 20mg at night
- Age from 16 years onwards
- Omeprazole 20mg capsules. Take one capsule at night; supply 28 capsules; NHS Cost £12.75.

Omeprazole tablets: 20mg at night
- Age from 16 years onwards
- Omeprazole 20mg tablets. Take one tablet at night; supply 28 tablets; NHS Cost £12.75.

Lansoprazole capsules: 30mg at night
- Age from 16 years onwards
- Lansoprazole 30mg capsules. Take one capsule at night; supply 28 capsules; NHS Cost £23.63.

Lansoprazole orodispersible tablets: 30mg at night
- Age from 16 years onwards
- Lansoprazole 30mg orodisp tabs. Take one tablet at night; supply 28 tablets; NHS Cost £19.88.

Pantoprazole e/c tablets: 40mg at night
- Age from 16 years onwards
- Pantoprazole 40mg e/c tablets. Take one tablet at night; supply 28 tablets; NHS Cost £21.69.

Rabeprazole e/c tablets: 20mg at night
- Age from 16 years onwards
- Rabeprazole 20mg e/c tabs. Take one tablet at night; supply 28 tablets; NHS Cost £21.16.

Esomeprazole tablets: 20mg at night
- Age from 16 years onwards
- Esomeprazole 20mg tablets. Take one tablet at night; supply 28 tablets; NHS Cost £18.50.

Nocturnal symptoms: low-dose PPI twice a day

Omeprazole capsules: 10mg twice a day
- Age from 16 years onwards
- Omeprazole 10mg capsules. Take one capsule twice a day; supply 56 capsules; NHS Cost £15.44.

Omeprazole tablets: 10mg twice a day
- Age from 16 years onwards
- Omeprazole 10mg tablets. Take one tablet twice a day; supply 56 tablets; NHS Cost £22.80.

Lansoprazole capsules: 15mg twice a day
- Age from 16 years onwards
- Lansoprazole 15mg capsules. Take one capsule twice a day (on an empty stomach); supply 56 capsules; NHS Cost £25.84.

Lansoprazole orodispersible tablets: 15mg twice a day
- Age from 16 years onwards
- Lansoprazole 15mg orodisp tabs. Take one tablet twice a day (on an empty stomach); supply 56 tablets; NHS Cost £21.72.

Pantoprazole e/c tablets: 20mg twice a day
- Age from 16 years onwards
- Pantoprazole 20mg e/c tablets. Take one tablet twice a day; supply 56 tablets; NHS Cost £24.62.

Rabeprazole e/c tablets: 10mg twice a day
- Age from 16 years onwards
- Rabeprazole 10mg e/c tabs. Take one tablet twice a day; supply 56 tablets; NHS Cost £23.12.

Nocturnal symptoms: add-on H_2-receptor antagonist

Cimetidine tablets: 400mg at night for 2 weeks
- Age from 16 years onwards
- Cimetidine 400mg tablets. Take one tablet at night for 2 weeks; supply 14 tablets; NHS Cost £1.30.

Ranitidine tablets: 150mg at night for 2 weeks
- Age from 16 years onwards
- Ranitidine 150mg tablets. Take one tablet at night for 2 weeks; supply 14 tablets; NHS Cost £1.68.

Nizatidine capsules: 150mg at night for 2 weeks
- Age from 16 years onwards
- Nizatidine 150mg capsules. Take one capsule at night for 2 weeks; supply 14 capsules; NHS Cost £2.86.

Famotidine tablets: 20mg at night for 2 weeks
- Age from 16 years onwards
- Famotidine 20mg tablets. Take one tablet at night for 2 weeks; supply 14 tablets; NHS Cost £5.82.

Maintenance treatment — proven GORD

Which therapy?

- **Review at least annually** all people with dyspepsia requiring long-term treatment.
- **Encourage people to step down treatment** to the lowest dose required to control symptoms.
- **Discuss using the treatment on an 'on-demand' basis** (i.e. waiting for symptoms to develop before taking treatment).
- Consider whether it is appropriate to stop current treatment (e.g. proton pump inhibitor, H_2-receptor antagonist, or prokinetic) and return to an antacid or alginate 'on demand'.
- **Do not step down or stop treatment with a PPI for:**
  - People with complicated oesophagitis (past strictures, ulcers, or haemorrhage).
- **Reinforce lifestyle advice:**
  - Healthy eating, weight loss, stopping smoking.
  - Avoiding precipitating factors, e.g. bending, alcohol, coffee, fatty foods.
  - Propping up the bed head, eating smaller meals, not eating close to bedtime.

Practical prescribing points

For further information please see the *Medicines Compendium* (www.medicines.org.uk) or the *British National Formulary* (www.bnf.org).

- **Proton pump inhibitors:** differences between the proton pump inhibitors in clinical efficacy and safety are minimal.
  - Omeprazole is currently cheapest.
  - Omeprazole and esomeprazole occasionally enhance the effects of warfarin and phenytoin. Monitor carefully if omeprazole or esomeprazole are started or stopped.
- **Cimetidine: avoid in people taking** erythromycin, warfarin, amiodarone, theophylline, carbamazepine, phenytoin, and sodium valproate as cimetidine inhibits hepatic drug metabolism by binding to microsomal cytochrome P450.
- **Prokinetics: avoid long-term use** of metoclopramide or domperidone.
- **Metoclopramide: avoid in young adults** as extrapyramidal adverse effects are more common in this age group.

Antacids and alginates are not suitable for long-term, frequent-dose, continuous use.
Antacids: combinations of aluminium salts with magnesium salts may be preferable to magnesium salts alone (may cause diarrhoea) or aluminium salts alone (may cause constipation).

Follow-up advice

All people with dyspepsia requiring long-term treatment should have an annual review of their condition, and lifestyle advice should be reinforced.
Follow-up for people with Barrett's oesophagus, severe ulcerative disease, stricture, ulcer, or haemorrhage should be guided by a specialist.

Should I refer or investigate?

Refer?

Indications for repeat endoscopy

Note: proton pump inhibitors and H_2-receptor antagonists should be stopped at least 2 weeks before endoscopy. Nonsteroidal anti-inflammatory drug use should also be suspended in all people requiring referral.
Consider managing previously investigated people without new alarm symptoms according to previous endoscopic findings. However, if an additional diagnosis is suspected, or if the person has been symptom-free for several years before symptoms recur, consider referring for a repeat endoscopy to confirm the diagnosis.
Immediate endoscopy (i.e. same day) is indicated for people presenting with dyspepsia together with significant acute gastrointestinal bleeding.
Anyone who develops ALARM symptoms should be referred urgently for endoscopy, or to a specialist. That is people with:

- Chronic gastrointestinal bleeding
- Progressive unintentional weight loss
- Progressive difficulty swallowing (dysphagia)
- Persistent vomiting
- Iron deficiency anaemia
- Epigastric mass
- Suspicious barium meal result

People 55 years and over, presenting with unexplained and persistent recent onset dyspepsia alone, should be referred for urgent endoscopy.
Urgent referral to a specialist should also be considered in a person (of any age) who has unexplained worsening of their dyspepsia and:

- Barrett's oesophagus
- Known dysplasia, atrophic gastritis, or intestinal metaplasia
- Peptic ulcer surgery over 20 years ago

If definite dysphagia or odynophagia is present with a suspicious history or regurgitation, it is appropriate to refer for a barium swallow.

Investigate?

When referring, consider a full blood count to assist specialist assessment. This should be carried out in accordance with local arrangements.

Patient information leaflets

The following PILs are available at www.prodigy.nhs.uk

- Acid Reflux & Oesophagitis
- Barium Swallow / Meal / Follow Through
- Barrett's Oesophagus
- Barrett's Oesophagus Foundation
- CORE, Fighting Gut and Liver Disease
- Gastroscopy (Endoscopy)
- Hiatus Hernia

Shared decision making

- Your symptoms of acid reflux have improved.
- If symptoms return after treatment has finished, options to consider are:
  - A daily dose of an acid-suppressing medicine. Start at full dose. But once symptoms have eased again, gradually reduce to the lowest dose needed to control symptoms, *or*
  - Short courses of an acid-suppressing medicine just when symptoms occur.
  - Trying a prokinetic medicine such as domperidone or metoclopramide, *or*
  - An antacid as required.
- Note: some people need long-term full-dose acid-suppressing medication, for example, if you have a stricture.
- Remember, lifestyle factors may also help to prevent reflux. For example:
  - Stop smoking if you are a smoker.
  - Cut down on alcohol if you drink heavily.
  - Don't eat too much fatty or spicy food.
  - Raise the head of the bed and avoid eating close to bedtime.
  - Avoid bending.
  - Lose weight if you are overweight.

Drug rationale

Drugs not included

- **Other antacid preparations** are not included. Products containing simeticone (activated dimeticone) are unlikely to confer any additional advantage. Products containing bismuth have not been included because of a high incidence of adverse effects. Many other products available to purchase over the counter are not prescribable on the NHS.
- **Other alginate preparations** are not included because they not available as sugar-free products.
- **Bismuth chelate, sucralfate, and misoprostol** are not included because their use is limited by their adverse effects and lack of proven usefulness in gastro-oesophageal reflux disease (GORD) [Galmiche et al, 1998; WeMeReC, 2002].

Drugs included

- **Proton pump inhibitors:** all currently available PPIs (omeprazole, lansoprazole, pantoprazole, rabeprazole, and esomeprazole) are licensed for maintenance treatment in GORD.
  - People should be encouraged to use the lowest dose that controls symptoms.
  - All PPIs have been studied as on-demand therapy, but only rabeprazole and esomeprazole are currently licensed for this indication.
  - Note: when undertaking meta-analysis of dose-related effects, NICE classed esomeprazole 20 mg as a full-dose equivalent to omeprazole 20 mg.
- **H_2-receptor antagonists** (cimetidine, famotidine, nizatidine, ranitidine) are an option for people who have an inadequate response to PPI therapy [NICE, 2004].
- **Prokinetic agents** (metoclopramide or domperidone) are also an option for people who have an inadequate response to PPI therapy [NICE, 2004]. They may improve symptoms such as bloating or early satiety [van Pinxteren et al, 2004].

D

- **Antacid and alginates** are included for on-demand use. Long-term, frequent-dose, continuous prescription of antacid therapy is inappropriate and only relieves symptoms in the short term, rather than preventing them [NICE, 2004]. However, they are a suitable 'on-demand' option, particularly for those people who are able to return to self-care.

Prescriptions

Proton pump inhibitors: full dose

Omeprazole capsules: 20mg once a day
- Age from 16 years onwards
- Omeprazole 20mg capsules. Take one capsule once a day; supply 28 capsules; NHS Cost £12.75.

Omeprazole tablets: 20mg once a day
- Age from 16 years onwards
- Omeprazole 20mg tablets. Take one tablet once a day; supply 28 tablets; NHS Cost £12.75.

Lansoprazole capsules: 30mg each morning
- Age from 16 years onwards
- Lansoprazole 30mg capsules. Take one capsule each morning (on an empty stomach); supply 28 capsules; NHS Cost £23.63.

Lansoprazole orodispersible tablets: 30mg each morning
- Age from 16 years onwards
- Lansoprazole 30mg orodisp tabs. Take one tablet each morning (on an empty stomach); supply 28 tablets; NHS Cost £19.88.

Pantoprazole e/c tablets: 40mg once a day
- Age from 16 years onwards
- Pantoprazole 40mg e/c tablets. Take one tablet once a day; supply 28 tablets; NHS Cost £21.69.

Rabeprazole e/c tablets: 20mg once a day
- Age from 16 years onwards
- Rabeprazole 20mg e/c tabs. Take one tablet once a day; supply 28 tablets; NHS Cost £21.16.

Esomeprazole tablets: 20mg once a day
- Age from 16 years onwards
- Esomeprazole 20mg tablets. Take one tablet once a day; supply 28 tablets; NHS Cost £18.50.

Proton pump inhibitors: low dose or on-demand

Omeprazole capsules: 10mg once a day
- Age from 16 years onwards
- Omeprazole 10mg capsules. Take one capsule once a day. If you are able to, try to take one capsule once a day only when your symptoms recur; supply 28 capsules; NHS Cost £7.72.

Omeprazole tablets: 10mg once a day
- Age from 16 years onwards
- Omeprazole 10mg tablets. Take one tablet once a day. If you are able to, try to take one tablet once a day only when your symptoms recur; supply 28 tablets; NHS Cost £11.40.

Lansoprazole capsules: 15mg each morning
- Age from 16 years onwards
- Lansoprazole 15mg capsules. Take one capsule each morning (on an empty stomach). If you are able to, try to take one capsule each morning only when your symptoms recur; supply 28 capsules; NHS Cost £12.92.

Lansoprazole orodispersible tablets: 15mg each morning
- Age from 16 years onwards
- Lansoprazole 15mg orodisp tabs. Take one tablet each morning (on an empty stomach). If you are able to, try to take one tablet each morning only when your symptoms recur; supply 28 tablets; NHS Cost £10.86.

Pantoprazole e/c tablets: 20mg once a day
- Age from 16 years onwards
- Pantoprazole 20mg e/c tablets. Take one tablet once a day. If you are able to, try to take one tablet once a day only when your symptoms recur; supply 28 tablets; NHS Cost £12.31.

Rabeprazole e/c tablets: 10mg once a day
- Age from 16 years onwards
- Rabeprazole 10mg e/c tabs. Take one tablet once a day If you are able to, try to take one tablet once a day only when your symptoms recur; supply 28 tablets; NHS Cost £11.56.

Esomeprazole e/c tablets: 20mg once a day
- Age from 16 years onwards
- Esomeprazole 20mg tablets. Take one tablet once a day If you are able to, try to take one tablet once a day only when your symptoms recur; supply 28 tablets; NHS Cost £18.50.

H_2-receptor antagonists: maintenance or on-demand

Cimetidine tablets: 400mg twice a day
- Age from 16 years onwards
- Cimetidine 400mg tablets. Take one tablet twice a day. If you are able to, reduce to one tablet at night. Alternatively, try taking these tablets only when your symptoms recur; supply 60 tablets; NHS Cost £5.58.

Ranitidine tablets: 150mg twice a day
- Age from 16 years onwards
- Ranitidine 150mg tablets. Take one tablet twice a day. you are able to, reduce to one tablet at night. Alternatively, try taking these tablets only when your symptoms recur; supply 60 tablets; NHS Cost £7.21.

Nizatidine capsules: 150mg twice a day
- Age from 16 years onwards
- Nizatidine 150mg capsules. Take one capsule twice a day. If you are able to, reduce to one cap at night. Alternatively, try taking these capsules only when your symptoms recur; supply 60 capsules; NHS Cost £12.26

Famotidine tablets: 20mg twice a day
- Age from 16 years onwards
- Famotidine 20mg tablets. Take one tablet twice a day. you are able to, reduce to one tablet at night. Alternatively, try taking these tablets only when your symptoms recur; supply 56 tablets; NHS Cost £23.28.

Prokinetics: on-demand (not suitable for long-term use)

Domperidone tablets: 10mg to 20mg four times a day
- Age from 16 years onwards
- Domperidone 10mg tablets. Take one to two tablets fo times a day (before meals and at bedtime). If you are ab to, try to take these tablets only when your symptoms recur; supply 200 tablets; NHS Cost £16.62.

Metoclopramide tablets: 10mg three times a day
- Age from 20 years onwards
- Metoclopramide 10mg tablets. Take one tablet three times a day. If you are able to, try to take one tablet three times a day only when your symptoms recur; supply 84 tablets; NHS Cost £2.61.

Antacids and alginates: on-demand

Antacids: co-magaldrox 195/220mg suspension
- Age from 16 years onwards
- Co-magald 195/220mg/5ml susp. Take two to four 5ml spoonfuls 20-60 minutes after food and at bedtime, when required to relieve dyspepsia; supply 1000 ml; NHS Cost £3.82; OTC Cost £6.74.

ıtacids: aluminium hydroxide 4% suspension

Age from 16 years onwards

Aluminium hydroxide 4% mixture. Take one to two 5ml spoonfuls four times a day (between meals and at bedtime) when required to relieve dyspepsia; supply 400 ml; NHS Cost £2.84; OTC Cost £3.32.

ıtacids: magnesium trisilicate mixture

Age from 16 years onwards

Magnesium trisilicate mixture. Take two 5ml spoonfuls (mixed in water) three times a day when required to relieve dyspepsia; supply 400 ml; NHS Cost £0.94; OTC Cost £1.10.

ginates: Gastrocote liquid (sugar-free)

Age from 16 years onwards

Gastrocote liquid. Take one to three 5ml spoonfuls four times a day (after meals and at bedtime) when required to relieve dyspepsia; supply 1000 ml; NHS Cost £5.58; OTC Cost £9.84.

ginates: Gaviscon Advance tablets (sugar-free)

Age from 16 years onwards

Gaviscon Advance tablets. Chew one to two tablets (followed by water) after meals and at bedtime, when required to relieve dyspepsia; supply 120 tablets; NHS Cost £6.48; OTC Cost £14.98.

ginates: Gaviscon Advance liquid (sugar-free)

Age from 16 years onwards

Gaviscon Advance s/f susp. Take one to two 5ml spoonfuls after meals and at bedtime, when required to relieve dyspepsia; supply 500 ml; NHS Cost £5.40; OTC Cost £9.95.

ginates: Peptac liquid (sugar-free)

Age from 16 years onwards

Peptac s/f liquid. Take two to four 5ml spoonfuls after meals and at bedtime, when required to relieve dyspepsia; supply 1000 ml; NHS Cost £4.32; OTC Cost £7.98.

ginates: Rennie Duo suspension (sugar-free)

Age from 16 years onwards

Rennie Duo oral suspension. Take two to four 5ml spoonfuls after meals and at bedtime, when required to relieve dyspepsia; supply 1000 ml; NHS Cost £5.34; OTC Cost £10.58.

ːxtended Information

ˌackground information

What is dyspepsia? p.657
What is GORD? p.657
How common is it? p.657
How do I know my patient has GORD? p.657
What else might it be? p.658
Complications and prognosis p.658

/hat is dyspepsia?

Dyspepsia is a term used to describe a group of symptoms that alert the clinician to consider the possibility of upper gastrointestinal tract disease. It is not a diagnosis. The group of symptoms includes epigastric pain, heartburn or acid regurgitation (with or without bloating), nausea, or vomiting.

/hat is GORD?

Gastro-oesophageal reflux disease (GORD) is a term used to describe diseases that cause reflux of gastric contents into the oesophagus, causing symptoms (e.g. heartburn or acid regurgitation) that are sufficient to interfere with quality of life.

- Endoscopy may reveal oesophageal mucosal breaks (oesophagitis), or may be normal (endoscopy-negative reflux disease).
- **Endoscopy-negative reflux disease** refers to people with predominant reflux symptoms and a normal endoscopy (i.e. without oesophagitis).
- There is no universally accepted definition of the grades of oesophagitis. The Los Angeles classification and the Savary–Miller classification are shown in Table 1.
- **Complications of GORD are rare and include** deep ulcers, strictures, or Barrett's oesophagus (columnar epithelium in the distal oesophagus). Barrett's oesophagus can be defined as long-segment disease (where the abnormal mucosa extends 3 cm or more above the gastro-oesophageal junction) or short-segment disease (where the abnormal muscosa extends less than 3 cm above the gastro-oesophageal junction).

Table 1: Classification of oesophagitis.

Los Angeles classification	Savary–Miller classification
Grade A: one or more mucosal breaks each no longer than 5 mm in length	Grade I: exhibits one or more supravestibular, non-confluent reddish spots, with or without exudate
Grade B: at least one mucosal break >5 mm long, but not continuous between the tops of adjacent mucosal folds	Grade II: demonstrates erosive and exudative lesions in the distal oesophagus which may be confluent, but not circumferential
Grade C: at least one mucosal break that is continuous between the tops of adjacent mucosal folds, but which is not circumferential	Grade III: is characterized by circumferential erosions in the distal oesophagus, covered by haemorrhagic and pseudomembranous exudate
Grade D: mucosal break that involves at least three-quarters of the luminal circumference	Grade IV: is defined by the presence of chronic complications such as deep ulcers, stenosis, or scarring with Barrett's metaplasia

How common is it?

- Heartburn and acid regurgitation are experienced by 5% of the population several times a month [DTB, 1996]. Most people treat themselves with over-the-counter preparations.
- About 4% of general practice consultations are for dyspepsia and about 10% of these lead to referral for further investigation [British Society of Gastroenterology, 2002].
- For those people investigated by endoscopy for dyspepsia, 30% have no abnormal findings (i.e. endoscopy-negative reflux disease or non-ulcer dyspepsia) and 10–17% have oesophagitis [British Society of Gastroenterology, 2002].
- A further 30% have either gastritis, duodenitis, or hiatus hernia; 10–15% have duodenal ulcer; 5–10% have gastric ulcer; and 2% have gastric cancer [British Society of Gastroenterology, 2002].
- Long-segment Barrett's oesophagus (a complication of GORD) is currently diagnosed in 1.4% of all endoscopies [NICE, 2004].

How do I know my patient has GORD?

History

- **Symptoms are variable:**
  - **Epigastric pain** often radiates to the throat and worsens when bending or lying flat.
  - **Heartburn,** oesophageal reflux, or oesophageal spasm (characterized by a sharp, stabbing substernal pain) commonly occurs at night or after consumption of a large meal.

- **Regurgitation** of acid and food into the mouth may occur.
- **Dysphagia** and pain on swallowing may accompany severe oesophagitis.
- **Symptoms are a poor predictor of disease severity or underlying pathology** (C). For example:
  - People with oesophagitis and Barrett's oesophagus may be asymptomatic.
  - People with severe heartburn may have a normal endoscopy.
  - The presence of heartburn does not exclude other pathology. For example, one study found that duodenal ulcer was as common in people with dominant heartburn as in those with epigastric pain [Chiba et al, 2003].

Investigations

- **Oesophagitis and endoscopy-negative reflux disease can only be diagnosed by endoscopy.** However, it is neither necessary nor practical to investigate a diagnosis in every patient with dyspepsia (in the absence of ALARM symptoms) if symptoms are controlled by empirical treatment [NICE, 2004].
  - This guidance deals with the management of people with endoscopically determined oesophagitis and endoscopy-negative reflux disease.
  - People with reflux-like symptoms who do *not* need an endoscopy (i.e. do not have ALARM symptoms) should be managed via the PRODIGY guidance *Dyspepsia — symptoms (uninvestigated by endoscopy)*.

Less common investigations

- **24-hour oesophageal pH testing** may be useful in people with reflux symptoms and a normal endoscopy to confirm the diagnosis of endoscopy-negative reflux disease. It is usually reserved for the investigation of persistent gastro-oesophageal reflux disease (GORD) that does not respond adequately to treatment.
- **Oesophageal manometry** does not diagnose GORD, but is used to evaluate peristalsis and to assess the function of the lower oesophageal sphincter. It is usually reserved for people who are going to undergo anti-reflux surgery.

What else might it be?

- **Cardiac or biliary disease** (C).
  - Cardiac pain may be clinically indistinguishable from dyspepsia.
  - Biliary colic occasionally presents with epigastric pain.
- **Oesophageal or gastric carcinoma.** Investigate for malignancy in the presence of any ALARM symptoms (chronic gastrointestinal bleeding; dysphagia; progressive unintentional weight loss; persistent vomiting; iron deficiency anaemia; an epigastric mass; or suspicious barium meal). Symptom severity is a poor indicator of an underlying disease.
- **Irritable bowel syndrome** may manifest as dyspepsia with bloating, but is usually associated with abnormal bowel habits.
- **Motility disorders** may also manifest as upper abdominal discomfort with bloating and early satiety. Gastroparesis should be suspected in people with diabetes mellitus, especially when peripheral neuropathy is present.
- **Non-ulcer dyspepsia** (also known as functional dyspepsia).
- **Peptic ulcer disease.**
- **Other causes of dysphagia include** peptic stricture, Schatzki ring, and (less commonly) achalasia, diffuse spasm, systemic sclerosis, bronchial carcinoma, enlarged mediastinal nodes, aortic aneurysm, post-cricoid web, or radiation stricture.

Table 2: Diagnostic tests for gastro-oesophageal reflux disease.

Investigation	Specificity (%)	Sensitiv (%)
Endoscopy with > grade I oesophagitis	96	68
24-hour oesophageal pH test	95	93
Oesophageal manometry with lower oesophageal sphincter pressure, <10 mmHg	84	58

Complications and prognosis

Complications

- Haemorrhage
- Anaemia
- Strictures
- Barrett's oesophagus (oesophageal columnar metaplasi — a premalignant condition

Prognosis

- **For people with gastro-oesophageal reflux disease** (GORD), symptoms are recurrent and intermittent; symptoms recur annually in about 50% of these people The lifetime risk of recurrence is about 80% [NICE, 2004].
- Heartburn is a major feature of GORD; 7% of adults have daily symptoms and 35% have monthly symptom but the degree of pain does not correspond well to the severity of oesophagitis [Moayyedi et al, 2004].
- People with endoscopy-negative reflux disease remain stable, with a minority of people developing oesophagit over time [Moayyedi et al, 2004].
- People with Barrett's oesophagus develop oesophageal cancer at a rate of 0.5% per year, a rate that is more than 30 times higher than in the general population, bu low in absolute terms [Spechler, 2003].

Management issues

- Overview of management p.659
- What general measures are useful? p.659
- What is first-line treatment? p.659
- What should I do if there is inadequate response to first line treatment? p.659
- What should I do if symptoms recur? p.659
- How should people with Barrett's oesophagus be managed? p.660
- How should people with other complications be managed? p.660
- Reviewing and stepping down treatment p.660
- When is repeat endoscopy indicated? p.660
- Supporting evidence for treatment strategies p.661
- Surgery p.661
- Medicines management p.662

This guidance covers the management of people with endoscopically determined oesophagitis or people with endoscopy-negative reflux disease.
People with uninvestigated 'reflux-like' symptoms should be managed as patients with uninvestigated dyspepsia (C) [NICE, 2004]. See the PRODIGY guidance *Dyspepsia — symptoms (uninvestigated by endoscopy)*. Consider managing previously investigated people without new ALARM symptoms according to previous endoscopic findings.

Overview of management

- Review medication that may be causing dyspepsia.
- Offer general lifestyle advice.
- Offer a full-dose proton pump inhibitor (PPI) for 1 month.
- If symptoms persist after the initial course of PPI:
  - Extend the course of PPI for a further month.
  - Or consider giving a double-dose PPI for 1 month if oesophagitis is severe.
  - Or consider switching to an H_2-receptor antagonist (H_2RA) or a prokinetic for people with mild oesophagitis or endoscopy-negative reflux disease.
- If symptoms were initially controlled by a course treatment but have now returned:
  - Re-start the treatment (e.g. a PPI or H_2RA) with a limited number of repeat prescriptions.
  - Step down to the lowest dose required to control symptoms.
  - Encourage people to use treatment on an 'on-demand' basis.
- All people with endoscopically determined oesophagitis or endoscopy-negative reflux disease requiring long-term treatment should have an annual review of their condition, and lifestyle advice should be reinforced.
- Anxiety regarding symptoms should be addressed. People who consult with dyspepsia are often more anxious about the significance of their symptoms than those who do not, but the symptoms are not generally more severe or longer lasting.

What general measures are useful?

Which medication might be causing dyspeptic symptoms?

- **Stop nonsteroidal anti-inflammatory drugs (NSAIDs) wherever possible (A).** If an NSAID is essential, consider gastric protection or substitution with a COX-2 selective NSAID.
- **Theophylline, nitrates, and calcium-channel blockers** may reduce lower oesophageal sphincter pressure. Consider withdrawing if there are predominant reflux symptoms.
- **Bisphosphonates and corticosteroids** commonly cause gastrointestinal adverse effects.

[MeReC, 1998; NICE, 2004]

What lifestyle advice is recommended?

- **Offer simple lifestyle advice,** including healthy eating, weight reduction, and smoking cessation (**B**). Although there is no clear evidence that lifestyle factors (such as smoking, alcohol, caffeine, and diet) affect dyspepsia, there are more important general health benefits.
- **If the person has identified a precipitating factor,** then it is sensible to advise them to avoid it (e.g. bending, alcohol, coffee, chocolate, fatty foods, spicy foods) (**C**).
- **Other suggestions for people with reflux symptoms include** eating smaller meals, not eating before going to bed, and propping up the bed head. (One possible cause of reflux disease is transient relaxation of the lower oesophageal sphincter: lying flat may therefore increase reflux episodes since gravity does not then prevent acid regurgitation.)
- **Provide people with patient information** to support the care they receive (**C**).

[MeReC, 1998; NICE, 2004]

What is first-line treatment?

- **Offer a full-dose proton pump inhibitor** (PPI) **for 1 month** to people with endoscopically determined oesophagitis or endoscopy-negative reflux disease [NICE, 2004].
- In the past either a step-up or a step-down strategy has been advocated [NICE, 2000]. However, NICE now recommends a step-down approach to PPI therapy.
- People with diagnosed gastro-oesophageal reflux disease (GORD) do *not* need to be routinely tested (and treated) for *Helicobacter pylori* because *H pylori* eradication does not improve outcomes in GORD [Delaney et al, 2004].

D

What should I do if there is inadequate response to first-line treatment?

- **If there is an inadequate initial response** to the first 4 weeks of proton pump inhibitor (PPI) treatment, extend the course for a further 4 weeks [NICE, 2004].
- **A minority of people have persistent symptoms despite PPI therapy,** and this group remain a challenge to treat.
  - For people with Los Angeles grade A or B oesophagitis or endoscopy-negative reflux disease, consider switching to an H_2-receptor antagonist (H_2RA) or a prokinetic (e.g. domperidone or metoclopramide) as some individuals may respond to these therapies [NICE, 2004]. (There is no evidence to guide which to offer first, but prokinetics may improve symptoms of bloating and early satiety.)
  - If the person has Los Angeles grade C or D oesophagitis (i.e. severe oesophagitis) and still remains symptomatic, offer a double-dose PPI for a further month [NICE, 2004], then encourage the person to step down treatment to the lowest dose required to control symptoms.
  - If the person has a problem with nocturnal symptoms that do not respond to PPI therapy, it may be worth adding an additional H_2RA at bedtime in the short term (e.g. intermittent 2-week courses).

What should I do if symptoms recur?

- Most people with gastro-oesophageal reflux disease (GORD) will experience a recurrence of symptoms within 1 year. While a trial without medication is appropriate, many people will need further courses of treatment.
- **If there was an initial response to treatment** but symptoms have now returned, offer maintenance treatment:
  - Re-start treatment (e.g. a proton pump inhibitor [PPI]) at full dose, with a limited number of repeat prescriptions.
  - Encourage people to step down treatment to the lowest dose required to control symptoms (**B**).
  - Discuss using the treatment on an 'on-demand' basis (i.e. waiting for symptoms to develop before taking treatment) (**B**).
- **Note that stepping down or stopping treatment with at PPI is not appropriate for:**
  - People with complicated oesophagitis (past strictures, ulcers, or haemorrhage).
  - People taking a PPI for gastroprotection against NSAIDs.
  - People with a previous bleeding peptic ulcer who remain *Helicobacter pylori* positive after at least two attempts at eradication.

How should people with Barrett's oesophagus be managed?

- Barrett's oesophagus is a risk factor for oesophageal cancer, but the absolute incidence of oesophageal cancer in people with Barrett's oesophagus is low (about 0.5% per year). There is also some evidence to suggest that Barrett's oesophagus does not shorten survival [Eckardt et al, 2001].
- Proton pump inhibitors (PPIs) are used for symptom control. It is unknown whether acid suppression can reduce the risk of developing oesophageal cancer, so it is currently unclear whether there is any value in continuing PPIs in people with asymptomatic Barrett's oesophagus.
- Many other strategies have been proposed to reduce the risk of developing oesophageal cancer, including double-dose PPI maintenance therapy (to normalize rather than just reduce gastric acid pH); anti-reflux surgery; endoscopic ablative therapy; and regular endoscopic surveillance [Spechler, 2003; Chang and Katzka, 2004].
- There is no consensus regarding which strategy to use since none has been shown to reduce mortality from oesophageal adenocarcinoma in people with Barrett's oesophagus. Therefore practice in the UK varies widely between specialist centres [Mandal et al, 2003].
- People with Barrett's oesophagus should therefore be managed on an individual basis, on the advice of a consultant gastroenterologist.

How should people with other complications be managed?

- **People with oesophageal strictures** are initially managed in secondary care. Once strictures have been successfully treated, these people should remain on long-term continuous full-dose proton pump inhibitor (PPI) therapy to prevent relapse, i.e. PPI therapy should *not* be stepped down [NICE, 2000]. People who experience recurrence of their strictures may benefit from long-term twice daily PPI therapy. If in doubt, seek specialist advice.
- **People with oesophageal ulcer or haemorrhage** should also be maintained on full-dose PPIs [NICE, 2000].

Reviewing and stepping down treatment

How should I follow up people whose symptoms respond to treatment?

- All people with gastro-oesophageal reflux disease requiring long-term treatment should have an annual review of their condition, and lifestyle advice should be reinforced [NICE, 2004] (C).
  - Encourage people to step down treatment to the lowest dose required to control symptoms (C).
  - Discuss using the treatment on an 'on-demand' basis (i.e. waiting for symptoms to develop before taking treatment) (C).
- Note that stepping down or stopping treatment is not appropriate for:
  - People with complicated oesophagitis (past strictures, ulcers, or haemorrhage).
  - People taking a proton pump inhibitor (PPI) for gastroprotection against nonsteroidal anti-inflammatory drugs.
  - People with a previous bleeding peptic ulcer who remain *Helicobacter pylori* positive after at least two attempts at eradication.

How should I manage people whose symptoms persist despite treatment?

- If there is an inadequate response to therapy or new emergent symptoms, it may become appropriate to refer to a specialist for a second opinion or endoscopy may become appropriate. See *When is repeat endoscopy indicated?*

When is repeat endoscopy indicated?

Note: proton pump inhibitors and H_2-receptor antagonists should be stopped at least 2 weeks before endoscopy (**B**). Nonsteroidal anti-inflammatory drug use should also be suspended in all people requiring referral (C).

- **Consider** managing previously investigated people without new ALARM symptoms according to previous endoscopic findings. However, if an additional diagnosis is suspected, or if the person has been symptom-free for several years before symptoms recur, consider referring for a repeat endoscopy to confirm the diagnosis.
- **Immediate endoscopy** (i.e. same day) is indicated for people presenting with dyspepsia together with significant acute gastrointestinal bleeding.
- **Anyone who develops ALARM symptoms should be referred urgently for endoscopy, or to a specialist** (C) [NICE, 2005]. That is people with:
  - Chronic gastrointestinal bleeding
  - Progressive unintentional weight loss
  - Progressive difficulty swallowing (dysphagia)
  - Persistent vomiting
  - Iron deficiency anaemia
  - Epigastric mass
  - Suspicious barium meal result
- **People 55 years and over, presenting with unexplained and persistent recent onset dyspepsia** alone, should be referred for urgent endoscopy (C) [NICE, 2004].
  - *Unexplained* is defined as a symptom(s) and/or sign(s) that has not led to a diagnosis being made by the primary care professional after initial assessment of the history, examination and primary care investigations (if any)'. In the context of this recommendation, the primary care professional should confirm that the dyspepsia is new rather than a recurrent episode and exclude common precipitants of dyspepsia such as ingestion of NSAIDs.
  - *Persistent* refers to the continuation of specified symptoms and/or signs beyond a period that would normally be associated with self-limiting problems. The precise period will vary depending on the severity of symptoms and associated features, as assessed by the healthcare professional. In many cases, the upper limit the professional will permit symptoms and/or signs to persist before initiating referral will be 4–6 weeks.
- **Urgent referral to a specialist should also be considered in** a person (of any age) who has unexplained worsening of their dyspepsia and Barrett's oesophagus; or known dysplasia, atrophic gastritis, or intestinal metaplasia; or peptic ulcer surgery over 20 years ago (C) [NICE, 2005].
- **If dysphagia is present** (interference with the swallowing mechanism that occurs within 5 seconds of starting the swallowing process) it is appropriate to refer for a barium swallow. There is a risk of perforation if an endoscope is pushed through a stricture. Before endoscopic examination, barium swallow will delineate the stricture to see how long it is.

[NICE, 2004; NICE, 2005]

Supporting evidence for treatment strategies

First-line treatment

Acute healing of oesophagitis

- Proton pump inhibitors (PPIs) are more effective than H_2-receptor antagonists (H_2RAs) at healing oesophagitis in trials [NICE, 2004]. Data pooled by NICE found that healing occurred in 22% of people taking placebo, 39% of people on H_2RAs, and 76% of people on PPIs (although there was considerable variation in the findings of individual studies). This equates to a number needed to treat of 6 for H_2RAs and 2 for PPIs.
- There is no evidence that any PPI is more effective than another for healing oesophagitis when PPIs are compared at equivalent doses [Edwards et al, 2001; Sharma et al, 2001].
- Antacids and alginates are widely used but there are few studies examining their efficacy for healing oesophagitis. Data pooled by NICE found that alginates do provide symptom relief. However, the limited available evidence also shows that antacids are no more effective than placebo for healing oesophagitis [NICE, 2004].

Endoscopy-negative reflux disease

- A recent Cochrane systematic review found that, on balance, PPIs appear more effective than H_2RAs in people with endoscopy-negative reflux disease [NICE, 2004; van Pinxteren et al, 2004].
- Meta-analysis of the head-to-head trials showed that 53% of people on a PPI became symptom-free compared with 42% of those on an H_2RA, although the difference was not statistically significant.

Inadequate response to first-line treatment

- Data pooled by NICE suggest that there may be additional benefit in increasing the duration of therapy from 4 to 8 weeks in people who do not initially respond to proton pump inhibitors (PPIs). The overall healing rates were 68% at 4 weeks and 85% at 8 weeks (although there was significant heterogeneity between the studies analysed).
- Doubling the dose of PPI has only a small effect in healing oesophagitis at 4 weeks. Pooled data found that the average healing rate in full-dose PPI groups was 72%, and doubling the dose resulted in an absolute increase of 5%. In other words, one extra person experienced healing for every 19 given the double-dose treatment compared to those given the full-dose treatment (NNT = 19, 95% CI 10 to 294). However, *post-hoc* subgroup analysis suggests that the absolute increase in healing is greatest in people with Los Angeles grade C and D oesophagitis [NICE, 2004].
- Prokinetic agents (domperidone or metoclopramide) increase lower oesophageal sphincter pressure and promote oesophageal and gastric emptying [DTB, 1996]. They may therefore improve symptoms such as bloating or early satiety. However, trials have been few, small-scale, and heterogeneous — most evidence for prokinetics is for cisapride which is no longer available [van Pinxteren et al, 2004].
- Additional H_2RA therapy may be of some benefit for people with nocturnal acid breakthrough in the short term. Although most people probably have some gastric acid breakthrough on PPI therapy, it is fortunately rare for transient oesophageal relaxation to occur at night (even in people with gastro-oesophageal reflux disease) [Xue et al, 2001]. Therefore most people do not experience nocturnal symptoms. Tachyphylaxis rapidly occurs with nocturnal H_2RA therapy so efficacy reduces over time [Fackler et al, 2002; Pan et al, 2004]. Intermittent 2-week courses of H_2RA therapy may be a pragmatic approach to avoid this problem, although use in this way has not been studied.

Maintenance treatment

- The relapse rate without treatment is estimated to be 60–80%. Data pooled by NICE found that over 6–12 months of follow-up [NICE, 2004]:
  - Full-dose proton pump inhibitors (PPIs) are more effective than placebo. The average relapse rate on placebo was 79% compared to 24% on full-dose PPIs. This represents an absolute risk reduction of 55%, so that for every two persons given full-dose treatment, one extra remained relapse-free compared to those taking placebo (NNT = 1.8, 95% CI 1.6 to 2.0).
  - Full-dose PPIs are slightly more effective than low-dose PPIs. The average remission rate was 72% on low-dose PPIs compared to 85% on full-dose PPIs (i.e. a relapse rate of 28% compared with 15%). This represents an absolute risk reduction of 13% (NNT = 7.8, 95% CI 5.8 to 11.9).
  - Full-dose PPIs are more effective than H_2-receptor antagonists (H_2RAs). The average relapse rate on H_2RAs was 59% compared to 20% on full-dose PPIs. This represents an absolute risk reduction of 39% (NNT = 2.6, 95% CI 2.0 to 3.6).

D

On-demand PPI therapy

- Most studies of on-demand therapy have evaluated people with endoscopy-negative reflux disease or Los Angeles grade A or B oesophagitis.
- Although it was not possible for NICE to combine the data for meta-analysis, the general trend of study outcomes suggests that on-demand or intermittent PPI therapy is superior to placebo. Studies that have compared intermittent to continuous therapy also suggest that there is little difference in 'willingness to continue' (80–90%) between these strategies.
- NICE recommends 'on-demand' therapy as this promotes patient involvement in the management of their disease, and should in theory be the most cost-effective as, on average, patients take therapy once every three days. However, therapy can (and should) be individualized as a proportion of people will continue to take their PPI daily.

Does *H pylori* play a role in GORD?

- *Helicobacter pylori* does not cause or aggravate gastro-oesophageal reflux disease (GORD) [Malfertheiner et al, 2002]. Eradication of *H pylori* does not improve symptoms of GORD [Delaney et al, 2004].
- There is consensus that *H pylori* eradication is not associated with the development of GORD in most cases, and does not exacerbate existing GORD [DTB, 2002; Malfertheiner et al, 2002].
- Some experts recommend eradication before starting long-term acid suppression [Malfertheiner et al, 2002]. PPI treatment in the presence of *H pylori* infection may accelerate the progression of atrophic gastritis, a risk factor for gastric cancer. However, there is no consensus on this issue, and *H pylori* testing is not routinely recommended for people with GORD. If there is an incidental positive result for *H pylori* in a person with GORD, any decision to eradicate should be based on the likely risk of gastric cancer in that particular person, and on the person's preference.

Surgery

- Surgery cannot be recommended for the routine management of persistent gastro-oesophageal reflux disease, although individual people whose quality of life remains significantly impaired may value this form of treatment (**A**).

- Surgery to prevent reflux (e.g. Nissen fundoplication), which is increasingly performed using laparoscopic techniques, improves oesophagitis and can control symptoms in around 90% of people.
- However, open surgery or laparoscopic surgery is no better than long-term medical therapy at achieving remission from symptoms. There is a small postoperative mortality associated with anti-reflux surgery.
- Surgery may be considered in young people with severe disease with poor quality of life due to symptoms or who require high doses of maintenance proton pump inhibitor to control their symptoms.

[DTB, 1996; NICE, 2004]

D

Medicines management

Which PPI?

- **Differences between the proton pump inhibitors (PPIs) in clinical efficacy and safety are minimal** [WeMeReC, 2002]. On present evidence, PPIs do not have any serious contraindications for the vast majority of users, and have been in common use for over a decade.
- All PPIs (omeprazole, lansoprazole, pantoprazole, rabeprazole, and esomeprazole) are currently licensed for treatment and maintenance in gastro-oesophageal reflux disease. All PPIs have been studied as on-demand therapy, but only rabeprazole and esomeprazole are currently licensed for this indication.
- **Omeprazole is currently the least expensive PPI,** although this may change when other PPIs become available generically.
- PPIs are generally well tolerated. Adverse effects include gastrointestinal disturbances (most commonly diarrhoea), headaches, and dizziness.
- PPIs should not be offered to people with ALARM symptoms prior to endoscopy as they may mask gastric cancer. If someone already taking a PPI needs an endoscopy, the PPI should be stopped at least 2 weeks before the endoscopy.
- PPIs undergo extensive hepatic metabolism. In liver disease, do not exceed the following doses: 20 mg daily for omeprazole, pantoprazole, and esomeprazole; 30 mg daily for lansoprazole. There are no data on the use of rabeprazole in people with severe hepatic impairment so the manufacturer advises caution.
- Omeprazole and esomeprazole occasionally enhance the effects of warfarin and phenytoin. Monitor people taking these drugs carefully if omeprazole or esomeprazole are started or stopped.

Which dose?

- Recommended doses of proton pump inhibitors are outlined in Table 3.

How should I advise people to take on-demand PPIs?

- 'On-demand' therapy is where treatment is taken only when symptoms recur. Once symptoms are relieved (often after a few days) treatment is stopped again.
- The PPI doses most commonly studied as on-demand therapy are rabeprazole 10 mg, pantoprazole 20 mg, esomeprazole 20 mg, omeprazole 20 mg, and lansoprazole 15 mg. Only rabeprazole and esomeprazole are licensed for this indication.
- Some people may prefer to use treatment intermittently, i.e. use a 2–4 week course of treatment when symptoms recur.

[Bardhan, 2003; NICE, 2004]

Table 3: PRODIGY-recommended proton pump inhibitor doses for GORD.

PPI	Full dose	Low dose	Double dose
Omeprazole	20 mg once a day	*10 mg once a day	40 mg once a da
Lansoprazole	30 mg once a day	15 mg once a day	*30 mg twice a day
Pantoprazole	40 mg once a day	20 mg once a day	*40 mg twice a day
Rabeprazole	20 mg once a day	10 mg once a day	*20 mg twice a day
Esomeprazole	†20 mg once a day	Not available	40 mg once a da

* Not licensed at this dose for GORD.
† Lower than the licensed starting dose for esomeprazole in GORD, but considere to be dose equivalent to other PPIs. When undertaking meta-analysis of dose-related effects, NICE classed esomeprazole 20 mg as a full-dose equivalent to omeprazole 20 mg.

H_2-receptor antagonists, prokinetics, antacids, and alginates

H_2-receptor antagonists

- **Cimetidine, famotidine, nizatidine, and ranitidine appea to be equally effective.** They have been demonstrated to be more effective than placebo in the management of gastro-oesophageal reflux disease.
- **Adverse effects are uncommon** and include diarrhoea, headache, dizziness, rash, and tiredness.
- **Cimetidine should be avoided in people taking** erythromycin, warfarin, amiodarone, theophylline, carbamazepine, phenytoin, and sodium valproate as cimetidine inhibits hepatic drug metabolism by binding to microsomal cytochrome P450.

Prokinetic agents

- **Domperidone and metoclopramide** are both used as prokinetic agents to reduce symptoms such as bloating and early satiety.
- **Long-term use should be avoided.** There is an increased risk of hyperprolactinaemia (e.g. galactorrhoea, gynaecomastia, and amenorrhoea) with both domperidone and metoclopramide. Chronic use of metoclopramide increases the risk of extrapyramidal adverse effects (i.e. drug-induced parkinsonism). Extrapyramidal adverse effects are very rare with domperidone as it does not cross the blood-brain barrier
- Encourage people using prokinetics to use them as on-demand or intermittent therapy.
- Metoclopramide should be avoided in young adults (under the age of 20 years) because of the increased risk of extrapyramidal adverse effects in this age group.

Antacids and alginates

- There is limited evidence on the efficacy of antacids in the management of dyspepsia; however, symptomatic relief is often reported with the use of an antacid or alginate.
- They are best given when symptoms occur or are expected, i.e. after meals and at bedtime. They also remain in the stomach for longer at these times, and therefore have longer to act.
- **Antacids should preferably not be taken at the same tim as other drugs** as they may impair absorption.
- Most antacids contain aluminium salts, magnesium salts or a combination of the two.
- **Combinations of aluminium salts with magnesium salts may be preferable** to magnesium salts alone (which may cause diarrhoea) or aluminium salts alone (which may cause constipation).
- **Alginates** form a 'raft' that floats on the surface of the stomach contents. They are most useful for people with mild reflux symptoms.

References

NHS staff in England can link, free of charge, from references to full text journals by clicking on [Full text] on the PRODIGY website.

1. Bardhan, K.D. (2003) Intermittent and on-demand use of proton pump inhibitors in the management of symptomatic gastroesophageal reflux disease. *American Journal of Gastroenterology* **98**(3 Suppl), S40-S48.
2. British Society of Gastroenterology (2002) *Dyspepsia management guidelines*. British Society of Gastroenterology. www.bsg.org.uk/clinical_prac/guidelines/dyspepsia.htm [Accessed: 20/08/2002].
3. Chang, J.T. and Katzka, D.A. (2004) Gastroesophageal reflux disease, Barrett esophagus, and esophageal adenocarcinoma. *Archives of Internal Medicine* **164**(14), 1482–1488. [Full text]
4. Chiba, N., Thompson, A.B.R. and Barkun, A.N. (2003) The Rome II definition of dyspepsia does not exclude patients with GERD in primary care. *Gastroenterology* **124**(4 Suppl 1), A223-A224.
5. Delaney, B., Moayyedi, P. and Forman, D. (2004) *Helicobacter pylori infection*. Volume 12. www.clinicalevidence.com [Accessed: 06/01/2005].
6. DTB (1996) Medical management of gastro-oesophageal reflux. *Drug & Therapeutics Bulletin* **34**(1), 1–4.
7. DTB (2002) Should *H. Pylori* be eradicated in non-ulcer dyspepsia? *Drug & Therapeutics Bulletin* **40**(3), 23–24. [Full text]
8. Eckardt, V.F., Kanzler, G. and Bernhard, G. (2001) Life expectancy and cancer risk in patients with Barrett's esophagus: a prospective controlled investigation. *American Journal of Medicine* **111**(1), 33–37.
9. Edwards, S.J., Lind, T. and Lundell, L. (2001) Systematic review of proton pump inhibitors for the acute treatment of reflux oesophagitis. *Alimentary Pharmacology & Therapeutics* **15**(11), 1729–1736.
10. Fackler, W.K., Ours, T.M., Vaezi, M.F. and Richter, J.E. (2002) Long-term effect of H2RA therapy on nocturnal gastric acid breakthrough. *Gastroenterology* **122**(3), 625–632.
11. Galmiche, J.P., Letessier, E. and Scarpignato, C. (1998) Treatment of gastro-oesophageal reflux disease in adults. *British Medical Journal* **316**(7146), 1720–1723. [Full text]
12. Malfertheiner, P., Megraud, F., O'Morain, C. et al (2002) Current concepts in the management of *Helicobacter pylori* infection – the Maastricht 2–2000 consensus report. *Alimentary Pharmacology & Therapeutics* **16**(2), 167–180.
13. Mandal, A., Playford, R.J. and Wicks, A.C. (2003) Current practice in surveillance strategy for patients with Barrett's oesophagus in the UK. *Alimentary Pharmacology & Therapeutics* **17**(10), 1319–1324.
14. MeReC (1998) Proton pump inhibitors: their role in dyspepsia. *MeReC Bulletin* **9**(11), 41–44.
15. Moayyedi, P., Delaney, B. and Forman, D. (2004) *Gastro-oesophageal reflux disease*. Clinical Evidence. Volume 12. www.clinicalevidence.com [Accessed: 06/01/2005].
16. NICE (2000) *Guidance on the use of proton pump inhibitors in the treatment of dyspepsia*. Technology appraisal guidance no. 7. National Institute for Clinical Excellence. www.nice.org.uk [Accessed: 16/10/2003].
17. NICE (2004) *Dyspepsia: management of dyspepsia in adults in primary care: NICE guideline*. Clinical guideline 17. National Institute for Clinical Excellence. www.nice.org.uk [Accessed: 27/08/2004].
18. NICE (2005) *Referral guidelines for suspected cancer – quick reference guide*. Clinical guideline 27. National Institute for Health and Clinical Excellence. www.nice.org.uk [Accessed: 01/07/2005].
19. Pan, T., Wang, Y., Guo, Z. and Wang, Q. (2004) *Additional bedtime H2-receptor antagonist for the control of nocturnal gastric acid breakthrough*. The Cochrane Library. Issue 3. Chichester, UK: John Wiley & Sons, Ltd. www.nelh.nhs.uk/cochrane.asp [Accessed: 21/04/2005]. [Full text]
20. Sharma, V.K., Leontiadis, G.I. and Howden, C.W. (2001) Meta-analysis of randomized controlled trials comparing standard clinical doses of omeprazole and lansoprazole in erosive oesophagitis. *Alimentary Pharmacology & Therapeutics* **15**(2), 227–231.
21. Spechler, S.J. (2003) Managing Barrett's oesophagus. *British Medical Journal* **326**(7395), 892–894. [Full text]
22. van Pinxteren, B., Numans, M.E., Bonis, P.A. and Lau, J. (2004) *Short-term treatment with proton pump inhibitors, H2-receptor antagonists and prokinetics for gastro-oesophageal reflux disease-like symptoms and endoscopy negative reflux disease (Cochrane Review)*. The Cochrane Library. Issue 3. Chichester, UK: John Wiley & Sons, Ltd. www.nelh.nhs.uk/cochrane.asp [Accessed: 21/04/2005]. [Full text]
23. WeMeReC (2002) Use of proton pump inhibitors in primary care. *WeMeReC Bulletin* **9**(2), 1–6.
24. Xue, S., Katz, P.O., Banerjee, P. et al (2001) Bedtime H2 blockers improve nocturnal gastric acid control in GERD patients on proton pump inhibitors. *Alimentary Pharmacology & Therapeutics* **15**(9), 1351–1356.

Evidence grading

Evidence grading is from the National Institute of Clinical Excellence guideline *Dyspepsia*, August 2004. The definitions of grades of recommendation used in this guideline are as follows:

A At least one randomized controlled trial as part of a body of literature of overall good quality and consistency addressing the specific recommendation without extrapolation.

B Well-conducted clinical studies but no randomized clinical trials on the topic of recommendation, or with extrapolation from evidence obtained from randomized trials of meta-analysis.

C Expert committee reports or opinions and/or clinical experiences of respected authorities. This grading indicates that directly applicable clinical studies of good quality are absent, or with extrapolation from higher levels of evidence.

GPP Good practice point. Recommended good practice based on the clinical experience of the guideline development group.

PRODIGY GUIDANCE

Dyspepsia — proven non-ulcer dyspepsia

Last revised in July 2005
www.prodigy.nhs.uk/guidance.asp?gt=Dyspepsia - proven non-ulcer

Applies to people over the age of 16 years

This guidance is based on the National Institute for Clinical Excellence (NICE) guideline on *Dyspepsia* (August 2004).

This guidance covers the management of adults with endoscopically determined non-ulcer dyspepsia. People with dyspepsia symptoms who have not had an endoscopy should be managed as people with 'uninvestigated dyspepsia'. See the PRODIGY guidance *Dyspepsia — symptoms (uninvestigated by endoscopy)*.

This guidance does not cover the management of pregnancy-associated dyspepsia, gastro-oesophageal reflux disease, or peptic ulcer disease.

There is separate PRODIGY guidance for *Dyspepsia — symptoms (uninvestigated by endoscopy)*; proven ulcers (*Dyspepsia — proven DU or GU*); proven gastro-oesophageal reflux disease (*Dyspepsia — proven GORD*), and pregnancy-associated dyspepsia (*Dyspepsia — pregnancy-associated*).

D

Goals

- To provide effective control of symptoms
- To identify and treat *Helicobacter pylori* infection
- To prevent relapse and complications
- To detect any serious diagnoses, including oesophageal or gastric carcinoma

Contents

Scenarios

- Initial endoscopy result — first-line treatment p.664
- *H pylori* test result — proven non-ulcer dyspepsia p.666
- Persistent symptoms — proven non-ulcer dyspepsia p.669

Extended Information, p. 671

Which scenario?

- **Initial endoscopy result — first-line treatment:** covers identification of *H pylori* infection in people with endoscopically determined non-ulcer dyspepsia, and advice regarding lifestyle factors which may help improve symptoms.
- ***H pylori* test result — proven non-ulcer dyspepsia:** covers treatment options for people with endoscopically determined non-ulcer dyspepsia who have been tested for *H pylori* and have been found to be *H pylori* positive or *H pylori* negative.
- **Persistent symptoms — proven non-ulcer dyspepsia:** covers the management of people with endoscopically determined non-ulcer dyspepsia whose symptoms persist despite treatment.

Initial endoscopy result — first-line treatment

Which therapy?

- **Reassure people** that no serious disease has been found.
- **Stop nonsteroidal anti-inflammatory drugs where possible.**
- **Review other medication that may be causing dyspepsia:** corticosteroids; bisphosphonates; medication that may lower oesophageal sphincter pressure (e.g. theophylline, nitrates, and calcium-channel blockers).
- **Test for *Helicobacter pylori* (usually done at endoscopy).**
  - **If *H pylori* test results are available:** see scenario *H pylori test result — proven non-ulcer dyspepsia* for treatment choices.
  - **If there is a delay in obtaining *H pylori* test results:**
    - Either, offer a 1-month course of a low-dose proton pump inhibitor (PPI).
    - Or, offer a 1-month course of a H_2-receptor antagonist (H_2RA).
- **If an *H pylori* test was not done at endoscopy:**
  - Use a carbon-13 urea breath test or the stool antigen test.
  - **Do not test within** 2 weeks of PPI therapy or within 4 weeks of antibiotic therapy as false-negative results may occur.
- **Give lifestyle advice:** healthy eating, weight loss, stopping smoking.

Practical prescribing points

For further information please see the *Medicines Compendium* (www.medicines.org.uk) or the *British National Formulary* (www.bnf.org).

- **Proton pump inhibitors (PPIs):** differences between the PPIs in clinical efficacy and safety are minimal.
  - Omeprazole is currently cheapest.
  - Omeprazole and esomeprazole occasionally enhance the effects of warfarin and phenytoin. Monitor carefully if omeprazole or esomeprazole are started or stopped.
- **Cimetidine: avoid in people taking** erythromycin, warfarin, amiodarone, theophylline, carbamazepine, phenytoin, and sodium valproate as cimetidine inhibits hepatic drug metabolism by binding to microsomal cytochrome P450.

H pylori tests

- **Carbon-13 urea breath tests:** advise the person to fast for at least 6 hours before the test and then (for all tests except diabact UBT®) ingest citric acid or orange juice just before the test to slow gastric emptying. (The diabact UBT® tablet contains citric acid.) The person then provides two or three breath samples before ingestion of the carbon-13 tablet, and again 30 minutes afterwards (only 10 minutes afterwards for diabact UBT®) by blowing through a straw into a series of glass, screw-top tubes. Breath samples are sent away for analysis by mass spectrometry.

- **Stool antigen tests:** these require the person to collect a stool sample (at least pea-sized). The sample is then sent to the laboratory for analysis.

Follow-up advice

- **Follow-up is guided by *H pylori* test results.** See scenario *H pylori test result — proven non-ulcer dyspepsia.*
- All people with dyspepsia requiring long-term treatment should have an annual review of their condition, and lifestyle advice should be reinforced.

Should I refer or investigate?

Refer?

Indications for repeat endoscopy

Note: proton pump inhibitors and H_2-receptor antagonists should be stopped at least 2 weeks before endoscopy. Nonsteroidal anti-inflammatory drug use should also be suspended in all people requiring referral.

- **Consider** managing previously investigated people without new ALARM symptoms according to previous endoscopic findings. However, if an additional diagnosis is suspected, or if the person has been symptom-free for several years before symptoms recur, consider referring for a repeat endoscopy to confirm the diagnosis.
- **Immediate endoscopy** (i.e. same day) is indicated for people presenting with dyspepsia together with significant acute gastrointestinal bleeding.
- **Anyone who develops ALARM symptoms should be referred urgently for endoscopy, or to a specialist.** That is people with:
  - Chronic gastrointestinal bleeding
  - Progressive unintentional weight loss
  - Progressive difficulty swallowing (dysphagia)
  - Persistent vomiting
  - Iron deficiency anaemia
  - Epigastric mass
  - Suspicious barium meal result
- **People 55 years and over, presenting with unexplained and persistent recent onset dyspepsia** alone, should be referred for urgent endoscopy.
- **Urgent referral to a specialist should also be considered** in a person (of any age) who has unexplained worsening of their dyspepsia and:
  - Barrett's oesophagus
  - Known dysplasia, atrophic gastritis, or intestinal metaplasia
  - Peptic ulcer surgery over 20 years ago
- **If definite dysphagia or odynophagia is present** with a suspicious history or regurgitation, it is appropriate to refer for a barium swallow.

Investigate?

- When referring, consider a full blood count to assist specialist assessment. This should be carried out in accordance with local arrangements.

Patient information leaflets

The following PILs are available at www.prodigy.nhs.uk

- CORE, Fighting Gut and Liver Disease
- Dyspepsia - Functional or Non-Ulcer
- Gastroscopy (Endoscopy)
- Helicobacter Pylori & Stomach Pain

Shared decision making

- Things to consider that may help if you have non-ulcer (functional) dyspepsia include:
  - **Changes to lifestyle:**
    - Stop smoking if you are a smoker.
    - Cut down on alcohol if you drink heavily.
    - Don't eat too much fatty or spicy food.
    - Eat healthily and try to lose weight if you are overweight.
  - **Your medication.** Some medicines may cause dyspepsia, for example anti-inflammatory painkillers (aspirin, ibuprofen, etc.), theophylline, nitrates, calcium-channel blockers, biphosphonates, steroids, and various others.
  - **Testing for bacteria called *H pylori*.** This is sometimes the underlying cause. If found, it can usually be cleared with treatment.
- Other treatment options include a month's course of:
  - **A PPI acid-suppressing medicine** (omeprazole, lansoprazole, esomeprazole, pantoprazole, or rabeprazole), OR
  - **An H_2-receptor antagonist acid-suppressing medicine** (cimetidine, famotidine, nizatidine, or ranitidine).
- See a doctor if symptoms persist or return after finishing treatment.

Drug rationale

Drugs not included

- **Antacid and alginates** are not included. Antacid therapy is no more effective than placebo in reducing the symptoms of non-ulcer dyspepsia [Moayyedi et al, 2003; NICE, 2004].
- **Prokinetic agents** (metoclopramide or domperidone) are not included. The evidence for prokinetic therapy is based on trials using cisapride (no longer commercially available) but publication bias is thought to have occurred and the data are considered unreliable. There are no studies examining the efficacy of domperidone or metoclopramide in non-ulcer dyspepsia [Moayyedi et al, 2003; NICE, 2004].

Drugs included

- ***H pylori* tests** are included for use if an *H pylori* test was not undertaken at endoscopy. Prescriptions for carbon-13 urea breath test kits and an advice note for the stool antigen test are offered.
- **Low-dose proton pump inhibitors (PPIs)** (omeprazole, lansoprazole, pantoprazole, and rabeprazole) are included for empirical acid-suppression therapy. Full-dose esomeprazole is also included because there is no low-dose equivalent available.
  - No PPIs are currently licensed for treatment of non-ulcer dyspepsia because the evidence is poor and only a small subset of people with non-ulcer dyspepsia seem to respond to acid suppression. However, the available evidence suggests that full-dose PPIs are no more effective than low-dose PPIs for non-ulcer dyspepsia [Moayyedi et al, 2003; NICE, 2004].
  - Note: when undertaking meta-analysis of dose-related effects, NICE classed esomeprazole 20mg as a full-dose equivalent to omeprazole 20mg.
- **H_2-receptor antagonists (H_2RAs)** (cimetidine, famotidine, nizatidine, and ranitidine) are included as an alternative to PPIs for empirical acid-suppression. No H_2RAs are currently licensed for this indication because the evidence is poor and publication bias may have occurred [Moayyedi et al, 2003; NICE, 2004].

D

Prescriptions

H pylori tests (if not already done during endoscopy)

Advice note: stool antigen test
- Age from 16 years onwards
- The stool antigen test is a way of testing whether you have a current infection with Helicobacter pylori. Put a pea-sized sample of your faeces (stools) into the container provided. Please return this sample to reception so that it can be sent to the laboratory for analysis. Acid suppressing medicines and antibiotics can affect the results of this test. If you have used an acid suppressing medicine within the last 2 weeks, or have taken antibiotics within the last 4 weeks, please check with your doctor before taking this test.

Carbon urea breath test: Diabact UBT H pylori test kit
- Age from 16 years onwards
- Diabact UBT tablet + kit. Follow the instructions given inside this pack; supply 1 kit; NHS Cost £12.75.

Carbon urea breath test: Helicobacter Test Hp-plus test kit
- Age from 16 years onwards
- Helicobacter Test Hp-plus. Follow the instructions given inside this pack; supply 1 kit; NHS Cost £19.75.

Carbon urea breath test: Helicobacter Test INFAI test kit
- Age from 16 years onwards
- Helicobacter test INFAI. Follow the instructions given inside this pack; supply 1 kit; NHS Cost £17.10.

Carbon urea breath test: Pylobactell H pylori test kit
- Age from 16 years onwards
- Pylobactell H pylori test kit. Follow the instructions given inside this pack; supply 1 kit; NHS Cost £20.75.

Low-dose proton pump inhibitors for 4 weeks

Omeprazole capsules: 10mg once a day
- Age from 16 years onwards
- Omeprazole 10mg capsules. Take one capsule once a day for 4 weeks; supply 28 capsules; NHS Cost £7.72.

Omeprazole tablets: 10mg once a day
- Age from 16 years onwards
- Omeprazole 10mg tablets. Take one tablet once a day for 4 weeks; supply 28 tablets; NHS Cost £11.40.

Lansoprazole capsules: 15mg each morning
- Age from 16 years onwards
- Lansoprazole 15mg capsules. Take one capsule each morning (on an empty stomach) for 4 weeks; supply 28 capsules; NHS Cost £12.92.

Lansoprazole orodispersible tablets: 15mg each morning
- Age from 16 years onwards
- Lansoprazole 15mg orodisp tabs. Take one tablet each morning (on an empty stomach) for 4 weeks; supply 28 tablets; NHS Cost £10.86.

Pantoprazole e/c tablets: 20mg once a day
- Age from 16 years onwards
- Pantoprazole 20mg e/c tablets. Take one tablet once a day for 4 weeks; supply 28 tablets; NHS Cost £12.31.

Rabeprazole e/c tablets: 10mg once a day
- Age from 16 years onwards
- Rabeprazole 10mg e/c tabs. Take one tablet once a day for 4 weeks; supply 28 tablets; NHS Cost £11.56.

Esomeprazole e/c tablets: 20mg once a day
- Age from 16 years onwards
- Esomeprazole 20mg tablets. Take one tablet once a day for 4 weeks; supply 28 tablets; NHS Cost £18.50.

H_2-receptor antagonists for 4 weeks

Cimetidine tablets: 400mg twice a day
- Age from 16 years onwards
- Cimetidine 400mg tablets. Take one tablet twice a day for 4 weeks; supply 60 tablets; NHS Cost £5.58.

Ranitidine tablets: 150mg twice a day
- Age from 16 years onwards
- Ranitidine 150mg tablets. Take one tablet twice a day for 4 weeks; supply 60 tablets; NHS Cost £7.21.

Nizatidine capsules: 150mg twice a day
- Age from 16 years onwards
- Nizatidine 150mg capsules. Take one capsule twice a day for 4 weeks; supply 60 capsules; NHS Cost £12.26.

Famotidine tablets: 20mg twice a day
- Age from 16 years onwards
- Famotidine 20mg tablets. Take one tablet twice a day for 4 weeks; supply 56 tablets; NHS Cost £23.28.

H pylori test result — proven non-ulcer dyspepsia

Which therapy?

- **If *H pylori* negative:**
  - Either, offer a 1-month course of a low-dose proton pump inhibitor (PPI)
  - Or, offer a 1-month course of a H_2-receptor antagonist
- **If *H pylori*-positive:** eradicate using a 1-week course of triple therapy.
  - **First-line triple therapy:** use a PPI plus amoxicillin 1 g and clarithromycin 500 mg, all given twice a day.
  - **For people with penicillin hypersensitivity:** use a PPI plus metronidazole 400 mg and clarithromycin 250 mg, all given twice a day.
- **If clarithromycin or metronidazole has previously been taken,** do not use that antibiotic in the triple therapy regimen. Choose an alternative from:
  - Amoxicillin, clarithromycin, metronidazole, or oxytetracycline.
- ***H pylori* re-testing after eradication therapy is not recommended** in people with non-ulcer dyspepsia.

Practical prescribing points

For further information please see the *Medicines Compendium* (www.medicines.org.uk) or the *British National Formulary* (www.bnf.org).

- **Remind people that it is important to complete the course** and warn about adverse effects.
- **Advise people taking metronidazole** to avoid alcohol for the duration of the course and for at least 48 hours afterwards, because of the possibility of a disulfiram-like (Antabuse) reaction.
- **Clarithromycin** inhibits the metabolism of other drugs and can prolong the QT interval. Check drug interactions before prescribing.
- **Proton pump inhibitors (PPIs):** differences between the PPIs in clinical efficacy and safety are minimal.
  - Omeprazole is currently cheapest.
  - Omeprazole and esomeprazole occasionally enhance the effects of warfarin and phenytoin. Monitor carefully if omeprazole or esomeprazole are started or stopped.
- **Cimetidine: avoid in people taking** erythromycin, warfarin, amiodarone, theophylline, carbamazepine, phenytoin, and sodium valproate as cimetidine inhibits hepatic drug metabolism by binding to microsomal cytochrome P450.

'ollow-up advice

If symptoms continue or recur after initial treatment (whether *H pylori* eradication or acid suppression was used) offer a low-dose proton pump inhibitor or an H_2-receptor antagonist with a limited number of repeat prescriptions, or consider switching to a prokinetic. See scenario *Persistent symptoms — proven non-ulcer dyspepsia.*

- Encourage people to use the lowest dose that controls symptoms.
- Discuss using the treatment on an 'on-demand' basis (i.e. waiting for symptoms to develop before taking treatment).

Do not re-test for *H pylori* unless there is a strong clinical need (e.g. family history of gastric cancer).

All people with dyspepsia requiring long-term treatment should have an annual review of their condition, and lifestyle advice should be reinforced.

hould I refer or investigate?

:efer?

ndications for repeat endoscopy

'ote: proton pump inhibitors and H_2-receptor antagonists ıould be stopped at least 2 weeks before endoscopy. 'onsteroidal anti-inflammatory drug use should also be ıspended in all people requiring referral.

Consider managing previously investigated people without new ALARM symptoms according to previous endoscopic findings. However, if an additional diagnosis is suspected, or if the person has been symptom-free for several years before symptoms recur, consider referring for a repeat endoscopy to confirm the diagnosis.

Immediate endoscopy (i.e. same day) is indicated for people presenting with dyspepsia together with significant acute gastrointestinal bleeding.

Anyone who develops ALARM symptoms should be referred urgently for endoscopy, or to a specialist. That is people with:

- Chronic gastrointestinal bleeding
- Progressive unintentional weight loss
- Progressive difficulty swallowing (dysphagia)
- Persistent vomiting
- Iron deficiency anaemia
- Epigastric mass
- Suspicious barium meal result

People 55 years and over, presenting with unexplained and persistent recent onset dyspepsia alone, should be referred for urgent endoscopy.

Urgent referral to a specialist should also be considered in a person (of any age) who has unexplained worsening of their dyspepsia and:

- Barrett's oesophagus
- Known dysplasia, atrophic gastritis, or intestinal metaplasia
- Peptic ulcer surgery over 20 years ago

If definite dysphagia or odynophagia is present with a suspicious history or regurgitation, it is appropriate to refer for a barium swallow.

ıvestigate?

When referring, consider a full blood count to assist specialist assessment. This should be carried out in accordance with local arrangements.

Patient information leaflets

The following PILs are available at www.prodigy.nhs.uk

- CORE, Fighting Gut and Liver Disease
- Dyspepsia - Functional or Non-Ulcer
- Gastroscopy (Endoscopy)
- Helicobacter Pylori & Stomach Pain

Shared decision making

Treatment options for non-ulcer (functional) dyspepsia include the following:

- If you are infected with bacteria called *H pylori* then:
  - This is sometimes the cause of symptoms.
  - It may be worth clearing the infection to see if symptoms go. It can usually be cleared with a one-week course of treatment of:
    - **An acid-suppressing medicine,** plus
    - **Two antibiotics.** Tell your doctor if you are allergic to any antibiotic. Some people develop side-effects with antibiotics. The most common are diarrhoea and feeling sick.
    - It is really important to take the whole course of treatment properly or it may not work.
- If you are not infected with *H Pylori*, options include a one-month trial of:
  - **A PPI acid-suppressing medicine** (omeprazole, lansoprazole, esomeprazole, pantoprazole, or rabeprazole), OR
  - **An H_2-receptor antagonist acid-suppressing medicine** (cimetidine, famotidine, nizatidine, or ranitidine).
- See a doctor if symptoms persist or return after finishing treatment.

D

Drug rationale

Drugs not included

- **Antacid and alginates** are not included. Antacid therapy is no more effective than placebo in reducing the symptoms of non-ulcer dyspepsia [Moayyedi et al, 2003; NICE, 2004].
- **Prokinetic agents** (metoclopramide or domperidone) are not included. The evidence for prokinetic therapy is based on trials using cisapride (no longer commercially available) but publication bias is thought to have occurred and the data are considered unreliable. There are no studies examining the efficacy of domperidone or metoclopramide in non-ulcer dyspepsia [Moayyedi et al, 2003; NICE, 2004].
- **Quadruple therapy** (a proton pump inhibitor [PPI], bismuth, tetracycline and metronidazole) is as effective as triple therapy for *H pylori* eradication, but taking 17 tablets per day does not make it a practical first-line option [Delaney et al, 2003].
- **Dual therapies** for *H pylori* eradication with PPIs and antibiotics are not recommended [NICE, 2004].
- **Triple therapies using ranitidine bismuth citrate instead of a PPI** are not recommended because evidence of efficacy is less strong than for PPI triple regimens [DTB, 1996; MeReC, 1997].
- **Two-week triple therapy** is no more effective than one-week triple therapy [NICE, 2004]. Longer regimens also cost more and have a longer duration of minor adverse effects.
- **Triple therapy using a PPI plus amoxicillin and metronidazole** is no longer recommended [NICE, 2004]. Pooled data from four randomized, controlled trials have shown that it is less effective than either of the two triple therapies that contain clarithromycin.

Drugs included

- **Low-dose proton pump inhibitors (PPIs)** (omeprazole, lansoprazole, pantoprazole, and rabeprazole) are included for empirical acid-suppression therapy. Full-dose esomeprazole is also included because there is no low-dose equivalent available.
  - No PPIs are currently licensed for treatment of non-ulcer dyspepsia because the evidence is poor and only a small subset of people with non-ulcer dyspepsia seem to respond to acid suppression. However, the available evidence suggests that full-dose PPIs are no more effective than low-dose PPIs for non-ulcer dyspepsia [Moayyedi et al, 2003; NICE, 2004].
  - Note: when undertaking meta-analysis of dose-related effects, NICE classed esomeprazole 20mg as a full-dose equivalent to omeprazole 20mg.
- **H_2-receptor antagonists (H_2RAs)** (cimetidine, famotidine, nizatidine, and ranitidine) are included as an alternative to PPIs for empirical acid-suppression. No H_2RAs are currently licensed for this indication because the evidence is poor and publication bias may have occurred [Moayyedi et al, 2003; NICE, 2004].
- **Triple therapy:** NICE recommends the following one-week triple therapy eradication regimens for *H pylori* eradication:
  - A 'PAC' regimen (a PPI plus amoxicillin 1 g and clarithromycin 500 mg, all given twice a day).
  - Or (for people with penicillin hypersensitivity) a 'PCM' regimen (a PPI plus metronidazole 400 mg and clarithromycin 250 mg, all given twice a day).
  - Pooled data for the recommended PAC and PCM regimens show no statistically significant difference in eradication rates: 82% for PAC, and 82.6% for PCM.
- Note: the dose of clarithromycin in the Helimet® packs (containing lansoprazole, metronidazole, and clarithromycin) is higher than that recommended by NICE for a PCM regimen. However, it is included because some people find the single-pack presentation helpful for compliance.

Prescriptions

H pylori positive: PPI + amoxicillin + clarithromycin

Omeprazole + amoxicillin + clarithromycin

- Age from 16 years onwards
- Amoxicillin 500mg capsules. Take two capsules twice a day for 7 days; supply 28 capsules; NHS Cost £1.44.
- Clarithromycin 500mg tablets. Take one tablet twice a day for 7 days; supply 14 tablets; NHS Cost £21.90.
- Omeprazole 20mg capsules. Take one capsule twice a day for 7 days; supply 14 capsules; NHS Cost £6.38.

Lansoprazole + amoxicillin + clarithromycin

- Age from 16 years onwards
- Lansoprazole 30mg capsules. Take one capsule twice a day (on an empty stomach) for 7 days; supply 14 capsules; NHS Cost £11.82.
- Clarithromycin 500mg tablets. Take one tablet twice a day for 7 days; supply 14 tablets; NHS Cost £21.90.
- Amoxicillin 500mg capsules. Take two capsules twice a day for 7 days; supply 28 capsules; NHS Cost £1.44.

HeliClear triple pack

- Age from 16 years onwards
- HeliClear triple pack. Take one lansoprazole capsule, one clarithromycin tablet, and two amoxicillin capsules twice a day for 7 days; supply 1 triple pack; NHS Cost £35.01.

Pantoprazole + amoxicillin + clarithromycin

- Age from 16 years onwards
- Pantoprazole 40mg e/c tablets. Take one tablet twice a day for 7 days; supply 14 tablets; NHS Cost £10.85.
- Amoxicillin 500mg capsules. Take two capsules twice a day for 7 days; supply 28 capsules; NHS Cost £1.44.
- Clarithromycin 500mg tablets. Take one tablet twice a day for 7 days; supply 14 tablets; NHS Cost £21.90.

Rabeprazole + amoxicillin + clarithromycin

- Age from 16 years onwards
- Amoxicillin 500mg capsules. Take two capsules twice a day for 7 days; supply 28 capsules; NHS Cost £1.44.
- Clarithromycin 500mg tablets. Take one tablet twice a day for 7 days; supply 14 tablets; NHS Cost £21.90.
- Rabeprazole 20mg e/c tabs. Take one tablet twice a day for 7 days; supply 14 tablets; NHS Cost £10.58.

Esomeprazole + amoxicillin + clarithromycin

- Age from 16 years onwards
- Amoxicillin 500mg capsules. Take two capsules twice a day for 7 days; supply 28 capsules; NHS Cost £1.44.
- Clarithromycin 500mg tablets. Take one tablet twice a day for 7 days; supply 14 tablets; NHS Cost £21.90.
- Esomeprazole 20mg tablets. Take one tablet twice a day for 7 days; supply 14 tablets; NHS Cost £9.25.

H pylori positive: PPI + metronidazole + clarithromycin

Omeprazole + metronidazole + clarithromycin

- Age from 16 years onwards
- Omeprazole 20mg capsules. Take one capsule twice a day for 7 days; supply 14 capsules; NHS Cost £6.38.
- Metronidazole 400mg tablets. Take one tablet twice a day for 7 days; supply 14 tablets; NHS Cost £1.03.
- Clarithromycin 250mg tablets. Take one tablet twice a day for 7 days; supply 14 tablets; NHS Cost £10.94.

Lansoprazole + metronidazole + clarithromycin

- Age from 16 years onwards
- Lansoprazole 30mg capsules. Take one capsule twice a day (on an empty stomach) for 7 days; supply 14 capsules; NHS Cost £11.82.
- Metronidazole 400mg tablets. Take one tablet twice a day for 7 days; supply 14 tablets; NHS Cost £1.03.
- Clarithromycin 250mg tablets. Take one tablet twice a day for 7 days; supply 14 tablets; NHS Cost £10.94.

HeliMet triple pack

- Age from 16 years onwards
- HeliMet triple pack. Take one lansoprazole capsule, one clarithromycin tablet and one metronidazole tablet twice a day for 7 days; supply 1 pack; NHS Cost £35.40.

Pantoprazole + metronidazole + clarithromycin

- Age from 16 years onwards
- Pantoprazole 40mg e/c tablets. Take one tablet twice a day for 7 days; supply 14 tablets; NHS Cost £10.85.
- Metronidazole 400mg tablets. Take one tablet twice a day for 7 days; supply 14 tablets; NHS Cost £1.03.
- Clarithromycin 250mg tablets. Take one tablet twice a day for 7 days; supply 14 tablets; NHS Cost £10.94.

Rabeprazole + metronidazole + clarithromycin

- Age from 16 years onwards
- Rabeprazole 20mg e/c tabs. Take one tablet twice a day for 7 days; supply 14 tablets; NHS Cost £10.58.
- Metronidazole 400mg tablets. Take one tablet twice a day for 7 days; supply 14 tablets; NHS Cost £1.03.
- Clarithromycin 250mg tablets. Take one tablet twice a day for 7 days; supply 14 tablets; NHS Cost £10.94.

Esomeprazole + metronidazole + clarithromycin

- Age from 16 years onwards
- Esomeprazole 20mg tablets. Take one tablet twice a day for 7 days; supply 14 tablets; NHS Cost £9.25.

Metronidazole 400mg tablets. Take one tablet twice a day for 7 days; supply 14 tablets; NHS Cost £1.03.
Clarithromycin 250mg tablets. Take one tablet twice a day for 7 days; supply 14 tablets; NHS Cost £10.94.

H pylori negative: low-dose PPIs for 4 weeks

Omeprazole capsules: 10mg once a day
Age from 16 years onwards
Omeprazole 10mg capsules. Take one capsule once a day for 4 weeks; supply 28 capsules; NHS Cost £7.72.

Omeprazole tablets: 10mg once a day
Age from 16 years onwards
Omeprazole 10mg tablets. Take one tablet once a day for 4 weeks; supply 28 tablets; NHS Cost £11.40.

Lansoprazole capsules: 15mg each morning
Age from 16 years onwards
Lansoprazole 15mg capsules. Take one capsule each morning (on an empty stomach) for 4 weeks; supply 28 capsules; NHS Cost £12.92.

Lansoprazole orodispersible tablets: 15mg each morning
Age from 16 years onwards
Lansoprazole 15mg orodisp tabs. Take one tablet each morning (on an empty stomach) for 4 weeks; supply 28 tablets; NHS Cost £10.86.

Pantoprazole e/c tablets: 20mg once a day
Age from 16 years onwards
Pantoprazole 20mg e/c tablets. Take one tablet once a day for 4 weeks; supply 28 tablets; NHS Cost £12.31.

Rabeprazole e/c tablets: 10mg once a day
Age from 16 years onwards
Rabeprazole 10mg e/c tabs. Take one tablet once a day for 4 weeks; supply 28 tablets; NHS Cost £11.56.

Esomeprazole tablets: 20mg once a day
Age from 16 years onwards
Esomeprazole 20mg tablets. Take one tablet once a day for 4 weeks; supply 28 tablets; NHS Cost £18.50.

H pylori negative: H_2-receptor antagonists for 4 weeks

Cimetidine tablets: 400mg twice a day
Age from 16 years onwards
Cimetidine 400mg tablets. Take one tablet twice a day for 4 weeks; supply 60 tablets; NHS Cost £5.58.

Ranitidine tablets: 150mg twice a day
Age from 16 years onwards
Ranitidine 150mg tablets. Take one tablet twice a day for 4 weeks; supply 60 tablets; NHS Cost £7.21.

Nizatidine capsules: 150mg twice a day
Age from 16 years onwards
Nizatidine 150mg capsules. Take one capsule twice a day for 4 weeks; supply 60 capsules; NHS Cost £12.26.

Famotidine tablets: 20mg twice a day
Age from 16 years onwards
Famotidine 20mg tablets. Take one tablet twice a day for 4 weeks; supply 56 tablets; NHS Cost £23.28.

Persistent symptoms — proven non-ulcer dyspepsia

Which therapy?

- **If symptoms continue or recur, reassure people** that no serious disease has been found.
- **Offer a low-dose proton pump inhibitor** (PPI) **or an H_2-receptor antagonist** (H_2RA) with a limited number of repeat prescriptions.
- **If low-dose PPIs or H_2RAs provide inadequate symptom relief,** offer a trial of a prokinetic.
- Full-dose PPIs are not recommended: they are no more effective than low-dose PPIs in non-ulcer dyspepsia.
- ***H pylori* re-testing after eradication therapy is not recommended** in people with non-ulcer dyspepsia.
- **If there is still an inadequate response** to therapy, or new emergent symptoms, consider referring to a specialist for a second opinion.
- **If symptoms respond to a treatment:**
  - Continue treatment with a limited number of repeat prescriptions.
  - **Encourage people to use the lowest dose that controls symptoms.**
  - **Discuss using the treatment on an 'on-demand' basis** (i.e. waiting for symptoms to develop before taking treatment).
  - Consider whether it is appropriate to stop current treatment (e.g. PPI, H_2RA, or prokinetic) and return to an antacid or alginate 'on demand'.

D

Practical prescribing points

For further information please see the *Medicines Compendium* (www.medicines.org.uk) or the *British National Formulary* (www.bnf.org).

- **Proton pump inhibitors (PPIs):** differences between the PPIs in clinical efficacy and safety are minimal.
  - Omeprazole is currently cheapest.
  - Omeprazole and esomeprazole occasionally enhance the effects of warfarin and phenytoin. Monitor carefully if omeprazole or esomeprazole are started or stopped.
- **Cimetidine: avoid in people taking** erythromycin, warfarin, amiodarone, theophylline, carbamazepine, phenytoin, and sodium valproate as cimetidine inhibits hepatic drug metabolism by binding to microsomal cytochrome P450.
- **Prokinetics: avoid long-term use** of metoclopramide or domperidone.
- **Metoclopramide: avoid in young adults** (under the age of 20 years) as extrapyramidal adverse effects are more common in this age group.
- **Antacids and alginates** are not suitable for long-term, frequent-dose, continuous use.
- **Antacids:** combinations of aluminium salts with magnesium salts may be preferable to magnesium salts alone (which may cause diarrhoea) or aluminium salts alone (which may cause constipation).

Follow-up advice

- **Do not re-test for *H pylori*** unless there is a strong clinical need (e.g. family history of gastric cancer).
- All people with dyspepsia requiring long-term treatment should have an annual review of their condition, and lifestyle advice should be reinforced.

Should I refer or investigate?

Refer?

Indications for repeat endoscopy

Note: proton pump inhibitors and H_2-receptor antagonists should be stopped at least 2 weeks before endoscopy. Nonsteroidal anti-inflammatory drug use should also be suspended in all people requiring referral.

- **Consider** managing previously investigated people without new ALARM symptoms according to previous endoscopic findings. However, if an additional diagnosis is suspected, or if the person has been symptom-free for

several years before symptoms recur, consider referring for a repeat endoscopy to confirm the diagnosis.
- **Immediate endoscopy** (i.e. same day) is indicated for people presenting with dyspepsia together with significant acute gastrointestinal bleeding.
- **Anyone who develops ALARM symptoms should be referred urgently for endoscopy, or to a specialist.** That is people with:
  - Chronic gastrointestinal bleeding
  - Progressive unintentional weight loss
  - Progressive difficulty swallowing (dysphagia)
  - Persistent vomiting
  - Iron deficiency anaemia
  - Epigastric mass
  - Suspicious barium meal result
- **People 55 years and over, presenting with unexplained and persistent recent onset dyspepsia** alone, should be referred for urgent endoscopy.
- **Urgent referral to a specialist should also be considered** in a person (of any age) who has unexplained worsening of their dyspepsia and:
  - Barrett's oesophagus
  - Known dysplasia, atrophic gastritis, or intestinal metaplasia
  - Peptic ulcer surgery over 20 years ago
- **If definite dysphagia or odynophagia is present** with a suspicious history or regurgitation, it is appropriate to refer for a barium swallow.

Investigate?

- When referring, consider a full blood count to assist specialist assessment. This should be carried out in accordance with local arrangements.

Patient information leaflets

The following PILs are available at www.prodigy.nhs.uk
- CORE, Fighting Gut and Liver Disease
- Dyspepsia - Functional or Non-Ulcer
- Gastroscopy (Endoscopy)
- Helicobacter Pylori & Stomach Pain

Shared decision making

- The symptoms of non-ulcer (functional) dyspepsia typically come and go. Treatment is sometimes not satisfactory and you may have to put up with symptoms from time to time.
- Medication that may help to ease symptoms include:
  - **An acid-suppressing medicine.** Once symptoms have eased, gradually reduce to the lowest dose needed to control symptoms, OR just use it when symptoms flare-up.
  - **A prokinetic medicine** such as domperidone or metoclopramide. These speed up the passage of food through the stomach and may particularly help to ease symptoms of bloating or feeling full soon after eating.

Drug rationale

Drugs not included

- **Other antacid preparations** are not included. Products containing simeticone (activated dimeticone) are unlikely to confer any additional advantage. Products containing bismuth have not been included because of a high incidence of adverse effects. Many other products available to purchase over the counter are not prescribable on the NHS.
- **Other alginate preparations** are not included because they not available as sugar-free products.

Drugs included

- **Low-dose proton pump inhibitors (PPIs)** (omeprazole, lansoprazole, pantoprazole, and rabeprazole) are included for empirical acid-suppression therapy. Full-dose esomeprazole is also included because there is no low-dose equivalent available.
  - No PPIs are currently licensed for treatment of non-ulcer dyspepsia because the evidence is poor and only a small subset of people with non-ulcer dyspepsia seem to respond to acid suppression. However, the available evidence suggests that full-dose PPIs are no more effective than low-dose PPIs for non-ulcer dyspepsia [Moayyedi et al, 2003; NICE, 2004].
  - Note: when undertaking meta-analysis of dose-related effects, NICE classed esomeprazole 20mg as a full-dose equivalent to omeprazole 20mg.
- **H_2-receptor antagonists** (H_2RAs) (cimetidine, famotidine, nizatidine, and ranitidine) are included as an alternative to PPIs for empirical acid-suppression. No H_2RAs are currently licensed for this indication because the evidence is poor and publication bias may have occurred [Moayyedi et al, 2003; NICE, 2004].
- **Prokinetic agents** (metoclopramide or domperidone) are an alternative if there is an inadequate response to a PPI or an H_2RA. However, there are no studies examining the efficacy of domperidone or metoclopramide in non-ulcer dyspepsia [Moayyedi et al, 2003; NICE, 2004].
- **Antacid and alginates** are included for on-demand use. Long-term, continuous use of frequent-dose antacid therapy is inappropriate and only relieves symptoms in the short term, rather than preventing them [NICE, 2004]. However, they are a suitable 'on-demand' option particularly for those people who are able to return to self-care.

Prescriptions

Proton pump inhibitors: low dose or on-demand

Omeprazole capsules: 10mg once a day
- Age from 16 years onwards
- Omeprazole 10mg capsules. Take one capsule once a day. If you are able to, try to take one capsule once a day only when your symptoms recur; supply 28 capsules; NHS Cost £7.72.

Omeprazole tablets: 10mg once a day
- Age from 16 years onwards
- Omeprazole 10mg tablets. Take one tablet once a day. If you are able to, try to take one tablet once a day only when your symptoms recur; supply 28 tablets; NHS Cost £11.40.

Lansoprazole capsules: 15mg each morning
- Age from 16 years onwards
- Lansoprazole 15mg capsules. Take one capsule each morning (on an empty stomach). If you are able to, try to take one capsule each morning only when your symptoms recur; supply 28 capsules; NHS Cost £12.92

Lansoprazole orodispersible tablets: 15mg each morning
- Age from 16 years onwards
- Lansoprazole 15mg orodisp tabs. Take one tablet each morning (on an empty stomach). If you are able to, try to take one tablet each morning only when your symptoms recur; supply 28 tablets; NHS Cost £10.86.

Pantoprazole e/c tablets: 20mg once a day
- Age from 16 years onwards
- Pantoprazole 20mg e/c tablets. Take one tablet once a day. If you are able to, try to take one tablet once a day only when your symptoms recur; supply 28 tablets; NHS Cost £12.31.

abeprazole e/c tablets: 10mg once a day
Age from 16 years onwards
Rabeprazole 10mg e/c tabs. Take one tablet once a day. If you are able to, try to take one tablet once a day only when your symptoms recur; supply 28 tablets; NHS Cost £11.56.

someprazole e/c tablets: 20mg once a day
Age from 16 years onwards
Esomeprazole 20mg tablets. Take one tablet once a day. If you are able to, try to take one tablet once a day only when your symptoms recur; supply 28 tablets; NHS Cost £18.50.

$_2$-receptor antagonists: maintenance or on-emand

imetidine tablets: 400mg twice a day
Age from 16 years onwards
Cimetidine 400mg tablets. Take one tablet twice a day. If you are able to, reduce to one tablet at night. Alternatively, try taking these tablets only when your symptoms recur; supply 60 tablets; NHS Cost £5.58.

anitidine tablets: 150mg twice a day
Age from 16 years onwards
Ranitidine 150mg tablets. Take one tablet twice a day. If you are able to, reduce to one tablet at night. Alternatively, try taking these tablets only when your symptoms recur; supply 60 tablets; NHS Cost £7.21.

izatidine capsules: 150mg twice a day
Age from 16 years onwards
Nizatidine 150mg capsules. Take one capsule twice a day. If you are able to, reduce to one cap at night. Alternatively, try taking these capsules only when your symptoms recur; supply 60 capsules; NHS Cost £12.26.

amotidine tablets: 20mg twice a day
Age from 16 years onwards
Famotidine 20mg tablets. Take one tablet twice a day. If you are able to, reduce to one tablet at night. Alternatively, try taking these tablets only when your symptoms recur; supply 56 tablets; NHS Cost £23.28.

rokinetics: on-demand (not suitable for long-term se)

omperidone tablets: 10mg to 20mg four times a day
Age from 16 years onwards
Domperidone 10mg tablets. Take one to two tablets four times a day (before meals and at bedtime). If you are able to, try to take these tablets only when your symptoms recur; supply 200 tablets; NHS Cost £16.62.

etoclopramide tablets: 10mg three times a day
Age from 20 years onwards
Metoclopramide 10mg tablets. Take one tablet three times a day. If you are able to, try to take one tablet three times a day only when your symptoms recur; supply 84 tablets; NHS Cost £2.61.

ntacids and alginates: on-demand

ntacids: co-magaldrox 195/220mg suspension
Age from 16 years onwards
Co-magald 195/220mg/5ml susp. Take two to four 5ml spoonfuls 20-60 minutes after food and at bedtime, when required to relieve dyspepsia; supply 1000 ml; NHS Cost £3.82; OTC Cost £6.74.

ntacids: aluminium hydroxide 4% suspension
Age from 16 years onwards
Aluminium hydroxide 4% mixture. Take one to two 5ml spoonfuls four times a day (between meals and at bedtime) when required to relieve dyspepsia; supply 400 ml; NHS Cost £2.84; OTC Cost £3.32.

Antacids: magnesium trisilicate mixture
- Age from 16 years onwards
- Magnesium trisilicate mixture. Take two 5ml spoonfuls (mixed in water) three times a day when required to relieve dyspepsia; supply 400 ml; NHS Cost £0.94; OTC Cost £1.10.

Alginates: Gastrocote liquid (sugar-free)
- Age from 16 years onwards
- Gastrocote liquid. Take one to three 5ml spoonfuls four times a day (after meals and at bedtime) when required to relieve dyspepsia; supply 1000 ml; NHS Cost £5.58; OTC Cost £9.84.

Alginates: Gaviscon Advance tablets (sugar-free)
- Age from 16 years onwards
- Gaviscon Advance tablets. Chew one to two tablets (followed by water) after meals and at bedtime, when required to relieve dyspepsia; supply 120 tablets; NHS Cost £6.48; OTC Cost £14.98.

Alginates: Gaviscon Advance liquid (sugar-free)
- Age from 16 years onwards
- Gaviscon Advance s/f susp. Take one to two 5ml spoonfuls after meals and at bedtime, when required to relieve dyspepsia; supply 500 ml; NHS Cost £5.40; OTC Cost £9.95.

Alginates: Peptac liquid (sugar-free)
- Age from 16 years onwards
- Peptac s/f liquid. Take two to four 5ml spoonfuls after meals and at bedtime, when required to relieve dyspepsia; supply 1000 ml; NHS Cost £4.32; OTC Cost £7.98.

Alginates: Rennie Duo suspension (sugar-free)
- Age from 16 years onwards
- Rennie Duo oral suspension. Take two to four 5ml spoonfuls after meals and at bedtime, when required to relieve dyspepsia; supply 1000 ml; NHS Cost £5.34; OTC Cost £10.58.

Extended Information

Background information

- What is dyspepsia? p.671
- What is non-ulcer dyspepsia? p.671
- How common is it? p.672
- How do I know my patient has non-ulcer dyspepsia? p.672
- What else might it be? p.672
- Complications and prognosis p.672

What is dyspepsia?

- **Dyspepsia is a term used to describe a group of symptoms** that alert the clinician to consider the possibility of upper gastrointestinal tract disease. It is not a diagnosis. The group of symptoms includes epigastric pain, heartburn or acid regurgitation (with or without bloating), nausea, or vomiting.

What is non-ulcer dyspepsia?

- **Non-ulcer dyspepsia** (also known as functional dyspepsia) is the most common diagnosis after endoscopy. It refers to people with dyspeptic symptoms and a normal endoscopy (i.e. endoscopy has excluded gastric or duodenal ulcer, oesophagitis, and malignancy).
- Non-ulcer dyspepsia includes people with simple gastritis or duodenitis, but erosive duodenitis and gastric erosions are considered to be part of the spectrum of peptic ulcer disease.

- The Rome II definition further excludes people with predominant heartburn but without oesophagitis and describes them as having 'endoscopy-negative reflux disease'.

[NICE, 2004]

How common is it?

- About 4% of general practice consultations are for dyspepsia and about 10% of these lead to referral for further investigation.
- For those people investigated by endoscopy for dyspepsia, 30% have no abnormal findings (i.e. have non-ulcer dyspepsia or endoscopy-negative reflux disease).
- A further 30% have gastritis, duodenitis, or hiatus hernia; 10–17% have oesophagitis; 10–15% have duodenal ulcer; 5–10% have gastric ulcer; and 2% have gastric cancer.

[British Society of Gastroenterology, 2002].

How do I know my patient has non-ulcer dyspepsia?

History

- **Symptoms are variable,** but may include upper abdominal pain or discomfort, retrosternal pain, heartburn, acid reflux, anorexia, nausea, vomiting, bloating, fullness, or early satiety.
- Pain in the right or left hypochondrium does not constitute dyspepsia [Hunt et al, 2002].

Investigations

- **Non-ulcer dyspepsia can only be diagnosed by endoscopy** because it is defined as people with dyspeptic symptoms and a normal endoscopy. However, it is neither necessary nor practical to investigate a diagnosis in every person with dyspepsia (in the absence of ALARM symptoms) if symptoms are controlled by empirical treatment [NICE, 2004].
  - People with predominant ulcer-like or dysmotility-like symptoms and a normal endoscopy have non-ulcer dyspepsia.
  - People with predominant heartburn and a normal endoscopy have endoscopy-negative reflux disease and should be managed via the separate PRODIGY guidance *Dyspepsia — proven GORD*.
  - People with dyspeptic symptoms who do *not* need an endoscopy should be managed via the separate PRODIGY guidance *Dyspepsia — symptoms (uninvestigated by endoscopy)*.
- ***Helicobacter pylori* testing** is commonly undertaken. Eradication is recommended in people with non-ulcer dyspepsia who test positive for *Helicobacter pylori* [Malfertheiner et al, 2002].

What else might it be?

- **Cardiac or biliary disease (C).**
  - Cardiac pain may be clinically indistinguishable from dyspepsia.
  - Biliary colic occasionally presents with epigastric pain.
- **Oesophageal or gastric carcinoma.** Investigate for malignancy in the presence of any ALARM symptoms (chronic gastrointestinal bleeding; dysphagia; progressive unintentional weight loss; persistent vomiting; iron deficiency anaemia; an epigastric mass; or suspicious barium meal). Symptom severity is a poor indicator of an underlying disease.
- **Gastro-oesophageal reflux disease** (GORD). GORD is a term used to describe diseases that cause reflux of gastric contents into the oesophagus, causing symptoms that a[re] sufficient to interfere with quality of life.
- **Peptic ulcer disease.**
- **Irritable bowel syndrome** may manifest as dyspepsia with bloating, but is usually associated with abnormal bowel habits.
- **Motility disorders** may also manifest as upper abdomi[nal] discomfort with bloating and early satiety. Gastropare[sis] should be suspected in people with diabetes mellitus, especially when peripheral neuropathy is present.
- **Other causes of dysphagia include** peptic stricture, Schatzki ring, and (less commonly) achalasia, diffuse spasm, systemic sclerosis, bronchial carcinoma, enlarge[d] mediastinal nodes, aortic aneurysm, post-cricoid web, [or] radiation stricture.

Complications and prognosis

Complications

- **There may be a missed diagnosis of oesophageal or gastric cancer.** Carcinoma at the site of a 'benign' ulcer may be a result of initial misdiagnosis, even if the ulcer seemed to respond to treatment.

Prognosis

- **For people with non-ulcer dyspepsia,** symptoms are recurrent and intermittent; symptoms recur annually in about 50% of these people. The lifetime risk of recurrence is about 80% [Graham, 1997; NICE, 2004]

Management issues

- Overview of management p.673
- What general measures are useful? p.673
- What is first-line treatment? p.673
- Which *H pylori* test should I use? p.673
- What should I do if symptoms persist or return? p.673
- Reviewing and stepping-down treatment p.674
- When is repeat endoscopy indicated? p.674
- Supporting evidence for treatment strategies p.674
- Psychological therapies p.675
- Medicines management p.675

This guidance covers the management of people with endoscopically determined non-ulcer dyspepsia. People with dyspepsia symptoms that have not been investigated by endoscopy should be managed as people with 'uninvestigated dyspepsia' (C) [NICE, 2004]. See the PRODIGY guidance *Dyspepsia — symptoms (uninvestigated by endoscopy)*. Consider managing previously investigated people without new ALARM symptoms according to previous endoscopic findings.

erview of management

Review medication that may be causing dyspepsia.
Offer general lifestyle advice.
Test for *H pylori* and, if the test is positive, eradicate it using triple therapy.
If *H pylori* has been excluded or has been treated but symptoms persist, offer a low-dose proton pump inhibitor or H_2-receptor antagonist for 1 month.
If symptoms persist or return, continue with acid-suppression therapy. Encourage people to:

- Step-down to the lowest dose required to control symptoms.
- Use treatment on an 'on-demand' basis.
- Return to self-care with an antacid or alginate.

All people with non-ulcer dyspepsia requiring long-term treatment should have an annual review of their condition, and lifestyle advice should be reinforced. Anxiety regarding symptoms should be addressed. It is important to reassure people with non-ulcer dyspepsia that no serious disease has been found.

hat general measures are useful?

'hich medication might be causing non-ulcer yspepsia?

top nonsteroidal anti-inflammatory drugs (NSAIDs) wherever possible (A).
Theophylline, nitrates, and calcium-channel blockers nay reduce lower oesophageal sphincter pressure. Consider withdrawing if there are predominant reflux symptoms.
Bisphosphonates and corticosteroids commonly cause gastrointestinal adverse effects.
eReC, 1998; NICE, 2004]

'hat lifestyle advice is recommended?

Offer simple lifestyle advice, including healthy eating, weight reduction, and smoking cessation (**B**). Although here is no clear evidence that lifestyle factors (such as smoking, alcohol, caffeine, and diet) affect dyspepsia, here are more important general health benefits.
f the person has identified a precipitating factor, then it s sensible to advise them to avoid it (e.g. bending, alcohol, coffee, chocolate, fatty foods, spicy foods) (**C**).
Other suggestions for people with reflux symptoms nclude eating smaller meals, not eating before going to bed, and propping up the bed head. (One possible cause of reflux disease is transient relaxation of the lower oesophageal sphincter: lying flat may therefore increase reflux episodes because gravity does not then prevent acid regurgitation.)
Provide people with patient information to support the care they receive (**C**).
[eReC, 1998; NICE, 2004]

hat is first-line treatment?

Initial treatment involves testing for *Helicobacter pylori* and, if the test is positive, eradicating it using triple therapy (**A**).
If *H pylori* has been excluded or has been treated but symptoms persist, (or if *H pylori* eradication therapy has recently been given) offer a low-dose proton pump inhibitor or a H_2-receptor antagonist for 1 month (**A**).
Note: there is insufficient evidence to guide whether *H pylori* testing or acid suppression should be offered first, but it seems practical to test for *H pylori* first because carbon-13 urea breath tests or stool antigen tests should not be performed within 2 weeks of acid-suppression therapy (or within 4 weeks of antimicrobial therapy) as false-negative results may occur.
[NICE, 2004]

Which *H pylori* test should I use?

If *Helicobacter pylori* testing has not already been undertaken during endoscopy (e.g. using a CLO [Campylobacter-like organism] test) consider the following:

- **A carbon-13 urea breath test or a stool antigen test is recommended** for pretreatment testing [NICE, 2004] (**A**).
- Neither type of test should be performed within 2 weeks of proton pump inhibitor therapy or within 4 weeks of antibiotic therapy, as false-negative results may occur [DTB, 2004].
- If the person is taking long-term antibiotics: phenoxymethylpenicillin, nitrofurantoin, and trimethoprim are not active against *H pylori*, so will not affect the test results. Advice should be sought from the local microbiology laboratory on when to test and test-interpretation if people are taking other long-term antibiotics [HPA Helicobacter Working Group, Personal Communication, 2005]. (Tetracyclines, macrolides, broad spectrum penicillins [e.g. amoxicillin], cephalosporins, and anti-tuberculosis drugs are all active against *H pylori*.)
- ***H pylori* re-testing after eradication therapy is not routinely recommended** in people with non-ulcer dyspepsia (**C**). However, they may value the information it provides.
- If post-eradication testing is appropriate, only a carbon-13 urea breath test should be used [NICE, 2004] (**A**).

How do I use a carbon-13 urea breath test?

- Carbon-13 urea breath tests involve a separate appointment at the practice because the manufacturers recommend that the performance of the test is supervised.
- The kits currently prescribable on the NHS for adults include diabact UBT®, Helicobacter Test Hp-Plus®, Helicobacter Test INFAI®, and Pylobactell®.
- The person should fast for at least 6 hours before the test and then (for all tests except diabact UBT®) ingest citric acid or orange juice just before the test to slow gastric emptying. (The diabact UBT® tablet contains citric acid.)
- The person then provides two or three breath samples before ingestion of the carbon-13 tablet, and again 30 minutes afterwards (only 10 minutes afterwards for diabact UBT®) by blowing through a straw into a series of glass, screw-top tubes.
- Breath samples are sent away for analysis by mass spectrometry and results are available within 24 hours of receipt.

[DTB, 2004]

How do I use a stool antigen test?

- Stool antigen tests require the person to collect a stool sample (at least pea-sized). The sample is then sent to the laboratory for analysis.
- Stool antigen tests do not require a separate appointment at the practice and are cheaper than carbon urea breath testing.

What should I do if symptoms persist or return?

- Consider managing previously investigated people without new ALARM symptoms according to previous endoscopic findings (**C**) [NICE, 2004].

- In people with non-ulcer dyspepsia, symptoms will naturally improve in 36% of the people, 7% will improve due to eradication therapy, but in 57% substantial symptoms will remain over a 3–12 month period [NICE, 2004].
- Unlike peptic ulcer disease, there is no 'one-off' cure, and treatment is often needed on a long-term basis. No drug therapies have been found to have a high success rate for relieving symptoms of non-ulcer dyspepsia. Although the mechanisms causing non-ulcer dyspepsia are unknown, symptoms are heterogeneous, suggesting that different therapies may be effective for different people. Reassurance that no serious disease has been found is important [SIGN, 2003].
- **Offer a low-dose proton pump inhibitor (PPI) or an H_2-receptor antagonist (H_2RA),** with a limited number of repeat prescriptions (C). There is no evidence to guide which of these therapies should be tried first. PPIs offer more powerful acid suppression but H_2RAs are cheaper [NICE, 2004].
- **Encourage people to use the lowest dose required to control symptoms** (C).
- **Discuss using the treatment on an 'on-demand' basis** (i.e. waiting for symptoms to develop before taking treatment) (B).
- **If PPIs or H_2RAs provide inadequate symptom relief,** offer a trial of a prokinetic.
- **Long-term, continuous antacid therapy is not recommended.** Long-term, continuous use of frequent-dose antacid therapy is inappropriate and only relieves symptoms in the short term, rather than preventing them (B) [NICE, 2004]. However, it is a suitable 'on-demand' option, particularly for those people who are able to return to self-care.

Reviewing and stepping-down treatment

- All people with non-ulcer dyspepsia requiring long-term treatment should have an annual review of their condition and medication, and lifestyle advice should be reinforced.
  - Encourage people to step-down treatment to the lowest dose required to control symptoms (C).
  - Discuss using the treatment on an 'on-demand' basis (i.e. waiting for symptoms to develop before taking treatment) (C).
  - It may be appropriate to stop current treatment (e.g. proton pump inhibitor, H_2-receptor antagonist, or prokinetic) and return to self-care with an antacid or alginate (C). (This may be prescribed or purchased over the counter.)
- If there is an inadequate response to therapy or new symptoms emerge, referral to a specialist for a second opinion or an endoscopy may become appropriate. See *When is repeat endoscopy indicated?*

[NICE, 2004]

When is repeat endoscopy indicated?

Note: proton pump inhibitors and H_2-receptor antagonists should be stopped at least 2 weeks before endoscopy (B). Nonsteroidal anti-inflammatory drug use should also be suspended in all people requiring referral (C).

- **Consider** managing previously investigated people without new ALARM symptoms according to previous endoscopic findings. However, if an additional diagnosis is suspected, or if the person has been symptom-free for several years before symptoms recur, consider referring for a repeat endoscopy to confirm the diagnosis.
- **Immediate endoscopy** (i.e. same day) is indicated for people presenting with dyspepsia together with significant acute gastrointestinal bleeding.
- **Anyone who develops ALARM symptoms should be referred urgently for endoscopy, or to a specialist** (C) [NICE, 2005]. That is people with:
  - Chronic gastrointestinal bleeding
  - Progressive unintentional weight loss
  - Progressive difficulty swallowing (dysphagia)
  - Persistent vomiting
  - Iron deficiency anaemia
  - Epigastric mass
  - Suspicious barium meal result
- **However, people 55 years and over,** presenting with unexplained and persistent recent onset dyspepsia alor should be referred for urgent endoscopy (C) [NICE, 2004].
  - *Unexplained* is defined as a symptom(s) and/or sign that has not led to a diagnosis being made by the primary care professional after initial assessment of the history, examination and primary care investigations (if any)'. In the context of this recommendation, the primary care professional sho confirm that the dyspepsia is new rather than a recurrent episode and exclude common precipitants dyspepsia such as ingestion of NSAIDs.
  - *Persistent* refers to the continuation of specified symptoms and/or signs beyond a period that would normally be associated with self-limiting problems. The precise period will vary depending on the severi of symptoms and associated features, as assessed by the healthcare professional. In many cases, the uppe limit the professional will permit symptoms and/or signs to persist before initiating referral will be 4–6 weeks.
- **Urgent referral to a specialist should also be considere in** a person (of any age) who has unexplained worseni of their dyspepsia and Barrett's oesophagus; or known dysplasia, atrophic gastritis, or intestinal metaplasia; o peptic ulcer surgery over 20 years ago (C) [NICE, 200
- **If dysphagia is present** (interference with the swallowi mechanism that occurs within 5 seconds of starting th swallowing process) it is appropriate to refer for a barium swallow. There is a risk of perforation if an endoscope is pushed through a stricture. Before endoscopic examination, a barium swallow will delineate the stricture to see how long it is.

[NICE, 2004; NICE, 2005]

Supporting evidence for treatment strategi

H pylori 'test and treat'

- Available evidence from trials indicates that eradicatio of *Helicobacter pylori* (if present) is an effective and cost-effective option in non-ulcer dyspepsia [NICE, 2004].
- Data pooled by NICE from 12 trials of 3 to 12 months duration found that *H pylori* eradication was more effective than placebo at reducing the risk of symptom persisting: the risk ratio for symptoms persisting was 0 (95% CI 0.86 to 0.95); for every 14 people treated the was one additional responder (NNT = 14).
- Benefit is obtained by a short course of therapy, while acid suppression requires long-term treatment. Thus eradication therapy is likely to be more cost-effective, i spite of the high number needed to treat for one persor to obtain benefit [SIGN, 2003; NICE, 2004].
- It is possible that the effect of *H pylori* eradication in non-ulcer dyspepsia is based on a sub-group of people with an 'ulcer diathesis' and treatment prevents development of peptic ulcers. This hypothesis is difficu to prove, but might explain why an effect is seen.

H pylori eradication regimens

- One-week triple therapy regimens (a proton pump inhibitor [PPI] plus two antibiotics) are recommended. Two-week regimens are no more effective than one-week regimens. Dual therapy is not as effective as triple therapy. Quadruple therapy (a PPI, bismuth, tetracycline, and metronidazole) is as effective as triple therapy, but taking 17 tablets per day does not make it a practical first-line option [Delaney et al, 2003].
- The recommended PAC regimen (a PPI plus amoxicillin 1 g and clarithromycin 500 mg, all given twice a day) and PCM regimen (a PPI plus metronidazole 400 mg and clarithromycin 250 mg, all given twice a day) are the optimum regimens on current evidence. Data pooled by NICE show that [NICE, 2004]:
  - Double-dose PPIs are more effective than single-dose PPIs in PAC regimens (eradication rate of 85.4% for double-dose PPIs and 78.5% for single-dose PPIs). The data were less clear for PCM regimens (due to much smaller patient numbers). Double-dose PPIs are therefore also recommended in PCM regimens as there is not enough data to clearly support single dose PPIs.
  - The dose of clarithromycin differs between the two regimens. Pooled data for PAC regimens show eradication rates of 79.8% with clarithromycin 250 mg compared with 89.6% with clarithromycin 500 mg. In PCM regimens, doubling the dose of clarithromycin had no statistically significant effect: eradication rates were 87.4% for clarithromycin 250 mg and 88.9% for clarithromycin 500 mg.
  - Pooled data for the recommended PAC and PCM regimens show no statistically significant difference in eradication rates: 82% for PAC, and 82.6% for PCM.
- Although triple therapy using a PPI plus amoxicillin and metronidazole has previously been recommended as a first-line therapy, pooled data from four randomized, controlled trials have shown that it is less effective than either of the two triple therapies that contain clarithromycin [NICE, 2004].

Acid suppression

- Long-term acid suppression is appropriate for *Helicobacter pylori*-negative people and those who fail to respond to eradication therapy, but the evidence is poor and only a small subset of people seem to respond [NICE, 2004].
- A systematic review of evidence from trials of 2 to 8 weeks' duration found that both proton pump inhibitors (PPIs) and H_2-receptor antagonists (H_2RAs) can reduce the symptoms of non-ulcer dyspepsia [Moayyedi et al, 2003; NICE, 2004].
  - PPIs were more effective than placebo at reducing dyspepsia: the relative risk for symptoms persisting was 0.86 (95% CI 0.77 to 0.95).
  - Full-dose PPIs are no more effective than low-dose PPIs: the relative risk for symptoms persisting was 0.98 (95% CI 0.92 to 1.05).
  - H_2RAs were more effective than placebo at reducing dyspepsia: the risk ratio for symptoms persisting was 0.76 (95% CI 0.70 to 0.82), but a funnel-plot suggested that this result could be due to publication bias.
  - Antacid therapy was no more effective than placebo in reducing the symptoms of non-ulcer dyspepsia.
- Although the efficacy of PPIs and H_2RAs cannot be compared directly, they both seem to work, but only for a small subset of people.
- On balance, low-dose PPIs are recommended in preference to H_2RAs as the data are more robust, although H_2RAs are cheaper.

On-demand PPI therapy

- There are no long-term treatment trials in dyspepsia, which is surprising given that it is a chronic, relapsing condition. It is argued that 'on-demand' proton pump inhibitor (PPI) therapy may be effective, but less costly than continuous therapy [NICE, 2004]. However, therapy can (and should) be individualized as a proportion of people will continue to take their PPI daily.
- The evidence for using 'on-demand' PPI therapy (i.e. waiting for symptoms to develop before taking treatment) in non-ulcer dyspepsia is extrapolated from studies looking at people with endoscopy-negative reflux disease. The patient populations are similar and, in the absence of ALARM symptoms, this extrapolation is a safe step [NICE, 2004].
- Although it was not possible for NICE to combine the data for meta-analysis, the general trend of study outcomes suggests that on-demand or intermittent PPI therapy is superior to placebo. Studies that have compared intermittent to continuous therapy also suggest that there is little difference in 'willingness to continue' (80–90%) between these strategies.

D

Prokinetics

- The evidence for prokinetic therapy is based on trials using cisapride (which is no longer commercially available), but publication bias is thought to have occurred and the data are considered unreliable. There are no studies examining the efficacy of domperidone or metoclopramide in non-ulcer dyspepsia.

Psychological therapies

- Non-ulcer dyspepsia is not usually caused by stress, anxiety, or depression, but these factors may worsen the symptoms and reduce an individual's ability to cope with them [SIGN, 2003].
- In people with non-ulcer dyspepsia, three small trials of psychological interventions (such as cognitive behaviour therapy or psychotherapy) showed decreases in dyspeptic symptoms after the intervention at 3 months, but this effect did not persist at 1 year.
- However, such interventions are intensive and relatively costly. Therefore they are not recommended for routine provision by primary care teams [NICE, 2004].

Medicines management

Which *H pylori* eradication regimen should I use?

- **NICE recommends that one of the following one-week eradication regimens is used:**
  - A 'PAC' regimen (a proton pump inhibitor [PPI], plus amoxicillin 1 g and clarithromycin 500 mg, all given twice a day)
  - Or (for people with penicillin hypersensitivity) a 'PCM' regimen (a PPI plus metronidazole 400 mg and clarithromycin 250 mg, all given twice a day)
- Note: NICE recommends that re-testing after eradication therapy is *not* required in people with non-ulcer dyspepsia, although they may value the information it provides (C) [NICE, 2004]. Second-line eradication regimens are therefore rarely required in people with non-ulcer dyspepsia. If they are required specialist advice should be sought.

Which eradication regimen should I use if my patient has had a recent course of antibiotics?

- **An alternative antibiotic should be used in the eradication regimen** if a course of clarithromycin or

metronidazole has previously been given (for any indication).
- The HPA Helicobacter Working Group recommends that two antibiotics are chosen from the following options: amoxicillin, clarithromycin, metronidazole, or oxytetracycline.
- Other antibiotics can be considered, but advice should be sought from the Helicobacter Reference Laboratory (telephone 0208 327 6538).

[HPA Helicobacter Working Group, Personal Communication, 2005]

Antibiotic resistance

- Laboratory testing suggests that *Helicobacter pylori* antibiotic resistance is around 15–66% for metronidazole, and 8–30% for clarithromycin [McLoughlin et al, 2004]. (Data on *H pylori* resistance to amoxicillin have not been published.)
- Treatment failure with a regimen containing clarithromycin is highly correlated with clarithromycin resistance. Clarithromycin is therefore best avoided if a recent course has been given.
- The association between metronidazole resistance and treatment failure is less clear cut.
  - Data pooled by NICE suggest that there is no significant difference in eradication rates between PAC and PCM regimens. NICE suggests that possible explanations are that PCM may be more effective than PAC in metronidazole-sensitive strains, or that the impact of metronidazole resistance may not be as marked as observational studies suggest [NICE, 2004].
  - Metronidazole could therefore be considered if a recent course had been taken and there was no suitable alternative.

[HPA Helicobacter Working Group, Personal Communication, 2005]

Which PPI?

- **Differences between the proton pump inhibitors (PPIs) in clinical efficacy and safety are minimal** [WeMeReC, 2002]. On present evidence, PPIs do not have any serious contraindications for most users, and have been in common use for over a decade.
- No PPIs (omeprazole, lansoprazole, pantoprazole, rabeprazole, and esomeprazole) are currently licensed for treatment and maintenance in non-ulcer dyspepsia.
- **Omeprazole is currently the least expensive PPI,** although this may change when other PPIs become available generically.
- PPIs are generally well tolerated. Adverse effects include gastrointestinal disturbances (mostly commonly diarrhoea), headaches, and dizziness.
- PPIs should not be offered to people with ALARM symptoms prior to endoscopy as they may mask gastric cancer. If someone already taking a PPI needs an endoscopy, the PPI should be stopped at least 2 weeks before the endoscopy.
- PPIs undergo extensive hepatic metabolism. In liver disease, do not exceed the following doses: 20 mg daily for omeprazole, pantoprazole, and esomeprazole; 30 mg daily for lansoprazole. There are no data on the use of rabeprazole in people with severe hepatic impairment so the manufacturer advises caution.
- Omeprazole and esomeprazole occasionally enhance the effects of warfarin and phenytoin. Monitor people taking these drugs carefully if omeprazole or esomeprazole are started or stopped.

Which dose?

- Recommended doses of proton pump inhibitors are outlined in Table 1.

Table 1: PRODIGY-recommended proton pump inhibitor doses for non-ulcer dyspepsia.

PPI	Low dose	*H pylori* eradication regimen dose (double dose)
Omeprazole	*10 mg once a day	20 mg twice a day
Lansoprazole	*15 mg once a day	30 mg twice a day
Pantoprazole	*20 mg once a day	40 mg twice a day
Rabeprazole	*10 mg once a day	20 mg twice a day
Esomeprazole	† Not available	20 mg twice a day

* Not licensed for non-ulcer dyspepsia.
† When undertaking meta-analysis of dose-related effects, NICE classed esomeprazole 20mg (the lowest available dose of esomeprazole) as a full-dose equivalent to omeprazole 20mg.

How should I advise people to take on-demand PPIs?

- 'On-demand' therapy is where treatment is taken only when symptoms recur. Once symptoms are relieved (often after a few days) treatment is stopped again.
- The PPI doses most commonly studied as on-demand therapy are rabeprazole 10mg, pantoprazole 20mg, esomeprazole 20mg, omeprazole 20mg, and lansoprazole 15mg. None are licensed for on-demand treatment in people with non-ulcer dyspepsia, but esomeprazole and rabeprazole are licensed for on-demand treatment in gastro-oesophageal reflux disease.
- Some people may prefer to use treatment intermittently, i.e. a 2–4 week course of treatment when symptoms recur.

[Bardhan, 2003; NICE, 2004]

H_2-receptor antagonists, prokinetics, antacids, and alginates

H_2-receptor antagonists

- **Cimetidine, famotidine, nizatidine, and ranitidine seem to be equally effective.** They have been shown to be more effective than placebo in the management of non-ulcer dyspepsia, although there are concerns that publication bias has occurred [Moayyedi et al, 2003].
- **Adverse effects are uncommon** and include diarrhoea, headache, dizziness, rash, and tiredness.
- **Cimetidine should be avoided in people taking** erythromycin, warfarin, amiodarone, theophylline, carbamazepine, phenytoin, and sodium valproate as cimetidine inhibits hepatic drug metabolism by binding to microsomal cytochrome P450.

Prokinetic agents

- **Domperidone and metoclopramide** are both used as prokinetic agents to reduce symptoms such as bloating and early satiety.
- **Long-term use should be avoided.** There is an increased risk of hyperprolactinaemia (e.g. galactorrhoea, gynaecomastia, and amenorrhoea) with both domperidone and metoclopramide. Chronic use of metoclopramide increases the risk of extrapyramidal adverse effects (i.e. drug-induced Parkinsonism). Extrapyramidal adverse effects are very rare with domperidone as it does not cross the blood-brain barrier
- Encourage people using prokinetics to use them as on-demand or intermittent therapy.
- Metoclopramide should be avoided in young adults (under the age of 20 years) because of the increased risk of extrapyramidal adverse effects in this age group.

Antacids and alginates

- There is limited evidence on the efficacy of antacids in the management of dyspepsia; however, symptomatic relief is often reported with the use of an antacid or alginate.
- They are best given when symptoms occur or are expected, i.e. after meals and at bedtime. They also

remain in the stomach for longer at these times, and therefore have longer to act.

Antacids should preferably not be taken at the same time as other drugs as they may impair absorption.

Most antacids contain aluminium salts, magnesium salts, or a combination of the two.

Combinations of aluminium salts with magnesium salts may be preferable to magnesium salts alone (which may cause diarrhoea) or aluminium salts alone (which may cause constipation).

Alginates form a 'raft' that floats on the surface of the stomach contents. They are most useful for people with mild reflux symptoms.

References

NHS staff in England can link, free of charge, from references to full text journals by clicking on [Full text] on the PRODIGY website.

1. Bardhan, K.D. (2003) Intermittent and on-demand use of proton pump inhibitors in the management of symptomatic gastroesophageal reflux disease. *American Journal of Gastroenterology* **98**(3 Suppl), S40-S48.
2. British Society of Gastroenterology (2002) *Dyspepsia management guidelines.* British Society of Gastroenterology. www.bsg.org.uk/clinical_prac/guidelines/dyspepsia.htm [Accessed: 20/08/2002].
3. Delaney, B.C., Moayyedi, P and Forman, D (2003) *Initial management strategies for dyspepsia (Cochrane Review).* The Cochrane Library. Issue 2. Chichester, UK: John Wiley & Sons, Ltd. www.nelh.nhs.uk/cochrane.asp [Accessed: 06/01/2005]. [Full text]
4. DTB (1996) Medical management of gastro-oesophageal reflux. *Drug & Therapeutics Bulletin* **34**(1), 1–4.
5. DTB (2004) Which test for *Helicobacter pylori* in primary care? *Drug & Therapeutics Bulletin* **42**(9), 71–72. [Full text]
6. Graham, D.Y. (1997) Can therapy even be denied for *Helicobacter pylori* infection? *Gastroenterology* **113**(Suppl 6), 113–117.
7. HPA Helicobacter Working Group (2005) *Personal communication. Antibiotic resistance and second-line antibiotics for eradication therapy.* Health Protection Agency: UK.
8. Hunt, R.H., Fallone, C., Veldhuyzen Van Zanten, S. et al (2002) Etiology of dyspepsia: implications for empirical therapy. *Canadian Journal of Gastroenterology* **16**(9), 635–641.
9. Malfertheiner, P., Megraud, F., O'Morain, C. et al (2002) Current concepts in the management of *Helicobacter pylori* infection – the Maastricht 2–2000 consensus report. *Alimentary Pharmacology & Therapeutics* **16**(2), 167–180.
10. McLoughlin, R., Racz, I., Buckley, M. et al (2004) Therapy of *Helicobacter pylori. Helicobacter* **9**(Suppl 1), 42–48.
11. MeReC (1997) Dyspepsia, peptic ulcer and *Helicobacter pylori. MeReC Bulletin* **8**(2), 5–8.
12. MeReC (1998) Proton pump inhibitors: their role in dyspepsia. *MeReC Bulletin* **9**(11), 41–44.
13. Moayyedi, P., Soo, S., Deeks, J. et al (2003) *Eradication of Helicobacter pylori for non-ulcer dyspepsia (Cochrane Review).* Issue 1. Chichester, UK: John Wiley & Sons, Ltd. www.nelh.nhs.uk/cochrane.asp [Accessed: 06/01/2005]. [Full text]
14. NICE (2004) *Dyspepsia: management of dyspepsia in adults in primary care: NICE guideline.* Clinical guideline 17. National Institute for Clinical Excellence. www.nice.org.uk [Accessed: 27/08/2004].
15. NICE (2005) *Referral guidelines for suspected cancer – quick reference guide.* Clinical guideline 27. National Institute for Health and Clinical Excellence. www.nice.org.uk [Accessed: 01/07/2005].
16. SIGN (2003) *Dyspepsia.* Report no. 68. Scottish Intercollegiate Guideline Network. www.sign.ac.uk [Accessed: 19/07/2003].
17. WeMeReC (2002) Use of proton pump inhibitors in primary care. *WeMeReC Bulletin* **9**(2), 1–6.

D

Evidence grading

Evidence grading is from the National Institute of Clinical Excellence guideline, *Dyspepsia,* August 2004. The definitions of grades of recommendation used in this guideline are as follows:

A — At least one randomized controlled trial as part of a body of literature of overall good quality and consistency addressing the specific recommendation without extrapolation.

B — Well-conducted clinical studies but no randomized clinical trials on the topic of recommendation, or with extrapolation from evidence obtained from randomized trials of meta-analysis.

C — Expert committee reports or opinions and/or clinical experiences of respected authorities. This grading indicates that directly applicable clinical studies of good quality are absent, or with extrapolation from higher levels of evidence.

GPP — Good practice point. Recommended good practice based on the clinical experience of the guideline development group.

PRODIGY GUIDANCE

Dyspepsia — symptoms (uninvestigated by endoscopy)

Last revised in July 2005
www.prodigy.nhs.uk/guidance.asp?gt=Dyspepsia - symptoms

Applies to people over the age of 16 years

This guidance is based on the National Institute for Clinical Excellence (NICE) guideline on *Dyspepsia* (August 2004). The section on managing dyspepsia associated with nonsteroidal inflammatory drugs is based on the New Zealand Guidelines Group guideline on *Management of dyspepsia and heartburn* (June 2004).

This guidance covers the management of adults with dyspepsia. It provides recommendations for managing undiagnosed dyspeptic problems.

This guidance does not cover the management of pregnancy-associated dyspepsia, gastric cancer, oesophageal cancer, pancreatic cancer, gallstones, or irritable bowel syndrome.

There is separate PRODIGY guidance for pregnancy-associated dyspepsia (*Dyspepsia — pregnancy associated*); proven ulcer (*Dyspepsia — proven DU or GU*); proven gastro-oesophageal reflux disease (*Dyspepsia — proven GORD*); and proven non-ulcer dyspepsia (*Dyspepsia — proven non-ulcer dyspepsia*). There is also separate PRODIGY guidance for *Irritable bowel syndrome*.

Goals

- To provide effective control of dyspeptic symptoms
- To identify and treat *Helicobacter pylori* infection
- To ensure appropriate use of endoscopy
- To promote healing of any mucosal lesions
- To prevent relapse and complications
- To detect any serious diagnoses, including oesophageal or gastric carcinoma

Contents

Scenarios

- Initial presentation — dyspepsia symptoms (no endoscopy) p.678
- Dyspepsia with ALARM symptoms p.680
- *H pylori* test result p.681
- Symptoms persist or return p.684
- Good response to treatment p.686
- Dyspepsia while taking NSAIDs p.689

Extended Information, p. 691

Which scenario?

- **Initial presentation — dyspepsia symptoms (no endoscopy):** covers the first-line management of people presenting with dyspepsia symptoms.
- **Dyspepsia with ALARM symptoms:** covers the management of people with ALARM symptoms (e.g. weight loss, gastrointestinal bleeding, anorexia).
- ***H pylori* test result:** covers the management of people who test positive for *H pylori* and who test negative for *H pylori*.
- **Symptoms persist or return:** covers the management of people when symptoms persist or return after first-line treatment.
- **Good response to treatment:** covers step-down strategies and use of on-demand treatment for people whose symptoms responded to treatment.
- **Dyspepsia while taking NSAIDs:** covers the management of people taking nonsteroidal anti-inflammatory drugs (NSAIDs).

Initial presentation — dyspepsia symptoms (no endoscopy)

Which therapy?

- **Refer urgently if the person has any ALARM symptoms** (See *Should I refer or investigate?*)
- **Address anxieties** about the significance of symptoms.
- **Stop nonsteroidal anti-inflammatory drugs (NSAIDs) where possible.** If this is not possible, see scenario *Dyspepsia while taking NSAIDs*.
- **Review other medication that may be causing dyspepsia** corticosteroids; bisphosphonates; medication that may lower oesophageal sphincter pressure (e.g. theophylline, nitrates, and calcium-channel blockers).
- **Choose a first-line treatment strategy.** Either:
  - **Test for *Helicobacter pylori* infection.**
  - **Or, offer a single course of** a full-dose proton pump inhibitor for 1 month.
- **If testing for *H pylori*:**
  - Use a carbon-13 urea breath test or the stool antigen test.
  - **Do not test within** 2 weeks of proton pump inhibitor therapy or within 4 weeks of antibiotic therapy as false-negative results may occur.
- **Give lifestyle advice:**
  - Healthy eating, weight loss, stopping smoking.
  - Avoiding precipitating factors, e.g. bending, alcohol, coffee, fatty foods.
  - For reflux symptoms: propping up the bed-head, eating smaller meals, not eating close to bedtime.

Practical prescribing points

For further information please see the *Medicines Compendium* (www.medicines.org.uk) or the *British National Formulary* (www.bnf.org).

- **Proton pump inhibitors (PPIs):** differences between the PPIs in clinical efficacy and safety are minimal.
  - Omeprazole is currently cheapest.
  - Omeprazole and esomeprazole occasionally enhance the effects of warfarin and phenytoin. Monitor carefully if omeprazole or esomeprazole are started or stopped.

pylori tests

Carbon-13 urea breath tests: advise the person to fast for at least 6 hours before the test and then (for all tests except diabact UBT®) ingest citric acid or orange juice just before the test to slow gastric emptying. (The diabact UBT® tablet contains citric acid.) The person then provides two or three breath samples before ingestion of the carbon-13 tablet, and again 30 minutes afterwards (only 10 minutes afterwards for diabact UBT®) by blowing through a straw into a series of glass, screw-top tubes. Breath samples are sent away for analysis by mass spectrometry.

Stool antigen tests: these require the person to collect a stool sample (at least pea-sized). The sample is then sent to the laboratory for analysis.

ollow-up advice

Follow-up is not usually needed unless symptoms are persistent or recurrent.

Note that re-testing after eradication therapy is *not* routinely recommended for people whose dyspepsia has not been investigated by endoscopy.

hould I refer or investigate?

efer?

Note: proton pump inhibitors and H_2-receptor antagonists hould be stopped at least 2 weeks before endoscopy. Nonsteroidal anti-inflammatory drug use should also be uspended in all people requiring referral.

Routine endoscopy of people of any age presenting with dyspepsia but *without* ALARM symptoms is not necessary.

Immediate endoscopy (i.e. same day) is indicated for people presenting with dyspepsia together with significant acute gastrointestinal bleeding.

Anyone who develops ALARM symptoms should be referred urgently for endoscopy, or to a specialist. That is people with:

- Chronic gastrointestinal bleeding
- Progressive unintentional weight loss
- Progressive difficulty swallowing (dysphagia)
- Persistent vomiting
- Iron deficiency anaemia
- Epigastric mass
- Suspicious barium meal result

People 55 years and over, presenting with unexplained and persistent recent onset dyspepsia alone, should be referred for urgent endoscopy.

Urgent referral to a specialist should also be considered in a person (of any age) who has unexplained worsening of their dyspepsia and:

- Barrett's oesophagus
- Known dysplasia, atrophic gastritis, or intestinal metaplasia
- Peptic ulcer surgery over 20 years ago

If definite dysphagia or odynophagia is present with a suspicious history or regurgitation, it is appropriate to refer for a barium swallow.

In people of *any age* with difficult to control or persistent dyspeptic symptoms consider referring those people with long-term, frequently recurring or poorly controlled symptoms: the endoscopy may clarify the diagnosis to exclude complicated gastro-oesophageal reflux disease (GORD) or peptic ulcer disease.

Urgent endoscopy should also be considered in people aged 55 years or over with unexplained and persistent recent-onset dyspepsia alone.

Investigate?

- **Consider a full blood count** in all people with new onset dyspepsia in order to detect iron deficiency anaemia.

Patient information leaflets

The following PILs are available at www.prodigy.nhs.uk

- Barium Swallow / Meal / Follow Through
- CORE, Fighting Gut and Liver Disease
- Dyspepsia (Indigestion)
- Gastroscopy (Endoscopy)
- Helicobacter Pylori & Stomach Pain

D

Shared decision making

- Things to consider that may help to ease symptoms include:
  - **Changes to lifestyle:**
    - Stop smoking if you are a smoker.
    - Cut down on alcohol if you drink heavily.
    - Don't eat too much fatty or spicy food.
    - Eat healthily and try to lose weight if you are overweight.
  - **Your current medication:** some medicines may cause dyspepsia such as anti-inflammatory painkillers (aspirin, ibuprofen etc.), steroids, bisphosphonates, and various others.
- Treatment options for recurring dyspepsia include:
  - **A 4-week course of a PPI acid-suppressing medicine** (omeprazole, lansoprazole, esomeprazole, pantoprazole, or rabeprazole), OR
  - **Testing for bacteria called *H pylori*.** This is often the underlying cause of dyspepsia. If found it can usually be cleared with a one-week course of treatment of:
    - An acid-suppressing medicine, plus
    - Two antibiotics. Tell your doctor if you are allergic to any antibiotic. Some people develop side-effects with antibiotics. The most common are diarrhoea and feeling sick.
    - It is really important to take the whole course of treatment properly or it may not work.
- See a doctor if symptoms persist or return after finishing treatment.

Drug rationale

Drugs not included

- **H_2-receptor antagonists, antacids, alginates, and prokinetics** are not included. They are widely used as over-the-counter remedies for self-care before presentation to the GP.

Drugs included

- ***H pylori* tests** are offered for the diagnosis of gastroduodenal infection with *H pylori* [NICE, 2004]. Prescriptions for carbon-13 urea breath-test kits and an advice note for the stool antigen test are included.
- **Empirical PPI therapy:** PPIs are an effective treatment for dyspepsia symptoms that have not been investigated by endoscopy [NICE, 2004]. Note: when undertaking meta-analysis of dose-related effects, NICE classed esomeprazole 20mg as a full-dose equivalent to omeprazole 20mg.

D

Prescriptions

H pylori tests

Advice note: stool antigen test
- Age from 16 years onwards
- The stool antigen test is a way of testing whether you have a current infection with Helicobacter pylori. Put a pea-sized sample of your faeces (stools) into the container provided. Please return this sample to reception so that it can be sent to the laboratory for analysis. Acid suppressing medicines and antibiotics can affect the results of this test. If you have used an acid suppressing medicine within the last 2 weeks, or have taken antibiotics within the last 4 weeks, please check with your doctor before taking this test.

Carbon urea breath test: Diabact UBT H pylori test kit
- Age from 16 years onwards
- Diabact UBT tablet + kit. Follow the instructions given inside this pack; supply 1 kit; NHS Cost £12.75.

Carbon urea breath test: Helicobacter Test Hp-plus test kit
- Age from 16 years onwards
- Helicobacter Test Hp-plus. Follow the instructions given inside this pack; supply 1 kit; NHS Cost £19.75.

Carbon urea breath test: Helicobacter Test INFAI test kit
- Age from 16 years onwards
- Helicobacter test INFAI. Follow the instructions given inside this pack; supply 1 kit; NHS Cost £17.10.

Carbon urea breath test: Pylobactell H pylori test kit
- Age from 16 years onwards
- Pylobactell H pylori test kit. Follow the instructions given inside this pack; supply 1 kit; NHS Cost £20.75.

Proton pump inhibitors for 4 weeks

Omeprazole capsules: 20mg once a day for 4 weeks
- Age from 16 years onwards
- Omeprazole 20mg capsules. Take one capsule once a day for 4 weeks; supply 28 capsules; NHS Cost £12.75.

Omeprazole tablets: 20mg once a day for 4 weeks
- Age from 16 years onwards
- Omeprazole 20mg tablets. Take one tablet once a day for 4 weeks; supply 28 tablets; NHS Cost £12.75.

Lansoprazole capsules: 30mg each morning for 4 weeks
- Age from 16 years onwards
- Lansoprazole 30mg capsules. Take one capsule each morning (on an empty stomach) for 4 weeks; supply 28 capsules; NHS Cost £23.63.

Lansoprazole orodisp tablets: 30mg each morning for 4 weeks
- Age from 16 years onwards
- Lansoprazole 30mg orodisp tabs. Take one tablet each morning (on an empty stomach) for 4 weeks; supply 28 tablets; NHS Cost £19.88.

Pantoprazole e/c tablets: 40mg once a day for 4 weeks
- Age from 16 years onwards
- Pantoprazole 40mg e/c tablets. Take one tablet once a day for 4 weeks; supply 28 tablets; NHS Cost £21.69.

Rabeprazole e/c tablets: 20mg once a day for 4 weeks
- Age from 16 years onwards
- Rabeprazole 20mg e/c tabs. Take one tablet once a day for 4 weeks; supply 28 tablets; NHS Cost £21.16.

Esomeprazole tablets: 20mg once a day for 4 weeks
- Age from 16 years onwards
- Esomeprazole 20mg tablets. Take one tablet once a day for 4 weeks; supply 28 tablets; NHS Cost £18.50.

Dyspepsia with ALARM symptoms

Which therapy?

- **Refer urgently if the person has any ALARM symptoms or any other suspicious symptoms.** (See *Should I refer or investigate?*)
  - Stop proton pump inhibitors (PPIs) or H_2-receptor antagonists (H_2RAs) at least 2 weeks before endoscopy.
  - Check pre-investigation requirements with your local endoscopy unit.
- **If symptom relief is needed:**
  - **Use antacids or alginates** — they do not need to be stopped before endoscopy.
  - If symptoms are poorly controlled and endoscopy cannot be performed urgently, a 2–4 week course of an H_2RA could be used, but it must be stopped at least 2 weeks before endoscopy.
  - PPIs should be avoided in this situation.

Practical prescribing points

For further information please see the *Medicines Compendium* (www.medicines.org.uk) or the *British National Formulary* (www.bnf.org).

- **Antacids:** combinations of aluminium salts with magnesium salts may be preferable to magnesium salts alone (which may cause diarrhoea) or aluminium salts alone (which may cause constipation).

Follow-up advice

- Follow-up should be guided by results of investigations.

Should I refer or investigate?

Refer?

Note: proton pump inhibitors and H_2-receptor antagonists should be stopped at least 2 weeks before endoscopy. Nonsteroidal anti-inflammatory drug use should also be suspended in all people requiring referral.

- **Routine endoscopy of people of any age presenting with dyspepsia but *without* ALARM symptoms is not necessary.**
- **Immediate endoscopy** (i.e. same day) is indicated for people presenting with dyspepsia together with significant acute gastrointestinal bleeding.
- **Anyone who develops ALARM symptoms should be referred urgently for endoscopy, or to a specialist.** That is people with:
  - Chronic gastrointestinal bleeding
  - Progressive unintentional weight loss
  - Progressive difficulty swallowing (dysphagia)
  - Persistent vomiting
  - Iron deficiency anaemia
  - Epigastric mass
  - Suspicious barium meal result
- **People 55 years and over, presenting with unexplained and persistent recent onset dyspepsia** alone, should be referred for urgent endoscopy.
- **Urgent referral to a specialist should also be considered** in a person (of any age) who has unexplained worsening of their dyspepsia and:
  - Barrett's oesophagus
  - Known dysplasia, atrophic gastritis, or intestinal metaplasia
  - Peptic ulcer surgery over 20 years ago

If definite dysphagia or odynophagia is present with a suspicious history or regurgitation, it is appropriate to refer for a barium swallow.

In people of *any* age with difficult to control or persistent dyspeptic symptoms consider referring those people with long-term, frequently recurring or poorly controlled symptoms: the endoscopy may clarify the diagnosis to exclude complicated gastro-oesophageal reflux disease (GORD) or peptic ulcer disease.

nvestigate?

Consider a full blood count to assist specialist assessment. This should be carried out in accordance with local arrangements.

?atient information leaflets

The following PILs are available at www.prodigy.nhs.uk

Barium Swallow / Meal / Follow Through
CORE, Fighting Gut and Liver Disease
Dyspepsia (Indigestion)
Gastroscopy (Endoscopy)
Helicobacter Pylori & Stomach Pain

;hared decision making

You are advised to have an endoscopy.

For this test you swallow a thin flexible telescope so a doctor or nurse can see into your oesophagus (gullet), stomach, and duodenum.

If you are taking:

- Acid-suppressing medication, you should stop it for 2 weeks before your endoscopy.
- Anti-inflammatory medication, you should stop it now.

If symptoms flare up after stopping acid-suppressing medication, you can take antacids up to the time of your endoscopy.

Drug rationale

Drugs not included

Proton pump inhibitors should be avoided because the healing of lesions may make diagnosis difficult at endoscopy.

H_2-receptor antagonist should ideally be avoided because the healing of lesions may make diagnosis difficult at endoscopy. A 2–4 week course of treatment is reasonable if endoscopy cannot be performed promptly and symptoms are poorly controlled on antacids. However, they should preferably be stopped at least 2 weeks prior to endoscopy.

- **Antacid preparations other than those containing aluminium hydroxide and/or magnesium trisilicate** are not included. Products containing simeticone (activated dimeticone) are unlikely to confer any additional advantage [BNF 48, 2004]. Products containing bismuth have not been included because of a high incidence of adverse effects. Many other products available to purchase over the counter are not prescribable on the NHS.
- **Alginate preparations that are not available as sugar-free products** are not included.

Drugs included

- **Antacids containing aluminium hydroxide and/or magnesium trisilicate** have been included. Antacids containing aluminium or magnesium are effective, long acting, and are not absorbed to a significant extent. Using them in combination minimizes the adverse effects of constipation (aluminium) and diarrhoea (magnesium).
- **Alginates** are effective and safe in most people. They should be used in people with symptoms of reflux. All alginates offered are sugar-free.

Prescriptions

Antacids

Co-magaldrox 195/220mg suspension (low sodium content)

- Age from 16 years onwards
- Co-magald 195/220mg/5ml susp. Take two to four 5ml spoonfuls 20-60 minutes after food and at bedtime, when required to relieve dyspepsia; supply 1000 ml; NHS Cost £3.82; OTC Cost £6.74.

Aluminium hydroxide 4% suspension

- Age from 16 years onwards
- Aluminium hydroxide 4% mixture. Take one to two 5ml spoonfuls four times a day (between meals and at bedtime) when required to relieve dyspepsia; supply 400 ml; NHS Cost £2.84; OTC Cost £3.32.

Magnesium trisilicate mixture

- Age from 16 years onwards
- Magnesium trisilicate mixture. Take two 5ml spoonfuls (mixed in water) three times a day when required to relieve dyspepsia; supply 400 ml; NHS Cost £0.94; OTC Cost £1.10.

Alginates

Gastrocote liquid (sugar-free)

- Age from 16 years onwards
- Gastrocote liquid. Take one to three 5ml spoonfuls four times a day (after meals and at bedtime) when required to relieve dyspepsia; supply 1000 ml; NHS Cost £5.58; OTC Cost £9.84.

Gaviscon Advance tablets (sugar-free)

- Age from 16 years onwards
- Gaviscon Advance tablets. Chew one to two tablets (followed by water) after meals and at bedtime, when required to relieve dyspepsia; supply 120 tablets; NHS Cost £6.48; OTC Cost £14.98.

Gaviscon Advance liquid (sugar-free)

- Age from 16 years onwards
- Gaviscon Advance s/f susp. Take one to two 5ml spoonfuls after meals and at bedtime, when required to relieve dyspepsia; supply 500 ml; NHS Cost £5.40; OTC Cost £9.95.

Peptac liquid (sugar-free)

- Age from 16 years onwards
- Peptac s/f liquid. Take two to four 5ml spoonfuls after meals and at bedtime, when required to relieve dyspepsia; supply 1000 ml; NHS Cost £4.32; OTC Cost £7.98.

Rennie Duo suspension (sugar-free)

- Age from 16 years onwards
- Rennie Duo oral suspension. Take two to four 5ml spoonfuls after meals and at bedtime, when required to relieve dyspepsia; supply 1000 ml; NHS Cost £5.34; OTC Cost £10.58.

H pylori test result

Which therapy?

- **If the result is negative:** offer a 1-month course of a full-dose proton pump inhibitor (PPI).

- **If the result is positive:** eradicate using a 1-week course of triple therapy.
  - **First-line triple therapy:** use a PPI plus amoxicillin 1 g and clarithromycin 500 mg, all given twice a day.
  - **For people with penicillin hypersensitivity:** use a PPI plus metronidazole 400 mg and clarithromycin 250 mg, all given twice a day.
- **If clarithromycin or metronidazole has previously been taken,** do not use that antibiotic in the triple therapy regimen. Choose an alternative from:
  - Amoxicillin, clarithromycin, metronidazole, or oxytetracycline.

D

Practical prescribing points

For further information please see the *Medicines Compendium* (www.medicines.org.uk) or the *British National Formulary* (www.bnf.org).

- **Remind people that it is important to complete the** course and warn about adverse effects.
- **Advise people taking metronidazole** to avoid alcohol for the duration of the course and for at least 48 hours afterwards, because of the possibility of a disulfiram-like (Antabuse) reaction.
- **Clarithromycin** inhibits the metabolism of other drugs and can prolong the QT interval. Check drug interactions before prescribing.
- **Proton pump inhibitors (PPIs):** differences between the PPIs in clinical efficacy and safety are minimal.
  - Omeprazole is currently cheapest.
  - Omeprazole and esomeprazole occasionally enhance the effects of warfarin and phenytoin. Monitor carefully if omeprazole or esomeprazole are started or stopped.

Follow-up advice

- **If symptoms persist or return after** *H pylori* **eradication,** do not re-test for *H pylori* unless there is a strong clinical need (e.g. family history of gastric cancer). See scenario *Symptoms persist or return* for further management.

Should I refer or investigate?

Refer?

Note: Proton pump inhibitors and H_2-receptor antagonists should be stopped at least 2 weeks before endoscopy. Nonsteroidal anti-inflammatory drug use should also be suspended in all people requiring referral.

- **Routine endoscopy of people of any age presenting with dyspepsia but** ***without*** **ALARM symptoms is not necessary.**
- **Immediate endoscopy** (i.e. same day) is indicated for people presenting with dyspepsia together with significant acute gastrointestinal bleeding.
- **Anyone who develops ALARM symptoms should be referred urgently for endoscopy, or to a specialist.** That is people with:
  - Chronic gastrointestinal bleeding
  - Progressive unintentional weight loss
  - Progressive difficulty swallowing (dysphagia)
  - Persistent vomiting
  - Iron deficiency anaemia
  - Epigastric mass
  - Suspicious barium meal result
- **People 55 years and over, presenting with unexplained and persistent recent onset dyspepsia** alone, should be referred for urgent endoscopy.
- **Urgent referral to a specialist should also be considered** in a person (of any age) who has unexplained worsening of their dyspepsia and:
  - Barrett's oesophagus
  - Known dysplasia, atrophic gastritis, or intestinal metaplasia
  - Peptic ulcer surgery over 20 years ago
- **If definite dysphagia or odynophagia is present** with a suspicious history or regurgitation, it is appropriate to refer for a barium swallow.
- **In people of** ***any age*** **with difficult to control or persistent dyspeptic symptoms** consider referring those people with long-term, frequently recurring or poorly controlled symptoms: the endoscopy may clarify the diagnosis to exclude complicated gastro-oesophageal reflux disease (GORD) or peptic ulcer disease.

Investigate?

- When referring, consider a full blood count to assist specialist assessment. This should be carried out in accordance with local arrangements.

Patient information leaflets

The following PILs are available at www.prodigy.nhs.uk

- Barium Swallow / Meal / Follow Through
- CORE, Fighting Gut and Liver Disease
- Dyspepsia (Indigestion)
- Gastroscopy (Endoscopy)
- Helicobacter Pylori & Stomach Pain

Shared decision making

- **If you are not infected with** ***H pylori*****:**
  - You will need to take a 4-week course of a PPI acid-suppressing medicine (omeprazole, lansoprazole, pantoprazole, or rabeprazole).
- **If you are infected with** ***H pylori*** the bacteria can usually be cleared with a one-week course of treatment of:
  - **An acid-suppressing medicine,** plus
  - **Two antibiotics.** Tell your doctor if you are allergic to any antibiotic. Some people develop side-effects with antibiotics. The most common are diarrhoea and feeling sick.)
  - It is really important to take the whole course of treatment properly or it may not work.
- See a doctor if symptoms persist or return after finishing treatment.

Drug rationale

Drugs not included

- **Quadruple therapy** (a proton pump inhibitor [PPI], bismuth, tetracycline and metronidazole) is as effective as triple therapy for *H pylori* eradication, but taking 17 tablets per day does not make it a practical first-line option [Delaney et al, 2003].
- **Dual therapies** for *H pylori* eradication with PPIs and antibiotics are not recommended [NICE, 2004].
- **Triple therapies using ranitidine bismuth citrate instead of a PPI are not** recommended because evidence of efficacy is less strong than for PPI triple regimens [DTB, 1996; MeReC, 1997].
- **Two-week triple therapy** is no more effective than one-week triple therapy [NICE, 2004]. Longer regimens also cost more and have a longer duration of minor adverse effects.
- **Triple therapy using a PPI plus amoxicillin and metronidazole** is no longer recommended [NICE, 2004]. Pooled data from four randomized, controlled trials have shown that it is less effective than either of the two triple therapies that contain clarithromycin.

rugs included

Empirical PPI therapy: PPIs are an effective treatment for dyspepsia symptoms that have not been investigated by endoscopy [NICE, 2004]. Note: when undertaking meta-analysis of dose-related effects, NICE classed esomeprazole 20mg as a full-dose equivalent to omeprazole 20mg.

Triple therapy: NICE recommends the following one-week triple therapy eradication regimens for *H pylori* eradication [NICE, 2004]:

- A 'PAC' regimen (a PPI plus amoxicillin 1 g and clarithromycin 500 mg, all given twice a day)
- Or (for people with penicillin hypersensitivity) a 'PCM' regimen (a PPI plus metronidazole 400 mg and clarithromycin 250 mg, all given twice a day)
- Pooled data for the recommended PAC and PCM regimens show no statistically significant difference in eradication rates: 82% for PAC, and 82.6% for PMC.

Note: the dose of clarithromycin in the Helimet® packs (containing lansoprazole, metronidazole, and clarithromycin) is higher than that recommended by NICE for a PCM regimen. However, it is included because some people find the single-pack presentation helpful for compliance.

rescriptions

I pylori positive: PPI + amoxicillin + clarithromycin

meprazole + amoxicillin + clarithromycin

- Age from 16 years onwards
- Amoxicillin 500mg capsules. Take two capsules twice a day for 7 days; supply 28 capsules; NHS Cost £1.44.
- Clarithromycin 500mg tablets. Take one tablet twice a day for 7 days; supply 14 tablets; NHS Cost £21.90.
- Omeprazole 20mg capsules. Take one capsule twice a day for 7 days; supply 14 capsules; NHS Cost £6.38.

ınsoprazole + amoxicillin + clarithromycin

- Age from 16 years onwards
- Lansoprazole 30mg capsules. Take one capsule twice a day (on an empty stomach) for 7 days; supply 14 capsules; NHS Cost £11.82.
- Clarithromycin 500mg tablets. Take one tablet twice a day for 7 days; supply 14 tablets; NHS Cost £21.90.
- Amoxicillin 500mg capsules. Take two capsules twice a day for 7 days; supply 28 capsules; NHS Cost £1.44.

eliClear triple pack

- Age from 16 years onwards
- HeliClear triple pack. Take one lansoprazole capsule, one clarithromycin tablet, and two amoxicillin capsules twice a day for 7 days; supply 1 triple pack; NHS Cost £35.01.

antoprazole + amoxicillin + clarithromycin

- Age from 16 years onwards
- Pantoprazole 40mg e/c tablets. Take one tablet twice a day for 7 days; supply 14 tablets; NHS Cost £10.85.
- Amoxicillin 500mg capsules. Take two capsules twice a day for 7 days; supply 28 capsules; NHS Cost £1.44.
- Clarithromycin 500mg tablets. Take one tablet twice a day for 7 days; supply 14 tablets; NHS Cost £21.90.

abeprazole + amoxicillin + clarithromycin

- Age from 16 years onwards
- Amoxicillin 500mg capsules. Take two capsules twice a day for 7 days; supply 28 capsules; NHS Cost £1.44.
- Clarithromycin 500mg tablets. Take one tablet twice a day for 7 days; supply 14 tablets; NHS Cost £21.90.
- Rabeprazole 20mg e/c tabs. Take one tablet twice a day for 7 days; supply 14 tablets; NHS Cost £10.58.

Esomeprazole + amoxicillin + clarithromycin

- Age from 16 years onwards
- Amoxicillin 500mg capsules. Take two capsules twice a day for 7 days; supply 28 capsules; NHS Cost £1.44.
- Clarithromycin 500mg tablets. Take one tablet twice a day for 7 days; supply 14 tablets; NHS Cost £21.90.
- Esomeprazole 20mg tablets. Take one tablet twice a day for 7 days; supply 14 tablets; NHS Cost £9.25.

H pylori positive: PPI + metronidazole + clarithromycin

Omeprazole + metronidazole + clarithromycin

- Age from 16 years onwards
- Omeprazole 20mg capsules. Take one capsule twice a day for 7 days; supply 14 capsules; NHS Cost £6.38.
- Metronidazole 400mg tablets. Take one tablet twice a day for 7 days; supply 14 tablets; NHS Cost £1.03.
- Clarithromycin 250mg tablets. Take one tablet twice a day for 7 days; supply 14 tablets; NHS Cost £10.94.

Lansoprazole + metronidazole + clarithromycin

- Age from 16 years onwards
- Lansoprazole 30mg capsules. Take one capsule twice a day (on an empty stomach) for 7 days; supply 14 capsules; NHS Cost £11.82.
- Metronidazole 400mg tablets. Take one tablet twice a day for 7 days; supply 14 tablets; NHS Cost £1.03.
- Clarithromycin 250mg tablets. Take one tablet twice a day for 7 days; supply 14 tablets; NHS Cost £10.94.

HeliMet triple pack

- Age from 16 years onwards
- HeliMet triple pack. Take one lansoprazole capsule, one clarithromycin tablet and one metronidazole tablet twice a day for 7 days; supply 1 pack; NHS Cost £35.40.

Pantoprazole + metronidazole + clarithromycin

- Age from 16 years onwards
- Pantoprazole 40mg e/c tablets. Take one tablet twice a day for 7 days; supply 14 tablets; NHS Cost £10.85.
- Metronidazole 400mg tablets. Take one tablet twice a day for 7 days; supply 14 tablets; NHS Cost £1.03.
- Clarithromycin 250mg tablets. Take one tablet twice a day for 7 days; supply 14 tablets; NHS Cost £10.94.

Rabeprazole + metronidazole + clarithromycin

- Age from 16 years onwards
- Rabeprazole 20mg e/c tabs. Take one tablet twice a day for 7 days; supply 14 tablets; NHS Cost £10.58.
- Metronidazole 400mg tablets. Take one tablet twice a day for 7 days; supply 14 tablets; NHS Cost £1.03.
- Clarithromycin 250mg tablets. Take one tablet twice a day for 7 days; supply 14 tablets; NHS Cost £10.94.

Esomeprazole + metronidazole + clarithromycin

- Age from 16 years onwards
- Esomeprazole 20mg tablets. Take one tablet twice a day for 7 days; supply 14 tablets; NHS Cost £9.25.
- Metronidazole 400mg tablets. Take one tablet twice a day for 7 days; supply 14 tablets; NHS Cost £1.03.
- Clarithromycin 250mg tablets. Take one tablet twice a day for 7 days; supply 14 tablets; NHS Cost £10.94.

H pylori negative: proton pump inhibitors for 4 weeks

Omeprazole capsules: 20mg once a day for 4 weeks

- Age from 16 years onwards
- Omeprazole 20mg capsules. Take one capsule once a day for 4 weeks; supply 28 capsules; NHS Cost £12.75.

Omeprazole tablets: 20mg once a day for 4 weeks

- Age from 16 years onwards
- Omeprazole 20mg tablets. Take one tablet once a day for 4 weeks; supply 28 tablets; NHS Cost £12.75.

Lansoprazole capsules: 30mg each morning for 4 weeks
- Age from 16 years onwards
- Lansoprazole 30mg capsules. Take one capsule each morning (on an empty stomach) for 4 weeks; supply 28 capsules; NHS Cost £23.63.

Lansoprazole orodisp tablets: 30mg each morning for 4 weeks
- Age from 16 years onwards
- Lansoprazole 30mg orodisp tabs. Take one tablet each morning (on an empty stomach) for 4 weeks; supply 28 tablets; NHS Cost £19.88.

Pantoprazole e/c tablets: 40mg once a day for 4 weeks
- Age from 16 years onwards
- Pantoprazole 40mg e/c tablets. Take one tablet once a day for 4 weeks; supply 28 tablets; NHS Cost £21.69.

Rabeprazole e/c tablets: 20mg once a day for 4 weeks
- Age from 16 years onwards
- Rabeprazole 20mg e/c tabs. Take one tablet once a day for 4 weeks; supply 28 tablets; NHS Cost £21.16.

Esomeprazole tablets: 20mg once a day for 4 weeks
- Age from 16 years onwards
- Esomeprazole 20mg tablets. Take one tablet once a day for 4 weeks; supply 28 tablets; NHS Cost £18.50.

Symptoms persist or return

Which therapy?

- **Refer urgently if the person has any ALARM symptoms or any other suspicious symptoms.** (See *Should I refer or investigate?*)
- **If symptoms persist or return** offer the alternative course of first-line treatment:
  - Either, a full-dose proton pump inhibitor (PPI) therapy for 1 month.
  - Or, test for *Helicobacter pylori* and (if the result is positive) eradicate using triple therapy. See scenario *H pylori test result* for triple therapy regimens,
- **If testing for *H pylori*:**
  - Use a carbon-13 urea breath test or the stool antigen test.
  - **Do not test within** 2 weeks of proton pump inhibitor therapy or within 4 weeks of antibiotic therapy as false-negative results may occur.
- **When both first-line treatment strategies have been tried:**
  - **If there was an initial response to a PPI** but symptoms have now returned:
    - Step-down the PPI to the lowest dose required to control symptoms.
    - Discuss using the treatment on an 'on-demand' basis.
  - **If the initial response to a PPI was inadequate:**
    - Consider offering an H_2-receptor antagonist or a prokinetic because some individuals may benefit.
    - Prokinetic agents may improve symptoms such as bloating or early satiety.
- **If symptoms remain difficult to control** consider referring for an endoscopy.

Practical prescribing points

For further information please see the *Medicines Compendium* (www.medicines.org.uk) or the *British National Formulary* (www.bnf.org).

- **Proton pump inhibitors (PPIs):** differences between the PPIs in clinical efficacy and safety are minimal.
  - Omeprazole is currently cheapest.
  - Omeprazole and esomeprazole occasionally enhance the effects of warfarin and phenytoin. Monitor carefully if omeprazole or esomeprazole are started o[r] stopped.
- **Cimetidine: avoid in people taking** erythromycin, warfarin, amiodarone, theophylline, carbamazepine, phenytoin, and sodium valproate as cimetidine inhibits hepatic drug metabolism by binding to microsomal cytochrome P450.
- **Prokinetics: avoid long-term use** of metoclopramide or domperidone.
- **Metoclopramide: avoid in young adults (under the age 20 years)**, as extrapyramidal adverse effects are more common in this age group.

H pylori tests

- **Carbon-13 urea breath tests:** advise the person to fast f[or] at least 6 hours before the test and then (for all tests except diabact UBT®) ingest citric acid or orange juice just before the test to slow gastric emptying. (The diabact UBT® tablet contains citric acid.) The person then provides two or three breath samples before ingestion of the carbon-13 tablet, and again 30 minutes afterwards (only 10 minutes afterwards for diabact UBT®) by blowing through a straw into a series of glas[s] screw-top tubes. Breath samples are sent away for analysis by mass spectrometry.
- **Stool antigen tests:** these require the person to collect a stool sample (at least pea-sized). The sample is then sen[t] to the laboratory for analysis.

Follow-up advice

- **If symptoms persist or return after *H pylori* eradication** do not re-test for *H pylori* unless there is a strong clinic[al] need (e.g. family history of gastric cancer).
- **All people with dyspepsia requiring long-term treatmen[t] should** have an annual review of their condition, and lifestyle advice should be reinforced.

Should I refer or investigate?

Refer?

Note: proton pump inhibitors and H_2-receptor antagonist[s] should be stopped at least 2 weeks before endoscopy. Nonsteroidal anti-inflammatory use should also be suspended in all people requiring referral.

- **Routine endoscopy of people of any age presenting wit[h] dyspepsia but *without* ALARM symptoms is not necessary.**
- **Immediate endoscopy** (i.e. same day) is indicated for people presenting with dyspepsia together with significant acute gastrointestinal bleeding.
- **Anyone who develops ALARM symptoms should be referred urgently for endoscopy, or to a specialist.** That is people with:
  - Chronic gastrointestinal bleeding
  - Progressive unintentional weight loss
  - Progressive difficulty swallowing (dysphagia)
  - Persistent vomiting
  - Iron deficiency anaemia
  - Epigastric mass
  - Suspicious barium meal result
- **People 55 years and over, presenting with unexplained and persistent recent onset dyspepsia** alone, should be referred for urgent endoscopy.
- **Urgent referral to a specialist should also be considered** in a person (of any age) who has unexplained worsenin[g] of their dyspepsia and:
  - Barrett's oesophagus
  - Known dysplasia, atrophic gastritis, or intestinal metaplasia

- Peptic ulcer surgery over 20 years ago

If definite dysphagia or odynophagia is present with a suspicious history or regurgitation, it is appropriate to refer for a barium swallow.

In people of *any age* with difficult to control or persistent dyspeptic symptoms consider referring those people with long-term, frequently recurring or poorly controlled symptoms: the endoscopy may clarify the diagnosis to exclude complicated gastro-oesophageal reflux disease (GORD) or peptic ulcer disease.

nvestigate?

When referring, consider a full blood count to assist specialist assessment. This should be carried out in accordance with local arrangements.

?atient information leaflets

he following PILs are available at www.prodigy.nhs.uk

Barium Swallow / Meal / Follow Through
CORE, Fighting Gut and Liver Disease
Dyspepsia (Indigestion)
Gastroscopy (Endoscopy)
Helicobacter Pylori & Stomach Pain

›hared decision-making

Treatment options for recurring dyspepsia include:

- **A 4-week course of a PPI acid-suppressing medicine** (omeprazole, lansoprazole, esomeprazole, pantoprazole, or rabeprazole), OR
- **Testing for bacteria called *H pylori*.** This is often the underlying cause of dyspepsia. If found it can usually be cleared with a one-week course of treatment of:
  - **An acid-suppressing medicine,** plus
  - **Two antibiotics.** Tell your doctor if you are allergic to any antibiotic. Some people develop side-effects with antibiotics. The most common are diarrhoea and feeling sick.
  - It is really important to take the whole course of treatment properly or it may not work.

If symptoms persist after trying one of these options, the other option is then advised.

If symptoms were helped by a PPI, but returned when you stopped it, then the options to consider are:

- Take the PPI regularly. But, when symptoms ease, gradually reduce the dose need to control symptoms, OR
- Take short courses of the PPI just when symptoms occur.

If symptoms persist despite all the above, then the options to consider are:

- **An alternative acid-suppressing medicine** such as cimetidine, famotidine, nizatidine, or ranitidine.
- **A prokinetic medicine** such as domperidone or metoclopramide. These speed up the passage of food through the stomach and may particularly help to ease symptoms of bloating or feeling full soon after eating.

Drug rationale

Drugs not included

Antacids and alginates are not included. They are widely used as over-the-counter remedies for self-care before presentation to the GP. They are also used as the final part of a step-down strategy once symptoms are controlled.

Drugs included

- ***H pylori* tests** are offered for the diagnosis of gastroduodenal infection with *H pylori* [NICE, 2004]. Prescriptions for carbon-13 urea breath-test kits and an advice note for the stool antigen test are included.
- **Proton pump inhibitors:** PPIs are an effective treatment for dyspepsia symptoms that have not been investigated by endoscopy [NICE, 2004]. Note: when undertaking meta-analysis of dose-related effects, NICE classed esomeprazole 20mg as a full-dose equivalent to omeprazole 20mg.
- **H_2-receptor antagonists:** cimetidine, famotidine, nizatidine, and ranitidine seem to be equally effective. They have been shown to be more effective than placebo in the management of people whose dyspepsia has not been investigated by endoscopy.
- **Prokinetic agents** (metoclopramide or domperidone) may improve symptoms such as bloating or early satiety, and may be most useful for people with predominant reflux symptoms. However, trials have been few, small-scale, and heterogeneous.

D

Prescriptions

H pylori tests

Advice note: stool antigen test

- Age from 16 years onwards
- The stool antigen test is a way of testing whether you have a current infection with Helicobacter pylori. Put a pea-sized sample of your faeces (stools) into the container provided. Please return this sample to reception so that it can be sent to the laboratory for analysis. Acid suppressing medicines and antibiotics can affect the results of this test. If you have used an acid suppressing medicine within the last 2 weeks, or have taken antibiotics within the last 4 weeks, please check with your doctor before taking this test.

Carbon urea breath test: Diabact UBT H pylori test kit

- Age from 16 years onwards
- Diabact UBT tablet + kit. Follow the instructions given inside this pack; supply 1 kit; NHS Cost £12.75.

Carbon urea breath test: Helicobacter Test Hp-plus test kit

- Age from 16 years onwards
- Helicobacter Test Hp-plus. Follow the instructions given inside this pack; supply 1 kit; NHS Cost £19.75.

Carbon urea breath test: Helicobacter Test INFAI test kit

- Age from 16 years onwards
- Helicobacter test INFAI. Follow the instructions given inside this pack; supply 1 kit; NHS Cost £17.10.

Carbon urea breath test: Pylobactell H pylori test kit

- Age from 16 years onwards
- Pylobactell H pylori test kit. Follow the instructions given inside this pack; supply 1 kit; NHS Cost £20.75.

Proton pump inhibitors: full dose

Omeprazole capsules: 20mg once a day

- Age from 16 years onwards
- Omeprazole 20mg capsules. Take one capsule once a day; supply 28 capsules; NHS Cost £12.75.

Omeprazole tablets: 20mg once a day

- Age from 16 years onwards
- Omeprazole 20mg tablets. Take one tablet once a day; supply 28 tablets; NHS Cost £12.75.

Lansoprazole capsules: 30mg each morning
- Age from 16 years onwards
- Lansoprazole 30mg capsules. Take one capsule each morning (on an empty stomach); supply 28 capsules; NHS Cost £23.63.

Lansoprazole orodispersible tablets: 30mg each morning
- Age from 16 years onwards
- Lansoprazole 30mg orodisp tabs. Take one tablet each morning (on an empty stomach); supply 28 tablets; NHS Cost £19.88.

Pantoprazole e/c tablets: 40mg once a day
- Age from 16 years onwards
- Pantoprazole 40mg e/c tablets. Take one tablet once a day; supply 28 tablets; NHS Cost £21.69.

Rabeprazole e/c tablets: 20mg once a day
- Age from 16 years onwards
- Rabeprazole 20mg e/c tabs. Take one tablet once a day; supply 28 tablets; NHS Cost £21.16.

Esomeprazole tablets: 20mg once a day
- Age from 16 years onwards
- Esomeprazole 20mg tablets. Take one tablet once a day; supply 28 tablets; NHS Cost £18.50.

Proton pump inhibitors: low dose or on-demand

Omeprazole capsules: 10mg once a day
- Age from 16 years onwards
- Omeprazole 10mg capsules. Take one capsule once a day. If you are able to, try to take one capsule once a day only when your symptoms recur; supply 28 capsules; NHS Cost £7.72.

Omeprazole tablets: 10mg once a day
- Age from 16 years onwards
- Omeprazole 10mg tablets. Take one tablet once a day. If you are able to, try to take one tablet once a day only when your symptoms recur; supply 28 tablets; NHS Cost £11.40.

Lansoprazole capsules: 15mg each morning
- Age from 16 years onwards
- Lansoprazole 15mg capsules. Take one capsule each morning (on an empty stomach). If you are able to, try to take one capsule each morning only when your symptoms recur; supply 28 capsules; NHS Cost £12.92.

Lansoprazole orodispersible tablets: 15mg each morning
- Age from 16 years onwards
- Lansoprazole 15mg orodisp tabs. Take one tablet each morning (on an empty stomach). If you are able to, try to take one tablet each morning only when your symptoms recur; supply 28 tablets; NHS Cost £10.86.

Pantoprazole e/c tablets: 20mg once a day
- Age from 16 years onwards
- Pantoprazole 20mg e/c tablets. Take one tablet once a day. If you are able to, try to take one tablet once a day only when your symptoms recur; supply 28 tablets; NHS Cost £12.31.

Rabeprazole e/c tablets: 10mg once a day
- Age from 16 years onwards
- Rabeprazole 10mg e/c tabs. Take one tablet once a day. If you are able to, try to take one tablet once a day only when your symptoms recur; supply 28 tablets; NHS Cost £11.56.

Esomeprazole e/c tablets: 20mg once a day
- Age from 16 years onwards
- Esomeprazole 20mg tablets. Take one tablet once a day. If you are able to, try to take one tablet once a day only when your symptoms recur; supply 28 tablets; NHS Cost £18.50.

H_2-receptor antagonists: maintenance or on-demand

Cimetidine tablets: 400mg twice a day
- Age from 16 years onwards
- Cimetidine 400mg tablets. Take one tablet twice a day. If you are able to, reduce to one tablet at night. Alternatively, try taking these tablets only when your symptoms recur; supply 60 tablets; NHS Cost £5.58.

Ranitidine tablets: 150mg twice a day
- Age from 16 years onwards
- Ranitidine 150mg tablets. Take one tablet twice a day. If you are able to, reduce to one tablet at night. Alternatively, try taking these tablets only when your symptoms recur; supply 60 tablets; NHS Cost £7.21.

Nizatidine capsules: 150mg twice a day
- Age from 16 years onwards
- Nizatidine 150mg capsules. Take one capsule twice a day. If you are able to, reduce to one cap at night. Alternatively, try taking these capsules only when your symptoms recur; supply 60 capsules; NHS Cost £12.26.

Famotidine tablets: 20mg twice a day
- Age from 16 years onwards
- Famotidine 20mg tablets. Take one tablet twice a day. If you are able to, reduce to one tablet at night. Alternatively, try taking these tablets only when your symptoms recur; supply 56 tablets; NHS Cost £23.28.

Prokinetics: on-demand (not suitable for long-term use)

Domperidone tablets: 10mg to 20mg four times a day
- Age from 16 years onwards
- Domperidone 10mg tablets. Take one to two tablets four times a day (before meals and at bedtime). If you are able to, try to take these tablets only when your symptoms recur; supply 200 tablets; NHS Cost £16.62.

Metoclopramide tablets: 10mg three times a day
- Age from 20 years onwards
- Metoclopramide 10mg tablets. Take one tablet three times a day. If you are able to, try to take one tablet three times a day only when your symptoms recur; supply 84 tablets; NHS Cost £2.61.

Good response to treatment

Which therapy?

- **Give lifestyle advice** (e.g. healthy eating, weight loss, stopping smoking).
- **Encourage people to step-down treatment** to the lowest dose required to control symptoms.
- **Discuss using treatments on an 'on-demand' basis.**
- **Consider** whether it is appropriate to stop current treatment (e.g. proton pump inhibitor [PPI] or H_2-receptor antagonist) and return to an antacid or alginate 'on demand'.
- **Do not step-down or stop treatment with a PPI for:**
  - People with complicated oesophagitis (past strictures, ulcers, or haemorrhage).
  - People taking a PPI for gastroprotection against nonsteroidal anti-inflammatory drugs.
  - People with a previous bleeding peptic ulcer who remain *H pylori* positive after at least two attempts at eradication.

Practical prescribing points

For further information please see the *Medicines Compendium* (www.medicines.org.uk) or the *British National Formulary* (www.bnf.org).

- **Proton pump inhibitors (PPIs):** differences between the PPIs in clinical efficacy and safety are minimal.
  - Omeprazole is currently cheapest.
  - Omeprazole and esomeprazole occasionally enhance the effects of warfarin and phenytoin. Monitor carefully if omeprazole or esomeprazole are started or stopped.
- **Cimetidine: avoid in people taking** erythromycin, warfarin, amiodarone, theophylline, carbamazepine, phenytoin, and sodium valproate as cimetidine inhibits hepatic drug metabolism by binding to microsomal cytochrome P450.
- **Prokinetics: avoid long-term use** of metoclopramide or domperidone.
- **Metoclopramide: avoid in young adults (under the age of 20 years)**, as extrapyramidal adverse effects are more common in this age group.
- **Antacids:** combinations of aluminium salts with magnesium salts may be preferable to magnesium salts alone (which may cause diarrhoea) or aluminium salts alone (which may cause constipation).

Follow-up advice

- **All people with dyspepsia requiring long-term treatment should have an annual review** of their condition, and lifestyle advice should be reinforced.

Should I refer or investigate?

Refer?

Note: proton pump inhibitors and H_2-receptor antagonists should be stopped at least 2 weeks before endoscopy. Nonsteroidal anti-inflammatory drug use should also be suspended in all people requiring referral.

- **Routine endoscopy of people of any age presenting with dyspepsia but *without* ALARM symptoms is not necessary.**
- **Immediate endoscopy** (i.e. same day) is indicated for people presenting with dyspepsia together with significant acute gastrointestinal bleeding.
- **Anyone who develops ALARM symptoms should be referred urgently for endoscopy, or to a specialist.** That is people with:
  - Chronic gastrointestinal bleeding
  - Progressive unintentional weight loss
  - Progressive difficulty swallowing (dysphagia)
  - Persistent vomiting
  - Iron deficiency anaemia
  - Epigastric mass
  - Suspicious barium meal result
- **People 55 years and over, presenting with unexplained and persistent recent onset dyspepsia** alone, should be referred for urgent endoscopy.
- **Urgent referral to a specialist should also be considered in** a person (of any age) who has unexplained worsening of their dyspepsia and:
  - Barrett's oesophagus
  - Known dysplasia, atrophic gastritis, or intestinal metaplasia
  - Peptic ulcer surgery over 20 years ago
- **If definite dysphagia or odynophagia is present** with a suspicious history or regurgitation, it is appropriate to refer for a barium swallow.

Investigate?

- When referring, consider a full blood count to assist specialist assessment. This should be carried out in accordance with local arrangements.

Patient information leaflets

The following PILs are available at www.prodigy.nhs.uk

- Barium Swallow / Meal / Follow Through
- CORE, Fighting Gut and Liver Disease
- Dyspepsia (Indigestion)
- Gastroscopy (Endoscopy)

Shared decision making

- **Your indigestion** (dyspepsia) has improved with treatment.
- **If symptoms return after treatment has finished** then options to consider are:
  - Antacids as required, OR, if symptoms are more troublesome.
  - A daily dose of an acid-suppressing medicine. Start at full dose. But when symptoms have eased again, gradually reduce to the lowest dose needed to control symptoms, OR
  - Short courses of an acid-suppressing medicine just when symptoms occur.
- Note: the above does not apply for some people who definitely need long-term, full-dose acid-suppressing medication. For example, if you are taking acid-suppressing medicine to prevent an ulcer caused by anti-inflammatory medication.
- **Remember,** lifestyle factors may also help to prevent indigestion. For example:
  - Stop smoking if you are a smoker.
  - Cut down on alcohol if you drink heavily.
  - Don't eat too much fatty or spicy food.
  - Eat healthily and try to lose weight if you are overweight.

Drug rationale

Drugs not included

- **Antacid preparations other than those containing aluminium hydroxide and/or magnesium trisilicate** are not included. Products containing simeticone (activated dimeticone) are unlikely to confer any additional advantage [BNF 48, 2004]. Products containing bismuth have not been included because of a high incidence of adverse effects. Many other products available to purchase over the counter are not prescribable on the NHS.
- **Alginate preparations that are not available as sugar-free products** are not included.
- **The use of bismuth chelate, sucralfate, and misoprostol** is limited by their adverse effects, and they have not been included [WeMeReC, 2002].

Drugs included

- **Proton pump inhibitors (PPIs):** PPIs are an effective treatment for dyspepsia symptoms that have not been investigated by endoscopy [NICE, 2004]. The lowest effective dose of a PPI should be used as 'on-demand' therapy or as a maintenance dose. Note: when undertaking meta-analysis of dose-related effects, NICE classed esomeprazole 20mg as a full-dose equivalent to omeprazole 20mg.
- **H_2-receptor antagonists:** cimetidine, famotidine, nizatidine, and ranitidine seem to be equally effective. They have been shown to be more effective than placebo in the management of people whose dyspepsia has not been investigated by endoscopy.
- **Prokinetic agents** (metoclopramide or domperidone) may improve symptoms such as bloating or early satiety, and may be most useful for people with predominant

D

reflux symptoms. However, trials have been few, small-scale, and heterogeneous.

- **Antacids containing aluminium hydroxide and/or magnesium trisilicate** have been included. Antacids containing aluminium or magnesium are effective, long acting, and are not absorbed to a significant extent. Using them in combination minimizes the adverse effects of constipation (aluminium) and diarrhoea (magnesium).
- **Alginates** are effective and safe in most people. They should be used in people with symptoms of reflux [WeMeReC, 2002]. All alginates offered are sugar-free.

D

Prescriptions

Proton pump inhibitors: full dose

Omeprazole capsules: 20mg once a day

- Age from 16 years onwards
- Omeprazole 20mg capsules. Take one capsule once a day; supply 28 capsules; NHS Cost £12.75.

Omeprazole tablets: 20mg once a day

- Age from 16 years onwards
- Omeprazole 20mg tablets. Take one tablet once a day; supply 28 tablets; NHS Cost £12.75.

Lansoprazole capsules: 30mg each morning

- Age from 16 years onwards
- Lansoprazole 30mg capsules. Take one capsule each morning (on an empty stomach); supply 28 capsules; NHS Cost £23.63.

Lansoprazole orodispersible tablets: 30mg each morning

- Age from 16 years onwards
- Lansoprazole 30mg orodisp tabs. Take one tablet each morning (on an empty stomach); supply 28 tablets; NHS Cost £19.88.

Pantoprazole e/c tablets: 40mg once a day

- Age from 16 years onwards
- Pantoprazole 40mg e/c tablets. Take one tablet once a day; supply 28 tablets; NHS Cost £21.69.

Rabeprazole e/c tablets: 20mg once a day

- Age from 16 years onwards
- Rabeprazole 20mg e/c tabs. Take one tablet once a day; supply 28 tablets; NHS Cost £21.16.

Esomeprazole tablets: 20mg once a day

- Age from 16 years onwards
- Esomeprazole 20mg tablets. Take one tablet once a day; supply 28 tablets; NHS Cost £18.50.

Proton pump inhibitors: low dose or on-demand

Omeprazole capsules: 10mg once a day

- Age from 16 years onwards
- Omeprazole 10mg capsules. Take one capsule once a day. If you are able to, try to take one capsule once a day only when your symptoms recur; supply 28 capsules; NHS Cost £7.72.

Omeprazole tablets: 10mg once a day

- Age from 16 years onwards
- Omeprazole 10mg tablets. Take one tablet once a day. If you are able to, try to take one tablet once a day only when your symptoms recur; supply 28 tablets; NHS Cost £11.40.

Lansoprazole capsules: 15mg each morning

- Age from 16 years onwards
- Lansoprazole 15mg capsules. Take one capsule each morning (on an empty stomach). If you are able to, try to take one capsule each morning only when your symptoms recur; supply 28 capsules; NHS Cost £12.92.

Lansoprazole orodispersible tablets: 15mg each morning

- Age from 16 years onwards
- Lansoprazole 15mg orodisp tabs. Take one tablet each morning (on an empty stomach). If you are able to, try t take one tablet each morning only when your symptoms recur; supply 28 tablets; NHS Cost £10.86.

Pantoprazole e/c tablets: 20mg once a day

- Age from 16 years onwards
- Pantoprazole 20mg e/c tablets. Take one tablet once a day. If you are able to, try to take one tablet once a day only when your symptoms recur; supply 28 tablets; NHS Cost £12.31.

Rabeprazole e/c tablets: 10mg once a day

- Age from 16 years onwards
- Rabeprazole 10mg e/c tabs. Take one tablet once a day. If you are able to, try to take one tablet once a day only when your symptoms recur; supply 28 tablets; NHS Cost £11.56.

Esomeprazole e/c tablets: 20mg once a day

- Age from 16 years onwards
- Esomeprazole 20mg tablets. Take one tablet once a day. If you are able to, try to take one tablet once a day only when your symptoms recur; supply 28 tablets; NHS Cost £18.50.

H_2-receptor antagonists: maintenance or on-demand

Cimetidine tablets: 400mg twice a day

- Age from 16 years onwards
- Cimetidine 400mg tablets. Take one tablet twice a day. If you are able to, reduce to one tablet at night. Alternatively, try taking these tablets only when your symptoms recur; supply 60 tablets; NHS Cost £5.58.

Ranitidine tablets: 150mg twice a day

- Age from 16 years onwards
- Ranitidine 150mg tablets. Take one tablet twice a day. I you are able to, reduce to one tablet at night. Alternatively, try taking these tablets only when your symptoms recur; supply 60 tablets; NHS Cost £7.21.

Nizatidine capsules: 150mg twice a day

- Age from 16 years onwards
- Nizatidine 150mg capsules. Take one capsule twice a day. If you are able to, reduce to one cap at night. Alternatively, try taking these capsules only when your symptoms recur; supply 60 capsules; NHS Cost £12.26.

Famotidine tablets: 20mg twice a day

- Age from 16 years onwards
- Famotidine 20mg tablets. Take one tablet twice a day. If you are able to, reduce to one tablet at night. Alternatively, try taking these tablets only when your symptoms recur; supply 56 tablets; NHS Cost £23.28.

Prokinetics: on-demand (not suitable for long-term use)

Domperidone tablets: 10mg to 20mg four times a day

- Age from 16 years onwards
- Domperidone 10mg tablets. Take one to two tablets four times a day (before meals and at bedtime). If you are able to, try to take these tablets only when your symptoms recur; supply 200 tablets; NHS Cost £16.62.

Metoclopramide tablets: 10mg three times a day

- Age from 20 years onwards
- Metoclopramide 10mg tablets. Take one tablet three times a day. If you are able to, try to take one tablet three times a day only when your symptoms recur; supply 84 tablets; NHS Cost £2.61.

Antacids and alginates: on-demand

ntacids: co-magaldrox 195/220mg suspension
Age from 16 years onwards
Co-magald 195/220mg/5ml susp. Take two to four 5ml spoonfuls 20-60 minutes after food and at bedtime, when required to relieve dyspepsia; supply 1000 ml; NHS Cost £3.82; OTC Cost £6.74.

ntacids: aluminium hydroxide 4% suspension
Age from 16 years onwards
Aluminium hydroxide 4% mixture. Take one to two 5ml spoonfuls four times a day (between meals and at bedtime) when required to relieve dyspepsia; supply 400 ml; NHS Cost £2.84; OTC Cost £3.32.

ntacids: magnesium trisilicate mixture
Age from 16 years onwards
Magnesium trisilicate mixture. Take two 5ml spoonfuls (mixed in water) three times a day when required to relieve dyspepsia; supply 400 ml; NHS Cost £0.94; OTC Cost £1.10.

ginates: Gastrocote liquid (sugar-free)
Age from 16 years onwards
Gastrocote liquid. Take one to three 5ml spoonfuls four times a day (after meals and at bedtime) when required to relieve dyspepsia; supply 1000 ml; NHS Cost £5.58; OTC Cost £9.84.

ginates: Gaviscon Advance tablets (sugar-free)
Age from 16 years onwards
Gaviscon Advance tablets. Chew one to two tablets (followed by water) after meals and at bedtime, when required to relieve dyspepsia; supply 120 tablets; NHS Cost £6.48; OTC Cost £14.98.

ginates: Gaviscon Advance liquid (sugar-free)
Age from 16 years onwards
Gaviscon Advance s/f susp. Take one to two 5ml spoonfuls after meals and at bedtime, when required to relieve dyspepsia; supply 500 ml; NHS Cost £5.40; OTC Cost £9.95.

ginates: Peptac liquid (sugar-free)
Age from 16 years onwards
Peptac s/f liquid. Take two to four 5ml spoonfuls after meals and at bedtime, when required to relieve dyspepsia; supply 1000 ml; NHS Cost £4.32; OTC Cost £7.98.

ginates: Rennie Duo suspension (sugar-free)
Age from 16 years onwards
Rennie Duo oral suspension. Take two to four 5ml spoonfuls after meals and at bedtime, when required to relieve dyspepsia; supply 1000 ml; NHS Cost £5.34; OTC Cost £10.58.

Dyspepsia while taking NSAIDs

Which therapy?

Stop nonsteroidal anti-inflammatory drugs (NSAIDs) wherever possible.

If this is not possible, consider using strategies to reduce NSAID use:

- Offer a trial of use on a limited 'as required' basis.
- Dose reduction.
- Switching to paracetamol.
- Switching to low-dose ibuprofen (400 mg three times a day).

Consider referral for endoscopy. (See *Refer or investigate?*).

If the NSAID has been *stopped* and endoscopy is *not* needed: manage in the usual way. See scenario *Initial presentation — dyspepsia symptoms (no endoscopy)*.

- **If continued NSAID use is still necessary** (and either endoscopy was not needed or it excluded NSAID-induced complications):
  - Remind people that NSAIDs should be taken with or after food.
  - **Test for *Helicobacter pylori*** and (if the result is positive) eradicate using triple therapy. See scenario *H pylori test result* for triple therapy regimens.
  - **Use gastroprotection** (a proton pump inhibitor [PPI] or full-dose misoprostol) combined with a standard NSAID in people *with* risk factors for NSAID complications. Alternatively, consider switching to a COX-2 selective NSAID alone.
  - Offer symptomatic treatment with a PPI to people *without* risk factors for NSAID complications if symptoms persist despite eradication therapy (or if the test is negative).
- **If testing for *H pylori*:**
  - Use a carbon-13 urea breath test or the stool antigen test.
  - **Do not test within** 2 weeks of PPI therapy or within 4 weeks of antibiotic therapy as false-negative results may occur.

Risk factors for NSAID-induced complications include:

- Age over 65 years
- Previous history of peptic ulcer disease, gastrointestinal bleeding or perforation
- Also taking corticosteroids, anticoagulants, or low-dose aspirin
- Taking maximum doses of NSAIDs for a long duration
- Serious comorbidity such as cardiovascular disease or diabetes

Practical prescribing points

For further information please see the *Medicines Compendium* (www.medicines.org.uk) or the *British National Formulary* (www.bnf.org).

- **Proton pump inhibitors (PPIs):** differences between the PPIs in clinical efficacy and safety are minimal.
  - Omeprazole is currently cheapest.
  - Omeprazole and esomeprazole occasionally enhance the effects of warfarin and phenytoin. Monitor carefully if omeprazole or esomeprazole are started or stopped.
- **Misoprostol:** diarrhoea and abdominal pain are common. Advise women of child-bearing age to use adequate contraception, because misoprostol increases the risk of miscarriage.

H pylori tests

- **Carbon-13 urea breath tests:** advise the person to fast for at least 6 hours before the test and then (for all tests except diabact UBT®) ingest citric acid or orange juice just before the test to slow gastric emptying. (The diabact UBT® tablet contains citric acid.) The person then provides two or three breath samples before ingestion of the carbon-13 urea tablet, and again 30 minutes afterwards (only 10 minutes afterwards for diabact UBT®) by blowing through a straw into a series of glass, screw-top tubes. Breath samples are sent away for analysis by mass spectrometry.
- **Stool antigen tests:** these require the person to collect a stool sample (at least pea-sized). The sample is then sent to the laboratory for analysis.

D

Follow-up advice

- **Review the need for nonsteroidal anti-inflammatory drug (NSAID) use regularly** (at least 6 monthly) and consider using strategies to reduce NSAID use. For example:
  - Offer a trial of use on a limited 'as required' basis.
  - Consider dose reduction.
  - Consider switching to paracetamol.
  - Consider switching to low-dose ibuprofen (400 mg three times a day).

Should I refer or investigate?

Refer?

Note: proton pump inhibitors and H_2-receptor antagonists should be stopped at least 2 weeks before endoscopy. Nonsteroidal anti-inflammatory drug use should also be suspended in all people requiring referral.

- **Consider referral for endoscopy if:**
  - There is a strong suspicion of ulcer.
  - Symptoms persist despite *H pylori* testing and acid suppression in a person over 55 years of age.
  - The person is aged over 65 years and has 1 additional risk factor for NSAID complications.
  - The person is aged under 65 years and has 2 additional risk factors for NSAID complications.
- **Risk factors for NSAID-induced complications include:**
  - Age over 65 years.
  - Previous history of peptic ulcer disease, gastrointestinal bleeding or perforation.
  - Also taking corticosteroids, anticoagulants, or low-dose aspirin.
  - Taking maximum doses of NSAIDs for a long duration.
  - Serious comorbidity such as cardiovascular disease or diabetes.

Investigate?

- All people taking nonsteroidal anti-inflammatory drugs with persistent or recurrent dyspepsia should be tested for *Helicobacter pylori*, preferably with a carbon-13 urea breath test or stool antigen test.
- When referring, consider a full blood count to assist specialist assessment. This should be carried out in accordance with local arrangements.

Patient information leaflets

The following PILs are available at www.prodigy.nhs.uk

- Barium Swallow / Meal / Follow Through
- CORE, Fighting Gut and Liver Disease
- Dyspepsia (Indigestion)
- Gastroscopy (Endoscopy)
- Helicobacter Pylori & Stomach Pain

Shared decision making

- **If you develop indigestion (dyspepsia) it may be caused by your anti-inflammatory medication.**
- If you are able to stop taking the anti-inflammatory medication, your indigestion may go.
- If you are not able to stop the medication, or if symptoms persist if you do stop it, you:
  - Should take acid-suppressing medication
  - Should have a test to see if your gut is infected with bacteria called *H pylori*
    - *H pylori* infection can cause ulcers in the gut, particularly if you take anti-inflammatory medicines
    - The infection can be cleared with a one-week course of treatment
  - May need to have an endoscopy to check for an ulce
- **Some people who take anti-inflammatory medication have an increased risk of developing a stomach ulcer.**
  - For example, if you:
    - Are over the age of 65
    - Have had an ulcer in the past
    - Are taking steroid tablets, anticoagulants, or low-dose aspirin
    - Take regular large doses of anti-inflammatory medication
    - Have certain other conditions such as heart disease or diabetes
- If you are at increased risk of developing an ulcer you can protect your stomach by taking:
  - An acid-suppressing medicine, or
  - Misoprostol, which can protect the stomach lining.

Drug rationale

Drugs not included

- **H_2-receptor antagonists (H_2RAs):** double doses of H_2RAs are effective at reducing the risk of endoscopic gastric and duodenal ulcers but this is an off-licence use [Rostom et al, 2002]. Standard doses only reduce the risk of endoscopic duodenal ulcers. They are therefore not included [SIGN, 2003].
- **Proton pump inhibitors: rabeprazole** is not currently licensed for preventing nonsteroidal anti-inflammatory drug-induced complications.
- **Low-dose misoprostol:** lower doses (e.g. 400 microgram per day) are less effective than proton pump inhibitors reducing the incidence of endoscopic lesions, and have greater adverse effects [NICE, 2004]. (Diarrhoea and abdominal pain are common.)

Drugs included

- **Proton pump inhibitors** (omeprazole, lansoprazole, pantoprazole, and esomeprazole) are generally the preferred choice for gastroprotection. They are effective and well tolerated; they reduce the risk of endoscopic gastric ulcers by 63% and the risk of duodenal ulcers b 81% [Rostom et al, 2002]. However there is a lack of data on prevention of ulcer complications.
- **Full-dose misoprostol** (200 micrograms four times a da is effective for the treatment and prophylaxis of nonsteroidal anti-inflammatory drug-associated ulcers, but it is not always well tolerated [Hawkey et al, 1998; Rostom et al, 2002].
- ***H pylori* tests** are offered for the diagnosis of gastroduodenal infection with *H pylori* [NICE, 2004]. Prescriptions for carbon-13 urea breath-test kits and an advice note for the stool antigen test are included.

Prescriptions

GI protection: proton pump inhibitors

Omeprazole capsules: 20mg once a day

- Age from 16 years onwards
- Omeprazole 20mg capsules. Take one capsule once a day; supply 28 capsules; NHS Cost £12.75.

Omeprazole tablets: 20mg once a day

- Age from 16 years onwards
- Omeprazole 20mg tablets. Take one tablet once a day; supply 28 tablets; NHS Cost £12.75.

Lansoprazole capsules: 30mg each morning
- Age from 16 years onwards
- Lansoprazole 30mg capsules. Take one capsule each morning (on an empty stomach); supply 28 capsules; NHS Cost £23.63.

Lansoprazole orodispersible tablets: 30mg each morning
- Age from 16 years onwards
- Lansoprazole 30mg orodisp tabs. Take one tablet each morning (on an empty stomach); supply 28 tablets; NHS Cost £19.88.

Pantoprazole e/c tablets: 20mg once a day
- Age from 16 years onwards
- Pantoprazole 20mg e/c tablets. Take one tablet once a day; supply 28 tablets; NHS Cost £12.31.

Esomeprazole tablets: 20mg once a day
- Age from 16 years onwards
- Esomeprazole 20mg tablets. Take one tablet once a day; supply 28 tablets; NHS Cost £18.50.

Lansoprazole capsules: 15mg each morning
- Age from 16 years onwards
- Lansoprazole 15mg capsules. Take one capsule each morning (on an empty stomach); supply 28 capsules; NHS Cost £12.92.

Lansoprazole orodispersible tablets: 15mg each morning
- Age from 16 years onwards
- Lansoprazole 15mg orodisp tabs. Take one tablet each morning (on an empty stomach); supply 28 tablets; NHS Cost £10.86.

GI protection: misoprostol

Misoprostol 200micrograms four times a day
- Age from 16 years onwards
- Misoprostol 200microgram tabs. Take one tablet four times a day; supply 112 tablets; NHS Cost £20.79.

H pylori tests

Advice note: stool antigen test
- Age from 16 years onwards
- The stool antigen test is a way of testing whether you have a current infection with Helicobacter pylori. Put a pea-sized sample of your faeces (stools) into the container provided. Please return this sample to reception so that it can be sent to the laboratory for analysis. Acid suppressing medicines and antibiotics can affect the results of this test. If you have used an acid suppressing medicine within the last 2 weeks, or have taken antibiotics within the last 4 weeks, please check with your doctor before taking this test.

Carbon urea breath test: Diabact UBT H pylori test kit
- Age from 16 years onwards
- Diabact UBT tablet + kit. Follow the instructions given inside this pack; supply 1 kit; NHS Cost £12.75.

Carbon urea breath test: Helicobacter Test Hp-plus test kit
- Age from 16 years onwards
- Helicobacter Test Hp-plus. Follow the instructions given inside this pack; supply 1 kit; NHS Cost £19.75.

Carbon urea breath test: Helicobacter Test INFAI test kit
- Age from 16 years onwards
- Helicobacter test INFAI. Follow the instructions given inside this pack; supply 1 kit; NHS Cost £17.10.

Carbon urea breath test: Pylobactell H pylori test kit
- Age from 16 years onwards
- Pylobactell H pylori test kit. Follow the instructions given inside this pack; supply 1 kit; NHS Cost £20.75.

Extended Information

Background information

- What is dyspepsia? p.691
- How common is it? p.691
- What are the common underlying causes of dyspepsia? p.691
- How do I know what is causing dyspepsia? p.692
- What else might it be? p.692
- Complications and prognosis p.692

D

What is dyspepsia?

- **Dyspepsia is a term used to describe a group of symptoms** that alert the clinician to consider the possibility of upper gastrointestinal tract disease. It is not a diagnosis.
- **There is no universally accepted definition** of dyspepsia.
- The Rome II criteria define dyspepsia as pain or discomfort centred predominantly in the upper abdomen for at least 12 weeks in the last 12 months.
- The British Society of Gastroenterology criteria are broader, and define dyspepsia as any symptom referable to the upper gastrointestinal tract, present for 4 weeks or more, including upper abdominal pain or discomfort, heartburn, acid reflux, nausea, and vomiting.
- NICE broadly defines dyspepsia in unselected patients in primary care to include people with recurrent epigastric pain, heartburn or acid regurgitation (with or without bloating), nausea, or vomiting (C).

How common is it?

- The prevalence of dyspeptic symptoms is between 23% and 41%, and about a quarter of sufferers will consult their general practitioner.
- About 4% of general practice consultations are for dyspepsia and about 10% of these lead to referral for further investigation.

[British Society of Gastroenterology, 2002]

What are the common underlying causes of dyspepsia?

- **Non-ulcer dyspepsia** (also known as functional dyspepsia) is the most common diagnosis after endoscopy. Non-ulcer dyspepsia refers to people with dyspeptic symptoms and a normal endoscopy (i.e. endoscopy has excluded gastric or duodenal ulcer, oesophagitis, and malignancy). It includes people with simple gastritis or duodenitis, but erosive duodenitis and gastric erosions are considered to be part of the spectrum of peptic ulcer disease.
- **Gastro-oesophageal reflux disease** (GORD) is a term used to describe diseases that cause reflux of gastric contents into the oesophagus, causing symptoms that are sufficient to interfere with quality of life. Endoscopy may reveal oesophageal mucosal breaks (oesophagitis), or may be normal (endoscopy-negative reflux disease).
- **Endoscopy-negative reflux disease** refers to people with predominant reflux symptoms and a normal endoscopy (i.e. without oesophagitis).
- **A hiatus hernia** occurs when part of the stomach moves up in the chest through a defect in the diaphragm. It commonly (but not always) causes GORD.
- **Peptic ulcer disease** is ulceration of the intestinal mucosa, commonly in the stomach (gastric ulcer) or in the duodenum (duodenal ulcer). Oesophageal ulceration can also occur. Peptic ulcer disease is difficult to discriminate clinically from non-ulcer (functional) dyspepsia.

[Logan and Delaney, 2001; NICE, 2004]

How do I know what is causing dyspepsia?

History

- **Symptoms are variable,** but may include upper abdominal pain or discomfort, retrosternal pain, heartburn, acid reflux, anorexia, nausea, vomiting, bloating, fullness, or early satiety.
- Pain in the right or left hypochondrium does not constitute dyspepsia [Hunt et al, 2002].
- **Dyspeptic symptoms are a poor predictor of disease severity or underlying pathology** (C). For example:
  - Only about 50% of individuals with 'classic' symptoms have a specific lesion identified by endoscopy [NICE, 2004].
  - Many people with peptic ulcers do not identify the epigastrium as the site of pain.
  - Heartburn is a major feature of gastro-oesophageal reflux disease, but one study found that duodenal ulcer was as common in people with dominant heartburn as epigastric pain [Chiba et al, 2003].

Examination

- **Other than epigastric tenderness, the physical examination is usually normal.** Epigastric tenderness is poorly discriminating.
- Hypotension or tachycardia may indicate acute blood loss from gastrointestinal bleeding.
- Weight loss, a palpable mass, enlarged supraclavicular nodes (Virchow's nodes) and acanthosis nigricans.
- Clinical signs of anaemia (due to a bleed), such as brittle nails, cheilosis, and pallor of the palpebral mucosa or nail beds may suggest malignancy.

Investigations

- **Endoscopy** is the gold standard test to exclude pathology or make a formal diagnosis. However, it is neither necessary nor practical to investigate a diagnosis in every person with dyspepsia (in the absence of ALARM symptoms) if symptoms are controlled by empirical treatment.
  - **Routine endoscopy is not necessary for people of any age presenting with dyspepsia who do not have ALARM symptoms (B)** [NICE, 2004].
  - For those people investigated by endoscopy for dyspepsia: 30% have no abnormal findings; 30% have either gastritis, duodenitis, or hiatus hernia; 10–17% have oesophagitis; 10–15% have duodenal ulcer; 5–10% have gastric ulcer; and 2% have gastric cancer [British Society of Gastroenterology, 2002].
- ***Helicobacter pylori* testing is commonly undertaken.** Eradication is recommended in people who test positive for *H pylori* with [Malfertheiner et al, 2002]:
  - Uninvestigated dyspepsia (i.e. endoscopy is not required)
  - Proven duodenal ulcer (newly diagnosed people and those who have been diagnosed previously but remain asymptomatic should all be treated)
  - Proven gastric ulcer (newly diagnosed)
  - People taking long-term nonsteroidal anti-inflammatory drugs (NSAIDs)
  - MALToma (mucosa-associated lymphoid tissue lymphoma)
  - Atrophic gastritis
  - Post-gastric cancer resection
  - People with first degree relatives with gastric cancer
  - Non-ulcer (functional) dyspepsia
- Note: *H pylori* eradication does not improve outcomes in gastro-oesophageal reflux disease.
- **Consider a full blood count** in all people with new onset dyspepsia in order to detect iron deficiency anaemia (D) [NICE, 2005].

What else might it be?

- **Cardiac or biliary disease (C).**
  - Cardiac pain may be clinically indistinguishable from dyspepsia.
  - Biliary colic occasionally presents with epigastric pain.
- **Oesophageal or gastric carcinoma.** Investigate for malignancy in the presence of any ALARM symptoms (chronic gastrointestinal bleeding; dysphagia; progressive unintentional weight loss; persistent vomiting; iron deficiency anaemia; an epigastric mass; or suspicious barium meal). Symptom severity is a poor indicator of an underlying disease.
- **An adverse drug reaction.** Nonsteroidal anti-inflammatory drugs (NSAIDs), bisphosphonates, opioid analgesics, metformin, orlistat, corticosteroids, theophylline, and iron or potassium salts commonly cause dyspepsia.
- **Irritable bowel syndrome** may manifest as dyspepsia with bloating, but is usually associated with abnormal bowel habits.
- **Motility disorders** may also manifest as upper abdominal discomfort with bloating and early satiety. Gastroparesis should be suspected in people with diabetes mellitus, especially when peripheral neuropathy is present.
- **Gastroenteritis, ileus, intestinal obstruction, cholecystitis, pancreatitis,** may present with nausea and vomiting.
- **Other causes of dysphagia include** peptic stricture, Schatzki ring, and (less commonly) achalasia, diffuse spasm, systemic sclerosis, bronchial carcinoma, enlarged mediastinal nodes, aortic aneurysm, post-cricoid web, or radiation stricture.
- **Rarely,** Crohn's disease, sarcoidosis, hepatoma, ischaemic bowel disease, intestinal parasites (*Giardia, Strongyloides*), abdominal cancer, carbohydrate malabsorption, Zollinger–Ellison syndrome.

Complications and prognosis

Complications

- **Depending on the underlying diagnosis,** the following can occur:
  - Recurrence
  - Haemorrhage
  - Perforation
  - Anaemia
  - Pyloric stenosis
  - Strictures
- **There may be a missed diagnosis of oesophageal or gastric cancer.** Carcinoma at the site of a 'benign' ulcer may be a result of initial misdiagnosis, even if the ulcer seemed to respond to treatment.

Prognosis

- **For people with non-ulcer dyspepsia or reflux disease,** symptoms are recurrent and intermittent; symptoms recur annually in about 50% of these people. The lifetime risk of recurrence is about 80%.
- **For people with gastric or duodenal ulceration** *Helicobacter pylori* eradication markedly reduces the risk of recurrence during their lifetime:
  - Lifetime risk of recurrence for gastric ulcer is 60% if *H pylori* positive, but 5% if *H pylori* negative.
  - Lifetime risk of recurrence for duodenal ulcer is 80% if *H pylori* positive, but 5% if *H pylori* negative.

[Graham, 1997; NICE, 2004]

Management issues

- Overview of management p.693
- Who needs an initial referral for endoscopy? p.693
- Should I offer treatment while the person is awaiting endoscopy? p.693
- What general measures are useful? p.693
- What is first-line treatment? p.694
- Which *H pylori* test should I use? p.694
- What should I do if symptoms persist or return? p.694
- Who needs to be referred for endoscopy if symptoms persist? p.694
- Reviewing and stepping-down treatment p.695
- How do I manage dyspepsia associated with nonsteroidal anti-inflammatory drugs? p.695
- Supporting evidence for treatment strategies p.696
- Medicines management p.698

If an endoscopic diagnosis of non-ulcer dyspepsia, peptic ulcer disease, or gastro-oesophageal reflux disease (GORD) has been made, then please see the relevant guidance (*Dyspepsia — proven non-ulcer dyspepsia; Dyspepsia — proven DU or GU*; or *Dyspepsia — proven GORD*). Consider managing previously investigated people without new ALARM symptoms according to previous endoscopic findings.

Overview of management

- Consider whether an endoscopy is needed. See *Who needs an initial referral for endoscopy?* for further information.
- If endoscopy is *not* needed, manage as follows:
  - Review medication that may be causing dyspepsia.
  - Offer general lifestyle advice.
  - Offer empirical treatment with either:
    - A course of a proton pump inhibitor (PPI) at full dose for one month, or
    - *H pylori* 'test and treat'
- If symptoms persist or return:
  - Offer the alternative empirical treatment.
  - Consider whether endoscopy is appropriate.
- If symptoms respond to treatment, encourage people (as appropriate) to:
  - Step-down the PPI to the lowest dose required to control symptoms.
  - Use treatment on an 'on-demand' basis.
  - Return to self-care with an antacid or alginate.
- All people with dyspepsia requiring long-term treatment should have an annual review of their condition, and lifestyle advice should be reinforced.
- Anxiety regarding symptoms should be addressed. People who consult with dyspepsia are often more anxious about the significance of their symptoms than those who do not, but the symptoms are not generally more severe or longer lasting.

Who needs an initial referral for endoscopy?

Note: proton pump inhibitors and H_2-receptor antagonists should be stopped at least 2 weeks before endoscopy (B). Nonsteroidal anti-inflammatory drug use should also be suspended in all people requiring referral (C).

- **Routine endoscopy of people of any age presenting with dyspepsia but *without* ALARM symptoms is not necessary (B).** These people can be managed successfully without a formal diagnosis, because endoscopic findings will not change management in most cases.
- **Immediate endoscopy** (i.e. same day) is indicated for people presenting with dyspepsia together with significant acute gastrointestinal bleeding (C).
- **Anyone who develops ALARM symptoms should be referred for an urgent endoscopy** (i.e. within 2 weeks) (B). That is people with:
  - Chronic gastrointestinal bleeding
  - Progressive unintentional weight loss
  - Progressive difficulty swallowing (dysphagia)
  - Persistent vomiting
  - Iron deficiency anaemia
  - Epigastric mass or suspicious barium meal
- **Urgent endoscopy should also be considered in** a person (of any age) who has a change in the character of their dyspepsia, if they have any of the following known risk factors: Barrett's oesophagus; known dysplasia, atrophic gastritis, or intestinal metaplasia; or peptic ulcer surgery over 20 years ago (C).
- **If dysphagia is present** (interference with the swallowing mechanism that occurs within 5 seconds of starting the swallowing process) it is appropriate to refer for a barium swallow. There is a risk of perforation if an endoscope is pushed through a stricture. Before endoscopic examination, a barium swallow will delineate the stricture to see how long it is.
- **Routine endoscopy should also be considered in people aged 55 years or over** when symptoms persist despite *H pylori* testing and acid-suppression therapy, and there is a raised risk of gastric cancer or anxiety about cancer (e.g. continuous symptoms, onset of symptoms of less than one year ago, family history, pernicious anaemia, previous gastric surgery or gastric ulcer).
- **Urgent endoscopy should also be considered in people aged 55 years or over with unexplained and persistent recent-onset dyspepsia alone (D).**

[NICE, 2004; NICE, 2005]

Should I offer treatment while the person is awaiting endoscopy?

- **Proton pump inhibitors (PPIs) and H_2-receptor antagonists (H_2RAs) should be stopped at least 2 weeks before endoscopy (B)** [NICE, 2004].
- Symptomatic treatment prior to endoscopy may mask active disease and result in an inaccurate diagnosis. Check pre-investigation requirements with your local endoscopy unit.
- If the person is not currently taking treatment but has to wait for investigation, it is reasonable to offer a single course of treatment.
  - Antacids or alginates are preferred. They do not need to be stopped before the endoscopy.
  - If symptoms are poorly controlled and endoscopy cannot be performed urgently, a 2–4 week course of an H_2RA could be used, but it must be stopped at least 2 weeks before endoscopy.
  - PPIs are probably best avoided in this situation. They must be stopped at least 2 weeks before endoscopy.

What general measures are useful?

Which medication might be causing dyspepsia?

- **Stop nonsteroidal anti-inflammatory drugs (NSAIDs) wherever possible (A).** With those people who require continued NSAID use, see *How do I manage dyspepsia associated with nonsteroidal anti-inflammatory drugs?*
- **Theophylline, nitrates, and calcium-channel blockers** may reduce lower oesophageal sphincter pressure. Consider withdrawing if there are predominant reflux symptoms.
- **Bisphosphonates and corticosteroids** commonly cause gastrointestinal adverse effects.

[MeReC, 1998; NICE, 2004]

What lifestyle advice is recommended?

- **Offer simple lifestyle advice,** including healthy eating, weight reduction, and smoking cessation (**B**). Although there is no clear evidence that lifestyle factors (such as smoking, alcohol, caffeine, and diet) affect dyspepsia, there are more important general health benefits.
- **If the person has identified a precipitating factor,** then it is sensible to advise them to avoid it (e.g. bending, alcohol, coffee, chocolate, fatty foods, spicy foods) (**C**).
- **Other suggestions for people with reflux symptoms include** eating smaller meals, not eating before going to bed, and propping up the bed head. (One possible cause of reflux disease is transient relaxation of the lower oesophageal sphincter: lying flat may therefore increase reflux episodes because gravity does not then prevent acid regurgitation.)
- **Provide people with patient information** to support the care they receive (**C**).

[MeReC, 1998; NICE, 2004]

What is first-line treatment?

Many people will already have tried a range of over-the-counter therapies (such as antacids, alginates, H_2-receptor antagonists, and omeprazole) before presenting to their GP.

- **First-line treatment for dyspepsia that does not need investigation by endoscopy is empirical (A).**
  - Either, offer full-dose proton pump inhibitor therapy for 1 month (**A**).
  - Or, offer *H pylori* 'test and treat' (**A**).
- **There is insufficient evidence to guide which should be offered first (A).** Dyspeptic symptoms are a poor predictor of underlying pathology or disease severity.
- It may be practical to test for *H pylori* first (i.e. before offering empirical acid suppression) because carbon-13 urea breath tests or stool antigen tests should not be performed within 2 weeks of acid-suppression therapy (or within 4 weeks of antimicrobial therapy), as false-negative results may occur.

[NICE, 2004]

Which *H pylori* test should I use?

- **A carbon-13 urea breath test or a stool antigen test is recommended** for pretreatment testing [NICE, 2004] (**A**).
- Neither type of test should be performed within 2 weeks of proton pump inhibitor therapy or within 4 weeks of antibiotic therapy, as false-negative results may occur [DTB, 2004].
- If the person is taking long-term antibiotics: phenoxymethylpenicillin, nitrofurantoin, and trimethoprim are not active against *Helicobacter pylori*, so will not affect the test results. Advice should be sought from the local microbiology laboratory on when to test and test interpretation if people are taking other long-term antibiotics [HPA Helicobacter Working Group, Personal Communication, 2005]. (Tetracyclines, macrolides, broad spectrum penicillins [e.g. amoxicillin], cephalosporins, and anti-tuberculosis drugs are all active against *H pylori*.)
- ***H pylori* re-testing after eradication therapy** is not routinely recommended in people with dyspepsia that has not been investigated by endoscopy unless there is a strong clinical need (e.g. family history of gastric cancer) [NICE, 2004].
- **If post-eradication testing is appropriate,** only a carbon-13 urea breath test should be used [NICE, 2004] (**A**).

How do I use a carbon-13 urea breath test?

- Carbon-13 urea breath tests involve a separate appointment at the practice because the manufacturers recommend that the performance of the test is supervised.
- The kits currently prescribable on the NHS for adults include diabact UBT®, Helicobacter Test Hp-Plus®, Helicobacter Test INFAI®, and Pylobactell®.
- **The person should fast for at least 6 hours before the test** and then (for all tests except diabact UBT®) ingest citric acid or orange juice just before the test to slow gastric emptying. (The diabact UBT® tablet contains citric acid.)
- The person then provides two or three breath samples before ingestion of the carbon-13 tablet, and again 30 minutes afterwards (only 10 minutes afterwards for diabact UBT®) by blowing through a straw into a series of glass, screw-top tubes.
- Breath samples are sent away for analysis by mass spectrometry and results are available within 24 hours of receipt.

[DTB, 2004]

How do I use a stool antigen test?

- Stool antigen tests require the person to collect a stool sample (at least pea-sized). The sample is then sent to the laboratory for analysis.
- Stool antigen tests do not require a separate appointment at the practice and are cheaper than carbon urea breath testing.

What should I do if symptoms persist or return?

- **If symptoms persist or return after the initial strategy,** offer the alternative first-line treatment strategy:
  - Either, offer full-dose proton pump inhibitor (PPI) therapy for 1 month.
  - Or, offer *H pylori* 'test and treat'.
- **If symptoms persist or return after *H pylori* eradication,** do not re-test for *H pylori* unless there is a strong clinical need (e.g. family history of gastric cancer).
- **When both first-line treatment strategies have been tried:**
  - **If there was an initial response to a PPI but symptoms have now returned:**
    - Re-start the PPI at full dose, with a limited number of repeat prescriptions.
    - Encourage people to step-down the PPI to the lowest dose required to control symptoms (**B**).
    - Discuss using the treatment on an 'on-demand' basis (i.e. waiting for symptoms to develop before taking treatment) (**B**).
  - **If there was an inadequate response to a PPI,** offer an H_2-receptor antagonist or prokinetic therapy (metoclopramine or domperidone) as some individuals may respond to these therapies (**B**).

[NICE, 2004]

Who needs to be referred for endoscopy if symptoms persist?

- **Routine endoscopy of people of any age presenting with dyspepsia but *without* ALARM symptoms is not necessary** (**C**) [NICE, 2004].
- **However, people 55 years and over,** presenting with unexplained and persistent recent onset dyspepsia alone, should be referred for urgent endoscopy (**C**) [NICE, 2004].
  - *Unexplained* is defined as a symptom(s) and/or sign(s) that has not led to a diagnosis being made by the primary care professional after initial assessment of

the history, examination and primary care investigations (if any)', In the context of this recommendation, the primary care professional should confirm that the dyspepsia is new rather than a recurrent episode and exclude common precipitants of dyspepsia such as ingestion of NSAIDs.
- *Persistent* refers to the continuation of specified symptoms and/or signs beyond a period that would normally be associated with self-limiting problems. The precise period will vary depending on the severity of symptoms and associated features, as assessed by the healthcare professional. In many cases, the upper limit the professional will permit symptoms and/or signs to persist before initiating referral will be 4–6 weeks.

- **Anyone who develops ALARM symptoms should be referred urgently for endoscopy, or to a specialist** (C) [NICE, 2005]. That is people with:
  - Chronic gastrointestinal bleeding
  - Progressive unintentional weight loss
  - Progressive difficulty swallowing (dysphagia)
  - Persistent vomiting
  - Iron deficiency anaemia
  - Epigastric mass
  - Suspicious barium meal result
- **Urgent referral to a specialist should also be considered** in a person (of any age) who has unexplained worsening of their dyspepsia and Barrett's oesophagus; or known dysplasia, atrophic gastritis, or intestinal metaplasia; or peptic ulcer surgery over 20 years ago (C) [NICE, 2005].
- **In people of any age with difficult to control or persistent dyspeptic symptoms** (i.e. both *H pylori* 'test and treat' and empirical acid suppression has been tried) endoscopy is not usually necessary in the absence of ALARM symptoms (D) [NICE, 2004]. However, PRODIGY suggests that it is sensible to refer those people with long-term, frequently recurring or poorly controlled symptoms: the endoscopy may clarify the diagnosis to exclude complicated gastro-oesophageal reflux disease (GORD) or peptic ulcer disease.
- **For people taking nonsteroidal anti-inflammatory drugs,** see the section *How do I manage dyspepsia associated with nonsteroidal anti-inflammatory drugs?*

Reviewing and stepping-down treatment

How should I follow up people whose symptoms respond to treatment?

- All people with dyspepsia requiring long-term treatment should have an annual review of their condition, and lifestyle advice should be reinforced (C).
- Encourage people to step-down treatment to the lowest dose required to control symptoms (C).
- Discuss using the treatment on an 'on-demand' basis (i.e. waiting for symptoms to develop before taking treatment) (C).
- It may be appropriate to stop current treatment (e.g. proton pump inhibitor, H_2-receptor antagonist, or prokinetic) and return to self-care with an antacid or alginate (C). (This may be prescribed or purchased over the counter.)
- Note that stepping-down or stopping treatment is not appropriate for:
  - People with complicated oesophagitis (past strictures, ulcers, or haemorrhage).
  - People taking a PPI for gastroprotection against nonsteroidal anti-inflammatory drugs.
  - People with a previous bleeding peptic ulcer who remain *H pylori* positive after at least two attempts at eradication.

[NICE, 2004]

How should I manage people whose symptoms persist despite treatment?

- An alternate treatment strategy may be appropriate. See *What should I do if symptoms persist or return?*
- Endoscopy may be appropriate. See *Who needs to be referred for endoscopy if symptoms persist?* [De Boer and Tytgat, 2000; SIGN, 2003]

How do I manage dyspepsia associated with nonsteroidal anti-inflammatory drugs?

There are few studies to guide recommendations. The following advice is predominantly based on recommendations from the New Zealand Guidelines Group guideline on the *Management of Dyspepsia and Heartburn* [NZGG, 2004].

- **Stop nonsteroidal anti-inflammatory drugs (NSAIDs) wherever possible.**
  - In many people, dyspepsia will resolve when NSAIDs are stopped.
  - NSAID-related complications (haemorrhage, ulceration, perforation) can occur in otherwise asymptomatic individuals.
- **If analgesia is still needed, try paracetamol instead** of an NSAID if possible.
- **Consider endoscopy for people taking NSAIDs who have dyspeptic symptoms if:**
  - There is a strong suspicion of ulcer.
  - The person is aged over 65 years and has 1 additional risk factor for NSAID complications.
  - The person is aged under 65 years and has 2 additional risk factors for NSAID complications.
  - Symptoms persist despite *H pylori* testing and acid suppression in a person over 55 years of age.
- **Risk factors for NSAID-induced complications include:**
  - Age over 65 years.
  - Previous history of peptic ulcer disease, gastrointestinal bleeding or perforation.
  - Also taking corticosteroids, anticoagulants, or low-dose aspirin.
  - Taking maximum doses of NSAIDs for a long duration.
  - A serious comorbidity such as cardiovascular disease, renal or hepatic impairment, diabetes, or hypertension.
- If ulceration is found, then a proton pump inhibitor should be prescribed, to heal the ulcer and prevent recurrence. See the PRODIGY guidance *Dyspepsia — proven DU or GU* for further information.
- **If endoscopy is not required and the person is no longer taking an NSAID:**
  - Either, offer full-dose proton pump inhibitor (PPI) therapy for 1 month [NICE, 2004].
  - Or, offer *H pylori* 'test and treat' [NICE, 2004].
- **If the person *still needs* an NSAID** (and either an endoscopy was not needed, or excluded NSAID-induced complications):
  - Remind the person that NSAIDs should be taken with or after food.
  - **Test for *H pylori*** and eradicate using triple therapy if the test is positive.
  - **Use gastroprotection** (a PPI or full-dose misoprostol) combined with a standard NSAID in people *with* risk factors for NSAID complications. Alternatively, consider switching to a COX-2 selective NSAID alone. Note: their place is currently uncertain after the recent withdrawal of rofecoxib due to an increased risk of cardiovascular events.
  - If symptoms persist despite eradication therapy (or if the initial test is *H pylori* negative) offer a full-dose proton pump inhibitor to relieve symptoms.

- H_2-receptor antagonists are an alternative, but are not recommended because the evidence that they provide symptomatic relief in this situation is weak [MeReC, 2002; Rostom et al, 2002].

Supporting evidence for treatment strategies

Endoscopy referral criteria

- For most people, endoscopic findings will not change the treatment received, and there is a small but definite risk of harm from the procedure (the rate of significant adverse events may be as high as 1 in 200 in the UK).
- In addition, retrospective studies show that upper gastrointestinal malignancy is uncommon in people with dyspepsia (especially below the age of 55 years) and when it is found, it is often associated with a poor prognosis. It is not clear whether early detection of upper gastrointestinal cancers improves outcomes.
- ALARM symptoms are present in 10% of people presenting with dyspepsia in primary care [Meineche-Schmidt and Jorgensen, 2002].
- A recent UK prospective observational study [Kapoor et al, 2005] examined the predictive value of the Department of Health *referral guidelines for suspected cancer* [DH, 2000]. The prevalence of gastric cancer was 4% in a cohort of people referred urgently for alarm symptoms. Dysphagia and weight loss were predictive of cancer, however existing criteria of age more than 55 years with new onset or continous epigastric pain was found to be negatively associated with cancer.
- Referral for dysphagia or significant weight loss at any age, or referral at age over 55 years plus ALARM symptoms, would have detected 99.8% of the cancers found in the cohort [Kapoor et al, 2005]. These findings are supported by other retrospective studies.

H pylori 'test and treat'

- In people with dyspepsia that has not been investigated by endoscopy (i.e. uninvestigated dyspepsia), *H pylori* testing and treatment is more effective than empirical acid suppression, and as effective as endoscopy-based management:
  - Data pooled by NICE from trials in selected people with uninvestigated dyspepsia who tested positive for *H pylori* found that the average response rate at 1 year for those receiving empirical acid suppression was 47% and *H pylori* eradication increased this to 60%; for every 7 people treated there was one additional responder (NNT = 7) [NICE, 2004].
  - There is no significant difference in symptom relief at 1 year between an *H pylori* 'test-and-treat' strategy compared with endoscopy-based management of uninvestigated dyspepsia in primary care (34% compared with 33%; RR 1.02, 95%, CI 0.85 to 1.23) [Delaney et al, 2004]. However, using a 'test and treat' strategy significantly reduces the number of people needing endoscopy [NICE, 2004].
- An *H pylori* 'test and treat' strategy is likely to have a positive effect on underlying pathology such as peptic ulcer disease:
  - *H pylori* infection is a recognised factor in the development of peptic ulceration; about 15% of people with *H pylori* will develop a peptic ulcer [Graham, 1997].
  - It is possible that the effect of *H pylori* eradication in non-ulcer dyspepsia is based on a sub-group of people with an 'ulcer diathesis' and treatment prevents development of peptic ulcers. This hypothesis is difficult to prove, but might explain why an effect is seen.
  - *H pylori* infection is associated with gastric B-cell lymphoma, and distal gastric cancer. About 1% of people with *H pylori* will develop gastric cancer during their lifetime [Graham, 1997]. Studies have shown that gastric atrophy and intestinal metaplasia may partially regress after *H pylori* eradication, and there is some evidence that eradicating *H pylori* helps to prevent gastric cancer [Uemura et al, 2001].
- An *H pylori* 'test and treat' strategy is unlikely to affect outcomes (either positive or negative) if the underlying pathology is gastro-oesophageal reflux disease (GORD).
  - *H pylori* does not cause or aggravate GORD [McColl, 2002]. Eradication does not improve symptoms of GORD [Delaney et al, 2003].
  - There is consensus that *H pylori* eradication is not associated with the development of GORD in most cases, and does not exacerbate existing GORD [DTB, 2002; Malfertheiner et al, 2002].
- An *H pylori* 'test and treat' strategy is appropriate for people with NSAID-induced dyspepsia or ulcers:
  - In people without previous ulcers, *H pylori* eradication reduces the risk of NSAID-induced peptic ulcers compared to placebo, and was as effective as acid suppression in reducing this risk [Delaney et al, 2003].
  - In people with previous peptic ulcers, *H pylori* eradication reduces the risk of peptic ulceration compared to omeprazole at 6 months [Delaney et al, 2003].
  - In people with a previous bleeding ulcer, *H pylori* eradication is less effective than omeprazole in preventing recurrence in people taking naproxen, but as effective in people taking low-dose aspirin [Delaney et al, 2003].

Which *H pylori* test?

Initial testing (pretreatment)

- **A carbon-13 urea breath test or a stool antigen test is recommended for pretreatment testing in primary care** [NICE, 2004].
  - Carbon-13 urea breath tests are consistently accurate with about 95% sensitivity and specificity reported in studies. Stool antigen tests seem to perform as well as carbon-13 urea breath tests [DTB, 2004; NICE, 2004].
  - Neither type of test should be performed within 2 weeks of proton pump inhibitor therapy or within 4 weeks of antibiotic therapy, as false-negative results may occur [DTB, 2004].
- Stool antigen tests using monoclonal antibodies seem to be more accurate (sensitivity of 96% and specificity of 97%) than tests using polyclonal antibodies (sensitivity of 90% and specificity 94%) [DTB, 2004].
- Laboratory-based serology is an alternative *if* it has been locally validated [NICE, 2004]. However, the sensitivity and specificity of serology varies in different populations. (The reason for this is unclear but may relate to different strains of *H pylori* or genetic differences in the population.) Because most laboratories receive samples from wide geographical areas it is likely that they will be covering populations that vary considerably in terms of age, social class, and ethnicity, making local validation difficult. In addition, serological findings only indicate exposure to *H pylori*, not necessarily active infection: antibody levels only fall slowly over several months after eradication. Use of serology leads to at least twice as many false positives as the carbon-13 urea breath test or the stool antigen test.
- Near-patient serology kits are not recommended because they have widely varying sensitivities and specificities. Studies of the accuracy of several new rapid whole-blood

test kits have shown sensitivity of 82–95% and specificity of 83–94% [SIGN, 2003].

- Carbon-14 urea breath tests are not appropriate for primary care as they involve a small dose of radiation.
- **If the person requires endoscopy,** then biopsies can be taken to test for *H pylori*, e.g. with the rapid urease test (the Campylobacter-like organism [CLO] test). This has a sensitivity of 85–90% and a specificity of 98–100% [Meurer and Bower, 2002].

Post-eradication testing

- *H pylori* re-testing is not recommended in people with dyspepsia that has not been investigated by endoscopy, unless there is a strong clinical need (e.g. family history of gastric cancer) [NICE, 2004].
- **If re-testing is appropriate, only a carbon-13 urea breath test should be used** [NICE, 2004].
- Serological tests are not reliable in determining eradication, unless more than 1 year has elapsed since eradication therapy was given [Feldman et al, 1998].
- Stool antigen tests are not currently recommended by NICE for post-eradication testing. However, there is increasing evidence that they are sensitive and specific to use for post-eradication testing and they are likely to become recommended for this purpose in the future [HPA Helicobacter Working Group, Personal Communication, 2005].

Empirical PPI therapy

- In the past either a step-up or a step-down strategy has been advocated [NICE, 2000]. NICE now recommend a step-down approach to proton pump inhibitor (PPI) therapy.
- PPIs are more effective than antacids or alginates at reducing dyspeptic symptoms in people whose dyspepsia has not been investigated by endoscopy (i.e. uninvestigated dyspepsia). In trials, the average response rate taking an antacid or alginate was 37%, and PPI therapy increased this to 55%: for every 6 people treated there was one additional repsonder (NNT = 6) [Delaney et al, 2003; NICE, 2004].
- PPIs are more effective than H_2-receptor antagonists (H_2RAs) at reducing dyspeptic symptoms in people with uninvestigated dyspepsia. In trials, the average response rate taking an H_2RA was 36%, and PPI therapy increased this to 58%: for every 5 people treated there was one additional responder (NNT = 5) [Delaney et al, 2003; NICE, 2004].
- Most studies did not include people with predominant bloating or dysmotility symptoms. This could possibly have exaggerated the treatment effect of PPIs.
- Early endoscopy has not been shown to produce better outcomes than empirical acid suppression [NICE, 2004].

H pylori eradication regimens

- One-week triple therapy regimens (a proton pump inhibitor [PPI] plus two antibiotics) are recommended. Two-week regimens are no more effective than one-week regimens. Dual therapy is not as effective as triple therapy. Quadruple therapy (a PPI, bismuth, tetracycline and metronidazole) is as effective as triple therapy, but taking 17 tablets per day does not make it a practical first-line option [Delaney et al, 2003].
- The recommended PAC regimen (a PPI plus amoxicillin 1 g and clarithromycin 500 mg, all given twice a day) and PCM regimen (a PPI plus metronidazole 400 mg and clarithromycin 250 mg, all given twice a day) are the optimum regimens on current evidence. Data pooled by NICE show that [NICE, 2004]:
    - Double-dose PPIs are more effective than single-dose PPIs in PAC regimens (eradication rate of 85.4% for double-dose PPIs and 78.5% for single-dose PPIs). The data were less clear for PCM regimens (due to much smaller patient numbers). Double-dose PPIs are therefore also recommended in PCM regimens as there is not enough data to clearly support single-dose PPIs.
    - The dose of clarithromycin differs between the two regimens. Pooled data for PAC regimens show eradication rates of 79.8% with clarithromycin 250 mg compared with 89.6% with clarithromycin 500 mg. In PCM regimens, doubling the dose of clarithromycin had no statistically significant effect: eradication rates were 87.4% for clarithromycin 250 mg and 88.9% for clarithromycin 500 mg.
    - Pooled data for the recommended PAC and PCM regimens show no statistically significant difference in eradication rates: 82% for PAC, and 82.6% for PCM.
- Although triple therapy using a PPI plus amoxicillin and metronidazole has previously been recommended as a first-line therapy, pooled data from four randomized, controlled trials have shown that it is less effective than either of the two triple therapies that contain clarithromycin [NICE, 2004].

On-demand PPI therapy

- There are no long-term treatment trials of dyspepsia, which is surprising given that it is a chronic, relapsing condition. It is argued that 'on-demand' PPI therapy may be effective, but less costly than continuous therapy [NICE, 2004]. However, therapy can (and should) be individualized as a proportion of people will continue to take their PPI daily.
- The evidence for using 'on-demand' PPI therapy (i.e. waiting for symptoms to develop before taking treatment) in people whose dyspepsia has not been investigated by endoscopy is extrapolated from studies looking at people with endoscopy-negative reflux disease. The patient populations are similar and, in the absence of ALARM symptoms, this extrapolation is a safe step [NICE, 2004].
- Although it was not possible for NICE to combine the data for meta-analysis, the general trend of study outcomes suggests that on-demand or intermittent PPI therapy is superior to placebo. Studies that have compared intermittent to continuous therapy also suggest that there is little difference in 'willingness to continue' (80–90%) between these strategies.
- There is a concern that many people with reflux symptoms will not have an endoscopy, and on-demand PPI therapy may be given to people with severe oesophagitis. However, severe oesophagitis is rare in primary care (less than 5% of all gastro-oesophageal reflux disease) and there is no evidence of harm of this approach, particularly as this group is more likely to take PPIs more often as symptoms recur more readily [Castell et al, 2002].

H_2-receptor antagonists and prokinetics

- Although proton pump inhibitors are more effective than H_2-receptor antagonists (H_2RAs) at reducing dyspeptic symptoms in trials in people whose dyspepsia has not been investigated by endoscopy, some individuals may respond better to H_2RA therapy [Delaney et al, 2003; NICE, 2004].
- Prokinetic agents (e.g. domperidone or metoclopramide) may improve symptoms such as bloating or early satiety, and may be most useful for people with predominant reflux symptoms. However, trials have been few, small-scale, and heterogeneous — most evidence for prokinetics is for cisapride, which is no longer available [Delaney et al, 2003].

Preventing NSAID-induced complications

- Nonsteroidal anti-inflammatory drug (NSAID) use and *H pylori* infection are synergistic for the development of peptic ulcer and ulcer bleeding [Huang et al, 2002].
- *H pylori* eradication reduces the risk of peptic ulceration compared to omeprazole at 6 months in NSAID users with previous peptic ulcers [Delaney et al, 2004]. However, it is less effective than omeprazole in preventing recurrence in people taking naproxen with a previous bleeding ulcer [Delaney et al, 2004].
- Proton pump inhibitors at full dose are generally the preferred choice for gastroprotection. They are effective and well tolerated; they reduce the risk of endoscopic gastric ulcers by 63% and the risk of duodenal ulcers by 81% [Rostom et al, 2002]. However there is a lack of data on prevention of ulcer complications.
- Misoprostol 800 micrograms per day has been shown to reduce the risk of endoscopic gastric and duodenal ulcers, and *clinically* important ulcer complications, but its place is limited by its adverse effects [Rostom et al, 2002]. Lower doses (e.g. 400 micrograms per day) are less effective than PPIs at reducing the incidence of endoscopic lesions, and have greater adverse effects [NICE, 2004]. (Diarrhoea and abdominal pain are common.)
- Double doses of H_2-receptor antagonists (H_2RAs) are also effective at reducing the risk of endoscopic gastric and duodenal ulcers but this is an off-licence use [Rostom et al, 2002]. Standard doses only reduce the risk of endoscopic duodenal ulcers [SIGN, 2003].

Medicines management

Which *H pylori* eradication regimen should I use?

- **NICE recommends that one of the following one-week eradication regimens is used:**
  - A 'PAC' regimen (a proton pump inhibitor [PPI], plus amoxicillin 1 g and clarithromycin 500 mg, all given twice a day)
  - Or (for people with penicillin hypersensitivity) a 'PCM' regimen (a PPI plus metronidazole 400 mg and clarithromycin 250 mg, all given twice a day)
- Note: NICE recommends that re-testing after eradication therapy is *not* required in people whose dyspepsia has not been investigated by endoscopy, unless there is a strong clinical need (e.g. family history of gastric cancer). Second-line eradication regimens are therefore rarely needed in people whose dyspepsia has not been investigated by endoscopy.

Which eradication regimen should I use if my patient has had a recent course of antibiotics?

- **An alternative antibiotic should be used in the eradication regimen** if a course of clarithromycin or metronidazole has previously been given (for any indication).
- The HPA Helicobacter Working Group recommends that two antibiotics are chosen from the following options: amoxicillin, clarithromycin, metronidazole, or oxytetracycline.
- Other antibiotics can be considered, but advice should be sought from the Helicobacter Reference Laboratory (telephone 0208 327 6538).

[HPA Helicobacter Working Group, Personal Communication, 2005]

Antibiotic resistance

- Laboratory testing suggests that *Helicobacter pylori* antibiotic resistance is around 15–66% for metronidazole, and 8–30% for clarithromycin [McLoughlin et al, 2004]. (Data on *H pylori* resistance to amoxicillin have not been published.)
- Treatment failure with a regimen containing clarithromycin is highly correlated with clarithromycin resistance. Clarithromycin is therefore best avoided if a recent course has been given.
- The association between metronidazole resistance and treatment failure is less clear cut.
  - Data pooled by NICE suggest that there is no significant difference in eradication rates between PAC and PCM regimens. NICE suggests that possible explanations are that PCM may be more effective than PAC in metronidazole-sensitive strains, or that the impact of metronidazole resistance may not be as marked as observational studies suggest [NICE, 2004].
  - Metronidazole could therefore be considered if a recent course had been taken and there was no suitable alternative.

[HPA Helicobacter Working Group, Personal Communication, 2005]

Which PPI?

- **Differences between the proton pump inhibitors (PPIs) in clinical efficacy and safety are minimal** [WeMeReC, 2002]. On present evidence, PPIs do not have any serious contraindications for most users, and have been in common use for over a decade.
- PPIs are an effective treatment for dyspepsia symptoms that have not been investigated by endoscopy [NICE, 2004].
- **Omeprazole is currently the least expensive PPI,** although this may change when other PPIs become available generically.
- PPIs are generally well tolerated. Adverse effects include gastrointestinal disturbances (most commonly diarrhoea), headaches, and dizziness.
- PPIs should not be offered to people with ALARM symptoms prior to endoscopy as they may mask gastric cancer. If someone already taking a PPI needs an endoscopy, the PPI should be stopped at least 2 weeks before the endoscopy.
- PPIs undergo extensive hepatic metabolism. In liver disease, do not exceed the following doses: 20 mg daily for omeprazole, pantoprazole, and esomeprazole; 30 mg daily for lansoprazole. There are no data on the use of rabeprazole in people with severe hepatic impairment so the manufacturer advises caution.
- Omeprazole and esomeprazole occasionally enhance the effects of warfarin and phenytoin. Monitor people taking these drugs carefully if omeprazole or esomeprazole are started or stopped.

Which dose?

- Recommended doses of proton pump inhibitors are outlined in Table 1.

How should I advise people to take on-demand therapy?

- 'On-demand' therapy is where treatment is taken only when symptoms recur. Once symptoms are relieved (often after a few days) treatment is stopped again.
- The PPI doses most commonly studied for on-demand PPI therapy are rabeprazole 10mg, pantoprazole 20mg, esomeprazole 20mg, omeprazole 20mg, and lansoprazole 15mg. None are licensed for on-demand treatment in people whose dyspepsia has not been investigated by endoscopy, but esomeprazole and rabeprazole are licensed for on-demand treatment in gastro-oesophageal reflux disease.

Table 1: PRODIGY-recommended proton pump inhibitor doses for dyspeptic symptoms that have not been investigated by endoscopy.

PPI	Full dose	Low dose	*H pylori* eradication regimen dose	Prophylaxis for NSAID-associated ulcer
Omeprazole	20 mg once a day	10 mg once a day	20 mg twice a day	20 mg once a day
Lansoprazole	30 mg once a day	15 mg once a day	30 mg twice a day	15–30 mg once a day
Pantoprazole	40 mg once a day	20 mg once a day	40 mg twice a day	20 mg once a day
Rabeprazole	20 mg once a day	10 mg once a day	20 mg twice a day	*
Esomeprazole	†20 mg once a day	Not available	20 mg twice a day	20 mg once a day

* Not licensed for this indication
†When undertaking meta-analysis of dose-related effects, NICE classed esomeprazole 20mg as a full-dose equivalent to omeprazole 20mg.

- Some people may prefer to use treatment intermittently, i.e. a 2–4 week course of treatment when symptoms recur.

[Bardhan, 2003; NICE, 2004]

Which agents are suitable for gastroprotection against NSAIDs?

- Proton pump inhibitors at full dose are generally the preferred choice for gastroprotection. Omeprazole, lansoprazole, pantoprazole, and esomeprazole are all licensed for prophylaxis of NSAID-associated ulcers. Rabeprazole is not licensed for this indication.
- Misoprostol is an alternative, but its place is limited by its adverse effects [Rostom et al, 2002]. The full dose (800 micrograms per day) should be used because lower doses (e.g. 400 micrograms per day) are less effective [NICE, 2004].

H_2-receptor antagonists, antacids, alginates, and prokinetics

H_2-receptor antagonists

- **Cimetidine, famotidine, nizatidine, and ranitidine seem to be equally effective.** They have been shown to be more effective than placebo in the management of people whose dyspepsia has not been investigated by endoscopy.
- **Adverse effects are uncommon** and include diarrhoea, headache, dizziness, rash, and tiredness.
- **Cimetidine should be avoided in people taking** erythromycin, warfarin, amiodarone, theophylline, carbamazepine, phenytoin, and sodium valproate as cimetidine inhibits hepatic drug metabolism by binding to microsomal cytochrome P450.

Antacids and alginates

- There is limited evidence on the efficacy of antacids in the management of dyspepsia; however, symptomatic relief is often reported with the use of an antacid or alginate.
- They are best given when symptoms occur or are expected, i.e. after meals and at bedtime. They also remain in the stomach for longer at these times, and therefore have longer to act.
- **Antacids should preferably not be taken at the same time as other drugs** as they may impair absorption.
- Most antacids contain aluminium salts, magnesium salts, or a combination of the two.
- **Combinations of aluminium salts with magnesium salts may be preferable** to magnesium salts alone (which may cause diarrhoea) or aluminium salts alone (which may cause constipation).
- **Alginates** form a 'raft' that floats on the surface of the stomach contents. They are most useful for people with mild reflux symptoms.

Prokinetic agents

- **Domperidone and metoclopramide** are both used as prokinetic agents to reduce symptoms such as bloating and early satiety.
- **Long-term use should be avoided.** There is an increased risk of hyperprolactinaemia (e.g. galactorrhoea, gynaecomastia, and amenorrhoea) with both domperidone and metoclopramide. Chronic use of metoclopramide increases the risk of extrapyramidal adverse effects (i.e. drug-induced Parkinsonism). Extrapyramidal adverse effects are very rare with domperidone as it does not cross the blood-brain barrier.
- Encourage people using prokinetics to use them as on-demand or intermittent therapy.
- Metoclopramide should be avoided in young adults (under the age of 20 years) because of the increased risk of extrapyramidal adverse effects in this age group.

References

NHS staff in England can link, free of charge, from references to full text journals by clicking on [Full text] on the PRODIGY website.
Note: users in England and Wales can access Cochrane Library full text free of charge without an Athens password.

1. Bardhan, K.D. (2003) Intermittent and on-demand use of proton pump inhibitors in the management of symptomatic gastroesophageal reflux disease. *American Journal of Gastroenterology* **98**(3 Suppl), S40-S48.
2. BNF 48 (2004) *British National Formulary.* 48th edn. London: British Medical Association and Royal Pharmaceutical Society of Great Britain.
3. British Society of Gastroenterology (2002) *Dyspepsia management guidelines.* British Society of Gastroenterology. www.bsg.org.uk/clinical_prac/guidelines/dyspepsia.htm [Accessed: 20/08/2002].
4. Castell, D.O., Kahrilas, P.J., Richter, J.E. et al (2002) Esomeprazole (40 mg) compared with lansoprazole (30 mg) in the treatment of erosive esophagitis. *American Journal of Gastroenterology* 97(3), 575–583.
5. Chiba, N., Thompson, A.B.R. and Barkun, A.N. (2003) The Rome II definition of dyspepsia does not exclude patients with GERD in primary care. *Gastroenterology* **124**(4 Suppl 1), A223-A224.
6. De Boer, W.A. and Tytgat, G.N.J. (2000) Treatment of *Helicobacter pylori* infection. *British Medical Journal* **320**(7226), 31–34. [Full text]
7. Delaney, B.C., Moayyedi, P and Forman, D (2003) *Initial management strategies for dyspepsia (Cochrane Review).* The Cochrane Library. Issue 2. Chichester, UK: John Wiley & Sons, Ltd. www.nelh.nhs.uk/cochrane.asp [Accessed: 06/01/2005]. [Full text]
8. Delaney, B., Moayyedi, P. and Forman, D. (2004) *Helicobacter pylori infection.* Volume 12. www.clinicalevidence.com [Accessed: 06/01/2005].
9. DH (2000) *Referral guidelines for suspected cancer.* Department of Health. www.dh.gov.uk [Accessed: 27/04/2004]. [Full text]

10. DTB (1996) Medical management of gastro-oesophageal reflux. *Drug & Therapeutics Bulletin* **34**(1), 1–4.
11. DTB (2002) Should *H. Pylori* be eradicated in non-ulcer dyspepsia? *Drug & Therapeutics Bulletin* **40**(3), 23–24. [Full text]
12. DTB (2004) Which test for *Helicobacter pylori* in primary care? *Drug & Therapeutics Bulletin* **42**(9), 71–72. [Full text]
13. Feldman, M., Cryer, B., Lee, E. and Peterson, W.L. (1998) Role of seroconversion in confirming cure of *Helicobacter pylori* infection. *Journal of the American Medical Association* **280**(4), 363–365. [Full text]
14. Graham, D.Y. (1997) Can therapy even be denied for *Helicobacter pylori* infection? *Gastroenterology* **113**(Suppl 6), 113–117.
15. Hawkey, C.J., Karrasch, J.A., Szczepanski, L. et al (1998) Omeprazole compared with misoprostol for ulcers associated with nonsterodial antiinflammatory drugs. *New England Journal of Medicine* **338**(11), 727–734. [Full text]
16. HPA Helicobacter Working Group (2005) *Personal communication. Antibiotic resistance and second-line antibiotics for eradication therapy.* Health Protection Agency: UK.
17. Huang, J.Q., Sridhar, S. and Hunt, R.H. (2002) Role of *Helicobacter pylori* infection and non-steroidal anti-inflammatory drugs in peptic-ulcer disease: a meta-analysis. *Lancet* **359**(9300), 14–22. [Full text]
18. Hunt, R.H., Fallone, C., Veldhuyzen Van Zanten, S. et al (2002) Etiology of dyspepsia: implications for empirical therapy. *Canadian Journal of Gastroenterology* **16**(9), 635–641.
19. Kapoor, N., Bassi, A., Sturgess, R. and Bodger, K. (2005) Predictive value of alarm features in a rapid access upper gastrointestinal cancer service. *Gut* **54**(1), 40–45.
20. Logan, R. and Delaney, B. (2001) ABC of the upper gastrointestinal tract: implications of dyspepsia for the NHS. *British Medical Journal* **323**(7314), 675–677. [Full text]
21. Malfertheiner, P., Megraud, F., O'Morain, C. et al (2002) Current concepts in the management of *Helicobacter pylori* infection – the Maastricht 2–2000 consensus report. *Alimentary Pharmacology & Therapeutics* **16**(2), 167–180.
22. McColl, K.E. (2002) Motion – *Helicobacter pylori* causes or worsens GERD: arguments against the motion. *Canadian Journal of Gastroenterology* **16**(9), 615–617.
23. McLoughlin, R., Racz, I., Buckley, M. et al (2004) Therapy of *Helicobacter pylori*. *Helicobacter* **9**(Suppl 1), 42–48.
24. Meineche-Schmidt, V. and Jorgensen, T. (2002) 'Alarm symptoms' in patients with dyspepsia: a three-year prospective study from general practice. *Scandinavian Journal of Gastroenterology* **37**(9), 999–1007.
25. MeReC (1997) Dyspepsia, peptic ulcer and *Helicobacter pylori*. *MeReC Bulletin* **8**(2), 5–8.
26. MeReC (1998) Proton pump inhibitors: their role in dyspepsia. *MeReC Bulletin* **9**(11), 41–44.
27. MeReC (2002) NSAIDs and gastroprotection, Cox-II selective inhibitors. *MeReC Briefing* **20**(Oct), 1–8.
28. Meurer, L.N. and Bower, D.J. (2002) Management of *Helicobacter pylori* infection. *American Family Physician* **65**(7), 1327–1336. [Full text]
29. NICE (2000) *Guidance on the use of proton pump inhibitors in the treatment of dyspepsia.* Technology appraisal guidance no. 7. National Institute for Clinical Excellence. www.nice.org.uk [Accessed: 16/10/2003].
30. NICE (2004) *Dyspepsia: management of dyspepsia in adults in primary care: NICE guideline.* Clinical guideline 17. National Institute for Clinical Excellence. www.nice.org.uk [Accessed: 27/08/2004].
31. NICE (2005) *Referral guidelines for suspected cancer – quick reference guide.* Clinical guideline 27. National Institute for Health and Clinical Excellence. www.nice.org.uk [Accessed: 01/07/2005].
32. NZGG (2004) *Management of dyspepsia and heartburn.* New Zealand Guidelines Group. www.nzgg.org.nz [Accessed: 06/01/2005].
33. Rostom, A., Wells, G., Tugwell, P. et al (2002) *Prevention of NSAID-induced gastroduodenal ulcers (Cochrane Review).* The Cochrane Library. Issue 4. Chichester, UK: John Wiley & Sons, Ltd. www.nelh.nhs.uk/cochrane.asp [Accessed: 04/04/2005]. [Full text]
34. SIGN (2003) *Dyspepsia.* Report no. 68. Scottish Intercollegiate Guideline Network. www.sign.ac.uk [Accessed: 19/07/2003].
35. Uemura, N., Okamoto, S., Yamamoto, S. et al (2001) *Helicobacter pylori* infection and the development of gastric cancer. *New England Journal of Medicine* **345**(11), 784–789. [Full text]
36. WeMeReC (2002) Use of proton pump inhibitors in primary care. *WeMeReC Bulletin* 9(2), 1–6.

Evidence grading

Evidence grading is from the National Institute of Clinical Excellence guideline, *Dyspepsia,* August 2004. The definitions of grades of recommendation used in this guideline are as follows:

A At least one randomized controlled trial as part of a body of literature of overall good quality and consistency addressing the specific recommendation without extrapolation.

B Well-conducted clinical studies but no randomized clinical trials on the topic of recommendation, or with extrapolation from evidence obtained from randomized trials of meta-analysis.

C Expert committee reports or opinions and/or clinical experiences of respected authorities. This grading indicates that directly applicable clinical studies of good quality are absent, or with extrapolation from higher levels of evidence.

GPP Good practice point. Recommended good practice based on the clinical experience of the guideline development group.

PRODIGY GUIDANCE

Earwax

Last revised in July 2004
www.prodigy.nhs.uk/guidance.asp?gt=Earwax

Applies to people over the age of 6 months

This guidance covers the management of earwax.

This guidance does not cover the management of other ear conditions.

There is separate PRODIGY guidance for *Otitis externa* and *Otitis media — acute*.

E

Goals

- To recognize the need for removal of earwax
- To remove earwax effectively and safely when indicated
- To refer appropriately for specialist assessment and management

Contents

Scenarios

- Earwax p.701

Extended Information, p. 702

Earwax

Which therapy?

- **Remove earwax only if it is causing symptoms** (i.e. discomfort, hearing loss), **or if a clear view of the eardrum is needed.**
- **Choice of treatment depends on patient preference, resources, and available skills.**
- Alternatives for treating impacted wax are:
  - **Ear drops to soften the wax** which then often spontaneously disperses. Tap water, sodium chloride 0.9%, or sodium bicarbonate are as effective as any other cerumenolytic ear drop. In resistant cases, the person may need to lie with the affected ear uppermost for a few minutes after a generous amount of the softening agent has been applied.
  - **Irrigation:** this could be done immediately or 15–30 minutes after ear drops. The pressure-controlled electronic irrigator is safer to use than the traditional syringe.
  - **Use of an ear curette** to hook out wax or microsuction. These are effective and safe in trained hands, but would usually be done in secondary care.

Practical prescribing points

For further information, please see the *Medicines Compendium* (www.medicines.org.uk) or the *British National Formulary* (www.bnf.org).

- **Avoid ear irrigation in the following circumstances:**
  - Perforation of the tympanic membrane (present, previous, suspected, or grommet)
- **Use ear drops if practical; otherwise irrigate with caution when:**
  - Previous middle ear or mastoid surgery
  - Recurrent otitis externa or chronic middle ear disease
  - Inability to cooperate
  - One ear is deaf and the other has impacted wax — there is a remote but unacceptable risk of causing bilateral deafness
- People with nut allergies should not use almond oil.

Should I refer or investigate?

Refer?

Consider referral to otolaryngology if:

- Wax remains impacted after appropriate treatment.
- Deafness or other symptoms remain after removal of earwax.
- Irrigation is followed by severe pain or deafness or vertigo.
- There are contraindications to irrigation (see cautions).

Patient information leaflets

The following PILs are available at www.prodigy.nhs.uk

- Ear Wax

Shared decision making

- **Earwax is normal.** It may build up and cause dulled hearing or mild discomfort.
- **Do not poke or clean the ears with cotton buds or similar objects.**
- **Ear drops alone** often cause wax to break up and come out of the ear by itself.
  - We recommend plain water, or sodium bicarbonate (but other drops such as olive oil, almond oil, and branded products may be just as good).
  - You can buy ear droppers in an empty bottle and ear drops from pharmacies.
  - Warm the drops to body temperature before using them; hold the bottle in your hand or put it in your pocket for a while.
  - Pour a few drops into the affected ear. Lie with that ear uppermost for a few minutes to allow the drops to soak into the wax.
  - Use the drops three to four times a day for 5 days.
- **You may need syringing of the ear** if ear drops alone fail to break up the wax plug. You may need to soften the wax with drops before the ears are syringed.

Drug rationale

Drugs not included

- **Propriety preparations of cerumenolytic ear drops** are not included. Many different preparations are available, none with any clear clinical advantage. Cerumenolytics with organic solvents may cause local irritation of the ear canal.

Drugs included

- **Sodium bicarbonate or sodium chloride 0.9% ear drops** are effective and cheap. There is some suggestion that plain water and sodium bicarbonate are particularly effective at disintegrating earwax.

- **Almond or olive oil** are also an effective and cheap means of softening earwax.

Prescriptions

Ear drops

Sodium chloride 0.9% ear drops

- Age from 6 months onwards
- Sodium chloride0.9% nose drops. Put 3 to 4 drops into the affected ear(s) 3 to 4 times a day for 3 to 5 days; supply 10 ml; NHS Cost £1.86; OTC Cost £2.99.

Sodium bicarbonate 5% ear drops

- Age from 6 months onwards
- Sodium bicarbonate ear drops. Put 3 to 4 drops into the affected ear(s) 3 to 4 times a day for 3 to 5 days; supply 10 ml; NHS Cost £1.18; OTC Cost £2.08.

Almond oil ear drops

- Age from 6 months onwards
- Almond oil. Put 3 to 4 drops into the affected ear(s) 3 to 4 times a day for 3 to 5 days; supply 10 ml; NHS Cost £0.09; OTC Cost £0.69.

Olive oil ear drops

- Age from 6 months onwards
- Olive oil. Put 3 to 4 drops into the affected ear(s) 3 to 4 times a day for 3 to 5 days; supply 10 ml; NHS Cost £0.07; OTC Cost £0.67.

Extended Information

Background information

- What is it? p.702
- How common is it? p.702
- How do I know my patient has it? p.702
- What else might it be? p.702
- Complications and prognosis p.702

What is it?

- **Cerumen** is the wax-like substance produced in the external auditory canal by the ceruminous glands.
- **Earwax** is a combination of cerumen, sebum, desquamated corneocytes (the dead, flattened cells on the outer layer of the skin), sweat, hair, and foreign matter (e.g. dust) that has been retained.
- **People with recurrent earwax impaction** may have a failure of the corneocytes in the external auditory canal to separate and migrate externally.
- **The colour and consistency** of earwax varies considerably between individuals: from yellow through brown to black, and from dry and flaky to moist and sticky. Soft cerumen is more common in children; hard cerumen is more common in adults.

[Hawke, 2002]

How common is it?

- **Impacted earwax is more common in older people** [Aung and Mulley, 2002].
- **It is more frequently found in people who use hearing aids and in those who use ear buds** [Aung and Mulley, 2002].
- A survey of 289 UK GPs reported that each saw an average of nine people a month requesting removal of earwax [Sharp et al, 1990].

How do I know my patient has it?

- The person may complain of ear discomfort, hearing loss, and occasionally tinnitus.
- Examination of the ear canal with an auriscope will reveal excessive wax.
- Raise the index of suspicion of impacted earwax in older people, in people wearing hearing aids, and in young children, because they may not complain of hearing loss. Impacted earwax with hearing loss is common in these groups, and the potential consequences of hearing loss are severe: depression and social isolation in the elderly; impaired development and difficulties at school in the young.

What else might it be?

- **Otitis externa** (inflammation of the auricle or external ear canal due to allergy or infection)
- **Foreign bodies** (particularly suspect in children)

Complications and prognosis

Complications

- **Hearing loss** is a common and reversible consequence of impacted earwax.
- **Complications of syringing** occur in about 1 in 1000 ears syringed [Bird, 2003]. These include bleeding (which is usually self-limited), perforation, otitis externa, or disturbance in balance (causing nausea and vomiting) [Grossan, 2000], and, rarely, deafness and balance difficulties.

[Sharp et al, 1990; Zivic and King, 1993; Bapat et al, 2001]

Management issues

- General issues p.702
- Ear drops to soften wax (cerumenolytics) p.702
- Ear irrigation p.703
- Other mechanical removal techniques (usually available only in secondary care) p.703

General issues

- **Earwax is a normal physiological substance** that protects the ear canal. The quantity produced varies greatly between individuals.
- **Earwax needs to be removed only if it causes symptoms** (i.e. discomfort, hearing loss) or if an unimpeded view of the eardrum is needed.
- The ear is a self-cleaning system and cotton buds should not be used to try to clear the ear canal, as wax is likely to be pushed back against the eardrum and become more impacted.
- Impacted earwax can be treated with ear drops alone, irrigation (with or without prior use of ear drops to soften the wax), microsuction, and curettage.
- **There is little good evidence on the relative effectiveness of the various treatment options** [Browning, 2003; Burton and Doree, 2004]. Thus the choice of strategy depends mainly on patient preferences, the ability of the person to cooperate, the practitioner's skills and available equipment, cost, and convenience.
- Often the appropriate first-line treatment is an ear drop to soften the wax.

Ear drops to soften wax (cerumenolytics)

- **Evidence from clinical trials:** a recent Cochrane systematic review of trials of cerumenolytics found eight clinical trials, all with small numbers of participants, and most of poor methodological quality. The reviewers concluded that there is no evidence to prefer one particular cerumenolytic to any other, and that water and sodium chloride 0.9% seem to be as effective as any

proprietary agent [Burton and Doree, 2004]. PRODIGY recommends the use of tap water, sodium chloride 0.9% or sodium bicarbonate ear drops. (Olive oil and almond oil are widely used and are therefore also included in the choice of prescriptions.)
- **Evidence from *in vitro* studies:** *in vitro* studies have shown that water-based cerumenolytics (e.g. water, sodium bicarbonate) cause moderate disintegration after 15 to 30 minutes, and complete disintegration in a few hours. Olive oil and other oil-based products have little or no effect on earwax *in vitro* [Somerville, 2002].
- **Adverse effects:** preparations containing organic solvents may cause irritation and inflammation of the external ear canal and do not offer any clear advantages [BNF 47, 2004]. People with nut allergies should not use almond oil.
- After instilling the ear drops, the person should lie with the affected ear uppermost for 5–10 minutes.

Ear irrigation

- **Ear irrigation is indicated** if impacted wax causes loss of hearing, discomfort, or, rarely, tinnitus.
- **Avoid ear irrigation in the following circumstances:**
  - Perforation of the tympanic membrane (present, previous, suspected, or grommet)
- **Use ear drops if practical, otherwise irrigate with caution, when:**
  - Previous middle ear or mastoid surgery
  - Unable to cooperate
  - Recurrent otitis externa or chronic middle ear disease
  - Deafness in one ear and impacted wax in the other ear — there is a remote but unacceptable risk of causing bilateral deafness
- **Tips on the technique of ear irrigation**
  - Consider softening the earwax by using ear drops about 30 minutes before irrigation.
  - An electronic irrigator is safer than a syringe because it provides better control of water pressure and flow direction.
  - Warm the water to body temperature to avoid inducing dizziness and vertigo by stimulating the caloric reflex.
  - Use a nozzle that can be inserted without occluding the ear canal, and that therefore will allow water and wax to flow out without excessive pressure.
  - Ensure that the nozzle is firmly attached to the syringe.
  - Take care not to hurt the person with the tip of the nozzle or by using water pressure that is too high.
  - Straighten the ear canal by pulling the pinna gently up and back.
  - Direct the water flow backwards along the roof of the ear canal.
  - Collect the out-flowing water in a kidney dish under the person's ear.
  - Repeat (up to about six times) if wax remains impacted.
  - When the wax is resistant to initial irrigation attempts, prescribe ear drops to be used several times a day for 3–5 days.

Full descriptions of techniques for ear examination and the use of syringes and electronic irrigators can be found on the ENT Nursing web site: www.entnursing.com.

[Lewis-Cullinan and Janken, 1990; Sharp et al, 1990; Aung and Mulley, 2002; Memel et al, 2002; Bird, 2003]

Other mechanical removal techniques (usually available only in secondary care)

Several other mechanical removal techniques are available, but usually only in secondary care, where they enable impacted wax to be removed under direct vision:
- Ear curettes and forceps
- Microsuction

[Aung and Mulley, 2002]

References

NHS staff in England can link, free of charge, from references to full text journals by clicking on [Full text] on the PRODIGY website.

1. Aung, T. and Mulley, G.P. (2002) Removal of ear wax: 10 minute consultation. *British Medical Journal* **325**(7354), 27–28. [Full text]
2. Bapat, U., Nia, J. and Bance, M. (2001) Severe audiovestibular loss following ear syringing for wax removal. *Journal of Laryngology & Otology* **115**(5), 410–411. [Full text]
3. Bird, S. (2003) Clinical practice: risk management. The potential pitfalls of ear syringing: minimising the risks. *Australian Family Physician* **32**(3), 150–151.
4. BNF 47 (2004) *British National Formulary*. 47th edn. London: British Medical Association and Royal Pharmaceutical Society of Great Britain.
5. Browning, G. (2003) Wax in ear. *Clinical Evidence* **10**(Dec), 490–497.
6. Burton, M.J. and Doree, C.J. (2004) *Ear drops for the removal of ear wax (Cochrane Review)*. The Cochrane Library. Issue 2. Chichester, UK: John Wiley & Sons, Ltd.
7. Grossan, M. (2000) Safe, effective techniques for cerumen removal. *Geriatrics* **55**(1), 80–86. [Full text]
8. Hawke, M. (2002) Update on cerumen and ceruminolytics. *Ear, Nose, & Throat Journal* **81**(8:Suppl 1), S1-S4.
9. Lewis-Cullinan, C. and Janken, J.K. (1990) Effect of cerumen removal on the hearing ability of geriatric patients. *Journal of Advanced Nursing* **15**(5), 594–600.
10. Memel, D., Langley, C., Watkins, C. et al (2002) Effectiveness of ear syringing in general practice: a randomised controlled trial and patients' experiences. *British Journal of General Practice* **52**(484), 906–911.
11. Sharp, J.F., Wilson, J.A., Ross, L. and Barr-Hamlington, R.M. (1990) Ear wax removal: a survey of current practice. *British Medical Journal* **301**(6763), 1251–1253.
12. Somerville, G. (2002) The most effective products available to facilitate ear syringing. *British Journal of Community Nursing* **7**(2), 94–101.
13. Zivic, R.C. and King, S. (1993) Cerumen-impaction management for clients of all ages. *Nurse Practitioner* **18**(3), 29–39.

PRODIGY GUIDANCE

Eating disorders

Last revised in November 2004
www.prodigy.nhs.uk/guidance.asp?gt=Eatingdisorders

Applies to people over the age of 12 years

This guidance is the PRODIGY implementation of the National Institute for Clinical Excellence (NICE) clinical guideline *Eating disorders — core interventions in the treatment and management of anorexia nervosa, bulimia nervosa, and related eating disorders* developed by the National Collaborating Centre for Mental Health (NCCMH) and commissioned by NICE. The NCCMH is funded by NICE and is led by a partnership between the Royal College of Psychiatrists' research unit (College Research Unit — CRU) and the British Psychological Society's equivalent unit (Centre for Outcomes Research and Effectiveness — CORE) [NICE, 2004].

This guidance covers the identification, treatment, and management of the eating disorders anorexia nervosa, bulimia nervosa, and related conditions in primary care.

This guidance does not cover the management of eating disorders associated with a separate physical or other primary mental disorder of which a disorder of eating is a symptom.

There is separate PRODIGY guidance for *Depression*.

Goals

- To identify and refer appropriately people who are showing psychological and physical signs of having an eating disorder

Contents

Scenarios
- Eating disorders p.704

Extended Information, p. 704

Eating disorders

Which therapy?

- Most people with an eating disorder present in primary care. Presenting features are given in the section *How do I know my patient has it?*
- Treatment requires expertise that is usually only available in secondary or tertiary care:
  - Psychological therapies are the treatment of first choice.
  - Pharmacological treatment is recommended as an adjunct for some people; however, initiation in primary care is not recommended.
- The role of primary care is therefore diagnosis and referral to the appropriate specialist for treatment.

Follow-up advice

- Follow-up will usually be provided by secondary care services.
- People with enduring anorexia nervosa not under the care of a secondary care service should be offered an annual physical and mental health review by their GP.

Should I refer or investigate?

Refer?

- **Referral of all people with an eating disorder to secondary care is recommended.** It is recognized, however, that at the present time there are wide variations in the provision of eating disorder service throughout the UK. Services range from outpatient treatment provided by community mental health teams, to specialist eating disorder units.

Investigate?

- **Anorexia nervosa** — laboratory investigations are not usually required for diagnosis. Most tests remain normal even with extreme weight loss and are a poor guide to physical risk.
- **Bulimia nervosa** — laboratory investigations are not usually required for diagnosis. If undertaken, they reveal abnormalities in about 10% of people with bulimia nervosa; these commonly include dehydration, hypokalaemia, hypochloraemia, and alkalosis. These abnormalities settle with the cessation of vomiting and the misuse of laxatives and diuretics.

Patient information leaflets

The following PILs are available at www.prodigy.nhs.uk
- Anorexia & Bulimia Care - ABC
- Anorexia Nervosa
- Bulimia Nervosa

Drug rationale

- No prescriptions are offered.

Extended Information

Background information

- What is it? p.704
- How common is it? p.705
- How do I know my patient has it? p.705
- What else might it be? p.706
- Complications and prognosis p.706

What is it?

Anorexia nervosa

- Anorexia nervosa is a syndrome in which the individual maintains a low bodyweight as a result of a preoccupation with weight, construed as either a fear of fatness or a pursuit of thinness.
- Weight is maintained at least 15% below the expected.

- In adults this represents a body mass index (BMI) of below 17.5 kg/m².
- In younger people, the diagnosis may be made in those who fail to gain weight during the expected growth spurt of puberty — they can become underweight without losing weight.

- Weight loss is self-induced by avoidance of foods thought to be fattening. One or more of the following may also be present:
  - Self-induced vomiting
  - Self-induced purging
  - Excessive exercise
  - Use of appetite suppressants
  - Use of diuretics
- Body image is distorted, with a dread of fatness.
- There is a widespread endocrine disorder involving the hypothalamic–pituitary–gonadal axis. This manifests in women as amenorrhoea, in men as loss of libido and potency, and before puberty as delayed puberty with stunted growth and physical development.

Bulimia nervosa

- Bulimia nervosa is characterized firstly by recurrent episodes of binge eating, and secondly by compensatory behaviour (any one or a combination of vomiting, purging, fasting, or excessive exercise) in order to prevent weight gain. Misuse of laxatives, diuretics, thyroxine, amphetamines, or other medication may occur.
- There is controversy over the diagnostic category for bulimia nervosa:
  - The World Health Organization stresses that purging behaviour (which encompasses self-induced vomiting and laxative misuse) should be categorized as bulimia nervosa.
  - The DSM-IV criteria distinguish between this type of behaviour and the non-purging type (i.e. excessive exercise and fasting).
- BMI is maintained above 17.5 kg/m².
- There is often a history of an earlier episode of anorexia nervosa.
- There is a morbid dread of fatness, with a sharply defined weight threshold set by the individual.

Atypical eating disorders

- These are defined as eating disorders which closely resemble anorexia nervosa or bulimia nervosa, but do not meet the precise diagnostic criteria for them. For example:
  - The person's weight may be just above the diagnostic threshold for anorexia nervosa.
  - Although the BMI is less than 17.5 kg/m², the woman may still be menstruating.
  - Binge eating and purging may occur less frequently than specified for a diagnosis of bulimia nervosa.
- Many people with atypical eating disorders have suffered with anorexia or bulimia nervosa in the past.
- They are also known as eating disorders not otherwise specified, and include binge eating.

Binge eating

- This is a recently described condition. Individuals engage in uncontrollable episodes of binge eating, but do not use compensatory purging behaviours. Binge eating episodes are associated with three or more of the following:
  - Eating more rapidly than normal.
  - Eating until feeling uncomfortably full.
  - Eating large amounts of food when not physically hungry.
  - Eating alone through embarrassment at the amount one is eating.
  - Feeling disgust or extreme guilt after overeating.

How common is it?

Anorexia nervosa

- The incidence of anorexia nervosa is 19 per 100,000 per year in females, and 2 per 100,000 per year in males.
- Female teenagers (aged between 13 and 19 years) showed the highest rates at 51 cases per 100,000 per year.
- The mean age of onset is 16–17 years.
- Anorexia nervosa is thought to be extremely rare in developing countries and black populations.

Bulimia nervosa

- Bulimia nervosa is more common in females (accounting for 90% of cases), affecting between 0.5% and 1.0% of young women, with an even social class distribution.
- The mean age of onset is 18–19 years.
- The full syndrome is rarely seen in young people below the age of 14 years.

Binge eating

- The prevalence of binge eating is more difficult to gauge because of the variability in the definition of this condition; it lies between 1% and 79%, depending on the definitions used.
- The onset of binge eating is usually in the teenage years or early 20s, but people may not present until later, typically in their 30s and 40s.
- The sex ratio is more evenly distributed than in other eating disorders.

How do I know my patient has it?

General points about diagnosing eating disorders

- The diagnosis of an eating disorder is made on the basis of the history. This is supported, where possible, by corroboration from a relative or friend.
- Eating disorders may be difficult to detect, as individuals are slow to present. The main obstacle to diagnosis is the person's own willingness or otherwise to disclose his or her motives, symptoms, and behaviours.
- People with an eating disorder do, however, present to primary care more frequently than controls. These presentations are particularly with psychological, gastrointestinal, and gynaecological problems.
- Healthcare professionals should be alert to the possibility of an eating disorder.

Anorexia nervosa

- **The first contact with primary care** is often made by a concerned family member, friend, or schoolteacher rather than the individual. Typical features that lead to this concern are:
  - Weight loss
  - Skipping meals, hiding food, or a restrictive diet
  - Mood changes
  - Altered sleep patterns
  - Increased activity
- **People with anorexia nervosa often present with non-specific physical symptoms:**
  - Abdominal pain
  - Amenorrhoea
  - Bloating
  - Constipation
  - Cold intolerance
  - Growth failure (in children)

  - Hair, nail, or skin changes
  - Light-headedness
- **Weight is maintained at least 15% below the expected.**
  - In adults this represents a BMI of below 17.5 kg/m^2.
  - In those under 18 years of age, BMI centile charts should be used, a cut-off of below the 2.4th centile indicating underweight.
- **Weight loss is self-induced** by avoidance of foods thought to be fattening. One or more of the following may also be present:
  - Self-induced vomiting
  - Self-induced purging
  - Excessive exercise
  - Use of appetite suppressants
  - Use of diuretics
- **Typical psychological features** (although these may be denied) include:
  - Denial of the seriousness of the weight loss or its consequences.
  - Disturbance in evaluating bodyweight or shape.
  - Fear of gaining weight or becoming fat, despite being underweight.
  - Preoccupation with shape- or weight-related matters.
  - Undue influence of eating or change in bodyweight on self-evaluation.
- **Laboratory investigations** are not usually required for diagnosis. Most tests remain normal even with extreme weight loss, and are a poor guide to physical risk.
- **Physical assessment** is to determine the presence and severity of emaciation, and physical consequences, rather than to aid diagnosis.
- **There are established risk factors** for the development of anorexia nervosa:
  - Family history of an eating disorder
  - Type 1 diabetes
  - Previous overweight
  - Occupation (e.g. athlete, dancer, model)

Bulimia nervosa

- A person with bulimia nervosa is more likely to be older, and to consult alone, than one with anorexia nervosa.
- There may be a history of previous anorexia nervosa, of unhappiness with weight, and of attempts to diet. There may be a request for help with weight loss.
- **People with bulimia nervosa commonly report more physical complaints than those with anorexia nervosa when they present.** Common symptoms are:
  - Abdominal pain
  - Bloating
  - Constipation
  - Diarrhoea
  - Fatigue
  - Irregular periods
  - Lethargy
  - Oesophagitis
  - Rectal prolapse
  - Sore throat
  - Swollen hands and feet
- **Typical psychological features** (although these may be denied) include:
  - Episodes of binge eating and purging associated with extreme guilt and shame.
  - Episodes of binge eating associated with loss of control over eating.
  - Morbid dread of fatness, with a sharply defined weight threshold set by the individual.
  - Preoccupation with thoughts of food (shopping, eating, and purging).
- **Mood disturbance is common in people with bulimia nervosa,** most frequently symptoms of anxiety and tension. Self-harm (commonly scratching or cutting) is common.
- **BMI is maintained above 17.5 kg/m^2.** There are recurrent episodes of binge eating, with compensatory behaviour in order to prevent weight gain:
  - Excessive exercise
  - Fasting
  - Misuse of laxatives, diuretics, thyroxine, or amphetamines
  - Purging
  - Vomiting
- **Examination is often normal.** However, the following signs may be found:
  - Calluses on the back of the hand (Russell's sign, from self-induced vomiting).
  - Enlarged salivary glands (particularly the parotids).
  - Erosion of dental enamel, mainly the lingual surface of the upper teeth.
  - Oedema (following abrupt withdrawal of laxatives or diuretics).
- **Laboratory investigations** reveal abnormalities in about 10% of people with bulimia nervosa; these commonly include:
  - Dehydration
  - Hypokalaemia
  - Hypochloraemia
  - Alkalosis

What else might it be?

- Other causes of weight loss:
  - Diabetes
  - Malabsorption
  - Neoplasm
  - Infection, e.g. tuberculosis
  - Hyperthyroidism
  - Autoimmune disease
- Other causes of amenorrhoea:
  - Pregnancy
  - Primary ovarian failure
  - Polycystic ovary syndrome
- Other psychological problems:
  - Depression
  - Obsessive–compulsive disorder
  - Somatization

Complications and prognosis

Complications

Anorexia nervosa

Physical

- Starvation affects every system in the body:
  - **Musculoskeletal system** — weakness, loss of muscle strength (including heart muscle), loss of bone density (with an increased risk of fractures in later life), and impairment of linear growth.
  - **Endocrine system** — low luteinizing hormone, follicle-stimulating hormone, suppressed thyroid-stimulating hormone, growth hormone resistance, and raised cortical levels. If pubertal development has not been completed, secondary sexual characteristics may not fully develop, and permanent stunting of growth is common.
  - **Reproductive system** — infertility, risk of polycystic ovaries. There is a higher risk of premature delivery and babies that are small for gestational age.
  - **Brain volume** — this is reduced and may be a permanent deficit despite full recovery from the eating disorder. People with eating disorders score greater than one standard deviation from the norm on tests of perceptual rigidity, preservation, and set shifting, and

may have the neurological sign dysdiadochokinesis. There may also be short- and long-term effects on cognitive functioning in children.
- Morbidity and mortality from coronary heart disease is increased.
- Death — people with anorexia nervosa have an almost 10-fold increased risk of dying compared to healthy people of the same age and sex.

Social and emotional

- **Emotional difficulties** leading to a range of physical and social problems, including becoming unable to adequately care for oneself, stopping leisure activities, interrupting educational goals, and losing personal autonomy.
- **Depression** is a common comorbid diagnosis (found to be as high as 63% in some studies). Obsessive–compulsive disorder has been found to be present in 35% of people.

Bulimia nervosa

Physical

- There is considerable overlap between the long-term disabling consequences of bulimia nervosa and those of anorexia nervosa.
- **Dental erosion** is the most common problem and is due to the frequent exposure of the dental enamel to the gastric acid. Teeth may become discoloured and change shape. There may also be tooth sensitivity and high levels of dental caries.
- **Loss of the gag reflex** and gastro-oesophageal reflux may occur. Frequent and severe vomiting may cause more serious complications such as oesophagitis, oesophageal tears, and perforation.
- Rarely, gastric dilatation may occur that poses the risk of gastric rupture and death.
- Long-term excessive laxative abuse can reduce the motility of the colon, resulting in constipation and an atonic cathartic colon.
- Fluid and electrolyte disturbances may occur as a result of laxative or diuretic abuse. The most common are dehydration, hypokalaemia, hypochloraemia, and alkalosis. Dehydration can cause volume depletion and consequently low blood pressure and a rapid pulse. Individuals may complain of dizziness because of orthostatic hypotension and weakness. Renal function can also be affected. Secondary hypoaldosteronism can lead to rebound fluid retention and peripheral oedema when laxatives and diuretics are withdrawn.
- Fasting and binge eating can also lead to high levels of insulin release with large fluctuations in blood sugar. There may also be abnormal levels of tryptophan, the precursor for serotonin. This may disrupt appetite control mechanisms and utilization and deposition of energy. There is also a suggestion that tryptophan (and hence serotonin) depletion may lead to increased irritability, depressed mood, increased rating in body image concern, and subjective loss of control of eating in people who have recovered from bulimia nervosa.
- Morbidity and mortality from coronary heart disease is increased.

Social and emotional

- Estimates of the prevalence of personality disorder in people with bulimia nervosa have ranged from 21% to 77%. Obsessive compulsive and avoidant personality disorders have been frequently described.

Atypical eating disorders

- Where atypical eating disorders are similar to the full syndromes of anorexia and bulimia nervosa, the physical dangers and psychosocial impairments closely resemble those of the diagnostic conditions.

Prognosis

Anorexia nervosa

- The course of anorexia nervosa is very variable. There is no good evidence on the prognosis of people with anorexia nervosa who do not access formal medical care.
- A summary of 68 treatment studies published before 1989 with a length of follow-up of between 1 and 33 years found that 43% of people recover completely, 36% improve, 20% develop a chronic eating disorder, and 5% die from anorexia nervosa.
- The vast majority of longer-term follow-up studies indicate that people with anorexia nervosa have an almost 10-fold increased risk of dying compared to healthy people of the same age and sex. The all-cause standard mortality ratio for anorexia nervosa has been estimated at 9.6% (95% CI 7.8 to 11.5), about three times higher than for other psychiatric illnesses.
- The average annual risk of mortality has been calculated at 0.59% per year in females.
- The mortality rate appears to be higher for people with lower weight during their illness, and for those presenting between 20 and 29 years of age.
- A BMI of less than 13 kg/m^2 in adults indicates a greater mortality risk.
- Among studies in which the cause of death is recorded, 54% of people died of eating disorder complications (i.e. malnutrition or methods of weight control), 27% committed suicide, and 19% died of unknown causes or other causes. Prolonged QT intervals may predispose a person to life-threatening arrhythmias and might be responsible for cases of sudden death.
- Some people with anorexia nervosa progress to other eating disorders, particularly bulimia nervosa.

Bulimia nervosa

- There have been few studies with a long follow-up period of the course and outcome of bulimia nervosa. Many people with bulimia nervosa are not receiving any help, and most of these will suffer a chronic or a relapsing course.
- With the most effective treatments, 50% of people can be expected to be asymptomatic between 2 and 10 years after assessment. About 20% are likely to continue with the full form of the illness. About 30% have a course of illness characterized by either remissions or relapses, or develop an atypical eating disorder (i.e. they have features of bulimia nervosa but do not fulfil the diagnostic criteria).
- The mortality rate associated with bulimia is uncertain.

Atypical eating disorders

- The prognosis depends largely on the severity of associated physical and psychological features. Sometimes there is movement between one diagnosis and another. Thus those with atypical eating disorder may go on to develop bulimia nervosa, or more rarely anorexia nervosa.

Binge eating disorder

- Those with binge eating disorder typically give long histories of being prone to binge eating, but these may alternate with extended periods free from binge eating. The spontaneous remission rate may be high.
- Short-term response rate appears to be better than for anorexia nervosa and bulimia nervosa, but there are no studies of long-term outcome.

E

Management issues

- Overview p.708
- What is the role of primary care? p.708
- How should anorexia nervosa be managed? p.708
- How should bulimia nervosa be managed? p.709
- How should atypical eating disorders be managed? p.710
- How should binge eating disorder be managed? p.710

Overview

- **Psychological therapies are the treatment of first choice for an eating disorder.**
- **Pharmacological treatment is recommended as an adjunct for some people:**
  - In anorexia nervosa, medication has been found to be disappointing in affecting symptoms, weight, or associated mood disturbance. There are considerable adverse effects (people with anorexia are particularly at risk of cardiac arrhythmias). It has been concluded that medication offers little advantage when added to standard treatment with psychological therapies.
  - In bulimia nervosa and binge eating disorder, whilst medication is not recommended first line, there is some evidence that antidepressants (particularly selective serotonin reuptake inhibitors) contribute to the cessation of binge eating and purging.
  - In atypical eating disorders, there is little evidence to guide treatment. It is recommended to follow the guidance for that condition which most closely resembles the person's eating disorder.
- Many people with an eating disorder are ambivalent about treatment, with consequent demands and challenges for the healthcare workers involved (C).

What is the role of primary care?

- **Most people with an eating disorder present in primary care. Treatment, however, requires expertise that is usually only available in secondary or tertiary care. The role of primary care is therefore diagnosis and referral to the appropriate specialist for treatment:**
  - Diagnosis is discussed in the section *How do I know my patient has it?*
  - **Referral of all people with an eating disorder to secondary care is recommended.** It is recognized, however, that at the present time there are wide variations in the provision of eating disorder service throughout the UK. Services range from outpatient treatment provided by community mental health teams, to specialist eating disorder units.
- People with enduring anorexia nervosa not under the care of a secondary care service should be offered an annual physical and mental health review by their GP (C).

How should anorexia nervosa be managed?

- Many people with anorexia nervosa find it hard to acknowledge that they have a problem and are ambivalent about change. They may place a high value on some of their symptoms and deny the potentially life-threatening nature of their disorder.
- Most people with anorexia nervosa should be managed on an outpatient basis, with psychological treatment (with physical monitoring) provided by a healthcare professional competent to give it and to assess the physical risk of people with eating disorders (C). However, a substantial minority receive inpatient treatment.
- Outpatient psychological treatment for anorexia nervosa should normally be of at least 6 months' duration (C). If there is any deterioration during this time or the completion of an adequate course of outpatient psychological treatment does not lead to significant improvement, more intensive forms of treatment (for example, a move from individual therapy to combined individual and family work; or day care or inpatient care) should be considered (C).
- The therapeutic involvement of siblings and other family members should be considered in all cases because of the effects of anorexia nervosa on other family members (C).
- Dietary counselling should not be provided as the sole treatment for anorexia nervosa (C).
- Body mass index is a better marker than weight alone as a proxy measure of physical risk, but a rigid cut off point is less good for the extremes of height as the relationship is non-linear.
- Regular monitoring of height as well as weight is important in children and adolescents with anorexia nervosa. Recommended weight ranges have to be regularly adjusted to take into account changes in height and age.
- If laxative abuse is present, this should be reduced gradually, and the person informed that laxative use does not reduce calorie absorption (C). Abrupt cessation can result in reflex fluid and sodium retention.

What is the role of psychological treatments in anorexia nervosa?

- The aims of psychological treatment are: (C)
  - To reduce risk.
  - To encourage weight gain and healthy eating.
  - To reduce other symptoms related to an eating disorder.
  - To facilitate psychological and physical recovery.
- Various forms of psychological treatment are associated with improvements in terms of weight gain and recovery; the long-term benefits, however, may not be sustained.
- Therapies to be considered for the psychological treatment of anorexia nervosa include cognitive analytic therapy, cognitive behaviour therapy, interpersonal psychotherapy, focal psychodynamic therapy, and family interventions focused explicitly on eating disorders (C).
- The focus of treatment should be on weight gain, healthy eating, and reducing other symptoms related to eating disorders.

What is the role of pharmacological treatments in anorexia nervosa?

- There is limited evidence for pharmacological treatments, and medication should not be used as the primary treatment for anorexia nervosa. Many people with anorexia nervosa have compromised cardiovascular function.
- Drugs that have been studied have not shown any significant benefit in terms of weight gain, relapse of clinical deterioration, acceptability, or tolerability. Drugs that have been studied in the treatment of anorexia nervosa are:
  - Antidepressants — tricyclic antidepressants (amitriptyline, clomipramine) and selective serotonin reuptake inhibitors (fluoxetine, citalopram)
  - Antihistamines (cyproheptadine)
  - Antipsychotics (pimozide, sulpiride)
- There may be no need to use medication for comorbid conditions such as depressive or obsessive–compulsive features as they may resolve with weight gain alone.
- All patients with a diagnosis of anorexia nervosa should have an alert placed in their prescribing record concerning the risk of adverse effects (C).

When should people with anorexia nervosa receive inpatient care?

- This should be considered for people with anorexia nervosa whose disorder has not improved with appropriate outpatient treatment, or for whom there is a significant risk of suicide or severe self-harm, or whose disorder is associated with high or moderate physical risk (C).
- In the UK, people with anorexia nervosa are often not admitted for inpatient treatment until the body mass index falls below 13 kg/m^2 or weight loss is greater than 20%. Here, the goal is full weight recovery and so admissions are longer-term. Managing such low-weight patients can be hazardous in an outpatient setting and should rarely be done without specialist advice.
- Compulsory admission may sometimes be required. Advice from an appropriate specialist should be sought in this situation.

How should physical complications and coexisting disease be managed in anorexia nervosa?

Weight gain

- A number of complications can occur during refeeding due to electrolyte abnormalities (the 'refeeding syndrome'), and thus physical monitoring is necessary. People most at risk are those with a body mass index of 12 kg/m^2 or less; those who vomit, abuse laxatives, and binge; and those with concurrent physical conditions. Hypophosphataemia may develop rapidly during refeeding, and if severe can cause cardiac and respiratory failure, delirium, and fits.
- In the first few weeks of refeeding, in patients who have had very low or absent intake for long periods, no attempt should be made to achieve a net weight gain. Instead they should receive energy and protein provision at levels at or less than their estimated basal requirements, with generous provision of balanced multi-vitamins and minerals, especially thiamine, potassium, magnesium, and phosphate.
- There is controversy, but little evidence, about the appropriate time course to achieve the goals of treatment. Some argue it is important to restore normal weight as soon as possible, others argue for a slower weight increase.
- In most people an average weekly weight gain of 0.5–1.0 kg for inpatients, and 0.5 kg for outpatients should be the aim of treatment. This requires about 3500–7000 extra calories a week (C).
- Total parenteral nutrition should not be used for people with anorexia nervosa, unless there is significant gastrointestinal dysfunction (C).

Osteoporosis and osteopenia

- The development of osteopenia and osteoporosis is a serious and long-term consequence of starvation. Oestrogen deficiency, malnutrition, low body mass, and hyperactivity all play a part in its development. Reduced bone mineral density is associated with an increased fracture rate and long-term disability such as pain, kyphosis, and loss of height. Osteoporosis is manifest in some people after a year of anorexia, and the severity increases over time if the illness remains untreated.
- In a study of adults (mean age 22 years) with severe anorexia (mean body mass index 13.9 kg/m^2) followed over 2 years (during which time body mass index increased to 17.1 kg/m^2) there was an overall 2% increase in bone density which related to weight gain.
- Full recovery from anorexia nervosa, with weight gain and return of menstruation, leads to a marked increase in bone density. However, in those that remain underweight with amenorrhoea, bone loss continues (III).
- The most effective treatment/preventative agent for osteoporosis in anorexia nervosa is not yet known. Adequate nutrition and weight are the most relevant factors but in some cases this is difficult to implement in the long term. Therefore there has been some interest in actively managing and preventing osteoporosis. Treatment agents include oestrogen (in the form of hormone replacement therapy or the contraceptive pill), which inhibits bone resorption; vitamin D; calcium; insulin-like growth factor (IGF); and dehydroepiandrosterone (DHEA). Bisphosphonates and fluoride have also been tried. Hormonal treatments have not been evaluated in adolescents with anorexia nervosa; there is a risk that oestrogen administration may cause premature epiphyseal fusion and stunt growth.

Diabetes

- Treatment of an eating disorder in people with diabetes is essential because of the greatly increased physical risk in this group (C).
- Patients with Type 1 diabetes and an eating disorder should have intensive regular physical monitoring as they are at high risk of retinopathy and other complications (C).

Reproductive system

- In adolescent anorexia nervosa there is a risk of pubertal delay and ultimately arrested pubertal development.

Pregnancy and the postnatal period

- It is unusual for women with anorexia nervosa to become pregnant.
- Pregnant women with either current or remitted anorexia nervosa should be considered for more intensive prenatal care to ensure adequate prenatal nutrition and fetal development (C).

How should bulimia nervosa be managed?

- Most people with bulimia nervosa are treated on an outpatient basis unless there is severe psychiatric comorbidity or physical complications.

What is the role of psychological treatments in bulimia nervosa?

- Cognitive behaviour therapy for bulimia nervosa (CBT-BN), a specifically adapted form of CBT, should be offered to adults with bulimia nervosa. The course of treatment should be for 16–20 sessions over 4–5 months (**A**).
- Interpersonal psychotherapy should be considered as an alternative to CBT, but people should be informed it takes 8–12 months to achieve results comparable with cognitive behaviour therapy (**B**).
- When people with bulimia nervosa have not responded to or do not want CBT, other psychological treatments should be considered (**B**).
- As a possible first step, people with bulimia nervosa should be encouraged to follow an evidence-based self-help programme (**B**).

What is the role of pharmacological treatments in bulimia nervosa?

- Drugs are not as acceptable or as well tolerated as psychological treatments in people with bulimia nervosa. Only short-term effects have been studied, and trials of pharmacological and psychological treatments are difficult to compare.
- As an alternative or additional first step to using an evidence-based self-help programme, adults with bulimia nervosa may be offered a trial of an antidepressant (**B**). Selective serotonin reuptake inhibitors (specifically

fluoxetine) are the only drugs recommended. The licensed dose of fluoxetine is 60–80 mg once daily (i.e. higher than for depression). It can reduce the frequency of binge eating and purging, but the long-term effects are unknown. Any beneficial effect will be rapidly apparent. It is often found that any beneficial effect is poorly sustained.
- Very few drugs are recommended for children and adolescents less than 18 years old.

When should people with bulimia nervosa receive inpatient care?

- Special inpatient programmes for the treatment of bulimia nervosa are unusual in the UK.
- For people with bulimia nervosa who are at risk of suicide or self-harm, admission as an inpatient or a day patient or the provision of more intensive outpatient care should be considered (C).
- Psychiatric admission for people with bulimia nervosa should normally be undertaken in a setting with experience of managing this disorder (C).

How should physical complications and coexisting disease be managed in bulimia nervosa?

Electrolyte disturbances

- Patients with bulimia nervosa who are vomiting frequently or taking large quantities of laxatives (especially if they are also underweight) should have their fluid and electrolyte balance assessed (C).
- Common disturbances are dehydration, hypokalaemia, hypochloraemia, and alkalosis.
- When electrolyte disturbance is detected, it is usually sufficient to focus on eliminating the behaviour responsible. In the small proportion of cases where supplementation is required to restore electrolyte imbalance, oral rather than intravenous administration is recommended, unless there are problems with gastrointestinal absorption (C).
- If laxative abuse is present, this should be reduced gradually, and the person informed that laxative use does not reduce calorie absorption (C). Abrupt cessation can result in reflex fluid and sodium retention.

Dental problems

- Dental erosion is the most common oral problem in people who make themselves vomit. It is important that clinicians advise patients on dental consequences and refer them to a dentist. Dental practitioners are advised to monitor dental erosion, to offer advice and provide treatment to prevent further erosion and improve appearance. Although any advice will aim to limit vomiting, patients should also be advised:
  - That brushing teeth after vomiting should be avoided as it may increase tooth damage.
  - That mouth rinsing after vomiting with water and sodium bicarbonate (or other non-acid mouth wash) will neutralize the acid environment. If this is not possible finishing meals with alkaline foods (milk or cheese) will help.
  - To visit the dentist regularly.
  - That fluoride mouth rinses and toothpastes may be helpful for desensitization.
- A high intake of acidic foods and drinks may increase dental erosion. These should be limited to meal times only and avoided last thing at night. Prolonged sipping, holding acidic beverages in the mouth, and 'frothing' before swallowing should all be avoided. Chewing sugar-free gum after meals will stimulate salivary flow.

Diabetes

- Women with Type 1 diabetes have an increased risk of bulimia nervosa, and poor adherence to insulin treatment is frequent in individuals with Type 1 diabetes. This comorbidity complicates psychological interventions. Psychoeducation may have some limited benefit on eating disorder symptoms but not on diabetic control. In the management of people with bulimia nervosa and Type 1 diabetes, close liaison and a shared knowledge base between the eating disorder and diabetes teams is essential.
- Treatment of an eating disorder in people with diabetes is essential because of the greatly increased physical risk in this group (C).
- People with Type 1 diabetes and an eating disorder should have intensive regular physical monitoring as they are at high risk of retinopathy and other complications (C).

Pregnancy and the postnatal period

- Pregnant women with eating disorders require careful monitoring throughout the pregnancy and the post-partum period (C).
- Most pregnant women with bulimia nervosa will have an uneventful pregnancy. For some, the post-partum period can present considerable challenges. The following points should be considered:
  - Women with bulimia nervosa may have more complications during pregnancy and the children are smaller at birth.
  - They may also have problematic interactions feeding their infants and children.
  - They tend to be more concerned about their child's weight and shape.
  - They tend to have more problematic interactions with their children.

How should atypical eating disorders be managed?

- In the absence of evidence to guide the management of atypical eating disorders other than binge eating disorder, it is recommended that the clinician considers following guidance on the treatment of the eating problem that most closely resembles the individual patient's eating disorder (C).

How should binge eating disorder be managed?

- In patients with binge eating disorder there is an apparently good short-term response to a range of psychological interventions including self-help. Given the lower level of acute physical and psychiatric risk compared with anorexia and bulimia nervosa, treatment of binge eating disorder may be deliverable in primary care through the use of evidence-based self-help manuals (B).
- Cognitive behaviour therapy for binge eating disorder (CBT-BED), a specifically adapted form of CBT, should be offered to people with persistent binge eating disorder (A).
- Other psychological treatments (interpersonal psychotherapy for binge eating disorder and modified dialectical behaviour therapy) may be offered to adults with persistent binge eating disorder (B).
- People should be informed that all psychological treatments for binge eating disorder have a limited effect on bodyweight (A).
- As an alternative, or additional first step to using an evidence-based self-help programme, consideration should be given to offering a trial of a selective serotonin reuptake inhibitor (SSRI) antidepressant drug (B).
- The use of an SSRI can reduce binge eating, but the long-term effects are unknown. An antidepressant may be sufficient treatment for a limited subset of people (B).

References

1. NICE (2004) *Eating disorders: core interventions in the treatment and management of anorexia nervosa, bulimia nervosa and related eating disorders*. Clinical guideline CG9. National Institute for Clinical Excellence. www.nice.org.uk [Accessed: 30/01/2004].

Evidence grading

Evidence grading is from the National Institute of Clinical Excellence guideline *Eating disorders*, January 2004. The definitions of grades of recommendation used in this guideline are as follows:

Grade	Evidence
A	At least one randomized controlled trial as part of a body of literature of overall good quality and consistency addressing the specific recommendation without extrapolation.
B	Well-conducted clinical studies but no randomized clinical trials on eating disorders (evidence levels II or III); or extrapolated form level I evidence.
C	Expert committee reports or opinions and/or clinical experiences of respected authorities (evidence level IV) or extrapolated from level I or II evidence. This grading indicates that directly applicable clinical studies of good quality are absent, or not readily available.

Level	Type of evidence
I	Evidence obtained from a single randomized controlled trial or a meta-analysis of randomized controlled trials.
IIa	Evidence obtained from at least one well-designed controlled study without randomization.
IIb	Evidence obtained from at least one other well-designed quasi-experimental study.
III	Evidence obtained from well-designed non experimental descriptive studies, such as comparative studies, correlation studies and case-control studies.
IV	Expert committee reports or opinions and/or clinical experiences of respected authorities (evidence level IV) or extrapolated from level I or II evidence. This grading indicates that directly applicable clinical studies of good quality are absent, or not readily available.

E

PRODIGY GUIDANCE

Eczema — atopic

Last revised in November 2004
www.prodigy.nhs.uk/guidance.asp?gt=Eczema - atopic

Applies to people over the age of 1 month

This guidance covers the assessment and management of atopic eczema in primary care.

This guidance does not cover the detailed management of second-line treatments for atopic eczema that can be managed by a healthcare professional with specialist expertise e.g. a general practitioner with a specialist interest in dermatology.

There is separate PRODIGY guidance for *Dermatitis — contact* and *Seborrhoeic dermatitis*.

E

Goals

- To treat atopic eczema in primary care with first-line treatments
- To identify factors triggering atopic eczema
- To refer people appropriately who require assessment and treatment by a specialist

Contents

Scenarios
- Dry skin — starting treatment p.712
- Dry skin — maintenance treatment p.714
- Localized flare-up p.717
- Widespread flare-up p.720
- Chronic lichenified eczema p.723
- Widespread flare-up — severe p.726

Extended Information, p. 727

Which scenario?

- **Dry skin — starting treatment:** covers the initial management of dry skin and provides advice on selecting appropriate products.
- **Dry skin — maintenance treatment:** covers the continuing management of dry skin.
- **Localized flare-up:** covers the management of acute localised flare-ups of atopic eczema.
- **Widespread flare-up:** covers the management of an acute widespread flare-up of atopic eczema. If the widespread flare-up is severe or is not responding well to topical corticosteroids of an appropriate strength, see scenario *Widespread flare-up — severe/not responding*.
- **Chronic lichenified eczema:** covers the management of lichenified lesions.
- **Widespread flare-up — severe:** covers the management of a severe widespread flare-up of atopic eczema that is severe or is not responding well to topical corticosteroids of an appropriate strength.

Dry skin — starting treatment

Which therapy?

Select an emollient

- **For hairy skin** — prescribe a lotion.
- **For weeping eczema** — prescribe a cream.
- **For mildly dry skin** — prescribe a cream or a lotion.
- **For moderate to severely dry skin, determine the person's preferred product by:**
    - **Explaining to the person** that effectiveness of emollients depends on their lipid content, the frequency of application, and the quantity applied.
    - **Explaining** that creams will need to be used more frequently and/or more generously than ointments to have the same effect.
    - **Ideally, prescribing small quantities of a selection of creams and ointments** to find the most acceptable treatment to the person. Where prescription charges apply, it may be cheaper for the person to buy the emollients.
- **Prescribe a bath emollient** for anyone with moderate, severe, or widespread dry skin. This can be either a purpose-made product or an ointment dispersed in the bath water.

Advise on avoiding environmental irritants

- Use an emollient soap substitute.
- Use gloves when unable to avoid handling irritants such as detergents.
- Avoid extremes of temperature and humidity.
- Use non-abrasive fabrics for clothing, such as cotton.
- Reapply emollients after wetting skin.

Practical prescribing points

For further information please see the *Medicines Compendium* (www.medicines.org.uk) or the *British National Formulary* (www.bnf.org).

- **Bath emollients create a slippery surface in the bath and on surrounding non-slip surfaces.** Users and family members need to take extra care in the bathroom, and the bath should be cleaned thoroughly after use to reduce the risk of slipping. A bath mat or hand rails may be useful.
- **Reactions to emollients** are most commonly due to preservatives, fragrances, lanolin, or arachis oil. If such a reaction is suspected, the person should switch to a product with different constituents. See Table 1 in *Management issues/What are the adverse effects of emollients, and how are they managed?*
- **Some emollients are classified as borderline substances** and can only be prescribed when endorsed as ACBS (Advisory Committee on Borderline Substances. These include: E45® lotion and bath oil; and Aveeno® cream, lotion and bath oil.

Follow-up advice

- **Review after a trial of treatment** and prescribe generous quantities of the product that is most acceptable to the person. More than one type of product may be required.
- **If treatment is not effective,** consider stepping up treatment by any or all of the following:

- Changing the emollient to one with a higher lipid content if that is tolerable (lotion to cream, or cream to ointment).
- Increasing the frequency of application.
- Increasing the quantity of emollient applied.
- **If the treatment is effective but not well tolerated,** consider stepping down treatment by any or all of the following:
  - Changing the emollient to one with a lower lipid content.
  - Reducing the frequency of application.
  - Reducing the quantity of emollient applied.

Should I refer or investigate?

Refer?

- Referral is rarely necessary for individuals with atopic eczema and dry skin without an acute flare-up.
- Consider if the diagnosis is uncertain.

Investigate?

- Investigations are rarely needed to establish a diagnosis of atopic eczema.
- Estimation of immunoglobulin E (IgE) and specific radioallergosorbant tests (RASTs) serve only to confirm the atopic nature of the individual, and are occasionally of value in confirming adult-onset eczema.

Patient information leaflets

The following PILs are available at www.prodigy.nhs.uk

- Eczema - Atopic
- Eczema - Emollients (Moisturisers)
- Eczema - Triggers and Irritants
- National Eczema Society
- Skin Care Campaign

Shared decision making

- **Emollients (moisturizers)** help to prevent flare-ups of eczema.
- **Apply liberally as often as you need** — commonly 2–3 times per day.
- **Many people use a variety of emollients.** For example:
  - A bath or shower additive for a background 'oiling' (but they make the bath slippery — be careful).
  - A thick ointment as a soap substitute.
  - A cream or ointment at other times.
    - Ointments work better and longer than creams do, but are messier to use.
    - Creams for mild dry skin, or for weepy eczema.
  - Lotions for hairy areas.
  - An ointment at bedtime.
- **Rarely, some people become sensitised to an ingredient in an emollient.**
- **Try to avoid skin irritants:**
  - Avoid normal soaps, bubble baths, etc.
  - Wear cotton clothes or other smooth fabrics next to the skin.
  - Avoid getting too hot or too cold.
  - Wear gloves when handling irritants such as detergents.
  - Reapply emollients after wetting skin.

Drug rationale

Many emollients are available and there is little evidence to support the use of one particular product over another. Emollients offered have been selected on the basis of their common usage and relative cost. However, some people may find that other preparations are more suitable for their personal needs.

Drugs not included

- **Emollients containing antiseptic agents,** such as triclosan and benzalkonium chloride have failed to show clearly enough that they improve clinical symptoms or reduce the load of *Staphylococcus aureus*. They may cause allergic contact dermatitis [DTB, 1998].
- **Emollients containing urea** are not offered; they should be reserved for use when standard emollients have proved ineffective [MeReC, 1998].
- **Emollients containing antipruritic agents,** such as lauromacrogols, are not offered. Evidence of additional benefits over standard emollients is limited [MeReC, 1998].

E

Drugs included

Small pack sizes of emollient are recommended at first on a trial basis; if they prove effective and acceptable to the person with dry skin, then larger pack sizes are recommended (see separate scenario *Dry skin — maintenance treatment*).

- **Ointments: emulsifying, hydrous, liquid and soft paraffin, Epaderm®, and Hydromol®** can be applied directly to skin, used as a soap substitute, or used as a bath emollient by dissolving in hot water.
- **Creams: aqueous, Aveeno®, Diprobase®, E45®, Oilatum®, and Unguentum M®** have lower lipid content than ointments, but are a good alternative for people who cannot tolerate ointments, or who want an additional emollient for regular use during the day (especially on the face and hands).
- **Lotions: Aveeno®, E45®, Keri®, Dermamist® and Lacticare®** are useful for regions of dry skin in hairy areas.
- **Bath additives: Alpha Keri Bath®, Aveeno®, Balneum®, Diprobath®, E45®, and Oilatum ®** are offered to help prevent dehydration of the skin caused by bathing, and can be used as soap substitutes.

Prescriptions

Ointments – trial pack sizes for dry skin

Emulsifying ointment BP

- All ages
- Emulsifying ointment BP. Apply to skin frequently and liberally, as often as required. Use as a bath additive by dissolving in hot water. Use as a soap substitute; supply 100 grams; NHS Cost £0.30.

Hydrous ointment BP

- All ages
- Hydrous ointment BP. Apply to skin frequently and liberally, as often as required. Use as a soap substitute; supply 100 grams; NHS Cost £0.40.

Liquid and white soft paraffin ointment NPF

- All ages
- Liquid+white soft paraffin. Apply to skin frequently and liberally, as often as required. Use as a bath additive by dissolving in hot water. Use as a soap substitute; supply 250 grams; NHS Cost £1.88.

Epaderm ointment

- All ages
- Epaderm ointment (125g). Apply to skin frequently and liberally, as often as required. Use as a bath additive by dissolving in hot water. Use as a soap substitute; supply 125 grams; NHS Cost £3.67; OTC Cost £6.45.

Hydromol ointment
- All ages
- Hydromol ointment (125g). Apply to skin frequently and liberally, as often as required. Use as a bath additive by dissolving in hot water. Use as a soap substitute; supply 125 grams; NHS Cost £3.30; OTC Cost £5.79.

Creams – trial pack sizes for dry skin

Aqueous cream BP
- All ages
- Aqueous cream BP. Apply to skin frequently and liberally, as often as required. Use as a soap substitute; supply 500 grams; NHS Cost £1.06.

E45 cream
- All ages
- E45 cream (125g). Apply to skin frequently and liberally, as often as required. Use as a soap substitute; supply 125 grams; NHS Cost £2.46; OTC Cost £3.75.

Diprobase cream
- All ages
- Diprobase cream (50g). Apply to skin frequently and liberally, as often as required. Use as a soap substitute; supply 50 grams; NHS Cost £1.54; OTC Cost £2.78.

Unguentum M cream
- All ages
- Unguentum M cream (100g). Apply to skin frequently and liberally, as often as required. Use as a soap substitute; supply 100 grams; NHS Cost £3.13; OTC Cost £6.13.

Oilatum cream
- All ages
- Oilatum cream (150g). Apply to skin frequently and liberally, as often as required. Use as a soap substitute; supply 150 grams; NHS Cost £3.38; OTC Cost £5.96.

Lotions for dry skin

E45 lotion
- All ages
- E45 lotion. Apply to skin frequently and liberally, as often as required; supply 200 ml; NHS Cost £2.40; OTC Cost £3.76.

Keri lotion
- All ages
- Keri lotion (190ml). Apply to skin frequently and liberally, as often as required; supply 190 ml; NHS Cost £6.27; OTC Cost £4.81.

Aveeno lotion
- All ages
- Aveeno lotion. Apply to skin frequently and liberally, as often as required; supply 400 ml; NHS Cost £6.02; OTC Cost £10.61.

Dermamist spray
- All ages
- Dermamist spray. Spray sparingly over clean, dry skin. Follow the instructions given inside the pack; supply 250 ml; NHS Cost £9.91; OTC Cost £17.46.

Lacticare lotion
- All ages
- Lacticare lotion. Apply to skin frequently and liberally, as often as required; supply 150 ml; NHS Cost £3.19; OTC Cost £5.62.

Bath additives for dry skin

Oilatum emollient bath additive
- All ages
- Oilatum Emollient (250ml). Add to bath water as directed; supply 250 ml; NHS Cost £2.75; OTC Cost £4.85.

Balneum bath oil
- All ages
- Balneum bath oil (200ml). Add to bath water as directed; supply 200 ml; NHS Cost £2.79; OTC Cost £4.92.

Diprobath bath additive
- All ages
- Diprobath bath additive. Add to bath water as directed; supply 500 ml; NHS Cost £7.50.

Alpha Keri Bath oil
- All ages
- Alpha Keri Bath oil (240ml). Add to bath water as directed; supply 240 ml; NHS Cost £3.45; OTC Cost £6.08.

Aveeno bath oil
- All ages
- Aveeno bath oil. Add to bath water as directed; supply 250 ml; NHS Cost £4.28; OTC Cost £7.54.

E45 emollient bath oil
- All ages
- E45 emollient bath oil (250ml). Add to bath water as directed; supply 250 ml; NHS Cost £2.95; OTC Cost £4.62.

Dry skin — maintenance treatment

Which therapy?

Maintenance emollient treatment

- **Select an emollient** based upon the areas to be treated, the severity of dry skin, and individual preference — see the scenario *Dry skin — starting treatment* for further information.
- **Prescribe generous quantities** of the product that is most acceptable to the person.
- **Emphasise the need for regular use** of emollients, and offer sufficient quantities for application at least three times a day.
- **Alter the intensity of treatment** in response to skin dryness and frequency of flare-ups.
- **If the skin is dry and flare-ups frequent,** increase the intensity of treatment by all or any of the following:
  - Changing to a product with a higher lipid content (lotion to cream, or cream to ointment).
  - Suggesting the use of ointments at night if daytime use is unacceptable.
  - Increasing the frequency of application.
  - Increasing the quantity of emollient applied.
- **If the skin is healthy and flare-ups infrequent,** consider reducing the intensity of treatment by any or all of the following:
  - Changing to a product with a lower lipid content.
  - Reducing the frequency of application.
  - Reducing the quantity of emollient applied.

Advise on avoiding environmental irritants

- Use an emollient soap substitute.
- Use gloves when unable to avoid handling irritants such as detergents.
- Avoid extremes of temperature and humidity.
- Use non-abrasive fabrics for clothing, such as cotton.
- Reapply emollients after wetting skin.

Practical prescribing points

For further information please see the *Medicines Compendium* (www.medicines.org.uk) or the *British National Formulary* (www.bnf.org).

A bath emollient may be an ointment mixed with the bath water or a product designed for use as a bath additive. Bath emollients create a slippery surface in the bath and on surrounding non-slip surfaces. Users and family members need to take extra care in the bathroom, and the bath should be cleaned thoroughly after use to reduce the risk of slipping. A bath mat or hand rails may be useful.

Reactions to emollients are most commonly due to preservatives, fragrances, lanolin, or arachis oil. If such a reaction is suspected, the person should switch to a product with different constituents. See Table 1 in *Management issues/What are the adverse effects of emollients and how are they managed?*

Some emollients are classified as borderline substances and can only be prescribed when endorsed as ACBS (Advisory Committee on Borderline Substances. These include: E45® lotion and bath oil; and Aveeno® cream, lotion and bath oil.

ollow-up advice

The frequency of review will depend on the severity of the problem and the person's experience of managing the condition.

If treatment is not effective, consider stepping up treatment by any or all of the following:

- Changing the emollient to one with a higher lipid content if that is tolerable (lotion to cream, or cream to ointment).
- Increasing the frequency of application of the emollient.
- Increasing the quantity of emollient applied.

If the treatment is effective but not well tolerated, consider stepping down treatment by any or all of the following:

- Changing the emollient to one with a lower lipid content.
- Reducing the frequency of application.
- Reducing the quantity of emollient applied.

hould I refer or investigate?

efer?

Referral is rarely necessary for individuals with atopic eczema and dry skin without an acute flare-up.

Consider referral if the diagnosis is uncertain.

nvestigate?

Investigations are rarely needed to establish a diagnosis of atopic eczema.

Estimation of immunoglobulin E (IgE) and specific radioallergosorbant tests (RASTs) serve only to confirm the atopic nature of the individual, and are occasionally of value in confirming adult-onset eczema.

atient information leaflets

he following PILs are available at www.prodigy.nhs.uk

Eczema - Atopic
Eczema - Emollients (Moisturisers)
Eczema - Triggers and Irritants
National Eczema Society
Skin Care Campaign

hared decision making

Emollients (moisturizers) help to prevent flare-ups of eczema.

- **Apply liberally as often as you need** — commonly 2–3 times per day.
- **Many people use a variety of emollients.** For example:
  - A bath or shower additive for a background 'oiling' (but they make the bath slippery–be careful).
  - A thick ointment as a soap substitute.
  - A cream or ointment at other times.
    - Ointments work better and longer than creams do, but are messier to use.
    - Creams for mild dry skin, or for weepy eczema.
  - Lotions for hairy areas.
  - An ointment at bedtime.
- **Rarely, some people become sensitised to an ingredient in an emollient.**
- **Try to avoid skin irritants:**
  - Avoid normal soaps, bubble baths, etc.
  - Wear cotton clothes or other smooth fabrics next to the skin.
  - Avoid getting too hot or too cold.
  - Wear gloves when handling irritants such as detergents.
  - Reapply emollients after wetting skin

Drug rationale

Many emollients are available, and there is little evidence to support the use of one particular product over another. Emollients offered have been selected on the basis of their common usage and relative cost. However, some people may find that other preparations are more suitable for their personal needs.

Drugs not included

- **Emollients containing antiseptic agents,** such as triclosan and benzalkonium chloride, have failed to show clearly enough that they improve clinical symptoms or reduce the load of *Staphylococcus aureus*. They may cause allergic contact dermatitis [DTB, 1998].
- **Emollients containing urea** are not offered; they should be reserved for use when standard emollients have proved ineffective [MeReC, 1998].
- **Emollients containing antipruritic agents,** such as lauromacrogols, are not offered. Evidence of additional benefits over standard emollients is limited [MeReC, 1998].

Drugs included

- During maintenance treatment for dry skin, it is preferable to use sizeable quantities of ointment on large areas of affected skin, such as the trunk or lower limbs. Creams are more suitable for smaller areas of sensitive skin, such as the face, particularly when application is required during the day. Therefore smaller quantities of creams are offered, but these should be increased should the person prefer using cream on widespread areas of dry skin.
- **Ointments: emulsifying, hydrous, liquid and soft paraffin, Epaderm®, and Hydromol®** can be applied directly to skin, used as a soap substitute, or used as a bath emollient by dissolving in hot water.
- **Creams: aqueous, Aveeno®, Diprobase®, E45®, Oilatum®, and Unguentum M®** have lower lipid content than ointments do, but are a good alternative for people who cannot tolerate ointments, or want an additional emollient for regular use during the day (especially on the face and hands).
- **Lotions: Aveeno®, E45®, Keri®, Dermamist® and Lacticare®** are useful for regions of dry skin in hairy areas.
- **Bath additives: Alpha Keri Bath®, Aveeno®, Balneum®, Diprobath®, E45®, and Oilatum®** are offered to help

prevent dehydration of the skin caused by bathing, and can be used as soap substitutes.

Prescriptions

Ointments – for localized dry skin

Emulsifying ointment BP
- All ages
- Emulsifying ointment BP. Apply to skin frequently and liberally, as often as required. Use as a bath additive by dissolving in hot water. Use as a soap substitute; supply 500 grams; NHS Cost £1.42.

Hydrous ointment BP
- All ages
- Hydrous ointment BP. Apply to skin frequently and liberally, as often as required. Use as a soap substitute; supply 500 grams; NHS Cost £1.99.

Liquid and white soft paraffin ointment NPF
- All ages
- Liquid+white soft paraffin. Apply to skin frequently and liberally, as often as required. Use as a bath additive by dissolving in hot water. Use as a soap substitute; supply 500 grams; NHS Cost £3.76.

Epaderm ointment
- All ages
- Epaderm ointment (500g). Apply to skin frequently and liberally, as often as required. Use as a bath additive by dissolving in hot water. Use as a soap substitute; supply 1 500 gram tub; NHS Cost £6.21; OTC Cost £10.95.

Hydromol ointment
- All ages
- Hydromol ointment (500g). Apply to skin frequently and liberally, as often as required. Use as a bath additive by dissolving in hot water. Use as a soap substitute; supply 1 500 gram tub; NHS Cost £5.64; OTC Cost £9.79.

Ointments – for widespread dry skin

Emulsifying ointment BP
- Age under 5 years
- Emulsifying ointment BP. Apply to skin frequently and liberally, as often as required. Use as a bath additive by dissolving in hot water. Use as a soap substitute; supply 500 grams; NHS Cost £1.42.

Emulsifying ointment BP
- Age from 6 to 11 years
- Emulsifying ointment BP. Apply to skin frequently and liberally, as often as required. Use as a bath additive by dissolving in hot water. Use as a soap substitute; supply 1000 grams; NHS Cost £2.84.

Emulsifying ointment BP
- Age from 12 years onwards
- Emulsifying ointment BP. Apply to skin frequently and liberally, as often as required. Use as a bath additive by dissolving in hot water. Use as a soap substitute; supply 2000 grams; NHS Cost £5.68.

Hydrous ointment BP
- Age under 5 years
- Hydrous ointment BP. Apply to skin frequently and liberally, as often as required. Use as a soap substitute; supply 500 grams; NHS Cost £1.99.

Hydrous ointment BP
- Age from 6 to 11 years
- Hydrous ointment BP. Apply to skin frequently and liberally, as often as required. Use as a soap substitute; supply 1000 grams; NHS Cost £3.98.

Hydrous ointment BP
- Age from 12 years onwards
- Hydrous ointment BP. Apply to skin frequently and liberally, as often as required. Use as a soap substitute; supply 2000 grams; NHS Cost £7.96.

Liquid and white soft paraffin ointment NPF
- Age under 5 years
- Liquid+white soft paraffin. Apply to skin frequently and liberally, as often as required. Use as a bath additive by dissolving in hot water. Use as a soap substitute; supply 500 grams; NHS Cost £3.76.

Liquid and white soft paraffin ointment NPF
- Age from 6 to 11 years
- Liquid+white soft paraffin. Apply to skin frequently and liberally, as often as required. Use as a bath additive by dissolving in hot water. Use as a soap substitute; supply 1000 grams; NHS Cost £7.52.

Liquid and white soft paraffin ointment NPF
- Age from 12 years onwards
- Liquid+white soft paraffin. Apply to skin frequently and liberally, as often as required. Use as a bath additive by dissolving in hot water. Use as a soap substitute; supply 2000 grams; NHS Cost £15.04.

Epaderm ointment
- Age under 5 years
- Epaderm ointment (500g). Apply to skin frequently and liberally, as often as required. Use as a bath additive by dissolving in hot water. Use as a soap substitute; supply 1 500 gram tub; NHS Cost £6.21; OTC Cost £10.95.

Epaderm ointment
- Age from 6 to 11 years
- Epaderm ointment (500g). Apply to skin frequently and liberally, as often as required. Use as a bath additive by dissolving in hot water. Use as a soap substitute; supply 2 500 gram tub; NHS Cost £12.42; OTC Cost £21.90.

Epaderm ointment
- Age from 12 years onwards
- Epaderm ointment (500g). Apply to skin frequently and liberally, as often as required. Use as a bath additive by dissolving in hot water. Use as a soap substitute; supply 4 500 gram tub; NHS Cost £24.84; OTC Cost £43.80.

Hydromol ointment
- Age under 5 years
- Hydromol ointment (500g). Apply to skin frequently and liberally, as often as required. Use as a bath additive by dissolving in hot water. Use as a soap substitute; supply 1 500 gram tub; NHS Cost £5.64; OTC Cost £9.79.

Hydromol ointment
- Age from 6 to 11 years
- Hydromol ointment (500g). Apply to skin frequently and liberally, as often as required. Use as a bath additive by dissolving in hot water. Use as a soap substitute; supply 2 500 gram tub; NHS Cost £11.28; OTC Cost £19.58.

Hydromol ointment
- Age from 12 years onwards
- Hydromol ointment (500g). Apply to skin frequently and liberally, as often as required. Use as a bath additive by dissolving in hot water. Use as a soap substitute; supply 4 500 gram tub; NHS Cost £22.56; OTC Cost £38.76.

Creams for dry skin

Aqueous cream BP
- All ages
- Aqueous cream BP. Apply to skin frequently and liberally, as often as required. Use as a soap substitute; supply 500 grams; NHS Cost £1.06; OTC Cost £1.87.

E45 cream
- All ages
- E45 cream (500g). Apply to skin frequently and liberally, as often as required. Use as a soap substitute; supply 500 grams; NHS Cost £9.69; OTC Cost £6.20.

Diprobase cream
- All ages
- Diprobase cream (500g). Apply to skin frequently and liberally, as often as required. Use as a soap substitute; supply 500 grams; NHS Cost £6.61; OTC Cost £11.63.

Unguentum M cream
- All ages
- Unguentum M cream (500g). Apply to skin frequently and liberally, as often as required. Use as a soap substitute; supply 500 grams; NHS Cost £9.55; OTC Cost £18.70.

Oilatum cream
- All ages
- Oilatum cream (500ml). Apply to skin frequently and liberally, as often as required. Use as a soap substitute; supply 500 ml; NHS Cost £6.35; OTC Cost £9.93.

Lotions for dry skin

E45 lotion
- All ages
- E45 lotion. Apply to skin frequently and liberally, as often as required; supply 500 ml; NHS Cost £4.50; OTC Cost £7.05.

Keri lotion
- All ages
- Keri lotion (380ml). Apply to skin frequently and liberally, as often as required; supply 380 ml; NHS Cost £5.81; OTC Cost £10.23.

Aveeno lotion
- All ages
- Aveeno lotion. Apply to skin frequently and liberally, as often as required; supply 400 ml; NHS Cost £6.02; OTC Cost £10.61.

Dermamist spray
- All ages
- Dermamist spray. Spray sparingly over clean, dry skin. Follow the instructions given inside the pack; supply 250 ml; NHS Cost £9.91; OTC Cost £17.46.

Lacticare lotion
- All ages
- Lacticare lotion. Apply to skin frequently and liberally, as often as required; supply 150 ml; NHS Cost £3.19; OTC Cost £5.62.

Bath additives for dry skin

Oilatum Emollient bath additive
- All ages
- Oilatum Emollient (500ml). Add to bath water as directed; supply 500 ml; NHS Cost £4.57; OTC Cost £8.06.

Balneum bath oil
- All ages
- Balneum bath oil (500ml). Add to bath water as directed; supply 500 ml; NHS Cost £6.06; OTC Cost £10.68.

Diprobath bath additive
- All ages
- Diprobath bath additive. Add to bath water as directed; supply 500 ml; NHS Cost £7.50; OTC Cost £13.21.

Alpha Keri Bath oil
- All ages
- Alpha Keri Bath oil (480ml). Add to bath water as directed; supply 400 ml; NHS Cost £6.43; OTC Cost £11.32.

Aveeno bath oil
- All ages
- Aveeno bath oil. Add to bath water as directed; supply 250 ml; NHS Cost £9.66; OTC Cost £15.98.

E45 emollient bath oil
- All ages
- E45 emollient bath oil (500ml). Add to bath water as directed; supply 500 ml; NHS Cost £4.70; OTC Cost £7.36.

Localized flare-up

Which therapy?

- **Settle inflammation with topical corticosteroids.**
- ***In adults***
  - **Face, genitals, and flexures** — treat with a mildly potent corticosteroid.
  - **The eyelids** — treat intermittently with a mildly potent corticosteroid for at most 14 days. Monitor intraocular pressure in people over the age of 35 years if the treatment is used frequently.
  - **The palms, soles of the feet, and scalp** — treat with potent corticosteroid.
  - **The trunk and limbs:**
    - Select the lowest potency of corticosteroid that is likely to work within 7–14 days of treatment, based upon the severity of inflammation and response to previous treatment.
    - Review if not showing significant signs of improvement within 7 days, and step up to a more potent steroid.
    - Alternatively, for mild to moderate eczema treat with a potent corticosteroid for 3 days (short-burst treatment).
- ***In children and infants***
  - Treat all skin areas with mildly potent corticosteroid as a first choice.
  - Occasional use of moderately potent preparations on areas other than the face, genitals or flexures may be used as an alternative treatment.
- **Treat visibly infected eczema with oral antibiotics.**
  - **Flucloxacillin or erythromycin** (if the person is allergic to penicillin) are first-line treatments.
- **Manage frequent flare-ups.**
  - **Review and emphasise the use of emollients.** Increase the intensity of emollient treatment, if acceptable to the person, by all or any of the following:
    - Changing the emollient to one with a higher lipid content (lotion to a cream, or a cream to an ointment).
    - Increasing the frequency of application of the emollient.
    - Increasing the quantity of emollient applied.
  - **Review factors that might be provoking flare-ups:**
    - Avoid environmental irritants or stresses.
    - Consider antigen avoidance measures if other measures fail.

E

Practical prescribing points

For further information please see the *Medicines Compendium* (www.medicines.org.uk) or the *British National Formulary* (www.bnf.org).

- **Frequency of application:** the evidence suggests that once-daily application of topical corticosteroids is as effective as more frequent application. Note that most manufacturers recommend two or three applications per day.
- **Give specific advice regarding the quantity of steroid to apply.** Where larger areas require treatment, explain and demonstrate the use of the fingertip unit (FTU).
  - **One FTU weighs about 500 mg.** It is roughly equivalent to the amount of cream or ointment that can be squeezed from a tube with a standard nozzle onto an adult index finger from the tip of the finger to the first crease.
  - **For an adult,** one FTU of topical corticosteroid is sufficient to treat a skin area about twice that of the flat of the hand with the fingers.
  - **For a child aged 6 months to 1 year,** apply a quarter of the adult amount.
  - **For a child from 1 year to 4 years,** apply a third of the adult amount.
- **Prescribe sufficient topical corticosteroid** to treat the flare-up until it is completely resolved.
- **Occlusion** increases both the absorption and effect of topical corticosteroids. If the area affected is occluded (e.g. the nappy area), use a weaker corticosteroid.

Follow-up advice

- Review after 7 days if the condition is not responding well to treatment.
- Review at any stage if the condition deteriorates despite treatment.

Should I refer or investigate?

Refer?

- **Disseminated herpes simplex virus infection** — arrange emergency admission for confirmation of the diagnosis and antiviral treatment.
- **Unresponsive severe disease,** including bacterially infected eczema unresponsive to treatment with oral antibiotics and topical corticosteroids — arrange emergency admission or urgent referral, depending on severity.
- **Eczema requiring a duration and potency of treatment with topical corticosteroids that risks skin thinning** (i.e. if a potent corticosteroid is required on the same area of skin of the trunk or limbs on average more frequently than 7 days within a 5-week period) — the risk is increased:
  - In thin skin and flexural areas.

Table 1: Suitable quantities of corticosteroid to prescribe for a flare-up in adults.

Body area	Amount of corticosteroid to prescribe
Face and neck	30g
Both hands	30g
Scalp	30g
Both arms	30 to 60g
Both legs	100g
Trunk	100g
Groins and genitalia	30g

[BNF 47, 2004]

  - With increasing duration of use.
  - When corticosteroids are used with occlusion.
- **Uncontrolled eczema where dietary factors are** suspected, requiring advice from a dietician.
- Where there is diagnostic uncertainty.

Investigate?

- **Microbiological investigation is indicated** to ascertain sensitivities when infected eczema does not respond to a first-line antibiotic.

Patient information leaflets

The following PILs are available at www.prodigy.nhs.uk

- Eczema - Atopic
- Eczema - Emollients (Moisturisers)
- Eczema - Fingertip Units for Topical Steroids
- Eczema - Topical Steroids
- National Eczema Society
- Skin Care Campaign

Shared decision making

- **Topical steroids** reduce inflammation in the skin. Apply daily until the flare-up of eczema has gone, and then sto[p] it.
  - In many cases, a 7–14 day course of a mild steroid is enough.
  - Return for a stronger steroid if there is no improvement in 5–7 days.
  - For adults, an alternative is to use a strong steroid from the outset for 3 days.
  - Apply the correct amount of each dose by using 'fingertip units'.
  - Side-effects are uncommon unless used long-term.
- **Also, keep using liberal amounts of emollients** (moisturizers). Many people use a variety. For example:
  - A bath or shower additive for a background 'oiling' (but they make the bath slippery — be careful).
  - A thick ointment as a soap substitute.
  - A cream or ointment at other times.
    - Ointments work better and longer than creams do, but are messier to use.
    - Use creams for mild dry skin, or for weepy eczema.
  - Lotions for hairy areas.
  - An ointment at bedtime.
- **An antibiotic** is sometimes needed if the eczema become[s] infected.

Drug rationale

Drugs not included

- **Topical tacrolimus and pimecrolimus** are not offered. NICE recommends that these should be initiated only by physicians (including general practitioners) with a specia[l] interest and experience in dermatology.
- **Oral corticosteroids** may be useful as 'rescue therapy' fo[r] particularly severe and widespread flares of eczema.
- **Very potent topical corticosteroids:** clobetasol propionate, difluocortolone valerate, and halcinonide ar[e] reserved for use under specialist supervision in eczema that has proved resistant to other topical corticosteroids
- **Topical corticosteroids with antibiotics:** there is a lack o[f] evidence that these products are more effective than topical corticosteroids alone, and there is a possibility that widespread use may contribute to the development of bacterial resistance.
- **Emollients** should be continued as usual during a flare-up of eczema. Details of initiating emollient treatment are given in the scenario *Dry skin — starting treatment.*

rugs included

The vehicle used for the corticosteroid is a matter of personal preference, but in general creams are favoured on wet or weeping eczema, and ointments are preferred for dry or lichenified skin.
Mildly potent topical corticosteroid: hydrocortisone is suitable for use in mild eczema, inflammation of sensitive areas such as the face or neck, and eczema in infants.
Moderately potent topical corticosteroids: aclometasone dipropionate, clobetasone butyrate, and dilute betamethasone valerate 0.025% are suitable for use in moderate to severe eczema.
Potent topical corticosteroids: betamethasone valerate 0.1%, betamethasone diproprionate, hydrocortisone butyrate, and mometasone furoate are suitable for use in severe flare-ups of eczema.
Lotions and foams are suitable vehicles for scalp applications and are usually easier to apply than are standard creams and ointments. Topical applications of bethamethasone valerate, betamethasone diproprionate, hydrocortisone butyrate, and mometasone furoate are recommended for eczema of the scalp. Note that some applications have an alcoholic base and application on broken skin may be painful.
Flucloxacillin has activity against Gram-positive organisms, including beta-lactamase-producing staphylococci and streptococci. It is licensed in the treatment of infected skin conditions, including eczema.
Erythromycin is suitable for people with infected eczema who have a known hypersensitivity to penicillin and related antibiotics.

rescriptions

Mildly potent corticosteroids

ydrocortisone 1% ointment
Age from 1 month onwards
Hydrocortisone 1% ointment (30g). Apply thinly to the affected area(s) once a day for up to 7 days; supply 30 grams; NHS Cost £0.72; OTC Cost £1.22.

ydrocortisone 1% cream
Age from 1 month onwards
Hydrocortisone 1% cream (30g). Apply thinly to the affected area(s) once a day for up to 7 days; supply 30 grams; NHS Cost £0.72; OTC Cost £1.22.

Moderately potent corticosteroids

etamethasone valerate 0.025% ointment
Age from 12 months onwards
Betamethasone val 0.025% ointment. Apply thinly to the affected area(s) once a day for up to 7 days; supply 100 grams; NHS Cost £3.59.

lobetasone butyrate 0.05% ointment
Age from 12 months onwards
Clobetasone butyrate 0.05% ointment. Apply thinly to the affected area(s) once a day for up to 7 days; supply 30 grams; NHS Cost £2.12.

lclometasone dipropionate 0.05% ointment
Age from 12 months onwards
Alclometasone 0.05% ointment. Apply thinly to the affected area(s) once a day for up to 7 days; supply 50 grams; NHS Cost £2.82.

etamethasone valerate 0.025% cream
Age from 12 months onwards
Betamethasone val 0.025% cream. Apply thinly to the affected area(s) once a day for up to 7 days; supply 100 grams; NHS Cost £3.59.

Clobetasone butyrate 0.05% cream
- Age from 12 months onwards
- Clobetasone butyrate 0.05% cream. Apply thinly to the affected area(s) once a day for up to 7 days; supply 30 grams; NHS Cost £2.12.

Alclometasone dipropionate 0.05% cream
- Age from 12 months onwards
- Alclometasone 0.05% cream. Apply thinly to the affected area(s) once a day for up to 7 days; supply 50 grams; NHS Cost £2.82.

Potent corticosteroids

Betamethasone valerate 0.1% ointment
- Age from 12 years onwards
- Betamethasone val 0.1% ointment. Apply thinly to the affected area(s) once a day for up to 7 days; supply 30 grams; NHS Cost £1.69.

Hydrocortisone butyrate 0.1% ointment
- Age from 12 years onwards
- Hydrocortisone butyr 0.1% ointment. Apply thinly to the affected area(s) once a day for up to 7 days; supply 30 grams; NHS Cost £2.46.

Betamethasone dipropionate 0.05% ointment
- Age from 12 years onwards
- Diprosone 0.05% ointment (30g). Apply thinly to the affected area(s) once a day for up to 7 days; supply 30 grams; NHS Cost £2.41.

Mometasone furoate 0.1% ointment
- Age from 12 years onwards
- Mometasone 0.1% furoate ointment. Apply thinly to the affected area(s) once a day for up to 7 days; supply 30 grams; NHS Cost £4.88.

Betamethasone valerate 0.1% cream
- Age from 12 years onwards
- Betamethasone val 0.1% cream. Apply thinly to the affected area(s) once a day for up to 7 days; supply 30 grams; NHS Cost £1.54.

Hydrocortisone butyrate 0.1% cream
- Age from 12 years onwards
- Hydrocortisone butyr 0.1% cream. Apply thinly to the affected area(s) once a day for up to 7 days; supply 30 grams; NHS Cost £2.46.

Betamethasone dipropionate 0.05% cream
- Age from 12 years onwards
- Diprosone 0.05% cream (30g). Apply thinly to the affected area(s) once a day for up to 7 days; supply 30 grams; NHS Cost £2.41.

Mometasone furoate 0.1% cream
- Age from 12 years onwards
- Mometasone 0.1% furoate cream. Apply thinly to the affected area(s) once a day for up to 7 days; supply 30 grams; NHS Cost £4.88.

Scalp applications

Betamethasone valerate 0.1% scalp application
- Age from 12 years onwards
- Betamethasone val 0.1% sca app. Apply to scalp once a day, for up to 7 days; supply 100 ml; NHS Cost £4.22.

Betamethasone valerate 0.1% lotion
- Age from 12 years onwards
- Betamethasone val 0.1% lotion. Apply to scalp once a day, for up to 7 days; supply 100 ml; NHS Cost £5.23.

Betamethasone valerate 0.12% foam
- Age from 12 years onwards
- Betamethasone val 0.12% foam. Apply to scalp once a day, for up to 7 days; supply 100 grams; NHS Cost £7.50.

Betamethasone dipropionate 0.05% lotion

- Age from 12 years onwards
- Diprosone 0.05% lotion (30ml). Apply to scalp once a day, for up to 7 days; supply 1 30ml applicator; NHS Cost £3.04.

Hydrocortisone butyrate 0.1% scalp application

- Age from 12 years onwards
- Hydrocortisone butyr scalp lotion. Apply to scalp once a day, for up to 7 days; supply 100 ml; NHS Cost £10.49.

Mometasone furoate 0.1% scalp application

- Age from 12 years onwards
- Mometasone 0.1% lotion. Apply to scalp once a day, for up to 7 days; supply 60 ml; NHS Cost £9.76.

Antibiotic for 7 days (if visibly infected)

Flucloxacillin syrup: 62.5mg four times a day

- Age from 1 month to 23 months
- Flucloxacillin 125mg/5ml syrup. Take 2.5ml four times a day for 7 days; supply 100 ml; NHS Cost £3.49.

Flucloxacillin syrup: 125mg four times a day

- Age from 2 to 4 years
- Flucloxacillin 125mg/5ml syrup. Take one 5ml spoonful four times a day for 7 days; supply 200 ml; NHS Cost £6.97.

Flucloxacillin syrup: 250mg four times a day

- Age from 5 to 11 years
- Flucloxacillin 250mg/5ml syrup. Take one 5ml spoonful four times a day for 7 days; supply 200 ml; NHS Cost £13.97.

Flucloxacillin capsules: 250mg four times a day

- Age from 12 years onwards
- Flucloxacillin 250mg capsules. Take one capsule four times a day for 7 days; supply 28 capsules; NHS Cost £2.93.

Flucloxacillin capsules: 500mg four times a day

- Age from 12 years onwards
- Flucloxacillin 500mg capsules. Take one capsule four times a day for 7 days; supply 28 capsules; NHS Cost £4.73.

Erythromycin s/f suspension: 125mg four times a day

- Age from 1 month to 23 months
- Erythromycin 125mg/5ml sf susp. Take one 5ml spoonful four times a day for 7 days; supply 200 ml; NHS Cost £2.22.

Erythromycin s/f suspension: 250mg four times a day

- Age from 2 to 11 years
- Erythromycin 250mg/5ml sf susp. Take one 5ml spoonful four times a day for 7 days; supply 200 ml; NHS Cost £3.80.

Erythromycin s/f suspension: 500mg four times a day

- Age from 9 to 11 years
- Erythromycin 500mg/5ml sf susp. Take one 5ml spoonful four times a day for 7 days; supply 200 ml; NHS Cost £6.44.

Erythromycin e/c tablets: 250mg four times a day

- Age from 12 years onwards
- Erythromycin 250mg e/c tablets. Take one tablet four times a day for 7 days; supply 28 tablets; NHS Cost £3.08.

Erythromycin e/c tablets: 500mg four times a day

- Age from 12 years onwards
- Erythromycin 250mg e/c tablets. Take two tablets four times a day for 7 days; supply 56 tablets; NHS Cost £6.16.

Widespread flare-up

Which therapy?

- **Settle inflammation with topical corticosteroids.**
- ***In adults***
  - **Face, genitals, and flexures** — treat with a mildly potent corticosteroid.
  - **The eyelids** — treat with a mildly potent corticosterc for at most 14 days. Monitor intraocular pressure in people over the age of 35 years if the treatment is use frequently.
  - **The palms, soles of the feet, and scalp** — treat with a potent corticosteroid.
  - **The trunk and limbs:**
    - Select the lowest potency of corticosteroid that is likely to work within 7–14 days of treatment, base upon the severity of inflammation and response to previous treatment.
    - Review if there are no significant signs of improvement within 7 days, and step up to a more potent steroid.
    - Alternatively, for mild to moderate eczema treat with a potent corticosteroid for 3 days (short-burst treatment).
- ***In children and infants***
  - Treat all skin areas with a mildly potent corticostero as a first choice.
  - Occasional use of moderately potent preparations on areas other than the face, genitals, or flexures may be used as an alternative treatment.
- **Treat visibly infected eczema with oral antibiotics.**
  - **Flucloxacillin or erythromycin** (if the person is allerg to penicillin) are first-line treatments.
- **Manage frequent flare-ups.**
  - **Review and emphasise the use of emollients.** Increase the intensity of emollient treatment, if acceptable to the person, by all or any of the following:
    - Changing the emollient to one with a higher lipid content (lotion to a cream, or a cream to an ointment).
    - Increasing the frequency of application of the emollient.
    - Increasing the quantity of emollient applied.
  - **Review factors that might be provoking flare-ups:**
    - Avoid environmental irritants or stresses.
    - Consider antigen avoidance measures if other measures fail.

Practical prescribing points

For further information please see the *Medicines Compendium* (www.medicines.org.uk) or the *British National Formulary* (www.bnf.org).

- **Frequency of application:** the evidence suggests that once-daily application of topical corticosteroids is as effective as more frequent application. Note that most manufacturers recommend two or three applications pe day.
- **Give specific advice regarding the quantity of steroid to apply.** Where larger areas require treatment, explain an demonstrate the use of the fingertip unit (FTU).
  - **One FTU weighs about 500 mg.** It is roughly equivalent to the amount of cream or ointment that can be squeezed from a tube with a standard nozzle onto an adult index finger from the tip of the finger to the first crease.
  - **For an adult,** one FTU of topical corticosteroid is sufficient to treat a skin area about twice that of the flat of the hand with the fingers.

- **For a child aged 6 months to 1 year,** use a quarter of the adult amount.
- **For a child from 1 year to 4 years,** use a third of the adult amount.

Prescribe sufficient topical corticosteroid to treat the flare-up until it is completely resolved.

Occlusion increases both the absorption and effect of topical corticosteroids. If the area affected is occluded (e.g. the nappy area), use a weaker corticosteroid.

hould I refer or investigate?

efer?

Disseminated herpes simplex virus infection — arrange emergency admission for confirmation of the diagnosis and antiviral treatment.

Unresponsive severe disease, including bacterially infected eczema unresponsive to treatment with oral antibiotics and topical corticosteroids — arrange emergency admission or urgent referral depending on severity.

Eczema requiring a duration and/or potency of treatment with topical corticosteroids that risks systemic adverse effects.

Eczema requiring a duration and potency of treatment with topical corticosteroids that risks skin thinning (i.e. if a potent corticosteroid is required on the same area of skin of the trunk or limbs on average more frequently than 7 days within a 5-week period) — the risk is increased:

- In thin skin and flexural areas.
- With increasing duration of use.
- When corticosteroids are used with occlusion.

Uncontrolled eczema where dietary factors are suspected, requiring advice from a dietician.

Where there is diagnostic uncertainty.

vestigate?

Microbiological investigation is indicated to ascertain sensitivities when infected eczema does not respond to first-line antibiotics.

atient information leaflets

ıe following PILs are available at www.prodigy.nhs.uk

Eczema - Atopic
Eczema - Emollients (Moisturisers)
Eczema - Fingertip Units for Topical Steroids
Eczema - Topical Steroids
Eczema - Triggers and Irritants
National Eczema Society
Skin Care Campaign

able 2: Suitable quantities of corticosteroid to prescribe r a flare-up in adults.

ody area	Amount of corticosteroid to prescribe
ce and neck	30g
th hands	30g
alp	30g
th arms	30 to 60g
th legs	100g
unk	100g
oins and genitalia	30g

NF 47, 2004]

Table 3: Weekly dose of corticosteroids unlikely to cause systemic adverse effects in adults.

Treatment period (months)	Mild and moderately potent	Potent	Very potent
<2 months	100 g	50 g	30 g
2–6 months	50 g	30 g	15 g
6–12 months	25 g	15 g	7.5 g

Shared decision making

- **Topical steroids** reduce inflammation in the skin. Apply daily until the flare-up of eczema has gone, and then stop it.
  - In many cases, a 7–14 day course of a mild steroid is enough.
  - Return for a stronger steroid if there is no improvement in 5–7 days.
  - For adults, an alternative is to use a strong steroid from the outset for 3 days.
  - Apply the correct amount of each dose by using 'fingertip units'.
  - Side-effects are uncommon unless the treatment is used long-term.
- **Also, keep using liberal amounts of emollients** (moisturizers). Many people use a variety. For example:
  - A bath or shower additive for a background 'oiling' (but they make the bath slippery — be careful).
  - A thick ointment as a soap substitute.
  - A cream or ointment at other times.
    - Ointments work better and longer than creams do, but are messier to use.
    - Creams for mild dry skin, or for weepy eczema.
  - Lotions for hairy areas.
  - An ointment at bedtime.
- **An antibiotic** is sometimes needed if the eczema becomes infected.

Drug rationale

Drugs not included

- **Antipruritic drugs:** oral antihistamines, topical calamine, topical antihistamines, local anaesthetics, or doxepin hydrochloride are not recommended in the management of flare-ups of eczema. Whilst some drugs may have a restricted role in preventing itchiness, the effectiveness of these agents are limited and often offset by adverse effects.
- **Wet-wrap bandages,** including those impregnated with zinc or ichthammol, are not offered. They can be useful to protect the skin, improve the hydrating action of emollients, increase the effect of topical corticosteroids, and cool the skin and reduce pruritus. However, they can be difficult to apply and are more suited to a secondary-care environment.
- **Topical tacrolimus and pimecrolimus** are not offered. NICE recommends that these should be initiated only by physicians (including general practitioners) with a special interest and experience in dermatology.
- **Oral corticosteroids** may be useful as 'rescue therapy' for particularly severe and widespread flares of eczema.
- **Very potent topical corticosteroids:** clobetasol propionate, difluocortolone valerate, and halcinonide, are reserved for use under specialist supervision in eczema that has proved resistant to other topical corticosteroids.
- **Topical corticosteroids with antibiotics:** there is a lack of evidence that these products are more effective than topical corticosteroids alone, and there is a possibility

that widespread use may contribute to the development of bacterial resistance.
- **Emollients** should be continued as usual during a flare-up of eczema. Details of initiating emollient treatment are given in the scenario *Dry skin — starting treatment.*

Drugs included

- The vehicle used for the corticosteroid is a matter of personal preference, but in general creams are favoured on wet or weeping eczema, and ointments are preferred for dry or lichenified skin
- **Mildly potent topical corticosteroid:** hydrocortisone is suitable for use in mild eczema, inflammation of sensitive areas such as the face or neck, and eczema in infants.
- **Moderately potent topical corticosteroids:** aclometasone dipropionate, clobetasone butyrate, and dilute betamethasone valerate 0.025% are suitable for use in moderate to severe eczema.
- **Potent topical corticosteroids:** betamethasone valerate 0.1%, betamethasone diproprionate, hydrocortisone butyrate, and mometasone furoate are suitable for use in severe flare-ups of eczema.
- **Lotions and foams are suitable vehicles for scalp applications** and are usually easier to apply than are standard creams and ointments. Topical applications of bethamethasone valerate, betamethasone diproprionate, hydrocortisone butyrate, and mometasone furoate are recommended for eczema of the scalp. Note that some applications have an alcoholic base and application on broken skin may be painful.
- **Flucloxacillin** has activity against Gram-positive organisms, including beta-lactamase-producing staphylococci and streptococci. It is licensed in the treatment of infected skin conditions, including eczema.
- **Erythromycin** is suitable for people with infected eczema who have a known hypersensitivity to penicillin and related antibiotics.

Prescriptions

Mildly potent corticosteroids

Hydrocortisone 1% ointment
- Age from 1 month onwards
- Hydrocortisone 1% ointment (100g). Apply thinly to the affected area(s) once a day for up to 7 days; supply 100 grams; NHS Cost £2.38; OTC Cost £1.22.

Hydrocortisone 1% cream
- Age from 1 month onwards
- Hydrocortisone 1% cream (100g). Apply thinly to the affected area(s) once a day for up to 7 days; supply 100 grams; NHS Cost £2.18.

Moderately potent corticosteroids

Betamethasone valerate 0.025% ointment
- Age from 12 months onwards
- Betamethasone val 0.025% ointment. Apply thinly to the affected area(s) once a day for up to 7 days; supply 100 grams; NHS Cost £3.59.

Clobetasone butyrate 0.05% ointment
- Age from 12 months onwards
- Clobetasone butyrate 0.05% ointment. Apply thinly to the affected area(s) once a day for up to 7 days; supply 100 grams; NHS Cost £6.20.

Alclometasone dipropionate 0.05% ointment
- Age from 12 months onwards
- Alclometasone 0.05% ointment. Apply thinly to the affected area(s) once a day for up to 7 days; supply 100 grams; NHS Cost £5.64.

Betamethasone valerate 0.025% cream
- Age from 12 months onwards
- Betamethasone val 0.025% cream. Apply thinly to the affected area(s) once a day for up to 7 days; supply 100 grams; NHS Cost £3.59.

Clobetasone butyrate 0.05% cream
- Age from 12 months onwards
- Clobetasone butyrate 0.05% cream. Apply thinly to the affected area(s) once a day for up to 7 days; supply 100 grams; NHS Cost £6.20.

Alclometasone dipropionate 0.05% cream
- Age from 12 months onwards
- Alclometasone 0.05% cream. Apply thinly to the affected area(s) once a day for up to 7 days; supply 100 grams; NHS Cost £5.64.

Potent corticosteroids

Betamethasone valerate 0.1% ointment
- Age from 12 years onwards
- Betamethasone val 0.1% ointment. Apply thinly to the affected area(s) once a day for up to 7 days; supply 100 grams; NHS Cost £4.35.

Hydrocortisone butyrate 0.1% ointment
- Age from 12 years onwards
- Hydrocortisone butyr 0.1% ointment. Apply thinly to the affected area(s) once a day for up to 7 days; supply 100 grams; NHS Cost £7.58.

Betamethasone dipropionate 0.05% ointment
- Age from 12 years onwards
- Diprosone 0.05% ointment(100g). Apply thinly to the affected area(s) once a day for up to 7 days; supply 100 grams; NHS Cost £6.84.

Mometasone furoate 0.1% ointment
- Age from 12 years onwards
- Mometasone 0.1% furoate ointment. Apply thinly to the affected area(s) once a day for up to 7 days; supply 100 grams; NHS Cost £14.05.

Betamethasone valerate 0.1% cream
- Age from 12 years onwards
- Betamethasone val 0.1% cream. Apply thinly to the affected area(s) once a day for up to 7 days; supply 100 grams; NHS Cost £4.35.

Hydrocortisone butyrate 0.1% cream
- Age from 12 years onwards
- Hydrocortisone butyr 0.1% cream. Apply thinly to the affected area(s) once a day for up to 7 days; supply 100 grams; NHS Cost £7.58.

Betamethasone dipropionate 0.05% cream
- Age from 12 years onwards
- Diprosone 0.05% cream (100g). Apply thinly to the affected area(s) once a day for up to 7 days; supply 100 grams; NHS Cost £7.58.

Mometasone furoate 0.1% cream
- Age from 12 years onwards
- Mometasone 0.1% furoate cream. Apply thinly to the affected area(s) once a day for up to 7 days; supply 100 grams; NHS Cost £14.05.

Scalp applications

Betamethasone valerate 0.1% scalp application
- Age from 12 years onwards
- Betamethasone val 0.1% sca app. Apply to scalp once a day, for up to 7 days; supply 100 ml; NHS Cost £4.22.

Betamethasone valerate 0.1% lotion
- Age from 12 years onwards
- Betamethasone val 0.1% lotion. Apply to scalp once a day, for up to 7 days; supply 100 ml; NHS Cost £5.23.

Betamethasone valerate 0.12% foam
- Age from 12 years onwards
- Betamethasone val 0.12% foam. Apply to scalp once a day, for up to 7 days; supply 100 grams; NHS Cost £7.50.

Betamethasone dipropionate 0.05% lotion
- Age from 12 years onwards
- Diprosone 0.05% lotion (30ml). Apply to scalp once a day, for up to 7 days; supply 1 30ml applicator; NHS Cost £3.04.

Hydrocortisone butyrate 0.1% scalp application
- Age from 12 years onwards
- Hydrocortisone butyr scalp lotion. Apply to scalp once a day, for up to 7 days; supply 100 ml; NHS Cost £10.49.

Mometasone furoate 0.1% scalp application
- Age from 12 years onwards
- Mometasone 0.1% lotion. Apply to scalp once a day, for up to 7 days; supply 60 ml; NHS Cost £9.76.

Antibiotic for 7 days (if visibly infected)

Flucloxacillin syrup: 62.5mg four times a day
- Age from 1 month to 23 months
- Flucloxacillin 125mg/5ml syrup. Take 2.5ml four times a day for 7 days; supply 100 ml; NHS Cost £3.49.

Flucloxacillin syrup: 125mg four times a day
- Age from 2 to 4 years
- Flucloxacillin 125mg/5ml syrup. Take one 5ml spoonful four times a day for 7 days; supply 200 ml; NHS Cost £6.97.

Flucloxacillin syrup: 250mg four times a day
- Age from 5 to 11 years
- Flucloxacillin 250mg/5ml syrup. Take one 5ml spoonful four times a day for 7 days; supply 200 ml; NHS Cost £13.97.

Flucloxacillin capsules: 250mg four times a day
- Age from 12 years onwards
- Flucloxacillin 250mg capsules. Take one capsule four times a day for 7 days; supply 28 capsules; NHS Cost £2.93.

Flucloxacillin capsules: 500mg four times a day
- Age from 12 years onwards
- Flucloxacillin 500mg capsules. Take one capsule four times a day for 7 days; supply 28 capsules; NHS Cost £4.73.

Erythromycin s/f suspension: 125mg four times a day
- Age from 1 month to 23 months
- Erythromycin 125mg/5ml sf susp. Take one 5ml spoonful four times a day for 7 days; supply 200 ml; NHS Cost £2.22.

Erythromycin s/f suspension: 250mg four times a day
- Age from 2 to 11 years
- Erythromycin 250mg/5ml sf susp. Take one 5ml spoonful four times a day for 7 days; supply 200 ml; NHS Cost £3.80.

Erythromycin s/f suspension: 500mg four times a day
- Age from 9 to 11 years
- Erythromycin 500mg/5ml sf susp. Take one 5ml spoonful four times a day for 7 days; supply 200 ml; NHS Cost £6.44.

Erythromycin e/c tablets: 250mg four times a day
- Age from 12 years onwards
- Erythromycin 250mg e/c tablets. Take one tablet four times a day for 7 days; supply 28 tablets; NHS Cost £3.08.

Erythromycin e/c tablets: 500mg four times a day
- Age from 12 years onwards
- Erythromycin 250mg e/c tablets. Take two tablets four times a day for 7 days; supply 56 tablets; NHS Cost £6.16.

Chronic lichenified eczema

Which therapy?

- **Settle the lichenified chronic lesion with a potent corticosteroid.**
  - Treat until the skin has returned to normal.
  - Most lesions will require 4–6 weeks of treatment.
- **Treat visibly infected eczema with oral antibiotics.**
  - Flucloxacillin or erythromycin (if the person is allergic to penicillin) are first-line treatments.
- **Prevent recurrence of chronic lesions.**
  - Settle further acute flare-ups with intermittent topical corticosteroids. Ideally, these treatments should be of sufficient potency to achieve this within 14 days.
  - If acute flare-ups are frequent:
    - Review and emphasis the regular use of emollients.
    - Review factors that might be provoking flare-ups.
- For further information on settling acute flare-ups and managing frequent flare-ups, see the scenario *Localized flare-up*.

Practical prescribing points

For further information please see the *Medicines Compendium* (www.medicines.org.uk) or the *British National Formulary* (www.bnf.org).

- **Frequency of application:** the evidence suggests that once-daily application of topical corticosteroids is as effective as more frequent application. Note that most manufacturers recommend two or three applications per day.
- **Give specific advice regarding the quantity of steroid to apply.** Where larger areas require treatment, explain and demonstrate the use of the fingertip unit (FTU).
  - **One FTU weighs about 500 mg.** It is roughly equivalent to the amount of cream or ointment that can be squeezed from a tube with a standard nozzle onto an adult index finger from the tip of the finger to the first crease.
  - **For an adult,** one FTU of topical corticosteroid is sufficient to treat a skin area about twice that of the flat of the hand with the fingers.
  - **For a child aged 6 months to 1 year,** use a quarter of the adult amount.
  - **For a child from 1 year to 4 years,** use a third of the adult amount.
- Prescribe a sufficient quantity to settle a lesion completely.

Follow-up advice

- **In view of the risk associated with prolonged use of potent topical corticosteroids,** keep the person under close review until these products are no longer required.
- **The exact frequency of review** will depend on the severity of the problem and the person's experience of managing the condition.

Should I refer or investigate?

Refer?

- **Disseminated herpes simplex virus infection** — arrange emergency admission for confirmation of the diagnosis and antiviral treatment.
- **Unresponsive severe disease,** including bacterially infected eczema unresponsive to treatment with oral antibiotics and topical corticosteroids — arrange emergency admission or urgent referral depending on severity.

- **Eczema requiring a duration and/or potency of treatment with topical corticosteroids that risks systemic adverse effects.**

Table 4: Weekly dose of corticosteroids unlikely to cause systemic adverse effects in adults.

Treatment period (months)	Mild and moderately potent	Potent	Very potent
<2 months	100 g	50 g	30 g
2–6 months	50 g	30 g	15 g
6–12 months	25 g	15 g	7.5 g

- **Eczema requiring a duration and potency of treatment with topical corticosteroids that risks skin thinning** (i.e. if a potent corticosteroid is required on the same area of skin of the trunk or limbs on average more frequently than 7 days within a 5-week period) — the risk is increased:
  - In thin skin and flexural areas.
  - With increasing duration of use.
  - When corticosteroids are used with occlusion.
- **Uncontrolled eczema where dietary factors** are suspected, requiring advice from a dietician.
- Where there is diagnostic uncertainty.

Investigate?

- **Microbiological investigation is indicated** to ascertain sensitivities when infected eczema does not respond to first-line antibiotics.

Patient information leaflets

The following PILs are available at www.prodigy.nhs.uk

- Eczema - Atopic
- Eczema - Emollients (Moisturisers)
- Eczema - Fingertip Units for Topical Steroids
- Eczema - Topical Steroids
- Eczema - Triggers and Irritants
- National Eczema Society
- Skin Care Campaign

Shared decision making

- **A 4–6 week course of a strong topical steroid** may be needed on clear patches of lichenified (thickened) inflamed skin.
  - Apply the correct amount of each dose by using 'fingertip units'.
  - Side-effects are uncommon unless used long-term.
  - Once it has cleared, stop the steroid.
- **Also, keep using liberal amounts of emollients** (moisturizers). Many people use a variety. For example:
  - A bath or shower additive for a background 'oiling' (but they make the bath slippery — be careful).
  - A thick ointment as a soap substitute.
  - A cream or ointment at other times.
    - Ointments work better and longer than creams do, but are messier to use.
    - Creams for mild dry skin, or for weepy eczema.
  - Lotions for hairy areas.
  - An ointment at bedtime.
- **An antibiotic** is sometimes needed if the eczema becomes infected.

Drug rationale

Drugs not included

- **Antipruritic drugs:** oral antihistamines, topical calamine, topical antihistamines, local anaesthetics or doxepin hydrochloride are not recommended in the management of flare-ups of eczema. Whilst some drugs may have a restricted role in preventing itchiness, the effectiveness of these agents are limited and often offset by adverse effects:
- **Wet-wrap bandages**, including those impregnated with zinc or ichthammol, are not offered. They can be useful to protect the skin, improve the hydrating action of emollients, increase the effect of topical corticosteroids, and cool the skin and reduce pruritus. However, they can be difficult to apply and are more suited to a secondary-care environment.
- **Topical tacrolimus and pimecrolimus** are not offered. NICE recommends that these should be initiated only by physicians (including general practitioners) with a special interest and experience in dermatology.
- **Oral corticosteroids** may be useful as 'rescue therapy' for particularly severe and widespread flares of eczema.
- **Very potent topical corticosteroids:** clobetasol propionate, difluocortolone valerate, and halcinonide are reserved for use under specialist supervision in eczema that has proved resistant to other topical corticosteroids.
- **Topical corticosteroids with antimicrobial agents:** there is a lack of evidence that these products are more effective than topical corticosteroids alone, and there is a possibility that widespread use may contribute to the development of bacterial resistance.
- **Emollients** should be continued as usual during a flare-up of eczema. Details of initiating emollient treatment are given in the scenario *Dry skin — starting treatment.*

Drugs included

- The vehicle used for the corticosteroid is a matter of personal preference, but in general creams are favoured on wet or weeping eczema, and ointments are preferred for dry or lichenified skin
- **Mildly potent topical corticosteroid:** hydrocortisone is suitable for use in mild eczema, inflammation of sensitive areas such as the face or neck, and eczema in infants.
- **Moderately potent topical corticosteroids:** aclometasone dipropionate, clobetasone butyrate, and dilute betamethasone valerate 0.025% are suitable for use in moderate to severe eczema.
- **Potent topical corticosteroids:** betamethasone valerate 0.1%, betamethasone diproprionate, hydrocortisone butyrate, and mometasone furoate are suitable for use in severe flare-ups of eczema.
- **Lotions and foams are suitable vehicles for scalp applications** and are usually easier to apply than are standard creams and ointments. Topical applications of bethamethasone valerate, betamethasone diproprionate, hydrocortisone butyrate, and mometasone furoate are recommended for eczema of the scalp. Note that some applications have an alcoholic base and application on broken skin may be painful.
- **Flucloxacillin** has activity against Gram-positive organisms including beta-lactamase-producing staphylococci and streptococci. It is licensed in the treatment of infected skin conditions, including eczema.
- **Erythromycin** is suitable for people with infected eczema who have a known hypersensitivity to penicillin and related antibiotics.

Prescriptions

Mildly potent corticosteroids

Hydrocortisone 1% ointment

- Age from 1 month onwards
- Hydrocortisone 1% ointment (100g). Apply thinly to the affected area(s) once a day, when required; supply 100 grams; NHS Cost £2.38; OTC Cost £1.22.

Hydrocortisone 1% cream
- Age from 1 month onwards
- Hydrocortisone 1% cream (100g). Apply thinly to the affected area(s) once a day, when required; supply 100 grams; NHS Cost £2.18.

Moderately potent corticosteroids

Betamethasone valerate 0.025% ointment
- Age from 12 months onwards
- Betamethasone val 0.025% ointment. Apply thinly to the affected area(s) once a day, when required; supply 100 grams; NHS Cost £3.59.

Clobetasone butyrate 0.05% ointment
- Age from 12 months onwards
- Clobetasone butyrate 0.05% ointment. Apply thinly to the affected area(s) once a day, when required; supply 100 grams; NHS Cost £6.20.

Alclometasone dipropionate 0.05% ointment
- Age from 12 months onwards
- Alclometasone 0.05% ointment. Apply thinly to the affected area(s) once a day, when required; supply 100 grams; NHS Cost £5.64.

Betamethasone valerate 0.025% cream
- Age from 12 months onwards
- Betamethasone val 0.025% cream. Apply thinly to the affected area(s) once a day, when required; supply 100 grams; NHS Cost £3.59.

Clobetasone butyrate 0.05% cream
- Age from 12 months onwards
- Clobetasone butyrate 0.05% cream. Apply thinly to the affected area(s) once a day, when required; supply 100 grams; NHS Cost £6.20.

Alclometasone dipropionate 0.05% cream
- Age from 12 months onwards
- Alclometasone 0.05% cream. Apply thinly to the affected area(s) once a day, when required; supply 100 grams; NHS Cost £5.64.

Potent corticosteroids

Betamethasone valerate 0.1% ointment
- Age from 12 years onwards
- Betamethasone val 0.1% ointment. Apply thinly to the affected area(s) once a day, when required; supply 100 grams; NHS Cost £4.35.

Betamethasone dipropionate 0.05% ointment
- Age from 12 years onwards
- Diprosone 0.05% ointment(100g). Apply thinly to the affected area(s) once a day, when required; supply 100 grams; NHS Cost £2.41.

Mometasone furoate 0.1% ointment
- Age from 12 years onwards
- Mometasone 0.1% furoate ointment. Apply thinly to the affected area(s) once a day, when required; supply 100 grams; NHS Cost £14.05.

Betamethasone valerate 0.1% cream
- Age from 12 years onwards
- Betamethasone val 0.1% cream. Apply thinly to the affected area(s) once a day, when required; supply 100 grams; NHS Cost £4.35.

Hydrocortisone butyrate 0.1% cream
- Age from 12 years onwards
- Hydrocortisone butyr 0.1% cream. Apply thinly to the affected area(s) once a day, when required; supply 100 grams; NHS Cost £7.58.

Betamethasone dipropionate 0.05% cream
- Age from 12 years onwards
- Diprosone 0.05% cream (100g). Apply thinly to the affected area(s) once a day, when required; supply 100 grams; NHS Cost £7.58.

Mometasone furoate 0.1% cream
- Age from 12 years onwards
- Mometasone 0.1% furoate cream. Apply thinly to the affected area(s) once a day, when required; supply 100 grams; NHS Cost £14.05.

Scalp applications

Betamethasone valerate 0.1% scalp application
- Age from 12 years onwards
- Betamethasone val 0.1% sca app. Apply to scalp once a day, for up to 7 days; supply 100 ml; NHS Cost £4.22.

Betamethasone valerate 0.1% lotion
- Age from 12 years onwards
- Betamethasone val 0.1% lotion. Apply to scalp once a day, for up to 7 days; supply 100 ml; NHS Cost £5.23.

Betamethasone valerate 0.12% foam
- Age from 12 years onwards
- Betamethasone val 0.12% foam. Apply to scalp once a day, for up to 7 days; supply 100 grams; NHS Cost £7.50.

Betamethasone dipropionate 0.05% lotion
- Age from 12 years onwards
- Diprosone 0.05% lotion (30ml). Apply to scalp once a day, for up to 7 days; supply 1 30ml applicator; NHS Cost £3.04.

Hydrocortisone butyrate 0.1% scalp application
- Age from 12 years onwards
- Hydrocortisone butyr scalp lotion. Apply to scalp once a day, for up to 7 days; supply 100 ml; NHS Cost £10.49.

Mometasone furoate 0.1% scalp application
- Age from 12 years onwards
- Mometasone 0.1% lotion. Apply to scalp once a day, for up to 7 days; supply 60 ml; NHS Cost £9.76.

Antibiotic for 7 days (if visibly infected)

Flucloxacillin syrup: 62.5mg four times a day
- Age from 1 month to 23 months
- Flucloxacillin 125mg/5ml syrup. Take 2.5ml four times a day for 7 days; supply 100 ml; NHS Cost £3.49.

Flucloxacillin syrup: 125mg four times a day
- Age from 2 to 4 years
- Flucloxacillin 125mg/5ml syrup. Take one 5ml spoonful four times a day for 7 days; supply 200 ml; NHS Cost £6.97.

Flucloxacillin syrup: 250mg four times a day
- Age from 5 to 11 years
- Flucloxacillin 250mg/5ml syrup. Take one 5ml spoonful four times a day for 7 days; supply 200 ml; NHS Cost £13.97.

Flucloxacillin capsules: 250mg four times a day
- Age from 12 years onwards
- Flucloxacillin 250mg capsules. Take one capsule four times a day for 7 days; supply 28 capsules; NHS Cost £2.93.

Flucloxacillin capsules: 500mg four times a day
- Age from 12 years onwards
- Flucloxacillin 500mg capsules. Take one capsule four times a day for 7 days; supply 28 capsules; NHS Cost £4.73.

Erythromycin s/f suspension: 125mg four times a day
- Age from 1 month to 23 months
- Erythromycin 125mg/5ml sf susp. Take one 5ml spoonful four times a day for 7 days; supply 200 ml; NHS Cost £2.22.

Erythromycin s/f suspension: 250mg four times a day
- Age from 2 to 11 years
- Erythromycin 250mg/5ml sf susp. Take one 5ml spoonful four times a day for 7 days; supply 200 ml; NHS Cost £3.80.

Erythromycin s/f suspension: 500mg four times a day
- Age from 9 to 11 years
- Erythromycin 500mg/5ml sf susp. Take one 5ml spoonful four times a day for 7 days; supply 200 ml; NHS Cost £6.44.

Erythromycin e/c tablets: 250mg four times a day
- Age from 12 years onwards
- Erythromycin 250mg e/c tablets. Take one tablet four times a day for 7 days; supply 28 tablets; NHS Cost £3.08.

Erythromycin e/c tablets: 500mg four times a day
- Age from 12 years onwards
- Erythromycin 250mg e/c tablets. Take two tablets four times a day for 7 days; supply 56 tablets; NHS Cost £6.16.

E

Widespread flare-up — severe

Which therapy?

- **Exclude eczema herpeticum;** if suspected, arrange emergency admission.
- **Arrange urgent referral or emergency admission,** depending on clinical judgement, if a widespread flare-up is:
  - Severe
  - Not responding well to topical corticosteroids of appropriate potency
  - Distressing to the person
- **Prescribe an antibiotic** if the person is awaiting urgent referral and there are *any* features of infection.
- **Consider prescribing oral prednisolone** if the person is awaiting urgent referral.
- **Oral corticosteroids should be continued until the individual is seen by a specialist,** as there is a risk of rebound flare-up when stopped. It is therefore important that the person is seen within 7 days, to avoid prolonged oral steroid use.
- **Flucloxacillin or erythromycin** are first-line antibiotics.

Practical prescribing points

For further information please see the *Medicines Compendium* (www.emc.vhn.net) or the *British National Formulary* (www.bnf.org).
- Start with 30 mg prednisolone once daily and reduce the dose by 5 mg a day as soon as inflammation settles. Continue on the lowest dose of oral corticosteroid that manages the inflammation adequately until the specialist sees the person.

Should I refer or investigate?

Refer?

- **Seek specialist help** if a widespread flare-up is:
  - Severe
  - Not responding well to topical corticosteroids of appropriate potency
  - Distressing to the person
- The decision to arrange emergency admission or urgent outpatient review for someone with unresponsive severe disease will depend on clinical judgement.
- **Disseminated herpes simplex virus infection** (eczema herpeticum) is potentially life-threatening, and if suspected should prompt emergency admission for confirmation of the diagnosis and anti-viral treatment.

Patient information leaflets

The following PILs are available at www.prodigy.nhs.uk
- Eczema - Atopic
- Eczema - Emollients (Moisturisers)
- Eczema - Fingertip Units for Topical Steroids
- Eczema - Topical Steroids
- Eczema - Triggers and Irritants
- National Eczema Society
- Skin Care Campaign

Shared decision making

- **You need to be seen by a specialist, as your eczema is severe.**
- **A course of steroid tablets** is an option to reduce the inflammation until you are seen by the specialist.
- **A course of antibiotics** may be needed too if the eczema is infected.

Drug rationale

Drugs not included

- **Topical corticosteroids** are not included. However, they can be used in conjunction with oral prednisolone to hasten the resolution of a severe widespread flare-up of eczema, but this increases the possibility of systemic adverse effects.
- **Topical corticosteroids with antimicrobial agents** are not recommended. There is a lack of evidence that these products are more effective than topical corticosteroids alone, and there are additional concerns over the possibility that they may result in bacterial resistance.

Drugs included

- **Oral corticosteroids** are recommended as 'rescue therapy' for someone with severe widespread flare-ups of eczema who is in considerable discomfort and requires immediate relief. A short course of prednisolone, taken as 30 mg once daily, is included for at most 7 days or until the person can be referred to a specialist.
- **Oral antibiotics** should always be prescribed for widespread and severe flare-ups of eczema.
  - **Flucloxacillin** is active against Gram-positive organisms, including beta-lactamase-producing staphylococci and streptococci. It is licensed in the treatment of infected skin conditions, including eczema.
  - **Erythromycin** is suitable for people with infected eczema who have a known hypersensitivity to penicillin and related antibiotics.

Prescriptions

Rescue therapy – oral prednisolone 30mg/day for 7 days

Plain prednisolone: 30mg each morning for 7 days
- Age from 16 years onwards
- Prednisolone 5mg tablets. Take six tablets each morning (as a single dose) for 7 days; supply 42 tablets; NHS Cost £1.02.

Antibiotic for 7 days (if visibly infected)

Flucloxacillin syrup: 62.5mg four times a day
- Age from 1 month to 23 months
- Flucloxacillin 125mg/5ml syrup. Take 2.5ml four times a day for 7 days; supply 100 ml; NHS Cost £3.49.

lucloxacillin syrup: 125mg four times a day
Age from 2 to 4 years
Flucloxacillin 125mg/5ml syrup. Take one 5ml spoonful four times a day for 7 days; supply 200 ml;
NHS Cost £6.97.

lucloxacillin syrup: 250mg four times a day
Age from 5 to 11 years
Flucloxacillin 250mg/5ml syrup. Take one 5ml spoonful four times a day for 7 days; supply 200 ml;
NHS Cost £13.97.

lucloxacillin capsules: 250mg four times a day
Age from 12 years onwards
Flucloxacillin 250mg capsules. Take one capsule four times a day for 7 days; supply 28 capsules;
NHS Cost £2.93.

lucloxacillin capsules: 500mg four times a day
Age from 12 years onwards
Flucloxacillin 500mg capsules. Take one capsule four times a day for 7 days; supply 28 capsules;
NHS Cost £4.73.

rythromycin s/f suspension: 125mg four times a day
Age from 1 month to 23 months
Erythromycin 125mg/5ml sf susp. Take one 5ml spoonful four times a day for 7 days; supply 200 ml;
NHS Cost £2.22.

rythromycin s/f suspension: 250mg four times a day
Age from 2 to 11 years
Erythromycin 250mg/5ml sf susp. Take one 5ml spoonful four times a day for 7 days; supply 200 ml;
NHS Cost £3.80.

rythromycin s/f suspension: 500mg four times a day
Age from 9 to 11 years
Erythromycin 500mg/5ml sf susp. Take one 5ml spoonful four times a day for 7 days; supply 200 ml;
NHS Cost £6.44.

rythromycin e/c tablets: 250mg four times a day
Age from 12 years onwards
Erythromycin 250mg e/c tablets. Take one tablet four times a day for 7 days; supply 28 tablets;
NHS Cost £3.08.

rythromycin e/c tablets: 500mg four times a day
Age from 12 years onwards
Erythromycin 250mg e/c tablets. Take two tablets four times a day for 7 days; supply 56 tablets;
NHS Cost £6.16.

Extended Information

Background information

What is atopic eczema? p.727
What causes atopic eczema? p.727
How common is it? p.727
How do I know my patient has it? p.728
What else might it be? p.728
Complications and prognosis p.728

What is atopic eczema?

Atopic eczema is a chronic, relapsing, inflammatory skin condition characterized by an itchy red rash that favours the skin creases such as the folds of the elbows or behind the knees.

Atopic eczema is associated with other atopic disease such as asthma and hay fever [Hoare et al, 2000].

A tendency to dry skin results from a reduced lipid barrier that increases transdermal water loss and lowers resistance to irritant substances.

- Intracellular oedema and white cell infiltrates occur in the dermis. Complex abnormalities of immunoregulation have been observed, as have raised serum immunoglobulin E (IgE) levels in 80% of people with atopic eczema, where the degree of elevation corresponds to the severity of the disease.

What causes atopic eczema?

Atopic eczema occurs in genetically susceptible individuals when exposed to environmental irritants and/or allergens. It may be accentuated, but not caused, by endogenous factors such as stress, or hormonal changes in women.

Genetic factors

- **The precise genetic cause is unknown** but is likely to be due to genetic abnormalities.
- Atopic eczema is present in about 80% of children where both parents are affected, and in 60% if only one parent is affected [Uehara and Kimura, 1993].

Environmental irritants

- **Irritants such as soap, detergents, and chemicals** are common triggers for atopic eczema. Soaps and detergents reduce the already depleted lipid barrier and may allow increased penetration of allergens. They may also have a direct irritant effect or be allergenic themselves.
- **Extremes of temperature and humidity** may exacerbate eczema. Most people are aware of seasonal variation in their atopic eczema; most improve in summer and worsen in winter. However, sweating induced by heat or exercise can provoke an exacerbation at any time of year [Beltrani and Boguneiwicz, 2003].
- **Abrasive fabrics** such as wool can exacerbate eczema.

Environmental allergens

- **Dietary factors** aggravate atopic eczema in about 10% of children, but in adults this is far less common [Holden and Parish, 1998].
- **Inhaled allergens** have been shown to exacerbate atopic eczema. The most commonly implicated allergens include house dust mites, pollens, pet dander, and moulds [Beltrani and Boguneiwicz, 2003].
- **The role of *Staphylococcus aureus* in triggering atopic eczema is uncertain.** It is present in 90% of atopic skin lesions, and the density of colonization tends to increase with the clinical severity. Whether the increase in colonization with the bacteria is the cause of the deterioration in the eczema or whether the deterioration in the eczema promotes colonization with bacteria is debatable. Certainly, eczema complicated by clinically apparent infection commonly leads to a worsening of the condition [Hoare et al, 2000].

Endogenous factors

- **Stress may exacerbate atopic eczema,** although this effect is highly variable between individuals. In addition, atopic eczema may be a cause of psychological distress [Beltrani and Boguneiwicz, 2003].
- **Hormonal changes in women** can exacerbate atopic eczema. Premenstrual flare-ups occur in 30% of young women with atopic eczema. Pregnancy is also noted to have an adverse effect in 50% of pregnant women with atopic eczema [Beltrani and Boguneiwicz, 2003].

How common is it?

- **Atopic eczema accounts for 30% of all dermatological consultations in general practice** [Holden and Parish, 1998].

E

- **Atopic eczema is common and the prevalence is increasing** [Williams, 1992].
- The prevalence of atopic eczema is 15–20% in children and 2–10% in adults [Holden and Parish, 1998].
- It is most common in children, with about 80% of cases starting before the age of 5 years [Wüthrich, 1996].

How do I know my patient has it?

Atopic eczema is likely if the person has an itchy skin condition and three or more of the following:

- A history of itching of skin creases (e.g. bends of elbows or behind knees) or cheeks in young children.
- A history or the presence of flexural eczema or eczema affecting the cheeks, forehead, or outer limbs in young children.
- A tendency towards dry skin.
- A personal or immediate family history of asthma or hay fever.
- Onset under the age of 2 years.

[MeReC, 2003]

Appearance and distribution

The distribution of lesions tends to vary with age, and the appearance of persistent lesions may alter with scratching. A tendency to dry skin persists throughout life even in people where the condition appears to have resolved.

- **Acute flare-ups** vary in appearance, from collections of fluid in the skin (vesicles) to areas of poorly demarcated redness. Other features may also be present, such as crusting, scaling, cracking, and swelling of the skin.
- **Chronic lesions** commonly become thickened (lichenified) as a result of repeated scratching.
- **During infancy,** atopic eczema primarily involves the face, the scalp, and the extensor surfaces of the limbs, and is more likely to be acute. The nappy area is usually spared.
- **In children and in adults with long-standing disease,** localization to the flexure of the limbs is more likely.
- **Adults commonly have generalized dryness and itching,** particularly with exposure to irritants. Chronic eczema on the hand may be the primary manifestation.

Investigations

- **Investigations are rarely required to establish the diagnosis.**
- Estimation of immunoglobulin E (IgE) and specific radioallergosorbant tests (RASTs) serve only to confirm the atopic nature of the individual, and are occasionally of value in confirming adult-onset eczema.

What else might it be?

Common differential diagnoses likely to be seen in general practice include:

- Psoriasis
- Contact dermatitis
- Seborrhoeic dermatitis
- Fungal infections
- Lichen simplex chronicus
- Scabies and other infestations

Complications and prognosis

Complications

Infection

- **Bacterial infection** with *Staphylococcus aureus* may present with typical impetigo or as worsening of the eczema with increased redness, oozing, and crusting.
- **Herpes simplex infection,** indicated by grouped vesicles and punched-out erosions, can also occur. Disseminated herpes simplex virus infection, eczema herpeticum, presents with widespread lesions that may coalesce to large, denuded, bleeding areas that can extend over the entire body.
- **Superficial fungal infections** are also more common in people with atopic eczema.

Psychosocial impact

Atopic eczema may have a profound effect on many aspects of life:

- **Disturbed sleep patterns.**
- **Reduced self-esteem** because of chronic visible disease.
- **Isolation of children from their peers** (e.g. by preventing them participating in swimming or because of dietary restrictions).
- **Significant effects on a child's behaviour and development,** because of poor sleep, reduced self-esteem and social isolation; this may persist into later life.

Prognosis

- **Atopic eczema generally runs a relapsing course,** with a tendency to gradual improvement in adult life.
- **Atopic eczema can be expected to clear in 60–70% of children by their early teens,** although relapses may occur. A tendency towards dry and irritable skin generally persists.
- **Predictors of a worse prognosis** include:
  - Onset at an age of 3–6 months
  - Severe disease in childhood
  - Associated asthma or hay fever
  - Small family size
  - High IgE serum levels

[Wüthrich, 1996]

Management issues

- Overview of managing atopic eczema in primary care p.728
- Emollients p.729
- Topical corticosteroids p.730
- Infected eczema p.732
- What are the trigger factors for eczema and how do I manage them? p.732
- Referral to a specialist p.734
- Which treatments have no proven value? p.734
- Can atopic eczema be prevented? p.734

Overview of managing atopic eczema in primary care

General

- **Management in primary care is based upon:**
  - Identifying and avoiding the provoking factors.
  - Using emollients regularly.
  - Using topical corticosteroids and oral antibiotics intermittently for flare-ups.
  - Referring selected people to a specialist.
- **Information** about the condition, the factors that may provoke it, the role of different treatments, and their effective and safe use, is required to manage eczema effectively.
- **Treatment should be planned** to balance the individual's goals of disease control against the safety and acceptability of treatment. Without this approach, compliance is likely to be poor and management less than optimal.
- **It is important to demonstrate how to use topical treatments,** particularly topical corticosteroids, and to emphasise the correct quantities to use.

Managing dry skin

- **The aim of management of eczema between flare-ups** is to control skin dryness and itching and reduce the frequency of flare-ups.
- **Establish a daily skin-care regime with emollients.** The type of emollient, its frequency, and the quantity to apply should be tailored to the individual's skin requirements and lifestyle.
- **Avoid irritation to the skin** by prescribing an emollient soap substitute, and advising the person to:
  - Use gloves when unable to avoid handling irritants such as detergents.
  - Avoid extremes of temperature and humidity.
  - Use non-abrasive clothing fabrics, such as cotton.
  - Reapply emollients after wetting the skin.

Managing flare-ups

- **Settle inflammation** with topical corticosteroids.
- **Treat clinically apparent bacterial infection** with oral antibiotics.
- **Urgently refer** or admit someone with severe unresponsive disease, and admit someone when you suspect herpes simplex virus of complicating the flare-up (eczema herpeticum).

Managing frequent flare-ups

- **Settle acute flare-up** as above.
- **Review and emphasise the use of emollients** to improve the skin's barrier function. Increase the intensity of emollient treatment, if acceptable to the individual, by all or any of the following:
  - Change the emollient to one with a higher lipid content.
  - Advise the person to apply the emollient more often.
  - Recommend applying more emollient each time.
- **Review the factors that might be provoking flare-ups:**
  - Are there environmental irritants or stresses that can be avoided?
  - Allergen avoidance is burdensome, but may be considered when other measures fail.
- **Refer to a specialist** if there is a risk of either systemic adverse effects or localized adverse effects due to topical corticosteroid use.
- **Refer to a dietician** when you are considering dietary intervention.

Managing chronic eczema in adults

- **Settle chronic lesions** with a potent corticosteroid.
- **Review and consider:**
  - The use of emollients.
  - The avoidance of environmental irritants and stress.
  - Antigen avoidance, if appropriate.
- **Settle further flare-ups** with intermittent use of a topical corticosteroid of an appropriate potency and duration of use.
- **Refer to a specialist** if there is a risk of either systemic adverse effects or localized adverse effects due to topical corticosteroid use.

Managing severe widespread eczema

- **Seek specialist help** if a flare-up is widespread, severe, and distressing to the individual.
- **Consider oral prednisolone and antibiotics** if there is a delay before specialist review.
- **There is a risk of rebound flare-up when oral corticosteroids are stopped.** The individual should stay on the oral corticosteroid until other measures are instituted. It is therefore important that the specialist sees the individual within 7 days, in order to avoid prolonged oral corticosteroid use.

Emollients

How do emollients work?

- **Good quality evidence for the use of emollients in treating atopic eczema is surprisingly lacking.** Despite this, emollients are almost universally recommended as first-line treatment in the treatment of atopic eczema.
- **The aim of treatment with emollients** is to reduce symptoms of skin dryness and reduce the frequency of flare-ups.
- **Emollients improve the depleted lipid barrier of the skin.** This reduces transdermal water loss and therefore reduces skin dryness and itch. The improved lipid barrier also increases the skin's resistance to irritants, so flare-ups occur less often.

What determines the effectiveness of emollients in practice?

- **The effectiveness of emollient treatment depends on how well the lipid barrier is restored.** The dryer the skin, the more lipid will need to be applied.
- **The amount of lipid applied to the skin is determined by:**
  - The proportion of lipid in the product used
  - How often the product is applied
  - How much is applied
- **Varying any of these factors will alter the intensity of treatment.**

What types of emollient are there?

- **Lotions, creams, and ointments** vary in the proportion of lipid to water.
- **The lipid content** is lowest in lotions, intermediate in creams, and highest in ointments.
- **The tolerability of a product is largely determined by its lipid content.** The higher the lipid content, the greasier and stickier it feels and the shinier its appearance.

How do I choose a suitable emollient?

Choose an emollient by considering the dryness of the skin, the type of skin, and individual preference. Individual preference is largely determined by the product's tolerability and convenience of use.

- **Areas of hairy skin** requiring an emollient are most acceptably treated with a lotion.
- **Weeping eczema** is best treated with a water-soluble cream or lotion, because ointments will tend to slough off and become unacceptably messy.
- **Low to moderate dryness of the skin:** when flare-ups are infrequent, a relatively low intensity of treatment will restore the skin's lipid-barrier function. If dryness is mild, a lotion may be sufficient, but more commonly a cream is required.
- **Moderately dry to very dry skin:** when flare-ups are more frequent, a higher intensity of treatment is required to restore the lipid-barrier function. Individual preference will determine the product to use:
  - Creams are generally better tolerated, but will need to be applied more frequently and generously to have the same effect as a single application of ointment.
  - The individual will need to balance the tolerability of a product against the convenience of its use and the acceptability of symptoms.
- **The tolerability and convenience of a product can only be determined by trying the treatment.** When more intense treatment is required, a trial of small quantities of several creams and ointments is often advocated in order to determine the most acceptable treatment.
- **More than one type of product may be required.** An ointment may be acceptable for night-time use and a cream preferred during the day. Different products may be preferred at different times, depending on the

intensity of treatment required and the area of skin to be treated.

How much emollient should I prescribe?

- **Prescribe generous quantities of emollient once a suitable product has been determined.** A common mistake is to prescribe insufficient emollient, which may lead to under-use. It is not unusual for an adult to require a 500 g tub of emollient per week and a child to require a 500 g tub every 2 weeks.

How often should an emollient be applied?

- **The intensity of treatment should be responsive** to the need to maintain symptoms and flare-ups at an acceptable level. It can vary markedly between individuals and for the same individual over time. Applying emollient generously three times a day is a good starting point, but this may need to be increased up to every hour if the skin is very dry.
- **Apply emollients as soon as possible after bathing or showering,** while water is still trapped in the skin for extra hydration.

Should I prescribe emollient soap substitute and/or bath emollients?

- **Emollient soap substitutes** are useful to avoid the drying effects of soaps, and should be considered for all people with eczema. They are particularly useful for people who are required to wash or wet their hands frequently.
- **Bath emollients** are a useful additional treatment to a lotion, cream, or ointment. They help to clean and hydrate the skin and provide a convenient method of covering the whole body. Purpose-made bath oils or ointments dispersed in the bath water can be used for this purpose.
- Bath emollients coat the bath, making it greasy. Warn about the risk that the individual or a family member could slip and fall in the bath or shower. Using a mat and grab rails may help to minimize the risk of slipping.
- The drying effects of bubble bath and shampoo can be avoided by not using these items in the bath.

How should emollients be applied with topical corticosteroids?

- Apply the corticosteroid to the eczematous areas and emollient to the rest of the skin *without mixing*, as this may dilute the effect of the corticosteroid.
- Between corticosteroid treatments, apply emollient to all areas including the areas previously treated with corticosteroid. Wait at least 30 minutes before applying the emollient over the corticosteroid.

What are the adverse effects of emollients, and how are they managed?

- **There may be sensitivity to constituents** such as the preservatives, fragrances, and biologically derived ingredients such as lanolin (see Table 5). If you suspect the preservative of causing problems, change to a product that has a different one. Alternatively, prescribe an ointment if this is acceptable, because it will not usually contain a preservative.
- **In children with moderate to severe eczema, aqueous cream** has been associated with an increased incidence of irritant skin reactions compared with other emollients [Cork et al, 2003]. The significance of this in older people or in people with mild eczema has not been established. As with any emollient, if it causes a reaction, offer an alternative.

Topical corticosteroids

What is the evidence for the effectiveness of topical corticosteroids?

- Randomized controlled trials of topical corticosteroids compared with placebo suggest a large treatment effect [Hoare et al, 2000]. Topical corticosteroids are the first-line treatment for settling the inflammation of a flare-up.

What potency of topical corticosteroid should I prescribe and for how long?

Acute flare up

- **For the face, genitals and flexures** where the skin is thin, prescribe a mildly potent topical corticosteroid. The absorption of corticosteroid is enhanced through thin skin and in flexures, owing to the self-occlusive effect of the skin fold.
- **The eyelids** should be treated only intermittently with a mildly potent topical corticosteroid, for at most 14 days. The person should take care to avoid getting corticosteroid on the surface of the eye. There is a slight risk of cataract formation, and in people over the age of 35 years there is a risk of glaucoma, necessitating regula monitoring of intraocular pressure by a specialist when more than 14 days of treatment is necessary.
- **The palms, soles of the feet, and scalp** require treatment with a potent corticosteroid, because the thick skin reduces the penetration of the corticosteroid and hence its effectiveness.
- **For children, where the surface area to be treated is relatively large** start treatment with a mildly potent topical corticosteroid. Treatment with a moderately potent corticosteroid should be used only infrequently. Where control of flare-ups requires frequent use of a moderately potent corticosteroid, seek specialist help.
- **Treatment of the trunk and limbs in adults:** select the lowest potency of corticosteroid that is likely to work within 7–14 days of starting treatment, based upon:
  - The severity of inflammation
  - Response to previous treatment
- **Review** if there is no significant sign of improvement within 7 days, and step up to a more potent corticosteroid.
- **Seek specialist help** if eczema requires a duration or potency of treatment with a topical corticosteroid that risks systemic or localized adverse effects.
- **Short-burst treatment for mild to moderate eczema** aims to resolve a flare-up with 3 days of treatment, using a potent topical corticosteroid. It is more convenient for the person and is supported by evidence as an effective and safe approach in the treatment of mild to moderate eczema flare-ups [Charman and Williams, 2003].

Chronic lichenified eczema

- **Chronic inflammation** that is untreated or undertreated may lead to ongoing itch, scratching, and subsequent lichenification that significantly reduces penetration of topical corticosteroids.
- **Settle the lichenified lesion with a potent topical corticosteroid.** Treatment for 4–6 weeks is commonly required to restore the skin back to normal. The exact duration will depend on the response to treatment.
- **Continue with maintenance treatment** with regular emollients and intermittent topical corticosteroids of adequate potency to prevent the problem recurring.

How much topical corticosteroid should be applied?

- **Give specific information regarding the quantity of topical corticosteroid to apply.** Advice from doctors is often vague or non-existent and may result in the person

ble 5: Ingredients and excipients that may make the skin sensitive.

nollient	Lanolin derivatives	Cetyl or cetostearyl alcohol	Benzyl alcohol	Isopropyl palmitate	Parabens	Fragrance	Other potential sensitizers
nulsifying ntment*		X					—
aderm®		X					—
dromol® ntment		X			X		—
drous ointment*	X						Phenoxy-ethanol
paraffin ntment*							—
ueous cream*		X					*May* contain chlorocresol
probase® cream		X					Chlorocresol
5® cream	X	X			X		—
latum® cream		X	X				Potassium sorbate
guentum M®		X					Propylene glycol, sorbic acid
eeno® lotion		X	X	X			—
rmamist®							Coconut oil
5® lotion	X		X	X	X		—
ri®	X				X	X	Propylene glycol, quatemium-15
ctiCare®		X		X		X	Imidurea
ha Keri Bath®	X					X	Oxybenzone
eeno® bath oil						X	Beeswax
lneum®						X	Propylene glycol, Hydoxytoluene
probath®							Laureth-4
5® bath oil							—
latum® bath ditive	X			X		X	—

he exact formulation of some generic emollients may vary.

using inappropriate quantities of corticosteroid [Long and Finlay, 1993]. Overuse may increase the risk of adverse effects of corticosteroid. Underuse may delay the settling of a flare-up, leading to the unnecessary use of a more potent preparation [Long et al, 1998].

A corticosteroid should be applied to the skin as a thin layer: for large areas, the quantity of corticosteroid to apply is expressed in terms of fingertip units (FTUs). **Use of FTUs is recommended and should be demonstrated** to avoid confusion. These units may be used together with body charts that show the number of FTUs required to cover each area of a child's or adult's body.

One FTU weighs about 500 mg. It is roughly equivalent to the amount of cream or ointment that can be squeezed from a tube with a standard nozzle onto an adult index finger from the tip of the finger to the first crease.

One FTU is sufficient to treat a skin area about twice that of the flat of the hand with the fingers together [MeReC, 1999].

Back this up with written information. There is a PRODIGY Patient Information Leaflet about this.

Vhat quantity of corticosteroid should I prescribe?

It is important to prescribe enough topical corticosteroid to treat the flare-up until it is completely resolved. The inconvenience of returning for a further prescription increases the risk of under-treatment and poor disease control.

- In a survey of 83 people with atopic eczema seen in an outpatient department, 25% felt that their GP did not prescribe enough topical corticosteroid. Of these, 75% were reluctant to attend for a further prescription [Long and Finlay, 1993].

Should corticosteroids be applied once a day or twice a day?

- **The National Institute for Clinical Excellence** has considered trial evidence, as well as expert opinion about the prescription of topical corticosteroids once or twice daily.
  - The committee was told that differences exist in clinical practice.
  - It concluded that there was no compelling evidence of a clinically significant difference between once-daily application and more frequent application of topical corticosteroids.
  - It was persuaded that current clinical practice would therefore support a recommendation for the use of topical corticosteroids no more frequently than twice a day.
- **The evidence included a systematic review that identified three good-quality randomized controlled trials**

Table 6: Suitable quantities of corticosteroid to prescribe for a flare-up in adults.

Body area	Amount of corticosteroid to prescribe
Face and neck	30g
Both hands	30g
Scalp	30g
Both arms	30–60g
Both legs	100g
Trunk	100g
Groins and genitalia	30g

[BNF 47, 2004]

comparing once-daily with twice-daily administration of topical corticosteroids.
  - In no study were more frequent applications better than once-daily application.
  - While the results suggested a small difference in favour of more frequent applications, these did not reach statistical significance.
  - No good-quality study could be identified that compared frequencies of application of a mildly potent topical corticosteroid [Hoare et al, 2000].
- **Using a once-daily application of a topical corticosteroid has some advantages:**
  - A lower risk of adverse effects
  - Greater convenience for the person
  - Lower cost to the NHS

What are the adverse effects of topical corticosteroids?

Systemic adverse effects

- **Systemic adverse effects are most likely with potent topical corticosteroids** when used in large quantities for prolonged periods. Mild reversible hypophyseal-pituitary-adrenal (HPA) suppression may occur, which may lead to the features of Cushing syndrome [Clement and Du Vivier, 1987].
- **Safe weekly doses for topical corticosteroids** based upon potency, quantity, and duration of use have been determined by studies on systemic absorption. It is important to realize that this does not mean that local adverse effects cannot occur with this level of use, only that HPA suppression is unlikely [Clement and Du Vivier, 1987].
- **Children and particularly infants** are much more susceptible to systemic adverse effects from topical corticosteroids, owing to their relatively large surface area in relation to bodyweight. In addition, the effects of HPA suppression in children may lead to retarded growth. It is strongly recommended that children requiring moderately potent topical corticosteroids on a regular basis be under the care of a specialist and have their growth carefully monitored.

[Coulson, 1996]

Localized adverse effects

- **Skin thinning is much more likely with potent topical corticosteroids.** The skin on the trunk and limbs may start to thin within 1–3 weeks of starting a potent topical corticosteroid, but reverses within 4 weeks if treatment is stopped. There is little risk of skin thinning with mild to moderate topical corticosteroids used for up to 4 weeks [DTB, 2003].
- **If a potent corticosteroid is required on the same area of skin of the trunk or limbs on average more frequently than 7 days within a 5-week period,** there is a risk of skin thinning and a specialist should review the person.
- The risk is increased:
  - In thin skin and flexural areas
  - With increasing duration of use
  - When corticosteroids are used with occlusion
- Topical corticosteroids may precipitate or worsen acne, worsen rosacea, or provoke perioral dermatitis.

Table 7: Weekly dose of corticosteroids unlikely to cause systemic adverse effects in adults.

Treatment period (months)	Mild and moderately potent	Potent	Very potent
<2 months	100 g	50 g	30 g
2–6 months	50 g	30 g	15 g
6–12 months	25 g	15 g	7.5 g

Infected eczema

How do I know when eczema is infected?

- **The diagnosis of bacterial infection relies on the visible appearance,** not on microbiological examination, because 90% of atopic eczema patches are colonized b *Staphylococcus aureus*. Microbiological investigations ascertain sensitivities are useful if visible infection fails respond to a first-line antibiotic. Swab severely infected eczema before treating, to reduce delay in switching to an appropriate antibiotic if the infection is not sensitive to the first-line treatment.
- **The typical appearance of impetigo** (crusted lesions tha may be yellow) may be difficult to distinguish from eczema. It is common practice, therefore, to assume th eczema that is severe or that unexpectedly deteriorates may have become infected, and to treat it with an oral antibiotic.
- **Herpes simplex** complicating atopic eczema (eczema herpeticum) may be misdiagnosed as a *S aureus* infection. The presence of punched-out erosions, vesicl or infected skin lesions that fail to respond to oral antibiotics should raise suspicion of a herpes simplex infection.

When should I prescribe an antibiotic?

- **Treat visibly infected eczema with oral antibiotics.**
  - The skin of most people with atopic eczema is colonized with *S aureus*, with colonization present in 90% of affected areas. In some cases clinically overt infection of the eczema develops.
  - Trials have shown that treatment of visibly infected eczema with oral antibiotics improves the rate of resolution of the flare-up.
- There is no evidence from a randomized controlled tria to support the use of oral antibiotics when there are no visible signs of infection. Colonization rates fall dramatically when the eczema is treated with topical corticosteroids alone.

[Hoare et al, 2000]

- **Flucloxacillin or erythromycin** (if the patient is allergic penicillin) are recommended as first-line oral antibiotic [HPA, 2003].
- **Topical antimicrobial/corticosteroid combinations** hav been shown to be no more effective than topical corticosteroid alone in treating either visibly infected o uninfected flare-ups [Hoare et al, 2000].

How do I manage someone with eczema infected with herpes simplex?

- **Life-threatening dissemination has been reported.** Therefore, arrange urgent admission for confirmation the diagnosis and antiviral treatment.

What are the trigger factors for eczema and how do I manage them?

Irritants

People with atopic eczema are more vulnerable to irritan than are normal individuals, and it is therefore important to identify and avoid irritants that trigger the itch–scratch cycle. These include:

- **Soaps and detergents** used on the skin remove the protective lipid barrier, increasing the tendency of the skin to be dry, itchy, and more permeable to allergens. These should be avoided where possible by means such as using emollient soap substitutes, avoiding the use of bubble bath and shampoos in the bath, and gloves to prevent exposure to detergents and other chemicals.

Toiletries commonly contain perfumes, preservatives, and alcohols, all of which may be irritating to the skin and should be avoided.

Abrasive clothing. Cottons are naturally fine-textured and breathe well and are therefore a good choice for someone with atopic eczema. However, limited evidence from two randomized controlled trials (RCTs) suggests that it is the texture of the fabric and not the actual type of fabric that is the important factor [Hoare et al, 2000].

Extremes of temperature and humidity can be managed with practical measures to reduce provocation of flare-up.

Psychological stress and habitual scratching

Psychological stress does not cause atopic eczema but will often exacerbate the problem. Some people respond to stress with habitual scratching that sets off the itch–scratch cycle, and in some instances the disease itself may be the source of the stress. Relaxation and behavioural techniques may prove useful in controlling the symptoms.

Prevention of habitual scratching using behavioural techniques has been shown to improve global eczema scores. Behavioural techniques combined with treatment with hydrocortisone cream have been studied in two RCTs, which showed a reduction of nearly 70% in global eczema scores compared to an improvement of 40% in the group using hydrocortisone alone. Despite shortcomings in the design of the study, it seems likely that these results were significant [Hoare et al, 2000].

The lack of availability of professionals able to offer this combination treatment means that it is rarely used. It may be worth consideration in someone with more severe disease when habitual scratching is considered a significant factor.

Food hypersensitivity and eczema

If a child's eczema is mild and easily managed with simple measures such as emollients and intermittent topical corticosteroid, there is no need to consider exclusion diets.

Diet is probably only a significant trigger for atopic eczema in 10% of children, and the likelihood of diet as a trigger factor decreases rapidly over the age of 3 years [Barnetson and Rogers, 2002].

Exclusion diets for selected people with demonstrable food sensitivity may benefit management of their eczema. The evidence for using exclusion diets for unselected people is inconclusive [Smethurst and Macfarlane, 2003].

- One RCT concluded that exclusion of egg from the diet of children with proven sensitivity to egg reduced the surface area affected by eczema.
- There are conflicting results from two RCTs examining the effect of excluding egg and cows' milk on the severity of eczema in unselected children.
- One RCT comparing a 'few-foods diet' with usual diet in unselected people found no significant difference in the severity of eczema.

Dietary manipulation is unlikely to replace the need for a regular skin-care regime with emollients and intermittent topical corticosteroids.

How do I know if diet is a significant trigger factor?

Itching and scratching may worsen shortly after eating certain foods. An obvious sign is redness, swelling, and irritation around the mouth.

Immediate food hypersensitivy occurs within 2 hours of eating certain foods. Skin symptoms include urticaria, swelling, and redness. Other symptoms may occur, such as abdominal pain, vomiting, wheezing, itchy eyes, and sneezing.

- **Delayed food hypersensitivity** occurs 6–24 hours after eating the food. Symptoms include worsening of itching and the eczema, possibly accompanied by abdominal pain and diarrhoea.
- **Suspicion of a food being responsible for deterioration in eczema is made by observation.** The association is usually obvious when there is an immediate type of food reaction. A diary, keeping a record of eczema, scratching, sleep, and all foods and drink eaten over a period of 4–6 weeks can be helpful in identifying a problem food. Often parents may have tried avoiding some foods, and this should be enquired about.
- **Confirmation of the diagnosis** is made with an exclusion-and-challenge procedure supervised by a dietician. This procedure involves:
  - Removing all sources of suspected food for 2–6 weeks to bring about an improvement in the eczema.
  - Reintroducing the suspected food to bring about a return of the eczema.
  - Removing the suspected food to bring about an improvement again.
- **Supervision by a dietician** is important to ensure that the procedure is carried out properly and that the diet used is nutritionally balanced.
- **The most common foods to trigger eczema** include cows' milk, eggs, soya, wheat, fish, and nuts.

House-dust mite and other inhalant allergens

- There is strong circumstantial evidence that house-dust mite antigens are an important precipitating factor for atopic eczema.
- Atopic eczema may be better controlled when house-dust mite allergen can be substantially reduced.
  - Modest but significant benefit was shown in three RCTs when house-dust mite levels were substantially reduced by measures such as using synthetic mattress covers, acaricidal spraying, and frequent high-filtration vacuuming.
  - In studies where house-dust mite levels were reduced only by 68%, no benefit was shown.

[Smethurst and Macfarlane, 2003]

How do I know if house-dust mite is a significant trigger factor?

- **House-dust mite is a common trigger factor** in many people with atopic eczema. It is more common than food sensitivity in older children and adults.
- **The benefit to an individual of reducing exposure to house-dust mites can be shown only by undertaking a trial period of reduced exposure.**
- A significant reduction in the exposure is worth considering when moderate to severe eczema proves difficult to control with regular emollients and intermittent topical corticosteroid.
- Specific radioallergosorbant tests (RASTs) and skin-prick testing have a high number of false positives and have little value in confirming whether house-dust mite is a significant trigger factor. However, if the results are positive it may be useful to consider a trial of reducing exposure to house-dust mite allergen [Sampson and Albergo, 1984].

How is house-dust mite managed?

- For the benefits to be seen, there must be an extreme reduction in house-dust mite allergen. The measures required for modest benefit to be achieved may be impracticable for many people.
- Daily dusting, vacuuming of carpets, and the use of Gortex bed covers seem to be the most effective measures to reduce the allergen load.

Other inhalant allergens

- Animal dander, moulds, and pollens have all been implicated in triggering flare-ups in atopic eczema. The principles of diagnosis and management are as for house-dust mite, although avoidance in many cases may be more easily achieved.

[Hoare et al, 2000]

Referral to a specialist

When should I refer to a specialist?

Most people with atopic eczema can be managed in primary care. In order of urgency, referral to a specialist is advised in the following situations.

- **Disseminated herpes simplex virus infection** (eczema herpeticum). This is potentially life-threatening, and if suspected should prompt emergency admission for confirmation of the diagnosis and antiviral treatment.
- **Unresponsive severe disease** (often causing sleep disturbance or absence from school or work), including bacterially infected eczema unresponsive to treatment with oral antibiotics and topical corticosteroids.
- **Eczema requiring a duration and/or potency of treatment** with topical corticosteroids that risks systemic or localized adverse effects.
- **Uncontrolled eczema where dietary factors** are suspected, requiring advice from a dietician.
- Where there is diagnostic uncertainty.

What treatments are available from specialists?

- **Topical immunosuppressant, tacrolimus, or pimecrolimus** are useful when there is a serious risk of systemic or localized adverse effects due to topical corticosteroid, or when eczema cannot be controlled with topical corticosteroid. The long-term safety of topical immunosuppressants has not been established, and treatment should therefore only by initiated by physicians (including general practitioners) with a special interest and experience in dermatology, and only after careful discussion with the patient about the potential risks and benefits of all appropriate second-line treatment options. Pimecrolimus is used to treat mild to moderate eczema, and tacrolimus is used to treat moderate to severe atopic eczema.
- **Wet-wraps are commonly used to manage severe eczema in young children.** A generous layer of emollient (or a low-potency topical corticosteroid in severe cases) is applied to the skin and a layer of pre-soaked bandages applied on top. A second layer of dry dressings then follows this. Close supervision is required in order to avoid systemic adverse effects when a topical corticosteroid is used.
- **Ultraviolet (UV) light treatment has clearly been shown to improve atopic eczema.** Issues regarding what type of UV light is most effective, the effects on chronicity, the duration of remission, and long-term safety are as yet not resolved [Hoare et al, 2000].
- **Hospitalization** without otherwise changing the prescribed treatment will often result in improvement when treatment has failed in the community. In many cases, a sustained improvement results from removing the person from environmental antigens or emotional stresses, providing intense education, and assuring compliance with treatment.

Which treatments have no proven value?

- **Antiseptic/emollient combinations are not recommended.** Two small randomized controlled trials (RCTs) of poor quality failed to show any significant benefit of using the combined products above that of an emollient alone [DTB, 1998].
- **Sedating antihistamines** are commonly prescribed to promote sleep and reduce scratching. However, studies have failed to show any clear benefit for itch or global improvement in eczema.
- **Topical doxepin** failed to show any sustained benefit compared with placebo in a review of four RCTs. In addition, systemic absorption of doxepin leads to drowsiness in up to 20% of people.
- **Dietary supplementation:** the evidence is either lacking or does not support the use of these treatments. Supplementation with essential fatty acids, pyridoxine, vitamin E, multivitamins, and zinc salts have all been suggested as treatments for atopic eczema.
- **Chinese herbal medicine** may include oral or topical Chinese herbs in combination with acupuncture, diet, or exercise to treat or prevent eczema. Evidence from different RCTs has been contradictory, and at present benefit is unproven. Some topical preparations contain potent topical steroids, and some of the oral preparations have been associated with serious toxicity.
- **Evening primrose oil,** oral and topical, has been widely used in atopic eczema, but two large trials have shown that evening primrose oil taken orally offers no benefit in atopic eczema.
- **Avoidance of biological washing powders shows no demonstrable benefit to the management of atopic eczema,** as shown by one small but well-designed RCT. The narrow confidence intervals in the results provide convincing evidence of the lack of harmful effect.
- **Probiotic (microorganism) oral supplements** such as Lactobacilli species have been studied in the primary prevention of atopic eczema in infants and may offer some benefit, although further large-scale studies are required.
- **Coal-tar topical products** have been used for decades to manage a variety of dry-skin conditions. Evidence of benefit in atopic eczema is lacking and coal tar may cause hypersensitivity reactions.

[DTB, 2000; Hoare et al, 2000].

Can atopic eczema be prevented?

- **Exclusive breastfeeding for at least 3 months may reduce the risk of eczema in infants with a family history of eczema.** A systematic review of prospective cohort studies (4158 infants) assessed the effects of exclusive breastfeeding during the first 3 months after birth on the development of atopic eczema. It found a significant reduction in the risk of atopic eczema developing after a mean of 4.5 years (OR 0.68, 95% CI 0.52 to 0.88). However, subgroup analysis found that the preventive effect was significant only in children with a family history of atopic eczema (OR 0.58, 95% CI 0.41 to 0.9[illegible] for children who had a first degree relative with an atopic condition) [Smethurst and Macfarlane, 2003].
- **Evidence does not support the use of an antigen-avoidance diet during pregnancy to reduce atopic eczema.** The evidence from four trials involving 451 participants does not suggest any protective effect from antigen avoidance during pregnancy, but did result in a statistically significant lower mean birth weight [Kramer and Kakuma, 2004].

References

NHS staff in England can link, free of charge, from references to full text journals by clicking on [Full text] on the PRODIGY website.

1. Barnetson, R.S. and Rogers, M. (2002) Childhood atopic eczema. *British Medical Journal* **324**(7350), 1376–1379. [Full text]
2. Beltrani, V.S. and Boguneiwicz, M. (2003) *Dermatology Online Journal* 9(2), 1.

BNF 47 (2004) *British National Formulary*. 47th edn. London: British Medical Association and Royal Pharmaceutical Society of Great Britain.

Charman, C. and Williams, H. (2003) The use of corticosteroids and corticosteroid phobia in atopic dermatitis. *Clinics in Dermatology* **21**(3), 193–200.

Clement, M. and Du Vivier, A. (1987) *Topical steroids for skin disorders*. Oxford: Blackwell Scientific Publications.

Cork, M.J., Timmins, J., Holden, C. et al (2003) An audit of adverse drug reactions to aqueous cream in children with atopic eczema. *Pharmaceutical Journal* **271**(7277), 747–748.

Coulson, I. (1996) Topical steroids for skin disease. *Dermatology in Practice* **March/April**, 5–8.

DTB (1998) Antiseptic/emollient combinations. *Drug & Therapeutics Bulletin* **36**(11), 84–86.

DTB (2000) Doxepin cream for eczema? *Drug & Therapeutics Bulletin* **38**(4), 31–32.

0. DTB (2003) Topical steroids for atopic dermatitis in primary care. *Drug & Therapeutics Bulletin* **41**(1), 5–8.

1. Hoare, C., Li Wan Po, A. and Williams, H. (2000) Systematic review of treatments for atopic eczema. *Health Technology Assessment* **4**(37), 1–191.

2. Holden, C.A. and Parish, W.E. (1998) Atopic dermatitis. In: Champion, R.H., Burton, J.L., Burns, D.A and Breathnach, S.M. (Eds.) *Rook/ Wilkinson/ Ebling Textbook of Dermatology: Volume 1*. 6th edn. Oxford: Blackwell Science. 681–708.

3. HPA (2003) *Management of infection guidance for primary care: for consultation and local adaptation*. Health Protection Agency. www.hpa.org.uk [Accessed: 26/02/2004]. [Full text]

14. Kramer, M.S. and Kakuma, R. (2004) *Maternal dietary antigen avoidance during pregnancy and/or lactation for preventing or treating atopic disease in the child (Cochrane Review)*. The Cochrane Library. Issue 1. Chichester, UK: John Wiley & Sons, Ltd.

15. Long, C.C. and Finlay, A.Y. (1993) Perceived underprescription of topical therapy. *British Journal of General Practice* **43**(372), 305.

16. Long, C.C., Mills, C.M. and Finlay, A.Y. (1998) A practical guide to topical therapy in children. *British Journal of Dermatology* **138**(2), 293–296.

17. MeReC (1998) The use of emollients in dry skin conditions. *MeReC Bulletin* **9**(12), 45–48.

18. MeReC (1999) Using topical corticosteroids in general practice. *MeReC Bulletin* **10**(6), 21–24.

19. MeReC (2003) Atopic eczema in primary care. *MeReC Bulletin* **14**(1), 1–4.

20. Sampson, H.A. and Albergo, R. (1984) Comparison of results of skin tests, RAST, and double-blind, placebo-controlled food challenges in children with atopic dermatitis. *Journal of Allergy & Clinical Immunology* **74**(1), 26–33.

21. Smethurst, D. and Macfarlane, S. (2003) Atopic eczema. *Clinical Evidence* **10**(Dec), 1785–1803.

22. Uehara, M. and Kimura, C. (1993) Descendant family history of atopic dermatitis. *Acta Dermato-Venereologica* **73**(1), 62–63.

23. Williams, H.C. (1992) Is the prevalence of atopic dermatitis increasing? *Clinical & Experimental Dermatology* **17**(6), 385–391.

24. Wüthrich, B. (1996) Epidemiology and natural history of atopic dermatitis. *Allergy and Clinical Immunology International* **8**(3), 77–82.

PRODIGY GUIDANCE

Endometriosis

Last revised in February 2003
www.prodigy.nhs.uk/guidance.asp?gt=Endometriosis

Applies to women over the age of 12 years

This guidance covers the management of endometriosis.

This guidance does not cover the management of dysmenorrhoea.

There is separate PRODIGY guidance for *Dysmenorrhoea* and *Menorrhagia*.

Goals

- Relieve pain
- Improve subfertility

Contents

Scenarios
- Analgesia and hormonal treatment p.736
- Oral contraception required p.739

Extended Information, p. 742

Which scenario?

- **Analgesia and hormonal treatment:** offers advice on pain relief in endometriosis and on the choices of hormonal treatments available.
- **Oral contraception required:** provides prescribing advice when it is appropriate to combine symptom management of endometriosis with oral contraception (off-licence use). More detailed advice and further choices are available in the PRODIGY *Contraception* guidance.

Analgesia and hormonal treatment

Which therapy?

- **Treatment is usually initiated on the advice of a specialist,** as a definitive diagnosis can only be made by laparoscopy.
- **Analgesics,** in particular nonsteroidal anti-inflammatory drugs (NSAIDs), may be adequate for symptom relief. Paracetamol with or without codeine may be useful when NSAIDs are not tolerated or are contraindicated.
- **Hormonal treatments are all equally effective at relieving symptoms,** and choice should usually be determined by patient preference and the duration of treatment required.
- Table 1 below summarises the treatment options available and whether their recommended use is for the short or the long term or both.
- **All hormonal treatments are contraindicated in pregnancy and breastfeeding.** Before any hormonal treatment is started, the possibility of pregnancy must b ruled out.
- **'Add-back' therapy,** using hormone replacement therap (HRT), may be recommended in conjunction with gonadotrophin-releasing hormone (GnRH) analogues; this has no effect on efficacy and helps to reduce advers effects on bone mineral density. For further informatio on HRT preparations, see PRODIGY *Menopause* guidance.
- **Surgery** is the preferred treatment option for endometriotic ovarian cysts or infertility.

Practical prescribing points

For further information, please see the *Medicines Compendium* (www.medicines.org.uk) or the *British National Formulary* (www.bnf.org).

NSAIDs

- People with a history of peptic ulcer disease should onl be given NSAIDs after other possibilities have been considered (CSM advice).
- Worsening of asthma may be related to the ingestion o NSAIDs (CSM warning).

Hormonal therapy

Adverse events

- **Progestogens:** contraindicated in pregnancy. Adverse effects include irregular bleeding, bloating, skin change mood changes, and weight gain. Depot medroxyprogesterone acetate causes a reduction in bor mineral density in many women who use it but the risk of osteoporosis and fractures in later life is not known.
- **Danazol and gestrinone:** contraindicated in pregnancy and breastfeeding. Adverse effects include weight gain; hirsutism; acne; mood changes; and occasionally deepening of the voice, which may be irreversible. Danazol is only licensed for use when other treatments have failed.

Table 1: Hormonal treatment options for treating endometriosis.

Therapy	Progestogens		Anti-progesterones	Gonadotrophin-releasing hormone antagonists	Combined oral contraceptive
	Norethisterone/ dydrogesterone	Medroxy-progesterone			
Short-term*	+	+	+	+	+
Long-term**	+	–	–	–	+

* Licensed treatment duration varies between 3 months and 9 months.
** Can be taken indefinitely.

GnRH analogues: contraindicated in pregnancy and breastfeeding. Adverse effects include hot flushes, insomnia, reduced libido, vaginal dryness, headaches, and reduced bone mineral density, all of which are helped by 'add-back' therapy

Buserelin and nafarelin nasal sprays

If **nasal decongestant** is required during treatment with either buserelin or nafarelin, it should be administered at least 30 minutes afterwards.

Nafarelin: sneezing during or immediately after dosing may impair absorption. If sneezing occurs, repeating the dose may be advisable.

Should I refer or investigate?

Refer?

Refer all women with suspected endometriosis: a definitive diagnosis can only be made by laparoscopy.

Investigate?

Primary care investigations are not helpful for making a diagnosis of endometriosis.

Vaginal swabs and endocervical swabs for chlamydia should be taken if pelvic inflammatory disease is suspected.

Patient information leaflets

The following PILs are available at www.prodigy.nhs.uk
- Endometriosis
- Endometriosis - Treatment Options
- Laparoscopy and Laparoscopic Surgery
- National Endometriosis Society

Shared decision making

Treatment options for endometriosis include:

Not treating if symptoms are mild and fertility is not an issue.

Painkillers such as paracetamol, anti-inflammatories, or codeine taken during your periods. This may be all that you need if symptoms are mild.

Hormone treatments: these work by reducing oestrogen, or its effect on endometrial cells which need oestrogen to survive. There are several types. One is usually started by a specialist.

Danazol, gestrinone, or gonadotrophin-releasing hormone (GnRH) analogues are usually taken for 6 months only.

A progestogen can be taken long-term.

On average, all hormone treatments work as well as each other. However:
- Some women respond to one treatment better than others.
- The treatments differ in their possible side-effects.
- So, it is not unusual to switch treatments if the first does not suit.

You should use condoms if you have sex whilst taking hormone treatments as there is a risk of affecting a developing baby.

The contraceptive pill: this often works well and can be taken long term.

Surgery: this can be done to remove larger patches of endometriosis. This may ease symptoms and improve fertility if this is a problem. Hysterectomy is an option if you have completed your family and other treatments have not helped.

Drug rationale

Drugs not included

- **'Add-back' regimens** (using hormone replacement therapy [HRT], or a progestogen with or without an oestrogen) can reduce the bone loss and hot flushes that accompany therapy with gonadotrophin-releasing hormone (GnRH) analogues. They do not interfere with the effectiveness of GnRH analogues in reducing pain and may protect against loss of bone mineral density [Farquhar and Sutton, 1998; Franke et al, 2000; Surrey and Hornstein, 2002]. There are many combinations of oestrogen and progestogen suitable for this purpose, but prescriptions have not been included, as most women will simply continue on medication started by or recommended by the specialist. See also the PRODIGY *Menopause* guidance.
- **Nonsteroidal anti-inflammatory drugs (NSAIDs) other than ibuprofen, naproxen, and diclofenac acid** are not included. Excluded drugs are either associated with a higher risk of gastrointestinal adverse events or there is insufficient data to reach clear conclusions regarding their safety [Henry et al, 1996; Hernández-Diaz and Rodriguez, 2000; BNF 43, 2002].
- **Progestogens** not licensed for use in endometriosis are excluded [BNF 43, 2002].

Drugs included

- **Ibuprofen, naproxen, and diclofenac** are all clinically effective at relieving pain and are prostaglandin inhibitors. Ibuprofen may be the preferred first choice because of its more favourable risk–benefit ratio [Bandolier, 1998; Zhang and Li Wan Po, 1998; BNF 43, 2002].
- **Paracetamol** may be effective, particularly when used regularly rather than as required.
- **The weak opioid, codeine** (alone or in combination with regular paracetamol), can be helpful when paracetamol alone is insufficient, especially when NSAIDs are not tolerated or are contraindicated.
- **Antiprogestogens, GnRH analogues, and some progestogens** are licensed for the treatment of endometriosis. There is a general lack of comparative efficacy data and choice will often be determined by patient preference according to their adverse event profile.
  - **Progestogens: medroxyprogesterone acetate, dydrogesterone, and norethisterone** are all offered as continuous therapy. Medroxyprogesterone is licensed for 90 consecutive days although some clinicians do use it for longer if adverse effects are minimal and symptoms are well controlled. This use would be off-licence. There is no licensed restriction on length of treatment for dydrogesterone and norethisterone. Dydrogesterone is also offered as a luteal phase therapy; however there are some doubts as to the efficacy of this regimen.
  - **Antiprogestogens: danazol and gestrinone** are particularly poorly tolerated due to androgenic adverse effects of weight gain; hirsutism; acne; and occasionally deepening of the voice, which may be irreversible [Prentice et al, 2002b; Selak et al, 2002]. However, they do not reduce bone mineral density, as the anabolic effects counteract the effect of lowered oestrogen levels. Gestrinone has a longer half-life than danazol and only needs to be taken twice a week. Danazol is included as a second-line option when other hormonal treatments have failed.
  - **GnRH analogues: buserelin and nafarelin (nasal sprays), goserelin implant, leuprorelin injection, and**

triptorelin injection are all included. The 3-monthly depot injection of goserelin is not offered as this is only licensed for prostate cancer. All these products will be specialist initiated and are only licensed for 6 months' use; further courses of treatment are not recommended. They are usually better tolerated than danazol, especially if 'add-back' therapy is offered to reduce hot flushes and other adverse effects [Farquhar and Sutton, 1998].

Prescriptions

E

Analgesia: use when required

Ibuprofen 400mg three times a day
- Age from 12 years onwards
- Ibuprofen 400mg tablets. Take one tablet three times a day; supply 84 tablets; NHS Cost £2.46; OTC Cost £4.34.

Ibuprofen 600mg three times a day
- Age from 16 years onwards
- Ibuprofen 600mg tablets. Take one tablet three times a day; supply 84 tablets; NHS Cost £3.35.

Naproxen 250mg three to four times a day
- Age from 16 years onwards
- Naproxen 250mg tablets. Take two tablets initially, then take one tablet 3 to 4 times a day. Maximum of 5 tablets in 24 hours; supply 60 tablets; NHS Cost £2.35.

Diclofenac sodium 25mg e/c three times a day
- Age from 16 years onwards
- Diclofenac 25mg e/c tablets. Take one tablet three times a day; supply 84 tablets; NHS Cost £2.45.

Diclofenac sodium 50mg e/c three times a day
- Age from 16 years onwards
- Diclofenac 50mg e/c tablets. Take one tablet three times a day; supply 84 tablets; NHS Cost £3.73.

Paracetamol 500mg to 1g up to four times a day
- Age from 12 to 15 years
- Paracetamol 500mg tablets. Take one to two tablets every 4 to 6 hours when required for pain relief. Maximum of 8 tablets in 24 hours; supply 100 tablets; NHS Cost £0.75; OTC Cost £1.32.

Paracetamol 1g up to four times a day
- Age from 16 years onwards
- Paracetamol 500mg tablets. Take two tablets every 4 to 6 hours when required for pain relief. Maximum of 8 tablets in 24 hours; supply 100 tablets; NHS Cost £0.75; OTC Cost £1.32.

Codeine 30mg tablets: add on to paracetamol if required
- Age from 16 years onwards
- Codeine 30mg tablets. Take one to two tablets every 4 to 6 hours when required for pain relief. Maximum of 8 tablets in 24 hours; supply 56 tablets; NHS Cost £2.04.

Progestogens

Medroxyprogesterone 10mg three times a day
- Age from 16 years onwards
- Medroxyprogesterone 10mg tabs. Take one tablet three times a day; supply 90 tablets; NHS Cost £22.16.

Norethisterone 5mg twice a day
- Age from 16 years onwards
- Norethisterone 5mg tablets. Take one tablet twice a day; supply 60 tablets; NHS Cost £4.30.

Norethisterone 5mg three times a day
- Age from 16 years onwards
- Norethisterone 5mg tablets. Take one tablet three times a day; supply 90 tablets; NHS Cost £6.45.

Dydrogesterone 10mg twice a day
- Age from 16 years onwards
- Dydrogesterone 10mg tablets. Take one tablet twice a day; supply 60 tablets; NHS Cost £4.49.

Dydrogesterone 10mg three times a day
- Age from 16 years onwards
- Dydrogesterone 10mg tablets. Take one tablet three times a day; supply 90 tablets; NHS Cost £6.74.

Less preferred: dydrogesterone 10mg twice a day (days 5-25)
- Age from 16 years onwards
- Dydrogesterone 10mg tablets. Take one tablet twice a day from day 5 to day 25 of cycle; supply 42 tablets; NHS Cost £3.14.

Less preferred: dydrogesterone 10mg x3 a day (days 5-25)
- Age from 16 years onwards
- Dydrogesterone 10mg tablets. Take one tablet three times a day from day 5 to day 25 of cycle; supply 63 tablets; NHS Cost £4.71.

Gestrinone or danazol (second line)

Gestrinone 2.5mg twice a week
- Age from 16 years onwards
- Gestrinone 2.5mg capsules. Take one capsule twice a WEEK; supply 8 capsules; NHS Cost £111.73.

Danazol 200mg once a day
- Age from 16 years onwards
- Danazol 200mg capsules. Take one capsule once a day supply 28 capsules; NHS Cost £13.23.

Danazol 200mg twice a day
- Age from 16 years onwards
- Danazol 200mg capsules. Take one capsule twice a da supply 56 capsules; NHS Cost £26.46.

Danazol 200mg three times a day
- Age from 16 years onwards
- Danazol 200mg capsules. Take one capsule three time day; supply 84 capsules; NHS Cost £39.69.

Danazol 400mg twice a day
- Age from 16 years onwards
- Danazol 200mg capsules. Take two capsules twice a d supply 112 capsules; NHS Cost £52.92.

GnRH analogues (nasal spray)

Buserelin 150microgram nasal spray
- Age from 16 years onwards
- Buserelin 150mcg nasal spray. Spray once into each nostril three times a day; supply 2 nasal sprays; NHS Cost £75.43.

Nafarelin 200microgram nasal spray
- Age from 18 years onwards
- Nafarelin 200mcg nasal spray. Spray once into one nostril each morning, and spray once into the other nostril at night; supply 1 spray; NHS Cost £53.01.

GnRH analogues (injection)

Goserelin 3.6mg subcutaneous injection
- Age from 16 years onwards
- Goserelin 3.6mg implant. For subcutaneous injection once every 4 weeks; supply 1 implant; NHS Cost £122.27.

Leuprorelin 3.75mg subcutaneous or intramuscular injection
- Age from 16 years onwards
- Leuprorelin 3.75mg injection. For intramuscular or subcutaneous injection, once every 4 weeks; supply 1 2ml vial; NHS Cost £125.40.

Triptorelin 4.2mg intramuscular injection
- Age from 16 years onwards
- Triptorelin 4.2mg inj powder. For intramuscular injection, once every 4 weeks; supply 1 ampoule; NHS Cost £105.05.

Oral contraception required

Which therapy?

- **Combined oral contraceptives** (COCs) provide contraception and seem to relieve symptoms of endometriosis, although this is off-licence use [Moore et al, 2003]. They offer the option of long-term symptom management.
- Choice should be based on suitability for the individual.
  - **Preparations containing 30–35 micrograms of oestrogen plus a low dosage of either levonorgestrel or norethisterone are a suitable first choice of pill.**
  - A range of 'first-choice' COCs is offered in this scenario with others offered in the PRODIGY *Contraception* guidance.
- Before prescribing the COC pill:
  - **Enquire about** personal and family history, current conditions and medications, any contraindications, cautions (first prescription particularly), and adverse effects (repeat prescriptions).
  - **Record blood pressure.**
  - **Measure** height and weight and calculate body mass index (BMI) if obesity is a concern.
  - **Breast or pelvic examination is unnecessary** unless clinically indicated by symptoms.
- **Women should be advised on how to take the pill** and this information is detailed on the right-hand side of the prescription and in the patient information leaflet.
- **Generally start on the first day of the menstrual cycle; no additional contraception is then necessary.** If started later, exclude the risk of pregnancy since the last menstrual period and advise the woman to use additional contraceptive precautions for 7 days.

Practical prescribing points

For further information please see the *Medicines Compendium* (www.medicines.org.uk) or the *British National Formulary* (www.bnf.org).

- **COCs do not protect against sexually transmitted infections (STIs) or human immunodeficiency virus (HIV).** If there is a risk of STIs or HIV, the correct and consistent use of condoms is recommended, either alone or with another contraceptive method. Male latex condoms are proven to protect against STIs and HIV [WHO, 1998].
- **The World Health Organization has published medical eligibility criteria for COC use.** For a full list of the World Health Organization (WHO) medical eligibility criteria, see www.who.int/reproductive-health/publications/mec/3_cocs.pdf. Not all uncommon medical conditions that might make COC use problematic are listed.
- **Conditions where COCs are either an unacceptable (category 4) health risk or where the risks usually outweigh the advantages (category 3)** are detailed in Table 2.
- A woman with conditions where the advantages of COCs generally outweigh the theoretical or proven risks (WHO category 2) requires careful follow-up, especially if two or more of these problems coexist.
- Many women will have no factors (WHO category 1) in their medical history that give concern about any increased individual risks for them with COCs. For any individual woman, the balance of clinical risks and benefits of COCs must be considered together with her situation, motivation, and concerns about her choice of method.

Follow-up advice

- **First follow-up appointment** is usually offered 10–12 weeks after initial visit to check blood pressure and to enquire about adverse effects. Also check correct and consistent pill use, and knowledge of what to do if a pill is missed.
- **Where there are medical or non-medical concerns,** follow-up after 6 weeks is usual.
- **For established users of combined oral contraceptive (COC) pills,** 6-monthly checks are accepted UK practice. Blood pressure, clinical history, and adverse effects should be checked together with correct and consistent pill use, and knowledge of what to do if a pill is missed.

Should I refer or investigate?

Refer?

- **All people with suspected endometriosis:** a definitive diagnosis can only be made by laparoscopy.
- If there is inadequate response to treatment.

Investigate?

- **Vaginal and endocervical swabs** for chlamydia should be taken if pelvic inflammatory disease is suspected.
- **Before commencing the combined oral contraceptive (COC) pill:**
  - Breast and pelvic examinations are unnecessary in asymptomatic women before first prescriptions of a COC pill.
  - Lipid screening:
    - There is little evidence to support screening for abnormal lipids as part of a strategy to improve COC safety.
    - It is appropriate to screen women who have one or more non-smoking siblings or parents who develop arterial disease prematurely, or who come from a family known to have a hereditary artherogenic disorder (if screening not previously performed).
  - Thrombophilia screening:
    - It is not appropriate to screen all women for thrombophilia prior to prescribing the COC pill.
    - Testing should be discussed with women who have a definite family history of thrombophilia or venous thromboembolic disease affecting first-degree relatives.

Patient information leaflets

The following PILs are available at www.prodigy.nhs.uk
- Endometriosis
- Endometriosis - Treatment Options
- Laparoscopy and Laparoscopic Surgery
- National Endometriosis Society

Shared decision making

Some points about most combined contraceptive pills include:
- Start the first pack on the first day of your next period — it is fully effective from then on.
- Take one pill a day for 21 days, at about the same time each day. Then stop for 7 days. You should have a period. Start the next pack after 7 days.

Table 2: Clinical conditions where COCs are considered either unacceptable (category 4), or where the risks usually outweigh the advantages (category 3) for use in contraception. Note: combined contraceptive patches have been assigned the same category ratings as COCs.

Condition	Category	Comment
<6 weeks postpartum	4	There is some theoretical concern that the neonate may be at risk because of exposure to steroid hormones during the first 6 weeks postpartum. There is also some theoretical concern regarding the association between COC use up to 3 weeks postpartum and risk of thrombosis in the mother.
>=6 weeks to <6 months postpartum (primarily breastfeeding)	3	In the first 6 months postpartum, use of COCs during breastfeeding diminishes the quantity of breast milk, decreases the duration of lactation, and may thereby adversely affect the growth of the infant.
Postpartum <21 days	3	Blood coagulation and fibrinolysis are essentially normalized by 3 weeks postpartum.
Aged >=35 years and smoking <15 cigarettes a day	3	COC users who smoked were at increased risk of cardiovascular diseases, especially myocardial infarction (MI), compared with those who did not smoke. Studies have also showed an increased risk of MI with increasing number of cigarettes smoked per day.
Aged >=35 years and smoking >15 cigarettes a day	4	
Cardiovascular disease — multiple risk factors for arterial cardiovascular disease	3/4	If a woman has multiple major risk factors, any of which alone would substantially increase the risk of cardiovascular disease, use of COCs may increase her risk to an unacceptable level. However, simple addition of categories for multiple risk factors is not intended; e.g. a combination of two risk factors assigned a category 2 may not necessarily warrant a higher category.
History of hypertension, where blood pressure (BP) *cannot* be evaluated (including hypertension during pregnancy)	3	Hypertension — classifications assume that no other risk factors for cardiovascular disease exist. Risk of cardiovascular disease may increase substantially when multiple risk factors exist. Evaluation of BP level and cause is recommended, as soon as feasible. Women who did not have a BP check before COC use have been found to have an increased risk of acute MI and stroke.
Adequately controlled hypertension, where BP *can* be evaluated	3	Women adequately treated for hypertension are at reduced risk of acute myocardial infarction (MI) and stroke as compared with untreated women. Although there are no data, COC users with adequately controlled and monitored hypertension should be at reduced risk of acute MI and stroke compared with untreated hypertensive COC users.
Elevated blood pressure levels (properly taken measurements) *systolic 140–159 or diastolic 90–99*	3	Among women with hypertension, COC users are at increased risk of stroke and MI compared with non-users. The risk increases with incremental rises in BP. A single BP reading of 140–159/ 90–99 is not sufficient to classify a woman as hypertensive.
Systolic >=160 or diastolic >=100	4	—
Vascular disease	4	Increased risk of arterial thrombosis associated with COC use should be avoided in women with underlying vascular disease.
Venous thromboembolism (VTE) — current or past history Major surgery with prolonged immobilization	4	The increased risk of VTE associated with COCs should have little impact on healthy women, but may have substantial impact on women with a history of thromboembolism.
Known thrombogenic mutations (e.g. Factor V Leiden; Prothrombin mutation; Protein S, Protein C and Antithrombin deficiencies)	4	Routine screening is not appropriate because of the rarity of the conditions and the high cost of screening. Among women with thrombogenic mutations, COC users have been found to have a two to twenty-fold higher risk of thrombosis than non-users.
Current ischaemic heart disease	4	Among women with underlying vascular disease, the increased risk associated with COC use should be avoided.
Stroke	4	Among women with underlying vascular disease, the increased risk associated with COC use should be avoided.
Known hyperlipidaemias	3/2	Routine screening is not appropriate because of the rarity of the conditions and the high cost of screening. While some types are risk factors for vascular disease, the category should be assessed according to the type, its severity and the presence of other cardiovascular risk factors.
Complicated valvular heart disease	4	Among women with valvular heart disease, COC use may further increase the risk of arterial thrombosis; women with complicated valvular heart disease are at greatest risk
Migraine with focal neurological symptoms at any age	4	Classification depends on accurate diagnosis of those severe headaches that are migrainous and those that are not. Any new headaches or marked changes in headaches should be evaluated. Classification is for women without any other risk factors for stroke. Risk of stroke increases with age, hypertension, and smoking.
Migraine without focal neurological symptoms <35 where continuous use	3	
Migraine without focal symptoms in women >=35 years, firstly in initiation and secondly with continuation	3 4	
Current breast disease	4	Breast cancer is a hormonally sensitive tumour, and the prognosis of women with current or recent breast cancer may worsen with COC use.
Past history of breast cancer and no evidence of recurrence for 5 years	3	
Nephropathy/retinopathy/ neuropathy	3/4	The category should be assessed according to the severity of the condition.

Condition	Category	Comment
Other vascular disease or diabetes of >20 years' duration	3/4	The category should be assessed according to the severity of the condition.
Gallbladder disease — symptomatic medically treated or current	3	COCs may cause a small increased risk of gall-bladder disease. There is also concern that COCs may worsen existing gall-bladder disease.
History of cholestasis — past COC-related	3	History of COC-related cholestasis predicts an increased risk with subsequent COC use.
Viral hepatitis — active	4	COCs are metabolized by the liver, and their use may adversely affect women whose liver function is already compromised.
Cirrhosis — mild compensated	3	COCs are metabolized by the liver, and their use may adversely affect women whose liver function is already compromised.
Cirrhosis — severe decompensated	4	
Liver tumours — benign and malignant	4	COCs are metabolized by the liver, and their use may adversely affect women whose liver function is compromised. In addition, COC use may enhance the growth of tumours.
Liver enzyme-inducing drugs	3	Although the interaction between commonly used liver enzyme-inducers and COCs is not harmful to women, it is likely to reduce the efficacy of COCs. Use of other contraceptives (e.g. progestogen-only injection) should be encouraged for women who are long-term users of any of these drugs. Whether increasing the hormone dose of COCs is of benefit remains unclear.

Category 4 — a condition that represents an unacceptable health risk if a COC is used.
Category 3 — a condition where the theoretical or proven risks usually outweigh the advantages of using a COC.

- Read and keep the information leaflet that comes in the packet. It will remind you about how to take the pill, possible side-effects, risks, what to do if you miss a pill, vomit, take other medication, etc. Briefly:
  - If you are more than 12 hours late in taking a pill — refer to the leaflet for advice on what to do.
  - If you are prescribed antibiotics or other medication — tell the prescribing doctor, nurse or dentist that you take the pill.
  - Possible side effects include headache, weight gain, nausea, breast tenderness, and mood changes. These are usually temporary.
  - Breakthrough bleeding (a light blood loss from time to time) is common. Do not stop taking the pill. It usually settles within 3 months but tell a doctor or practice nurse if it persists.
- **The risk of serious problems is small** — though more common in smokers. Serious problems include a slight increased risk of a blood clot in a leg vein (deep vein thrombosis) or in an artery, which may cause a heart attack or stroke. There is also a slight increased risk of cancer of the breast, cervix, and liver.

Drug rationale

Drugs not included

- **Combined oral contraceptives (COCs) containing desogestrel or gestodene** are not included as they are probably associated with an increased risk of venous thromboembolism compared with preparations containing levonorgestrel.
- **Higher dosages of levonorgestrel or norethisterone** are not included since there is no evidence that the COCs with higher dosages of norethisterone and levonorgestrel offer any advantages over preparations with lower dosages of these progestogens.
- **Preparations containing 20 micrograms of oestrogen** have not been shown to offer any advantage over preparations containing 30–35 micrograms of oestrogen, and some women may not achieve good cycle control with them.
- **Preparations containing high-dosage (50 micrograms) oestrogen** are only indicated for women concurrently taking hepatic enzyme-inducing drugs.
- **Biphasic preparations** offer no advantage over monophasic preparations [Van Vliet et al, 2001]. It is uncertain whether triphasic preparations offer any advantage.
- **'Every day' preparations** are not routinely used in the UK but can be useful to help women who have difficulty starting the next packet at the correct time.
- **Dianette** (cyproterone acetate and ethinylestradiol) is not licensed solely for use as a contraceptive. It should be reserved for selected women requiring treatment for severe acne, refractory to prolonged antibiotic therapy, or with moderately severe hirsutism.

Drugs included

- **Preparations containing low-dosage oestrogen (30-35 micrograms), oestrogen plus low-dosage progestogen (levonorgestrel 150 micrograms or norethisterone 500 micrograms)** are therefore included.
- Note: both Microgynon-30 and Ovranette contain ethinylestradiol 30 micrograms plus levonorgestrel 150 micrograms. Both Brevinor and Ovysmen contain ethinylestradiol 35 micrograms plus norethisterone 500 micrograms.
- For detailed information on the choice of COC and prescribing advice see the PRODIGY guidance on *Contraception*.

Prescriptions

COC containing levonorgestrel or norethisterone

Microgynon 30 (levonorgestrel 150micrograms)

- Age from 12 to 60 years
- Microgynon 30 tablets. Take one tablet once a day for 21 days. Start the next packet after a 7-day break. See package insert for full instructions; supply 63 tablets; NHS Cost £2.13.

Ovranette (levonorgestrel 150micrograms)

- Age from 12 to 60 years
- Ovranette tablets. Take one tablet once a day for 21 days. Start the next packet after a 7-day break. See package insert for full instructions; supply 63 tablets; NHS Cost £2.05.

Brevinor (norethisterone 500micrograms)

- Age from 12 to 60 years
- Brevinor tablets. Take one tablet once a day for 21 days. Start the next packet after a 7-day break. See package insert for full instructions; supply 63 tablets; NHS Cost £1.67.

Ovysmen (norethisterone 500micrograms)
- Age from 12 to 60 years
- Ovysmen tablets. Take one tablet once a day for 21 days. Start the next packet after a 7-day break. See package insert for full instructions; supply 63 tablets; NHS Cost £1.70.

Extended Information

Background information

- What is it? p.742
- How common is it? p.742
- How do I know my patient has it? p.742
- What else might it be? p.742
- Complications and prognosis p.742

E

What is it?

- **Endometriosis is defined as the presence of endometrial tissue outside the uterine cavity and musculature,** most often in the pelvis and abdomen. Other sites are rarely involved but include the pleura, pericardium, and the central nervous system.
- **Pathogenesis is uncertain.** The most widely held view is that spread of endometrial tissue outside the uterine cavity occurs due to retrograde menstruation, possibly with coexisting abnormal immune function. This ectopic endometrium responds to hormonal changes during the menstrual cycle, with subsequent bleeding, inflammation, and, if the ovaries are affected, the development of endometriotic ovarian cysts (endometriomas).

[Olive and Schwartz, 1993; Giudice et al, 1998; DTB, 1999]

How common is it?

- **Endometriosis is found almost exclusively in women of reproductive age,** with an average age at diagnosis of 25–29 years [Olive and Schwartz, 1993]. Subclinical disease may be present in even younger women [Edmonds, 1999]. Risk factors are thought to include an early menarche and late menopause [Farquhar, 2001].
- **Estimates of prevalence in premenopausal women vary from 1% to 15%** [Moore et al, 2003], although even wider ranges have been proposed. All estimates are speculative as diagnosis can only be confirmed by laparoscopy, which tends to be performed on a highly selected population [McPherson and Waller, 1997]. Up to 87% of women with a gynaecological cause of chronic pelvic pain will have the presence of endometrial implants confirmed by laparoscopy [Winkel and Scialli, 2001].
- **Endometriosis is found in 15–50% of women presenting with infertility** [Olive and Schwartz, 1993; Giudice et al, 1998].
- **There is debate as to whether there is a genetic basis to endometriosis.** There is some evidence of a familial tendency, with endometriosis being more common among first-degree relatives of affected women [Olive and Schwartz, 1993; Kennedy, 1998]. However, studies are poorly controlled and often do not include laparoscopic assessment. Biased selection is also common, as an affected mother is likely to advise her daughter to seek early gynaecological assessment for any number of symptoms that may or may not be related to the disease.

How do I know my patient has it?

History

- **Women with endometriosis may have no symptoms.**
- **Symptoms are most commonly** cyclical or chronic pelvic pain, dysmenorrhoea, and deep dyspareunia. The appearance or worsening of symptoms at the time of menstruation suggests endometriosis [Brosens, 1997].
- **Other symptoms may include:** lower abdominal pain; backache; menstrual irregularity, such as premenstrual spotting; menstrual haematuria or lower abdominal pain on urination; rectal bleeding or pain on defecation; and cyclical pain at extrapelvic sites [Brosens, 1997; Moore et al, 2003]. The severity of symptoms is not necessarily indicative of the degree of severity of endometriosis.
- **There may be a history of difficulty in conceiving** [Hughes et al, 2002].

Examination

- **Examination is often normal.** Rarely, localized tenderness and nodular lesions in the fornices or cystic lesions on the ovaries may be palpable on bimanual examination, and 'blueberry' haemorrhagic lesions may be visible in the posterior fornix or at other sites on speculum examination [Brosens, 1997].

Investigations

- **Investigations routinely available** to primary care cannot make a diagnosis of endometriosis.
- **Ultrasound scans** may detect ovarian cysts, but this is not specific for endometriotic cysts (endometriomas).
- **Laparoscopy** is the usual way of confirming the diagnosis, by direct inspection and biopsy [Brosens, 1997; Bergqvist, 1999; Moore et al, 2003].

What else might it be?

- Pelvic inflammatory disease
- Primary dysmenorrhoea
- Adenomyosis
- Irritable bowel disease
- Uterine fibroids

Complications and prognosis

Complications

- **Infertility:** moderate to severe endometriosis can cause tubal damage leading to infertility. Lesser degrees of endometriosis, even in the absence of any obvious tubal damage, are also associated with subfertility, although the reason for this is not known [Hughes et al, 2002].
- **Adhesion formation may occur,** either due to the endometriosis or due to surgery, although this is less likely with laparoscopic surgery [DTB, 1999].

Prognosis

- **The natural course of the disease is still uncertain.** It has been suggested that only about 30% of women experience progressive disease while in the remainder the endometriosis either remains in a steady state or deteriorates [Farquhar, 2001].
- **Relapse is common once hormonal treatment is discontinued.** In trials of treatment with a gonadotrophin-releasing hormone (GnRH) analogue or danazol, about 10–20% of women required further treatment within 12 months. Uncontrolled cohort studies report recurrence rates of about 50% at 5 years. Trials with an extended follow-up period are required to determine the likelihood of relapse in the long term [Farquhar and Sutton, 1998].

Surgical treatment: surgical cohort studies report 20% recurrence at 5 years after surgery [Farquhar and Sutton, 1998].

Management issues

General issues p.743
Drug treatments p.743
Surgical treatments p.744
Pre- and postoperative hormonal treatment p.744
Infertility p.744

General issues

- The need for and the choice of treatment depends on the presence and severity of symptoms, pregnancy plans, age, and the extent of the disease.
- There is a lack of comparative data between the various hormonal options and between hormonal treatment and surgical treatment [Prentice et al, 2002a]. Surgery is generally considered when medical treatments fail or the woman is having difficulty conceiving.
- Pain relief with analgesics, in particular nonsteroidal anti-inflammatory drugs (NSAIDs), may be adequate for some women [Olive and Schwartz, 1993; Bergqvist, 1999].
- Education about the condition and the different treatments available is important, as with any potentially chronic condition. Patient support groups may be helpful.

Drug treatments

Analgesia

- **Analgesia** is usually the preferred therapy. There is a suggestion that, because of the established association between prostaglandin release and dysmenorrhoea, a similar association exists in endometriosis [Shaw, 1997]. Even if this is not the case, nonsteroidal anti-inflammatory drugs (NSAIDs) remain the first choice because they inhibit the inflammatory processes that occur during endometriosis. Paracetamol with or without added codeine may be an alternative if NSAIDs are poorly tolerated or contraindicated.

Hormonal treatment

- **Hormonal treatment aims to induce atrophy of ectopic endometrium,** either by altering the effect of oestrogen on the endometriotic tissue or by reducing oestrogen levels.
- **Recurrence after discontinuation of hormonal treatment commonly occurs.** It is likely that between 25–60% of women will have recurrence of the disease within 1 year of finishing their treatment [Edmonds, 1999; Winkel and Scialli, 2001].
- **Currently available treatments are** danazol, gestrinone, gonadotrophin-releasing hormone (GnRH) analogues, the combined oral contraceptive (COC), and progestogens.
- **All these treatments are probably equally effective at relieving symptoms** of endometriosis [Farquhar, 2001; Hughes et al, 2002; Prentice et al, 2002a]. Those treatments that induce amenorrhoea are, not surprisingly, particularly successful at treating dysmenorrhoea [Farquhar and Sutton, 1998; DTB, 1999; Moore et al, 2003].

Types of hormonal treatment

- **Progestogens and antiprogestogens** include the progestogens (medroxyprogesterone acetate, dydrogesterone, and norethisterone) and antiprogestogens (danazol and gestrinone). Medroxyprogesterone acetate and norethisterone are taken continuously and dydrogesterone can be taken cyclically or continuously. Danazol and gestrinone are both taken continuously.
  - **Progestogens** induce endometrial atrophy and also inhibit ovulation with reduction in oestrogen levels. Adverse effects are most commonly irregular bleeding, bloating, mood changes, and weight gain [Vercellini et al, 1997; Bergqvist, 1999].
  - **The antiprogestogen danazol** inhibits secretion of pituitary gonadotrophins. It also has androgenic, anti-oestrogenic, and antiprogestogenic activity, and usually causes amenorrhoea (a pseudo-menopause). It is poorly tolerated because of androgenic adverse effects of weight gain; hirsutism; acne; mood changes; and occasionally deepening of the voice, which may be irreversible [Prentice et al, 2002b; Selak et al, 2002]. It does not reduce bone mineral density, as its anabolic effects counteract the effect of lowered oestrogen levels [Stevenson, 1995; Bergqvist, 1999]. It is only licensed for use in women who have not responded to other treatments.
  - **The antiprogestogen gestrinone** has similar actions to danazol but has a longer half-life, allowing twice weekly instead of daily dosing. It is also better tolerated because it is less androgenic [DTB, 1999].
  - **Progestogens and antiprogestogens** were compared with other hormonal therapies in a Cochrane review of their efficacy for the relief of pain associated with endometriosis [Prentice et al, 2002b]. There was found to be a general lack of data, and none of the studies included enough women to reach any firm conclusions. The authors cautiously concluded that treatment with antiprogestogens or continuous progestogens is likely to be effective. However, there appears to be some doubt with respect to the efficacy of luteal phase progestogens — only dydrogesterone is licensed for use in this way.
- **The COC:**
  - **The COC is commonly used to relieve symptoms of endometriosis,** although this is off-licence use. A Cochrane review looking at the efficacy of COCs for reducing the pain of endometriosis found only one study that satisfied the inclusion criteria [Moore et al, 2003].
    - At the end of the study period the low-dosage COC (ethinylestradiol 0.02 mg plus desogestrel 0.15 mg taken cyclically) was as effective as a GnRH analogue (goserelin 3.6 mg subcutaneously once a month) for the relief of dyspareunia and non-menstrual pelvic pain. In addition, the COC reduced dysmenorrhoea, but the GnRH analogue was more effective as it induced amenorrhoea. After 6 months' follow-up (i.e. 6 months after the intervention period had ended), there was a trend towards the COC being more effective for relieving dysmenorrhoea and the GnRH analogue being more effective for dyspareunia.
    - The advantage of the COC is that, unlike the GnRH analogues, it can be taken indefinitely.
  - There is a lack of comparative data about the effectiveness of different COCs for the management of endometriosis and the choice of preparation should be guided by safety and patient choice.
- **GnRH analogues:**
  - **GnRH analogues** (buserelin, goserelin, nafarelin, leuprorelin, and triptorelin) initially stimulate pituitary secretion and then rapidly inhibit secretion due to 'pituitary down-regulation' — anovulation, markedly reduced oestrogen levels, and amenorrhoea then follow (i.e. they induce a postmenopausal state).

- **Adverse effects** include hot flushes, insomnia, reduced libido, vaginal dryness, headaches, and reduced bone mineral density.
- **GnRH analogues are only licensed for 6 months' use,** principally because of the effects on bone mineral density, which typically falls by 4–6% during this time [DTB, 1999]. Some small studies have looked at the possibility of re-treating women after several months' break from a 6-month course of GnRH analogue. The results have been promising, with women reporting a decline in symptom severity. Although there is insufficient evidence to recommend this at present, using shorter repeated doses of GnRH analogue (e.g. a repeated 3-month treatment course) offers the theoretical possibility of a sustained beneficial effect combined with less impact on bone mineral density and fewer hypo-oestrogenic effects [Rice, 2002].
- **'Add-back' therapy** with hormonal replacement therapy (HRT) during treatment with GnRH analogues reduces adverse effects, in particular hot flushes, without affecting efficacy of treatment [Moghissi et al, 1998; Franke et al, 2000]. 'Add-back' therapy may also protect against loss of bone mineral density, although there is doubt about how much benefit is obtained. It should also be noted that HRT is not licensed for the prevention of osteoporosis alone [CSM, 2003]. Some investigators claim that bone density 6 months after GnRH analogue therapy is similar whether 'add-back' therapy is given or not [Farquhar and Sutton, 1998; Bergqvist, 1999] and others that several regimens have been shown to be effective for reducing bone loss [Irahara et al, 2001; Rice, 2002; Surrey and Hornstein, 2002].
  - The use of other bone-sparing agents such as the bisphosphonates has also been proposed [Child and Tan, 2001] but at present no therapy is licensed for this indication.

Choice of hormonal treatment

- **Adverse effects mainly determine choice of drug,** as all the available hormonal treatments seem to be equally effective for relieving the symptoms of endometriosis. However, there is a lack of data on patient satisfaction and compliance with the various treatments available [Selak et al, 2002]. Patient preference, after an explanation of the likely adverse effects, should usually guide treatment choice.
- **Duration of treatment needed is also an important determining factor.** For women who need long-term treatment, options include the progestogens norethisterone or dydrogesterone, or the COCs (off-licence use) — all can be used indefinitely. Medroxyprogesterone is licensed for 90 consecutive days although some clinicians do use it for longer if adverse effects are minimal and symptoms are well controlled. This use is off-licence. Danazol is licensed for up to 9 months and gestrinone for 6 months. GnRH analogues are licensed for up to 6 months of treatment and further courses of treatment after this are not recommended.

Surgical treatments

- **Surgical treatment aims to remove areas of endometriosis** in order to relieve symptoms or remove physical barriers, such as adhesions, that are preventing conception. Surgical treatment may be categorized as conservative or radical. Surgery is the treatment of choice for endometriotic ovarian cysts (endometriomas) and infertility.
- **The main conservative surgical techniques performed by laparoscopy are** thermal or laser ablation, excision, ovarian cystectomy and denervation procedures.
  - **Laparoscopic ablation of endometrial deposits may** relieve pain in some women. However there has only been one small prospective randomized trial in 74 women with follow-up for just 1 year, which showed inconclusive results [Farquhar, 2001; Winkel and Scialli, 2001; Jacobson et al, 2002]. There have been no randomized controlled trials comparing laser with diathermy ablation.
  - **Laparoscopic excision of endometriomas** seems to relieve pain, although there are no randomized controlled trials that have looked at this. A retrospective review found that 74% of people reported improvement or resolution in pain after surgery [DTB, 1999].
  - **Denervation procedures** — presacral neurectomy or laparascopic uterine nerve ablation (LUNA) — are poorly supported by evidence, and there is a risk of complications [DTB, 1999; Farquhar, 2001]. There is only one review of two randomized controlled trials of LUNA compared with a sham operation. No significant difference in patient satisfaction was found between the groups. There was no report of follow-up or adverse effects [Farquhar, 2001].
  - **Laparoscopic drainage was compared with cystectomy** in one randomized controlled trial of 64 women. Relief of pain and subfertility both appeared to be improved more in the women undergoing cystectomy [Farquhar, 2001].
- **Hysterectomy with salpingo-oophorectomy** is a radical solution reserved for women as a last resort. It is often referred to as 'definitive' treatment despite the fact that there is evidence that endometriosis may recur [Winkel and Scialli, 2001].

Pre- and postoperative hormonal treatment

- **Preoperative hormonal treatment with GnRH analogue** compared with placebo was assessed in one randomized controlled study in 75 women. There was found to be no significant difference in ease of surgery, although the trial was probably insufficiently powered to exclude a clinically significant effect [Farquhar, 2001].
- **Postoperative hormonal treatment** is of uncertain value, with conflicting results from different studies [Farquhar and Sutton, 1998; DTB, 1999; Busacca et al, 2001].
- **Postoperative treatment** with danazol, medroxyprogesterone acetate, GnRH analogues or COCs compared with placebo or expectant management has been assessed in six randomized controlled trials [Farquhar, 2001]. Pain was not significantly relieved by 3 months' postoperative therapy but was significantly reduced by 6 months' therapy in all cases except with COCs. Three of the trials also looked at effects on fertility and found no difference in pregnancy rates.

Infertility

- **Hormonal treatments for endometriosis do not improve fertility** [Hughes et al, 2002].
- **Surgery improves fertility in women with severe endometriosis,** particularly with ovarian endometriomas because of the gross distortion in pelvic anatomy and improvement in tubal function after treatment [Farquhar and Sutton, 1998].
- **Surgery may also improve fertility rates in women with mild to moderate endometriosis,** with one study showing that 31% of women who had laparoscopic ablation of endometrial deposits were pregnant within 36 weeks compared with 18% of the control group who only had diagnostic laparoscopy [DTB, 1999]. Other studies, however, did not find benefit [Italian Endometriosis Study Group, 1999]. A Cochrane review is underway to assess the effectiveness of laparoscopic surgery for the

treatment of subfertility associated with endometriosis [Jacobson, 2002].

- **Specialized infertility treatments (such as in vitro fertilization) may need to be considered in some women.** For further information, see the separate PRODIGY guidance on *Infertility*.

References

NHS staff in England can link, free of charge, from references to full text journals by clicking on [Full text] on the PRODIGY website.

1. Bandolier (1998) *Analgesics for dysmenorrhoea*. Bandolier. www.jr2.ox.ac.uk/bandolier/booth/painpag/Chronrev/Analges/CP066.html [Accessed: 09/08/2002].
2. Bergqvist, A. (1999) Current drug therapy recommendations for the treatment of endometriosis. *Drugs* **58**(1), 39–50.
3. BNF 43 (2002) *British National Formulary*. 43rd edn. London: British Medical Association and Royal Pharmaceutical Society of Great Britain.
4. Brosens, I. (1997) Diagnosis of endometriosis. *Seminars in Reproductive Endocrinology* **15**(3), 229–233.
5. Busacca, M., Somigliana, E., Bianchi, S. et al (2001) Post-operative GnRH analogue treatment after conservative surgery for symptomatic endometriosis stage III-IV: a randomized controlled trial. *Human Reproduction* **16**(11), 2399–2402. [Full text]
6. Child, T.J. and Tan, S.L. (2001) Endometriosis: aetiology, pathogenesis and treatment. *Drugs* **61**(12), 1735–1750.
7. CSM (2003) *Further advice on safety of HRT: risk/benefit unfavourable for first-line use in prevention of osteoporosis*. CEM/CMO/2003/19. Committee on Safety of Medicines. www.mca.gov.uk/aboutagency/regframework/csm/csmhome.htm [Accessed: 09/01/2004].
8. DTB (1999) Managing endometriosis. *Drug & Therapeutics Bulletin* **37**(4), 25–32.
9. Edmonds, D.K. (1999) Endometriosis. In: Edmonds, D.K. (Ed.) *Dewhurst's textbook of obstetrics and gynaecology for postgraduates*. 6th edn. Oxford: Blackwell Science. 420–431.
10. Farquhar, C. (2001) Endometriosis. *Clinical Evidence* 7(Jun), 1654–1662.
11. Farquhar, C. and Sutton, C. (1998) The evidence for the management of endometriosis. *Current Opinion in Obstetrics & Gynaecology* **10**(4), 321–332.
12. Franke, H.R., van de Weijer, P.H., Pennings, T.M. and van der Mooren, M.J. (2000) Gonadotropin-releasing hormone agonist plus "add-back" hormone replacement therapy for treatment of endometriosis: a prospective, randomized, placebo-controlled, double-blind trial. *Fertility and Sterility* **74**(3), 534–539.
13. Giudice, L.C., Tazuke, S.I. and Swiersz, L. (1998) Status of Current Research on Endometriosis. *Journal of Reproductive Medicine* **43**(3 Suppl), 252–262.
14. Henry, D., Lim, L.L., Garcia-Rodriguez, L.A. et al (1996) Variability in risk of gastrointestinal complications with individual non-steroidal anti-inflammatory drugs: results of a collaborative meta-analysis. *British Medical Journal* **312**(7046), 1563–1566. [Full text]
15. Hernández-Diaz, S. and Rodriguez, L.A. (2000) Association between nonsteroidal anti-inflammatory drugs and upper gastrointestinal tract bleeding/perforation: an overview of epidemiologic studies published in the 1990s. *Archives of Internal Medicine* **160**(14), 2093–2099. [Full text]
16. Hughes, E., Fedorkow, D., Collins, J. and Vandekerckhove, P. (2002) *Ovulation suppression for endometriosis (Cochrane Review)*. The Cochrane Library. Issue 3. Oxford: Update Software.
17. Irahara, M., Uemura, H., Yasui, T. et al (2001) Efficacy of every-other-day administration of conjugated equine estrogen and medroxyprogesterone acetate on gonadotropin-releasing hormone agonists treatment in women with endometriosis. *Gynecologic & Obstetric Investigation* **52**(4), 217–222.
18. Italian Endometriosis Study Group (1999) Ablation of lesions or no treatment in minimal-mild endometriosis in infertile women: a randomised trial. *Human Reproduction* **14**(5), 1332–1334. [Full text]
19. Jacobson, T (2002) *Laparoscopic surgery for subfertility associated with endometriosis (Protocol for a Cochrane Review)*. The Cochrane Library. Issue 3. Oxford: Update Software.
20. Jacobson, T.Z., Barlow, D.H., Garry, R. and Koninckx, P. (2002) *Laparoscopic surgery for pelvic pain associated with endometriosis (Cochrane Review)*. The Cochrane Library. Issue 3. Oxford: Update Software.
21. Kennedy, S. (1998) The genetics of endometriosis. *Journal of Reproductive Medicine* **43**(3 Suppl), 263–268.
22. McPherson, A. and Waller, D. (Eds.) (1997) *Women's health*. 4th edn. Oxford: Oxford University Press.
23. Moghissi, K.S., Schiaff, W.D., Olive, D.L. et al (1998) Goserelin acetate (Zoladex) with or without hormone replacement therapy for the treatment of endometriosis. *Fertility & Sterility* **69**(6), 1056–1062.
24. Moore, J., Kennedy, S. and Prentice, A. (2003) *Modern combined oral contraceptives for pain associated with endometriosis (Cochrane Review)*. The Cochrane Library. Issue 4. Oxford: Update Software.
25. Olive, D.L. and Schwartz, L.B. (1993) Medical Progress: endometriosis. *New England Journal of Medicine* **328**(24), 1759–1769.
26. Prentice, A., Deary, A.J., Goldbeck-Wood, S. et al (2002a) *Gonadotrophin-releasing hormone analogues for pain associated with endometriosis (Cochrane Review)*. The Cochrane Library. Issue 3. Oxford: Update Software.
27. Prentice, A., Deary, A.J. and Bland, E. (2002b) *Progestagens and anti-progestagens for pain associated with endometriosis (Cochrane Review)*. The Cochrane Library. Issue 3. Oxford: Update Software.
28. Rice, V.M. (2002) Conventional medical therapies for endometriosis. *Annals of the New York Academy of Sciences* **955**(March), 343–352.
29. Selak, V., Farquhar, C., Prentice, A. and Singla, A. (2002) *Danazol for pelvic pain associated with endometriosis (Cochrane Review)*. The Cochrane Library. Issue 3. Oxford: Update Software.
30. Shaw, R.W. (1997) Endometriosis. In: Shaw, R.W., Soutter, W.P., Stanton, S.L. et al (Eds.) *Gynaecology*. 2nd edn. London: Churchill Livingstone. 457–474.
31. Stevenson, J.C. (1995) The impact of bone loss in women with endometriosis. *International Journal of Gynaecology & Obstetrics* **50**(Suppl 1), S11-S15.
32. Surrey, E.S. and Hornstein, M.D. (2002) Prolonged GnRH agonist and add-back therapy for symptomatic endometriosis: long-term follow-up. *Obstetrics & Gynecology* **99**(5), 709–719.
33. Van Vliet, H.A.A.M., Grimes, D.A., Helmerhorst, F.M. and Schulz, K.F. (2001) *Biphasic versus monophasic oral contraceptives for contraception (Cochrane Review)*. The Cochrane Library. Issue 2. Oxford: Update Software.
34. Vercellini, P., Cortesi, I. and Crosignani, P.G. (1997) Progestins for symptomatic endometriosis – a critical

analysis of the evidence. *Fertility & Sterility* 68(3), 393–401.
35. WHO (1998) *Cardiovascular disease and steroid hormone contraception.* WHO Technical Report Series 877. Geneva: World Health Organisation.
36. Winkel, C.A. and Scialli, A.R. (2001) Medical and surgical therapies for pain associated with endometriosis. *Journal of Women's Health and Gender Based Medicine* 10(2), 137–162.
37. Zhang, W.Y. and Li Wan Po, A. (1998) Efficacy of minor analgesics in primary dysmenorrhoea: a systematic review. *British Journal of Obstetrics & Gynaecology* 105(7), 780–789.

E

PRODIGY GUIDANCE

Enuresis — nocturnal

Last revised in July 2005
www.prodigy.nhs.uk/guidance.asp?gt=Enuresis - nocturnal

Applies to people from the age of 2 to 20 years

This guidance covers the management of nocturnal enuresis in children. However, similar principles apply to adults who are still bedwetting.

This guidance does not cover other forms of incontinence, such as daytime wetting in children.

Goals

- To reduce the frequency of wet beds
- To attain sustained night-time dryness (so-called 'complete success')
- To avoid the anxiety and emotional stress that nocturnal enuresis causes in children and their parents

Contents

Scenarios
- Enuresis – nocturnal p.747

Extended Information, p. 749

Enuresis — nocturnal

Which therapy?

- Explain that it is usually possible to help the child to achieve dryness even if previous attempts have failed.
- **Simple practical advice includes:**
  - Make sure that the child empties the bladder at bedtime.
  - Improve the child's access to the toilet (e.g. if the child sleeps in a bunk bed, make sure that they sleep in the bottom one; leave a light on at night; place a child seat on the toilet).
  - Involve the child in cleaning up after wetting, so they can share the responsibility (but not as a punishment).
  - Do not restrict fluids. The child should have about eight drinks a day, spaced out throughout the day, the last one about 1 hour before bed. Avoid caffeine in night-time food and drink (e.g. tea, coffee, cola, chocolate).
  - Use waterproof covers for the mattress and duvet, and absorbent, quilted sheets.
  - Wash the child thoroughly before dressing them, including their hair if they are very wet.
  - Use simple emollients to protect the skin.
  - Rinse bedding and nightclothes in cold water or mild bleach.
  - Use room deodorizers.
  - 'Lifting' the child at night is useful only as a short-term or occasional measure.
- Treat constipation if present (see PRODIGY guidance *Constipation*).
- It may be appropriate to give no active treatment if the child and parents do not find the symptoms bothersome, or if the child is under 7 years of age.
- **If active treatment is appropriate:**
  - **Enuresis alarms are the first line treatment** in motivated children over 7 years. Warn parents about the possibility of relapse, but reassure them about success rates of retreatment.
  - **Reward systems are an alternative form of treatment.** The system needs to be tailored to the individual child:
    - Goals must be well-defined and achievable.
    - Rewards must have some value to the child.
    - Achievements must be rewarded immediately and consistently.
    - As the frequency of wetting declines, so the goals for dryness can be gradually raised.
    - Wetting should be treated in a matter-of-fact way. Wetting should not be punished; nor should it elicit some kind of 'lesser' reward.
  - **Drug treatment for short periods** is appropriate to allow the child to recover confidence, or as a temporary measure to tide them over nights spent away from home (e.g. school trips). However, the relapse rate is high once treatment is discontinued.
    - Desmopressin and imipramine are of equal efficacy. Imipramine is associated with a higher risk of adverse effects, however, and can be fatal in overdose.
  - Whichever form of treatment is used, it is important to treat relapses promptly.

Practical prescribing points

For further information, see the *Medicines Compendium* (www.medicines.org.uk) or the *British National Formulary* (www.bnf.org).

- **Adverse effects of desmopressin** include the potential to develop hyponatraemia. Warn caregivers to avoid fluid overload — not more than one mug of liquid should be drunk from 1 hour before administration of desmopressin to 8 hours afterwards.
  - Caution should be exercised in children with cystic fibrosis [Mark and Frank, 1995; BNF 49, 2005].
  - Desmopressin should not be used in children with heart failure or other conditions requiring treatment with diuretics, or in people with hypertension. Caution is required in people with conditions that are characterized by fluid and/or electrolyte imbalance.
  - After 3 months' treatment, desmopressin should be withdrawn for at least 1 week for reassessment of the enuresis [Glazener and Evans, 2002].
  - Do not exceed the recommended dose.
- **Intranasal desmopressin may be ineffective** in children with allergic rhinitis or viral rhinitis.
- **Adverse effects of tricyclic antidepressants** include anxiety, insomnia, dry mouth, and personality changes. Tricyclic antidepressants should not be used in patients with arrhythmias. They can be fatal in overdose and caregivers should be warned to store them out of children's reach [Mark and Frank, 1995; BNF 49, 2005].

Follow-up advice

- **Review** all children at intervals to provide encouragement and to monitor the response to treatment.
- **Reassess at 3-monthly intervals** all children who are prescribed drug treatments for extended periods. Stop

E

the treatment for at least 1 week and review the situation [BNF 49, 2005].

Should I refer or investigate?

Refer?

- Refer the child to the local enuresis advisor or enuresis clinic.
- **Some children may need to be referred to secondary care:**
  - If an enuresis advisor is not available, and if there is no response to treatment undertaken in the primary-care setting.
  - If a urinary tract infection has been detected at the initial assessment (see PRODIGY guidance *Urinary tract infection — children*).
  - If daytime wetting occurs.
  - If an organic cause of enuresis is suspected (e.g. diabetes mellitus, renal disease, spinal dysraphism, neuropathy).
  - If psychological problems are associated with the enuresis (either as a cause or as an effect).
- Advise the family to consult Education and Resources for Improving Childhood Continence (telephone 0117 960 3060, www.eric.org.uk/). This organization provides information (CD-ROM, DVD, video) and support, and sells a wide range of products, including alarms, covers for mattresses and bedding, and waterproof duvets and mattresses.

Investigate?

- **Urine dipstick and urine culture** (to exclude diabetes mellitus and urinary tract infection).

Patient information leaflets

The following PILs are available at www.prodigy.nhs.uk

- Bedwetting - Alarms
- Bedwetting.co.uk
- Bedwetting (Enuresis)
- Bedwetting - Medicine Treatments
- Bedwetting - Reward Systems
- Education & Resources for Improving Childhood Continence

Shared decision making

- **Bedwetting is common.** One in five 5-year-olds and at least one in twenty 10-year-olds are bedwetters.
- General tips include:
  - **Be patient** — many children are not dry until school years.
  - **Be sensitive** — bedwetting is sometimes due to stress or worries at school or home.
  - **Encourage** — praise and reward children who show signs of improvement.
  - **Do not punish** — a child cannot help bedwetting.
  - **Responsibility** — children who are old enough should be given responsibility for changing bedclothes and nightclothes (but not as a punishment).
  - **Drinks** — the child should drink normally (e.g. seven to eight drinks) during the day, but do not give them a drink within 30 minutes of bedtime.
- **Alarm treatment** usually cures motivated children aged 7 years and older. An alarm is usually needed for 3–5 months to 'condition' the child to wake and go to the toilet.
- **Medication** usually works well but may cause side-effects. In addition, the bedwetting usually returns when medication is stopped. It can be useful for short spells, such as holidays, or to allow a child to recover confidence.
- **Education and Resources for Improving Childhood Continence (ERIC)** provides information and support (telephone 0117 960 3060, www.eric.org.uk/). They provide information (CD-ROM, DVD, video) and support, and sell a wide range of products, including alarms, covers for mattresses and bedding, and waterproof duvets and mattresses.

Drug rationale

Drugs not included

- **Oxybutynin** treatment in nocturnal enuresis is not supported by clinical trials [Glazener et al, 2003a]. It may be useful in people with daytime wetting that is suggestive of bladder overactivity [Mark and Frank, 1995].
- **Other antimuscarinic drugs,** for example propiverine, propantheline, and tolterodine, are not included because they are licensed for daytime urinary incontinence (usually due to bladder overactivity) in adults only.
- **Amitriptyline and nortriptyline** are not offered. Neither of these has been as well studied as imipramine and they do not offer any benefits in terms of improved safety. In addition, amitriptyline is more sedating than imipramine [BNF 49, 2005].
- **Other drugs,** including anxiolytics (e.g. diazepam) or sympathomimetics (e.g. ephedrine), appear to have no value [Miller et al, 1992; Glazener et al, 2003a]. Indometacin has shown some benefit in one small placebo-controlled trial but more evidence is needed [Sener et al, 1998].

Drugs included

- **Desmopressin** has been shown to be an effective treatment for nocturnal enuresis [Glazener and Evans, 2002]. The oral and intranasal routes appear to be equally effective. [Janknegt et al, 1997; Miller et al, 1992]. If an extended course is given, the need for continued treatment must be reassessed after 3 months by stopping desmopressin for at least 1 week [BNF 49, 2005].
- **Imipramine** is effective in the treatment of nocturnal enuresis and is the most widely used and studied tricyclic agent [Glazener et al, 2003b]. It is also less sedating than amitriptyline. Tricyclic antidepressants have similar efficacy to desmopressin and are considerably cheaper. However, this must be weighed against their many adverse effects and the potentially fatal consequences of overdose. For this reason, only a short course of imipramine tablets is offered. (Imipramine syrup is less widely available, but can be ordered from a specials manufacturer.)

Prescriptions

Non-drug management

Advice only: enuresis management

- Age from 7 to 20 years
- Practical tips to help bedwetting: Make sure your child empties their bladder just before going to bed. Avoid drinking for half an hour before bedtime. Make sure your child has easy access to the toilet in the night. This might mean leaving a light on for them, or leaving the door open. Let the child help and get involved in the cleaning up after wetting. Encourage your child to have 8 drinks a day, spaced out throughout the day. Avoid drinks containing caffeine, such as cola, coffee, tea, hot

chocolate or chocolate milk, as these cause extra urine to be produced. If your child is still bedwetting, a common practice is to use an alarm or buzzer to help. This works by waking the child when they start to wet the bed. It takes several months to work but is often effective. Alarms can be borrowed from a local continence clinic or advisor, who can provide support while they are being used. More information can be obtained from Enuresis Resource and Information Centre (ERIC) Tel: 0117 960 3060, http://www.eric.org.uk/. ERIC is a national registered charity that provides advice and information on all aspects of bedwetting.

Desmopressin: for short-term use

Desmopressin nasal spray: 20mcg at night (6ml)
- Age from 7 to 20 years
- Desmopressin 10mcg nasal spray. Spray once into each nostril at bedtime; supply 1 6ml spray; NHS Cost £28.00.

Desmopressin nasal spray: 20mcg at night (5ml)
- Age from 7 to 20 years
- Desmopressin 10mcg nasal spray. Spray once into each nostril at bedtime; supply 1 5ml spray; NHS Cost £21.17.

Desmopressin nasal spray: 40mcg at night IF needed (6ml)
- Age from 7 to 20 years
- Desmopressin 10mcg nasal spray. Spray twice into each nostril at bedtime; supply 1 6ml spray; NHS Cost £28.00.

Desmopressin nasal spray: 40mcg at night IF needed (5ml)
- Age from 7 to 20 years
- Desmopressin 10mcg nasal spray. Spray twice into each nostril at bedtime; supply 1 5ml spray; NHS Cost £21.17.

Desmopressin tablets: 200mcg at night
- Age from 7 to 20 years
- Desmopressin 200microgram tabs. Take one tablet at bedtime; supply 7 tablets; NHS Cost £7.25.

Desmopressin tablets: 400mcg at night IF needed
- Age from 7 to 20 years
- Desmopressin 200microgram tabs. Take two tablets at bedtime; supply 14 tablets; NHS Cost £14.50.

Desmopressin: for long-term use

Desmopressin nasal spray: 20mcg at night (30 days)
- Age from 7 to 20 years
- Desmopressin 10mcg nasal spray. Spray once into each nostril at bedtime; supply 1 6ml spray; NHS Cost £28.00.

Desmopressin nasal spray: 20mcg at night (25 days)
- Age from 7 to 20 years
- Desmopressin 10mcg nasal spray. Spray once into each nostril at bedtime; supply 1 5ml spray; NHS Cost £21.17.

Desmopressin nasal spray: 40mcg at night IF needed (30 days)
- Age from 7 to 20 years
- Desmopressin 10mcg nasal spray. Spray twice into each nostril at bedtime; supply 2 6ml spray; NHS Cost £56.00.

Desmopressin nasal spray: 40mcg at night IF needed (25 days)
- Age from 7 to 20 years
- Desmopressin 10mcg nasal spray. Spray twice into each nostril at bedtime; supply 2 5ml spray; NHS Cost £42.34.

Desmopressin tablets: 200mcg at night (30days)
- Age from 7 to 20 years
- Desmopressin 200microgram tabs. Take one tablet at bedtime; supply 30 tablets; NHS Cost £30.34.

Desmopressin tablets: 400mcg tablets at night (30 days)
- Age from 7 to 20 years
- Desmopressin 200microgram tabs. Take two tablets at bedtime; supply 60 tablets; NHS Cost £60.68.

Imipramine: for short-term use

Imipramine tablets: 25mg at night (7 days)
- Age from 7 to 10 years
- Imipramine 25mg tablets. Take one tablet 30 minutes before bedtime; supply 7 tablets; NHS Cost £0.25.

Imipramine tablets: 50mg at night (7 days)
- Age from 8 to 20 years
- Imipramine 25mg tablets. Take two tablets 30 minutes before bedtime; supply 14 tablets; NHS Cost £0.50.

Imipramine tablets: 75mg at night (7 days)
- Age from 11 to 20 years
- Imipramine 25mg tablets. Take three tablets 30 minutes before bedtime; supply 21 tablets; NHS Cost £0.75.

Extended Information

Background information

- What is it? p.749
- How common is it? p.750
- How do I know my patient has it? p.750
- What else might it be? p.750
- Complications and prognosis p.751

What is it?

Definitions

- **Enuresis** is the 'involuntary discharge of urine by day or night or both, in a child aged 5 years or older, in the absence of congenital or acquired defects of the nervous system or urinary tract'. However, most management strategies are aimed at children of 7 years or older.
- **Nocturnal enuresis** or **bedwetting** is the lack of night-time bladder control. Nocturnal enuresis accounts for 85% of people with enuresis.
  - **'Primary nocturnal enuresis'** is the term used when bladder control has never been gained.
  - **'Secondary nocturnal enuresis'** is the term used when bladder control has been gained for at least 6 months and then lost.

[Hjalmas et al, 2004]

Model of the cause of nocturnal enuresis

- **Nocturnal enuresis is a heterogeneous disorder. A 'three systems' model of the cause has been proposed:**
  - **Sleep polyuria** caused by altered antidiuretic hormone (ADH) secretion. Usually, ADH secretion increases during sleep and low volumes of urine are produced at night. It has been suggested (but not proved) that children with nocturnal enuresis do not experience an increase in ADH secretion at night and therefore produce relatively large volumes of urine.
  - **Reduced night-time bladder capacity** has been found in children with nocturnal enuresis, in comparison with controls. Detrusor overactivity has been shown to be related to reduced night-time bladder capacity in children with nocturnal enuresis.
  - **Lack of arousal from sleep** before micturition begins. There is no evidence, however, of any difference in

sleep patterns in children with enuresis, compared with controls.

[van Dyk et al, 2003; Butler et al, 2004; Hjalmas et al, 2004]

Causative factors and associations

- **Genetic:** studies have found a positive family history in up to 70% of children with nocturnal enuresis.
- **Stressful life events:** the birth of a younger sibling, hospital admission with separation from the mother, discord within the family, starting a new school, bullying, moving house, and (rarely) sexual abuse are associated with nocturnal enuresis.
- **Diuretic drinks:** bedwetting may be associated with food and drinks containing caffeine, such as tea, coffee, cola, or chocolate.
- **Constipation:** nocturnal enuresis has been reported to occur in a third of chronically constipated children. In one study, the treatment of chronic constipation led to the resolution of nocturnal enuresis in 63% of affected children [Loening-Baucke, 1997].
- **Urinary tract infection:** this may be a cause of secondary nocturnal enuresis or of daytime wetting.
- **Upper airway obstruction:** sleep apnoea due to upper airway obstruction is a rare cause of bedwetting.
- **Organic pathology:** nocturnal enuresis is rarely due to any other organic disease. (In contrast, daytime wetting has a stronger association with organic pathology.)
- **Attention deficit hyperactivity disorder (ADHD):** enuresis has been reported to be more common in children with ADHD — the odds ratio is 2.7 times higher than in controls.

[Dobson and Blackwell, 1995; Mikkelsen, 2001; Hjalmas et al, 2004; Glazener et al, 2005a]

Uncertain or controversial associations

- **Developmental delay:** there is conflicting evidence on the association (or lack of association) between developmental delay and enuresis.
- **Behavioural problems:** behavioural problems may be more common in girls and in children who wet both day and night.
- **Toilet-training practice:** there is no evidence that early potty training prevents bedwetting.

[Mikkelsen, 2001; Hjalmas et al, 2004; Glazener et al, 2005a]

How common is it?

- **Nocturnal enuresis** affects about:
  - 15% of 5-year-olds
  - 7% of 8-year-olds
  - 5% of 10-year-olds
  - 2% of 15-year-olds
  - 0.5% of adults aged 18–64 years
- **The spontaneous cure rate** for nocturnal enuresis is about 15% per annum and is independent of age.
- **Fewer than half of parents with a bedwetting child** consult a doctor about the problem.
- **There are cultural and social differences** in both the prevalence of nocturnal enuresis and in how likely it is that professional help will be sought. For example, the prevalence of bedwetting is lower in UK Asians; and children from socially deprived areas are less likely to be brought to medical attention.

[Hjalmas et al, 2004]

How do I know my patient has it?

History

- Distinguish between children with nocturnal enuresis (the majority) and children who also have episodes of enuresis during the daytime.
- Distinguish between primary and secondary nocturnal enuresis.
- Ask about:
  - The number of dry nights in the past week or month.
  - The pattern of micturition (strength of stream, hesitation, dribbling).
  - Fluid intake at bedtime.
  - Intake of diuretics at bedtime (e.g. tea, coffee, cola, chocolate).
  - Practical issues:
    - Can the child get to the toilet easily during the night (e.g. if they sleep in a bunk bed, ask if they sleep in the bottom one)?
    - Does the child need a light to be left on at night to get to the toilet?
    - Can the child sit on the toilet comfortably, or do they need a child seat?
    - Does the child have any fears associated with the toilet?
  - The impact the nocturnal enuresis has on the child and the family, including the attitudes of the parents.
  - Any possible stresses at home or school that may be affecting the child.
  - Any suggestion of sleep apnoea.
  - Constipation and soiling.
  - Treatment strategies already tried (including punishments and rewards).
- Take a past medical history, including:
  - Any previous urinary tract infections.
  - The child's general developmental history.

[Hjalmas et al, 2004]

Examination

- Examination is (by definition) normal in children with nocturnal enuresis. Examine the abdomen, perineum, spine, and nervous system for obvious signs of other possible conditions.

Investigations

- **Urinalysis and urine culture** to exclude diabetes mellitus and a urinary tract infection. These are the only investigations required in primary nocturnal enuresis.
- **Ultrasound examination of the kidneys and urinary tract** is recommended in children who are wet during the daytime to exclude anatomical abnormalities, stones, renal cysts, or dilatation of the ureter and renal pelvis. Ultrasound examination of the bladder before and after micturition can help to identify abnormal bladder structure and to measure the residual urine after voiding.

[Cayan et al, 2001; Mikkelsen, 2001; Hjalmas et al, 2004]

What else might it be?

- **Urinary tract infection and other acute illness** can cause short periods of bedwetting in someone who has previously been dry.
- **Chronic constipation.**
- **Diabetes mellitus, renal failure:** there are usually other symptoms (e.g. polyuria, excessive thirst).
- **Bladder overactivity** or another cause of daytime incontinence with a nocturnal component.
- **Congenital abnormality of the urinary tract,** such as an ectopic ureter (girls) or posterior urethral valves (boys).

- **Neurological disorder** (e.g. neuropathy, spinal dysraphism).

[Dobson and Blackwell, 1995; Hjalmas et al, 2004]

Complications and prognosis

Complications

- **Child:** the older the child, the more distressing and disabling bedwetting is. Social isolation, bullying, and low self-esteem may result. Successful treatment of nocturnal enuresis has been shown to lead to an increase in self-esteem.
- **Enuresis that persists into adult life:** this is associated with severe psychosocial problems affecting self-esteem, careers, social life, and personal relationships.
- **Parent/caregiver:** the work and cost of extra laundry and the additional stress of caring for a child with enuresis cause parental anxiety. This may have adverse consequences on their ability to support the child. Up to 30% of parents become intolerant of the enuresis and consequently also of their child.

[Butler and Stenberg, 2001; Hjalmas et al, 2004]

Prognosis

- **Spontaneous remission** (without treatment) occurs in about 15% of children each year. Spontaneous remission is more likely if there is a family history of nocturnal enuresis [Mikkelsen, 2001].
- **Relapse rate** after all forms of treatment (overall) is 10–20%.

Management issues

- Is there any simple advice that can be given to the parents of a child with nocturnal enuresis? p.751
- At what age should treatment for nocturnal enuresis be initiated? p.751
- Where and by whom should a child with nocturnal enuresis be managed? p.751
- Which non-drug treatments are recommended for nocturnal enuresis? p.751
- Which drug treatments are recommended for nocturnal enuresis? p.752
- Which treatments are not recommended for nocturnal enuresis? p.753
- What is the supporting evidence for drug treatment? p.753
- Medicines management p.753

Is there any simple advice that can be given to the parents of a child with nocturnal enuresis?

- **Explain that it is usually possible to help the child achieve dryness** even if previous attempts have failed.
- **Simple practical advice includes:**
  - Ensure that the child empties the bladder at bedtime.
  - Improve the child's access to the toilet (e.g. if the child sleeps in a bunk bed, make sure that they sleep in the bottom one; leave a light on at night; place a child seat on the toilet).
  - Involve the child in cleaning up after wetting, so that they can share the responsibility (but not as a punishment).
  - **Do *not* restrict fluids.** The child should have about eight drinks a day, spaced out throughout the day, the last one about 1 hour before bed. Avoid caffeine in night-time food and drink (e.g. tea, coffee, cola, chocolate).
  - Use waterproof covers for the mattress and duvet, and absorbent, quilted sheets.
  - Wash the child thoroughly before dressing them, including their hair if they are very wet.
  - Use simple emollients to protect the skin.
  - Rinse bedding and nightclothes in cold water or mild bleach.
  - Use room deodorizers.
  - 'Lifting' the child at night is useful only as a short-term or occasional measure.
- Treat constipation if present (see PRODIGY guidance *Constipation*).

[Canadian Paediatric Society, 2002]

At what age should treatment for nocturnal enuresis be initiated?

- There are no studies of the best age at which to start treatment for nocturnal enuresis [Lyth and Bosson, 2004]. It is generally accepted, however, that treatment should begin between 6 years and 8 years of age.
- It may be appropriate to give no active treatment if the child and parents do not find the symptoms bothersome, or if the child is under 7 years of age.
- The severity of the impact of nocturnal enuresis determines the urgency of referral and intensity of treatment. Urgent referral and treatment are usually indicated for children over the age of 10 years.

[Hjalmas et al, 2004]

Where and by whom should a child with nocturnal enuresis be managed?

- A child with nocturnal enuresis should be managed in the community.
- Refer the child to the local enuresis advisor or enuresis clinic.
- **Some children may need to be referred to secondary care:**
  - If an enuresis advisor is not available and there is no response to treatment undertaken in the primary-care setting.
  - If a urinary tract infection has been detected at the initial assessment (see PRODIGY guidance *Urinary tract infection — children*).
  - If daytime wetting occurs.
  - If an organic cause of enuresis is suspected (e.g. diabetes mellitus, renal disease, spinal dysraphism, neuropathy).
  - If psychological problems are associated with the enuresis (either as a cause or as an effect).
- **Advise the family to consult Education and Resources for Improving Childhood Continence** (telephone 0117 960 3060, www.eric.org.uk/). This organization provides information (CD-ROM, DVD, video) and support, and sells a wide range of products, including alarms, covers for mattresses and bedding, and waterproof duvets and mattresses.

[Dobson and Blackwell, 1995; DTB, 2004]

Which non-drug treatments are recommended for nocturnal enuresis?

- Reward systems and enuresis alarms are recommended.

Reward systems

- **The theory of reward systems** is that a child will respond, over a period of time, to extra attention or treats awarded for dryness. Implementing a reward system successfully requires more time and effort than simply putting up a star chart:
  - **Goals** must be well-defined and achievable.
  - **Rewards** must have some value to the child.

E

- **Achievements** must be rewarded immediately and consistently.
- **As the frequency of wetting declines,** so the goals for dryness can be gradually raised.
- **Wetting should be treated in a matter-of-fact way.** Wetting should not be punished; nor should it elicit some kind of 'lesser' reward.

- A recent Cochrane systematic review found that, in comparison with controls, the use of reward systems was associated with significantly fewer wet nights, higher cure rates, and lower relapse rates [Glazener and Evans, 2004].

Enuresis alarms

E

- **Enuresis alarms are the first-line treatment** in motivated children over the age of 7 years, as a certain level of maturity is required before the child is able to cooperate fully.
  - Enuresis alarms have an initial success rate of 65–80%. The relative risk of failure to achieve 14 consecutive dry nights is 0.27 (95% CI 0.19 to 0.39).
  - Withdrawal rates are about 40%.
  - Relapse rates are 30–50%. The relative risk of failure to remain dry is 0.58 (95% CI 0.46 to 0.74).
  - Enuresis alarms are associated with a lower relapse rate than drugs, although alarms are slower to take effect. Compared with relapse after desmopressin, there is limited evidence to suggest a relative risk of 0.11 (95% CI 0.02 to 0.78).
  - Failure rates are higher in children with behavioural or family difficulties.
- **Alarms are usually needed for 3–5 months.** To be effective, alarms need regular supervision (every few weeks) by an experienced professional. Alarms can be borrowed from the local enuresis advisor or can be bought privately from Education and Resources for Improving Childhood Continence (telephone 0117 960 3060, www.eric.org.uk/).
- **Discontinue** use of the alarm when there have been 14 consecutive dry nights.
- **Treat relapses promptly:**
  - Retreatment after relapse has a success rate similar to that of initial treatment with an alarm.
  - Relapse after initial success is a great disappointment to children. They need to be warned about this possibility before it occurs and encouraged by giving them information about the success rates achieved with retreatment.
  - 'Overlearning' may reduce the rate of relapse: once dryness has been achieved for 14 consecutive nights, the child is encouraged to drink extra fluid to 'over-condition' the bladder. This is continued until there have been 7–14 consecutive dry nights.
- **Several types of alarm are available:** pad-and-bell alarms (where the sensor pad is positioned under the child in the bed); **body-worn alarms** (where the tiny sensor is attached to the child's pants and the alarm is worn on the pyjamas); and **vibrating alarms.** There is no evidence that any one type is more effective than the others, but some children or parents will have a particular preference.
- **The mode of action** is as follows:
  - An alarm sounds when the child passes urine.
  - The control is placed so that the child must get out of bed to switch the alarm off.
  - He or she should then go to the toilet, empty the bladder and dry off.
  - Wet bedding or clothes should be changed by the child (with help if necessary).
  - In time, the child usually learns either to awaken before the alarm sounds, or to sleep through the night without the need to pass urine.
  - With the pad-and-bell system, the child should sleep naked below the waist to ensure that the alarm is triggered promptly on urination.
- **Enuresis alarms are *not* advised in the following situations:**
  - If the child is not motivated to use one.
  - If the child shares a bed.
  - If more than one child in a family is being treated simultaneously.
  - If the parents are unable to give sufficient support.
  - If the parents are taking a blaming or punitive approach (alarms can exacerbate this).
  - If transient stress is the precipitating factor.
  - If the child is unduly frightened or embarrassed by the alarm.
  - If the child also has daytime symptoms.

[Dobson and Blackwell, 1995; Glazener et al, 2005a]

Which drug treatments are recommended for nocturnal enuresis?

- **The role of drug treatment** is as a short-term treatment to allow the child to recover confidence, or as a temporary measure to tide the child over nights spent away from home (e.g. school trips).
- **Drug treatments may also be useful as an adjunct** to alarm treatment, as a way of easing the initial week of alarm treatment.
- **Drugs act more quickly** than the alarm systems, but the relapse rate is higher once treatment has stopped.
- Drug treatment may be used in the longer term if an enuresis alarm is inappropriate. When used in this way, the drug should be stopped for a week every 3 months to check whether it is still needed.

Desmopressin

- Desmopressin is licensed for the treatment of nocturnal enuresis.
- Night-time administration of desmopressin increases water reabsorption in the collecting ducts of the kidneys resulting in a low nocturnal urine volume. However, this action is not sufficient to explain its action in nocturnal enuresis, because restriction of fluid intake alone does not appear to help, and not all children with nocturnal enuresis respond to desmopressin.
- Desmopressin is associated with a response rate of about 70% and has a rapid onset of action. However, its effect may not be maintained on discontinuing treatment, and symptoms have been found to recur in 50–95% after stopping treatment.
- There is some evidence that taking desmopressin intermittently after an initial 3-month treatment period [Akbal et al, 2004] or continuously over 12 months [Wolfish et al, 2003] may prevent relapse.
- For CSM advice and more information see *Medicines Management section.*

[Gimpel et al, 1998; Glazener and Evans, 2002; van Kerrebroeck, 2002; Akbal et al, 2004; Ng et al, 2005]

Tricyclic antidepressants

- Amitriptyline, imipramine, and nortriptyline are all licensed for use in nocturnal enuresis in children aged 7 years and over. Their mode of action is related to their antimuscarinic activity.
- Evidence of efficacy is lacking for other tricyclic antidepressants and related antidepressant drugs.

- **Compared with desmopressin,** tricyclic antidepressants have similar efficacy and are less expensive, but cause more adverse effects.
[Lackgren et al, 1999; Glazener et al, 2003b]

Which treatments are not recommended for nocturnal enuresis?

- Complex behavioural and educational interventions (dry-bed training and full-spectrum home training) have not been found to be more effective than the use of an enuresis alarm alone. There is insufficient evidence to recommend them in the treatment of nocturnal enuresis [Glazener et al, 2004; Hjalmas et al, 2004].
- 'Lifting' (taking the child to the toilet without waking before enuresis occurs) is not recommended. It encourages the child to empty the bladder while asleep, and stops the child from developing an association between a full bladder and the need to wake [DTB, 2004].
- Traditional Chinese acupuncture has been studied in small trials. There is insufficient evidence to recommend it for the treatment of nocturnal enuresis [Mikkelsen, 2001; Hjalmas et al, 2004].
- Laser acupuncture has been studied in small trials. There is insufficient evidence to recommend it for the treatment of nocturnal enuresis [Radmayr et al, 2001].
- Acupressure has been studied in small trials. There is insufficient evidence to recommend it for the treatment of nocturnal enuresis [Yuksek et al, 2003].
- Acupuncture has been studied in small trials. There is insufficient evidence to recommend it for the treatment of nocturnal enuresis [Glazener et al, 2005b].
- Chiropractic has been studied in small trials. There is insufficient evidence to recommend it for the treatment of nocturnal enuresis [Glazener et al, 2005b].
- Hypnosis has been studied in small trials. There is insufficient evidence to recommend it for the treatment of nocturnal enuresis [Mikkelsen, 2001; Glazener et al, 2005b].
- Psychotherapy has been studied in small trials. There is insufficient evidence to recommend it for the treatment of nocturnal enuresis [Glazener et al, 2005b].
- Other drugs used to treat nocturnal enuresis include oxybutynin and ephedrine, but there is limited evidence to support their effectiveness and safety [Glazener et al, 2003a; Mikkelsen, 2001; Hjalmas et al, 2004; Müller et al, 2004].

What is the supporting evidence for drug treatment?

Desmopressin

- A recent Cochrane review showed that desmopressin rapidly reduces the number of wet nights per week experienced by children, although there is some evidence that this was not sustained after treatment stopped [Glazener and Evans, 2002].
- A number of studies have been published since this Cochrane review:
  - A randomized controlled trial compared enuretic alarms, oral desmopressin, and combined treatment in 105 Chinese children [Ng et al, 2005]. A significant reduction in the mean number of wet nights per week occurred in all three groups. However, this was only sustained after treatment in the children who were using enuretic alarms.
  - A prospective study in 123 young people (mean age 12.5 years, range 6–22 years) found that taking oral desmopressin intermittently after an initial 3-month treatment period is effective in preventing relapse [Akbal et al, 2004]. Of the 92 participants who completed the study, 45 responded to a daily dose of 0.2 mg desmopressin, while the dose was titrated to 0.4 mg for the remaining 47; 23 did not respond to 0.4 mg.
  - A long-term observational trial carried out over 12 months in 256 children found that oral desmopressin was effective at reducing the frequency of wet nights and increased the response rate over a longer treatment period [Wolfish et al, 2003].
  - A large open trial in 399 children (age range 6–12 years) demonstrated that desmopressin nasal spray halved the number of wet nights per month by the end of the 12-month period [Hjalmas et al, 1998].
  - A second open, nonrandomized trial in 237 children found desmopressin to be effective in 70–75% of children treated using different regimens of intranasal application, with a dose range of 20–40 micrograms [Chiozza et al, 1999].

E

Tricyclic antidepressants

- A recent Cochrane review found that although tricyclic antidepressants are effective in reducing the frequency of wet nights, most children relapse after stopping active treatment [Glazener et al, 2003b].
- A more recent review showed a significant reduction of wet nights when compared with baseline values in all of the studies [Müller et al, 2004]. On average, the reduction of wet nights was about 50%.
  - The review included 11 placebo-controlled trials with a total of 386 children, in which at least one arm was treated with imipramine and one with placebo.
  - The incidence of adverse effects in the imipramine group was double that found in the placebo group. The incidence of adverse effects was similar in the imipramine and desmopressin groups.

Medicines management

How should drug treatment be prescribed?

Desmopressin

- **Desmopressin is available in oral and intranasal preparations** but there are insufficient data to compare the efficacy of the two dosage forms.
- **Oral preparations** are initially given in a dose of 200 micrograms at bedtime in children over 5 years (preferably over 7 years); the dose is only increased to 400 micrograms if the lower dose is not effective [BNF 49, 2005]. Treatment should be withdrawn for at least 1 week for reassessment after 3 months.
- **Intranasal preparations are** initially given in a dose of 20 micrograms at bedtime, increased to 40 micrograms if the lower dose is not effective. Treatment should be withdrawn for at least 1 week for reassessment after 3 months.
- **Avoid the use of intranasal preparations** if the child has inflamed nasal mucous membranes, nasal congestion, or an upper respiratory tract infection.
- Fluid intake should be limited to 240 ml from 1 hour before medication until 8 hours afterwards.
- **Counsel children and parents:**
  - During a course of desmopressin treatment, children should be advised not to drink more than 240 ml (8 fluid ounces) of fluid on any night that desmopressin is given, in order to avoid the possible risk of water intoxication [Glazener and Evans, 2002].
  - Stop desmopressin treatment during periods of vomiting or diarrhoea.
  - The presence of food may reduce the absorption of desmopressin. If this is suspected, the oral dose should

be given at least 1.5 hours after a meal, or the intranasal preparation should be considered.

Tricyclic antidepressants

- Tricyclic antidepressants such as imipramine and, less often, amitriptyline and nortriptyline are also used but behaviour disturbances may occur and relapse is common after withdrawal.
- Treatment should not normally be given for more than 3 months without assessing the child for adverse effects.
- Toxicity after overdosage with tricyclic antidepressants is of particular concern.
- **Imipramine** hydrochloride is given at bedtime in the following doses: 25 mg for children aged 7 years, 25–50 mg for children aged 8–11 years, and 50–75 mg for children over 11 years.

[BNF 49, 2005]

E

How safe is drug treatment?

Desmopressin

- **Adverse effects** include fluid retention, hyponatraemia (associated with convulsions in more serious cases), stomach pain, headache, nausea, vomiting, and allergic reactions. Emotional disturbance has also been reported in children.
- **In addition, adverse effects with the nasal preparation** are related to the site of delivery and include epistaxis, nasal congestion, and rhinitis. Long-term safety of the intranasal preparation (up to 1 year) was confirmed in a Swedish study [Hjalmas et al, 1998]. It can be used in children over 5 years of age, but preferably should be used in children over the age of 7 years.
- **CSM advice:** people being treated for primary nocturnal enuresis should be warned to avoid fluid overload (including during swimming) in the 8-hour period after taking desmopressin. They should stop taking desmopressin during an episode of vomiting or diarrhoea (until fluid balance has returned to normal). The risk of hyponatraemic convulsions can also be minimized by keeping to the recommended starting doses and by avoiding concomitant use of drugs which increase secretion of antidiuretic hormone (e.g. tricyclic antidepressants).

Tricyclic antidepressants

- **Minor adverse effects** of tricyclic antidepressants are related to their antimuscarinic actions, and include postural hypotension, dry mouth, constipation, urinary retention, perspiration, tachycardia, nausea, lethargy, and insomnia.
- **Other adverse effects** include anorexia, anxiety, depression, and diarrhoea.
- **Overdose** of a tricyclic antidepressant drug can be fatal, so parents should be urged to keep these drugs stored well away from young children.
- This has led some specialist centres to reduce the frequency with which they prescribe tricyclic antidepressants for enuresis.

[Glazener et al, 2003b; BNF 49, 2005]

References

NHS staff in England can link, free of charge, from references to full text journals by clicking on [Full text] on the PRODIGY website.

1. Akbal, C., Ekici, S., Erkan, I. and Tekgul, S. (2004) Intermittent oral desmopressin therapy for monosymptomatic primary nocturnal enuresis. *Journal of Urology* **171**(6 Pt 2), 2603–2606.
2. BNF 49 (2005) *British National Formulary.* 49th edn. London: British Medical Association and Royal Pharmaceutical Society of Great Britain.
3. Butler, R.J. (1991) Establishment of working definitions in nocturnal enuresis. *Archives of Disease in Childhood* **66**(2), 267–271.
4. Butler, R. and Stenberg, A. (2001) Treatment of childhood nocturnal enuresis: an examination of clinically relevant principles. *BJU International* **88**(6), 563–571.
5. Butler, R.J., Robinson, J.C., Holland, P. and Doherty-Williams, D. (2004) Investigating the three systems approach to complex childhood nocturnal enuresis: medical treatment interventions. *Scandinavian Journal of Urology and Nephrology* **38**(2), 117–121.
6. Canadian Paediatric Society (2002) *Enuresis.* Canadian Paediatric Society. www.cps.ca [Accessed: 31/01/2005]. [Full text]
7. Cayan, S., Doruk, E., Bozlu, M. et al (2001) Is routine urinary tract investigation necessary for children with monosymptomatic primary nocturnal enuresis? *Urology* **58**(4), 598–602.
8. Chiozza, M.L., del Gado, R., di Toro, R. et al (1999) Italian multicentre open trial on DDAVP spray in nocturnal enuresis. *Scandinavian Journal of Urology and Nephrology* **33**(1), 42–48.
9. Dobson, P. and Blackwell, C.L. (Eds.) (1995) *A guide to enuresis: a guide to the treatment of enuresis for professionals.* Bristol: Enuresis Resource and Information Centre.
10. DTB (2004) Management of bedwetting in children. *Drug & Therapeutics Bulletin* **42**(5), 33–37.
11. Gimpel, G.A., Warzak, W.J., Kuhn, B.R. and Walburn, J.N. (1998) Clinical perspectives in primary nocturnal enuresis. *Clinical Pediatrics* **37**(1), 23–29. [Full text]
12. Glazener, C.M.A. and Evans, J.H.C. (2002) *Desmopressin for nocturnal enuresis in children (Cochrane Review).* The Cochrane Library. Issue 3. Chichester, UK: John Wiley & Sons, Ltd. www.nelh.nhs.uk/cochrane.asp [Accessed: 01/04/2005]. [Full text]
13. Glazener, C.M.A. and Evans, J.H.C. (2004) *Simple behavioural and physical interventions for nocturnal enuresis in children (Cochrane Review).* The Cochrane Library. Issue 2. Chichester, UK: John Wiley & Sons, Ltd. www.nelh.nhs.uk/cochrane.asp [Accessed: 15/06/2005]. [Full text]
14. Glazener, C.M.A., Evans, J.H.C. and Peto, R.E. (2003a) *Drugs for nocturnal enuresis in children (other than desmopressin and tricyclics) (Cochrane Review).* The Cochrane Library. Issue 4. Chichester, UK: John Wiley & Sons, Ltd. www.nelh.nhs.uk/cochrane.asp [Accessed: 01/04/2005]. [Full text]
15. Glazener, C.M.A., Evans, J.H.C. and Peto, R.E. (2003b) *Tricyclic and related drugs for nocturnal enuresis in children (Cochrane Review).* The Cochrane Library. Issue 3. Chichester, UK: John Wiley & Sons, Ltd. www.nelh.nhs.uk/cochrane.asp [Accessed: 14/06/2005]. [Full text]
16. Glazener, C.M.A., Evans, J.H.C. and Peto, R.E. (2004) *Complex behavioural and educational interventions for nocturnal enuresis in children (Cochrane Review).* The Cochrane Library. Issue 1. Chichester, UK: John Wiley & Sons, Ltd. www.nelh.nhs.uk/cochrane.asp [Accessed: 14/06/2005]. [Full text]
17. Glazener, C.M.A., Evans, J.H.C. and Peto, R.E. (2005a) *Alarm interventions for nocturnal enuresis in children (Cochrane Review).* The Cochrane Library. Issue 2. Chichester, UK: John Wiley & Sons, Ltd. www.nelh.nhs.uk/cochrane.asp [Accessed: 01/04/2005]. [Full text]
18. Glazener, C.M.A., Evans, J.H.C. and Cheuk, D.K.L. (2005b) *Complementary and miscellaneous interventions for nocturnal enuresis in children.* The Cochrane Library. Issue 2. Chichester, UK: John Wiley

& Sons, Ltd. www.nelh.nhs.uk/cochrane.asp [Accessed: 14/06/2005]. [Full text]
19. Hjalmas, K., Hanson, E., Hellstrom, A.L. et al (1998) Long-term treatment with desmopressin in children with primary monosymptomatic nocturnal enuresis: an open multicentre study. Swedish Enuresis Trial (SWEET) Group. *British Journal of Urology* **82**(5), 704–709.
20. Hjalmas, K., Arnold, T., Bower, W. et al (2004) Nocturnal enuresis: an international evidence based management strategy. *Journal of Urology* **171**(6 Pt 2), 2545–2561.
21. Janknegt, R.A., Zweers, H.M., Delaere, K.P. et al (1997) Oral desmopressin as a new treatment modality for primary nocturnal enuresis in adolescents and adults: a double-blind, randomized, multicenter study. Dutch Enuresis Study Group. *Journal of Urology* **157**(2), 513–517.
22. Lackgren, G., Hjalmas, K., van Gool, J. et al (1999) Nocturnal enuresis: a suggestion for a European treatment strategy. *Acta Paediatrica* **88**(6), 679–690.
23. Loening-Baucke, V. (1997) Urinary incontinence and urinary tract infection and their resolution with treatment of chronic constipation of childhood. *Pediatrics* **100**(2), 228–232. [Full text]
24. Lyth, N. and Bosson, S. (2004) *Nocturnal enuresis.* Clinical Evidence. Volume 12. www.clinicalevidence.com [Accessed: 28/02/2005].
25. Mark, S.D. and Frank, J.D. (1995) Nocturnal enuresis. *British Journal of Urology* **75**(4), 427–434.
26. Mikkelsen, E.J. (2001) Enuresis and encopresis: ten years of progress. *Journal of the American Academy of Child & Adolescent Psychiatry* **40**(10), 1146–1158.
27. Miller, K., Atkin, B. and Moody, L. (1992) Drug therapy for nocturnal enuresis. *Drugs* **44**(1), 47–56.
28. Müller, D., Roehr, C.C. and Eggert, P. (2004) Comparative tolerability of drug treatment for nocturnal enuresis in children. *Drug Safety* **27**(10), 717–727.
29. Ng, C.F.-N., Wong, S.-N., Chang, S. et al (2005) Comparing alarms, desmopressin, and combined treatment in Chinese enuretic children. *Pediatric Nephrology* **20**(2), 163–169.
30. Radmayr, C., Schlager, A., Studen, M. and Bartsch, G. (2001) Prospective randomized trial using laser acupuncture versus desmopressin in the treatment of nocturnal enuresis. *European Urology* **40**(2), 201–205.
31. Sener, F., Hasanoglu, E. and Soylemezoglu, O. (1998) Desmopressin versus indomethacin treatment in primary nocturnal enuresis and the role of prostaglandins. *Urology* **52**(5), 878–881.
32. van Dyk, J.C., Duvenhage, F., Coetzee, L.J.E. et al (2003) South African guidelines for the management of nocturnal enuresis. *South African Medical Journal* **93**(5), 338–340.
33. van Kerrebroeck, P.E. (2002) Experience with the long-term use of desmopressin for nocturnal enuresis in children and adolescents. *BJU International* **89**(4), 420–425.
34. Wolfish, N.M., Barkin, J., Gorodzinsky, F. and Schwarz, R. (2003) The Canadian enuresis study and evaluation: short and long-term safety and efficacy of an oral desmopressin preparation. *Scandinavian Journal of Urology and Nephrology* **37**(1), 22–27.
35. Yuksek, M.S., Erdem, A.F., Atalay, C. and Demirel, A. (2003) Acupressure versus oxybutinin in the treatment of enuresis. *Journal of International Medical Research* **31**(6), 552–556.

PRODIGY GUIDANCE

Epilepsy

Last revised in November 2004
At the time of print this topic was being updated. The newly revised guidance will be issued on to the website in 2006.
www.prodigy.nhs.uk/guidance.asp?gt=Epilepsy

Applies to people of all ages

This guidance is based on the Scottish Intercollegiate Guidelines Network (SIGN) Guideline *Diagnosis and Management of Epilepsy in Adults* (April 2003). The guidance also incorporates guidelines published by the National Institute of Clinical Excellence (NICE) in April 2004, technology appraisal number 79 *Newer drugs for epilepsy in children*; and in March 2004, technology appraisal number 76 *Newer drugs for epilepsy in adults.*

This guidance covers the initial management of epilepsy and the continued management of epilepsy with monotherapy. It also covers the emergency management of prolonged seizures (status epilepticus).

This guidance does not cover the management of people who are uncontrolled on monotherapy, who require combination therapy under the supervision of a specialist, or who have complicated paediatric epilepsy syndromes such as infantile spasms (West's syndrome) or Lennox–Gastaut syndrome.

There is separate PRODIGY guidance for *Alcohol — problem drinking* and *Febrile convulsion.*

Goals

- To ensure correct diagnosis and seizure classification
- To stop seizures or, if this is not possible, reduce their frequency and severity
- To minimize adverse effects on lifestyle
- To provide information to people with epilepsy and their carers

Contents

Scenarios

- Primary generalized tonic-clonic p.756
- Partial seizures p.760
- Myoclonic p.764
- Absences (rarely adults) p.767
- Status epilepticus p.770

Extended Information, p. 771

Which scenario?

- **Primary generalized tonic-clonic:** covers the management of people diagnosed as having primary generalized tonic-clonic seizures (previously called grand mal or major seizures).
- **Partial seizures:** covers the management of people diagnosed as having simple partial seizures (previously called focal or Jacksonian seizures; i.e. consciousness not impaired) or complex partial seizures (previously called psychomotor or temporal lobe seizures; i.e. consciousness impaired).
- **Myoclonic:** covers the management of people diagnosed as having myoclonic seizures.
- **Absences (rarely adults):** covers the management of people diagnosed as having absences (previously called petit mal seizures).
- **Status epilepticus:** covers the management of people presenting with seizure lasting more than 5 minutes; therefore at risk of status epilepticus (defined as seizure or a series of series lasting more than 30 minutes).

Primary generalized tonic-clonic

Which therapy?

- **Urgently refer people with suspected recent-onset seizures to a neurologist.**
  - Consider urgent outpatient referral or admission depending on local policy.
  - If unacceptable delay is expected then seek telephone advice.
- **Education, information, and support for affected people and their carers are vital.**
- **Self-help organizations** can often give valuable support and information.
- **Prescriptions offered are for initiation and maintenance doses of monotherapy only** — they do not cover dosage regimens that may be necessary for adding in a second drug.
- **Sodium valproate** is preferred monotherapy.
- **Carbamazepine or lamotrigine** are alternatives.

Practical prescribing points

For further information please see the *Medicines Compendium* (www.medicines.org.uk) or the *British National Formulary* (www.bnf.org).

General points

- **Avoid interchanging formulations of antiepileptic drugs (AEDs) where possible.**
- **Avoid sudden withdrawal of an AED** unless adverse effects make this essential as there is an increased risk of seizure recurrence with rapid withdrawal. Sudden AED withdrawal has been associated with sudden unexpected death (see *How and when should antiepileptic drug withdrawal be managed?*).
- **AEDs interact with many drugs** and it is advisable to check possible interactions before other drugs are initiated.
- **If contraception is required,** use sodium valproate or lamotrigine. If carbamazepine is needed, use barrier methods or an intra-uterine device. Alternatively, use a combined oral contraceptive (COC) with at least 50 micrograms of oestrogen, or give Depo-Provera at 10-week intervals. Do not use other progestogen-only preparations. See PRODIGY *Contraception* guidance for further information.

- **Pregnancy:** the UK reported risk rate of major congenital malformation in women with epilepsy:
  - Not exposed to AEDs during pregnancy was 0.9% (95% CI 0.2 to 4.7)
  - Taking carbamazepine during pregnancy was 2.3% (95% CI 1.4 to 4.0)
  - Taking lamotrigine during pregnancy was 3% (95% CI 1.5 to 5.7)
  - Taking sodium valproate during pregnancy was 7.2% (95% CI 5.2 to 10)

Sodium valproate

- **Common dose-dependent adverse effects** are weight gain, tremor, transient hair loss (usually temporary), and menstrual irregularities in adolescent girls.
- **Rare and unpredictable serious adverse effects include:** hepatotoxicity (in children below 3 years old or those with severe learning difficulties), thrombocytopenia, and pancreatitis.
- **Advise people to seek immediate medical attention** if symptoms develop such as:
  - Vomiting, anorexia, jaundice, drowsiness, or loss of seizure control; these are signs of blood or liver disorders.
  - Abdominal pain, nausea, and vomiting; these are signs of pancreatitis.

Carbamazepine

- **Avoid generic substitution with modified-release carbamazepine preparations.**
- **Common dose-dependent adverse effects** are dizziness, headaches, diplopia, insomnia, ataxia, and hyponatraemia. Hyponatraemia usually resolves with fluid intake restriction.
- **The likelihood of dose-related adverse effects may be reduced** by altering the timing of the medication or using modified-release tablets.
- **Rash develops in 10% of people;** if this is persistent or severe, stop treatment.
- **Falls in elderly people** may result from high blood levels of carbamazepine causing ataxia.
- **Advise people to seek immediate medical attention** if fever, sore throat, mouth ulcers, bruising, or bleeding develop.
- **Agranulocytosis** is a rare idiosyncratic reaction and is not predictable by routine blood monitoring.
- **St John's wort has the potential to reduce the plasma concentration of carbamazepine** if used concomitantly.

Lamotrigine

- **Common dose-dependent adverse effects** are sedation, ataxia, diplopia, nausea, and vomiting.
- **CSM advises:** be alert for symptoms and signs suggestive of bone marrow failure such as anaemia, bruising, or infection.
- **Advise people to seek immediate medical attention** if fever, sore throat, mouth ulcers, bruising, or bleeding develop.
- **Rash is idiosyncratic** but can be severe. It is more likely to occur when dose titration is more rapid than recommended and with concomitant use of sodium valproate. The drug should be withdrawn unless the rash is clearly not drug-related (a mild maculopapular rash develops in about 10% of people).

Follow-up advice

- **Monitoring of plasma drug concentration is unnecessary in most people** because seizure control and the development of adverse effects determine the dose.
- **People on sodium valproate — liver function monitoring is important** in the first 6 months of treatment in children under 3 years old and in people with metabolic, degenerative, and developmental conditions:
  - Discontinue treatment if there is an abnormally prolonged prothrombin time.
  - Avoid concomitant use of salicylates as they are broken down via the same metabolic pathway.
- **Routine biochemical and haematological monitoring is not usually necessary.**

Should I refer or investigate?

Refer?

- **Referral guidelines for suspected cancer** published by the National Institute for Health and Clinical Excellence (NICE) recommend that people with suspected recent-onset seizures should be urgently referred to a neurologist.
- **Specialist referral is also recommended:**
  - **If seizures continue** on maximal tolerated monotherapy — to check the diagnosis is correct and advise on whether add-on therapy is needed.
  - **If there is a sudden unexplained deterioration in seizure control.**
  - **If there is diagnostic doubt.**
  - **If a woman on antiepileptic medication becomes (or intends to become) pregnant** — to advise on whether a dosage reduction or even discontinuation of treatment should be considered.
  - **If changing to an alternative drug or if withdrawal of treatment is considered.**
  - **In people with an established diagnosis of epilepsy who have never had a specialist assessment** — up to a third may be wrongly diagnosed.

Investigate?

Initial primary care investigations are usually negative, but the following should be considered (mainly applies to adults):

- **Routine blood tests to exclude underlying metabolic problems** (full blood count, erythrocyte sedimentation rate, electrolytes, renal function, liver function tests, calcium, and glucose); abnormal liver function tests and raised mean corpuscular volume may indicate alcohol problems.
- **Chest X-ray,** if clinically indicated (e.g. in smokers, or if there are chest symptoms) to exclude malignancy.

For people on treatment

- **Regular monitoring of plasma drug concentration is unnecessary in most people** because seizure control and the development of adverse effects determine the dose. Monitoring may be indicated in the following situations: to check on compliance; seizures in a person with previously well-controlled epilepsy; suspected toxicity; and severely disabled people in whom toxicity may be difficult to assess.
- **Routine biochemical and haematological monitoring is not usually necessary.**

Patient information leaflets

The following PILs are available at www.prodigy.nhs.uk

- Epilepsy - A General Introduction
- Epilepsy - Could It Be?
- Epilepsy - Dealing With a Seizure
- Epilepsy - Living With Epilepsy
- Epilepsy Scotland
- Epilepsy - Tonic Clonic Seizures

- Epilepsy - Treatments
- Epilepsy Wales

Shared decision making

- **Medication can prevent seizures.** A low dose is started, but increased if necessary.
- **Side-effects.** Most people have none, or only minor ones. They are more likely at higher doses. A switch to another medicine may be possible if troublesome side-effects occur.
- **Sodium valproate** is commonly used. Possible side-effects include: tremor, weight gain, hair thinning (reversible), and menstrual problems. Serious liver trouble is a rare problem.
- **Carbamazepine** is an alternative. Possible side-effects include: drowsiness, double vision, headache, and sickness. A serious blood disorder is a rare problem. Tell a doctor urgently if you get a sore throat, bruising, mouth ulcers, or fever whilst taking this medicine.
- **Lamotrigine** is an alternative. Possible side-effects include: drowsiness, double vision, sickness, unsteadiness, and a rash.
- **Other medication** — bought or prescribed — may interact with medication for seizures. Check with the doctor or pharmacist before taking any other medication.
- **Contraception.** Carbamazepine interferes with 'the pill'. Either a high-dose pill or two low-dose pills taken together are needed.
- **Pregnancy.** Tell a doctor if you intend to become pregnant whilst taking medication for seizures.

Drug rationale

Drugs not included

- **Newer antiepileptic drugs (other than lamotrigine and topiramate)** are not licensed as monotherapy for primary generalized tonic-clonic seizures. Topiramate is not included, as larger trial data are needed to confirm benefits of efficacy and it is very costly.
- **Phenytoin** is no longer considered a preferred monotherapy choice owing to its poor adverse effect profile, narrow therapeutic index, and titration difficulties due to its saturation pharmacokinetics.
- **Phenobarbital and primidone** are no longer considered as preferred monotherapy choices due to their adverse effect profiles.
- **Clonazepam and clobazam** are occasionally used, but sedation and the development of tolerance limit their use. In addition, clobazam is licensed only as an add-on treatment.
- **Ethosuximide** is licensed only for the treatment of absence seizures, and is rarely used for the treatment of other types of seizure.

[MeReC, 1995]

Drugs included

- **Sodium valproate** is effective against all the generalized seizures and is preferred monotherapy.
- **Modified-release sodium valproate preparations** are offered as their use has notably increased in secondary care, resulting in many people requiring repeat prescriptions in primary care. However, there is limited evidence to support the use of modified-release sodium valproate except for improved patient convenience and compliance.
- **Carbamazepine** is effective for the treatment of primary generalized tonic-clonic seizures.
- **Both branded and generic carbamazepine preparations** are offered. Changing the formulation or brand of AED is not recommended because different preparations may vary in bioavailability or have different pharmacokinetic profiles and, thus, increased potential for reduced effect or excessive side effects [NICE, 2004c].
- **Modified-release carbamazepine preparations** may occasionally be useful in some people who are taking high doses and who suffer from peak concentration adverse effects, as an alternative to more frequent daily dosing [Feely, 1999].
- **Lamotrigine** is a more recent antiepileptic drug that is licensed for monotherapy of primary generalized tonic-clonic seizures in people 12 years and over. It is more expensive than the older antiepileptic drugs.

[MeReC, 1995; Brodie and Dichter, 1997; Brown et al, 1998; BNF 45, 2003; SIGN, 2003]

Prescriptions

Start doses of antiepileptic drugs

Valproate: titrate from 600mg to 1g per day (1st choice)
- Age from 12 years onwards
- Sod valproate 100mg crush tabs. Take three tablets twice a day for 3 days, then take four tablets twice a day for 3 days, then take five tablets twice a day; supply 122 tablets; NHS Cost £4.75.

Valproate s/f liquid: 10mg/kg x2 a day (child up to 20kg)
- Age under 11 years
- Sod valproate 200mg/5ml sf liquid. *WEIGHT REQUIRED* Take 10mg per kg bodyweight TWICE a day; supply 300 ml; NHS Cost £5.42.

Valproate crushable tabs: 10mg/kg x2 a day(child up to 20kg)
- Age under 11 years
- Sod valproate 100mg crush tabs. *WEIGHT REQUIRED* Take 10mg per kg bodyweight TWICE a day; supply 100 tablets; NHS Cost £3.89.

Valproate s/f liquid: 200mg twice a day (child over 20kg)
- Age under 11 years
- Sod valproate 200mg/5ml sf liquid. Take one 5ml spoonful twice a day; supply 600 ml; NHS Cost £10.84.

Valproate crushable tabs: 200mg x2 a day (child over 20kg)
- Age under 11 years
- Sod valproate 100mg crush tabs. Take two tablets twice a day; supply 200 tablets; NHS Cost £7.78.

Carbamazepine: titrate from 200mg to 600mg per day
- Age from 10 years onwards
- Carbamazepine 100mg tablets. Take one tablet twice a day for 2 weeks, then take two tablets twice a day for 2 weeks, then take 3 tablets twice a day; supply 168 tablets; NHS Cost £4.86.

Carbamazepine: titrate from 200mg to 800mg per day
- Age from 10 years onwards
- Carbamazepine 100mg tablets. Take one tablet twice a day for 2 weeks, then take two tablets twice a day for 2 weeks, then take 3 tablets twice a day for 2 weeks; supply 168 tablets; NHS Cost £4.86.
- Carbamazepine 400mg tablets. Take one tablet twice a day; supply 28 tablets; NHS Cost £3.70.

Carbamazepine liquid: 50mg twice a day
- Age under 11 months
- Carbamazepine 100mg/5ml sf liquid. Take 2.5ml twice a day; supply 150 ml; NHS Cost £3.43.

Carbamazepine liquid: titrate from 50mg to 100mg twice a day
- Age from 12 months to 4 years
- Carbamazepine 100mg/5ml sf liquid. Take 2.5ml twice a day for 2 weeks, then take 5ml twice a day; supply 300 ml; NHS Cost £6.86.

Carbamazepine liquid:titrate from 100mg to 200mg twice a day
- Age from 5 to 9 years
- Carbamazepine 100mg/5ml sf liquid. Take one 5ml spoonful twice a day for 2 weeks, then take two 5ml spoonfuls twice a day; supply 600 ml; NHS Cost £13.72.

Tegretol: titrate from 200mg to 600mg per day
- Age from 10 years onwards
- Tegretol 100mg tablets. Take one tablet twice a day for 2 weeks, then take two tablets twice a day for 2 weeks, then take 3 tablets twice a day; supply 168 tablets; NHS Cost £4.86.

Tegretol: titrate from 200mg to 800mg per day
- Age from 10 years onwards
- Tegretol 100mg tablets. Take one tablet twice a day for 2 weeks, then take two tablets twice a day for 2 weeks, then take 3 tablets twice a day for 2 weeks; supply 168 tablets; NHS Cost £4.86.
- Tegretol 400mg tablets. Take one tablet twice a day; supply 28 tablets; NHS Cost £3.70.

Tegretol liquid: 50mg twice a day
- Age under 11 months
- Tegretol 100mg/5ml s/f liquid. Take 2.5ml twice a day; supply 150 ml; NHS Cost £3.43.

Tegretol liquid: titrate from 50mg to 100mg twice a day
- Age from 12 months to 4 years
- Tegretol 100mg/5ml s/f liquid. Take 2.5ml twice a day for 2 weeks, then take 5ml twice a day; supply 300 ml; NHS Cost £6.86.

Tegretol liquid: titrate from 100mg to 200mg twice a day
- Age from 5 to 9 years
- Tegretol 100mg/5ml s/f liquid. Take one 5ml spoonful twice a day for 2 weeks, then take two 5ml spoonfuls twice a day; supply 600 ml; NHS Cost £13.72.

Lamotrigine: titrate from 25mg to 50mg once a day
- Age from 12 years onwards
- Lamotrigine 25mg tablets. Take one tablet once a day for 2 weeks, then take two tablets once a day; supply 42 tablets; NHS Cost £16.45.

Maintenance doses: sodium valproate

Valproate e/c tablets: 500mg twice a day
- Age from 12 years onwards
- Sod valproate 500mg e/c tabs. Take one tablet twice a day; supply 56 tablets; NHS Cost £6.48.

Valproate e/c tablets: 600mg twice a day
- Age from 12 years onwards
- Sod valproate 200mg e/c tabs. Take three tablets twice a day; supply 168 tablets; NHS Cost £9.42.

Valproate e/c tablets: 700mg twice a day
- Age from 12 years onwards
- Sod valproate 500mg e/c tabs. Take one tablet twice a day; supply 56 tablets; NHS Cost £7.26.
- Sod valproate 200mg e/c tabs. Take one tablet twice a day; supply 56 tablets; NHS Cost £3.14.

Valproate e/c tablets: 800mg twice a day
- Age from 12 years onwards
- Sod valproate 200mg e/c tabs. Take four tablets twice a day; supply 224 tablets; NHS Cost £12.57.

Valproate e/c tablets: 600mg three times a day
- Age from 12 years onwards
- Sod valproate 200mg e/c tabs. Take three tablets three times a day; supply 252 tablets; NHS Cost £14.14.

Valproate e/c tablets: 1g twice a day
- Age from 12 years onwards
- Sod valproate 500mg e/c tabs. Take two tablets twice a day; supply 112 tablets; NHS Cost £14.52.

Weight up to 20kg: 10mg/kg twice a day (s/f liquid)
- Age under 11 years
- Sod valproate 200mg/5ml sf liquid. *WEIGHT REQUIRED* Take 10mg per kg bodyweight TWICE a day; supply 300 ml; NHS Cost £5.42.

Weight up to 20kg: 10mg/kg twice a day (crushable tablets)
- Age under 11 years
- Sod valproate 100mg crush tabs. *WEIGHT REQUIRED* Take 10mg per kg bodyweight TWICE a day; supply 100 tablets; NHS Cost £3.89.

Weight over 20kg: 200mg twice a day (s/f liquid)
- Age under 11 years
- Sod valproate 200mg/5ml sf liquid. Take one 5ml spoonful twice a day; supply 600 ml; NHS Cost £12.96.

Weight over 20kg: 240mg twice a day (s/f liquid)
- Age under 11 years
- Sod valproate 200mg/5ml sf liquid. Take 6ml twice a day; supply 600 ml; NHS Cost £12.96.

Weight over 20kg: 300mg twice a day (s/f liquid)
- Age under 11 years
- Sod valproate 200mg/5ml sf liquid. Take 7.5ml twice a day; supply 600 ml; NHS Cost £12.96.

Weight over 20kg: 200mg twice a day (crushable tablets)
- Age under 11 years
- Sod valproate 100mg crush tabs. Take two tablets twice a day; supply 200 tablets; NHS Cost £7.78.

Weight over 20kg: 250mg twice a day (crushable tablets)
- Age under 11 years
- Sod valproate 100mg crush tabs. Take two and a half tablets twice a day; supply 200 tablets; NHS Cost £7.78.

Weight over 20kg: 300mg twice a day (crushable tablets)
- Age under 11 years
- Sod valproate 100mg crush tabs. Take three tablets twice a day; supply 200 tablets; NHS Cost £7.78.

Maintenance doses: generic and branded carbamazepine

Carbamazepine tablets: 300mg twice a day
- Age from 10 years onwards
- Carbamazepine 100mg tablets. Take three tablets twice a day; supply 168 tablets; NHS Cost £4.86.

Carbamazepine tablets: 400mg twice a day
- Age from 10 years onwards
- Carbamazepine 400mg tablets. Take one tablet twice a day; supply 56 tablets; NHS Cost £5.90.

Carbamazepine tablets: 400mg twice a day + 200mg once a day
- Age from 10 years onwards
- Carbamazepine 200mg tablets. Take two tablets each morning and night, and take one tablet each lunchtime; supply 140 tablets; NHS Cost £7.50.

Carbamazepine tablets: 400mg three times a day
- Age from 15 years onwards
- Carbamazepine 400mg tablets. Take one tablet three times a day; supply 84 tablets; NHS Cost £8.85.

Tegretol tablets: 300mg twice a day
- Age from 10 years onwards
- Tegretol 100mg tablets. Take three tablets twice a day; supply 168 tablets; NHS Cost £4.86.

Tegretol tablets: 400mg twice a day
- Age from 10 years onwards
- Tegretol 400mg tablets. Take one tablet twice a day; supply 56 tablets; NHS Cost £5.90.

Tegretol tablets: 400mg twice a day + 200mg once a day
- Age from 10 years onwards
- Tegretol 200mg tablets. Take two tablets each morning and night, and take one tablet each lunchtime; supply 140 tablets; NHS Cost £7.50.

Tegretol tablets: 400mg three times a day
- Age from 15 years onwards
- Tegretol 400mg tablets. Take one tablet three times a day; supply 84 tablets; NHS Cost £8.85.

Carbamazepine s/f liquid: 50mg twice a day
- Age under 11 months
- Carbamazepine 100mg/5ml sf liquid. Take 2.5ml twice a day; supply 150 ml; NHS Cost £3.34.

Carbamazepine s/f liquid: 100mg twice a day
- Age under 4 years
- Carbamazepine 100mg/5ml sf liquid. Take one 5ml spoonful twice a day; supply 300 ml; NHS Cost £6.86.

Carbamazepine s/f liquid: 200mg twice a day
- Age from 12 months to 9 years
- Carbamazepine 100mg/5ml sf liquid. Take two 5ml spoonfuls twice a day; supply 600 ml; NHS Cost £13.72.

Carbamazepine s/f liquid: 200mg three times a day
- Age from 5 to 9 years
- Carbamazepine 100mg/5ml sf liquid. Take two 5ml spoonfuls three times a day; supply 900 ml; NHS Cost £20.58.

Tegretol s/f liquid: 50mg twice a day
- Age under 11 months
- Tegretol 100mg/5ml s/f liquid. Take 2.5ml twice a day; supply 150 ml; NHS Cost £3.34.

Tegretol s/f liquid: 100mg twice a day
- Age under 4 years
- Tegretol 100mg/5ml s/f liquid. Take one 5ml spoonful twice a day; supply 300 ml; NHS Cost £6.86.

Tegretol s/f liquid: 200mg twice a day
- Age from 12 months to 9 years
- Tegretol 100mg/5ml s/f liquid. Take two 5ml spoonfuls twice a day; supply 600 ml; NHS Cost £13.72.

Tegretol s/f liquid: 200mg three times a day
- Age from 5 to 9 years
- Tegretol 100mg/5ml s/f liquid. Take two 5ml spoonfuls three times a day; supply 900 ml; NHS Cost £20.58.

Maintenance doses: m/r carbamazepine and m/r valproate

Valproate m/r tablets: 500mg twice a day
- Age from 12 years onwards
- Sod valproate 500mg m/r tabs. Take one tablet twice a day; supply 56 tablets; NHS Cost £6.79.

Valproate m/r tablets: 600mg twice a day
- Age from 12 years onwards
- Sod valproate 300mg m/r tabs. Take two tablets twice a day; supply 112 tablets; NHS Cost £13.59.

Valproate m/r tablets: 700mg twice a day
- Age from 12 years onwards
- Sod valproate 200mg m/r tabs. Take one tablet twice a day; supply 56 tablets; NHS Cost £4.53.
- Sod valproate 500mg m/r tabs. Take one tablet twice a day; supply 56 tablets; NHS Cost £11.32.

Valproate m/r tablets: 800mg twice a day
- Age from 12 years onwards
- Sod valproate 200mg m/r tabs. Take four tablets twice a day; supply 224 tablets; NHS Cost £18.12.

Valproate m/r tablets: 900mg twice a day
- Age from 12 years onwards
- Sod valproate 300mg m/r tabs. Take three tablets twice a day; supply 168 tablets; NHS Cost £20.38.

Valproate m/r tablets: 1g twice a day
- Age from 12 years onwards
- Sod valproate 500mg m/r tabs. Take two tablets twice a day; supply 56 tablets; NHS Cost £11.31.

Tegretol Retard tablets: 400mg twice a day
- Age from 10 years onwards
- Tegretol Retard 400mg m/r tabs. Take one tablet twice a day; supply 56 tablets; NHS Cost £10.34.

Tegretol Retard tablets: 600mg twice a day
- Age from 15 years onwards
- Tegretol Retard 200mg m/r tabs. Take three tablets twice a day; supply 168 tablets; NHS Cost £15.78.

Maintenance doses: lamotrigine

Lamotrigine tablets: 100mg once a day
- Age from 12 years onwards
- Lamotrigine 100mg tablets. Take one tablet once a day; supply 28 tablets; NHS Cost £32.19.

Lamotrigine tablets: 150mg once a day
- Age from 12 years onwards
- Lamotrigine 50mg tablets. Take three tablets once a day; supply 84 tablets; NHS Cost £55.97.

Lamotrigine tablets: 200mg once a day
- Age from 12 years onwards
- Lamotrigine 200mg tablets. Take one tablet once a day; supply 28 tablets; NHS Cost £54.71.

Partial seizures

Which therapy?

The following applies to people with simple and complex partial seizures, with or without secondary generalization.

- **Urgently refer people with suspected recent-onset seizures to a neurologist.**
  - Consider urgent outpatient referral or admission depending on local policy.
  - If unacceptable delay is expected then seek telephone advice.
- **Education, information, and support for affected people and their carers are vital.**
- **Self-help organizations** can often give valuable support and information.
- **Prescriptions offered are for initiation and maintenance doses of monotherapy only** — they do not cover dosage regimens that may be necessary for adding in a second drug.
- Carbamazepine, sodium valproate, or lamotrigine are preferred monotherapies.
- **Women of childbearing potential** — sodium valproate should not be started without specialist neurological advice, and for partial seizures, sodium valproate should be used only in women found to be resistant to other treatments.

Practical prescribing points

For further information please see the *Medicines Compendium* (www.medicines.org.uk) or the *British National Formulary* (www.bnf.org).

General points

- **Avoid interchanging formulations of antiepileptic drugs (AEDs) where possible.**
- **Avoid sudden withdrawal of an AED** unless adverse effects make this essential as there is an increased risk of seizure recurrence with rapid withdrawal. Sudden AED withdrawal has been associated with sudden unexpected death (see *Antiepileptic drug withdrawal*).

- **AEDs interact with many drugs** and it is advisable to check possible interactions before initiating other drugs.
- **Contraception required:** use sodium valproate or lamotrigine. If carbamazepine is needed, use barrier methods or an intra-uterine device. Alternatively, use a combined oral contraceptive (COC) with at least 50 micrograms of oestrogen, or give Depo-Provera at 10-week intervals. Do not use other progestogen-only preparations. See PRODIGY *Contraception* guidance for further information.
- **Pregnancy: the UK reported risk rate of major congenital malformation in women with epilepsy:**
  - Not exposed to AEDs during pregnancy was 0.9% (95% CI 0.2 to 4.7)
  - Taking carbamazepine during pregnancy was 2.3% (95% CI 1.4 to 4.0)
  - Taking lamotrigine during pregnancy was 3% (95% CI 1.5 to 5.7)
  - Taking sodium valproate during pregnancy was 7.2% (95% CI 5.2 to 10)

Sodium valproate

- **Common dose-dependent adverse effects** are weight gain, tremor, transient hair loss (usually temporary), and menstrual irregularities in adolescent girls.
- **Rare and unpredictable serious adverse effects include:** hepatotoxicity (in children below 3 years old or those with severe learning difficulties), thrombocytopenia, and pancreatitis.
- **Advise people to seek immediate medical attention** if symptoms develop such as:
  - Vomiting, anorexia, jaundice, drowsiness, or loss of seizure control; these are signs of blood or liver disorders.
  - Abdominal pain, nausea, and vomiting; these are signs of pancreatitis.

Carbamazepine

- **Avoid generic substitution with modified-release carbamazepine preparations.**
- **Common dose-dependent adverse effects** are dizziness, headaches, diplopia, insomnia, ataxia, and hyponatraemia. Hyponatraemia usually resolves with fluid intake restriction.
- **The likelihood of dose-related adverse effects may be** reduced by altering the timing of the medication or using modified-release tablets.
- **Rash develops in 10% of people;** if this is persistent or severe, stop treatment.
- **Falls in elderly people** may result from high blood levels of carbamazepine causing ataxia.
- **Advise people to seek immediate medical attention** if fever, sore throat, mouth ulcers, bruising, or bleeding develop.
- **Agranulocytosis** is a rare idiosyncratic reaction and is not predictable by routine blood monitoring.
- **St John's wort has the potential to reduce the plasma concentration of carbamazepine** if used concomitantly.

Lamotrigine

- **Common dose-dependent adverse effects** are sedation, ataxia, diplopia, nausea, and vomiting.
- **CSM advises:** be alert for symptoms and signs suggestive of bone marrow failure such as anaemia, bruising, or infection.
- **Advise people to seek immediate medical attention** if fever, sore throat, mouth ulcers, bruising, or bleeding develop.
- **Rash is idiosyncratic** but can be severe. It is more likely to occur when dose titration is more rapid than recommended and with concomitant use of sodium valproate. The drug should be withdrawn unless the rash is clearly not drug-related (a mild maculopapular rash develops in about 10% of people).

Follow-up advice

- **Monitoring of plasma drug concentration is unnecessary in most people** because seizure control and the development of adverse effects determine the dose.
- **People on sodium valproate — liver function monitoring is important** in the first 6 months of treatment in children under 3 years old and in people with metabolic, degenerative, and developmental conditions:
  - Discontinue treatment if there is an abnormally prolonged prothrombin time.
  - Avoid concomitant use of salicylates as they are broken down via the same metabolic pathway.
- **Routine biochemical and haematological monitoring is not usually necessary.**

E

Should I refer or investigate?

Refer?

- **Referral guidelines for suspected cancer** published by the National Institute for Health and Clinical Excellence (NICE) recommend that people with suspected recent-onset seizures should be urgently referred to a neurologist.
- **Specialist referral is also recommended:**
  - **If seizures continue** on maximal tolerated monotherapy — to check the diagnosis is correct and advise on whether add-on therapy is needed.
  - **If there is a sudden unexplained deterioration in seizure control.**
  - **If there is diagnostic doubt.**
  - **If a woman on antiepileptic medication becomes** (or intends to become) **pregnant** — to advise on whether a dosage reduction or even discontinuation of treatment should be considered.
  - **If changing to an alternative drug or if withdrawal of treatment is considered.**
  - **In people with an established diagnosis of epilepsy who have never had a specialist assessment** — up to a third may be wrongly diagnosed.

Investigate?

Initial primary care investigations are usually negative, but the following should be considered (mainly applies to adults):

- **Routine blood tests to exclude underlying metabolic problems** (full blood count, erythrocyte sedimentation rate, electrolytes, renal function, liver function tests, calcium, and glucose); abnormal liver function tests and raised mean corpuscular volume may indicate alcohol problems.
- **Chest X-ray,** if clinically indicated (e.g. in smokers, or if there are chest symptoms) to exclude malignancy.

For people on treatment

- **Regular monitoring of plasma drug concentration is unnecessary in most people** because seizure control and the development of adverse effects determine the dose. Monitoring may be indicated in the following situations: to check on compliance; seizures in a person with previously well-controlled epilepsy; suspected toxicity; and severely disabled people in whom toxicity may be difficult to assess.
- **Routine biochemical and haematological monitoring is not usually necessary.**

Patient information leaflets

The following PILs are available at www.prodigy.nhs.uk

- Epilepsy - A General Introduction
- Epilepsy - Could It Be?
- Epilepsy - Living With Epilepsy
- Epilepsy - Partial Seizures
- Epilepsy Scotland
- Epilepsy - Treatments
- Epilepsy Wales

Shared decision making

E

- **Medication can prevent seizures.** A low dose is started, but increased if necessary.
- **Side-effects.** Most people have none, or only minor ones. They are more likely at higher doses. A switch to another medicine may be possible if troublesome side-effects occur.
- **Sodium valproate** is commonly used. Possible side-effects include: tremor, weight gain, hair thinning (reversible), and menstrual problems. Serious liver trouble is a rare problem.
- **Carbamazepine** is an alternative. Possible side-effects include: drowsiness, double vision, headache, and sickness. A serious blood disorder is a rare problem. Tell a doctor urgently if you get a sore throat, bruising, mouth ulcers, or fever whilst taking this medicine.
- **Lamotrigine** is an alternative. Possible side-effects include: drowsiness, double vision, sickness, unsteadiness, and a rash.
- **Other medication** — bought or prescribed — may interact with medication for seizures. Check with the doctor or pharmacist before taking any other medication.
- **Contraception.** Carbamazepine interferes with 'the pill'. Either a high-dose pill or two low-dose pills taken together are needed.
- **Pregnancy.** Tell a doctor if you intend to become pregnant whilst taking medication for seizures.

Drug rationale

Drugs not included

- **Most recent antiepileptic drugs (other than lamotrigine, oxcarbazepine, and topiramate)** are not licensed as monotherapy for partial seizures.
- **Oxcarbazepine** is not offered as it is a black triangle drug and remains under the surveillance of the CSM. The potential for drug interactions appears to be less with oxcarbazepine than carbamazepine, but larger trial data are needed to confirm benefits of efficacy [Gloaguen et al, 1998].
- **Phenytoin** is no longer considered a preferred monotherapy choice owing its poor adverse effect profile, narrow therapeutic index, and titration difficulties due to its saturation pharmacokinetics.
- **Phenobarbital and primidone** are no longer considered as preferred monotherapy choices due to their adverse effect profiles.
- **Clonazepam and clobazam** are occasionally used, but sedation and the development of tolerance limit their use. In addition, clobazam is licensed only as an add-on treatment.
- **Ethosuximide** is licensed only for the treatment of absence seizures and is rarely used for the treatment of other types of seizure.

[MeReC, 1995]

Drugs included

- **Sodium valproate** is effective treatment for partial seizures and is a good preferred monotherapy.
- **Modified-release sodium valproate preparations** are offered as their use has notably increased in secondary care, resulting in many people requiring repeat prescriptions in primary care. However, there is limited evidence to support the use of modified-release sodium valproate except for improved patient convenience and compliance.
- **Carbamazepine** is effective for the treatment of partial seizures.
- **Both branded and generic carbamazepine preparations** are offered. Changing the formulation or brand of AED is not recommended because different preparations may vary in bioavailability or have different pharmacokinetic profiles and, thus, increased potential for reduced effect or excessive side effects [NICE, 2004c].
- **Modified-release preparations** of carbamazepine may occasionally be useful in some people who are taking high doses and who suffer from peak concentration adverse effects, as an alternative to more frequent daily dosing [Feely, 1999].
- **Lamotrigine** is a more recent antiepileptic drug that is licensed for monotherapy of partial seizures. It is more expensive than the older antiepileptic drugs.

[MeReC, 1995; Brodie and Dichter, 1997; Brown et al, 1998; BNF 45, 2003; SIGN, 2003]

Prescriptions

Start doses of antiepileptics

Valproate: titrate from 600mg to 1g per day (1st choice)
- Age from 12 years onwards
- Sod valproate 100mg crush tabs. Take three tablets twice a day for 3 days, then take four tablets twice a day for 3 days, then take five tablets twice a day; supply 122 tablets; NHS Cost £4.75.

Valproate s/f liquid: 10mg/kg x2 a day (child up to 20kg)
- Age under 11 years
- Sod valproate 200mg/5ml sf liquid. *WEIGHT REQUIRED* Take 10mg per kg bodyweight TWICE a day; supply 300 ml; NHS Cost £5.42.

Valproate crushable tabs: 10mg/kg x2 a day(child up to 20kg)
- Age under 11 years
- Sod valproate 100mg crush tabs. *WEIGHT REQUIRED* Take 10mg per kg bodyweight TWICE a day; supply 100 tablets; NHS Cost £3.89.

Valproate s/f liquid: 200mg twice a day (child over 20kg)
- Age under 11 years
- Sod valproate 200mg/5ml sf liquid. Take one 5ml spoonful twice a day; supply 600 ml; NHS Cost £10.84.

Valproate crushable tabs: 200mg x2 a day (child over 20kg)
- Age under 11 years
- Sod valproate 100mg crush tabs. Take two tablets twice a day; supply 200 tablets; NHS Cost £7.78.

Carbamazepine: titrate from 200mg to 600mg per day
- Age from 10 years onwards
- Carbamazepine 100mg tablets. Take one tablet twice a day for 2 weeks, then take two tablets twice a day for 2 weeks, then take 3 tablets twice a day; supply 168 tablets; NHS Cost £4.86.

Carbamazepine: titrate from 200mg to 800mg per day
- Age from 10 years onwards
- Carbamazepine 100mg tablets. Take one tablet twice a day for 2 weeks, then take two tablets twice a day for 2

weeks, then take 3 tablets twice a day for 2 weeks; supply 168 tablets; NHS Cost £4.86.
- Carbamazepine 400mg tablets. Take one tablet twice a day; supply 28 tablets; NHS Cost £3.70.

Carbamazepine liquid: 50mg twice a day
- Age under 11 months
- Carbamazepine 100mg/5ml sf liquid. Take 2.5ml twice a day; supply 150 ml; NHS Cost £3.43.

Carbamazepine liquid: titrate from 50mg to 100mg twice a day
- Age from 12 months to 4 years
- Carbamazepine 100mg/5ml sf liquid. Take 2.5ml twice a day for 2 weeks, then take 5ml twice a day; supply 300 ml; NHS Cost £6.86.

Carbamazepine liquid:titrate from 100mg to 200mg twice a day
- Age from 5 to 9 years
- Carbamazepine 100mg/5ml sf liquid. Take one 5ml spoonful twice a day for 2 weeks, then take two 5ml spoonfuls twice a day; supply 600 ml; NHS Cost £13.72.

Tegretol: titrate from 200mg to 600mg per day
- Age from 10 years onwards
- Tegretol 100mg tablets. Take one tablet twice a day for 2 weeks, then take two tablets twice a day for 2 weeks, then take 3 tablets twice a day; supply 168 tablets; NHS Cost £4.86.

Tegretol: titrate from 200mg to 800mg per day
- Age from 10 years onwards
- Tegretol 100mg tablets. Take one tablet twice a day for 2 weeks, then take two tablets twice a day for 2 weeks, then take 3 tablets twice a day for 2 weeks; supply 168 tablets; NHS Cost £4.86.
- Tegretol 400mg tablets. Take one tablet twice a day; supply 28 tablets; NHS Cost £3.70.

Tegretol liquid: 50mg twice a day
- Age under 11 months
- Tegretol 100mg/5ml s/f liquid. Take 2.5ml twice a day; supply 150 ml; NHS Cost £3.43.

Tegretol liquid: titrate from 50mg to 100mg twice a day
- Age from 12 months to 4 years
- Tegretol 100mg/5ml s/f liquid. Take 2.5ml twice a day for 2 weeks, then take 5ml twice a day; supply 300 ml; NHS Cost £6.86.

Tegretol liquid: titrate from 100mg to 200mg twice a day
- Age from 5 to 9 years
- Tegretol 100mg/5ml s/f liquid. Take one 5ml spoonful twice a day for 2 weeks, then take two 5ml spoonfuls twice a day; supply 600 ml; NHS Cost £13.72.

Lamotrigine: titrate from 25mg to 50mg once a day
- Age from 12 years onwards
- Lamotrigine 25mg tablets. Take one tablet once a day for 2 weeks, then take two tablets once a day; supply 42 tablets; NHS Cost £16.45.

Maintenance doses: sodium valproate

Valproate e/c tablets: 500mg twice a day
- Age from 12 years onwards
- Sod valproate 500mg e/c tabs. Take one tablet twice a day; supply 56 tablets; NHS Cost £6.48.

Valproate e/c tablets: 600mg twice a day
- Age from 12 years onwards
- Sod valproate 200mg e/c tabs. Take three tablets twice a day; supply 168 tablets; NHS Cost £9.42.

Valproate e/c tablets: 700mg twice a day
- Age from 12 years onwards
- Sod valproate 500mg e/c tabs. Take one tablet twice a day; supply 56 tablets; NHS Cost £7.26.
- Sod valproate 200mg e/c tabs. Take one tablet twice a day; supply 56 tablets; NHS Cost £3.14.

Valproate e/c tablets: 800mg twice a day
- Age from 12 years onwards
- Sod valproate 200mg e/c tabs. Take four tablets twice a day; supply 224 tablets; NHS Cost £12.57.

Valproate e/c tablets. 600mg three times a day
- Age from 12 years onwards
- Sod valproate 200mg e/c tabs. Take three tablets three times a day; supply 252 tablets; NHS Cost £14.14.

Valproate e/c tablets: 1g twice a day
- Age from 12 years onwards
- Sod valproate 500mg e/c tabs. Take two tablets twice a day; supply 112 tablets; NHS Cost £14.52.

Weight up to 20kg: 10mg/kg twice a day (s/f liquid)
- Age under 11 years
- Sod valproate 200mg/5ml sf liquid. *WEIGHT REQUIRED* Take 10mg per kg bodyweight TWICE a day; supply 300 ml; NHS Cost £5.42.

Weight up to 20kg: 10mg/kg twice a day (crushable tablets)
- Age under 11 years
- Sod valproate 100mg crush tabs. *WEIGHT REQUIRED* Take 10mg per kg bodyweight TWICE a day; supply 100 tablets; NHS Cost £3.89.

Weight over 20kg: 200mg twice a day (s/f liquid)
- Age under 11 years
- Sod valproate 200mg/5ml sf liquid. Take one 5ml spoonful twice a day; supply 600 ml; NHS Cost £12.96.

Weight over 20kg: 240mg twice a day (s/f liquid)
- Age under 11 years
- Sod valproate 200mg/5ml sf liquid. Take 6ml twice a day; supply 600 ml; NHS Cost £12.96.

Weight over 20kg: 300mg twice a day (s/f liquid)
- Age under 11 years
- Sod valproate 200mg/5ml sf liquid. Take 7.5ml twice a day; supply 600 ml; NHS Cost £12.96.

Weight over 20kg: 200mg twice a day (crushable tablets)
- Age under 11 years
- Sod valproate 100mg crush tabs. Take two tablets twice a day; supply 200 tablets; NHS Cost £7.78.

Weight over 20kg: 250mg twice a day (crushable tablets)
- Age under 11 years
- Sod valproate 100mg crush tabs. Take two and a half tablets twice a day; supply 200 tablets; NHS Cost £7.78.

Weight over 20kg: 300mg twice a day (crushable tablets)
- Age under 11 years
- Sod valproate 100mg crush tabs. Take three tablets twice a day; supply 200 tablets; NHS Cost £7.78.

Maintenance doses: generic and branded carbamazepine

Carbamazepine tablets: 300mg twice a day
- Age from 10 years onwards
- Carbamazepine 100mg tablets. Take three tablets twice a day; supply 168 tablets; NHS Cost £4.86.

Carbamazepine tablets: 400mg twice a day
- Age from 10 years onwards
- Carbamazepine 400mg tablets. Take one tablet twice a day; supply 56 tablets; NHS Cost £5.90.

Carbamazepine tablets: 400mg twice a day + 200mg once a day
- Age from 10 years onwards
- Carbamazepine 200mg tablets. Take two tablets each morning and night, and take one tablet each lunchtime; supply 140 tablets; NHS Cost £7.50.

Carbamazepine tablets: 400mg three times a day
- Age from 15 years onwards
- Carbamazepine 400mg tablets. Take one tablet three times a day; supply 84 tablets; NHS Cost £8.85.

Tegretol tablets: 300mg twice a day
- Age from 10 years onwards
- Tegretol 100mg tablets. Take three tablets twice a day; supply 168 tablets; NHS Cost £4.86.

Tegretol tablets: 400mg twice a day
- Age from 10 years onwards
- Tegretol 400mg tablets. Take one tablet twice a day; supply 56 tablets; NHS Cost £5.90.

Tegretol tablets: 400mg twice a day + 200mg once a day
- Age from 10 years onwards
- Tegretol 200mg tablets. Take two tablets each morning and night, and take one tablet each lunchtime; supply 140 tablets; NHS Cost £7.50.

E

Tegretol tablets: 400mg three times a day
- Age from 15 years onwards
- Tegretol 400mg tablets. Take one tablet three times a day; supply 84 tablets; NHS Cost £8.85.

Carbamazepine s/f liquid: 50mg twice a day
- Age under 11 months
- Carbamazepine 100mg/5ml sf liquid. Take 2.5ml twice a day; supply 150 ml; NHS Cost £3.34.

Carbamazepine s/f liquid: 100mg twice a day
- Age under 4 years
- Carbamazepine 100mg/5ml sf liquid. Take one 5ml spoonful twice a day; supply 300 ml; NHS Cost £6.86.

Carbamazepine s/f liquid: 200mg twice a day
- Age from 12 months to 9 years
- Carbamazepine 100mg/5ml sf liquid. Take two 5ml spoonfuls twice a day; supply 600 ml; NHS Cost £13.72.

Carbamazepine s/f liquid: 200mg three times a day
- Age from 5 to 9 years
- Carbamazepine 100mg/5ml sf liquid. Take two 5ml spoonfuls three times a day; supply 900 ml; NHS Cost £20.58.

Tegretol s/f liquid: 50mg twice a day
- Age under 11 months
- Tegretol 100mg/5ml s/f liquid. Take 2.5ml twice a day; supply 150 ml; NHS Cost £3.34.

Tegretol s/f liquid: 100mg twice a day
- Age under 4 years
- Tegretol 100mg/5ml s/f liquid. Take one 5ml spoonful twice a day; supply 300 ml; NHS Cost £6.86.

Tegretol s/f liquid: 200mg twice a day
- Age from 12 months to 9 years
- Tegretol 100mg/5ml s/f liquid. Take two 5ml spoonfuls twice a day; supply 600 ml; NHS Cost £13.72.

Tegretol s/f liquid: 200mg three times a day
- Age from 5 to 9 years
- Tegretol 100mg/5ml s/f liquid. Take two 5ml spoonfuls three times a day; supply 900 ml; NHS Cost £20.58.

Maintenance doses: m/r carbamazepine and m/r valproate

Valproate m/r tablets: 500mg twice a day
- Age from 12 years onwards
- Sod valproate 500mg m/r tabs. Take one tablet twice a day; supply 56 tablets; NHS Cost £6.79.

Valproate m/r tablets: 600mg twice a day
- Age from 12 years onwards
- Sod valproate 300mg m/r tabs. Take two tablets twice a day; supply 112 tablets; NHS Cost £13.59.

Valproate m/r 700mg twice a day
- Age from 12 years onwards
- Sod valproate 500mg m/r tabs. Take one tablet twice a day; supply 56 tablets; NHS Cost £11.32.
- Sod valproate 200mg m/r tabs. Take one tablet twice a day; supply 56 tablets; NHS Cost £4.53.

Valproate m/r tablets: 800mg twice a day
- Age from 12 years onwards
- Sod valproate 200mg m/r tabs. Take four tablets twice a day; supply 224 tablets; NHS Cost £18.12.

Valproate m/r tablets: 900mg twice a day
- Age from 12 years onwards
- Sod valproate 300mg m/r tabs. Take three tablets twice a day; supply 168 tablets; NHS Cost £20.38.

Valproate m/r tablets: 1g twice a day
- Age from 12 years onwards
- Sod valproate 500mg m/r tabs. Take two tablets twice a day; supply 56 tablets; NHS Cost £11.31.

Tegretol Retard tablets: 400mg twice a day
- Age from 10 years onwards
- Tegretol Retard 400mg m/r tabs. Take one tablet twice a day; supply 56 tablets; NHS Cost £15.78.

Tegretol Retard tablets: 600mg twice a day
- Age from 12 years onwards
- Tegretol Retard 200mg m/r tabs. Take three tablets twice a day; supply 168 tablets; NHS Cost £10.34.

Maintenance doses: lamotrigine

Lamotrigine tablets: 100mg once a day
- Age from 12 years onwards
- Lamotrigine 100mg tablets. Take one tablet once a day; supply 28 tablets; NHS Cost £32.19.

Lamotrigine tablets: 150mg once a day
- Age from 12 years onwards
- Lamotrigine 50mg tablets. Take three tablets once a day; supply 84 tablets; NHS Cost £55.97.

Lamotrigine tablets: 200mg once a day
- Age from 12 years onwards
- Lamotrigine 200mg tablets. Take one tablet once a day; supply 28 tablets; NHS Cost £54.71.

Myoclonic

Which therapy?

- **Urgently refer people with suspected recent-onset seizures to a neurologist.**
  - Consider urgent outpatient referral or admission depending on local policy.
  - If unacceptable delay is expected then seek telephone advice.
- **Education, information, and support for affected people and their carers are vital.**
- **Self-help organizations** can often give valuable support and information.
- **Prescriptions offered are for initiation and maintenance doses of monotherapy only** — they do not cover dosage regimens that may be necessary for adding in a second drug.
- **Sodium valproate** is preferred monotherapy.
- **Lamotrigine** (off-licence use) or **clonazepam** are alternatives.

Practical prescribing points

For further information please see the *Medicines Compendium* (www.medicines.org.uk) or the *British National Formulary* (www.bnf.org).

General points

- **Avoid interchanging formulations of antiepileptic drugs (AEDs) where possible.**
- **Avoid sudden withdrawal of an AED** unless adverse effects make this essential as there is an increased risk of seizure recurrence with rapid withdrawal. Sudden AED

withdrawal has been associated with sudden unexpected death (see *How and when should antiepileptic drug withdrawal be managed?*).
- **AEDs interact with many drugs** and it is advisable to check possible interactions before initiating other drugs.
- **Pregnancy: the UK reported risk rate of major congenital malformation in women with epilepsy:**
  - Not exposed to AEDs during pregnancy was 0.9% (95% CI 0.2 to 4.7)
  - Taking carbamazepine during pregnancy was 2.3% (95% CI 1.4 to 4.0)
  - Taking sodium valproate during pregnancy was 7.2% (95% CI 5.2 to 10)
  - Taking lamotrigine during pregnancy was 3% (95% CI 1.5 to 5.7)

Sodium valproate

- **Common dose-dependent adverse effects** are weight gain, tremor, transient hair loss (usually temporary), and menstrual irregularities in adolescent girls.
- **Rare and unpredictable serious adverse effects include:** hepatotoxicity (in children below 3 years old or those with severe learning difficulties), thrombocytopenia, and pancreatitis.
- **Advise people to seek immediate medical attention** if symptoms develop such as:
  - Vomiting, anorexia, jaundice, drowsiness, or loss of seizure control; these are signs of blood or liver disorders.
  - Abdominal pain, nausea, and vomiting; these are signs of pancreatitis.

Lamotrigine

- **Common dose-dependent adverse effects** are sedation, ataxia, diplopia, nausea, and vomiting.
- **CSM advises:** be alert for symptoms and signs suggestive of bone marrow failure such as anaemia, bruising, or infection.
- **Advise people to seek immediate medical attention** if fever, sore throat, mouth ulcers, bruising, or bleeding develop.
- **Rash is idiosyncratic** but can be severe. It is more likely to occur when dose titration is more rapid than recommended and with concomitant use of sodium valproate. The drugs should be withdrawn unless the rash is clearly not drug-related (a mild maculopapular rash develops in about 10% of people).

Clonazepam

- **Sedative adverse effects** may be significant, but tolerance is common. Warn the person that alcohol will enhance sedative effects.
- **Elderly people are particularly sensitive** to the effects of centrally depressant drugs and may experience confusion.
- **Withdrawal** may be difficult because of the risk of dependence.

Follow-up advice

- **Monitoring of plasma drug concentration is unnecessary in most people** because seizure control and the development of adverse effects determine the dose.
- **People on sodium valproate — liver function monitoring is important** in the first 6 months of treatment in children under 3 years old and in people with metabolic, degenerative, and developmental conditions:
  - Discontinue treatment if there is an abnormally prolonged prothrombin time.
  - Avoid concomitant use of salicylates as they are broken down via the same metabolic pathway.
- **Routine biochemical and haematological monitoring is not usually necessary.**

Should I refer or investigate?

Refer?

- **Referral guidelines for suspected cancer** published by the National Institute for Health and Clinical Excellence (NICE) recommend that people with suspected recent-onset seizures should be urgently referred to a neurologist.
- **Specialist referral is also recommended:**
  - **If seizures continue** on maximal tolerated monotherapy — to check the diagnosis is correct and advise on whether add-on therapy is needed.
  - **If there is a sudden unexplained deterioration in seizure control.**
  - **If there is diagnostic doubt.**
  - **If a woman on antiepileptic medication becomes** (or **intends to become) pregnant** — to advise on whether a dosage reduction or even discontinuation of treatment should be considered.
  - **If changing to an alternative drug or if withdrawal of treatment is considered.**
  - **In people with an established diagnosis of epilepsy who have never had a specialist assessment** — up to a third may be wrongly diagnosed.

Investigate?

Initial primary care investigations are usually negative, but the following should be considered (mainly applies to adults):
- **Routine blood tests to exclude underlying metabolic problems** (full blood count, erythrocyte sedimentation rate, electrolytes, renal function, liver function tests, calcium, and glucose); abnormal liver function tests and raised mean corpuscular volume may indicate alcohol problems.
- **Chest X-ray,** if clinically indicated (e.g. in smokers, or if there are chest symptoms) to exclude malignancy.

For people on treatment
- **Regular monitoring of plasma drug concentration is unnecessary in most people** because seizure control and the development of adverse effects determine the dose. Monitoring may be indicated in the following situations: to check on compliance; seizures in a person with previously well-controlled epilepsy; suspected toxicity; and severely disabled people in whom toxicity may be difficult to assess.
- **Routine biochemical and haematological monitoring is not usually necessary.**

Patient information leaflets

The following PILs are available at www.prodigy.nhs.uk
- Epilepsy - A General Introduction
- Epilepsy - Could It Be?
- Epilepsy - Living With Epilepsy
- Epilepsy Scotland
- Epilepsy - Treatments
- Epilepsy Wales

Shared decision making

- **Medication can prevent seizures.** A low dose is started, but increased if necessary.
- **Side-effects.** Most people have none, or only minor ones. They are more likely at higher doses. A switch to another medicine may be possible if troublesome side-effects occur.

E

- **Sodium valproate** is commonly used for myoclonic seizures. Possible side-effects include: tremor, weight gain, hair thinning (reversible), and menstrual problems. A serious liver problem is a rare problem.
- **Lamotrigine** is an alternative. Possible side-effects include: drowsiness, double vision, sickness, unsteadiness, and a rash.
- **Clonazepam** is another option but may cause drowsiness.
- **Other medication** — bought or prescribed — may interact with medication for seizures. Check with the doctor or pharmacist before taking any other medication.
- **Pregnancy.** Tell a doctor if you intend to become pregnant whilst taking medication for seizures.

E

Drug rationale

Drugs not included

- **Most recent antiepileptic drugs** are not licensed as monotherapy for the treatment of myoclonic seizures.
- **Carbamazepine** may worsen myoclonic seizures.
- **Phenytoin** is no longer considered a preferred monotherapy choice owing its poor adverse effect profile, narrow therapeutic index, and titration difficulties due to its saturation pharmacokinetics.
- **Phenobarbital and primidone** are no longer considered as preferred monotherapy choices due to their adverse effect profiles.
- **Clobazam** is not indicated in the treatment of myoclonic seizures. In addition, it is licensed only as add-on treatment for seizures.
- **Ethosuximide** is licensed only for the treatment of absence seizures and is rarely used for the treatment of other types of seizure.

[MeReC, 1995]

Drugs included

- **Sodium valproate** is the preferred treatment for myoclonic seizures.
- **Modified-release sodium valproate preparations** are offered as its use has notably increased in secondary care resulting in many people requiring repeat prescriptions in primary care. However, there is limited evidence to support the use of modified-release sodium valproate except for improved patient convenience and compliance.
- **Lamotrigine** is a newer antiepileptic drug that is licensed for monotherapy of partial and generalized seizures. Although not specifically licensed for myoclonic seizures, it is increasingly used for this indication and appears to be effective.
- **Clonazepam** is occasionally used for the treatment of myoclonic seizures, but sedation and the development of tolerance limit its use. Clonazepam tablets are the only licensed oral preparation available in the UK, but liquid preparations on a named patient basis can be obtained through a pharmacy. Please contact your local pharmacist for advice on this.

[MeReC, 1995; Brodie and Dichter, 1997; Brown et al, 1998; Feely, 1999; BNF 45, 2003; SIGN, 2003]

Prescriptions

Start doses of antiepileptic drugs

Valproate: titrate from 600mg to 1g per day (1st choice)
- Age from 12 years onwards
- Sod valproate 100mg crush tabs. Take three tablets twice a day for 3 days, then take four tablets twice a day for 3 days, then take five tablets twice a day; supply 122 tablets; NHS Cost £5.37.

Weight up to 20kg: 10mg/kg twice a day (s/f liquid)
- Age under 11 years
- Sod valproate 200mg/5ml sf liquid. *WEIGHT REQUIRED* Take 10mg per kg bodyweight TWICE a day; supply 300 ml; NHS Cost £5.89.

Weight up to 20kg: 10mg/kg twice a day (crushable tablets)
- Age under 11 years
- Sod valproate 100mg crush tabs. *WEIGHT REQUIRED* Take 10mg per kg bodyweight TWICE a day; supply 100 tablets; NHS Cost £4.40.

Weight over 20kg: 200mg twice a day (s/f liquid)
- Age under 11 years
- Sod valproate 200mg/5ml sf liquid. Take one 5ml spoonful twice a day; supply 600 ml; NHS Cost £11.78.

Weight over 20kg: 200mg twice a day (crushable tablets)
- Age under 11 years
- Sod valproate 100mg crush tabs. Take two tablets twice a day; supply 200 tablets; NHS Cost £8.80.

Lamotrigine: titrate from 25mg to 50mg once a day
- Age from 12 years onwards
- Lamotrigine 25mg tablets. Take one tablet once a day for 2 weeks, then take two tablets once a day; supply 42 tablets; NHS Cost £14.97.

Clonazepam: titrate from 500mcg to 3mg per day
- Age from 5 to 11 years
- Clonazepam 500microgram tabs. Take 1 tab at night for 4 nights, then take 1 tab twice a day for 7 days, then take 2 tabs twice a day for 7 days, then take 2 tabs three times a day; supply 106 tablets; NHS Cost £4.49.

Clonazepam: titrate from 1mg to 4mg per day
- Age from 12 to 64 years
- Clonazepam 500microgram tabs. Take 2 tablets at night for 4 nights, then take 2 tablets twice a day for 7 days, then take 2 tablets twice a day and 4 tablets at night; supply 172 tablets; NHS Cost £7.22.

Clonazepam: titrate from 500mcg to 4mg per day
- Age from 65 years onwards
- Clonazepam 500microgram tabs. Take 1 tab at night for 4 nights, then 1 tab twice a day for 7 days, then 2 tabs twice a day for 7 days, then 2 tabs twice a day and 4 tabs at night; supply 126 tablets; NHS Cost £5.29.

Maintenance doses: sodium valproate

Valproate e/c tablets: 500mg twice a day
- Age from 12 years onwards
- Sod valproate 500mg e/c tabs. Take one tablet twice a day; supply 56 tablets; NHS Cost £9.03.

Valproate e/c tablets: 600mg twice a day
- Age from 12 years onwards
- Sod valproate 200mg e/c tabs. Take three tablets twice a day; supply 168 tablets; NHS Cost £10.25.

Valproate e/c tablets: 700mg twice a day
- Age from 12 years onwards
- Sod valproate 500mg e/c tabs. Take one tablet twice a day; supply 56 tablets; NHS Cost £9.03.
- Sod valproate 200mg e/c tabs. Take one tablet twice a day; supply 56 tablets; NHS Cost £3.42.

Valproate e/c tablets: 800mg twice a day
- Age from 12 years onwards
- Sod valproate 200mg e/c tabs. Take four tablets twice a day; supply 224 tablets; NHS Cost £13.66.

Valproate e/c tablets: 600mg three times a day
- Age from 12 years onwards
- Sod valproate 200mg e/c tabs. Take three tablets three times a day; supply 252 tablets; NHS Cost £16.66.

Valproate e/c tablets: 1g twice a day
- Age from 12 years onwards
- Sod valproate 500mg e/c tabs. Take two tablets twice a day; supply 112 tablets; NHS Cost £18.05.

Weight up to 20kg: 10mg/kg twice a day (s/f liquid)
- Age under 11 years
- Sod valproate 200mg/5ml sf liquid. *WEIGHT REQUIRED* Take 10mg per kg bodyweight TWICE a day; supply 300 ml; NHS Cost £5.89.

Weight up to 20kg: 10mg/kg twice a day (crushable tablets)
- Age under 11 years
- Sod valproate 100mg crush tabs. *WEIGHT REQUIRED* Take 10mg per kg bodyweight TWICE a day; supply 100 tablets; NHS Cost £4.40.

Weight over 20kg: 200mg twice a day (s/f liquid)
- Age under 11 years
- Sod valproate 200mg/5ml sf liquid. Take one 5ml spoonful twice a day; supply 600 ml; NHS Cost £11.78.

Weight over 20kg: 240mg twice a day (s/f liquid)
- Age under 11 years
- Sod valproate 200mg/5ml sf liquid. Take 6ml twice a day; supply 600 ml; NHS Cost £12.96.

Weight over 20kg: 300mg twice a day (s/f liquid)
- Age under 11 years
- Sod valproate 200mg/5ml sf liquid. Take 7.5ml twice a day; supply 600 ml; NHS Cost £12.96.

Weight over 20kg: 200mg twice a day (crushable tablets)
- Age under 11 years
- Sod valproate 100mg crush tabs. Take two tablets twice a day; supply 200 tablets; NHS Cost £8.80.

Weight over 20kg: 250mg twice a day (crushable tablets)
- Age under 11 years
- Sod valproate 100mg crush tabs. Take two and a half tablets twice a day; supply 200 tablets; NHS Cost £7.78.

Weight over 20kg: 300mg twice a day (crushable tablets)
- Age under 11 years
- Sod valproate 100mg crush tabs. Take three tablets twice a day; supply 200 tablets; NHS Cost £7.78.

Maintenance doses: m/r sodium valproate

Valproate m/r tablets: 500mg twice a day
- Age from 12 years onwards
- Sod valproate 500mg m/r tabs. Take one tablet twice a day; supply 56 tablets; NHS Cost £11.31.

Valproate m/r tablets: 600mg twice a day
- Age from 12 years onwards
- Sod valproate 300mg m/r tabs. Take two tablets twice a day; supply 112 tablets; NHS Cost £13.59.

Valproate m/r tablets: 700mg twice a day
- Age from 12 years onwards
- Sod valproate 500mg m/r tabs. Take one tablet twice a day; supply 56 tablets; NHS Cost £11.00.
- Sod valproate 200mg m/r tabs. Take one tablet twice a day; supply 56 tablets; NHS Cost £4.00.

Valproate m/r tablets: 800mg twice a day
- Age from 12 years onwards
- Sod valproate 200mg m/r tabs. Take four tablets twice a day; supply 224 tablets; NHS Cost £18.00.

Valproate m/r tablets: 900mg twice a day
- Age from 12 years onwards
- Sod valproate 300mg m/r tabs. Take three tablets twice a day; supply 168 tablets; NHS Cost £20.38.

Valproate m/r tablets: 1g twice a day
- Age from 12 years onwards
- Sod valproate 500mg m/r tabs. Take two tablets twice a day; supply 56 tablets; NHS Cost £11.31.

Maintenance doses: lamotrigine

Lamotrigine tablets: 100mg once a day
- Age from 12 years onwards
- Lamotrigine 100mg tablets. Take one tablet once a day; supply 28 tablets; NHS Cost £29.29.

Lamotrigine tablets: 150mg once a day
- Age from 12 years onwards
- Lamotrigine 50mg tablets. Take three tablets once a day; supply 84 tablets; NHS Cost £50.93.

Lamotrigine tablets: 200mg once a day
- Age from 12 years onwards
- Lamotrigine 200mg tablets. Take one tablet once a day; supply 28 tablets; NHS Cost £49.78.

Maintenance doses: clonazepam

Clonazepam tablets: 3mg daily (1.5mg twice a day)
- Age from 5 to 12 years
- Clonazepam 500microgram tabs. Take three tablets twice a day; supply 168 tablets; NHS Cost £7.43.

Clonazepam tablets: 4mg daily (2mg twice a day)
- Age from 5 years onwards
- Clonazepam 2mg tablets. Take one tablet twice a day; supply 56 tablets; NHS Cost £3.29.

Clonazepam tablets: 6mg daily (2mg am and 4mg pm)
- Age from 5 years onwards
- Clonazepam 2mg tablets. Take one tablet in the morning and take two tablets at night; supply 84 tablets; NHS Cost £4.94.

Clonazepam tablets: 8mg daily (4mg twice a day)
- Age from 12 years onwards
- Clonazepam 2mg tablets. Take two tablets twice a day; supply 112 tablets; NHS Cost £6.59.

Absences (rarely adults)

Which therapy?

- **Urgently refer people with suspected recent-onset seizures to a neurologist.**
  - Consider urgent outpatient referral or admission depending on local policy.
  - If unacceptable delay is expected then seek telephone advice.
- **Education, information, and support for affected people and their carers are vital.**
- **Self-help organizations** can often give valuable support and information.
- **Prescriptions offered are for initiation and maintenance doses of monotherapy only** — they do not cover dosage regimens that may be necessary for adding in a second drug.
- **Sodium valproate** is preferred monotherapy.
- **Ethosuximide** (not if generalized tonic-clonic seizures also occur) or lamotrigine (off-licence use) are alternatives.

Practical prescribing points

For further information please see the *Medicines Compendium* (www.medicines.org.uk) or the *British National Formulary* (www.bnf.org).

General points

- **Avoid interchanging formulations of antiepileptic drugs (AEDs) where possible.**
- **Avoid sudden withdrawal of an AED** unless adverse effects make this essential as there is an increased risk of seizure recurrence with rapid withdrawal. Sudden AED withdrawal has been associated with sudden unexpected

death (see *How and when should antiepileptic drug withdrawal be managed?*).

- **AEDs interact with many drugs** and it is advisable to check possible interactions before initiating other drugs.
- **Pregnancy: the UK reported risk rate of major congenital malformation in women with epilepsy:**
  - Not exposed to AEDs during pregnancy was 0.9% (95% CI 0.2 to 4.7)
  - Taking carbamazepine during pregnancy was 2.3% (95% CI 1.4 to 4.0)
  - Taking lamotrigine during pregnancy was 3% (95% CI 1.5 to 5.7)
  - Taking sodium valproate during pregnancy was 7.2% (95% CI 5.2 to 10)

Sodium valproate

- **Liver function monitoring is important** in the first 6 months of therapy in children under 3 years old and in people with metabolic, degenerative, and developmental conditions:
  - Discontinue treatment if there is an abnormally prolonged prothrombin time.
  - Avoid concomitant use of salicylates as they are broken down via the same metabolic pathway.
- **Advise people to seek immediate medical attention** if symptoms develop such as:
  - Vomiting, anorexia, jaundice, drowsiness, or loss of seizure control; these are signs of blood or liver disorders.
  - Abdominal pain, nausea, and vomiting; these are signs of pancreatitis.
- **Common dose-dependent adverse effects** are weight gain, tremor, transient hair loss (usually temporary), and menstrual irregularities in adolescent girls.
- **Rare and unpredictable serious adverse effects include:** hepatotoxicity (in children below 3 years old or those with severe learning difficulties), thrombocytopenia, and pancreatitis.

Ethosuximide

- Agranulocytosis is a rare idiosyncratic reaction that is not predictable by blood monitoring.
- People should be advised to report symptoms such as fever, sore throat, mouth ulcers, and bruising.
- Ethosuximide is not advised for people with a past history of bone marrow suppression.

Lamotrigine

- **CSM advises:** be alert for symptoms and signs suggestive of bone marrow failure such as anaemia, bruising, or infection.
- **Advise people to seek immediate medical attention** if fever, sore throat, mouth ulcers, bruising, or bleeding develop.
- **Common dose-dependent adverse effects** are sedation, ataxia, diplopia, nausea, and vomiting.
- **Rash is an idiosyncratic adverse effect,** and the drug should be withdrawn unless the rash is clearly not drug-related (a mild maculopapular rash develops in about 10% of people). Factors associated with the risk of serious skin reactions include:
  - Initial lamotrigine dosing higher than recommended.
  - More rapid dose escalation than recommended.
  - Concomitant use of sodium valproate.

Follow-up advice

- **Monitoring of plasma drug concentration is unnecessary in most people** because seizure control and the development of adverse effects determine the dose.
- **People on sodium valproate — liver function monitoring is important** in the first 6 months of treatment in children under 3 years old and in people with metabolic, degenerative, and developmental conditions:
  - Discontinue treatment if there is an abnormally prolonged prothrombin time.
  - Avoid concomitant use of salicylates as they are broken down via the same metabolic pathway.
- **Routine biochemical and haematological monitoring is not usually necessary.**

Should I refer or investigate?

Refer?

- **Referral guidelines for suspected cancer** published by the National Institute for Health and Clinical Excellence (NICE) recommend that people with suspected recent-onset seizures should be urgently referred to a neurologist.
- **Specialist referral is also recommended:**
  - **If seizures continue** on maximal tolerated monotherapy — to check the diagnosis is correct and advise on whether add-on therapy is needed.
  - **If there is a sudden unexplained deterioration in seizure control.**
  - **If there is diagnostic doubt.**
  - **If a woman on antiepileptic medication becomes (or intends to become) pregnant** — to advise on whether a dosage reduction or even discontinuation of treatment should be considered.
  - **If changing to an alternative drug or if withdrawal of treatment is considered.**
  - **In people with an established diagnosis of epilepsy who have never had a specialist assessment** — up to a third may be wrongly diagnosed.

Investigate?

Initial primary care investigations are usually negative, but the following should be considered (mainly applies to adults):

- **Routine blood tests to exclude underlying metabolic problems** (full blood count, erythrocyte sedimentation rate, electrolytes, renal function, liver function tests, calcium, and glucose); abnormal liver function tests and raised mean corpuscular volume may indicate alcohol problems.
- **Chest X-ray,** if clinically indicated (e.g. in smokers, or if there are chest symptoms) to exclude malignancy.

For people on treatment

- **Regular monitoring of plasma drug concentration is unnecessary in most people** because seizure control and the development of adverse effects determine the dose. Monitoring may be indicated in the following situations: to check on compliance; seizures in persons with previously well-controlled epilepsy; suspected toxicity; and severely disabled people in whom toxicity may be difficult to assess.
- **Routine biochemical and haematological monitoring is not usually necessary.**

Patient information leaflets

The following PILs are available at www.prodigy.nhs.uk

- Epilepsy - A General Introduction
- Epilepsy - Childhood Absence Seizures
- Epilepsy - Could It Be?
- Epilepsy - Living With Epilepsy
- Epilepsy Scotland
- Epilepsy - Treatments
- Epilepsy Wales

Shared decision making

- **Medication can prevent absence seizures.** A low dose is started, but increased if necessary.
- **Side-effects.** Most people have none, or only minor ones. They are more likely at higher doses. A switch to another medicine may be possible if troublesome side-effects occur.
- **Sodium valproate** is commonly used. Possible side-effects include: tremor, weight gain, hair thinning (reversible), and menstrual problems. Serious liver trouble is a rare problem.
- **Ethosuximide** is an alternative. Possible side-effects include drowsiness, double vision, headache, and sickness. A serious blood disorder is a rare problem. Tell a doctor urgently if you get a sore throat, bruising, mouth ulcers, or fever while taking this medicine.
- **Lamotrigine** is an alternative. Possible side-effects include: drowsiness, double vision, sickness, unsteadiness, and a rash.
- **Other medication** — bought or prescribed — may interact with medication for seizures. Check with the doctor or pharmacist before taking any other medication.
- **Pregnancy.** Tell a doctor if you intend to become pregnant whilst taking medication for seizures.

Drug rationale

Drugs not included

- **Newer antiepileptic drugs** are not licensed as monotherapy for the treatment of absence seizures.
- **Carbamazepine** may worsen absence seizures.
- **Phenytoin** is no longer considered a preferred monotherapy choice owing to its poor adverse effect profile, narrow therapeutic index, and titration difficulties due to its saturation pharmacokinetics.
- **Phenobarbital and primidone** are no longer considered as preferred monotherapy choices due to their adverse effect profiles.
- **Clonazepam,** although effective in the treatment of absence seizures, is not a preferred option owing to problems with sedation and tolerance.
- **Clobazam** is licensed only as an add-on treatment for seizures.

[MeReC, 1995]

Drugs included

- There does not appear to be a bioavailability problem with different preparations of sodium valproate or ethosuximide [BNF 45, 2003].
- **Sodium valproate** is the preferred treatment for absence seizures, particularly if these are associated with generalized tonic-clonic seizures.
- **Modified-release sodium valproate preparations** are offered as their use has notably increased in secondary care, resulting in many people requiring repeat prescriptions in primary care. However, there is limited evidence to support the use of modified-release sodium valproate except for improved patient convenience and compliance.
- **Ethosuximide** is licensed for the treatment of absence seizures, and is rarely used for the treatment of other types of seizure.
- **Lamotrigine** is a newer antiepileptic drug that is now licensed for monotherapy of partial and primary and secondarily generalized seizures. Although not specifically licensed for absence seizures, it is increasingly used for this indication and appears to be effective.
  Lamotrigine is not recommended for monotherapy in children aged under 12 years.

[MeReC, 1995; Brodie and Dichter, 1997; Feely, 1999; Brown et al, 1998; BNF 45, 2003; SIGN, 2003]

Prescriptions

Start doses of antiepileptic drugs

Valproate: titrate from 600mg to 1g per day (1st choice)
- Age from 12 years onwards
- Sod valproate 100mg crush tabs. Take three tablets twice a day for 3 days, then take four tablets twice a day for 3 days, then take five tablets twice a day; supply 122 tablets; NHS Cost £5.37.

Weight up to 20kg: 10mg/kg twice a day (s/f liquid)
- Age under 11 years
- Sod valproate 200mg/5ml sf liquid. *WEIGHT REQUIRED* Take 10mg per kg bodyweight TWICE a day; supply 300 ml; NHS Cost £5.89.

Weight up to 20kg: 10mg/kg twice a day (crushable tablets)
- Age under 11 years
- Sod valproate 100mg crush tabs. *WEIGHT REQUIRED* Take 10mg per kg bodyweight TWICE a day; supply 100 tablets; NHS Cost £4.40.

Weight over 20kg: 200mg twice a day (s/f liquid)
- Age under 11 years
- Sod valproate 200mg/5ml sf liquid. Take one 5ml spoonful twice a day; supply 600 ml; NHS Cost £11.78.

Weight over 20kg: 200mg twice a day (crushable tablets)
- Age under 11 years
- Sod valproate 100mg crush tabs. Take two tablets twice a day; supply 200 tablets; NHS Cost £8.80.

Ethosuximide syrup: 10mg/kg twice a day
- Age under 5 years
- Ethosuximide 250mg/5ml syrup. *WEIGHT REQUIRED* Take 10mg per kg bodyweight TWICE a day; supply 200 ml; NHS Cost £3.73.

Ethosuximide syrup: titrate from 500mg to 1g per day
- Age from 6 years onwards
- Ethosuximide 250mg/5ml syrup.; supply 600 ml; NHS Cost £13.20.

Ethosuximide capsules: titrate from 500mg to 1g per day
- Age from 6 years onwards
- Ethosuximide 250mg capsules. Take 2 capsules at night for 1 week, then take 1 capsule in the morning and 2 capsules at night for 1 week, then take 2 capsules twice a day; supply 91 capsules; NHS Cost £7.33.

Lamotrigine: titrate from 25mg to 50mg once a day
- Age from 12 years onwards
- Lamotrigine 25mg tablets. Take one tablet once a day for 2 weeks, then take two tablets once a day; supply 42 tablets; NHS Cost £14.97.

Maintenance doses: sodium valproate

Valproate e/c tablets: 500mg twice a day
- Age from 12 years onwards
- Sod valproate 500mg e/c tabs. Take one tablet twice a day; supply 56 tablets; NHS Cost £9.03.

Valproate e/c tablets: 600mg twice a day
- Age from 12 years onwards
- Sod valproate 200mg e/c tabs. Take three tablets twice a day; supply 168 tablets; NHS Cost £10.25.

Valproate e/c tablets: 700mg twice a day
- Age from 12 years onwards
- Sod valproate 500mg e/c tabs. Take one tablet twice a day; supply 56 tablets; NHS Cost £9.03.

- Sod valproate 200mg e/c tabs. Take one tablet twice a day; supply 56 tablets; NHS Cost £3.42.

Valproate e/c tablets: 800mg twice a day
- Age from 12 years onwards
- Sod valproate 200mg e/c tabs. Take four tablets twice a day; supply 224 tablets; NHS Cost £13.66.

Valproate e/c tablets: 600mg three times a day
- Age from 12 years onwards
- Sod valproate 200mg e/c tabs. Take three tablets three times a day; supply 252 tablets; NHS Cost £16.66.

Valproate e/c tablets: 1g twice a day
- Age from 12 years onwards
- Sod valproate 500mg e/c tabs. Take two tablets twice a day; supply 112 tablets; NHS Cost £18.05.

E

Weight up to 20kg: 10mg/kg twice a day (s/f liquid)
- Age under 11 years
- Sod valproate 200mg/5ml sf liquid. *WEIGHT REQUIRED* Take 10mg per kg bodyweight TWICE a day; supply 300 ml; NHS Cost £5.89.

Weight up to 20kg: 10mg/kg twice a day (crushable tablets)
- Age under 11 years
- Sod valproate 100mg crush tabs. *WEIGHT REQUIRED* Take 10mg per kg bodyweight TWICE a day; supply 100 tablets; NHS Cost £4.40.

Weight over 20kg: 200mg twice a day (s/f liquid)
- Age under 11 years
- Sod valproate 200mg/5ml sf liquid. Take one 5ml spoonful twice a day; supply 600 ml; NHS Cost £11.78.

Weight over 20kg: 240mg twice a day (s/f liquid)
- Age under 11 years
- Sod valproate 200mg/5ml sf liquid. Take 6ml twice a day; supply 600 ml; NHS Cost £12.96.

Weight over 20kg: 300mg twice a day (s/f liquid)
- Age under 11 years
- Sod valproate 200mg/5ml sf liquid. Take 7.5ml twice a day; supply 600 ml; NHS Cost £12.96.

Weight over 20kg: 200mg twice a day (crushable tablets)
- Age under 11 years
- Sod valproate 100mg crush tabs. Take two tablets twice a day; supply 200 tablets; NHS Cost £8.80.

Weight over 20kg: 250mg twice a day (crushable tablets)
- Age under 11 years
- Sod valproate 100mg crush tabs. Take two and a half tablets twice a day; supply 200 tablets; NHS Cost £7.78.

Weight over 20kg: 300mg twice a day (crushable tablets)
- Age under 11 years
- Sod valproate 100mg crush tabs. Take three tablets twice a day; supply 200 tablets; NHS Cost £7.78.

Maintenance doses: m/r sodium valproate

Valproate m/r tablets: 500mg twice a day
- Age from 12 years onwards
- Sod valproate 500mg m/r tabs. Take one tablet twice a day; supply 56 tablets; NHS Cost £11.31.

Valproate m/r tablets: 600mg twice a day
- Age from 12 years onwards
- Sod valproate 300mg m/r tabs. Take two tablets twice a day; supply 112 tablets; NHS Cost £13.59.

Valproate m/r tablets: 700mg twice a day
- Age from 12 years onwards
- Sod valproate 500mg m/r tabs. Take one tablet twice a day; supply 56 tablets; NHS Cost £11.00.
- Sod valproate 200mg m/r tabs. Take one tablet twice a day; supply 56 tablets; NHS Cost £4.00.

Valproate m/r tablets: 800mg twice a day
- Age from 12 years onwards
- Sod valproate 200mg m/r tabs. Take four tablets twice a day; supply 224 tablets; NHS Cost £18.00.

Valproate m/r tablets: 900mg twice a day
- Age from 12 years onwards
- Sod valproate 300mg m/r tabs. Take three tablets twice a day; supply 168 tablets; NHS Cost £20.38.

Valproate m/r tablets: 1g twice a day
- Age from 12 years onwards
- Sod valproate 500mg m/r tabs. Take two tablets twice a day; supply 56 tablets; NHS Cost £11.31.

Maintenance doses: ethosuximide

Ethosuximide syrup: 10mg/kg twice a day
- Age under 5 years
- Ethosuximide 250mg/5ml syrup. *WEIGHT REQUIRED* Take 10mg per kg bodyweight TWICE a day; supply 200 ml; NHS Cost £3.73.

Ethosuximide syrup: 500mg twice a day
- Age from 6 to 10 years
- Ethosuximide 250mg/5ml syrup. Take two 5ml spoonfuls twice a day; supply 600 ml; NHS Cost £13.20

Ethosuximide syrup: 500mg each morning + 750mg at night
- Age from 6 to 10 years
- Ethosuximide 250mg/5ml syrup. Take two 5ml spoonfuls in the morning and take three 5ml spoonfuls at night; supply 800 ml; NHS Cost £14.92.

Ethosuximide syrup: 750mg twice a day
- Age from 6 to 10 years
- Ethosuximide 250mg/5ml syrup. Take three 5ml spoonfuls twice a day; supply 900 ml; NHS Cost £16.80

Ethosuximide capsules: 500mg twice a day
- Age from 6 years onwards
- Ethosuximide 250mg capsules. Take two capsules twice a day; supply 112 capsules; NHS Cost £9.02.

Ethosuximide capsules: 500mg each morning + 750mg at night
- Age from 6 years onwards
- Ethosuximide 250mg capsules. Take two capsules each morning and take three capsules at night; supply 140 capsules; NHS Cost £11.28.

Ethosuximide capsules: 750mg twice a day
- Age from 6 years onwards
- Ethosuximide 250mg capsules. Take three capsules twice a day; supply 168 capsules; NHS Cost £13.53.

Maintenance doses: lamotrigine

Lamotrigine tablets: 100mg once a day
- Age from 12 years onwards
- Lamotrigine 100mg tablets. Take one tablet once a day; supply 28 tablets; NHS Cost £29.29.

Lamotrigine tablets: 150mg once a day
- Age from 12 years onwards
- Lamotrigine 50mg tablets. Take three tablets once a day; supply 84 tablets; NHS Cost £50.93.

Lamotrigine tablets: 200mg once a day
- Age from 12 years onwards
- Lamotrigine 200mg tablets. Take one tablet once a day; supply 28 tablets; NHS Cost £49.78.

Status epilepticus

Which therapy?

- **Prolonged generalized tonic-clonic seizures cause significant morbidity and mortality. If a generalized tonic-clonic seizure (or serial seizures) has lasted longer than 5 minutes, then emergency medical treatment is necessary.** Other types of status epilepticus have a much lower risk of morbidity.

- **Immediate measures include the basic ABC (airway, breathing, circulation) of resuscitation.**
- **In primary care diazepam** can be conveniently and safely administered as a rectal solution, which may be a more practical treatment option than intravenous administration of lorazepam.
- **Urgent admission** is required if the person does not respond.
- **It may be useful for a carer to be able to administer rectal diazepam** to a person who is prone to frequent seizures, providing he or she is willing and suitable training is provided.
- The Summary of Products Characteristics for diazepam rectal tubules recommends the following doses of rectal diazepam, calculated from the person's weight:
  - **Adult and child: 500 micrograms/kg**
  - **Elderly and frail people: 250 micrograms/kg**

Practical prescribing points

For further information please see the *Medicines Compendium* (www.medicines.org.uk) or the *British National Formulary* (www.bnf.org).

Should I refer or investigate?

Refer?

- **Emergency admission** is required for all seizures that are prolonged and that are not terminated by the rectal administration of diazepam.
- **Admission may also be required** if the person responds to emergency primary care treatment but has adverse social circumstances (e.g. no carer).
- **Referral guidelines for suspected cancer** published by the National Institute for Health and Clinical Excellence (NICE) recommend that people with suspected recent-onset seizures should be urgently referred to a neurologist.

Patient information leaflets

The following PILs are available at www.prodigy.nhs.uk

- Epilepsy - A General Introduction
- Epilepsy - Could It Be?
- Epilepsy - Living With Epilepsy
- Epilepsy Scotland
- Epilepsy - Treatments
- Epilepsy Wales

Shared decision making

Drug rationale

Drugs not included

- **Preparations of diazepam other than rectal diazepam:** although intravenous diazepam is more effective than rectal diazepam, it should be used only if resuscitation facilities are available, owing to the risk of respiratory depression and hypotension.
- **All other antiepileptic drugs:** although the intravenous use of other antiepileptic drugs (e.g. phenytoin, lorazepam) is effective in the management of status epilepticus, their use in primary care is not appropriate.

Drugs included

- **Rectal diazepam** is a standard, relatively safe, and rapidly acting treatment for seizures. A selection of doses is offered, based on weight as recommended by the *British National Formulary.*

[DTB, 1996; BNF 45, 2003]

Prescriptions

Adults and children > 10kg

Diazepam 5mg rectal tubes

- Age from 12 months to 64 years
- Diazepam 5mg/2.5ml rectal tube. *WEIGHT REQUIRED* Give 500micrograms per kg bodyweight as a single dose. Insert into the rectum as directed; supply 5 rectal tubes; NHS Cost £6.38.

Diazepam 10mg rectal tubes

- Age from 12 months to 64 years
- Diazepam 10mg/2.5ml rectal tube. *WEIGHT REQUIRED* Give 500micrograms per kg bodyweight as a single dose. Insert into the rectum as directed; supply 5 rectal tubes; NHS Cost £8.12.

Elderly or frail – lower dose

Diazepam 5mg rectal tubes

- Age from 65 years onwards
- Diazepam 5mg/2.5ml rectal tube. *WEIGHT REQUIRED* Give 250micrograms per kg bodyweight as a single dose. Insert into the rectum as directed; supply 5 rectal tubes; NHS Cost £6.38.

Diazepam 10mg rectal tubes

- Age from 65 years onwards
- Diazepam 10mg/2.5ml rectal tube. *WEIGHT REQUIRED* Give 250micrograms per kg bodyweight as a single dose. Insert into the rectum as directed; supply 5 rectal tubes; NHS Cost £8.12.

Extended Information

Background information

- What is it? p.771
- How common is it? p.772
- How do I know my patient has it? p.772
- What else might it be? p.773
- Complications and prognosis p.773

What is it?

- **Epilepsy is a condition characterized by recurrent, unprovoked seizures,** i.e. not an isolated event or due to an underlying acute reversible medical problem such as meningitis or alcohol withdrawal.
- **An epileptic seizure** is a brief disturbance of consciousness, behaviour, emotion, motor function, or sensation that is due to abnormal electrical discharge in the brain.
- **There are a number of different epileptic syndromes,** which differ in aetiology, prognosis, and treatment. Classification of seizure types and epilepsy syndromes is important, as these have implications for management and prognosis. The international classification of epileptic seizures lists them as **partial or generalized seizures.** Note: some people have seizures that cannot be classified in this way.
- **Partial seizures** may be one of three types:
  - Simple partial seizures with no loss of consciousness (previously called focal or Jacksonian seizures).
  - Complex partial seizures (previously called psychomotor or temporal lobe seizures):
    - With impairment of consciousness at onset

  - Simple partial onset followed by impairment of consciousness
  - Partial seizures evolving to generalized tonic-clonic seizures if the neuronal discharge spreads to involve the entire brain.
- **Generalized seizures** may be convulsive or non-convulsive. There are six types:
  - Tonic-clonic (previously called grand mal seizures)
  - Absence (previously called petit mal seizures)
  - Myoclonic
  - Tonic
  - Clonic
  - Atonic
- **Seizure types occur with the following frequency:**
  - 60% tonic-clonic
  - 20% complex partial
  - 12% mixed tonic-clonic and partial
  - 3% simple partial
  - Less than 5% absence, myoclonic, and other seizure types
- **Status epilepticus** is a seizure or a series of seizures that lasts for 30 minutes or longer.
- **Aetiology:** recent advances in neuroimaging mean that a cause is now found in over two-thirds of people with epilepsy. Of defined causes, the most common are: cerebrovascular disease; cerebral tumours; genetic, congenital, or hereditary conditions; alcohol; drugs and other toxic causes; head trauma (including neurosurgery); and post-infective causes (encephalitis and meningitis).

[MeReC, 1995; Burn et al, 1997; Hall et al, 1997; Brown et al, 1998; SIGN, 2003]

- **In children,** epilepsy is often considered in terms of the epileptic syndrome — that is an epileptic disorder characterised by a set pattern of seizure type(s) possibly associated with other features, such as a particular physical appearance or learning disability.
- If a syndrome can be identified (and sometimes it may take months to evolve), this allows clarification of the cause, severity and prognosis of epilepsy. However, for 30% of children with epilepsy, it is not possible to designate a specific syndrome. The most common are:
  - Benign childhood epilepsy with centrotemporal spikes (benign rolandic epilepsy)
  - Juvenile myoclonic epilepsy
  - Childhood absence epilepsy
  - Localisation-related epilepsies categorised as symptomatic (known underlying cause) or cryptogenic (symptomatic cause suspected but not found)
- **Compared with adults, epilepsy in children differs in several important respects:**
  - There are more epilepsy syndromes and causes of epilepsy.
  - There is greater heterogeneity with respect to syndrome type, causes and prognoses.
  - The usual refractory seizure type is generalised rather than partial.
  - One syndrome may evolve into another with increasing age.
  - It has more potential for impact on social, educational and behavioural aspects of life.

[NICE, 2004a]

How common is it?

- **Epilepsy is a common neurological condition.** The prevalence of individuals on treatment for epilepsy is about 1 in 200, and lifetime prevalence is between 2% and 5% of the population.
- One study found that the reported prevalence rate increased with age, from 3.9 per 1000 population at the age of 7 years, to 4.9 per 1000 population at 16 years [NICE, 2004b].
- **Up to a half of institutionalized people with multiple disabilities and up to a third of people with a learning difficulty have epilepsy.**
- **The annual incidence rate in developed countries has been estimated to be around 50/100,000 people (range 40–70/100,000) [NICE, 2004b]. The highest rates are in young children and elderly people.**
- **A typical GP will:**
  - **Be treating 10 people for epilepsy.**
  - **Diagnose one or two new cases each year.**
  - **Care for about 15–25 people who have had seizures in the past,** but who have either not been treated or have stopped treatment.

[MeReC, 1995; Hall et al, 1997; Sunder, 1997; Wallace et al, 1997; Brown et al, 1998]

How do I know my patient has it?

Misdiagnosis is common; specialist assessment should usually be obtained both to confirm the type of seizure(s) and to determine whether the person has a recognized epileptic syndrome.

History

- **A clear history from the patient and an eyewitness to the attack give the most important diagnostic information and should be the mainstay of the diagnosis (C).**
- Enquire about a family history of epilepsy, a past history of seizures, and a history of neurological or developmental problems, all of which make a diagnosis of epilepsy more likely.
- **Generalized tonic-clonic seizures:** the person falls to the ground and becomes rigid and cyanotic, followed by rhythmic contractions of the limbs and trunk. Incontinence of urine or faeces, and tongue biting may occur. The seizure usually lasts for 2–3 minutes. Drowsiness and confusion follow prior to regaining full consciousness.
- **Simple partial seizures:** consciousness is not impaired. There may be localized motor, sensory (may include olfactory, visual, or auditory symptoms), autonomic, or psychic and déjà vu phenomena. Simple partial seizures are sometimes described as 'auras', particularly if they then lead to a complex partial or generalized seizure.
- **Complex partial seizures:** consciousness is impaired, with inattention or staring for some minutes. Automatisms such as chewing, lip-smacking, or plucking at clothing may occur. There are often preceding symptoms of a simple partial seizure (e.g. sensory aura or déjà vu).
- **Secondarily generalized seizures:** there is a history of a simple (aura) or complex seizure, followed by a tonic-clonic seizure.
- **Myoclonic seizures:** there are involuntary single or multiple muscle jerks. A brief loss of consciousness can occur, and may be followed by a tonic-clonic seizure. Myoclonic seizures tend to occur on waking or falling asleep. There is often a history of morning clumsiness (e.g. dropping a cup when a myoclonic jerk occurs). Most cases develop between the ages of 12 and 18 years, and there is often a strong family history.
- **Absence seizures:** there is a brief episode of inattention lasting seconds. There is no aura. 'Atypical' absence seizures have a slower onset and longer duration. With absence seizures, there is a high incidence of associated generalized tonic-clonic seizures. Both typical and atypical absence seizures start in childhood (usually between 3 and 12 years of age) and rarely persist into adulthood, but may develop into other generalized seizures.

- **Benign childhood epilepsy with centrotemporal spikes** (benign rolandic epilepsy) involves partial seizures arising in the rolandic (centrotemporal or midtemporal) area of the brain and most commonly arises between the ages of 7 and 9 years. Secondary generalisation to tonic–clonic seizures may occur. Seizures are most frequent on falling asleep and more than half of children have seizures only during sleep. Seizures almost always resolve during puberty. The decision to use drug treatment depends on the frequency and severity of the seizures.
- **Juvenile myoclonic epilepsy (JME)** is the most common generalised seizure syndrome in young people and the onset is usually between 10 and 16 years of age. Lifelong treatment is usually required. It is characterised by myoclonic seizures which commonly affect the arms and/or trunk, typically on waking. Tonic–clonic seizures are associated with the myoclonic jerks in 90% of people with JME, and about 25% have brief absence seizures. Photosensitivity occurs in around 50% of people with JME.
- **Childhood absence epilepsy** involves brief (4–20 seconds) and frequent (50–100 per day) absence seizures with abrupt loss of consciousness. It may be associated with learning problems. Other types of epileptic seizures are not part of childhood absence epilepsy, although a proportion of children will develop them later. Most children enter a permanent remission before puberty, but a significant proportion continue to have absences or go on to develop tonic–clonic or myoclonic seizures that persist into adult life. About 15% of children with childhood absence epilepsy later exhibit JME. Childhood absence epilepsy is classified as an idiopathic generalised epilepsy (probably of genetic origin).
- **Localisation-related epilepsies** — symptomatic (known underlying cause) or cryptogenic (symptomatic cause suspected but not found). These involve partial (focal) seizures. The clinical features, accompanying disabilities and prognosis of these epilepsies depend on the cause and location of the brain abnormality.

[SIGN, 2003; NICE, 2004a]

Examination

- **Physical examination should always be performed** in order to detect: developmental abnormalities; neurological signs (may indicate cerebrovascular disease or cerebral tumour); or signs of an underlying condition such as the Sturge–Weber syndrome, neurofibromatosis, or tuberous sclerosis. However, physical examination is usually negative.

Investigation

- **Primary care investigations seldom give useful information.** If clinically indicated, chest X-ray should be performed to exclude malignancy (e.g. in smokers, or if there are chest symptoms). Blood tests (e.g. full blood count, erythrocyte sedimentation rate, electrolytes, renal function, liver function, calcium, and glucose) may indicate an underlying disorder or metabolic disturbance.
- **Secondary care investigations,** such as electroencephalography, neuroimaging, and metabolic screening in children, may aid seizure classification and help to determine the aetiology but they have limitations.
  - Magnetic resonance imaging (MRI) scanning is the current standard of reference in the investigation of people with epilepsy.
  - Computed tomography scanning (CT) has a role in the urgent assessment of seizures or when MRI is contraindicated, but it is less effective in detecting lesions.
  - Electroencephalography (EEG) is not routinely indicated and should not be performed to 'exclude' a diagnosis of epilepsy (C).
  - EEG can be used to support the diagnosis in people in whom the clinical history indicates a significant probability of an epileptic seizure or epilepsy (C).
  - EEG should be used to support the classification of epileptic seizures and epilepsy syndromes when there is clinical doubt (C).
  - EEG should be performed in young people with generalized seizures to aid classification and to detect a photoparoxysmal response (C).

[Hall et al, 1997; Brown et al, 1998; Scheepers et al, 1998; SIGN, 2003]

What else might it be?

The differential diagnosis of seizures is large and includes:

- Vaso-vagal syncope (faint)
- Cardiac arrhythmia
- Transient ischaemic attack
- Hyperventilation or panic attacks
- Hypoglycaemia
- Complex migraine
- Vertigo
- Drop attacks
- Tics
- Alcohol abuse or withdrawal
- Drug-induced (e.g. antihypertensives, antidepressants, drug overdose, substance abuse)
- Infectious (meningitis, encephalitis)
- Concussive convulsion
- Psychogenic (pseudo-seizures) — 50% of those affected also have true epilepsy
- Narcolepsy and catalepsy
- Dissociative disorder
- Transient global amnesia
- Hypnic jerks (on falling asleep)
- Sleep paralysis
- Night terrors (child)
- Breath-holding attack (child)
- Febrile convulsion (child)
- Munchausen syndrome by proxy (child)

[Neville, 1997; Sander and O'Donoghue, 1997; Bowman, 1998; Brown et al, 1998; Appleton and Neville, 1999; SIGN, 2003]

Complications and prognosis

Complications

- **Social stigmatization** (perceived or experienced) may occur, with employment, educational, driving, and social difficulties [Chaplin et al, 1992; Collings and Chappell, 1994; Scambler, 1994; Thapar, 1996; Hall et al, 1997].
- **Psychosocial problems** may be evident, including lack of confidence (e.g. in work or leisure situations), poor self-esteem, dependence on others, anxiety, and depression [Chaplin et al, 1992; O'Donoghue et al, 1999]. Social development may be a particular issue in children.
- **Adverse effects of antiepileptic drugs** are a significant problem for many people [Hall et al, 1997; Mills et al, 1997]. Rash is the most common, occurring in up to 10% of people on carbamazepine, phenytoin, or lamotrigine.
- **Physical trauma** may occur as a result of having a seizure [Hall et al, 1997; Mills et al, 1997].
- **There is an increased risk of fetal malformations** for pregnant women taking antiepileptic drugs [DTB, 1994b]. See the *Pregnancy* section for more information.
- **Developmental problems** are common in some children with early onset seizures, such as infantile spasms

(West's syndrome) and Lennox–Gastaut syndrome [Neville, 1997].
- **Specific cognitive difficulties** (e.g. with reading or arithmetic) can occur and may have a serious impact on a child's education if not recognized [Brown et al, 1998].

Prognosis

- **Recurrence risk after a first seizure varies greatly.** The risk is lowest (13–40%) for provoked seizures, or in people with a normal electroencephalogram (EEG) and no identifiable cause. The risk is highest (up to 90%) in people with epileptic discharges on EEG, or with congenital neurological defects. Overall the risk is 30–40%. Recurrence is most likely in the first 12 months, and falls to less than 10% after 2 years. Treatment with antiepileptic drugs halves the recurrence risk.
- **Remission of seizures is common.** At 9 years after diagnosis about 70% of those affected will have been seizure-free for the preceding 3 years and only about 30% will still be on medication [Cockerell et al, 1995; Cockerell et al, 1997]. Of those who continue to have seizures, some will have recognizable cerebral abnormalities and severe and persistent types of epilepsy [Wallace et al, 1997].
- **Medication can often be withdrawn successfully,** although the risk of seizure recurrence increases in people who are not receiving treatment. For people who have been seizure-free for 2 years, if treatment is stopped the average relapse rate is 41%, compared with 22% if treatment is continued [Bessant et al, 1991]. See *Antiepileptic drug withdrawal* for more information.
- **Mortality is increased in all people with epilepsy** (especially in children with symptomatic epilepsy and those with learning or physical disabilities), with a risk approximately 2–3 times that of the general population [NICE, 2004b]. Some of these deaths may be related to an underlying condition, suicide, accidents, or status epilepticus. Sudden unexplained death in epilepsy (SUDEP) can occur and is probably due to central respiratory arrest during a seizure [Coyle et al, 1994; Cockerell et al, 1997; Hall et al, 1997; Brown et al, 1998].

Management issues

- General issues p.774
- To whom should a person with a seizure be referred? p.774
- What are the drug treatments for epilepsy? p.775
- How should provoked seizures be managed? p.777
- Which issues are important for a woman with epilepsy who requires contraception? p.777
- How do epilepsy and antiepileptic drugs affect pregnancy? p.777
- Which issues are important for a woman with epilepsy who is breastfeeding? p.778
- Which issues are important for a woman with epilepsy who is postpartum? p.778
- How does hormone replacement therapy (HRT) affect epilepsy and antiepileptic drugs? p.778
- Which issues are particular to children with epilepsy? p.778
- Which issues are particular to people with learning difficulties who have epilepsy? p.779
- Which issues are particular to elderly people with epilepsy? p.779
- How is a person's driving licence affected by epilepsy? p.779
- What is the role of surgical treatment for epilepsy? p.779
- Which other treatments are recommended for epilepsy? p.779
- How should status epilepticus be managed? p.779
- Medicines management p.780

General issues

- **The diagnosis of epilepsy** should be made by a neurologist or other epilepsy specialist (C).
- **The seizure type(s) and epilepsy syndrome** should be identified (C).
- **A clear history from the patient and an eyewitness to the attack** give the most important diagnostic information and should be the mainstay of the diagnosis (C).
- **Education, information, and support for affected people and their carers is vital,** particularly covering issues (depending upon age) such as medication, driving, safe and risky leisure activities, education, employment, contraception, and pregnancy [Chappell, 1992; Betts and Smith, 1994; Webb et al, 1998].
- **Self-help organizations** can often give valuable support and information, and people should be informed of these [Ridsdale et al, 1999].
- **Provoking factors,** such as alcohol, tiredness, menstruation, and flashing lights or video games (photosensitivity), should be identified and discussed [Binnie et al, 1994].

To whom should a person with a seizure be referred?

- **Referral guidelines for suspected cancer** published by the National Institute for Health and Clinical Excellence (NICE) recommend that people with suspected new-onset seizures should be urgently referred to a neurologist [NICE, 2005].
- **Specialist assessment** is important as soon as possible after a first seizure in order to confirm the diagnosis, obtain advice on treatment, and provide appropriate information to them and their carers. Up to a third of people with an initial diagnosis of epilepsy are subsequently found to have been misdiagnosed [Wallace et al, 1997; Scheepers et al, 1998]. If access to a specialized service is limited then refer to a physician or paediatrician with a special interest in epilepsy [The Epilepsy Task Force, 1995; Hall et al, 1997]. Local referral guidelines may be available.
- **Epilepsy in children** — a paediatrician or a paediatric neurologist under shared care protocols with primary care should oversee the management in such cases [NICE, 2004a].
- **The involvement of an epilepsy nurse specialist,** if available, is recommended, especially while the person is waiting to be seen by a specialist [Betts and Smith, 1994].
- **If started on medication, people are usually discharged back to the care of their GP when the condition becomes stable:**
  - A structured management system for epilepsy should be established in primary care and an annual review of people with epilepsy is desirable **(D)**.
  - The annual review would be facilitated and enhanced by the development of specialist epilepsy nurses, linking primary care to the hospital system, resulting in a *shared care management system* **(D)**.
  - The shared care management system adopted should seek to:
    - Identify all people with epilepsy, register/record basic demographic data, validate the classification of seizures and syndromes.
    - Make the provisional diagnosis in new people, provide appropriate information, and refer to a specialist centre.

- Monitor seizures, aiming to improve control by adjustment of medication or referral to hospital services.
- Minimize adverse effects of medications and their interactions.
- Facilitate structured withdrawal from medication where appropriate, and if agreed by the patient.
- Introduce non-clinical interventions, and disseminate information to help improve quality of life for people with epilepsy.
- Address specific women's issues and needs of people with learning disabilities (D).

- **Referral of all patients to an epilepsy nurse specialist,** if available, is recommended. One study has shown that people seen by an epilepsy nurse specialist were more likely to have discussed general epilepsy topics and less likely to report missing taking their medication [Mills et al, 1999]. Another study showed that 70% of people with epilepsy had previously unidentified problems successfully resolved by the nurse, including misdiagnosis, overmedication, and lack of awareness of drug adverse effects.

What are the drug treatments for epilepsy?

What general drug issues are important in epilepsy?

- **The decision to start antiepileptic drugs (AEDs)** should be made by an epilepsy specialist together with the person concerned (B). AED treatment should be supervised by an epilepsy specialist as part of an agreed patient treatment plan [NICE, 2004c].
  - In adults, this should be a medical practitioner with training and expertise in epilepsy.
  - In children, this should be a paediatrician with epilepsy training and expertise.
- **If delay is expected and treatment is considered necessary,** then telephone advice should be obtained from an epilepsy specialist or a specialist epilepsy liaison nurse [Brown et al, 1998; Mills et al, 1999].
- **As part of shared care management plans,** GPs and other primary care team members should review and ensure that AEDs are continued, and check for any signs of adverse effects, drug interactions and non-adherence to medication regimens.
- **Treatment is not usually required after a first seizure.** Whether to treat or not is largely decided by the risk of further seizures and how acceptable this is. Estimates of recurrence risk vary: overall the risk is 30–40%, and it is greatest in the first 12 months, falling to less than 10% after 2 years [Hopkins et al, 1988; Berg and Shinnar, 1991].
- **Treatment with AEDs reduces the recurrence risk by half.** Early treatment with AEDs does not, however, appear to alter the prognosis of epilepsy (best predicted by the number of seizures in the first 6 months after diagnosis, and the response to the first AED).
- **AEDs should be offered after a first tonic-clonic seizure if:**
  - The person has had previous myoclonic, absence, or partial seizures.
  - The person has a congenital neurological deficit.
  - The person considers the risk of recurrence unacceptable.
- **Monotherapy** is effective in controlling the majority of seizures, and all AEDs licensed for monotherapy have similar efficacy in newly diagnosed epilepsy when the AED is prescribed for an appropriate seizure type. Adverse effects and interactions are less likely than with multidrug regimens [Brown et al, 1998; Stephen and Brodie, 1998; Tanaka, 1999].
- **Treatment recommendations for different antiepileptic monotherapy agents are shown in Table 1.**
- **The adverse effect and interaction profiles** should direct the choice of drug for the individual person (A).
- **In selecting AED for girls** who are likely to need continued treatment into adulthood, safety in pregnancy needs to be considered. See *How do epilepsy and antiepiletic drugs affect pregnancy?* for more information.
- **Failure to respond to appropriate AEDs** should prompt a review of the diagnosis of epilepsy and adherence to medication (C).
- **The majority of patients with newly diagnosed epilepsy respond well to AEDs.** Failure to do so may be due to:
  - An incorrect diagnosis of epilepsy.
  - An inappropriate choice of AED for the type of epilepsy.
  - Failure to take the prescribed AED.
  - An underlying cerebral neoplasm.

Table 1: Antiepileptic drug monotherapy recommendations for different seizure types.

Antiepileptic drug	Recommendations
Sodium valproate	First-line option for the treatment of partial and secondary generalized seizures as well as for primary generalized seizures (A). Drug of choice (as is lamotrigine) if any doubt about seizure type and/or syndrome classification (A). Note: women of childbearing potential should not be started on sodium valproate without specialist neurological advice, and that for partial seizures, sodium valproate should be used only in women found to be resistant to other treatments.
Carbamazepine	First-line option in partial and secondary generalized seizures (A).
Lamotrigine	First-line option in partial and primary and secondary generalized seizures (in people 12 years and older) (A). Lamotrigine has efficacy for absence and myoclonic seizures but use here is off-licence. Drug of choice (as is sodium valproate) if any doubt about seizure type and/or syndrome classification (A).
Clonazepam	An option for the treatment of refractory myoclonic seizures. An option for use in tonic-clonic or partial seizures.
Ethosuximide	An option for the treatment of absence seizures but when other types of seizure co-exist sodium valproate is generally preferred because of its broader spectrum.
Oxcarbazepine	An option for the treatment of partial and secondary generalized seizures (in adults and children aged 6 years and older) (A). Currently a black triangle drug under the surveillance of the Committee on Safety of Medicines. Larger trial data are needed to confirm benefits of efficacy.
Phenobarbital	Effective for most seizure types, but sedating adverse effects have made it a less preferred option.
Phenytoin	Effective for most seizure types, but complications with titrating doses have made it a less preferred option.
Primidone	Effective for most seizure types, but sedating adverse effects have made it a less preferred option.
Topiramate	An option for the treatment of primary generalized, partial, and secondary generalized seizures (in adults and children aged 6 years and older with newly diagnosed epilepsy). Larger trial data are needed to confirm benefits of efficacy.

- Covert drug or alcohol abuse.
- **Combination therapy should be considered** when treatment with two first-line AEDs has failed, or when the first well-tolerated drug substantially improves seizure control but fails to produce seizure freedom at maximal dosage (A).
- **The choice of drugs in combination** should be matched to the person's seizure type(s), and the number should be limited to two or at most three AEDs (B).
- **If the person has a good response to the second drug,** then the original drug can be gradually withdrawn [Wallace et al, 1997].
- **If the second drug is not effective,** this should be slowly withdrawn and simultaneously replaced with another add-on drug. This process can be repeated with other possible options [Wallace et al, 1997]. If an encouraging but suboptimal effect is obtained with a particular combination, it may be worthwhile trying the addition of a small dose of a third AED.
- **If trials of combination therapy do not bring about worthwhile benefits,** treatment should revert to the regimen (monotherapy or combination therapy) that has provided the best balance between effectiveness in reducing seizure frequency and tolerability of adverse effects [NICE, 2004b; NICE, 2004a].
- **People taking AEDs should receive dietary and other lifestyle advice** to minimize the risk of osteoporosis (D). Osteopenia, osteomalacia, and increased risk of hip fracture have been associated with AEDs, but their aetiology is likely to be multifactorial.
- **Alcohol consumption of 1–2 units per day** is usually safe for most people taking AEDs, but excessive alcohol intake and binge drinking should be avoided [DTB, 1996].
  - Those who drink heavily may not respond to standard dosages of some AEDs, and in particular may need to be prescribed higher doses of phenytoin and possibly carbamazepine to maintain adequate serum levels.
  - Alcohol withdrawal may trigger idiopathic generalized epileptic seizures in some people.
- Hypoglycaemia commonly presents after a binge in people with epilepsy who abuse alcohol, causing stupor, confusion, bizarre behaviour, tremulousness, and occasionally seizures [SIGN, 2003].

[MeReC, 1995; Brodie and Dichter, 1997; Brown et al, 1998; Heaney et al, 1998; Feely, 1999]

In what way are drug formulations important in epilepsy?

- **Changing the formulation or brand of AED is not recommended** because different preparations may vary in bioavailability or have different pharmacokinetic profiles and, thus, increased potential for reduced effect or excessive side effects [NICE, 2004c].

Which drug interactions are important in epilepsy?

- **Drug interactions commonly occur with antiepileptic drugs (AEDs),** with interactions between themselves and other medication taken concurrently.
- **Hepatic enzyme induction** occurs with carbamazepine, oxcarbazepine, phenobarbital, phenytoin, primidone, and topiramate, which therefore interact with a large number of drugs, particularly hormonal contraceptive products [MeReC, 1995; Feely, 1999].
- **Carbamazepine** is the only AED that significantly induces its own metabolism [Tanaka, 1999].
- **Phenytoin** has a narrow therapeutic index, and concomitant use with some drugs results in an increase in the plasma phenytoin concentration with acute toxic adverse effects.
- **After an AED is withdrawn** enzyme induction persists for up to 4 weeks.
- **The following AEDs do not induce hepatic enzymes:** acetazolamide, benzodiazepines, ethosuximide, gabapentin, lamotrigine, levetiracetam, sodium valproate, tiagabine, and vigabatrin.

When should drug monitoring be undertaken in epilepsy?

- **Routine monitoring of antiepileptic drug (AED) concentrations is not indicated (D).** In most people seizure control and the development of adverse effects determine the dose.
- **Phenytoin is the exception** because a small increase in dose can result in a large increase in the serum level (saturation kinetics). Even then, the reference range is only a rough guide to dose, because some people will have good control with lower levels and a few require and tolerate higher levels.
- Measurement can sometime be useful in the following circumstances:
  - Assessment of compliance
  - Seizures in a previously well-controlled person
  - Suspected toxicity
  - Severely disabled people in whom toxicity may be difficult to assess
- Assay of vigabatrin, lamotrigine, gabapentin, topiramate, tiagabine, oxcarbazepine, and levetiracetam concentrations should not be undertaken routinely (D).
- **Interpretation of AED blood levels is best done by an epilepsy specialist.**

How and when should antiepileptic drug withdrawal be managed?

- **The question of whether to continue treatment or withdraw antiepileptic drugs (AEDs)** should be discussed between the person with epilepsy (who has been seizure-free for at least 2 years), their carers and an epilepsy specialist, so that an informed choice can be made [NICE, 2004c].
- **Factors to be discussed include:** driving, employment, fear and risks of further seizures, and concerns about prolonged AED treatment. The Driver and Vehicle Licensing Agency recommends that driving should cease during the period of AED withdrawal and for 6 months afterwards.
- **AED withdrawal is associated with an increased risk of seizure recurrence** [Medical Research Council Antiepileptic Drug Withdrawal Study Group, 1991]. This has been found to depend on various factors including: the age when epilepsy started, taking more than one drug, and the type of seizures experienced.
- In an observational study of 564 people on AEDs, about 70% were seizure-free after 5 years [Cockerell et al, 1997].
- **In women of child-bearing age,** any changes to medication should be completed prior to conception, where possible, and the number and dose of drugs should be minimized [Crawford et al, 1999]. See the *Pregnancy* section for more information.
- **Withdrawal of AEDs must be managed by, or be under the guidance of, the specialist** [NICE, 2004c].
- When AED treatment is being discontinued in an individual who has been seizure free, it should be carried out slowly (at least 2–3 months) and one drug should be withdrawn at a time [NICE, 2004c]. One month should be left between completing withdrawal of one drug and beginning withdrawal of the next.
- **Benzodiazepine and barbiturate withdrawal** may take up to 6 months or longer and requires particular care

because of the possibility of drug-related withdrawal symptoms and/or seizure recurrence [NICE, 2004c].

- There should be a failsafe plan agreed with individuals and their families and/or carers as appropriate, whereby if seizures recur, the last dose reduction is reversed and medical advice is sought [NICE, 2004c].
- **Prognostic index indicators** can be used to give an estimate of the risk of seizure recurrence with continued treatment compared with slow AED withdrawal (A). The prognostic index can only be used as a guide to help patients and healthcare professionals as the tool has not been systematically validated. For more information see www.sign.ac.uk/pdf/sign70.pdf(Tables 2 and 3, pages 14 and 15).

How should provoked seizures be managed?

- Seizures can be provoked by:
  - Acute metabolic disturbances
  - Treatment with certain drugs (e.g. antidepressants, antimuscarinics, anti-emetics, antipsychotics, bupropion, lithium, mefloquine, nonsteroidal anti-inflammatory drugs, especially in combination with quinolone antibiotics, opioids, and oral contraceptives)
  - Drug withdrawal (e.g. alcohol, benzodiazepines, and barbiturates)
  - Drug abuse (e.g. amphetamines, cocaine, ecstasy, heroin, and methadone)
- When seizures are provoked by metabolic disturbances or drugs, attention should be directed to correction or withdrawal of the provocative factor.
- **Short-term benzodiazepine treatment may be given** to reduce the risk of seizures in the context of acute alcohol withdrawal and delirium tremens (B).
- **Following an acute brain insult or neurosurgery,** prophylactic antiepileptic drug (AED) treatment is not indicated (B).
- **Following an acute brain insult,** AEDs used to treat the provoked seizures should be withdrawn (unless unprovoked seizures occur later) (C).
- **AED treatment is not indicated for concussive convulsions (D).**

Which issues are important for a woman with epilepsy who requires contraception?

See PRODIGY *Contraception* guidance for more information.

- **Advice on contraception should be given before women are sexually active.** Women with epilepsy should be encouraged to plan their pregnancies, as many pregnancies are unplanned. All opportunities to reinforce this advice should be taken.
- **When antiepileptic drug (AED) therapy is being initiated,** if a woman is already taking an oral contraceptive or using the combined transdermal contraceptive patch, then an AED that does not induce hepatic enzymes is preferable (e.g. sodium valproate, lamotrigine, ethosuximide). These AEDs do not alter the efficacy of the COC.
- **If a woman taking AED therapy requires contraception** then the method selected should take into consideration whether the AED may interact with the contraceptive preparation.
- **When the COC (or contraceptive patch) is given with an enzyme-inducing AED** (i.e. carbamazepine, oxcarbazepine, phenobarbital, phenytoin, primidone, or topiramate), a COC containing a minimum of 50 micrograms of oestrogen should be used. Women should be warned that the efficacy of the combined contraceptive preparation is reduced, and barrier methods of contraception should also be used until 4 weeks after cessation of the liver enzyme-inducer.
- **A regimen containing 50 micrograms of ethinylestradiol (EE) may be achieved** by either taking either one of the following options:
  - Norinyl-1 (containing mestranol 50 micrograms, a prodrug of EE).
  - Two low-dose COCs providing a total daily dose of 50–60 micrograms EE.
- **If breakthrough bleeding occurs with 50 micrograms of oestrogen,** the dose should be increased to 80 or 100 micrograms and tricycling of the COC should be considered (D). Tricycling means taking three packs of the high-dose COC without interruption followed by a reduced pill-free interval of 4 days after the final pack.
- **The oral progesterone-only contraceptive is not recommended for women taking enzyme-inducing AEDs** (D), as these increase the metabolism of progesterone.
- **Depot injections of progestogen-only contraceptives — medroxyprogesterone (Depo-Provera)** may be used with hepatic enzyme-inducing AEDs, but for long-term contraception should be given every 10 weeks (D). The Summary of Product Characteristics, however, recommends that injections should be repeated every 12 weeks for long-term contraception and does not discuss this specific scenario. The risk of interaction appears to be just a theoretical one and may be related to how potent the enzyme inducer is.
- **Note: depot norethisterone (Noristerat) injection** is only licensed for short-term use (two injections) in the UK and so no formal recommendations are available.
- **Progesterone implants are not suitable** for women taking enzyme-inducing AEDs (D), as they are ineffective when these AEDs are used.
- **For emergency contraception,** the dose of levonorgestrel should be increased to 1.5 mg and 750 micrograms 12 hours apart in women taking enzyme-inducing AEDs (D).

How do epilepsy and antiepileptic drugs affect pregnancy?

- **Reassure women with epilepsy that most have a normal pregnancy and delivery.**
- Epilepsy is common in women of child-bearing age and exposure to antiepileptic drugs (AEDs) occurs in approximately 1 in 250 pregnancies [Wallace et al, 1998].
- **Before becoming pregnant,** women should have their epilepsy treatment reviewed by an epilepsy specialist, where possible. Urgent referral to an epilepsy specialist is advised once pregnancy is confirmed.
- Any woman who has given birth to a child with a malformation while taking AEDs should be offered review by an epilepsy specialist before becoming pregnant again (D).
- **Women should be made aware of the risks of uncontrolled seizures both to themselves and to the fetus** (D).
- **If epilepsy is in remission, withdrawal of AEDs prior to conception may be considered by an epilepsy specialist** — the risk of recurrent seizures is low, and the consequences of recurrent seizures must be understood.
- **If AEDs are to be used in pregnancy,** the relative risks of seizures and fetal malformation should be discussed with the woman (C).
- **Ideally, a woman should conceive on the lowest effective dose of one AED** appropriate for her epilepsy syndrome. If she has good seizure control and presents already pregnant, there is probably little to be gained by altering her AEDs (C).

- **Crude rates for risk of major congenital malformation are** 4% (95% CI 3.3 to 5.3) in women taking one antiepileptic drug and 6.3% (95% CI 4.3 to 9.1) in women taking more than one based on information collated in a UK database. The risk may be as high as 24% in women who are taking four drugs [Scottish Obstetric Guidelines Audit Project, 1997]. The UK reported risk rate in women with epilepsy:
  - Not exposed to AEDs during pregnancy was 0.9% (95% CI 0.2 to 4.7)
  - Taking carbamazepine during pregnancy was 2.3% (95% CI 1.4 to 4.0)
  - Taking lamotrigine during pregnancy was 3% (95% CI 1.5 to 5.7)
  - Taking sodium valproate during pregnancy was 7.2% (95% CI 5.2 to 10)

E

[NICE, 2004b]

- **Sodium valproate** — the Summary of Product Characteristics recommends that women of childbearing potential should not be started on sodium valproate without specialist neurological advice, and that for partial seizures, sodium valproate should be used only in women found to be resistant to other treatments [ABPI Medicines Compendium, 2004].
- The most common major malformations associated with established AEDs are neural tube defects (sodium valproate 3%, carbamazepine 1%), orofacial defects, congenital heart abnormalities, and hypospadias.
- **There is insufficient evidence on which to base advice about the risks of most of the newer AEDs.** Lamotrigine has been reported as having an associated major malformation rate of 3% (95% CI 1.5 to 5.7).
- **Whether AEDs taken during pregnancy can affect the child's intellectual development** is uncertain, but currently there are particular concerns about the effects of sodium valproate on infant development [CSM, 2003a].
- **Folic acid 5 mg daily should be prescribed to all women with epilepsy from before conception up to the end of the first trimester (D).** Although there is no direct evidence of benefit in women on AEDs, folate supplementation has been shown to reduce the incidence of neural tube defects in the offspring of non-epileptic women [Wald, 1991], and so current guidelines recommend 5 mg daily [Crawford et al, 1999].
- **The risk of offspring developing epilepsy (inheritance)** is often a major concern to parents who have epilepsy. The level of risk varies with the type of epilepsy, and advice is best obtained from an epilepsy specialist. For example:
  - The risk of any type of seizure in a child of a mother with idiopathic generalized epilepsy (IGE) is 4–8%.
  - In a child of a father with IGE the risk is only slightly higher than that of the general population.
- All pregnant women with epilepsy, whether or not they are on medication, should be notified, with their consent, to the UK Pregnancy Register (Tel: 0800 389 1248).

[SIGN, 2003]

Which issues are important for a woman with epilepsy who is breastfeeding?

- **Breastfeeding by mothers taking antiepileptic drugs** (AEDs) is relatively safe provided that the infant is healthy and born close to term.
- **All mothers should be encouraged to breastfeed** and receive support from their health visitor, midwife, and GP.
- **The possibility of sedation** should be considered in infants of mothers taking phenobarbital [DTB, 1994b; Scottish Obstetric Guidelines Audit Project, 1997; Quality Standards Subcommittee of the American Academy of Neurology, 1998].

Which issues are important for a woman with epilepsy who is postpartum?

- **All infants born to mothers taking antiepileptic drugs (AEDs) should be given vitamin K_1 1 mg intramuscularly at birth (C).**
- If there are additional risk factors for haemorrhagic disease of the newborn (e.g. maternal liver disease, anticipated premature delivery), oral vitamin K_1 (phytomenadione 10 mg daily) should also be given in the last month of pregnancy (**D**).
- Following delivery, a review of the mother's AEDs should be undertaken by an epilepsy specialist. As the physiological changes associated with pregnancy gradually remit, blood levels of AEDs may rise. This review also gives the opportunity to discuss contraception and preconception advice for future pregnancies.
- The fatigue and sleep deprivation associated with caring for a new baby can provoke seizures.
- Babies of women with epilepsy, especially those with myoclonic seizures, are at risk of injury; advice on safety aspects of caring for the baby should be given by the GP and health visitor. Bathing infants is potentially hazardous if the mother has seizures associated with loss of awareness.

How does hormone replacement therapy (HRT) affect epilepsy and antiepileptic drugs?

- Women should be aware that their seizure pattern may change at the time of the menopause (**D**).
- HRT should be prescribed for the same indications as in women who do not have epilepsy (**D**), primarily for management of menopausal symptoms.
- Osteopenia, osteomalacia, and increased risk of hip fracture have been associated with antiepileptic drugs (AEDs), but their aetiology is likely to be multifactorial.
- However, HRT is no longer recommended as a first-line therapy for the long-term prevention of osteoporosis [CSM, 2003b]. Women should be aware of other measures to reduce osteoporosis, including a good calcium intake, exercise, and stopping smoking.
- Enzyme-inducing AEDs (carbamazepine, oxcarbazepine, phenobarbital, phenytoin, primidone, and topiramate) reduce the efficacy of standard doses of HRT.

Which issues are particular to children with epilepsy?

- **Antiepileptic treatment** for children is less well supported by clinical trial data than antiepileptic treatment for adults, and drugs are more likely to be used off-licence [Neville, 1997].
- **There are a number of epileptic syndromes that are specific to children.** Although most of these are 'benign' and usually remit (e.g. the benign childhood partial epilepsies and childhood absence epilepsy), there are some that have a poor prognosis (e.g. infantile spasms and Lennox–Gastaut syndrome), and close specialist supervision is necessary.
- **Twenty-five per cent of children with epilepsy have special educational needs,** and at least 20% have moderate or severe learning difficulties [Hall et al, 1997; Brown et al, 1998].

Which issues are particular to people with learning difficulties who have epilepsy?

- **In people with learning difficulties and epilepsy, adequate time should be allowed for the consultation (D).**
- **The carer should know the person** and bring relevant information on seizure type, frequency, possible adverse effects of medication, general health, and behaviour to the consultation (D).
- **Information** in an accessible form should be available to patients and carers (D).
- **There should be a multidisciplinary approach to treatment,** delivered by professionals with an expertise in epilepsy, to improve quality of life. Community learning disability nurses have an important role in liaising between the specialist services, patients, and carers (D).

Which issues are particular to elderly people with epilepsy?

- **The diagnosis of epilepsy in the elderly can be particularly challenging.** There may be no eyewitness account, and other comorbidity may mimic or coexist with epilepsy. The presentation may be with unexplained cuts, bruising, or burns; with unexplained incontinence; with confusion or drowsiness; or simply having been found on the floor by a carer. Syncope is the most common differential diagnosis. A high index of suspicion is vital, with appropriate referral to secondary care for investigation and consideration of the diagnosis.
- **The majority of elderly people who develop epilepsy have partial seizures with or without secondary generalization.**
- **Cerebrovascular disease is the most common cause of epilepsy in the elderly.**
- **The management of epilepsy in the elderly may also be challenging.** Polypharmacy is common in the elderly, with a consequent increase in the risk of drug interactions; this is coupled with the increased chance of adverse drug effects in the elderly.

[Tallis et al, 2002]

How is a person's driving licence affected by epilepsy?

- **For group 1 entitlement,** driving must be avoided for 1 year after the occurrence of an epileptic seizure while the person was awake. This also applies to a seizure occurring while the person was asleep. However, if seizures have occurred only during sleep for a period of at least 3 years, then a group 1 driving licence can be held.
- **For group 2 entitlement** (light goods vehicle or public service vehicle), a licence may be reissued only if the person has had no seizure for at least 10 years while having no treatment.
- **If treatment is withdrawn,** the current Driver and Vehicle Licensing Agency (DVLA) recommendation is that the person should not drive while the treatment is being withdrawn or for 6 months afterwards. If a person has a seizure, then the usual rules apply.
- **For seizures where there is a clear provoking factor** (e.g. due to a tricyclic antidepressant), special consideration may be given by the DVLA.

[DVLA, 1999]

What is the role of surgical treatment for epilepsy?

- **Surgery may be appropriate for people with drug-resistant epilepsy** when an anatomical abnormality can be localized. The aim of surgery is either to cure by the removal of epileptogenic tissue, or to reduce seizure activity by separating epileptogenic tissue from the remainder of the cortex. Implantation of a vagus nerve stimulator is a newer technique that has been shown to be effective in some people, although its current place in therapy is uncertain [Hall et al, 1997; Herman and Pedley, 1998].
- **Complications of surgery are rare;** overall mortality is less than 1%, and postoperative neurological deficit is usually transient and occurs in less than 5% of those undergoing surgery. Some people will have a persistent minor memory disturbance [Engel, 1996; Wallace et al, 1997].

Which other treatments are recommended for epilepsy?

- **Psychological treatments** are not an alternative to pharmacological treatments, but their use can be considered in people with poorly controlled seizures (B).
- **A ketogenic diet** is effective in some children and adults with refractory epilepsy [Bazil and Pedley, 1998; Brown et al, 1998].
- **Behavioural therapy,** including biofeedback, may be effective in some people, although there is a lack of trial data to support its use [Brown et al, 1998].
- **Complementary medicine** (e.g. acupuncture, yoga) is increasingly popular with people who use this in addition to conventional medicine. There is no evidence that these improve seizure control [Ramaratnam and Sridharan, 2004]. In addition, some aromatherapy preparations have an alerting effect on the brain and may exacerbate seizures.

How should status epilepticus be managed?

- Status epilepticus has been defined as the persistence of epileptic activity for more than 30 minutes.
- **Prolonged generalized tonic-clonic seizures cause significant morbidity and mortality.** If a generalized tonic-clonic seizure (or serial seizures) has lasted longer than 5 minutes, then emergency medical treatment is necessary. Other types of status epilepticus have a much lower risk of morbidity.
- **Immediate measures include the basic ABC (airway, breathing, circulation) of resuscitation.**
- **Intravenous diazepam or lorazepam are both effective and safe** when controlling tonic-clonic status epilepticus. Lorazepam has the advantage over diazepam of a much shorter duration of action, but its use in the community is limited by the need for refrigerated storage. Intravenous administration should ideally only be performed where resuscitation facilities are available due to the risk of respiratory depression and hypotension [DTB, 1996].
- **In primary care diazepam** can be conveniently and safely administered as a rectal solution, which may be a more practical treatment option.
- **Urgent admission** is required if the person does not respond.
- **People with recurrent prolonged or serial seizures in the community** should be initially managed by carers who should use diazepam 10–20 mg rectal solution, according to an agreed protocol (A). This may prevent or even terminate the development of status epilepticus. The protocol must include advice on when to transfer to hospital.
- **Buccal or intranasal midazolam** has also been used off-licence as a more convenient alternative, mainly in children, and it may also be safer. Use of midazolam in this way needs further assessment and it is not currently recommended in PRODIGY.

Medicines management

General issues

- **Avoid sudden withdrawal of an antiepileptic drug (AED)** unless adverse effects make this essential, as rapid AED withdrawal is associated with seizure recurrence [Medical Research Council Antiepileptic Drug Withdrawal Study Group, 1991; DTB, 2003] (see *Antiepileptic drug withdrawal*).
- **People should be warned of potential adverse effects** and given clear instructions to seek medical attention urgently for symptoms including rash, bruising, or somnolence with vomiting, especially in the first few weeks of treatment (C).
- **Regular structured reviews should be conducted with all patients** to ensure that they are not maintained for long periods in treatment that is ineffective or poorly tolerated, and to check that concordance with prescribed medication is maintained.
  - For adults, this can be done by the GP.
  - For children, this should be done by a paediatrician with expertise in epilepsy.
- **Routine monitoring of AED concentrations is not recommended as AED plasma concentrations are not a useful index of efficacy.** Measurement can sometimes be useful in the following circumstances: adjustment of phenytoin dosage and assessment of adherence and toxicity (D).
- **Routine monitoring of liver function and full blood count is not recommended for adverse drug reaction assessment (C).**
- **Many adverse effects of AEDs are dose-related** and may occur at therapeutic doses. In order to help minimize adverse effects, the drug should be introduced at a dose recommended by the manufacturer and slowly increased to the minimum dose that achieves seizure control.
- **All AEDs are associated with and often cause:**
  - Central nervous system (CNS) adverse effects, which include behavioural effects and cognitive dysfunction and are probably associated more with polytherapy than monotherapy. Note: it can be difficult to distinguish between adverse effects and the consequences of the condition.
  - Idiosyncratic adverse reactions — which very occasionally may be serious.
- **CNS adverse effects** — children may be particularly susceptible to these effects and this has consequences in terms of difficulties with behaviour, learning and development [NICE, 2004a].
- Note: only drugs recommended for use as monotherapy in this guidance are discussed in this section.

Sodium valproate

- **Before initiating therapy** (and also before surgery), blood cell count, bleeding time, and coagulation tests should be performed to establish that there is no undue potential for bleeding complications. Sodium valproate inhibits platelet aggregation leading to prolongation of bleeding time and frequently to thrombocytopenia [DTB, 1994a].
- Plasma drug levels may be useful when prescribing child doses.
- **Sodium valproate may cause liver damage,** and therefore monitoring of liver function is important, mainly in the first 6 months of therapy in children under 3 years of age and those with metabolic, degenerative, or developmental conditions [BNF 45, 2003]. In these people:
  - Discontinue treatment if there is an abnormally prolonged prothrombin time.
  - Avoid concomitant use of salicylates as they are metabolized via the same metabolic pathway.
- Advise people with epilepsy to seek immediate medical attention if symptoms develop, such as:
  - Vomiting, anorexia, jaundice, drowsiness, or loss of seizure control; these are signs of blood or liver disorders.
  - Abdominal pain, nausea, and vomiting; these are sigr of pancreatitis.
- **Adverse effects which may occur include** [Mattson et al 1992; Richens et al, 1994]:
  - Weight gain (12%), usually after at least 3 months' treatment, partly due to increased appetite.
  - Tremor, at higher doses (5%).
  - Transient hair loss (2.9%); regrowth may be curly.
  - Menstrual irregularities may occur in adolescent girls (common).
- **Rare serious adverse effects** [DTB, 1994a] **include:**
  - Hepatotoxicity (mainly in children below the age of 3 and those with severe learning difficulties, many of whom have a coexisting metabolic disorder)
  - Thrombocytopenia
  - Pancreatitis

Lamotrigine

- **Lamotrigine monotherapy is not licensed in children younger than 12 years of age.**
- **The Committee on Safety of Medicines (CSM) advice regarding blood disorders:** prescribers should be alert fo symptoms and signs suggestive of bone marrow failure such as anaemia, bruising, or infection. Aplastic anaemia, bone marrow depression, and pancytopenia have been associated rarely with lamotrigine.
- **Serious skin reactions** including Stevens–Johnson syndrome and toxic epidermal necrolysis have been found to develop mainly within the first 8 weeks of use, especially in children. The CSM has advised that factors associated with the risk of serious skin reactions include
  - Initial lamotrigine dosing higher than recommended
  - More rapid dose escalation than recommended
  - Concomitant use of sodium valproate
- Advise people with epilepsy to seek immediate medical attention if symptoms develop such as skin rash or influenza-like symptoms, as these may be associated wit hypersensitivity.
- **A mild maculopapular rash develops in about 10% of people.** The incidence can be reduced by beginning with a low dose [DTB, 1994a] and avoiding rapid increase of the initial dose [Guberman et al, 1999].
- **Avoid sudden withdrawal of lamotrigine,** unless a serious skin reaction develops (see *How and when should antiepileptic drug withdrawal be managed?*). Ideally withdrawal should be tapered off over 2 weeks c longer.

Carbamazepine

- **Advise people on carbamazepine to seek immediate medical attention** if they develop symptoms indicative o blood, hepatic, or skin disorders, e.g. fever, sore throat, rash, mouth ulcers, bruising, or bleeding.
- **Avoid abrupt withdrawal of carbamazepine** as this has been found to enhance sympathetic activity during non-REM sleep, which could predispose to sudden unexpected death in epilepsy [Hennessy et al, 2001].
- **Idiosyncratic and rare but serious adverse effects** include Stevens–Johnson syndrome, exfoliative dermatitis, and hepatitis [DTB, 1994a].
- **Skin rash** develops in 10% of people [Mattson et al, 1992] and people should be advised to seek immediate medical attention if symptoms develop [Richens et al, 1994; BNF 45, 2003].

Reversible dizziness (7%), headaches (6%), diplopia (4%), insomnia (4%), and ataxia (2%) are dose-related and may be dose-limiting.

Ataxia may occur from high blood levels of carbamazepine and this may result in falls, especially in elderly people.

Hyponatraemia is found in 20% of people [van Amelsvoort et al, 1994] but is usually well tolerated and usually of no importance (except where combined with trauma or high fluid intake, for example). If the hyponatraemia is problematic, such as in an elderly person, restriction of fluid intake or a slight reduction in the carbamazepine dose usually resolves the issue.

Carbamazepine induces liver microsomal enzymes and interacts with many drugs, including speeding up its own metabolism as well as that of oestrogens and progestogens (see *Which issues are important for a woman with epilepsy who requires contraception?*).

St John's wort has the potential to reduce the plasma concentration of carbamazepine if used concomitantly [Cott, 2001].

The incidence of dose-related adverse effects may be reduced [SIGN, 2003] **by:**

- Altering the timing of the medication.
- Use of modified-release tablets (i.e. reducing the frequency of giving the daily dose).

Ethosuximide

Advise people with epilepsy and their carers to seek immediate medical attention if symptoms indicative of blood disorders develop, such as: fever, sore throat, rash, mouth ulcers, bruising, or bleeding.

Idiosyncratic rare but serious adverse effects include Stevens–Johnson syndrome, exfoliative dermatitis, and hepatitis.

Clonazepam

Sedative adverse effects may be significant, but tolerance is common. Warn the person that alcohol will enhance sedative effects (see *How is a person's driving licence affected by epilepsy?*).

Elderly people are particularly sensitive to the effects of centrally depressant drugs and may experience confusion.

Withdrawal may be difficult because of the risk of dependence (*How and when should antiepileptic drug withdrawal be managed?*).

References

NHS staff in England can link, free of charge, from references to full text journals by clicking on [Full text] on the PRODIGY website.

1. ABPI Medicines Compendium (2004) *Summary of product characteristics for Epilim.* Electronic Medicines Compendium. Datapharm Communications Ltd. www.emc.medicines.org.uk [Accessed: 01/07/2004].
2. Appleton, R.E. and Neville, B.G.R. (1999) Teenagers with epilepsy. *Archives of Disease in Childhood* **81**(1), 76–79. [Full text]
3. Bazil, C.W. and Pedley, T.A. (1998) Advances in the medical treatment of epilepsy. *Annual Review of Medicine* **49**, 135–162. [Full text]
4. Berg, A.T. and Shinnar, S. (1991) The risk of seizure recurrence following a first unprovoked seizure: a quantitative review. *Neurology* **41**(7), 965–972.
5. Bessant, P., Chadwick, D.W. and Easton, B. (1991) Randomised study of antiepileptic drug withdrawal in patients in remission. *Lancet* **337**(8751), 1175–1180. [Full text]
6. Betts, T. and Smith, K. (1994) New departures in epilepsy care: an epilepsy liaison service. *Seizure* **3**(4), 301–308.
7. Binnie, C.D., Harding, G.F., Richens, A. and Wilkins, A. (1994) Video games and epileptic seizures – a consensus statement. Video-Game Epilepsy Consensus Group. *Seizure* **3**(4), 245–246.
8. BNF 45 (2003) *British National Formulary.* 45th edn. London: British Medical Association and Royal Pharmaceutical Society of Great Britain.
9. Bowman, E.S. (1998) Pseudoseizures. *Psychiatric Clinics of North America* **21**(3), 649–657.
10. Brodie, M.J. and Dichter, M.A. (1997) Established antiepileptic drugs. *Seizure* **6**(3), 159–174.
11. Brown, S., Betts, T., Crawford, P. et al (1998) Epilepsy needs revisited: a revised epilepsy needs document for the UK. *Seizure* **7**(6), 435–436.
12. Burn, J., Dennis, M., Bamford, J. et al (1997) Epileptic seizures after first stroke; the Oxfordshire community stroke project. *British Medical Journal* **315**(7122), 1582–1587. [Full text]
13. Chaplin, J.E., Lasso, R.Y. and Shorvon, S.D. (1992) National general practice study of epilepsy: the social and psychological effects of a recent diagnosis of epilepsy. *British Medical Journal* **304**(6839), 1416–1418.
14. Chappell, B. (1992) Epilepsy: patient views on their condition and teatment. *Seizure* **1**(2), 103–109.
15. Cockerell, O.C., Johnson, A.L., Sander, J.W.A.S. et al (1995) Remission of epilepsy: results from the national general practice study of epilepsy. *Lancet* **346**(8968), 140–144. [Full text]
16. Cockerell, O.C., Johnson, A.L., Sander, J.W.A.S. and Shorvon, S.D. (1997) Prognosis of epilepsy: a review and further analysis of the first nine years of the British national general practice study of epilepsy, a prospective population-based study. *Epilepsia* **38**(1), 31–46.
17. Collings, J.A. and Chappell, B. (1994) Correlates of employment history and employability in a British epilepsy sample. *Seizure* **3**(4), 255–262.
18. Cott, J.M. (2001) Herb-drug interactions. *CNS Spectrums* **6**(10), 827–832.
19. Coyle, H.P., Baker-Brian, N. and Brown, S.W. (1994) Coroners' autopsy reporting of sudden unexplained death in epilepsy (SUDEP) in the UK. *Seizure* **3**(4), 247–254.
20. Crawford, P., Appleton, R., Betts, T. et al (1999) Best practice guidelines for the management of women with epilepsy. *Seizure* **8**(4), 201–217.
21. CSM (2003a) Sodium valproate and prescribing in pregnancy. *Current Problems in Pharmacovigilance* **29**(Sept), 6.
22. CSM (2003b) *Further advice on safety of HRT: risk/benefit unfavourable for first-line use in prevention of osteoporosis.* CEM/CMO/2003/19. Committee on Safety of Medicines. www.mhra.gov.uk [Accessed: 09/01/2004].
23. DTB (1994a) Drug treatment of epilepsy. *Drug & Therapeutics Bulletin* **32**(6), 45–48. [Full text]
24. DTB (1994b) Epilepsy and pregnancy. *Drug & Therapeutics Bulletin* **32**(7), 49–51.
25. DTB (1996) Stopping status epileptics. *Drug & Therapeutics Bulletin* **34**(10), 73–75.
26. DTB (2003) When and how to stop antiepileptic drugs in adults. *Drug & Therapeutics Bulletin* **41**(6), 41–43.
27. DVLA (1999) *At a glance guide to current medical standards of fitness to drive. Neurological disorders.* Drivers Medical Group, Driver and Vehicle Licensing Authority. www.dvla.gov.uk/at_a_glance/content.htm [Accessed: 27/01/2003].

E

28. Engel, J., Jr. (1996) Surgery for seizures. *New England Journal of Medicine* **334**(10), 647–652.
29. Feely, M. (1999) Fortnightly review: drug treatment of epilepsy. *British Medical Journal* **318**(7176), 106–109. [Full text]
30. Gloaguen, V., Cottraux, J., Cucherat, M. and Blackburn, I.M. (1998) A meta analysis of the effects of cognitive therapy in depressed patients. *Journal of Affective Disorders* **49**(1), 59–72.
31. Guberman, A.H., Besag, F.M., Brodie, M.J. et al (1999) Lamotrigine-associated rash: risk/benefit considerations in adults and children. *Epilepsia* **40**(7), 985–991.
32. Hall, B., Martin, E. and Smithson, H. (Eds.) (1997) *Epilepsy: a general practice problem.* 3rd edn. London: The Royal College of General Practitioners.
33. Heaney, D.C., Shorvon, S.D. and Sander, J.W.A.S. (1998) An economic appraisal of carbamazepine, lamotrigine, phenytoin and valproate as initial treatment in adults with newly diagnosed epilepsy. *Epilepsia* **39**(Suppl 3), S19-S25.
34. Hennessy, M.J., Tighe, M.G., Binnie, C.D. and Nashef, L. (2001) Sudden withdrawal of carbamazepine increases cardiac sympathetic activity in sleep. *Neurology* **57**(9), 1650–1654.
35. Herman, S.T. and Pedley, T.A. (1998) New options for the treatment of epilepsy. *Journal of the American Medical Association* **280**(8), 693–694. [Full text]
36. Hopkins, A., Garman, A. and Clarke, C. (1988) The first seizure in adult life. Value of clinical features, electroencephalography, and computerised tomographic scanning in prediction of seizure recurrence. *Lancet* **1**(8588), 721–726.
37. Mattson, R.H., Cramer, J.A. and Collins, J.F. (1992) A comparison of valproate with carbamazepine for the treatment of complex partial seizures and secondarily generalized tonic-clonic seizures in adults. *New England Journal of Medicine* **327**(11), 765–771.
38. Medical Research Council Antiepileptic Drug Withdrawal Study Group (1991) Randomised study of antiepileptic drug withdrawal in patients in remission. *Lancet* **337**(8751), 1175–1180. [Full text]
39. MeReC (1995) The treatment of epilepsy (part 1). *MeReC Bulletin* **6**(5), 17–20.
40. Mills, N., Bachmann, M., Harvey, I. et al (1997) Patients' experience of epilepsy and health care. *Family Practice* **14**(2), 117–123.
41. Mills, N., Bachmann, M.O., Harvey, I. et al (1999) Effect of a primary-care-based epilepsy specialist nurse service on quality of care from the patients' perspective: quasi-experimental evaluation. *Seizure* **8**(1), 1–7.
42. Neville, B.G.R. (1997) Epilepsy in childhood. *British Medical Journal* **315**(7113), 924–930. [Full text]
43. NHS Confederation and BMA (2005) *New GMS contract.* Department of Health. www.dh.gov.uk [Accessed: 27/09/2005]. [Full text]
44. NICE (2004a) *Newer drugs for epilepsy in children.* Technology appraisal no. 79. National Institute for Clinical Excellence. www.nice.org.uk [Accessed: 28/04/2004].
45. NICE (2004b) *Newer drugs for epilepsy in adults.* Technology appraisal no. 76. National Institute for Clinical Excellence. www.nice.org.uk [Accessed: 01/07/2004].
46. NICE (2004c) *The epilepsies: the diagnosis and management of the epilepsies in adults and children in primary and secondary care – NICE guideline.* Clinical guideline 20. National Institute for Health and Clinical Excellence. www.nice.org.uk [Accessed: 27/10/2004]. [Full text]
47. NICE (2005) *Referral guidelines for suspected cancer quick reference guide.* Clinical guideline 27. National Institute for Health and Clinical Excellence. www.nice.org.uk [Accessed: 01/07/2005].
48. O'Donoghue, M.F., Goodridge, D.M.G., Redhead, K. et al (1999) Assessing the psychosocial consequences o epilepsy: a community-based study. *British Journal of General Practice* **49**(440), 211–214.
49. Quality Standards Subcommittee of the American Academy of Neurology (1998) Practice parameter: management issues for women with epilepsy (summar statement). *Neurology* **51**(4), 944–948.
50. Ramaratnam, S. and Sridharan, K. (2004) *Yoga for epilepsy (Cochrane Review).* The Cochrane Library. Issue 4. Chichester, UK: John Wiley & Sons, Ltd.
51. Richens, A., Davidson, D.L., Cartlidge, N.E. and Easter, D.J. (1994) A multicentre comparative trial of sodium valproate and carbamazepine in adult onset epilepsy. *Journal of Neurology, Neurosurgery & Psychiatry* **57**(6), 682–687.
52. Ridsdale, L., Kwan, I. and Cryer, C. (1999) The effect of a special nurse on patients' knowledge of epilepsy and their emotional state. *British Journal of General Practice* **49**(441), 285–289.
53. Sander, J.W.A.S. and O'Donoghue, M.F. (1997) Epilepsy: getting the diagnosis right. *British Medical Journal* **314**(7075), 158–159. [Full text]
54. Scambler, G. (1994) Patient perceptions of epilepsy an of doctors who manage epilepsy. *Seizure* **3**(4), 287–293.
55. Scheepers, B., Clough, P. and Pickles, C. (1998) The misdiagnosis of epilepsy: findings of a population study. *Seizure* **7**(5), 403–406.
56. Scottish Obstetric Guidelines Audit Project (1997) *The management of pregnancy in women with epilepsy.* Scottish Programme for Clinical Effectiveness in Reproductive Health. www.sign.ac.uk [Accessed: 10/12/2003].
57. SIGN (2003) *Diagnosis and management of epilepsy i adults.* Report no. 70. Scottish Intercollegiate Guidelines Network. www.sign.ac.uk [Accessed: 30/05/2003].
58. Stephen, L.J. and Brodie, M.J. (1998) New drug treatments for epilespsy. *Prescribers' Journal* **38**(2), 98–106.
59. Sunder, T.R. (1997) Meeting the challenge of epilepsy in persons with multiple handicaps. *Journal of Child Neurology* **12**(Suppl 1), S38-S43. [Full text]
60. Tallis, R., Boon, P., Perucca, E. and Stephen, L. (2002 Epilepsy in the elderly people: management issues. *Epileptic Disorders* **4**(Suppl 2), S33-S39.
61. Tanaka, E. (1999) Clinically significant pharmacokinetic drug interactions between antiepileptic drugs. *Journal of Clinical Pharmacy & Therapeutics* **24**(2), 87–92.
62. Thapar, A.K. (1996) Care of patients with epilepsy in the community: will new initiatives address old problems? *British Journal of General Practice* **46**(37), 42.
63. The Epilepsy Task Force (1995) *Specification for epilepsy services.* London: The Epilepsy Task Force.
64. van Amelsvoort, T., Bakshi, R., Devaux, C.B. and Schwabe, S. (1994) Hyponatremia associated with carbamazepine and oxcarbazepine therapy: a review. *Epilepsia* **35**(1), 181–188.
65. Wald, N. (1991) Prevention of neural tube defects: results of the medical research council vitamin study. *Lancet* **338**(8760), 131–137. [Full text]
66. Wallace, H., Shorvon, S.D., Hopkins, A. and O'Donoghue, M. (Eds.) (1997) *Adults with poorly controlled epilepsy. Part 1 – clinical guidelines for treatment. Part 2 – practical tools for aiding epilepsy*

management. London: The Royal College of Physicians.

7. Wallace, H., Shorvon, S. and Tallis, R. (1998) Age-specific incidence and prevalence rates of treated epilepsy in an unselected population of 2, 052, 922 and age-specific fertility rates of women with epilepsy. *Lancet* 352(9145), 1970–1973. [Full text]

8. Webb, D.W., Coleman, H., Fielder, A. and Kennedy, C.R. (1998) An audit of paediatric epilepsy care. *Archives of Disease in Childhood* 79(2), 145–148. [Full text]

vidence grading

vidence grading is from the Scottish Intercollegiate uidelines Network (SIGN) Guideline *Diagnosis and anagement of Epilepsy in Adults*, April 2003. The finitions of grades of recommendation used in this uideline are as follows:

A	At least one meta-analysis, systematic review, or randomized controlled trial (RCT) rated as 1++ and directly applicable to the target population or A systematic review of RCTs or a body of evidence consisting principally of studies rated as 1+ directly applicable to the target population and demonstrating overall consistency of results
B	A body of evidence including studies rated as 2++ directly applicable to the target population and demonstrating overall consistency of results or Extrapolated evidence from studies rated as 1++ or 1+
C	A body of evidence including studies rated as 2+ directly applicable to the target population and demonstrating overall consistency of results or Extrapolated evidence from studies rated as 2++
D	Evidence level 3 or 4 or Extrapolated evidence from studies rated as 2+

PRODIGY GUIDANCE

Febrile convulsion

Last revised in April 2005
www.prodigy.nhs.uk/guidance.asp?gt=Febrile convulsion

Applies to children from the age of 6 months to 6 years

This guidance covers the management of a child who presents having had a febrile convulsion.

This guidance does not cover the emergency management of a child who is still convulsing, or the management of a child who has epilepsy or other seizure disorder.

There is separate PRODIGY guidance for *Epilepsy*.

Goals

- To make an accurate diagnosis of febrile convulsion
- To identify children who should be admitted to hospital for further assessment
- To reassure and inform parents about the benign nature of febrile convulsions
- To inform parents about the immediate home treatment of possible future febrile convulsions

Contents

Scenarios
- Febrile convulsions p.784

Extended Information, p. 785

Febrile convulsions

Which therapy?

- **Consider admission** — see *Should I refer or investigate?*
- **Reassure carers and inform them that:**
  - Febrile convulsions do not harm the child. They do not cause brain damage. And, they are not the same as epilepsy.
  - Epilepsy can develop later, but this is rare — the chance is about 1 in 100 for children who have had two or more febrile convulsions.
  - Febrile convulsions may recur — the chance is about 1 in 3.
    - Treatment to prevent febrile convulsions is seldom needed, and would only be started after assessment by a specialist.
- **Advise on controlling fever in the future.**
  - Treating a fever will not prevent febrile convulsions from recurring, but it will ease symptoms of fever.
  - High temperatures are best reduced by giving paracetamol or ibuprofen, and by removing excess clothing and bedding.
  - Fanning and tepid sponging can distress the child, and are of no benefit.
- **Teach parents to manage a recurrent convulsion. They should:**
  - Place the child in the recovery position on a soft surface, lying semi-prone with the face turned to the side. This prevents the inhalation of vomit, keeps the airways open, and prevents the child from hurting him- or herself.
  - Not force anything into the mouth.
  - Note the time that the convulsion started, and stay with the child.
  - Wait few minutes for the convulsions to stop and then phone the GP or NHS Direct.
  - Dial 999 and request ambulance transport to the nearest hospital accident and emergency department the convulsions continue for more than 5 minutes.
- **Advise on immunization**
  - A febrile convulsion only rarely follows a immunization. The excess risks are:
    - **For diphtheria, tetanus toxoid, and whole cell pertussis (DTP) immunization:** 6–9 children per 100,000 immunizations; risk increased on the day vaccination, but not subsequently.
    - **For measles, mumps, and rubella (MMR):** 25–34 children per 100,000 vaccinations; risk increased 8–14 days after vaccination.
  - The vaccination schedule should be completed as th is no increased risk of febrile convulsions with futur vaccinations.
  - The risk of neurological and developmental problem is not increased when a febrile convulsion is associat with a vaccination.

Practical prescribing points

For further information see the *Medicines Compendium* (www.medicines.org.uk) or the *British National Formul* (www.bnf.org).

Should I refer or investigate?

Refer?

- **Most children who have had a febrile convulsion do n need to be admitted.**
  - The main concern is the possibility of missing a mor serious diagnosis such as meningitis.
- **Strongly consider admission** for observation, lumbar puncture or treatment if any of the following factors a present:
  - Age under 18 months (may have meningitis without meningeal signs)
  - Signs of meningitis
  - Child was drowsy before the seizure, or is irritable, systemically unwell or 'toxic'
  - Petechial rash
  - Recent or current treatment with antibiotics (partial treated meningitis may not have meningeal signs)
  - Complex convulsion (i.e. lasting longer than 10 minutes, or focal, or repeated in the same episod of illness, or with incomplete recovery within 1 hou
  - Early review by a doctor not possible
  - Inadequate home circumstances
  - Parents anxious or unable to cope
  - The cause of the fever requires hospital managemen in its own right
- **Consider referral if:**
  - The diagnosis of febrile convulsion is in doubt.

- Febrile convulsions have been severe, or complicated and prophylactic treatment might be indicated.
- The child might be at increased risk for epilepsy, for example, having a neurological or developmental condition or because there is a history of epilepsy in parents or siblings.

vestigate?

Blood glucose. Rule out hypoglycaemia in a child who convulses for more than 5 minutes, or who is excessively drowsy after the convulsion.
Urine microscopy and culture. If no cause for the fever is found, and the child is not to be admitted, take a urine specimen (clean catch, suprapubic aspirate, or catheter specimen) for microscopy and culture.
Other investigations should be guided by the cause of the fever rather than by the febrile convulsion.

atient information leaflets

ie following PILs are available at www.prodigy.nhs.uk
Febrile Convulsion
Paracetamol
Temperatures (Fevers) in Children

hared decision making

Febrile convulsions occur in about 3 in 100 children under the age of 6 years. They usually last less than 5 minutes.

- They are not epilepsy.
- They do not cause brain damage.

Any illness that causes a fever ('temperature') may cause a febrile convulsion. The common causes are viral infections causing coughs, colds, 'flu, etc.
Try to keep a fever down when your child has a feverish illness.

- **Paracetamol or ibuprofen** reduce fever. Always have some in the home.
- **Remove the child's clothes.**

Only one convulsion occurs in most cases. In about 3 in 10 cases another occurs with a future feverish illness.
Learn how to put a child in the 'recovery position' — lay him or her on their side with their head to one side. Do not put anything into the mouth but remove anything that could interfere with breathing (such as vomit or food).
Call a doctor or ambulance if the child does not recover quickly or if you feel that the illness causing the fever is more serious than a common viral infection.
A febrile convulsion very occasionally follows a vaccination.

rug rationale

rugs not included

Intravenous diazepam for seizure termination is not practical for use in primary care.
Midazolam for seizure termination is not included as it is not licensed for use in febrile convulsions in the UK.
Diazepam in the rectal or oral form for prevention of recurrent febrile convulsions: this treatment should only be initiated by a specialist. Diazepam in the oral form is not licensed for use in febrile convulsions.
Other benzodiazepines are not included, as they are not licensed for use in febrile convulsions.
Oral anticonvulsants for prevention of recurrent febrile convulsions: this treatment should only be initiated by a specialist.

Drugs included

- **Paracetamol** is an effective and safe antipyretic and analgesic for children.
- **Ibuprofen** is an effective and safe antipyretic and analgesic for children over the age of 12 months.

Prescriptions

Antipyretics: use when required

Paracetamol s/f susp: 60mg to 120mg up to four times a day

- Age from 6 to 11 months
- Paracetamol 120mg/5ml s/f susp. Take 2.5ml to 5ml every 4 to 6 hours when required for relief of high temperature. Maximum of 4 doses in 24 hours; supply 150 ml; NHS Cost £0.65; OTC Cost £1.14.

Paracetamol s/f susp: 120mg to 240mg up to four times a day

- Age from 12 months to 6 years
- Paracetamol 120mg/5ml s/f susp. Take one to two 5ml spoonfuls every 4 to 6 hours when required for relief of high temperature. Maximum of 4 doses in 24 hours; supply 300 ml; NHS Cost £1.30; OTC Cost £2.28.

Ibuprofen s/f susp: 50mg three to four times a day

- Age from 12 months to 2 years
- Ibuprofen 100mg/5ml s/f susp. Take 2.5ml three to four times a day when required for relief of high temperature. Do not exceed the stated dose; supply 100 ml; NHS Cost £1.79; OTC Cost £3.15.

Ibuprofen s/f susp: 100mg three to four times a day

- Age from 3 to 6 years
- Ibuprofen 100mg/5ml s/f susp. Take one 5ml spoonful 3 to 4 times a day when required for relief of high temperature. Do not exceed the stated dose; supply 150 ml; NHS Cost £2.81; OTC Cost £4.95.

Extended Information

Background information

- What is it? p.785
- How common is it? p.786
- How do I know my patient has it? p.786
- What else might it be? p.786
- Complications and prognosis p.787

What is it?

What is a febrile convulsion (or febrile seizure)?

- **A febrile convulsion** is a seizure occurring in a child aged 6 months to 5 years, associated with fever arising from infection or inflammation outside the central nervous system in a child who is otherwise neurologically normal [Offringa and Moyer, 2001].
- A Delphi consensus development process failed to reach agreement on what threshold temperature could be regarded as defining a fever. The final consensus was that fever should be assumed to be present if the 'history and examination were indicative' [Armon et al, 2003].
    - The age limits are arbitrary and should be used as guidelines in clinical practice.
- **Simple febrile convulsions** are isolated, generalized, tonic–clonic seizures lasting less than 10–15 minutes.
- **Complex febrile convulsions** last about 15–30 minutes, or are focal, or recur during the febrile illness, or are not followed by full consciousness within an hour.

What causes febrile convulsions?

- The mechanisms causing febrile convulsions are not known. It may not be the fever that causes the seizure, but release of cytokines, as a consequence of infection, that (a) cause fever and (b) cause seizures. The risk of febrile convulsions depends upon the age of the child, so reflecting maturational sensitivity to the cytokines with respect to seizure induction. Consequently, much of the debate over the presence, height, or rate of rise of the fever may be irrelevant [Stern, Personal Communication, 2005].

What conditions cause the fever in a child with febrile convulsions?

Viral infections and otitis media are the most common sources of fever in children with febrile convulsions.

- A comprehensive review of the literature identified the conditions usually associated with febrile convulsions [Armon et al, 2003]. In decreasing order of frequency they are:
  - Viral infections
  - Otitis media
  - Tonsillitis
  - Urinary tract infection
  - Gastroenteritis
  - Lower respiratory tract infection
  - Meningitis
  - Post-immunization
- The table below presents evidence of a low prevalence of serious bacterial illness in children with febrile convulsions.

Bacterial meningitis

A main concern when assessing children who have had a febrile convulsion is to detect and manage bacterial meningitis.

- Bacterial meningitis can be effectively treated, and the consequences of delayed treatment can be devastating.
- The risk of bacterial meningitis is low in children with febrile convulsions [Trainor et al, 2001; Armon et al, 2003]. However, it is difficult to estimate the prevalence of bacterial meningitis accurately because:
  - Many studies are hospital-based, but some children with febrile convulsions are managed in primary care.
  - In many children a firm diagnosis of bacterial meningitis is frequently not possible, either because a lumbar puncture to obtain cerebrospinal fluid (CSF) was not done, or because the CSF culture and microscopy result was not definitive.

How common is it?

- Between 2% and 4% of children have a febrile seizure [Smith, 1994; Armon et al, 2001; Waruiru and Appleton, 2004].
- The peak incidence is at 18 months [Waruiru and Appleton, 2004].

Table 1: Prevalence of serious bacterial illness in 455 children admitted to hospital with a diagnosis of a first-time febrile convulsion [Trainor et al, 2001].

Test	Number performed	Number positive
Chest X-rays	208	26 pneumonia
Urine cultures	171	10
Blood culture	315	4 (all *Streptococcus pneumoniae*)
Stool cultures	14	2 (both *Shigella sonnei*)
Cerebrospinal fluid cultures	135	0

- About 4% of febrile convulsions occur in the first 6 months of life, 90% between 6 months and 3 years, and 6% after 3 years of age [Smith, 1994]. (The cited study had age criteria that differed from those used in this guidance.)
- About 5% of all paediatric medical attendances to an accident and emergency department in Nottingham we for febrile convulsions [Armon et al, 2001]. About 70% of these children were admitted.

How do I know my patient has it?

History

- **Age:** 6 months to 5 years old (approximately)
- **Convulsion:**
  - **Duration** — usually no longer than 3–6 minutes; clas as complex if prolonged more than 10–15 minutes
  - **Pattern** — usually generalized tonic–clonic; class as complex if focal
  - **Recovery of level of consciousness** — usually comple within an hour; class as complex if not fully recovere within an hour
- **Temperature** — fever around the time of the convulsio
- **Previous febrile convulsion** — class as complex if convulsions recur in the same febrile illness
- **Recent immunization** — it is rare for a febrile convulsi to be precipitated by a immunization; see *Does immunization increase the risk of febrile convulsions a other complications?* in *Complications and prognosis*, below

Examination

- **Level of consciousness.**
- **Focus of infection.** An infection is usually found to be t source of the fever. Check for viral infections, otitis media, tonsillitis, urinary tract infection (UTI), gastroenteritis, lower respiratory tract infection, and meningitis.

Investigations

- Investigations should be directed towards identifying th source of the fever.
  - **UTI.** When no focus of infection is found, and admission is not planned, take a urine sample (clean catch, suprapubic aspirate, or catheter specimen) for microscopy and culture.
  - **Bacterial meningitis.** A main concern is to identify children with bacterial meningitis. Criteria for referr for investigation are fully detailed in the section *Whe should I admit or refer a child who has had a febrile convulsion?* in *Management issues*, below.
- Blood tests, electroencephalograms (EEGs), and neuroimaging are not required in the evaluation of simple febrile convulsions.

[American Academy of Pediatrics, 1996; Armon et al, 2003]

What else might it be?

- **Epilepsy**
- **Any other cause of convulsion with fever, or without fever, for example:**
  - Meningitis (including partially treated bacterial meningitis)
  - Encephalitis
  - Cerebral palsy with intercurrent infection
  - Hypoglycaemia or other metabolic disorder
  - Neurodegenerative disorders
  - Poisoning
  - Non-accidental shaking injury, rarely

Note that complex febrile convulsions are more likely tha simple febrile convulsions to be provoked by a serious condition. Therefore, suspect serious pathology in a child who has had a prolonged or focal febrile convulsion, or who has not recovered within an hour of a febrile convulsion.

[Royal College of Physicians and the British Paediatric Association, 1991; Fukuyama et al, 1996]

Complications and prognosis

Complications

- **Long-term adverse effects are rare.**
  - There is no evidence of subsequent impaired intelligence or poorer academic achievement [Verity et al, 1998].
  - There is a slightly increased risk of epilepsy — see under *Prognosis* below.

Prognosis

What is the risk of recurrence after a febrile convulsion?

- **Febrile convulsions recur** in subsequent febrile illnesses in about 30% of children. Only 9% have more than three seizures [Smith, 1994; Fukuyama et al, 1996].
- **Recurrence is most common within a year** of the first febrile convulsion (70%) [Fukuyama et al, 1996].
- **Recurrence is more likely if:**
  - The first febrile convulsion occurs under the age of 15 months.
  - The first convulsion is complex.
  - There is a family history of febrile convulsions or epilepsy in a first-degree relative.
  - The child attends day nursery (due to increased frequency of febrile illnesses).
- The recurrence rate is 10% in the absence of these risk factors; 25% with one risk factor; 50% with two risk factors; and approaches 100% with three or more risk factors.

[Knudsen, 1996; Armon et al, 2003]

What is the risk of epilepsy developing after a febrile convulsion?

- The risk of subsequent epilepsy is rare but increases with each of the following factors:
  - Neurological abnormalities or developmental delay before the onset of febrile convulsions
  - Atypical seizures
  - Family history of epilepsy
  - Complex convulsions
- In the absence of these risk factors only 1% of children go on to develop epilepsy (compared with 0.4% of children without a history of febrile convulsion) [Stenklyft and Carmona, 1994; Knudsen, 1996; Berg et al, 1999].
- A Danish study found that children who had febrile convulsions after measles, mumps, and rubella (MMR) immunization were not at increased risk of later epilepsy (0.23% compared with 0.60%; not statistically significantly different) [Vestergaard et al, 2004].

Does immunization increase the risk of febrile convulsions and other complications?

- **Immunization is rarely followed by a febrile convulsion.**
  - A large cohort study estimated the risks of a febrile convulsion following immunization with diphtheria, tetanus toxoid, and whole cell pertussis (DTP) and MMR [Barlow et al, 2001]. Excess rates of febrile convulsions were:
    - **For DTP:** 6–9 children per 100,000 immunizations; risk increased on the day of immunization, but not subsequently. However, acellular DTPa is now used. We found no study measuring the rate of febrile convulsions after immunization with acellular pertussis, but since other reactions are generally fewer than with whole cell preparations, it is likely to be no higher.
    - **For MMR:** 25–34 children per 100,000 immunizations; risk increased 8–14 days after immunization
  - A recent study from Denmark of the relationship between MMR and febrile convulsions, based on a larger number of immunized children than Barlow's gives similar relative risks. The authors also found that children who had febrile convulsions after MMR immunization were at slightly increased risk of further febrile convulsions. [Vestergaard et al, 2004]
- **Immunization-associated febrile convulsions are not likely to cause recurrent febrile convulsions with future immunizations.**
  - Children who had a febrile seizure following immunization were no more likely to have a subsequent seizure than children who had a febrile seizure not associated with immunization [Barlow et al, 2001].
- **Immunization-associated febrile convulsions are not likely to cause neurobehavioural disorders.**
  - The relative risk of developing one or more learning or developmental disabilities after a febrile convulsion associated with immunization was 0.56 (95% confidence interval 0.07 to 4.2) [Barlow et al, 2001].

Management issues

- Overview of the management of febrile convulsions p.787
- When should I admit or refer a child who has had a febrile convulsion? p.787
- How do I manage the fever? p.788
- What measures should I consider to prevent febrile convulsions? p.788
- How should I counsel parents? p.788

Overview of the management of febrile convulsions

- Reassure carers that febrile convulsions do not harm the child.
- Advise on controlling fever in the future: an antipyretic, cool clothing, no physical cooling.
- Teach parents to manage a recurrent convulsion: recovery position, nothing forced into mouth.
- Recommend that immunization schedules be completed.
- Admit children who need observation, investigation, or treatment of the underlying condition: the main concern is to detect children at increased risk of meningitis.
- Consider referral for children who are at increased risk for epilepsy.

When should I admit or refer a child who has had a febrile convulsion?

Criteria for admission

- **Most children with a first febrile convulsion do not need to be admitted.** *The main concern is the possibility of missing a more serious diagnosis such as meningitis.*
- **Strongly consider admission** for observation, lumbar puncture or treatment if any of the following factors are present:
  - **Age under 18 months** (may have meningitis without meningeal signs)

- **Signs of meningitis** (neck stiffness; photophobia; Kernig's sign; Brudzinski's signs; bulging fontanelle; depressed level of consciousness, for example, Glasgow Coma scale <15 at 1 hour after the convulsion):
  - **Kernig's sign:** pain restricts leg straightening when supine and holding the thigh flexed to a right angle
  - **Brudzinski sign 1** (contralateral reflex, contralateral sign): when lying supine, passive flexion of one leg results in a similar movement in the opposite leg
  - **Brudzinski sign 2** (neck sign): knees and hips flex involuntarily when the neck is flexed while supine
  - **Test for meningism gently and considerately, as this can be painful**
- **Child was drowsy before the seizure, or is irritable, systemically unwell or 'toxic'**
- **Petechial rash**
- **Recent or current treatment with antibiotics** (because partially treated meningitis may not have meningeal signs)
- **Complex convulsion** (i.e. lasting longer than 10 minutes; or with focal features, e.g. jerking affecting only one limb; or repeated in the same episode of illness; or with incomplete recovery within 1 hour)
- **Early review by a doctor not possible**
- **Inadequate home circumstances**
- **Carer anxious** or unable to cope
- **The cause of the fever requires hospital management in its own right**

[Royal College of Physicians and the British Paediatric Association, 1991; American Academy of Pediatrics, 1999; Armon et al, 2003; Warden et al, 2003; Waruiru and Appleton, 2004]

When should I refer a child who has had a febrile convulsion?

Consider referral if:

- The diagnosis of febrile convulsion is in doubt.
- The cause of the fever is in doubt (see below).
- Febrile convulsions have been severe, or complicated and prophylactic treatment might be indicated.
- The child might be at increased risk for epilepsy, for example, having a neurological or developmental condition or because there is a history of epilepsy in parents or siblings [Fukuyama et al, 1996].
- The parents require additional reassurance that the child is not at risk of dying or of serious complications.

How do I manage the fever?

Diagnose the cause of the fever

- **Seek the source of the fever.**
  - Consider the following differential diagnosis: viral infection, otitis media, tonsillitis, urinary tract infection (UTI), gastroenteritis, lower respiratory tract infection, meningitis, post-immunization, post-ictal fever [Baumer and Paediatric Accident and Emergency Research Group, 2004].
- When no focus of infection is found, and admission is not planned, a urine sample should be taken for dipstick test, microscopy, and culture [Armon et al, 2003].
  - Ideally the urine specimen should be from a suprapubic aspirate or catheter sample, which may need to be obtained in hospital. If this is impractical, urine may be collected by bag, clean catch, or pad, bearing in mind that contamination of the urine may make interpretation of culture results unreliable [Verrier-Jones, Personal Communication, 2005]. The likelihood of urinary tract infection is very high if a dipstick test of the urine is positive for both nitrite and leucocyte esterase [Centre for Reviews and Dissemination, 2004].

Treat the fever to ease symptoms

- Prescribe paracetamol or ibuprofen.
- Remove excessive clothing and bedding.
- Avoid physical methods such as fanning, cold bathing, and tepid sponging — their use is controversial as they are felt to cause some discomfort and minimal benefit.

[Royal College of Physicians and the British Paediatric Association, 1991; Fukuyama et al, 1996; Meremikwu and Oyo-Ita, 2003; Watts et al, 2003]

What measures should I consider to prevent febrile convulsions?

- **Treatment to prevent recurrence of febrile convulsions is rarely necessary** and should only be prescribed after specialist assessment.
- **Treating fevers with antipyretics does not prevent febrile convulsions** [Offringa and Moyer, 2001].
- **Intermittent rectal diazepam** given at the onset of a fever to prevent febrile convulsions may be a suitable option, depending on home circumstances, for a child at high risk of recurrence of severe or complicated seizures.
  - Diazepam (oral and rectal) at relatively high doses may prevent febrile convulsions in subsequent illness if given at the onset of a febrile episode [Offringa and Moyer, 2001; Masuko et al, 2003].
  - Rectal diazepam is safe for home use, providing parents are properly educated in its use [Royal College of Physicians and the British Paediatric Association, 1991; Knudsen, 1996].
  - Adverse effects have been reported with intermittent use of diazepam; these included ataxia (31.1%), lethargy (28.8%), and irritability (24.4%), but lasted no more than 36 hours [Verrotti et al, 2004].
  - Treatment to prevent febrile seizures should only be prescribed after specialist assessment.
- **Continuous prophylaxis is controversial.** Anticonvulsants such as phenobarbital are minimally effective in preventing febrile convulsions — on average 8 children would need to be treated for 2 years to prevent 1 febrile convulsion — and the benefits of prophylaxis are outweighed by the risk of adverse effects [Offringa and Moyer, 2001].
- **No treatment is available to reduce the rare risk of subsequent epilepsy.**
- **Immunization is not contraindicated after a febrile convulsion.**
  - There is evidence to suggest that immunizations do not increase the risk of recurrent febrile convulsions [Offringa and Moyer, 2001].

How should I counsel parents?

- **Inform parents** that:
  - Although febrile convulsions are frightening to watch, they are not harmful to the child, do not cause brain damage, and will not cause the child to die.
  - The child will be sleepy for up to an hour after the convulsion.
  - Febrile convulsions are not the same as epilepsy.
  - Epilepsy can develop later, but this is rare — the chance is about 1 in 100 for children who have had two or more febrile convulsions.
  - Febrile convulsions may recur — about 1 in 3 children will have another febrile convulsion.
  - Treatment to prevent febrile convulsions recurring is seldom necessary, nor is it worth having to put up with the side effects or taking the risk of serious adverse effects.

  - If the child is at high risk for further seizures (e.g. having a neurological condition or because there is a family history of epilepsy in parents or siblings), referral to a specialist might be useful.
- **Advise parents on controlling high temperatures**
  - The aim of controlling fever is to ease symptoms, not to prevent febrile convulsions.
  - High temperature is best reduced by giving paracetamol or ibuprofen, and by removing excessive clothing and bedding.
  - Fanning and tepid sponging are likely to cause discomfort and are of little benefit.
- **Teach parents to manage a recurrent convulsion. They should:**
  - Place the child in the recovery position on a soft surface, lying semi-prone with the face turned to the side. This prevents the inhalation of vomit, keeps the airways open, and prevents the child from hurting him- or herself.
  - Not force anything into the mouth.
  - Note the time that the convulsion started, and stay with the child.
  - Wait a few minutes for the convulsions to stop, then phone their GP or NHS Direct.
  - Dial 999 if the convulsions continue more than 5 minutes, and request ambulance transport to the nearest hospital accident and emergency department.
- **Counsel parents about immunization**
  - Immunization is still advised after a febrile convulsion, even if, as rarely happens, the febrile convulsion followed a immunization.

[Baumer et al, 1981; Gordon et al, 2001; Huang, 2001; Parmar et al, 2001; Huang et al, 2002; Armon et al, 2003; Warden et al, 2003; Waruiru and Appleton, 2004]

References

NHS staff in England can link, free of charge, from references to full text journals by clicking on [Full text] on the PRODIGY website.

1. American Academy of Pediatrics (1996) Practice parameter: the neurodiagnostic evaluation of the child with a first simple febrile seizure. *Pediatrics* **97**(5), 769–772.
2. American Academy of Pediatrics (1999) Practice parameter: long-term treatment of the child with simple febrile seizures. *Pediatrics* **103**(6 Pt 1), 1307–1309. [Full text]
3. Armon, K., Stephenson, T., Gabriel, V. et al (2001) Determining the common medical presenting problems to an accident and emergency department. *Archives of Disease in Childhood* **84**(5), 390–392. [Full text]
4. Armon, K., Stephenson, T., Hemingway, P. et al (2003) An evidence and consensus based guideline for the management of a child after a seizure. *Emergency Medicine Journal* **20**(1), 13–20.
5. Barlow, W.E., Davis, R.L., Glasser, J.W. et al (2001) The risk of seizures after receipt of whole-cell pertussis or measles, mumps, and rubella vaccine. *New England Journal of Medicine* **345**(9), 656–661. [Full text]
6. Baumer, J.H. and Paediatric Accident and Emergency Research Group (2004) Evidence based guideline for post-seizure management in children presenting acutely to secondary care. *Archives of Disease in Childhood* **89**(3), 278–280.
7. Baumer, J.H., David, T.J., Valentine, S.J. et al (1981) Many parents think their child is dying when having a first febrile convulsion. *Developmental Medicine & Child Neurology* **23**(4), 462–464.
8. Berg, A.T., Shinnar, S., Levy, S.R. and Testa, F.M. (1999) Childhood-onset epilepsy with and without preceding febrile seizures. *Neurology* **53**(8), 1742–1748.
9. Centre for Reviews and Dissemination (2004) Diagnosing urinary tract infection (UTI) in the under fives. *Effective Health Care Bulletin* 8(6), 1–12.
10. Fukuyama, Y., Seki, T., Ohtsuka, C. et al (1996) Practical guidelines for physicians in the management of febrile seizures. *Brain and Development* **18**(6), 479–484.
11. Gordon, K.E., Dooley, J.M., Camfield, P.R. et al (2001) Treatment of febrile seizures: the influence of treatment efficacy and side-effect profile on value to parents. *Pediatrics* **108**(5), 1080–1088. [Full text]
12. Huang, M.C. (2001) Parental concerns for the child with febrile convulsion: long-term effects of educational interventions. *Acta Neurologica Scandinavica* **103**(5), 288–293.
13. Huang, M.C., Liu, C.C., Huang, C.C. and Thomas, K. (2002) Parental responses to first and recurrent febrile convulsions. *Acta Neurologica Scandinavica* **105**(4), 293–299.
14. Knudsen, F.U. (1996) Febrile seizures – treatment and outcome. *Brain and Development* **18**(6), 438–449.
15. Masuko, A.H., Castro, A.A., Santos, G.R. et al (2003) Intermittent diazepam and continuous phenobarbital to treat recurrence of febrile seizures: a systematic review with meta-analysis. *Arquivos de Neuro-Psiquiatria* **61**(4), 897–901.
16. Meremikwu, M. and Oyo-Ita, A. (2003) *Physical methods for treating fever in children (Cochrane Review)*. The Cochrane Library. Issue 2. Chichester, UK: John Wiley & Sons, Ltd. www.nelh.nhs.uk/cochrane.asp [Accessed: 01/12/2004]. [Full text]
17. Offringa, M. and Moyer, V.A. (2001) Evidence based paediatrics: Evidence based management of seizures associated with fever. *British Medical Journal* **323**(7321), 1111–1114. [Full text]
18. Parmar, R.C., Sahu, D.R. and Bavdekar, S.B. (2001) Knowledge, attitude and practices of parents of children with febrile con vulsion. *Journal of Postgraduate Medicine* **47**(1), 19–23.
19. Royal College of Physicians and the British Paediatric Association (1991) Guidelines for the management of convulsions with fever. *British Medical Journal* **303**(6803), 634–636.
20. Smith, M.C. (1994) Febrile seizures. Recognition and management. *Drugs* **47**(6), 933–944.
21. Stenklyft, P.H. and Carmona, M. (1994) Febrile seizures. *Emergency Medicine Clinics of North America* **12**(4), 989–999.
22. Stern, C. (2005) *Personal communication. The mechanisms of febrile convulsions*. Consultant in Neurology, St. Thomas' Hospital: London.
23. Trainor, J.L., Hampers, L.C., Krug, S.E. and Listernick, R. (2001) Children with first-time simple febrile seizures are at low risk of serious bacterial illness. *Academic Emergency Medicine* 8(8), 781–787. [Full text]
24. Verity, C.M., Greenwood, R. and Golding, J. (1998) Long-term intellectual and behavioral outcomes of children with febrile convulsions. *New England Journal of Medicine* 338(24), 1723–1728. [Full text]
25. Verrier-Jones, K. (2005) *Personal communication. Diagnosis of urinary tract infection in children presenting with a febrile convulsion*. Reader in Child Health, University of Cardiff: Cardiff, UK.
26. Verrotti, A., Latini, G., di Corcia, G. et al (2004) Intermittent oral diazepam prophylaxis in febrile convulsions: its effectiveness for febrile seizure recurrence. *European Journal of Paediatric Neurology* 8(3), 131–134.

27. Vestergaard, M., Hviid, A., Madsen, K.M. et al (2004) MMR vaccination and febrile seizures: Evaluation of susceptible subgroups and long-term prognosis. *Journal of the American Medical Association* **292**(3), 351–357. [Full text]
28. Warden, C.R., Zibulewsky, J., Mace, S. et al (2003) Evaluation and management of febrile seizures in the out-of-hospital and emergency department settings. *Annals of Emergency Medicine* **41**(2), 215–222.
29. Waruiru, C. and Appleton, R. (2004) Febrile seizures: an update. *Archives of Disease in Childhood* **89**(8), 751–756.
30. Watts, R., Robertson, J. and Thomas, G. (2003) Nursing management of fever in children: a systematic review. *International Journal of Nursing Practice* **9**(1), S1-S8.

F

PRODIGY GUIDANCE

Fungal (dermatophyte) infections — skin and nails

Last revised in February 2003
www.guidance.prodigy.nhs.uk/guidance.asp?gt=Fungal - skin and nails

Applies to people over the age of 2 months

This guidance covers fungal dermatophyte infections of the skin, nails, and scalp.

This guidance does not cover the management of patients with *Candida* infection of the skin and nail folds (paronychia) with or without nail involvement. It also does not cover the management of oral or systemic candidiasis, nappy rash, erythrasma, pityriasis versicolor, bacterial skin infections, or candidal balanitis.

There is separate PRODIGY guidance for *Candida — skin and nails.*

F

Goals

- To relieve itchiness and irritation due to infection
- To prevent spread of fungal infections
- To reduce scarring and loss of hair resulting from scalp ringworm
- To manage fungal nail infection appropriately, identifying those people who require no treatment and those who would benefit from oral antifungal therapy
- To improve the cosmetic appearance of nails
- To reduce severe sequelae and secondary bacterial infection in those with compromised circulation or sensation, such as in diabetic neuropathy

Contents

Scenarios

- Skin — ringworm p.791
- Skin — athlete's foot p.792
- Skin — fungal groin infection p.794
- Scalp — ringworm p.795
- Nails — fungal infection p.796

Extended Information, p. 797

Which scenario?

- **Skin — ringworm:** covers the management of fungal skin infection (tinea corporis).
- **Skin — athlete's foot:** covers the management of athlete's foot (tinea pedis).
- **Skin — fungal groin infection:** covers the management of fungal groin infection (tinea cruris).
- **Scalp — ringworm:** covers the management of fungal infection of the scalp (tinea capitis).
- **Nails — fungal infection:** covers the management of dermatophyte nail infection (tinea ungium or onychomycosis).

Note: *Candida* skin and nail infections are covered in the PRODIGY guidance *Candida — skin and nails.*

Skin — ringworm

Which therapy?

- **Send skin scrapings samples to the laboratory before starting treatment.**
- Treatment should not be delayed while waiting for mycology results.
- **Topical treatment with an imidazole or terbinafine is recommended.** They are similarly effective. (Imidazoles include clotrimazole, econazole, ketoconazole, miconazole, and sulconazole.)
  - **Imidazoles:** treat for 2–4 weeks to *clear* the lesions.
  - **Terbinafine** (adults only): treat for 1 week to *clear* the lesions.
  - **Topical clotrimazole is recommended if pregnant or breastfeeding** (topical terbinafine should not be used).
- Exclusion from school is unnecessary, once treatment has been established.
- **Continue treatment for 1–2 weeks after the skin has healed.**
- Combining a topical antifungal agent with corticosteroid preparations is usually unnecessary. Consider if the infection is particularly inflamed and irritated.
- **Oral treatments are not recommended unless** the skin is widely affected or there is severe, non-resolving infection.

Practical prescribing points

For further information please see the *Medicines Compendium* (www.medicines.org.uk) or the *British National Formulary* (www.bnf.org).

Should I refer or investigate?

Refer?

- **Referral is rarely necessary,** unless the appearance is unusual or the diagnosis is unclear.
- Seek specialist advice if there is no response to treatment or if infection is severe (oral treatment may be advised).
- **Where infection is occurring in schools,** it may be necessary to involve the local Consultant in Communicable Disease Control.

Investigate?

- **Skin-scraping samples should be collected and sent to the laboratory before starting treatment.** All samples should be put onto black card so that the material is easily visible.
- **If culture indicates that the source is an animal,** advise the family to investigate pets (with help from the vet, if necessary).
- **If culture indicates a human source,** family members and school friends should be examined for signs of ringworm and investigated if appropriate. Note: clinical symptoms may be minimal.

Patient information leaflets

The following PILs are available at www.prodigy.nhs.uk

- Antibiotics - Why No Antibiotic?
- Ringworm (Fungal Rash)

Shared decision making

- **An antifungal cream** will usually clear ringworm. You can buy one from a pharmacy, or get one on prescription.
- **When using the cream:**
  - Apply it to the surrounding 4–6 cm of normal skin in addition to the rash itself.
  - Apply it for a further 1–2 weeks after the rash has gone.
- **Antifungal tablets** are sometimes needed if the infection is widespread.
- **Sometimes the infection comes from a pet.** If you suspect this, check other family members for the rash.
- **Children do not need to stay off school once treatment has started.**

F

Drug rationale

Drugs not included

- **Oral (systemic) treatment** is only indicated in severe, extensive skin infection, or in the rare patient who is unresponsive to topical treatment. Specialist assessment should usually be considered in such cases.
- **Amorolfine cream** is not offered. There is insufficient data comparing it to topical imidazoles.
- **Nystatin** is not effective against dermatophyte skin infections.
- **Topical combination products containing an antifungal plus a corticosteroid** are usually unnecessary. However they are an option if the infection is particularly inflamed and irritated.

Drugs included

- **Imidazole creams** are effective against dermatophytes. All the imidazoles currently available (clotrimazole, econazole, ketoconazole, miconazole, and sulconazole) are included, as there is little evidence of difference between them. Product selection will depend on the area to be treated and prescriber/user preference.
- **Terbinafine cream** appears to be similarly effective to imidazoles in achieving mycological and symptom cure against dermatophytes.

Prescriptions

Topical imidazoles

Clotrimazole 1% cream

- Age from 2 months onwards
- Clotrimazole 1% cream. Apply to the affected area and the surrounding skin two to three times a day; supply 50 grams; NHS Cost £3.80; OTC Cost £7.99.

Econazole 1% cream

- Age from 2 months onwards
- Econazole 1% cream. Apply to the affected area and the surrounding skin twice a day; supply 30 grams; NHS Cost £2.75; OTC Cost £2.46.

Ketoconazole 2% cream

- Age from 2 months onwards
- Ketoconazole 2% cream. Apply to the affected area and the surrounding skin twice a day; supply 30 grams; NHS Cost £3.81.

Miconazole 2% cream

- Age from 2 months onwards
- Miconazole 2% cream. Apply to the affected area and the surrounding skin twice a day; supply 30 grams; NHS Cost £2.12; OTC Cost £3.65.

Sulconazole 1% cream

- Age from 2 months onwards
- Sulconazole 1% cream. Apply to the affected area and the surrounding skin twice a day; supply 30 grams; NHS Cost £3.00; OTC Cost £5.29.

Topical terbinafine

Terbinafine 1% cream

- Age from 12 years onwards
- Terbinafine 1% cream. Apply thinly to the affected area and the surrounding skin twice a day for 7 days; supply 15 grams; NHS Cost £4.86; OTC Cost £9.98.

Skin — athlete's foot

Which therapy?

- **Offer advice on hygiene measures** and the risks of passing on infection (see Patient Information Leaflet). In particular:
  - There is no need to avoid school or sports.
  - Feet should be covered in communal changing areas.
- **Treat with a topical imidazole, undecenoates, or terbinafine.** (Imidazoles include clotrimazole, econazole, ketoconazole, miconazole, and sulconazole.)
  - **Imidazoles:** treat for 2–4 weeks to *clear* the lesions.
  - **Terbinafine** (adults only): treat for 1 week to *clear* the lesions.
  - **Undecenoates** (adults only): treat for 2–4 weeks to *clear* the lesions.
  - **Topical clotrimazole is recommended if pregnant or breastfeeding** (oral and topical terbinafine should not be used).
- **Continue treatment for 1–2 weeks after the skin has healed.**
- Combining a topical antifungal agent with corticosteroid preparations is usually unnecessary. Consider doing this if the infection is particularly inflamed and irritated.
- **Consider oral terbinafine if there is:**
  - Moccasin pattern tinea pedis
  - Severe or non-resolving infection
  - Associated nail infection (see scenario *Fungal infection — nails*)
- **Send skin scrapings samples to the laboratory before starting oral treatment** — treatment can be started while waiting for results. Stop if results do not confirm the diagnosis.

Practical prescribing points

For further information please see the *Medicines Compendium* (www.medicines.org.uk) or the *British National Formulary* (www.bnf.org).

Oral terbinafine

- **Severe liver reactions have been reported with oral terbinafine use.**
- **Terbinafine can affect taste,** which may be an unsatisfactory adverse effect in some patients.

Should I refer or investigate?

Refer?

- Referral is rarely necessary for athlete's foot.
- Seek specialist advice if there is no response to treatment.

Investigate?

- Investigation is rarely necessary for athlete's foot.

Patient information leaflets

The following PILs are available at www.prodigy.nhs.uk

- Antifungal Medicines
- Athlete's Foot (Tinea Pedis)

Shared decision making

- **An antifungal cream** will usually clear athlete's foot. You can buy one from a pharmacy, or get one on prescription.
- **When using the cream:**
  - Apply to the surrounding 4–6 cm of normal skin in addition to the rash.
  - Apply for a further 1–2 weeks after the rash has gone.
- **You do not need to stay away from school or sports.** Try to keep your feet covered in communal changing areas until the rash is gone.
- **Antifungal tablets** may be needed if a nail becomes infected too, or if the infection is severe.
- **To prevent athlete's foot recurring:**
  - Wash your feet and toes daily, and dry them thoroughly.
  - Do not share towels in communal changing rooms. Wash towels often.
  - Change your socks daily. Cotton socks are best.

Drug rationale

Drugs not included

- **Nystatin** is not effective against dermatophyte skin infections.
- **Antiperspirant dusting powders** require further evidence of effectiveness before they can be included as treatment options. They may have a role in preventing infection.
- **Amorolfine cream** is available for the treatment of fungal skin infections, but there is insufficient data to support its routine use in the management of athlete's foot.
- **Topical combination products containing an antifungal plus a corticosteroid** are usually unnecessary. However they are an option if the infection is particularly inflamed and irritated.
- **Oral griseofulvin** is no longer a first-line treatment for athlete's foot, groin fungal infection, and skin ringworm because it is no longer available in the UK as a licensed product. Note: griseofulvin tablets can be imported on a named-patient basis, or alternatively griseofulvin suspension (available from Specials Manufacturer's) can be used.

Drugs included

- **Imidazole creams** are effective against dermatophytes. All the imidazoles currently available (clotrimazole, econazole, ketoconazole, miconazole, and sulconazole) are included, as there is little evidence of difference between them. Product selection will depend on the area to be treated and prescriber/user preference.
- **Terbinafine cream** appears to be similarly effective to imidazoles in achieving mycological and symptom cure against dermatophytes. It is not licensed for use in children.
- **Undecenoate cream** has demonstrated a greater reduction in treatment failure when trialled against a placebo. However, relative efficacy has only been assessed between topical imidazoles and topical terbinafine. It is not licensed for use in children.
- **Oral terbinafine** (systemic treatment) is offered for mycologically proven moccasin pattern tinea pedis; severe, extensive skin infection; or in the rare patient unresponsive to topical treatment. Specialist assessment should usually be considered in the latter cases. Note: it is not licensed for use in children.

Prescriptions

Topical imidazoles

Clotrimazole 1% cream

- Age from 2 months onwards
- Clotrimazole 1% cream. Apply to the affected area and the surrounding skin two to three times a day; supply 50 grams; NHS Cost £3.80; OTC Cost £7.99.

Econazole 1% cream

- Age from 2 months onwards
- Econazole 1% cream. Apply to the affected area and the surrounding skin twice a day; supply 30 grams; NHS Cost £2.75; OTC Cost £2.46.

Ketoconazole 2% cream

- Age from 2 months onwards
- Ketoconazole 2% cream. Apply to the affected area and the surrounding skin twice a day; supply 30 grams; NHS Cost £3.81.

Miconazole 2% cream

- Age from 2 months onwards
- Miconazole 2% cream. Apply to the affected area and the surrounding skin twice a day; supply 30 grams; NHS Cost £2.12; OTC Cost £3.65.

Sulconazole 1% cream

- Age from 2 months onwards
- Sulconazole 1% cream. Apply to the affected area and the surrounding skin twice a day; supply 30 grams; NHS Cost £3.00; OTC Cost £5.29.

Topical terbinafine

Terbinafine 1% cream

- Age from 12 years onwards
- Terbinafine 1% 30g. Apply thinly to the affected area and the surrounding skin twice a day for 7 days; supply 30 grams; NHS Cost £9.72; OTC Cost £19.96.

Topical undecenoates

Zinc undecenoate 20% + undecenoic acid 5% cream

- Age from 12 years onwards
- Mycota cream. Apply to the affected area and the surrounding skin twice a day; supply 50 grams; NHS Cost £2.34; OTC Cost £4.10.

Oral terbinafine (only if moccasin pattern or severe)

Terbinafine tablets: 250mg once a day for 2 weeks

- Age from 12 years onwards
- Terbinafine 250mg tablets. Take one tablet once a day for 2 weeks; supply 14 tablets; NHS Cost £23.00.

Terbinafine tablets: 250mg once a day for 4 weeks

- Age from 12 years onwards
- Terbinafine 250mg tablets. Take one tablet once a day for 4 weeks; supply 28 tablets; NHS Cost £44.66.

Terbinafine tablets: 250mg once a day for 6 weeks

- Age from 12 years onwards
- Terbinafine 250mg tablets. Take one tablet once a day for 6 weeks; supply 42 tablets; NHS Cost £67.82.

Skin — fungal groin infection

Which therapy?

- **Offer advice on hygiene measures** and the risks of passing on infection (see Patient Information Leaflet).
- **Treat with a topical imidazole or terbinafine.** They are similarly effective. (Imidazoles include clotrimazole, econazole, ketoconazole, miconazole, and sulconazole.)
  - **Imidazoles:** treat for 2–4 weeks to *clear* the lesions.
  - **Terbinafine** (adults only): treat for 1 week to *clear* the lesions.
  - **Topical clotrimazole is recommended if pregnant or breastfeeding** (topical terbinafine should not be used).
- **Continue treatment for 1–2 weeks after the skin has healed.**
- Combining topical antifungal agent with corticosteroid preparations is usually unnecessary. Consider doing this if the infection is particularly inflamed and irritated.
- Oral treatments are not recommended unless there is severe, non-resolving infection.
- **Treat any associated athlete's foot similarly.**

F

Practical prescribing points

For further information please see the *Medicines Compendium* (www.medicines.org.uk) or the *British National Formulary* (www.bnf.org).

Should I refer or investigate?

Refer?

- Referral is rarely necessary for fungal groin infection.
- Seek specialist advice if there is no response to treatment, or if the infection is severe (oral treatment may be advised).

Investigate?

- Investigation is rarely necessary for fungal groin infection.

Patient information leaflets

The following PILs are available at www.prodigy.nhs.uk

- Antifungal Medicines
- Tinea Cruris

Shared decision making

- **An antifungal cream** will usually clear a fungal rash in the groin. You can buy one from a pharmacy, or get one on prescription.
- **When using the cream:**
  - Apply to the surrounding 4–6 cm of normal skin in addition to the rash.
  - Apply for 1–2 weeks after the rash has gone.
- **An antifungal medicine** taken by mouth is sometimes needed if the infection is widespread or severe.
- **To prevent this rash recurring:**
  - Wash your groin daily, then dry it thoroughly (a hairdryer may help).
  - Change your underwear daily.
  - Check for athlete's foot (fungi from toes may spread to the groin).
  - Do not share towels in communal changing rooms. Wash towels often.

Drug rationale

Drugs not included

- **Oral (systemic) treatment** is indicated only in severe, extensive skin infection, or in the rare patient who is unresponsive to topical treatment. Specialist assessment should usually be considered in such cases.
- **Nystatin** is not effective against dermatophyte skin infections.
- **Antiperspirant dusting powders** require further evidence of effectiveness before they can be included as treatment options. They may have a role in preventing infection.
- **Topical combination products containing an antifungal plus a corticosteroid** are usually unnecessary. However they are an option if the infection is particularly inflamed and irritated.

Drugs included

- **Imidazole creams** are effective against dermatophytes. All the imidazoles currently available (clotrimazole, econazole, ketoconazole, miconazole, and sulconazole) are included, as there is little evidence of difference between them. Product selection will depend on the area to be treated and prescriber/user preference.
- **Terbinafine cream** appears to be similarly effective to imidazoles in achieving mycological and symptom cure against dermatophytes.

Prescriptions

Topical imidazoles

Clotrimazole 1% cream

- Age from 2 months onwards
- Clotrimazole 1% cream. Apply to the affected area and the surrounding skin two to three times a day; supply 50 grams; NHS Cost £3.80; OTC Cost £7.99.

Econazole 1% cream

- Age from 2 months onwards
- Econazole 1% cream. Apply to the affected area and the surrounding skin twice a day; supply 30 grams; NHS Cost £2.75; OTC Cost £2.46.

Miconazole 2% cream

- Age from 2 months onwards
- Miconazole 2% cream. Apply to the affected area and the surrounding skin twice a day; supply 30 grams; NHS Cost £2.12; OTC Cost £3.65.

Ketoconazole 2% cream

- Age from 2 months onwards
- Ketoconazole 2% cream. Apply to the affected area and the surrounding skin twice a day; supply 30 grams; NHS Cost £3.81.

Sulconazole 1% cream

- Age from 2 months onwards
- Sulconazole 1% cream. Apply to the affected area and the surrounding skin twice a day; supply 30 grams; NHS Cost £3.00; OTC Cost £5.29.

Topical terbinafine

Terbinafine 1% cream

- Age from 12 years onwards
- Terbinafine 1% cream. Apply thinly to the affected area and the surrounding skin twice a day for 7 days; supply 15 grams; NHS Cost £4.86; OTC Cost £9.98.

Scalp — ringworm

Which therapy?

- **Send samples for culture in all suspected cases.**
- Treatment for scalp ringworm should not be delayed while waiting for mycology results.
- **Oral terbinafine (off-licence use) or griseofulvin (unlicensed product) is recommended.**
  - **Terbinafine:** treat for 2–4 weeks.
  - **Griseofulvin:** treat for 8–10 weeks (usually). The optimal duration of treatment depends on the infecting fungal type.
- **Seek specialist advice for women who are pregnant or breastfeeding.** Terbinafine and griseofulvin should not be used.
- **Weigh children to determine the appropriate daily dose** (see *Prescribing points*).
- **Consider selenium shampoo or povidone-iodine shampoo** (used twice weekly) to reduce the risk of spread to others.
- **Kerions can be soaked and their crusts removed;** this may be soothing.
- Exclusion from school is unnecessary, once oral treatment has been established.

Practical prescribing points

For further information, please see the *Medicines Compendium* (www.medicines.org.uk) or the *British National Formulary* (www.bnf.org).

Oral terbinafine

- **Severe liver reactions have been reported with terbinafine use.**
- **Terbinafine can affect taste,** which may be an unsatisfactory adverse effect in some patients.
- Terbinafine is not licensed for the treatment of scalp ringworm and there are no licensed doses for children. The following are suggested dosage regimes for children over 2 years old: bodyweight 10–20 kg, 62.5 mg once per day; bodyweight 21–40 kg, 125 mg once per day; bodyweight over 40 kg, 250 mg once per day.

Oral griseofulvin

- **Oral griseofulvin is no longer available in the UK as a licensed product.** However, griseofulvin tablets can be imported on a named-patient basis, or alternatively griseofulvin suspension (available from Specials Manufacturer's) can be used.
- The recommended dose for children over 1 month of age is 10 mg/kg once a day, or 5 mg/kg twice a day. For adults and children over the age of 12 years, use 500 mg once a day or 250–500 mg twice a day.
- **Men should not father a child within 6 months of treatment.**
- **Griseofulvin can reduce the effectiveness of both combined and progestogen-only oral contraceptives.**
- Griseofulvin may impair performance of skilled tasks (e.g. driving); effects of alcohol are enhanced.

Should I refer or investigate?

Refer?

- **Dermatology referral is not recommended unless the** response to treatment is poor, the diagnosis is difficult, or the infection recurs.
- Seek specialist advice for treatment options during pregnancy and breastfeeding.
- **Where infection is occurring in schools,** it may be necessary to involve the local Consultant in Communicable Disease Control.

Investigate?

- **Samples should be collected and sent to the laboratory before starting treatment.**
- **Scale and plucked hairs** are suitable samples. *Cut hair is of no value.* Scrape the affected area with a scalpel or glass slide, and ensure that some complete or broken-off hairs are included for culture. All samples should be put onto black card so that the material is easily visible.
- **In children, specimens can also be obtained using a scalp-massage brush.** The scalp is brushed 10 times and the contaminated brush sent off for analysis. Local laboratories may provide information on the availability of scalp-massage brushes.
- **If culture indicates that the source is an animal,** advise the family to investigate pets (with help from the vet, if necessary).
- **If culture indicates a human source,** family members and school friends should be examined for signs of ringworm and investigated if appropriate. Note: clinical symptoms may be minimal.

Patient information leaflets

The following PILs are available at www.prodigy.nhs.uk

- Antifungal Medicines
- Ringworm of the Scalp

Shared decision making

- **Antifungal** medication (terbinafine or griseofulvin) taken by mouth will usually clear a fungal infection of the scalp.
  - 8–10 weeks of treatment is usually needed.
  - You should not take antifungals if you are pregnant.
  - Men should not father a child within 6 months of treatment with griseofulvin.
  - **Side effects are uncommon,** but include rashes and feeling sick.
- **Selenium shampoo, or povidone-iodine shampoo** used twice weekly may be advised in addition. This reduces the risk of spreading the infection to others.
- **Sometimes the infection comes from a family pet.** If you suspect this, check other family members for scalp or skin rashes. The family pet may need to be checked by a vet.
- **Children do not need to stay off school once treatment has started.**

Drug rationale

Drugs not included

- **Topical antifungal preparations used as sole therapy** are not appropriate for the treatment of ringworm on the scalp [Higgins et al, 2000].
- **Oral antifungals other than griseofulvin or terbinafine** are not offered, as they are not licensed for use in children and there is insufficient data to recommend their use in adults.

Drugs included

- **Terbinafine** (off-licence) is offered. Shorter treatment courses are required than with griseofulvin therapy. The following are suggested dosage regimes for children over 2 years old: bodyweight 10–20 kg, 62.5 mg once per day, bodyweight 21–40 kg, 125 mg once per day; bodyweight over 40 kg, 250 mg once per day.

F

- **Griseofulvin (unlicensed)** is no longer available in the UK as a licensed product. However, griseofulvin tablets can be imported on a named-patient basis, or alternatively griseofulvin suspension (available from Specials Manufacturer's) can be used. The optimal duration of treatment depends on the infecting fungal type. For most infections, 8–10 weeks' treatment will suffice.

Prescriptions

Oral terbinafine (off-licence use)

Terbinafine tablets: 250mg once a day
- Age from 12 years onwards
- Terbinafine 250mg tablets. Take one tablet once a day; supply 14 tablets; NHS Cost £23.16.

F

Child weighs 10-20kg: terbinafine 62.5mg once a day
- Age from 12 months to 10 years
- Terbinafine 250mg tablets. *WEIGHT REQUIRED* Take a quarter of a tablet ONCE a day; supply 14 tablets; NHS Cost £23.16.

Child weighs 21-40kg: terbinafine 125mg once a day
- Age from 5 to 11 years
- Terbinafine 250mg tablets. *WEIGHT REQUIRED* Take a half a tablet ONCE a day; supply 14 tablets; NHS Cost £23.16.

Child weighs 41kg or more: terbinafine 250mg once a day
- Age from 8 to 11 years
- Terbinafine 250mg tablets. *WEIGHT REQUIRED* Take one tablet once a day; supply 14 tablets; NHS Cost £23.16.

Oral griseofulvin (unlicensed)

Griseofulvin suspension: prescribe by body-weight
- Age from 2 months to 11 years
- Griseofulvin suspension is available from 'Specials manufacturers'. The strength of the formulation is made to order. Weigh the child and prescribe a daily dose of 10mg per kg bodyweight. The dose may be administered once a day or in divided doses. Treatment needs to be taken for 8-10 weeks.

Griseofulvin tablets: 500mg once a day
- Age from 12 years onwards
- Griseofulvin 500mg tablets. Take one tablet once a day; supply 28 tablets; NHS Cost £2.62.

Griseofulvin tablets: 250mg twice a day
- Age from 12 years onwards
- Griseofulvin 125mg tablets. Take two tablets twice a day; supply 112 tablets; NHS Cost £2.80.

Griseofulvin tablets: 500mg twice a day
- Age from 12 years onwards
- Griseofulvin 500mg tablets. Take one tablet twice a day; supply 56 tablets; NHS Cost £5.24.

Topical antifungal shampoo

Povidone-iodine 4% shampoo
- Age from 2 years onwards
- Povidone-iodine 4% shampoo. Shampoo the scalp twice a week for 4 weeks; supply 250 ml; NHS Cost £2.32; OTC Cost £4.10.

Selenium sulphide 2.5% shampoo
- Age from 5 years onwards
- Selenium sulphide 2.5% shampoo. Shampoo the scalp twice a week for 4 weeks; supply 50 ml; NHS Cost £1.44; OTC Cost £2.50.

Nails — fungal infection

Which therapy?

- **Consider whether investigation/treatment is appropriate**
  - Treatment may not be needed if it is a long-standing fungal infection of the toenails (change in appearance only). Consider possible complications of systemic therapy against benefits of treatment.
  - But, investigate/treat people with diabetes or peripheral vascular disease to avoid complications.
- **Start treatment only when the results of mycological examination are available.** A positive microscopy result, where hyphae are seen, is an indication for starting treatment before culture results.
- For the treatment of *Candida* infections, see separate PRODIGY guidance for *Candida — skin and nails.*
- **Oral terbinafine is recommended for dermatophyte nail infections.**
  - **Infection of fingernails** requires oral terbinafine for between 6 weeks and 3 months.
  - **Toenail infection** requires treatment for 3 months, occasionally up to 6 months.
- **Oral itraconazole is an alternative (usually taken for 2–3 months):**
  - When terbinafine is not tolerated.
  - If mixed infection with *Candida* is found on mycology
  - For severe nail disease in immunocompromised patients (longer courses may be needed).
- **Seek specialist advice for women who are pregnant or breastfeeding.** Terbinafine and itraconazole should not be used.

Practical prescribing points

For further information, please see the *Medicines Compendium* (www.medicines.org.uk) or the *British National Formulary* (www.bnf.org).

Oral terbinafine

- **Severe liver reactions have been reported with terbinafine use.**
- **Terbinafine can affect taste,** which may be an unsatisfactory adverse effect in some patients.

Oral itraconazole

- The anticoagulant effect of warfarin may be enhanced by oral itraconazole.
- **Do not give itraconazole to patients at high risk of heart failure.** Those at highest risk are the elderly, patients taking high doses or receiving longer treatment courses, patients with cardiac disease, and patients taking negative inotropic drugs.
- **Liver function tests are recommended if there is a history of liver disease or if treatment is to exceed 1 month.** Tests should also be undertaken if anorexia, nausea, vomiting, fatigue, abdominal pain, or dark urine develops.

Follow-up advice

- **If still taking treatment at 3 months, consider a repeat culture.** A positive culture at this stage would indicate that a longer course was required.

Should I refer or investigate?

Refer?

Referral is rarely necessary.
Seek specialist advice if there is no response to treatment or for treatment options during pregnancy and breastfeeding.

Investigate?

Mycological investigation is necessary before starting treatment.
Nail clippings and subungual debris are required.

- Proximal samples are preferable.
- Nail clippings taken with 'heavy-duty' chiropodist toenail clippers may be necessary for thick toenails.
- All samples should be put onto black card so that the material is easily visible.

Patient information leaflets

The following PILs are available at www.prodigy.nhs.uk
Antifungal Medicines
Nail Infection - Fungal

Shared decision making

Not treating a fungal nail infection is an option if it is mild.
Antifungal tablets usually work well, but the course of treatment is at least 6–12 weeks, and may be longer.

- Terbinafine clears the infection in up to 19 in 20 cases.
- Itraconazole clears the infection in up to 16 in 20 cases; but you can take this *one week on, three weeks off*. It may also be the best treatment if *Candida* is causing the infection.

Tablets will also clear any associated athlete's foot.
Antifungal nail paint does not work as well as tablets do. It is an option if the infection does not involve the skin around the nail. In this situation it works in up to half of cases, with 6–12 months of treatment.
To prevent further nail infection, treat athlete's foot as early as possible.

Drug rationale

Drugs not included

Topical antifungal agents are inappropriate for the treatment of fungal nail infections. Topical applications of amorolfine or itraconazole have demonstrated effectiveness in the treatment of early distal onychomycosis involving only one or two nails.
Oral griseofulvin is not offered. Griseofulvin has proven effectiveness in fingernail fungal infection, but requires longer treatment periods than do terbinafine or itraconazole. Treatment of fungal toenail infection with griseofulvin has been less successful.

Drugs included

Oral terbinafine is offered as first-line treatment in the treatment of mycologically proven fungal nail infection. Infection of fingernails requires oral terbinafine for between 6 weeks and 3 months. Toenail infection requires treatment for 3 months, occasionally up to 6 months.
Oral itraconazole is offered as an alternative first line treatment for people unable to tolerate terbinafine. Oral itraconazole has not demonstrated cure rates that are as good as those for terbinafine, but it may be useful in people with severe immunosuppression who have suspected counter-infection with yeasts. Itraconazole prescriptions are offered for once-a-day continuous therapy or twice-a-day intermittent therapy. Both regimens appear similarly effective, and the choice should be guided by the person with the infection.

Prescriptions

Oral terbinafine

Terbinafine tablets: 250mg once a day

- Age from 12 years onwards
- Terbinafine 250mg tablets. Take one tablet once a day; supply 28 tablets; NHS Cost £44.66.

Oral itraconazole

Continuous therapy: itraconazole 200mg once a day

- Age from 12 years onwards
- Itraconazole 100mg capsules. Take two capsules once a day; supply 56 capsules; NHS Cost £58.80.

Pulse therapy: itraconazole 200mg twice a day for 7 days

- Age from 12 years onwards
- Itraconazole 100mg capsules. Take two capsules twice a day for 7 days. Repeat the course after a 21-day break; supply 28 capsules; NHS Cost £29.35.

Extended Information

Background information

- What is it? p.797
- How common is it? p.798
- How do I know my patient has it? p.798
- What else might it be? p.798
- Complications and prognosis p.799

What is it?

- **The important causative agents** in fungal skin infections are the dermatophyte fungi (*Trichophyton*, *Microsporum*, and *Epidermophyton* species) and yeasts.
- **Dermatophytes are responsible for 90% of fungal infections of the skin, hair, and nails** [Higgins et al, 2000].
- **Superficial dermatophyte infection may occur at different sites:**
  - **Athlete's foot** (also known as tinea pedis), commonly affecting the interdigital space of the fourth and fifth toes, and possibly spreading to the skin of the plantar surface of the foot or the dorsum and between other toes.
  - **Moccasin-type athlete's foot.**
  - **Fungal infection of the groin and genital area** (also known as tinea cruris or 'jock itch').
  - **Ringworm of the skin** (also known as tinea corporis).
  - **Scalp ringworm** (also known as tinea capitis).
  - **Fungal infections of the nail** (also known as tinea ungium or onychomycosis).
- **About 5% of cases of fungal nail infections are due to non-dermatophyte moulds,** such as *Scopulariopsis*, which almost exclusively affect nails and which may not respond to conventional therapy.
- **Yeast species** (*Malassezia furfur* and *Candida*) typically affect the mucous membranes, but may also be responsible for infection of the skin and nails. Candidal skin and nail infections are covered in separate PRODIGY guidance *Candida — skin and nails*.

How common is it?

- **Fungal foot infection** was identified in 17% of regular attendees at communal swimming baths in a survey in 1973. With increased use of communal sports facilities, it is likely that prevalence remains high in people sharing changing rooms for sports activity. The term 'athlete's foot' reflects the fact that infection is common in young people who use these facilities. The prevalence in the wider population is unknown; many people treat themselves, though the condition is a common reason for attending GP surgeries in the UK.
- **Fungal nail infection** is more frequently seen in toenails, rather than fingernails. In one survey it was identified in 2.7% of adults assessed and in 4.7% of those over the age of 55 years [Roberts et al, 1992]. Thirty-eight percent of those with infection had not sought advice for the condition. Another estimate is that it occurs in 20-30% of people with athlete's foot, which would make the prevalence much higher [Denning et al, 1995]. Fungal nail infection is more common where there has been nail trauma or diabetes, with increasing age, and where there is athlete's foot.
- **Fungal infection of the groin area is a common infection seen in younger people,** particularly if they are frequently involved in sweaty activity (hence the expression 'jock itch'). It is most common in men, and often seen in association with athlete's foot.
- **Ringworm of the skin,** or tinea corporis, is a relatively common infection, usually caught from animals such as dogs, cats, and cattle, but it can also be caught from humans.
- **Ringworm of the scalp occurs most commonly in children.**
  - Until recently it was commonly caused by zoophilic fungi, spread from cats or dogs, or more rarely cattle.
  - It has increased in prevalence over the last two decades, owing to increasing infection from human spread. It is sometimes found as epidemics in inner-city schools. It particularly affects those of Afro-Caribbean origin. The reason for this change is unknown.

How do I know my patient has it?

History and examination

- **Athlete's foot (tinea pedis)** is a cutaneous fungal infection that causes the skin to itch, flake, and fissure. It commonly affects the interdigital space of the fourth and fifth toes. It may spread to the skin of the plantar surface of the foot, the dorsum of the foot, and between other toes.
- **Moccasin-type athlete's foot** (also known as dry-type), appears as a diffuse, somewhat thick, erythema and scaling over the entire sole (like a moccasin or slipper).
- **Fungal infection of the groin and genital area (also known as tinea cruris or 'jock itch')** causes an itchy rash affecting the groin creases. It is commonly associated with athlete's foot.
- **Ringworm of the skin (also known as tinea corporis)** occurs over flatter, exposed areas of skin, and the rash often has a raised circular shape. The rash typically begins as an erythematous raised area; as it spreads, the interior inflammation resolves, forming the ring-like shape. Sometimes several rings develop and merge. Swelling and blisters may also appear. Generalized rashes and scaling can also appear.
- **Scalp ringworm (also known as tinea capitis)** causes circular patchy hair loss (alopecia) with a scaly rash. Small spots of hair may remain in a random pattern in the bare areas. The lymph nodes in the back of the neck are often tender and swollen.
  - Infections with fungi of animal origin classically present as discrete, circular patches of hair loss with scaling, itching, and inflammation, and occasionally pustules.
  - Infections from fungi of human origin are difficult to diagnose by simple inspection. The inflammation and scaling are generally mild, often looking like localised dandruff, although pustules may still occur.
  - A more severe form of tinea capitis involves a mass called a kerion. The kerion is a large, oozing lesion. The person experiences pain, swelling, and sometimes fever. Without treatment, a kerion can leave permanent scarring and hair loss.
- **Fungal infections of the nail (also known as tinea ungium or onychomycosis)** is characterised by nail thickening and discolouration. The texture of the nail changes and the nail may be soft and easily broken. Often the adjacent skin is infected; if the skin is treated in isolation the nail can be the source of reinfection.

Investigations

- **Uncomplicated, typical athlete's foot and fungal infections in the groin area may justifiably be treated without microbiological investigation.**
- **For other conditions, diagnosis should ideally be confirmed by taking skin, hair, or nail samples for mycology.** The samples should be sent to the laboratory so that causative fungus can be identified by microscopy and culture. In more severe infections (e.g. moccasin or dry-type athlete's foot) or in situations where the diagnosis is suspected but not certain (e.g. nail or scalp disease), samples should always be obtained.
- Wood's light examination is often, erroneously, thought to be important — it is only useful as a screening test for scalp ringworm due to cat and dog species (*Trichophyton canis*).
- **Samples appropriate in nature and size must be sent to the laboratory.** All samples should be put onto black card so that the material is easily visible. Transport materials are available from most laboratories.
  - **For skin infections,** skin scale should be obtained.
  - **For scalp disease,** scale and, most importantly, plucked hairs are essential. Cut hair is of no value. Collect specimens by scraping the affected area with a scalpel or glass slide, ensuring that some complete or broken-off hairs are included for culture.
  - **Where scalp infection is suspected in children,** specimens can also be obtained using a scalp-massage brush. The scalp is brushed 10 times and the contaminated brush pressed into the surface of an agar-coated Petri dish, which is then incubated for up to 3 weeks.
  - **In the case of nail disease,** both nail clippings and subungual debris are required, with more proximal samples being ideal. 'Heavy-duty' chiropodist toenail clippers may be necessary for thick toenails.

What else might it be?

- **Athlete's foot** may resemble:
  - Gram-negative bacterial infection of the toe cleft
  - Erythrasma
  - Pustular psoriasis
  - Dermatitis
- **Ringworm of the skin** is similar to skin disease that produces discoid or annular lesions:
  - Psoriasis
  - Pitryasis rosea
  - Granuloma annulare
  - Annular erythemas
- **Ringworm of the scalp** can look similar to:
  - Seborrhoeic dermatitis of the scalp

- Atopic dermatitis affecting the scalp
- Psoriasis of the scalp
- Alopecia areata (patches of hair missing)
- Bacterial folliculitis (particularly difficult to distinguish from kerion)

Fungal nail infections often resemble other nail conditions:

- Nail after trauma.
- Psoriasis — yellow, friable nails with pitting and onycholysis (lifting of nail from nail-bed). Usually evidence of psoriasis is found elsewhere.
- Eczema — irregular pitted dystrophy of nail. Usually adjacent skin is eczematous.
- Onychogryposis — failure to cut toenails, with overgrowth and distortion. However, this condition may be complicated by fungal infection.
- Candidal skin and nail infection. This usually affects the fingers, and occurs in those who frequently get their hands wet. The infection usually occurs in the distal parts of the nail and is often associated with pus collecting around the nail (paronychia). Paronychia is rarely seen in other fungal infections. See separate PRODIGY guidance *Candida — skin and nails.*

Complications and prognosis

Itching and irritation, which may affect quality of life, occur in most fungal infections of the skin.

Infection may spread to other parts of the body or to other people. Fungal infections and lesions may persist, and recurrence is common. Lesions can also become secondarily infected.

Cosmetic problems may occur. The change in the appearance of the nail is considered unsightly and embarrassing by many of those with the condition.

Pain on walking may occur with toenail infections.

Immunocompromised patients with superficial fungal infection are at increased risk of the infection developing into an invasive form.

There is some evidence that those with peripheral vascular disease and diabetes may have more severe problems related to fungal infections; particularly as cracked skin may act as a portal for severe bacterial infection. Also, peripheral neuropathy and sensory loss may lead to increased trauma in diabetic patients. Vascular insufficiency may compound this further and lead to serious sequelae.

Scarring and permanent hair loss may occur in severe scalp ringworm infection.

Management issues

Athlete's foot, groin infection, or ringworm of the skin p.799
Scalp ringworm p.800
Fungal infection of the nails p.800

Athlete's foot, groin infection, or ringworm of the skin

General measures

It is important to prevent infection if possible and to treat early disease whenever it is suspected.

Fungal groin infection is often found in association with athlete's foot, and similar general measures can be adopted to prevent infection and spread to others.

Ringworm infections are sometimes associated with contact with animals — cattle or household pets, such as cats and dogs. If infections in pets are suspected, veterinary inspection may be advised. In many instances there is no obvious source for the infection.

Hygiene measures

There is no need for people with fungal infection to avoid school or sports, but care should be taken to avoid transmission to others, by careful hygiene and by ensuring that appropriate treatment is being used.

- **Athlete's foot (tinea pedis).**
  - Use appropriate footwear in changing areas, use foot powders and sprays, and in particular clean and dry the feet properly.
  - Do not share towels in communal changing rooms and wash personal towels frequently.
  - Wash feet daily and dry them thoroughly, especially between the toes.
  - Minimize foot perspiration.
  - Avoid tight footwear, especially in summer.
  - Wear cotton socks that keep the feet dry. Change them frequently, especially if the feet tend to sweat heavily.
- **Groin infection (tinea cruris).**
  - Good hygiene helps to prevent infection.
  - Wash the groin area daily.
  - Be scrupulous about drying after bathing or showering.
  - Change underwear daily, as fungi may persist in skin debris.
  - Treat athlete's foot carefully. Avoid scratching at feet and groin.
  - Use one's own towels and wash them after use.
- **Ringworm of the skin (tinea corporis).**
  - Other children and adults in the family should be asked to look for signs of ringworm.

Treatment of athlete's foot, groin infection, or ringworm

- **Many people purchase topical treatments** (clotrimazole, econazole, ketoconazole, miconazole, and terbinafine) from a pharmacy for athlete's foot and fungal groin infection, without consulting a doctor or nurse. However, for skin ringworm the diagnosis should ideally be confirmed by taking skin scrapings for mycology.
- **Topical imidazoles and terbinafine appear to be similarly effective** in achieving mycological and symptom cure.
- There is evidence to suggest that treatment of athlete's foot with the older topical undecenoates (Monphytol and Mycota) and tolfanate may also be effective, but relative efficacy has only been assessed between imidazoles and terbinafine.
- **Topical treatment is usually necessary for 2–4 weeks with imidazoles or undecenoates, and for one week with terbinafine,** to clear lesions. Generally, topical treatment should be used for 1–2 weeks after the skin has healed to eradicate any residual fungal material, which lodges in the keratin layer.
- **Combining topical antifungal agent with corticosteroid preparations is unnecessary.** It may be useful over a short period if the infection is particularly inflamed and irritant.
- **Inappropriate or mistaken use of topical corticosteroids may suppress and disguise the infection,** and can sometimes make the infection worse ('tinea incognito').
- **Oral treatments are rarely needed.**
  - Oral terbinafine and itraconazole are effective in athlete's foot, groin fungal infection, and skin ringworm, but systemic therapy is usually needed only in very severe or non-resolving infection. However, involvement of the sole of the foot (moccasin pattern) commonly requires systemic treatment.
  - Oral griseofulvin is no longer a first-line treatment for athlete's foot, groin fungal infection, and skin ringworm because it is no longer available in the UK as a licensed product. Note: griseofulvin tablets can be imported on a named-patient basis, or alternatively

griseofulvin suspension (available from Specials Manufacturer's) can be used.

[Crawford et al, 2000; Crawford et al, 2001; DTB, 2002]

Scalp ringworm

General measures

- Recent reports show a trend change in pathogenic fungi identified in primary care, with an increase in the frequency of fungi of human origin. This infection, which was previously sporadic and associated with exposure to infected animals, is now spreading within families and in schools.
- **If cultures show that the infecting organism is of human origin,** other members of the family and school friends should be examined and specimens taken for culture, bearing in mind that clinical symptoms may be minimal.
- **If the source is an animal, the family should investigate family pets.** Other children and adults in the family should be asked to look for signs of scalp infection or ringworm.

Hygiene measures

- Human-source fungi can be transmitted between children at school, but exclusion is unnecessary.
- There is no evidence that shaving the head aids therapy or reduces the risk of transmission.

Treatment of scalp ringworm

- **Oral antifungal treatment is necessary** to obtain an effective clinical and mycological cure.
  - **Terbinafine.** There is some evidence that terbinafine is effective for common types of scalp ringworm, but use for this condition would be off-licence. Terbinafine has demonstrated efficacy, with shorter treatment courses than griseofulvin (2–4 weeks), in the treatment of scalp ringworm in children [Jones, 1995]. Adverse effects reported in trials appear to be low, but only small trials have been published. Prescriptions are offered for children in line with BNF-recommended doses.
  - **Griseofulvin** is no longer available in the UK as a licensed product. However, griseofulvin tablets can be imported on a named-patient basis, or alternatively griseofulvin suspension (available from Specials Manufacturer's) can be used. The optimal duration of treatment depends on the infecting fungal type. For most infections, 8–10 weeks' treatment will suffice. For some infections, such as those caused by *Tricophyton tonsurans*, the response may be slower, and treatment may need to be given for as long as 12 weeks.
  - **Itraconazole.** There is some evidence that itraconazole is effective for common types of scalp ringworm, but use for this condition would be off-licence.
- A generalized reaction of itchy papules, particularly around the ear, may occur as a reactive phenomenon (an id response) at the onset of treatment. This is sometimes mistaken for a drug reaction.
- **Kerions can be soaked and their crusts removed;** this may be soothing. The use of oral or topical corticosteroids to reduce scarring, or to reduce the id reaction that may occur with treatment of kerion, is controversial.
- Referral to a specialist is needed only if the response to treatment is poor, if the diagnosis is difficult, or if infection recurs.
- **Topical therapy alone is not recommended, but when combined with oral therapy it may have value in reducing the risk of transmission.**
  - Selenium sulphide lotion (used as a shampoo) may be useful in limiting the spread of infection when given t an infected child as an adjunctive treatment to oral griseofulvin. It has been shown to kill fungal spores o scalp hair when applied twice weekly for 2 weeks. A recent guideline for dermatologists by the British Association of Dermatologists advised that those wit mycological evidence of carriage should be given either povidone-iodine shampoo or selenium sulphid shampoo to use twice weekly in addition to oral antifungal therapy.
  - One open study in animal-source ringworm suggeste that adding topical 2% ketoconazole lotion once dail or 1% clotrimazole lotion twice daily, in addition to oral griseofulvin may produce a faster cure rate than griseofulvin given alone. It is not known if adjunctive use of either of these preparations reduces the length of treatment needed or the carriage of human-source fungi.

[DTB, 1996; Higgins et al, 2000]

Fungal infection of the nails

General issues

- Toenails are more commonly infected than fingernails b dermatophytes. *Candida* infections are more likely to affect the fingernails and fingernail folds. See the separa PRODIGY guidance *Candida — skin and nails*. There i wide geographical and ethnic variation in the causative species.
- **Whether to investigate and treat.** Many people have long-standing fungal infection of their toenails, but may have no symptoms apart from the change in appearanc of the nail. In these instances it may be entirely appropriate to give no treatment, so as to avoid the complications associated with systemic therapy.
- **Investigation and treatment is recommended in those with poor or diminished circulation** (e.g. where there is diabetes or peripheral vascular disease) in order to avoi complications. This advice is based on consensus, rathe than any particular evidence (such patients tend to be excluded from drug trials).
- **Treatment should be started only when results of mycological examination are available:**
  - It is easy to misdiagnose fungal nail infections.
  - Long-term oral therapy is needed for dermatophyte nail infections.
  - However, *Candida* infections can generally be treated with topical therapies.
- **A positive microscopy result, where hyphae are seen, is an indication for starting treatment but,** ideally, a cultu result should be awaited as visualised hyphae do not distinguish between pathogenic dermatophyte fungi and commensals.
- Results of culture are usually not available for two to three weeks, but are sometimes available earlier.
- In the UK about 5% of cases are due to non-dermatophyte moulds, such as *Scopulariopsis*, which almost exclusively affect nails, and which may not respond to conventional therapy.

[Denning et al, 1995; MeReC, 1997]

Treatment of fungal infection of the nails

Topical therapy with tioconazole or amorolfine:

- **Proximal nail disease or severe nail-bed involvement is extremely unlikely to respond to topical treatment.** Cur rates for toenail infections are poor.
- The BNF suggests that they be used for early fungal nai infection with mild distal disease and limited to up to two nails [BNF 44, 2002].

A 40% cure rate with 28% tioconazole with undecylenic acid (Trosyl) may be possible, especially with dermatophyte and *Candida* species.
A similar cure rate for toenails can be obtained with amorolfine, but with affected fingernails a rather better cure rate of 50% after 6 months is likely.
Treatment needs to be continued for at least 6 months for fingernails and for 12 months or longer for toenails.
)enning et al, 1995; MeReC, 1997; BNF 44, 2002]

ral therapy with terbinafine:

Cure rates of 80% to 95% with terbinafine in dermatophyte nail infection are seen in clinical trials.
A recent systematic review concluded that terbinafine was more effective for long-term resolution than was continuous itraconazole therapy, based on mycological cure assessed at 11 or 12 months. The NNT to have an additional cure, if using terbinafine rather than itraconazole, was 5 (95% CI 4 to 8) [Crawford et al, 2002].
Treatment with oral terbinafine will also treat associated skin infection without the need for additional topical treatment.
Oral terbinafine may be used in children aged 12 and over when other options are unsuitable or have failed.
Infection of fingernails requires oral terbinafine for between 6 weeks and 3 months. Toenail infection requires treatment for 3 months, occasionally up to 6 months.
From a clinical viewpoint, it may be difficult to assess whether a fingernail or toenail is free of infection at 3 months, since the distal dystrophic part of the nail may not have grown out. A repeat culture at 3 months may be useful in patients undergoing treatment, since a positive culture at this stage would indicate whether a longer course was required.
)enning et al, 1995; MeReC, 1997; BNF 44, 2002]

ral therapy with itraconazole

Itraconazole has slightly lower cure rates compared to terbinafine for dermatophyte nail infection.
Itraconazole is indicated if mixed fungal and yeast infection is found. Up to 5% of cases of infected nails have mixed fungal and yeast cultures. Itraconazole is active against most *Candida* species, and is also effective in dermatophyte infection.
It can be used as continuous therapy or as 'pulsed treatment' (in which a week of treatment is alternated with 3 weeks without treatment for several cycles) for 2–3 months. Cure rates are similar for these regimens.
Itraconazole daily for at least 3 months may be the most appropriate treatment for severe nail disease in immunocompromised patients, especially when non-dermatophyte moulds such as *Aspergillus* species are implicated.
For people still taking treatment at 3 months, consider a repeat culture. A positive culture at this stage would indicate whether a longer course was required.
)enning, 1995; MeReC, 1997; BNF 44, 2002]

Oral therapy with griseofulvin

- **Griseofulvin is no longer a first-line treatment for fungal nail infections and** it is no longer available in the UK as a licensed product.
- It has proven effectiveness in fingernail fungal infection (it can cure up to 90% of fingernail infections in 4 to 8 months) but requires longer treatment periods than do terbinafine or itraconazole.
- Griseofulvin has a low cure rate of 40% in toenail infections. Treatment with terbinafine or itraconazole gives more than double this cure rate.

[Denning et al, 1995; MeReC, 1997; BNF 44, 2002]

References

NHS staff in England can link, free of charge, from references to full text journals by clicking on [Full text] on the PRODIGY website.

1. BNF 44 (2002) *British National Formulary*. 44th edn. London: British Medical Association and Royal Pharmaceutical Society of Great Britain.
2. Crawford, F., Hart, R., Bell-Syer, S. et al (2000) *Topical treatments for fungal infections of the skin and nails of the foot (Cochrane Review)*. The Cochrane Library. Issue 2. Oxford: Update Software.
3. Crawford, F., Hart, R., Bell-Syer, S.E.M. et al (2001) Extracts from "Clinical Evidence": athlete's foot and fungally infected toenails. *British Medical Journal* **322**(7281), 288–289. [Full text]
4. Crawford, F., Young, P., Godfrey, C. et al (2002) Oral treatments for toenail onychomycosis: a systematic review. *Archives of Dermatology* **138**(6), 811–816. [Full text]
5. Denning, D.W. (1995) Can we prevent azole resistance in fungi? *Lancet* **346**, 454.
6. Denning, D.W., Evans, E.G.V., Kibbler, C.C. et al (1995) Fortnightly review: fungal nail disease: a guide to good practice (report of a Working Group of the British Society for Medical Mycology). *British Medical Journal* **311**(7015), 1277–1281. [Full text]
7. DTB (1996) Management of scalp ringworm. *Drug & Therapeutics Bulletin* **34**(1), 5–6.
8. DTB (2002) Getting rid of athlete's foot. *Drug & Therapeutics Bulletin* **40**(7), 55–56.
9. Higgins, E.M., Fuller, L.C. and Smith, C.H. (2000) Guidelines for the management of tinea capitis. *British Journal of Dermatology* **143**(1), 53–58.
10. Jones, T.C. (1995) Overview of the use of terbinafine (Lamisil) in children. *British Journal of Dermatology* **132**(5), 683–689.
11. MeReC (1997) Fungal nail infections (onychomycosis). *MeReC Bulletin* **8**(12), 45–48.
12. Roberts, D.T., Richardson, M.D., Dwyer, P.K. and Donegan, R. (1992) Terbinafine in chronic paronychia and candida onychomycosis. *Journal of Dermatological Treatment* **3**(Suppl 1), 39–42.

F

PRODIGY GUIDANCE

Gastroenteritis

Last revised in October 2003
www.prodigy.nhs.uk/guidance.asp?gt=Gastroenteritis

Applies to people over the age of 1 month

This guidance covers the management of acute infective gastroenteritis.

This guidance does not cover the management of other causes of acute diarrhoea. It does not cover the prevention of gastroenteritis, including antibiotic chemoprophylaxis of travellers' diarrhoea, or the management of gastroenteritis in neonates less than 1 month of age.

There is separate PRODIGY guidance on *Irritable bowel syndrome*.

G

Goals

- To alleviate symptoms
- To reduce length of illness
- To avoid dehydration and electrolyte imbalance
- To reduce infectious period
- To reduce risk of transmission to others

Contents

Scenarios

- Gastroenteritis in children — no confirmed cause p.802
- Gastroenteritis in adults — no confirmed cause p.804
- Travellers' diarrhoea p.807
- Confirmed *Campylobacter* p.810
- Confirmed *Salmonella* p.813
- Confirmed *Shigella* p.815
- Confirmed giardiasis p.818

Extended Information, p. 821

Which scenario?

- **Gastroenteritis in children — no confirmed cause:** covers the management of gastroenteritis in children up to the age of 12 years where the cause is unknown.
- **Gastroenteritis in adults — no confirmed cause:** covers the management of gastroenteritis in people aged 12 years or older where the cause is unknown.
- **Travellers' diarrhoea:** covers the management of traveller's diarrhoea in children and adults.
- **Confirmed *Campylobacter*:** covers the management of gastroenteritis in children and adults where stool culture has shown *Campylobacter*.
- **Confirmed *Salmonella*:** covers the management of gastroenteritis in children and adults where stool culture has shown *Salmonella*.
- **Confirmed *Shigella*:** covers the management of gastroenteritis in children and adults where stool culture has shown *Shigella*.
- **Confirmed giardiasis:** covers the management of gastroenteritis in children and adults where stool culture has shown *Giardia*.

Gastroenteritis in children — no confirmed cause

Which therapy?

General issues

- **Notify cases of dysentery (bloody stools) or suspected food poisoning** to the local consultant in Communicabl Disease Control.
- **Advise on how to prevent transmission** (e.g. hand washing and other hygienic measures).
- **Children should usually be excluded from nursery or school until:**
  - Free of diarrhoea and vomiting.
  - A satisfactory fluid intake and urine output is maintained.
- **Normal feeding should be restarted as soon as possible** in children, as there is no evidence that fasting will have any benefit.
- **Many people can simply be advised to increase their intake of fluids,** which should ideally include soups and pure fruit juices. Early feeding is now recommended, if tolerated, especially with foods high in carbohydrates, such as bread, pasta, potatoes, or rice.
- **Young children** are particularly prone to becoming dehydrated, and the use of oral rehydration therapy (ORT) alternating with normal fluids is advisable.

Treatment of dehydration

- **Mild dehydration** can often be treated outside hospital, provided social circumstances are appropriate and early review of the person can be guaranteed.
- **Mild dehydration** can often be managed at home with ORT, providing there are no complicating comorbiditie social circumstances are appropriate, and early review can be guaranteed.
- **For children:** give 30–50 ml/kg of ORT over 3–4 hours. Follow this with unrestricted fluids, either normal fluids or alternating with ORT.

Antimotility drugs

- **Antimotility drugs** must be avoided in young children.

Antibiotic treatment

- **Antibiotic therapy should usually be reserved for children with positive stool cultures,** particularly if symptoms are severe or not settling. In many people the illness may be resolved by the time a report is received.
- **Seek specialist advice on appropriate antibiotic treatme in children.**

Practical prescribing points

For further information, please see the *Medicines Compendium* (www.medicines.org.uk) or the *British National Formulary* (www.bnf.org).

- **When oral rehydration therapy is used in people with diabetes,** blood glucose levels need to be monitored more carefully.

Follow-up advice

- **If symptoms are not improving within 48 hours,** then a further review and stool investigation is advisable.
- **Children with mild dehydration who are being treated at home** require early review.

Should I refer or investigate?

Refer?

- **Admit children who are 5% or more dehydrated.**
- **Consider admission if:**
  - Severe gastroenteritis and systemic upset (severe abdominal pain, clear tenderness on abdominal palpation)
  - Vomiting and unable to retain oral rehydration therapy
  - Colicky, abdominal pain and sudden ceasing of the diarrhoea — indicative of intussusception
  - Immunocompromised
  - Taking immunosuppressants or systemic corticosteroids
  - Typhoid syndrome

Investigate?

- **Stool culture (and if recent foreign travel, examination for ova, cysts, and parasites, with at least three samples, ideally obtained on three separate days)** should be carried out immediately in the following circumstances:
  - Bloody diarrhoea
  - Severe gastroenteritis and systemic upset
  - Symptoms do not improve within 48 hours
  - Persistent diarrhoea for more than 5 days
  - Suspected food poisoning
  - Suspected travellers' diarrhoea
  - Child is irate
- **Laboratory testing may be carried out for pathogens not routinely sought, depending on information provided on the request form.** Relevant information, such as duration of the symptoms, the presence of bloody diarrhoea, recent foreign travel, recent antibiotic therapy, and suspected food poisoning, must be clearly documented. In many laboratories, routine testing for rotavirus in children under 5 years old may be carried out.
- **Consider testing stool samples for *Clostridium difficile* toxin in people with severe symptoms,** especially if they have been recently hospitalized, or have received antibiotic therapy within the previous 6 weeks (in particular lincomycins, broad-spectrum penicillins, or cephalosporins).
- **Persistent diarrhoea for more than 14 days requires further stool investigation** to exclude parasitic infections such as *Giardia*, *Entamoeba*, and *Cryptosporidium*. Specialist advice should be considered.

Patient information leaflets

The following PILs are available at www.prodigy.nhs.uk

- Gastroenteritis in Children

Shared decision making

- **Most bouts of gastroenteritis settle within a few days.**
- **Give plenty to drink** to prevent dehydration.
- **Encourage normal eating as much as possible.** Try to include fruit juices and soups (for sugar and salt), and foods high in carbohydrate such as bread, pasta, potatoes or rice.
  - Breastfed babies — continue to breastfeed.
  - Bottle-fed babies — continue with normal feeds.
- **Rehydration solutions** may be useful in addition, if there is concern about dehydration. They provide a perfect balance of water, salt, and sugar.
- **Antidiarrhoeal medication** should not be given to young children.
- **Antibiotics** are not normally advised, but may be needed in certain severe infections.
- **Good hygiene prevents spread** (washing hands after changing nappies, etc.).
- **Use a barrier cream** in infants wearing nappies.
- **See a doctor if the symptoms do not improve soon** — in particular if there is:
  - Persistent vomiting
  - Blood in vomit or diarrhoea
  - Drowsiness or confusion
  - Concern about dehydration

Drug rationale

Drugs not included

- **Other oral rehydration therapy (ORT):** the World Health Organization formulation is not recommended. It has a higher sodium and glucose content than the formulations commonly used in the UK, and people here generally suffer less severe sodium loss [Murphy, 1998; BNF 45, 2003].
- **Anti-emetics:** there is a lack of evidence to support the use of anti-emetics. They are of little value and may cause significant adverse effects, particularly in children. Sedation may interfere with ORT [WHO, 1993a]. Nausea and vomiting often improve after adequate rehydration.
- **Antispasmodics** are not recommended in children because they are rarely effective and have troublesome adverse effects [American Academy of Pediatrics, 1996; BNF 45, 2003].
- **Antimotility drugs** are not recommended for children [WHO, 1993a; Murphy, 1998; BNF 45, 2003].
- **Bismuth subsalicylate** (available as Pepto-Bismol) has been shown to reduce stool frequency, but it is available only over the counter and is not available on prescription. Large quantities of this liquid preparation may be needed to control symptoms, making it a less practical option [WHO, 1993b; BNF 45, 2003].
- **Antibiotics** are not included. They are rarely indicated in gastroenteritis, because it is usually a self-limiting condition and may not be bacterial in origin. If an antibiotic is deemed necessary, seek specialist advice on appropriate antibiotic treatment in children.

Drugs included

- **Oral rehydration therapy (ORT)** is indicated for the prevention of dehydration in young children, and for the treatment of mild dehydration. The products included here are also available over the counter from pharmacies for people who may wish to purchase them. They are available in a selection of flavours and pack sizes [Murphy, 1998; BNF 45, 2003].
- **Rice-based ORTs** (e.g. Dioralyte Relief) have been shown to reduce stool output in people with cholera, but

not in infants or children with non-cholera diarrhoea [Fontaine et al, 2003]. Prescriptions are included, but currently it is not clear whether they offer any advantages over glucose-based solutions for routine use.

- **Loperamide** has a low incidence of adverse effects on the central nervous system. However, it should be avoided in children under 4 years of age and in people with severe symptoms or dysentery, owing to a risk of precipitating ileus or toxic megacolon [WHO, 1993b; Farthing et al, 1996; BNF 45, 2003].

Prescriptions

Non-drug management

Advice only: preventing dehydration

- Age from 1 month to 11 years
- Most bouts of gastroenteritis settle within a few days. Aim to prevent dehydration by drinking plenty of normal drinks if possible. The child should eat as normal a diet as possible for their age and as soon as possible. Where appropriate, include fruit juices and soups which contain sugar and salt and also foods high in carbohydrate such as bread and pasta. Rehydration solutions may be useful in addition to normal drinks if there is concern about dehydration. They provide a perfect balance of water, salt and sugar and can be bought at a pharmacy and the pharmacist can advise you on their use. Breastfed babies should continue to breastfeed. Antidiarrhoeal medication should not be given to young children.

G

Acute oral rehydration therapy

Dioralyte sachets: 30-50ml/kg over 3 to 4 hours

- Age from 1 month to 11 years
- Dioralyte sachets. *WEIGHT REQUIRED* Take 30 to 50ml per kg bodyweight over 3 to 4 hours; supply 20 sachets; NHS Cost £5.68; OTC Cost £10.01.

Dioralyte tablets: 30-50ml/kg over 3 to 4 hours

- Age from 1 month to 11 months
- Dioralyte effervescent tablets. *WEIGHT REQUIRED* Take 30 to 50ml per kg bodyweight over 3 to 4 hours; supply 40 tablets; NHS Cost £5.16; OTC Cost £9.10.

Dioralyte tablets: 30-50ml/kg over 3 to 4 hours

- Age from 12 months to 11 years
- Dioralyte effervescent tablets. *WEIGHT REQUIRED* Take 30 to 50ml per kg bodyweight over 3 to 4 hours; supply 40 tablets; NHS Cost £5.16; OTC Cost £9.09.

Electrolade sachets: 30-50ml/kg over 3 to 4 hours

- Age from 1 month to 11 years
- Electrolade multiflavour sachets. *WEIGHT REQUIRED* Take 30 to 50ml per kg bodyweight over 3 to 4 hours; supply 20 sachets; NHS Cost £4.99; OTC Cost £7.99.

Oral rehydration therapy

Dioralyte sachets: 1 to 1.5 times usual 24 hour feed volume

- Age from 1 month to 11 months
- Dioralyte sachets. *WEIGHT REQUIRED* Give 150ml per kg bodyweight per day in divided doses OR one to one and a half times usual 24 hour feed volume; supply 20 sachets; NHS Cost £5.68; OTC Cost £10.01.

Dioralyte sachets: 200ml after each loose stool

- Age from 12 months to 11 years
- Dioralyte sachets. *WEIGHT REQUIRED* Take 10ml per kg bodyweight after each loose stool OR the contents of one sachet (dissolved in water) after each loose stool; supply 20 sachets; NHS Cost £5.68; OTC Cost £10.01.

Dioralyte tablets: 1 to 1.5 times usual 24 hour feed volume

- Age from 1 month to 11 months
- Dioralyte effervescent tablets. *WEIGHT REQUIRED* Give 150ml per kg bodyweight per day in divided doses OR one to one and a half times usual 24 hour feed volume; supply 40 tablets; NHS Cost £5.16; OTC Cost £9.10.

Dioralyte tablets: 200ml after each loose stool

- Age from 12 months to 11 years
- Dioralyte effervescent tablets. *WEIGHT REQUIRED* Take 10ml per kg bodyweight after each loose stool OR two tablets (dissolved in water) after each loose stool; supply 40 tablets; NHS Cost £5.16; OTC Cost £9.10.

Electrolade sachets: 1 to 1.5 times usual 24 hr feed volume

- Age from 1 month to 11 months
- Electrolade multiflavour sachets. *WEIGHT REQUIRED* Give 150ml per kg bodyweight per day in divided doses OR one to one and a half times usual 24 hour feed volume; supply 20 sachets; NHS Cost £4.99; OTC Cost £7.99.

Electrolade sachets: 200ml after each loose stool

- Age from 12 months to 11 years
- Electrolade multiflavour sachets. *WEIGHT REQUIRED* Take 10ml per kg bodyweight after each loose stool OR the contents of one sachet (dissolved in water) after each loose stool; supply 20 sachets; NHS Cost £4.99; OTC Cost £7.99.

Gastroenteritis in adults — no confirmed cause

Which therapy?

General issues

- **Notify cases of dysentery (bloody stools) or suspected food poisoning** to the local consultant in Communicable Disease Control.
- **Advise on how to prevent transmission** (e.g. hand washing and other hygienic measures).
- **People should usually be excluded from school or work until free of diarrhoea and vomiting.**
- **Normal feeding should be started as soon as possible,** as there is no evidence that fasting will have any benefit.
- **Many people can simply be advised to increase their intake of fluids,** which should ideally include fruit juices and soups. Early feeding is now recommended, if tolerated, especially with foods high in carbohydrates, such as bread, pasta, potatoes, or rice.
- **Frail, elderly people** are particularly prone to becoming dehydrated, and the use of oral rehydration therapy (ORT), alternating with normal fluids, is advisable.

Treatment of dehydration

- **Mild dehydration** can often be treated outside hospital, provided social circumstances are appropriate and early review of the person can be guaranteed.
- **For adults/people over 12 years of age:** give 2 litres of ORT in the first 24 hours, followed by unrestricted normal fluids with 200 ml of ORT per loose stool or vomit.

Antimotility drugs

- **Antimotility drugs are occasionally beneficial in adults** with mild to moderate diarrhoea. These drugs must be avoided in people with severe gastroenteritis or dysentery, owing to the risk of precipitating ileus or toxi megacolon.

Antibiotic treatment

- **Antibiotic therapy should usually be reserved for people with positive stool cultures,** particularly if symptoms are severe or not settling. In many people the illness may be resolved by the time a report is received.
- **However, empirical antibiotic therapy with a quinolone may be appropriate** for high-risk people (e.g. immunosuppressed) or those presenting with dysentery (which is often due to locally invasive bacterial infection). If a quinolone is contraindicated, then seek specialist advice on appropriate treatment.

Practical prescribing points

For further information, please see the *Medicines Compendium* (www.medicines.org.uk) or the *British National Formulary* (www.bnf.org).

Ciprofloxacin

- **Tendon damage** (including rupture) has been reported rarely in people receiving quinolones. Tendon rupture may occur within 48 hours of starting treatment. The CSM has advised that:
  - Quinolones are contraindicated in people with a history of tendon disorders related to quinolone use.
  - Elderly people are more prone to tendonitis.
  - The risk of tendon rupture is increased by the concomitant use of corticosteroid.
  - If tendonitis is suspected, the quinolone should be discontinued immediately.
- **The CSM has also warned that quinolones may induce convulsions** in people with or without a history of epilepsy, or in conditions that predispose to seizures, or where the person is concurrently taking nonsteroidal anti-inflammatory drugs (NSAIDs).
- **Quinolones are contraindicated in all three trimesters of pregnancy and in breastfeeding women** because they can be excreted in breast milk. They are not recommended for growing adolescents, because of concerns that they may cause arthropathy.

Loperamide

- **Loperamide** should be avoided in people with severe gastroenteritis or dysentery, because of the risk of precipitating ileus or toxic megacolon.

Oral rehydration therapy

- **When oral rehydration therapy is used in people with diabetes,** blood glucose levels may need to be monitored more carefully.

Follow-up advice

- **If symptoms are not improving within 48 hours,** then further review and stool investigation is advisable.
- **People with mild dehydration who are being treated at home** require an early review.

Should I refer or investigate?

Refer?

- **Admit people who are 5% or more dehydrated.**
- **Consider admission if:**
  - Severe gastroenteritis and systemic upset (severe abdominal pain, clear tenderness on abdominal palpation)
  - Vomiting and unable to retain oral rehydration therapy (ORT)
  - Typhoid syndrome
  - Elderly
  - Inflammatory bowel disease
  - Renal failure
  - Immunocompromised
  - Taking immunosuppressants or systemic corticosteroids
  - Arthritis with severe symptoms (diarrhoea often precedes arthritis by 2–4 weeks)
  - Carditis
  - Pancreatitis
- **Mild dehydration** may be managed at home with ORT, providing there are no complicating comorbidities, social circumstances are appropriate, and early review can be guaranteed.
- **Specialist advice** should be sought from an infectious disease specialist or gastroenterologist if homosexual men or people with AIDS develop acute, severe, or persistent diarrhoea.

Investigate?

- **Stool culture (and examination for ova, cysts, and parasites if there has been recent foreign travel)** should be carried out immediately in the following circumstances:
  - Bloody diarrhoea
  - Severe gastroenteritis and systemic upset
  - Symptoms do not improve within 48 hours
  - Persistent diarrhoea for more than 5 days
  - Suspected food poisoning
  - Suspected travellers' diarrhoea
- **Laboratory testing may be carried out for pathogens not routinely sought, depending on information provided on the request form.** Relevant information, such as duration of the symptoms, the presence of bloody diarrhoea, recent foreign travel, recent antibiotic therapy, and suspected food poisoning, must be clearly documented.
- **Consider testing stool samples for *Clostridium difficile* toxin in people with severe symptoms,** especially if they have been recently hospitalized, or have received antibiotic therapy within the previous 6 weeks (in particular lincomycins, broad-spectrum penicillins, or cephalosporins).
- **Persistent diarrhoea for more than 14 days requires further stool investigation** to exclude parasitic infections such as *Giardia*, *Entamoeba*, and *Cryptosporidium*. Specialist advice should be considered.

Patient information leaflets

The following PILs are available at www.prodigy.nhs.uk

- Gastroenteritis in Adults

Shared decision making

- **Most bouts of gastroenteritis settle within a few days.**
- **Drink plenty** of normal drinks if possible. The aim is to prevent dehydration.
- **Eat as normally as possible.** Ideally include fruit juices and soups, which will provide sugar and salt, and also foods that are high in carbohydrate, such as bread, pasta, potatoes or rice.
- **Rehydration solutions** may be useful in addition, if there is concern about dehydration. They provide a perfect balance of water, salt, and sugar.
- **Antidiarrhoeal medication** may sometimes be beneficial to adults.
- **Antibiotics** are not normally advised, but they may help in certain severe infections.
- **Good hygiene prevents spread** (washing hands after going to toilet, etc.).

G

- **Does your job involve handling food?** You will need special advice.
- **See a doctor if the symptoms do not improve soon.** In particular if there is:
  - Persistent vomiting
  - Blood in vomit or diarrhoea
  - Drowsiness or confusion
  - Concern about dehydration

Drug rationale

Drugs not included

- **Other oral rehydration therapy (ORT):** the World Health Organization formulation is not recommended. It has a higher sodium and glucose content than the formulations commonly used in the UK, because people here generally suffer less severe sodium loss [Murphy, 1998; BNF 45, 2003].
- **Anti-emetics:** there is a lack of evidence to support the use of anti-emetics. They are of little value and may cause significant adverse effects. Sedation may interfere with ORT [WHO, 1993a]. Nausea and vomiting often improve after adequate rehydration. Anti-emetics may be of help in an adult who is vomiting severely (e.g. metoclopramide 10 mg intramuscularly) [Dwight and Collier, 2001a].
- **Antispasmodics** are not recommended, as there are few data to support their use in older people [BNF 45, 2003].
- **Antimotility drugs** (other than loperamide) are not included. These preparations have a limited adjunctive role for symptom control, but many have adverse effects on the central nervous system, including sedation, and are considered less suitable for prescribing.
- **Bismuth subsalicylate** (available as Pepto-Bismol) has been shown to reduce stool frequency, but it is available only over the counter and is not available on prescription. Large quantities of this liquid preparation may be needed to control symptoms, making it a less practical option [WHO, 1993b; BNF 45, 2003].
- **Antibiotics** (other than ciprofloxacin and trimethoprim) are not included. They are rarely indicated in gastroenteritis, because it is usually a self-limiting condition and may not be bacterial in origin. There is resistance in many of the more common infecting organisms to older antibiotics, and there are reports of increasing resistance to quinolones [Farthing et al, 1996; DH and SMAC, 1998; Hoge et al, 1998; Murphy, 1998;]. Those quinolones not licensed for treatment of gastrointestinal infections are not included. Nalidixic acid is licensed, but treatment failure and relapse rate may be more common.

Drugs included

- **Oral rehydration therapy (ORT)** is indicated for the prevention of dehydration in frail elderly people, and for the treatment of mild dehydration. The products included here are also available over the counter from pharmacies for people who may wish to purchase them. They are available in a selection of flavours and pack sizes [Murphy, 1998; BNF 45, 2003].
- **Rice-based ORTs** (e.g. Dioralyte Relief) have been shown to reduce stool output in children with cholera, but not in people with non-cholera diarrhoea [Fontaine et al, 2003]. Prescriptions are included, but currently it is not clear whether they offer any advantages over glucose-based solutions for routine use.
- **Loperamide** may be a useful adjunct for symptom control in some adults, but it should not be used routinely. It has a low incidence of adverse effects on the central nervous system, but should be avoided in people with severe symptoms or dysentery, because of the risk of precipitating ileus or toxic megacolon [WHO, 1993b Farthing et al, 1996; BNF 45, 2003].
- **Ciprofloxacin** may occasionally be required, such as for those who are at high risk or who present with dysenter [Farthing et al, 1996].
- **A short course of trimethoprim** is an option in pregnant women.
- If an antibiotic is considered necessary and the person cannot take a quinolone or trimethoprim, seek specialis advice on appropriate treatment.

Prescriptions

Non-drug management

Advice only: preventing dehydration
- Age from 12 years onwards
- Most bouts of gastroenteritis settle within a few days. Aim to prevent dehydration by drinking plenty of normal drinks if possible. Eat as normal a diet as possible and as soon as possible. Include fruit juices and soups which contain sugar and salt and also foods high in carbohydrate such as bread and pasta. Rehydration solutions may be useful in addition to normal drinks if there is concern about dehydration. They provide a perfect balance of water, salt and sugar and can be bought at a pharmacy and the pharmacist can advise yo on their use. Antidiarrhoeal medication may sometimes benefit. You can buy a suitable preparation from a pharmacy and the pharmacist can advise you on its use.

Acute oral rehydration therapy

Dioralyte sachets: 2L over 24 hours then 200ml after stoo
- Age from 12 years onwards
- Dioralyte sachets. Take two litres in divided doses over 24 hours, then 200ml after each loose stool; supply 20 sachets; NHS Cost £5.68; OTC Cost £10.01.

Dioralyte tablets: 2L over 24 hours then 200ml after stool
- Age from 12 years onwards
- Dioralyte effervescent tablets. Take two litres in divided doses over 24 hours, then 200ml after each loose stool; supply 40 tablets; NHS Cost £5.16; OTC Cost £9.09.

Electrolade sachets: 2L over 24 hours then 200ml after stool
- Age from 12 years onwards
- Electrolade multiflavour sachets. Take two litres in divided doses over 24 hours, then 200ml after each loos stool; supply 20 sachets; NHS Cost £4.99; OTC Cost £7.99.

Oral rehydration therapy

Dioralyte sachets: 200-400ml after each loose stool
- Age from 12 years onwards
- Dioralyte sachets. Take the contents of one to two sachets (dissolved in water) after each loose stool; supply 20 sachets; NHS Cost £5.68; OTC Cost £10.01.

Dioralyte tablets: 200-400ml after each loose stool
- Age from 12 years onwards
- Dioralyte effervescent tablets. Take two to four tablets (dissolved in water) after each loose stool; supply 40 tablets; NHS Cost £5.16; OTC Cost £9.10.

Electrolade sachets: 200-400ml after each loose stool
- Age from 12 years onwards
- Electrolade multiflavour sachets. Take the contents of one to two sachets (dissolved in water) after each loose stool; supply 20 sachets; NHS Cost £4.99; OTC Cost £7.99.

Loperamide: not for routine use

Loperamide: 4mg now, then 2mg after stool. Max 16mg/24hours
- Age from 12 years onwards
- Loperamide 2mg capsules. Take TWO capsules initially, then take ONE capsule after each loose stool for up to 5 days. Maximum of 8 capsules in 24 hours; supply 30 capsules; NHS Cost £1.22; OTC Cost £13.38.

Antibiotics for 3 days: rarely appropriate

Ciprofloxacin tablets: 500mg twice a day (NOT if pregnant)
- Age from 16 years onwards
- Ciprofloxacin 500mg tablets. Take one tablet twice a day for 3 days; supply 6 tablets; NHS Cost £8.00.

Trimethoprim: 200mg twice a day
- Age from 12 years onwards
- Trimethoprim 200mg tablets. Take one tablet twice a day for 3 days; supply 6 tablets; NHS Cost £0.25.

Travellers' diarrhoea

Which therapy?

Antibiotic treatment

- **Empirical antibiotic treatment is unnecessary in the majority of people.** It should usually be reserved for people with severe symptoms or those with medical conditions (e.g. diabetes) for whom an episode of infective diarrhoea would be dangerous, and when illness causes serious disruption to a person's activities.

Antimotility drugs

- **Antimotility drugs are occasionally beneficial in adults** with mild to moderate diarrhoea. They must not be prescribed for children under 4 years old, or for people with severe gastroenteritis or dysentery, because of the risk of severe colitis and toxic dilation of the colon.

General issues

- **Notify cases of dysentery (bloody stools) or suspected food poisoning** to the local consultant in Communicable Disease Control.
- **Advise on how to prevent transmission** (e.g. hand washing and other hygienic measures).
- **People should usually be excluded from school or work** until they are free of diarrhoea and vomiting and are able to maintain a satisfactory fluid intake.
- **Normal feeding should be restarted as soon as possible** in both children and adults. There is no evidence that fasting will have any benefit.

Prevention of dehydration

- **Many people can simply be advised to increase their intake of fluids** — usually glucose-containing fluids and soups are sufficient for adults. Infants, young children, and frail elderly people are particularly prone to becoming dehydrated. Early feeding is now recommended, if tolerated, especially with foods high in carbohydrates, such as bread, pasta, potatoes, or rice.

Treatment of dehydration

- **Mild dehydration** can often be treated outside hospital, provided social circumstances are appropriate, and early review of the person can be guaranteed.
- **For children:** give 30–50 ml/kg of oral rehydration therapy (ORT) over 3–4 hours. Follow this with unrestricted fluids, either with normal fluids or alternating with ORT.
- **For adults:** give 2 litres of ORT in the first 24 hours, followed by unrestricted normal fluids, with 200 ml of ORT per loose stool or vomit.

Practical prescribing points

For further information, please see the *Medicines Compendium* (www.medicines.org.uk) or the *British National Formulary* (www.bnf.org).

Ciprofloxacin

- **Tendon damage** (including rupture) has been reported rarely in people receiving quinolones. Tendon rupture may occur within 48 hours of starting treatment. The CSM has advised that:
  - Quinolones are contraindicated in people with a history of tendon disorders related to quinolone use.
  - Elderly people are more prone to tendonitis.
  - The risk of tendon rupture is increased by the concomitant use of corticosteroids.
  - If tendonitis is suspected, the quinolone should be discontinued immediately.
- **The CSM has also warned that quinolones may induce convulsions** in people with or without a history of epilepsy, or in conditions that predispose to seizures, or where the person is concurrently taking nonsteroidal anti-inflammatory drugs (NSAIDs).
- **Quinolones are contraindicated in all three trimesters of pregnancy and in breastfeeding women** because they can be excreted in breast milk. They are not recommended for growing adolescents, because of concerns that they may cause arthropathy.

Trimethoprim

- **Trimethoprim** is a folate antagonist. Its use should be avoided in women either with known folate deficiency, or taking folate antagonists (e.g. antiepileptics or proguanil), unless a folate supplement is taken. For further information, telephone the National Teratology Information Service (0191 2321525).

Loperamide

- **Loperamide** should be avoided in children under 4 years of age and in people with severe gastroenteritis or dysentery, because of the risk of severe colitis and toxic megacolon.

Oral rehydration therapy

- **When oral rehydration therapy is used in people with diabetes,** blood glucose levels may need to be monitored more carefully.

Follow-up advice

- **If symptoms are not improving within 48 hours,** then further review and stool investigation is advisable.
- **People with mild dehydration who are being treated at home** require an early review.

Should I refer or investigate?

Refer?

- **Admit people who are 5% or more dehydrated.**
- **Consider admission if:**
  - Severe gastroenteritis and systemic upset (severe abdominal pain, clear tenderness on abdominal palpation)

- Vomiting and unable to retain oral rehydration therapy (ORT)
- Colicky, abdominal pain and sudden ceasing of the diarrhoea — indicative of intussusception
- Elderly
- Inflammatory bowel disease
- Renal failure
- Immunocompromised
- Taking immunosuppressants or systemic corticosteroids
- Arthritis with severe symptoms (diarrhoea often precedes arthritis by 2–4 weeks)
- Carditis
- Pancreatitis

- **Mild dehydration** may be managed at home with ORT, providing there are no complicating comorbidities, social circumstances are appropriate, and early review can be guaranteed.
- **Specialist advice** should be sought from an infectious disease specialist or gastroenterologist if homosexual men or people with AIDS develop acute, severe, or persistent diarrhoea.

G

Investigate?

- **Returning travellers with diarrhoea should have:**
  - Blood tests for liver function, electrolytes, and renal function
  - A full blood count
  - Analysis of plasma/serum chemistry
- **Stool culture and examination for ova, cysts, and parasites (with at least three samples, ideally obtained on three separate days)** should be carried out immediately if there is bloody diarrhoea or severe symptoms, or if the person is not improving within 48 hours.
- **Laboratory testing may be carried out for pathogens not routinely sought, depending on information provided on the request form.** Relevant information, such as location of foreign travel, duration of the symptoms, the presence of bloody diarrhoea, recent antibiotic therapy, and suspected food poisoning, must be clearly documented. In many laboratories routine testing for rotavirus in children under 5 years old may be carried out.
- **Consider testing stool samples for *Clostridium difficile* toxin in people with severe symptoms,** especially if they have been recently hospitalized, or have received antibiotic therapy within the previous 6 weeks (in particular lincomycins, broad-spectrum penicillins, or cephalosporins).
- **Persistent diarrhoea for more than 14 days, despite treatment, requires further stool investigation** to exclude parasitic infections such as *Giardia*, *Entamoeba*, *Cryptosporidium*, and *Cyclospora*. Specialist advice should be considered.

Patient information leaflets

The following PILs are available at www.prodigy.nhs.uk

- Gastroenteritis in Adults
- Gastroenteritis in Children

Shared decision making

- **Most bouts of travellers' diarrhoea settle within a few days.**
- **Drink plenty** of normal drinks if possible. The aim is to prevent dehydration.
- **Eat as normally as possible.** Ideally include fruit juices and soups, which will provide sugar and salt, and also foods that are high in carbohydrate, such as bread, pasta, potatoes, or rice.
- **Rehydration solutions** may be useful in addition, if there is concern about dehydration. They provide a perfect balance of water, salt, and sugar.
- **Antidiarrhoeal medication** should not be given to young children. Adults may sometimes benefit from this.
- **Antibiotics** are not normally advised, but they may help in certain severe infections.
- **Always wash your hands** after going to the toilet (or changing nappies).
- **Does your job involve handling food?** You will need special advice.
- **See a doctor if the symptoms do not improve soon** — in particular if there is:
  - Persistent vomiting
  - Blood in vomit or diarrhoea
  - Drowsiness or confusion
  - Concern about dehydration

Drug rationale

Drugs not included

- **Other oral rehydration therapy (ORT):** the World Health Organization formulation of this is not recommended. It has a higher sodium content than the formulations commonly used in the UK, because people here generally suffer less severe sodium loss [Murphy, 1998; BNF 45, 2003].
- **Anti-emetics:** there is a lack of evidence to support the use of anti-emetics. They are of little value and may cause significant adverse effects, particularly in children. Sedation may interfere with ORT [WHO, 1993a]. Nausea and vomiting often improve after adequate rehydration. In adults, anti-emetics may be of help if the person is vomiting severely (e.g. metoclopramide 10 mg intramuscularly) [Dwight and Collier, 2001a].
- **Antispasmodics** are not recommended in children, because they are rarely effective and have troublesome adverse effects. There are also few data to support their use in older people [American Academy of Pediatrics, 1996; BNF 45, 2003].
- **Antimotility drugs** (other than loperamide) are not included. These preparations have a limited adjunctive role for symptom control, but many have adverse effects on the central nervous system, including sedation, and are considered to be less suitable for prescribing. They may cause paralytic ileus, and are not recommended for use in children [WHO, 1993b; Murphy, 1998; BNF 45, 2003].
- **Bismuth subsalicylate** (available as Pepto-Bismol) has been shown to reduce stool frequency, but it is only available for purchase over the counter in the UK in a liquid form. Large quantities may be needed to control symptoms, making it a less practical option for travellers [WHO, 1993b; BNF 45, 2003].
- **Antibiotics** (other than ciprofloxacin and trimethoprim) are not included. They are rarely indicated in travellers' diarrhoea, because it is usually a mild, self-limiting condition. They should be reserved to preserve their efficacy and limit the development of resistance, which is known to be increasing [Farthing et al, 1996; DH and SMAC, 1998; Murphy, 1998]. Those quinolones not licensed for treatment of gastrointestinal infections are not included. Nalidixic acid is licensed, but treatment failure and relapse rate may be more common.

Drugs included

- **Oral rehydration therapy (ORT)** is indicated for the prevention of dehydration in young children and frail elderly people, and for the treatment of mild dehydration. The products included here are also available over the counter from pharmacies for people who may wish to purchase them. They are available in a selection of flavours and pack sizes [Murphy, 1998; BNF 45, 2003].

- **Rice-based ORT** (e.g. Dioralyte Relief) has been shown to reduce stool output in people with cholera, but not in infants or children with non-cholera diarrhoea [Fontaine et al, 2003]. Prescriptions are included, but currently it is not clear whether they offer any advantages over glucose-based solutions for routine use.
- **Loperamide** is effective in reducing stool frequency and increasing stool consistency. It may be a useful adjunct for symptom control in some adults, but it should not be used routinely. It has a low incidence of adverse effects on the central nervous system, but should be avoided in children under 4 years of age and people with severe symptoms or dysentery, because of the risk of precipitating ileus or toxic megacolon [WHO, 1993b; Farthing et al, 1996; BNF 45, 2003].
- **Antibiotics: ciprofloxacin** may occasionally be required, such as for those who are at high risk or who present with severe symptoms or dysentery, or when illness causes serious disruption to the person's activities [Farthing et al, 1996]. There are reports of increasing resistance to quinolones, and indiscriminate use of antibiotics should be avoided [DH and SMAC, 1998].
- **Trimethoprim** may be a suitable alternative, and a short course of trimethoprim is the antibiotic of choice in pregnant women.
- If an antibiotic is considered necessary and the person cannot take a quinolone or trimethoprim, seek specialist advice on appropriate treatment.

Prescriptions

Non-drug management

Advice only: preventing dehydration
- Age from 1 month onwards
- Most bouts of gastroenteritis settle within a few days. Aim to prevent dehydration by drinking plenty of normal drinks if possible. The child should eat as normal a diet as possible for their age and as soon as possible. Where appropriate, include fruit juices and soups which contain sugar and salt and also foods high in carbohydrate such as bread and pasta. Rehydration solutions may be useful in addition to normal drinks if there is concern about dehydration. They provide a perfect balance of water, salt and sugar and can be bought at a pharmacy and the pharmacist can advise you on their use. Breastfed babies should continue to breastfeed. Antidiarrhoeal medication should not be given to young children. Adults may sometimes benefit. You can buy a suitable preparation from a pharmacy and the pharmacist can advise you on its use.

Acute oral rehydration therapy

Dioralyte sachets: 30-50ml/kg over 3 to 4 hours
- Age from 1 month to 11 years
- Dioralyte sachets. *WEIGHT REQUIRED* Take 30 to 50ml per kg bodyweight over 3 to 4 hours; supply 20 sachets; NHS Cost £5.68; OTC Cost £10.01.

Dioralyte sachets: 2L over 24 hours then 200ml after stool
- Age from 12 years onwards
- Dioralyte sachets. Take two litres in divided doses over 24 hours, then 200ml after each loose stool; supply 20 sachets; NHS Cost £5.68; OTC Cost £10.01.

Dioralyte tablets: 30-50ml/kg over 3 to 4 hours
- Age from 1 month to 11 months
- Dioralyte effervescent tablets. *WEIGHT REQUIRED* Take 30 to 50ml per kg bodyweight over 3 to 4 hours; supply 40 tablets; NHS Cost £5.16; OTC Cost £9.10.

Dioralyte tablets: 30-50ml/kg over 3 to 4 hours
- Age from 12 months to 11 years
- Dioralyte effervescent tablets. *WEIGHT REQUIRED* Take 30 to 50ml per kg bodyweight over 3 to 4 hours; supply 40 tablets; NHS Cost £5.16; OTC Cost £9.09.

Dioralyte tablets: 2L over 24 hours then 200ml after stool
- Age from 12 years onwards
- Dioralyte effervescent tablets. Take two litres in divided doses over 24 hours, then 200ml after each loose stool; supply 40 tablets; NHS Cost £5.16; OTC Cost £9.09.

Electrolade sachets: 30-50ml/kg over 3 to 4 hours
- Age from 1 month to 11 years
- Electrolade multiflavour sachets. *WEIGHT REQUIRED* Take 30 to 50ml per kg bodyweight over 3 to 4 hours; supply 20 sachets; NHS Cost £4.99; OTC Cost £7.99.

Electrolade sachets: 2L over 24 hours then 200ml after stool
- Age from 12 years onwards
- Electrolade multiflavour sachets. Take two litres in divided doses over 24 hours, then 200ml after each loose stool; supply 20 sachets; NHS Cost £4.99; OTC Cost £7.99.

Oral rehydration therapy

Dioralyte sachets: 1 to 1.5 times usual 24 hour feed volume
- Age from 1 month to 11 months
- Dioralyte sachets. *WEIGHT REQUIRED* Give 150ml per kg bodyweight per day in divided doses OR one to one and a half times usual 24 hour feed volume; supply 20 sachets; NHS Cost £5.68; OTC Cost £10.01.

Dioralyte sachets: 200ml after each loose stool
- Age from 12 months to 11 years
- Dioralyte sachets. *WEIGHT REQUIRED* Take 10ml per kg bodyweight after each loose stool OR the contents of one sachet (dissolved in water) after each loose stool; supply 20 sachets; NHS Cost £5.68; OTC Cost £10.01.

Dioralyte sachets: 200-400ml after each loose stool
- Age from 12 years onwards
- Dioralyte sachets. Take the contents of one to two sachets (dissolved in water) after each loose stool; supply 20 sachets; NHS Cost £5.68; OTC Cost £10.01.

Dioralyte tablets: 1 to 1.5 times usual 24 hour feed volume
- Age from 1 month to 11 months
- Dioralyte effervescent tablets. *WEIGHT REQUIRED* Give 150ml per kg bodyweight per day in divided doses OR one to one and a half times usual 24 hour feed volume; supply 40 tablets; NHS Cost £5.16; OTC Cost £9.10.

Dioralyte tablets: 200ml after each loose stool
- Age from 12 months to 11 years
- Dioralyte effervescent tablets. *WEIGHT REQUIRED* Take 10ml per kg bodyweight after each loose stool OR two tablets (dissolved in water) after each loose stool; supply 40 tablets; NHS Cost £5.16; OTC Cost £9.10.

Dioralyte tablets: 200-400ml after each loose stool
- Age from 12 years onwards
- Dioralyte effervescent tablets. Take two to four tablets (dissolved in water) after each loose stool; supply 40 tablets; NHS Cost £5.16; OTC Cost £9.10.

Electrolade sachets: 1 to 1.5 times usual 24 hr feed volume

- Age from 1 month to 11 months
- Electrolade multiflavour sachets. *WEIGHT REQUIRED* Give 150ml per kg bodyweight per day in divided doses OR one to one and a half times usual 24 hour feed volume; supply 20 sachets; NHS Cost £4.99; OTC Cost £7.99.

Electrolade sachets: 200ml after each loose stool

- Age from 12 months to 11 years
- Electrolade multiflavour sachets. *WEIGHT REQUIRED* Take 10ml per kg bodyweight after each loose stool OR the contents of one sachet (dissolved in water) after each loose stool; supply 20 sachets; NHS Cost £4.99; OTC Cost £7.99.

Electrolade sachets: 200-400ml after each loose stool

- Age from 12 years onwards
- Electrolade multiflavour sachets. Take the contents of one to two sachets (dissolved in water) after each loose stool; supply 20 sachets; NHS Cost £4.99; OTC Cost £7.99.

G

Loperamide: not for routine use

Loperamide: 4mg now, then 2mg after stool. Max 16mg/24hours

- Age from 12 years onwards
- Loperamide 2mg capsules. Take TWO capsules initially, then take ONE capsule after each loose stool for up to 5 days. Maximum of 8 capsules in 24 hours; supply 30 capsules; NHS Cost £1.22; OTC Cost £13.38.

Antibiotics for 3 days: rarely appropriate

Ciprofloxacin tablets: 500mg twice a day (NOT if pregnant)

- Age from 16 years onwards
- Ciprofloxacin 500mg tablets. Take one tablet twice a day for 3 days; supply 6 tablets; NHS Cost £7.43.

Trimethoprim s/f suspension: 50mg twice a day

- Age from 6 months to 5 years
- Trimethoprim 50mg/5ml s/f susp. Take one 5ml spoonful twice a day for 3 days; supply 30 ml; NHS Cost £0.53.

Trimethoprim s/f suspension: 100mg twice a day

- Age from 6 to 11 years
- Trimethoprim 50mg/5ml s/f susp. Take two 5ml spoonfuls twice a day for 3 days; supply 60 ml; NHS Cost £1.06.

Trimethoprim: 200mg twice a day

- Age from 12 years onwards
- Trimethoprim 200mg tablets. Take one tablet twice a day for 3 days; supply 6 tablets; NHS Cost £0.29.

Confirmed *Campylobacter*

Which therapy?

Antibiotic treatment

- **Erythromycin or ciprofloxacin** are advised for people with severe symptoms of dysentery. Early treatment is likely to be most effective.

Antimotility drugs

- **Antimotility drugs are occasionally beneficial in adults** with mild to moderate diarrhoea. They must be not be prescribed for children under 4 years old, or for people with severe gastroenteritis or dysentery, owing to the risk of severe colitis and toxic dilation of the colon.

General issues

- **Notify cases of dysentery (bloody stools) or suspected food poisoning** to the local consultant in Communicable Disease Control.
- **Advise on how to prevent transmission** (e.g. hand washing and other hygienic measures).
- **People should usually be excluded from school or work** until they are free of diarrhoea and vomiting, and are able to maintain a satisfactory fluid intake.
- **Normal feeding should be restarted as soon as possible** in both children and adults. There is no evidence that fasting will have any benefit.

Prevention of dehydration

- **Many people can simply be advised to increase their intake of fluids** — usually glucose-containing fluids and soups are sufficient for adults. Infants, young children, and frail elderly people are particularly prone to becoming dehydrated. Early feeding is now recommended, if tolerated, especially with foods high in carbohydrates, such as bread, pasta, potatoes, or rice.

Treatment of dehydration

- **Mild dehydration** can often be treated outside hospital, provided social circumstances are appropriate and an early review of the person can be guaranteed.
- **For children:** give 30–50 ml/kg of oral rehydration therapy (ORT) over 3–4 hours. Follow this with unrestricted fluids, either with normal fluids or alternating with ORT.
- **For adults:** give 2 litres of ORT in the first 24 hours, followed by unrestricted normal fluids with 200 ml of ORT per loose stool or vomit.

Practical prescribing points

For further information, please see the *Medicines Compendium* (www.medicines.org.uk) or the *British National Formulary* (www.bnf.org).

Ciprofloxacin

- **Tendon damage** (including rupture) has been reported rarely in people receiving quinolones. Tendon rupture may occur within 48 hours of starting treatment. The CSM has advised that:
  - Quinolones are contraindicated in people with a history of tendon disorders related to quinolone use.
  - Elderly people are more prone to tendonitis.
  - The risk of tendon rupture is increased by the concomitant use of corticosteroids.
  - If tendonitis is suspected, the quinolone should be discontinued immediately.
- **The CSM has also warned that quinolones may induce convulsions** in people with or without a history of epilepsy, or in conditions that predispose to seizures, or where the person is concurrently taking nonsteroidal anti-inflammatory drugs (NSAIDs).
- **Quinolones are contraindicated in all three trimesters of pregnancy and in breastfeeding women** because they can be excreted in breast milk. They are not recommended for growing adolescents, because of concerns that they may cause arthropathy.

Loperamide

- **Loperamide** should be avoided in children under 4 years of age and in people with severe gastroenteritis or dysentery, because of the risk of severe colitis and toxic megacolon.

Oral rehydration therapy

- **When oral rehydration therapy is used in people with diabetes,** blood glucose levels may need to be monitored more carefully.

Follow-up advice

- **People with mild dehydration who are being treated at home** require an early review.

Should I refer or investigate?

Refer?

- **People with severe gastroenteritis and systemic upset may require admission.**
- **Admit people who are 5% or more dehydrated.**
- **Mild dehydration** may be managed at home with ORT, providing there are no complicating comorbidities, social circumstances are appropriate, and early review can be guaranteed.

Investigate?

- No further investigation is usually necessary.

Patient information leaflets

The following PILs are available at www.prodigy.nhs.uk

- Gastroenteritis in Adults
- Gastroenteritis in Children

Shared decision making

- ***Campylobacter*** is a common cause of gastroenteritis.
- **Drink plenty** of normal drinks if possible. The aim is to prevent dehydration.
- **Eat as normally as possible.** Ideally include fruit juices and soups, which will provide sugar and salt, and also foods that are high in carbohydrate, such as bread, pasta, potatoes, or rice.
- **Rehydration solutions** may be useful in addition, if there is concern about dehydration. They provide a perfect balance of water, salt, and sugar.
- **Breastfed babies** should continue to breastfeed.
- **Antidiarrhoeal medication** should not be given to young children. Adults may sometimes benefit from this.
- **Antibiotics** are not normally advised, but they may help if the illness is severe.
- **Always wash your hands** after going to the toilet (or changing nappies).
- **Does your job involve handling food?** You will need special advice.
- **See a doctor if the symptoms do not improve soon** — in particular if there is:
  - Persistent vomiting
  - Blood in vomit or diarrhoea
  - Drowsiness or confusion
  - Concern about dehydration

Drug rationale

Drugs not included

- **Other oral rehydration therapy (ORT):** the World Health Organization formulation of this is not recommended. It has a higher sodium content than the formulations commonly used in the UK, because people here generally suffer less severe sodium loss [Murphy, 1998; BNF 45, 2003].
- **Anti-emetics:** there is a lack of evidence to support the use of anti-emetics. They are of little value and may cause significant adverse effects, particularly in children. Sedation may interfere with ORT [WHO, 1993b]. Nausea and vomiting often improve after adequate rehydration. In adults, anti-emetics may be of help if vomiting is severe (e.g. metoclopramide 10 mg intramuscularly) [Dwight and Collier, 2001a].
- **Antispasmodics** are not recommended in children because they are rarely effective and have troublesome adverse effects. There are also few data to support their use in older people [American Academy of Pediatrics, 1996; BNF 45, 2003].
- **Antimotility drugs** (other than loperamide) are not included. These preparations have a limited adjunctive role for symptom control, but many have adverse effects on the central nervous system, including sedation, and are considered to be less suitable for prescribing. They may cause paralytic ileus, and are not recommended for use in children [WHO, 1993b; Murphy, 1998; BNF 45, 2003].
- **Bismuth subsalicylate** (available as Pepto-Bismol) has been shown to reduce stool frequency, but it is available for purchase only over the counter in the UK in a liquid form. Large quantities may be needed to control symptoms, making it a less practical option [WHO, 1993b; BNF 45, 2003].
- **Antibiotics** (other than erythromycin and ciprofloxacin) are not included because they are not indicated for *Campylobacter* [Murphy, 1998; BNF 45, 2003]. There is controversy over the usefulness of antibiotic therapy in this condition, because it is self-limiting.

Drugs included

- **Oral rehydration therapy (ORT)** is indicated for the prevention of dehydration in young children and frail elderly people, and for treatment of mild dehydration. The products included here are also available over the counter from pharmacies for people who may wish to purchase them. They are available in a selection of flavours and pack sizes [Murphy, 1998; BNF 45, 2003].
- **Rice-based ORT** (e.g. Dioralyte Relief) has been shown to reduce stool output in people with cholera, but not in infants or children with non-cholera diarrhoea [Fontaine et al, 2003]. Prescriptions are included, but currently it is not clear whether they offer any advantages over glucose-based solutions for routine use.
- **Loperamide** is effective in reducing stool frequency and increasing stool consistency. It may be a useful adjunct for symptom control in some adults, but it should not be used routinely. It has a low incidence of adverse effects on the central nervous system, but should be avoided in children under 4 years of age and in people with severe symptoms or dysentery, because of the risk of precipitating ileus or toxic megacolon [WHO, 1993b; Farthing et al, 1996; BNF 45, 2003].
- **Antibiotics: erythromycin or ciprofloxacin** may be required occasionally, such as for those who are at high risk or who present with dysentery. There is little to guide the choice of preferred treatment clinically, although there may be greater resistance to ciprofloxacin in some geographical areas. Treatment courses of 5 to 7 days are currently recommended [Tompkins, Personal Communication, 2003].
- If an antibiotic is considered necessary, it may be appropriate to seek local specialist advice on appropriate treatment.

Prescriptions

Non-drug management

Advice only: preventing dehydration
- Age from 1 month onwards
- Most bouts of gastroenteritis settle within a few days. Aim to prevent dehydration by drinking plenty of normal drinks if possible. The child should eat as normal a diet as possible for their age and as soon as possible. Where appropriate, include fruit juices and soups which contain sugar and salt and also foods high in carbohydrate such as bread and pasta. Rehydration solutions may be useful in addition to normal drinks if there is concern about dehydration. They provide a perfect balance of water, salt and sugar and can be bought at a pharmacy and the pharmacist can advise you on their use. Breastfed babies should continue to breastfeed. Antidiarrhoeal medication should not be given to young children. Adults may sometimes benefit. You can buy a suitable preparation from a pharmacy and the pharmacist can advise you on its use.

G

Acute rehydration therapy

Dioralyte sachets: 30-50ml/kg over 3 to 4 hours
- Age from 1 month to 11 years
- Dioralyte sachets. *WEIGHT REQUIRED* Take 30 to 50ml per kg bodyweight over 3 to 4 hours; supply 20 sachets; NHS Cost £5.68; OTC Cost £10.01.

Dioralyte sachets: 2L over 24 hours then 200ml after stool
- Age from 12 years onwards
- Dioralyte sachets. Take two litres in divided doses over 24 hours, then 200ml after each loose stool; supply 20 sachets; NHS Cost £5.68; OTC Cost £10.01.

Dioralyte tablets: 30-50ml/kg over 3 to 4 hrs
- Age from 1 month to 11 months
- Dioralyte effervescent tablets. *WEIGHT REQUIRED* Take 30 to 50ml per kg bodyweight over 3 to 4 hours; supply 40 tablets; NHS Cost £5.16; OTC Cost £9.10.

Dioralyte tablets: 30-50ml/kg over 3 to 4 hrs
- Age from 12 months to 11 years
- Dioralyte effervescent tablets. *WEIGHT REQUIRED* Take 30 to 50ml per kg bodyweight over 3 to 4 hours; supply 40 tablets; NHS Cost £5.16; OTC Cost £9.09.

Dioralyte tablets: 2L over 24 hours then 200ml after stool
- Age from 12 years onwards
- Dioralyte effervescent tablets. Take two litres in divided doses over 24 hours, then 200ml after each loose stool; supply 40 tablets; NHS Cost £5.16; OTC Cost £9.09.

Electrolade sachets: 30-50ml/kg over 3 to 4 hrs
- Age from 1 month to 11 years
- Electrolade multiflavour sachets. *WEIGHT REQUIRED* Take 30 to 50ml per kg bodyweight over 3 to 4 hours; supply 20 sachets; NHS Cost £4.99; OTC Cost £7.99.

Electrolade sachets: 2L over 24 hours then 200ml after stool
- Age from 12 years onwards
- Electrolade multiflavour sachets. Take two litres in divided doses over 24 hours, then 200ml after each loose stool; supply 20 sachets; NHS Cost £4.99; OTC Cost £7.99.

Oral rehydration therapy

Dioralyte sachets: 1 to 1.5 times usual 24 hour feed volume
- Age from 1 month to 11 months
- Dioralyte sachets. *WEIGHT REQUIRED* Give 150ml per kg bodyweight per day in divided doses OR one to one and a half times usual 24 hour feed volume; supply 20 sachets; NHS Cost £5.68; OTC Cost £10.01.

Dioralyte sachets: 200ml after each loose stool
- Age from 12 months to 11 years
- Dioralyte sachets. *WEIGHT REQUIRED* Take 10ml per kg bodyweight after each loose stool OR the contents of one sachet (dissolved in water) after each loose stool; supply 20 sachets; NHS Cost £5.68; OTC Cost £10.01.

Dioralyte sachets: 200-400ml after each loose stool
- Age from 12 years onwards
- Dioralyte sachets. Take the contents of one to two sachets (dissolved in water) after each loose stool; supply 20 sachets; NHS Cost £5.68; OTC Cost £10.01.

Dioralyte tablets: 1 to 1.5 times usual 24 hour feed volum
- Age from 1 month to 11 months
- Dioralyte effervescent tablets. *WEIGHT REQUIRED* Give 150ml per kg bodyweight per day in divided doses OR one to one and a half times usual 24 hour feed volume; supply 40 tablets; NHS Cost £5.16; OTC Cost £9.10.

Dioralyte tablets: 200ml after each loose stool
- Age from 12 months to 11 years
- Dioralyte effervescent tablets. *WEIGHT REQUIRED* Take 10ml per kg bodyweight after each loose stool OR two tablets (dissolved in water) after each loose stool; supply 40 tablets; NHS Cost £5.16; OTC Cost £9.10.

Dioralyte tablets: 200-400ml after each loose stool
- Age from 12 years onwards
- Dioralyte effervescent tablets. Take two to four tablets (dissolved in water) after each loose stool; supply 40 tablets; NHS Cost £5.16; OTC Cost £9.10.

Electrolade sachets: 1 to 1.5 times usual 24 hr feed volume
- Age from 1 month to 11 months
- Electrolade multiflavour sachets. *WEIGHT REQUIRED* Give 150ml per kg bodyweight per day in divided doses OR one to one and a half times usual 24 hour feed volume; supply 20 sachets; NHS Cost £4.99; OTC Cost £7.99.

Electrolade sachets: 200ml after each loose stool
- Age from 12 months to 11 years
- Electrolade multiflavour sachets. *WEIGHT REQUIRED* Take 10ml per kg bodyweight after each loose stool OR the contents of one sachet (dissolved in water) after each loose stool; supply 20 sachets; NHS Cost £4.99; OTC Cost £7.99.

Electrolade sachets: 200-400ml after each loose stool
- Age from 12 years onwards
- Electrolade multiflavour sachets. Take the contents of one to two sachets (dissolved in water) after each loose stool; supply 20 sachets; NHS Cost £4.99; OTC Cost £7.99.

Loperamide: not for routine use

Loperamide: 4mg now, then 2mg post stool. Max 16mg/24hours
- Age from 12 years onwards
- Loperamide 2mg capsules. Take TWO capsules initially, then take ONE capsule after each loose stool for up to 5 days. Maximum of 8 capsules in 24 hours; supply 30 capsules; NHS Cost £1.22; OTC Cost £13.38.

Antibiotics for 5 days or 7 days: rarely appropriate

Erythromycin e/c tablets: 250mg four times a day x 5 day
- Age from 12 years onwards
- Erythromycin 250mg e/c tablets. Take one tablet four times a day for 5 days; supply 20 tablets; NHS Cost £2.20.

Erythromycin e/c tablets: 250mg four times a day x 7 days
Age from 12 years onwards
Erythromycin 250mg e/c tablets. Take one tablet four times a day for 7 days; supply 28 tablets;
NHS Cost £3.08.

Erythromycin s/f suspension: 125mg four times a day x 5 days
Age from 1 month to 23 months
Erythromycin 125mg/5ml sf susp. Take one 5ml spoonful four times a day for 5 days; supply 100 ml;
NHS Cost £1.12.

Erythromycin s/f suspension: 125mg four times a day x 7 days
Age from 1 month to 23 months
Erythromycin 125mg/5ml sf susp. Take one 5ml spoonful four times a day for 7 days; supply 140 ml;
NHS Cost £2.24.

Erythromycin s/f suspension: 250mg four times a day x 5 days
Age from 2 to 11 years
Erythromycin 250mg/5ml sf susp. Take one 5ml spoonful four times a day for 5 days; supply 100 ml;
NHS Cost £1.97.

Erythromycin s/f suspension: 250mg four times a day x 7 days
Age from 2 to 11 years
Erythromycin 250mg/5ml sf susp. Take one 5ml spoonful four times a day for 7 days; supply 140 ml;
NHS Cost £3.96.

Ciprofloxacin tabs:500mg x2 a day for 5 days NOT if pregnant
Age from 16 years onwards
Ciprofloxacin 500mg tablets. Take one tablet twice a day for 5 days; supply 10 tablets; NHS Cost £12.38.

Ciprofloxacin tabs:500mg x2 a day for 7 days NOT if pregnant
Age from 16 years onwards
Ciprofloxacin 500mg tablets. Take one tablet twice a day for 7 days; supply 14 tablets; NHS Cost £17.33.

Confirmed *Salmonella*

Which therapy?

Antibiotic treatment

Antibiotic therapy is rarely appropriate in otherwise healthy individuals, and may prolong the excretion of *Salmonella*. Treatment is usually recommended only for the very young, for immunocompromised people, and for those who are systemically ill. If antibiotics are thought to be necessary, then trimethoprim or ciprofloxacin are suitable choices.

At the time of diagnosis, anyone who is either moderately ill or who has been excreting *Salmonella* for one month or longer may need to be treated with an antibiotic.

Antimotility drugs

Antimotility drugs are occasionally beneficial in adults with mild to moderate diarrhoea. They must be not be prescribed for children under 4 years old, or for people with severe gastroenteritis or dysentery, owing to the risk of severe colitis and toxic dilation of the colon.

General issues

Notify cases of dysentery (bloody stools) or suspected food poisoning to the local consultant in Communicable Disease Control.

- **Advise on how to prevent transmission** (e.g. hand washing and other hygienic measures).
- **People should usually be excluded from school or work** until they are free of diarrhoea and vomiting and are able to maintain a satisfactory fluid intake.
- **Normal feeding should be restarted as soon as possible** in both children and adults. There is no evidence that fasting will have any benefit.

Prevention of dehydration

- **Many people can simply be advised to increase their intake of fluids** — usually glucose-containing fluids and soups are sufficient for adults. Infants, young children, and frail elderly people are particularly prone to becoming dehydrated. Early feeding is now recommended, if tolerated, especially with foods high in carbohydrates, such as bread, pasta, potatoes, or rice.

Treatment of dehydration

- **Mild dehydration** can often be treated outside hospital, provided social circumstances are appropriate and early review of the person can be guaranteed.
- **For children:** give 30–50 ml/kg of oral rehydration therapy (ORT) over 3–4 hours. Follow this with unrestricted fluids, either with normal fluids or alternating with ORT.
- **For adults:** give 2 litres of ORT in the first 24 hours, followed by unrestricted normal fluids with 200 ml of ORT per loose stool or vomit.

Practical prescribing points

For further information, please see the *Medicines Compendium* (www.medicines.org.uk) or the *British National Formulary* (www.bnf.org).

- **Loperamide** should be avoided in people with severe gastroenteritis or dysentery, owing to the risk of severe colitis and toxic dilation of the colon.
- **When oral rehydration therapy is used in people with diabetes,** blood glucose levels may need to be monitored more carefully.

Follow-up advice

- **People with mild dehydration who are being treated at home** require an early review.

Should I refer or investigate?

Refer?

- **Admit people who are 5% or more dehydrated.**
- **People with severe gastroenteritis and systemic upset may require admission.**
- **Mild dehydration** may be managed at home with ORT, providing there are no complicating comorbidities, social circumstances are appropriate, and early review can be guaranteed.
- **Visible symptoms of typhoid fever** — high fever which has slowly increased, general weakness, and a rash of 2–3 mm pink-red spots on the chest or abdomen — require admission [EBM, 2000].

Investigate?

- **In the first week of illness, blood culture** may be useful to aid diagnosis.
- **After this time, stool and bone marrow cultures** are more helpful in confirming the diagnosis.

G

Patient information leaflets

The following PILs are available at www.prodigy.nhs.uk

- Gastroenteritis in Adults
- Gastroenteritis in Children

Shared decision making

- *Salmonella* is one cause of gastroenteritis.
- **Drink plenty** of normal drinks if possible. The aim is to prevent dehydration.
- **Eat as normally as possible.** Ideally include fruit juices and soups, which will provide sugar and salt, and also foods that are high in carbohydrate, such as bread, pasta, potatoes, or rice.
- **Rehydration solutions** may be useful in addition, if there is concern about dehydration. They provide a perfect balance of water, salt, and sugar.
- **Breastfed babies should continue to breastfeed.**
- **Antidiarrhoeal medication** should not be given to young children. Adults may sometimes benefit from this.
- **Antibiotics** are not normally advised. They are occasionally used in severely ill people.
- **Always wash your hands** after going to the toilet (or changing nappies).
- **Does your job involve handling food?** You will need special advice.
- **See a doctor if the symptoms do not improve soon** — in particular if there is:
  - Persistent vomiting
  - Blood in vomit or diarrhoea
  - Drowsiness or confusion
  - Concern about dehydration

G

Drug rationale

Drugs not included

- **Other oral rehydration therapy (ORT):** the World Health Organization formulation of this is not recommended. It has a higher sodium content than the formulations commonly used in the UK, because people here generally suffer less severe sodium loss [Murphy, 1998; BNF 45, 2003].
- **Anti-emetics:** there is a lack of evidence to support the use of anti-emetics. They are of little value and may cause significant adverse effects, particularly in children. Sedation may interfere with ORT [WHO, 1993b]. Nausea and vomiting often improve after adequate rehydration. In adults, anti-emetics may be of help if vomiting is severe (e.g. metoclopramide 10 mg intramuscularly) [Dwight and Collier, 2001a].
- **Antispasmodics** are not recommended in children because they are rarely effective and have troublesome adverse effects. There are also few data to support their use in older people [American Academy of Pediatrics, 1996; BNF 45, 2003].
- **Antimotility drugs** (other than loperamide) are not included. These preparations have a limited adjunctive role for symptom control, but many have adverse effects on the central nervous system, including sedation, and are considered to be less suitable for prescribing. They may cause paralytic ileus, and are not recommended for use in children [WHO, 1993b; Murphy, 1998; BNF 45, 2003].
- **Bismuth subsalicylate** (available as Pepto-Bismol) has been shown to reduce stool frequency, but it is only available for purchase over the counter in the UK in a liquid form. Large quantities may be needed to control symptoms, making it a less practical option for travellers [WHO, 1993b; BNF 45, 2003].
- **Antibiotics** are not included, because there is no evidence of clinical benefit for antibiotic therapy in the majority of otherwise healthy people [Sirinavin and Garner, 1999]. They may prolong elimination of the infecting organism from the gut.

Drugs included

- **Oral rehydration therapy (ORT)** is indicated for the prevention of dehydration in young children and frail elderly people, and for the treatment of mild dehydration. The products included here are also available over the counter from pharmacies for people who may wish to purchase them. They are available in a selection of flavours and pack sizes [Murphy, 1998; BNF 45, 2003].
- **Rice-based ORT** (e.g. Dioralyte Relief) has been shown to reduce stool output in people with cholera, but not in infants or children with non-cholera diarrhoea [Fontaine et al, 2003]. Prescriptions are included, but currently it is not clear whether they offer any advantages over glucose-based solutions for routine use.
- **Loperamide** is effective in reducing stool frequency and increasing stool consistency. It may be a useful adjunct for symptom control in some adults, but it should not be used routinely. It has a low incidence of adverse effects on the central nervous system, but should be avoided in children under 4 years of age and people with severe symptoms or dysentery, because of the risk of precipitating ileus or toxic megacolon [WHO, 1993b; Farthing et al, 1996; BNF 45, 2003].

Prescriptions

Non-drug management

Advice only: preventing dehydration

- Age from 1 month onwards
- Salmonella is one cause of gastroenteritis. Drink plenty of normal drinks if possible. The aim is to prevent dehydration. Eat as normally as possible as soon as possible. Ideally include fruit juices and soups which contain sugar and salt. Also, foods high in carbohydrate such as bread and pasta. Rehydration solutions may be useful in addition to normal drinks if there is concern about dehydration. They provide a perfect balance of water, salt and sugar. These can be bought at a pharmacy and the pharmacist can advise you on their use. Breastfed babies should continue to breastfeed. Antidiarrhoeal medication should not be given to young children. Adults may sometimes benefit. You can buy a suitable preparation from a pharmacy and the pharmacist can advise you on its use.

Acute rehydration therapy

Dioralyte sachets: 30-50ml/kg over 3 to 4 hrs

- Age from 1 month to 11 years
- Dioralyte sachets. *WEIGHT REQUIRED* Take 30 to 50ml per kg bodyweight over 3 to 4 hours; supply 20 sachets; NHS Cost £5.68; OTC Cost £10.01.

Dioralyte sachets: 2L over 24 hours then 200ml after stoo

- Age from 12 years onwards
- Dioralyte sachets. Take two litres in divided doses over 24 hours, then 200ml after each loose stool; supply 20 sachets; NHS Cost £5.68; OTC Cost £10.01.

Dioralyte tablets: 30-50ml/kg over 3 to 4 hours

- Age from 1 month to 11 months
- Dioralyte effervescent tablets. *WEIGHT REQUIRED* Take 30 to 50ml per kg bodyweight over 3 to 4 hours; supply 40 tablets; NHS Cost £5.16; OTC Cost £9.10.

Dioralyte tablets: 30-50ml/kg over 3 to 4 hours

- Age from 12 months to 11 years
- Dioralyte effervescent tablets. *WEIGHT REQUIRED* Take 30 to 50ml per kg bodyweight over 3 to 4 hours; supply 40 tablets; NHS Cost £5.16; OTC Cost £9.09.

Dioralyte tablets: 2L over 24 hours then 200ml after stool

- Age from 12 years onwards
- Dioralyte effervescent tablets. Take two litres in divided doses over 24 hours, then 200ml after each loose stool; supply 40 tablets; NHS Cost £5.16; OTC Cost £9.09.

Electrolade sachets: 30-50ml/kg over 3 to 4 hours

- Age from 1 month to 11 years
- Electrolade multiflavour sachets. *WEIGHT REQUIRED* Take 30 to 50ml per kg bodyweight over 3 to 4 hours; supply 20 sachets; NHS Cost £4.99; OTC Cost £7.99.

Electrolade sachets: 2L over 24 hours then 200ml after stool

- Age from 12 years onwards
- Electrolade multiflavour sachets. Take two litres in divided doses over 24 hours, then 200ml after each loose stool; supply 20 sachets; NHS Cost £4.99; OTC Cost £7.99.

Oral rehydration therapy

Dioralyte sachets: 1 to 1.5 times usual 24 hour feed volume

- Age from 1 month to 11 months
- Dioralyte sachets. *WEIGHT REQUIRED* Give 150ml per kg bodyweight per day in divided doses OR one to one and a half times usual 24 hour feed volume; supply 20 sachets; NHS Cost £5.68; OTC Cost £10.01.

Dioralyte sachets: 200ml after each loose stool

- Age from 12 months to 11 years
- Dioralyte sachets. *WEIGHT REQUIRED* Take 10ml per kg bodyweight after each loose stool OR the contents of one sachet (dissolved in water) after each loose stool; supply 20 sachets; NHS Cost £5.68; OTC Cost £10.01.

Dioralyte sachets: 200-400ml after each loose stool

- Age from 12 years onwards
- Dioralyte sachets. Take the contents of one to two sachets (dissolved in water) after each loose stool; supply 20 sachets; NHS Cost £5.68; OTC Cost £10.01.

Dioralyte tablets: 1 to 1.5 times usual 24 hour feed volume

- Age from 1 month to 11 months
- Dioralyte effervescent tablets. *WEIGHT REQUIRED* Give 150ml per kg bodyweight per day in divided doses OR one to one and a half times usual 24 hour feed volume; supply 40 tablets; NHS Cost £5.16; OTC Cost £9.10.

Dioralyte tablets: 200ml after each loose stool

- Age from 12 months to 11 years
- Dioralyte effervescent tablets. *WEIGHT REQUIRED* Take 10ml per kg bodyweight after each loose stool OR two tablets (dissolved in water) after each loose stool; supply 40 tablets; NHS Cost £5.16; OTC Cost £9.10.

Dioralyte tablets: 200-400ml after each loose stool

- Age from 12 years onwards
- Dioralyte effervescent tablets. Take two to four tablets (dissolved in water) after each loose stool; supply 40 tablets; NHS Cost £5.16; OTC Cost £9.10.

Electrolade sachets: 1 to 1.5 times usual 24 hr feed volume

- Age from 1 month to 11 months
- Electrolade multiflavour sachets. *WEIGHT REQUIRED* Give 150ml per kg bodyweight per day in divided doses OR one to one and a half times usual 24 hour feed volume; supply 20 sachets; NHS Cost £4.99; OTC Cost £7.99.

Electrolade sachets: 200ml after each loose stool

- Age from 12 months to 11 years
- Electrolade multiflavour sachets. *WEIGHT REQUIRED* Take 10ml per kg bodyweight after each loose stool OR the contents of one sachet (dissolved in water) after each loose stool; supply 20 sachets; NHS Cost £4.99; OTC Cost £7.99.

Electrolade sachets: 200-400ml after each loose stool

- Age from 12 years onwards
- Electrolade multiflavour sachets. Take the contents of one to two sachets (dissolved in water) after each loose stool; supply 20 sachets; NHS Cost £4.99; OTC Cost £7.99.

Loperamide: not for routine use

Loperamide: 4mg now, then 2mg after stool. Max 16mg/24hours

- Age from 12 years onwards
- Loperamide 2mg capsules. Take TWO capsules initially, then take ONE capsule after each loose stool for up to 5 days. Maximum of 8 capsules in 24 hours; supply 30 capsules; NHS Cost £1.22; OTC Cost £6.35.

Confirmed *Shigella*

Which therapy?

Antibiotic treatment

- **People with persistent or severe symptoms should be treated with ciprofloxacin** to shorten the clinical illness and duration of pathogen excretion. Nalidixic acid is an alternative for children. Trimethoprim is an alternative for pregnant women, but resistance is an increasing problem and specialist advice should usually be sought in such cases.

Antimotility drugs

- **Antimotility drugs are occasionally beneficial in adults** with mild to moderate diarrhoea. They must be not be prescribed for children under 4 years old, or for people with severe gastroenteritis or dysentery, owing to the risk of severe colitis and toxic dilation of the colon.

General issues

- **Notify cases of dysentery (bloody stools) or suspected food poisoning** to the local consultant in Communicable Disease Control.
- **Advise on how to prevent transmission** (e.g. hand washing and other hygienic measures).
- **People should usually be excluded from school or work** until they are free of diarrhoea and vomiting and are able to maintain a satisfactory fluid intake.
- **Normal feeding should be restarted as soon as possible** in both children and adults. There is no evidence that fasting will have any benefit.

Prevention of dehydration

- **Many people can simply be advised to increase their intake of fluids** — usually glucose-containing fluids and soups are sufficient for adults. Infants, young children, and frail elderly people are particularly prone to becoming dehydrated. Early feeding is now recommended, if tolerated, especially with foods high in carbohydrates, such as bread, pasta, potatoes, or rice.

Treatment of dehydration

- **Mild dehydration** can often be treated outside hospital, provided social circumstances are appropriate and early review of the person can be guaranteed.
- **For children:** give 30–50 ml/kg of oral rehydration therapy (ORT) over 3–4 hours. Follow this with unrestricted fluids, either with normal fluids or alternating with ORT.
- **For adults:** give 2 litres of ORT in the first 24 hours, followed by unrestricted normal fluids with 200 ml of ORT per loose stool or vomit.

Practical prescribing points

For further information, please see the *Medicines Compendium* (www.medicines.org.uk) or the *British National Formulary* (www.bnf.org).

Quinolones

G

- **Tendon damage** (including rupture) has been reported rarely in people receiving quinolones. Tendon rupture may occur within 48 hours of starting treatment. The CSM has advised that:
  - Quinolones are contraindicated in people with a history of tendon disorders related to quinolone use.
  - Elderly people are more prone to tendonitis.
  - The risk of tendon rupture is increased by the concomitant use of corticosteroids.
  - If tendonitis is suspected, the quinolone should be discontinued immediately.
- **The CSM has also warned that quinolones may induce convulsions** in people with or without a history of epilepsy, or in conditions that predispose to seizures, or where the person is concurrently taking nonsteroidal anti-inflammatory drugs (NSAIDs).
- **Quinolones are contraindicated in all three trimesters of pregnancy and in breastfeeding women** because they can be excreted in breast milk. They are not recommended for growing adolescents, owing to concerns that they may cause arthropathy.

Trimethoprim

- **Trimethoprim** is a folate antagonist. Its use should be avoided in women either with known folate deficiency, or taking folate antagonists (e.g. antiepileptics, proguanil), unless a folate supplement is taken. For further information, telephone the National Teratology Information Service (0191 2321525).

Loperamide

- **Loperamide** should be avoided in children under 4 years of age and in people with severe gastroenteritis or dysentery, owing to the risk of severe colitis and toxic megacolon.

Oral rehydration therapy

- **When oral rehydration therapy is used in people with diabetes,** blood glucose levels may need to be monitored more carefully.

Follow-up advice

- **People with mild dehydration who are being treated at home** require an early review.

Should I refer or investigate?

Refer?

- **Admit people who are 5% or more dehydrated.**
- **People with severe gastroenteritis and systemic upset may require admission.**
- **Mild dehydration** may be managed at home with ORT, providing there are no complicating comorbidities, socia circumstances are appropriate, and early review can be guaranteed.

Investigate?

- No further investigation is necessary.

Patient information leaflets

The following PILs are available at www.prodigy.nhs.uk

- Gastroenteritis in Adults
- Gastroenteritis in Children

Shared decision making

- ***Shigella*** is one cause of gastroenteritis.
- **Drink plenty** of normal drinks if possible. The aim is to prevent dehydration.
- **Eat as normally as possible.** Ideally include fruit juices and soups, which will provide sugar and salt, and also foods high in carbohydrate, such as bread, pasta, potatoes, or rice.
- **Rehydration solutions** may be useful in addition, if there is concern about dehydration. They provide a perfect balance of water, salt, and sugar.
- **Breastfed babies should continue to breastfeed.**
- **Antidiarrhoeal medication** should not be given to young children. Adults may sometimes benefit from this.
- **Antibiotics** are not normally advised. They may help if the infection is severe.
- **Always wash your hands** after going to the toilet (or changing nappies).
- **Does your job involve handling food?** You will need special advice.
- **See a doctor if the symptoms do not improve soon** — in particular if there is:
  - Persistent vomiting
  - Blood in vomit or diarrhoea
  - Drowsiness or confusion
  - Concern about dehydration

Drug rationale

Drugs not included

- **Other oral rehydration therapy (ORT):** the World Health Organization formulation of this is not recommended. It has a higher sodium content than the formulations commonly used in the UK, because people here generally suffer less severe sodium loss [Murphy, 1998; BNF 45, 2003].
- **Anti-emetics:** there is a lack of evidence to support the use of anti-emetics. They are of little value and may cause significant adverse effects, particularly in children. Sedation may interfere with ORT [WHO, 1993b]. Nausea and vomiting often improve after adequate rehydration. Anti-emetics may be of help in an adult who is vomiting severely (e.g. metoclopramide 10 mg intramuscularly) [Dwight and Collier, 2001a].
- **Antispasmodics** are not recommended in children because they are rarely effective and have troublesome adverse effects. There are also few data to support their

use in older people [American Academy of Pediatrics, 1996; BNF 45, 2003].

- **Antimotility drugs** (other than loperamide) are not included. These preparations have a limited adjunctive role for symptom control, but many have adverse effects on the central nervous system, including sedation, and are considered to be less suitable for prescribing. They may cause paralytic ileus, and are not recommended for use in children [WHO, 1993b; Murphy, 1998; BNF 45, 2003].
- **Bismuth subsalicylate** (available as Pepto-Bismol) has been shown to reduce stool frequency, but it is only available for purchase over the counter in the UK in a liquid form. Large quantities may be needed to control symptoms, making it a less practical option for travellers [WHO, 1993b; BNF 45, 2003].
- **Antibiotics** other than ciprofloxacin, nalidixic acid, and trimethoprim are not indicated in this condition, owing to the increasing problem of antibiotic resistance [Cheasty et al, 1998; DH and SMAC, 1998; BNF 45, 2003].

Drugs included

- **Oral rehydration therapy** (ORT) is indicated for the prevention of dehydration in young children and frail elderly people, and for the treatment of mild dehydration. The products included here are also available over the counter from pharmacies for people who may wish to purchase them. They are available in a selection of flavours and pack sizes [Murphy, 1998; BNF 45, 2003].
- **Rice-based ORT** (e.g. Dioralyte Relief) has been shown to reduce stool output in people with cholera, but not in infants or children with non-cholera diarrhoea [Fontaine et al, 2003]. Prescriptions are included, but currently it is not clear whether they offer any advantages over glucose-based solutions for routine use.
- **Loperamide** is effective in reducing stool frequency and increasing stool consistency. It may be a useful adjunct for symptom control in some adults, but it should not be used routinely. It has a low incidence of adverse effects on the central nervous system, but should be avoided in children under 4 years of age and people with severe symptoms or dysentery, owing to a risk of precipitating ileus or toxic megacolon [WHO, 1993b; Farthing et al, 1996; BNF 45, 2003].
- **Antibiotics: ciprofloxacin** may occasionally be required, such as for those who are at high risk or who present with severe symptoms or dysentery, or when illness causes serious disruption to the person's activities [Farthing et al, 1996].
- **Nalidixic acid** is an alternative for children.
- **A short course of trimethoprim** is an option for pregnant women, but resistance is increasing. Where this is a problem, specialist advice should be sought [WHO, 1993b; Cheasty et al, 1998].

Prescriptions

Non-drug management

Advice only: preventing dehydration

- Age from 1 month onwards
- Shigella is one cause of gastroenteritis. Drink plenty of normal drinks if possible. The aim is to prevent dehydration. Eat as normally as possible as soon as possible. Ideally include fruit juices and soups which contain sugar and salt. Also, foods high in carbohydrate such as bread and pasta. Rehydration solutions may be useful in addition to normal drinks if there is concern about dehydration. They provide a perfect balance of water, salt and sugar. These can be bought at a pharmacy and the pharmacist can advise you on their use. Breastfed babies should continue to breastfeed. Antidiarrhoeal medication should not be given to young children. Adults may sometimes benefit. You can buy a suitable preparation from a pharmacy and the pharmacist can advise you on its use.

Acute rehydration therapy

Dioralyte sachets: 30-50ml/kg over 3 to 4 hours

- Age from 1 month to 11 years
- Dioralyte sachets. *WEIGHT REQUIRED* Take 30 to 50ml per kg bodyweight over 3 to 4 hours; supply 20 sachets; NHS Cost £5.68; OTC Cost £10.01.

Dioralyte sachets: 2L over 24 hours then 200ml after stool

- Age from 12 years onwards
- Dioralyte sachets. Take two litres in divided doses over 24 hours, then 200ml after each loose stool; supply 20 sachets; NHS Cost £5.68; OTC Cost £10.01.

Dioralyte tablets: 30-50ml/kg over 3 to 4 hours

- Age from 1 month to 11 months
- Dioralyte effervescent tablets. *WEIGHT REQUIRED* Take 30 to 50ml per kg bodyweight over 3 to 4 hours; supply 40 tablets; NHS Cost £5.16; OTC Cost £9.10.

Dioralyte tablets: 30-50ml/kg over 3 to 4 hours

- Age from 12 months to 11 years
- Dioralyte effervescent tablets. *WEIGHT REQUIRED* Take 30 to 50ml per kg bodyweight over 3 to 4 hours; supply 40 tablets; NHS Cost £5.16; OTC Cost £9.09.

Dioralyte tablets: 2L over 24 hours then 200ml after stool

- Age from 12 years onwards
- Dioralyte effervescent tablets. Take two litres in divided doses over 24 hours, then 200ml after each loose stool; supply 40 tablets; NHS Cost £5.16; OTC Cost £9.09.

Electrolade sachets: 30-50ml/kg over 3 to 4 hours

- Age from 1 month to 11 years
- Electrolade multiflavour sachets. *WEIGHT REQUIRED* Take 30 to 50ml per kg bodyweight over 3 to 4 hours; supply 20 sachets; NHS Cost £4.99; OTC Cost £7.99.

Electrolade sachets: 2L over 24 hours then 200ml after stool

- Age from 12 years onwards
- Electrolade multiflavour sachets. Take two litres in divided doses over 24 hours, then 200ml after each loose stool; supply 20 sachets; NHS Cost £4.99; OTC Cost £7.99.

Oral rehydration therapy

Dioralyte sachets: 1 to 1.5 times usual 24 hour feed volume

- Age from 1 month to 11 months
- Dioralyte sachets. *WEIGHT REQUIRED* Give 150ml per kg bodyweight per day in divided doses OR one to one and a half times usual 24 hour feed volume; supply 20 sachets; NHS Cost £5.68; OTC Cost £10.01.

Dioralyte sachets: 200ml after each loose stool

- Age from 12 months to 11 years
- Dioralyte sachets. *WEIGHT REQUIRED* Take 10ml per kg bodyweight after each loose stool OR the contents of one sachet (dissolved in water) after each loose stool; supply 20 sachets; NHS Cost £5.68; OTC Cost £10.01.

Dioralyte sachets: 200-400ml after each loose stool

- Age from 12 years onwards
- Dioralyte sachets. Take the contents of one to two sachets (dissolved in water) after each loose stool; supply 20 sachets; NHS Cost £5.68; OTC Cost £10.01.

Dioralyte tablets: 1 to 1.5 times usual 24 hour feed volume
- Age from 1 month to 11 months
- Dioralyte effervescent tablets. *WEIGHT REQUIRED* Give 150ml per kg bodyweight per day in divided doses OR one to one and a half times usual 24 hour feed volume; supply 40 tablets; NHS Cost £5.16; OTC Cost £9.10.

Dioralyte tablets: 200ml after each loose stool
- Age from 12 months to 11 years
- Dioralyte effervescent tablets. *WEIGHT REQUIRED* Take 10ml per kg bodyweight after each loose stool OR two tablets (dissolved in water) after each loose stool; supply 40 tablets; NHS Cost £5.16; OTC Cost £9.10.

Dioralyte tablets: 200-400ml after each loose stool
- Age from 12 years onwards
- Dioralyte effervescent tablets. Take two to four tablets (dissolved in water) after each loose stool; supply 40 tablets; NHS Cost £5.16; OTC Cost £9.10.

Electrolade sachets: 1 to 1.5 times usual 24 hr feed volume
- Age from 1 month to 11 months
- Electrolade multiflavour sachets. *WEIGHT REQUIRED* Give 150ml per kg bodyweight per day in divided doses OR one to one and a half times usual 24 hour feed volume; supply 20 sachets; NHS Cost £4.99; OTC Cost £7.99.

Electrolade sachets: 200ml after each loose stool
- Age from 12 months to 11 years
- Electrolade multiflavour sachets. *WEIGHT REQUIRED* Take 10ml per kg bodyweight after each loose stool OR the contents of one sachet (dissolved in water) after each loose stool; supply 20 sachets; NHS Cost £4.99; OTC Cost £7.99.

Electrolade sachets: 200-400ml after each loose stool
- Age from 12 years onwards
- Electrolade multiflavour sachets. Take the contents of one to two sachets (dissolved in water) after each loose stool; supply 20 sachets; NHS Cost £4.99; OTC Cost £7.99.

Loperamide: not for routine use

Loperamide: 4mg now, then 2mg after stool. Max 16mg/24 hours
- Age from 12 years onwards
- Loperamide 2mg capsules. Take TWO capsules initially, then take ONE capsule after each loose stool for up to 5 days. Maximum of 8 capsules in 24 hours; supply 30 capsules; NHS Cost £1.22; OTC Cost £6.35.

Antibiotics for 3 days or 7 days: rarely appropriate

Ciprofloxacin tablets: 500mg twice a day (NOT if pregnant)
- Age from 16 years onwards
- Ciprofloxacin 500mg tablets. Take one tablet twice a day for 3 days; supply 6 tablets; NHS Cost £8.52.

Nalidixic acid tablets:1g four times a day (NOT if pregnant)
- Age from 12 to 16 years
- Nalidixic acid 500mg tablets. Take two tablets four times a day for 7 days; supply 56 tablets; NHS Cost £12.83.

Nalidixic acid s/f suspension: 12.5mg/kg four times a day
- Age from 3 months to 5 years
- Nalidixic acid 300mg/5ml s/f. *WEIGHT REQUIRED* Take 12.5mg per kg bodyweight FOUR times a day for 7 days; supply 150 ml; NHS Cost £12.85.

Nalidixic acid s/f suspension: 12.5mg/kg four times a day
- Age from 6 to 11 years
- Nalidixic acid 300mg/5ml s/f. *WEIGHT REQUIRED* Take 12.5mg per kg bodyweight FOUR times a day for 7 days; supply 300 ml; NHS Cost £25.70.

Trimethoprim: 200mg twice a day
- Age from 12 years onwards
- Trimethoprim 200mg tablets. Take one tablet twice a day for 3 days; supply 6 tablets; NHS Cost £0.29.

Trimethoprim s/f suspension: 50mg twice a day
- Age from 6 months to 5 years
- Trimethoprim 50mg/5ml s/f susp. Take one 5ml spoonful twice a day for 3 days; supply 30 ml; NHS Cost £0.53.

Trimethoprim s/f suspension: 100mg twice a day
- Age from 6 to 11 years
- Trimethoprim 50mg/5ml s/f susp. Take two 5ml spoonfuls twice a day for 3 days; supply 60 ml; NHS Cost £1.06.

Confirmed giardiasis

Which therapy?

Antibiotic treatment

- **Treat people with giardiasis with metronidazole.** If symptoms persist after treatment with metronidazole, *and* repeat stool culture remains positive, seek specialist advice, as *Giardia* resistant to metronidazole have been reported.

Antimotility drugs

- **Antimotility drugs are occasionally beneficial in adults** with mild to moderate diarrhoea. They must not be prescribed for children under 4 years old, or for people with severe gastroenteritis or dysentery, owing to the risk of severe colitis and toxic dilation of the colon.

General issues

- **Notify cases of giardiasis** to the local consultant in Communicable Disease Control.
- **Advise on how to prevent transmission** (e.g. hand washing and other hygienic measures).
- **People should usually be excluded from school or work** until they are free of diarrhoea and are able to maintain a satisfactory fluid intake.
- **Normal feeding should be restarted as soon as possible** in both children and adults. There is no evidence that fasting will have any benefit.

Prevention of dehydration

- **Many people can simply be advised to increase their intake of fluids** — usually glucose-containing fluids and soups are sufficient for adults. Infants, young children, and frail elderly people are particularly prone to becoming dehydrated. Early feeding is now recommended, if tolerated, especially with foods high in carbohydrates, such as bread, pasta, potatoes, or rice.

Treatment of dehydration

- **Mild dehydration** can often be treated outside hospital, provided social circumstances are appropriate and early review of the person can be guaranteed.
- **For children:** give 30–50 ml/kg of oral rehydration therapy (ORT) over 3–4 hours. Follow this with unrestricted fluids, either with normal fluids alternating with ORT, or just normal fluids.

- **For adults:** give 2 litres of ORT in the first 24 hours, followed by unrestricted normal fluids with 200 ml of ORT per loose stool or vomit.

Practical prescribing points

For further information, please see the *Medicines Compendium* (www.medicines.org.uk) or the *British National Formulary* (www.bnf.org).

Metronidazole

- **Metronidazole:** advise avoidance of alcohol for the duration of treatment and for at least 48 hours afterwards, because of the possibility of a disulfiram-like (Antabuse) reaction.

Loperamide

- **Loperamide** should be avoided in children under 4 years of age and in people with severe gastroenteritis or dysentery, owing to the risk of severe colitis and toxic megacolon.

Oral rehydration therapy

- **When oral rehydration therapy is used in people with diabetes,** blood glucose levels may need to be monitored more carefully.

Follow-up advice

- **People with mild dehydration who are being treated at home** require an early review.

Should I refer or investigate?

Refer?

- **Admit people who are 5% or more dehydrated.**
- **People with severe gastroenteritis may require admission.**
- **Mild dehydration** may be managed at home with ORT, providing there are no complicating comorbidities, social circumstances are appropriate, and early review can be guaranteed.

Investigate?

- **No further investigation is necessary following the initial diagnosis.** Cases of giardiasis resistant to metronidazole have been reported; if symptoms persist after treatment with metronidazole, three further samples should be analysed on consecutive days.

Patient information leaflets

The following PILs are available at www.prodigy.nhs.uk

- Gastroenteritis in Adults
- Gastroenteritis in Children

Shared decision making

- *Giardia* is is one cause of gastroenteritis.
- **Drink plenty** of normal drinks if possible. The aim is to prevent dehydration.
- **Eat as normally as possible.** Ideally include fruit juices and soups, which will provide sugar and salt, and also foods high in carbohydrate, such as bread, pasta, potatoes, or rice.
- **Rehydration solutions** may be useful in addition, if there is concern about dehydration. They provide a perfect balance of water, salt, and sugar.
- **Breastfed babies should continue to breastfeed.**
- **Antidiarrhoeal medication** should not be given to young children. Adults may sometimes benefit from this.
- **An antibiotic called metronidazole** is advised for **giardiasis.**
  - Do not drink alcohol whilst taking metronidazole and for 48 hours after stopping the drug. The two together can make you quite ill.
  - Metronidazole may give a short-term metallic taste.
- **Always wash your hands** after going to the toilet (or changing nappies).
- **Does your job involve handling food?** You will need special advice.
- **See a doctor if the symptoms do not improve** after the course of metronidazole has finished.

Drug rationale

Drugs not included

- **Other oral rehydration therapy:** the World Health Organization formulation of this is not recommended. It has a higher sodium content than the formulations commonly used in the UK, because people here generally suffer less severe sodium loss [Murphy, 1998; BNF 45, 2003].
- **Antispasmodics** are not recommended in children because they are rarely effective and have troublesome adverse effects. There are also few data to support their use in older people [American Academy of Pediatrics, 1996; BNF 45, 2003].
- **Antimotility drugs (other than loperamide)** are not included. These preparations have a limited adjunctive role for symptom control, but many have adverse effects on the central nervous system, including sedation, and are considered to be less suitable for prescribing. They may cause paralytic ileus, and are not recommended for use in children [WHO, 1993b; Murphy, 1998; BNF 45, 2003].
- **Bismuth subsalicylate** (available as Pepto-Bismol) has been shown to reduce stool frequency, but it is only available for purchase over the counter in the UK in a liquid form. Large quantities may be needed to control symptoms, making it a less practical option for travellers [WHO, 1993b; BNF 45, 2003].
- **Antibiotics (other than metronidazole)** are not included. Tinidazole is probably as effective as metronidazole; but it is more expensive and, belonging to the same class as metronidazole, appears to offer no clinical advantage. Mepacrine hydrochloride is not licensed for the treatment of giardiasis, and is very rarely used in primary care [BNF 45, 2003].

Drugs included

- **Oral rehydration therapy** (ORT) is indicated for the prevention of dehydration in young children and frail elderly people, and for the treatment of mild dehydration. The products included here are also available over the counter from pharmacies for people who may wish to purchase them. They are available in a selection of flavours and pack sizes [Murphy, 1998; BNF 45, 2003].
- **Rice-based ORT** (e.g. Dioralyte Relief) has been shown to reduce stool output in people with cholera, but not in infants or children with non-cholera diarrhoea [Fontaine et al, 2003]. Prescriptions are included, but currently it is not clear whether they offer any advantages over glucose-based solutions for routine use.
- **Loperamide** is effective in reducing stool frequency and increasing stool consistency. It may be a useful adjunct for symptom control in some adults, but it should not be used routinely. It has a low incidence of adverse effects on the central nervous system, but should be avoided in children under 4 years of age and people with severe

symptoms or dysentery, because of the risk of precipitating ileus or toxic megacolon [WHO, 1993b; Farthing et al, 1996; BNF 45, 2003].

- **Antibiotics: metronidazole** is recommended for all people who have a diagnosis of giardiasis. Cases of giardiasis resistant to metronidazole have been reported; if symptoms persist after treatment with metronidazole, and repeat stool culture remains positive, specialist advice should be sought.

Prescriptions

Non-drug management

Advice only: preventing dehydration

- Age from 1 month onwards
- Giardiasis is one cause of gastroenteritis. Drink plenty of normal drinks if possible. The aim is to prevent dehydration. Eat as normally as possible as soon as possible. Ideally include fruit juices and soups which contain sugar and salt. Also, foods high in carbohydrate such as bread and pasta. Rehydration solutions may be useful in addition to normal drinks if there is concern about dehydration. They provide a perfect balance of water, salt and sugar. These can be bought at a pharmacy and the pharmacist can advise you on their use. Breastfed babies should continue to breastfeed. Antidiarrhoeal medication should not be given to young children. Adults may sometimes benefit. You can buy a suitable preparation from a pharmacy and the pharmacist can advise you on its use.

G

Acute rehydration therapy

Dioralyte sachets: 30-50ml/kg over 3 to 4 hours

- Age from 1 month to 11 years
- Dioralyte sachets. *WEIGHT REQUIRED* Take 30 to 50ml per kg bodyweight over 3 to 4 hours; supply 20 sachets; NHS Cost £5.68; OTC Cost £10.01.

Dioralyte sachets: 2L over 24 hours then 200ml after stool

- Age from 12 years onwards
- Dioralyte sachets. Take two litres in divided doses over 24 hours, then 200ml after each loose stool; supply 20 sachets; NHS Cost £5.68; OTC Cost £10.01.

Dioralyte tablets: 30-50ml/kg over 3 to 4 hours

- Age from 1 month to 11 months
- Dioralyte effervescent tablets. *WEIGHT REQUIRED* Take 30 to 50ml per kg bodyweight over 3 to 4 hours; supply 40 tablets; NHS Cost £5.16; OTC Cost £9.10.

Dioralyte tablets: 30-50ml/kg over 3 to 4 hours

- Age from 12 months to 11 years
- Dioralyte effervescent tablets. *WEIGHT REQUIRED* Take 30 to 50ml per kg bodyweight over 3 to 4 hours; supply 40 tablets; NHS Cost £5.16; OTC Cost £9.09.

Dioralyte tablets: 2L over 24 hours then 200ml after stool

- Age from 12 years onwards
- Dioralyte effervescent tablets. Take two litres in divided doses over 24 hours, then 200ml after each loose stool; supply 40 tablets; NHS Cost £5.16; OTC Cost £9.09.

Electrolade sachets: 30-50ml/kg over 3 to 4 hours

- Age from 1 month to 11 years
- Electrolade multiflavour sachets. *WEIGHT REQUIRED* Take 30 to 50ml per kg bodyweight over 3 to 4 hours; supply 20 sachets; NHS Cost £4.99; OTC Cost £7.99.

Electrolade sachets: 2L over 24 hours then 200ml after stool

- Age from 12 years onwards
- Electrolade multiflavour sachets. Take two litres in divided doses over 24 hours, then 200ml after each loose stool; supply 20 sachets; NHS Cost £4.99; OTC Cost £7.99.

Oral rehydration therapy

Dioralyte sachets: 1 to 1.5 times usual 24 hour feed volume

- Age from 1 month to 11 months
- Dioralyte sachets. *WEIGHT REQUIRED* Give 150ml per kg bodyweight per day in divided doses OR one to one and a half times usual 24 hour feed volume; supply 20 sachets; NHS Cost £5.68; OTC Cost £10.01.

Dioralyte sachets: 200ml after each loose stool

- Age from 12 months to 11 years
- Dioralyte sachets. *WEIGHT REQUIRED* Take 10ml per kg bodyweight after each loose stool OR the contents of one sachet (dissolved in water) after each loose stool; supply 20 sachets; NHS Cost £5.68; OTC Cost £10.01.

Dioralyte sachets: 200-400ml after each loose stool

- Age from 12 years onwards
- Dioralyte sachets. Take the contents of one to two sachets (dissolved in water) after each loose stool; supply 20 sachets; NHS Cost £5.68; OTC Cost £10.01.

Dioralyte tablets: 1 to 1.5 times usual 24 hour feed volume

- Age from 1 month to 11 months
- Dioralyte effervescent tablets. *WEIGHT REQUIRED* Give 150ml per kg bodyweight per day in divided doses OR one to one and a half times usual 24 hour feed volume; supply 40 tablets; NHS Cost £5.16; OTC Cost £9.10.

Dioralyte tablets: 200ml after each loose stool

- Age from 12 months to 11 years
- Dioralyte effervescent tablets. *WEIGHT REQUIRED* Take 10ml per kg bodyweight after each loose stool OR two tablets (dissolved in water) after each loose stool; supply 40 tablets; NHS Cost £5.16; OTC Cost £9.10.

Dioralyte tablets: 200-400ml after each loose stool

- Age from 12 years onwards
- Dioralyte effervescent tablets. Take two to four tablets (dissolved in water) after each loose stool; supply 40 tablets; NHS Cost £5.16; OTC Cost £9.10.

Electrolade sachets: 1 to 1.5 times usual 24 hr feed volume

- Age from 1 month to 11 months
- Electrolade multiflavour sachets. *WEIGHT REQUIRED* Give 150ml per kg bodyweight per day in divided doses OR one to one and a half times usual 24 hour feed volume; supply 20 sachets; NHS Cost £4.99; OTC Cost £7.99.

Electrolade sachets: 200ml after each loose stool

- Age from 12 months to 11 years
- Electrolade multiflavour sachets. *WEIGHT REQUIRED* Take 10ml per kg bodyweight after each loose stool OR the contents of one sachet (dissolved in water) after each loose stool; supply 20 sachets; NHS Cost £4.99; OTC Cost £7.99.

Electrolade sachets: 200-400ml after each loose stool

- Age from 12 years onwards
- Electrolade multiflavour sachets. Take the contents of one to two sachets (dissolved in water) after each loose stool; supply 20 sachets; NHS Cost £4.99; OTC Cost £7.99.

Loperamide: not for routine use

Loperamide: 4mg now, then 2mg after stool. Max 16mg/24 hours

- Age from 12 years onwards
- Loperamide 2mg capsules. Take TWO capsules initially, then take ONE capsule after each loose stool for up to 5

days. Maximum of 8 capsules in 24 hours; supply 30 capsules; NHS Cost £1.22; OTC Cost £6.35.

Metronidazole (NOT if pregnant)

Metronidazole suspension: 500mg once a day for 3 days
- Age from 12 months to 2 years
- Metronidazole 200mg/5ml susp. Take 12.5ml once a day for three days; supply 50 ml; NHS Cost £7.70.

Metronidazole suspension: 600mg once a day for 3 days
- Age from 3 to 6 years
- Metronidazole 200mg/5ml susp. Take three 5ml spoonfuls once a day for three days; supply 45 ml; NHS Cost £7.70.

Metronidazole suspension: 700mg once a day for 3 days
- Age from 3 to 6 years
- Metronidazole 200mg/5ml susp. Take 17.5ml once a day for three days; supply 55 ml; NHS Cost £7.70.

Metronidazole suspension: 800mg once a day for 3 days
- Age from 3 to 6 years
- Metronidazole 200mg/5ml susp. Take four 5ml spoonfuls once a day for three days; supply 60 ml; NHS Cost £7.70.

Metronidazole suspension: 1g once a day for 3 days
- Age from 7 to 9 years
- Metronidazole 200mg/5ml susp. Take five 5ml spoonfuls once a day for 3 days; supply 75 ml; NHS Cost £7.70.

Metronidazole tablets: 2g once a day for 3 days
- Age from 10 years onwards
- Metronidazole 400mg tablets. Take five tablets once a day for three days; supply 15 tablets; NHS Cost £0.37.

Metronidazole tablets: 400mg three times a day for 5 days
- Age from 10 years onwards
- Metronidazole 400mg tablets. Take one tablet three times a day for 5 days; supply 15 tablets; NHS Cost £0.73.

Metronidazole tablets: 500mg twice a day for 7 days
- Age from 10 years onwards
- Metronidazole 500mg tablets. Take one tablet twice a day for 7 days; supply 0 tablets.

Metronidazole tablets: 500mg twice a day for 10 days
- Age from 10 years onwards
- Metronidazole 500mg tablets. Take one tablet twice a day for 10 days; supply 20 tablets; NHS Cost £3.33.

Extended Information

Background information

- What is it? p.821
- How common is it? p.821
- How do I know my patient has it? p.822
- How do I know my patient is dehydrated? p.822
- What else might it be? p.823
- Complications and prognosis p.823

What is it?

- **Infective gastroenteritis** is characterized by a rapid onset of diarrhoea, and is often accompanied by one or more of the following: nausea, vomiting, fever, anorexia, abdominal cramps, flatulence, or bloating [Dalby-Payne and Elliott, 2002]. Acute symptoms last up to 14 days.
- **Diarrhoea** is defined as the passage of watery stools with an increase in stool frequency — at least three times in a 24-hour period [WHO, 1993b; De Bruyn, 2002].
- **Travellers' diarrhoea** is a type of gastroenteritis, which most commonly results from intestinal infection with international travel (especially between developed and developing countries). Symptoms typically last around 4 days.
- **Dysentery** is infective gastroenteritis characterized by loose, small-volume stools with blood and mucus. Pyrexia and abdominal cramps often accompany dysentery.
- **The cause of gastroenteritis may be bacteria, protozoa, toxins, or viruses.** Infection is often obtained from ingestion of contaminated food and water, although viruses are usually transmitted directly from person to person.
- **The aetiology of gastroenteritis** has been investigated, and in England it has been found that:
  - **In children under 5 years of age,** viruses cause about 80% of episodes. The rotavirus species is the most common, and it is estimated that this virus results in about 18,000 children under 5 years of age being admitted to hospital in England and Wales each year [Tompkins et al, 1999].
  - **In adults,** *Campylobacter* was most commonly identified, followed by rotavirus.
  - **Other less common causes** included: *Escherichia coli, Salmonella, Shigella, Clostridium perfringens* enterotoxin (bacteria); adenovirus, astrovirus (viruses); *Cryptosporidium, Giardia, Entamoeba* (protozoa) [Tompkins et al, 1999].
- **Travellers' diarrhoea is most commonly caused by bacteria:**
  - The most common bacterial cause worldwide is enterotoxigenic *E coli* [von Sonnenburg et al, 2000; Jiang et al, 2002].
  - *Cyclospora* is a relatively new protozoal agent that has been found in biopsies of the small intestine of people who have travelled to Nepal.
- **Some organisms found in contaminated food (e.g. *Staphylococcus aureus* and *Bacillus cereus*) produce enterotoxins,** which, on ingestion, result in a rapid onset of diarrhoea and vomiting, with symptoms usually lasting less than 12 hours [Tauxe and Hughes, 1995].
- **No pathogen is identified in about half the cases investigated** [Tompkins et al, 1999; de Wit et al, 2001]. This may be because of clearance of the pathogen before resolution of symptoms, technical problems with culture, taking of inappropriate specimens, or, possibly, the presence of an unidentifiable infective agent.

[Farthing et al, 1992; DTB, 2002; De Bruyn et al, 2003; Farthing, 2003]

How common is it?

Children

- **Acute gastroenteritis occurs most commonly in children,** and accounts for over 20% of GP consultations for children aged less than 5 years in the UK [Dalby-Payne and Elliott, 2002]. Many cases are not reported, but it is estimated that the range is from one to three illnesses per year for children aged less than 5 years.

Adults

- **Gastroenteritis has been estimated to occur in 1 in 5 people of all ages each year.** Of the people infected, only 1 in 6 presents to a GP [Wheeler et al, 1999].
- **Many people do not seek medical attention.** Of those who do, only a proportion will have a stool specimen submitted for investigation.
- **Suspected 'food poisoning' is common.** In one study, 9% of those in a community survey who reported symptoms of gastroenteritis, and 22% of those consulting their GP for such illness, thought they definitely or probably had 'food poisoning' [Farthing et al, 1996].

G

Travellers' diarrhoea

- **The risk of developing travellers' diarrhoea** depends upon the destination, mode of travel [DTB, 2002], and duration of visit. The chance of a UK person developing travellers' diarrhoea is:
  - Greater than 20% in high-risk destinations (e.g. Africa, South America, some parts of the Middle East, and most of Asia)
  - 15–20% in intermediate-risk areas (e.g. southern Europe, Israel, Japan, South Africa, and some of the Caribbean islands)
  - Less than 8% in low-risk areas (e.g. North America, northern Europe, Australia, and New Zealand)
- **10% of people affected have dysentery** (bloody diarrhoea), which may persist for weeks.

How do I know my patient has it?

History

G

- **The history may include identifying the following features** if appropriate:
  - The onset of illness — abrupt or gradual.
  - The duration and sequence of the symptoms
  - Whether family members or other contacts are also ill
  - Details of any foreign travel — travel duration, destinations, diet
  - Consumption of unsafe foods — possible sources of food poisoning
  - Use of recent medication (e.g. antibiotic use)
  - Any weight loss, especially in children
  - Sexual practices (homosexual men are at particular risk of infective proctitis)
  - The immune status
  - Underlying conditions predisposing to infectious diarrhoea (e.g. AIDS)
  - Recent contact with pets with diarrhoea or animals external to the home
  - Occupation as a food-handler or care-giver
  - Attendance at a day-care centre

Symptoms and signs

- **Nausea, vomiting, fever, anorexia, abdominal cramps, flatulence, and bloating** may accompany the acute onset of diarrhoea [Dalby-Payne and Elliott, 2002].
- **Bloody diarrhoea and mucus (dysentery)** strongly suggests the presence of an invasive organism (e.g. *Campylobacter, Salmonella, Shigella,* or *Escherichia coli* 0157).
- **Travellers' diarrhoea** may begin at any time during travel or shortly after return, but it most commonly occurs early in the trip and lasts around 4 days.
- **Signs of dehydration** may be visibly apparent.

Investigations

- **Stool culture is necessary when the person:**
  - Has stools that contain blood
  - Is febrile
  - Appears systemically unwell
  - Has watery diarrhoea present for longer than 4 days
  - Has recently returned from abroad
  - Attends a nursery/child-minder/play-group/school or a day centre
  - Has suspected food poisoning or gastroenteritis
  - Is either a food handler putting other people at risk, or lives with people who handle food for the public
  - Is taking or has recently taken a broad-spectrum antibiotic (request *Clostridium difficile* toxin detection), in particular lincomycins, broad-spectrum penicillins, or cephalosporins [Dwight and Collier, 2001a]
  - Is taking or has recently taken chemotherapy
- **A negative stool culture does not exclude infection.** In a large general-practice study, no enteropathogens were detected from a large proportion of samples, despite comprehensive testing [Tompkins et al, 1999].
- **Policy varies between laboratories as to which cultures and other investigations are routinely undertaken on each sample.** Specific investigations required should be requested. Laboratory testing may be done for pathogens not routinely sought, depending on information provided on the request form. Relevant information, such as the presence of bloody diarrhoea, recent foreign travel, recent antibiotic therapy, and suspected food poisoning, must be clearly documented. In many laboratories, routine testing for rotavirus in children under 5 years old may be carried out, but it is not known how many laboratories currently undertake this particular investigation [Tompkins, Personal Communication, 2003; Wright, Personal Communication, 2003].
- **Consider testing for *Clostridium difficile* toxin if symptoms are severe,** especially if the person has been recently hospitalized, or has received antibiotic therapy within the previous 4 or 6 weeks (in particular, lincomycins, broad-spectrum penicillins, or cephalosporins).
- **Persistent diarrhoea (e.g. for more than 14 days) requires further stool investigation** to exclude parasitic infections such as *Giardia, Entamoeba, Cryptosporidium,* and *Cyclospora*. Specialist advice should be considered.
- **Specialist advice should be sought if homosexual men or people with AIDS** develop acute severe diarrhoea or persistent diarrhoea.

[Farthing, 1998; Dwight and Collier, 2001a; Guerrant et al, 2002]

How do I know my patient is dehydrated?

- **It is important to exclude dehydration,** especially in children or in people with severe or prolonged symptoms.
- **A baby who is seriously dehydrated may continue to feed well,** so feeding should not be used as an indication of well-being [Dwight and Collier, 2001b]. Acute weight change may be a useful measure of dehydration in a child, provided that a recent accurate weight has been recorded. Dehydration signs are not usually present until there is a weight loss of about 5% [Cincinnati Children's Hospital Medical Center, 2002].
- **Table 1 summarizes some of the more common features associated with different degrees of dehydration in children.** In the UK, people with gastroenteritis will rarely exhibit anything more than mild losses.
- **In mild dehydration,** symptoms are frequently absent, or include tiredness, anorexia, nausea, and light-headedness. Physical examination is normal.
- **In moderate dehydration,** symptoms become more prominent. Findings include decreased skin turgor, dry mucous membranes, sunken eyes, sunken fontanelle (in infants), absence of tears when crying, absence of urinating in several hours, postural hypotension, tachycardia, and oliguria.
- **In severe dehydration,** the person may develop signs of hypovolaemic shock, including a low level of consciousness, oliguria or anuria, cool extremities, a rapid and feeble pulse, low or undetectable blood pressure, and peripheral cyanosis. Death follows if rehydration is not started quickly.

[WHO, 1993b; Farthing et al, 1996; Dwight and Collier, 2001b; Cincinnati Children's Hospital Medical Center, 2002]

Table 1: Clinical features associated with degree of dehydration in children.

Clinical features	Mild (<5%)	Moderate (5–10%)	Severe (>10%)
Dry mouth	Moist	Dry	Very dry
Extremities	Warm, good refill	Delayed refill	Mottled, poor refill
Tears	Normal	Normal to absent	Absent
Sunken eyes	Normal	Sunken	Very sunken and dry
Level of consciousness	Well, alert	Restless, irritable	Lethargic, unconscious (floppy)
Skin pinch	Goes back quickly	Goes back slowly	Considerable decrease
Tachycardia	Normal	Moderate increase	Major increase
Decreased urine output	Slight decrease	Moderate decrease	Major decrease

What else might it be?

- **Drug-induced diarrhoea** may occur as a result of taking antibiotics, anti-malarials, magnesium-containing antacids, or antimotility drugs; or as result of inappropriate laxative use. The condition normally reverses upon withdrawal of the drug.
- **Pseudomembranous colitis:** due to toxin-producing *Clostridium difficile* — consider in a case where a recent course of antibiotic (in particular lincomycins, broad-spectrum penicillins, or cephalosporins) has been taken.
- **Systemic infection** may present non-specifically with diarrhoea, especially in neonates and infants.
- **Malaria** — diarrhoea may be a symptom.
- **First presentation of any cause of chronic diarrhoea [Walker-Smith and Murch, 2003]:**
  - Motility disorders — constipation and bypass diarrhoea, toddler diarrhoea, or chronic non-specific diarrhoea (often responds to dietary changes)
  - Chronic inflammatory bowel disease (ulcerative colitis or Crohn's disease)
  - Other bowel disease (diverticulitis, cancer etc.)
  - Food-sensitive enteropathy — lactose intolerance
  - Coeliac disease
  - Pancreatic disorders — consider cystic fibrosis
  - Surgical disorders and complications
  - Congenital inborn errors of metabolism

Complications and prognosis

Complications

- **The risk of complications is greatest** at the extremities of life, in people with concurrent chronic disease, and in those who are immunocompromised.
- **Dehydration and electrolyte disturbance** can occur. If severe, these can result in acidosis and circulatory failure, with hypoperfusion of vital organs, renal failure, and eventual death.
- **People with travellers' diarrhoea may be vulnerable to complications for which they were taking drugs.** Some of these may be poorly absorbed during diarrhoea (e.g. antimalarials, antiepileptics, antidiabetics, anticoagulants, and contraceptives) [Spira, 2003].
- **Reactive complications** such as arthritis, carditis, urticaria, erythema nodosum, conjunctivitis, and Reiter's syndrome are associated with *Salmonella*, *Campylobacter*, *Yersinia enterocolitica* and *Shigella* [EBM, 2000]. In contrast, there are usually no reactive complications associated with viral and parasitic gastroenteritis.
- **Systemic invasion by *Salmonella* species** may result in localized infections in bones, joints, meninges, and the gallbladder.
- Enteropathogenic *Escherichia coli* infection may be complicated by the development of haemolytic uraemic syndrome (HUS) and thrombotic thrombocytopenic purpura, which may cause permanent kidney failure. Children are especially vulnerable, and 5–10% develop HUS.
- **Toxic megacolon** due to fulminant infective colitis occurs rarely.
- **Guillain–Barré syndrome** may complicate *Campylobacter* infection.
- **Typhoid syndrome may occur in *Salmonella*, *Campylobacter*, and mixed infections** caused by intestinal bacterial pathogens. The syndrome usually needs to be treated in hospital [EBM, 2000].
- **Malnutrition,** with or without diarrhoea, may follow some infections and is a common risk in developing countries [Guerrant et al, 2002].
- **Rare intractable diarrhoea syndromes** may require long-term parenteral nutrition or even small intestinal transplantation [Walker-Smith and Murch, 2003].
- **Disorders of the gall bladder** may prevent pathogens from being detected [EBM, 2000].
- **Schistosomiasis** may occur as a result of travel to tropical locations. There is also an association between schistosomiasis and chronic salmonellosis [Spira, 2003].

[Crowley et al, 1997; Farthing, 1998; EBM, 2000]

Prognosis

- **Acute gastroenteritis is usually a mild self-limiting illness,** but if untreated can result in morbidity and mortality secondary to water and electrolyte losses.
- **In developed countries,** dehydration secondary to gastroenteritis may cause hospital admission, but death is uncommon.

Management issues

- General issues p.823
- Feeding during gastroenteritis p.824
- Prevention of dehydration p.824
- Treatment of dehydration p.824
- Antimotility drugs p.824
- Anti-emetics p.825
- Antibiotic treatment p.825
- Chronic diarrhoea p.826

General issues

- **Most cases of mild to moderate diarrhoea are self-limiting,** are of short duration, and do not require laboratory investigation.
- **It is a statutory obligation to notify all cases of dysentery and suspected or confirmed food poisoning.** An initial telephone or fax communication to the local Consultant in Communicable Disease Control (CCDC) or public-health consultant should be followed by written notification on the standard certificate. This should not await laboratory identification of a cause [Farthing et al, 1996].
- **People should be advised on how to prevent transmission** to other family members or contacts. Recommendations include:
  - Personal hygiene with hand washing
  - Prompt disinfection of contaminated surfaces
  - Prompt washing of soiled clothes
  - Avoidance of food/water if there is a chance of contamination

G

- **A recent systematic review found that interventions to promote washing hands with soap** were associated with a decrease in risk of diarrhoeal disease of 47% (95% CI 24% to 63%) [Curtis and Cairncross, 2003].
- **All those affected should usually be excluded from school or work until free of diarrhoea and vomiting.** Food handlers and staff of healthcare facilities should be symptom-free for at least 48 hours before returning to work [DH, 1995]. Sick leave of one week is necessary for a person suffering from diarrhoea and working as a food-handler. Further leave may be necessary for people diagnosed with *Salmonella* or *Shigella* — until three consecutive faecal specimens have been confirmed [EBM, 2000].
- **Official Department of Health policy regarding food handlers** is that anyone who has diarrhoea or vomiting must immediately leave the food-handling area. For the majority, no measures other than temporary exclusion are required. Prior to returning to work:
  - Employees should have had no diarrhoea or vomiting for 48 hours after any treatment has ceased.
  - Good hygiene practice, especially hand washing, should be maintained.
  - Negative stool samples are not a necessary condition for return to work. Occasionally, employers wrongly insist on this, in which case the CCDC should usually be involved [Tompkins, Personal Communication, 2003].
  - If diarrhoea is due to hepatitis A infection, then employees should remain off work until 7 days after the onset of symptoms (usually jaundice).
  - Specialist advice should be sought in all cases of enteric fever (typhoid) and haemorrhagic *Escherichia coli* [DH, 1995].
- **Particular care is needed in people with risk factors for poor outcome,** such as:
  - The very young or elderly
  - Those with pre-existing medical conditions (e.g. immunodeficiency, gastric hypochlorhydria, inflammatory bowel disease, valvular heart disease, or diabetes mellitus)
  - Those taking certain drugs (e.g. systemic corticosteroids, acid suppressant agents, angiotensin-converting enzyme [ACE] inhibitors, or diuretics).

Feeding during gastroenteritis

- **Normal feeding should be restarted as soon as possible in both children and adults** — there is no evidence that fasting will have any benefit [Farthing et al, 1992; American Academy of Pediatrics, 1996; Farthing, 1998; Murphy, 1998; Nutrition Committee, 2002].
- In a study of children admitted to hospital with gastroenteritis, normal feeding after 4 hours of oral rehydration therapy (ORT) administration was compared with normal feeding after 24 hours of ORT. Early feeding resulted in greater weight gain after rehydration and during hospitalization, with no worsening of diarrhoea, prolongation of diarrhoea, increased vomiting, or lactose intolerance [Sandhu et al, 1997].
- **Continued feeding is particularly important in breastfeeding infants,** because cessation of feeding may lead to reduction in milk supply [WHO, 1993b; Wan, 1999].
- **If the child is vomiting,** very frequent small feedings (every 10–60 minutes) of regular diet or ORT may be better tolerated [Cincinnati Children's Hospital Medical Center, 2002].
- **A systematic review has found that lactose-free feeds were superior to lactose-containing feeds** in reducing the duration of diarrhoea in children with mild to severe dehydration. However, because lactose intolerance is rare, the use of lactose-free foods is seldom required [Brown et al, 1994; Sandhu et al, 1997].

Prevention of dehydration

- **Many people can safely be advised to increase their intake of fluids.** Usually glucose-containing fluids and soups are sufficient for adults [Wingate et al, 2001]. Eating foods that are high in carbohydrates (such as bread, pasta, potatoes, or rice) helps to promote glucose and sodium co-transport, and should be encouraged.
- **Young children and frail elderly people** are particularly prone to becoming dehydrated, and the use of a proprietary oral rehydration therapy, alternating with normal fluids, is advisable [Murphy, 1998].
- **The child's preferred, usual, and age-appropriate diet should be encouraged,** to prevent or limit dehydration. This approach has been reported to reduce the duration of the diarrhoea and to speed recovery [Cincinnati Children's Hospital Medical Center, 2002].

Treatment of dehydration

- **Mild dehydration** (less than 5%) can often be treated outside of hospital, provided social circumstances are appropriate and early review of the person can be guaranteed. More severe dehydration usually requires admission.
  - **Oral rehydration therapy (ORT) should be used in all cases.** Soft drinks, such as lemonade, cola, Lucozade, etc., alone are inappropriate and may cause osmotic diarrhoea — they have low electrolyte concentrations and are hypertonic, owing to their high carbohydrate content [American Academy of Pediatrics, 1996].
  - **For children,** 30–50 ml/kg of ORT should be given over 3–4 hours. If the child is breastfed, then alternate normal feeds with feeds of ORT. Otherwise rehydrate the child first over 3–4 hours and then recommence the normal diet [Dwight and Collier, 2001b].
  - **For adults,** 2 litres of ORT should be given in the first 24 hours, followed by unrestricted normal fluids with 200 ml of ORT per loose stool or vomit thereafter [Farthing et al, 1996].
- **If the child is breastfed, alternate normal feeds with feeds of ORT.** Otherwise, rehydrate the child first (over 3–4 hours), then recommence the child's normal diet.
- **Once rehydration has been achieved,** restart maintenance fluids such as breast milk, bottle/formula milk, or other fluids appropriate for the child's age. Normal fluid requirements can be calculated from Table 2.
- **A person with moderate dehydration (5–10%) or severe dehydration (>10%) should be admitted to hospital.**

[Dwight and Collier, 2001b]

Antimotility drugs

- **Antimotility drugs are not recommended for acute diarrhoea in young children.** Such drugs do not prevent dehydration, and older agents have the potential to cause central nervous system (CNS) adverse effects such as toxicity and ileus [WHO, 1993b; American Academy of Pediatrics, 1996; Farthing, 1998].

Table 2: Bodyweight and associated fluid maintenance requirements per day for children.

Bodyweight increments	Fluid required per day
First 10 kg	100 ml/kg
Second 10 kg	50 ml/kg
Subsequent kg	25 ml/kg

- **Antimotility drugs are occasionally useful for symptomatic control in adults** with mild to moderate diarrhoea. However, such drugs should be avoided if diarrhoea is bloody (in severe gastroenteritis or dysentery), because of the risk of precipitating severe colitis and toxic dilation of the colon [Farthing et al, 1996; Farthing, 1998]. Loperamide is the preferred choice because of its low incidence of CNS adverse effects.
- **Loperamide can be used in children over 4 years of age.** Limited trial data have found that loperamide significantly reduced the time to relief of symptoms of acute diarrhoea in children with mild to moderate dehydration, but may cause constipation [Dalby-Payne and Elliott, 2002].

Anti-emetics

- **There is a lack of evidence to support the use of anti-emetics in primary care.** Consensus opinion appears to be that they are of little value and may cause significant adverse effects, particularly in children. Nausea and vomiting often improve after adequate rehydration with oral rehydration therapy.
- **In adults,** anti-emetics may be of help if the person is vomiting severely (e.g. metoclopramide 10 mg intramuscularly) [Dwight and Collier, 2001a].

Antibiotic treatment

- **Antibiotic therapy is seldom indicated** in acute infective gastroenteritis. Its indiscriminate use is likely to increase the prevalence of resistant organisms, which is already a major problem in many developing countries and an increasing problem in the UK [Farthing et al, 1996; DH and SMAC, 1998; Murphy, 1998].
- **Antibiotic therapy should usually be reserved for people with positive stool cultures,** particularly if symptoms are severe or not settling. In many people the symptoms of gastroenteritis may be resolved by the time a report is received [Farthing et al, 1996].
- **Empirical antibiotic therapy with a quinolone may be appropriate** for high-risk people or those presenting with dysentery, as this is often due to locally invasive bacterial infection [Farthing et al, 1996].
- **In community-acquired diarrhoea:** ciprofloxacin has been found in randomized controlled trials to reduce the duration of community-acquired diarrhoea by 1 to 2 days [De Bruyn, 2002; Farthing et al, 1996].

Travellers' diarrhoea

- **Routine use of antibiotics is not recommended,** as most people will be only mildly affected, and there are potential risks of adverse effects and an unnecessary build-up of resistance [Hoge et al, 1998].
- **A systematic review has found that empirical use of antibiotics** significantly increases the cure rate of travellers' diarrhoea at 72 hours (OR 5.9, 95% CI 4.1 to 8.6) [De Bruyn et al, 2003].
- **Antibiotic treatment is appropriate for people:**
  - With severe symptoms
  - When the illness causes serious disruption (e.g. a short business trip)
  - With medical conditions (e.g. diabetes) for whom an episode of infective diarrhoea would be dangerous [DTB, 2002]
- **Where antibiotics are necessary, recommended treatment is:**
  - Ciprofloxacin — drug of choice
  - Trimethoprim — for children, adolescents, and pregnant and breastfeeding women
- **There is still debate about the optimum duration of antibiotic therapy.**
- **A broad-spectrum antibiotic is preferable,** because the symptoms tend to be non specific, thus making it difficult to target treatment to a single pathogen. However, there is widespread bacterial resistance to macrolides, penicillins, and tetracyclines [Wingate et al, 2001].
- **Prophylactic antibiotic prescriptions** are not available on the NHS to people travelling abroad. It may be reasonable for people travelling to remote, high-risk areas where medical services are not easily available to purchase a private prescription before departure. People prescribed antibiotics should be advised to seek medical advice if their condition does not improve within 48 hours [Wingate et al, 2001].

[Farthing et al, 1996; De Bruyn, 2002]

- The Department of Health has freely made available two information sources on health advice for travellers:
  - A booklet, *Health Advice for travellers*, can be obtained from travel agents, from post-offices, by telephoning 0800 555 777, or via the Internet at www.dh.gov.uk/PolicyAndGuidance/HealthAdviceForTravellers/fs/en.
  - A handbook, *Health Information for Overseas Travel*, can be obtained by phoning 0870 600 5522 or via the Internet at www.tso.co.uk.

Campylobacter

- **Usually self limiting,** and people often recover without intervention.
- **People with severe symptoms or dysentery** should be treated with erythromycin or ciprofloxacin. Early treatment is likely to be most effective [Cheasty et al, 1998].
- **Treatment courses of from 5 to 7 days** are currently recommended [Tompkins, Personal Communication, 2003].

Salmonella

- **Antibiotics are of no benefit in healthy individuals** and may prolong excretion of *Salmonella*.
- Usually, treatment is recommended only for the very young, immunocompromised people, and those who are systemically ill.
- **In the first week of illness, blood culture** may be useful to aid diagnosis.
- After this time, stool and bone marrow cultures are more helpful in confirming the diagnosis.

[Murphy, 1998; Sirinavin and Garner, 1999; Spira, 2003]

Shigella

- ***Shigella dysenteriae* should be treated with antibiotics** [EBM, 2000].
- **Antibiotics have no effect** on the disease caused by *Shigella flexneri*.
- **People with severe symptoms or dysentery** should be treated with ciprofloxacin.
- **Nalidixic acid is an alternative for children.**
- **Trimethoprim is an alternative for pregnant women,** but resistance is an increasing problem and specialist advice should usually be sought in such cases.

[WHO, 1993b; Murphy, 1998; Cheasty et al, 1998; EBM, 2000; BNF 45, 2003]

Enterohaemorrhagic *Escherichia coli infection* (e.g. 0157 serotype)

- **The use of antibiotics is controversial,** because there is some evidence that antibiotic therapy used for this condition may increase the risk of developing haemolytic uraemic syndrome (HUS). A recent meta-analysis, however, did not show any increase in the risk of HUS associated with antibiotic use [Safdar et al, 2002].

G

Protozoa

- **Amoebic dysentery is treated with metronidazole, followed by a course of diloxanide** to ensure eradication of intestinal disease. Metronidazole is the drug of choice for treating giardiasis [BNF 45, 2003]. No specific therapy is currently recommended for the treatment of cryptosporidiosis in immunocompetent individuals — symptoms usually settle within 2 weeks [DH, 1998].
- **Giardiasis is the most common protozoal infection in returning travellers,** and typically presents after an incubation period of 1–3 weeks. Another risk group is children who attend day nurseries.
- **Giardiasis has a variety of presentations:** acute diarrhoea, chronic diarrhoea that can last several months with malabsorption, weight loss, and failure to thrive in children. Many people are asymptomatic carriers. Vomiting and fever are rare.
- **Giardiasis is diagnosed by the recognition of trophozoites or cysts on microscopy of faeces.** Shedding can be intermittent, leading to false negative results. Microscopy of one sample detects 60–80% of infections; it is therefore recommended that three samples are analysed on consecutive days [Vesy and Peterson, 1999; Gardner and Hill, 2001; Zaat et al, 2003].

Chronic diarrhoea

- **Chronic diarrhoea is defined** as the production of loose stools with or without increased stool frequency for more than 4 weeks [American Gastroenterological Association, 1999].
- **The differential diagnosis of chronic diarrhoea is extensive and often requires specialist investigation.** Infective causes include persistent *Shigella* and *Salmonella* infections, *Giardia*, *Cryptosporidium*, tropical sprue-like syndromes, and syndromes of bacterial overgrowth. The management of these is outside the scope of this guidance.

References

NHS staff in England can link, free of charge, from references to full text journals by clicking on [Full text] on the PRODIGY website.

1. American Academy of Pediatrics (1996) Practice parameter: the management of acute gastroenteritis in young children. *Pediatrics* **97**(3), 424–435.
2. American Gastroenterological Association (1999) American Gastroenterological Association medical position statement: guidelines for the evaluation and management of chronic diarrhoea. *Gastroenterology* **116**(6), 1451–1463.
3. BNF 45 (2003) *British National Formulary*. 45th edn. London: British Medical Association and Royal Pharmaceutical Society of Great Britain.
4. Brown, K.H., Peerson, J.M. and Fontaine, O. (1994) Use of nonhuman milks in the dietary management of young children with acute diarrhoea: a meta-analysis of clinical trials. *Pediatrics* **93**(1), 17–27.
5. Cheasty, T., Skinner, J.A., Rowe, B. and Threlfall, E.J. (1998) Increasing incidence of antibiotic resistance in sheigellas from humans in England and Wales: recommendations for therapy. *Microbial Drug Resistance* **4**(1), 57–60.
6. Cincinnati Children's Hospital Medical Center (2002) *Evience based clinical practice guideline for children with acute gastroenteritis (AGE)*. Guideline 5. Cincinnati: Cincinnati Children's Hospital Medical Center. www.cincinnatichildrens.org [Accessed: 20/12/2002].
7. Crowley, D.S., Ryan, M.J. and Wall, P.G. (1997) Gastroenteritis in children under 5 years of age in England and Wales. *Communicable Disease Report* 7(6), 82–86.
8. Curtis, V. and Cairncross, S. (2003) Effect of washing hands with soap on diarrhoea risk in the community: a systematic review. *Lancet Infectious Diseases* 3(5), 275–281.
9. Dalby-Payne, J. and Elliott, E. (2002) Acute gastroenteritis in children. *Clinical Evidence* 7, 227–235.
10. De Bruyn, G. (2002) Diarrhoea. *Clinical Evidence* 7, 1–2.
11. De Bruyn, G., Hahn, S. and Borwick, A. (2003) *Antibiotic treatment for travellers' diarrhoea*. The Cochrane Library. Issue 3. Oxford: Update Software.
12. de Wit, M.A., Koopmans, M.P., Kortbeek, L.M. et al (2001) Gastroenteritis in sentinel general practices, The Netherlands. *Emerging Infectious Diseases* 7(1), 82–91.
13. DH (1995) *Food handlers fitness to work: guidance for food businesses, enforcement officers and health professionals*. London: Department of Health.
14. DH (1998) *Cryptosporidium in water supplies: third report of the group of experts*. London: Department of the Environment and the Regions & Department of Health.
15. DH and SMAC (1998) *The path of least resistance*. Department of Health. www.dh.gov.uk [Accessed: 27/04/2004]. [Full text]
16. DTB (2002) What to do about traveller's diarrhoea. *Drug & Therapeutics Bulletin* **40**(5), 36–38.
17. Dwight, O. and Collier, J (2001a) *Food poisoning/gastroenteritis in adults*. National Patients' Access Team. http://nelhpc.sghms.ac.uk/orangebook/infections.html [Accessed: 19/12/2002].
18. Dwight, O. and Collier, J (2001b) *Gastroenteritis in infants and young children*. National Patients' Access Team. http://nelhpc.sghms.ac.uk/orangebook/paediatrics.html [Accessed: 19/12/2002].
19. EBM (2000) *Clinical features and treatment of diarrhoea in adults according to aetiology*. Helsinki: Duodecim Medical Publications Ltd. www.ebm-guidelines.com [Accessed: 20/12/2002].
20. Farthing, M. (1998) Treatment and prevention of diarrhoea. *Practitioner* **242**(1586), 388–394. [Full text]
21. Farthing, M.J.G. (2003) Travellers' diarrhoea. *Medicine* **31**(1), 35–40.
22. Farthing, M.J.G., Du Pont, H.L., Guandalini, S. et al (1992) Treatment and prevention of travellers' diarrhoea. *Gastroenterology International* 5(3), 162–175.
23. Farthing, M., Feldman, R., Finch, R. et al (1996) The management of infective gastroenteritis in adults. A consensus statement by an expert panel convened by the British Society for the Study of Infection. *Journal of Infection* **33**(3), 143–152.
24. Fontaine, O., Gore, S.M. and Pierce, N.F. (2003) *Rice based oral rehydration solution for treating diarrhoea (Cochrane Review)*. The Cochrane Library. Issue 3. Oxford: Update Software.
25. Gardner, T.B. and Hill, D.R. (2001) Treatment of giardiasis. *Clinical Microbiology Reviews* **14**(1), 114.
26. Guerrant, R.L., Van Gilder, T., Steiner, T.S. et al (2002) Practice guidelines for the management of infectious diarrhea. *Clinical Infectious Diseases* **32**(3), 331–351.
27. Hoge, C.W., Gambel, J.M., Srijan, A. et al (1998) Trends in antibiotic resistance among diarrheal pathogens isolated in Thailand over 15 years. *Clinical Infectious Diseases* **26**(2), 341–345.

28. Jiang, Z.D., Lowe, B., Verenkar, M.P. et al (2002) Prevalence of enteric pathogens among international travelers with diarrhea acquired in Kenya (Mombasa), India (Goa), or Jamaica (Montego Bay). *Journal of Infectious Diseases* **185**(4), 497–502. [Full text]
29. Murphy, M.S. (1998) Guidelines for managing acute gastroenteritis based on a systematic review of published research. *Archives of Disease in Childhood* **79**(3), 279–284. [Full text]
30. Nutrition Committee, C.P.S. (2002) *Oral rehydration therapy and early refeeding in the management of childhood gastroenteritis*. Ottawa: Canadian Paediatric Society. www.cps.ca/english/statements/N/n94-03.htm [Accessed: 19/12/2002].
31. Safdar, N., Said, A., Gangnon, R.E. and Maki, D.G. (2002) Risk of hemolytic uremic syndrome after antibiotic treatment of Escherichia coli O157:H7 enteritis: a meta-analysis. *Journal of the American Medical Association* **288**(8), 996–1001. [Full text]
32. Sandhu, B.K., Isolauri, E., Walker-Smith, J.A. et al (1997) A multicentre study on behalf of the European Society of Paediatric Gastroenterology and Nutrition Working Group on Acute Diarrhoea: early feeding in childhood gastroenteritis. *Journal of Pediatric Gastroenterology & Nutrition* **24**(5), 522–527.
33. Sirinavin, S. and Garner, P. (1999) *Antibiotics for treating salmonella gut infections (Cochrane Review)*. The Cochrane Library. Issue 4. Oxford:Update Software.
34. Spira, A.M. (2003) Assessment of travellers who return home ill. *Lancet* **361**(9367), 1459–1469. [Full text]
35. Tauxe, R.V. and Hughes, J.M. (1995) Food borne disease. In: Mandell, G.L., Bennet, J.E., Dolin, R. et al (Eds.) *Principles and Practice of Infectious Diseases*. 4th edn. New York: Churchill Livingstone. 1012–1025.
36. Tompkins, D. (2003) *Personal communication*. Public Health Laboratory Service: London.
37. Tompkins, D.S., Hudson, M.J., Smith, H.R. et al (1999) A study of infectious intestinal disease in England: microbiological findings in cases and controls. *Communicable Disease & Public Health* **2**(2), 108–113.
38. Vesy, C.J. and Peterson, W.L. (1999) Review article: the management of giardiasis. *Alimentary Pharmacology & Therapeutics* **13**(7), 843–850.
39. von Sonnenburg, F., Tornieporth, N., Waiyaki, P. et al (2000) Risk and aetiology of diarrhoea at various tourist destinations. *Lancet* **356**(9224), 133–134. [Full text]
40. Walker-Smith, J.A. and Murch, S.H. (2003) Diarrhoea in childhood. *Medicine* **31**(1), 41–44.
41. Wan, C. (1999) Randomised trial of different rates of feeding in acute diarrhoea. *Archives of Disease in Childhood* **81**(6), 487–491. [Full text]
42. Wheeler, J.G., Sethi, D., Cowden, J.M. et al (1999) Study of infectious intestinal disease in England: rates in the community, presenting to general practice, and reported to national surveillance. *British Medical Journal* **318**(7190), 1046–1050. [Full text]
43. WHO (Ed.) (1993a) *Insomnia in general practice*. Geneva: Division of Mental Health, World Health Organisation.
44. WHO (1993b) *The treatment of diarrhoea: practical guidelines*. 3rd ed. Geneva: World Health Organisation.
45. Wingate, D., Phillips, S.F., Lewis, S.J. et al (2001) Guidelines for adults on self-medication for the treatment of acute diarrhoea. *Alimentary Pharmacology and Therapeutics* **15**(6), 773–782.
46. Wright, P. (2003) *Personal communication*. Public Health Laboratory Service: London.
47. Zaat, J.O., Mank, T. and Assendelft, W.J. (2003) *Drugs for treating giardiasis (Cochrane review)*. The Cochrane Library. Issue 2. Oxford: Update Software.

PRODIGY GUIDANCE

Gingivitis and periodontitis — plaque-associated

Last revised in July 2005
www.prodigy.nhs.uk/guidance.asp?gt=Gingivitis

Applies to people over the age of 12 years

This guidance mainly covers plaque-associated gingivitis and periodontitis. The treatment of acute necrotizing ulcerative gingivitis is briefly reviewed.

There is separate guidance for several related conditions: *Dental abscess, Candida — oral, Aphthous ulcer, Herpes simplex — oral.*

This guidance does not cover forms of gingivitis and periodontitis that are not associated with plaque.

This guidance does not cover systemic conditions that also have oral manifestations (e.g. lichen planus, pemphigus, or pemphigoid).

Goals

- Relief of symptoms such as pain, bleeding gums, halitosis, gum hypertrophy
- Prevention of tooth decay, tooth loosening, and tooth loss

Contents

Scenarios

- Plaque-associated gingivitis and periodontitis p.828
- Acute necrotizing ulcerative gingivitis (ANUG) p.830

Extended Information, p. 831

Which scenario?

- **Plaque-associated gingivitis and periodontitis:** covers the initial treatment in general medical practice and recommendations for referral for dental assessment and treatment.
- **Acute necrotizing ulcerative gingivitis (ANUG):** covers the immediate management of acute necrotizing ulcerative gingivitis in general medical practice whilst the person is awaiting urgent dental referral.

Plaque-associated gingivitis and periodontitis

Which therapy?

- Advise the patient that:
  - Oral hygiene with tooth brushing and flossing can control and treat plaque and gingivitis.
  - Antiseptic toothpastes and mouthwashes are not generally recommended for people with healthy gums.
  - Antiseptic toothpastes and mouthwashes are recommended when tooth brushing and flossing are impractical or insufficient on their own.
  - Oral hygiene on its own is not sufficient to treat periodontitis; referral to a dentist is necessary.
  - Smoking is an important risk factor for periodontal disease; smokers should be encouraged to stop smoking.
- In the presence of clinically apparent plaque-associated gingivitis or periodontitis:
  - Recommend good oral hygiene: daily flossing, twice daily brushing of the teeth with an antiseptic toothpaste, and twice daily use of an antiseptic mouthwash.
    - Chlorhexidine is the most effective oral antiseptic available — see note under *Prescribing points* below about managing discoloration.
    - Triclosan is an alternative for people who experience problems with tooth staining due to chlorhexidine.
    - Hexetidine is an option for people who prefer not to use chlorhexidine and triclosan.
    - Antiseptic toothpastes containing phenolic compounds and triclosan are widely available for people to purchase.
  - Refer to a dentist for additional measures, including:
    - Scaling and polishing of teeth to remove plaque and calculus above and below the gum margin.
    - Surgical removal of pocket walls and diseased tissue (rarely required).

Practical prescribing points

For further information please see the *Medicines Compendium* (www.medicines.org.uk) or the *British National Formulary* (www.bnf.org).

- **Chlorhexidine preparations** can stain teeth brown when used regularly. The stain is not permanent, and can be reduced by brushing teeth before (but not after) use, and avoiding drinks that contain tannin (e.g. tea, coffee, and red wine). Staining is less likely with lower concentrations of chlorhexidine, i.e. 0.12%. The mouth should be rinsed well between brushing and using chlorhexidine, as some ingredients in toothpaste can inactivate chlorhexidine. Staining can be easily removed by a dentist or dental hygienist.

Should I refer or investigate?

Refer?

- Refer all people with clinically apparent gingivitis for a dental check-up once they are better (if they do not already have a follow-up appointment).
- Refer all people with periodontitis or gingivitis that does not respond adequately. They require dental assessment and treatment within a few weeks.
- Refer acute necrotizing gingivitis, early-onset periodontitis, and other acute or progressive oral conditions.

Referral guidelines for suspected cancer published by the National Institute for Health and Clinical Excellence (NICE) [NICE, 2005] recommend referral or follow-up for people with persistent symptoms or signs related to the oral cavity in whom a definitive diagnosis of a benign lesion cannot be made. If the symptoms and signs have not disappeared after 6 weeks refer urgently.

NICE recommends urgent referral for people with:

- Unexplained ulceration of the oral mucosa or mass persisting for more than 3 weeks.
- Unexplained red and white patches (included suspected lichen planus) of the oral mucosa that *are* painful or swollen or bleeding.
- Unexplained tooth mobility persisting for more than 3 weeks (to a dentist).

NICE recommend non-urgent referral for people with unexplained red and white patches (included suspected lichen planus) of the oral mucosa that are *not* painful or swollen or bleeding.

nvestigate?

Special investigations such as dental probing to measure depth of gingival pockets and X-rays to assess damage to teeth and alveolar bone require referral to a dentist.

ʔatient information leaflets

The following PILs are available at www.prodigy.nhs.uk

- British Dental Association
- British Dental Health Foundation
- Dental Plaque and Gum Disease

Shared decision making

- **Good oral hygiene** helps to prevent and treat gum disease.
  - Brush teeth to clear plaque and debris — at least twice a day. Use a fluoride toothpaste.
  - Floss daily to remove plaque from between teeth. You may find it useful to get advice from a dentist or dental hygienist on how to floss.
  - Use an antiseptic mouthwash twice a day if it is not practical to brush the teeth
  - Have regular dental checks to detect plaque, remove scaling, and treat any gum disease.
  - If you smoke, stopping smoking also helps.
- If you have more marked gum disease your dentist or doctor may advise an antiseptic mouthwash such as chlorhexidine (and/or antiseptic toothpaste, gel, or spray).
- Dental treatment may be needed for more severe gum disease.

Drug rationale

Drugs not included

- **Antibiotic dental gels** — there is no clear evidence that local treatment with antibiotic dental gels adds to the benefit achieved by conventional debridement alone [DTB, 1994].
- **Oral antibiotics** — although gingivitis has a bacterial component, systemic antibiotics have only transient benefit and therefore do not routinely have a place in the treatment of gingivitis or periodontitis [Coventry et al, 2000].
- **Povidone-iodine mouthwash** is useful for mucosal infections but does not inhibit plaque formation [BNF 47, 2004].

Drugs included

- **Chlorhexidine gluconate** is effective in reducing the gingival inflammation, bleeding, and dental plaque, but it can stain the teeth [Barnett, 2003]. Chlorhexidine 0.2% mouthwash, 1% gel, and 0.2% spray are licensed as an aid in the treatment and prevention of gingivitis. Mouthwash is recommended, as it is more likely to come into contact with a larger affected area.
- **Chlorhexidine 0.12% mouthwash** is available over the counter; an advice note is provided for people wishing to buy this product (it does not currently have a Clinical Terms (Read) code and therefore cannot be prescribed through PRODIGY).
- **Hexetidine** is effective in reducing the gingival inflammation, bleeding, and dental plaque. A 0.1% mouthwash is licensed as an aid in the treatment and prevention of gingivitis. This is a useful alternative for people who experience staining with chlorhexidine, but it may be less effective.
- **Triclosan** is used in many over-the-counter dental preparations; an advice note is provided for people wishing to buy these products.
- **Mouthwashes containing phenolic essential oil compounds** are widely available; an advice note is provided for people wishing to buy these products.

G

Prescriptions

Advice note: oral hygiene

Advice only: good oral hygiene

- Age from 12 years onwards
- Good oral hygiene helps to prevent and treat gum disease. Brush teeth to clear plaque and debris – at least twice a day. Use fluoride toothpaste if your water supply is low in fluoride. Floss daily to remove plaque from between teeth. For those who are unable to use a toothbrush, use an antiseptic mouthwash each day. Have regular dental checks to detect and clear excessive build up of plaque, and to detect and treat early gum disease. If you smoke, stopping smoking also helps.

Antiseptic mouthwash or toothpaste

Advice only: OTC antiseptic mouthwash/toothpaste

- Age from 12 years onwards
- If you have more marked gum disease your dentist or doctor may advise an antiseptic mouthwash (and/or antiseptic toothpaste, gel, or spray). Many of these are available for you to buy over the counter – ask your pharmacist to advise you on which one you should buy.

Chlorhexidine 0.2% mouthwash: rinse with 10ml twice a day

- Age from 12 years onwards
- Chlorhexidine 0.2% mouthwash. Rinse the mouth with 10ml for about 1 minute twice a day; supply 300 ml; NHS Cost £1.82; OTC Cost £4.15.

Chlorhexidine 1% dental gel: use once or twice a day

- Age from 12 years onwards
- Chlorhexidine 1% dental gel. Brush the teeth thoroughly with one inch of gel on a moistened toothbrush for about 1 minute once or twice a day; supply 50 grams; NHS Cost £1.21; OTC Cost £2.65.

Chlorhexidine 0.2% spray: use twice a day

- Age from 12 years onwards
- Chlorhexidine 0.2% spray. Spray up to 12 sprays onto the teeth and gums twice a day; supply 60 ml; NHS Cost £4.10, OTC Cost £6.69.

Hexetidine 0.1% mouthwash: rinse with 15ml twice a day

- Age from 12 years onwards
- Hexetidine 0.1% mouthwash. Rinse the mouth with 15ml for about 1 minute twice a day; supply 400 ml; NHS Cost £4.04; OTC Cost £6.78.

Acute necrotizing ulcerative gingivitis (ANUG)

Which therapy

- **Refer for urgent dental assessment and management.**
- **Initiate treatment immediately with:**
  - **Metronidazole** 200 mg three times a day or **amoxicillin** 250-500mg three times a day.
  - **An analgesic** such as paracetamol or ibuprofen.
  - **An antiseptic mouthwash** until the condition has cleared.
- **Advise on the general preventative oral hygiene measures** such as flossing and brushing, which should be adopted as soon as they can be tolerated.
- **Offer advice on smoking cessation** (if relevant).

Practical prescribing points

For further information please see the *Medicines Compendium* (www.medicines.org.uk) or the *British National Formulary* (www.bnf.org).

- **Chlorhexidine preparations** can stain teeth brown when used regularly. The stain is not permanent, and can be reduced by brushing teeth before (but not after) use, and avoiding drinks that contain tannin (e.g. tea, coffee, and red wine). Staining is less likely with lower concentrations of chlorhexidine, i.e. 0.12%. The mouth should be rinsed well between brushing and using chlorhexidine, as some ingredients in toothpaste can inactivate chlorhexidine. Staining can be easily removed by a dentist or dental hygienist.
- **Ibuprofen** may cause gastrointestinal irritation and occasionally gastrointestinal haemorrhage. Avoid if there is a history of peptic ulceration. Ibuprofen may worsen asthma, hypertension, renal impairment, or cardiac failure.

Should I refer or investigate?

Refer?

- Refer for urgent dental assessment.

Patient information leaflets

The following PILs are available at www.prodigy.nhs.uk

- British Dental Association
- British Dental Health Foundation

Shared decision making

- You have a severe gum infection and should see a dentist urgently.
- Until seen by a dentist you should:
  - Use an antiseptic mouthwash twice a day.
  - Take an antibiotic (metronidazole or amoxicillin).
  - Take painkillers if it is painful.
- **Good oral hygiene** will help to prevent further gum disease when this episode has settled.
  - Brush teeth to clear plaque and debris — at least twice a day. Use a fluoride toothpaste if your water supply is low in fluoride.
  - Floss daily to remove plaque from between teeth.
  - Use an antiseptic mouthwash twice a day if it is not practical to brush the teeth
  - Have regular dental checks to detect plaque, remove scaling, and treat any gum disease.
  - If you smoke, stopping smoking also helps.

Drug rationale

Drugs not included

- **Oral antibiotics other than metronidazole or amoxicillin** are not recommended for the treatment of acute ulcerative necrotizing gingivitis.

Drugs included

- **Metronidazole** given as a 3-day course is recommended for the treatment of acute necrotizing ulcerative gingivitis.
- **Amoxicillin** is an alternative to metronidazole.
- **Paracetamol** is included for simple analgesia.
- **Ibuprofen** is included as an alternative to paracetamol for analgesia.
- **Chlorhexidine gluconate 0.2% and hexetidine 0.1% mouthwashes** are included, they should be used until the condition clears. Chlorhexidine 0.12% mouthwash is available over the counter (it does not currently have a Clinical Terms [Read] code and therefore cannot be prescribed through PRODIGY).
- **Hydrogen peroxide:** mouthwashes containing an oxidizing agent (e.g. hydrogen peroxide) may be useful in the treatment of acute necrotizing ulcerative gingivitis [BNF 47, 2004]

Prescriptions

Analgesia: use when required

Paracetamol tablets: 500mg to 1g up to four times a day

- Age from 12 to 15 years
- Paracetamol 500mg tablets. Take one to two tablets every 4 to 6 hours when required for pain relief. Maximum of 8 tablets in 24 hours; supply 100 tablets; NHS Cost £0.75; OTC Cost £1.32.

Paracetamol tablets: 1g up to four times a day

- Age from 16 years onwards
- Paracetamol 500mg tablets. Take two tablets every 4 to 6 hours when required for pain relief. Maximum of 8 tablets in 24 hours; supply 100 tablets; NHS Cost £0.75; OTC Cost £1.32.

Ibuprofen tablets: 400mg three times a day

- Age from 12 years onwards
- Ibuprofen 400mg tablets. Take one tablet three times a day when required for pain relief. Do not exceed the stated dose; supply 24 tablets; NHS Cost £0.70; OTC Cost £1.23.

Antiseptic mouthwash

Chlorhexidine 0.2% mouthwash: rinse with 10ml twice a day

- Age from 12 years onwards
- Chlorhexidine 0.2% mouthwash. Rinse the mouth with 10ml for about 1 minute twice a day; supply 300 ml; NHS Cost £1.84; OTC Cost £4.15.

Hexetidine 0.1% mouthwash: rinse with 15ml twice a day

- Age from 12 years onwards
- Hexetidine 0.1% mouthwash. Rinse the mouth with 15ml for about 1 minute twice a day; supply 400 ml; NHS Cost £4.04; OTC Cost £6.78.

Hydrogen peroxide 6% (20 vol) mouthwash: use 2-3 times a day

- Age from 12 years onwards
- Hydrogen peroxide 6% mouthwash. Rinse the mouth with 15ml (diluted in half a glass of warm water) for about 2 minutes two to three times a day; supply 500 ml; NHS Cost £0.85; OTC Cost £1.51.

Preferred antibiotic: metronidazole for 3 days

Metronidazole 200mg three times a day

- Age from 12 years onwards
- Metronidazole 200mg tablets. Take one tablet three times a day for 3 days; supply 9 tablets; NHS Cost £0.18.

Alternative antibiotic: amoxicillin for 5 days

Amoxicillin 250mg three times a day for five days

- Age from 12 years onwards
- Amoxicillin 250mg capsules. Take one capsule three times a day for 5 days; supply 15 capsules; NHS Cost £0.89.

Amoxicillin 500mg three times a day for five days

- Age from 12 years onwards
- Amoxicillin 500mg capsules. Take one capsule three times a day for 5 days; supply 15 capsules; NHS Cost £1.32.

Advice note: oral hygiene

Advice only: good oral hygiene

- Age from 12 years onwards
- Good oral hygiene will help to prevent further gum disease when this episode has settled. Brush teeth to clear plaque and debris – at least twice a day. Use a fluoride toothpaste if your water supply is low in fluoride. Floss daily to remove plaque from between teeth. For those who are unable to use a toothbrush, use an antiseptic mouthwash regularly. Have regular dental checks to detect and clear excessive build up of plaque, and to detect and treat early gum disease. If you smoke, stopping smoking also helps.

Extended Information

Background information

- What is it? p.831
- How common is it? p.832
- How do I know my patient has plaque-associated gingivitis? p.832
- How do I know my patient has acute necrotizing ulcerative gingivitis? p.832
- What else might it be? p.832
- Complications and prognosis p.832

What is it?

- **Gingivitis** is inflammation of the gums due to any cause.
- **Plaque-associated gingivitis** is inflammation of the interdental and marginal gingiva associated with dental plaque, although, as is explained below, the mechanisms of cause and effect are not yet fully understood. The gum bleeds easily (e.g. on brushing the teeth), but gingivitis is otherwise asymptomatic.
  - The term 'gingivitis' is often loosely used to mean 'plaque-associated gingivitis', which is by far the most common form of gingivitis.
- **Periodontitis** occurs when inflammation of the gingiva involves the periodontal ligament. The periodontal ligament is a dense connective tissue that surrounds the root of the tooth and attaches it to the alveolar bone. In periodontitis the periodontal ligament is progressively destroyed, the gum recesses, loss of gum attachment to teeth becomes clinically apparent, and alveolar bone is lost. Teeth become loose, and may eventually fall out. *Pyorrhoea* is a synonym for periodontitis but has fallen out of use.
- For the purposes of this guidance, plaque-associated gingivitis is staged as:
  - Subclinical gingivitis
  - Clinically apparent gingivitis (without periodontitis)
  - Periodontitis
- **Dental plaque** is a soft bacterial deposit that readily forms on exposed surfaces of teeth and is easily removed by brushing and flossing the teeth.
- **Calculus** (or tartar) is calcified plaque. It sticks firmly to teeth. Generally, it can only be removed by a dentist or dental hygienist with special instruments.

[Bral and Brownstein, 1988]

G

What causes plaque-associated gingivitis and periodontitis?

The pathology of gingivitis and periodontitis are graphically illustrated at: www.nlm.nih.gov/medlineplus/ency/images/ency/fullsize/1136.jpg.

The pathogenesis of plaque-associated gingivitis and periodontitis is not yet fully understood, but it is known that:

- The pathophysiology of gingivitis is complex and seems to involve an immunological reaction in the gums to bacteria and bacterial products present in dental plaque.
- Plaque contains huge numbers of bacteria in a complex mixture of up to 400 different species. A few of these species have been implicated in plaque-associated gingivitis and periodontitis, including the Gram-positive rod *Actinomyces viscosus*, and Gram-negative anaerobes *Porphyromonas gingivalis*, *Actinobacillus actinomycetemcomitans*, *Fusobacterium* species, and *Capnocytophaga* species.
- Host factors, innate and acquired, may be more important in the aetiology of gingivitis than specific bacteria. Risk factors for gingivitis and periodontitis include:
  - Poor oral hygiene
  - Socioeconomic deprivation
  - Cigarette smoking
  - Immune depression
  - Diabetes mellitus
  - Osteoporosis (there is debate about its role in gum disease)
- Periodontitis is an episodic event, but what triggers this deterioration is not clearly understood.

[Slots, 1979; Bral and Brownstein, 1988; Schroeder and Listgarten, 1997]

What other important kinds of gingivitis are there?

- **Acute necrotizing ulcerative gingivitis** (ANUG, or Vincent's gingivitis, or trench mouth) is a progressive, painful, acute infection of the gums with ulceration, swelling, and sloughing off of dead tissue. It is associated with fusiform bacteria and spirochaetes. Stress, smoking, and a compromised host immune response are risk factors.
- **Early-onset periodontitis** and **accelerated periodontitis** are forms of plaque-associated gingivitis that progress rapidly over several months or a few years. *Actinobacillus actinomycetemcomitans* has been implicated.

[Bral and Brownstein, 1988; Coventry et al, 2000; Lehner, 2003]

How common is it?

- Studies in the USA and the UK suggest that gingivitis or periodontitis affects 50–90% of the adult population [Albandar and Kingman, 1999; Coventry et al, 2000].
- A survey in the United Kingdom in 1998 found that in dentate adults:
  - Plaque was visible in 72%
  - Calculus was visible in 73%
  - Periodontal pocketing was present in 54%
  - Loss of attachment >=4 mm was present in 43%
  - Loss of attachment >=6 mm was present in 8%

[Office for National Statistics, 2000]
- A survey in the United Kingdom of the dental health of children in 1997 found:
  - Plaque in 43% of 15–18 year olds.
  - Gingivitis (indicated by bleeding on probing the gums) in 40% of 15–18 year-olds.
  - Periodontal pocketing in 17% of 15–18 year-olds.
  - The prevalence of dental conditions increased with age and was significantly higher in boys than girls.

[Office for National Statistics et al, 2001]
- The incidence of new diagnoses of gingivitis or periodontitis in Dutch general practice is about 4 per 10,000 people per year [Deconinck et al, 2003].

How do I know my patient has plaque-associated gingivitis?

The main features of plaque-associated gingivitis are:

- **Subclinical gingivitis**
  - No symptoms
  - Gum margins slightly swollen and reddened
- **Clinically apparent gingivitis**
  - Discomfort from gums
  - Reddening and swelling of the gum margins
  - Bleeding of gums when teeth cleaned or gently probed
- **Periodontitis**
  - **Symptoms** commonly are absent, but some people have:
    - Halitosis
    - Foul taste
    - Difficulty in eating
  - **Signs** include signs of gingivitis, plus:
    - Pus and debris expressible from gingival pockets
    - Loosening and drifting of teeth; eventual loss of teeth
    - Gum abscess
  - Confirmation of the diagnosis of periodontitis may require dental examination with periodontal probing and radiography.

[Coventry et al, 2000; Lehner, 2003]

How do I know my patient has acute necrotizing ulcerative gingivitis?

- Sudden onset.
- Malaise (in a few).
- Characteristic halitosis.
- Acute pain, bleeding.
- Metallic taste.
- Fever (in a few).
- Punched-out gingival ulcers covered with a white pseudomembrane. Ulcers occur in the interdental papillae and are not found on other parts of the oral mucosa; this helps distinguish acute necrotizing ulcerative gingivitis from conditions such herpetic gingivostomatitis.

[Keys and Bartold, 2000]

What else might it be?

- **Herpetic gingivostomatitis**
  - Occurs predominantly in children.
  - There is acute onset, fever, malaise, pain, and ulceration of both gingiva and oral mucosa.
  - Caused by primary infection with herpes simplex virus.
- **Desquamative gingivitis (which my be due to lichen planus, pemphigoid or pemphigus)**
  - White and erythematous or erosive areas on the whole of the gingiva and/or buccal mucosa; full thickness inflammation of the gums (not just the margins); bullae in oral mucosa; may be ulcerative; sometimes bilateral; skin may be involved in lichen planus; conjunctiva may be involved in pemphigoid [Scully and Porter, 1997].
- **Other causes of gingival bleeding** include platelet disorders, vascular conditions, leukaemia, HIV infection but note that:
  - Bleeding from the gingiva due to gingivitis may be more obvious in women taking oral contraceptives, during pregnancy, and on stopping smoking.
- **Gum hypertrophy**
  - Most commonly caused by phenytoin, calcium-channel blockers, or ciclosporin.
    - About 50% of people taking phenytoin, 30% of those taking ciclosporin, and 10% of those taking nifedipine will experience gum hypertrophy [Meraw and Sheridan, 1998; Lee and Morris, 2001].
  - Rarer causes include:
    - **Other drugs** including other antiepileptics (carbamazepine, phenobarbital, ethosuximide)
    - **Hormonal changes** in pregnancy, puberty, with oral contraceptives
    - **Malignancy**, e.g. Langerhans cell histiocytoma, leukaemia
- **Denture-associated** trauma or candidiasis

'Red flags'

- **Rapid progression**
  - If periodontitis presents in children or young adults, or if it progresses rapidly, the possibility of serious conditions such as early-onset periodontitis, immunosuppression, and malignancy should be ruled out.
- **Suspected oral malignancy** — signs include:
  - Ulceration of the oral mucosa persisting for more than 3 weeks.
  - Oral swellings persisting for more than 3 weeks.
  - All red or red and white patches of the oral mucosa, particularly if they are painful or swollen or bleeding.
  - Unexplained tooth mobility persisting for more than 3 weeks.
  - The level of suspicion is further increased if the patient is a heavy smoker or heavy alcohol drinker and is aged over 45 years and male; other forms of tobacco use and chewing betel, gutkha, or pan also raise suspicion.

[Coventry et al, 2000; Lehner, 2003; British Association of Oral and Maxillofacial Surgeons, 2004; NICE, 2005]

Complications and prognosis

Complications

- Chronic periodontal disease, if untreated, can progressively lead to:
  - Damage to the periodontal membrane and alveolar bone
  - Recurrent gum abscesses
  - Detachment of the gum from the tooth with formation of periodontal pockets

- Progressive deepening of pockets and recession of the gums
- Drifting and loosening of teeth
- Loss of multiple teeth

[Lehner, 2003; Coventry et al, 2000]

- Periodontal disease may be a risk factor for cardiovascular disease and low birth weight and premature birth. But the evidence is conflicting and further studies are required [Madianos et al, 2002; Moore et al, 2004].

Management issues

- How can gingivitis and periodontitis be prevented? p.833
- What is the management of plaque-associated gingivitis and periodontitis? p.833
- What is the management of acute necrotizing ulcerative gingivitis (ANUG)? p.834
- Medicines management p.834

How can gingivitis and periodontitis be prevented?

- **Oral hygiene** prevents caries and helps to prevent gingivitis and periodontitis.
- Oral hygiene measures include tooth brushing, flossing, and, for those who are unable to use a toothbrush, rinsing with an effective mouthwash.
  - Children should be introduced to dental hygiene practices as early as possible.
  - Fluoridated toothpaste is recommended [British Society of Paediatric Dentistry, 1996; Health Development Agency, 2001].
    - Fluoridated toothpastes are available in three concentration ranges: low-fluoride paste with less than 600 ppm; standard pastes with about 1000 ppm; high-concentration pastes with about 1500 ppm.
    - From the age of 6 years the anterior teeth are not at risk of opacities caused by fluoride ingestion and toothpastes with higher concentrations of fluoride should be used.
    - Children under the age of 6 and at low risk of caries should use a low-fluoride toothpaste. The risk for caries is considered to be low in children who live in areas with fluoridated water or use fluoride supplements, have regular dental check-ups, have no or well-controlled caries, and have parents motivated to supervise tooth brushing and exercise dietary control.
    - Children with a higher risk of dental caries should use a standard paste.
    - Children up to the age of 6 years should be supervised by an adult when they are cleaning their teeth. This is to ensure that only small amounts of toothpaste are used and that as little toothpaste as possible is swallowed.
  - Antiseptic toothpastes and mouthwashes are widely available. However, there is some debate about the appropriateness of their use in people with healthy gums [Hoang, 2000]. Some people fear that widespread use could promote the development of bacterial resistance, although there is no evidence for this.
- Periodic review by a dentist ensures timely detection and treatment of problems such as excessive plaque and calculus that can lead to or aggravate periodontal disease.
- Smokers should be encouraged to quit because they have significantly increased risks of periodontal disease, oral cancer and other diseases. (For guidance on helping people to quit smoking see separate PRODIGY guidance *Smoking cessation*).

[American Academy of Periodontology, 2000; Coventry et al, 2000; Hoang, 2000; Barnett, 2003]

What is the management of plaque-associated gingivitis and periodontitis?

- **Oral hygiene** with tooth brushing, flossing, and rinsing with mouthwashes can control and treat gingivitis.
- **Antiseptic toothpaste and mouthwashes** are effective in controlling plaque and gingivitis.
  - Chlorhexidine is the most effective at reducing plaque, gingivitis, and gingival bleeding [Grossman et al, 1989; Overholser et al, 1990]. In the UK, products available for the prevention and treatment of gingivitis include chlorhexidine gluconate mouthwash (0.12% and 0.2%), spray (0.2%), and gel (1%). Chlorhexidine discolours the teeth, but if this is not removed by usual tooth brushing it can be easily removed by a dentist or dental hygienist.
  - Triclosan is a broad-spectrum antiseptic effective against plaque bacteria. It is marketed in toothpastes and pre-brush mouthwashes, which are widely available [Worthington et al, 1993; Ayad et al, 1995; Triratana et al, 2002].
  - Hexetidine is also effective in reducing gingival inflammation, gingival bleeding, and plaque [Sharma et al, 2003]. A 0.1% mouthwash is licensed in the UK as an aid in the prevention and treatment of gingivitis.
  - Phenolic compounds have been employed as antiseptics since Lister used phenol as a surgical antiseptic in the 1860s. Phenolic/essential oil compounds have been shown to have moderate plaque inhibitory effects, and to reduce gingival inflammation [Gordon et al, 1985; DePaola et al, 1989]. Many widely available mouthwashes contain phenolic/essential oil compounds.
- **Advise smokers on support services that could help them stop smoking** (see separate PRODIGY guidance *Smoking cessation*).

Criteria for referral the maxillofacial department of the local hospital

- Referral guidelines for suspected cancer published by the National Institute for Health and Clinical Excellence (NICE) [NICE, 2005] recommend referral or follow-up for people with persistent symptoms or signs related to the oral cavity in whom a definitive diagnosis of a benign lesion cannot be made. If the symptoms and signs have not disappeared after 6 weeks refer urgently.
- NICE recommends urgent referral for people with:
  - Unexplained ulceration of the oral mucosa or mass persisting for more than 3 weeks.
  - Unexplained red and white patches (included suspected lichen planus) of the oral mucosa that *are* painful or swollen or bleeding.
- NICE recommends non-urgent referral for people with:
  - Unexplained red and white patches (included suspected lichen planus) of the oral mucosa that are *not* painful or swollen or bleeding.

Criteria for referral to a dentist

- **Clinically apparent gingivitis not responding to standard oral hygiene**
  - Refer for dental check-up to detect plaque and remove calculus by scaling and polishing teeth.
- **Periodontitis**
  - Refer for scaling and polishing, and assessment of need for specialist treatment.
- **Suspicion of oral cancer**

G

- NICE recommends urgent referral of people with unexplained tooth mobility persisting for more than 3 weeks [NICE, 2005].
- **Other conditions** such as early-onset periodontitis and acute necrotizing ulcerative gingivitis
  - Refer for dental assessment and treatment, with an urgency according to the severity of the case.

[Coventry et al, 2000; Hoang, 2000; Barnett, 2003; Lehner, 2003; Bral and Brownstein, 1988]

What is the management of acute necrotizing ulcerative gingivitis (ANUG)?

- Treatment should be initiated immediately with:
  - **Metronidazole** 200 mg three times a day for 3 days for an adult [BNF 47, 2004] or **amoxicillin** 250–500 mg three times a day for 5 days is an alternative.
  - **An analgesic** such as paracetamol or ibuprofen.
  - **An antiseptic mouthwash** (e.g. chlorhexidine) until the condition has cleared.
  - **Advice on the general preventative oral hygiene measures** such as flossing and brushing, which should be adopted as soon as the mouth is sufficiently comfortable.
  - Advice on smoking cessation (if appropriate).
- Referral for urgent dental assessment and management is required.
  - Professional cleaning is required as the gums are uncomfortable.
  - Referral is especially important since ANUG can be mimicked by other conditions such as necrotizing periodontitis, which can be seen in AIDS and which should be suspected if ANUG does not respond to treatment.

Medicines management

- **Chlorhexidine preparations** can stain teeth brown when used regularly. The stain is not permanent, and can be reduced by brushing teeth before (but not after) use, and avoiding drinks that contain tannin (e.g. tea, coffee, and red wine). Staining is less likely with lower concentrations of chlorhexidine, i.e. 0.12%. The mouth should be rinsed well between brushing and using chlorhexidine, as some ingredients in toothpaste can inactivate chlorhexidine. Staining can be easily removed by a dentist or dental hygienist.

References

NHS staff in England can link, free of charge, from references to full text journals by clicking on [Full text] on the PRODIGY website.

1. Albandar, J.M. and Kingman, A. (1999) Gingival recession, gingival bleeding, and dental calculus in adults 30 years of age and older in the United States, 1988–1994. *Journal of Periodontology* **70**(1), 30–43.
2. American Academy of Periodontology (2000) Parameters of care. *Journal of Periodontology* **71**(5 Suppl), 847–883.
3. Ayad, F., Berta, R., Petrone, M. et al (1995) Effect on plaque removal and gingivitis of a triclosan-copolymer pre-brush rinse: a six-month clinical study in Canada. *Journal of the Canadian Dental Association* **61**(1), 53–56. [erratum appears in: J Can Dent Assoc (1995) 61(3), 184].
4. Barnett, M.L. (2003) The role of therapeutic antimicrobial mouthrinses in clinical practice: control of supragingival plaque and gingivitis. *Journal of the American Dental Association* **134**(6), 699–704.
5. BNF 47 (2004) *British National Formulary*. 47th edn. London: British Medical Association and Royal Pharmaceutical Society of Great Britain.
6. Bral, M. and Brownstein, C.N. (1988) Antimicrobial agents in the prevention and treatment of periodontal diseases. *Dental Clinics of North America* **32**(2), 217–241.
7. British Association of Oral and Maxillofacial Surgeons (2004) *Clinical guidelines for the referral of oral squamous cell carcinoma*. British Association of Oral and Maxillofacial Surgeons. www.baoms.org.uk/ce/ce_oralscc_guidelines.html [Accessed: 18/06/2004].
8. British Society of Paediatric Dentistry (1996) Fluoride dietary supplements and fluoride toothpastes for children. *International Journal of Paediatric Dentistry* **6**(3), 139–142.
9. Coventry, J., Griffiths, G., Scully, C. and Tonetti, M. (2000) ABC of oral health: periodontal disease. *British Medical Journal* **321**(7252), 36–39. [erratum appears in BMJ (2000) 321(7260), 526]. [Full text]
10. Deconinck, S., Boeke, A.J.P., van der Waal, I. and van der Windt, A.W.M. (2003) Incidence and management of oral conditions in general practice. *British Journal of General Practice* **53**(487), 130–132.
11. DePaola, L.G., Overholser, C.D., Meiller, T.F. et al (1989) Chemotherapeutic inhibition of supragingival dental plaque and gingivitis development. *Journal of Clinical Periodontology* **16**(5), 311–315.
12. DTB (1994) Antibiotic gels for periodontal disease. *Drug & Therapeutics Bulletin* **32**(6), 43–44.
13. Gordon, J.M., Lamster, I.B. and Seiger, M.C. (1985) Efficacy of Listerine antiseptic in inhibiting the development of plaque and gingivitis. *Journal of Clinical Periodontology* **12**(8), 697–704.
14. Grossman, E., Meckel, A.H., Isaacs, R.L. et al (1989) A clinical comparison of antibacterial mouthrinses: effects of chlorhexidine, phenolics, and sanguinarine on dental plaque and gingivitis. *Journal of Periodontology* **60**(8), 435–440.
15. Health Development Agency (2001) *The scientific basis of dental health education: a policy document (revised fourth edition)*. Health Development Agency. www.dpb.nhs.uk/archives/other/sci_basis_dental_health2.pdf [Accessed: 29/09/2004].
16. Hoang, T.Q. (2000) The use of triclosan in supportive treatment of gingivitis and periodontitis. *Journal of the Western Society of Periodontology – Periodontal Abstracts* **48**(4), 101–108.
17. Keys, D. and Bartold, M. (2000) Periodontal conditions of relevance to the Australian Dental Force. *Australian Dental Force Health* **1**(Sep), 114–118.
18. Lee, A. and Morris, J. (2001) Gastrointestinal disorders. In: Lee, A. (Ed.) *Adverse drug reactions*. London: Pharmaceutical Press. 45–75.
19. Lehner, T. (2003) The mouth and salivary glands. In: Warrell, D.A., Cox, T.M., Firth, J.D. and Benz, E.J.Jr (Eds.) *Oxford textbook of medicine. Volume 2*. 4th edn. Oxford: Oxford University Press. Section 14.5.
20. Madianos, P.N., Bobetsis, G.A. and Kinane, D.F. (2002) Is periodontitis associated with an increased risk of coronary heart disease and preterm and/or low birth weight births? *Journal of Clinical Periodontology* **29**(Suppl 3), 22–36.
21. Meraw, S.J. and Sheridan, P.J. (1998) Medically induced gingival hyperplasia. *Mayo Clinic Proceedings* **73**(12), 1196–1199. [Full text]
22. Moore, S., Ide, M., Coward, P.Y. et al (2004) A prospective study to investigate the relationship between periodontal disease and adverse pregnancy outcome. *British Dental Journal* **197**(5), 251–258.
23. NICE (2005) *Referral guidelines for suspected cancer – quick reference guide*. Clinical guideline 27. National

Institute for Health and Clinical Excellence. www.nice.org.uk [Accessed: 01/07/2005].
24. Office for National Statistics (2000) *Adult dental health survey, oral health in the United Kingdon 1998.* Office for National Statistics. www.statistics.gov.uk [Accessed: 15/06/2004]. [Full text]
25. Office for National Statistics, Medical Research Council, Ministry of agriculture fisheries and food and Department of Health (2001) *National diet and nutrition survey: young people aged 4 to 18 years, 1997.* London: The Stationary Office.
26. Overholser, C.D., Meiller, T.F., DePaola, L.G. et al (1990) Chemotherapeutic inhibition of supragingival dental plaque and gingivitis development. *Journal of Clinical Periodontology* **17**(8), 575–579.
27. Schroeder, H.E. and Listgarten, M.A. (1997) The gingival tissues: the architecture of periodontal protection. *Periodontology 2000* **13**, 91–120.
28. Scully, C. and Porter, S.R. (1997) The clinical spectrum of desquamative gingivitis. *Seminars in Cutaneous Medicine & Surgery* **16**(4), 308–313.
29. Sharma, N.C., Galustians, H.J., Qaqish, J. et al (2003) Antiplaque and antigingivitis effectiveness of a hexetidine mouthwash. *Journal of Clinical Periodontology* **30**(7), 590–594.
30. Slots, J. (1979) Subgingival microflora and periodontal disease. *Journal of Clinical Periodontology* **6**(5), 351–382.
31. Triratana, T., Rustogi, K.N., Volpe, A.R. et al (2002) Clinical effect of a new liquid dentifrice containing triclosan/copolymer on existing plaque and gingivitis. *Journal of the American Dental Association* **133**(2), 219–225.
32. Worthington, H.V., Davies, R.M., Blinkhorn, A.S. et al (1993) A six-month clinical study of the effect of a pre-brush rinse on plaque removal and gingivitis. *British Dental Journal* **175**(9), 322–326.

PRODIGY GUIDANCE

Glaucoma

Last revised in December 2002
www.prodigy.nhs.uk/guidance.asp?gt=Glaucoma

Applies to people of all ages

This guidance provides information on the management of primary open-angle glaucoma and acute angle-closure glaucoma.

This guidance does not cover other rare forms of glaucoma, for example congenital glaucoma or pigmentary glaucoma.

Goals

- Early detection of disease
- Arrest progression of disease to:
  - Reduce loss of visual field/vision
  - Protect against blindness

G

Contents

Scenarios

- Primary open-angle glaucoma p.836
- Acute angle-closure glaucoma p.836

Extended Information, p. 837

Which scenario?

- **Primary open-angle glaucoma:** covers the management of people who are found to have raised intraocular pressure (IOP) or visual field defects (or other features) suggestive of 'chronic' primary open-angle glaucoma.
- **Acute angle-closure glaucoma:** offers advice where acute angle-closure glaucoma is suspected.

Primary open-angle glaucoma

Which therapy?

- **In order to initiate therapy,** specialist assessment is necessary and referral to secondary care is required.
- **The maintenance of drug therapy** should be guided by advice from secondary care.

Should I refer or investigate ?

Refer?

- If primary closed-angle glaucoma is suspected, people should be referred for assessment and management by an ophthalmologist.

Investigate?

- **A family history of glaucoma** should prompt regular monitoring of intraocular pressure (IOP), ophthalmoscopic examination, and perimetry by an optometrist.
- **People aged over 40 years with a first-degree relative with glaucoma** are eligible for free eye tests. These are generally recommended annually.

Patient information leaflets

The following PILs are available at www.prodigy.nhs.uk

- Glaucoma (Primary Open Angle)
- International Glaucoma Association

Shared decision making

- **Glaucoma** is a condition where the nerve at the back of the eye (the optic nerve) becomes damaged.
- **Primary open-angle glaucoma** is the common type.
  - It is usually due to an increase in the eye pressure.
  - There are usually no symptoms at first.
  - If left untreated, the pressure in the eye can gradually damage the back of the eye to cause visual loss or even blindness.
- **Referral to an eye specialist** is usual if glaucoma is found on eye testing.
- **Eye drops** can reduce the eye pressure, which prevents damage. Use the drops exactly as advised to keep the eye pressure down.
- **Eye surgery** is an option, particularly if drops fail to control the eye pressure.
- **All people over 40** should have regular eye checks to detect early glaucoma — especially close relatives of people with glaucoma.

Drug rationale

- Drug treatment should be initiated only after specialist assessment in secondary care. Therefore no prescriptions are included. Maintenance therapy should be guided by advice from secondary care.

Acute angle-closure glaucoma

Which therapy?

- **Suspected acute angle-closure glaucoma** requires immediate referral (for example to an eye casualty department), or admission, according to local arrangements and severity, for assessment with consideration of urgent reduction of intraocular pressure (IOP).
- **An ophthalmologist** should guide subsequent drug therapy.

Should I refer or investigate ?

Refer?

- Suspected acute angle-closure glaucoma requires immediate referral (for example to an eye casualty department), or admission, according to local arrangements and severity, for assessment with consideration of urgent reduction of intraocular pressure (IOP).

Patient information leaflets

The following PILs are available at www.prodigy.nhs.uk

- International Glaucoma Association

Shared decision making

Drug rationale

- Drug treatment should be initiated only after specialist assessment in secondary care. Therefore no prescriptions are included. Maintenance therapy should be guided by advice from secondary care.

Extended Information

Background information

- What is it? p.837
- How common is it? p.837
- How do I know my patient has it? p.837
- What else might it be? p.837
- Complications and prognosis p.837

What is it?

- **Glaucoma is a group of eye diseases commonly associated with an increase in intraocular pressure (IOP),** although in some people the IOP is found to be within the normal range. Glaucoma leads to optic disc damage and consequently to typical visual field defects. Ultimately it can lead to impaired vision and disability.
- **Glaucoma can be broadly classified into open-angle ('chronic'), acute angle-closure, and the much rarer congenital type.**
- **Primary open-angle glaucoma** is caused by a blockage within the trabecular meshwork, restricting the drainage of aqueous humour. Optic disc damage results, mainly as a consequence of increased IOP, but there may be other mechanisms of damage, particularly ischaemia. Some sufferers have an IOP within the normal range, i.e. below 21 mmHg (normal-tension glaucoma). Risk factors for primary open-angle glaucoma include increasing age, a family history of glaucoma, and diabetes. It is more common in Afro-Caribbean people.
- **Acute angle-closure glaucoma** is a rapid and severe rise in IOP caused by physical obstruction of the anterior chamber drainage angle. It usually results from apposition of the lens to the back of the iris, preventing the flow of aqueous humour from the posterior chamber to the anterior chamber. Risk factors for acute angle-closure glaucoma include hypermetropia (long sight — spectacle lenses are thick centrally and magnify images), eyes with shallow anterior chambers, increasing age, family history, and a previous attack in the other eye. It is more common in people of Asian descent.

[DTB, 1997]

How common is it?

- **Primary open-angle glaucoma:**
  - In the UK, about 1–2% of people aged over 40 years have primary open-angle glaucoma; this rises to about 7% in people over 75 years [DTB, 1997].
  - Primary open-angle glaucoma is the cause of visual impairment in 13% of those who are registered blind [DTB, 1997].
- **Acute angle-closure glaucoma:**
  - The condition is rare; the prevalence is about 1 in 1000 over the age of 40 [Anand and Cunliffe, 1998].

How do I know my patient has it?

Primary open-angle glaucoma

- **Primary open angle glaucoma, if suspected, requires referral to an ophthalmologist for assessment.**
- **Most people will not notice any symptoms until severe visual damage has occurred.** The diagnosis of primary open-angle glaucoma therefore usually occurs during routine eye testing by an optometrist or an ophthalmologist (over 90% of cases) [Crick and Tuck, 1995]. The management of primary open-angle glaucoma is initiated in secondary care.
- The most reliable method for diagnosing primary open-angle glaucoma is through a combination of ophthalmoscopy, tonometry (IOP measurement), and perimetry (visual field assessment) [DTB, 1997].
- **Signs include:**
  - **Visual field loss** is often unnoticed by the person, and it is difficult to pick up clinically in the early stages. The pattern of field loss is characteristic (arcuate scotoma). Central vision is spared until relatively late in the disease [Khaw and Elkington, 1999]. Visual field loss is irreversible once established.
  - **Disc changes** are the most reliable sign of disease — the cup:disc ratio increases as nerve fibres atrophy. Asymmetry of disc changes is also important. Disc haemorrhages can also be a sign of glaucomatous disc damage.
  - **The intraocular pressure (IOP) is usually raised.** However, 20% of people with primary open-angle glaucoma have a normal IOP, and a raised IOP (above 21 mmHg) can occur in those without primary open-angle glaucoma [DTB, 1997].

Acute angle-closure glaucoma

- **Acute angle-closure glaucoma requires emergency treatment and admission.**
- **Signs and symptoms include:**
  - Acute onset, often in the evening, when reduced light levels cause pupil dilation (mydriasis) (consequently it more commonly presents in the winter).
  - Red eye, which is exquisitely painful.
  - Pain, often severe; may be accompanied by vomiting.
  - Cloudy cornea (due to oedema) resulting in transient episodes of severely blurred vision; person may describe haloes when viewing lights.
  - Pupil semidilated, large and oval, and fixed to light.
  - Iris may appear bowed forward (rather than flat) if a torch light is projected across the anterior chamber.

What else might it be?

Acute angle-closure glaucoma can mimic other causes of red eye:

- Conjunctivitis
- Iritis (anterior uveitis)
- Episcleritis or scleritis
- Herpes simplex infection (corneal ulceration)
- Acute abdomen — where nausea and vomiting predominate

Complications and prognosis

- **Primary open-angle glaucoma** slowly progresses, when untreated, with increasing visual field loss. Long-term control of intraocular pressure is needed to prevent recurrence.
- **Acute angle-closure glaucoma** can rapidly result in blindness if untreated. Recurrence is rare if peripheral iridotomy or iridectomy is performed.

Management issues

- Primary open-angle glaucoma p.838
- Acute angle-closure glaucoma p.838

G

Primary open-angle glaucoma

General

- **A family history** of glaucoma should prompt regular monitoring of intraocular pressure (IOP), ophthalmoscopic examination, and perimetry. People aged over 40 years with a first-degree relative with glaucoma are eligible for free eye tests.
- **Early diagnosis** of primary open-angle glaucoma is the key to effective management, and is essential in preventing or halting irreversible visual loss.
- **The focus of management** is on lowering the IOP because, in general, the lower the IOP, the better the prognosis [DTB, 1997].

Drug treatment

- **No drug treatment** is offered in Prodigy as drug treatment is always initiated and subsequently guided by secondary care.
- **Most treatments** for primary open-angle glaucoma are intended to lower the IOP to generally as low a pressure as possible with minimum adverse effects. There is an extensive range of topical agents, each of which either suppresses aqueous humour production or improves its outflow.
- **Recently, the prostaglandin analogue latanoprost has been shown to be effective in lowering intraocular pressure** [Zhang et al, 2001; Heijl et al, 2002].
- **Many specialists are now commonly using prostaglandin analogues as the preferred treatment before a beta-blocker.** Other specialists are only using them if a beta-blocker is not suitable. There is still debate about the role of beta-blockers for initial monotherapy [Goldberg, 2002].
- **Prostaglandin analogues appear to have very few systemic adverse effects** and they are safer to use than beta-blockers [Goldberg, 2002]. Nevertheless they currently have a Committee on Safety of Medicines (CSM) black triangle status and other adverse effects could become evident in the future.
- **Topical beta-blockers have traditionally been the mainstay of initial treatment.** They have excellent pressure-lowering efficacy, long duration of action, and relatively few ocular adverse effects [Alward, 1998]. Several preparations can be used (betaxolol, carteolol, levobunolol, and timolol) — all are equally effective and are given once or twice daily. However, for sufficient drug to enter the eye the solutions used are relatively concentrated and therefore can have systemic activity.
- **Topical beta-blockers should be used with care in people at risk of heart failure or heart block.** The CSM has advised that beta-blockers, even those with apparent cardioselectivity, should not be used in people with asthma or a history of obstructive airways disease, unless no alternative treatment is available. In such cases the risk of inducing bronchospasm should be appreciated and appropriate precautions taken.
- **Other drugs, if needed, can be selected from:**
  - Alternative topical prostaglandin analogues: travoprost and bimatoprost
  - A topical sympathomimetic, such as brimonidine
  - A topical carbonic anhydrase inhibitor (CAI), such as dorzolamide or brinzolamide
  - A topical miotic, such as pilocarpine
  - An oral CAI, the diuretic acetazolamide: may be used in severe cases
- **Increasingly drugs are used in combination,** usually given separately. Combination preparations of timolol with latanoprost (Xalacom), and timolol with dorzolamide (Cosopt), are now available.
- Recent observational data suggest that the use of these drugs can reduce, or delay, subsequent progression to surgery [Bateman et al, 2001].

Surgical procedures

Trabeculectomy

- This involves the creation of a channel between the inside of the eye and the subconjunctival space, thus bypassing the blocked trabecular meshwork. Early surgery is often advocated for primary open-angle glaucoma if a trial of medical treatment has failed to meet target pressures, especially in younger people or those presenting with a high IOP [DTB, 1997].

Laser trabeculoplasty

- Direct application of laser energy to the trabecular meshwork can produce a fall in IOP in people with primary open-angle glaucoma; this is comparable with that achieved by drug treatment. It is rarely used but may be useful in older people with a moderately raised IOP who are unable to instil drops, but the effects are sometimes transient [DTB, 1997].

Acute angle-closure glaucoma

General

- **Presentation with acute angle-closure glaucoma is a medical emergency.**
- **Emergency admission** is required to preserve the sight of the eye.
- **If admission is not immediately possible** (in remote places, for example) parenteral anti-emetic and analgesia should be considered.
- **The diagnosis should be considered** in any person presenting with an acute, painful red eye.

Treatment

- **A reduction in IOP** is achieved first medically and then surgically.
- **In the acute situation,** intravenous (IV) or oral administration of a CAI is used to reduce IOP.
- **Topical pilocarpine** (usually the preferred miotic agent) may then be used to constrict the pupil and break pupil block (this is where aqueous fluid unable to drain away builds up posterior to the iris, pushing it forward to block the trabecular meshwork).
- **An IV hyperosmotic agent** is only rarely used when these measures do not work.
- **For long-term benefit** to prevent an attack from occurring, surgical lowering of IOP is then achieved through the creation of a hole in the iris. More recently this has been carried out by laser (laser iridotomy) treatment, which has largely replaced conventional surgery (iridectomy). The other eye is usually treated also, as a prophylactic measure. The person may require supplementary topical treatment or trabeculectomy if some of the angle is permanently closed by an attack.

References

NHS staff in England can link, free of charge, from references to full text journals by clicking on [Full text] on the PRODIGY website.

1. Alward, W.L.M. (1998) Medical management of glaucoma. *New England Journal of Medicine* 339(18), 1298–1307. [Full text]
2. Anand, N. and Cunliffe, I.A. (1998) Glaucoma: the aetiology and pathology of glaucoma. *Hospital Pharmacist* 5(March), 73–80.
3. Bateman, D.N., Clark, R., Azuara-Blanco, A. et al (2001) The impact of new drugs on management of

glaucoma in Scotland: observational study. *British Medical Journal* **323**(7326), 1401–1402. [Full text]
4. Crick, R.P. and Tuck, M.W. (1995) How can we improve the detection of glaucoma? Thorough testing and better targeting. *British Medical Journal* **310**(6979), 546–547. [Full text]
5. DTB (1997) The management of primary open angle glaucoma. *Drug & Therapeutics Bulletin* **35**(1), 4–6.
6. Goldberg, I. (2002) Should beta blockers be abandoned as initial monotherapy in chronic open angle glaucoma? The controversy. *British Journal of Ophthalmology* **86**(6), 691–692. [Full text]
7. Heijl, A., Leske, M.C., Bengtsson, B. et al (2002) Reduction of intraocular pressure and glaucoma progression: results from the early manifest glaucoma trial. *Archives of Ophthalmology* **120**(10), 1268–1279. [Full text]
8. Khaw, P.T. and Elkington, A.R. (Eds.) (1999) *ABC of eyes.* 3rd edn. London: BMJ Publishing Group.
9. Zhang, W.Y., Po, A.L., Dua, H.S. and Azuara-Blanco, A. (2001) Meta-analysis of randomised controlled trials comparing latanoprost with timolol in the treatment of patients with open angle glaucoma or ocular hypertension. *British Journal of Ophthalmology* **85**(8), 983–990. [Full text]

G

PRODIGY GUIDANCE

Glue ear

Last revised in February 2004
www.prodigy.nhs.uk/guidance.asp?gt=Glue ear

Applies to people of all ages

This guidance covers the management of glue ear (otitis media with effusion).

This guidance does not cover the management of other ear disorders.

There is separate PRODIGY guidance for *Otitis media — acute* and *Otitis externa*.

Goals

- To decide whether or not the person has glue ear.
- To refer appropriately to specialist services.

G

Contents

Scenarios

- Glue ear p.840

Extended Information, p. 841

Glue ear

Which therapy?

- **Give clear verbal and written information (e.g. PRODIGY patient information leaflets) to parents or carers.** Knowledge about glue ear varies considerably, and many parents are extremely concerned about the possible impact of the condition on their child.
- **Advise parents or carers not to expose the child to tobacco smoke,** as this is a recognized risk factor for glue ear.
- **In children with glue ear,** nothing worthwhile is gained by prescribing an antibiotic, corticosteroid, decongestant, or antihistamine.
- **Children less than 4 years old with glue ear** should be referred to an ear, nose, and throat (ENT) specialist. Watchful waiting is not appropriate in this age group, as a reliable level of hearing loss cannot be obtained.
- **Children who are 4 years and older and present with glue ear** can be safely managed with watchful waiting, repeat audiometry being performed in 3 months. Watchful waiting is not appropriate for children who have significant disability or who have associated high-risk conditions, such as cleft palate or Down's syndrome — such children should be referred to an ENT specialist.
- **Children who are 4 years and older with persistent glue ear,** or who have problems with speech and language, development, or behaviour, should be referred to an ENT specialist.
- **Suggested referral advice** from NICE is outlined in the section *Should I refer or investigate?*

Follow-up advice

- Review the child at 3 months, ideally with repeat audiometry, to determine whether hearing loss is still a problem.

Should I refer or investigate?

Refer?

- The National Institute for Clinical Excellence in *Referral advice: a guide to appropriate referral from general to specialist services* [NICE, 2001] gives the advice in Table 1. for glue ear in children. The referral advice is meant to encourage local health communities to discuss referral issues and enable local referral guidelines and protocols to be produced (for further information see, www.nice.org.uk).

Investigate?

Detection of middle-ear fluid

- **Otosocopy** may be useful, although a normal-looking eardrum does not exclude glue ear. One or more of the following may be seen if glue ear is present:
  - Opacification of the drum (other than due to scarring)
  - Loss of the light reflex, or a more diffused light reflex
  - Indrawn, retracted, or concave drum
  - Decreased or absent mobility of the drum
  - Presence of bubbles or fluid level
  - Yellow or amber colour change to the drum
  - Fullness or bulging of the drum, though this is not typical
- **Pneumatic otoscopy** (if available) assesses eardrum mobility. An immobile or sluggishly mobile eardrum is suggestive of glue ear.
- **Tympanometry** (if available) is a useful confirmatory diagnostic test. A flat curve indicates fluid behind the eardrum.

Assessment of hearing

- **Accurate hearing assessment** of a child with suspected hearing loss usually requires referral to specialist services, such as local audiology clinics.

Table 1: When to refer a child with persistent glue ear to an ear, nose and throat (ENT) specialist.

	Referral timing
The otoscopic features are atypical and are accompanied by a persistent foul-smelling discharge suggestive of cholesteatoma.	***
The child has excessive hearing loss suggestive of additional sensori-neural deafness.	***
The child has proven hearing loss, plus difficulties with speech, language, cognition, or behaviour.	**
The child has proven hearing loss, plus a second disability, such as Down's syndrome.	**
The child has proven hearing loss, together with frequent episodes of acute otitis media.	**
The child has proven persistent hearing loss detected on two occasions separated by 3 months or more (results of formal testing should be included in the referral letter).	*

Arrangements should be made so that the child:
*** is seen urgently (maximum wait of 2 weeks recommended but to be agreed locally)
** is seen soon (maximum waiting time to be agreed locally)
* has a routine appointment (maximum waiting time to be agreed locally)

- **When to refer a child for formal hearing assessment** varies according to the presentation. If the hearing loss has lasted for more than a month, referral is usually appropriate. If the history is shorter than this, the parents should be advised to bring their child back if the problem seems to be persisting for more than a month, so that a hearing test can be arranged.
- **Pure-tone audiometry** is the best way to assess hearing. However, pure-tone audiometry is only suitable for children who are 4 years and older, as those younger than this are not old enough to cooperate. The following tests are suitable for children younger than 4 years; however, these tests do not provide a quantitative level of loss, and are therefore less useful:
  - **Distraction tests** are usually suitable for children aged 6–18 months.
  - **The McCormick Toy Test** is usually suitable for children aged 2–5 years.

Patient information leaflets

The following PILs are available at www.prodigy.nhs.uk

- Glue Ear

Shared decision making

- **Glue ear** causes dulled hearing because of a build-up of fluid in the middle ear.
- **It is usually best to 'wait and see'** whether it will clear by itself. Glue ear clears without treatment in most cases over a few weeks or months.
- **There are no medicines** that make the fluid clear faster.
- **Referral to an Ear, Nose, and Throat (ENT) specialist** may be needed if hearing does not improve.
- **An operation (grommets and/or removal of adenoids)** may be advised if glue ear persists.
- **A child with dulled hearing may become frustrated** at not following all that is going on. This frustration may lead to poor school performance, behaviour problems, irritability, etc. Younger children may be slower than average to develop speech.
- **Speak louder, more clearly, and face-to-face to children with glue ear.** Make sure teachers are aware of the problem too.
- **Do not let anyone smoke** in the same home as the child. Passive smoking can make glue ear worse.

Drug rationale

- **No drugs are recommended for the management of glue ear.**
- **Antibiotics do not provide any worthwhile benefit** [SIGN, 2003]; there is evidence of some short-term benefit but this is not maintained. A systematic review found that by 1 month the absolute risk difference for clearance of glue ear was 14% (95% CI 4% to 24%; for every seven children given antibiotics, one extra child will have clearance of glue ear after 4 weeks compared with those taking placebo, NNT = 7) However, by 6 weeks after treatment there was no significant difference [Williamson, 2003]. Antibiotics may be of some value in treating superadded acute infection.
- **Corticosteroids (topical or systemic) are of uncertain value and are not recommended** [SIGN, 2003]. A Cochrane systematic review suggests that oral steroids give some short-term benefit, but that this has to be balanced against the known risks of systemic steroids [Butler and Van Der Voort, 2002]. A small, randomized controlled trial suggests that intranasal steroids may give some short-term benefit, but more data are needed [Tracy et al, 1998].
- **Antihistamines, decongestants, and mucolytics are of no proven benefit** [SIGN, 2003; Williamson, 2003].

Extended Information

Background information

- What is it? p.841
- How common is it? p.841
- How do I know my patient has it? p.842
- What else might it be? p.842
- Complications and prognosis p.842

What is it?

- **Glue ear is the common term for otitis media with effusion.** Other terms include secretory otitis media and serous otitis media.
- **Glue ear is defined as inflammation of the middle ear, accompanied by the accumulation of fluid in the middle-ear cleft, without the symptoms and signs of acute inflammation** [SIGN, 2003].
- **Glue ear often results in conductive hearing loss,** and is the commonest cause of hearing loss and elective surgery in childhood. In ears with documented fluid, the average hearing loss is 20 decibels (dB), but may be as high as 50 dB. A deficit of more than 25 dB in the better ear is usually important, but a deficit of 20 dB or even 15 dB does not mean that important hearing loss has not been or will not be suffered at some point. Spontaneous resolution is common, but if episodes are frequent or persistent, speech, language development, and behaviour may be adversely affected.
- **The causes of glue ear are uncertain.** Viral or bacterial infections, abnormal mucus viscosity, and Eustachian tube dysfunction have all been implicated. Risk factors include:
  - Male sex
  - Exposure to tobacco smoke
  - Younger age (peaks at 2 years)
  - Formula feeding as an infant
  - Sibling history of glue ear
  - Season (more prevalent in winter months)
  - Attendance at a day care centre
  - Recurrent upper respiratory tract infections [Freemantle et al, 1992; AHCPR, 1994; Kubba et al, 2000; SIGN, 2003].

How common is it?

- **Glue ear is common.** Many children, however, do not present for medical attention, as they have unrecognized symptoms (even if symptoms have been present for a considerable length of time).
- **Incidence** in young children is high, with most having at least one episode of glue ear during early childhood.
- **Prevalence** is significantly lower than incidence, owing to the short duration of episodes of glue ear. There is a peak of 20% at 2 years of age, with a second peak in the sixth year [Freemantle et al, 1992].
- **Studies have varied in their findings, owing to different case mixes, sample sizes, and definitions of glue ear.**
  - **Zeisel et al followed 108 children from the age of 6 months to 2 years.** Every child except one had evidence of glue ear on at least one occasion. At least one episode of glue ear occurred in 76% of children aged 6–12 months and in 30% of children aged 21–24 months [Zeisel et al, 1995].
  - **Hogan et al followed 95 children from birth to 3 years.** Frequent episodes of glue ear were common, although the mean duration of episodes was only

8 weeks for bilateral effusion. In 17% of children, glue ear was present for more than half of their first 3 years of life. More severely affected children tended to have more frequent rather than longer episodes of glue ear [Hogan et al, 1997].
- **Zielhuis et al followed 1338 children from the age of 2 years to 4 years,** with tympanometry every 3 months on nine consecutive occasions [Zielhuis et al, 1989]. Of the 593 children with complete data, 18% had bilateral glue ear on two or more consecutive occasions and about 7% on more than half of the test occasions [Stephenson et al, 1993].
- **Williamson et al followed 856 children aged 5–8 years until they left primary school.** At least one episode of glue ear occurred in 27% of children. The annual incidence was 27% for children aged 5 years, which dropped to 7% for children aged 8 years [Williamson et al, 1994].

How do I know my patient has it?

G

History

- **The usual presenting feature is hearing loss,** which may be noticed by the child's carer or teacher.
- **Concern regarding speech and language, social interaction, behaviour, or education** may be a presenting feature.
- **There may be a history of clumsiness or balance problems.**
- **There may be a history of associated problems,** such as recurrent upper respiratory infections, otitis media, and nasal catarrh.
- **There may be no history to indicate the presence of glue ear,** and hearing loss may be picked up on child health surveillance.

[SIGN, 2003]

General examination

- **Be alert to the child's response when spoken to** (e.g. an excessively fixed stare at the person talking may indicate hearing difficulty). Non-distraction by incidental faint sounds also indicates the possibility of hearing loss.
- **Ideally, assess whether or not the child is achieving appropriate developmental milestones.** This may be better done by another appropriately trained health professional, such as a health visitor.
- **Look for wax blocking the ear canal.**

Detection of middle ear fluid

- **Otosocopy** may be useful, although a normal-looking eardrum does not exclude glue ear. One or more of the following may be seen if glue ear is present:
  - Opacification of the drum (other than due to scarring)
  - Loss of the light reflex, or a more diffused light reflex
  - Indrawn, retracted, or concave drum
  - Decreased or absent mobility of the drum
  - Presence of bubbles or fluid level
  - Yellow or amber colour change to the drum
  - Fullness or bulging of the drum, though this is not typical
- **Pneumatic otoscopy** assesses eardrum mobility. Its use increases the sensitivity of diagnosing glue ear, but it is not widely available in primary care in the UK. An immobile or sluggishly mobile eardrum is suggestive of glue ear. For skilled users, the positive predictive value of an abnormal finding (i.e. the likelihood that an effusion is present if the drum is poorly mobile) is about 90%. The negative predictive value of a normal finding (i.e. the likelihood that no effusion is present if the drum moves normally) is about 80% [AHCPR, 1994].
- **Tympanometry** is a useful confirmatory diagnostic test, but is not widely available in primary care in the UK. The test measures the ability of the eardrum to react to sound. A flat curve indicates fluid behind the eardrum. The positive predictive value of an abnormal tympanogram is reported to vary between 49% and 99%, and the negative predictive value between 64% and 93% [AHCPR, 1994].

[SIGN, 2003]

Assessment of hearing

- **Accurate hearing assessment of a child with suspected hearing loss usually requires referral to specialist services, such as local audiology clinics.**
- **When to refer a child for formal hearing assessment varies according to the presentation.** If the hearing loss has lasted for more than a month, referral is usually appropriate. If the history is shorter than this, the parents should be advised to bring their child back if the problem seems to be persisting for more than a month, so that a hearing test can be arranged.
- **Pure-tone audiometry** is the best way to assess hearing. However, pure-tone audiometry is only suitable for children who are 4 years and older, as those younger than this are not old enough to cooperate. The following tests are suitable for children younger than 4 years; however, these tests do not provide a quantitative level of loss, and are therefore less useful:
  - **Distraction tests** are usually suitable for children aged 6–18 months.
  - **The McCormick Toy Test** is usually suitable for children aged 2–5 years.
- **A hearing loss of 25 decibels (dB) or greater in the better ear is usually important.** With a hearing loss of 30 dB, normal conversation may sound like a soft whisper.

[SIGN, 2003]

What else might it be?

- Hearing loss due to other causes (e.g. earwax, foreign body, or hereditary condition).
- Behaviour disturbance unrelated to any underlying hearing problem.

Complications and prognosis

Complications

- **Glue ear may adversely affect speech, language development, behaviour, and education.** However, the evidence regarding this is inconsistent, with only a weak association between glue ear and delayed speech and language development. Most studies suggest that for most children any adverse effect is temporary.
- **Some studies have shown an association between glue ear and clumsiness or balance problems.** This result has not been confirmed by other studies.

[SIGN, 2003]

Prognosis

- **Spontaneous resolution of glue ear is common in community cohort studies;** 50% resolve within 3 months and 95% within a year [Zielhuis et al, 1989]. In most children, problems with glue ear do not persist beyond early childhood.
- **Resolution seems to be less common in children attending Ear, Nose, and Throat (ENT) clinics,** probably because such children have already been through a period of watchful waiting and have been found to have persistent middle ear fluid.

Management issues

- Initial management and indications for referral p.843
- Surgical treatment p.843
- Autoinflation p.843
- Medical treatments (none recommended) p.843

Initial management and indications for referral

- **Give clear verbal and written information (e.g. PRODIGY patient information leaflets) to parents or carers.** Knowledge about glue ear varies considerably, and many parents are extremely concerned about the possible impact of the condition on their child.
- **Advise parents or carers not to expose the child to tobacco smoke,** as this is a recognized risk factor for glue ear.
- **Children less than 4 years old with glue ear** should be referred to an ear, nose, and throat (ENT) specialist. Watchful waiting is not appropriate in this age group, as a reliable level of hearing loss cannot be obtained.
- **Children who are 4 years and older and present with glue ear** can be safely managed with watchful waiting, repeat audiometry being performed in 3 months. Watchful waiting is not appropriate for children who have significant disability or who have associated high-risk conditions, such as cleft palate or Down's syndrome — such children should be referred to an ENT specialist.
- **Children who are 4 years and older with persistent glue ear,** or who have problems with speech and language, development, or behaviour, should be referred to an ENT specialist.
- The National Institute for Clinical Excellence in *Referral advice: a guide to appropriate referral from general to specialist services* [NICE, 2001] gives the advice in Table 2 for glue ear in children. The referral advice is meant to encourage local health communities to discuss referral issues and enable local referral guidelines and protocols to be produced (for further information, see www.nice.org.uk).

Surgical treatment

- **Surgery may resolve glue ear and improve hearing in the short term,** but there is less certainty about long-term outcomes. There is large variation in effect between children.

Table 2: When to refer a child with persistent glue ear to an ear, nose and throat (ENT) specialist.

	Referral timing
The otoscopic features are atypical and are accompanied by a persistent foul-smelling discharge suggestive of cholesteatoma.	***
The child has excessive hearing loss suggestive of additional sensori-neural deafness.	***
The child has proven hearing loss, plus difficulties with speech, language, cognition, or behaviour.	**
The child has proven hearing loss, plus a second disability, such as Down's syndrome.	**
The child has proven hearing loss, together with frequent episodes of acute otitis media.	**
The child has proven persistent hearing loss detected on two occasions separated by 3 months or more (results of formal testing should be included in the referral letter).	*

Arrangements should be made so that the child:
*** is seen urgently (maximum wait of 2 weeks recommended but to be agreed locally)
** is seen soon (maximum waiting time to be agreed locally)
* has a routine appointment (maximum waiting time to be agreed locally)

- **There continues to be debate about how best to select children for surgery.** The issue is complicated by the high rate of resolution of glue ear, particularly in younger children.
- **Timing of surgery may not be critical.** A recent trial compared 'watchful waiting' for 9 months with immediate surgery for children with persistent bilateral glue ear, hearing loss, and problems with speech, language, learning, or behaviour [Maw et al, 1999]. Early surgery improved verbal comprehension and expressive language, but by 18 months these were similar in both groups. By this time, however, 85% of children in the watchful waiting group had been treated with grommets.
- **Treatment options are grommet insertion, adenoidectomy, or both.** Adenoidectomy with grommet insertion seems to provide more prolonged improvement than either alone.
  - A systematic review found that surgery (insertion of grommets, adenoidectomy, or both) improved short-term outcomes, with an average improvement in hearing of 12 decibels (dB) with little difference between any of the treatments [Freemantle et al, 1992].
  - A subsequent trial found that grommets and adenoidectomy combined were more effective at maintaining improvement. The median duration of glue ear was reduced from 8 years without treatment to 5 years with grommets, 4 years with adenoidectomy, and 3 years with adenoidectomy and grommets combined [Maw and Bawden, 1993]. Over a third of children who had grommet insertion alone required further surgery within the year, compared with less than 10% of those treated with both adenoidectomy and grommet insertion.
- **The benefits of surgery have to be balanced against possible harms.** Tympanosclerosis frequently occurs after grommet insertion, although the long-term consequences of this are uncertain. Infection after grommet insertion may occur, and there is also a slightly increased incidence of chronic perforation. There is a slight risk of haemorrhage after adenoidectomy. There are also the slight risks of general anaesthesia and the psychological trauma of hospitalization and operation [Freemantle et al, 1992].
- **Advice on swimming and bathing after grommet insertion** is based on a small number of trials of poor quality, but grommet insertion does not seem to be a contraindication to swimming. Soap reduces the surface tension of water, theoretically increasing the risk of water entering the middle-ear cavity. We could find no trials covering this issue, but it is advised to avoid immersion of the head in soapy water [SIGN, 2003].

Autoinflation

- **Autoinflation may be of benefit in older, motivated children** [SIGN, 2003]. It is difficult, however, to make firm recommendations, owing to the poor quality of trial data [Reidpath et al, 1999; Williamson, 2003].
- **The recommended method is with an otovent device.** A balloon is inflated by blowing into it from one nostril, while sealing the other nostril with a finger. This action results in an increase in intranasal pressure and opening of the Eustachian tube (i.e. a Valsalva manoeuvre). The otovent device is not available on prescription.

Medical treatments (none recommended)

- **Antibiotics do not provide any worthwhile benefit** [SIGN, 2003]; there is evidence of some short-term benefit, but this is not maintained. A systematic review found that by 1 month the absolute risk difference for clearance of glue ear was 14% (95% CI 4% to 24%; for every seven children given antibiotics, one extra child will have clearance of glue ear after 4 weeks compared with those taking placebo, NNT = 7). However, by 6 weeks after treatment there was no significant difference [Williamson, 2003]. Antibiotics may be of some value in treating superadded acute infection.

- **Corticosteroids (topical or systemic) are of uncertain value and are not recommended** [SIGN, 2003]. A Cochrane systematic review suggests that oral steroids give some short-term benefit, but that this has to be balanced against the known risks of systemic steroids [Butler and Van Der Voort, 2002]. A small, randomized controlled trial suggests that intranasal steroids may give some short-term benefit, but more data are needed [Tracy et al, 1998].
- **Antihistamines, decongestants, and mucolytics are of no proven benefit** [SIGN, 2003; Williamson, 2003].

G

References

NHS staff in England can link, free of charge, from references to full text journals by clicking on [Full text] on the PRODIGY website.

1. AHCPR (1994) *Otitis media with effusion in young children: clinical practice guideline2*. Agency for Health Care Policy and Research.
2. Butler, C.C. and Van Der Voort, J.H. (2002) *Oral or topical nasal steroids for hearing loss associated with otitis media with effusion in children. [update of Cochrane Database Syst Rev. 2000(4): CD001935; PMID: 11034736]*. The Cochrane Library. Issue 3. Oxford: Update Software.
3. Freemantle, N., Long, A., Mason, J. et al (1992) The treatment of persistent glue ear in children. *Effective Health Care Bulletin* 4, 1–15.
4. Hogan, S.C., Stratford, K.J. and Moore, D.R. (1997) Duration and recurrence of otitis media with effusion in children from birth to 3 years: prospective study using monthly otoscopy and tympanometry. *British Medical Journal* 314(7077), 350–353.
5. Kubba, H., Pearson, J.P. and Birchall, J.P. (2000) The aetiology of otitis media with effusion: a review. *Clinical Otolaryngology* 25(3), 181–194.
6. Maw, R. and Bawden, R. (1993) Spontaneous resolution of severe chronic glue ear in children and the effect of adenoidectomy, tonsillectomy, and insertion of ventilation tubes (grommets). *British Medical Journal* 306(6880), 756–760.
7. Maw, R., Wilks, J., Harvey, I. et al (1999) Early surgery compared with watchful waiting for glue ear and effect on language development in preschool children: a randomised trial [published erratum appears in Lancet 1999 Oct 16;354(9187):1392]. *Lancet* 353(9157), 960–963.
8. NICE (2001) *Referral advice – a guide to appropriate referral from general to specialist services*. National Institute for Clinical Excellence. www.nice.org.uk [Accessed: 11/08/2002].
9. Reidpath, D.D., Glasziou, P.P. and Del Mar, C. (1999) Systematic review of autoinflation for treatment of glue ear in children. *British Medical Journal* 318(7192), 1177–1178.
10. SIGN (2003) *Diagnosis and management of childhood otitis media in primary care*. Report No. 66. Scottish Intercollegiate Guidelines Network. www.sign.ac.uk [Accessed: 02/06/2003].
11. Stephenson, H., Haggard, M., Zielhuis, G. et al (1993) Prevalence of tympanogram asymmetries and fluctuations in otitis media with effusion: implications for binaural hearing. *Audiology* 32(3), 164–174.
12. Tracy, J.M., Demain, J.G., Hoffman, K.M. and Goetz, D.W. (1998) Intranasal beclomethasone as an adjunct to treatment of chronic middle ear effusion. *Annals of Allergy, Asthma, & Immunology* 80(2), 198–206.
13. Williamson, I. (2003) Otitis media with effusion. *Clinical Evidence* 9(June), 577–584.
14. Williamson, I.G., Dunleavey, J., Bain, J. and Robinson, D. (1994) The natural history of otitis media with effusion – a three-year study of the incidence and prevalence of abnormal tympanograms in four south west Hampshire infant and first schools. *Journal of Laryngology & Otology* 108(11), 930–934.
15. Zeisel, S.A., Roberts, J.E., Gunn, E.B. et al (1995) Prospective surveillance for otitis media with effusion among black infants in group child care. *Journal of Pediatrics* 127(6), 875–880.
16. Zielhuis, G.A., Rach, G.H. and van den Broek, P. (1989) Screening for otitis media with effusion in pre-school children. *Lancet* 333(1), 311–313.

PRODIGY GUIDANCE

Gout

Last revised in July 2005
www.prodigy.nhs.uk/guidance.asp?gt=Gout

Applies to people over the age of 16 years

This guidance covers gouty arthritis and asymptomatic hyperuricaemia.

This guidance does not cover the management of other crystal-related arthropathies (e.g. pseudogout), gout in children, uric acid renal stones, urate nephropathy, or the prevention of hyperuricaemia in people who are being treated for haematological malignancies.

There is separate PRODIGY guidance for *Osteoarthritis* and for *Rheumatoid arthritis*.
This version of the guidance has limited details on the evidence to support the recommendations. The version that includes a detailed review of the evidence is available on request from prodigy-enquiries@schin.ncl.ac.uk.

Goals

The goals in treating someone with gout are to:

- Enable the person to understand the nature of the condition, and the risks and benefits of the various drug and dietary treatment options
- Promptly relieve the pain and inflammation of an acute attack of gout
- Reduce the risk of recurrent attacks of gout — if not outweighed by the risks of treatment
- Minimize the risks of developing new tophi, and to resolve existing tophi
- Minimize the risks of developing joint damage, renal stones, and urate nephropathy
- Identify and modify risk factors for gout that may have other adverse effects on the person's health

Contents

Scenarios

- Acute monoarticular gout p.845
- Acute polyarticular gout p.849
- Introduction of long-term urate-lowering therapy p.853
- Gout despite use of urate-lowering therapy p.856
- Asymptomatic hyperuricaemia p.858

Extended Information, p. 858

Which scenario?

Acute monoarticular gout: covers the management of an acute attack of gout affecting only one joint or extra-articular structure.

Acute polyarticular gout: covers the management of an acute attack of gout affecting more than one joint or extra-articular structure.

Introduction of long-term urate-lowering therapy: covers the introduction of urate-lowering therapy.

Gout despite use of urate-lowering therapy: covers the management of an acute attack of gout in a person who is being treated with urate-lowering therapy.

Asymptomatic hyperuricaemia: covers the management of a person with a raised plasma level of urate who has never had gout.

Acute monoarticular gout

Which therapy?

Always consider the possibility of sepsis in an acute hot joint.

- **Rule out, or manage, secondary causes of gout** (for details, see Table 1 in *Background information*).
- **Suggest cautious use of an ice pack.** The pack should be wrapped in a towel to avoid direct skin contact and ice-burn.
- **Start drug treatment as soon as possible,** preferably within 24 hours of the onset of the attack.
  - Prompt treatment is facilitated if people with gout have a supply of medicine at home and they understand the disadvantages of delaying treatment.
- **Treat an acute attack** of gout with a nonsteroidal anti-inflammatory drug (NSAID), colchicine, corticosteroid, or analgesic.
- **Treatment with an NSAID is the generally preferred option** unless there are contraindications.
- **Systemic corticosteroids and oral colchicine** are options if NSAIDs are not suitable.
- **Intra-articular corticosteroids** are an option to use as sole therapy or adjunctive therapy if the joint is suitable for injecting *and* the expertise to inject the joint is available.
- **Analgesics** are sometimes required in addition to other therapy for acute gout. They may also be used alone if NSAIDs, corticosteroids, and colchicine are all contraindicated.
- **Do not introduce urate-lowering therapy during an acute attack** — see *Urate-lowering therapy* scenario.
- **Suggest a prudent diet and lifestyle.**
  - Moderate ingestion of alcohol.
  - Restrict dietary energy intake to limit weight gain, or, in the obese, to lose weight.
  - Limit ingestion of heart, herring, sardines, and mussels (very high purine content).
  - Moderate ingestion of other meat and seafood (high purine content).
  - Consider moderating ingestion of yeast extracts, pulses, and other vegetables high in purines (less evidence of risk).
- **Manage any risk factors** for gout and associated conditions that are present, including:
  - Drugs (e.g. diuretics)
  - Obesity
  - Hypertension
  - Renal impairment
  - Myeloproliferative disease
  - Hyperlipidaemia (especially hypertriglyceridaemia)
  - Vascular disease
  - Psoriasis
  - Enzyme deficiencies such as hypoxanthine guanine phosphoribosyltransferase deficiency

Practical prescribing points

For further information, see the *Medicines Compendium* (www.medicines.org.uk) or the *British National Formulary* (www.bnf.org).

NSAIDs

- **Only one NSAID should be prescribed at a time.**
- **NSAIDs may worsen asthma, hypertension, renal impairment, or heart failure.**
- Do not give diclofenac, indometacin, or naproxen without gastroprotection if there is a history of peptic ulceration.
- Do not give etoricoxib if there is active peptic ulceration, or to people with uncontrolled hypertension.
- **People with cardiovascular disease:**
  - Do not give etoricoxib to people with established ischaemic heart disease, cerebrovascular disease, peripheral arterial disease, or moderate or severe heart failure due to the small increased risk of thrombotic events.
  - Do not use etoricoxib with low-dose aspirin. (Gastrointestinal protective effects of etoricoxib are reduced.)
- **In people with risk factors for gastrointestinal NSAID complications:**
  - Use paracetamol (with or without codeine) instead of a NSAID if possible.
  - Or, use gastroprotection (a PPI or full-dose misoprostol) combined with a standard NSAID.
  - Or, consider switching to etoricoxib alone (COX-2 selective).
- **Risk factors for gastrointestinal NSAID complications include:**
  - Age of 65 years and over.
  - Previous history of gastroduodenal ulcer, gastrointestinal (GI) bleeding, or gastroduodenal perforation.
  - Concomitant use of medications that are known to increase the likelihood of upper-GI adverse events, e.g. anticoagulants, aspirin (even a low dose), and corticosteroids.
  - Presence of serious comorbidity, such as cardiovascular disease, renal or hepatic impairment, diabetes, or hypertension.
  - Requirement for prolonged duration of NSAID use.
  - Use of maximum recommended doses of NSAIDs.

Colchicine

- **Diarrhoea** is common at full dose, especially in old people. Consider giving less frequently to avoid severe gastrointestinal toxicity.
- **Avoid in serious gastrointestinal or cardiac disorders.** Toxicity is more likely to occur with underlying renal impairment. Reduce the dose accordingly (see the BNF section on renal impairment).

Corticosteroids

- **Corticosteroids may worsen diabetic control or heart failure.**

Intra-articular corticosteroids

- **Atrophy of subcutaneous tissues and local skin depigmentation** may occur from periarticular leakage of corticosteroid. The risk is greatest if large or repeated doses of a long-acting, potent corticosteroid are given. In general, hydrocortisone, dexamethasone, or prednisolone is recommended for injection of small joints, and triamcinolone or methylprednisolone for injection of large joints.

Codeine

- Codeine may cause nausea, vomiting, constipation, and drowsiness. A regular laxative is often needed when it is used long-term.

Misoprostol

- Diarrhoea and abdominal pain are common. Advise women of child-bearing age to use adequate contraception, because misoprostol increases the risk of miscarriage.

Follow-up advice

- **If risk factors are found** (e.g. renal impairment, alcohol excess), further assessment and treatment or modification are required.
- **Advise the person to return if** the joint is more inflamed 24 hours after an intra-articular injection, or if there are systemic symptoms of infection, or adverse effects from the medication.
- **Review if long-term urate-lowering therapy is being considered.**
- **Indications for urate-lowering therapy:**
  - **Recurrent attacks of gouty arthritis** despite attempts to reduce risk factors
  - **Polyarticular gout**
  - **The presence of tophi**
  - **Clinical or radiological signs of chronic gouty arthritis**
  - **Uric acid renal stones or gouty nephropathy** (outside the scope of this guidance)

Should I refer or investigate?

Refer?

Refer if:

- **Sepsis** is suspected.
- **The diagnosis is in doubt.**
- **Intra-articular steroid injection** is indicated and facilities or expertise for this are unavailable.
- **Usual anti-inflammatory therapy is ineffective or contraindicated** (for example, renal failure or inability to tolerate usual drugs).

Investigate?

- **Joint aspiration and polarized-light microscopy** of synovial fluid for urate crystals — note that:
  - It is desirable to establish the diagnosis of gout by joint aspiration, but aspiration of small joints, and in particular the first metatarsophalangeal joint, may not be practical.
- **Plasma urate level** — note that:
  - Not all people with hyperuricaemia have gout.
  - Not all people with gout have hyperuricaemia.
- **Renal function** (plasma creatinine).
- **Full blood count** — could indicate inflammation or an underlying myeloproliferative disorder.
- Also consider:
  - **Liver-function tests,** including gamma-glutamyl transferase (GGT) — could help assess alcohol intake.
  - **X-ray** of the affected joint if recurrent or chronic gout is thought to have resulted in joint damage, or if pseudogout is suspected.

Patient information leaflets

The following PILs are available at www.prodigy.nhs.uk

- Anti-inflammatory Painkillers
- Arthritis Research Campaign - ARC
- Blood Test - General

Gout
Medicines Name Changes of Medicines
UK Gout Society

Shared decision making

Gout attacks are due to a build-up of uric acid (urate) in the joint.

An anti-inflammatory painkiller will usually ease a gout attack within 12–24 hours.

- Some people need a medicine to 'protect the stomach' if gut side-effects occur while they are taking anti-inflammatories.

Colchicine is an option if you have side-effects with anti-inflammatories.

Steroids are an option if you have side-effects with anti-inflammatories and colchicine.

Paracetamol, codeine, or other painkillers can be taken as well, to help ease pain.

An ice pack can also help to ease pain. Use a bag of frozen peas or ice cubes wrapped in a towel. Do not put ice directly against the skin, as it may cause 'ice-burn'.

Gout attacks in some people may be triggered by excess alcohol, by being overweight, and by certain medicines such as some 'water tablets' (diuretics) or low-dose aspirin.

A medicine can be taken each day to prevent gout attacks if they recur.

Drug rationale

Drugs not included

Urate-lowering therapy should not be started until the acute attack of gout has resolved. See the scenario *Introduction of urate-lowering therapy*.

Standard nonsteroidal anti-inflammatory drugs (NSAIDs), other than diclofenac, indometacin, and naproxen, are not generally recommended:

- **Ibuprofen** and some other NSAIDs are not licensed for the treatment of acute gout.
- **Ketoprofen, piroxicam, and sulindac** are licensed for the treatment of acute gout, but are less frequently used and are associated with an increased risk and range of adverse effects.
- **Azapropazone** should be reserved for use on specialist advice where other less toxic treatments have proved ineffective.
- **Modified-release NSAIDs:** no improvement in efficacy or reduction in adverse events has been found. These drugs are also relatively expensive.

[Henry et al, 1996; Hernández-Diaz and Rodriguez, 2000; CSM, 2002]

Analgesics, other than paracetamol and codeine taken separately, are not recommended:

- **Strong opioids** (e.g. morphine, pethidine) should be avoided because of the risk of dependence if they are used inappropriately.
- **Weak opioids,** other than codeine, have either not been shown to be more effective than codeine (when used in combination with paracetamol) or are more expensive.
- **Low-dose weak opioids with paracetamol** (combination products), e.g. co-codamol 8/500 mg: There is no evidence that these offer any clinical benefit over paracetamol alone and they are likely to lead to opioid adverse effects [MeReC, 1993; De Craen et al, 1996; Moore and McQuay, 1997].
- **High-dose weak opioids with paracetamol** (combination products), e.g. co-codamol 30/500 mg: These do not allow titration to the most effective and safe analgesic dose to match individual requirements.
- **Co-proxamol** (dextropropoxyphene 32.5 mg/ paracetamol 325 mg) has been withdrawn by the Committee on Safety of Medicines because of its unfavourable risk/benefit ratio; it is associated with an unacceptable risk of overdose [CSM, 2005].

- **Gastroprotective agents** are sometimes needed, but not all are recommended:
  - **H_2-receptor antagonists (H_2RAs).** At standard doses, H_2RAs reduce the risk of duodenal ulceration, and there is some evidence that double doses reduce the risk of gastric ulceration [Rostom et al, 2002]. However, no H_2RA is currently licensed for the prevention of gastric ulceration induced by NSAIDs [BNF 48, 2004], which is more common than duodenal ulceration.
  - **Rabeprazole** is not included, as it is not specifically licensed for the prevention of NSAID-induced GI ulcers [BNF 48, 2004].
  - **Fixed-dose combinations of standard NSAIDs with misoprostol.** The optimum dose of misoprostol (i.e. 800 micrograms daily) cannot be reached using these preparations. In particular, only 400 micrograms daily of misoprostol is given with the higher doses of NSAID in these preparations.

G

Drugs included

Anti-inflammatory drugs

- **Standard nonsteroidal anti-inflammatory drugs (NSAIDs): diclofenac, indometacin, and naproxen** have a reasonable balance of efficacy against adverse-effect profile [CSM, 1994; Henry et al, 1996; Hernández-Diaz and Rodriguez, 2000] and are licensed for the treatment of acute gout [BNF 48, 2004]. The risk of gastrointestinal adverse events is highest with indometacin [Hernández-Diaz and Rodriguez, 2000].
- **Etoricoxib,** a COX-2 selective NSAID, is licensed for acute gout and is currently undergoing post-market surveillance (black triangle). It causes fewer GI adverse effects, but may be associated with an increased risk of cardiovascular toxicity. The safety of COX-2 selective NSAIDs is currently being evaluated by the European Medicines Evaluation Agency (EMEA). Note: there is no evidence to suggest that using etoricoxib with a gastroprotective agent further reduces the risk of GI adverse effects than etoricoxib alone.
- **Colchicine** is included for use when an NSAID is contraindicated. Its use is limited by the high incidence of diarrhoea, which can be profuse and often occurs within the first 24 hours of use, before symptomatic relief is obtained [Ahern et al, 1987].
- **Systemic corticosteroids** can be used in an acute attack if NSAIDs and colchicine are contraindicated:
  - **Triamcinolone acetonide or methyl prednisolone** can be given as a one-off intramuscular injection.
  - **Oral corticosteroids:** low-dose prednisolone is relatively safe and convenient to use in short courses.
- **Intra-articular corticosteroids.** Hydrocortisone acetate, dexamethasone sodium phosphate, and prednisolone acetate are recommended for injection of small joints, and triamcinolone acetonide and methylprednisolone for injection of large joints. They vary in their potency and duration of effect [DTB, 1995]. Lidocaine (lignocaine) is also available for local anaesthesia.

Gastroprotective agents

- **Proton pump inhibitors (PPIs): lansoprazole, omeprazole, esomeprazole, and pantoprazole** are licensed for the prevention of gastroduodenal ulceration induced by standard NSAIDs [BNF 48, 2004]. PPIs reduce the risk of endoscopic ulcers, but there are no data on prevention of ulcer complications [Rostom et al, 2002]. However, they are generally considered the preferred choice for gastroprotection, as they are better tolerated than misoprostol.

- **Misoprostol** is licensed for prevention of gastroduodenal ulceration induced by standard NSAIDs [BNF 48, 2004]. It reduces the risk of endoscopically proven ulcers, and has also been shown to reduce the risk of ulcer complications [Rostom et al, 2002]. It is less well tolerated than PPIs owing to gastrointestinal adverse effects, particularly diarrhoea.

Analgesia

- **Paracetamol** is included for additional analgesia.
- **Codeine (in combination with paracetamol).** Higher-dose codeine is included for use with regular paracetamol for additional pain relief. Codeine 60 mg plus paracetamol has been shown to provide more pain relief than either codeine 60 mg alone or paracetamol 1000 mg alone [Moore et al, 1997]. Codeine should be prescribed separately from paracetamol to allow flexibility of dosing and titration of analgesic effect.

G

Prescriptions

NSAIDs (maximum doses) and colchicine

Diclofenac sodium e/c tablets: 50mg three times a day
- Age from 16 years onwards
- Diclofenac 50mg e/c tablets. Take one tablet three times a day; supply 84 tablets; NHS Cost £1.45.

Naproxen tablets: 500mg twice a day
- Age from 16 years onwards
- Naproxen 500mg tablets. Take one tablet twice a day; supply 56 tablets; NHS Cost £4.90.

Indometacin capsules: 50mg three times a day
- Age from 16 years onwards
- Indometacin 50mg capsules. Take one capsule three times a day; supply 84 capsules; NHS Cost £5.97.

Indometacin capsules: 50mg four times a day
- Age from 16 years onwards
- Indometacin 50mg capsules. Take one capsule four times a day; supply 112 capsules; NHS Cost £7.96.

Etoricoxib: if HIGH RISK of NSAID-induced ulcer
- Age from 16 years onwards
- Etoricoxib 120mg tablets. Take one tablet once a day; supply 28 tablets; NHS Cost £24.11.

Colchicine tablets: 500mcg three times a day (recommended)
- Age from 16 years onwards
- Colchicine 500microgram tabs. Take one tablet three times a day until pain relief is achieved; supply 9 tablets; NHS Cost £1.49.

Colchicine tablets: 500mcg every 2 to 3 hours (maximum dose)
- Age from 16 years onwards
- Colchicine 500microgram tabs. Take TWO tablets now, then take ONE tablet every 2 to 3 hours until pain relief is achieved or until vomiting or diarrhoea occurs; supply 12 tablets; NHS Cost £1.99.

GI protection: use ONLY with a standard NSAID

Omeprazole capsules: 20mg once a day
- Age from 16 years onwards
- Omeprazole 20mg capsules. Take one capsule once a day; supply 28 capsules; NHS Cost £12.75.

Omeprazole tablets: 20mg once a day
- Age from 16 years onwards
- Omeprazole 20mg tablets. Take one tablet once a day; supply 28 tablets; NHS Cost £12.75.

Lansoprazole capsules: 15mg each morning
- Age from 16 years onwards
- Lansoprazole 15mg capsules. Take one capsule each morning (on an empty stomach); supply 28 capsules; NHS Cost £12.92.

Lansoprazole capsules: 30mg each morning
- Age from 16 years onwards
- Lansoprazole 30mg capsules. Take one capsule each morning (on an empty stomach); supply 28 capsules; NHS Cost £23.63.

Pantoprazole e/c tablets: 20mg once a day
- Age from 16 years onwards
- Pantoprazole 20mg e/c tablets. Take one tablet once a day; supply 28 tablets; NHS Cost £12.31.

Esomeprazole tablets: 20mg once a day
- Age from 16 years onwards
- Esomeprazole 20mg tablets. Take one tablet once a day supply 28 tablets; NHS Cost £18.50.

Lansoprazole orodispersible tablets: 15mg each morning
- Age from 16 years onwards
- Lansoprazole 15mg orodisp tabs. Take one tablet each morning (on an empty stomach); supply 28 tablets; NHS Cost £10.86.

Lansoprazole orodispersible tablets: 30mg each morning
- Age from 16 years onwards
- Lansoprazole 30mg orodisp tabs. Take one tablet each morning (on an empty stomach); supply 28 tablets; NHS Cost £21.38.

Misoprostol tablets: 200micrograms four times a day
- Age from 16 years onwards
- Misoprostol 200microgram tabs. Take one tablet four times a day; supply 120 tablets; NHS Cost £18.72.

Additional analgesia

Paracetamol tablets: 1g up to four times a day
- Age from 16 years onwards
- Paracetamol 500mg tablets. Take two tablets every 4 to 6 hours when required for pain relief. Maximum of 8 tablets in 24 hours; supply 200 tablets; NHS Cost £1.50 OTC Cost £2.50.

Add on if required: codeine 30-60mg up to four times a day
- Age from 16 years onwards
- Codeine 30mg tablets. Take one to two tablets every 4 to 6 hours when required for pain relief. Maximum of 8 tablets in 24 hours; supply 84 tablets; NHS Cost £6.87.

Paracetamol 500mg tablets + codeine 30mg tablets
- Age from 16 years onwards
- Paracetamol 500mg tablets. Take two tablets every 4 to 6 hours when required for pain relief. Maximum of 8 tablets in 24 hours; supply 200 tablets; NHS Cost £1.50 OTC Cost £2.50.
- Codeine 30mg tablets. Take one to two tablets every 4 to 6 hours when required for pain relief. Maximum of 8 tablets in 24 hours; supply 84 tablets; NHS Cost £6.87.

Intra-articular corticosteroids

Large joint: triamcinolone acetonide 40mg/ml + lidocaine 1%
- Age from 16 years onwards
- Triamcinolone acet 40mg/ml inj. Inject into large joint: 0.25ml (10mg) to 1ml (40mg), according to joint size; supply 1 1ml vial; NHS Cost £1.70.
- Lidocaine 1% injection (2ml). For local anaesthetic injection; supply 1 2ml ampoule; NHS Cost £0.28.

arge joint: methylprednisolone 80mg/2ml + lidocaine 1%
Age from 16 years onwards
Depo-Medrone+lidocaine 80/20mg. Inject into large joint: 0.5ml (20mg) to 2ml (80mg), according to joint size; supply 1 2ml vial; NHS Cost £5.88.

ledium joint: methylprednisolone 40mg/ml + lidocaine %
Age from 16 years onwards
Depo-Medrone+lidocaine 40/10mg. Inject into medium joint: 0.25ml (10mg) to 1ml (40mg), according to joint size; supply 1 1ml vial; NHS Cost £3.28.

mall joint: dexamethasone sod phos 5mg/ml + lidocaine %
Age from 16 years onwards
Dexamethasone sod phos 5mg/ml. Inject into small joint: 0.16ml (0.8mg) to 0.2ml (1mg), according to joint size; supply 1 1ml ampoule; NHS Cost £0.83.
Lidocaine 1% injection (2ml). For local anaesthetic injection; supply 1 2ml ampoule; NHS Cost £0.28.

mall joint: prednisolone acetate 25mg/ml + lidocaine 1%
Age from 16 years onwards
Prednisolone acet 25mg/ml inj. Inject into small joint: 0.2ml (5mg) to 0.4ml (10mg), according to joint size; supply 1 1ml ampoule; NHS Cost £4.77.
Lidocaine 1% injection (2ml). For local anaesthetic injection; supply 1 2ml ampoule; NHS Cost £0.28.

mall joint: hydrocortisone acetate 25mg/ml + lidocaine %
Age from 16 years onwards
Hydrocortisone 25mg/ml inj. Inject into small joint: 0.2ml (5mg) to 0.5ml (12.5mg), according to joint size; supply 1 1ml vial; NHS Cost £4.77.
Lidocaine 1% injection (2ml). For local anaesthetic injection; supply 1 2ml ampoule; NHS Cost £0.28.

Systemic corticosteroids

riamcinolone acetonide 40mg/ml intramuscular injection
Age from 16 years onwards
Triamcinolone ace 40mg/ml inj. For deep intramuscular injection: 1ml (40mg) to 2ml (80mg), into gluteal muscle; supply 2 1ml pre-filled syringe; NHS Cost £4.22.

lethylprednisolone 40mg/ml intramuscular injection
Age from 16 years onwards
Methylprednisolone 40mg/ml inj. For deep intramuscular injection: 1ml (40mg) to 3ml (120mg), into gluteal muscle; supply 3 1ml vial; NHS Cost £8.61.

rednisolone e/c tablets: 15mg each morning for 10 days
Age from 16 years onwards
Prednisolone 5mg e/c tablets. Take three tablets each morning for ten days; supply 30 tablets;
NHS Cost £0.51.

rednisolone e/c tablets: 7.5mg each morning for 10 days
Age from 16 years onwards
Prednisolone 2.5mg e/c tablets. Take three tablets each morning for ten days; supply 30 tablets;
NHS Cost £0.31.

Acute polyarticular gout

Vhich therapy?

- **Rule out, or manage, secondary causes of gout** (for details, see Table 1 in *Background information*).
- **Suggest cautious use of an ice pack.** The pack should be wrapped in a towel to avoid direct skin contact and ice-burn.
- **Start drug treatment as soon as possible,** preferably within 24 hours of the onset of the attack.
  - Prompt treatment is facilitated if people with gout have a supply of medicine at home and they understand the disadvantages of delaying treatment.
- **Treat an acute attack** of gout with a nonsteroidal anti-inflammatory drug (NSAID), colchicine, corticosteroid, or analgesic.
- **Treatment with an NSAID is the generally preferred option** unless there are contraindications.
- **Systemic corticosteroids and oral colchicine** are options if NSAIDs are not suitable.
- **Intra-articular corticosteroids** are an option to use as sole therapy or adjunctive therapy *if* only one or two joints are affected, *and* they are suitable for injecting, *and* the expertise to inject the joint (s) is available.
- **Analgesics** are sometimes given in addition to other therapy for acute gout. They may also be used alone if NSAIDs, corticosteroids, and colchicine are all contraindicated.
- **Do not introduce urate-lowering therapy during an acute attack** — see *Urate-lowering therapy* scenario.
- **Suggest a prudent diet and lifestyle:**
  - Moderate ingestion of alcohol.
  - Restrict dietary energy intake to limit weight gain, or, in the obese, to lose weight.
  - Limit ingestion of heart, herring, sardines, and mussels (very high purine content).
  - Moderate ingestion of other meat and seafood (high purine content).
  - Consider moderating ingestion of yeast extracts, pulses, and other vegetables high in purines (less evidence of risk).
- **Manage any risk factors** for gout and associated conditions that are present, including:
  - Drugs (e.g. diuretics)
  - Obesity
  - Hypertension
  - Renal impairment
  - Myeloproliferative disease
  - Hyperlipidaemia (especially hypertriglyceridaemia)
  - Vascular disease
  - Psoriasis
  - Enzyme deficiencies such as hypoxanthine guanine phosphoribosyltransferase deficiency

Practical prescribing points

For further information, see the *Medicines Compendium* (www.medicines.org.uk) or the *British National Formulary* (www.bnf.org).

NSAIDs

- **Only one NSAID should be prescribed at a time.**
- **NSAIDs may worsen asthma, hypertension, renal impairment, or heart failure.**
- Do not give diclofenac, indometacin, or naproxen without gastroprotection if there is a history of peptic ulceration.
- Do not give etoricoxib if there is active peptic ulceration, or to people with uncontrolled hypertension.
- **People with cardiovascular disease:**
  - Do not give etoricoxib to people with established ischaemic heart disease, cerebrovascular disease, peripheral arterial disease, or moderate or severe heart failure due to the small increased risk of thrombotic events.
  - Do not use etoricoxib with low-dose aspirin. (Gastrointestinal protective effects of etoricoxib are reduced.)
- **In people with risk factors for gastrointestinal NSAID complications:**

- Use paracetamol (with or without codeine) instead of a NSAID if possible.
- Or, use gastroprotection (a PPI or full-dose misoprostol) combined with a standard NSAID.
- Or, consider switching to etoricoxib alone (COX-2 selective).

- **Risk factors for gastrointestinal NSAID complications include:**
  - Age of 65 years and over.
  - Previous history of gastroduodenal ulcer, gastrointestinal (GI) bleeding, or gastroduodenal perforation.
  - Concomitant use of medications that are known to increase the likelihood of upper-GI adverse events, e.g. anticoagulants, aspirin (even a low dose), and corticosteroids.
  - Presence of serious comorbidity, such as cardiovascular disease, renal or hepatic impairment, diabetes, or hypertension.
  - Requirement for prolonged duration of NSAID use.
  - Use of maximum recommended doses of NSAIDs.

G

Colchicine

- **Diarrhoea** is common at full dose, especially in elderly people. Consider giving colchicine less frequently to avoid severe gastrointestinal toxicity.
- **Avoid colchicine in serious gastrointestinal or cardiac disorders.** Toxicity is more likely to occur with underlying renal impairment. Reduce the dose accordingly (see the BNF section on renal impairment).

Corticosteroids

- **Corticosteroids may worsen diabetic control or heart failure.**
- **Document the history of chickenpox,** because there is a risk of potentially fatal disseminated chickenpox in non-immune people being treated with corticosteroids. Advise these people to avoid close contact with anyone who has chickenpox or shingles, and to seek urgent medical advice if they are exposed.
- **Atrophy of subcutaneous tissues and local skin depigmentation** may occur from periarticular leakage of corticosteroid. The risk is greatest if large or repeated doses of a long-acting, potent corticosteroid are given. In general, hydrocortisone, dexamethasone, or prednisolone is recommended for injection of small joints, and triamcinolone or methylprednisolone for injection of large joints.

Codeine

- Codeine may cause nausea, vomiting, constipation, and drowsiness. A regular laxative is often needed when it is used long-term.

Misoprostol

- Diarrhoea and abdominal pain are common. Advise women of child-bearing age to use adequate contraception, because misoprostol increases the risk of miscarriage.

Follow-up advice

- **People suffering from polyarticular gout will need long-term urate-lowering therapy** after the acute attack has settled.
- **If risk factors are found** (e.g. renal impairment, alcohol excess), further assessment and treatment or modification are required.
- **Advise the person to return if** a joint is more inflamed 24 hours after an intra-articular injection, or there are systemic symptoms of infection, or adverse effects from the medication.

Should I refer or investigate?

Refer?

Refer if:

- **Sepsis** is suspected.
- **The diagnosis is in doubt** — gout rarely presents with polyarticular involvement, and conditions such as rheumatoid arthritis need to be excluded.
- **Intra-articular steroid injection** is indicated and facilities or expertise for this are unavailable.
- **Usual anti-inflammatory therapy is ineffective or contraindicated** (for example, renal failure, or inability to tolerate usual drugs).

Investigate?

- **Joint aspiration and microscopy of synovial fluid** for urate crystals — note that:
  - It is desirable to establish the diagnosis of gout; but aspiration of small joints, and in particular the first metatarsophalangeal joint, may not be practical.
- **Plasma urate level** — note that:
  - Not all people with hyperuricaemia have gout.
  - Not all people with gout have hyperuricaemia.
- **Renal function** (plasma creatinine).
- **Full blood count** — could indicate inflammation or an underlying myeloproliferative disorder.
- Also consider:
  - **Liver-function tests,** including gamma-glutamyl transferase (GGT) — could help assess alcohol intake.
  - **X-ray,** if recurrent or chronic gout is thought to have resulted in joint damage.

Patient information leaflets

The following PILs are available at www.prodigy.nhs.uk

- Anti-inflammatory Painkillers
- Arthritis Research Campaign - ARC
- Blood Test - General
- Gout
- Medicines - Name Changes of Medicines
- UK Gout Society

Shared decision making

- Gout attacks are due to a build-up of uric acid (urate) in the joint.
- **An anti-inflammatory painkiller** will usually ease a gout attack within 12–24 hours.
  - Some people need a medicine to 'protect the stomach' if gut side-effects occur while they are taking anti-inflammatories.
- **Colchicine** is an option if you have side-effects with anti-inflammatories.
- **Steroids** are an option if you have side-effects with anti-inflammatories and colchicine.
- **Paracetamol, codeine,** or other painkillers can be taken as well, to help ease pain.
- **An ice pack** can also help to ease pain. Use a bag of frozen peas or ice cubes wrapped in a towel. Do not put ice directly against the skin, as it may cause 'ice-burn'.
- Gout attacks in some people may be triggered by excess alcohol, being overweight, and certain medicines such as some 'water tablets' (diuretics) or low-dose aspirin.
- A medicine can be taken each day to prevent gout attacks if they recur.

Drug rationale

Drugs not included

- **Urate-lowering therapy** should not be started until the acute attack of gout has resolved. See the scenario *Introduction of urate-lowering therapy*.
- **Standard nonsteroidal anti-inflammatory drugs** (NSAIDs) other than diclofenac, indometacin, and naproxen are not generally recommended:
  - **Ibuprofen** and some other NSAIDs are not licensed for the treatment of acute gout.
  - **Ketoprofen, piroxicam, and sulindac** are licensed for the treatment of acute gout, but are less frequently used and are associated with an increased risk and range of adverse effects.
  - **Azapropazone** should be reserved for use on specialist advice where other less toxic treatments have proved ineffective.
  - **Modified-release NSAIDs:** no improvement in efficacy or reduction in adverse events has been found. These drugs are also relatively expensive.

[Henry et al, 1996; Hernández-Diaz and Rodriguez, 2000; CSM, 2002]

- **Analgesics,** other than paracetamol and codeine taken separately, are not recommended:
  - **Strong opioids** (e.g. morphine, pethidine) should be avoided because of the risk of dependence if they are used inappropriately.
  - **Weak opioids,** other than codeine, have either not been shown to be more effective than codeine (when used in combination with paracetamol), or are more expensive.
  - **Low-dose weak opioids with paracetamol** (combination products), e.g. co-codamol 8/500 mg: There is no evidence that these offer any clinical benefit over paracetamol alone, and they are likely to lead to opioid adverse effects [MeReC, 1993; De Craen et al, 1996; Moore and McQuay, 1997].
  - **High-dose weak opioids with paracetamol** (combination products), e.g. co-codamol 30/500 mg: These do not allow titration to the most effective and safe analgesic dose to match individual requirements.
  - **Co-proxamol** (dextropropoxyphene 32.5 mg/ paracetamol 325 mg) has been withdrawn by the Committee on Safety of Medicines due to its unfavourable risk/benefit ratio; it is associated with an unacceptable risk of overdose [CSM, 2005].
- **Gastroprotective agents** are sometimes needed, but not all are recommended:
  - **H_2-receptor antagonists (H_2RAs).** At standard doses, H_2RAs reduce the risk of duodenal ulceration, and there is some evidence that double doses reduce the risk of gastric ulceration [Rostom et al, 2002]. However, no H_2RA is currently licensed for the prevention of gastric ulceration induced by NSAIDs [BNF 48, 2004], which is more common than duodenal ulceration.
  - **Rabeprazole** is not included, as it is not specifically licensed for the prevention of NSAID-induced GI ulcers [BNF 48, 2004].
  - **Fixed-dose combinations of standard NSAIDs with misoprostol.** The optimum dose of misoprostol (i.e. 800 micrograms daily) cannot be reached using these preparations. In particular, only 400 micrograms daily of misoprostol is given with the higher doses of NSAID in these preparations.

Drugs included

Anti-inflammatory drugs

- **Standard nonsteroidal anti-inflammatory drugs (NSAIDs): diclofenac, indometacin, and naproxen** have a reasonable balance of efficacy against adverse-effect profile [CSM, 1994; Henry et al, 1996; Hernández-Diaz and Rodriguez, 2000] and are licensed for the treatment of acute gout [BNF 48, 2004]. The risk of gastrointestinal adverse events is highest with indometacin [Hernández-Diaz and Rodriguez, 2000].
- **Etoricoxib,** a COX-2 selective NSAID, is licensed for acute gout and is currently undergoing post-market surveillance (black triangle). It causes fewer GI adverse effects, but may be associated with an increased risk of cardiovascular toxicity. The safety of COX-2 selective NSAIDs is currently being evaluated by the European Medicines Evaluation Agency (EMEA). Note: there is no evidence to suggest that using etoricoxib with a gastroprotective agent further reduces the risk of GI adverse effects than etoricoxib alone.
- **Colchicine** is included for use when an NSAID is contraindicated. Its use is limited by the high incidence of diarrhoea, which can be profuse and often occurs within the first 24 hours of use, before symptomatic relief is obtained [Ahern et al, 1987].
- **Systemic corticosteroids** can be used in an acute attack if NSAIDs and colchicine are contraindicated:
  - **Triamcinolone acetonide or methyl prednisolone** can be given as a one-off intramuscular injection.
  - **Oral corticosteroids:** low-dose prednisolone is relatively safe and convenient to use in short courses.
- **Intra-articular corticosteroids:** Hydrocortisone acetate, dexamethasone sodium phosphate, and prednisolone acetate are recommended for injection of small joints, and triamcinolone acetonide and methylprednisolone for injection of large joints. They vary in their potency and duration of effect [DTB, 1995]. Lidocaine (lignocaine) is also available for local anaesthesia.

Gastroprotective agents

- **Proton pump inhibitors (PPIs): lansoprazole, omeprazole, esomeprazole, and pantoprazole** are licensed for the prevention of gastroduodenal ulceration induced by standard NSAIDs [BNF 48, 2004]. PPIs reduce the risk of endoscopic ulcers, but there are no data on prevention of ulcer complications [Rostom et al, 2002]. However, they are generally considered the preferred choice for gastroprotection, as they are better tolerated than misoprostol.
- **Misoprostol** is licensed for prevention of gastroduodenal ulceration induced by standard NSAIDs [BNF 48, 2004]. It reduces the risk of endoscopically proven ulcers and has also been shown to reduce the risk of ulcer complications [Rostom et al, 2002]. It is less well tolerated than PPIs owing to gastrointestinal adverse effects, particularly diarrhoea.

Analgesia

- **Paracetamol** is included for additional analgesia.
- **Codeine (in combination with paracetamol).** Higher-dose codeine is included for use with regular paracetamol for additional pain relief. Codeine 60 mg plus paracetamol has been shown to provide more pain relief than either codeine 60 mg alone or paracetamol 1000 mg alone [Moore et al, 1997]. Codeine should be prescribed separately from paracetamol to allow flexibility of dosing and titration of analgesic effect.

Prescriptions

NSAIDs (maximum doses) and colchicine

Diclofenac sodium e/c tablets: 50mg three times a day
- Age from 16 years onwards
- Diclofenac 50mg e/c tablets. Take one tablet three times a day; supply 84 tablets; NHS Cost £1.45.

Naproxen tablets: 500mg twice a day
- Age from 16 years onwards
- Naproxen 500mg tablets. Take one tablet twice a day; supply 60 tablets; NHS Cost £4.90.

Indometacin capsules: 50mg three times a day
- Age from 16 years onwards
- Indometacin 50mg capsules. Take one capsule three times a day; supply 84 capsules; NHS Cost £5.97.

Indometacin capsules: 50mg four times a day
- Age from 16 years onwards
- Indometacin 50mg capsules. Take one capsule four times a day; supply 112 capsules; NHS Cost £7.96.

Etoricoxib: if HIGH RISK of NSAID-induced ulcer
- Age from 16 years onwards
- Etoricoxib 120mg tablets. Take one tablet once a day; supply 28 tablets; NHS Cost £24.11.

Colchicine tablets: 500mcg three times a day (recommended)
- Age from 16 years onwards
- Colchicine 500microgram tabs. Take one tablet three times a day until pain relief is achieved; supply 9 tablets; NHS Cost £1.49.

Colchicine tablets: 500mcg every 2 to 3 hours (maximum dose)
- Age from 16 years onwards
- Colchicine 500microgram tabs. Take TWO tablets now, then take ONE tablet every 2 to 3 hours until pain relief is achieved or until vomiting or diarrhoea occurs; supply 12 tablets; NHS Cost £1.99.

GI protection: use ONLY with a standard NSAID

Omeprazole capsules: 20mg once a day
- Age from 16 years onwards
- Omeprazole 20mg capsules. Take one capsule once a day; supply 28 capsules; NHS Cost £12.75.

Omeprazole tablets: 20mg once a day
- Age from 16 years onwards
- Omeprazole 20mg tablets. Take one tablet once a day; supply 28 tablets; NHS Cost £12.75.

Lansoprazole capsules: 15mg each morning
- Age from 16 years onwards
- Lansoprazole 15mg capsules. Take one capsule each morning (on an empty stomach); supply 28 capsules; NHS Cost £12.92.

Lansoprazole capsules: 30mg each morning
- Age from 16 years onwards
- Lansoprazole 30mg capsules. Take one capsule each morning (on an empty stomach); supply 28 capsules; NHS Cost £23.63.

Pantoprazole e/c tablets: 20mg once a day
- Age from 16 years onwards
- Pantoprazole 20mg e/c tablets. Take one tablet once a day; supply 28 tablets; NHS Cost £12.31.

Esomeprazole tablets: 20mg once a day
- Age from 16 years onwards
- Esomeprazole 20mg tablets. Take one tablet once a day; supply 28 tablets; NHS Cost £18.50.

Lansoprazole orodispersible tablets: 15mg each morning
- Age from 16 years onwards
- Lansoprazole 15mg orodisp tabs. Take one tablet each morning (on an empty stomach); supply 28 tablets; NHS Cost £10.86.

Lansoprazole orodispersible tablets: 30mg each morning
- Age from 16 years onwards
- Lansoprazole 30mg orodisp tabs. Take one tablet each morning (on an empty stomach); supply 28 tablets; NHS Cost £21.38.

Misoprostol tablets: 200micrograms four times a day
- Age from 16 years onwards
- Misoprostol 200microgram tabs. Take one tablet four times a day; supply 120 tablets; NHS Cost £18.72.

Additional analgesia

Paracetamol tablets: 1g up to four times a day
- Age from 16 years onwards
- Paracetamol 500mg tablets. Take two tablets every 4 to 6 hours when required for pain relief. Maximum of 8 tablets in 24 hours; supply 200 tablets; NHS Cost £1.50; OTC Cost £2.50.

Add on if required: codeine 30-60mg up to four times a day
- Age from 16 years onwards
- Codeine 30mg tablets. Take one to two tablets every 4 to 6 hours when required for pain relief. Maximum of 8 tablets in 24 hours; supply 84 tablets; NHS Cost £6.87.

Paracetamol 500mg tablets + codeine 30mg tablets
- Age from 16 years onwards
- Paracetamol 500mg tablets. Take two tablets every 4 to 6 hours when required for pain relief. Maximum of 8 tablets in 24 hours; supply 200 tablets; NHS Cost £1.50; OTC Cost £2.50.
- Codeine 30mg tablets. Take one to two tablets every 4 to 6 hours when required for pain relief. Maximum of 8 tablets in 24 hours; supply 84 tablets; NHS Cost £6.87.

Intra-articular corticosteroids

Large joints: triamcinolone acetonide 40mg/ml + lidocaine 1%
- Age from 16 years onwards
- Triamcinolone acet 40mg/ml inj. Inject into large joint: 0.25ml (10mg) to 1ml (40mg), according to joint size; supply 1 1ml vial; NHS Cost £1.70.
- Lidocaine 1% injection (2ml). For local anaesthetic injection; supply 1 2ml ampoule; NHS Cost £0.28.

Large joints: methylprednisolone 80mg/2ml + lidocaine 1%
- Age from 16 years onwards
- Depo-Medrone+lidocaine 80/20mg. Inject into large joint: 0.5ml (20mg) to 2ml (80mg), according to joint size; supply 1 2ml vial; NHS Cost £5.88.

Medium joints: methylprednisolone 40mg/ml + lidocaine 1%
- Age from 16 years onwards
- Depo-Medrone+lidocaine 40/10mg. Inject into medium joint: 0.25ml (10mg) to 1ml (40mg), according to joint size; supply 1 1ml vial; NHS Cost £3.28.

Small joints: dexamethasone sod phos 5mg/ml + lidocaine 1%
- Age from 16 years onwards
- Dexamethasone sod phos 5mg/ml. Inject into small joint 0.16ml (0.8mg) to 0.2ml (1mg), according to joint size; supply 1 1ml ampoule; NHS Cost £0.83.
- Lidocaine 1% injection (2ml). For local anaesthetic injection; supply 1 2ml ampoule; NHS Cost £0.28.

Small joints: prednisolone acetate 25mg/ml + lidocaine 1%

- Age from 16 years onwards
- Prednisolone acet 25mg/ml inj. Inject into small joint: 0.2ml (5mg) to 0.4ml (10mg), according to joint size; supply 1 1ml ampoule; NHS Cost £4.77.
- Lidocaine 1% injection (2ml). For local anaesthetic injection; supply 1 2ml ampoule; NHS Cost £0.28.

Small joints: hydrocortisone acetate 25mg/ml + lidocaine 1%

- Age from 16 years onwards
- Hydrocortisone 25mg/ml inj. Inject into small joint: 0.2ml (5mg) to 0.5ml (12.5mg), according to joint size; supply 1 1ml vial; NHS Cost £4.77.
- Lidocaine 1% injection (2ml). For local anaesthetic injection; supply 1 2ml ampoule; NHS Cost £0.28.

Systemic corticosteroids

Triamcinolone acetonide 40mg/ml intramuscular injection

- Age from 16 years onwards
- Triamcinolone ace 40mg/ml inj. For deep intramuscular injection: 1ml (40mg) to 2ml (80mg), into gluteal muscle; supply 2 1ml pre-filled syringe; NHS Cost £4.22.

Methylprednisolone 40mg/ml intramuscular injection

- Age from 16 years onwards
- Methylprednisolone 40mg/ml inj. For deep intramuscular injection: 1ml (40mg) to 3ml (120mg), into gluteal muscle; supply 3 1ml vial; NHS Cost £8.61.

Prednisolone e/c tablets: 15mg each morning for 10 days

- Age from 16 years onwards
- Prednisolone 5mg e/c tablets. Take three tablets each morning for ten days; supply 30 tablets; NHS Cost £0.51.

Prednisolone e/c tablets: 7.5mg each morning for 10 days

- Age from 16 years onwards
- Prednisolone 2.5mg e/c tablets. Take three tablets each morning for ten days; supply 30 tablets; NHS Cost £0.31.

Introduction of long-term urate-lowering therapy

Which therapy?

Consider whether urate-lowering therapy is indicated (see *Management issues*).

Allopurinol

- **Do not start until after an acute attack of gout has completely resolved.**
- **Start at low dose** (100 mg daily) and, if the person has satisfactory renal function, increase gradually to 300 mg daily over 4–6 weeks. Use a lower maintenance dose in renal impairment. The aim is initially to reduce the plasma urate level to the normal range (i.e. less than 0.42 mmol/l). If this does not control acute attacks or if tophi are troublesome, then a lower target (e.g. 0.36 mmol/l) and higher doses of allopurinol should be considered.
- **Co-prescribe an anti-inflammatory drug for 3 months** while allopurinol is being introduced, in order to reduce the risk of allopurinol-induced attacks of gout. For this purpose, use a nonsteroidal anti-inflammatory drug (NSAID) or a low dose of colchicine. If these are not tolerated or are contraindicated, low-dose oral prednisolone (7.5 mg daily) for 3 months can be considered.
- **Gastroprotection should be considered** in people at high risk of NSAID upper-gastrointestinal toxicity (i.e. those over 65 years of age, or with a history of peptic ulcer or gastrointestinal bleeding).
- **Warn the person that acute attacks of gout may occur** while starting allopurinol; if this happens, the allopurinol should be continued and the attack treated in the usual way.
- **Advise also that gout attacks may take months to stop,** even if plasma urate reaches its target.
- **Suggest a prudent diet and lifestyle.**
  - Moderate ingestion of alcohol.
  - Restrict dietary energy intake to limit weight gain, or, in the obese, to lose weight.
  - Limit ingestion of heart, herring, sardines, and mussels (very high purine content).
  - Moderate ingestion of other meat and seafood (high purine content).
  - Consider moderating ingestion of yeast extracts, pulses, and other vegetables high in purines (less evidence of risk).
- **Manage any risk factors** for gout and associated conditions that are present, including:
  - Drugs (e.g. diuretics)
  - Obesity
  - Hypertension
  - Renal impairment
  - Myeloproliferative disease
  - Hyperlipidaemia (especially hypertriglyceridaemia)
  - Vascular disease
  - Psoriasis
  - Enzyme deficiencies such as hypoxanthine guanine phosphoribosyltransferase deficiency

G

Practical prescribing points

For further information, see the *Medicines Compendium* (www.medicines.org.uk) or the *British National Formulary* (www.bnf.org).

Allopurinol

- **A pruritic, maculopapular rash** occurs in about 2% of people.
- **Allopurinol increases the risk of toxicity from azathioprine and mercaptopurine.**
- **Toxicity is more likely to occur with underlying renal impairment.** Reduce the dose accordingly (see the BNF section on renal impairment).
- **A hypersensitivity reaction** occurs rarely, which can include rash, fever, hepatitis, renal impairment, leucocytosis, and eosinophilia.

Colchicine

- **Diarrhoea** is common at full dose, especially in elderly people. Consider giving less frequently to avoid severe gastrointestinal toxicity.
- **Avoid in serious gastrointestinal or cardiac disorders.** Toxicity is more likely to occur with underlying renal impairment. Reduce the dose accordingly (see the BNF section on renal impairment).

Nonsteroidal anti-inflammatory drugs

- **Only one NSAID should be prescribed at a time.**
- **NSAIDs may worsen asthma, hypertension, renal impairment, or heart failure.**
- Do not give ibuprofen, diclofenac, or naproxen without gastroprotection if there is a history of peptic ulceration.
- **People with cardiovascular disease:** ibuprofen may reduce the cardiovascular protective effect of low-dose aspirin.
- **In people with risk factors for gastrointestinal NSAID complications:**

- Use paracetamol (with or without codeine) instead of a NSAID if possible.
- Or, use gastroprotection (a PPI or full-dose misoprostol) combined with a standard NSAID.
- Or, consider switching to a COX-2 selective NSAID alone.

- **Risk factors for gastrointestinal NSAID complications include:**
  - Age of 65 years and over.
  - Previous history of gastroduodenal ulcer, gastrointestinal (GI) bleeding, or gastroduodenal perforation.
  - Concomitant use of medications that are known to increase the likelihood of upper-GI adverse events, e.g. anticoagulants, aspirin (even a low dose), and corticosteroids.
  - Presence of serious comorbidity, such as cardiovascular disease, renal or hepatic impairment, diabetes, or hypertension.
  - Requirement for prolonged duration of NSAID use.
  - Use of maximum recommended doses of NSAIDs.

G

Misoprostol

- Diarrhoea and abdominal pain are common. Advise women of child-bearing age to use adequate contraception, because misoprostol increases the risk of miscarriage.

Follow-up advice

- **Check plasma urate at 3 months** and review with results.
- **Advise the person to return if** recurrent attacks are still occurring despite treatment, or adverse effects have arisen from the medication.

Should I refer or investigate?

Refer?

Refer if:

- **The diagnosis is in doubt.**
- **Usual therapy for gout is ineffective or contraindicated** (for example renal failure, or inability to tolerate usual drugs).

Investigate?

- **Test plasma urate after 3 months** and review with results. The aim is to reduce the plasma urate level to the normal range (i.e. less than 0.42 mmol/l). If this does not control gout, or if tophi are troublesome, a lower target (e.g. 0.36 mmol/l) could be considered.

Patient information leaflets

The following PILs are available at www.prodigy.nhs.uk

- Anti-inflammatory Painkillers
- Arthritis Research Campaign - ARC
- Blood Test - General
- Gout
- UK Gout Society

Shared decision making

- **Allopurinol** is a medicine taken every day to prevent gout attacks. It works by lowering the level of uric acid (urate) in the blood.
- **Allopurinol takes 2–3 months to work fully.** It can sometimes cause a gout attack when first taken. Therefore:
  - **An anti-inflammatory painkiller** is often prescribed for the first 3 months after starting allopurinol, just in case the allopurinol causes a gout attack.
    - Some people need a medicine to 'protect the stomach' if gut side-effects occur while they are taking anti-inflammatories.
  - **Colchicine** is an option if you have side-effects with anti-inflammatories.
- **A blood test after three months** will check that the level of uric acid has come down. If not, the dose of allopurinol may need to be increased.
- **If you have a gout attack while taking allopurinol,** you can still take anti-inflammatories to ease pain. But let a doctor know, as the dose of allopurinol may need to be increased.

Drug rationale

Drugs not included

- **Sulfinpyrazone** is an effective uricosuric agent but is not included here, owing to:
  - The need to maintain adequate urinary volume.
  - The need initially to alkalinize the urine to reduce the risk of stone formation.
  - The increased risk of uric acid stones in the urinary tract.
  - The relative ineffectiveness of sulfinpyrazone in the presence of renal impairment.

[Conaghan and Day, 1994; Emmerson, 1996; van Doornum and Ryan, 2000]

- **Probenecid,** another uricosuric drug, is no longer available in the United Kingdom [BNF 48, 2004].
- **Standard nonsteroidal anti-inflammatory drugs** (NSAIDs), other than ibuprofen, diclofenac, and naproxen, are not generally recommended:
  - **Ketoprofen, piroxicam, indometacin, sulindac, and azopropazone** are licensed for the treatment of acute gout (though not the prophylaxis of gout), but are associated with an increased risk and range of adverse effects compared withthe NSAIDs that are included.
  - **Etoricoxib,** a COX-2 selective NSAID, may have greater cardiovascular risks when taken for extended periods. The safety of COX-2 selective NSAIDs is currently being evaluated by the European Medicines Evaluation Agency (EMEA).
  - **Modified-release NSAIDs:** no improvement in efficacy or reduction in adverse events has been found. These drugs are also relatively expensive.

[Henry et al, 1996; Hernández-Diaz and Rodriguez, 2000; CSM, 2002]

- **Analgesics,** other than paracetamol and codeine taken separately, are not recommended:
  - **Strong opioids** (e.g. morphine, pethidine) should be avoided because of the risk of dependence if they are used inappropriately.
  - **Weak opioids,** other than codeine, have either not been shown to be more effective than codeine (when used in combination with paracetamol), or are more expensive.
  - **Low-dose weak opioids with paracetamol** (combination products), e.g. co-codamol 8/500 mg: There is no evidence that these offer any clinical benefit over paracetamol alone and they are likely to lead to opioid adverse effects [MeReC, 1993; De Craen et al, 1996; Moore and McQuay, 1997].
  - **High-dose weak opioids with paracetamol** (combination products), e.g. co-codamol 30/500 mg: These do not allow titration to the most effective and safe analgesic dose to match individual requirements.

- **Co-proxamol** (dextropropoxyphene 32.5 mg/ paracetamol 325 mg) has been withdrawn by the Committee on Safety of Medicines due to its unfavourable risk/benefit ratio; it is associated with an unacceptable risk of overdose [CSM, 2005].
- **Gastroprotective agents** are sometimes needed, but not all are recommended:
  - **H_2-receptor antagonists (H_2RAs).** At standard doses, H_2RAs reduce the risk of duodenal ulceration, and there is some evidence that double doses reduce the risk of gastric ulceration [Rostom et al, 2002]. However, no H_2RA is currently licensed for the prevention of gastric ulceration induced by NSAIDs [BNF 48, 2004], which is more common than duodenal ulceration.
  - **Rabeprazole** is not included, as it is not specifically licensed for the prevention of NSAID-induced GI ulcers [BNF 48, 2004].
  - **Fixed-dose combinations of standard NSAIDs with misoprostol.** The optimum dose of misoprostol (i.e. 800 micrograms daily) cannot be reached using these preparations. In particular, only 400 micrograms daily of misoprostol is given with the higher doses of NSAID in these preparations.

Drugs included

- **Allopurinol** is effective in reducing the plasma urate level and subsequent attacks of gout. It should be introduced gradually, starting at low dose to reduce the chance of inducing acute gout [Kot et al, 1993].
- **Low-dose colchicine (0.5–1.5 mg daily)** is effective as anti-inflammatory prophylaxis. Treatment should begin at the lower dose in elderly people or people with renal impairment [Kot et al, 1993]. Gastrointestinal adverse effects are less common, at the low doses used for prophylaxis.
- **Standard nonsteroidal anti-inflammatory drugs (NSAIDs). Ibuprofen, diclofenac, and naproxen** have a good balance of efficacy against adverse-effect profile [CSM, 1994; Henry et al, 1996; Hernández-Diaz and Rodriguez, 2000]. Standard doses are offered, as these are generally accepted to be sufficient for anti-inflammatory prophylaxis, although data are lacking.
- **Proton pump inhibitors (PPIs): lansoprazole, omeprazole, esomeprazole, and pantoprazole** are licensed for the prevention of gastroduodenal ulceration induced by NSAIDs [BNF 48, 2004]. PPIs reduce the risk of endoscopic ulcers, but there are no data on prevention of ulcer complications [Rostom et al, 2002]. However, they are generally considered the preferred choice for gastroprotection, as they are better tolerated than misoprostol.
- **Misoprostol** is licensed for the prevention of gastroduodenal ulceration induced by NSAIDs [BNF 48, 2004]. It reduces the risk of endoscopically proven ulcers and has also been shown to reduce the risk of ulcer complications [Rostom et al, 2002]. It is less well tolerated than PPIs owing to gastrointestinal adverse effects, particularly diarrhoea.

Prescriptions

Anti-inflammatory prophylaxis with NSAIDs

Ibuprofen tablets: 400mg three times a day

- Age from 16 years onwards
- Ibuprofen 400mg tablets. Take one tablet three times a day; supply 84 tablets; NHS Cost £2.74; OTC Cost £4.83.

Ibuprofen tablets: 600mg three times a day

- Age from 16 years onwards
- Ibuprofen 600mg tablets. Take one tablet three times a day; supply 84 tablets; NHS Cost £4.02.

Diclofenac sodium e/c tablets: 25mg three times a day

- Age from 16 years onwards
- Diclofenac 25mg e/c tablets. Take one tablet three times a day; supply 84 tablets; NHS Cost £1.72.

Diclofenac sodium e/c tablets: 50mg three times a day

- Age from 16 years onwards
- Diclofenac 50mg e/c tablets. Take one tablet three times a day; supply 84 tablets; NHS Cost £1.45.

Naproxen tablets: 250mg twice a day

- Age from 16 years onwards
- Naproxen 250mg tablets. Take one tablet twice a day; supply 56 tablets; NHS Cost £2.68.

Naproxen tablets: 500mg twice a day

- Age from 16 years onwards
- Naproxen 500mg tablets. Take one tablet twice a day; supply 56 tablets; NHS Cost £4.90.

GI protection: if at high risk of NSAID complications

Omeprazole capsules: 20mg once a day

- Age from 16 years onwards
- Omeprazole 20mg capsules. Take one capsule once a day; supply 28 capsules; NHS Cost £12.75.

Omeprazole tablets: 20mg once a day

- Age from 16 years onwards
- Omeprazole 20mg tablets. Take one tablet once a day; supply 28 tablets; NHS Cost £12.75.

Lansoprazole capsules: 15mg each morning

- Age from 16 years onwards
- Lansoprazole 15mg capsules. Take one capsule each morning (on an empty stomach); supply 28 capsules; NHS Cost £12.92.

Lansoprazole capsules: 30mg each morning

- Age from 16 years onwards
- Lansoprazole 30mg capsules. Take one capsule each morning (on an empty stomach); supply 28 capsules; NHS Cost £23.63.

Pantoprazole e/c tablets: 20mg once a day

- Age from 16 years onwards
- Pantoprazole 20mg e/c tablets. Take one tablet once a day; supply 28 tablets; NHS Cost £12.31.

Esomeprazole tablets: 20mg once a day

- Age from 16 years onwards
- Esomeprazole 20mg tablets. Take one tablet once a day; supply 28 tablets; NHS Cost £18.50.

Lansoprazole orodispersible tablets: 15mg each morning

- Age from 16 years onwards
- Lansoprazole 15mg orodisp tabs. Take one tablet each morning (on an empty stomach); supply 28 tablets; NHS Cost £10.86.

Lansoprazole orodispersible tablets: 30mg each morning

- Age from 16 years onwards
- Lansoprazole 30mg orodisp tabs. Take one tablet each morning (on an empty stomach); supply 28 tablets; NHS Cost £21.38.

Misoprostol tablets: 200micrograms four times a day

- Age from 16 years onwards
- Misoprostol 200microgram tabs. Take one tablet four times a day; supply 120 tablets; NHS Cost £18.72.

Anti-inflammatory prophylaxis with colchicine

Colchicine 500mcg twice a day (usual maintenance dose)

- Age from 16 years onwards
- Colchicine 500microgram tabs. Take one tablet twice a day; supply 56 tablets; NHS Cost £9.30.

Colchicine 500mcg once a day (elderly/renal impairment)
- Age from 16 years onwards
- Colchicine 500microgram tabs. Take one tablet once a day; supply 28 tablets; NHS Cost £4.65.

Colchicine 500mcg three times a day
- Age from 16 years onwards
- Colchicine 500microgram tabs. Take one tablet three times a day; supply 84 tablets; NHS Cost £13.94.

Start allopurinol (normal renal function)

Allopurinol: titrate from 100mg up to 300mg daily
- Age from 16 years onwards
- Allopurinol 100mg tablets. Take one tablet once a day for 2 weeks, then take two tablets once a day for 2 weeks, then take three tablets once a day; supply 48 tablets; NHS Cost £2.19.

Allopurinol tablets: 300mg once a day (usual target dose)
- Age from 16 years onwards
- Allopurinol 300mg tablets. Take one tablet once a day; supply 28 tablets; NHS Cost £1.84.

G

Adjust dose of allopurinol (urate level/renal function)

Allopurinol tablets: 300mg once a day (usual target dose)
- Age from 16 years onwards
- Allopurinol 300mg tablets. Take one tablet once a day; supply 28 tablets; NHS Cost £2.17.

Allopurinol tablets: 400mg per day (200mg twice a day)
- Age from 16 years onwards
- Allopurinol 100mg tablets. Take two tablets twice a day; supply 112 tablets; NHS Cost £3.64.

Allopurinol tablets: 500mg per day (300mg am and 200mg pm)
- Age from 16 years onwards
- Allopurinol 300mg tablets. Take one tablet each morning; supply 28 tablets; NHS Cost £2.17.
- Allopurinol 100mg tablets. Take two tablets together at night; supply 56 tablets; NHS Cost £1.82.

Allopurinol tablets: 600mg per day (300mg twice a day)
- Age from 16 years onwards
- Allopurinol 300mg tablets. Take one tablet twice a day; supply 56 tablets; NHS Cost £4.34.

Allopurinol tablets: 200mg once a day
- Age from 16 years onwards
- Allopurinol 100mg tablets. Take two tablets once a day; supply 56 tablets; NHS Cost £1.82.

Allopurinol tablets: 100mg once a day
- Age from 16 years onwards
- Allopurinol 100mg tablets. Take one tablet once a day; supply 28 tablets; NHS Cost £0.91.

Gout despite use of urate-lowering therapy

Which therapy?

- **Treat the acute attack** (see the acute scenarios).
- **Check for the presence of secondary causes** of gout, and ensure that they are effectively managed (see below for details).
- **Check compliance** with urate-lowering therapy and response of plasma urate.
- **If compliance has been poor,** recommence allopurinol after the acute attack has settled. Use the normal regimen (see *Urate-lowering therapy* scenario) with prophylactic anti- inflammatory treatment of either low-dose colchicine or a nonsteroidal anti-inflammatory drug (NSAID) for 3 months. Consider referral if both are contraindicated.
- **If the person has complied** with allopurinol treatment, do not alter the maintenance dose during an attack of gout. Consider further modification of risk factors. If this is not possible, increase the dose of allopurinol gradually up to 900 mg daily if necessary (as long as the person has normal renal function) and consider referral to secondary care. While increasing the allopurinol dose, anti-inflammatory therapy will again be required for up to 3 months as prophylaxis against allopurinol-induced attacks of gout. The aim is to reduce the plasma urate level to the normal range (i.e. less than 0.42 mmol/l). If this does not control gout, or if tophi are troublesome, consider lowering the target level of urate (e.g. to 0.36 mmol/l), and increasing the dose of allopurinol.
- **Reinforce the desirability of adopting a prudent diet and lifestyle.**
  - Moderate ingestion of alcohol.
  - Restrict dietary energy intake to limit weight gain, or, in the obese, to lose weight.
  - Limit ingestion of heart, herring, sardines, and mussels (very high purine content).
  - Moderate ingestion of other meat and seafood (high purine content).
  - Consider moderating ingestion of yeast extracts, pulses, and other vegetables high in purines (less evidence of risk).
- **Review and manage any risk factors** for gout and associated conditions that are present, including:
  - Drugs (e.g. diuretics)
  - Obesity
  - Hypertension
  - Renal impairment
  - Myeloproliferative disease
  - Hyperlipidaemia (especially hypertriglyceridaemia)
  - Vascular disease
  - Psoriasis
  - Enzyme deficiencies such as hypoxanthine guanine phosphoribosyltransferase deficiency

Practical prescribing points

For further information, see the *Medicines Compendium* (www.medicines.org.uk) or the *British National Formulary* (www.bnf.org).

Allopurinol

- **A pruritic, maculopapular rash** occurs in about 2% of people.
- **Allopurinol increases the risk of toxicity from azathioprine and mercaptopurine.**
- **Toxicity is more likely to occur with underlying renal impairment.** Reduce the dose accordingly (see the BNF section on renal impairment).
- **A hypersensitivity reaction** occurs rarely, which can include rash, fever, hepatitis, renal impairment, leucocytosis, and eosinophilia.

Follow-up advice

- **Check plasma urate at 3 months** and review with results.
- **Advise the person to return if** recurrent attacks are still occurring despite treatment, or adverse effects have arisen from the medication.

Should I refer or investigate?

Refer?

Refer if:

- The person is still having attacks of gout on the maximum tolerated dose of allopurinol.
- The person is still having attacks of gout when the plasma urate level has been reduced below 0.42 mmol/l.
- The diagnosis is in doubt.
- The person is unable to use or tolerate their medication.

Investigate?

- **Check the plasma urate level before and after alteration of the allopurinol dose.** Reduction of the plasma urate level to the normal range (i.e. less than 0.42 mmol/l) is the aim. (If gout is not controlled, or tophi are troublesome, consider lowering the target level of plasma urate — e.g. to 0.36 mmol/l.)
- **If the person becomes unwell,** check the full blood count, creatinine and electrolytes, and liver-function tests, in view of possible hypersensitivity reaction to allopurinol.
- **Check liver-function tests,** including gamma-glutamyl transferase (GGT), and consider alcohol excess.
- **X-ray** may be required if recurrent or chronic gout is thought to have resulted in joint damage.

Patient information leaflets

The following PILs are available at www.prodigy.nhs.uk

- Anti-inflammatory Painkillers
- Arthritis Research Campaign - ARC
- Blood Test - General
- Gout
- UK Gout Society

Shared decision making

If your gout is still occurring despite treatment, it is important to make sure that:

- **You are taking the allopurinol tablets every day.**
- **You are doing all you can to reduce your risk** of getting more gout, by altering your lifestyle (e.g. drinking less alcohol and reducing your weight).
- **Your doctor may want to increase the dose** of your allopurinol.
- **Your doctor may want to refer you to a specialist** in joint problems (a rheumatologist) to help confirm the diagnosis and plan your future treatment.

Drug rationale

Drugs not included

- **Sulfinpyrazone** is an effective uricosuric agent, but is not included, owing to:
  - The need to maintain adequate urinary volume.
  - The need initially to alkalinize the urine to reduce the risk of stone formation.
  - The increased risk of uric acid stones in the urinary tract.
  - The relative ineffectiveness of sulfinpyrazone in the presence of renal impairment.

[Conaghan and Day, 1994; Emmerson, 1996; van Doornum and Ryan, 2000].

- **Probenecid,** another uricosuric drug, is no longer available in the United Kingdom [BNF 48, 2004].
- For prescriptions for anti-inflammatory prophylaxis, see the scenario *Urate-lowering therapy.*

Drugs included

- **Allopurinol** is effective in reducing the plasma urate level and subsequent attacks of gout. It should be introduced gradually, starting at low dose to reduce the chance of inducing acute gout [Kot et al, 1993].

Prescriptions

Allopurinol 100-300mg per day

Allopurinol tablets: 100mg once a day

- Age from 16 years onwards
- Allopurinol 100mg tablets. Take one tablet once a day; supply 28 tablets; NHS Cost £1.28.

Allopurinol tablets: 200mg once a day

- Age from 16 years onwards
- Allopurinol 100mg tablets. Take two tablets once a day; supply 56 tablets; NHS Cost £2.56.

Allopurinol tablets: 300mg once a day

- Age from 16 years onwards
- Allopurinol 300mg tablets. Take one tablet once a day; supply 28 tablets; NHS Cost £1.84.

Allopurinol 400-600mg per day

Allopurinol tablets: 400mg per day (200mg twice a day)

- Age from 16 years onwards
- Allopurinol 100mg tablets. Take two tablets twice a day; supply 112 tablets; NHS Cost £7.36.

Allopurinol tablets: 500mg per day (300mg am and 200mg pm)

- Age from 16 years onwards
- Allopurinol 100mg tablets. Take two tablets together at night; supply 56 tablets; NHS Cost £2.56.
- Allopurinol 300mg tablets. Take one tablet each morning; supply 28 tablets; NHS Cost £1.84.

Allopurinol tablets: 600mg per day (300mg twice a day)

- Age from 16 years onwards
- Allopurinol 300mg tablets. Take one tablet twice a day; supply 56 tablets; NHS Cost £3.68.

Allopurinol 700-900mg per day

Allopurinol tablets: 700mg per day (300mg am and 400mg pm)

- Age from 16 years onwards
- Allopurinol 300mg tablets. Take one tablet twice a day; supply 56 tablets; NHS Cost £3.68.
- Allopurinol 100mg tablets. Take one tablet at night; supply 28 tablets; NHS Cost £1.28.

Allopurinol tablets: 800mg per day (400mg twice a day)

- Age from 16 years onwards
- Allopurinol 300mg tablets. Take one tablet twice a day; supply 56 tablets; NHS Cost £3.68.
- Allopurinol 100mg tablets. Take one tablet twice a day; supply 56 tablets; NHS Cost £2.56.

Allopurinol tablets: 900mg per day (400mg am and 500mg pm)

- Age from 16 years onwards
- Allopurinol 300mg tablets. Take one tablet twice a day; supply 56 tablets; NHS Cost £3.68.
- Allopurinol 100mg tablets. Take one tablet each morning and take two tablets at night; supply 84 tablets; NHS Cost £3.84.

Asymptomatic hyperuricaemia

Which therapy?

- **Asymptomatic hyperuricaemia does not require treatment with drugs,** but steps should be taken to reduce the urate level by other means.
- **Suggest a prudent diet and lifestyle.**
  - Moderate ingestion of alcohol.
  - Restrict dietary energy intake to limit weight gain, or, in the obese, to lose weight.
  - Limit ingestion of heart, herring, sardines, and mussels (very high purine content).
  - Moderate ingestion of other meat and seafood (high purine content).
  - Consider moderating ingestion of yeast extracts, pulses, and other vegetables high in purines (less evidence of risk).
- **Manage any risk factors** for gout and associated conditions that are present, including:
  - Drugs (e.g. diuretics)
  - Obesity
  - Hypertension
  - Renal impairment
  - Myeloproliferative disease
  - Hyperlipidaemia (especially hypertriglyceridaemia)
  - Vascular disease
  - Psoriasis
  - Enzyme deficiencies such as hypoxanthine guanine phosphoribosyltransferase deficiency

G

Follow-up advice

- **Pursue further the assessment and adjustment of risk factors if found** (e.g. renal impairment, alcohol excess).
- **Advise the person to attend if a hot swollen joint develops.**

Should I refer or investigate?

Refer?

- Referral is not required unless clinically significant co-existent pathology is found.

Investigate?

- **Renal function:** plasma creatinine and electrolytes.
- **Full blood count,** looking for myeloproliferative disease.
- **Liver-function tests,** including gamma-glutamyl transferase (GGT), in view of possible alcohol excess.

Patient information leaflets

The following PILs are available at www.prodigy.nhs.uk

- Arthritis Research Campaign - ARC
- Blood Test - General
- Gout
- UK Gout Society

Shared decision making

- **You have a raised level of uric acid (urate) in your blood,** which sometimes leads to attacks of gout and, more rarely, kidney stones.
- **This does not require any tablets at present but the urate level can be reduced in some cases by lifestyle changes.** Mainly by:
  - Reducing the amount of alcohol if you drink heavily.
  - Losing some weight if you are overweight.
  - Cutting back on eating purine rich foods if you eat a lot of them (liver, kidney, brain, heart, herring, sardines, mussels, meat extracts, meats, and shellfish).
- Your doctor may want to take some blood samples to look for other problems that may be causing a raised urate level. For example, a kidney problem.

Drug rationale

- No drugs are offered.

Prescriptions

Advice note

Advice only: raised uric acid levels

- Age from 16 years onwards
- You have a raised level of urate in your blood which sometimes leads to attacks of gout and more rarely, kidney stones. This does not require any tablets at present but the level can be improved by changing your lifestyle e.g. reducing the amount of alcohol you drink or losing some weight. Your doctor may want to take some blood samples to look for other problems which may be why you have the raised urate level , e.g. your kidney function.

Extended Information

Background information

- What is it? p.858
- What causes gout? p.858
- How common is it? p.859
- How do I know my patient has it? p.859
- What else might it be? p.860
- Complications and prognosis p.861

What is it?

- **Gout** is a condition in which monosodium urate crystals deposit in joints and other tissues, such as soft connective tissues or the urinary tract.
  - **Gouty arthritis** is arthritis due to urate crystals in joints.
  - **Podagra** is gouty arthritis of the big toe.
  - **Tophi** are observable nodules caused by urate deposits in soft connective tissues.
  - **Chronic tophaceous gout** is the combination of tophi and a chronic destructive arthritis.
  - **Gouty urinary lithiasis** is the presence of urate-containing stones (calculi) in the urinary tract.
  - **Urate nephropathy** is an interstitial nephritis caused by the formation of urate crystals in the kidney.
- The natural history of gout has three phases:
  - A long period of asymptomatic hyperuricaemia before gout manifests.
  - A period during which acute attacks of gouty arthritis are followed by variable intervals (months to years) when there are no symptoms: so-called interval gout, or intercritical gout.
  - The final period of chronic tophaceous gout.

What causes gout?

Gout is the end result of a complex chain of events, which has been worked out in some detail. The most important gaps in knowledge are how urate crystals stimulate the inflammatory responses that result in gout, and how this is interrupted by anti-inflammatory drugs.

Table 1: Secondary causes of hyperuricaemia.

Urate under-excretion	Urate overproduction
Alcohol ingestion	Excessive dietary intake of purines
Renal impairment	Myeloproliferative diseases
Hypertension	Administration of cytotoxic drugs (tumour lysis syndrome)
Drugs	Psoriasis
Lead toxicity	Inherited enzyme deficiencies: hypoxanthine guanine phosphoribosyltransferase deficiency (Lesch–Nyhan syndrome and less severe variants), glucose-6-phosphate dehydrogenase deficiency, phosphoribosyl pyrophosphate synthetase variant (with increased activity)

- Urate crystals can form in any tissue (except brain). Urate crystals are found in joints affected by gout, but they have also been found in asymptomatic joints.
  - Inflammation associated with urate crystals in joints causes a sterile arthritis.
  - Inflammation associated with urate crystals in soft tissues causes a sterile cellulitis.
  - Inflammation associated with urate crystals in the kidneys causes interstitial nephritis.
- The origin of urate crystals is uric acid produced in the metabolism of purine compounds (adenine and guanine, which are found in DNA and RNA). At physiological pH, uric acid is 98% ionized. Thus, in extracellular fluid where sodium is the major cation, uric acid effectively exists as a solution of sodium urate.
- There are three sources of purines in humans: the diet, degradation of endogenous purines, and *de novo* synthesis. Dietary purines account for about 30% of excreted urate, but adopting a purine-free diet typically reduces plasma urate concentrations by only 10–20%.
- Urate has low solubility, and in humans statistically normal urate levels are close to saturation levels.
  - In the UK the upper limit of the reference range for plasma urate is usually taken as 0.42 mmol/l for males and 0.36 mmol/l for premenopausal females. The maximum solubility of monosodium urate in plasma is about 0.57 mmol/l at 37°C.
  - At 37°C the solubility of urate in physiological saline is 0.41 mmol/l, but at 30°C it is only 0.27 mmol/l.
  - The fact that urate levels are higher in men than women explains why more men than women suffer from gout. The fact that temperatures in the feet and hands can be low enough to precipitate urate from plasma explains why gout tends to attack joints in the extremities. Similar reasoning explains why tophi typically form in the helix of the ear, finger tips, olecranon bursae and other cool anatomical sites.
- Urate excretion is two-thirds by the kidneys and one third by the gastrointestinal tract.
- About 90% of people with primary hyperuricaemia are under-excretors of urate; about 10% are overproducers of urate; and a few have combined under-excretion and overproduction of urate.
- Often no cause can be identified for hyperuricaemia. However, hyperuricaemia and gout can be secondary to several factors. These are classified in Table 1 according to their effect on urate physiology.
- (The classification in Table 1 has been used to match the mechanism of therapy with the mechanism of hyperuricaemia — urate 'under-excretors' to be given a uricosuric drug; urate 'over-producers' to be treated with a xanthine oxidase inhibitor. However, in practice when treating gout it is not necessary to differentiate urate under-excretion from urate overproduction [Schlesinger and Schumacher, 2004].)

Cohen and Emmerson, 1998; Marshall, 2000; Nuki, 2002; Rott and Agudelo, 2003; Terkeltaub, 2003; Dutch College of General Practitioners, 2004]

How common is it?

- A study of UK general practice found that:
  - The prevalence of gout in people registered in the General Practice Research Database (GPRD) was 1.4%.
  - The overall ratio of men to women was 3.6:1.
  - The annual incidence of gout ranged from 1.19–1.80 cases per 1000 person-years [Mikuls et al, 2005].
- The risk of gout increases with plasma urate level — see Table 2 [Campion et al, 1987].
- Although gout is more likely to occur in people with hyperuricaemia, it can occur in people with normal plasma urate levels; and many people with hyperuricaemia never develop gout.
- Gout is rare in premenopausal women, except in the case of a genetic abnormality in urate handling.

How do I know my patient has it?

- **Ask about:**
  - **Previous attacks of gouty arthritis,** and which joints are (and have been) involved
    - Acute attacks of gout become less frequent as the disease progresses.
  - **Arthritis in the big toe**
    - The initial attack of gout affects the first metacarpophalangeal joint in 70% of people, and this joint is affected in 90% of cases at some time.
  - **Rapidity of onset**
    - Inflammation usually reaches maximum intensity within 24 hours.
  - **Alcohol ingestion**
  - **Dietary intake of purines, particularly from meat and seafood**
  - **Use of drugs that can raise plasma urate levels:**
    - Ciclosporin
    - Cytotoxic drugs
    - Diuretics, thiazide and loop
    - Ethambutol
    - Low-dose aspirin
    - Nicotinic acid
    - Pyrazinamide
    - Tacrolimus
  - **Comorbidity that can increase the risk of gout**
    - Obesity, hypertension, renal impairment, myeloproliferative disease, hyperlipidaemia (especially hypertriglyceridaemia), vascular disease,

Table 2: Five-year cumulative incidence of gout categorised by plasma urate level.

Plasma urate (mmol/l)	5-year cumulative incidence (per 1000)
<0.42	5
0.42–0.47	20
0.48–0.53	41
0.54–0.59	198
>=0.60	305

severe psoriasis, enzyme defects such as hypoxanthine guanine phosphoribosyltransferase (HGPRT) deficiency and glucose-6-phosphate dehydrogenase (G6PD) deficiency.
  - **Exposure to lead**
- **Look for evidence of:**
  - **Arthritis** (swelling, redness, warmth, pain on passive movement)
    - The big toe, i.e. first metatarsophalangeal (MTP) joint, is the site most frequently affected in gout.
    - Other joints affected are in the instep, heel, ankle, knee, finger, wrist, and elbow (listed in order of decreasing frequency).
    - Lower limb joints are affected more frequently than upper limb joints.
  - **Tophi** (firm, white, translucent nodules)
    - It usually takes at least 10 years after the first attack of acute gout for tophi to develop.
    - Tophi are most commonly found on fingers, toes, ulnar side of forearms, olecranon bursae, prepatella bursae, Achilles tendons, and the helix of the ears; but they can occur anywhere (e.g. in spinal canal, vocal cords).
    - The pattern of tophi and joint involvement is characteristically asymmetric.
    - In postmenopausal women who are taking diuretics, tophi can form over Heberden's nodes [O'Dell, 1983].
- **Consider the following tests:**
  - **Plasma urate**
    - **To confirm hyperuricaemia.** Note that gout may present without hyperuricaemia, and hyperuricaemia may be present without gout. Note also that plasma levels of urate *fall* during an acute attack. The level of plasma urate at which gout can be safely ruled out is taken to be 0.38 mmol/l by the Dutch Gout Guidelines. However, during an acute attack a level as low as 0.33 mmol/l may be more appropriate. [Dutch College of General Practitioners, 2004; Logan et al, 1997].
    - **To follow progress while on urate-lowering therapy.**
  - **Joint fluid microscopy and culture**
    - Presence of urate crystals confirms diagnosis of gout.
    - Absence of evidence of infection rules out septic arthritis.
    - Aspiration of joint fluid is not indicated if the diagnosis of gout is not in doubt and septic arthritis is not suspected.
    - A review rated as 'Bronze' the quality of evidence supporting use of microscopy to detect urate crystals. No randomized controlled trial (RCT) has studied the effect on clinical outcomes of testing for urate crystals in synovial fluid or tophi. The test can have false positives and false negatives. The quality of the test depends on the quality of the laboratory providing the test and the quality of the specimen sent for testing. [Schlesinger and Schumacher, 2004].
  - **Joint X-ray**
    - Suspect pseudogout if there are more than three attacks a year despite treatment. Consider an X-ray of an affected joint (especially if wrist or knee) to look for chondrocalcinosis. If found, the probability of pseudogout is increased; if not found, pseudogout can be excluded. [Bencardino and Hassankhani, 2003].
  - **Erythrocyte sedimentation rate**
    - A raised erythrocyte sedimentation rate (ESR) increases the likelihood of septic arthritis; but a normal ESR does not completely rule out sepsis.

[Cohen and Emmerson, 1998; Nuki, 2002; Dutch College of General Practitioners, 2004; Schlesinger and Schumacher, 2004]

American College of Rheumatology criteria for the diagnosis of gout

The American College of Rheumatology (ACR) published in 1977 'preliminary' criteria for the diagnosis of acute gouty arthritis [Wallace et al, 1977]. These criteria have been widely accepted and are used currently [Schlesinger and Schumacher, 2004; Underwood, 2004].

- The 'gold standard' for diagnosing gout is demonstration by microscopy of urate crystals in synovial fluid or in a tophus.
- However, testing for urate crystals in joint fluid or tophi is often not practical. The ACR criteria thus also allow gout to be diagnosed if six or more of the following criteria are met:
  - More than one attack of acute arthritis.
  - Maximal inflammation developing within 1 day.
  - Monoarthritis attack (90% of initial attacks are monoarticular).
  - Redness over affected joint (s).
  - Unilateral attack on the first metatarsophalangeal (MTP) joint.
  - Unilateral attack on the tarsal joint.
  - Tophus (proven or suspected).
  - Hyperuricaemia.
  - Asymmetric swelling within a joint on X-ray. Asymmetric swelling can also be found on examination, but the data from which the ACR criteria were derived did not include this.
  - Subcortical cysts without erosions on X-ray.
  - No organisms found on culture of synovial fluid.

Further information to aid diagnosis

- An acute attack may be accompanied by raised temperature, white blood cell count, platelet count, erythrocyte sedimentation rate (ESR), and C-reactive protein (CRP) level.
- **Patterns of disease**
  - Recurrent episodes can affect the same or other joints. Polyarticular attacks become more likely as the disease progresses.
  - Gout presenting in the second or third decade of life suggests the possibility of a genetic enzyme disorder such as hypoxanthine guanine phosphoribosyltransferase deficiency.
  - Older people with gout tend to present differently from younger people. In older people with gout:
    - The onset is more likely to be polyarticular.
    - The upper limb is more likely to be involved than the lower; fingers are often affected.
    - Women are affected more commonly than men.
    - Tophi can occur early in the course of the disease, sometimes without previous attacks of gout, and may be found in atypical sites.
  - Gout is often associated with the use of diuretics.

[Cohen and Emmerson, 1998; Terkeltaub, 2003]

What else might it be?

- **Septic arthritis**
  - Septic arthritis must be considered in any acute hot joint. Septic arthritis is important to diagnose, as late recognition can be fatal. If suspected, refer for emergency joint aspiration and culture.
- **Osteoarthritis with coincidental hyperuricaemia**
- **Non-urate crystal-induced arthropathy,** such as:
  - Pseudogout, i.e. calcium pyrophosphate deposition disease (CPPD)
  - Hydroxyapatite crystal deposition disease (basic calcium phosphate crystallopathy)
  - Combined CPPD and hydroxyapatite crystallopathy
- **Psoriatic arthritis**

Reactive arthritis
Rheumatoid arthritis
Seronegative spondyloarthropathy

Complications and prognosis

Complications

Tophi may create a physical hindrance, become inflamed, exude tophaceous material, or develop secondary infection.

Urinary stones. The annual incidence of urinary stones in people suffering from gout is 1% [Fessel, 1979]. The incidence of uric acid stones (with and without a calcium component) varies between countries and accounts for 5% to 40% of all urinary calculi [Shekarriz and Stoller, 2002].

Interstitial nephropathy is a rare complication of gout [Schlesinger and Schumacher, 2004]. It can be familial [Stavrou et al, 1998].

Prognosis

Acute attacks of gout are generally thought to be self-limited [Terkeltaub, 2003]. However, this opinion has little data to support it [Schlesinger and Schumacher, 2004; Underwood, 2004].

Recurrent acute episodes and the development of chronic gout lead to progressive joint damage, pain, and disability.

Before urate-lowering therapy became available, a study of rate of development of tophi followed 1195 people with gout. Multiple tophi were present in 40% of people 5 years after the first attack, in 50% after 10 years, and in 70% after 20 years.[Yu and Gutman, 1967], cited in [Dutch College of General Practitioners, 2004].

Management issues

Overview of the management of gout p.861
How do I treat an acute attack of gout? p.861
What steps should I take to prevent future attacks of gout? p.862
How should I manage people with tophi? p.863
Medicines management p.863
What is the supporting evidence? p.864

Information that would be useful when prescribing is given in the *Medicines management* section.

The evidence that supports the recommendations is reviewed in the section *What is the supporting evidence?*. This version of the guidance has limited details on the evidence to support the recommendations. The version that includes a detailed review of the evidence is available on request from prodigy-enquiries@schin.ncl.ac.uk.

Overview of the management of gout

- **How do I manage an acute attack of gout?**
  - Help the person with gout to understand and manage the condition.
  - Suggest cautious use of an ice pack.
  - Start drug treatment with a nonsteroidal anti-inflammatory drug (NSAID) (or corticosteroid or colchicine) as soon as possible, preferably within 24 hours of the onset of the attack.
  - Offer additional analgesia if needed.
- **How do I prevent further attacks of gout?**
  - Suggest a sensible diet and lifestyle — moderate use of alcohol and limited dietary purines.
  - Manage any risk factors for gout that are present (e.g. drugs, obesity, hypertension).
  - Start urate-lowering therapy in the following circumstances:
    - Recurrent attacks
    - Tophi
    - Urate nephropathy
  - Wait until the acute attack has resolved before starting urate-lowering therapy, *and*
  - Co-prescribe an anti-inflammatory medication (NSAID, colchicine, or corticosteroid).

How do I treat an acute attack of gout?

What information is someone with gout likely to need?

A person with gout needs information to understand and manage their condition. Points to discuss include the following.

- Acute gout is a self-limited condition that, if untreated, will spontaneously resolve in 1–3 weeks in most people.
- Options for treatment include:
  - Physical interventions to alleviate pain (e.g. ice).
  - Drugs to alleviate pain and inflammation.
  - Diet and lifestyle measures to prevent further attacks.
  - Drugs to prevent further attacks.
- Drug treatment should be introduced rapidly at the onset of symptoms.
- The risks and benefits of treatment need to be balanced — drugs may have adverse effects.
- Patient support is provided by the UK Gout Society: www.ukgoutsociety.org/about.htm.

What should I consider before initiating treatment?

- **Always consider the possibility of sepsis in an acute hot joint.** If septic arthritis is suspected, then either refer urgently, or aspirate the joint and arrange urgent microscopy and culture.
- Rule out, or manage, any secondary causes of hyperuricaemia (see Table 1 in the section *What is it?*).

What treatment should I use?

- **Suggest cautious use of an ice pack.**
  - A pack of frozen peas is convenient to use, as it moulds to fit the affected part.
  - The pack should be wrapped in a towel to avoid direct skin contact and ice-burn.
  - Apply for about 20 minutes.
  - Ensure that the temperature of the affected part has returned to normal before repeating the application. Repeat as often as required.
- **Start drug treatment with an NSAID, colchicine, or corticosteroid as soon as possible, preferably within 24 hours of the onset of the attack.**
  - Prompt treatment is facilitated if people with gout have a supply of medicine at home and they understand the disadvantages of delaying treatment.
  - **An NSAID is the generally preferred option,** unless there are contraindications.
    - Marked symptomatic relief occurs within 24 hours.
    - **The full licensed dose of the NSAID should be used.** Higher doses are no longer recommended, as the risk of adverse effects outweighs any benefit.
    - **Which NSAID?** As no important difference in efficacy has been shown between different NSAIDs, the choice depends on the risk of adverse effects,

convenience, and cost. If the person is not at high risk for gastrointestinal bleeding, a non-COX-selective NSAID is cost-effective. If gastroprotection is required, the preferred option is to use a non-COX-selective NSAID together with a proton pump inhibitor.

- **Oral colchicine is an option if NSAIDs are contraindicated.**
  - Colchicine relieves symptoms within hours, but most people taking it at therapeutic doses suffer from nausea, vomiting, and/or diarrhoea.
- **Systemic corticosteroids are also an option if NSAIDs are not suitable.**
  - Oral and intramuscular corticosteroids are effective if given in adequate doses.
  - Adjunctive low-dose colchicine has been advocated by some experts because rebound flares of arthritis have occurred on withdrawal of systemic corticosteroids [Terkeltaub, 2003], but there is no published evidence to support this.
- **Intra-articular corticosteroids** are an option to use as sole therapy or adjunctive therapy *if* only one or two joints are affected, *and* they are suitable for injecting, *and* the expertise to inject the joint (s) is available.
  - For more information, see the sections *Intra-articular corticosteroids* in the *Medicines management* section and *Intra-articular corticosteroids* in the *What is the supporting evidence*? section.

- **Analgesics** are sometimes required in addition to other therapy for acute gout. They may also be used alone if NSAIDs, corticosteroids, and colchicine are all contraindicated.

What steps should I take to prevent future attacks of gout?

- **Suggest a sensible diet and lifestyle.**
  - Moderate ingestion of alcohol.
  - Restrict dietary energy intake to limit weight gain, or, in an obese person, to lose weight.
  - Restrict dietary intake of purines.
    - Limit ingestion of heart, herring, sardines, or mussels (very high purine content).
    - Moderate ingestion of other meat and seafood (high purine content).
    - Consider moderating ingestion of yeast extracts and vegetables with high purine content: e.g. peas, beans, lentils, oatmeal, spinach, asparagus, cauliflower, mushrooms (less evidence of risk).
- **Manage any risk factors for gout that are present,** including:
  - Drugs (e.g. diuretics)
  - Obesity
  - Hypertension
  - Renal impairment
  - Myeloproliferative disease
  - Hyperlipidaemia (especially hypertriglyceridaemia)
  - Vascular disease
  - Psoriasis
  - Enzyme deficiencies such as hypoxanthine guanine phosphoribosyltransferase deficiency
- **Start urate-lowering therapy (if indicated) after the acute attack has resolved, and co-prescribe an anti-inflammatory medication** (NSAID or low-dose colchicine) as prophylaxis against a recurrent attack.
  - Advise the person that urate-lowering therapy may at first exacerbate gout.
  - Advise also that gout attacks may take months to stop, even if plasma urate is within the target range. This is presumably because mobilisation of tissue urate stores takes so long [Grove, Personal Communication, 2005].
  - Tell them how to deal with an acute attack if it occurs: start treatment with an anti-inflammatory (NSAID, corticosteroid, or colchicine) as soon as possible, and continue the urate-lowering therapy.

What are the indications for starting urate-lowering therapy?

- Urate-lowering therapy should be started when there are:
  - Recurrent attacks of gouty arthritis despite attempts to reduce risk factors (e.g. after more than two attacks in one year or more than three attacks in total), *or*
  - One or more tophi, *or*
  - Clinical or radiological signs of chronic gouty arthritis *or*
  - Recurrent uric acid renal stones (other aspects of the management of urinary lithiasis are out of the scope of this guidance)
- People with raised plasma urate levels who do not have gout do not need to be treated with urate-lowering therapy, as gout is not an inevitable consequence of hyperuricaemia.
  - People with asymptomatic hyperuricaemia should be advised to follow the non-drug strategies used by people with gout (i.e. adopt a prudent diet and lifestyle and ensure that any risk factors for gout are managed).

What urate-lowering treatments should I use?

- Available options for urate-lowering therapy are allopurinol (a xanthine oxidase inhibitor) and sulfinpyrazone (a uricosuric agent).
  - **Allopurinol** is the preferred option for urate-lowering therapy (unless contraindicated)].
  - **Sulfinpyrazone** is less effective than allopurinol, and administration is less convenient, as steps have to be taken to avoid formation of uric acid calculi. It is therefore not generally recommended.
  - (Febuxostat, a novel inhibitor of xanthine oxidase/dehydrogenase, is currently undergoing phase III clinical trials and may become available in the near future [Schlesinger, 2004].)
- **Aim initially to reduce the plasma urate level to the normal range** (i.e. less than 0.42 mmol/l).
  - Periodically test the plasma urate (e.g. every 6 months until stable) and, if on allopurinol, adjust the dose accordingly [Mikuls et al, 2004].
  - If attacks recur, or tophi are troublesome, it may be appropriate to set a lower target level (e.g. 0.36 mmol/l) and increase the dose of allopurinol.
- **If concurrent low-dose aspirin is required,** use allopurinol (unless contraindicated).
- **Options for anti-inflammatory prophylaxis** during the introduction of urate-lowering therapy are a nonsteroidal anti-inflammatory drug (NSAID), low-dose colchicine, or low-dose prednisolone.
  - Lower doses of NSAIDs are generally advised for anti-inflammatory prophylaxis.
  - Low-dose colchicine (0.5–1.5 mg daily) may be as effective as anti-inflammatory prophylaxis. Gastrointestinal adverse effects are less common at the low doses used for prophylaxis.
  - When neither an NSAID nor colchicine is tolerated, or both are contraindicated, consider low-dose oral prednisolone (7.5 mg daily) for 3 months. However, it may be preferable to refer the person to a specialist.
- Anti-inflammatory prophylaxis for 3 months is generally accepted UK practice [BNF 48, 2004]. However, the duration of prophylaxis recommended by experts ranges from 1 to 12 months [Kot et al, 1993].

How should I manage people with tophi?

The principles of management of people with tophi (and other complications of gout) are similar to those for managing people with frequent recurrences of gout — see the *Medicines management* section for details on dietary management and options for drug treatments.

Rarely, a tophus may be so disabling that referral for assessment for surgical removal is indicated.

People with complications of gout such as urate kidney stones or urate nephropathy should be referred for specialist advice.

Medicines management

Nonsteroidal anti-inflammatory drugs p.863
Colchicine p.863
Systemic corticosteroids p.863
Intra-articular corticosteroids p.864
Allopurinol p.864
Which analgesic should I use? p.864
Drug regimens for the prevention of gout p.864
Drug regimens for acute gout p.864

Nonsteroidal anti-inflammatory drugs

A full discussion on the contraindications, adverse effects, monitoring issues, and interactions of NSAIDs is beyond the scope of this guidance. For further information, see the separate PRODIGY guidance on *Nonsteroidal anti-inflammatory drugs (NSAIDs)*.

Diclofenac, naproxen, indometacin, and etoricoxib are licensed for the treatment of acute gout.

Ibuprofen, diclofenac, and naproxen are generally preferred for preventing gout while urate-lowering therapy is initiated, owing to their more favourable adverse-effect profile. Note: this is an off-licence use.

Consider patient comorbidity when prescribing nonsteroidal anti-inflammatory drugs (NSAIDs).

- NSAIDs commonly cause gastrointestinal adverse effects, and can worsen asthma, hypertension, renal impairment, and heart failure.
- There is a small increased risk of cardiovascular events with coxibs (which seems highest in people who already have cardiovascular disease).

For people with gout at high risk of gastrointestinal adverse events, we recommend the following options:

- Use paracetamol (with or without codeine) instead of a NSAID if possible.
- Or, use a gastroprotective agent with a standard NSAID [NICE, 2001].
- Or, use a COX-2 selective NSAID alone [NICE, 2001].

For advice on the management of dyspepsia due to NSAIDs, see the separate PRODIGY guidance on *Dyspepsia — symptoms (uninvestigated by endoscopy)* and *Dyspepsia — proven DU, GU, or NSAID-associated ulcer*.

Colchicine

Colchicine should be reserved for use when treatment with an NSAID is contraindicated or poorly tolerated.

What dosing regimen of colchicine should I use?

Acute gout: there is little evidence as to what is the optimal dosing strategy to treat acute attacks of gout, despite widespread usage of the drug over several decades. Most experts now agree that the present licensed dose of colchicine is too high for many individuals and may result in an unnecessary degree of GI-related adverse effects:

- An initial starting dose of 500 micrograms three times a day or less frequently is recommended (based on case reports and other empirical evidence) [Morris et al, 2003].
- If the initial dose proves ineffective, the dose can be gradually increased up to the licensed dose. This consists of an initial dose of 1 mg, followed by 500 micrograms every 2–3 hours until relief of pain is achieved, or vomiting or diarrhoea occurs. A maximum of 6 mg should be used, and treatment should not be repeated within 3 days [BNF 48, 2004].
- Treatment should begin at the lower dose in elderly people or those with renal impairment [Kot et al, 1993].

- **Prophylaxis of gout** (during urate-lowering therapy): low doses (0.5–1.5 mg daily) are effective. Treatment should begin at the lower dose in elderly people or those with renal impairment [Kot et al, 1993].

What are the main adverse effects associated with colchicine?

- **Gastrointestinal adverse effects,** such as nausea and vomiting, diarrhoea, and abdominal cramps or pains, are common with colchicine use, and can be severe enough to limit treatment. One study found that, although colchicine was effective at relieving symptoms of gout in most people, more than half experienced diarrhoea within 24 hours of use [Ahern et al, 1987].
- **Other adverse effects are much less common,** and include blood disorders with prolonged usage.

Who should avoid taking colchicine?

- **Avoid use** in people with serious gastrointestinal or cardiac disorders. Toxicity is more likely in people with renal impairment and may necessitate the use of lower doses [Conaghan and Day, 1994].
- **Colchicine is contraindicated in pregnant women,** who should be referred to a specialist if they require treatment. It should also be avoided in breastfeeding women.

Systemic corticosteroids

What is the role of systemic corticosteroids in treating gout?

- Systemic corticosteroids can be used as an alternative to NSAIDs or colchicine if these are contraindicated.
  - Corticosteroids are not specifically licensed for the treatment of gout.
- **Long-term use of corticosteroids,** such as for prophylaxis of gout, should be generally be avoided, owing to the potential for serious adverse effects.
  - Consider referral to a specialist if treatment with corticosteroids for more than 2 months seems necessary. This could occur if the person with gout requires prophylaxis of inflammation during the initiation period of urate-lowering therapy, and neither an NSAID nor colchicine is suitable.

What systemic corticosteroids are available?

- **Intramuscular corticosteroids:** triamcinolone acetonide or methyl prednisolone can be given as a one-off intramuscular injection (40 mg) to relieve symptoms of acute gout.
- **Oral corticosteroids:** low-dose prednisolone is relatively safe and convenient to use in short courses.
  - A dose of 15 mg a day (taken in the morning) for 10 days, tapering to 7.5 mg for 10 days, is usually adequate.
  - Higher doses, up to 40 mg each morning for a few days before tapering, may be considered if a rapid response is required [Grove, Personal Communication, 2005].

G

Intra-articular corticosteroids

What is the role of intra-articular corticosteroids in treating gout?

- Intra-articular corticosteroids can be used to treat an acute flare-up of gout in one, or at most, two, joints. They should only be given by healthcare professionals with experience of giving intra-articular injections [DTB, 1995].
  - Intra-articular corticosteroids are not specifically licensed in the treatment of gout.

Which injectable corticosteroid should I use?

- **Specific corticosteroids are recommended for different joints according to their size.** Atrophy of subcutaneous tissues and local skin depigmentation may occur from periarticular leakage of corticosteroid. The risk is greatest if large or repeated doses of a long-acting, potent corticosteroid are given:
  - **Smaller joints:** hydrocortisone, dexamethasone, or prednisolone is recommended.
  - **Larger joints:** triamcinolone or methylprednisolone is recommended.

When should I avoid injecting a joint?

- **Avoid injecting:**
  - Prosthetic joints
  - When there is any possibility of sepsis
  - An acutely inflamed, gouty first metatarsal pharyngeal joint — this is not only difficult, but also so painful that it is unlikely to be tolerated by the person with gout
  - Joints within 3 months of a previous injection
- **Inject with caution if:**
  - The person is taking anticoagulants

Allopurinol

Allopurinol is a xanthine oxidase inhibitor that reduces uric acid formation by blocking the final step in urate synthesis. It is used to lower plasma urate levels and consequently prevent attacks of gout.

What regimen of allopurinol should I use?

- **Allopurinol should be introduced gradually,** starting at low dosage to reduce the chance of inducing acute gout [Kot et al, 1993]. For adults with normal renal function, the starting dosage should be 100 mg daily, gradually building up to a usual maintenance dosage of 300 mg daily over about 4 weeks [Emmerson, 1996]. The maintenance dosage should be adjusted according to the plasma urate level, aiming for a level of less than 0.42 mmol/l. Some people may require only 100 mg daily but others may need as much as 900 mg daily. Dosages over 300 mg daily should be given in divided doses [BNF 48, 2004]. If gout is not controlled or tophi are troublesome, the target plasma urate level should be lowered (e.g. to 0.36 mmol/l) and the dose of allopurinol increased.
- **The dosage should be reduced in renal impairment.** Many of the common adverse effects relate to inappropriate dosage in people with renal impairment [Conaghan and Day, 1994]. See the BNF section on prescribing in renal impairment for details.

What are the adverse effects of allopurinol?

- **In up to 2% of people, a pruritic, maculopapular rash occurs;** concurrent ampicillin may increase the frequency of this rash. Exfoliative dermatitis is a rare but serious adverse effect, occurring in less than 1 in 1000 people; it is often accompanied by vasculitis, fever, liver dysfunction, eosinophilia, and renal impairment [Conaghan and Day, 1994; Emmerson, 1996].
- Gastrointestinal adverse effects can occur, but are usually mild.

What drugs can I use to prevent acute attacks of gout during treatment with allopurinol?

- **The use of allopurinol can paradoxically precipitate an acute attack of gout** while the target urate level is being reached. These attacks can be avoided by using a prophylactic drug during the first 3 months of treatmen
  - Lower doses of NSAIDs (possibly with a gastroprotective agent) are preferred.
  - Colchicine can be used if NSAIDs are contraindicated Low doses (typically 0.5–1.5 mg per day) should be used, depending on renal function.
  - If both NSAIDs and colchicine are contraindicated, low doses of oral prednisolone (7.5 mg per day) can b used, but this should be done under expert supervision.
- Alternatively, a supply of drugs for acute attacks can be prescribed and used 'as required'. This approach may b particularly suitable for individuals receiving low doses of allopurinol [Grove, Personal Communication, 2005].

Which analgesic should I use?

- **Analgesics will aid pain relief** but have no effect on the course of the attack of gout.
- **Codeine in combination with regular paracetamol** is more effective than either paracetamol or codeine used alone for acute pain [Moore et al, 1997].

Paracetamol

- Paracetamol is safe and effective for the treatment of mild to moderate pain when used correctly, and is well tolerated at the recommended daily dose.
- It is more likely to be effective for acute gout pain when used regularly rather than 'as required'.

Codeine

- Codeine may be added to paracetamol if more pain reli is required.
- Paracetamol and codeine should be prescribed separate so they can be individually titrated; combination products such as co-codamol are not recommended.
- Codeine may cause nausea, vomiting, constipation, and drowsiness. A regular laxative is often needed when it is used long-term.

Drug regimens for the prevention of gout

Drug regimens for preventing attacks of gout are listed in Table 3. Note that not all the drugs listed are recommended by PRODIGY.

Drug regimens for acute gout

Drug regimens used for an acute attack of gout are listed i Table 4. Note that not all the drugs listed are recommended by PRODIGY.

What is the supporting evidence?

Abbreviations used in this section

CI	Confidence interval
NNT	Number needed to treat
OR	Odds ratio
RCT	Randomized controlled trial
SD	Standard deviation

What is the evidence supporting the use of non-drug treatments during an acute attack of gout?

Application of an ice pack

- An RCT with 19 subjects found that pain was reduced i 48% (95% CI 8 to 67) of people who used an ice pack; the NNT was 3 (95% CI 2 to 13) [Schlesinger et al, 2002].

'able 3: Drug therapy options for the prevention of acute gout [Terkeltaub, 2003; BNF 48, 2004].

rug	Typical regimens	Comments
rate-lowering therapy		
llopurinol	100 mg once a day, gradually titrated to 300 mg once a day (normal target dose).	Dosage depends on renal function.
ulfinpyrazone	100–200 mg once a day, gradually titrated to 600 mg once a day.	Sulfinpyrazone is not usually recommended, owing to its adverse-effects profile.
SAIDs (prophylaxis) *		
uprofen	400–600 mg three times a day	Ibuprofen, diclofenac, and naproxen probably have the best safety profiles of the NSAIDs and are the most commonly used in the prevention of gout.
iclofenac	25–50 mg three times a day	
aproxen	250–500 mg twice a day	
olchicine rophylaxis)	500 micrograms twice a day	Exact dosage depends on renal function.

NSAIDs are not licensed for the prevention of gout. NSAID usage may require the use of gastroprotective agents.

esting affected joints

Motion was found to exacerbate inflammation in joints with gout experimentally induced in dogs [Agudelo et al, 1972].

pplication of heat

Heat was found to aggravate inflammation in joints with gout experimentally induced in dogs [Dorwart et al, 1974].

What is the evidence supporting the use of NSAIDs for an acute attack of gout?

ffectiveness of NSAIDs

One placebo-controlled trial of 30 people with acute gout has compared an NSAID, tenoxicam, with placebo [Garcia de la Torre, 1987; Underwood, 2004].

- After 1 day, tenoxicam compared with placebo significantly increased the proportion of people who reported at least 50% reduction in pain.
- After 4 days, the response to tenoxicam was rated by the treating physician as 'good or excellent' more often than with placebo.

There is no RCT comparing an NSAID with colchicine in the treatment of gout [Schlesinger and Schumacher, 2004; Underwood, 2004].

We found 12 clinical trials that compared two different NSAIDs 'head-to-head'.

- No study reported any clinical advantage of one NSAID over another in terms of effectiveness.
- Evidence on adverse effects was inconsistent, although the largest study reported that indometacin (a non-selective inhibitor of COX) was associated with more drug-related adverse events than etoricoxib (a COX-2 selective inhibitor).

A review of RCTs comparing NSAIDs used for acute gout reported that in most reviewed studies recovery was faster in people treated with an NSAID than in a historical series of untreated people [Schlesinger and Schumacher, 2004].

ffect of aspirin on plasma urate

There is some concern about the use of aspirin in people with hyperuricaemia and/or gout [Schlesinger and Schumacher, 2004].

A review found that results from three observational studies are inconsistent, and concluded that there are no major concerns with the use of aspirin in people with gout [Schlesinger and Schumacher, 2004]. Case series have found that:

- Aspirin at more than 3 g/day is uricosuric [Yu and Gutman, 1959].
- Aspirin 1–2 g/day causes uric acid retention [Yu and Gutman, 1959].
- Aspirin 75–325 mg/day has variable effects on uric acid excretion [Caspi et al, 2000; Harris et al, 2000].

Which NSAID should I use?

- **There are eight NSAIDs licensed** in the United Kingdom for the treatment of acute gout.
  - **Diclofenac, naproxen, and indometacin** are recommended as preferred choices. They have a favourable adverse effect profile compared with other NSAIDs [CSM, 2002]. Naproxen and diclofenac are the most commonly used NSAIDs as reflected by their usage data [Prescription Pricing Authority, 2002]. Indometacin is associated with more GI adverse events than is naproxen or diclofenac, but has been the most widely studied in acute gout.
  - **Ketoprofen, piroxicam, and sulindac** are less preferred options, owing to their greater potential for GI toxicity, although they may prove effective in some individuals.
  - **Azapropazone** has a strong anti-inflammatory action but also is associated with the most GI toxicity [Hernández-Diaz and Rodriguez, 2000]. It should only be used on specialist advice, and when other less toxic drugs have proved ineffective.
  - **Etoricoxib,** a COX-2 selective NSAID, is licensed but is currently undergoing post-market surveillance (black triangle). It is associated with less GI toxicity than other NSAIDs licensed for gout, but there are concerns regarding the cardiovascular toxicities of this drug group, particularly when used for extended periods. The safety of COX-2 selective NSAIDs is currently being evaluated by the European Medicines Evaluation Agency (EMEA).

What is the evidence supporting the use of colchicine for an acute attack of gout?

Oral colchicine

- A review [Schlesinger and Schumacher, 2004] found one placebo-controlled RCT of colchicine treatment for acute gout [Ahern et al, 1987].
  - Colchicine (1 mg, then 0.5 mg every 2 hours until complete response or toxicity) was given to 22 people with acute gout. A placebo was given to 21 people. NSAIDs were not given.
  - After 48 hours, two-thirds of the people treated with colchicine had improved, whereas one third of the people taking placebo had improved.
  - Colchicine treatment resulted in more rapid improvement.
  - Colchicine was more effective when taken within 24 hours of the onset of an attack.
  - All people taking colchicine developed diarrhoea and/or vomiting: median time 24 hours (range 12–36); mean total dose 6.7 mg. People taking placebo did not experience diarrhoea or vomiting, although five of them became nauseous.

Table 4: Drug therapy options for the treatment of acute gout [Terkeltaub, 2003; BNF 48, 2004].

Drug	Typical regimen	Comments
NSAIDs*		
Diclofenac	50 mg three times a day	Diclofenac, naproxen, and indometacin are preferred NSAIDs, as they have relatively good safety profiles.
Naproxen	750 mg initially, followed by 250 mg three times a day	
Indometacin	50 mg three or four times a day	
Ketoprofen	100–200 mg daily in divided doses	Ketoprofen, piroxicam, and sulindac are less preferre NSAIDs, owing to potentially worse adverse-effect profiles.
Piroxicam	40 mg daily in divided doses	
Sulindac	200 mg twice a day	
Azapropazone	600 mg three times a day initially (then reduce to 1.2 g daily in divided doses)	Azapropazone should be used only on specialist advice, and when less toxic drugs have proved ineffective.
Etoricoxib	120 mg once a day	Black triangle — its place in treatment is currently unclear.
Colchicine	1 mg initially, followed by 500 micrograms every 2–3 hours until relief of pain is attained or vomiting or diarrhoea occurs, or until a total dose of 6 mg has been reached	Use only if there is a contraindication to NSAIDs. Lower doses may be as effective, and may be required in people with renal impairment.
Systemic corticosteroids		
Oral prednisolone	15 or 7.5 mg in the morning for 10 days	Suitable for acute gout where NSAIDs are contraindicated or ineffective
Intramuscular (IM) triamcinolone acetonide	40 mg injection	
IM methylprednisolone	40 mg injection	
Intra-articular (IA) corticosteroids†		
IA triamcinalone acetonide	40 mg/ml (large joints)	Suitable for acute gout where NSAIDs are contra-indicated or ineffective. Do not use in multiple joints (maximum of *two* joints should be treated at any one time), and exclude the possibility of septic arthritis.
IA methylprednisolone	40 mg/ml (large or medium joints)	
IA dexamethasone sodium phosphate	5 mg/ml (small joints)	
IA prednisolone acetate	25 mg/ml (small joints)	
IA hydrocortisone acetate	25 mg/ml (small joints)	
Analgesics		
Paracetamol	1 g up to four times a day	Paracetamol and codeine should be given separately s they can be titrated separately.
Codeine	20–60 mg up to four times a day	

* All NSAIDs have the potential to cause GI adverse effects and may require the addition of gastroprotective agents.
† Injection of joints should only be carried out by experienced healthcare professionals.

- Data from uncontrolled trials are consistent with the placebo-controlled RCT [Schlesinger and Schumacher, 2004].

Intravenous colchicine

- A review concluded that the risk of serious adverse events is so great that intravenous colchicine should not be used for acute gout [Schlesinger and Schumacher, 2004].

What is the evidence supporting the use of corticosteroids for an acute attack of gout?

Oral corticosteroids

- A prospective case series compared intravenous methylprednisolone with oral prednisone for treating people with acute gout who had contraindications to the use of NSAIDs [Groff et al, 1990].
  - Complete resolution of symptoms occurred within 7 days for 11 of 13 people, and within 10 days for the remaining 2 people.
  - In the 9 people who had fewer than 6 affected joints, doses of corticosteroid ranged from 20 to 50 mg/day and were tapered over 4–20 days.
  - No rebound attacks occurred when the steroids were stopped.
- Different dosing regimens have not been tested in clinical trials [Schlesinger and Schumacher, 2004].
- Accepted clinical practice in the UK is to use short courses of lower doses (e.g. prednisolone 15 mg daily or less) [BNF 48, 2004].
- Doses of 40–60 mg of prednisone are recommended to treat acute gout in people who are being treated with ciclosporin [Terkeltaub, 2003].

Intramuscular corticosteroids

- A review found one non-randomized clinical trial of treatments for acute gout that compared an intramuscular corticosteroid with an NSAID [Schlesing and Schumacher, 2004].
  - Oral indometacin 50 mg three times a day was compared with intramuscular triamcinolone acetate 50 mg in a clinical trial of 27 people presenting withi 5 days of an attack of gouty arthritis [Alloway et al, 1993].
  - People with contraindications to therapy with indometacin received triamcinolone acetonide.
  - The mean time to resolution of symptoms was 8 days for people treated with indometacin and 7 days for people treated with triamcinolone acetate.
  - No adverse effects or episodes of rebound gout attack occurred with the triamcinolone acetonide therapy.

Intra-articular corticosteroids

- There is no controlled trial of intra-articular corticosteroids for acute attacks of gout [Schlesinger an Schumacher, 2004; Underwood, 2004].
- The use of intra-articular steroids in acute gouty arthrit is supported by expert opinion, based on clinical experience reported as case series [Gray et al, 1981; Fernandez et al, 1999; Nuki, 2002; Schlesinger and Schumacher, 2004].

Adrenocorticotropic hormone

- A review found three small clinical trials of adrenocorticotropic hormone (ACTH) for acute gout [Schlesinger and Schumacher, 2004].
- The evidence, although meagre, does not suggest that ACTH is superior to corticosteroids.

What is the evidence supporting dietary measures to prevent recurrent attacks of gout?

Moderating alcohol ingestion

- A study that followed 47,000 men over 12 years found that alcohol intake was strongly associated with an increased relative risk of gout. The risk varied according to type of alcoholic beverage: beer conferred a larger risk than spirits. Moderate wine drinking did not increase the risk [Choi et al, 2004a].
- A population survey found alcohol consumption to be predictive of gout in hyperuricaemic people irrespective of the level of plasma uric acid (OR 2.31, 95% CI 1.04 to 5.54) [Lin et al, 2000a].
- A prospective observational study of 233 men with raised plasma uric acid found that alcohol consumption was an independent predictor of the onset of gout (OR 3.45, 95% CI 1.58 to 7.56) [Lin et al, 2000b].

Moderating dietary ingestion of purines

- A study that followed 47,000 men over 12 years found increased relative risks (RR) for gout associated with high levels of consumption of meat and seafood (RR 1.41, 95% CI 1.07 to 1.86) and (RR 1.51, 95% CI 1.17 to 1.95) [Choi et al, 2004b].
  - The study found no evidence for increased risk of gout from eating vegetables with high purine content (peas, beans, lentils, spinach, mushrooms, oatmeal, and cauliflower) and concluded that moderate intake of purine-rich vegetables or protein is not associated with an increased risk of gout.
  - The study found that high levels of consumption of dairy products are associated with a decreased risk for gout.
- A case series of 15 people with gout found that a strict purine-free diet can reduce plasma uric acid by 15–20% [Nicholls and Scott, 1972] (cited in [Schlesinger and Schumacher, 2004]).

Avoiding weight gain, losing weight

- A prospective cohort study followed 12,150 men over 12 years and confirmed 730 cases of gout [Choi et al, 2005]. The authors concluded that higher adiposity and weight gain are strong risk factors for gout in men, while weight loss is protective.
- Table 5 and Table 6 outline the multivariate relative risks of gout associated with adiposity and weight gain respectively.
- A population survey found central obesity to be predictive of gout in hyperuricaemic people irrespective of the level of plasma uric acid (OR 2.43, 95% CI 1.14 to 5.29) [Lin et al, 2000a].
- A prospective observational study of 233 men with raised plasma uric acid found that excessive weight gain was an independent predictor of the onset of gout (OR 1.91, 95% CI 0.98 to 4.01) [Lin et al, 2000b].
- An observational study of a diet with restricted energy and high in complex carbohydrates and mono- and polyunsaturated fats was made in 13 non-diabetic obese men with gout [Dessein et al, 2000].

What is the evidence supporting the use of colchicine to prevent recurrent attacks of gout?

- Using colchicine to prevent recurrent attacks of gout was first advocated in 1936 [Cohen, 1936] (cited in [Schlesinger and Schumacher, 2004]).
- Several clinical trials of prophylactic colchicine have been reported, but all have methodological weaknesses [Schlesinger and Schumacher, 2004].
- No RCT has tested the use of colchicine alone for preventing recurrent gout [Schlesinger and Schumacher, 2004].
- The best evidence comes from an RCT of 51 people with recurrent gout [Paulus et al, 1974] (cited in [Schlesinger and Schumacher, 2004]).
  - Subjects were treated either with probenecid 1.5 g/day plus colchicine 1.5 mg/day, or with probenecid 1.5 g/day plus placebo.
  - Results were reported only for the 38 people who had a sustained reduction in plasma uric acid (on the grounds that the others were unlikely to be compliant).
  - There were 23 attacks of acute gout during the 109 person-months of therapy with probenecid plus colchicine, and 35 attacks of acute gout during the 94 person-months of therapy with probenecid plus placebo.

What is the evidence supporting the use of urate-lowering therapy to prevent recurrent attacks of gout?

Frequency of acute gout during the first months of urate-lowering therapy

- It has been postulated that treatments that lower plasma urate levels can precipitate an acute attack of gout, or prolong an attack in progress [Schlesinger and Schumacher, 2004].
- Published evidence to support this comes from case reports in three articles [Thompson et al, 1962; Yu and Gutman, 1964; Delbarre et al, 1966] (cited in [Schlesinger and Schumacher, 2004]). Most of the episodes of acute gout occurred while colchicine was being taken and/or dietary interventions were being applied.

Effects of urate-lowering therapy

- An open randomised trial followed 86 men with chronic gout who were given either allopurinol 300 mg/day or benzbromarone 100 mg/day [Perez-Ruiz et al, 1998]. (Note: benzbromarone is available only on a named-patient basis for people with moderate renal impairment and contraindications to allopurinol [Nuki, 2002].)
  - Plasma urate was reduced by 2.75 mg/dl in the allopurinol group and 5.04 mg/dl in the benzbromarone group.

Table 5: Multivariate relative risks of gout associated with adiposity.

body mass index (BMI)	Relative risk	95% confidence interval
21 to 22.9	1	—
25 to 29.9	1.95	1.44–2.65
30 to 34.9	2.33	1.62–3.36
35 or greater	2.97	1.73–5.10

p <0.001 for trend

Table 6: Multivariate relative risks of gout associated with weight gain.

Change in weight	Relative risk	95% confidence interval
Lost 10 lb or more since study baseline	0.61	0.40–0.92
Stable within 4 lb since 21 years old	1	—
Gained 30 lb or more since 21 years old	1.99	1.49–2.66

- Optimal plasma urate levels were achieved by 53% of the allopurinol group and 100% of the benzbromarone group.
- A trial (randomization unclear) in 183 people with gout compared allopurinol with uricosuric treatment [Weinberger et al, 1975] (cited in [Schlesinger and Schumacher, 2004]).
  - Attacks of gout ceased after at most 4 years in people treated with allopurinol; uricosuric treatment was not as effective.
- A clinical quasi-randomized trial in 37 people compared allopurinol with uricosuric treatment [Scott, 1966] (cited in [Schlesinger and Schumacher, 2004]).
  - The daily dose of allopurinol (300 mg, 12 men; 400 mg, 6 men; and 600 mg, 2 men) was determined by the plasma uric acid level.
  - Probenecid was started at 1 g/day and increased to 2 g/day after 2 weeks.
  - Sulfinpyrazone was switched for probenecid in 5 people who had adverse effects.
  - All people also received colchicine 0.5 mg 2–3 times a day for the first few months.
  - Mean plasma uric acid fell to 4.7 mg/dl (range 2.6–5.5) in the allopurinol group and 5.2 mg/dl (range 3.8–73) in the uricosuric group.
  - Clinical response was equivalent in the two groups; half of the people were free of acute gout at the final assessment.

How low should the target be for lowering plasma urate?

- Urate crystals persist in 58% of asymptomatic knees of people with non-tophaceous gout, despite lowering plasma uric acid to 0.43 mmol/l (7.1 mg/dl) [Bomalaski et al, 1986].
- A case series of 57 people with recurrent gout compared the clinical response to urate-lowering therapy in people whose plasma uric acid remained above (group A) or below (group B) the target of 0.36 mmol/l (6 mg/dl) [Li-Yu et al, 2001].
  - Urate crystals in joint aspirates were found in 14/16 people in group A, and in 7/16 people in group B.
  - The mean number of acute attacks of gout in the last year of follow-up was 6 for group A and 1 for group B.
- A cohort study found that attacks diminished once allopurinol was started, even before plasma uric acid levels returned to normal [Beutler et al, 2001] (cited in [Schlesinger and Schumacher, 2004]).

For how long should urate-lowering treatment be continued?

- Urate lowering on treatment with allopurinol is dose-dependent, yet many people are maintained on a fixed dose of allopurinol, usually 100 mg/day or 300 mg/day irrespective of plasma urate levels [Schlesinger and Schumacher, 2004].
- When allopurinol is stopped, urate levels rise, and acute attacks and tophi can occur [Levinson and Becker, 1993].
- An RCT that followed 50 people with gout for 2–4 years compared the use of continuous allopurinol with allopurinol used for 2 months a year [Bull and Scott, 1989].
  - From the third year of treatment, no further attack occurred in the continuously treated group, while gout recurred in people treated intermittently.

Why are sulfinpyrazone and probenecid not recommended?

Sulfinpyrazone

- **Sulfinpyrazone** lowers plasma urate by increasing renal excretion of uric acid, but is less favoured than allopurinol because of:
  - The greater effectiveness of allopurinol.
  - The increased risk of uric acid stones in the urinary tract (particularly if urinary volume is less than 1 ml/min).
  - The need to maintain adequate urinary volume and, initially, to alkalinize the urine to reduce the risk of stones.
  - The relative ineffectiveness of sulfinpyrazone in the presence of renal impairment [Conaghan and Day, 1994; Emmerson, 1996; van Doornum and Ryan, 2000].
- **Concurrent use of aspirin may reduce the effect of sulfinpyrazone.** Doses of aspirin as low as 700 mg when taken concurrently with sulfinpyrazone can cause an appreciable fall in uric acid excretion [Stockley, 2002]. The effect of lower doses is less certain; however, if low-dose aspirin is required, allopurinol should be used unless contraindicated.

Probenecid

- Probenecid is not specifically licensed for the management of gout. It is available in the United Kingdom on a named-patient basis only.

When is surgery required for tophi?

- A case report describes successful surgical removal of a large painful tophaceous nodule on the plantar aspect of the first metatarsophalangeal joint [Naas and Sanders, 1998]. Surgery relieved the pain and restored the ability to wear shoes and walk without discomfort.

References

NHS staff in England can link, free of charge, from references to full text journals by clicking on [Full text] on the PRODIGY website.

1. Agudelo, C.A., Schumacher, H.R. and Phelps, P. (1972) Effect of exercise on urate crystal-induced inflammation in canine joints. *Arthritis & Rheumatism* 15(6), 609–616.
2. Ahern, M.J., Reid, C., Gordon, T.P. et al (1987) Does colchicine work? The results of the first controlled study in acute gout. *Australian & New Zealand Journal of Medicine* 17(3), 301–304.
3. Alloway, J.A., Moriarty, M.J., Hoogland, Y.T. and Nashel, D.J. (1993) Comparison of triamcinolone acetonide with indomethacin in the treatment of acute gouty arthritis. *Journal of Rheumatology* 20(1), 111–113.
4. Bencardino, J.T. and Hassankhani, A. (2003) Calcium pyrophosphate dihydrate crystal deposition disease. *Seminars in Musculoskeletal Radiology* 7(3), 175–185.
5. Beutler, A.M., Rull, M., Schlesinger, N. et al (2001) Treatment with allopurinol decreases the number of acute gout attacks despite persistently elevated serum uric acid levels. *Clinical & Experimental Rheumatology* 19(5), 595.
6. BNF 48 (2004) *British National Formulary*. 48th edn. London: British Medical Association and Royal Pharmaceutical Society of Great Britain.
7. Bomalaski, J.S., Lluberas, G. and Schumacher, H.R., Jr. (1986) Monosodium urate crystals in the knee joint of patients with asymptomatic nontophaceous gout. *Arthritis & Rheumatism* 29(12), 1480–1484.
8. Bull, P.W. and Scott, J.T (1989) Intermittent control of hyperuricamia in the treatment of gout. *Journal of Rheumatology* 16(9), 1246–1248.
9. Campion, E.W., Glynn, R.J. and DeLabry, L.O. (1987) Asymptomatic hyperuricemia: risks and consequences in the Normative Aging Study. *American Journal of Medicine* 82(3), 421–426.

10. Caspi, D., Lubart, E., Graff, E. et al (2000) The effect of mini-dose aspirin on renal function and uric acid handling in elderly patients. *Arthritis & Rheumatism* **43**(1), 103–108.
11. Choi, H.K., Atkinson, K., Karlson, E.W. et al (2004a) Alcohol intake and risk of incident gout in men: a prospective study. *Lancet* **363**(9417), 1277–1281. [Full text]
12. Choi, H.K., Atkinson, K., Karlson, E.W. et al (2004b) Purine-rich foods, dairy and protein intake, and the risk of gout in men. *New England Journal of Medicine* **350**(11), 1093–1103. [Full text]
13. Choi, H.K., Atkinson, K., Karlson, E.W. and Curhan, G. (2005) Obesity, weight change, hypertension, diuretic use, and risk of gout in men: the health professionals follow-up study. *Archives of Internal Medicine* **165**(7), 742–748. [Full text]
14. Cohen, A. (1936) Gout. *American Journal of the Medical Sciences* **192**, 448–493.
15. Cohen, M.G. and Emmerson, B.T. (1998) Gout. In: Klippel, J.H., Dieppe, P., Arnett, F.C. et al (Eds.) *Rheumatology*. 2nd edn. London: St Louis, Mosby. 14.1–14.14.
16. Conaghan, P.G. and Day, R.O. (1994) Risks and benefits of drugs used in the management and prevention of gout. *Drug Safety* **11**(4), 252–258.
17. CSM (1994) Relative safety of oral non-aspirin NSAIDs. *Current Problems in Pharmacovigilance* **20**(Aug), 9–11.
18. CSM (2002) Non-steroidal anti-inflammatory drugs (NSAIDs) and gastrointestinal (GI) safety. *Current Problems in Pharmacovigilance* **28**(Apr), 5.
19. CSM (2005) *Withdrawal of co-proxamol products and interim updated prescribing information*. Committee on Safety of Medicines. www.mca.gov.uk [Accessed: 24/03/2005].
20. De Craen, A.J., Di Giulio, G., Lampe-Schoenmaeckers, J.E. et al (1996) Analgesic efficacy and safety of paracetamol-codeine combinations versus paracetamol alone: a systematic review. *British Medical Journal* **313**(7053), 321–325. [Full text]
21. Delbarre, F., Amor, B., Auscher, C. and de Gery, A. (1966) Treatment of gout with allopurinol. A study of 106 cases. *Annals of the Rheumatic Diseases* **25**(6), 627–633.
22. Dessein, P.H., Shipton, E.A., Stanwix, A.E. et al (2000) Beneficial effects of weight loss associated with moderate calorie/carbohydrate restriction, and increased proportional intake of protein and unsaturated fat on serum urate and lipoprotein levels in gout: a pilot study. *Annals of the Rheumatic Diseases* **59**(7), 539–543. [Full text]
23. Dorwart, B.B., Hansell, J.R. and Schumacher, H.R., Jr. (1974) Effects of cold and heat on urate crystal-induced synovitis in the dog. *Arthritis & Rheumatism* **17**(5), 563–571.
24. DTB (1995) Articular and periarticular corticosteroid injections. *Drug & Therapeutics Bulletin* **33**(9), 67–70. [Full text]
25. Dutch College of General Practitioners (2004) *NHG practice guideline 'gout'*. Dutch College of General Practitioners. http://nhg.artsennet.nl/upload/104/guidelines2/E72.htm [Accessed: 28/10/2004]. [Full text]
26. Emmerson, B.T. (1996) The management of gout. *New England Journal of Medicine* **334**(7), 445–451.
27. Fernandez, C., Noguera, R., Gonzalez, J.A. and Pascual, E. (1999) Treatment of acute attacks of gout with a small dose of intraarticular triamcinolone acetonide. *Journal of Rheumatology* **26**(10), 2285–2286.
28. Fessel, W.J. (1979) Renal outcomes of gout and hyperuricaemia. *American Journal of Medicine* **67**(1), 74–82.
29. Garcia de la Torre, I. (1987) Estudio doble-ciego paralelo, comparativo con tenoxicam vs placebo en artritis gotosa aguda [Spanish, double-blind parallel study comparing tenoxicam and placebo in acute gouty arthritis]. *Investigacion Medica Internacional* **14**, 92–97.
30. Gray, R.G, Tenenbaum, J. and Gottlieb, N.L. (1981) Local corticosteroid injection treatment in rheumatic disorders. *Seminars in Arthritis & Rheumatism* **10**(4), 231–254.
31. Groff, G.D., Franck, W.A. and Raddatz, D.A. (1990) Systemic steroid therapy for acute gout: a clinical trial and review of the literature. *Seminars in Arthritis & Rheumatism* **19**(6), 329–336.
32. Grove, M.L. (2005) *Personal communication. Target plasma urate levels*. Consultant rheumatologist, North Tyneside General Hospital: North Shields, UK.
33. Harris, M., Bryant, L.R., Danaher, P. and Alloway, J. (2000) Effect of low dose daily aspirin on serum urate levels and urinary excretion in patients receiving probenecid for gouty arthritis. *Journal of Rheumatology* **27**(12), 2873–2876.
34. Henry, D., Lim, L.L., Garcia-Rodriguez, L.A. et al (1996) Variability in risk of gastrointestinal complications with individual non-steroidal anti-inflammatory drugs: results of a collaborative meta-analysis. *British Medical Journal* **312**(7046), 1563–1566. [Full text]
35. Hernández-Diaz, S. and Rodriguez, L.A. (2000) Association between nonsteroidal anti-inflammatory drugs and upper gastrointestinal tract bleeding/perforation: an overview of epidemiologic studies published in the 1990s. *Archives of Internal Medicine* **160**(14), 2093–2099. [Full text]
36. Kot, T.V., Day, R.O. and Brooks, P.M. (1993) Preventing acute gout when starting allopurinol therpay: colchicine or NSAIDS? *Medical Journal of Australia* **159**(3), 182–184.
37. Levinson, D.J. and Becker, M.A. (1993) Clinical gout and the pathogenesis of hyperuricemia. In: McCarty, D.J. and Koopman, W.J. (Eds.) *Arthritis and allied conditions*. 12th edn. Philadelphia: Lea and Febriger. 1773–1818.
38. Lin, K.C., Lin, H.Y. and Chou, P. (2000a) Community based epidemiological study on hyperuricemia and gout in Kin-Hu, Kinmen. *Journal of Rheumatology* **27**(4), 1045–1050.
39. Lin, K.C., Lin, H.Y. and Chou, P. (2000b) The interaction between uric acid level and other risk factors on the development of gout among asymptomatic hyperuricemic men in a prospective study. *Journal of Rheumatology* **27**(6), 1501–1505.
40. Li-Yu, J., Clayburne, G., Sieck, M. et al (2001) Treatment of chronic gout. Can we determine when urate stores are depleted enough to prevent attacks of gout? *Journal of Rheumatology* **28**(3), 577–580.
41. Logan, J.A., Morrison, E. and McGill, P.E. (1997) Serum uric acid in acute gout. *Annals of the Rheumatic Diseases* **56**(11), 696–697. [Full text]
42. Marshall, W.J. (2000) *Clinical chemistry*. 4th edn. London: Mosby.
43. MeReC (1993) Combination analgesics. *MeReC Bulletin* **4**(12), 45–48.
44. Mikuls, T.R., MacLean, C.H., Olivieri, J. et al (2004) Quality of care indicators for gout management. *Arthritis & Rheumatism* **50**(3), 937–943.
45. Mikuls, T.R., Farrar, J.T., Bilker, W.B. et al (2005) Gout epidemiology: results from the UK General

Practice Research Database, 1990–1999. *Annals of the Rheumatic Diseases* **64**(2), 267–272.

46. Moore, R.A. and McQuay, H.J. (1997) Single-patient data meta-analysis of 3453 postoperative patients: oral tramadol versus placebo, codeine and combination analgesics. *Pain* **69**(3), 287–294.
47. Moore, A., Collins, S., Carroll, D. and McQuay, H. (1997) Paracetamol with and without codeine in acute pain: a quantitative systematic review. *Pain* **70**(2–3), 193–201.
48. Morris, I., Varughese, G. and Mattingly, P. (2003) Colchicine in acute gout. *British Medical Journal* **327**(7426), 1275–1276. [Full text]
49. Naas, J.E. and Sanders, L.J. (1998) Chronic tophaceous gout in a patient with a history of allopurinol toxicity. *Cutis* **62**(5), 239–241. [Full text]
50. NICE (2001) *Guidance on the use of cyclo-oxygenase (Cox) II selective inhibitors, celecoxib, rofecoxib, meloxicam and etodolac for osteoarthritis and rheumatoid arthritis*. Technology appraisal no. 27. National Institute for Health and Clinical Excellence. www.nice.org.uk [Accessed: 16/10/2003].
51. Nicholls, A. and Scott, J.T. (1972) Effect of weight-loss on plasma and urinary levels of uric acid. *Lancet* **2**(7789), 1223–1224.
52. Nuki, G. (2002) Gout. *Medicine* **30**(9), 71–77.
53. O'Dell, J.R. (1983) Gout in Heberden's nodes. *Arthritis & Rheumatism* **26**(11), 1413–1414.
54. Paulus, H.E., Schlosstein, L.H., Godfrey, R.G. et al (1974) Prophylactic colchicine therapy of intercritical gout. A placebo-controlled study of probenecid-treated patients. *Arthritis & Rheumatism* **17**(5), 609–614.
55. Perez-Ruiz, F., Alonso-Ruiz, A., Calabozo, M. et al (1998) Efficacy of allopurinol and benzbromarone for the control of hyperuricaemia. A pathogenic approach to the treatment of primary chronic gout. *Annals of the Rheumatic Diseases* **57**(9), 545–549. [Full text]
56. Prescription Pricing Authority (2002) *Analgesics and NSAIDs prescribing*. Prescription Pricing Authority. www.ppa.org.uk [Accessed: 21/01/2005].
57. Rostom, A., Wells, G., Tugwell, P. et al (2002) *Prevention of NSAID-induced gastroduodenal ulcers (Cochrane Review)*. The Cochrane Library. Issue 4. Chichester, UK: John Wiley & Sons, Ltd. www.nelh.nhs.uk/cochrane.asp [Accessed: 04/04/2005]. [Full text]
58. Rott, K.T. and Agudelo, C.A. (2003) Gout. *Journal of the American Medical Association* **289**(21), 2857–2860. [Full text]
59. Schlesinger, N. (2004) Management of acute and chronic gouty arthritis: present state-of-the-art. *Drugs* **64**(21), 2399–2416.
60. Schlesinger, N. and Schumacher, R. (2004) Gout. In: Tugwell, P., Shea, B., Boers, M. et al (Eds.) *Evidence-based rheumatology*. London: BMJ Books. 65–95.
61. Schlesinger, N., Detry, M.A., Holland, B.K. et al (2002) Local ice therapy during bouts of acute gouty arthritis. *Journal of Rheumatology* **29**(2), 331–334.
62. Scott, J.T. (1966) Comparison of allopurinol and probenecid. *Annals of the Rheumatic Diseases* **25**(6), 623–626.
63. Shekarriz, B. and Stoller, M. (2002) Uric acid nephrolithiasis: current concepts and controversies. *Journal of Urology* **168**(4 Pt 1), 1307–1314.
64. Stavrou, C., Pierides, A., Zouvani, I. et al (1998) Medullary cystic kidney disease with hyperuricemia and gout in a large Cypriot family: no allelism with nephronophthisis type 1. *American Journal of Medical Genetics* **77**(2), 149–154.
65. Stockley, I.H. (Ed.) (2002) *Drug interactions*. 6th edn. London: The Pharmaceutical Press.
66. Terkeltaub, R.A. (2003) Gout. *New England Journal of Medicine* **349**(17), 1647–1655. [Full text]
67. Thompson, G.R., Duff, I.F., Robinson, W.D. et al (1962) Long term uricosuric therapy in gout. *Arthritis & Rheumatism* **5**, 384–396.
68. Underwood, M. (2004) *Gout*. Clinical Evidence. Volume 11. www.clinicalevidence.com [Accessed: 03/02/2005].
69. van Doornum, S. and Ryan, P.F. (2000) Clinical manifestations of gout and their management. *Medical Journal of Australia* **172**(10), 493–497.
70. Wallace, S.L., Robinson, H., Masi, A.T. et al (1977) Preliminary criteria for the classification of the acute arthritis of primary gout. *Arthritis & Rheumatism* **20**(3), 895–900.
71. Weinberger, A., Schreiber, M., Sperling, O. and DeVeris, A. (1975) Comparative evaluation of uricosuric and allopurinol treatment in a series of 183 gouty patients. *International Reviews in Rheumatolog* **5**, 681–685.
72. Yu, T.F. and Gutman, A.B. (1959) Study of the paradoxical effects of salicylate in low, intermediate and high dosage on the renal mechanisms for excretior of urate in man. *Journal of Clinical Investigation* **38**(8 1298–1315.
73. Yu, T.F. and Gutman, A.B. (1964) Effect of allopurinc (4-hydroxypyrazolo(3, 4-d)pyrimidine) on serum and urinary uric acid in primary and secondary gout. *American Journal of Medicine* **37**, 885–898.
74. Yu, T.F. and Gutman, A.B. (1967) Principles of curren management of primary gout. *American Journal of the Medical Sciences* **254**(6), 893–907.

PRODIGY GUIDANCE

Haemorrhoids

Last revised in July 2005
www.prodigy.nhs.uk/guidance.asp?gt=Haemorrhoids

Applies to people over the age of 16 years

This guidance covers the primary care management of simple (first- and second-degree) haemorrhoids.

This guidance does not cover the management of other perianal conditions, or the treatment of other causes of rectal bleeding, or offer detailed surgical information.

There is separate PRODIGY guidance for *Anal fissure, Constipation,* and *Pruritus ani.*

Goals

- To relieve the symptoms of haemorrhoids
- To prevent worsening of symptomatic haemorrhoids, including prolapse, where possible
- To prevent recurrence of the symptoms of haemorrhoids

Contents

Scenarios

- Haemorrhoids p.871

Extended Information, p. 873

Haemorrhoids

Which therapy?

- **Relieve constipation and ensure soft stools:**
  - Recommend an increase in dietary fibre and fluid intake (wholemeal foods, bran, vegetables, etc., with 8 glasses/12 cups or more of caffeine-free fluid a day).
  - Consider fibre supplements (bulk-forming agents) to enhance the dietary fibre.
- **Consider symptomatic treatment:**
  - Soothing preparations (e.g. bismuth oxide, bismuth subgallate, peru balsam, zinc oxide, and witch-hazel) may help to relieve local irritation.
  - Preparations containing anaesthetics may help relieve pain, burning, and itching.
  - Preparations containing topical corticosteroids reduce inflammation and pain.
- **For painful thrombosed haemorrhoids:**
  - Presenting within 72 hours of onset of pain: consider urgent referral for excision.
  - Presenting more than 72 hours after onset of pain: recommend analgesia, bed rest, cold compresses, or warm baths.
  - Recommend a high-fibre diet and increased fluid intake to prevent recurrence.
- **Prescribe paracetamol or ibuprofen** if the haemorrhoids are painful.

Practical prescribing points

For further information see the *Medicines Compendium* (www.medicines.org.uk) or the *British National Formulary* (www.bnf.org).

Bulk-forming laxatives

- Advise the person that bulk-forming agents will take 2–3 days to relieve constipation and may take up to 6 weeks to improve symptoms of haemorrhoids.
- Advise an adequate fluid intake for people taking bulk-forming agents. Powder and granule forms should be mixed with at least 250 ml of fluid and taken immediately; an additional 250 ml of fluid is recommended to increase efficacy and prevent intestinal obstruction.
  - Ensure that there is adequate supervision of fluid intake in frail elderly or immobile people.
- Advise people not to take bulk-forming agents before going to bed.

Topical preparations

- Exclude local infection before recommending products containing a topical corticosteroid.
- Advise people that they should limit the use of anaesthetics and corticosteroids to a maximum of 7 days, to minimize skin sensitization and allergic reactions.

Analgesia

- Ibuprofen may cause gastrointestinal irritation and occasionally gastrointestinal haemorrhage — avoid if there is a history of peptic ulceration. Ibuprofen may worsen asthma, hypertension, renal impairment, or cardiac failure.

Follow-up advice

- Follow-up in primary care is not usually necessary.

Should I refer or investigate?

Refer?

- **Urgent referral is recommended for:**
  - Profuse bleeding
  - Severely painful thrombosed haemorrhoids
  - Diagnostic uncertainty
- **Routine referral is recommended for:**
  - Persistent bleeding
  - Severe prolapse
  - Haemorrhoids affecting daily living
  - Note: haemorrhoids in pregnancy usually resolve after the baby is born; reassessment for referral may be necessary if they persist after the delivery.
- **Referral guidelines for suspected cancer** published by the National Institute for Health and Clinical Excellence (NICE) [NICE, 2005] recommend that people who present with symptoms and signs suggestive of colorectal or anal cancer (see Table 1) are urgently referred to a team specialising in the management of lower gastrointestinal cancer (depending on local arrangements).

Patient information leaflets

The following PILs are available at www.prodigy.nhs.uk

- Constipation in Adults

Table 1: Guidelines for urgent referral of suspected lower gastrointestinal cancer.

Person	Symptoms and signs
Aged 40 years and older	Rectal bleeding with a change in bowel habit towards looser stools and/or increased stool frequency persisting 6 weeks or more.
Aged 60 years and older	Rectal bleeding persisting for 6 weeks or more without a change in bowel habit and without anal symptoms. A change in bowel habit to looser stools and/or more frequent stools persisting for 6 weeks or more without rectal bleeding.
Of any age	A right abdominal mass consistent with involvement of the large bowel. A palpable rectal mass (intraluminal and not pelvic; a pelvic mass outside the bowel would warrant an urgent referral to a urologist or gynaecologist).
Woman (not menstruating)	Unexplained iron deficiency anaemia and a haemoglobin 10 g/100 ml or below.*
Man of any age	Unexplained iron deficiency anaemia and a haemoglobin 11 g/100 ml or below.*

*Anaemia considered on the basis of history and examination in primary care not to be related to other sources of blood loss (e.g. ingestions of NSAIDs) or blood dyscrasia.

H

- Fibre in the Diet
- Haemorrhoids (Piles)
- Medicines - Name Changes of Medicines

Shared decision making

- Haemorrhoids (piles) often improve if you are not constipated or do not strain on the toilet.
- **To keep the faeces soft** and to avoid constipation:
  - **Take in plenty of fibre** by eating lots of fruit, vegetables, cereals, wholemeal bread, etc.
  - **Have lots to drink.** Adults should aim to drink at least two litres (10–12 cups) of fluid per day. (Preferably, these should be mostly non-caffeine drinks, that is, not much tea or coffee.)
  - **Fibre supplements** and 'bulk-forming' agents such as bran, ispaghula, methylcellulose, or sterculia can help, if a high-fibre diet is not bringing about improvement.
  - **Avoid painkillers that contain codeine** such as co-codamol.
- **To ease any pain or other symptoms:**
  - **Warm baths** are soothing.
  - **Bland soothing creams, ointments, or suppositories** may ease discomfort. They can be used as often as needed.
  - **An anaesthetic cream or ointment** may ease the pain. Use for no more than 5–7 days.
  - **A steroid cream or ointment** is sometimes used if there is a lot of inflammation around the haemorrhoid.
  - **Paracetamol** or ibuprofen may help to ease any pain.
- Very painful haemorrhoids may be eased by an ice pack or strong painkillers or both.
- Surgery may be needed if haemorrhoids remain troublesome.

Drug rationale

Drugs not included

- **Bran supplements** are no longer included as the only commercially available medicinal product containing bran (Trifyba) has been discontinued.
- **Stimulant laxatives** are not appropriate for treating chronic constipation associated with haemorrhoids. They are indicated only for intermittent or short-term relief, as chronic use can lead to fluid and electrolyte imbalance, colonic atony, and tolerance to their effects.
- **Osmotic laxatives** are reserved for second-line use when other laxatives have failed to produce an effect. In addition to being expensive, they commonly cause flatulence, bloating, and cramping. Many people find them unpalatable.

Drugs included

- **Bulk-forming agents** including ispaghula husk, sterculia, and methylcellulose are included. Clinically there is little to choose between the different products.
  - Ispaghula and sterculia are the bulk-forming agents of choice.
    - Since convenience of use is important if people are to adhere to long-term treatment, only products available in sachets are included.
    - Ispaghula sachets are available in a variety of flavours — a generic prescription is included so that the person can choose the flavour at the time of dispensing.
  - Methylcellulose is less preferred because the large number of tablets that need to be taken may reduce compliance.
- **All topical product combinations** available on prescription as ointments, creams, or suppositories, and containing varying amounts of astringent, steroid, or local anaesthetic are offered. Where identical products are available, the least expensive is offered. There is no good evidence to recommend one product above another, and choice will be governed by the patient's preference and any previous sensitivity reactions.

Prescriptions

Non-drug management

Advice only: high-fibre diet and OTC purchase

- Age from 16 years onwards
- Food rich in fibre taken with plenty to drink, prevents constipation and helps haemorrhoids to settle. Every day, eat more cereals, wholemeal bread, potatoes, fruit and vegetables (with their skins on if possible), and pulses (peas, beans, lentils). Build fibre intake up gradually until it is right for you. Always drink plenty of liquid. Try to drink at least 12 cups (8 glasses or mugs) of liquid a day. There are lots of products available from the Pharmacist which may help your problem. They are: a) Soothing medicines b) Soothing medicines with an anaesthetic c) Soothing medicines with an anti-inflammatory (steroid). You should only use these for a few days at a time.

Bulk-forming agents

Ispaghula 3.5g s/f sachets (Fybogel or Ispagel Orange)

- Age from 16 years onwards
- Ispaghula husk 3.5g s/f granules. Take the contents of one sachet (mixed in a glass of water) each morning and evening; supply 60 sachets; NHS Cost £4.24; OTC Cost £7.74.

Ispaghula 3.4g s/f sachets (Regulan)

- Age from 16 years onwards
- Ispaghula husk 3.4g s/f powder. Take the contents of one sachet (mixed in a glass of water) 1 to 3 times a day; supply 60 sachets; NHS Cost £3.94; OTC Cost £6.94.

Sterculia 62% sachets (Normacol)

- Age from 16 years onwards
- Sterculia 62% granules. Take the contents of one to two sachets, once or twice a day after meals. Wash down with plenty of water without chewing; supply 60 sachets NHS Cost £5.19; OTC Cost £9.15.

Sterculia 62% and frangula 8% sachets (Normacol Plus)
- Age from 16 years onwards
- Sterculia62%+frangula8% granules. Take the contents of one to two sachets, once or twice a day after meals. Wash down with plenty of water without chewing; supply 60 sachets; NHS Cost £5.56; OTC Cost £9.80.

Methylcellulose 500mg tablets
- Age from 16 years onwards
- Methylcellulose 500mg tablets. Take three to six tablets (with two glasses of water) each morning and evening; supply 224 tablets; NHS Cost £5.38; OTC Cost £9.50.

Bland soothing products

Anusol cream
- Age from 16 years onwards
- Anusol cream. Apply each morning and night, and after a bowel movement; supply 23 grams; NHS Cost £1.88; OTC Cost £3.15.

Anusol ointment
- Age from 16 years onwards
- Anusol ointment. Apply each morning and night, and after a bowel movement; supply 25 grams; NHS Cost £1.88; OTC Cost £3.15.

Anusol suppositories
- Age from 16 years onwards
- Anusol suppositories. Insert one suppository into the rectum each morning and night, and after a bowel movement; supply 24 suppositories; NHS Cost £3.15; OTC Cost £5.29.

Topicals: steroid (S) / steroid+local anaesthetic (S+A)

Anusol-HC ointment (S)
- Age from 16 years onwards
- Anusol-HC ointment. Apply each morning and night, and after a bowel movement; supply 30 grams; NHS Cost £2.66.

Anugesic-HC cream (S+A)
- Age from 16 years onwards
- Anugesic-HC cream. Apply each morning and night, and after a bowel movement; supply 30 grams; NHS Cost £3.71.

Proctosedyl ointment (S+A)
- Age from 16 years onwards
- Proctosedyl ointment. Apply twice a day, and after a bowel movement; supply 30 grams; NHS Cost £7.00.

Scheriproct ointment (S+A)
- Age from 16 years onwards
- Scheriproct ointment. Apply twice a day until symptoms improve, then reduce to once a day; supply 30 grams; NHS Cost £3.00.

Ultraproct ointment (S+A)
- Age from 16 years onwards
- Ultraproct ointment. Apply twice a day until symptoms improve, then reduce to once a day; supply 30 grams; NHS Cost £4.57.

Uniroid-HC ointment (S+A)
- Age from 16 years onwards
- Uniroid-HC ointment. Apply each morning and night, and after a bowel movement; supply 30 grams; NHS Cost £4.23.

Xyloproct ointment (S+A)
- Age from 16 years onwards
- Xyloproct ointment. Apply 2 to 3 times a day until symptoms improve; supply 20 grams; NHS Cost £2.26.

Suppositories: steroid (S) / steroid+local anaesthetic (S+A)

Anusol-HC suppositories (S)
- Age from 16 years onwards
- Anusol-HC suppositories. Insert one suppository into the rectum each morning and night, and after a bowel movement; supply 12 suppositories; NHS Cost £1.87.

Anugesic-HC suppositories (S+A)
- Age from 16 years onwards
- Anugesic-HC suppositories. Insert one suppository into the rectum each morning and night, and after a bowel movement; supply 12 suppositories; NHS Cost £2.69.

Proctosedyl suppositories (S+A)
- Age from 16 years onwards
- Proctosedyl suppositories. Insert one suppository into the rectum each morning and night, and after a bowel movement; supply 12 suppositories; NHS Cost £3.00.

Scheriproct suppositories (S+A)
- Age from 16 years onwards
- Scheriproct suppositories. Insert one suppository into the rectum once a day (after a bowel movement); supply 12 suppositories; NHS Cost £1.41.

Ultraproct suppositories (S+A)
- Age from 16 years onwards
- Ultraproct suppositories. Insert one suppository into the rectum once a day (after a bowel movement) for up to 7 days. Then reduce to one on alternate days for 7 days; supply 12 suppositories; NHS Cost £2.15.

Uniroid-HC suppositories (S+A)
- Age from 16 years onwards
- Uniroid-HC suppositories. Insert one suppository into the rectum each morning and night, and after a bowel movement; supply 12 suppositories; NHS Cost £1.91.

Extended Information

Background information

- What is it? p.873
- How common is it? p.874
- How do I know my patient has it? p.874
- What else might it be? p.874
- Complications and prognosis p.875

What is it?

- **Haemorrhoidal tissues** are part of the normal anatomy of the distal rectum and anal canal. They originate either above the dentate line (internal) or below the dentate line (external).
  - Internal haemorrhoids (originating from the internal haemorrhoidal plexus) are cushions of vascular and connective tissue that are lined with rectal mucosa.
  - External haemorrhoids (originating from the external haemorrhoidal plexus) are vascular complexes underlying the richly innervated anoderm.
- **Normal haemorrhoidal tissue** is thought to contribute to anal continence by acting as a compressible lining that allows the anus to close completely, and to protect the anal canal from direct trauma by engorging with blood during defecation.
- **The disease state of 'haemorrhoids'** occurs when haemorrhoids become symptomatic as a result of enlargement or pathological change.
- **Haemorrhoids become symptomatic** as the result of chronic engorgement of the internal complex which causes enlarged, displaced vascular cushions within the anal canal and distal rectum. The exact cause of the pathological changes to the haemorrhoidal tissues that

H

lead to symptoms is uncertain. Proposed factors include constipation, diarrhoea, prolonged straining, pregnancy, derangement of the internal sphincter, hereditary factors, and diet.

- **Internal haemorrhoids** are classified according to the degree of prolapse, although this may not always reflect the severity of symptoms:
  - First-degree (project into the lumen of the anal canal but do not prolapse)
  - Second-degree (prolapse on straining with spontaneous reduction)
  - Third-degree (prolapse on straining and require manual reduction)
  - Fourth-degree (prolapsed and incarcerated, and cannot be reduced)
- **External haemorrhoids** lie under the perianal skin just inside and outside the anal verge below the dentate line. They may be visible on external examination. External haemorrhoids become symptomatic as a result of thrombosis (perianal haematoma).
- **People can have internal and external haemorrhoids at the same time.**
- **Skin tags** may result from repeated episodes of dilatation and thrombosis of external haemorrhoids causing enlargement of the overlying skin. They are common and should not be confused with external haemorrhoids as they do not contain dilated blood vessels. They may trap moisture and cause perianal irritation as well as interfering with anal hygiene.

[Grendell et al, 1996; Nisar and Scholefield, 2003; American Gastroenterological Association, 2004a; Kann and Whitlow, 2004]

How common is it?

- **Estimates of prevalence vary widely,** as anorectal symptoms are often wrongly attributed to haemorrhoids.
- **Nearly half the population** will experience at least one haemorrhoidal episode at some point during their lives [Hussain, 2001].
- **Prevalence is equal between the sexes,** although men are more likely to report haemorrhoids to their GP.
- **Prevalence generally increases with age** until the seventh decade.
- **Prevalence is higher in pregnant women** than in non-pregnant women of the same age [Quijano and Abalos, 2003].

[Alonso-Coello and Castillejo, 2003; Quijano and Abalos, 2003]

How do I know my patient has it?

Assessment

- **Most people with anorectal symptoms will ascribe their symptoms to haemorrhoids.** A thorough history and physical examination is therefore necessary to rule out other diagnoses (see *What else might it be?*).
- **A detailed history should include:** the colour and character of bleeding, temporal relationships between symptoms and defecation, bowel symptoms (e.g. constipation, diarrhoea), presence of mucus, exacerbating factors, and factors related to the relief of symptoms.
- **Assessment should include** a visual inspection with the person in the prone jack-knife or left lateral decubitus position, and a digital rectal examination.
- **Proctoscopy (or anoscopy) should be performed to confirm or refute the diagnosis of haemorrhoids,** unless there is isolated rectal bleeding in small amounts in an otherwise fit young person only associated with straining at stool or significant constipation, or a previous diagnosis of haemorrhoids with no new symptoms.
  - Where the facilities or expertise are not available to perform these investigations in primary care, the person may need to be referred for assessment.

[Nisar and Scholefield, 2003; Kann and Whitlow, 2004]

Internal haemorrhoids

Symptoms

- Symptoms experienced depend on the severity or degree of the haemorrhoid.
  - First-degree: painless bleeding
  - Second-degree: mild discomfort, bleeding
  - Third-degree: pain, bleeding, mucus discharge
  - Fourth-degree: pain, bleeding, possible thrombosis, and strangulation
- **Bleeding** often occurs with defecation, and is bright red. It can vary from streaks on the toilet paper to blood dripping into the toilet. Blood may be seen on the outside of the stool but is not mixed in with the stool.
- **Anal itching and irritation** may result from chronic mucus discharge irritating the perianal skin.
- **A sense of rectal fullness or discomfort** may result when prolapse occurs with bowel movement.
- **Pain** is rarely experienced, unless the haemorrhoid prolapses into the anal canal and becomes swollen, incarcerated, and thrombosed.
- **Soiling** may occur with third- or fourth-degree haemorrhoids as a result of impaired continence or mucus discharge.

Signs

- **The perineum may appear normal** if there is a non-prolapsed internal haemorrhoid. These haemorrhoids are also difficult to feel on digital rectal examination.
- **The perineum may be macerated** from chronic mucus discharge causing local irritation.
- **Proctoscopy** may reveal tissue with evidence of chronic venous dilatation, friability, mobility, and squamous metaplasia.
- **Bluish, soft bulging** vessels covered by mucosa may be seen on examination if internal haemorrhoids have prolapsed.

External haemorrhoids

Symptoms

- **External haemorrhoids do not usually cause symptoms** unless thrombosis occurs, in which case they may cause acute severe pain.
- **The pain of a thrombosed haemorrhoid** usually peaks 48–72 hours after onset, and is self-limited to 7–10 days.
- **Bleeding** may occur if the clot erodes through the skin. This may be infrequent and is often evident on underwear.

Signs

- **Bluish, soft bulging** vessels covered by skin (anoderm) may be seen.

[Eastwood and Avunduk, 1994; Orkin et al, 1999; Hussain, 1999; Hussain, 2001; Balasubramaniam and Kaiser, 2003; Nisar and Scholefield, 2003]

What else might it be?

It is important to exclude other causes of rectal bleeding, particularly:

- Colorectal malignancy — see *When should I refer someone with haemorrhoids?*
- Inflammatory bowel disease
- Diverticular disease
- Adenomatous polyps
- Ulcer
- Anal fissure

Other differential diagnoses include:

- Obstruction

- Rectal prolapse
- Condylomata acuminata (warts)
- Abscess
- Fistula
- Other causes of pruritus ani (e.g. threadworms, contact dermatitis)

[Grendell et al, 1996]

Complications and prognosis

Complications

Complications of haemorrhoids may form part of the presenting symptoms.

- **Ulceration** may result from the thrombosis of external haemorrhoids.
- **Skin tags** may result from repeated episodes of dilatation and thrombosis causing enlargement of the overlying skin.
- **Maceration** may occur due to mucus discharge.
- **Ischaemia, thrombosis, or gangrene** may develop from internal haemorrhoids that remain prolapsed.
- **Perianal sepsis** may occur rarely.
- **Anaemia** may rarely result from severe or persistent bleeding.

[Grendell et al, 1996; Kann and Whitlow, 2004]

Prognosis

- Haemorrhoids are a chronic problem; most people will have several episodes during their lifetime.
- Episodes tend to worsen with time, but it is generally considered a benign disorder with only about 10% of people needing surgery to alleviate symptoms.

[Alonso-Coello and Castillejo, 2003]

- **Thrombosed external haemorrhoids (perianal haematomas):** if not treated in 2–4 weeks the clot in the thrombosed vessels will either spontaneously drain through the thinned overlying skin, or be gradually reabsorbed, and the discomfort will gradually diminish [Kann and Whitlow, 2004].

Management issues

- How should I manage someone with haemorrhoids? p.875
- What conservative measures should I recommend? p.875
- How should I manage haemorrhoids in pregnant women? p.876
- When should I refer someone with haemorrhoids? p.876

How should I manage someone with haemorrhoids?

Management of a person with haemorrhoids will be largely governed by both the degree and severity of symptoms.

Internal haemorrhoids

- **First- or second-degree haemorrhoids** can usually be treated in primary care with conservative measures, as long as symptoms are minor and do not interfere with daily activities.
- **If symptoms are severe,** particularly if there is profuse bleeding, extreme pain, or severely affected daily living, refer to a colorectal surgeon.
- **Third- and fourth-degree haemorrhoids** will usually require surgery, and the person should be referred to a colorectal surgeon.

[Nagle and Rolandelli, 1996; Hussain, 2001; Nisar and Scholefield, 2003]

External haemorrhoids

- **If diagnosed within 72 hours of onset of pain,** severely painful thrombosed external haemorrhoids are best managed by excision under local anaesthetic. This will usually require urgent referral.
- **Incision and drainage of clot does relieve the pain but is not generally recommended** because the thrombosis commonly recurs and there may be persistent bleeding.
- **For thrombosed haemorrhoids presenting more than 72 hours after the onset of pain,** conservative measures should be recommended. Analgesia, bed rest, and cold compresses or warm baths may help relieve symptoms in people who have mild to moderate discomfort with symptoms that do not warrant referral.

[Orkin et al, 1999; American Gastroenterological Association, 2004b; Kann and Whitlow, 2004]

What conservative measures should I recommend?

Increased fibre intake

- **General measures to prevent constipation** will help to decrease straining during defecation and ease the symptoms of haemorrhoids, as well as reducing recurrence.
- **A high-fibre diet is recommended in people with haemorrhoidal symptoms.** Increasing fibre intake, together with increasing liquid intake, is an effective way of softening the stool and reducing constipation.
  - Increased dietary fibre can be achieved by eating more fruit, vegetables, bran, and wholemeal bread.
- **Fibre supplementation** with bulk-forming agents (e.g. ispaghula husk, sterculia, methylcellulose) can be used to enhance a high-fibre diet.
  - There is little to choose between the products in terms of efficacy, but a careful choice of product (based on formulation and flavour) will help compliance and therefore improve outcome.
- High-fibre diet and fibre supplements have been shown to reduce episodes of bleeding and discomfort in people with haemorrhoids, compared with placebo.
  - Increased fibre intake should *always* be accompanied by increased fluid intake. Advise the person to drink at least eight glasses (or 2 litres) of caffeine-free liquid per day.
  - Advise the person that bulk-forming agents will take 2–3 days to relieve constipation and may take up to 6 weeks to improve symptoms of haemorrhoids.

[Alonso-Coello and Castillejo, 2003; Balasubramaniam and Kaiser, 2003; Nisar and Scholefield, 2003]

Symptomatic relief with topical therapies

- **A wide range of topical preparations is available for the treatment of haemorrhoids.**
  - There is a general lack of controlled clinical trials of effectiveness for any of the topical products licensed for symptomatic treatment of haemorrhoids.
  - Many people report some empirical benefit with their use, especially local anaesthetics and topical corticosteroids.
- **Bland, soothing (astringent) preparations** (e.g. allantoin, bismuth oxide, bismuth subgallate, peru balsam, zinc oxide, and witch-hazel) may help to relieve local irritation.
- **Anaesthetic preparations** (e.g. lidocaine [lignocaine], cinchocaine, benzocaine, pramocaine) may alleviate pain, burning, and itching. They should be used for a few days only, because they may cause sensitization of the anal skin.

- **Products containing topical corticosteroids** may reduce inflammation and, consequently, pain.
  - Local infection must be excluded before use.
  - Short courses of up to 7 days only should be used. Prolonged use may lead to skin atrophy, contact dermatitis, and skin sensitization.
- **The cream or ointment base** may confer an additional emollient and soothing effect.
- **Sitz baths** (warm-water baths taken in the sitting position that cover only the hips and buttocks) are often recommended. Although there is no evidence to support their use, many people find that they have a soothing effect.

[Alonso-Coello and Castillejo, 2003; Nisar and Scholefield, 2003; BNF 48, 2004; Kann and Whitlow, 2004]

Behaviour modification

- **Advice on avoiding straining** should be emphasized.
- **Losing weight and increasing exercise** are thought to contribute to a healthier bowel habit, although there is no evidence that they relieve the symptoms of haemorrhoids.
- **Good perianal hygiene** may be helpful in providing symptomatic relief and preventing perineal dermatitis.
- There is no evidence for the role of certain foods in the pathogenesis or exacerbation of haemorrhoids.

[Nisar and Scholefield, 2003; Kann and Whitlow, 2004]

Phlebotonics

- Dietary supplementation with semi-synthetic flavonoids has been assessed in several studies. Flavonoids act primarily to increase venous tone, lymphatic drainage, and capillary resistance, and to normalize capillary permeability.
  - Results are currently inconsistent for micronized purified flavonoid fraction (MPFF), and further studies are needed to determine its place in therapy [Thanapongsathorn and Vajrabukka, 1992; Ho et al, 2000].
  - MPFF does not have a licence for use in the UK.

[Nisar and Scholefield, 2003; American Gastroenterological Association, 2004a]

How should I manage haemorrhoids in pregnant women?

- **If symptoms develop during pregnancy,** they usually resolve after delivery.
- Conservative measures are usually sufficient in the interim.
- Pregnant women with severe symptoms or haemorrhoidal complications should be referred.

When should I refer someone with haemorrhoids?

- Consider referral for sigmoidoscopy/colonoscopy in younger people with symptoms suggestive of alternative disease processes, for example altered bowel habit (especially diarrhoea), weight loss, or abnormal blood counts.
- People with extremely painful acutely thrombosed external haemorrhoids require urgent referral for excision under local anaesthetic.
- People with thrombosed haemorrhoids should also be referred when excessive bleeding is problematic, when there is chronic irritation or leakage, or when there is evidence of secondary infection.
- People with internal haemorrhoids that have prolapsed and become swollen, incarcerated, and thrombosed, should be referred for haemorrhoidectomy.
- People with first- or second-degree haemorrhoids that do not respond to conservative treatment should be referred for non-operative techniques (e.g. rubber band ligation, sclerotherapy, or infa-red photocoagulation) or surgery (haemorrhoidectomy).
- Referral guidelines for suspected cancer published by the National Institute for Health and Clinical Excellence (NICE) [NICE, 2005] recommend that people who present with symptoms and signs suggestive of colorectal or anal cancer (see Table 2) are urgently referred to a team specialising in the management of lower gastrointestinal cancer (depending on local arrangements).

Table 2: Guidelines for urgent referral of suspected lower gastrointestinal cancer.

Person	Symptoms and signs
Aged 40 years and older	Rectal bleeding with a change in bowel habit towards looser stools and/or increased stool frequency persisting 6 weeks or more.
Aged 60 years and older	Rectal bleeding persisting for 6 weeks or more without a change in bowel habit and without anal symptoms. A change in bowel habit to looser stools and/or more frequent stools persisting for 6 weeks or more without rectal bleeding.
Of any age	A right abdominal mass consistent with involvement of the large bowel. A palpable rectal mass (intraluminal and not pelvic; a pelvic mass outside the bowel would warrant an urgent referral to a urologist or gynaecologist).
Woman (not menstruating)	Unexplained iron deficiency anaemia and a haemoglobin 10 g/100 ml or below.*
Man of any age	Unexplained iron deficiency anaemia and a haemoglobin 11 g/100 ml or below.*

*Anaemia considered on the basis of history and examination in primary care not to be related to other sources of blood loss (e.g. ingestions of NSAIDs) or blood dyscrasia.

References

NHS staff in England can link, free of charge, from references to full text journals by clicking on [Full text] on the PRODIGY website.

1. Alonso-Coello, P. and Castillejo, M.M. (2003) Office evaluation and treatment of hemorrhoids. *Journal of Family Practice* **52**(5), 366–374.
2. American Gastroenterological Association (2004a) American Gastroenterological Association technical review on the diagnosis and treatment of hemorrhoids. *Gastroenterology* **126**(5), 1463–1473.
3. American Gastroenterological Association (2004b) American Gastroenterological Association medical position statement: diagnosis and treatment of hemorrhoids. *Gastroenterology* **126**(5), 1461–1462.
4. Balasubramaniam, S. and Kaiser, A.M. (2003) Management options for symptomatic hemorrhoids. *Current Gastroenterology Reports* **5**(5), 431–437.
5. BNF 48 (2004) *British National Formulary*. 48th edn. London: British Medical Association and Royal Pharmaceutical Society of Great Britain.
6. Eastwood, G.L. and Avunduk, C. (1994) Hemorrhoids and other anorectal disorders. In: *Manual of gastroenterology*. 2nd edn. Boston: Little, Brown and Co. 267–270.
7. Grendell, J.H., McQuaid, R. and Friedman, S.L. (1996) Anorectal diseases: hemorrhoids13. In: Grendell, J.H., McQuaid, R., Friedman, S.L. et al (Eds.) *Current diagnosis and treatment in gastroenterology*. Stamford, Conn.: Appleton & Lange. 415–418.
8. Ho, Y.H., Tan, M. and Seow-Choen, F. (2000) Micronized purified flavonidic fraction compared

favorably with rubber band ligation and fiber alone in the management of bleeding hemorrhoids: randomized controlled trial. *Diseases of the Colon & Rectum* **43**(1), 66–69.

. Hussain, J.N. (1999) Hemorrhoids. *Primary Care: Clinics in Office Practice* **26**(1), 35–51.

0. Hussain, J.N. (2001) Haemorrhoids: essentials of clinical management. *Australian Family Physician* **30**(1), 29–35.

1. Kann, B.R. and Whitlow, C.B. (2004) Hemorrhoids: diagnosis and management. *Techniques in Gastrointestinal Endoscopy* **6**(1), 6–11.

2. Nagle, D. and Rolandelli, R.H. (1996) Primary care office management of perianal and anal disease. *Primary Care; Clinics in Office Practice* **23**(3), 609–620.

3. NICE (2005) *Referral guidelines for suspected cancer – quick reference guide.* Clinical guideline 27. National Institute for Health and Clinical Excellence. www.nice.org.uk [Accessed: 01/07/2005].

14. Nisar, PJ. and Scholefield, J.H. (2003) Managing haemorrhoids. *British Medical Journal* **327**(7419), 847–851. [Full text]

15. Orkin, B.A, Schwartz, A.M. and Orkin, M. (1999) Hemorrhoids: what the dermatologist should know. *Journal of the American Academy of Dermatology* **43**(3 (Pt 1)), 449–456.

16. Quijano, C.E. and Abalos, E. (2003) *Conservative management of symptomatic and/or complicated haemorrhoids in pregnancy and the puerperium (Protocol for a Cochrane Review).* The Cochrane Library. Issue 1. Chichester, UK: John Wiley & Sons, Ltd. [Accessed: 20/04/2005]. [Full text]

17. Thanapongsathorn, W. and Vajrabukka, T. (1992) Clinical trial of oral diosmin (Daflon) in the treatment of hemorrhoids. *Diseases of the Colon & Rectum* **35**(11), 1085–1088.

H

PRODIGY GUIDANCE

Head lice

Last revised in February 2004
www.prodigy.nhs.uk/guidance.asp?gt=Head lice

Applies to people of all ages

This guidance covers the management of head lice infestation (pediculosis capitis).

There is separate PRODIGY guidance on the management of *Pubic lice* and *Scabies*.

Goals

- To eradicate live head lice and viable eggs

Contents

Scenarios

- First-line treatment p.878
- Treatment failure p.880

Extended Information, p. 882

Which scenario?

- **First-line treatment:** covers the management of people presenting for the first time.
- **Treatment failure:** covers the therapy options for people in whom first treatment failed.

First-line treatment

Which therapy?

- **ONLY treat if a live louse is found.**
- Check family and friends who may have had close head-to-head contact.
- **Advise the family that for treatment to be successful:**
  - The treatment must be used correctly.
  - All infested contacts must be treated simultaneously.
- **EITHER give two applications of insecticide, used 7 days apart.**
  - Use malathion, phenothrin, or permethrin.
  - Give one bottle per application. Give 2–3 bottles per application if the hair is thick.
  - Advise the family to inspect the hair and scalp (by detection combing) 2–3 days after the final application to check that treatment has been successful.
- **OR use wet combing (e.g. using the 'Bug Busting' method).** The family must be well motivated because of the time involved: it must be undertaken meticulously every 4 days for at least 2 weeks. If lice are found on the second, third, or fourth session, it should be continued until no lice have been seen for three consecutive sessions.
- **You may need to prescribe according to local policy.**

Factors affecting choice of insecticide

- **Product application time:** we suggest that products with a 12-hour application time (liquids and lotions) should be preferred, rather than those with very short application times (cream rinse or mousse).
- **Normal healthy skin:** use an alcohol-based product.
- **Asthma:** use an aqueous product, or a low-alcohol product.
- **Eczema or other broken skin conditions:** use an aqueous product. If there is other infestation present, this should be treated separately.
- **Pregnancy and breastfeeding:** use wet combing if possible. If an insecticide is necessary, use malathion (in an aqueous base).
- **Children under 2 years of age:** use wet combing if possible. Use an aqueous product if an insecticide is necessary (prescription-only for children under 6 months).

Practical prescribing points

For further information please see the *Medicines Compendium* (www.medicines.org.uk) or the *British National Formulary* (www.bnf.org). For further information regarding pregnancy, contact the National Teratology Information Service (telephone 0191 232 1525).

- **Lotions** (both alcohol-based and aqueous-based) need to be applied for 12 hours to be effective.
- **Advise patients that alcohol-based lotions are flammable.** Alcoholic lotions must be allowed to dry naturally. People should not use a hair dryer and must keep away from open fires, flames, and cigarettes while the lotion is on.

Follow-up advice

- **Insecticides:** advise the person to inspect the hair and scalp (by detection combing) 2–3 days after the second application to check for reinfestation or unsuccessful eradication. See the patient information leaflet *Checking for head lice* for information on how to carry out detection combing.
- **Wet combing** should be repeated every 4 days for at least 2 weeks. If lice are found on the second, third, or fourth session, it should be continued until no lice have been seen for three consecutive sessions.

Patient information leaflets

The following PILs are available at www.prodigy.nhs.uk

- Community Hygiene Concern
- Head Lice - Detection
- Head Lice - Full Overview
- Head Lice - Medicated Treatment
- Head Lice - Wet Combing Treatment

Shared decision making

- **Medicated treatments** for head lice include malathion, permethrin, and phenothrin. They come in various brands.
  - Follow the instructions on how to apply and how long to leave on the hair.
  - Do not go swimming before applying (chlorine may stop it working).
  - Do not use a hairdryer to dry hair after applying treatment.
  - Re-apply the same treatment after 7 days.

- Check that there are no lice 2–3 days after the second application.

Wet combing ('Bug Busting') is an alternative option:

- You need to do this twice a week for at least 2 weeks.
- It takes about 15 minutes each session.

Other points about treatment:

Check for lice in household members and close contacts. All infested contacts should be treated at the same time, to prevent reinfestation.

Alcohol-based lotions:

- Should not be used if you have asthma, eczema, or broken skin.
- Are flammable so do not use near fires or flames.

Pregnant or breastfeeding women — 'Bug Busting' is preferred. If a medicated treatment is needed, use water-based malathion lotion.

Children under 2 years — 'Bug Busting' is preferred. If a medicated treatment is needed, use a water-based lotion.

Drug rationale

Drugs not included

Shampoos are diluted too much in use to be effective and are therefore not included [BNF 45, 2003].

Carbaryl is no longer recommended as first-line therapy following reports of carcinogenicity in rodents after continuous dosing [Chief Medical Officer, 1995]. It should only be considered in cases of suspected resistance to all other insecticides [DTB, 1998].

Drugs included

Malathion, permethrin, and phenothrin are included. The current strategy to use two applications of insecticide 7 days apart is a pragmatic approach (off-licence). The second application of insecticide is used to kill nymphs emerging from eggs that survived the first application.

We suggest that the products with a shorter application time are less preferred. Although they are more convenient, there are concerns that shorter application times may help to promote the emergence of resistance. However, no clinical studies have been conducted to confirm that this is the case.

A prescription for wet combing using the Bug Buster kit is included in this scenario. Families using this method must be well motivated as it must be undertaken meticulously and regularly to be successful [DH, 2000]. It is suitable for people who do not wish to use insecticides.

Prescriptions

Usual treatment options

Alcohol-based lotion: malathion

- Age from 2 years onwards
- Malathion 0.5% alcoholic lotion. Apply to dry hair and scalp. Leave to dry naturally. Wash off after 12 hours. Repeat after 7 days; supply 100 ml; NHS Cost £4.44; OTC Cost £7.78.

Alcohol-based lotion: phenothrin

- Age from 2 years onwards
- Phenothrin 0.2% lotion. Apply to dry hair and scalp. Leave to dry naturally. Wash off after 12 hours. Repeat after 7 days; supply 100 ml; NHS Cost £4.44; OTC Cost £7.78.

Alcohol-based mousse: phenothrin (less preferred)

- Age from 2 years onwards
- Phenothrin 0.5% aerosol foam. Massage onto dry hair and scalp. Do not dry hair. Wash off after 30 minutes. Repeat after 7 days; supply 50 g; NHS Cost £2.27; OTC Cost £4.15.

Alcohol-based cream rinse: permethrin (less preferred)

- Age from 2 years onwards
- Permethrin 1% cream rinse. Apply to clean damp hair. Leave on for 10 minutes then wash off. Repeat after 7 days; supply 118 ml; NHS Cost £4.52; OTC Cost £7.58.

Wet combing (using the Bug Buster kit)

- Age from 2 years onwards
- Bug Buster kit. Use as directed on the right hand side of the prescription; supply 1 kit; NHS Cost £4.31; OTC Cost £7.59.

People with asthma

Aqueous-based liquid: malathion

- Age from 2 years onwards
- Malathion 0.5% aqueous liquid. Apply to dry hair and scalp. Leave to dry naturally. Wash off after 12 hours. Repeat after 7 days; supply 100 ml; NHS Cost £4.44; OTC Cost £7.78.

Aqueous-based liquid: phenothrin

- Age from 2 years onwards
- Phenothrin 0.5% aqueous liquid. Apply to dry hair and scalp. Leave to dry naturally. Wash off after 12 hours. Repeat after 7 days; supply 100 ml; NHS Cost £4.44; OTC Cost £7.78.

Alcohol-based cream rinse: permethrin (less preferred)

- Age from 2 years onwards
- Permethrin 1% cream rinse. Apply to clean damp hair. Leave on for 10 minutes then wash off. Repeat after 7 days; supply 118 ml; NHS Cost £4.52; OTC Cost £7.58.

Wet combing (using the Bug Buster kit)

- Age from 2 years onwards
- Bug Buster kit. Use as directed on the right hand side of the prescription; supply 1 kit; NHS Cost £4.31; OTC Cost £7.59.

People with eczema or broken skin

Aqueous-based liquid: malathion

- Age from 2 years onwards
- Malathion 0.5% aqueous liquid. Apply to dry hair and scalp. Leave to dry naturally. Wash off after 12 hours. Repeat after 7 days; supply 100 ml; NHS Cost £4.44; OTC Cost £7.78.

Aqueous-based liquid: phenothrin

- Age from 2 years onwards
- Phenothrin 0.5% aqueous liquid. Apply to dry hair and scalp. Leave to dry naturally. Wash off after 12 hours. Repeat after 7 days; supply 100 ml; NHS Cost £4.44; OTC Cost £7.78.

Wet combing (using the Bug Buster kit)

- Age from 2 years onwards
- Bug Buster kit. Use as directed on the right hand side of the prescription; supply 1 kit; NHS Cost £4.31; OTC Cost £7.59.

Pregnancy and breastfeeding

Wet combing (using the Bug Buster kit)

- Age from 12 to 60 years
- Bug Buster kit. Use as directed on the right hand side of the prescription; supply 1 kit; NHS Cost £4.31; OTC Cost £7.59.

Aqueous-based liquid: malathion

- Age from 12 to 60 years
- Malathion 0.5% aqueous liquid. Apply to dry hair and scalp. Leave to dry naturally. Wash off after 12 hours. Repeat after 7 days; supply 100 ml; NHS Cost £4.44.

Children under 2 years of age

Wet combing (using the Bug Buster kit)

- Age under 23 months
- Bug Buster kit. Use as directed on the right hand side of the prescription; supply 1 kit; NHS Cost £4.31; OTC Cost £7.59.

Aqueous-based liquid: malathion

- Age from 1 month to 23 months
- Malathion 0.5% aqueous liquid. Apply to dry hair and scalp. Leave to dry naturally. Wash off after 12 hours. Repeat after 7 days; supply 50 ml; NHS Cost £1.85.

Aqueous-based liquid: phenothrin

- Age from 1 month to 23 months
- Phenothrin 0.5% aqueous liquid. Apply to dry hair and scalp. Leave to dry naturally. Wash off after 12 hours. Repeat after 7 days; supply 50 ml; NHS Cost £2.22.

Treatment failure

Which therapy?

- **ONLY re-treat if a live louse is found.**
- Check family and friends who may have had close head-to-head contact.
- **Advise the family that for treatment to be successful:**
  - The treatment must be used correctly.
  - All infested contacts must be treated simultaneously.
- **Consider whether treatment failure could be due to:** inadequate treatment, incorrectly applied treatment, misdiagnosis, reinfestation, or resistance.
- **EITHER give two applications of insecticide, used 7 days apart:**
  - **Use a different class of insecticide for the second course of treatment.** Options are carbaryl, malathion, or phenothrin (permethrin and phenothrin are both pyrethroids).
  - Give one bottle per application. Give 2–3 bottles per application if the hair is thick.
  - Advise the family to inspect the hair and scalp (by detection combing) 2–3 days after the final application to check that treatment has been successful.
- **OR use wet combing (e.g. using the 'Bug Busting' method).** The family must be well motivated because of the time involved: it must be undertaken meticulously every 4 days for at least 2 weeks. If lice are found on the second, third, or fourth session, it should be continued until no lice have been seen for three consecutive sessions.
- **You may need to prescribe according to local policy for treatment failure.**

Factors affecting choice of insecticide

- **Normal healthy skin:** use an alcohol-based product.
- **Asthma:** use an aqueous product, or a low-alcohol product.
- **Eczema or other broken skin conditions:** use an aqueous product. If there is other infestation present, this should be treated separately.
- **Pregnancy and breastfeeding:** use wet combing if possible. If an insecticide is necessary, use malathion (in an aqueous base).
- **Children under 2 months of age:** use wet combing if possible. Use an aqueous product if an insecticide is necessary (prescription-only for children under 6 months).

Practical prescribing points

For further information please see the *Medicines Compendium* (www.medicines.org.uk) or the *British National Formulary* (www.bnf.org). For further information regarding pregnancy, contact the National Teratology Information Service (telephone 0191 232 1525).

- **Lotions** (both alcohol-based and aqueous-based) need to be applied for 12 hours to be effective.
- **Advise patients that alcohol-based lotions are flammable.** Alcoholic lotions must be allowed to dry naturally. People should not use a hair dryer and must keep away from open fires, flames, and cigarettes while the lotion is on.
- **Malathion, phenothrin, and carbaryl** should not be used more than once a week for more than 3 consecutive weeks.

Follow-up advice

- **Insecticides:** advise the person to inspect the hair and scalp (by detection combing) 2–3 days after the second application to check for reinfestation or unsuccessful eradication. See the patient information leaflet *Checking for head lice* for information on how to carry out detection combing.
- **Wet combing** should be repeated every 4 days for at least 2 weeks. If lice are found on the second, third, or fourth session, it should be continued until no lice have been seen for three consecutive sessions.

Patient information leaflets

The following PILs are available at www.prodigy.nhs.uk

- Community Hygiene Concern
- Head Lice - Detection
- Head Lice - Full Overview
- Head Lice - Medicated Treatment
- Head Lice - Wet Combing Treatment

Shared decision making

- **Medicated treatments** for head lice include malathion, permethrin, and phenothrin. They come in various brands. Carbaryl is an option if others have been tried and failed.
  - Follow the instructions on how to apply and how long to leave on the hair.
  - Do not go swimming before applying (chlorine may stop it working).
  - Do not use a hairdryer to dry hair after applying treatment.
  - Re-apply the same treatment after 7 days.
  - Check that there are no lice 2-3 days after the second application.
- **Wet combing ('Bug Busting')** is an alternative option:
  - You need to do this twice a week for at least 2 weeks.
  - It takes about 15 minutes each session.

Other points about treatment:

- Check for lice in household members and close contacts. All infested contacts should be treated at the same time, to prevent reinfestation.
- Alcohol-based lotions:
  - Should not be used if you have asthma, eczema, or broken skin.
  - Are flammable, so do not use near fires or flames.

Pregnant or breastfeeding women — 'Bug Busting' is preferred. If a medicated treatment is needed, use water-based malathion lotion.
Children under 2 years — 'Bug Busting' is preferred. If a medicated treatment is needed, use a water-based lotion.

Drug rationale

Drugs not included

Shampoos are diluted too much in use to be effective and are therefore not included [BNF 45, 2003].
Products with a short application time (permethrin 1% cream rinse and phenothrin mousse) are not included. Although they are more convenient, there are concerns that shorter application times may help to promote the emergence of resistance. However, no clinical studies have been conducted to confirm that this is the case.

Drugs included

Malathion and phenothrin are included. The current strategy to use two applications of insecticide 7 days apart is a pragmatic approach (off-licence). The second application of insecticide is used to kill nymphs emerging from eggs that survived the first application.
Carbaryl is now a prescription-only medicine following reports of carcinogenicity in rodents after continuous dosing [Chief Medical Officer, 1995]. It should only be considered in cases of suspected resistance to all other insecticides [DTB, 1998].
A prescription for wet combing using the Bug Buster kit is included in this scenario. Families using this method must be well motivated as it must be undertaken meticulously and regularly to be successful [DH, 2000]. It is suitable for people who do not wish to use insecticides.

Prescriptions

Usual treatment options

Alcohol-based lotion: malathion
- Age from 2 years onwards
- Malathion 0.5% alcoholic lotion. Apply to dry hair and scalp. Leave to dry naturally. Wash off after 12 hours. Repeat after 7 days; supply 100 ml; NHS Cost £4.44; OTC Cost £7.78.

Alcohol-based lotion: phenothrin
- Age from 2 years onwards
- Phenothrin 0.2% lotion. Apply to dry hair and scalp. Leave to dry naturally. Wash off after 12 hours. Repeat after 7 days; supply 100 ml; NHS Cost £4.44; OTC Cost £7.78.

Alcohol-based lotion: carbaryl
- Age from 2 years onwards
- Carbaryl 0.5% alcoholic lotion. Apply to dry hair and scalp. Leave to dry naturally. Wash off after 12 hours. Repeat after 7 days; supply 100 ml; NHS Cost £4.55.

Wet combing (using the Bug Buster kit)
- Age from 2 years onwards
- Bug Buster kit. Use as directed on the right hand side of the prescription; supply 1 kit; NHS Cost £4.31; OTC Cost £7.59.

People with asthma

Aqueous-based liquid: malathion
- Age from 2 years onwards
- Malathion 0.5% aqueous liquid. Apply to dry hair and scalp. Leave to dry naturally. Wash off after 12 hours. Repeat after 7 days; supply 100 ml; NHS Cost £4.44; OTC Cost £7.78.

Aqueous-based liquid: phenothrin
- Age from 2 years onwards
- Phenothrin 0.5% aqueous liquid. Apply to dry hair and scalp. Leave to dry naturally. Wash off after 12 hours. Repeat after 7 days; supply 100 ml; NHS Cost £4.44; OTC Cost £7.78.

Aqueous-based liquid: carbaryl
- Age from 2 years onwards
- Carbaryl 1% aqueous liquid. Apply to dry hair and scalp. Leave to dry naturally. Wash off after 12 hours. Repeat after 7 days; supply 100 ml; NHS Cost £4.55.

Wet combing (using the Bug Buster kit)
- Age from 2 years onwards
- Bug Buster kit. Use as directed on the right hand side of the prescription; supply 1 kit; NHS Cost £4.31; OTC Cost £7.59.

People with eczema or broken skin

Aqueous-based liquid: malathion
- Age from 2 years onwards
- Malathion 0.5% aqueous liquid. Apply to dry hair and scalp. Leave to dry naturally. Wash off after 12 hours. Repeat after 7 days; supply 100 ml; NHS Cost £4.44; OTC Cost £7.78.

Aqueous-based liquid: phenothrin
- Age from 2 years onwards
- Phenothrin 0.5% aqueous liquid. Apply to dry hair and scalp. Leave to dry naturally. Wash off after 12 hours. Repeat after 7 days; supply 100 ml; NHS Cost £4.44; OTC Cost £7.78.

Aqueous-based liquid: carbaryl
- Age from 2 years onwards
- Carbaryl 1% aqueous liquid. Apply to dry hair and scalp. Leave to dry naturally. Wash off after 12 hours. Repeat after 7 days; supply 100 ml; NHS Cost £4.55.

Wet combing (using the Bug Buster kit)
- Age from 2 years onwards
- Bug Buster kit. Use as directed on the right hand side of the prescription; supply 1 kit; NHS Cost £4.31; OTC Cost £7.59.

Pregnancy and breastfeeding

Wet combing (using the Bug Buster kit)
- Age from 12 to 60 years
- Bug Buster kit. Use as directed on the right hand side of the prescription; supply 1 kit; NHS Cost £4.31; OTC Cost £7.59.

Aqueous-based liquid: malathion
- Age from 12 to 60 years
- Malathion 0.5% aqueous liquid. Apply to dry hair and scalp. Leave to dry naturally. Wash off after 12 hours. Repeat after 7 days; supply 100 ml; NHS Cost £4.44.

Children under 2 years of age

Wet combing (using the Bug Buster kit)
- Age from 1 month to 23 months
- Bug Buster kit. Use as directed on the right hand side of the prescription; supply 1 kit; NHS Cost £4.31; OTC Cost £7.59.

Aqueous-based liquid: malathion
- Age from 1 month to 23 months
- Malathion 0.5% aqueous liquid. Apply to dry hair and scalp. Leave to dry naturally. Wash off after 12 hours. Repeat after 7 days; supply 50 ml; NHS Cost £1.85.

Aqueous-based liquid: phenothrin

- Age from 1 month to 23 months
- Phenothrin 0.5% aqueous liquid. Apply to dry hair and scalp. Leave to dry naturally. Wash off after 12 hours. Repeat after 7 days; supply 50 ml; NHS Cost £2.22.

Aqueous-based liquid: carbaryl

- Age from 1 month to 23 months
- Carbaryl 1% aqueous liquid. Apply to dry hair and scalp. Leave to dry naturally. Wash off after 12 hours. Repeat after 7 days; supply 50 ml; NHS Cost £2.27.

Extended Information

Background information

- What is it? p.882
- How common is it? p.882
- How is it transmitted? p.882
- How do I know my patient has it? p.882
- Who else should be checked? p.882
- What else might it be? p.882

What is it?

- The head louse (*Pediculus capitis*) is grey/brown in colour and about 1–3 mm long. Head lice feed by sucking blood from the scalp of their host. The female louse lays her eggs (smaller than a pinhead) on the hair shaft near the scalp surface. The eggs shells are firmly attached to the hair and are not washed off by regular shampooing. The eggs hatch in about 7 days, and the egg shells are left empty (nits). The young lice (nymphs) take 9–12 days to become adults.
- Adult lice are about the size of a sesame seed. Young lice are about the size of a pinhead.

[Aston et al, 1998; MeReC, 1999; DH, 2000]

How common is it?

- For every 1000 patients, a practice can expect to have about three people consult with head lice per year. This figure does not include consultations with the practice nurse or self-treatment from a pharmacy.
- It is most common in children aged 4–11, but all ages are at risk of infestation.
- Head lice have no preference for hair type and can infest short, long, clean, or dirty hair.
- It is generally more common in girls than boys and in those from urban rather than rural areas.

[Downs et al, 1999b; MeReC, 1999]

How is it transmitted?

- **Transmission of head lice requires close head-to-head contact** (lice cannot jump, fly, or swim).
- There is no need to wash clothing or bedding that has been in contact with lice; head lice that fall off the head or clamber onto hats or pillows are likely to die quite soon because they need a host for warmth and to feed.

[DH, 2000]

How do I know my patient has it?

- **A live louse must be found to confirm head louse infestation.**
- Louse specimens found at home can be attached to sticky tape and brought to the consultation to aid identification.
- **Detection combing should be used to identify lice.** See the patient information leaflet *Checking for head lice* for information on how to carry out detection combing.
- Live lice can be found anywhere on the scalp. Hatched lice live close to the scalp unless approaching death (after about 20 days), or if the host sweats. (Sweat drives them further out on the hair to avoid the moisture.) Lice that involuntarily fall off the head or clamber onto hats or pillows are usually dying or harmless.
- Nits (empty egg shells) are usually found above the ears and around the hairline. The presence of nits alone does not indicate active infestation — it is difficult to distinguish them from live eggs with the naked eye.
- Many people are asymptomatic, the lice and nits only being detected by careful examination of the scalp.
- Itching is a common presenting symptom, but can take up to 3 months to develop after a first infestation. Excoriations may lead to impetigo and furunculosis.

[Aston et al, 1998; DTB, 1998; Ibarra, 1998; MeReC, 1999; Dodd, 2003]

Who else should be checked?

- **Contact tracing of family and friends** who may have had close head-to-head contact is vital to prevent reinfestation.
- **Detection combing should be used to identify lice.** See the patient information leaflet *Checking for head lice* for information on how to carry out detection combing.
- For large families, detection combing is very time-consuming. Help with detection combing by the health visitor or practice nurse may be useful in this situation.

[Aston et al, 1998; Ibarra, 1998; MeReC, 1999; DH, 2000]

What else might it be?

- **Seborrhoeic scales, hair casts, and hair spray** (which can all be brushed off) may be confused with nits (which stick to the hair like glue).
- **Pubic lice** (*Phthirus pubis*) may be found in any coarse hair, such as eyebrows, eyelashes, axillary hair, moustaches and beards, as well as pubic hair.
- **Body lice** (*Pediculus humanus*) are usually found on clothes, although they feed on the body.

[Aston et al, 1998]

Management issues

- How should I treat head lice? p.882
- Do children with head lice need to be kept off school? p.883
- Resistance to insecticides p.883
- Treatment failure p.883
- Can head lice infestation be prevented? p.883
- Medicines management p.884

How should I treat head lice?

- **Treatment is not necessary unless a live louse is found.**
- **There are two treatment strategies that can be used.**
  - **Insecticides:** two applications of an insecticide are used 7 days apart (Note: this is different to the packaging information, which states that a single application is sufficient). Success is checked by detection combing 2–3 days after the final application. The first choice of insecticide will be determined by local resistance patterns. (For further information, see section *Resistance to insecticides* below.) If treatment fails or reinfestation occurs, a course of a *different* insecticide is used [Aston et al, 1998].
  - **Wet combing:** this must be undertaken meticulously to be successful. It must be undertaken every 4 days for at least 2 weeks. If lice are found on the second, third, or fourth session, it should be continued until no lice have been seen for three consecutive sessions [Ibarra,

1998]. Families using this method must be well motivated because of the time involved. See the *Patient information leaflets* for a more detailed explanation for wet combing using the 'Bug Busting' method.
- **For either treatment strategy to be successful,** it must be used correctly, and all *infested* contacts must be treated simultaneously. Note that close contacts should be checked for head lice (by detection combing) but only treated if a live louse is found.
- **There is no need to wash or fumigate clothing or bedding** that has been in contact with lice.

Availability of insecticides

- **Malathion, permethrin, and phenothrin are available** over the counter in the UK in a variety of formulations (e.g. lotions, liquids, cream rinse) for the treatment of head lice.
- **Carbaryl** is a prescription-only medicine.

Supporting evidence for head lice treatments

- **Experts continue to debate the relative effectiveness of insecticides and the wet combing method.**
- **Most studies of treatments for head lice are of poor quality.** This was highlighted by a recent Cochrane review where, out of 71 trials identified, only four were considered suitable for inclusion [Dodd, 2003].
- The studies included in the Cochrane review evaluated malathion, permethrin, and wet combing using the 'Bug Busting' method [Dodd, 2003]. Permethrin and malathion, but not wet combing, were effective for the treatment of head lice in these studies.
- However, three of the four studies included in the Cochrane review were conducted in populations with no previous exposure to insecticide. Resistance has since emerged, so first choice will depend on local resistance patterns [Dodd, 2003].
- There were no trials of phenothrin or carbaryl of sufficient quality to be included in the Cochrane review.
- **The current strategy to use two applications of insecticide seven days apart is a pragmatic approach** — the second application of insecticide is used to kill nymphs emerging from eggs that survived the first application.
- This strategy has been compared to wet combing in one randomised controlled trial in the UK. It was conducted in an area of intermediate malathion resistance (with 74 children), and found that malathion 0.5% (given as two applications seven days apart) was twice as effective as 'Bug Busting' at eradicating head lice [Roberts et al, 2000]. However, neither treatment was 100% effective: the overall cure rate was 38% for 'Bug Busting' and 78% for malathion lotion.
- 'Bug Busting' was more effective than phenothrin at eradicating head lice in a further study of 30 children. Again, neither treatment was 100% effective: by day 14, the overall cure rate was 53% for 'Bug Busting' and 13% for phenothrin [Plastow et al, 2001]. Treatment was undertaken by trained nurses in this study, and it is uncertain if similar results would be obtained if 'Bug Busting' is carried out by parents. In addition, resistance to phenothrin has been widely documented in the UK.
- A 3-year randomized controlled trial evaluating the 'Bug Busting' method against insecticides is currently being undertaken by the London School of Hygiene and Tropical Medicine [Bingham et al, 2000].

Other products

- **Tea tree oil, quassia, other essential oils, herbal remedies, and petrol** have not been shown to be effective, and should not be assumed to be safe because they are 'natural'. Petrol is a fire hazard and potentially dangerous [MeReC, 1999].
- **Electric combs** are available but there is only anecdotal evidence of both their success and their failure.

Do children with head lice need to be kept off school?

- **There is no need for children with head lice to stay away from school.**
- A child with lice will generally have had them for several weeks before diagnosis, so keeping them away from school is unlikely to affect transmission.
- Letters notifying other parents of cases have not been found to prevent the spread of head lice, but often provoke itching and anxiety as a psychological response.

[Aston et al, 1998; PHLS, 1999]

Resistance to insecticides

- **Resistance of lice to malathion, permethrin, or phenothrin has been documented in many areas of the UK** [Burgess et al, 1995; Downs et al, 2002]. Lice that are resistant to both malathion and permethrin have been identified [Downs et al, 1999a]. Nearly all lice remain susceptible to carbaryl, although resistance to *in vitro* testing has occasionally been identified.
- **The first choice of insecticide will vary between different localities,** as resistance has been found to vary between geographical locations [Downs et al, 2002]. Further information on local policies can be obtained from the health visitor, the primary care organization medical or pharmaceutical advisors, or contact the local Health Protection Agency team.

Treatment failure

- **Before using another course of treatment, consider** whether treatment failure could be due to inadequate treatment, incorrectly applied treatment, misdiagnosis, or reinfestation (e.g. were all infested contacts treated?) [Aston et al, 1998].
- **Use a different class of insecticide for the second course of treatment.** This reduces repeated exposure to the same insecticide, and it is hoped that resistance will emerge more slowly as a result. Note: permethrin and phenothrin are from the same chemical class (pyrethroids) [Aston et al, 1998].
- Genuine resistance is likely if both young and adult lice are seen 24 hours after insecticide use. Eggs can still hatch following treatment; therefore the presence of only young lice does not indicate resistance [MeReC, 1999]. If only older lice are seen, reinfestation from another contact is likely. Adult lice are about the size of a sesame seed. Young lice are about the size of a pinhead [DH, 2000].
- **Wet combing is an alternative to insecticides, but it must be undertaken meticulously and regularly to be successful:** it must be undertaken every 4 days for at least 2 weeks. If lice are found on the second, third, or fourth session, it should be continued until no lice have been seen for three consecutive sessions [Ibarra, 1998].

Can head lice infestation be prevented?

- Reinfestation shortly after successful treatment can be prevented by treatment of all *infested* contacts.
- Insecticides have no place in preventing a new head lice infestation The only indication for using an insecticide is if a live louse has been found on the head.
- Wet combing does not prevent infestation, but it can help identify the presence of a new infestation (detection combing). If parents are concerned because there is an 'outbreak' of head lice at school, regular wet combing

H

(e.g. weekly) will identify any new infestation, which can then be treated by continued wet combing or by using an insecticide.
- Piperonal 2% is a head lice repellent available on sale (over the counter) from pharmacies. Its place in therapy is unclear since it is not intended for routine prophylactic use and does not treat existing infestation.

[Aston et al, 1998; Ibarra, 1998]

Medicines management

Insecticides

- **Lotions and liquids should be applied for 12 hours before being washed off** [BNF 45, 2003]. (Note that this is an off-licence use of phenothrin 0.2% lotion, which is only licensed for a 2-hour application time).
- We suggest that the products with a shorter application time are less preferred. Although they are more convenient, there are concerns that shorter application times may help to promote the emergence of resistance. However, no clinical studies have been conducted to confirm that this is the case.
- **Alcoholic lotions are preferred to aqueous liquids** as they may be slightly more effective.
- **However, aqueous preparations are preferred for small children, or people with asthma, eczema, or broken skin** since alcoholic lotions may cause wheezing or skin irritation [BNF 45, 2003].
- **Patients should be advised that alcohol-based lotions are flammable.** Alcoholic lotions must be allowed to dry naturally. People should not use a hair dryer and must keep away from open fires, flames, and cigarettes while the lotion is on.
- Carbaryl is now a prescription-only medicine following reports of carcinogenicity in rodents after continuous dosing [Chief Medical Officer, 1995]. It should only be considered in cases of suspected resistance to all other insecticides [DTB, 1998].
- Concerns have been raised in the past that topical malathion (an organophosphate) could potentially cause serious systemic adverse effects. However a recent Committee on Safety of Medicines review concluded there is no evidence to suggest that this is the case [CSM, 2000].
- **Pregnancy and breastfeeding:** use the wet combing method ('Bug Busting') if possible. If an insecticide is necessary, the National Teratology Information Service currently recommends malathion because it is poorly absorbed and rapidly eliminated (telephone 0191 232 1525 for further information) [National Teratology Information Service, 1999].
- **Children under 2 years of age:** use the wet combing method ('Bug Busting') if possible. Use an aqueous-based product if an insecticide is needed. Note: children under 6 months of age can only be treated under medical supervision. (Insecticides are not available over the counter for this age group.)

Wet combing

- **Wet combing can be undertaken using** a 'Bug Busting' kit (available on prescription or over the counter), or alternatively using a detection comb plus conditioner. Metal nit combs are not suitable for removing lice. Detection combs are made of plastic and have wider spaced teeth than nit combs. They are available from pharmacies.
- Information about how to perform wet combing using the 'Bug Busting' method can be found in the *Patient information leaflets*.

References

NHS staff in England can link, free of charge, from references to full text journals by clicking on [Full text] on the PRODIGY website.

1. Aston, R., Duggal, H., Simpson, J. and Burgess, I. (1998) *Head lice: a report for consultants in communicable disease control (CCDCs).* Public Health Medicine Environmental Group Executive Committee. www.phmeg.org.uk [Accessed: 14/10/2003].
2. Bingham, P., Kirk, S., Hill, N. and Figueroa, J. (2000) The methodology and operation of a pilot randomized control trial of the effectiveness of the Bug Busting method against a single application insecticide product for head louse treatment. *Public Health* **114**(4), 265–268.
3. BNF 45 (2003) *British National Formulary.* 45th edn. London: British Medical Association and Royal Pharmaceutical Society of Great Britain.
4. Burgess, I.F., Brown, C.M., Peock, S. and Kaufman, J. (1995) Head lice resistant to pyrethroid insecticides in Britain. *British Medical Journal* **311**(7007), 752.
5. Chief Medical Officer (1995) *New advice to government on use of insecticide as a treatment for lice: experts advise restricted use of carbaryl.* London: Department of Health.
6. CSM (2000) Safety of malathion for the treatment of louse and scabies infestation. *Current Problems in Pharmacovigilance* **26**(May), 2.
7. DH (2000) *The prevention and treatment of head lice.* Department of Health. www.dh.gov.uk [Accessed: 08/06/2004]. [Full text]
8. Dodd, C.S. (2003) *Interventions for treating head lice (Cochrane Review).* The Cochrane Library. Issue 3. Oxford: Update Software.
9. Downs, A.M.R., Stafford, K.A., Harvey, I. and Coles, G.C. (1999a) Evidence for double resistance to permethrin and malathion in head lice. *British Journal of Dermatology* **141**(3), 508–511.
10. Downs, A.M.R., Harvey, I. and Kennedy, C.T.C. (1999b) The epidemiology of head lice and scabies in the UK. *Epidemiology and Infection* **122**(3), 471–477.
11. Downs, A.M.R., Stafford, K.A., Hunt, L.P. et al (2002) Widespread insecticide resistance in head lice to the over-the-counter pediculocides in England, and the emergence of carbaryl resistance. *British Journal of Dermatology* **146**(1), 88–93.
12. DTB (1998) Treating head louse infections. *Drug & Therapeutics Bulletin* **36**(6), 45–46.
13. Ibarra, J. (1998) Pediculosis. In: Figueroa, J., Hall, S., Ibarra, J. et al (Eds.) *Primary health care guide to common UK parasitic diseases.* London: Community Hygiene Concern. 1–16.
14. MeReC (1999) Management of head louse infection. *MeReC Bulletin* **10**(5), 17–20.
15. National Teratology Information Service (1999) *Management of scabies and head lice in pregnancy.* NHS Northern and Yorkshire: Regional Drug and Therapeutics Centre.
16. PHLS (1999) *Head lice (pediculosis) factsheets for school – wired for health.* Public Health Laboratory Service. www.hpa.org.uk [Accessed: 14/10/2003].
17. Plastow, L., Luthra, M., Powell, R. et al (2001) Head lice infestation: bug busting vs. traditional treatment. *Journal of Clinical Nursing* **10**(6), 775–783.
18. Roberts, R.J., Casey, D., Morgan, D.A. and Petrovic, M. (2000) Comparison of wet combing with malathion for treatment of head lice in the UK: a pragmatic randomised controlled trial. *Lancet* **356**(9229), 540–544. [Full text]

PRODIGY GUIDANCE

Headache

Last revised in July 2005
www.prodigy.nhs.uk/guidance.asp?gt=Headache

Applies to people over the age of 16 years

This guidance covers the management of episodic tension-type headache, chronic tension-type headache, cluster headache, and medication overuse headache.

This guidance does not cover migraine. It also does not cover the diagnosis and treatment of all of the causes of headache.

There is separate PRODIGY guidance for *Brain tumour — suspected, Glaucoma, Glue ear, Hypertension, Migraine, Neck pain, Otitis media — acute, Shingles and postherpetic neuralgia, Sinusitis,* and *Trigeminal neuralgia.*

Goals

- To reduce the severity and frequency of headache
- To exclude serious pathology
- To avoid the development of medication overuse headache

Contents

Scenarios

- Episodic tension-type headache p.885
- Chronic tension-type headache p.887
- Medication overuse headache p.888
- Cluster headache p.889

Extended Information, p. 890

Which scenario?

- **Episodic tension-type headache:** covers the management of episodic tension-type headache. The features of this type of headache include:
  - Often stress-related.
  - Lasts from 30 minutes to 7 days.
  - Usually bilateral.
  - Pressing or tightening, but not pulsating.
  - Mild to moderate severity.
  - May arise from, or spread into, the neck.
  - Not worsened by routine activity.
  - Photophobia or phonophobia may be present, but are mild.
  - Nausea is not present.
  - The only significant finding on examination is increased pericranial muscle tenderness (frontal, temporal, masseter, pterygoid, sternocleidomastoid, splenius, and trapezius).
- **Chronic tension-type headache:** covers the management of chronic tension-type headache. This type of headache occurs on 15 days or more each month. Otherwise, it has all of the features of episodic tension-type headache. Chronic tension-type headache evolves over time in people who originally suffered from episodic tension-type headache.
- **Medication overuse headache:** covers the management of headache that results from the chronic overuse of medication used to treat headache. Chronic medication overuse headache is associated with aspirin, paracetamol (especially when combined with codeine), nonsteroidal anti-inflammatory drugs (NSAIDs), triptans, opioids, and ergotamine. It should be considered in a person with a pre-existing primary headache (particularly migraine or tension-type headache, sometimes present for years) who reports that their headaches have worsened (also, the frequency of headache, and medication use, has increased). The features of this type of headache include:
  - Develops (or markedly worsens) during the period of medication overuse.
  - Pre-emptive use of medication is common, i.e. the medication that is causing the headache is taken in anticipation of the headache's occurring.
  - Present on more than 15 days every month.
  - Usually present (and often at its worst) on waking.
  - Location, character, and intensity of the headache are highly variable (between different people, and in the same person).
  - Usually increases after physical exertion.
  - Nausea and vomiting are rare.
  - Temporarily worsens on discontinuation of the causative medication.
- **Cluster headache:** covers the management of cluster headache. This type of headache consists of attacks of severe unilateral pain. The features of this type of headache include:
  - Felt in or around the eye or temple (but may spread to other areas of the head).
  - Excruciating, and described as boring or burning.
  - Each attack lasts 15–180 minutes, and may occur from once every other day to 8 times daily.
  - Each attack is associated with one or more of the following ipsilateral features:
    - Conjunctival injection
    - Lacrimation
    - Nasal congestion
    - Rhinorrhoea
    - Forehead and facial sweating
    - Miosis
    - Ptosis
    - Eyelid oedema
  - The person is typically restless or agitated, unable to lie down, and typically paces the floor, or may even bang their head against the wall.
  - Often occur at night, typically waking the person after 1–2 hours sleep.

Episodic tension-type headache

Which therapy?

- Reassure the person that episodic tension-type headache is self-limiting. Reassurance may be the only therapy that is needeed.
- Manage stress, anxiety, or depression appropriately. Episodic tension-type headache may be stress-related. See the separate PRODIGY guidance for *Depression* and *Stress — acute reaction.*
- Give advice on exercise and posture.

- If analgesia is required:
  - Nonsteroidal anti-inflammatory drugs (NSAIDs) are recommended as first-line therapy, as they are more effective than paracetamol.
  - Paracetamol is recommended for people intolerant of NSAIDs.
  - Avoid opioids (including codeine) because of the risk of developing medication overuse headache (the risk is much higher with opioids than with NSAIDs or paracetamol).
- Ask about the use of over-the-counter medications, especially as many contain codeine.

Practical prescribing points

For further information please see the *Medicines Compendium* (www.medicines.org.uk) or the *British National Formulary* (www.bnf.org).

NSAIDs

- NSAIDs may cause gastrointestinal irritation and occasionally gastrointestinal haemorrhage. Do not give without gastroprotection if there is a history of peptic ulceration.
- NSAIDs may worsen asthma, hypertension, renal impairment, or heart failure.
- Cardiovascular disease: avoid ibuprofen — it may reduce the cardiovascular protective effect of low-dose aspirin.

Follow-up advice

- It is not usually necessary to follow up people with episodic tension-type headache.

Should I refer or investigate?

Refer?

- Consider referral to a physiotherapist for advice about posture.

Investigate?

- Investigations are not required for episodic tension-type headache.

Patient information leaflets

The following PILs are available at www.prodigy.nhs.uk

- Headaches - A Summary
- Headaches - Tension Type

Shared decision making

- Most tension-type headaches occur for no apparent reason. Anxiety, stress, emotion, or other factors may trigger some headaches.
- If stress is a cause, learning to relax (with the help of books or tapes) may help to ease stress and prevent headaches.
- **Regular exercise** such as brisk walks, cycling, jogging, swimming, etc., may reduce the number of headaches.
- **Anti-inflammatory painkillers** such as ibuprofen usually ease tension-type headaches.
  - Side-effects sometimes occur. Stomach pain and bleeding from the stomach are the most serious.
  - Some people with asthma, high blood pressure, kidney failure, and heart failure may not be able to take these tablets.
- **Paracetamol** is an alternative if you have side-effects or problems taking anti-inflammatory painkillers.
- Do not take painkillers for headache on more than 15 days in any month, or for more than two consecutive days. Overuse of painkillers is one cause of frequent headaches.

Drug rationale

Drugs not included

- **Opioids (including codeine)** must be avoided due to the risk of developing medication overuse headache.

Drugs included

- **Nonsteroidal anti-inflammatory drugs (NSAIDs), including ibuprofen, naproxen, and diclofenac,** are recommended as first-line therapy.
  - They have a good balance of efficacy against adverse effect profile.
  - Ibuprofen is associated with the lowest risk of gastrointestinal adverse effects and should be tried first before diclofenac and naproxen, which are associated with intermediate risk.
- **Paracetamol** is recommended for people intolerant of NSAIDs.

Prescriptions

1st choice: ibuprofen

Ibuprofen tablets: 400mg up to three times a day

- Age from 16 years onwards
- Ibuprofen 400mg tablets. Take one tablet three times a day when required for pain relief. Do not exceed the stated dose; supply 48 tablets; NHS Cost £1.37; OTC Cost £2.42.

Ibuprofen tablets: 600mg up to three times a day

- Age from 16 years onwards
- Ibuprofen 600mg tablets. Take one tablet three times a day when required for pain relief. Do not exceed the stated dose; supply 48 tablets; NHS Cost £2.01.

Ibuprofen tablets: 800mg up to three times a day

- Age from 16 years onwards
- Ibuprofen 400mg tablets. Take two tablets three times a day when required for pain relief. Do not exceed the stated dose; supply 84 tablets; NHS Cost £2.74.

Alternative: other NSAIDs

Diclofenac sodium e/c tablets: 25mg up to three times a day

- Age from 16 years onwards
- Diclofenac 25mg e/c tablets. Take one tablet three times a day when required for pain relief. Do not exceed the stated dose; supply 84 tablets; NHS Cost £1.72.

Diclofenac sodium e/c tablets: 50mg up to three times a day

- Age from 16 years onwards
- Diclofenac 50mg e/c tablets. Take one tablet three times a day when required for pain relief. Do not exceed the stated dose; supply 84 tablets; NHS Cost £1.45.

Naproxen tablets: 250mg up to twice a day

- Age from 16 years onwards
- Naproxen 250mg tablets. Take one tablet twice a day when required for pain relief. Do not exceed the stated dose; supply 56 tablets; NHS Cost £2.68.

Naproxen tablets: 500mg up to twice a day

- Age from 16 years onwards
- Naproxen 500mg tablets. Take one tablet twice a day when required for pain relief. Do not exceed the stated dose; supply 56 tablets; NHS Cost £4.90.

Paracetamol: use if NSAID intolerant

Paracetamol: 1g up to four times a day
- Age from 16 years onwards
- Paracetamol 500mg tablets. Take two tablets every 4 to 6 hours when required for pain relief. Maximum of 8 tablets in 24 hours; supply 50 tablets; NHS Cost £0.64; OTC Cost £1.12.

Chronic tension-type headache

Which therapy?

- **Amitriptyline is the treatment of choice for chronic tension-type headache.**
- The starting dose should be 10–25 mg at night, and increased every few days by 10 mg increments to a target dose of 75–150 mg at night.
- Withdraw gradually (by 10 mg every few days) after improvement has been maintained for 4–6 months.
- If the headaches worsen during the withdrawal period, increase the dose of amitriptyline again to the target previously attained, and continue at this dose for a further 4–6 months before attempting gradual withdrawal again.

Practical prescribing points

For further information please see the *Medicines Compendium* (www.medicines.org.uk) or the *British National Formulary* (www.bnf.org).

Amitriptyline

- Driving: the Driver and Vehicle Licensing Authority (DVLA) recommends avoiding drugs that have antimuscarinic effects, such as tricyclic antidepressants (TCAs). All people taking TCAs should be advised not to drive if adversely affected, particularly during the first month of starting the medication or increasing the dose (tolerance develops within a week or two of a stable dose).
- Other cautions include: cardiac disease, particularly with arrhythmias; epilepsy; pregnancy and breastfeeding; glaucoma; prostatism; bipolar disorder; urinary retention; and suspected risk of overdosing.
- Contraindications: recent myocardial infarction, arrhythmias, and hepatic impairment.
- Adverse effects commonly include dry mouth, sedation, constipation, postural hypotension, confusion (particularly in elderly people), urinary retention, and weight gain.

Follow-up advice

- Regular follow-up should be tailored to the individual during the period of amitriptyline therapy.

Should I refer or investigate?

Refer?

- Chronic tension-type headache may be refractory to treatment. If this appears to be the case, referral to a neurologist or pain clinic is advised.

Investigate?

- Investigations are not required for chronic tension-type headache.

Patient information leaflets

The following PILs are available at www.prodigy.nhs.uk
- Headache - Chronic Tension-Type
- Headaches - A Summary

Shared decision making

- **Amitriptyline** may reduce the duration and frequency of headaches if you have lots of headaches ('chronic tension-type headache').
  - Take amitriptyline every day at bedtime.
  - You may notice it causes a dry mouth. Extra drinks will help.
  - Start with a low dose. Gradually increase the dose as directed.
  - Stop it 4–6 months after headaches have improved.
- **Other things that may reduce headaches include:**
  - Regular exercise such as brisk walks, cycling, jogging, etc.
  - If stress is a cause, learning to relax (with the help of books or tapes) may help to ease stress and prevent headaches.
  - It may help to keep a diary. Note when, where, how bad, and how long each headache lasts. Also note anything that may have caused it. A pattern may emerge and you may find a trigger to avoid. For example, hunger, bad posture, anger, etc.

Drug rationale

Drugs not included

- **Antidepressants other than amitriptyline** (tricyclic and selective serotonin reuptake inhibitors) have not been shown to be effective in treating chronic tension-type headache. Coexistent depression should, however, be treated appropriately; see the separate PRODIGY guidance for *Depression*.
- There is insufficient evidence of the efficacy of acupuncture or homeopathy to recommend their use in chronic tension-type headache.

Drugs included

- **Amitriptyline is the treatment of choice.** The starting dose should be 10–25 mg at night, and increased every few days by 10 mg increments to a target dose of 75–150 mg at night.

Prescriptions

Amitriptyline

Amitriptyline: initial titration from 10mg to 40mg at night
- Age from 16 years onwards
- Amitriptyline 10mg tablets. Take 1 tab at night for 7 nights, then 2 tabs at night for 7 nights, then 3 tabs at night for 7 nights, then 4 tabs at night for 7 nights; supply 70 tablets; NHS Cost £2.50.

Amitriptyline tablets: 50mg at night
- Age from 16 years onwards
- Amitriptyline 50mg tablets. Take one tablet at night; supply 28 tablets; NHS Cost £1.60.

Amitriptyline tablets: 75mg at night
- Age from 16 years onwards
- Amitriptyline 25mg tablets. Take three tablets at night; supply 84 tablets; NHS Cost £5.13.

Amitriptyline tablets: 100mg at night
- Age from 16 years onwards
- Amitriptyline 50mg tablets. Take two tablets at night; supply 56 tablets; NHS Cost £3.20.

Amitriptyline tablets: 125mg at night
- Age from 16 years onwards
- Amitriptyline 25mg tablets. Take one tablet at night; supply 28 tablets; NHS Cost £1.71.
- Amitriptyline 50mg tablets. Take two tablets at night; supply 56 tablets; NHS Cost £3.20.

Amitriptyline tablets: 150mg at night
- Age from 16 years onwards
- Amitriptyline 50mg tablets. Take three tablets at night; supply 84 tablets; NHS Cost £4.80.

Medication overuse headache

Which therapy?

- **Stop the therapy causing medication overuse headache.**
- **Replace the causative medication with a regular nonsteroidal anti-inflammatory drug (NSAID)** unless the causative medication is actually an NSAID.
- **If the causative medication is an NSAID (or if the person is intolerant of NSAIDs), replace it with amitriptyline.**
- Continue treatment until the medication overuse headache improves (this may take up to 6 months).

H

Practical prescribing points

For further information please see the *Medicines Compendium* (www.medicines.org.uk) or the *British National Formulary* (www.bnf.org).

NSAIDs

- **Only one NSAID should be prescribed at a time.**
- **NSAIDs may worsen asthma, hypertension, renal impairment, or heart failure.**
- Do not give ibuprofen, diclofenac, or naproxen without gastroprotection if there is a history of peptic ulceration.
- **People with cardiovascular disease:** ibuprofen may reduce the cardiovascular protective effect of low-dose aspirin.
- **In people with risk factors for gastrointestinal NSAID complications:**
  - Use paracetamol instead of a NSAID if possible.
  - Or, use gastroprotection (a PPI or full-dose misoprostol) combined with a standard NSAID.
- **Risk factors for gastrointestinal NSAID complications include:**
  - Age of 65 years and over.
  - Previous history of gastroduodenal ulcer, gastrointestinal (GI) bleeding, or gastroduodenal perforation.
  - Concomitant use of medications that are known to increase the likelihood of upper-GI adverse events, e.g. anticoagulants, aspirin (even a low dose), and corticosteroids.
  - Presence of serious comorbidity, such as cardiovascular disease, renal or hepatic impairment, diabetes, or hypertension.
  - Requirement for prolonged duration of NSAID use.
  - Use of maximum recommended doses of NSAIDs.

Amitriptyline

- Driving: the Driver and Vehicle Licensing Authority (DVLA) recommends avoiding drugs that have antimuscarinic effects, such as tricyclic antidepressants (TCAs). All people taking TCAs should be advised not to drive if adversely affected, particularly during the first month of starting the medication or increasing the dose (tolerance develops within a week or two of a stable dose).
- Other cautions include: cardiac disease, particularly with arrhythmias; epilepsy; pregnancy and breastfeeding; glaucoma; prostatism; bipolar disorder; urinary retention; and suspected risk of overdosing.
- Contraindications: recent myocardial infarction, arrhythmias, and hepatic impairment.
- Adverse effects commonly include dry mouth, sedation, constipation, postural hypotension, confusion (particularly in elderly people), urinary retention, and weight gain.

Follow-up advice

- Regular follow-up should be tailored to the individual during the management of medication overuse headache.

Should I refer or investigate?

Refer?

- Referral to a neurologist is advised if management of medication overuse headache fails in primary care.

Investigate?

- Investigations are not required for medication overuse headache.

Patient information leaflets

The following PILs are available at www.prodigy.nhs.uk
- Headache - Medication Induced

Shared decision making

- If you have medication overuse headache:
  - You must stop the causative painkillers completely.
  - When you stop the painkillers, the headaches will get worse until the painkillers are 'out of your system'.
  - Your doctor will prescribe an alternative for the headache. Do not take any other painkiller, including any that you may buy at a chemist or other shop.
  - Your headaches should then gradually go back to a 'normal' frequency. However, in some cases it takes months for the headaches to ease off after stopping the painkillers.
- Once the headaches are back to 'normal':
  - Do not take painkillers for headache on more than 15 days in any month, or
  - For more than two consecutive days.

Drug rationale

Drugs not included

- **Paracetamol and opioid analgesics (including codeine)** are not recommended.

Drugs included

- **Nonsteroidal anti-inflammatory drugs (NSAIDs) such as ibuprofen, diclofenac, or naproxen** are the treatment of choice for medication overuse headache.
- **Amitriptyline** may be considered if the causative agent is an NSAID (or if the person is intolerant of NSAIDs). The starting dose should be 10–25 mg at night, and increased every few days by 10 mg increments to a target dose of 75–150 mg at night.
- **Proton pump inhibitors and misoprostol** are included for gastroprotection against NSAIDs for people at high risk of gastrointestinal complications.

Prescriptions

1st choice: ibuprofen

Ibuprofen tablets: 400mg three times a day
- Age from 16 years onwards
- Ibuprofen 400mg tablets. Take one tablet three times a day; supply 84 tablets; NHS Cost £2.74; OTC Cost £4.83.

Ibuprofen tablets: 600mg three times a day
- Age from 16 years onwards
- Ibuprofen 600mg tablets. Take one tablet three times a day; supply 84 tablets; NHS Cost £4.02.

Ibuprofen tablets: 800mg three times a day
- Age from 16 years onwards
- Ibuprofen 400mg tablets. Take two tablets three times a day; supply 168 tablets; NHS Cost £5.48.

Alternative: other NSAIDs

Diclofenac sodium e/c tablets: 25mg three times a day
- Age from 16 years onwards
- Diclofenac 25mg e/c tablets. Take one tablet three times a day; supply 84 tablets; NHS Cost £1.72.

Diclofenac sodium e/c tablets: 50mg three times a day
- Age from 16 years onwards
- Diclofenac 50mg e/c tablets. Take one tablet three times a day; supply 84 tablets; NHS Cost £1.45.

Naproxen tablets: 250mg twice a day
- Age from 12 years onwards
- Naproxen 250mg tablets. Take one tablet twice a day; supply 56 tablets; NHS Cost £2.68.

Naproxen tablets: 500mg twice a day
- Age from 16 years onwards
- Naproxen 500mg tablets. Take one tablet twice a day; supply 56 tablets; NHS Cost £4.90.

GI protection: ONLY if at high risk of NSAID-induced ulcer

Omeprazole capsules: 20mg once a day
- Age from 16 years onwards
- Omeprazole 20mg capsules. Take one capsule once a day; supply 28 capsules; NHS Cost £12.75.

Omeprazole tablets: 20mg once a day
- Age from 16 years onwards
- Omeprazole 20mg tablets. Take one tablet once a day; supply 28 tablets; NHS Cost £12.75.

Lansoprazole capsules: 30mg each morning
- Age from 16 years onwards
- Lansoprazole 30mg capsules. Take one capsule each morning (on an empty stomach); supply 28 capsules; NHS Cost £23.63.

Lansoprazole orodispersible tablets: 30mg each morning
- Age from 16 years onwards
- Lansoprazole 30mg orodisp tabs. Take one tablet each morning (on an empty stomach); supply 28 tablets; NHS Cost £19.88.

Pantoprazole e/c tablets: 20mg once a day
- Age from 16 years onwards
- Pantoprazole 20mg e/c tablets. Take one tablet once a day; supply 28 tablets; NHS Cost £12.31.

Esomeprazole tablets: 20mg once a day
- Age from 16 years onwards
- Esomeprazole 20mg tablets. Take one tablet once a day; supply 28 tablets; NHS Cost £18.50.

Lansoprazole capsules: 15mg each morning
- Age from 16 years onwards
- Lansoprazole 15mg capsules. Take one capsule each morning (on an empty stomach); supply 28 capsules; NHS Cost £12.92.

Lansoprazole orodispersible tablets: 15mg each morning
- Age from 16 years onwards
- Lansoprazole 15mg orodisp tabs. Take one tablet each morning (on an empty stomach); supply 28 tablets; NHS Cost £10.86.

Amitriptyline: if NSAID causative agent

Amitriptyline: initial titration from 10mg to 40mg at night
- Age from 16 years onwards
- Amitriptyline 10mg tablets. Take 1 tab at night for 7 nights, then 2 tabs at night for 7 nights, then 3 tabs at night for 7 nights, then 4 tabs at night for 7 nights; supply 70 tablets; NHS Cost £1.95.

Amitriptyline tablets: 50mg at night
- Age from 16 years onwards
- Amitriptyline 50mg tablets. Take one tablet at night; supply 28 tablets; NHS Cost £1.60.

Amitriptyline tablets: 75mg at night
- Age from 16 years onwards
- Amitriptyline 25mg tablets. Take three tablets at night; supply 84 tablets; NHS Cost £2.43.

Amitriptyline tablets: 100mg at night
- Age from 16 years onwards
- Amitriptyline 50mg tablets. Take two tablets at night; supply 56 tablets; NHS Cost £3.20.

Amitriptyline tablets: 125mg at night
- Age from 16 years onwards
- Amitriptyline 25mg tablets. Take one tablet at night; supply 28 tablets; NHS Cost £1.71.
- Amitriptyline 50mg tablets. Take two tablets at night; supply 56 tablets; NHS Cost £3.20.

Amitriptyline tablets: 150mg at night
- Age from 16 years onwards
- Amitriptyline 50mg tablets. Take three tablets at night; supply 84 tablets; NHS Cost £4.80.

Cluster headache

Which therapy?

- **Sumatriptan is the treatment of choice.**
  - **Subcutaneous injection** is the only formulation of any of the triptans licensed for use in cluster headache.
- **Alcohol (and other vasodilators) should be avoided during a cluster period,** as their ingestion triggers attacks in some people.

Practical prescribing points

For further information please see the *Medicines Compendium* (www.medicines.org.uk) or the *British National Formulary* (www.bnf.org).

Sumatriptan

- **'Triptan sensations'** include a warm–hot sensation, tightness, tingling, flushing, and feelings of heaviness or pressure in areas such as the face, limbs, and occasionally the chest.
  - If the person is forewarned of these symptoms they may cause less distress should they occur.
  - Discontinue and review if there are particularly intense sensations or chest pain.
- **Sumatriptan should not be taken by the following people:**
  - People with uncontrolled hypertension.
  - People with coronary heart disease or cerebrovascular disease.
  - People with coronary vasospasm (including Prinzmetal's angina)

- People with risk factors for coronary heart disease or cerebrovascular disease.
- Sumatriptan may cause drowsiness.
- Subcutaneous sumatriptan is administered via an auto-injector, and care should be taken when administering the injection.
  - It must be administered as directed, and not administered into a vein.
  - No more than two injections should be administered in 24 hours, and at least 1 hour should have passed between the two doses.

Follow-up advice

- Follow-up should be tailored to the requirements of the person with cluster headache.

Should I refer or investigate?

Refer?

- Referral to a neurologist or pain clinic is advised.

Investigate?

- Investigations are not required for cluster headache.

Patient information leaflets

The following PILs are available at www.prodigy.nhs.uk
- Headache - Cluster Headache
- OUCH (UK) (cluster headache support)

Shared decision making

- **Sumatriptan** given by injection under the skin is the usual treatment to abort a cluster headache.
  - It usually eases a headache in about 10 minutes.
  - The adult dose is a 6 mg injection for each headache. The maximum dose in 24 hours is two 6 mg injections (12 mg) with a minimum interval of 1 hour between the two doses.
  - Side-effects sometimes occur, but if they do they are generally mild. They include feeling sick, dizziness, tiredness, and dry mouth. A minority of people also develop a warm–hot sensation, tightness, tingling, flushing, and feelings of heaviness or pressure in the face, arms, legs, and occasionally the chest.
  - Some people should not take sumatriptan. For example, some people with heart disease, stroke disease, or peripheral vascular disease.
- **Avoid alcohol** for the duration of the cluster of headaches as it can trigger a headache.
- Other medicines are sometimes tried in order to *prevent* cluster headaches. These are usually prescribed under the supervision of a specialist.

Drug rationale

Drugs not included

- **Standard analgesics, such as paracetamol and nonsteroidal anti-inflammatory drugs,** are not recommended for cluster headache.
- **Oral triptans** are not absorbed rapidly enough to be of use in the treatment of cluster headache.
- **Nasal sumatriptan and zolmitriptan** have evidence of efficacy in the treatment of cluster headache, but are not licensed for this indication.

Drugs included

- **Sumatriptan given by subcutaneous injection is the treatment of choice,** and is the only formulation of the triptans that is licensed for cluster headache.

Prescriptions

Sumatriptan injection

Sumatriptan s/c injection: 6mg if required, max twice a day
- Age from 18 years onwards
- Sumatriptan 6mg/0.5ml inj. Inject the contents of one syringe (6mg) subcutaneously at onset of cluster headache. Maximum of 2 doses (12mg) in 24 hours; supply 2 pre-filled syringes; NHS Cost £44.19.

Extended Information

Background information

- What is it? p.890
- How common is it? p.890
- How do I know my patient has it? p.891
- What else might it be? p.892
- Complications p.892

What is it?

- **Headache is a symptom that has many causes.**
- In 2003 The International Headache Society published the second edition of *The International Classification of Headache Disorders*. This classifies and defines all of the causes of headache in the following sections:
  - Migraine
  - Tension-type headache
  - Cluster headache and other trigeminal autonomic cephalalgias
  - Other primary headaches
  - Headache attributed to head and/or neck trauma
  - Headache attributed to cranial or cervical vascular disorder
  - Headache attributed to non-vascular intracranial disorder
  - Headache attributed to a substance or its withdrawal
  - Headache attributed to infection
  - Headache attributed to disorder of homeostasis
  - Headache or facial pain attributed to disorder of cranium, neck, eyes, ears, nose, sinuses, teeth, mouth, or other facial or cranial structures
  - Headache attributed to psychiatric disorder
  - Cranial neuralgias and central causes of facial pain
- The full classification can be viewed at http://216.25.100.131/ihscommon/guidelines/pdfs/ihc_II_main_no_print.pdf.

[Headache Classification Subcommittee of the International Headache Society, 2004]

How common is it?

- **The lifetime prevalence of headache is 96%;** it is higher in females (99%) than males (93%) [Rasmussen et al, 1991].
- **Tension-type headache is the most common type of headache. The lifetime prevalence of tension-type headache ranges from 30% to 78% in different studies;** it is more common in women than in men; the prevalence declines with age. Chronic tension-type headache (occurring on >=15 days each month) affects 3% of adults [Silberstein et al, 2002; BASH, 2004;

Headache Classification Subcommittee of the International Headache Society, 2004].

- **The lifetime prevalence of migraine is 16%;** it is higher in females (25%) than males (8%) [Rasmussen et al, 1991].
- People who suffer from migraine have an increased prevalence of tension-type headache (87% compared with 78% of the general population) [Rasmussen et al, 1991].
- **Medication overuse headache is the most common cause of intractable headache.** Up to 1 in 50 people suffer from medication overuse headache. It is five times more common in women then in men [BASH, 2004].

How do I know my patient has it?

Overview

- **An accurate diagnosis is vital in order that the correct treatment can be given.**
- **The history is the most important factor in reaching a diagnosis.** A full history may be time-consuming, but enough time must be given otherwise misdiagnosis (and hence incorrect treatment) may result. A headache diary is a particularly useful tool to aid diagnosis.
- **It is important to remember that people may suffer from more than one type of headache.** A separate history must be taken for each type.
- **A central nervous system and general examination,** as guided by the history, should be performed in all cases. It is likely to be normal in most people, but is essential in order to exclude serious causes of headache and to allay the person's anxiety. Of people referred to outpatients because of headache, less than 1% had an intracranial lesion, and each person with an intracranial lesion had physical signs of it.
  - Fundoscopy and blood pressure measurement must always be performed to exclude papilloedema and hypertension. It is often sensible to repeat fundoscopy at review appointments. Hypertension does not cause headache (unless it is malignant hypertension), but medication used to treat headache (especially migraine) may adversely affect blood pressure.
- **Most people need no investigation.** There are no diagnostic tests for the most common causes of headache.
  - Neuroimaging is unlikely to be helpful unless the history suggests a serious cause of headache, or there are abnormal clinical signs.

Migraine

- **Migraine** is usually easily diagnosed from the history. See the separate PRODIGY guidance for *Migraine*.

Tension-type headache

- **Tension-type headache** is divided into episodic or chronic subtypes:
  - **Episodic tension-type headache** lasts from 30 minutes to 7 days. It is usually bilateral. It is described as pressing or tightening (but not pulsating), and is of mild to moderate intensity. It may arise from, or spread into, the neck. It is not worsened by routine physical activity. Photophobia or phonophobia may be present, but are mild. Nausea is not a feature of episodic tension-type headache. The only significant finding on examination is increased pericranial muscle tenderness (frontal, temporal, masseter, pterygoid, sternocleidomastoid, splenius, and trapezius).
  - **Chronic tension-type headache** occurs on 15 days or more each month. Otherwise, it has all of the features of episodic tension-type headache. Chronic tension-type headache evolves over time in people who originally suffered from episodic tension-type headache.
- Tension-type headache is mild to moderate, but seldom severe.
- Tension-type headache is often stress-related.
- Tension-type headache is more common in sedentary people.
- People who suffer from tension-type headache often suffer from migraine without aura.
- People who suffer from tension-type headache may develop medication overuse headache.

Medication overuse headache

- **Medication overuse headache** results from the chronic overuse of medication used to treat headache. It is associated with aspirin, paracetamol (especially when combined with codeine), nonsteroidal anti-inflammatory drugs (NSAIDs), triptans, opioids, and ergotamine. It does not develop when the same analgesia is used for other chronic conditions; the reason for this is not known.
- Medication overuse headache should be considered in a person with a pre-existing primary headache (particularly migraine or tension-type headache, sometimes present for years) who reports that their headaches have worsened. The frequency of headache, and medication use, has increased.
- The headache develops (or markedly worsens) during the period of medication overuse.
- The development of medication overuse headache requires the following frequency of medication use:
  - Aspirin, paracetamol (not combined with codeine), NSAIDs — used for 15 days or more every month for more than 3 months.
  - Triptans, opioids, ergotamine — used for 10 days or more every month for more than 3 months.
- Pre-emptive use of medication is common, i.e. the medication that is causing the headache is taken in anticipation of the headache's occurring.
- **The features of medication overuse headache include:**
  - The headache is present on more than 15 days every month.
  - The headache is usually present (and often at its worst) on waking.
  - The location, character, and intensity of the headache are highly variable (between different people, and in the same person).
  - The headache usually increases after physical exertion.
  - Nausea and vomiting are rare.
  - The headache temporarily worsens on discontinuation of the causative medication.

Cluster headache

- **Cluster headache** consists of attacks of severe unilateral pain. The pain is felt in or around the eye or temple (but may spread to other areas of the head). The pain is excruciating, and is described as boring or burning. Each attack lasts 15–180 minutes, and may occur from once every other day to 8 times daily.
- Each attack is associated with one or more of the following ipsilateral features:
  - Conjunctival injection
  - Lacrimation
  - Nasal congestion
  - Rhinorrhoea
  - Forehead and facial sweating
  - Miosis
  - Ptosis
  - Eyelid oedema
- During an attack the person is typically restless or agitated, unable to lie down, and typically paces the

floor, or may even bang their head against the wall. Attacks often occur at night, typically waking the person after 1–2 hours sleep.

- Attacks occur in clusters lasting for weeks or months, separated by remission periods lasting months or years. However, 10–15% of sufferers have no remission periods.
- During a cluster period the pain almost invariably occurs on the same side.
- During a cluster period an attack can be precipitated by alcohol or other vasodilators.
- The onset of cluster headache is usually 20–40 years of age. It is 3–4 times more common in men.
- Cluster headache is inherited as an autosomal dominant condition in 5% of cases.

[Silberstein et al, 2002; BASH, 2004]

What else might it be?

- The list of causes of headache is extensive and can be viewed at http://216.25.100.131/ihscommon/guidelines/pdfs/ihc_II_main_no_print.pdf.
- Conditions that are frequently thought to cause headache, but are actually rarely a cause, include:
  - **Sinus disease** — sinusitis is overdiagnosed as a cause of headache; in particular, frontal headache is more commonly due to migraine or tension-type headache than sinusitis.
    - Acute sinusitis may cause headache, and is accompanied by purulent nasal discharge.
    - Chronic sinusitis only causes headache if there is an acute exacerbation.
  - **Errors of refraction** — these are rarely a cause of headache. If so, the headache is mild, felt in the eyes or frontal area, and is absent on waking.

[Silberstein et al, 2002; BASH, 2004]

Complications

- Depression secondary to chronic headache.
- Medication overuse headache.

Management issues

- How do I manage episodic tension-type headache? p.892
- How do I manage chronic tension-type headache? p.892
- How do I manage medication overuse headache? p.892
- How do I manage cluster headache? p.893
- Medicines management p.893

How do I manage episodic tension-type headache?

- **Reassurance may be the only management that is needed.** Episodic tension-type headache is self-limiting, and an explanation of its benign nature should always be given.
- **Manage stress, anxiety, or depression appropriately.** Episodic tension-type headache may be stress-related. See the separate PRODIGY guidance for *Depression* and *Stress — acute reaction.*
- **Physical exercise may be beneficial.** Tension-type headache is more common in sedentary people. Referral to a physiotherapist may be beneficial for advice about posture.
- **Symptomatic medication** may be necessary for people with episodic tension-type headache. It is appropriate if the headache occurs on average less than 2 days per week.
  - Nonsteroidal anti-inflammatory drugs (NSAIDs) are recommended as first-line therapy, as they appear to be more effective than paracetamol.
  - Paracetamol is recommended for people intolerant of NSAIDs.
  - Opioids (including codeine) must be avoided due to the risk of developing medication overuse headache (the risk is much higher with opioids than with NSAIDs or paracetamol).
  - It is important to ask about the use of over-the-counter medications, especially as many contain codeine.

[Silberstein et al, 2002; BASH, 2004]

How do I manage chronic tension-type headache?

- **Amitriptyline is the treatment of choice for chronic tension-type headache.** One systematic review and three RCTs found that amitriptyline significantly improved headache duration and frequency of chronic tension-type headache.
- There is insufficient evidence of the efficacy of other antidepressants (tricyclic and selective serotonin reuptake inhibitors) to recommend their use in chronic tension-type headache. Other tricyclic antidepressants may be used if the person is intolerant of amitriptyline, but there are no studies to support this or to guide the choice of antidepressant. Coexistent depression should, however, be treated appropriately; see the separate PRODIGY guidance for *Depression.*
- Cognitive behavioural therapy has limited evidence of efficacy in reducing the intensity of chronic tension-type headache.
- There is insufficient evidence of the efficacy of acupuncture or homeopathy to recommend their use in chronic tension-type headache.
- Chronic tension-type headache may be refractory to treatment. If this appears to be the case, referral to a neurologist or pain clinic is advised.

[Silberstein et al, 2002; BASH, 2004; Goadsby, 2004]

How do I manage medication overuse headache?

- **Stopping the therapy causing medication overuse headache is imperative.** Cessation, however, will initially cause the headaches to worsen; subsequent improvement usually occurs within several weeks, but may take several months. There is no consensus over whether to advise abrupt or gradual (over several weeks) cessation of the suspected drug.
- **Replace the causative medication with a regular nonsteroidal anti-inflammatory drug (NSAID)** (unless the causative medication is actually an NSAID, or the person is intolerant of NSAIDs):
  - There is no evidence to guide the choice of NSAID; PRODIGY recommends the use of standard NSAIDs at standard doses.
  - Continue the NSAID until the medication overuse headache improves — this may take up to 6 months — then stop the NSAID.
  - If the headaches worsen upon stopping the NSAID, it is advised to restart the NSAID at the same dose as previously taken, and to take it for a further 6 months before stopping again.
- **If the causative agent is an NSAID (or the person is intolerant of NSAIDs), replace it with amitriptyline.**
- Regular review and repeated explanation of the cause of medication overuse headache, and the management plan, is advised during this withdrawal period.
  - The headaches will initially worsen before any improvement is noticed.
  - Many people will be tempted to use over-the-counter analgesia. It is vital that they are strongly advised against this.

H

- Referral to a neurologist is advised if management fails in primary care.

[Zed et al, 1999; Silberstein et al, 2002]

How do I manage cluster headache?

- **Sumatriptan given by subcutaneous injection is the treatment of choice for acute cluster headache.** This is the only formulation of any of the triptans that is licensed for cluster headache.
- Sumatriptan and zolmitriptan given by nasal spray have shown evidence of efficacy in the treatment of acute cluster headache, but are not licensed for this indication.
- **Alcohol should be avoided during a cluster period,** as its ingestion triggers attacks in some people.
- There is little evidence to govern the prophylactic treatment of cluster headache. Management is empirical, and includes corticosteroids, ergotamine, lithium, methysergide, and verapamil. Referral to a neurologist or pain clinic is advised.

[Silberstein et al, 2002; BNF 48, 2004]

Medicines management

Nonsteroidal anti-inflammatory drugs (NSAIDs)

A full discussion on the contraindications, adverse effects, monitoring issues, and interactions of NSAIDs is beyond the scope of this guidance. For further information, see the separate PRODIGY guidance on *Nonsteroidal anti-inflammatory drugs (NSAIDs)*.

- Consider patient comorbidity when prescribing nonsteroidal anti-inflammatory drugs (NSAIDs).
- NSAIDs commonly cause gastrointestinal adverse effects, and can worsen asthma, hypertension, renal impairment, and heart failure.
- For people at high risk of gastrointestinal adverse events, we recommend the following options:
  - Use paracetamol instead of a NSAID if possible.
  - Or, use a gastroprotective agent with a standard NSAID.
- For advice on the management of dyspepsia due to NSAIDs, see the separate PRODIGY guidance on *Dyspepsia — symptoms (uninvestigated by endoscopy)* and *Dyspepsia — proven DU, GU, or NSAID-associated ulcer*.

Amitriptyline

What is the initial dose and how should this be increased?

- Amitriptyline should be taken at night.
- Therapy should be started with a low dose and increased gradually, according to the clinical response and any evidence of intolerance.
- The starting dose should be 10–25 mg at night, and increased every few days by 10 mg increments to a target dose of 75–150 mg at night.
- Improvement should be noticed within a few days of reaching the target dose.

How should amitriptyline be withdrawn?

- Withdrawal should be gradual (by 10 mg every few days) after improvement has been maintained for 4–6 months.
- If the headaches worsen during the withdrawal period, it is advised to increase the dose of amitriptyline again to the target previously attained, and continue at this dose for a further 4–6 months before attempting gradual withdrawal again.

What monitoring is recommended?

- Electrocardiogram should be carried out in patients with cardiac disease and in the elderly.

Which potentially hazardous interactions should be avoided or monitored carefully?

- Amitriptyline may cause drowsiness which may affect the performance of skilled tasks (e.g. driving).
- Amitriptyline should not be used in patients:
  - During the recovery phase after myocardial infarction.
  - Who have arrhythmias, particularly heart block of any degree.
  - Who have mania.
  - Who have severe liver disease.
  - Who are pregnant.
  - Who are breastfeeding.
- Concomitant administration of the following is contraindicated:
  - Monoamine oxidase inhibitors (MAOIs); amitriptyline must also not be used within 2 weeks of discontinuation of therapy with an MAOI.
  - Alcohol, barbiturates, and other CNS depressants, the effects of which may be enhanced by amitriptyline therapy.

Sumatriptan

Which formulation of sumatriptan should be used?

- Oral absorption is poor, nasal and subcutaneous formulations have a faster onset of action.
- Only subcutaneous sumatriptan is licensed for use in cluster headache; however, sumatriptan nasal spray is licensed for use in migraine.

How should subcutaneous sumatriptan be administered?

- Sumatriptan should not be used prophylactically.
- **The recommended adult dose is a single 6 mg** subcutaneous injection for each cluster attack.
- **No more than two doses** should be taken in 24 hours, with a **minimum interval of 1 hour** between the two doses.
- **If more than two doses are taken in 24 hours,** the patient should contact their doctor or attend an accident and emergency department.

What are the adverse effects of sumatriptan?

- **Adverse effects** of sumatriptan are generally mild and self-limiting. They include nausea, dizziness, somnolence, and dry mouth [Fox, 2000].
- **'Triptan sensations'** include a warm–hot sensation, tightness, tingling, flushing, and feelings of heaviness or pressure in areas such as the face and limbs, and occasionally the chest. They occur in less than 3% of people in clinical studies of the use of triptans for migraine.
- **Sumatriptan should not be given intravenously** because of its potential to cause vasospasm.
- **People with ischaemic heart disease, cerebrovascular disease, peripheral vascular disease, or uncontrolled hypertension should not use sumatriptan.** Chest pain can occur, but has only occasionally been associated with the electrocardiogram or enzyme changes seen in myocardial infarction. Myocardial infarction has been reported in rare cases [Welch et al, 2000].
- People with risk factors for ischaemic heart disease should be evaluated carefully before starting sumatriptan [Evans and Martin, 2000; Welch et al, 2000].
- Sumatriptan should not be used in people:
  - Who have coronary vasospasm (Prinzmetal's angina).
  - Who have severe hepatic impairment.
  - Who are pregnant.
  - Who are breastfeeding.
- Concomitant administration of the following is contraindicated:
  - Ergotamine or derivatives of ergotamine (including methysergide).

- Monoamine oxidase inhibitors (MAOIs); amitriptyline must also not be used within 2 weeks of discontinuation of therapy with an MAOI.

References

1. BASH (2004) *Guidelines for all doctors in the diagnosis and management of migraine and tension-type headache*. British Association for the Study of Headache. www.bash.org.uk [Accessed: 21/09/2004].
2. BNF 48 (2004) *British National Formulary*. 48th edn. London: British Medical Association and Royal Pharmaceutical Society of Great Britain.
3. Evans, R.W. and Martin, V. (2000) Expert opinion: assessing cardiac risk prior to use of triptans. *Headache* 40(7), 599–602.
4. Fox, A.W. (2000) Comparative tolerability of oral 5-HT1B/1D agonists. *Headache* 40(7), 521–527.
5. Goadsby, P.J. (2004) *Headache (chronic tension-type)*. Clinical Evidence. Volume 12. www.clinicalevidence.com [Accessed: 02/02/2005].
6. Headache Classification Subcommittee of the International Headache Society (2004) The international classification of headache disorders. 2nd edition. *Cephalalgia* 24(Suppl 1), 1–150.
7. Rasmussen, B.K., Jensen, R., Schroll, M. and Olesen, J. (1991) Epidemiology of headache in a general population – a prevalence study. *Journal of Clinical Epidemiology* 44(11), 1147–1157.
8. Silberstein, S.D., Lipton, R.B. and Goadsby, P.J. (2002) *Headache in clinical practice*. 2nd edn. London: Martin Dunitz.
9. Welch, K.M., Mathew, N.T., Stone, P. et al (2000) Tolerability of sumatriptan: clinical trials and post-marketing experience. *Cephalalgia* 20(8), 687–695. [erratum appears in *Cephalalgia* (2001) 21(2), 164–5].
10. Zed, P.J., Loewen, P.S. and Robinson, G. (1999) Medication-induced headache: overview and systematic review of therapeutic approaches. *Annals of Pharmacotherapy* 33(1), 61–72.

PRODIGY GUIDANCE

Heart failure

Last revised in June 2004
At the time of print this topic was being updated. The newly revised guidance will be issued on to the website in 2006.
www.prodigy.nhs.uk/guidance.asp?gt=Heart failure

Applies to people over the age of 16 years

This guidance covers the initiation and continuing treatment of people with heart failure and the emergency management of acute pulmonary oedema.

This guidance does not cover the management of people with predominant diastolic dysfunction, as shown by echocardiography (impaired diastolic filling and with normal or elevated left ventricular ejection fraction), predominant right heart failure (as in cor pulmonale), or children with heart failure.

There is separate PRODIGY guidance for *Angina, Hyperlipidaemia, Hypertension,* and *Prior myocardial infarction — prophylactic treatments.*

Goals

- To diagnose correctly
- To improve symptoms and slow their deterioration
- To improve long-term survival

Contents

Scenarios

- Initial Management — ACE inhibitor and diuretic p.895
- Increase ACE inhibitor p.898
- Increase diuretic (if needed) p.899
- Addition of beta-blocker p.901
- Addition of spironolactone p.903
- Addition of digoxin p.904
- Intolerant of ACE inhibitor p.905
- Acute heart failure (pulmonary oedema) p.907

Extended Information, p. 907

Which scenario?

- **Initial Management — ACE inhibitor and diuretic:** covers the initiation of ACE inhibitor and/or diuretic.
- **Increase ACE inhibitor:** covers the titration to an optimum 'target' dose of ACE inhibitor (or to the maximum tolerated dose if lower).
- **Increase diuretic (if needed):** covers the management of people with persisting symptoms and signs of fluid overload.
- **Addition of beta-blocker:** covers the management of people on adequate doses of ACE inhibitor.
- **Addition of spironolactone:** covers the management of people with moderate to severe heart failure on adequate doses of ACE inhibitor and diuretic.
- **Addition of digoxin:** covers the management of people in sinus rhythm on adequate doses of ACE inhibitor and diuretic but still symptomatic. For people in atrial fibrillation see separate PRODIGY guidance *Atrial fibrillation.*
- **Intolerant of ACE inhibitor:** covers the initiation of angiotensin-II receptor antagonist or isosorbide dinitrate/hydralazine as an alternative to an ACE.
- **Acute heart failure:** covers the management of acute heart failure.

Initial Management — ACE Inhibitor and Diuretic

Which therapy?

- **Asymptomatic people or people with mild symptoms (NYHA grades I–II)** — consider ACE inhibitor alone.
- **Otherwise first treat with a diuretic and once stable initiate an ACE inhibitor.**
- **Initiate treatment with a low dose of an ACE inhibitor** and advise the person to sit or lie down for 2–4 hours after this initial dose.
- **If at risk of first-dose hypotension** (see *Prescribing points*) it is preferable to withdraw or reduce diuretics temporarily for at least 24 hours prior to starting an ACE inhibitor, initiate treatment with a very low dose of a short-acting ACE inhibitor (captopril 6.25 mg), and monitor carefully for 2 hours. Alternatively, consider initiating treatment in hospital.
- **If tolerated, increase the dose of ACE inhibitor** over 4 weeks, with the goal of reaching the doses used in clinical trials:
  - Captopril 50 mg three times daily
  - Enalapril 10–20 mg twice daily
  - Lisinopril 30–35 mg daily
  - Ramipril 5 mg twice daily
- **Increase more cautiously in those at increased risk of first-dose hypotension.**
- **Higher doses of an ACE inhibitor may be necessary** in people who remain symptomatic.

Practical prescribing points

For further information please see the *Medicines Compendium* (www.medicines.org.uk) or the *British National Formulary* (www.bnf.org).

- **The risk of ACE inhibitor-induced first-dose hypotension or renal impairment is increased in the following high-risk groups of people:**
  - Creatinine >150 micromol/l
  - Urea >12 mmol/l
  - Sodium <130 mmol/l
  - Systolic blood pressure <100 mmHg
  - Diuretic dose > furosemide (frusemide) 80 mg or bumetanide 2 mg daily
  - Known or suspected renal artery stenosis, e.g. if peripheral vascular disease
  - People aged 70 years and over or who are frail
  - Hypovolaemia
  - With unstable heart failure

- Receiving high-dose vasodilator therapy
- **Avoid potassium-sparing diuretics (except spironolactone) or potassium supplements** in people on ACE inhibitors (other than in exceptional cases) due to the risk of hyperkalaemia.
- **Stop nonsteroidal anti-inflammatory drugs (if possible)** as they reduce the effectiveness of diuretics and increase the risk of renal impairment with ACE inhibitors.
- **Avoid ACE inhibitors if significant cardiac outflow tract obstruction** (e.g. due to aortic stenosis or hypertrophic obstructive cardiomyopathy).
- **Liver disease**
  - ACE inhibitors that are in the form of prodrugs, such as enalapril and ramipril, require close monitoring in people with impaired liver function.
  - Loop diuretics cause hypokalaemia that may precipitate coma.
- **Pregnancy and breastfeeding:** avoid — potential adverse defects in pregnancy include problems with fetal and neonatal blood pressure control and renal function.

Follow-up advice

H

- **ACE inhibitors can cause renal failure as well as hyperkalaemia, therefore, renal function should be monitored (blood pressure, renal function, serum potassium) before and during treatment — one week after each dose increase.**
- **Repeat serum electrolytes and renal function within one week** of starting an ACE inhibitor or diuretic, and review the person to assess response to treatment and to check BP.
- **Check for adverse effects,** such as symptomatic hypotension, renal dysfunction or hyperkalaemia (i.e. a rise in urea to 12 mmol/l, creatinine to 200 micromol /l, or potassium to 5.5 mmol/l). If these occur either stop or reduce the dose of ACE inhibitor, and consider specialist referral.
- **If tolerated, increase the dose of the ACE inhibitor** over 4 weeks, with the goal of reaching the doses used in clinical trials:
  - Captopril 50 mg three times daily
  - Enalapril 10–20 mg twice daily
  - Lisinopril 30–35 mg daily
  - Ramipril 5 mg twice daily
- **At the end of this titration period** check serum electrolytes, renal function, BP, and response to treatment.
- **Once on a stable dose** serum electrolytes and renal function should be checked at least annually.
- **Cough** is common in heart failure but is also caused by an ACE inhibitor in a small percentage of people. Cough is not an indication to stop an ACE inhibitor unless it is troublesome.
- **Monitor regularly all people taking loop diuretics** for hypovolaemia, renal failure, and electrolyte imbalances.

Should I refer or investigate?

Refer?

- **Consider hospital initiation of an ACE inhibitor if:**
  - Creatinine >150 micromol/l
  - Urea >12 mmol/l
  - Sodium <130 mmol/l
  - Systolic blood pressure <100 mmHg
  - Diuretic dose > furosemide (frusemide) 80 mg or bumetanide 2 mg daily
  - Known or suspected renal artery stenosis, e.g. if peripheral vascular disease
  - People aged 70 years and over or who are frail
  - Hypovolaemia
  - With unstable heart failure
  - Receiving high-dose vasodilator therapy
- **Refer if unsure of the diagnosis.**
- Any person with a potentially reversible cause of heart failure (e.g. a valve lesion) should be referred to a cardiologist.

Investigate?

- **Echocardiography:** should be performed in all people with suspected heart failure to confirm the diagnosis and exclude underlying causes (e.g. valvular heart disease).
- **Full blood count:** to detect anaemia (may exacerbate or precipitate heart failure).
- **Serum electrolytes and renal function:** as a baseline and to exclude renal impairment.
- **Liver function tests:** deranged in hepatic congestion and may indicate possibility of alcohol-related cardiomyopathy.
- **Blood glucose:** to detect diabetes mellitus.
- **Blood lipids:** to detect hyperlipidaemia.
- **Thyroid function tests:** hyperthyroidism or hypothyroidism may exacerbate or precipitate heart failure.
- **Urinalysis:** suspect renal impairment if proteinuria or haematuria are detected.
- **ECG:** look for signs of previous MI, ischaemia, left ventricular hypertrophy, arrhythmias. **Heart failure is unlikely if the ECG is normal,** and the diagnosis should be reconsidered in this situation.
- **B-type natriuretic peptide (BNP) or its N-terminal fragment (NTproBNP):** a raised concentration of either has been shown to have a sensitivity of greater than 90% and a specificity of 80–90% for the diagnosis of heart failure. *Heart failure is unlikely if the level of BNP or NTproBNP is normal, especially if the ECG is also normal,* and the diagnosis should be reconsidered in this situation.
- **CXR:** to look for signs of heart failure (upper lobe diversion, interstitial oedema, effusions) and to help exclude pulmonary disease.

Patient information leaflets

The following PILs are available at www.prodigy.nhs.uk

- Blood Test - General
- Blood Test - Kidney Function
- British Cardiac Patients Association
- British Heart Foundation
- Cardiomyopathy Association
- Heart Failure
- How the Heart Works
- Medicines - Name Changes of Medicines

Shared decision making

- **An ACE inhibitor** (Angiotensin Converting Enzyme Inhibitor) is the usual treatment for heart failure. These medicines help to prevent a build up of body fluid, and have a protective effect on the heart muscle.
- When you first start an ACE inhibitor:
  - Lie or sit down for 2–4 hours after the very first dose.
  - Start with a low dose at first, and gradually increase the dose over 4 weeks.
  - A blood test is usual before, and about a week after, starting an ACE inhibitor.
  - If you take a diuretic ('water tablet') you may be advised not to take it for a day or so before an ACE inhibitor is started.

- **A diuretic** ('water tablet') may be prescribed as well. It will make you pass out extra urine. This helps you to clear excess body fluid that builds up.

Drug rationale

Drugs not included

- **ACE inhibitors other than captopril, enalapril, lisonopril, and ramipril** are not offered. ACE inhibitors not licensed for initiating heart failure treatment in primary care [BNF 47, 2004] and those that have not been studied in large clinical trials to examine outcomes such as their effect on mortality, are not offered.
- **Loop diuretics other than bumetanide and furosemide (frusemide)** are not included. Torasemide offers no clinical benefit and is also excluded on cost grounds.
- **Diuretics other than furosemide and bumetanide. Thiazides** are not as effective as effective in heart failure as loop diuretics, especially if renal function is impaired. Combination with a loop diuretic may be valuable in some people with oedema but this should usually only be initiated under specialist supervision [DTB, 1994]. **Torasemide** offers no clinical advantage to furosemide or bumetanide and is significantly more expensive. **Potassium-sparing diuretics** are not usually effective for heart failure. They should only be added to a loop or thiazide diuretic if a person cannot tolerate an ACE inhibitor and caution is required.
- **Beta-blockers** should be considered for people who are clinically stable and taking an ACE inhibitor and/or diuretic, as they further improve prognosis (see *Addition of beta-blocker* scenario) [Heart Failure Society of America, 1999; Krum, 2001; Remme et al, 2001].
- **Spironolactone** should be considered for people with moderate to severe heart failure already taking a combination of an ACE inhibitor, diuretic and/or digoxin, as this further improves prognosis (see *Addition of spironolactone* scenario) [SIGN, 1999; DH, 2000; Samuel, 2003].
- **Digoxin** should be considered for people in sinus rhythm who continue to be symptomatic despite adequate doses of diuretic and ACE inhibitor (see *Addition of digoxin* scenario) [DH, 2000]. Digoxin can improve symptoms and, when combined with a diuretic and ACE inhibitor, has been shown to reduce the risk of hospitalization and clinical deterioration, but not mortality [Hood et al, 2002].
- **Angiotensin-II receptor antagonists** are not currently licensed for the treatment of heart failure, although trial data appear comparable with ACE inhibitors [Pitt et al, 2000; Cohn and Tognoni, 2001]. The National Service Framework and SIGN guidance suggest considering an angiotension-II receptor antagonist if ACE inhibitors are not tolerated, particularly due to cough (see *Intolerant of ACE inhibitor* scenario).
- **Hydralazine/isosorbide dinitrate in combination** might be considered in people unable to tolerate an ACE inhibitor (see *Intolerant of ACE inhibitor* scenario) but evidence indicates that improvement in survival is more effective with ACE inhibitors [Cohn et al, 1991]. Hydralazine is only licensed for initiation in hospital for people in heart failure, and requires careful titration.

Drugs included

- **ACE inhibitors — captopril, enalapril, lisinopril, and ramipril** are licensed for initiation in the community. They have all been studied in large clinical trials and there is good evidence that they reduce mortality, hospital admission and improve symptoms and exercise tolerance in all grades of symptomatic heart failure [Garg and Yusuf, 1995; Eccles et al, 1998; Flather et al, 2000]. Careful monitoring of people on ACE inhibitors is essential.
- **Loop diuretics** are effective for increasing renal sodium and fluid excretion and giving symptom relief in left heart failure.
  - **Furosemide (frusemide)** is the most commonly used diuretic in the UK.
  - **Bumetanide** is an effective alternative to furosemide [DTB, 1994]. Bumetanide is thought to be less ototoxic than furosemide, and therefore preferred in people with hearing problems or receiving other ototoxic medication [MeReC, 1990].

Prescriptions

Start enalapril/lisinopril/ramipril: first 2-week titration

Enalapril: initial titration from 2.5mg to 5mg per day
- Age from 16 years onwards
- Enalapril 2.5mg tablets. Take one tablet once a day for 7 days (take the FIRST dose at night). Then take two tablets once a day for 7 days; supply 21 tablets; NHS Cost £1.96.

Lisinopril: initial titration from 2.5mg to 5mg per day
- Age from 16 years onwards
- Lisinopril 2.5mg tablets. Take one tablet once a day for 7 days (take the FIRST dose at night). Then take two tablets once a day for 7 days; supply 21 tablets; NHS Cost £4.70.

Ramipril: initial titration from 1.25mg to 2.5mg per day
- Age from 16 years onwards
- Ramipril 1.25mg tablets. Take one tablet once a day for 7 days (take the FIRST dose at night). Then take two tablets once a day for 7 days; supply 21 tablets; NHS Cost £3.98.

Enalapril/lisinopril/ramipril: second 2-week titration

Enalapril: further titration from 10mg to 20mg per day
- Age from 16 years onwards
- Enalapril 10mg tablets. Take one tablet once a day for 7 days, then take one tablet twice a day for 7 days; supply 21 tablets; NHS Cost £4.00.

Lisinopril: further titration from 10mg to 20mg per day
- Age from 16 years onwards
- Lisinopril 10mg tablets. Take one tablet once a day for 7 days, then take two tablets once a day for 7 days; supply 21 tablets; NHS Cost £7.28.

Ramipril: further titration from 5mg to 10mg per day
- Age from 16 years onwards
- Ramipril 5mg tablets. Take one tablet once a day for 7 days, then take two tablets once a day for 7 days; supply 21 tablets; NHS Cost £7.16.

Start captopril: titration over 8 weeks

Weeks 1 and 2: titrate captopril from 6.25mg to 25mg per day
- Age from 16 years onwards
- Captopril 12.5mg tablets. Take half a tablet at night on day 1, then take one tablet twice a day for 14 days; supply 29 tablets; NHS Cost £1.19.

Weeks 3 and 4: captopril 25mg twice a day
- Age from 16 years onwards
- Captopril 25mg tablets. Take one tablet twice a day; supply 28 tablets; NHS Cost £1.61.

Weeks 5 and 6: captopril 50mg twice a day
- Age from 16 years onwards
- Captopril 50mg tablets. Take one tablet twice a day; supply 28 tablets; NHS Cost £2.04.

Weeks 7 and 8: captopril 50mg three times a day

- Age from 16 years onwards
- Captopril 50mg tablets. Take one tablet three times a day; supply 42 tablets; NHS Cost £3.05.

Start loop diuretic

Bumetanide 1mg each morning

- Age from 16 years onwards
- Bumetanide 1mg tablets. Take one tablet each morning; supply 14 tablets; NHS Cost £0.85.

Furosemide (frusemide) 40mg each morning

- Age from 16 years onwards
- Furosemide 40mg tablets. Take one tablet each morning; supply 14 tablets; NHS Cost £0.39.

Increase ACE inhibitor

Which therapy?

- If tolerated, increase the dose of ACE inhibitor over 4 weeks to a dose equivalent to those used in clinical trials:
  - Captopril 50 mg three times daily
  - Enalapril 10–20 mg twice daily
  - Lisinopril 30–35 mg daily
  - Ramipril 5 mg twice daily
- Even higher doses may be necessary in people who remain symptomatic.

H

Practical prescribing points

For further information please see the *Medicines Compendium* (www.medicines.org.uk) or the *British National Formulary* (www.bnf.org).

- **Avoid potassium-sparing diuretics (except spironolactone) or potassium supplements** in people on ACE inhibitors (other than in exceptional cases) due to the risk of hyperkalaemia.
- **Stop nonsteroidal anti-inflammatory drugs (if possible)** as they reduce the effectiveness of diuretics and increase the risk of renal impairment with ACE inhibitors.
- **Avoid ACE inhibitors if significant cardiac outflow tract obstruction** (e.g. due to aortic stenosis or hypertrophic obstructive cardiomyopathy).
- **Liver disease**
  - ACE inhibitors that are in the form of prodrugs, such as enalapril and ramipril, require close monitoring in people with impaired liver function.
  - Loop diuretics cause hypokalaemia which may precipitate coma.

Follow-up advice

- **ACE inhibitors can cause renal failure as well as hyperkalaemia, therefore, renal function should be monitored (blood pressure, renal function, serum potassium) during treatment — one week after each dose increase.**
- Review after 1 month; check for adverse effects, such as symptomatic hypotension, renal dysfunction, or hyperkalaemia (i.e. a rise in urea to >=12 mmol/l, creatinine to >=200 micromol /l, or potassium to >=5.5 mmol/l). If these occur either stop or reduce the dose of ACE inhibitor and consider specialist referral.
- **Once on a stable dose,** serum electrolytes and renal function should be checked at least annually.
- **Cough** is common in heart failure but is also caused by an ACE inhibitor in a small percentage of people. Cough is not an indication to stop an ACE inhibitor unless it is troublesome.
- **Monitor regularly all people taking loop diuretics** for hypovolaemia, renal failure, and electrolyte imbalances.

Should I refer or investigate?

Refer?

Consider referral if:

- **Poor response to treatment** with adequate doses of an ACE inhibitor (e.g. captopril 50 mg three times daily, enalapril 10–20 mg twice daily, lisinopril 30–35 mg daily, ramipril 5 mg twice daily) and a diuretic (e.g. 80 mg furosemide [frusemide] or 2 mg bumetanide daily). Alternatively, consider beta-blockers, spironolactone, and digoxin.
- **Unable to tolerate an ACE inhibitor.** Alternatively, consider an angiotensin-II receptor antagonist or isosorbide dinitrate/hydralazine.
- **Deteriorating renal function or hyperkalaemia.**
- Any person with a potentially reversible cause of heart failure (e.g. a valve lesion) should be referred to a cardiologist.

Investigate?

If not previously done, the following should be considered:

- **Echocardiography:** should be performed in all people with suspected heart failure to confirm the diagnosis and exclude underlying causes (e.g. valvular heart disease).
- **Full blood count:** to detect anaemia (may exacerbate or precipitate heart failure).
- **Serum electrolytes and renal function:** as a baseline and to exclude renal impairment.
- **Liver function tests:** deranged in hepatic congestion and may indicate possibility of alcohol-related cardiomyopathy.
- **Blood glucose:** to detect diabetes mellitus.
- **Blood lipids:** to detect hyperlipidaemia.
- **Thyroid function tests:** hyperthyroidism or hypothyroidism may exacerbate or precipitate heart failure.
- **Urinalysis:** suspect renal impairment if proteinuria or haematuria are detected.
- **ECG:** look for signs of previous MI, ischaemia, left ventricular hypertrophy, arrhythmias. Heart failure is unlikely if the ECG is normal, and the diagnosis should be reconsidered in this situation.
- **B-type natriuretic peptide (BNP) or its N-terminal fragment (NTproBNP):** a raised concentration of either has been shown to have a sensitivity of greater than 90% and a specificity of 80–90% for the diagnosis of heart failure. *Heart failure is unlikely if the level of BNP or NTproBNP is normal,* especially if the ECG is also normal, and the diagnosis should be reconsidered in this situation.
- **CXR:** to look for signs of heart failure (upper lobe diversion, interstitial oedema, effusions) and to help exclude pulmonary disease.

Patient information leaflets

The following PILs are available at www.prodigy.nhs.uk

- Blood Test - General
- Blood Test - Kidney Function
- British Cardiac Patients Association
- British Heart Foundation
- Cardiomyopathy Association
- Heart Failure
- How the Heart Works

Shared decision making

- **An ACE inhibitor** (Angiotensin Converting Enzyme Inhibitor) is the usual treatment for heart failure. These

medicines help to prevent a build up of body fluid, and have some protective effect on the heart muscle.
- A low dose of an ACE inhibitor is started at first, and then gradually increased to a usual regular dose.
- You need a blood test at least once a year when you take an ACE inhibitor medicine.

Drug rationale

Drugs not included

- **ACE inhibitors other than captopril, enalapril, lisonopril, and ramipril** are not offered. ACE inhibitors not licensed for initiating heart failure treatment in primary care [BNF 47, 2004] and those that have not been studied in large clinical trials to examine outcomes such as their effect on mortality, are not offered.

Drugs included

- **ACE inhibitors — captopril, enalapril, lisinopril, and ramipril** are licensed for initiation in the community. They have all been studied in large clinical trials and there is good evidence that they reduce mortality, hospital admission and improve symptoms and exercise tolerance in all grades of symptomatic heart failure [Garg and Yusuf, 1995; Eccles et al, 1998; Flather et al, 2000]. Careful monitoring of people on ACE inhibitors is essential.

Prescriptions

Enalapril

Enalapril 2.5mg twice a day
- Age from 16 years onwards
- Enalapril 2.5mg tablets. Take one tablet twice a day; supply 56 tablets; NHS Cost £5.22.

Enalapril 5mg twice a day
- Age from 16 years onwards
- Enalapril 5mg tablets. Take one tablet twice a day; supply 56 tablets; NHS Cost £7.54.

Enalapril 10mg twice a day (minimum target dose)
- Age from 16 years onwards
- Enalapril 10mg tablets. Take one tablet twice a day; supply 56 tablets; NHS Cost £10.66.

Enalapril 15mg twice a day
- Age from 16 years onwards
- Enalapril 5mg tablets. Take three tablets twice a day; supply 168 tablets; NHS Cost £22.56.

Enalapril 20mg twice a day
- Age from 16 years onwards
- Enalapril 20mg tablets. Take one tablet twice a day; supply 56 tablets; NHS Cost £12.24.

Lisinopril

Lisinopril 2.5mg once a day
- Age from 16 years onwards
- Lisinopril 2.5mg tablets. Take one tablet once a day; supply 28 tablets; NHS Cost £6.26.

Lisinopril 5mg once a day
- Age from 16 years onwards
- Lisinopril 5mg tablets. Take one tablet once a day; supply 28 tablets; NHS Cost £7.86.

Lisinopril 10mg once a day
- Age from 16 years onwards
- Lisinopril 10mg tablets. Take one tablet once a day; supply 28 tablets; NHS Cost £9.70.

Lisinopril 20mg once a day (minimum target dose)
- Age from 16 years onwards
- Lisinopril 20mg tablets. Take one tablet once a day; supply 28 tablets; NHS Cost £10.97.

Lisinopril 30mg once a day
- Age from 16 years onwards
- Lisinopril 10mg tablets. Take three tablets once a day; supply 84 tablets; NHS Cost £29.10.

Lisinopril 35mg once a day
- Age from 16 years onwards
- Lisinopril 10mg tablets. Take three tablets once a day; supply 84 tablets; NHS Cost £29.10.
- Lisinopril 5mg tablets. Take one tablet once a day; supply 28 tablets; NHS Cost £7.86.

Ramipril

Ramipril 1.25mg twice a day
- Age from 16 years onwards
- Ramipril 1.25mg tablets. Take one tablet twice a day; supply 56 tablets; NHS Cost £10.60.

Ramipril 2.5mg twice a day
- Age from 16 years onwards
- Ramipril 2.5mg tablets. Take one tablet twice a day; supply 56 tablets; NHS Cost £15.02.

Ramipril 5mg twice a day (minimum target dose)
- Age from 16 years onwards
- Ramipril 5mg tablets. Take one tablet twice a day; supply 56 tablets; NHS Cost £19.10.

Captopril

Captopril 12.5mg twice a day
- Age from 16 years onwards
- Captopril 12.5mg tablets. Take one tablet twice a day; supply 56 tablets; NHS Cost £2.22.

Captopril 25mg twice a day
- Age from 16 years onwards
- Captopril 25mg tablets. Take one tablet twice a day; supply 56 tablets; NHS Cost £2.95.

Captopril 25mg three times a day
- Age from 16 years onwards
- Captopril 25mg tablets. Take one tablet three times a day; supply 84 tablets; NHS Cost £4.82.

Captopril 50mg twice a day
- Age from 16 years onwards
- Captopril 50mg tablets. Take one tablet twice a day; supply 56 tablets; NHS Cost £3.75.

Captopril 50mg three times a day (target dose)
- Age from 16 years onwards
- Captopril 50mg tablets. Take one tablet three times a day; supply 84 tablets; NHS Cost £6.09.

Increase diuretic (if needed)

Which therapy?

- **Use the lowest dose of diuretic necessary** to relieve fluid overload and breathlessness.
- **People with mild to moderate heart failure and preserved renal function,** who also receive an ACE inhibitor, rarely need more than 80 mg of furosemide (frusemide) or 2 mg of bumetanide daily.
- **People with mild to moderate renal impairment** rarely need more than 160 mg of furosemide or 4 mg of bumetanide daily.
- **People with severely impaired renal function** often require very high doses of diuretic (specialist supervision strongly recommended).

Practical prescribing points

For further information please see the *Medicines Compendium* (www.medicines.org.uk) or the *British National Formulary* (www.bnf.org).

- **Hyponatraemia and hypokalaemia** can occur with diuretic therapy, particularly at higher doses.
- **Liver disease** — loop diuretics cause hypokalaemia that may precipitate coma.

Follow-up advice

- **Repeat serum electrolytes within one week of increasing the dose,** and review people to assess response to treatment.
- **Once on a stable dose,** serum electrolytes should be checked at least annually.
- **Monitor regularly all people taking loop diuretics** for hypovolaemia, renal failure, and electrolyte imbalances, especially if they are also taking ACE inhibitors.

H

Should I refer or investigate?

Refer?

Consider referral if:

- **Poor response to treatment** with adequate doses of an ACE inhibitor (e.g. captopril 50 mg three times daily, enalapril 10–20 mg twice daily, lisinopril 30–35 mg daily, ramipril 5 mg twice daily) and a diuretic (e.g. 80 mg furosemide [frusemide] or 2 mg bumetanide daily). Alternatively, consider spironolactone and digoxin.
- **Unable to tolerate an ACE inhibitor.** Alternatively, consider an angiotensin-II receptor antagonist or isosorbide dinitrate/hydralazine.
- **Deteriorating renal function.**
- Any person with a potentially reversible cause of heart failure (e.g. a valve lesion) should be referred to a cardiologist.

Investigate?

If not previously done, the following should be considered:

- **Echocardiography:** should be performed in all people with suspected heart failure to confirm the diagnosis and exclude underlying causes (e.g. valvular heart disease).
- **Full blood count:** to detect anaemia (may exacerbate or precipitate heart failure).
- **Serum electrolytes and renal function:** as a baseline and to exclude renal impairment.
- **Liver function tests:** deranged in hepatic congestion and may indicate possibility of alcohol-related cardiomyopathy.
- **Blood glucose:** to detect diabetes mellitus.
- **Blood lipids:** to detect hyperlipidaemia.
- **Thyroid function tests:** hyperthyroidism or hypothyroidism may exacerbate or precipitate heart failure.
- **Urinalysis:** suspect renal impairment if proteinuria or haematuria are detected.
- **ECG:** look for signs of previous MI, ischaemia, left ventricular hypertrophy, arrhythmias. Heart failure is unlikely if the ECG is normal, and the diagnosis should be reconsidered in this situation.
- **B-type natriuretic peptide (BNP) or its N-terminal fragment (NTproBNP):** a raised concentration of either has been shown to have a sensitivity of greater than 90% and a specificity of 80–90% for the diagnosis of heart failure. *Heart failure is unlikely if the level of BNP or NTproBNP is normal,* especially if the ECG is also normal, and the diagnosis should be reconsidered in this situation.
- **CXR:** to look for signs of heart failure (upper lobe diversion, interstitial oedema, effusions) and to help exclude pulmonary disease.

Patient information leaflets

The following PILs are available at www.prodigy.nhs.uk

- Blood Test - General
- British Cardiac Patients Association
- British Heart Foundation
- Cardiomyopathy Association
- Heart Failure
- How the Heart Works
- Medicines - Name Changes of Medicines

Shared decision making

- **A diuretic ('water tablet')** is commonly prescribed if you have heart failure. It will make you pass out extra urine. This helps you to clear excess body fluid that builds up.
- The dose of the diuretic is usually increased if you still retain fluid.
- **An ACE inhibitor** (Angiotensin Converting Enzyme Inhibitor) is commonly prescribed in addition to a diuretic. These medicines help to prevent a build up of body fluid, and have a protective effect on the heart muscle.
- You need a blood test at least once a year when you take a diuretic.

Drug rationale

Drugs not included

- **Loop diuretics other than bumetanide and furosemide (frusemide)** are not included. Torasemide offers no clinical benefit and is also excluded on cost grounds.
- **Diuretics other than furosemide and bumetanide.** **Thiazides** are not as effective as effective in heart failure as loop diuretics, especially if renal function is impaired. Combination with a loop diuretic may be valuable in some people with oedema but this should usually only be initiated under specialist supervision [DTB, 1994]. **Torasemide** offers no clinical advantage to furosemide or bumetanide and is significantly more expensive. **Potassium-sparing diuretics** are not usually effective for heart failure. They should only be added to a loop or thiazide diuretic if a person cannot tolerate an ACE inhibitor and caution is required.
- **Spironolactone** should be considered for people with moderate to severe heart failure already taking a combination of an ACE inhibitor, diuretic and/or digoxin, as this further improves prognosis (see *Addition of spironolactone* scenario) [SIGN, 1999; DH, 2000; Samuel, 2003].

Drugs included

- **Loop diuretics** are effective for increasing renal sodium and fluid excretion and giving symptom relief in left heart failure.
  - **Furosemide (frusemide)** is the most commonly used diuretic in the UK.
  - **Bumetanide** is an effective alternative to furosemide [DTB, 1994]. Bumetanide is thought to be less ototoxic than furosemide, and may be preferred in people with hearing problems or receiving other ototoxic medication [MeReC, 1990].

Prescriptions

Bumetanide

Bumetanide 1mg each morning
- Age from 16 years onwards
- Bumetanide 1mg tablets. Take one tablet each morning; supply 28 tablets; NHS Cost £1.67.

Bumetanide 2mg each morning
- Age from 16 years onwards
- Bumetanide 1mg tablets. Take two tablets each morning; supply 56 tablets; NHS Cost £3.34.

Bumetanide 3mg each morning
- Age from 16 years onwards
- Bumetanide 1mg tablets. Take three tablets each morning; supply 84 tablets; NHS Cost £5.01.

Bumetanide 4mg each morning
- Age from 16 years onwards
- Bumetanide 1mg tablets. Take four tablets each morning; supply 112 tablets; NHS Cost £6.68.

Furosemide (frusemide)

Furosemide (frusemide) 40mg each morning
- Age from 16 years onwards
- Furosemide 40mg tablets. Take one tablet each morning; supply 28 tablets; NHS Cost £1.80.

Furosemide (frusemide) 80mg each morning
- Age from 16 years onwards
- Furosemide 40mg tablets. Take two tablets each morning; supply 56 tablets; NHS Cost £3.60.

Furosemide (frusemide) 120mg each morning
- Age from 16 years onwards
- Furosemide 40mg tablets. Take three tablets each morning; supply 84 tablets; NHS Cost £5.40.

Furosemide (frusemide) 160mg each morning
- Age from 16 years onwards
- Furosemide 40mg tablets. Take four tablets each morning; supply 112 tablets; NHS Cost £7.20.

Addition of beta-blocker

Which therapy?

- **Beta-blockers are recommended for all people with heart failure (NYHA grades I–IV),** unless there is a contraindication.
- **People should be in a stable condition, and taking an ACE inhibitor (unless contraindicated) before treatment with a beta-blocker is initiated.**
- **The beta-blocker should be started at low doses and slowly increased.**
  - The starting dose of bisoprolol is 1.25 mg once daily — the target dose is 10 mg once daily.
  - The starting dose of carvedilol is 3.125 mg once daily — the target dose is 25 mg twice daily.

Practical prescribing points

For further information please see the *Medicines Compendium* (www.medicines.org.uk) or the *British National Formulary* (www.bnf.org).
- **Adverse effects of the initiation of treatment are common** and include:
  - Symptomatic hypotension
  - Worsening of underlying disease (due to withdrawal of sympathetic drive)
  - Bradycardia
- People who develop adverse effects during initiation or titration of treatment may require adjustment of concomitant therapy. Adverse effects are, however, usually transitory and rarely necessitate cessation of the beta-blocker.
- **CSM advice** — beta-blockers should not be given to people with a history of asthma or bronchospasm.

Follow-up advice

- **Review after initiation and after each dose increase;** check for adverse effects, such as symptomatic hypotension, worsening of underlying disease, and bradycardia.

Should I refer or investigate?

Refer?

Consider referral if:
- **The GP does not feel confident** about initiating beta-blocker therapy.
- **Unable to tolerate beta-blockers.**
- Any person with a potentially reversible cause of heart failure (e.g. a valve lesion) should be referred to a cardiologist.

H

Investigate?

If not previously done, the following should be considered:
- **Echocardiography:** should be performed in all people with suspected heart failure to confirm the diagnosis and exclude underlying causes (e.g. valvular heart disease).
- **Full blood count:** to detect anaemia (may exacerbate or precipitate heart failure).
- **Serum electrolytes and renal function:** as a baseline and to exclude renal impairment.
- **Liver function tests:** deranged in hepatic congestion and may indicate possibility of alcohol-related cardiomyopathy.
- **Blood glucose:** to detect diabetes mellitus.
- **Blood lipids:** to detect hyperlipidaemia.
- **Thyroid function tests:** hyperthyroidism or hypothyroidism may exacerbate or precipitate heart failure.
- **Urinalysis:** suspect renal impairment if proteinuria or haematuria are detected.
- **ECG:** look for signs of previous MI, ischaemia, left ventricular hypertrophy, arrhythmias. Heart failure is unlikely if the ECG is normal, and the diagnosis should be reconsidered in this situation.
- **B-type natriuretic peptide (BNP) or its N-terminal fragment (NTproBNP):** a raised concentration of either has been shown to have a sensitivity of greater than 90% and a specificity of 80–90% for the diagnosis of heart failure. *Heart failure is unlikely if the level of BNP or NTproBNP is normal, especially if the ECG is also normal,* and the diagnosis should be reconsidered in this situation.
- **CXR:** to look for signs of heart failure (upper lobe diversion, interstitial oedema, effusions) and to help exclude pulmonary disease.

Patient information leaflets

The following PILs are available at www.prodigy.nhs.uk
- Blood Test - General
- British Cardiac Patients Association
- British Heart Foundation
- Cardiomyopathy Association
- Heart Failure
- How the Heart Works

Shared decision making

- **A beta-blocker medicine,** such as **bisoprolol** or **carvedilol,** is commonly prescribed if you have heart failure. These medicines have a protective effect on the heart muscle.
- A beta-blocker is usually taken in addition to an ACE inhibitor medicine.
- A low dose of beta-blocker is started at first, and then increased every few weeks until a regular dose is reached.
- When the beta-blocker is first started, some people develop side effects (which are often just temporary) such as:
  - Low blood pressure (you may feel faint or dizzy).
  - An increase in breathlessness or tiredness.
  - A slow pulse.

Drug rationale

Drugs not included

- **All beta-blockers other than bisoprolol and carvedilol** are not included as they are not licensed for the treatment of heart failure. There are trial data to support the use of modified-release metoprolol but it is not licensed.

Drugs included

- **Bisoprolol and carvedilol** have been found to reduce the rate of death and hospitalization in people with mild to moderate stable heart failure [Dargie and Lechat, 1999; Brophy et al, 2001; Packer et al, 2001; Yancy et al, 2001]. Bisoprolol and carvedilol are the only beta-blockers that are licensed for the treatment of heart failure.

Prescriptions

Start bisoprolol: titration over 12 weeks

Week 1: bisoprolol 1.25mg each morning
- Age from 16 years onwards
- Bisoprolol 1.25mg tablets. Take one tablet each morning; supply 7 tablets; NHS Cost £2.14.

Week 2: bisoprolol 2.5mg each morning
- Age from 16 years onwards
- Bisoprolol 2.5mg tablets. Take one tablet each morning; supply 7 tablets; NHS Cost £2.14.

Week 3: bisoprolol 3.75mg each morning
- Age from 16 years onwards
- Bisoprolol 3.75mg tablets. Take one tablet each morning; supply 7 tablets; NHS Cost £2.14.

Weeks 4 to 7: bisoprolol 5mg each morning
- Age from 16 years onwards
- Bisoprolol 5mg tablets. Take one tablet each morning; supply 28 tablets; NHS Cost £8.56.

Weeks 8 to 11: bisoprolol 7.5mg each morning
- Age from 16 years onwards
- Bisoprolol 7.5mg tablets. Take one tablet each morning; supply 28 tablets; NHS Cost £9.09.

Week 12 onwards: bisoprolol 10mg each morning
- Age from 16 years onwards
- Bisoprolol 10mg tablets. Take one tablet each morning; supply 28 tablets; NHS Cost £9.61.

Start carvedilol: titration over 7 or 9 weeks

Weeks 1 and 2: carvedilol 3.125mg twice a day
- Age from 16 years onwards
- Carvedilol 3.125mg tablets. Take one tablet twice a day with food; supply 28 tablets; NHS Cost £8.14.

Weeks 3 and 4: carvedilol 6.25mg twice a day
- Age from 16 years onwards
- Carvedilol 6.25mg tablets. Take one tablet twice a day with food; supply 28 tablets; NHS Cost £9.04.

Weeks 5 and 6: carvedilol 12.5mg twice a day
- Age from 16 years onwards
- Carvedilol 12.5mg tablets. Take one tablet twice a day with food; supply 28 tablets; NHS Cost £10.05.

People > 85kg – weeks 7 to 8: carvedilol 25mg twice a day
- Age from 16 years onwards
- Carvedilol 25mg tablets. Take one tablet twice a day with food; supply 28 tablets; NHS Cost £12.56.

People < 85kg – week 7 onwards: carvedilol 25mg twice a day
- Age from 16 years onwards
- Carvedilol 25mg tablets. Take one tablet twice a day with food; supply 28 tablets; NHS Cost £12.56.

People > 85kg – week 9 onwards: carvedilol 50mg twice a day
- Age from 16 years onwards
- Carvedilol 25mg tablets. Take two tablets twice a day with food; supply 56 tablets; NHS Cost £25.12.

Bisoprolol: maintenance doses

Bisoprolol 1.25mg each morning
- Age from 16 years onwards
- Bisoprolol 1.25mg tablets. Take one tablet each morning; supply 28 tablets; NHS Cost £8.56.

Bisoprolol 2.5mg each morning
- Age from 16 years onwards
- Bisoprolol 2.5mg tablets. Take one tablet each morning; supply 28 tablets; NHS Cost £8.56.

Bisoprolol 3.75mg each morning
- Age from 16 years onwards
- Bisoprolol 3.75mg tablets. Take one tablet each morning; supply 28 tablets; NHS Cost £8.56.

Bisoprolol 5mg each morning
- Age from 16 years onwards
- Bisoprolol 5mg tablets. Take one tablet each morning; supply 28 tablets; NHS Cost £8.56.

Bisoprolol 7.5mg each morning
- Age from 16 years onwards
- Bisoprolol 7.5mg tablets. Take one tablet each morning; supply 28 tablets; NHS Cost £9.09.

Bisoprolol 10mg each morning
- Age from 16 years onwards
- Bisoprolol 10mg tablets. Take one tablet each morning; supply 28 tablets; NHS Cost £9.61.

Carvedilol: maintenance doses

Carvedilol 3.125mg twice a day
- Age from 16 years onwards
- Carvedilol 3.125mg tablets. Take one tablet twice a day with food; supply 56 tablets; NHS Cost £16.28.

Carvedilol 6.25mg twice a day
- Age from 16 years onwards
- Carvedilol 6.25mg tablets. Take one tablet twice a day with food; supply 56 tablets; NHS Cost £18.08.

Carvedilol 12.5mg twice a day
- Age from 16 years onwards
- Carvedilol 12.5mg tablets. Take one tablet twice a day with food; supply 56 tablets; NHS Cost £20.10.

Carvedilol 25mg twice a day: people less than 85kg
- Age from 16 years onwards
- Carvedilol 25mg tablets. Take one tablet twice a day with food; supply 56 tablets; NHS Cost £25.12.

Carvedilol 50mg twice a day: people more than 85kg

- Age from 16 years onwards
- Carvedilol 25mg tablets. Take two tablets twice a day with food; supply 112 tablets; NHS Cost £50.24.

Addition of spironolactone

Which therapy?

- **Consider low-dose spironolactone (25 mg daily)** for people with moderate to severe heart failure (NYHA grades III–IV) who are already on a combination of an ACE inhibitor and a loop diuretic, as this further improves symptoms and prognosis.
- **Optimum doses of the ACE inhibitor** (captopril 50 mg three times daily, enalapril 10–20 mg twice daily, lisinopril 30–35 mg daily, ramipril 5 mg twice daily) **and loop diuretic** (at least furosemide [frusemide] 40 mg daily or bumetanide 1 mg) should ideally be reached prior to considering spironolactone.
- **Careful monitoring for hyperkalaemia and hypovolaemia is required.** However, safety data are reassuring; in a large trial the median potassium concentration increased by only 0.3 mmol/l, and there was no increased risk of serious hyperkalaemia.

Practical prescribing points

For further information please see the *Medicines Compendium* (www.medicines.org.uk) or the *British National Formulary* (www.bnf.org).

- **Hyperkalaemia** — close monitoring is required, particularly if people are also on ACE inhibitors or other drugs that conserve potassium.
- **Renal failure** — avoid in moderate renal failure.

Follow-up advice

- **Check serum electrolytes within one week of starting spironolactone** to exclude hyperkalaemia. There are no clear recommendations available on how often to check thereafter; it would be sensible to repeat electrolytes one month later and a week after any change in concomitant medication.

Should I refer or investigate?

Refer?

Consider referral if:

- **Unable to tolerate spironolactone.**
- **Deteriorating renal function or hyperkalaemia.**
- Any person with a potentially reversible cause of heart failure (e.g. a valve lesion) should be referred to a cardiologist.

Investigate?

If not previously done, the following should be considered:

- **Echocardiography:** should be performed in all people with suspected heart failure to confirm the diagnosis and exclude underlying causes (e.g. valvular heart disease).
- **Full blood count:** to detect anaemia (may exacerbate or precipitate heart failure).
- **Serum electrolytes and renal function:** as a baseline and to exclude renal impairment.
- **Liver function tests:** deranged in hepatic congestion and may indicate possibility of alcohol-related cardiomyopathy.
- **Blood glucose:** to detect diabetes mellitus.
- **Blood lipids:** to detect hyperlipidaemia.
- **Thyroid function tests:** hyperthyroidism or hypothyroidism may exacerbate or precipitate heart failure.
- **Urinalysis:** suspect renal impairment if proteinuria or haematuria are detected.
- **ECG:** look for signs of previous MI, ischaemia, left ventricular hypertrophy, arrhythmias. Heart failure is unlikely if the ECG is normal, and the diagnosis should be reconsidered in this situation.
- **B-type natriuretic peptide (BNP) or its N-terminal fragment (NTproBNP):** a raised concentration of either has been shown to have a sensitivity of greater than 90% and a specificity of 80–90% for the diagnosis of heart failure. *Heart failure is unlikely if the level of BNP or NTproBNP is normal, especially if the ECG is also normal,* and the diagnosis should be reconsidered in this situation.
- **CXR:** to look for signs of heart failure (upper lobe diversion, interstitial oedema, effusions) and to help exclude pulmonary disease.

Patient information leaflets

The following PILs are available at www.prodigy.nhs.uk

- Blood Test - General
- British Cardiac Patients Association
- British Heart Foundation
- Cardiomyopathy Association
- Heart Failure
- How the Heart Works

Shared decision making

- **Spironolactone** is used to treat heart failure if symptoms persist despite taking an ACE inhibitor medicine and a diuretic (water tablet).
- Spironolactone works to help clear the body of excess fluid.
- You should carry on with your ACE inhibitor and diuretic as well.
- You should have a blood test about a week after starting spironolactone. You may then need a blood test every so often, as advised by your doctor.

Drug rationale

Drugs not included

- There are no aldosterone antagonists other than spironolactone available in the UK.

Drugs included

- **Spironolactone** has been found to further decrease mortality in severe heart failure when used in combination with an ACE inhibitor and a loop diuretic. Spironolactone is recommended for use in people with moderate to severe heart failure (NYHA grades III–IV) who are symptomatic on usual treatment [Pitt et al, 1999].

Prescriptions

Spironolactone

Spironolactone 25mg each morning

- Age from 16 years onwards
- Spironolactone 25mg tablets. Take one tablet each morning; supply 28 tablets; NHS Cost £2.34

Addition of digoxin

Which therapy?

- **Consider digoxin for people in sinus rhythm** if they continue to have symptoms (NYHA grades II–IV) despite adequate doses of an ACE inhibitor and a diuretic (this has been shown to improve symptoms although it does not improve prognosis).
- **Give digoxin to all people with atrial fibrillation** who need control of the ventricular rate (see PRODIGY *Atrial fibrillation* guidance).
- **For people in sinus rhythm, aim for a plasma concentration of about 0.89 ng/ml** (measured at least 6 hours post-dose). Higher doses, up to a maximum of 2 ng/ml, may be worth trying in people who continue to have severe symptoms.

Suggested regime for initiation and maintenance of treatment:

H

- **Loading doses of digoxin are not generally needed** for people in sinus rhythm.
- **The recommended starting dose is 125 micrograms daily,** or 62.5 micrograms daily for those with renal impairment. The usual maintenance dose is 125–250 micrograms daily.
- **In people with normal renal function,** check levels about one week after starting treatment or changing the dose. Measure the level at least 6 hours post-dose.
- **In people with impaired renal function,** it may be advisable to do a further check a week later as they take longer to reach steady state concentrations.
- **Monitoring of plasma digoxin levels** may be of benefit while adjusting the dose, for checking compliance, and for assessing possible toxicity.
- For the use of digoxin in atrial fibrillation, see the PRODIGY *Atrial fibrillation* guidance.

Practical prescribing points

For further information please see the *Medicines Compendium* (www.medicines.org.uk) or the *British National Formulary* (www.bnf.org).

- **Digoxin has a narrow therapeutic window.** The usual therapeutic plasma concentration ranges between 1–2 ng/ml.
- **Toxicity may be precipitated by** metabolic disturbances (e.g. hypokalaemia, hypercalcaemia, hypoxia and acidosis, renal impairment, dehydration, and hypothyroidism) or by drugs that increase plasma levels (e.g. verapamil, amiodarone, and quinidine).
- Quinidine, verapamil, and amiodarone increase plasma digoxin levels.
- **Suspect toxicity if** anorexia, nausea, vomiting, diarrhoea, mental confusion, or blurred vision.
- **Toxicity may cause a variety of arrhythmias,** and apparent return of sinus rhythm may be due to digoxin toxicity (e.g. atrial tachycardia with AV block, junctional tachycardia, or atrial fibrillation with complete AV block). At toxic doses, digoxin may cause or worsen heart failure.
- **Monitoring levels may be of benefit to assess for possible toxicity,** to check on adherence to treatment, or while adjusting the dose. Plasma levels must be measured at least 6 hours after the last dose.
  - Levels less than 1.5 micrograms/litre, in the absence of hypokalaemia, indicate that digoxin toxicity is unlikely.
  - Levels greater than 3.0 micrograms/litre indicate that toxicity is likely.
  - With levels between 1.5 and 3.0 micrograms/litre digoxin toxicity should be considered a possibility.
- **Avoid in Wolff-Parkinson-White syndrome,** as may cause the ventricular rate to accelerate.

Follow-up advice

- **Monitoring of plasma digoxin levels** may be of benefit while adjusting the dose, for checking compliance, and for assessing possible toxicity.
- **In people with normal renal function,** check levels about one week after starting treatment or changing the dose. Measure the level at least 6 hours post-dose.
- **In people with impaired renal function,** it may be advisable to do a further check a week later as they take longer to reach steady state concentrations.

Should I refer or investigate?

Refer?

Consider referral if:

- **Unable to tolerate digoxin.**
- **Deteriorating renal function.**
- Any person with a potentially reversible cause of heart failure (e.g. a valve lesion) should be referred to a cardiologist.

Investigate?

If not previously done, the following should be considered:

- **Echocardiography:** should be performed in all people with suspected heart failure to confirm the diagnosis and exclude underlying causes (e.g. valvular heart disease).
- **Full blood count:** to detect anaemia (may exacerbate or precipitate heart failure).
- **Serum electrolytes and renal function:** as a baseline and to exclude renal impairment.
- **Liver function tests:** deranged in hepatic congestion and may indicate possibility of alcohol-related cardiomyopathy.
- **Blood glucose:** to detect diabetes mellitus.
- **Blood lipids:** to detect hyperlipidaemia.
- **Thyroid function tests:** hyperthyroidism or hypothyroidism may exacerbate or precipitate heart failure.
- **Urinalysis:** suspect renal impairment if proteinuria or haematuria are detected.
- **ECG:** look for signs of previous MI, ischaemia, left ventricular hypertrophy, arrhythmias. Heart failure is unlikely if the ECG is normal, and the diagnosis should be reconsidered in this situation.
- **B-type natriuretic peptide (BNP) or its N-terminal fragment (NTproBNP):** a raised concentration of either has been shown to have a sensitivity of greater than 90% and a specificity of 80–90% for the diagnosis of heart failure. *Heart failure is unlikely if the level of BNP or NTproBNP is normal, especially if the ECG is also normal,* and the diagnosis should be reconsidered in this situation.
- **CXR:** to look for signs of heart failure (upper lobe diversion, interstitial oedema, effusions) and to help exclude pulmonary disease.

Patient information leaflets

The following PILs are available at www.prodigy.nhs.uk

- Blood Test - General
- British Cardiac Patients Association
- British Heart Foundation
- Cardiomyopathy Association

- Heart Failure
- How the Heart Works

Shared decision making

- **Digoxin** is used to treat heart failure if symptoms persist despite taking an ACE inhibitor medicine and a diuretic (water tablet).
- Digoxin works by helping the heart muscle to contract more strongly. (It also has another action to regulate the heart rate if you also have atrial fibrillation.)
- You should carry on with your ACE inhibitor and diuretic as well.
- You should have a blood test about a week after starting digoxin. You may then need a blood test every so often, as advised by your doctor.

Drug rationale

Drugs not included

- **Cardiac glycosides other than digoxin** — digitoxin is more expensive than digoxin, and is not widely used in the UK.

Drugs included

- **Digoxin,** given in combination with a diuretic and an ACE inhibitor to people with heart failure (NYHA grades II–IV) in normal sinus rhythm, has been found to reduce hospitalization and clinical deterioration, but not mortality [Hood et al, 2002].

Prescriptions

Digoxin

Digoxin 62.5micrograms once a day
- Age from 16 years onwards
- Digoxin 62.5microgram tablets. Take one tablet once a day; supply 28 tablets; NHS Cost £0.72.

Digoxin 125micrograms once a day
- Age from 16 years onwards
- Digoxin 125microgram tablets. Take one tablet once a day; supply 28 tablets; NHS Cost £0.56.

Digoxin 250micrograms once a day
- Age from 16 years onwards
- Digoxin 250microgram tablets. Take one tablet once a day; supply 28 tablets; NHS Cost £0.56.

Intolerant of ACE inhibitor

Which therapy?

- **If the person is truly intolerant of an ACE inhibitor, then the Department of Health recommends** considering either an angiotensin-II receptor antagonist or a combination of hydralazine and isosorbide dinitrate.
- **Angiotensin-II receptor antagonists (AIIRAs):** candesartan, losartan (off-licence), and valsartan are recommended in PRODIGY for people intolerant of an ACE inhibitor (in particular intolerance due to ACE inhibitor-induced cough). AIIRAs and their future role will be reviewed, and the guidance will be updated to reflect further evidence with publication of more trial data and changes in licensing.
- **Hydralazine and isosorbide dinitrate in combination:** this has been shown to improve prognosis, although less than with an ACE inhibitor. Hydralazine is only licensed for initiation in hospital for people in heart failure, and the dose has to be carefully increased. No prescriptions are offered within PRODIGY.
- **Referral for a specialist opinion** may be considered in some people unable to tolerate an ACE inhibitor. A person who develops renal impairment on an ACE inhibitor is also likely to develop renal impairment on an AIIRA.

Practical prescribing points

For further information please see the *Medicines Compendium* (www.medicines.org.uk) or the *British National Formulary* (www.bnf.org).

- **High-risk groups:** consider a lower starting dose when starting an AIIRA and increase the dose more cautiously.
- **Avoid potassium-sparing diuretics (except spironolactone) or potassium supplements** in people on AIIRAs (other than in exceptional cases) due to the risk of hyperkalaemia.
- **Stop nonsteroidal anti-inflammatory drugs (if possible)** as they reduce the effectiveness of diuretics and increase the risk of renal impairment with AIIRAs.
- **Avoid AIIRAs if significant cardiac outflow tract obstruction** (e.g. due to aortic stenosis or hypertrophic obstructive cardiomyopathy).
- **Liver disease:** monitor effects closely in people with impaired liver function and consider using a lower dose.
- **Renal impairment:** close monitoring of plasma potassium concentration and renal function is advised.
- **Pregnancy and breastfeeding:** avoid — potential adverse defects in pregnancy include problems with fetal and neonatal blood pressure control and renal function.

Follow-up advice

- **AIIRAs require the same monitoring as for an ACE inhibitor, therefore renal function should be monitored (blood pressure, renal function, serum potassium) during treatment — one week after each dose increase.**
- **Repeat serum electrolytes and renal function within one week** of starting an AIIRA, and review the person to assess response to treatment and to check BP.
- **Check for adverse effects,** such as symptomatic hypotension, renal dysfunction, or hyperkalaemia (i.e. a rise in urea to 12 mmol/l, creatinine to 200 micromol /l, or potassium to 5.5 mmol/l). If these occur either stop or reduce the dose of AIIRA, and consider specialist referral.
- **Once on a stable dose** serum electrolytes and renal function should be checked at least annually.
- **Monitor regularly all people taking loop diuretics** for hypovolaemia, renal impairment, and electrolyte imbalances.

Should I refer or investigate?

Refer?

- **Referral for a specialist opinion** may be considered in some people unable to tolerate an ACE inhibitor.
  - Angiotensin-II receptor antagonists (AIIRAs) are not currently licensed for use in heart failure.
  - A person who develops renal impairment on an ACE inhibitor is also likely to develop renal impairment on an AIIRA.
  - Hydralazine/isosorbide dinitrate combination is difficult to titrate, and hydralazine is only licensed for initiation in hospital for people with heart failure.
- Any person with a potentially reversible cause of heart failure (e.g. a valve lesion) should be referred to a cardiologist.

Investigate?

If not previously done, the following should be considered:

- **Echocardiography:** should be performed in all people with suspected heart failure to confirm the diagnosis and exclude underlying causes (e.g. valvular heart disease).
- **Full blood count:** to detect anaemia (may exacerbate or precipitate heart failure).
- **Serum electrolytes and renal function:** as a baseline and to exclude renal impairment.
- **Liver function tests:** deranged in hepatic congestion and may indicate possibility of alcohol-related cardiomyopathy.
- **Blood glucose:** to detect diabetes mellitus.
- **Blood lipids:** to detect hyperlipidaemia.
- **Thyroid function tests:** hyperthyroidism or hypothyroidism may exacerbate or precipitate heart failure.
- **Urinalysis:** suspect renal impairment if proteinuria or haematuria are detected.
- **ECG:** look for signs of previous MI, ischaemia, left ventricular hypertrophy, arrhythmias. **Heart failure is unlikely if the ECG is normal,** and the diagnosis should be reconsidered in this situation.
- **B-type natriuretic peptide (BNP) or its N-terminal fragment (NTproBNP):** a raised concentration of either has been shown to have a sensitivity of greater than 90% and a specificity of 80–90% for the diagnosis of heart failure. *Heart failure is unlikely if the level of BNP or NTproBNP is normal, especially if the ECG is also normal,* and the diagnosis should be reconsidered in this situation.
- **CXR:** to look for signs of heart failure (upper lobe diversion, interstitial oedema, effusions) and to help exclude pulmonary disease.

Patient information leaflets

The following PILs are available at www.prodigy.nhs.uk

- Blood Test - General
- Blood Test - Kidney Function
- British Cardiac Patients Association
- British Heart Foundation
- Cardiomyopathy Association
- Heart Failure
- How the Heart Works

Shared decision making

- **An ACE inhibitor** (Angiotensin Converting Enzyme Inhibitor) is the usual treatment for heart failure. These medicines help to prevent a build up of body fluid, and have a protective effect on the heart muscle.
- Some people cannot take an ACE inhibitor for various reasons. There are other medicines that may help. One of these is an AIIRA (angiotensin-II receptor antagonist). Some people who cannot tolerate an ACE inhibitor may need to be referred to a specialist for advice.

Drug rationale

Drugs not included

- **Angiotensin-II receptor antagonists (AIIRAs) other than candesartan, losartan, and valsartan** are not currently recommended for people intolerant of an ACE inhibitor in heart failure. Eprosartan and irbesartan are not included, as there are insufficient trial data published of their use in heart failure. Olmesartan and telmisartan are also not offered, as they remain under the surveillance of the Committee on Safety of Medicines.
- **Hydralazine and isosorbide dinitrate in combination** has been shown to improve prognosis but evidence indicates that improvement in survival is more effective with ACE inhibitors [Cohn et al, 1991]. Hydralazine is only licensed for initiation in hospital for people in heart failure, and the dose has to be carefully increased. Therefore no prescriptions for hydralazine and isosorbide dinitrate in combination are offered.

Drugs included

- **Candesartan, losartan, and valsartan** are the only angiotensin-II receptor antagonists recommended for people intolerant of an ACE inhibitor in heart failure.
  - Candesartan is now licensed for heart failure and impaired left ventricular dysfunction. Valsartan is now licensed for heart failure in post myocardial infarction patients. Losartan is not currently licensed for the treatment of heart failure.
  - Trial data suggest AIIRAs have prognostic benefit comparable to that of ACE inhibitors [Pitt et al, 2000; Cohn and Tognoni, 2001; Dickstein and Kjekshus, 2002; Granger et al, 2003; Pfeffer et al, 2003a; Pfeffer et al, 2003b].
  - Prescriptions for titration and target doses are included reflecting those used in trials.

Prescriptions

Losartan: titrate up

Losartan: titrate up from 25mg to 50mg per day

- Age from 16 years onwards
- Losartan 25mg tablets. Take one tablet once a day for 7 days, then take two tablets once a day for 7 days; supply 21 tablets; NHS Cost £12.93.

Losartan: ideal target

Losartan 50mg once a day

- Age from 16 years onwards
- Losartan 50mg tablets. Take one tablet once a day; supply 28 tablets; NHS Cost £17.33.

Candesartan and valsartan: titrate up

Candesartan: initial titration from 4mg to 8mg per day

- Age from 16 years onwards
- Candesartan 4mg tablets. Take one tablet once a day for 2 weeks, then take two tablets once a day; supply 42 tablets; NHS Cost £19.43.

Candesartan: further titration from 8mg to 16mg per day

- Age from 16 years onwards
- Candesartan 8mg tablets. Take one tablet once a day for 2 weeks, then take two tablets once a day; supply 42 tablets; NHS Cost £22.43.

Candesartan: further titration from 16mg to 32mg per day

- Age from 16 years onwards
- Candesartan 16mg tablets. Take one tablet once a day for 2 weeks, then take two tablets once a day; supply 42 tablets; NHS Cost £26.63.

Valsartan 20mg twice a day: first 4-week titration step

- Age from 16 years onwards
- Valsartan 40mg tablets. Take half a tablet twice a day for 4 weeks; supply 28 tablets; NHS Cost £14.76.

Valsartan 40mg twice a day: second 4-week titration step

- Age from 16 years onwards
- Valsartan 40mg capsules. Take one capsule twice a day for 4 weeks; supply 56 capsules; NHS Cost £29.52.

Valsartan 80mg twice a day: third 4-week titration step
- Age from 16 years onwards
- Valsartan 80mg capsules. Take one capsule twice a day for 4 weeks; supply 56 capsules; NHS Cost £32.88.

Valsartan 160mg twice a day: last 4-week titration step
- Age from 16 years onwards
- Valsartan 160mg capsules. Take one capsule twice a day; supply 56 capsules; NHS Cost £43.32.

Candesartan and valsartan: ideal target doses

Candesartan 32mg once a day
- Age from 16 years onwards
- Candesartan 32mg tablets. Take one tablet once a day; supply 28 tablets; NHS Cost £16.13.

Valsartan 160mg twice a day
- Age from 16 years onwards
- Valsartan 160mg capsules. Take one capsule twice a day; supply 56 capsules; NHS Cost £43.32.

Acute heart failure (pulmonary oedema)

Which therapy?

- **Emergency admission** is required in most cases.
- **Intravenous diuretics and diamorphine** are essential emergency treatments:
  - Furosemide (frusemide) 20–50 mg by slow iv. injection.
  - Diamorphine 2.5–5 mg by slow iv. injection (caution if coexisting chronic obstructive pulmonary disease).
- **An iv. anti-emetic should also be given (not cyclizine).**
- **Sublingual and buccal nitrates are also effective in the treatment of acute heart failure.**
- **Oxygen** (high-flow, unless coexisting chronic obstructive pulmonary disease) should be given if available.
- **If acute MI is suspected, give aspirin 300 mg.**
- **If the person is known to have chronic heart failure** and this is thought to be a minor exacerbation, an increase in the usual dose of diuretic and monitoring at home may suffice.

Practical prescribing points

For further information please see the *Medicines Compendium* (www.medicines.org.uk) or the *British National Formulary* (www.bnf.org).

Patient information leaflets

The following PILs are available at www.prodigy.nhs.uk
- British Cardiac Patients Association
- British Heart Foundation
- Cardiomyopathy Association
- Heart Failure
- How the Heart Works
- Medicines - Name Changes of Medicines

Shared decision making

Drug rationale

Drugs not included

- **Cyclizine** has not been included because it can aggravate heart failure and counteract the haemodynamic effects of diamorphine. The combination product, **cyclimorph**, has therefore not been included.
- **Prochlorperazine** has not been included because it is only licensed for intramuscular injection, which is not recommended for people with suspected myocardial infarction as it can cause a haematoma in those who receive thrombolysis, and may alter cardiac enzyme results.

[DTB, 1995; BNF 47, 2004;]

Drugs included

- The GP would usually treat acute heart failure using their own supply of emergency drugs. Prescriptions are included, however, so that the GP can generate a prescription afterwards.
- **Intravenous diamorphine** is appropriate and effective for symptomatic relief in most people. It may be reconstituted with 5 ml of water for injection, to give 1 mg in 1 ml dilution for ease of administration by slow intravenous injection.
- **Intravenous metoclopramide** is an effective anti-emetic. It is licensed for intravenous use.
- **Furosemide (frusemide)** given intravenously is effective for the relief of pulmonary oedema in acute heart failure.

[DTB, 1995]

H

Prescriptions

For generation of script after emergency IV treatment

CD – Diamorphine + water for injection
- Age from 16 years onwards
- Water for injection (5ml). For reconstitution; supply 1 5ml ampoule; NHS Cost £0.22.

Furosemide (frusemide) 20mg/2ml injection
- Age from 16 years onwards
- Furosemide 20mg/2ml injection. For intravenous injection; supply 3 2ml ampoules; NHS Cost £2.64.

Metoclopramide 10mg/2ml injection
- Age from 16 years onwards
- Metoclopramide 10mg/2ml inj. For intravenous injection; supply 1 2ml ampoules; NHS Cost £0.27.

Extended Information

Background information

- What is it? p.907
- How common is it? p.908
- How do I know my patient has it? p.908
- What else might it be? p.908
- Complications and prognosis p.908

What is it?

- **Heart failure is a clinical syndrome usually due to left ventricular dysfunction,** resulting in acute or chronic symptoms of cardiac pump failure.
- **The most common causes of heart failure are** coronary heart disease, hypertension, alcohol abuse, and idiopathic dilated cardiomyopathy [AHCPR, 1994; Bandolier, 1997; McKelvie et al, 1998; DH, 2000].
- **Other causes are** valvular and pericardial disease; or non-cardiac diseases causing high-output cardiac failure, such as anaemia, thyrotoxicosis, septicaemia, Paget's disease of bone, and arteriovenous fistulae. Any person with a potentially reversible cause of heart failure (e.g. a valve lesion) should be referred to a cardiologist [McDonagh and Dargie, 1998].

How common is it?

- **The incidence** is about one new case per 1000 population per year, and is increasing by about 10% every year. The incidence increases with age to more than 10 cases per 1000 in people aged 85 years and over [DH, 2000].
- **The prevalence** ranges from 3–20 cases per 1000 population, increasing to at least 80 cases per 1000 in people aged 75 years and over [DH, 2000].
- **The male to female ratio** is about 2:1.
- **The median age of presentation is 76 years.**
- **An average GP (list size 2000) will see about 20 people with heart failure each year.** Four people will be admitted to hospital, and 2 of these will die within the next four years [Eccles et al, 1998].
- **Heart failure accounts for** more than 4% of all general medical and cardiology admissions, and more than 1% of the total NHS budget (hospitalization accounts for almost 60% of this and drug costs about 7.5%) [Medicines Resource, 1996; McDonagh and Dargie, 1998].
- **The prevalence of heart failure is increasing** because of the improved treatment of coronary heart disease (e.g. thrombolysis resulting in more people surviving a myocardial infarct but left with residual left ventricular dysfunction), and the ageing population [Medicines Resource, 1996; Bandolier, 1997; McDonagh and Dargie, 1998].

How do I know my patient has it?

Acute heart failure

- Often precipitated by a myocardial infarction.
- **Signs include:**
  - Severe breathlessness
  - Frothy pink sputum
  - Cold clammy skin
  - Tachycardia
  - Low blood pressure
  - Lung crepitations
  - Raised jugular venous pressure
  - Third heart sound
  - Confusion

Chronic heart failure

- **Making an accurate diagnosis of heart failure and determining its cause can be difficult** because the signs and symptoms are often non-specific. People with even severely impaired left ventricular function may have no symptoms or signs of heart failure. Clinical diagnosis is confirmed to be accurate in approximately half of cases when investigated by echocardiography.
- **The likelihood of heart failure in the presence of suggestive symptoms and signs is increased if** there is a history of myocardial infarction (MI) or angina, an abnormal ECG, or a chest X-ray showing pulmonary congestion or cardiomegaly.
- **Symptoms include:**
  - Shortness of breath on exertion (sensitivity 66%, specificity 52%)
  - Decreased exercise tolerance (often simply 'fatigue')
  - Paroxysmal nocturnal dyspnoea (sensitivity 33%, specificity 76%)
  - Orthopnoea (sensitivity 21%, specificity 81%)
  - Ankle swelling (sensitivity 23%, specificity 80%)
- **The most specific signs are:**
  - Laterally displaced apex beat
  - Elevated jugular venous pressure
  - Third heart sound
- **Less specific signs include:**
  - Tachycardia
  - Lung crepitations
  - Hepatic engorgement (tender hepatomegaly)
  - Peripheral oedema
- **Electrocardiogram (ECG)** may show acute ischaemia, arrhythmias, left ventricular hypertrophy, left bundle branch block, or prior MI. **Heart failure is unlikely if the ECG is normal,** and the diagnosis should be reconsidered in this situation.
- **Chest X-ray (CXR)** may show signs of heart failure, and helps to exclude pulmonary causes of dyspnoea. Radiological features of heart failure are pulmonary vascular congestion (upper lobe diversion), pulmonary oedema, effusions, or cardiomegaly. A CXR may not be carried out the same day however, and any features of pulmonary oedema may have resolved with treatment.
- **B-type natriuretic peptide (BNP) and its N-terminal fragment (NTproBNP)** have recently emerged as diagnostic blood tests for heart failure. A raised concentration of either has been shown to have a sensitivity of greater than 90% and a specificity of 80–90% for the diagnosis of heart failure, whether this is systolic or diastolic failure [de Lemos et al, 2003]. Heart failure is unlikely if the level of BNP or NTproBNP is normal, especially if the ECG is also normal, and the diagnosis should be reconsidered in this situation.
- **Echocardiography or radionuclide measurements should be carried out in all people with suspected heart failure to evaluate left ventricular function.** If availability of these investigations is limited, a decision may need to be made on clinical grounds.

[AHCPR, 1994; Badgett et al, 1997; NZMJ, 1997; Eccles et al, 1998; McDonagh and Dargie, 1998; SIGN, 1999; DH, 2000]

Diastolic heart failure

- **A diagnosis of diastolic heart failure requires the presence of all the following features:**
  - The presence of symptoms or signs of heart failure.
  - The presence of normal or slightly reduced left ventricular (LV) systolic function.
  - Evidence of abnormal LV relaxation and filling, diastolic distensibility, and diastolic stiffness.
- The second feature is readily diagnosed by routine echocardiography. The third, however, can only be diagnosed by Doppler echocardiography, which is not routinely available, or by cardiac catheterization.

[European Study Group on Diastolic Heart Failure (ESGDHF), 1998; Lainchbury and Redfield, 1999; Mandinov et al, 2000]

What else might it be?

- **Other causes of shortness of breath on exertion** — e.g. pulmonary disease, obesity, unfitness, volume overload from renal failure or nephrotic syndrome, angina, anxiety.
- **Other causes of peripheral oedema** — e.g. dependent oedema, nephrotic syndrome.
- **Non-cardiac diseases causing high-output cardiac failure** — e.g. anaemia, thyrotoxicosis, septicaemia, Paget's disease of bone, arteriovenous fistulae.

It is usually possible to differentiate between cardiac and pulmonary causes on the basis of history, examination, electrocardiography, chest X-ray, and echocardiography.

Complications and prognosis

Complications

- **Quality of life** is worse than with many other common medical conditions. Psychosocial functioning is impaired with over a third of people experiencing severe and prolonged depressive illness [DH, 2000].

Prognosis

- **Heart failure has a prognosis worse than most cancers.** Average annual mortality rates range from 10% to over 50% depending on severity [DH, 2000].

Management issues

- General issues in chronic heart failure p.909
- Recommended drug treatments for left ventricular systolic dysfunction p.909
- Other potentially useful drug treatments p.911
- Treatments of no proven benefit p.911
- Surgical treatments p.912
- Diastolic heart failure p.912
- Medicines management p.912

The following applies to chronic heart failure only.

General issues in chronic heart failure

- **Manage other risk factors** (e.g. hypertension, diabetes, smoking, obesity, inactivity).
- **Manage coexisting coronary heart disease** in line with standard practice (i.e. symptom relief, secondary prevention measures such as aspirin and hyperlipidaemia).
- **Avoid aggravating factors.** Try to avoid drugs that may exacerbate heart failure, such as nonsteroidal anti-inflammatory drugs and short-acting calcium-channel blockers. Advise low salt diet. Advise a moderate alcohol intake (21 units weekly for men, 14 units weekly for women), unless alcoholic cardiomyopathy is present when complete avoidance of alcohol should be recommended. Limiting fluid intake may be appropriate in advanced heart failure, but care is needed to avoid dehydration.
- **Vaccinate people against influenza annually and pneumococcus as a one-off,** as they are at increased risk of infective complications.
- **Consider cardiac rehabilitation, palliative care, and long-term social support** if appropriate.
- Any person with a potentially reversible cause of heart failure (e.g. a valve lesion) should be referred to a cardiologist.
- **The New York Heart Association (NYHA) has classified chronic heart failure** according to the following functional criteria:
  - Grade I — no limitation of physical activity; ordinary physical activity does not cause undue fatigue, palpitation, or dyspnoea.
  - Grade II — slight limitation of physical activity; comfortable at rest, but ordinary physical activity results in fatigue, palpitation, or dyspnoea.
  - Grade III — marked limitation of physical activity; comfortable at rest, but less than ordinary activity causes fatigue, palpitation, or dyspnoea.
  - Grade IV — unable to carry out any physical activity without discomfort; symptoms of cardiac insufficiency at rest; if any physical activity is undertaken.

[European Heart Journal, 1997; NZMJ, 1997; NHS CRD, 1998; DH, 2000]

Recommended drug treatments for left ventricular systolic dysfunction

- **Drug treatments should be initiated in the following order:**
  - ACE inhibitor — with diuretic if needed — for NYHA Grades I–IV.
  - Angiotensin-II receptor antagonist — if intolerant of ACE inhibitor.
  - Beta-blocker — for NYHA Grades I–IV.
  - Spironolactone — for NYHA Grades III–IV.
  - Digoxin — for NYHA Grades II–IV.

ACE inhibitors

- **Angiotensin-converting enzyme inhibitors (ACE inhibitors) relieve symptoms and improve prognosis** and should be considered in all people with heart failure [Eccles et al, 1998; SIGN, 1999; DH, 2000]. Twenty-six people need to be treated for 3 years to prevent one death [SIGN, 1999].
- **ACE inhibitors are cost-effective** [Andersson and Swedberg, 1998; Eccles et al, 1998]. In a health authority of 250,000 people, around 40 deaths and 300 hospital admissions could be prevented each year using ACE inhibitors [Bandolier, 1997].
- **All ACE inhibitors are effective in treating heart failure,** although most evidence is from clinical trials of enalapril [Medicines Resource, 1996; Eccles et al, 1998].
- **Treatment with an ACE inhibitor alone** can be considered in people with NYHA grades I–II who do not have symptoms or signs of fluid overload. Diuretics should be added if fluid overload is present [Eccles et al, 1998].
- **Cough** is common in heart failure but is also caused by an ACE inhibitor in a small percentage of people. Cough is not a reason to stop an ACE inhibitor unless it is troublesome [SIGN, 1999; DTB, 2000].

Initiation of treatment

- **Treatment with an ACE inhibitor can be started in the community in the majority of people** with heart failure [Bandolier, 1997].
- **It is not usually necessary to stop or decrease the dose of diuretic** when starting an ACE inhibitor [SIGN, 1999]. However, particular care is necessary in high-risk groups.
- **Be aware of potential drug interactions** — stop potassium-sparing diuretics (except spironolactone) and potassium supplements because of the risk of hyperkalaemia, and stop nonsteroidal anti-inflammatory drugs (if possible) because of the risk of renal impairment.
- **Initiate treatment with a low dose of an ACE inhibitor.** The person should be advised to sit or lie down for 2–4 hours after this initial dose, as there is a risk of first-dose hypotension [Medicines Resource, 1996].
- **If tolerated, increase the dose of ACE inhibitor** over a minimum of 4 weeks, with the goal of reaching the 'target' doses used in clinical trials:
  - Captopril 50 mg three times daily
  - Enalapril 10–20 mg twice daily
  - Lisinopril 30–35 mg daily
  - Ramipril 5 mg twice daily

[Eccles et al, 1998; SIGN, 1999; DTB, 2000]

- Increase the dose more cautiously in high-risk groups.

High-risk groups

- **Consider hospital referral for initiation of ACE inhibitor treatment if any of the following apply** (due to the risk of first-dose hypotension or precipitating renal failure) [SIGN, 1999]:
  - Creatinine >150 micromol/l
  - Urea >12 mmol/l
  - Sodium <130 mmol/l
  - Systolic blood pressure <100 mmHg
  - Diuretic dose > furosemide (frusemide) 80 mg or bumetanide 2 mg daily
  - Known or suspected renal artery stenosis, e.g. if peripheral vascular disease
  - People aged 70 years and over or who are frail

- Hypovolaemia
- With unstable heart failure
- Receiving high-dose vasodilator therapy
- **If this is not possible then initiate treatment at home with a low dose of a short-acting ACE inhibitor** (captopril 6.25 mg) and monitor the person's blood pressure carefully for 2 hours [Eccles et al, 1998]. If possible, withhold diuretics for a brief period (at least 24 hours) to allow any volume depletion to resolve, as this reduces the risk of first-dose hypotension.

[Heart Failure Society of America, 1999; Krum, 2001; Remme et al, 2001]

Diuretics — loop and thiazide

- **Diuretics give rapid symptom relief** and should be started early in symptomatic people with signs of fluid overload. Their long-term effects on mortality rates and other endpoints when given alone are not known (excluding spironolactone). An ACE inhibitor should always be added to diuretic therapy, unless contraindicated, as this improves prognosis.
- **Loop diuretics are usually preferred to thiazide diuretics.** Thiazides may be as effective as loop diuretics in treating oedema in people with mild failure who have preserved renal function.
- **The combination of a thiazide with a loop diuretic** gives a synergistic effect and may be useful in people with severe, persistent symptoms. Close monitoring of electrolytes is required and such treatment should usually be specialist initiated.

[MeReC, 1990; DTB, 1994; European Heart Journal, 1997; NZMJ, 1997; Andersson and Swedberg, 1998; Eccles et al, 1998; Heart Failure Society of America, 1999; SIGN, 1999; DH, 2000; DTB, 2000; Krum, 2001; Remme et al, 2001]

Beta-blockers

- **Beta-blockers are recommended for all people with heart failure (NYHA grades I–IV) whose failure is stable,** on standard treatment, unless there is a contraindication.
- **Beta-blockers in combination with other treatments,** such as ACE inhibitors, diuretics and digoxin, improve survival by more than 30% compared to standard treatment alone in people with stable heart failure.
- **Bisoprolol, carvedilol, and modified-release metoprolol have been shown to be beneficial.** Bisoprolol and carvedilol are the only beta-blockers that are licensed for the treatment of heart failure.

Initiation of treatment

- **Treatment should usually be started under specialist supervision.** There may, however, be GPs with sufficient expertise who feel confident to initiate beta-blocker therapy in primary care.
- **People should be in a stable condition, and taking an ACE inhibitor (unless contraindicated) before treatment is initiated.**
- **The beta-blocker should be started at low doses and slowly increased.**
  - The starting dose of bisoprolol is 1.25 mg once daily — the target dose is 10 mg once daily.
  - The starting dose of carvedilol is 3.125 mg twice daily — the target dose is 25 mg twice daily for people less than 85 kg, and 50 mg twice daily for people more than 85 kg.
- **Adverse effects of the initiation of treatment are common** and include:
  - Symptomatic hypotension
  - Worsening of underlying disease (due to withdrawal of sympathetic drive)
  - Bradycardia
- People who develop adverse effects during initiation or titration of treatment may require adjustment of concomitant therapy. It may be necessary to reduce the dose of the beta-blocker by one titration step, and reconsider a further increase when the adverse effects have resolved. Adverse effects are, however, usually transitory and rarely necessitate cessation of the beta-blocker.
- If a person who is already taking a beta-blocker for another indication (e.g. atenolol for hypertension) develops heart failure, the decision about which beta-blocker to use (i.e. to continue the one for the pre-existing condition, or to change to bisoprolol or carvedilol) has not been studied. Expert opinion, however, suggests that it depends on whether the person is stable:
  - If stable, the previous drug should be continued.
  - If not stable, the previous beta-blocker should be stopped until the person becomes stable (this may require hospital admission) and then bisoprolol or carvedilol should be started.

[Heidenreich et al, 1997; Heart Failure Society of America, 1999; SIGN, 1999; Krum, 2001; MeReC, 2001; Remme et al, 2001; WeMeReC, 2001]

Spironolactone

- **Spironolactone,** an aldosterone antagonist, should be considered for people with moderate to severe heart failure (NYHA grades III–IV) who are already on an ACE inhibitor and a loop diuretic [SIGN, 1999; DH, 2000; Samuel, 2003].
- **The Randomised Aldactone Evaluation Study (RALES)** compared treatment with low-dose spironolactone (25 mg daily) added to standard care with other diuretics, ACE inhibitors and digoxin against standard care alone, in people with moderate to severe heart failure (NYHA III–IV) [Pitt et al, 1999]. Mortality was reduced by 30%, the risk of hospitalization for worsening heart failure was reduced by 35%, and there was a significant improvement in symptoms. Over 2 years, one death was avoided for every 9 people treated with spironolactone in addition to standard therapy.
- **Careful monitoring for hyperkalaemia and hypovolaemia is required.** However, safety data from RALES are reassuring; the median potassium concentration increased by only 0.3 mmol/l and there was no increased risk of serious hyperkalaemia.

[Heart Failure Society of America, 1999; Krum, 2001; Remme et al, 2001]

Digoxin

- **Digoxin,** given in combination with a diuretic and an ACE inhibitor to people with heart failure (NYHA grades II–IV) in normal sinus rhythm, has been found to reduce hospitalization and clinical deterioration, but not mortality [Hood et al, 2002].
- **Consider digoxin** if the person continues to be symptomatic despite adequate doses of diuretic and ACE inhibitor [DH, 2000].
- **Aim for a plasma concentration of about 0.89 ng/ml** (measured at least 6 hours post-dose), as this was the mean plasma concentration achieved in the DIG trial [DIG, 1997; SIGN, 1999]. In the majority of people, the dose of digoxin should be 125–250 micrograms daily. Higher doses, up to a maximum concentration of 2 ng/ml, may be worth trying in people who continue to be very symptomatic [SIGN, 1999].
- **Give digoxin to all people with heart failure and atrial fibrillation** who need control of the ventricular rate.

[Heart Failure Society of America, 1999]

Angiotensin-II receptor antagonists

- **Candesartan, losartan, and valsartan are recommended in PRODIGY for people intolerant of an ACE inhibitor** (especially when that intolerance is due to ACE inhibitor-induced cough). Initial trial data appear comparable with ACE inhibitors.
  - Candesartan was studied in 7601 people with heart failure in the CHARM study, and significantly reduced cardiovascular deaths and admissions due to heart failure compared with placebo. Notably, one of its three arms, CHARM-Alternative, studied 2028 people with heart failure who had previously been unable to tolerate an ACE inhibitor — for cardiovascular death or admission due to heart failure, this arm found that the numbers needed to treat = 14 [Granger et al, 2003; Pfeffer et al, 2003a].
  - Losartan was compared with captopril in 3152 people with heart failure in the ELITE study; there was no significant difference in all-cause mortality [Pitt et al, 2000]. Losartan was also compared with captopril in 5477 people in the OPTIMAAL trial; there was a non-significant difference in all-cause mortality in favour of captopril [Dickstein and Kjekshus, 2002].
  - Valsartan was compared with captopril in 14,808 people with heart failure in the VALIANT trial; there was no significant difference in all cause mortality, fatal and nonfatal cardiovascular events [Pfeffer et al, 2003b].
- Candesartan is now licensed for heart failure and impaired left ventricular dysfunction. Valsartan is now licensed for heart failure in post myocardial infarction patients. Losartan is not currently licensed for the treatment of heart failure.
- **Other AIIRAs** have either insufficient trial data published of their use in heart failure, or remain under the surveillance of the Committee on Safety of Medicines.
- **AIIRAs and their future role will be reviewed** and the PRODIGY guidance will be updated to reflect further evidence with the publication of more trial data.

Initiation of treatment

- **Treatment with an AIIRA is only recommended where a person is intolerant of an ACE inhibitor.**
- **Treatment with an AIIRA can be started in the community in the majority of people with heart failure.**
- **It is not usually necessary to stop or decrease the dose of diuretic** when starting an AIIRA. However, particular care is necessary in high-risk groups.
- **Be aware of potential drug interactions** — stop potassium-sparing diuretics (except spironolactone) and potassium supplements because of the risk of hyperkalaemia, and stop nonsteroidal anti-inflammatory drugs (if possible) because of the risk of renal impairment.
- **Initiate treatment with a low dose of an AIIRA.** The person should be advised to sit or lie down for 2–4 hours after this initial dose, as there is a risk of first-dose hypotension.
- **If tolerated, increase the dose of the AIIRA** over a minimum of 4 weeks, with the goal of reaching the 'target' doses:
  - Candesartan 32 mg once daily
  - Losartan 50 mg once daily
  - Valsartan 160 mg twice daily
- Increase the dose more cautiously in high-risk groups.
- **People on AIIRAs require the same monitoring as that required with an ACE inhibitor** and the same adverse effects, with the exception of cough, should be anticipated.

[Pitt et al, 1997; Krum, 2001; Remme et al, 2001]

High-risk groups

- **Consider hospital referral for initiation of AIIRA treatment if any of the following apply** (due to the risk of first-dose hypotension or precipitating renal failure):
  - Creatinine >150 micromol/l
  - Urea >12 mmol/l
  - Sodium <130 mmol/l
  - Systolic blood pressure <100 mmHg
  - Diuretic dose > furosemide (frusemide) 80 mg or bumetanide 2 mg daily
  - Known or suspected renal artery stenosis, e.g. if peripheral vascular disease
  - People aged 70 years and over or who are frail
  - Hypovolaemia
  - With unstable heart failure
  - Receiving high-dose vasodilator therapy
- **If this is not possible then initiate treatment at home with a low dose of an AIIRA** and monitor the person's blood pressure carefully for 2 hours. If possible, withhold diuretics for a brief period (at least 24 hours) to allow any volume depletion to resolve, as this reduces the risk of first-dose hypotension.

Other potentially useful drug treatments

- **Hydralazine and isosorbide dinitrate in combination** improve symptoms and prognosis, and might be considered for people unable to tolerate an ACE inhibitor or an angiotensin-II receptor antagonist [AHCPR, 1994].
- **The National Service Framework** and SIGN guidance suggest considering hydralazine/isosorbide dinitrate if ACE inhibitors and angiotension-II receptor antagonists are not tolerated [DH, 2000].

[Heart Failure Society of America, 1999; Krum, 2001; Remme et al, 2001]

Treatments of no proven benefit

Combination of ACE and angiotensin-II receptor antagonists

- **Combination treatment with an ACE and angiotensin-II receptor antagonist (AIIRA) can not currently recommended.** Subgroup analysis from large trials has found inconsistent risk/benefit with this combination strategy and therefore it seems prudent to optimize the management of treatment for heart failure where there is good evidence whilst more trial evidence is awaited [MeReC, 2003].
- **Alpha-blockers** should be used with caution in people with heart failure, following the decision to discontinue the doxazosin-treatment arm of the Antihypertensive and Lipid-lowering Treatment to Prevent Heart Attack Trial (ALLHAT). An interim analysis showed that people on doxazosin had a significantly increased incidence of heart failure [ALLHAT Officers, 2000; Messerli, 2000].
- **Anti-arrhythmic agents** have been used to try to reduce the high risk of ventricular arrhythmias in people with heart failure. Amiodarone has a modest effect in reducing mortality but is poorly tolerated and its place in the management of heart failure is still uncertain. Other anti-arrhythmic agents are either ineffective or increase mortality [Andersson and Swedberg, 1998; EBM, 1998; Lau, 1998; Samuel, 2003].
- **Anticoagulants** are not recommended, unless the person also has atrial fibrillation [European Heart Journal, 1997].
- **Calcium-channel blockers** are of no proven benefit in heart failure. Verapamil and diltiazem may worsen heart failure due to their negative inotropic effect [Andersson and Swedberg, 1998, Coats, 1998] However, there are

some trial data suggesting that these may be of benefit in people with heart failure due to idiopathic dilated cardiomyopathy, although more data are needed [Figulla et al, 1996]. Long-acting dihydropyridine calcium-channel blockers are unlikely to exacerbate heart failure, but early suggestions that dihydropyridines may improve outcome in heart failure have not been backed up by subsequent studies [Littler and Sheridan, 1995; Cohn et al, 1997; Thackray et al, 2000].

Surgical treatments

Revascularisation surgery

- **There are no randomised-controlled trials** that have evaluated the outcomes of revascularisation in heart failure.
- **Cohort studies have shown benefit** in people with coexisting angina.
- **More evidence of effectiveness is required** before revascularisation can be recommended as a routine treatment for ischaemic heart failure [DH, 2000].

Other surgical procedures

- **These are highly specialist procedures, which are rarely carried out.** They include cardiac transplantation, cardiomyoplasty, implantable mechanical support devices, and left ventricular volume reduction procedures.

Diastolic heart failure

- **There have been no large, randomised trials of the treatment of diastolic heart failure** [Vasan and Benjamin, 2001].
- **Treatment is therefore empirical,** and includes diuretics, beta-blockers, calcium-channel blockers, ACE inhibitors, and angiotensin-II receptor antagonists. There is little clinical evidence of the efficacy of any drug in the treatment of diastolic heart failure [Mandinov et al, 2000; Vasan and Benjamin, 2001].

Medicines management

ACE inhibitors and angiotensin-II receptor antagonists

- **In all people,** measure serum creatinine and electrolytes 1 week after initiating ACE therapy and 1 week after each increase in dosage.
- **Avoid ACE inhibitors or angiotensin-II receptor antagonists (AIIRAs) in all three trimesters of pregnancy** because of the potential for abnormalities in fetal and neonatal blood pressure (BP) control and renal function.
- **Avoid ACE inhibitors or AIIRAs also in:**
  - Breastfeeding — traces of ACE inhibitors have been detected in breast milk.
  - Critical renovascular disease in the form of bilateral renal artery stenosis or severe renal artery stenosis supplying a single functioning kidney — due to the risk of renal impairment, which may cause severe and progressive renal failure.
  - Significant cardiac outflow tract obstruction (e.g. due to aortic stenosis or hypertrophic obstructive cardiomyopathy) — because of the risk of hypotension and syncope due to vasodilatory effects.
- **Stop nonsteroidal anti-inflammatory drugs (NSAIDs)** if possible as they increase the risk of renal impairment with ACE inhibitors or AIIRAs.
- **Concomitant use with low-dose spironolactone** requires careful monitoring because of the risk of hyperkalaemia. Other potassium-sparing diuretics or potassium supplements should be avoided.
- **A cough may develop** in someone using an ACE inhibitor — where this persists, angiotensin-II receptor antagonists (AIIRAs) are recommended as an alternative

Diuretics

- **Diuretics are best avoided in someone with gout.** If a diuretic is deemed necessary, consider prophylaxis with allopurinol. See separate PRODIGY guidance on *Gout*.
- **Acute hypotension** may be induced as a result of vigorous diuresis especially following administration of a loop diuretic or where combination diuretic therapy is being taken. The diuresis associated with diuretics is dose related.
- **Hypokalaemia may occur** with both thiazide and loop diuretics; therefore renal function needs to be monitored Hypokalaemia may be particularly dangerous in people also being treated with a cardiac glycoside.

Beta-blockers

- **Avoid beta-blockers in someone with asthma, or with chronic obstructive airways disease that has an asthmatic component,** as they can precipitate bronchospasm that is unresponsive to beta$_2$-agonists.
- **People with diabetes** should be advised that beta-blockers may slightly raise their blood glucose levels, and their response to hypoglycaemia may be delayed or symptoms of hypoglycaemia may not occur in the usual way. Bisoprolol is cardioselective and may be preferable Avoid beta-blockers in someone who experiences frequent hypoglycaemia [BNF 47, 2004].
- **Sleep disturbance or nightmares** are more likely with a lipid-soluble beta-blockers as they more easily cross the blood-brain barrier [BNF 47, 2004]. Bisoprolol is moderately lipid soluble and carvedilol is highly lipid soluble.
- **A recent meta-analysis** highlighted that there is no significant increased risk of depressive symptoms while taking beta-blockers, and only a small increase in the risk of fatigue (18 per 1000 patients, 95% CI 5 to 30) or sexual dysfunction (5 per 1000 patients, 95% CI 2 to 8) [Ko et al, 2002].
- **Assess** objective signs of peripheral vascular disease in someone who experiences cold extremities with beta-blockers.

Spironolactone

- **There is a risk of severe hyperkalaemia,** especially as the person is likely to already be on an ACE inhibitor. Therefore careful monitoring of serum creatinine and potassium is necessary, in particular with any change in treatment or in the patient's condition.
- **Additional use** of other potassium-sparing diuretics or potassium supplements should be avoided.
- **Concomitant use of digoxin also requires careful monitoring.** If hypokalaemia occurs, spironolactone may increase the toxicity of digoxin.

Digoxin

- **Digoxin toxicity** is the most serious, and avoidable, adverse effect of digoxin therapy (digoxin has a narrow therapeutic window).
- Toxicity may be precipitated by:
  - **Metabolic disturbances** (e.g. hypokalaemia, hypercalcaemia, hypoxia and acidosis, renal impairment, dehydration, and hypothyroidism)
  - **Drugs that increase digoxin levels** (e.g. verapamil, amiodarone, and quinidine)
- **It is important to check serum electrolytes and creatinine** in people taking digoxin, to assess renal function and potassium levels. The frequency of this should be according to individual patient requirements and in this

population, monitoring is likely to be conducted at regular intervals because of the different therapies (e.g. ACE inhibitors, diuretics etc.) that people are likely to be taking.

Suspect digoxin toxicity if there is anorexia, nausea, vomiting, diarrhoea, mental confusion, or blurred vision. At toxic levels, digoxin may cause or worsen heart failure and it may cause a variety of arrhythmias.

Check levels only to assess possible toxicity, or adherence to treatment. Plasma levels must be measured at least 6 hours after the last dose [BNF 47, 2004].

- Levels less than 1.5 micrograms/litre, in the absence of hypokalaemia, indicate that digoxin toxicity is unlikely.
- Levels greater than 3.0 micrograms/litre indicate that toxicity is likely.
- With levels between 1.5 and 3.0 micrograms/litre, digoxin toxicity should be considered a possibility.

References

NHS staff in England can link, free of charge, from references to full text journals by clicking on [Full text] on the PRODIGY website.

1. AHCPR (1994) *Heart failure: evaluation and care of patients with left ventricular systolic dysfunction.* Clinical Practice Guideline No. 11. Rockville, MD: Agency for Health Care Policy & Research.
2. ALLHAT Officers (2000) Major cardiovascular events in hypertensive patients randomized to doxazosin vs chlorthalidone. *Journal of the American Medical Association* **283**(15), 1967–1975. [Full text]
3. Andersson, B. and Swedberg, K. (1998) Management of overt heart failure. In: Yusuf, S. (Ed.) *Evidence based cardiology*. London: BMJ Books. 647–673.
4. Badgett, R.G., Lucey, C.R. and Mulrow, C.D. (1997) Can the clinical examination diagnose left-sided heart failure in adults? *Journal of the American Medical Association* **277**(21), 1712–1719. [Full text]
5. Bandolier (1997) *ACE Inhibitors in the treatment of chronic heart failure: effective and cost effective.* Bandolier. www.jr2.ox.ac.uk/bandolier/band8/b8-1.html [Accessed: 26/02/2002].
6. BNF 47 (2004) *British National Formulary.* 47th edn. London: British Medical Association and Royal Pharmaceutical Society of Great Britain.
7. Brophy, J.M., Joseph, L. and Rouleau, J.L. (2001) Beta-blockers in congestive heart failure. A Bayesian meta-analysis. *Annals of Internal Medicine* **134**(7), 550–560.
8. Coats, A.J.S. (1998) Investigation and medical treatment of heart failure. *Medicine* **26**(1), 116–121.
9. Cohn, J.N. and Tognoni, G. (2001) A randomized trial of the angiotensin-receptor blocker valsartan in chronic heart failure. *New England Journal of Medicine* **345**(23), 1667–1675. [Full text]
10. Cohn, J.N., Johnson, G., Ziesche, S. et al (1991) A comparison of enalapril with hydralazine-isosorbide dinitrate in the treatment of chronic congestive heart failure. *New England Journal of Medicine* **325**(5), 303–310.
11. Cohn, J.N., Ziesche, S., Smith, R. et al (1997) Effect of the calcium antagonist felodipine as supplementary vasodilator therapy in patients with chronic heart failure treated with enalapril: V-HeFT III. *Circulation* **96**(3), 856–863. [Full text]
12. Dargie, H.J. and Lechat, P. (1999) The Cardiac Insufficiency Bisoprolol Study II (CIBIS -II) beta blockers for mild to moderate heart failure. *Lancet* **353**(9146), 9–13. [Full text]
13. de Lemos, J.A., McGuire, D.K. and Drazner, M.H. (2003) B-type natriuretic peptide in cardiovascular disease. *Lancet* **362**(9380), 316–322. [Full text]
14. DH (2000) *NSF for CHD: Coronary heart disease. Chapter 6: heart failure.* Department of Health. www.dh.gov.uk [Accessed: 16/06/2004]. [Full text]
15. Dickstein, K. and Kjekshus, J. (2002) Effects of losartan and captopril on mortality and morbidity in high-risk patients after acute myocardial infarction: the OPTIMAAL randomised trial. *Lancet* **360**(9335), 752–760. [Full text]
16. DIG (1997) The effect of digoxin on mortality and morbidity in patients with heart failure. *New England Journal of Medicine* **336**(8), 525–533. [Full text]
17. DTB (1994) Diuretics for heart failure. *Drug & Therapeutics Bulletin* **32**(11), 83–85.
18. DTB (1995) Left heart failure (drugs for the doctor's bag). *Drug & Therapeutics Bulletin* **33**(1), 3–5.
19. DTB (2000) Heart failure drugs: what's new? *Drug & Therapeutics Bulletin* **38**(4), 25–27.
20. EBM (1998) Review: amiodarone reduces mortality after MI and for congestive heart failure. *Evidence Based Medicine* 3(4), 112–112.
21. Eccles, M., Freemantle, N. and Mason, J. (1998) North of England evidence based development project: guideline for angiotensin converting enzyme inhibitors in primary care management of adults with symptomatic heart failure. *British Medical Journal* **316**(7141), 1369–1375. [Full text]
22. European Heart Journal (1997) The treatment of heart failure. Task Force of the Working Group on Heart Failure of the European Society of Cardiology. *European Heart Journal* **18**(5), 736–753.
23. European Study Group on Diastolic Heart Failure (ESGDHF) (1998) How to diagnose diastolic heart failure. *European Heart Journal* **19**(7), 990–1003.
24. Figulla, H.R., Gietzen, F., Zeymer, U. et al (1996) Diltiazem improves cardiac function and exercise capacity in patients with idiopathic dilated cardiomyopathy: results of the Diltiazem in Dilated Cardiomyopathy Trial. *Circulation* **94**(3), 346–352. [Full text]
25. Flather, M.D., Yusuf, S., Kober, L. et al (2000) Longterm ACE-inhibitor therapy in patients with heart failure or left-ventricular dysfunction: a systematic overview of data from individual patients. *Lancet* 355(9215), 1575–1581. [Full text]
26. Garg, R. and Yusuf, S. (1995) Overview of randomized trials of angiotensin-converting enzyme inhibitors on mortality and morbidity in patients with heart failure. Collaborative Group on ACE Inhibitor Trials. *Journal of the American Medical Association* 273(18), 1450–1456. [published erratum appears in *JAMA* (1995) 274(6), 462]. [Full text]
27. Granger, C.B., McMurray, J.J., Yusuf, S. et al (2003) Effects of candesartan in patients with chronic heart failure and reduced left-ventricular systolic function intolerant to angiotensin-converting-enzyme inhibitors: the CHARM-alternative trial. *Lancet* **362**(9386), 772–776. [Full text]
28. Heart Failure Society of America (1999) Heart Failure Society of America (HFSA) practice guidelines. HFSA guidelines for management of patients with heart failure caused by left ventricular systolic dysfunction – pharmacological approaches. *Journal of Cardiac Failure* 5(4), 357–382. [erratum appears in *J Card Fail* (2000) 6(1), 74].
29. Heidenreich, P.A., Lee, T.T. and Massie, B.M. (1997) Effect of beta-blockade on mortality in patients with heart failure: a meta-analysis of randomized clinical trials. *Journal of the American College of Cardiology* **30**(1), 27–34.

30. Hood, W.B.Jr, Dans, A.L., Guyatt, G.H. et al (2002) *Digitalis for treatment of congestive heart failure in patients in sinus rhythm (Cochrane Review)*. The Cochrane Library. Issue 1. Oxford: Update Software.
31. Ko, D.T., Hebert, P.R., Coffey, C.S. et al (2002) Beta-blocker therapy and symptoms of depression, fatigue and sexual dysfunction. *Journal of the American Medical Association* **288**(3), 351–352. [Full text]
32. Krum, H. (2001) Guidelines for management of patients with chronic heart failure in Australia. *Medical Journal of Australia* **174**(9), 459–466.
33. Lainchbury, J.G. and Redfield, M.M. (1999) Doppler echocardiographic-guided diagnosis and therapy of heart failure. *Current Cardiology Reports* **1**(1), 55–66.
34. Lau, J. (1998) Commentary on: review: amiodarone reduces mortality after MI and for congestive heart failure. *Evidence Based Medicine* **3**(4), 112–113.
35. Littler, W.A. and Sheridan, D.J. (1995) Placebo controlled trial of felodipine in patients with mild to moderate heart failure. *British Heart Journal* **73**(5), 428–433.
36. Mandinov, L., Eberli, F.R., Seiler, C. and Hess, O.M. (2000) Diastolic heart failure. *Cardiovascular Research* **45**(4), 813–825.
37. McDonagh, T.A. and Dargie, H.J. (1998) Epidemiology and pathophysiology of heart failure. *Medicine* **26**(1), 111–115.
38. McKelvie, R.S., Benedict, C.R. and Yusuf, S. (1998) Prevention of congestive heart failure and treatment of asymptomatic left ventricular dysfunction. In: Yusuf, S., Cairns, J.A., Camm, A.J. et al (Eds.) *Evidence based cardiology*. London: BMJ Publishing Group. 703–721.
39. Medicines Resource (1996) The use of ACE inhibitors in the treatment and prevention of heart failure. *Medicines Resource*(28), 107–110.
40. MeReC (1990) Diuretics. *MeReC Bulletin* **2**, 1–8.
41. MeReC (2001) The diagnosis and drug treatment of heart failure. *MeReC Briefing* **15**(Aug), 1–8.
42. MeReC (2003) Is there a place for combination treatment with an ACE inhibitor and an angiotension II receptor antagonist? *MeReC Extra* **11**(Dec), 1.
43. Messerli, F.H. (2000) Implications of discontinuation of doxazosin arm of ALLHAT. *Lancet* **355**(9207), 863–864. [Full text]
44. NHS CRD (1998) Cardiac rehabilitation. *Effective Health Care Bulletin* **4**(4), 1–12.
45. NZMJ (1997) New Zealand guidelines for the management of chronic heart failure. The National Heart Foundation of New Zealand Cardiac Society of Australia and New Zealand and the Royal New Zealand College of General Practitioners Working Party. *New Zealand Medical Journal* **110**(1040), 99–107.
46. Packer, M., Coats, A.J.S., Fowler, M.B. et al (2001) Effect of carvedilol on survival in severe chronic heart failure. *New England Journal of Medicine* **344**(22), 1651–1658. [Full text]
47. Pfeffer, M.A., Swedberg, K., Granger, C.B. et al (2003a) Effects of candesartan on mortality and morbidity in patients with chronic heart failure: the CHARM-overall programme. *Lancet* **362**(9386), 759–766. [Full text]
48. Pfeffer, M.A., McMurray, J.J., Velazquez, E.J. et al (2003b) Valsartan, captopril, or both in myocardial infarction complicated by heart failure, left ventricular dysfunction, or both. *New England Journal of Medicine* **349**(20), 1893–1906. [Full text]
49. Pitt, B., Segal, R., Martinez, F.A. et al (1997) Randomised trial of losartan versus captopril in patients over 65 with heart failure (Evaluation of Losartan in the Elderly Study, ELITE). *Lancet* **349**(9054), 747–752. [Full text]
50. Pitt, B., Zannad, F., Remme, W.J. et al (1999) The effect of spironolactone on morbidity and mortality in patients with severe heart failure. *New England Journal of Medicine* **341**(10), 709–717. [Full text]
51. Pitt, B., Poole-Wilson, P.A., Segal, R. et al (2000) Effec of losartan compared with captopril on mortality in patients with symptomatic heart failure: randomised trial – the Losartan Heart Failure Survival Study ELIT II. *Lancet* **355**(9215), 1582–1587. [Full text]
52. RCGP Effective Clinical Practice Unit (2000) *Evidence based review criteria for the primary care managemen of coronary heart disease*. Sheffield: University of Sheffield.
53. Remme, W.J., Swedberg, K. and Task Force for the Diagnosis and Treatment of Chronic Heart Failure, European Society of Cardiology (2001) Guidelines for the diagnosis and treatment of chronic heart failure. *European Heart Journal* **22**(17), 1527–1560.
54. Samuel, R. (2003) Heart failure. *Clinical Evidence* **10**(Dec), 30–46.
55. SIGN (1999) *Diagnosis and treatment of heart failure due to left ventricular systolic dysfunction*. Report no. 35. Scottish Intercollegiate Guidelines Network. www.sign.ac.uk [Accessed: 26/02/2003].
56. Thackray, S., Witte, K., Clark, A.L. and Cleland, J.G. (2000) Clinical trials update: OPTIME-CHF, PRAISE-2, ALL-HAT. *European Journal of Heart Failure* **2**(2), 209–212.
57. Vasan, R.S. and Benjamin, E.J. (2001) Diastolic heart failure–no time to relax. *New England Journal of Medicine* **344**(1), 56–59. [Full text]
58. WeMeReC (2001) Drug management of heart failure. *WeMeReC Bulletin* **8**(5), 1–6.
59. Yancy, C.W., Fowler, M.B., Colucci, W.S. et al (2001) Race and the response to adrenergic blockade with carvedilol in patients with chronic heart failure. *New England Journal of Medicine* **344**(18), 1358–1365. [Full text]

PRODIGY GUIDANCE

Herpes simplex — genital

Last revised in April 2002
At the time of print this topic was being updated. The newly revised guidance will be issued on to the website in late 2005.
www.prodigy.nhs.uk/guidance.asp?gt=Herpes simplex - genital

Applies to people over the age of 14 years

This guidance covers the management of genital herpes in adults.
This guidance does not cover the management of immunocompromised individuals, but gives some general management information. It also does not cover neonatal herpes, genital herpes in children, or other genital infections.

There is separate PRODIGY guidance for *Bacterial vaginosis*, *Candida — female genital*, *Chlamydia*, *Herpes simplex — oral*, *Herpes simplex — ocular*, *Herpes zoster*, *Pruritus vulvae*, *Trichomoniasis*, *Urinary tract infection — children*, *Urinary tract infection (lower) — men*, and *Urinary tract infection (lower) — women*.

Goals

- To provide information, support, and counselling to affected people
- To reduce the risk of transmission
- To reduce the severity and duration of episodes, especially first episodes
- To reduce the frequency of recurrent episodes with suppressive therapy where appropriate

Contents

Scenarios

- First episode p.915
- Recurrent episode p.917
- Suppressive therapy p.918
- Pregnancy p.919

Extended Information, p. 920

Which scenario?

- **First episode:** covers the management of people presenting with a first clinical episode of genital herpes (this may be a primary infection or a non-primary first symptomatic episode).
- **Recurrent episode:** covers the management of people presenting with an episode of genital herpes who have a history of one or more previous symptomatic episodes.
- **Suppressive therapy:** covers the management of individuals who would benefit from treatment to reduce the frequency of recurrences (e.g. those with six or more recurrences per year, severe episodes, or significant psychological morbidity).
- **Pregnancy:** offers advice on the referral of women to specialists, and gives information on the subsequent management.

First episode

Which therapy?

- **Referral to a genito-urinary medicine clinic** is preferred, to ensure accurate diagnosis, to exclude other sexually transmitted infections, to discuss partner notification, and for expert counselling.
- **Oral antiviral treatment** should be given to people presenting within 5 days of the start of the episode or while new lesions are still forming. Seek specialist advice for pregnant women and immunocompromised patients.
- **Oral analgesics** help to relieve pain.
- **Topical anaesthetics** help to relieve pain but may cause skin sensitization, so limit continuous use to 5–7 days.
- **Other general measures** that may help include:
  - **Bathing in salt water** (e.g. half a cup of ordinary household salt in the bath) to ease pain.
  - **Vaseline** on affected skin may give some protection.
  - **Urinating sitting in warm water** to relieve dysuria.
  - **Increased intake of oral fluids** to reduce the risk of urinary retention.
- **Education and counselling** are important and should include an explanation of the disease's natural history and recurrences, management with antiviral drugs, transmission risks, pregnancy issues, and partner notification.
- **Self-help groups** may provide valuable support and information.

Practical prescribing points

For further information, please see the *Medicines Compendium* (www.medicines.org.uk) or the *British National Formulary* (www.bnf.org).

Follow-up advice

Follow-up at 5–7 days for individuals with first episode genital herpes allows for:

- **Assessment of the skin lesions.** If vesicles are still *appearing* a further 5-day course of antiviral drugs can be prescribed. Note: vesicles will not necessarily have healed completely at this stage.
- **Further counselling and advice** on the natural history of herpes, recurrences, management with antiviral drugs, transmission risks, pregnancy issues, and partner notification.

Should I refer or investigate?

Refer?

- **Referral to a genito-urinary medicine clinic** is preferable for first episodes.
- **If the person is pregnant,** specialist advice should be obtained.
- **If the person is immunocompromised,** specialist advice should be obtained.
- If acute urinary retention occurs, admission is necessary.
- If the person is psychologically affected, professional counselling, where available, should be offered to them.

Investigate?

- **Confirmation of the diagnosis** at a genito-urinary medicine clinic is preferred.
- **Viral culture and typing** is the recommended investigation; swabs should be taken as soon as possible, as sensitivity is greatest early in the illness when vesicles are present.
- **Correct collection of specimens is essential:** swab the lesion firmly, to collect any vesicle fluid and also to pick up virus-infected cells from the base of the lesion. Use viral transport medium and swabs, which are usually available from local virology laboratories. Ensure rapid transport to the laboratory.

Patient information leaflets

The following PILs are available at www.prodigy.nhs.uk

- Herpes (Genital)
- Herpes (Genital) - Antiviral Medication
- Herpes Viruses Association
- Medicines - Name Changes of Medicines

H

Shared decision making

- Genital herpes is caused by a virus that is passed on by vaginal or anal sex. You can also get genital herpes by having oral sex with a person who has a cold sore.
- The first episode of genital herpes is usually the worst. Once this has gone, the virus settles in a nearby nerve. Further symptoms may then occur from time to time. These 'recurrences' tend to be less severe than the first episode.
- **The following may help ease symptoms:**
  - **Painkillers** such as paracetamol taken regularly.
  - **An anaesthetic ointment** containing lidocaine (lignocaine).
  - **Salt baths** (half a cup of salt in the bath water).
  - **An ice pack** (ice wrapped in a tea towel) on the sores for 5–10 minutes.
  - **Passing urine whilst sitting in warm water** if it is painful to pass urine.
  - **Drinking plenty of fluids.**
- **Antiviral medication** is often taken for 5 days. This does not clear the virus from the body. It works by stopping the virus from multiplying. It reduces the severity and duration of symptoms if started within 5 days of the onset of symptoms.

Drug rationale

Drugs not included

- **Inosine pranobex** has been shown to be less effective than aciclovir [Mindel et al, 1987; BNF 42, 2001].
- **Amantadine** is licensed for herpes zoster infection, not herpes simplex.
- **Topical antivirals** are not recommended in genital herpes as they are less effective than oral antiviral treatments [White and Wardropper, 1997; MMWR, 1998; Short, 1998; AGUM, 2001].
  - **Topical aciclovir** is licensed but less effective than oral treatment.
  - **Topical penciclovir** is only licensed for treatment of herpes labialis (cold sores).
  - **Idoxuridine** (in dimethyl sulfoxide) has had variable results, and is only effective if started at onset of infection. It was used in the past but therapy is messy, malodorous, and potentially toxic [Conlon, 1995; BNF 42, 2001].
- There is no evidence to support the combined use of both oral and topical antiviral treatment [AGUM, 2001].
- **Famciclovir** is as effective as aciclovir and valaciclovir [Mindel, 1998; AGUM, 2001]. At the recommended dose of 250 mg three times per day for 5 days, famciclovir is considerably more expensive than the other antiviral agents.
- **Aciclovir in daily doses of greater than 1 g per day** is not included, as the standard doses are effective (higher doses are sometimes used in immunocompromised patients).

Drugs included

- **Paracetamol and ibuprofen** are effective analgesics. They may provide relief from the pain of acute herpes infection. Codeine phosphate may be added to paracetamol or ibuprofen if necessary.
- **Topical anaesthetics** may relieve pain but there is the potential for developing skin sensitization [BNF 42, 2001; AGUM, 2001].
- **Aciclovir** 200 mg five times a day for 5 days effectively treats first episode genital herpes. Reduced duration of viral shedding, time to crusting, and time to healing have been demonstrated.
- **Valaciclovir** is a prodrug of aciclovir and has demonstrated equivalent effectiveness to aciclovir. Administration is only required twice each day.

Prescriptions

Advice note

Advice only: symptom management

- Age from 14 years onwards
- Recurring infections of genital herpes tend to be less severe and usually last just a few days (like recurring cold sores). The following is often all that is needed to ease symptoms when they occur; painkillers such as paracetamol taken regularly; an anaesthetic ointment containing lidocaine (lignocaine); vaseline applied over the sores may ease pain due to friction; a salt bath (half a cup of salt in the bath water); an ice pack (ice wrapped in a tea towel) placed over the sores for 5-10 minutes; passing urine whilst sitting in warm water may help if passing urine is painful; drink plenty of fluids.

Analgesia: use when required

Paracetamol 1g up to four times a day

- Age from 14 years onwards
- Paracetamol 500mg tablets. Take two tablets every 4 to 6 hours when required for pain relief. Maximum of 8 tablets in 24 hours; supply 100 tablets; NHS Cost £0.75; OTC Cost £1.50.

Ibuprofen 400mg three times a day

- Age from 14 years onwards
- Ibuprofen 400mg tablets. Take one tablet three times a day when required for pain relief. Do not exceed the stated dose; supply 84 tablets; NHS Cost £2.46.

Paracetamol 500mg tablets + codeine 30mg tablets

- Age from 14 years onwards
- Paracetamol 500mg tablets. Take two tablets every 4 to 6 hours when required for pain relief. Maximum of 8 tablets in 24 hours; supply 100 tablets; NHS Cost £0.75; OTC Cost £1.50.
- Codeine 30mg tablets. Take one to two tablets every 4 to 6 hours when required for pain relief. Maximum of 8 tablets in 24 hours; supply 28 tablets; NHS Cost £1.45.

Topical anaesthetics

Lidocaine (lignocaine) 2% gel

- Age from 14 years onwards
- Lidocaine 2% gel. Apply to the lesions to ease pain. Use 5 minutes before urinating to ease pain associated with passing urine; supply 12 tubes; NHS Cost £8.38.

Lidocaine (lignocaine) 5% ointment

- Age from 14 years onwards
- Lidocaine 5% ointment. Apply to the lesions to ease pain. Use 5 minutes before urinating to ease pain associated with passing urine; supply 15 grams; NHS Cost £0.85; OTC Cost £1.40.

Antivirals for 5 days

Aciclovir 200mg five times a day

- Age from 14 years onwards
- Aciclovir 200mg tablets. Take one tablet five times a day for 5 days; supply 25 tablets; NHS Cost £4.97.

Valaciclovir 500mg twice a day

- Age from 14 years onwards
- Valaciclovir 500mg tablets. Take one tablet twice a day for 5 days; supply 10 tablets; NHS Cost £23.50.

Recurrent episode

Which therapy?

- **Supportive measures** may be all that is required as recurrent episodes are usually of shorter duration and are less severe than first episodes. These include:
  - **Oral analgesics** to relieve pain.
  - **Topical anaesthetic** to relieve pain — but can cause skin sensitization so limit continuous use to 5–7 days.
  - **Bathing in salt water** (e.g. half a cup of ordinary household salt in the bath) to relieve pain.
  - **Vaseline** on affected skin may give some relief.
  - **Urinating sitting in warm water** to relieve dysuria.
  - **Increased intake of oral fluids** to reduce the risk of urinary retention.
- **Oral antiviral treatment** may be useful for severely affected people or those with a history of previous severe, prolonged, or frequent episodes. Seek specialist advice for pregnant women and immunocompromised patients.
- **Episodic patient-initiated antiviral treatment** may be appropriate for suitably counselled people. Treatment at the onset of prodromal symptoms or within 24 hours of the onset of lesions is most likely to be effective.
- **Continuous suppressive antiviral treatment** — see scenario *Suppressive therapy*.
- **Education and counselling** is important and should include an explanation of the disease's natural history and recurrences, management with antiviral drugs, transmission risks, pregnancy issues, and partner notification.
- **Self-help groups** may provide valuable support and information.

Practical prescribing points

For further information, please see the *Medicines Compendium* (www.medicines.org.uk) or the *British National Formulary* (www.bnf.org).

Should I refer or investigate?

Refer?

- **If the person is pregnant,** specialist advice should be obtained.
- **If the person is immunocompromised,** specialist advice should be obtained.
- If acute urinary retention occurs (rare), admission is necessary.
- If the person is psychologically affected, professional counselling, where available, should be offered to them.

Investigate?

- **If there is no previous virological confirmation** of the diagnosis, then this should be sought. Referral to a genito-urinary medicine clinic may be preferred in order to do this.
- **Viral culture and typing is the recommended investigation:** swabs should be taken as soon as possible as sensitivity is greatest early in the illness when vesicles are present.
- **Correct collection of specimens is essential:** swab the lesion firmly, to collect any vesicle fluid and also to pick up virus-infected cells from the base of the lesion. Use viral transport medium and swabs, which are usually available from local virology laboratories. Ensure rapid transport to the laboratory.

Patient information leaflets

The following PILs are available at www.prodigy.nhs.uk

- Herpes (Genital)
- Herpes (Genital) - Antiviral Medication
- Herpes Viruses Association
- Medicines - Name Changes of Medicines

Shared decision making

- Recurrent episodes of genital herpes are usually less severe than the first episode.
- **The following may be all that is needed to ease symptoms of a recurrence:**
  - **Painkillers** such as paracetamol taken regularly.
  - **An anaesthetic ointment** containing lidocaine (lignocaine).
  - **Salt baths** (half a cup of salt in the bath water).
  - **An ice pack** (ice wrapped in a tea towel) on the sores for 5–10 minutes.
  - **Passing urine whilst sitting in warm water** if it is painful to pass urine.
  - **Drinking plenty of fluids.**
- **Antiviral medication** may be needed if recurrences are severe. It works by stopping the virus from multiplying. It reduces the severity and duration of symptoms if started soon after the onset of symptoms.
- A 5-day course of antiviral medication is an option to have on 'standby' to take as soon as possible after symptoms begin.

Drug rationale

Drugs not included

- **Inosine pranobex** has been shown to be less effective than aciclovir [Mindel et al, 1987; BNF 42, 2001].
- **Amantadine** is licensed for herpes zoster infection, not herpes simplex.
- **Topical antivirals** are not recommended in genital herpes as they are less effective than oral antiviral treatments [White and Wardropper, 1997; MMWR, 1998; Short, 1998; AGUM, 2001].
  - **Topical aciclovir** is licensed but less effective than oral treatment.
  - **Topical penciclovir** is only licensed for the treatment of herpes labialis (cold sores).

- **Idoxuridine** (in dimethyl sulfoxide) has had variable results, and is only effective if started at onset of infection. It was used in the past but therapy is messy, malodorous, and potentially toxic [Conlon, 1995; BNF 42, 2001].
- There is no evidence to support the combined use of both oral and topical antiviral treatment [AGUM, 2001].

Drugs included

- **Paracetamol and ibuprofen** are effective and safe for most people. They may provide relief from the pain of the acute herpes infection. Codeine phosphate may be added to paracetamol or ibuprofen if necessary.
- **Topical anaesthetics** may relieve pain but there is the potential for developing skin sensitization [AGUM, 2001; BNF 42, 2001].
- **Aciclovir** 200 mg five times a day for 5 days effectively treats first episode genital herpes. Reduced duration of viral shedding, time to crusting, and time to healing have been demonstrated.
- **Valaciclovir** is a prodrug of aciclovir and has demonstrated equivalent effectiveness to aciclovir.
- **Famciclovir** 125 mg twice daily for 5 days has demonstrated equivalent effectiveness to aciclovir in the episodic treatment of recurrent episodes of genital herpes.

Prescriptions

Advice note

Advice only: symptom management
- Age from 14 years onwards
- Recurring infections of genital herpes tend to be less severe and usually last just a few days (like recurring cold sores). The following is often all that is needed to ease symptoms when they occur; painkillers such as paracetamol taken regularly; an anaesthetic ointment containing lidocaine (lignocaine); vaseline applied over the sores may ease pain due to friction; a salt bath (half a cup of salt in the bath water); an ice pack (ice wrapped in a tea towel) placed over the sores for 5-10 minutes; passing urine whilst sitting in warm water may help if passing urine is painful; drink plenty of fluids.

Analgesia: use when required

Paracetamol 1g up to four times a day
- Age from 14 years onwards
- Paracetamol 500mg tablets. Take two tablets every 4 to 6 hours when required for pain relief. Maximum of 8 tablets in 24 hours; supply 100 tablets; NHS Cost £0.75; OTC Cost £1.50.

Ibuprofen 400mg three times a day
- Age from 14 years onwards
- Ibuprofen 400mg tablets. Take one tablet three times a day when required for pain relief. Do not exceed the stated dose; supply 84 tablets; NHS Cost £2.46.

Paracetamol 500mg tablets + codeine 30mg tablets
- Age from 14 years onwards
- Paracetamol 500mg tablets. Take two tablets every 4 to 6 hours when required for pain relief. Maximum of 8 tablets in 24 hours; supply 50 tablets; NHS Cost £0.36; OTC Cost £0.75.
- Codeine 30mg tablets. Take one to two tablets every 4 to 6 hours when required for pain relief. Maximum of 8 tablets in 24 hours; supply 28 tablets; NHS Cost £1.45.

Topical anaesthetics

Lidocaine (lignocaine) 2% gel
- Age from 14 years onwards
- Lidocaine 2% gel. Apply to the lesions to ease pain. Use 5 minutes before urinating to ease pain associated with passing urine; supply 12 tubes; NHS Cost £8.38.

Lidocaine (lignocaine) 5% ointment
- Age from 14 years onwards
- Lidocaine 5% ointment. Apply to the lesions to ease pain. Use 5 minutes before urinating to ease pain associated with passing urine; supply 15 grams; NHS Cost £0.85; OTC Cost £1.40.

Antivirals for 5 days

Aciclovir 200mg five times a day
- Age from 14 years onwards
- Aciclovir 200mg tablets. Take one tablet five times a day for 5 days; supply 25 tablets; NHS Cost £9.00.

Valaciclovir 500mg twice a day
- Age from 14 years onwards
- Valaciclovir 500mg tablets. Take one tablet twice a day for 5 days; supply 10 tablets; NHS Cost £23.50.

Famciclovir 125mg twice a day
- Age from 14 years onwards
- Famciclovir 125mg tablets. Take one tablet twice a day for 5 days; supply 10 tablets; NHS Cost £28.12.

Episodic antivirals for patient initiation (5 days)

Aciclovir 200mg five times a day
- Age from 14 years onwards
- Aciclovir 200mg tablets. Take one tablet five times a day for 5 days; supply 25 tablets; NHS Cost £9.00.

Valaciclovir 500mg twice a day
- Age from 14 years onwards
- Valaciclovir 500mg tablets. Take one tablet twice a day for 5 days; supply 10 tablets; NHS Cost £23.50.

Famciclovir 125mg twice a day
- Age from 14 years onwards
- Famciclovir 125mg tablets. Take one tablet twice a day for 5 days; supply 10 tablets; NHS Cost £28.12.

Suppressive therapy

Which therapy?

- **Aciclovir and valaciclovir are equally effective** for the suppression of genital herpes.
- **Continuous suppressive antiviral therapy** should be considered in individuals with a virologically confirmed diagnosis of genital herpes if recurrences are frequent (particularly if more than six times a year), severe, or associated with significant psychological morbidity.
- **Intermittent suppressive antiviral therapy** may be an option for some people, for example to reduce the chance of an attack during a specified period (e.g. a holiday).
- **Seek specialist advice for pregnant women or immunocompromised patients.**
- **Supportive treatments,** for example analgesics and saline baths, may help pain relief should an acute episode break through.

Practical prescribing points

For further information, please see the *Medicines Compendium* (www.medicines.org.uk) or the *British National Formulary* (www.bnf.org).

Follow-up advice

- Treatment should be discontinued after a maximum of 1 year to reassess recurrence frequency.
- While not receiving treatment, the minimum period for assessment should include two recurrences.
- People who continue to have unacceptable high rates of recurrence may need continued suppressive treatment.

Should I refer or investigate?

Refer?

- **Specialist advice** regarding the need for suppressive therapy may be preferred.
- **If the person is pregnant,** specialist advice should be obtained.
- **If the person is immunocompromised,** specialist advice should be obtained.
- If the person is psychologically affected, professional counselling, where available, should be offered to them.

Investigate?

- **If there is no previous virological confirmation** of the diagnosis, then this should be obtained before initiating suppressive treatment; this usually requires virological testing at the next recurrence. Referral to a genito-urinary medicine clinic may be preferred in order to do this.
- **Viral culture and typing is the recommended investigation:** swabs should be taken as soon as possible as sensitivity is greatest early in the illness when vesicles are present.
- **Correct collection of specimens is essential:** swab the lesion firmly, to collect any vesicle fluid and also to pick up virus-infected cells from the base of the lesion. Use viral transport medium and swabs, which are usually available from local virology laboratories. Ensure rapid transport to the laboratory.

Patient information leaflets

The following PILs are available at www.prodigy.nhs.uk
- Herpes (Genital)
- Herpes (Genital) - Antiviral Medication
- Herpes Viruses Association

Shared decision making

- **Regular antiviral medication** is an option if you have frequent recurrences of genital herpes. It will usually reduce the number and severity of recurrences.
- A reduced 'maintenance' dose rather than the full treatment dose is usual.
- A typical plan is to take a 6–12 month course. Medication can then be stopped to see whether recurrences have become less frequent. This can be repeated if necessary.
- **Treatment for special events:** a course of medication helps to prevent a recurrence during special times. This is an option even if you do not have frequent recurrences but want to have the least chance of symptoms occurring during a special time; for example, during a holiday.

Drug rationale

Drugs not included

- **Inosine pranobex** has been shown to be less effective than aciclovir [Mindel et al, 1987; BNF 42, 2001].
- **Amantadine** is licensed for herpes zoster infection, not herpes simplex.
- **Topical antivirals** are not recommended in genital herpes as they are less effective than oral antiviral treatments [White and Wardropper, 1997; MMWR, 1998; Short, 1998; AGUM, 2001].
  - **Idoxuridine** (in dimethyl sulfoxide) has had variable results, and is only effective if started at onset of infection. It was used in the past but therapy is messy, malodorous, and potentially toxic [Conlon, 1995; BNF 42, 2001].
  - **Topical aciclovir** is licensed but less effective than oral treatment.
  - **Topical penciclovir** is only licensed for the treatment of herpes labialis (cold sores).
- There is no evidence to support the combined use of both oral and topical antiviral treatment [AGUM, 2001].
- **Famciclovir** 250 mg twice a day is as effective and safe as aciclovir and valaciclovir [Mindel, 1998; AGUM, 2001]. At the recommended dose of 250 mg twice a day famciclovir is considerably more expensive than the other antiviral agents.

Drugs included

- **Aciclovir** 400 mg twice a day reduces the frequency and severity of recurrences and reduces the frequency of asymptomatic viral shedding. Aciclovir 200 mg four times a day is an alternative dosing regimen.
- **Valaciclovir** 500 mg daily is a prodrug of aciclovir and has demonstrated equivalent effectiveness to aciclovir. Valaciclovir 250 mg twice daily is an alternative dosing regimen.

[AGUM, 2001]

Prescriptions

Antivirals

Aciclovir 400mg twice a day
- Age from 14 years onwards
- Aciclovir 400mg tablets. Take one tablet twice a day; supply 56 tablets; NHS Cost £12.03.

Aciclovir 200mg four times a day
- Age from 14 years onwards
- Aciclovir 200mg tablets. Take one tablet four times a day; supply 112 tablets; NHS Cost £22.26.

Valaciclovir 500mg once a day
- Age from 14 years onwards
- Valaciclovir 500mg tablets. Take one tablet once a day; supply 28 tablets; NHS Cost £65.66.

Valaciclovir 250mg twice a day
- Age from 16 years onwards
- Valaciclovir 500mg tablets. Take half a tablet twice a day; supply 28 tablets; NHS Cost £65.66.

Pregnancy

Which therapy?

- **Pregnant women should be referred for specialist advice and management.**
- **First episode genital herpes in the first and second trimester:** oral aciclovir is usually given. Vaginal delivery should be anticipated. Continuous aciclovir in the last 4 weeks of pregnancy modestly reduces the risk of recurrence at term.
- **First episode genital herpes in the third trimester:** Caesarean section should be considered for all women, particularly those developing symptoms after 34 weeks of gestation, as the risk of viral shedding in labour is very

H

high. If vaginal delivery is unavoidable, aciclovir treatment of mother and baby may be indicated.
- **Recurrent genital herpes:** Caesarean section is not indicated in women who do not have genital lesions at delivery. Continuous aciclovir in the last 4 weeks of pregnancy may modestly reduce the risk of recurrence at term. If lesions are present at the onset of labour, then Caesarean section is an option, although there is a lack of evidence for its effectiveness: the risks of vaginal delivery for the fetus are small (0.25–3% risk of transmission) and they should be weighed against the risks to the mother of Caesarean section.

Should I refer or investigate?

Refer?

- **Pregnant women should be referred for specialist advice and management.** A summary of recommended treatment is given in the section *Which therapy?*
- **If the person is immunocompromised,** specialist advice should be obtained.
- If the person is psychologically affected, professional counselling, where available, should be offered to them.

H

Investigate?

- **If there is no previous virological confirmation** of the diagnosis, then this should be sought. Referral to a genito-urinary medicine or obstetric clinic as appropriate may be preferred at this stage.
- **Viral culture and typing is the recommended investigation:** swabs should be taken as soon as possible, as sensitivity is greatest early in the illness when vesicles are present.
- **Correct collection of specimens is essential:** swab the lesion firmly, to collect any vesicle fluid and also to pick up virus-infected cells from the base of the lesion. Use viral transport medium and swabs, which are usually available from local virology laboratories. Ensure rapid transport to the laboratory.

Patient information leaflets

The following PILs are available at www.prodigy.nhs.uk
- Herpes (Genital)
- Herpes (Genital) - Antiviral Medication
- Herpes Viruses Association

Shared decision making

- **Advice from a specialist** is best if you have genital herpes and are pregnant or planning to have a baby. The advice will be for your own circumstances but the following is the kind of advice that may be given.
- **If you have a first episode of genital herpes:**
  - **Late in pregnancy,** a Caesarean section may be advised (particularly if it occurs after 34 weeks as there is a high risk of passing the virus on to the baby during vaginal delivery). A serious infection of the baby may occur.
  - **Early in pregnancy,** symptoms should have settled by the time of childbirth. Antiviral medication may be advised in the last 4 weeks of pregnancy to prevent a recurrence of symptoms during childbirth, and a Caesarean section is not usually necessary.
- **If you have recurrent genital herpes:**
  - Caesarean section is not usually necessary so long as you do not have symptoms during childbirth.
  - Some specialists advise antiviral medication in the last 4 weeks of pregnancy, which may reduce the risk of a recurrence.

Drug rationale

- Pregnant women should be managed by specialists, so no prescriptions are included. Aciclovir is the antiviral of choice during pregnancy. Although it is not licensed for use in pregnancy, there is substantial experience of its use and to date there is no evidence of harm [Smith et al, 1998; AGUM, 2001].

Extended Information

Background information

- What is it? p.920
- How common is it? p.920
- How do I know my patient has it? p.921
- What else might it be? p.921
- Complications and prognosis p.921

What is it?

- **Genital herpes** is an infection caused by herpes simplex virus (HSV), encompassing lesions on the genitals and nearby areas (e.g. buttocks, anal area). There are two types of HSV: type 1 and type 2. HSV-1 usually causes oral herpes (cold sores), but can also cause up to half of genital disease. HSV-2 infection nearly always causes genital disease.
- **Infectivity** is greatest with direct contact with an infected blister or sore. However, most cases are acquired from a partner shedding virus asymptomatically. HSV-2 is usually acquired after vaginal or anal sex, while HSV-1 infection is usually acquired after orogenital sex.
- **The primary infection** is defined as the first time a person is infected with genital herpes. After primary infection the virus becomes latent in dorsal root ganglia. Recurrence is due to reactivation of the virus, causing either symptomatic lesions or asymptomatic viral shedding.
- **If the person has symptoms at primary infection it is known as a primary first episode.**
- If they do not have symptoms the disease will go unrecognized until they get a recurrence that is symptomatic, and the first symptomatic episode is called a non-primary first episode. People with non-primary first episodes have evidence of previous infection, as shown by the presence of type-specific antibodies at the time of presentation.

[Thin, 1996; Brugha et al, 1997; White and Wardropper, 1997; NZHF, 2000; AGUM, 2001]

How common is it?

- **At least 1 in 10 people** may be infected with genital herpes simplex, and up to 80% of these will have asymptomatic or unrecognized disease. Prevalence varies with the population studied, with serological examination showing low rates in blood donors, intermediate rates in pregnant women, and high rates in genito-urinary medicine clinic attenders.
- **HSV-2 virus causes the majority of genital disease, but HSV-1 can cause 25–50% of genital disease.**
- **More than 20,000 cases** of genital herpes are reported annually from genito-urinary clinics in the UK, of which over 60% are first episodes. This number is likely to be considerably greater as many cases are not seen in clinics and are not reported.
- **The mean number of genital herpes cases seen by a GP is** 1.37 first episodes per year, and 0.96 recurrent episodes per year, according to one questionnaire survey [Woolley and Chandiok, 1996].

- **During pregnancy,** primary infection is very rare. Recurrent disease is more common, although it is unusual for a woman with genital herpes to have an outbreak during the last weeks of pregnancy.

[Brugha et al, 1997; Mindel, 1998; Drake et al, 2000; NZHF, 2000]

How do I know my patient has it?

- **Confirmation of the diagnosis at a genito-urinary medicine clinic** is preferred, to ensure accurate diagnosis, to exclude other sexually transmitted infections, and to offer expert counselling and partner notification.
- **The diagnosis is often missed,** as many people are asymptomatic or have atypical presentations.
- **Examination** of the genital area, and the rest of the skin including the oral cavity, will help to rule out, or confirm, differential diagnoses (see *What else might it be?* below).
- **Immunocompromised patients** may have prolonged and severe infection and are at increased risk of disseminated infection.

Symptoms and signs of first episode genital herpes

- **Symptoms** are similar with both types of HSV.
- **Prodromal symptoms** may occur in some people. They include influenza-like symptoms and tingling or irritation in the genital area.
- **Areas of genital erythema then develop into clusters of small vesicles** that occur in crops over the next 1–2 weeks. They contain clear or cloudy fluid, which rupture to form painful, shallow ulcers that then crust except in moist mucosal areas. By the third week most have healed.
- **Less classically,** there may be only a small fissure or raw area, a painless ulcer, a small area of erythema, or an area of irritation with no visible abnormality.
- **Extragenital sites** may be affected, particularly the buttocks and perianal area.
- **Vaginal or urethral discharge** may be present.
- **Inguinal lymph nodes** may become swollen and tender.
- **Dysuria** is common and acute retention of urine can occur.

Symptoms and signs of recurrent genital herpes

- Recurrent symptoms of both HSV-I and HSV-2 infections are much milder and of shorter duration than the first episode.
- Recurrences are usually less severe and less frequent with HSV-1 infection when compared with HSV-2.
- Lesions are usually unilateral and often recur at the same site.

Diagnostic procedures

- **Viral culture** is the 'gold standard' method.
- **Correct collection of specimens for culture is essential.** Blister lesions are the best source of virus. Swab the lesion firmly to collect any vesicle fluid and scrape virus-infected cells from the base of the lesion. Use viral transport medium and swabs, which are usually available from local virology or microbiology laboratories. Ensure rapid transport to the laboratory (within 24 hours), otherwise the sample should be stored in the refrigerator after collection. A commercial medium and swab called Virocult may be used as an alternative.
- **Culture results** are usually available within 3 to 4 days but can take up to 2 weeks. Sensitivity is highest in first episode infections, if vesicles are present, and in immunocompromised patients. Typing results are not routinely available.
- **Direct viral antigen detection tests and detection of virus by polymerase chain reaction** are not widely available.
- **Type-specific serology** is not yet widely available, and should not usually be used as a replacement for culture in people with active lesions.

[Slomka, 1996; Thin, 1996; Brugha et al, 1997; Scott et al, 1997; NZHF, 2000; AGUM, 2001]

What else might it be?

- **Candidiasis** and **scabies** excoriations may be confused with genital herpes, but vesicles are not present.
- **Rarer infectious causes** of genital ulceration in the UK are syphilis, chancroid, lymphogranuloma venereum, granuloma inguinale, herpes zoster virus, and Epstein–Barr virus.
- **Non-infectious causes include** Reiter's syndrome, Behcet's syndrome, drug reactions, lichen planus, lichen simplex, lichen sclerosus, trauma (including dermatitis artefacta), and malignancy.
- More than one cause of genital ulceration may be present and genital herpes may coexist with other sexually transmitted infections.

[White and Wardropper, 1997; MMWR, 1998]

Complications and prognosis

Immediate complications

- **Urinary retention** due to dysuria or, less commonly, autonomic neuropathy [AGUM, 2001].
- **Secondary infection** with *Staphylococcus* may give the appearance of folliculitis.
- **Aseptic meningitis** is more likely to occur during primary infection [AGUM, 2001; Wald et al, 2001]. In one study, 36% of women and 13% of men developed symptoms of fever, headache, neck stiffness, and photophobia. In another study, 8 out of 189 people with genital herpes were hospitalized with aseptic meningitis [White and Wardropper, 1997]. Symptoms usually develop 3 to 12 days from onset of genital lesions and settle over 2 to 3 days, usually with full recovery.
- **Encephalitis or disseminated infection** are rare complications that are more likely in immunocompromised patients.

Longer-term complications

- **Risk of transmission to a sexual partner** over a 1-year period (not using condoms but avoiding skin contact when symptoms are present) is 10%. Transmission is most likely to occur during sex, when the skin is broken, and when there are lesions present. However, transmission can occur when there are no symptoms present by 'asymptomatic shedding'. Genital herpes may increase the risk of transmission and acquisition of human immunodeficiency virus (HIV).
- **Psychological and psychosexual problems** are common, for example, fear of social stigma and rejection, difficulty with relationships, and depression.
- **Vaginal adhesions** after severe infection are very rare but may result in obstructive dyspareunia.
- **Neonatal herpes infection,** after maternal transmission, is a serious complication; fortunately numbers are low, with less than 2 per 100,000 live births in the UK.

Prognosis

- **Symptomatic recurrence is likely** in most people after first episode symptomatic disease. Recurrences are usually of shorter duration and are less severe.
- **Recurrence is more likely with HSV-2.** The median rate of recurrence for HSV-2 is approximately once every 3 months, compared with once per year for HSV-1.

[Tookey and Peckham, 1996; Brugha et al, 1997; NZHF, 2000; Diaz-Mitoma et al, 1998; Mindel, 1998; Smith et al, 1998; AGUM, 2001]

Management issues

- General issues and patient education p.922
- Supportive measures p.922
- Antiviral medication p.922
- Antiviral treatment of first episode p.922
- Antiviral treatment of recurrences p.923
- Antiviral suppression therapy p.923
- Management of genital herpes in pregnancy p.923
- Management of genital herpes in immunocompromised people p.923

General issues and patient education

- **Genito-urinary medicine clinics:** it is preferable that people with suspected genital herpes attend a genito-urinary medicine clinic to ensure accurate diagnosis, to exclude other sexually transmitted infections, to discuss partner notification, and to obtain expert counselling [Barton, 1996; White and Wardropper, 1997; Mindel, 1998].
- **Education and counselling:** people with genital herpes are often upset and distressed. Guilt, depression, lowered self-esteem, and fear of rejection are common reactions.
    - An explanation should be given about the disease's natural history, together with the likelihood and nature of recurrences.
    - It is important to explain that recurrent symptoms, if they are a problem, can be controlled.
    - Information about management with antiviral drugs, transmission risks, pregnancy issues, and partner notification is important.
    - Reading material that can be taken away allows the person the opportunity to absorb the information and formulate questions that can be raised at follow-up consultations.
- **Partner notification** is best done through genito-urinary medicine clinics. It can clarify whether a partner or ex-partner is infected or not.
- **People in long-term relationships** often assume that their partner has been unfaithful. An explanation that genital herpes can be acquired but not clinically evident for some time (e.g. months or years) may be helpful. Further, the genital herpes episode may be due to herpes simplex virus 1 (HSV-1, the main cause of cold sores) from their partner.
- **Self-help groups:** groups can often provide valuable support and information.
- **Advice on transmission:** transmission is most likely to occur during sexual contact, when the skin is broken, and when there are lesions present, so sex should be avoided if prodromal symptoms or lesions are present.
    - Infection can sometimes be acquired from people with asymptomatic viral shedding or from individuals who are unaware that they are infected.
    - Asymptomatic viral shedding particularly occurs in the first 6 to 12 months after a primary infection, with HSV-2 infection, and immediately before and after symptomatic recurrences.
    - Condoms have been shown to reduce transmission from men to women, particularly when the herpes lesions are confined to the penis, which can be totally covered by the condom [Wald et al, 2001]. Condoms may not reduce the risk of transmission from women to men, because lesions on the vulval area cannot be totally covered.
    - It is possible to get a coinfection of HSV-1 and HSV-2 [MMWR, 1998; NZHF, 2000; AGUM, 2001].
- **Advice on pregnancy:** genital herpes can be managed during pregnancy, but it is best for pregnant women to be managed by a specialist to minimize the likelihood of uterine infection or neonatal transmission (see *Management of genital herpes in pregnancy* below).
- **Advice on recurrence:** recurrent episodes are usually less severe than the primary episode. HSV-2 infections recur more often (on average, once every 3 months) than HSV 1 infections (on average, once per year).

Supportive measures

- **Oral analgesics** and **topical anaesthetics** may relieve pain, although there is a risk of skin sensitization with topical products.
- **Bathing in salt water** may ease pain, for example half a cup of ordinary household salt in the bath [NZHF, 2000; AGUM, 2001].
- **Dysuria** may be relieved by urinating while sitting in warm water. Application of a topical anaesthetic 5 minutes before urinating may also help, but there is a risk of skin sensitization. Increasing oral fluid intake will dilute urine, making it less painful to void, and reduces the risk of urinary retention [NZHF, 2000; White and Wardropper, 1997].
- **Ice packs** or application of **vaseline** onto infected skin may temporarily reduce pain.

Antiviral medication

- **Antiviral therapy** targets the viral replication process in herpes-infected cells.
- **Oral antiviral medications** are effective in both first and recurrent episodes of herpes.
- **Currently available licensed oral antivirals** are aciclovir, valaciclovir (a prodrug of aciclovir), and famciclovir (a prodrug of penciclovir).
- **Resistance** to these agents is not a significant problem in immunocompetent people. Cross-resistance between aciclovir, valaciclovir, and famciclovir is common [DTB 1998].
- **Topical antiviral agents** are less effective than oral agents and are not recommended. There is no benefit to be gained from the combined use of oral and topical antivirals [Short, 1998; AGUM, 2001].
- **Intravenous (IV) antiviral agents** are only indicated when the person cannot swallow or tolerate oral medication. IV antivirals may be used in pregnancy or in immunocompromised people under specialist management.

Antiviral treatment of first episode

- **Oral antivirals** reduce the duration and severity of symptoms, reduce the duration of viral shedding, and hasten the time to healing in first episodes of genital herpes.
- **Oral antiviral treatment** should be given to people presenting within 5 days of the start of the episode or while new lesions are still forming [AGUM, 2001].
- **Courses of 5 days are recommended,** but it may be prudent to continue therapy beyond 5 days if new lesions are still appearing at this time [AGUM, 2001].
- Aciclovir 200 mg five times a day for 5 days, or valaciclovir 500 mg twice a day for 5 days, are equally effective [DTB, 1998; AGUM, 2001]. Famciclovir 250 mg three times a day for 5 days is also effective, but is a much more expensive option.

Antiviral treatment of recurrences

- The best strategy for managing an individual will change over time according to recurrence frequency, symptom severity, and relationship status [AGUM, 2001].
- **Oral antivirals** taken when recurrent symptoms appear will reduce the duration and severity of symptoms, reduce the duration of viral shedding, and hasten the time to healing in recurrent episodes of genital herpes.
- Aciclovir 200 mg five times a day for 5 days, famciclovir 125 mg twice a day for 5 days, or valaciclovir 500 mg twice a day for 5 days are all effective.
- **Antiviral treatment is not always necessary** as episodes are usually of shorter duration and are less severe than first episodes; analgesia and saline baths may be adequate [NZHF, 2000; AGUM, 2001].
- **Episodic antiviral treatment** (i.e. treatment as new episode begins) may be useful for people with a history of prolonged recurrences. Patient-initiated treatment early in the episode is most likely to be effective [Brugha et al, 1997; AGUM, 2001].
- **Short courses of antivirals for recurrences** will not affect the natural history or frequency of recurrences. If the frequency or severity of recurrences are a problem, continuous suppressive antiviral therapy may be needed (see below).

Antiviral suppression therapy

- **Continuous suppressive antiviral therapy** greatly reduces the frequency and severity of recurrences and reduces the frequency of asymptomatic viral shedding, but it is not known whether the risk of transmission is also reduced [Brugha et al, 1997; NZHF, 2000; Diaz-Mitoma et al, 1998; MMWR, 1998; Short, 1998; AGUM, 2001]. In one study recurrence was reduced from 12.5 to 1.7 recurrences in the first year, and then stayed at 0.8 recurrences per year for the next 4 years of treatment [Goldberg et al, 1993] .
- **Continuous suppressive antiviral therapy** should be considered if recurrences are frequent (particularly if more than six times a year), severe, or associated with significant psychological morbidity [Brugha et al, 1997]. Treatment should be discontinued after a maximum of 1 year to reassess the frequency of recurrences. While not receiving treatment, the minimum period for assessment should include two recurrences, in order to properly assess recurrence rates. People who continue to have unacceptable high rates of recurrence may need continued suppressive treatment [AGUM, 2001].
- **Intermittent suppressive therapy** may be an option for some people, for example to ensure they do not have an attack during a specified period, for example a holiday.
- Aciclovir 400 mg twice a day, aciclovir 200 mg four times day, valaciclovir 250 mg twice daily, or valaciclovir 500 mg daily are equally effective for suppression of genital herpes. Safety and resistance data on long-term aciclovir therapy extends to 15 years. Famciclovir 250 mg twice a day is also effective, but is a much more expensive option.

Management of genital herpes in pregnancy

- **Specialist supervision is necessary** for the treatment of genital herpes during pregnancy.
- **Neonatal herpes** is a rare but potentially serious infection, which may be acquired during labour through direct contact with infected genital secretions. Rarely there may be disseminated maternal or fetal infection or intra-uterine infection.
- **Greatest risk to the newborn infant occurs with vaginal delivery during a primary infection,** when about 50% of infants become infected. Transmission rates are lowest for women who acquire herpes before pregnancy; even if recurrent lesions are present at the time of delivery the risk of transmission is only 0.25–3%, possibly because of maternal antibodies passed through the placenta [NZHF, 2000; Smith et al, 1998].
- **Management depends upon** the stage of pregnancy and whether it is a first or recurrent episode [NZHF, 2000; Smith et al, 1998; AGUM, 2001].
- **First episode genital herpes in the first and second trimester:** oral aciclovir is usually given. It is not licensed for use in pregnancy, but there is substantial experience of its use and, to date, there is no evidence of harm [Smith et al, 1998; AGUM, 2001]. Vaginal delivery should be anticipated. Continuous aciclovir in the last 4 weeks of pregnancy is an option, as there is limited evidence that it can reduce the rate of recurrence at term [NZHF, 2000; AGUM, 2001; Wald, 2001].
- **First episode genital herpes in the third trimester:** the risk of viral shedding in labour is very high, and the risk of transmission to the baby is up to 50%. Caesarean section should be considered for all women, particularly those developing symptoms after 34 weeks of gestation. Caesarean section carries an increased morbidity and mortality risk to the mother. If vaginal delivery is unavoidable, aciclovir treatment of mother and baby may be indicated [NZHF, 2000; AGUM, 2001].
- **Recurrent genital herpes:** Caesarean section is not indicated in women who do not have recurrent genital lesions at delivery. There is limited evidence that continuous aciclovir in the last 4 weeks of pregnancy may modestly reduce the risk of recurrence, but will not totally eliminate viral shedding [Wald, 2001]. If lesions are present at the onset of labour, then Caesarean section is an option, although there is a lack of evidence for its effectiveness: the risks of vaginal delivery for the fetus are small (0.25–3% risk of transmission) and they should be weighed against the risks to the mother of Caesarean section [NZHF, 2000; AGUM, 2001].

Management of genital herpes in immunocompromised people

- **Immunocompromised patients with genital herpes simplex** should be referred to the appropriate specialist for management.
- **Clinically refractory lesions due to genital HSV** are a major problem in people with severe immunodeficiency, including late stage human immunodeficiency virus (HIV) disease.
- **A standard suppressive regimen** is usually used for those immunocompromised people with frequently recurring genital herpes. Under specialist care, lesions that fail to respond to standard therapy are usually treated with an increased dose of aciclovir. If that is unsuccessful, specialists may change the treatment to either topical trifluridine or cidofovir gel for accessible lesions, or IV foscarnet for inaccessible lesions [AGUM, 2001].

H

References

NHS staff in England can link, free of charge, from references to full text journals by clicking on [Full text] on the PRODIGY website.

1. AGUM (2001) *National guideline for the management of genital herpes.* Clinical Effectiveness Group (Association for Genitourinary Medicine and the MedicalSociety for the Study of Venereal Diseases). www.bashh.org [Accessed: 22/04/2005].
2. Barton, S. (1996) Sharing care in genital herpes: new guidelines for the GP/GUM interface. *British Journal of Sexual Medicine* **23**(3), 13–15.

3. BNF 42 (2001) *British National Formulary*. 42nd edn. London: British Medical Association and Royal Pharmaceutical Society of Great Britain.
4. Brugha, R., Keersmaekers, K., Renton, A. and Meheus, A. (1997) Genital herpes infection: a review. *International Journal of Epidemiology* 26(4), 698–709.
5. Conlon, C.P. (1995) Herpes zoster. *Prescribers' Journal* 35(2), 46–52.
6. Diaz-Mitoma, F., Sibbald, G.R., Shafran, S.D et al (1998) Oral famciclovir for the suppression of recurrent genital herpes. *Journal of the American Medical Association* 280(10), 887–892. [Full text]
7. Drake, S., Taylor, S., Brown, D. and Pillay, D. (2000) Improving the care of patients with genital herpes. *British Medical Journal* 321(7261), 619–623. [Full text]
8. DTB (1998) Update on drugs for herpes zoster and genital herpes. *Drug & Therapeutics Bulletin* 36(10), 77–79. [Full text]
9. Goldberg, L.H., Kaufman, R.H., Kurtz, T.O. et al (1993) Continuous five year treatment of patients with frequently recurring genital herpes simplex virus. *Journal of Medical Virology* 41(Suppl. 1), 45–50.
10. Mindel, A. (1998) Genital herpes – how much of a public -health problem? *Lancet* 351(Suppl III), 16–18. [Full text]
11. Mindel, A., Kinghorn, G., Allason-Jones, E. et al (1987) Treatment of first-attack genital herpes – acyclovir versus inosine pranobex. *Lancet* 1(8543), 1171–1173. [published erratum appears in *Lancet* (1987) 2(8558), 584].
12. MMWR (1998) Guidelines for treatment of sexually transmitted diseases. *Morbidity & Mortality Weekly Report* 47(RR-1), 1–118.
13. NZHF (2000) *2000 guidelines for the management of genital herpes in New Zealand*. 5th Edition 2000. New Zealand: New Zealand Herpes Foundation.
14. Scott, L.L., Hollier, L.M. and Dias, K. (1997) Perinata herpesvirus infections. *Infectious Disease Clinics of North America* 11(1), 27–53.
15. Short, L. (1998) Recommended dosing regimens in genital herpes. *Prescriber*, 44–51.
16. Slomka, M.J. (1996) Seroepidemiology and control of genital herpes: the value of type specific antibodies to herpes simplex virus. *Communicable Disease Report* 6(3), R41-R45.
17. Smith, J.R., Cowan, F.M. and Munday, P. (1998) The management of herpes simplex virus infection in pregnancy. *British Journal of Obstetrics & Gynaecology* 105(3), 255–260.
18. Thin, R.N. (1996) Diagnosis of genital herpes simplex infections. *Current Problems in Dermatology* 24, 50–56.
19. Tookey, P. and Peckham, C.S. (1996) Neonatal herpes simplex virus infection in the British isles. *Paediatric & Perinatal Epidemiology* 10(4), 432–442.
20. Wald, A., Langenberg, A.G., Link, K. et al (2001) Effect of condoms on reducing the transmission of herpes simplex virus type 2 from men to women. *Journal of the American Medical Association* 285(24), 3100–3106. [Full text]
21. White, C. and Wardropper, A.G. (1997) Genital herpe simplex infection in women. *Clinics in Dermatology* 15(1), 81–91.
22. Woolley, P.D. and Chandiok, S. (1996) Survey of the management of genital herpes in general practice. *International Journal of STD & AIDS* 7(3), 206–211.

PRODIGY GUIDANCE

Herpes simplex — ocular

Last revised in February 2005
www.prodigy.nhs.uk/guidance.asp?gt=Herpessimplex - ocular

Applies to people of all ages

This guidance covers the management of ocular herpes simplex.

This guidance does not cover the management of herpes zoster ophthalmicus.

There is separate PRODIGY guidance for *Herpes simplex — genital, Herpes simplex — oral,* and *Shingles and postherpetic neuralgia.*

Goals

To reduce symptoms
To reduce the complications of herpes simplex virus keratitis and iritis (e.g. blindness and decreased visual acuity due to corneal scarring and glaucoma)
To reduce the risk of recurrence
To improve corneal graft survival after penetrating keratoplasty
[Barker, 2004]

Contents

Scenarios

- Herpes simplex — ocular p.925

Extended Information, p. 925

Herpes simplex — ocular

Which therapy?

If ocular herpes simplex is suspected, patients should be sent immediately to the eye casualty department, unless there is access to a slit lamp and the necessary expertise is available in the practice. This is a sight-threatening condition and diagnosis can be difficult.
Staining with fluorescein may reveal dendritic ulceration. However, the absence of dendritic ulceration does not exclude corneal herpes simplex disease; if dendritic ulceration is suspected on clinical grounds, patients should always be referred to an ophthalmologist.
Corticosteroids should never be given for an undiagnosed red eye, when visual acuity is impaired, or if there is a history of ocular herpes infection.
Contact lenses should not be worn whilst symptomatic.

Patient information leaflets

The following PILs are available at www.prodigy.nhs.uk
Herpes Simplex Eye Infection
Herpes Viruses Association

Shared decision making

You may have an infection of the eye caused by the cold sore virus. Sometimes this is mild and clears quickly. However, it may become severe and lead to serious eye problems.
It is important for you to see an eye specialist as soon as possible.
There are good treatments available, even for severe infection. These treatments (usually tablets or eye drops) are usually prescribed by eye specialists.

- **Do not wear contact lenses** until the symptoms have gone completely.
- In the future you may have a slightly higher than average risk of getting this type of eye infection again. You should report any future eye symptoms promptly to a doctor.

Drug rationale

- There are no prescriptions included. If ocular herpes simplex is suspected, patients should be sent immediately to the eye casualty department, unless there is access to a slit lamp and the necessary expertise is available in the practice.

Extended Information

Background information

- What is it? p.925
- How common is it? p.926
- How do I know my patient has it? p.926
- What else might it be? p.926
- Complications and prognosis p.926

What is it?

- **Ocular herpes simplex is usually caused by infection with herpes simplex virus (HSV) type 1** (HSV-1) and occasionally by HSV type 2 (HSV-2).
- **Primary infection** occurs when there is HSV infection in people with no previous viral exposure. Up to 90% of cases are subclinical. It occurs most often in childhood and adolescence, and does not usually affect the eye. There is, however, a trend for young adults to present with ocular herpes as a primary infection.
- **Recurrent ocular infection is due to reactivation of virus** lying dormant in the trigeminal ganglion and represents 95% of cases.
- **Neonatal eye disease** is most commonly caused by HSV-2, which is transmitted during vaginal delivery.
- **Ocular manifestations of herpes simplex infection are varied** and include:
  - **Keratitis:**
    - Epithelial keratitis — involvement of the superficial layer of the cornea is the most common ocular manifestation (63% of episodes) and is typified by a dendritic ulcer.
    - Stromal keratitis — involvement of the middle layer of the cornea is less common (6% of initial episodes and 17% of recurrent episodes). Stromal disease occurs when viral antigen passes to the stroma and induces an immunological reaction. Usually this induces a disciform oedema but a more severe

inflammatory response can cause necrotizing stromal keratitis.
- Iritis or uveitis (6% of cases)
- Blepharitis
- Conjunctivitis
- Retinitis
- Periorbital vesicular skin rash

[Frith et al, 2001]

How common is it?

- **Incidence of new cases** of ocular herpes simplex is 8.4 per 100,000 person-years.
- **Overall incidence of new and recurrent ocular herpes simplex** is 21 per 100,000 person-years.
- **Prevalence of ocular herpes simplex** is 1.5 cases per 1,000 population.
- **Males and females are affected equally.**
- **The highest incidence of initial presentation is in middle-aged people** (mean age 37 years). There is some evidence that the mean age at first presentation is increasing.
- Ocular herpes simplex disease is the most common infective cause of corneal blindness in high-income countries.

[Liesegang, 1989]

How do I know my patient has it?

Recurrent ocular herpes simplex

General points
- **The manifestations of recurrent ocular herpes simplex are varied;** they include epithelial keratitis resulting in the classic lesion of a branching dendritic ulcer (most common), stromal keratitis, punctate keratitis, iritis, conjunctivitis, and blepharitis. A vesicular rash on the eyelids is uncommon in recurrent disease and suggests primary infection [Baum, 1995; Seal and Bron, 1997; Thielen et al, 2000; Frith et al, 2001].
- **Symptoms and signs are usually unilateral** in immunocompetent persons. Bilateral disease is seen in about 12% of cases [Liesegang, 1989; Liesegang, 1991].
- **The diagnosis is generally made clinically** and laboratory testing is seldom necessary.

Trigger factors

Trigger factors cause the virus to be reactivated and it may then migrate to the cornea, resulting in ocular herpes simplex. Trigger factors include:
- Fever
- Ultraviolet light
- Cold wind
- Systemic illness
- Menstruation
- Emotional stress
- Local trauma
- Immunosuppression
- Trigeminal nerve manipulation

Symptoms
- Redness of the eye
- Ache/pain in the eye
- Photophobia
- Watering of the eye
- Blurring of vision — depending on the site of ulceration

Signs
- Red eye — maximally around the cornea
- Dendritic ulcer — often obvious only after staining with fluorescein
- Hazy cornea — due to oedema or scarring from a previous episode
- Localized 'creamy' corneal opacity — indicative of stromal keratitis
- Reduced visual acuity
- Reduced corneal sensation (test with a wisp of tissue)
- Vesicles or pustules along the lid margin and/or periocular skin
- Erosions and/or ulceration of the eyelid margin
- Swollen pre-auricular nodes
- Swelling and redness of the eyelid

Primary ocular herpes simplex disease

General points
- Primary disease may be asymptomatic.
- Usual manifestations are periocular dermatitis, follicular conjunctivitis, and an ulcerative blepharitis.

Symptoms
- Generally unwell
- Red eye
- Rash on the eyelid
- Photophobia and watering of the eye (indicative of corneal involvement)

Signs
- Vesicles or pustules along the lid margin and/or periocular skin
- Swelling and redness of the eyelid
- Erosions and/or ulceration of the eyelid margin
- Red eye — maximally around the cornea
- Multiple small epithelial lesions or small dendritic ulcers
- Swollen pre-auricular nodes

[Baum, 1995; Lee and Laibson, 1996; Seal and Bron, 1997; Thielen et al, 2000; Frith et al, 2001]

What else might it be?

- **Herpes zoster ophthalmicus** — associated vesicular rash in the distribution of the ophthalmic division of the fifth cranial nerve, seldom recurrent, typically affecting elderly people.
- **Orbital cellulitis** — unwell, tender sinuses, restriction of eye movements; admit urgently if suspected.
- **Bacterial conjunctivitis** — bilateral red eyes with purulent discharge.
- **Adenovirus conjunctivitis/keratoconjunctivitis** — often occurs in epidemics and associated with upper respiratory tract infection.
- **Chlamydial conjunctivitis** — chronic mucopurulent conjunctivitis.
- **Corneal abrasion** — history of trauma.
- **Pseudo-dendritic ulcer** secondary to acanthamoeba infection.
- **Episcleritis** — usually relatively asymptomatic, localized redness in one or both eyes.
- **Scleritis** — localized area of inflammation associated with severe pain.
- **Acute glaucoma** — painful, red eye and blurring of vision in a person aged over 50 years; pupil usually mid-dilated, oval and non-reactive to light.
- **Subconjunctival haemorrhage** — red eye without any visual discomfort or disturbance.
- **Iritis/uveitis of other cause.**

Complications and prognosis

Complications

- **Recurrence is common,** and reported as 20% by 2 years 40% by 5 years, and 67% by 7 years. Recurrence rates increase with subsequent episodes [Liesegang, 2001].
- **Corneal scarring and visual loss** may require corneal transplantation. Even after a corneal transplant the risk of ocular herpes simplex remains and may result in corneal scarring and graft failure. There is also an increased risk of allograft rejection [Tambasco et al, 1999].
- **Perforated corneal ulcer.**

Secondary infection with bacteria or fungi.
Secondary glaucoma.
Systemic involvement (if immunity impaired).

Prognosis

Epithelial keratitis tends to resolve in 1–2 weeks. It has a good prognosis.
Stromal keratitis is more likely to result in corneal scarring and loss of vision. An Australian study found that 5% of corneal grafts were carried out in people with visual disability, or with impending corneal perforation, after stromal ocular herpes simplex [Barker, 2004]. Overall 90% of 'involved eyes' maintain a visual acuity of 20/40 or 6/12 (driving level acuity) or better, and only 3% develop vision worse than 20/100 or 6/30 [Liesegang, 1991].

Management issues

How is ocular herpes simplex managed in primary care? p.927
How is ocular herpes simplex managed in secondary care? p.927

How is ocular herpes simplex managed in primary care?

If ocular herpes simplex is suspected, the person should be sent immediately to the eye casualty department, unless there is access to a slit lamp and the necessary expertise is available in the practice. This is a sight-threatening condition and diagnosis can be difficult. **Corticosteroids should never be given for an undiagnosed red eye, when visual acuity is impaired, or if there is a history of ocular herpes simplex infection** [Watson and Coroneo, 2001]. Corticosteroids can transform a simple herpetic dendritic ulcer into an extensive amoeboid ulcer involving all layers of the cornea, with resultant corneal scarring and visual loss [Frith et al, 2001].

How is ocular herpes simplex managed in secondary care?

Specialist management may include:

Diagnostic tests if required: diagnosis is usually made clinically (e.g. swabs for virus culture, immunofluoresence, or nucleic acid amplification by polymerase chain reaction).
Conservative management for uncomplicated herpes simplex eyelid lesions, blepharitis, and conjunctivitis: these are usually self-limiting conditions, resolving within 2–3 weeks [Lee and Laibson, 1996]. However there is high risk of corneal infection, which may appear as late as 10 days after eyelid lesions.

Treatment of epithelial ocular herpes simplex

Topical antivirals: these improve cure rates and reduce recurrence [Wilhelmus, 2004]. More trials are needed to investigate if there are any therapeutic differences between the topical antiviral agents.
Topical interferons (alpha or beta): a systematic review has found that they are as effective as an antiviral agent in healing after 7 days, but increased healing after 14 days compared with an antiviral [Wilhelmus, 2004].
Topical antivirals plus interferon: studies have shown that epithelial disease heals faster with topical antiviral treatment plus interferon compared with treatment with a topical antiviral alone, after 14 days [Barker, 2004; Wilhelmus, 2004].

- **Debridement:** in people with epithelial ocular herpes simplex, a systematic review has found no significant difference between debridement and no treatment. The review also found that debridement plus antiviral treatment improves healing at 7 days compared with either treatment alone [Wilhelmus, 2004]. One limitation of this review is that a variety of treatments were used, therefore these findings have to be interpreted with caution.

Treatment of stromal ocular herpes simplex

- **Topical corticosteroids with prophylactic topical antiviral therapy:** this may reduce the progression and shorten the duration of stromal keratitis [Wilhelmus et al, 1994; Barker, 2004].
- **Oral aciclovir:** a randomized controlled trial (104 people) compared time to treatment failure with oral aciclovir compared with placebo [Barron et al, 1994]. Both groups also received a standard regimen of topical corticosteroids and a topical antiviral over 10 weeks. The trial found no significant difference between oral aciclovir and placebo in rates of treatment failure at 16 weeks.

Prevention of ocular herpes simplex

- **Long-term oral aciclovir** significantly reduced the risk of any type of recurrence in people who had epithelial or stromal ocular herpes simplex virus in one or both eyes within the 12 months preceding treatment [Herpetic Eye Disease Group, 1998].
  - Stromal keratitis is associated with corneal scarring and visual loss and people with recurrent stromal disease are especially likely to benefit from long-term oral aciclovir [Jabs, 1998; Herpetic Eye Disease Study Group, 2000]. Note: treatment of epithelial keratitis with topical antivirals is usually successful and the probability of visual loss is low.
- **Short-term oral aciclovir** in people with epithelial keratitis produced no significant difference in the rate of stromal keratitis or iritis and no significant difference in the cumulative risk of developing stromal keratitis or iritis at 1 year of follow-up [Herpetic Eye Disease Study Group, 1997].
- **In people with corneal grafts:** one small (53 people) retrospective study showed that postoperative oral aciclovir given after a corneal graft for ocular herpes simplex disease may reduce the rate of recurrent dendritic keratitis and improve graft survival [Tambasco et al, 1999]. More trial data is needed, as there is limited evidence to support this approach.

References

NHS staff in England can link, free of charge, from references to full text journals by clicking on [Full text] on the PRODIGY website.

1. Barker, N. (2004) Ocular herpes simplex. *Clinical Evidence* **11**(June), 871–879.
2. Barron, B.A., Gee, L., Hauck, W.W. et al (1994) Herpetic Eye Disease Study. A controlled trial of oral acyclovir for herpes simplex stromal keratitis. *Ophthalmology* **101**(12), 1871–1882.
3. Baum, J. (1995) Infections of the eye. *Clinical Infectious Diseases* **21**(3), 479–486.
4. Frith, P., Gray, R., MacLennan, A.H. and Ambler, P. (Eds.) (2001) *The eye in clinical practice.* 2nd edn. London: Blackwell Science.
5. Herpetic Eye Disease Group (1998) Acyclovir for the prevention of recurrent herpes simplex virus eye disease. *New England Journal of Medicine* **339**(5), 300–306. [Full text]

H

6. Herpetic Eye Disease Study Group (1997) A controlled trial of oral acyclovir for the prevention of stromal keratitis or iritis in patients with herpes simplex virus epithelial keratitis. The Epithelial Keratitis Trial. *Archives of Ophthalmology* **115**(6), 703–712. [Full text]
7. Herpetic Eye Disease Study Group (2000) Oral acyclovir for herpes simplex virus eye disease: effect on prevention of epithelial keratitis and stromal keratitis. Herpetic Eye Disease Study Group. *Archives of Ophthalmology* **118**(8), 1030–1036. [Full text]
8. Jabs, D.A. (1998) Acyclovir for recurrent herpes simplex virus ocular disease. *New England Journal of Medicine* **339**(5), 340–341. [Full text]
9. Lee, S.Y. and Laibson, P.R. (1996) Medical management of herpes simplex ocular infections. *International Ophthalmology Clinics* **36**(2), 85–97.
10. Liesegang, T.J. (1989) Epidemiology of ocular herpes simplex. Natural history in Rochester, Minn, 1950 through 1982. *Archives of Ophthalmology* **107**(8), 1160–1165.
11. Liesegang, T.J. (1991) A community study of ocular herpes simplex. *Current Eye Research* **10**(Suppl), 111–115.
12. Liesegang, T.J. (2001) Herpes simplex virus epidemiology and ocular importance. *Cornea* **20**(1), 1–13.
13. Seal, D.V. and Bron, A.J. (1997) Infections of the eye. Herpes simplex virus eye disease. In: O'Grady, F., Finch, R., Lambert, H.P. and Greenwood, D. (Eds.) *Antibiotic and chemotherapy: Anti-infective agents a their use in therapy*. 7th edn. Edinburgh: Churchill Livingstone. 780–782.
14. Tambasco, F.P., Cohen, E.J., Nguyen, L.H. et al (199 Oral acyclovir after penetrating keratoplasty for herp simplex keratitis. *Archives of Ophthalmology* **117**(4) 445–449. [Full text]
15. Thielen, T.L., Castle, S.S. and Terry, J.E. (2000) Anterior ocular infections: an overview of pathophysiology and treatment. *Annals of Pharmacotherapy* **34**(2), 235–246.
16. Watson, S. and Coroneo, M. (2001) Steroids and the eye. *Medicine Today* **2**(3), 79–85.
17. Wilhelmus, K.R. (2004) *Interventions for herpes simplex virus epithelial keratitis (Cochrane Review)*. The Cochrane Library. Issue 3. Chichester, UK: John Wiley & Sons, Ltd.
18. Wilhelmus, K.R., Gee, L., Hauck, W.W. et al (1994) Herpetic eye disease study: a controlled trial of topica corticosteroids for herpes simplex stromal keratitis. *Ophthalmology* **101**(12), 1883–1895.

H

PRODIGY GUIDANCE

Herpes simplex — oral

Last revised in July 2005
www.prodigy.nhs.uk/guidance.asp?gt=Herpes simplex - oral

Applies to people of all ages

This guidance covers the management of oral herpes simplex (oral herpes labialis), including gingivostomatitis and cold sores.

This guidance does not cover neonatal herpes simplex, herpetic whitlow, eczema herpeticum, or other herpes infections such as herpes zoster.

There is separate PRODIGY guidance for *Aphthous ulcer*, *Chickenpox*, *Herpes simplex — genital*, *Herpes simplex — ocular*, *Palliative care — oral problems*, *Shingles and postherpetic neuralgia*, and *Trigeminal neuralgia*.

Goals

To minimize the symptoms of oral herpes simplex
To avoid development of complications

Contents

Scenarios

- Herpes simplex gingivostomatitis p.929
- Herpes simplex cold sores p.930

Extended Information, p. 931

Which scenario?

Herpes simplex gingivostomatitis: covers the management of gingivostomatitis, either as a feature of primary herpes simplex infection, or less commonly as a feature of severe recurrence.
Herpes simplex cold sores: covers the management of herpes simplex cold sores.

Herpes simplex gingivostomatitis

Which therapy?

Soft diet and adequate fluid intake are important. In severe cases, intravenous hydration may be required.
Paracetamol or ibuprofen is effective in treating pain and fever.
Chlorhexidine mouthwash helps to prevent plaque accumulation if brushing teeth is painful.
Oral antivirals are not usually needed in uncomplicated primary gingivostomatitis. They are useful in severe cases or in immunocompromised people. (Hospital admission may be needed.)
Discuss the course of the disease, the possibility of recurrence, transmission risks (advise people to avoid kissing and to wash their hands often), and stress the importance of avoiding immunocompromised people and neonates.

Practical prescribing points

For further information please see the *Medicines Compendium* (www.medicines.org.uk) or the *British National Formulary* (www.bnf.org).

- **Chlorhexidine mouthwash:** this can stain teeth brown when used regularly. The stain is not usually permanent, and can be reduced by avoiding drinks that contain tannin (e.g. tea, coffee, or red wine), and by brushing teeth before use. Note: rinse the mouth well after brushing as chlorhexidine can be inactivated by some ingredients in toothpaste.)
- **Ibuprofen:** may cause gastrointestinal irritation and occasionally gastrointestinal haemorrhage. Avoid if there is a history of peptic ulceration. Ibuprofen may worsen asthma, hypertension, renal impairment, or cardiac failure.

Should I refer or investigate?

Refer?

- **Admit for intravenous hydration if severe oropharyngeal lesions limit drinking** (be particularly vigilant with children).
- **A specialist should supervise the care of immunocompromised individuals or those with severe infection.** Oral or intravenous antiviral therapy is usually indicated. Refer immediately so that maximum antiviral effect is obtained.

Patient information leaflets

The following PILs are available at www.prodigy.nhs.uk

- Cold Sores - Primary Infection
- Herpes Viruses Association

Shared decision making

- The infection in your mouth is caused by the cold sore virus. The sores normally go within 1–3 weeks.
- **Paracetamol or ibuprofen** will ease pain or fever.
- **Drink plenty.** It may be painful to swallow. Ice pops and sloppy food are tips to try with children. Tell a doctor if a child stops drinking because of the pain.
- **Chlorhexidine mouthwashes** may be useful to clean your teeth with if brushing is too painful.
- Cold sores are now likely to occur from time to time, but this first infection is usually the worst.
- When you have a primary or recurring cold sore, you should:
  - **Not kiss anyone.**
  - **Wash your hands regularly.**
  - **Avoid newborn babies and anyone who has a poor immune system,** such as someone on chemotherapy or with AIDS.
- However, when you have no symptoms (when the virus is dormant), you are not usually infectious.

H

Drug rationale

Drugs not included

- **Topical antivirals (aciclovir and penciclovir):** there is no evidence available for the effects of topical agents on the duration or severity of symptoms of the first attack of oral herpes simplex, which usually presents as gingivostomatitis [Worrall, 2004]. Topical antiviral preparations are not recommended for application to mucous membranes such as in the mouth, as they are difficult to apply and may be irritant.
- **Oral antivirals** are not usually needed in uncomplicated primary gingivostomatitis. They marginally reduce the duration of pain and the time to healing, especially if taken early in the attack.
  - **Aciclovir and valaciclovir** are licensed for the treatment of herpes simplex infections and have been most widely studied.
  - **Famciclovir** is not licensed for the treatment of oral herpes simplex.
  - **Inosine pranobex** tablets are licensed for the treatment of mucocutaneous herpes simplex, but there is little evidence of symptom relief or reduction in time to healing in immunocompetent people.
- **Idoxuridine 5% in dimethyl sulfoxide** (Herpid paint): early application of higher concentrations (idoxuridine 15% in dimethyl sulfoxide) has been shown to shorten the course of oral herpes simplex, but there is little evidence of benefit with idoxuridine 5% paint [Spruance et al, 1990a].
- **Other topical, soothing remedies** are available in a wide variety of formulations. Evidence of their effectiveness is scarce, although they are frequently used and some people may find benefit.

H

Drugs included

- **Paracetamol and ibuprofen** are effective for analgesia and for the relief of fever.
- **Chlorhexidine mouthwash** helps to prevent plaque accumulation if brushing teeth is painful, and may reduce the risk of secondary bacterial infection.

Prescriptions

Analgesia/antipyretics: use when required

Paracetamol s/f susp: 60mg to 120mg up to four times a day
- Age from 3 to 11 months
- Paracetamol 120mg/5ml s/f susp. Take 2.5ml to 5ml every 4 to 6 hours when required for relief of pain or high temperature. Maximum of 4 doses in 24 hours; supply 150 ml; NHS Cost £0.65; OTC Cost £1.14.

Paracetamol s/f susp: 120mg to 240mg up to four times a day
- Age from 12 months to 5 years
- Paracetamol 120mg/5ml s/f susp. Take one to two 5ml spoonfuls every 4 to 6 hours when required for relief of pain or high temperature. Maximum of 4 doses in 24 hours; supply 300 ml; NHS Cost £1.30; OTC Cost £2.28.

Paracetamol s/f susp: 250mg to 500mg up to four times a day
- Age from 6 to 11 years
- Paracetamol 250mg/5ml s/f susp. Take one to two 5ml spoonfuls every 4 to 6 hours when required for relief of pain or high temperature. Maximum of 4 doses in 24 hours; supply 300 ml; NHS Cost £1.59; OTC Cost £2.80.

Paracetamol tablets: 500mg to 1g up to four times a day
- Age from 12 to 15 years
- Paracetamol 500mg tablets. Take one to two tablets every 4 to 6 hours when required for relief of pain or high temperature. Maximum of 8 tablets in 24 hours; supply 100 tablets; NHS Cost £0.75; OTC Cost £1.32.

Paracetamol tablets: 1g up to four times a day
- Age from 16 years onwards
- Paracetamol 500mg tablets. Take two tablets every 4 to 6 hours when required for relief of pain or high temperature. Maximum of 8 tablets in 24 hours; supply 100 tablets; NHS Cost £0.75; OTC Cost £1.32.

Ibuprofen s/f susp: 50mg three to four times a day
- Age from 12 months to 2 years
- Ibuprofen 100mg/5ml s/f susp. Take 2.5ml three to four times a day when required for relief of pain or high temperature. Do not exceed the stated dose; supply 100 ml; NHS Cost £2.00; OTC Cost £3.52.

Ibuprofen s/f susp: 100mg three to four times a day
- Age from 3 to 7 years
- Ibuprofen 100mg/5ml s/f susp. Take one 5ml spoonful 3 to 4 times a day when required for relief of pain or high temperature. Do not exceed the stated dose; supply 150 ml; NHS Cost £2.73; OTC Cost £4.81.

Ibuprofen s/f susp: 200mg three to four times a day
- Age from 8 to 11 years
- Ibuprofen 100mg/5ml s/f susp. Take two 5ml spoonfuls 3 to 4 times a day when required for relief of pain or high temperature. Do not exceed the stated dose; supply 300 ml; NHS Cost £5.46; OTC Cost £9.62.

Ibuprofen tablets: 400mg three times a day
- Age from 12 years onwards
- Ibuprofen 400mg tablets. Take one tablet three times a day when required for relief of pain or high temperature. Do not exceed the stated dose; supply 24 tablets; NHS Cost £0.70; OTC Cost £1.23.

Chlorhexidine mouthwash

Chlorhexidine 0.2% mouthwash: rinse with 10ml twice a day
- Age from 7 years onwards
- Chlorhexidine 0.2% mouthwash. Rinse the mouth with 10ml for about 1 minute twice a day; supply 300 ml; NHS Cost £1.93; OTC Cost £4.15.

Herpes simplex cold sores

Which therapy?

- **Topical antivirals are not usually needed:**
  - They only reduce the duration of symptoms by half to one day.
  - For there to be any benefit, they must be started as soon as symptoms begin.
- **Oral antivirals are reserved for** severe cases or immunocompromised people. (Hospital admission may be needed.)
- **Topical analgesia** can be given for local pain relief, but is short-acting. Consider:
  - Choline salicylate gel for mildly painful lesions.
  - Lidocaine (lignocaine) ointment or spray for extremely painful lesions.
- **Discuss** the course of the disease, transmission risks (advise people to avoid kissing and to wash their hands often), and stress the importance of avoiding immunocompromised people and neonates.
- **People who can identify sunlight as a trigger** may find sunscreen (sun protection factor 15 or more) useful for reducing recurrence.

Practical prescribing points

For further information please see the *Medicines Compendium* (www.medicines.org.uk) or the *British National Formulary* (www.bnf.org).

Should I refer or investigate?

Refer?

- **Immunocompromised individuals:** seek specialist advice promptly when treating these people.

Patient information leaflets

The following PILs are available at www.prodigy.nhs.uk

- Cold Sores
- Herpes Viruses Association

Shared decision making

- Cold sores recur, as the virus lies dormant in the body and 'activates' from time to time — commonly 2–3 times a year. Each episode lasts 5–10 days.
- **Soothing creams** can be bought from the pharmacist.
- **An antiviral cream** may reduce the duration and severity of a cold sore. Start as soon as the tingle or itch occurs. You can buy a cream at a pharmacy or get one on prescription. Some people find that antiviral creams have no effect.
- **Sunscreen lip balm** may help to prevent cold sores, as strong sunlight may trigger the virus to activate and cause a cold sore in some people.
- When you have a cold sore, you should:
  - **Not kiss anyone.**
  - **Wash your hands regularly.**
  - **Avoid newborn babies and anyone who has a poor immune system,** such as someone on chemotherapy or with AIDS.
- However, when you have no symptoms (when the virus is dormant), you are not usually infectious.

Drug rationale

Drugs not included

- **Paracetamol and ibuprofen** are effective for analgesia and for the relief of fever, but are usually needed only in gingivostomatitis.
- **Chlorhexidene mouthwash** helps to prevent plaque accumulation if brushing teeth is painful and may reduce the risk of secondary bacterial infection, but is usually needed only in gingivostomatitis.
- **Idoxuridine 5% in dimethyl sulfoxide (Herpid paint):** early application of higher concentrations (idoxuridine 15% in dimethyl sulfoxide) has been shown to shorten the course of oral herpes simplex. There is little evidence of benefit of idoxuridine 5% paint [Spruance et al, 1990a].
- **Oral antivirals:** oral antivirals are not usually needed in primary care. There is limited evidence that oral aciclovir or valaciclovir can reduce the duration of symptoms by about 1 day if taken early in the attack (that is, at prodrome) [Jensen et al, 2004; Worrall, 2004]. Any effect on the duration of pain is very small [Spruance et al, 1990b; Rooney et al, 1993; Whitley et al, 1998]. Famciclovir has not been shown to improve the time to healing in recurrent attacks [Worrall, 2004].
- **Sunscreen:** there is some evidence that sunscreen reduces the rate of recurrence of oral herpes simplex [Rooney et al, 1991; Duteil et al, 1998]. Sunscreen products are readily available in the shops.

Drugs included

- **Topical antivirals (aciclovir and penciclovir)** are not usually needed. Research has shown that penciclovir may promote marginally faster healing and pain resolution, and reduction in time to healing by 1 day [Spruance et al, 1997; Boon et al, 2000]. Topical aciclovir cream offers very limited benefits.
- **Choline salicylate dental gel** (Bonjela or Dinnefords Teejel) may provide analgesia for some people, but excessive application can cause ulceration.
- **Lidocaine (lignocaine) 5% ointment** should be reserved for severe pain.

Prescriptions

Topical analgesia (use when required)

Choline salicylate: use 1/4 inch of gel up to 6 times a day

- Age from 4 months to 11 years
- Choline salicylate oral gel. Gently massage 1/4 inch of gel onto the affected area when required for pain relief. Maximum of 6 applications in 24 hours; supply 15 grams; NHS Cost £1.70; OTC Cost £2.65.

Choline salicylate: use 1/2 inch of gel up to 6 times a day

- Age from 12 years onwards
- Choline salicylate oral gel. Gently massage 1/2 inch of gel onto the affected area when required for pain relief. Maximum of 6 applications in 24 hours; supply 15 grams; NHS Cost £1.70; OTC Cost £2.65.

Lidocaine 5% ointment: use when required

- Age from 12 years onwards
- Lidocaine 5% ointment. Apply a small amount of ointment to the affected area when required for pain relief; supply 15 grams; NHS Cost £0.85.

Selected cases – topical antivirals

Penciclovir 1% cream: apply every 2 hours for 4 days

- Age from 16 years onwards
- Penciclovir 1% cream. Apply to cold sore every 2 hours (during waking hours) for 4 days; supply 2 grams; NHS Cost £4.20.

Aciclovir 5% cream: apply five times a day for 5 days

- Age from 3 months onwards
- Aciclovir 5% cream (2g). Apply to cold sore five times a day for 5 days; supply 2 grams; NHS Cost £2.68; OTC Cost £4.25.

Extended Information

Background information

- What is it? p.931
- How common is it? p.932
- How do I know my patient has it? p.932
- How is it transmitted? p.932
- What else might it be? p.932
- Complications and prognosis p.932

What is it?

- Infection with herpes simplex virus (HSV) can cause pain and blistering within the mouth (gingivostomatitis or recurrent oral ulceration), or on or around the lips (cold sores or herpes labialis).
- Herpes simplex virus type 1 (HSV-1) is usually the cause.
- After primary infection, the HSV-1 virus ascends through sensory neurones and becomes latent in the dorsal root ganglia of the trigeminal nerve. Occasionally, the cervical or other ganglia may be affected. The virus

lies dormant until triggered by a stimulus such as a viral infection (e.g. the common cold), sunlight, trauma, or impaired immunity.

- Rarely, HSV-2 may cause primary infection of the oral cavity, typically in association with orogenital sex, but recurrent disease in this location is rare [Esmann, 2001].

How common is it?

- 80% of the population are asymptomatic carriers of the virus.
- 20–40% of people have experienced cold sores at some time.
- Less than 1% of primary care consultations each year in the UK are for oral herpes simplex.

[Barbarash, 2001; Worrall, 2004]

How do I know my patient has it?

Primary infection

- **Primary infection most often occurs in infancy or childhood.** It typically follows viral entry into the oral mucosa, and may be symptomatic, unnoticed, unrecognized, or asymptomatic.
- **Gingivostomatitis is the most common presentation in young children,** and typically presents with vesicles and ulcers on the tongue, lips, gums, buccal mucosa, and hard and soft palates. Pain, inability to swallow, drooling, and dehydration are common. There may be associated fever, cervical lymphadenopathy, halitosis, lethargy, loss of appetite and irritability.
- **Pharyngitis is a more common presentation in adolescents,** with lesions in the throat and accompanying viral symptoms similar to those of glandular fever.
- **Herpetic whitlow** may occasionally occur via autoinoculation to the fingers.

[Bader et al, 1978; Barbarash, 2001; Worrall, 2004]

Recurrent disease

- After primary infection, the virus may reactivate from time to time, causing recurrent disease.
- **Cold sore lesions are the most common form of recurrent disease.** They tend to occur in the same location, be unilateral, and recur two or three times a year on average.
- **Cold sores are usually seen on the lips** and extend to the skin around the mouth. Other areas on the face, chin, or nose are sometimes involved. Lesions begin as erythematous areas that swell into papules. These fill with fluid to become vesicles, which then collapse into ulcers. This takes 1–3 days. The ulcers crust over and the skin returns to normal within about 2 weeks.
- **Prodromal symptoms may occur** 6–24 hours before the appearance of a lesion. Prodromal symptoms include tingling, pain, and/or itching in the perioral area.
- **Oral mucosal lesions are rare** and not generally associated with fever. They are usually restricted to small clusters of microvesicles that rupture to leave punctate ulcers, typically on the palatal gingiva. (In immunocompromised people, they can form chronic ulcers, often on the tongue.)

[Bader et al, 1978; Birek, 2000; Barbarash, 2001]

Possible triggers of recurrent disease

- **Factors that may trigger a recurrence** of oral herpes simplex include immunosuppression (e.g. corticosteroids), upper respiratory tract infections, fatigue, emotional stress, physical trauma, exposure to sun (ultraviolet light), trauma, and menstruation.

Diagnostic tests

- **Tests are not usually necessary** in immunocompetent people, as history and examination will usually confirm the diagnosis.
- **Viral culture from swabs of lesions** has been considered the gold standard, but the usefulness of this method is limited by the relatively short time period of viral shedding and the relatively low number of viral particles present in samples.

How is it transmitted?

- **Transmission is due to viral shedding into saliva,** and can occur by direct contact with saliva (e.g. kissing).
- **The risk of transmission is highest for 1–4 days from the onset of symptoms,** but may be prolonged in immunocompromised people. (Advise people to avoid contact during this time with neonates or immunocompromised people, as they are at greater risk of severe disease.)
- Viral shedding into saliva may occur during asymptomatic infection, but it is thought that the risk of infection is much smaller than during symptomatic infection.

[Birek, 2000]

What else might it be?

Differential diagnosis of herpes simplex gingivostomatitis

- Aphthous ulcers — do not cause fever, and lesions are more likely to be on non-keratinized mucosa
- Hand, foot, and mouth disease — lesions may also be seen on hands or feet; positive Coxsackie virus culture from lesions or stool
- Herpes zoster of second or third division of the trigeminal nerve
- Infectious mononucleosis
- Erythema multiforme
- Stevens–Johnson syndrome
- Behçet's disease
- Leukaemia

Differential diagnosis of cold sores

- Aphthous ulcers — are not unilateral and are more likely to be on non-keratinized mucosa
- Chickenpox
- Impetigo
- Lip cancer
- Primary oral chancre of syphilis

Red flags

- **Signs of possible oral cancer include:**
  - Ulceration of the oral mucosa persisting for more than 3 weeks.
  - Oral swellings persisting for more than 3 weeks.
  - Red or red and white patches of the oral mucosa particularly if they are painful or swollen or bleeding.
- The level of suspicion is further increased if the person is a heavy smoker or heavy alcohol drinker and is aged over 45 years and male; other forms of tobacco use and chewing betel, gutkha, or pan also raise suspicion.

Complications and prognosis

Complications

- **Dehydration** is a complication of severe gingivostomatitis, especially in children.
- **Recurrent lesions** at the same site may occasionally cause atrophy and scarring.

- **Secondary bacterial infection,** including impetigo, can occur.
- **Eczema herpeticum** can complicate atopic eczema.
- **Bell's palsy** is possibly a complication of herpes simplex infection [Schirm and Mulkens, 1997].
- **Rare complications** include dissemination, herpes encephalitis, meningitis, corneal dendritic ulcers (ocular herpes simplex) and erythema multiforme. (Note: most recurrent erythema multiforme is a reaction to herpes simplex.)

Prognosis

- Oral herpes simplex is usually a self-limiting disease.
- Lesions (whether due to primary infection or recurrent disease) usually heal in 1–3 weeks.

Management issues

- How should I treat cold sores or gingivostomatitis? p.933
- Do I need to use antiviral treatment? p.933
- Can cold sores be prevented? p.933
- Other treatments p.933

How should I treat cold sores or gingivostomatitis?

- **Most people with cold sores or gingivostomatitis can be managed symptomatically,** as the disease is usually mild and self-limiting.
- **Paracetamol and ibuprofen** are effective in relieving pain and pyrexia.
- **Local analgesics may also be useful,** although their duration of action is short and they do not provide continuous analgesia throughout the day [Scully et al, 2003]. Choline salicylate gel or lidocaine (lignocaine) ointment can be used on discrete lesions such as a cold sore. Choline salicylate gel is probably sufficient for mildly painful lesions.
- **Chlorhexidine mouthwash helps to prevent plaque accumulation** if brushing teeth is painful.
  - Chlorhexidine can stain teeth brown when used regularly.
  - The stain is not usually permanent, and can be reduced by avoiding drinks that contain tannin (e.g. tea, coffee, or red wine), and by brushing teeth before use. However, the mouth should be rinsed well afterwards, as some ingredients in toothpaste can inactivate chlorhexidine.
- **A soft diet may be needed in children with painful gingivostomatitis.** Drinking should also be encouraged to prevent dehydration in children who are avoiding eating or drinking because of the pain.
- **To reduce the risk of transmission to others,** advise people to avoid kissing, and to wash their hands regularly. The risk of transmission is highest during the first 1–4 days of symptoms.

Do I need to use antiviral treatment?

First attack (gingivostomatitis)

- **Topical antivirals: there is no evidence available** on the effects of topical antivirals on the duration or severity of symptoms of the first attack of oral herpes simplex [Worrall, 2004].
- **Oral antivirals: there is no consensus** on whether or not to treat immunocompetent people with oral antivirals. Limited evidence from small randomized controlled trials in children with gingivostomatitis suggests that oral aciclovir may marginally reduce the duration of pain and time to healing [Amir et al, 1997; Worrall, 2004]. There may be some groups in whom treatment may be beneficial (for example, children with severe infection who are identified early enough during the first attack). However, most children with primary disease are not diagnosed [Amir et al, 1997].

Recurrent attacks (cold sores)

- **Topical antivirals: there is no consensus** on whether or not to treat immunocompetent people with topical antivirals, but studies have found only modest benefits. Topical penciclovir or aciclovir must be started as soon as symptoms begin to be of any benefit:
  - A systematic review found weak evidence that topical penciclovir or aciclovir reduces the duration of pain compared with placebo, but slightly stronger evidence that these drugs reduce healing time [Worrall, 2004].
  - Both pain and healing may be reduced by about half a day if topical penciclovir or aciclovir is applied at the *first symptom or sign* of recurrence, whether this is prodromal or a later stage [Spruance et al, 1997; Spruance et al, 2002].
  - Idoxuridine 5% in dimethyl sulfoxide (Herpid paint) has little evidence of benefit, and consensus is that it is of little value in practice. Early application of a higher concentration (idoxuridine 15% in dimethyl sulfoxide) was shown to shorten the course of oral herpes simplex, but this strength is not available [Spruance et al, 1990a].
- **Oral antivirals: there is no consensus** on whether or not to treat immunocompetent people with oral antivirals, but they may be of most use in severe cases. There is limited evidence that oral aciclovir or valaciclovir can reduce the duration of symptoms by about 1 day if taken early in the attack (that is, at prodrome) [Jensen et al, 2004; Worrall, 2004]. Any effect on the duration of pain is very small [Spruance et al, 1990b; Rooney et al, 1993; Whitley et al, 1998].

Immunocompromised people

- **Specialist advice should be sought.** Disease can be more severe in immunocompromised people, and antiviral treatment is required. These individuals may need admission to hospital for treatment.

Can cold sores be prevented?

- **Sunscreen may be useful for people who can identify sunlight as a trigger;** there is some evidence that sunscreen reduces the rate of recurrence of cold sores [Rooney et al, 1991; Duteil et al, 1998; Worrall, 2004].
- There is no evidence available to support the use of topical antivirals for the prevention of cold sores [Worrall, 2004].
- **Prophylactic oral antivirals are not generally recommended** for immunocompetent individuals. There is only limited evidence that prophylactic oral aciclovir or valaciclovir reduces the frequency and severity of attacks of cold sores. In addition, it is not clear whether oral antivirals should be used continuously, or restricted to high-risk periods (e.g. during exposure to intense sunlight) [Whitley et al, 1998; Worrall, 2004].
- **Specialist advice should be sought for immunocompromised people.** Oral antivirals have a role in prophylaxis of recurrence and prevention of disease in this group of people.

Other treatments

- **Tetracaine 1.8% cream (a topical anaesthetic)** may reduce the time to scab loss and improve symptoms such as pain, although the evidence for this is limited [Kaminester et al, 1999]. However, this product is not

H

commercially available in the UK. Tetracaine 4% gel is available, but is unsuitable for this purpose, as it must not be applied to inflamed or broken skin.

- **Balm mint extract, tea tree oil, and other palliative topical agents** may have an effect on pain, dryness, and itching. There is not enough evidence to assess whether they have an effect on healing, time to crusting, severity of an attack, or rate of recurrence [Koytchev et al, 1999; Barbarash, 2001; Carson et al, 2001].
- **Low-intensity infrared laser treatment** may have an effect on cold sores, although currently there is not enough evidence available [Schindl and Neumann, 1999; Dougal and Kelly, 2001].

References

NHS staff in England can link, free of charge, from references to full text journals by clicking on [Full text] on the PRODIGY website.

1. Amir, J., Harel, L., Smetana, Z. and Varsano, I. (1997) Treatment of herpes simplex gingivostomatitis with aciclovir in children: a randomised double blind placebo controlled study. *British Medical Journal* **314**(7097), 1800–1803. [Full text]
2. Bader, C., Crumpacker, C.S., Schnipper, L.E. et al (1978) The natural history of recurrent facial-oral infection with herpes simplex virus. *Journal of Infectious Diseases* **138**(6), 897–905.
3. Barbarash, R.A (2001) Update on treatment for oral herpes simplex viral infections (cold sores and fever blisters). *Today's Therapeutic Trends* **19**(1), 39–57.
4. Birek, C. (2000) Herpes virus-induced diseases: oral manifestations and current treatment options. *Journal of the Californian Dental Association* **28**(12), 911–921.
5. Boon, R., Goodman, J.J., Martinez, J. et al (2000) Penciclovir cream for the treatment of sunlight-induced herpes simplex labialis: a randomized, double-blind, placebo-controlled trial. Penciclovir Cream Herpes Labialis Study Group. *Clinical Therapeutics* **22**(1), 76–90.
6. Carson, C.F., Ashton, L., Dry, L. et al (2001) Melaleuca alternifolia (tea tree) oil gel (6%) for the treatment of recurrent herpes labialis. *Journal of Antimicrobial Chemotherapy* **48**(3), 450–451. [Full text]
7. Dougal, G. and Kelly, P. (2001) A pilot study of treatment of herpes labialis with 1072 nm narrow waveband light. *Clinical and Experimental Dermatology* **26**(2), 149–154.
8. Duteil, L., Queille-Roussel, C., Loesche, C. and Verschoore, M. (1998) Assessment of the effect of sunblock stick in the prevention of solar-simulating ultraviolet light-induced herpes labialis. *Journal of Dermatological Treatment* **9**(1), 11–14.
9. Esmann, J. (2001) The many challenges of facial herpes simplex virus infection. *Journal of Antimicrobial Chemotherapy* **47**(Suppl T1), 17–27.
10. Jensen, L.A., Hoehns, J.D. and Squires, C.L. (2004) Oral antivirals for the acute treatment of recurrent herpes labialis. *Annals of Pharmacotherapy* **38**(4), 705–709.
11. Kaminester, L.H., Pariser, R.J., Pariser, D.M. et al (1999) A double-blind, placebo-controlled study of topical tetracaine in the treatment of herpes labialis. *Journal of the American Academy of Dermatology* **41**(6), 996–1001.
12. Koytchev, R., Alken, R.G. and Dundarov, S. (1999) Balm mint extract (Lo-701) for topical treatment of recurring herpes labialis. *Phytomedicine* **6**(4), 225–230.
13. Rooney, J.F., Bryson, Y., Mannix, M.L. et al (1991) Prevention of ultraviolet-light-induced herpes labialis by sunscreen. *Lancet* **338**(8780), 1419–1422. [Full text]
14. Rooney, J.F., Straus, S.E., Mannix, M.L. et al (1993) Oral acyclovir to suppress frequently recurrent herpes labialis. A double-blind, placebo-controlled trial. *Annals of Internal Medicine* **118**(4), 268–272. [Full text]
15. Schindl, A. and Neumann, R. (1999) Low intensity laser therapy is an effective treatment for recurrent herpes simplex infection. Results from a randomized double-blind placebo-controlled study. *Journal of Investigative Dermatology* **113**(2), 221–223.
16. Schirm, J. and Mulkens, P.S.J.Z. (1997) Bell's palsy and herpes simplex virus. *Acta Pathologica Microbiologica et Immunologica Scandinavica* **105**(11), 815–823.
17. Spruance, S.L., Stewart, J.C.B., Freeman, D.J. et al (1990a) Early application of topical 15% idoxuridine in dimethyl sulfoxide shortens the course of herpes simplex labialis: a multicentre placebo-controlled trial. *Journal of Infectious Diseases* **161**(2), 191–197.
18. Spruance, S.L., Stewart, J.C.B., Rowe, N.H. et al (1990b) Treatment of recurrent herpes simplex labialis with oral acyclovir. *Journal of Infectious Diseases* **161**(2), 185–190.
19. Spruance, S.L., Rea, T.L., Thoming, C. et al (1997) Penciclovir cream for the treatment of herpes simplex labialis. A randomized, multicenter, double-blind, placebo-controlled trial. *Journal of the American Medical Association* **277**(17), 1374–1379. [Full text]
20. Spruance, S.L., Nett, R., Marbury, T. et al (2002) Acyclovir cream for treatment of herpes simplex labialis: results of two randomized, double-blind, vehicle-controlled, multicenter clinical trials. *Antimicrobial Agents & Chemotherapy* **46**(7), 2238–2243.
21. Whitley, R.J., Kimberlin, D.W. and Roizmann, B. (1998) Herpes simplex viruses. *Clinical Infectious Diseases* **26**(3), 541–555.
22. Worrall, G. (2004) Herpes labialis. *Clinical Evidence* **11**(June), 2174–2181.

PRODIGY GUIDANCE

Hiccups

Last revised in April 2002
At the time of print this topic was being updated. The newly revised guidance will be issued on to the website in late 2005.
www.prodigy.nhs.uk/guidance.asp?gt=Hiccups

Applies to people of all ages

This guidance covers the management of transient, persistent, and intractable hiccups.

Goals

- To establish, where possible, a cause for persistent or intractable hiccups
- To stop or alleviate persistent or intractable hiccups

Contents

Scenarios
- Hiccup p.935

Extended Information, p. 936

Hiccup

Which therapy?

- **Most hiccups will stop spontaneously** and rarely require treatment other than simple physical manoeuvres, e.g. sipping ice water, swallowing granulated sugar, biting on a lemon, breath holding, hyperventilating, breathing into a paper bag, gasping induced by a sudden fright, pulling knees to the chest.
- **If hiccups are persistent or intractable, then an underlying organic cause should always be considered.**
- **Drug therapy is worth trying for persistent or intractable hiccups:**
  - Chlorpromazine and haloperidol are both licensed for the treatment of intractable hiccups.
  - Metoclopramide may be particularly useful for people with gastric stasis (common in palliative care).
  - Unlicensed options include baclofen, nifedipine, carbamazepine, amitriptyline, and sodium valproate. Some experts recommend baclofen as a first line option when a cause cannot be identified and corrected.

Practical prescribing points

For further information please see the *Medicines Compendium* (www.medicines.org.uk) or the *British National Formulary* (www.bnf.org).

- Metoclopramide should not be given to children or young adults due to the increase risk of extrapyramidal adverse effects.

Should I refer or investigate?

Refer?

- All cases of recurrent, persistent or intractable hiccups should be referred for further investigation, unless a correctable metabolic problem is identified or the patient is terminally ill.
- If hiccups are difficult to control in a terminally ill patient consider obtaining advice from a palliative care specialist.

Investigate?

- If hiccups are persistent or intractable check electrolytes, serum calcium, and blood glucose to exclude metabolic causes.

Patient information leaflets

The following PILs are available at www.prodigy.nhs.uk

- Hiccough

Shared decision making

- Hiccups usually go without treatment. They can sometimes be stopped by:
  - Sipping ice water
  - Swallowing granulated sugar
  - Biting on a lemon
  - Breath holding, hyperventilating, or breathing into a paper bag
  - Gasping after a sudden fright
  - Pulling your knees to your chest
- Hiccups that do not go are sometimes due to an underlying cause. Many illnesses can cause hiccups. Tests or a referral to a specialist may be needed to find the cause.
- Medication such as **chlorpromazine, haloperidol**, or **metoclopramide** is sometimes needed to stop hiccups. If one does not work, switching to another may work.

Drug rationale

Drugs not included

- **Baclofen, nifedipine, carbamazepine, amitriptyline, and sodium valproate** have been used for the treatment of persistent or intractable hiccups. However, they are not licensed for this indication and evidence for their effectiveness is limited [Friedman, 1996].

Drugs included

- **Chlorpromazine and haloperidol** are both licensed for the treatment of intractable hiccups.
- **Metoclopramide** restores normal co-ordination and tone to the upper digestive tract and may be particularly useful to relieve hiccup associated with gastric stasis [Friedman, 1996]. This is not licensed specifically for the management of hiccup.

Prescriptions

Anti-hiccup treatment

Chlorpromazine 25mg three times a day

- Age from 16 years onwards
- Chlorpromazine 25mg tablets. Take one tablet three times a day. If hiccups are not relieved, increase the dose

by one tablet each day up to a maximum of 8 tablets in 24 hours; supply 70 tablets; NHS Cost £0.53.

Haloperidol 1.5mg three times a day

- Age from 16 years onwards
- Haloperidol 1.5mg tablets. Take one tablet three times a day. If hiccups are not relieved, increase the dose by one tablet each day up to a maximum of 6 tablets in 24 hours; supply 50 tablets; NHS Cost £2.76.

Metoclopramide 10mg three times a day

- Age from 20 years onwards
- Metoclopramide 10mg tablets. Take one tablet three times a day; supply 28 tablets; NHS Cost £0.86.

Extended Information

Background information

- What is it? p.936
- How common is it? p.936
- What might the underlying cause of persistent or intractable hiccups be? p.936
- Complications and prognosis p.936

H

What is it?

- A hiccup is an involuntary, spasmodic contraction of the diaphragm causing an initial inspiration that is suddenly checked by the closure of the glottis, which results in the typical sound [Friedman, 1996].
- A hiccup reflex arc has been described. The afferent limb is composed of the vagus and phrenic nerves and the sympathetic chain arising from T6–T12, with a hiccup centre located in the upper spinal cord (C3–C5). The efferent limb of the reflex is primarily the phrenic nerve with involvement of the nerves to the glottis and accessory muscles of respiration. Unlike many other reflexes (e.g. coughing, sneezing) hiccups do not have a protective or useful function [Rousseau, 1995; Lewis, 2000].
- **Most hiccups occur as brief, self-limited episodes lasting up to a few minutes** and are of no clinical significance [Lewis, 2000]. The most frequent identifiable causes are gastric distension (overeating or eating too fast, drinking carbonated drinks, aerophagia), sudden change in temperature (very hot or cold food or drinks, a cold shower), alcohol, excess smoking, psychogenic (sudden excitement, emotional stress) [Friedman, 1996; Lewis, 2000].
- **Persistent hiccups,** that last for more than 48 hours or recur at frequent intervals, and **intractable hiccups,** which persist for more than a month, are often due to an underlying disease process. There are more than a hundred reported causes of persistent or intractable hiccup [Rousseau, 1995].
- **Psychogenic hiccups** should only be diagnosed with extreme caution and after ruling out an organic cause. They can result from stress, excitement, and grief reactions, and anorexia nervosa [Launois et al, 1993; Friedman, 1996].

How common is it?

- Short self-limiting, episodes of hiccups are commonly experienced by healthy children and adults. They occur frequently in young children, and particularly in premature babies [Launois et al, 1993].
- Persistent and intractable hiccups occur more frequently in adults and in men [Launois et al, 1993; Rousseau, 1995].
- Intractable hiccups are rare. It is estimated that seven cases per year could be expected in a large tertiary care setting [Friedman, 1996].

What might the underlying cause of persistent or intractable hiccups be?

Persistent and intractable hiccups are often caused by an underlying structural, metabolic, chemical, inflammatory, demyelinating, neoplastic, or infectious disorder stimulating the nerves involved in the hiccup reflex arc. Examples include:

- **Disorders of the gastrointestinal tract:** particularly gastrointestinal reflux, achalasia, and oesophageal or small bowel obstruction. One study showed that 76% of 72 patients with persistent or intractable hiccup of no apparent cause had gastroesophageal disease, which was in most cases clinically silent [Guelaud et al, 1995]. Gastric distension is probably the most frequent underlying cause in people with terminal cancer [Wilcock and Twycross, 1996].
- **Pathology of the central nervous system:** particularly lesions of the medulla including infarction, tumour, tuberculoma, abscess, haematoma, and demyelination.
- **Diaphragmatic irritation** caused by subphrenic or hepatic disease, pleural or pericardial effusion.
- **Postoperative:** intra-abdominal (cholecystectomy, gastrectomy, etc.), thoracotomy, craniotomy.
- **Toxic/metabolic:** uraemia, diabetes mellitus, alcohol, fever, hypokalaemia, hypocalcaemia, hyponatraemia, hypocarbia (hyperventilation), Addison's disease.
- **Drugs:** corticosteroids, benzodiazepines, methyldopa, and antibiotics have been linked to hiccups [Prescrire International, 1999].

[Howard, 1992; Launois et al, 1993; Lewis, 2000]

Complications and prognosis

Persistent and intractable hiccups may have a considerable impact on general health through disturbance of eating, sleeping, and drinking. They can cause:

- Exhaustion
- Malnutrition and weight loss
- Dehydration
- Wound dehiscence
- Death — in extreme cases

[Howard, 1992; Launois et al, 1993; Lewis, 2000]

Management issues

- Most hiccups will stop spontaneously and rarely require treatment.
- **If hiccups are persistent or intractable,** then an underlying organic cause should always be considered. If a cause is established, treatment should be directed to the underlying disorder.
- Case studies or anecdotal reports provide the evidence base for guidance in the management of hiccup. There is a lack of controlled clinical trials to adequately assess any of the treatments discussed.
- **Simple physical manoeuvres** that attempt to interrupt the hiccup reflex include:
  - Stimulation of the nasopharynx, e.g. sipping ice water, swallowing granulated sugar, crushed ice or stale bread, inhaling smelling salts, tasting vinegar or angostura bitters, biting on a lemon or forcible traction of the tongue.
  - Interruption of normal respiratory function, e.g. Valsalva manoeuvre, breath holding, hyperventilating, breathing into a paper bag, gasping induced by a sudden fright, sneezing.
  - Counterirritation of the diaphragm, e.g. pulling knees to the chest, leaning forward to compress the chest.

[Launois et al, 1993]

- **Drug therapy** works on the hiccup reflex arc by blocking transmitting nerve impulses, counter stimulating impulses, or affecting the cause. Persistent or intractable hiccups usually justify an attempt with drug therapy.
  - Chlorpromazine and haloperidol are both licensed for the treatment of intractable hiccups.
  - Metoclopramide may be particularly useful for people with gastric stasis (common in palliative care).
  - *Unlicensed* options include baclofen, nifedipine, carbamazepine, amitriptyline, and sodium valproate. Some experts regard baclofen as an appropriate first line option when a cause cannot be identified and corrected [DTB, 1990; Ramirez and Graham, 1992; Guelaud et al, 1995; Friedman, 1996].
- **Acupuncture and hypnotherapy** have been reported to be effective.
- **Electrical stimulation, or surgical or chemical disruption of the phrenic nerve** may be considered if hiccups remain unresponsive to drug treatment and cause significant discomfort or morbidity. Glossopharyngeal nerve blocks have been reported to be effective and are less invasive than phrenic nerve disruption [Okuda et al, 1998; Dobelle, 1999; Lewis, 2000].

References

1. Dobelle, W.H. (1999) Use of breathing pacemakers to suppress intractable hiccups of up to thirteen years duration. *ASAIO Journal* 45(6), 524–525.
2. DTB (1990) Intractable hiccup: baclofen and nifedipine are worth trying. *Drug & Therapeutics Bulletin* 28(9), 36.
3. Friedman, N.L. (1996) Hiccups: a treatment review. *Pharmacotherapy* 16(6), 986–995.
4. Guelaud, C., Similowski, T., Bizec, J.L. et al (1995) Baclofen therapy for chronic hiccup. *European Respiratory Journal* 8(2), 235–237.
5. Howard, R.S. (1992) Persistent hiccups. *British Medical Journal* 305(6864), 1237–1238.
6. Launois, S., Bizec, J.L., Whitelaw, W.A. et al (1993) Hiccup in adults: an overview. *European Respiratory Journal* 6(4), 563–575.
7. Lewis, J.H. (2000) Hiccups and their cures. *Clinical Perspectives in Gastroenterology* 3(5), 277–283.
8. Okuda, Y., Kitajima, T. and Asai, T. (1998) Use of a nerve stimulator for phrenic nerve block in treatment of hiccups. *Anesthesiology* 88(2), 525–527.
9. Prescrire International (1999) Drug-induced hiccups. *Prescrire International* 8(39), 23–23.
10. Ramirez, F.C. and Graham, D.Y. (1992) Treatment of intractable hiccup with baclofen: results of a double-blind randomized, controlled, cross-over study. *American Journal of Gastroenterology* 87(12), 1789–1791.
11. Rousseau, P. (1995) Hiccups. *Southern Medical Journal* 88(2), 175–181.
12. Wilcock, A. and Twycross, R. (1996) Midazolam for intractable hiccup. *Journal of Pain and Symptom Management* 12(1), 59–61.

H

PRODIGY GUIDANCE

Hyperlipidaemia

Last revised in April 2005
www.prodigy.nhs.uk/guidance.asp?gt=Hyperlipidaemia

Applies to people over the age of 16 years

This guidance covers the management of hyperlipidaemia, including targeting treatment towards people at highest risk of coronary heart disease (CHD), and people with familial dyslipidaemias.

This guidance does not cover in detail the management of any of the risk factors for CHD other than hyperlipidaemia. It also does not cover the use of antithrombotic agents such as aspirin.

There is separate PRODIGY guidance for *Coronary heart disease risk — identification and management, Angina, Atrial fibrillation, Diabetes Type 2 — lipid management, Heart failure, Hypertension, Obesity, Prior myocardial infarction — prophylactic treatments,* and *Smoking cessation.*

Goals

- Target lipid-lowering treatment at all people who have a 30% or more risk of coronary heart disease (CHD) over 10 years, and all people with diabetes whose 10-year CHD risk is more than 15%
- Identify and treat people with common familial dyslipidaemias
- Following a decision to start treatment, aim to lower:
  - Serum total cholesterol to below 5.0 mmol/l or to reduce it by 20–25%, whichever would result in the lower level
  - Serum low-density lipoprotein cholesterol to below 3.0 mmol/l or to reduce it by 30%, whichever would result in the lower level
- Where raised triglycerides require treatment, aim to lower levels below 2.3 mmol/l

[DH, 2000]

Contents

Scenarios
- Who should be screened for hyperlipidaemia? p.938
- Fasting triglyceride >10: refer for specialist care p.939
- Initial total cholesterol <5 mmol/l p.941
- Initial total cholesterol >5 (and triglyceride <5) p.942
- Initial total cholesterol >5 and triglyceride >5 p.944
- Managing statin therapy p.947
- Managing fibrate therapy p.949

Extended Information, p. 951

Which scenario?

- **Who should be screened for hyperlipidaemia?** This scenario explains which groups of people should be targeted for hyperlipidaemia screening.
- **Fasting triglyceride (TG) >10: refer for specialist care:** covers the management of those who have very severe hypertriglyceridaemia (i.e. serum TG >10 mmol/l).
- **Initial total cholesterol <5 mmol/l:** covers the management of people with initial total cholesterol of less than 5 mmol/l.
- **Initial total cholesterol >5 (and triglyceride <5):** covers the management of people with an initial total cholesterol level of *greater* than 5 mmol/l and a triglyceride level *less* than 5 mmol/l.
- **Initial total cholesterol >5 and triglyceride >5:** covers the management of people with an initial total cholesterol level of *greater* than 5 mmol/l and a triglyceride level *greater* than 5 mmol/l.
- **Managing statin therapy:** provides advice on titrating the dose of statin according to response and adverse effects.
- **Managing fibrate therapy:** provides advice on titrating the dose of fibrate according to response and adverse effects.

Who should be screened for hyperlipidaemia?

Which therapy?

- The decision to screen for hyperlipidaemia depends on the person's 10-year risk of CHD.
- **Non-fasting total cholesterol (TC) and HDL-C is adequate as an initial screening test.**
- People whose TC is raised should have a *fasting* lipid profile to confirm the results before a decision about treatment is made (i.e. TC, LDL-C, HDL-C, and triglycerides).
- **Check lipid levels in anyone with established CHD, ischaemic stroke, transient ischaemic attack, or peripheral vascular disease.**
- **The second priority** (once these people are being effectively managed) is people whose 10-year risk of CHD is >30%, but who *do not* have CHD or other occlusive arterial disease.
  - Target people who have diabetes, hypertension, or a family history of premature CHD first.
  - Calculate initial 10-year risk of CHD using average lipid levels for age and sex. If CHD risk is >30% over 10 years, check lipid levels.
- **Check lipid levels in someone with suspected familial dyslipidaemia.** Family screening and counselling of people with a familial dyslipidaemia is also important as they have an increased risk of CHD.
- **Screen for familial hypercholesterolaemia if:**
  - Family history of premature CHD, tendon xanthomata, or TC >7.5 mmol/l, OR
  - Personal history of premature CHD or tendon xanthoma, OR
  - Corneal arcus in people under 45 years
- **Screen for familial combined hyperlipidaemia if:**
  - Family history of hyperlipidaemia or premature CHD (not due to familial hypercholesterolaemia)

Follow-up advice

Total cholesterol (TC) >5 mmol/l

- **People with established CHD, ischaemic stroke, transient ischaemic attack, or peripheral vascular disease** should have a *fasting* lipid profile repeated before a decision

about treatment is made (i.e. TC, LDL-C, HDL-C, and triglycerides).
- **People whose 10-year risk of CHD is >30%** should have a *fasting* lipid profile repeated before a decision about treatment is made.
- **People with Type 2 diabetes and a 15–30% risk of CHD over 10 years** should have a *fasting* lipid level repeated.
- Other people whose CHD risk is <30% over 10 years are at lower risk of CHD. Consider checking *fasting* lipid profile if familial hypercholesterolaemia suspected.

TC <5 mmol/l

- **People whose TC is <5 mmol/l should be reassured and offered diet and lifestyle advice** for CHD prevention.
- If they have established CHD, other occlusive artery disease, diabetes, or hypertension, re-check non-fasting TC and HDL-C annually.
- For men aged over 60 years, or men aged over 50 years who smoke, re-check annually.
- For none of the above risk factors, re-check in 3–5 years.

Should I refer or investigate?

Refer?

- **Severe hypercholesterolaemia,** i.e. total cholesterol (TC) >10 mmol/l.
- **Severe hypertriglyceridaemia,** i.e. triglycerides >10 mmol/l.
- **Suspected familial hypercholesterolaemia:** TC >7.5 mmol/l (or LDL-C >4.9 mmol/l) *and* at least one of the following:
  - Tendon xanthomata in themselves or in a first- or second-degree relative.
  - Family history of premature coronary heart disease or other atherosclerotic disease in a male first-degree relative before the age of 55 years, or in a female first-degree relative before the age of 65 years.
  - Family history of TC >7.5 mmol/l in a first- or second-degree relative.
- Reasons for referral are to make a firm diagnosis, to initiate treatment if required, and to counsel and screen the family.
- **Referral may be unnecessary for someone with suspected familial combined hyperlipidaemia** if they qualify for treatment according to risk assessment. Family screening and counselling, however, should not be forgotten.

Investigate?

- **Non-fasting total cholesterol (TC) and HDL-C is adequate as an initial screening test** (TC and HDL-C are not affected by meals).
- The averages of at least two (and preferably three) measurements of blood pressure and lipids should be used to calculate coronary heart disease risk.
- A fasting specimen should be taken prior to starting treatment to get an accurate assessment of LDL-C and triglyceride levels.

Patient information leaflets

The following PILs are available at www.prodigy.nhs.uk
- Alcohol and Sensible Drinking
- British Heart Foundation
- British Nutrition Foundation
- Cholesterol
- Cholesterol - A Summary
- Eat More Fruit and Vegetables
- Exercise for Health
- Healthy Eating
- Healthy Lifestyle - Five Choices
- Smokeline
- Smoking - Help to Stop with Bupropion
- Smoking - Nicotine Replacement Therapy
- Smoking - The Facts
- Smoking - Tips on Stopping
- Weight Reduction - A Summary
- Weight Reduction - How to Lose Weight

Shared decision making

- A high cholesterol level is a risk factor for heart disease.
- Other risk factors include smoking, being overweight, high blood pressure, and diabetes.
- **Only people who are at high risk of heart disease need to have their cholesterol checked.** Such high-risk people include:
  - People who already have heart disease, or people who have had a stroke.
  - People who have a family history of high cholesterol.
  - People who have diabetes.
- People who originally come from India, Pakistan, Bangladesh, or Sri Lanka also need to have their cholesterol checked, as they have a higher risk of heart disease than white people do.
- People who do not have any other risk factors for heart disease do not usually need to have their cholesterol levels checked.

Drug rationale

- No prescriptions are offered in this scenario.

Fasting triglyceride >10: refer for specialist care

Which therapy?

- **Referral for specialist care is usually indicated.**
- If very severe hypertriglyceridaemia (>10 mmol/l) is left untreated, there is a significant risk of pancreatitis (as well as an increased risk of coronary heart disease).
- **Start fibrate treatment while waiting for referral appointment** (if there is no significant abnormality in the liver-function tests and no severe renal impairment).
  - Check CK, AST/ALT, and serum creatinine before starting treatment.
- **If the person has renal impairment:**
  - Consider seeking specialist advice before starting treatment with a fibrate.
  - Modified-release preparations of fibrates are contraindicated in people with renal impairment. Use standard preparations and start at low doses. Increase dose slowly, while carefully monitoring lipid levels, CK, AST or ALT, and renal function (e.g. every 4 weeks).
- **If practical,** stop any treatment with oestrogens, corticosteroids, or thiazides while waiting for specialist assessment.
- **Rule out or manage secondary causes of hypertriglyceridaemia:** hepatitis, or hepatobiliary disease; alcoholism; diabetes mellitus; pregnancy (due to raised oestrogens); other drugs, including isotretinoin, and tamoxifen; renal failure; lipodystrophies; glycogen storage disease; and systemic lupus erythematosus.
- **Offer lifestyle advice:** Mediterranean diet, weight, exercise, smoking, alcohol.

H

Practical prescribing points

For further information please see the *Medicines Compendium* (www.medicines.org.uk) or the *British National Formulary* (www.bnf.org).

- **Hepatotoxicity is rare,** but is thought to be dose-dependent.
- **Advise people to report muscle pain, aches, or cramps.** Withdraw statin while checking CK level. (A non-significant increase in CK is common.)
- **Myopathy is rare, but the risk is increased in the presence of:**
    - Renal impairment, hypothyroidism, alcohol abuse, underlying muscle disorders, or age >70 years.
    - Co-prescription of statins with fibrates (do not use gemfibrozil), or nicotinic acid (>1 g).
    - A past history of myopathy with any lipid-lowering drug.
- **Warfarin and fibrates:** reduce the dose of warfarin by about a third and make further adjustments according to changes in the international normalized ratio.
- **Stop fibrate treatment if:**
    - Serum creatinine increases progressively.
    - There is a strong suspicion of myopathy, or CK level >5 times upper limit of normal.
    - Myalgic symptoms persist despite a normal CK level — a trial off treatment may be needed.
    - AST or ALT level persists above 3 times upper limit of normal.

H

Follow-up advice

People with very severe hypertriglyceridaemia will usually be followed up by, or in shared care with, specialist services.

Monitoring fibrate therapy

- **Advise the person to report any muscular pains immediately.** Check the CK level.
- **Discontinue fibrate if** there is a strong suspicion of myopathy, if CK exceeds 5 times upper limit of normal range, if transaminases *persist* above 3 times upper limit of normal range, or if serum creatinine continues to rise progressively.
- **12 weeks after starting:** check fasting serum lipid profile and AST or ALT. Dose titration is not possible for most fibrates — the starting dose is the usual maintenance dose.
- **Annual checks:** fasting serum lipid profile, AST or ALT, and serum creatinine.
- **If the person has renal impairment,** consider specialist referral before starting treatment with a fibrate. Titrate the dose slowly, while carefully monitoring lipid levels, CK, AST or ALT, and renal function (e.g. every 4 weeks).

Should I refer or investigate?

Refer?

- **Referral for specialist care is usually indicated if hypertriglyceridaemia >10 mmol/l** — if untreated, there is a significant risk of pancreatitis.
- **Start fibrate treatment while waiting for referral appointment** (if there is no significant abnormality in the liver function tests and no severe renal impairment).

Investigate?

- If referring, no further investigations are necessary (avoid duplication).
- **If secondary hypertriglyceridaemia is suspected after history and examination, tests to investigate this are indicated.** Causes of severe hypertriglyceridaemia include: hepatitis, or hepatobiliary disease; alcoholism; diabetes mellitus; pregnancy (due to raised oestrogens); drugs, including oestrogens (oral contraceptives), and isotretinoin; and renal failure.

Patient information leaflets

The following PILs are available at www.prodigy.nhs.uk

- Alcohol and Sensible Drinking
- Blood Test - General
- British Heart Foundation
- British Nutrition Foundation
- Cholesterol
- Cholesterol - A Summary
- Eat More Fruit and Vegetables
- Exercise for Health
- Healthy Eating
- Healthy Lifestyle - Five Choices
- Smokeline
- Smoking - Help to Stop with Bupropion
- Smoking - Nicotine Replacement Therapy
- Smoking - The Facts
- Smoking - Tips on Stopping
- Weight Reduction - A Summary
- Weight Reduction - How to Lose Weight

Shared decision making

- You have a triglyceride (blood fat) level that is very high.
- Referral to a specialist may be recommended.
- A high triglyceride level sometimes runs in families.
- In some cases, a high triglyceride level is made worse by taking other medicines for other conditions.

Drug rationale

Drugs not included

- **Statins** are not included in this scenario, because fibrates produce greater reductions in triglyceride (TG) levels.
- **Omega-3 polyunsaturated fatty acids** (omega-3 PUFAs) reduce serum TG levels, and can therefore be a useful adjunct in the treatment of hypertriglyceridaemia. They can increase LDL-C levels, so both LDL-C and TG levels should be monitored. A large number of capsules are needed for a therapeutic dose, and they are expensive.
- **High doses of nicotinic acid** can produce large increases in HDL-C, as well as lowering cholesterol and TG levels. However, it is rarely used because of its adverse effects, especially vasodilation [BNF 44, 2002].

Drugs included

- **Fibrates: bezafibrate, ciprofibrate, fenofibrate, or gemfibrozil** may be initiated while waiting for referral appointment.
- Modified-release preparations of fibrates are contraindicated in someone with renal impairment. Low doses of standard-release preparations are offered in this case. Note: bezafibrate is not offered for people with renal impairment because it becomes contraindicated at a milder degree of renal impairment than other fibrates.
- A non-drug prescription giving diet and lifestyle advice is offered.

Prescriptions

Non-drug management

Advice only: diet and lifestyle
- Age from 16 years onwards
- Your cholesterol level is high. Lifestyle and dietary changes can sometimes reduce the cholesterol level and other risk factors for heart disease. You should aim to eat and live healthily. This means: No smoking. Regular exercise. Moderate alcohol consumption. Lose weight if you are overweight or obese. MORE vegetables, fruit, cereals, wholegrain bread, poultry, fish, rice, skimmed or semi-skimmed milk, grilled food, lean meat, pasta etc. LESS fatty meats, fatty cheeses, full cream milk, fried food, lard, etc. If you do fry, choose a vegetable oil such as sunflower or rapeseed. Use low fat spreads. Add less salt to food, and avoid foods that are very salty. Have your cholesterol level checked again in 3 months time.

Start fibrate (normal renal function)

Bezafibrate 400mg m/r once a day
- Age from 16 years onwards
- Bezafibrate 400mg m/r tablets. Take one tablet once a day; supply 30 tablets; NHS Cost £8.70.

Bezafibrate 200mg three times a day
- Age from 16 years onwards
- Bezafibrate 200mg tablets. Take one tablet three times a day; supply 84 tablets; NHS Cost £8.24.

Ciprofibrate 100mg once a day
- Age from 16 years onwards
- Ciprofibrate 100mg tablets. Take one tablet once a day; supply 28 tablets; NHS Cost £14.72.

Fenofibrate 160mg m/r once a day (equiv to 200mg std daily)
- Age from 16 years onwards
- Fenofibrate 160mg m/r tablets. Take one tablet once a day; supply 28 tablets; NHS Cost £14.75.

Fenofibrate 200mg once a day (equivalent to 160mg m/r daily)
- Age from 16 years onwards
- Fenofibrate 200mg capsules. Take one capsule once a day; supply 28 capsules; NHS Cost £17.95.

Fenofibrate 267mg once a day
- Age from 16 years onwards
- Fenofibrate 267mg capsules. Take one capsule once a day; supply 28 capsules; NHS Cost £21.75.

Gemfibrozil 600mg twice a day
- Age from 16 years onwards
- Gemfibrozil 600mg tablets. Take one tablet twice a day; supply 56 tablets; NHS Cost £19.79.

Start fibrate (mild/moderate renal impairment)

Fenofibrate 67mg once a day
- Age from 16 years onwards
- Fenofibrate 67mg capsules. Take one capsule once a day; supply 30 capsules; NHS Cost £7.77.

Gemfibrozil 300mg twice a day
- Age from 16 years onwards
- Gemfibrozil 300mg capsules. Take one capsule twice a day; supply 56 capsules; NHS Cost £12.14.

Ciprofibrate 100mg on alternate days
- Age from 16 years onwards
- Ciprofibrate 100mg tablets. Take one tablet on alternate days; supply 14 tablets; NHS Cost £7.36.

Initial total cholesterol <5 mmol/l

Which therapy?

- **Reassure and offer diet and lifestyle advice if total cholesterol (TC) is <5 mmol/l.**
- **Re-check non-fasting TC annually in:**
  - Established CHD or other occlusive artery disease, diabetes, or hypertension.
  - Men aged over 60 years, or men aged over 50 years who smoke.
- If the person has none of the above risk factors, re-check TC in 5 years.
- **Consideration can be given to offering treatment with a statin to** people with established CHD or other occlusive artery disease, or people whose 10-year CHD risk is >30%. There is some evidence that reducing serum cholesterol has a preventative effect on CHD, whatever the baseline cholesterol level.

Follow-up advice

- Re-check non-fasting total cholesterol and HDL-C annually if the person has established coronary heart disease, other occlusive artery disease, diabetes, or hypertension.
- For men aged over 60 years, or men aged over 50 years who smoke, re-check annually.
- For none of the above risk factors, re-check in 3–5 years.

Patient information leaflets

The following PILs are available at www.prodigy.nhs.uk
- Alcohol and Sensible Drinking
- Blood Test - General
- British Heart Foundation
- British Nutrition Foundation
- Cholesterol
- Cholesterol - A Summary
- Eat More Fruit and Vegetables
- Exercise for Health
- Healthy Eating
- Healthy Lifestyle - Five Choices
- Smokeline
- Smoking - Help to Stop with Bupropion
- Smoking - Nicotine Replacement Therapy
- Smoking - The Facts
- Smoking - Tips on Stopping
- Weight Reduction - A Summary
- Weight Reduction - How to Lose Weight

Shared decision making

- **Your cholesterol level is less than 5**, which is good.
- You do not need a cholesterol-lowering medicine.
- **You should continue to eat and live healthily.** Follow this regime:
  - No smoking.
  - Regular exercise.
  - Lose weight if you are overweight or obese.
  - MORE vegetables, fruit, cereals, wholegrain bread, poultry, fish, rice, skimmed or semi-skimmed milk, grilled food, lean meat, pasta, etc.
  - LESS fatty meats, fatty cheeses, full cream milk, fried food, lard, etc.
  - If you do fry, choose a vegetable oil such as sunflower or rapeseed.
  - Use low fat spreads.
  - Add less salt to food, and avoid prepared foods that are very salty.

- Moderate alcohol consumption.
- If you have diabetes or high blood pressure or are taking any medicines for other conditions, be sure to follow advice for keeping these conditions under best possible control.

Drug rationale

- A non-drug prescription giving diet and lifestyle advice is offered.

Prescriptions

Non-drug management

Advice only: diet and lifestyle

- Age from 16 years onwards
- Your cholesterol level is now less than 5, which is GOOD. You should continue to eat and live healthily. No smoking. Regular exercise. Moderate alcohol consumption. Lose weight if you are overweight or obese. MORE vegetables, fruit, cereals, wholegrain bread, poultry, fish, rice, skimmed or semi-skimmed milk, grilled food, lean meat, pasta etc. LESS fatty meats, fatty cheeses, full cream milk, fried food, lard, etc. If you do fry, choose a vegetable oil such as sunflower or rapeseed. Use low fat spreads. Add less salt to food, and avoid foods that are very salty.

H

Initial total cholesterol >5 (and triglyceride <5)

Which therapy?

- Arrange for the person to have a *fasting* lipid profile to confirm results.
- **Rule out or manage secondary causes** of hypercholesterolaemia or mixed hyperlipidaemia.
- **Calculate baseline CHD risk using the average of 2–3 lipid and blood pressure results.** (Not needed if established CHD, ischaemic stroke, transient ischaemic attack (TIA), peripheral vascular disease (PVD), or familial dyslipidaemia.)
- **Statin therapy is indicated if** total cholesterol (TC) >5.0 mmol/l, or LDL-C >3.0 mmol/l, but triglycerides (TG) <5.0 mmol/l *and* the person has:
  - Established CHD, ischaemic stroke, TIA, PVD, or a familial dyslipidaemia (risk calculation not required).
  - 10-year CHD risk >30% (but no CHD, stroke, TIA, or PVD).
  - Type 2 diabetes and 10-year CHD risk of 15–30%.
- **Aim to lower TC by** 20–25%, or to below 5 mmol/l (whichever is the lower). Aim to lower LDL-C by 30%, or to below 3 mmol/l (whichever gives the lower level).
- **Review every 4–8 weeks and adjust dose until the target lipid level is reached.**
- **Reinforce lifestyle advice:** Mediterranean diet, weight, exercise, smoking, alcohol.
- **Manage coexisting diseases rigorously:** diabetes, hypertension, established occlusive artery disease, left ventricular dysfunction, prior myocardial infarction, and atrial fibrillation.
- **Refer someone with** very severe hypercholesterolaemia or hypertriglyceridaemia (usually >10 mmol/l), or suspected familial hypercholesterolaemia.
- **Family screening and counselling** of people with familial combined hyperlipidaemia is important. It is not always necessary to refer these people if they already qualify for treatment.

Practical prescribing points

For further information please see the *Medicines Compendium* (www.medicines.org.uk) or the *British National Formulary* (www.bnf.org).

- **Check CK and AST or ALT** before starting drugs.
- **Hepatotoxicity is rare**, but is thought to be dose-dependent.
- **Advise people to report muscle pain, aches, or cramps. Withdraw statin while checking CK level.** (A non-significant increase in CK is common.)
- **Myopathy is rare, but the risk is increased in the presence of:**
  - Renal impairment, hypothyroidism, alcohol abuse, underlying muscle disorders, or age >70 years.
  - Co-prescription of statins with fibrates (do not use gemfibrozil), or nicotinic acid (>1 g).
  - A past history of myopathy with any lipid-lowering drug.
  - Co-prescription of drugs that increase simvastatin or atorvastatin levels. (Avoid ciclosporin, clarithromycin, erythromycin, HIV protease inhibitors, itraconazole, or ketoconazole.)
- **Use a lower starting dose of statins in people at increased risk of myopathy.** (Do not start treatment if baseline CK >5 times upper limit of normal.)
- **Warfarin and simvastatin or fluvastatin:** monitor INR closely until stable — INR *occasionally* increases significantly.
- **Stop statin treatment if:**
  - There is a strong suspicion of myopathy, or CK level >5 times upper limit of normal.
  - Myalgic symptoms persist despite a normal CK level — a trial off treatment may be needed.
  - AST or ALT level persists above 3 times upper limit of normal.

Follow-up advice

Monitoring statin therapy

- **Aim to lower total cholesterol** (TC) **by** 20–25%, or to below 5 mmol/l (whichever is the lower).
- **Advise the person to report any muscular pains immediately.** Check the CK level.
- **Discontinue statin if** there is a strong suspicion of myopathy, if CK exceeds 5 times upper limit of normal range, or if transaminases *persist* above 3 times upper limit of normal range.
- **4–8 weeks after starting, or after a dose increase:** check non-fasting TC and AST or ALT. A fasting sample is needed only if a LDL-C level is required.
- **Annual checks:** non-fasting TC, and AST or ALT.

Ask about family history (if this has not already been done)

- **Consider familial combined hyperlipidaemia if:** TC 6.5–8.0 mmol/l and triglycerides 2.3–5.0 mmol/l AND family history of hyperlipidaemia or premature CHD.
- **Consider familial hypercholesterolaemia when the person has** serum TC >7.5 mmol/l (or LDL-C >4.9 mmol/l) and any of the following:
  - Tendon xanthomata in himself/herself or in a first- or second-degree relative.
  - Family history of premature CHD or other atherosclerotic disease in a male first-degree relative before the age of 55 years, or in a female first-degree relative before the age of 65 years.
  - Family history of TC >7.5 mmol/l in a first- or second-degree relative.

Should I refer or investigate?

Refer?

- **Severe hypercholesterolaemia,** i.e. total cholesterol (TC) >10 mmol/l.
- **Severe hypertriglyceridaemia,** i.e. triglycerides >10 mmol/l.
- **Target lipid levels are not achieved** despite maximum tolerated doses.
- **Suspected familial hypercholesterolaemia:** TC >7.5 mmol/l (or LDL-C >4.9 mmol/l) AND at least one of the following:
  - Tendon xanthomata in themselves or in a first- or second-degree relative.
  - Family history of premature coronary heart disease or other atherosclerotic disease in a male first-degree relative before the age of 55 years, or in a female first-degree relative before the age of 65 years.
  - Family history of TC >7.5 mmol/l in a first- or second-degree relative.
- Reasons for referral are to make a firm diagnosis, to initiate treatment if required, and to counsel and screen the family.
- **Referral may be unnecessary for someone with suspected familial combined hyperlipidaemia** if they qualify for treatment according to risk assessment. Family screening and counselling, however, should not be forgotten.

Investigate?

Pretreatment tests

- Fasting lipid profile (total cholesterol, LDL-C, HDL-C, triglycerides) — at least 2 (preferably 3) measurements for final coronary heart disease risk calculation with mean levels.
- Baseline CK and AST/ALT.
- Rule out secondary causes of hypercholesterolaemia, e.g. drugs (ciclosporin), hypothyroidism, obstructive jaundice, nephrotic syndrome.
- Rule out secondary causes of combined hyperlipidaemia, e.g. pregnancy, drugs (oral corticosteroids, oral contraceptives, high doses of thiazides), multiple myeloma.

Monitoring response to treatment and toxicity

- **Check CK if muscle symptoms occur.**
- **4–8 weeks after starting, or after a dose increase:** check non-fasting total cholesterol and AST or ALT. A fasting sample is only needed if an LDL-C or triglyceride level is required.
- **Annual checks:** non-fasting TC, and AST or ALT.

Patient information leaflets

The following PILs are available at www.prodigy.nhs.uk

- Alcohol and Sensible Drinking
- Blood Test - General
- British Heart Foundation
- British Nutrition Foundation
- Cholesterol
- Cholesterol - A Summary
- Eat More Fruit and Vegetables
- Exercise for Health
- Healthy Eating
- Healthy Lifestyle - Five Choices
- Smokeline
- Smoking - Help to Stop with Bupropion
- Smoking - Nicotine Replacement Therapy
- Smoking - The Facts
- Smoking - Tips on Stopping
- Weight Reduction - A Summary
- Weight Reduction - How to Lose Weight

Shared decision making

- **Your cholesterol level remains high.**
- **A 'statin' medicine is recommended.**
- **Side effects are uncommon.**
  - A few people develop mild headaches, mild upset stomach, dizziness, or itch. These often go with continued treatment.
  - A very rare, but more serious, side effect is a muscle problem. Tell a doctor if you develop muscle pains whilst taking a statin medicine.
- **You will need a blood test** before starting a statin, and about 6 weeks later.
- **You should still eat and live healthily.** Follow this regime:
  - No smoking.
  - Regular exercise.
  - Lose weight if you are overweight or obese.
  - MORE vegetables, fruit, cereals, wholegrain bread, poultry, fish, rice, skimmed or semi-skimmed milk, grilled food, lean meat, pasta, etc.
  - LESS fatty meats, fatty cheeses, full cream milk, fried food, lard, etc.
  - If you do fry, choose a vegetable oil such as sunflower or rapeseed.
  - Use low fat spreads.
  - Add less salt to food, and avoid foods that are very salty.
  - Moderate alcohol consumption.
- If you have diabetes or high blood pressure or are taking any medicines for other conditions, be sure to follow advice for keeping these conditions under best possible control.

Drug rationale

Drugs not included

- **Lipid-lowering agents other than statins are not included in this scenario, because evidence for their benefit is not as strong as that for the statins.**
- **Ezetimibe** (a novel cholesterol absorption inhibitor) is not offered as a first-line treatment for hyperlipidaemia because it is a black triangle drug, and post-marketing data are needed to confirm its safety. Its effect on clinical end points has not yet been assessed. It may be considered as an adjunct to other lipid-lowering therapy in people unable to achieve target lipid levels on statins or fibrates alone, or for people unable to tolerate higher doses of statins. It is also an alternative for people unable to tolerate other lipid-lowering drugs.
- **Rosuvastatin** is not offered as a first-line treatment for hyperlipidaemia because it is a black triangle drug, and post-marketing data are needed to confirm its safety. Unlike other statins, its effect on clinical end points has not yet been assessed. It is an alternative option for people unable to achieve target lipid levels with high doses of other statins.

Drugs included

- **Statins: simvastatin, pravastatin, atorvastatin, and fluvastatin** are offered. Pravastatin has been shown to reduce the overall number of coronary heart disease events in one large primary prevention study [Shepherd et al, 1995]. Atorvastatin, simvastatin, and pravastatin have been shown in large-scale secondary prevention trials to reduce deaths from all causes, the most conservative measure of clinical outcome [LaRosa et al,

1999; Athyros et al, 2002; Heart Protection Study Collaborative Group, 2002]. Fluvastatin given to people after their first percutaneous coronary intervention has been shown to reduce the risk of major adverse coronary events [Serruys et al, 2002].
- A non-drug prescription giving diet and lifestyle advice is offered.

Prescriptions

Non-drug management

Advice only: diet and lifestyle
- Age from 16 years onwards
- Your cholesterol level is high. Lifestyle and dietary changes can sometimes reduce the cholesterol level and other risk factors for heart disease. You should aim to eat and live healthily. This means: No smoking. Regular exercise. Moderate alcohol consumption. Lose weight if you are overweight or obese. MORE vegetables, fruit, cereals, wholegrain bread, poultry, fish, rice, skimmed or semi-skimmed milk, grilled food, lean meat, pasta etc. LESS fatty meats, fatty cheeses, full cream milk, fried food, lard, etc. If you do fry, choose a vegetable oil such as sunflower or rapeseed. Use low fat spreads. Add less salt to food, and avoid foods that are very salty. Have your cholesterol level checked again in 3 months time.

H

Start statin (PRODIGY start doses)

Simvastatin 20mg at night
- Age from 16 years onwards
- Simvastatin 20mg tablets. Take one tablet at night; supply 28 tablets; NHS Cost £7.80.

Atorvastatin 10mg once a day
- Age from 16 years onwards
- Atorvastatin 10mg tablets. Take one tablet once a day; supply 28 tablets; NHS Cost £18.03.

Fluvastatin 40mg at night
- Age from 16 years onwards
- Fluvastatin 40mg capsules. Take one capsule at night; supply 28 capsules; NHS Cost £12.72.

Pravastatin 40mg at night
- Age from 16 years onwards
- Pravastatin 40mg tablets. Take one tablet at night; supply 28 tablets; NHS Cost £29.69.

Start statin (high start doses)

Simvastatin 40mg at night
- Age from 16 years onwards
- Simvastatin 40mg tablets. Take one tablet at night; supply 28 tablets; NHS Cost £15.60.

Atorvastatin 20mg once a day
- Age from 16 years onwards
- Atorvastatin 20mg tablets. Take one tablet once a day; supply 28 tablets; NHS Cost £29.69.

Pravastatin 40mg at night
- Age from 16 years onwards
- Pravastatin 40mg tablets. Take one tablet at night; supply 28 tablets; NHS Cost £29.69.

Fluvastatin 80mg m/r at night
- Age from 16 years onwards
- Fluvastatin 80mg m/r tablets. Take one tablet at night; supply 28 tablets; NHS Cost £16.00.

Start statin (low start doses)

Simvastatin 10mg at night
- Age from 16 years onwards
- Simvastatin 10mg tablets. Take one tablet at night; supply 28 tablets; NHS Cost £5.78.

Atorvastatin 10mg once a day
- Age from 16 years onwards
- Atorvastatin 10mg tablets. Take one tablet once a day; supply 28 tablets; NHS Cost £18.03.

Fluvastatin 20mg at night
- Age from 16 years onwards
- Fluvastatin 20mg capsules. Take one capsule at night; supply 28 capsules; NHS Cost £12.72.

Pravastatin 10mg at night
- Age from 16 years onwards
- Pravastatin 10mg tablets. Take one tablet at night; supply 28 tablets; NHS Cost £16.18.

Pravastatin 20mg at night
- Age from 16 years onwards
- Pravastatin 20mg tablets. Take one tablet at night; supply 28 tablets; NHS Cost £29.69.

Initial total cholesterol >5 and triglyceride >5

Which therapy?

- Arrange for the person to have a *fasting* lipid profile to confirm results.
- **Rule out or manage secondary causes of mixed hyperlipidaemia.**
- **Calculate baseline CHD risk using the average of 2–3 lipid and blood pressure results.** (Not needed if established CHD, ischaemic stroke, transient ischaemic attack (TIA), peripheral vascular disease (PVD), or familial dyslipidaemia.)
- **A statin or a fibrate is indicated if** total cholesterol (TC) >5.0 mmol/l, or LDL-C >3.0 mmol/l, *and* triglycerides (TG) >5.0 mmol/l *and* the person has:
  - Established CHD, ischaemic stroke, TIA, or PVD, or a familial dyslipidaemia (risk calculation not required).
  - 10-year CHD risk >30% (but no CHD, stroke, TIA, or PVD).
  - People with Type 2 diabetes with a 10-year CHD risk of 15–30%.
- **Fibrates lower TG better, but statins have more evidence for preventing CHD.**
- **Before prescribing a fibrate for a person with renal impairment:**
  - Consider seeking specialist advice.
  - Modified-release preparations of fibrates are contraindicated in people with renal impairment. Use standard preparations and start at low doses. Increase dose slowly, while carefully monitoring lipid levels, CK, AST or ALT, and renal function (e.g. every 4 weeks).
- **Aim to lower TC by** 20–25%, or to below 5 mmol/l (whichever is the lower). Aim to lower LDL-C by 30%, or to below 3 mmol/l (whichever gives the lower level).
- **Aim to lower TG below 2.3 mmol/l.**
- **Review statins every 4–8 weeks and adjust dose until the target lipid level is reached.** Review fibrates after 12 weeks. (Dose titration is not possible for most fibrates — the starting dose is the usual maintenance dose.)
- **Reinforce lifestyle advice:** Mediterranean diet, weight, exercise, smoking, alcohol.
- **Manage coexisting diseases rigorously:** diabetes, hypertension, established occlusive artery disease, left ventricular dysfunction, prior myocardial infarction, and atrial fibrillation.
- **Refer people with** very severe hypercholesterolaemia or hypertriglyceridaemia (usually >10 mmol/l), or suspected familial hypercholesterolaemia.
- **Family screening and counselling** of people with familial combined hyperlipidaemia is important. It is not always

necessary to refer these people if they already qualify for treatment.

Practical prescribing points

For further information please see the *Medicines Compendium* (www.medicines.org.uk) or the *British National Formulary* (www.bnf.org).

- **Check CK and AST or ALT** before starting drugs. Check serum creatinine before starting a fibrate.
- **Hepatotoxicity is rare,** but is thought to be dose-dependent.
- **Advise people to report muscle pain, aches, or cramps.** Withdraw statin while checking CK level. (A non-significant increase in CK is common.)
- **Myopathy is rare, but the risk is increased in the presence of:**
  - Renal impairment, hypothyroidism, alcohol abuse, underlying muscle disorders, or age >70 years.
  - Co-prescription of statins with fibrates (do not use gemfibrozil), or nicotinic acid (>1 g).
  - A past history of myopathy with any lipid-lowering drug.
  - Co-prescription of drugs that increase simvastatin or atorvastatin levels. (Avoid ciclosporin, clarithromycin, erythromycin, HIV protease inhibitors, itraconazole, or ketoconazole.)
- **Use a lower starting dose of statins in people at increased risk of myopathy.** (Do not start treatment if baseline CK >5 times upper limit of normal.)
- **Warfarin and simvastatin or fluvastatin:** monitor INR closely until stable — INR *occasionally* increases significantly.
- **Warfarin and fibrates:** reduce the dose of warfarin by about a third and make further adjustments according to changes in the INR.
- **Stop treatment if:**
  - Serum creatinine increases progressively (with fibrates).
  - There is a strong suspicion of myopathy, or CK level >5 times upper limit of normal.
  - Myalgic symptoms persist despite a normal CK level — a trial off treatment may be needed.
  - AST or ALT level persists above 3 times upper limit of normal.

Follow-up advice

- **Advise the person to report any muscular pains immediately.** Check the CK level.
- **Discontinue lipid-lowering therapy if** there is a strong suspicion of myopathy, if CK exceeds 5 times upper limit of normal range, or if transaminases *persist* above 3 times upper limit of normal range.
- Also, discontinue fibrate therapy if serum creatinine continues to rise.
- **Aim to lower total cholesterol (TC) by** 20–25%, or to below 5 mmol/l (whichever is the lower). Aim to lower LDL-C by 30%, or to below 3 mmol/l (whichever gives the lower level).
- **Aim to lower triglycerides below 2.3 mmol/l.**

Statins

- **Check fasting serum lipids profile every 4–8 weeks** and titrate dose until target or maximum tolerated dose is reached, and then annually. Note: fasting lipid profile is needed to give an accurate assessment of triglyceride levels.
- **Check AST or ALT** every 4–8 weeks until dose is stable, and then annually.

Fibrates

- **Check fasting serum lipid profile after 12 weeks.** Dose titration is not possible for most fibrates — the starting dose is the usual maintenance dose.
- **Check AST or ALT after 12 weeks,** and then annually.
- **If the person has renal impairment,** consider specialist referral before starting treatment with a fibrate. Titrate the dose slowly, while carefully monitoring lipid levels, CK, AST or ALT and renal function (e.g. every 4 weeks).

Ask about family history (if this has not already been done)

- **Consider familial combined hyperlipidaemia if:** TC 6.5–8.0 mmol/l and triglycerides 2.3–5.0 mmol/l AND family history of hyperlipidaemia or premature CHD.
- **Consider familial hypercholesterolaemia when the person has** serum TC >7.5 mmol/l (or LDL-C >4.9 mmol/l) AND any of the following:
  - Tendon xanthomata in himself/herself or in a first- or second-degree relative.
  - Family history of premature coronary heart disease or other atherosclerotic disease in a male first-degree relative before the age of 55 years, or in a female first-degree relative before the age of 65 years.
  - Family history of TC >7.5 mmol/l in a first- or second-degree relative.

Should I refer or investigate?

Refer?

- **Severe hypercholesterolaemia,** i.e. total cholesterol TC >10 mmol/l.
- **Severe hypertriglyceridaemia,** i.e. triglycerides >10 mmol/l.
- **Target lipid levels are not achieved despite maximum tolerated doses.**
- **Suspected familial hypercholesterolaemia:** TC >7.5 mmol/l (or LDL-C >4.9 mmol/l) AND at least one of the following:
  - Tendon xanthomata in themselves or in a first- or second-degree relative.
  - Family history of premature coronary heart disease or other atherosclerotic disease in a male first-degree relative before the age of 55 years, or in a female first-degree relative before the age of 65 years.
  - Family history of TC >7.5 mmol/l in a first- or second-degree relative.
- Reasons for referral are to make a firm diagnosis, to initiate treatment if required, and to counsel and screen the family.
- **Referral may be unnecessary for someone with suspected familial combined hyperlipidaemia** if they qualify for treatment according to risk assessment. Family screening and counselling, however, should not be forgotten.

Investigate?

Pretreatment tests

- **Fasting lipid profile** (total cholesterol, LDL-C, HDL-C, triglycerides) — at least 2 (preferably 3) measurements for final coronary heart disease risk calculation with mean levels.
- **Baseline CK and AST/ALT** (and serum creatinine if taking a fibrate).
- Rule out secondary causes of combined hyperlipidaemia, e.g. pregnancy, drugs (oral corticosteroids, oral contraceptives, high doses of thiazides), multiple myeloma.

H

Monitoring response to treatment and toxicity

- **Check CK if muscle symptoms occur.**
- **4–8 weeks after starting statin, or after a dose increase:** check fasting TC and AST or ALT.
- **12 weeks after starting fibrate:** check fasting serum lipid profile, serum creatinine, and AST or ALT. Dose titration is not possible for most fibrates — the starting dose is the usual maintenance dose.
- **Annual checks:** fasting TC, and AST or ALT (and serum creatinine if taking a fibrate).

Patient information leaflets

The following PILs are available at www.prodigy.nhs.uk

- Alcohol and Sensible Drinking
- Blood Test - General
- British Heart Foundation
- British Nutrition Foundation
- Cholesterol
- Cholesterol - A Summary
- Eat More Fruit and Vegetables
- Exercise for Health
- Healthy Eating
- Healthy Lifestyle - Five Choices
- Smokeline
- Smoking - Help to Stop with Bupropion
- Smoking - Nicotine Replacement Therapy
- Smoking - The Facts
- Smoking - Tips on Stopping
- Weight Reduction - A Summary
- Weight Reduction - How to Lose Weight

H

Shared decision making

- **Your cholesterol and triglyceride (blood fat) levels remain high.**
- **A 'statin' or a 'fibrate' medicine is recommended.**
- Side effects are uncommon.
  - A few people develop mild headaches, mild upset stomach, dizziness, or itch. These often go away with continued treatment.
  - A very rare, but serious, side effect is a muscle problem. Tell a doctor if you develop muscle pains whilst taking one of these medicines.
- **You will need a blood test from time to time.**
- **You should still eat and live healthily.** Follow this regime:
  - No smoking.
  - Regular exercise.
  - Lose weight if you are overweight or obese.
  - MORE vegetables, fruit, cereals, wholegrain bread, poultry, fish, rice, skimmed or semi-skimmed milk, grilled food, lean meat, pasta, etc.
  - LESS fatty meats, fatty cheeses, full cream milk, fried food, lard, etc.
  - If you do fry, choose a vegetable oil such as sunflower or rapeseed.
  - Use low fat spreads.
  - Add less salt to food, and avoid prepared foods that are very salty.
  - Moderate alcohol consumption.
- **If you have diabetes or high blood pressure or are taking any medicines for other conditions,** be sure to follow advice for keeping these conditions under best possible control.

Drug rationale

Drugs not included

- **Rosuvastatin** is not offered as a first-line treatment for hyperlipidaemia because it is a black triangle drug, and post-marketing data are needed to confirm its safety. Unlike other statins, its effect on clinical end points has not yet been assessed. It is an alternative option for people unable to achieve target lipid levels with high doses of other statins.
- **Omega-3 polyunsaturated fatty acids** (omega-3 PUFAs) reduce serum triglyceride (TG) levels, and can therefore be a useful adjunct in the treatment of hypertriglyceridaemia. They can increase LDL-C levels, so both LDL-C and TG levels should be monitored. A large number of capsules are needed for a therapeutic dose, and they are expensive.
- **Anion-exchange resins** are very inconvenient to take, and are therefore reserved as adjunctive therapy for people who are unable to achieve target lipid levels on the maximum tolerated dose of a statin or fibrate.
- **High doses of nicotinic acid** can produce large increases in , as well as lowering cholesterol and TG levels. However, it is rarely used because of its adverse effects, especially vasodilation [BNF 44, 2002].
- **Ezetimibe** (a novel cholesterol absorption inhibitor) is not offered as a first-line treatment for hyperlipidaemia because it is a black triangle drug, and post-marketing data are needed to confirm its safety. Its effect on clinical end points has not yet been assessed. It may be considered as an adjunct to other lipid-lowering therapy in people unable to achieve target lipid levels on statins or fibrates alone, or for people unable to tolerate higher doses of statins. It is also an alternative for people unable to tolerate other lipid-lowering drugs.

Drugs included

- **Statins: simvastatin, atorvastatin, and fluvastatin** are licensed for use in mixed hyperlipidaemia. They are the treatment of choice for hypercholesterolaemia with raised triglycerides (TGs) up to 5.0 mmol/l [Wood et al, 1998]. Pravastatin is not currently licensed for this indication, but is included because there is evidence that it reduces overall coronary heart disease event rates in people with raised cholesterol levels [Shepherd et al, 1995]. In addition, TG lowering is a class effect: reduction in TG levels is related to low-density lipoprotein cholesterol-lowering, but significant reductions only occur in people with high baseline TG levels [Stein et al, 1998].
- **Fibrates: bezafibrate, ciprofibrate, fenofibrate, and gemfibrozil** are included. Compared with statins, fibrates can achieve greater reductions in TGs, and greater increases in HDL-C. They are an alternative to statins for treating mixed hyperlipidaemia (hypercholesterolaemia together with TG levels greater than 5.0 mmol/l).
- Modified-release preparations of fibrates are contraindicated in people with renal impairment. Low doses of standard-release preparations are offered for these people. Note: bezafibrate is not offered for people with renal impairment because it becomes contraindicated at a milder degree of renal impairment than other fibrates.
- A non-drug prescription giving diet and lifestyle advice is offered.

Prescriptions

Start statin (PRODIGY start doses)

Simvastatin 20mg at night
- Age from 16 years onwards
- Simvastatin 20mg tablets. Take one tablet at night; supply 28 tablets; NHS Cost £7.80.

Atorvastatin 10mg once a day
- Age from 16 years onwards
- Atorvastatin 10mg tablets. Take one tablet once a day; supply 28 tablets; NHS Cost £18.03.

Fluvastatin 40mg at night
- Age from 16 years onwards
- Fluvastatin 40mg capsules. Take one capsule at night; supply 28 capsules; NHS Cost £12.72.

Pravastatin 40mg at night
- Age from 16 years onwards
- Pravastatin 40mg tablets. Take one tablet at night; supply 28 tablets; NHS Cost £29.69.

Start statin (high start doses)

Simvastatin 40mg at night
- Age from 16 years onwards
- Simvastatin 40mg tablets. Take one tablet at night; supply 28 tablets; NHS Cost £15.60.

Atorvastatin 20mg once a day
- Age from 16 years onwards
- Atorvastatin 20mg tablets. Take one tablet once a day; supply 28 tablets; NHS Cost £29.69.

Pravastatin 40mg at night
- Age from 16 years onwards
- Pravastatin 40mg tablets. Take one tablet at night; supply 28 tablets; NHS Cost £29.69.

Fluvastatin 80mg m/r at night
- Age from 16 years onwards
- Fluvastatin 80mg m/r tablets. Take one tablet at night; supply 28 tablets; NHS Cost £16.00.

Start statin (low start doses)

Simvastatin 10mg at night
- Age from 16 years onwards
- Simvastatin 10mg tablets. Take one tablet at night; supply 28 tablets; NHS Cost £5.78.

Atorvastatin 10mg once a day
- Age from 16 years onwards
- Atorvastatin 10mg tablets. Take one tablet once a day; supply 28 tablets; NHS Cost £18.03.

Fluvastatin 20mg at night
- Age from 16 years onwards
- Fluvastatin 20mg capsules. Take one capsule at night; supply 28 capsules; NHS Cost £12.72.

Pravastatin 10mg at night
- Age from 16 years onwards
- Pravastatin 10mg tablets. Take one tablet at night; supply 28 tablets; NHS Cost £16.18.

Pravastatin 20mg at night
- Age from 16 years onwards
- Pravastatin 20mg tablets. Take one tablet at night; supply 28 tablets; NHS Cost £29.69.

Start fibrate (normal renal function)

Bezafibrate 400mg m/r once a day
- Age from 16 years onwards
- Bezafibrate 400mg m/r tablets. Take one tablet once a day; supply 30 tablets; NHS Cost £8.70.

Bezafibrate 200mg three times a day
- Age from 16 years onwards
- Bezafibrate 200mg tablets. Take one tablet three times a day; supply 84 tablets; NHS Cost £8.24.

Ciprofibrate 100mg once a day
- Age from 16 years onwards
- Ciprofibrate 100mg tablets. Take one tablet once a day; supply 28 tablets; NHS Cost £14.72.

Fenofibrate 160mg m/r once a day (equiv to 200mg std daily)
- Age from 16 years onwards
- Fenofibrate 160mg m/r tablets. Take one tablet once a day; supply 28 tablets; NHS Cost £14.75.

Fenofibrate 200mg once a day (equivalent to 160mg m/r daily)
- Age from 16 years onwards
- Fenofibrate 200mg capsules. Take one capsule once a day; supply 28 capsules; NHS Cost £17.95.

Fenofibrate 267mg once a day
- Age from 16 years onwards
- Fenofibrate 267mg capsules. Take one capsule once a day; supply 28 capsules; NHS Cost £21.00.

Gemfibrozil 600mg twice a day
- Age from 16 years onwards
- Gemfibrozil 600mg tablets. Take one tablet twice a day; supply 56 tablets; NHS Cost £19.79.

Start fibrate (mild/moderate renal impairment)

Fenofibrate 67mg once a day
- Age from 16 years onwards
- Fenofibrate 67mg capsules. Take one capsule once a day; supply 30 capsules; NHS Cost £7.77.

Gemfibrozil 300mg twice a day
- Age from 16 years onwards
- Gemfibrozil 300mg capsules. Take one capsule twice a day; supply 56 capsules; NHS Cost £12.14.

Ciprofibrate 100mg on alternate days
- Age from 16 years onwards
- Ciprofibrate 100mg tablets. Take one tablet on alternate days; supply 14 tablets; NHS Cost £7.36.

Managing statin therapy

Which therapy?

- **Aim to lower total cholesterol by** 20–25%, or to below 5 mmol/l (whichever is the lower). Aim to lower LDL-C by 30%, or to below 3 mmol/l (whichever gives the lower level).
- **Review every 4–8 weeks and adjust dose until the target lipid level is reached.**
- **If the target cholesterol level is not reached at maximum titration,** consider: compliance; using an alternative statin (e.g. simvastatin or atorvastatin); referral to a specialist lipid clinic; or combination therapy, e.g. with a statin and a bile acid sequestrant, or both a statin and a fibrate.
- **A prescription for combination therapy is not available through PRODIGY,** as it is often initiated in secondary care. (The risk of myopathy is increased if a statin and a fibrate are used together.)
- **Reinforce lifestyle advice:** Mediterranean diet, weight, exercise, smoking, alcohol.
- **Manage coexisting diseases rigorously:** diabetes, hypertension, established occlusive artery disease, left ventricular dysfunction, prior myocardial infarction, and atrial fibrillation.
- **Rule out or manage secondary causes of hyperlipidaemia.**

- **Consider familial conditions if suggested by clinical features.**
- **Stop treatment if:**
  - Strong suspicion of myopathy, or CK level greater than 5 times upper limit of normal.
  - Myalgic symptoms persist despite a normal CK level — a trial off treatment may be needed.
  - AST or ALT level persists above 3 times upper limit of normal.

Practical prescribing points

For further information please see the *Medicines Compendium* (www.medicines.org.uk) or the *British National Formulary* (www.bnf.org).

- **Hepatotoxicity is rare, but is thought to be dose-dependent.**
- **Advise people to report muscle pain, aches, or cramps. Withdraw statin while checking CK level.** (A non-significant increase in CK is common.)
- **Myopathy is rare, but the risk is increased in the presence of:**
  - Renal impairment, hypothyroidism, alcohol abuse, underlying muscle disorders, or age >70 years.
  - Co-prescription of statins with fibrates (do not use gemfibrozil), or nicotinic acid (>1 g).
  - A past history of myopathy with any lipid-lowering drug.
  - Co-prescription of drugs that increase simvastatin or atorvastatin levels. (Avoid ciclosporin, clarithromycin, erythromycin, HIV protease inhibitors, itraconazole, or ketoconazole.)
- **Use a lower starting dose of statins in people at increased risk of myopathy.** (Do not start treatment if baseline CK >5 times upper limit of normal.)
- **Warfarin and simvastatin or fluvastatin:** monitor INR closely until stable — INR *occasionally* increases significantly.

Follow-up advice

Monitoring statin therapy

- **Aim to lower total cholesterol (TC) by 20–25%, or to below 5 mmol/l (whichever is the lower).**
- **Advise the person to report any muscular pains immediately.** Check the CK level.
- **Discontinue statin if** strong suspicion of myopathy, if CK exceeds 5 times upper limit of normal range, or if transaminases *persist* above 3 times upper limit of normal range.
- **4–8 weeks after starting, or after a dose increase:** check non-fasting TC and AST or ALT. A fasting sample is needed only if a LDL-C or triglyceride level is required.
- **Annual checks:** non-fasting TC, and AST or ALT.
- **If the person has renal impairment,** consider specialist referral before starting treatment with a fibrate. Titrate the dose slowly, while carefully monitoring lipid levels, CK, AST or ALT and renal function, e.g. every 4 weeks.

Should I refer or investigate?

Refer?

- If the target cholesterol level is not reached at maximum tolerated titration, consider referral to a specialist lipid clinic.
- Other options include assessing compliance, using an alternative statin (e.g. atorvastatin or simvastatin), or using combination therapy (e.g. with both a statin and a bile acid sequestrant, or both a statin and a fibrate).
- A prescription for combination therapy is not available through PRODIGY, as it is often initiated in secondary care.

Investigate?

- Once stabilized, review annually with non-fasting total cholesterol, and AST/ALT.

Patient information leaflets

The following PILs are available at www.prodigy.nhs.uk

- Blood Test - General
- Blood Test - Liver Function Tests
- British Heart Foundation
- British Nutrition Foundation
- Cholesterol
- Cholesterol - A Summary
- Eat More Fruit and Vegetables
- Healthy Eating
- Healthy Lifestyle - Five Choices
- Weight Reduction - A Summary

Shared decision making

- The dose of your medicine needs adjusting.
- Most people who take these medicines have no side effects. A few people may experience mild side effects. These include mild upset stomach or gut, itching, or a rash. Tell your doctor immediately if you have any muscle pains.
- Continue with the dietary advice previously given.
- Drink alcohol in moderation, exercise regularly, and do not smoke.
- If you have diabetes or high blood pressure or are taking any medicines for other conditions, be sure to follow advice for keeping these conditions under best possible control.

Drug rationale

Drugs not included

- This scenario is for the management of statin therapy: other classes of lipid lowering drugs are therefore not included.
- **Rosuvastatin** is not offered as a first-line treatment for hyperlipidaemia because it is a black triangle drug, and post-marketing data are needed to confirm its safety. Unlike other statins, its effect on clinical end points has not yet been assessed. It is an alternative option for people unable to achieve target lipid levels with high doses of other statins.

Drugs included

- Maintenance doses/dose adjustments are offered for atorvastatin, fluvastatin, pravastatin, and simvastatin.
- A non-drug prescription giving diet and lifestyle advice is offered.

Prescriptions

Non-drug management

Advice only: diet and lifestyle

- Age from 16 years onwards
- Your cholesterol level is high. Lifestyle and dietary changes can sometimes reduce the cholesterol level and other risk factors for heart disease. You should aim to eat and live healthily. This means: No smoking. Regular exercise. Moderate alcohol consumption. Lose weight if you are overweight or obese. MORE vegetables, fruit,

cereals, wholegrain bread, poultry, fish, rice, skimmed or semi-skimmed milk, grilled food, lean meat, pasta etc. LESS fatty meats, fatty cheeses, full cream milk, fried food, lard, etc. If you do fry, choose a vegetable oil such as sunflower or rapeseed. Use low fat spreads. Add less salt to food, and avoid foods that are very salty. Have your cholesterol level checked again in 3 months time.

Simvastatin

Simvastatin 10mg at night
- Age from 16 years onwards
- Simvastatin 10mg tablets. Take one tablet at night; supply 28 tablets; NHS Cost £5.78.

Simvastatin 20mg at night
- Age from 16 years onwards
- Simvastatin 20mg tablets. Take one tablet at night; supply 28 tablets; NHS Cost £7.80.

Simvastatin 40mg at night
- Age from 16 years onwards
- Simvastatin 40mg tablets. Take one tablet at night; supply 28 tablets; NHS Cost £15.60.

Simvastatin 80mg at night
- Age from 16 years onwards
- Simvastatin 80mg tablets. Take one tablet at night; supply 28 tablets; NHS Cost £28.77.

Atorvastatin

Atorvastatin 10mg once a day
- Age from 16 years onwards
- Atorvastatin 10mg tablets. Take one tablet once a day; supply 28 tablets; NHS Cost £18.03.

Atorvastatin 20mg once a day
- Age from 16 years onwards
- Atorvastatin 20mg tablets. Take one tablet once a day; supply 28 tablets; NHS Cost £29.69.

Atorvastatin 40mg once a day
- Age from 16 years onwards
- Atorvastatin 40mg tablets. Take one tablet once a day; supply 28 tablets; NHS Cost £29.69.

Atorvastatin 80mg once a day
- Age from 16 years onwards
- Atorvastatin 80mg tablets. Take one tablet once a day; supply 28 tablets; NHS Cost £29.69.

Pravastatin

Pravastatin 10mg at night
- Age from 16 years onwards
- Pravastatin 10mg tablets. Take one tablet at night; supply 28 tablets; NHS Cost £16.18.

Pravastatin 20mg at night
- Age from 16 years onwards
- Pravastatin 20mg tablets. Take one tablet at night; supply 28 tablets; NHS Cost £29.69.

Pravastatin 40mg at night
- Age from 16 years onwards
- Pravastatin 40mg tablets. Take one tablet at night; supply 28 tablets; NHS Cost £29.69.

Fluvastatin

Fluvastatin 20mg at night
- Age from 16 years onwards
- Fluvastatin 20mg capsules. Take one capsule at night; supply 28 capsules; NHS Cost £12.72.

Fluvastatin 40mg at night
- Age from 16 years onwards
- Fluvastatin 40mg capsules. Take one capsule at night; supply 28 capsules; NHS Cost £12.72.

Fluvastatin 80mg m/r at night
- Age from 16 years onwards
- Fluvastatin 80mg m/r tablets. Take one tablet at night; supply 28 tablets; NHS Cost £16.00.

Managing fibrate therapy

Which therapy?

- **Aim to lower total cholesterol by** 20–25%, or to below 5 mmol/l (whichever is the lower). Aim to lower LDL-C by 30%, or to below 3 mmol/l (whichever gives the lower level).
- **Aim to lower triglycerides** below 2.3 mmol/l.
- **Dose titration is needed only if there is impaired renal function** — the recommended starting dose is the usual maintenance dose. Note: it can take 3 to 4 months before maximum effects are seen.
- **If the target cholesterol level is not reached,** consider: compliance, changing to a statin, referral to a specialist lipid clinic, or using combination therapy.
- **A prescription for combination therapy is not available through PRODIGY,** as it is often initiated in secondary care. (The risk of myopathy is increased if a statin and a fibrate are used together.)
- **Reinforce lifestyle advice:** Mediterranean diet, weight, exercise, smoking, alcohol.
- **Manage coexisting diseases rigorously:** diabetes, hypertension, established occlusive artery disease, left ventricular dysfunction, prior myocardial infarction, or atrial fibrillation.
- **Rule out or manage secondary causes of hyperlipidaemia.**
- **Consider familial conditions** if suggested by clinical features.
- **When prescribing a fibrate for a person with renal impairment:**
  - Consider seeking specialist advice before adjusting the dose of a fibrate in renal impairment.
  - Modified-release preparations of fibrates are contraindicated in people with renal impairment. Use standard preparations and start at low doses. Increase dose slowly, while carefully monitoring lipid levels, CK, AST or ALT and renal function (e.g. every 4 weeks).
- **Stop fibrate treatment if:**
  - Serum creatinine increases progressively.
  - There is a strong suspicion of myopathy, or CK level >5 times upper limit of normal.
  - Myalgic symptoms persist despite a normal CK level — a trial off treatment may be needed.
  - AST or ALT level persists above 3 times upper limit of normal.

Practical prescribing points

For further information please see the *Medicines Compendium* (www.medicines.org.uk) or the *British National Formulary* (www.bnf.org).

- **Hepatotoxicity is rare,** but is thought to be dose-dependent.
- **Advise people to report muscle pain, aches, or cramps.** Withdraw statin while checking CK level. (A non-significant increase in CK is common.)
- **Myopathy is rare, but the risk is increased in the presence of:**
  - Renal impairment, hypothyroidism, alcohol abuse, underlying muscle disorders, or age >70 years.
  - Co-prescription of statins with fibrates (do not use gemfibrozil), or nicotinic acid (>1 g).

H

- A past history of myopathy with any lipid-lowering drug.
- **Warfarin and fibrates:** reduce the dose of warfarin by about a third and make further adjustments according to changes in the international normalized ratio.

Follow-up advice

Monitoring fibrate therapy

- **Advise the person to report any muscular pains immediately.** Check the CK level.
- **Discontinue fibrate if** there is a strong suspicion of myopathy, if CK exceeds 5 times upper limit of normal range, if transaminases *persist* above 3 times upper limit of normal range, or if serum creatinine continues to rise progressively.
- **12 weeks after starting:** check fasting serum lipid profile and AST or ALT. Dose titration is not possible for most fibrates — the starting dose is the usual maintenance dose.
- **Annual checks:** fasting serum lipid profile, AST or ALT, and serum creatinine.
- **If the person has renal impairment,** consider specialist referral before starting treatment with a fibrate. Titrate the dose slowly, while carefully monitoring lipid levels, CK, AST or ALT and renal function (e.g. every 4 weeks).

Should I refer or investigate?

Refer?

- Consider referral to a specialist lipid clinic if the target cholesterol or triglyceride level is not reached at maximum tolerated titration.
- Other options include assessing compliance, changing to a statin, or using combination therapy.
- A prescription for combination therapy is not available through PRODIGY, as it is often initiated in secondary care. (The risk of myopathy is increased if a statin and a fibrate are used together.)

Investigate?

- Once stabilized, review annually with fasting lipid profile, AST or ALT, and serum creatinine.

Patient information leaflets

The following PILs are available at www.prodigy.nhs.uk

- Blood Test - General
- British Heart Foundation
- British Nutrition Foundation
- Cholesterol
- Cholesterol - A Summary
- Eat More Fruit and Vegetables
- Healthy Eating
- Healthy Lifestyle - Five Choices
- Weight Reduction - A Summary
- Weight Reduction - How to Lose Weight

Shared decision making

- The dose of your medicine needs adjusting.
- Most people who take these medicines have no side effects. A few people may experience mild side effects. These include mild upset stomach or gut, itching or a rash. Tell your doctor immediately if you have any muscle pains.
- Continue with the dietary advice previously given.
- Drink alcohol in moderation, exercise regularly, and do not smoke.
- If you have diabetes or high blood pressure or are taking any medicines for other conditions, be sure to follow advice for keeping these conditions under best possible control.

Drug rationale

Drugs not included

- This scenario is for the management of fibrate therapy: other classes of lipid lowering drugs are therefore not included.

Drugs included

- Maintenance doses/dose adjustments are offered for bezafibrate, ciprofibrate, fenofibrate, and gemfibrozil.
- A non-drug prescription giving diet and lifestyle advice is also offered.

Prescriptions

Non-drug management

Advice only: diet and lifestyle

- Age from 16 years onwards
- Your cholesterol level is high. Lifestyle and dietary changes can sometimes reduce the cholesterol level and other risk factors for heart disease. You should aim to eat and live healthily. This means: No smoking. Regular exercise. Moderate alcohol consumption. Lose weight if you are overweight or obese. MORE vegetables, fruit, cereals, wholegrain bread, poultry, fish, rice, skimmed or semi-skimmed milk, grilled food, lean meat, pasta etc. LESS fatty meats, fatty cheeses, full cream milk, fried food, lard, etc. If you do fry, choose a vegetable oil such as sunflower or rapeseed. Use low fat spreads. Add less salt to food, and avoid foods that are very salty. Have your cholesterol level checked again in 3 months time.

Step-up fenofibrate (mild/moderate renal impairment)

Fenofibrate 67mg once a day

- Age from 16 years onwards
- Fenofibrate 67mg capsules. Take one capsule once a day; supply 30 capsules; NHS Cost £7.77.

Fenofibrate 67mg twice a day

- Age from 16 years onwards
- Fenofibrate 67mg capsules. Take one capsule twice a day; supply 60 capsules; NHS Cost £15.53.

Fenofibrate 67mg three times a day

- Age from 16 years onwards
- Fenofibrate 67mg capsules. Take one capsule three times a day; supply 90 capsules; NHS Cost £23.30.

Step-up gemfibrozil (mild/moderate renal impairment)

Gemfibrozil 300mg twice a day

- Age from 16 years onwards
- Gemfibrozil 300mg capsules. Take one capsule twice a day; supply 56 capsules; NHS Cost £12.14.

Gemfibrozil 300mg three times a day

- Age from 16 years onwards
- Gemfibrozil 300mg capsules. Take one capsule three times a day; supply 84 capsules; NHS Cost £18.21.

Gemfibrozil 600mg twice a day

- Age from 16 years onwards
- Gemfibrozil 600mg tablets. Take one tablet twice a day; supply 56 tablets; NHS Cost £19.79.

Table 1: Classification of the common primary hyperlipidaemias (units are in mmol/l).

Hypercholesterolaemia
Common hypercholesterolaemia — Polygenic; TC >6.5, LDL-C >4.0, TG <2.3
Familial hypercholesterolaemia — Autosomal dominant; TC >7.5, LDL-C >5.0, TG <2.3
Hypertriglyceridaemia: *Moderate*: TG >2.3 and <5; *Severe*: TG >5 and <10; *Very severe*: TG >10
Non-familial hypertriglyceridaemia
Familial hypertriglyceridaemia
Familial lipoprotein lipase deficiency
Familial apolipoprotein C-II deficiency
Combined hypertriglyceridaemia and hypercholesterolaemia
Non-familial combined hyperlipidaemia — TC >7.0, LDL-C >4.0, HDL-C <1.0, TG >3.5
Familial combined hyperlipidaemia — TC >7.0, LDL-C >5.0, HDL-C <1.0, TG >3.5
Familial Type III hyperlipoproteinaemia — TC >8.0, TC >TG >5.0

Note: the lipid levels in the table are a guide to the patterns found in the dyslipidaemias. Diagnosis is made by taking into account the person's sex, age, ethnic origin, family history, and physical findings, and other laboratory tests such as apolipoproteins. Desirable levels of serum cholesterol and LDL-C are specified in the National Service Framework for Coronary Heart Disease.
TC = total cholesterol
LDL-C = low-density lipoprotein cholesterol
TG = triglycerides
HDL-C = high-density lipoprotein

Step-up ciprofibrate (mild/moderate renal impairment)

Ciprofibrate 100mg on alternate days
- Age from 16 years onwards
- Ciprofibrate 100mg tablets. Take one tablet on alternate days; supply 14 tablets; NHS Cost £7.36.

Ciprofibrate 100mg once a day
- Age from 16 years onwards
- Ciprofibrate 100mg tablets. Take one tablet once a day; supply 28 tablets; NHS Cost £14.72.

Fibrate maintenance doses (normal renal function)

Bezafibrate 400mg m/r once a day
- Age from 16 years onwards
- Bezafibrate 400mg m/r tablets. Take one tablet once a day; supply 30 tablets; NHS Cost £8.70.

Bezafibrate 200mg three times a day
- Age from 16 years onwards
- Bezafibrate 200mg tablets. Take one tablet three times a day; supply 84 tablets; NHS Cost £8.24.

Ciprofibrate 100mg once a day
- Age from 16 years onwards
- Ciprofibrate 100mg tablets. Take one tablet once a day; supply 28 tablets; NHS Cost £14.72.

Fenofibrate 160mg m/r once a day (equiv to 200mg std daily)
- Age from 16 years onwards
- Fenofibrate 160mg m/r tablets. Take one tablet once a day; supply 28 tablets; NHS Cost £14.75.

Fenofibrate 200mg once a day (equivalent to 160mg m/r daily)
- Age from 16 years onwards
- Fenofibrate 200mg capsules. Take one capsule once a day; supply 28 capsules; NHS Cost £17.95.

Fenofibrate 267mg capsules
- Age from 16 years onwards
- Fenofibrate 267mg capsules. Take one capsule once a day; supply 28 capsules; NHS Cost £21.00.

Gemfibrozil 600mg twice a day
- Age from 16 years onwards
- Gemfibrozil 600mg tablets. Take one tablet twice a day; supply 56 tablets; NHS Cost £19.79.

Extended Information

Background information

- What is it? p.951
- How common is it? p.951
- How do I know my patient has hyperlipidaemia? p.951
- Does my patient have a familial dyslipidaemia? p.952
- What else might it be? p.952
- Complications and prognosis p.952

What is it?

- **Hyperlipidaemia** is the term used to denote raised serum levels of one or more of the lipids: total cholesterol (TC), low-density lipoprotein cholesterol, or triglycerides (TG), or both TC and TG (combined hyperlipidaemia).
- **Dyslipidaemia** is a wider term that also includes low levels of high-density lipoprotein cholesterol.
- **It is not a simple matter to define what is a high, normal, or low serum lipid level.** Lipid levels in an individual vary from day to day, and the distribution of lipid levels varies with age, sex, ethnicity, and country (e.g. average cholesterol levels in Japan are very low compared with levels in the UK) [Durrington, 1995].

H

How common is it?

- **The UK population has one of the highest average serum cholesterol levels in the world.** Two-thirds of people have a serum cholesterol level greater than 5.2 mmol/l. For men aged between 45 and 75 years, the median serum cholesterol is 6.2 mmol/l. For women aged 45–55 years, it is 6.1 mmol/l, and it is 6.8 mmol/l for women aged over 55 years.
- **Low levels of high-density lipoprotein cholesterol** can occur as an isolated abnormality, but they frequently occur with raised triglyceride levels (e.g. in familial combined hyperlipidaemia, and in dyslipidaemia in Type 2 diabetes).
- **Familial hypercholesterolaemia** is the most important clinical syndrome leading to premature coronary heart disease (CHD). Heterozygous familial hypercholesterolaemia is one of the most common familial conditions, with a prevalence of about 1 in 500. (Homozygous familial hypercholesterolaemia is rare, and is not considered here.)
- **Familial combined hyperlipidaemia** is more common than heterozygous familial hypercholesterolaemia, occurring in about 1 in 100 people. People with familial combined hyperlipidaemia tend to develop CHD later in life than do those with familial hypercholesterolaemia.

[Bild et al, 1993; Durrington, 1995; Wood et al, 1998; Defesche, 2000]

How do I know my patient has hyperlipidaemia?

- **Table 1 shows the classification** of common hyperlipidaemias in the UK.
- Hyperlipidaemia increases a person's risk of coronary heart disease (CHD), and hyperlipidaemia is treated in order to lower this risk.
- **Lipid levels, on their own, are a poor predictor of CHD outcome.** Therefore, treatment in the UK is targeted towards those at highest risk of CHD. See *Who should be treated for hyperlipidaemia?*

[Bild et al, 1993; Durrington, 1995; Wood et al, 1998; DH, 2000]

Does my patient have a familial dyslipidaemia?

Familial hypercholesterolaemia

- **Tendon xanthomata are virtually diagnostic** of heterozygous familial hypercholesterolaemia. However, they may not be apparent in younger people. Their prevalence increases with age. About 30% of all people with heterozygous familial hypercholesterolaemia have tendon xanthomata; 50% have some sign of hyperlipidaemia.
- **Xanthelasma and premature corneal arcus are also commonly found,** but are not specific for familial hypercholesterolaemia.
- **Measure fasting serum lipids if any of the following is present:**
  - Family history of premature coronary heart disease (CDH), hyperlipidaemia, or tendon xanthomata, OR
  - Personal history of premature cardiovascular disease, or tendon xanthomata, OR
  - Corneal arcus in people under 45 years
- **Refer for assessment if:**
  - Suggestive family history, personal history, or physical examination AND
  - Total cholesterol above 7.5 mmol/l or low-density lipoprotein cholesterol above 4.9 mmol/l (in adults)

[Bild et al, 1993; Durrington, 1995; Simon Broome Register Group, 1999; Defesche, 2000]

Familial combined hyperlipidaemia

- **Familial combined hyperlipidaemia should be suspected** in an individual with moderate to severe mixed hyperlipidaemia (typically serum total cholesterol 6.5–8.0 mmol/l and serum triglycerides [TG] 2.3–5.0 mmol/l), AND a family history of hyperlipidaemia or premature CHD (not due to familial hypercholesterolaemia).
- **Screened family members** may be found to have isolated raised TG; mixed or lone hypercholesterolaemia; or hypertension with hypercholesterolaemia (familial dyslipidaemic hypertension).

[Durrington, 1995]

What else might it be?

- **Secondary causes of hyperlipidaemia** should be excluded or identified and managed, particularly if total serum cholesterol is greater than 6.5 mmol/l, or serum triglycerides exceed 8.0 mmol/l.
- Important causes of secondary hyperlipidaemia are listed in Table 2.

[Stone, 1994; Durrington, 1995]

Table 2: Important causes of secondary hyperlipidaemia.

Lipid abnormality	Cause
Hypercholesterolaemia	Hypothyroidism Obstructive jaundice Anorexia nervosa Nephrotic syndrome Drugs*: ciclosporin
Hypertriglyceridaemia	Hepatitis, hepatobiliary disease Alcohol abuse Diabetes mellitus Drugs*: isotretinoin, oral contraceptives (oestrogens), high doses of beta-blockers, anion-exchange resins Pregnancy Obesity Renal failure
Combined hypertriglyceridaemia and hypercholesterolaemia	Drugs*: oral contraceptives (progestogens and oestrogens), corticosteroids, high doses of thiazides Pregnancy Multiple myeloma Conditions that predominately cause hypertriglyceridaemia can also result in combined hyperlipidaemia in some individuals (e.g. Type 2 diabetes mellitus, obesity)

Secondary causes should (usually) be addressed first and then the need for specific lipid-lowering therapy reassessed.
* If a drug is thought to be the cause of clinically significant hyperlipidaemia, review the indications for the drug, and consider alternative treatments, or reduction of dose. Consider also the addition of a lipid-lowering diet with or without lipid-lowering drug therapy.

Complications and prognosis

Raised serum cholesterol

- **About 46% of deaths due to coronary heart disease (CHD) may be attributable to raised serum cholesterol** [Magnus and Beaglehole, 2001].
- **CHD is a leading cause of death in the UK.** One in four deaths in men, and one in six deaths in women, are due to CHD [British Heart Foundation, 2003].
- **People with heterozygous familial hypercholesterolaemia** have a fourfold increased risk of CHD. Men are at greater risk than women are, and, if untreated, 50–75% will have a myocardial infarction by the age of 60 years.
- **People with familial combined hyperlipidaemia** also have an increased risk of CHD, but CHD usually only manifests after 60 years of age.
- **Lipid-lowering therapy reduces the risk of CHD in high-risk individuals.** Clinical trials have shown reductions of about 30% in relative risk of CHD events and 20% for relative risk of death.

[Bild et al, 1993; Durrington, 1995; Simon Broome Register Group, 1999; Defesche, 2000]

Raised serum triglycerides

- **A raised serum triglyceride (TG) level is an independent risk factor for CHD,** but because it is subject to huge biological variation, it makes a poor predictor of CHD outcome. People with both raised total cholesterol (TC) and raised TG are at greater risk of CHD than are people who just have raised TC.
- **Very severe hypertriglyceridaemia (more than 10 mmol/l) is a risk factor for pancreatitis.** The most common associations of very severe hypertriglyceridaemia and pancreatitis are in:
  - Diabetes mellitus
  - Alcohol abuse
  - Pregnancy
  - Adverse effects of drugs (see list in Table 2)

[Durrington, 1995]

Decreased serum high-density lipoprotein

- Decreased levels of serum high-density lipoprotein cholesterol (HDL-C) are also an independent risk factor for CHD. A 0.026 mmol/l increase in HDL-C is associated with a relative risk reduction of 2% in men and 3% in women.

Management issues

- Who should be screened for hyperlipidaemia? p.953
- How do I calculate coronary heart disease risk? p.953
- Who should be treated for hyperlipidaemia? p.953
- Indications for specialist referral p.954
- Goals for lowering serum lipids p.954
- How should hyperlipidaemia be treated? p.955
- Dietary management of hyperlipidaemia p.955

- Measuring lipid levels and monitoring toxicity p.956
- Supporting evidence for statins p.956
- Supporting evidence for fibrates p.956
- Supporting evidence for other lipid-lowering agents p.957
- Medicines management: statins and fibrates p.957

Who should be screened for hyperlipidaemia?

- Raised serum cholesterol is an important risk factor for coronary heart disease (CHD). However, when it is used on its own, it is a relatively poor predictor of who will go on to have a CHD event — only 42% of those who will suffer a CHD event over 15 years will have a serum cholesterol greater than 6.5 mmol/l [NHS CRD, 1998].
- About 5% of the population currently have CHD. A further 3% of people aged 35–69 years have a 30% risk of a CHD event within 10 years.
- If the threshold is lowered to a 15% risk of a CHD event within 10 years, about 30% of men and 10% of women are at risk. A large proportion of the population is therefore at risk. Consequently, the *National Service Framework for Coronary Heart Disease* has prioritized who should be screened for hyperlipidaemia.
- **The decision to measure serum lipids therefore depends on the person's absolute risk of CHD.**
- **The first priority is people with established CHD, ischaemic stroke, transient ischaemic attack, or peripheral vascular disease.** These people are already at high risk of a further cardiovascular event.
- **The second priority** (once the first-priority people are being effectively managed) is people whose 10-year risk of CHD is greater than 30%, but who *do not* have CHD or other occlusive arterial disease.
  - Unselected screening of the whole population is not recommended.
  - Targeted screening should begin with people who have diabetes or hypertension.
- **The National Institute for Clinical Excellence (NICE) now recommends that all people with Type 2 diabetes should have their lipid levels checked annually** [NICE, 2002b].
- **Family screening and counselling of people with a familial dyslipidaemia is also important,** as these people have an increased risk of CHD [Durrington, 1995]. The National Screening Committee supports case-finding among relatives of familial hyperlipidaemia cases as a cost-effective strategy [Marks et al, 2000].

[DH, 2000]

What about people at lower risk of CHD?

- **It is not worthwhile to measure cholesterol concentrations in people whose risk, assuming that they have average values of serum cholesterol, is less than 15% over 10 years.** The reason for this is that very few people would have serum cholesterol levels so high (more than 3 standard deviations greater than the average) that they would qualify for treatment under current criteria (i.e. CHD risk over 10 years greater than 30%) [Robson et al, 2000].
- **For people without diabetes or occlusive vascular disease, and whose blood pressure is 140/85 mmHg or less, and whose cholesterol levels are average:**
  - Women do not exceed 15% 10-year risk for CHD even if they smoke. Therefore *in the absence of other risk factors*, women do not need to have lipid levels screened.
  - Men exceed 15% 10-year risk for CHD at 50 years if they smoke and at 60 years if they do not smoke.
- There is a case for screening these men whose 10-year risk of CHD is greater than 15%, but the NHS budget cannot yet support this level of prescribing [Robson et al, 2000].
- **If people with significant hyperlipidaemia and a 10-year CHD risk of over 15% are discovered opportunistically, they should be offered treatment.**

How do I calculate coronary heart disease risk?

- **Calculate 10-year coronary heart disease (CHD) risk using the Joint British Societies risk assessment charts** (printed at the back of the *British National Formulary*) or use the online calculator:
  - www.bhsoc.org/Cardiovascular_Risk_Charts_and_Calculators.htm
- **There are other CHD risk calculators available.** For further information, see the separate PRODIGY guidance on *Coronary heart disease risk — identification and management.*
- **If cholesterol results are not available,** use average values depending on age and sex.
- **If the calculated risk is greater than 15%, recalculate risk** with the averages of at least two (and preferably three) measurements of blood pressure (BP) and lipids.
- **Use baseline BP and lipid measurements for risk calculation** if the person is already on antihypertensive or lipid-lowering drugs.
- Note: antihypertensive drugs or lipid-lowering therapy should still be started (or continued) if modification of risk factors results in the calculated risk falling below the threshold for drug treatment. Such modification might reflect, for instance, that the person has quit smoking, or has started treatment for hypertension.
- **If lifestyle advice results in BP or lipid levels falling below treatment targets, drug treatment is not needed.** However, results should be re-checked annually, as they are likely to alter with time.
- **Certain individuals are at higher risk than the risk tools predict.** Higher risk occurs in:
  - Family history of premature CHD — adjust risk upwards by a factor of 1.5.
  - Familial dyslipidaemia (e.g. hypercholesterolaemia, familial combined hyperlipidaemia, or other inherited dyslipidaemia).
  - People with raised triglyceride levels.
  - Those who are not yet diabetic, but have impaired fasting glucose (6.1–6.9 mmol/l).
  - People with Type 1 diabetes. The risk is often greater than that predicted by the ratio of cholesterol to high-density lipoprotein cholesterol (HDL-C) in Type 1 diabetes. It may be more accurate to ignore HDL-C and use the lipid scale for total serum cholesterol alone, but there is no direct evidence for this approach.
  - Women with premature menopause.
  - People having the lowest incomes.
  - Increasing age. Risk increases exponentially with age, so the risk will be closer to the next age category on the risk prediction charts for the last four years of each decade.
  - People of south Asian descent, i.e. originating from the Indian subcontinent (the risk charts have not been validated in ethnic minority populations).
- **CHD risk-assessment tools should be used to supplement, not replace, clinical judgement.**

[Wood et al, 1998]

Who should be treated for hyperlipidaemia?

- **The decision to treat hyperlipidaemia depends on both the lipid profile and the 10-year risk of coronary heart disease (CHD).**

H

Table 3: Who should be offered treatment for hyperlipidaemia?

10-year risk of CHD	Treat hyperlipidaemia if:
Established CHD	TC >5.0 mmol/l, LDL-C >3.0 mmol/l, or TG >2.3 mmol/l
>30% but no CHD	TC >5.0 mmol/l, LDL-C >3.0 mmol/l, or TG >2.3 mmol/l
<30%	Most people are at lower risk of CHD. Only consider treatment for hyperlipidaemia if familial hypercholesterolaemia is suspected (e.g. TC >7.5 mmol/l *and* physical signs of hyperlipidaemia or family history of premature CHD — refer for specialist assessment).
15–30% and diabetes	TC >5.0 mmol/l, LDL-C >3.0 mmol/l, or TG >2.3 mmol/l
-	TG >10 mmol/l (refer for specialist assessment)

CHD = coronary heart disease TC = total cholesterol TG = triglycerides

- Table 3 outlines who should be offered treatment for hyperlipidaemia.

[DH, 2000; NICE, 2002b]

- **There is a case for lowering lipid levels in people with established CHD and in people who are at high risk of CHD, whatever their baseline lipid level.** The Heart Protection Study recently found that lowering low-density lipoprotein cholesterol (LDL-C) levels by 1 mmol/l from 4 mmol/l to 3 mmol/l reduced the risk of CHD by about 25% [Heart Protection Study Collaborative Group, 2002]. This result is close to the 30% reduction in cardiovascular risk achieved by previous studies, all of which had higher baseline cholesterol levels (generally between 5.5 mmol/l and 7 mmol/l) [LaRosa et al, 1999].
- **These findings are also supported by the ASCOT-LLA study,** which again found that lowering LDL-C levels by 1 mmol/l from 3.4 mmol/l to 2.3 mmol/l in people at high risk of CHD reduced the risk of CHD by 36% [Sever et al, 2003].
- **The findings of these studies are not reflected in the National Service Framework for Coronary Heart Disease and National Institute for Clinical Excellence (NICE) guidelines** on prior myocardial infarction [DH, 2000; NICE, 2002a]. There are significant financial implications of implementing this policy. Consider seeking local primary care trust advice.

Additional information

- **Management decisions should be based on the average of at least two measurements** (three if possible), because lipid levels are subject to variation. The second sample should preferably be taken after a few weeks. TC and high-density lipoprotein cholesterol (HDL-C) can be determined from a non-fasting sample. LDL-C and triglycerides (TG) require a fasting specimen.
- **People with both raised TC and raised TG are at greater risk of CHD** than are people who just have raised TC.
- **Very severe isolated hypertriglyceridaemia** (fasting serum TG levels greater than 10 mmol/l) should be treated to reduce the risk of pancreatitis.
- **A low HDL-C level is a strong predictor of CHD.** The ratio of TC to HDL-C is a more accurate predictor of risk than is serum TC level (and the ratio is used in the risk calculations). However, it is no longer used on its own as a treatment threshold for hyperlipidaemia. For instance, someone with a TC greater than 5 mmol/l (and who is at high risk of CHD) should be offered lipid-lowering treatment, even if the ratio of TC to HDL-C is satisfactory.

Table 4: Treatment targets for different baseline total cholesterol levels.

Baseline total cholesterol	Treatment goal
6.5 mmol/l or above	5 mmol/l
6 mmol/l	4.5 mmol/l
5.5 mmol/l	4.1 mmol/l
5 mmol/l	3.8 mmol/l

- **The combination of raised LDL-C, low HDL-C (less than 1 mmol/l), and raised TG levels appears to be particularly atherogenic.** This combination is often found in people with Type 2 diabetes.
- **Diabetes increases the risk of developing and dying from heart disease** by two- to five-fold. This finding is reflected in the recent NICE guideline *Management of Type 2 diabetes — management of blood pressure and blood lipids*. The guideline recommends that people with Type 2 diabetes who have a 10-year CHD risk greater than 15% and a serum TC greater than 5 mmol/l should be offered treatment [NICE, 2002b].
- **People with Type 1 diabetes** often have raised HDL-C, but unusually this does not seem to protect against CHD.
- **Clinical judgement should be used when interpreting specified action thresholds, limits, and typical levels.**

[Durrington, 1995; DH, 2000; NICE, 2002b]

Indications for specialist referral

Referral is usually appropriate in cases of:

- **Suspected familial hypercholesterolaemia,** i.e. when the person has total cholesterol (TC) greater than 7.5 mmol/l (or low-density lipoprotein cholesterol [LDL-C] greater than 4.9 mmol/l) AND at least one of the following:
  - Tendon xanthomata in himself/herself or in a first- or second-degree relative.
  - Family history of premature coronary heart disease (CHD).
  - Family history of TC greater than 7.5 mmol/l.
- **Suspected familial combined hyperlipidaemia,** i.e. the individual has a mixed hyperlipidaemia and a family history of hyperlipidaemia or premature CHD.
- **Failure of therapy:** failure to meet target lipid reduction despite maximally tolerated therapy.
- **Severe hypercholesterolaemia:** initial TC greater than 10 mmol/l.
- **Very severe hypertriglyceridaemia:** triglycerides greater than 10 mmol/l.

Goals for lowering serum lipids

- Although the Heart Protection Study may ultimately alter the threshold for treatment, the goals of treatment remain the same:
  - **Total serum cholesterol** — aim to lower by 20–25% of baseline or to below 5.0 mmol/l, whichever would result in the lower level.
  - **Serum low-density lipoprotein cholesterol** — aim to lower by 30% of baseline or to below 3.0 mmol/l, whichever would result in the lower level.
- Treatment targets are outlined in Table 4.
- **Serum triglycerides (TG) level** — aim to lower below 2.3 mmol/l if serum TG level is raised.
- Few studies examine the effect on cardiovascular risk of raising high-density lipoprotein cholesterol (HDL-C) levels. Generally, HDL-C less than 1 mmol/l is considered to be low.
- Note: the target for audit recommended by the National Service Framework for Coronary Heart Disease is total cholesterol less than 5 mmol/l.

[DH, 2000]

How should hyperlipidaemia be treated?

- **All people with hyperlipidaemia should be given diet and lifestyle advice** to reduce hyperlipidaemia and the risk of coronary heart disease (CHD). This advice should be followed as an adjunct to drug treatment.
- **Advice should be personalized** and cover Mediterranean diet, weight, exercise, stopping smoking, and moderate alcohol consumption. For further information about lifestyle advice, see the separate PRODIGY guidance on *Coronary heart disease risk — identification and management.*
- **Hypercholesterolaemia:** statins are the treatment of choice for hypercholesterolaemia. Statins reduce cardiovascular risk by about 30% in people with established CHD. Adherence to treatment is essential to reduce this risk; benefit is not substantial until after 1–2 years of statin therapy. Evidence from the major statin trials is summarized in Table 6.
- **Combined hyperlipidaemia** (raised cholesterol and raised triglycerides): statins are the treatment of choice for combined hyperlipidaemia when triglycerides (TG) are moderately raised (i.e. in the range 2.3–5 mmol/l).
- **For combined hyperlipidaemia with levels of TG above 5.0 mmol/l** there is uncertainty about the best management. Choices are to use a fibrate or a statin. Simvastatin, atorvastatin, fluvastatin, and rosuvastatin are currently licensed for combined hyperlipidaemia. Statins at high doses can achieve reductions in TG approaching that of fibrates, and many feel that the evidence best supports the use of statins in the prevention of CHD. However, fibrates achieve greater reductions in TG and greater increases in high-density lipoprotein cholesterol.
- **Hypertriglyceridaemia:** again, a statin can be used if the level is less than 5 mmol/l. Otherwise a fibrate or a statin can be used.
- **Very severe isolated hypertriglyceridaemia** (fasting serum TG levels greater than 10 mmol/l) should be treated to reduce the risk of pancreatitis. Someone with this condition should be prescribed a fibrate and referred for specialist assessment. Fibrates, nicotinic acid, acipimox, and omega-3 fatty acids are the usual treatments considered in secondary care.

[Durrington, 1995; DH, 2000; NICE, 2002b]

Should I use a 3-month trial of dietary management before starting drug treatment?

- **Dietary management can reduce baseline lipid levels by 1–5%.** It can be effective as a sole treatment in a small number of well-motivated people [NHS CRD, 1998].
- **Someone with established CHD, ischaemic stroke, transient ischaemic attack, peripheral vascular disease, or a familial dyslipidaemia should be started on treatment** (with a statin) as soon as possible. A trial of dietary management before treatment is not necessary, because the person is at high risk of further CHD events. However, dietary management should still be used in conjunction with statins to reduce lipid levels.
- A statin is often prescribed before discharge for people admitted with unstable angina or myocardial infarction. Although cholesterol lowering takes 1–2 years before it reduces CHD risk, studies have found that long-term use of statins improves outcomes if they are prescribed on discharge [Fonarow and Ballantyne, 2001]. If someone with a recent myocardial infarction was not started on a statin while an in-patient, wait 6 weeks before checking lipid levels. (Lipid levels decrease in people after acute myocardial infarction and take about 6 weeks to return to baseline levels.)
- **Other people with a 10-year CHD risk of over 30% (but no CHD) may benefit from a 3-month trial of dietary management.** A short delay in initiating therapy is unlikely to have measurable effects on a chronic disease such as CHD. However, it would be reasonable to start treatment earlier, particularly if cholesterol levels are very high.
- **People whose 10-year risk of CHD is less than 30%** are at lower risk of a CHD event occurring. For those who require treatment (e.g. suspected familial hypercholesterolaemia), a 3-month trial of dietary management is recommended — a short delay in initiating therapy is unlikely to have measurable effects on a chronic disease such as CHD.

[Durrington, 1995; Wood et al, 1998; DH, 2000; NICE, 2002b;]

Is there an age limit for offering treatment?

- **There is no upper age limit for offering treatment.** Until the Heart Protection Study, trials included few people over the age of 70 years. Previous guidelines have recommended age limits of 70 or 75 years for initiation of statin therapy. However, the Heart Protection Study provides evidence that statin drugs reduce the risk of developing CHD irrespective of age, sex, or cholesterol level [Heart Protection Study Collaborative Group, 2002].

How long should people be treated for?

- **Benefit from statins does not become substantial until after 1–2 years of therapy.**
- The National Service Framework for Coronary Heart Disease recommends that treatment be continued indefinitely, given the absence of studies on stopping treatment with lipid-lowering drugs [DH, 2000].
- Long-term (up to 8 years) treatment with statins produces sustained benefits [LIPID Study Group, 2002].

What is the place of over-the-counter simvastatin?

- Some people may wish to buy simvastatin over the counter for *primary prevention* of CHD. Simvastatin 10 mg at night can be bought by people with a 10–15% CHD risk over 10 years. This applies to:
  - All men aged 55 years and over.
  - Men aged 45–55 and women aged over 55 who have a family history of CHD, are smokers, are obese, or are of south Asian descent.
- People with CHD or diabetes cannot buy simvastatin over the counter and will be referred back to their GP by the pharmacist.
- Higher doses of simvastatin cannot be bought from a pharmacy.

Does hormone replacement therapy prevent CHD?

- **Hormone replacement therapy (HRT) has *not* been shown to be beneficial** in preventing CHD in women both with and without CHD. In fact, studies have shown a slight tendency to *increased rates* of CHD in women with 1–2 years of treatment with HRT.
- **HRT should not be initiated for prevention of CHD,** and consideration should be given to stopping HRT after any cardiovascular disease event [CSM, 2002b].

Dietary management of hyperlipidaemia

- **As dietary management alone results in only small reductions in cholesterol levels (1–5%), it is generally most useful as an adjunct to drug treatment** [NHS CRD, 1998].
- **However, people should be advised to adopt a healthier overall diet,** as up to 30% of all deaths from coronary heart disease (CHD) have been attributed to unhealthy

diets. The focus should not just be on reducing fat intake [MeReC, 2002].

- **A Mediterranean diet** contains many of the dietary elements that are thought to be protective in CHD [British Heart Foundation, 1999]:
  - Replace butter with olive oil and mono-unsaturated margarine (e.g. based on rape-seed or olive oil).
  - Eat less red meat (replace beef, lamb, and pork with poultry).
  - Eat more fish, including at least one portion of oily fish per week (e.g. mackerel, herring, kipper, pilchard, sardine, salmon, or trout).
  - Eat more bread (especially whole-grain bread).
  - Eat more root vegetables and green vegetables.
  - Eat fruit every day.
- **Also encourage people to eat fewer commercial bakery and deep-fried foods (these contain high levels of sugar and trans-fats), and to aim to eat five portions of fruit and vegetables every day.** Note: tinned and frozen fruit and vegetables are as good as fresh vegetables. A glass of fruit juice also counts as a portion.
- **Margarine containing sitostanol ester may help some people** reduce the cholesterol intake from their diet. It has been shown to reduce total cholesterol by about 10% when substituted for part of the daily fat intake. Adding 2 g of plant sterol to an average daily portion of margarine reduces serum low-density lipoprotein cholesterol by an average of 0.54 mmol/l in people aged 50–59, 0.43 mmol/l in people aged 40–49, and 0.33 mmol/l in those aged 30–39 [Law, 2000].
- **The place of margarine containing sitostanol ester in the management of people with hypercholesterolaemia is uncertain.** There are no randomized controlled trials with clinical outcome data, and there is limited information on safety. It is an option as part of a cholesterol-lowering diet, although its cost could deter some people.

H

Measuring lipid levels and monitoring toxicity

- **Serum lipid measurements are subject to biological variation** and ideally require at least three measurements (with a minimum of two) to assess their true mean levels.
- **Levels of triglyceride (TG) are raised by fat in recent meals.** Therefore, a fasting TG result is needed to calculate low-density lipoprotein cholesterol (LDL-C) levels accurately.
- Levels of serum total cholesterol (TC), LDL-C, and high-density lipoprotein cholesterol (HDL-C) decrease in people with acute myocardial infarction and take about 6 weeks to return to baseline levels.
- Table 5 outlines how to monitor for response to treatment and for toxicity.

[Wood et al, 1998]

Other tests

- Assays of apolipoproteins are increasingly used for assessment and monitoring, because apolipoprotein B is more reliable than LDL-C and does not require fasting.
- Genetic tests are used when investigating familial dyslipidaemias, but these tests are usually done in specialist clinics.

Supporting evidence for statins

- **Statins are potent low-density lipoprotein cholesterol (LDL-C) cholesterol-lowering agents.** They have shown clear benefit in trials of both primary and secondary prevention of coronary heart disease (CHD).
- **Statins inhibit the enzyme HMG-CoA reductase.** This inhibition limits the synthesis of cholesterol and increases the numbers of LDL-C receptors. Statins also decrease triglyceride (TG) levels, and this is in proportion to their cholesterol-lowering effect. Most statins reduce LDL-C by 25–45%, and total cholesterol by 20–40% at *maximum* doses. TG are lowered by 10–30%. High-density lipoprotein cholesterol (HDL-C) is increased by 5–10%, but the change can be less in those with very low initial levels of HDL-C [Probstfield and Brunzell, 1998].
- **Lipid-lowering therapy reduces the risk of CHD in high-risk individuals.** A systematic review of clinical trials has shown reductions of about 30% in relative risk of CHD events, and 20% for relative risk of death [LaRosa et al, 1999].
- **Four statins on the UK market have been shown in randomized controlled trials (RCTs) to improve a variety of clinical outcomes.** Simvastatin, pravastatin, and atorvastatin have been shown in large RCTs to reduce deaths from all causes. Fluvastatin given to people after their first percutaneous coronary intervention has been shown to reduce the risk of major adverse coronary events. Illustrative results in terms of NNTs have been calculated from reports of the major trials of the statins, and are summarized in Table 6.
- Early trials of statins selected mostly mature men under the age of 75 years with raised lipid levels. The Heart Protection Study and a recent systematic review [LaRosa et al, 1999] provide good evidence that:
  - The protective effect of statins extends to women, older, and younger people.
  - Statins are protective against CHD, even at low baseline cholesterol levels.
  - Statins also protect against cerebrovascular disease and peripheral vascular disease.
  - Statins are safe when prescribed under conditions where clinicians and users are alert to the possibility of adverse events such as rhabdomyolysis. (However, continued surveillance is always necessary with a new product to determine its safety when used without the close supervision that a clinical trial provides.)
- Until recently there was no data on clinical outcomes with atorvastatin. However, the recent GREACE study found that atorvastatin prevented more CHD events than did 'usual care' in people with established CHD [Athyros et al, 2002]. In addition, the ASCOT-LLA study found that more CHD events were prevented by atorvastatin than by placebo in people with hypertension and at least three additional risk factors for CHD [Sever et al, 2003].
- **Rosuvastatin is the latest addition to the UK statin market.** Rosuvastatin 10 mg has been shown to lower LDL-C more than do atorvastatin 10 mg, simvastatin 20 mg, or pravastatin 20 mg after 12–52 weeks of treatment [Brown et al, 2002; Olsson et al, 2002; Blasetto et al, 2003]. Both rosuvastatin and the comparator statins were well tolerated. We have found no studies assessing the impact of rosuvastatin on clinical end points.
- Note: the outcome 'death from all causes' shown in Table 6 was chosen for illustrative purposes because it is a conservative measure of overall benefit. Other outcomes such as 'major adverse coronary event' have lower NNTs, but exclude possible adverse events from the intervention.

Supporting evidence for fibrates

- **Fibrates have a much smaller effect on low-density lipoprotein cholesterol (LDL-C) cholesterol than do statins, but have a greater effect on triglyceride (TG) and high-density lipoprotein cholesterol (HDL-C) levels.** They reduce LDL-C by 7–11% and TG by 20–35%, and increase HDL-C by 10–15%. Greater reductions in TG (40–60%) may be seen in people with moderate to severe hypertriglyceridaemia [Probstfield and Brunzell, 1998].

- **Fibrates are mainly used to treat significant hypertriglyceridaemia.** Fibrates may also have a role in treating people with low HDL-C, those who cannot tolerate statins, and people with combined hyperlipidaemia with significantly raised TG levels.
- **Fibrates have been shown on systematic review to improve outcome in people with hyperlipidaemia.** However, the evidence is not as strong as that from statin trials [Gould et al, 1998; NHS CRD, 1998; Wood et al, 1998].
- **Gemfibrozil** has been shown to improve clinical outcome in one large primary prevention study, the Helsinki Heart Study. NNTs were calculated from the published data: 592 to prevent one death (not statistically significant) and 71 to prevent one major cardiovascular event [Frick et al, 1987].
- **Conversely, bezafibrate** was not found to reduce mortality in another large secondary prevention study, which recruited people with raised LDL-C. Subgroup analysis identified a significant risk reduction in people with raised TG levels, but this requires confirmation [BIP Study Group, 2000].
- **There are several fibrate trials currently in progress,** which should clarify the place of fibrates in the management of hyperlipidaemia. An angiographic study using fenofibrate to correct dyslipidaemia in Type 2 diabetes found that fenofibrate, compared with placebo, was associated with less angiographic progression in coronary artery stenosis [Diabetes Atherosclerosis Intervention Study Investigators, 2001]. The Fenofibrate Intervention and Event Lowering in Diabetes (FIELD) study, which is designed to assess clinical endpoints, should provide additional useful evidence.

Supporting evidence for other lipid-lowering agents

- **Ezetimibe** is a novel cholesterol absorption inhibitor that prevents the absorption of dietary and biliary cholesterol without affecting the absorption of triglycerides (TG) or fat-soluble vitamins. Unlike bile-acid sequestrants, it does not affect the absorption of other drugs.
- Ezetimibe monotherapy lowers low-density lipoprotein cholesterol (LDL-C) by about 15–20%. Addition of ezetimibe to simvastatin, atorvastatin, and pravastatin therapy increased LDL-C reductions at all doses of statin used. Simvastatin 10 mg plus ezetimibe 10 mg produced a 44% reduction in LDL-C, similar to that of simvastatin 80 mg alone [Davidson et al, 2002]. Ezetimibe was well tolerated in clinical studies; however, it is a novel compound, and a black triangle drug, and so post-marketing data are needed to confirm this. It effects on clinical end points has not yet been assessed.
- **Omega-3 polyunsaturated fatty acids** (omega-3 PUFAs) reduce serum TG levels, and can therefore be a useful adjunct in the treatment of hypertriglyceridaemia. They can increase LDL-C levels, so both LDL-C and TG levels should be monitored. A large number of capsules are needed for a therapeutic dose, which may not be acceptable to some. (The daily dose of Omacor is 4 capsules a day, while for Maxepa it is 10 capsules per day.) Breath and burps that smell of fish are a relatively common 'adverse effect'.
- Omega-3 PUFAs have also been shown to reduce the risk of death in men who have survived a myocardial infarction. Studies have found a 15–30% reduction in the risk of death, mostly accounted for by a reduction in sudden deaths [GISSI-Prevenzione Investigators, 1999; Ness et al, 2002]. It is thought that they reduce the risk of sudden death by preventing cardiac arrhythmias, and stabilizing atherosclerotic plaques [Hu and Willett, 2002].
- There are many dietary sources of omega-3 PUFAs, including oily fish, canola oil, flaxseed oil, walnuts, and leafy green vegetables.
- **Anion-exchange resins** prevent reabsorption of bile acids. Consequently, the liver is forced to convert cholesterol into new bile acids, thereby increasing the amount of LDL-C removed from circulation by the liver. These resins are very inconvenient to take, and are therefore reserved as adjunctive therapy for people who are unable to achieve target lipid levels on the maximum tolerated dose of a statin.
- **High doses of nicotinic acid** can produce large increases in high-density lipoprotein cholesterol, as well as lowering cholesterol and TG levels. However, it is rarely used because of its adverse effects, especially vasodilation [BNF 44, 2002].

Medicines management: statins and fibrates

Which statin?

- **Five statins are licensed in the UK** for prevention of coronary heart disease (CHD) and/or treatment of hyperlipidaemia: atorvastatin, fluvastatin, pravastatin,

Table 5: Monitoring response to treatment and toxicity [Pasternak et al, 2002].

Timescale	Tests	
Initial screening		Non-fasting TC and HDL-C
Pretreatment	Baseline lipid profile	Fasting full lipid profile: TC, LDL-C, HDL-C and TG
	Baseline tests for toxicity	Creatine kinase (CK) AST or ALT Creatinine (only needed if using a fibrate)
	Exclude hypothyroidism as a secondary cause	Thyroid simulating hormone (TSH)
8–12 weeks after the start of treatment OR an increase in dose	Lipid levels Liver function tests	Usually non-fasting TC and HDL-C* AST or ALT
Annually	Lipid levels Liver function tests	Usually non-fasting TC and HDL-C* AST or ALT
If muscle symptoms suspected	Check CK	CK

TC = total cholesterol
LDL-C = low-density lipoprotein cholesterol
TG = triglycerides
HDL-C = high-density lipoprotein
ALT = alanine aminotransferase
AST = aspartate aminotransferase
*If LDL-C or TG levels are needed, a fasting sample must be taken.

Table 6: Summary of evidence from the major trials of statins for an outcome 'death from all causes'.

Study/reference	Size	Drug	Dose	Prevention aim	NNT
WOSCOPS [PROSPER study group, 2002]	6595	pravastatin	40 mg	primary	45 (over 4.9 years)
AFCAPS/TexCAPS [AF/TexCAPS, 1998]	6605	lovastatin	20–40 mg	primary	-
4S [Pedersen et al, 1998]	4444	simvastatin	20–40 mg	secondary	30 (over 5.4 years)
CARE [Sacks et al, 1996]	4159	pravastatin	40 mg	secondary	128 (over 5 years)
LIPID [LIPID Study Group, 1998]	9014	pravastatin	40 mg	secondary	33 (over 6.1 years)
Systematic review of above studies [LaRosa et al, 1999]	30817	statins	—	primary + secondary	61 (over 5 years)
Heart Protection Study Collaborative Group, 2002	20536	simvastatin	40 mg	high-risk primary + secondary	57 (over at least 5 years)
GREACE [Athyros et al, 2002]	1600	atorvastatin	10–80 mg	secondary	47 (over 3 years)
ASCOT-LLA [Sever et al, 2003]	10305	atorvastatin	10 mg	primary	200 (over 3.3 years)
FLARE [Serruys et al, 1999]	1054	fluvastatin	40 mg twice a day	secondary	—
LIPS [Serruys et al, 2002]	1677	fluvastatin	40 mg twice a day	secondary	62 (over 3.9 years)

rosuvastatin, and simvastatin. Simvastatin and pravastatin have the most solid body of evidence for efficacy and safety (see Table 6).
- A recent cross-sectional survey of 17 UK general practices found that more people were likely to achieve a total cholesterol of less than 5 mmol/l if they were taking atorvastatin or simvastatin [Hippisley-Cox et al, 2003]. Note: this study was conducted before the launch of rosuvastatin.

What starting dose?

The rationale for selecting the starting dose depends on the risks and benefits of several alternative strategies.
- **The 'evidence-based dose' strategy** uses the doses used in the major trials as the starting dose. The rationale is that the best evidence of efficacy is for these doses (i.e. atorvastatin 10–20 mg, fluvastatin 80 mg, pravastatin 40 mg, and simvastatin 20–40 mg). Note: for fluvastatin and pravastatin the evidence-based doses are the maximum licensed doses.
- **The 'fire and forget' strategy** aims to use only the starting doses of a statin in all individuals whose CHD risk over 10 years is more than 15%, i.e. to give lower doses to more people [PROSPER study group, 2002]. Once the statin is prescribed, people are expected to return for assessment only if they have symptoms or worries. Advantages include significantly lower total costs and smaller demands on resources such as primary care clinician time. Disadvantages include the lack of trial evidence to support the safety and efficacy of the strategy — reduced monitoring may lead to increased rates of toxicity and non-adherence to treatment.
- **The 'titrate to target' strategy** uses lower starting doses to minimize the risk of toxicity. Many people will not need a higher dose to achieve treatment targets of cholesterol; and doubling the dose only reduces cholesterol levels by a further 5–6%. The National Service Framework for Coronary Heart Disease currently recommends this approach [DH, 2000; Shepherd, 2002].
- **In the absence of other specific UK guidance, we recommend the following starting doses:** atorvastatin 10 mg, fluvastatin 40 mg, pravastatin 40 mg, and simvastatin 20 mg.
- Lower starting doses should be considered for people at increased risk of myopathy (see below).
- Higher starting doses could be considered in younger, large, otherwise healthy people with high cholesterol levels.

Tolerability of statins and fibrates

- **Gastrointestinal adverse effects are the most common** adverse effects, but rarely require treatment to stop.
- **Hepatotoxicity is rare,** and is thought to be dose-dependent. Progression to liver failure specifically due to statins occurs exceedingly rarely, if ever [Pasternak et al, 2002]. Reversal of transaminase elevation is frequently noted with a reduction in dose, and elevations do not often recur with either re-challenge or selection of another statin.
- **Non-specific muscle aches or joint pains are common.** Advise anyone starting a statin or fibrate that it is important to report muscle symptoms (pain, tenderness, soreness) without delay.
- **Measure serum creatine kinase (CK) if muscle symptoms occur.** (Regular monitoring of serum CK is unnecessary.) Fortunately, the increase in CK is not usually significant.
- **Myositis and rhabdomyolysis associated with statins and fibrates is rare** (approximately 1 case in every 100,000 treatment years). Although the exact mechanism is unclear, it appears to be a dose-dependent effect.
- (Note: the start dose of rosuvastatin must not exceed 10 mg. The 40 mg dose is contraindicated in people with predisposing factors for myopathy, and also in people of Asian descent [due to increased bioavailability in this group of people].)
- **The Committee on the Safety of Medicines advises that the risk of myopathy is increased:**
  - In the presence of underlying muscle disorders, renal impairment, untreated hypothyroidism, alcohol abuse, or age over 70 years.
  - When statins are co-prescribed with other lipid-lowering drugs, e.g. fibrates (e.g. gemfibrozil, fenofibrate), or nicotinic acid.

- If there is a past history of myopathy with any lipid-lowering drug.
- With co-prescrition of drugs that increase simvastatin or atorvastatin levels. (Avoid other drugs that inhibit cytochrome P450 CYP3A4, see *Significant interactions* below.)

- **If CK is more than 5 times the upper limit of normal at baseline, do not start treatment.**
- **Withold treatment** until the CK level has been investigated if the individual reports muscle pain, muscle weakness, or cramps.
- **Stop fibrate/statin treatment if:**
  - Serum creatinine increases progressively (with fibrates).
  - Strong suspicion of myopathy, or CK level greater than 5 times upper limit of normal.
  - Myalgic symptoms persist despite a normal CK level — a trial off treatment may be necessary.
  - Alanine aminotransferase (ALT) or aspartate aminotransferase (AST) level persists above 3 times upper limit of normal.
- **Consider seeking specialist advice if symptoms and elevated CK levels do not rapidly return to normal.**

[CSM, 2001; CSM, 2002a; Pasternak et al, 2002; CSM, 2004]

Significant interactions

- **Warfarin and fibrates:** reduce the dose of warfarin by about a third and make further adjustments according to changes in the international normalized ratio (INR) [Stockley, 1999].
- **Warfarin and simvastatin, fluvastatin, or rosuvastatin:** monitor INR closely until stable — the INR *occasionally* increases significantly with these statins.
- **Statins and cytochrome P450 interactions:** simvastatin and atorvastatin are metabolised by cytochrome P450 CYP3A4. Inhibition of this enzyme can increase the plasma levels of these statins, and therefore increase the risk of dose-related adverse effects, including rhabdomyolysis. Fluvastatin is metabolised by a different cytochrome P450 enzyme (CYP2C9), and pravastatin and rosuvastatin are not substantially metabolised by cytochrome P450 [CSM, 2004].
  - **Potent inhibitors of CYP3A4:** avoid azole antifungals (itraconazole and ketoconazole); macrolide antibiotics (erythromycin, clarithromycin, telithromycin); and HIV protease inhibitors. If co-prescribing ciclosporin, do not exceed simvastatin 10 mg. In addition, advise people taking simvastatin or atorvastatin to avoid grapefruit juice.
  - **Less potent inhibitors of CYP3A4:** do not exceed simvastatin 20 mg with verapamil or amiodarone. Do not exceed simvatatin 40 mg with diltiazem. Also exercise caution if using atorvastatin with these drugs.
  - **Other metabolic interactions:** if co-prescribing gemfibrozil or nicotinic acid (>1 g per day), do not exceed simvastatin 10 mg, and use atorvastatin with caution.

References

NHS staff in England can link, free of charge, from references to full text journals by clicking on [Full text] on the PRODIGY website.

1. AF/TexCAPS (1998) Primary prevention of acute coronary events with lovastatin in men and women with average cholesterol levels: results of Air Force/ Texas Coronary Atherosclerosis Prevention Study. *Journal of the American Medical Association* **279**(20), 1615–1622. [Full text]
2. Athyros, V.G., Papageorgiou, A.A., Mercouris, B.R. et al (2002) Treatment with atorvastatin to the national cholesterol educational program goal versus 'usual' care secondary coronary heart disease prevention. The Greek atorvastatin and coronary-heart-disease evaluation (GREACE) study. *Current Medical Research & Opinion* **18**(4), 220–228. [Full text]
3. Bild, D.E., Williams, R.R., Brewer, B. et al (1993) Identification and management of heterozygous familial hypercholesterolaemia: summary and recommendations from an NHLBI workshop. *American Journal of Cardiology* **72**(10), 1D-5D.
4. BIP Study Group (2000) Secondary prevention by raising HDL cholesterol and reducing triglycerides in patients with coronary artery disease: the Bezafibrate Infarction Prevention (BIP) study. *Circulation* **102**(1), 21–27. [Full text]
5. Blasetto, J.W., Stein, E.A., Brown, W.V. et al (2003) Efficacy of rosuvastatin compared with other statins at selected starting doses in hypercholesterolemic patients and in special population groups. *American Journal of Cardiology* **91**(5A), 3C-10C.
6. BNF 44 (2002) *British National Formulary*. 44th edn. London: British Medical Association and Royal Pharmaceutical Society of Great Britain.
7. British Heart Foundation (1999) *Fish, fruit, vegetables and mediterranean diet*. Factfile 2/1999. British Heart Foundation. www.bhf.org.uk [Accessed: 12/01/2003].
8. British Heart Foundation (2003) *Coronary heart disease statistics 2003*. British Heart Foundation. www.heartstats.org//datapage.asp?id=1652 [Accessed: 07/02/2003].
9. Brown, W.V., Bays, H.E., Hassman, D.R. et al (2002) Efficacy and safety of rosuvastatin compared with pravastatin and simvastatin in patients with hypercholesterolemia: a randomized, double-blind, 52-week trial. *American Heart Journal* **144**(6), 1036–1043.
10. CSM (2001) Cerivastatin (Lipobay) withdrawn. *Current Problems in Pharmacovigilance* **27**(Aug), 9.
11. CSM (2002a) HMG CoA reductase inhibitors (statins) and myopathy. *Current Problems in Pharmacovigilance* **28**(Oct), 8.
12. CSM (2002b) New product information for hormone replacement therapy. *Current Problems in Pharmacovigilance* **28**(April), 1–2.
13. CSM (2004) Statins and cytochrome P450 interactions. *Current Problems in Pharmacovigilance* **30**(Oct), 1–2.
14. Davidson, M.H., McGarry, T., Bettis, R. et al (2002) Ezetimibe coadministered with simvastatin in patients with primary hypercholesterolemia. *Journal of the American College of Cardiology* **40**(12), 2125–2134.
15. Defesche, J.C. (2000) Familial hypercholesterolaemia. In: Betteridge, D.J. (Ed.) *Lipids and vascular disease: current issues*. London: Martin Dunitz. 65–76.
16. DH (2000) *National service framework for coronary heart disease*. Department of Health. www.dh.gov.uk [Accessed: 15/07/2005]. [Full text]
17. Diabetes Atherosclerosis Intervention Study Investigators (2001) Effect of fenofibrate on progression of coronary-artery disease in type 2 diabetes: the diabetes atherosclerosis intervention study, a randomised study. *Lancet* **357**(9260), 905–910. [Full text]
18. Durrington, P.N. (Ed.) (1995) *Hyperlipidaemia: diagnosis and management*. 2nd edn. Oxford: Butterworth-Heinemann.
19. Fonarow, G.C. and Ballantyne, C.M. (2001) In-hospital initiation of lipid-lowering therapy for patients with coronary heart disease: the time is now. *Circulation* **103**(23), 2768–2770. [Full text]

H

20. Frick, M.H., Elo, O., Haapa, K. et al (1987) Helsinki Heart Study: primary-prevention trial with gemfibrozil in middle-aged men with dyslipidemia. Safety of treatment, changes in risk factors, and incidence of coronary heart disease. *New England Journal of Medicine* **317**(20), 1237–1245.
21. GISSI-Prevenzione Investigators (1999) Dietary supplementation with n-3 polyunsaturated fatty acids and vitamin E after myocardial infarction: results of the GISSI-Prevenzione trial. *Lancet* **354**(9177), 447–445. [Full text]
22. Gould, A.L., Rossouw, J.E., Santanello, N.C. et al (1998) Cholesterol reduction yields clinical benefit: impact of statin trials. *Circulation* **97**(10), 946–952. [Full text]
23. Heart Protection Study Collaborative Group (2002) MRC/BHF heart protection study of cholesterol lowering with simvastatin in 20536 high-risk individuals: a randomised placebo-controlled trial. *Lancet* **360**(9326), 7–22. [Full text]
24. Hippisley-Cox, J., Cater, R., Pringle, M. and Coupland, C. (2003) Cross-sectional survey of effectiveness of lipid lowering drugs in reducing serum cholesterol concentration in patients in 17 general practices. *British Medical Journal* **326**(7391), 689–693. [Full text]
25. Hu, F.B. and Willett, W.C. (2002) Optimal diets for prevention of coronary heart disease. *Journal of the American Medical Association* **288**(20), 2569–2578. [Full text]
26. LaRosa, J.C., Jiang, H.E. and Vupputuri, S. (1999) Effect of statins on risk of coronary disease. *Journal of the American Medical Association* **282**(24), 2340–2346. [Full text]
27. Law, M. (2000) Plant sterol and stanol margarines and health. *British Medical Journal* **320**(7238), 861–864. [Full text]
28. LIPID Study Group (1998) Prevention of cardiovascular events and death with pravastatin in patients with coronary heart disease and a broad range of initial cholesterol levels. The long-term intervention with pravastatin in ischaemic disease. *New England Journal of Medicine* **339**(19), 1349–1357. [Full text]
29. LIPID Study Group (2002) Long-term effectiveness and safety of pravastatin in 9014 patients with coronary heart disease and average cholesterol concentrations: the LIPID trial follow-up. *Lancet* **359**(9315), 1379–1387. [Full text]
30. Magnus, P. and Beaglehole, R. (2001) The real contribution of the major risk factors to the coronary epidemics: time to end the "only-50%" myth. *Archives of Internal Medicine* **161**(22), 2657–2660. [Full text]
31. Marks, D., Wonderling, D., Thorogood, M. et al (2000) Screening for hypercholesterolaemia versus case finding for familial hypercholesterolaemia: a systematic review and cost-effectiveness analysis. *Health Technology Assessment* **4**(29), 1–129.
32. MeReC (2002) Lifestyle measures to reduce cardiovascular risk. *MeReC Briefing* **19**(July), 1–8.
33. Ness, A.R., Hughes, J., Elwood, P.C. et al (2002) The long-term effect of dietary advice in men with coronary disease: follow-up of the Diet and Reinfarction trial (DART). *European Journal of Clinical Nutrition* **56**(6), 512–518.
34. NHS CRD (1998) Cholesterol and coronary heart disease: screening and treatment. *Effective Health Care Bulletin* **4**(1), 1–16.
35. NICE (2002a) *Audit of the management of post-MI patients in primary care.* National Institute for Clinical Excellence. www.nice.org.uk [Accessed: 04/11/2002].
36. NICE (2002b) *Management of type 2 diabetes – management of blood pressure and blood lipids.* Inherited clinical guideline H. National Institute for Clinical Excellence. www.nice.org.uk [Accessed: 28/01/2003].
37. Olsson, A.G., Istad, H., Luurila, O. et al (2002) Effects of rosuvastatin and atorvastatin compared over 52 weeks of treatment in patients with hypercholesterolemia. *American Heart Journal* **144**(6), 1044–1051.
38. Pasternak, S., Smith, S.C., Bairey-Merz, C.N. et al (2002) ACC/AHA/NHLBI clinical advisory on the use and safety of statins. *Journal of the American College of Cardiology* **40**(3), 568–573.
39. Pedersen, T.R., Olsson, A.G., Faergeman, O. et al (1998) Lipoprotein changes and reduction in the incidence of major coronary heart disease events in the Scandinavian Simvastatin Survival Study (4S). *Circulation* **97**(15), 1453–1460. [Full text]
40. Probstfield, J.L. and Brunzell, J.D. (1998) Use of lipid lowering agents in the prevention of cardiovascular disease. In: Yusuf, S., Cairns, J.A., Camm, A.J. et al (Eds.) *Evidence based cardiology*. London: BMJ Books. 206–225.
41. PROSPER study group (2002) Pravastatin in elderly individuals at risk of vascular disease (PROSPER): a randomised controlled trial. *Lancet* **360**(9346), 1623–1630. [Full text]
42. Robson, J., Boomla, K., Hart, B. and Feder, G. (2000) Estimating cardiovascular risk for primary prevention: outstanding questions for primary care. *British Medical Journal* **320**(7236), 702–704. [Full text]
43. Sacks, F.M., Pfeffer, M.A., Moye, L.A. et al (1996) The effect of pravastatin on coronary events after myocardial infarction in patients with average cholesterol levels. The Cholesterol and Recurrent Events trial investigators (CARE). *New England Journal of Medicine* **335**(14), 1001–1009. [Full text]
44. Serruys, P.W., Foley, D.P., Jackson, G. et al (1999) A randomized placebo-controlled trial of fluvastatin for prevention of restenosis after successful coronary balloon angioplasty; final results of the fluvastatin angiographic restenosis (FLARE) trial. *European Heart Journal* **20**(1), 58–69.
45. Serruys, P.W., de Feyter, P., Macaya, C. et al (2002) Fluvastatin for prevention of cardiac events following successful first percutaneous coronary intervention: a randomized controlled trial. *Journal of the American Medical Association* **287**(24), 3215–3222. [Full text]
46. Sever, P.S., Dahlof, B., Poulter, N.R. et al (2003) Prevention of coronary and stroke events with atorvastatin in hypertensive patients who have average or lower-than-average cholesterol concentrations, in the Anglo-Scandinavian Cardiac Outcomes Trial – Lipid Lowering Arm (ASCOT-LLA): a multicentre randomised controlled trial. *Lancet* **361**(9364), 1149–1158. [Full text]
47. Shepherd, J. (2002) Resource management in prevention of coronary heart disease: optimising prescription of lipid-lowering drugs. *Lancet* **359**(9325) 2271–2273. [Full text]
48. Shepherd, J., Cobbe, S.M., Ford, I. et al (1995) Prevention of coronary heart disease with pravastatin in men with hypercholesterolemia. The West of Scotland Coronary Prevention Study (WOSCOPS). *New England Journal of Medicine* **333**(20), 1301–1308.
49. Simon Broome Register Group (1999) Mortality in treated heterozygous familial hypercholesterolaemia: implications for clinical management. *Atherosclerosis* **142**(1), 105–112.
50. Stein, A.A., Lane, M. and Laskarzewski, P. (1998) Comparison of statins in hypertriglyceridemia. *American Journal of Cardiology* **81**(4A), 66B-69B.

51. Stockley, I.H. (Ed.) (1999) *Drug interactions*. 5th edn. London: The Pharmaceutical Press.
52. Stone, N.J. (1994) Secondary causes of hyperlipidemia. *Medical Clinics of North America* 78(1), 117–141.
53. Wood, D., Durrington, D., Poulter, N. et al (1998) Joint British recommendations on prevention of coronary heart disease in clinical practice. *Heart* 80(Suppl 2), S1-S29. [Full text]

H

PRODIGY GUIDANCE

Hypertension

Last revised in July 2005
www.prodigy.nhs.uk/guidance.asp?gt=Hypertension

Applies to people over the age of 16 years

This guidance covers the management of hypertension in people without diabetes. It is based on both the NICE (2004) and the BHS (2004) management guidelines. The guidance also includes evidence from recently published systematic reviews and meta-analyses.
This guidance contains information which has been adapted by PRODIGY from guidelines produced by NICE, with the intention of disseminating and facilitating its implementation. However, NICE has not checked the information to confirm that it does accurately reflect and implement the guidelines and therefore no guarantees are given either by NICE or PRODIGY in this regard.

This guidance does not cover the management of hypertension in people with diabetes, hypertension in children, hypertension during pregnancy, or malignant hypertension (hypertensive crises).

There is separate PRODIGY guidance on *Hypertension in pregnancy, Diabetes Type 1 and 2 — hypertension, Coronary heart disease risk — identification and management, Hyperlipidaemia, Obesity and Smoking cessation.* This guidance may require calculation of cardiovascular risk.

H

Goals

- To identify people with hypertension
- To treat hypertension adequately to reduce the risk of cardiovascular morbidity and mortality
- To identify other cardiovascular risk factors and manage them as appropriate

Contents

Scenarios

- 140–159/90–99 mmHg — initiate treatment? p.962
- 160/100 mmHg or more — initiate treatment p.966
- Change to or add thiazide p.969
- Change to, increase, or add beta-blocker p.971
- Change to, increase, or add ACE inhibitor p.972
- Change to, increase, or add calcium-channel blocker p.975
- Change to, increase, or add alpha-blocker p.977
- Intolerant of ACE inhibitor p.979
- Aspirin — who to treat? p.981

Extended Information, p. 982

Which scenario?

- **140–159/90–99 mmHg — initiate treatment?:** provides advice on how to decide whether to treat with antihypertensive medication and which drug to use.
- **160/100 mmHg or more — initiate treatment:** covers the management of people with a blood pressure (BP) of 160/100 mmHg or more.
- **Change to or add thiazide:** a thiazide-type diuretic is best combined with angiotensin-converting enzyme (ACE) inhibitors or beta-blockers; generally the preferred monotherapy choice, particularly for people 55 years and over.
- **Change to, increase, or add beta-blocker:** beta-blockers are best combined with thiazides or calcium-channel blockers (CCBs) (not verapamil); a preferred choice if there is angina or a history of myocardial infarction (MI), and may be considered in people with heart failure under close specialist supervision.
- **Change to, increase, or add ACE inhibitor:** ACE inhibitors are best combined with thiazides or CCBs; a preferred choice in heart failure, left ventricular dysfunction, Type 1 or Type 2 diabetic nephropathy, or chronic renal disease (usually following specialist advice). Some ACE inhibitors are also used in post MI and in established heart failure.
- **Change to, increase, or add calcium-channel blocker:** CCBs are best combined with ACE-inhibitors or beta-blockers (but never verapamil); dihydropyridine CCBs are an alternative to thiazides in elderly people; rate-limiting CCBs are an alternative to beta-blockers in people with angina.
- **Change to, increase, or add alpha-blocker:** alpha-blockers have a role in more resistant hypertension as an option in someone already on three antihypertensive drugs; they can be added to any major class of antihypertensive. Alpha-blockers may be especially useful in men with prostatism.
- **Intolerant of ACE inhibitor:** covers the initiation of an angiotensin-II receptor antagonist (AIIRA) as an alternative to an ACE inhibitor.
- **Aspirin — who to treat?:** provides advice on when to consider aspirin in people with hypertension.

140–159/90–99 mmHg — initiate treatment?

Which therapy?

General

- **Assess BP at two or more subsequent consultations if an initial BP measurement is raised.**
  - Check two readings at each visit.
  - Measurements should normally be made at monthly intervals.
  - Measure more frequently if BP is very high (e.g. systolic >=180 or diastolic >=110).
- **Important lifestyle interventions that reduce BP** — regular exercise, weight reduction, healthy diet, limiting alcohol, coffee and salt intake and relaxation.
- **Identify and treat cardiovascular risk factors** as appropriate, such as hyperlipidaemia and smoking (see separate PRODIGY guidance on *Hyperlipidaemia and Smoking cessation*).
- **Start drug treatment in people with sustained BP of 140/90 mmHg or more if:**
  - There is any complication of hypertension or target organ damage.
  - The 10-year cardiovascular disease (CVD) risk is >=20%. Calculate CVD risk using the Joint British

Societies risk charts www.bhsoc.org/Cardiovascular_Risk_Charts_and_Calculators.htm or the back of the BNF www.bnf.org.

- **A thiazide-type diuretic** is generally the drug of choice for people of any age or ethnic origin.
- **A beta-blocker** is an alternative option for people <55 years old.

Factors affecting preferred choice of treatment

- **Afro-Caribbean people:** a thiazide-type diuretic is preferred, but a calcium-channel blocker (CCB) is an alternative option.
- **Age >=55 years old: a thiazide-type diuretic is preferred** and a long-acting dihydropyridine CCB is an alternative option.
- **Angina:** a beta-blocker is preferred, but either a long-acting dihydropyridine or a rate-limiting CCB is an alternative option if a beta-blocker is not tolerated or contraindicated.
- **Asthma or a history of bronchospasm:** do not use beta-blockers (Committee on Safety of Medicines warning).
- **Diabetes:** see separate PRODIGY guidance on *Diabetes Type 1 and 2 — hypertension.*
- **Gout:** generally avoid using a thiazide-type diuretic — if one is necessary, consider prophylaxis with allopurinol (see separate PRODIGY guidance on *Gout*).
- **Heart failure, left ventricular dysfunction:** an angiotensin-converting enzyme (ACE) inhibitor is the first choice or if not tolerated an angiotensin-II receptor antagonist (AIIRA).
- **Isolated systolic hypertension: a thiazide-type diuretic is preferred** and a long-acting dihydropyridine CCB is an alternative option.
- **Post myocardial infarction (MI):** a beta-blocker is preferred, note: an appropriately licensed ACE inhibitor may be added in haemodynamically stable patients with LV dysfunction or heart failure.
- **Stroke secondary prophylaxis: combining a thiazide-type diuretic with an ACE is preferred.**

Practical prescribing points

For further information please see the *Medicines Compendium* (www.medicines.org.uk) or the *British National Formulary* (www.bnf.org).

Beta-blockers

- **Heart failure (HF):** if uncontrolled, generally avoid beta-blockers, except for bisoprolol and carvedilol which are licensed for use in stable HF; see the PRODIGY *Heart failure* guidance.
- **Depression, fatigue, and sexual dysfunction:** very small associations found in trial data.

ACE inhibitors

- **Avoid potassium-sparing diuretics or potassium supplements** (other than in exceptional cases e.g. low-dose spironolactone for severe heart failure) due to the risk of hyperkalaemia.
- **Monitor renal function carefully with** peripheral vascular disease (risk of renovascular disease) and raised serum creatinine.
- **The risk of either ACE inhibitor-induced or AIIRA-induced first-dose hypotension or renal impairment is increased in the following high-risk groups of people:**
  - Creatinine higher than 150 micromol/l
  - Urea higher than 12 mmol/l
  - Sodium less than 130 mmol/l
  - Systolic BP less than 100 mmHg
  - Diuretic dosage greater than furosemide (frusemide) 80 mg or bumetanide 2 mg daily
  - Known or suspected renal artery stenosis, for example if peripheral vascular disease
  - People aged 70 years and over or who are frail
  - Hypovolaemia
  - With unstable heart failure
  - Receiving high-dosage vasodilator treatment

Calcium-channel blockers (dihydropyridines)

- **Ankle swelling** (due to the vasodilatory action of dihydropyridines). Diuretics should not be routinely prescribed but they may help if there is marked oedema.
- **Facial flushing, headaches and palpitations** (often improves with continued use).

Calcium-channel blockers (rate limiting)

- **Verapamil:** never use with beta-blockers.
- **Diltiazem:** may cause bradycardia when used in combination with beta-blockers and careful monitoring is required, therefore use with caution.
- **Verapamil commonly causes constipation** (advise consuming more fluids and fibre).
- **Vasodilatory adverse effects** are less common with rate-limiting than dihydropyridine CCBs.

Concomitant use of drug formulations with a high sodium content

- Many effervescent drug formulations (e.g. compound analgesics) contain high sodium content. They should therefore be avoided where possible as they may aggravate hypertension. Note: soluble aspirin tablets have very low sodium content.

Follow-up advice

- **Advise lifestyle interventions whether treatment is started or not.**
- **If treatment is not started,** review annually to check BP, reassess CV risk and discuss lifestyle.
- **If treatment is started,** reassess response after an interval of at least 4 weeks, unless it is necessary to lower the BP more urgently.
  - **People receiving thiazides** need serum potassium checked within 4–6 weeks of start.
  - **People receiving ACE inhibitors** need monitoring of renal function, BP, and serum potassium) before and during treatment — within 1 week of starting and 1 week after each dosage increase to assess response to treatment.
  - **Check for adverse effects with an ACE** e.g. symptomatic hypotension, renal dysfunction, or hyperkalaemia i.e. if creatinine >=150 micromol /l, urea >=12 mmol/l, or potassium >=5.5 mmol/l, either stop or reduce the dose, and consider referral.
- **Optimum target BP** is =<140/90 mmHg (GMS contract audit standard is =<150/90 mmHg).
- **Once stable,** review annually and test urine for protein and blood as well as checking serum electrolytes and renal function (especially in people taking diuretics, ACE inhibitors or AIIRAs). More frequent review may be necessary in some people and other authorities would recommend at least a 6-monthly review.

Should I refer or investigate?

Refer?

Urgent assessment and treatment if:

- People present with signs of papilloedema and/or retinal haemorrhage or suspected phaeochromocytoma (possible signs include labile or postural hypotension, headache, palpitations, pallor and excess sweating).
- Impending cardiovascular complications, e.g. transient ischaemic attack (TIA), left ventricular failure.

Consider referral:

- In people <35 years of age where treatment is indicated to exclude a secondary cause.
- Where signs and symptoms suggest secondary causes of hypertension including:
  - Hypokalaemia/increased plasma sodium (Conn's syndrome?)
  - Elevated serum creatinine
  - Proteinuria or haematuria (after excluding urinary tract infection)
  - Sudden onset or worsening of hypertension
- Of people with documented postural hypotension (i.e. a fall in systolic BP when standing of >=20 mmHg) or symptoms of it, to a specialist.
- To a smoking cessation service where appropriate.
- Of people who do not reach targets or whose high-density lipoprotein cholesterol or triglyceride levels remain abnormal (e.g. <1.0 or >2.3 mmol/l, respectively).
- Of people with unusual BP variability.
- Where isolated clinic hypertension (white-coat hypertension) is a possibility: unless access is available to ambulatory BP monitoring or home monitoring and confidence in interpreting values (see section *How do I measure blood pressure?*).
- For secondary care initiation of an ACE inhibitor in high-risk groups; see section *Prescribing points*.

Investigate?

Recommended routine investigations include:

- Urine test strip to measure the presence of protein and blood.
- Blood sample to measure:
  - Plasma glucose (ideally fasted level).
  - Electrolytes.
  - Creatinine.
  - Serum total cholesterol and high-density lipoprotein. Note: fasting is only necessary where a triglyceride level is required.
- Electrocardiogram using a 12 lead electrocardiograph—to help exclude left ventricular hypertrophy.

Patient information leaflets

The following PILs are available at www.prodigy.nhs.uk

- Blood Pressure Association
- Blood Test - General
- Blood Test - Kidney Function
- High Blood Pressure - A Summary
- High Blood Pressure Foundation
- High Blood Pressure (Hypertension)
- High Blood Pressure - Medication
- Medicines - Name Changes of Medicines

Shared decision making

- The higher your blood pressure, the greater the risk of developing heart disease, a stroke, and kidney problems. You have mildly raised BP.
- You can lower your BP by:
  - **Losing weight** if you are overweight.
  - **Reducing your alcohol intake** if you drink a lot.
  - **A low salt diet.**
  - **Regular exercise** such as swimming, cycling, jogging, dancing, brisk walking, or anything that causes mild breathlessness. At least 30 minutes' exercise, at least five times a week, is best.
  - **Eating lots of fruit and vegetables** and a low-fat diet.
- **Smoking** makes the risk from high BP much worse.
- **If you have mildly raised BP:**
  - Regular checks is all that you need if other risk factors are low.
  - Medication may be advised if you also have other risk factors.
- **Various medicines** can lower BP. The one chosen depends on such things as whether you have other medical problems, whether you take other medication, your age, etc.

Drug rationale

Drugs not included

- **Fixed-dosage combinations** are not recommended when initiating treatment because they do not allow for flexible dosage titrations. In people taking multiple drugs, they may have a role in improving compliance by reducing the number of drugs.
- **Thiazide-type diuretics other than bendroflumethiazide (bendrofluazide)** are not included as they do not offer any significant advantages. There is good evidence for efficacy of chlortalidone at lowering BP and improving cardiovascular outcomes [ALLHAT Officers, 2002] but PACT data indicates that culturally there are few prescriptions for this in England and therefore clinicians are less familiar with the drug's profile.
- **Beta-blockers other than atenolol** have not been included. There is little to choose between them in terms of efficacy. Cardioselective agents are preferred because they have a better safety profile.
- **ACE inhibitors other than enalapril, lisinopril, perindopril, ramipril, and trandolapril** are not recommended. Captopril has a shorter half-life than other ACE inhibitors, it needs to be taken in divided doses, and is no longer recommended as a first-choice ACE inhibitor. Cilazapril, fosinopril, imidapril, moexipril, and quinapril are alternative options but there is less trial data of their use.
- **Angiotensin-II receptor antagonists (AIIRAs)** are not offered but may be used as an alternative to ACE inhibitors in people with a persistent ACE inhibitor-induced cough.
- **Dihydropyridine calcium-channel blockers (CCBs) other than nifedipine, felodipine and amlodipine** are not included. Short-acting and immediate-release formulations are associated with large variations in BP and reflex tachycardia.
- **Verapamil modified-release formulations** are expensive and have not been included.
- **Alpha-blockers** are generally used less often than the other classes of agent and so are not included in this scenario. See scenario *Change to, increase, or add alpha-blocker* for prescriptions.
- **Centrally acting antihypertensive drugs:** there is no evidence from large-scale trials to support use of centrally acting drugs (methyldopa, clonidine, or moxonidine, or older vasodilators, for example hydralazine and minoxidil) in the initial treatment of hypertension [N England Hypertension GDG, 2004].
- **Adrenergic neurone blocking drugs** are considered less suitable for prescribing and have largely fallen from use,

but may be necessary with other treatment in resistant hypertension [BNF 49, 2005].

Drugs included

- **Thiazide-type diuretics: bendroflumethiazide (bendrofluazide)** is the diuretic of choice in the UK and is cost-effective, safe, and well tolerated. It has a shallow dose response curve and therefore low-dose bendroflumethiazide should be used. Also low dosages cause little disturbance to glucose and lipids [Sweetman, 2002; BNF 49, 2005].
- **Beta-blockers: atenolol** is an effective, well established, inexpensive cardioselective beta-blocker which can be given once daily [BNF 49, 2005]. Atenolol 50 mg is the usual starting dose but a 25 mg dose might achieve a therapeutic response in some people. Despite recent controversy questioning the effectiveness of atenolol [Carlberg et al, 2004], it remains the beta-blocker of choice until more conclusive evidence proves otherwise.
- **ACE inhibitors: enalapril, lisinopril, perindopril, ramipril, and trandolapril are included.** They have comparable efficacy profiles, reputable safety records, and can be taken once a day.
    - Enalapril: people at risk of an excessive fall in BP after the initial dose may best start on 2.5 mg each day.
    - Ramipril: 1.25 mg each day may achieve a therapeutic response in some people, for others the dose should be increased every 1–2 weeks until the desired effect is achieved up to a maximum of 10 mg once a day.
    - Perindopril: people at risk of an excessive fall in BP after the initial dose may best start on 2 mg each day.
    - Trandolapril: 500 mcg each day may achieve a therapeutic response in some people, for others the dose should be increased incrementally every 2–4 weeks until the desired effect is achieved up to either a maximum of 4 mg once a day.
    - Note: initiation doses may differ to those offered in this scenario where ACE inhibitors are used in addition to a diuretic or in renal impairment.
    - All ACE inhibitors are licensed for the treatment of other cardiovascular morbidity (although starting regimens may different to those offered here).
- **Long-acting dihydropyridine calcium-channel blockers (CCBs): nifedipine, felodipine and amlodipine** are included. Nifedipine and amlodipine have both been studied in large double-blind RCTs [ALLHAT Officers, 2002] and felodipine featured in the HOT research [Hansson et al, 1998; Brown et al, 2000]. They are an alternative option to thiazide-type diuretics in elderly people and have evidence of improved outcomes in those with isolated systolic hypertension [Systolic Hypertension-Europe (Syst-Eur) Trial Investigators, 1997]. They have once-daily dosage regimens are also licensed for use in angina.
- **Rate-limiting CCBs: diltiazem and verapamil** are an option in those with angina. The diltiazem modified-release formulations offered are included by brand name because of potential problems caused by switching brands [BNF 49, 2005]. The least expensive, once-daily formulations in a range of strengths and dosages for use in hypertension are included.

Prescriptions

Start thiazide diuretic

Bendroflumethiazide (bendrofluazide) 2.5mg each morning
- Age from 16 years onwards
- Bendroflumethiazide 2.5mg tabs. Take one tablet each morning; supply 28 tablets; NHS Cost £1.17.

Start beta-blocker

Atenolol 25mg once a day
- Age from 16 years onwards
- Atenolol 25mg tablets. Take one tablet once a day; supply 28 tablets; NHS Cost £1.12.

Atenolol 50mg once a day
- Age from 16 years onwards
- Atenolol 50mg tablets. Take one tablet once a day; supply 28 tablets; NHS Cost £0.84.

Start ACE inhibitor

Enalapril 2.5mg once a day
- Age from 16 years onwards
- Enalapril 2.5mg tablets. Take one tablet once a day; supply 28 tablets; NHS Cost £0.95.

Enalapril 5mg once a day
- Age from 16 years onwards
- Enalapril 5mg tablets. Take one tablet once a day; supply 28 tablets; NHS Cost £1.28.

Lisinopril 2.5mg once a day
- Age from 16 years onwards
- Lisinopril 2.5mg tablets. Take one tablet once a day; supply 28 tablets; NHS Cost £1.17.

Ramipril: initial titration from 1.25mg to 2.5mg per day
- Age from 16 years onwards
- Ramipril 1.25mg capsules. Take one capsule once a day for 2 weeks, then take two capsules once a day; supply 42 capsules; NHS Cost £2.70.

Ramipril 1.25mg once a day
- Age from 16 years onwards
- Ramipril 1.25mg capsules. Take one capsule once a day; supply 28 capsules; NHS Cost £1.80.

Perindopril 2mg once a day
- Age from 16 years onwards
- Perindopril 2mg tablets. Take one tablet each morning on an empty stomach; supply 30 tablets; NHS Cost £10.95.

Perindopril 4mg once a day
- Age from 16 years onwards
- Perindopril 4mg tablets. Take one tablet each morning on an empty stomach; supply 30 tablets; NHS Cost £10.95.

Trandolapril: initial titration from 0.5mg to 1mg per day
- Age from 16 years onwards
- Trandolapril 500mcg capsules. Take one capsule once a day for 2 weeks, then take two capsules once a day; supply 42 capsules; NHS Cost £5.13.

Trandolapril 500micrograms once a day
- Age from 16 years onwards
- Trandolapril 500mcg capsules. Take one capsule once a day; supply 28 capsules; NHS Cost £3.42.

Start calcium-channel blocker (dihydropyridine)

Felodipine m/r 2.5mg each morning
- Age from 60 years onwards
- Felodipine 2.5mg m/r tablets. Take one tablet each morning; supply 28 tablets; NHS Cost £6.70.

Felodipine m/r 5mg each morning
- Age from 16 years onwards
- Felodipine 5mg m/r tablets. Take one tablet each morning; supply 28 tablets; NHS Cost £8.93.

Nifedipine m/r: Adalat LA 20mg each morning
- Age from 16 years onwards
- Adalat LA 20mg m/r tablets. Take one tablet each morning; supply 28 tablets; NHS Cost £5.27.

H

Nifedipine m/r: Adalat LA 30mg each morning
- Age from 16 years onwards
- Adalat LA 30mg m/r tablets. Take one tablet each morning; supply 28 tablets; NHS Cost £7.59.

Nifedipine m/r: Coracten XL 30mg each morning
- Age from 16 years onwards
- Coracten XL 30mg m/r capsules. Take one capsule each morning; supply 28 capsules; NHS Cost £6.06.

Amlodipine 5mg once a day
- Age from 16 years onwards
- Amlodipine 5mg tablets. Take one tablet once a day; supply 28 tablets; NHS Cost £8.89.

Start calcium-channel blocker (rate-limiting)

Diltiazem m/r: Slozem 120mg once a day
- Age from 60 years onwards
- Slozem 120mg m/r capsules. Take one capsule once a day; supply 28 capsules; NHS Cost £7.00.

Diltiazem m/r: Slozem 180mg once a day
- Age from 16 years onwards
- Slozem 180mg m/r capsules. Take one capsule once a day; supply 28 capsules; NHS Cost £7.80.

Diltiazem m/r: Slozem 240mg once a day
- Age from 16 years onwards
- Slozem 240mg m/r capsules. Take one capsule once a day; supply 28 capsules; NHS Cost £8.20.

Diltiazem m/r: Viazem XL 120mg once a day
- Age from 60 years onwards
- Viazem XL 120mg capsules. Take one capsule once a day; supply 28 capsules; NHS Cost £6.60.

Diltiazem m/r: Viazem XL 180mg once a day
- Age from 16 years onwards
- Viazem XL 180mg capsules. Take one capsule once a day; supply 28 capsules; NHS Cost £7.36.

Verapamil 120mg twice a day
- Age from 16 years onwards
- Verapamil 120mg tablets. Take one tablet twice a day; supply 56 tablets; NHS Cost £3.14.

160/100 mmHg or more — initiate treatment

Which therapy?

General

- **Advise about lifestyle interventions that reduce BP** — regular exercise, weight reduction, healthy diet, limiting alcohol, coffee and salt intake and relaxation.
- **Identify and treat cardiovascular risk factors** as appropriate, such as hyperlipidaemia and smoking (see separate PRODIGY guidance on *Hyperlipidaemia and Smoking cessation*).
- **Treat all people with sustained systolic BPs of 160 mmHg or more, or diastolic BPs of 100 mmHg or more, or both.**
  - **A thiazide-type diuretic** is generally the drug of choice for people of any age or ethnic origin.
  - **A beta-blocker** is an alternative option for people <55 years old.

Factors affecting preferred choice of treatment

- **Afro-Caribbean people:** a thiazide-type diuretic is preferred, but a calcium-channel blocker (CCB) is an alternative option.
- **Age >=55 years old:** a thiazide-type diuretic is preferred and a long-acting dihydropyridine CCB is an alternative option.
- **Angina:** a beta-blocker is preferred, but either a long-acting dihydropyridine or a rate-limiting CCB is an alternative option if a beta-blocker is not tolerated or contraindicated.
- **Asthma or a history of bronchospasm:** do not use beta-blockers (Committee on Safety of Medicines warning).
- **Diabetes:** see separate PRODIGY guidance on *Diabetes Type 1 and 2 — hypertension.*
- **Gout:** generally avoid using a thiazide-type diuretic — if one is necessary, consider prophylaxis with allopurinol (see separate PRODIGY guidance on *Gout*).
- **Heart failure, left ventricular dysfunction:** an angiotensin-converting enzyme (ACE) inhibitor is the first choice or if not tolerated an angiotensin-II receptor antagonist (AIIRA).
- **Isolated systolic hypertension:** a thiazide-type diuretic is preferred and a long-acting dihydropyridine CCB is an alternative option.
- **Post myocardial infarction (MI):** a beta-blocker is preferred, note: an appropriately licensed ACE inhibitor may be added in haemodynamically stable patients with LV dysfunction or heart failure.
- **Stroke secondary prophylaxis:** combining a thiazide-type diuretic with an ACE is preferred.

Practical prescribing points

For further information please see the *Medicines Compendium* (www.medicines.org.uk) or the *British National Formulary* (www.bnf.org).

Beta-blockers

- **Heart failure (HF):** if uncontrolled, generally avoid beta-blockers, except for bisoprolol and carvedilol which are licensed for use in HF; see the PRODIGY guidance on *Heart failure.*
- **Depression, fatigue, and sexual dysfunction:** very small associations found in trial data.

ACE inhibitors

- **Avoid potassium-sparing diuretics or potassium supplements** (other than in exceptional cases e.g. low-dose spironolactone for severe heart failure) due to the risk of hyperkalaemia.
- **Monitor renal function carefully with** peripheral vascular disease (risk of renovascular disease) and raised serum creatinine.
- **The risk of either ACE inhibitor-induced or AIIRA-induced first-dose hypotension or renal impairment is increased in the following high-risk groups of people:**
  - Creatinine higher than 150 micromol/l
  - Urea higher than 12 mmol/l
  - Sodium less than 130 mmol/l
  - Systolic BP less than 100 mmHg
  - Diuretic dosage greater than furosemide (frusemide) 80 mg or bumetanide 2 mg daily
  - Known or suspected renal artery stenosis, for example if peripheral vascular disease
  - People aged 70 years and over or who are frail
  - Hypovolaemia
  - With unstable heart failure
  - Receiving high-dosage vasodilator treatment

Calcium-channel blockers (dihydropyridines)

- **Ankle swelling** (due to the vasodilatory action of dihydropyridines). Diuretics should not be routinely prescribed but they may help if there is marked oedema.

- **Facial flushing, headaches and palpitations** (often improves with continued use).

Calcium-channel blockers (rate limiting)

- **Verapamil:** never use with beta-blockers.
- **Diltiazem:** may cause bradycardia when used in combination with beta-blockers and careful monitoring is required, therefore use with caution.
- **Verapamil commonly causes constipation** (advise consuming more fluids and fibre).
- **Vasodilatory adverse effects** are less common with rate-limiting than dihydropyridine CCBs.

Concomitant use of drug formulations with a high sodium content

- Many effervescent drug formulations (e.g. compound analgesics) contain high sodium content. They should therefore be avoided where possible as they may aggravate hypertension. Note: soluble aspirin tablets have very low sodium content.

Follow-up advice

- **Advise lifestyle interventions whether treatment is started or not.**
- **Reassess response to treatment after an interval of at least 4 weeks,** unless it is necessary to lower the BP more urgently.
- **Optimum target BP** is =<140/90 mmHg (GMS contract audit standard is =<150/90 mmHg).
- **People receiving ACE inhibitors** need monitoring of renal function, BP, and serum potassium) before and during treatment — within 1 week of starting and 1 week after each dosage increase to assess response to treatment.
- **Check for adverse effects,** for example symptomatic hypotension, renal dysfunction, or hyperkalaemia (i.e. a rise in urea to 12 mmol/l, creatinine to 200 micromol/l, or potassium to 5.5 mmol/l). If these occur either stop or reduce the dosage of ACE inhibitor, and consider specialist referral.
- **Once stable,** review annually and test urine for protein and blood as well as checking serum electrolytes and renal function (especially in people taking diuretics, ACE inhibitors or AIIRAs). More frequent review may be necessary in some people and other authorities would recommend at least a 6-monthly review.

Should I refer or investigate?

Refer?

Urgent assessment and treatment is recommended if:

- People present with accelerated (malignant) hypertension (BP >=180/110 mmHg with signs of papilloedema and/or retinal haemorrhage) or suspected phaeochromocytoma (possible signs include labile or postural hypotension, headache, palpitations, pallor and excessive sweating).
- Impending cardiovascular complications, e.g. transient ischaemic attack (TIA), left ventricular failure.

Consider referral:

- In people <35 years of age where treatment is indicated to exclude a secondary cause.
- Where signs and symptoms suggest secondary causes of hypertension including:
  - Hypokalaemia/increased plasma sodium (Conn's syndrome?)
  - Elevated serum creatinine
  - Proteinuria or haematuria (after excluding urinary tract infection)
  - Sudden onset or worsening of hypertension
- Of people with documented postural hypotension (i.e. a fall in systolic BP when standing of >=20 mmHg) or symptoms of it, to a specialist.
- To a smoking cessation service where appropriate.
- Of people who do not reach targets or whose high-density lipoprotein cholesterol or triglyceride levels remain abnormal (e.g. <1.0 or >2.3 mmol/l, respectively).
- Of people with unusual BP variability.
- Where isolated clinic hypertension (white-coat hypertension) is a possibility: unless access is available to ambulatory BP monitoring or home monitoring and confidence in interpreting values (see section *How do I measure blood pressure?*).
- For secondary care initiation of an ACE inhibitor in high-risk groups; see section *Prescribing points*.

Investigate?

- **Consider the need for specialist investigation** of people with unusual signs and symptoms, or whose management depends critically on the accurate estimation of their BP.
- **Routine investigations that should be performed include:**
  - Urine test strip to measure the presence of protein and blood.
  - Blood sample to measure:
    - Plasma glucose (ideally fasted level).
    - Electrolytes.
    - Creatinine.
    - Serum total cholesterol and high-density lipoprotein. Note: fasting is only necessary where a triglyceride level is required.
  - Electrocardiogram using a 12 lead electrocardiograph — to help exclude left ventricular hypertrophy.

Patient information leaflets

The following PILs are available at www.prodigy.nhs.uk

- Blood Pressure Association
- Blood Test - General
- Blood Test - Kidney Function
- High Blood Pressure - A Summary
- High Blood Pressure Foundation
- High Blood Pressure (Hypertension)
- High Blood Pressure - Medication
- Medicines - Name Changes of Medicines

Shared decision making

- The higher your blood pressure, the greater the risk of developing heart disease, a stroke, and kidney problems.
- You can lower your BP by:
  - **Losing weight** if you are overweight.
  - **Reducing alcohol intake** if you drink a lot.
  - **A low salt diet.**
  - **Regular exercise** such as swimming, cycling, jogging, dancing, brisk walking, or anything that causes mild breathlessness. At least 30 minutes' exercise, at least five times a week, is best.
  - **Eating lots of fruit and vegetables** and a low-fat diet.
- **Smoking** makes the risk from high BP much worse.
- **Medication** is advised if your BP stays at 160/100 or above.
- **Ideally,** your BP should be less than 140/90.
- **Various medicines** can lower BP. The one chosen depends on such things as whether you have other medical problems, whether you take other medication, your age, etc.

Drug rationale

Drugs not included

- **Fixed-dosage combinations** are not recommended when initiating treatment because they do not allow for flexible dosage titrations. In people taking multiple drugs, they may have a role in improving compliance by reducing the number of drugs.
- **Thiazide-type diuretics other than bendroflumethiazide (bendrofluazide)** are not included as they do not offer any significant advantages. There is good evidence for efficacy of chlortalidone at lowering BP and improving cardiovascular outcomes [ALLHAT Officers, 2002] but PACT data indicates that culturally there are few prescriptions for this in England and therefore clinicians are less familiar with the drugs profile.
- **Beta-blockers other than atenolol** have not been included. There is little to choose between them in terms of efficacy. Cardioselective agents are preferred because they have a better safety profile.
- **ACE inhibitors other than enalapril, lisinopril, perindopril, ramipril, and trandolapril** are not recommended. Captopril has a shorter half-life than other ACE inhibitors, it needs to be taken in divided doses, and is no longer recommended as a first-choice ACE inhibitor. Cilazapril, fosinopril, imidapril, moexipril, and quinapril are alternative options but there is less trial data of their use.
- **Angiotensin-II receptor antagonists (AIIRAs)** are not offered but may be used as an alternative to ACE inhibitors in people with a persistent ACE inhibitor-induced cough.
- **Dihydropyridine calcium-channel blockers (CCBs) other than nifedipine, felodipine, and amlodipine** are not included. Short-acting and immediate-release formulations are associated with large variations in BP and reflex tachycardia.
- **Verapamil modified-release formulations** are expensive and have not been included.
- **Alpha-blockers** are generally used less often than the other classes of agent and so are not included in this scenario. See scenario *Change to, increase, or add alpha-blocker* for prescriptions.
- **Centrally acting antihypertensive drugs:** there is no evidence from large-scale trials to support use of centrally acting drugs (methyldopa, clonidine, or moxonidine, or older vasodilators, for example hydralazine and minoxidil) in the initial treatment of hypertension [N England Hypertension GDG, 2004].
- **Adrenergic neurone blocking drugs** are considered less suitable for prescribing and have largely fallen from use, but may be necessary with other treatment in resistant hypertension [BNF 49, 2005].

Drugs included

- **Thiazide-type diuretics: bendroflumethiazide (bendrofluazide)** is the diuretic of choice in the UK and is cost-effective, safe, and well tolerated. It has a shallow dose response curve and therefore low-dose bendroflumethiazide should be used. Also low dosages cause little disturbance to glucose and lipids [Sweetman, 2002; BNF 49, 2005].
- **Beta-blockers: atenolol** is an effective, well established, inexpensive cardioselective beta-blocker which can be given once daily [BNF 49, 2005]. Atenolol 50 mg is the usual starting dose but a 25 mg dose might achieve a therapeutic response in some people. Despite recent controversy questioning the effectiveness of atenolol [Carlberg et al, 2004], it remains the beta-blocker of choice until more conclusive evidence proves otherwise.
- **ACE inhibitors: enalapril, lisinopril, perindopril, ramipril, and trandolapril** are included. They have comparable efficacy profiles, reputable safety records, and can be taken once a day.
  - Enalapril: people at risk of an excessive fall in BP after the initial dose may best start on 2.5 mg each day.
  - Ramipril: 1.25 mg each day may achieve a therapeutic response in some people, for others the dose should be increased every 1–2 weeks until the desired effect is achieved up to a maximum of 10 mg once a day.
  - Perindopril: people at risk of an excessive fall in BP after the initial dose may best start on 2 mg each day.
  - Trandolapril: 500 mcg each day may achieve a therapeutic response in some people, for others the dose should be increased incrementally every 2–4 weeks until the desired effect is achieved up to either a maximum of 4 mg once a day.
  - Note: initiation doses may differ to those offered in this scenario where ACE inhibitors are used in addition to a diuretic or in renal impairment.
  - All ACE inhibitors are licensed for the treatment of other cardiovascular morbidity (although starting regimens may different to those offered here).
- **Long-acting dihydropyridine calcium-channel blockers (CCBs): nifedipine, felodipine and amlodipine** are included. Nifedipine and amlodipine have both been studied in large double-blind RCTs [ALLHAT Officers, 2002] and felodipine featured in the HOT research [Hansson et al, 1998; Brown et al, 2000]. They are an alternative option to thiazide-type diuretics in elderly people and have evidence of improved outcomes in those with isolated systolic hypertension [Systolic Hypertension-Europe (Syst-Eur) Trial Investigators, 1997]. They have once-daily dosage regimens are also licensed for use in angina.
- **Rate-limiting CCBs: diltiazem and verapamil** are an option in those with angina. The diltiazem modified-release formulations offered are included by brand name because of potential problems caused by switching brands [BNF 49, 2005]. The least expensive, once-daily formulations in a range of strengths and dosages for use in hypertension are included.

Prescriptions

Start thiazide diuretic

Bendroflumethiazide (bendrofluazide) 2.5mg each morning

- Age from 16 years onwards
- Bendroflumethiazide 2.5mg tabs. Take one tablet each morning; supply 28 tablets; NHS Cost £1.17.

Start beta-blocker

Atenolol 25mg once a day

- Age from 16 years onwards
- Atenolol 25mg tablets. Take one tablet once a day; supply 28 tablets; NHS Cost £0.74.

Atenolol 50mg once a day

- Age from 16 years onwards
- Atenolol 50mg tablets. Take one tablet once a day; supply 28 tablets; NHS Cost £0.85.

Start ACE inhibitor

Enalapril 2.5mg once a day

- Age from 16 years onwards
- Enalapril 2.5mg tablets. Take one tablet once a day; supply 28 tablets; NHS Cost £0.95.

Enalapril 5mg once a day
- Age from 16 years onwards
- Enalapril 5mg tablets. Take one tablet once a day; supply 28 tablets; NHS Cost £1.28.

Lisinopril 2.5mg once a day
- Age from 16 years onwards
- Lisinopril 2.5mg tablets. Take one tablet once a day; supply 28 tablets; NHS Cost £1.17.

Ramipril: initial titration from 1.25mg to 2.5mg per day
- Age from 16 years onwards
- Ramipril 1.25mg capsules. Take one capsule once a day for 2 weeks, then take two capsules once a day; supply 42 capsules; NHS Cost £2.70.

Ramipril 1.25mg once a day
- Age from 16 years onwards
- Ramipril 1.25mg capsules. Take one capsule once a day; supply 28 capsules; NHS Cost £1.80.

Perindopril 2mg once a day
- Age from 16 years onwards
- Perindopril 2mg tablets. Take one tablet each morning on an empty stomach; supply 30 tablets; NHS Cost £10.95.

Perindopril 4mg once a day
- Age from 16 years onwards
- Perindopril 4mg tablets. Take one tablet each morning on an empty stomach; supply 30 tablets; NHS Cost £10.95.

Trandolapril: initial titration from 0.5mg to 1mg per day
- Age from 16 years onwards
- Trandolapril 500mcg capsules. Take one capsule once a day for 2 weeks, then take two capsules once a day; supply 42 capsules; NHS Cost £5.13.

Trandolapril 500micrograms once a day
- Age from 16 years onwards
- Trandolapril 500mcg capsules. Take one capsule once a day; supply 28 capsules; NHS Cost £3.42.

Start calcium-channel blocker (dihydropyridine)

Felodipine m/r 2.5mg each morning
- Age from 60 years onwards
- Felodipine 2.5mg m/r tablets. Take one tablet each morning; supply 28 tablets; NHS Cost £6.70.

Felodipine m/r 5mg each morning
- Age from 16 years onwards
- Felodipine 5mg m/r tablets. Take one tablet each morning; supply 28 tablets; NHS Cost £8.93.

Nifedipine m/r: Adalat LA 20mg each morning
- Age from 16 years onwards
- Adalat LA 20mg m/r tablets. Take one tablet each morning; supply 28 tablets; NHS Cost £5.27.

Nifedipine m/r: Adalat LA 30mg each morning
- Age from 16 years onwards
- Adalat LA 30mg m/r tablets. Take one tablet each morning; supply 28 tablets; NHS Cost £7.59.

Nifedipine m/r: Coracten XL 30mg each morning
- Age from 16 years onwards
- Coracten XL 30mg m/r capsules. Take one capsule each morning; supply 28 capsules; NHS Cost £6.06.

Amlodipine 5mg once a day
- Age from 16 years onwards
- Amlodipine 5mg tablets. Take one tablet once a day; supply 28 tablets; NHS Cost £8.89.

Start calcium-channel blocker (rate-limiting)

Diltiazem m/r: Slozem 120mg once a day
- Age from 60 years onwards
- Slozem 120mg m/r capsules. Take one capsule once a day; supply 28 capsules; NHS Cost £7.00.

Diltiazem m/r: Slozem 180mg once a day
- Age from 16 years onwards
- Slozem 180mg m/r capsules. Take one capsule once a day; supply 28 capsules; NHS Cost £7.80.

Diltiazem m/r: Slozem 240mg once a day
- Age from 16 years onwards
- Slozem 240mg m/r capsules. Take one capsule once a day; supply 28 capsules; NHS Cost £8.20.

Diltiazem m/r: Viazem XL 120mg once a day
- Age from 60 years onwards
- Viazem XL 120mg capsules. Take one capsule once a day; supply 28 capsules; NHS Cost £6.60.

Diltiazem m/r: Viazem XL 180mg once a day
- Age from 16 years onwards
- Viazem XL 180mg capsules. Take one capsule once a day; supply 28 capsules; NHS Cost £7.36.

Verapamil 120mg twice a day
- Age from 16 years onwards
- Verapamil 120mg tablets. Take one tablet twice a day; supply 56 tablets; NHS Cost £3.14.

Change to or add thiazide

Which therapy?

A stepwise approach to adding drugs is recommended in an attempt to achieve the target BP.

- **Drug treatment should normally begin with a low-dose thiazide-type diuretic.**
- In people <55 years old, with moderately raised BP, consider beginning with a beta-blocker.
- **If a drug is tolerated but target BP is not achieved** — add second line treatment.
- **If a drug is *not* tolerated** — discontinue and proceed to second line treatment.
- **Second line treatment should be selected according to whether the person has a raised risk of new-onset Type 2 diabetes:**
- **In people at risk of Type 2 diabetes:**
  - Add an angiotensin-converting enzyme (ACE) inhibitor
  - Consider substituting an angiotensin-receptor II antagonist in people who do not tolerate an ACE inhibitor due to cough
- **In people *not* at risk of Type 2 diabetes:**
  - Add a beta-blocker or,
  - Add a thiazide-type diuretic if a beta-blocker was used first line
- **If a thiazide is not tolerated and the person is *not* at risk of Type 2 diabetes:**
  - Prescribe a beta-blocker
- **If a third line treatment is required:**
  - Add a calcium-channel blocker.
- **If further BP lowering is indicated consider:**
  - An ACE inhibitor or beta-blocker (if not yet used)
  - Another antihypertensive drug
  - Referring to a specialist
- **In people at high risk of developing Type 2 diabetes the combination of a thiazide-type diuretic with a beta-blocker may be appropriate** to manage treatment resistant hypertension or if cardiovascular disease develops.

Practical prescribing points

For further information please see the *Medicines Compendium* (www.medicines.org.uk) or the *British National Formulary* (www.bnf.org)

Thiazide diuretics

- Avoid using a thiazide-type diuretic in people with gout — if one is necessary, consider prophylaxis with allopurinol (see separate PRODIGY guidance on *Gout*).

Concomitant use of drug formulations with a high sodium content

- Many effervescent drug formulations (e.g. compound analgesics) contain high sodium content. They should therefore be avoided where possible as they may aggravate hypertension. Note: soluble aspirin tablets have very low sodium content.

Follow-up advice

- **Reassess response to treatment after an interval of at least 4 weeks,** unless it is necessary to lower the BP more urgently.
- **People receiving thiazides** need serum potassium checked within 4–6 weeks of start.
- **Optimum target BP** is =<140/90 mmHg (GMS contract audit standard is =<150/90 mmHg).
- **Once stable,** review annually and test urine for protein and blood as well as checking serum electrolytes and renal function (especially in people taking diuretics, ACE inhibitors or AIIRAs). More frequent review may be necessary in some people and other authorities would recommend at least a 6-monthly review.

Should I refer or investigate?

Refer?

Urgent assessment and treatment is recommended if:

- People present with accelerated (malignant) hypertension (BP >=180/110 mmHg with signs of papilloedema and/or retinal haemorrhage) or suspected phaeochromocytoma (possible signs include labile or postural hypotension, headache, palpitations, pallor and excessive sweating).
- Impending cardiovascular complications, e.g. transient ischaemic attack (TIA), left ventricular failure.

Consider referral:

- In people <35 years of age where treatment is indicated to exclude a secondary cause.
- Where signs and symptoms suggest secondary causes of hypertension including:
  - Hypokalaemia/increased plasma sodium (Conn's syndrome?)
  - Elevated serum creatinine
  - Proteinuria or haematuria (after excluding urinary tract infection)
  - Sudden onset or worsening of hypertension
- Of people with documented postural hypotension (i.e. a fall in systolic BP when standing of >=20 mmHg) or symptoms of it, to a specialist.
- To a smoking cessation service where appropriate.
- Of people who do not reach targets or whose high-density lipoprotein cholesterol or triglyceride levels remain abnormal (e.g. <1.0 or >2.3 mmol/l, respectively).
- Of people with unusual BP variability.
- Where isolated clinic hypertension (white-coat hypertension) is a possibility: unless access is available to ambulatory BP monitoring or home monitoring and confidence in interpreting values (see section *How do I measure blood pressure?*).
- For secondary care initiation of an ACE inhibitor in high-risk groups; see section *Prescribing points*.

Investigate?

- **Consider the need for specialist investigation** of people with unusual signs and symptoms, or whose management depends critically on the accurate estimation of their BP.

Patient information leaflets

The following PILs are available at www.prodigy.nhs.uk

- Blood Pressure Association
- Blood Test - General
- Blood Test - Kidney Function
- High Blood Pressure - A Summary
- High Blood Pressure Foundation
- High Blood Pressure (Hypertension)
- High Blood Pressure - Medication
- Medicines - Name Changes of Medicines

Shared decision making

- **A thiazide-type diuretic** ('water tablet') such as bendroflumethiazide (bendrofluazide) is commonly prescribed to lower blood pressure (BP).
- Ideally, your BP should be less than 140/90.
- Sometimes a thiazide is used alone. Sometimes one is combined with another medicine if BP is not well controlled with one medicine alone.
- The dose needed to treat high BP is low, so you will not notice much diuretic effect (passing extra urine).
- Thiazides can sometimes cause gout, or can make gout worse.
- You should have a blood test 4–6 weeks after starting a diuretic, and then annually.

Drug rationale

Drugs not included

- **Thiazide-type diuretics other than bendroflumethiazide (bendrofluazide)** are not included as they do not offer any significant advantages. There is good evidence for efficacy of chlortalidone at lowering BP and improving cardiovascular outcomes [ALLHAT Officers, 2002] but PACT data indicates that culturally there are few prescriptions for this in England and therefore clinicians are less familiar with the drugs profile.

Drugs included

- **Thiazide-type diuretics: bendroflumethiazide (bendrofluazide)** is the diuretic of choice in the UK and is cost-effective, safe, and well tolerated. It has a shallow dose response curve and therefore low-dose bendroflumethiazide should be used. Also low dosages cause little disturbance to glucose and lipids [Sweetman, 2002; BNF 49, 2005].

Prescriptions

Start thiazide diuretic

Bendroflumethiazide (bendrofluazide) 2.5mg each morning

- Age from 16 years onwards
- Bendroflumethiazide 2.5mg tabs. Take one tablet each morning; supply 28 tablets; NHS Cost £1.17.

Change to, increase, or add beta-blocker

Which therapy?

A stepwise approach to adding drugs is recommended in an attempt to achieve the target BP.

- **Drug treatment should normally begin with a low-dose thiazide-type diuretic.**
- In people <55 years old, with moderately raised BP, consider beginning with a beta-blocker.
- **If a drug is tolerated but target BP is not achieved** — add second line treatment.
- **If a drug is *not* tolerated** — discontinue and proceed to second line treatment.
- **Second line treatment should be selected according to whether the person has a raised risk of new-onset Type 2 diabetes:**
- **In people at risk of Type 2 diabetes:**
  - Add an angiotensin-converting enzyme (ACE) inhibitor.
  - Consider substituting an angiotensin-receptor II antagonist in people who do not tolerate an ACE inhibitor due to cough.
- **In people *not* at risk of Type 2 diabetes:**
  - Add a beta-blocker or,
  - Add a thiazide-type diuretic if a beta-blocker was used first line.
- **If a thiazide is *not* tolerated and the person is not at risk of Type 2 diabetes:**
  - Prescribe a beta-blocker.
- **If a third line treatment is required:**
  - Add a calcium-channel blocker.
- **If further BP lowering is indicated consider:**
  - An ACE inhibitor or beta-blocker (if not yet used).
  - Another antihypertensive drug.
  - Referring to a specialist.
- **In people at high risk of developing Type 2 diabetes the combination of a thiazide-type diuretic with a beta-blocker may be appropriate** to manage treatment resistant hypertension or if cardiovascular disease develops.

Practical prescribing points

For further information please see the *Medicines Compendium* (www.medicines.org.uk) or the *British National Formulary* (www.bnf.org).

Beta-blockers

- **Beta-blockers should be avoided in people with either asthma or those with chronic obstructive pulmonary disease (COPD) that has an asthmatic component** as bronchospasm may be precipitated that is unresponsive to beta-2 agonists.
- **Heart failure (HF):** if uncontrolled, generally avoid beta-blockers, except for bisoprolol and carvedilol which are licensed for use in HF; see the PRODIGY guidance on *Heart failure.*

Concomitant use of drug formulations with a high sodium content

- Many effervescent drug formulations (e.g. compound analgesics) contain high sodium content. They should therefore be avoided where possible as they may aggravate hypertension. Note: soluble aspirin tablets have very low sodium content.

Follow-up advice

- **If treatment is started, reassess response after an interval of at least 4 weeks,** unless it is necessary to lower the BP more urgently.
- **Optimum target BP** is =<140/90 mmHg (GMS contract audit standard is =<150/90 mmHg).
- **Once stable,** review annually and test urine for protein and blood as well as checking serum electrolytes and renal function (especially in people taking diuretics, ACE inhibitors or AIIRAs). More frequent review may be necessary in some people and other authorities would recommend at least a 6-monthly review.

Should I refer or investigate?

Refer?

Urgent assessment and treatment if:

- People present with accelerated (malignant) hypertension (BP >=180/110 mmHg with signs of papilloedema and/or retinal haemorrhage) or suspected phaeochromocytoma (possible signs include labile or postural hypotension, headache, palpitations, pallor and excessive sweating).
- Impending cardiovascular complications, e.g. transient ischaemic attack (TIA), left ventricular failure.

Consider referral:

- In people <35 years of age where treatment is indicated to exclude a secondary cause.
- Where signs and symptoms suggest secondary causes of hypertension including:
  - Hypokalaemia/increased plasma sodium (Conn's syndrome?)
  - Elevated serum creatinine
  - Proteinuria or haematuria (after excluding urinary tract infection)
  - Sudden onset or worsening of hypertension
- Of people with documented postural hypotension (i.e. a fall in systolic BP when standing of >=20 mmHg) or symptoms of it, to a specialist.
- To a smoking cessation service where appropriate.
- Of people who do not reach targets or whose high-density lipoprotein cholesterol or triglyceride levels remain abnormal (e.g. <1.0 or >2.3 mmol/l, respectively).
- Of people with unusual BP variability.
- Where isolated clinic hypertension (white-coat hypertension) is a possibility: unless access is available to ambulatory BP monitoring or home monitoring and confidence in interpreting values (see section *How do I measure blood pressure?*).
- For secondary care initiation of an ACE inhibitor in high-risk groups; see section *Prescribing points.*

Investigate?

- **Consider the need for specialist investigation** of people with unusual signs and symptoms, or whose management depends critically on the accurate estimation of their BP.

Patient information leaflets

The following PILs are available at www.prodigy.nhs.uk

- Blood Pressure Association
- Blood Test - General
- Blood Test - Kidney Function
- High Blood Pressure - A Summary
- High Blood Pressure Foundation
- High Blood Pressure (Hypertension)
- High Blood Pressure - Medication

Shared decision making

- **A beta-blocker medicine** such as atenolol is commonly prescribed to lower blood pressure (BP).
- Ideally, your BP should be less than 140/90.
- A beta-blocker may be used alone. Sometimes one is combined with another medicine if BP is not well controlled with one medicine alone.
- Beta-blockers are particularly useful if you also have angina.
- You should not take a beta-blocker if you have asthma, chronic obstructive pulmonary disease, or certain types of heart or blood vessel problems.
- Some people develop side-effects with beta-blockers. These include: cool hands and feet, poor sleep, tiredness, and impotence.
- If side-effects occur, a different medicine may suit better. But...
- *Do not suddenly stop taking a beta-blocker medicine.*

Drug rationale

H

Drugs not included

- **Beta-blockers other than atenolol** have not been included. There is little to choose between them in terms of efficacy. Cardioselective agents are preferred because they have a better safety profile.

Drugs included

- **Beta-blockers: atenolol** is an effective, well established, inexpensive cardioselective beta-blocker which can be given once daily [BNF 49, 2005]. Atenolol 50 mg is the usual starting dose but a 25 mg dose might achieve a therapeutic response in some people. Despite recent controversy questioning the effectiveness of atenolol [Carlberg et al, 2004], it remains the beta-blocker of choice until more conclusive evidence proves otherwise.

Prescriptions

Start or increase atenolol

Atenolol 25mg once a day
- Age from 16 years onwards
- Atenolol 25mg tablets. Take one tablet once a day; supply 28 tablets; NHS Cost £1.12.

Atenolol 50mg once a day
- Age from 16 years onwards
- Atenolol 50mg tablets. Take one tablet once a day; supply 28 tablets; NHS Cost £0.85.

Change to, increase, or add ACE inhibitor

Which therapy?

A stepwise approach to adding drugs is recommended in an attempt to achieve the target BP.

- **Drug treatment should normally begin with a low-dose thiazide-type diuretic.**
- In people <55 years old, with moderately raised BP, consider beginning with a beta-blocker.
- **If a drug is tolerated but target BP is not achieved** — add second line treatment.
- **If a drug is *not* tolerated** — discontinue and proceed to second line treatment.
- **Second line treatment should be selected according to whether the person has a raised risk of new-onset Type 2 diabetes:**
- **In people at risk of Type 2 diabetes:**
  - Add an angiotensin-converting enzyme (ACE) inhibitor.
  - Consider substituting an angiotensin-receptor II antagonist in people who do not tolerate an ACE inhibitor due to cough.
- **In people *not* at risk of Type 2 diabetes:**
  - Add a beta-blocker or,
  - Add a thiazide-type diuretic if a beta-blocker was used first line.
- **If a thiazide-type is not tolerated and the person is *not* at risk of Type 2 diabetes:**
  - Prescribe a beta-blocker.
- **If a third line treatment is required:**
  - Add a calcium-channel blocker.
- **If further BP lowering is indicated consider:**
  - An ACE inhibitor or beta-blocker (if not yet used).
  - Another antihypertensive drug.
  - Referring to a specialist.
- **In people at high risk of developing Type 2 diabetes the combination of a thiazide-type diuretic with a beta-blocker may be appropriate** to manage treatment resistant hypertension or if cardiovascular disease develops.

Practical prescribing points

For further information please see the *Medicines Compendium* (www.medicines.org.uk) or the *British National Formulary* (www.bnf.org).

ACE inhibitor

- **Avoid potassium-sparing diuretics or potassium supplements** (other than in exceptional cases e.g. low-dose spironolactone for severe heart failure) due to the risk of hyperkalaemia.
- **Monitor renal function carefully with** peripheral vascular disease (risk of renovascular disease) and raised serum creatinine.
- **The risk of ACE inhibitor-induced first-dose hypotension or renal impairment is increased in the following high-risk groups of people:**
  - Creatinine higher than 150 micromol/l
  - Urea higher than 12 mmol/l
  - Sodium less than 130 mmol/l
  - Systolic BP less than 100 mmHg
  - Diuretic dosage greater than furosemide (frusemide) 80 mg or bumetanide 2 mg daily
  - Known or suspected renal artery stenosis, for example if peripheral vascular disease
  - People aged 70 years and over or who are frail
  - Hypovolaemia
  - With unstable heart failure
  - Receiving high-dosage vasodilator therapy

Concomitant use of drug formulations with a high sodium content

- Many effervescent drug formulations (e.g. compound analgesics) contain high sodium content. They should therefore be avoided where possible as they may aggravate hypertension. Note: soluble aspirin tablets have very low sodium content.

Follow-up advice

- **People receiving ACE inhibitors** need monitoring of renal function, BP, and serum potassium) before and during treatment — within 1 week of starting and 1 week after each dosage increase to assess response to treatment.

Check for adverse effects, for example symptomatic hypotension, renal dysfunction, or hyperkalaemia (i.e. a rise in urea to 12 mmol/l, creatinine to 200 micromol /l, or potassium to 5.5 mmol/l). If these occur either stop or reduce the dosage of ACE inhibitor, and consider specialist referral.
Once the person is receiving a stable dosage serum electrolytes and renal function should be checked at least annually.
Reassess response to treatment after an interval of at least 4 weeks, unless it is necessary to lower the BP more urgently.
Optimum target BP is =<140/90 mmHg (GMS contract audit standard is =<150/90 mmHg).
Once stable, review annually and test urine for protein and blood as well as checking serum electrolytes and renal function (especially in people taking diuretics, ACE inhibitors or AIIRAs). More frequent review may be necessary in some people and other authorities would recommend at least a 6-monthly review.

Should I refer or investigate?

Refer?

Urgent assessment and treatment if:
People present with accelerated (malignant) hypertension (BP >=180/110 mmHg with signs of papilloedema and/ or retinal haemorrhage) or suspected phaeochromocytoma (possible signs include labile or postural hypotension, headache, palpitations, pallor and excessive sweating).
Impending cardiovascular complications, e.g. transient ischaemic attack (TIA), left ventricular failure.
Consider referral:
In people <35 years of age where treatment is indicated to exclude a secondary cause.
Where signs and symptoms suggest secondary causes of hypertension including:
- Hypokalaemia/increased plasma sodium (Conn's syndrome?)
- Elevated serum creatinine
- Proteinuria or haematuria (after excluding urinary tract infection)
- Sudden onset or worsening of hypertension

Of people with documented postural hypotension (i.e. a fall in systolic BP when standing of >=20 mmHg) or symptoms of it, to a specialist.
To a smoking cessation service where appropriate.
Of people who do not reach targets or whose high-density lipoprotein cholesterol or triglyceride levels remain abnormal (e.g. <1.0 or >2.3 mmol/l, respectively).
Of people with unusual BP variability.
Where isolated clinic hypertension (white-coat hypertension) is a possibility: unless access is available to ambulatory BP monitoring or home monitoring and confidence in interpreting values (see section *How do I measure blood pressure?*).
For secondary care initiation of an ACE inhibitor in high-risk groups; see section *Prescribing points*.

Investigate?

Serum electrolytes within 1 week of starting or increasing the dosage of an ACE inhibitor.
Consider the need for specialist investigation of patients with unusual signs and symptoms, or whose management depends critically on the accurate estimation of their BP.

Patient information leaflets

The following PILs are available at www.prodigy.nhs.uk
- Blood Pressure Association
- Blood Test - General
- Blood Test - Kidney Function
- High Blood Pressure - A Summary
- High Blood Pressure Foundation
- High Blood Pressure (Hypertension)
- High Blood Pressure - Medication

Shared decision making

- **An ACE inhibitor** is often prescribed to lower blood pressure (BP).
- Ideally, your BP should be less than 140/90.
- An ACE inhibitor may be used alone. Sometimes one is combined with another medicine if BP is not well controlled with one medicine alone.
- ACE inhibitors are particularly useful if you also have heart failure or diabetes.
- ACE inhibitors should not be taken by people with: certain types of kidney problems; some types of artery problems; and in pregnancy.
- You should have a blood test before starting an ACE inhibitor, and within a week after starting it, and within a week of any increase of dose. Then, a yearly blood test is usual.

Drug rationale

Drugs not included

- **ACE inhibitors other than enalapril, lisinopril, perindopril, ramipril, and trandolapril** are not recommended. Captopril has a shorter half-life than other ACE inhibitors, it needs to be taken in divided doses, and is no longer recommended as a first-choice ACE inhibitor. Cilazapril, fosinopril, imidapril, moexipril, and quinapril are alternative options but there is less trial data of their use.

Drugs included

- All ACE inhibitors are licensed for the treatment of other cardiovascular morbidity (although starting regimens are different to those offered here).
- **ACE inhibitors: enalapril, lisinopril, perindopril, ramipril, and trandolapril** are included. They have comparable efficacy profiles, reputable safety records, and can be taken once a day.
  - Enalapril: people at risk of an excessive fall in BP after the initial dose may best start on 2.5 mg each day.
  - Ramipril: 1.25 mg each day may achieve a therapeutic response in some people, for others the dose should be increased every 1–2 weeks until the desired effect is achieved up to a maximum of 10 mg once a day.
  - Perindopril: people at risk of an excessive fall in BP after the initial dose may best start on 2 mg each day.
  - Trandolapril: 500 mcg each day may achieve a therapeutic response in some people, for others the dose should be increased incrementally every 2–4 weeks until the desired effect is achieved up to either a maximum of 4 mg once a day.
  - Note: initiation doses may differ to those offered in this scenario where ACE inhibitors are used in addition to a diuretic or in renal impairment.
  - All ACE inhibitors are licensed for the treatment of other cardiovascular morbidity (although starting regimens may different to those offered here).

[Systolic Hypertension-Europe (Syst-Eur) Trial Investigators, 1997; Hansson et al, 1999; The Heart

Outcomes Prevention Evaluation Study Investigators, 2000; Progress Collaborative Group, 2001; ALLHAT Officers, 2002; Wing et al, 2003; BNF 49, 2005]

Prescriptions

Start or increase enalapril

Start enalapril: 2.5mg once a day
- Age from 16 years onwards
- Enalapril 2.5mg tablets. Take one tablet once a day; supply 28 tablets; NHS Cost £0.95.

Start enalapril: 5mg once a day
- Age from 16 years onwards
- Enalapril 5mg tablets. Take one tablet once a day; supply 28 tablets; NHS Cost £1.28.

Enalapril 2.5mg once a day
- Age from 16 years onwards
- Enalapril 2.5mg tablets. Take one tablet once a day; supply 28 tablets; NHS Cost £0.95.

Enalapril 5mg once a day
- Age from 16 years onwards
- Enalapril 5mg tablets. Take one tablet once a day; supply 28 tablets; NHS Cost £1.28.

Enalapril 10mg once a day
- Age from 16 years onwards
- Enalapril 10mg tablets. Take one tablet once a day; supply 28 tablets; NHS Cost £1.38.

Enalapril 20mg once a day
- Age from 16 years onwards
- Enalapril 20mg tablets. Take one tablet once a day; supply 28 tablets; NHS Cost £1.54.

Enalapril 40mg once a day
- Age from 16 years onwards
- Enalapril 20mg tablets. Take two tablets once a day; supply 56 tablets; NHS Cost £3.08.

Start or increase lisinopril

Start lisinopril: 2.5mg once a day
- Age from 16 years onwards
- Lisinopril 2.5mg tablets. Take one tablet once a day; supply 28 tablets; NHS Cost £1.17.

Lisinopril 2.5mg once a day
- Age from 16 years onwards
- Lisinopril 2.5mg tablets. Take one tablet once a day; supply 28 tablets; NHS Cost £1.17.

Lisinopril 5mg once a day
- Age from 16 years onwards
- Lisinopril 5mg tablets. Take one tablet once a day; supply 28 tablets; NHS Cost £1.34.

Lisinopril 10mg once a day
- Age from 16 years onwards
- Lisinopril 10mg tablets. Take one tablet once a day; supply 28 tablets; NHS Cost £1.70.

Lisinopril 20mg once a day
- Age from 16 years onwards
- Lisinopril 20mg tablets. Take one tablet once a day; supply 28 tablets; NHS Cost £2.22.

Lisinopril 40mg once a day
- Age from 16 years onwards
- Lisinopril 20mg tablets. Take two tablets once a day; supply 56 tablets; NHS Cost £4.44.

Start or increase ramipril

Start ramipril: 1.25mg once a day
- Age from 16 years onwards
- Ramipril 1.25mg capsules. Take one capsule once a day; supply 28 capsules; NHS Cost £1.80.

Ramipril: initial titration from 1.25mg to 2.5mg per day
- Age from 16 years onwards
- Ramipril 1.25mg capsules. Take one capsule once a day for 2 weeks, then take two capsules once a day; supply 42 capsules; NHS Cost £2.70.

Ramipril 1.25mg once a day
- Age from 16 years onwards
- Ramipril 1.25mg capsules. Take one capsule once a day; supply 28 capsules; NHS Cost £1.80.

Ramipril 2.5mg once a day
- Age from 16 years onwards
- Ramipril 2.5mg capsules. Take one capsule once a day; supply 28 capsules; NHS Cost £1.63.

Ramipril 5mg once a day
- Age from 16 years onwards
- Ramipril 5mg capsules. Take one capsule once a day; supply 28 capsules; NHS Cost £2.32.

Ramipril 10mg once a day
- Age from 16 years onwards
- Ramipril 10mg capsules. Take one capsule once a day; supply 28 capsules; NHS Cost £2.68.

Start or increase perindopril

Start perindopril: 2mg once a day
- Age from 16 years onwards
- Perindopril 2mg tablets. Take one tablet each morning on an empty stomach; supply 30 tablets; NHS Cost £10.95.

Start perindopril: 4mg once a day
- Age from 16 years onwards
- Perindopril 4mg tablets. Take one tablet each morning on an empty stomach; supply 30 tablets; NHS Cost £10.95.

Perindopril 2mg once a day
- Age from 16 years onwards
- Perindopril 2mg tablets. Take one tablet each morning on an empty stomach; supply 30 tablets; NHS Cost £10.95.

Perindopril 4mg once a day
- Age from 16 years onwards
- Perindopril 4mg tablets. Take one tablet each morning on an empty stomach; supply 30 tablets; NHS Cost £10.95.

Perindopril 8mg once a day
- Age from 16 years onwards
- Perindopril 8mg tablets. Take one tablet each morning on an empty stomach; supply 30 tablets; NHS Cost £10.95.

Start or increase trandolapril

Start trandolapril: 500micrograms once a day
- Age from 16 years onwards
- Trandolapril 500mcg capsules. Take one capsule once a day; supply 28 capsules; NHS Cost £3.42.

Trandolapril: initial titration from 0.5mg to 1mg per day
- Age from 16 years onwards
- Trandolapril 500mcg capsules. Take one capsule once a day for 2 weeks, then take two capsules once a day; supply 42 capsules; NHS Cost £5.13.

Trandolapril 500micrograms once a day
- Age from 16 years onwards
- Trandolapril 500mcg capsules. Take one capsule once a day; supply 28 capsules; NHS Cost £3.42.

Trandolapril 1mg once a day
- Age from 16 years onwards
- Trandolapril 1mg capsules. Take one capsule once a day supply 28 capsules; NHS Cost £9.62.

randolapril 2mg once a day
Age from 16 years onwards
Trandolapril 2mg capsules. Take one capsule once a day; supply 28 capsules; NHS Cost £8.39.
randolapril 4mg once a day
Age from 16 years onwards
Trandolapril 4mg capsules. Take one capsule once a day; supply 28 capsules; NHS Cost £14.24.

Change to, increase, or add calcium-channel blocker

Which therapy?

stepwise approach to adding drugs is recommended in n attempt to achieve the target BP.

Drug treatment should normally begin with a low-dose thiazide-type diuretic.

In people <55 years old, with moderately raised BP, consider beginning with a beta-blocker.

If a drug is tolerated but target BP is not achieved — add second line treatment.

If a drug is *not* tolerated — discontinue and proceed to second line treatment.

Second line treatment should be selected according to whether the person has a raised risk of new-onset Type 2 diabetes:

In people at risk of Type 2 diabetes:

- Add an angiotensin-converting enzyme (ACE) inhibitor.
- Consider substituting an angiotensin-receptor II antagonist in people who do not tolerate an ACE inhibitor due to cough.

In people *not* at risk of Type 2 diabetes:

- Add a beta-blocker or,
- Add a thiazide-type diuretic if a beta-blocker was used first line.

If a thiazide-type is not tolerated and the person is *not* at risk of Type 2 diabetes:

- Prescribe a beta-blocker.

If a third line treatment is required:

- Add a calcium-channel blocker.

If further BP lowering is indicated consider:

- An ACE inhibitor or beta-blocker (if not yet used).
- Another antihypertensive drug.
- Referring to a specialist.

In people at high risk of developing Type 2 diabetes the combination of a thiazide-type diuretic with a beta-blocker may be appropriate to manage treatment resistant hypertension or if cardiovascular disease develops.

Practical prescribing points

or further information please see the *Medicines Compendium* (www.medicines.org.uk) or the *British National Formulary* (www.bnf.org).

Calcium-channel blockers (dihydropyridines)

Ankle swelling (due to the vasodilatory action of dihydropyridines). Diuretics should not be routinely prescribed but they may help if there is marked oedema.

Facial flushing, headaches and palpitations (often improves with continued use).

Calcium-channel blockers (rate limiting)

Verapamil: do not use with beta-blockers.

Diltiazem: may cause bradycardia when used in combination with beta-blockers and careful monitoring is required, therefore use with caution

- **Verapamil commonly causes constipation** (advise consuming more fluids and fibre).
- **Vasodilatory adverse effects** are less common with rate-limiting than dihydropyridine CCBs.

Concomitant use of drug formulations with a high sodium content

- Many effervescent drug formulations (e.g. compound analgesics) contain high sodium content. They should therefore be avoided where possible as they may aggravate hypertension. Note: soluble aspirin tablets have very low sodium content.

Follow-up advice

- **Reassess response to treatment after an interval of at least 4 weeks,** unless it is necessary to lower the BP more urgently.
- **Optimum target BP** is =<140/90 mmHg (GMS contract audit standard is =<150/90 mmHg).
- **Once stable,** review annually and test urine for protein and blood as well as checking serum electrolytes and renal function (especially in people taking diuretics, ACE inhibitors or AIIRAs). More frequent review may be necessary in some people and other authorities would recommend at least a 6-monthly review.

H

Should I refer or investigate?

Refer?

Urgent assessment and treatment is recommended if:

- People present with accelerated (malignant) hypertension (BP >=180/110 mmHg with signs of papilloedema and/or retinal haemorrhage) or suspected phaeochromocytoma (possible signs include labile or postural hypotension, headache, palpitations, pallor and excessive sweating).
- Impending cardiovascular complications, e.g. transient ischaemic attack (TIA), left ventricular failure.

Consider referral:

- In people <35 years of age where treatment is indicated to exclude a secondary cause.
- Where signs and symptoms suggest secondary causes of hypertension including:
  - Hypokalaemia/increased plasma sodium (Conn's syndrome?)
  - Elevated serum creatinine
  - Proteinuria or haematuria (after excluding urinary tract infection)
  - Sudden onset or worsening of hypertension
- Of people with documented postural hypotension (i.e. a fall in systolic BP when standing of >=20 mmHg) or symptoms of it, to a specialist.
- To a smoking cessation service where appropriate.
- Of people who do not reach targets or whose high-density lipoprotein cholesterol or triglyceride levels remain abnormal (e.g. <1.0 or >2.3 mmol/l, respectively).
- Of people with unusual BP variability.
- Where isolated clinic hypertension (white-coat hypertension) is a possibility: unless access is available to ambulatory BP monitoring or home monitoring and confidence in interpreting values (see section *How do I measure blood pressure?*).
- For secondary care initiation of an ACE inhibitor in high-risk groups; see section *Prescribing points*.

Urgent assessment and treatment needed if:

- People present with accelerated (malignant) hypertension (BP >=180/110 mmHg with signs of papilloedema and/or retinal haemorrhage) or suspected phaeochromocytoma (possible signs include labile or postural hypotension, headache, palpitations, pallor and excessive sweating).

- **Impending cardiovascular complications,** for example transient ischaemic attack (TIA), left ventricular failure.

Consider referral if:

- In people <35 years of age where treatment is indicated to exclude a secondary cause.
- **Where signs and symptoms suggest other secondary causes:**
  - Hypokalaemia/increased plasma sodium (Conn's syndrome?)
  - Elevated serum creatinine
  - Proteinuria or haematuria (after excluding urinary tract infection)
  - Sudden onset or worsening of hypertension
- Of people with documented postural hypotension (i.e. a fall in systolic BP when standing of >=20mmHg) or symptoms of it, to a specialist.
- To a smoking cessation service where appropriate.
- Of people who do not reach targets or whose high-density lipoprotein cholesterol or triglyceride levels remain abnormal (e.g. <1.0 or >2.3 mmol/l, respectively).
- **Of people with unusual BP variability.**
- **Where isolated clinic hypertension** (white-coat hypertension) is a possibility: unless access is available to ambulatory BP monitoring or home monitoring and confidence in interpreting values (see section *How do I measure blood pressure?*).

Investigate?

- **Consider the need for specialist investigation** of patients with unusual signs and symptoms, or whose management depends critically on the accurate estimation of their BP.

Patient information leaflets

The following PILs are available at www.prodigy.nhs.uk

- Blood Pressure Association
- Blood Test - General
- Blood Test - Kidney Function
- High Blood Pressure - A Summary
- High Blood Pressure Foundation
- High Blood Pressure (Hypertension)
- High Blood Pressure - Medication

Shared decision making

- **A calcium-channel blocker** (CCB) is often prescribed to lower blood pressure (BP). There are several types and brands.
- Ideally, your BP should be less than 140/90.
- Sometimes a CCB is used alone. Sometimes one is combined with another medicine if BP is not well controlled with one medicine alone.
- A CCB may be particularly useful if you also have angina.
- Some people develop side-effects with a CCB. These include: swollen ankles, facial flushing, headaches, palpitations and constipation. If these occur, they may ease off with continued use.
- If side-effects remain troublesome, a different medicine may suit better.

Drug rationale

Drugs not included

- **Dihydropyridine calcium-channel blockers (CCBs) other than nifedipine, felodipine, and amlodipine** are not included. Short-acting and immediate-release formulations are associated with large variations in BP and reflex tachycardia.
- **Verapamil modified-release formulations** are expensive and have not been included.

Drugs included

- **Long-acting dihydropyridine calcium-channel blockers (CCBs): nifedipine, felodipine and amlodipine** are included. Nifedipine and amlodipine have both been studied in large double-blind RCTs [ALLHAT Officers, 2002] and felodipine featured in the HOT research [Hansson et al, 1998; Brown et al, 2000]. They are an alternative option to thiazide-type diuretics in elderly people and have evidence of improved outcomes in those with isolated systolic hypertension [Systolic Hypertension-Europe (Syst-Eur) Trial Investigators, 1997]. They have once-daily dosage regimens are also licensed for use in angina.
- **Rate-limiting CCBs: diltiazem and verapamil** are an option in those with angina. The diltiazem modified-release formulations offered are included by brand name because of potential problems caused by switching brands [BNF 49, 2005]. The least expensive, once-daily formulations in a range of strengths and dosages for use in hypertension are included.

Prescriptions

Start or increase felodipine

Start felodipine m/r: 2.5mg each morning
- Age from 60 years onwards
- Felodipine 2.5mg m/r tablets. Take one tablet each morning; supply 28 tablets; NHS Cost £6.70.

Start felodipine m/r: 5mg each morning
- Age from 16 years onwards
- Felodipine 5mg m/r tablets. Take one tablet each morning; supply 28 tablets; NHS Cost £8.93.

Felodipine m/r 2.5mg each morning
- Age from 16 years onwards
- Felodipine 2.5mg m/r tablets. Take one tablet each morning; supply 28 tablets; NHS Cost £6.70.

Felodipine m/r 5mg each morning
- Age from 16 years onwards
- Felodipine 5mg m/r tablets. Take one tablet each morning; supply 28 tablets; NHS Cost £8.93.

Felodipine m/r 10mg each morning
- Age from 16 years onwards
- Felodipine 10mg m/r tablets. Take one tablet each morning; supply 28 tablets; NHS Cost £12.01.

Start or increase nifedipine

Start Adalat LA 20mg each morning
- Age from 16 years onwards
- Adalat LA 20mg m/r tablets. Take one tablet each morning; supply 28 tablets; NHS Cost £5.27.

Start Adalat LA 30mg each morning
- Age from 16 years onwards
- Adalat LA 30mg m/r tablets. Take one tablet each morning; supply 28 tablets; NHS Cost £7.59.

Adalat LA 20mg each morning
- Age from 16 years onwards
- Adalat LA 20mg m/r tablets. Take one tablet each morning; supply 28 tablets; NHS Cost £5.27.

Adalat LA 30mg each morning
- Age from 16 years onwards
- Adalat LA 30mg m/r tablets. Take one tablet each morning; supply 28 tablets; NHS Cost £7.59.

dalat LA 60mg each morning
- Age from 16 years onwards
- Adalat LA 60mg m/r tablets. Take one tablet each morning; supply 28 tablets; NHS Cost £9.69.

tart Coracten XL 30mg each morning
- Age from 16 years onwards
- Coracten XL 30mg m/r capsules. Take one capsule each morning; supply 28 capsules; NHS Cost £6.06.

oracten XL 30mg each morning
- Age from 16 years onwards
- Coracten XL 30mg m/r capsules. Take one capsule each morning; supply 28 capsules; NHS Cost £6.06.

oracten XL 60mg each morning
- Age from 16 years onwards
- Coracten XL 60mg m/r capsules. Take one capsule each morning; supply 28 capsules; NHS Cost £9.01.

tart or increase amlodipine

tart amlodipine 5mg once a day
- Age from 16 years onwards
- Amlodipine 5mg tablets. Take one tablet once a day; supply 28 tablets; NHS Cost £8.89.

mlodipine 5mg once a day
- Age from 16 years onwards
- Amlodipine 5mg tablets. Take one tablet once a day; supply 28 tablets; NHS Cost £8.89.

mlodipine 10mg once a day
- Age from 16 years onwards
- Amlodipine 10mg tablets. Take one tablet once a day; supply 28 tablets; NHS Cost £12.25.

tart or increase diltiazem

iazem XL 120mg once a day
- Age from 60 years onwards
- Viazem XL 120mg capsules. Take one capsule once a day; supply 28 capsules; NHS Cost £6.60.

iazem XL 180mg once a day
- Age from 16 years onwards
- Viazem XL 180mg capsules. Take one capsule once a day; supply 28 capsules; NHS Cost £7.36.

iazem XL 240mg once a day
- Age from 16 years onwards
- Viazem XL 240mg capsules. Take one capsule once a day; supply 28 capsules; NHS Cost £7.74.

iazem XL 300mg once a day (do not use as start dose)
- Age from 16 years onwards
- Viazem XL 300mg capsules. Take one capsule once a day; supply 28 capsules; NHS Cost £8.03.

lozem 120mg once a day
- Age from 16 years onwards
- Slozem 120mg m/r capsules. Take one capsule once a day; supply 28 capsules; NHS Cost £7.00.

lozem 180mg once a day
- Age from 16 years onwards
- Slozem 180mg m/r capsules. Take one capsule once a day; supply 28 capsules; NHS Cost £7.80.

lozem 240mg once a day
- Age from 16 years onwards
- Slozem 240mg m/r capsules. Take one capsule once a day; supply 28 capsules; NHS Cost £8.20.

lozem 360mg once a day (do not use as start dose)
- Age from 16 years onwards
- Slozem 180mg m/r capsules. Take two capsules once a day; supply 56 capsules; NHS Cost £15.60.

Start or increase verapamil

Start verapamil: 120mg twice a day
- Age from 16 years onwards
- Verapamil 120mg tablets. Take one tablet twice a day; supply 56 tablets; NHS Cost £3.14.

Verapamil 120mg twice a day
- Age from 16 years onwards
- Verapamil 120mg tablets. Take one tablet twice a day; supply 56 tablets; NHS Cost £3.14.

Verapamil 160mg twice a day
- Age from 16 years onwards
- Verapamil 160mg tablets. Take one tablet twice a day; supply 56 tablets; NHS Cost £4.75.

Verapamil 240mg twice a day
- Age from 16 years onwards
- Verapamil 120mg tablets. Take two tablets twice a day; supply 112 tablets; NHS Cost £6.28.

Change to, increase, or add alpha-blocker

H

Which therapy?

Note: current evidence does not support the use of alpha-blockers for the initial treatment of hypertension

A stepwise approach to adding drugs is recommended in an attempt to achieve the target BP.

- **Drug treatment should normally begin with a low-dose thiazide-type diuretic.**
- In people <55 years old, with moderately raised BP, consider beginning with a beta-blocker.
- **If a drug is tolerated but target BP is not achieved** — add second line treatment.
- **If a drug is *not* tolerated** — discontinue and proceed to second line treatment.
- **Second line treatment should be selected according to whether the person has a raised risk of new-onset Type 2 diabetes:**
- **In people at risk of Type 2 diabetes:**
  - Add an angiotensin-converting enzyme (ACE) inhibitor.
  - Consider substituting an angiotensin-receptor II antagonist in people who do not tolerate an ACE inhibitor due to cough.
- **In people *not* at risk of Type 2 diabetes:**
  - Add a beta-blocker or,
  - Add a thiazide-type diuretic if a beta-blocker was used first line.
- **If a thiazide is not tolerated and the person is *not* at risk of Type 2 diabetes:**
  - Prescribe a beta-blocker.
- **If a third line treatment is required:**
  - Add a calcium-channel blocker.
- **If further BP lowering is indicated consider:**
  - An ACE inhibitor or beta-blocker (if not yet used).
  - Another antihypertensive drug.
  - Referring to a specialist.
- **In people at high risk of developing Type 2 diabetes the combination of a thiazide diuretic with a beta-blocker may be appropriate** to manage treatment resistant hypertension or if cardiovascular disease develops.

Practical prescribing points

For further information please see the *Medicines Compendium* (www.medicines.org.uk) or the *British National Formulary* (www.bnf.org).

Alpha-blockers

- **Avoid in people with heart failure or impaired left ventricular function,** The doxazosin treatment arm of the ALLHAT trial was stopped because of an increase in cases of new onset heart failure in people assigned to doxazosin compared with chlortalidone [ALLHAT Officers, 2000].
- **Micturition syncope:** alpha-blockers may impair blood pressure responsiveness, increasing the risk of micturition syncope in susceptible individuals.
- **Gastrointestinal obstruction, oesophageal obstruction, or any degree of stricture:** doxazosin MR should be avoided, as the outer membrane of the formulation is not digested.

Concomitant use of drug formulations with a high sodium content

- Many effervescent drug formulations (e.g. compound analgesics) contain high sodium content. They should therefore be avoided where possible as they may aggravate hypertension. Note: soluble aspirin tablets have very low sodium content.

Follow-up advice

- **Reassess response to treatment after an interval of at least 4 weeks,** unless it is necessary to lower the BP more urgently.
- **Optimum target BP** is =<140/90 mmHg (GMS contract audit standard is =<150/90 mmHg).
- **Once stable,** review annually and test urine for protein and blood as well as checking serum electrolytes and renal function (especially in people taking diuretics, ACE inhibitors or AIIRAs). More frequent review may be necessary in some people and other authorities would recommend at least a 6-monthly review.

Should I refer or investigate?

Refer?

Urgent assessment and treatment is recommended if:

- People present with accelerated (malignant) hypertension (BP >=180/110 mmHg with signs of papilloedema and/or retinal haemorrhage) or suspected phaeochromocytoma (possible signs include labile or postural hypotension, headache, palpitations, pallor and excessive sweating).
- Impending cardiovascular complications, e.g. transient ischaemic attack (TIA), left ventricular failure.

Consider referral:

- In people <35 years of age where treatment is indicated to exclude a secondary cause.
- Where signs and symptoms suggest secondary causes of hypertension including:
  - Hypokalaemia/increased plasma sodium (Conn's syndrome?)
  - Elevated serum creatinine
  - Proteinuria or haematuria (after excluding urinary tract infection)
  - Sudden onset or worsening of hypertension
- Of people with documented postural hypotension (i.e. a fall in systolic BP when standing of >=20 mmHg) or symptoms of it, to a specialist.
- To a smoking cessation service where appropriate.
- Of people who do not reach targets or whose high-density lipoprotein cholesterol or triglyceride levels remain abnormal (e.g. <1.0 or >2.3 mmol/l, respectively).
- Of people with unusual BP variability.
- Where isolated clinic hypertension (white-coat hypertension) is a possibility: unless access is available t ambulatory BP monitoring or home monitoring and confidence in interpreting values (see section *How do I measure blood pressure?*).
- For secondary care initiation of an ACE inhibitor in high-risk groups; see section *Prescribing points*.

Investigate?

- **Consider the need for specialist investigation** of patients with unusual signs and symptoms, or whose management depends critically on the accurate estimation of their BP.

Patient information leaflets

The following PILs are available at www.prodigy.nhs.uk

- Blood Pressure Association
- Blood Test - General
- Blood Test - Kidney Function
- High Blood Pressure - A Summary
- High Blood Pressure Foundation
- High Blood Pressure (Hypertension)
- High Blood Pressure - Medication

Shared decision making

- **An alpha-blocker medicine** may be prescribed to lower blood pressure (BP).
- Ideally, your BP should be less than 140/90.
- An alpha-blocker is usually added to other medicine(s) i BP is not well controlled.
- An alpha-blocker may be particularly useful for men with high BP who also have prostatism.
- An alpha-blocker should not be taken by people with heart failure.

Drug rationale

Drugs not included

- **Tamsulosin and alfuzosin** are not included as they are only licensed for prostatic hyperplasia, not hypertensio
- **Standard release doxazosin** is not included as the modified-release doxazosin formulation has a better adverse effect profile, is easier to initiate and only slight more expensive.

[BNF 49, 2005]

Drugs included

- **Once-daily doxazosin MR and terazosin are recommended as first-choice alpha-blockers.** They offer simple dose titrations, the once-daily dosing may be convenient and improve compliance, and they are simil in price to other alpha-blockers (other than prazosin).
- **Prazosin** is much less expensive than other alpha-blockers but is more likely to cause symptomatic first-dose hypotension, requires careful dose titration, and needs to be taken 2–3 times daily.
- **Indoramin** is also included and needs to be taken in twc or three divided doses.

[BNF 49, 2005]

Prescriptions

Start or increase doxazosin m/r

Start doxazosin: 4mg m/r once a day

- Age from 16 years onwards
- Doxazosin 4mg m/r tablets. Take one tablet once a day supply 28 tablets; NHS Cost £6.33.

Doxazosin 4mg m/r once a day

- Age from 16 years onwards
- Doxazosin 4mg m/r tablets. Take one tablet once a day; supply 28 tablets; NHS Cost £6.33.

Doxazosin 8mg m/r once a day

- Age from 16 years onwards
- Doxazosin 8mg m/r tablets. Take one tablet once a day; supply 28 tablets; NHS Cost £12.67.

Start or increase terazosin

Start terazosin: starter pack

- Age from 16 years onwards
- Terazosin starter pack. Take one tablet once a day. See package insert for full instructions; supply 28 tablets; NHS Cost £13.00.

Terazosin 2mg once a day

- Age from 16 years onwards
- Terazosin 2mg tablets. Take one tablet once a day; supply 28 tablets; NHS Cost £5.64.

Terazosin 4mg once a day

- Age from 16 years onwards
- Terazosin 2mg tablets. Take two tablets once a day; supply 56 tablets; NHS Cost £11.28.

Terazosin 5mg once a day

- Age from 16 years onwards
- Terazosin 5mg tablets. Take one tablet once a day; supply 28 tablets; NHS Cost £9.59.

Terazosin 10mg once a day

- Age from 16 years onwards
- Terazosin 10mg tablets. Take one tablet once a day; supply 28 tablets; NHS Cost £20.16.

Terazosin 20mg once a day

- Age from 16 years onwards
- Terazosin 10mg tablets. Take two tablets once a day; supply 56 tablets; NHS Cost £40.32.

Start or increase indoramin

Start indoramin 25mg twice a day (2-week supply)

- Age from 16 years onwards
- Indoramin 25mg tablets. Take one tablet twice a day; supply 28 tablets; NHS Cost £3.00.

Indoramin 25mg twice a day

- Age from 16 years onwards
- Indoramin 25mg tablets. Take one tablet twice a day; supply 56 tablets; NHS Cost £6.00.

Indoramin 50mg twice a day

- Age from 16 years onwards
- Indoramin 25mg tablets. Take two tablets twice a day; supply 112 tablets; NHS Cost £12.00.

Indoramin 100mg twice a day

- Age from 16 years onwards
- Indoramin 25mg tablets. Take four tablets twice a day; supply 224 tablets; NHS Cost £24.00.

Start or increase prazosin

Start prazosin: titrate from 1mg to 4mg/day (2-week supply)

- Age from 16 years onwards
- Prazosin 500microgram tablets. Take one tablet twice a day for four days. Take the first dose in the evening; supply 8 tablets; NHS Cost £0.36.
- Prazosin 1mg tablets. Start, in the evening once the prazosin 500mcg tablets are finished. Take one tablet twice a day for four days, then take two tablets twice a day; supply 32 tablets; NHS Cost £1.43.

Prazosin 1mg twice a day

- Age from 16 years onwards
- Prazosin 1mg tablets. Take one tablet twice a day; supply 56 tablets; NHS Cost £3.23.

Prazosin 2mg twice a day

- Age from 16 years onwards
- Prazosin 2mg tablets. Take one tablet twice a day; supply 56 tablets; NHS Cost £4.39.

Prazosin 4mg twice a day

- Age from 16 years onwards
- Prazosin 2mg tablets. Take two tablets twice a day; supply 112 tablets; NHS Cost £8.78.

Prazosin 5mg three times a day

- Age from 16 years onwards
- Prazosin 5mg tablets. Take one tablet three times a day; supply 84 tablets; NHS Cost £13.13.

Prazosin 10mg twice a day

- Age from 16 years onwards
- Prazosin 5mg tablets. Take two tablets twice a day; supply 112 tablets; NHS Cost £17.50.

Intolerant of ACE inhibitor

Which therapy?

- **If the person is truly intolerant of an ACE inhibitor,** consider an angiotensin-II receptor antagonist (AIIRA).
- **Effect of an AIIRA compared with an ACE inhibitor:** no published trials have reported a comparison of the long-term renal effects and mortality.
- **Referral for a specialist opinion** may be considered in some people unable to tolerate an ACE inhibitor. A person who develops renal impairment when receiving an ACE inhibitor is also likely to develop renal impairment when receiving an AIIRA.

Practical prescribing points

For further information please see the *Medicines Compendium* (www.medicines.org.uk) or the *British National Formulary* (www.bnf.org).

Angiotensin-II receptor antagonist

- **Avoid potassium-sparing diuretics or potassium supplements** (other than in exceptional cases e.g. low-dose spironolactone for severe heart failure) due to the risk of hyperkalaemia.
- **Monitor renal function carefully with** peripheral vascular disease (risk of renovascular disease) and raised serum creatinine.
- **The risk of angiotensin-II receptor antagonist (AIIRA)-induced first-dose hypotension or renal impairment is increased in the following high-risk groups of people:**
    - Creatinine higher than 150 micromol/l
    - Urea higher than 12 mmol/l
    - Sodium less than 130 mmol/l
    - Systolic BP less than 100 mmHg
    - Diuretic dosage greater than furosemide (frusemide) 80 mg or bumetanide 2 mg daily
    - Known or suspected renal artery stenosis, for example if peripheral vascular disease
    - People aged 70 years and over or who are frail
    - Hypovolaemia
    - With unstable heart failure
    - Receiving high-dosage vasodilator therapy
- Stop nonsteroidal anti-inflammatory drugs (NSAIDs) (if possible) as they increase the risk of renal impairment with AIIRAs.

Concomitant use of drug formulations with a high sodium content

- Many effervescent drug formulations (e.g. compound analgesics) contain high sodium content. They should therefore be avoided where possible as they may aggravate hypertension. Note: soluble aspirin tablets have very low sodium content.

Follow-up advice

- **Angiotensin-II receptor antagonists (AIIRAs) require the same monitoring as for an ACE inhibitor,** therefore renal function should be monitored (BP, renal function, serum potassium) during treatment — 1 week after each dosage increase.
- **Repeat serum electrolytes and renal function within 1 week** of starting an AIIRA, and review the person to assess response to treatment and to check BP.
- **Check for adverse effects,** such as symptomatic hypotension, renal dysfunction, or hyperkalaemia (i.e. a rise in urea to 12 mmol/l, creatinine to 200 micromol /l, or potassium to 5.5 mmol/l). If these occur either stop or reduce the dosage of AIIRA, and consider specialist referral.
- **Once stable,** review annually and test urine for protein and blood as well as checking serum electrolytes and renal function (especially in people taking diuretics, ACE inhibitors or AIIRAs). More frequent review may be necessary in some people and other authorities would recommend at least a 6-monthly review.
- **Monitor regularly all people taking loop diuretics** for hypovolaemia, renal impairment, and electrolyte imbalances.
- **Liver disease:** monitor effects closely in people with impaired liver function and consider using a lower dosage.
- **Renal impairment:** close monitoring of plasma potassium concentration and renal function is advised.

Should I refer or investigate?

Refer?

Urgent assessment and treatment if:

- People present with accelerated (malignant) hypertension (BP >=180/110 mmHg with signs of papilloedema and/ or retinal haemorrhage) or suspected phaeochromocytoma (possible signs include labile or postural hypotension, headache, palpitations, pallor and excessive sweating).
- Impending cardiovascular complications, e.g. transient ischaemic attack (TIA), left ventricular failure.

Consider referral:

- In people <35 years of age where treatment is indicated to exclude a secondary cause.
- Where signs and symptoms suggest secondary causes of hypertension including:
  - Hypokalaemia/increased plasma sodium (Conn's syndrome?)
  - Elevated serum creatinine
  - Proteinuria or haematuria (after excluding urinary tract infection)
  - Sudden onset or worsening of hypertension
- Of people with documented postural hypotension (i.e. a fall in systolic BP when standing of >=20 mmHg) or symptoms of it, to a specialist.
- To a smoking cessation service where appropriate.
- Of people who do not reach targets or whose high-density lipoprotein cholesterol or triglyceride levels remain abnormal (e.g. <1.0 or >2.3 mmol/l, respectively).
- Of people with unusual BP variability.
- Where isolated clinic hypertension (white-coat hypertension) is a possibility: unless access is available to ambulatory BP monitoring or home monitoring and confidence in interpreting values (see section *How do I measure blood pressure?*).
- For secondary care initiation of an ACE inhibitor in high-risk groups; see section *Prescribing points.*

Investigate?

- **Consider the need for specialist investigation** of patients with unusual signs and symptoms, or whose management depends critically on the accurate estimation of their BP.

Patient information leaflets

The following PILs are available at www.prodigy.nhs.uk

- Blood Pressure Association
- Blood Test - General
- Blood Test - Kidney Function
- High Blood Pressure - A Summary
- High Blood Pressure Foundation
- High Blood Pressure (Hypertension)
- High Blood Pressure - Medication

Shared decision making

- **An angiotensin-II receptor antagonist (AIIRA)** is sometimes used to lower blood pressure (BP). There are various brands.
- Ideally, your BP should be less than 140/90.
- Sometimes an AIIRA is used alone. Sometimes one is combined with another medicine if BP is not well controlled with one medicine alone.
- AIIRAs are particularly useful if you also have diabetes or heart failure.
- You will need a blood test before starting an AIIRA, and within a week after starting one. Then, a yearly blood test is usual.

Drug rationale

Drugs not included

- **Angiotensin-II receptor antagonists (AIIRAs) other than candesartan, irbesartan, losartan, and valsartan** are not offered. Eprosartan, olmesartan and telmisartan have been introduced more recently and their efficacy has not been published in as large trials as those for other AIIRAs. They are all licensed for use in hypertension and there is probably a class effect, so they are alternative options. Olmesartan and telmisartan are also black triangle drugs and remain under the surveillance of the Committee on Safety of Medicines [BNF 49, 2005].

Drugs included

- **AIIRAs: candesartan, irbesartan, losartan, and valsartan** are offered and have all been assessed in large trials [Parving et al, 2001; Dahlof et al, 2002; Lindholm et al, 2002; Lithell et al, 2003; Schrader et al, 2003; Julius et al, 2004; N England Hypertension GDG, 2004]. They may be used as an alternative to ACE inhibitors in people with a persistent ACE inhibitor-induced cough [N England Hypertension GDG, 2004]. Losartan and valsartan are the most expensive AIIRAs.

Prescriptions

Start angiotensin-II receptor antagonist: low dose

Candesartan 2mg once a day

- Age from 16 years onwards
- Candesartan 2mg tablets. Take one tablet once a day; supply 28 tablets; NHS Cost £11.96.

Candesartan 4 mg once a day
- Age from 16 years onwards
- Candesartan 4mg tablets. Take one tablet once a day; supply 28 tablets; NHS Cost £8.15.

Irbesartan 75mg once a day
- Age from 16 years onwards
- Irbesartan 75mg tablets. Take one tablet once a day; supply 28 tablets; NHS Cost £10.29.

Losartan 25mg once a day
- Age from 16 years onwards
- Losartan 25mg tablets. Take one tablet once a day; supply 28 tablets; NHS Cost £18.12.

Valsartan 40mg once a day
- Age from 16 years onwards
- Valsartan 40mg capsules. Take one capsule once a day; supply 28 capsules; NHS Cost £14.76.

Start angiotensin-II receptor antagonist: standard dose

Candesartan 8mg once a day
- Age from 16 years onwards
- Candesartan 8mg tablets. Take one tablet once a day; supply 28 tablets; NHS Cost £9.89.

Irbesartan 150mg once a day
- Age from 16 years onwards
- Irbesartan 150mg tablets. Take one tablet once a day; supply 28 tablets; NHS Cost £12.57.

Losartan 50mg once a day
- Age from 16 years onwards
- Losartan 50mg tablets. Take one tablet once a day; supply 28 tablets; NHS Cost £18.09.

Valsartan 80mg once a day
- Age from 16 years onwards
- Valsartan 80mg capsules. Take one capsule once a day; supply 28 capsules; NHS Cost £16.44.

Usual maintenance dose or increase dose: AIIRA

Candesartan 8mg once a day
- Age from 16 years onwards
- Candesartan 8mg tablets. Take one tablet once a day; supply 28 tablets; NHS Cost £9.89.

Candesartan 16mg once a day
- Age from 16 years onwards
- Candesartan 16mg tablets. Take one tablet once a day; supply 28 tablets; NHS Cost £12.72.

Irbesartan 150mg once a day
- Age from 16 years onwards
- Irbesartan 150mg tablets. Take one tablet once a day; supply 28 tablets; NHS Cost £12.57.

Irbesartan 300mg once a day
- Age from 16 years onwards
- Irbesartan 300mg tablets. Take one tablet once a day; supply 28 tablets; NHS Cost £16.91.

Losartan 50mg once a day
- Age from 16 years onwards
- Losartan 50mg tablets. Take one tablet once a day; supply 28 tablets; NHS Cost £18.09.

Losartan 100mg once a day
- Age from 16 years onwards
- Losartan 100mg tablets. Take one tablet once a day; supply 28 tablets; NHS Cost £24.20.

Valsartan 80mg once a day
- Age from 16 years onwards
- Valsartan 80mg capsules. Take one capsule once a day; supply 28 capsules; NHS Cost £16.44.

Valsartan 160mg once a day
- Age from 16 years onwards
- Valsartan 160mg capsules. Take one capsule once a day; supply 28 capsules; NHS Cost £21.66.

Aspirin — who to treat?

Which therapy?

In people *without* cardiovascular disease

- Recommend/prescribe aspirin 75 mg daily for people with a 10 year CVD risk of >=20% and in whom BP is controlled to <145/90 mmHg with no contraindications to aspirin use.

In people *with* cardiovascular disease

- Recommend/prescribe aspirin 75 mg daily if there is evidence of established ischaemic cardiovascular disease:
  - Angina
  - Myocardial infarction
  - Non-haemorrhagic cerebrovascular disease
  - Peripheral vascular disease
  - Atherosclerotic renovascular disease

H

Practical prescribing points

For further information please see the *Medicines Compendium* (www.medicines.org.uk) or the *British National Formulary* (www.bnf.org).

Low-dosage aspirin

- **Concurrent nonsteroidal anti-inflammatory drugs (NSAIDs):** the risk of serious gastrointestinal complications doubles in people who regularly take low-dose aspirin and another NSAID. If possible, stop the second NSAID.
- **Avoid ibuprofen, if a second NSAID must be used concomitantly** — it may reduce the cardiovascular protective effect of low-dose aspirin. Consider using naproxen or diclofenac if a second NSAID must be used.
- **Asthma:** aspirin can induce bronchospasm in people who are hypersensitive to aspirin, but this is rare.
- For more information, see the PRODIGY guidance on:
  - *Dyspepsia — symptoms (uninvestigated by endoscopy)*
  - *Nonsteroidal anti-inflammatory drugs (NSAIDs)*

Concomitant use of effervescent drug formulations

- Many effervescent drug formulations (e.g. compound analgesics) contain high sodium content. They should therefore be avoided where possible as they may aggravate hypertension. Note: soluble aspirin tablets have very low sodium content.

Patient information leaflets

The following PILs are available at www.prodigy.nhs.uk
- Blood Pressure Association
- High Blood Pressure - A Summary
- High Blood Pressure Foundation
- High Blood Pressure (Hypertension)
- High Blood Pressure - Medication

Shared decision making

- **Aspirin** (low-dosage) is often prescribed:
  - If you have heart disease, stroke, or other vascular disease, or

- If you have an increased risk of developing these diseases.
- Aspirin:
  - Reduce the 'stickiness' of the blood, which
  - Reduces the chance of a blood clot forming, which
  - Reduces your chance of having a heart attack or stroke.
- Aspirin may not be advisable if you have asthma, or duodenal or stomach ulcers.
- It is uncommon to have side-effects with low-dosage aspirin. It causes some bleeding in the stomach in a few people. So:
- **Tell a doctor if you develop stomach pains, black faeces (motions), or notice blood in your faeces whilst taking aspirin.**
- Your risk of bleeding complications is increased if you also take other anti-inflammatory medicines or anticoagulants.

Drug rationale

Drugs not included

- **Enteric-coated preparations are not offered** as there is no convincing evidence that this reduces toxicity at a dosage of 75 mg [DTB, 1997]. Evidence is greatest for low-dose aspirin, therefore higher doses of aspirin are not included.

Drugs included

- **Aspirin (75 mg daily)** is included because studies have shown that low-dosage aspirin reduces the risk of subsequent cardiovascular events in people with established cardiovascular disease [Hayden et al, 2002]. Soluble aspirin produces less occult bleeding.

Prescriptions

Aspirin

Aspirin 75mg dispersible once a day

- Age from 16 years onwards
- Aspirin 75mg dispersible tabs. Take one tablet once a day; supply 28 tablets; NHS Cost £0.87; OTC Cost £1.00.

Extended Information

Background information

- What is hypertension? p.982
- How common is it? p.982
- How do I measure blood pressure? p.982
- How do I confirm that the blood pressure is raised? p.984
- What are the causes of secondary hypertension? p.984
- Complications and prognosis p.985

What is hypertension?

- **Hypertension (in people without diabetes) is defined as a sustained systolic blood pressure (BP) of >=140 mmHg, or sustained diastolic BP of >=90 mmHg** [Chobanian et al, 2003; European Society of Hypertension & European Society of Cardiology Guidelines Committee, 2003; N England Hypertension GDG, 2004; Williams et al, 2004].
  - Hypertension is considered to be *sustained* if an initial raised BP measurement persists at two or more subsequent consultations.
- Hypertension is a risk factor for the development of cardiovascular disease. Systolic and diastolic BPs are continuously related to the risk of developing cardiovascular disease, with a gradient of risk that extends into the range of BP that is described as 'normal'.
- **Hypertension may:**
  - Have no identifiable cause (in 95% of people) — essential or primary hypertension.
  - Be the result of an underlying cause — secondary hypertension, see *What are the causes of secondary hypertension?*
- **Table 1 shows how The British Hypertensive Society has classified different BP levels.**

How common is it?

- **In England, 40% of the adult population** have a sustained BP of >=140/90 mmHg and this is the threshold for the diagnosis of hypertension that is most commonly used [Brown, 1997]. The proportion of people with hypertension increases with age.
  - About one third of people in middle age have hypertension.
  - About two thirds in old age have hypertension.
- **Afro-Caribbean men and women** are consistently reported as having higher prevalence rates of hypertension than their Caucasian counterparts [Agyemang and Bhopal, 2003].
- **People of South Asian origin** also have a high prevalence of hypertension. They are commonly insulin resistant, and have a high prevalence of Type 2 diabetes.

[Primatesta and Brookes, 2001]

How do I measure blood pressure?

What equipment and training do I need to measure blood pressure?

- The National Institute of Clinical Excellence (NICE) recommends that healthcare professionals taking blood pressure (BP) measurements need adequate initial training and periodic review of their performance (C).
- Healthcare providers must ensure that BP measuring devices are properly validated, maintained and regularly recalibrated according to manufacturers' instructions (C).
- The mercury sphygmomanometer has been routinely used for BP measurement in clinical practice for many years and if properly maintained, remains the gold standard. However, due to health and safety concerns over environmental mercury, alternative measurement devices are required.
- Further information on BP devices can be obtained from the British Hypertension Society (BHS) Information Service (telephone: 020 8725 3412, e-mail: bhsis@sghms.ac.uk, website: www.bhsoc.org).

Table 1: Classification of BP levels (mmHg) in people without diabetes.

Category*	Systolic BP	Diastolic BP
Optimal	<120	<80
Normal	<130	<85
High normal	130–139	85–89
Mild hypertension	140–159	90–99
Moderate hypertension	160–179	100–109
Severe hypertension	>=180	>=110
Isolated systolic hypertension	>=140	<90

*When systolic and diastolic readings fall into different categories, the higher BP category should apply.

- Information on BP monitors validated to the BHS standard, and recommended are also available at www.bhsoc.org or www.dableducational.org.

How should I measure BP in the consultation?

- Ideally, standardise the environment when measuring BP: provide a relaxed, temperate setting, with the person quiet and seated with their arm outstretched and supported (C).
- When measuring BP, by auscultation (with a mercury sphygmomanometer or semiautomated device):
  - **Routinely measure sitting BP except:**
    - Record the standing BP in people with symptoms of postural hypotension (C). This is more common in elderly and diabetic people.
  - **Select cuff of appropriate size** (as if the cuff is too small it may overestimate BP) and wrap around the upper arm and connect to a manometer. Cuffs should already be marked to indicate the arm circumference for which they are suitable. These marks should be easily seen when the cuff is applied to an arm.
  - Palpate the brachial pulse in the antecubital fossa of that arm.
  - Rapidly inflate cuff to 20 mmHg above the point where the brachial pulse disappears.
  - Deflate the cuff and note the pressure where pulse reappears.
  - Re-inflate the cuff to 20 mmHg above the point where the brachial pulse disappears.
  - Using one hand, place the stethoscope over the brachial artery ensuring complete skin contact with no clothing in between.
  - Slowly deflate the cuff at 2–3 mmHg per second listening for Korotkoff sounds as detailed in Table 2.
  - When the sounds have disappeared, deflate the cuff — make sure that this is completed quickly if repeating the measurement.
- The systolic pressure is the pressure when faint repetitive tapping sounds that gradually increase in intensity are first heard.
- The diastolic pressure is the pressure when all the sounds disappear.
- **NICE recommends** that ideally, a second confirmatory reading should be taken at the end of the consultation the first blood pressure (BP) measurement >=140/90 mmHg (C).

[N England Hypertension GDG, 2004]

Ambulatory blood pressure monitoring

When is ambulatory blood pressure monitoring recommended?

- **Routine use of automated ambulatory BP monitoring (ABPM) in primary care is not recommended** as there is debate about how to accurately interpret ABPM data (B).
- **ABPM should be considered:**
  - When the BP shows unusual variability.
  - When hypertension seems to be resistant to drug treatment.
  - If 'White-coat hypertension' (clinic: high BP and ABMP: normal BP) is suspected.
  - If hypotensive symptoms are present in people with hypertensive clinic values.
  - To identify nocturnal hypertension.
  - To determine the efficacy of drug treatment over 24 hours.

How should ABPM be performed?

- ABPM devices are relatively expensive and vary markedly in their accuracy, size, weight and noise level, as well as ease of use and information provided by the accompanying software.

Table 2: Outline of Korotkoff Phases and when to record the systolic and diastolic BPs

BP to record	Phase	Description
Systolic	I	First occurrence of faint repetitive tapping sounds that gradually increase in intensity and last 2 consecutive beats
	II	Brief period may follow when the sounds soften and/or 'swish'
	Ausculatory gap	Sounds may disappear altogether in some people
	III	Return of sharper sounds becoming crisper for a short time
	IV*	Distinct, abrupt muffling of sounds: soft and blowing-like*
Diastolic	V	When all sounds disappear completely

* Note: record diastolic BP at Phase IV if sounds audible to zero cuff pressure

- For currently available, validated, and recommended devices, see www.bhsoc.org or www.dableducational.org.
- **When measuring BP by ABPM:**
  - Relax person in a quiet room.
  - Enter person's details on monitor.
  - Measure BP in both arms.
    - If systolic BP difference is <10 mmHg use non-dominant arm.
    - If systolic BP difference is >=10 mmHg use higher pressure arm.
  - Select cuff of appropriate size.
  - Select frequency of measurements — usually 30 minute intervals day and night.
  - Inactivate LCD display.
  - Give written instructions and a diary card.
  - Instruct the person how to remove and inactivate monitor after 24 hours.

How should ABPM values be interpreted?

- **Typically average daily ABPM values tend to be lower than their clinic readings.**
- Therefore to compare the two methods treatment thresholds and targets should probably be adjusted downwards, although evidence for true equivalence is lacking and will be variable [Williams et al, 2004].
- **The British Hypertensive Society recommends a downward correction of 10/5 mmHg when converting clinic to ambulatory values.** Note: both ambulatory and clinic values are useful as a minority of patients record higher ambulatory than clinic values.
- **The threshold for the upper limit of normality most commonly recommended is 135/85 mmHg** [O'Brien et al, 2001b].
- **Evidence is limited** on the degree to which ABPM can be used to determine cardiovascular prognosis [N England Hypertension GDG, 2004].
- **Threshold ABPM values to guide interpretation of readings** have been proposed (Table 3).
  - The definition of normal and abnormal ABPM levels remains controversial.
  - Evidence is not available to support recommendations in the range between 'normal' and 'abnormal' levels nor for levels lower then given.
  - Lower levels may be taken as abnormal in people whose risk factor profile is high and in whom there is concomitant disease such as diabetes mellitus.

[O'Brien et al, 2001b]

What are the advantages and disadvantages of ABPM?

- **Ambulatory monitoring is regarded as superior to home BP monitoring** because it allows for measurements over a full 24 hour period. However home BP monitoring is more appropriate than ambulatory for the long-term

H

Table 3: Recommended threshold levels of ambulatory blood pressure measurement.

Time period	Normal	Abnormal
Daytime	=<135/85	>140/90
Night time	=<120/70	>125/75
24 hour	=<130/80	>135/85

follow-up of treated people because of the greater convenience for repeated measurements [O'Brien et al, 2003].

- **Their use requires trained staff and patients also need adequate instruction.** People using ABPM may need to keep a diary of events that are known to affect BP, so that readings can be related to them, for example, periods of sleep [N England Hypertension GDG, 2004].

Blood pressure monitoring at home

When is blood pressure monitoring at home recommended?

- **Routine use of home monitoring devices in primary care is not recommended (B).**
  - **Finger and wrist monitors are not recommended** as they are generally not as accurate as upper arm devices [N England Hypertension GDG, 2004; Williams et al, 2004].
- **There is less evidence for home than ambulatory BP monitoring.** However, it is less costly, more convenient and accurate and validated devices are now available [O'Brien et al, 2001a].

How should home monitoring be performed?

- **Many people purchase BP monitoring devices, and these should be independently validated.** Fully automated memory equipped electronic devices are preferable because they require less training, prevent observer and reporter bias, and allow for average readings over defined intervals and comparison with previous periods [O'Brien et al, 2003].
- For currently available, validated, and recommended devices, see www.bhsoc.org and www.dableducational.org.
- **There is currently no consensus about how to calculate a home measurement mean value** in terms of frequency, timing or number of measurements to be taken [N England Hypertension GDG, 2004]. One suggestion [O'Brien et al, 2003] is to:
  - Systolic BP monitoring should be performed after a period of 5 minutes' rest.
  - Device cuff must be at heart level on the arm with the highest BP.
  - Take the average of measurements over 7 days with morning and evening recordings.
  - Discard measurements of the first day as they may not be representative.
  - Average measurements from 6 days (i.e. 12 readings) to calculate the home BP level.
  - Repeat measurements for one week every three months for long term observation.
  - Avoid overuse of the method and self modification of treatment.

How should the results of home monitoring be interpreted?

- **Typically values from home monitoring tend to be lower than their clinic readings.**
- Therefore to compare the two methods treatment thresholds and targets should probably be adjusted downwards, although evidence for true equivalence is lacking and will be variable [Williams et al, 2004].
- The British Hypertensive Society recommends a downward correction of 10/5 mmHg when converting clinic to home values.
- **The threshold for the upper limit of normality most commonly recommended is 135/85 mmHg,** identical to mean daytime ambulatory BP [O'Brien et al, 2001c].
- Evidence is limited on the degree to which home monitoring BP can be used to determine cardiovascular prognosis [N England Hypertension GDG, 2004].
- Higher readings need to be assessed as part of the overall cardiovascular risk profile.

What are the advantages and disadvantages of home monitoring?

- **Advantages** of home BP monitoring are potentially similar to ABPM including that:
  - Frequent measurement produces average values that may be more reproducible and reliable than traditional clinic measurement.
  - Self monitoring may improve BP control by improving compliance as people become more involved in their care [Cappuccio et al, 2004].
  - Two outcome studies have shown that self monitoring predicts cardiovascular outcome better than clinic measurements [Bobrie et al, 2004; Kizer et al, 2005] but more evidence is needed to confirm this.
- **Disadvantages** are mainly that it is essential to train people in the appropriate use of devices and data interpretation, to avoid measurement bias. Several studies have highlighted inconsistent measuring techniques.

How do I confirm that the blood pressure is raised?

- **NICE recommends that ideally, a second confirmatory reading should be taken at the end of the consultation if the first blood pressure (BP) measurement >=140/90 mmHg (C).**
  - From a pragmatic perspective, it is a good idea to taken several readings over several weeks following a BP measurement >=140/90 mmHg.
- **Measure BP on both of the person's arms** with the higher value identifying the reference arm for future measurement (C). This is only necessary at the first consultation.
- **To confirm/identify hypertension (sustained raised BP >=140/90 mmHg),** ask the individual to return for at least two subsequent clinics where BP is assessed from two readings under the best conditions available (C).
- **In people with arrhythmia type disorders e.g. atrial fibrillation (AF), auscultatory measurements and multiple readings are recommended** — marked beat-to-beat variability associated with AF can make the use of semiautomatic or automated devices difficult.
- **Measurements should normally be made at monthly intervals. However, people with more severe hypertension (and cardiovascular risk) should be re-evaluated more urgently (C).**
- **The duration of monitoring** to establish the BP depends on the initial value.
- **The threshold level for a diagnosis of hypertension is arbitrary and there is no precise level** [MacMahon et al, 1990; Lewington et al, 2002].

[N England Hypertension GDG, 2004]

What are the causes of secondary hypertension?

About 5% of cases of hypertension in the community are secondary to an underlying condition. A minority of these can be reversed, with cure or easier control of hypertension being achieved subsequently. The results of physical examination and *routine tests* will help identify a few of the causes — most will be missed unless routine tests include the estimation of renin and catecholamine secretion.

Renal disorder

Renal disorders as a group are possibly the most common secondary cause of hypertension but they are rarely amenable to surgical cure.

- **Chronic pyelonephritis:** usually picked up unexpectedly on ultrasound when investigating hypertension. A history of vesicoureteric reflux, or recurrent urinary tract infections is less likely.
- **Diabetic kidney disease:** indicated by microalbuminuria or proteinuria.
- **Glomerulonephritis:** often indicated by microscopic haematuria.
- **Polycystic kidney disease:** suggested by abdominal or flank mass, microscopic haematuria, family history.
- **Obstructive uropathy:** may have abdominal or flank mass.
- **Renal cell carcinoma.**

Vascular disorder

- **Coarctation of the aorta:** usually results in upper limb hypertension, and there may be a significant difference in BP between the left and right arm. Other signs include absent or weak femoral pulses, radio-femoral delay, palpable collateral blood vessels in the back muscles, and a suprasternal murmur radiating through to the back.
- **Renal artery stenosis:** suspect if peripheral vascular disease and presence of abdominal bruit. Most cases are clinically silent (other than hypertension), but may be suspected from an increased level of plasma renin.

Endocrine disorder

- **Primary hyperaldosteronism (Conn's syndrome) usually presents with:** hypokalaemia, alkalosis (elevated bicarbonate) and plasma sodium >140 mmol/L. It may rarely present with tetany, muscle weakness, polyuria. All features may be completely masked by treatment with a calcium-channel blocker. Conn's syndrome is probably the commonest curable cause of hypertension. After identification of a possible adrenal adenoma on computed tomography (CT) or magnetic resonance (MR) scan, patients require tertiary referral for confirmation of unilateral aldosterone excess and laparoscopic adrenalectomy.
- **Phaeochromocytoma:** may present with intermittent high BP, headaches, sweating attacks, and palpitations, or unexplained fever and abdominal pains. Alternatively people may be asymptomatic. It is the rarest but most important cause of hypertension to diagnose because malignant transformation or catastrophic haemorrhage from the tumour can be fatal complications.
- **Cushing's syndrome:** suspect when clinical features are present (e.g. truncal obesity and striae). It rarely presents as hypertension alone.
- **Acromegaly:** suspect if clinical features are present (e.g. enlargement of hands and feet, facial changes, sweating, etc).

Miscellaneous

- **Connective tissue disorders:** scleroderma, systemic lupus erythematosus (SLE), polyarteritis nodosa.
- **Retroperitoneal fibrosis.**

Drug or toxin-induced

- **Alcohol may be the commonest individual secondary cause of hypertension.** Features include variable hypertension, resistant to commonly used drugs, which disappears within a week or two of complete abstinence.
- Others include:
  - Ciclosporin
  - Cocaine and other substances of abuse
  - Combined oral contraceptive pill
  - Corticosteroids
  - Erythropoietin
  - Leflunomide
  - Nonsteroidal anti-inflammatory drugs (NSAIDs)
  - Sympathomimetics (may be found in over-the-counter cough and cold remedies) e.g. ephedrine and phenylpropanolamine etc.
  - Liquorice (may be present in herbal medicines)

Complications and prognosis

Complications

- Stroke, transient ischaemic attack, dementia
- Left ventricular hypertrophy and/or left ventricular strain on electrocardiogram, heart failure
- Myocardial infarction, angina
- Peripheral vascular disease
- Fundal hemorrhages or exudates, papillodema
- Renal impairment (associated with raised serum creatinine)

[Williams et al, 2004]

Prognosis

- **Hypertension is a contributory factor in cardiovascular diseases which account for 30% of all deaths annually** [N England Hypertension GDG, 2004].
- The cardiovascular prognosis of hypertension is worse in the presence of:
  - Certain comorbidities (e.g. diabetes, obesity)
  - Lifestyle risk factors (e.g. high dietary salt intake, smoking, lack of exercise)
  - Other risk factors (e.g. family history, male sex, Afro-Caribbean or South Asian ethnic origin)
- The relative risk reduction with antihypertensive treatment is approximately constant — predictions from epidemiological data indicate that a reduction of 5–6 mmHg in diastolic BP sustained over at least 5 years produces a 35–40% relative risk reduction in stroke and a 20–25% relative risk reduction in coronary heart disease [Collins and Peto, 1994]. Greatest absolute benefits will be seen in those at highest risk.

[Padwal et al, 2001]

Management issues

- Overview of management of hypertension p.986
- What routine investigations should be done? p.986
- Cardiovascular risk assessment in people with hypertension p.986
- Lifestyle interventions in people with hypertension p.987
- When should I recommend starting antihypertensive medication? p.987
- What drug should I start treatment with? p.988
- What target blood pressure should I aim for? p.989
- What should I do if the target BP is not achieved with one drug? p.989
- When can antihypertensive treatment be stopped or reduced? p.991
- Should beta-blockers or thiazide diuretics be prescribed for people at high risk of Type 2 diabetes? p.991
- How should I manage older people? p.992
- What issues should I bear in mind when treating people of Afro-Caribbean or South Asian ethnic origin? p.992
- When should I recommend low-dose aspirin? p.992
- How should I manage hyperlipidaemia? p.992
- Should I prescribe hormone replacement therapy? p.993

- Medicines management p.993

Overview of management of hypertension

- **Blood pressure (BP) reduction** should be part of a general cardiovascular risk reduction strategy (along with raised lipids management, antiplatelet use, maintaining regular exercise, smoking cessation, eating a healthy diet, and minimising alcohol, coffee and salt intake).
- **Offer advice about lifestyle interventions** initially and then periodically to people undergoing assessment or treatment of hypertension.
- **Refer immediately** people with accelerated (malignant) hypertension (BP >=180/110 mmHg with signs of papilloedema and/or retinal haemorrhage) or suspected phaeochromocytoma (possible signs include labile or postural hypotension, headache, palpitations, pallor and excessive sweating) (C).
- **NICE recommends that** specialist referral should be considered for people with documented postural hypotension (i.e. a fall in systolic BP when standing of >=20 mmHg) or symptoms of it (C).
- **If raised BP is sustained, assess cardiovascular risk using the Joint British Societies new risk charts.** Cardiovascular risk should guide treatment.
- **Discuss all treatment options** and fully involve people in decisions about their care as attitudes to benefits and risks will vary. Consider providing PRODIGY patient information leaflets (PILs) as appropriate.
- **People with sustained:**
  - **Systolic BPs of 140–159 mmHg or diastolic BPs of 90–99 mmHg, or both,** may require treatment, depending upon their absolute level of risk of developing cardiovascular disease (A).
  - **Systolic BPs of >=160 mmHg, or diastolic BPs >=100 mmHg, or both, all** require drug treatment and lifestyle advice (A).
- **Drug treatment should normally begin with a low dose thiazide diuretic** (A).
- **Consider initiating with a beta-blocker** in people <55 years old, with moderately raised BP.
- **Consider adding in drugs in a stepwise approach** to achieve a target of =<140/90 mmHg Titrate drug doses as according to the manufacturer's instructions noting any cautions and contraindications (A).
- **Select second-line drugs according to whether or not the person has a raised risk of new-onset Type 2 diabetes:**
  - People not at raised risk — add a beta-blocker (A).
  - People at raised risk — add an angiotensin-converting enzyme (ACE) inhibitor (A), or an angiotensin-II receptor antagonist (AIIRA).
- **For third line selection,** add a calcium-channel blocker (A).
- **If further BP lowering is warranted,** consider an ACE inhibitor or beta-blocker (if not yet used), another antihypertensive drug, or referring to a specialist (A).
- **Provide appropriate guidance and materials** about the benefits of drugs and the unwanted adverse effects sometimes experienced in order to help people make informed choices (C).
- **Once BP is managed adequately,** provide an annual review of care to monitor BP, provide support and discuss lifestyle, symptoms and medication (C). More frequent review may be necessary in some people and other authorities would recommend at least a 6-monthly review [Williams et al, 2004].

H

What routine investigations should be done?

- **The following routine tests should be performed:** (C)
  - Urine test strip — to measure presence of protein and blood.
  - Blood sample — to measure:
    - Plasma glucose (ideally fasted level).
    - Electrolytes.
    - Creatinine.
    - Serum total cholesterol and high-density lipoprotein. Note: fasting is only necessary where a triglyceride level is required.
  - Electrocardiogram using a 12 lead electrocardiograph — to help exclude severe left ventricular hypertrophy and ischaemia.
- Tests may help identify diabetes, evidence of hypertensive damage to the heart and kidneys, and secondary causes of hypertension such as kidney disease.

Cardiovascular risk assessment in people with hypertension

Why is cardiovascular risk assessed?

- **Cardiovascular risk should be assessed to discuss prognosis and healthcare** options with people, who have a raised BP and other modifiable risk factors for cardiovascular disease (CVD) (B) [N England Hypertension GDG, 2004].
  - Factors such as older age, smoking and high cholesterol levels increase a person's cardiovascular disease (CVD) risk associated with any BP.
  - It is important to offer treatment to people based on their profile of cardiovascular risk rather than focusing on BP in isolation.

When should I assess cardiovascular risk?

- **If raised blood pressure (BP) is sustained and the individual does not have established cardiovascular disease (CVD), or other major atherosclerotic disease,** a formal assessment of CVD risk may help to guide the treatment choice (C) [N England Hypertension GDG, 2004].
- **There is no need to assess risk in high risk groups** (people with sustained BP >=160/100 mmHg, a previous myocardial infarction, angina, non-haemorrhagic cerebrovascular disease, peripheral vascular disease, diabetes, or atherosclerotic renovascular disease) as there is already >20% (CVD risk).

How should I assess cardiovascular risk?

- **New risk charts have been produced by the Joint British Societies (JBS)** to help determine CVD risk and support treatment decisions for people with mild hypertension, The proposed new charts:
  - Assess 10 year risk of CVD (non-fatal myocardial infarction and stroke, coronary and stroke death and new angina pectoris) for individuals who have not already developed coronary heart disease (CHD) or other major atherosclerotic disease. They have been proposed to replace the former CHD risk assessment charts.
  - Can be accessed via: www.bhsoc.org/Cardiovascular_Risk_Charts_and_Calculators.htm or the back of the BNF www.bnf.org.
- For each person choose the table matching their gender, age and smoking status (smoker = current smoker or a person who has stopped smoking within the past 5 years). If no high-density lipoprotein (HDL) cholesterol result is available for the total cholesterol (TC) to HDL ratio, use the total serum cholesterol value (TC) as this assumes HDL is 1.00 mmol/l.

- **If only the CHD risk score is known multiply it by 4/3** to approximate the CVD risk score.
- A variety of international risk models have been developed and many provide a useful prognostic tool for clinicians and patients in primary care. However they all have limitations and so PRODIGY only specifically recommends use of the JBS new risk charts.

When do the cardiovascular risk charts incorrectly estimate risk and how should I manage this?

- **The charts predict only 10 years risk** and therefore grossly underestimate lifetime risk in younger people. Therefore the new charts have been modified so that anyone below 50 years of age is assessed on the basis of risk if aged 49 years old.
- **In men aged 40–59 years,** the charts may overestimate CVD risk.
- **The charts will overestimate current risk most in people aged less than 40 years.**
  - Clinical judgement must be exercised in deciding on treatment in younger people.
  - In people less than 40 years of age with hypertension, the risks and benefits of drug treatment need to be discussed and weighed up when considering the lifetime cardiovascular risk.
  - Refer for specialist review those people where a secondary cause of hypertension is suspected.
- **The charts may underestimate CVD risk in people being treated with antihypertensive drugs** as the charts are based on groups of people with untreated BP, total cholesterol and HDL cholesterol. However the charts may still act as a guide when augmenting treatment.
- **The JBS recommend to multiply the risk by approximately 1.5 in people:**
  - With family histories of premature CVD or stroke.
  - Of ethnic backgrounds originating from the Indian subcontinent.
- **In other circumstances where the charts underestimate CVD risk, there is currently no quantifiable way of assessing the extent.** However, an awareness of these scenarios may support practical decision making where the assessment is borderline, such as in people with:
  - Raised triglyceride levels.
  - Premature menopause.
  - An impaired fasting glucose (6.1–6.9 mmol/l), who are not yet diabetic.

Lifestyle interventions in people with hypertension

When should I recommend lifestyle interventions?

- **Lifestyle interventions should be encouraged as an integral part of the management of all people with hypertension,** either alone in mild hypertension or as adjunct to drug treatment.
- A healthier lifestyle (including a healthy diet and regular exercise) can reduce, delay or remove the need for long-term drug treatment in some people by lowering BP and CVD risk [N England Hypertension GDG, 2004] but regular follow-up is required.

What lifestyle interventions are recommended?

- **Offer appropriate guidance and written or audiovisual materials to promote lifestyle changes (B).** Provide patients with PRODIGY patient information leaflets (PILs) as appropriate.
- **The most important lifestyle recommendations include:**
  - **Encourage people to keep their dietary sodium intake low,** either by reducing or substituting sodium salt, as this can reduce BP (**B**).
  - **Offer advice and help to smokers to stop smoking (A).** Smoking cessation has been associated with improvements in morbidity and mortality but the benefit cannot easily be quantified in terms of any BP reductions that may follow. For more information, see the PRODIGY guidance on *Smoking cessation.*
  - **Ask about alcohol consumption** and encourage a reduced intake where the individual drinks excessively (men: >21 units per week, and women: >14 units per week) as this can reduce BP and has broader health benefits (**B**).
  - **Encourage people to reduce calorie intake,** and bodyweight reduction should follow as well as BP reduction, see Table 4.
- **Other lifestyle recommendations include:**
  - **Discourage excessive consumption of coffee** (>=5 cups per day) and other caffeine-rich products (**B**). Excessive coffee intake is associated with small increases in BP.
  - **Relaxation therapies** (e.g. stress management, meditation, cognitive therapies, muscle relaxation and biofeedback) can reduce BP and individuals may wish to pursue these as part of their treatment. However routine provision by primary care teams is neither widely available, nor currently recommended (**B**).
  - **Do not offer calcium, magnesium or potassium supplements** (alone or in combination) as a method for reducing BP (**B**).
  - **Inform people about local initiatives** to provide support and promote healthy lifestyle by, e.g. healthcare teams or patient organizations.

[N England Hypertension GDG, 2004]

What changes in BP can be expected from lifestyle interventions?

- Changes in BP that might be achievable from lifestyle interventions are given in Table 4.
- Data are summarised from randomised controlled trials of lifestyle interventions where follow-up was for 8 weeks or more.
- Combinations of two or more lifestyle interventions can achieve even greater reductions.
- About one quarter of people with hypertension will achieve a reduction in systolic BP of at least 10 mmHg with a combined diet and exercise intervention, [N England Hypertension GDG, 2004].

[Whelton et al, 2002; N England Hypertension GDG, 2004; Williams et al, 2004]

When should I recommend starting antihypertensive medication?

- The thresholds for intervention and recommendations for review are displayed in Table 5.
- **Drug treatment should be offered to people with a** sustained (**A**):
  - Systolic BP of 140–159 mmHg, or diastolic BP 90–99 mmHg, or both, in the presence of existing CVD, or target organ damage, or an estimated CVD risk >=20% over 10 years.
  - Systolic BP of >=160 mmHg, or diastolic BP >=100 mmHg or more, or both.
- Note: the 10 year risk of CVD >=20% is equivalent to coronary heart disease (CHD) >=15% over 10 years. For more information, see *How should I assess cardiovascular risk?*
- **Treatment should be offered to people regardless of age.**
- **People with isolated systolic hypertension (systolic BP >=160 mmHg)** should be offered the same treatment as people with raised systolic *and* diastolic BP (**A**). Therefore generally initiate someone with thiazide-type diuretic, even if the diastolic BP is normal. The following

H

Table 4: Lifestyle interventions for BP reduction.

Intervention	Recommendation	Approximate systolic BP reduction anticipated
Physical activity	Engage in regular aerobic physical activity, for example, brisk walking for at least 30 minutes most days	Up to 10 mmHg
Weight reduction including the Dietary Approaches to Stop Hypertension (DASH) eating plan*	Maintain ideal body mass index (20–25 kg/m²). Consume diet rich in fruit, and vegetables (at least 5 portions per day) and in low-fat dairy products with a reduced content of saturated and total fat.	Up to 14 mmHg
Dietary sodium restriction	Reduce dietary sodium intake to <100 mmol/day (<2.4 g sodium or <6 g sodium chloride)	Up to 10 mmHg
Alcohol moderation	Men =<21 units per week Women =<14 units per week	Up to 10 mmHg
Relaxation	Structured interventions	Up to 10 mmHg

* The DASH eating plan can be downloaded from www.nhlbi.nih.gov/health/public/heart/hbp/dash

trials provide evidence that ISH should be treated in the same way as essential hypertension:

- SHEP (Systolic Hypertension in Elderly Program) was a randomized controlled trial (RCT) involving 4736 people with ISH followed up for approximately 5 years [Systolic Hypertension-Europe (Syst-Eur) Trial Investigators, 1997]. The trial found antihypertensive stepped care with low-dose chlortalidone as step 1 found 5 year absolute benefit of 30 stroke events per 1000 participants and 5 year absolute benefit of 55 major cardiovascular events per 1000.
- SYST-EUR (Systolic Hypertension in Europe) was an RCT of 4695 people with ISH randomly assigned to nitrendipine 10–40 mg daily with the possible addition of enalapril and hydrochlorothiazide, or matching placebos. At a median of 2 years follow-up, the difference between drug and placebo groups were systolic 10.1 mmHg and diastolic 4.5 mmHg. Active treatment reduced the total rate of stroke from 13.7 to 7.9 endpoints per 1000 patient years. Cardiovascular mortality was slightly lower on active treatment but all-cause mortality was not influenced. The researchers concluded that treatment of 1000 patients for 5 years with this type of regimen may prevent 29 strokes or 53 major cardiovascular endpoints. However there is no reason why any other antihypertensive regimen would not produce this effect.
- ISH drug treatment has been investigated in Trial [Systolic Hypertension-Europe (Syst-Eur) Trial Investigators, 1997].

[N England Hypertension GDG, 2004; Williams et al, 2004]

What drug should I start treatment with?

- **In general, the main determinant of benefit from BP-lowering drugs is the achieved BP, rather than the choice of treatment** — this has been confirmed by head to head studies that indicate similar benefits irrespective of which major antihypertensive drug class is used to begin treatment [Blood Pressure Lowering Treatment Trialists Collaboration, 2000; Staessen et al, 2001].
- However the blood pressure lowering arm of the Anglo-Scandinavian Cardiac Outcomes Trial (ASCOT), a large trial (19,000 people) comparing BP lowering treatments, has recently been halted. Significant cardiovascular benefits were seen using a calcium-channel blocker (amlodipine) and/or an angiotensin enzyme inhibitor (perindopril) compared to a beta-blocker (atenolol) and/or a thiazide diuretic (**bendroflumethiazide**

Table 5: Thresholds for intervention and recommendations for review following BP measurement.

Blood Pressure Level	Recommendation
Systolic BP <130 mmHg and/or Diastolic BP <85 mmHg	Review within 5 years
Systolic BP 130–139 mmHg and/or Diastolic BP 85–89 mmHg and/or people who have had high BP at any time previously	Review annually
Systolic BP 140–159 mmHg and/or Diastolic BP 90–99 mmHg	Cardiovascular complications/ target organ damage or diabetes* present: confirm within 12 weeks, and then treat.
	Re-measure at monthly intervals if cardiovascular complications/target organ damage or diabetes is absent.
Systolic BP >=160–179 mmHg and/or Diastolic BP >=100–109 mmHg	Cardiovascular complications/target organ damage or diabetes* present: confirm over 3–4 weeks, then treat.
	Cardiovascular complications/ target organ damage or diabetes absent: lifestyle measures, re-measure weekly initially, and treat if BP persists at these levels over 4–12 weeks.
Systolic BP >=180–219 mmHg and/or Diastolic BP 110–119 mmHg	Confirm over 1–2 weeks, and then treat.
Systolic BP >=220 mmHg and/or Diastolic BP >=120 mmHg	Repeat on same day and treat immediately if confirmed.
Secondary hypertension	Specialist referral is appropriate. (Admission for immediate treatment is unnecessary for most with secondary hypertension.)

* For more information about people with diabetes, see the PRODIGY guidance on *Diabetes Type 1 and 2 — hypertension.*

[Williams et al, 2004]

[bendrofluazide]). The results of this trial are expected to be published in the second half of 2005 [ASCOT, 2004].

Comorbidity will often influence the choice of antihypertensive treatment selection.

What does NICE currently recommend?

Drug treatment should normally begin with a low dose thiazide diuretic (A).

In people <55 years old, with moderately raised BP, consider beginning with a beta-blocker.

[N England Hypertension GDG, 2004]

What is the rationale for this approach by NICE?

In the Antihypertensive and Lipid-Lowering Treatment to Prevent Heart Attack Trial (ALLHAT), 33,357 people aged >=55 years with hypertension and at least one other coronary heart disease (CHD) risk factor were randomly allocated to treatment with chlortalidone, amlodipine, or lisinopril [ALLHAT Officers, 2002]. Follow up took place over 4 to 8 years. No difference was found in the rate of fatal CHD, non-fatal myocardial infarction or in all-cause mortality. However, compared with people allocated to chlortalidone:

- People taking amlodipine had an increased incidence of heart failure (10.2% compared with 7.7%; RR 1.38, 95% CI 1.25 to 1.52).
- People taking lisinopril had an increased incidence of combined cardiovascular disease (33% compared with 31%; RR 1.1, 95% CI 1.05 to 1.16); stroke (6.3% compared with 5.6%; RR 1.15, 95% CI 1.02 to 1.3); and heart failure (8.7% compared with 7.7%; RR 1.19, 95% CI, 1.07 to 1.31).

A meta-analysis of data from 42 long term randomised controlled trials (n = 192,478) confirmed that none of the other antihypertensive drug classes were significantly better than low-dose thiazide diuretics for preventing any major cardiovascular disease outcome [Psaty et al, 2003].

Given the full evidence profile, there seems to be no justification for routinely beginning an ACE inhibitor or calcium-channel blocker.

The beta blocker option in people <55 years of age came from acceptance of the argument for choosing a drug that suppresses the renin system (as well as acceptance that the sequence of giving a thiazide diuretic and then a beta-blocker could be reversed).

What does the BHS currently recommend?

Antihypertensive drugs should be selected by considering compelling indications and contraindications. Table 6 represents a summary of compelling indications for antihypertensive drug groups and evidence from trial data regarding individual drug use.

Where no compelling circumstances apply, drug treatment should be initiated based on the age and ethnicity of the person using the AB/CD treatment plan. Each letter refers to an antihypertensive drug class:

- A: either an ACE inhibitor or an angiotensin-II receptor antagonist (AIIRA)
- B: a beta-blocker
- C: a calcium-channel blocker (CCB)
- D: a diuretic (thiazide-type)

In Caucasian people <55 years old — prescribe A or B.

In Caucasian people >=55 years or people of African descent of any age — prescribe C or D.

[Williams et al, 2004]

What is the rationale for this approach by the BHS?

This AB/CD rule is based on a theoretical assumption that hypertension can be classed as 'high or low renin' [Brown et al, 2003]. Treatment should begin with a category of drug that either inhibits the renin-angiotensin system or not:

- ACE inhibitors, AIIRAs, or beta-blocker drugs being more effective in Caucasian people less than 55 years old who have high renin concentrations.
- CCBs or thiazide diuretic drugs being more effective in Caucasian people 55 years or over, or people of African descent of any age who have low renin concentrations [Dickerson et al, 1999].

- The initial antihypertensive selection in the AB/CD approach was based on the findings of:
  - A randomised double blind trial (n = 1292) that compared BP lowering by different drugs. It found D to be less effective in young Caucasians and C was more effective (at all ages) than A or B in the black population [Materson et al, 1993].
  - Two small (n = 34, n = 56) drug rotation studies [Dickerson et al, 1999; Deary et al, 2002].
  - Renin profiling studies.
- Cardiovascular outcome study data is limited to support the AB/CD treatment plan.
- Indications for the antihypertensive drug groups and the supporting evidence is outlined in Table 6.

H

What target blood pressure should I aim for?

Cardiovascular risk is directly related to both systolic and diastolic BP levels without any evidence of a threshold down to at least 115/75 mmHg.

- **The National Institute of Clinical Excellence** (NICE) **recommends a target of =<140/90 mmHg** for non-diabetic people with hypertension [N England Hypertension GDG, 2004].
- **The British Hypertensive Society (BHS) recommends a target of <140/85 mmHg** in non-diabetic people with hypertension [Williams et al, 2004].

What should I do if the target BP is not achieved with one drug?

In the clinical trial environment between 50–75% people have been found to achieve a target BP of <140/90 mmHg [Turnbull et al, 2003] but for the general population this percentage will be lower. In practice under treated hypertension is common, with up to half of all people with diagnosed hypertension not reaching recommended targets.

- **Additional drugs should be added in order to achieve a target of =<140/90 mmHg or until further treatment is inappropriate or declined.** Many people require two or more drugs to achieve current blood pressure (BP) targets and up to a third of people will require three or more drugs [Williams et al, 2004].
  - **Antihypertensives from different classes generally have an additive effect when prescribed together.** Sub maximal dosages of two drugs may result in larger falls in BP and fewer adverse effects than maximal dosages of a single drug.
  - Titrate drug doses according to the manufacturer's instructions noting any cautions and contraindications (**A**). For information on what dose of drug to use, see the *Medicines management* section.
- **Sometimes a clinical decision may have to be made whether to intensify drug treatment to achieve target or settle for a BP which is less than target.** People not achieving their target BP, or for whom further treatment is inappropriate or declined, will still receive worthwhile benefit from any reductions in BP (**B**) [N England Hypertension GDG, 2004].
  - Larger reductions in BP are associated with larger reductions in risk.
  - In the Hypertension Optimal Trial (HOT), BP levels of around 160 mmHg systolic and 90 mmHg diastolic

Table 6: Compelling indications for antihypertensive drug groups and evidence from trial data.

Drug groups, indications and recommendations	Key trial data
Thiazide-type diuretics: a relatively low dose of a thiazide-type diuretic is first choice in most people, especially >=55 years as well as people with isolated systolic hypertension (ISH), heart failure and in secondary prevention of stroke.	This is strongly supported by the ALLHAT trial, which found chlortalidone to have slightly better cardiovascular outcomes compared with other antihypertensive drugs [ALLHAT Officers, 2002 and a recent meta-analysis [Psaty et al, 2003].
Beta-blockers: first choice if angina or history of myocardial infarction (MI). Consider appropriately licensed drugs in people with heart failure.	Have proven morbidity and mortality benefits [Messerli et al, 1998].
ACE inhibitors: first choice in heart failure, left ventricular dysfunction, and Type 1 diabetic nephropathy. Also used in post MI or established coronary heart disease and secondary stroke prevention.	Clinical trials have found them to be effective at improving outcomes, [Hansson et al, 1999; Sleight, 2000] and the ALLHAT trial confirms that an ACE or a CCB are possible alternative choices to diuretic treatment [Hansson et al, 1999; ALLHAT Officers, 2002]. The PROGRESS (Perindopril Protection Against Recurrent Stroke) trial randomized people following stroke to perindopril alone or with addition of indapamide if necessary or placebo [Progress Collaborativ Group, 2001]. The trial did not find an overall reduction in mortality but found statistically significant reductions in coronary events (RR 0.76, 95% CI 0.60 to 0.96) and stroke (RR 0.73, 95% CI 0.64 to 0.84) with combined use of perindopril and thiazide, endorsing combination treatment as soon as possible to achieve improved clinica benefit.
Angiotensin-II receptor antagonists (AIIRAs): alternative option in people where ACE inhibitor is not tolerated. AIIRAs are indicated in Type 2 diabetic nephropathy, hypertension with left ventricular hypertrophy, heart failure in ACE-intolerant people and post MI.	Losartan and candesartan have evidence for improved cardiovascular outcomes in people with hypertension. Losartan has only been studied in very high-risk individuals with left ventricular hypertrophy [Dahlof et al, 2002]. Candesartan has been randomised to elderly people with mild to moderate hypertension and without cardiovascular disease in the preceding 6 months to candesartan or placebo [Lithell et al, 2003]. The results did not show an overall reduction in mortality or coronary events but a borderline statistically significant reduction in stroke (RR 0.77, 95% CI 0.59 to 1.01), primarily due to reduced non-fatal stroke Valsartan has been compared with amlodipine, each drug being randomized to people over 50 with hypertension and high risk of cardiovascular events [Julius et al, 2004]. The main outcome, a composite of cardiac morbidity and mortality did not differ significantly between the two. MI (a secondary outcome) was significantly more frequent in the valsartan group (Hazard ratio 1.19, 95% CI 1.02 to 1.38). However the incidence of diabetes was significantly lower in people on valsartan, similar to the apparent difference between lisinopril and amlodipine in ALLHAT. More studies are required before they can be recommended over other antihypertensives.
Calcium-channel blockers (CCBs) (dihydropyridines): a long-acting dihydropyridine is an alternative to a thiazide-type diuretic in elderly people, especially those with isolated systolic hypertension. Consider as an alternative to a beta-blocker or a rate-limiting CCB in angina.	Meta-analyses have not demonstrated any convincing evidence that any one class has benefit over other antihypertensive drugs [Blood Pressure Lowering Treatment Trialists Collaboration, 2000; Pahor et al, 2000; Opie and Schall, 2002]. Trial evidence supports the role of long-acting dihydropyridine CCBs in elderly hypertensive populations especially in those with isolated systolic hypertension [SIGN, 2002], although higher doses are likely to be required to achieve target BP [Systolic Hypertension-Europe (Syst-Eur) Trial Investigators, 1997]. Results from the ALLHAT trial confirm that CCBs remain one of the main drug groups for treating hypertension [ALLHAT Officers, 2002]
CCBs (rate limiting): alternative to a beta-blocker or a dihydropyridine CCB in people with angina. Also an option post MI only in people who cannot tolerate beta-blockers.	
Alpha-blockers: benign prostatic hypertrophy	Have been shown to be less effective than other classes as monotherapy in reducing BP, but useful as a fourth-line drug. Doxazosin was found in the ALLHAT trial to be as effective as diuretics in preventing the primary outcome of coronary events, despit being less effective to reducing BP, however the doxazosin treatment arm in the trial was stopped because of an increase in cases of new onset heart failure compared with people in the chlortalidone treatment arm [ALLHAT Officers, 2000].

conferred only slightly worse outcomes than the target levels [Hansson et al, 1998].

What does NICE recommend for add-on treatment?

- **A stepwise approach to adding drugs is recommended in an attempt to achieve the target BP.**
  - If a drug is tolerated but target BP is not achieved — add second line treatment.
  - If a drug is *not* tolerated — discontinue and proceed to second line treatment.
- **ACE inhibitors and beta-blockers** whose mode of action is to suppress renin production may not be effective in lowering BP in patients of Afro-caribbean descent, when used as monotherapy, however these drugs may be effective in combination with a thiazide diuretic.
- **Second line treatment should be selected according to whether the person has a raised risk of new-onset Type 2 diabetes:**
  - In people at risk of Type 2 diabetes:
    - Add an angiotensin-converting enzyme (ACE) inhibitor (A).
    - Consider substituting an angiotensin-receptor II antagonist (AIIRA) in people who do not tolerate an ACE inhibitor due to cough (A).
  - In people *not* at risk of Type 2 diabetes:
    - Add a beta-blocker (A) or,

- Add a thiazide if a beta-blocker was used first line.
- Note: depending on patient comorbidity and the results of ASCOT [ASCOT, 2004], it may be best to explore alternative options to a thiazide combined with a beta-blocker where possible.
- If a thiazide is not tolerated and the person is *not* at risk of Type 2 diabetes:
  - NICE recommends that a beta-blocker should be prescribed.

If a third line treatment is required:
- Add a calcium-channel blocker (**A**).

If further BP lowering is indicated consider (A):
- An ACE inhibitor or beta-blocker (if not yet used).
- Another antihypertensive drug.
- Referring to a specialist.

In people at high risk of developing Type 2 diabetes the combination of a thiazide diuretic with a beta-blocker may be appropriate to manage treatment resistant hypertension or if cardiovascular disease develops (**B**). If this combination is necessary, it should only be a fourth line strategy.
[N England Hypertension GDG, 2004]

What does the BHS recommend for add-on treatment?

If hypertension is mild and uncomplicated and if a first drug is well tolerated but the target BP is not achieved:
- Substitute an alternative drug.

In more severe or complicated hypertension and if a drug is tolerated but the target BP is not achieved:
- Use a stepwise approach to adding drugs until BP is controlled.
- Treatment can be stepped down later if BP falls substantially below the target level.

The AB/CD treatment plan can be used as a guide. Each letter refers to an antihypertensive drug class:
- A or B translates to either an ACE inhibitor/an angiotensin-II receptor antagonist or a beta-blocker respectively.
- C or D meaning either a calcium-channel blocker (CCB) or a diuretic (thiazide-type).

If two drugs are required logical combinations are: A (or B) * + C or D.

If BP is still insufficiently controlled, the combination of A (or B) * + C + D is recommended.

When hypertension remains resistant, A + B + C + D or the addition of an alpha-blocker or low dose spironolactone may be effective.

Avoid B + D in those people at high risk of developing Type 2 diabetes, unless there are compelling indications.

Beta-blockers combined with diuretics may lead to a greater incidence of diabetes mellitus compared with other antihypertensive drug combinations.
[Williams et al, 2004]

When can antihypertensive treatment be stopped or reduced?

People with a low cardiovascular risk and well controlled BP may be offered a trial reduction or withdrawal of treatment with appropriate lifestyle guidance and ongoing review (B) [N England Hypertension GDG, 2004].

Withdrawal of antihypertensive drugs has a much better chance of being successful:
- In people who are relatively young, with lower on-treatment BP, taking only one drug and who adopt lifestyle changes.
- When supported by structured interventions to encourage people to restrict their salt intake and to lose weight, if overweight.

- **Patients who reach 80 years of age while on antihypertensives** should probably remain on drug treatment especially if there is evidence of target organ damage or if there are other significant cardiovascular disease risk factors such as diabetes.

Should beta-blockers or thiazide diuretics be prescribed for people at high risk of Type 2 diabetes?

Who is at high risk of developing Type 2 diabetes?

- **People at high risk of Type 2 diabetes have:**
  - A strong family history of Type 2 diabetes.
  - Impaired glucose tolerance (fasting plasma glucose >=6.5 mmol/l).
  - Clinical obesity (Body Mass Index >=30).
  - South Asian or Afro-Caribbean ethnic origin.

[N England Hypertension GDG, 2004]

What does NICE recommend?

- **The National Institute of Clinical Evidence (NICE) recommend either a thiazide diuretic or a beta-blocker for people (including those at risk of Type 2 diabetes) requiring first line treatment of hypertension.**
- **NICE do not recommend a beta-blocker and thiazide as an initial combination in people at risk of developing Type 2 diabetes;** however this combination may be necessary when hypertension is resistant to treatment or if cardiovascular disease develops (**B**).
- At review, consider modifying the medication of people who are at risk of Type 2 diabetes and are currently using only a thiazide diuretic and beta-blocker combination and at raised risk of diabetes (**B**). A change of treatment is unlikely to be appropriate in people taking three or more antihypertensive drugs.

[N England Hypertension GDG, 2004]

What does the BHS recommend?

- The British Hypertension Society recommends the AB/CD treatment plan in which a thiazide diuretic *or* a beta-blocker may be given to people at high risk of diabetes
- BHS advise against the *routine* use of a thiazide diuretic and beta-blocker combination in people at high risk of developing diabetes.

[Williams et al, 2004]

What is the evidence?

- Trial evidence suggests that the onset of Type 2 diabetes is greater in people taking a beta-blocker and thiazide combination compared with other drug combinations and may lead to an increased incidence of diabetes of 0.4% per year of treatment i.e. one additional case of diabetes for 250 people treated every year.
- A meta analysis of seven trials (almost 77,000 people) showed a significantly higher incidence of diabetes in people taking beta-blockers and/or thiazide diuretics (about half received a beta-blocker *and* a thiazide) compared to people taking other antihypertensive drugs (risk ratio 1.23, 95% CI 1.16 to 1.30). The increased risk was thought to be due to the combination of beta-blocker and thiazide diuretic rather than the use of the drugs separately [N England Hypertension GDG, 2004].
- Trial data from the blood pressure lowering arm of the Anglo-Scandinavian Cardiac Outcomes Trial (ASCOT) comparing blood pressure lowering treatments may provide more information. The results of this trial are expected to be published in the second half of 2005 [ASCOT, 2004]

How should I manage older people?

The absolute benefit from treatment is greater in older people than in younger people with hypertension, because of their higher absolute risk. The benefit has to be balanced against possible hazards of prescribing, such as postural hypotension and risk of falling.

- **Offer people over 80 years of age the same treatment as younger people, taking into account any comorbidity and current medication** (B) [N England Hypertension GDG, 2004].
  - People over 80 years of age are poorly represented in clinical trials and the effectiveness of treatment in this group is less certain. However, it is reasonable to assume that older people will receive worthwhile benefits from drug treatment, particularly in terms of reduced risk of stroke.
  - Patients who reach 80 years of age while on antihypertensives should probably remain on drug treatment especially if there is evidence of target organ damage or if there are other significant cardiovascular disease risk factors such as diabetes.

H

What issues should I bear in mind when treating people of Afro-Caribbean or South Asian ethnic origin?

- UK-based studies show that people of Afro-Caribbean and South Asian ethnic origin have higher rates of hypertension and Type 2 diabetes than Caucasians.
- **People of African descent may be more sensitive to dietary salt restriction and have been found to a thiazide diuretic or a calcium-channel blocker** than an angiotensin converting enzyme inhibitor, angiotensin-receptor II antagonist, or beta-blocker, whose mechanism of action is to suppress renin production [Williams et al, 2004].
- **Cardiovascular risk assessment charts are likely to underestimate cardiovascular disease** (CVD) risk in people originating from South Asia as they have not been validated in these populations. The risk should be multiplied by approximately 1.5.
- **People from South Asia have high rates of Type 2 diabetes and dyslipidaemia** and these coexisting conditions may influence drug choice. There is no good evidence that they respond to antihypertensive drugs differently than Caucasians [Williams et al, 2004].

When should I recommend low-dose aspirin?

In people *without* cardiovascular disease

- The risk/benefit ratio for prescribing aspirin is most favourable in people at high risk of cardiovascular disease (CVD).
- **The National Institute of Clinical Excellence (NICE)** recommend aspirin 75 mg daily for people with a 10 year CVD risk of >=20% (**A**) and in whom blood pressure (BP) is controlled to <145/90 mmHg (**B**) with no contraindications to aspirin use [NICE, 2002].
- **The British Hypertensive Society (BHS) recommend** aspirin 75 mg daily for people who are 50 years old and over with a 10 year CVD risk of >=20% and in whom BP is controlled to <150/90 mmHg with no contraindications to aspirin use [Williams et al, 2004].

In people *with* cardiovascular disease

- **Both NICE and BHS recommend** aspirin 75 mg daily if there is evidence of established ischaemic cardiovascular disease (myocardial infarction, angina, non-haemorrhagic cerebrovascular disease, peripheral vascular disease, or atherosclerotic renovascular disease (**B**).

[N England Hypertension GDG, 2004; Williams et al, 2004]

How should I manage hyperlipidaemia?

When should I start a statin in people *with* cardiovascular disease?

- See the separate PRODIGY guidance on *Hyperlipidaemia* for more detailed information.
- **The National Service Framework (NSF) for coronary heart disease (CHD) recommends** starting a statin in people with high blood pressure (BP) and CHD when:
  - Total cholesterol (TC) is >=5 mmol/l.
  - Low-density lipoprotein cholesterol (LDL-C) is >=3 mmol/l.
- **The BHS recommends** starting a statin in all people up to the age of at least 80, with TC >3.5 mmol/l and CHD peripheral arterial disease or a history of ischaemic stroke.

[DH, 2000]

When should I start a statin in people *without* cardiovascular disease?

- See the separate PRODIGY guidance on *Hyperlipidaemia* for more detailed information.
- **The NSF for CHD** recommends starting a statin to lower serum cholesterol concentrations in people with high BP who have a 10 year CHD risk >=30% when:
  - TC is >=5 mmol/l.
  - LDL-C is >=3 mmol/l.
- Note: the 10 year risk of CHD >=15% is equivalent to CVD >=20% over 10 years). For more information, see *How should I assess cardiovascular risk?*
- **The British Hypertensive Society (BHS)** recommend starting a statin in people who are aged up to at least 80 years old, with a 10 year CVD risk >=20% and with TC concentration >=3.5 mmol/l.
  - In reality, this would mean considering a statin in most people with hypertension (especially men) over the age of 50 years.

[DH, 2000; Williams et al, 2004]

What are target levels of total cholesterol, low-density lipoprotein cholesterol and total triglyceride should I aim for?

- See the separate PRODIGY guidance on *Hyperlipidaemia* for more detailed information.
- **The NSF for CHD recommends** aiming at a *minimum* to achieve one of the following:
  - A reduction in TC to <5.0 mmol/l or by 30%, whichever is lower.
  - A reduction in LDL-C to below 3.0 mmol/l or by 30% whichever is lower.
  - Note: further reductions increase benefit.
- **BHS recommends** aiming:
  - To either lower TC by 25% or LDL-C by 30% (whichever represents the greatest reduction), or
  - To reach a TC of either <4.0 mmol/l or an LDL-C of <2.0 mmol/l (whichever represents the greatest reduction). Note: audit targets are <5.0 mmol/l and <3.0 mmol/l respectively.
- **Consider referral to a lipid specialist for people who do not reach targets** or whose high-density lipoprotein cholesterol (HDL-C) or triglyceride (TG) levels remain abnormal (e.g. <1.0 or >2.3 mmol/l, respectively).

[DH, 2000; Williams et al, 2004]

Should I prescribe hormone replacement therapy?

Hypertension is not a contraindication to the use of hormone replacement therapy (HRT). There is no evidence that HRT elevates blood pressure (BP) or has an adverse effect in women with hypertension [Rees and Purdie, 2002].

HRT should not be prescribed for either primary or secondary prevention of coronary heart disease (CHD) or stroke [CSM, 2004]. Consideration should be given to stopping HRT in any woman who has experienced a cardiovascular event. However, for some women with severe menopausal symptoms, the benefits of symptom relief may outweigh the possible increase in CHD events.

HRT may increase the risk of CHD in women with or without a history of CHD, particularly in the first year of use (oestrogen-only HRT does not seem to increase or decrease the risk of CHD). Observational studies have actually indicated that HRT might prevent CHD [Grodstein et al, 2000] but this finding has been refuted by randomized controlled trials [Grady et al, 2002; Manson et al, 2003].

Medicines management

General principles of drug treatment

Where possible recommend treatment with drugs taken only once a day (A).

- A meta-analysis found that people adhered to once-daily blood pressure (BP) lowering regimens better than to regimens requiring two or more doses a day (91% compared with 83%) [Iskedjian et al, 2002]. Similarly once-daily regimens were better adhered to than twice daily regimens (93% compared with 87%).

Prescribe non-proprietary drugs where these are appropriate and minimise cost (B).

An interval of at least four weeks is generally recommended after initiating treatment to evaluate response [Williams et al, 2004]. A shorter interval may be appropriate if urgent lowering of BP is required.

It is good clinical practice to assess serum electrolytes in all people on antihypertensive drugs every 6 to 12 months.

Drugs in the main antihypertensive drug classes are similarly well tolerated — withdrawal occurs typically at rates of 5–10% per year.

Thiazide-type diuretics

Which diuretics are indicated for the treatment of hypertension?

PRODIGY recommends bendroflumethiazide (bendrofluazide) as the first-choice diuretic. Chlortalidone is an alternative option.

Bendroflumethiazide is widely used in the UK, and is effective, safe, well tolerated, and economical.

Chlortalidone has good evidence for efficacy at lowering BP and improving cardiovascular outcomes [ALLHAT Officers, 2002].

What dose of diuretic should I use?

Use relatively low doses for the treatment of hypertension — thiazides have a shallow dose response curve. Higher doses are unlikely to have additional clinical benefits and are more likely to cause marked changes in blood glucose and lipid levels with an associated increased risk of morbidity and mortality [Sweetman, 2002; BNF 49, 2005].

Bendroflumethiazide (bendrofluazide) is initiated and maintained at a dose of 2.5 mg/day.

- **Chlortalidone** is initiated at a dose of 25 mg/day and if inadequate response (according to the Summary of Product Characteristics) the dose can be increased to 50 mg/day [ABPI Medicines Compendium, 2003].

What are the key adverse effects of thiazides?

- **Thiazides in combination with a beta-blocker:**
  - May lead to one additional case of diabetes for each 250 people treated every year [N England Hypertension GDG, 2004].
- **In people with gout** — thiazides may cause hyperuricaemia (raised serum uric acid levels) and gout. If a thiazide is necessary, consider prophylaxis with allopurinol.
- **Impotence** — is a relatively common adverse effect.

Which key drug interactions are relevant for thiazides?

- **There is an increased risk of cardiac toxicity if thiazide-induced hypokalaemia** occurs with digoxin use — monitor serum potassium.

How should I monitor a person taking a thiazide?

- **Reassess response to treatment after an interval of at least 4 weeks.**
- **Serum potassium levels should be checked:**
  - Within 4–6 weeks of starting a thiazide, although electrolyte disturbances are unlikely to occur with low-doses [UKMI, 2002].
  - If the person's condition changes or a potentially interacting drug is added.
  - Annually [UKMI, 2002].

Beta-blockers

Which beta-blockers are indicated for the treatment of hypertension?

- **PRODIGY recommends atenolol as a first-choice beta-blocker.** It has good trial data for effectiveness in reducing BP and improving cardiovascular outcomes. It is cardioselective, has a simple once-daily dosing, is inexpensive, and is widely used in the UK.
- Many other beta-blockers are licensed for the treatment of hypertension and these vary in cardioselectivity, intrinsic sympathomimetic activity and cost but there is no evidence that any individual beta-blocker is more effective at lowering BP, better tolerated or improves morbidity greater than the others.

What dose of beta-blocker should I use?

- **Atenolol:** initiate and maintain with atenolol 50 mg/day. For people responding inadequately to 50 mg/day, an increase to 100 mg/day can be considered. However, because of a shallow dose response for antihypertensive effectiveness, adding another antihypertensive drug may be a better option than increasing the dose of atenolol.

What are the key adverse effects of, and contraindications to, beta-blockers?

- **Beta-blockers should be avoided in people with either asthma or those with chronic obstructive pulmonary disease (COPD) that has an asthmatic component** as bronchospasm may be precipitated that is unresponsive to beta-2 agonists.
- **Cold extremities, paraesthesia, and numbness may occur,** and are more common in people with **peripheral vascular disease. If troublesome,** beta-blockers may need to be stopped — this is most likely in severe peripheral vascular disease.
- **Sleep disturbance or nightmares** may occur, but are less likely with water-soluble beta-blockers such as atenolol (less likely to cross the blood-brain barrier).
- **Fatigue** (incidence approximately 18 per 1000 people treated with a beta-blocker) [Ko et al, 2002].
- **Sexual dysfunction** (5 per 1000 people treated with a beta-blocker). The patient should be directly questioned

whether they are having sexual problems, as this adverse effect is often not volunteered due to embarrassment.

- **Depression** has been claimed to be an adverse effect of beta-blockers, but a recent meta-analysis found no significant increased risk of depressive symptoms in people taking beta-blockers [Ko et al, 2002].

Which key drug interactions are common/potentially hazardous?

- **Do not prescribe a beta-blocker with verapamil,** as severe bradycardia, asystole, severe hypotension and/or heart failure may occur.
- **Caution is needed if a beta-blocker is taken with diltiazem** — monitor carefully (pulse, BP) as bradycardia and AV block with diltiazem. Asystole/sudden death has also been reported.
- **Bradycardia can be caused** by beta-blockers in combination with anti-arryhythmics, diltiazem and digoxin. Monitor BP and pulse, and adjust treatment as necessary.

How should I monitor a patient taking beta-blocker?

- **Reassess response to treatment after an interval of at least 4 weeks,** unless it is necessary to lower the blood pressure (BP) more urgently.
- **There are no specific monitoring requirements for beta-blockers.**

H

ACE inhibitors and angiotensin-II receptor antagonists (AIIRAs)

Which ACE inhibitors are indicated for the treatment of hypertension?

- There are several ACE inhibitors that are licensed for the treatment of hypertension. All ACE inhibitors seem to have comparable BP-lowering efficacy.
- **PRODIGY recommends enalapril, lisinopril, perindopril, ramipril, or trandolapril as first-choice ACE inhibitors.** These are established ACE inhibitors with trial data for improving cardiovascular outcomes in hypertensive populations and can all be taken once a day.
- **Captopril is no longer recommended as a first-choice ACE inhibitor** — it has a shorter half-life than other ACE inhibitors and needs to be taken in divided doses.
- Cilazapril, fosinopril, imidapril, moexipril, and quinapril are alternative options but there is less trial data of their use.

What dose of ACE inhibitor should I use?

- The doses of ACE inhibitor that are recommended for initiation and maintenance are outlined in Table 7.

Which AIIRAs are indicated for the treatment of hypertension?

- **PRODIGY recommends candesartan, irbesartan, losartan or valsartan** for hypertension.
- **Losartan** was found to improve cardiovascular outcomes in people with hypertension in the Losartan Intervention For Endpoint Reduction in Hypertension (LIFE) trial, although this was in high-risk people with left ventricular hypertrophy [Dahlof et al, 2002].
- **Candesartan** was not found to significantly reduce the incidence of a first major cardiovascular event, myocardial infarction, or cardiovascular mortality in the SCOPE (Study on Cognition and Prognosis in the Elderly) trial. However subgroup analysis has found improved outcomes in elderly people with hypertension in terms of reduction in non-fatal stroke compared to people in the placebo group, although the 95% confidence interval was wide and this has to be interpreted with caution [Lithell et al, 2003].
- **Irbesartan** when directly compared with losartan has shown at least comparable efficacy in BP reduction [Kassler-Taub et al, 1998]. It has also been found to be effective in protecting against the progression of nephropathy in Type 2 diabetes [Lewis et al, 2001] — this effect is independent of its antihypertensive effect, and the degree of effective is dose-dependent [Parving et al, 2001].
- **Valsartan** has been compared with amlodipine, each drug being randomized to people over 50 with hypertension and high risk of cardiovascular events [Julius et al, 2004]. Significantly lower BP levels were achieved with amlodipine in the first three months but levels became similar with time. Both drugs were found to offer benefit, the composite of cardiac morbidity and mortality did not differ significantly between the two. Myocardial infarction (a secondary outcome) was significantly more frequent in the valsartan group (Hazard ratio 1.19, 95% CI 1.02 to 1.38). However the incidence of diabetes was significantly lower in people on valsartan, similar to the difference found between lisinopril and amlodipine in ALLHAT.

What dose of AIIRA should I use?

- **Losartan**
  - Elderly over 75 years, hepatic or renal impairment, or intravascular volume depletion (e.g. taking diuretics): initiate with 25 mg/day.
  - Standard initiation dose is 50 mg/day.
  - Usual maintenance dose is 50 mg/day.
  - Maximum daily dose is 100 mg/day.
- **Candesartan**
  - If hepatic impairment, initiate with 2 mg/day.
  - If renal impairment, initiate with 4 mg/day.
  - Standard initiation dose is 8 mg/day.
  - Usual maintenance dose is 8 mg/day.
  - Maximum daily dose is 16 mg/day.
- **Valsartan**
  - Elderly over 75 years, mild to moderate renal impairment, moderate to severe renal impairment or intravascular volume depletion: initially 40 mg/day.
  - Standard 80 mg once a day.
  - Maximum 160 mg once a day.

What are the key adverse effects of, and contraindication to, ACE inhibitors and AIIRAs?

- **Avoid ACE inhibitors and AIIRAs in renovascular disease:** they may cause acute renal failure. People with pre-existing renal disease are in particular danger.
- **Avoid ACE inhibitors and AIIRAs in people with severe renal failure:** they may cause renal insufficiency as there is a risk of irreversible renal interstitial fibrosis, oliguria or azotemia requiring dialysis, or renal artery thrombosis.
- **There is an increased risk of severe first-dose hypotension** in people with hypovolaemia, hyponatraemia, on a low sodium diet, or taking high-

Table 7: Initiation, maintenance and maximum doses for ACE inhibitors.

Dose of drug	Enalapril	Lisinopril	Perindopril	Ramipril	Trandolapril
Elderly initiation*	5mg/day*	2.5 mg/day*	2 mg/day*	1.25 mg/day*	500 mcg/day*
Standard initiation*	5 mg/day*	2.5 mg/day*	4 mg/day*	1.25 mg/day*	500 mcg/day*
Usual maintenance	20 mg/day	20 mg/day	4 mg/day	2.5–5 mg/day	1–2 mg/day
Max/day	40 mg/day	Carace® 40 mg /day, Zestril® 80 mg/day	8 mg/day	10 mg/day	4 mg/day

* Initiation doses may differ if used in addition to a diuretic or in renal impairment

dose diuretics (i.e. furosemide [frusemide] 80 mg/day, bumetanide 2 mg/day).

- **Persistent dry cough** occurs in 10–20% people taking ACE inhibitors but is much less common with AIIRA use. Pooled trial data suggests a 4% incidence of cough with ACE inhibitors, although the incidence may be higher in routine clinical practice [Law et al, 2003].
- **Dizziness and headaches** (are the most common reported adverse effects with ACE inhibitors, whereas with AIIRAs their prevalence is very low).
- **First-dose hypotension** (most commonly in people who are hypovolaemic or hyponatraemic, often as a result of taking high-doses of diuretics).
- **Syncope:** particularly in people with cardiac outflow tract obstruction, (e.g. significant aortic stenosis or obstructive hypertrophic cardiomyopathy,) as vasodilatation leads to reduced cardiac output).

Which key drug interactions are relevant for ACE inhibitors and AIIRAs?

- **Avoid concomitant use of potassium-sparing diuretics and potassium salts** (other than in exceptional cases e.g. low dose spironolactone for severe heart failure) because of increased risk of hyperkalaemia. Careful monitoring of serum potassium is required. Concomitant use of ciclosporin, epoetin, and possibly drospirenone should also be avoided.
- **Monitor people concomitantly using heparin** as there is a danger of hyperkalaemia which should be avoided.

How should I monitor a patient taking an ACE inhibitor or AIIRA?

- **Check BP and serum creatinine and electrolytes prior to starting treatment, a week after starting treatment, and a week after any subsequent dose increase.** If the serum creatinine increases by 50 micromol/l or serum potassium is 5.5 mmol/l or more, either stop or reduce the dose of drug [UKMI, 2002]. These increases may not be a problem unless progressive.
- **Reassess response to treatment after an interval of at least 4 weeks,** unless it is necessary to lower the blood pressure (BP) more urgently.
- **Once on a stable dose, serum electrolytes should be checked at least annually.**

Dihydropyridine calcium-channel blockers

Which dihydropyridine calcium-channel blockers CCBs are indicated for the treatment of hypertension?

- **PRODIGY recommends amlodipine, or once-daily modified-release nifedipine or felodipine as first-choices of a dihydropyridine CCB.**
- Amlodipine and modified-release nifedipine have both been studied in large double-blind, randomised controlled trials (RCTs):
  - **Amlodipine** was compared with chlortalidone (thiazide) and lisinopril (ACE inhibitor) in the ALLHAT study. There was no difference between any of the treatments in the primary endpoint (fatal coronary heart disease or non-fatal myocardial infarction) or in overall mortality [ALLHAT Officers, 2002]. However, people taking amlodipine had an increased risk of heart failure compared with chlortalidone in ALLHAT.
  - **Nifedipine MR once daily** was compared with co-amilozide (hydrochlorothiazide/amiloride) in the INSIGHT study. No significant difference was found in the incidence of cardiovascular events [Brown et al, 2000].
  - **Felodipine** featured in the HOT research [Hansson et al, 1998].
- There are many other dihydropyridine CCBs licensed for the treatment of hypertension but short-acting and immediate-release dihydropyridine formulations are associated with large variations in blood pressure (BP) and reflex tachycardia, and should be avoided.

What dose of dihydropyridine CCB should I use?

- **Amlodipine:**
  - Standard initiation dose is 5 mg/day.
  - Usual maintenance dose is 5–10 mg/day.
  - Maximum daily dose is 10 mg/day.
- **Nifedipine MR once daily**
  - Standard initiation doses range from 20–30 mg/day.
  - Usual maintenance dose is 20–30 mg/day.
  - Maximum daily dose is 90 mg/day.
- **Felodipine MR once daily**
  - Standard initiation doses range from 2.5–5 mg/day.
  - Usual maintenance dose is 5–10 mg/day.
  - Maximum daily doses above 20 mg/day are rarely needed.

What are the key adverse effects of, and contraindications to, dihydropyridine CCBs?

- **Uncontrolled heart failure:** although dihydropyridines rarely aggravate heart failure (any negative inotropic effect is offset by a reduction in left ventricular work), they should not be initiated in people with uncontrolled heart failure. (Amlodipine may be used cautiously in stable heart failure [Littler and Sheridan, 1995; Packer et al, 1996; Cohn et al, 1997; Thackray et al, 2000].)
- **Cardiac outflow obstruction (significant aortic stenosis, obstructive hypertrophic cardiomyopathy): vasodilatation may result in reduced cardiac output.**
- **Hepatic impairment:** the manufacturers of nifedipine MR recommend that this be avoided in people with hepatic impairment, as the duration of effect is considerably prolonged.
- **Facial flushing and headaches** (due to the vasodilatory action of dihyropyridines, often improve with continued use).
- **Ankle swelling (due to the vasodilatory action of dihydropyridines).** Diuretics should not be routinely prescribed but they may help if there is marked oedema.
- **Other common adverse effects include:**
  - Dizziness
  - Fatigue
  - Palpitations
  - Postural hypotension
  - Skin rashes
- **Gum hyperplasia** has occasionally been reported.

Which key drug interactions are relevant for dihydropyridine CCBs?

- **Cimetidine (with nifedipine)** — increased hypotensive effect due to inhibition of the metabolism of dihydropyridine, monitor BP and consider reducing the dihydropyridine dose.
- **Enzyme inducing drugs increase elimination of dihyropyridines** — reduced hypotensive effect. Monitor clinical response to dihydropyridine and increase the dose if necessary. Consider reducing dihydropyridine dose if enzyme-inducing drug discontinued.
- **Nifedipine may increase the plasma concentration of digoxin** and cause possible toxicity. Monitor digoxin levels and reduce the dose of digoxin if necessary.

How should I monitor a patient taking a dihydropyridine CCB?

- **Reassess response to treatment after an interval of at least 4 weeks,** unless it is necessary to lower the blood pressure (BP) more urgently.
- **No specific monitoring is required for people taking dihydropyridine CCBs.** Important comorbidities and drug interactions may prompt more frequent follow-up (see appropriate sections).

H

Rate-limiting calcium-channel blockers (CCBs)

Which rate-limiting CCBs are indicated for the treatment of hypertension?

- **Diltiazem and verapamil are currently the only available rate-limiting CCBs, and are both licensed for the treatment of hypertension.**
- **Diltiazem or verapamil are an alternative to beta-blockers in people with coronary heart disease** (e.g. if a beta-blocker is contraindicated). They are effective anti-anginal drugs, and there is evidence that they reduce the risk of non-fatal MI in people with a history of previous myocardial infarction [NICE, 2001].
- **PRODIGY recommends once-daily formulations of diltiazem** — there is little difference in cost compared to twice-daily formulations and once-daily dosage regimens may be more convenient for some people.
- **PRODIGY recommends non-proprietary verapamil** — this is markedly less expensive than modified-release (MR) formulations of verapamil. Both non-proprietary verapamil and higher doses of the MR formulations need to be taken twice daily.

H

What dose of rate-limiting CCB should I use?

- **Doses vary depending on the product chosen (of which there are many)**
- **Once-daily MR diltiazem products:**
  - Elderly, hepatic or renal impairment: initiation dose ranges from 120–200 mg/day.
  - The standard initiation dose ranges from 180–240 mg/day.
  - The maximum dose ranges from 200–360 mg/day.
- **Verapamil (non-proprietary):**
  - Standard initiation dose is 120 mg twice a day.
  - Maximum dose is 240 mg twice a day.

What are the key adverse effects of, and contraindications to, rate-limiting CCBs?

- **Marked bradycardia, sick sinus syndrome, second or third degree atrioventricular (AV) block:** may cause AV block, resulting in severe bradycardia and hypotension.
- **Heart failure:** may cause bradycardia and myocardial depression, further reducing cardiac output.
- **Atrial flutter or fibrillation complicating Wolff-Parkinson-White syndrome:** avoid verapamil, as may precipitate ventricular tachycardia due to increased conduction across the anomalous pathway.
- **Patient taking a beta-blocker:** do not prescribe verapamil and a beta-blocker together, as severe bradycardia, asystole, severe hypotension, and/or heart failure may occur.
- **Hepatic impairment:** the half-life of diltiazem and verapamil is prolonged in people with impaired liver function. Low doses should be used.
- **First-degree atrioventricular (AV) block:** increased AV block may result in bradycardia.
- **Renal impairment:** although diltiazem and verapamil are extensively metabolised in the liver, the manufacturers recommend dosage reduction in people with renal impairment.
- **Verapamil commonly causes constipation** (advise people to eat more fibre and drink plenty of fluid).
- **Bradycardia** may result from taking diltiazem or verapamil.
- **Vasodilatory adverse effects** (flushing, headaches, ankle swelling) are less common with rate-limiting CCBs than with dihydropyridine CCBs.

Which key drug interactions are relevant for rate-limiting CCBs?

- **Do not prescribe verapamil and a beta-blocker together** as severe bradycardia, asystole, severe hypotension and/or heart failure with verapamil.
- **Caution is needed if diltiazem is taken with a beta-blocker** — monitor carefully (pulse, BP) as bradycardia and AV block with diltiazem. Asystole/sudden death has also been reported.
- **Anti-arrhythmics** — monitor carefully (ideally avoid, or consider seeking specialist advice) as additive cardiovascular effects.
- **Cimetidine** — increased hypotensive effect due to inhibition of the metabolism of dihydropyridine, monitor BP and consider reducing the CCB dose.
- **Enzyme inducing drugs increase elimination of CCB** — reduced hypotensive effect. Monitor clinical response to CCB and increase the dose if necessary. Consider reducing CCB dose if enzyme-inducing drug discontinued.
- **Digoxin** — increased plasma concentration of interacting drug, with possible toxicity. Monitor *digoxin* levels and reduce the dose of digoxin if necessary.

How should I monitor a patient taking a rate-limiting CCB?

- **Reassess response to treatment after an interval of at least 4 weeks,** unless it is necessary to lower the blood pressure (BP) more urgently.
- **No specific monitoring is required for people taking rate-limiting CCBs.** Important comorbidities and drug interactions may prompt more frequent follow-up (see appropriate sections).

Alpha-blockers

Which alpha-blockers are indicated for the treatment of hypertension?

- **PRODIGY recommends once-daily doxazosin MR and terazosin as first-choice alpha-blockers.** They offer simple dose titrations, the once-daily dosing may be convenient and improve compliance, and they are similar in price to other alpha-blockers (other than prazosin).
- **Prazosin and indoramin are alternative options:**
  - Prazosin is much less expensive than other alpha-blockers but is more likely to cause symptomatic first-dose hypotension, requires careful dose titration, and needs to be taken 2–3 times daily.
  - Indoramin also needs to be taken in two or three divided doses.

What dose of alpha-blocker should I use?

- **Doxazosin MR:**
  - Standard initiation dose is 4 mg/day (optimal effect may take up to 4 weeks).
  - Usual maintenance dose is 4 mg/day.
  - Maximum dose is 8 mg/day.
- **Terazosin**
  - Standard initiation dose is 1 mg at bedtime.
  - Titrate dose if necessary after 7 days to 2 mg/day.
  - Usually maintain between 2–10 mg/day.

What are the key adverse effects of, and contraindications to, alpha blockers

- **Micturition syncope:** alpha-blockers may impair blood pressure (BP) responsiveness, increasing the risk of micturition syncope in susceptible individuals.
- **Heart failure:** alpha-blockers may exacerbate heart failure. The doxazosin treatment arm of the ALLHAT trial was stopped because of an increase in cases of new onset heart failure in people assigned to doxazosin compared with chlortalidone [ALLHAT Officers, 2000].
- **Gastrointestinal obstruction, oesophageal obstruction, or any degree of stricture:** doxazosin MR should be avoided, as the outer membrane of the formulation is not digested.
- **Elderly, hepatic or renal impairment:** alpha-blockers are renally excreted and are also excreted via the gut following hepatic metabolism. Caution is necessary in elderly people or people with hepatic or renal impairment, with careful dose titration.

- **Parkinson's disease:** there have been case reports of extrapyramidal disorders in people taking indoramin, and the manufacturer suggests caution in people with Parkinson's disease.
- **Epilepsy:** animal studies suggest an increased risk of seizures with indoramin, and the manufacturer advises caution in people with epilepsy.
- **First-dose hypotension** (vasodilatory effects may cause a rapid reduction in blood pressure after the first dose, particularly in elderly people).
- **Other cardiovascular related adverse effects include:** dizziness, palpitations, peripheral oedema, and, rarely, angina.
- **Central nervous system adverse effects include:** weakness, tiredness, headache, somnolence and sweating.
- In most instances adverse effects will disappear with continued treatment or may be tolerated with no decrease in dosage of the drug required.

Which drug interactions are relevant for alpha-blockers?

- Prazosin increases the plasma concentration of digoxin, prescribe a different alpha-blocker, or monitor digoxin levels and adjust dose of digoxin as appropriate.

How should I monitor a patient taking an alpha blocker?

- **Reassess response to treatment after an interval of at least 4 weeks,** unless it is necessary to lower the BP more urgently.
- There are no specific monitoring requirements for alpha-blockers.

Antiplatelet drugs

- **Aspirin use is associated with adverse gastrointestinal (GI) effects.** A meta-analysis involving over 66,000 people found a two-fold greater risk of GI bleeding for those taking long-term low-dose aspirin compared with those who did not take aspirin [Derry and Loke, 2000; North of England Dyspepsia Guideline Development Group, 2004].
- **There is no robust evidence that different formulations of aspirin are associated with different degrees of risk of GI adverse effects** [Kelly et al, 1996; CSM, 2002]. Enteric-coated are more expensive than standard aspirin preparations.
- Consider prescribing a gastroprotective agent for people who experience dyspepsia with aspirin.
- **There is concern that ibuprofen may reduce the cardioprotective effect of low-dose aspirin in people with cardiovascular disease** by antagonizing the irreversible platelet inhibition induced by aspirin [British Heart Foundation, 2002; NHS CRD, 2003]. Although the interaction of ibuprofen with aspirin is potentially clinically important, the current level of evidence is not sufficient to make clear recommendations for or against the use of concomitant ibuprofen for people requiring prophylactic low-dose aspirin therefore:
  - **It would seem prudent to avoid taking concomitant low-dose aspirin with regular ibuprofen in people with cardiovascular disease risk factors** including diabetes, hyperlipidaemia and obesity.
  - Either naproxen or diclofenac may be a better option if an NSAID is required.
  - Ibuprofen used occasionally is considered to pose less of a risk than regular ibuprofen for people also taking low-dose aspirin.
- For more information, see the PRODIGY guidance on:
  - *Dyspepsia — symptoms (uninvestigated by endoscopy)*
  - *Nonsteroidal anti-inflammatory drugs (NSAIDs)*
- **Clopidogrel** is an alternative for the small number of people genuinely hypersensitive to aspirin (i.e. for whom aspirin induces angio oedema or bronchospasm). This is an off-licence use of clopidogrel. Dyspepsia is also a common adverse effect of clopidogrel.

References

NHS staff in England can link, free of charge, from references to full text journals by clicking on [Full text] on the PRODIGY website.
Note: all users can access the full texts of DH papers without an Athens password.

1. ABPI Medicines Compendium (2003) *Summary of product characteristics for Hygroton tablets 50mg.* Electronic Medicines Compendium. Datapharm Communications Ltd. www.emc.medicines.org.uk [Accessed: 14/01/2005].
2. Agyemang, C. and Bhopal, R. (2003) Is the blood pressure of people from African origin adults in the UK higher or lower than that in European origin white people? A review of cross-sectional data. *Journal of Human Hypertension* **17**(8), 523–534.
3. ALLHAT Officers (2000) Major cardiovascular events in hypertensive patients randomized to doxazosin vs chlorthalidone. *Journal of the American Medical Association* **283**(15), 1967–1975. [Full text]
4. ALLHAT Officers (2002) Major outcomes in high-risk hypertensive patients randomized to angiotensin-converting enzyme inhibitor or calcium channel blocker vs diuretic. The Antihypertensive and Lipid-Lowering Treatment to Prevent Heart Attack Trial (ALLHAT). *Journal of the American Medical Association* **288**(23), 2981–2997. [Full text]
5. ASCOT (2004) *Success of new treatment halts international blood pressure drug trial.* Imperial College London. www.ascotstudy.org [Accessed: 26/01/2005].
6. Blood Pressure Lowering Treatment Trialists Collaboration (2000) Effects of ACE inhibitors, calcium antagonists, and other blood-pressure-lowering drugs: results of prospectively designed overviews of randomised trials. *Lancet* **356**(9246), 1955–1964. [Full text]
7. BNF 49 (2005) *British National Formulary.* 49th edn. London: British Medical Association and Royal Pharmaceutical Society of Great Britain.
8. Bobrie, G., Chatellier, G., Genes, N. et al (2004) Cardiovascular prognosis of "masked hypertension" detected by blood pressure self-measurement in elderly treated hypertensive patients. *Journal of the American Medical Association* **291**(11), 1342–1349. [Full text]
9. British Heart Foundation (2002) *Aspirin and ibuprofen.* Factfile 11/2002. British Heart Foundation. www.bhf.org.uk [Accessed: 01/12/2002].
10. Brown, M.J. (1997) Science, medicine, and the future. Hypertension. *British Medical Journal* **314**(7089), 1258–1261. [Full text]
11. Brown, M.J., Palmer, C.R., Castaigne, A. et al (2000) Morbidity and mortality in patients randomised to double-blind treatment with a long-acting calcium-channel blocker or diuretic in the international nifedipine GITS study: intervention as a goal in hypertension treatment (INSIGHT). *Lancet* **356**(9227), 366–372. [Full text]
12. Brown, M.J., Cruickshank, J.K., Dominiczak, A.F. et al (2003) Better blood pressure control: how to combine drugs. *Journal of Human Hypertension* **17**(2), 81–86.
13. Cappuccio, F.P., Kerry, S.M., Forbes, L. and Donald, A. (2004) Blood pressure control by home monitoring: meta-analysis of randomised trials. *British Medical Journal* **329**(7458), 145–150.

14. Carlberg, B., Samuelsson, O. and Lindholm, L.H. (2004) Atenolol in hypertension: is it a wise choice? *Lancet* **364**(9446), 1684–1689. [Full text]
15. Chobanian, A.V., Bakris, G.L., Black, H.R. et al (2003) The seventh report of the joint national committee on prevention, detection, evaluation, and treatment of high blood pressure: the JNC 7 report. *Journal of the American Medical Association* **289**(19), 2560–2572. [Full text]
16. Cohn, J.N., Ziesche, S., Smith, R. et al (1997) Effect of the calcium antagonist felodipine as supplementary vasodilator therapy in patients with chronic heart failure treated with enalapril: V-HeFT III. *Circulation* **96**(3), 856–863. [Full text]
17. Collins, R. and Peto, R. (1994) Antihypertensive drug therapy: effects on stroke and coronary heart disease. In: Swales, J.D. (Ed.) *Textbook of hypertension.* Oxford: Blackwell Scientific Publications. 1156–1164.
18. CSM (2002) Non-steroidal anti-inflammatory drugs (NSAIDs) and gastrointestinal (GI) safety. *Current Problems in Pharmacovigilance* **28**(Apr), 5.
19. CSM (2004) Review of the evidence regarding long-term safety of HRT. *Current Problems in Pharmacovigilance* **30**(Oct), 4–7.
20. Dahlof, B., Devereux, R.B., Kjeldsen, S.E. et al (2002) Cardiovascular morbidity and mortality in the Losartan Intervention For Endpoint reduction in hypertension study (LIFE): a randomised trial against atenolol. *Lancet* **359**(9311), 995–1003. [Full text]
21. Deary, A.J., Schumann, A.L., Murfet, H. et al (2002) Double-blind, placebo-controlled crossover comparison of five classes of antihypertensive drugs. *Journal of Hypertension* **20**(4), 771–777.
22. Derry, S. and Loke, Y.K. (2000) Risk of gastrointestinal haemorrhage with long term use of aspirin: meta-analysis. *British Medical Journal* **321**(7270), 1183–1187. [Full text]
23. DH (2000) *National service framework for coronary heart disease.* Department of Health. www.dh.gov.uk [Accessed: 15/07/2005]. [Full text]
24. Dickerson, J.E.C., Hingorani, A.D., Ashby, M.J. et al (1999) Optimisation of antihypertensive treatment by crossover rotation of four major classes. *Lancet* **353**(9169), 2008–2013. [Full text]
25. DTB (1997) Which prophylactic aspirin? *Drug & Therapeutics Bulletin* **35**(1), 7–8. [Full text]
26. European Society of Hypertension & European Society of Cardiology Guidelines Committee (2003) 2003 European Society of Hypertension & European Society of Cardiology guidelines for the management of arterial hypertension. *Journal of Hypertension* **21**(6), 1011–1053.
27. Grady, D., Herrington, D., Bittner, V. et al (2002) Cardiovascular disease outcomes during 6.8 years of hormone therapy. Heart and Estrogen/Progestin Replacement Study Follow-up (HERSII). *Journal of the American Medical Association* **288**(1), 49–57. [Full text]
28. Grodstein, F., Manson, J.E., Colditz, G.A. et al (2000) A prospective, observational study of postmenopausal hormone therapy and primary prevention of cardiovascular disease. *Annals of Internal Medicine* **133**(12), 933–941.
29. Hansson, L., Zanchetti, I., Carruthers, S.G. et al (1998) Effects of intensive blood-pressure lowering and low-dose aspirin in patients with hypertension: Principal results of the Hypertension Optimal Treatment (HOT) randomised trial. *Lancet* **351**(9118), 1755–1762. [Full text]
30. Hansson, L., Lindholm, L.H., Niskanen, L. et al (1999) Effect of angiotensin-converting-enzyme inhibition compared with conventional therapy on cardiovascular morbidity and mortality in hypertension: the Captopril Prevention Project (CAPPP) randomised trial. *Lancet* **353**(9153), 611–615. [Full text]
31. Hayden, M., Pignone, M., Phillips, C. and Mulrow, C. (2002) Aspirin for the primary prevention of cardiovascular events: a summary of the evidence for the U.S. Preventive Services Task Force. *Annals of Internal Medicine* **136**(2), 161–172.
32. Iskedjian, M., Einarson, T.R., MacKeigan, L.D. et al (2002) Relationship between daily dose frequency and adherence to antihypertensive pharmacotherapy: evidence from a meta-analysis. *Clinical Therapeutics* **24**(2), 302–316.
33. Julius, S., Kjeldsen, S.E., Weber, M. et al (2004) Outcomes in hypertensive patients at high cardiovascular risk treated with regimens based on valsartan or amlodipine: the VALUE randomised trial. *Lancet* **363**(9426), 2022–2031. [Full text]
34. Kassler-Taub, K., Littlejohn, T., Elliott, W. et al (1998) Comparative efficacy of two angiotensin II receptor antagonists, irbesartan and losartan, in mild-to-moderate hypertension. *American Journal of Hypertension* **11**(4), 445–453.
35. Kelly, J.P., Kaufman, D.W., Jurgelon, J.M. et al (1996) Risk of aspirin-associated major upper-gastrointestinal bleeding with enteric-coated or buffered product. *Lancet* **348**(9039), 1413–1416. [Full text]
36. Kizer, J.R., Dahlof, B., Kjeldsen, S.E. et al (2005) Stroke reduction in hypertensive adults with cardiac hypertrophy randomized to losartan versus atenolol: the losartan intervention for endpoint reduction in hypertension study. *Hypertension* **45**(1), 46–52.
37. Ko, D.T., Hebert, P.R., Coffey, C.S. et al (2002) Beta-blocker therapy and symptoms of depression, fatigue and sexual dysfunction. *Journal of the American Medical Association* **288**(3), 351–352. [Full text]
38. Law, M.R., Wald, N.J., Morris, J.K. and Jordan, R.E. (2003) Value of low dose combination treatment with blood pressure lowering drugs: analysis of 354 randomised trials. *British Medical Journal* **326**(7404), 1427–1434. [Full text]
39. Lewington, S., Clarke, R., Qizilbash, N. et al (2002) Age-specific relevance of usual blood pressure to vascular mortality: a meta-analysis of individual data for one million adults in 61 prospective studies. *Lancet* **360**(9349), 1903–1913. [Full text]
40. Lewis, E.J., Hunsicker, L.G., Clarke, W.R. et al (2001) Renoprotective effect of the angiotensin-receptor antagonist irbesartan in patients with nephropathy due to type 2 diabetes. *New England Journal of Medicine* **345**(12), 851–860. [Full text]
41. Lindholm, L.H., Ibsen, H., Dahlof, B. et al (2002) Cardiovascular morbidity and mortality in patients with diabetes in the Losartan Intervention For Endpoint reduction in hypertension study (LIFE): a randomised trial against atenolol. *Lancet* **359**(9311), 1004–1010. [Full text]
42. Lithell, H., Hansson, L., Skoog, I. et al (2003) The Study on Cognition and Prognosis in the Elderly (SCOPE): principal results of a randomized double-blind intervention trial. *Journal of Hypertension* **21**(5), 875–886.
43. Littler, W.A. and Sheridan, D.J. (1995) Placebo controlled trial of felodipine in patients with mild to moderate heart failure. *British Heart Journal* **73**(5), 428–433.
44. MacMahon, S., Peto, R., Cutler, J. et al (1990) Blood pressure, stroke, and coronary heart disease. Part 1, Prolonged differences in blood pressure: prospective observational studies corrected for the regression dilution bias. *Lancet* **335**(8692), 765–774. [Full text]

45. Manson, J.E., Hsia, J., Johnson, K.C. et al (2003) Estrogen plus progestin and the risk of coronary heart disease. *New England Journal of Medicine* **349**(6), 523–534. [Full text]
46. Materson, B.J., Reda, D.J., Cushman, W.C. et al (1993) Single-drug therapy for hypertension in men. A comparison of six antihypertensive agents with placebo. The Department of Veterans Affairs Cooperative Study Group on Antihypertensive Agents. *New England Journal of Medicine* **328**(13), 914–921.
47. Messerli, F.H., Grossman, E. and Goldbourt, U. (1998) Are beta-blockers efficacious as first-line therapy for hypertension in the elderly? A systematic review. *Journal of the American Medical Association* **279**(23), 1903–1907. [Full text]
48. N England Hypertension GDG (2004) *Essential hypertension: managing adult patients in primary care: full guideline.* North of England Hypertension Guideline Development Group, Centre for Health Services Research. www.nice.org.uk [Accessed: 25/11/2004].
49. NHS Confederation and BMA (2005) *New GMS contract.* Department of Health. www.dh.gov.uk [Accessed: 27/09/2005]. [Full text]
50. NHS CRD (2003) *Ibuprofen may reduce the protective benefits of aspirin on cardiovascular disease.* Hitting the Headlines Archive. National Electronic Library for Health. www.nelh.nhs.uk/hth/ibuprofen.asp [Accessed: 15/07/2005].
51. NICE (2001) *Prophylaxis for patients who have experienced a myocardial infarction.* Inherited clinical guideline A. National Institute for Clinical Excellence. www.nice.org.uk [Accessed: 28/01/2003].
52. NICE (2002) *Management of type 2 diabetes – management of blood pressure and blood lipids.* Inherited clinical guideline H. National Institute for Clinical Excellence. www.nice.org.uk [Accessed: 28/01/2003].
53. North of England Dyspepsia Guideline Development Group (2004) *Dyspepsia: managing dyspepsia in adults in primary care: full guideline.* Centre for Health Services Research. www.nice.org.uk [Accessed: 27/08/2004].
54. O'Brien, E., Waeber, B., Parati, G. et al (2001a) Blood pressure measuring devices: recommendations of the European Society of Hypertension. *British Medical Journal* **322**(7285), 531–536. [Full text]
55. O'Brien, E., Beevers, G. and Lip, G.Y.H (2001b) ABC of hypertension: blood pressure measurement. Part III – automated sphygmomanometry: ambulatory blood pressure measurement. *British Medical Journal* **322**(7294), 1110–1114. [Full text]
56. O'Brien, E., Beevers, G. and Lip, G.Y.H. (2001c) ABC of hypertension: blood pressure measurement. Part IV – automated sphygmomanometry: self blood pressure measurement. *British Medical Journal* **322**(7295), 1167–1170. [Full text]
57. O'Brien, E., Asmar, R., Beilin, L. et al (2003) European Society of Hypertension recommendations for conventional, ambulatory and home blood pressure measurement. *Journal of Hypertension* **21**(5), 821–848.
58. Opie, L.H. and Schall, R. (2002) Evidence-based evaluation of calcium channel blockers for hypertension. *Journal of the American College of Cardiology* **39**(2), 315–322.
59. Packer, M., O'Connor, C.M., Ghali, J.K. et al (1996) Effect of amlodipine on morbidity and mortality in severe chronic heart failure. Prospective Randomized Amlodipine Survival Evaluation Study Group. *New England Journal of Medicine* **335**(15), 1107–1114. [Full text]
60. Padwal, R., Straus, S.E. and McAlister, F.A. (2001) Evidence based management of hypertension: cardiovascular risk factors and their effects on the decision to treat hypertension: evidence based review. *British Medical Journal* **322**(7292), 977–980. [Full text]
61. Pahor, M., Psaty, B.M., Alderman, M.H. et al (2000) Health outcomes associated with calcium antagonists compared with other first-line antihypertensive therapies: a meta-analysis of randomised controlled trials. *Lancet* **356**(9246), 1949–1954. [Full text]
62. Parving, H.H., Lehnert, H., Brochner-Mortensen, J. et al (2001) The effect of irbesartan on the development of diabetic nephropathy in patients with type 2 diabetes. *New England Journal of Medicine* **345**(12), 870–878. [Full text]
63. Primatesta, P. and Brookes, M. (2001) Cardiovascular disease: prevalence and risk factors. In: Erens, B., Primatesta, P., Prior, G. et al (Eds.) *Health survey for England – the health of minority ethnic groups '99.* London: The Stationery Office.
64. Progress Collaborative Group (2001) Randomised trial of a perindopril-based blood-pressure-lowering regimen among 6105 individuals with previous stroke or transient ischaemic attack. *Lancet* **358**(9287), 1033–1041. [Full text]
65. Psaty, B.M., Lumley, T., Furberg, C.D. et al (2003) Health outcomes associated with various antihypertensive therapies used as first-line agents: a network meta-analysis. *Journal of the American Medical Association* **289**(19), 2534–2544. [Full text]
66. Rees, M. and Purdie, D.W (Eds.) (2002) *Management of the menopause: the handbook of the British Menopause Society.* 3rd edn. London: BMS Publications Ltd.
67. Schrader, J., Luders, S., Kulschewski, A. et al (2003) The ACCESS study: evaluation of acute candesartan cilexetil therapy in stroke survivors. *Stroke* **34**(7), 1699–1703.
68. SIGN (2002) *Hypertension in older people.* Report no. 49. Scottish Intercollegiate Guidelines Network. www.sign.ac.uk [Accessed: 12/12/2002].
69. Sleight, P. (2000) The HOPE study (Heart Outcomes Prevention Evaluation). *Journal of the Renin-Angiotensin-Aldosterone System* **1**(1), 18–20.
70. Staessen, J.A., Wang, J.G. and Thijs, L. (2001) Cardiovascular protection and blood pressure reduction: a meta-analysis. *Lancet* **358**(9290), 1305–1315. [Full text]
71. Sweetman, S.C. (Ed.) (2002) *Martindale: the complete drug reference.* 33rd edn. London: Pharmaceutical Press.
72. Systolic Hypertension-Europe (Syst-Eur) Trial Investigators (1997) Randomised double blind comparison of placebo and active treatment for older patients with isolated systolic hypertension. *Lancet* **350**(9080), 757–764. [Full text]
73. Thackray, S., Witte, K., Clark, A.L. and Cleland, J.G. (2000) Clinical trials update: OPTIME-CHF, PRAISE-2, ALL-HAT. *European Journal of Heart Failure* **2**(2), 209–212.
74. The Heart Outcomes Prevention Evaluation Study Investigators (2000) Effects of an angiotensin-converting-enzyme inhibitor, ramipril, on cardiovascular events in high-risk patients. *New England Journal of Medicine* **342**(3), 145–153. [Full text]
75. Turnbull, F., Neal, B., Algert, C. et al (2003) Effects of different blood-pressure-lowering regimens on major cardiovascular events: results of prospectively-designed overviews of randomised trials. *Lancet* **362**(9395), 1527–1535. [Full text]

76. UKMI (2002) *Drug monitoring requirements in primary care: prepared by Croydon PCT and London-South Thames Medicine Information Service.* UK Medicines Information. www.ukmi.nhs.uk [Accessed: 01/10/2003].
77. Whelton, P.K., He, J., Appel, L.J. et al (2002) Primary prevention of hypertension. *Journal of the American Medical Association* 288(15), 1882–1888. [Full text]
78. Williams, B., Poulter, N.R., Brown, M.J. et al (2004) Guidelines for management of hypertension: report of the fourth working party of the British Hypertension Society, 2004-BHS IV. *Journal of Human Hypertension* 18(3), 139–185.
79. Wing, L.M.H., Reid, C.M., Ryan, P. et al (2003) A comparison of outcomes with angiotensin-converting-enzyme inhibitors and diuretics for hypertension in the elderly. *New England Journal of Medicine* 348(7), 583–592. [Full text]

Evidence grading

Evidence grading is from the National Institute of Clinical Excellence guideline on *Essential hypertension: managing adult patients in primary care* (written by the North of England Hypertension Guideline Development Group), 2004. The definitions of grades of recommendation used in this guideline are as follows:

A	There is robust evidence to recommend a pattern of care
B	On balance of evidence, a pattern of care is recommended with caution
C	Evidence being inadequate, a pattern of care is recommended by consensus

H

PRODIGY GUIDANCE

Hypertension in pregnancy

Last revised in April 2003
www.prodigy.nhs.uk/guidance.asp?gt=Hypertension in pregnancy

Applies to women from the age of 14 to 60 years

This guidance covers the management of pregnant women with chronic (pre-existing) hypertension, gestational hypertension (pregnancy-induced hypertension), or pre-eclampsia.

There is separate PRODIGY guidance for the management of hypertension in other groups (see *Hypertension*).

Goals

- Early detection of raised blood pressure during pregnancy
- Control of raised blood pressure during pregnancy, if necessary
- Avoidance of maternal morbidity and mortality
- Avoidance of fetal complications

Contents

Scenarios
- Hypertension in pregnancy p.1001

Extended Information, p. 1002

Hypertension in pregnancy

Which therapy?

- **Only prescribe antihypertensive medication after specialist advice.** The antihypertensive prescriptions offered are for the three main treatments used during pregnancy. Standard doses only are offered, but higher doses may be required in some women.
- **Expert assessment is required for a pregnant woman with a blood pressure (BP) of 140/90 mmHg or more.** This usually requires immediate contact with the local obstetric unit.
- **Urgent admission is indicated for** a pregnant woman with BP greater than 160/100 mmHg, or BP greater than or equal to 140/90 mmHg with proteinuria or symptoms such as headache, visual disturbance, or epigastric pain.
- **Antihypertensive medication is not always required,** particularly for mild chronic (pre-existing) hypertension or gestational hypertension.
- **If a woman with chronic (pre-existing) hypertension has her antihypertensive treatment continued during pregnancy,** it is advisable to switch to one that is recommended for use during pregnancy. In particular, ACE inhibitors and angiotensin-II receptor antagonists must be stopped. *If the woman is concerned about medicines she has taken in early pregnancy, further information can be obtained from the National Teratology Information Service on 0191 232 1525.*

Factors affecting choice of treatment

- **Depression:** do not use methyldopa.
- **Asthma or a history of bronchospasm:** do not use labetalol (Committee on Safety of Medicines warning).
- **Severe peripheral vascular disease:** avoid labetalol.
- **Diabetes:** do not use labetalol (it is not a cardioselective beta-blocker).
- **Liver disease:** do not use methyldopa or labetalol.

Practical prescribing points

For further information, please see the *Medicines Compendium* (www.medicines.org.uk) or the *British National Formulary* (www.bnf.org).

Methyldopa

- Drowsiness and tiredness are common and dose-related.

Labetalol

- Severe hepatocellular damage has been reported after both short-term and long-term treatment. If liver dysfunction is suspected, check liver function tests. Labetalol must be stopped and not restarted if there is evidence of damage, or if jaundice is present.

Follow-up advice

- **Close specialist follow-up is necessary** for any woman with raised blood pressure during pregnancy.

Should I refer or investigate?

Refer?

- **Expert assessment** is required for a pregnant woman with a blood pressure (BP) of 140/90 mmHg or more. This usually requires immediate contact with the local obstetric unit.
- **Urgent admission** is indicated for a pregnant woman with BP greater than 160/100 mmHg, or with signs of pre-eclampsia, such as proteinuria, or suggestive symptoms, such as visual disturbance or severe headache.

Investigate

- **Check urine for proteinuria** (1+ or more indicates possible pre-eclampsia).
- **Other investigations are usually carried out in secondary care** (e.g. full blood count, electrolytes, uric acid, liver function tests, and 24-hour urinary protein level).

Patient information leaflets

The following PILs are available at www.prodigy.nhs.uk

- APEC - Action on Pre-Eclampsia
- Blood Test - General
- Blood Test - Kidney Function
- High Blood Pressure of Pregnancy
- Pre-Eclampsia

Shared decision making

- **High blood pressure in pregnancy is common.** There are usually no symptoms and the risk is small if it remains mildly raised. Make sure you have regular checks.

- **There are risks to both mother and baby** if high blood pressure becomes more severe.
- **See a doctor if any of the following occur:**
  - Headaches
  - Swelling (puffiness) of the feet, face, or hands
  - Blurring of vision, or other visual problems
  - Stomach pain
  - Vomiting
  - Simply not feeling right
- **If the high blood pressure becomes severe,** the only complete cure is to induce the birth. This may mean that the baby is born prematurely.
- **Medication may be an option** for moderate or severe high blood pressure. It can lower blood pressure and reduce the risk of complications. You may be advised for a while to allow the pregnancy to progress further before the birth is induced.

Drug rationale

Drugs not included

H

- **Diuretics** are seldom used, because of theoretical concerns that they may further reduce the already decreased circulatory blood volume in women with pre-eclampsia. However, low-dose thiazide diuretics in women with pre-existing hypertension are not thought to be harmful, and may be continued throughout pregnancy [Ramsay et al, 1999].
- **ACE inhibitors** must be avoided, as they may cause oligohydramnios, renal failure, and intra-uterine death [Magee, 2001b]. There is little data on the use of angiotensin-II receptor antagonists during pregnancy, but adverse effects are likely to be similar to those of ACE inhibitors.
- **Hydralazine** is usually reserved for intravenous use in severe hypertension.
- **Calcium antagonists, other than nifedipine,** are not offered, as there is less information available on their use in pregnancy.
- **There is a lack of data on beta-blockers other than labetalol.** Atenolol should be avoided, as there is some evidence that its use is linked to fetal growth retardation [Onwude et al, 1995].
- **There is a lack of data on the use of alpha-blockers** in pregnancy.
- **Preventative treatments including calcium supplements or low-dose aspirin** are of uncertain benefit. They may be considered by specialists in women at high risk of pre-eclampsia [Atallah et al, 2002; Knight et al, 2002].

Drugs included

- Standard doses only are offered but higher doses may be required in some women. Antihypertensive medication should only be prescribed *after* specialist advice.
- **Methyldopa** (a centrally acting antihypertensive) is usually the drug of choice, because of its long and extensive use without reports of serious adverse effects on the fetus [National Teratology Information Service, 1998; Ramsay et al, 1999; Magee, 2001a; Rosenthal and Oparil, 2002]. It is not specifically licensed for hypertension in pregnancy.
- **Labetalol** (an alpha- and beta-blocker) is often used as a second-line agent, although clinical experience is not as extensive as with methyldopa [Khedun et al, 2000]. It is the only drug specifically licensed for hypertension in pregnancy.
- **Nifedipine** (a calcium-channel blocker) is a third-line drug to methyldopa and labetalol. There is more evidence available on the use of nifedipine in pregnancy than for the other calcium-channel blockers [Ramsay et al, 1999]. Modified-release preparations are offered, as they avoid the precipitous fall in blood pressure (BP) that may occur with standard-release products. Once-daily preparations of nifedipine are offered on grounds of concordance. No nifedipine product is specifically licensed for hypertension in pregnancy.

Prescriptions

Methyldopa

Methyldopa 250mg twice a day
- Age from 14 to 60 years
- Methyldopa 250mg tablets. Take one tablet twice a day; supply 28 tablets; NHS Cost £0.85.

Methyldopa 250mg three times a day
- Age from 14 to 60 years
- Methyldopa 250mg tablets. Take one tablet three times a day; supply 42 tablets; NHS Cost £1.27.

Methyldopa 500mg twice a day
- Age from 14 to 60 years
- Methyldopa 500mg tablets. Take one tablet twice a day; supply 28 tablets; NHS Cost £1.73.

Methyldopa 500mg three times a day
- Age from 14 to 60 years
- Methyldopa 500mg tablets. Take one tablet three times a day; supply 42 tablets; NHS Cost £2.59.

Labetalol

Labetalol 100mg twice a day
- Age from 14 to 60 years
- Labetalol 100mg tablets. Take one tablet twice a day; supply 28 tablets; NHS Cost £2.38.

Labetalol 150mg twice a day
- Age from 14 to 45 years
- Labetalol 50mg tablets. Take one tablet twice a day; supply 28 tablets; NHS Cost £2.50.
- Labetalol 100mg tablets. Take one tablet twice a day; supply 28 tablets; NHS Cost £2.00.

Labetalol 200mg twice a day
- Age from 14 to 60 years
- Labetalol 200mg tablets. Take one tablet twice a day; supply 28 tablets; NHS Cost £3.22.

Nifedipine

Adalat LA 20mg once a day
- Age from 14 to 60 years
- Adalat LA 20mg m/r tablets. Take one tablet once a day; supply 14 tablets; NHS Cost £4.08.

Adalat LA 30mg once a day
- Age from 14 to 60 years
- Adalat LA 30mg m/r tablets. Take one tablet once a day; supply 14 tablets; NHS Cost £4.95.

Coracten XL 30mg once a day
- Age from 14 to 60 years
- Coracten XL 30mg m/r capsules. Take one capsule once a day; supply 14 capsules; NHS Cost £3.36.

Extended Information

Background information

- What is it? p.1003
- How common is it? p.1003
- How do I know my patient has it? p.1003
- What else might it be? p.1003
- Complications and prognosis p.1004

What is it?

Several different hypertensive disorders can complicate pregnancy, and numerous different terms and definitions are used. The following terms and definitions are used throughout this guidance:

- **Hypertension:** systolic blood pressure (BP) greater than or equal to 140 mmHg, or diastolic BP greater than or equal to 90 mmHg.
- **Chronic (pre-existing) hypertension:** hypertension diagnosed before pregnancy or during the first 20 weeks of gestation. Hypertension that is diagnosed for the first time during pregnancy and that does not resolve post-partum is also classified as chronic hypertension.
- **Gestational hypertension (pregnancy-induced hypertension):** hypertension detected for the first time after 20 weeks' gestation *without* proteinuria. Gestational hypertension is a provisional diagnosis: some women may go on to develop proteinuria (pre-eclampsia), whilst others may have pre-existing hypertension that has been masked by the physiological drop in BP in the early part of pregnancy. The diagnosis of gestational hypertension is confirmed if pre-eclampsia has not developed and the BP has returned to normal by 12 weeks post-partum.
- **Pre-eclampsia:** a multisystem disorder that is associated with hypertension and proteinuria, and rarely presents before 20 weeks' gestation. The pathological changes seen in pre-eclampsia are primarily ischaemic, affecting the placenta, kidney, liver, brain, and other organs. The cause of pre-eclampsia is unknown; abnormal implantation of the placenta, endothelial dysfunction, and abnormal immune responses have all been suggested as possible factors.
- **Pre-eclampsia superimposed upon chronic hypertension:** pre-eclampsia may occur in women with chronic hypertension, and the outlook is much worse than with either condition alone.
- **Eclampsia:** one or more seizures in association with pre-eclampsia. This is an obstetric emergency, with a high risk to the mother and fetus.

[Ramsay et al, 1999; National High Blood Pressure Education Program, 2000; Beevers et al, 2001]

How common is it?

- **Hypertensive disorders occur in up to 10% of all pregnancies;** rates vary according to the population studied and the criteria used for confirming the diagnosis [American College of Obstetricians and Gynecologists, 2001].
- **Chronic (pre-existing) hypertension** occurs in up to 5% of pregnant women [American College of Obstetricians and Gynecologists, 2001].
- **Gestational hypertension** occurs in 5–6% of all pregnancies [Magee, 2001a; DH, 2002].
- **Pre-eclampsia** occurs in 1–4% of first pregnancies and in about 15% of women with chronic hypertension.
  - For women without a history of pre-eclampsia in the first pregnancy, the risk of developing pre-eclampsia falls in subsequent pregnancies. However, the risk of developing pre-eclampsia approaches that of primigravidae if a pregnancy occurs with a different partner [Beevers et al, 2001].
  - Women with a history of pre-eclampsia in the first pregnancy have a recurrence risk of 10–20% in a subsequent pregnancy.
- **Eclampsia** complicates about 1 in 2000 pregnancies; 44% of seizures occur postnatally, 38% antepartum, and 18% during delivery [Royal College of Obstetricians & Gynaecologists, 1999].

How do I know my patient has it?

- **During pregnancy, routine monitoring of blood pressure (BP) and urine for proteinuria is necessary** in order to detect gestational hypertension or pre-eclampsia, as most women will be asymptomatic. Follow local guidance on the frequency of monitoring.
- **Hypertension is diagnosed if** systolic BP is greater than or equal to 140 mmHg or diastolic BP is greater than or equal to 90 mmHg. The criteria for chronic hypertension, gestational hypertension, and pre-eclampsia are covered in *What is it?*
- **Diastolic BP should be recorded at the disappearance of sounds (Korotkoff phase V),** not at muffling of sounds (Korotkoff phase IV) as recommended in the past [Ramsay et al, 1999; National High Blood Pressure Education Program, 2000].
- **It may be difficult to determine which type of hypertensive disorder is present if pre-pregnancy BP measurements are not available.** An apparent onset of hypertension after 20 weeks of gestation may reflect hypertension that was undetected prior to pregnancy and disguised by the BP fall of early to mid-pregnancy. A definite diagnosis may be possible only after the pregnancy [National High Blood Pressure Education Program, 2000].
- **In pre-eclampsia, symptoms and signs are poorly specific and may be absent.** When present, the most frequent symptoms are headache, visual disturbance, vomiting, epigastric pain, and oedema (weight gain). Any of these symptoms combined with an increase in BP should alert one to the possibility of pre-eclampsia [Ramsay et al, 1999].
- **Risk factors associated with pre-eclampsia include:**
  - First pregnancy
  - Teenage pregnancy
  - Increasing maternal age
  - Change of partner
  - Long interval between pregnancies
  - Low social class
  - Personal or family history of pre-eclampsia
  - Essential hypertension
  - Chronic renal disease
  - Diabetes
  - Systemic lupus erythematosus
  - Multiple pregnancy
  - Molar pregnancy
  - Obesity
  - Rhesus isoimmunization

[Ramsay et al, 1999; Beevers et al, 2001]

What else might it be?

- **Secondary hypertension is rare in pregnancy,** and a full description of the possible causes is outside the scope of this guidance; for further information see the separate PRODIGY guidance for *Hypertension*. Phaeochromocytoma, in particular, should be excluded if there are any suggestive features, as it may cause sudden death in pregnancy [Ramsay et al, 1999].
- **Conditions sometimes confused with pre-eclampsia or eclampsia** (e.g. because of clinical presentation or abnormal blood tests) include:
  - Viral hepatitis
  - Acute fatty liver of pregnancy
  - Acute pancreatitis
  - Gallbladder disease
  - Appendicitis
  - Kidney stones
  - Glomerulonephritis
  - Haemolytic-uraemic syndrome
  - Exacerbation of systemic lupus erythematosus

H

- Autoimmune thrombocytopaenia
- Thrombotic thrombocytopaenic purpura
- Cerebral venous thrombosis
- Encephalitis of various causes
- Cerebral haemorrhage
- Thyrotoxicosis
- Phaeochromocytoma
- Microangiopathies

[Magee, 2001a]

Complications and prognosis

Chronic hypertension

- **Most women with chronic hypertension will have mild-to-moderate hypertension (Blood pressure [BP] less than 160/110 mmHg) and are at low risk of perinatal complications** [National High Blood Pressure Education Program, 2000].
- **The likelihood of complications is increased in women with severe hypertension or with pre-existing cardiovascular or renal disease** [Ferrer et al, 2000]. Complications such as pre-eclampsia, placental abruption, impaired fetal growth, and premature birth result in an increased risk of perinatal morbidity and mortality [Ramsay et al, 1999; Ferrer et al, 2000].

H

Gestational hypertension

- **Women with gestational hypertension have perinatal risks similar to those of normotensive women.** However, women who present at less than 34 weeks' gestation are likely to be at increased risk of perinatal complications, as up to 40% will go on to develop pre-eclampsia [Magee, 2001a].

Pre-eclampsia

- **Pre-eclampsia is associated with the highest risk of perinatal complications.** Although the risk of complications is low in women with mild pre-eclampsia, it is not possible to predict who is at risk of developing complications, and close monitoring is necessary.
- **Women with pre-eclampsia are at increased risk** of placental abruption, cerebral haemorrhage, hepatic and renal impairment, disseminated intravascular coagulation, pulmonary oedema, circulatory collapse, and eclampsia (seizures) [National High Blood Pressure Education Program, 2000].
- **Hypertension during pregnancy is the most common cause of maternal death after thromboembolism,** with a rate of 10 per million pregnancies in the UK [DH, 1998]. Pre-eclampsia and eclampsia are likely to account for most of these.
- **Fetal complications** include low birth weight, premature delivery, and perinatal death.
- **Prognosis is particularly poor in** pre-eclampsia occurring before 34 weeks of gestation, eclampsia, and the syndrome of haemolysis, elevated serum liver enzymes and low platelet counts (HELLP).

Management issues

- General issues p.1004
- Non-drug measures p.1004
- Chronic hypertension p.1004
- Gestational hypertension p.1005
- Pre-eclampsia p.1005
- Antihypertensive drugs used during pregnancy p.1005
- Antihypertensive drugs to avoid p.1005
- Prevention of gestational hypertension and pre-eclampsia p.1005
- Management of severe hypertension and prevention of eclampsia p.1006

General issues

- **A key recommendation from the latest Confidential Enquiry into Maternal Deaths is that all women should receive antenatal education so that they are aware of the symptoms associated with pre-eclampsia** (e.g. headache or epigastric pain), its importance, and the need to obtain medical advice [DH, 1998].
- **Expert assessment is required for all pregnant women with a blood pressure (BP) of 140/90 mmHg or more.** This usually requires immediate contact with the local obstetric unit.
- **The role of antihypertensive medication in pregnant women with mild-to-moderate hypertension (diastolic pressure 90 to 109 mmHg) is uncertain** [Abalos et al, 2002]. A Cochrane Review found that antihypertensive medication reduced the risk of progressing to severe hypertension, but did not reduce the incidence of pre-eclampsia or improve perinatal outcomes [Magee, 2001a].

Non-drug measures

- **Non-pharmacological methods (including bed rest, psychosocial support, and stress management) do not reduce BP in gestational hypertension or pre-eclampsia, or reduce the risk of complications** [Scottish Obstetric Guidelines Audit Project, 1997; Magee, 2001a]. Most clinicians, however, would advise reduced physical activity. Weight reduction during pregnancy, even in obese women, is not recommended — although obesity may be a risk factor for the development of pre-eclampsia, there is no evidence that limiting weight gain reduces its occurrence [National High Blood Pressure Education Program, 2000].
- **The use of alcohol and tobacco during pregnancy should be strongly discouraged.** Excessive alcohol consumption can worsen maternal hypertension, and smoking is associated with placental abruption and fetal growth restriction [National High Blood Pressure Education Program, 2000].

Chronic hypertension

- **Prior to becoming pregnant, women with a history of hypertension should have their diagnosis and management reviewed.** Although most women will have essential hypertension, some may have undiagnosed secondary hypertension, which can rapidly deteriorate during pregnancy.
- **Most women with chronic hypertension will have mild-to-moderate hypertension (BP less than 160/110 mmHg and are at low risk of pregnancy complications.** BP falls during the first trimester, returning to non-pregnant values by the end of the third trimester. If chronic hypertension is newly diagnosed during pregnancy and the woman is not taking any medication, close monitoring without antihypertensive medication may be appropriate. If she is already taking antihypertensive medication, some specialists stop or reduce treatment under close observation. Threshold BPs for restarting treatment vary, but antihypertensive medication would usually be restarted if the systolic pressure exceeded 150 to 160 mmHg, or the diastolic exceeded 100 to 110 mmHg.
- **If antihypertensive medication is continued during pregnancy, it is advisable to switch to one that is recommended for use during pregnancy.** In particular, angiotensin-converting enzyme inhibitors (ACE inhibitors) and angiotensin-II receptor antagonists must

be stopped (see *Antihypertensive drugs to avoid*). After delivery, the previous antihypertensive medication can be restarted.

[Ramsay et al, 1999; National High Blood Pressure Education Program, 2000; Magee, 2001a; Kean, 2002]

Gestational hypertension

- **Antihypertensive medication is not usually indicated for women with gestational hypertension,** as most are at low risk of pregnancy complications. However, severe hypertension always requires treatment. Guidelines usually recommend antihypertensive treatment if the systolic pressure exceeds 150 to 160 mmHg, or the diastolic exceeds 100 to 110 mmHg [Magee, 2001a].
- **Careful monitoring is required to detect the onset of pre-eclampsia** (i.e. the presence of proteinuria).

Pre-eclampsia

- **Urgent specialist assessment is indicated for women presenting with possible pre-eclampsia** (hypertension with proteinuria, with or without symptoms — see *How do I know my patient has it?*).
- **The only curative treatment of pre-eclampsia is delivery,** but stabilization with antihypertensive treatment may allow time for a safe delivery to take place. Severe hypertension always requires antihypertensive treatment. After delivery, the hypertension and end-organ complications of pre-eclampsia usually settle over days to weeks.

Antihypertensive drugs used during pregnancy

- **Antihypertensive medication should only be initiated after specialist advice.**
- **There is insufficient evidence** to make firm recommendations on the choice of antihypertensive medication in pregnancy [Ramsay et al, 1999; Magee, 2001a].
- **Methyldopa** is usually the drug of first choice because of its long and extensive use without reports of serious adverse effects on the fetus [Ramsay et al, 1999; Magee, 2001a; Rosenthal and Oparil, 2002; National Teratology Information Service, 1998]. Methyldopa does not alter maternal cardiac output or blood flow to the uterus or kidneys.
- **Labetalol** (a combined alpha- and beta-blocker) is also often used. Atenolol should be avoided, as there is some evidence that its use may be linked to fetal growth retardation when given in early pregnancy [Onwude et al, 1995]. Other beta-blockers are seldom used, as there is little data on their safety during pregnancy.
- **Nifedipine** is the most extensively used calcium-channel blocker in pregnancy. There is no evidence of harm to the fetus, but in view of limited safety data it is recommended as an alternative to more established treatments only if these are ineffective. The modified-release preparation is recommended in preference to the standard-release product, which may cause a precipitous fall in BP [National Teratology Information Service, 2002]. There is less experience with other calcium-channel blockers.
- **Hydralazine** seems to be safe for use during pregnancy, although a few cases of fetal thrombocytopenia have been reported [Khedun et al, 2000]. Use in pregnancy is normally restricted to intravenous treatment for hypertensive emergencies. Less commonly, it is used orally for mild to moderate hypertension. Taken orally as monotherapy, it is poorly tolerated because of adverse effects such as palpitations, headache, and dizziness. It is therefore usually combined with methyldopa or labetalol [Awad et al, 2000; Drugs & Therapy Perspectives, 2001].
- **Diuretics** are little used, owing to theoretical concerns that they may further reduce the already decreased circulatory blood volume in women with pre-eclampsia. However, low-dose thiazide diuretics in women with pre-existing hypertension are not thought to be harmful, and may be continued throughout pregnancy [Ramsay et al, 1999].

Antihypertensive drugs to avoid

- **ACE inhibitors and angiotensin-II receptor antagonists must not be used during pregnancy.** ACE inhibitors when taken during the second and third trimester cause fetal renal dysfunction, with oligohydramnios, intra-uterine death, and neonatal death from renal failure [Magee, 2001b]. There is little data on the effects of angiotensin-II receptor antagonists, but adverse effects are likely to be similar to those of ACE inhibitors. Accidental exposure of the fetus to ACE inhibitors or angiotensin-II receptor antagonists in the *first trimester* is not grounds for termination of the pregnancy [Magee, 2001b; McElhatton, 2001].

H

Prevention of gestational hypertension and pre-eclampsia

- **No strategies are currently *routinely* recommended** for the prevention of gestational hypertension and pre-eclampsia.
- **Low-dose aspirin (50–75 mg):** a Cochrane Review of 39 randomized controlled studies, including more than 30,000 women, found aspirin to offer small to moderate benefits [Knight et al, 2002].
    - 8% reduction in the risk of delivery before 37 weeks' gestation (RR 0.92, 95% CI 0.88 to 0.97; NNT = 72, 95% CI 44 to 200).
    - 14% reduction in neonatal deaths (RR 0.86, CI 0.75 to 0.98; NNT = 250, 95% CI 95 to more than 10,000).
    - 15% reduction in the risk of developing pre-eclampsia (RR 0.85, 95% CI 0.78 to 0.92; NNT = 89, 95% CI 59 to 167).
    - No significant difference in other important outcomes.
    - No evidence of increased risk of bleeding for mother or baby.
- The reviewers concluded that the evidence for aspirin should be discussed with women at increased risk of pre-eclampsia (e.g. those with a history of pre-eclampsia in a previous pregnancy). The decision about whether to take aspirin should then be made in consultation between the woman and her doctor.
- **Calcium supplementation (1 g/day or more):** a Cochrane Review of 11 randomized controlled trials, including nearly 7000 women, found that calcium supplementation reduced the risk of developing pre-eclampsia by 32% (RR 0.68, 95% CI 0.57 to 0.81; NNT = 36, 95% CI 25 to 63). The effect was greatest for women at high risk of hypertension and those with low baseline calcium intake [Atallah et al, 2002]. It was noted that the largest trial to date [Levine et al, 1997] did not find any convincing evidence of benefit. However, this trial included women at low risk of hypertension with adequate dietary calcium, and all women received low-dose calcium supplementation as part of their routine antenatal care. The reviewers concluded that calcium supplementation might be of benefit in women at high risk of pre-eclampsia and in communities with low dietary calcium intake.
- **Other measures:** the effects of other dietary interventions on the risk of pre-eclampsia are unclear, owing to a lack of sufficient trial data. Interventions that have been

investigated include fish oil and evening primrose oil; protein, fish oil and calcium; vitamins C and E; reduced sodium intake; and magnesium supplements [Duley, 2002].

Management of severe hypertension and prevention of eclampsia

- The management of severe hypertension during pregnancy, and measures to reduce the risk of eclampsia, are outside the scope of this guidance — all cases require admission and close specialist supervision.
- The definition of severe hypertension in pregnancy varies, but is usually defined as systolic BP greater than 170 mmHg, or diastolic BP greater than 110 mmHg, or both [Magee, 2001b].

References

NHS staff in England can link, free of charge, from references to full text journals by clicking on [Full text] on the PRODIGY website.

H

1. Abalos, E., Duley, L., Steyn, D.W. and Henderson-Smart, D.J. (2002) *Antihypertensive drug therapy for mild to moderate hypertension during pregnancy (Cochrane Review)*. The Cochrane Library. Issue 3. Oxford: Update Software.
2. American College of Obstetricians and Gynecologists (2001) Chronic hypertension in pregnancy. *Obstetrics & Gynecology* **98**(1), 177–185.
3. Atallah, A.N., Hofmeyr, G.J. and Duley, L. (2002) *Calcium supplementation during pregnancy for preventing hypertensive disorders and related problems (Cochrane Review)*. The Cochrane Library. Issue 3. Oxford: Update Software.
4. Awad, K., Ali, P., Frishman, W.H. and Tejani, N. (2000) Pharmacologic approaches for the management of systemic hypertension in pregnancy. *Heart Disease* **2**(2), 124–132.
5. Beevers, G., Lip, G.Y.H. and O'Brien, E. (Eds.) (2001) *ABC of hypertension*. 4th edn. London: BMJ Books.
6. DH (1998) *Why mothers die: report on confidential enquiries into maternal deaths in the United Kingdom 1994–1996*. Department of Health. [Accessed: 24/05/2002]. [Full text]
7. DH (2002) *NHS maternity statistics, England: 1998–99 to 2000–01*. Report no.11. Department of Health.
8. Drugs & Therapy Perspectives (2001) Consider both the unborn child and the mother when treating hypertension in pregnancy. *Drugs & Therapy Perspectives* **17**(18), 11–15.
9. Duley, L. (2002) Pre-eclampsia and hypertension in pregnancy. *Clinical Evidence* 7, 1296–1309.
10. Ferrer, R.L., Sibai, B.M., Mulrow, C.D. et al (2000) Management of mild chronic hypertension during pregnancy: a review. *Obstetrics & Gynecology* **96**(5 Pt 2), 849–860.
11. Kean, L. (2002) Managing hypertension in pregnancy. *Current Obstetrics & Gynaecology* **12**(2), 104–110.
12. Khedun, S.M., Maharaj, B. and Moodley, J. (2000) Effects of antihypertensive drugs on the unborn child: what is known, and how should this influence prescribing? *Paediatric Drugs* **2**(6), 419–436.
13. Knight, M., Duley, L., Henderson-Smart, D.J. and King, J.F. (2002) *Antiplatelet agents for preventing and treating pre-eclampsia (Cochrane Review)*. The Cochrane Library. Issue 4. Oxford: Update Software.
14. Levine, R.J., Hauth, J.C., Curet, L.B. et al (1997) Trial of calcium to prevent preeclampsia. *New England Journal of Medicine* **337**(2), 69–76. [Full text]
15. Magee, L.A. (2001a) Treating hypertension in women of child-bearing age and during pregnancy. *Drug Safety* **24**(6), 457–474.
16. Magee, L.A. (2001b) Drugs in pregnancy: Antihypertensives. *Best Practice & Research in Clinical Obstetrics & Gynaecology* **15**(6), 827–845.
17. McElhatton, P.R. (2001) Heart and circulatory system drugs. In: Schaefer, C. (Ed.) *Drugs during pregnancy and lactation*. Amsterdam: Elsevier Science. 116–131.
18. National High Blood Pressure Education Program (2000) *Working group report on high blood pressure in pregnancy*. National High Blood Pressure Education Program. www.nhlbi.nih.gov/health/prof/heart/ [Accessed: 15/11/2002].
19. National Teratology Information Service (1998) *Methyldopa in pregnancy*. NHS Northern and Yorkshire: Regional Drug and Therapeutics Centre.
20. National Teratology Information Service (2002) *Use of nifedipine during pregnancy*. NHS Northern and Yorkshire: Regional Drug and Therapeutics Centre.
21. Onwude, J.L., Lilford, R.J., Hjartardottir, H. et al (1995) A randomised double blind placebo controlled trial of fish oil in high risk pregnancy. *British Journal of Obstetrics & Gynaecology* **102**(2), 95–100.
22. Ramsay, L.E., Williams, B., Johnston, G. et al (1999) Guidelines for management of hypertension: report of the third working party of the British Hypertension Society. *Journal of Human Hypertension* **13**(9), 569–592.
23. Rosenthal, T. and Oparil, S. (2002) The effect of antihypertensive drugs on the fetus. *Journal of Human Hypertension* **16**(5), 293–298.
24. Royal College of Obstetricians & Gynaecologists (1999) *Management of eclampsia*. Royal College of Obstetricians and Gynaecologists. www.rcog.org.uk/guidelines.asp?PageID=106&GuidelineID=9 [Accessed: 10/11/2002].
25. Scottish Obstetric Guidelines Audit Project (1997) *The management of mild non-proteinuric hypertension in pregnancy*. Scottish Obstetric Guidelines Audit Project.

PRODIGY GUIDANCE

Hyperthyroidism

Last revised in February 2005
www.prodigy.nhs.uk/guidance.asp?gt=Hyperthyroidism

Applies to people over the age of 16 years
This guidance covers the management of hyperthyroidism.

This guidance does not cover the management of children with hyperthyroidism, of Graves' ophthalmopathy, or the management of other thyroid disorders.

There is separate PRODIGY guidance for *Hypothyroidism*.

Goals

- To establish the diagnosis
- To treat effectively while waiting for specialist opinion

Contents

Scenarios

- Hyperthyroidism p.1007

Extended Information, p. 1008

Hyperthyroidism

Which therapy?

- **All people with hyperthyroidism should be referred to an endocrinologist.** If the person has no features of hyperthyroidism, treatment does not need to be initiated in primary care. If the person has features of hyperthyroidism, treatment may be initiated in primary care while waiting for the specialist assessment:
  - Beta-blockers are first choice unless contraindicated. They reduce the risk of tachyarrhythmias in people with hyperthyroidism. They also give symptomatic relief (e.g. for anxiety and tremor).
  - Antithyroid drugs may be initiated at a low dose in primary care in certain circumstances:
    - If beta-blockers are contraindicated.
    - In addition to beta-blockers if features of hyperthyroidism are marked.
    - This should always be discussed with the endocrinologist to whom the person has been referred before a prescription for antithyroid drugs is issued.
- **Following assessment by an endocrinologist,** treatment options are antithyroid drugs (carbimazole, propylthiouracil), radioactive iodine, and surgery (thyroidectomy).
- **Treatment for pregnant or breastfeeding women should only be initiated by specialists.**

Practical prescribing points

For further information, please see the *Medicines Compendium* (www.medicines.org.uk) or the *British National Formulary* (www.bnf.org).

Antithyroid drugs (carbimazole and propylthiouracil)

- **Advise people to** stop taking the medication, and seek an urgent blood count if they develop a fever, sore throat, mouth ulcers, or other symptoms of infection while taking antithyroid drugs.
- **Pruritus and rashes** are common, but often resolve with continued treatment. If a change in treatment is thought to be necessary, then changing carbimazole to propylthiouracil (or vice versa) can often be effective.

Beta-blockers

- **Heart failure:** seek specialist advice — low start doses must be used, and different beta-blockers (bisoprolol and carvedilol) are licensed for heart failure.
- **Asthma or a history of bronchospasm:** do not use beta-blockers (Committee on Safety of Medicines warning).
- **Severe peripheral vascular disease:** avoid beta-blockers.
- **Diabetes:** if using a beta-blocker, use atenolol or metoprolol (cardioselective). Avoid beta-blockers in people who experience frequent hypoglycaemia. Advise people that beta-blockers may slightly raise their blood glucose levels, and their response to hypoglycaemia may be delayed or symptoms of hypoglycaemia may not occur in the usual way.

Follow-up advice

- People will usually be under specialist supervision and closely monitored.

Should I refer or investigate?

Refer?

- All people with hyperthyroidism (overt or subclinical) should be referred to an endocrinologist.

Investigate?

- **Thyroid function tests (TFTs):**
  - In overt hyperthyroidism typically show a suppressed thyroid-stimulating hormone (TSH) level with raised free thyroxine (T_4) and free tri-iodothyronine (T_3) levels. A raised level of free T_3 can occur, however, with a normal level of free T_4 in 1% of people with hyperthyroidism (T_3 toxicosis).
  - In subclinical hyperthyroidism show a suppressed TSH level with normal levels of free T_4 and free T_3.
  - A raised free T_4 level with a normal or raised TSH level may indicate a TSH-secreting pituitary tumour (rare).
- **Secondary care investigations** may include an ultrasound scan and a thyroid uptake scan.

Patient information leaflets

The following PILs are available at www.prodigy.nhs.uk

- Antibody and Antigen Tests
- Biopsy
- Blood Test - General
- British Thyroid Foundation

H

- Goitre (Thyroid Swelling)
- Hyperthyroidism - Overactive Thyroid
- Medicines - Name Changes of Medicines
- Thyroid Eye Disease (TED) Charitable Trust

Shared decision making

- **Carbimazole or propylthiouracil** are 'antithyroid' medicines that reduce the level of thyroxine. They take several weeks to become fully effective.
- Rarely, antithyroid medicines can cause serious side effects to the blood. Report promptly to a doctor if you develop a sore throat or any other sign of infection.
- Regular blood checks are usual whilst taking antithyroid medication.
- **Beta-blocker medication,** such as propranolol, may also be advised for a few weeks. This helps to reduce symptoms while the antithyroid medication is building up its effect.

H

Drug rationale

Drugs not included

- **Beta-blockers other than atenolol, metoprolol and propranolol:** all beta-blockers are equally effective in alleviating the effects of hyperthyroidism and so the least expensive agents have been selected [Gittoes and Franklyn, 1998].

Drugs included

- **Beta-blockers: atenolol, metoprolol and propranolol** are selected as they are all equally effective in alleviating symptoms and are the least expensive agents. Larger doses may be required because people with hyperthyroidism may be relatively resistant to the effects of beta-blockers. Propranolol and metoprolol are widely used but, because hepatic metabolism is increased in the hyperthyroid state, they need to be given three to four times a day. Atenolol only needs to be taken once a day (as it is mainly excreted by the kidneys) but is not licensed for this use [Geffner and Hershman, 1992].
- **Antithyroid drugs: carbimazole and propylthiouracil** are the antithyroid drugs commonly used in the UK. Both drugs can be given either once daily or in divided doses, and prescribing practice seems to vary with personal preference. Carbimazole has a more acceptable dosage regimen, as a smaller number of tablets are required to be taken [Cooper, 2003]. If a GP is initiating an antithyroid drug while waiting for a specialist opinion, they should discuss this with the specialist concerned.

Prescriptions

Start beta-blocker (for symptomatic relief)

Propranolol 40mg three times a day
- Age from 16 years onwards
- Propranolol 40mg tablets. Take one tablet three times a day; supply 84 tablets; NHS Cost £1.95.

Metoprolol 50mg four times a day
- Age from 16 years onwards
- Metoprolol 50mg tablets. Take one tablet four times a day; supply 112 tablets; NHS Cost £4.88.

Atenolol 50mg once a day
- Age from 16 years onwards
- Atenolol 50mg tablets. Take one tablet once a day; supply 28 tablets; NHS Cost £0.73.

Atenolol 100mg once a day
- Age from 16 years onwards
- Atenolol 100mg tablets. Take one tablet once a day; supply 28 tablets; NHS Cost £0.91.

Start antithyroid drug (ONLY on specialist advice)

Carbimazole 20mg once a day
- Age from 16 years onwards
- Carbimazole 20mg tablets. Take one tablet once a day; supply 28 tablets; NHS Cost £4.46.

Propylthiouracil 100mg three times a day
- Age from 16 years onwards
- Propylthiouracil 50mg tablets. Take two tablets three times a day; supply 168 tablets; NHS Cost £74.79.

Extended Information

Background information

- What is it? p.1008
- How common is it? p.1008
- How do I know my patient has it? p.1009
- What else might it be? p.1009
- Complications and prognosis p.1009

What is it?

- **Hyperthyroidism** is an excess of thyroid hormones. The commonest cause is autoimmune (Graves' disease) characterized by the presence of antibodies directed against the thyroid-stimulating hormone (TSH) receptor, and causing a toxic diffuse goitre.
- **Other causes** of hyperthyroidism are:
  - Toxic multinodular goitre
  - Toxic nodule (adenoma)
  - Thyroiditis — frequently presents with hyperthyroidism, hypothyroidism then follows for several months, resolution then follows; thyroiditis can be classified as:
    - Infectious thyroiditis
    - Silent thyroiditis — usually painless, commonly occurs postpartum
    - Subacute thyroiditis (de Quervain's) — usually painful
  - Drug-induced hyperthyroidism (amiodarone)
  - Excessive ingestion of levothyroxine (thyroxine)
  - High levels of human chorionic gonadotrophin (HCG) as this is similar to TSH, and can stimulate the thyroid gland (and suppress TSH); examples include:
    - The end of the first trimester of pregnancy
    - Hyperemesis gravidarum
    - Trophoblastic disease
  - Pituitary adenoma secreting excess TSH
- **Hyperthyroidism can be differentiated into overt and subclinical:**
  - **Overt hyperthyroidism** is diagnosed when the TSH level is suppressed, with free thyroxine (T_4) and/or tri-iodothyronine (T_3) levels above the normal reference range, in a person with symptoms of hyperthyroidism.
  - **Subclinical hyperthyroidism** is diagnosed when the TSH level is suppressed, with free T_4 and T_3 levels within the normal reference range, in an asymptomatic person.

[Vanderpump et al, 1996; AACE Thyroid Task Force, 2002; Cooper, 2003]

How common is it?

- **The prevalence of overt hyperthyroidism** is about 20 per 1000 women and 2 per 1000 men (including previously treated cases) [Tunbridge et al, 1977].

- **The annual incidence of overt hyperthyroidism** is about 1 per 1000 women and is negligible for men [Vanderpump et al, 1995].
- **The prevalence of subclinical hyperthyroidism** is 1–2% in adults [AACE Thyroid Task Force, 2002], and 3% in those older than 80 years [Cooper, 2003].

How do I know my patient has it?

- **Symptoms are many and include:**
  - Changes in vision, photophobia, eye irritation, and diplopia (with Graves' ophthalmopathy)
  - Dyspnoea, palpitations
  - Emotional lability, insomnia, irritability, nervousness
  - Exercise intolerance, fatigue
  - Frequent bowel movements or diarrhoea
  - Heat intolerance, increased sweating
  - Increased appetite, weight loss
  - Infertility, oligomenorrhoea
- **Signs include:**
  - Agitation
  - Atrial fibrillation, heart failure, resting tachycardia
  - Conjunctival oedema, lid lag, and proptosis (with Graves' ophthalmopathy)
  - Dependent oedema
  - Pretibial myxoedema
  - Proximal myopathy
  - Thyroid enlargement
  - Tremor
  - Warm, moist hands
- **In the elderly, hyperthyroidism may present atypically;** common features in the elderly include:
  - Anorexia
  - Apathy
  - Atrial fibrillation (which is often resistant to digoxin)
  - Depression
  - Heart failure
  - Proximal myopathy
  - Weight loss
- **Thyroid function tests (TFTs):**
  - In overt hyperthyroidism typically show a suppressed thyroid-stimulating hormone (TSH) level with raised free thyroxine (T_4) and free tri-iodothyronine (T_3) levels. A raised level of free T_3 can occur, however, with a normal level of free T_4 in 1% of people with hyperthyroidism (T_3 toxicosis).
  - In subclinical hyperthyroidism show a suppressed TSH level with normal levels of free T_4 and free T_3.
  - A raised free T_4 level with a normal or raised TSH level may indicate a TSH-secreting pituitary tumour (rare).

[Singer et al, 1995; AACE Thyroid Task Force, 2002; Leonhardt and Heymann, 2002; Cooper, 2003]

What else might it be?

- **A suppressed thyroid-stimulating hormone (TSH) level in the absence of hyperthyroidism can occur in:**
  - Severe illness (the sick euthyroid state)
  - Corticosteroid therapy
  - Central hypothyroidism (due to hypothalamic or pituitary dysfunction)

[AACE Thyroid Task Force, 2002; Cooper, 2003]

Complications and prognosis

Complications

- Angina
- Atrial fibrillation
- Cardiomyopathy
- Graves' ophthalmopathy
- Heart failure
- Osteoporosis
- **In pregnancy, untreated hyperthyroidism is associated** with an increased risk of miscarriage, eclampsia, premature labour, low birth weight, fetal loss, and possibly congenital abnormality

Prognosis

- The prognosis after treatment is good; however, relapse may occur after cessation of therapy (see *Management issues*).

[AACE Thyroid Task Force, 2002; Cooper, 2003]

Management issues

- Overview p.1009
- What is the role of antithyroid drugs in hyperthyroidism? p.1009
- What is the role of radioactive iodine in hyperthyroidism? p.1010
- What is the role of surgery in hyperthyroidism? p.1010
- What is the role of beta-blockers in hyperthyroidism? p.1010
- How do I treat hyperthyroidism during pregnancy and breastfeeding? p.1010
- How do I treat subclinical hyperthyroidism? p.1011
- How do I treat Graves' ophthalmopathy? p.1011
- Medicines management p.1011

Overview

- **All people with hyperthyroidism should be referred to an endocrinologist.** If the person has no features of hyperthyroidism, treatment does not need to be initiated in primary care. If the person has features of hyperthyroidism, treatment may be initiated in primary care while waiting for the specialist assessment:
  - Beta-blockers are first choice unless contraindicated. They reduce the risk of tachyarrhythmias in people with hyperthyroidism.
  - Antithyroid drugs may be initiated in primary care in certain circumstances:
    - If beta-blockers are contraindicated.
    - In addition to beta-blockers if features of hyperthyroidism are marked.
- **There are three treatments used by specialists for hyperthyroidism,** all of which are associated with similar improvements in quality of life and patient satisfaction [Cooper, 2003]:
  - Antithyroid drugs
  - Radioactive iodine
  - Surgery — frequently used in the past, uncommonly now
- Treatment is initially monitored by free thyroxine (T_4) values, as suppression of thyroid-stimulating hormone (TSH) may persist for months despite adequate management [Franklyn, 1999].

What is the role of antithyroid drugs in hyperthyroidism?

- **Carbimazole and propylthiouracil** are both effective, but carbimazole is more widely used in the UK.
- **Two different treatment regimens may be used:**
  - Titration regimen, to try to achieve a euthyroid state.
  - Block-replace regimen, with the use of concomitant thyroid replacement therapy. This has the advantage of avoiding iatrogenic hypothyroidism and the need for frequent biochemical monitoring. This regimen is contraindicated during pregnancy.
  - There is no clear advantage of one regimen over the other in terms of outcome.

H

- Evidence from three randomised controlled trials suggests that the optimal duration of treatment for the titration regimen is 12–18 months, and for the block-replace regimen is 6–12 months [Abraham et al, 2004]. However, people frequently relapse when treatment is stopped. People most likely to achieve remission are those with mild disease and small goitres.
- **Hyperthyroidism during pregnancy** is a clear indication for choosing propylthiouracil.
- Relapsed Graves' disease or toxic nodular hyperthyroidism is occasionally treated with long-term carbimazole.

[Singer et al, 1995; Vanderpump et al, 1996; Gittoes and Franklyn, 1998; AACE Thyroid Task Force, 2002; Cooper, 2003; Miehle and Paschke, 2003]

What is the role of radioactive iodine in hyperthyroidism?

- **Radioactive iodine (Iodine-131)** is a radioactive isotope of iodine, usually taken in an oral solution formulation.
- **Most people with hyperthyroidism due to Graves' disease who receive radioactive iodine will eventually become hypothyroid,** usually within three to six months, and require lifelong thyroid replacement therapy. The likelihood of developing hypothyroidism after radioactive iodine treatment is low if the hyperthyroidism is due to toxic multinodular goitre or to a toxic nodule (adenoma).
- **It is the treatment of choice in:**
  - Adults
  - Toxic multinodular goitre
  - Toxic nodule
  - People relapsing after a course of antithyroid medication
- Although there are theoretical concerns, there is no evidence of adverse effects, in particular on fertility, incidence of congenital malformations, or incidence of cancer outside the thyroid either in the person or their children.
- **It is contraindicated in pregnancy and during breastfeeding.** It is advised that women should avoid becoming pregnant for at least four months following treatment. Men are advised not to father children for at least four months following treatment.
- **Pretreatment with antithyroid drugs** is necessary to avoid the risk of 'thyroid storm' (exacerbation of hyperthyroidism with fever and tachycardia) in the following groups:
  - The elderly
  - People with cardiac disease
  - People with severe hyperthyroidism
- **Antithyroid drugs should be stopped** at least 4 days before radioactive iodine is given, and restarted no sooner than 3 days after, to permit uptake of the iodine into the thyroid gland. Antithyroid drugs can usually be stopped after 2–6 weeks as the radioactive iodine takes effect.

[Vanderpump et al, 1996; Gittoes and Franklyn, 1998; AACE Thyroid Task Force, 2002; Cooper, 2003; Miehle and Paschke, 2003].

What is the role of surgery in hyperthyroidism?

- **Surgery** is usually a total thyroidectomy.
- **The main indications are:**
  - Suspected coexistent thyroid carcinoma
  - Solitary toxic nodule
  - Large goitre
  - Failed medical treatment
  - Patient preference
  - Pregnancy if adverse effects from antithyroid drugs occur
- **Complications are** haemorrhage, wound infection, recurrent laryngeal nerve damage, and transient (up to 20% of cases) and permanent (2%) hypocalcaemia.
- **Relapse of hyperthyroidism** occurs in 10% of people over a period of 10 years.

[Vanderpump et al, 1996; Gittoes and Franklyn, 1998; AACE Thyroid Task Force, 2002; Cooper, 2003; Miehle and Paschke, 2003]

What is the role of beta-blockers in hyperthyroidism?

- **Beta-blockers give symptomatic relief** (e.g. for anxiety, palpitations, tachycardia, tremor), and are often used while waiting for antithyroid drugs or radioactive iodine treatment to start working.
- Beta-blockers are often the only treatment required in hyperthyroidism secondary to thyroiditis.
- Larger and more frequent doses may be required because people with hyperthyroidism may be relatively resistant to the effects of beta-blockers.
- Propranolol and metoprolol are widely used but, because hepatic metabolism is increased in the hyperthyroid state, they need to be given three to four times a day. Atenolol only needs to be taken once a day (as it is mainly excreted by the kidneys) but is not licensed for this use.
- Seek specialist advice before starting beta-blockers in hyperthyroid people with heart failure — much lower starting doses should be used, and different beta-blocker (bisoprolol and carvedilol) are licensed for heart failure.

[Vanderpump et al, 1996; Gittoes and Franklyn, 1998; AACE Thyroid Task Force, 2002; Cooper, 2003; Miehle and Paschke, 2003]

How do I treat hyperthyroidism during pregnancy and breastfeeding?

- **For women planning pregnancy within the next 2–3 years,** initial treatment with radioactive iodine or surgery may be best.
- **Specialist advice should be sought** for treating hyperthyroidism in pregnancy.
- **Antithyroid drugs are the treatment of choice during pregnancy** with little evidence of teratogenicity, although there is a possible association of carbimazole with fetal aplasia cutis (a rare congenital scalp defect) and oesophageal atresia. Thyroid function should be monitored every 4–6 weeks during pregnancy to maintain optimum control, and also because both drugs cross the placenta and overtreatment can cause fetal goitre and hypothyroidism. If it is clinically possible, the dose may be reduced or discontinued 3–4 weeks before delivery, to reduce the risk of neonatal complications. There is a higher incidence of malformations and other forms of fetal toxicity if the maternal hyperthyroidism remains untreated.
  - **Block-replace regimens must not be used,** as the higher doses of antithyroid drugs used in block-replace regimens result in an increased risk of fetal goitre and hypothyroidism.
  - Graves' disease often improves during pregnancy, and in some cases drug treatment can be withdrawn in the third trimester.
  - Antithyroid drugs may be used during breastfeeding as long as neonatal development is closely monitored and the lowest effective dose is used.
- **Beta-blockers** can be used for symptomatic relief until antithyroid drugs start working, but specialist advice should be sought before initiation. Propranolol and

metoprolol can be used during breastfeeding, but atenolol should be avoided [UKMiCentral, 2003].

- **Radioactive iodine is contraindicated in pregnancy and during breastfeeding.** It is advised that women should avoid becoming pregnant for at least four months following treatment.

[Singer et al, 1995; Vanderpump et al, 1996; Gittoes and Franklyn, 1998; O'Doherty et al, 1999; AACE Thyroid Task Force, 2002; Cooper, 2003; Miehle and Paschke, 2003]

How do I treat subclinical hyperthyroidism?

- There is no consensus on the management of subclinical hyperthyroidism. Some specialists initiate antithyroid treatment, others review the individual every six months. Referral for specialist opinion is recommended.

[AACE Thyroid Task Force, 2002; Surks et al, 2004]

How do I treat Graves' ophthalmopathy?

- **Severe eye changes occur in about 5% of people with Graves' disease.** Minor changes can be found in up to 50% of people, increasing to 90% if investigated with ultrasound or CT scan. Smokers are more likely to develop ophthalmopathy.
- **Graves' ophthalmopathy may not occur at the same time as the hyperthyroidism:** the ophthalmopathy occurs before the hyperthyroidism in 20% of people, at the same time in 40%, and after the hyperthyroidism in 40% of people [Hanna et al, 1999]. Ophthalmopathy can also develop after the successful treatment of hyperthyroidism.
- **People may present with** excess tear production, photophobia, and grittiness, or with more severe symptoms such as diplopia, eye pain, and reduced visual acuity (due to optic nerve compression). Signs include eyelid retraction, conjunctival redness and swelling, proptosis (either unilateral or bilateral), periorbital oedema, and ophthalmoplegia.
- **Simple measures** can improve symptoms:
  - Avoiding dust
  - Sunglasses
  - Artificial tears
  - Elevation of the head of the bed to reduce periorbital oedema
  - Eye protectors while sleeping
- **Treatment of more severe disease** is complicated and may include corticosteroids, retro-orbital irradiation, and surgery.
- Hypothyroidism, persistent hyperthyroidism, and smoking aggravate Graves' ophthalmopathy.
- Radioactive iodine treatment for Graves' disease may aggravate ophthalmopathy, although this is often transient.

[Singer et al, 1995; Bartalena et al, 1998; AACE Thyroid Task Force, 2002; Cawood et al, 2004]

Medicines management

- **Initial doses** of carbimazole range from 15–40 mg once a day, and initial doses of propylthiouracil range from 200–400 mg per day in divided doses. If a GP is initiating an antithyroid drug while waiting for a specialist opinion, it is suggested that they use a starting dose of carbimazole 20 mg once a day, or propylthiouracil 100 mg three times a day. However, the decision to start an antithyroid drug in primary care should be discussed with the specialist concerned.
- Therapy is continued at the initial dose for 4–8 weeks until the person becomes euthyroid (based on the free thyroxine [T_4] level). There are then two options:
  - Titration regimen — the dose is gradually reduced to a maintenance dose of 5–15 mg per day for carbimazole, or 50–150 mg per day for propylthiouracil.
  - Block-replace regimen — levothyroxine is added to the antithyroid drug.
- Adverse effects occur in about 5% of people treated with antithyroid drugs and include rashes and pruritus, fever, arthralgia, headache, nausea, and mild gastrointestinal upset [Streetman and Khanderia, 2003].
- **Rashes and pruritus can be treated with an antihistamine** without discontinuing therapy Streetman, 2003. [Streetman and Khanderia, 2003]. Alternatively, therapy can be switched from carbimazole to propylthiouracil, or vice versa [Weetman, 2003].
- **Agranulocytosis is rare** (3 per 10,000 patient years of treatment), but if it does occur, it usually develops within the first 3 months of treatment. Advise people to stop taking the antithyroid drug, and seek an urgent blood count if they develop a fever, sore throat, mouth ulcers, or other symptoms of infection [CSM, 1999].

References

1. AACE Thyroid Task Force (2002) *American Association of Clinical Endocrinologists medical guidelines for the evaluation and treatment of hyperthyroidism and hypothyroidism.* American Association of Clinical Endocrinologists. www.aace.com/clin/guidelines [Accessed: 18/08/2004].
2. Abraham, P., Avenell, A., Watson, W.A. et al (2004) *Antithyroid drug regimen for treating Graves' hyperthyroidism (Cochrane Review).* The Cochrane Library. Issue 2. Chichester, UK: John Wiley & Sons, Ltd.
3. Bartalena, L., Marcocci, C., Bogazzi, F. et al (1998) Relation between therapy for hyperthyroidism and the course of Graves' ophthalmopathy. *New England Journal of Medicine* **338**(2), 73–78. [Full text]
4. Cawood, T., Moriarty, P. and O'Shea, D. (2004) Recent developments in thyroid eye disease. *British Medical Journal* **329**(7462), 385–390.
5. Cooper, D.S. (2003) Hyperthyroidism. *Lancet* **362**(9382), 459–468. [Full text]
6. CSM (1999) Reminder: agranulocytosis with anti-thyroid drugs. *Current Problems in Pharmacovigilance* **25**(Feb), 3.
7. Franklyn, J. (1999) Thyrotoxicosis. *Prescribers' Journal* **39**(1), 1–9.
8. Geffner, D.L. and Hershman, J.M. (1992) Beta-adrenergic blockade for the treatment of hyperthyroidism. *American Journal of Medicine* **93**(1), 61–68.
9. Gittoes, N.J.L. and Franklyn, J.A. (1998) Hyperthyroidism: current treatment guidelines. *Drugs* **55**(4), 555–562.
10. Hanna, F.W.F., Lazarus, J.H. and Scanlon, M.F. (1999) Controversial aspects of thyroid disease. *British Medical Journal* **319**(7214), 894–899. [Full text]
11. Leonhardt, J.M. and Heymann, W.R. (2002) Thyroid disease and the skin. *Dermatologic Clinics* **20**(3), 473–481.
12. Miehle, K. and Paschke, R. (2003) Therapy of hyperthyroidism. *Experimental & Clinical Endocrinology & Diabetes* **111**(6), 305–318.
13. O'Doherty, M.J., McElhatton, P.R. and Thomas, S.H.L. (1999) Treating thyrotoxicosis in pregnant or potentially pregnant women. The risk to the fetus is very low. *British Medical Journal* **318**(7175), 5–6. [Full text]
14. Singer, P.A., Cooper, D.S., Levy, E.G. et al (1995) Treatment guidelines for patients with hyperthyroidism

H

and hypothyroidism. *Journal of the American Medical Association* **273**(10), 808–812.
15. Streetman, D.D. and Khanderia, U. (2003) Diagnosis and treatment of Graves disease. *Annals of Pharmacotherapy* **37**(7–8), 1100–1109.
16. Surks, M.I., Ortiz, E., Daniels, G.H. et al (2004) Subclinical thyroid disease: scientific review and guidelines for diagnosis and management. *Journal of the American Medical Association* **291**(2), 228–238.
17. Tunbridge, W.M.G., Evered, D.C., Hall, R. et al (1977) The spectrum of thyroid disease in a community: the Whickham survey. *Clinical Endocrinology* **7**(6), 481–493.
18. UKMiCentral (2003) *Drugs in breast milk – quick reference guide*. UK Medicines Information. http://www.ukmicentral.nhs.uk/drugpreg/guide.htm [Accessed: 10/11/2003].
19. Vanderpump, M.P.J., Tunbridge, W.M.G., French, J.M. et al (1995) The incidence of thyroid disorders in the community: a twenty-year follow-up of the Whickham Survey. *Clinical Endocrinology* **43**(1), 55–68.
20. Vanderpump, M.P.J., Ahlquist, J.A.O., Franklyn, J.A. and Clayton, R.N. (1996) Consensus statement for good practice and audit measures in the management of hypothyroidism and hyperthyroidism. *British Medical Journal* **313**(7056), 539–544. [Full text]
21. Weetman, A.P. (2003) The thyroid gland and disorders of thyroid function. In: Warrell, D.A., Cox, T.M., Firth, J.D. and Benz, E.J.Jr (Eds.) *Oxford Textbook of Medicine*. 4th edn. Oxford: Oxford University Press. Section 12.4.

PRODIGY GUIDANCE

Hypnotic or anxiolytic dependence

Last revised in February 2003
www.prodigy.nhs.uk/guidance.asp?gt=Hypnotic/anxiolytic dependence

Applies to people over the age of 16 years

This guidance covers the management of hypnotic or anxiolytic dependence.

This guidance does not cover the management of overdose; dependence on other drugs (including alcohol dependence); or the management of dependence in neonates, children, or pregnancy.

There is separate PRODIGY guidance for *Alcohol — problem drinking, Depression, Insomnia, Opioid dependence, Smoking cessation,* and *Stress — acute reaction.*

Goals

- To guide withdrawal from long-term hypnotic or anxiolytic use

Contents

Scenarios
- Dependent on therapeutic dosages p.1013
- Dependent on high dosages p.1015

Extended Information, p. 1016

Which scenario?

- **Dependent on therapeutic dosages:** covers the management of people who are dependent on therapeutic dosages of prescribed hypnotics or anxiolytics.
- **Dependent on high dosages:** covers the management of people who are dependent on supratherapeutic dosages of hypnotics or anxiolytics, for example those obtained illegally and used intravenously.

Dependent on therapeutic dosages

Which therapy?

- **Educate** about problems of taking benzodiazepines long-term.
- **Motivate and encourage** people to take some responsibility for their situation and its solution. Give non-drug advice simultaneously. This alone may be adequate for some people.
- **If the person is taking a hypnotic or anxiolytic other than diazepam,** change them to the equivalent dosage of diazepam. Aim for the lowest dosage that will prevent withdrawal symptoms. Dose equivalents are given in Table 1.
- **The daily dose** may need to be divided in order to avoid intoxication or daytime drowsiness.
- **Reduce diazepam,** for example, initially in fortnightly steps of 5 mg, and then 2.5 mg, according to clinical judgement of the individual's needs and withdrawal symptoms. The final suggested steps are from 2.5 mg to 1 mg daily, then stopping.

Practical prescribing points

For further information, please see the *Medicines Compendium* (www.medicines.org.uk) or the *British National Formulary* (www.bnf.org).

Table 1: Doses of benzodiazepines that are equivalent to diazepam 5 mg.

Benzodiazepines	Approximate equivalent doses to diazepam 5 mg
Temazepam	10 mg
Nitrazepam	5 mg
Loprazolam	500 micrograms – 1 mg
Lorazepam	500 micrograms
Chlordiazepoxide	15 mg
Oxazepam	15 mg
Clonazepam	250 micrograms
Lormetazepam	500 micrograms – 1 mg
Clobazam	10 mg
'z' drugs	
Zopiclone	7.5 mg
Zolpidem	10 mg
Zaleplon	10 mg

- **Diazepam causes drowsiness** that may affect performance of skilled tasks (e.g. driving); the effects of alcohol are enhanced.
- **Abrupt or too rapid withdrawal of diazepam** can cause serious adverse reactions including rebound insomnia, severe anxiety, and seizures. Re-establishment of drug maintenance will usually reverse these effects.
- **Small doses of diazepam** can be administered by cutting tablets into two halves. This can be done by the person if the tablets are scored, or by the pharmacist otherwise.

Follow-up advice

- **It is important to review regularly** (at least every 3 months, or more frequently, according to clinical judgement) in order to monitor withdrawal symptoms, ensure compliance with withdrawal regimen, offer support and encouragement, reinforce non-drug techniques, and clarify goals and targets met.
- **If withdrawal symptoms occur,** maintain this dosage until symptoms improve. Further reductions may need to be taken in smaller fortnightly steps.
- **Aim to stop the drug completely.** This can take from 4 weeks to over a year.

Should I refer or investigate?

Refer?

- **Referral to a local drugs and alcohol mental health team, clinical psychologist, or trained counsellor may be appropriate:**
  - For more specialized and intensive behavioural therapies.

- For those people who fail to achieve withdrawal after repeated treatment and advice.
- If severe complications develop after withdrawal.
- If the person is simultaneously dependent on other drugs or alcohol.
- If there is coexisting physical or psychiatric morbidity.

- **Sleep laboratory referral** is not usually required, but the investigations conducted at these centres (electroencephalography and electro-oculography) may be useful in the following cases:
  - Insomnia that is exaggerated by the person.
  - Other unusual features of sleep (e.g. epilepsy during sleep, sleep apnoea).

Patient information leaflets

The following PILs are available at www.prodigy.nhs.uk

- Battle Against Tranquillisers - BAT
- Benzodiazepines
- CITA (Council for Involuntary Tranquilizer Addiction)
- Cognitive Behaviour Therapy (CBT)

H

Shared decision making

- When stopping a benzodiazepine which you have been taking long-term, it is best to do it gradually.
- If you are taking a benzodiazepine other than diazepam, at first it is best to switch to the equivalent dosage of diazepam.
- **Diazepam** is the easiest benzodiazepine to gradually reduce the dose and eventually stop.
- The aim is to reduce the dose of diazepam by about 2 mg every 2–4 weeks.
- If withdrawal symptoms are troublesome, a more gradual reduction of dose may be better.

Drug rationale

Drugs not included

- **Benzodiazepines other than diazepam** are not recommended for reduction protocols [Scottish Health Service Advisory Council, 1994; BNF 43, 2002]. Alprazolam and lorazepam, in particular, have the reputation of presenting particular withdrawal problems. Chlordiazepoxide has a more variable half-life than diazepam, and it is more difficult to halve small dosages [Russell and Lader, 1997].
- **Zaleplon, zolpidem, and zopiclone** (the 'z' drugs) are newer hypnotics reputed to cause less dependence than benzodiazepines. However, several studies and case reports contradict this, and they are only licensed for the short-term treatment of insomnia. Their use in benzodiazepine withdrawal is therefore not recommended [MeReC, 2002].
- **Buspirone** is a newer anxiolytic with a mechanism of action unrelated to that of the benzodiazepines. It does not alleviate the symptoms of benzodiazepine withdrawal and therefore must not be used for this purpose [BNF 43, 2002].

Drugs included

- **Diazepam** is a long-acting anxiolytic that causes less marked symptoms of withdrawal than other benzodiazepines. It has a quick onset of action, has been well studied, and is available in several different formulations and strengths.
- **Benzodiazepine withdrawal protocols** suggest transferring the person to diazepam and then reducing the dosage in fortnightly steps of 5 mg initially, and then by 2.5 mg every 2 weeks.
- Other than diazepam, the three most commonly prescribed benzodiazepines are temazepam, nitrazepam, and loprazolam [Prescription Pricing Authority, 2001]. Prescriptions for switching from these drugs to diazepam are included.

[Scottish Health Service Advisory Council, 1994; BNF 43, 2002].

Prescriptions

Advice notes

Advice only: good sleep hygiene

- Age from 16 years onwards
- Some poor nights sleep may occur at first. General tips to help with sleep include: Body rhythm – get up at the same time each day and never sleep in the day. Routines – are useful before bedtime e.g. a warm drink, hot bath and reading. Bedroom – should be free of noise and don't use for watching TV, eating, work. Stimulants – such as alcohol, caffeine and smoking should be avoided in the evening. Exercise – regularly during the day but not within a few hours of bedtime. Eat – only a light snack before bedtime and not a large meal. Relaxation – may be improved by using a relaxation tape in the evening.

Advice only: gradual dose reduction

- Age from 16 years onwards
- You are aiming to come off your benzodiazepine medicine. A gradual reduction in the dose is the usual method. Your medicine will be changed to the equivalent dose of diazepam. Diazepam is the easiest benzodiazepine to gradually reduce the dose and eventually stop. The aim is to reduce the dose of diazepam by about 2 mg every 2 weeks.

Change to diazepam maintenance

Change from temazepam 40mg (maximum licensed use)

- Age from 16 years onwards
- Diazepam 10mg tablets. Take two tablets at night; supply 28 tablets; NHS Cost £0.84.

Change from nitrazepam 10mg (maximum licensed dose)

- Age from 16 years onwards
- Diazepam 5mg tablets. Take two tablets at night; supply 28 tablets; NHS Cost £0.58.

Change from loprazolam 2mg (maximum licensed dose)

- Age from 16 years onwards
- Diazepam 10mg tablets. Take two tablets at night; supply 28 tablets; NHS Cost £0.84.

Change from other hypnotic/anxiolytic drug or dose

- Age from 16 years onwards
- Diazepam 5mg tablets. Take as directed; supply 56 tablets; NHS Cost £1.16.

Reduce from diazepam 20mg

Maintain on diazepam 20mg

- Age from 16 years onwards
- Diazepam 10mg tablets. Take two tablets at night; supply 28 tablets; NHS Cost £0.84.

First reduction: diazepam 15mg at night

- Age from 16 years onwards
- Diazepam 5mg tablets. Take three tablets at night; supply 42 tablets; NHS Cost £0.87.

Second reduction: diazepam 10mg at night

- Age from 16 years onwards
- Diazepam 5mg tablets. Take two tablets at night; supply 28 tablets; NHS Cost £0.58.

Third reduction: diazepam 7.5mg at night
- Age from 16 years onwards
- Diazepam 5mg tablets. Take one and a half tablets at night; supply 21 tablets; NHS Cost £0.39.

Fourth reduction: diazepam 5mg at night
- Age from 16 years onwards
- Diazepam 5mg tablets. Take one tablet at night; supply 14 tablets; NHS Cost £0.29.

Fifth reduction: diazepam 2.5mg at night
- Age from 16 years onwards
- Diazepam 5mg tablets. Take half a tablet at night; supply 7 tablets; NHS Cost £0.15.

Final reduction: diazepam 1mg at night
- Age from 16 years onwards
- Diazepam 2mg tablets. Take half a tablet at night; supply 7 tablets; NHS Cost £0.14.

Reduce from diazepam 10mg

Maintain on diazepam 10mg
- Age from 16 years onwards
- Diazepam 5mg tablets. Take two tablets at night; supply 28 tablets; NHS Cost £0.58.

First reduction: diazepam 7.5mg at night
- Age from 16 years onwards
- Diazepam 5mg tablets. Take one and a half tablets at night; supply 21 tablets; NHS Cost £0.39.

Second reduction: diazepam 5mg at night
- Age from 16 years onwards
- Diazepam 5mg tablets. Take one tablet at night; supply 14 tablets; NHS Cost £0.29.

Third reduction: diazepam 2.5mg at night
- Age from 16 years onwards
- Diazepam 5mg tablets. Take half a tablet at night; supply 7 tablets; NHS Cost £0.15.

Final reduction: diazepam 1mg at night
- Age from 16 years onwards
- Diazepam 2mg tablets. Take half a tablet at night; supply 7 tablets; NHS Cost £0.14.

Dependent on high dosages

Which therapy?

- **Use a multidisciplinary, shared-care approach.**
- **Carry out a detailed initial assessment.**
- **Give advice** on harm minimization (use of sterile needles and condoms) where appropriate.
- **Educate** about problems with taking benzodiazepines long-term, determine the goals of treatment with the person, motivate and encourage the person to take some responsibility for the situation and its solution, and give simultaneous non-drug advice.
- **If the person is taking a hypnotic or anxiolytic other than diazepam,** change them to the equivalent dosage of diazepam.
- **Aim for the lowest dosage of diazepam that will prevent withdrawal symptoms.**
- **For people who are misusing high dosages,** the amount prescribed should be substantially less than the amount they claim to be taking.
- **Titrate the diazepam dosage** according to withdrawal symptoms. Illicit users may often only need a low dosage — such as 30 mg of diazepam — to gain relief from withdrawal symptoms, even though they may have been using much higher dosages to obtain an intoxicating effect. Dose equivalents are given in Table 2.
- **The daily dose** may need to be divided in order to avoid intoxication or daytime drowsiness.

Table 2: Doses of benzodiazepines that are equivalent to diazepam 5 mg.

Benzodiazepines	Approximate equivalent doses to diazepam 5 mg
Temazepam	10 mg
Nitrazepam	5 mg
Loprazolam	500 micrograms – 1 mg
Lorazepam	500 micrograms
Chlordiazepoxide	15 mg
Oxazepam	15 mg
Clonazepam	250 micrograms
Lormetazepam	500 micrograms – 1 mg
Clobazam	10 mg
'z' drugs	
Zopiclone	7.5 mg
Zolpidem	10 mg
Zaleplon	10 mg

- **Reduce the dosage of diazepam in fortnightly or monthly steps** by around 5–10 mg per month, with smaller reductions when lower dosages are reached, according to clinical judgement of the individual's needs and withdrawal symptoms. The final suggested steps are from 2.5 mg to 1 mg daily, then stopping.

H

Practical prescribing points

For further information, please see the *Medicines Compendium* (www.medicines.org.uk) or the *British National Formulary* (www.bnf.org).
- **Diazepam causes drowsiness** that may affect performance of skilled tasks (e.g. driving); effects of alcohol are enhanced.
- **Abrupt or too rapid withdrawal of diazepam** can cause serious adverse reactions including rebound insomnia, severe anxiety, and seizures. Re-establishment of drug maintenance will usually reverse these effects.
- **Small doses of diazepam** can be administered by cutting tablets into two halves. This can be done by the person if the tablets are scored, or by the pharmacist otherwise.

Follow-up advice

- It is important to review regularly (at least every 3 months, or more frequently according to clinical judgement) in order to monitor withdrawal symptoms, ensure compliance with the withdrawal regimen, offer support and encouragement, reinforce non-drug techniques, and clarify goals and targets met.
- **If withdrawal symptoms occur,** maintain the dosage until symptoms improve. Further reductions may need to be taken in smaller fortnightly steps.
- **Aim to stop the drug completely.** This can take from 4 weeks to over a year.
- **If the person is also receiving a long-term prescription for methadone** for concomitant opiate dependency, the methadone should be kept stable during the benzodiazepine reduction period. Concurrent detoxification of both drugs is not recommended in the community.

Should I refer or investigate?

Refer?

- **Referral to a local drugs and alcohol mental health team, clinical psychologist, or trained counsellor may be appropriate:**

- For more specialized and intensive behavioural therapies.
- If high-dosage prescribing is required.
- For those people who fail to achieve withdrawal after repeated treatment and advice.
- If severe complications develop after withdrawal.
- If the person is simultaneously dependent on other drugs or alcohol.
- If there is coexisting physical or psychiatric morbidity.

- **Sleep laboratory referral is not usually required,** but the investigations conducted at these centres (electroencephalography and electro-oculography) may be useful in the following cases:
  - Insomnia that is exaggerated by the person.
  - Other unusual features of sleep (e.g. epilepsy during sleep, sleep apnoea).

Investigate?

- **Blood tests** (liver function tests, hepatitis B and C tests, and HIV tests) should be done according to clinical judgement based on the individual situation. Counselling is important before testing for hepatitis or HIV.
- **Urine analysis** to confirm drug use should be obtained at the outset of prescribing and randomly throughout treatment. Results should be interpreted in the light of clinical findings, as false negatives and false positives can occur.

H

Patient information leaflets

The following PILs are available at www.prodigy.nhs.uk

- Battle Against Tranquillisers - BAT
- Benzodiazepines
- CITA (Council for Involuntary Tranquilizer Addiction)
- Cognitive Behaviour Therapy (CBT)

Shared decision making

- When stopping a benzodiazepine which you have been taking long-term, it is best to do it gradually.
- If you are taking a benzodiazepine other than diazepam, at first it is best to switch to diazepam.
- **Diazepam** is the easiest benzodiazepine to gradually reduce the dose and eventually stop.
- The initial dose of diazepam should be the lowest to prevent withdrawal symptoms.
- The aim is then to reduce the dose of diazepam by about 2 mg every 2–4 weeks.
- If withdrawal symptoms are troublesome, a more gradual reduction of dose may be better.

Drug rationale

Drugs not included

- **Benzodiazepines other than diazepam** are not recommended for reduction protocols [Scottish Health Service Advisory Council, 1994; BNF 43, 2002]. Alprazolam and lorazepam, in particular, have the reputation of presenting particular withdrawal problems. Chlordiazepoxide has a more variable half-life than diazepam, and it is more difficult to halve small dosages [Russell and Lader, 1997].
- **Zaleplon, zolpidem, and zopiclone** (the 'z' drugs) are newer hypnotics reputed to cause less dependency than benzodiazepines. However, several studies and case reports contradict this, and they are only licensed for the short-term treatment of insomnia. Their use in benzodiazepine withdrawal is therefore not recommended [MeReC, 2002].
- **Buspirone** is a newer anxiolytic with a mechanism of action unrelated to that of the benzodiazepines. It does not alleviate the symptoms of benzodiazepine withdrawal and therefore must not be used for this purpose [BNF 43, 2002].

Drugs included

- **Diazepam** is a long-acting anxiolytic that causes less marked symptoms of withdrawal than other benzodiazepines. It has a quick onset of action, has been well studied, and is available in several different formulations and strengths.
- **Benzodiazepine withdrawal protocols** suggest transferring the person to diazepam and then reducing the dosage in steps. Initially, the dosage can be reduced by about 10% (up to a reduction of 10 mg) in fortnightly steps, and then by smaller steps of 2 mg or 2.5 mg every 2 weeks. This should be done according to the individual's needs and withdrawal symptoms.

[Scottish Health Service Advisory Council, 1994; BNF 43, 2002]

Prescriptions

Advice notes

Advice only: good sleep hygiene

- Age from 16 years onwards
- Some poor nights sleep may occur at first. General tips to help with sleep include: Body rhythm – get up at the same time each day and never sleep in the day. Routines – are useful before bedtime e.g. a warm drink, hot bath and reading. Bedroom – should be free of noise and don't use for watching TV, eating, work. Stimulants – such as alcohol, caffeine and smoking should be avoided in the evening. Exercise – regularly during the day but not within a few hours of bedtime. Eat – only a light snack before bedtime and not a large meal. Relaxation – may be improved by using a relaxation tape in the evening.

Advice only: gradual dose reduction

- Age from 16 years onwards
- You are aiming to come off your benzodiazepine medicine. A gradual reduction in the dose is the usual method. Your medicine will be changed to the equivalent dose of diazepam. Diazepam is the easiest benzodiazepine to gradually reduce the dose and eventually stop. The aim is to reduce the dose of diazepam by about 2 mg every 2 weeks.

Diazepam

Diazepam 10mg tablets

- Age from 16 years onwards
- Diazepam 10mg tablets. Take as directed; supply 28 tablets; NHS Cost £0.84.

Diazepam 5mg tablets

- Age from 16 years onwards
- Diazepam 5mg tablets. Take as directed; supply 28 tablets; NHS Cost £0.58.

Diazepam 2mg tablets

- Age from 16 years onwards
- Diazepam 2mg tablets. Take as directed; supply 28 tablets; NHS Cost £0.53.

Extended Information

Background information

- What is it? p.1017
- How common is it? p.1017

- How do I know my patient has it? p.1017
- Complications and prognosis p.1017

What is it?

- **The 1993 World Health Organization definition of drug dependence is:** 'a cluster of physiological, behavioural, and cognitive phenomena of variable intensity, in which the use of a psychoactive drug takes on a high priority. The necessary descriptive characteristics are a preoccupation with the desire to obtain the drug, and persistent drug seeking behaviour. Determinants and the problematic consequences of drug dependence may be biological, psychological, or social, and usually interact'.
- **The degree of psychological dependence** can be equated to the amount of negative effect (anxiety or depression, or both) experienced in the absence of the desired drug, and related behaviours.
- **Physical dependence** is significant chemical dependence on the drug, in addition to any psychological dependence: repeated doses of the drug may lead to a physiological modification of the drug taker so that relatively normal function can only take place with the drug being present in the body. When it is not, a range of physiological withdrawal symptoms result. These are rapidly relieved by further use of the drug. The relief of uncomfortable withdrawal symptoms is powerfully rewarding.
- **Patients may have become dependent on medication that has been prescribed for the treatment of anxiety or insomnia.** Physical and psychological dependence can occur with all benzodiazepines, after even a short-term treatment [Scottish Health Service Advisory Council, 1994; Medicines Resource, 1995a].
- **Alternatively, they may have become dependent on hypnotics or anxiolytics that they obtained through illicit means.** Benzodiazepines are often taken in combination with opiates [DH et al, 1999].
- **Not all drug misusers are drug-dependent.**
- **Those who misuse hypnotics and anxiolytics illicitly often misuse other drugs,** including alcohol, concurrently.
- **The following are classed as anxiolytics:** alprazolam, chlordiazepoxide, clobazam, clonazepam, clorazepate, diazepam, lorazepam, and oxazepam.
- **The following are classed as hypnotics:** flunitrazepam, flurazepam, loprazolam, lormetazepam, nitrazepam, temazepam, zaleplon, zolpidem, and zopiclone.

[Council of the Royal Pharmaceutical Society, 1998]

How common is it?

- **The number of prescriptions issued per year for benzodiazepines** dropped significantly after 1988, reflecting the Committee on Safety of Medicines warning regarding dependence on these drugs at this time [Scottish Health Service Advisory Council, 1994; Wright et al, 1994]. Unfortunately, however, this reduction has not continued, and benzodiazepine prescribing changed little between 1996 and 2001. In England in 2001 a total of 16 million prescriptions for hypnotics and anxiolytics were issued, at a cost of 35.6 million pounds [Prescription Pricing Authority, 2001].
- **Up to 90% of attendees at drug-misuse centres** reported use of benzodiazepines in a 1-year period, and 49% had injected them [DH et al, 1999].

[Russell and Lader, 1997]

How do I know my patient has it?

- **People with dependency may present in a variety of ways.** For example:
  - **At a routine review of their prescribed medication.**
  - **An active request for help** with dependency — the person is motivated to change their behaviour.
  - **A request for a further prescription** of hypnotics or anxiolytics, or a request for an increased dosage owing to tolerance (e.g. complaining of return of insomnia symptoms, or withdrawal symptoms).
  - **With features of withdrawal.** These may occur on sudden cessation of use of benzodiazepines and include:
    - **Anxiety symptoms:** anxiety, sweating, insomnia, headache, tremor, nausea, palpitations, vertigo, muscle spasms, panic attacks
    - **Disordered perceptions:** depersonalization, derealization, abnormal body sensations, abnormal sensation of movement, hypersensitivity to stimuli
    - **Major complications:** psychosis, convulsions

[DH et al, 1999]

Complications and prognosis

- **The risk of a road traffic accident** is increased when certain hypnotics or anxiolytics are used [Hemmelgarn et al, 1997; Barbone et al, 1998], and this is more likely if there is dependence. The drugs in these studies that increased the risk were the long half-life benzodiazepines chlordiazepoxide, clonazepam, clorazepate, diazepam, flurazepam, and nitrazepam; and the non-benzodiazepine zopiclone.
- **The risk of falls in the elderly** is increased by the use of hypnotics and anxiolytics [MeReC, 2002].
- **The success of withdrawal and detoxification regimens** is low unless they are linked to long-term rehabilitation.
- **The likelihood of clinical improvement is poor** if the person does not agree with the withdrawal regimen.
- **Failure to identify and address non compliance** at an early stage can result in a loss of motivation and drive, both for the patient and the clinician. Non-compliance with medication can actually aggravate a drug problem.
- **There is a risk of the drug getting into the wrong hands** in cases of non-compliance; for example, the person may sell the drug to purchase other illicit drugs, thereby perpetuating controlled drug misuse and contributing towards the illicit market.

Management issues

- General issues for those dependent on therapeutic dosages p.1017
- General issues for those dependent on high dosages p.1018
- Initial assessment of those dependent on therapeutic dosages p.1018
- Initial assessment of those dependent on high dosages p.1018
- Non-drug treatments for those dependent on therapeutic dosages p.1018
- Non-drug treatments for those dependent on high dosages p.1019
- Drug treatments for those dependent on therapeutic dosages p.1019
- Drug treatments for those dependent on high dosages p.1020
- Useful contacts p.1021

General issues for those dependent on therapeutic dosages

- **Relatively easy withdrawal** is possible in many people if the problems of continuing drug usage are explained to them. At least 50% of elderly benzodiazepine users would like to discontinue use [King et al, 1990; Barter and Cormack, 1996]. With help, 40% of people can

H

come off hypnotics or anxiolytics without difficulty; 40% may have some difficulty; and the remainder may opt to remain on benzodiazepines.
- **It is important to identify any potential causes of insomnia or anxiety states** (including exacerbating factors); these should be treated if possible.
- **Hypnotics started in hospital** to cover a sleepless night on a busy ward should not be continued by general practitioners [Medicines Resource, 1995a].
- **The placebo effect** in the treatment of chronic insomnia is 33% [Therapeutics Initiative, 1995].

General issues for those dependent on high dosages

- **Shared care:** the structure of shared care will vary between regions, depending on expertise in primary and secondary care, numbers of drug misusers, and the provision of treatment facilities. However, in all circumstances, co-ordination and communication between the health professionals involved is crucial in order to meet the multiple needs of the person [DH et al, 1999].
- **Prevention:** a recent government publication highlights the importance of prevention of drug dependence and rehabilitation, particularly in young people [Hellawell, 1999]. Local community involvement is important when developing drug prevention programmes [Central Drugs Prevention Unit, 1999]. This is not discussed in detail in this guidance.

H

Initial assessment of those dependent on therapeutic dosages

The assessment of the person should include, as appropriate:

History

- **Assess the degree of dependence: consider past and current (last 4 weeks) drug history.** This should be easily obtained from the individual's medical record of repeat prescriptions.
- **Assess the motivation to stop or change the pattern of drug use.**
- **Assess psychiatric history,** including overdoses, previous depression, or psychosis.

Examination

- **Assess mental health,** including general behaviour, mood, and cognitive state.

[DH et al, 1999]

Initial assessment of those dependent on high dosages

The assessment of the person should include, as appropriate:

History

- **Assess the degree of dependence: consider past and current (last 4 weeks) drug history** (e.g. age of starting; types, frequency and cost of drug misuse; overdoses; periods of abstinence; and symptoms when the person is unable to obtain the drug).
- **Assess the motivation to stop or change the pattern of drug misuse.**
- **Assess history of injecting, and risk of HIV and hepatitis** (e.g. supply of needles; sharing habits; knowledge of hepatitis B and C, HIV, and issues of transmission; and use of condoms).
- **Assess medical history** for complications of drug use (e.g. abscess, thrombosis; hepatitis B, C, and HIV status if known).
- **Assess psychiatric history,** including overdoses, previous depression, or psychosis.
- **Assess forensic history** (e.g. past custodial sentences, probation, or community service).
- **Assess social history** (e.g. family, employment, accommodation, financial situation).

Examination

- **Physical examination:**
  - To assess general health, for example anaemia, poor nutrition, or dental caries.
  - To confirm drug misuse, for example needle tracks, skin abscess, or signs of withdrawal:
    - Anxiety: sweating, insomnia, headache, tremor, nausea, palpitations, vertigo, muscle spasms, panic attacks
    - Disordered perceptions: depersonalization, derealization, abnormal body sensations, abnormal sensation of movement, hypersensitivity to stimuli
    - Major complications: psychosis, convulsions
- **Mental health assessment** should include general behaviour, mood, delusions or hallucinations, and confusional states.

Investigations (as appropriate, depending on clinical judgement of risk)

- **Blood tests** (liver function tests, hepatitis B and C, and HIV tests) should be done according to clinical judgement based on the individual situation. Counselling is important before testing for hepatitis or HIV.
- **Urine analysis** to confirm drug use should be obtained prior to prescribing and randomly throughout treatment. Results should be interpreted in the light of clinical findings, as false negatives and false positives can occur. Drugs that can be detected in urine include amphetamines, barbiturates, benzodiazepines, cannabis, cocaine, opiates, and phencyclidine.
- **Hair analysis:** a single strand of hair can give information about drug use over several weeks or months, although this is not a routine investigation.

[DH et al, 1999]

Non-drug treatments for those dependent on therapeutic dosages

- **Non-drug treatments are the mainstay of treatment for anxiety and insomnia states** — see the appropriate PRODIGY guidance on *Depression, Insomnia, Panic disorder*, and *Stress — acute reaction.*
- **Education** about the risks and benefits of benzodiazepines is effective in reducing their usage [Cormack et al, 1994].
- **If hypnotics or anxiolytics are being taken for insomnia or anxiety,** introduce non-drug treatments (tailored to the individual) at the same time as withdrawal from therapy. Interventions such as a purpose-designed letter sent to long-term benzodiazepine users have been found to be effective (20–40% of people stop or at least halve their intake). Specimen letters can be found in the Medicines Resource publication on the management of anxiety and insomnia [Bashir et al, 1994; Cormack et al, 1994; Hawley et al, 1994; Scottish Health Service Advisory Council, 1994; Medicines Resource, 1995a; Gilhooly et al, 1998], and at www.nyrdtc.nhs.uk/docs/dud/Managing.pdf (produced by the Northern and Yorkshire Regional Drug and Therapeutics Centre).

Non-drug treatments for those dependent on high dosages

- **Advise on harm minimization,** including, if appropriate, access to sterile needles and syringes, testing for hepatitis and HIV, and immunization against hepatitis B. This should be addressed at the time of the initial assessment [DH et al, 1999].
- **Set goals** with the person to identify the changes hoped for (e.g. lifestyle changes) and how the prescription can help these changes [DH et al, 1999].
- **Keep clear, concise notes,** and inform other doctors who may see the person of the current treatment, in order to ease continuity of care [DH et al, 1999].

Drug treatments for those dependent on therapeutic dosages

General issues regarding drugs

- **Hypnotics and anxiolytics should be avoided where possible** and be reserved for short courses to alleviate acute conditions after causal factors have been established. When used, they should be an adjunct to non-drug treatment. If used, the lowest effective dosage should be prescribed for the shortest possible time [WHO, 1993; Medicines Resource, 1995a; Medicines Resource, 1995b].
- **There is no evidence that the long-term substitution of one benzodiazepine for another is of any benefit.** The only benefit is obtained by changing the benzodiazepine to an equivalent dosage of diazepam, and then reducing the dosage as described in withdrawal regimens below [DH et al, 1999].

Benzodiazepines

- **Indications are limited** to use only where insomnia is severe, disabling, or subjecting the individual to extreme distress, in which case the lowest possible dosages are recommended and the treatment should be tapered off gradually [MeReC, 1995]; Therapeutics Initiative, 1995; [CSM, 1988; Therapeutics Initiative, 1995].
- **Long-term use is strongly discouraged,** as it can lead to addiction and dependence. Use for insomnia should be restricted to 1 week [DTB, 1993].
- **Driving impairment:** people using hypnotics may feel drowsy during the day, in which case they should always be advised not to drive or operate machinery [BNF 43, 2002]. In addition, any person suffering from excessive awake-time sleepiness, regardless of cause (e.g. due to the insomnia itself), should cease driving until there is satisfactory control of symptoms [Hemmelgarn et al, 1997; Barbone et al, 1998; DVLA, 2003].
- **Withdrawal symptoms** may occur if drugs are suddenly discontinued, even after taking benzodiazepines for short periods of time (3–14 days) [MeReC, 1995]. Short-acting benzodiazepines are more likely to lead to a withdrawal syndrome than long-acting drugs [Scottish Health Service Advisory Council, 1994]. Symptoms tend to occur shortly after abruptly stopping a benzodiazepine with a short half-life, or up to several days after stopping one with a long half-life. Rebound phenomena are not related to the particular drug prescribed, nor to the duration of prescribing [Scottish Health Service Advisory Council, 1994].

Newer hypnotics (the 'z' drugs)

- **Zaleplon, zolpidem, and zopiclone** are newer non-benzodiazepine hypnotics that are claimed to have lower dependence potential than benzodiazepines.
- **The dependence potential of zolpidem and zopiclone, however, seems to be no different from benzodiazepines,** and there is emerging anecdotal evidence of illegal abuse of zolpidem 'on the street' [Medicines Resource, 1995b; MeReC, 2002]. **Zaleplon** has only been available in the UK since March 2000, and its place in therapy and its dependence potential have not yet been established [MeReC, 2002]. The half-life of zaleplon is 1 hour, the shortest of any currently used hypnotic.
- **As the dependence potential of the 'z' drugs seems to be no different from benzodiazepines,** and the 'z' drugs are much more expensive, there is no evidence that the 'z' drugs should be prescribed instead of a benzodiazepine for short-term use.
- Zopiclone is associated with an increased risk of road traffic accidents, possibly explained by residual effects that impair car-driving performance [Barbone et al, 1998]. Zolpidem is associated with an increased risk of hip fracture [MeReC, 2002].

Buspirone

- **Buspirone** is a newer anxiolytic with a mechanism of action unrelated to that of the benzodiazepines. It does not alleviate the symptoms of benzodiazepine withdrawal and therefore must not be used for this purpose [BNF 43, 2002].

H

Withdrawal regimens for drug treatments

- **Prior to commencing withdrawal regimens,** it is important to determine the individual's expectations of treatment and degree of motivation to change [DH et al, 1999].
- **Withdrawal schedules:** diazepam is known to be much less addictive than lorazepam and other short-acting drugs; therefore, the first step in withdrawal is to change the drug to diazepam. Dose equivalents are given in Table 3. Note that this table is based on expert experience and best practice.
- **Aim for the lowest dosage of diazepam that will prevent withdrawal symptoms.**
- **The daily dosage of diazepam** may need to be divided in order to avoid intoxication or daytime drowsiness.
- **The dosage of diazepam should then be reduced in fortnightly or monthly steps,** according to clinical judgement of the individual's needs and withdrawal symptoms, rather than by immediate cessation, in order to avoid severe withdrawal effects [Scottish Health Service Advisory Council, 1994; Medicines Resource, 1995a]. The final suggested steps are from 2.5 mg to 1 mg daily, then stopping.

Table 3: Doses of benzodiazepines that are equivalent to diazepam 5 mg.

Benzodiazepines	Approximate equivalent doses to diazepam 5 mg
Temazepam	10 mg
Nitrazepam	5 mg
Loprazolam	500 micrograms – 1 mg
Lorazepam	500 micrograms
Chlordiazepoxide	15 mg
Oxazepam	15 mg
Clonazepam	250 micrograms
Lormetazepam	500 micrograms – 1 mg
Clobazam	10 mg
'z' drugs	
Zopiclone	7.5 mg
Zolpidem	10 mg
Zaleplon	10 mg

- **Replacement of benzodiazepines with alternative hypnotics or anxiolytics** can, in some people, lead to long-term use of the alternative drug instead and is not recommended [Gilhooly et al, 1998]. The only acceptable strategy for stopping benzodiazepine use seems to be gradual withdrawal and replacement with non-drug therapy.

Drug treatments for those dependent on high dosages

General issues regarding drugs

- **There is no evidence that the long-term substitution of one benzodiazepine for another is of any benefit.** The only benefit is obtained by changing the benzodiazepine to an equivalent dosage of diazepam, and then reducing the dosage as described in withdrawal regimens below [DH et al, 1999].
- **Misuse:** some misused temazepam comes from drugs prescribed directly to addicts, and also from the misappropriation of medication prescribed to other people, and from theft. Capsules, tablets, and liquid preparations of temazepam are all misused (as with all forms of benzodiazepines); hence the need to be vigilant whenever prescribing a benzodiazepine (particularly if the person is temporarily registered or unknown) [Scottish Health Service Advisory Council, 1994; Medicines Resource, 1995a; MeReC, 1995].
- **If the person is also receiving a long-term prescription of methadone** for concomitant opiate dependency, the methadone should be kept stable throughout the benzodiazepine reduction period. Concurrent detoxification is not recommended in the community [DH et al, 1999].

Benzodiazepines

- **Driving impairment:** people using hypnotics may feel drowsy during the day, in which case they should always be advised not to drive or operate machinery [BNF 43, 2002]. In addition, any person suffering from excessive awake-time sleepiness, regardless of cause (e.g. due to the insomnia itself), should stop driving until there is satisfactory control of symptoms. Persistent use of, or dependency on, benzodiazepines will lead to licence refusal or revocation for a minimum period of 1 year [Hemmelgarn et al, 1997; Barbone et al, 1998; DVLA, 2003].
- **Withdrawal symptoms** may occur if drugs are suddenly discontinued, even after taking benzodiazepines for relatively short periods of time (3–14 days) [MeReC, 1995]. Short-acting benzodiazepines are more likely to lead to a withdrawal syndrome than long-acting drugs [Scottish Health Service Advisory Council, 1994]. Symptoms tend to occur shortly after abruptly stopping a benzodiazepine with a short half-life, or up to several days after stopping one with a long half-life. Rebound phenomena are not related to the particular drug prescribed, nor to the duration of prescribing [Scottish Health Service Advisory Council, 1994].

Newer hypnotics (the 'z' drugs)

- **Zaleplon, zolpidem, and zopiclone** are newer non-benzodiazepine hypnotics that are claimed to have lower dependence potential than benzodiazepines.
- **The dependence potential of zolpidem and zopiclone, however, seems to be no different from benzodiazepines,** and there is emerging anecdotal evidence of illegal abuse of zolpidem 'on the street' [Medicines Resource, 1995b; MeReC, 2002]. **Zaleplon** has only been available in the UK since March 2000, and its place in therapy and its dependence potential have not yet been established [MeReC, 2002]. The half-life of zaleplon is 1 hour, the shortest of any currently used hypnotic.

Buspirone

- **Buspirone** is a newer anxiolytic with a mechanism of action unrelated to that of the benzodiazepines. It does not alleviate the symptoms of benzodiazepine withdrawal and therefore must not be used for this purpose [BNF 43, 2002].

Withdrawal regimens for drug treatments

- **A multidisciplinary approach is essential.**
- **Assess the most appropriate level of expertise required** to manage the person, and refer or liaise appropriately (i.e. shared care, specialist care, specialist generalist care, or other forms of psychosocial care) [Gerada and Tighe, 1999].
- **Prior to commencing withdrawal regimens,** it is important to determine the individual's expectations of treatment and degree of motivation to change [DH et al, 1999].
- **Once the assessment has been made,** consideration should be given to the possibility that psychosocial rehabilitation may be required. In such circumstances, further assessment (Community Care Assessment) should be sought [Gerada and Tighe, 1999].
- **Withdrawal schedules:** diazepam is known to be much less addictive than lorazepam and other short-acting drugs; therefore, the first step in withdrawal is to change the drug to diazepam. Dose equivalents are given in Table 4. Note that this table is based on expert experience and best practice.
- **Aim for the lowest dosage of diazepam that will prevent withdrawal symptoms.**
- **For people who are misusing high dosages,** the amount prescribed should be substantially less than the amount they claim to be taking. They may only need a dosage as low as 30 mg of diazepam to relieve withdrawal symptoms.
- **The daily dose of diazepam** may need to be divided in order to avoid intoxication or daytime drowsiness.
- **The dosage of diazepam should then be reduced in fortnightly or monthly steps,** according to clinical judgement of the individual's needs and withdrawal symptoms, rather than by immediate cessation, in order to avoid severe withdrawal effects. Those accustomed to a higher dosage over a longer period of time may require a longer period during which dosages are reduced, as they are likely to suffer greater withdrawal symptoms

Table 4: Doses of benzodiazepines that are equivalent to diazepam 5 mg.

Benzodiazepines	Approximate equivalent doses to diazepam 5 mg
Temazepam	10 mg
Nitrazepam	5 mg
Loprazolam	500 micrograms – 1 mg
Lorazepam	500 micrograms
Chlordiazepoxide	15 mg
Oxazepam	15 mg
Clonazepam	250 micrograms
Lormetazepam	500 micrograms – 1 mg
Clobazam	10 mg
'z' drugs	
Zopiclone	7.5 mg
Zolpidem	10 mg
Zaleplon	10 mg

H

[Scottish Health Service Advisory Council, 1994; Medicines Resource, 1995a]. The final suggested steps are from 2.5 mg to 1 mg daily, then stopping.

- **Replacement of benzodiazepines with alternative hypnotics or anxiolytics** can, in some people, lead to long-term use of the alternative drug instead and is not recommended [Gilhooly et al, 1998]. The only acceptable strategy for stopping benzodiazepine use seems to be gradual withdrawal and replacement with non-drug therapy.

Useful contacts

- Department of Health Drug Dependency web site: www.dh.gov.uk
- The National Drugs Helpline provides free and confidential advice, including information on local services. Telephone: 0800 776600.
- Also see annex 19 of the Department of Health 'Orange Book', *Drug misuse and dependence — guidelines on clinical management* www.dh.gov.uk [DH et al, 1999].

References

NHS staff in England can link, free of charge, from references to full text journals by clicking on [Full text] on the PRODIGY website.

1. Barbone, F., McMahon, A.D., Davey, P.G. et al (1998) Association of road-traffic accidents with benzodiazepine use. *Lancet* **352**(9137), 1331–1336. [Full text]
2. Barter, G. and Cormack, M. (1996) The long term use of benzodiazepines: patients' views, accounts and experiences. *Family Practice* **13**(6), 491–497.
3. Bashir, K., King, M. and Ashworth, M. (1994) Controlled evaluation of brief intervention by general practitioners to reduce chronic use of benzodiazepines. *British Journal of General Practice* **44**(386), 408–412.
4. BNF 43 (2002) *British National Formulary.* 43rd edn. London: British Medical Association and Royal Pharmaceutical Society of Great Britain.
5. Central Drugs Prevention Unit (1999) *The drugs prevention inititave 1989–1999.* The Home Office.
6. Cormack, M.A., Sweeney, K.G., Hughes-Jones, H. and Foot, G.A. (1994) Evaluation of an easy, cost-effective strategy for cutting benzodiazepine use in general practice. *British Journal of General Practice* **44**(378), 5–8.
7. Council of the Royal Pharmaceutical Society (1998) *Report of the Working Party on Pharmaceutical Services for Drug Misusers.* London: Royal Pharmaceutical Society of Great Britain.
8. CSM (1988) Benzodiazepines, dependence and withdrawal symptoms. *Current Problems in Pharmacovigilance* **21**(Jan), 1–2.
9. DH, Scottish Office DH, Welsh Office and DH and Social Services of NI (1999) *Drug misuse and dependence – guidelines on clinical management.* Department of Health. www.dh.gov.uk [Accessed: 27/04/2004]. [Full text]
10. DTB (1993) Benzodiazepine dependence – a helpful new report. *Drug & Therapeutics Bulletin* **31**(June), 52.
11. DVLA (2003) *At a glance guide to current medical standards of fitness to drive. Drug and alcohol misuse and dependency.* Drivers Medical Group, Driver and Vehicle Licensing Authority. www.dvla.gov.uk [Accessed: 29/01/2004].
12. Gilhooly, T.C., Webster, M.G.O., Poole, N.W. and Ross, S. (1998) What happens when doctors stop prescribing temazepam? Use of alternative therapies. *British Journal of General Practice* **48**(434), 1601–1602.
13. Hawley, C.J., Tattersall, M., Dellaportas, C. and Hallstrom, C. (1994) Comparison of long-term benzodiazepine users in three settings. *British Journal of Psychiatry* **165**(6), 792–796.
14. Hellawell, K. (1999) *Tackling drugs to build a better Britain.* London: The Stationary Office.
15. Hemmelgarn, B., Suissa, S., Huang, A. et al (1997) Benzodiazepine use and the risk of motor vehicle crash in the elderly. *Journal of the American Medical Association* **278**(1), 27–31. [Full text]
16. King, M.B., Gabe, J., Williams, P. and Rodrigo, E.K. (1990) Long term use of benzodiazepines: the views of patients. *British Journal of General Practice* **40**(334), 194–196.
17. Medicines Resource (1995a) Management of anxiety and insomnia (I). *Medicines Resource* **22**(May), 83–86.
18. Medicines Resource (1995b) Management of anxiety and insomnia (II). *Medicines Resource* **23**(June), 87–90.
19. MeReC (1995) Management of anxiety and insomnia. *MeReC Bulletin* **6**(10),
20. MeReC (2002) An update on benzodiazepines and non-benzodiazepine hypnotics. *MeReC Briefing* **17**(Apr), 6–8.
21. Prescription Pricing Authority (2001) *Prescribing of mental health drugs.* Prescription Pricing Authority. www.ppa.org.uk [Accessed: 29/08/2002].
22. Russell, J. and Lader, M. (1997) *Guidelines for the prevention and treatment of benzodiazepine dependence.* London: Mental Health Foundation.
23. Scottish Health Service Advisory Council (1994) *The management of anxiety and insomnia.* Edinburgh: HMSO.
24. Therapeutics Initiative (1995) To sleep or not to sleep: here are your questions. *Therapeutics Letter* **11**(Nov/Dec.),
25. WHO (Ed.) (1993) *Insomnia in general practice.* Geneva: Division of Mental Health, World Health Organisation.
26. Wright, N., Caplan, R. and Payne, S. (1994) Community survey of long term daytime use of benzodiazepines. *British Medical Journal* **309**(6946), 27–28. [Full text]

PRODIGY GUIDANCE

Hypothyroidism

Last revised in February 2005
www.prodigy.nhs.uk/guidance.asp?gt=Hypothyroidism

Applies to people over the age of 16 years

This guidance covers the management of hypothyroidism.

This guidance does not cover the management of children with hypothyroidism or of other thyroid disorders.

There is separate PRODIGY guidance for *Hyperthyroidism*.

Goals

- To establish the diagnosis
- To treat the condition effectively

Contents

Scenarios
- Hypothyroidism — initial treatment p.1022
- Hypothyroidism — maintenance treatment p.1023

Extended Information, p. 1024

Which scenario?

- **Hypothyroidism — initial treatment:** covers the initiation of levothyroxine (thyroxine) in a person recently diagnosed as having hypothyroidism.
- **Hypothyroidism — maintenance treatment:** covers the maintenance therapy in a person established on levothyroxine, including titration of doses after initiation.

Hypothyroidism — initial treatment

Which therapy?

- **Overt hypothyroidism (raised TSH, low thyroxine [T_4], characteristic features):**
  - **Low-risk people (i.e. younger, no coronary heart disease):**
    - Start with levothyroxine (thyroxine) 50–100 micrograms daily.
  - **Coexistent coronary heart disease or elderly:**
    - Start with 25 micrograms daily and increase cautiously.
- **Subclinical hypothyroidism (raised TSH, normal thyroxine [T_4], no convincing features):**
  - There is no consensus on the management of subclinical hypothyroidism. Some specialists recommend initiating levothyroxine treatment, others recommend annual review. PRODIGY recommends that advice is sought from local endocrinologists as shared care guidelines may exist.
  - If initiating treatment, this should only be undertaken if diagnosis is confirmed on repeat testing 3 months later. Start with levothyroxine 25–50 micrograms daily.

Practical prescribing points

For further information, please see the *Medicines Compendium* (www.medicines.org.uk) or the *British National Formulary* (www.bnf.org).

- **Adverse effects occur if the levothyroxine dose is excessive,** or if the initial increase in metabolism is too rapid:
  - Symptomatic hyperthyroidism (e.g. anginal pain, tachycardia, weight loss, heat intolerance, and hyperactivity).
  - Subclinical hyperthyroidism (increased risk of bone loss and atrial fibrillation).
- **Advise people to take levothyroxine before breakfast,** and to avoid taking iron and calcium supplements at this time.
- **People taking carbamazepine, phenytoin, or rifampicin:** check TSH level (and adjust levothyroxine dose accordingly) 6 weeks after dose changes to enzyme-inducing drugs.
- **People taking concomitant warfarin:** monitor international normalized ratio (INR) if the levothyroxine dose is altered. Dose reduction of warfarin is often needed.

Follow-up advice

- **Check thyroid-stimulating hormone (TSH)** 6 weeks after starting levothyroxine (thyroxine) or after any change in dose.
- **In low-risk people,** adjust levothyroxine dose by 25–50 micrograms every 6 weeks with the aim of returning the TSH level to normal.
- **In high-risk people** (coronary heart disease or elderly), increase by only 25 micrograms, but at 4-week intervals. Once the individual is clinically euthyroid, it is then advised to wait for 6 weeks before checking the TSH level.

Should I refer or investigate?

Refer?

- Refer if there is evidence of pituitary disease (low thyroid-stimulating hormone [TSH] and low thyroxine [T_4]).
- Consider referral in:
  - People less than 16 years.
  - Pregnant and post-partum women.
  - People presenting with particular management problems (e.g. coronary heart disease, on amiodarone or lithium).

Patient information leaflets

The following PILs are available at www.prodigy.nhs.uk

- Antibody and Antigen Tests
- Blood Test - General
- British Thyroid Foundation
- Hypothyroidism - Underactive Thyroid
- Medicines - Name Changes of Medicines

Shared decision-making

- **Levothyroxine (thyroxine)** is the treatment for an underactive thyroid.
- Ideally, take it before breakfast (and not with any iron or calcium tablets).
- A low dose is started at first and gradually built up every few weeks.
- A blood test is taken every few weeks at first, until the correct dose is found.
- A yearly blood test is then usual.
- Side effects are unusual. If you have angina you may notice more pains after starting levothyroxine. If this happens, tell a doctor.
- If you also take carbamazepine, phenytoin, rifampicin or warfarin, doses may need to be adjusted.

Drug rationale

Drugs not included

- **Levothyroxine (thyroxine [T_4]) plus liothyronine sodium (tri-iodothyronine [T_3]) therapy** is not routinely recommended. One small small-scale study suggested there might be some benefit from combination therapy but it was methodologically flawed, and two subsequent studies failed to confirm its findings [Bunevicius et al, 1999; Sawka et al, 2003; Walsh et al, 2003].

Drugs included

- **Levothyroxine (thyroxine)** is the standard thyroid replacement therapy.

Prescriptions

Heart disease/elderly (8-week supply)

Levothyroxine 25mcg daily for 4 weeks, then 50mcg daily
- Age from 16 years onwards
- Levothyroxine 25microgram tabs. Take one tablet each morning for 4 weeks, then take two tablets each morning for 4 weeks; supply 84 tablets; NHS Cost £2.55.

Standard initial therapy (8-week supply)

Levothyroxine (thyroxine) 50micrograms each morning
- Age from 16 years onwards
- Levothyroxine 50microgram tabs. Take one tablet each morning; supply 56 tablets; NHS Cost £1.14.

Levothyroxine (thyroxine) 100micrograms each morning
- Age from 16 to 50 years
- Levothyroxine 100microgram tab. Take one tablet each morning; supply 56 tablets; NHS Cost £1.72.

Hypothyroidism — maintenance treatment

Which therapy

All people on maintenance therapy:
- **Levothyroxine (thyroxine)** is the standard replacement therapy.
- The dose should be adjusted to maintain the thyroid-stimulating hormone (TSH) level in the normal range.
- Annual monitoring is advised when the dose is stable.

Practical prescribing points

For further information, please see the *Medicines Compendium* (www.medicines.org.uk) or the *British National Formulary* (www.bnf.org).
- **Adverse effects occur if the levothyroxine dose is excessive,** or if the initial increase in metabolism is too rapid:
  - Symptomatic hyperthyroidism (e.g. anginal pain, tachycardia, weight loss, heat intolerance, and hyperactivity).
  - Subclinical hyperthyroidism (increased risk of bone loss and atrial fibrillation).
- **Advise people to take levothyroxine before breakfast,** and to avoid taking iron and calcium supplements at this time.
- **People taking carbamazepine, phenytoin, or rifampicin:** check thyroid-stimulating hormone (TSH) level (and adjust levothyroxine dose accordingly) 6 weeks after dose changes to enzyme-inducing drugs.
- **People taking concomitant warfarin:** monitor international normalised ratio (INR) if the levothyroxine dose is altered. Dose reduction of warfarin is often needed.

H

Follow-up advice

- **Check thyroid-stimulating hormone** (TSH) level 6 weeks after any change in levothyroxine (thyroxine) dose.
- **Once stable,** annual checks are adequate.

Should I refer or investigate?

Refer?

- Consider referral in:
  - People less than 16 years.
  - Pregnant and post-partum women.
  - People presenting with particular management problems (e.g. coronary heart disease, on amiodarone or lithium).
  - People whose thyroid-stimulating hormone (TSH) level fails to return to normal, despite a dose of 200 micrograms or more of levothyroxine (thyroxine) — check compliance.
  - People who continue to be symptomatic, despite apparently adequate levothyroxine replacement.

Patient information leaflets

The following PILs are available at www.prodigy.nhs.uk
- Blood Test - General
- British Thyroid Foundation
- Hypothyroidism - Underactive Thyroid
- Medicines - Name Changes of Medicines

Shared decision-making

- **Levothyroxine (thyroxine)** is the treatment for an underactive thyroid.
- Ideally, take it before breakfast (and not with any iron or calcium tablets).
- Once the correct dose is found, most people have no problems while taking levothyroxine. It is best to take the tablet each day, but the occasional forgotten dose will not do any harm.
- A yearly blood test is usual to check that the dose is correct.
- If you also take carbamazepine, phenytoin, rifampicin or warfarin, doses may need to be adjusted.

Drug rationale

Drugs not included

- **Levothyroxine (thyroxine [T_4]) plus liothyronine sodium (tri-iodothyronine, [T_3]) therapy** is not routinely recommended. One small-scale study suggested there might be some benefit from combination therapy but it was methodologically flawed, and two subsequent studies failed to confirm its findings [Bunevicius et al, 1999; Sawka et al, 2003; Walsh et al, 2003].

Drugs included

- **Levothyroxine (thyroxine)** is the standard replacement therapy for hypothyroidism.

Prescriptions

Levothyroxine (thyroxine): lower doses (<100mcg)

Levothyroxine (thyroxine) 25micrograms each morning

- Age from 16 years onwards
- Levothyroxine 25microgram tabs. Take one tablet each morning; supply 84 tablets; NHS Cost £2.55.

Levothyroxine (thyroxine) 50micrograms each morning

- Age from 16 years onwards
- Levothyroxine 50microgram tabs. Take one tablet each morning; supply 84 tablets; NHS Cost £1.71.

Levothyroxine (thyroxine) 75micrograms each morning

- Age from 16 years onwards
- Levothyroxine 25microgram tabs. Take three tablets each morning; supply 252 tablets; NHS Cost £7.65.

Levothyroxine (thyroxine): higher doses (>=100mcg)

Levothyroxine (thyroxine) 100micrograms each morning

- Age from 16 years onwards
- Levothyroxine 100microgram tab. Take one tablet each morning; supply 84 tablets; NHS Cost £2.58.

Levothyroxine (thyroxine) 125micrograms each morning

- Age from 16 years onwards
- Levothyroxine 100microgram tab. Take one tablet each morning; supply 84 tablets; NHS Cost £2.58.
- Levothyroxine 25microgram tabs. Take one tablet each morning; supply 84 tablets; NHS Cost £2.55.

Levothyroxine (thyroxine) 150micrograms each morning

- Age from 16 years onwards
- Levothyroxine 50microgram tabs. Take three tablets each morning; supply 252 tablets; NHS Cost £5.13.

Levothyroxine (thyroxine) 175micrograms each morning

- Age from 16 years onwards
- Levothyroxine 100microgram tab. Take one tablet each morning; supply 84 tablets; NHS Cost £2.58.
- Levothyroxine 25microgram tabs. Take three tablets each morning; supply 252 tablets; NHS Cost £7.65.

Levothyroxine (thyroxine) 200micrograms each morning

- Age from 16 years onwards
- Levothyroxine 100microgram tab. Take two tablets each morning; supply 168 tablets; NHS Cost £5.16.

Extended Information

Background information

- What is it? p.1024
- How common is it? p.1024
- How do I know my patient has it? p.1025
- What else might it be? p.1025
- Complications and prognosis p.1025

What is it?

- **Hypothyroidism** results from undersecretion of thyroid hormone. This is usually due to primary thyroid gland failure secondary to chronic autoimmune thyroiditis (Hashimoto's disease), or follows radioactive iodine therapy or thyroidectomy.
- **Other causes of hypothyroidism are:**
  - Congenital hypothyroidism
  - Drug adverse effects (e.g. amiodarone, lithium, interferon alpha)
  - Irradiation of the head or neck
  - Secondary hypothyroidism due to pituitary or hypothalamic disease
  - Thyroiditis — frequently presents with hyperthyroidism, hypothyroidism then follows for several months, resolution then follows; thyroiditis can be classified as:
    - Infectious thyroiditis
    - Silent thyroiditis — usually painless, commonly occurs postpartum
    - Subacute thyroiditis (de Quervain's) — usually painful
- **Hypothyroidism can be differentiated into overt and subclinical:**
  - **Overt hypothyroidism** is diagnosed on the basis of characteristic clinical features, with a raised serum thyroid-stimulating hormone (TSH) level, and a low serum free thyroxine (T_4) level.
  - **Subclinical hypothyroidism** is diagnosed when the TSH level is raised, but the free T_4 level is normal, and there are no specific symptoms or signs of thyroid dysfunction.

[Weetman, 1997; AACE Thyroid Task Force, 2002; Nygaard, 2004; Roberts and Ladenson, 2004]

Which conditions are associated with hypothyroidism?

- Type 1 diabetes mellitus (10% will develop hypothyroidism)
- Addison's disease
- Coeliac disease
- Down's syndrome (a third will develop hypothyroidism before the age of 25 years)
- Pernicious anaemia
- Primary hypogonadism
- Rheumatoid arthritis
- Sjögren's syndrome
- Turner's syndrome
- Vitiligo

How common is it?

- **The prevalence of overt hypothyroidism** in women is 19 per 1000 population, and in men is 1 per 1000 population [Tunbridge et al, 1977].
- **The annual incidence of overt hypothyroidism** in women is 4 per 1000 population, and in men is 0.6 per 1000 population [Vanderpump et al, 1995].
- **Subclinical hypothyroidism** is more common in women. The incidence increases with age, with up to 10% of women over the age of 55–60 years having a raised thyroid-stimulating hormone (TSH) level [DTB, 1998; Helfand and Redfern, 1998]. It is more common in people who have been treated for hyperthyroidism, either with radioactive iodine or surgery, and in those with organ-specific autoimmune diseases, such as pernicious anaemia, Type 1 diabetes mellitus, or Addison's disease.

- Hypothyroidism is more common in women, with a female to male ratio of 7:1.
- It is more common in people with a family history of Hashimoto's disease.

[AACE Thyroid Task Force, 2002; Nygaard, 2004; Roberts and Ladenson, 2004]

How do I know my patient has it?

- **Symptoms develop insidiously and include:**
  - Carpal tunnel syndrome, muscle stiffness and pain
  - Cold intolerance
  - Constipation
  - Dementia, depression, mental slowing, poor concentration
  - Dry skin, hair loss
  - Hoarse voice
  - Infertility, irregular or heavy menstruation
  - Lethargy
  - Weight gain
- **Signs also develop insidiously and include:**
  - Ataxia, carpal tunnel syndrome, slowly relaxing reflexes
  - Bradycardia, heart failure, pleural effusion
  - Deep voice or hoarseness
  - Dry, pale or yellowish skin, generalised myxoedema (non-pitting oedema), sparse coarse hair
  - Goitre
  - Hypothermia
  - Toad-like face
- **Thyroid function tests (TFTs):**
  - In overt hypothyroidism show a raised thyroid-stimulating hormone (TSH) and a reduced free thyroxine (T_4) level.
  - In subclinical hypothyroidism show a raised TSH and a normal free T_4 level.
  - In secondary hypothyroidism (pituitary or hypothalamic disease) show a low or low–normal TSH and a reduced free T_4.
  - The use of corticosteroids in a person with hypothyroidism can reduce the TSH level.
- **Antithyroid antibodies are positive** in 95% of people with autoimmune thyroiditis. They are a useful test in people with subclinical hypothyroidism to decide whether to initiate treatment. Overt hypothyroidism develops in a high proportion of subclinical cases who have positive thyroid autoantibodies.
- **A full blood count** may show a normocytic normochromic anaemia or a mild macrocytosis.
- **A raised cholesterol level** may be found. Hypothyroidism is one of the causes of secondary hypercholesterolaemia, and 4–14% of people with hypercholesterolaemia have hypothyroidism. The cholesterol level falls as the hypothyroidism is treated.

[AACE Thyroid Task Force, 2002; Leonhardt and Heymann, 2002; Nygaard, 2004; Roberts and Ladenson, 2004]

What else might it be?

- **A raised thyroid-stimulating hormone (TSH) level in the absence of hypothyroidism can occur in:**
  - Adrenal failure
  - Renal failure
  - Exposure to cold
- The sick euthyroid state or non-thyroidal illness syndrome. This refers to the presence of a low free thyroxine (T_4) level and a normal or a low thyroid-stimulating hormone (TSH) level in a person with a chronic physical illness. The hormone levels return to normal following resolution of the illness.

[AACE Thyroid Task Force, 2002; Roberts and Ladenson, 2004]

Complications and prognosis

Complications

- There is an increased risk of coronary heart disease (due to increased levels of blood lipids).
- In pregnancy, untreated hypothyroidism is associated with an increased risk of pre-eclampsia, anaemia, premature labour, low birth weight, fetal loss, stillbirth, and postpartum haemorrhage.
- Hypothyroid coma (myxoedema coma) may occur, but this is now very rare.

Prognosis

- The prognosis with treatment is excellent.

[AACE Thyroid Task Force, 2002 ;Roberts and Ladenson, 2004]

Management issues

- Overview p.1025
- How do I treat overt hypothyroidism? p.1025
- How do I treat subclinical hypothyroidism? p.1026
- How do I treat hypothyroidism during pregnancy and breastfeeding? p.1026
- Medicines management p.1026

Overview

- **Indiscriminate use of the thyroid-stimulating hormone (TSH) level as a screening test is not effective.** The greater the clinical suspicion of hypothyroidism, the more useful a TSH value [Vanderpump et al, 1996; Bandolier, 1997; Weetman, 1997; US Preventive Services Task force, 2004].
- **Monitor the response to treatment with the TSH level.** The aim is to maintain the TSH level in the normal range. **The frequency of monitoring** is usually every 6 weeks after a change in dose, then yearly once stable.
- Studies of people on stable doses of treatment have shown that a fifth are taking insufficient, and a fifth are taking excessive, doses of thyroid replacement therapy.
- Refer for specialist advice if there is evidence of pituitary disease (low TSH and low T_4).
- Consider referral for specialist advice in:
  - People less than 16 years.
  - Pregnant and post-partum women.
  - People presenting with particular management problems (e.g. coronary heart disease, on amiodarone or lithium).

[Vanderpump et al, 1996; AACE Thyroid Task Force, 2002; Roberts and Ladenson, 2004]

How do I treat overt hypothyroidism?

- **Overt hypothyroidism is defined as** a raised thyroid-stimulating hormone (TSH) level with a reduced free thyroxine (T_4) level and characteristic clinical features.
- **The management is usually straightforward** with levothyroxine (thyroxine) replacement therapy.
- **The aim is to return the TSH level to the normal range.**
- Coexistent coronary heart disease requires careful initiation of levothyroxine, and gradual titration of dose with vigilant monitoring, as there is a risk of worsening angina, myocardial infarction, and sudden death [Vanderpump et al, 1996].
- Treatment with a combination of levothyroxine and tri-iodothyronine (T_3) has been studied. Its benefit remains unproven and it is not recommended.

[AACE Thyroid Task Force, 2002; Nygaard, 2004; Roberts and Ladenson, 2004]

H

How do I treat subclinical hypothyroidism?

- **Subclinical hypothyroidism is defined as** a raised thyroid-stimulating hormone (TSH) level with a normal free thyroxine (T_4) level and no specific clinical features.
- There is no consensus on the management of subclinical hypothyroidism. Some specialists recommend initiating levothyroxine (thyroxine) treatment, others recommend annual review. If initiating treatment, this should only be undertaken if diagnosis is confirmed on repeat testing 3 months later. PRODIGY recommends that advice is sought from local endocrinologists as shared care guidelines may exist.
- Subclinical hypothyroidism is more likely to develop into overt hypothyroidism if the person has positive antithyroid antibodies. In one large community study, the annual rate of progression from subclinical to overt hypothyroidism in women was 4.3% if the TSH level was raised and antibodies were present, 2.6% if the TSH level alone was raised, and 2.1% if antibodies were present but the serum TSH level was normal [Vanderpump et al, 1996]. Men with subclinical hypothyroidism are even more likely to develop overt disease [DTB, 1998].

H

[AACE Thyroid Task Force, 2002; Nygaard, 2004; Roberts and Ladenson, 2004; Surks et al, 2004]

How do I treat hypothyroidism during pregnancy and breastfeeding?

- In pregnancy untreated hypothyroidism is associated with an increased risk of pre-eclampsia, anaemia, premature labour, low birth weight, fetal loss, stillbirth, and postpartum haemorrhage.
- **The treatment is the same as when not pregnant,** although some women may need an increase in the daily dose of levothyroxine (thyroxine) by around 25–50 micrograms, usually in the later stages of pregnancy. The thyroid-stimulating hormone (TSH) level should be checked every 6 weeks and the dose of levothyroxine adjusted accordingly.
- Treatment with levothyroxine is safe while breastfeeding [UKMiCentral, 2003].

[AACE Thyroid Task Force, 2002; Nygaard, 2004; Roberts and Ladenson, 2004]

Medicines management

- **In the elderly and those with coronary heart disease,** a starting dose of 25 micrograms levothyroxine (thyroxine) daily is recommended; the dose is then titrated by 25 micrograms every 4 weeks [ABPI Medicines Compendium, 2004]. (A smaller dose increase at a more frequent interval balances the need to introduce treatment gradually against the need to reach a therapeutic dose.) Once the individual is clinically euthyroid, it is then advised to wait for 6 weeks before checking the thyroid-stimulating hormone (TSH) level.
- **In younger adults,** treatment is started with 50–100 micrograms levothyroxine daily, and titrated by 25–50 micrograms every 6 weeks until the TSH level is in the normal range. Once the appropriate dose has been established, it remains constant in most people.
- **Adverse effects occur if the levothyroxine dose is excessive,** or if the initial increase in metabolism is too rapid, and include symptomatic hyperthyroidism (e.g. anginal pain, tachycardia, weight loss, heat intolerance, and hyperactivity). Subclinical hyperthyroidism also has an increased risk of bone loss and atrial fibrillation [Roberts and Ladenson, 2004].
- Levothyroxine has a narrow therapeutic range, and small changes in absorption or metabolism can result in clinical or subclinical hypo- or hyperthyroidism [AACE Thyroid Task Force, 2002].
  - Its absorption is reduced by calcium, iron and anion-exchange resins. It is therefore best taken on an empty stomach, preferably before breakfast.
  - Its metabolism is accelerated by enzyme-inducing drugs (e.g. carbamazepine, phenytoin, phenobarbital, and rifampicin). Close monitoring and levothyroxine dose adjustment are needed when dose changes are made to these medicines.
- **People taking concomitant warfarin** need careful monitoring and adjustment of the warfarin dose if the levothyroxine dose is altered. Warfarin dose reduction is often needed.

References

1. AACE Thyroid Task Force (2002) *American Association of Clinical Endocrinologists medical guidelines for the evaluation and treatment of hyperthyroidism and hypothyroidism.* American Association of Clinical Endocrinologists. www.aace.com/clin/guidelines [Accessed: 18/08/2004].
2. ABPI Medicines Compendium (2004) *Thyroxine tablets BP 25 micrograms.* Electronic Medicines Compendium. Datapharm Communications Ltd. www.emc.medicines.org.uk [Accessed: 01/09/2004].
3. Bandolier (1997) *Signs and symptoms predict thyroid disease.* Bandolier. www.jr2.ox.ac.uk/bandolier/band46/b46-5.html [Accessed: 01/09/2004].
4. Bunevicius, R., Kazanavicius, G., Zalinkevicius, R. and Prange, A.J.Jr. (1999) Effects of thyroxine as compared with thyroxine plus triiodothyronine in patients with hypothyroidism. *New England Journal of Medicine* **340**(6), 424–429. [Full text]
5. DTB (1998) Managing subclinical hypothyroidism. *Drug & Therapeutics Bulletin* **36**(1), 1–3.
6. Helfand, M. and Redfern, C.C. (1998) Screening for Thyroid disease: An update clinical guideline part 2. *Annals of Internal Medicine* **129**(2), 144–158.
7. Leonhardt, J.M. and Heymann, W.R. (2002) Thyroid disease and the skin. *Dermatologic Clinics* **20**(3), 473–481.
8. Nygaard, B. (2004) Primary hypothyroidism. *Clinical Evidence* **11**, 807–812.
9. Roberts, C.G. and Ladenson, P.W. (2004) Hypothyroidism. *Lancet* **363**(9411), 793–803. [Full text]
10. Sawka, A.M., Gerstein, H.C., Marriott, M.J. et al (2003) Does a combination regimen of thyroxine (T4) and 3, 5, 3'-triiodothyronine improve depressive symptoms better than T4 alone in patients with hypothyroidism? Results of a double-blind, randomized, controlled trial. *Journal of Clinical Endocrinology & Metabolism* **88**(10), 4551–4555.
11. Surks, M.I., Ortiz, E., Daniels, G.H. et al (2004) Subclinical thyroid disease: scientific review and guidelines for diagnosis and management. *Journal of the American Medical Association* **291**(2), 228–238.
12. Tunbridge, W.M.G., Evered, D.C., Hall, R. et al (1977 The spectrum of thyroid disease in a community: the Whickham survey. *Clinical Endocrinology* **7**(6), 481–493.
13. UKMiCentral (2003) *Drugs in breast milk – quick reference guide.* UK Medicines Information. http://www.ukmicentral.nhs.uk/drugpreg/guide.htm [Accessed: 10/11/2003]. [Full text]
14. US Preventive Services Task force (2004) *Screening for thyroid disease: recommendation statement.* Agency for Healthcare Research and Quality. www.ahrq.gov/clinic/uspstf/uspsthyr.htm [Accessed: 19/08/2004].

15. Vanderpump, M.P.J., Tunbridge, W.M.G., French, J.M. et al (1995) The incidence of thyroid disorders in the community: a twenty-year follow-up of the Whickham Survey. *Clinical Endocrinology* **43**(1), 55–68.
16. Vanderpump, M.P.J., Ahlquist, J.A.O., Franklyn, J.A. and Clayton, R.N. (1996) Consensus statement for good practice and audit measures in the management of hypothyroidism and hyperthyroidism. *British Medical Journal* **313**(7056), 539–544. [Full text]
17. Walsh, J.P., Shiels, L., Lim, E.M. et al (2003) Combined thyroxine/liothyronine treatment does not improve well-being, quality of life, or cognitive function compared to thyroxine alone: a randomized controlled trial in patients with primary hypothyroidism. *Journal of Clinical Endocrinology & Metabolism* **88**(10), 4543–4550.
18. Weetman, A.P. (1997) Hypothyroidism: screening and subclinical disease. *British Medical Journal* **314**(7088), 1175–1178. [Full text]

PRODIGY GUIDANCE

Immunizations — childhood vaccination programme

Last revised in July 2005
www.prodigy.nhs.uk/guidance.asp?gt=Immunizations - childhood

Applies to people under the age of 25 years

This guidance is based on the childhood vaccination programme as directed by the Joint Committee on Vaccination and Immunization, an independent expert advisory committee of the Department of Health (DH). The schedule for immunization is available at www.immunisations.org.uk and further information is available in a DH publication *Immunization against Infectious Disease*, commonly referred to as the 'Green book' available at www.dh.gov.uk.

This guidance covers childhood immunization against infectious diseases, and provides information about vaccines, benefits, and risks.

This guidance does not cover the treatment of anaphylaxis.

There is separate PRODIGY guidance for *Immunization — travel vaccinations*, *Immunization — pneumococcal vaccine*, and *Influenza*.

I

Goals

- To immunize all children in line with the Department of Health childhood immunization schedule
- To immunize children who may have missed scheduled vaccinations
- To educate and inform parents and carers of the benefits of vaccination

Contents

Scenarios

- Immunizations in the first year of life p.1028
- Immunizations in the second year of life p.1030
- Pre-school vaccinations p.1030
- Tuberculosis BCG vaccine p.1031
- School leaver's vaccination p.1032
- Incomplete vaccination history, age 1–4 yrs p.1033
- Incomplete vaccination history, age 4–10 years p.1034
- Incomplete vaccination history, age over 10 years p.1036

Extended Information, p. 1037

Which scenario?

- **Immunizations in the first year of life:** covers advice for primary immunization.
- **Immunizations in the second year of life:** covers advice for immunization required beyond the first year of life following on from successful primary immunization.
- **Pre-school vaccinations:** covers advice for immunization required before a child's fifth birthday.
- **Tuberculosis BCG vaccine:** covers information related to Tuberculin testing and BCG vaccination.
- **School leaver's vaccination:** covers advice for immunization required before leaving school.
- **Incomplete vaccination history, age 1–4 yrs:** covers advice for a child with incomplete or with no history of immunization.
- **Incomplete vaccination history, age 4–10 years:** covers advice for a child with incomplete or with no history of immunization.
- **Incomplete vaccination history, age over 10 years:** covers advice for someone with incomplete or with no history of immunization.

Immunizations in the first year of life

Which therapy?

- **Obtain consent and check suitability for immunization.** See *Suitability for vaccination* for further information.
- **Starting at 2 months of age:** give three doses, with an interval of 1 month between doses, of:
  - **Pediacel®** vaccine (DTaP/IPV/Hib), which contains diphtheria, tetanus, acellular pertussis, inactivated poliomyelitis, and *Haemophilus influenzae* type b
  - **And, meningococcal C** vaccine (Men C)
- Offer paracetamol or ibuprofen to manage post-immunization pyrexia.

Additional advice

- **If a course is interrupted,** it may be resumed; there is no need to start again.
- **If the child is receiving the first dose of Men C after 4 months of age,** use only two doses.

Practical prescribing points

For further information please see the *Medicines Compendium* (www.medicine.org.uk) or the *British National Formulary* (www.bnf.org).

- **Pediacel® and Men C can be given on the same day.** Use different syringes/needles and inject into different sites.
- Give Pediacel® and Men C by intramuscular injection. In infants, use the antero-lateral aspects of the thigh. Use a 25G needle.
- **Delay vaccination during an acute febrile illness.** Wait until symptoms have resolved before vaccinating.
- **If there is an evolving neurological problem,** defer pertussis immunization (Pediacel®).
- **Advise parents:**
  - To give a dose of paracetamol or ibuprofen if fever develops, and keep the child cool (remove excess clothing or bedding). If fever persists after a second dose, they should seek medical advice.
  - To seek urgent medical advice if their child develops breathlessness, swelling of the mouth and throat, or a rash within a few days of immunization.

Should I refer or investigate?

Refer?

- **Neurological problems:** if immunization is to be deferred or if there is doubt, seek advice from a consultant paediatrician, immunization coordinator, or consultant in communicable disease.

Patient information leaflets

The following PILs are available at www.prodigy.nhs.uk
- Childhood Immunisation
- DTP-Hib Immunisation
- Meningococcal group C Immunisation

Shared decision making

- At age 2 months, most babies should have:
  - An injection of DTaP/IPV/Hib vaccine.
  - An injection of Meningococcus group C vaccine.
- This is repeated twice more at monthly intervals.
  - The immunizations will still work if they are given late, but for best protection for your baby, try to keep to the schedule.
- In most babies there are no problems. Serious reactions are very rare.
  - Slight swelling, redness, and firmness may occur for a short while at the injection sites.
  - A mild fever may occur a few hours after the injections.
- Give paracetamol or ibuprofen if:
  - The baby seems hot or irritable following immunization.
  - The baby has a history of febrile convulsions.
  - There is a family history of epilepsy.

Drug rationale

- **Paracetamol** is an effective and safe analgesic and antipyretic agent for most people.
- **Ibuprofen** is an effective alternative to paracetamol if there are no contraindications.
- **Pediacel® vaccine (DTaP/IPV/Hib),** which contains diphtheria, tetanus, acellular pertussis, inactivated poliomyelitis, and *Haemophilus influenzae* type b, is recommended for primary immunizations.
- **Meningococcal Group C conjugate vaccine** is offered for all children from 2 months of age. Vaccine is normally administered intramuscularly. Meningitec may be given by deep subcutaneous injection for children with haemophilia. NeisVac-C may be given by subcutaneous injection if there is thrombocytopenia or haemophilia.
- **Hiberix®** (*H influenzae*) vaccine is offered for use when Hib immunization has not been synchronized with the primary immunizations for tetanus, diphtheria, pertussis and poliomyelitis.

Prescriptions

Diphtheria+tetanus+pertussis+poliomyelitis+Hib vaccine

Diphtheria+tetanus+pertussis+polio+Hib (Pediacel)
- Age from 2 to 12 months
- Pediacel injection. Give 0.5ml by intramuscular injection. For primary immunization, give three doses at intervals of 1 month between doses; supply 1 0.5ml vial.

Meningococcal group C conjugate vaccine

Meningitec vaccine
- Age from 2 to 12 months
- Meningitec vaccine. Give 0.5ml by intramuscular injection. For primary immunization, give three doses at intervals of 1 month between doses; supply 1 0.5ml vial; NHS Cost £19.00.

NeisVac-C vaccine
- Age from 2 to 12 months
- NeisVac-C vaccine. Give 0.5ml by intramuscular injection. For primary immunization, give three doses at intervals of 1 month between doses; supply 1 0.5ml prefilled syringe; NHS Cost £15.00.

Menjugate vaccine
- Age from 2 to 12 months
- Menjugate vaccine. Give 0.5ml by intramuscular injection. For primary immunization, give three doses at intervals of 1 month between doses; supply 1 0.5ml vial; NHS Cost £16.00.

Hib (ONLY if not previously given)

Haemophilus influenzae type b vaccine (Hiberix)
- Age from 2 to 12 months
- Hiberix vaccine. Give 0.5ml by intramuscular injection. For primary immunization, give three doses at intervals of 1 month between doses; supply 1 0.5ml vial + diluent; NHS Cost £9.00.

Antipyretics: use when required

Paracetamol s/f susp: 10-15 mg/kg up to four times a day
- Age from 1 month to 2 months
- Paracetamol 120mg/5ml s/f susp. *WEIGHT REQUIRED* Give 10-15 mg per kg bodyweight every 4 to 6 hours. Max of 4 doses (or 60mg per kg) in 24 hours; supply 100 ml; NHS Cost £0.43; OTC Cost £1.95.

Paracetamol s/f susp: 60mg to 120mg up to four times a day
- Age from 3 to 11 months
- Paracetamol 120mg/5ml s/f susp. Take 2.5ml to 5ml every 4 to 6 hours when required for relief of high temperature. Maximum of 4 doses in 24 hours; supply 100 ml; NHS Cost £0.43; OTC Cost £1.95.

Paracetamol s/f susp: 120mg to 240mg up to four times a day
- Age from 12 to 13 months
- Paracetamol 120mg/5ml s/f susp. Take one to two 5ml spoonfuls every 4 to 6 hours when required for relief of high temperature. Maximum of 4 doses in 24 hours; supply 100 ml; NHS Cost £0.43; OTC Cost £1.95.

Ibuprofen s/f susp: 5mg/kg three to four times a day
- Age from 1 month to 11 months
- Ibuprofen 100mg/5ml s/f susp. *WEIGHT REQUIRED* Take 5mg per kg bodyweight three to four times a day when required for high temperature; supply 100 ml; NHS Cost £1.82; OTC Cost £3.59.

Ibuprofen s/f susp: 50mg three to four times a day
- Age from 12 to 13 months
- Ibuprofen 100mg/5ml s/f susp. Take 2.5ml three to four times a day when required for relief of high temperature. Do not exceed the stated dose; supply 100 ml; NHS Cost £1.82; OTC Cost £3.59.

Immunizations in the second year of life

Which therapy

- **Obtain consent and check suitability for immunization.** See *Suitability for vaccination* for further information.
- **Shortly after the first birthday:**
  - Give the first dose of measles, mumps, and rubella (MMR) vaccine.
  - If not previously immunized, offer a single dose of *Haemophilus influenzae* type b vaccine (Hib).
- Offer paracetamol or ibuprofen to manage post-immunization pyrexia.

Additional advice

- Give MMR vaccine irrespective of a history of measles, mumps, or rubella infection.
- Re-immunization is necessary when MMR vaccine has been given before 12 months of age.

Practical prescribing points

For further information please see the *Medicines Compendium* (www.medicine.org.uk) or the *British National Formulary* (www.bnf.org).

- **MMR and Hib can be given on the same day.** Use different syringes/needles and inject into different sites.
- Give MMR by intramuscular or deep subcutaneous injection. Give Hib by intramuscular injection. In children, use the deltoid muscle. Use a 23G needle.
- **Delay vaccination during an acute febrile illness.** Wait until symptoms have resolved before vaccinating.
- **Advise parents:**
  - To give a dose of paracetamol or ibuprofen if fever develops, and keep the child cool (remove excess clothing or bedding). If fever persists after a second dose, they should seek medical advice.
  - That malaise, fever, or a rash may occur, most commonly about a week after MMR immunization, and last about 2–3 days.
  - To seek urgent medical advice if their child develops breathlessness, swelling of the mouth and throat, or a rash within a few days of immunization.

Patient information leaflets

The following PILs are available at www.prodigy.nhs.uk

- Childhood Immunisation
- Measles/Mumps/Rubella Immunisation

Shared decision making

- The first dose of MMR immunization is offered to children soon after their first birthday.
- In most children, there are no problems with MMR vaccine. Serious reactions are very rare.
  - Some children develop a mild fever and a faint rash, a week to 10 days after the injection.
  - A few children develop a mild swollen face about 3 weeks later.
  - Neither of these reactions is infectious or serious.
- You can give **paracetamol or ibuprofen** if necessary.
- Is your child up-to-date with their other immunizations? They can catch up if necessary.

Drug rationale

Drugs not included

- **Measles, mumps, and rubella monovalent vaccines** are not available for the childhood vaccination programme.

Drugs included

- **Measles, mumps, and rubella (MMR) vaccine.**
- **Paracetamol** is an effective and safe analgesic and antipyretic agent for most people.
- **Ibuprofen** is an effective alternative to paracetamol if there are no contraindications.
- **Hiberix** (*Haemophilus influenzae*) type b vaccine, is offered for use when Hib immunization has not been synchronized with the primary immunizations for tetanus, diphtheria, and pertussis.

Prescriptions

Primary immunization: measles+mumps+rubella (MMR)

Measles+mumps+rubella vaccine (MMR) Priorix
- Age from 12 months to 2 years
- Priorix MMR vaccine. Give 0.5ml by intramuscular or deep subcutaneous injection; supply 1 0.5ml vial + diluent; NHS Cost £4.00.

Measles+mumps+rubella vaccine (MMR) MMRII
- Age from 12 months to 2 years
- MMRII MMR vaccine. Give 0.5ml by intramuscular or deep subcutaneous injection; supply 1 0.5ml injection; NHS Cost £4.00.

Hib (ONLY if not previously given)

Haemophilus influenzae type b vaccine (Hiberix)
- Age from 13 months to 2 years
- Hiberix vaccine. Give a single 0.5ml dose by intramuscular injection for primary immunization; supply 1 0.5ml vial + diluent; NHS Cost £9.00.

Antipyretics: use when required

Paracetamol s/f susp: 120mg to 240mg up to four times a day
- Age from 12 months to 2 years
- Paracetamol 120mg/5ml s/f susp. Take one to two 5ml spoonfuls every 4 to 6 hours when required for relief of high temperature. Maximum of 4 doses in 24 hours; supply 100 ml; NHS Cost £0.43; OTC Cost £1.95.

Ibuprofen s/f susp: 50mg three to four times a day
- Age from 12 months to 2 years
- Ibuprofen 100mg/5ml s/f susp. Take 2.5ml three to four times a day when required for relief of high temperature. Do not exceed the stated dose; supply 100 ml; NHS Cost £1.82; OTC Cost £3.59.

Pre-school vaccinations

Which therapy

- **Obtain consent and check suitability for immunization.** See *Suitability for vaccination* for further information.
- **If vaccinations are up-to-date:**
  - Give the second dose of measles, mumps, and rubella vaccine (MMR).
  - Give a booster dose of diphtheria, tetanus, acellular pertussis, and inactivated poliomyelitis as either dTaP/IPV (Repevax®) or DTaP/IPV (Infanrix IPV®).

- Offer paracetamol or ibuprofen to manage post-immunization pyrexia.
- **If vaccination history is incomplete,** see scenario *Incomplete vaccination history, age 4–10 years.*

Additional advice

- Give MMR vaccine irrespective of a history of measles, mumps, or rubella infection.

Practical prescribing points

For further information please see the *Medicines Compendium* (www.medicine.org.uk) or the *British National Formulary* (www.bnf.org).

- **MMR and Repevax® or Infanrix IPV® can be given on the same day.** Use different syringes/needles and inject into different sites.
- Give MMR by intramuscular or deep subcutaneous injection. Give Repevax® or Infanrix IPV® by intramuscular injection. In children, use the deltoid muscle. Use a 23G needle.
- **Delay vaccination during an acute febrile illness.** Wait until symptoms have resolved before vaccinating.
- **If there is an evolving neurological problem,** defer pertussis immunization (Repevax® or Infanrix IPV®).
- **Advise parents:**
  - To give a dose of paracetamol or ibuprofen if fever develops, and keep the child cool (remove excess clothing or bedding). If fever persists after a second dose, they should seek medical advice.
  - That malaise, fever, or a rash may occur, most commonly about a week after MMR immunization, and last about 2–3 days.
  - To seek urgent medical advice if their child develops breathlessness, swelling of the mouth and throat, or a rash within a few days of immunization.

Patient information leaflets

The following PILs are available at www.prodigy.nhs.uk

- Childhood Immunisation
- DTP-Hib Immunisation
- Measles/Mumps/Rubella Immunisation
- Meningococcal group C Immunisation

Shared decision making

- Most children have a pre-school booster of:
  - An injection of DTaP/IPV vaccine.
  - An injection of MMR vaccine.
- In most children, there are no problems. Serious reactions are very rare.
  - Slight swelling, redness, and firmness may occur for a short while at the injection sites.
  - A mild fever may occur a few hours after the injections.
- Following the MMR injection:
  - Some children develop a mild fever and a faint rash, a week to 10 days later.
  - A few children develop a mild swollen face about 3 weeks later.
  - Neither of these reactions is infectious or serious.
- You can give **paracetamol or ibuprofen** if necessary.

Drug rationale

Drugs not included

- **Pediacel® (DTaP/IPV/Hib)**, which contains diphtheria, tetanus, acellular pertussis, inactivated poliomyelitis, and *Haemophilus influenzae* type b, is not recommended for pre-school vaccination. A pre-school booster dose of Hib vaccine is not currently routinely recommended.
- **Hiberix®** (*H influenzae*) vaccine is not offered. A pre-school booster dose of Hib vaccine is not currently routinely recommended.

Drugs included

- **Measles, mumps, and rubella (MMR) vaccine.**
- **Repevax® (dTaP/IPV) or Infanrix IPV® (DTaP/IPV)** is recommended for pre-school booster immunizations. These vaccines contain diphtheria, tetanus, acellular pertussis, and inactivated poliomyelitis.
- **Paracetamol** is an effective and safe analgesic and antipyretic agent for most people.
- **Ibuprofen** is an effective alternative to paracetamol if there are no contraindications.

Prescriptions

Pre-school booster: diphtheria + tetanus + pertussis + polio

Low-dose diphtheria+tetanus+pertussis+polio (Repevax)

- Age from 3 to 6 years
- Repevax injection. Give 0.5ml by intramuscular injection; supply 1 0.5ml prefilled syringe.

Diphtheria+tetanus+pertussis+poliomyelitis (Infanrix IPV)

- Age from 3 to 6 years
- Infanrix IPV 0.5ml syringe. Give 0.5ml by intramuscular injection; supply 1 0.5ml prefilled syringe.

Primary immunization: measles+mumps+rubella (MMR)

Measles+mumps+rubella vaccine (MMR) Priorix

- Age from 12 months to 2 years
- Priorix MMR vaccine. Give 0.5ml by intramuscular or deep subcutaneous injection; supply 1 0.5ml vial + diluent; NHS Cost £4.00.

Measles+mumps+rubella vaccine (MMR) MMRII

- Age from 12 months to 2 years
- MMRII MMR vaccine. Give 0.5ml by intramuscular or deep subcutaneous injection; supply 1 0.5ml injection; NHS Cost £4.00.

Antipyretics: use when required

Paracetamol s/f susp: 120mg to 240mg up to four times a day

- Age from 3 to 6 years
- Paracetamol 120mg/5ml s/f susp. Take one to two 5ml spoonfuls every 4 to 6 hours when required for relief of high temperature. Maximum of 4 doses in 24 hours; supply 100 ml; NHS Cost £0.43; OTC Cost £1.95.

Ibuprofen s/f susp: 100mg three to four times a day

- Age from 3 to 6 years
- Ibuprofen 100mg/5ml s/f susp. Take one 5ml spoonful 3 to 4 times a day when required for relief of high temperature. Do not exceed the stated dose; supply 100 ml; NHS Cost £1.82; OTC Cost £3.59.

Tuberculosis BCG vaccine

Which therapy

- **Obtain consent and check suitability for immunization.** See *Suitability for vaccination* for further information.
- **Always carry out a tuberculin skin test before immunization** (unless under 3 months of age and no known recent contact with tuberculosis).

- Refer children with a positive tuberculin test to a chest clinic.
- **Children who would previously have been offered BCG vaccine at 10–14 years of age will now be screened for TB risk factors,** and tested and vaccinated if appropriate.
- **Those now recommended to routinely receive BCG vaccine are:**
  - Infants living in area where the incidence of tuberculosis (TB) is 40/100,000 or greater.
  - Infants whose parents or grandparents were born in a country with a TB incidence of 40/100,000 or greater.
  - Previously unvaccinated new immigrants from high prevalence countries for TB.
  - Note: the Department of Health with shortly be issuing guidance on high incidence areas in England and high incidence countries. See www.dh.gov.uk for further information.
- **The dose of BCG vaccine for children under 12 months of age is different:**
  - Children over 12 months of age, and adults: 0.1 ml dose by intradermal injection.
  - Children 12 months and under: 0.05 ml dose by intradermal injection.
- A child may receive BCG at any age at the request of a parent.

Practical prescribing points

For further information please see the *Medicines Compendium* (www.medicine.org.uk) or the *British National Formulary* (www.bnf.org).

- **BCG vaccine must *only* be given intradermally.** Use a 25G needle.
- Give BCG at the insertion of the deltoid muscle near the middle of the upper arm; avoid the tip of the shoulder because of the increased risk of keloid formation at this site.
- **BCG can be given on the same day as other childhood vaccines.** Use different syringes/needles and inject into different sites.
- **If MMR and BCG are not given on the same day,** leave an interval of at least 3 weeks between vaccinations.
- **Delay vaccination during an acute febrile illness.** Wait until symptoms have resolved before vaccinating.
- **Advise the child or parents:**
  - That it is quite normal to have a small amount of swelling at the injection site that can form a small ulcer that lasts for several weeks. This usually heals and leaves a small, flat scar.
  - To give a dose of paracetamol or ibuprofen if fever develops, and keep the child cool (remove excess clothing or bedding). If fever persists after a second dose, they should seek medical advice.
  - To seek urgent medical advice if their child develops breathlessness, swelling of the mouth and throat, or a rash within a few days of immunization.

Should I refer or investigate?

Refer?

- Refer new immigrants who show a Mantoux response with induration of at least 15 mm diameter to a chest clinic further investigation and supervision.
- Refer contacts of tuberculosis to a chest clinic for further investigation and supervision. A prophylactic course of isoniazid may be appropriate before vaccination is undertaken.

Investigate?

Tuberculin skin test

- **Use the Mantoux test.** This test uses Purified Protein Derivative (PPD).
- The Mantoux test uses PPD 100 units/ml. Use a preparation containing PPD 10 units/ml if tuberculosis is suspected, or if known to be hypersensitive to tuberculin.
- Test on the flexor surface of the left forearm at the junction of the upper third with the lower two-thirds.
- Read results 48–72 hours later.
- **Negative Mantoux response:** induration with a transverse diameter of 0–4 mm.
- **Positive Mantoux response:** induration with a transverse diameter of 5–14 mm. (The area of flare is irrelevant.) Do not give BCG vaccine.
- If the induration has a transverse diameter of more than 15 mm, refer to chest clinic for further investigation and supervision.

Factors affecting the tuberculin test

The reaction to tuberculin protein may be suppressed by the following:

- Infectious mononucleosis.
- Viral infections in general, including those of the upper respiratory tract.
- Live viral vaccines. Tuberculin testing should not be carried out within 3 weeks of receiving a live viral vaccine.
- Hodgkin's disease.
- Sarcoidosis.
- Corticosteroid therapy.
- Immunosuppressing treatment or diseases, including HIV.

Patient information leaflets

The following PILs are available at www.prodigy.nhs.uk

- BCG Immunisation
- Childhood Immunisation

Shared decision making

Drug rationale

- **Bacillus Calmette-Guérin vaccine** is available for intradermal injection.

Prescriptions

Any age child at high risk of TB

BCG vaccine

- Age under 11 months
- Bacillus Calmete-Guerin vaccin. FOR INTRADERMAL INJECTION. Inject 0.05ml at the site of the insertion of deltoid muscle onto the humerus; supply 1 injection.

BCG vaccine

- Age from 12 months to 25 years
- Bacillus Calmete-Guerin vaccin. FOR INTRADERMAL INJECTION. Inject 0.1ml at the site of the insertion of deltoid muscle onto the humerus; supply 1 injection.

School leaver's vaccination

Which therapy

- **Obtain consent and check suitability for immunization.** See *Suitability for vaccination* for further information.
- **If vaccinations are up-to-date:**

- Give a booster vaccine of Revaxis® vaccine (Td/IPV), which contains diphtheria (low dose), tetanus, and inactivated poliomyelitis.
- **If vaccination history is incomplete,** see scenario *Incomplete vaccination history, age over 10 years.*

Practical prescribing points

For further information please see the *Medicines Compendium* (www.medicine.org.uk) or the *British National Formulary* (www.bnf.org).

- Give Revaxis® by intramuscular injection. In children and adults, use the deltoid muscle. Use a 23G needle.
- **Delay vaccination during an acute febrile illness.** Wait until symptoms have resolved before vaccinating.
- **Advise people:**
    - To give a dose of paracetamol or ibuprofen if fever develops, and keep the child cool (remove excess clothing or bedding). If fever persists after a second dose, they should seek medical advice.
    - To seek urgent medical advice if their child develops breathlessness, swelling of the mouth and throat, or a rash within a few days of immunization.

Patient information leaflets

The following PILs are available at www.prodigy.nhs.uk

- Childhood Immunisation
- Polio Immunisation
- Tetanus Immunisation

Shared decision making

- Most teenagers, before they leave school, have a booster of:
    - Tetanus, diphtheria and poliomyelitis vaccine (a combined injection).
- In most people, there are no problems. Serious reactions are very rare.
    - Slight swelling, redness, and firmness may occur for a short while at the injection site.
    - A mild fever may occur a few hours after the injection.
    - You can take paracetamol or ibuprofen if necessary.

Drug rationale

- **Revaxis® vaccine (Td/IVP),** which contains low-dose diphtheria, tetanus, and inactivated poliomyelitis, is recommended for school leavers' booster immunizations.
- **Paracetamol** is an effective and safe analgesic and antipyretic agent for most people.
- **Ibuprofen** is an effective alternative to paracetamol if there are no contraindications.

Prescriptions

School leavers' booster: tetanus+diphtheria+polio vaccine

Low-dose diphtheria+tetanus+polio (Revaxis)

- Age from 12 to 25 years
- Revaxis injection. Give 0.5ml by intramuscular injection; supply 1 0.5ml prefilled syringe.

Antipyretic: use when required

Paracetamol tablets: 500mg to 1g up to four times a day

- Age from 12 to 15 years
- Paracetamol 500mg tablets. Take one to two tablets every 4 to 6 hours when required for relief of high temperature. Maximum of 8 tablets in 24 hours; supply 16 tablets; NHS Cost £0.21; OTC Cost £0.40.

Paracetamol tablets: 1g up to four times a day

- Age from 16 to 25 years
- Paracetamol 500mg tablets. Take two tablets every 4 to 6 hours when required for relief of high temperature. Maximum of 8 tablets in 24 hours; supply 16 tablets; NHS Cost £0.21; OTC Cost £0.40.

Ibuprofen tablets: 400mg three times a day

- Age from 12 to 25 years
- Ibuprofen 400mg tablets. Take one tablet three times a day when required for relief of high temperature. Do not exceed the stated dose; supply 12 tablets; NHS Cost £0.35; OTC Cost £0.62.

Incomplete vaccination history, age 1–4 yrs

Which therapy

- **Obtain consent and check suitability for immunization.** See *Suitability for vaccination* for further information.

Diphtheria, tetanus, pertussis, *Haemophilus influenzae* (Hib), poliomyelitis

- **Ensure that primary immunization is complete:** give three doses at monthly intervals of Pediacel® vaccine (DTaP/IPV/Hib), which contains diphtheria, tetanus, acellular pertussis, inactivated poliomyelitis, and Hib.
- **If immunization status is unknown:** ensure that no vaccine has been given in the last month before proceeding with primary immunization.
- **If Hib immunization status is unknown or incomplete** but other immunizations are up-to-date: offer a single dose of Hib.

Measles, mumps, and rubella (MMR)

- **Give the first dose of MMR vaccine** shortly after the first birthday.
- **If immunization status is unknown,** ensure that MMR has not been given within the last 3 months.

Meningococcal C

- If immunization status is unknown or incomplete, offer a single dose of vaccine.

Tuberculosis (BCG)

- If the child has risk factors for TB and there is no obvious scar from tuberculosis immunization, use a tuberculin test to assess immunity. See scenario *Tuberculosis BCG vaccine* for further information.

Practical prescribing points

For further information please see the *Medicines Compendium* (www.medicine.org.uk) or the *British National Formulary* (www.bnf.org).

- **Pediacel® (or Hib), Men C, and MMR can be given on the same day.** Use different syringes/needles and inject into different sites.
- Give Pediacel®, Men C, and Hib by intramuscular injection. Give MMR by intramuscular or deep subcutaneous injection.
- In infants, use the antero-lateral aspects of the thigh and use a 25G needle. In children, use the deltoid muscle and a 23G needle.
- **Delay vaccination during an acute febrile illness.** Wait until symptoms have resolved before vaccinating.
- **If there is an evolving neurological problem,** defer pertussis immunization.
- **Advise parents:**

- To give a dose of paracetamol or ibuprofen if fever develops, and keep the child cool (remove excess clothing or bedding). If fever persists after a second dose, they should seek medical advice.
- That malaise, fever, or a rash may occur, most commonly about a week after MMR immunization and lasting about 2–3 days.
- To seek urgent medical advice if their child develops breathlessness, swelling of the mouth and throat, or a rash within a few days of immunization.

Patient information leaflets

The following PILs are available at www.prodigy.nhs.uk

- DTP-Hib Immunisation
- Measles/Mumps/Rubella Immunisation
- Meningococcal group C Immunisation

Shared decision making

Drug rationale

Drugs not included

- **Repevax® vaccine (dTaP/IPV) or Infanrix IPV® vaccine** (DTaP/IPV), which contains diphtheria, tetanus, acellular pertussis, and inactivated poliomyelitis, is recommended for pre-school booster immunizations.
- **Bacillus Calmette-Guérin vaccine** is available for intradermal injection from the scenario *Tuberculosis BCG vaccine*.

Drugs included

- **Pediacel® vaccine (DTaP/IPV/Hib)**, which contains diphtheria, tetanus, acellular pertussis, inactivated poliomyelitis, and *Haemophilus influenzae* type b, is recommended for primary immunizations in all children under 10 years of age.
- **Hiberix®** (*H influenzae*) vaccine is offered for use when Hib immunization has not been synchronized with the primary immunizations for tetanus, diphtheria and pertussis. A single dose of Hib vaccine provides suitable protection.
- **Meningococcal Group C conjugate vaccine** is offered. Vaccine is normally administered intramuscularly. Meningitec may be given by deep subcutaneous injection for children with haemophilia. NeisVac-C may be given by subcutaneous injection if there is thrombocytopenia or haemophilia.
- **Measles, mumps, and rubella (MMR) vaccine.**
- **Paracetamol** is an effective and safe analgesic and antipyretic agent for most people.
- **Ibuprofen** is an effective alternative to paracetamol if there are no contraindications.

Prescriptions

Primary immunization: diphtheria+tetanus+pertussis+polio+Hib

Diphtheria+tetanus+pertussis+polio+Hib (Pediacel)

- Age from 13 months to 3 years
- Pediacel injection. Give 0.5ml by intramuscular injection. For primary immunization, give three doses at intervals of 1 month between doses; supply 1 0.5ml vial.

Primary immunization: Hib (ONLY if not previously given)

Haemophilus influenzae type b vaccine (Hiberix)

- Age from 13 months to 3 years
- Hiberix vaccine. Give a single 0.5ml dose by intramuscular injection for primary immunization; supply 1 0.5ml vial + diluent; NHS Cost £9.00.

Primary immunization: measles+mumps+rubella (MMR)

Measles+mumps+rubella vaccine (MMR) Priorix

- Age from 13 months to 3 years
- Priorix MMR vaccine. Give 0.5ml by intramuscular or deep subcutaneous injection; supply 1 0.5ml vial + diluent; NHS Cost £4.00.

Measles+mumps+rubella vaccine (MMR) MMRII

- Age from 13 months to 3 years
- MMRII MMR vaccine. Give 0.5ml by intramuscular or deep subcutaneous injection; supply 1 0.5ml injection; NHS Cost £4.00.

Primary immunization: meningococcal C conjugate vaccine

Meningitec vaccine

- Age from 13 months to 3 years
- Meningitec vaccine. Give a single 0.5ml dose by intramuscular injection for primary immunization; supply 1 0.5ml vial; NHS Cost £19.00.

NeisVac-C vaccine

- Age from 13 months to 3 years
- NeisVac-C vaccine. Give a single 0.5ml dose by intramuscular injection for primary immunization; supply 1 0.5ml prefilled syringe; NHS Cost £15.00.

Menjugate vaccine

- Age from 13 months to 3 years
- Menjugate vaccine. Give a single 0.5ml dose by intramuscular injection for primary immunization; supply 1 0.5ml vial; NHS Cost £16.00.

Antipyretics: use when required

Paracetamol s/f susp: 120mg to 240mg up to four times a day

- Age from 13 months to 3 years
- Paracetamol 120mg/5ml s/f susp. Take one to two 5ml spoonfuls every 4 to 6 hours when required for relief of high temperature. Maximum of 4 doses in 24 hours; supply 100 ml; NHS Cost £0.45; OTC Cost £1.95.

Ibuprofen s/f susp: 50mg three to four times a day

- Age from 13 months to 2 years
- Ibuprofen 100mg/5ml s/f susp. Take 2.5ml three to four times a day when required for relief of high temperature. Do not exceed the stated dose; supply 100 ml; NHS Cost £1.82; OTC Cost £3.59.

Ibuprofen s/f susp: 100mg three to four times a day

- Age from 3 to 3 years
- Ibuprofen 100mg/5ml s/f susp. Take one 5ml spoonful 3 to 4 times a day when required for relief of high temperature. Do not exceed the stated dose; supply 100 ml; NHS Cost £1.82; OTC Cost £3.59.

Incomplete vaccination history, age 4–10 years

Which therapy

- **Obtain consent and check suitability for immunization.** See *Suitability for vaccination* for further information.

Diphtheria, tetanus, pertussis, poliomyelitis

- **Ensure that primary immunization is complete:** give three doses at monthly intervals of Pediacel® vaccine (DTaP/IPV/Hib), which contains diphtheria, tetanus, acellular pertussis, inactivated poliomyelitis, and *Haemophilus influenzae* type b.
- **Give a booster dose** of Repevax® (dTaP/IPV) or Infanrix IPV® (DTaP/IPV) at least 1 year after the last dose of the primary course (ideally 3 years if possible).
- **If immunization status is unknown,** ensure that no vaccine has been given in the last month before proceding with primary immunization.

Measles, mumps, and rubella

- **Give one dose of MMR vaccine immediately,** and a second, (booster) dose at least 3 months later but preferably before school entry.
- If immunization status is unknown, ensure that MMR has not been given within the last three months.

Meningococcal C

- **If immunization status is unknown or incomplete,** offer a single dose of vaccine.

Tuberculosis (BCG)

- If the child has risk factors for TB and there is no obvious scar from tuberculosis immunization, use a tuberculin test to assess immunity. See scenario *Tuberculosis BCG vaccine* for further information.

Practical prescribing points

For further information please see the *Medicines Compendium* (www.medicine.org.uk) or the *British National Formulary* (www.bnf.org).

- **Pediacel® (or Repevax®, Infanrix IPV®, or Hib), Men C, or MMR can be given on the same day.** Use different syringes/needles and inject into different sites.
- Give Pediacel®, Repevax®, Infanrix IPV®, Men C, and Hib by intramuscular injection. Give MMR by intramuscular or deep subcutaneous injection. In children, use the deltoid muscle and a 23G needle.
- **Delay vaccination during an acute febrile illness.** Wait until symptoms have resolved before vaccinating.
- **If there is an evolving neurological problem,** defer pertussis immunization.
- **Advise parents:**
  - To give a dose of paracetamol or ibuprofen if fever develops, and keep the child cool (remove excess clothing or bedding). If fever persists after a second dose, they should seek medical advice.
  - That malaise, fever, or a rash may occur, most commonly about a week after MMR immunization and lasting about 2–3 days.
  - To seek urgent medical advice if their child develops breathlessness, swelling of the mouth and throat, or a rash within a few days of immunization.

Patient information leaflets

The following PILs are available at www.prodigy.nhs.uk

- DTP-Hib Immunisation
- Measles/Mumps/Rubella Immunisation
- Meningococcal group C Immunisation

Shared decision making

Drug rationale

Drugs not included

- **Bacillus Calmette-Guérin vaccine** is available for intradermal injection from the scenario *Tuberculosis BCG vaccine.*

Drugs included

- **Pediacel® vaccine (DTaP/IPV/Hib),** which contains diphtheria, tetanus, acellular pertussis, inactivated poliomyelitis, and *Haemophilus influenzae* type b, is recommended for primary immunizations in all children under 10 years of age.
- **Repevax® vaccine (dTaP/IPV) or Infanrix IPV® vaccine (DTaP/IPV),** which contains diphtheria, tetanus, acellular pertussis, and inactivated poliomyelitis, is recommended for booster immunizations for children under 10 years of age.
- **Measles, mumps, and rubella (MMR) vaccine.**
- **Meningococcal Group C conjugate vaccine** is offered. Vaccine is normally administered intramuscularly. Meningitec may be given by deep subcutaneous injection for children with haemophilia. NeisVac-C may be given by subcutaneous injection if there is thrombocytopenia or haemophilia.
- **Paracetamol** is an effective and safe analgesic and antipyretic agent for most people.
- **Ibuprofen** is an effective alternative to paracetamol if there are no contraindications.

Prescriptions

Primary immunization: diphtheria+tetanus+pertussis+polio+Hib

Diphtheria+tetanus+pertussis+polio+Hib (Pediacel)

- Age from 4 to 9 years
- Pediacel injection. Give 0.5ml by intramuscular injection. For primary immunization, give three doses at intervals of 1 month between doses; supply 1 0.5ml vial.

Booster dose: diphtheria + tetanus + pertussis + polio

Low-dose diphtheria+tetanus+pertussis+polio (Repevax)

- Age from 4 to 9 years
- Repevax injection. Give 0.5ml by intramuscular injection; supply 1 0.5ml prefilled syringe.

Diphtheria+tetanus+pertussis+polio (Infanrix IPV)

- Age from 4 to 9 years
- Infanrix IPV 0.5ml syringe. Give 0.5ml by intramuscular injection; supply 1 0.5ml prefilled syringe.

Primary immunization: measles+mumps+rubella vaccine (MMR)

Measles+mumps+rubella vaccine (MMR) Priorix

- Age from 4 to 9 years
- Priorix MMR vaccine. Give 0.5ml by intramuscular or deep subcutaneous injection; supply 1 0.5ml vial + diluent; NHS Cost £4.00.

Measles+mumps+rubella vaccine (MMR) MMRII

- Age from 4 to 9 years
- MMRII MMR vaccine. Give 0.5ml by intramuscular or deep subcutaneous injection; supply 1 0.5ml injection; NHS Cost £4.00

Primary immunization: meningococcal C conjugate vaccine

Meningitec vaccine
- Age from 4 to 9 years
- Meningitec vaccine. Give a single 0.5ml dose by intramuscular injection for primary immunization; supply 1 0.5ml vial; NHS Cost £19.00.

NeisVac-C vaccine
- Age from 4 to 9 years
- NeisVac-C vaccine. Give a single 0.5ml dose by intramuscular injection for primary immunization; supply 1 0.5ml prefilled syringe; NHS Cost £15.00.

Menjugate vaccine
- Age from 4 to 9 years
- Menjugate vaccine. Give a single 0.5ml dose by intramuscular injection for primary immunization; supply 1 0.5ml vial; NHS Cost £16.00.

Antipyretic: use when required

Paracetamol s/f susp: 120mg to 240mg up to four times a day
- Age from 4 to 5 years
- Paracetamol 120mg/5ml s/f susp. Take one to two 5ml spoonfuls every 4 to 6 hours when required for relief of high temperature. Maximum of 4 doses in 24 hours; supply 100 ml; NHS Cost £0.45; OTC Cost £1.95.

Paracetamol s/f susp: 250mg to 500mg up to four times a day
- Age from 6 to 9 years
- Paracetamol 250mg/5ml s/f susp. Take one to two 5ml spoonfuls every 4 to 6 hours when required for relief of high temperature. Maximum of 4 doses in 24 hours; supply 100 ml; NHS Cost £0.73; OTC Cost £3.52.

Ibuprofen s/f susp: 100mg three to four times a day
- Age from 4 to 7 years
- Ibuprofen 100mg/5ml s/f susp. Take one 5ml spoonful 3 to 4 times a day when required for relief of high temperature. Do not exceed the stated dose; supply 100 ml; NHS Cost £1.82; OTC Cost £3.59.

Ibuprofen s/f susp: 200mg three to four times a day
- Age from 8 to 9 years
- Ibuprofen 100mg/5ml s/f susp. Take two 5ml spoonfuls 3 to 4 times a day when required for relief of high temperature. Do not exceed the stated dose; supply 100 ml; NHS Cost £1.82; OTC Cost £3.59.

Incomplete vaccination history, age over 10 years

Which therapy

- **Obtain consent and check suitability for immunization.** See *Suitability for vaccination* for further information.

Diphtheria, tetanus and poliomyelitis

- **Ensure that primary immunization is complete:** give three doses at monthly intervals of Revaxis® vaccine (Td/IPV), which contains tetanus, low-dose diphtheria, and inactivated poliomyelitis, for primary immunization.
- **Give the first booster dose** of Revaxis® vaccine at least 5 years after the last dose of the primary course.
- **Give the second booster dose** of Revaxis® vaccine after a further 10 years.

Measles, mumps, and rubella (MMR)

- **Give one dose of MMR vaccine immediately,** and a second (booster) dose, at least 3 months later.
- If immunization status is unknown, ensure that MMR has not been given within the last 3 months.

Meningococcal C

- If immunization status is unknown or incomplete, offer a single dose of Men C vaccine.

Tuberculosis (BCG)

- If the child has risk factors for TB and there is no obvious scar from tuberculosis immunization, use a tuberculin test to assess immunity. See scenario *Tuberculosis BCG vaccine* for further information.

Practical prescribing points

For further information please see the *Medicines Compendium* (www.medicine.org.uk) or the *British National Formulary* (www.bnf.org).

- **Revaxis®, Men C, Hib, or MMR can be given on the same day.** Use different syringes/needles and inject into different sites.
- Give Revaxis®, Men C, and Hib by intramuscular injection. Give MMR by intramuscular or deep subcutaneous injection. In children and adults, use the deltoid muscle and a 23G needle.
- **Delay vaccination during an acute febrile illness.** Wait until symptoms have resolved before vaccinating.
- **If there is an evolving neurological problem,** defer pertussis immunization.
- **Advise parents:**
  - To give a dose of paracetamol or ibuprofen if fever develops, and keep the child cool (remove excess clothing or bedding). If fever persists after a second dose, they should seek medical advice.
  - That malaise, fever, or a rash may occur, most commonly about a week after MMR immunization and lasting about 2–3 days.
  - To seek urgent medical advice if their child develops breathlessness, swelling of the mouth and throat, or a rash within a few days of immunization.

Patient information leaflets

The following PILs are available at www.prodigy.nhs.uk
- BCG Immunisation
- Measles/Mumps/Rubella Immunisation
- Meningococcal group C Immunisation
- Polio Immunisation
- Tetanus Immunisation

Shared decision making

Drug rationale

Drugs not included

- **Hiberix** (*Haemophilus influenzae*) vaccine is not offered. Vaccination is not routinely recommended in this age group.
- **Bacillus Calmette-Guérin vaccine** is available for intradermal injection from the scenario *Tuberculosis BCG vaccine.*

Drugs included

- **Measles, mumps, and rubella (MMR) vaccine.**
- **Revaxis® vaccine (Td/IPV),** which contains diphtheria (low dose), tetanus, and inactivated poliomyelitis vaccine, is offered for children over 10 years of age for primary immunization and for booster doses.

- **Meningococcal Group C conjugate vaccine** is offered. Vaccine is normally administered intramuscularly. Meningitec may be given by deep subcutaneous injection for children with haemophilia. NeisVac-C may be given by subcutaneous injection if there is thrombocytopenia or haemophilia.
- **Paracetamol** is an effective and safe analgesic and antipyretic agent for most people.
- **Ibuprofen** is an effective alternative to paracetamol if there are no contraindications.

Prescriptions

Primary immunization: diphtheria + tetanus + polio

Low-dose diphtheria+tetanus+polio (Revaxis)
- Age from 10 to 25 years
- Revaxis injection. Give 0.5ml by intramuscular injection. For primary immunization, give three doses at intervals of 1 month between doses; supply 1 0.5ml prefilled syringe.

Primary immunization: measles+mumps+rubella vaccine (MMR)

Measles+mumps+rubella vaccine (MMR) Priorix
- Age from 10 to 25 years
- Priorix MMR vaccine. Give 0.5ml by intramuscular or deep subcutaneous injection; supply 1 0.5ml vial + diluent; NHS Cost £4.00.

Measles+mumps+rubella vaccine (MMR) MMRII
- Age from 10 to 25 years
- MMRII MMR vaccine. Give 0.5ml by intramuscular or deep subcutaneous injection; supply 1 0.5ml injection; NHS Cost £4.00.

Primary immunization: meningococcal C conjugate vaccine

Meningitec vaccine
- Age from 10 to 25 years
- Meningitec vaccine. Give a single 0.5ml dose by intramuscular injection for primary immunization; supply 1 0.5ml vial; NHS Cost £19.00.

NeisVac-C vaccine
- Age from 10 to 25 years
- NeisVac-C vaccine. Give a single 0.5ml dose by intramuscular injection for primary immunization; supply 1 0.5ml prefilled syringe; NHS Cost £15.00.

Menjugate vaccine
- Age from 10 to 25 years
- Menjugate vaccine. Give a single 0.5ml dose by intramuscular injection for primary immunization; supply 1 0.5ml vial; NHS Cost £16.00.

Antipyretic: use when required

Paracetamol s/f susp: 250mg to 500mg up to four times a day
- Age from 10 to 11 years
- Paracetamol 250mg/5ml s/f susp. Take one to two 5ml spoonfuls every 4 to 6 hours when required for relief of high temperature. Maximum of 4 doses in 24 hours; supply 100 ml; NHS Cost £0.73; OTC Cost £3.52.

Paracetamol tablets: 500mg to 1g up to four times a day
- Age from 12 to 15 years
- Paracetamol 500mg tablets. Take one to two tablets every 4 to 6 hours when required for relief of high temperature. Maximum of 8 tablets in 24 hours; supply 16 tablets; NHS Cost £0.21; OTC Cost £0.40.

Paracetamol tablets: 1g up to four times a day
- Age from 16 to 25 years
- Paracetamol 500mg tablets. Take two tablets every 4 to 6 hours when required for relief of high temperature. Maximum of 8 tablets in 24 hours; supply 16 tablets; NHS Cost £0.21; OTC Cost £0.40.

Ibuprofen s/f susp: 200mg three to four times a day
- Age from 10 to 11 years
- Ibuprofen 100mg/5ml s/f susp. Take two 5ml spoonfuls 3 to 4 times a day when required for relief of high temperature. Do not exceed the stated dose; supply 100 ml; NHS Cost £1.82; OTC Cost £3.59.

Ibuprofen tablets: 400mg three times a day
- Age from 12 to 25 years
- Ibuprofen 400mg tablets. Take one tablet three times a day when required for relief of high temperature. Do not exceed the stated dose; supply 12 tablets; NHS Cost £0.35; OTC Cost £0.62.

Extended Information

Background information

- What are the diseases covered by the childhood vaccination programme? p.1037
- How common are these diseases? p.1038
- How does vaccination lead to immunity? p.1038
- What types of vaccines are available? p.1039
- Complications of vaccination p.1039

What are the diseases covered by the childhood vaccination programme?

- **Diphtheria** is an acute infectious disease caused by toxigenic strains of *Corynebacterium diphtheriae*. Diphtheria is characterized by the formation of a tough membrane (pseudomembrane) attached firmly to underlying tissue that will bleed if forcibly removed. In the most serious infections the membrane begins on one tonsil and may spread to involve the other tonsil, uvula, soft palate, and pharyngeal wall. It may extend to the larynx, trachea, and bronchial tree, causing bronchial obstruction and death by hypoxia. Diphtheria also occurs in a cutaneous form and may rarely involve the eyes, middle ear, buccal mucosa, genitalia, and umbilical stump, usually secondarily. Systemic effects, chiefly myocarditis and peripheral neuritis, are caused by the exotoxin produced by *C diphtheriae*.
- ***Haemophilus influenzae*** is mainly associated with respiratory infections such as exacerbations of chronic bronchitis and otitis media. Infection with an encapsulated strain of the organism *H influenzae* type b (Hib) commonly leads to meningitis accompanied with bacteraemia.
- **Measles** is an acute viral infection with clinical features that may include coryza, conjunctivitis, bronchitis, Koplik spots, rash, and fever. Complications include otitis media, bronchitis, pneumonia, convulsions, or encephalitis.
- **Mumps** is an acute viral infection that usually presents with unilateral or bilateral parotid swelling but occasionally may be asymptomatic. Complications include pancreatitis, oophoritis, orchitis, male sterility, meningitis, and encephalitis. Mumps may cause permanent unilateral deafness.
- **Rubella (German measles)** is a mild infectious disease that causes a transient erythematous rash and lymphadenopathy involving post-auricular and sub-occipital glands. Maternal infection in the first 8–10 weeks of pregnancy may have serious consequences: fetal

damage occurs in up to 90% of infants, resulting in multiple defects.

- **Meningococcal meningitis and septicaemia** are caused by *Neisseria meningitides*. Meningococci are distinguished by antigenic grouping such as A, B, C, Y, and W135. The most common types in the United Kingdom are B and C. They are further subdivided by type and sulphonamide sensitivity.
- **Pertussis (whooping cough)** is a bacterial infection caused by *Bordetella pertussis*. Usual symptoms are a paroxysmal cough or coughing spasm followed by apnoea. Repeated post-tussive vomiting may lead to weight loss. Possible complications are pneumonia or cerebral hypoxia resulting in brain damage.
- **Poliomyelitis** is a viral infection (poliomyelitis virus type 1, 2, or 3) that attacks the motor neurones of the anterior horns in the brainstem and spinal cord. Acute disease is characterized clinically by fever, sore throat, headache, and vomiting, often with stiffness of the neck and back. Major illness, which may or may not be preceded by the minor illness, is characterized by involvement of the central nervous system, stiff neck, and perhaps paralysis. There may be subsequent atrophy of groups of muscles, ending in contraction and permanent deformity.
- **Tetanus** is an acute infectious disease caused by the anaerobic, spore-forming bacillus *Clostridium tetani*. Characteristic symptoms are muscle rigidity superimposed with agonising contractions.
- **Tuberculosis (TB)** is a bacterial infection caused by *Mycobacterium tuberculosis*, *M bovis*, or *M africanum*. Most cases of TB in the United Kingdom affect the respiratory system, with non-respiratory forms presenting more commonly in immigrants and in those with impaired immunity.

[DH, 1996]

How common are these diseases?

- **Diphtheria:** owing to a successful vaccination programme introduced in the 1950s, diphtheria and the causative organism *Corynebacteria diphtheriae* have been virtually eliminated from the United Kingdom. It is, therefore, not possible to acquire natural immunity from a sub-clinical infection. High immunization uptake must be maintained to prevent a resurgence of diphtheria, which could follow the introduction of cases or carriers from overseas.
- ***Haemophilus influenzae* type b (Hib):** before the introduction of the vaccine in 1992, one in 600 children developed some form of invasive Hib disease before their fifth birthday. Laboratory reports of Hib infection in England and Wales fell from 627 in 1992 to 39 in 1995. Notifications (all ages) of *H influenzae* meningitis declined from 484 to 60 in the same period.
- **Measles:** before the introduction of measles vaccine in 1968, annual notification of measles infection in England and Wales varied between 160,000 and 800,000. By 1980, notifications had only reduced to 50,000–100,000. When the combined measles, mumps, and rubella (MMR) vaccine was introduced in 1988 and coverage exceeded 90%, notifications fell dramatically. Incidence of measles continued to fall after the introduction of a second dose of MMR into the childhood vaccination programme in 1996. However, after persistent media attention to misleading misinformation on the safety of MMR and a decrease in uptake, notifications of measles are no longer decreasing. In the first quarter of 2003, 151 cases of confirmed measles were reported. Only seven cases had a history of vaccination, including a one-year-old known to have received single-antigen measles vaccine. The majority of cases were in London (75), which is also associated with the lowest uptake of MMR. Latest figures on uptake of MMR are available from the Health Protection Agency.
- **Mumps:** before the introduction of the MMR vaccine, about 1200 hospital admissions annually were due to mumps. Notification of mumps has fallen progressively and the incidence of the disease in all ages has fallen dramatically. After the recent falls in the level of MMR uptake, however, there has been a slight increase in notifications of mumps infection.
- **Rubella (German measles):** up to 70 cases of Congenital Rubella Syndrome per year were reported before rubella vaccination was introduced for pre-pubertal girls in 1970. The number of women with rubella antibodies increased from 85–90% before 1970 to 97–98% by 1987. However, outbreaks in males continued, with associated peaks in reports of maternal rubella disease. High coverage of MMR for all children should eliminate these outbreaks in the future.
- **Meningococcal meningitis and septicaemia:** notifications of meningococcal disease increased from 1555 in 1994–1995 to 2962 in 1998–1999 (June to July, epidemiological years). Group C disease has been responsible for recent increases in notifications. Incidence of infection is highest in young children, but fatality is greatest in teenagers.
- **Pertussis (whooping cough):** before the introduction of vaccine, average annual notifications of pertussis in England and Wales exceeded 100,000 cases. Following reductions in coverage because of public anxiety about vaccine safety, notifications increased to similar figures. Continual high coverage, above 90%, is required to prevent outbreaks, particularly in epidemic years.
- **Poliomyelitis:** annual incidence of infection due to wild poliomyelitis virus has gradually fallen from nearly 4000 cases in 1955 to zero, following the introduction of a poliomyelitis vaccine in 1956. In June 2002, the European Regional Commission of the World Health Organization for the Certification of Poliomyelitis Eradication declared all 51 member states of the European region to be free of poliomyelitis.
- **Tetanus:** tetanus spores are present in soil, and thus tetanus can never be eradicated. Notifications, deaths, and laboratory reports of tetanus are mainly from people over the age of 45 years who have not been immunized. Between 1984 and 1995 there were 145 notifications of tetanus in England and Wales.
- **Tuberculosis (TB):** notifications of TB fell significantly throughout the twentieth century until 1987, since when small year-on-year increases have been observed. Approximately 400 deaths a year in the United Kingdom are attributed to TB. TB is now largely concentrated in the major conurbations, with over 40% of cases in London. The highest rates are in particular risk groups: 60% of reported cases are in people born abroad, the rate being higher in certain ethnic groups in the first few years after they enter the country, and rates remain high in the children of these immigrants, wherever born. Other risk groups include contacts of cases, the homeless, and those with HIV infection.

[DH, 1996; CMO, 2005]

How does vaccination lead to immunity?

- Immunity can be induced against a variety of bacterial and viral agents, either actively or by passive transfer. A newborn baby has passive immunity to several diseases, from antibodies passed from its mother via the placenta. Passive immunity usually lasts for only a few weeks or months, but for measles, mumps, and rubella it lasts up to 1 year. The childhood vaccination programme aims to deliver long-term immunity.

- **Active immunity** provides long-term immunity, and is induced by administering inactivated or attenuated live organisms or their products.
- **Cell-mediated immunity and serum antibodies** are induced by vaccines to produce a protective effect.
- **The primary response** occurs after the first administration of inactivated vaccine or toxin to someone who has had no prior exposure to the antigen. A slow antibody or antitoxin response of predominantly immunoglobulin M antibody is produced.
- **The secondary response** occurs when further administrations increase the antibody or antitoxin titre (immunoglobulin G) to a higher level. Depending on the potency of the product and on the time interval, further injections lead to an accelerated response.
- **Antibody or antitoxin levels remain high for months or years following a full course,** but even if the level of detectable antibody falls, the immune mechanism has been sensitized and a further dose (booster) of vaccine reinforces immunity.
- Some people may not produce sufficient levels of antibodies after exposure to an antigen; however, achieving immunization targets in excess of 90% of a population should lead to herd immunity. Individuals who have not produced sufficient antibodies are at risk of infection; this risk is greater with lower uptake of immunization in a community.
- **Herd immunity** develops when resistance of a group to a pathogen is due to immunity of a large proportion of the group to that pathogen.
- Some inactivated vaccines contain adjuvant (substances that enhance the antibody response).

What types of vaccines are available?

- **Inactivated vaccines:** diphtheria, tetanus, pertussis, poliomyelitis, *Haemophilus influenzae* type b (Hib), and meningococcal C conjugate vaccine.
- Inactived vaccines are produced by exposing toxoid to a denaturing agent, resulting in loss of infectivity without loss of antigenicity. Inactivated vaccines have the following advantages and disadvantages:
  - Little or no risk of infection (if properly inactivated).
  - Not possible for all viruses; denaturizing may lead to loss of antigenicity (e.g. as in measles).
  - Not as effective at preventing infection as live virus (mucosal immunity, IgA).
  - May not protect for a long period.
- **Live-virus vaccines:** measles, mumps, rubella.

Table 1: Vaccines used in the UK childhood immunization programme.

Vaccine	Components	Brand name
DTaP/IPV/Hib	Diphtheria, tetanus, pertussis, poliomyelitis, and *H influenzae*	Pediacel
DTaP/IPV	Diphtheria, tetanus, pertussis, and poliomyelitis	Infanrix IPV
dTaP/IPV	Low-dose diphtheria, tetanus, pertussis, and poliomyelitis	Repevax
Td/IPV	Low-dose diphtheria, tetanus, and poliomyelitis	Revaxis
MMR	Measles, mumps, and rubella (live vaccine)	MMR-II or Priorix
Hib	*Haemophilus influenzae*	Hiberix
Men C	Meningococcal Group C	Meningitec, NeisVac-C, or Menjugate
BCG	Bacillus Calmette-Guérin vaccine (live) given for TB immunization	-

- These vaccines use a virus with reduced pathogenicity to provide immune response without disease and have the following advantages and disadvantages:
  - Good immunogens.
  - Induce long-lived immunity.
  - Unstable: biochemically (live virus) and genetically (reversion to virulence).
  - Contamination possible.
  - Inappropriate vaccination with live vaccine (e.g. immunocompromised hosts, or rubella in pregnancy) may theoretically lead to disease.

Complications of vaccination

General information

- **Pain, swelling, or redness at the injection site** are common and may persist for several days.
- **Malaise, transient fever, and headache** may also occur.
- **Anaphylactic reactions to vaccines are very rare,** but they cannot be predicted and have the potential to be fatal.
  - Most anaphylactic reactions occur in individuals who have no known risk factors, making it difficult to advise on special precautions. It is uncertain whether a history of hypersensitivity significantly increases the risk of anaphylaxis.
  - Anaphylaxis is typically rapid and unpredictable, with variable severity and clinical features. However, the time of onset of anaphylaxis may be delayed for up to 72 hours.
  - Serious features include cardiovascular collapse, bronchospasm, angio-oedema, pulmonary oedema, loss of consciousness, and urticaria. People with asthma often develop bronchospasm during anaphylaxis.
  - Anaphylaxis generally responds promptly to parenteral adrenaline.
  - All cases of anaphylaxis should be reported using the Yellow Card scheme.
- **Febrile convulsions are rare** in the first six months of life and most common in the second year of life. After this age the frequency falls and they are rare after 5 years of age. Following diphtheria, tetanus, and pertussis, 6–9 children per 100,000 vaccinations may have febrile convulsion on the day of vaccination; and following measles, mumps, and rubella (MMR) 25–34 children per 100,000 vaccinations may have febrile convulsions 8–14 days after vaccination.
- **Cot deaths (Sudden Infant Death Syndrome — SIDS)** occur most commonly during the first year of life and may therefore coincide with the giving of primary immunization vaccinations. Studies have established that this association is coincidence rather than causal. The incidence of SIDS appears to be lower in children who have had pertussis vaccine than in those who have not.
- **Mercury (in a preservative called thiomersal) is not present in any vaccines recommended in the UK childhood vaccination programme.**

[DH, 1996]

Combined vaccines containing pertussis

- **Adverse reactions:** severe reactions to vaccination such as fever, convulsions, high-pitched screaming, and episodes of pallor, cyanosis, and limpness (hypotonic-hyporesponsive episodes) are rare. Experience from Canada suggests that they are less common with DTaP/IPV/Hib vaccines (which contain acellular pertussis) than those containing whole cell pertussis. They also seem to occur with equal frequency after vaccination with DTP containing acellular pertussis, or DT alone. Note: all DTP vaccines available in the UK now contain only acellular pertussis.

I

- **Neurological conditions:** very rarely, severe neurological conditions, including encephalopathy and prolonged convulsions, resulting in permanent brain damage and death have been reported after pertussis vaccine; but similar illnesses can develop from a variety of causes in the first year of life in both immunized and non-immunized children.
  - In a British study, children with a family or personal history of epilepsy were immunized with pertussis vaccine without any significant adverse events, and their developmental progress has been normal [Ramsay et al, 1994]. In children with a close family history (first-degree relatives) of idiopathic epilepsy, there may be a risk of developing a similar condition, irrespective of vaccine.
  - The National Childhood Encephalopathy Study (NCES) examined 1182 children with serious acute neurological illnesses reported in Great Britain between 1976 and 1979. Only 39 had recently had pertussis vaccine, and in many of these the association of the neurological illnesses with immunization could have occurred by chance.
  - Analysis of the results of the NCES showed that the vaccine may very rarely be associated with the development of severe acute neurological illness in children who were previously apparently normal; most children suffered no apparent harm. The number of cases of severe acute neurological illness reported in the NCES, even after three years of intensive case-finding, was too small to show conclusively whether or not the vaccine could cause permanent brain damage, if such damage occurs at all.
  - These conclusions have been confirmed in a study that found no significant increased risk of serious acute neurological illness in the 7 days after DTP vaccine in children less than 2 years of age [DH, 1996].
- **Asthma:** it has been suggested that pertussis vaccine is linked with the development of asthma. A double-blind study of pertussis vaccines found no significant differences between DTP-immunized children and controls for reported wheezing, itchy rash, or sneezing. The results suggest that there is no reason to withhold pertussis immunization because of fear of subsequent asthma or allergy.

[DH, 1996; DH, 2004e]

MMR vaccine

- **Adverse reactions:** after the first dose of MMR vaccine malaise, fever, and/or rash commonly occur about a week after immunization and last about 2–3 days.
  - Parotid swelling occurs in about 1% of children of all ages up to 4 years, usually in the third week and occasionally later.
  - Thrombocytopenia, which usually resolves spontaneously, occurs in about 1 in 24,000 children given a first dose of MMR at 12–15 months of age.
  - Arthropathy (arthralgia or arthritis), has been reported to occur rarely after MMR immunization — if arthropathy develops other than 14–21 days after immunization, it is unlikely to have been caused by the vaccine.
- **Evidence is convincing that MMR does not cause autism** or any particular subtypes of autistic spectrum disorder.
  - A hypothesis published in 1998 suggested that measles, mumps, and rubella (MMR) vaccine may cause autism as a result of persistent measles-virus infection of the gastrointestinal tract. Studies published since 1998 have continued not to find an increased risk of autistic spectrum disorder associated with MMR [CSM, 2002]. The vaccine also has not been found to be associated with developmental regression or gastrointestinal disorders.
  - Randomized controlled trials comparing harms of MMR compared with placebo have shown no evidence that MMR is associated with developmental regression [Virtanen et al, 2000]. In a retrospective cohort study, 537,303 children were traced for 7 years. The study found no association between MMR vaccination and autistic disorder of any kind.
  - Data from a national United Kingdom general practic[e] registry found that the risk of autism among boys increased in the period 1988–1993, whereas MMR coverage remained almost constant at about 97% ove[r] the same period. A long-term prospective population-based passive surveillance study from Finland similarl[y] reported no cases of developmental regression in 1.8 million people vaccinated with MMR [Patja et al, 2000; Madsen et al, 2002].
  - Further information on the safety of MMR is availabl[e] on the NHS website at www.mmrthefacts.nhs.uk.
- **Inflammatory bowel disease:** MMR vaccine has not bee[n] found to be associated with gastrointestinal disorders. A systematic review of six large observational studies fro[m] different developed countries found no evidence of an association between inflammatory bowel disease and MMR or measles vaccines [Taylor et al, 2002]. The long-term, prospective population-based passive surveillance study from Finland reported no cases of inflammatory bowel disease after 14 years of follow-up [Peltola et al, 1998].
- **Encephalitis and encephalopathy:** MMR vaccine contains live attenuated virus; it is therefore biologically plausible for it to cause encephalitis. A review of the published evidence on encephalitis and measles or MM[R] immunization concluded that the evidence is inadequate to accept or reject a causal relationship between measles or mumps vaccine and encephalitis or encephalopathy. [If] there is a risk, it is exceptionally small.

[DH, 1996]

BCG vaccine

- **Injection site reactions to BCG vaccine are rare if attention is paid to the techniques** for both tuberculin testing and BCG immunization. All personnel performing these tests must be properly instructed, and observed to be using the correct techniques.
  - It is quite normal to have a small amount of swelling at the injection site that can form a small ulcer. This usually heals eventually and leaves a small, flat scar.
  - There may be some swelling of glands in the armpit (less than 1 cm across), which is a natural reaction to the vaccine.
  - Injections made too deeply may increase the risk of lymphadenitis and abscess formation.
  - Keloid formation is uncommon, and largely avoidabl[e] if the recommended injection sites are used (the mid-upper arm or the thigh). Most experience is with the upper arm, and it is know that the risk of keloid formation is greatly increased if the injection is given at a site higher than the insertion of the deltoid muscl[e] near the middle of the upper arm.
- **Extremely rarely,** infection with the bacteria in the vaccine (*Mycobacterium bovis*) has been reported, whic[h] can spread through the body, including to the bones. These infections need to be treated in a similar way to the treatment of tuberculosis.

[DH, 1996]

Management issues

Childhood immunization programme p.1041
Can I give more than one vaccine at the same time? p.1042
What advice should I give about post-immunization pyrexia? p.1042
What if the vaccination history is unknown or incomplete? p.1042
What if a child has a tetanus-prone wound? p.1043
Consent to vaccination p.1043
Vaccination procedures p.1044
Suitability for vaccination p.1044

Childhood immunization programme

Diphtheria, tetanus, pertussis, poliomyelitis and *Haemophilus* influenzae type b

Diptheria (D or d), tetanus (T), acellular pertussis (aP), and inactivated poliomyelitis (IPV) are only available in combined vaccines. Vaccines containing whole cell pertussis, and the live poliomyelitis vaccine (oral) are no longer used in the UK for the childhood immunization programme. The diphtheria component of these combined vaccines is produced in two strengths:

- Vaccines containing the higher dose of diphtheria toxoid (abbreviated to 'D') contain not less than 30 IU.
- Vaccines containing the lower dose of diphtheria toxoid (abbreviated to 'd') contain approximately 2 IU.

Vaccines containing the higher dose of diphtheria toxoid (D) are used to achieve satisfactory primary immunization of children up to ten years of age. The lower dose of diphtheria toxoid (d) is used for booster doses and for primary immunization in individuals aged 10 years and over.

Haemophilus influenza type B (Hib) is available in a combined vaccine (DTaP/IPV) or as a single component vaccine.

At 2–4 months of age: give the primary course (three doses of DTaP/IPV/Hib) ideally starting at 2 months of age, with an interval of 1 month between each dose.

- If a course is interrupted, it may be resumed; there is no need to start again.
- **Before school entry: give a booster dose of dTaP/IPV or DTaP/IPV,** preferably at least 3 years after the last dose of the primary course. A reinforcing (booster) dose of Hib is not recommended for children who have received three injections at the appropriate times.
- **At 13–18 years of age: give a booster dose of Td/IPV** before leaving school.

[DH, 2004b; DH, 2004c; DH, 2004e; DH, 2004f; DH, 2004g]

Meningococcal C

- **At 2–4 months of age: give a primary course** (three doses of Men C) ideally starting at 2 months of age, with an interval of 1 month between each dose.
- If a course is interrupted, it may be resumed; there is no need to start again.
- A booster dose is not needed.
- The meningococcal C conjugate vaccine protects against Group C disease only. Children at risk whilst travelling abroad should also be immunized with the quadrivalent meningococcal meningitis (A, C, W135, Y) vaccine, even if they have received the meningococcal C conjugate vaccine before.
- Children aged less than 18 months of age should not be given meningococcal plain polysaccharide A&C vaccine except for protection against Group A meningitis. Efficacy is established for serogroup A, but the response to the serogroup C component is only transitory.

[DH, 2004d]

Measles, Mumps, and Rubella

- **Give MMR vaccine irrespective of a history of measles, mumps, or rubella infection.**
- **Single-antigen measles, mumps, or rubella vaccines are not available in the UK.**
- **Offer all children two doses of MMR vaccine:**
  - **The first dose is given shortly after the first birthday.** (Passive immunity from antibodies passed on by the mother via the placenta usually lasts only for a few weeks or months, but for measles, mumps, and rubella it may last up to one year.)

'able 2: Childhood immunization programme.

ge	Immunization	Vaccine	Notes
months	Primary course: 1st dose of DTaP/IPV/Hib	Pediacel®	If the primary course of DTaP/IPV/Hib or Men C is interrupted, it may be resumed; there is no need to start again.
	Primary course: 1st dose of Men C	Meningitec®, NeisVac-C®, or Menjugate®	
months	Primary course: 2nd dose of DTaP/IPV/Hib	Pediacel®	-
	Primary course: 2nd dose of Men C	Meningitec®, NeisVac-C®, or Menjugate®	
months	Primary course: 3rd dose of DTaP/IPV/Hib	Pediacel®	If the primary course of Men C is delayed, for children over 4 months and under 12 months of age receiving their first dose, only two doses are required.
	Primary course: 3rd dose of Men C	Meningitec®, NeisVac-C®, or Menjugate®	
2–15 ıonths	MMR	MMR-II® or Priorix®	Other live vaccines must be given at the same time or at least 3 weeks later.
	Hib (if not given previously with the primary course of DTaP/IPV)	Hiberix®	Only a single dose of Hib is needed if immunization is started at this age.
–5 years	Booster dose: dTaP/IPV or DTaP/IPV	Repevax® (dTaP/IPV) or Infanrix IPV® (DTaP/IPV)	Give the booster dose 3 years after the 3rd dose of DTaP/IPV/Hib.
	Booster dose: MMR	MMR-II® or Priorix®	-
0–14 years	Screen for risk factors for tuberculosis (TB). BCG vaccine is now only indicated for those with risk factors for TB.	BCG vaccine	Only give if indicated by tuberculin skin test. Other live vaccines must be given at the same time or at least 3weeks later.
3–18 years	Booster dose: Td/IPV	Revaxis®	-

- **A booster dose is given before school entry** to achieve maximum coverage.
- A single dose of MMR vaccine confers protection in around 90% of individuals for measles and mumps and 95% for rubella. Therefore, if 92% of children are given MMR vaccine, with 90% efficacy for the measles component, only 83% are protected from each year's birth cohort. The accumulation over time of these susceptible children is sufficient to allow the re-emergence of epidemics of measles. This potential for epidemics should be prevented with a two-dose programme.
- **MMR vaccine can be given to children of any age** whose parents request it. Re-immunization is necessary when vaccine has been given before 12 months of age.
- **Children in the following groups are at particular risk from measles infection:**
  - Children with chronic conditions such as cystic fibrosis, congenital heart or kidney disease, failure to thrive, Down's syndrome.
  - Children from the age of 1 year upwards in residential or day care, including playgroups and nursery schools.

[DH, 1996]

Tuberculosis

- The recommended BCG (Bacillus Calmette-Guérin) vaccination programme has recently changed.
- **Those now recommended to routinely receive BCG vaccine are:**
  - Infants living in area where the incidence of tuberculosis (TB) is 40/100,000 or greater.
  - Infants whose parents or grandparents were born in a country with a TB incidence of 40/100,000 or greater.
  - Previously unvaccinated new immigrants from high prevalence countries for TB.
  - Note: the Department of Health with shortly be issuing guidance on high incidence areas in England and high incidence countries. See www.dh.gov.uk for further information.
- **Children who would previously have been offered BCG vaccine at 10–14 years of age will now be screened for TB risk factors,** and tested and vaccinated if appropriate.
- A child may receive BCG at any age at the request of a parent.
- **The dose of BCG vaccine for children under 12 months is different from that for adults.**
  - Children over 12 months of age, and adults: a single 0.1 ml dose by intradermal injection
  - Children 12 months and under: 0.05 ml dose by intradermal injection
- Revaccination is not recommended if initial vaccine is given after 12 months of age.
- The duration of immunity after BCG vaccination is not known. People normally become tuberculin-positive 6 weeks after vaccination.
- Refer contacts of tuberculosis to a chest clinic for further investigation and supervision. A prophylactic course of isoniazid may be appropriate before vaccination is undertaken.

[DH, 1996; CMO, 2005]

Tuberculin testing

- **Always carry out a tuberculin skin test before BCG immunization.** The only exception to this rule is for infants up to 3 months of age, who may be immunized without a prior test providing that they have had no known recent contact with tuberculosis.
- The test assesses the individual's sensitivity to tuberculin protein: the greater the strength of the tuberculin reaction, the more likely an individual is to have active disease.
- People with a positive test should not be given BCG — it is unnecessary and may cause a larger reaction.
- **Those with a strong positive test need to be referred to a chest clinic** for assessment of the need for further investigation and treatment.
- **The Mantoux test will replace the Heaf test** as the standard method of tuberculin testing. (Supplies of Heaf strength tuberculin PPD are no longer available.) An intradermal injections are given in the middle of the flexor surface of the forearm. This site should not be used for injecting vaccines.

[DH, 1996; CMO, 2005]

Can I give more than one vaccine at the same time?

- **Inactivated vaccines** (e.g. diphtheria, tetanus, pertussis, poliomyelitis, *Haemophilus influenza*, and meningococcal C conjugate vaccine) can be given at the same time as each other. However, they should be given using separate syringes and at different sites. If inactivated vaccines are *not* administered on the same day, there is no need to observe a specific interval between administering them.
- **Live vaccines** (e.g. MMR, BCG vaccine) can be given at the same time as each other (using separate syringes and at different sites). If live vaccines are *not* administered on the same day, they should be separated from other live vaccines by an interval of at least 3 weeks. However, no interval need be observed between the administration of live vaccines and inactivated vaccines.
- If parents do not wish MMR vaccine to be given at the same time as other injected vaccines, give MMR and recall the child for the other vaccines as soon as possible.

[DH, 1996]

What advice should I give about post-immunization pyrexia?

- **Advise all parents that a febrile period may follow immunization.** Transient fever usually occurs within a few days of immunization with most vaccines. However with MMR vaccine, fever does not usually develop until 1–2 weeks after vaccination.
- **Advise parents to give a dose of paracetamol or ibuprofen** if fever develops, and keep the child cool by removing excessive clothing and bedding. If fever persists after a second dose, they should seek medical advice. Fanning and tepid sponging are likely to cause discomfort and are of little benefit.
- The aim of controlling fever is to ease symptoms; it does not prevent febrile seizures. Note: febrile seizures are very rare following immunization.

What if the vaccination history is unknown or incomplete?

- Unless there is a reliable history of previous immunization, individuals should be assumed to be unimmunized and the full UK recommendations should be followed.
- If the primary immunizations of DTaP/IPV/Hib have not been completed by the time that MMR vaccine is due, they can be given at the same time using separate syringes and different sites.
- There is also an opportunity to check that all recommended immunizations have been completed when children attend for pre-school boosters or their school-leaving immunizations.

Diphtheria, tetanus, pertussis, and poliomyelitis

- **Incomplete primary course:** complete the course of three doses at monthly intervals. If a course is interrupted, it may be resumed; there is no need to start again.
  - Children under the age of 10 years: use DTaP/IPV/Hib vaccine (Pediacel®)
  - Children over the age of 10 years and adults: use Td/IPV (Revaxis®)
- **Booster doses: two booster doses are needed to complete the recommended schedule.**
  - For children starting their boosters *under* the age of 10 years:
    - Give routine pre-school and subsequent boosters as per the UK schedule.
    - The first booster dose should ideally be given 3 years after completion of the primary course, but may be given as early as 1 year after the third primary dose (to re-establish them on the routine schedule).
    - The second booster should be given at the time of school leaving. Wherever possible a minimum of 5 years (ideally 10 years if possible) should be left between the first and second boosters.
  - For children starting their booster doses *over* the age of 10 years (and adults):
    - Give the first booster dose 5–10 years after completion of the primary course.
    - Give the second booster dose 10 years after the previous dose.
  - Children under the age of 10 years: use DTaP/IPV (Infanrix IPV®) or dTaP/IPV (Repevax®) for the booster dose.
  - Children over the age of 10 years and adults: use Td/IPV for the booster dose (Revaxis®).
- Children coming to the UK may have had a fourth dose of a diphtheria-containing vaccine that is given at around 18 months of age in some countries. This dose should be discounted as it may not provide satisfactory protection until the time of the teenage booster.

[DH, 2004b; DH, 2004e; DH, 2004f; DH, 2004g]

Haemophilus influenzae (type b)

- **Children under the age of 13 months** are at high risk of disease. Give three doses of Hib vaccine, even if the child has already commenced or completed their immunizations against diphtheria, tetanus, pertussis, and poliomyelitis.
- **Non-immunized children aged 13–48 months** are at lower risk of disease, and the vaccine is effective after a single dose. Offer one dose of Hib vaccine, either simultaneously with MMR, or singly if the MMR has already been given.
- **Older children and adults:** because the incidence of invasive disease falls sharply after 4 years, routine immunization of older children and adults is not recommended.
- However, people with asplenia are at increase risk of invasive Hib infection. Offer a single dose of Hib vaccine, irrespective of age or the interval from splenectomy. Those under 1 year should be given two further doses. At present, there are no data to indicate a need for further booster doses. When splenectomy is performed electively, the vaccine should be given ideally at least 2 weeks before splenectomy.

[DH, 2004c]

Meningococcal C

- **Incomplete primary course:** give the outstanding doses at monthly intervals. If a course is interrupted, it may be resumed; there is no need to start again.
- **For children aged 4–12 months** receiving their first dose, only two doses are required.
- **Older children and adults up to the age of 24 years** receiving their first dose, only a single dose is required. Note: if an individual has received the polysaccharide vaccine previously, they should now receive the conjugate vaccine, providing that 3 years have elapsed between doses.
- Routine immunization of adults over the aged 25 years and over is not recommended as the risk of meningococcal infection is much lower. However, people with asplenia are at greater risk of meningococcal infection and should be offered the conjugate vaccine.

[DH, 1996; CMO, 2002]

Measles, mumps, and rubella (MMR)

- **Children over the age of 12 months and adults:** give one dose of MMR vaccine immediately, and a second (booster) dose, at least 3 months later.
- If immunization status is unknown, ensure that MMR has not been given within the last 3 months.

[DH, 1996]

Tuberculosis (BCG)

- If the child has risk factors for TB and there is no obvious scar from tuberculosis immunization, use a tuberculin test to assess immunity. If there is a negative tuberculin test, offer a single dose of BCG vaccine.

[DH, 1996; CMO, 2005]

What if a child has a tetanus-prone wound?

A tetanus-prone wound may be defined as: a puncture wound; a significant degree of devitalized tissue; contaminated with soil or manure; containing foreign bodies; compound fractures; clinical signs of sepsis; wounds or burns sustained more than 6 hours before surgical treatment.

- **Person fully immunized, i.e. has received five doses of vaccine at appropriate intervals:** tetanus booster not needed. Consider giving human tetanus immunoglobulin for tetanus-prone wounds where the risk of infection is especially high, e.g. those contaminated with manure or extensive devitalized tissue.
- **Primary immunization complete, boosters incomplete but up-to-date:** tetanus booster not needed but may be given if booster is due and it is convenient to give now. Consider giving human tetanus immunoglobulin for tetanus-prone wounds where the risk of infection is especially high, e.g. those contaminated with manure or extensive devitalized tissue.
- **Primary immunization incomplete, or boosters not up-to-date:** give tetanus booster and further doses as needed to complete the recommended schedule (Note: if the primary course is interrupted it should be resumed but not repeated). Add human tetanus immunoglobulin if it is a tetanus-prone wound. Note: inject tetanus vaccine and immunoglobulin at different sites.
- **Not immunized or immunization status uncertain:** give an immediate dose of vaccine followed by completion of the full primary course if records confirm the need. Add human tetanus immunoglobulin if it is a tetanus-prone wound (see above).

[DH, 2004g]

Consent to vaccination

- **People must be given adequate information before they can give consent.** This should include written or verbal information about the process, benefits and risks of the immunization. Ensure that parents feel that their questions have been adequately answered and that their concerns about vaccination have been considered.
- **Obtain written or verbal consent for vaccination at each vaccination visit.** Written consent provides a permanent

record, but there is no legal requirement for consent to be in writing. Consent obtained before the occasion upon which a child is brought for vaccination is only an agreement for the child to be included in the vaccination programme, and does not mean that consent is in place for each future vaccination.
- **Adults** (aged 18 years and over) must consent to their own treatment.

Immunizations in schools

- **Children aged 16 or 17** are entitled to consent to their own medical treatment.
- **In younger children,** consent should be obtained from the parent or person with parental responsibility. A child under 16 years of age may give consent for vaccination, provided he or she understands fully the benefits and risks involved. However, the child should be encouraged to involve a parent or guardian, if possible, in the decision.
- In the absence of any reservation expressed to the contrary, the attendance of a child at school on the day that the parent or guardian has been advised that the child will be immunized may also be viewed as acceptance that the child may be immunized.

Immunization of younger children

- Consent should be obtained from the parent or person with parental responsibility, provided that person is capable of consenting to the immunization in question and is able to communicate their decision.
- Where this person brings the child in response to an invitation for immunization, and. Following an appropriate consultation presents the child for that immunization, these actions may be considered evidence of consent.

[DH, 2004a]

Vaccination procedures

Record taking

- **Obtain written or verbal consent** at the time of vaccination from the parent or person with parental responsibility. Ensure that parents feel that their questions have been adequately answered, and that their concerns about vaccination have been considered.
- **Establish suitability for immunization.** If the individual's fitness and suitability cannot be established, vaccination should be delayed. See *Suitability for vaccination* for further information.
- **Check** the identity of the vaccine, usage instructions, and its expiry date.
- **Record** the date of immunization, title of vaccine, and batch number on the recipient's record. If two vaccines are given simultaneously, the relevant sites should be recorded to allow any reactions to be related to the causative vaccine.

Storage and reconstitution of vaccines

- **Store vaccines and diluents at 2–8°C, protected from light** in a designated refrigerator. Vaccine (including diluent) that has been frozen or has thawed should not be used. Freeze-dried vaccines must be stored in the dry state. A maximum–minimum thermometer should be used to check that the temperature has not gone out of the intended range.
- **Reconstitute** freeze-dried vaccine with the diluent supplied. This should be done slowly to avoid frothing, with a sterile 21G needle. Before injection, the colour of the product must be checked with that stated by the manufacturer in the package insert.

Administration of vaccines

- **Swab the skin with alcohol** if the skin is dirty, but allow it to evaporate before injecting. Live vaccines can be destroyed by coming into contact with alcohol.
- **Use the appropriate route of injection.**
  - Most childhood vaccines should be given only by intramuscular injection. (MMR-II or Priorix can be given by intramuscular or deep subcutaneous injection.)
  - In patients with thrombocytopenia or bleeding disorders, however, the subcutaneous route should be used.
  - BCG vaccine must *only* be given intradermally.
- **Use an appropriate site for injecting.**
  - In infants, use the antero-lateral aspect of the thigh.
  - In older children and adults, use the deltoid muscle. (The buttocks are not recommended as an injection site for any of the childhood vaccines. If the buttock is to be used, injection into the upper, outer quadrant minimizes the possibility of damage to the sciatic nerve.)
  - BCG vaccine should be given at the insertion of the deltoid muscle near the middle of the upper arm; avoid the tip of the shoulder because of the increased risk of keloid formation at this site.
- **Ensure the correct needle is used.** A 25G needle is suitable for deep subcutaneous or intramuscular injections in infants. A 23G needle is appropriate for deep subcutaneous or intramuscular injections in older children and adults. A 25G needle should be used for intradermal injections.
- **If more than one vaccine is being given,** use different syringes/needles and inject into different sites.
- **Ask the parents to wait after immunization** to ensure that the child is not experiencing an immediate adverse reaction (e.g. for 10 minutes). Anaphylaxis is rare, and typically occurs within minutes. However, the time of onset may be variable because of delayed absorption from an intramuscular injection (e.g. within 72 hours of immunization).
- **Parents should also be advised:**
  - To seek urgent medical advice if their child develops early symptoms such as breathlessness, swelling of the mouth and throat, or rash within the following 72 hours.
  - To give a dose of paracetamol or ibuprofen if fever develops, and keep the child cool by removing excessive clothing and bedding. If fever persists after a second dose, they should seek medical advice.
  - That, following the first dose of MMR vaccine, malaise, fever, or a rash may occur, most commonly about a week after immunization, and lasts about 2–3 days.
  - That it is quite normal for BCG vaccination to cause a small amount of swelling at the injection site that can form a small ulcer. This usually heals eventually and leaves a small, flat scar.

[DH, 1996; DH, 2004b; DH, 2004c; DH, 2004d; DH, 2004e; DH, 2004f; DH, 2004g]

Suitability for vaccination

Contraindications to vaccination

- **Anaphylaxis:** vaccines should not be given to those who have had a confirmed anaphylactic reaction within 72 hours of a previous dose of the same vaccine. In addition:
  - Tetanus-, diphtheria-, pertussis-, poliomyelitis-, or Hib- containing vaccines should not be given if there is a confirmed anaphylactic reaction to neomycin,

streptomycin or polymyxin B (which may be present in trace amounts).
  - MMR vaccine should not be given if there is a confirmed anaphylactic reaction to neomycin.
  - Meningococcal C conjugate vaccine should not be given if there is a confirmed anaphylactic rection to a previous dose of diphtheria or tetanus toxoid. (It uses the carrier proteins of the variant diphtheria toxin or tetanus toxoid.)
- **Other severe adverse reactions.** (Severe in this context means an extensive area of redness and swelling affecting large areas of the arm, leg, or other injection site, or a fever equal to or in excess of 39.5°C within 48 hours of injection):
  - Meningococcal C conjugate vaccine should not be given if is a definite history of a *severe* reaction to a previous dose, or to diphtheria or tetanus toxoid.
  - However, tetanus-, diphtheria-, pertussis-, poliomyelitis-, or Hib- containing vaccines *should* still be given to children with a severe reaction within 72 hours of a preceding dose.
- **Tuberculin positive:** BCG vaccine should not be administered to individuals who are tuberculin-positive (that is, an induration of 5 mm or greater in diameter in the Mantoux test, or a Heaf grade 2 to 4).

[DH, 1996; DH, 2004b; DH, 2004c; DH, 2004d; DH, 2004e; DH, 2004f; DH, 2004g]

Reasons to delay vaccination

Where there is doubt, seek appropriate advice from a consultant paediatrician, District Immunization Coordinator or Consultant in Communicable Disease Control, rather than withholding vaccine.

- **Acute illness:** if a child is suffering from any acute illness, postpone immunization until the child has fully recovered. Minor infections without fever or systemic upset are not reasons to postpone immunization.
- **Pregnancy:**
  - Tetanus, diphtheria, acellular pertussis, inactivated poliomyelitis, and Hib may be given to pregnant women when clinically indicated. There is no evidence of risk from vaccinating pregnant women or those who are breastfeeding with inactivated virus or bacterial vaccines or toxoids.
  - Although there is no information to suggest that meningococcal C conjugate vaccine is unsafe in pregnancy, it should not be given unless there is a high risk of the individual developing the disease.
  - Pregnancy should be avoided for 1 month after MMR vaccine, as for rubella vaccine. (Although there is no evidence to suggest that rubella vaccine is teratogenic, live vaccines should not be given to pregnant women because of the theoretical possibility of harm to the fetus.)
  - Do not offer BCG vaccine (live) to women who are pregnant or who are breastfeeding, unless it is thought that they are at high risk of catching TB.
- **People with an evolving neurological problem** (including uncontrolled epilepsy): defer immunization until the condition is stable.
- **Encephalopathy or encephalitis that occurred within 7 days of immunization** is unlikely to have been caused by the vaccine, but should be investigated by a specialist. Immunization should be deferred in children where no underlying cause was found (*and* the child did not recover completely within seven days) until the condition has stabilised. If a cause is identified or the child recovers within seven days, immunization should proceed as recommended.

[DH, 1996; DH, 2004b; DH, 2004c; DH, 2004d; DH, 2004e; DH, 2004f; DH, 2004g]

Can a child with a personal or close family history of febrile seizures be vaccinated?

- Febrile seizures are rare following immunization. When there is a personal or family history of febrile seizures, there is an increased risk of these occurring after any fever, including that caused by immunization.
- **Personal history of febrile seizures:** immunization should be carried out after advice on the prevention of pyrexia has been given (provided there was complete recovery after the previous febrile seizure). The aim of controlling fever is to ease symptoms; it does not prevent febrile seizures. If there is uncertainty, seek specialist paediatric advice rather than refuse immunization.
- **Close family history of febrile seizures** (e.g. in parents or siblings): give advice about post-immunization pyrexia before administering the vaccine.

[DH, 1996; DH, 2004b; DH, 2004c; DH, 2004d; DH, 2004e; DH, 2004f; DH, 2004g]

Can people with immunosuppression or HIV infection be vaccinated?

- **Inactivated vaccines: people with immunosuppression or HIV infection** (regardless of CD4 count) should be given inactivated vaccines (e.g. tetanus, diphtheria, pertussis, poliomyelitis, Hib, meningococcal C conjugate vaccine) in accordance with the recommended schedule. However these individuals may not make a full antibody response. Re-immunization should be considered after treatment is finished and recovery has occurred.
- **Live vaccines: immunosuppressed people** taking *live* vaccines (e.g. MMR, BCG) may not have a normal immune response and may suffer severe adverse reactions to live vaccines. The following people are potentially at risk:
  - **People taking cancer chemotherapy or generalized radiotherapy,** or people who have had such therapy in the preceding 6 months.
  - **People on immunosuppressive treatment** for an organ transplant.
  - **People who have had a bone marrow transplant** in the previous 6 months.
  - **People on systemic corticosteroid treatment** for at least one week (high-dose), or on low-dose systemic corticosteroid treatment combined with cytotoxic drugs, or people on long-term low-dose corticosteroid treatment.
  - **In addition, BCG vaccine should not be given to** people with a malignant condition such as lymphoma, Hodgkin's disease, or other tumour of the reticuloendothelial system.
- **Live vaccines: people with HIV infection** can receive MMR vaccine (but not while severely immunosuppressed). The Joint Committee on Vaccination and Immunization advises that BCG should *not* be administered to HIV-positive people.

[DH, 1996]

Can MMR vaccine be given to children with allergy to egg?

- There is increasing evidence that MMR vaccine can be given safely to children even when they have previously had an anaphylactic reaction (generalized urticaria, swelling of the mouth and throat, difficulty in breathing, hypotension, or shock) following food containing egg.
- A combined total of 1265 people were involved in 16 studies that have shown that none of 284 people with histories of egg hypersensitivity confirmed by oral challenge had any adverse reactions to MMR. In a further study, MMR was administered safely to 1209 people with positive skin-tests to egg. There were

only two reports of symptoms suggestive of anaphylaxis (0.16%).
- The combined data indicate that over 99% of children who are allergic to eggs can safely receive MMR vaccine. Dislike of egg, or refusal to eat it, is not a contraindication. If there is concern, seek paediatric advice with a view to immunization under controlled conditions such as admission to hospital as a day case.

[DH, 1996]

NOT contraindications to vaccination

The following are *not* reasons to delay or avoid vaccination, and the recommended immunization schedule should be followed:

- Previous history of pertussis, measles, rubella or mumps infection.
- A personal or family history of allergy, asthma, eczema, hay fever, or 'snuffles'.
- Prematurity: immunization should not be postponed.
- Stable neurological conditions such as cerebral palsy, Down's syndrome, spina bifida, or well-controlled epilepsy.
- Contact with an infectious disease.
- Treatment with antibiotics or local corticosteroids (e.g. topical or inhaled).
- The child to be immunized is being breastfed or their mother is pregnant.
- History of jaundice after birth.
- Under a certain weight.
- Taking 'replacement' corticosteroids.

[DH, 1996]

References

NHS staff in England can link, free of charge, from references to full text journals by clicking on [Full text] on the PRODIGY website.

1. CMO (2002) *Extending meningitis C vaccine to 20–24 year olds*. PL/CMO/2002/1. Department of Health. www.dh.gov.uk [Accessed: 22/06/2005]. [Full text]
2. CMO (2005) *Changes to the BCG vaccination programme*. PL/CMO/2005/3. Department of Health. www.dh.gov.uk [Accessed: 11/07/2005]. [Full text]
3. CSM (2002) *New research shows no link between MMR and autism or bowel disease according to the Committee on Safety in Medicines*. Current Problems in Pharmacovigilance. Committee on Safety in Medicines. www.mca.gov.uk/whatsnew/pressreleases/mmr.pdf [Accessed: 16/02/2004].
4. DH (1996) *Immunisation against infectious disease*. Department of Health. www.dh.gov.uk [Accessed: 18/05/2004]. [Full text]
5. DH (2004a) *New (November 2004) chapter 3 – consent to immunisation*. Immunisation against infectious disease. Department of Health. www.dh.gov.uk [Accessed: 22/06/2005]. [Full text]
6. DH (2004b) *New (August 2004) chapter 15 – diphtheria*. Immunisation against infectious disease. Department of Health. www.dh.gov.uk [Accessed: 22/06/2005]. [Full text]
7. DH (2004c) *New (August 2004) chapter 16 – haemophilus influenzae b (hib)*. Immunisation against infectious disease. Department of Health. www.dh.gov.uk [Accessed: 22/06/2005]. [Full text]
8. DH (2004d) *New (April 2004) chapter 23 – meningococcal*. Immunisation against infectious disease. Department of Health. www.dh.gov.uk [Accessed: 22/06/2005]. [Full text]
9. DH (2004e) *New (August 2004) chapter 24 – pertussis*. Immunisation against infectious disease. Department of Health. www.dh.gov.uk [Accessed: 22/06/2005]. [Full text]
10. DH (2004f) *New (August 2004) chapter 26 – poliomyelitis*. Immunisation against infectious disease. Department of Health. www.dh.gov.uk [Accessed: 22/06/2005]. [Full text]
11. DH (2004g) *New (August 2004) chapter 30 – tetanus*. Immunisation against infectious disease. Department of Health. www.dh.gov.uk [Accessed: 22/06/2005]. [Full text]
12. Madsen, K.M., Hviid, A., Vestergaard, M. et al (2002) A population-based study of measles, mumps, and rubella vaccination and autism. *New England Journal of Medicine* **347**(19), 1477–1482. [Full text]
13. Patja, A., Davidkin, I., Kurki, T. et al (2000) Serious adverse events after measles-mumps-rubella vaccination during a fourteen-year prospective follow-up. *Pediatric Infectious Disease Journal* **19**(12), 1127–1134.
14. Peltola, H., Patja, A., Leinikki, P. et al (1998) No evidence for measles, mumps, and rubella vaccine-associated inflammatory bowel disease or autism in a 14-year prospective study. *Lancet* **351**(9112), 1327–1328. [Full text]
15. Ramsay, M., Begg, N., Holland, B. and Dalphinis, J. (1994) Pertussis immunisation in children with a family or personal history of convulsions: a review of children referred for specialist advice. *Health Trends* **26**(1), 23–24.
16. Taylor, B., Miller, E., Lingam, R. et al (2002) Measles, mumps, and rubella vaccination and bowel problems or developmental regression in children with autism: population study. *British Medical Journal* **324**(7334), 393–396. [Full text]
17. Virtanen, M., Peltola, H., Paunio, M. and Heinonen, O.P. (2000) Day-to-day reactogenicity and the healthy vaccinee effect of measles-mumps-rubella vaccination. *Pediatrics* **106**(5), 62.

PRODIGY GUIDANCE

Immunizations — pneumococcal vaccine

Last revised in October 2005
www.prodigy.nhs.uk/guidance.asp?gt=Immunizations - pneumococcal

Applies to people of all ages

This guidance covers immunization of people in whom pneumococcal infection (bacteraemic pneumonia, bacteraemia, or meningitis) is likely to be more common or more serious.

This guidance does not cover childhood vaccinations or travel vaccinations.

There is separate PRODIGY guidance for *Immunizations — childhood vaccination program, Immunizations — travel vaccinations, Influenza*, and *Chest infections.*

Goals

- Vaccination of those at highest risk from pneumococcal pneumonia, pneumococcal bacteraemia, and pneumococcal meningitis

Contents

Scenarios

- Pneumococcal vaccination p.1047

Extended Information, p. 1048

Pneumococcal vaccination

Which therapy?

- **Obtain consent and check suitability for immunization.** See *Suitability for vaccination* for further information.
- **Vaccinate all those aged 65 and over** (this programme is currently being phased in).
- **Vaccinate the following high-risk groups** (aged 2 months and over):
  - Asplenia or severe dysfunction of the spleen (including homozygous sickle-cell disease and coeliac syndrome).
  - Chronic lung disease. Note: asthma is an indication if it is so severe as to require continuous or frequently repeated use of *systemic* corticosteroids, i.e. at a dose equivalent to prednisolone 20 mg or more per day (any age) or, for children under 20 kg, at a dose of 1 mg or more per kilogram bodyweight per day, for more than a month.
  - Chronic heart disease.
  - Nephrotic syndrome or chronic renal disease.
  - Chronic liver disease (including cirrhosis).
  - Diabetes mellitus.
  - Immunosuppression due to disease or treatment.
  - HIV infection (at all stages).
  - Those with cochlear implants.
  - Those with CSF shunts.
  - Children under 5 years of age who have previously had pneumococcal meningitis or pneumococcal bacteraemia.
- **Age over 5 years:** give a single 0.5 ml dose of polysaccharide vaccine (Pneumovax II®).
- **Age under 5 years:** give a primary series of conjugate vaccine (Prevenar®), followed by a booster dose of polysaccharide vaccine (Pneumovax II®) once over the age of 2 years.
- **Only certain groups need revaccination every 5 years with Pneumovax II®, that is people with:**
  - Splenic dysfunction or no spleen
  - Nephrotic syndrome
- **Other individuals do not usually need revaccination.** If in any doubt, seek specialist advice.

Practical prescribing points

For further information please see the *Medicines Compendium* (www.medicines.org.uk) or the *British National Formulary* (www.bnf.org).

- Give Pneumovax II® by subcutaneous or intramuscular injection. Give Prevenar® by intramuscular injection. In infants use the antero-lateral aspects of the thigh and a 25G needle. In older children and adults use the upper arm and a 23G needle.
- **Delay vaccination during an acute febrile illness.** Wait until symptoms have resolved before vaccinating.
- Pneumovax II® can be given on the same day as influenza vaccine. Prevenar® can be given on the same day as other childhood vaccines.
- **If more than one vaccine is being given,** use different needles/syringes and inject into different sites.
- **Advise people to seek urgent medical advice** if they develop breathlessness, swelling of the mouth or throat, or a rash within a few days of immunization.
- **Advise parents to** give a dose of paracetamol or ibuprofen if a child develops a fever, and keep the child cool (remove excess clothing or bedding). If a fever persists after a second dose, they should seek medical advice.

Patient information leaflets

The following PILs are available at www.prodigy.nhs.uk

- Immunisation - UK Schedule/ General
- Pneumococcal Immunisation

Shared decision making

- **For pneumococcal immunization:**
  - Most people need just one injection which lasts for life.
  - If your child is under five, he or she will need several injections over time.
  - If you have no spleen, a non-functioning spleen, or have nephrotic syndrome, you may need boosters every 5 years.
- **After the injection:**
  - Wait in for 10 minutes before leaving to check you have not reacted to the vaccine.
  - If a high temperature develops in a child, give them a dose of paracetamol or ibuprofen. If the temperature persists after a second dose 4–6 hours later, then seek medical advice.
  - If you become breathless, develop swelling, or a rash within a few days, seek medical help urgently. (This is very rare.)

Drug rationale

Both pneumococcal vaccinations currently available in the UK are included:

- **Pneumococcal polysaccharide vaccine (Pneumovax II®)** is included for use in adults and children over 2 years of age at high risk of pneumococcal infection.
- **Pneumococcal conjugate vaccine (Prevenar®)** is included for use in children under 5 years of age at high risk of pneumococcal infection.

Prescriptions

Individuals at high risk of pneumococcal infection

All adults over 65 years of age

- Age from 65 years onwards
- Pneumovax II vaccine. Give 0.5ml by intramuscular or subcutaneous injection; supply 1 0.5 ml vial; NHS Cost £9.49.

High-risk individuals over 5 years of age

- Age from 5 to 64 years
- Pneumovax II vaccine. Give 0.5ml by intramuscular or subcutaneous injection; supply 1 0.5 ml vial; NHS Cost £9.49.

Children aged 12 to 59 months at high-risk

- Age from 12 months to 4 years
- Prevenar vaccine. Give two doses (each of 0.5ml) by intramuscular injection, separated by an interval of at least 2 months; supply 2 0.5ml vial; NHS Cost £78.50.

Children aged 7 to 11 months at high-risk

- Age from 7 to 11 months
- Prevenar vaccine. Give two doses (each of 0.5ml) by intramuscular injection, with at least 1 month between doses. Then give a third dose after the first birthday; supply 3 0.5ml vial; NHS Cost £117.75.

Children aged 2 to 6 months at high-risk

- Age from 2 to 6 months
- Prevenar vaccine. Give three doses (each of 0.5ml) by intramuscular injection, with at least 1 month between doses. Then give a fourth dose after the first birthday; supply 4 0.5ml vial; NHS Cost £157.00.

Extended Information

Background information

- What diseases does invasive pneumococcal infection cause? p.1048
- How common is invasive pneumococcal disease? p.1048
- How does vaccination with pneumococcal vaccine lead to immunity? p.1048
- What types of pneumococcal vaccines are available? p.1048
- Complications of vaccination p.1049

What diseases does invasive pneumococcal infection cause?

- Pneumococcal disease is caused by infection with *Streptococcus pneumoniae* (an encapsulated Gram-positive coccus).
- Invasive infection with *S pneumoniae* can cause bacteraemic pneumonia, bacteraemia, or meningitis.
- It is a major cause of morbidity and mortality, especially in the very young, the elderly, and the immunocompromized [DH, 2004].
- Ninety types of encapsulated *S pneumoniae* have been characterized.
- Only 8–10 of these cause two-thirds of the serious infections in adults and about 80% of infections in children [CDSC, 2002].

How common is invasive pneumococcal disease?

- Pneumococcal pneumonia is estimated to affect 1 in 1000 adults each year and to have a mortality of 10–20% [World Health Organization, 1999].
- During the year 2000, 4744 laboratory isolates of *Streptococcus pneumoniae* from blood, cerebrospinal fluid (CSF), or other normally sterile sites were reported to the Health Protection Agency [CDR, 2003].
- Although the average reporting rate of 9 per 100,000 population was low, it varied markedly with age. The highest reporting rates were seen in the very young and the very old (e.g. 73/100,000 for infants under 1 month of age, and 41/1000 for adults over 75 years).

How does vaccination with pneumococcal vaccine lead to immunity?

- Pneumococcal vaccines use organism products (purified capsular polysaccharide from several strains of *Streptococcus pneumoniae*) to achieve active immunity.
  - These organism products produce a protective effect by inducing cell-mediated immunity and serum antibodies.
  - The primary response occurs after the first administration of organism products to a person without prior exposure to the antigen. A slow antibody response (predominantly immunoglobulin M) is produced.
  - The secondary response occurs when further administrations increase the antibody titre (immunoglobulin G) to a higher level.
- Most adults will have had some previous exposure to *S pneumoniae,* and so will develop a good immunoglobulin G antibody response to a single dose of pneumococcal vaccine by the third week following immunization.
- Children, however, need a primary series of injections to produce immunity; the number of doses required varies with age. See *What is the schedule for administration?* for further information.

[DH, 2004]

What types of pneumococcal vaccines are available?

- There are two types of pneumococcal vaccine available in the UK:
  - 23-valent pneumococcal polysaccharide vaccine (Pneumovax II®)
  - 7-valent pneumococcal conjugate vaccine (Prevenar®)
- Both pneumococcal vaccines available in the UK are inactivated vaccines.
- The polysaccharide vaccine contains purified capsular protein from 23 types of *Streptococcus pneumoniae.* These account for 96% of the isolates that cause serious pneumococcal infections in the UK.
- The conjugate vaccine contains polysaccharide antigens from seven common types of *S pneumoniae,* conjugated to a carrier protein and adsorbed onto aluminium phosphate. These serotypes account for about 80% of invasive pneumococcal infections in children under 5 years of age, but only for about 65% of all serious pneumococcal infections in the UK.

[DH, 2004]

Complications of vaccination

- Severe anaphylactic reactions are rare.
- Injection site reactions (e.g. pain, redness, and swelling) and low-grade fever are amongst the most commonly reported adverse effects. More severe systemic reactions are infrequent.
- No increased local or systemic reactions have been reported with repeated doses of pneumococcal conjugate vaccine throughout the primary course. However more children seem to experience transient tenderness with the booster dose.

[DH, 1996; ABPI Medicines Compendium, 2002; ABPI Medicines Compendium, 2003]

Management issues

- Who should receive pneumococcal vaccine? p.1049
- Which vaccine should I use? p.1049
- What is the schedule for immunizing high-risk groups? p.1049
- Can I give pneumococcal vaccine at the same time as other vaccines? p.1049
- Should pneumococcal vaccine be re-administered? p.1050
- Vaccination procedures p.1050
- Suitability for vaccination p.1051

Who should receive pneumococcal vaccine?

- **All those aged 65 and over** should receive pneumococcal vaccine.
- **All those aged 2 months and over in the following high-risk groups** should also be vaccinated:
  - **Asplenia or severe dysfunction of the spleen** (including homozygous sickle-cell disease and coeliac syndrome).
  - **Chronic lung disease** (including individuals with chronic obstructive pulmonary disease; bronchiectasis; cystic fibrosis; interstitial lung fibrosis; pneumoconiosis; children with respiratory conditions caused by aspiration, or a neuromuscular disease, e.g. cerebral palsy, with a risk of aspiration). Asthma is *not* an indication, unless so severe as to require continuous or frequently repeated use of *systemic* corticosteroids, as defined in *Immunosupression* below.
  - **Chronic heart disease** (including those requiring regular medication and/or follow-up for ischaemic heart disease, congenital heart disease, hypertensive heart disease [excluding uncomplicated, controlled hypertension], and chronic heart failure).
  - **Chronic renal disease** (including nephrotic syndrome, or chronic renal failure, or renal transplantation).
  - **Chronic liver disease** (including cirrhosis).
  - **Diabetes mellitus** (requiring insulin or oral hypoglycaemic drugs).
  - **Immunosuppression due to disease or treatment** (including asplenia or splenic dysfunction; and also including those on or likely to be on systemic corticosteroids for more than a month at a dose equivalent to prednisolone 20 mg or more per day [any age] or, for children under 20 kg, a dose of 1 mg or more per kilogram bodyweight per day). Note: the antibody response may not be as good in people who are immunosuppressed. Seek specialist advice if this is of particular concern.
  - **HIV infection** (at all stages).
  - **Those with cochlear implants.**
  - **Those with CSF shunts.**
  - **Children under 5 years of age who have previously had invasive pneumococcal disease** (e.g. pneumococcal meningitis or pneumococcal bacteraemia).

[CMO, 2005]

Which vaccine should I use?

- **Pneumococcal polysaccharide vaccine (Pneumovax II®) is the vaccine routinely used.** However, children under 2 years of age show little antibody response to immunization with this vaccine.
- **Pneumococcal conjugate vaccine (Prevenar®) should only be used for children under 5 years of age in the high-risk groups** listed above.
- Children who have previously received the conjugate vaccine should also receive the polysaccharide vaccine after the age of 2 years. (The polysaccharide vaccine protects against more types of *Streptococcus pneumoniae* than the conjugate vaccine.)

Supporting evidence

- **Pneumococcal polysaccharide vaccine:** current evidence suggests that immunization with this vaccine probably prevents 50–70% of cases of pneumococcal bacteraemia [DH, 2004]. There is conflicting evidence regarding its efficacy in protecting against non-bacteraemic pneumococcal pneumonia [Jackson, 2003; Christenson et al, 2004]. The polysaccharide vaccine is less effective in those with immunosuppression and in children under 2 years of age. Since pneumococcal meningitis is most common in young children, the polysaccharide vaccine has little scope for preventing this disease [DH, 2004].
- **Pneumococcal conjugate vaccine:** efficacy data come from a large randomized study in the United States [Black, 2000]. Children were vaccinated at 2, 4, and 6 months of age, with a further dose at 15 months of age. After the first dose, the vaccine was 94% effective at preventing infection due to one of the seven serotypes of *S pneumoniae* covered by the vaccine. This rose to 97% after the fourth dose. The vaccine protected against meningitis, bacteraemia, pneumonia, and otitis media.

What is the schedule for immunizing high-risk groups?

See Table 1.
[CMO, 2004]

Special groups

- **At-risk children under 5 years of age who** have already received a single dose of the polysaccharide vaccine (Pneumovax II®), should also now receive two doses of the conjugate vaccine (Prevenar®). The Prevenar® doses should be separated by an interval of at least 1 month, and should be started at least 2 months after the last dose Pneumovax II® [CMO, 2004].
- **Asplenic people:** where possible, give the vaccine 4–6 weeks (but at least 2 weeks) before splenectomy. If this is not possible, vaccinate 14 days after recovery from the operation (although it can be given sooner if there are concerns that vaccination might be missed).
- **Patients requiring chemotherapy or radiotherapy:** where possible, give the vaccine 4–6 weeks (but at least 2 weeks) before chemotherapy or radiotherapy is started. If this is not possible, vaccinate 3 months after completion of chemotherapy or radiotherapy.

Can I give pneumococcal vaccine at the same time as other vaccines?

- **Inactivated vaccines** (e.g. pneumococcal vaccines, influenza vaccine, diphtheria, tetanus, pertussis, poliomyelitis, *Haemophilus influenza*, and meningococcal C conjugate vaccine) can be given at the same time as each other. However, they should be given using separate syringes and at different sites. If inactivated vaccines are *not* administered on the same

Table 1.

Age at start	Vaccine	Immunization schedule
5 years onwards	Polysaccharide vaccine (Pneumovax II®)	Single 0.5 ml dose
12 months to 5 years*	Primary series: conjugate vaccine (Prevenar®)	Two doses, each of 0.5 ml, separated by an interval of at least 2 months.
	Booster dose: polysaccharide vaccine (Pneumovax II®)	Once over 2 years of age, give a single 0.5 ml dose (at least 2 months after last injection of Prevenar®).
7 to 11 months*	Primary series: conjugate vaccine (Prevenar®)	Two doses, each of 0.5 ml, separated by an interval of at least 1 month *plus* a third dose after the first birthday
	Booster dose: polysaccharide vaccine (Pneumovax II®)	Once over 2 years of age, give a single 0.5 ml dose (at least 2 months after last injection of Prevenar®).
2 to 6 months*	Primary series: conjugate vaccine (Prevenar®)	Three doses, each of 0.5 ml, separated by an interval of at least 1 month (the first dose is usually given at age 2 months) *plus* a fourth dose after the first birthday
	Booster dose: polysaccharide vaccine (Pneumovax II®)	Once over 2 years of age, give a single 0.5 ml dose (at least 2 months after last injection of Prevenar®).
Under 2 months	Vaccination not recommended	

* Children who have previously received the conjugate vaccine should also receive the polysaccharide vaccine after the age of 2 years. (The polysaccharide vaccine protects against more types of *S pneumoniae* than the conjugate vaccine.)

day, there is no need to observe a specific interval between administering them.

- **Live vaccines** (e.g. MMR, BCG vaccine) can be given at the same time as each other (using separate syringes and at different sites). If live vaccines are *not* administered on the same day, they should be separated from other live vaccines by an interval of at least 3 weeks. However, no interval need be observed between the administration of live vaccines and inactivated vaccines (e.g. pneumococcal vaccines).

[DH, 1996]

Should pneumococcal vaccine be re-administered?

- **Revaccination is not routinely recommended.** A single dose of pneumococcal polysaccharide vaccine provides sufficient cover for most people.
- Revaccination less than 3 years after the first injection can produce severe local reactions in some people [BNF 46, 2003]. In general, adverse reactions are more common in people with higher concentrations of antibodies to pneumococcal polysaccharides.
- **Revaccination every 5 years is recommended for individuals in whom antibodies are likely to have declined more rapidly,** for example, those with:
  - No spleen
  - Splenic dysfunction
  - Nephrotic syndrome
- Antibody concentration may decline more rapidly in children, and revaccination after 3 years may be considered for children under 10 years of age [BNF 46, 2003]. People who are immunosuppressed may have a smaller antibody response to vaccination, also resulting in lower antibody concentrations.
- If there is doubt, the need for revaccination should be discussed with a haematologist, immunologist, or microbiologist, and measurement of antibody concentration considered [BNF 46, 2003].

Vaccination procedures

Record taking

- **Obtain written or verbal consent** at the time of vaccination. Adults (aged over 18 years) must consent to their own treatment. For children, consent should be sought from the parent or person with parental responsibility. Ensure that the individual (or the parents) feel that their questions have been adequately answered, and that their concerns about vaccination have been considered.
- **Establish suitability for immunization.** If the individual's fitness and suitability cannot be established, vaccination should be delayed. See *Suitability for vaccination* for further information.
- **Check** the identity of the vaccine, usage instructions, and its expiry date.
- **Record** the date of immunization, title of vaccine, and batch number on the recipient's record. If two vaccines are given simultaneously, the relevant sites should be recorded to allow any reactions to be related to the causative vaccine.

Storage and reconstitution of vaccines

- **Store vaccines and diluents at 2–8°C, protected from light** in a designated refrigerator. Vaccine (including diluent) that has been frozen or has thawed should not be used. Freeze-dried vaccines must be stored in the dry state. A maximum–minimum thermometer should be used to check that the temperature has not gone out of the intended range.
- **Both types of pneumococcal vaccine are supplied ready for use;** no dilution or reconstitution is needed.
- **Check for the absence of suspended particles or changes in colour** before using either vaccine (see the manufacturer's leaflet). Do not use if particles or colour changes are observed.

Administration of vaccines

- **Swab the skin with alcohol** if the skin is dirty, but allow it to evaporate before injecting. Live vaccines can be destroyed by coming into contact with alcohol.
- **Use the appropriate route of injection.**
  - Pneumococcal polysaccharide vaccine (Pneumovax II®) can be given by subcutaneous or intramuscular injection.
  - Pneumococcal conjugate vaccine (Prevenar®) should be given by intramuscular injection.
- **Use an appropriate site for injecting.**
  - In infants, use the antero-lateral aspect of the thigh.
  - In older children and adults, use the deltoid muscle. (If the buttock is used, injection into the upper, outer quadrant minimizes the possibility of damage to the sciatic nerve.)

- **Ensure the correct needle is used.** A 25G needle is suitable for deep subcutaneous or intramuscular injections in infants. A 23G needle is appropriate for deep subcutaneous or intramuscular injections in older children and adults.
- **If more than one vaccine is being given,** use different syringes/needles and inject into different sites.
- **Ask the person to wait after immunization** to ensure that they are not experiencing an immediate adverse reaction (e.g. for 10 minutes). Anaphylaxis is rare, and typically occurs within minutes. However, the time of onset may be variable because of delayed absorption from an intramuscular injection (e.g. within 72 hours of immunization).
- **People should also be advised:**
  - To seek urgent medical advice if their child develops early symptoms such as breathlessness, swelling of the mouth and throat, or rash within the following 72 hours.
  - To give a dose of paracetamol or ibuprofen if a child develops a fever after immunization, and keep them cool by removing excessive clothing and bedding. If fever persists after a second dose, they should seek medical advice.

[DH, 1996; ABPI Medicines Compendium, 2002; ABPI Medicines Compendium, 2003; DH, 2004]

Suitability for vaccination

Contraindications to vaccination

- **Anaphylaxis:** vaccines should not be given to those who have had a confirmed anaphylactic reaction within 72 hours of a previous dose of the same vaccine. In addition, pneumococcal conjugate vaccine (Prevenar®) should not be given if there is a confirmed anaphylactic reaction to diphtheria toxoid. (The carrier protein in the conjugate vaccine is derived from diphtheria toxoid, so there may be cross-reactivity.)
- **Other severe adverse reactions.** (Severe in this context means an extensive area of redness and swelling affecting large areas of the arm, leg, or other injection site, or a fever equal to or in excess of 39.5°C within 48 hours of injection):
  - Do not give vaccine if there is a definite history of a *severe* reaction to a previous dose.
  - Do not give pneumococcal conjugate vaccine (Prevenar®) if there is a definite history of a *severe* reaction to a previous dose of diphtheria-containing vaccine.

[DH, 1996; ABPI Medicines Compendium, 2003; DH, 2004]

Reasons to delay vaccination

Where there is doubt, seek appropriate advice from a consultant paediatrician, District Immunization Coordinator, or Consultant in Communicable Disease Control, rather than withholding vaccine.

- **Acute illness:** if a child is suffering from any acute illness, postpone immunization until the child has fully recovered. Minor infections without fever or systemic upset are not reasons to postpone immunization.
- **Pregnancy:** inactivated vaccines such as pneumococcal conjugate vaccine and pneumococcal polysaccharide vaccine are probably safe in pregnancy (the risks to the fetus are likely to be negligible), but use only if a clear indication exists and the benefits clearly outweigh the risks.

[DH, 1996; DH, 2004]

Can a child with a personal or close family history of febrile seizures be vaccinated?

- Febrile seizures are rare following immunization. When there is a personal or family history of febrile seizures, there is an increased risk of these occurring after any fever, including that caused by immunization.
- **Personal history of febrile seizures:** immunization should be carried out after advice on the prevention of pyrexia has been given (provided there was complete recovery after the previous febrile seizure). The aim of controlling fever is to ease symptoms; it does not prevent febrile seizures. If there is uncertainty, seek specialist paediatric advice rather than refuse immunization.
- **Close family history of febrile seizures** (e.g. in parents or siblings): give advice about post-immunization pyrexia before administering the vaccine.

[DH, 1996]

NOT contraindications to vaccination

- A personal or family history of allergy, asthma, eczema, hay fever, or 'snuffles'.
- Prematurity: immunization should not be postponed.
- Stable neurological conditions such as cerebral palsy and Down's syndrome.
- Contact with an infectious disease.
- Treatment with antibiotics or local corticosteroids (e.g. topical or inhaled).
- The child to be immunized is being breastfed or their mother is pregnant.
- History of jaundice after birth.
- Under a certain weight.
- Taking 'replacement' corticosteroids.
- Close family history of febrile convulsions (e.g. in parents or siblings) — give advice about post-immunization pyrexia before administering the vaccine.

[DH, 1996]

I

References

NHS staff in England can link, free of charge, from references to full text journals by clicking on [Full text] on the PRODIGY website.

1. ABPI Medicines Compendium (2002) *Summaries of product characteristics for Pneumovax II*. Electronic Medicines Compendium. Datapharm Communications Ltd.. www.emc.medicines.org.uk [Accessed: 01/02/2004].
2. ABPI Medicines Compendium (2003) *Summary of product characteristics for Prevenar*. Electronic Medicines Compendium. Datapharm Communications Ltd.. www.emc.medicines.org.uk [Accessed: 01/02/2004].
3. Black, S. (2000) Efficacy, safety, and immunogenicity of heptavalent pneumococcal vaccine in older adults. *Pediatric Infectious Disease Journal* 19(3), 187–195.
4. BNF 46 (2003) *British National Formulary*. 46th edn. London: British Medical Association and Royal Pharmaceutical Society of Great Britain.
5. CDR (2003) Invasive pneumonococcal infection. *Communicable Disease Report*(13), 21.
6. CDSC (2002) *Streptococcus pneumoniae*. Communicable Disease Surveillance Centre.
7. Christenson, B., Hedlund, J., Lundbergh, P. and Ortqvist, A. (2004) Additive preventive effect of influenza and pneumococcal vaccines in elderly persons. *European Respiratory Journal* 23(3), 363–368.
8. CMO (2004) *Update on the influenza and pneumococcal immunisation programmes*. PL/CMO/

2004/4. Department of Health. www.dh.gov.uk [Accessed: 11/08/2004]. [Full text]
9. CMO (2005) *The pneumococcal immunisation programme for older people and risk groups.* Department of Health. www.dh.gov.uk [Accessed: 04/10/2005].
10. DH (1996) *Immunisation against infectious disease.* Department of Health. www.dh.gov.uk [Accessed: 18/05/2004]. [Full text]
11. DH (2004) *New (September 2004) chapter 25 – pneumococcal.* Immunisation against infectious disease. Department of Health. www.dh.gov.uk [Accessed: 04/07/2005]. [Full text]
12. Jackson, L.A. (2003) Effectiveness of pneumococcal polysaccharide pneumococcal vaccine in older adults. *New England Journal of Medicine* **348**(18), 1747–1755. [Full text]
13. World Health Organization (1999) Pneumococcal vaccines. *WHO Position Papers* **74**(23), 177–183.

PRODIGY GUIDANCE

Immunizations — travel vaccinations

Last revised in July 2005
www.prodigy.nhs.uk/guidance.asp?gt=Immunization - travel

Applies to people of all ages

This guidance is based on the Department of Health publication *Immunisation against Infectious Disease*, commonly referred to as the 'green book', and its accompanying supplement, *Health Information for Overseas Travel*, also commonly known as the 'yellow book'. The current version of the green book can be found at www.dh.gov.uk, and the yellow book can be found at www.the-stationery-office.co.uk/doh/hinfo/index.htm.

This guidance covers the use of vaccinations required or recommended for travel overseas. The following vaccinations are covered: typhoid fever, tetanus, hepatitis A, yellow fever, meningococcal meningitis, poliomyelitis, rabies, Japanese encephalitis, tick-borne encephalitis, and cholera.

This guidance does not cover other vaccinations available on the childhood vaccination programme, or occupational vaccinations, such as hepatitis B. This guidance does not give advice on the management of anaphylaxis following vaccination.

There is separate PRODIGY guidance for *Malaria prophylaxis*, *Immunizations — childhood vaccination programme*, and *Immunizations — pneumococcal vaccine*.

Goals

- To provide advice on the dangers of infectious diseases abroad
- To ensure standard childhood vaccinations are up-to-date and provide general vaccination cover
- To provide specific vaccinations for people travelling to endemic areas or engaging in particularly high-risk work overseas

Contents

Scenarios

- Typhoid fever immunization p.1053
- Tetanus immunization p.1054
- Hepatitis A immunization p.1055
- Yellow fever immunization p.1056
- Meningococcal meningitis immunization p.1057
- Poliomyelitis immunization p.1058
- Rabies immunization p.1059
- Japanese encephalitis immunization p.1060
- Tick-borne encephalitis immunization p.1061

Extended Information, p. 1062

Which scenario?

- **Typhoid fever immunization:** covers advice for people travelling to areas endemic with typhoid fever.
- **Tetanus immunization:** covers advice for people travelling to areas with poor healthcare provision where post-exposure treatment might be unavailable or difficult to obtain.
- **Hepatitis A immunization:** covers advice for people travelling to areas endemic with hepatitis A.
- **Yellow fever immunization:** covers advice for people travelling to areas endemic with yellow fever (Africa and South America), and details of where to find yellow fever vaccination centres.
- **Meningococcal meningitis immunization:** covers advice for people travelling to areas endemic with meningococcal group A strain, as well as Muslims undergoing the Hajj (annual pilgrimage to Mecca).
- **Poliomyelitis immunization:** covers advice for people who are not immunized against poliomyelitis and are travelling to endemic areas.
- **Rabies immunization:** covers advice for people whose travel puts them at risk of exposure to rabies.
- **Japanese encephalitis immunization:** covers advice for people travelling to areas endemic with Japanese encephalitis.
- **Tick-borne encephalitis immunization:** covers advice for people travelling to areas endemic with tick-borne encephalitis.

Typhoid fever immunization

Which therapy?

- **Travellers are advised to undergo vaccination against typhoid fever if they are travelling to areas with poor sanitation and hygiene.** Africa, Asia, Central and South America, and the Caribbean are the worst affected areas.
- **Vaccination is probably unnecessary for short stays (1–2 weeks) in good accommodation** (including most 'package holidays').
- **There are two inactive vaccines available:** a capsular polysaccharide typhoid vaccine and a combined vaccine for hepatitis A and typhoid fever. Children under the age of 18 months to 2 years may show a suboptimal response to typhoid vaccination.
- **Vaccination for typhoid fever should be carried out 2 weeks before travel** to allow immunity to develop.
- **Typhoid vaccination gives protection for 3 years** before another dose is required. The combined vaccine also gives protection against hepatitis A for 1 year.
- **Typhoid vaccination is not 100% effective.**
- **Advise people to** observe scrupulous water, food, and personal hygiene even if they are vaccinated.
- **Obtain consent and check suitability for immunization.** See *Suitability for vaccination* for further information.

Practical prescribing points

For further information please see the *Medicines Compendium* (www.medicines.org.uk) or the *British National Formulary* (www.bnf.org).

- Give inactivated typhoid vaccine by intramuscular injection. In infants, use the antero-lateral aspects of the thigh and use a 25G needle. In older children and adults, use the deltoid muscle and a 23G needle.
- **Delay vaccination during an acute febrile illness.** Wait until symptoms have resolved before vaccinating.

- **If more than one vaccine is being given,** use different needles/syringes and inject into different sites.
- **Advise people to seek urgent medical advice if** they develop breathlessness, swelling of the mouth or throat, or a rash within a few days of immunization.
- **Advise parents** to give a dose of paracetamol or ibuprofen if a child develops a fever, and keep the child cool (remove excess clothing or bedding). If a fever persists after a second dose, they should seek medical advice.

Follow-up advice

- **Immunization with typhoid fever vaccination gives protection for 3 years.** If the person is at continued risk of contracting the illness after this time, advise a follow-up appointment where a reinforcing dose can be given.

Patient information leaflets

The following PILs are available at www.prodigy.nhs.uk
- Travel Advice Unit, Consular Directorate, Foreign & Commonwealth Office
- TravelHealth.co.uk
- Typhoid Immunisation

Shared decision making

- **You may need typhoid immunization** if you go to an 'at risk' country, particularly where sanitation is poor. You may not need it for short stays in good accommodation. To be immunized, you need:
  - One injection (ideally at least 2 weeks before travel).
  - A booster every 3 years if you remain at risk.
- **An option** is a combined injection against typhoid and hepatitis A if you require both.
- **Tell us before these injections if you:**
  - Are pregnant.
  - Had a reaction to typhoid vaccine in the past.
- **Immunization is only one aspect of travel health.** Get the free booklet *Health Advice for Travellers* from a main post office.

Drug rationale

- **An *inactivated* vaccine, Vi polysaccharide typhoid vaccine, is included.** It is taken as an intramuscular injection at least 2 weeks before travel, and confers immunity for 3 years. It has a good safety profile and is essential in areas that are endemic with typhoid fever [BNF 46, 2003]. Typhim Vi® is licensed for use in all ages, although children under 18 months of age may show a suboptimal response. Typherix® is licensed for adults and children over 2 years of age. It can be used for children under 2 years of age, but this is an off-licence use.
- **A combined vaccine giving immunity against hepatitis A and typhoid fever is included.** It is taken as a single intramuscular injection and confers immunity against hepatitis A and typhoid for 1 and 3 years respectively. It has a good safety profile and is useful in areas that are endemic with both hepatitis A and typhoid fever [BNF 46, 2003].

Table 1: Recommended five-dose immunization schedule for tetanus.

Schedule	Children under the age of 10 years	Adults and children over 10 years
Primary course	3 doses of vaccine (usually as DTaP/IPV/Hib) at 2, 3, and 4 months of age*	3 doses of vaccine (as Td/IPV), each one month apart*
Fourth dose	At least 3 years after the last dose of the primary course, usually pre-school entry (as dTaP/IPV or DTaP/IPV)	5–10 years after the last dose of the primary course (as Td/IPV)
Fifth dose	Aged 13–18 years or before leaving school (as Td/IPV)	10 years after fourth dose (as Td/IPV)

* If the full primary course cannot be completed before departure, complete the course on return.
DTaP/IPV/Hib = Diphtheria, tetanus, acellular pertussis, inactivated poliomyelitis, and *Haemophilus influenzae* type b vaccine (Pediacel®)
dTaP/IPV = Low-dose diphtheria, tetanus, acellular pertussis, and inactivated poliomyelitis vaccine (Repevax®)
DTaP/IPV = Diphtheria, tetanus, acellular pertussis, and inactivated poliomyelitis vaccine (Infanrix IPV®)
Td/IPV = Low-dose diphtheria, tetanus, and inactivated poliomyelitis vaccine for adults and children over 10 years of age (Revaxis®)

Prescriptions

Single component typhoid fever vaccine (inactivated)

Vi polysaccharide typhoid vaccine (Typhim Vi)
- Age from 2 months onwards
- Typhim Vi vaccine. Give 0.5ml by intramuscular injection; supply 1 0.5ml prefilled syringe; NHS Cost £9.49.

Vi polysaccharide typhoid vaccine (Typherix)
- Age from 2 months onwards
- Typherix vaccine. Give 0.5ml by intramuscular injection; supply 1 0.5ml prefilled syringe; NHS Cost £9.93.

Combined typhoid fever and hepatitis A vaccine (inactivated)

Hepatitis A+typhoid vaccine (Hepatyrix)
- Age from 15 years onwards
- Hepatyrix vaccine. Give 1ml by intramuscular injection; supply 1 1ml prefilled syringe; NHS Cost £34.49.

Hepatitis A+typhoid vaccine (ViATIM)
- Age from 16 years onwards
- ViATIM vaccine. Give 1ml by intramuscular injection; supply 1 1ml prefilled syringe; NHS Cost £32.49.

Tetanus immunization

Which therapy

- **Check that ALL people are up-to-date with the recommended five-dose schedule for tetanus immunization,** regardless of travel arrangements.
  - People who have not been vaccinated require a primary course of tetanus vaccine.
  - People who have not received adequate reinforcing doses require a booster dose.
  - A booster is not routinely needed if they are up-to-date with the recommended five-dose schedule (e.g. adults have received 5 doses at appropriate intervals).
- **ALL people travelling to countries where tetanus immunoglobulin may not be available require a booster dose of tetanus, regardless of immunization status** (i.e. even if they have previously had five doses).
- **Obtain consent and check suitability for immunization.** See *Suitability for vaccination* for further information.

Practical prescribing points

For further information please see the *Medicines Compendium* (www.medicines.org.uk) or the *British National Formulary* (www.bnf.org).
- Give tetanus-containing vaccines by intramuscular injection. In infants, use the antero-lateral aspects of the thigh and use a 25G needle. In older children and adults, use the deltoid muscle and a 23G needle.

- **Delay vaccination during an acute febrile illness.** Wait until symptoms have resolved before vaccinating.
- **If more than one vaccine is being given,** use different needles/syringes and inject into different sites.
- **Advise people to seek urgent medical advice if** they develop breathlessness, swelling of the mouth or throat, or a rash within a few days of immunization.
- **Advise parents** to give a dose of paracetamol or ibuprofen if a child develops a fever, and keep the child cool (remove excess clothing or bedding). If a fever persists after a second dose, they should seek medical advice.

Follow-up advice

- **Primary immunization** requires three doses of tetanus-containing vaccine spaced 4 weeks apart. Schedule appointments accordingly.
- Full, permanent protection is achieved once the recommended five dose schedule has been completed (i.e. a primary course and two further booster doses 10 years apart).

Patient information leaflets

The following PILs are available at www.prodigy.nhs.uk

- Tetanus Immunisation
- Travel Advice Unit, Consular Directorate, Foreign & Commonwealth Office
- TravelHealth.co.uk

Shared decision making

- **You should be up-to-date with tetanus immunization** if you go abroad. Most people are immunized as children, but some older adults are not. Fully immunized against tetanus means:
  - A primary course of three doses, 4 weeks apart.
  - Two further booster doses. These are given at 10 year intervals in adults.
- **Tell us before these injections if you:**
  - Are pregnant.
  - Had a reaction to tetanus vaccine in the past.
- **Immunization is only one aspect of travel health.** Get the free booklet *Health Advice for Travellers* from a main post office.

Drug rationale

Drugs not included

- **The adsorbed tetanus and diphtheria (low-dose) vaccine (Td) is not included.** It has been superseded by combined tetanus, low-dose diphtheria, and inactivated poliomyelitis vaccine.

Drugs included

- **Revaxis® vaccine** (Td/IPV), which contains diphtheria (low dose), tetanus, and inactivated poliomyelitis, is offered for adults and children over 10 years of age for primary immunization and for booster doses.
- **Pediacel® vaccine (DTaP/IPV/Hib),** which contains diphtheria, tetanus, aceullular pertussis, inactivated poliomyelitis, and *Haemophilus influenzae* type b, is recommended for primary immunizations in all children under 10 years of age.
- **Repevax® vaccine (dTaP/IPV) or Infanrix IPV® vaccine (DTaP/IPV),** which contains diphtheria, tetanus, aceullular pertussis, and inactivated poliomyelitis, is recommended for booster doses for children under 10 years of age.

[DH, 1996; DH, 2001; BNF 46, 2003]

Prescriptions

Tetanus-containing vaccines (inactivated)

Primary course: diphtheria+tetanus+pertussis+polio+Hib

- Age from 2 months to 9 years
- Pediacel injection. Give 0.5ml by intramuscular injection. For primary immunization, give three doses at intervals of 1 month between doses; supply 1 0.5ml vial.

Booster: low-dose diphtheria+tetanus+pertussis+polio

- Age from 3 to 9 years
- Repevax injection. Give 0.5ml by intramuscular injection; supply 1 0.5ml prefilled syringe.

Primary course: low-dose diphtheria+tetanus+polio

- Age from 10 years onwards
- Revaxis injection. Give 0.5ml by intramuscular injection. For primary immunization, give three doses at intervals of 1 month between doses; supply 1 0.5ml prefilled syringe.

Booster: low-dose diphtheria+tetanus+polio

- Age from 10 years onwards
- Revaxis injection. Give 0.5ml by intramuscular injection; supply 1 0.5ml prefilled syringe.

Hepatitis A immunization

Which therapy

- **People travelling *outside* the Western world are at increased risk of contracting hepatitis A** (i.e. in places other than Western Europe, North America, Australia, and New Zealand).
- **Consider vaccinating ALL people travelling to high-risk areas,** irrespective of the duration of travel.
- **Consider testing for hepatitis A antibodies** (to assess immunization status) in:
  - People 50 years of age and older.
  - People who were born or have lived in areas of high endemicity.
  - People with a history of jaundice.
- **The primary immunization** consists of a single dose of *inactivated* hepatitis A vaccine. Coverage lasts for about one year.
- **A booster dose** 6–12 months later gives protection for up to 10 years.
- **A combined vaccine for hepatitis A and typhoid fever is also available,** and may be useful for people requiring simultaneous coverage of both illnesses, especially since they are frequently endemic in the same areas. Both components are *inactive*. The hepatitis A component gives protection for one year and the typhoid component gives immunity for 3 years.
- **Obtain consent and check suitability for immunization.** See *Suitability for vaccination* for further information.

Practical prescribing points

For further information please see the *Medicines Compendium* (www.medicines.org.uk) or the *British National Formulary* (www.bnf.org).

- Give hepatitis A vaccine by intramuscular injection. In children and adults, use the deltoid muscle and a 23G needle.
- **Delay vaccination during an acute febrile illness.** Wait until symptoms have resolved before vaccinating.

- **If more than one vaccine is being given, use different needles/syringes and inject into different sites.**
- **Advise people to seek urgent medical advice** if they develop breathlessness, swelling of the mouth or throat, or a rash within a few days of immunization.
- **Advise parents** to give a dose of paracetamol or ibuprofen if a child develops a fever, and keep the child cool (remove excess clothing or bedding). If a fever persists after a second dose, they should seek medical advice.

Follow-up advice

- **Immunization with hepatitis A vaccine gives immunity for one year.** A reinforcing dose can be given after 6–12 months that will extend immunity to 10 years.

Patient information leaflets

The following PILs are available at www.prodigy.nhs.uk

- Hepatitis A
- Hepatitis A Immunisation
- Immunisation - UK Schedule/ General
- Travel Advice Unit, Consular Directorate, Foreign & Commonwealth Office
- TravelHealth.co.uk

Shared decision making

- **Hepatitis A immunization** is advised if you are travelling to a high-risk area, and especially if you are travelling to:
  - High-risk areas often.
  - A high risk area for 3 or more months.
  - A high-risk area for any length of time and have chronic liver disease.
- **One injection protects for 1 year.** A booster 6–12 months later protects for up to 10 years.
- **An option is a combined injection** against hepatitis A and typhoid and if you require both.
- **Tell us before these injections if you:**
  - Are pregnant.
  - Had a reaction to hepatitis vaccine in the past.
- **Side-effects?** The injection site may be sore for a few days. You may feel sick, have a mild fever, or headache for a day or so. Severe reactions are rare.
- **Immunization is only one aspect of travel health.** Get the free booklet *Health Advice for Travellers* from a main post office.

Drug rationale

Drugs not included

- **Human normal immunoglobulin** (HNIG) is not offered. Immunity conferred against hepatitis A by HNIG is short-lived (typically lasting 3 months), and it may interfere with the immunization process of other vaccines and affect antibody assays. However, HNIG has a role in protecting immunosuppressed people who may not become sufficiently immunized with the vaccine alone, and for giving immediate protection during outbreaks of the virus [DH, 1996; BNF 46, 2003].

Drugs included

- **Single-dose hepatitis A vaccine is included.** It is safe and effective. Hepatitis A vaccine is *inactive* and is given as a single intramuscular injection. It confers immunity for one year, and a reinforcing dose can be given after 6–12 months that extends immunity up to 10 years.
- **A combined vaccine giving immunity against hepatitis A and typhoid fever is offered.** It is taken as a single intramuscular injection and confers immunity against hepatitis A and typhoid for 1 and 3 years respectively. It has a good safety profile and is useful in areas that are endemic with both hepatitis A and typhoid fever.

[DH, 1996; BNF 46, 2003]

Prescriptions

Adults: single component hepatitis A vaccine (inactivated)

Hepatitis A vaccine (Avaxim)
- Age from 16 years onwards
- Avaxim vaccine. Give 0.5ml by intramuscular injection; supply 1 0.5ml prefilled syringe; NHS Cost £20.63.

Hepatitis A vaccine (Epaxal)
- Age from 16 years onwards
- Epaxal vaccine. Give 0.5ml by intramuscular injection; supply 1 0.5ml prefilled syringe; NHS Cost £23.81.

Hepatitis A vaccine (Havrix Monodose)
- Age from 16 years onwards
- Havrix Monodose. Give 1ml by intramuscular injection; supply 1 1ml prefilled syringe; NHS Cost £23.81.

Children: single component hepatitis A vaccine (inactivated)

Hepatitis A vaccine (Epaxal)
- Age from 12 months to 15 years
- Epaxal vaccine. Give 0.5ml by intramuscular injection; supply 1 0.5ml prefilled syringe; NHS Cost £23.81.

Hepatitis A vaccine (Havrix Junior Monodose)
- Age from 12 months to 15 years
- Havrix Junior Monodose. Give 0.5ml by intramuscular injection; supply 1 0.5ml prefilled syringe; NHS Cost £18.03.

Hepatitis A vaccine (Vaqta Paediatric)
- Age from 2 to 17 years
- Vaqta Paediatric vaccine. Give 0.5ml by intramuscular injection; supply 1 0.5ml vial; NHS Cost £15.65.

Combined typhoid fever and hepatitis A vaccine (inactivated)

Hepatitis A+typhoid vaccine (Hepatyrix)
- Age from 15 years onwards
- Hepatyrix vaccine. Give 1ml by intramuscular injection; supply 1 1ml prefilled syringe; NHS Cost £34.49.

Hepatitis A+typhoid vaccine (ViATIM)
- Age from 16 years onwards
- ViATIM vaccine. Give 1ml by intramuscular injection; supply 1 1ml prefilled syringe; NHS Cost £32.49.

Yellow fever immunization

Which therapy

- **Yellow fever is endemic in tropical South America and sub-Saharan Africa.**
- **Travellers to affected countries MUST be vaccinated against the illness:**
  - **It is a serious disease,** is frequently fatal, and there is no cure.
  - **Many countries require an International Certificate of Vaccination** as proof of immunity from the disease.
  - If the vaccination is contraindicated in the traveller, a medical letter of exemption signed by a medical practitioner should be obtained.
- **Yellow fever vaccine can only be administered at** specialist centres designated by the national health administration and recorded with the World Health

Organization. A list of the nearest available centres can be found at www.nathnac.org.

Yellow fever immunization is by *live* vaccine and confers immunity for 10 years. After this a reinforcing dose is required for re-certification.

Travellers to endemic regions are also advised to use standard precautions to prevent mosquito bites.

Obtain consent and check suitability for immunization. See *Suitability for vaccination* for further information.

Advise people that yellow fever vaccine is **not** routinely available on the NHS for overseas travel. Payment is at the discretion of the specialist centre.

Practical prescribing points

For further information please see the *Medicines Compendium* (www.medicines.org.uk) or the *British National Formulary* (www.bnf.org).

Follow-up advice

Yellow fever immunization lasts for 10 years, after which a reinforcing dose is required for full immunity and re-certification.

Should I refer or investigate?

Refer?

Yellow fever vaccine can only be administered at specialist centres designated by the national health administration and recorded with the World Health Organization. A list of the nearest available centres can be found at www.nathnac.org.

Patient information leaflets

The following PILs are available at www.prodigy.nhs.uk

Travel Advice Unit, Consular Directorate, Foreign & Commonwealth Office

TravelHealth.co.uk

Yellow Fever Immunisation

Shared decision making

A certificate of immunization against yellow fever is compulsory for entry to some countries:

- One injection protects for 10 years. Have this at least 10 days before travel.
- Have a booster every 10 years if you are still at risk.

Tell us before having the injection if you:

- Are pregnant.
- Had a severe reaction to yellow fever vaccine in the past.
- Have a poor immune system (on chemotherapy, take steroids, have HIV, etc).

Side-effects? About 1 in 20 people have headache, aches, mild fever, or soreness at the injection site. These may develop several days after the injection but soon pass. Severe reactions are rare.

Immunization is only one aspect of travel health. For example, protect yourself from mosquito bites. Get the free booklet *Health Advice for Travellers* from a main post office.

Drug rationale

No vaccines are included. The yellow fever vaccine is only available at designated centres.

Meningococcal meningitis immunization

Which therapy

- **Consider immunizing people if they are travelling to areas where meningococcal group A is prevalent.** This includes areas of sub-Saharan Africa, the Middle East, and the Indian subcontinent.
- **The following people should be vaccinated:**
  - People staying for extended time periods, such as one month or more in a high-risk area.
  - People engaging in high-risk holidays or work, such as backpacking or living in rural communities in a high-risk area.
  - People attending the Hajj (Mecca) and Umrah pilgrames in Saudi Arabia.
  - Seasonal workers to the Hajj area.
- **A quadrivalent vaccine, ACWY Vax®,** is presently the only vaccine recommended for travellers.
  - It provides protection against A, C, W135, and Y strains of the infection.
  - Children under the age of 2 years may show a suboptimal response to the vaccine (off-licence use).
- **Vaccination for meningococcal meningitis should be carried out 2–3 weeks before travel** to allow immunity to develop.
- **Saudi Arabia now requires proof of vaccination** with ACWY Vax® for visitors arriving for the Hajj and Umrah pilgrimages, or for seasonal working in the Hajj areas.
- **A booster dose** may be given after 5 years if continued immunity is needed.
- Immunity lasts for a shorter period in children under 5 (especially those under 2 years). Consider giving a booster after 2–3 years.
- **Obtain consent and check suitability for immunization.** See *Suitability for vaccination* for further information.
- **Advise people that** meningococcal meningitis vaccine is **not routinely available on the NHS for overseas travel. Payment is at the discretion of the practice.**

Practical prescribing points

For further information please see the *Medicines Compendium* (www.medicines.org.uk) or the *British National Formulary* (www.bnf.org).

- Give ACWY Vax® vaccine by deep subcutaneous injection. In infants, use the antero-lateral aspects of the thigh and use a 25G needle. In older children and adults, use the antero-lateral aspect of the thigh, the upper arm or buttocks, and use a 23G needle.
- **Delay vaccination during an acute febrile illness.** Wait until symptoms have resolved before vaccinating.
- **If more than one vaccine is being given,** use different needles/syringes and inject into different sites.
- **Advise people to seek urgent medical advice** if they develop breathlessness, swelling of the mouth or throat, or a rash within a few days of immunization.
- **Advise parents** to give a dose of paracetamol or ibuprofen if a child develops a fever, and keep the child cool (remove excess clothing or bedding). If a fever persists after a second dose, they should seek medical advice.

Follow-up advice

- **Immunization lasts for about 5 years,** after which a reinforcing dose is necessary, although this interval may be shorter in children. A reinforcing dose after this time

is necessary as a visa requirement for Muslims undergoing the Hajj for a repeat time.
- Immunity lasts for a shorter period in children under 5 (especially those under 2 years). Consider giving a booster after 2–3 years for this age group.

Patient information leaflets

The following PILs are available at www.prodigy.nhs.uk
- Immunisation - UK Schedule/ General
- Meningococcal group C Immunisation
- Meningococcal Immunisation
- Travel Advice Unit, Consular Directorate, Foreign & Commonwealth Office
- TravelHealth.co.uk

Shared decision making

- **You should be immunized against the meningococcus** if you travel to 'at risk' areas, particularly if your stay is for a month or more.
- **One injection protects for 5 years.** Have a booster after 5 years if you are still at risk.
- **Muslims undergoing the Hajj** (pilgrimage to Mecca) need a certificate of this immunization to get a visa to go to Saudi Arabia.
- **Tell us before having the injection if you:**
  - Are pregnant.
  - Had a severe reaction to meningococcal vaccine in the past.
- **Side-effects?** Pain and redness occur at the injection site in about 1 in 10 people and last 1–2 days. A mild fever sometimes occurs. Severe reactions are rare.
- **Immunization is only one aspect of travel health.** Get the free booklet *Health Advice for Travellers* from a main post office.

Drug rationale

Drugs not included

- **Meningococcal C conjugate vaccine** (MenC) is not offered. This vaccine is now part of the childhood vaccination programme, but only confers immunity against group C, which is common in the United Kingdom but less prevalent abroad. Children who have received the MenC vaccination are NOT covered for travel to high-risk areas abroad [DH, 1996].
- **Meningococcal plain polysaccharide A&C vaccine is now NOT recommended** for travellers at risk from infection. This follows a recent change in the national guidelines and reflects the growing number of meningococcal infections that are not caused by the A or C strains, particularly the rise in prevalence of W135. The A&C vaccine has consequently been withdrawn and has been unavailable since May 2004 [NaTHNaC, 2003a].

Drugs included

- **The ACWY vax vaccine is offered.** This is an *inactive* quadrivalent vaccine that confers immunity against groups A, C, Y, and W135. This vaccine is necessary for Muslims undergoing the Hajj (pilgrimage to Mecca), as there have been outbreaks of the W135 strain there in recent years [BNF 46, 2003; NaTHNaC, 2004a]. It can be given to children under the age of 2 years, but the antibody response may be suboptimal and it is not licensed for this age group.

Prescriptions

Meningococcal meningitis quadrivalent vaccine (inactivated)

Quadrivalent meningococcal vaccine (ACWY Vax)
- Age from 2 to 23 months
- ACWY Vax injection. Give 0.5ml by deep subcutaneous injection; supply 1 0.5ml vial+diluent;
NHS Cost £17.99.

Quadrivalent meningococcal vaccine (ACWY Vax)
- Age from 2 years onwards
- ACWY Vax injection. Give 0.5ml by deep subcutaneous injection; supply 1 0.5ml vial+diluent;
NHS Cost £17.99.

Poliomyelitis immunization

Which therapy

- **Check that ALL people are up-to-date with the recommended five-dose schedule for poliomyelitis immunization,** regardless of travel arrangements.
- Travellers born before 1958 may not have been immunized.
- **Travellers to polio-endemic regions (e.g. Nigeria, Pakistan, India) are advised to have an additional booster** dose of vaccine if they have not previously had one in the last 10 years, particularly if they are living or working in high-risk conditions (e.g. health workers).
- **Obtain consent and check suitability for immunization.** See *Suitability for vaccination* for further information.

Practical prescribing points

For further information please see the *Medicines Compendium* (www.medicines.org.uk) or the *British National Formulary* (www.bnf.org).
- Give poliomyelitis-containing vaccines by intramuscular injection. In infants, use the antero-lateral aspects of the thigh and use a 25G needle. In older children and adults use the deltoid muscle and a 23G needle.
- **Delay vaccination during an acute febrile illness.** Wait until symptoms have resolved before vaccinating.
- **If more than one vaccine is being given,** use different needles/syringes and inject into different sites.
- **Advise people to seek urgent medical advice if** they develop breathlessness, swelling of the mouth or throat, or a rash within a few days of immunization.

Table 2: Recommended five-dose immunization schedule for poliomyelitis.

Schedule	Children under the age of 10 years	Adults and children over 10 years
Primary course	3 doses of vaccine (usually as DTaP/IPV/Hib) at 2, 3, and 4 months of age*	3 doses of vaccine (as Td/IPV), each one month apart*
Fourth dose	At least 3 years after the last dose of the primary course, usually pre-school entry (as dTaP/IPV or DTaP/IPV)	5–10 years after the last dose of the primary course (as Td/IPV)
Fifth dose	Aged 13–18 years or before leaving school (as Td/IPV)	10 years after fourth dos (as Td/IPV)

* If the full primary course cannot be completed before departure, complete the course on return.
DTaP/IPV/Hib = Diphtheria, tetanus, acellular pertussis, inactivated poliomyelitis, and *Haemophilus influenzae* type b vaccine (Pediacel®)
dTaP/IPV = Low-dose diphtheria, tetanus, acellular pertussis, and inactivated poliomyelitis vaccine (Repevax®)
DTaP/IPV = Diphtheria, tetanus, acellular pertussis, and inactivated poliomyelitis vaccine (Infanrix IPV®)
Td/IPV = Low-dose diphtheria, tetanus, and inactivated poliomyelitis vaccine for adults and children over 10 years of age (Revaxis®)

- **Advise parents** to give a dose of paracetamol or ibuprofen if a child develops a fever, and keep the child cool (remove excess clothing or bedding). If a fever persists after a second dose, they should seek medical advice.

Follow-up advice

- **Primary immunization** requires three doses of Td/IPV vaccine (tetanus, low-dose diphtheria, and inactivated poliomyelitis vaccine) spaced 4 weeks apart. Schedule appointments accordingly.
- Two further booster doses 10 years apart are needed to complete the recommended five-dose schedule.

Patient information leaflets

The following PILs are available at www.prodigy.nhs.uk

- Polio Immunisation
- Travel Advice Unit, Consular Directorate, Foreign & Commonwealth Office
- TravelHealth.co.uk

Shared decision making

- **All people should be immunized against polio.**
  - Many people are fully immunized from childhood immunizations.
  - If you are not fully immunized, you should be:
    - The primary course is three doses, 4 weeks apart.
    - Two booster doses are then given at 10-year intervals.
    - If you have not had a booster within the past 10 years, you should have one before you travel to 'at risk' areas.
- **Immunization is only one aspect of travel health.** Get the free booklet *Health Advice for Travellers* from a main post office.

Drug rationale

Drugs not included

- **Oral poliomyelitis vaccine** (a *live* attenuated vaccine) is now only available for outbreak control.

Drugs included

- **Revaxis® vaccine (Td/IPV),** which contains diphtheria (low dose), tetanus, and inactivated poliomyelitis, is offered for adults and children over 10 years of age for primary immunization and for booster doses.
- **Pediacel® vaccine (DTaP/IPV/Hib),** which contains diphtheria, tetanus, aceullular pertussis, inactivated poliomyelitis, and *Haemophilus influenzae* type b, is recommended for primary immunizations in all children under 10 years of age.
- **Repevax® vaccine (dTaP/IPV) or Infranrix IPV® vaccine (DTaP/IPV),** which contains diphtheria, tetanus, aceullular pertussis, and inactivated poliomyelitis, is recommended for booster doses for children under 10 years of age.

[DH, 1996; DH, 2001]

Prescriptions

Poliomyelitis-containing vaccines (inactivated)

Primary course: diphtheria+tetanus+pertussis+polio+Hib

- Age from 2 months to 9 years
- Pediacel injection. Give 0.5ml by intramuscular injection. For primary immunization, give three doses at intervals of 1 month between doses; supply 1 0.5ml vial.

Booster: low-dose diphtheria+tetanus+pertussis+polio

- Age from 3 to 9 years
- Repevax injection. Give 0.5ml by intramuscular injection; supply 1 0.5ml prefilled syringe.

Primary course: low-dose diphtheria+tetanus+polio

- Age from 10 years onwards
- Revaxis injection. Give 0.5ml by intramuscular injection. For primary immunization, give three doses at intervals of 1 month between doses; supply 1 0.5ml prefilled syringe.

Booster: low-dose diphtheria+tetanus+polio

- Age from 10 years onwards
- Revaxis injection. Give 0.5ml by intramuscular injection; supply 1 0.5ml prefilled syringe.

Rabies immunization

Which therapy

- **Rabies vaccination is not necessary for the average traveller.** Though the disease is endemic worldwide, post-exposure vaccination is available and the risks to the traveller are slight.
- **The following travellers should be offered pre-exposure immunization** (prophylaxis) against rabies:
  - **People travelling in enzootic areas,** where there is an unusually high risk of infection.
  - **People travelling in very remote areas,** where medical care may not be immediately available.
  - **People who are working abroad** with, or in close contact to, animals (e.g. veterinarians, zoologists).
- **Currently there are two rabies vaccines** available in the United Kingdom. Both are inactivated.
- **The recommended schedule** is three doses on days 0, 7, and 28.
- **A booster dose** can be given from 2 years after the primary course was completed. Further doses can be given at 2–3 year intervals if needed.
- **Obtain consent and check suitability for immunization.** See *Suitability for vaccination* for further information.
- **Advise people that** rabies vaccine is **not** routinely available on the NHS for overseas travel except for travellers working overseas whose occupation puts them at high risk of exposure to the virus. Payment is at the discretion of the practice.

Practical prescribing points

For further information please see the *Medicines Compendium* (www.medicines.org.uk) or the *British National Formulary* (www.bnf.org).

- Give rabies vaccine by intramuscular injection. In infants, use the antero-lateral aspects of the thigh and use a 25G needle. In older children and adults, use the deltoid muscle and a 23G needle.
- **Delay vaccination during an acute febrile illness.** Wait until symptoms have resolved before vaccinating.
- **If more than one vaccine is being given,** use different needles/syringes and inject into different sites.
- **Advise people to seek urgent medical advice if** they develop breathlessness, swelling of the mouth or throat, or a rash within a few days of immunization.
- **Advise parents** to give a dose of paracetamol or ibuprofen if a child develops a fever, and keep the child cool (remove excess clothing or bedding). If a fever persists after a second dose, they should seek medical advice.

Follow-up advice

- **Primary immunization** against rabies requires two or three doses of vaccine over one month. Schedule appointments accordingly.
- **A reinforcing dose of rabies vaccine** is required after 2–3 years in people at continued risk of exposure.

Should I refer or investigate?

- A person presenting with a suspicious animal bite contracted from abroad should be immediately referred for post-exposure prophylaxis.

Patient information leaflets

The following PILs are available at www.prodigy.nhs.uk

- Rabies Immunisation
- Travel Advice Unit, Consular Directorate, Foreign & Commonwealth Office
- TravelHealth.co.uk

Shared decision making

- **You should have rabies immunization** if you travel to remote parts of the world where medical treatment might not be available.
- Three doses of vaccine are usually given — the first, then the others 7 and 28 days later.
- Booster doses are needed after 2–3 years if you continue to be at risk.
- **Tell us before you have these injections if you:**
  - Are pregnant.
  - Had a severe reaction to rabies vaccine in the past.
- **Side-effects?** You may get redness and swelling at the injection site for 1–2 days. Severe reactions are rare.
- **Immunization is only one aspect of travel health.** Get the free booklet *Health Advice for Travellers* from a main post office.

Drug rationale

Drugs not included

- **Human rabies-specific immunoglobulin** (HRIG) is not included. It is only indicated as an adjuvant in the post-exposure prophylaxis of rabies when there is a high risk that the virus has been contracted [DH, 1996].

Drugs included

- **Rabies human diploid cell vaccine** (HDCV) is offered for pre-exposure prophylaxis of rabies. It is administered by intramuscular, intradermal (expert use required), or deep subcutaneous injection. It is safe and effective when properly used, and confers protection for 2–3 years. There are two regimens available for primary immunization:
  - **A complete course** consisting of three doses of HDCV given on days 0, 7, and 28, which confers complete immunity.
  - **An alternative course** consisting of two doses 4 weeks apart, which gives 98% immunity.

[DH, 1996; DH, 2001; BNF 46, 2003]

Prescriptions

Rabies vaccine (inactivated)

Primary course: rabies vaccine BP (Aventis Pasteur brand)

- Age from 12 months onwards
- Rabies inactive vaccine. Give 1ml by intramuscular or deep subcutaneous injection. For primary immunization give three doses on days 0, 7, and 28; supply 1 1ml vial; NHS Cost £22.15.

Booster: rabies vaccine BP (Aventis Pasteur brand)

- Age from 3 years onwards
- Rabies inactive vaccine. Give 1ml by intramuscular or deep subcutaneous injection; supply 1 1ml vial; NHS Cost £22.15.

Primary course: Rabipur

- Age from 2 months onwards
- Rabipur vaccine. Give 1ml by intramuscular injection. For primary immunization give three doses on days 0, 7, and 28; supply 1 1ml vial+diluent; NHS Cost £22.15.

Booster: Rabipur

- Age from 2 years onwards
- Rabipur vaccine. Give 1ml by intramuscular injection; supply 1 1ml vial+diluent; NHS Cost £22.15.

Japanese encephalitis immunization

Which therapy

- **People travelling to South-East Asia and the Far East may need to be vaccinated against Japanese encephalitis.** Vaccination is recommended in the following people:
  - People staying for longer periods (i.e. over a month).
  - People travelling in rural areas (especially in areas with rice paddies).
  - People doing extensive outdoor activities in endemic areas.
  - People travelling at the end of the monsoon season (roughly June–September).
- **There are two *inactive* vaccines** (unlicensed and named patient only) currently available for Japanese encephalitis.
- **The recommended schedule for optimum protection is:**
  - **A primary course** of three doses, given on days 0, 7, and 28 (JE-Vax® vaccine only).
  - **A booster dose** can be given every 2–3 years following the third dose if at continued risk.
  - Note: children under 3 years of age should receive half the adult dose.
- **Immunity to Japanese encephalitis takes one month to develop.**
- **Anaphylaxis** is more common with Japanese encephalitis vaccine than other vaccines. People receiving the vaccination should be observed for 30 minutes and be warned of the potential for severe delayed reactions.
- **Regardless of immunization status,** travellers to endemic regions are also advised to use standard precautions to prevent mosquito bites.
- **Obtain consent and check suitability for immunization.** See *Suitability for vaccination* for further information.
- **Advise people that** Japanese encephalitis vaccine is **not** routinely available on the NHS for overseas travel. Payment is at the discretion of the practice.

Practical prescribing points

For further information please see the *Medicines Compendium* (www.medicines.org.uk) or the *British National Formulary* (www.bnf.org).

- Give Japanese encephalitis vaccine by deep subcutaneous injection. In infants, use the antero-lateral aspects of the thigh and use a 25G needle. In older children and adults, use the antero-lateral aspect of the thigh, the upper arm or buttocks, and use a 23G needle.
- **Immunization is not advised in pregnancy or in people with cardiac, renal or hepatic disorders, leukaemia, or lymphoma** because of a lack of data on the vaccine's efficacy and safety in these individuals. Use only if absolutely necessary.
- **Delay vaccination during an acute febrile illness.** Wait until symptoms have resolved before vaccinating.
- **If more than one vaccine is being given,** use different needles/syringes and inject into different sites.
- **Advise people to seek urgent medical advice if** they develop breathlessness, swelling of the mouth or throat, or a rash within a few days of immunization.
- **Advise parents** to give a dose of paracetamol or ibuprofen if a child develops a fever, and keep the child cool (remove excess clothing or bedding). If a fever persists after a second dose, they should seek medical advice.

Follow-up advice

- Japanese encephalitis vaccine is administered as two or three doses over a one-month period. Follow-up appointments should be arranged accordingly.
- The exact interval that the Japanese encephalitis vaccine provides immunity for after primary immunization is unknown, but is likely to be at least 2 years. Therefore, people who are at continued risk of exposure to Japanese encephalitis should have a reinforcing dose after 2 years.

Patient information leaflets

The following PILs are available at www.prodigy.nhs.uk

- Japanese Encephalitis Immunisation
- Travel Advice Unit, Consular Directorate, Foreign & Commonwealth Office
- TravelHealth.co.uk

Shared decision making

- **You should be immunized against Japanese encephalitis** if you stay for a month or longer in 'at risk' areas — or if you have a shorter trip but:
  - Travel in rural areas (especially in areas of rice farming), or
  - Do a lot of outdoor activities, or
  - Travel at the end of the rainy season (roughly June–September)
- Three doses of vaccine are usually given — the first, then the others 7 and 28 days later.
- An alternative is two injections, 7 days apart. But this only gives 80% immunity for a shorter period.
- **Complete the course at least 10–14 days before departure (preferably 1 month before).**
- Have a booster after 3 years if you remain 'at risk'.
- **Tell us before these injections if you:**
  - Are pregnant.
  - Have conditions of the heart, kidney, or liver, or if you have leukaemia or lymphoma.
  - Had a reaction to this vaccine in the past.
- **Side-effects?** An allergic reaction occasionally occurs. This can cause a rash, swelling of the face, and breathing problems. The allergic reaction can occur within minutes, but can be delayed for up to 2 weeks. Severe reactions are rare.
- **Immunization is only one aspect of travel health.** For example, protect yourself from mosquito bites. Get the free booklet *Health Advice for Travellers* from a main post office.

Drug rationale

- **Japanese encephalitis vaccine** is included, as it is the only protection against the disease. It is an inactive vaccine given as a deep subcutaneous injection and confers effective immunity if the schedules are adhered too. However, it takes one month for immunity to develop, and there is also the potential for serious adverse effects during this period [DH, 1996].
- Note: the two vaccines available (JE-Vax® (Biken) or Japanese encephalitis Green Cross brand) are not licensed in the UK and are only available on a named-patient basis. Only JE-Vax® is licensed (in Japan) for the immunization schedule recommended in the UK. [DH, 2001]

Prescriptions

Japanese encephalitis vaccine (inactivated)

Primary course: Japanese encephalitis vaccine

- Age from 3 years onwards
- Japanese encephalitis vaccine. Give 1ml by deep subcutaneous injection. For primary immunization, give three doses on days 0,7, and 28; supply 1 1ml vial.

Primary course: Japanese encephalitis vaccine

- Age from 12 months to 2 years
- Japanese encephalitis vaccine. Give 0.5ml by deep subcutaneous injection. For primary immunization, give three doses on days 0, 7, and 28; supply 1 1ml vial.

Booster: Japanese encephalitis vaccine

- Age from 3 years onwards
- Japanese encephalitis vaccine. Give 1ml by deep subcutaneous injection; supply 1 1ml vial.

Booster: Japanese encephalitis vaccine

- Age from 12 months to 2 years
- Japanese encephalitis vaccine. Give 0.5ml by deep subcutaneous injection; supply 1 1ml vial.

Tick-borne encephalitis immunization

Which therapy

- **Vaccination against tick-borne encephalitis is rarely necessary.** Consider vaccination for people walking, camping, or working in forested areas of Western Europe, Scandinavia, and the former Soviet Union in summer.
- **Immunization for tick-borne encephalitis** is provided by an *inactive* vaccine (only available on a named-patient basis):
  - **Primary immunization** consists of two intramuscular injections given 4–12 weeks apart. This gives protection for one year.
  - For children aged 3–15 years: give 0.25 ml (half the adult dose) for the first dose. However give 0.5 ml (usual adult dose) for the second and third doses.
  - **A booster dose** at 9–12 months extends immunity to 3 years. Booster doses are required every 3 years for people at continued risk of infection.
- **Regardless of immunization status,** people travelling in affected areas are also advised to cover arms, legs and

ankles, and use insect repellent on socks and outer clothing. Unpasteurized milk should also be avoided.
- **Obtain consent and check suitability for immunization.** See *Suitability for vaccination* for further information.
- **Advise people that** tick-borne encephalitis vaccine is **not** routinely available on the NHS for overseas travel. Payment is at the discretion of the practice.

Practical prescribing points

For further information please see the *Medicines Compendium* (www.medicines.org.uk) or the *British National Formulary* (www.bnf.org).
- Give tick-borne encephalitis vaccine by intramuscular injection. In infants, use the antero-lateral aspects of the thigh and use a 25G needle. In older children and adults, use the deltoid muscle and a 23G needle.
- **Delay vaccination during an acute febrile illness.** Wait until symptoms have resolved before vaccinating.
- **If more than one vaccine is being given,** use different needles/syringes and inject into different sites.
- **Advise people to seek urgent medical advice if** they develop breathlessness, swelling of the mouth or throat, or a rash within a few days of immunization.
- **Advise parents** to give a dose of paracetamol or ibuprofen if a child develops a fever, and keep the child cool (remove excess clothing or bedding). If a fever persists after a second dose, they should seek medical advice.

Follow-up advice

- **Tick-borne encephalitis** vaccine is administered as two doses over a 4–12 week period. Follow up appointments should be arranged accordingly. A third dose can be given after 9–12 months and will extend immunity.
- Reinforcing doses are required every 3 years for those at continued risk of exposure to the disease.

Patient information leaflets

The following PILs are available at www.prodigy.nhs.uk
- Tick Borne Encephalitis Immunisation
- Travel Advice Unit, Consular Directorate, Foreign & Commonwealth Office
- TravelHealth.co.uk

Shared decision making

- **Immunization against tick-borne encephalitis** may be advised if you walk, camp, or work in forested areas of 'at risk' countries in late spring or summer.
  - Two injections 4–12 weeks apart protect for one year.
  - A third injection at 9–12 months extends immunity to 3 years.
  - Have booster doses every 3 years if you continue to be at risk.
- **Tell us before these injections if you:**
  - Are pregnant.
  - Have conditions of the heart, kidney, or liver, or if you have leukaemia or lymphoma.
  - Had a reaction to this vaccine in the past.
- **Side effects?** Mild pain and redness may occur at the injection site. Tiredness, mild fever, feeling sick, an itchy rash, and headache sometimes occur for a short time. Severe reactions are rare.
- **Immunization is only one aspect of travel health.** For example, protect yourself from tick bites. Get the free booklet *Health Advice for Travellers* from a main post office.

Drug rationale

Drugs not included

- **Tick-borne encephalitis immunoglobulin** is not included. This is only indicated for post-exposure prophylaxis of tick-borne encephalitis [DH, 1996; DH, 2001].

Drugs included

- **Tick-borne encephalitis vaccine** is offered. This is an *inactive* vaccine administered as an intramuscular injection, and is effective in preventing the disease. Primary immunization consists of two doses spaced at least 4 weeks apart, which confers immunity for one year. Reinforcing doses can be taken after one year and then after 3 years for those at continued exposure.

[DH, 1996; DH, 2001]

Prescriptions

Tick-borne encephalitis vaccine (inactivated)

Primary course: tick-borne encephalitis vaccine (FSME-Immun)
- Age from 16 years onwards
- FSME-Immun. Give 0.5ml by intramuscular injection. For primary immunization, give two doses, 4-12 weeks apart; supply 1 0.5ml prefilled syringe.

Primary course: tick-borne encephalitis vaccine (FSME-Immun)
- Age from 3 to 15 years
- FSME-Immun. Give by intramuscular injection. For primary immunization, give 0.25ml for the first dose. Give a second dose of 0.5ml after 4-12 weeks; supply 1 0.5ml prefilled syringe.

Booster: tick-borne encephalitis vaccine (FSME-Immun)
- Age from 3 years onwards
- FSME-Immun. Give 0.5ml by intramuscular injection; supply 1 0.5ml prefilled syringe.

Extended Information

Background information

- Why are travel vaccinations necessary? p.1062
- Which diseases commonly require vaccination? p.1063
- What other diseases may require vaccination? p.1063
- Where are these diseases prevalent? p.1064

Why are travel vaccinations necessary?

- **Health advice for travellers is becoming increasingly complex** owing to the increasing number of people travelling overseas for work or leisure:
  - **Travel to sub-tropical or tropical destinations is becoming more common,** and potentially dangerous diseases are more likely to be endemic in these areas.
  - **Extended holidays abroad are becoming more popular,** and these may increase exposure to tropical diseases accordingly. In addition, holidays involving travel in rural areas can increase the likelihood of contracting an infection, and medical treatment may be scarce.
- **Many infectious diseases endemic in foreign countries can be vaccinated against.** A traveller can greatly reduce the risk of contracting an infection by taking the relevant vaccines before travelling.
- **Some countries require an International Certification of Vaccination as a condition of entry.** Most notably, many tropical countries in Africa and South America will not

accept travellers unless they can prove they have been vaccinated against yellow fever.

- **Travellers contracting tropical diseases abroad and importing them back to the United Kingdom pose a significant problem.** Many diseases, such as typhoid fever, are occasionally notified in the United Kingdom but are usually contracted abroad. Often the symptoms of tropical diseases may not be recognized by a GP in the United Kingdom, making diagnosis difficult.

[DH, 1996; DH, 2001]

Which diseases commonly require vaccination?

The following diseases are endemic in many regions of the world, particularly in hotter or less well-developed countries. Vaccination against some or all of these illnesses will provide adequate cover for most travellers.

Typhoid fever

- **Typhoid fever is a systemic infection caused by the Gram-negative bacillus *Salmonella typhi*.** Most salmonella infections only result in local infection of the gastrointestinal tract (i.e. 'food poisoning'), but some serotypes can cause systemic infection, resulting in serious illness with prolonged pyrexia and prostration.
- **The incubation period for the disease is usually 1–3 weeks.** Some 10% of people with the infection excrete the organism for up to 3 months after infection, and up to half of these may become permanent carriers.
- **Typhoid fever is spread by the faecal–oral route.** It is therefore principally a disease associated with poor sanitation and personal hygiene. Around 200 cases are notified in the United Kingdom each year, and of these 80% are contracted from abroad (principally the Indian subcontinent).

Tetanus

- **Tetanus is caused by spores of the anaerobic tetanus bacillus,** which is found ubiquitously in soil. It is contracted by infection through skin wounds, including superficial injuries (which may go unnoticed). Incubation of the spores occurs at the site of the wound and typically takes 4–21 days, during which time exotoxins are produced.
- **The symptoms of tetanus** are characterized by muscular rigidity with superimposed agonising contractions. It is rare, but frequently fatal once contracted.
- Between 1984 and 1995 there were 145 cases of tetanus in England and Wales. It is more common in the elderly and in women, who are less likely to be immunized.

Hepatitis A

- **Hepatitis A is caused by a virus transmitted by the faecal–oral route.** It is spread by person-to-person contact and through contaminated food or drink, and has an incubation time of 15–40 days.
- **Hepatitis A is usually a mild disease** and chronic liver damage is rare, although it may have serious complications in people with pre-existing liver disease. It is often asymptomatic in children, and the severity of the illness tends to increase with age. Its incidence is generally sporadic in nature, although outbreaks do occur.
- **Most cases (about 80%) of hepatitis A are contracted in the United Kingdom.** However, the incidence of the illness is higher in less developed countries, including those in Africa, South America, Central America, the Indian subcontinent, and Eastern Europe.

Yellow fever

- **Yellow fever is caused by an acute flavivirus infection spread by the bite of infected mosquitoes.** The incubation period of the virus is usually 3–6 days, after which symptoms become apparent.
- **Yellow fever is potentially a very severe disease.** Early symptoms may be non-specific in nature, or there may be a sudden onset of fever, vomiting, and prostration, followed by haemorrhage and jaundice. Over 50% of non-immunized adults may die of the illness, and there is no specific treatment once symptoms have started.
- **There are two variants of the disease,** known as 'urban' yellow fever and 'jungle' yellow fever. These are clinically and aetiologically identical, but have different patterns of spread. Jungle yellow fever is endemic in rural areas, whereas urban yellow fever appears episodically in cities as an epidemic.
- **Yellow fever is exclusively found in sub-Saharan Africa and South America.** There have been no cases in North America, Europe, or Asia in recent times.

Meningococcal meningitis

- **Meningococcal meningitis is caused by the Gram-negative diplococcus *Neisseria meningitides*.** It is divided into subgroups, which are antigenetically distinct. The most commonly contracted strains in the United Kingdom are groups B and C, with group A being relatively rare. However, prevalence of these groups, particularly group A, is different in other parts of the world.
- Meningococci are carried by 10–25% of the United Kingdom population and are transmitted by droplet spread or direct contact from carriers or individuals in the early stages of the disease. It has an incubation rate of 2–3 days in susceptible people.
- **Meningococcal meningitis is a very serious disease.** Early symptoms and signs are usually malaise, pyrexia, and vomiting, which may progress to headache, photophobia, joint pains, or confusion. A characteristic haemorrhagic rash indicating septicaemia may also develop. Even with antibiotic treatment, the disease may then progress to coma and death.

Poliomyelitis

- **Poliomyelitis is an acute illness caused by invasion of the gastrointestinal tract by one of three types of polio virus (I, II, and III).** The virus is transmitted through faeces and pharyngeal secretions and has an incubation period of about 3–21 days.
- **Polio primarily attacks the nervous system.** Symptoms include gastrointestinal disturbances, headache, malaise, and stiffness of the neck and back. A small number of people infected will go on to develop flaccid paralysis, most commonly affecting the legs, although the facial nerves may also be affected. In most people this paralysis is not permanent and diminishes with time, although they are at risk of developing post-polio syndrome (reoccurrence of the disease) 10–40 years later.
- Since the introduction of effective vaccines in the mid-1950s, polio has been eradicated from the developed world and is becoming less prevalent in the developing world. However, it is still endemic in some areas, including sub-Saharan Africa and the Indian subcontinent.

[DH, 1996; DH, 2001]

What other diseases may require vaccination?

The following diseases are endemic in parts of the world, but do not usually pose a serious risk to travellers overseas.

However, in particular circumstances, where there is a specific risk of contracting one or more of these diseases, vaccinations are available and may be recommended.

Rabies

- **Rabies is caused by a rhabdovirus and is potentially transmitted by all mammals.** It has a very variable incubation period, but symptoms usually present 2–8 weeks after infection, which is nearly always from an animal bite.
- **Rabies is a very serious illness.** Early symptoms include paraesthesiae around the site of the wound, fever, headache, and malaise. It can then progress in one of three ways: spasms; hydrophobia, hallucinations, and maniacal behaviour progressing to paralysis and coma; or an ascending flaccid paralysis and sensory disturbance. Rabies is nearly always fatal, with death resulting from respiratory paralysis.
- The last case of indigenous rabies in the United Kingdom was of the non-classical lyssavirus type, and caused the death of a bat handler in 2002 [Pounder, 2003]. The United Kingdom is still regarded as being rabies-free, however, with the last case previous to this occurring in 1902.
- **The rabies virus is endemic in most countries,** and all continents of the world, except Australasia and Antarctica, are affected. The principal carriers in Europe are thought to be foxes, although domestic pets, cattle, horses, and deer have all been implicated. In the United States, skunks, racoons, and bats account for 95% of cases.

Japanese encephalitis

- **Japanese encephalitis is caused by a flavivirus that is spread by the bite of infected mosquitoes.** It has an incubation time of 2–8 days.
- **Japanese encephalitis is a mild disease in most people** and is often completely asymptomatic. However, in a small proportion of people (estimated at about 1 in 200) the disease is much more serious. In these people, the infection may present as a flu-like illness, with fever, chills, tiredness, headache, nausea, and vomiting, and possibly confusion and agitation. Encephalitis may follow from this, and this is fatal in 30% of affected people. It causes permanent brain damage, including paralysis, in a further 30%.
- **Japanese encephalitis occurs throughout South-East Asia and the Far East.** It is particularly common in rural agricultural areas, and is associated with the rainy season in some countries.

Tick-borne encephalitis

- **Tick-borne encephalitis is caused by a flavivirus from the same family as yellow fever and Japanese encephalitis.** It is usually spread by tick bites, although unpasteurized milk is also thought to be a source of the disease.
- **The incubation time of the disease is usually 7–14 days,** although the chances of being infected from a single bite are slight. Affected people may initially develop a flu-like illness that lasts about a week, before going on to develop encephalitis. It is fatal in 1–5% of cases.
- **Tick-borne encephalitis occurs** in warm forested parts of Western Europe, Scandinavia, and the former Soviet Union, including western Russia. It is not found in the United Kingdom.

Cholera

- **Cholera is an acute diarrhoeal illness** caused by an enterotoxin produced by *Vibrio cholera* that have colonized the small bowel. It is a water-borne disease, being solely transmitted through contaminated water or food (especially shellfish).
- **The incubation period of cholera is usually 2–5 days, but the disease may become symptomatic in only a few hours.** It is characterized by profuse watery stools and possibly vomiting, and can rapidly lead to dehydration, metabolic acidosis, and circulatory collapse. Cholera is a very dangerous disease if not adequately treated, but mortality is less than 1% with prompt, correct management.
- **Cholera is endemic in areas with poor sanitation and hygiene.** The Indian subcontinent, the Far East, Africa, and South America are particularly affected. However, with adequate precautions, the risk to the traveller is low.

[DH, 1996; DH, 2001; DH, 2001]

Where are these diseases prevalent?

The regions that are affected by the diseases covered in this guidance are listed in Table 3. This is only an approximate guide; a more exact country-by-country guide to disease prevalence can be found in the Department of Health 'yellow book', *Health Information for Overseas Travel.* It should also be kept in mind that the regional prevalence of these diseases is not constant, but can fluctuate rapidly (for instance during epidemics).

[DH, 2001]

Management issues

- General advice for the overseas traveller p.1064
- Information sources p.1065
- Vaccinations commonly recommended for overseas travel p.1065
- Vaccinations that may be recommended for extended holidays or work overseas p.1067
- Scheduling of vaccinations p.1068
- Vaccination procedures p.1069
- Reasons to delay vaccination p.1070

General advice for the overseas traveller

- **Attendance for immunization** provides an excellent opportunity to discuss the issues below. It may also prove an opportune time to review the person's childhood vaccinations, and check that they are up-to-date. Many vaccinations presently on the childhood vaccination programme are necessary for overseas travel.
- **People should be reassured** that the overall risk of contracting infectious diseases from abroad is very low if safeguards are taken. Vaccinations are a sensible precaution for some diseases in some countries abroad.
- **The risk of contracting an infectious disease abroad** is subject to several factors:
  - **The region visited.** The risk may vary from country by country, or prevalence may vary within countries.
  - **The length of stay.** The longer the stay, the greater the risk of exposure.
  - **The time of stay.** Some diseases are more prevalent at certain times of the year (e.g. the rainy season).
  - **The type of holiday or work.** In general, people are more at risk in rural areas than in urbanized or developed areas. Hence backpacking may be more dangerous than a 'package' holiday, and work in rural or wild areas is often particularly high in risk.
  - **The age and health of the traveller.** Some people may be more susceptible to infections, and some vaccines have contraindications.
- **The consequence of contracting an infectious disease abroad** should also be considered. Health provision in developing countries may be inadequate or difficult to

Table 3: Diseases that may require vaccination and their regional prevalence.

Disease	Regions primarily affected	Comments
Typhoid fever	Developing world, particularly the Indian subcontinent	Mainly transmitted through contaminated water or food (avoidable)
Tetanus	Found ubiquitously throughout the world	Treatment for a suspected tetanus wound may be difficult in some developing countries
Hepatitis A	Worldwide, but prevalence greater in the developing world	Vaccination recommended outside Western Europe, North America, and Australasia
Yellow fever	Sub-Saharan Africa and tropical South America	An International Certificate of Vaccination is a condition of entry for some countries
Meningococcal meningitis	Worldwide, but some strains (especially A) are much more common outside the United Kingdom	Saudi Arabia requires proof of vaccination with a quadrivalent vaccine (ACWY vax) for visitors arriving for the Hajj (Mecca) and Umrah pilgrimages, or for seasonal working in the Hajj areas
Poliomyelitis	Largely eradicated, but still endemic in some areas — 98% of new cases are from Nigeria, Pakistan, and India	Complete eradication of the poliovirus is expected before the end of the decade
Rabies	Endemic in most regions of the world. Exceptions include the British Isles, Scandinavia, Japan, and Australasia	Treatment for a suspected rabies wound may be difficult in some developing countries
Japanese encephalitis	South-East Asia and the Far East	Most at risk in rural and agricultural areas, and there may be seasonal variations
Tick-borne encephalitis	Forested areas of Western Europe, Scandinavia, and the former Soviet Union	Risk is small for short stays
Cholera	Endemic in developing countries, especially the Indian subcontinent, Africa, the Far East and South America	Transmitted through contaminated water or food (avoidable). An oral vaccine is now available.

access, and diseases normally treatable in the United Kingdom may have a more serious outcome.

- **Practical and conservative measures** should be taken where possible. For example, bottled water should be used, and suitable measures to protect against insect bites may be important.
- **The most common infectious diseases** contracted abroad *cannot* effectively be vaccinated against:
  - **Travellers' diarrhoea** occurs in up to 50% of visitors abroad and can generally be prevented by avoiding contaminated food and drink. This is covered in the separate PRODIGY guidance available for *Gastroenteritis*.
  - **Malaria** is probably the most serious acute infectious disease commonly contracted from abroad. About 2000 people return to the United Kingdom with the illness each year, and most of these could be avoided with the proper use of chemoprophylaxis. There is a separate PRODIGY guidance for *Malaria Prophylaxis*.
  - **Sexually transmitted infections** are commonly contracted abroad. Some areas such as Thailand and sub-Saharan Africa are endemic with HIV.
  - **Parasitic infestations,** for instance roundworm, are among the most common infectious diseases bought back to the United Kingdom from abroad.

[DH, 1996; DH, 2001]

Information sources

This guidance gives a summary of advice for the immunization of overseas travellers, but it is not intended to be comprehensive or exhaustive. In addition, although this guidance is correct at the time of writing, prevalence of infectious diseases abroad and guidelines for travel immunization can change in short periods of time. If in any doubt, further advice should be consulted. Table 4 gives information on the main sources of up-to-date advice available in the United Kingdom.

Vaccinations commonly recommended for overseas travel

The following vaccines are available for overseas travellers, and should adequately cover most people's needs and requirements. They are mainly useful for travel to subtropical and tropical regions, which often have a poor medical infrastructure. This guidance does not cover routine childhood immunizations (e.g. tuberculosis) or occupational immunizations (e.g. hepatitis B), which should be up-to-date. Poliomyelitis-containing and tetanus-containing vaccinations are included, however, as reinforcing doses may be necessary.

Typhoid fever

- **Typhoid is endemic in areas with poor sanitation and hygiene** (e.g. Africa, Asia, Central and South America, and the Caribbean). Although it can be prevented by avoiding contaminated food and drink, this can be difficult in practice, and vaccination when travelling in these areas is strongly recommended.
- **Two vaccines are available that offer protection against typhoid fever:**
  - **An inactive capsular polysaccharide typhoid vaccine.**
  - **A combined vaccine for hepatitis A and typhoid fever is also available,** and may be useful for people requiring simultaneous coverage of both illnesses. Both components are inactive.
- **Vaccination for typhoid fever should be carried out 2 weeks before travel,** to allow immunity to develop.
- **Typhoid vaccination gives protection for 3 years** before another dose is required. The combined vaccine also gives protection against hepatitis A for 1 year.
- **Typhoid vaccine is not 100% effective,** particularly if the traveller is exposed to large doses of typhoid. Therefore scrupulous attention to personal, food, and water hygiene should be maintained at all times when travelling in endemic areas. In addition, children under the age of 18 months to 2 years may show a suboptimal response to typhoid vaccination.

[DH, 1996]

Tetanus

- **Tetanus vaccination is part of the childhood vaccination programme,** so many travellers will already be immunized. Check that ALL people are up-to-date with the recommended five-dose schedule for tetanus

Table 4: The main sources of information available on the current recommendations or requirements for immunization for travel abroad.

Information source	Information provided and contact details
Immunization against Infectious Disease, DH 'green book'	Invaluable source of information on all vaccinations. Available as a booklet from post offices (or phone 0800 555 777), or online at www.dh.gov.uk.
Health Information for Overseas Travel, DH 'yellow book'	Supplement for overseas travel, especially for a country-by-country guide of vaccination requirements. Available online at www.the-stationery-office.co.uk/doh/hinfo.
British National Formulary	Updated biannually. Available as a book, compact disc, or online at www.bnf.org.
Travax	Scottish Centre for Infection and Environmental Health website. Registration is required, and there is a fee for non-Scottish NHS workers. Available at www.travax.scot.nhs.uk.
Traveller	This is a computer database of travel information that needs to be installed on a computer. It is updated monthly for a subscription fee. Telephone 0114 282 3488.
National Travel Health Network and Centre (NaTHNaC)	Provides advice on travel immunizations to healthcare professionals *only*, weekdays 9–12 am and 2–4.30 pm. Phone (020) 7380 9234. There is also a useful website on travel requirements, including latest news, available at www.nathnac.org.
Monthly Index of Medical Specialities (MIMS)	MIMS has a comprehensive country-by-country list of immunizations required for foreign travel. Updated monthly.
Community pharmacists	Pharmacists can provide up-to-date information on vaccine requirements.

immunization, regardless of travel arrangements, see Table 3.

- **Children under 10 years:** offer immunization for tetanus according to the childhood vaccination programme, see Table 3.
- **Children over the age of 10 years and adults:**
  - **People who have not been vaccinated** require a primary course of tetanus vaccine (followed by two boosters at appropriate intervals) regardless of their travel destination. Elderly people, especially women and men who have not been in the armed forces, are especially likely to fall into this category.
  - **People who are not fully immunized** (i.e. have not received adequate reinforcing doses) require a booster dose regardless of their travel destination. Full, permanent protection is achieved once the recommended five dose schedule has been completed (i.e. a primary course and two further booster doses 10 years apart).
- **ALL people travelling to developing countries** (where access to tetanus immunoglobulin may be limited) should receive an additional tetanus booster regardless of their immunization status (i.e. even if they have had the full complement of five tetanus vaccinations).

[CMO, 2002; DH, 2004c]

Hepatitis A

- **Most cases of hepatitis A are contracted at home,** but the prevalence of the disease, and risk of contracting it, is significantly higher outside Western Europe, North America, or Australia and New Zealand. The highest-risk areas include the Indian subcontinent, the Far East, and Eastern Europe.
- **Vaccination should be considered for all people travelling to high-risk areas,** irrespective of the duration of travel. Frequent travellers, people travelling for extended periods, or people with chronic liver disease are especially at risk, and vaccination in these groups is essential.
- **Testing for hepatitis A antibodies** (to assess immunization status) may be worthwhile in the following individuals:
  - People 50 years of age and older.
  - People who were born or have lived in areas of high endemicity.
  - People with a history of jaundice.
- **The primary immunization** consists of an *inactivated* hepatitis A vaccine, administered as a single intramuscular injection (in the deltoid). Coverage lasts for about one year.
- **A booster dose** 6–12 months later gives protection for up to 10 years.
- **A combined vaccine for hepatitis A and typhoid fever is also available,** and may be useful for people requiring simultaneous coverage of both illnesses, especially since they are frequently endemic in the same areas. Both components are *inactive*. The hepatitis A component gives protection for one year and the typhoid component gives immunity for 3 years.

[DH, 1996]

Yellow fever

- Yellow fever is endemic in a strip that runs from tropical areas of South America to sub-Saharan Africa. A full list of countries affected can be found in the Department of Health y book, *Health Information for Overseas Travel*.

Table 5: Recommended five-dose immunization schedule for tetanus, poliomyelitis, and diphtheria.

Schedule	Children under the age of 10 years	Adults and children over 10 years
Primary course	3 doses of vaccine (usually as DTaP/IPV/Hib) at 2, 3, and 4 months of age*	3 doses of vaccine (as Td/IPV), each one month apart*
Fourth dose	At least 3 years after the last dose of the primary course, usually pre-school entry (as dTaP/IPV or DTaP/IPV)	5–10 years after the last dose of the primary course (as Td/IPV)
Fifth dose	Aged 13–18 years or before leaving school (as Td/IPV)	10 years after fourth dose (as Td/IPV)

* If the full primary course cannot be completed before departure, complete the course on return.
DTaP/IPV/Hib = Diphtheria, tetanus, acellular pertussis, inactivated poliomyelitis, and *Haemophilus influenzae* type b vaccine (Pediacel®)
dTaP/IPV = Low-dose diphtheria, tetanus, acellular pertussis, and inactivated poliomyelitis vaccine (Repevax®)
DTaP/IPV = Diphtheria, tetanus, acellular pertussis, and inactivated poliomyelitis vaccine (Infanrix IPV®)
Td/IPV = Low-dose diphtheria, tetanus, and inactivated poliomyelitis vaccine for adults and children over 10 years of age (Revaxis®)

When travelling to these destinations vaccination is essential:

- **Yellow fever is a serious illness** that can result in death in 50% of non-immunized adults.
- **There is no treatment** for yellow fever once infected.
- **Many countries require an International Certificate of Vaccination** against the disease, either for all travellers or for travellers entering from endemic countries.

The yellow fever vaccine is a *live* attenuated preparation. It is administered as a single dose by the deep subcutaneous route. It confers immunity in close to 100% of recipients.

Immunity probably persists for life. However, a reinforcing dose after 10 years is recommended for those at persisting risk of contracting the disease, and is necessary for re-certification.

The yellow fever vaccine can only be administered at specialist centres designated by the national health administration and recorded with the World Health Organization. A list of the nearest available centres, and other useful information, can be found at www.nathnac.org.

DH, 1996]

Meningococcal meningitis

Meningococcal meningitis is endemic in all regions of the world, but the risk of contacting the disease is greater in some regions than in the United Kingdom. In particular, the prevalence of Group A meningococcal meningitis is very low in the United Kingdom but has been responsible for several epidemics recently elsewhere in the world.

High-risk areas for contracting Group A meningococcal meningitis include much of sub-Saharan Africa (the 'meningitis belt'), Northern India, Nepal, Bhutan, Pakistan, and Saudi Arabia.

Vaccination is recommended for the following people travelling to high-risk areas for contracting Group A menincococcal meningitis:

- People staying for extended time periods, such as one month or more.
- People engaging in high-risk holidays or work, such as backpacking or living in rural communities.
- People attending the Hajj (Mecca) and Umrah pilgrames in Saudi Arabia. (There have been epidempics in recent years in these areas.)
- Seasonal working in the Hajj area.

A quadrivalent vaccine, ACWY Vax®, is now recommended for travellers. A single dose provides cover against strains A, C, Y, and W135 of the disease. It can be used in children under the age of 2 years (off-licence use) but they may show a suboptimal response to the vaccine.

- **Vaccination with ACWY Vax® should be carried out 2–3 weeks before travel,** to allow immunity to develop.
- **Immunity typically lasts for** 5 years in adults before requiring a reinforcing dose. In children and infants (especially those under 2 years) immunity lasts for a shorter period, particularly against the Group C strain.

Saudi Arabia now requires proof of vaccination with ACWY Vax® for visitors arriving for the Hajj and Umrah pilgrimages, or for seasonal working in the Hajj areas.

Meningococcal conjugate C vaccine (Men C) is now part of the childhood vaccination programme. However, this DOES NOT protect against Group A meningococcal meningitis, and therefore people who have received MenC are not suitably immunized for travel abroad.

NaTHNaC, 2003a; DH, 2004a; NaTHNaC, 2004a]

Poliomyelitis

- **Poliomyelitis has been eliminated from much of the world,** and complete eradication is expected in this decade. However, there is still a risk of contracting the disease in some regions, and 98% of new infections occur in Nigeria, Pakistan, and India. It is essential that travellers to these regions are fully immunized.
- **Check that ALL people are up-to-date with the recommended five-dose schedule for poliomyelitis immunization,** regardless of travel arrangements, see Table 3. **Inactivated poliomyelitis-containing vaccines** are now recommended for immunization in the UK. Oral poliomyelitis vaccine (a *live* attenuated vaccine) is now only available for outbreak control.
- **Children under 10 years:** offer immunization for poliomyelitis according to the childhood vaccination programme, see Table 3.
- **Children over the age of 10 years and adults:**
    - **People who have not been vaccinated** required a primary course of poliomyelitis vaccine (followed by two boosters at appropriate intervals, see Table 3) regardless of their travel destination. Travellers born before 1958 may not have been immunized, and these people should be immunized as a matter of course in any event.
    - **People who are not fully immunized** (i.e. have not received two booster doses at appropriate intervals) require a booster dose regardless of their travel destination.
- **Travellers to polio-endemic regions** are advised to have an additional booster dose of vaccine if they have not previously had one in the last 10 years. This is particularly important for health workers in endemic regions.

[DH, 2001; DH, 2004b; NaTHNaC, 2004c]

Vaccinations that may be recommended for extended holidays or work overseas

The following vaccines are not usually necessary for travellers overseas, but are available in the UK if required for special circumstances. Travellers taking extended holidays in areas endemic with these diseases may be advised to take these vaccinations, particularly if they are travelling in remote areas (e.g. 'backpacking'). Overseas workers, especially those working closely with indigenous rural populations, or health workers, may also require immunization.

Rabies

- **Rabies is endemic throughout the world,** with a few exceptions, such as the British Isles, Scandinavia, and Australasia. However, the risk to travellers is relatively slight, and post-exposure treatment of the disease (after a bite has occurred) is available, BUT needs to be administered quickly.
- **The following travellers should be offered pre-exposure immunization** (prophylaxis) against rabies:
    - **People travelling in enzootic areas** (e.g. jungle habitat), where there is an unusually high risk of infection.
    - **People travelling in very remote areas,** where medical care may not be immediately available.
    - **People who are working abroad with, or in close contact to, animals** (e.g. veterinarians, zoologists). People working with animals in the United Kingdom should also be immunized.
- **Currently there are two rabies vaccines** available in the United Kingdom, made from human diploid cells or chick embryo cells. Both are inactivated.
- **The recommended schedule** is three doses on days 0, 7, and 28.

  - The third dose can be given from day 21 if there is insufficient time before travel.
  - If it is not possible to administer three doses of vaccine, it is likely that, in the majority of cases, two doses will confer protection provided they are given at least 28 days apart.
  - If there are time constraints to the full pre-exposure course, two doses given at least 1 week apart will confer some protection. A single dose is likely to prime the immune system, but will obviously offer less protection than the recommended schedule. Travellers should be aware that if they are bitten, a full course of post-exposure prophylaxis will be needed.
- **A booster dose** can be given from 2 years after the primary course was completed. Further doses can be given at 2–3 year intervals if needed.
- **Post-exposure vaccination** (i.e. after a bite has occurred) depends on the immunization status of the person affected. Expert advice should be sought immediately, even if the person has been fully immunized. A rabies-specific immunoglobulin is also available for post-exposure treatment as an adjuvant to vaccination.

[NaTHNaC, 2003b; DH, 2005]

Japanese encephalitis

- **Japanese encephalitis is endemic in South-East Asia and the Far East.** Vaccination is recommended for the following travellers to this region:
  - People staying for longer periods (i.e. over a month).
  - People travelling in rural areas (especially in areas where rice and pig farming coexist).
  - People doing extensive outdoor activities in endemic areas.
  - People travelling at the end of the monsoon season (roughly June–September).
- **Japanese encephalitis vaccine is not licensed in the UK,** and therefore must be given on a named-patient basis. There are two *inactive* vaccines currently available for Japanese encephalitis.
- **The recommended schedule for optimum protection is:**
  - **A primary course** of three doses, given on days 0, 7, and 28 (JE-Vax® vaccine only).
  - **A booster dose** can be given every 2–3 years following the third dose if at continued risk.
  - Note: children under 3 years of age should receive half the adult dose.
- **An alternative schedule is:**
  - A two-dose regimen given on days 0 and 7, but this only provides 80% of vaccines with immunity for about 3 months (JE-Vax® or Japanese encephalitis Green Cross vaccine).
  - A booster dose after 3 months is recommended for this schedule.
- **Allergic or anaphylactic events** occur more frequently with the Japanese encephalitis vaccine than with other vaccines, and may be delayed by up to 2 weeks. Serious systemic reactions include urticaria, angioedema, and cardiovascular collapse, and occur in about 0.6% of vaccine recipients. People receiving the vaccine should be observed for 30 minutes (in a place with resuscitation equipment and expertise), and warned of the possibilities of severe, delayed reactions. The vaccine should be taken at least 10–14 days before commencement of travel.
- Travellers to endemic regions are also advised to use standard precautions to prevent mosquito bites, as it is transmitted to humans by *Culex* mosquitoes.

[DH, 1996; NaTHNaC, 2004b]

Tick-borne encephalitis

- **Tick-borne encephalitis is endemic to forested areas of Western Europe, Scandinavia, and the former Soviet Union.** Although the risk to the average traveller is small, vaccination is recommended for people who intend to walk, camp, or work in heavily forested regions during late spring or summer, especially if there is heavy undergrowth.
- **Immunization for tick-borne encephalitis** is provided by an *inactive* vaccine.
  - **Primary immunization** consists of two intramuscular injections given 4–12 weeks apart. This gives protection for one year. Note that the dose is different for children aged 3–15 years: give 0.25 ml (half the adult dose) for the first dose. However give 0.5 ml (usual adult dose) for the second and third doses.
  - **A booster dose** at 9–12 months extends immunity to 3 years. Booster doses are required every 3 years for people at continued risk of infection.
- People travelling in affected areas are also advised to cover arms, legs, and ankles, and use insect repellent on socks and outer clothing. Unpasteurized milk should also be avoided. This applies whether they have been vaccinated or not.

Cholera

- **Cholera is endemic in regions of poor sanitation and hygiene,** with the Indian subcontinent, the Far East, Africa and South America being particularly affected. Travellers are advised that the illness is best prevented by avoiding contaminated food and water.
- **An oral vaccine for cholera** has recently been developed and approved by the European Medicines Agency (EMEA). *Dukoral* protects against disease caused by *Vibrio cholerae* serogroup O1, and is licensed for use in adults and children over 2 years of age visiting cholera endemic areas. It currently has black triangle status and is not available on the NHS [EMEA, 2003].
- **Cholera vaccination should not be required by any traveller.** Some border officials may occasionally ask travellers for evidence of immunization if they are travelling from an endemic area. If this is anticipated, a signed statement on official paper advising that cholera vaccination is not indicated should be supplied.

[DH, 1996; DH, 2001]

Scheduling of vaccinations

- **Scheduling of travel vaccinations needs to be taken with care.** Wherever possible, the recommended intervals between doses and between vaccines should be adhered to. The current immunization status of the traveller, the time before travel is due to commence, and the number of live vaccines required need to be taken into consideration.
- **The traveller's current immunization status** needs to be assessed. Many vaccinations may have already been given in childhood, for occupational reasons, or for previous trips abroad. Only single reinforcing doses may be necessary.
- **The time interval** before travelling may be important:
  - **Some vaccinations require multiple doses** spread over days, weeks, or months for primary immunization. Sometimes, shorter dosing schedules can be given at the expense of the traveller acquiring full immunity (e.g. rabies), or resulting in immunity lasting for less time (e.g. tick-borne encephalitis). This may be a necessary or desirable trade off if there is limited time before travel commences.
  - **Most vaccines do not confer protection immediately,** but take time to become fully effective. In particular, immunization with typhoid fever vaccine takes 2 weeks, and that with Japanese encephalitis takes over a month to become effective.

- **Some vaccines have short-lived responses,** and immunity may diminish after extended periods overseas, particularly if they are taken far in advance before commencement of travel (e.g. hepatitis A).

Most travellers' needs can be accommodated in two visits with careful planning, spaced about one month apart. Table 4 summarizes the schedules for each vaccine.

Can I give more than one vaccine at the same time?

Inactivated vaccines (e.g. tetanus, poliomyelitis, injectable typhoid, hepatitis A, quadrivalent meningococcal meningitis vaccine, rabies, Japanese encephalitis, tick-borne encephalitis)and can be given at the same time as each other. However, they should be given using separate syringes and at different sites. If inactivated vaccines are *not* administered on the same day, there is no need to observe a specific interval between administering them.

Live vaccines (e.g. yellow fever, BCG, MMR) can be given at the same time as each other (using separate syringes and at different sites). If live vaccines are *not* administered on the same day, they should be separated from other live vaccines by an interval of at least 3 weeks. However, no interval need be observed between the administration of live vaccines and inactivated vaccines.

If in doubt, seek expert opinion.

DH, 1996; Goodyer, 2000; DH, 2001; BNF 46, 2003]

Vaccination procedures

Consent and record taking

Obtain written or verbal consent at the time of vaccination. Adults (Aged over 18 years) must consent to their own treatment. For children, consent should be sought from the parent or person with parental responsibility. Ensure that the individual (or their parents) feel that their questions have been adequately answered, and that their concerns about vaccination have been considered.

Establish suitability for immunization. If the individual's fitness and suitability cannot be established, vaccination should be delayed. See *Suitability for vaccination* for further information.

Check the identity of the vaccine, usage instructions, and its expiry date.

Record the date of immunization, title of vaccine, and batch number on the recipient's record. If two vaccines are given simultaneously, the relevant sites should be recorded to allow any reactions to be related to the causative vaccine.

Storage and reconstitution of vaccines

- **Store vaccines and diluents at 2–8°C, protected from light** in a designated refrigerator. Vaccine (including diluent) that has been frozen or has thawed should not be used. Freeze-dried vaccines must be stored in the dry state. A maximum–minimum thermometer should be used to check that the temperature has not gone out of the intended range.
- **Reconstitute** freeze-dried vaccine with the diluent supplied. This should be done slowly to avoid frothing, with a sterile 21G needle. Before injection, the colour of the product must be checked with that stated by the manufacturer in the package insert.

Administration of vaccines

- **Swab the skin with alcohol** if the skin is dirty, but allow it to evaporate before injecting. Live vaccines can be destroyed by coming into contact with alcohol.
- **Use the appropriate route of injection.**
  - Tetanus, poliomyelitis, injectable typhoid, hepatitis A, rabies, and tick-borne encephalitis should be given only by intramuscular injection. In patients with thrombocytopenia or bleeding disorders, however, the subcutaneous route should be used.
  - ACWY Vax® (meningococcal meningitis) and Japanese encephalitis vaccine should be given by deep subcutaneous injection.
- **Use an appropriate site for injecting.**
  - In infants, use the antero-lateral aspect of the thigh.
  - In older children and adults, use the deltoid muscle for tetanus, poliomyelitis, injectable typhoid, hepatitis A, and tick-borne encephalitis vaccines. (The buttocks should not be used as the injection site for typhoid or hepatitis A.) Use the antero-lateral aspect of the thigh, the upper arm or buttocks for ACWY Vax® and Japanese encephalitis vaccine. If the buttock is to be used, injection into the upper, outer quadrant minimizes the possibility of damage to the sciatic nerve.
- **Ensure the correct needle is used.** A 25G needle is suitable for deep subcutaneous or intramuscular injections in infants. A 23G needle is appropriate for deep subcutaneous or intramuscular injections in older children and adults.
- **If more than one vaccine is being given,** use different syringes/needles and inject into different sites.
- **Ask the person to wait after immunization** to ensure that they are not experiencing an immediate adverse reaction (generally for about 10 minutes, but 30 minutes for Japanese encephalitis vaccine). Anaphylaxis is rare, and typically occurs within minutes. However, the time of

able 6: Summary of vaccination schedules.

accine	Vaccine type	Interval between doses*	Immunization period**	Time taken until maximal immunity+
yphoid fever	Inactivated	Single dose	3 years	2 weeks
etanus	Inactivated	Booster dose	10 years	4 weeks
epatitis A	Inactivated	Single dose	1 year	90% immunity in 2 weeks
ellow fever	Live	Single dose	10 years	10 days
leningococcal meningitis	Inactivated	Single dose	5 years	90% immunity in 2–3 weeks
oliomyelitis	Inactivated	Booster dose	10 years	4 weeks
abies	Inactivated	4 weeks	3 years	After third dose
panese encephalitis	Inactivated	4 weeks	3 years	4 weeks
ick-borne encephalitis	Inactivated	4–12 weeks	1 year	One week after second dose

Interval between first and last dose if more than one dose required for full primary immunization. Tetanus and poliomyelitis assume primary immunizations have been mpleted (i.e. are reinforcing doses).

* Average interval until a reinforcing dose is necessary in adults. May differ in children and elderly people.

Immunity usually develops gradually after vaccination. May differ in children and elderly people.

H, 1996]

onset may be variable because of delayed absorption from an intramuscular injection (e.g. within 72 hours of immunization).

- **People should also be advised:**
  - To seek urgent medical advice if they develop early symptoms such as breathlessness, swelling of the mouth and throat, or rash within the following 72 hours.
  - To give a dose of paracetamol or ibuprofen if a child develops a fever after immunization, and keep them cool by removing excessive clothing and bedding. If fever persists after a second dose, they should seek medical advice.

[DH, 1996; DH, 2004a; DH, 2004b; DH, 2004c; DH, 2005]

Payment and availability of travel vaccinations

- **Some vaccines necessary for travel overseas are available on the NHS,** whatever the purpose for travel is. These include the following vaccinations: typhoid fever, tetanus, hepatitis A, and poliomyelitis. Rabies is available only for travellers working overseas whose occupation puts them at high risk of exposure to the virus.
- **The following are not routinely available on the NHS for overseas travel:** meningococcal vaccines, yellow fever, Japanese encephalitis, and tick-borne encephalitis.
- **Payment for the prescribing of vaccines for travel purposes is at the discretion of the practice.** Sometimes an administration charge may be made; therefore, the exact cost of immunization may vary between practices as well as between vaccination centres.
- **Japanese encephalitis and tick-borne encephalitis vaccines** can be obtained on a named-patient basis only. In addition, Japanese encephalitis vaccine is not licensed in the UK.

[DH, 1996; Goodyer, 2000]

Contraindications to vaccination

- **Anaphylaxis:** vaccines should not be given to those who have had a confirmed anaphylactic reaction within 72 hours of a previous dose of the same vaccine. In addition:
  - Tetanus- or poliomyelitis-containing vaccines should not be given if there is a confirmed anaphylactic reaction to neomycin, streptomycin or polymyxin B (which may be present in trace amounts).
  - Avaxim® (contains hepatitis A) and Hepatyrix® or ViATIM® (contain typhoid and hepatitis A) should not be given if there is a confirmed anaphylactic reaction to neomycin.
  - Epaxal® (contains hepatitis A) should not be given to people who are allergic to eggs.
  - Rabipur® (rabies vaccine) should not be given to people who are allergic to eggs, neomycin, chlorotetracycline, or amphotericin B.
  - Tick-borne encephalitis vaccine should not be given if there is a confirmed anaphylactic reaction to neomycin or eggs.
- **Other severe adverse reactions.** (Severe in this context means an extensive area of redness and swelling affecting large areas of the arm, leg, or other injection site, or a fever equal to or in excess of 39.5°C within 48 hours of injection):
  - Do not give vaccine if there is a definite history of a *severe* reaction to a previous dose.
  - However, tetanus- or poliomyelitis-containing vaccines *should* still be given to people with a severe reaction within 72 hours of a preceding dose.
- **Japanese encephalitis vaccine is not advised in** pregnancy or in people with cardiac, renal or hepatic disorders, leukaemia, or lymphoma because of a lack of data on the vaccine's efficacy and safety in these individuals.

[DH, 1996; DH, 2004a; DH, 2004b; DH, 2004c; DH, 2005]

Reasons to delay vaccination

Where there is doubt, seek appropriate advice from a consultant paediatrician, District Immunization Coordinator or Consultant in Communicable Disease Control, rather than withholding vaccine.

- **Acute illness:** if a person is suffering from any acute illness, postpone immunization until the child has fully recovered. Minor infections without fever or systemic upset are not reasons to postpone immunization.
- **Pregnancy:**
  - Tetanus, diphtheria, acellular pertussis, inactivated poliomyelitis, and Hib may be given to pregnant women when clinically indicated. There is no evidence of risk from vaccinating pregnant women or those who are breastfeeding with inactivated virus or bacterial vaccines or toxoids.
  - Other inactivated vaccines (e.g. injectable typhoid, hepatitis A, quadrivalent meningococcal meningitis, rabies, tick-borne encephalitis) are probably safe in pregnancy (the risks to the fetus are likely to be negligible), but use only if a clear indication exists and the benefits clearly outweigh the risks.
  - Japanese encephalitis vaccine is not advised in pregnancy.
  - Live vaccines (e.g. yellow fever) should be used in pregnancy only when the benefits clearly outweigh the risks, because of theoretical possibility of harm to the fetus.

[DH, 1996; DH, 2004a; DH, 2004b; DH, 2004c; DH, 2005]

Can people with immunosuppression or HIV infection be vaccinated?

- **Inactivated vaccines: people with immunosuppression or HIV infection** (regardless of CD4 count) can be given inactivated vaccines (e.g. tetanus, injectable poliomyelitis, injectable typhoid, hepatitis A, meningococcal meningitis, rabies, japanse encephalitis, tick-borne encephalitis). However these individuals may not make a full antibody response. Re-immunization should be considered after treatment is finished and recovery has occurred.
- **Human normal immunoglobulin (HNIG) is a possible alternative to the hepatitis A inactivated vaccine** in immunosuppressed individuals, whose response to the vaccine may be inadequate [BNF 46, 2003], or for immediate protection for people coming into contact with people with hepatitis A:
  - HNIG provides protection against hepatitis A for relatively short periods of time (about 4 months). It is therefore suitable for short or occasional trips to endemic areas, but not for prolonged or frequent stays abroad.
  - It may interfere with the development of immunity conferred by some live virus vaccines (e.g. yellow fever vaccine). The live virus vaccine should be given 3 weeks before HNIG or 3 months afterwards. However, the yellow fever vaccine is not affected.
- **Live vaccines: immunosuppressed people** taking *live* vaccines (e.g. yellow fever) may not have a normal immune response and may suffer severe adverse reactions to live vaccines. The following people are potentially at risk:
  - **People taking cancer chemotherapy or generalized radiotherapy,** or people who have had such therapy in the preceding 6 months.

- **People on immunosuppressive treatment** for an organ transplant.
- **People who have had a bone marrow transplant** in the previous 6 months.
- **People on systemic corticosteroid treatment** for at least one week (high-dose), or on low-dose systemic corticosteroid treatment combined with cytotoxic drugs, or people on long-term low-dose corticosteroid treatment.

- **Live vaccines: people with HIV infection** should *not* receive yellow fever vaccination (Joint Committee on Vaccination and Immunization advice).

[DH, 1996; DH, 2004a; DH, 2004b; DH, 2004c; DH, 2005]

Conditions that are NOT contraindications

The following are *not* reasons to delay or avoid vaccination, but if in doubt consult expert opinion:

- A personal or family history of allergy, asthma, eczema, hay fever, or 'snuffles'.
- Prematurity: immunization should not be postponed.
- Stable neurological conditions such as cerebral palsy, Down's syndrome, spina bifida, or well-controlled epilepsy.
- Contact with an infectious disease.
- Treatment with antibiotics or local corticosteroids (e.g. topical or inhaled).
- The child to be immunized is being breastfed or their mother is pregnant.
- History of jaundice after birth.
- Under a certain weight.
- Taking 'replacement' corticosteroids.

[DH, 1996]

References

NHS staff in England can link, free of charge, from references to full text journals by clicking on [Full text] on the PRODIGY website.

1. BNF 46 (2003) *British National Formulary*. 46th edn. London: British Medical Association and Royal Pharmaceutical Society of Great Britain.
2. CMO (2002) *Update on immunisation issues: replacement of single antigen tetanus vaccine (T) by combined tetanus/low dose diphtheria vaccine for adults and adolescents (Td) and advice for tetanus immunisation following injuries*. PL/CMO/2002/4. Department of Health. www.dh.gov.uk [Accessed: 30/04/2004].
3. DH (1996) *Immunisation against infectious disease*. Department of Health. www.dh.gov.uk [Accessed: 18/05/2004]. [Full text]
4. DH (2001) *Health information for overseas travel*. Department of Health. www.dh.gov.uk [Accessed: 03/06/2004]. [Full text]
5. DH (2004a) *New (April 2004) chapter 23 – meningococcal*. Immunisation against infectious disease. Department of Health. www.dh.gov.uk [Accessed: 22/06/2005]. [Full text]
6. DH (2004b) *New (August 2004) chapter 26 – poliomyelitis*. Immunisation against infectious disease. Department of Health. www.dh.gov.uk [Accessed: 22/06/2005]. [Full text]
7. DH (2004c) *New (August 2004) chapter 30 – tetanus*. Immunisation against infectious disease. Department of Health. www.dh.gov.uk [Accessed: 22/06/2005]. [Full text]
8. DH (2005) *New (May 2005) chapter 27 – rabies*. Immunisation against infectious disease. Department of Health. www.dh.gov.uk [Accessed: 28/06/2005]. [Full text]
9. EMEA (2003) *Committee for proprietary medicinal products summary of opinion for Dukoral*. Pre-Authorisation Evaluation of Medicines for Human Use: CPMP/3947/03. The European Agency for the Evaluation of Medicinal Products. www.emea.eu.int [Accessed: 04/06/2004].
10. Goodyer, L. (2000) Travel vaccinations. *Pharmaceutical Journal* **265**(7124), 792–797.
11. NaTHNaC (2003a) *Changes to meningococcal meningitis recommendations for travellers*. Department of Health. [Accessed: 07/04/2004]. [Full text]
12. NaTHNaC (2003b) *Health professionals, travel health information sheets. Rabies vaccine information*. Department of Health. www.nathnac.org/pro/factsheets/rabies_vaccine.htm [Accessed: 28/06/2005]. [Full text]
13. NaTHNaC (2004a) *Meningococcal meningitis ACWY vaccine*. Department of Health. http://www.nathnac.org/healthprofessionals/menigitis-vaccine.html [Accessed: 11/02/2004].
14. NaTHNaC (2004b) *Japanese encephalitis vaccine information*. Department of Health. http://www.nathnac.org/healthprofessionals/Japanese encephalitis-vaccine.html [Accessed: 11/02/2004].
15. NaTHNaC (2004c) *Health professionals, clinical updates. 19 August 2004: poliomyelitis and changes to recommendations for travellers*. Department of Health. www.nathnac.org/pro/clinical_updates/polio_recommendations.htm [Accessed: 28/06/2005].
16. Pounder, D. (2003) Bat rabies. *British Medical Journal* **326**(7392), 726. [Full text]

PRODIGY GUIDANCE

Impetigo

Last revised in December 2002
www.prodigy.nhs.uk/guidance.asp?gt=Impetigo

Applies to people over the age of 1 month

This guidance covers the treatment of impetigo.

This guidance does not cover infected wounds and burns, infected eczema, or cellulitis.

There is separate PRODIGY guidance for *Acne vulgaris, Burns and scalds, Bites — human and animal, Herpes simplex — oral, Lacerations*, and *Fungal — skin and nails.*

Goals

- Alleviate symptoms and limit the duration of infection
- Minimize the risks of complications
- Reduce contagious spread
- Identify any contributory cause

Contents

Scenarios
- Impetigo p.1072

Extended Information, p. 1073

Impetigo

Which therapy?

- **Oral flucloxacillin for 7 days is the first choice oral antibiotic.**
- Erythromycin is an alternative oral antibiotic if the patient is hypersensitive to penicillins.
- **For a small, localized patch of impetigo, topical fusidic acid is an alternative to an oral antibiotic.**
- Offer advice on how to reduce transmission, e.g. hand washing, not sharing towels.
- Recommend that children stay away from nursery or school until there is no further crusting.

Practical prescribing points

For further information, please see the *Medicines Compendium* (www.medicines.org.uk) or the *British National Formulary* (www.bnf.org).

Follow-up advice

- Follow up is generally not necessary.
- Advise follow-up appointment if impetigo does not resolve with treatment.

Should I refer or investigate?

- Bacterial swabs for culture and sensitivity should be obtained before referral is considered.
- Referral is rarely necessary. It may be indicated in severe impetigo or impetigo unresponsive to treatment.
- If there is a significant local outbreak, it is advisable to involve the local Consultant in Communicable Disease Control.

Patient information leaflets

The following PILs are available at www.prodigy.nhs.uk

- Impetigo

Shared decision making

- Impetigo is not usually serious, but can spread if not treated.
- **An antibiotic cream** may be used for a small patch of impetigo.
- **Antibiotic liquid, tablets or capsules** are used if the infection is more widespread.
- **Impetigo is contagious:**
  - Try not to touch patches of impetigo.
  - Wash your hands if you do touch a patch of impetigo, and after applying antibiotic cream.
  - Do not share towels, flannels, etc, until the infection has gone.
  - Change towels frequently to stop spread of infection.
  - Children with impetigo should stay off school or nursery until there is no further crusting.

Drug rationale

Drugs not included

- **Broad-spectrum antibiotics** are not offered. As the pathogen is known, a narrow spectrum antibiotic active against *Staphylococcus aureus* is sufficient.
- **Topical corticosteroid/antibiotic combinations** are not recommended; they should be avoided as they may aggravate infection.
- **Mupirocin** remains an essential therapy for the treatmen of methicillin-resistant *S aureus* (MRSA) and prescriptions are not offered for first-line use.
- **Topical preparations containing chlortetracycline hydrochloride, gramicidin, tetracycline, polymixin B sulphate, neomycin, bacitracin, or combinations of topical antibiotics or antifungal agents** are not offered. Broad-spectrum agents are unnecessary in bullous impetigo. Topical neomycin or topical bacitracin are particularly likely to cause skin sensitization.
- **Hydrogen peroxide cream** is not recommended; this was found to be effective in one small trial, but there is insufficient evidence to recommend routine use [Christensen and Anehus, 1994].
- **Antibacterial skin cleansers** are not recommended. Antibacterial cleansers have been used to remove crusts and to reduce the spread of infection, but there is no evidence that they have any greater effect than washing with soapy water.

Drugs included

- **Oral flucloxacillin** is effective against *Staphylococcus aureus* infection. At least 7 days of treatment is required
- **Topical fusidic acid preparations** are offered for the treatment of localized superficial infection. To prevent the development of resistance, topical antibiotic agents should not be used to treat widespread lesions and treatment courses should be limited to 5 days.

- **Erythromycin** is effective against *S aureus*. It is offered for people with penicillin hypersensitivity.

Prescriptions

Oral flucloxacillin for 7 days

Flucloxacillin syrup: 62.5mg four times a day
- Age from 1 month to 23 months
- Flucloxacillin 125mg/5ml syrup. Take 2.5ml four times a day for 7 days; supply 200 ml; NHS Cost £6.46.

Flucloxacillin syrup: 125mg four times a day
- Age from 2 to 4 years
- Flucloxacillin 125mg/5ml syrup. Take one 5ml spoonful four times a day for 7 days; supply 200 ml; NHS Cost £6.46.

Flucloxacillin syrup: 250mg four times a day
- Age from 5 to 11 years
- Flucloxacillin 250mg/5ml syrup. Take one 5ml spoonful four times a day for 7 days; supply 200 ml; NHS Cost £13.94.

Flucloxacillin capsules: 250mg four times a day
- Age from 12 years onwards
- Flucloxacillin 250mg capsules. Take one capsule four times a day for 7 days; supply 28 capsules; NHS Cost £2.93.

Flucloxacillin capsules: 500mg four times a day
- Age from 12 years onwards
- Flucloxacillin 500mg capsules. Take one capsule four times a day for 7 days; supply 28 capsules; NHS Cost £4.73.

Oral erythromycin for 7 days (if penicillin allergy)

Erythromycin s/f suspension: 125mg four times a day
- Age from 1 month to 23 months
- Erythromycin 125mg/5ml sf susp. Take one 5ml spoonful four times a day for 7 days; supply 140 ml; NHS Cost £2.32.

Erythromycin s/f suspension: 250mg four times a day
- Age from 2 to 11 years
- Erythromycin 250mg/5ml sf susp. Take one 5ml spoonful four times a day for 7 days; supply 140 ml; NHS Cost £3.90.

Erythromycin s/f suspension: 500mg four times a day
- Age from 9 to 11 years
- Erythromycin 500mg/5ml sf susp. Take one 5ml spoonful four times a day for 7 days; supply 140 ml; NHS Cost £6.70.

Erythromycin e/c tablets: 250mg four times a day
- Age from 12 years onwards
- Erythromycin 250mg e/c tablets. Take one tablet four times a day for 7 days; supply 28 tablets; NHS Cost £3.08.

Erythromycin e/c tablets: 500mg four times a day
- Age from 12 years onwards
- Erythromycin 250mg e/c tablets. Take two tablets four times a day for 7 days; supply 56 tablets; NHS Cost £6.16.

Topical fusidic acid for 5 days

Fusidic acid ointment
- Age from 1 month onwards
- Sodium fusidate 2% w/v ointmen. Apply to the affected area three times a day for 5 days; supply 15 grams; NHS Cost £2.23.

Fusidic acid cream
- Age from 1 month onwards
- Fusidic acid 2% w/v cream. Apply to the affected area three times a day for 5 days; supply 15 grams; NHS Cost £2.74.

Extended Information

Background information

- What is it? p.1073
- How common is it? p.1073
- How do I know my patient has it? p.1073
- What else might it be? p.1074
- Complications and prognosis p.1074

What is it?

- **Impetigo is a superficial, contagious skin infection** occurring in the epidermis and/or dermis.
- The infection can result from direct invasion of healthy tissue, or it may occur secondarily to an underlying skin disease.
- Impetigo is associated with the formation of blisters (bullae), and in its classic form is often known as bullous impetigo. It usually occurs following close contact with an infected person or carrier.
- Impetigo can affect clusters such as family or schoolmates.
- Staphylococci or streptococci alone or together can cause impetigo. Bullous impetigo is always due to *Staphylococcus aureus*. Non-bullous impetigo is predominantly due to infection with *S aureus*, although pathogenic beta-haemolytic strains of streptococci may be isolated.

How common is it?

- Impetigo occurs sporadically, most often in infants and young children. It occurs more commonly during the summer months.
- **Impetigo is the most common skin infection in children.** The prevalence in general practice has been reported as being 2.8% of all children aged 4 years and under, and 1.6 % of all children aged between 5 and 15 years [McCormick et al, 1995]. Peak incidence occurs between the ages of 2 and 6 years [Bruijnzeels et al, 1993].
- **Some conditions predispose to colonization with *Staphylococcus aureus*,** e.g. atopic dermatitis, Type 2 diabetes mellitus; haemodialysis and peritonealdialysis; intravenous drug use; and human immunodeficiency virus (HIV) infection.
- **Impetigo-like infections (sometimes called non-bullous impetigo) may affect skin that has been traumatized,** such as varicella lesions, insect bites, abrasions, lacerations, and burns. This guidance does not cover such infections.

How do I know my patient has it?

- **Crusted lesions, usually yellow in colour,** most commonly on the face.
- **Typically there may be scattered surrounding lesions,** known as 'satellite lesions'.
- **Lesions are associated with little or no pain.** Occasionally there may be pruritus.
- **Usually, there is no surrounding erythema,** but, under the crusts, the base of the lesion is red. The person is not systemically unwell.
- **More severe impetigo is commonly associated with lymphadenopathy and malaise.**

What else might it be?

- Acute non-infective dermatitis
- Acute dermatophyte infection
- Herpetic infection
- Scabies, or impetigo secondary to scabies
- Wound infections with impetigo-like lesions

Complications and prognosis

Complications

- Impetigo commonly spreads to other areas of the body if not treated.
- Scarring and pigment changes are occasionally seen following severe impetigo. However, these may resolve over time.
- **The condition is contagious** and can be passed to other family members or close contacts of the infected individual.
- **Involvement of deeper tissues,** with cellulitis, suppurative lymphadenitis, furunculosis, abscess formation, or septicaemia, is rare but may occur, especially with immunosuppression.
- **Exotoxins** produced by some strains of *Staphylococcus aureus* may rarely result in staphylococcal toxic shock syndrome or scalded skin syndrome.
- Non-infectious complications of *Streptococcus pyogenes* infection include guttate psoriasis, scarlet fever or acute glomerulonephritis. Streptococcal infections are not associated with bullous impetigo and streptococcal impetigo is uncommon in the UK.

Management issues

- General issues p.1074
- Drug treatment p.1074

General issues

- Information on the natural history of impetigo is not available, and active treatment is usually given. In some cases impetigo may be self-limiting [Resnick, 2000].
- It is commonly recommended that crusting skin lesions be softened and removed by soaking in warm soapy water or povidone-iodine prior to applying topical treatments [BNF 43, 2002]. It should be noted that systemic antibiotic penetration into crusting is poor.
- Care should be taken to avoid contagious spread of impetigo. It is generally suggested that advice to families should recommend:
  - Careful hand washing after touching a patch of impetigo, and after applying antibiotic cream.
  - Avoidance of sharing towels, flannels, etc, until the infection has gone.
  - That children should stay away from nursery or school until there is no further crusting.
- If more than one household member is infected it is particularly important to obtain swabs for culture to define the organism precisely. An appropriate oral antibiotic should be prescribed and patients followed up to ensure elimination of infection.

Drug treatment

- **It is generally advocated that antibiotic therapy should be prescribed** to eradicate infection, relieve symptoms, and reduce the risk of transmission to others.
- **Impetigo should be treated with oral antibiotics.** Oral antibiotics are definitely indicated if there is associated lymphadenopathy or systemic illness.
- **It seems reasonable to treat a small, localized patch of impetigo with a topical antibiotic;** this will avoid possible adverse effects from taking systemic antibiotics.
- There are several studies indicating that the effectiveness of topical therapy with fusidic acid or mupirocin is similar to that of oral antibiotic therapy [Britton et al, 1990; Bass et al, 1997].
- There is debate about whether all impetigo should be treated with systemic antibiotics, to minimize the risk of development of resistant organisms. Topical antibiotic treatment is associated with greater antibiotic resistance than systemic (oral) treatment [Brown and Wise, 2002; Owen and Cheesbrough, 2002; Stoddart et al, 2002; Sule et al, 2002; Weston et al, 2002; Zadik and Young, 2002].

Oral antibiotics

- **Flucloxacillin or erythromycin** are typically used to treat impetigo, as they are usually effective against *Staphylococcus aureus* infections. Optimal treatment length is not evident from the literature but commonly 7 days treatment is prescribed [PHLS, 2002].

Topical antibiotics

- **Fusidic acid (sodium fusidate).** A recent study confirms that topical fusidic acid is more effective than placebo [Koning et al, 2002]. Topical fusidic acid and topical mupirocin seem to be equally effective [Sutton, 1992]. Some argue that the use of topical fusidic acid should be restricted. Widespread indiscriminate use may give rise to resistant *Staphylococcus aureus* and reduce the value of the systemic formulation of the drug, which is used in hospital practice for the management of severe staphylococcal infections. [Brown and Wise, 2002; Owen and Cheesbrough, 2002; Stoddart et al, 2002; Sule et al, 2002; Weston et al, 2002; Zadik and Young, 2002]
- **Mupirocin.** The BNF advises that mupirocin should not be used for more than 10 days, and that it should not be used in hospital other than for the treatment of methicillin-resistant *S aureus* (MRSA), to reduce the risk of development of resistance [BNF 43, 2002]. In line with current PHLS guidance, PRODIGY recommends that mupirocin be reserved for second-line therapy.

Antiseptic washes and cleansers

- Antibacterial cleansers, such as povidone-iodine, have been used to remove crusts and to reduce the spread of infection, but there is no evidence that they have any greater effect than washing with soapy water [Dagan and Bar-David, 1992; Koning et al, 2002].
- Povidone-iodine plus placebo was less effective than povidone-iodine plus topical fusidic acid in a recently published study [Koning et al, 2002].
- Chlorhexidine and hydrogen peroxide are often used as cleansing agents in impetigo and skin infections. There is some evidence that hydrogen peroxide cream has some effect in healing impetigo [Christensen and Anehus, 1994].

References

NHS staff in England can link, free of charge, from references to full text journals by clicking on [Full text] on the PRODIGY website.

1. Bass, J.W., Chan, D.S., Creamer, K.M. et al (1997) Comparison of oral cephalexin, topical mupirocin and topical bacitracin for treatment of impetigo. *Pediatric Infectious Disease Journal* **16**(7), 708–710.

2. BNF 43 (2002) *British National Formulary*. 43rd edn. London: British Medical Association and Royal Pharmaceutical Society of Great Britain.
3. Britton, J.W., Fajardo, J.E and Krafte-Jacobs, B. (1990) Comparison of mupirocin and erythromycin in the treatment of impetigo. *Journal of Pediatrics* **117**(5), 827–829.
4. Brown, E.M. and Wise, R. (2002) Fusidic acid cream for impetigo. Fusidic acid should be used with restraint. *British Medical Journal* **324**(7350), 1394. [Full text]
5. Bruijnzeels, M.A., Van Suijlekom-Smit, L.W.A., Van der Velden, J. and van der Wouden, J.C. (1993) *The child in general practice. Dutch national survey of morbidity and interventions in general practice.* Rotterdam: Erasmus University.
6. Christensen, O.B. and Anehus, S. (1994) Hydrogen peroxide cream: an alternative to topical antibiotics in the treatment of impetigo contagiosa. *Acta Dermato Venereologica* **74**(6), 460–462.
7. Dagan, R. and Bar-David, Y. (1992) Double-blind study comparing erythromycin and mupirocin for treatment of impetigo in children: implications of a high prevalence of erythromycin-resistant Staphylococcus aureus strains. *Antimicrobial Agents and Chemotherapy* **36**(2), 287–290.
8. Koning, S., Suijlekom-Smit, L.W., Nouwen, J.L. et al (2002) Fusidic acid cream in the treatment of impetigo in general practice: double blind randomised placebo controlled trial. *British Medical Journal* **324**(7331), 203–206. [Full text]
9. McCormick, A., Fleming, D. and Charlton, J. (1995) *Morbidity statistics from general practice. Fourth national study 1991–1992.* Office of Population Censuses and Surveys. www.statistics.gov.uk [Accessed: 03/05/2005].
10. Owen, S.E. and Cheesbrough, J.S. (2002) Fusidic acid cream for impetigo. Findings cannot be extrapolated. *British Medical Journal* **324**(7350), 1396. [Full text]
11. PHLS (2002) *Management of infection guidance for primary care.* PHLS. www.hpa.org.uk [Accessed: 05/09/2002].
12. Resnick, D.S (2000) Staphylococcal and streptococcal skin infections: pyodermas and toxin-mediated syndromes. In: Harper, J., Oranje, A., Prose, N. et al (Eds.) *Textbook of pediatric dermatology*. Oxford: Blackwell Science. 369–372.
13. Stoddart, B., Collyns, T. and Denton, M. (2002) Fusidic acid cream for impetigo. Problem may be clinically important. *British Medical Journal* **324**(7350), 1395–1396. [Full text]
14. Sule, O., Brown, N., Brown, D.F. and Burrows, N. (2002) Fusidic acid cream for impetigo. Judicious use is advisable. *British Medical Journal* **324**(7350), 1394–1395. [Full text]
15. Sutton, J. (1992) Efficacy and acceptability of fusidic acid cream and mupirocin ointment in facial impetigo. *Current Therapeutic Research* **51**(5), 673–678.
16. Weston, V.C., Boswell, T.C., Finch, R.G. and Perkins, W. (2002) Fusidic acid cream for impetigo. Emergence of resistance to fusidic acid limits its use. *British Medical Journal* **324**(7350), 1395. [Full text]
17. Zadik, P. and Young, N. (2002) Fusidic acid cream for impetigo. Resistance trends must be monitored. *British Medical Journal* **324**(7350), 1396. [Full text]

PRODIGY GUIDANCE

Infertility

Last revised in July 2004
www.prodigy.nhs.uk/guidance.asp?gt=Infertility

Applies to people over the age of 16 years

This guidance is based on the National Institute for Clinical Excellence (NICE) guideline, *Fertility: assessment and treatment for people with fertility problems* (February 2004).

This guidance covers the primary care management of infertile and subfertile couples.

This guidance does not cover secondary and tertiary care management of infertility but outlines the treatment that is offered. It only gives brief information on ovulation induction agents, *in vitro* fertilization (IVF), and other forms of assisted conception. It does not cover the treatment of impotence. It does not cover surrogacy, or issues around sperm and egg banking.

There is separate PRODIGY guidance for *Amenorrhoea, Contraception, Endometriosis, Menopause*, and *Preconceptual counselling*.

Goals

- To guide initial management of the infertile couple and suggest appropriate referral and investigation criteria

Contents

Scenarios

- Infertility p.1076

Extended Information, p. 1078

Infertility

Which therapy?

For all women trying to conceive

- **Folic acid** supplements are recommended.
- **Check rubella status.** If seronegative, rubella vaccine (as MMR) is indicated. Advise the woman not to get pregnant within 1 month of the vaccination.
- **Check that the cervical smear** is up-to-date.
- **Advise regular sex** two to three times a week throughout the cycle.

Managing infertility

- Investigations and referral for infertility are not generally advised until the couple have been unable to achieve a pregnancy after 1 year of unprotected intercourse. Reassure that 84% of couples will conceive within 12 months of trying.
- Assess all couples who are concerned about their fertility:
  - **Ask both partners about medical history,** including drugs and surgery; length of time trying to conceive; frequency and difficulties of sexual intercourse; previous children born; sexually transmitted diseases, and occupation and lifestyle factors, such as smoking and alcohol. In addition for women, record menstrual history and previous contraception.
  - **Examine:** including a pelvic examination (for women) and scrotum and penis examination (for men).
- For couples who have not conceived after 1 year of regular unprotected sexual intercourse or have been identified as less likely to conceive:
  - **Arrange semen analysis.** For details see *Should I refer or investigate?*
  - **Measure mid-luteal phase progesterone in the woman.** Sample at day 21 (or 7 days before next period starts). For details see *Should I refer or investigate?*
- **Provide educational materials and lifestyle advice if appropriate,** on:
  - Stopping smoking
  - Alcohol (1–2 units once or twice a week for women, reduce excessive drinking for men)
  - Weight (in particular, women with body mass index greater than 29 should lose weight)
  - A well-balanced diet
- **Generally refer couples who have not managed to conceive after 18 months,** if history, examination, and investigations are normal in both partners, and the woman is under the age of 35 years.
- **Consider early referral** using the criteria in *Should I refer or investigate?*

Practical prescribing points

For further information, please see the *Medicines Compendium* (www.medicines.org.uk) or the *British National Formulary* (www.bnf.org).

Should I refer or investigate?

Refer?

When to refer to a fertility clinic/secondary care:

- **Follow local protocols** and make the decision to refer with the couple.
- **Deferred referral is acceptable if infertility duration is less than 18 months** and the history, examination, and initial investigations are normal, if the couple are satisfied with this plan.
- **Earlier referral may be prompted by factors including:**
  - Maternal age greater than 35 years
  - Previous surgery (woman, abdominal or pelvic; man, urogenital)
  - Irregular menstrual cycle
  - Previous sexually transmitted disease (man and woman) or pelvic inflammatory disease (woman)
  - Abnormal pelvic (woman) or genital (man) examination, varicocele (man)
  - Abnormalities in initial investigation
  - Known reason for infertility, e.g. prior treatment for cancer

Other referrals:

- **Referral to a counsellor** may be appropriate for some people for help with the psychological and emotional distress of infertility.
- **Referral to a psychosexual counsellor** may be appropriate for those people in whom sexual problems may be contributing to infertility.
- Refer people with chronic viral infections (e.g. hepatitis B, hepatitis C and HIV) to the appropriate specialist centre to provide advice about risk reduction, investigation and treatment.

Investigate?

- **Chlamydia screening** should be part of the assessment of all women presenting with infertility.
- **Check the rubella status** in all women who are trying to conceive. If seronegative, rubella vaccination (as MMR) is indicated and the woman should be advised not to become pregnant within 1 month of the vaccination. Do not give the vaccine if the woman is already pregnant.
- **Arrange a semen specimen for all men prior to referral.** The sample should be taken after 2 to 3 days of abstinence (but not more than 7 days) prior to the collection of the sample. Collection should be by masturbation rather than coitus interruptus, without the use of condoms or jellies, and taken to the laboratory as quickly as possible, preferably within 1 hour, in a container labelled with date and time of production, and date of immediate preceding ejaculation.
- **If the semen analysis is normal** then a repeat confirmatory test should be taken 3 months after the initial test.
- **If the result of the first semen sample is abnormal** then a repeat test should be done. If azoospermia or severe oligospermia has been found then the repeat test should be done as soon as possible.
- **Mid-luteal phase progesterone** should be measured to confirm ovulation in all women prior to referral. A sample should be taken 7 days before expected period (day 21 in a 28 day cycle) and the date of next period recorded (to confirm that sample is mid-luteal). Values range from 16–28 nanomols/litre as the lowest limit indicative of ovulation.

Patient information leaflets

The following PILs are available at www.prodigy.nhs.uk

- Biopsy
- Blood Test - General
- Donor Conception Network
- Human Fertilisation & Embryology Authority
- Infertility - a Basic Understanding
- Infertility Network UK
- Laparoscopy and Laparoscopic Surgery
- National Gamete Donation Trust
- Rubella Immunisation
- Semen Analysis

Shared decision making

- **About 1 in 7 couples have difficulty conceiving.** There are various causes.
- More than half of couples who have been trying for a baby for a year will become pregnant in the second year without treatment. However, it is common to start tests after about a year of trying for a baby.
- **Initial tests** include a semen test for the man and a blood test to check for ovulation in the woman.
- **Folic acid** is recommended for all women trying to conceive.
- **Rubella** immunity should also be checked.

- **Referral to a specialist** is an option after the results of the initial tests are back. However, waiting times are sometimes long.

Drug rationale

Drugs not included

- **Infertility drugs:** in most cases prescribing is initiated and maintained by secondary care. In some situations these drugs will need to be prescribed in primary care and it is appropriate in this situation to liaise with the gynaecologist to whom the couple has been referred, in order to establish the exact dose of drug and number of cycles required.

Drugs included

- **Folic acid 400 micrograms daily** until week 12 of pregnancy is recommended to reduce the risk of neural tube defects.
- **Folic acid 5 mg daily** is recommended for people taking anticonvulsants, who have coeliac disease, who have previously had a child with a neural tube defect, or have a family history of neural tube defect [Wald, 1991; Lumley et al, 2003]. Women with sickle cell anaemia (HbS/S), HbH disease, or HbS/C disease should also take 5 mg folic acid daily for life and continue to do so during pregnancy [Taylor, Personal Communication, 2004].
- **Rubella vaccine** (as MMR) is included if the women is seronegative.
    - **A pregnancy test must be carried out initially** to confirm that the woman is not pregnant. As there have not been any cases of congenital rubella syndrome reported after inadvertent immunization shortly before or during pregnancy, routine termination of the pregnancy should not be recommended if conception occurs.
- Note: the Department of Health has advised that seronegative women should be vaccinated using MMR (measles, mumps, and rubella) since the Department is no longer able to secure supplies of licensed rubella vaccine [CMO, 2003].

Prescriptions

Folic acid tablets

Folic acid 400micrograms once a day

- Age from 16 years onwards
- Folic acid 400microgram tabs. Take one tablet once a day; supply 90 tablets; NHS Cost £2.24; OTC Cost £4.05.

Folic acid 5mg once a day (special cases)

- Age from 16 years onwards
- Folic acid 5mg tablets. Take one tablet once a day; supply 84 tablets; NHS Cost £1.32.

Rubella vaccine (NOT if pregnant)

Rubella vaccine (as MMR) – NOT if pregnant

- Age from 16 years onwards
- MMR vaccine. Give 0.5ml by deep subcutaneous or intramuscular injection. Read attached information; supply 1 0.5ml injection; NHS Cost £2.53.

Advice note: sperm sample collection

Advice only

- Age from 16 years onwards
- Collection of a sperm sample 1. Your doctor will give you a special pot for collection of the sperm sample and also a form which must be handed in to the laboratory.

2. Do not have sex for 2 or 3 days before collection of the sperm sample. 3. Collect the sample by masturbation, not by withdrawal, and without using any jellies or condoms. 4. Collect the sperm sample into the container and write on the label :– – the time and date of collection of your sperm sample, – the date of your previous ejaculation. 5. It is important that you take the sperm sample to the laboratory very quickly, within 1 hour of collection.

Extended Information

Background information

- What is it? p.1078
- How common is it? p.1078
- What causes it? p.1078
- Likely outcomes of infertility p.1079

What is it?

- **Infertility is the inability to conceive, but a couple are regarded as infertile if after regular sexual intercourse they have not conceived in 2 years** [National Collaborating Centre for Women's and Children's Health, 2004].
- Infertility is classed as primary in couples who have never conceived and secondary in couples who have previously conceived [National Collaborating Centre for Women's and Children's Health, 2004].
- **Infertility may be categorized** into unexplained (30%), or secondary to ovulatory failure (27%), male factors (19%), tubal factors (14%), or endometriosis (5%) [NHS CRD, 1992; De Kretser, 1997; Templeton, 2000]. The presence of disorders in both the man and the woman has been reported to occur in about 39% of cases [Thonneau et al, 1991; National Collaborating Centre for Women's and Children's Health, 2004].

How common is it?

- **The prevalence of infertility is around 14% in European countries, affecting one in seven couples** [National Collaborating Centre for Women's and Children's Health, 2004].
- **Of all couples attempting to conceive, 16% are unsuccessful after 1 year.** This reduces to 8% after 2 years and 7% after 3 years [National Collaborating Centre for Women's and Children's Health, 2004].
- **Infertility is more common with increasing age:** female fertility declines with age although the effect on male fertility is less clear. With regular sexual intercourse only 6% women aged 35 years and 23% of those aged 38 years will have failed to conceive after 3 years [National Collaborating Centre for Women's and Children's Health, 2004].
- **The number of couples seeking help has increased** although it is not thought that there has been a major increase in the prevalence of infertility. Theories such as a decline in sperm count due to environmental factors are controversial. Behavioural factors such as a tendency to delay childbearing may play a role [Himmel et al, 1997; Templeton, 2000].

What causes it?

Causes of infertility in women

Disorders of ovulation

- **Premature ovarian failure**
- **Polycystic ovarian syndrome:** often associated with hirsutism, obesity, acne, and menstrual irregularity.
- **Hypothalamic-pituitary causes:**
  - **Anterior pituitary macro or microadenoma** may alter prolactin secretion and lead to amenorrhoea and anovulation. Although stress may cause a transient rise in prolactin, levels higher than 1000 ml/litre suggest an adenoma.
  - **Hypogonadotrophic hypogonadism:** the commonest cause is excessive exercising, being underweight or both. People with anorexia nervosa are normally amenorrhoeic.
  - **Sheehan's syndrome** (panhypopituitarism most often following massive postpartum haemorrhage or trauma) is now very rare.
  - **Kallmann's syndrome** (amenorrhoea and anosmia due to congenital lack of hypothalamic production of gonadotrophin-releasing hormone) is rare.
- **Thyroid:** hyperthyroidism and hypothyroidism may lead to menstrual disorders and ovulatory dysfunction.
- **Adrenal:** Cushing's syndrome and congenital adrenal hyperplasia may cause anovulation.

Tubal, uterine and cervical factors

- **Genital tract infection causing tubal damage:** chlamydial infection is a major risk factor [Land and Evers, 2002].
- **Previous pelvic surgery** causing tubal damage or adhesions, or previous cervical surgery causing scarring or shortening of cervix and, rarely, cervical stenosis.
- **Submucosal fibroids may** distort the uterine cavity and impair implantation [Campbell and Monga, 2000].
- **Previous sterilization.**
- **Cervical mucus defect or dysfunction.**
- **Endometriosis:** tubal distortion and limitation of fimbrial motility due to pelvic adhesions.

Drugs

- **Nonsteroidal anti-inflammatory drugs,** in particular indometacin, can inhibit ovulation.
- **Chemotherapy with cytotoxic drugs** can induce ovarian failure, which may be permanent.
- **Recreational drugs, such as marijuana and cocaine,** have also been associated with impaired ovulatory and tubal function.

[Dukes, 1996; Janssen and Genta, 2000; National Collaborating Centre for Women's and Children's Health, 2004]

Other factors

- **Occupational/environmental factors** which may affect fertility include shift work, intense physical workload, pesticides, solvents and formaldehyde [National Collaborating Centre for Women's and Children's Health, 2004].
- **Psychogenic** factors may affect fertility but studies have not consistently shown this [Himmel et al, 1997].
- **Significant systemic illness** e.g. thyroid problems.

[Cooke, 1996; Hargreave and Mills, 1998; Chambers, 1999; Chen and Brzyski, 1999; Campbell and Monga, 2000; Hamilton-Fairley and Taylor, 2003; HFEA, 2004a; National Collaborating Centre for Women's and Children's Health, 2004; Symonds and Symonds, 2004]

Causes of infertility in men

Defective spermatogenesis

- Commonest cause of male subfertility: reduced count of mainly dysfunctional spermatozoa (oligoasthenoteratozoospermia) of unknown cause
- Congenital, e.g. Klinefelter's syndrome (karyotype 47 XXY, small testes and sterility)
- Hypogonadotrophic hypogonadism, e.g. Kallmann's syndrome
- Pituitary causes, e.g. hyperprolactinaemia from a pituitary adenoma

Genital tract abnormalities

- **Previous vasectomy.**
- **Past history of infection,** e.g. mumps orchitis; epididymitis and prostatovesiculitis may also lead to infertility.
- **Congenital absence of vas deferens:** 1–2% of infertile men.
- **Testicular tumour:** may be palpable on examination.
- **Maldescended testes:** absence of testes on examination.
- **Varicocele:** present in up to approximately 25%–40% of subfertile men, although its association with infertility is not clear [Wong et al, 2000].

Drugs

- **Sulfasalazine, neuroleptics, and nitrofurantoin** can affect semen quality and cause oligospermia. The effect is usually reversible on withdrawal of medication [Dukes, 1996; National Collaborating Centre for Women's and Children's Health, 2004].
- **Chemotherapy with cytotoxic drugs** can induce permanent azoospermia [National Collaborating Centre for Women's and Children's Health, 2004].
- **Beta-blockers, cimetidine, psychotrophic drugs, and spironolactone** can cause impotence or ejaculatory dysfunction [National Collaborating Centre for Women's and Children's Health, 2004].
- **The use of drugs such as anabolic steroids and cocaine** can adversely affect the quality of semen.

[Dukes, 1996; National Collaborating Centre for Women's and Children's Health, 2004]

Other factors

- **Ejaculation disorders,** e.g. retrograde ejaculation, impotence.
- **Environmental factors** which may affect fertility include agricultural chemicals, X-ray exposure, solvents, and heavy metals [National Collaborating Centre for Women's and Children's Health, 2004].
- **Antibodies against spermatozoa,** e.g. post vasectomy.
- **Exposure of testes to heat.**
- **Psychogenic** stress and its association with infertility in men is not clear. A higher incidence of male sexual disturbances has been observed in couples undergoing fertility investigation and treatment [National Collaborating Centre for Women's and Children's Health, 2004; Saleh et al, 2003].
- **Significant systemic illness,** e.g. cardiac failure, chronic renal failure, neoplasia, uncontrolled diabetes, liver cirrhosis, thyrotoxicosis.

[Wu, 1996; De Kretser, 1997; Himmel et al, 1997; Hargreave and Mills, 1998; Chambers, 1999; Hirsh, 2003]

Likely outcomes of infertility

Without treatment

- For couples who have been trying for less than a year, the conception rate is between 80% and 90%.
- For couples who have been trying to conceive for up to 3 years, the conception rate is about 40% in a 1-year period (equivalent to a monthly fecundity rate of 4–5%) if the woman is aged about 30 years.
- For couples who have been trying for more than 3 years, the conception rate is still up to 25% in a 1-year period.
- If a male or female subfertility factor has been identified, there is still a likelihood of spontaneous conception, although the success rates may be lower.

[NHS CRD, 1992; Himmel et al, 1997; Hargreave and Mills, 1998; Te Velde and Cohlen, 1999].

With treatment

- ***In vitro* fertilization (IVF):** the overall live birth rate per treatment cycle is 21.8% (25.1% for women aged less than 38 years). If frozen embryos are used the success rate is about 12% per treatment cycle. After five attempts, just over half of women aged under 34 years will have conceived [HFEA, 2004a; HFEA, 2004b]. One in 20 pregnancies that result in a live birth will be a multiple pregnancy. Twins are much are more common than triplets (ratio of 15:1) [National Collaborating Centre for Women's and Children's Health, 2004].
- **Intracytoplasmic sperm injection (ICSI):** the overall live birth rate per embryo transfer is 28.7% (25.7% for women over 38 years) [HFEA, 2004b].
- **Intrauterine insemination (IUI)** has a pregnancy rate of 9% per treatment cycle using ovulation stimulation in couples with unexplained infertility [National Collaborating Centre for Women's and Children's Health, 2004].
- **Donor insemination (DI)** has a live birth rate of about 10–12% with each attempt in women under 30 years, and 9% in women aged 35–39 years [HFEA, 2004a].
- **Oocyte donation** has a live birth rate of 25–40% with each attempt (eggs donated by women under 36 years)[HFEA, 2004a].
- **Embryo donation** has a live birth rate of 16.8% using frozen embryos and 27.3% using fresh embryos [Lee and Yap, 2003].
- **Gamete intrafallopian transfer (GIFT)** has a pregnancy rate of 25–30% in any one treatment cycle [HFEA, 2004a].
- **Tubal surgery:** reported pregnancy rates range between 5% and 50%, with the severity of tubal damage being closely linked to outcome [National Collaborating Centre for Women's and Children's Health, 2004].
- **Reversal of sterilization:** pregnancy rates of up to 85.7% have been reported, although rates depend on the type of previous surgery and age. A successful outcome is more likely in younger women [Cohen et al, 1999; Yoon et al, 1999; Tourgeman et al, 2001; Hanafi, 2003].
- **Reversal of vasectomy** results in subsequent pregnancy rates ranging between 35% and 71% [Himmel et al, 1997].
- **Medical treatment for male factor infertility** is effective only if the cause is hypogonadotrophic hypogonadism, where 80% of men have achieved a positive sperm count [National Collaborating Centre for Women's and Children's Health, 2004].
- **Medical treatments for ovulatory dysfunction** caused by hyperprolactinaemia results in an ovulation rate of 70–80% [Hamilton-Fairley and Taylor, 2003].
- **Pulsatile gonadotrophin-releasing hormone for hypothalamic amenorrhoea** results in conception rates of 80–90% after 12 months' use [Hamilton-Fairley and Taylor, 2003].

Management issues

- General issues p.1079
- Assessment of the infertile couple in primary care p.1080
- Lifestyle advice p.1081
- Referring the couple for specialist help p.1082
- Secondary and tertiary care management p.1082
- Problems with assisted conception p.1084
- Counselling and information on infertility p.1084
- Anonymity of donors p.1084

General issues

- **Assessment and investigations for infertility are not generally advised until the couple have been unable to achieve a pregnancy after a year of unprotected intercourse.** Some people who present with concerns about their fertility need only simple reassurance that the chance of conception is 84% in the first year if they do not use contraception and have regular sexual intercourse. About half of couples who do not conceive in the first year will conceive in the second year (a cumulative pregnancy rate of 92%) [National Collaborating Centre for Women's and Children's Health, 2004].

- **Regular sexual intercourse (two or three times a week) throughout the cycle** should ensure that intercourse falls within the fertile period. Timing of intercourse using temperature charts and luteinizing hormone detection methods causes stress and has not been shown to improve conception rates. They are therefore not recommended [Hargreave and Mills, 1998; National Collaborating Centre for Women's and Children's Health, 2004].
- **Folic acid supplements** should be taken whilst trying to conceive and for the first 12 weeks of pregnancy in order to reduce the risk of neural tube defects. Most women should take 400 micrograms daily. A higher dose of 5 mg daily is recommended for women who either have a family history of neural tube defect, who have had a baby with a neural tube defect, who are taking antiepileptic medication, or who have coeliac disease [Wald, 1991; Lumley et al, 2003; National Collaborating Centre for Women's and Children's Health, 2004].
- **Rubella status** should be checked. If seronegative, rubella vaccination is indicated and the woman should be advised not to become pregnant within 1 month of the vaccination. Note: the Department of Health has advised that seronegative women should be vaccinated using MMR (measles, mumps, and rubella) since the Department is no longer able to secure supplies of licensed rubella vaccine [CMO, 2003].
- **Cervical screening** should be offered in accordance with the national cervical screening programme guidance [National Collaborating Centre for Women's and Children's Health, 2004].
- For further information see the PRODIGY *Preconceptual counselling* guidance.

Assessment of the infertile couple in primary care

When should I assess?

- Couples who are concerned about their fertility should be offered an initial assessment (history and examination) in primary care. Specifically enquire about lifestyle and sexual history to identify couples who may be less likely to conceive [National Collaborating Centre for Women's and Children's Health, 2004].
- Couples who have not conceived after 1 year of regular unprotected sexual intercourse, or have been identified as less likely to conceive, should also be offered initial investigations, e.g. semen analysis, assessment of ovulation, or both [National Collaborating Centre for Women's and Children's Health, 2004].

How should I assess the woman?

History

A full medical, sexual, and social history should include:

- **Maternal age** (fertility decreases with age).
- **Previous children** born to the woman, previous pregnancies and miscarriages (with same or different partner).
- **Length of time** trying to conceive, and frequency and difficulties of sexual intercourse.
- **Length of time since stopping contraception** and type of contraception.
- **Menstrual cycle details:** including length of cycle and symptoms and signs of ovulation, e.g. ovulatory discomfort, changes in cervical mucus.
- **Cervical smear history and previous pelvic surgery,** e.g. appendicitis.
- **Symptoms of pelvic inflammatory disease or endometriosis,** e.g. dyspareunia and dysmenorrhoea.
- **Past history of sexually transmitted diseases or pelvic inflammatory disease** [World Health Organization Task Force on the Prevention and Management of Infertility, 1995].
- **Systemic or debilitating diseases** including thyroid dysfunction, diabetes, inflammatory bowel disease, and anorexia nervosa.
- **Drug history:** see *Causes of infertility in women/Drugs*.
- **Details of occupation** for possible exposure to hazards that can reduce fertility, e.g. pesticides, nitrous oxide, formaldehyde and solvents [National Collaborating Centre for Women's and Children's Health, 2004].
- **Lifestyle factors** that may affect fertility, e.g. smoking, alcohol intake, excessive exercise, stress. Excessive travelling that limits optimal coital timing may indirectly affect fertility.

[Chambers, 1999; Symonds and Symonds, 2004]

Examination

- **Pelvic examination** may identify factors causing infertility, such as vaginal infection or tenderness indicating endometriosis or pelvic inflammatory disease. Bimanual examination may reveal fibroids or an ovarian cyst [Hargreave and Mills, 1998; Chambers, 1999].
- **Also look for obesity** (associated with lower fertility), hirsutism, acne, or both (associated with polycystic ovary syndrome), and galactorrhoea (suggestive of hyperprolactinaemia) [Chambers, 1999].

Initial investigations

- **Mid-luteal phase progesterone levels should be checked in all women to confirm ovulation.** The sample should be taken 7 days before the expected period (day 21 in a 28-day cycle) [National Collaborating Centre for Women's and Children's Health, 2004].
- **In women with prolonged irregular menstrual cycles,** depending on the timing of menstrual periods, serum progesterone may need to be taken later in the cycle, and repeated weekly thereafter until the next menstrual cycle starts [National Collaborating Centre for Women's and Children's Health, 2004].
- **Serum gonadotrophins (follicle-stimulating hormone and luteinizing hormone) should be measured in all women with irregular menstrual cycles.** Women with high levels of gonadotrophins are likely to have reduced fertility [National Collaborating Centre for Women's and Children's Health, 2004].
- **Thyroid function tests should only be undertaken in women with symptoms of thyroid disease.** Women with possible fertility problems are no more likely than the general population to have thyroid disease [National Collaborating Centre for Women's and Children's Health, 2004].
- **Prolactin estimation** should be reserved for women with an ovulatory disorder, galactorrhoea or a suspected pituitary tumour [National Collaborating Centre for Women's and Children's Health, 2004].
- **Chlamydia screening.** NICE recommends that all women who will be undergoing uterine instrumentation should be tested for chlamydia, as infertility investigations may result in iatrogenic pelvic inflammatory disease. Although the prevalence of *Chlamydia trachomatis* is only 1.9% in subfertile women, the number of people diagnosed with uncomplicated chlamydia infection has risen steadily since 1993 particularly in the 16–19-year-old age group. We would therefore recommend that

chlamydia screening should be part of the assessment of all women presenting with infertility. If the test is positive, women and their partners should be referred for appropriate management and contact tracing [PHLS et al, 2000; National Collaborating Centre for Women's and Children's Health, 2004].

How should I assess the man?

History

A full medical, sexual, and social history should include:

- **Previous children** born to the man (with same or different partner).
- **Length of time** trying to conceive, and frequency and difficulties of sexual intercourse.
- **Past history of mumps, sexually transmitted diseases, or testicular trauma** [World Health Organization Task Force on the Prevention and Management of Infertility, 1995; Kennedy, Personal Communication, 2004].
- **Previous surgery** e.g. herniorrhaphy.
- **Previous urogenital pathology and treatment,** e.g. undescended testis or orchidopexy.
- **Systemic or debilitating diseases, e.g. cardiac failure, chronic renal failure, neoplasia, uncontrolled diabetes liver cirrhosis, thyrotoxicosis** [Wu, 1996].
- **Drug history:** see *Causes of infertility in men/Drugs*.
- **Details of occupation** for possible exposure to pesticides, X-rays, solvents, paints, chemicals from smelting or welding [National Collaborating Centre for Women's and Children's Health, 2004].
- **Lifestyle factors** that may affect fertility, e.g. smoking, alcohol intake, excessive travelling that limits optimal coital timing, excess exercise, stress, social or occupational situations that may cause testicular hyperthermia.

[Chambers, 1999; Symonds and Symonds, 2004]

Examination

- Scrotal examination may reveal lumps (cancer, varicocele, or hernia), small, soft testes, or undescended testes in some cases.
- The penis should be examined, including a check of the position of the urethral meatus, for structural abnormalities and signs of infection.
- Assess secondary sexual characteristics.
- Look for gynaecomastia.

[Cooke, 1996; Hargreave and Mills, 1998; Chambers, 1999]

Initial investigations

- **One fresh semen specimen** should be taken during the initial investigation. The specimen should be produced after 2–3 days abstinence from sex. The specimen should be sent to the laboratory as quickly as possible as analysis should be carried out preferably within 1 hour of production [Chambers, 1999; National Collaborating Centre for Women's and Children's Health, 2004].
- **Interpret using the World Health Organization (WHO) normal values:**
  - Volume 2 ml or more.
  - Liquefaction time within 60 minutes.
  - pH 7.2 or more.
  - Sperm concentration greater than 20 million/ml.
  - Motility: 50% or more motile (grades a and b) or 25% or more with progressive motility (grade a) within 60 minutes of ejaculation. (Grade a is rapid progressive motility, with sperm moving swiftly, usually in a straight line; grade b is slow or sluggish progressive motility and sperm may be less linear in their progression.)
  - Vitality: 75% or more live.
  - White blood cells: fewer than 1 million per ml.
  - Morphology >30% normal forms (or >15% based on strict morphological criteria).
- **If the result of the first semen sample is normal, a repeat confirmatory test should ideally be taken 3 months after the initial test as this allows time for the cycle of spermatozoa to be completed.**
- **If the result of the first semen sample is abnormal then a repeat test should be done.** If there is a gross spermatozoa deficiency (azoospermia or severe oligospermia) then the repeat test should be done as soon as possible.

[National Collaborating Centre for Women's and Children's Health, 2004]

Which investigations are not generally recommended?

- Basal body temperature charts do not reliably predict ovulation and are not recommended [National Collaborating Centre for Women's and Children's Health, 2004; Guermandi et al, 2001].
- Ovulation predictor kits are widely available but there is no evidence that attempts to time intercourse to the menstrual cycle will result in improved conception rates and they are not recommended [Hargreave and Mills, 1998; Chambers, 1999].
- The routine use of postcoital testing has no predictive value for pregnancy rates [National Collaborating Centre for Women's and Children's Health, 2004].
- Screening for antisperm antibodies should not be offered, as there is no evidence of effective treatment to improve fertility [National Collaborating Centre for Women's and Children's Health, 2004].

Lifestyle advice

Smoking

- **Smoking cessation is advisable for both men and women.** Smoking, including passive smoking has been shown to be detrimental to fertility in women [Hughes and Brennan, 1996; Augood et al, 1998; Hull et al, 2000; BMA, 2004]. In men, although there is no clear evidence that smoking delays conception or affects fertility, it may affect sperm quality and general health [BMA, 2004].

Alcohol limitation

- **Women should be advised to limit alcohol to 1 to 2 units once or twice a week.** The evidence for a link between alcohol and female infertility is conflicting, and the limits for safe consumption are not known, but until more is known, low consumption of alcohol when trying to become pregnant and during pregnancy is advisable [DH, 2003; National Collaborating Centre for Women's and Children's Health, 2004].
- **Men should be informed that alcohol consumption within the Department of Health's recommendations of 3 to 4 units a day is unlikely to affect their fertility.** Excessive alcohol consumption can be detrimental to semen quality [National Collaborating Centre for Women's and Children's Health, 2004].

Weight

- **Weight loss should be encouraged in women with a body mass index (BMI) greater than 29,** as this is likely to increase their chance of ovulation and therefore conception. There is no proven association between male obesity and infertility, although obesity is associated with poorer general health, a reduction in sperm motility and increased DNA fragmentation [Rich-Edwards et al, 2002; Kort et al, 2003; Kort et al, 2003; National Collaborating Centre for Women's and Children's Health, 2004].
- **Women who have a body mass index of less than 19** and either amenorrhoea or irregular menstruation should be

advised that gaining weight is likely to increase their chance of conception [National Collaborating Centre for Women's and Children's Health, 2004].

Nutrition

- **A well-balanced diet** will contribute to general good health for both partners. Although there is little research on nutritional factors in infertility, there have been studies suggesting that nutritional deficiencies may play a role; e.g. vitamins C, D, E, selenium, zinc, and folate deficiencies may affect sperm quality [Wong et al, 2000].
- There is no consistent evidence to link consumption of caffeinated beverages (tea, coffee, and cola) and infertility [National Collaborating Centre for Women's and Children's Health, 2004].

Clothing

- Men should be informed that although there is an association between an elevated scrotal temperature and reduced semen quality, it is uncertain whether wearing loose-fitting underwear improves semen quality [Tiemessen et al, 1996; Munkelwitz and Gilbert, 1998; National Collaborating Centre for Women's and Children's Health, 2004].

Referring the couple for specialist help

- Referral criteria for people presenting with infertility may vary between health authorities.
- Decision to refer should always be based on the individual couple's concerns and preferences. Even after referral to secondary care, continuing support in primary care is needed.
- **Generally consider referral if the couple have not managed to conceive after 18 months,** if history, examination, and investigations are normal in both partners, and the woman is under the age of 35 years [Chambers, 1999].
- **Abnormality of any initial tests** suggests that earlier secondary care involvement is required [Chambers, 1999].
- **Earlier referral** (i.e. duration of infertility less than 18 months) may also be prompted by factors listed in Table 1.

[Chambers, 1999; National Collaborating Centre for Women's and Children's Health, 2004]

- **People who experience fertility problems should be treated by a specialist team** as this is likely to improve the effectiveness and efficiency of treatment and is known to improve patients' satisfaction [National Collaborating Centre for Women's and Children's Health, 2004]. The exception is where there are obvious abnormalities of the male genitalia, when men may be more appropriately referred to a urologist as well [Chambers, 1999].

Table 1: Factors that may prompt an early referral to a specialist infertility centre.

Woman	Man
Aged over 35 years	Previous genital pathology
Amenorrhoea/oligomenorrhoea	Previous urogenital surgery
Previous abdominal/pelvic surgery	Previous sexually transmitted infection
Previous pelvic inflammatory disease	Varicocele
Previous sexually transmitted infection	Significant systemic illness
Abnormal pelvic examination	Abnormal genital examination
Known reason for infertility, e.g. prior treatment for cancer	Known reason for infertility, e.g. prior treatment for cancer

- **Information about the likely treatments in secondary care,** should they be needed, may be of great help to the couple. See *Likely outcomes of infertility with treatment.*
- **Refer people with chronic viral infections** (e.g. hepatitis B, hepatitis C and HIV) to the appropriate specialist centre to provide advice about risk reduction, investigation and treatment [National Collaborating Centre for Women's and Children's Health, 2004].

Secondary and tertiary care management

General issues

- Specialist infertility clinics are the referral centres of choice. While many secondary care centres carry out a range of infertility treatments, *in vitro* fertilization (IVF), intracytoplasmic sperm injection (ICSI), and donor insemination (DI) are usually only offered in tertiary care.
- General practitioners may find that because of the strict confidentiality of the Human Fertilisation and Embryology Act, that they may not be sent information about their patient's assisted conception treatment. Sometimes letters will be set from the unit to the patient for them to release to their doctor as they see fit [Braude and Muhammed, 2003].

National recommendations

- The Department of Health recommends that each primary care trust offer:
  - All women aged 23–39 who meet the NICE clinical criteria (see below) a minimum of one full cycle of IVF from April 2005. In the longer term it is expected that primary care trusts will progress towards fully implementing NICE guidance.
  - Priority to couples who do not already have a child living with them.
- NICE recommends that all couples where the woman is aged 23–39 years at the time of treatment and who have an identified cause for their fertility problems (such as azoospermia or bilateral tubal occlusion) or who have infertility for at least 3 years' duration should be offered up to three stimulated cycles of *in vitro* fertilization treatment [National Collaborating Centre for Women's and Children's Health, 2004].

Assessment in secondary care

- **Investigations in women** normally include tubal patency tests. Women who are not known to have comorbidities (e.g. pelvic inflammatory disease, endometriosis, or previous ectopic pregnancy) should be offered a hysterosalpingogram or hysterosalpingo-contrast-ultrasonography. Women thought to have comorbidities should be offered diagnostic laparoscopy and dye so that tubal and other pelvic pathologies can be assessed at the same time [National Collaborating Centre for Women's and Children's Health, 2004].
- **Investigations in men** include an assessment of the sperm, starting with a review of results obtained from primary care investigations. In men with abnormal sperm, a more detailed examination is carried out which may include microbiological tests, sperm culture, endocrine tests, imaging of the urogenital tract, and testicular biopsy.

Types of fertility treatment

Medical treatment

- **Ovulation induction with clomifene:** clomifene is an effective treatment for anovulation, and may be used in selected women [Hughes et al, 2004]. The following needs to be noted:

  - The Committee on Safety of Medicines (CSM) recommend that no more than six cycles are given. Long-term cyclical therapy is also not recommended [CSM, 1995; ABPI Medicines Compendium, 2002].
  - NICE recommends treatment for up to 12 cycles. Use beyond this has been associated with an increased risk of ovarian cancer [Rossing et al, 1994; National Collaborating Centre for Women's and Children's Health, 2004].
  - Ovarian ultrasound monitoring of at least the first cycle where clomifene is prescribed is important, to titrate the drug to an appropriate dose and reduce the likelihood of multiple pregnancy [National Collaborating Centre for Women's and Children's Health, 2004].
  - Counselling, with regard to the risks of multiple pregnancy, ovarian hyperstimulation, foetal reduction, and possible risk of ovarian cancer, should be given.
- **Metformin** or laparoscopic ovarian drilling may be offered to women with polycystic ovary syndrome who have not responded to clomifene [National Collaborating Centre for Women's and Children's Health, 2004]
- **Gonadotrophins** may be offered to women with clomiphene-resistant anovulatory infertility, but carry a significant risk of multiple pregnancy. Careful monitoring with ultrasound is needed [Kennedy, Personal Communication, 2004].
- **Pulsatile gonadotrophin-releasing hormone and dopamine agonists** are other treatments for the induction of ovulation.
- **Drug-induced ovarian suppression is no longer recommended for women with endometriosis** because it does not improve pregnancy rates [Duckitt, 2003; National Collaborating Centre for Women's and Children's Health, 2004].
- **Dopamine agonists** should be offered to women with ovulatory disorders secondary to hyperprolactinaemia. Investigations should be done to exclude a pituitary adenoma or extrapituitary tumour before proceeding with infertility treatment [Hamilton-Fairley and Taylor, 2003; National Collaborating Centre for Women's and Children's Health, 2004].
- **Gonadotrophin drugs** are effective in improving fertility in men with hypogonadotrophic hypogonadism [National Collaborating Centre for Women's and Children's Health, 2004].

Surgical treatment

- **Tubal surgery** may be effective in women with mild tubal disease. Tubal catheterization or cannulation improves the chance of pregnancy in women with proximal tubal obstruction [National Collaborating Centre for Women's and Children's Health, 2004].
- **Laparoscopic surgery** appears to improve the chance of pregnancy in women with all grades of endometriosis [National Collaborating Centre for Women's and Children's Health, 2004], although the evidence from some of the studies is conflicting [Duckitt, 2003].
- **Surgery for fibroids** should be considered if there is no other explanation for infertility. It is essential for intracavity fibroids [Hart, 2003] and should be considered for intramural fibroids >5 cm in diameter, particularly when they are encroaching on the cavity [Kennedy, Personal Communication, 2004].
- **Surgery for varicoceles** should not be offered, as it does not improve pregnancy rates [National Collaborating Centre for Women's and Children's Health, 2004].
- **Surgical correction of epididymal blockage** in men with obstructive azoospermia is likely to restore fertility [National Collaborating Centre for Women's and Children's Health, 2004].

Assisted conception

- **Intrauterine insemination** (IUI) is the process, timed to coincide with ovulation, by which sperm is placed in the woman's uterus using a fine plastic tube. Low doses of ovary-stimulating hormones are usually also given, to maximize pregnancy rates. If IUI does not work, people move on to try IVF, or ICSI. Ovarian stimulation combined with IUI increases pregnancy rates in subfertile women with mild endometriosis [National Collaborating Centre for Women's and Children's Health, 2004].
- **Donor insemination** (DI) is the insemination of sperm from a donor into a woman, via her vagina into the cervical canal or into the uterus itself (IUI). Sometimes low doses of ovary-stimulating hormones are used in conjunction with DI, with the aim of increasing pregnancy rates. DI should be considered as an option when the man has no or very few sperm on testicular biopsy or surgical extraction; has had a vasectomy, and reversal has failed or not been tried; or has an infectious disease such as HIV, or where there is a high risk of transmitting a genetic disorder to the offspring [National Collaborating Centre for Women's and Children's Health, 2004].
- ***In vitro* fertilization** (IVF) involves retrieval of the egg(s), which is mixed with sperm and incubated for 2–3 days; the resultant embryo(s) is then injected into the uterus via the cervix. The Human Fertilisation and Embryology Authority recommends that only two embryos be implanted, to reduce the risk of multiple pregnancy [Braude and Rowell, 2003b; National Collaborating Centre for Women's and Children's Health, 2004].
- **Intracytoplasmic sperm injection** (ICSI) involves an individual sperm being injected directly into the egg, to bypass natural barriers that prevent fertilization. ICSI is used for couples who have failed to achieve successful fertilization through conventional IVF, or where the quality or numbers of sperm is too low for normal IVF to be likely to succeed. ISCI is now the treatment of choice in severe male factor infertility [Kennedy, Personal Communication, 2004]. It may be worth re-referring to specialist clinics men with very low sperm counts who have been told in the past they cannot be helped [Chambers, 1999; Braude and Rowell, 2003b].
- **Oocyte donation** involves stimulation of the donor's ovaries and collection of eggs, which are then fertilized by the recipient's husband's sperm. After 2–3 days the embryos are transferred to the uterus of the recipient via the cervix, following hormonal preparation of the endometrium. This method is suitable for women who have ovarian failure (either premature, or following radiotherapy or chemotherapy); who have had bilateral oophorectomy; where there is gonadal dysgenesis, including Turner's syndrome, or where there is a high risk of transmitting a genetic disorder. It is also used in certain cases of IVF failure [National Collaborating Centre for Women's and Children's Health, 2004].
- **Embryo donation.** Couples who have had successful IVF or ICSI treatment may decide to donate their spare embryos to help other infertile couples [HFEA, 2004a].
- **Gamete intrafallopian transfer** (**GIFT**) involves egg retrieval, mixing the eggs with the prepared sperm, and then injecting the eggs (maximum of three) with the sperm into the fallopian tube [Chambers, 1999; HFEA, 2004a]. There is insufficient evidence to recommend its use in preference to IVF in couples with unexplained infertility problems or male factor fertility problems [National Collaborating Centre for Women's and Children's Health, 2004].

[DH, 2004a]

Problems with assisted conception

Ovulation hyperstimulation syndrome

- **Ovarian hyperstimulation syndrome** (OHSS) generally develops if a woman has had an excessive response to gonadotrophins and has produced a large number of follicles (over 20). It is particularly severe in people with polycystic ovary syndrome who have been treated with human gonadotrophin-releasing hormone analogues. It can follow the use of clomifene in sensitive people, e.g. those with polycystic ovarian syndrome.
- **OHSS presents:**
  - **Early:** within 1–5 days of human gonadotrophin injection, soon after egg collection and embryo transfer
  - **Late:** 7–14 days after embryo transfer when endogenous human chorionic gonadotrophin (HCG) rises after successful implantation
- **Symptoms and signs include:**
  - Feeling unwell, nausea, vomiting
  - Abdominal pain, distension, or both caused by enlarged ovaries and acute ascites
  - Bowel disturbance—constipation or diarrhoea
  - Dark concentrated urine due to reduced renal perfusion and low urine output
  - Dyspnoea due to splinting of the diaphragm secondary to ascites or pleural effusion
  - Leg and vulval oedema
- **Seek urgent advice from a specialist unit if OHSS is suspected.**

Ectopic pregnancy

- **Ectopic pregnancy** occurs in about 4% of pregnancies that occur after assisted conception. Heterotopic (one embryo in the uterus and one in the tube) pregnancy is extremely rare naturally (one in 30,000 pregnancies) but the rate may be as high as one in 100 pregnancies in women who have had assisted conception [Tal et al, 1996].

[Braude and Rowell, 2003a]

Counselling and information on infertility

- **It is important to involve both partners in all aspects of management.** Discussion of wishes, plans, beliefs, and motives are important [Himmel et al, 1997].
- **Counselling** should be made available to all infertile couples, and may cover these different aspects:
  - Implications of investigations and treatments.
  - Emotional support for social and psychological issues such as stress.
  - Help with ethical and legal issues, especially for assisted conception.
  - Therapeutic counselling to help people accommodate the feelings they have about their infertility.
- **Information on infertility** is often available locally and should be provided to the couple. National sources of up-to-date information include the Human Fertilisation and Embryology Authority (www.hfea.gov.uk) and the patient organizations CHILD (www.child.org.uk), ISSUE (www.issue.co.uk) and BICA (www.bica.net).

Anonymity of donors

- Children born as a result of sperm, eggs, or embryos donated after 1 April 2005 will be able to access the identity of their donor when they reach the age of 18 years. This change in the regulation will not be retrospective. Anybody donating before April 2005 will remain anonymous.
- Under existing regulations, when they reach the age of 18 years, people may ask the HFEA to confirm whether they were born as a result of donated sperm, eggs or embryos. Those intending to marry, including those who plan to do so before they reach the age of 18 years, may also ask whether the HFEA register shows that they are related to the person they intend to marry.

[DH, 2004b]

References

NHS staff in England can link, free of charge, from references to full text journals by clicking on [Full text] on the PRODIGY website.

1. ABPI Medicines Compendium (2002) *Summary of product characteristics for Clomid.* Electronic Medicines Compendium. Datapharm Communications Ltd. www.emc.medicines.org.uk [Accessed: 08/04/2002].
2. Augood, C., Duckitt, K. and Templeton, A.A. (1998) Smoking and female infertility: a systematic review and meta-analysis. *Human Reproduction* **13**(6), 1532–1539.
3. BMA (2004) *Smoking and reproductive life. The impact of smoking on sexual, reproductive and child health.* British Medical Association. www.bma.org.uk [Accessed: 11/02/2004].
4. Braude, P. and Muhammed, S. (2003) ABC of subfertility. Assisted conception and the law in the United Kingdom. *British Medical Journal* **327**(7421), 978–981. [Full text]
5. Braude, P. and Rowell, P. (2003a) ABC of subfertility. Assisted conception. III–Problems with assisted conception. *British Medical Journal* **327**(7420), 920–923. [Full text]
6. Braude, P. and Rowell, P. (2003b) ABC of subfertility. Assisted conception. II–In vitro fertilisation and intracytoplasmic sperm injection. *British Medical Journal* **327**(7419), 852–855. [Full text]
7. Campbell, S. and Monga, A.; (Eds.) (2000) Infertility. In: *Gynaecology by ten teachers.* London: Arnold. 83–89.
8. Chambers, R. (Ed.) (1999) *Fertility problems: a simple guide.* Abingdon: Radcliffe Medical Press.
9. Chen, E.C. and Brzyski, R.G. (1999) Exercise and reproductive dysfunction. *Fertility and Sterility* **71**(1), 1–6.
10. CMO (2003) *Protecting women against rubella: switch from rubella vaccine to MMR.* Department of Health. www.dh.gov.uk [Accessed: 27/04/2004].
11. Cohen, M.A., Chang, P.L., Uhler, M. et al (1999) Reproductive outcome after sterilization reversal in women of advanced reproductive age. *Journal of Assisted Reproduction & Genetics* **16**(8), 402–404. [Full text]
12. Cooke, S. (1996) Treatment of infertility: the general approach to the infertile couple. *Prescribers' Journal* **36**(1), 42–45.
13. CSM (1995) Drug safety issues in obstetrics and gynaecology. *Current Problems in Pharmacovigilance* **21**(2), 7.
14. De Kretser, D.M. (1997) Male infertility. *Lancet* **349**(9054), 787–790. [Full text]
15. DH (2003) *Alcohol and health.* Department of Health. www.dh.gov.uk [Accessed: 26/02/2004]. [Full text]
16. DH (2004a) *Health secretary welcomes new fertility guidance.* Press Release Notice 2004/0069. Department of Health. www.dh.gov.uk [Accessed: 05/03/2004]. [Full text]
17. DH (2004b) *Anonymity to be removed from future sperm, egg and embryo donors.* Department of Health. www.dh.gov.uk [Accessed: 14/05/2004]. [Full text]

18. Duckitt, K. (2003) Infertility and subfertility. *Clinical Evidence* **10**(Dec), 2108–2135.
19. Dukes, M.N.G. (Ed.) (1996) *Meyler's side effects of drugs*. 13th edn. New York: Elsevier.
20. Guermandi, E., Vegetti, W., Bianchi, M.M. et al (2001) Reliability of ovulation tests in infertile women. *Obstetrics & Gynecology* **97**(1), 92–96.
21. Hamilton-Fairley, D. and Taylor, A. (2003) ABC of subfertility. Anovulation. *British Medical Journal* **327**(7414), 546–549. [Full text]
22. Hanafi, M.M. (2003) Factors affecting the pregnancy rate after microsurgical reversal of tubal ligation. *Fertility and Sterility* **80**(2), 434–440.
23. Hargreave, T.B. and Mills, J.A. (1998) Investigating and managing infertility in general practice. *British Medical Journal* **316**(7142), 1438–1441. [Full text]
24. Hart, R. (2003) ABC of subfertility. Unexplained infertility, endometriosis, and fibroids. *British Medical Journal* **327**(7417), 721–724.
25. HFEA (2004a) *Your guide to infertility. HFEA directory of clinics 2003/04*. London: Human Fertilisation & Embryology Authority.
26. HFEA (2004b) *Facts and figures*. Human Fertilisation & Embryology Authority. www.hfea.gov.uk [Accessed: 12/03/2004].
27. Himmel, W., Ittner, E., Kochen, M.M. et al (1997) Management of involuntary childlessness. *British Journal of General Practice* **47**(415), 111–118.
28. Hirsh, A. (2003) ABC of subfertility. Male subfertility. *British Medical Journal* **327**(7416), 669–672. [Full text]
29. Hughes, E.G. and Brennan, B.G. (1996) Does cigarette smoking impair natural or assisted fecundity? *Fertility and Sterility* **66**(5), 679–689.
30. Hughes, E., Collins, J. and Vandekerckhove, P. (2004) *Clomiphene citrate for ovulation induction in women with oligo-amenorrhoea (Cochrane Review)*. The Cochrane Library. Issue 1. Chichester, UK: John Wiley & Sons, Ltd.
31. Hull, M.G., North, K., Taylor, H. et al (2000) Delayed conception and active and passive smoking. The Avon Longitudinal Study of Pregnancy and Childhood Study Team. *Fertility and Sterility* **74**(4), 725–733.
32. Janssen, N.M. and Genta, M.S. (2000) The effects of immunosuppressive and anti-inflammatory medications on fertility, pregnancy, and lactation. *Archives of Internal Medicine* **160**(5), 610–619. [Full text]
33. Kennedy, R. (2004) *Personal communication*. Secretary, British Fertility Society: Bradley Stoke, UK.
34. Land, A. and Evers, J.L. (2002) Chlamydia infection and subfertility. *Best Practice Research in Clinical Obstetrics and Gynaecology* **16**(6), 901–912.
35. Lee, J. and Yap, C. (2003) Embryo donation: a review. *Acta Obstetricia et Gynecologica Scandinavica* **82**(11), 991–996.
36. Lumley, J., Watson, L., Watson, M. and Bower, C. (2003) *Periconceptional supplementation with folate and/or multivitamins for preventing neural tube defects (Cochrane Review)*. The Cochrane Library. Issue 4. Oxford: Update Software.
37. Munkelwitz, R. and Gilbert, B.R. (1998) Are boxer shorts really better? A critical analysis of the role of underwear type in male subfertility. *Journal of Urology* **160**(4), 1329–1333.
38. National Collaborating Centre for Women's and Children's Health (2004) *Fertility: assessment and treatment for people with fertility problems – full guideline*. Royal College of Obstetricians and Gynaecologists. www.rcog.org.uk [Accessed: 02/03/2004].
39. NHS CRD (1992) The management of subfertility. *Effective Health Care Bulletin* **1**(3), 1–24.
40. PHLS, DHSS&PS and Scottish ISD(D)5 Collaborative Group (2000) *Trends in sexually transmitted infections in the United Kingdom 1990–1999. New episodes seen at genitourinary medicine clinics*. Public Health Laboratory Service. www.hpa.org.uk [Accessed: 20/05/2004].
41. Rossing, M.A., Daling, J.R., Weiss, N.S. et al (1994) Ovarian tumors in a cohort of infertile women. *New England Journal of Medicine* **331**(12), 771–776.
42. Saleh, R.A., Ranga, G.M., Raina, R. et al (2003) Sexual dysfunction in men undergoing infertility evaluation: a cohort observational study. *Fertility and Sterility* **79**(4), 909–912.
43. Symonds, E.M. and Symonds, I.M. (2004) Infertility and disorders of sexual function. In: *Essential obstetrics and gynaecology*. 4th edn. London: Churchill Livingstone. 261–265.
44. Tal, J., Haddad, S., Gordon, N. and Timor-Tritsch, I. (1996) Heterotopic pregnancy after ovulation induction and assisted reproductive technologies: a literature review from 1971 to 1993. *Fertility and Sterility* **66**(1), 1–12.
45. Taylor, P. (2004) *Personal communication*. Consultant Hematologist, Royal Victoria Infirmary: Newcastle upon Tyne.
46. Templeton, A. (2000) Infertility and the establishment of pregnancy – overview. *British Medical Bulletin* **56**(3), 577–587.
47. Te Velde, E.R. and Cohlen, B.J. (1999) The management of infertility. *New England Journal of Medicine* **340**(3), 224–226. [Full text]
48. Thonneau, P., Marchand, S., Tallec, A. et al (1991) Incidence and main causes of infertility in a resident population (1, 850, 000) of three French regions (1988–1989). *Human Reproduction* **6**(6), 811–816.
49. Tiemessen, C.H., Evers, J.L. and Bots, R.S. (1996) Tight-fitting underwear and sperm quality. *Lancet* **347**(9018), 1844–1845. [Full text]
50. Tourgeman, D.E., Bhaumik, M., Cooke, G.C. et al (2001) Pregnancy rates following fimbriectomy reversal via neosalpingostomy: a 10-year retrospective analysis. *Fertility & Sterility* **76**(5), 1041–1044.
51. Wald, N. (1991) Prevention of neural tube defects: results of the medical research council vitamin study. *Lancet* **338**(8760), 131–137. [Full text]
52. Wong, W.Y., Thomas, C.M., Merkus, J.M. et al (2000) Male factor subfertility: possible causes and the impact of nutritional factors. *Fertility and Sterility* **73**(3), 435–442.
53. World Health Organization Task Force on the Prevention and Management of Infertility (1995) Tubal infertility: serologic relationship to past chlamydial and gonococcal infection. *Sexually Transmitted Diseases* **22**(2), 71–77.
54. Wu, F.C.W. (1996) Disorders of male reproduction. In: Weatherall, D.J., Leadingham, J.G.G., Warrell, D.A. et al (Eds.) *Oxford textbook of medicine*. 3rd edn. Oxford: Oxford University Press and Electronic Publishing BV. Section 12.8.2.
55. Yoon, T.K., Sung, H.R., Kang, H.G. et al (1999) Laparoscopic tubal anastomosis: fertility outcome in 202 cases. *Fertility and Sterility* **72**(6), 1121–1126.

PRODIGY GUIDANCE

Influenza

Last revised in July 2005
www.prodigy.nhs.uk/guidance.asp?gt=Influenza

Applies to people of all ages

This guidance covers the treatment and prevention of influenza.

This guidance does not cover the management of complications of influenza, such as chest infections, pneumonia, and otitis media. It also does not cover the circumstances of a pandemic, impending pandemic, or a widespread epidemic of a new strain of influenza to which there is little or no community resistance.

There is separate PRODIGY guidance for the management of *Otitis media — acute*, pneumonia during an influenza epidemic (within the *Chest infections* PRODIGY guidance), *Sinusitis*, and *Sore throat — acute*.

Goals

- To reduce symptoms
- To reduce the risk of complications of influenza, for example pneumonia and otitis media
- To reduce hospitalization
- To reduce deaths from influenza
- To promote appropriate self-management of future episodes
- To prevent influenza in at-risk adults and children

Contents

Scenarios

- Influenza — treatment p.1086
- Prevention — influenza vaccination p.1088
- Post-exposure prophylaxis of influenza p.1089

Extended Information, p. 1091

Which scenario?

- **Influenza — treatment:** covers the treatment of acute influenza.
- **Prevention — influenza vaccination:** covers the indications and administration of influenza vaccine.
- **Post-exposure prophylaxis:** covers the post-exposure prophylaxis of influenza.

Influenza — treatment

Which therapy?

- **Advise self-management strategies for otherwise healthy people with uncomplicated influenza:**
  - Rest
  - Drink plenty of fluids
  - Symptomatic relief with analgesics and antipyretics such as paracetamol, or ibuprofen to relieve discomfort and fever
- **Zanamivir or oseltamivir** is recommended when influenza is circulating in the community, for the treatment of at-risk adults and children. They must be able to commence treatment within 48 hours of the onset of symptoms.
- **GPs will be informed when influenza is considered to be circulating in the community** through community-based virological surveillance schemes.
- **At-risk people are defined as those who:**
  - Have chronic respiratory disease (including chronic obstructive pulmonary disease and asthma)
  - Have significant cardiovascular disease (excluding individuals with hypertension)
  - Are immunocompromised
  - Have diabetes mellitus
  - Have chronic renal disease
  - Are aged 65 years or over
- **Zanamivir or oseltamivir are *not* recommended** for otherwise healthy children or adults under 65 years with influenza.
- **Clinical discretion should be exercised when people who are not considered to be at risk request antiviral medication,** bearing in mind the National Institute for Clinical Excellence (NICE) recommendations.

Practical prescribing points

For further information please see the *Medicines Compendium* (www.medicines.org.uk) or the *British National Formulary* (www.bnf.org).

Analgesia/antipyretic

- **Ibuprofen:** as with other nonsteroidal anti-inflammatory drugs (NSAIDs), ibuprofen may worsen or precipitate gastrointestinal haemorrhage, asthma, hypertension, renal impairment, or cardiac failure. Avoid if there is a history of peptic ulcers, and in pregnant women.

Antiviral use

- This is not a substitute for influenza vaccination.
- The protection lasts only as long as the antiviral therapy is administered.

Zanamivir

- **Zanamivir is administered as a dry-powder inhaler** (Diskhaler). Instructions and demonstration of the correct use of the device are likely to be beneficial.
- **People with asthma or chronic obstructive pulmonary disease:**
  - Should be informed of the risk of bronchospasm
  - Should have a fast-acting bronchodilator available
  - Should be advised to use their bronchodilators before taking zanamivir if they are taking regular bronchodilator therapy
- **People with severe underlying airways disease** should only take zanamivir if it is possible to closely monitor them, and appropriate facilities are available to treat bronchospasm.
- **Pregnancy and breastfeeding:** there is no information available on the effects of zanamivir in pregnancy or breastfeeding. Zanamivir should only be used in pregnant women where the potential benefit justifies the risk to the fetus. For further advice, phone the National Teratology Information Service (0191 232 1525).

Oseltamivir

- **Capsule and suspension formulations** are available. Capsules are recommended in adults, adolescents or children greater than 40 kg in weight who are able to swallow them.
- **Renal impairment**
  - The following dosages are recommended for people with renal impairment (as measured by creatinine clearance), prescribed oseltamivir for the treatment of influenza:
    - Creatinine greater than 30 ml/min: 75 mg twice a day (no dosage adjustment)
    - Creatinine 10–30 ml/min: 75 mg once a day
    - Creatinine less than 10 ml/min: not recommended
    - Renal dialysis: not recommended
  - Measuring creatinine clearance prior to commencing oseltamivir is not practical. If severe renal impairment is suspected from previous tests consider prescribing half the standard dose (75 mg once a day) or seeking specialist advice.
- **Pregnancy and breastfeeding:** there is no information available on the effects of oseltamivir in pregnancy or breastfeeding. Oseltamivir should only be used in pregnant women where the potential benefit justifies the risk to the fetus. For further advice, phone the National Teratology Information Service (0191 232 1525).
- **Committee on Safety of Medicines (CSM) information:** oseltamivir is a black triangle drug and is currently under the surveillance of the CSM.

Follow-up advice

- Follow-up is generally not necessary.

Should I refer or investigate?

Refer?

- **Admission** is indicated if symptoms or severe complications develop, for example pneumonia or encephalitis.
- **If serious alternative diagnoses are suspected** (e.g. malaria in a person who has recently travelled to a malaria area), consider admission/referral to a specialist.
- **If there is an exacerbation or a problem with underlying disease** consider admission/referral to a specialist.

Investigate?

- **The diagnosis of influenza is made on clinical grounds.**
- **The principal role of laboratory diagnosis is for influenza surveillance** — to indicate when influenza is circulating in the community, and to identify the predominant circulating types, subtypes, and strains.
- **Diagnostic tests available include:**
  - **Viral culture:** nasopharyngeal swabs or aspirates in appropriate transport medium can reliably obtain virus material for culture. Viral culture is necessary for information on influenza subtypes and strains. Results are available after 3–7 days (sometimes longer).
  - **Serology:** acute and convalescent sera are tested for rises in either complement-fixing or haemagglutination-inhibiting antibodies. The convalescent sample is usually taken 10–14 days after the acute sample.
  - **Immunofluorescence:** viral antigen can be detected directly with immunofluorescence using nasopharyngeal swabs or aspirates. Results are available within 24 hours.
  - **Polymerase chain reaction.**
  - **Rapid antigen testing.**

Patient information leaflets

The following PILs are available at www.prodigy.nhs.uk

- Antibiotics - Why No Antibiotic?
- Flu Like Illness
- Flu - Preventing
- Influenza Immunisation
- Paracetamol

Shared decision making

- Flu usually lasts 3–5 days, but cough and tiredness may persist for 3 weeks. Treatment aims to ease symptoms until you recover.
  - **Paracetamol or ibuprofen** will lower your temperature, and ease aches and pains.
  - Have lots to drink to prevent mild dehydration.
- Complications such as a chest infection are unusual if you are normally well and are under 65.
- Antibiotics are not usually prescribed as they do not kill viruses.
- **An antiviral medicine such as zanamivir or oseltamivir** may be prescribed if you are at increased risk of complications (aged over 65 or have certain diseases). These do not cure flu, but may reduce the severity and duration of symptoms, and may prevent complications.
- Note: malaria causes similar symptoms to flu. Have you been abroad to a 'malaria country' within the last year?

Drug rationale

Drugs not included

- **Antibiotics** are not effective against influenza virus or other upper respiratory tract virus infections [Arroll and Kenealy, 2002].
- **Aspirin** is not included because of its adverse effect profile. It is no longer recommended for use in children under the age of 16 with a febrile illness.
- **Amantadine:** there is a lack of data to indicate whether amantadine is effective in treating at-risk people with influenza, or whether it reduces the incidence of serious complications and death. The usefulness of amantadine is limited by adverse reactions, a limited spectrum of activity, and drug resistance. It is therefore not recommended.

Drugs included

- **Paracetamol** is an effective and safe analgesic and antipyretic agent for most people.
- **Ibuprofen** is an effective alternative to paracetamol if there are no contraindications.
- **Zanamivir or oseltamivir** are recommended by the National Institute for Clinical Excellence (NICE) for the treatment of at-risk adults who present with influenza-like illness (ILI) and who can start therapy within 48 hours of the onset of symptoms, when influenza A or B is circulating in the community [NICE, 2003a].
  - They are available on an NHS prescription for treating influenza only under these circumstances, and the prescription must be endorsed 'SLS'.
  - These drugs reduce the duration of symptoms by approximately 1 day, and there is increasing evidence to indicate that they reduce complications in at-risk individuals [Burls et al, 2002; Turner et al, 2002]. It is assumed that the use of zanamivir or oseltamivir will reduce the incidence of hospitalization and death in at-risk persons with influenza, although currently this linkage is not proven because of a lack of data.
- **Note: antiviral therapy is not recommended for the treatment of otherwise healthy adults with influenza.**

Prescriptions

Advice note

Advice only: symptom management

- All ages
- Virus infections such as flu are normally cleared by the body's immune system. Antibiotics do not kill viruses. Treatments aim to ease symptoms: paracetamol or ibuprofen taken regularly lower the temperature of a fever and ease pains and headaches. Have lots to drink to prevent mild dehydration. Complications are unusual in people who are normally well. Consult a doctor if symptoms change or become worse.

Analgesia/antipyretics: use when required

Paracetamol s/f susp: 60mg to 120mg up to four times a day

- Age from 3 to 11 months
- Paracetamol 120mg/5ml s/f susp. Take 2.5ml to 5ml every 4 to 6 hours when required for relief of pain or high temperature. Maximum of 4 doses in 24 hours; supply 150 ml; NHS Cost £0.65; OTC Cost £1.15.

Paracetamol s/f susp: 120mg to 240mg up to four times a day

- Age from 12 months to 5 years
- Paracetamol 120mg/5ml s/f susp. Take one to two 5ml spoonfuls every 4 to 6 hours when required for relief of pain or high temperature. Maximum of 4 doses in 24 hours; supply 300 ml; NHS Cost £1.24; OTC Cost £2.18.

Paracetamol s/f susp: 250mg to 500mg up to four times a day

- Age from 6 to 11 years
- Paracetamol 250mg/5ml s/f susp. Take one to two 5ml spoonfuls every 4 to 6 hours when required for relief of pain or high temperature. Maximum of 4 doses in 24 hours; supply 300 ml; NHS Cost £1.53; OTC Cost £2.70.

Paracetamol tablets: 500mg to 1g up to four times a day

- Age from 12 to 15 years
- Paracetamol 500mg tablets. Take one to two tablets every 4 to 6 hours when required for relief of pain or high temperature. Maximum of 8 tablets in 24 hours; supply 50 tablets; NHS Cost £0.38; OTC Cost £0.66.

Paracetamol tablets: 1g up to four times a day

- Age from 16 years onwards
- Paracetamol 500mg tablets. Take two tablets every 4 to 6 hours when required for relief of pain or high temperature. Maximum of 8 tablets in 24 hours; supply 50 tablets; NHS Cost £0.38; OTC Cost £0.66.

Ibuprofen s/f susp: 50mg three to four times a day

- Age from 12 months to 2 years
- Ibuprofen 100mg/5ml s/f susp. Take 2.5ml three to four times a day when required for relief of pain or high temperature. Do not exceed the stated dose; supply 100 ml; NHS Cost £2.00; OTC Cost £3.53.

Ibuprofen s/f susp: 100mg three to four times a day

- Age from 3 to 7 years
- Ibuprofen 100mg/5ml s/f susp. Take one 5ml spoonful 3 to 4 times a day when required for relief of pain or high temperature. Do not exceed the stated dose; supply 150 ml; NHS Cost £2.73; OTC Cost £4.81.

Ibuprofen s/f susp: 200mg three to four times a day

- Age from 8 to 11 years
- Ibuprofen 100mg/5ml s/f susp. Take two 5ml spoonfuls 3 to 4 times a day when required for relief of pain or high temperature. Do not exceed the stated dose; supply 300 ml; NHS Cost £5.46; OTC Cost £9.62.

Ibuprofen tablets: 400mg three times a day

- Age from 12 years onwards
- Ibuprofen 400mg tablets. Take one tablet up to three times a day when required for relief of pain or high temperature. Do not exceed the stated dose; supply 24 tablets; NHS Cost £0.70; OTC Cost £1.75.

At-risk people: zanamivir or oseltamivir (within 48 hours)

Zanamivir Diskhaler: 10mg twice a day for 5 days (SLS)

- Age from 12 years onwards
- Zanamivir 5mg disks+Diskhaler. Inhale the contents of two blisters twice a day for 5 days; supply 1 20 dose diskhaler; NHS Cost £24.00.

Oseltamivir susp: child weighs 15kg or less (SLS)

- Age from 12 months to 12 years
- Oseltamivir 12mg/ml suspension. Using the oral dispenser provided, take 30mg twice a day for 5 days; supply 63 ml; NHS Cost £18.18.

Oseltamivir susp: child weighs 15.1 to 23kg (SLS)

- Age from 12 months to 12 years
- Oseltamivir 12mg/ml suspension. Using the oral dispenser provided, take 45mg twice a day for 5 days; supply 63 ml; NHS Cost £18.18.

Oseltamivir susp: child weighs 23.1 to 40kg (SLS)

- Age from 12 months to 12 years
- Oseltamivir 12mg/ml suspension. Using the oral dispenser provided, take 60mg twice a day for 5 days; supply 63 ml; NHS Cost £18.18.

Oseltamivir susp: child weighs 40kg or more (SLS)

- Age from 12 months to 12 years
- Oseltamivir 12mg/ml suspension. Using the oral dispenser provided, take 75mg twice a day for 5 days; supply 63 ml; NHS Cost £18.18.

Oseltamivir capsules: 75mg twice a day (SLS)

- Age from 13 years onwards
- Oseltamivir 75mg capsules. Take one capsule twice a day for 5 days; supply 10 capsules; NHS Cost £18.18.

Prevention — influenza vaccination

Which therapy?

- **Annual influenza vaccine is strongly recommended for:**
  - All aged 65 years and over
  - All aged over 6 months with the following:
    - Chronic respiratory disease, including asthma
    - Chronic heart disease
    - Chronic renal disease
    - Diabetes
    - Immunosuppression
  - Those living in long-stay residential and nursing homes or other long-stay facilities
- **Vaccination is also recommended for** NHS employees directly involved in patient care, if sufficient supplies of vaccine are available.
- The two types of influenza vaccine currently available in the UK ('split virus' and 'surface antigen' vaccine) are equally effective and have a similar adverse reaction rate.
- **The preferred time for vaccination is October/early November.**
- **In children under 12 years who have not previously been vaccinated in a past year,** should receive a second dose after at least 4 weeks.
- **Consider pneumococcal vaccine** as the target groups for both vaccines overlap. Note: pneumococcal vaccine is generally administered only once.

Practical prescribing points

For further information please see the *Medicines Compendium* (www.medicines.org.uk) or the *British National Formulary* (www.bnf.org).

- Give influenza vaccine by intramuscular or deep subcutaneous injection. In infants use the antero-lateral aspect of the thigh and a 25G needle. In older children and adults use the deltoid and a 23G needle.
- **Do not give influenza vaccine to people who** have had an anaphylactic reaction to eggs or a previous dose of the vaccine.
- **Delay vaccination during an acute febrile illness.** Wait until symptoms have resolved before vaccinating.
- **Pregnancy:** avoid giving influenza vaccine unless the woman is at risk of serious illness or death should she develop influenza. However, there is no evidence that influenza vaccine prepared from inactivated virus harms the fetus.
- Influenza vaccine can be given on the same day as pneumococcal vaccine.
- **If more than one vaccine is being given,** use different needles/syringes and inject into different sites.
- **Advise people to seek urgent medical advice** if they develop breathlessness, swelling of the mouth or throat, or a rash within a few days of immunization.
- **Advise parents** to give a dose of paracetamol or ibuprofen if a child develops a fever, and keep the child cool (remove excess clothing or bedding). If a fever persists after a second dose, they should seek medical advice.

Follow-up advice

- Follow-up is generally not necessary.

Patient information leaflets

The following PILs are available at www.prodigy.nhs.uk

- Antibiotics - Why No Antibiotic?
- Flu Like Illness
- Flu - Preventing
- Influenza Immunisation
- Paracetamol

Shared decision making

- You should be immunized against flu each autumn if:
  - You have a lung disease such as asthma, emphysema, chronic bronchitis, etc.
  - You have heart disease, a serious kidney disease, or diabetes.
  - You have a poor immune system. (For example, if you have no spleen, are taking chemotherapy or steroid treatment, if you have HIV or AIDS, etc.)
  - You are aged 65 or over.
  - You live in a nursing home or residential accommodation.
- Flu immunization does not prevent coughs and colds. It protects only against the true influenza virus that is expected in the coming winter.
- You may have a temporary slight soreness at the injection site. Serious allergic reactions to the vaccine are rare.

Drug rationale

- Prescriptions for the two types of inactivated influenza vaccine ('split virus' and 'surface antigen' vaccine) available in the UK are offered for immunization in all aged over 6 months considered at risk of serious illness or death should they develop influenza, all people aged 65 years and over, and those living in long-stay residential and nursing homes or other long-stay facilities.

Prescriptions

Influenza vaccine: if at risk of complications of influenza

Inactivated influenza vaccine (surface antigen)

- Age from 6 months to 2 years
- Inact influenza vacc-s.antigen. Give 0.25ml to 0.5ml as a single dose by IM or deep SC injection; supply 1 0.5ml prefilled syringe; NHS Cost £3.98.

Inactivated influenza vaccine (surface antigen)

- Age from 3 to 11 years
- Inact influenza vacc-s.antigen. Give 0.5ml as a single dose by IM or deep SC injection; supply 1 0.5ml prefilled syringe; NHS Cost £3.98.

Inactivated influenza vaccine (surface antigen)

- Age from 12 years onwards
- Inact influenza vacc-s.antigen. Give 0.5ml as a single dose by IM or deep SC injection; supply 1 0.5ml prefilled syringe; NHS Cost £3.98.

Inactivated influenza vaccine (split virion)

- Age from 6 months to 2 years
- Inact influenza vacc-split virion. Give 0.25ml to 0.5ml as a single dose by IM or deep SC injection; supply 1 0.5ml prefilled syringe; NHS Cost £5.91.

Inactivated influenza vaccine (split virion)

- Age from 3 to 11 years
- Inact influenza vacc-split virion. Give 0.5ml as a single dose by IM or deep SC injection; supply 1 0.5ml prefilled syringe; NHS Cost £5.91.

Inactivated influenza vaccine (split virion)

- Age from 12 years onwards
- Inact influenza vacc-split virion. Give 0.5ml as a single dose by IM or deep SC injection; supply 1 0.5ml prefilled syringe; NHS Cost £5.91.

Post-exposure prophylaxis of influenza

Which therapy?

Note: post-exposure prophylaxis is not a substitute for vaccination.

General population

- **Post-exposure prophylaxis with oseltamivir** is recommended by the National Institute for Clinical Excellence (NICE) for people who are:
  - Aged 13 years and older, *and*
  - At-risk, *and*
  - Not effectively protected by vaccination, *and*
  - In close contact (i.e. someone who lives in the same house environment as a person suffering from symptoms of influenza-like illness [ILI]), *and*
  - Able to begin prophylaxis within 48 hours of exposure
- NICE does not recommend post-exposure prophylaxis in healthy people up to the age of 65 years.
- Consider offering influenza vaccination to unvaccinated individuals (unless contraindicated).

Residential care establishment

- **Post-exposure prophylaxis with oseltamivir** is recommended by NICE for people living in a residential care establishment where a resident or staff member has

I

ILI, *whether or not they have been vaccinated,* if they are:
 - Aged 13 years and older, *and*
 - At-risk, *and*
 - Able to begin prophylaxis within 48 hours of exposure
- In addition if an outbreak of ILI occurs in a residential care establishment consider:
 - **Separating** people with ILI from people without if possible.
 - **Restricting contact** between ill staff/visitors and residents.
 - **Offering influenza vaccination to unvaccinated staff and residents** (unless contraindicated).

Who is at risk?

- **At-risk persons are defined as those who:**
 - Have chronic respiratory disease (including chronic obstructive pulmonary disease and asthma)
 - Have significant cardiovascular disease (excluding individuals with hypertension)
 - Are immunocompromised
 - Have diabetes mellitus
 - Have chronic renal disease
 - Are aged 65 years or over

Practical prescribing points

For further information please see the *Medicines Compendium* (www.medicines.org.uk) or the *British National Formulary* (www.bnf.org).

Antiviral use

- Antiviral drugs offer protection against influenza for as long as they are administered.
- For post-exposure prophylaxis, treatment with antiviral drugs is usually for 7–10 days.

Oseltamivir

- **Capsule and suspension formulations** are available. Capsules are recommended in adults, adolescents, or children greater than 40 kg in weight who are able to swallow them.
- **Renal impairment:**
 - The following dosages are recommended for people with renal impairment (as measured by creatinine clearance), prescribed oseltamivir for the treatment of influenza:
   - Creatinine greater than 30 ml/min: 75 mg once a day (no dosage adjustment)
   - Creatinine 10–30 ml/min: 75 mg alternate days
   - Creatinine less than 10 ml/min: not recommended
   - Renal dialysis: not recommended
 - Measuring creatinine clearance prior to commencing oseltamivir is not practical. If severe renal impairment is suspected from previous tests consider prescribing half the standard dose (75 mg once a day) or seeking specialist advice.
- **Pregnancy and breastfeeding:** there is no information available on the effects of oseltamivir in pregnancy or breastfeeding. Oseltamivir should only be used in pregnant women where the potential benefit justifies the risk to the fetus. For further advice, phone the National Teratology Information Service (0191 232 1525).
- **CSM information:** oseltamivir is a black triangle drug and is currently under the surveillance of the Committee of Safety of Medicines (CSM).

Influenza vaccination

- Give influenza vaccine by intramuscular or deep subcutaneous injection. In infants use the antero-lateral aspect of the thigh and a 25G needle. In older children and adults use the deltoid and a 23G needle.
- **Do not give influenza vaccine to people who have had an anaphylactic reaction to eggs or a previous dose of the vaccine.**
- **Delay vaccination during an acute febrile illness.** Wait until symptoms have resolved before vaccinating.
- **Pregnancy:** avoid giving influenza vaccine unless the woman is at risk of serious illness or death should she develop influenza. However, there is no evidence that influenza vaccine prepared from inactivated virus harms the fetus.
- Influenza vaccine can be given on the same day as pneumococcal vaccine.
- **If more than one vaccine is being given,** use different needles/syringes and inject into different sites.
- **Advise people to seek urgent medical advice** if they develop breathlessness, swelling of the mouth or throat, or a rash within a few days of immunization.
- **Advise parents to** give a dose of paracetamol or ibuprofen if a child develops a fever, and keep the child cool (remove excess clothing or bedding). If a fever persists after a second dose, they should seek medical advice.

Follow-up advice

- Follow-up is generally not necessary.

Should I refer or investigate?

Refer?

- **Admission** is indicated if symptoms or severe complications develop, for example pneumonia or encephalitis.
- **If serious alternative diagnoses are suspected,** for example malaria in a person who has recently travelled to a malaria area, consider admission/referral to a specialist.
- **If there is an exacerbation or a problem with underlying disease** consider admission/referral to a specialist.

Investigate?

- **The diagnosis of influenza is made on clinical grounds.**
- **The principal role of laboratory diagnosis is for influenza surveillance** — to indicate when influenza is circulating in the community, and to identify the predominant circulating types, subtypes, and strains.
- **Diagnostic tests available include:**
 - **Viral culture:** nasopharyngeal swabs or aspirates in appropriate transport medium can reliably obtain virus material for culture. Viral culture is necessary for information on influenza subtypes and strains. Results are available after 3–7 days (sometimes longer).
 - **Serology:** acute and convalescent sera are tested for rises in either complement-fixing or haemagglutination-inhibiting antibodies. The convalescent sample is usually taken 10–14 days after the acute sample.
 - **Immunofluorescence:** viral antigen can be detected directly with immunofluorescence using nasopharyngeal swabs or aspirates. Results are available within 24 hours.
 - **Polymerase chain reaction.**
 - **Rapid antigen testing.**

Patient information leaflets

The following PILs are available at www.prodigy.nhs.uk
- Antibiotics - Why No Antibiotic?

- Flu Like Illness
- Flu - Preventing
- Influenza Immunisation
- Paracetamol

Drug rationale

Drugs not included

- **Zanamivir** does not currently have a licence for the prophylaxis of influenza.
- **Amantadine** has been shown to be effective in the prevention of influenza A in healthy adults; however, there is a lack of data about its effectiveness in at-risk individuals, and at the currently licensed dose of 100 mg daily. It is therefore not recommended.

Drugs included

- **Prescriptions for the two types of inactivated influenza vaccine** ('split virus' and 'surface antigen' vaccine) available in the UK are offered for immunization in all aged over 6 months considered at risk of serious illness or death should they develop influenza, all people aged 65 years and over, and those living in long-stay residential and nursing homes or other long-stay facilities.
- **Oseltamivir** has been shown to effective in preventing influenza in unvaccinated healthy adults and adolescents [NICE, 2003b]. The National Institute for Clinical Excellence recommends oseltamivir for post-exposure prophylaxis of influenza in at-risk people, aged 13 years and older, who can begin prophylaxis within 48 hours:
  - *If they are not effectively protected by vaccination*, and have been exposed to someone with influenza-like illness.
  - *Whether or not they have been vaccinated*, if they live in a residential care establishment where a resident or staff member has influenza-like illness.
- Oseltamivir is available on an NHS prescription for post-exposure prophylaxis under these circumstances, and the prescription must be endorsed 'SLS'.

Prescriptions

Oseltamivir: if at risk of complications of influenza

Oseltamivir capsules: 75mg once a day for 10 days (SLS)
- Age from 13 years onwards
- Oseltamivir 75mg capsules. Take one capsule once a day for 10 days; supply 10 capsules; NHS Cost £16.36.

Influenza vaccine: if at risk of complications of influenza

Inactivated influenza vaccine (surface antigen)
- Age from 6 months to 2 years
- Inact influenza vacc-s.antigen. Give 0.25ml to 0.5ml as a single dose by IM or deep SC injection; supply 1 0.5ml prefilled syringe; NHS Cost £3.98.

Inactivated influenza vaccine (surface antigen)
- Age from 3 to 11 years
- Inact influenza vacc-s.antigen. Give 0.5ml as a single dose by IM or deep SC injection; supply 1 0.5ml prefilled syringe; NHS Cost £3.98.

Inactivated influenza vaccine (surface antigen)
- Age from 12 years onwards
- Inact influenza vacc-s.antigen. Give 0.5ml as a single dose by IM or deep SC injection; supply 1 0.5ml prefilled syringe; NHS Cost £3.98.

Inactivated influenza vaccine (split virion)
- Age from 6 months to 2 years
- Inact influenza vacc-split virion. Give 0.25ml to 0.5ml as a single dose by IM or deep SC injection; supply 1 0.5ml prefilled syringe; NHS Cost £5.91.

Inactivated influenza vaccine (split virion)
- Age from 3 to 11 years
- Inact influenza vacc-split virion. Give 0.5ml as a single dose by IM or deep SC injection; supply 1 0.5ml prefilled syringe; NHS Cost £5.91.

Inactivated influenza vaccine (split virion)
- Age from 12 years onwards
- Inact influenza vacc-split virion. Give 0.5ml as a single dose by IM or deep SC injection; supply 1 0.5ml prefilled syringe; NHS Cost £5.91.

Extended Information

Background information

- What is it? p.1091
- How common is it? p.1092
- What are the risk factors for contracting influenza? p.1092
- How do I know my patient has it? p.1092
- What else might it be? p.1093
- Complications and prognosis p.1093
- How and why is influenza monitored? p.1093

What is it?

Influenza is an acute respiratory illness caused by the influenza virus. It occurs all over the world and is responsible for considerable morbidity and mortality each year.

Influenza virus

- **There are three serotypes of influenza virus: A, B, and C.** Influenza A viruses are further categorized into subtypes based on the surface antigens, neuraminidase (N antigen) and haemagglutinin (H antigen). Additionally, strains are classified on geographical location of first isolation, serial number, and year of isolation.
- **Influenza A and B cause most clinical disease.** Influenza A occurs more frequently and is more virulent. It is responsible for most major epidemics and pandemics. Influenza B often cocirculates with influenza A during the yearly outbreaks. Generally, influenza B causes less severe clinical illness, although it can still be responsible for outbreaks. Influenza C usually causes a mild or asymptomatic infection similar to the common cold.
- The influenza virus is made up of a lipid membrane that surrounds a protein shell and a core of RNA. Three proteins are embedded in the lipid membrane of influenza types A and B; two *glycoproteins* that act as the major antigenic determinant of influenza type A and B — N antigen and H antigen — and *a membrane channel protein*. Neuraminidase is an enzyme that facilitates the release of new virions from infected host cells, while haemagglutinin facilitates the entry of virus into respiratory epithelial cells. The membrane channel for influenza A is known as the M2 protein, and for influenza B is known as the NB protein. Differences in the structure of the membrane channel are associated with different susceptibility to the antiviral agent, amantadine.
- The influenza virus attaches to epithelial cells of the upper and lower respiratory tract, invades the host cell and then uses it to reproduce. Virions are released when the host cell is lysed. The subsequent breaches in the

respiratory epithelium result in an increased susceptibility to secondary viral and bacterial infection.

Transmission

- Influenza is primarily transmitted by respiratory secretions through coughing or sneezing.
- Direct nasal or eye contact with hands contaminated with the virus can also result in infection.

Incubation period

- The incubation period is 1 to 4 days (average 2 days).

Period of infectivity

- People with influenza are usually infectious a day before symptoms begin and remain infectious for about 5 days after the onset of the illness.
- Children can remain infectious for up to 2 weeks.
- Severely immunocompromised people can shed virus for weeks.

Antigenic drift and shift

- The physical structure of the influenza virus makes it prone to minor changes (point mutations) to one or both surface antigens during replication. This is known as antigenic drift and results in seasonal epidemics as it enables the virus to infect people who have only partial immunity from exposure to influenza in previous years.
- Influenza B viruses undergo less rapid antigenic drift than influenza A viruses.
- Major changes in the H and N antigens (probably as a result of genetic recombination when two strains of influenza A coinfect a single host) lead to a new virus subtype to which there is little population immunity. This is known as antigenic shift and has the potential to cause major epidemics and pandemics.
- Antigenic shift only occurs in influenza A viruses.

[WHO, 2000; CDC, 2002; Turner et al, 2002]

How common is it?

- Influenza usually occurs during the winter months, from October to April in the UK.
- **Up to 15% of the population may develop influenza in any one year.**
- The number of people who consult their GP with influenza-like illness (ILI) during the influenza season varies considerably from year to year. In an average year, GP consultations for new episodes of influenza and ILI rise from a baseline of less than 50/100,000 of the population per week to up to 200/100,000 per week [Dedman and Watson, 1997; Fleming et al, 1999].
- **An epidemic can be declared if the GP consultation rates for new episodes of influenza and ILI exceed 400/ 100,000 of the population per week** [Dedman and Watson, 1997]. The last epidemic in England and Wales occurred in 1989–1990.
- Pandemics (worldwide epidemics) occur infrequently and independently of season. Three pandemics occurred in the twentieth century — 1918, 1957, and 1967. The pandemic of 1918, also known as 'Spanish flu', killed an estimated 40 million people worldwide [WHO, 2000].

What are the risk factors for contracting influenza?

The risk of an individual contracting disease when influenza virus is circulating depends on a number of factors:

- **The infectivity and virulence of the circulating strain.**
- **The natural level of immunity:** depends on past exposure to influenza virus or vaccination, and the degree of cross-immunity from these to the circulating strain.
- **General nutritional and health status.**
- **Living arrangements:** much greater risk of transmission in closed environments such as residential homes, schools, and prisons.
- **Age:** influenza occurs most frequently in school-age children because of a lack of immunity from previous exposure and because of the opportunity for transmission in school. Being 65 years or over, or very young, are not risk factors for contracting influenza. However, individuals in these groups are more at risk of serious illness or death should they develop influenza.

[Burls et al, 2002]

How do I know my patient has it?

Clinical features

- **A broad spectrum of disease is associated with influenza,** ranging from asymptomatic infection; through a febrile illness with mild respiratory symptoms; a respiratory illness with systemic features; to an illness with multisystem complications affecting lung, heart, brain, liver, kidney, and muscle.
- **Influenza commonly presents abruptly** with anorexia, malaise, headache, fever in the range 38–40 °Celsius, myalgia, non-productive cough, sore throat, nasal discharge or obstruction, and sneezing.
- **Clinical features typically last for 3–5 days,** although cough, tiredness, and malaise may last for 1–2 weeks.
- **Infection in neonates and infants may present non-specifically** with lethargy, poor feeding, apnoea, or unexplained fever, or pneumonia, or otitis media.
- **Drowsiness is uncommon in adults,** but occurs in 10% of children aged 4–15 years, and in half of children under the age of 4 years.
- **Gastrointestinal features are rarely prominent,** although nausea, vomiting, and diarrhoea can sometimes accompany influenza infection, especially in children.
- **Fever may be absent in the elderly.**
- **The accuracy of a diagnosis of influenza based on clinical features is limited** as symptoms overlap considerably with those caused by other organisms, in particular adenovirus, rhinovirus, respiratory syncytial virus, parainfluenza virus, and bacterial infections.
- **Influenza surveillance information can aid clinical judgement.** The specificity of a clinical diagnosis is greater when the prevalence of influenza is above the winter baseline rate. One in three people who present with an ILI have true influenza when the levels of GP consultations for new episodes of influenza and ILI are above 50/100,000 of the population per week. However, only one in seven people have true influenza when the 50/100,000 threshold is not reached [Burls et al, 2002].

[Wiselka, 1994; CDC, 2002; Turner et al, 2002]

Diagnostic tests

- **The diagnosis of influenza is made on clinical grounds.**
- **The principal role of laboratory diagnosis is for influenza surveillance** — to indicate when influenza is circulating in the community, and to identify the predominant circulating types, subtypes, and strains.
- **Diagnostic tests available include:**
  - **Viral culture:** nasopharyngeal swabs or aspirates in appropriate transport medium can reliably obtain virus material for culture. Viral culture is necessary for information on influenza subtypes and strains. Results are available after 3–7 days (sometimes longer).
  - **Serology:** acute and convalescent sera are tested for rises in either complement-fixing or haemagglutination-inhibiting antibodies. The convalescent sample is usually taken 10–14 days after the acute sample.

    - **Immunofluorescence:** viral antigen can be detected directly with immunofluorescence using nasopharyngeal swabs or aspirates. Results are available within 24 hours.
    - **Polymerase chain reaction.**
    - **Rapid antigen testing.**
- **Near-patient rapid diagnostic testing** of nasopharyngeal, nasal, or throat swabs can detect influenza virus within 30 minutes. These tests currently lack sensitivity and specificity, and are probably no better at diagnosing influenza than the experienced clinician.

[Turner et al, 2002]

What else might it be?

There are a large number of differential diagnoses for people presenting with influenza-like illness. These include:

- The 'common cold'
- Streptococcal pharyngitis
- Meningitis
- Bacterial pneumonia
- Other respiratory viral infections, for example respiratory syncytial virus, coronavirus, rhinovirus
- Malaria: suspect in people who have recently travelled to a malaria area
- 'Prodromal flu-like illness' on contraction of HIV infection

Complications and prognosis

Complications

- Most complications of influenza in adults are respiratory.
- **Respiratory complications include:**
    - Acute bronchitis in about 20% of cases, with an increased risk in the elderly and in those with chronic medical conditions
    - Secondary bacterial pneumonia, particularly *Staphylococcus aureus*
    - Primary viral pneumonia
    - Exacerbations of asthma
    - Exacerbations of chronic obstructive pulmonary disease
    - Lung abscess
    - Empyema
    - Pulmonary aspergillosis
    - Sinusitis
- **Non-respiratory complications include:**
    - Febrile convulsions
    - Otitis media
    - Toxic shock syndrome
    - Myositis and myoglobinaemia
    - Heart failure
    - Myocarditis
    - Reye's syndrome
    - Guillain–Barré syndrome
    - Transverse myelitis
    - Encephalitis
- **Influenza infection of pregnant women is associated with early and late fetal deaths and increased perinatal mortality.** The perinatal mortality rate increased 1.6-fold during the 1989–1990 epidemic compared with a similar period in 1985–1986. Influenza in pregnancy has also been linked to a variety of congenital abnormalities; however, no consistent association with specific abnormalities has been found, and the influenza virus has not been conclusively implicated. [Turner et al, 2002]
- **Time off work** due to influenza infection has considerable economic implications — 150 million working days lost to influenza in the UK costs the economy about £6.75 billion each year [Voelker, 1999].

Prognosis

- **Most people recover completely within 1–2 weeks.**
- **The risks for complications, hospitalizations, and deaths** are higher among people aged 65 years and older, very young children, and those with underlying conditions compared with healthy older children and adults under 65 years. (Underlying conditions could include chronic respiratory disease, including asthma and chronic obstructive pulmonary disease; chronic heart disease; chronic renal disease; diabetes mellitus; and immunosuppression due to disease or treatment.)
- **Residents of nursing homes are at particular risk of serious influenza complications** — they are older, have a higher rate of chronic disease and may respond less well to influenza vaccination than the general population. Additionally, living in close proximity increases transmission of the influenza virus.
- **Women who are pregnant have a small increased absolute risk of severe pulmonary complications, hospitalization, and death** during the second and third trimesters following influenza [Turner et al, 2002].
- **Between 3000 and 4000 deaths are attributed to influenza each year in the UK.** The number of excess deaths attributable to influenza in epidemic years can be much higher; for example there may have been nearly 30,000 excess deaths in 1989–1990. More than 85% of these deaths are in people over 65 years. [NHS CRD, 1996]

How and why is influenza monitored?

- **The World Health Organization (WHO) has had responsibility for administrating an international network for influenza surveillance** since 1948. The network consists of four International WHO Collaborating Centres for Reference and Research on Influenza (located in Atlanta, London, Melbourne, and Tokyo), and 110 National Influenza Reference Centres in 82 countries. The National Influenza Reference Centre for the UK is based at the Specialist Reference Microbiology Division of the Health Protection Agency, Colindale.
- **Monitoring of clinical influenza activity** in the UK includes surveillance of GP consultations for influenza and ILI, for example the RCGP network of 70 spotter practices in England, ILI among children in boarding schools, mortality data provided by the Office for National Statistics, and NHS Direct calls.
- **Virological data** for the UK are obtained from samples from community and hospital sources, and specimens from laboratories from across the country.
- By monitoring the circulating strains of influenza virus, the WHO can make recommendations for the antigenic composition of next year's influenza vaccine.
- Influenza surveillance data are also important to guide decisions regarding antiviral treatment and prophylaxis; to monitor the emergence of antiviral resistance; to compare circulating influenza strains with vaccine strains; and to monitor the emergence of new influenza A subtypes that could cause a pandemic.

[WHO, 2000; Health Protection Agency, 2003]

Management issues

- Influenza vaccination p.1094
- Treatment of influenza in otherwise healthy individuals p.1095
- Antiviral drugs — general p.1095
- Antiviral drugs for the treatment of influenza p.1095
- Antiviral agents for the prophylaxis of influenza p.1096
- Management of outbreaks of influenza in long-stay residential care settings where influenza could spread

rapidly among people at high risk of complications p.1097

Influenza vaccination

General

- **Influenza vaccine is prepared each year** using virus strains (which are inactivated) recommended by the World Health Organization.
- **Two types of influenza vaccine are currently available in the UK** ('split virus' and 'surface antigen' vaccine). These are equally effective and have a similar adverse reaction rate [DH, 1996].
- A live attenuated influenza vaccine is also produced, but is not licensed in the UK. A potential advantage is that this is administered intranasally.
- Influenza immunization provides protection against strains related to those in the vaccine for about 1 year and should be repeated annually [DH, 1996].

Effectiveness

- **The effectiveness of influenza vaccine** depends primarily on the age and immunocompetence of the individual receiving the vaccine, and the similarity between the virus strains used to develop the vaccine and those in circulation.
- **Influenza immunization is highly effective in preventing influenza in healthy adults under the age of 65 years.** When the vaccine and circulating viruses are antigenically similar, immunization in this group:
  - Prevents influenza illness in 68% of individuals (95% CI 49% to 79%) [Demicheli et al, 2002].
  - Results in decreased time off work and decreased use of healthcare resources, including antibiotics.
- **In older people, protection against infection may be less, but immunization has been shown to reduce significantly the incidence of pneumonia, hospital admissions, and mortality.** When the vaccine and circulating viruses are antigenically similar, immunization:
  - Prevents influenza illness in around 60% of individuals over the age of 60 years who do not live in residential care settings.
  - Prevents influenza illness in 30–40% of elderly people living in nursing homes.
  - Is up to 60% effective at preventing hospitalization or pneumonia in elderly persons living in nursing homes, and 80% effective at preventing death.
- **Influenza vaccination is also effective in preventing influenza in children from the age of 6 months** and:
  - Is up to 90% effective at preventing influenza-associated respiratory illness among children aged 1–15 years.
  - May reduce the incidence of influenza-associated otitis media in children by 30%.

[CDC, 2002]

National policy for influenza immunization

- **Selective immunization** is recommended to protect those who are most at risk of serious illness or death should they develop influenza.
- **National policy in the UK is that influenza immunization should be offered to:**
  - All aged 65 years and over
  - All aged over 6 months in the following groups (see Table 1 for representative examples):
    - Chronic respiratory disease, including asthma
    - Chronic heart disease
    - Chronic renal disease
    - Diabetes
    - Immunosuppression
  - Those living in long-stay residential and nursing homes or other long-stay facilities

[CMO, 2003; CMO, 2004]

Note: clinicians should use their clinical judgment to decide whether a person is considered to be at risk of serious illness or death should they develop influenza.

- **The national policy for influenza vaccination was changed in 2000 to include otherwise fit people aged 65–74 years.** Evidence has shown that immunizing this group leads to improved life expectancy, as well as reductions in hospital admissions and complications. Previously, vaccination was recommended to everyone over 75 years.
- **Target groups for influenza and pneumococcal vaccination overlap considerably.** Both vaccines can be administered at the same time, at different sites. Note: for most people pneumococcal vaccine is given only once and re-immunization may cause adverse reactions [DH, 1996].

[CMO, 2003; CMO, 2004]

Influenza immunization for health and social care staff

- Influenza immunization of healthcare workers may reduce the transmission of influenza to vulnerable patients, some of whom may have impaired immunity and thus reduced protection from any influenza vaccine they have received themselves.
- **The Department of Health recommends that NHS employers should offer influenza immunization to employees directly involved in patient care.** Social care employers should consider similar action.
- **Occupational influenza immunization should be provided through an occupational health service** and is the responsibility of the employer.
- **Staff should not be asked to go to their GP for their immunization** unless they fall within one of the

Table 1: This shows the clinical risk categories with representative examples.

Clinical risk category	Representative examples
Chronic respiratory disease, including asthma	This includes chronic obstructive pulmonary disease, including chronic bronchitis and emphysema, bronchiectasis, cystic fibrosis, interstitial lung fibrosis, pneumoconiosis, asthma requiring continuous or repeated use of inhaled or systemic steroids or with previous exacerbations requiring hospital admission, and children who have previously been admitted to hospital for lower respiratory tract disease.
Chronic heart disease	This includes chronic ischaemic heart disease, congenital heart disease and hypertensive heart disease requiring regular medication and follow-up (but excluding uncomplicated controlled hypertension), and chronic heart failure.
Chronic renal disease	This includes nephrotic syndrome, chronic renal failure, and renal transplantation.
Diabetes	Diabetes mellitus requiring insulin or oral hypoglycaemic drugs.
Immunosuppression	Due to disease or treatment, including asplenia or splenic dysfunction, HIV infection at all stage, and also including systemic steroids for more than a month equivalent to 20 mg prednisolone daily (any age) or, for children under 20 kg, a dose of 1 mg or more per kg per day. Note: some immunocompromised people may have a suboptimal immunological response to vaccine.

recommended high-risk groups, or GPs have been contracted specifically to provide this service.
- Vaccine for staff should not be obtained at the expense of vaccine for the risk groups.
- Employers are recommended to keep records of staff immunized and monitor the effectiveness of their programme.

[CMO, 2003; CMO, 2004]

Suitability for vaccination

- Vaccines should not be given to those who have had a confirmed anaphylactic reaction to a previous dose of the same vaccine. Influenza vaccines should not be given if there is a confirmed anaphylactic reaction to other components of the vaccine or to eggs (as the vaccine is prepared in hens' eggs.
- Reasons to delay vaccination:
  - Acute illness: if an individual is suffering from any acute febrile illness, postpone immunization until they have fully recovered. Minor infections without fever or systemic upset are not reasons to postpone immunization.
  - Pregnancy: inactivated vaccines such as influenza are probably safe in pregnancy (the risks to the fetus are likely to be negligible), but use only if a clear indication exists and the benefits clearly outweigh the risks (e.g. if there is a risk of serious illness or death should they develop influenza [as in Table 1]).

[DH, 1996]

Adverse effects

- **Influenza vaccine is usually well tolerated.**
- **Soreness at the vaccination site is the most common adverse reaction,** affecting 24–64% of individuals. This is usually mild and lasts less than 2 days. It rarely interferes with daily activities.
- **Fever, malaise, myalgia, and arthralgia** can occur. These reactions occur 1–12 hours after immunization and last up to 2 days.
- **Immediate allergic reactions such as urticaria, angio-oedema, bronchospasm, and anaphylaxis are rare.** These are most likely to result from hypersensitivity to residual egg protein.
- Note: currently available influenza vaccines in the UK contain inactivated virus and cannot cause influenza.

[DH, 1996; CDC, 2002]

Treatment of influenza in otherwise healthy individuals

- **Otherwise healthy individuals with uncomplicated influenza-like illness (ILI) should be advised to follow self-management strategies** such as resting, increasing their fluid intake, and using analgesics and antipyretics. Influenza for most people is an unpleasant but self-limiting illness.

Antiviral drugs — general

- **Mode of action:**
  - **Zanamivir and oseltamivir** inhibit the influenza virus enzyme neuraminidase, which is involved in the release of new virions from infected host cells. Zanamivir and oseltamivir are active against both influenza A and influenza B.
  - **Amantadine** affects virus cell membrane ion channel activity and interferes with viral replication. It is only active against influenza A.
- **Formulation:**
  - **Zanamivir is administered as a dry-powder inhaler (Diskhaler),** which the elderly may find difficult to use [Diggory et al, 2001].
  - **Oseltamivir and amantadine are administered orally** and each is available as a hard capsule and an oral solution.
- **Adverse effects:**
  - **Zanamivir is generally well tolerated and the frequency of adverse events is similar to placebo.** However, studies have shown that people with asthma and other chronic respiratory diseases may experience bronchospasm or a decline in respiratory function. Clinicians should carefully consider the risks and benefits before recommending zanamivir for such people. The individual should be made aware of and accept the risks before zanamivir is prescribed, and they should have a fast-acting bronchodilator available when taking it [CDC, 2002; NICE, 2002; NICE, 2003a].
  - **Oseltamivir is well tolerated.** Nausea and vomiting are the most frequent adverse effects and can occur in up to 10% of people treated with oseltamivir. However, only 1% of participants in trials discontinued the drug because of this adverse effect [UKMI, 2001; Turner et al, 2002].
  - **Amantadine can cause significant adverse effects.** The most commonly reported are gastrointestinal disturbances (e.g. nausea, anorexia), neurological symptoms (loss of concentration, dizziness, agitation, nervousness, depression, insomnia, fatigue, weakness), and myalgia [ABPI Medicines Compendium, 2002].
- **Drug resistance:**
  - **Currently in the UK, 2.3% of circulating influenza A virus is resistant to amantadine.** When amantadine is used to treat influenza A, drug-resistant viruses can appear in up to a third of patients. The drug-resistant strains can replace sensitive strains within 2–3 days of starting therapy, but treatment remains beneficial even when drug-resistant strains emerge. The frequency of transmission of drug-resistant virus and the impact on the control of infection are unknown. [CDC, 2002]
  - **Development of resistance to oseltamivir and zanamivir occurs infrequently** [CDC, 2002].

Antiviral drugs for the treatment of influenza

- **Currently (October 2003) there are three drugs** that are licensed in the UK for the treatment of influenza — zanamivir, oseltamivir, and amantadine.
- **Evidence for the effectiveness** of these drugs is based principally on studies of otherwise healthy people with influenza.
- **Data are limited** regarding the effectiveness of antiviral drugs for the treatment of influenza among people at high risk of serious complications.

Zanamivir

- **Zanamivir is licensed for the treatment of influenza A and B in people aged 12 years or older,** if given within 48 hours of the onset of symptoms, when influenza is circulating.
- **Zanamivir has modest benefit in reducing the duration of symptoms when used early to treat influenza types A and B.**
  - **A meta-analysis of otherwise healthy adults** (12–65 years) with ILI showed that zanamivir reduces the duration of symptoms by 0.78 days. For people with confirmed influenza in this group, zanamivir reduces the duration of symptoms by 1.26 days [Turner et al, 2002].
  - **A meta-analysis of at-risk individuals** (aged 12 years or above) with ILI showed that zanamivir might reduce the duration of symptoms by 0.93 days (not statistically significant). For at-risk adults with

confirmed influenza, zanamivir reduces the duration of symptoms by 1.99 days [Turner et al, 2002].

- Pooled data indicate a reduction of complications requiring antibiotics in people treated with zanamivir compared with placebo. This was statistically significant for all (healthy and at-risk) individuals with ILI and healthy individuals with confirmed influenza. A more recent pooled analysis of high-risk individuals (adults and children) with ILI recruited into trials indicates that zanamivir reduces antibiotic prescribing for complications (OR 0.57, 95% CI 0.32 to 1.03) [Turner et al, 2002].
- **The effectiveness of zanamivir at reducing serious complications of influenza is uncertain.** Data are limited and inconclusive regarding hospitalization rates for individuals treated with zanamivir compared with placebo. Similarly there are limited data regarding death rates, as the trials were not powered to demonstrate differences for either group [Turner et al, 2002].
- **The National Institute for Clinical Excellence (NICE) recommends the use of zanamivir** for the treatment of at-risk adults who present with ILI and who can start therapy within 48 hours of the onset of symptoms, when influenza A or B is circulating in the community [NICE, 2003a]. Zanamivir is available on an NHS prescription for treating influenza only under these circumstances, and the prescription must be endorsed 'SLS'.

Oseltamivir

- **Oseltamivir is licensed for the treatment of influenza A and B in people aged 1 year or more,** within 48 hours of the onset of symptoms, when influenza is circulating in the community. It is also licensed for the prophylaxis of influenza A and B in people aged 13 years or more when influenza is circulating. (See section *Antiviral agents for the prophylaxis of influenza.*)
- **Oseltamivir is likely to be beneficial in reducing the duration of symptoms when used early to treat influenza types A and B.**
  - **A meta-analysis of otherwise healthy adults** (12–65 years) with ILI showed that oseltamivir reduces the duration of symptoms by 0.86 days. For people with confirmed influenza in this group, oseltamivir reduces the duration of symptoms by 1.38 days [Turner et al, 2002].
  - **A meta-analysis of at-risk individuals** (aged 12 years or above) with ILI showed that oseltamivir might reduce the duration of symptoms by 0.35 days (not statistically significant). For at-risk adults with confirmed influenza, oseltamivir might reduce the duration of symptoms by 0.45 days (not statistically significant) [Turner et al, 2002].
  - One study of children aged 1–12 years with ILI showed that oseltamivir reduces the duration of symptoms by 0.87 days. For children with confirmed influenza in this group, oseltamivir reduces the symptoms by 1.49 days [Turner et al, 2002].
- Pooled analysis of data indicates a statistically significant reduction of lower respiratory tract complications requiring antibiotics in people treated with oseltamivir compared with placebo [Turner et al, 2002].
- Oseltamivir has been shown (in a single study) to reduce the incidence of otitis media in children aged 1–12 years with confirmed influenza (OR 0.50, 95% CI 0.29 to 0.87) [Turner et al, 2002].
- **The effectiveness of oseltamivir at reducing serious complications of influenza is uncertain.** Data are very limited regarding hospitalization rates for individuals treated with oseltamivir compared with placebo. Similarly there are limited data regarding death rates, as the trials were not powered to demonstrate differences for either group [Turner et al, 2002].
- **NICE recommends the use of oseltamivir** for the treatment of at-risk adults and children who present with ILI and who can start therapy within 48 hours of the onset of symptoms, when influenza A or B is circulating in the community [NICE, 2003a]. Oseltamivir is available on an NHS prescription for treating influenza only under these circumstances, and the prescription must be endorsed 'SLS'.

Amantadine

- **Amantadine is licensed for the treatment of (and prophylaxis against) influenza A in people at risk of complications.** It should be commenced within 48 hours of the onset of influenza symptoms.
- **Treatment with amantadine 200 mg has been shown to shorten duration of influenza by about 1 day in healthy adults** (95% CI 0.7 to 1.3) [Jefferson et al, 2002]. Zanamivir and oseltamivir are similarly effective. Note: trials included in this systematic review used amantadine 200 mg daily, whereas the licensed dose for the treatment of influenza is currently 100 mg daily.
- **The benefits of treating children and at-risk persons suffering from influenza with amantadine are uncertain.**
  - Studies investigating the effectiveness of treating influenza with amantadine in children and the elderly are of poor quality and difficult to generalize.
  - We could find no randomized controlled trials of amantadine 100 mg for treatment of influenza in people with chronic disease.
- **Amantadine has been used infrequently** because of concerns about adverse reactions, its limited spectrum of activity, and drug resistance.
- Amantadine is not recommended for the treatment of influenza [NICE, 2003a].

[Turner et al, 2002]

Antiviral agents for the prophylaxis of influenza

- **Antiviral drugs are *not* a substitute for vaccination, but should be regarded as an adjunct in the prevention and control of influenza.**
- Currently two drugs are licensed in the UK for the prophylaxis of influenza — oseltamivir and amantadine.
- There are two ways of providing prophylaxis:
  - **Post-exposure prophylaxis,** which involves starting antiviral drugs after an individual has come into close contact with someone who is suspected of having influenza. Treatment is usually for 7–10 days.
  - **Seasonal prophylaxis,** which involves prescribing antiviral drugs throughout the time that influenza is circulating in the community. Treatment is usually for around 6 weeks.

Oseltamivir

- **Oseltamivir is licensed for the prophylaxis of influenza A and B in people aged 13 years or more,** following a contact with a person with clinically diagnosed influenza, when influenza is circulating in the community.
- **Oseltamivir is likely to be beneficial for the prevention and control of influenza.**
  - Pooled data of two trials shows that oseltamivir is 75% effective at preventing influenza in healthy unvaccinated adults (18–65 years), when local influenza activity is increased [Turner et al, 2002].
  - A single trial showed that oseltamivir was 90% effective at preventing influenza in elderly people (64–96 years) in residential care, during the influenza season. Nearly all (98%) of the participants had

Table 2: This summarizes the clinical effectiveness of antiviral agents at reducing duration of symptoms and the time taken to return to normal activities.

	Reduction in the median time to alleviation of symptoms compared with placebo		Reduction in the median time to return to normal activities compared with placebo	
	Influenza positive	Influenza-like illness (ILI)	Influenza positive	Influenza-like illness (ILI)
Zanamivir in otherwise healthy adults aged 12–65 years	1.26 days (95% CI 0.59 to 1.93)	0.78 days (95% CI 0.26 to 1.3)	0.46 days (95% CI 0.02 to 0.90)	0.51 days (95% CI –0.02 to +1.04)
Zanamivir in at-risk adults	1.99 days (95% CI 0.90 to 3.08)	0.93 days (95% CI –0.05 to +1.90)	0.20 days (95% CI –0.79 to +1.19)	0.09 days (95% CI –0.78 to +0.95)
Oseltamivir in otherwise healthy adults aged 12–65 years	1.38 days (95% CI 0.80 to 1.96)	0.86 days (95% CI 0.31 to 1.41)	1.64 days (95 % CI 0.69 to 2.58)	1.33 days (95% CI 0.71 to 1.96)
Oseltamivir in at-risk adults	0.45 days (95% CI –0.97 to +1.88)	0.35 days (95% CI –0.71 to +1.40)	3.00 days (95% CI 0.13 to 5.88)	2.45 days (95% CI 0.05 to 4.86)
Oseltamivir in otherwise healthy children	1.49 days (95% CI 0.76 to 2.22)	0.87 days (95% CI 0.25 to 1.49)	1.86 days (95% CI 1.06 to 2.65)	1.25 days (95% CI 0.70 to 1.80)
Amantadine in otherwise healthy adults aged 14–60 years	1 day (fever) (95% CI 0.7 to 1.3)	Not applicable	Not applicable	Not applicable
Amantadine in elderly and children	Poor quality data. Cochrane systematic review in progress	Poor quality data. Cochrane systematic review in progress	Poor quality data. Cochrane systematic review in progress	Poor quality data. Cochrane systematic review in progress

coexisting medical conditions, and 80% had received influenza vaccination [Peters et al, 2001].
- A single trial showed that oseltamivir was 90% effective at preventing influenza in household contacts of people with influenza [Welliver et al, 2001]. This is the only study that has specifically looked at post-exposure prophylaxis.

- **NICE recommends oseltamivir for post-exposure prophylaxis** [NICE, 2003b] in people who are:
  - Aged 13 years and older, *and*
  - At-risk, *and*
  - Not effectively protected by vaccination, *and*
  - In close contact (i.e. someone who lives in the same house environment as a person suffering from symptoms of ILI, *and*
  - Able to begin prophylaxis within 48 hours of exposure
- Oseltamivir is available on an NHS prescription for post-exposure prophylaxis under these circumstances, and the prescription must be endorsed 'SLS'.
- NICE does not recommend post-exposure prophylaxis in healthy people up to the age of 65 years [NICE, 2003b].
- **NICE does not recommend oseltamivir for seasonal prophylaxis** of influenza [NICE, 2003b].

Zanamivir

- Zanamivir does not currently have a licence for the prophylaxis of influenza.
- It appears to be between 70% and 90% effective at preventing influenza [CDC, 2002].
- Although it is likely to be as effective as oseltamivir in preventing influenza, it is not currently recommended for this indication.

[Turner et al, 2002; NICE, 2003b]

Amantadine

- Amantadine is licensed for the prophylaxis of influenza A for at-risk people.
- **Amantadine has been shown to be effective in the prevention of influenza A in healthy adults.** It can prevent 23% of ILI cases and 63% of serologically confirmed influenza A cases [Jefferson et al, 2002]. However, the majority of trials included in this systematic review used amantadine 200 mg daily, whereas the licensed dosage of amantadine for the prophylaxis of influenza is 100 mg daily. One study comparing amantadine *100 mg* daily with placebo in healthy unvaccinated adults indicates that amantadine 100 mg is effective for the prophylaxis of influenza in this group (OR 0.44, 95% CI 0.27 to 0.71).
- There is a lack of high-quality data regarding the effectiveness of amantadine for the prophylaxis of influenza in the elderly, children, and at-risk adults [Turner et al, 2002].
- Amantadine is not recommended for either post-exposure or seasonal prophylaxis of influenza [NICE, 2003b].

Table 3: Summary of the effectiveness of oseltamivir and zanamivir for the prophylaxis of influenza

Situation	Odds ratio (95% CI)	
	Zanamivir	Oseltamivir
Post-exposure prophylaxis in households	0.19 (0.09 to 0.38) Based on two trials	0.20 (0.05 to 0.74) Based on 2 trials (one not published)
Seasonal prophylaxis — healthy	0.31 (0.14 to 0.64) Based on one trial	0.26 (0.08 to 0.84) Based on two trials
Seasonal prophylaxis — elderly	No data available	0.08 (0.01 to 0.61) Based on one trial
Outbreak prophylaxis — elderly	0.11 (0.00 to 2.91) for influenza A Based on one trial 0.15 (0.00 to 4.01) for influenza B Based on one trial	No data available

Management of outbreaks of influenza in long-stay residential care settings where influenza could spread rapidly among people at high risk of complications

- **To minimize the transmission of influenza virus to uninfected residents the following measures should be considered:**
  - Offering influenza vaccinations to unvaccinated staff and residents (unless contraindicated).
  - Separation of people with confirmed or suspected influenza from individuals who do not clinically have ILI.
  - Restriction of contact between ill staff/visitors and residents.

- Restriction of staff movements between wards or buildings.

[CDC, 2002]

- **NICE recommends oseltamivir for post-exposure prophylaxis in people who live in a residential care establishment where a resident or staff member has ILI, *whether or not they have been vaccinated,* if they are:**
  - Aged 13 years and older, *and*
  - At-risk, *and*
  - Able to begin prophylaxis within 48 hours of exposure
- Oseltamivir is available on an NHS prescription for post-exposure prophylaxis under these circumstances, and the prescription must be endorsed 'SLS'.
- Note: a residential care establishment is defined (for the purposes of the NICE guidance) as a place where the person resides in the long term in order to be provided with continuing care alongside a number of other individuals.

[NICE, 2003b]

- Treatment should be for at least 2 weeks or until 1 week after the end of the outbreak if new cases continue to occur [CDC, 2002].

References

NHS staff in England can link, free of charge, from references to full text journals by clicking on [Full text] on the PRODIGY website.

1. ABPI Medicines Compendium (2002) *Summary of product characteristics for Lysovir 100mg capsules.* Electronic Medicines Compendium. Datapharm Communications Ltd. www.emc.medicines.org.uk [Accessed: 10/10/2002].
2. Arroll, B. and Kenealy, T. (2002) *Antibiotics for the common cold (Cochrane Review).* The Cochrane Library. Issue 3. Oxford: Update Software.
3. Burls, A., Clark, W., Stewart, T. et al (2002) Zanamivir for the treatment of influenza in adults: a systematic review and economic evaluation. *Health Technology Assessment* 6(9),
4. CDC (2002) *Prevention and control of influenza: recommendations of the advisory committee on immunization practices (ACIP).* Centers for Disease Control and Prevention. 51(RR03). www.cdc./gov/mmwr/preview/mmwrhtml/rr5103a1.htm [Accessed: 29/09/2002].
5. CMO (2003) *Adult immunisation update.* Department of Health. www.dh.gov.uk [Accessed: 27/04/2004].
6. CMO (2004) *Update on the influenza and pneumococcal immunisation programmes.* PL/CMO/2004/4. Department of Health. www.dh.gov.uk [Accessed: 11/08/2004]. [Full text]
7. Dedman, D.J. and Watson, J.M. (1997) The use of thresholds to describe levels of influenza activity. *PHLS Microbiology Digest* 14(4), 206–208.
8. Demicheli, V., Rivetti, D., Deeks, J.J. and Jefferson, T.O. (2002) *Vaccines for preventing influenza in healthy adults (Cochrane Review).* The Cochrane Library. Issue 3. Oxford: Update Software.
9. DH (1996) *Influenza.* The Green Book: Chapter 20. Department of Health. www.dh.gov.uk [Accessed: 27/04/2004]. [Full text]
10. Diggory, P., Fernandez, C., Humphrey, A. et al (2001) Comparison of elderly people's technique in using two dry powder inhalers to deliver zanamivir: randomised controlled trial. *British Medical Journal* 322(7286), 577–579. [Full text]
11. Fleming, D.M., Zambon, M., Bartelds, A.I. and De Jong, J.C. (1999) The duration and magnitude of influenza epidemics: a study of surveillance data from sentinel general practices in England, Wales and the Netherlands. *European Journal of Epidemiology* 15(5), 467–473. [Full text]
12. Health Protection Agency (2003) *Sources of data for influenza surveillance in the United Kingdom.* Health Protection Agency. www.hpa.org.uk [Accessed: 21/10/2003].
13. Jefferson, T.O., Demicheli, V., Deeks, J.J. and Rivetti, D. (2002) *Amantadine and Rimantadine for preventing and treating influenza A in adults (Cochrane Review).* Issue 3. Oxford: Update Software.
14. NHS Confederation and BMA (2005) *New GMS contract.* Department of Health. www.dh.gov.uk [Accessed: 27/09/2005]. [Full text]
15. NHS CRD (1996) Influenza vaccination and older people. *Effectiveness Matters* 2(1),
16. NICE (2002) *Appraisal consultation document: the clinical and cost effectiveness of zanamivir, oseltamivir and amantadine for the treatment and prophylaxis of influenza.* National Institute for Clinical Excellence. www.nice.org.uk [Accessed: 08/08/2002].
17. NICE (2003a) *Guidance on the the use of zanamivir, oseltamivir and amantadine for the treatment of influenza.* Health technology appraisal no. 58. National Institute for Clinical Excellence. www.nice.org.uk [Accessed: 01/09/2003].
18. NICE (2003b) *Guidance on the use of oseltamivir and amantadine for the prophylaxis of influenza.* Technology appraisal guidance no. 67. National Institute for Clinical Excellence. www.nice.org.uk [Accessed: 01/10/2003].
19. Peters, P.H., Jr., Gravenstein, S., Norwood, P. et al (2001) Long-term use of oseltamivir for the prophylaxis of influenza in a vaccinated frail older population. *Journal of the American Geriatrics Society* 49(8), 1025–1031.
20. Turner, D., Wailoo, A., Nicholson, K. et al (2002) *Systematic review and economic decision modelling for the prevention and treatment of influenza A and B.* Leicester: University of Leicester.
21. UKMI (2001) *New drugs in clinical development: oseltamivir.* UK Medicines Information. www.ukmi.nhs.uk/Newmaterial/html/docs/29100101.pdf [Accessed: 12/08/2002].
22. Voelker, R. (1999) Fighting the flu. *Journal of the American Medical Association* 281(2), 123–123. [Full text]
23. Welliver, R., Monto, A.S., Carewicz, O. et al (2001) Effectiveness of oseltamivir in preventing influenza in household contacts: a randomized controlled trial. *Journal of the American Medical Association* 285(6), 748–754. [Full text]
24. WHO (2000) *WHO report on global surveillance of epidemic-prone infectious diseases. Chapter 7 – influenza.* WHO/CDS/CSR/ISR/2000.1. WHO Department of Communicable Disease Surveillance and Response. www.who.int/emc-documents/surveillance/whocdscsrisr20001c.html [Accessed: 11/10/2002].
25. Wiselka, M. (1994) Influenza: diagnosis, management, and prophylaxis. *British Medical Journal* 308(6940), 1341–1345. [Full text]

PRODIGY GUIDANCE

Insect bites and stings

Last revised in February 2004
www.prodigy.nhs.uk/guidance.asp?gt=Insect bites and stings

Applies to people over the age of 1 month

This guidance covers insect bites and stings, including bites from ticks and mites.

This guidance does not cover spider bites or bites from insects that are not indigenous to the UK.

There is separate PRODIGY guidance for *Bites — human and animal, Head lice, Malaria prophylaxis, Pubic lice,* and *Scabies.*

Goals

- To relieve symptoms
- To prevent reinfestation
- To prevent secondary infection
- To treat anaphylaxis promptly
- To minimize the risk of future anaphylactic reactions

Contents

Scenarios

- Insect bites p.1099
- Insect stings p.1101
- Previous anaphylactic reaction p.1102

Extended Information, p. 1103

Which scenario?

- **Insect bites:** covers the acute symptomatic management of uncomplicated insect bites and the prevention of reinfestation.
- **Insect stings:** covers the acute symptomatic management of uncomplicated insect stings including the removal of the sting, and local and mild systemic allergic reactions.
- **Previous anaphylactic reaction:** covers the future management of patients who have had a moderate to severe anaphylactic reaction.

Insect bites

Which therapy?

- **Treat local itching** with a topical antipruritic such as crotamiton. A short course of sedative antihistamine at night may be helpful to break the itch–scratch cycle.
- **If there is localized inflammation,** topical corticosteroids may be helpful.
- **If there is an urticarial reaction,** consider a short course of an oral antihistamine.
- **If possible determine the cause of infestation and prevent recurrence:**
  - The distribution of bites may help determine the type of insect.
  - A careful history may highlight the source of the infection.
- **Eliminate the source of infestation:**
  - Cat and dog fleas — direct insecticides at the pet, its bedding, household carpets, soft furnishings.
  - Bedbugs — apply insecticide to walls and furniture.
  - Cheyletiella mite — seek local veterinary advice.

Practical prescribing points

For further information please see the *Medicines Compendium* (www.medicines.org.uk) or the *British National Formulary* (www.bnf.org).

Antihistamines

- **Sedative antihistamines** cause drowsiness that may persist the next day. Advise people not to drive or operate machinery if affected.
- **Second-generation (non-sedating) oral antihistamines.** Although drowsiness is rare, it can occur and may affect performance of skilled tasks such as driving.
- **In people with moderate renal impairment** the dose of cetirizine should be halved.

Follow-up advice

- It is not generally necessary to follow up people who have had an insect bite.
- Ensure that measures have been undertaken to prevent reinfestation where appropriate.
- People who have removed a tick should be advised to seek medical advice promptly if they develop a skin lesion or become pyrexial within a month of the bite, because of the possibility of Lyme disease.

Should I refer or investigate?

Investigate?

- Investigate potential sources of reinfestation.

Patient information leaflets

The following PILs are available at www.prodigy.nhs.uk

- Insect Bites
- Medicines - Name Changes of Medicines

Shared decision making

- Treatment options following an insect bite include:
  - Crotamiton ointment to soothe itch.
  - **A mild steroid cream** such as hydrocortisone to reduce any inflammation.
  - **Antihistamine tablets** to reduce itch and inflammation if you have a lot of bites.
- Repeated bites usually come from insects that infest a pet, furnishing, bedding, etc. You may need to find the cause of an infestation and treat it with insecticide.

Drug rationale

Drugs not included

- **Topical antihistamines** are of limited efficacy and may cause sensitization.
- **Calamine lotion** generally soothes itch, although the residue (when dried) can exacerbate itch in some people.
- **Non-sedating oral antihistamines, desloratadine** (a metabolite of loratadine), **levocetirizine** (an isomerof cetirizine), and **mizolastine** are more recently marketed products that are still under close post-marketing surveillance.

Drugs included

- **Crotamiton** cream or lotion has soothing qualities and may help to relieve the itch caused by insect bites, although there is no objective proof of its anti-pruritic activity. It is licensed for the relief of itching and skin irritation caused by insect bites and stings.
- **Betamethasone valerate** is a potent topical corticosteroid, which may be useful in short courses when there is an inflammatory local reaction to the bite.
- **The combination of hydrocortisone 0.25% with crotamiton 10%** is licensed for the treatment of insect bite reactions.
- **Hydroxyzine** is specifically licensed for pruritus and is sedating. It is offered as a night-time dose for temporary help with sleeping, to help break the itch–scratch cycle.
- **Chlorphenamine (chlorpheniramine)** is also included because it is inexpensive and is an effective sedating antihistamine of intermediate duration.
- **Non-sedating antihistamines: cetirizine, loratadine, and fexofenadine** are available for once-daily administration where there is an urticarial reaction.

Prescriptions

Topical antipruritic

Crotamiton 10% cream: apply 2 to 3 times a day
- Age from 1 month onwards
- Crotamiton 10% cream. Apply to the affected area 2 to 3 times a day when required for relief of itching; supply 30 grams; NHS Cost £2.27; OTC Cost £3.55.

Crotamiton 10% lotion: apply 2 to 3 times a day
- Age from 1 month onwards
- Crotamiton 10% lotion. Apply to the affected area 2 to 3 times a day when required for relief of itching; supply 100 ml; NHS Cost £2.99; OTC Cost £4.69.

Topical corticosteroid

Betamethasone 0.1% cream: apply once or twice a day
- Age from 12 months onwards
- Betamethasone val 0.1% cream. Apply thinly to the affected area once or twice a day. Use for a maximum of 7 days unless otherwise directed; supply 30 grams; NHS Cost £1.54.

Betamethasone 0.1% ointment: apply once or twice a day
- Age from 12 months onwards
- Betamethasone val 0.1% ointment. Apply thinly to the affected area once or twice a day. Use for a maximum of 7 days unless otherwise directed; supply 30 grams; NHS Cost £1.69.

Topical antipruritic + hydrocortisone

Crotamiton + hydrocortisone cream
- Age from 1 month onwards
- Eurax-Hydrocortisone cream. Apply thinly to the affected area 2 to 3 times a day. Use for a maximum of 7 days unless otherwise directed; supply 15 grams; NHS Cost £1.98; OTC Cost £3.09.

Oral antihistamines: non-sedating

Cetirizine s/f solution: 5mg once a day
- Age from 2 to 5 years
- Cetirizine 5mg/5ml s/f sol. Take one 5ml spoonful once a day; supply 100 ml; NHS Cost £5.25; OTC Cost £8.78.

Cetirizine s/f solution: 10mg once a day
- Age from 6 to 11 years
- Cetirizine 5mg/5ml s/f sol. Take two 5ml spoonfuls once a day; supply 100 ml; NHS Cost £5.25; OTC Cost £8.78.

Cetirizine tablets: 10mg once a day
- Age from 12 years onwards
- Cetirizine 10mg tablets. Take one tablet once a day; supply 7 tablets; NHS Cost £1.66; OTC Cost £4.45.

Fexofenadine tablets: 180mg once a day
- Age from 12 years onwards
- Fexofenadine 180mg tablets. Take one tablet once a day; supply 7 tablets; NHS Cost £2.25.

Loratadine syrup: 5mg once a day
- Age from 2 to 5 years
- Loratadine 5mg/5ml syrup. Take one 5ml spoonful once a day; supply 100 ml; NHS Cost £2.85; OTC Cost £4.99.

Loratadine syrup: 10mg once a day
- Age from 6 to 11 years
- Loratadine 5mg/5ml syrup. Take two 5ml spoonfuls once a day; supply 100 ml; NHS Cost £2.85; OTC Cost £4.99.

Loratadine tablets: 10mg once a day
- Age from 12 years onwards
- Loratadine 10mg tablets. Take one tablet once a day; supply 7 tablets; NHS Cost £1.47; OTC Cost £4.45.

Oral antihistamines: sedating

Chlorphenamine (chlorpheniramine) syrup: 1mg at night prn
- Age from 12 to 23 months
- Chlorphenamine 2mg/5ml syrup. Take 2.5ml at night when required for relief of itching; supply 50 ml; NHS Cost £0.72; OTC Cost £1.26.

Chlorphenamine (chlorpheniramine) syrup: 1-2mg at night prn
- Age from 2 to 5 years
- Chlorphenamine 2mg/5ml syrup. Take 2.5ml to 5ml at night when required for relief of itching; supply 100 ml; NHS Cost £1.43; OTC Cost £2.53.

Chlorphenamine (chlorpheniramine) syrup: 2-4mg at night prn
- Age from 6 to 11 years
- Chlorphenamine 2mg/5ml syrup. Take one to two 5ml spoonfuls at night when required for relief of itching; supply 100 ml; NHS Cost £1.43; OTC Cost £2.53.

Chlorphenamine (chlorpheniramine) tablets: 4mg at night prn
- Age from 12 years onwards
- Chlorphenamine 4mg tablets. Take one tablet at night when required for relief of itching; supply 14 tablets; NHS Cost £0.22; OTC Cost £1.40.

Hydroxyzine syrup: 5mg to 15mg at night when required
- Age from 6 months to 6 years
- Hydroxyzine 10mg/5ml syrup. Take 2.5ml to 7.5ml at night when required for relief of itching; supply 100 ml; NHS Cost £0.96.

Hydroxyzine syrup: 15mg to 25mg at night when required
- Age from 7 to 11 years
- Hydroxyzine 10mg/5ml syrup. Take 7.5ml to 12.5ml at night when required for relief of itching; supply 200 ml; NHS Cost £1.91.

Hydroxyzine tablets: 25mg at night when required
- Age from 12 years onwards
- Hydroxyzine 25mg tablets. Take one tablet at night when required for relief of itching; supply 14 tablets; NHS Cost £0.51.

Insect stings

Which therapy?

- **Remove the sting as quickly as possible.**
- **Treat localized pain, swelling, and erythema** at the site of the sting with simple analgesics and cold compresses (e.g. ice packs).
- **If the sting is associated with local inflammation** consider a short course of topical corticosteroids.
- **If a large local or mild systemic (mild urticaria without hypotension or breathing difficulties) reaction develops,** give an oral antihistamine.
- **Systemic reactions with respiratory difficulty and/or hypotension (anaphylaxis) need prompt treatment of laryngeal oedema, bronchospasm, and hypotension.**

Practical prescribing points

For further information please see the *Medicines Compendium* (www.medicines.org.uk) or the *British National Formulary* (www.bnf.org).

Analgesia

- **Ibuprofen:** as with other nonsteroidal anti-inflammatory drugs, ibuprofen may worsen or precipitate gastrointestinal haemorrhage, asthma, hypertension, renal impairment, or cardiac failure. Avoid if there is a history of peptic ulcers and in pregnant women.

Antihistamines

- **Sedative antihistamines** cause drowsiness that may persist the next day. Advise people not to drive or operate machinery if affected.
- **Second-generation (non-sedating) oral antihistamines.** Although drowsiness is rare, it can occur and may affect performance of skilled tasks such as driving.
- **In people with moderate renal impairment** the dose of cetirizine should be halved.

Follow-up advice

- It is not generally necessary to follow up people who have had an insect sting without a generalized systemic reaction.

Should I refer or investigate?

Refer?

- Refer someone who has had a generalized allergic reaction to an allergy clinic or allergist (ideally one with expertise in anaphylaxis) if available to confirm the cause and give advice on prevention of further reactions.

Patient information leaflets

The following PILs are available at www.prodigy.nhs.uk
- Insect Stings
- Medicines - Name Changes of Medicines

Shared decision making

- Treatment options following an insect sting include:
  - **A cold compress** (for example, a cold flannel or an ice pack) to ease the pain and help to minimize any swelling.
  - **A painkiller** such as paracetamol or ibuprofen to ease the pain.
  - **A steroid cream** such as hydrocortisone to reduce any inflammation.
  - **Antihistamines tablets,** if you have swelling.
- If you are stung again remember to:
  - Scrape out the sting as quickly as possible with a knife, the edge of a credit card, or similar.
  - Call an ambulance if you develop any allergy symptoms such as wheezing, blotchy skin rash, facial swelling, or dizziness.

Drug rationale

Drugs not included

- **Calamine lotion** should not be used on insect stings [BNF 46, 2003].
- **Topical antihistamines** are of limited efficacy and may cause sensitization.
- **Non-sedating oral antihistamines: desloratadine** (a metabolite of loratadine), **levocetirizine** (an isomer of cetirizine), and **mizolastine** are more recently marketed products that are still under close post-marketing surveillance.

Drugs included

- **Paracetamol** is usually effective for pain relief.
- **Ibuprofen** is offered as alternative pain relief for people with no contraindications.
- **Betamethasone valerate** is a potent topical corticosteroid, which may be useful in short courses when there is an inflammatory local reaction to the sting.
- **Non-sedating antihistamines: cetirizine, loratadine, and fexofenadine** are available for once-daily administration if there is large local swelling or a mild urticarial reaction.
- **Sedating antihistamines: chlorphenamine (chlorpheniramine)** is an inexpensive alternative for people who prefer a sedating antihistamine.

Prescriptions

Analgesia: use when required

Paracetamol s/f susp: 60mg to 120mg up to four times a day
- Age from 3 to 11 months
- Paracetamol 120mg/5ml s/f susp. Take 2.5ml to 5ml every 4 to 6 hours when required for pain relief. Maximum of 4 doses in 24 hours; supply 150 ml; NHS Cost £0.65; OTC Cost £1.14.

Paracetamol s/f susp: 120mg to 240mg up to four times a day
- Age from 12 months to 5 years
- Paracetamol 120mg/5ml s/f susp. Take one to two 5ml spoonfuls every 4 to 6 hours when required for pain relief. Maximum of 4 doses in 24 hours; supply 300 ml; NHS Cost £1.30; OTC Cost £2.28.

I

Paracetamol s/f susp: 250mg to 500mg up to four times a day
- Age from 6 to 11 years
- Paracetamol 250mg/5ml s/f susp. Take one to two 5ml spoonfuls every 4 to 6 hours when required for pain relief. Maximum of 4 doses in 24 hours; supply 300 ml; NHS Cost £1.59; OTC Cost £2.80.

Paracetamol tablets: 500mg to 1g up to four times a day
- Age from 12 to 15 years
- Paracetamol 500mg tablets. Take one to two tablets every 4 to 6 hours when required for pain relief. Maximum of 8 tablets in 24 hours; supply 100 tablets; NHS Cost £0.75; OTC Cost £1.32.

Paracetamol tablets: 1g up to four times a day
- Age from 16 years onwards
- Paracetamol 500mg tablets. Take two tablets every 4 to 6 hours when required for pain relief. Maximum of 8 tablets in 24 hours; supply 100 tablets; NHS Cost £0.75; OTC Cost £1.32.

Ibuprofen s/f susp: 50mg three to four times a day
- Age from 12 months to 2 years
- Ibuprofen 100mg/5ml s/f susp. Take 2.5ml three to four times a day when required for pain relief. Do not exceed the stated dose; supply 100 ml; NHS Cost £2.00; OTC Cost £3.52.

Ibuprofen s/f susp: 100mg three to four times a day
- Age from 3 to 7 years
- Ibuprofen 100mg/5ml s/f susp. Take one 5ml spoonful 3 to 4 times a day when required for pain relief. Do not exceed the stated dose; supply 150 ml; NHS Cost £2.73; OTC Cost £4.81.

Ibuprofen s/f susp: 200mg three to four times a day
- Age from 8 to 11 years
- Ibuprofen 100mg/5ml s/f susp. Take two 5ml spoonfuls 3 to 4 times a day when required for pain relief. Do not exceed the stated dose; supply 300 ml; NHS Cost £5.46; OTC Cost £9.62.

Ibuprofen tablets: 400mg three times a day
- Age from 12 years onwards
- Ibuprofen 400mg tablets. Take one tablet three times a day when required for pain relief. Do not exceed the stated dose; supply 24 tablets; NHS Cost £0.70; OTC Cost £1.23.

Topical corticosteroid

Betamethasone 0.1% cream: apply once or twice a day
- Age from 12 months onwards
- Betamethasone val 0.1% cream. Apply thinly to the affected area once or twice a day. Use for a maximum of 7 days unless otherwise directed; supply 30 grams; NHS Cost £1.54.

Betamethasone 0.1% ointment: apply once or twice a day
- Age from 12 months onwards
- Betamethasone val 0.1% ointment. Apply thinly to the affected area once or twice a day. Use for a maximum of 7 days unless otherwise directed; supply 30 grams; NHS Cost £1.69.

Oral antihistamines: non-sedating

Cetirizine s/f solution: 5mg once a day
- Age from 2 to 5 years
- Cetirizine 5mg/5ml s/f sol. Take one 5ml spoonful once a day; supply 100 ml; NHS Cost £5.25; OTC Cost £8.78.

Cetirizine s/f solution: 10mg once a day
- Age from 6 to 11 years
- Cetirizine 5mg/5ml s/f sol. Take two 5ml spoonfuls once a day; supply 100 ml; NHS Cost £5.25; OTC Cost £8.78.

Cetirizine tablets: 10mg once a day
- Age from 12 years onwards
- Cetirizine 10mg tablets. Take one tablet once a day; supply 7 tablets; NHS Cost £1.66; OTC Cost £4.45.

Fexofenadine tablets: 180mg once a day
- Age from 12 years onwards
- Fexofenadine 180mg tablets. Take one tablet once a day; supply 7 tablets; NHS Cost £2.25.

Loratadine syrup: 5mg once a day
- Age from 2 to 5 years
- Loratadine 5mg/5ml syrup. Take one 5ml spoonful once a day; supply 100 ml; NHS Cost £2.85; OTC Cost £4.99.

Loratadine syrup: 10mg once a day
- Age from 6 to 11 years
- Loratadine 5mg/5ml syrup. Take two 5ml spoonfuls once a day; supply 100 ml; NHS Cost £2.85; OTC Cost £4.99.

Loratadine tablets: 10mg once a day
- Age from 12 years onwards
- Loratadine 10mg tablets. Take one tablet once a day; supply 7 tablets; NHS Cost £1.47; OTC Cost £4.45.

Oral antihistamines: sedating

Chlorphenamine (chlorpheniramine) syrup: 1mg twice a day
- Age from 12 to 23 months
- Chlorphenamine 2mg/5ml syrup. Take 2.5ml twice a day; supply 50 ml; NHS Cost £0.72; OTC Cost £1.26.

Chlorphenamine (chlorpheniramine): 1-2mg three times a day
- Age from 2 to 5 years
- Chlorphenamine 2mg/5ml syrup. Take 2.5ml to 5ml three times a day; supply 100 ml; NHS Cost £1.43; OTC Cost £2.53.

Chlorphenamine (chlorpheniramine) syrup: 2mg 3-4 times a day
- Age from 6 to 11 years
- Chlorphenamine 2mg/5ml syrup. Take one 5ml spoonful 3 to 4 times a day; supply 100 ml; NHS Cost £1.43; OTC Cost £2.53.

Chlorphenamine (chlorpheniramine)tabs: 4mg three times a day
- Age from 12 years onwards
- Chlorphenamine 4mg tablets. Take one tablet three times a day; supply 21 tablets; NHS Cost £0.33; OTC Cost £2.10.

Previous anaphylactic reaction

Which therapy?

- **Consider referral to an allergy clinic or immunologist for all people who have had any systemic reaction to an insect sting.**
- Seek specialist advice from an allergy clinic or immunologist regarding local recommendations for interim management of these people.
- The allergy clinic will give people appropriate drugs to manage a future reaction themselves:
    - Those who are at risk of further moderate to severe reactions may be given a pre-loaded adrenaline syringe and a written treatment plan.
    - It is very important that the person (and relatives/carers) is taught how and when to use the treatments provided.
- Advise people who have had allergic reactions to insect stings to avoid subsequent stings by wearing long-sleeved clothes and gloves, and avoiding brightly-coloured

clothes, cosmetics, perfumes, or hair sprays that attract insects.

Practical prescribing points

For further information please see the *Medicines Compendium* (www.medicines.org.uk) or the *British National Formulary* (www.bnf.org).

Adrenaline

- **Beta blockers:** reduce the dose of adrenaline by 50% in people who are known to be on a beta-blocker. Consider withdrawing and substituting beta-blockers (including eye drops) in a person who is considered at risk of anaphylaxis.
- **Tricyclic antidepressants and monoamine oxidase inhibitors (MAOIs):** reduce the dose of adrenaline by 50%.
- **Cocaine** sensitizes the heart to catecholamines and adrenaline and is therefore relatively contraindicated in people taking cocaine.
- **Auto-injection devices:** specify the brand of auto-injection device (Epipen or Anapen) as there are important differences between the triggering mechanisms.

Should I refer or investigate?

Refer?

- Refer someone who has had a generalized allergic reaction to an allergy clinic or allergist (ideally one with expertise in anaphylaxis) if available, to confirm the cause and give advice on prevention of further reactions.

Patient information leaflets

The following PILs are available at www.prodigy.nhs.uk

- Anaphylaxis Campaign
- Insect Bites
- Insect Stings

Shared decision making

- If you have a severe allergic reaction to an insect sting, you may be advised to always carry an adrenaline injection for use in an emergency.
- You (and close family or carers) should be trained how to use the adrenaline. Make sure you know exactly how to use it.
- Make sure the adrenaline you have does not pass the expiry date.
- If you are stung again, you should still go to hospital immediately, even if you use the adrenaline injection.
- Try to avoid further stings. For example, when you are in a place where stinging insects may be present then:
  - Wear long-sleeved clothes and gloves.
  - Avoid brightly coloured clothes, cosmetics, perfumes, or hair sprays, which may attract insects.
  - Be alert when you cook or eat outdoors as food attracts insects, especially wasps.

Drug rationale

Drugs not included

- Drugs for the future management of people with previous anaphylaxis may be initiated or recommended by your local allergy clinic or immunologist.

Drugs included

- **Adrenaline** for self-administration will usually be prescribed by the local allergist. If there is no local allergist available, or the person has to wait to see them, the GP may need to provide these drugs for self-administration, but it is essential that they are given with the appropriate advice and training.

Prescriptions

Adrenaline for self management

Child weighs 15-30kg: Epipen 150mcg for self administration

- Age from 3 to 12 years
- Epipen 150micrograms. Inject into the muscle on the outer part of the thigh; supply 2 2ml autoinjector device; NHS Cost £56.38.

Child weighs 15-30kg: Anapen 150mcg for self administration

- Age from 3 to 12 years
- Anapen junior 150micrograms. Inject into the muscle on the outer part of the thigh; supply 2 1.05ml autoinjector device; NHS Cost £50.74.

Adult/child >30kg: Epipen 300mcg for self administration

- Age from 6 years onwards
- Epipen 300micrograms. Inject into the muscle on the outer part of the thigh; supply 2 2ml autoinjector device; NHS Cost £56.38.

Adult/child >30kg: Anapen 300mcg for self administration

- Age from 6 years onwards
- Anapen 300micrograms. Inject into the muscle on the outer part of the thigh; supply 2 1.05ml auto-injector; NHS Cost £50.74.

Extended Information

Background information

- What is it? p.1103
- How common is it? p.1104
- How do I know my patient has it? p.1104
- What else might it be? p.1104
- Complications and prognosis p.1104

What is it?

Insect bites

- **Trauma produced by a biting insect seldom causes serious problems,** however, the biting insect deposits salivary gland secretions, which contain various antigenic substances that may provoke a reaction in the person who has been bitten.
- **The type of reaction provoked mainly depends on previous exposure to the same or related species** [Burns, 1998]:
  - The first time a person is bitten there is commonly no reaction unless the salivary secretions of the insect contain a directly injurious substance.
  - After repeated bites, as sensitivity occurs, an itchy papule develops about 24 hours after each bite and this persists for several days.
  - After further bites, an extremely itchy weal develops immediately. This lasts about 2 hours, and is followed by a firm pruritic papule about 24 hours later, which usually persists for several days.

- With continued and repeated exposure, the delayed papule reaction no longer occurs and eventually there is no reaction at all.
- Biting insects commonly encountered in the UK include: midges, gnats and mosquitoes; flies; fleas; mites; ticks; and bedbugs [Millikan, 1993].

Insect stings

- The stinging apparatus of stinging insects consists of a sac of venom attached to a barbed stinger. The sting occurs when the sac contracts and venom is deposited in the tissue. The venom contains allergens, which cause a reaction in the person who has been stung.
- This reaction ranges from localized pain, erythema, and swelling at the site of the sting, to a severe systemic reaction (anaphylaxis).
- Stinging insects commonly encountered in the UK include: honeybees, bumblebees, wasps, and hornets.

[Reisman, 1994; Burns, 1998; Ewan, 1998b]

How common is it?

- The incidence and prevalence of insect bites and stings is uncertain.

How do I know my patient has it?

Insect bites

- **Irritation** is an almost constant symptom, and rubbing and scratching may increase the inflammatory changes and eczematization [Burns, 1998].
- **Papular urticaria** is a common presentation in children, especially those between 2 and 7 years old, and those with a history of atopic dermatitis. It is less common in adults. Papular urticaria is caused by a sensitivity reaction to the bites of fleas, lice, bedbugs, gnats, mites, and other insects and consists of groups or lines of intensely itchy indurated papules which persist for up to 2 weeks [Millikan, 1993; Stibich and Schwartz, 2001].
- **Bullous reactions** are common on the lower legs but may occur at other sites, particularly in children [Burns, 1998].
- Chronic cases in adults may present as a lichen simplex chronicus or a prurigo-type picture.
- Typical presentations of different biting insects are shown in Table 1.

[Inskip et al, 1996; Burns, 1998; Wilson and King, 2003].

Insect stings

- Insect stings typically produce intense, burning pain, followed by erythema and a small area (up to 1 cm) of oedema, which usually subsides within a few hours.
- Allergic reactions can be either local or systemic:
  - Local reactions involve oedema that extends beyond the site of the sting, evolving over several hours and lasting up to 7 days. Such oedema is not dangerous unless it affects the airway.
  - Generalized (systemic) reactions vary in severity. The onset of generalized reactions is usually rapid and features may include:
    - Rhinitis and conjunctivitis
    - Abdominal pain, vomiting, and diarrhoea
    - Erythema
    - Generalized pruritus followed by urticaria
    - Facial or generalized angio-oedema
    - A sense of impending doom
    - Abdominal cramps and nausea
    - Tachycardia
    - Hypotension (causing light-headedness, giddiness, and fainting)
    - Difficulty in breathing due to severe asthma or throat swelling

Table 1: Typical presentations of common insect bites.

Biting insect	Presentation
Midges, mosquitoes, and gnats	Bites usually cause small papular lesions. Weals and bullae (large blisters) may form in sensitized individuals.
Fleas — animal/human	Bites may be grouped in lines or in irregular clusters. Bites usually cause papular urticaria in sensitized individuals. Occasionally bullae may occur.
Horseflies	Bites are often very painful and urticaria, dizziness, weakness, wheezing, or angio-oedema may accompany the resulting cutaneous weal. Secondary infection is common.
Bedbugs	Bites are painless and there may be no symptoms if the individual has not previously been bitten. Sensitized people characteristically develop intensely irritating weals or papules surmounted by haemorrhagic puncta.
The Blandford fly (found in an arc running from East Anglia through Oxfordshire into Dorset)	Bites occur most frequently on the legs and are very painful. The reaction to them can vary from a small blister to a large, haemorrhagic, indurated lesion and may be accompanied by fever or pain in the joints.
Ticks	Bites are not usually painful and there may only be a red papule at the bite site that may progress to local swelling and erythema. In some cases blistering, severe pruritus, and bruising develop.
Cheyletiella mites (frequently harboured by dogs and cats)	Intensely itchy papules appear where the mites have fed on skin. There may be a tiny vesicle surmounting the papule, and older lesions may show necrosis.
Mites that occur in stored products (e.g. grain, flour, dried meat, cheese, and fruit)	Bites cause intensely itchy minute pruritic papules or papulovesicles on exposed parts of the body.

    - Collapse and unconsciousness

Note: not all these symptoms are necessarily present, depending on the severity of the reaction.

[Burns, 1998; Ewan, 1998b]

What else might it be?

- Cellulitis — large local reactions to an insect bite may occasionally be confused with cellulitis. The presence of ascending lymphangitis and lymphadenopathy suggest an infectious cause.
- Chickenpox.
- Urticaria.
- Contact dermatitis.
- Scabies.
- Pubic lice.

[Millikan, 1993; Reisman, 1994].

Complications and prognosis

Complications

Infection

- **Bacterial infection** may occur as a result of scratching or may be introduced at the time of the bite [Burns, 1998]. It can present as impetigo, folliculitis, cellulitis, or lymphangitis [Burns, 1998].

Systemic reactions

- **Urticarial reaction** may develop in some people several hours after the bite or sting.
- **Fever and malaise** may occur if the local reaction is severe or if bites are numerous.
- **Multiple bee or wasp stings may cause systemic toxic effects** including hypotension, diarrhoea, vomiting, headache, generalized vasodilatation, and shock. In children this may be fatal [Burns, 1998].
- **A serum sickness-like reaction** with urticaria, joint swelling, and arthralgia may occur very rarely 7–10 days after a sting [Reisman, 1994].
- **The prevalence of systemic allergic reaction to an insect sting was** found to be 3.3% in one study [Golden et al, 1989].

Anaphylaxis

- **Anaphylaxis can occur after an insect sting,** particularly from a bee or wasp. Anaphylaxis after an insect bite is rare [Burns, 1998].
- **The incidence of anaphylaxis** due to insect stings in the general population is not reliably known, but has been estimated to be between 0.3% and 3% [Reisman, 1994]. Every year in the UK there are 2–9 deaths of people who have become severely allergic to bee or wasp stings [The Anaphylaxis Campaign, 2003].
- **Anaphylaxis from insect stings is most common in people under 20 years of age** and occurs more frequently in males than females, probably reflecting exposure rather than any predisposition towards age or sex [Reisman, 1994].
- The proportion of people with a history of anaphylaxis who have an anaphylactic reaction to a subsequent sting is very variable (20–80%)[Ewan, 1998b]. One study showed that many people (40%) had only a local reaction after a previous generalized systemic reaction [Settipane and Chafee, 1979]. People allergic to wasp venom are rarely allergic to bee venom [Ewan, 1998b].

Diseases transmitted by bites

- **Lyme disease** (caused by *Borrelia burgdorferi*) is transmitted by the tick *Ixodes ricinus*. It is uncommon in the UK, but the incidence is rising and there are now over 200 cases diagnosed annually [McGarry et al, 2001]. Untreated Lyme disease can result in arthritis, meningitis, neuropathies, carditis, and encephalopathy.
- **West Nile virus** is unlikely to be transmitted in the UK because the population density of mosquitoes is relatively low, but clinicians are advised to consider West Nile virus as a differential diagnosis in people over 50 years old with a clinical picture of viral encephalitis or aseptic meningitis. In the majority of people the infection is asymptomatic or causes a mild influenza-like illness [Crook et al, 2002; PHLS, 2003].

Prognosis

- **Bite reactions may persist for months.** This is particularly likely with tick bites, as persistent granulomatous papules or nodules may be provoked by retained mouthparts, although most tick bites will heal within 3 weeks [Wilson and King, 2003].
- **Insect stings:** swelling may extend over a large area, often peaking within 48 hours and lasting as long as 7 days [Reisman, 1994].

Management issues

Insect bites p.1105
Insect stings p.1106

Insect bites

There is a general lack of good quality evidence regarding the management of insect bites.

Acute management

- Bites from midges, gnats, mosquitoes, horseflies, ticks, and the Blandford fly are usually a one-off occurrence and symptomatic treatment will be sufficient.
- In the case of bites from fleas, mites, and bedbugs infestation is likely to be present. In this case symptomatic treatment may be of some help, but the ultimate solution is to trace the source of the bites and eliminate the infestation (see section *Preventing reinfestation*) [Hunter et al, 2002].
- **Symptomatic treatments for itching include:**
  - **Crotamiton cream or lotion.** This has soothing qualities and may help to relieve itching, although there is no objective proof of its anti-pruritic activity.
  - **Antihistamines.** These are of minimal help in treating pruritus [Klein and Clark, 1999; DTB, 2002]. However, a short course of a sedative oral antihistamine at night may be useful to break the itch–scratch cycle and help with sleep.
- **If there is local inflammation,** consider using a topical corticosteroid. This may also help to relieve itching, although there is little objective evidence to support this.
- **If there is an urticarial reaction,** consider giving a short course of an oral antihistamine. No published randomized controlled trials have assessed the efficacy of oral antihistamines in the treatment of acute urticaria although they are widely recognized as the mainstay of treatment. In chronic urticaria second-generation antihistamines have been shown to be more effective than placebo in controlling itch and the appearance of weals, reducing sleeplessness, and lessening interference with daily activities [DTB, 2002].
- **Tick:** remove the tick as soon as possible after the bite using fine-point tweezers to grasp the tick as close to the skin as possible. Pull gently, avoiding squeezing the body of the tick. Clean the site of the bite with disinfectant. Traditional methods of tick removal using a burned match, petroleum jelly, or nail polish are ineffective [FDA, 2001].
- *Borrelia* infection (Lyme disease) is uncommon in the UK. Routine use of either antimicrobial prophylaxis or serological tests after a tick bite is not recommended. People who develop a skin lesion or pyrexia within 1 month of removing a tick should be advised to seek medical advice promptly [ATTRACT, 2003].

Preventing reinfestation

Discovering the source of infestation

- **The distribution of the bite(s) may suggest their origin:**
  - Localization to the abdomen or thighs (e.g. from an animal sitting on a person's lap) — cheyletiella mite [Parish and Schwartzman, 1993].
  - Lesions below the knees and most profuse around the ankles — cat or dog fleas. Clusters of bites can be found elsewhere on the body if the person has lain on an infested rug or sofa [Parish and Schwartzman, 1993].
  - Scattered all over the body — bird fleas, bird mites, or bedbugs [Burns, 1998].
  - Patterned areas around the elastic of the clothing — lice or fleas [Millikan, 1993].
  - Primarily on exposed areas — mosquito and fly bites [Millikan, 1993].
- **A careful history may reveal the origin of infestation.** Factors in the history to consider include:

- **Domestic pets:** not only in the person's home but also those in homes frequently visited are often the source of persistent flea bites [Burns, 1998].
- **Recent move:** a history of recently moving to a new house (even if it has remained empty for some time) suggests bites from animal fleas, which can survive for a few months in the absence of their natural host.
- **Living environment:** infestation with the human flea occurs mainly in overcrowded communities with low standards of hygiene.
- Presence of nests or nest boxes on or near the house may cause household infestations with bird fleas.
- **Old houses, poultry houses, birds' nests, furniture, and upholstery** may harbour bedbugs, which may travel great distances to reach a suitable host.
- **Occupation:** people who handle stored products (e.g. dockworkers, warehouse workers) are most at risk from mite dermatitis, but shopkeepers and domestic workers may occasionally be affected.
- **Recent travel:** the bite may be due to a foreign insect.

[Burns, 1998; Wilson and King, 2003]

Confirming the source of infestation

- **The principal sign of flea infestation in an affected animal** is the presence of dried masses of flea faeces on the animal's coat. A flea spends only 20 minutes a day on the animal and for every flea seen on an animal there will be 10–100 fleas in the environment [Parish and Schwartzman, 1993].
- **Fleas live primarily in furnishings and only visit the animal for blood meals** [Parish and Schwartzman, 1993]. Flea eggs are often laid in cracks in floors and walls and under furniture [Parish and Schwartzman, 1993].
- **Dog and cat fleas can often be detected from the animal's bedding.** Macroscopically flea eggs and faeces have a 'pepper and salt' appearance. In cases where diagnosis is extremely difficult it may be necessary to confirm diagnosis by placing the bedding in a polythene bag and shaking vigorously for a few minutes. The bedding can then be removed and the contents of the bag sent for microscopic examination [Burns, 1998].
- **Excessive dandruff, 'walking dandruff'**, especially on the back of a cat or dog, is a sign of infestation with cheyletiella mites [Burns, 1998].
- **Pet animals should be examined for signs of skin disease.** If diagnosis is difficult the pet should be brushed vigorously whilst standing on a polythene sheet. Enough dandruff-like material in which cheyletiella mites may be found can be obtained to send to a laboratory [Hunter et al, 2002].
- **If bird fleas or bird mites are suspected, it may be valuable to examine the dust vacuumed from bedrooms,** although this is a time-consuming exercise [Burns, 1998].

Eliminating the infestation

- **Domestic cat and dog flea infestations** — treatment with insecticides should be directed at both the pet and its bedding, and at household carpets and soft furnishings. Rugs and furniture should be thoroughly vacuumed. Contact with other pets should be limited. [Parish and Schwartzman, 1993; Burns, 1998; Stibich et al, 2001]. Other upholstery may also need treatment.
- **Cheyletiella mite** — seek local veterinary advice as aggressive treatment is needed [Parish and Schwartzman, 1993; Burns, 1998].
- **Bedbugs** — apply insecticide to walls and furniture likely to be harbouring the bugs [Hunter et al, 2002].

Preventing bites

- A recent study found that currently available repellents that do not contain diethyltoluamide (DEET) do not provide protection for as long as those containing DEET, and cannot be relied upon to provide protection in environments where mosquito-borne diseases are a substantial threat [Fradin and Day, 2002].
- We found no evidence that ingested compounds including garlic and thiamine (vitamin B_1) are capable of repelling biting arthropods [Khan et al, 1969; Fradin and Day, 2002].

Insect stings

Acute management

- **A bee sting should be removed as quickly as possible.** Traditional advice regarding bee stings is that the sting should be scraped off and never pinched. However, one study found that the method of removal was irrelevant, speed being more important, as even slight delays can increase the amount of venom received [Visscher et al, 1996].

Local reactions

- Localized pain, swelling, and erythema at the site of the sting usually subsides within several hours, and needs only treatment with analgesics and cold compresses (e.g. ice packs) [Reisman, 1994]. A short course of topical corticosteroids may be helpful [BNF 46, 2003].

Large local reactions

- Local allergic reactions to a sting (involving oedema that extends beyond the site of the sting) will usually respond to a short course of oral antihistamine [Ewan, 1998b].
- Such oedema is not dangerous unless it affects the airway [Ewan, 1998b]. If the airway is affected, treat as anaphylaxis.

Systemic reactions

- Generalized urticaria may be treated with an oral antihistamine and a corticosteroid. People who develop any progression of symptoms should seek medical help.
- It is important to be aware that mild symptoms may progress to a severe reaction. Clinical judgement will need to be exercised depending on the type of reaction, social circumstances, and access to local medical facilities. If there is any doubt then admit for observation.
- Symptoms that occur as part of a severe generalized reaction (e.g. vomiting, abdominal or uterine cramps, or wheezing) should be treated with intramuscular adrenaline and admitted to hospital urgently for observation. It should be noted that people with asthma are particularly at risk.

[Spickett, Personal Communication, 2003]

- **Systemic reactions with respiratory difficulty and/or hypotension (anaphylaxis) need prompt treatment of laryngeal oedema, bronchospasm, and hypotension.**
  - Call an ambulance.
  - Secure the airway.
  - Give oxygen if available — administer at high flow rates (10–15 litres/min).
  - Lying flat with or without leg elevation may be helpful for hypotension, but unhelpful for breathing difficulties.
  - Intramuscular (IM) adrenaline should be given to all people with clinical signs of shock, airway swelling, or definite breathing difficulty. Manifestations likely to alert the physician to a severe reaction include inspiratory stridor, wheeze, cyanosis, pronounced tachycardia, and decreased capillary filling. The dose of IM adrenaline recommended by the UK Resuscitation Council is shown in Table 2.
    - The preferred site for IM adrenaline in the initial treatment of anaphylaxis is the midpoint of the thigh, anterolateral aspect [Simons et al, 2001].
    - Adrenaline should *not* be given intravenously (IV) for the treatment of anaphylaxis in a general practice setting.

  - Use a suitable technique for measuring small doses (e.g. insulin syringe).
  - Adrenaline can be repeated after about 5 minutes if no clinical improvement or if deterioration occurs after the initial injection.
- Antihistamines (chlorphenamine [chlorpheniramine]) should be used routinely in the management of all anaphylactic reactions to help counter histamine-mediated vasodilation:
  - >12 years: chlorphenamine 10–20 mg IM (or slow IV)
  - 6–12 years [unlicensed]: chlorphenamine 5–10 mg IM (or slow IV)
  - 1–6 years [unlicensed]: chlorphenamine 2.5–5 mg IM (or slow IV)
  - <1 year [unlicensed]: chlorphenamine 250 micrograms/kg slow IV
- Corticosteroid (hydrocortisone as sodium succinate) helps in an acute attack and has a role in late reactions due to the production of leukotrienes: these occur 4–6 hours after the initial reaction, which may have been successfully treated. This is of particular importance in people with asthma (who are at increased risk of severe or fatal anaphylaxis) if they have been treated with corticosteroids previously.
  - >12 years: hydrocortisone (as sodium succinate) 100–500 mg IM (or slow IV)
  - 6–12 years: hydrocortisone (as sodium succinate) 100 mg IM (or slow IV)
  - <6 years: hydrocortisone (as sodium succinate) 50 mg IM (or slow IV)
- If severe hypotension does not respond rapidly to drug treatment, infusion of fluid may be required (e.g. sodium chloride).
- An inhaled $beta_2$-agonist is useful as an adjunctive measure if bronchospasm is a major feature that does not respond rapidly to other treatment.

[Resuscitation Council, 1999; Royal College of Paediatrics and Child Health, 1999]

Future management

- Consider referral to an allergy clinic or immunologist for all people who have had any systemic reaction to an insect sting.
- Seek specialist advice from an allergy clinic or immunologist regarding local recommendations for interim management of these people.
- The options for future management are:
  - Desensitization: the indications for desensitization in Britain are conservative because of the high incidence of spontaneous improvement and the adverse effects of desensitization treatment [Ewan, 1998b].
  - The person being given appropriate drugs to initiate management of the reaction himself or herself. People who have had systemic reactions may be given a pre-loaded adrenaline syringe and a written treatment plan and the patient (and relatives) taught how and when to use the treatments provided [Ewan, 1998a].
- People who have had allergic reactions to insect stings should avoid subsequent stings by wearing long-sleeved clothes and gloves, and avoiding brightly-coloured clothes, cosmetics, perfumes, or hair sprays that attract insects [Reisman, 1994].

Table 2: Dose of adrenaline.

Age	Dose of adrenaline
Adults	500 micrograms IM (0.5 ml of a 1:1000 [1 mg/ml] solution)
Adolescents >11 years	Up to 500 micrograms IM (0.5 ml of a 1:1000 [1 mg/ml] solution)
Children 6–11 years	250 micrograms IM (0.25 ml of a 1:1000 [1 mg/ml] solution)
Children 6 months to 6 years	120 micrograms IM (0.12 ml of a 1:1000 [1 mg/ml] solution)
Children <6 months	50 micrograms IM (0.05 ml of a 1:1000 [1 mg/ml] solution)

IM = intramuscular

Medicines management

Oral antihistamines

- **Sedative antihistamines** cause drowsiness that may persist the next day. People should not drive or operate machinery if affected.
- **Second-generation (non-sedating) oral antihistamines:** although drowsiness is rare, it can occur and may affect performance of skilled tasks such as driving.

Topical corticosteroids

- **Moderate or mild potency topical steroids** are rarely associated with adverse effects, especially if only used for short periods. Potential local problems associated with excessive use may include thinning of the skin, irreversible striae atrophicae and telangiectasia, contact dermatitis, or mild depigmentation.

Adrenaline

- **Beta-blockers** may increase the severity of an anaphylactic reaction and may antagonize some of the beneficial actions of adrenaline. However, because the beta-blockers block only the beta effects of the adrenaline and not the alpha effects, the effect on blood pressure (acute hypertension) can be appreciably enhanced, and there is evidence that this can be dangerous. The Resuscitation Council (UK) recommend reducing the dose of adrenaline by 50% in people who are known to be on a beta-blocker.
  - Consider withdrawing and substituting beta-blockers (including eye drops) in a person who is considered at risk of anaphylaxis.
- **Tricyclic antidepressants and monoamine oxidase inhibitors (MAOIs)** may increase susceptibility to arrhythmias. The dose of adrenaline should be reduced by 50%.
- **Cocaine** sensitizes the heart to catecholamines and adrenaline and is therefore relatively contraindicated in people taking cocaine.
- **Auto-injection devices:** care should be taken in choosing an appropriate auto-injection device (Epipen or Anapen) as there are important differences between the triggering mechanisms. The brand of auto-injection device should be specified.

[Resuscitation Council, 1999; McLean-Tooke et al, 2003]

Parenteral chlorphenamine (chlorpheniramine)

- During anaphylaxis, chlorphenamine may be given intramuscularly, or by slow IV injection over 1–2 minutes.
- Chlorphenamine is not licensed to be given to children less than 12 years old, other than by the oral route [Royal College of Paediatrics and Child Health, 1999; BNF 46, 2003].

References

NHS staff in England can link, free of charge, from references to full text journals by clicking on [Full text] on the PRODIGY website.

1. ATTRACT (2003) *Question: I have a patient with possible tick bites.* NHS Wales. www.attract.wales.nhs.uk [Accessed: 09/10/2003].

2. BNF 46 (2003) *British National Formulary*. 46th edn. London: British Medical Association and Royal Pharmaceutical Society of Great Britain.
3. Burns, D.A (1998) Diseases caused by arthropods and other noxious animals. In: Champion, R.H., Burton, J.L., Breathnach, S.M. and Burns, D.A. (Eds.) *Textbook of dermatology*. 6th edn. Oxford: Blackwell Science. 1423–1447.
4. Crook, P.D., Crowcroft, N.S. and Brown, D.W. (2002) West Nile virus and the threat to the UK. *Communicable Disease & Public Health* 5(2), 138–143.
5. DTB (2002) Oral antihistamines for allergic disorders. *Drug & Therapeutics Bulletin* 40(8), 59–62. [Full text]
6. Ewan, P.W. (1998a) ABC of allergies: anaphylaxis. *British Medical Journal* **316**(7142), 1442–1445. [Full text]
7. Ewan, P.W. (1998b) ABC of allergies: venom allergy. *British Medical Journal* **316**(7141), 1365–1368. [Full text]
8. FDA (2001) *How to remove a tick*. U.S. Food and Drug Administration. www.fda.gov [Accessed: 01/08/2003].
9. Fradin, M.S. and Day, J.F. (2002) Comparative efficacy of insect repellents against mosquito bites. *New England Journal of Medicine* **347**(1), 13–18. [Full text]
10. Golden, D.B., Marsh, D.G., Kagey-Sobotka, A. et al (1989) Epidemiology of insect venom sensitivity. *Journal of the American Medical Association* **262**(2), 240–244.
11. Hunter, J.A.A, Savin, J.A. and Dahl, M.V. (Eds.) (2002) Infestations. In: *Clinical dermatology*. 3rd edn. Oxford: Blackwell Science.
12. Inskip, H., Campbell, L., Godfrey, K. and Coggon, D. (1996) A survey of the prevalence of biting by the Blandford fly during 1993. *British Journal of Dermatology* **134**(4), 696–699.
13. Khan, A.A., Maibach, H.I., Strauss, W.G. and Fenley, W.R. (1969) Vitamin B1 is not a systemic mosquito repellent in man. *Transactions of the St Johns Hospital Dermatological Society* 55(1), 99–102.
14. Klein, P.A. and Clark, R.A. (1999) An evidence-based review of the efficacy of antihistamines in relieving pruritus in atopic dermatitis. *Archives of Dermatology* **135**(12), 1522–1525. [Full text]
15. McGarry, J.W., McCall, P.J. and Welby, S. (2001) Arthropod dermatoses acquired in the UK and overseas. *Lancet* 357(9274), 2105–2106. [Full text]
16. McLean-Tooke, A.P.C., Bethune, C.A., Fay, A.C. and Spickett, G.P. (2003) Adrenaline in the treatment of anaphylaxis: what is the evidence? *British Medical Journal* **327**(7427), 1332–1335. [Full text]
17. Millikan, L.E. (1993) Papular urticaria. *Seminars in Dermatology* **12**(1), 53–56.
18. Parish, L.C. and Schwartzman, R.M. (1993) Zoonoses of dermatological interest. *Seminars in Dermatology* **12**(1), 57–64.
19. PHLS (2003) *West Nile virus – response to the CMO's annual report – 3 July 2003*. Public Health Laboratory Service. www.phls.org.uk/press_media/id_bulletins/archive/2003/030703id.htm [Accessed: 26/08/2003].
20. Reisman, R.E. (1994) Insect stings. *New England Journal of Medicine* **331**(8), 523–527.
21. Resuscitation Council (1999) Emergency medical treatment of anaphylactic reactions. *Journal of Accident and Emergency Medicine* **16**(4), 243–247.
22. Royal College of Paediatrics and Child Health (Ed.) (1999) *Medicines for children*. London: RCPCH Publications.
23. Settipane, G.A. and Chafee, F.H. (1979) Natural history of allergy to Hymenoptera. *Clinical Allergy* 9(4), 385–390.
24. Simons, F.E.R., Gu, X. and Simons, K.J. (2001) Epinephrine absorption in adults: intramuscular versus subcutaneous injection. *Journal of Allergy & Clinical Immunology* **108**(5), 871–873.
25. Spickett, G.P. (2003) *Personal communication*. Immunologist, Newcastle General Hospital: Newcastle upon Tyne.
26. Stibich, A.S. and Schwartz, R.A. (2001) Papular urticaria. *Pediatric Dermatology* **68**(2), 89–91.
27. Stibich, A.S., Carbonaro, P.A. and Schwartz, R.A. (2001) Insect bite reactions: an update. *Dermatology* **202**(3), 193–197.
28. The Anaphylaxis Campaign (2003) *Allergy to bee and wasp stings*. The Anaphylaxis Campaign. www.anaphylaxis.org.uk/ [Accessed: 06/10/2003].
29. Visscher, P.K., Vetter, R.S. and Camazine, S. (1996) Removing bee stings. *Lancet* **348**(9023), 301–302. [Full text]
30. Wilson, D.C. and King, Jr, L.E. (2003) Arthropod bites and stings. In: Freedberg, I.M., Eisen, A.Z., Wolff, K. et al (Eds.) *Fitzpatrick's dermatology in general medicine*. 5th edn. London: McGraw-Hill. 2685–2695.

PRODIGY GUIDANCE

Insomnia

Last revised in July 2003
www.prodigy.nhs.uk/guidance.asp?gt=Insomnia

Applies to people over the age of 16 years

This guidance covers the management of transient, short-term, and chronic insomnia.

This guidance does not cover the management of narcolepsy.

There is separate PRODIGY guidance for *Hypnotic/anxiolytic dependence*, *Leg cramps*, and *Stress — acute reaction*.

Goals

- To improve quality and duration of sleep
- To improve quality of life
- To reinstate a normal sleep pattern without medication
- To reduce the need for hypnotics and avoid dependence on these drugs
- To guide withdrawal from long-term hypnotic use

Contents

Scenarios

- Anticipated transient insomnia (3 days or less) p.1109
- Short-term insomnia (more than 3 days, less than 3 weeks) p.1111
- Chronic insomnia (more than 3 weeks' duration) p.1112
- Chronic hypnotic drug usage p.1114

Extended Information, p. 1116

Which scenario?

- **Anticipated transient insomnia (3 days or less):** covers the management of insomnia, often caused by an acute event that is anticipated not to last for more than 2–3 nights.
- **Short-term insomnia (more than 3 days, less than 3 weeks):** covers the management of insomnia that is anticipated to last for more that a few days but for less than 3 weeks.
- **Chronic insomnia (more than 3 weeks' duration):** covers the management of insomnia lasting longer than 3 weeks.
- **Chronic hypnotic drug usage:** covers management in people taking hypnotic medication over a long term.

Anticipated transient insomnia (3 days or less)

Which therapy?

- **Identify any potential causes of insomnia or exacerbating factors** and treat where possible.
- **Use non-drug treatments** where possible, including simple advice and counselling. Use available PRODIGY Patient Information Leaflets.
- **If the insomnia is severe, disabling, or subjecting the individual to extreme distress,** consider prescribing a hypnotic as an adjunct to non-drug treatment:
  - **Use the lowest effective dose for 1–3 nights** maximum.
  - **Temazepam, loprazolam, or lormetazepam** are the preferred choices. Zopiclone, zolpidem, or zaleplon are possible alternatives.
- **Be careful whenever prescribing a hypnotic,** particularly if the person is temporarily registered or unknown, as these drugs are commonly misused.

Practical prescribing points

For further information please see the *Medicines Compendium* (www.medicines.org.uk) or the *British National Formulary* (www.bnf.org).

- **The Committee on the Safety of Medicines** advises benzodiazepines should only be used when insomnia is severe, disabling, or subjecting the individual to extreme stress. They should only be used for short-term relief of insomnia (2–4 weeks maximum).
- **Benzodiazepines may cause drowsiness** the following day and impair skilled tasks (e.g. driving). Elderly people, and people with hepatic impairment, may require lower doses.
- **Benzodiazepines enhance the effect of alcohol** and other depressants: concomitant use should be avoided.
- **Zopiclone, zolpidem, and zaleplon** should be treated with the same caution as benzodiazepines.

Follow-up advice

- **Follow-up is not usually required.** Ask the person to return if the insomnia continues and is causing distress.

Should I refer or investigate?

Refer?

- Referral is not usually necessary.

Patient information leaflets

The following PILs are available at www.prodigy.nhs.uk

- Insomnia - Poor Sleep
- Insomnia (Poor Sleep) - A Summary
- Insomnia - Sleeping Tablets
- Relaxation Exercises

Shared decision making

- Most bouts of poor sleep soon pass.
- **Tips to help with sleep include:**
  - Get up at the same time each day.
  - Never sleep during the daytime.
  - Routines are useful before bedtime, such as a warm drink, a hot bath, and reading.
  - The bedroom should be quiet and not used for TV, work, etc.
  - Avoid stimulants in the evening such as alcohol, caffeine, and smoking.
  - Exercise during the day, but not just before bedtime.
  - Eat only a light snack before bedtime and not a large meal.

  - A relaxation tape in the evening can help you to relax.
- **Sleeping tablets** are occasionally advised for a few days. But:
  - They may cause 'hangover' drowsiness the next day.
  - They can make you feel drowsy if you get up in the night — which may lead to falls.

Drug rationale

Drugs not included

- **Barbiturates** are only indicated in insomnia for treatment of severe intractable insomnia in people already taking barbiturates. They have unacceptably high risks of tolerance, dependence, and other adverse effects [BNF 44, 2002].
- **Sedative antidepressants,** such as amitriptyline, are sometimes useful for people with coexisting psychiatric disorders, such as depression. However, they are more toxic than benzodiazepines, and should be reserved for people who have disorders for which they are specifically indicated [Ashton, 1994; Scottish Health Service Advisory Council, 1994].
- **Some sedative antihistamines (e.g. diphenhydramine and promethazine)** are available without a prescription for the self-treatment of occasional insomnia. However, they are not as effective as benzodiazepines, have more adverse effects, and are more toxic in overdose [Maczaj, 1993; Scottish Health Service Advisory Council, 1994; Therapeutics Initiative, 1995].
- **Antipsychotic drugs** are not licensed for insomnia and should not be used for this purpose. They may have a place in the management of insomnia secondary to an underlying psychiatric condition, but treatment should not be initiated without specialist advice or supervision [BNF 44, 2002].
- **Chloral derivatives** have only a limited role as hypnotics, as they have a high incidence of gastric irritation [Scottish Health Service Advisory Council, 1994; BNF 44, 2002].
- **Chlormethiazole** may be useful for elderly people if confusion has been found to be a problem with other hypnotics. However, it is associated with unpleasant adverse effects, including nasal and gastric irritation [Gilhooly et al, 1998; BNF 44, 2002].
- **Long-acting and medium-acting benzodiazepines** are considered unsuitable as hypnotics due to their prolonged action, which causes hangover effects the following day, and doses can be cumulative. However, diazepam, taken at night, may be useful when insomnia is related to daytime anxiety [Ashton, 1994; BNF 44, 2002].
- **Lorazepam,** a short-acting benzodiazepine, is primarily used as an anxiolytic. It is associated with a greater risk of withdrawal problems [BNF 44, 2002].

Drugs included

- **Temazepam, loprazolam, and lormetazepam** are short-acting benzodiazepines recommended for 'one-off' use in the treatment of insomnia. They have short half-lives and are metabolized to inactive compounds, which leads to minimal hangover effects the following day. They have good safety profiles when used correctly. A maximum of three minimal effective doses is offered, which minimizes the potential for dependence [Ashton, 1994; Grad, 1995; Therapeutics Initiative, 1995; BNF 44, 2002].
- **The newer 'Z' drug hypnotics** are as effective as the short-acting benzodiazepines, but offer few proven advantages over them. In addition, they are more expensive. They are offered as alternatives if benzodiazepines are not well tolerated.
  - **Zopiclone** has similar efficacy to the benzodiazepines, and has similar adverse effects, and the potential for dependence with prolonged use.
  - **Zolpidem** has a shorter duration of action than the short-acting benzodiazepines, and has been reported to have less hangover effects the following day.
  - **Zaleplon** is the shortest-acting hypnotic. It reduces time taken to sleep but not duration, and may have some benefit as an 'as required' hypnotic.

[Kirkwood, 1999; Chow et al, 2000; BNF 44, 2002; MeReC, 2002]

Prescriptions

Non-drug management

Advice only: good sleep hygiene
- Age from 16 years onwards
- General tips to help with sleep include: Body rhythm – get up at the same time each day and never sleep in the day. Routines – are useful before bedtime e.g. a warm drink, hot bath and reading. Bedroom – should be free of noise and don't use for watching TV, eating, work. Stimulants – such as alcohol, caffeine and smoking should be avoided in the evening. Exercise – regularly during the day but not within a few hours of bedtime. Eat – only a light snack before bedtime and not a large meal. Relaxation – may be improved by using a relaxation tape in the evening. Depression is a common cause of poor sleep. Is this or another illness making things worse?

Short-acting benzodiazepine

Temazepam 10mg at night (if required)
- Age from 16 years onwards
- Temazepam 10mg tablets. Take one tablet at night if required; supply 3 tablets; NHS Cost £0.10.

Loprazolam 1mg at night (if required)
- Age from 16 years onwards
- Loprazolam 1mg tablets. Take one tablet at night if required; supply 3 tablets; NHS Cost £0.48.

Lormetazepam 500micrograms at night (if required)
- Age from 16 years onwards
- Lormetazepam 500mcg tablets. Take one tablet at night if required; supply 3 tablets; NHS Cost £0.36.

Alternative therapy: Z drugs

Zopiclone 7.5mg at night (if required)
- Age from 16 to 70 years
- Zopiclone 7.5mg tablets. Take one tablet at night if required; supply 3 tablets; NHS Cost £0.48.

Zolpidem 10mg at night (if required)
- Age from 16 to 70 years
- Zolpidem 10mg tablets. Take one tablet at night if required; supply 3 tablets; NHS Cost £0.47.

Zaleplon 10mg at night (if required)
- Age from 16 to 70 years
- Zaleplon 10mg capsules. Take one capsule at night if required; supply 3 capsules; NHS Cost £0.87.

Z drugs in the elderly or hepatically impaired

Zopiclone 3.75mg at night (if required)
- Age from 16 years onwards
- Zopiclone 3.75mg tablets. Take one tablet at night if required; supply 3 tablets; NHS Cost £0.33.

Zolpidem 5mg at night (if required)
- Age from 16 years onwards
- Zolpidem 5mg tablets. Take one tablet at night if required; supply 3 tablets; NHS Cost £0.32.

Zaleplon 5mg at night (if required)
- Age from 16 years onwards
- Zaleplon 5mg capsules. Take one capsule at night if required; supply 3 capsules; NHS Cost £0.72.

Short-term insomnia (more than 3 days, less than 3 weeks)

Which therapy?

- **Identify any potential causes of insomnia or exacerbating factors** and treat where possible.
- **Use non-drug treatments** where possible, including simple advice and counselling. Use available PRODIGY Patient Information Leaflets.
- **Sleep diaries** may be used to assess the degree of insomnia and monitor treatment progress.
- **If the insomnia is severe, disabling, or subjecting the individual to extreme distress,** consider prescribing a hypnotic as an adjunct to non-drug treatment:
  - **Use the lowest effective dose** for a maximum of 1 week.
  - **Consider using intermittently** (e.g. once every other day, every third day).
  - **Temazepam, loprazolam, or lormetazepam** are the preferred choices. Zopiclone, zolpidem, or zaleplon are possible alternatives.
- **Be careful whenever prescribing a hypnotic,** particularly if the person is temporarily registered or unknown, as these drugs are commonly misused.

Practical prescribing points

For further information please see the *Medicines Compendium* (www.medicines.org.uk) or the *British National Formulary* (www.bnf.org).

- **The Committee on the Safety of Medicines** advises benzodiazepines should only be used when insomnia is severe, disabling, or subjecting the individual to extreme stress. They should only be used for short-term relief of insomnia (2–4 weeks maximum).
- **Benzodiazepines may cause drowsiness** the following day and impair skilled tasks (e.g. driving). Elderly people, and people with hepatic impairment, may require lower doses.
- **Benzodiazepines enhance the effect of alcohol** and other depressants: concomitant use should be avoided.
- **Zopiclone, zolpidem, and zaleplon** should be treated with the same caution as benzodiazepines.

Follow-up advice

- **Follow-up is not usually necessary.** Ask the person to return if the insomnia continues and is causing distress.
- **If the cause of insomnia is known,** review treatment of the underlying condition as appropriate.

Should I refer or investigate?

Refer?

- Referral is not usually necessary.

Patient information leaflets

The following PILs are available at www.prodigy.nhs.uk
- Insomnia - Poor Sleep
- Insomnia (Poor Sleep) - A Summary
- Insomnia - Sleeping Tablets
- Relaxation Exercises
- Sleep Council
- Sleep Diary

Shared decision making

- Is depression or another illness the cause of your poor sleeping?
- **A sleep diary** may help to identify the extent of the problem.
- **Tips to help with sleep include:**
  - Get up at the same time each day.
  - Never sleep during the daytime.
  - Routines are useful before bedtime, such as a warm drink, a hot bath, and reading.
  - The bedroom should be quiet and not used for TV, work, etc.
  - Avoid stimulants in the evening such as alcohol, caffeine, and smoking.
  - Exercise during the day, but not just before bedtime.
  - Eat only a light snack before bedtime and not a large meal.
  - A relaxation tape in the evening can help you to relax.
- **Sleeping tablets** are sometimes advised.
  - They should not be taken for more than one week. If you take them for longer they stop working so well and you may become dependent on them.
  - They may cause 'hangover' drowsiness the next day.
  - They can make you feel drowsy if you get up in the night — which may lead to falls.

Drug rationale

Drugs not included

- **Barbiturates** are only indicated in insomnia for treatment of severe intractable insomnia in people already taking barbiturates. They have unacceptably high risks of tolerance, dependence, and other adverse effects [BNF 44, 2002].
- **Sedative antidepressants,** such as amitriptyline, are sometimes useful for people with coexisting psychiatric disorders, such as depression. However, they are more toxic than benzodiazepines, and should be reserved for people who have disorders for which they are specifically indicated [Ashton, 1994; Scottish Health Service Advisory Council, 1994].
- **Antipsychotic drugs** are not licensed for insomnia and should not be used for this purpose. They may have a place in the management of insomnia secondary to an underlying psychiatric condition, but treatment should not be initiated without specialist advice or supervision [BNF 44, 2002].
- **Some sedative antihistamines (e.g. diphenhydramine and promethazine)** are available without a prescription for the self-treatment of occasional insomnia. However, they are not as effective as benzodiazepines, have more adverse effects, and are more toxic in overdose [Maczaj, 1993; Scottish Health Service Advisory Council, 1994; Therapeutics Initiative, 1995].
- **Chloral derivatives** have only a limited role as hypnotics, as they have a high incidence of gastric irritation [Scottish Health Service Advisory Council, 1994; BNF 44, 2002].
- **Chlormethiazole** may be useful for elderly people if confusion has been found to be a problem with other hypnotics. However, it is associated with unpleasant adverse effects, including nasal and gastric irritation [Gilhooly et al, 1998; BNF 44, 2002].
- **Long-acting and medium-acting benzodiazepines** are considered unsuitable as hypnotics due to their prolonged action, which causes hangover effects the

following day, and doses can be cumulative. However, diazepam, taken at night, may be useful when insomnia is related to daytime anxiety [Ashton, 1994; BNF 44, 2002].
- **Lorazepam,** a short-acting benzodiazepine, is primarily used as an anxiolytic. It is associated with a greater risk of withdrawal problems [BNF 44, 2002].

Drugs included

- **Temazepam, loprazolam, and lormetazepam** are short-acting benzodiazepines recommended for use in the treatment of short-term insomnia. They have short half-lives and are metabolized to inactive compounds, which leads to minimal hangover effects the following day. They have good safety profiles when used correctly. A 1-week course is offered, which minimizes the potential for dependence [Ashton, 1994; Grad, 1995; BNF 44, 2002].
- **The newer 'Z' drug hypnotics** are as effective as the short-acting benzodiazepines, but offer few proven advantages over them. In addition, they are more expensive. They are offered as alternatives if benzodiazepines are not well tolerated.
  - **Zopiclone** has similar efficacy to the benzodiazepines, and has similar adverse effects, and the potential for dependence with prolonged use.
  - **Zolpidem** has a shorter duration of action than the short-acting benzodiazepines, and has been reported to have less hangover effects the following day.
  - **Zaleplon** is the shortest-acting hypnotic. It reduces time taken to sleep but not duration, and may have some benefit as an 'as required' hypnotic.

[Kirkwood, 1999; Chow et al, 2000; BNF 44, 2002; MeReC, 2002]

Prescriptions

Non-drug management

Advice only: good sleep hygiene
- Age from 16 years onwards
- General tips to help with sleep include: Body rhythm – get up at the same time each day and never sleep in the day. Routines – are useful before bedtime e.g. a warm drink, hot bath and reading. Bedroom – should be free of noise and don't use for watching TV, eating, work. Stimulants – such as alcohol, caffeine and smoking should be avoided in the evening. Exercise – regularly during the day but not within a few hours of bedtime. Eat – only a light snack before bedtime and not a large meal. Relaxation – may be improved by using a relaxation tape in the evening. Depression is a common cause of poor sleep. Is this or another illness making things worse?

Short-acting benzodiazepine

Temazepam 10mg at night when required (x7 doses)
- Age from 16 years onwards
- Temazepam 10mg tablets. Take one tablet at night ONLY if required; supply 7 tablets; NHS Cost £0.23.

Loprazolam 1mg at night when required (x7 doses)
- Age from 16 years onwards
- Loprazolam 1mg tablets. Take one tablet at night ONLY if required; supply 7 tablets; NHS Cost £1.16.

Lormetazepam 500micrograms at night when required (x7 doses)
- Age from 16 years onwards
- Lormetazepam 500mcg tablets. Take one tablet at night ONLY if required; supply 7 tablets; NHS Cost £0.85.

Alternative therapy: Z drugs

Zopiclone 7.5mg at night when required (x7 doses)
- Age from 16 to 70 years
- Zopiclone 7.5mg tablets. Take one tablet at night ONLY if required; supply 7 tablets; NHS Cost £1.12.

Zolpidem 10mg at night when required (x7 doses)
- Age from 16 to 70 years
- Zolpidem 10mg tablets. Take one tablet at night ONLY if required; supply 7 tablets; NHS Cost £1.09.

Zaleplon 10mg at night when required (x7 doses)
- Age from 16 to 70 years
- Zaleplon 10mg capsules. Take one capsule at night ONLY if required; supply 7 capsules; NHS Cost £2.02.

Z drugs in the elderly or hepatically impaired

Zopiclone 3.75mg at night when required (x7 doses)
- Age from 16 years onwards
- Zopiclone 3.75mg tablets. Take one tablet at night ONLY if required; supply 7 tablets; NHS Cost £0.77.

Zolpidem 5mg at night when required (x7 doses)
- Age from 16 years onwards
- Zolpidem 5mg tablets. Take one tablet at night ONLY if required; supply 7 tablets; NHS Cost £0.75.

Zaleplon 5mg at night when required (x7 doses)
- Age from 16 years onwards
- Zaleplon 5mg capsules. Take one capsule at night ONLY if required; supply 7 capsules; NHS Cost £1.68.

Chronic insomnia (more than 3 weeks' duration)

Which therapy?

- **Identify any potential causes of insomnia or exacerbating factors.** If it is suspected the person is depressed, consider prescribing a trial course of low-dose sedative antidepressants.
- **Use non-drug treatments** where possible, including simple advice and counselling. Use available PRODIGY Patient Information Leaflets.
- **Sleep diaries** may be used to assess the degree of insomnia and monitor treatment progress.
- **Assessment in a sleep laboratory** may be advisable for people with suspected sleep apnoea or snoring problems.
- **Drug treatment is generally not advised.** However, there may be some situations, for example acute exacerbation of insomnia during a crisis, where a short course of hypnotics may be beneficial:
  - **Use the lowest effective dose** for a maximum of 1 week.
  - **Consider using intermittently** (e.g. once every other day, every third day).
  - **Temazepam, loprazolam, or lormetazepam** are the preferred choices. Zopiclone, zolpidem, or zaleplon are possible alternatives.
- **Long-term treatment of chronic insomnia with drugs is *not* effective.** Tolerance and dependence to hypnotics can occur rapidly, which will complicate the prognosis. The maximum length of treatment with hypnotics should be 2 weeks, and additional or repeat prescriptions should NOT be given.
- **Be careful whenever prescribing a hypnotic,** particularly if the person is temporarily registered or unknown, as these drugs are commonly misused.

Practical prescribing points

For further information please see the *Medicines Compendium* (www.medicines.org.uk) or the *British National Formulary* (www.bnf.org).

- **The Committee on the Safety of Medicines** advises benzodiazepines should only be used when insomnia is severe, disabling, or subjecting the individual to extreme stress. They should only be used for short-term relief of insomnia (2–4 weeks maximum).
- **Benzodiazepines may cause drowsiness** the following day and impair skilled tasks (e.g. driving). Elderly people, and people with hepatic impairment, may require lower doses.
- **Benzodiazepines enhance the effect of alcohol** and other depressants: concomitant use should be avoided.
- **Zopiclone, zolpidem, and zaleplon** should be treated with the same caution as benzodiazepines.

Follow-up advice

- **Review the patient at regular intervals,** to reinforce and encourage.
- **If the cause of insomnia is known,** review treatment of the underlying condition as appropriate.

Should I refer or investigate?

Refer?

- **Referral to a clinical psychologist or specially trained counsellor** may be appropriate for more specialized and intensive behavioural therapies.
- **Sleep laboratory referral is not usually required,** but the investigations conducted at these centres (electroencephalography, electromyography, and electrooculography) may be useful in the following cases:
  - **Longstanding chronic insomnia,** resistant to treatment.
  - **Insomnia in which there is suspicion of exaggeration** by the patient.
  - **Other unusual features of sleep** (e.g. epilepsy during sleep, sleep apnoea).

Patient information leaflets

The following PILs are available at www.prodigy.nhs.uk

- Insomnia - Poor Sleep
- Insomnia (Poor Sleep) - A Summary
- Insomnia - Sleeping Tablets
- Relaxation Exercises
- Sleep Council
- Sleep Diary

Shared decision making

- About 1 in 5 adults do not get as much sleep as they would like.
- Is depression or another illness the cause of your poor sleeping?
- **A sleep diary** may help to identify the extent of the problem.
- **Tips to help with sleep include:**
  - Get up at the same time each day.
  - Never sleep during the daytime.
  - Routines are useful before bedtime, such as a warm drink, a hot bath, and reading.
  - The bedroom should be quiet and not used for TV, eating, work, etc.
  - Avoid stimulants in the evening such as alcohol, caffeine, and smoking.
  - Exercise during the day, but not just before bedtime.
  - Eat only a light snack before bedtime and not a large meal.
  - A relaxation tape in the evening can help you to relax.
- **Sleeping tablets** are not advised because if you take them for more than a week they stop working so well and you are likely to become dependent on them ('addicted').
- **Referral** to a psychologist or counsellor may be advised in some cases.

Drug rationale

Drugs not included

- **Barbiturates** are only indicated in insomnia for treatment of severe intractable insomnia in people already taking barbiturates. They have unacceptably high risks of tolerance, dependence, and other adverse effects [BNF 44, 2002].
- **Sedative antidepressants,** such as amitriptyline, are sometimes useful for people with coexisting psychiatric disorders, such as depression. However, they are more toxic than benzodiazepines, and should be reserved for people who have disorders for which they are specifically indicated [Ashton, 1994; Scottish Health Service Advisory Council, 1994].
- **Some sedative antihistamines (e.g. diphenhydramine and promethazine)** are available without a prescription for the self-treatment of occasional insomnia. However, they are not as effective as benzodiazepines, have more adverse effects, and are more toxic in overdose [Maczaj, 1993; Scottish Health Service Advisory Council, 1994; Therapeutics Initiative, 1995].
- **Antipsychotic drugs** are not licensed for insomnia and should not be used for this purpose. They may have a place in the management of insomnia secondary to an underlying psychiatric condition, but treatment should not be initiated without specialist advice or supervision [BNF 44, 2002].
- **Chloral derivatives** have only a limited role as hypnotics, as they are associated with a high incidence of gastric irritation [Scottish Health Service Advisory Council, 1994; BNF 44, 2002].
- **Chlormethiazole** may be useful for elderly people if confusion has been found to be a problem with other hypnotics. However, it leads to unpleasant adverse effects, including nasal and gastric irritation [Gilhooly et al, 1998].
- **Long-acting and medium-acting benzodiazepines** are considered unsuitable as hypnotics due to their prolonged action, which causes hangover effects the following day, and doses can be cumulative. However, diazepam, taken at night, may be useful when insomnia is related to daytime anxiety [Ashton, 1994; BNF 44, 2002].
- **Lorazepam,** a short-acting benzodiazepine, is primarily used as an anxiolytic. It is associated with a greater risk of withdrawal problems [BNF 44, 2002].

Drugs included

- **Temazepam, loprazolam, and lormetazepam** are short-acting benzodiazepines recommended for use in the treatment of short-term insomnia. They have short half-lives and are metabolized to inactive compounds, leading to minimal hangover effects the following day. They have good safety profiles when used correctly. A 1-week course is offered, which minimizes the potential for dependence [Ashton, 1994; Grad, 1995; Therapeutics Initiative, 1995; BNF 44, 2002].
- **The newer 'Z' drug hypnotics** are as effective as the short-acting benzodiazepines, but offer few proven advantages over them. In addition, they are more

expensive. They are offered as alternatives if benzodiazepines are not well tolerated.

- **Zopiclone** has similar efficacy to the benzodiazepines, and has similar adverse effects, and the potential for dependence with prolonged use.
- **Zolpidem** has a shorter duration of action than the short-acting benzodiazepines, and has been reported to have less hangover effects the following day.
- **Zaleplon** is the shortest-acting hypnotic. It reduces time taken to sleep but not duration, and may have some benefit as an 'as required' hypnotic.

[Kirkwood, 1999; Chow et al, 2000; BNF 44, 2002; MeReC, 2002]

Prescriptions

Non-drug management

Advice only: good sleep hygiene

- Age from 16 years onwards
- General tips to help with sleep include: Body rhythm – get up at the same time each day and never sleep in the day. Routines – are useful before bedtime e.g. a warm drink, hot bath and reading. -Bedroom – should be free of noise and don't use for watching TV, eating, work. Stimulants – such as alcohol, caffeine and smoking should be avoided in the evening. Exercise – regularly during the day but not within a few hours of bedtime. Eat – only a light snack before bedtime and not a large meal. Relaxation – may be improved by using a relaxation tape in the evening. Depression is a common cause of poor sleep. Is this or another illness making things worse?

Short-acting benzodiazepine

Temazepam 10mg at night when required (x7 doses)

- Age from 16 years onwards
- Temazepam 10mg tablets. Take one tablet at night ONLY if required; supply 7 tablets; NHS Cost £0.23.

Loprazolam 1mg at night when required (x7 doses)

- Age from 16 years onwards
- Loprazolam 1mg tablets. Take one tablet at night ONLY if required; supply 7 tablets; NHS Cost £1.16.

Lormetazepam 500micrograms at night when required (x7 doses)

- Age from 16 years onwards
- Lormetazepam 500mcg tablets. Take one tablet at night ONLY if required; supply 7 tablets; NHS Cost £0.85.

Alternative therapy: Z drugs

Zopiclone 7.5mg at night when required (x7 doses)

- Age from 16 to 70 years
- Zopiclone 7.5mg tablets. Take one tablet at night ONLY if required; supply 7 tablets; NHS Cost £1.12.

Zolpidem 10mg at night when required (x7 doses)

- Age from 16 to 70 years
- Zolpidem 10mg tablets. Take one tablet at night ONLY if required; supply 7 tablets; NHS Cost £1.09.

Zaleplon 10mg at night when required (x7 doses)

- Age from 16 to 70 years
- Zaleplon 10mg capsules. Take one capsule at night ONLY if required; supply 7 capsules; NHS Cost £2.02.

Z drugs in the elderly or hepatically impaired

Zopiclone 3.75mg at night when required (x7 doses)

- Age from 16 years onwards
- Zopiclone 3.75mg tablets. Take one tablet at night ONLY if required; supply 7 tablets; NHS Cost £0.77.

Zolpidem 5mg at night when required (x7 doses)

- Age from 16 years onwards
- Zolpidem 5mg tablets. Take one tablet at night ONLY if required; supply 7 tablets; NHS Cost £0.75.

Zaleplon 5mg at night when required (x7 doses)

- Age from 16 years onwards
- Zaleplon 5mg capsules. Take one capsule at night ONLY if required; supply 7 capsules; NHS Cost £1.68.

Chronic hypnotic drug usage

Which therapy?

Note that this scenario gives advice and prescriptions on the initial treatment of hypnotic dependence only. For more detailed information on diazepam withdrawal, see the separate PRODIGY guidance on *Hypnotic/anxiolytic dependence*.

- **Educate** people about the problems of taking benzodiazepines long-term.
- **Motivate and encourage** people to take some responsibility for their situation and its solution. Give non-drug advice simultaneously. This alone may be adequate for some people.
- **Calculate the dosage of hypnotics, and change to the equivalent dosage of diazepam.** Aim for the lowest dosage that will prevent withdrawal symptoms. Dose equivalents are given in Table 1.
- **The daily dosage** may need to be divided in order to avoid intoxication or daytime drowsiness.

Practical prescribing points

For further information, please see the *Medicines Compendium* (www.medicines.org.uk) or the *British National Formulary* (www.bnf.org).

- **Diazepam causes drowsiness** that may affect performance of skilled tasks (e.g. driving); the effects of alcohol are enhanced.
- **Abrupt or too rapid withdrawal of diazepam** can cause serious adverse reactions including rebound insomnia, severe anxiety, and seizures. Re-establishment of drug maintenance will usually reverse these effects.
- **Small doses of diazepam** can be administered by cutting tablets into two halves. This can be done by the person if the tablets are scored, or by the pharmacist otherwise.

Follow-up advice

- **Review the patient 2 weeks after they have been maintained on diazepam.** Check for withdrawal symptoms and associated complications.

Table 1: Doses of benzodiazepines that are equivalent to diazepam 5 mg.

Benzodiazepines	Approximate equivalent doses to diazepam 5 mg
Temazepam	10 mg
Nitrazepam	5 mg
Loprazolam	500 micrograms to 1 mg
Lorazepam	500 micrograms
Oxazepam	15 mg
Lormetazepam	500 micrograms to 1 mg
Z drugs	
Zopiclone	7.5 mg
Zolpidem	10 mg
Zaleplon	10 mg

After successful diazepam maintenance has been achieved, begin reducing the dose of diazepam. For more detailed information on diazepam withdrawal, see the separate PRODIGY guidance on *Hypnotic/anxiolytic dependence*.

hould I refer or investigate?

efer?

Referral to a local drugs and alcohol mental health team, clinical psychologist, or trained counsellor may be appropriate:

- For more specialized and intensive behavioural therapies.
- For those people who fail to achieve withdrawal after repeated treatment and advice.
- If severe complications develop after withdrawal.
- If the person is simultaneously dependent on other drugs or alcohol.
- If there is coexisting physical or psychiatric morbidity.

Sleep laboratory referral is not usually required, but the investigations conducted at these centres (electroencephalography, electromyography and electrooculography) may be useful in the following cases:

- Insomnia that is exaggerated by the person.
- Other unusual features of sleep (e.g. epilepsy during sleep, sleep apnoea).

atient information leaflets

ıe following PILs are available at www.prodigy.nhs.uk

Insomnia - Poor Sleep
Insomnia (Poor Sleep) - A Summary
Insomnia - Sleeping Tablets
Relaxation Exercises
Sleep Council
Sleep Diary

hared decision making

Diazepam can be used as a substitute to help you come off sleeping tablets.

- Diazepam prevents the withdrawal symptoms which commonly occur if you stop sleeping tablets suddenly.
- With diazepam, it is then easier to gradually reduce the dose and stop.
- The aim is to reduce the dose by about 2 mg every 2–4 weeks.
- If withdrawal symptoms are troublesome, a more gradual reduction of dose may be better.

Some poor nights' sleep may occur when you first switch to diazepam.

Tips to help with sleep include:

- Get up at the same time each day.
- Never sleep during the daytime.
- Routines are useful before bedtime such as a warm drink, a hot bath, and reading.
- The bedroom should be quiet and not used for TV, work, etc.
- Avoid stimulants in the evening such as alcohol, caffeine, and smoking.
- Exercise during the day, but not just before bedtime.
- Eat only a light snack before bedtime and not a large meal.
- A relaxation tape in the evening can help you to relax.

Drug rationale

Drugs not included

- **Benzodiazepines other than diazepam** are not recommended for reduction protocols [Scottish Health Service Advisory Council, 1994; BNF 44, 2002]. Alprazolam and lorazepam, in particular, have the reputation of presenting particular withdrawal problems. Chlordiazepoxide has a more variable half-life than diazepam, and it is more difficult to halve small dosages [Russell and Lader, 1997].
- **Zaleplon, zolpidem, and zopiclone** (the 'Z' drugs) are newer hypnotics reputed to cause less dependence than benzodiazepines. However, several studies and case reports contradict this, and they are only licensed for the short-term treatment of insomnia. Their use in benzodiazepine withdrawal is therefore not recommended [MeReC, 2002].
- **Buspirone** is a newer anxiolytic with a mechanism of action unrelated to that of the benzodiazepines. It does not alleviate the symptoms of benzodiazepine withdrawal and therefore must not be used for this purpose [BNF 44, 2002].

Drugs included

- **Benzodiazepine** withdrawal protocols suggest substituting diazepam for the drug the patient is currently using, and then reducing the dose in small steps of 2 mg or 2.5 mg every 2 weeks [Scottish Health Service Advisory Council, 1994; BNF 44, 2002].
- **Diazepam** has a quick onset of action, has been well studied, and is available in several different formulations and strengths [BNF 44, 2002].
- **Temazepam, nitrazepam, and loprazolam** are the three most commonly prescribed benzodiazepine hypnotics [Prescription Pricing Authority, 2001]. Prescriptions for switching from these drugs to diazepam are included.

Prescriptions

Non-drug management

Advice only: good sleep hygiene

- Age from 16 years onwards
- Some poor nights sleep may occur at first. General tips to help with sleep include: Body rhythm – get up at the same time each day and never sleep in the day. Routines – are useful before bedtime e.g. a warm drink, hot bath and reading. Bedroom – should be free of noise and don't use for watching TV, eating, work. Stimulants – such as alcohol, caffeine and smoking should be avoided in the evening. Exercise – regularly during the day but not within a few hours of bedtime. Eat – only a light snack before bedtime and not a large meal. Relaxation – may be improved by using a relaxation tape in the evening.

Change to diazepam maintenance

Change from temazepam 40mg (maximum licensed use)

- Age from 16 years onwards
- Diazepam 10mg tablets. Take two tablets at night; supply 28 tablets; NHS Cost £0.84.

Change from nitrazepam 10mg (maximum licensed dose)

- Age from 16 years onwards
- Diazepam 5mg tablets. Take two tablets at night; supply 28 tablets; NHS Cost £0.58.

I

Change from loprazolam 2mg (maximum licensed dose)
- Age from 16 years onwards
- Diazepam 10mg tablets. Take two tablets at night; supply 28 tablets; NHS Cost £0.84.

Change from other hypnotic/anxiolytic drug or dose
- Age from 16 years onwards
- Diazepam 5mg tablets. Take as directed; supply 56 tablets; NHS Cost £1.16.

Extended Information

Background information

- What is it? p.1116
- How common is it? p.1116
- How do I know my patient has it? p.1116
- Complications and prognosis p.1116

What is it?

- **Insomnia** refers to complaints involving the inability to obtain adequate sleep [WHO, 1993].
- **It is not possible to define 'normal sleep'.** People's perception of what is normal varies considerably. They may complain of difficulty getting to sleep, waking during the night, waking early in the morning, or non-refreshing sleep.
- **Insomnia has been classified in several different ways:** by duration, severity, or comorbidity. The *Diagnostic and Statistical Manual of Mental disorders* (DSM-IV) and the *International Classification of Disease,* 10th edition (ICD-10), are descriptive, whereas the International Classification of Sleep Disorders Revised (ICSD-R) classifies insomnia according to presumed underlying pathology. These classifications are useful for research purposes but are not really suitable for primary care.
- **The 1983 Consensus conference** on insomnia from the National Institutes of Health, USA, classified insomnia into three major categories. The categories were based on the duration of symptoms, and these still constitute the most practical framework for primary care:
  - **Transient insomnia** lasts for 2–3 days.
  - **Short-term insomnia** lasts for more than a few days but less than 3 weeks.
  - **Chronic insomnia** can be defined as insomnia most nights for 3 weeks or longer.

[Freedman et al, 1984]

- However, this framework has the disadvantage that the categories of transient and short-term insomnia can only be made retrospectively.
- **There is no identifiable cause** in 29% of cases of chronic insomnia [Lamberg, 1997].

How common is it?

- **About 9–31%** of all people have sleep problems in any given year [WHO, 1993; Lamberg, 1997].
- **In a UK study,** 36% of people reported insomnia symptoms, but only 76% of these reported sleep dissatisfaction [Ohayon et al, 1997].
- **Prevalence** seems to be greater in women, older people, and those who are socio-economically disadvantaged [WHO, 1993].
- Insomnia typically develops at times of increased life stress [WHO, 1993].

How do I know my patient has it?

History

The following three components should be looked for:

- **Sleep disturbance,** which can be subdivided into the following:
  - **Sleep-onset insomnia** (i.e. difficulty in falling asleep). This is the most prevalent complaint. Younger peopl are more likely to have this problem.
  - **Frequent nocturnal awakening** (i.e. difficulty in maintaining sleep). Older people are more likely to have this problem.
  - **Early morning awakening** (i.e. waking up early in th morning and being unable to get back to sleep). This the least prevalent complaint.

[WHO, 1993]

- **Difficulty in functioning during the daytime** (e.g. fatigu irritability, difficulty concentrating), in addition to slee disturbance [WHO, 1993].
- **The presence of a recognized cause of insomnia** should be identified and treated. Consider underlying causes a conditions that may present as insomnia, easily remembered as 'the five Ps' — physical, physiological, psychological, psychiatric, and pharmacological [Ashton, 1994]. Some of the most common causes are listed in Table 2. However, this is not an exhaustive list

[WHO, 1993; Ashton, 1994; Kupfer and Reynolds, 1997 Lamberg, 1997; Kirkwood, 1999]

Physical examination

- Exclude obvious physical causes [WHO, 1993].

Complications and prognosis

- **Chronic insomnia** may lead to:
  - Psychiatric problems (e.g. depression, panic disorder [Lamberg, 1997].
  - Abuse of alcohol or other drugs [Lamberg, 1997].
- **Misdiagnosis** can lead to the failure to treat potentially curable conditions (e.g. depression).
- **The use of hypnotics** to treat insomnia can lead to:
  - **Drug-induced 'hangover'** the following day, causing daytime drowsiness and consequently an increased risk of accidents.
  - **Drug tolerance and dependence,** even after a short course of treatment.
  - **Adverse effects from drug withdrawal** following dependence, including acute rebound insomnia.

[Ashton, 1994; MeReC, 2002]

Management issues

- General issues p.1116
- Non-drug treatments p.1117
- Standard drug treatments p.1118
- Other drug treatments p.1119
- Alternative remedies p.1119
- Chronic hypnotic usage p.1120

General issues

- **Treating any identified potential causes** of insomnia or exacerbating factors, where possible, may alleviate the insomnia (see *How do I know my patient has it?*).
- **Hypnotics started in hospital** to cover a sleepless night on a busy ward should not be continued following discharge [Medicines Resource, 1995].
- **People taking hypnotics should be warned** that these may impair alertness, concentration, and driving performance, particularly at the start of treatment or when the dose has been increased. Affected people

ble 2: Common underlying causes of insomnia.

e 'P's	Type of disorder	Examples and comments
ysical	Movement disorders	Restless legs syndrome, periodic leg movements can cause inability to fall asleep
	Respiratory disorders	Obstructive sleep apnoea, dyspnoea, and coughing can cause frequent awakening
	Painful conditions	Arthritis, headaches
	Diseases of the prostate gland	Benign prostatic hyperplasia and prostatic carcinoma can cause nocturia
	Endocrine causes	Hyperthyroidism (sweats), diabetes mellitus (nocturia), diabetes insipidus (nocturia)
	Perimenopausal symptoms	Hot flushes
	Other physical illnesses	Pruritus, nocturia, Parkinson's disease, and leg cramps
ysiological	The sleeping environment	Noise, light, a partner's snoring
	Disturbed sleep routine	Napping during the day, getting up at different times, shift work, jetlag. Intellectual or physical activity immediately prior to going to bed may lead to difficulty in sleeping
	Bedtime routine	This may be the real problem in children with sleep difficulties
chological	Loss, crisis, worry	Bereavement, relationships, home circumstances, work difficulties
	Conditioned insomnia	Excessive worrying about not sleeping and behaviour that is destructive to sleep (e.g. an irregular schedule, or lying in bed ruminating)
chiatric	Underlying depression	Depression often presents with insomnia as a symptom
	Dementia	May lead to reversal of normal sleep patterns, causing insomnia
	Anxiety states	May present with insomnia
armacological	Drug withdrawal symptoms	Ceasing medication (e.g. hypnotics) may induce rebound insomnia
	Alcohol	Can reduce the quality of sleep: sends to sleep but wakes up quickly
	Drugs	Appetite suppressants, chronic benzodiazepine misuse, certain antidepressants can cause sleep problems, discontinuation of antidepressants, thyroid hormones, sympathomimetics (agitation), diuretics (nocturia), corticosteroids (agitation), and beta-blockers (bad dreams).

should not drive. In addition, alcohol and other depressants will potentiate the effects of hypnotics [DVLA, 1999].

on-drug treatments

In most people, insomnia can be managed using non-pharmacological methods.

- **Addressing the underlying cause of insomnia** is more likely to be successful in the long term, although it may be more time-consuming than simply giving a prescription for a hypnotic.
- **Non-drug strategies** may involve behavioural therapy, anxiety management, self-monitoring, and counselling.
- **Problem-solving approaches** may enable the person to manage the problem, and consequently be more likely to feel in control.

shton, 1994; Medicines Resource, 1995].

atient advice and self-management

Lifestyle advice is important, regarding the restriction of caffeine, nicotine, and alcohol; exercise; regular sleep and awakening times; and maintenance of a good sleeping environment [WHO, 1993; Therapeutics Initiative, 1995; Kupfer and Reynolds, 1997]. A Cochrane Review found one study that suggested exercise in people over 60 years may be useful in enhancing sleep and contribute to increased quality of life [Montgomery and Dennis, 2003a]. However, it is generally recognised that exercise near bedtime can prevent sleep.

- **Educating both the person and carer about sleep is sometimes required** (e.g. reminding patients that less sleep may be needed by the elderly). For an advice sheet, see the PRODIGY Patient Information Leaflet, *Insomnia — Poor Sleep*. For carers see the PRODIGY Patient Information Leaflet, *Insomnia — Information for Carers*.
- **Sleep diaries** can be useful for assessment and monitoring [Medicines Resource, 1995; MeReC, 1995]. Self-monitoring in this way makes it possible to assess the person's motivation and also gives the person responsibility over his or her own health [Scottish Health Service Advisory Council, 1994]. For a specimen diary, see the PRODIGY Patient Information Leaflet, *Sleep Diary*.
- **Patient guides,** which should include tips on sleeping, may be helpful. There is a large range of written and audio material available in bookshops [MeReC, 1995]. For an example of an advice sheet on promoting sleep, relaxation, and information for patients or their carers, see the PRODIGY Patient Information Leaflet, *Insomnia — Ten Tips to Help Poor Sleep*.

Counselling and behavioural therapies

- **In more difficult cases** a person may benefit from referral to a clinical psychologist or trained counsellor.

- **Cognitive behavioural therapies:** there is limited evidence for the effectiveness of cognitive behavioural therapies and hypnotherapy [Complementary and Alternative Medicine, 2001; Bazian Ltd., 2002].
  - **Cognitive behavioural therapies for sleep problems in people aged over 60 years are mildly effective** for some aspects of sleep in the short term, according to a Cochrane Review [Montgomery and Dennis, 2003b].

Standard drug treatments

General issues in standard drug treatment

- **Before a hypnotic is prescribed,** the cause of insomnia should be investigated and treated; non-drug treatment should be used wherever possible. Treatment with hypnotics is only indicated in anticipated transient or short-term insomnia [BNF 44, 2002]:
  - **Transient insomnia** typically lasts 2–3 days and is often caused by extraneous factors such as noise, shift work, or jetlag. Treatment should consist of only one or two single doses of a hypnotic, at the minimal effective dose.
  - **Short-term insomnia** lasts for more than a few days but less than 3 weeks, and may be caused by emotional problems or physical illness. If indicated, only short courses of hypnotics should be used, at the minimal effective dose, usually for less than 1 week. Intermittent doses should also be considered to minimize the potential for drug tolerance and dependence.

[BNF 44, 2002]

- **Hypnotics should NOT be prescribed for long-term use,** and repeat prescribing should be avoided. Hypnotics are only licensed for the short-term treatment of insomnia; tolerance and dependence can occur rapidly with all hypnotics [Ashton, 1994; Angst, 1997; Eccles et al, 1998; DH, 1999].
- **All hypnotics have the potential for misuse and abuse;** hence there is a need to be vigilant when prescribing these drugs, particularly if the patient is temporarily registered or unknown. Temazepam is the most commonly abused drug, but other benzodiazepines, and more recently zopiclone, have all been implicated in illicit drug use [Scottish Health Service Advisory Council, 1994; Medicines Resource, 1995; MeReC, 1995; Prescribe International, 2001].
- The use of hypnotics is rarely justified in children, and care should be taken when prescribing to elderly people, due to the potential for ataxia and consequent falls [BNF 44, 2002].
- **Short-acting benzodiazepines** are regarded as the drugs of choice when drug treatment for insomnia is indicated. The newer 'Z drugs' are indicated in specific clinical instances or when benzodiazepines are poorly tolerated [Ashton, 1994; BNF 44, 2002; MeReC, 2002; NICE, 2004].

Benzodiazepines compared with Z drugs

- **Zopiclone, zolpidem, and zaleplon** are newer, non-benzodiazepine hypnotics developed in the last decade. Although they are not a distinct drug class, they are often collectively referred to as the 'Z' drugs [Kirkwood, 1999; Chow et al, 2000].
- **Z drugs are structurally unrelated to the benzodiazepines or one another,** and have different receptor affinities and pharmacokinetics from the classical benzodiazepines. However, the hypnotic effect and related adverse effects of Z drugs are broadly similar to those of the short-acting benzodiazepines [Kirkwood, 1999; Chow et al, 2000].
- **At present, there seem to be few advantages or disadvantages of Z drugs compared with benzodiazepines.** Claims of reduced adverse effects, tolerance, and dependency (compared with benzodiazepines) have not been substantiated by later studies and case reports [Kirkwood, 1999; Chow et al, 2000]. Until proven otherwise, the Z drugs should be treated with the same caution as benzodiazepines [MeReC, 2002]. In particular, they should only be prescribed for short-term management of insomnia [BN 44, 2002].
- **The National Institute for Clinical Evidence** states that when a hypnotic is required, the drug with the lowest cost should be prescribed. The only circumstance when more expensive hypnotic should be used is when the initial drug was poorly tolerated. People who have not responded to one hypnotic should not be prescribed any of the others [NICE, 2004].
- **The decision to use Z drugs should be based on each individual drug's merits** (see Zopiclone, Zolpidem, and Zaleplon). However, it should be taken into account th these drugs are more expensive than their benzodiazepine counterparts.

Benzodiazepines

- **Benzodiazepines** should only be considered where insomnia is severe, disabling, or subjecting the individu to extreme distress. Treatment should be short-term (nc more than a week), with the lowest effective dose being used. Intermittent dosing should also be considered where possible [Ashton, 1994; MeReC, 1995; CSM, 1988].
- **A recent systematic review** found that benzodiazepines were effective in increasing sleep duration, but did not significantly decrease the time taken to fall asleep. They were also associated with an increase in hangover-relat adverse effects compared with placebo [Holbrook et al, 2000].
- **All benzodiazepines have both anxiolytic and hypnotic effects.** The predominant effect, and consequent license indication, is dependent on their duration of action:
  - **Loprazolam, lormetazepam, and temazepam** are classed as short-acting, and are recommended for use as hypnotics. They have little or no hangover effect, but are more associated with acute withdrawal symptoms.
  - **Nitrazepam, flunitrazepam, and flurazepam** are licensed as hypnotics and have an intermediate duration of effect. However, they are not recommended as they may have residual effects the following day.
  - **Diazepam** is a long-acting benzodiazepine mainly use for its anxiolytic properties. It is associated with an increase in adverse effects, particularly in the elderly. However, it has a place in the treatment of insomnia related to daytime anxiety.

[Grad, 1995; Medicines Resource, 1995; Therapeutics Initiative, 1995; BNF 44, 2002]

Adverse effects of benzodiazepines

- **Long-acting benzodiazepines** have been associated with an increased risk of road traffic accidents in both adult and elderly populations [Hemmelgarn et al, 1997; Barbone et al, 1998]. There is no evidence that intermediate or short-acting benzodiazepines are associated with increased risk, but nevertheless caution should be taken when any benzodiazepine is used, as drowsiness may continue the next day.
  - Patients affected by drowsiness should be advised not to drive or operate machinery [BNF 44, 2002].

- In addition, any person suffering from excessive awake-time sleepiness, regardless of cause (e.g. due to the insomnia itself) should cease driving until there is satisfactory control of symptoms [DVLA, 1999].

An increased risk of falls has been associated with benzodiazepine use in elderly people [Wang et al, 2001], although there is conflicting evidence about this [Pierfitte et al, 2001]. The potential risk of hip fracture in elderly people taking benzodiazepines needs to be taken into consideration [MeReC, 2002].

Physical and psychological dependence can occur after even short-term treatment with all benzodiazepines. Withdrawal symptoms may occur if the drug is suddenly discontinued, even after taking it for a short period of time (3–14 days) [MeReC, 1995]. Symptoms tend to occur shortly after abruptly stopping a benzodiazepine with a short half-life, or up to several days after stopping one with a long half-life. Rebound phenomena are not related to the particular drug prescribed, or to the length of prescribing.

;cottish Health Service Advisory Council, 1994]

:opiclone

A systematic review found that zopiclone was as effective as short-acting benzodiazepines in the treatment of insomnia. There was no difference in reported adverse effects [Holbrook et al, 2000; NICE, 2004].

Zopiclone causes hangovers and impaired psychomotor performance, similarly to temazepam [Wagner et al, 1998]. Its use has been linked to an increased risk of road traffic accidents [Barbone et al, 1998].

Zopiclone use has been associated with tolerance, dependence, and misuse. Loss of efficacy due to tolerance has been reported, causing patients to increase the dose, resulting in dependence [Jones and Sullivan, 1998; Prescribe International, 2001]. Withdrawal symptoms have also been reported, even with correctly prescribed doses [Medicines Resource, 1995; MeReC, 2002].

:olpidem

Zolpidem is considered to be as effective as benzodiazepines in terms of time taken to fall asleep and sleep duration [Wagner et al, 1998; Holm and Goa, 2000; Lader, 2001; NICE, 2004].

Zolpidem has a shorter duration of action than zopiclone, and is consequently thought to have minimal hangover-related adverse effects the following day [Lader, 2001]. However, an increased risk of hip fracture in elderly people, caused by falls, has been reported [Wang et al, 2001].

Zolpidem is reputed to have less tolerance, dependence, and abuse potential than benzodiazepines [Lader, 2001], although cases of misuse leading to dependence and withdrawal problems have been documented [Holm and Goa, 2000; Prescribe International, 2001]. In addition, delirium, nightmares, and hallucinations have been reported at licensed doses [Toner et al, 2000].

aleplon

Zaleplon has a very short duration of action, with a half-life of about 1 hour [Doghramji, 2001]. It is as effective as zolpidem or triazolam (now discontinued) in reducing the time taken to fall asleep, but has little effect on sleep duration, and the quality of sleep achieved is variable. Zaleplon may have a role as an 'as required' hypnotic when people are having difficulty falling asleep [UK Medicines Information Pharmacists Group, 2000].

Zaleplon causes less hangover effects (such as impaired psychomotor, cognitive, and memory abilities) than benzodiazepines. It is also reported as having less potential for dependence and abuse, and is less likely to cause rebound insomnia upon discontinuation [UK Medicines Information Pharmacists Group, 2000; Doghramji, 2001]. However, until more is known it should be treated with caution because, as with all hypnotics, there is the potential for abuse [MeReC, 2002].

- **Zaleplon is licensed for the treatment of insomnia when there is difficulty falling asleep.** Note: the maximum licensed length of treatment with zaleplon is 2 weeks, compared to 4 weeks for zopiclone and zolpidem [ABPI Medicines Compendium, 2003].

Other drug treatments

- **A variety of drugs have sedative properties** and have been used historically, or are still used, in the treatment of insomnia. However, only the short-acting benzodiazepines and the Z drugs are recommended for treatment of primary insomnia (i.e. without comorbidity), as these drugs are effective and have relatively good safety profiles.
- **Barbiturates** are only indicated in insomnia for treatment of severe intractable insomnia in people already taking barbiturates. They have unacceptably high risks of tolerance, dependence, and other adverse effects [BNF 44, 2002].
- **Sedative antidepressants,** such as amitriptyline, are sometimes useful for people with coexisting psychiatric disorders, such as depression, and are often used in general practice for their hypnotic effect. However, they are more toxic than benzodiazepines, and should be reserved for people who have disorders for which they are specifically indicated [Ashton, 1994; Scottish Health Service Advisory Council, 1994].
- **Antipsychotic drugs** are not licensed for insomnia and should not be used for this purpose. They may have a place in the management of insomnia secondary to an underlying psychiatric condition, but treatment should not be initiated without specialist advice or supervision [BNF 44, 2002].
- **Chloral derivatives** have only a limited role as hypnotics, as they have a high incidence of gastric irritation [Scottish Health Service Advisory Council, 1994; BNF 44, 2002].
- **Chlormethiazole** may be useful for elderly people if confusion has been found to be a problem with other hypnotics. However, it is associated with unpleasant adverse effects, including nasal and gastric irritation [Gilhooly et al, 1998; BNF 44, 2002].
- **Various sedative antihistamines are available,** both on prescription and over the counter, but evidence for their effectiveness is limited:
  - **Diphenhydramine,** on sale to the public as *Dreemon®*, *Medinex®*, *Nightcalm®*, and *Nytol®*, causes daytime sedation, psychomotor impairment, and antimuscarinic adverse effects [Wagner et al, 1998]. It is not recommended in elderly people [Ancoli-Israel, 2000].
  - **Promethazine,** available as *Phenergan Nightime®* and *Sominex®*, also causes daytime sedation [BNF 44, 2002].

Alternative remedies

- **Valerian** is a herbal medicine that has been promoted for improving sleep. There is some evidence that it may have a small benefit in the treatment of insomnia, but there is a general lack of available data. A number of adverse effects have also been reported. In addition, valerian should not be used in pregnant or breastfeeding women, or people with hepatic impairment [Bandolier, 2000; Wagner et al, 1998; Complementary and Alternative Medicine, 2001].

- **Kava-kava** is reputed to have sedative properties, but its use has been prohibited due to reports of associated hepatotoxicity [CSM, 2002].
- **Melatonin** has not been proven to be effective, and is currently unavailable in the UK [Wagner et al, 1998].

Chronic hypnotic usage

- **Long-term use of hypnotics can lead to tolerance and dependence,** and is associated with a range of adverse effects. The majority of prescriptions for hypnotic drugs are to chronic users, often on repeat prescriptions. The *National Service Framework for Mental Health* states that, where possible, chronic users of hypnotics should be encouraged to stop their medication, with the aid of withdrawal programmes [DH, 1999; Regional Drug and Therapeutics Centre, 2001].
- **Management in people who chronically use hypnotic drugs may be problematic.** See the separate PRODIGY guidance on *Hypnotic or anxiolytic dependence.*
- **There is little good evidence on the best way to withdraw from benzodiazepines.** Expert opinion and theory suggest switching to an equivalent dose of diazepam taken at night, and, once the patient is stabilized, reducing the dose sequentially in small steps according to clinical judgement of the individual's needs and withdrawal symptoms:
  - **Small fortnightly reductions** of 2–2.5 mg diazepam are recommended. It is better to withdraw too slowly than too rapidly.
  - **If withdrawal symptoms develop,** the dose of diazepam should be maintained or temporarily increased until they abate.
  - **The final reduction of diazepam is often hardest to achieve.** Smaller doses of diazepam can be prescribed by cutting scored tablets in half.

[Ashton, 1994; Scottish Health Service Advisory Council, 1994; BNF 44, 2002]

- **Chronic users of Z drugs** should also be encouraged to stop taking the drug. Withdrawal by switching to diazepam is advised, though there is little evidence on the equivalent doses of these drugs [BNF 44, 2002].

References

NHS staff in England can link, free of charge, from references to full text journals by clicking on [Full text] on the PRODIGY website.

1. ABPI Medicines Compendium (2003) *Summary of product characteristics for Sonata 5mg & 10mg hard capsules.* Electronic Medicines Compendium. Datapharm Communications Ltd. www.emc.medicines.org.uk [Accessed: 25/03/2003].
2. Ancoli-Israel, S. (2000) Insomnia in the elderly: a review for the primary care practitioner.. *Sleep* **23**(Suppl. 1), S23-S30.
3. Angst, J. (1997) A regular review of the long term follow up of depression. *British Medical Journal* **315**(7116), 1143–1146. [Full text]
4. Ashton, H. (1994) Guidelines for the rational use of benzodiazepines. When and what to use. *Drugs* **48**(1), 25–40.
5. Bandolier (2000) *Valerian for insomnia.* Bandolier. www.jr2.ox.ac.uk/bandolier/band81/b81-7.html [Accessed: 01/04/2003].
6. Barbone, F., McMahon, A.D., Davey, P.G. et al (1998) Association of road-traffic accidents with benzodiazepine use. *Lancet* **352**(9137), 1331–1336. [Full text]
7. Bazian Ltd. (2002) Insomnia. *Clinical Evidence* **9**, 1896–1899.
8. BNF 44 (2002) *British National Formulary.* 44th edn London: British Medical Association and Royal Pharmaceutical Society of Great Britain.
9. Chow, S.L., Tomlinson, B. and Chow, M.S.S. (2000) Pharmacologic management of insomnia: assessing the nonbenzodiazepine hypnotics. *Hospital Formulary* **35**(11), 894–903.
10. Complementary and Alternative Medicine (2001) *Insomnia.* The Desktop Guide to Complementary and Alternative Medicine [CD-ROM]. Mosby.
11. CSM (1988) Benzodiazepines, dependence and withdrawal symptoms. *Current Problems in Pharmacovigilance* **21**(Jan), 1–2.
12. CSM (2002) *CSM advice on liver toxicity associated with kava-kava and proposed regulatory action by the Government.* Committee on Safety of Medicines. www.dhsspsni.gov.uk/ [Accessed: 09/04/2003].
13. DH (1999) *National service framework for mental health.* Department of Health. www.dh.gov.uk [Accessed: 26/04/2004]. [Full text]
14. Doghramji, P.P. (2001) Treatment of insomnia with zaleplon, a novel sleep medication. *International Journal of Clinical Practice* 55(5), 329–334.
15. DVLA (1999) *At a glance guide to current medical standards of fitness to drive. Renal disorders, respiratory disorders, sleep disorders.* Swansea: Drivers Medical Group, Driver and Vehicle Licensing Authority. www.dvla.gov.uk/at_a_glance/content.ht [Accessed: 27/01/2003].
16. Eccles, M., Freemantle, N. and Mason, J. (1998) *The choice of antidepressants for depression in primary care.* Newcastle upon Tyne: Centre for Health Servic Research.
17. Freedman, D.X., Derryberry, J.S., Federman, D.D. et (1984) Consensus conference. Drugs and insomnia. The use of medications to promote sleep. *Journal of American Medical Association* **251**(18), 2410–2414.
18. Gilhooly, T.C., Webster, M.G.O., Poole, N.W. and Ross, S. (1998) What happens when doctors stop prescribing temazepam? Use of alternative therapies. *British Journal of General Practice* **48**(434), 1601–1602.
19. Grad, R.M. (1995) Benzodiazepines for insomnia in community-dwelling elderly: a review of benefit and risk. *Journal of Family Practice* **41**(5), 473–481.
20. Hemmelgarn, B., Suissa, S., Huang, A. et al (1997) Benzodiazepine use and the risk of motor vehicle cra in the elderly. *Journal of the American Medical Association* **278**(1), 27–31. [Full text]
21. Holbrook, A.M., Crowther, R., Lotter, A. et al (200 Meta-analysis of benzodiazepine use in the treatmen of insomnia. *Canadian Medical Association Journal* **162**(2), 225–233. [Full text]
22. Holm, K.J. and Goa, K.L. (2000) Zolpidem: an upda of its pharmacology, therapeutic efficacy and tolerability in the treatment of insomnia. *Drugs* **59**(4 865–889.
23. Jones, I.R. and Sullivan, G. (1998) Physical dependa on zopiclone: case reports. *British Medical Journal* **316**(7125), 117–117. [Full text]
24. Kirkwood, C.K. (1999) Management of insomnia. *Journal of the American Pharmaceutical Association* **39**(5), 688–696.
25. Kupfer, D.J. and Reynolds, C.F. (1997) Managemen of insomnia. *New England Journal of Medicine* **336**(341–346. [Full text]
26. Lader, M.H. (2001) Implications of hypnotic flexibil on patterns of clinical use. *International Journal of Clinical Practice* **Suppl 116.**(Jan), 14–19.
27. Lamberg, L. (1997) Sleep specialists weigh hypnotics behavioral therapies for insomnia. *Journal of the*

American Medical Association **278**(20), 1647–1649. [Full text]

Maczaj, M. (1993) Pharmacological treatment of insomnia. *Drugs* **45**(1), 44–55.

Medicines Resource (1995) Management of anxiety and insomnia (I). *Medicines Resource* **22**(May), 83–86.

MeReC (1995) Management of anxiety and insomnia. *MeReC Bulletin* **6**(10),

MeReC (2002) An update on benzodiazepines and non-benzodiazepine hypnotics. *MeReC Briefing* **17**(Apr), 6–8.

Montgomery, P. and Dennis, J. (2003a) *Physical exercise for sleep problems in adults aged 60+ (Cochrane Review)*. The Cochrane Library. Issue 1. Oxford: Update Software.

Montgomery, P. and Dennis, J. (2003b) *Cognitive behavioural interventions for sleep problems in adults aged 60+ (Cochrane Review)*. The Cochrane Library. Issue 1. Oxford: Update Software.

NICE (2004) *Guidance on the use of zaleplon, zolpidem and zopiclone for the short-term management of insomnia.* Technology appraisal no. 77. National Institute for Clinical Excellence. www.nice.org.uk [Accessed: 28/04/2004].

Ohayon, M.M., Caulet, M., Priest, R.G. and Guilleminault, C. (1997) DSM-IV and ICSD-90 insomnia symptoms and sleep dissatisfaction. *British Journal of Psychiatry* **171**(10), 382–388.

Pierfitte, C., Macouillard, G., Thicoipe, M. et al (2001) Benzodiazepines and hip fractures in elderly people: case-control study. *British Medical Journal* **322**(7288), 704–708. [Full text]

Prescribe International (2001) Hypnotic dependence: zolpidem and zopiclone too. *Prescrire International* **10**(51), 15.

38. Prescription Pricing Authority (2001) *Prescribing of mental health drugs.* Prescription Pricing Authority. www.ppa.org.uk [Accessed: 29/08/2002].
39. Regional Drug and Therapeutics Centre (2001) *Managing hypnotic and anxiolytic withdrawal in primary care.* NHS Northern and Yorkshire: Regional Drug and Therapeutics Centre.
40. Russell, J. and Lader, M. (1997) *Guidelines for the prevention and treatment of benzodiazepine dependence.* London: Mental Health Foundation.
41. Scottish Health Service Advisory Council (1994) *The management of anxiety and insomnia.* Edinburgh: HMSO.
42. Therapeutics Initiative (1995) To sleep or not to sleep: here are your questions. *Therapeutics Letter* **11**(Nov/Dec.),
43. Toner, L.C., Tsambiras, B.M., Catalano, G. et al (2000) Central nervous system side effects associated with zolpidem treatment. *Clinical Neuropharmacology* **23**(1), 54–58.
44. UK Medicines Information Pharmacists Group (2000) *Zaleplon.* UK Medicines Information. Department of Health. www.ukmi.nhs.uk/med_info/stage4.asp [Accessed: 10/03/2003].
45. Wagner, J., Wagner, M.L. and Hening, W.A. (1998) Beyond benzodiazepines: alternative pharmacologic agents for the treatment of insomnia. *Annals of Pharmacotherapy* **32**(6), 680–691.
46. Wang, P.S., Bohn, R.L., Glynn, R.J. et al (2001) Zolpidem use and hip fractures in older people. *Journal of the American Geriatrics Society* **49**(12), 1685–1690.
47. WHO (Ed.) (1993) *Insomnia in general practice.* Geneva: Division of Mental Health, World Health Organisation.

PRODIGY GUIDANCE

Irritable bowel syndrome

Last revised in July 2002
At the time of print this topic was being updated. The newly revised guidance will be issued on to the website in late 2005.
www.prodigy.nhs.uk/guidance.asp?gt=Irritable bowel syndrome

Applies to people of all ages

This guidance covers the management of irritable bowel syndrome.
There is separate PRODIGY guidance for *Constipation, Dyspepsia — proven gastro-oesophageal reflux disease, Dyspepsia — symptoms (uninvestigated by endoscopy), Dyspepsia — proven DU, GU, or NSAID-associated ulcer, Dyspepsia — proven non-ulcer dyspepsia* and *Gastroenteritis*.

Goals

- To reduce symptoms
- To improve quality of life

Contents

Scenarios
- Mild IBS p.1122
- Moderate / severe IBS p.1123

Extended Information, p. 1125

Which scenario?

- **Mild IBS:** covers the management of adults and children with mild IBS who do not require drug treatments.
- **Moderate/severe IBS:** covers the management of adults with moderate to severe IBS who require drug treatments. Children are not included in this scenario since treatment with drugs is not recommended.

Mild IBS

Which therapy?

- **Exclude other conditions** such as inflammatory bowel disease, neoplasia, and psychological problems. These may also coexist with IBS and should be treated appropriately.
- **Explain the diagnosis;** reassure that symptoms may be long-lived but are never life threatening, do not indicate further disease, are intermittent, and generally improve with time.
- **Non-drug options include:**
  - **Simple dietary advice** may be helpful to all sufferers of IBS.
  - **Constipation** — try an increase in dietary fibre and fluid intake. Fibre, particularly bran, sometimes worsens symptoms, and should be tailored to the individual.
  - **Diarrhoea** — try a reduction in dietary fat, tea, coffee, and cigarette smoking.
  - **Pain and spasm** — try a reduction in tea and coffee or other triggers.
  - **Stress management** may be effective in some people.
  - **Drug treatments** are rarely required if symptoms are mild and people are adequately counselled.

Should I refer or investigate?

Refer?

- **Exclude serious alternative diagnoses** — such as neoplasia and inflammatory bowel disease — particularly if there are sinister symptoms or signs.
- **Whether or not this necessitates referral depends on:**
  - Clinical judgement of the individual person's risks (such as age over 45 years at presentation; family history of cancer of colon, breast, ovary, or uterus; new symptoms; failure of standard treatment; siniste symptoms — e.g. rectal bleeding, weight loss, anorexia).
  - Whether or not there is open access to appropriate investigations.
  - The degree of expertise available within the practice
- **Referral to a dietician may be appropriate,** particularly exclusion diets are being considered.

Investigate?

Consider the following investigations to exclude other causes of symptoms:

- **Blood tests** — full blood count, erythrocyte sedimentation rate, C-reactive protein, thyroid functio liver function, endomysial autoantibodies (for coeliac disease) — all normal in IBS.
- **Stool examination and culture** (particularly if persister diarrhoea) — to exclude occult blood, ova and parasit
- **Sigmoidoscopy** — to exclude inflammation and melanosis coli (laxative abuse).
- **Whether or not to proceed to colonoscopy or barium enema** depends on the individual person's risk (see *Ref* above). Specialist advice should be sought at this stage [Francis and Whorwell, 1997; Maxwell et al, 1997].

Patient information leaflets

The following PILs are available at www.prodigy.nhs.uk

- Barium Enema
- Barium Swallow / Meal / Follow Through
- Biopsy
- Blood Test - Blood Count and Smear
- Blood Test - Detecting Inflammation
- Blood Test - General
- Constipation in Adults
- Eat More Fruit and Vegetables
- Faecal Occult Blood Test
- Fibre in the Diet
- Irritable Bowel Syndrome
- Irritable Bowel Syndrome Network
- Medicines - Name Changes of Medicines

Shared decision making

- Irritable bowel syndrome is common. Symptoms vary, and flare up from time to time, but often settle for long periods without any treatment.
- **If constipation is a main symptom** — eating more fibre and drinking more fluid may help. (Extra fibre makes symptoms worse in some people, but it is worth a try.)
- **If diarrhoea is a main symptom** — reducing tea, coffee, dietary fat (and stopping smoking) may help.
- **Pain and spasm** — tea, coffee, dairy foods, and other foods may trigger these symptoms in some people. Try keeping a food diary. It may be worth cutting out a suspected food for a while.
- **Stress** such as family problems, exams, etc, may trigger symptoms. Some people find relaxation techniques, stress counselling, and similar therapies help to control symptoms.

Drug rationale

- There are no prescriptions offered. People with mild symptoms usually respond to education and reassurance and do not require prescription medication [AGA, 1996].

Prescriptions

Non-drug management

Advice only: symptom management

- All ages
- Irritable bowel syndrome (IBS) Small but frequent meals and a diet low in caffeine and alcohol may help. If constipation is a main symptom then eating more fibre and lots to drink may help. If diarrhoea is a main symptom then reducing tea, coffee and dietary fat (and stopping smoking) may help. Pain and spasm may be caused by dietary 'triggers' such as tea, coffee, and some dairy products. It may be worth keeping a food diary for a couple of weeks and cutting out suspected foods for a while. Stress (e.g. family problems, exams) may also trigger symptoms.

Moderate / severe IBS

Which therapy?

- **Exclude other conditions** such as inflammatory bowel disease, neoplasia, and psychological problems. These may also coexist with IBS and should be treated appropriately.
- **Explain the diagnosis;** reassure that symptoms may be long-lived but are never life threatening, do not indicate further disease, are intermittent, and generally improve with time.
- **Simple dietary advice may be helpful to all sufferers of IBS.**
- **If explanation, reassurance, and dietary advice are not effective, consider drug treatments** according to the symptoms experienced by the individual person.
- **Drug options for:**
  - **Pain and spasm** — antispasmodic medication may give symptom relief.
    - If no response to antispasmodics, consider low dose amitriptyline.
  - **Diarrhoea** — loperamide is effective in reducing stool frequency, and increasing stool consistency.
  - **Constipation** — bulk-forming laxatives may ease symptoms. A high fibre diet helps some people (but bran can make some worse).
- If symptoms are intermittent, dose 'as required' rather than regularly.
- Because antidepressants must be used on a continual rather than an as needed basis, they are generally reserved for people having frequently recurrent or continual symptoms.

Practical prescribing points

For further information please see the *Medicines Compendium* (www.medicines.org.uk) or the *British National Formulary* (www.bnf.org).

Pregnancy and breastfeeding

- Alverine and mebeverine are not recommended, but there is no actual evidence of increased foetal toxicity at normal therapeutic doses.
- If amitriptyline is required throughout pregnancy, it is recommended that the dose be tapered 3–4 weeks prior to delivery to reduce the likelihood of neonatal withdrawal symptoms occurring.
- Telephone the National Teratology Information Service for further information (0191 2321525).

Follow-up advice

- Try treating with appropriate explanation, reassurance, dietary changes, and at least one drug treatment for at least 6 weeks, before classing the condition as resistant to treatment.

Should I refer or investigate?

Refer?

- **If the person has severe or intractable symptoms,** depending on skills within the practice, consider referral for psychotherapy, centrally acting drugs (e.g. antidepressants), or to a pain clinic.
- **Exclude serious alternative diagnoses** — such as neoplasia and inflammatory bowel disease — particularly if there are sinister symptoms or signs.
- **Whether or not this necessitates referral depends on:**
  - Clinical judgement of the individual person's risks (such as age over 45 years at presentation; family history of cancer of colon, breast, ovary, or uterus; new symptoms; failure of standard treatment; sinister symptoms — e.g. rectal bleeding, weight loss, anorexia).
  - Whether or not there is open access to appropriate investigations.
  - The degree of expertise available within the practice.
- **Referral to a dietician may be appropriate,** particularly if exclusion diets are being considered.

Investigate?

Consider the following investigations to exclude other causes of symptoms:

- **Blood tests** — full blood count, erythrocyte sedimentation rate, C-reactive protein, thyroid function, liver function, endomysial autoantibodies (for coeliac disease) — all normal in IBS.
- **Stool examination and culture** (particularly if persistent diarrhoea) — to exclude occult blood, ova and parasites.
- **Sigmoidoscopy** — to exclude inflammation and melanosis coli (laxative abuse).
- **Whether or not to proceed to colonoscopy or barium enema** depends on the individual person's risk (see *referral* above). Specialist advice should be sought at this stage.

Patient information leaflets

The following PILs are available at www.prodigy.nhs.uk

- Barium Enema
- Barium Swallow / Meal / Follow Through
- Biopsy
- Blood Test - Blood Count and Smear
- Blood Test - Detecting Inflammation
- Blood Test - General
- Constipation in Adults
- Eat More Fruit and Vegetables
- Faecal Occult Blood Test
- Fibre in the Diet
- Irritable Bowel Syndrome
- Irritable Bowel Syndrome Network

Shared decision making

- Irritable bowel syndrome is common. Symptoms vary, and flare up from time to time, but often settle for long periods without any treatment.
- **If constipation is a main symptom:**
  - Eating more fibre and drinking more fluid may help. (extra fibre makes symptoms worse in some people, but it is worth a try.)
  - A fibre supplement is an option if the above is not sufficient.
- **If diarrhoea is a main symptom:**
  - Reducing tea, coffee, dietary fat (and stopping smoking) may help.
  - A short courses of loperamide is an option.
- **For pain and spasm:**
  - Tea, coffee, dairy foods, and other foods may trigger these symptoms in some people. Try keeping a food diary. It may be worth cutting out a suspected food for a while.
  - An antispasmodic medicine is an option to take 'as required' when symptoms flare up.
  - An antidepressant is another option. You need to take this regularly. It is used for its pain relieving effect, not to treat depression.
- **Stress** such as family problems, exams, etc, may trigger symptoms. Some people find relaxation techniques, stress counselling, and similar therapies help to control symptoms.

Drug rationale

Drugs not included

For children, dietary changes alone are recommended, as the evidence for drug treatment is even poorer than in adults, and laxatives are more likely to cause dependence in children.

Bulk-forming agents

- **Bran supplements** are no longer included as the only commercially available medicinal product containing bran (Trifyba) has recently been discontinued.

Laxatives

- **Senna and bisacodyl** — there is lack of evidence of their efficacy in IBS, and chronic use of stimulant laxatives should be avoided [Drossman and Thompson, 1992; Pattee and Thompson, 1992].
- **Lactulose** can be sickly, and sometimes exacerbates abdominal distension [Francis and Whorwell, 1997; Maxwell et al, 1997].

Antimotility agents

- **Metoclopramide** does not act on the lower intestine [Drossman and Thompson, 1992].
- **Domperidone** has not been found to be any more effective than placebo in IBS [Fielding, 1982; Farthing, 1998].

Antispasmodics

- **Atropine** is poorly selective with a high potential for anticholinergic adverse effects.
- **Propantheline** is an alternative to hyoscine, but it is not available without a prescription and has not been studied in IBS.

Antidiarrhoeal agents

- **Codeine** is more likely to cause sedation and should not be used long-term because of the risk of dependence.
- **Diphenoxylate** is only prescribable as a combination product with atropine (co-phenotrope) and has not been studied in IBS.
- **Colestyramine** is poorly tolerated, and many people prefer loperamide which is equally effective.

[Pattee and Thompson, 1992]

Antidepressants

- **The role of specific serotonin re-uptake inhibitors** has not yet been evaluated [Francis and Whorwell, 1997; Farthing, 1998].
- **Other tricyclics** have been less well studied than amitriptyline, and have therefore not been included [Lynn and Friedman, 1993; AGA, 1996; Francis and Whorwell, 1997; Farthing, 1998].

Anxiolytics

- These are not recommended because of weak efficacy, potential for dependence, and interaction with other drugs and alcohol [AGA, 1996].

Drugs included

General issues

- Dosing 'as required' rather than regular treatment may be more suitable for those with intermittent symptoms [Francis and Whorwell, 1997].
- Because antidepressants must be used on a continual rather than an as needed basis, they are generally reserved for people having frequently recurrent or continual symptoms [Camilleri, 1999].

Laxatives

- **Bulk-forming laxatives** (e.g. ispaghula — a soluble fibre) are recommended only for people who have a predominant component of constipation. They are generally effective and well tolerated [Francis and Whorwell, 1997].

Antidiarrhoeal agents

- **Loperamide** is effective for treating people with predominantly loose, frequent stools, and urgency of defecation. It reduces stool frequency and urgency, and improves stool consistency [Cann et al, 1984; Lynn and Friedman, 1993; Maxwell et al, 1997; Farthing, 1998].

Antispasmodics

- **Direct intestinal smooth muscle relaxants such as mebeverine or alverine** may be superior to placebo for reducing abdominal pain and spasm. They have some selectivity for smooth intestinal muscle, and relatively few adverse effects [Tudor, 1986; Pittler and Ernst, 1998].

- **Peppermint oil** may be superior to placebo for improving abdominal pain, distension, and stool frequency [Liu et al, 1997]. It is thought to act by causing relaxation of smooth muscle, and has few adverse effects [Pittler and Ernst, 1998].

Antimuscarinics/anticholinergics

- **Dicycloverine (dicyclomine)** is thought to act more selectively on gastrointestinal smooth muscle, and therefore has fewer adverse effects than other antimuscarinics [Lynn and Friedman, 1993].
- **Hyoscine butylbromide** is sometimes helpful, but has the potential for more antimuscarinic adverse effects than dicycloverine [Maxwell et al, 1997].

Antidepressants — (not for treatment of depression)

- Amitriptyline has been better studied in the treatment of pain and spasm in IBS than other tricyclic antidepressant drugs and is offered here [Jailwala et al, 2000; Jones et al, 2000].
- Lower therapeutic doses than for depression are suggested for use for IBS (providing there is no coexisting depression). Nocturnal dosing produces the best response [Jones et al, 2000].

Prescriptions

Non-drug management

Advice only: symptom management
- All ages
- Irritable bowel syndrome (IBS) Small but frequent meals and a diet low in caffeine and alcohol may help. If constipation is a main symptom then eating more fibre and lots to drink may help. If diarrhoea is a main symptom then reducing tea, coffee and dietary fat (and stopping smoking) may help. Pain and spasm may be caused by dietary 'triggers' such as tea, coffee, and some dairy products. It may be worth keeping a food diary for a couple of weeks and cutting out suspected foods for a while. Stress (e.g. family problems, exams) may also trigger symptoms.

Pain & spasm: antispasmodics

Mebeverine 135mg three times a day
- Age from 16 years onwards
- Mebeverine 135mg tablets. Take one tablet three times a day, preferably 20 minutes before meals; supply 168 tablets; NHS Cost £12.77; OTC Cost £40.00.

Alverine 60mg to 120mg up to three times a day
- Age from 16 years onwards
- Alverine 60mg capsules. Take one to two capsules up to three times a day when required; supply 168 capsules; NHS Cost £18.34; OTC Cost £20.00.

Dicycloverine (dicyclomine) 10mg to 20mg three times a day
- Age from 16 years onwards
- Dicycloverine 10mg tablets. Take one to two tablets three times a day; supply 168 tablets; NHS Cost £9.54; OTC Cost £11.36.

Hyoscine butylbromide 20mg four times a day
- Age from 16 years onwards
- Hyoscine butylbromide 10mg tab. Take one tablet three times a day. Increase up to two tablets four times a day if required; supply 448 tablets; NHS Cost £20.72.

Peppermint oil: 1-2 caps three times a day (no peanut oil)
- Age from 16 years onwards
- Peppermint oil 0.2ml capsules. Take one to two capsules three times a day; supply 168 capsules; NHS Cost £21.50; OTC Cost £37.90.

Peppermint oil: 1-2 caps three times a day (with peanut oil)
- Age from 16 years onwards
- Peppermint oil 0.2ml m/r caps. Take one to two capsules three times a day; supply 168 capsules; NHS Cost £18.34; OTC Cost £38.00.

Diarrhoea predominant

Loperamide 2mg to 4mg up to four times a day
- Age from 16 years onwards
- Loperamide 2mg capsules. Take one to two capsules up to four times a day; supply 56 capsules; NHS Cost £3.14; OTC Cost £5.53.

Constipation predominant

Ispaghula 3.5g s/f sachets (Fybogel or Ispagel Orange)
- Age from 16 years onwards
- Ispaghula husk 3.5g s/f granules. Take the contents of one sachet (mixed in a glass of water) each morning and evening; supply 60 sachets; NHS Cost £4.24; OTC Cost £9.30.

Ispaghula 3.4g s/f sachets (Regulan)
- Age from 16 years onwards
- Ispaghula husk 3.4g s/f powder. Take the contents of one sachet (mixed in a glass of water) 1 to 3 times a day; supply 60 sachets; NHS Cost £3.14; OTC Cost £7.50.

Sterculia 62% sachets (Normacol)
- Age from 16 years onwards
- Sterculia 62% granules. Take the contents of one to two sachets, once or twice a day after meals. Wash down with plenty of water without chewing; supply 60 sachets; NHS Cost £5.11; OTC Cost £9.01.

Amitriptyline (not for depression)

Amitriptyline 10mg at night (1-week supply)
- Age from 16 years onwards
- Amitriptyline 10mg tablets. Take one tablet at night; supply 7 tablets; NHS Cost £0.06.

Amitriptyline 25mg at night (4-week supply)
- Age from 16 years onwards
- Amitriptyline 25mg tablets. Take one tablet at night. Increase at weekly intervals if needed to a maximum of 3 tablets in 24 hours; supply 63 tablets; NHS Cost £1.80.

Extended Information

Background information

- What is it? p.1125
- How common is it? p.1126
- How do I know my patient has it? p.1126
- What else might it be? p.1126
- Complications and prognosis p.1126

What is it?

- **Irritable bowel syndrome (IBS) is a chronic, relapsing functional disorder of the gut,** characterised by abdominal pain, abdominal distension, and some abnormality of bowel habit [Francis and Whorwell, 1997; Maxwell et al, 1997].
- **More precise definitions of IBS vary.** Some perceive it to be a grouping together of all unknown causes of abdominal symptoms. Others adhere to criteria such as

the Rome II Criteria for IBS (see *How do I know my patient has it?*), which provide the current standard definition [Thompson, 1998], the Manning criteria, Drossman's consensus, or several other definitions [Maxwell et al, 1997; Kay et al, 1998].

- **The pathophysiology behind IBS is unclear.** Suggestions include gastrointestinal motility abnormalities, smooth muscle abnormalities not specific to the gastrointestinal tract, sensory abnormalities (visceral hypersensitivity), and imbalances in neurotransmitters [Maxwell et al, 1997; Horwitz and Fisher, 2001].
- **Psychosocial factors** are also thought to play a role in the pathology of IBS. The hospital anxiety and depression scale shows higher anxiety scores in hospital attenders with IBS than in controls (40–60% of people with IBS who seek medical help have symptoms of anxiety or depression or both) [Farthing, 1998]. Stressful life events sometimes worsen symptoms, and abnormal illness attitudes (such as hypochondriacal beliefs, disease phobia, bodily preoccupation) are significantly more intense among outpatients with IBS than those who have organic bowel disease, normal controls, and people with depression. Whether psychopathology is a cause or a result of the bowel symptoms is unclear [Maxwell et al, 1997]. It is likely that psychological factors exacerbate and perpetuate IBS symptoms [Francis and Whorwell, 1997].
- **Other theories of causation** include infection (e.g. following gastroenteritis [Neal et al, 1997; Garcia and Ruig¢mez, 1999]), inflammation, diet, antibiotics (leading to overgrowth of *Candida*), post-surgery, and heredity. There is no conclusive evidence as to which of these is truly causal, or the extent to which they may be causal. It is likely that the cause of IBS is multi-factorial [Francis and Whorwell, 1997; Maxwell et al, 1997].

How common is it?

- **The prevalence** in the UK varies from 5–22%, depending on the criteria used [Maxwell et al, 1997].
- **The incidence** over 5 years ranges from 1%–36%, depending on the criteria used [Maxwell et al, 1997].
- **Women are affected more commonly than men** (studies suggest male: female ratio varies from 1:1.1 to 1:2.6) [Francis and Whorwell, 1997; Maxwell et al, 1997; Jones et al, 2000].
- **20–50% of referrals to gastroenterology clinics** are for people ultimately diagnosed with IBS [Maxwell et al, 1997].
- **Most people with IBS do not seek medical advice.** In one study of people with IBS, only 33% had sought medical advice for it during the preceding 2 years [Maxwell et al, 1997]. IBS sufferers with more severe pain, greater concern about the serious nature of symptoms, higher anxiety and depression scores, and more negative life events may be more likely to consult than other IBS sufferers [Kettell et al, 1992].
- **Symptoms consistent with a diagnosis of IBS** have been reported in between 6% of 12–13 year olds and 14% of 15–16 year olds [Hyams et al, 1996].

How do I know my patient has it?

General

- **There are no pathognomonic features** of IBS, therefore it is a diagnosis of exclusion. However, diagnosis does not have to be exclusive — there may be coexisting morbidity, such as inflammatory bowel disease [Maxwell et al, 1997].
- **Children** may be less likely than adults to describe alterations in bowel habit, their pain symptoms being more predominant [McWade, 1992].
- **Examination may be normal,** or may reveal abdominal tenderness and/or distension.
- **Gastrointestinal symptoms** include recurrent abdominal pain, abdominal distension and some degree of disturbed bowel habit.

Rome II criteria

The Rome II criteria for IBS provide the current standard definition:

- **At least 12 weeks, which need not be consecutive, in the preceding 12 months of abdominal discomfort or pain that has two of three features:**
  - Relieved by defaecation
  - Onset associated with a change in frequency of stool
  - Onset associated with a change in form (appearance) of stool
- **The following symptoms cumulatively support the diagnosis of IBS:**
  - Abnormal stool frequency (for research purposes abnormal may be defined as more than 3 stools daily)
  - Abnormal stool form (lumpy/hard or loose/watery stool)
  - Abnormal stool passage (straining, urgency, or feeling of incomplete evacuation)
  - Passage of mucous
  - Bloating or feeling of abdominal distension

[Thompson, 1998]

- **IBS does not cause rectal bleeding.**
- **Non-gastrointestinal symptoms** such as lethargy, poor sleep, fybromyalgia, backache, urinary frequency, and dyspareunia are more frequent in people with IBS, and support the diagnosis [Francis and Whorwell, 1997; Jones et al, 2000].
- **Diagnosis should be confirmed** in general practice by observation over time.

Onset

- **IBS can occur in children,** and many people can trace the onset of their symptoms back to childhood.
- Symptoms begin before the age of 35 years in 50% of people, and 40% of people with IBS are aged from 35–50 years.
- Onset in old age is rare.

[Maxwell et al, 1997]

What else might it be?

- **Always exclude serious causes,** according to the presenting symptoms. Those with presenting features most similar to IBS include:
  - Gastrointestinal neoplasia
  - Inflammatory bowel disease (e.g. Crohn's disease, ulcerative colitis)
  - Malabsorption (e.g. Coeliac disease)
  - Gastrointestinal infection (e.g. giardiasis)
- In addition, many other gastrointestinal disorders (e.g. diverticulosis), gynaecological (e.g. premenstrual syndrome, endometriosis), urological, endocrine (e.g. thyrotoxicosis), and psychological disorders (e.g. anxiety, depression, laxative abuse) can present with similar symptoms to IBS.
- **Symptoms similar to IBS may also present as a somatisation** of psychological disturbance, for example due to sexual and emotional abuse [Talley et al, 1996].

Complications and prognosis

Complications

- Failure to manage symptoms adequately can reduce quality of life, and may lead to social problems and psychiatric morbidity (depression, anxiety).

Prognosis

- **IBS is not life-threatening,** and does not indicate development of serious disease [Maxwell et al, 1997].
- Symptoms are usually long-lived, with periods of exacerbation and remission likely, and generally tend to improve with time [Francis and Whorwell, 1997; Maxwell et al, 1997].
- 40–70% of people will improve with placebo alone [Maxwell et al, 1997].
- 25% of people will have no response to, or even deteriorate despite, appropriate treatment [Francis and Whorwell, 1997].

Management issues

- General issues p.1127
- Simple non-drug treatments p.1127
- Drug treatments p.1127
- Psychological treatments p.1128
- Other treatments p.1128
- Referral p.1129

General issues

- **There is no easy treatment or cure for IBS.**
- The appropriate treatment depends on the symptoms experienced by the individual (i.e. whether constipation, diarrhoea, pain, or spasms are the predominant symptom), and should be tailored accordingly.
- **It is important to exclude serious alternative diagnoses.** Whether or not this necessitates referral depends on clinical judgement.
- **Management tends to be approached by considering either:**
  - **End-organ treatment** — aimed at relieving specific symptoms (diet, laxatives, antidiarrhoeals, and antispasmodics), or
  - **Central treatments** — aimed at modifying pain pathways in the CNS (counselling, psychotherapy, hypnotherapy, cognitive therapy, antidepressants)
  - The choice between these two treatments depends upon the preferences of the individual clinician. However, the 2 approaches are not mutually exclusive [Farthing, 1998].

Simple non-drug treatments

Explanation and reassurance

- **The most important part of management is explanation of the diagnosis, with reassurance** that although symptoms may be long-lived, they do not indicate the development of further disease, are paroxysmal (with periods of exacerbation and remission likely), and generally tend to improve with time [Francis and Whorwell, 1997; Maxwell et al, 1997].
- **Finding out why the person is presenting at this moment in time** may provide useful clues regarding exacerbating factors, psychiatric comorbidity, and anxieties the person may have about the symptoms [Drossman and Thompson, 1992].

Diet and lifestyle

- **Simple dietary advice** such as correcting excesses of caffeine and alcohol may be helpful to all sufferers of IBS. A balanced, healthy diet taken as small, regular meals is recommended. Some people may benefit from an increase in dietary fibre, whilst others may benefit from a reduction [British Society for Gastroenterology, 1998].
- **Triggers to symptoms may be identifiable** in some people (e.g. lactose, dairy products, high-fat foods, rich or spicy foods, bread and cereals) in which case a therapeutic trial of withholding that food could be tried, although the extent to which any benefits are placebo-effect is unclear [Maxwell et al, 1997; Farthing, 1998]. Strict exclusion diets, however, have low success rates in the majority of people, should be supervised by a dietician, and can be difficult for the individual [Thompson, 1998].
- **Constipation** may respond to increased intake of a range of dietary fibres (e.g. cereals, grain, fruits and vegetables) and an increase in fluid intake. Wheat bran has been shown to increase stool weight and decrease gut transit time. However, some people with IBS are intolerant of bran and experience a worsening of symptoms, notably wind, distension, and pain. Diet should therefore be tailored to the individual [Farthing, 1998]. The recommended daily fibre intake, regardless of whether IBS is present or not, is 20–35 grams per day [Hwang, 1999]. Fibre supplements may be helpful initially [Jones et al, 2000].
- **Diarrhoea** may respond to a reduction in dietary fat, tea, and coffee intake, and reduced cigarette smoking.
- **Pain and spasm** may respond to a reduction in tea and coffee intake.

[Maxwell et al, 1997]

Drug treatments

- **People with mild symptoms usually respond to education and reassurance and do not require prescription medication** [AGA, 1996].
- **The role of drugs in IBS is not curative;** their aim is to counteract specific symptoms when non-drug treatments have failed [Thompson, 1998].
- Poor trial design, lack of definitive diagnosis, and a high placebo response contribute to the poor evidence base for IBS treatments. Current drug treatments are of limited value, but specific symptoms may respond to targeted treatment [Jones et al, 2000; MeReC, 2000].
- **Most drugs used to treat IBS are not studied specifically for this condition,** and where they are, the effect tends to be only slightly greater than the placebo effect of up to 70%. This, together with the adverse effect profile of the drug, should be considered when deciding whether or not to initiate treatment [Francis and Whorwell, 1997; Thompson, 1998].
- **Dosing 'as required'** rather than regular treatment may be more suitable for those with intermittent symptoms [Francis and Whorwell, 1997].
- **For children,** dietary changes alone are recommended, as the evidence for drug treatment is even poorer than in adults, and laxatives are more likely to cause dependence in children [NIDDKD, 2003].

Laxatives

- **Bulk-forming laxatives (e.g. ispaghula)** are recommended only for people who have a predominant component of constipation. Although proven as laxatives in the general population, there is a lack of evidence regarding their efficacy in IBS [Jailwala et al, 2000].
- **Bran may cause distension and worsen pain** when used indiscriminately, with up to 55% of people with IBS who take bran experiencing worse rather than improved symptoms [Francis and Whorwell, 1994].
- **Ispaghula is less likely than bran to cause these adverse effects** [Heaton, 1997; Farthing, 1998].
- **Lactulose is sometimes effective,** although has a sickly taste, and may exacerbate abdominal distension [Francis and Whorwell, 1997; Maxwell et al, 1997].

- There is a lack of evidence for the efficacy of stimulant laxatives in the treatment of IBS and their chronic use should be discouraged [Drossman and Thompson, 1992; Pattee and Thompson, 1992].

Antidiarrhoeal agents

- **Loperamide** slows small and large intestinal transit, reduces stool frequency and urgency, and improves stool consistency in people with IBS who have a predominant component of diarrhoea [Farthing, 1998; Jailwala et al, 2000; Jones et al, 2000]. No consistent improvement in abdominal pain and distension has been shown with loperamide [Jailwala et al, 2000].
- **The dose required varies considerably** between people and 'as required' use may be appropriate [Francis and Whorwell, 1997; Maxwell et al, 1997].
- **Other antimotility drugs** include codeine phosphate and diphenoxylate [Francis and Whorwell, 1997; Maxwell et al, 1997].
- **Colestyramine** is effective in treating bile salt induced diarrhoea. About 10% of people with diarrhoea predominant IBS have evidence of bile salt malabsorption, and may respond to colestyramine. It is, however, poorly tolerated, and many people prefer loperamide which is equally effective [Jailwala et al, 2000].

Antispasmodics

- **Smooth muscle relaxants** were shown to be superior to placebo in a recent meta-analysis, especially in reducing abdominal pain [Jailwala et al, 2000; Poynard et al, 2001].
- **Direct acting smooth muscle relaxants such as mebeverine and alverine** have some selectivity for smooth intestinal muscle and have relatively few adverse effects.
- **Antimuscarinics such as hyoscine and dicycloverine (dicyclomine)** are sometimes helpful, but are poorly selective and have potential for anticholinergic adverse effects.
- **Peppermint oil** is a common component of over-the-counter preparations for IBS, and is thought to act by causing relaxation of smooth muscle. It is thought to be effective in improving symptoms of abdominal pain, distension, and stool frequency [Liu et al, 1997], although more high quality randomised studies are needed [Pittler and Ernst, 1998].
- **There is no consensus on duration of treatment** with antispasmodics, although the majority of studies published seem to use used trials of one month [Tudor, 1986; Liu et al, 1997; Poynard et al, 2001] .

Antidepressants

- **Tricyclic antidepressants** are now frequently used to treat people with diarrhoea and pain-predominant IBS, particularly those with more severe or refractory symptoms [Camilleri, 1999; Jones et al, 2000].
- **Tricyclic antidepressants** may help to relieve pain and spasm via activity independent of their antidepressant effect. In addition, their antidiarrhoeal properties may be of benefit to some people [Francis and Whorwell, 1997; Maxwell et al, 1997].
- **A recent meta-analysis suggests that tricyclic and related antidepressants produce improvements** in abdominal pain and diarrhoea and in global symptoms in people with IBS [Jackson et al, 2000; Jailwala et al, 2000] although evidence is inconclusive.
- **Lower therapeutic doses than for depression** are suggested for use for IBS (providing there is no coexisting depression) with an effect on pain occurring at 1–7 days [Farthing, 1998]. Nocturnal dosing produces the best response [Jones et al, 2000].
- Because antidepressants must be used on a continual rather than an as needed basis, they are generally reserved for people having frequently recurrent or continual symptoms [Camilleri, 1999].
- **The role of specific serotonin re-uptake inhibitors** has not yet been evaluated.
- **Anxiolytics** are not recommended because of weak efficacy, potential for dependence, and interaction with other drugs and alcohol [AGA, 1996].

Psychological treatments

- **Psychotherapy (dynamic), cognitive therapy, and hypnotherapy** have been shown to be of benefit in some clinical trials of IBS [Farthing, 1998], although methodological inaccuracies in many trials mean that the degree of efficacy has not yet been established [Talley et al, 1996]. There is also a lack of comparative data to determine which treatments are most effective [AGA, 1996].
- **Limits on resources** usually mean that the more time-consuming techniques should be restricted to the most difficult cases, when symptoms are resistant to treatment, or symptoms are severe enough to impair quality of life [AGA, 1996]; and to those most likely to benefit substantially [Jones et al, 2000].
- **In people without marked psychiatric abnormalities,** relaxation therapy, biofeedback, and hypnotherapy may be considered. In people with marked psychiatric illness, cognitive behavioural therapy, dynamic psychotherapy, and psychiatric referral may be more appropriate [Jones et al, 2000].
- **Relaxation therapy**
  - May be useful for those suffering from stress and anxiety.
  - Can be easily taught through audiotapes.
- **Biofeedback**
  - Involves measurement and explanation of normal physiology so the person becomes more aware of rectal sensations and avoids inappropriate straining.
  - Has been used most commonly for treating incontinence and constipation.
- **Hypnotherapy**
  - Is used to induce a state of relaxation with the ultimate aim of enabling people to control symptoms on their own.
  - Is time-consuming and expensive, but may be cost effective in severe refractory cases.
- **Cognitive behaviour therapy**
  - Teaches people to recognise the association between their symptoms and the way they respond to life events.
  - Then focuses treatment on identifying and solving their problems.
- **Dynamic psychotherapy**
  - Attempts to relate particular symptoms to significant life changes.
  - May be useful for improving symptoms of abdominal pain and altered bowel habit, particularly in women and people with overt psychiatric symptoms or stress-related pain.

Other treatments

- **Transcutaneous nerve stimulation** may be effective in treating the pain of IBS, although usually has no effect on other symptoms.
- **Chinese herbal medicine** has been shown to significantly improve bowel symptoms and global symptoms, with no loss of effect 14 weeks after completion of treatment [Bensoussan et al, 1998].

Referral

- **If symptoms are constant, more severe, there is poor response to standard treatment, or the person requires further reassurance,** referral for specialist opinion is appropriate [Francis and Whorwell, 1997]. Any change of symptoms should be re-evaluated [Thompson, 1998].
- **People with atypical symptoms, or symptoms and signs suggesting high risk of neoplasia** (such as age over 45 years at presentation; family history of cancer of colon, breast, ovary, or uterus; new symptoms; sinister symptoms — e.g. rectal bleeding, weight loss, anorexia) should always be referred [Francis and Whorwell, 1997].
- **In secondary care, further investigations** such as barium enemas and sigmoidoscopy are considered, and more specialist treatments such as exclusion diets, hypnotherapy, psychotherapy, transcutaneous nerve stimulation, and use of tricyclic antidepressants may be tried [Francis and Whorwell, 1997]. Some specialist centres, where available, may carry out motility and visceral sensitivity testing to help clarify the diagnosis [Francis and Whorwell, 1997].

References

NHS staff in England can link, free of charge, from references to full text journals by clicking on [Full text] on the PRODIGY website.

1. AGA (1996) *Irritable bowel syndrome.* Bethesda, MD: American Gastroenterological Association.
2. Bensoussan, A., Talley, N.J., Hing, M. et al (1998) Treatment of irritable bowel syndrome with Chinese herbal medicine: a randomized controlled trial. *Journal of the American Medical Association* **280**(18), 1585–1589. [Full text]
3. Camilleri, M. (1999) Therapeutic approach to the patient with irritable bowel syndrome. *American Journal of Medicine* **107**(5A), 27S-32S.
4. Cann, P.A., Read, N.W., Holdsworth, C.D. and Barends, D. (1984) Role of loperamide and placebo in management of irritable bowel syndrome (IBS). *Digestive Diseases & Sciences* **29**(3), 239–247.
5. Drossman, D.A. and Thompson, W.G. (1992) The irritable bowel syndrome: review and a graduated multicomponent treatment approach. *Annals of Internal Medicine* **116**(12 Pt 1), 1009–1016.
6. Farthing, M.J.G. (1998) New drugs in the management of the irritable bowel syndrome. *Drugs* **56**(1), 11–21.
7. Fielding, J.F. (1982) Domperidone treatment in the irritable bowel syndrome. *Digestion* **23**(2), 125–127.
8. Francis, C.Y. and Whorwell, P.J. (1994) Bran and irritable bowel syndrome: time for reappraisal. *Lancet* **344**(8914), 39–40. [Full text]
9. Francis, C.Y. and Whorwell, P.J. (1997) The irritable bowel syndrome. *Postgraduate Medical Journal* **73**(855), 1–7.
10. Garcia, L.A. and Ruig¢mez, A. (1999) Increased risk of irritable bowel syndrome after bacterial gastroenteritis: cohort study. *British Medical Journal* **318**(7183), 565–566. [Full text]
11. Heaton, K.W. (1997) Irritable bowel syndrome. *Prescribers' Journal* **37**(4), 199–205.
12. Horwitz, B.J. and Fisher, R.S. (2001) The irritable bowel syndrome. *New England Journal of Medicine* **344**(24), 1846–1850. [Full text]
13. Hyams, J.S., Burke, G., Davis, P.M. et al (1996) Abdominal pain and irritable bowel syndrome in adolescents: a community-based study. *Journal of Pediatrics* **129**(2), 220–226.
14. Jackson, J.L., O'Malley, P.G., Tomkins, G. et al (2000) Treatment of functional gastrointestinal disorders with antidepressant medications: a meta-analysis. *American Journal of Medicine* **108**(1), 65–72.
15. Jailwala, J., Imperiale, T.F. and Kroenke, K. (2000) Pharmacologic treatment of the irritable bowel syndrome: a systematic review of randomized, controlled trials. *Annals of Internal Medicine* **133**(2), 136–147.
16. Jones, J., Boorman, J., Cann, P. et al (2000) *British Society of Gastroenterology guidelines for the management of the irritable bowel syndrome.* British Society of Gastroenterology. www.bsg.org.uk [Accessed: 12/05/2005].
17. Kay, L., Jorgensen, T. and Lanng, C. (1998) Irritable bowel syndrome: which definitions are consistent? *Journal of Internal Medicine* **244**(6), 489–494.
18. Kettell, J., Jones, R. and Lydeard, S. (1992) Reasons for consultation in irritable bowel syndrome: symptoms and patient characteristics. *British Journal of General Practice* **42**(364), 459–461.
19. Liu, J.H., Chen, G.H., Yeh, H.Z. et al (1997) Enteric-coated peppermint-oil capsules in the treatment of irritable bowel syndrome: a prospective, randomized trial. *Journal of Gastroenterology* **32**(6), 765–768.
20. Lynn, R.B. and Friedman, L.S. (1993) Irritable bowel syndrome. *New England Journal of Medicine* **329**(26), 1940–1945.
21. Maxwell, P.R., Mendall, M.A. and Kumar, D. (1997) Irritable bowel syndrome. *Lancet* **350**(9092), 1691–1695. [Full text]
22. McWade, L.J. (1992) Irritable bowel syndrome: diagnosis and management in school-aged children and adolescents. *Journal of Pediatric Health Care* **6**(2), 82–83.
23. MeReC (2000) Irritable bowel syndrome. *MeReC Bulletin* **11**(11), 41–44.
24. Neal, K.R., Hebden, J. and Spiller, R. (1997) Prevalence of gastointestional symptoms six months after bacterial gastroenteritis and risk factors for developement of the irritable bowel syndrome: postal survey of patients. *British Medical Journal* **314**(7083), 779–782. [Full text]
25. NIDDKD (2003) *Irritable bowel syndrome in children.* National Institute of Diabetes and Digestive and Kidney Diseases. http://digestive.niddk.nih.gov [Accessed: 29/06/2005].
26. Pattee, P.L. and Thompson, W.G. (1992) Drug treatment of the irritable bowel syndrome. *Drugs* **44**(2), 200–206.
27. Pittler, M.H. and Ernst, E. (1998) Peppermint oil for irritable bowel syndrome: a critical review and metaanalysis. *American Journal of Gastroenterology* **93**(7), 1131–1135.
28. Poynard, T., Regimbeau, C. and Benhamou, Y. (2001) Meta-analysis of smooth muscle relaxants in the treatment of irritable bowel syndrome. *Alimentary Pharmacology & Therapeutics* **15**(3), 355–361.
29. Talley, N.J., Owen, B.K., Boyce, P. and Paterson, K. (1996) Psychological treatments for irritable bowel syndrome: a critique of controlled treatment trials. *American Journal of Gastroenterology* **91**(2), 277–283.
30. Thompson, D.G. (1998) Irritable bowel syndrome. *Medicine* **26**(9), 102–104.
31. Tudor, G.J. (1986) A general practice study to compare alverine citrate with mebeverine hydrochloride in the treatment of irritable bowel syndrome. *British Journal of Clinical Practice* **40**(7), 276–278.

PRODIGY GUIDANCE

Lacerations

Last revised in September 2004
www.prodigy.nhs.uk/guidance.asp?gt=Lacerations

Applies to people of all ages

This guidance covers minor lacerations and abrasions.

This guidance does not include detailed guidance on local anaesthesia or suturing of wounds.

There is separate PRODIGY guidance for *Bites — human & animal* and *Burns and scalds.*

Goals

- To offer immediate first aid
- To reduce risk of infection
- To treat any established infection
- To achieve satisfactory wound healing with good cosmetic outcome
- To prevent tetanus

Contents

Scenarios
- Clean and not infected p.1130
- Contaminated but not infected p.1132
- Infected p.1135

Extended Information, p. 1139

L

Which scenario?

- **Clean and not infected:** covers the management of lacerations that are not dirty, contaminated, or infected.
- **Contaminated but not infected:** covers the management of lacerations that are at higher risk of infection, particularly puncture wounds; wounds with a significant degree of devitalized tissue; and wounds contaminated with soil, manure, or faeces.
- **Infected:** covers the management of lacerations that show signs of infection (usually late presentations).

Clean and not infected

Which therapy?

General

- **Apply pressure** to control bleeding.
- **Establish** when and how the injury occurred, and the likelihood of a penetrating foreign body (which will require exploration).
- **Examine** for damage to the arteries, nerves, muscles, and tendons.
- **Irrigate thoroughly** with sodium chloride 0.9% or tap water, using a 30–60 ml syringe, to clean the wound. Gravel grazes need to be carefully cleaned to prevent permanent tattooing of the skin.
- **Close wounds** as soon as possible. Clean wounds can be closed up to 24 hours after the injury. Consider delayed closure after 3–5 days for people in whom antibiotic prophylaxis should be considered (see below).
  - **Suturing** is generally required for lacerations that involve the dermal layer (full thickness).
  - **Sterile skin-closure strips** can be applied to 'v'-flap lacerations on thin skin on the legs in the elderly and in some lacerations in children.
  - **Tissue adhesives** are an alternative to sutures for clean, simple wounds.
- **Cover sutures** with a sterile, non-adherent dressing to protect the wound.
- **Give paracetamol or ibuprofen** for pain relief.
- **Check tetanus immunization status** and give vaccine where appropriate (see section *Tetanus prophylaxis*).

Antibiotic prophylaxis

- **Antibiotics are not usually required** for simple, clean lacerations in healthy people.
- **Consider antibiotic prophylaxis for:**
  - Wounds that are extensive intra-oral lacerations, wounds to the feet, or stellate lesions.
  - People with diabetes mellitus, alcohol dependency, peripheral vascular disease, asplenism, or immunosuppression, including those on oral corticosteroids or chemotherapy.
- **Flucloxacillin or erythromycin** (for penicillin-allergic people) are suitable first-line choices for simple lacerations in people who require antibiotic prophylaxis. If the person is known not to tolerate erythromycin because of adverse effects, consider giving clarithromycin as an alternative.
- **For advice on antibiotic prophylaxis** for wounds with a significant degree of devitalized tissue; puncture wounds; or wounds contaminated with soil, manure, or faeces, see scenario *Contaminated but not infected.*

Practical prescribing points

For further information, please see the *Medicines Compendium* (www.medicines.org.uk) or the *British National Formulary* (www.bnf.org).

- **Ibuprofen:** may cause gastrointestinal irritation and occasionally gastrointestinal haemorrhage. Avoid if there is a history of peptic ulceration. May worsen asthma, hypertension, renal impairment, or cardiac failure.
- **Tissue adhesives should not be used on** joints, hands, feet, lips, mucosa, infected wounds, puncture wounds, bite wounds, or stellate wounds.
- **Tetanus immunoglobulin:** the Blood Transfusion Service distributes tetanus immunoglobulin to general practitioners on demand.

Follow-up advice

- **Advise the person to keep the wound dry** for the first 3 days and to return if the wound becomes infected (e.g. if they notice signs any erythema, warmth, swelling, or drainage).
- **Advise** on future safety measures, and provide education about the importance of thoroughly cleaning wounds and managing simple cuts at home.
- **Remove sutures** of the face after 3–5 days, of joints after 10–14 days, and of other sites after 7–10 days.

Should I refer or investigate?

Refer?

- **Referral** to accident and emergency/plastic surgery is usually indicated for:
  - Lacerations involving arteries, nerves, muscles, tendons, or bones
  - Facial lacerations (excluding very minor cuts)
  - Lip lacerations, particularly if the vermilion border is breached
  - Lacerations requiring complicated sutures
  - Suspected penetrating foreign body (e.g. glass/metal), for exploration under anaesthetic
  - Devitalized wounds where debridement is required

Patient information leaflets

The following PILs are available at www.prodigy.nhs.uk

- Cuts (Lacerations)
- Tetanus Immunisation

Shared decision making

- How did this injury happen? Can any changes be made to prevent this happening again?
- **Wounds must be cleaned thoroughly.** (You can do this with tap water at home for any future small cuts that do not need medical attention.)
- **Keep the repaired wound dry for 3 days.**
- If you have stitches they normally need removing:
  - After 3–5 days for facial wounds.
  - After 10–14 days for joint wounds.
  - After 7–10 days for other sites.
- **Paracetamol** or **ibuprofen** will help to ease pain.
- **Are you up-to-date with tetanus immunizations?**
- Come back if the wound area becomes more tender, swollen, or red.
- High-factor sunscreen used for 6–12 months on healing wounds that are exposed to sunshine may prevent unwanted permanent colour changes to the skin.

Drug rationale

Drugs not included

- **Oral antibiotics other than flucloxacillin and erythromycin,** are not included. As they are generally either less active against the bacteria that commonly cause wound infections, or more expensive, or both.
- **Topical antibiotics** are not effective in the treatment of lacerations [DTB, 1991].

Drugs included

- **Paracetamol** is included for simple analgesia.
- **Ibuprofen** is included as an alternative to paracetamol for analgesia.
- **Non-adherent dressings** protect the wound after suturing.
- **When tetanus vaccination is indicated** (see section *Tetanus prophylaxis* [DH, 2004]:
  - Children aged under 10 years: DTaP/IPV/Hib (combined diphtheria, tetanus, acellular pertussis, inactivated poliomyelitis, and *Haemophilus influenzae* type b vaccine) is recommended for primary immunization. dTaP/IPV (combined low-dose diphtheria, tetanus, acellular pertussis, and inactivated poliomyelitis vaccine) is recommended for booster doses.
  - People aged 10 years or over: Td/IPV (combined low-dose diphtheria, tetanus, and inactivated poliomyelitis vaccine) is recommended for both primary immunizations and booster doses.
- **When antibiotics are indicated** (see *Which therapy?*):
  - **Flucloxacillin** is included as it is active against the bacteria that commonly cause wound infections (e.g. *Staphylococcus aureus* and Group A streptococcus).
  - **Erythromycin** is also active against these bacteria and is a suitable alternative to flucloxacillin for people who are allergic to penicillin. If the person is known not to tolerate erythromycin because of its adverse effects, consider giving clarithromycin as an alternative.

Prescriptions

Analgesia: use when required

Paracetamol s/f susp: 60mg to 120mg up to four times a day

- Age from 3 to 11 months
- Paracetamol 120mg/5ml s/f susp. Take 2.5ml to 5ml every 4 to 6 hours when required for pain relief. Maximum of 4 doses in 24 hours; supply 150 ml; NHS Cost £0.65; OTC Cost £1.14.

Paracetamol s/f susp: 120mg to 240mg up to four times a day

- Age from 12 months to 5 years
- Paracetamol 120mg/5ml s/f susp. Take one to two 5ml spoonfuls every 4 to 6 hours when required for pain relief. Maximum of 4 doses in 24 hours; supply 300 ml; NHS Cost £1.30; OTC Cost £2.28.

Paracetamol s/f susp: 250mg to 500mg up to four times a day

- Age from 6 to 11 years
- Paracetamol 250mg/5ml s/f susp. Take one to two 5ml spoonfuls every 4 to 6 hours when required for pain relief. Maximum of 4 doses in 24 hours; supply 300 ml; NHS Cost £1.70; OTC Cost £2.99.

Paracetamol tablets: 500mg to 1g up to four times a day

- Age from 12 to 15 years
- Paracetamol 500mg tablets. Take one to two tablets every 4 to 6 hours when required for pain relief. Maximum of 8 tablets in 24 hours; supply 100 tablets; NHS Cost £0.75; OTC Cost £1.32.

Paracetamol tablets: 1g up to four times a day

- Age from 16 years onwards
- Paracetamol 500mg tablets. Take two tablets every 4 to 6 hours when required for pain relief. Maximum of 8 tablets in 24 hours; supply 100 tablets; NHS Cost £0.75; OTC Cost £1.32.

Ibuprofen s/f susp: 50mg three to four times a day

- Age from 12 months to 2 years
- Ibuprofen 100mg/5ml s/f susp. Take 2.5ml three to four times a day when required for pain relief. Do not exceed the stated dose; supply 100 ml; NHS Cost £1.82; OTC Cost £3.21.

Ibuprofen s/f susp: 100mg three to four times a day

- Age from 3 to 7 years
- Ibuprofen 100mg/5ml s/f susp. Take one 5ml spoonful 3 to 4 times a day when required for pain relief. Do not exceed the stated dose; supply 150 ml; NHS Cost £2.73; OTC Cost £4.81.

Ibuprofen s/f susp: 200mg three to four times a day

- Age from 8 to 11 years
- Ibuprofen 100mg/5ml s/f susp. Take two 5ml spoonfuls 3 to 4 times a day when required for pain relief. Do not exceed the stated dose; supply 300 ml; NHS Cost £5.46; OTC Cost £9.62.

Ibuprofen tablets: 400mg three times a day
- Age from 12 years onwards
- Ibuprofen 400mg tablets. Take one tablet three times a day when required for pain relief. Do not exceed the stated dose; supply 24 tablets; NHS Cost £0.70; OTC Cost £1.23.

Antibiotics (IF indicated): flucloxacillin for 5 days

Flucloxacillin syrup: 62.5mg four times a day
- Age from 1 month to 11 months
- Flucloxacillin 125mg/5ml syrup. Take 2.5ml four times a day for 5 days; supply 100 ml; NHS Cost £3.49.

Flucloxacillin syrup: 125mg four times a day
- Age from 12 months to 4 years
- Flucloxacillin 125mg/5ml syrup. Take one 5ml spoonful four times a day for 5 days; supply 100 ml; NHS Cost £3.49.

Flucloxacillin syrup: 250mg four times a day
- Age from 5 to 11 years
- Flucloxacillin 250mg/5ml syrup. Take one 5ml spoonful four times a day for 5 days; supply 100 ml; NHS Cost £6.97.

Flucloxacillin capsules: 250mg four times a day
- Age from 12 years onwards
- Flucloxacillin 250mg capsules. Take one capsule four times a day for 5 days; supply 20 capsules; NHS Cost £2.09.

Flucloxacillin capsules: 500mg four times a day
- Age from 12 years onwards
- Flucloxacillin 500mg capsules. Take one capsule four times a day for 5 days; supply 20 capsules; NHS Cost £3.38.

Penicillin allergy: erythromycin for 5 days

Erythromycin s/f suspension: 125mg four times a day
- Age from 1 month to 23 months
- Erythromycin 125mg/5ml sf susp. Take one 5ml spoonful four times a day for 5 days; supply 100 ml; NHS Cost £1.12.

Erythromycin s/f suspension: 250mg four times a day
- Age from 2 to 11 years
- Erythromycin 250mg/5ml sf susp. Take one 5ml spoonful four times a day for 5 days; supply 100 ml; NHS Cost £1.84.

Erythromycin s/f suspension: 500mg four times a day
- Age from 9 to 11 years
- Erythromycin 500mg/5ml sf susp. Take one 5ml spoonful four times a day for 5 days; supply 100 ml; NHS Cost £2.86.

Erythromycin e/c tablets: 250mg four times a day
- Age from 12 years onwards
- Erythromycin 250mg e/c tablets. Take one tablet four times a day for 5 days; supply 20 tablets; NHS Cost £2.20.

Erythromycin e/c tablets: 500mg four times a day
- Age from 12 years onwards
- Erythromycin 250mg e/c tablets. Take two tablets four times a day for 5 days; supply 40 tablets; NHS Cost £4.40.

Erythromycin intolerant: clarithromycin for 5 days

Clarithromycin suspension: 62.5mg twice a day
- Age from 12 months to 2 years
- Clarithromycin 125mg/5ml susp. Take 2.5ml twice a day for 5 days; supply 70 ml; NHS Cost £6.00.

Clarithromycin suspension: 125mg twice a day
- Age from 3 to 6 years
- Clarithromycin 125mg/5ml susp. Take one 5ml spoonful twice a day for 5 days; supply 70 ml; NHS Cost £6.00.

Clarithromycin suspension: 187.5mg twice a day
- Age from 7 to 9 years
- Clarithromycin 125mg/5ml susp. Take 7.5ml twice a day for 5 days; supply 100 ml; NHS Cost £10.32.

Clarithromycin suspension: 250mg twice a day
- Age from 10 to 11 years
- Clarithromycin 250mg/5ml susp. Take one 5ml spoonful twice a day for 5 days; supply 70 ml; NHS Cost £12.00.

Clarithromycin tablets: 250mg twice a day
- Age from 12 years onwards
- Clarithromycin 250mg tablets. Take one tablet twice a day for 5 days; supply 10 tablets; NHS Cost £8.03.

Dressings and tetanus prophylaxis

5cm x 5cm Absorbent perforated plastic film faced dressing
- All ages
- Perforated FA 5x5cm dressing. Apply to the affected area as directed; supply 5 single dressings; NHS Cost £0.45; OTC Cost £0.80.

10cm x 10cm Absorbent perforated plastic film faced dressing
- All ages
- Perforated FA 10x10cm dressing. Apply to the affected area as directed; supply 5 single dressings; NHS Cost £0.75; OTC Cost £1.32.

20cm x 10cm Absorbent perforated plastic film faced dressing
- All ages
- Perforated FA 10x20cm dressing. Apply to the affected area as directed; supply 5 single dressings; NHS Cost £1.60; OTC Cost £2.82.

Permeable non-woven synthetic adhesive tape
- All ages
- Perm non-wvn tape 1.25cmx5m. Apply as required; supply 1 5metre roll; NHS Cost £0.35; OTC Cost £0.69.

Primary course: diphtheria+tetanus+pertussis+polio+Hib
- Age from 2 months to 9 years
- Pediacel injection. Give 0.5ml by intramuscular injection. For primary immunization, give three doses at intervals of 1 month between doses; supply 1 0.5ml vial.

Booster: low-dose diphtheria+tetanus+pertussis+polio
- Age from 3 to 9 years
- Repevax injection. Give 0.5ml by intramuscular injection; supply 1 0.5ml prefilled syringe.

Primary course: low-dose diphtheria+tetanus+polio
- Age from 10 years onwards
- Revaxis injection. Give 0.5ml by intramuscular injection. For primary immunization, give three doses at intervals of 1 month between doses; supply 1 0.5ml prefilled syringe.

Booster: low-dose diphtheria+tetanus+polio
- Age from 10 years onwards
- Revaxis injection. Give 0.5ml by intramuscular injection; supply 1 0.5ml prefilled syringe.

Contaminated but not infected

Which therapy?

General

- **Apply pressure** to control bleeding.
- **Establish** when and how the injury occurred, and the likelihood of a penetrating foreign body (which will require exploration).
- **Examine** for damage to the arteries, nerves, muscles, and tendons.

- **Irrigate thoroughly** with sodium chloride 0.9% or tap water, using a 30–60 ml syringe, to clean the wound. Gravel grazes need to be carefully cleaned to prevent permanent tattooing of the skin.
- **Do not close** wounds contaminated with soil, manure, faeces, saliva, or vaginal secretions, or wounds that are clinically infected. Do not close other contaminated wounds that are more than 6 hours old. Consider delayed closure after 3–5 days if there is no evidence of infection.
  - **Suturing** is generally required in lacerations that involve the dermal layer (full thickness).
  - **Sterile skin-closure strips** can be applied to 'v'-flap lacerations on thin skin on legs in the elderly and in some lacerations in children.
- **Cover sutures** with a sterile, non-adherent dressing to protect the wound.
- **Give paracetamol or ibuprofen** for pain relief.
- **Check tetanus immunization status** and give vaccine or immunoglobulin where appropriate (see section *Tetanus prophylaxis*).

Antibiotic prophylaxis

- **Antibiotics are not usually required** for simple lacerations in healthy people, even if they are contaminated.
- **Consider antibiotic prophylaxis for:**
  - Wounds that have a significant degree of devitalized tissue; puncture wounds; or wounds that are contaminated with soil, manure, or faeces.
  - People with diabetes mellitus, alcohol dependency, peripheral vascular disease, asplenism, or immunosuppression, including those on oral corticosteroids or chemotherapy.
- **Co-amoxiclav, or erythromycin plus metronidazole** (for penicillin-sensitive people) are suitable first-line choices for contaminated wounds. If the person is known not to tolerate erythromycin because of adverse effects, consider giving clarithromycin plus metronidazole as an alternative.

Practical prescribing points

For further information, please see the *Medicines Compendium* (www.medicines.org.uk) or the *British National Formulary* (www.bnf.org).

- **Ibuprofen:** may cause gastrointestinal irritation and occasionally gastrointestinal haemorrhage. Avoid if there is a history of peptic ulceration. May worsen asthma, hypertension, renal impairment, or cardiac failure.
- **Tetanus immunoglobulin:** the Blood Transfusion Service distributes tetanus immunoglobulin to general practitioners on demand.

Follow-up advice

- **Advise the person to keep the wound dry** for the first 3 days and to return if the wound becomes infected (e.g. if the person notices any erythema, warmth, swelling, or drainage).
- **Advise** on future safety measures, and provide education about the importance of thoroughly cleaning wounds and managing simple cuts at home.
- **Remove sutures** of the face after 3–5 days, of joints after 10–14 days, and of other sites after 7–10 days.

Should I refer or investigate?

Refer?

- **Referral** to accident and emergency/plastic surgery is usually indicated for:
  - Lacerations involving arteries, nerves, muscles, tendons, or bones
  - Facial lacerations (excluding very minor cuts)
  - Lip lacerations, particularly if the vermilion border is breached
  - Lacerations requiring complicated sutures
  - Suspected penetrating foreign body (e.g. glass/metal) for exploration under anaesthetic
  - Devitalized wounds where debridement is required

Investigate?

- **Routine swabbing** of wounds is not recommended. However, sending swabs for sensitivities should be considered for infected wounds and for heavily contaminated wounds.
- **Therapy** should be reviewed according to the results.
- **Swabs** should be taken if there is no response to initial treatment.

Patient information leaflets

The following PILs are available at www.prodigy.nhs.uk

- Cuts (Lacerations)
- Tetanus Immunisation

Shared decision making

- How did this injury happen? Can any changes be made to prevent this happening again?
- **Wounds must be cleaned thoroughly.** (You can do this with tap water at home for any future small cuts that do not need medical attention.)
- If you have stitches, they normally need removing:
  - After 3–5 days for facial wounds.
  - After 10–14 days for joint wounds.
  - After 7–10 days for other sites.
- **Antibiotics** to prevent infection may be advised in certain situations.
- **Paracetamol** or **ibuprofen** will help to ease any pain.
- **Are you up-to-date with tetanus immunizations?**
- Come back if the wound area becomes more tender, swollen, or red.
- High-factor sunscreen used for 6–12 months on healing wounds that are exposed to sunshine may prevent unwanted permanent colour changes to the skin.

Drug rationale

Drugs not included

- **Topical antibiotics are not effective** in the treatment of lacerations [DTB, 1991].
- **Oral antibiotics other than co-amoxiclav, or erythromycin plus metronidazole,** are not included as they are generally either less active against the bacteria that commonly cause wound infections, or do not cover anaerobes, and may be more expensive.

Drugs included

- **Paracetamol** is included for simple analgesia.
- **Ibuprofen** is included as an alternative to paracetamol for analgesia.
- **When antibiotics are indicated** for contaminated wounds:
  - **Co-amoxiclav** is included, as it is active against staphylococci, streptococci, and anaerobic bacteria. Note: anaerobic infections are more common in these types of wound.
  - **Erythromycin** plus metronidazole is included to cover these bacteria for people who are allergic to penicillin. If the person is known not to tolerate erythromycin

L

because of adverse effects, consider giving clarithromycin plus metronidazole as an alternative.

- **Non-adherent dressings** protect the wound after suturing.
- **When tetanus vaccination is indicated** (see section *Tetanus prophylaxis*) [DH, 2004]:
  - Children aged under 10 years: DTaP/IPV/Hib (combined diphtheria, tetanus, acellular pertussis, inactivated poliomyelitis, and *Haemophilus influenzae* type b vaccine) is recommended for primary immunization. dTaP/IPV (combined low-dose diphtheria, tetanus, acellular pertussis, and inactivated poliomyelitis vaccine) is recommended for booster doses for both primary immunizations and booster doses.
  - People aged 10 years or over: Td/IPV (combined low-dose diphtheria, tetanus, and inactivated poliomyelitis vaccine) is recommended.

Prescriptions

Analgesia: use when required

Paracetamol s/f susp: 60mg to 120mg up to four times a day

- Age from 3 to 11 months
- Paracetamol 120mg/5ml s/f susp. Take 2.5ml to 5ml every 4 to 6 hours when required for pain relief. Maximum of 4 doses in 24 hours; supply 150 ml; NHS Cost £0.65; OTC Cost £3.19.

Paracetamol s/f susp: 120mg to 240mg up to four times a day

- Age from 12 months to 5 years
- Paracetamol 120mg/5ml s/f susp. Take one to two 5ml spoonfuls every 4 to 6 hours when required for pain relief. Maximum of 4 doses in 24 hours; supply 300 ml; NHS Cost £1.30; OTC Cost £2.28.

Paracetamol s/f susp: 250mg to 500mg up to four times a day

- Age from 6 to 11 years
- Paracetamol 250mg/5ml s/f susp. Take one to two 5ml spoonfuls every 4 to 6 hours when required for pain relief. Maximum of 4 doses in 24 hours; supply 300 ml; NHS Cost £1.70; OTC Cost £2.99.

Paracetamol tablets: 500mg to 1g up to four times a day

- Age from 12 to 15 years
- Paracetamol 500mg tablets. Take one to two tablets every 4 to 6 hours when required for pain relief. Maximum of 8 tablets in 24 hours; supply 100 tablets; NHS Cost £0.75; OTC Cost £1.32.

Paracetamol tablets: 1g up to four times a day

- Age from 16 years onwards
- Paracetamol 500mg tablets. Take two tablets every 4 to 6 hours when required for pain relief. Maximum of 8 tablets in 24 hours; supply 100 tablets; NHS Cost £0.75; OTC Cost £1.32.

Ibuprofen s/f susp: 50mg three to four times a day

- Age from 12 months to 2 years
- Ibuprofen 100mg/5ml s/f susp. Take 2.5ml three to four times a day when required for pain relief. Do not exceed the stated dose; supply 100 ml; NHS Cost £1.82; OTC Cost £3.21.

Ibuprofen s/f susp: 100mg three to four times a day

- Age from 3 to 7 years
- Ibuprofen 100mg/5ml s/f susp. Take one 5ml spoonful 3 to 4 times a day when required for pain relief. Do not exceed the stated dose; supply 150 ml; NHS Cost £2.73; OTC Cost £4.81.

Ibuprofen s/f susp: 200mg three to four times a day

- Age from 8 to 11 years
- Ibuprofen 100mg/5ml s/f susp. Take two 5ml spoonfuls 3 to 4 times a day when required for pain relief. Do not exceed the stated dose; supply 300 ml; NHS Cost £5.46; OTC Cost £9.62.

Ibuprofen tablets: 400mg three times a day

- Age from 12 years onwards
- Ibuprofen 400mg tablets. Take one tablet three times a day when required for pain relief. Do not exceed the stated dose; supply 24 tablets; NHS Cost £0.70; OTC Cost £1.23.

1st-line antibiotic (IF indicated): co-amoxiclav for 5 days

Co-amoxiclav 125/31mg/5ml susp: 0.25ml/kg three times a day

- Age from 1 month to 11 months
- Co-amoxiclav 125/31mg/5ml susp. *WEIGHT REQUIRED* Take 0.25ml per kg bodyweight THREE times a day for 5 days; supply 100 ml; NHS Cost £4.57.

Co-amoxiclav s/f suspension: 125/31mg three times a day

- Age from 12 months to 6 years
- Co-amoxiclav 125/31mg/5ml susp. Take one 5ml spoonful three times a day for 5 days; supply 100 ml; NHS Cost £4.57.

Co-amoxiclav s/f suspension: 250/62mg three times a day

- Age from 7 to 11 years
- Co-amoxiclav 250/62mg/5ml susp. Take one 5ml spoonful three times a day for 5 days; supply 100 ml; NHS Cost £6.42.

Co-amoxiclav tablets: 250/125mg three times a day

- Age from 12 years onwards
- Co-amoxiclav 375mg tablets. Take one tablet three times a day for 5 days; supply 15 tablets; NHS Cost £7.08.

Co-amoxiclav tablets: 500/125mg three times a day

- Age from 12 years onwards
- Co-amoxiclav 625mg tablets. Take one tablet three times a day for 5 days; supply 15 tablets; NHS Cost £11.24.

Penicillin allergy (IF indicated): erythro + met for 5 days

Erythromycin 125mg/5ml + metronidazole 200mg/5ml suspension

- Age from 1 month to 23 months
- Erythromycin 125mg/5ml sf susp. Take one 5ml spoonful four times a day for 5 days; supply 100 ml; NHS Cost £1.05.
- Metronidazole 200mg/5ml susp. *WEIGHT REQUIRED* Take 7.5mg per kg bodyweight THREE times a day for 5 days. (Max 400mg per dose.); supply 100 ml; NHS Cost £7.66.

Erythromycin 250mg/5ml + metronidazole 200mg/5ml suspension

- Age from 2 to 11 years
- Erythromycin 250mg/5ml sf susp. Take one 5ml spoonful four times a day for 5 days; supply 100 ml; NHS Cost £1.84.
- Metronidazole 200mg/5ml susp. *WEIGHT REQUIRED* Take 7.5mg per kg bodyweight THREE times a day for 5 days. (Max 400mg per dose.); supply 100 ml; NHS Cost £7.66.

Erythromycin 500mg/5ml + metronidazole 200mg/5ml suspension

- Age from 9 to 11 years
- Erythromycin 500mg/5ml sf susp. Take one 5ml spoonful four times a day for 5 days; supply 100 ml; NHS Cost £2.86.

- Metronidazole 200mg/5ml susp. *WEIGHT REQUIRED* Take 7.5mg per kg bodyweight THREE times a day for 5 days. (Max 400mg per dose.); supply 200 ml; NHS Cost £15.32.

Erythromycin 250mg e/c + metronidazole 400mg tablets
- Age from 12 years onwards
- Erythromycin 250mg e/c tablets. Take one tablet four times a day for 5 days; supply 20 tablets; NHS Cost £2.72.
- Metronidazole 400mg tablets. Take one tablet three times a day for 5 days; supply 15 tablets; NHS Cost £0.71.

Erythromycin 500mg e/c + metronidazole 400mg tablets
- Age from 12 years onwards
- Erythromycin 250mg e/c tablets. Take two tablets four times a day for 5 days; supply 40 tablets; NHS Cost £5.44.
- Metronidazole 400mg tablets. Take one tablet three times a day for 5 days; supply 15 tablets; NHS Cost £0.71.

Erythromycin intolerant: clarithro + met for 5 days

Clarithromycin 125mg/5ml + metronidazole 200mg/5ml susp
- Age from 12 months to 2 years
- Metronidazole 200mg/5ml susp. *WEIGHT REQUIRED* Take 7.5mg per kg bodyweight THREE times a day for 5 days. (Max 400mg per dose.); supply 100 ml; NHS Cost £7.66.
- Clarithromycin 125mg/5ml susp. Take 2.5ml twice a day for 5 days; supply 70 ml; NHS Cost £6.00.

Clarithromycin 125mg/5ml + metronidazole 200mg/5ml susp
- Age from 3 to 6 years
- Clarithromycin 125mg/5ml susp. Take one 5ml spoonful twice a day for 5 days; supply 70 ml; NHS Cost £6.00.
- Metronidazole 200mg/5ml susp. *WEIGHT REQUIRED* Take 7.5mg per kg bodyweight THREE times a day for 5 days. (Max 400mg per dose.); supply 100 ml; NHS Cost £7.66.

Clarithromycin 125mg/5ml + metronidazole 200mg/5ml susp
- Age from 7 to 9 years
- Clarithromycin 125mg/5ml susp. Take 7.5ml twice a day for 5 days; supply 100 ml; NHS Cost £10.32.
- Metronidazole 200mg/5ml susp. *WEIGHT REQUIRED* Take 7.5mg per kg bodyweight THREE times a day for 5 days. (Max 400mg per dose.); supply 200 ml; NHS Cost £15.32.

Clarithromycin 250mg/5ml + metronidazole 200mg/5ml susp
- Age from 10 to 11 years
- Clarithromycin 250mg/5ml susp. Take one 5ml spoonful twice a day for 5 days; supply 70 ml; NHS Cost £12.00.
- Metronidazole 200mg/5ml susp. *WEIGHT REQUIRED* Take 7.5mg per kg bodyweight THREE times a day for 5 days. (Max 400mg per dose.); supply 200 ml; NHS Cost £15.32.

Clarithromycin 250mg + metronidazole 400mg tablets
- Age from 12 years onwards
- Clarithromycin 250mg tablets. Take one tablet twice a day for 5 days; supply 10 tablets; NHS Cost £8.40.
- Metronidazole 400mg tablets. Take one tablet three times a day for 5 days; supply 15 tablets; NHS Cost £0.71.

Dressings and tetanus prophylaxis

5cm x 5cm Absorbent perforated plastic film faced dressing
- All ages
- Perforated FA 5x5cm dressing. Apply to the affected area as directed; supply 5 single dressings; NHS Cost £0.45; OTC Cost £0.79.

10cm x 10cm Absorbent perforated plastic film faced dressing
- All ages
- Perforated FA 10x10cm dressing. Apply to the affected area as directed; supply 5 single dressings; NHS Cost £0.75; OTC Cost £1.32.

20cm x 10cm Absorbent perforated plastic film faced dressing
- All ages
- Perforated FA 10x20cm dressing. Apply to the affected area as directed; supply 5 single dressings; NHS Cost £1.60; OTC Cost £2.82.

Permeable non-woven synthetic adhesive tape
- All ages
- Perm non-wvn tape 1.25cmx5m. Apply as required; supply 1 5metre roll; NHS Cost £0.35; OTC Cost £0.69.

Primary course: diphtheria+tetanus+pertussis+polio+Hib
- Age from 2 months to 9 years
- Pediacel injection. Give 0.5ml by intramuscular injection. For primary immunization, give three doses at intervals of 1 month between doses; supply 1 0.5ml vial.

Booster: low-dose diphtheria+tetanus+pertussis+polio
- Age from 3 to 9 years
- Repevax injection. Give 0.5ml by intramuscular injection; supply 1 0.5ml prefilled syringe.

Primary course: low-dose diphtheria+tetanus+polio
- Age from 10 years onwards
- Revaxis injection. Give 0.5ml by intramuscular injection. For primary immunization, give three doses at intervals of 1 month between doses; supply 1 0.5ml prefilled syringe.

Booster: low-dose diphtheria+tetanus+polio
- Age from 10 years onwards
- Revaxis injection. Give 0.5ml by intramuscular injection; supply 1 0.5ml prefilled syringe.

Infected

Which therapy?

General

- **Establish** when and how the injury occurred, and the likelihood of a penetrating foreign body (which will require exploration).
- **Examine** for damage to the arteries, nerves, muscles, and tendons.
- **Irrigate thoroughly** with sodium chloride 0.9% or tap water, using a 30–60 ml syringe, to clean the wound. Gravel grazes need to be carefully cleaned to prevent permanent tattooing of the skin.
- **Do not close** wounds that are clinically infected. Seek advice or consider delayed closure after 3–5 days.
- **All infected wounds should be treated with antibiotics:**
  - If the original laceration was 'clean', treat with flucloxacillin or erythromycin (if penicillin-sensitive).
  - If the original laceration was a puncture wound; had a significant degree of devitalized tissue; or was contaminated with soil, manure, or faeces, treat with co-amoxiclav, or erythromycin plus metronidazole (if penicillin-sensitive)

L

    - If the person is known not to tolerate erythromycin because of adverse effects, consider giving clarithromycin (with or without metronidazole) as an alternative.
- **Cover** with a sterile, non-adherent dressing to protect the wound.
- **Give paracetamol or ibuprofen** for pain relief.
- **Check tetanus immunization status** and give vaccine where appropriate (see section *Tetanus prophylaxis*).

Practical prescribing points

For further information, please see the *Medicines Compendium* (www.medicines.org.uk) or the *British National Formulary* (www.bnf.org).

- **Ibuprofen:** may cause gastrointestinal irritation and occasionally gastrointestinal haemorrhage. Avoid if there is a history of peptic ulceration. May worsen asthma, hypertension, renal impairment, or cardiac failure.
- **Tetanus immunoglobulin:** the Blood Transfusion Service distributes tetanus immunoglobulin to general practitioners on demand.

Follow-up advice

- **Review** the wound in 24–48 hours to check that the infection is clearing.
- **Advise** that if signs of infection worsen or if the person is feeling increasingly ill, an urgent review is needed.
- **Advise** on future safety measures, and provide education about the importance of thoroughly cleaning wounds if appropriate.

L

Should I refer or investigate?

Refer?

- **Referral** to accident and emergency/plastic surgery is usually indicated for:
    - Lacerations involving arteries, nerves, muscles, tendons, or bones
    - Facial lacerations (excluding very minor cuts)
    - Lip lacerations, particularly if the vermilion border is breached
    - Lacerations requiring complicated sutures
    - Suspected penetrating foreign body (e.g. glass/metal) for exploration under anaesthetic
    - Devitalized wounds where debridement is required
- **Admit if:**
    - There are signs of worsening infection or if the person is deteriorating clinically. Intravenous antibiotic therapy may be required.
    - Systemic symptoms are present (e.g. rigors, malaise, high temperature, confusion).

Investigate?

- **Swab the wound** and send for culture and sensitivity.
- **Therapy** should be reviewed according to the results.

Patient information leaflets

The following PILs are available at www.prodigy.nhs.uk

- Cuts (Lacerations)
- Tetanus Immunisation

Shared decision making

- How did this injury happen? Can any changes be made to prevent this happening again?
- **Wounds must be cleaned thoroughly.** (You can do this with tap water at home for any future small cuts that do not need medical attention.)
- **You need antibiotics, as the wound is infected.**
- If the wound needs stitches or similar, it is best to wait a few days until the infection has cleared.
- **Paracetamol or ibuprofen** will ease pain.
- **Are you up-to-date with tetanus immunizations?**
- See a doctor soon if the infection gets worse or does not get better.
- High-factor sunscreen used for 6–12 months on healing wounds that are exposed to sunshine may prevent unwanted permanent colour changes to the skin.

Drug rationale

Drugs not included

- **Topical antibiotics** are not effective in the treatment of lacerations [DTB, 1991].
- **Oral antibiotics other than flucloxacillin, erythromycin, co-amoxiclav, and metronidazole** are not included for empirical treatment as they are generally either less active against the bacteria that commonly cause wound infections, or do not cover anaerobic infections, or both, and may be more expensive.

Drugs included

- **Paracetamol** is included for simple analgesia.
- **Ibuprofen** is included as an alternative to paracetamol for analgesia.
- **For lacerations that were originally 'clean':**
    - **Flucloxacillin** is included, as it is active against the bacteria that commonly cause wound infections (e.g. *Staphylococcus aureus* and Group A streptococcus).
    - **Erythromycin** is also active against these bacteria, and is a suitable alternative to flucloxacillin for people who are allergic to penicillin. If the person is known not to tolerate erythromycin because of adverse effects, consider giving clarithromycin as an alternative.
- **For lacerations that were originally puncture wounds; had a significant degree of devitalized tissue; or were contaminated with soil, manure or faeces:**
    - **Co-amoxiclav** is included, as it is active against staphylococci, streptococci, and anaerobic bacteria. Note: anaerobic infections are more common in these types of wound.
    - **Erythromycin plus metronidazole** is included to cover these bacteria for people who are allergic to penicillin. If the person is known not to tolerate erythromycin because of adverse effects, consider giving clarithromycin plus metronidazole as an alternative.
- **Non-adherent dressings** protect the wound.
- **When tetanus vaccination is indicated** (see section *Tetanus prophylaxis*) [DH, 2004]:
    - Children aged under 10 years: DTaP/IPV/Hib (combined diphtheria, tetanus, acellular pertussis, inactivated poliomyelitis, and *Haemophilus influenzae* type b vaccine) is recommended for primary immunization. dTaP/IPV (combined low-dose diphtheria, tetanus, acellular pertussis, and inactivated poliomyelitis vaccine) is recommended for booster doses for both primary immunizations and booster doses.
    - People aged 10 years or over: Td/IPV (combined low-dose diphtheria, tetanus, and inactivated poliomyelitis vaccine) is recommended.

Prescriptions

Analgesia: use when required

Paracetamol s/f susp: 60mg to 120mg up to four times a day
- Age from 3 to 11 months
- Paracetamol 120mg/5ml s/f susp. Take 2.5ml to 5ml every 4 to 6 hours when required for pain relief. Maximum of 4 doses in 24 hours; supply 150 ml; NHS Cost £0.65; OTC Cost £1.14.

Paracetamol s/f susp: 120mg to 240mg up to four times a day
- Age from 12 months to 5 years
- Paracetamol 120mg/5ml s/f susp. Take one to two 5ml spoonfuls every 4 to 6 hours when required for pain relief. Maximum of 4 doses in 24 hours; supply 300 ml; NHS Cost £1.30; OTC Cost £2.28.

Paracetamol s/f susp: 250mg to 500mg up to four times a day
- Age from 6 to 11 years
- Paracetamol 250mg/5ml s/f susp. Take one to two 5ml spoonfuls every 4 to 6 hours when required for pain relief. Maximum of 4 doses in 24 hours; supply 300 ml; NHS Cost £1.70; OTC Cost £2.99.

Paracetamol tablets: 500mg to 1g up to four times a day
- Age from 12 to 15 years
- Paracetamol 500mg tablets. Take one to two tablets every 4 to 6 hours when required for pain relief. Maximum of 8 tablets in 24 hours; supply 100 tablets; NHS Cost £0.75; OTC Cost £1.32.

Paracetamol tablets: 1g up to four times a day
- Age from 16 years onwards
- Paracetamol 500mg tablets. Take two tablets every 4 to 6 hours when required for pain relief. Maximum of 8 tablets in 24 hours; supply 100 tablets; NHS Cost £0.75; OTC Cost £1.32.

Ibuprofen s/f susp: 50mg three to four times a day
- Age from 12 months to 2 years
- Ibuprofen 100mg/5ml s/f susp. Take 2.5ml three to four times a day when required for pain relief. Do not exceed the stated dose; supply 100 ml; NHS Cost £1.82; OTC Cost £3.21.

Ibuprofen s/f susp: 100mg three to four times a day
- Age from 3 to 7 years
- Ibuprofen 100mg/5ml s/f susp. Take one 5ml spoonful 3 to 4 times a day when required for pain relief. Do not exceed the stated dose; supply 150 ml; NHS Cost £2.73; OTC Cost £4.81.

Ibuprofen s/f susp: 200mg three to four times a day
- Age from 8 to 11 years
- Ibuprofen 100mg/5ml s/f susp. Take two 5ml spoonfuls 3 to 4 times a day when required for pain relief. Do not exceed the stated dose; supply 300 ml; NHS Cost £5.46; OTC Cost £9.62.

Ibuprofen tablets: 400mg three times a day
- Age from 12 years onwards
- Ibuprofen 400mg tablets. Take one tablet three times a day when required for pain relief. Do not exceed the stated dose; supply 24 tablets; NHS Cost £0.70; OTC Cost £1.23.

Clean wound: flucloxacillin or erythromycin for 5 days

Flucloxacillin syrup: 62.5mg four times a day
- Age from 1 month to 11 months
- Flucloxacillin 125mg/5ml syrup. Take 2.5ml four times a day for 5 days; supply 100 ml; NHS Cost £3.49.

Flucloxacillin syrup: 125mg four times a day
- Age from 12 months to 4 years
- Flucloxacillin 125mg/5ml syrup. Take one 5ml spoonful four times a day for 5 days; supply 100 ml; NHS Cost £3.49.

Flucloxacillin syrup: 250mg four times a day
- Age from 5 to 11 years
- Flucloxacillin 250mg/5ml syrup. Take one 5ml spoonful four times a day for 5 days; supply 100 ml; NHS Cost £6.97.

Flucloxacillin capsules: 250mg four times a day
- Age from 12 years onwards
- Flucloxacillin 250mg capsules. Take one capsule four times a day for 5 days; supply 20 capsules; NHS Cost £2.08.

Flucloxacillin capsules: 500mg four times a day
- Age from 12 years onwards
- Flucloxacillin 500mg capsules. Take one capsule four times a day for 5 days; supply 20 capsules; NHS Cost £3.38.

Erythromycin s/f suspension: 125mg four times a day
- Age from 1 month to 23 months
- Erythromycin 125mg/5ml sf susp. Take one 5ml spoonful four times a day for 5 days; supply 100 ml; NHS Cost £1.12.

Erythromycin s/f suspension: 250mg four times a day
- Age from 2 to 11 years
- Erythromycin 250mg/5ml sf susp. Take one 5ml spoonful four times a day for 5 days; supply 100 ml; NHS Cost £1.84.

Erythromycin s/f suspension: 500mg four times a day
- Age from 9 to 11 years
- Erythromycin 500mg/5ml sf susp. Take one 5ml spoonful four times a day for 5 days; supply 100 ml; NHS Cost £2.86.

Erythromycin e/c tablets: 250mg four times a day
- Age from 12 years onwards
- Erythromycin 250mg e/c tablets. Take one tablet four times a day for 5 days; supply 20 tablets; NHS Cost £2.20.

Erythromycin e/c tablets: 500mg four times a day
- Age from 12 years onwards
- Erythromycin 250mg e/c tablets. Take two tablets four times a day for 5 days; supply 40 tablets; NHS Cost £4.40.

Contaminated: co-amoxiclav or erythromycin + metronidazole

Co-amoxiclav 125/31mg/5ml susp: 0.25ml/kg three times a day
- Age from 1 month to 11 months
- Co-amoxiclav 125/31mg/5ml susp. *WEIGHT REQUIRED* Take 0.25ml per kg bodyweight THREE times a day for 5 days; supply 100 ml; NHS Cost £4.57.

Co-amoxiclav suspension: 125/31mg three times a day
- Age from 12 months to 6 years
- Co-amoxiclav 125/31mg/5ml susp. Take one 5ml spoonful three times a day for 5 days; supply 100 ml; NHS Cost £4.57.

Co-amoxiclav suspension: 250/62mg three times a day
- Age from 7 to 11 years
- Co-amoxiclav 250/62mg/5ml susp. Take one 5ml spoonful three times a day for 5 days; supply 100 ml; NHS Cost £6.42.

Co-amoxiclav tablets: 250/125mg three times a day
- Age from 12 years onwards
- Co-amoxiclav 375mg tablets. Take one tablet three times a day for 5 days; supply 15 tablets; NHS Cost £7.08.

Co-amoxiclav tablets: 500/125mg three times a day
- Age from 12 years onwards
- Co-amoxiclav 625mg tablets. Take one tablet three times a day for 5 days; supply 15 tablets; NHS Cost £11.23.

Erythromycin 125mg/5ml + metronidazole 200mg/5ml suspension
- Age from 1 month to 23 months
- Erythromycin 125mg/5ml sf susp. Take one 5ml spoonful four times a day for 5 days; supply 100 ml; NHS Cost £1.05.
- Metronidazole 200mg/5ml susp. *WEIGHT REQUIRED* Take 7.5mg per kg bodyweight THREE times a day for 5 days. (Max 400mg per dose.); supply 100 ml; NHS Cost £7.66.

Erythromycin 250mg/5ml + metronidazole 200mg/5ml suspension
- Age from 2 to 11 years
- Erythromycin 250mg/5ml sf susp. Take one 5ml spoonful four times a day for 5 days; supply 100 ml; NHS Cost £1.84.
- Metronidazole 200mg/5ml susp. *WEIGHT REQUIRED* Take 7.5mg per kg bodyweight THREE times a day for 5 days. (Max 400mg per dose.); supply 100 ml; NHS Cost £7.66.

Erythromycin 500mg/5ml + metronidazole 200mg/5ml suspension
- Age from 9 to 11 years
- Erythromycin 500mg/5ml sf susp. Take one 5ml spoonful four times a day for 5 days; supply 100 ml; NHS Cost £2.86.
- Metronidazole 200mg/5ml susp. *WEIGHT REQUIRED* Take 7.5mg per kg bodyweight THREE times a day for 5 days. (Max 400mg per dose.); supply 200 ml; NHS Cost £15.34.

Erythromycin 250mg e/c + metronidazole 400mg tablets
- Age from 12 years onwards
- Erythromycin 250mg e/c tablets. Take one tablet four times a day for 5 days; supply 20 tablets; NHS Cost £2.72.
- Metronidazole 400mg tablets. Take one tablet three times a day for 5 days; supply 17 tablets; NHS Cost £0.71.

Erythromcyin 500mg e/c + metronidazole 400mg tablets
- Age from 12 years onwards
- Erythromycin 250mg e/c tablets. Take two tablets four times a day for 5 days; supply 40 tablets; NHS Cost £5.44.
- Metronidazole 400mg tablets. Take one tablet three times a day for 5 days; supply 17 tablets; NHS Cost £0.71.

Erythromycin intolerant: clarithromycin or clarith + metron

Clarithromycin suspension: 62.5mg twice a day
- Age from 12 months to 2 years
- Clarithromycin 125mg/5ml susp. Take 2.5ml twice a day for 5 days; supply 70 ml; NHS Cost £6.00.

Clarithromycin suspension: 125mg twice a day
- Age from 3 to 6 years
- Clarithromycin 125mg/5ml susp. Take one 5ml spoonful twice a day for 5 days; supply 70 ml; NHS Cost £6.00.

Clarithromycin suspension: 187.5mg twice a day
- Age from 7 to 9 years
- Clarithromycin 125mg/5ml susp. Take 7.5ml twice a day for 5 days; supply 100 ml; NHS Cost £10.32.

Clarithromycin suspension: 250mg twice a day
- Age from 10 to 11 years
- Clarithromycin 250mg/5ml susp. Take one 5ml spoonful twice a day for 5 days; supply 70 ml; NHS Cost £12.00.

Clarithromycin tablets: 250mg twice a day
- Age from 12 years onwards
- Clarithromycin 250mg tablets. Take one tablet twice a day for 5 days; supply 10 tablets; NHS Cost £8.03.

Clarithromycin tablets: 500mg twice a day (severe infection)
- Age from 12 years onwards
- Clarithromycin 500mg tablets. Take one tablet twice a day for 5 days; supply 10 tablets; NHS Cost £16.06.

Clarithromycin 125mg/5ml + metronidazole 200mg/5ml susp
- Age from 12 months to 2 years
- Clarithromycin 125mg/5ml susp. Take 2.5ml twice a day for 5 days; supply 70 ml; NHS Cost £6.00.
- Metronidazole 200mg/5ml susp. *WEIGHT REQUIRED* Take 7.5mg per kg bodyweight THREE times a day for 5 days. (Max 400mg per dose.); supply 100 ml; NHS Cost £7.66.

Clarithromycin 125mg/5ml + metronidazole 200mg/5ml susp
- Age from 3 to 6 years
- Clarithromycin 125mg/5ml susp. Take one 5ml spoonful twice a day for 5 days; supply 70 ml; NHS Cost £6.00.
- Metronidazole 200mg/5ml susp. *WEIGHT REQUIRED* Take 7.5mg per kg bodyweight THREE times a day for 5 days. (Max 400mg per dose.); supply 100 ml; NHS Cost £7.66.

Clarithromycin 125mg/5ml + metronidazole 200mg/5ml susp
- Age from 7 to 9 years
- Clarithromycin 125mg/5ml susp. Take 7.5ml twice a day for 5 days; supply 100 ml; NHS Cost £10.32.
- Metronidazole 200mg/5ml susp. *WEIGHT REQUIRED* Take 7.5mg per kg bodyweight THREE times a day for 5 days. (Max 400mg per dose.); supply 200 ml; NHS Cost £15.32.

Clarithromycin 250mg/5ml + metronidazole 200mg/5ml susp
- Age from 10 to 11 years
- Clarithromycin 250mg/5ml susp. Take one 5ml spoonful twice a day for 5 days; supply 70 ml; NHS Cost £12.00.
- Metronidazole 200mg/5ml susp. *WEIGHT REQUIRED* Take 7.5mg per kg bodyweight THREE times a day for 5 days. (Max 400mg per dose.); supply 200 ml; NHS Cost £15.32.

Clarithromycin 250mg + metronidazole 400mg tablets
- Age from 12 years onwards
- Clarithromycin 250mg tablets. Take one tablet twice a day for 5 days; supply 10 tablets; NHS Cost £8.40.
- Metronidazole 400mg tablets. Take one tablet three times a day for 5 days; supply 15 tablets; NHS Cost £0.71.

Clarithromycin 500mg + metronidazole 400mg tablets
- Age from 12 years onwards
- Clarithromycin 500mg tablets. Take one tablet twice a day for 5 days; supply 10 tablets; NHS Cost £16.82.
- Metronidazole 400mg tablets. Take one tablet three times a day for 5 days; supply 15 tablets; NHS Cost £0.71.

Dressings and tetanus prophylaxis

5cm x 5cm Absorbent perforated plastic film faced dressing
- All ages
- Perforated FA 5x5cm dressing. Apply to the affected area as directed; supply 5 single dressings; NHS Cost £0.45; OTC Cost £0.79.

10cm x 10cm Absorbent perforated plastic film faced dressing
- All ages
- Perforated FA 10x10cm dressing. Apply to the affected area as directed; supply 5 single dressings; NHS Cost £0.75; OTC Cost £1.32.

20cm x 10cm Absorbent perforated plastic film faced dressing
- All ages
- Perforated FA 10x20cm dressing. Apply to the affected area as directed; supply 5 single dressings; NHS Cost £1.60; OTC Cost £2.82.

Permeable non-woven synthetic adhesive tape
- All ages
- Perm non-wvn tape 1.25cmx5m. Apply as required; supply 1 5metre roll; NHS Cost £0.39; OTC Cost £0.69.

Primary course: diphtheria+tetanus+pertussis+polio+Hib
- Age from 2 months to 9 years
- Pediacel injection. Give 0.5ml by intramuscular injection. For primary immunization, give three doses at intervals of 1 month between doses; supply 1 0.5ml vial.

Booster: low-dose diphtheria+tetanus+pertussis+polio
- Age from 3 to 9 years
- Repevax injection. Give 0.5ml by intramuscular injection; supply 1 0.5ml prefilled syringe.

Primary course: low-dose diphtheria+tetanus+polio
- Age from 10 years onwards
- Revaxis injection. Give 0.5ml by intramuscular injection. For primary immunization, give three doses at intervals of 1 month between doses; supply 1 0.5ml prefilled syringe.

Booster: low-dose diphtheria+tetanus+polio
- Age from 10 years onwards
- Revaxis injection. Give 0.5ml by intramuscular injection; supply 1 0.5ml prefilled syringe.

Extended Information

Background information

- What is it? p.1139
- How common is it? p.1139
- Complications and prognosis p.1139

What is it?

- **A laceration** is a tearing or splitting of the skin commonly caused by blunt trauma, or an incision of the skin caused by a sharp object such as a knife or broken glass.
- **An abrasion or graze** is a minor wound in which the surface of the skin is worn away by rubbing or friction. This wound can be very painful and may have dirt embedded in it.

[DTB, 1991; Capellan and Hollander, 2003; Cole, 2003]

How common is it?

- Skin wounds are common, accounting for 15% of attendances at accident and emergency departments.
- Lacerations occur predominantly in young adults. About a third of lacerations occur in adults between the ages of 19 and 35 years.
- Lacerations are more common in men than in women.

[Hollander and Singer, 1999; Bradley, 2001]

Complications and prognosis

- **Foreign bodies** within the wound may result in chronic infection and delay healing [Capellan and Hollander, 2003].
- **Crush injuries** cause a greater degree of devitalization and are more prone to infection [Capellan and Hollander, 2003].
- **Wound infection** occurs in 1–12% of non-bite wounds managed in accident and emergency departments [Cummings and Del Baccaro, 1995]. By way of comparison, 2–50% of bite wounds become infected [Dire, 1992; Cummings, 1994; Monteiro, 1995].
- **Pre-tibial lacerations** heal slowly in older people and may become necrotic, because of poor blood supply to the pre-tibial area [Cole, 2003].
- **Other complications include** unsightly scars; blood loss if vessels are severed; damage to underlying nerves, muscles, or tendons; fractures; and tetanus.

Management issues

- Initial management p.1139
- Timing of wound closure p.1140
- Suturing p.1140
- Choice of suture material p.1140
- Sterile skin-closure strips p.1140
- Tissue adhesives p.1140
- Tetanus prophylaxis p.1140
- Antibiotic prophylaxis p.1141
- Antibiotic treatment p.1141

Initial management

- **Apply pressure to control bleeding.** If blood loss is heavy or does not stop, maintain pressure and refer urgently to accident and emergency.
- **Establish** when and how the injury occurred, and the likelihood of a suspected penetrating foreign body.
- **Referral to accident and emergency/plastic surgery is usually indicated for:**
  - Lacerations involving arteries, nerves, muscles, tendons, or bones
  - Facial lacerations (excluding very minor cuts)
  - Lip lacerations, particularly if the vermilion border is breached
  - Lacerations requiring complicated sutures
  - Suspected penetrating foreign body (e.g. glass/metal), for X-ray or exploration under anaesthetic
  - Devitalized wounds where extensive debridement is required
- **For lacerations managed in primary care:**
  - **Irrigate the wound thoroughly** using sodium chloride 0.9% or tap water to remove debris and reduce bacterial contamination, thus minimizing the risk of infection.
  - Although comparative evidence is limited, results from a recent Cochrane review suggest that using tap water to cleanse acute wounds is at least as efficacious as using sodium chloride 0.9% in terms of reducing infection rates and improving healing rates [Fernandez et al, 2004]. The quality of tap water should be at least drinkable.
  - **High-pressure irrigation is more effective** than low-pressure irrigation at reducing bacterial wound counts and wound infection rates. However, sustained high-pressure irrigation may be associated with increased tissue damage and should be used with caution, especially in highly vascularized areas. Adequate high pressure can be achieved using a 30–60 ml syringe and a 16–19 gauge needle. More gentle irrigation can be achieved using a saline aerosol, a Steripod, or, if water is used, a syringe without a needle [Singer et al, 1997; Hollander and Singer, 1999; Capellan and Hollander, 2003; Cole, 2003].

L

- The role of antiseptics in wound cleansing is uncertain. There are some concerns that they damage tissue and delay wound healing, and they are not generally recommended.
- **Gravel abrasions need to be carefully cleaned** to reduce the risk of infection and permanent tattooing of the skin from subcutaneous grit.

[Castille, 1998; Hollander and Singer, 1999; Knapp, 1999; Wilson et al, 2000; Cole, 2003]

Timing of wound closure

- **Wounds that have been contaminated** with faeces, saliva, vaginal secretions, soil, or manure should not be closed, as they are at high risk of infection. Consider delayed primary closure (usually 3–5 days after the initial injury if there is no evidence of infection).
- **Other wounds that are less than 6 hours old** may be closed after sufficient irrigation and debridement.
- **Other wounds that are more than 6 hours old** may be closed after sufficient irrigation and debridement unless there is considered to be a high risk of infection. A decision on whether or not it is safe to close the wound depends on location, causation, and host factors. Wounds that are at high risk of infection include:
  - Wounds that are heavily contaminated
  - Extensive intra-oral lacerations
  - Wounds to the feet
  - Stellate lesions
  - Devitalized wounds
  - Wounds in people with diabetes mellitus; alcohol dependency; peripheral vascular disease; asplenism; or immunosuppression, including those on oral corticosteroids or chemotherapy
  - Wounds caused by compression or tension (crush injuries)
- **Wounds that are more than 24 hours old** should be treated by delayed primary closure (usually 3–5 days after the initial injury if there is no evidence of infection).
- **Infected wounds should not be closed.** Seek advice or consider delayed closure after 3–5 days, provided no infection remains.

[Singer et al, 1997; Edlich and Reddy, 2001]

Suturing

- **Simple non-facial lacerations** may be sutured in primary care.
- **Lacerations that involve the dermal layer** (i.e. full skin thickness) generally require suturing.
- **After suturing, cover the wound** with a protective, sterile, non-adherent dressing for 24–48 hours.
- **Wounds should be kept dry for 3 days.** After 24–48 hours the wound can be gently washed, but should not be scrubbed or soaked.
- **Remove sutures** of the face after 3–5 days, of joints after 10–14 days, and of other sites after 7–10 days.

[Singer et al, 1997]

Choice of suture material

- **Synthetic monofilament materials** such as nylon or polypropylene are inert and preferable to silk, which may cause tissue reaction.
- **The smallest size of suture material** that is practical for a wound should be used.
- For small, simple wounds the most frequently used sizes of suture material range from 3/0 (large) to 6/0 (fine). As a general guide:
  - Trunk and lower limbs — 3/0
  - Scalp — 3/0, 4/0
  - Upper limbs — 4/0
  - Face — 5/0, 6/0
- **Reduce the recommended adult sizes** by one size when suturing children's wounds.

[Castille, 1998; Whiteside and Moorehead, 1998]

Sterile skin-closure strips

- **Sterile skin-closure strips** can be applied to 'v'-flap lacerations on thin skin on the legs in the elderly, and to some lacerations in children.
- **Such strips should not be used** in areas subject to tension (e.g. joints) or on oily, moist, or hairy areas.
- **Protective dressings are not usually necessary.**
- **Advise the person that the wound must be kept dry** until the closure strips are removed.
- **Sterile skin-closure strips can be removed** after 5–7 days (or for pre-tibial lacerations, after 10–14 days).

[Singer et al, 1997; Hollander and Singer, 1999; Cole, 2003; Richardson, 2003]

Tissue adhesives

- **Tissue adhesives can be applied rapidly and painlessly.**
- **They are as effective as sutures for the repair of simple, clean wounds** [Simon et al, 1997], with similar cosmetic results [Bruns et al, 1998; Singer et al, 1998; Singer et al, 2002].
- **They should not be used** on joints, hands, feet, lips, mucosa, infected wounds, puncture wounds, bite wounds, or stellate wounds.
- **Hold the skin edges together** and then apply the tissue adhesive in thin layers. (This action reduces the amount of heat felt as the adhesive is applied.)
- **Do not get adhesive in the wound,** as this will impair wound healing.
- **After application, no dressing is required.**
- **The wound should be kept dry for 5 days.** The person may shower, although prolonged contact with water (e.g. a bath or swimming) should be avoided [Richardson, 2003].
- **The adhesive will slough off after 7–10 days.**
- There is a small but significant increased risk of the wound re-opening with tissue adhesives; 25 people would need to be treated with standard wound closure to prevent one incident wound re-opening using tissue adhesive (Number Needed to Harm (NNH) = 25, 95% CI 14 to 100) [Farion et al, 2004].
- **Tissue adhesives containing** enbucrilate (Histoacryl and Indermil), ethyl-2-cyanoacrylate (Epiglu), 2-octylcyanoacrylates (Dermabond) and butylcyanoacrylate (LiquaBond) are available in the UK [BNF 47, 2004].

[Singer et al, 1997; Hollander and Singer, 1999; Bruns and Worthington, 2000; Wilson et al, 2000]

Tetanus prophylaxis

- **Check tetanus immunization status for all laceration wounds.** A total of five doses of vaccine, administered at the appropriate intervals, is considered to give lifelong immunity (see Table 1).
- Note: existing stocks of Td (adsorbed diphtheria [low-dose] and tetanus vaccine) can be used for administration at the time of a tetanus-prone wound if appropriate. However, if the polio, or polio, and diphtheria vaccination needs to be updated at the same time then Td/IPV should be used.
- **Following a laceration, tetanus prophylaxis should be given as follows:**
  - **Person fully immunized, i.e. has received five doses of vaccine at appropriate intervals:** tetanus booster not needed. Consider giving human tetanus immunoglobulin for tetanus-prone wounds where the risk of infection is especially high, e.g. those

Table 1: Immunization schedule for tetanus.

Schedule	Children	Adults and children over 10 years
Primary course	3 doses of vaccine (usually as DTaP/IPV/Hib) at 2, 3, and 4 months of age	3 doses of vaccine (as Td/IPV), each one month apart
Fourth dose	At least 3 years after the last dose of the primary course, usually pre-school entry (as dTaP/IPV)	5–10 years after the last dose of the primary course (as Td/IPV)
Fifth dose	Aged 13–18 years or before leaving school (as Td/IPV)	10 years after fourth dose (as Td/IPV)

DTaP/IPV/Hib = Diphtheria, tetanus, acellular pertussis, inactivated poliomyelitis, and *Haemophilus influenzae* type b vaccine
dTaP/IPV = Low-dose diphtheria, tetanus, acellular pertussis, and inactivated poliomyelitis vaccine
Td/IPV = Low-dose diphtheria, tetanus, and inactivated poliomyelitis vaccine for adults and children over 10 years of age

contaminated with manure or extensive devitalized tissue.
- **Primary immunization complete, boosters incomplete but up-to-date:** tetanus booster not needed but may be given if booster is due and it is convenient to give now. Consider giving human tetanus immunoglobulin for tetanus-prone wounds where the risk of infection is especially high, e.g. those contaminated with manure or extensive devitalized tissue.
- **Primary immunization incomplete, or boosters not up-to-date:** give tetanus booster and further doses as needed to complete the recommended schedule (note: if the primary course is interrupted it should be resumed but not repeated). Add human tetanus immunoglobulin if it is a tetanus-prone wound (defined as: a puncture wound; a significant degree of devitalized tissue; contaminated with soil or manure; containing foreign bodies; compound fractures; clinical signs of sepsis; wounds or burns sustained more than 6 hours before surgical treatment). Note: inject tetanus vaccine and immunoglobulin at different sites.
- **Not immunized or immunization status uncertain:** give an immediate dose of vaccine. Add human tetanus immunoglobulin if it is a tetanus-prone wound (see above). Arrange further doses of tetanus vaccine as needed to complete the recommended five-dose schedule.

[DH, 2004]

Antibiotic prophylaxis

- **Antibiotic prophylaxis is not usually required for simple lacerations.** A meta-analysis of antibiotics to prevent infection in simple wounds found no evidence of benefit [Cummings and Del Baccaro, 1995].
- **Antibiotic prophylaxis may be appropriate in some circumstances:**
  - **For wounds to the feet, extensive intra-oral lacerations, or stellate lesions:** consider flucloxacillin (or erythromycin if the person is allergic to penicillin) [Edlich et al, 1986; Rodgers, 1992; Courand and Ward, 1996; Hollander and Singer, 1999].
  - For lacerations that are contaminated with soil, manure, or faeces; puncture wounds; or lacerations that have a significant degree of devitalized tissue: consider co-amoxiclav, or erythromycin plus metronidazole (if penicillin-allergic).
  - **For people with diabetes mellitus; alcohol dependency; peripheral vascular disease; asplenism; or immunosuppression,** including those on oral corticosteroids or chemotherapy: consider flucloxacillin or (or erythromycin if the person is allergic to penicillin). For contaminated wounds (see above), puncture wounds, or wounds that have a significant degree of devitalized tissue, consider co-amoxiclav (or erythromycin plus metronidazole if the person is allergic to penicillin) [Rodgers, 1992; Hollander and Singer, 1999].
  - **For antibiotic prophylaxis after animal or human bites,** see the separate PRODIGY guidance *Bites — human & animal.*

Antibiotic treatment

- **Clean lacerations that have become infected** should be treated with flucloxacillin (or erythromycin if the person is allergic to penicillin). They are likely to be infected with staphylococci or streptococci (i.e. normal skin commensals), so flucloxacillin or erythromycin is a suitable first-line treatment.
- **Lacerations that have become infected and were originally contaminated with soil, manure, or faeces; puncture wounds; or lacerations that have a significant degree of devitalized tissue** should be treated with co-amoxiclav (or erythromycin plus metronidazole if the person is allergic to penicillin). Antibiotic treatment should cover staphylococci, streptococci, and anaerobic bacteria. Note: anaerobic infection is more likely in these types of wound.

References

NHS staff in England can link, free of charge, from references to full text journals by clicking on [Full text] on the PRODIGY website.

1. BNF 47 (2004) *British National Formulary.* 47th edn. London: British Medical Association and Royal Pharmaceutical Society of Great Britain.
2. Bradley, L. (2001) Pretibial lacerations in older patients: the treatment options. *Journal of Wound Care* **10**(1), 521–523.
3. Bruns, T.B. and Worthington, J.M. (2000) Using tissue adhesive for wound repair: a practical guide to dermabond. *American Family Physician* **61**(5), 1383–1388. [Full text]
4. Bruns, T.B., Robinson, B.S., Smith, R.J. et al (1998) A new tissue adhesive for laceration repair in children. *Journal of Pediatrics* **132**(6), 1067–1070.
5. Capellan, O. and Hollander, J.E. (2003) Management of lacerations in the emergency department. *Emergency Medicine Clinics of North America* **21**(1), 205–231.
6. Castille, K. (1998) Suturing. *Nursing Standard* **12**(41), 41–48. [Full text]
7. Cole, E. (2003) Wound management in the A&E department. *Nursing Standard* **17**(46), 45–52. [Full text]
8. Courand, J.A. and Ward, M. (1996) Prevention of infection in the management of minor lacerations and puncture wounds. *Seminars in Pediatric Infectious Diseases* **7**(1), 71–77.
9. Cummings, P. (1994) Antibiotics to prevent infection in patients with dog bite wounds: a meta-analysis of randomized trials. *Annals of Emergency Medicine* **23**(3), 535–540.
10. Cummings, P. and Del Baccaro, M.A. (1995) Antibiotics to prevent infection of simple wounds: a meta-analysis of randomised studies. *American Journal of Emergency Medicine* **13**(4), 396–400.
11. DH (2004) *New (August 2004) chapter 30 – tetanus.* Immunisation against infectious disease. Department of Health. www.dh.gov.uk [Accessed: 22/06/2005]. [Full text]
12. Dire, D.J. (1992) Emergency management of dog and cat bite wounds. *Emergency Medicine Clinics of North America* **10**(4), 719–736.

L

13. DTB (1991) Local applications to wounds – I: cleansers, antibacterials, debriders. *Drug & Therapeutics Bulletin* 29(24), 93–95.
14. Edlich, R.F. and Reddy, V.R. (2001) 5th annual David R. Boyd, MD lecture: revolutionary advances in wound repair in emergency medicine during the last three decades. A view toward the new millennium. *Journal of Emergency Medicine* 20(2), 167–193.
15. Edlich, R.F., Kenney, J.G., Morgan, R.F. et al (1986) Antimicrobial treatment of minor soft tissue lacerations: a critical review. *Emergency Medicine Clinics of North America* 4(3), 561–580.
16. Farion, K., Osmond, M.H., Hartling, L. et al (2004) *Tissue adhesives for traumatic lacerations in children and adults (Cochrane Review)*. The Cochrane Library. Issue 1. Chichester, UK: John Wiley & Sons, Ltd.
17. Fernandez, R., Griffiths, R. and Ussia, C. (2004) *Water for wound cleansing (Cochrane Review)*. The Cochrane Library. Issue 1. Chichester, UK: John Wiley & Sons, Ltd.
18. Hollander, J.E. and Singer, A.J. (1999) Laceration management. *Annals of Emergency Medicine* 34(3), 356–367.
19. Knapp, J.F. (1999) Updates in wound management for the pediatrician. *Emergency Medicine Clinics of North America* 46(6), 1201–1213.
20. Monteiro, J.A. (1995) Human and animal bite wound infections. *European Journal of Internal Medicine* 6(4), 209–215.
21. Richardson, M. (2003) Wound closure.. *Emergency Nurse* 11(3), 25–32. [Full text]
22. Rodgers, K.G. (1992) The rational use of antimicrobial agents in simple wounds. *Emergency Medicine Clinics of North America* 10(4), 753–766.
23. Simon, H.K., McLario, D.J., Bruns, T.B. et al (1997) Long-term appearance of lacerations repaired using a tissue adhesive. *Pediatrics* 99(2), 193–195. [Full text]
24. Singer, A.J., Hollander, J.E. and Quinn, J.V. (1997) Evaluation and management of traumatic lacerations. *New England Journal of Medicine* 337(16), 1142–1148. [Full text]
25. Singer, A.J., Hollander, J.E., Valentine, S.M. et al (1998) Prospective, randomized, controlled trial of tissue adhesive (2-octylcyanoacrylate) vs standard wound closure techniques for laceration repair. *Academic Emergency Medicine* 5(2), 94–99.
26. Singer, A.J., Quinn, J.V., Clark, R.E. et al (2002) Closure of lacerations and incisions with octylcyanoacrylate: a multicenter randomized controlled trial. *Surgery* 131(3), 270–276.
27. Whiteside, M.R.C. and Moorehead, R.J. (1998) Management of traumatic wounds. In: Leaper, D.J. and Harding, K.G. (Eds.) *Wounds: biology and management*. Oxford: Oxford University Press. 88–99.
28. Wilson, J.L., Kocurek, K. and Doty, B.J. (2000) A systematic approach to laceration repair. *Postgraduate Medicine* 107(4), 1–10.

PRODIGY GUIDANCE

Leg cramps — unknown cause

Last revised in July 2005
www.prodigy.nhs.uk/guidance.asp?gt=Leg cramps

Applies to people over the age of 16 years

This guidance covers the management of idiopathic leg cramps occurring in the calf, thigh or foot.

This guidance does not cover exercise-induced cramp, restless-leg syndrome, tetany, contracture, dystonia or the management of secondary causes of leg cramps.

There is separate PRODIGY guidance for *Deep vein thrombosis, Sprains and strains* and *Thrombophlebitis.*

Goals

- To reassure the person of the benign nature of leg cramps
- To prevent or reduce the number of attacks of cramp

Contents

Scenarios
- Leg cramps p.1143

Extended Information, p. 1144

Leg cramps

Which therapy?

- **Identify and treat any predisposing causes:** for example metabolic disturbances, peripheral vascular disease.
- **Discontinue drugs** associated with leg cramps (where appropriate) for example, salbutamol, terbutaline, raloxifene, alcohol, diuretics, nifedipine, phenothiazines, penicillamine, nicotinic acid.
- **Reassurance** that idiopathic leg cramps are benign may be all that is required.
- **Consider recommending simple measures, although there is a lack of evidence of benefit for these.** Stretching exercises are commonly advised. Stretching the muscle with active contraction of the opposing muscle may relieve symptoms during an attack and prevent recurrences.
- **Consider prescribing quinine** for people with regular cramps who are not helped by non-drug treatments and whose quality of life is significantly affected. Do not use quinine in pregnancy. If prescribing quinine:
  - Discuss the risks of quinine with the person prior to prescribing.
  - Review medication to identify potentially serious drug interactions (see *Prescribing points*).
  - Monitor taking quinine for benefits and adverse effects.
  - Emphasise the importance of review after 4 weeks and explain that quinine should be continued if there is evidence of benefit.

Practical prescribing points

For further information please see the *Medicines Compendium* (www.medicines.org.uk) or the *British National Formulary* (www.bnf.org).

- **Adverse effects** of quinine have been reported, but these do appear to be dose-related.
  - Tinnitus may occur at the low doses used for leg cramp.
  - Cinchonism may occur at usual therapeutic doses. Symptoms include tinnitus, impaired hearing, visual disturbances, headache, hot and flushed skin, nausea; and in severe cases abdominal pain, vomiting, diarrhoea, rashes, and confusion.
- Hypersensitivity reactions such as thrombocytopenic purpura and thrombocytopenia have been reported.
- **Quinine has cardiovascular effects,** so use with caution in people with heart disease.
- There are a number of potentially serious drug interactions with quinine.
  - **Monitor digoxin plasma levels** as there is a likely but variable increase with concomitant use of quinine. Halving the digoxin maintenance dose may be necessary.
  - **There is an increased risk of ventricular arrhythmias** if quinine is taken with certain drugs, including amiodarone, moxifloxacin, terfenadine, pimozide and thioridazine. Avoid concomitant prescribing.
  - **There is an increased risk of convulsions** if quinine is taken with mefloquine.
- **Quinine is very toxic in overdose,** and may lead to permanent visual impairment, cardiac arrhythmias, and death.

Follow-up advice

- Monitor benefits and adverse effects of quinine treatment at 4 weeks.
- If relief is obtained at 4 weeks, continue quinine treatment, unless adverse effects are unacceptable.
- Attempt to stop quinine treatment every 3 months in order to assess whether it is still beneficial.

Should I refer or investigate?

Refer?

- Referral is rarely required unless indicated by a specific underlying cause, or if the symptoms are unbearable and not responsive to appropriate therapies.

Investigate?

- **Investigations are not routinely recommended** unless the history and examination raise suspicion of an underlying cause, or the symptoms are atypical or particularly severe.
- **The following investigations may be appropriate to exclude secondary causes of leg cramps:**
  - **Urea, electrolyte, and calcium** measurements — if electrolyte disturbance is suspected
  - **Thyroid function tests** — if thyroid disease is suspected
  - **Fasting blood glucose and/or oral glucose tolerance test** — if diabetes mellitus is suspected
  - **Liver function tests** — if cirrhosis is suspected

L

- **Magnesium levels** — if hypomagnesaemia is suspected (chronic malabsorption)
- **Creatinine kinase levels and electromyogram** — if a muscle disorder is suspected
- **Lead levels** — if lead toxicity is suspected

Patient information leaflets

The following PILs are available at www.prodigy.nhs.uk

- Cramps in the Leg

Shared decision making

- Leg cramps are common, particularly in older people.
- **Stretching exercises** of the calf muscles may prevent leg cramps. Aim for about 5 minutes' exercise, three times a day. Stand facing a wall about 1 metre away, then lean forward keeping the soles of your feet flat on the ground. Hold for about 10 seconds and then repeat after a period of 5 seconds relaxation.
- **Quinine tablets** are the usual treatment if stretching exercises do not help.
- **A 4-week course of quinine is often tried.** If it helps, it can be continued. Leg cramps may not go completely but they often become less frequent.
- **Quinine is dangerous in overdose** — keep it away from children.
- Do not take quinine if you are pregnant or may become pregnant.

L

Drug rationale

Drugs not included

- **Quinine salts other than the sulphate and bisulphate** (i.e. hydrochloride and dihydrochloride) are not included because they are used less frequently than quinine sulphate and bisulphate, and it will be more difficult for the person to secure a supply.
- **Vitamin E** has not been shown to be effective for the prevention and/or treatment of leg cramps [Connolly et al, 1992; Roca et al, 1992].
- **Naftidrofuryl, verapamil, and diltiazem** are not included because trials have been small and unconvincing [Baltodano et al, 1988; Young and Connolly, 1993; Voon and Sheu, 2001].
- **Calcium salts and sodium chloride** are possibly beneficial for the treatment of leg cramps in pregnancy, according to some small trials. However, they are not included because there is a lack of good-quality data [Young and Jewell, 2002]. The study investigating the use of sodium chloride is more than 50 years old and less relevant today, given our higher intake of dietary sodium.
- **Magnesium** citrate or magnesium lactate taken as 5 mmol in the morning and 10 mmol in the evening may be beneficial to some pregnant women who get leg cramps, but products containing these salts are not available on prescription [Young and Jewell, 2002].

Drugs included

- **Quinine** is the only drug to have been studied in any detail. Quinine sulphate was the salt used in a meta-analysis of published trials showing efficacy of quinine in leg cramps [Man-Son-Hing and Wells, 1995; Diener et al, 2002].
- Quinine sulphate and bisulphate are included because they are the most frequently prescribed quinine salts and will be most readily available to the person.

Prescriptions

1st line: non-drug management

Advice only: stretching exercises

- Age from 16 years onwards
- Stretching exercises for leg cramps: Stretching exercises of the calf muscle will prevent cramps in many people. Aim to do 5 minutes of stretching exercises, 3 times a day. Leaning forward on a wall with the soles of the feet flat on the ground is one way of stretching the calf muscle.

Non-drug management failed: quinine tablets

Quinine sulphate 200mg at night

- Age from 16 years onwards
- Quinine sulphate 200mg tablets. Take one tablet at night; supply 28 tablets; NHS Cost £1.47.

Quinine sulphate 300mg at night

- Age from 16 years onwards
- Quinine sulphate 300mg tablets. Take one tablet at night; supply 28 tablets; NHS Cost £1.30.

Quinine bisulphate 300mg at night

- Age from 16 years onwards
- Quinine bisulphate 300mg tabs. Take one tablet at night; supply 28 tablets; NHS Cost £1.45.

Extended Information

Background information

- What are idiopathic leg cramps? p.1144
- What are the secondary causes of leg cramps? p.1144
- How common are idiopathic leg cramps? p.1145
- How do I know my patient has idiopathic leg cramps? p.1145
- What else might it be? p.1145
- Complications and prognosis p.1145

What are idiopathic leg cramps?

- **A cramp is a transient, involuntary episode of pain,** usually sustained for minutes (up to 10 minutes), in which whole muscles or muscle groups go into spasm.
- **Idiopathic leg cramps** are the most common type of cramps and involve the calf muscle, thigh muscle, and small muscles of the foot. They occur at rest and usually at night.
- **It is probable that leg cramps occur when a muscle that is already in a shortened position is involuntarily stimulated.** This commonly happens at night where the plantar flexed foot places the calf and ventral foot muscles in the most shortened and vulnerable position.

[McGee, 1990; Riley and Antony, 1995; Kanaan and Sawaya, 2001; Salih, 2001]

What are the secondary causes of leg cramps?

Medical conditions

- **Conditions that may cause cramps include:**
  - Metabolic disturbance (e.g. hyponatraemia, hypokalaemia, hyperkalaemia, hypocalcaemia, hypomagnesaemia, hypoglycaemia).
  - Chronic diarrhoea.
  - Severe acute diarrhoea.
  - Excessive heat causing volume depletion and hyponatraemia.
  - Pregnancy, especially in the late months.

- Cirrhosis of the liver.
- Renal dialysis, possibly owing to plasma volume contraction.
- Thyroid disease:
  - Hyperthyroid myopathy may be associated with cramps.
  - Hypothyroidism is associated with weakness, enlarged muscles and painful muscle spasms.
- Heavy alcohol ingestion, which may induce severe muscle cramps.
- Lead toxicity.
- Sarcoidosis.
- Disorders of the lower motor neurone, including amyotrophic lateral sclerosis, polyneuropathies involving the motor neurone, recovered poliomyelitis, peripheral nerve injury and nerve root compression.

Drugs

- Certain drugs are known to be associated with leg cramps, although expert opinion varies on the strength of this association. In a study investigating quinine prescriptions in general practice, 37 out of 70 (53%) people who were prescribed quinine were also taking other drugs known to be associated with leg cramps [Mackie and Davidson, 1995].
- **Drugs that may cause cramps include:**
  - Salbutamol
  - Terbutaline
  - Raloxifene
  - Morphine (withdrawal)
  - Diuretics (owing to electrolyte loss)
  - Nifedipine
  - Phenothiazines
  - Penicillamine
  - Nicotinic acid

[McGee, 1990; Riley and Antony, 1995; DTB, 1996; Abdulla et al, 1999; Kanaan and Sawaya, 2001; Butler et al, 2002; Sweny, 2003]

How common are idiopathic leg cramps?

- **The prevalence of idiopathic leg cramps increases with age.** About one third of people over 60 years and half of people over 80 years suffer from cramp at rest.
- Forty per cent of people with leg cramps have more than three episodes per week and 6% have episodes at least once every 24 hours.

[McGee, 1990; Naylor and Young, 1994]

How do I know my patient has idiopathic leg cramps?

Symptoms

- **The main symptom is pain,** which varies in severity and is often described as sharp. The pain is localized to one muscle or muscle group, is usually unilateral, and most commonly affects the calf.
- **The duration of the pain varies from seconds to many minutes,** but the muscle may remain tender for up to 24 hours after the acute pain.
- **Onset is at rest and occurs suddenly,** often causing the person to be woken from sleep.

Signs

- During the cramp there is palpable hardening of the affected muscle.
- Otherwise examination is unremarkable.

Investigations

- **Investigations are not routinely recommended** unless the history and examination raise suspicion of an underlying cause, or the symptoms are atypical or particularly severe.
- **The following investigations may be appropriate to exclude secondary causes of leg cramps:**
  - **Urea, electrolyte, and calcium** measurements — if electrolyte disturbance is suspected
  - **Thyroid function tests** — if thyroid disease is suspected
  - **Fasting blood glucose and/or oral glucose tolerance test** — if diabetes mellitus is suspected
  - **Liver function tests** — if cirrhosis is suspected
  - **Magnesium levels** — if hypomagnesaemia is suspected (chronic malabsorption)
  - **Creatinine kinase levels and electromyogram** — if a muscle disorder is suspected
  - **Lead levels** — if lead toxicity is suspected

[McGee, 1990; Riley and Antony, 1995; Kanaan and Sawaya, 2001; Butler et al, 2002; Pagana and Pagana, 2002; Thakker, 2003]

What else might it be?

- **Differential diagnosis includes:**
  - Simple muscle strain.
  - Restless legs (Ekbom's) syndrome.
  - Hypnagogic muscle jerking.
  - Intermittent claudication and ischaemic rest pain.
  - Tetany.
  - Dystonia.
  - Contracture.
  - Lumbar nerve root entrapment.
  - Ruptured Baker's cyst.
  - Deep vein thrombosis/thrombophlebitis.
  - Peripheral neuropathy.
  - Occupational cramps, which are thought to be a focal dystonia (e.g. writer's, pianist's, typist's and cobbler's cramp).

[McGee, 1990; Riley and Antony, 1995]

Complications and prognosis

Complications

- Idiopathic nocturnal leg cramps have a relatively benign natural history, with no serious complications.
- Sleep disturbance may affect quality of life.

Prognosis

- Cramps may occur intermittently during one day or they may persist over several weeks. Most cases will resolve spontaneously [Salih, 2001].

Management issues

- How should I assess someone with leg cramps? p.1145
- How should an acute attack of leg cramp be managed? p.1146
- How should recurrent leg cramps be managed? p.1146
- How should I manage leg cramps in pregnancy? p.1146
- What evidence is there for other drug treatments? p.1147
- Medicines management p.1147

How should I assess someone with leg cramps?

- Exclude medical conditions that are known to cause leg cramps.
- Review medication to identify drugs that may cause leg cramps.

How should an acute attack of leg cramp be managed?

- **Passive stretching and massage** of the affected muscles can relieve an acute attack of cramp. Passive stretching should be performed with active contraction of the opposing muscle (e.g. in cramp affecting the calf, dorsiflex the ankle whilst extending the knee) [Weiner and Weiner, 1980].
- **Simple analgesia** — is unlikely to be useful for relieving the pain of an acute attack of leg cramps that last only seconds or minutes. Analgesics may help relief if muscle tenderness follows the cramp.

How should recurrent leg cramps be managed?

- **Reassurance** that idiopathic leg cramps are benign may be all that is required.
- **Consider recommending simple measures, although here is a lack of evidence of benefit for these.**
  - **Stretching exercises** are commonly advised. It is recommended that stretching exercises should be carried out three times daily initially, and then continued at a frequency that maintains a cramp-free state. Stretching the calf muscles before going to bed may help some people [Daniell, 1979; Postgraduate Medicine, 2002].
  - **Other measures** e.g. raising the foot or the head of the bed to maintain dorsiflexion; using a pillow to prop the feet up in bed while sleeping in the supine position; hanging the feet over the end of the bed while sleeping in the prone position; and keeping blankets loose at the foot of the bed to prevent toes and feet from pointing downwards during sleep have not been investigated in trials but are thought by experts to be helpful in preventing leg cramps [Weiner and Weiner, 1980; Warburton et al, 1987; Kanaan and Sawaya, 2001].
- **Quinine should be considered if the leg cramps are frequent, troublesome and affecting quality of life.** It is the only drug that has been shown to be effective in the treatment and prevention of nocturnal cramps.

What is the supporting evidence for stretching exercises?

- There is a lack of good evidence to suggest that stretching exercises are effective and some evidence to suggest that they are ineffective.
- An observational study was carried out on 44 people with frequent cramps who were instructed to carry out simple stretching exercises (see Patient Information Leaflets) three times a day until their cramps disappeared. The characteristics of the people who were investigated were not reported including whether they were taking quinine. All reported cure within a week (21 people within 72 hours) and most remained cramp-free for follow-up periods as long as one year [Daniell, 1979].
- A recent randomised controlled trial investigated the effectiveness of stretching exercise in 191 people who were already taking quinine. Half of the people in the study were advised to discontinue their quinine and the other half to continue, and both groups were advised to undertake either stretching or non-stretching exercises. This study did not confirm that stretching exercises were effective strategy to reduce the frequency or severity of night cramps [Coppin et al, 2005].
- Until further evidence is available, it seems reasonable to consider a trial of stretching exercises to prevent leg cramps.

What is the supporting evidence for quinine?

- **Quinine sulphate reduced the frequency and also the severity** [Man-Son-Hing et al, 1998] of attacks of leg cramps, but did not seem to reduce the duration [Diener et al, 2002].
- There was a significant reduction in leg cramps in people treated with quinine sulphate 200 mg twice a day for 2 weeks compared with placebo [Diener et al, 2002]. This was a double-blind, placebo-controlled, parallel-group, multi-centre trial including 98 participants. Adverse effects were reported in both the treatment and placebo groups, but were not statistically significant.
- Treatment with quinine sulphate (200 mg or 300 mg at night) resulted in a significant reduction (8.83; 95% CI 3.85 to 2.75) in the number of cramps in 4 weeks compared with placebo in a meta-analysis of six randomised, double-blind, crossover trials [Man-Son-Hing and Wells, 1995]. The number of nights with cramps was also reduced by 27%.
- The meta-analysis referred to in the previous bullet later included unpublished data that reduced the estimate of efficacy of quinine to 3.60 fewer cramps (95% CI 2.15 to 5.05) in a 4-week period [Man-Son-Hing et al, 1998]. There were 2.45 fewer cramps in 4 weeks reported in the unpublished data (95% CI 1.03 to 3.87).
- **Long-term efficacy of quinine** has not been evaluated in published trials to date.

How should I manage leg cramps in pregnancy?

- **Massage and stretching the affected muscle** remained the treatment of choice in pregnant women in a Cochrane review in the management of leg cramps during pregnancy [Young and Jewell, 2002].
- **Quinine is not recommended for the management of leg cramps in pregnancy.** Large amounts of quinine can induce miscarriage and congenital malformations (particularly of the optic and auditory nerves) [ABPI Medicines Compendium, 2003].

What is the supporting evidence for drug therapy in pregnancy?

- A recent Cochrane review found the following results [Young and Jewell, 2002].
  - **Magnesium** (lactate or citrate) was found to alleviate leg cramps in doses of 5 mmol in the morning and 10 mmol in the evening taken for 3 weeks (OR 0.18, 95% CI 0.05 to 0.60) [Dahle et al, 1995]. Leg cramps ceased in a third of women and reduced the frequency of attacks in others.
  - **Calcium lactate** showed no clear benefit in reducing leg cramps.
  - **Sodium chloride** showed a possible reduction in the number of leg cramps experienced by pregnant women. However the trial was carried out over 50 years ago and the results may no longer be relevant because of dietary changes, which include an increased sodium intake in the general population. However, sodium chloride cannot be recommended as there was a high relapse rate on stopping treatment and there may an adverse effect on blood pressure from such high doses (45–60 gm daily).
  - **Multivitamin** preparations may be helpful but the data were difficult to interpret as it was unclear which ingredient, if any, was effective, or if indeed if this was a placebo effect.

What evidence is there for other drug treatments?

The following drug treatments are not currently recommended for use in primary care, as most of the studies involving them included only a small number of participants and have limited evidence of effectiveness.

Double-blind, randomised placebo-controlled crossover trials

- **Naftidrofuryl significantly reduced the frequency of leg cramps** in 14 people compared with placebo [Young and Connolly, 1993]. People in the naftidrofuryl group also reported an increased number of cramp-free days per month.
- **Diltiazem (30 mg) reduced the frequency,** but not the intensity, of leg cramps in 12 people compared with placebo [Voon and Sheu, 2001].
- **Vitamin B complex significantly reduced** the frequency, intensity, and duration of leg cramps in 28 elderly people with hypertension [Chan, 1998]. Of the people taking vitamin B complex, 28% had almost complete remission of leg cramps, and 57% showed significant reduction in leg cramps. Improvement was seen after 4 weeks and persisted for 12 weeks.
- **Vitamin E (800 iu) did not significantly improve** the frequency or severity of night cramps or sleep disturbance in 27 men compared with quinine [Connolly et al, 1992]. They found that quinine significantly improved the frequency and severity of night cramps within 4 weeks of initiating treatment, compared with vitamin E and placebo.
- **Magnesium.** Two trials in men and non-pregnant women gave contradictory results.
  - One trial of 46 people suggested that 300 mg magnesium may be effective in reducing the number of cramps [Roffe et al, 2002]. However, 56% of these people were also taking quinine and 23% had peripheral vascular disease, a predisposing factor for leg cramps.
  - The second trial of 42 people found no evidence of effectiveness of 900 mg of magnesium [Frusso et al, 1999].
- **Orphenadrine.** A trial in 59 people suggested that orphenadrine reduced the frequency of nocturnal leg cramps [Latta, 1989]. The frequency of leg cramp in the treated group was 39% less than that experienced in the placebo group. However, the results are difficult to interpret, as almost half the people were either lost to follow-up or discontinued the orphenadrine.

Open-labelled trials

- **Verapamil resolved nocturnal leg cramps** within 8 weeks in eight elderly people whose cramps were unresponsive to quinine [Baltodano et al, 1988].

Medicines management

How should quinine be prescribed?

- **Quinine 200–300 mg at bedtime** is effective in reducing the frequency of nocturnal leg cramps. It may take up to 4 weeks for improvement to become apparent, and the treatment is then given regularly if there is benefit [BNF 49, 2005].
- **Treatment should be interrupted at intervals** of about 3 months to assess the need for further quinine treatment [BNF 49, 2005]. Some people who found quinine beneficial were able to stop it without any major problems [Coppin et al, 2005].
- **People should be monitored** closely during the early stages for adverse effects as well as for benefit [BNF 49, 2005].

How safe is quinine?

- **Adverse effects** of quinine have been reported, but these do appear to be dose-related.
  - There is no good study of the risk of adverse effects when using the *low doses* that are prescribed for leg cramps, although a recent meta-analysis showed that tinnitus was the only adverse effect occurring with significantly greater frequency than found with placebo [Man-Son-Hing et al, 1998].
  - Adverse effects of quinine are reported at the *high doses* received during treatment of malaria namely tinnitus, headache, nausea, visual disturbance, fever, digestive disorders, thrombocytopenia, and pruritus [Mackie and Davidson, 1995; DTB, 1996; Reddy et al, 2004].
- **Hypersensitivity reactions** are not uncommon, with symptoms usually limited to fever and rashes. However, angioedema, thrombocytopenia and asthma have been reported [Dukes and Aronson, 2000; Brasic, 2001].
- Drinking tonic water is unlikely to be effective in managing leg cramps, as large quantities would need to be consumed to achieve therapeutic levels. Tonic water contains up to 80 mg/l, and other soft drinks (e.g. bitter lemon) contain up to 40 mg/l, of quinine hydrochloride [Worden et al, 1987].
- **Prolonged QT interval** has been noted with quinine. However, clinically significant effects are generally only seen with very high doses or following overdose [Thomas, 1997; Dukes and Aronson, 2000]. Consider the risk–benefit ratio when prescribing quinine with other drugs that may prolong the QT interval, as they may have a synergistic effect.
- **Overdose** of quinine may lead to permanent visual impairment, cardiac arrhythmias, and death [DTB, 1996; BNF 49, 2005].

Who should not be prescribed quinine for leg cramps?

- A woman who is pregnant or who might become pregnant. Pregnancy in someone with malaria is not generally regarded as a contraindication to the use of quinine. As malaria infection is potentially serious during pregnancy and poses a threat to the mother and fetus, there is little justification in withholding treatment in the absence of a suitable alternative. However, quinine should not be used for cramps during pregnancy.
- Someone who has previously had a hypersensitive reaction to quinine or who has had thrombocytopenic purpura associated with quinine.
- Quinine is contraindicated in someone with a history of haemolytic anaemia, G6PD deficiency, haemoglobinuria, myasthenia gravis, or optic neuritis.
- Quinine should only be used after a risk–benefit assessment in a person with heart disease.

[DTB, 1996; ABPI Medicines Compendium, 2003; BNF 49, 2005]

Are there any significant drug interactions associated with quinine?

There are several potentially serious drug interactions with quinine and these should be identified before prescribing.

- **Cardiac glycosides:** the concomitant use of quinine may increase the plasma level of digoxin. Halving the maintenance dose of digoxin may be necessary.
- **Anti-arrhythmics:** there is an increased risk of ventricular arrhythmias if quinine is taken with *amiodarone*.

L

- **Antipsychotics:** there is an increased risk of ventricular arrhythmias, and concomitant use should be avoided with *pimozide* or *thioridazine*.
- **Antihistamines:** concomitant use of *terfenadine* should be avoided, owing to the increased risk of ventricular arrhythmias.
- **Antibiotics:** there is an increased risk of ventricular arrhythmias, and concomitant use should be avoided with *moxifloxacin*.
- **Other antimalarials:** quinine should not be prescribed for people taking *mefloquine*, as there is an increased risk of convulsions.

[ABPI Medicines Compendium, 2003; BNF 49, 2005]

References

NHS staff in England can link, free of charge, from references to full text journals by clicking on [Full text] on the PRODIGY website.

1. Abdulla, A.J., Jones, P.W. and Pearce, V.R. (1999) Leg cramps in the elderly: prevalence, drug and disease associations. *International Journal of Clinical Practice* 53(7), 494–496.
2. ABPI Medicines Compendium (2003) *Summary of product characteristics for Quinine sulphate tablets 200mg*. Electronic Medicines Compendium. Datapharm Communications Ltd. www.emc.medicines.org.uk [Accessed: 07/03/2005].
3. Baltodano, N., Gallo, B.V. and Weidler, D.J. (1988) Verapamil vs quinine in recumbent nocturnal leg cramps in the elderly. *Archives of Internal Medicine* 148(9), 1969–1970.
4. BNF 49 (2005) *British National Formulary*. 49th edn. London: British Medical Association and Royal Pharmaceutical Society of Great Britain.
5. Brasic, J.R. (2001) Quinine-induced thrombocytopenia in a 64-year-old man who consumed tonic water to relieve nocturnal leg cramps. *Mayo Clinic Proceedings* 76(8), 863–864. [Full text]
6. Butler, J.V., Mulkerrin, E.C. and O'Keeffe, S.T. (2002) Nocturnal leg cramps in older people. *Postgraduate Medical Journal* 78(924), 596–598. [Full text]
7. Chan, P. (1998) Randomized, double-blind, placebo-controlled study of the safety and efficacy of vitamin B complex in the treatment of nocturnal leg cramps in elderly patients with hypertension. *Journal of Clinical Pharmacology* 38(12), 1151–1154.
8. Connolly, P.S., Shirley, E.A., Wasson, J.H. and Nierenberg, D.W. (1992) Treatment of nocturnal leg cramps. A crossover trial of quinine vs. vitamin E. *Archives of Internal Medicine* 152(9), 1877–1880.
9. Coppin, R.J., Wicke, D.M. and Little, P.S. (2005) Managing nocturnal leg cramps – calf-stretching exercises and cessation of quinine treatment: a factorial randomised controlled trial. *British Journal of General Practice* 55(512), 186–191.
10. Dahle, L.O., Berg, G., Hammar, M. et al (1995) The effect of oral magnesium substitution on pregnancy-induced leg cramps. *American Journal of Obstetrics and Gynecology* 173(1), 175–180.
11. Daniell, H.W. (1979) Simple cure for nocturnal leg cramps. *New England Journal of Medicine* 301(4), 216.
12. Diener, H.C., Dethlefsen, U., Dethlefsen-Gruber, S. and Verbeek, P. (2002) Effectiveness of quinine in treating muscle cramps: a double-blind, placebo-controlled, parallel-group, multicentre trial. *International Journal of Clinical Practice* 56(4), 243–246.
13. DTB (1996) Quinine for nocturnal leg cramps? *Drug & Therapeutics Bulletin* 34(Jan), 7–8. [Full text]
14. Dukes, M.N.G. and Aronson, J.K. (Eds.) (2000) *Meyler's side effects of drugs*. 14th edn. Oxford: Elsevier.
15. Frusso, R., Zarate, M., Augustovski, F. and Rubinstein, A. (1999) Magnesium for the treatment of nocturnal leg cramps: a crossover randomized trial. *Journal of Family Practice* 48(11), 868–871.
16. Kanaan, N. and Sawaya, R. (2001) Nocturnal leg cramps. Clinically mysterious and painful – but manageable. *Geriatrics* 56(6), 34–42. [Full text]
17. Latta, D. (1989) An alternative to quinine in nocturnal leg cramps. *Current Therapeutic Research* 45(5), 833–837.
18. Mackie, M.A. and Davidson, J. (1995) Prescribing of quinine and cramp inducing drugs in general practice. *British Medical Journal* 311(7019), 1541. [Full text]
19. Man-Son-Hing, M. and Wells, G. (1995) Meta-analysis of efficacy of quinine for treatment of nocturnal leg cramps in elderly people. *British Medical Journal* 310(6971), 13–17. [Full text]
20. Man-Son-Hing, M., Wells, G. and Lau, A. (1998) Quinine for nocturnal leg cramps a meta-analysis including unpublished data. *Journal of General Internal Medicine* 13(9), 600–606.
21. McGee, S.R. (1990) Muscle cramps. *Archives of Internal Medicine* 150(3), 511–518.
22. Naylor, J.R. and Young, J.B. (1994) A general population survey of rest cramps. *Age and Ageing* 23(5), 418–420.
23. Pagana, K.D. and Pagana, T.J. (Eds.) (2002) *Mosby's manual of diagnostic and laboratory tests*. 2nd edn. London: Mosby.
24. Postgraduate Medicine (2002) Patient notes: nocturnal leg cramps. *Postgraduate Medicine* 111(2), 125–126. [Full text]
25. Reddy, J.C.M., Shuman, M.A.M. and Aster, R.H.M. (2004) Quinine/Quinidine-induced thrombocytopenia: a great imitator. *Archives of Internal Medicine* 164(2), 218–220. [Full text]
26. Riley, J.D. and Antony, S.J. (1995) Leg cramps: differential diagnosis and management. *American Family Physician* 52(6), 1794–1798.
27. Roca, A.O., Jarjoura, D., Blend, D. et al (1992) Dialysis leg cramps. Efficacy of quinine versus vitamin E. *ASAIO Journal* 38(3), M481-M485.
28. Roffe, C., Sills, S., Crome, P. and Jones, P. (2002) Randomised, cross-over, placebo controlled trial of magnesium citrate in the treatment of chronic persistent leg cramps. *Medical Science Monitor* 8(5), CR326-CR330.
29. Salih, A. (2001) Treating leg cramps and restless syndrome. *Prescriber* 12(3), 93–97.
30. Sweny, P. (2003) Renal transplantation. In: Warrell, D.A., Cox, T.M., Firth, J.D. and Benz, E.J.Jr (Eds.) *Oxford textbook of medicine*. 4th edn. Oxford: Oxford University Press. 20.6.3.
31. Thakker, R.V. (2003) Parathyroid disorders and diseases altering calcium metabolism. In: Warrell, D.A., Cox, T.M., Firth, J.D. and Benz, E.J.Jr (Eds.) *Oxford textbook of medicine*. 4th edn. Oxford: Oxford University Press. Section 12.6.
32. Thomas, S.H.L. (1997) Drugs and the QT interval. *Adverse Drug Reaction Bulletin* 182(Feb), 691–694.
33. Voon, W.C. and Sheu, S.H (2001) Diltiazem for nocturnal leg cramps. *Age & Ageing* 30(1), 91–92. [Full text]
34. Warburton, A., Royston, J.P., O'Neill, C.J. et al (1987) A quinine a day keeps the leg cramps away? *British Journal of Clinical Pharmacology* 23(4), 459–465.
35. Weiner, I.H and Weiner, H.L (1980) Nocturnal leg muscle cramps. *Journal of the American Medical Association* 244(20), 2332–2333.

36. Worden, A.N., Frape, D.L. and Shephard, N.W. (1987) Consumption of quinine hydrochloride in tonic water. *Lancet* 1(8527), 271–272.
37. Young, J.B. and Connolly, M.J. (1993) Naftidrofuryl treatment for rest cramp. *Postgraduate Medical Journal* **69**(814), 624–626.
38. Young, G.L. and Jewell, D. (2002) *Interventions for leg cramps in pregnancy (Cochrane Review)*. The Cochrane Library. Issue 1. Chichester, UK: John Wiley & Sons, Ltd. www.nelh.nhs.uk/cochrane.asp [Accessed: 10/02/2005]. [Full text]

L

PRODIGY GUIDANCE

Leg ulcer — venous

Last revised in November 2004
www.prodigy.nhs.uk/guidance.asp?gt=Legulcer - venous

Applies to people over the age of 16 years

This guidance is based on the clinical practice guideline, '*The management of patients with venous leg ulcers*', produced by the Royal College of Nursing institute (1998).

This guidance covers the management of venous leg ulcers: assessment, cleansing, debridement, dressing, compression therapy, and preventing recurrence. Management of infection is covered, and complications such as pain and associated dermatitis are discussed.

This guidance does not cover the management of leg ulcers with an arterial component or skin ulcers due to pressure.

There is separate PRODIGY guidance for *Palliative care — malodorous malignant ulcer of the skin* and *Diabetes Type 1 and 2 — foot disease.*

Goals

- To provide optimal conditions for ulcer healing, including general health promotion and education
- To manage complications of venous leg ulcers such as oedema, infection, and contact dermatitis
- To identify possible arterial insufficiency that requires assessment and treatment in secondary care
- To minimize or prevent the recurrence of leg ulcers

Contents

Scenarios

- Uncomplicated venous leg ulcer p.1150
- Leg ulcer with heavy exudate p.1153
- Infected venous leg ulcer p.1156
- 12-week follow-up assessment of venous leg ulcer p.1158
- Healed venous leg ulcer p.1160

Extended Information, p. 1161

Which scenario?

- **Uncomplicated venous leg ulcer:** covers the intial management of of simple venous leg ulcers (with or without slough) that are not infected and do not have heavy exudate or odour.
- **Leg ulcer with heavy exudate:** covers the initial management of venous leg ulcers with heavy exudates or associated odour.
- **Infected venous leg ulcer:** covers the management of venous leg ulcers that show clinical signs and symptoms of infection.
- **12-week follow-up assessment of venous leg ulcer:** covers the formal reassessment of venous leg ulcers. This should be carried out 12 weeks after the start of treatment, and every 12 weeks thereafter until healed.
- **Healed venous leg ulcer:** covers measures to prevent recurrence of venous ulcers.

Uncomplicated venous leg ulcer

Which therapy?

Assess the ulcerated area

- **Record length and width of ulcer:** trace the margins or photograph.
- **Document the ulcer site:** appearance of the ulcer edge, ulcer base, and surrounding skin.
- **Measure the ankle brachial pressure index (ABPI).**

Clean and dress the leg ulcer

- Consider bed rest or leg elevation to reduce oedema before applying compression bandages.
- **Measure ankle circumference** 2 cm above the malleolus.
- **Wash leg ulcers with clean tap water** and dry carefully.
- **Dress the wound with a low-adherent dressing.**
- **Apply 4-layer graduated compression bandaging.**
- For active people or people unable to tolerate 4-layer bandaging, consider using 2-layer short-stretch bandaging.

Manage associated symptoms

- **Offer oral analgesia** such as paracetamol for associated pain.
- **Consider topical analgesia** if there is pain during dressing changes.
- **Routine wound swabs are not recommended.** Only use if there is evidence of clinical infection.

Follow-up advice

- **Re-dress the leg ulcer** with compression bandages every week.
- **Reassess ulcers after 12 weeks** and every 12 weeks thereafter until healed.
  - Reasses Doppler ABPI at 12 weeks if the ulcer is not fully healed or is deteriorating.
  - Refer complications such as non-healing ulcers after 12 weeks of adequate treatment.
  - Refer if suspected malignancy, or if the diagnosis is uncertain (e.g. if the ulcer is not healing or has an atypical appearance or distribution).
- **Regularly assess concordance with treatment,** and the effect of pain and mobility on quality of life.
- **Provide written patient information.** People are more likely to comply with treatment regimes if they are fully informed of the rationale and options for their management.
- **Give general health promotion advice** regarding regular walking and mobility, avoiding prolonged standing, leg elevation when immobile, stopping smoking, and good foot-care.
- **Recommend graduated compression stockings for at least 5 years after ulcer healing,** in order to minimize the risk of recurrence.

Should I refer or investigate?

Refer?

- **ABPI less than 0.8:** assume to have arterial disease, and refer to a vascular clinic for further assessment. Compression bandaging in such instances may further compromise arterial blood supply, and should be generally avoided.
- **ABPI less than 0.5:** urgent vascular referral. Compression bandaging in such instances should be avoided.
- **Suspected malignancy,** or if the diagnosis is uncertain (e.g. if the ulcer is not healing or has an atypical appearance or distribution).
- **Acute ischaemic changes** as a consequence of compression bandaging.
- **Rapidly deteriorating ulcer.**
- **Non-healing ulcer** after 12 weeks of adequate treatment.
- **Pain management** is inadequate.
- Healed ulcers with a view to venous surgery if appropriate.

Investigate?

Rule out an arterial component.

- **Check pedal pulses,** as they may indicate arterial insufficiency.
- **Measure the ankle brachial pressure index (ABPI).**

Other investigations to consider:

- **Full blood count** to check for anaemia, infection.
- **Erythrocyte sedimentation rate, C-reactive protein:** inflammatory markers.
- **Fasting blood glucose and urinalysis** to screen for diabetes mellitus.
- **Urea, electrolytes, and creatinine** to check for renal impairment.
- **Wound swab only if clinical evidence of infection:** pyrexia, increasing pain, enlarging ulcer or cellulitis.

Shared decision making

- **A leg ulcer is normally washed with tap water before a dressing is put on.**
- **A nurse will usually apply compression bandages over the dressing.** This is the most important part of treatment to help the ulcer to heal.
- **The dressing and bandaging are normally changed every week.**
- Other measures that may promote healing include:
  - **Keep as active as possible.**
  - **Do not stand for long periods.**
  - **If possible, elevate your leg when you are resting.**
  - **If you smoke, try to stop.**
- **Painkillers** may be helpful if the ulcer is painful.
- Once the ulcer has healed, if you wear a support stocking each day it will help to prevent a recurrence.

Drug rationale

Drugs not included

- **Hydrogel sheets, pastes, and products that require premixing** are not offered.
- **Low-adherent dressings other than knitted viscose primary dressings** are not required as the wound contact layer for uncomplicated ulcers.
- **Adhesive bordered dressings** are not offered, as people with venous leg ulcer tend to have sensitive skin, and because dressings under high compression multi-layer bandages do not tend to slip.
- **Multi-layer compression bandaging: individual bandages** for multi-layer bandaging are offered as part of a kit and not separately in this scenario.
- **Compression hosiery** is reserved for people with healed ulcers, to prevent recurrence.

Drugs included

- **Ready-mixed hydrogel dressings** are offered to help with desloughing ulcers. A range of sizes and application packs appropriate for venous leg ulcers are offered.
- **Multi-layer compression bandaging: 4-layer kits** (K-Four®, Profore®, System 4®, Ultra-Four®) are offered, appropriate to ankle circumference. They contain:
  - **Low-adherent dressings** for the wound contact layer.
  - **Wadding bandages** (the first layer applied), which are used to reshape the leg in people with a narrow ankle circumference.
  - **Light support bandages,** used at layers 2 and 3.
  - **Cohesive bandages,** used at layer 4.
- **Two-layer short-stretch bandaging** may be preferred in an active, younger person, or if concordance with 4-layer bandaging is a problem. These are generally offered as a multiple-item prescription containing:
  - **Low-adherent dressings:** knitted viscose primary dressings (e.g. N-A Dressings®) are suitable for a wound contact layer beneath compression bandaging.
  - **Wadding bandages** (the first layer applied) are used to reshape the leg in people with a narrow ankle circumference.
  - **Short-stretch compression bandages** are the second layer applied.
  - Note: Proguide® is the only 2-layer system available as a kit.
- **Paracetamol** is offered as a first-line analgesic. Manage pain according to response and associated comorbidities.

L

Prescriptions

Hydrogel for sloughy wounds

15g size: Aquaform hydrogel

- Age from 16 years onwards
- Aquaform hydrogel (15g). Apply to dry sloughy wounds when required to help autolytic debridement; supply 4 15g packs; NHS Cost £7.20.

15g size: Granugel hydrogel

- Age from 16 years onwards
- Granugel hydrogel (15g). Apply to dry sloughy wounds when required to help autolytic debridement; supply 4 15g tubes; NHS Cost £7.92.

15g size: Intrasite hydrogel

- Age from 16 years onwards
- Intrasite gel (15g). Apply to dry sloughy wounds when required to help autolytic debridement; supply 4 15g sachets; NHS Cost £8.24.

15g size: Nu-Gel hydrogel

- Age from 16 years onwards
- Nu-Gel hydrogel (15g). Apply to dry sloughy wounds when required to help autolytic debridement; supply 4 15g packs; NHS Cost £7.72.

15g size: Purilon hydrogel

- Age from 16 years onwards
- Purilon gel (15g). Apply to dry sloughy wounds when required to help autolytic debridement; supply 4 15g packs; NHS Cost £7.92.

8g size: Intrasite hydrogel
- Age from 16 years onwards
- Intrasite gel (8g). Apply to dry sloughy wounds when required to help autolytic debridement; supply 4 8g sachets; NHS Cost £6.12.

8g size: Purilon hydrogel
- Age from 16 years onwards
- Purilon gel (8g). Apply to dry sloughy wounds when required to help autolytic debridement; supply 4 8g packs; NHS Cost £6.00.

25g size: Intrasite hydrogel
- Age from 16 years onwards
- Intrasite gel (25g). Apply to dry sloughy wounds when required to help autolytic debridement; supply 4 25g sachets; NHS Cost £12.20.

4-layer bandage kits (measure ankle circumference:)

Ankle circumference <18cm: Profore kit
- Age from 16 years onwards
- Profore 4 layer kit ankle<18cm. Follow the instructions given inside this pack; supply 1 kit; NHS Cost £9.41.

Ankle circumference 18-25cm: Ultra four kit
- Age from 16 years onwards
- Ultra four kit 18-25cm. Follow the instructions given inside this pack; supply 1 kit; NHS Cost £6.16.

Ankle circumference 18-25cm: K-Four kit
- Age from 16 years onwards
- Use the following information to write a prescription: supply one K-Four multilayer compression bandaging kit for ankle circumference 18-25cm. Follow the instructions given inside the pack. (Price £6.55)

Ankle circumference 18-25cm: System 4 kit
- Age from 16 years onwards
- Use the following information to write a prescription: supply one System 4 multilayer compression bandaging kit for ankle circumference 18-25cm. Follow the instructions given inside the pack. (Price £8.15)

Ankle circumference 18-25cm: Profore kit
- Age from 16 years onwards
- Profore 4 layer kit 18-25cm. Follow the instructions given inside this pack; supply 1 kit; NHS Cost £8.77.

Ankle circumference 25-30cm: Profore kit
- Age from 16 years onwards
- Profore 4 layer kit 25-30cm. Follow the instructions given inside this pack; supply 1 kit; NHS Cost £7.27.

Ankle circumference >30cm: Profore kit
- Age from 16 years onwards
- Profore 4 layer kit ankle>30cm. Follow the instructions given inside this pack; supply 1 kit; NHS Cost £10.89.

2-layer short-stretch bandages

2-layer dressing: Actiban short-stretch bandage + wadding
- Age from 16 years onwards
- Soft absorbent bandage 10cm. Use for two-layer compression bandaging; supply 6 3.5m bandages; NHS Cost £2.52.
- Knit viscose dress 9.5x9.5cm. Use for two-layer compression bandaging; supply 6 dressings; NHS Cost £1.98.
- Actiban sht-stretch band 10cm. Use for two-layer compression bandaging; supply 6 5m bandages; NHS Cost £20.40.

2-layer dressing: Actico short-stretch bandage + wadding
- Age from 16 years onwards
- Actico cohesive bandage 10cm. Use for two-layer compression bandaging; supply 6 6m bandages; NHS Cost £18.60.
- Soft absorbent bandage 10cm. Use for two-layer compression bandaging; supply 6 3.5m bandages; NHS Cost £2.52.
- Knit viscose dress 9.5x9.5cm. Use for two-layer compression bandaging; supply 6 dressings; NHS Cost £1.98.

2-layer dressing: Comprilan short-stretch bandage + wadding
- Age from 16 years onwards
- Soft absorbent bandage 10cm. Use for two-layer compression bandaging; supply 6 3.5m bandages; NHS Cost £2.52.
- Knit viscose dress 9.5x9.5cm. Use for two-layer compression bandaging; supply 6 dressings; NHS Cost £1.98.
- Comprilan short-stretch 10cm. Use for two-layer compression bandaging; supply 6 5m bandages; NHS Cost £19.98.

2-layer dressing: Rosidal K short-stretch bandage + wadding
- Age from 16 years onwards
- Soft absorbent bandage 10cm. Use for two-layer compression bandaging; supply 6 3.5m bandages; NHS Cost £2.52.
- Rosidal K short-stretch 10cm. Use for two-layer compression bandaging; supply 6 5m bandages; NHS Cost £20.16.
- Knit viscose dress 9.5x9.5cm. Use for two-layer compression bandaging; supply 6 dressings; NHS Cost £1.98.

2-layer dressing: Silkolan short-stretch bandage + wadding
- Age from 16 years onwards
- Soft absorbent bandage 10cm. Use for two-layer compression bandaging; supply 6 3.5m bandages; NHS Cost £2.52.
- Silkolan short stretch 10cm. Use for two-layer compression bandaging; supply 6 5m bandages; NHS Cost £21.72.
- Knit viscose dress 9.5x9.5cm. Use for two-layer compression bandaging; supply 6 dressings; NHS Cost £1.98.

Proguide (Red) 2-layer kit: ankle circumference 18-22cm
- Age from 16 years onwards
- Proguide 18-22cm red kit. Follow the instructions given inside this pack; supply 6 kits; NHS Cost £54.42.

Proguide (Yellow) 2-layer kit: ankle circumference 22-28cm
- Age from 16 years onwards
- Proguide 22-28cm yellow kit. Follow the instructions given inside this pack; supply 6 kits; NHS Cost £57.42.

Proguide (Green) 2-layer kit: ankle circumference 28-32cm
- Age from 16 years onwards
- Proguide 28-32cm green kit. Follow the instructions given inside this pack; supply 6 kits; NHS Cost £60.36.

Analgesia: use when required

Paracetamol tablets: 1g up to four times a day
- Age from 16 years onwards
- Paracetamol 500mg tablets. Take two tablets every 4 to 6 hours when required for pain relief. Maximum of 8 tablets in 24 hours; supply 100 tablets; NHS Cost £0.75; OTC Cost £1.32.

Leg ulcer with heavy exudate

Which therapy?

Assess the ulcerated area

- **Record length and width of ulcer:** trace the margins or photograph.
- **Document the ulcer site:** appearance of the ulcer edge, ulcer base, and surrounding skin.
- **Measure the ankle brachial pressure index (ABPI).**

Clean and dress the wound

- **Measure ankle circumference** 2 cm above the malleolus.
- **Wash leg ulcers with clean tap water** and dry carefully.
- **Compression is the mainstay of treatment,** as a reduction in oedema will reduce subsequent exudate formation. If exudate is not controlled by compression:
  - **For sloughy wounds** consider an alginate dressing.
  - **For 'clean' wounds** use a polyurethane foam dressing.
  - **If there is associated odour,** consider an odour absorbent dressing.

Apply compression bandaging

- Consider bed rest or leg elevation to reduce oedema before applying compression bandages.
- **Apply 4-layer graduated compression bandaging.**
- For active people or people unable to tolerate 4-layer bandaging, consider using 2-layer short-stretch bandaging.

Manage associated symptoms

- **Offer oral analgesia** such as paracetamol for associated pain.
- **Consider topical analgesia** if there is pain during dressing changes.
- **Routine wound swabs are not recommended.** Only use if there is evidence of clinical infection.
- **Involve other health professionals.** If available, consider dermatology specialist nurses, community leg-ulcer clinics, and leg-ulcer nurse specialists.
- Ensure direct access to specialised services for the management of specific complications.

Follow-up advice

- **Re-dress leg ulcer** with compression bandages every week.
- **Reassess ulcers after 12 weeks** and every 12 weeks thereafter until healed.
  - Reasses Doppler ABPI at 12 weeks if the ulcer is not fully healed or is deteriorating.
  - Refer complications such as non-healing ulcers after 12 weeks of adequate treatment.
  - Refer if suspected malignancy, or if the diagnosis is uncertain (e.g. if the ulcer is not healing or has an atypical appearance or distribution).
- **Regularly assess patient concordance with treatment,** and the effect of pain and mobility on quality of life.
- **Provide written patient information.** People are more likely to comply with treatment regimes if they are fully informed of the rationale and options for their management.
- **Give general health promotion advice** regarding regular walking and mobility, avoiding prolonged standing, leg elevation when immobile, stopping smoking, and good foot-care.
- **Recommend graduated compression stockings for at least 5 years after ulcer healing,** in order to minimise the risk of recurrence.

Refer or investigate

Refer?

- **ABPI less than 0.8:** assume to have arterial disease, and refer to a vascular clinic for further assessment. Compression bandaging in such instances may further compromise arterial blood supply, and should be generally avoided.
- **ABPI less than 0.5:** urgent vascular referral. Compression bandaging in such instances should be avoided.
- **Suspected malignancy,** or if the diagnosis is uncertain (e.g. if the ulcer is not healing or has an atypical appearance or distribution).
- **Acute ischaemic changes** as a consequence of compression bandaging.
- **Rapidly deteriorating ulcer.**
- **Non-healing ulcer** after 12 weeks of adequate treatment.
- **Pain management** inadequate.
- Healed ulcers with a view to venous surgery if appropriate.

Investigate?

Rule out an arterial component.

- **Check pedal pulses,** as they may indicate arterial insufficiency.
- **Measure the ankle brachial pressure index (ABPI).**

Other investigations to consider

- **Full blood count** to check for anaemia, infection.
- **Erythrocyte sedimentation rate, C-reactive protein:** inflammatory markers.
- **Fasting blood glucose and urinalysis** to screen for diabetes mellitus.
- **Urea, electrolytes, and creatinine** to check for renal impairment.
- **Wound swab only if clinical evidence of infection:** pyrexia, increasing pain, enlarging ulcer, or cellulitis

Patient information leaflets

The following PILs are available at www.prodigy.nhs.uk

- Leg Ulcers - Venous

Shared decision making

- **A leg ulcer is normally washed with tap water before a dressing is put on.**
- **Sometimes dead tissue needs to be cleared** from the wound before it is dressed.
- **A nurse will usually apply compression bandages over the dressing.** This is the most important part of treatment to help the ulcer to heal.
- **The dressing and bandaging are normally changed every week.**
- Other measures that may promote healing include:
  - **Keep as active as possible.**
  - **Do not stand for long periods.**
  - **If possible, elevate your leg when you are resting.**
  - **If you smoke, try to stop.**
- **Painkillers** may be helpful if the ulcer is painful.
- Once the ulcer has healed, if you wear a support stocking each day it will help to prevent a recurrence.

Drug rationale

Drugs not included

- **Dressings** that are not recommended for heavily exuding ulcers are not included.
- **Cavity dressings** are not offered.
- **Low-adherent dressings other than knitted viscose primary dressings** are not required as the wound contact layer for uncomplicated ulcers.
- **Adhesive bordered dressings** are not offered as people with venous leg ulcer tend to have sensitive skin, and because dressings under high compression multi-layer bandages do not tend to slip.
- **Multi-layer compression bandaging: individual bandages** for multi-layer bandaging are offered as part of a kit and not separately in this scenario.
- **Compression hosiery** is reserved for people with healed ulcers, to prevent recurrence.

Drugs included

- **Polyurethane foam dressings** are useful for absorbing exudates from wounds and are suitable for a wound contact layer beneath compression bandaging.
- **Alginate dressings** are useful for wounds with heavy exudates and slough.
- **Odour absorbent dressings** may be useful if there is odour associated with the leg ulcer.
- **Multi-layer compression bandaging: 4-layer kits** (K-Four®, Profore®, System 4®, Ultra-Four®) are offered, appropriate to ankle circumference. They contain:
  - **Low-adherent dressings** for the wound contact layer.
  - **Wadding bandages** (the first layer applied), which are used to reshape the leg in people with a narrow ankle circumference.
  - **Light support bandages,** used at layers 2 and 3.
  - **Cohesive bandages,** used at layer 4.
- **Two-layer short-stretch bandaging** may be preferred in an active, younger person, or if concordance with 4-layer bandaging is a problem. These are generally offered as a multiple-item prescription containing:
  - **Low-adherent dressings:** knitted viscose primary dressings (e.g. N-A Dressings®) are suitable for a wound contact layer beneath compression bandaging. Note: use a foam dressing instead if this is more clinically appropriate.
  - **Wadding bandages** (the first layer applied) are used to reshape the leg in people with a narrow ankle circumference.
  - **Short-stretch compression bandages,** are the second layer applied.
  - Note: Proguide® is the only 2-layer system available as a kit.
- **Paracetamol** is offered as a first-line analgesic. Manage pain according to response and associated comorbidities.

Prescriptions

Polyurethane foam dressings

5cmx5cm Allevyn dressing
- Age from 16 years onwards
- Allevyn 5cmx5cm dressing. Apply directly to the venous ulcer to absorb excess exudate underneath compression bandages; supply 5 dressings; NHS Cost £5.40.

5cmx7.5cm Advazorb dressing
- Age from 16 years onwards
- Advazorb 5cmx7.5cm dressing. Apply directly to the venous ulcer to absorb excess exudate underneath compression bandages; supply 5 dressings; NHS Cost £2.25.

6cmx6cm Curafoam Plus dressing
- Age from 16 years onwards
- Curafoam Plus 6cmx6cm dressing. Apply directly to the venous ulcer to absorb excess exudate underneath compression bandages; supply 5 dressings; NHS Cost £5.30.

10cmx10cm Advazorb dressing
- Age from 16 years onwards
- Advazorb 10cmx10cm dressing. Apply directly to the venous ulcer to absorb excess exudate underneath compression bandages; supply 5 dressings; NHS Cost £4.00.

10cmx10cm Curafoam Plus dressing
- Age from 16 years onwards
- Curafoam Plus 10cmx10cm dressing. Apply directly to the venous ulcer to absorb excess exudate underneath compression bandages; supply 5 dressings; NHS Cost £8.25.

10cmx10cm Allevyn dressing
- Age from 16 years onwards
- Allevyn 10cmx10cm dressing. Apply directly to the venous ulcer to absorb excess exudate underneath compression bandages; supply 5 dressings; NHS Cost £10.65.

10cmx10cm Biatain non-adhesive dressing
- Age from 16 years onwards
- Biatain non-adhesive 10cmx10cm. Apply directly to the venous ulcer to absorb excess exudate underneath compression bandages; supply 5 dressings; NHS Cost £10.20.

11cmx11cm Tielle Plus dressing
- Age from 16 years onwards
- Tielle Plus borderless 11x11cm. Apply directly to the venous ulcer to absorb excess exudate underneath compression bandages; supply 5 dressings; NHS Cost £14.65.

10cmx10cm Lyofoam C odour absorbent foam/charcoal dressing
- Age from 16 years onwards
- Lyofoam C 10cmx10cm dressing. Apply directly to the venous ulcer to absorb excess exudate underneath compression bandages; supply 5 dressings; NHS Cost £13.45.

Alginate dressings

5cmx5cm Curasorb dressing
- Age from 16 years onwards
- Curasorb 5x5cm alginate dressing. Apply directly to the venous ulcer to absorb excess exudate underneath compression bandages; supply 5 dressings; NHS Cost £3.45.

5cmx5cm Sorbsan dressing
- Age from 16 years onwards
- Sorbsan 5x5cm dressing x10. Apply directly to the venous ulcer to absorb excess exudate underneath compression bandages; supply 1 box of ten dressings; NHS Cost £7.40.

7.5cmx12cm Kaltostat dressing
- Age from 16 years onwards
- Kaltostat 7.5cmx12cm dressing. Apply directly to the venous ulcer to absorb excess exudate underneath compression bandages; supply 5 dressings; NHS Cost £8.85.

10cmx10cm Curasorb dressing
- Age from 16 years onwards
- Curasorb 10cmx10cm dressing. Apply directly to the venous ulcer to absorb excess exudate underneath compression bandages; supply 5 dressings; NHS Cost £7.30.

10cmx10cm Sorbalgon dressing
- Age from 16 years onwards
- Sorbalgon 10cmx10cm dressing. Apply directly to the venous ulcer to absorb excess exudate underneath compression bandages; supply 5 dressings; NHS Cost £7.50.

10cmx10cm Sorbsan dressing
- Age from 16 years onwards
- Sorbsan 10x10cm dressing x10. Apply directly to the venous ulcer to absorb excess exudate underneath compression bandages; supply 1 box of ten dressings; NHS Cost £7.75.

10cmx10cm Algisite M dressing
- Age from 16 years onwards
- Algisite M 10cmx10cm dressing. Apply directly to the venous ulcer to absorb excess exudate underneath compression bandages; supply 5 dressings; NHS Cost £8.15.

10cmx10cm Melgisorb dressing
- Age from 16 years onwards
- Melgisorb 10cmx10cm dressing. Apply directly to the venous ulcer to absorb excess exudate underneath compression bandages; supply 5 dressings; NHS Cost £8.20.

10cmx10cm Carboflex odour absorbent charcoal dressing
- Age from 16 years onwards
- Carboflex 10cmx10cm dressing. Apply directly to the venous ulcer to absorb excess exudate underneath compression bandages; supply 5 dressings; NHS Cost £13.70.

4-layer bandage kits (measure ankle circumference:)

Ankle circumference <18cm: Profore kit
- Age from 16 years onwards
- Profore 4 layer kit ankle<18cm. Follow the instructions given inside this pack; supply 1 kit; NHS Cost £9.41.

Ankle circumference 18-25cm: Ultra four kit
- Age from 16 years onwards
- Ultra four kit 18-25cm. Follow the instructions given inside this pack; supply 1 kit; NHS Cost £6.16.

Ankle circumference 18-25cm: K-Four kit
- Age from 16 years onwards
- Use the following information to write a prescription: supply one K-Four multilayer compression bandaging kit for ankle circumference 18-25cm. Follow the instructions given inside the pack. (Price £6.55)

Ankle circumference 18-25cm: System 4 kit
- Age from 16 years onwards
- Use the following information to write a prescription: supply one System 4 multilayer compression bandaging kit for ankle circumference 18-25cm. Follow the instructions given inside the pack. (Price £8.15)

Ankle circumference 18-25cm: Profore kit
- Age from 16 years onwards
- Profore 4 layer kit 18-25cm. Follow the instructions given inside this pack; supply 1 kit; NHS Cost £8.77.

Ankle circumference 25-30cm: Profore kit
- Age from 16 years onwards
- Profore 4 layer kit 25-30cm. Follow the instructions given inside this pack; supply 1 kit; NHS Cost £7.27.

Ankle circumference >30cm: Profore kit
- Age from 16 years onwards
- Profore 4 layer kit ankle>30cm. Follow the instructions given inside this pack; supply 1 kit; NHS Cost £10.89.

2-layer short-stretch bandages

2-layer dressing: Actiban short-stretch bandage + wadding
- Age from 16 years onwards
- Soft absorbent bandage 10cm. Use for two-layer compression bandaging; supply 6 3.5m bandages; NHS Cost £2.52.
- Knit viscose dress 9.5x9.5cm. Use for two-layer compression bandaging; supply 6 dressings; NHS Cost £1.98.
- Actiban sht-stretch band 10cm. Use for two-layer compression bandaging; supply 6 5m bandages; NHS Cost £20.40.

2-layer dressing: Actico short-stretch bandage + wadding
- Age from 16 years onwards
- Soft absorbent bandage 10cm. Use for two-layer compression bandaging; supply 6 3.5m bandages; NHS Cost £2.52.
- Knit viscose dress 9.5x9.5cm. Use for two-layer compression bandaging; supply 6 dressings; NHS Cost £1.98.
- Actico cohesive bandage 10cm. Use for two-layer compression bandaging; supply 6 6m bandages; NHS Cost £18.60.

2-layer dressing: Comprilan short-stretch bandage + wadding
- Age from 16 years onwards
- Soft absorbent bandage 10cm. Use for two-layer compression bandaging; supply 6 3.5m bandages; NHS Cost £2.52.
- Comprilan short-stretch 10cm. Use for two-layer compression bandaging; supply 6 5m bandages; NHS Cost £19.98.
- Knit viscose dress 9.5x9.5cm. Use for two-layer compression bandaging; supply 6 dressings; NHS Cost £1.98.

2-layer dressing: Rosidal K short-stretch bandage + wadding
- Age from 16 years onwards
- Soft absorbent bandage 10cm. Use for two-layer compression bandaging; supply 6 3.5m bandages; NHS Cost £2.52.
- Knit viscose dress 9.5x9.5cm. Use for two-layer compression bandaging; supply 6 dressings; NHS Cost £1.98.
- Rosidal K short-stretch 10cm. Use for two-layer compression bandaging; supply 6 5m bandages; NHS Cost £20.16.

2-layer dressing: Silkolan short-stretch bandage + wadding
- Age from 16 years onwards
- Soft absorbent bandage 10cm. Use for two-layer compression bandaging; supply 6 3.5m bandages; NHS Cost £2.52.
- Silkolan short stretch 10cm. Use for two-layer compression bandaging; supply 6 5m bandages; NHS Cost £21.72.
- Knit viscose dress 9.5x9.5cm. Use for two-layer compression bandaging; supply 6 dressings; NHS Cost £1.98.

Proguide (Red) 2-layer kit: ankle circumference 18-22cm
- Age from 16 years onwards
- Proguide 18-22cm red kit. Follow the instructions given inside this pack; supply 6 kits; NHS Cost £54.42.

Proguide (Yellow) 2-layer kit: ankle circumference 22-28cm
- Age from 16 years onwards
- Proguide 22-28cm yellow kit. Follow the instructions given inside this pack; supply 6 kits; NHS Cost £57.42.

Proguide (Green) 2-layer kit: ankle circumference 28-32cm

- Age from 16 years onwards
- Proguide 28-32cm green kit. Follow the instructions given inside this pack; supply 6 kits; NHS Cost £60.36.

Analgesia: use when required

Paracetamol tablets: 1g up to four times a day

- Age from 16 years onwards
- Paracetamol 500mg tablets. Take two tablets every 4 to 6 hours when required for pain relief. Maximum of 8 tablets in 24 hours; supply 100 tablets; NHS Cost £0.75; OTC Cost £1.32.

Infected venous leg ulcer

Which therapy?

IMPORTANT: only take wound swabs and offer treatment if there is evidence of clinical infection (e.g. pyrexia, increasing pain, enlarging ulcer, or cellulitis). Routine wound swabs are not recommended.

Investigate cause of infection and start empirical therapy

- **Offer empirical treatment** with oral flucloxacillin 500 mg four times a day for 14 days.
- If the person is hypersensitive to penicillin, offer oral empirical treatment with erythromycin 500 mg four times a day for 14 days.
- **Clean the ulcer and take a wound swab.**
- **Review after 3 days** and after swab results are available.
- Start new antibiotic appropriate to sensitivities for 14 days.

Clean and dress the leg ulcer

- Consider bed rest or leg elevation to reduce oedema before applying compression bandages.
- **Measure ankle circumference** 2 cm above the malleolus.
- **Wash leg ulcers with clean tap water** and dry carefully.
- **Dress the wound with a low-adherent dressing.**
- **Apply 4-layer graduated compression bandaging.**
- For active people or people unable to tolerate 4-layer bandaging, use 2-layer short-stretch bandaging.
- **Re-dress daily or on alternate days** if there is evidence of infection, to avoid exudates seeping through.

Manage associated symptoms

- **Offer oral analgesia** for associated pain.
- **Consider topical analgesia** if there is pain during dressing changes.
- **Involve other health professionals.** If available, consider dermatology specialist nurses and vascular teams, community leg-ulcer clinics and leg-ulcer nurse specialists.
- Ensure direct access to specialised services for the management of specific complications.

Practical prescribing points

For further information please see the *Medicines Compendium* (www.medicines.org.uk) or the *British National Formulary* (www.bnf.org).

Follow-up advice

- **Review empirical treatment once the sensitivity of the infective organism is known.**
- **Re-dress daily or on alternate days** if there is evidence of infection, to avoid exudates seeping through.
- **Regularly assess patient concordance with treatment,** and the effect of pain and mobility on quality of life.
- **Provide written patient information.** People are more likely to comply with treatment regimes if they are fully informed of the rationale and options for their management.
- **Give general health promotion advice regarding regular** walking and mobility, avoiding prolonged standing, leg elevation when immobile, stopping smoking, and good foot-care.

Should I refer or investigate?

Refer?

- **Referral may be necessary if clinical infection does not improve with oral antibiotics or if there is rapid ulcer deterioration.**
- **Refer if suspected malignancy,** or if the diagnosis is uncertain (e.g. if the ulcer is not healing or has an atypical appearance or distribution).

Investigate?

Other investigations to consider:

- **Full blood count** to check for anaemia.
- **Erythrocyte sedimentation rate, C-reactive protein:** inflammatory markers.
- **Fasting blood glucose and urinalysis** to screen for diabetes mellitus.
- **Urea, electrolytes, and creatinine** to check for renal impairment.

Patient information leaflets

The following PILs are available at www.prodigy.nhs.uk

- Leg Ulcers - Venous

Shared decision making

- **A leg ulcer is normally washed with tap water before a dressing is put on.**
- **A course of antibiotics** is needed if the ulcer becomes infected.
- **A nurse will usually apply compression bandages over the dressing.** This is the most important part of treatment to help the ulcer to heal.
- **The dressing and bandaging** are normally changed every week — but more frequently if the ulcer is infected.
- Other measures that may promote healing include:
  - **Keep as active as possible.**
  - **Do not stand for long periods.**
  - **If possible, elevate your leg when you are resting.**
  - **If you smoke, try to stop.**
- **Painkillers** may be helpful if the ulcer is painful.
- Once the ulcer has healed, if you wear a support stocking each day it will help to prevent a recurrence.

Drug rationale

Drugs not included

- **Antibiotics other than flucloxacillin and erythromycin** are not offered. An antistaphylococcal antibiotic is appropriate for empirical therapy. Review treatment when the results of microbiological investigation are available.
- **Topical antibiotics** should be avoided unless used under specialist recommendation against an identified microorganism, and for a short duration.

- **Adhesive bordered dressings** are not offered, as people with venous leg ulcer tend to have sensitive skin, and because dressings under high compression multi-layer bandages do not tend to slip.
- **Multi-layer compression bandaging: individual bandages** for multi-layer bandaging are offered as part of a kit and not separately in this scenario.
- **Compression hosiery** is reserved for people with healed ulcers, to prevent recurrence.

Drugs included

- **Oral antibiotics** are offered, but intravenous antibiotics may be required, depending on the severity of infection.
  - **Flucloxacillin** is offered for first-line empirical treatment of infection.
  - **Erythromycin** is offered as an alternative for people with penicillin hypersensitivity.
- **Multi-layer compression bandaging: 4-layer kits** (K-Four®, Profore®, System 4®, Ultra-Four®) are offered, appropriate to ankle circumference. They contain:
  - **Low-adherent dressings** for the wound contact layer.
  - **Wadding bandages** (the first layer applied), which are used to reshape the leg in people with a narrow ankle circumference.
  - **Light support bandages,** used at layers 2 and 3.
  - **Cohesive bandages,** used at layer 4.
- **Two layer short-stretch bandaging** may be preferred in an active, younger person, or if concordance with 4-layer bandaging is a problem. These are generally offered as a multiple-item prescription containing:
  - **Low-adherent dressings:** knitted viscose primary dressings (e.g. N-A Dressings®) are suitable for a wound contact layer beneath compression bandaging.
  - **Wadding bandages** (the first layer applied) are used to reshape the leg in people with a narrow ankle circumference.
  - **Short-stretch compression bandages** are the second layer applied.
  - Note: Proguide® is the only 2-layer system available as a kit.
- **Paracetamol** is offered as a first-line analgesic. Manage pain according to response and associated comorbidities.

Prescriptions

Empirical antibiotic for 14 days

Flucloxacillin capsules: 500mg four times a day

- Age from 16 years onwards
- Flucloxacillin 500mg capsules. Take one capsule four times a day for 14 days; supply 56 capsules; NHS Cost £9.46.

Erythromycin e/c tablets: 500mg four times a day

- Age from 16 years onwards
- Erythromycin 250mg e/c tablets. Take two tablets four times a day for 14 days; supply 112 tablets; NHS Cost £12.32.

4-layer bandage kits (measure ankle circumference:)

Ankle circumference <18cm: Profore kit

- Age from 16 years onwards
- Profore 4 layer kit ankle<18cm. Follow the instructions given inside this pack; supply 1 kit; NHS Cost £9.41.

Ankle circumference 18-25cm: Ultra four kit

- Age from 16 years onwards
- Ultra four kit 18-25cm. Follow the instructions given inside this pack; supply 1 kit; NHS Cost £6.16.

Ankle circumference 18-25cm: K-Four kit

- Age from 16 years onwards
- Use the following information to write a prescription: supply one K-Four multilayer compression bandaging kit for ankle circumference 18-25cm. Follow the instructions given inside the pack. (Price £6.55)

Ankle circumference 18-25cm: System 4 kit

- Age from 16 years onwards
- Use the following information to write a prescription: supply one System 4 multilayer compression bandaging kit for ankle circumference 18-25cm. Follow the instructions given inside the pack. (Price £8.15)

Ankle circumference 18-25cm: Profore kit

- Age from 16 years onwards
- Profore 4 layer kit 18-25cm. Follow the instructions given inside this pack; supply 1 kit; NHS Cost £8.77.

Ankle circumference 25-30cm: Profore kit

- Age from 16 years onwards
- Profore 4 layer kit 25-30cm. Follow the instructions given inside this pack; supply 1 kit; NHS Cost £7.27.

Ankle circumference >30cm: Profore kit

- Age from 16 years onwards
- Profore 4 layer kit ankle>30cm. Follow the instructions given inside this pack; supply 1 kit; NHS Cost £10.89.

2-layer short-stretch bandages

2-layer dressing: Actiban short-stretch bandage + wadding

- Age from 16 years onwards
- Soft absorbent bandage 10cm. Use for two-layer compression bandaging; supply 6 3.5m bandages; NHS Cost £2.52.
- Knit viscose dress 9.5x9.5cm. Use for two-layer compression bandaging; supply 6 dressings; NHS Cost £1.98.
- Actiban sht-stretch band 10cm. Use for two-layer compression bandaging; supply 6 5m bandages; NHS Cost £20.40.

2-layer dressing: Actico short-stretch bandage + wadding

- Age from 16 years onwards
- Soft absorbent bandage 10cm. Use for two-layer compression bandaging; supply 6 3.5m bandages; NHS Cost £2.52.
- Knit viscose dress 9.5x9.5cm. Use for two-layer compression bandaging; supply 6 dressings; NHS Cost £1.98.
- Actico cohesive bandage 10cm. Use for two-layer compression bandaging; supply 6 6m bandages; NHS Cost £18.60.

2-layer dressing: Comprilan short-stretch bandage + wadding

- Age from 16 years onwards
- Soft absorbent bandage 10cm. Use for two-layer compression bandaging; supply 6 3.5m bandages; NHS Cost £2.52.
- Comprilan short-stretch 10cm. Use for two-layer compression bandaging; supply 6 5m bandages; NHS Cost £19.98.
- Knit viscose dress 9.5x9.5cm. Use for two-layer compression bandaging; supply 6 dressings; NHS Cost £1.98.

2-layer dressing: Rosidal K short-stretch bandage + wadding

- Age from 16 years onwards
- Soft absorbent bandage 10cm. Use for two-layer compression bandaging; supply 6 3.5m bandages; NHS Cost £2.52.
- Knit viscose dress 9.5x9.5cm. Use for two-layer compression bandaging; supply 6 dressings; NHS Cost £1.98.

L

- Rosidal K short-stretch 10cm. Use for two-layer compression bandaging; supply 6 5m bandages; NHS Cost £20.16.

2-layer dressing: Silkolan short-stretch bandage + wadding
- Age from 16 years onwards
- Soft absorbent bandage 10cm. Use for two-layer compression bandaging; supply 6 3.5m bandages; NHS Cost £2.52.
- Silkolan short stretch 10cm. Use for two-layer compression bandaging; supply 6 5m bandages; NHS Cost £21.72.
- Knit viscose dress 9.5x9.5cm. Use for two-layer compression bandaging; supply 6 dressings; NHS Cost £1.98.

Proguide (Red) 2-layer kit: ankle circumference 18-22cm
- Age from 16 years onwards
- Proguide 18-22cm red kit. Follow the instructions given inside this pack; supply 6 kits; NHS Cost £54.42.

Proguide (Yellow) 2-layer kit: ankle circumference 22-28cm
- Age from 16 years onwards
- Proguide 22-28cm yellow kit. Follow the instructions given inside this pack; supply 6 kits; NHS Cost £57.42.

Proguide (Green) 2-layer kit: ankle circumference 28-32cm
- Age from 16 years onwards
- Proguide 28-32cm green kit. Follow the instructions given inside this pack; supply 6 kits; NHS Cost £60.36.

Analgesia: use when required

L

Paracetamol tablets: 1g up to four times a day
- Age from 16 years onwards
- Paracetamol 500mg tablets. Take two tablets every 4 to 6 hours when required for pain relief. Maximum of 8 tablets in 24 hours; supply 100 tablets; NHS Cost £0.75; OTC Cost £1.32.

12-week follow-up assessment of venous leg ulcer

Which therapy?

Assess the ulcerated area

- **Record length and width of ulcer:** trace the margins or photograph.
- **Document the ulcer site:** appearance of the ulcer edge, ulcer base, and surrounding skin.
- **Reasses ankle brachial pressure index** (ABPI) at 12 weeks if the ulcer is not fully healed or is deteriorating.

Clean and dress the leg ulcer

- Consider bed rest or leg elevation to reduce oedema before applying compression bandages.
- **Measure ankle circumference** 2 cm above the malleolus.
- **Wash leg ulcers with clean tap water** and dry carefully.
- **Dress the wound with a low-adherent dressing.**
- **Apply 4-layer graduated compression bandaging.**
- For active people or people unable to tolerate 4-layer bandaging, use 2-layer short-stretch bandaging.

Manage associated symptoms

- **Continue analgesia** such as paracetamol for associated pain when required.
- **Routine wound swabs are not recommended.** Only use if there is evidence of clinical infection.

Follow-up advice

- **Re-dress the leg ulcer with compression bandages every week.**
- **Reassess ulcers after 12 weeks and every 12 weeks thereafter until healed.**
  - Reasses Doppler ABPI at 12 weeks if the ulcer is not fully healed or is deteriorating.
  - Refer complications such as non-healing ulcers after 12 weeks of adequate treatment.
  - Refer if suspected malignancy, or if the diagnosis is uncertain (e.g. if the ulcer is not healing or has an atypical appearance or distribution).
- **Regularly assess concordance with treatment,** and the effect of pain and mobility on quality of life.
- **Provide written patient information.** People are more likely to comply with treatment regimes if they are fully informed of the rationale and options for their management.
- **Give general health promotion advice** regarding regular walking and mobility, avoiding prolonged standing, leg elevation when immobile, stopping smoking, and good foot-care.
- **Recommend graduated compression stockings for at least 5 years after ulcer healing,** in order to minimize the risk of recurrence.

Should I refer or investigate?

Refer?

- **Refer if suspected malignancy,** or if the diagnosis is uncertain (e.g. if the ulcer is not healing or has an atypical appearance or distribution).
- Consider referral for healed ulcers, with a view to venous surgery if appropriate.

Investigate?

- **Routine wound swabs are not recommended,** and should be used only if there is evidence of clinical infection.

Patient information leaflets

The following PILs are available at www.prodigy.nhs.uk
- Leg Ulcers - Venous

Shared decision making

- **A leg ulcer is normally washed with tap water before a dressing is put on.**
- **A nurse will usually apply compression bandages over the dressing.** This is the most important part of treatment to help the ulcer to heal.
- **The dressing and bandaging** are normally changed every week.
- Other measures that may promote healing include:
  - **Keep as active as possible.**
  - **Do not stand for long periods.**
  - **If possible, elevate your leg when you are resting.**
  - **If you smoke, try to stop.**
- **Painkillers** may be helpful if the ulcer is painful.
- Once the ulcer has healed, if you wear a support stocking each day it will help to prevent a recurrence.

Drug rationale

Drugs not included

- **Multi-layer compression bandages 4-layer kits** are not offered, as the light support bandages are reusable and a full kit may not be required at each dressing change.

However, wadding bandages and cohesive bandages are single-use dressings.

Drugs included

- **Low-adherent wound contact dressing;** knitted viscose dressing size 9.5 cm x 9.5 cm is offered.
- **Wadding bandages** are the first layer to be applied in multi-layer compression and are used to reshape the leg.
- **Light support bandages** are used at layers two and three in 4-layer compression. Profore +® is offered for use on larger limbs. The light support bandages are reusable, and washing instructions should be followed.
- **Cohesive bandages** are the outer layer of a 4-layer dressing; they adhere to themselves and cannot be reused.
- **Short-stretch bandages** are offered for use with wadding bandages in a 2-layer dressing for more active people who cannot tolerate 4-layer dressings.

Prescriptions

Non-reusable first-layer wadding + wound contact dressings

Wound contact layer: knitted viscose dressing 9.5cmx9.5cm
- Age from 16 years onwards
- Knit viscose dress 9.5x9.5cm. Use as the wound contact dressing; supply 6 dressings; NHS Cost £1.98.

Wadding layer for shaping the leg and for absorption
- Age from 16 years onwards
- Soft absorbent bandage 10cm. Apply as the first layer in multi-layer compression bandaging; supply 6 3.5m bandages; NHS Cost £2.52.

Washable layer two: 4-layer bandage system

10cmx4.5m cotton+polyamide+elastane bandage
- Age from 16 years onwards
- Cotton+polyamide+elastane 10cm. Follow the instructions given inside this pack; supply 4 4.5m bandages; NHS Cost £3.96.

K-Four #2 (K-lite 10cm bandage)
- Age from 16 years onwards
- K-Four #2 10cmx4.5m bandage. Follow the instructions given inside this pack; supply 4 bandages; NHS Cost £3.84.

Profore #2 (Soffcrepe 10cm bandage)
- Age from 16 years onwards
- Profore #2 10cmx4.5m bandage. Follow the instructions given inside this pack; supply 4 4.5m bandages; NHS Cost £4.96.

System 4 #2 (Setocrepe 10cm bandage)
- Age from 16 years onwards
- System 4 #2 10cmx4.5m bandage. Follow the instructions given inside this pack; supply 4 4.5m bandages; NHS Cost £4.72.

Ultra Four #2 (Ultra Lite 10cm bandage)
- Age from 16 years onwards
- Ultra Four#2 10cmx4.5m bandage. Follow the instructions given inside this pack; supply 4 4.5m bandages; NHS Cost £3.68.

Washable layer three: 4-layer bandage system

10cmx6m elastomer+viscose type 3a bandage
- Age from 16 years onwards
- Elastomer+viscose 10cmx6m. Follow the instructions given inside this pack; supply 4 6m bandages; NHS Cost £10.20.

10cmx8.7m elastomer+viscose type 3a bandage
- Age from 16 years onwards
- Elastomer+viscose 10cmx8.7m. Follow the instructions given inside this pack; supply 4 8.7m bandages; NHS Cost £8.52.

K-four #3 (K-plus 10cm bandage)
- Age from 16 years onwards
- K-Four #3 10cmx8.7m bandage. Follow the instructions given inside this pack; supply 4 bandages; NHS Cost £18.48.

Profore #3 (Litepress 10cm bandage)
- Age from 16 years onwards
- Profore #3 10cmx8.7m bandage. Follow the instructions given inside this pack; supply 4 8.7m bandages; NHS Cost £14.48.

System 4 #3 (Elset 10cm bandage)
- Age from 16 years onwards
- System 4 #3 10cmx8m bandage. Follow the instructions given inside this pack; supply 4 8m bandages; NHS Cost £13.04.

Ultra Four #3 (Ultra plus 10cm bandage)
- Age from 16 years onwards
- Ultra Four#3 10cmx8.7m bandage. Follow the instructions given inside this pack; supply 4 8.7m bandages; NHS Cost £8.20.

Profore + (10cm bandage)
- Age from 16 years onwards
- Profore+ 10cmx3m bandage. Follow the instructions given inside this pack; supply 4 3m bandages; NHS Cost £13.60.

Non-reusable outer layer for 4-layer compression system

10cmx2.5m cohesive type 3a bandage
- Age from 16 years onwards
- Cohesive type 3a 10cm x 2.5m. Follow the instructions given inside this pack; supply 6 2.5m bandages; NHS Cost £18.00.

10cmx6m cohesive type 3a bandage
- Age from 16 years onwards
- Cohesive type 3a 10cm x 6m. Follow the instructions given inside this pack; supply 6 6m bandages; NHS Cost £17.10.

10cmx6.3m cohesive type 3a bandage
- Age from 16 years onwards
- Cohesive type 3a 10cm x 6.3m. Follow the instructions given inside this pack; supply 6 6.3m bandages; NHS Cost £16.92.

K-Four #4 (Ko-flex 10cm x 6m bandage)
- Age from 16 years onwards
- K-Four #4 10cmx6m bandage. Follow the instructions given inside this pack; supply 6 bandages; NHS Cost £17.40.

Profore #4 (Co-plus 10cmx2.5m bandage)
- Age from 16 years onwards
- Profore #4 10cmx2.5m bandage. Follow the instructions given inside this pack; supply 6 2.5m bandages; NHS Cost £18.00.

System 4 #4 (Coban 10cm x 6m bandage)
- Age from 16 years onwards
- System 4 #4 10cmx6m bandage. Follow the instructions given inside this pack; supply 6 6m bandages; NHS Cost £17.70.

Ultra Four #4 (Ultra Fast 10cm x 6.3m bandage)
- Age from 16 years onwards
- Ultra Four#4 10cmx6.3m bandage. Follow the instructions given inside this pack; supply 6 6.3m bandages; NHS Cost £16.92.

Washable short-stretch bandages

Actico 10cmx6m bandage
- Age from 16 years onwards
- Actico cohesive bandage 10cm. Follow the instructions given inside this pack; supply 4 6m bandages; NHS Cost £12.60.

Actiban 10cmx5m bandage
- Age from 16 years onwards
- Actiban sht-stretch band 10cm. Follow the instructions given inside this pack; supply 4 5m bandages; NHS Cost £13.60.

Comprilan 10cmx5m bandage
- Age from 16 years onwards
- Comprilan short-stretch 10cm. Follow the instructions given inside this pack; supply 4 5m bandages; NHS Cost £13.32.

Rosidal K 10cmx5m bandage
- Age from 16 years onwards
- Rosidal K short-stretch 10cm. Follow the instructions given inside this pack; supply 4 5m bandages; NHS Cost £13.44.

Silkolan 10cmx5m bandage
- Age from 16 years onwards
- Silkolan short stretch 10cm. Follow the instructions given inside this pack; supply 4 5m bandages; NHS Cost £14.48.

Proguide (Red) 2-layer kit: ankle circumference 18-22cm
- Age from 16 years onwards
- Proguide 18-22cm red kit. Follow the instructions given inside this pack; supply 4 kits; NHS Cost £36.28.

Proguide (Yellow) 2-layer kit: ankle circumference 22-28cm
- Age from 16 years onwards
- Proguide 22-28cm yellow kit. Follow the instructions given inside this pack; supply 4 kits; NHS Cost £38.28.

Proguide (Green) 2-layer kit: ankle circumference 28-32cm
- Age from 16 years onwards
- Proguide 28-32cm green kit. Follow the instructions given inside this pack; supply 4 kits; NHS Cost £40.24.

Healed venous leg ulcer

Which therapy?
- **Continue graduated compression stockings** for at least 5 years after ulcer healing.
- Consider the use of lifelong compression stockings with 6-monthly Doppler ABPI checks, to reduce the risk of recurrence further.
- **Offer** the strongest compression with which the person can comply.
- **Identify any at-risk areas early** to prevent further skin breakdown, as chronic venous hypertension may result in delayed healing if the leg is injured.
- **Give general health promotion advice** regarding regular walking and mobility, avoiding prolonged standing, leg elevation when immobile, stopping smoking and foot-care.
- **Encourage optimum nutrition and reduce obesity** where appropriate.

Follow-up advice
- **Provide written patient information.** People are more likely to comply with treatment regimes if they are fully informed of the rationale and options for their management.
- **Give general health promotion advice** regarding regular walking and mobility, avoiding prolonged standing, leg elevation when immobile, stopping smoking, and good foot-care.

Should I refer or investigate?

Refer?
- Consider referral for healed ulcers, with a view to venous surgery if appropriate.

Patient information leaflets
The following PILs are available at www.prodigy.nhs.uk
- Leg Ulcers - Venous

Shared decision making
- Once a venous leg ulcer has healed, if you wear a support stocking each day it will help to prevent a recurrence.
- **Ideally, wear class III compression stockings.** However, some people find class III stockings too tight, but class II may be fine.
- Other measures that may help prevent recurrences include:
  - **Keep as active as possible.**
  - **Do not stand for long periods.**
  - **If possible, elevate your leg when you are resting.**
  - **If you smoke, try to stop.**
  - **If you are overweight, try to lose some weight.**

Drug rationale

Drugs not included
- **Class I light support** stockings are not offered. Greater support is required for the prevention of recurrent venous leg ulcers.

Drugs included
- **Class II medium support** below-knee stocking are offered.
- **Class III strong support** below-knee stockings are offered.

Prescriptions

Class III below knee stockings

Class III knee-length stockings
- Age from 16 years onwards
- Class III knee-length stocking. One pair of circular knit, knee length class III compression stockings to be measured and fitted in the pharmacy; supply 2 single stockings; NHS Cost £10.44.

Class II below knee stockings

Class II knee-length stockings
- Age from 16 years onwards
- Class II knee-length stocking. One pair of circular knit, knee length class II compression stockings to be measured and fitted in the pharmacy; supply 2 single stockings; NHS Cost £9.21.

Extended Information

Background information

- What is it? p.1161
- How common is it? p.1161
- How do I know my patient has a venous leg ulcer? p.1161
- What are the risk factors for venous leg ulcer? p.1161
- What else might it be? p.1161
- Complications and prognosis p.1162

What is it?

- Chronic venous insufficiency and venous hypertension result from damage to the valves in the veins of the leg and inadequate functioning of the calf muscle pump [Nelson et al, 2004]. This leads to oedema and skin breakdown.
- A leg ulcer may be defined as the 'loss of skin below the knee on the leg or foot, which takes more than six weeks to heal' [NHS CRD, 1997].

How common is it?

- Venous leg ulcers are a common, chronic, recurring condition.
- **Venous leg ulcers have a prevalence estimated at 1.5–3 per 1000** of the UK population [NHS CRD, 1997].
- **Prevalence increases with age,** rising to 20 per 1000 aged over 80 years [Royal College of Nursing, 2000a]. The incidence of venous leg ulcers is expected to rise further, with demographic changes of increasing numbers of older people in the population.
- **Incidence is spread evenly across different socio-economic groups,** but ulcers take longer to heal and recurrence rates are higher in classes IV and V [SIGN, 1998].
- **Most people with ulceration (estimated at 80%) are managed solely in the community** [SIGN, 1998].
- Venous, stasis, or varicose ulcers represent 80–85% of all leg ulcers [Simon et al, 2004].
- **The economic cost** of leg ulcers to the NHS is estimated at £300–£600 million a year [Simon et al, 2004].

How do I know my patient has a venous leg ulcer?

History

Record any aspects of the past medical history that may suggest venous or non-venous disease.

Table 1: Past medical history that may suggest venous disease or non-venous disease.

History suggesting venous disease	History suggesting arterial disease
Varicose veins	Ischaemic heart disease
Proven deep vein thrombosis in the affected leg	Stroke
Phlebitis in the affected leg	Transient ischaemic attack
Previous fracture, trauma, or surgery	Diabetes mellitus
Family history of venous disease	Peripheral vascular disease
Symptoms of venous insufficiency: leg pain, heavy legs, aching, itching, swelling, skin breakdown, pigmentation, and eczema.	Intermittent claudication

[Royal College of Nursing, 2000a]

Examination

- Oedema of the lower leg.
- Varicose veins.
- Varicose eczema.
- Hyperpigmentation: haemosiderin deposition or iron pigments in the skin.
- Lipodermatosclerosis: dermatitis followed by induration and dermal fibrosis.
- Atrophie blanche: smooth, ivory-white plaques stippled with telangiectasia and surrounded by hyperpigmentation.

Investigations to exclude an arterial component to the ulcer

- Venous, stasis, or varicose ulcers represent 80–85% of all leg ulcers [Simon et al, 2004].
- The absence of pedal pulses may indicate arterial insufficiency; however, palpation alone is inadequate to rule this out.
- The ankle brachial pressure index (ABPI) is the most reliable way to detect arterial insufficiency [SIGN, 1998]. If ABPI is less than 0.8, assume arterial disease.
- Assessment of capillary refill.

Other investigations to consider

- Diabetes mellitus: fasting blood glucose and urinalysis.
- Renal function: urea, electrolytes, and creatinine [Royal College of Nursing, 2000b].
- Anaemia: full blood count.
- Inflammatory disease: erythrocyte sedimentation rate (ESR) or C-reactive protein.
- Infection: full blood count, ESR. Swab if there is clinical evidence of infection, such as pyrexia, increasing pain, enlarging ulcer, and cellulitis [SIGN, 1998].

What are the risk factors for venous leg ulcer?

At least two causative factors can be identified in a third of leg ulcers [London and Donnelly, 2000]. Risk factors include:

- Previous history of venous leg ulcer
- Increasing age
- Obesity
- Immobility
- Peripheral oedema
- Varicose veins
- Deep venous thrombosis

What else might it be?

- **Arterial ulcer** has a punched-out appearance, with ischaemia and necrosis. This is typical in a person with atherosclerosis, with pale or blue, mottled, shiny, cold skin; prolonged capillary refill; nail dystrophy; reduced hair growth; and calf muscle wasting of the limb.
- **Combined arterial and venous insufficiency** may be seen in 10–20% of leg ulcers [SIGN, 1998].
- **Rheumatoid ulcer** (vasculitic) is typically deep, well-demarcated and punched-out on the dorsum of foot or calf. People with rheumatoid arthritis might also have venous disease due to reduced mobility, neuropathy, and possibly impaired healing due to systemic corticosteroids.
- **Systemic vasculitis** often causes multiple leg ulcers that are necrotic and deep. There is usually an atypical distribution with vasculitic lesions elsewhere (e.g. nail-fold infarcts and splinter haemorrhages). This may be associated with systemic lupus erythematosus,

L

scleroderma, polyarteritis nodosa, or Wegener's granulomatosis.
- **Diabetic ulcer** is typically on the foot over a bony prominence. This may have neuropathic, arterial, and/or venous components.
- **Hypertensive ulcer** (due to arteriolar occlusion) is painful with necrotic edges, and is usually sited on the lateral aspect of the lower leg.
- **Malignant ulcer** (due to basal or squamous cell carcinoma, melanoma, or Bowen's disease) are rare, but must be considered if ulceration does not respond to conventional treatment or if the appearance is unusual.
- **Other possible causes** include traumatic ulcer, sarcoidosis, tropical ulcer, or pyoderma gangrenosum.

Complications and prognosis

Complications

- **Pain.**
- **Oedema.**
- **Immobility.**
- **Infection** may present as inflammation, redness, purulent exudate, pyrexia, increased pain, or the person becoming systemically unwell [Royal College of Nursing, 2000a]. More than 80% of chronic leg ulcers may be colonized with bacteria such as *Staphylococcus aureus* and *Pseudomonas aeruginosa* [O'Meara and Ovington, 2004]. The presence of bacterial contamination (non-replicating micro-organisms on the surface) does not appear to affect ulcer healing [Royal College of Nursing, 1998; O'Meara and Ovington, 2004].
- **Contact dermatitis** due to sensitivity to topical treatments.
- **Quality of life and daily functioning:** the negative impacts of chronic venous ulcers have been quoted in several studies [Budgen, 2004; Persoon et al, 2004] prescription costs of bandages and dressings, time off work, pain, psychological distress, loss of independence and social isolation [Simon et al, 2004].

Venous ulcers may deteriorate quickly after presentation, and it is important for health professionals to act quickly to minimise venous insufficiency and aid the healing process.

Prognosis

- **Venous leg ulcers cause significant morbidity and reduction in quality of life.**
- Twelve-month recurrence rates of 26–69% have been reported [Nelson et al, 2004].
- Poor healing rates may be exacerbated by poor patient concordance with treatment regimes.
- Healing rates of 70% at 12 weeks have been achieved for small ulcers managed in specialist clinics [SIGN, 1998].

Management issues

- How is a venous leg ulcer assessed? p.1162
- Who needs to be referred to a specialist clinic for further assessment? p.1162
- How is a venous leg ulcer managed? p.1163
- Who should be involved in the management of venous leg ulcers? p.1163
- What treatments are available? p.1163
- How are complications managed? p.1164
- What follow-up is necessary? p.1165
- How can recurrence be prevented? p.1165
- Dressings information p.1165

How is a venous leg ulcer assessed?

Initial assessment must exclude an arterial component to the ulcer, as compression bandaging may be inappropriate in such cases (see section on *Ankle Brachial Pressure Index*).

- Assess features of the ulcerated area:
  - Serial measurement (length and width) is an indicator of the healing process.
  - Tracing of the margins and photography may be helpful.
  - Note the site of the ulcer (usually on the gaiter area of the leg, above the medial or lateral malleoli).
  - Assess the edge of the ulcer (shallow, punched out, rolling).
  - Assess the base of the ulcer (granulating, sloughy, necrotic) and its position.
  - Note the condition of surrounding skin, odour, and signs of infection.
- Offer a full examination, including pulse, blood pressure, and body mass index calculation.
- Measure the ankle brachial pressure index (ABPI) to help detect arterial insufficiency.

[SIGN, 1998]

Ankle Brachial Pressure Index

- **Ankle brachial pressure index (ABPI) is an objective assessment of the ulcer to identify arterial disease** that may warrant referral to specialist vascular clinics. It provides an index of vessel competency by measuring the ratio of systolic blood pressure at the ankle to that in the arm, with a value of 1 being normal.
- It is important to be aware that ABPI measurements in patients with diabetes or atherosclerosis may not be reliable. Patients with these conditions may have falsely high (and misleading) pressure readings due to calcification of the vessels [SIGN, 1998]. In addition, microvascular disease associated with rheumatoid arthritis and systemic vasculitis cannot be assessed by ABPI. Therefore, if there is any doubt, such patients should be referred for specialist assessment.
- **ABPI less than 0.5:** arterial ulcers are likely and compression treatment is contraindicated, requiring urgent referral to a specialist vascular clinic for further assessment and possible revascularisation.
- **ABPI between 0.5 and 0.8:** assume that the person has arterial disease, and refer to a vascular clinic for further assessment. Compression bandaging in such instances may further compromise arterial blood supply, and should be generally avoided. However, if the ABPI is between 0.5 and 0.8, reduced compression can be used under strict supervision if the ulcer is clinically venous [SIGN, 1998; Royal College of Nursing, 2000b]. Clinical progress should be checked daily initially and compression modified according to clinical response.
- **ABPI greater than 0.8:** graduated compression bandages may be applied safely.
- **Arterial disease may develop in people with venous disease,** and health professionals should be aware that the ABPI may drop after the initial measurement [Royal College of Nursing, 2000a].

Who needs to be referred to a specialist clinic for further assessment?

If there is any doubt about the cause of the ulcer, specialist assessment is recommended.

- **Suspected arterial ulcer:** refer people with an ABPI of less than 0.8 for further assessment of arterial disease. If the ABPI is les than 0.5, refer urgently.
- **Suspected malignant ulcer,** a rapidly deteriorating ulcer, or diagnostic uncertainty: an atypical appearance or

- distribution of ulcers may require biopsy by dermatology.
- **Suspected rheumatoid ulcer,** or ulcers associated with systemic vasculitis.
- **People with diabetes with an ulcer on the foot** should be referred according to local arrangements.
- Note: acute ischaemic changes because of compression bandaging require urgent vascular referral.

How is a venous leg ulcer managed?

- **Involve appropriate health professionals,** as a multi-disciplinary approach is often needed.
- **Clean with water** initially. Debridement is not usually necessary; however, it is important to maintain a moist wound environment and any slough should be removed. If surgical debridement is necessary, a topical anaesthetic may reduce associated pain.
- **Apply a low-adherent dressing** to the ulcer.
- **Use compression bandaging** to heal the leg ulcer.
- **Reassess ulcers after 12 weeks** and every 12 weeks thereafter until healed.
- **Prevent recurrence of ulcers with compression stockings** for at least 5 years.

Who should be involved in the management of venous leg ulcers?

Organization of care

- **A co-ordinated multidisciplinary team approach** is vital, as a variety of health professionals including practice nurses, district nurses, general practitioners, dermatology specialist nurses and teams, and vascular teams may be involved. Direct access to specialised hospital services is vital in the management of specific complications.
- **Community leg-ulcer clinics** may significantly improve healing and recurrence rates, and are more cost-effective when they have close liaison with secondary care [NHS CRD, 1997; SIGN, 1998].
- **Leg-ulcer nurse specialists in dedicated clinics** can promote and maintain standards of care and cost-effectiveness, and provide training of hospital and community teams [Simon et al, 2004].
- **Future management** should focus on preventing ulceration by identifying populations at risk [Simon et al, 2004].

What treatments are available?

Cleansing and debridement

- **Leg ulcers should first be washed in tap water,** with bathing or showering at dressing changes, and dried carefully at each assessment [SIGN, 1998].
- Saline washes are not better than tap water in cleaning soft tissue wounds [SIGN, 1998].
- Antiseptics: there is no evidence that the use of antiseptics provides additional protection against infection [Royal College of Nursing, 2000a]. Research results are conflicting regarding the use of antimicrobial silver-based products to promote ulcer healing [O'Meara et al, 2000].
- **Debridement is only needed if** slough or necrotic tissue is not removed from the ulcer by gentle washing. There is no clear evidence as to the optimal method for debridement. However, there is consensus that chemical agents such as iodine, acetic acid, hydrogen peroxide, or hypochlorite should not be used [Royal College of Nursing, 1998].
- Sharp mechanical debridement (with a scalpel or sharp blade) may delay healing because of the risk of damaging healthy tissue and underlying blood vessels [Briggs and Nelson, 2004].
- There is increasing use of maggots as biological debriding agents. However, there have been few controlled trials of their use in treating venous leg ulcers thus far [Royal College of Nursing, 1998; Courtenay et al, 2000]. LarvE (sterile maggots of *Lucilia sericata*, the common greenbottle) secrete a mixture of proteolytic enzymes that break down slough and necrotic tissue that is then ingested. This provides an improved environment for healing to take place, particularly where conventional treatments have failed [Thomas, 2004]. Referral to a specialist clinic or team for assessment may be necessary before this debridement method is initiated.

Wound contact dressings

- **Wound contact dressings can be changed weekly** if there are no signs of infection.
- No specific dressing has been shown to improve healing rates in venous leg ulcer [SIGN, 1998; Bradley et al, 1999a; Bradley et al, 1999b].
- **Uncomplicated venous ulcers** require a simple low-adherent dressing. The dressing keeps the ulcer clean and allows excess exudate to be removed from the surface, reducing the risk of cross-infection and providing a moist micro-environment that promotes healing [Royal College of Nursing, 1998; Bradley et al, 1999b].
- **Sloughy venous leg ulcers** can be dressed with hydrogels to provide moisture that helps to liquefy slough [National Prescribing Centre, 1999].
- **Moderate to heavily exuding venous leg ulcers** are less common: an alginate or foam dressing may be useful for absorbing exudates [National Prescribing Centre, 1999].
- **Painful ulcers** may benefit from occlusive hydrocolloid or foam dressings [Royal College of Nursing, 2000a].

Compression dressings

- **Compression reduces high venous pressure in superficial veins,** aiding venous return of blood to the heart by increasing the velocity of flow in the deep veins. It reduces oedema by reducing the pressure difference between the capillaries and the tissues. This promotes transport of metabolic products away from tissues, allowing ulcers to heal. A variety of high compression products are available, which seem to have similar efficacy in encouraging ulcer healing [Fletcher et al, 1997; NHS CRD, 1997; Cullum et al, 2004].
- **Below-knee graduated compression is the mainstay of treatment** to improve venous return, and to reduce venous stasis and hypertension in uncomplicated venous leg ulcers. Graduated compression delivers the highest pressure at the ankle and gaiter area, and pressure progressively reduces towards the knee and thigh where less external pressure is needed.

Multi-layer compression

- **High compression multi-layer bandaging is recommended** (e.g. 4-layer or 3-layer bandaging). It has an improved ulcer healing rate compared to single-layer compression [NHS CRD, 1997; SIGN, 1998]. Trials generally favour multi-layer compression over 2-layer short-stretch bandages [SIGN, 1998]. However [Cullum et al, 2004], a recent study has found similar ulcer healing rates for both 4-layer and 2 layer short-stretch systems [Moffatt et al, 2003; Iglesias et al, 2004].
- An appropriately trained person should apply high compression multi-layer bandaging, to avoid the risk of pressure ulceration over bony points [Simon et al, 2004].
- Four-layer bandaging has sufficient absorption capacity to manage exudates, and to maintain application pressure for up to a week without needing re-application.

Other compression methods

- **Compression stockings** provide graduated pressure that may be better tolerated than multi-layer compression bandaging, but current evidence only supports the use of compression stockings for preventing ulcer recurrence [SIGN, 1998].
- **Intermittent pneumatic compression (IPC) may improve healing rates further** [NHS CRD, 1997]. An air pump periodically inflates and deflates bladders incorporated into sleeves that envelop the affected limb [Mani et al, 2004]. A systematic review has recommended pneumatic compression devices for people with refractory oedema and significant ulceration, where a 6-month trial of standard compression has failed, or where people are unwilling or unable to tolerate this [Berliner et al, 2003]. Overall, however, a recent Cochrane review found only small trials of IPC, which were not directly comparable, with two trials reporting improved ulcer healing with IPC [Mani et al, 2004]. There was no clear evidence that IPC improves healing when compared with compression alone or when added to standard compression regimes, and further research is needed. Higher concordance rates with IPC than with other compression methods have been quoted in other studies [Berliner et al, 2003].

Problems associated with compression

- **Adverse effects** may include reduced blood supply to the skin and pressure damage.
- **Arterial blood supply may be compromised.** Compression bandages should be removed immediately and medical advice sought if the person experiences a change in foot colour and/or temperature, or increased pain. An acute ischaemic complication from compression should prompt an urgent vascular referral [Royal College of Nursing, 2000a].
- **Other contraindications** to compression include active phlebitis, deep vein thrombosis, localized infection, or cellulitis [Ilsley, 2001].
- **Concordance with treatment should be assessed and encouraged regularly.** Compression bandaging may be uncomfortable, and the needs of the individual must be addressed to ensure that the maximum level of compression with the most appropriate dressing is applied.

Medicines to improve ulcer healing

- **Pentoxifylline should be reserved for** ulcers that do not heal with compression bandaging. A systematic review of eight randomized controlled trials suggests that pentoxifylline is more effective than placebo in reducing time to complete healing, and gives additional benefit to compression. However, further studies are required before pentoxifylline can be recommended as a routine treatment for venous leg ulcers [Jull et al, 2002].
- Small trial evaluations of prostaglandins and aspirin have not shown convincing evidence of improved ulcer healing compared with no drug treatment [Simon et al, 2004].

Other treatment options

- **Superficial venous surgery** may be considered in someone with chronic venous ulceration and superficial valvular incompetence, refractory to other treatment. This may involve removing superficial and/or perforating veins, or blocking incompetent veins by injecting irritant solution (sclerotherapy) [Nelson et al, 2004].
- **Skin grafting** may accelerate the speed of closure of the ulcer if other treatment modalities have failed. Pinch skin grafts (which provide epithelial islands from which epithelial growth may spread) have been highlighted in recent studies, and may be done in the community in association with multi-layer compression bandaging [Jones and Nelson, 2004; Simon et al, 2004].
- **Low-level laser therapy** is sometimes used. However, there is no significant evidence of any benefit [Flemming and Cullum, 2004b; Franek et al, 2002]. Combination laser and infrared light may promote healing further, but more research is needed [Flemming and Cullum, 2004b].
- **Therapeutic ultrasound, electromagnetic therapy, electrical stimulation, and hyperbaric oxygen** have similarly been suggested to stimulate healing. However, studies are generally small and the extent to which they have an impact is unclear [Fernandez-Chimeno et al, 2004; Flemming and Cullum, 2004a; Flemming and Cullum, 2004c; Kranke et al, 2004].

How are complications managed?

Leg oedema

- Limb dependency, immobility, and oedema all contribute to venous hypertension [Simon et al, 2004].
- **Leg elevation** encourages venous return and may reduce pain and leg swelling [Royal College of Nursing, 2000a]. Raising the legs above hip level for 30 minutes three to four times a day will allow swelling to subside and improve microcirculation in people with venous insufficiency. Placing several pillows under the bed mattress will assist leg elevation at night. However, there is insufficient evidence to recommend regular leg elevation as a routine intervention.
- Bed rest and elevation may reduce oedema of the ankle and leg before compression bandages are applied [SIGN, 1998].

Infection

- **Antibiotics should be used only if there is evidence of cellulitis or active infection** (e.g. pyrexia, increasing pain, enlarging ulcer, or cellulitis).
- The organisms most likely to be involved in cellulitis include *Staphylococcus aureus*, MRSA (methicillin-resistant *Staphylococcus aureus*), and Group A beta-haemolytic streptococci. Anaerobes may sometimes be involved.
- Empirical treatment with an anti-staphylococcal antibiotic should be used while awaiting wound swab results. Flucloxacillin 500 mg four times a day or erythromycin 500 mg four times a day for 14 days are suitable first choices for empirical therapy. Clarithromycin 250–500 mg twice a day is an alternative for people who are unable to tolerate erythromycin.
- Oral or intravenous antibiotics may be required, depending on the severity of the infection.
- **Routine wound swabs are not recommended,** as there is no evidence for their use [SIGN, 1998]. Antibiotics have little effect on wound healing generally [O'Meara et al, 2000], so there is no value in using them to treat organisms that have colonized a wound but are not causing clinical signs or symptoms of infection.
- **Topical antibiotics are frequent sensitizers** and should be avoided if possible [SIGN, 1998].
- Compression bandaging should not be used if there is evidence of cellulitis.
- **Dressings should be reapplied daily or on alternate days** to allow assessment of the infected area.

Dermatitis

- **Venous eczema is commonly associated with chronic venous ulcers.**
- Typical features of venous eczema include diffuse erythema, scaling, haemosiderin pigmentation, and exudate with crusting if there is superadded infection.

Frequent emollient application plus a short course of mild topical corticosteroid ointment should be the mainstay of treatment.

Allergic contact dermatitis may complicate venous eczema in 60–80% of patients [SIGN, 1998].

Common sensitisers include wool alcohols, topical antibiotics, topical corticosteroids, cetylstearyl alcohols, parabens, and rubber mixes. See Table 2.

Referral for dermatological patch testing may be appropriate if the dermatitis does not settle, or if there are concerns about sensitivity to a topical agent, dressing, or bandage used. Ideally a specific leg ulcer patch-test series should be used [SIGN, 1998].

People may become sensitized to components of their topical treatment at any time [Royal College of Nursing, 1998].

Pain

Venous disease and venous leg ulcers are frequently painful. The pain experienced may be constant or intermittent. Constant pain can originate from vascular structures (superficial, deep phlebitis), pitting oedema, collagen (lipodermatosclerosis), or infection. Ulcer pain is often episodic and may be due to surgical or other debridement procedures. Intermittent pain is often related to dressing removal or recent applications of new dressings.

Poor ulcer healing, arterial disease, or infection may also cause increased pain [Royal College of Nursing, 2000a], and this may be due to both inflammatory processes and nerve damage [Briggs and Nelson, 2004].

Between 17% and 65% of people with a leg ulcer experience severe or continuous pain with a major impact on quality of life [Briggs and Nelson, 2004]. Pain relief is important to maximise quality of life, to enable mobilization, and improve appetite.

A pain assessment may be helpful, particularly for pain related to dressing adherence and wound cleansing. Some guidelines suggest that these should be performed routinely [Royal College of Nursing, 1998].

Leg elevation and compression may reduce pain associated with leg swelling and reduced venous return [Heinen et al, 2004].

Manage pain with oral paracetamol initially, and adjust treatment according to response and associated comorbidities.

Topical analgesia may also be considered to reduce pain during debridement, although there is less evidence for these treatments [Briggs and Nelson, 2004], and use of topical analgesics on wounds is an off-licence indication.

What follow-up is necessary?

Formal reassessment is recommended 12 weeks after treatment is commenced and at subsequent 12-week intervals, unless there are concerns of ulcer deterioration before this time.

Serial measurement (length and width) is an indicator of the healing process.

Tracing of the margins and photography may be helpful.

Reassess the appearance of the ulcer: its edge (shallow, punched out, rolling), base (granulating, sloughy, necrotic), position, surrounding skin, odour, and signs of infection [SIGN, 1998].

Reassess the ankle brachial pressure index at 12 weeks if the ulcer is not fully healed or if it is deteriorating.

Patient concordance with treatment and the effect of pain and mobility on quality of life should be assessed regularly.

Written patient information should be provided when available, as people are more likely to comply with treatment regimes if they are fully informed of the rationale and options for their management.

How can recurrence be prevented?

- **Twelve-month recurrence rates vary widely** between different studies, and have been quoted as 26–69% [Nelson et al, 2004].
- **Graduated compression stockings** should ideally be used for at least 5 years after ulcer healing, in order to minimise the risk of recurrence [SIGN, 1998]. Some health professionals advocate the use of lifelong compression stockings with 6-monthly Doppler ankle brachial pressure index checks, to reduce this risk further.
- **Class III (high) compression stockings** are associated with less recurrence than Class II (medium) compression stockings. However, the strong-support Class III stockings are less well tolerated [Royal College of Nursing, 2000a].
- **Identify any at-risk areas early** to prevent further skin breakdown, as chronic venous hypertension may result in delayed healing if the leg is injured.
- **Offer general health promotion advice** regarding regular walking and mobility, avoiding prolonged standing, leg elevation when immobile, stopping smoking, and foot care.
- **Encourage optimum nutrition and reduce obesity** [Simon et al, 2004].

Medicines to prevent recurrence

- **Oxerutins or rutosides (Paroven capsules)** decrease capillary permeability and have been suggested for reducing ulcer recurrence, but have not shown any greater effect in preventing recurrence compared with placebo [NHS CRD, 1997; Simon et al, 2004].
- **Oral zinc sulfate supplements** are only useful to prevent recurrence of ulcers in people with low serum zinc levels. There is no evidence of benefit to support the general use of zinc supplements [Wilkinson and Hawke, 1998].

L

Dressings information

Wound dressings

- **Dressings should keep the wound moist and warm to promote granulation.**
- **Granulation tissue** is the outgrowth of new capillaries and connective tissue from the surface of an open wound. It is light red or dark pink in colour, soft to the touch, and 'bumpy' in appearance. It is very delicate and must be carefully supported while the wound heals.
- **Knitted viscose dressings** (e.g. N-A dressings, Tricotex) remain on the surface of a wound for several days, allowing exudate to pass through to an absorbent secondary dressing. Under high compression bandages, a knitted viscose dressing will suffice to produce a microenvironment to promote granulation. The absorbent layer above the dressing can be easily changed with minimal disturbance to the wound surface.
- **Hydrogel dressings** facilitate autolytic debridement of wounds and may be useful to maintain a moist wound environment in dry, sloughy wounds.
- **Hydrocolloid dressings** generally consist of a wafer constructed from a thin layer of polyurethane film (which is impermeable to water and microorganisms) with an adhesive that contains gelatine, pectin, and carboxymethylcellulose. Wound exudate combines with the ingredients of the adhesive to form a gel, which promotes moist wound healing.
- **Foam dressings** offer advantages in terms of speed of dressing change, comfort, and low odour potential compared with other dressing types. Foam dressings

contain absorbent hydrophilic foam and allow evaporation of water through the backing to give extra potential for fluid management. They are generally comfortable, soft, and well tolerated.
- **Alginate dressings** may be useful to absorb exudates if the ulcer is sloughy.

Allergens in dressings

- People with venous leg ulcers have high rates of skin sensitivity to allergens. Common allergens may be present in dressings for venous leg ulcers, as listed in Table 2.

Compression bandaging

- **Multi-layer '4-layer' compression** consists of four levels of bandage applied over a wound contact dressing in the following order:
  - Sub-compression wadding bandage.
  - Light support bandage, such as cotton crepe bandage.
  - Light compression bandage, such as knitted elastomer and viscose bandage.
  - Cohesive bandage (a bandage that adheres to itself to prevent movement of dressing).
- **Two-layer compression** is the application of a short-stretch bandage over a sub-compression wadding bandage, and may be useful for more active people or people for whom it is important to be able to wear their normal footwear.
- Only suitably trained practitioners should apply compression bandages. Inappropriate application may lead to uneven and inadequate pressures or too great a pressure being exerted, causing tissue damage or even necrosis.

Compression hosiery

Three different classes of stocking or graduated compression hosiery are available:
- **Medium to high compression stockings are recommended for prophylaxis** for 5 years after healing of a venous ulcer.

Table 2: Common allergens in the management of venous leg ulcers.

	Common allergen	Potential source
Lanolin	Wool alcohols, amerchol L101	Bath additives, creams, emollients, barrier preparations
Antibiotic	Neomycin, framycetin, bacitracin	Tulle dressings, topical antibiotics
Preservative	Parabens	Topical preparations, paste bandages
Vehicle	Cetyl alcohol, stearyl alcohol, cetylstearyl alcohol, cetostearyl alcohol	Most creams, emulsifying ointment, and some paste bandages
Adhesive	Colophony/ester of rosin	Adhesive-backed bandages and dressings, hydrocolloids
Rubber	Mercapto/carba/thiuram mix	Elastic bandages and supports, elastic stockings, latex gloves worn by carer
Biocide	Chlorocresol, quinoline mix, chlorhexidine	Antiseptics and dressings
Corticosteroid	Tixocortal pivalate	Topical corticosteroid preparations
Fragrance	Fragrance mix/balsam of Peru	Bath additives, emollients

[Royal College of Nursing, 2000a]

Table 3: Compression hosiery.

Class	Type	Ankle compression	Indication
I	Light	14–17 mmHg	Superficial/early varicose veins, mild oedema, venous ulcers
II	Medium	18–24 mmHg	Moderate varicosities, post-operative prevention and treatment
III	High	25–35 mmHg	Severe varicose veins, ankle oedema, venous ulcers

- **A range of styles and colours are available** to encourage concordance with prophylaxis.
- **Compression hosiery is available in two lengths, 'below the knee' and 'thigh'** length. Socks are available, as are suspenders for use with thigh-length stockings.
- **Hosiery may have an open or closed toe.** For open-toe hosiery, a heel may or may not be present.
- Graduated compression tights are not available for prescription on the NHS.

References

NHS staff in England can link, free of charge, from references to full text journals by clicking on [Full text] on the PRODIGY website.

1. Berliner, E., Ozbilgin, B. and Zarin, D.A. (2003) A systematic review of pneumatic compression for treatment of chronic venous insufficiency and venous ulcers. *Journal of Vascular Surgery* 37(3), 539–544.
2. Bradley, M., Cullum, N., Nelson, E.A. et al (1999a) Systematic reviews of wound care management: (2) Dressings and topic agents used in the healing of chronic wounds. Executive summary. *Health Technology Assessment* 3(17 Pt 2), 1–4.
3. Bradley, M., Cullum, N., Nelson, E.A. et al (1999b) Systematic reviews of wound care management: (2) Dressings and topic agents used in the healing of chronic wounds. *Health Technology Assessment* 3(17 Pt 2), 1–143.
4. Briggs, M. and Nelson, E.A. (2004) *Topical agents or dressings for pain in venous leg ulcers (Cochrane Review)*. The Cochrane Library. Issue 1. Chichester, UK: John Wiley & Sons, Ltd..
5. Budgen, V. (2004) Evaluating the impact on patients of living with a leg ulcer. *Nursing Times* 100(7), 30–31.
6. Courtenay, M., Church, J.C. and Ryan, T.J. (2000) Larva therapy in wound management. *Journal of the Royal Society of Medicine* 93(2), 72–74.
7. Cullum, N., Nelson, E.A., Fletcher, A.W. and Sheldon, T.A. (2004) *Compression for venous leg ulcers (Cochrane Review)*. The Cochrane Library. Issue 1. Chichester: John Wiley & Sons, Ltd..
8. Fernandez-Chimeno, M., Houghton, P. and Holey, L. (2004) *Electrical stimulation for chronic wounds (Protocol for a Cochrane Review)*. The Cochrane Library. Issue 1. Chichester, UK: John Wiley & Sons, Ltd..
9. Flemming, K. and Cullum, N. (2004a) *Therapeutic ultrasound for venous leg ulcers (Cochrane Review)*. The Cochrane Library. Issue 1. Chichester, UK: John Wiley & Sons, Ltd..
10. Flemming, K. and Cullum, N. (2004b) *Laser therapy for venous leg ulcers (Cochrane Review)*. The Cochrane Library. Issue 1. Chichester, UK: John Wiley & Sons, Ltd..
11. Flemming, K. and Cullum, N. (2004c) *Electromagnetic therapy for treating venous leg ulcers (Cochrane Review)*. The Cochrane Library. Issue 1. Chichester, UK: John Wiley & Sons, Ltd..

2. Fletcher, A., Cullum, N. and Sheldon, T.A. (1997) A systematic review of compression treatment for venous leg ulcer. *British Medical Journal* **315**(7108), 576–580. [Full text]
3. Franek, A., Krol, P. and Kucharzewski, M. (2002) Does low output laser stimulation enhance the healing of crural ulceration? Some critical remarks. *Medical Engineering & Physics* **24**(9), 607–615.
4. Heinen, M.M., van Achterberg, T., op Reimer, W.S. et al (2004) Venous leg ulcer patients: a review of the literature on lifestyle and pain-related interventions. *Journal of Clinical Nursing* **13**(3), 355–366.
5. Iglesias, C., Nelson, E.A., Cullum, N.A. and Torgerson, D.J. (2004) VenUS I: a randomised controlled trial of two types of bandage for treating venous leg ulcers. *Health Technology Assessment* **8**(29), 1–134.
6. Ilsley, K. (2001) *Practice devises an effective strategy for venous leg ulceration.* eGuidelines. www.eguidelines.co.uk [Accessed: 26/01/2004].
7. Jones, J.E. and Nelson, E.A. (2004) *Skin grafting for venous leg ulcers (Cochrane Review).* The Cochrane Library. Issue 1. Chichester, UK: John Wiley & Sons, Ltd..
8. Jull, A., Waters, J. and Arroll, B. (2002) Pentoxifylline for treatment of venous leg ulcers: a systematic review. *Lancet* **359**(9317), 1550–1554. [Full text]
9. Kranke, P., Bennett, M., Roeckl-Wiedmann, I. and Debus, S. (2004) *Hyperbaric oxygen for chronic wounds (Protocol for a Cochrane Review).* The Cochrane Library. Issue 1. Chichester, UK: John Wiley & Sons, Ltd..
0. London, N.J.M. and Donnelly, R. (2000) ABC of arterial and venous disease: ulcerated lower limb. *British Medical Journal* **320**(7249), 1589–1591. [Full text]
1. Mani, R., Vowden, K. and Nelson, E.A. (2004) *Intermittent pneumatic compression for treating venous leg ulcers (Cochrane Review).* The Cochrane Library. Isuue 1. Chichester, UK: John Wiley & Sons, Ltd..
2. Moffatt, C.J., McCullagh, L., O'Connor, T. et al (2003) Randomized trial of four-layer and two-layer bandage systems in the management of chronic venous ulceration. *Wound Repair & Regeneration* **11**(3), 166–171.
3. National Prescribing Centre (1999) Modern wound management dressings. *Prescribing Nurse Bulletin* **1**(2), 5–8.
24. Nelson, E.A., Bell-Syer, S. and Cullum, N.A. (2004) *Compression for preventing recurrence of venous ulcers (Cochrane Review).* The Cochrane Library. Issue 1. Chichester, UK: John Wiley & Sons, Ltd.
25. NHS CRD (1997) Compression therapy for venous leg ulcers. *Effective Health Care Bulletin* **3**(4), 1–12.
26. O'Meara, S. and Ovington, L. (2004) *Antibiotics and antiseptics for venous leg ulcers (Protocol for a Cochrane Review).* The Cochrane Library. Issue 1. Chichester, UK: John Wiley & Sons, Ltd..
27. O'Meara, S., Cullum, N., Majid, M. and Sheldon, T. (2000) Systematic reviews of wound care management: (3) antimicrobial agents for chronic wounds; (4) diabetic foot ulceration. Executive summary. *Health Technology Assessment* **4**(21), 1–4.
28. Persoon, A., Heinen, M.M., van der Vleuten, C.J. et al (2004) Leg ulcers: a review of their impact on daily life. *Journal of Clinical Nursing* **13**(3), 341–354.
29. Royal College of Nursing (1998) *The management of patients with venous leg ulcers. Recommendations for assessment, compression therapy, cleansing, debridement, dressing, contact sensitivity, training/education and quality assurance.* Royal College Of Nursing. www.rcn.org.uk [Accessed: 02/04/2004].
30. Royal College of Nursing (2000a) *The management of patients with venous leg ulcers. Audit protocol.* Royal College of Nursing. www.rcn.org.uk [Accessed: 02/04/2004].
31. Royal College of Nursing (2000b) *The management of patients with venous leg ulcers. Implementation guide.* Royal College of Nursing. www.rcn.org.uk [Accessed: 02/04/2004].
32. SIGN (1998) *The care of patients with chronic leg ulcer.* Report No. 26. Scottish Intercollegiate Guidelines Network. www.sign.ac.uk [Accessed: 26/03/2004].
33. Simon, D.A., Dix, F.P. and McCollum, C.N. (2004) Management of venous leg ulcers. *British Medical Journal* **328**(7452), 1358–1362.
34. Thomas, S. (2004) Advice for community pharmacists on how to order and dispose of maggots. *Pharmaceutical Journal* **272**(7287), 222–223.
35. Wilkinson, E.A. and Hawke, C.I. (1998) Does oral zinc aid the healing of chronic leg ulcers? A systematic literature review. *Archives of Dermatology* **134**(12), 1556–1560. [Full text]

L

PRODIGY GUIDANCE

Malaria prophylaxis

Last revised in November 2004
www.prodigy.nhs.uk/guidance.asp?gt=Malaria prophylaxis

Applies to people of all ages

This guidance covers the management of a person travelling to a malarious area and is based on Department of Health and Health Protection Agency (formerly Public Health Laboratory Service) recommendations.

This guidance does not cover the management of other tropical diseases or offer general travel advice.

There is separate guidance for *Immunizations — travel vaccinations.*

Goals

- To advise on preventing mosquito bites
- To prevent acquisition of malaria

Contents

Scenarios
- Malaria prophylaxis p.1168

Extended Information, p. 1171

Malaria prophylaxis

Which therapy?

- **Assess the degree of risk** (e.g. destination, duration of travel, business, backpacking etc.).
- **Stress the importance of adequate protection against mosquito bites.** Give advice on how to reduce the risk of being bitten. See *Patient information leaflets*.
- **Recommend chemoprophylaxis appropriate to the destination and risk,** taking into account the person's general health and past medical history. For example:
  - **Children:** weight is a better guide than age to dosage.
  - **Pregnancy:** avoid travel if possible. Chloroquine and/or proguanil are safe to use. (Give folic acid 5 mg daily if proguanil or pyrimethamine is used.)
  - **Breastfeeding:** chloroquine and/or proguanil may be used by breastfeeding mothers.
  - **Depression, or other psychiatric disorders:** do not use mefloquine (CSM advice).
  - **Epilepsy:** give folic acid 5 mg daily if proguanil is required. Do not use mefloquine (CSM advice) or chloroquine. Avoid doxycycline in people taking enzyme-inducing drugs (i.e. carbamazepine, phenytoin, or phenobarbital).
  - **Absence of a functional spleen:** compliance with prophylaxis is paramount. Avoid travel to a malarious area if possible.
  - **People intending to sunbathe:** avoid doxycycline as photosensitivity reactions can occur.
- **Give advice on how to recognize breakthrough malaria** and the importance of seeking immediate medical attention.
- **Up-to-date information on the correct choice of chemoprophylaxis should be obtained,** because of the complex picture of developing resistance.

Sources of information on chemoprophylaxis:

Table 1: Main sources of information for up-to-date guidance on malaria chemoprophylaxis.

Advice for healthcare professionals	
British National Formulary	Updated biannually. Also available on the Internet at www.bnf.org .
Health Protection Agency Malaria Reference Laboratory	020 7636 3924 Available on the Internet at www.hpa.org.uk
National Travel Health Network and centre	020 7380 9234
Travax. Scottish Centre for Infection and Environmental Health	Registration is required to use the website or access telephone advice. This is free to NHS users in Scotland; there is a token charge fc NHS users in other parts of the United Kingdom. www.travax.scot.nhs.uk 0141 300 1130
London, Northwick Park Hospital	020 7387 9300 (treatment)
Birmingham Heartlands Hospital (Infectious Diseases Unit)	0121 424 0357
Liverpool School of Tropical Medicine	0151 708 9393
Oxford	01865 225430
National Travel Health Network and Centre (NaTHNaC)	020 7380 9234

Practical prescribing points

For further information see the *Medicines Compendium* (www.medicines.org.uk) or the *British National Formula* (www.bnf.org).

- **Advise women of childbearing potential that adequate contraception must be used until:**
  - Three months after discontinuing mefloquine.
  - One week after discontinuing doxycycline.
  - Two weeks after discontinuing atovaquone/proguanil
- **Advise people taking mefloquine that neuropsychiatric adverse effects are uncommon.** If they do occur, the person should seek medical advice on alternative antimalarials, before the next dose is due (CSM advice) Advise travellers that dizziness or a disturbed sense of balance may affect the performance of skilled tasks (e.g driving); effects may persist for up to 3 weeks.
- **Advise people taking chloroquine** that it sometimes has temporary effect on visual accommodation. People should not drive if they are affected.

Advise people taking doxycycline that photosensitivity reactions sometimes occur. Wear full-length clothing, a hat, and high-factor sunscreen.

Malaria chemoprophylaxis is not recommended for prescription on FP10 by the Department of Health. Private prescriptions for mefloquine, doxycycline, and the combination of atovaquone with proguanil are offered. Chloroquine and proguanil tablets should be purchased over the counter from a pharmacist.

atient information leaflets

ie following PILs are available at www.prodigy.nhs.uk

Malaria Prevention

Malaria Reference Laboratory

MASTA (Travellers Health Line)

hared decision making

Take antimalarial medication exactly as advised. This will usually include a period before and after a visit to a 'malaria risk' country.

Avoid mosquito bites as much as possible. For example:

- Sleep in screened rooms; spray the bedroom with insecticide before sleeping.
- Use mosquito nets (impregnated with insecticide) if you sleep outside.
- Don't go out in the evening, or cover up well if you do (long sleeves, etc.).
- Use insect repellent on clothes and exposed skin.
- Use an electric mat or mosquito coil to vaporize insecticide overnight.
- Spray the bedroom with insecticide just before evening.

Malaria causes fever, shivers, and sweating, and can be very serious. Consult a doctor as soon as possible if you develop these symptoms:

- When in a 'malaria risk' country
- Within a year of returning (especially within 3 months)
- Even if you are taking antimalarial tablets — they are not 100% effective

rug rationale

ugs not included

Pyrimethamine with dapsone (Maloprim®) is no longer available in the UK and is only used on specialist advice. It can be imported (as Deltaprim®) if it is the only suitable regimen for a traveller.

ugs included

Up-to-date information on the correct choice of chemoprophylaxis should be obtained, because of the complex picture of developing resistance.

Malaria chemoprophylaxis is not recommended for prescription on FP10 by the Department of Health. Private prescriptions for mefloquine, doxycycline, and the combination of atovaquone with proguanil (Malarone®) are offered.The prescriptions offered are for 1, 2, 3 and 4 weeks' duration of travel.

Chloroquine and proguanil tablets should be purchased over the counter from a pharmacist.

Prescriptions

Chloroquine and proguanil (OTC advice)

OTC purchase advice: chloroquine + proguanil

- All ages
- Your anti-malarial tablets are not available on prescription but you can buy them from a pharmacy. Adults need to take: TWO proguanil tablets each DAY AND TWO chloroquine tablets ONCE a WEEK (on the same day each week). Children: the exact dose depends on their weight. You should start your tablets one week before you depart. They must be taken whilst you are away and continued for 4 weeks after you return to the UK. This is VERY important. It is important to still try and prevent mosquito bites from happening, even though you are taking anti-malarial tablets. See your doctor if you develop any flu-like illness within 1 year of travel, and especially within 3 months.

OTC purchase advice: chloroquine only

- All ages
- Your anti-malarial tablets are not available on prescription but you can buy them from a pharmacy. Adults need to take: TWO chloroquine tablets ONCE a WEEK (on the same day each week). Children: the exact dose depends on their weight. You should start your tablets one week before you depart. They must be taken whilst you are away and continued for 4 weeks after you return to the UK. This is VERY important. It is important to still try and prevent mosquito bites from happening, even though you are taking anti-malarial tablets. See your doctor if you develop any flu-like illness within 1 year of travel, and especially within 3 months.

OTC purchase advice: proguanil only

- All ages
- Your anti-malarial tablets are not available on prescription but you can buy them from a pharmacy. Adults need to take: TWO proguanil tablets each DAY. Children: the exact dose depends on their weight. You should start your tablets one week before you depart. They must be taken whilst you are away and continued for 4 weeks after you return to the UK. This is VERY important. It is important to still try and prevent mosquito bites from happening, even though you are taking anti-malarial tablets. See your doctor if you develop any flu-like illness within 1 year of travel, and especially within 3 months.

Mefloquine

1-week holiday: child weighs 6 to 15.9kg

- Age from 3 months to 5 years
- Mefloquine 250mg tablets. Take a quarter of a tablet once a WEEK (on the same day each week). Start taking 3 weeks before travel and continue for 4 weeks after return to UK; supply 2 tablets.

1-week holiday: child weighs 16 to 24.9kg

- Age from 2 to 9 years
- Mefloquine 250mg tablets. Take half a tablet once a WEEK (on the same day each week). Start taking 3 weeks before travel and continue for 4 weeks after return to UK; supply 4 tablets.

1-week holiday: child weighs 25 to 44.9kg

- Age from 6 to 13 years
- Mefloquine 250mg tablets. Take three quarters of a tablet once a WEEK (on the same day each week). Start 3 weeks before travel and continue for 4 weeks after return to UK; supply 6 tablets.

M

1-week holiday: child weighs > 45kg
- Age from 10 to 15 years
- Mefloquine 250mg tablets. Take one tablet once a WEEK (on the same day each week). Start taking 3 weeks before travel and continue for 4 weeks after return to UK; supply 8 tablets.

1-week holiday: adult
- Age from 16 years onwards
- Mefloquine 250mg tablets. Take one tablet once a WEEK (on the same day each week). Start taking 3 weeks before travel and continue for 4 weeks after return to UK; supply 8 tablets.

2-week holiday: child weighs 6 to 15.9kg
- Age from 3 months to 5 years
- Mefloquine 250mg tablets. Take a quarter of a tablet once a WEEK (on the same day each week). Start taking 3 weeks before travel and continue for 4 weeks after return to UK; supply 3 tablets.

2-week holiday: child weighs 16 to 24.9kg
- Age from 2 to 9 years
- Mefloquine 250mg tablets. Take half a tablet once a WEEK (on the same day each week). Start taking 3 weeks before travel and continue for 4 weeks after return to UK; supply 5 tablets.

2-week holiday: child weighs 25 to 44.9kg
- Age from 6 to 13 years
- Mefloquine 250mg tablets. Take three quarters of a tablet once a WEEK (on the same day each week). Start 3 weeks before travel and continue for 4 weeks after return to UK; supply 7 tablets.

2-week holiday: child weighs > 45kg
- Age from 10 to 15 years
- Mefloquine 250mg tablets. Take one tablet once a WEEK (on the same day each week). Start taking 3 weeks before travel and continue for 4 weeks after return to UK; supply 9 tablets.

2-week holiday: adult
- Age from 16 years onwards
- Mefloquine 250mg tablets. Take one tablet once a WEEK (on the same day each week). Start taking 3 weeks before travel and continue for 4 weeks after return to UK; supply 9 tablets.

3-week holiday: child weighs 6 to 15.9kg
- Age from 3 months to 5 years
- Mefloquine 250mg tablets. Take a quarter of a tablet once a WEEK (on the same day each week). Start taking 3 weeks before travel and continue for 4 weeks after return to UK; supply 3 tablets.

3-week holiday: child weighs 16 to 24.9kg
- Age from 2 to 9 years
- Mefloquine 250mg tablets. Take half a tablet once a WEEK (on the same day each week). Start taking 3 weeks before travel and continue for 4 weeks after return to UK; supply 5 tablets.

3-week holiday: child weighs 25 to 44.9kg
- Age from 6 to 13 years
- Mefloquine 250mg tablets. Take three quarters of a tablet once a WEEK (on the same day each week). Start 3 weeks before travel and continue for 4 weeks after return to UK; supply 8 tablets.

3-week holiday: child weighs > 45kg
- Age from 10 to 15 years
- Mefloquine 250mg tablets. Take one tablet once a WEEK (on the same day each week). Start taking 3 weeks before travel and continue for 4 weeks after return to UK; supply 10 tablets.

3-week holiday: adult
- Age from 16 years onwards
- Mefloquine 250mg tablets. Take one tablet once a WEEK (on the same day each week). Start taking 3 weeks before travel and continue for 4 weeks after retu to UK; supply 10 tablets.

4-week holiday: child weighs 6 to 15.9kg
- Age from 3 months to 5 years
- Mefloquine 250mg tablets. Take a quarter of a tablet once a WEEK (on the same day each week). Start takir 3 weeks before travel and continue for 4 weeks after return to UK; supply 3 tablets.

4-week holiday: child weighs 16 to 24.9kg
- Age from 2 to 9 years
- Mefloquine 250mg tablets. Take half a tablet once a WEEK (on the same day each week). Start taking 3 weeks before travel and continue for 4 weeks after retu to UK; supply 6 tablets.

4-week holiday: child weighs 25 to 44.9kg
- Age from 6 to 13 years
- Mefloquine 250mg tablets. Take three quarters of a tablet once a WEEK (on the same day each week). Star 3 weeks before travel and continue for 4 weeks after return to UK; supply 9 tablets.

4-week holiday: child weighs > 45kg
- Age from 10 to 15 years
- Mefloquine 250mg tablets. Take one tablet once a WEEK (on the same day each week). Start taking 3 weeks before travel and continue for 4 weeks after retu to UK; supply 11 tablets.

4-week holiday: adult
- Age from 16 years onwards
- Mefloquine 250mg tablets. Take one tablet once a WEEK (on the same day each week). Start taking 3 weeks before travel and continue for 4 weeks after retu to UK; supply 11 tablets.

Atovaquone + proguanil (Malarone)

1-week holiday: child weighs 11 to 20.9kg
- Age from 6 months to 7 years
- Malarone Paediatric tablets. Take one tablet once a da Start taking 1-2 days before travel and continue for 1 week after return to the UK; supply 16 tablets.

1-week holiday: child weighs 21 to 30.9kg
- Age from 5 to 8 years
- Malarone Paediatric tablets. Take two tablets once a day. Start taking 1-2 days before travel and continue f 1 week after return to the UK; supply 32 tablets.

1-week holiday: child weighs 31 to 40kg
- Age from 8 to 13 years
- Malarone Paediatric tablets. Take three tablets once a day. Start taking 1-2 days before travel and continue f 1 week after return to the UK; supply 48 tablets.

1-week holiday: child weighs > 40kg
- Age from 9 to 15 years
- Malarone. Take one tablet once a day. Start taking 1-2 days before travel and continue for 1 week after returr to the UK; supply 16 tablets.

1-week holiday: adult
- Age from 16 years onwards
- Malarone. Take one tablet once a day. Start taking 1-2 days before travel and continue for 1 week after returr to the UK; supply 16 tablets.

2-week holiday: child weighs 11 to 20.9kg
- Age from 6 months to 7 years
- Malarone Paediatric tablets. Take one tablet once a da Start taking 1-2 days before travel and continue for 1 week after return to the UK; supply 23 tablets.

2-week holiday: child weighs 21 to 30.9kg
- Age from 5 to 8 years
- Malarone Paediatric tablets. Take two tablets once a day. Start taking 1-2 days before travel and continue f 1 week after return to the UK; supply 46 tablets.

2-week holiday: child weighs 31 to 40kg
- Age from 8 to 13 years
- Malarone Paediatric tablets. Take three tablets once a day. Start taking 1-2 days before travel and continue for 1 week after return to the UK; supply 69 tablets.

2-week holiday: child weighs > 40kg
- Age from 9 to 15 years
- Malarone. Take one tablet once a day. Start taking 1-2 days before travel and continue for 1 week after return to the UK; supply 23 tablets.

2-week holiday: adult
- Age from 16 years onwards
- Malarone. Take one tablet once a day. Start taking 1-2 days before travel and continue for 1 week after return to the UK; supply 23 tablets.

3-week holiday: child weighs 11 to 20.9kg
- Age from 6 months to 7 years
- Malarone Paediatric tablets. Take one tablet once a day. Start taking 1-2 days before travel and continue for 1 week after return to the UK; supply 30 tablets.

3-week holiday: child weighs 21 to 30.9kg
- Age from 5 to 8 years
- Malarone Paediatric tablets. Take two tablets once a day. Start taking 1-2 days before travel and continue for 1 week after return to the UK; supply 60 tablets.

3-week holiday: child weighs 31 to 40kg
- Age from 8 to 13 years
- Malarone Paediatric tablets. Take three tablets once a day. Start taking 1-2 days before travel and continue for 1 week after return to the UK; supply 90 tablets.

3-week holiday: child weighs > 40kg
- Age from 9 to 15 years
- Malarone. Take one tablet once a day. Start taking 1-2 days before travel and continue for 1 week after return to the UK; supply 30 tablets.

3-week holiday: adult
- Age from 16 years onwards
- Malarone. Take one tablet once a day. Start taking 1-2 days before travel and continue for 1 week after return to the UK; supply 30 tablets.

4-week holiday: child weighs 11 to 20.9kg
- Age from 6 months to 7 years
- Malarone Paediatric tablets. Take one tablet once a day. Start taking 1-2 days before travel and continue for 1 week after return to the UK; supply 37 tablets.

4-week holiday: child weighs 21 to 30.9kg
- Age from 5 to 8 years
- Malarone Paediatric tablets. Take two tablets once a day. Start taking 1-2 days before travel and continue for 1 week after return to the UK; supply 74 tablets.

4-week holiday: child weighs 31 to 40kg
- Age from 8 to 13 years
- Malarone Paediatric tablets. Take three tablets once a day. Start taking 1-2 days before travel and continue for 1 week after return to the UK; supply 111 tablets.

4-week holiday: child weighs > 40kg
- Age from 9 to 15 years
- Malarone. Take one tablet once a day. Start taking 1-2 days before travel and continue for 1 week after return to the UK; supply 37 tablets.

4-week holiday: adult
- Age from 16 years onwards
- Malarone. Take one tablet once a day. Start taking 1-2 days before travel and continue for 1 week after return to the UK; supply 37 tablets.

Doxycycline

1-week holiday
- Age from 12 years onwards
- Doxycycline 100mg capsules. Take one capsule once a day. Start taking 1 week before travel and continue for 4 weeks after return to UK; supply 42 capsules.

2-week holiday
- Age from 12 years onwards
- Doxycycline 100mg capsules. Take one capsule once a day. Start taking 1 week before travel and continue for 4 weeks after return to UK; supply 49 capsules.

3-week holiday
- Age from 12 years onwards
- Doxycycline 100mg capsules. Take one capsule once a day. Start taking 1 week before travel and continue for 4 weeks after return to UK; supply 56 capsules.

4-week holiday
- Age from 12 years onwards
- Doxycycline 100mg capsules. Take one capsule once a day. Start taking 1 week before travel and continue for 4 weeks after return to UK; supply 63 capsules.

Extended Information

Background information

- What is it? p.1171
- What is the lifecycle of the malarial parasite? p.1171
- How common is it? p.1172
- What is the likelihood of a traveller contracting malaria? p.1172
- How do I know my patient has malaria? p.1172
- What else might it be? p.1172
- Complications and prognosis p.1172

M

What is it?

- **Malaria is a tropical disease caused by infection of red blood cells by *Plasmodium*,** a protozoan parasite which is transmitted to humans following a bite from its vector, the *Anopheles* mosquito.
- **There are four species that affect humans.** Most cases of malaria imported into the UK are due to *Plasmodium falciparum*, followed in order of frequency by *Plasmodium vivax*. The other two species, *Plasmodium ovale* and *Plasmodium malariae*, are less commonly seen. *P falciparum* has no dormant stage. The other species have dormant stages in the liver (*P vivax* and *P ovale*) or may persist for many years in the blood (*P malariae*), although they should not if treated: late malariae relapses are usually in untreated people whose original symptoms were missed.
- **Falciparum malaria is the most likely to result in severe illness and death.**

What is the lifecycle of the malarial parasite?

- **The infecting agent is called the sporozoite and is present in the female mosquito's saliva:** in most cases relatively few (8–15) sporozoites may be injected into the blood stream in a single bite [White, 2003].
- Sporozoites disappear from the blood within 8 hours. Successful ones enter liver cells where they multiply asexually to form a schizont which contains tens of thousands of merozoites. In *P vivax* and *P ovale* infection only, some sporozoites develop into hypnozoites, which are a dormant stage which may start multiplying up to a year or more after being acquired.
- The schizont matures, ruptures, and the merozoites are released into the blood stream. They penetrate red blood

cells where they initiate the cycle of development and multiplication that brings about the clinical symptoms of the disease. As numbers rise very rapidly people can become very ill quickly after the appearance of symptoms. Some of the merozoites form male and female gametocytes instead — these may persist in the circulation for several weeks and are the forms infective to the female mosquito.
- The malaria parasite matures and reproduces sexually in the female mosquito of the genus *Anopheles*.

[Eddleston and Pierini, 1999; Gill and Beeching, 2004]

How common is it?

- **It is estimated that worldwide there are 300–500 million cases of clinical malaria each year.** About 40% of the world's population is at risk of acquiring the disease [Croft, 2003].
- **Over 2000 cases of malaria are imported into the UK each year.**
- ***P falciparum*** (which is potentially fatal) accounts for over half of these cases.
- The greatest number of falciparum infections imported into the UK are contracted in West Africa by people whose ethnic origin is in that region [CDR, 2004].

What is the likelihood of a traveller contracting malaria?

- **The risk of contracting malaria is roughly proportional to the length of time spent in a malarious place.** A visit of 3 months carries about six times the risk of a visit that lasts 2 weeks [Bradley and Bannister, 2003]. This may not be true for longer stays in the tropics [Schneider, Personal Communication, 2004].
- **The risk also varies with the region visited.** For example, in West Africa up to 6% of travellers taking no chemoprophylaxis acquire malaria due to *P falciparum* each month. In East Africa, about 1% of travellers taking no prophylaxis acquire malaria each month [Bradley and Bannister, 2003]. The risk is lower in much of South Asia.
- **Other factors that influence the risk of contracting malaria include:**
  - Timing of visit (mosquitoes are most numerous during the rainy season)
  - Duration of visit (the longer the duration, the greater the risk of being bitten by an infected mosquito)
  - Pattern of activity: indoor or outdoor activities, living conditions, urban or rural stay
  - Timing of outdoor activities (the *Anopheles* mosquito bites between dusk and dawn)
  - Mode of travel (e.g. backpackers may be more exposed)
- **Many cases of falciparum malaria are due to either:**
  - Taking no chemoprophylaxis (and this is commonest among fatal cases)
  - Taking a drug not considered effective for the prevention of malaria in the area visited
  - Poor compliance
  - High-risk activity

[Hughes et al, 2003; Schwartz et al, 2003].

How do I know my patient has malaria?

- **Any fever in a traveller returning from a malarious area should be considered to be indicative of malaria until proved otherwise** [White, 2003].
- **The first symptoms of uncomplicated malaria are non-specific and resemble influenza.** Headache, muscular ache, vague abdominal discomfort, lassitude, and lethargy may precede the fever by up to 2 days. The temperature rises erratically initially with shivering, mild chills, worsening headache, malaise, and loss of appetite. Children are irritable, lethargic, and anorexic [White, 2003].
- **Get a blood smear examined promptly. The diagnosis of malaria is made by examination of stained blood smears** for the presence of malarial parasites. A negative result does not exclude malaria, and the test should be repeated if clinically indicated, ideally three times [Eddleston and Pierini, 1999].
- **A person with symptomatic malaria infection may be afebrile at any one time** but very rarely may be persistently afebrile in the presence of a very severe *P falciparum* infection [White, 2003].
- ***P falciparum* infection can progress to severe malaria.** The onset can be gradual or sudden and begin within hours or days of the first febrile symptoms of malaria. Features of severe malaria include an unrousable coma not attributable to other causes, severe anaemia, jaundice, renal failure, circulatory collapse, pulmonary oedema, acidosis, and death [Eddleston and Pierini, 1999; Gill and Beeching, 2004].
- **Death due to *P falciparum* infection may occur within a few hours, particularly in children.** A child may become comatose without any preceding fever or other symptoms [Gill and Beeching, 2004].

Timing of symptoms

- **Symptoms can occur any time after the first week of exposure.** Malaria should therefore be suspected in any person with a febrile illness who has travelled to a malarious area within the past year, especially if symptoms occur within 3 months. Recurring bouts of unexplained fever may be due to malaria.
- **First attacks of malaria due to *P falciparum* usually occur within 3 months of leaving a malarious area,** as *P falciparum* has no dormant stage [Bradley and Bannister, 2003]. However, people who have used mefloquine for prophylaxis tend to become unwell on average later than those who have taken other antimalarials.
- **Malaria can present up to a year or more following initial exposure,** as *P vivax*, *ovale*, and *malariae* (the 'benign' malarias) have dormant stages that can then become active; these malariae may persist for many years undiagnosed [Bradley and Bannister, 2003].

What else might it be?

- Any other febrile illness prevalent in the any of the areas visited.
- The normal differential diagnosis for any illness that normally presents with a fever in the UK.

Complications and prognosis

- **On average, nine people die from malaria** each year in the UK. Most of these deaths are preventable [Bradley and Bannister, 2003].
- **In the UK, the mortality of people who have contracted falciparum malaria is between 0.5% and 1%** [Bradley and Bannister, 2003].
- **Falciparum malaria can result in death within 24 hours of onset of symptoms,** for example, due to cerebral malaria or 'blackwater fever' (massive intravascular haemolysis with haemoglobinuria and acute renal failure).

Management issues

- What advice do travellers need about the risk of malaria? p.1173
- What advice do travellers need about preventing mosquito bites? p.1173
- Which chemoprophylaxis regimen is suitable? p.1174
- How should chemoprophylaxis be taken? p.1175
- Who needs to carry emergency standby treatment? p.1176
- Advice for foreign nationals returning to a malarious area p.1176

What advice do travellers need about the risk of malaria?

- **Travellers should be aware of** the risk of malaria in the area(s) they are visiting, know how to avoid being bitten by mosquitoes, and understand the importance of complying with chemoprophylaxis. They should know when to suspect breakthrough malaria, and understand the need to obtain treatment promptly.
- **Ideally, travel to malarious areas should be avoided by** pregnant women, infants and young children, and people without spleens (including functional asplenia). These groups are at particular risk of severe malaria. If travel is unavoidable, it is essential that strict precautions are taken to avoid mosquito bites, and adequate chemoprophylaxis is taken [Hughes et al, 2003].
- **Advise travellers to consult a doctor if** a febrile illness develops 7 or more days after entering a malarious area, or within 3 months of return. Malaria can occur for the first time over a year after visiting a malarious area, although presentation within the first 3 months is more likely.
- **Travellers should be aware that no chemoprophylaxis regime gives 100% protection.** Both compliance with chemoprophylaxis and preventing mosquito bites are therefore essential.
  - **For areas without drug resistance,** chloroquine 300 mg weekly or proguanil 200 mg daily are suitable, although they will not prevent the development of dormant liver stages of *P vivax* and *P ovale* malaria.
  - The combination of proguanil with chloroquine is also used.
  - **In falciparum resistant areas,** mefloquine, doxycycline, and atovaquone with proguanil (Malarone®) are usually recommended, depending on local resistance patterns.
  - There is a limited amount of data available on the protective efficacy of atovaquone with proguanil in non-immune travellers [Bradley and Bannister, 2003]. There is evidence of high protective efficacy in people living in *P falciparum*-endemic areas. However, such people are likely to be partially immune to malaria, and whether the trial results can be extrapolated to non-immune travellers from the UK is unclear.
  - Note: see Table 1 for the main sources of up-to-date guidance on chemoprophylaxis regimens.

What advice do travellers need about preventing mosquito bites?

- Reducing the number of mosquito bites significantly reduces the risk of contracting malaria [Bradley and Bannister, 2003].
- There is a lack of good evidence regarding the effectiveness of most personal protection measures [Croft, 2003] except for insecticide-treated bed nets, which have been clearly shown to reduce clinical attacks and deaths from malaria in children of countries where malaria is endemic [Abdulla et al, 2001; Lengeler, 2004]. Current UK guidelines recommend that the risk of being bitten by mosquitoes may be reduced by the following measures [Bradley and Bannister, 2003]:
  - Sleep in rooms that are properly screened (close-fitting gauze over windows and doors).
  - Spray the room at dusk with a knockdown insecticide to kill any mosquitoes that may have entered the room during the day.
  - Use mosquito nets impregnated with an insecticide (permethrin) if sleeping outdoors or in an unscreened or partly screened room. Nets should be treated every 6 months.
  - Vaporize insecticides overnight using an electrically heated mat or by burning a mosquito coil.
  - If going out at sunset and in the evening (when mosquitoes are most active), protect all exposed parts with an effective repellent and wear loose long-sleeved clothing, trousers, and socks. Light colours are less attractive to mosquitoes.
  - Use insect repellent applied to clothing or skin.

Mosquito repellants

- **Diethyltoluamide (DEET) should always be used first line** for preventing mosquito bites. It has a remarkable safety record during over 40 years of use by millions of people. There have been occasional reports of encephalopathy in children, usually after excessive, inappropriate use [Bradley and Bannister, 2003]. The following advice is based on expert opinion [Fradin, 1998; ; Stürchler, 2001]:
  - Adults should use products with a DEET concentration of 10% to 35%, although products containing up to 50% DEET can be used.
  - Children should use products containing 10% DEET or less (because of a larger surface-to-volume ration compared to adults).
  - Do not exceed the manufacturer's recommendations for product application.
  - It is important to avoid ingestion of DEET. In children who are likely to suck their hands, it may be sensible to avoid applying DEET to the hands.
- **Lemon eucalyptus oil is an alternative in people who are allergic to DEET.** In a study in the Bolivian Amazon, it offered good (97%) protection over a 4-hour period, compared to 15% DEET (85%), 2% neem oil (57%), and citronella (19%) [Moore et al, 2002]. However, its efficacy has not been studied in other areas of the world.
- A systematic review found that repellents containing citronella do not provide protection for as long as those containing DEET, and cannot be relied upon to provide protection in environments where mosquito-borne diseases are a substantial threat [Fradin, 1998].
- We found no evidence that ingested compounds including garlic and thiamine (vitamin B_1) are capable of repelling biting arthropods [Khan et al, 1969; Fradin and Day, 2002].

Sunscreens and DEET

- Sunscreens and DEET are often applied together. Results of a small study suggest that there is a significant decrease in sun protection factor when sunscreen is applied with DEET and additional measures to protect from ultraviolet radiation should be used, such as avoiding direct sunlight during peak hours and wearing protective clothing and headgear [Montemarano et al, 1997].
- Limited data suggest that the use of sunscreen does not compromise the protection that 35% DEET provides, but further studies on different combination of sunscreen

and insect repellent are needed in order to reach definite conclusions for different products [Murphy et al, 2000].
- If sunscreen and DEET are used at the same time, apply DEET *after* the sunscreen [Stürchler, 2001].

Which chemoprophylaxis regimen is suitable?

- **Assess the risk of malaria to the traveller.** Consider:
  - Countries and locations to be visited, and the risk in each place at that time of year
  - Duration of stay in malarious area (risk increases with length of stay)
  - Style of travel (e.g. backpacking, business, visiting relative, package tour)
  - Intended activities (e.g. safaris, beach, jungle explorations), especially if between dusk and dawn when mosquitoes are more active
- **The risks of malaria need to be balanced against the risks of chemoprophylaxis.** Chemoprophylaxis is not recommended where there is a very low risk of acquiring multi-drug-resistant malaria as the risk of adverse effects is higher than the risk of contracting malaria [Bradley and Bannister, 2003].
- **Adverse effects of antimalarial drugs** (if they occur) tend to present after the first few doses — the incidence of later-onset events is very low [Bradley and Bannister, 2003]. Note: since mefloquine only requires once-weekly dosing, it needs to be started at least two and a half weeks before travel so that there is sufficient time to change chemoprophylaxis if adverse events occur (over 75% of adverse reactions occur by the third dose). See the section *Adverse effects of chemoprophylaxis* for further information.
- **Follow up-to-date guidance when advising chemoprophylaxis,** as the pattern of drug resistance is changing. Table 2 highlights the main sources of information.
- **Malaria chemoprophylaxis is not prescribable on an FP10 prescription** [DH, 1995]. Chloroquine and proguanil can be obtained over the counter from a pharmacist. Mefloquine, doxycycline, and atovaquone with proguanil (Malarone®) can be obtained on private prescription.

Factors affecting the final choice of antimalarial

- **A past history of a psychiatric disorder, depression, or anxiety requiring treatment** is a contraindication to mefloquine. Doxycycline or atovaquone with proguanil (Malarone®)are useful alternatives [Bradley and Bannister, 2003].
- **In people with epilepsy:**
  - Mefloquine and chloroquine are contraindicated.
  - Proguanil alone is recommended for travel to malarious areas without chloroquine resistance.
  - Doxycycline or atovaquone with proguanil (Malarone®) are options for areas where there is a high risk of chloroquine-resistant malaria. However, the serum half-life of doxycycline is shortened by enzyme-inducing drugs (i.e. carbamazepine, phenytoin, and phenobarbital). As there is no information regarding doxycycline dosage in this situation, atovaquone with proguanil is recommended.
  - Dapsone with pyrimethamine (Maloprim®) is also suitable for children with epilepsy: although it is no longer available in the UK, it can be imported as Deltaprim®.
- **Hepatic dysfunction.** Mefloquine and doxycycline are not suitable for use in hepatic impairment because they are excreted solely via the liver. Proguanil and chloroquine are mainly used in mild impairment, and proguanil or atovaquone/proguanil in moderate impairment. Seek specialist advice for people with severe liver failure [Bradley and Bannister, 2003].
- **Renal impairment.** Proguanil is excreted by the kidney and the prophylactic dose will need to be reduced depending on the serum creatinine levels (see appendix 3 BNF). Do not use Malarone® (atovaquone with proguanil) in people with severe renal impairment (creatinine clearance <30 ml/minute): it is not possible to reduce the dose of proguanil because it is a fixed combination tablet. Dose reduction of chloroquine is only needed in severe renal impairment. Mefloquine or doxycycline may be used in areas with a high risk of chloroquine-resistant malaria, or with caution where there is severe renal impairment [Bradley and Bannister, 2003].
- **Cardiac conduction disturbances** may be potentiated by chloroquine or mefloquine, particularly if they are co-administered with other drugs with arrhythmogenic potential (e.g. amiodarone, digoxin).

Infants and children

- **Weight is a better guide than age** for the dose of antimalarials in children over 6 months of age [Bradley and Bannister, 2003].
- **Doxycycline is contraindicated** in children under the age of 12 years.
- **Chloroquine is the only antimalarial available as a suspension.** Mefloquine, proguanil, and atovaquone with proguanil (Malarone®) are only available as tablets. Paediatric Malarone® tablets are available and each contains one quarter of the adult tablet dose. If children are unable to swallow tablets, proguanil tablets and Malarone® tablets can be crushed and given with food [Hughes et al, 2003].
- **Chloroquine should be stored safely out of reach of children** as it is extremely dangerous in overdose [Hughes et al, 2003].

Women

- **Women capable of childbearing** should take contraceptive precautions while taking mefloquine and for 3 months after the last dose but should be advised that inadvertent use prior to or during the first trimester is not an indication for termination. It is best avoided unless there is a strong clinical indication for using it [Hughes et al, 2003].
- **Women wishing to become pregnant** should also avoid conception until 1 week after discontinuing doxycycline, and 2 weeks after stopping atovaquone with proguanil [Hughes et al, 2003].
- **Pregnant women** can take the usual doses of chloroquine and proguanil. (Proguanil and pyrimethamine are folate inhibitors and should therefore be taken with folic acid 5 mg daily [Bradley and Bannister, 2003].) Seek specialist advice for women travelling to *P falciparum*-resistant areas, as the choice is difficult: doxycycline is contraindicated; mefloquine may be associated with an increased risk of stillbirth and miscarriage (although it can be used if the need for it is great); and there is a lack of safety data for atovaquone with proguanil (Malarone®).
- **Breastfeeding mothers** can take the usual dose of antimalarial appropriate for the country to be visited except that doxycycline is contraindicated, and atovaquone with proguanil is not recommended due to absence of data regarding safety [Hughes et al, 2003].
- **Malaria prophylaxis taken by a breastfeeding mother does not protect the newborn** and therefore prophylaxis must be started for the newborn after birth if there is a risk of mosquito bites [Schneider, Personal Communication, 2004].

M

Table 2: Main sources of information for up-to-date guidance on malaria chemoprophylaxis.

Advice for healthcare professionals	
British National Formulary	Updated biannually. Also available on the Internet at www.bnf.org .
Health Protection Agency Malaria Reference Laboratory	020 7636 3924 Available on the Internet at www.hpa.org.uk
National Travel Health Network and centre	020 7380 9234
Travax. Scottish Centre for Infection and Environmental Health	Registration is required to use the website or access telephone advice. This is free to NHS users in Scotland; there is a token charge for NHS users in other parts of the United Kingdom. www.travax.scot.nhs.uk 0141 300 1130
London, Northwick Park Hospital	020 7387 9300 (treatment)
Birmingham Heartlands Hospital (Infectious Diseases Unit)	0121 424 0357
Liverpool School of Tropical Medicine	0151 708 9393
Oxford	01865 225430
National Travel Health Network and Centre (NaTHNaC)	020 7380 9234
Telephone advice lines for travellers	
Health Protection Agency (HPA), Malaria Reference Laboratory (at London School of Hygiene and Tropical Medicine)	09065 508 908 Recorded advice for travellers (calls charged at £1 per minute – September 2004)
Hospital for Tropical Diseases Travel Health line	09061 337733 Website: www.fitfortravel.scot.nhs.uk
World Health Organization advice on international travel and health	www.who.int/ith

Long-term travellers

- **Travellers are exposed to a steadily increasing cumulative risk of acquiring malaria.** Advise meticulous attention to avoiding mosquito bites. The longer the stay, the more important it is to use a regimen that gives a high level of protection.
- **Stress the importance of good compliance.** Compliance tends to be inversely related to the duration of travel [Hughes et al, 2003].
- **Seek specialist advice** on which antimalarial is most suitable for long-term chemoprophylaxis in the area(s) visited.
- Although no antimalarials are licensed for long-term use, the Advisory Committee on Malaria Prevention for UK Travellers advises [Hughes et al, 2003] that:
  - **Chloroquine and proguanil** — although there is no problem with long-term use, there is concern about the level of protective effect in certain geographical areas.
  - **Mefloquine** — can be used long-term safely for up to 3 years in the absence of adverse effects.
  - **Doxycycline** — there is no evidence of harm in the long term and it may be used for at least 2 years.
  - **Atovaquone with proguanil** — there is no evidence of harm with long-term use. May be used confidently for up to 3 months and possibly up to 6 months or longer with caution until more post-licensing data is available.

Adverse effects of chemoprophylaxis

- **The overall level of adverse events for mefloquine is comparable with that for chloroquine plus proguanil,** but the types of adverse effects differ [Barrett et al, 1996; Bradley and Bannister, 2003].
- **The neuropsychiatric adverse effects of mefloquine have been well publicized,** and have reduced its popularity. They include convulsions, paraesthesia, vertigo, headache, insomnia, vivid and unpleasant dreams, agitation, anxiety, irritability, depression, feelings of unreality, panic attacks, hallucinations, and psychotic episodes.
  - Mefloquine may cause dizziness or a disturbed sense of balance (particularly within the first 3 weeks of therapy). Advise travellers not to drive or do tasks requiring fine coordination if affected.
  - Serious adverse effects are rare, and most people have no adverse effects — only about 1 in 140 travellers can expect to have a neuropsychiatric adverse event unpleasant enough to temporarily prevent them from carrying out their day-to-day activities [Barrett et al, 1996; Bradley and Bannister, 2003].
- **Chloroquine plus proguanil can have unpleasant gastrointestinal adverse effects.** Mouth ulcers can be a particular problem, mainly due to the proguanil. Chloroquine can also exacerbate psoriasis and has a temporary effect on visual accommodation. Travellers should be advised not to drive if affected.
- **Photosensitivity occurs in 3% of people taking doxycycline;** this is usually mild although severe reactions can occur, so it is best avoided by travellers intending to sunbathe on holiday. Vaginal thrush can also be a problem (consider giving a one-dose treatment in case of need). Although doxycycline may cause diarrhoea, it may protect against some bacterial causes of traveller's diarrhoea [Bradley and Bannister, 2003].
- **The adverse effect profile of atovaquone with proguanil (Malarone®) seems comparable with that of other antimalarials,** and serious adverse effects are rare. There are fewer gastrointestinal side effects than with chloroquine plus proguanil, and fewer neuropsychiatric adverse events than with mefloquine [McKeage and Scott, 2003; Schlagenhauf et al, 2003].

How should chemoprophylaxis be taken?

- Chemoprophylaxis needs to be started before travel, to allow adequate levels to build up before entering a malarious area. It must be continued after returning from a malarious area (for 4 weeks for most antimalarials) to ensure that all the blood stages of malaria parasites have been eradicated.
- **Chloroquine alone, proguanil alone, or chloroquine with proguanil:** treatment should be started 1 week before travelling and continued for 4 weeks on returning. Proguanil is taken daily, while chloroquine is taken once

weekly. Compliance may be an issue with the combination as 16 tablets need to be taken each week.

- **Mefloquine** has the advantage of simple once-weekly dosing. It should be started at least two and a half weeks before travelling abroad and continued for 4 weeks after return [Bradley and Bannister, 2003]. The reason for starting at least two and a half weeks before travel is to have taken three doses before travelling, in order to see if there are any problems with side effects.
- **Doxycycline** is taken daily (at a dose of 100 mg). Treatment should be started 1 week before travelling and continued for 4 weeks on returning. Meticulous compliance appears to be of particular importance with this regime [Bradley, Personal Communication, 2004].
- **Atovaquone with proguanil** (**Malarone®**) is taken once daily with food or milk (to increase its absorption). This combination only needs to be started 1 or 2 days before departure, and need only be taken for 1 week after leaving a malarious area, as there is good evidence that the combination kills the developing liver stages of *P falciparum*. However, it is only licensed for travel for up to 28 days in a malarious area [Bradley and Bannister, 2003].

Who needs to carry emergency standby treatment?

- **Emergency standby treatment is rarely necessary.** It is *not* a substitute for regular chemoprophylaxis. Regular chemoprophylaxis should be taken as usual, and additional emergency standby treatment is carried to treat suspected breakthrough malaria.
- Travellers may benefit from carrying emergency standby treatment with them if they are:
  - Visiting remote malarious areas, or a remote area anywhere after being in a malarious area in the preceding 3 months and are unlikely to be within 24 hours' reach of a doctor or are in a place where suitable drugs are unavailable.
  - Undertaking multiple short visits to or residing in a low-risk area with highly drug-resistant malaria.
  - Taking sub-optimal chemoprophylaxis in a high-risk area.
- **Standby treatment is not needed for trips of less than a week,** because the interval between getting an infective bite and becoming ill with malaria is at least that long.
- **Treatment choice is determined by the travel destination and likely resistance rates.** It is recommended that expert advice be obtained when advising emergency standby treatment. (It should rarely need to be prescribed and up-to-date information on resistance is required.)
- **Careful counselling** regarding its use is necessary as it is often used inappropriately.

Advice for foreign nationals returning to a malarious area

- People who live in a malarious area gradually build up incomplete immunity following continuous exposure to malaria throughout their lifetime.
- People who have been away from a highly endemic area for malaria lose much of their acquired immunity relatively rapidly, so that if they revisit (or are repatriated to) a highly endemic area they are liable to attacks of malaria [Bradley, Personal Communication, 2004].
- Children who have been born in the UK will have no immunity whatsoever, and are therefore at high risk of severe infection.
- Those returning to a malarious area need to be fully aware of the malaria risk (especially to children) and seek extremely prompt treatment for any fevers. They may also consider chemoprophylaxis for a period [Bradley, Personal Communication, 2004].
- Immigrants to the UK from Asia are at special risk as many left during the malarial eradication campaigns and will visit places where malaria has re-emerged [Bradley and Bannister, 2003].

References

NHS staff in England can link, free of charge, from references to full text journals by clicking on [Full text] on the PRODIGY website.

1. Abdulla, S., Armstrong-Schellenberg, J., Nathan, R. et al (2001) Impact on malaria morbidity of a programme supplying insecticide treated nets in children aged under 2 years in Tanzania: community cross sectional study. *British Medical Journal* **322**(7281), 270–273. [Full text]
2. Barrett, P.J., Emmins, P.D., Clarke, P.D. and Bradley, D.J. (1996) Comparison of adverse events associated with use of mefloquine and combination of chloroquine and proguanil as antimalarial prophylaxis: postal and telephone survey of travellers. *British Medical Journal* **313**(7056), 525–528. [Full text]
3. Bradley, D.J. (2004) *Personal communication.* Ross Professor of Tropical Hygiene Emeritus, London School of Hygiene and Tropical Medicine: London.
4. Bradley, D.J. and Bannister, B. (2003) Guidelines for malaria prevention in travellers from the United Kingdom for 2003. *Communicable Disease and Public Health* **6**(3), 180–199.
5. CDR (2004) Malaria imported into the UK, 2003: implications for those advising travellers. *Communicable Disease Report* **14**(35), 18–23.
6. Croft, A. (2003) Malaria: prevention in travellers. *Clinical Evidence* **10**(Dec), 911–930.
7. DH (1995) *Malaria prophylaxis regulation permitting GPs to charge for prescribing or providing anti-malarial drugs.* London: Department of Health.
8. Eddleston, M. and Pierini, S. (Eds.) (1999) Malaria. In: *Oxford handbook of tropical medicine.* Oxford: Oxford University Press. 20–44.
9. Fradin, M.S. (1998) Mosquitoes and mosquito repellents: a clinician's guide. *Annals of Internal Medicine* **128**(11), 931–940.
10. Fradin, M.S. and Day, J.F. (2002) Comparative efficacy of insect repellents against mosquito bites. *New England Journal of Medicine* **347**(1), 13–18. [Full text]
11. Gill, G. and Beeching, N. (Eds.) (2004) Malaria. In: *Tropical Medicine.* 5th edn. Oxford: Blackwell Science Ltd. 55–72.
12. Hughes, C., Tucker, R., Bannister, B. and Bradley, D.J. (2003) Malaria prophylaxis for long-term travellers. *Communicable Disease and Public Health* **6**(3), 200–208.
13. Khan, A.A., Maibach, H.I., Strauss, W.G. and Fenley, W.R. (1969) Vitamin B1 is not a systemic mosquito repellent in man. *Transactions of the St Johns Hospital Dermatological Society* **55**(1), 99–102.
14. Lengeler, C. (2004) *Insecticide-treated bed nets and curtains for preventing malaria (Cochrane Review).* The Cochrane Library. Issue 2. Chichester, UK: John Wiley & Sons, Ltd.
15. McKeage, K. and Scott, L.J. (2003) Atovaquone/proguanil: a review of its use for the prophylaxis of Plasmodium falciparum malaria. *Drugs* **63**(6), 597–623.
16. Montemarano, A.D., Gupta, R.K., Burge, J.R. and Klein, K. (1997) Insect repellents and the efficacy of sunscreens. *Lancet* **349**(9066), 1670–1671. [Full text]

M

17. Moore, S.J., Lenglet, A. and Hill, N. (2002) Field evaluation of three plant-based insect repellents against malaria vectors in Vaca Diez Province, the Bolivian Amazon. *Journal of the American Mosquito Control Association* **18**(2), 107–110.
18. Murphy, M.E., Montemarano, A.D., Debboun, M. and Gupta, R. (2000) The effect of sunscreen on the efficacy of insect repellent: a clinical trial. *Journal of the American Academy of Dermatology* **43**(2 pt 1), 219–222.
19. Schlagenhauf, P., Tschopp, A., Johnson, R. et al (2003) Tolerability of malaria chemoprophylaxis in non-immune travellers to sub-Saharan Africa: multicentre, randomised, double blind, four arm study. *British Medical Journal* **327**(7423), 1078–1083. [Full text]
20. Schneider, G. (2004) *Personal communication.* International Medical Advisor, WEC International: Dusslingen, Germany.
21. Schwartz, E., Parise, M., Kozarsky, P. and Cetron, M. (2003) Delayed onset of malaria – implications for chemoprophylaxis in travellers. *New England Journal of Medicine* **349**(16), 1510–1516. [Full text]
22. Stürchler, M.P. (2001) The vector and measures against mosquito bites. In: Schlagenahauf-Lawlor, P. (Ed.) *Travellers' malaria.* London: BC Decker Inc.. 119–148.
23. White, N.J. (2003) Malaria. In: Cook, G.C. and Zumla, A.I. (Eds.) *Manson's tropical diseases*. 21st edn. London: W.B. Saunders. 1225–1235.

PRODIGY GUIDANCE

Meniere's disease

Last revised in July 2004
www.prodigy.nhs.uk/guidance.asp?gt=Meniere's disease

Applies to people over the age of 16 years

This guidance covers the management of Meniere's disease.

This guidance does not cover the management of other causes of vertigo, dizziness, nausea, deafness, or tinnitus.

Goals

- To stop or reduce the symptoms during acute attacks of vertigo
- To reduce the frequency and severity of acute attacks
- To optimize hearing and to control tinnitus
- To maximize quality of life and ability to cope with residual symptoms

Contents

Scenarios
- Meniere's disease p.1178

Extended Information, p. 1180

Meniere's disease

Which therapy?

- **Discuss the disorder and its anticipated fluctuant, unpredictable, and progressive course.**
- **Acute attacks of vertigo:** prescribe a short course of prochlorperazine or cinnarizine.
- **Consider prophylaxis with betahistine** for 6–12 months. Stop for a period to assess whether it is necessary to continue long-term treatment.
- Consider a hearing aid, sound therapy for tinnitus, balance training (if available), counselling, and lifestyle change such as reduction of salt intake.
- **Drivers with Meniere's disease are obliged to inform the Driver and Vehicle Licensing Agency.**
- **People prone to sudden attacks of vertigo should:**
  - Always have their medication readily accessible
  - Consider the risks before undertaking potentially dangerous activities such as operating machinery, climbing scaffolding, and swimming

Useful information can be obtained from:

- Meniere's Society www.menieres.org.uk/
- Royal National Institute for Deaf and Hard of Hearing People www.rnid.org.uk/
- British Tinnitus Association www.tinnitus.org.uk/

Practical prescribing points

For further information please see the *Medicines Compendium* (www.medicines.org.uk) or the *British National Formulary* (www.bnf.org).

Short-term treatment of acute attacks

- **Prochlorperazine:** extrapyramidal adverse effects have occurred, especially in the elderly. Avoid in hepatic or renal dysfunction, epilepsy, Parkinson's disease, and hypothyroidism.
- **Cinnarizine:** sedation, epigastric discomfort, rarely extrapyramidal symptoms in elderly people on prolonged therapy.

Long-term prophylactic treatment

- **Betahistine:** caution in peptic ulcer and asthma. Can cause indigestion. Headaches are common.

Follow-up advice

- **People should be followed up to assess:**
  - Vertigo control
  - Hearing loss and tinnitus
  - Disease activity and progression

Should I refer or investigate?

Refer?

- **Refer to an ear, nose and throat specialist:**
  - People regarding whom there is diagnostic doubt, for further assessment and investigations
  - People whose vertigo is refractory to medical treatments
  - For hearing, tinnitus, and balance assessment when necessary
- **Consider referral for cranial imaging** in people with:
  - Sudden onset of new severe symptoms (? bleed)
  - Dizziness and hearing loss lasting more than 2 weeks (? acoustic neuroma)

Investigate?

- **Audiography is usually indicated to assess hearing** (low-tone sensorineural hearing loss, fluctuating over time). This is the only test that is indicated routinely.
- Further tests are sometimes appropriate, usually because other causes of dizziness must be excluded. Referral to secondary care may be required for the tests, which include:
  - Computed tomography (CT) of the head, to exclude bone abnormalities
  - Magnetic resonance imaging (MRI) of the head, to exclude brain stem and cranial nerve disorders
  - Angiographic imaging to exclude vascular conditions
  - Swab of ear canal, aspiration of middle ear to exclude ear infection
  - Lumbar puncture to exclude multiple sclerosis, meningitis, encephalitis
  - Specific blood tests to exclude anaemia, hypothyroidism, diabetes mellitus, autoimmune disease, syphilis
  - Glycerol dehydration test, electrocochleography, to confirm Meniere's disease

Patient information leaflets

The following PILs are available at www.prodigy.nhs.uk

- Medicines - Name Changes of Medicines
- Meniere's Disease
- Meniere's Society

Shared decision making

- Meniere's disease causes attacks of vertigo (dizziness with nausea and vomiting), hearing loss, and tinnitus (noises in the ear).
- **Cinnarizine** or **prochlorperazine** ease nausea, vomiting, and dizziness.
  - Take a dose as soon as an attack begins.
  - They come as tablets, tablets to dissolve in the mouth, or suppositories.
  - Consider carrying some medication at all times in case it is needed suddenly.
- **Betahistine** aims to prevent attacks. If you take this medicine every day you may have fewer attacks or the attacks may not be as bad. However the attacks may not stop completely.
- Lifestyle changes such as stopping smoking, cutting out certain foods, salt restriction, and relaxation techniques may help some people, but there is little proof for this.
- Drivers with Meniere's disease must inform the DVLA.
- Referral to an ear specialist may be advised depending on the severity of symptoms, for example, for hearing aids, to help with tinnitus, or to consider surgery in severe cases.

Drug rationale

Drugs not included

- **Vestibular suppressants** other than prochlorperazine and cinnarizine for acute attacks of nausea and vertigo, have not been included although all may have a place in the treatment of individual people.
- **Thiazide diuretics** have not been included as there is inadequate evidence of benefit in Meniere's disease.
- **Trimetazidine** is not available in the UK.
- **Propranolol, diazepam, corticosteroids, and furosemide (frusemide)** have been used in the treatment of Meniere's disease. There is little evidence to support the use of these products.

[Brookes, 1996; Saeed, 1998]

Drugs included

- **Cinnarizine** has been shown to be effective for alleviating acute attacks and is offered as a short course.
- **Prochlorperazine** is included as an alternative to cinnarizine for acute attacks. Rectal, buccal, and intramuscular preparations are included as they offer alternative routes of absorption when a person is vomiting.
- **Betahistine** is the only prophylactic treatment licensed for Meniere's disease. A variety of doses have been used in randomized controlled trials. Maintenance dosages are usually in the range of 24–48 mg daily. We offer the recommended initial dose of 16 mg three times a day and lower maintenance dose of 8 mg three times a day.

Prescriptions

Acute attack: short-term prochlorperazine

7-day supply: prochlorperazine 5mg three times a day
- Age from 16 years onwards
- Prochlorperazine 5mg tablets. Take one tablet three times a day during an acute attack, increase to a maximum of two tablets three times a day if required; supply 42 tablets; NHS Cost £2.47.

7-day supply: prochlorperazine buccal 3mg twice a day
- Age from 16 years onwards
- Prochlorperazine 3mg buccal. Use one to two tablets twice a day during an acute attack. Place high up between the upper lip and gum and leave to dissolve; supply 30 tablets; NHS Cost £3.45.

14-day supply: prochlorperazine 5mg three times a day
- Age from 16 years onwards
- Prochlorperazine 5mg tablets. Take one tablet three times a day during an acute attack, increase to a maximum of two tablets three times a day if required; supply 84 tablets; NHS Cost £4.94.

14-day supply: prochlorperazine buccal 3mg twice a day
- Age from 16 years onwards
- Prochlorperazine 3mg buccal. Use one to two tablets twice a day during an acute attack. Place high up between the upper lip and gum and leave to dissolve; supply 50 tablets; NHS Cost £5.75.

If vomiting: prochlorperazine 25mg suppository when required
- Age from 16 years onwards
- Prochlorperazine 25mg suppositories. Insert one suppository into the rectum during an acute attack; supply 10 suppositories; NHS Cost £12.32.

If vomiting: prochlorperazine 12.5mg IM inj when required
- Age from 16 years onwards
- Prochlorperazine 12.5mg/ml inj. Give 12.5mg by deep intramuscular injection if required; supply 1 1ml ampoule; NHS Cost £0.59.

Acute attack: short-term cinnarizine

7-day supply: cinnarizine 30mg three times a day
- Age from 16 years onwards
- Cinnarizine 15mg tablets. Take two tablets three times a day during an acute attack; supply 42 tablets; NHS Cost £2.29.

14-day supply: cinnarizine 30mg three times a day
- Age from 16 years onwards
- Cinnarizine 15mg tablets. Take two tablets three times a day during an acute attack; supply 84 tablets; NHS Cost £4.58.

M

Maintenance treatment

Betahistine 16mg three times a day
- Age from 16 years onwards
- Betahistine 16mg tablets. Take one tablet three times a day; supply 84 tablets; NHS Cost £13.56.

Low dose: betahistine 8mg three times a day
- Age from 16 years onwards
- Betahistine 8mg tablets. Take one tablet three times a day; supply 84 tablets; NHS Cost £3.27.

Non-drug management

Advice only: tinnitus management
- Age from 16 years onwards
- Try these different ways to help cope with tinnitus: Avoid silence. Use pleasant background noises in the house. You can buy background noise cassettes, baby soothing sounds, or 'sound machines' from shops. Do pleasant activities that improve your well-being. Some people find that when they are relaxed, tinnitus improves. Ask about relaxation therapy. Tinnitus maskers may help break up the ringing in your ears. Pillow maskers may help you sleep. Go to bed when you are tired. Avoid watching TV in bed, drinking alcohol, tea or coffee late in the evening. Tinnitus is distressing, but trying to reduce the negative ideas and associations with tinnitus will help you to cope with it.

Extended Information

Background information

- What is it? p.1180
- How common is it? p.1180
- How do I know my patient has it? p.1180
- What else might it be? p.1180
- Complications and prognosis p.1181

What is it?

- **Meniere's disease is a progressive disorder of the inner ear of unknown aetiology. It can affect one or both ears initially; unilateral disease can progress to bilateral disease.**
- Meniere's disease causes recurrent episodes of vertigo, hearing loss, tinnitus and a sense of pressure in the ear. Vertigo (causing dizziness, nausea and vomiting) is often the most prominent symptom.
- The structures that make up the inner ear are the cochlea, which is responsible for hearing, and the vestibular apparatus, which is responsible for balance. The cochlea and the vestibular apparatus are a complex set of tubes enclosed by the membranous labyrinth. The membranous labyrinth is filled with a fluid called endolymph. In Meniere's disease there is a progressive distension of the membranous labyrinth, which is called 'endolymphatic hydrops'.
- Injury to the vestibular system causes vertigo and balance problems. Injury to the cochlea results in hearing loss.
- A number of theories have been put forward to explain Meniere's disease, but they have little scientific evidence to support them. Viral, vascular (ischaemia), genetic, immune, anatomical, and metabolic mechanisms for Meniere's disease have been proposed.

[Bandolier, 1995; Ludman, 1997; Corbridge, 1998; Saeed, 1998]

How common is it?

- The prevalence in the UK is between 1 in 1000 to 1 in 20,000 of the population. Estimates vary widely because different criteria have been used for diagnosing Meniere's disease [Bandolier, 1995].
- Men and women are equally affected.
- Peak onset is 20–50 years; although it can occur at any age it is uncommon in children [Bachor and Karmody, 1995].
- It sometimes (about 8%) runs in families [Bandolier, 1995].
- It is commonly associated with headache (70%) and sometimes with migraine (6%) [Eklund, 1999].

How do I know my patient has it?

- Meniere's disease is diagnosed on clinical grounds, simple audiometric tests and the exclusion of other causes of dizziness, hearing loss and tinnitus (see *What else might it be?*).
- **A firm diagnosis of Meniere's disease requires all three of the following criteria:**
  - At least two spontaneous episodes of vertigo lasting at least 20 minutes
  - Sensorineural hearing loss confirmed by audiometry
  - Tinnitus and/or perception of aural fullness
- Acute episodes of vertigo usually last from 20 minutes to 24 hours, and tend to occur in clusters, with a mean frequency of between 6 and 11 clusters per year.
- Periods of remission last from a few days to many months or, even years.
- Hearing loss initially affects the lower tones.
- Distinct features are recognised in early, middle and late stages of Meniere's disease (for details see *Complications and prognosis*).

[Committee on Hearing & Equilibrium of the American Academy of Otolaryngology – Head & Neck Foundation, 1995; Bondesson et al, 1998; Saeed, 1998]

What else might it be?

Meniere's disease is often difficult to distinguish from other diseases causing vertigo or dizziness.

- **Benign paroxysmal positional vertigo** is the commonest cause of vertigo. It is typically provoked by a change in the position of the head (e.g. to one side or when looking up), and usually lasts a few seconds.
- People with anaemia, hypothyroidism, diabetes mellitus, autoimmune disease, and syphilis rarely can have symptoms similar to Meniere's disease.
- General unsteadiness and vertigo have numerous other possible causes including:
  - Adverse effects of drugs
  - Functional (non-organic) dizziness; hyperventilation
  - Otitis media, otitis externa
  - Labyrinthitis, neuronitis
  - Vascular disturbances including vertebrobasilar insufficiency, thrombosis of labyrinthine artery, infarction of the lateral medulla
  - Head injury, or labyrinthine fistula
  - Tumours in or impinging on the ear, cerebellum or pons, e.g. acoustic neuroma

[Saeed, 1998]

Table 1: Investigations which can be used in determining the cause of vertigo.

Investigation	Condition
Computed tomography (CT) of the head	Abnormalities in bone, such as mastoiditis, fractures at the base of the skull, erosion of bone by tumours, and Paget's disease
Magnetic resonance imaging (MRI) of the head	Brain stem and cranial nerve disorders
Angiography, magnetic resonance angiography (MRA), or Doppler ultrasonography of the head	Vascular disturbances including vertebrobasilar insufficiency, thrombosis of labyrinthine artery, infarction of the lateral medulla
Swab of ear canal; aspiration of middle ear	Ear infections
Lumbar puncture	Multiple sclerosis, meningitis, encephalitis
Blood test	Anaemia, hypothyroidism, diabetes mellitus, autoimmune disease, syphilis
Glycerol dehydration test	Meniere's disease
Electrocochleography	Meniere's disease

M

Complications and prognosis

Complications

- **Quality of life,** for example travelling and employment, can be severely affected in some people because of the fluctuant, unpredictable, and progressive nature of the condition.
- **Psychological distress, anxiety,** and **depression.**
- **Loss of driving licence** if symptoms are sudden and disabling.

Prognosis

The disease progresses through the following stages:
- **Early-stage disease:** episodes, predominantly of rotatory vertigo, are sudden and unpredictable. Vertigo is accompanied by nausea and vomiting, and sometimes pallor and sweating. Attacks last from 20 minutes to 24 hours, and may be preceded by a feeling (aura) of fullness in the ear. During attacks hearing deteriorates and tinnitus increases, but between attacks hearing reverts to normal and tinnitus reduces or disappears.
- **Middle-stage disease:** sensorineural hearing loss (affecting lower pitches initially) becomes established and progresses, but continues to fluctuate. Paroxysms of vertigo are at their maximum severity. Periods of remission are variable, often lasting up to several months. Tinnitus progresses.
- **Late-stage disease:** the prime symptom is hearing loss that is non-fluctuant and progressively deteriorates. Episodes of vertigo diminish and disappear. However, general balance problems develop and the person may be unsteady, particularly in the dark. Tinnitus may be a significant symptom.

[Saeed, 1998]

Management issues

- Drugs for acute attacks of vertigo p.1181
- Drugs for prophylaxis p.1181
- Treatments available in secondary care p.1181
- Supportive measures p.1181
- Medicines management p.1182

The natural history of Meniere's disease involves fluctuating symptoms with periods of remission that are often long or even permanent. This pattern complicates treatment.

Drugs for acute attacks of vertigo

- **The phenothiazine, prochlorperazine, and the antihistamine, cinnarizine,** are effective treatments for the vertigo and nausea associated with Meniere's disease. These are useful during the period of the acute attacks.
- There are a variety of other drugs that may be suitable for individual circumstances, although most will have significant adverse effects that should be checked first.
- Consider the person's preferences when choosing the buccal, rectal, oral, or intramuscular route for drug delivery.

[BNF 46, 2003]

Drugs for prophylaxis

- A Cochrane systematic review found no evidence that tinnitus or deafness is alleviated or prevented by betahistine, diuretics, trimetazidine, or lithium (which has significant adverse effects) [James and Burton, 2004].
- Evaluation of treatments for prophylaxis of vertigo in Meniere's disease is difficult, owing to chronic course, fluctuating symptoms, variable remission periods and significant placebo responses [James and Thorp, 2003].
- **No treatment:** some people with infrequent mild attacks, or in whom the disease has 'burnt out' may prefer not to take any maintenance treatments.
- **Betahistine** (a vasodilator and histamine agonist with virtually exclusive H1 activity) is sometimes used long-term, although a Cochrane systematic review concluded that there was insufficient evidence to assess its effectiveness [James and Burton, 2004]. It is thought to work by reducing the pressure of fluid in the membrane of the inner ear. More recently, a randomized controlled trial (RCT) of 81 people with Meniere's disease found statistically significant and clinically important improvements with regard to frequency, intensity, and duration of vertigo attacks with treatment with betahistine 16 mg twice daily for 3 months [Mira et al, 2003]. Headache was a common adverse effect. A variety of betahistine doses have been studied in trials; the dosing in common use in the UK is 16 mg taken three times a day.
- **Trimetazidine** is one of a new class of anti-ischaemia drugs [Stanley and Marzilli, 2003]. It is not yet available in the UK. Two small RCTs in people with Meniere's disease found no significant difference between trimetazidine and betahistine in hearing, tinnitus, aural fullness, or quality of life. The two studies had conflicting results for vertigo [James and Thorp, 2003].
- **Diuretics alone or in combination with salt restriction:** the few controlled trials that exist are not conclusive [James and Thorp, 2003]. The proposed mechanism behind this treatment is that diuretics modify the endolymph (which has become potassium-rich resulting in intoxication of the hair cells). Salt restriction, which is more popular abroad than in the UK, is often tried, although it can be hard to sustain.
- **A variety of other treatments** are sometimes used in Meniere's disease, for example anti-anxiety drugs (vestibular suppressants such as diazepam), corticosteroids, and anti-allergy therapy [Slattery and Fayad, 1997; Bandolier, 2000; Derebery, 2000], but these are usually best tried with the advice of an ear, nose and throat consultant.
- **As different people respond variably to different treatments,** and as there is little evidence on which to base strong recommendations, a number of different therapies may have to be tried until one that suits the individual is found.

Treatments available in secondary care

Although in four out of five people the condition is controlled by medical treatments, a few individuals with severe Meniere's disease may need an ablative medical or surgical procedure to manage their vertigo. Ablative interventions aim to selectively destroy vestibular function (balance) while preserving cochlear function (hearing). Ablative procedures may be medical or surgical:
- **Gentamicin given locally into the middle ear** can reduce and control vertigo in about 90% of instances hearing deteriorates in about 40% [Assimakopoulos and Patrikakos, 2003].
- **Surgical treatments that are not destructive to hearing** include endolymphatic sac surgery and vestibular nerve section/neurectomy.
- **Surgical treatments that are destructive to hearing** such as labyrinthectomy have occasionally been used.

[Saeed, 1998]

Supportive measures

Loss of hearing

- **Hearing loss** is usually in the low-frequency range. Hearing and tinnitus fluctuate in the early stages of

M

disease, but in the later stages they may become permanent. Meniere's disease can result in marked intolerance to loud sounds.

- Compression hearing aids can compensate for the hearing loss in Meniere's disease by making quiet sounds louder and compressing loud sounds. These are now available within the range of standard National Health Service hearing aids.
- The Royal National Institute for Deaf and Hard of Hearing People (RNID) has helpful general information about deafness and also specific information about Meniere's disease on its web site (www.rnid.org.uk/).

Tinnitus

- **Tinnitus** can be annoying and distressing.
- Sound therapy, avoidance of silent environments, and relaxation techniques can help.
- The British Tinnitus Association has much information online (www.tinnitus.org.uk/).

Psychological distress

- **Distress is common in people with Meniere's disease,** as it is a difficult and unpredictable disease. Counselling, information, adaptation of lifestyle, and regular relaxation can be beneficial to some [Saeed, 1998]. Information about the disease to help people understand the condition is available from the Meniere's Society (www.menieres.org.uk), and also from the RNID (www.rnid.org.uk/).
- **Psychological support** is thought to positively affect subsequent management. An important goal of management is the ability to cope with residual symptoms and thus maximize the quality of life. As with other distressing conditions for which there is no ready cure, there are a number of alternative/complementary therapies, but the placebo response is significant. The Meniere's Society (www.menieres.org.uk/) and the Royal National Institute for Deaf and Hard of Hearing People (RNID) (www.rnid.org.uk/) are useful sources of information and support for both the patient and the practitioner

Impaired balance control

- **After an acute attack of vertigo,** the individual's natural tendency is to sit still. People should be encouraged to move around to promote central compensation: the brain uses vision and other senses to compensate for the loss of vestibular function.
- **Vestibular rehabilitation** (balance training) was effective in a small, randomized controlled trial of people suffering from uncontrolled dizziness or vertigo [Yardley et al, 1998]. It may only be suitable for people in whom acute attacks of vertigo are far apart and who suffer from motion-provoked symptoms between attacks, or for those who have had treatment to stabilize their balance organ and who are still experiencing motion-provoked imbalance [Beynon and Bottrill, 1997]. People should be taught by trained health professionals (ask at the local ear, nose and throat department).

[Bottrill, 1998; Cohen, 2000]

Lifestyle measures and alternative therapies

- **Drivers** with Meniere's disease are responsible for informing the Driver and Vehicle Licensing Agency (DVLA) about their condition. The DVLA will send a questionnaire to the person and ask for consent to contact their general practitioner or consultant. Generally, those people with sudden and disabling attacks that are not preceded by aura or warning signs may have their driving licence revoked [DVLA, 2003]. Once the condition is controlled, re-application for a licence can be made to the DVLA. The DVLA website (www.dvla.gov.uk) gives details on how to inform the DVLA of the person's medical condition and how to re-apply for a new licence once the condition is stable.
- **Sudden attacks of vertigo** mean that the person should consider the risks before activities such as operating dangerous machinery, using ladders or scaffolding, or going swimming.
- There is currently no evidence that avoidance of certain foods (e.g. salt, caffeine, nicotine, or alcohol) will help Meniere's disease [Bandolier, 1995; James and Thorp, 2003]. However, some people do report such lifestyle changes as being helpful.
- Transcutaneous electrical nerve stimulation (TENS), acupuncture, and spinal manipulation have been tried in people with Meniere's disease, but there is no evidence and little rationale to support their use.

Medicines management

- Vestibular suppressants such as prochlorperazine and cinnarizine should only be used short-term because prolonged use can lead to continued dizziness.
- Long-term use may also cause extrapyramidal symptoms such as involuntary movements (tardive dyskinesia), tremors and rigidity (Parkinsonism), restlessness (akathisia), muscle contractions (dystonia) and changes in temperature, breathing and heart rate.
- The elderly are at most risk for adverse effects from drug treatments.

Cinnarizine

- **Cinnarizine may cause drowsiness,** especially at the start of treatment. Warn people that if they are affected, they should avoid driving or operating heavy machinery.
- **Taking cinnarizine after meals** may reduce any epigastric discomfort.
- **Concurrent use of alcohol, central nervous system depressants or tricyclic antidepressants** may potentiate the sedative effects of these drugs or cinnarizine.
- Extrapyramidal symptoms are rare with cinnarizine. At most risk are elderly people receiving prolonged treatment.

[ABPI Medicines Compendium, 2004b]

Prochlorperazine

- **Prochlorperazine is contraindicated** in a large number of conditions, including liver or renal dysfunction and Parkinson's disease. If the person has any conditions in addition to Meniere's disease, check that it is safe to prescribe.
- **Elderly people** are particularly susceptible to its adverse effects, although some of these will only occur with prolonged use (e.g. drug-induced Parkinsonism). Be aware that, particularly in elderly individuals, prochlorperazine may cause postural hypotension, and it should also be used with caution in hot and cold weather (risk of hyper- and hypothermia).
- **Prochlorperazine may lower the seizure threshold** in people with epilepsy or history of seizures. Close monitoring is required.
- **Acute dystonia or dyskinesia,** usually transitory, are more common in children and young adults (usually occur within the first 4 days of treatment).
- The risk–benefit profile of prescribing prochlorperazine should be carefully assessed in people with a predisposition towards ventricular arrhythmias, e.g. those with cardiac disease; metabolic disorders such as hypokalaemia, hypocalcaemia or hypomagnesaemia; starvation; alcohol abuse, or concomitant therapy with other drugs known to increase the QT interval. Prochlorperazine has the potential to increase the QT

M

interval and close monitoring is advised (biochemical status and electrocardiogram) which may make it a second-line choice, cinnarizine being preferred.

- Neuroleptic malignant syndrome (NMS) is rare but life-threatening. The cardinal features are hyperthermia, rigidity, autonomic instability (labile blood pressure, tachycardia, sweating, incontinence, flushing and pallor), and altered level of consciousness. Onset can be slow or sudden. When NMS is suspected, stop treatment and monitor closely. When NMS is likely, stop treatment and admit urgently [Susman, 2001].

[Lee A, 2001; ABPI Medicines Compendium, 2004a]

Betahistine

- **Betahistine** does not affect driving or psychomotor ability.
- **Caution is advised** in people who have asthma (because of H_1-receptor activity), although clinical intolerance is relatively rare.
- **Caution is also advised** in people with a history of peptic ulcer, although there is virtually no H_2-receptor activity.
- Betahistine should be used for a sufficient length of time to cover anticipated future attacks, for example, for at least 6–12 months. After a period of 6–12 months some people may wish to attempt a withdrawal of betahistine, restarting it if and when attacks start again.

[ABPI Medicines Compendium, 2004c]

References

NHS staff in England can link, free of charge, from references to full text journals by clicking on [Full text] on the PRODIGY website.

1. ABPI Medicines Compendium (2004a) *Summary of product characteristics for Stemetil (prochlorperazine).* Electronic Medicines Compendium. Datapharm Communications Ltd. www.emc.medicines.org.uk [Accessed: 01/03/2004].
2. ABPI Medicines Compendium (2004b) *Summary of product characteristics for Stugeron (cinnarazine).* Electronic Medicines Compendium. Datapharm Communications Ltd. www.emc.medicines.org.uk [Accessed: 01/03/2004].
3. ABPI Medicines Compendium (2004c) *Summary of product characteristics for Betahistine.* Electronic Medicines Compendium. Datapharm Communications Ltd. www.emc.medicines.org.uk [Accessed: 01/03/2004].
4. Assimakopoulos, D. and Patrikakos, G. (2003) Treatment of Meniere's disease by intratympanic gentamicin application. *Journal of Laryngology & Otology* **117**(1), 10–16. [Full text]
5. Bachor, E. and Karmody, C.S. (1995) Endolymphatic hydrops in children. *Orl; Journal of Oto-Rhino-Laryngology & its Related Specialties* **57**(3), 129–134.
6. Bandolier (1995) *Meniere's disease.* Bandolier. 13. www.jr2.ox.ac.uk/bandolier/band13/b13-1.html [Accessed: 01/03/2004].
7. Bandolier (2000) *Tinnitus and Meniere's update.* Bandolier. 74. 2. www.jr2.ox.ac.uk/bandolier/band74/b74-2.html [Accessed: 01/03/2004].
8. Beynon, G. and Bottrill, I. (1997) *Vestibular rehabilitation in Meniere's disease.* Woking, Surrey: The Meniere's Society.
9. BNF 46 (2003) *British National Formulary.* 46th edn. London: British Medical Association and Royal Pharmaceutical Society of Great Britain.
10. Bondesson, E., Friberg, K., Soliman, S. and Lofdahl, C.G. (1998) Safety and efficacy of a high cumulative dose of salutamol inhaled via turbahaler or via a pressurized metered-dose inhaler in patients with asthma. *Respiratory Medicine* **92**(2), 325–330.
11. Bottrill, I. (1998) Diagnosing and treating Meniere's disease. *Practitioner* **242**(1587), 482–484. [Full text]
12. Brookes, G.B. (1996) The pharmacological treatment of Meniere's disease. *Clinical Otolaryngology & Allied Sciences* **21**(1), 3–11.
13. Cohen, H.S. (2000) Vertigo and balance disorders. Vestibular rehabilitation. *OT Practice* **5**(4), 14–18.
14. Committee on Hearing & Equilibrium of the American Academy of Otolaryngology – Head & Neck Foundation, Inc. (1995) Guidelines for the diagnosis and evaluation of therapy in Meniere's disease. *Otolaryngology – Head and Neck Surgery* **113**(3), 181–185.
15. Corbridge, R.J. (Ed.) (1998) *Essential ENT Practice.* London: Arnold.
16. Derebery, M.J. (2000) Allergic management of Meniere's disease: an outcome study. *Otolaryngology – Head & Neck Surgery* **122**(2), 174–182.
17. DVLA (2003) *At a glance guide to the current medical standards of fitness to drive: neurological disorders.* Drivers Medical Group, Driver and Vehicle Licensing Authority. http://www.dvla.gov.uk/at_a_glance/ch1_neurological.htm [Accessed: 27/02/2004].
18. Eklund, S. (1999) Headache in Meniere's disease. *Auris Nasus Larynx* **26**(4), 427–433.
19. James, A.L. and Burton, M.J. (2004) *Betahistine for Meniere's disease or syndrome (Cochrane Review).* The Cochrane Library. Issue 2. Chichester, UK: John Wiley & Sons Ltd.
20. James, A. and Thorp, M. (2003) Meniere's disease. *Clinical Evidence* **10**(Dec), 593–601.
21. Lee A (2001) Mental health disorders. In: Lee A (Ed.) *Adverse Drug Reactions.* London: Pharmaceutical Press. 195–199.
22. Ludman, H. (Ed.) (1997) *ABC of otolaryngology.* 4th edn. London: BMJ Publishing Group.
23. Mira, E., Guidetti, G., Ghilardi, L. et al (2003) Betahistine dihydrochloride in the treatment of peripheral vestibular vertigo. *European Archives of Oto-Rhino-Laryngology* **260**(2), 73–77.
24. Saeed, S.R. (1998) Diagnosis and treatment of Meniere's disease. *British Medical Journal* **316**(7128), 368–372. [Full text]
25. Slattery, W.H. and Fayad, J.N. (1997) Medical treatment of Meniere's disease. *Otolaryngologic Clinics of North America* **30**(6), 1027–1037.
26. Stanley, C.C. and Marzilli, M. (2003) Metabolic therapy in the treatment of ischaemic heart disease: the pharmacology of trimetazidine. *Fundamental and Clinical Pharmacology Online* **17**(2), 133–145.
27. Susman, V.L. (2001) Clinical management of neuroleptic malignant syndrome. *Psychiatric Quarterly* **72**(4), 325–336.
28. Yardley, L., Beech, S., Zander, L. et al (1998) A randomized controlled trial of exercise therapy for dizziness and vertigo in primary care. *British Journal of General Practice* **48**(429), 1136–1140.

PRODIGY GUIDANCE

Menopause

Last revised in July 2005
www.prodigy.nhs.uk/guidance.asp?gt=Menopause

Applies to women over the age of 25 years

This guidance covers the management of the menopause, including the place of both hormone replacement therapy (HRT) and alternatives to HRT. It deals with HRT in detail and provides HRT prescriptions. Prescriptions for alternative treatments are not included.
This guidance only gives brief information on the management of the menopause in women with venous thromboembolism, breast cancer, and other comorbidities.

There is separate PRODIGY guidance for *Osteoporosis treatment*, *Amenorrhoea*, *Menorrhagia*, *Contraception*, *Endometriosis*, *Urinary tract infection (lower) — women*; there are also Department of Health referral guidelines *Gynaecological cancer — suspected* and *Breast cancer — suspected*.

Goals

- To manage menopausal symptoms

Contents

Scenarios

- Options for managing menopausal symptoms p.1184
- Work-up for starting HRT p.1185
- Peri- or postmenopause — cyclical combined HRT tablets p.1187
- Peri- or postmenopause — cyclical combined HRT patches p.1189
- Postmenopause only — no-bleed continuous HRT tabs or patches p.1191
- Hysterectomy — oestrogen-only tablets p.1193
- Hysterectomy — oestrogen-only patch, gel, implant, spray p.1194
- Urogenital symptoms — vaginal oestrogens p.1196
- Adjunct progestogens (tablets or IUS) p.1198

Extended Information, p. 1199

Which scenario?

- **Options for managing menopausal symptoms:** advice on the place of hormone replacement therapy (HRT), and alternatives to HRT.
- **Work-up for starting HRT:** covers the initial work-up, and advises which HRT regimens to use.
- **Peri- or postmenopause — cyclical combined HRT tablets: covers** the use of combined oestrogen and progestogen tablets that will protect the uterus and produce a withdrawal bleed.
- **Peri- or postmenopause — cyclical combined HRT patches:** covers the use of combined oestrogen and progestogen patches that will protect the uterus and produce a withdrawal bleed.
- **Postmenopause only — no-bleed continuous HRT tabs or patches: covers** the use of combined oestrogen and progestogen tablets and patches that will protect the uterus and do not produce a withdrawal bleed.
- **Hysterectomy — oestrogen-only tablets:** covers the management of peri- or postmenopausal women without a uterus.
- **Hysterectomy — oestrogen-only patch, gel, implant, nasal:** covers the management of peri- or postmenopausal women without a uterus.
- **Urogenital symptoms — vaginal oestrogens:** covers the use of topical oestrogens for the local treatment of urogenital symptoms such as atrophic vaginitis. These products do not provide systemic HRT.
- **Adjunct progestogens (tablets or IUS):** covers the use of progestogens for endometrial protection in women with a uterus when the oestrogen and progestogen are delivered by different routes. The oestrogen component can be found in the 'oestrogen-only' (hysterectomy) scenarios.

Options for managing menopausal symptoms

Which therapy?

- **For many women, menopausal symptoms are mild and of short duration,** and do not require management beyond lifestyle adjustments, education, and reassurance.
- **For others, these symptoms may be distressing and require short-term treatment.**
- **All women should receive** lifestyle advice on preventing cardiovascular disease and osteoporosis. See *patient information leaflets*.

Hot flushes and night sweats

- **Offer lifestyle advice,** e.g. exercise, lighter clothing, sleeping in a cooler room, and reducing stress. Avoiding triggers like spicy foods, caffeine, smoking, or alcohol may help.
- **Consider using HRT.** It is the most effective way of relieving hot flushes. (Tibolone is an alternative.)
- **Other options include** (prescriptions not included in this guidance):
  - **Paroxetine 20 mg daily or venlafaxine 75 mg daily.** Some benefit shown in small studies, but off-licence use.
  - **Norethisterone 5 mg daily or megestrol acetate 40 mg daily.** Sometimes used by women with contraindications to oestrogen, but the risks of long-term progestogen-only treatment are unknown.
  - **Clonidine 50–75 micrograms twice a day** is less useful. It generally causes unacceptable adverse effects.
  - **Complementary therapies.** Widely used, but there is little evidence on efficacy or safety, and so are not recommended. Many products used have estrogenic properties (e.g. red clover, black cohosh, ginseng, isoflavones, phytoestrogens).

Mood or sleep disturbances

- **HRT will often improve sleep by alleviating night sweats.**

Psychological symptoms should be managed in the usual way. HRT is most likely to be useful if there are other menopausal symptoms present.

rogenital symptoms

Urogenital atrophy often responds well to local low-dose vaginal oestrogen.
Urge incontinence (e.g. urgency, frequency, nocturia) can respond to local oestrogen.
The place of oestrogens for treating stress incontinence or recurrent urinary tract infection is unclear. Other treatments should generally be explored.

ecreased libido and sexual dysfunction

Dyspareunia as a result of vaginal dryness can be relieved by HRT or tibolone.
Loss of libido may be improved by tibolone, although multiple factors are usually involved. Testosterone supplementation (most useful for women with surgical menopause) should only be undertaken on specialist advice.

ractical prescribing points

or further information, please see the *Medicines ompendium* (www.medicines.org.uk) or the *British lational Formulary* (www.bnf.org).

atient information leaflets

he following PILs are available at www.prodigy.nhs.uk
Menopause - Alternatives to HRT
Menopause and HRT
Menopause and HRT - A Summary
Menopause and Sex
Osteoporosis
Women's Health
Women's Health Concern

hared decision making

The menopause can cause many symptoms, such as hot flushes, night sweats, sleep disturbance, vaginal dryness, and discomfort.
Hormone replacement therapy (HRT) is a way of replacing the female hormone, oestrogen, which falls to low levels at the menopause.
HRT treats many symptoms of the menopause.
Other options for hot flushes:

- SSRIs are a class of antidepressant. It has been noticed that a 'side effect' of these medicines is to reduce hot flushes.
- Progestogen hormones alone sometimes help reduce hot flushes, but the long-term risks are unknown.
- Clonidine is not often used as it causes lots of side effects, but may be worth a try if all else fails.
- Some herbal treatments used for the menopause (like black cohosh, isoflavones, red clover, and ginseng) contain plant oestrogens. It is not known whether they are any safer than HRT (which also contains oestrogens).

Other options for vaginal dryness and discomfort:

- Vaginal lubricants and vaginal moisturizers can help ease vaginal dryness. (You can buy these from a pharmacy.)
- Some women only notice the dryness when they have sex. In this situation, if you place a small dose of lubricant inside the vagina before having sex it will usually help.

- **There are many things you can do to stay healthy.** Exercise and a healthy diet (vegetables, whole-grain cereals, calcium) are important.
- **Breast screening:** mammography is a test to check your breasts are healthy; it is available to women aged 50 to 64 years. If you are over 65 years, you can still take part in the national screening programme at your request. Make sure you are 'breast aware' — know what is normal for you (the look and feel of your breasts), know what changes to look for, and report any changes without delay.
- **Cervical screening:** it is also important to have a regular cervical smear test.

Drug rationale

- There are no prescriptions offered in this scenario.

Work-up for starting HRT

Which therapy?

- **HRT is primarily used to treat menopausal symptoms.** It is no longer recommended as a first-line therapy for preventing or treating osteoporosis.
- **Ask about symptoms and other illnesses, check contraindications, and investigate if appropriate** (see section *Should I refer or investigate?* for investigations).
- **Discuss the benefits and risks of HRT with the woman** (see section *Shared decision making* for risks and benefits of HRT).
- For alternatives to HRT, see scenario *Options for managing menopausal symptoms.*
- **Discuss lifestyle changes to prevent osteoporosis and cardiovascular disease.**
- **If the woman requires contraception:**
  - **Continue contraception for** 1 year after the last menstrual period in women over 50 years old, or for 2 years in women under 50 years old.
  - Women taking HRT should use barrier methods, an intra-uterine device, or the levonorgestrel-releasing intra-uterine system (IUS).
  - Women taking combined oral contraception do not need to have HRT added.

Choice of preparation

- **Discuss choice of preparation** (detailed below; see other scenarios for prescriptions):
- **Women with a uterus take oestrogen plus progestogen.**
  - **Perimenopausal** women usually take cyclical regimens. They cause a monthly bleed, and come as tablets or patches.
  - **Postmenopausal women** (i.e. 12 months or more since last menstrual period) have the option of either 'no bleed' (continuous combined) or cyclical regimens. Both regimens are available as tablets or patches.
  - Oestrogen-only is occasionally used if this has a better risk–benefit profile for an individual. Seek specialist advice if this is being considered. Advise the woman to report any unexpected vaginal bleeding promptly.
- **Women without a uterus only need to take oestrogen.** Tablets and patches are available (tablets are cheaper but patches have wider range of doses). Oestrogen-only gel, nasal spray implants, and the Menoring 50® vaginal ring are useful for some women.
- **Vaginal oestrogen is effective for urogenital symptoms.** Systemic oestrogen is also effective, but is only needed in women who have other menopausal symptoms requiring treatment.

M

Practical prescribing points

For further information please see the *Medicines Compendium* (www.medicines.org.uk) or the *British National Formulary* (www.bnf.org).

- **Coronary heart disease or stroke:** do not start HRT.
- **Diabetes:** transdermal HRT may have less impact on lipids. Advise women that the risk of coronary heart disease seems higher in women with diabetes who take HRT.
- **Fibroids:** HRT can be taken, but it may cause heavy or painful periods.
- **Gallstones:** transdermal preparations are preferred.
- **Migraine:** often improves after menopause; however HRT sometimes aggravates migraine.
- **Strong family history of breast cancer, or a personal history of benign breast disease:** avoid HRT if possible, or monitor closely.
- **Seek specialist advice for women with** breast cancer, endometrial cancer, undiagnosed vaginal bleeding, liver disease, endometriosis, or a personal or family history of venous thromboembolic disease. See *Should I refer or investigate?*

Follow-up advice

- **Follow up in 3 months if a new HRT product has been started.** Management of adverse effects is covered in each scenario.
- **Subsequent follow-up is usually 6-monthly,** but should be at least annual.
- **Follow-up investigations should be guided by clinical need:**
  - **Blood pressure** is only needed for women with pre-existing hypertension.
  - **Breast examination** should be carried out if indicated by personal or family history. Give advice about breast awareness and encourage participation in the national breast-screening programme, as appropriate for the woman's age.
  - **Pelvic examination** should be carried out if indicated by personal history. Encourage participation in the national cervical cancer screening programme, as appropriate for the woman's age.

Should I refer or investigate?

Refer?

- **Abnormal vaginal bleeding** (e.g. a sudden change in menstrual pattern, intermenstrual bleeding, postcoital bleeding, or a postmenopausal bleed): refer for endometrial assessment.
- **Current or past breast or endometrial cancer:** seek specialist advice.
- **Personal history of venous thromboembolism (VTE):** avoid HRT if possible. Refer to a specialist in thrombophilia if the woman requests HRT.
- **Family history of VTE:** screen for thrombophilia. Avoid HRT in women with thrombotic defects, or refer to a specialist in thrombophilia if the woman requests HRT.
- **Liver disease:** seek specialist advice. If HRT is used, transdermal preparations are advised.
- **Endometriosis:** seek specialist advice. HRT can exacerbate symptoms.

Investigate?

Investigations before starting HRT

- **Check body mass index and blood pressure.**
- **Other investigations should be guided by clinical need:**
  - **Breast examination:** if indicated by personal or family history.
  - **Pelvic examination:** if indicated by personal history.
  - **Mammography:** indicated for women at high risk of breast cancer.
  - **Thyroid function tests:** if symptoms suspected to be due to hypothyroidism.
- **In perimenopausal women, follicle-stimulating hormone (FSH) levels fluctuate and can be misleading.**
  - FSH levels may be useful in confirming premature menopause. (Note: hysterectomy with ovarian conservation is a risk factor for premature menopause).
  - Stop HRT or oestrogen-containing contraception for 6–8 weeks before checking FSH levels. Two readings 4–8 weeks apart are more reliable than a single reading.

Patient information leaflets

The following PILs are available at www.prodigy.nhs.uk

- Blood Test - General
- Menopause - Alternatives to HRT
- Menopause and HRT
- Menopause and HRT - A Summary
- Osteoporosis
- Women's Health
- Women's Health Concern

Shared decision making

- **Hormone replacement therapy (HRT)** is a way of replacing the female hormone, oestrogen, which falls to low levels at the menopause.
- **Is HRT suitable for you?** HRT is suitable for most women who are going through the menopause. It may not be suitable if you have had breast cancer, endometrial cancer, a severe blood clot, or severe liver disease. Your doctor will explain if you have a condition that makes HRT less suitable for you.
- **HRT is used to control symptoms** such as hot flushes, night sweats, sleep disturbance, vaginal dryness, and discomfort.
- **Risks:** there is a small increased risk of developing a blood clot, breast cancer, or a stroke if you use HRT for several years, compared with women of the same age who have not used HRT. See the patient information leaflet *The Menopause and HRT* for more information.
- **Which HRT?** Women who have not had a hysterectomy take HRT that contains oestrogen plus progestogen (the progestogen reduces the risk of endometrial cancer but increases the risk of breast cancer). Women who have had a hysterectomy take HRT that just contains oestrogen.
  - **Tablets** are taken every day.
  - **Patches** release oestrogen through the skin. They are worn all the time and are changed once or twice a week (they are usually stuck to the buttocks).
  - **Other forms of HRT:** occasionally your doctor may suggest you take your HRT in the form of an implant or vaginally. Vaginal creams and pessaries are useful if you only want help for vaginal symptoms.
- **Whether or not you decide to take HRT,** there are many things you can do to stay healthy. Exercise and a healthy diet (vegetables, whole-grain cereals, calcium) are important.
- **Breast screening:** mammography is a test to check your breasts are healthy; it is available to women aged 50 to 64 years. If you are 65 years or over, you can still take part in the national screening programme at your request. Make sure you are 'breast aware' — know what is normal for you (the look and feel of your breasts),

know what changes to look for, and report any changes without delay.

- **Cervical screening:** it is also important to have a regular cervical smear test.

Drug rationale

- There are no prescriptions offered in this scenario.

Peri- or postmenopause — cyclical combined HRT tablets

Which therapy?

- **For advice about deciding whether HRT is suitable, or which regimen to use, see the scenario *Work-up for starting HRT*.**
- **Cyclical products are designed to give regular bleeds.** (Most products give monthly bleeds, one product gives 3-monthly bleeds.)
- **Cyclical HRT is only suitable for women with a uterus.**
- **Use the lowest dose that controls menopausal symptoms.**
  - Younger women may need higher doses of oestrogen to control symptoms.
  - Older women need lower doses to control symptoms and their tolerance of oestrogen may be reduced.
  - Women with menopausal symptoms who are also at risk of osteoporosis can use HRT for both indications. When treatment is no longer needed for symptom control, therapy should be reviewed and HRT considered a second-line choice for osteoporosis.
- **Products should normally be used for 3 months before any decision is made that they are unsuitable** and for change to another product. Adverse effects are often transient.

Duration of HRT

- **Consider a trial withdrawal of HRT** after 1–2 years if the woman is no longer bothered by symptoms. Consider a trial withdrawal in all women after 5 years of use.
- **For women with a premature menopause,** consider stopping HRT when the woman reaches 50 years.
- **Advise women that symptoms sometimes recur after stopping HRT.** Women can choose to restart HRT, but should be counselled about the risks and benefits of long-term HRT.
- **In all women, assess risk factors for osteoporosis and discuss alternatives** to HRT (including diet and lifestyle advice) for preventing osteoporosis at this time.

Practical prescribing points

For further information please see the *Medicines Compendium* (www.medicines.org.uk) or the *British National Formulary* (www.bnf.org).

Managing progestogen-related adverse effects

- Oral progestogens can cause premenstrual syndrome-type symptoms, breast tenderness, backache, depression, and pelvic pain.
- **For bleeding problems** (pathology excluded) the options are:
  - Increase progestogen duration or dosage.
  - Change progestogen type, for example from less androgenic (medroxyprogesterone, dydrogesterone) to more androgenic (norethisterone, levonorgestrel).
  - In difficult cases consider using the levonorgestrel-releasing intra-uterine system (IUS) combined with an oestrogen delivered either orally or transdermally.
- **For other progestogen-related adverse effects** (occur cyclically) the options are:
  - Reduce progestogen dosage or duration (e.g. from 14 to 12 days).
  - Change progestogen type, for example from more androgenic (norethisterone, levonorgestrel) to less androgenic (medroxyprogesterone, dydrogesterone).
  - Change to 3-monthly regimen (Tridestra®). Most suitable for women with scanty periods (as irregular bleeding is less common in this group).
  - Change route to HRT patches.
  - In difficult cases, progestogen can also be given via the levonorgestrel-releasing IUS combined with an oestrogen delivered either orally or transdermally.

Managing oestrogen-related adverse effects

- Oral oestrogens can cause nausea, breast tenderness, leg cramps, bloating, and headaches, but these are often transient.
- **For oestrogen-related adverse effects** (occur constantly or randomly) the options are:
  - Reduce oestrogen dosage.
  - Change oestrogen type (swap between estradiol and conjugated oestrogens).
  - Change route of delivery (e.g. to patches which are less likely to cause nausea).

Follow-up advice

- **Follow up in 3 months if a new HRT product has been started.** For management of adverse effects, see *Which therapy?*
- **Subsequent follow-up is usually 6-monthly,** but should be at least annual. Discuss risks and benefits with the woman annually, as they will change over time.
- **Follow-up investigations should be guided by clinical need:**
  - **Blood pressure measurement** is only needed for women with pre-existing hypertension.
  - **Breast examination** should be carried out if indicated by personal or family history. Give advice about breast awareness and encourage participation in the national breast-screening programme, as appropriate for the woman's age.
  - **Pelvic examination** should be carried out if indicated by personal history. Encourage participation in the national cervical cancer screening programme, as appropriate for the woman's age.
- **Consider stopping HRT to assess abnormal bleeding,** for example, a change in the pattern of withdrawal bleeds, or breakthrough bleeding. Review 4 weeks later. If problems continue, see section *Should I refer or investigate?*

Should I refer or investigate?

Refer?

- Referral guidelines for suspected cancer recommend that women who have persistent or unexplained postmenopausal bleeding after stopping HRT for 6 weeks should be referred urgently to a team specialising in the management of gynaecological cancer, depending on local arrangements [NICE, 2005].

Investigate?

- Routine investigations are not normally indicated.
- Abnormal bleeding that occurs while taking cyclical HRT should be investigated, for example, a change in the pattern of withdrawal bleeds, or breakthrough bleeding.

M

Patient information leaflets

The following PILs are available at www.prodigy.nhs.uk

- Menopause - Alternatives to HRT
- Menopause and HRT
- Menopause and HRT - A Summary
- Menopause and Sex
- Osteoporosis
- Women's Health
- Women's Health Concern

Shared decision making

- **Hormone replacement therapy (HRT)** is a way of replacing the female hormone, oestrogen, which falls to low levels at the menopause.
- **Which HRT?** Women who have not had a hysterectomy take HRT that contains oestrogen plus progestogen (the progestogen keeps the uterus healthy).
- **Tablets** are taken every day. Follow the instructions on the packet carefully.
- **Monthly bleeds** will happen with most of these tablets.
- **Side effects** sometimes occur. They include nausea, breast tenderness, bloating, and premenstrual syndrome-type symptoms. Try to keep taking the HRT, because often the side effects disappear after a few weeks. If they don't disappear, you should tell your doctor.
- **HRT tablets are not contraceptives.** It is possible to get pregnant if your natural periods have not stopped completely. Tell your doctor if you need contraception.
- **Whether or not you decide to take HRT,** there are many things you can do to stay healthy. Exercise and a healthy diet (vegetables, whole-grain cereals, calcium) are important.
- **Breast screening:** mammography is a test to check your breasts are healthy — it is available to women aged 50 to 64 years. If you are 65 years or over, you can still take part in the national screening programme at your request. Make sure you are 'breast aware' — know what is normal for you (the look and feel of your breasts), know what changes to look for, and report any changes without delay.
- **Cervical screening:** it is also important to have a regular cervical smear test.

M

Drug rationale

Drugs not included

- **Products which provide varying oestrogen doses or oestrogen-free intervals** are not included. It is generally accepted that oestrogen replacement therapy should be taken continuously throughout the month. There is no evidence that varying oestrogen doses or oestrogen-free intervals are of benefit, and re-emergence of symptoms (e.g. flushing) may be seen during the low-dose or oestrogen-free interval of such products.
- **Continuous combined hormone replacement therapy (HRT)** can be found in the scenario *Postmenopause only – no-bleed continuous HRT tablets or patches.*
- **Tibolone** is an alternative to continuous combined HRT and can be found in the scenario *Postmenopause only – no-bleed continuous HRT tablets or patches.*

Drugs included

- **All currently available tablets containing continuous oestrogen plus a progestogen for 12–14 days of the cycle** have been included.
- **The 3-monthly regimen (Tridestra®) is also included.** It is most suitable for women with scanty periods (as irregular bleeding is less common in this group), and is generally used when progestogen adverse effects are a problem.

Prescriptions

Estradiol 1mg + cyclical progestogen

Climagest 1mg tablets (norethisterone 1mg x12 days)

- Age from 25 years onwards
- Climagest 1mg tablets. Take one tablet once a day. (Take in the order shown on the packet); supply 84 tablets; NHS Cost £13.91.

Elleste-Duet 1mg tablets (norethisterone 1mg x12 days)

- Age from 25 years onwards
- Elleste-Duet 1mg tablets. Take one tablet once a day. (Take in the order shown on the packet); supply 84 tablets; NHS Cost £9.72.

Femoston 1/10mg tablets (dydrogesterone 10mg x14 days)

- Age from 25 years onwards
- Femoston 1/10mg tablets. Take one tablet once a day. (Take in the order shown on the packet); supply 84 tablets; NHS Cost £14.97.

Novofem 1mg tablets (norethisterone 1mg x12 days)

- Age from 25 years onwards
- Novofem 1mg tablets. Take one tablet once a day. (Take in the order shown on the packet); supply 84 tablets; NHS Cost £13.50.

Estradiol 2mg + cyclical progestogen

Climagest 2mg tablets (norethisterone 1mg x12 days)

- Age from 25 years onwards
- Climagest 2mg tablets. Take one tablet once a day. (Take in the order shown on the packet); supply 84 tablets; NHS Cost £13.91.

Elleste-Duet 2mg tablets (norethisterone 1mg x12 days)

- Age from 25 years onwards
- Elleste-Duet 2mg tablets. Take one tablet once a day. (Take in the order shown on the packet); supply 84 tablets; NHS Cost £9.72.

Femoston 2/10mg tablets (dydrogesterone 10mg x14 days)

- Age from 25 years onwards
- Femoston 2/10mg tablets. Take one tablet once a day. (Take in the order shown on the packet); supply 84 tablets; NHS Cost £14.97.

FemTab Sequi (levonorgestrel 75mcg x12 days)

- Age from 25 years onwards
- FemTab Sequi tablets. Take one tablet once a day. (Take in the order shown on the packet); supply 84 tablets; NHS Cost £15.15.

Nuvelle 2mg tablets (levonorgestrel 75mcg x12 days)

- Age from 25 years onwards
- Nuvelle tablets. Take one tablet once a day. (Take in the order shown on the packet); supply 84 tablets; NHS Cost £15.15.

Conjugated oestrogens + cyclical progestogen

Prempak-C 625mcg tablets (norgestrel 150mcg x12 days

- Age from 25 years onwards
- Prempak-C 0.625 tablets. Take one maroon tablet once a day. In addition, take one light brown tablet once a day for 12 days, as shown on the packet; supply 1 3-month pack; NHS Cost £17.67.

Prempak C 1.25mg tablets (norgestrel 150mcg x12 days)

- Age from 25 years onwards
- Prempak-C 1.25 tabs. Take one yellow tablet once a day In addition, take one light brown tablet once a day for

12 days, as shown on the packet; supply 1 3-month pack; NHS Cost £17.67.

Premique Cycle 625mcg tabs (medroxyprogest 10mg x14 days)

- Age from 25 years onwards
- Premique Cycle tablets. Take one tablet once a day. (Take in the order shown on the packet); supply 84 tablets; NHS Cost £24.87.

Estradiol 2mg + 3-monthly cyclical progestogen + 7-day break

Tridestra 2mg tablets (medroxyprogest 20mg)

- Age from 25 years onwards
- Tridestra tablets. Take one tablet once a day. (Take in the order shown on the packet); supply 91 tablets; NHS Cost £23.78.

Peri- or postmenopause — cyclical combined HRT patches

Which therapy?

- **For advice about deciding whether HRT is suitable, or which regimen to use see the scenario *Work-up for starting HRT*.**
- **Cyclical patches are designed to give regular monthly bleeds.**
- **Cyclical HRT is only suitable for women with a uterus.**
- **Use the lowest dose that controls menopausal symptoms.**
  - Younger women may need higher doses of oestrogen to control symptoms.
  - Older women need lower doses to control symptoms and their tolerance of oestrogen may be reduced.
  - Women with menopausal symptoms who are also at risk of osteoporosis can use HRT for both indications. When treatment is no longer needed for symptom control, therapy should be reviewed and HRT considered to be a second-line choice for osteoporosis.
- **Products are available as** patches only (Estracombi®, Evorel Sequi®, FemSeven Sequi®), or estradiol patches plus progestogen tablets (Femapak®, Evorel Pak®).
- **Products should normally be used for 3 months before any decision is made that they are unsuitable,** and before changing to another product. Adverse effects are often transient.

Duration of HRT

- **Consider a trial withdrawal of HRT** after 1–2 years if the woman is no longer bothered by symptoms. Consider a trial withdrawal in all women after 5 years of use.
- **For women with a premature menopause,** consider stopping HRT when the woman reaches 50 years.
- **Advise women that** symptoms sometimes recur after stopping HRT. Women can choose to restart HRT, but should be counselled about the risks and benefits of long-term HRT.
- **In all women, assess risk factors for osteoporosis and discuss alternatives** to HRT (including diet and lifestyle advice) for preventing osteoporosis at this time.

Practical prescribing points

For further information please see the *Medicines Compendium* (www.medicines.org.uk) or the *British National Formulary* (www.bnf.org).

- **Advise women that patches should be applied to the buttocks** (never on the breasts).
- **Patch adhesiveness varies** on different skin types.
- **Skin reactions** are less common with matrix patches than reservoir patches (Estracombi®).

Managing progestogen-related adverse effects

- Transdermal or oral progestogens can cause premenstrual syndrome-type symptoms, breast tenderness, backache, depression, or pelvic pain.
- **For bleeding problems** (pathology excluded) the options are:
  - Increase progestogen duration or dosage.
  - Change progestogen type, for example from less androgenic (medroxyprogesterone, dydrogesterone) to more androgenic (norethisterone, levonorgestrel).
  - In difficult cases consider using the levonorgestrel-releasing intra-uterine system (IUS) combined with an oestrogen delivered either orally or transdermally.
- **For progestogen-related adverse effects** (occur cyclically) the options are:
  - Reduce progestogen duration (e.g. from 14 to 12 days) or dosage.
  - Change progestogen type, for example from more androgenic (norethisterone, levonorgestrel) to less androgenic (medroxyprogesterone, dydrogesterone).
  - Swap progestogen route between patches and tablets.
  - In difficult cases, consider changing route of delivery to the levonorgestrel-releasing IUS. Oestrogen must be given separately. See *Oestrogen-only* and *Adjunct progestogens* scenarios.

Managing oestrogen-related adverse effects

- Transdermal oestrogens can cause breast tenderness, leg cramps, bloating and headaches, but these are often transient.
- **For oestrogen-related adverse effects** (occur constantly or randomly) the options are:
  - Reduce oestrogen dosage (25 microgram patches are available in the scenario *Hysterectomy — oestrogen-only patch, gel implant, nasal*; these must be combined with a progestogen).
  - Change oestrogen type (swap between estradiol and conjugated oestrogens).
  - Change route of delivery (but tablets are more likely to cause nausea).

Follow-up advice

- **Follow up in 3 months if a new HRT product has been started.** For management of adverse effects, see *Which therapy?*
- **Subsequent follow-up is usually 6-monthly,** but should be at least annual. Discuss risks and benefits with the woman annually, as they will change over time.
- **Follow-up investigations should be guided by clinical need:**
  - **Blood pressure** is only needed for women with pre-existing hypertension.
  - **Breast examination** should be carried out if indicated by personal or family history. Give advice about breast awareness and encourage participation in the national breast-screening programme as appropriate for the woman's age.
  - **Pelvic examination** should be carried out if indicated by personal history. Encourage participation in the national cervical cancer screening programme as appropriate for the woman's age.
- **Consider stopping HRT to assess abnormal bleeding,** for example, a change in the pattern of withdrawal bleeds, or breakthrough bleeding. Review 4 weeks later. If problems continue, see section *Should I refer or investigate?*

Should I refer or investigate?

Refer?

- Referral guidelines for suspected cancer recommend that women who have persistent or unexplained postmenopausal bleeding after stopping HRT for 6 weeks should be referred urgently to a team specialising in the management of gynaecological cancer, depending on local arrangements [NICE, 2005].

Investigate?

- Routine investigations are not normally indicated.
- Abnormal bleeding that occurs while taking cyclical HRT should be investigated; for example, a change in the pattern of withdrawal bleeds, or breakthrough bleeding.

Patient information leaflets

The following PILs are available at www.prodigy.nhs.uk

- Menopause - Alternatives to HRT
- Menopause and HRT
- Menopause and HRT - A Summary
- Menopause and Sex
- Osteoporosis
- Women's Health
- Women's Health Concern

Shared decision making

- **Hormone replacement therapy** (HRT) is a way of replacing the female hormone, oestrogen, which falls to low levels at the menopause.
- **Which HRT?** Women who have not had a hysterectomy take HRT that contains oestrogen plus progestogen (the progestogen keeps the uterus healthy).
- **Patches** are worn all the time and are changed once or twice a week (they are usually stuck to the buttocks). Follow the instructions on the packet carefully.
- **You have a choice of patches alone or patches plus tablets** (you take the tablets for 12–14 days of the month only).
- **Monthly bleeds** will happen with all of these patches.
- **Side effects** sometimes occur. They include breast tenderness, bloating, and premenstrual syndrome-type symptoms. Try to keep taking the HRT, because often the side effects disappear after a few weeks. If they don't disappear, you should tell your doctor.
- **HRT patches are not contraceptives.** It is possible to get pregnant if your natural periods have not stopped completely. Tell your doctor if you need contraception.
- **Whether or not you decide to take HRT,** there are many things you can do to stay healthy. Exercise and a healthy diet (vegetables, whole-grain cereals, calcium) are important.
- **Breast screening:** mammography is a test to check your breasts are healthy — it is available to women aged 50 to 64 years. If you are over 65 years, you can still take part in the national screening programme at your request. Make sure you are 'breast aware' — know what is normal for you (the look and feel of your breasts), know what changes to look for, report any changes without delay.
- **Cervical screening:** it is also important to have a regular cervical smear test.

Drug rationale

Drugs not included

- **Products which provide varying oestrogen dosages** are not included. It is generally accepted that oestrogen replacement therapy should be taken continuously throughout the month. There is no evidence that varyin oestrogen doses are of benefit, and re-emergence of symptoms (e.g. flushing) may be seen during the low-dose or oestrogen-free interval of such products.
- **Continuous combined hormone replacement therapy (HRT)** can be found in the scenario *Postmenopause onl – no-bleed continuous HRT tablets or patches.*
- **Tibolone** is an alternative to continuous combined HRT and can be found in the scenario *Postmenopause only – no-bleed continuous HRT tablets or patches.*

Drugs included

- **All currently available packs that contain continuous oestrogen and a progestogen for 12–14 days of the cycl** are included.
- Estracombi combination pack contains reservoir patches. All other patches in this scenario are matrix patches.

Prescriptions

Once-weekly patch (estradiol 50mcg + cyclical progestogen)

FemSeven Sequi combination pack (levonorgest 10mcg x14 days)

- Age from 25 years onwards
- FemSeven Sequi patches. Apply one patch once a week to the trunk, below the waistline. Apply in the order shown; supply 1 3-month pack; NHS Cost £28.44.

Twice-weekly patch (estradiol 50mcg + cyclical progestogen)

Estracombi combination pack (norethisterone 250mcg x14 days)

- Age from 25 years onwards
- Estracombi TTS patches. Apply one patch twice a week to the trunk, below the waistline. Apply in the order shown; supply 1 3-month pack; NHS Cost £33.42.

Evorel Sequi combination pack (norethist 170mcg x14 days)

- Age from 25 years onwards
- Evorel Sequi patches. Apply one patch twice a week to the trunk, below the waistline. Apply in the order show supply 24 patches; NHS Cost £33.00.

Twice-weekly estradiol patch + cyclical progestogen tablets

Femapak 40mcg (dydrogesterone 10mg x14 days)

- Age from 25 years onwards
- Femapak 40 patches + tablets. Apply one patch twice a week to the trunk, below the waistline. In addition, tak one tablet once a day for 14 days, as shown on the packet; supply 3 one-month packs; NHS Cost £25.35.

Femapak 80mcg (dydrogesterone 10mg x14 days)

- Age from 25 years onwards
- Femapak 80 patches + tablets. Apply one patch twice a week to the trunk, below the waistline. In addition, tak one tablet once a day for 14 days, as shown on the packet; supply 3 one-month packs; NHS Cost £26.85.

Evorel Pak 50mcg (norethisterone 1mg x12 days)
Age from 25 years onwards
Evorel Pak patches + tablets. Apply one patch twice a week to the trunk, below the waistline. In addition, take one tablet once a day for 12 days, as shown on the packet; supply 3 one-month packs; NHS Cost £25.35.

Evorel Pak 2x50mcg (norethisterone 1mg x12 days)
Age from 25 years onwards
Evorel Pak patches + tablets. Apply two patches twice a week to the trunk, below the waistline. In addition, take one tablet once a day for 12 days, as shown on the packet; supply 6 one-month packs; NHS Cost £50.70.

Postmenopause only — no-bleed continuous HRT tabs or patches

Which therapy?

For advice about deciding whether HRT is suitable, or which regimen to use see the scenario *Work-up for starting HRT*.

Continuous combined regimens do not produce a withdrawal bleed and are only suitable for postmenopausal women (i.e. at least 12 months after the last spontaneous menstrual period). **Indivina®** must not be started until the woman is 3 years postmenopausal.

Advise women that irregular bleeding or spotting can occur in the first 4–6 months of treatment.

Continuous combined regimens are not suitable for women without a uterus.

Use the lowest dose that controls menopausal symptoms.

- Younger women may need higher doses of oestrogen to control symptoms.
- Older women need lower doses to control symptoms and their tolerance of oestrogen may be reduced.
- Women with menopausal symptoms who are also at risk of osteoporosis can use HRT for both indications. When treatment is no longer needed for symptom control, therapy should be reviewed and HRT considered as second-line choice for osteoporosis.

Products are available as tablets or patches.

Tibolone is an alternative to continuous oestrogen/progestogen hormone replacement therapy (HRT). It comes in tablet form and is taken continuously.

Products should normally be used for 3 months before any decision is made that they are unsuitable and before changing to another product. Adverse effects are often transient.

Duration of HRT

Consider a trial withdrawal of HRT after 1–2 years if the woman is no longer bothered by symptoms. Consider a trial withdrawal in all women after 5 years of use.

For women with a premature menopause, consider stopping HRT when the woman reaches 50 years.

Advise women that symptoms sometimes recur after stopping HRT. Women can choose to restart HRT, but should be counselled about the risks and benefits of long-term HRT.

In all women, assess risk factors for osteoporosis and discuss alternatives to HRT (including diet and lifestyle advice) for preventing osteoporosis at this time.

Practical prescribing points

For further information please see the *Medicines Compendium* (www.medicines.org.uk) or the *British National Formulary* (www.bnf.org).

- Oestrogens can cause nausea, breast tenderness, leg cramps, bloating, and headaches, but these are often transient.
- Progestogens can cause premenstrual syndrome-type symptoms, breast tenderness, backache, depression, and pelvic pain.

Managing adverse effects

- **Adverse effects are less likely at low doses.**
- **If they do occur, the following options can be tried:**
  - Reduce oestrogen dosage
  - Change oestrogen type (swap between estradiol and conjugated oestrogens)
  - Reduce progestogen dosage
  - Change progestogen type, for example from more androgenic (norethisterone, levonorgestrel) to less androgenic (medroxyprogesterone acetate, dydrogesterone)
  - Change route of delivery between patches and tablets
- **In difficult cases,** consider changing route of delivery to the levonorgestrel-releasing IUS. Oestrogen must be given separately. See the *Oestrogen-only* and *Adjunct progestogens* scenarios.

Follow-up advice

- **Follow up in 3 months if a new HRT product has been started.** For management of adverse effects, see *Which therapy?*
- **Subsequent follow-up is usually 6-monthly,** but should be at least annual. Discuss risks and benefits with the woman annually, as they will change over time.
- **Follow-up investigations should be guided by clinical need:**
  - **Blood pressure** is only needed for women with pre-existing hypertension.
  - **Breast examination** should be carried out if indicated by personal or family history. Give advice about breast awareness and encourage participation in the national breast-screening programme as appropriate for the woman's age.
  - **Pelvic examination** should be carried out if indicated by personal history. Encourage participation in the national cervical cancer screening programme as appropriate for the woman's age.
- **Consider stopping HRT to assess abnormal bleeding,** for example, if it persists beyond 6 months after starting HRT, or if it occurs after amenorrhoea. Review 4 weeks later. If problems continue, see section *Should I refer or investigate?*

Should I refer or investigate?

Refer?

- Referral guidelines for suspected cancer recommend that women who have persistent or unexplained postmenopausal bleeding after stopping HRT for 6 weeks should be referred urgently to a team specialising in the management of gynaecological cancer, depending on local arrangements [NICE, 2005].

Investigate?

- Routine investigations are not normally indicated.
- Bleeding on continuous combined regimens should be investigated if it persists beyond 6 months, if it becomes heavier rather than less, or it if occurs after amenorrhoea.

M

Patient information leaflets

The following PILs are available at www.prodigy.nhs.uk

- Menopause - Alternatives to HRT
- Menopause and HRT
- Menopause and HRT - A Summary
- Menopause and Sex
- Osteoporosis
- Women's Health
- Women's Health Concern

Shared decision making

- **Hormone replacement therapy (HRT)** is a way of replacing the female hormone, oestrogen, which falls to low levels at the menopause.
- **Which HRT?** Women who have not had a hysterectomy take HRT that contains oestrogen plus progestogen (the progestogen keeps the uterus healthy).
- **This type of HRT does not cause monthly bleeds.** Spotting may occur in the first few months, but should settle down within 4–6 months. Tell your doctor if bleeding persists, or if you get any new bleeding.
- **Tablets** are taken every day.
- **There is a patch you could use instead** of a tablet. Patches are worn all the time and are changed twice a week (they are usually stuck to the buttocks).
- **Tibolone** is an alternative to the standard HRT.
- Nausea, breast tenderness, bloating, and premenstrual syndrome-type symptoms may occur. Try to keep taking the HRT, because often the side effects disappear after a few weeks. If they don't disappear, you should tell your doctor.
- **HRT tablets are not contraceptives.** Contraception should be used for 1 year after your last natural period if you are more than 50 years old, or for 2 years after your last natural period if you are under 50 years old.
- **Whether or not you decide to take HRT,** there are many things you can do to stay healthy. Exercise and a healthy diet (vegetables, whole-grain cereals, calcium) are important.
- **Breast screening:** mammography is a test to check your breasts are healthy — it is available to women aged 50 to 64 years. If you are over 65 years, you can still take part in the national screening programme at your request. Make sure you are 'breast aware' — know what is normal for you (the look and feel of your breasts), know what changes to look for, and report any changes without delay.
- **Cervical screening:** it is also important to have a regular cervical smear test.

Drug rationale

Drugs not included

- **Cyclical hormone replacement therapy (HRT) products** can be found in the *Peri- or postmenopause — cyclical combined HRT tablets* scenario and the *Peri- or postmenopause — cyclical continuous HRT patches* scenario.

Drugs included

- **All currently available products containing continuous oestrogen and progestogen** are included. These products should not be used during the perimenopause or within 12 months of the last menstrual period, since the incidence of irregular vaginal bleeding is higher in these women. Indivina® is not licensed for use during the perimenopause or within 3 years of the last menstrual period.
- **Tibolone** is an alternative to continuous combined HRT for women who do not wish to have monthly withdrawal bleeds.

Prescriptions

Tablets: estradiol 1mg + continuous progestogen

Femoston-conti 1mg tablets (dydrogesterone 5mg)
- Age from 25 years onwards
- Femoston-conti tablets. Take one tablet once a day; supply 84 tablets; NHS Cost £22.62.

Kliovance 1mg tablets (norethisterone 500mcg)
- Age from 25 years onwards
- Kliovance tablets. Take one tablet once a day; supply 84 tablets; NHS Cost £15.45.

3 years postmenopause: Indivina 1/2.5mg (medroxyp 2.5mg)
- Age from 25 years onwards
- Indivina 1/2.5mg tablets. Take one tablet once a day; supply 84 tablets; NHS Cost £22.62.

3 years postmenopause: Indivina 1/5mg (medroxyp 5mg)
- Age from 25 years onwards
- Indivina 1/5mg tablets. Take one tablet once a day; supply 84 tablets; NHS Cost £22.62.

Tablets: estradiol 2mg + continuous progestogen

Climesse 2mg tablets (norethisterone 700mcg)
- Age from 25 years onwards
- Climesse tablets. Take one tablet once a day; supply 84 tablets; NHS Cost £25.86.

Elleste-Duet Conti 2mg tablets (norethisterone 1mg)
- Age from 25 years onwards
- Elleste-Duet Conti tablets. Take one tablet once a day; supply 84 tablets; NHS Cost £17.97.

Kliofem 2mg tablets (norethisterone 1mg)
- Age from 25 years onwards
- Kliofem tablets. Take one tablet once a day; supply 84 tablets; NHS Cost £15.45.

Nuvelle Continuous 2mg tablets (norethisterone 1mg)
- Age from 25 years onwards
- Nuvelle Continuous tablets. Take one tablet once a day; supply 84 tablets; NHS Cost £18.02.

3 years postmenopause: Indivina 2/5mg (medroxyp 5mg)
- Age from 25 years onwards
- Indivina 2/5mg tablets. Take one tablet once a day; supply 84 tablets; NHS Cost £22.62.

Tablets: conjugated oestrogens + continuous progestogen

Premique 625mcg tabs (medroxyprogesterone 5mg)
- Age from 25 years onwards
- Premique tablets. Take one tablet once a day; supply 84 tablets; NHS Cost £27.14.

Premique 300mcg tabs (medroxyprogesterone 1.5mg)
- Age from 25 years onwards
- Premique Low Dose tablets. Take one tablet once a day supply 84 tablets; NHS Cost £29.85.

Patches: estradiol 50mcg + continuous progestogen

Once-weekly patches: FemSeven Conti 50mcg (levonorgest 7mcg)
- Age from 25 years onwards
- FemSeven Conti patches. Apply one patch once a week to the trunk, below the waistline; supply 12 patches; NHS Cost £36.77.

Twice-weekly patches: Evorel Conti 50mcg (norethist 170mcg)

- Age from 25 years onwards
- Evorel Conti patches. Apply one patch twice a week to the trunk, below the waistline; supply 24 patches; NHS Cost £38.70.

Tibolone tablets

Tibolone 2.5mg tablets

- Age from 25 years onwards
- Tibolone 2.5mg tablets. Take one tablet once a day; supply 84 tablets; NHS Cost £39.14.

Hysterectomy — oestrogen-only tablets

Which therapy?

- **For advice about deciding whether HRT is suitable, or which regimen to use see the scenario *Work-up for starting HRT*.**
- **Oestrogen-only products are suitable for women without a uterus.** Tablets are taken continuously.
- **Use the lowest dose that controls menopausal symptoms.**
  - Younger women may need higher doses of oestrogen to control symptoms.
  - Older women need lower doses to control symptoms and their tolerance of oestrogen may be reduced.
  - Women with menopausal symptoms who are also at risk of osteoporosis can use HRT for both indications. When treatment is no longer needed for symptom control, therapy should be reviewed and HRT considered as a second-line choice for osteoporosis.
- **Products should usually be used for 3 months before deciding they are unsuitable** and swapping to another product. Adverse effects are often transient.

Duration of HRT

- **Consider stopping HRT** when a woman with a hysterectomy reaches 50 years.
- **Advise women that** symptoms sometimes recur after stopping HRT. Women can choose to restart HRT, but should be counselled about the risks and benefits of long-term HRT.
- **Assess the risk of osteoporosis and discuss alternatives to HRT** for preventing osteoporosis (including diet and lifestyle advice) at this time.

Practical prescribing points

For further information please see the *Medicines Compendium* (www.medicines.org.uk) or the *British National Formulary* (www.bnf.org).

Managing oestrogen-related adverse effects

- **Oral oestrogens** can cause nausea, breast tenderness, leg cramps, bloating, and headaches, but these are often transient.
- **For oestrogen-related adverse effects the options are:**
  - Consider reducing the dosage.
  - Consider changing the oestrogen type (swap between estradiol and conjugated oestrogens).
  - Consider changing the route of delivery (e.g. to patches, which are less likely to cause nausea — see separate scenario).

Follow-up advice

- **Follow up in 3 months if a new HRT product has been started.** For management of adverse effects, see *Which therapy?*
- **Subsequent follow-up is usually 6-monthly,** but should be at least annual. Discuss risks and benefits with the woman annually, as they will change over time.
- **Follow-up investigations should be guided by clinical need:**
  - **Blood pressure** is only needed for women with pre-existing hypertension.
  - **Breast examination** should be carried out if indicated by personal or family history. Give advice about breast awareness and encourage participation in the national breast-screening programme as appropriate for the woman's age.
  - **Pelvic examination** should be carried out if indicated. Women without a uterus will not be part of the national cervical cancer screening programme.

Patient information leaflets

The following PILs are available at www.prodigy.nhs.uk

- Menopause - Alternatives to HRT
- Menopause and HRT
- Menopause and HRT - A Summary
- Menopause and Sex
- Osteoporosis
- Women's Health
- Women's Health Concern

Shared decision making

- **Hormone replacement therapy** (**HRT**) is a way of replacing the female hormone, oestrogen, which falls to low levels at the menopause.
- **Which HRT?** If you have had a hysterectomy you only need oestrogen replacement. (Most women with a uterus take a progestogen as well to keep the uterus healthy.)
- **Tablets containing oestrogen** are taken every day. Follow the instructions on the packet carefully.
- **Side effects** sometimes occur. They include nausea and breast tenderness. Try to keep taking the HRT, because often the side effects disappear after a few weeks. If they don't disappear, you should tell your doctor.
- **Whether or not you decide to take HRT,** there are many things you can do to stay healthy. Exercise and a healthy diet (vegetables, whole grain cereals, calcium) are important.
- **Breast screening:** mammography is a test to check your breasts are healthy — it is available to women aged 50 to 64 years. If you are over 65 years, you can still take part in the national screening programme at your request. Make sure you are 'breast aware' — know what is normal for you (the look and feel of your breasts), know what changes to look for, and report any changes without delay.

Drug rationale

Drugs not included

- **Ethinylestradiol** is now considered less suitable than natural oestrogens for replacement therapy during the menopause and is therefore not included [Rees and Purdie, 2002].
- **Ovestin®** tablets (containing estriol only) are not licensed for complete menopausal management and are not included in this scenario.

M

- **Oestrogen-only HRT patches, and other non-oral formulations** are included in the scenario *Hysterectomy – oestrogen-only patch, gel, implant, nasal.*

Drugs included

- **All oestrogen-only** tablets that are licensed for relief of menopausal symptoms containing estradiol only, conjugated equine oestrogens only, estropipate only, or a combination of estradiol, estriol, and estrone, are included.

Prescriptions

Tablets: estradiol 1mg

Climaval 1mg tablets
- Age from 25 years onwards
- Climaval 1mg tablets. Take one tablet once a day; supply 84 tablets; NHS Cost £7.66.

Elleste-Solo 1mg tablets
- Age from 25 years onwards
- Elleste-Solo 1mg tablets. Take one tablet once a day; supply 84 tablets; NHS Cost £5.34.

FemTab 1mg tablets
- Age from 25 years onwards
- FemTab 1mg tablets. Take one tablet once a day; supply 84 tablets; NHS Cost £7.72.

Progynova 1mg tablets
- Age from 25 years onwards
- Progynova 1mg tablets. Take one tablet once a day; supply 84 tablets; NHS Cost £7.72.

Zumenon 1mg tablets
- Age from 25 years onwards
- Zumenon 1mg tablets. Take one tablet once a day; supply 84 tablets; NHS Cost £7.65.

M

Tablets: estradiol 2mg

Climaval 2mg tablets
- Age from 25 years onwards
- Climaval 2mg tablets. Take one tablet once a day; supply 84 tablets; NHS Cost £7.66.

Elleste-Solo 2mg tablets
- Age from 25 years onwards
- Elleste-Solo 2mg tablets. Take one tablet once a day; supply 84 tablets; NHS Cost £5.34.

FemTab 2mg tablets
- Age from 25 years onwards
- FemTab 2mg tablets. Take one tablet once a day; supply 84 tablets; NHS Cost £7.72.

Progynova 2mg tablets
- Age from 25 years onwards
- Progynova 2mg tablets. Take one tablet once a day; supply 84 tablets; NHS Cost £7.72.

Zumenon 2mg tablets
- Age from 25 years onwards
- Zumenon 2mg tablets. Take one tablet once a day; supply 84 tablets; NHS Cost £7.65.

Tablets: conjugated oestrogens

Premarin 625mcg tablets
- Age from 25 years onwards
- Conj oestrogens 625mcg tablets. Take one tablet once a day; supply 84 tablets; NHS Cost £9.72.

Premarin 1.25mg tablets
- Age from 25 years onwards
- Conj oestrogen 1.25mg tablets. Take one tablet once a day; supply 84 tablets; NHS Cost £13.19.

Tablets: other oestrogens

Hormonin: one tablet daily (estradiol + estriol + estrone)
- Age from 25 years onwards
- Hormonin tablets. Take one tablet once a day; supply 84 tablets; NHS Cost £6.61.

Hormonin: two tablets daily (estradiol + estriol + estrone)
- Age from 25 years onwards
- Hormonin tablets. Take two tablets once a day; supply 180 tablets; NHS Cost £13.22.

Harmogen 1.5mg tablets (estropipate)
- Age from 25 years onwards
- Harmogen 1.5mg tablets. Take one tablet once a day; supply 84 tablets; NHS Cost £11.31.

Harmogen 3mg once a day (estropipate)
- Age from 25 years onwards
- Harmogen 1.5mg tablets. Take two tablets once a day; supply 168 tablets; NHS Cost £22.62.

Hysterectomy — oestrogen-only patch, gel, implant, spray

Which therapy?

- **For advice about deciding whether HRT is suitable, or which regimen to use see the scenario *Work-up for starting HRT.***
- **Oestrogen-only products are suitable for women without a uterus** and are taken continuously.
- **Use the lowest dose that controls menopausal symptoms**
  - Younger women may need higher doses of oestrogen to control symptoms.
  - Older women need lower doses to control symptoms and their tolerance of oestrogen may be reduced.
  - Women with menopausal symptoms who are also at risk of osteoporosis can use HRT for both indications When treatment is no longer needed for symptom control, therapy should be reviewed and HRT considered a second-line choice for osteoporosis.
- **Application frequency:**
  - **Patches** are applied either once or twice a week.
  - **Gel or nasal spray is used daily.**
  - **Vaginal ring** is replaced every 3 months. (Only Menoring 50® gives systemic HRT.)
  - **Implants usually last for between 4 and 8 months.** Check plasma estradiol levels before re-implantation. Do not re-implant if levels are >1000 pmol/L, to avoid build up of supraphysiological levels of oestrogen.
- **Products should normally be used for 3 months before a decision is made that they are unsuitable** and changing to another product. Adverse effects are often transient.

Duration of HRT

- **Consider stopping HRT** when a woman with a hysterectomy reaches 50 years.
- **Advise women that** symptoms sometimes recur after stopping HRT. Women can choose to restart HRT, but should be counselled about the risks and benefits of long term HRT.
- **Assess the risk of osteoporosis and discuss alternatives to** HRT for preventing osteoporosis (including diet and lifestyle advice) at this time.

Practical prescribing points

For further information please see the *Medicines Compendium* (www.medicines.org.uk) or the *British National Formulary* (www.bnf.org).

- **Advise women that patches should be stuck on the buttocks** (never on the breasts).

- **Patch adhesiveness varies** on different skin types.
- **Skin reactions** are less common with matrix than reservoir patches (Estraderm TTS®).

Managing oestrogen-related adverse effects

- Oestrogens can cause breast tenderness, leg cramps, bloating, and headaches, but these are often transient.
- **Options include** reducing the dose, or changing the route of delivery (although tablets are more likely than patches to cause adverse effects such as nausea).

Follow-up advice

- **Follow up in 3 months if a new HRT product has been started.** For management of adverse effects, see *Which therapy?*
- **Subsequent follow-up is usually 6-monthly,** but should be at least annual. Discuss risks and benefits with the woman annually, as they will change over time.
- **Follow-up investigations should be guided by clinical need:**
  - **Blood pressure** is only needed for women with pre-existing hypertension.
  - **Breast examination** should be carried out if indicated by personal or family history. Give advice about breast awareness and encourage participation in the national breast-screening programme as appropriate for the woman's age.
  - **Pelvic examination** should be carried out if indicated. Women without a uterus will not be part of the national cervical cancer screening programme.

Patient information leaflets

The following PILs are available at www.prodigy.nhs.uk

- Menopause - Alternatives to HRT
- Menopause and HRT
- Menopause and HRT - A Summary
- Menopause and Sex
- Osteoporosis
- Women's Health
- Women's Health Concern

Shared decision making

- **Hormone replacement therapy (HRT)** is a way of replacing the female hormone, oestrogen, which falls to low levels at the menopause.
- **Which HRT?** If you have had a hysterectomy you only need oestrogen replacement. (Most women with a uterus take a progestogen as well to keep the uterus healthy.)
- **Patches** are worn all the time. You have a choice of patches that are changed once a week, or twice a week. Follow the instructions on the packet carefully.
- **Gel** is rubbed into the skin every day. You must be careful not to wash it off before it has been absorbed. Follow the instructions on the packet carefully.
- **Nasal spray** is used every day.
- **Vaginal rings** need to be changed every 3 months.
- **Implants** are put under the skin, and usually last for between 4 and 8 months. They are not used very often.
- **Side effects** sometimes occur. They include nausea and breast tenderness. Try to keep taking the HRT, because often the side effects disappear after a few weeks. If they don't disappear, you should tell your doctor.
- **Whether or not you decide to take HRT,** there are many things you can do to stay healthy. Exercise and a healthy diet (vegetables, whole-grain cereals, calcium) are important.
- **Breast screening:** mammography is a test to check your breasts are healthy — it is available to women aged 50 to 64 years. If you are over 65 years, you can still take part in the national screening programme at your request. Make sure you are 'breast aware' — know what is normal for you (the look and feel of your breasts), know what changes to look for, and report any changes without delay.

Drug rationale

Drugs not included

- **Oestrogen-only HRT tablets** are included in the scenario *Hysterectomy – oestrogen-only tablets.*

Drugs included

- **All oestrogen-only patches, implants, gels, nasal sprays, and vaginal rings that are currently licensed for relief of menopausal symptoms** are included in this scenario.
- Estraderm TTS® is a reservoir patch. All other patches in this scenario are matrix patches.

Prescriptions

Twice-weekly patch: usual start doses

Estraderm MX 50microgram patches
- Age from 25 years onwards
- Estraderm MX 50 patches. Apply one patch twice a week to the trunk, below the waistline; supply 24 patches; NHS Cost £15.65.

Evorel 50microgram patches
- Age from 25 years onwards
- Evorel 50 patches. Apply one patch twice a week to the trunk, below the waistline; supply 24 patches; NHS Cost £10.45.

Elleste Solo MX 40microgram patches
- Age from 25 years onwards
- Elleste Solo MX 40 patches. Apply one patch twice a week to the trunk, below the waistline; supply 24 patches; NHS Cost £15.57.

Estraderm TTS 50microgram patches
- Age from 25 years onwards
- Estraderm TTS 50mcg patches. Apply one patch twice a week to the trunk, below the waistline; supply 24 patches; NHS Cost £18.69.

Fematrix 40microgram patches
- Age from 25 years onwards
- Fematrix 40mcg patches. Apply one patch twice a week to the trunk, below the waistline; supply 24 patches; NHS Cost £16.50.

Twice-weekly patch: higher doses

Estraderm MX 75microgram patches
- Age from 25 years onwards
- Estraderm MX 75 patches. Apply one patch twice a week to the trunk, below the waistline; supply 24 patches; NHS Cost £18.25.

Estraderm MX 100microgram patches
- Age from 25 years onwards
- Estraderm MX 100 patches. Apply one patch twice a week to the trunk, below the waistline; supply 24 patches; NHS Cost £18.94.

Evorel 75microgram patches
- Age from 25 years onwards
- Evorel 75 patches. Apply one patch twice a week to the trunk, below the waistline; supply 24 patches; NHS Cost £11.10.

Evorel 100microgram patches
- Age from 25 years onwards
- Evorel 100 patches. Apply one patch twice a week to the trunk, below the waistline; supply 24 patches; NHS Cost £11.52.

Elleste Solo MX 80microgram patches
- Age from 25 years onwards
- Elleste Solo MX 80 patches. Apply one patch twice a week to the trunk, below the waistline; supply 24 patches; NHS Cost £17.97.

Estraderm TTS 100microgram patches
- Age from 25 years onwards
- Estraderm TTS 100mcg patches. Apply one patch twice a week to the trunk, below the waistline; supply 24 patches; NHS Cost £22.63.

Fematrix 80microgram patches
- Age from 25 years onwards
- Fematrix 80mcg patches. Apply one patch twice a week to the trunk, below the waistline; supply 24 patches; NHS Cost £18.00.

Twice-weekly patch: lower doses

Estraderm MX 25microgram patches
- Age from 25 years onwards
- Estraderm MX 25 patches. Apply one patch twice a week to the trunk, below the waistline; supply 24 patches; NHS Cost £15.59.

Evorel 25microgram patches
- Age from 25 years onwards
- Evorel 25 patches. Apply one patch twice a week to the trunk, below the waistline; supply 24 patches; NHS Cost £9.21.

Estraderm TTS 25microgram patches
- Age from 25 years onwards
- Estraderm TTS 25mcg patches. Apply one patch twice a week to the trunk, below the waistline; supply 24 patches; NHS Cost £18.63.

Once-weekly patches: all strengths

FemSeven 50microgram patches (usual start dose)
- Age from 25 years onwards
- FemSeven 50microgram patches. Apply one patch once a week to the trunk, below the waistline; supply 12 patches; NHS Cost £15.02.

FemSeven 75microgram patches
- Age from 25 years onwards
- FemSeven 75microgram patches. Apply one patch once a week to the trunk, below the waistline; supply 12 patches; NHS Cost £17.46.

FemSeven 100microgram patches
- Age from 25 years onwards
- FemSeven 100microgram patches. Apply one patch once a week to the trunk, below the waistline; supply 12 patches; NHS Cost £18.21.

Progynova TS 50microgram patches (usual start dose)
- Age from 25 years onwards
- Progynova TS 50mcg patch. Apply one patch once a week to the trunk, below the waistline; supply 12 patches; NHS Cost £17.88.

Progynova TS Forte 100microgram patches
- Age from 25 years onwards
- Progynova TS Forte 100mcg ptch. Apply one patch once a week to the trunk, below the waistline; supply 12 patches; NHS Cost £19.68.

Other non-oral products

Oestrogel (estradiol 0.06% gel)
- Age from 25 years onwards
- Oestrogel 0.06% gel. Apply two measures once a day to the arms, shoulders or inner thighs as directed; supply 240 grams; NHS Cost £23.85.

Sandrena (estradiol 0.1% gel)
- Age from 25 years onwards
- Sandrena 1mg gel. Apply the contents of one sachet once a day to the lower trunk or thighs as directed; supply 84 1mg sachets; NHS Cost £19.62.

Aerodiol 150microgam nasal spray
- Age from 25 years onwards
- Aerodiol 150mcg nasal spray. Spray once into ONE nostril once a day; supply 3 nasal sprays; NHS Cost £21.75.

Menoring 50 (estradiol 50microgram/24hours vaginal ring)
- Age from 25 years onwards
- Menoring 50 50mcg vaginal ring. Insert one ring high into the vagina and wear continuously for 3 months; supply 1 vaginal ring; NHS Cost £29.50.

Estradiol 25mg implant
- Age from 25 years onwards
- Estradiol 25mg implant. For subcutaneous implantation; supply 1 implant; NHS Cost £9.59.

Estradiol 50mg implant
- Age from 25 years onwards
- Estradiol 50mg implant. For subcutaneous implantation; supply 1 implant; NHS Cost £19.16.

Estradiol 100mg implant
- Age from 25 years onwards
- Estradiol 100mg implant. For subcutaneous implantation; supply 1 implant; NHS Cost £33.40.

Urogenital symptoms — vaginal oestrogens

Which therapy?

- **Low-dose vaginal oestrogens are only suitable for treating urogential symptoms.**
- **Urogenital atrophy often responds well** to local low-dose vaginal oestrogen.
- **Urge incontinence** (e.g. urgency, frequency, nocturia) can respond to local oestrogen.
- **The place of oestrogens for treating stress incontinence or recurrent urinary tract infection is unclear. Other treatments should generally be explored.**
- **Application frequency:**
  - **Creams or pessaries:** use daily for 2–3 weeks, then reduce to twice a week.
  - **Vaginal ring:** replace every 3 months for up to 2 years.
- **The CSM advises that treatment should be interrupted at least annually** to reassess the need for continued treatment.

Practical prescribing points

For further information, please see the *Medicines Compendium* (www.medicines.org.uk) or the *British National Formulary* (www.bnf.org).

- **Advise women to report** unexplained vaginal bleeding or spotting promptly.

Follow-up advice

- **Follow up in 1–3 months if a new low-dose vaginal HRT product has been started,** and consider the need to continue the product.
- **Use the lowest effective dose** to minimize systemic absorption, e.g. twice-weekly application of cream or pessaries.
- **Interrupt treatment at least annually** to reassess the need for continued treatment.
- **Follow-up investigations should be guided by clinical need:**
  - **Blood pressure** is only needed for women with pre-existing hypertension.
  - **Breast examination** should be carried out if indicated by personal or family history. Give advice about breast awareness and encourage participation in the national breast-screening programme as appropriate for the woman's age.
  - **Pelvic examination** should be carried out if indicated by personal history. Encourage participation in the national cervical cancer screening programme as appropriate for the woman's age.

Should I refer or investigate?

Investigate?

- Routine investigations are not normally indicated.
- Investigate any unexplained vaginal discharge, bleeding, or pain. Consider other causes, for example malignancy, infections, cervical erosion or strictures, or foreign bodies.

Patient information leaflets

The following PILs are available at www.prodigy.nhs.uk

- Menopause - Alternatives to HRT
- Menopause and HRT
- Menopause and HRT - A Summary
- Osteoporosis
- Women's Health
- Women's Health Concern

Shared decision making

- **After the menopause,** a reduction in the amount of the female hormone, oestrogen, can affect the tissues around the vagina.
- **Vaginal problems** often respond well to creams or medicines put directly into the vagina.
- **Problems passing urine** may also be helped by vaginal medicines.
- **Vaginal creams** come with special applicators to insert into the vagina.
- **Vaginal tablets (pessaries)** are an alternative and are inserted with an applicator.
- **A vaginal ring** can be left in the vagina for 3 months. If it is needed for longer, it is replaced every 3 months for up to 2 years.
- **Breast screening:** mammography is a test to check your breasts are healthy — it is available to women aged 50 to 64 years. If you are over 65 years, you can still take part in the national screening programme at your request. Make sure you are 'breast aware' — know what is normal for you (the look and feel of your breasts), know what changes to look for, and report any changes without delay.
- **Cervical screening:** it is also important to have a regular cervical smear test.

Drug rationale

Drugs not included

- **Topical conjugated equine oestrogens** are not included. Higher systemic absorption may potentially result in endometrial stimulation. If used on a long-term basis, an oral progestogen should be taken for 12–14 days of each month for endometrial protection [BNF 48, 2004].
- **The Menoring 50® vaginal ring** is not included because it has sufficient systemic absorption to treat vasomotor symptoms such as hot flushes and sweats, and urogenital symptoms.
- **Non-vaginal products** are not included in this scenario. Oral low-potency estriol products are licensed for genito-urinary symptoms associated with oestrogen deficiency states; but use of these products is thought to be associated with an increased relative risk of developing endometrial cancer when compared with vaginal products [Weiderpass et al, 1999a].

Drugs included

- **All vaginal preparations containing estriol and estradiol for intravaginal use** have been included.
- **Estriol preparations** are available as 0.01% intravaginal cream, 0.1% intravaginal cream, and 500 microgram pessaries. Due to different applicator sizes, both strengths of cream deliver a dose of 500 micrograms estradiol.
- **Estradiol preparations** are available as modified-release estradiol 25 microgram intravaginal tablets, or as an intravaginal ring releasing 7.5 micrograms of estradiol per 24 hours. Systemic levels of estradiol are not significantly raised by the estradiol-releasing intravaginal ring, and co-prescribing of a progestogen is not required for this product.

M

Prescriptions

Intravaginal cream: estriol

Estriol 0.01% cream (500mcg estriol per application)

- Age from 25 years onwards
- Ortho-Gynest cream. Insert one applicatorful into the vagina each evening until improvement occurs. Then reduce to one applicatorful twice a week; supply 80 grams; NHS Cost £2.72.

Estriol 0.1% cream (500mcg estriol per application)

- Age from 25 years onwards
- Ovestin 0.1% vaginal cream. Insert one applicatorful into the vagina each evening until improvement occurs. Then reduce to one applicatorful twice a week; supply 15 grams; NHS Cost £4.98.

Pessaries: estriol or estradiol

Estradiol 25microgram m/r pessaries

- Age from 25 years onwards
- Vagifem 25mcg pessaries. Insert one pessary into the vagina each evening for 2 weeks, then reduce to one pessary twice a week; supply 30 pessaries; NHS Cost £14.56.

Estriol 500microgram pessaries

- Age from 25 years onwards
- Ortho-Gynest 500mcg pessaries. Insert one pessary into the vagina each evening, until improvement occurs. Then reduce to one pessary twice a week; supply 30 pessaries; NHS Cost £10.58.

Vaginal ring: estradiol

Estradiol 2mg vaginal ring (7.5mcg estradiol/24 hours)
- Age from 25 years onwards
- Estring 2mg vaginal ring. Insert one ring high into the vagina and wear continuously for 3 months; supply 1 vaginal ring; NHS Cost £31.42.

Adjunct progestogens (tablets or IUS)

Which therapy?

- **If oestrogen and progestogen have to be delivered by different routes, separate progestogens** can be used for endometrial protection in women with a uterus.
- **Prescriptions for oestrogen-only products** can be found in the 'oestrogen-only' scenarios.
- **The minimum number of days** for cyclical endometrial protection are:
  - Norethisterone 1 mg for last 12–14 days of 28-day cycle
  - Medroxyprogesterone acetate 10 mg for last 14 days of 28-day cycle
  - Dydrogesterone 10 mg for last 14 days of 28-day cycle
- **The levonorgestrel intra-uterine system (LNG-IUS)** is appropriate for perimenopausal women who need contraception, and it will also protect the endometrium if the woman takes oestrogen hormone replacement therapy (HRT).
  - For the World Health Organization medical eligibility criteria for the LNG-IUS, see www.who.int/reproductive-health/publications/mec
  - The LNG-IUS should only be fitted by professionals trained to do so. Insertion may require local anaesthesia and dilatation of the cervical canal.

M

Practical prescribing points

For further information, please see the *Medicines Compendium* (www.medicines.org.uk) or the *British National Formulary* (www.bnf.org).

Managing progestogen-related adverse effects

- **For bleeding problems** (pathology excluded) either increase progestogen duration or dosage, or change progestogen type (e.g. from less androgenic to more androgenic).
- **For progestogen-related adverse effects** (occur cyclically) options are as follows:
  - Reduce progestogen dosage or duration.
  - Change progestogen type, for example from more androgenic to less androgenic.
  - In difficult cases try swapping route of delivery between tablets, patches, or LNG-IUS.

Follow-up advice

- **Follow up in 3 months if a new HRT product has been started.** For management of adverse effects, see *Which therapy?*
- **Subsequent follow-up is usually 6-monthly,** but should be at least annual. Discuss risks and benefits with the woman annually, as they will change over time.
- **Follow-up investigations should be guided by clinical need:**
  - **Blood pressure measurement** is only needed for women with pre-existing hypertension.
  - **Breast examination** should be carried out if indicated by personal or family history. Give advice about breast awareness and encourage participation in the national breast-screening programme as appropriate for the woman's age.
  - **Pelvic examination** should be carried out if indicated. Women without a uterus will not be part of the national cervical cancer screening programme.
- **Consider stopping HRT to assess abnormal bleeding** (e.g. change in pattern of withdrawal bleeds, or breakthrough bleeding). Review 4 weeks later. If problems continue see *Should I refer or investigate?*

Should I refer or investigate?

Refer?

- Referral guidelines for suspected cancer recommend that women who have persistent or unexplained postmenopausal bleeding after stopping HRT for 6 weeks should be referred urgently to a team specialising in the management of gynaecological cancer, depending on local arrangements [NICE, 2005].

Investigate?

- Routine investigations are not normally indicated.

Patient information leaflets

The following PILs are available at www.prodigy.nhs.uk
- Menopause - Alternatives to HRT
- Menopause and HRT
- Menopause and HRT - A Summary
- Menopause and Sex
- Osteoporosis
- Women's Health
- Women's Health Concern

Shared decision making

- **Hormone replacement therapy (HRT)** is a way of replacing the female hormone, oestrogen, which falls to low levels at the menopause.
- **Women who have not had a hysterectomy** take a progestogen as well as an oestrogen. Progestogens keep the uterus healthy, by stopping oestrogen from over-stimulating the lining of the uterus.
- **It is important** to make sure you take your progestogens correctly. Usually HRT is taken as a combined tablet, where the oestrogen and progestogen are mixed together. In a few women these hormones are given separately, which means you must pay more attention to when and how to take them.
- **Progestogen tablets** are usually taken for part of the month only (usually the last 12–14 days of a 28-day month). Follow the instructions on the packet carefully. Monthly bleeds will happen with most of these tablets.
- **A progestogen-releasing system** can be put into your uterus (like a coil). It will provide contraception.
- **Whether or not you decide to take HRT,** there are many things you can do to stay healthy. Exercise and a healthy diet (vegetables, whole-grain cereals, calcium) are important.
- **Breast screening:** mammography is a test to check your breasts are healthy — it is available to women aged 50 to 64 years. If you are over 65 years, you can still take part in the national screening programme at your request. Make sure you are 'breast aware' — know what is normal for you (the look and feel of your breasts), know what changes to look for, and report any changes without delay.

- **Cervical screening:** it is also important to have a regular cervical smear test.

Drug rationale

Drugs not included

- **Progestogen-only products that are not licensed for endometrial protection during oestrogen replacement therapy** are not included.

Drugs included

- **All progestogen-only tablets that are licensed for endometrial protection during oestrogen replacement therapy** are included. Note: some doses recommended for endometrial protection [Rees and Purdie, 2002] are not available as licensed progestogen-only products.
- **The levonorgestrel-releasing intra-uterine system (LNG-IUS)** is included. It is an alternative route for delivery of progestogen, particularly if the woman requires ongoing contraception [Rees and Purdie, 2002].

Prescriptions

Cyclical progestogen tablets (less androgenic)

Dydrogesterone 10mg once a day x14 days

- Age from 25 years onwards
- Duphaston HRT 10mg tablets. Take one tablet once a day on days 15-28 of each 28-day oestrogen HRT cycle; supply 42 tablets; NHS Cost £3.14.

Dydrogesterone 10mg twice a day x14 days

- Age from 25 years onwards
- Duphaston HRT 10mg tablets. Take one tablet twice a day on days 15-28 of each 28-day oestrogen HRT cycle; supply 84 tablets; NHS Cost £6.28.

Medroxyprogesterone 10mg once a day x14 days

- Age from 25 years onwards
- Medroxyprogesterone 10mg tabs. Take one tablet once a day on days 15-28 of each 28-day oestrogen HRT cycle; supply 42 tablets; NHS Cost £10.34.

Cyclical progestogen tablets (more androgenic)

Norethisterone 1mg once a day x14 days

- Age from 25 years onwards
- Micronor HRT 1mg tablets. Take one tablet once a day on days 15-28 of each 28-day oestrogen HRT cycle; supply 42 tablets; NHS Cost £4.37.

Norethisterone 1mg once a day x12 days

- Age from 25 years onwards
- Micronor HRT 1mg tablets. Take one tablet once a day on days 15-26 of each 28-day oestrogen HRT cycle; supply 36 tablets; NHS Cost £3.75.

Levonorgestrel intra-uterine system

Levonorgestrel-releasing intra-uterine system

- Age from 25 years onwards
- Levonorgestrel 52mg i-u system. For insertion into the uterine cavity; supply 1 device; NHS Cost £98.18.

Extended Information

Background information

- Definitions p.1199
- What causes the menopause? p.1199
- What causes premature menopause? p.1200
- How do I know my patient has it? p.1200
- How common are menopausal symptoms? p.1200
- Long-term health implications of the menopause p.1201

Definitions

- **Menopause** is the point in time when menstruation ceases permanently. It occurs with the final menstrual period, and can therefore only be diagnosed with certainty after 12 months' spontaneous amenorrhoea. The mean age of the menopause is 51 years.
- **Perimenopause** is the time period from when the ovaries start to fail (and symptoms such as irregular periods or hot flushes may begin) until 12 months after the final menstrual period.
- **Menopausal transition** is the period of time from when the ovaries start to fail (when symptoms may begin) until the final menstrual period. This transition period lasts about 4 years (shorter in smokers), starting on average at age 47.5 years. About 10% of women will not experience this transition, but will cease menstruation abruptly.
- **Postmenopause** is the time after the permanent cessation of menstruation. It can only be known with certainty after 12 months of spontaneous amenorrhoea. In practice this definition is difficult to apply, especially in women who have started hormone replacement therapy (HRT) in the perimenopause. It has been estimated that by the age of 54 years, 80% of women are postmenopausal [McKinlay et al, 1992].
- **Premature menopause** is defined as menopause that occurs before the age of 40 years.

[Rees and Purdie, 2002]

What causes the menopause?

Hormones and the normal menstrual cycle

- The menstrual cycle begins with the onset of bleeding, and lasts about 28 days. It is controlled by a complex system of hormones and feedback mechanisms.
- Gonadotrophin-releasing hormone (GnRH) stimulates the pituitary to release follicle-stimulating hormone (FSH) and luteinizing hormone (LH). In the first half of the cycle, these both act on the ovaries and stimulate ovarian follicular development. A group of follicles initially develops, and then a single follicle matures as a result of the action of FSH and LH.
- Near midcycle, there is a rise is oestrogen secretion from the follicle. This rise augments the response of the pituitary to GnRH, and triggers a burst of LH secretion, which stimulates ovulation.
- The ovulated follicle differentiates into the corpus luteum during the second half of the cycle (days 14–28). Initially there is a drop in oestrogen secretion, but then progesterone and oestrogen levels rise together, along with inhibin.
- The raised oestrogen level has a negative feedback effect on the pituitary, reducing the levels of FSH and LH that are produced as the cycle progresses. FSH levels are also reduced by inhibin.
- The raised progesterone level maintains the proliferated endometrium ready for implantation.
- If, towards the end of the 28-day cycle, the follicle has not been fertilized and does not implant, it begins to degenerate and the progesterone level falls, causing the endometrium to shed (menstruation).

Changes to hormones and the menstrual cycle at the menopause

- Some experts believe that the menopause evolved to protect women from the dangers of late childbirth. Others believe that the number of oocytes in a woman's ovaries is finite and that menopause occurs when there are none left.

- In premenopausal women, the predominating circulating oestrogen is estradiol (secreted by the ovaries). The ovaries also produce estrone, but this is about 10 times less potent than estradiol. As the ovaries fail, oestrogen production becomes dependent on peripheral conversion of testosterone to estrone in fat tissue. Some estrone is then converted into estradiol.
- During the menopause, as ovarian follicular activity begins to fail, oestrogen levels fall and reduced negative feedback to the pituitary causes FSH and LH levels to rise.
- Falling oestrogen levels begin to disrupt the menstrual cycle, and may cause other menopausal symptoms.
- Eventually the menopausal pattern of low oestrogen and high FSH and LH is established.

What causes premature menopause?

- **Primary premature menopause** may occur at any age and present as amenorrhoea. Not all women have acute symptoms. FSH levels are elevated. Spontaneous fertility may recur. Consider chromosome abnormalities such as Turner's syndrome. For the investigation and treatment of amenorrhoea, see the PRODIGY *Amenorrhoea* guidance.
- **Surgical menopause** occurs after bilateral oophorectomy. Abrupt falls in estradiol levels cause a higher frequency of symptoms.
- **Radiation-induced** menopause is caused by radiation to the pelvic area.
- **Chemotherapy-induced** menopause may occur after cancer treatment, with ovarian failure more common in women aged more than 30 years at the time of treatment.
- **Premature menopause after hysterectomy with ovarian conservation** can occur in the postoperative period, where it may be temporary, or at a later stage when it occurs sooner than the time of the natural menopause. It may depend on ovarian function preceding hysterectomy. Note: the diagnosis can be difficult as not all women suffer acute symptoms — some experts recommend annual FSH testing in this situation to determine whether HRT might be appropriate.

[Rees and Purdie, 2002]

M

How do I know my patient has it?

Signs and symptoms of the menopause

- **The perimenopause is usually diagnosed clinically** when the woman presents with symptoms and signs of reducing oestrogen levels.
- **Change to menstrual pattern:** menstrual cycle lengths may shorten to 2–3 weeks or lengthen to many months. The amount of menstrual blood loss may alter, and most commonly increases slightly.
- **Hot flushes and sweats (including night sweats)** are classical symptoms that occur in 70–80% of perimenopausal women [Rees and Purdie, 2002]. Hot flushes most commonly affect the face, head, neck, and chest. They generally only last a few minutes. Although their occurrence is not related directly to plasma estradiol levels, their onset may be related to falls in oestrogen levels.
- **Sleep disturbance** may occur. This is often due to night sweats, but may also be due to mood disorders, or primary sleep disorders. Chronically disturbed sleep can lead to insomnia, irritability, and difficulties with short-term memory and concentration.
- **Urinary and vaginal symptoms** such as vaginal discomfort and dryness, dyspareunia, recurrent lower urinary tract infection, and urinary incontinence are common in the menopause. Symptoms of urogenital atrophy may appear for the first time more than 10 years after the last menstrual period [Robinson and Cardozo, 2003].
- **Mood changes,** including nervousness, anxiety, irritability, depression, forgetfulness, and difficulty concentrating, have all been associated with the menopause. These symptoms are more likely to be associated with past problems and life stresses than attributable to the menopause alone. General population studies suggest that the majority of women do not experience major changes in mood during the menopause transition.
- **Loss of libido** can be attributed to androgen deficiency. However, non-hormonal factors such as conflict between partners, insomnia, inadequate stimulation, life stresses, or depression are also important contributors, and should not be overlooked.
- **Thinning of the skin, brittle nails, hair loss, and generalized aches and pains** are associated with reduced oestrogen levels.

[Rees and Purdie, 2002]

Investigations

- **Investigations are of limited value for diagnosing the menopause.**
- **Follicle-stimulating hormone (FSH) levels fluctuate markedly** during the perimenopause and so are of limited value in symptomatic women, in whom clinical history can form the basis of a diagnosis. A therapeutic trial of HRT may be more helpful.
- **However, serial FSH levels should be taken in women with suspected premature menopause** (symptoms under the age of 40 years) because of the implications of premature ovarian failure, and in women who have had a hysterectomy with ovarian conservation as they are at risk of an early menopause.
  - FSH levels should be measured when the woman is taking neither HRT nor oestrogen-based contraception.
  - FSH levels of greater than 30 IU/L are generally considered to be in the postmenopausal range.
  - Measurement of FSH levels should usually be repeated 4–8 weeks later to confirm this.
  - In women still experiencing menstrual bleeding, FSH levels measured on day 2 or 3 after the onset of bleeding are considered to be raised when they exceed 10–12 IU/L, and are an indication of diminished ovarian response [American Association of Clinical Endocrinologists, 1999].
- There is little place for measuring luteinizing hormone (LH), estradiol, and progesterone levels in clinical practice [Rees and Purdie, 2002].
- **Thyroid function tests** for free thyroxine (T_4) and thyroid-stimulating hormone (TSH) will distinguish thyroid disease symptoms from menopausal symptoms, particularly if there is inadequate symptomatic response to HRT [Rees and Purdie, 2002].

How common are menopausal symptoms?

- About 80% of women experience menopausal symptoms, and 45% of them find the symptoms distressing.
- Although menopausal symptoms are usually self-limiting (2–5 years), some women experience symptoms for many years.

[RCPE, 2003]

Long-term health implications of the menopause

- **The long-term consequences of the menopause remain clinically silent for many years.**
  - **Osteoporosis, urogenital atrophy, cardiovascular disease, and stroke** all increase after the menopause. They are all associated with, but not necessarily caused by, the menopausal drop in oestrogen levels. It is unclear whether dementia is associated directly with a fall in oestrogen levels.
  - **Women with premature menopause** are at increased risk of developing osteoporosis and cardiovascular disease, but are at lower risk of breast cancer.
- **Women show an increase in bodyweight with age,** and this tends to begin at or near menopause. Body fat redistribution to the abdomen also occurs with age (independently of weight gain). This centralized abdominal fat distribution is recognised as an independent risk factor for cardiovascular disease in women [Norman et al, 2004].

Management issues

- What are the options for managing menopausal symptoms? p.1201
- What are the long-term benefits and risks of HRT? p.1202
- HRT for women with a premature menopause p.1204
- Is there a place for HRT in long-term disease prevention? p.1204
- What are the options for managing the long-term health implications of the menopause? p.1205
- HRT and contraception p.1205
- HRT use in women with comorbidity p.1205
- Starting HRT p.1206
- Which hormones, which regimen, which route, which dose? p.1207
- Managing the adverse effects of HRT p.1209
- Monitoring and follow-up of women receiving HRT p.1210
- Changing HRT p.1210
- Stopping HRT p.1211

What are the options for managing menopausal symptoms?

General points

- **For many women, menopausal symptoms are mild and of short duration,** and do not require management beyond lifestyle adjustments, education, and reassurance [ICSI, 2003].
- **For others, these symptoms may be distressing and require short-term treatment with hormone replacement therapy (HRT).**
  - HRT is the provision of oestrogen (with a progestogen in women with a uterus).
  - HRT is highly effective for the relief of vasomotor symptoms and urogenital symptoms, and alleviates hormone-related mood changes and insomnia [RCPE, 2003]. Irregular menstrual pattern is not always improved by HRT, as underlying natural cycles may persist.
  - When HRT is stopped, symptoms may return, and some women may wish to restart HRT after reassessment and counselling.
- **Non-hormonal alternatives** may be suitable for women not wishing to take oestrogen-based therapy, or with a contraindication to HRT.

Hot flushes and night sweats

- **Lifestyle** modifications such as exercise, lighter clothing, sleeping in a cooler room, and reducing stress may be sufficient to manage hot flushes for many women [ICSI, 2003]. Avoidance of possible triggers, including spicy foods, caffeine, smoking, and alcohol may help.
- **HRT is the most effective way of relieving hot flushes** [Rees and Purdie, 2002; ICSI, 2003; MacLennan et al, 2004].
- **Tibolone** is a synthetic oral steroid with mixed oestrogenic, progestogenic, and androgenic actions that can be used to treat vasomotor symptoms [Modelska and Cummings, 2002].
- **Progestogen-only therapy** has also been shown to reduce flushing, although to a markedly lesser extent than oestrogen-based HRT [ICSI, 2003]. Norethisterone 5 mg daily or megestrol acetate 40 mg daily has been used [Rees and Purdie, 2002].
- **Non-hormonal alternatives, such as selective serotonin reuptake inhibitors,** may be helpful. Small studies suggest that paroxetine 20 mg daily or venlafaxine 75 mg daily may be effective for treating hot flushes [Barton et al, 2002; Stearns et al, 2003].
- Clonidine 50–75 mg twice daily is of limited value, as it generally causes unacceptable adverse effects [Rees and Purdie, 2002].
- **Complementary therapies are widely used by women, but they cannot currently be recommended** because there are few efficacy or safety data available [Ernst, 2001; Kronenberg and Fugh-Berman, 2002; Huntley and Ernst, 2003; ICSI, 2003].
  - **Many products contain phytoestrogens** (e.g. isoflavones and lignans) which are plant substances that are structurally similar to estradiol. Isoflavones are found in soy beans, chick peas, and red clover. Lignans are present in whole grains, seeds (especially flaxseed), vegetables, and fruit.
  - **Black cohosh** (contains phytoestrogens) may be of benefit, but the long-term effects of its oestrogenic properties are unknown. There have been very rare reports of hepatotoxicity with black cohosh [CSM, 2004b].
  - **Red clover** (contains phytoestrogens) may be of benefit but the studies are conflicting. In addition, some species contain coumarins, making them unsuitable for women taking anticoagulants.
  - **Soy foods** (contain phytoestrogens) seem to have a modest benefit for hot flushes, but the studies are not conclusive. They have been a staple part of Asian cuisine for thousands of years and are presumed to be safe.
  - **Other commonly used products include** dong quai, evening primrose oil, kava, and ginseng. The only studies of dong quai, evening primrose oil, and ginseng found no superiority over placebo. Dong quai extracts also contain coumarins. Women should avoid kava products as they have been linked to cases of liver toxicity [CSM, 2003e].
  - **Herbal products should be used with care** in women with contraindications to oestrogen, as some herbs (e.g. gingseng, black cohosh, and red clover) have oestrogenic properties. Their long-term effects on the breast and endometrium have not been assessed.

Mood or sleep disturbances

- **Lifestyle** changes, including regular physical activity and relaxation exercises, may help with anxiety symptoms. However, exercising late in the day may promote sleeplessness.
- **HRT will often improve sleep by alleviating night sweats.** In addition, women frequently report an

M

Table 1: Long-term benefits of HRT: results from the Women's Health Initiative study [CSM, 2004a].

Condition	Age	Oestrogen-only arm*		Combined HRT arm*	
		No. of cases per 1000 *non-HRT users* over 5 years	No. of cases per 1000 women who *used HRT for 5 years* over the same period	No. of cases per 1000 *non-HRT users* over 5 years	No. of cases per 1000 women who *used HRT for 5 years* over the same period
Colorectal cancer	50–59 60–69	6 10	No significant effect	3 8	2 (+/–1) 5 (+/–2)
Fracture of neck of femur	50–59 60–69	0.5 5.5	0.2 (+/–0.5) 2.5 (+/–2)	1.5 5.5	1.2 (+/–1) 2.5 (+/–2)

* The oestrogen-only arm used conjugated equine oestrogens alone. The combined HRT arm used conjugated equine oestrogens plus continuous medroxyprogesterone acetate.

improvement in sleep patterns with HRT, even if hot flushes or night sweats are not prominent features of their menopausal symptoms [ICSI, 2003].

- It is not known whether HRT has a direct effect on mood, irritability, or anxiety, or whether these effects are due solely to the alleviation of hot flushes and sleep disturbances.
- **Psychological symptoms should be managed on an individual basis,** and may need to be addressed via self-help groups, psychotherapy, other forms of counselling, or antidepressants [Rees and Purdie, 2002]. HRT should not be used as monotherapy for depression.
- **HRT is most likely to be useful if there are other menopausal symptoms present.** There is some evidence that oestrogen may potentiate the effects of antidepressants, possibly by increasing or maintaining serotonin levels. Conversely, progestogens may aggravate mood disturbances [ICSI, 2003].

Urogenital symptoms

M

- **HRT alleviates urogenital atrophy** [Robinson and Cardozo, 2003]. Local low-dose vaginal oestrogen is generally preferred: it is as effective as systemic HRT (oral, patches, or implant), but systemic absorption is low. Maximal benefit of HRT takes between 1 and 3 months of therapy, but may take up to 1 year of treatment [Cardozo et al, 1998]. (See *Vaginal oestrogens* for further details about vaginal products.)
- **Non-hormonal alternatives for urogential atrophy** include vaginal lubricants and vaginal moisturizers, but they are less effective than HRT [ICSI, 2003].
- **The place of HRT for treating urinary symptoms is less clear.**
  - **Urge incontinence** (e.g. urgency, frequency, nocturia) can respond to low-dose vaginal oestrogens [Robinson and Cardozo, 2003]. Combined oestrogen and progestogen therapy seems to reduce the likelihood of success [Moehrer et al, 2004].
  - **Stress incontinence** cannot be treated by oestrogens alone, although there is limited evidence that it may be alleviated by a combination of oestrogen and an alpha-adrenergic agonist [Robinson and Cardozo, 2003].
  - **Recurrent urinary tract infections** may be prevented by oestrogen replacement therapy, but there are no trial data on the appropriate dose and duration [Rees and Purdie, 2002]. See the PRODIGY guidance *Urinary tract infection (lower) — women* for treatment of active infection.

Decreased libido and sexual dysfunction

- Dyspareunia as a result of vaginal dryness can be relieved by HRT. While this will improve sexual functioning for many women, HRT has no proven direct effect on sexuality or libido [ICSI, 2003]. Generally, the quality of the relationship, and the health and interest of the male partner are more important in achieving a good sex life [Rees and Purdie, 2002].
- Loss of libido can be improved by testosterone supplementation, particularly after surgical menopause. Specialist advice should be sought as a wide range of doses, with potentially serious adverse effects, are quoted in the literature [ICSI, 2003]. The partial androgenic effects of tibolone may be useful for some women.
- Tibolone is an alternative to HRT for relieving vaginal dryness. It may also be useful for managing loss of libido [Modelska and Cummings, 2002].

What are the long-term benefits and risks of HRT?

Long-term benefits

- **The long-term benefits of HRT are a decreased risk of osteoporosis (with both oestrogen-only and combined HRT [oestrogen plus progestogen therapy]) and a decreased risk of colorectal cancer (with combined HRT only).** Other benefits are controversial and are discussed in *Unproven benefits*.
- The risk of colorectal cancer and osteoporosis increases with increasing age. HRT, therefore, produces a greater potential reduction in the number of cases of colorectal cancer or hip fracture in older women, than in younger women (see Table 1). However, some of the potential risks of HRT also increase with age (see ***Risks***).
- Osteoporotic fractures are a major cause of morbidity and mortality in the elderly. However, the most recent epidemiological studies suggest that for HRT to be an effective method of preventing hip fractures, continuous lifelong use is required, i.e. bone protection lasts as long as HRT is taken, but begins to decline as soon as HRT is stopped [Michaelsson et al, 1998].
- Although the recent Women's Health Initiative study confirmed that combined HRT (but not oestrogen-only HRT) reduces the risk of colorectal cancer, little is known about colorectal cancer risk when treatment is stopped [British Menopause Society, 2003].

Risks

- **The absolute increase in risks is small:** the extra number of cases of each of the conditions discussed below associated with HRT is typically smaller than the health risks associated with smoking or being very overweight [CSM, 2002].

Breast cancer

- **There is only a small increased risk of breast cancer for women taking short-term HRT;** typically 1–3 years' use for many women (Table 2).
  - **For oestrogen-only HRT the short-term risk is very small.**

Table 2: Increased risk of breast cancer associated with taking HRT [CSM, 2004a].

Study	Age	Oestrogen-only HRT		Combined HRT	
		No. of cases per 1000 *non-HRT users* over 5 years	No. of cases per 1000 women who *used HRT for 5 years* over the same period	No. of cases per 1000 *non-HRT users* over 5 years	No. of cases per 1000 women who *used HRT for 5 years* over the same period
Million Women Study*	50–64	14	15.5 (+/–1.5)	14	20 (+/–1)
Women's Health Initiative**	50–79	15	No significant effect	16	20 (+/–4)

* The Million Women Study was an observational study, so all types of HRT were included. The CSM have provided a cumulative risk of 14 cases/1000 non-HRT users over 5 years to facilitate comparison with the Women's Health Initiative study.
** The Women's Health Initiative was a randomised controlled trial. The oestrogen-only arm used conjugated equine oestrogens alone. The combined HRT arm used conjugated equine oestrogens plus continuous medroxyprogesterone acetate.

- **For combined HRT** (oestrogen plus progestogen therapy) the short-term risk of breast cancer is slightly higher.
- **The risk of breast cancer increases with duration of use** [Collaborative Group on Hormonal Factors in Breast Cancer, 1997; Women's Health Initiative, 2002; Million Women Study Collaborators, 2003].
  - Data from recent randomized controlled trials showed that the risk of breast cancer with combined HRT did not start to increase until 4 years after starting HRT. Although observational data from the Million Women Study suggest that the risk starts to increase after 1–2 years, many experts have criticised this study because many women had been taking HRT for several years before entering the study.
  - The oestrogen-only arm of the Women's Health Initiative has reported no increase in the risk of breast cancer over 7 years of use.
  - Observational data for longer-term use suggest that the risk of breast cancer increases with long-term use (e.g. >15 years). However insufficient data on the type of HRT used were collected, so it was not possible to analyse the difference in risk between oestrogen-only and combined HRT in this study.
- Observational data from the Million Women Study suggest that using a different preparation or route of delivery does not alter the increased risk of breast cancer with oestrogen-only HRT, or with combined HRT [Million Women Study Collaborators, 2003].
- Follow-up from large randomized controlled trials is not yet long enough to determine whether HRT decreases or increases mortality from breast cancer.
- **There is probably only a small increased risk of breast cancer for women taking tibolone.** Observational data suggest that it increases the risk of breast cancer more than oestrogen-only therapy, but less than combined HRT [Million Women Study Collaborators, 2003].
- **With all types of HRT, the risk of breast cancer begins to decline when HRT is stopped** and, by 5 years, it reaches the same level as in women who have never taken HRT [CSM, 2003a].

Endometrial cancer

- Unopposed oestrogen therapy enhances the development of endometrial hyperplasia and increases the risk of endometrial cancer in women with a uterus (Table 3) [Writing Group for the PEPI Trial, 1996; Rees and Purdie, 2002].
- Addition of progestogen reduces the risk of endometrial cancer. The Committee on Safety of Medicines has recently advised that adding a progestogen to oestrogen therapy (combined HRT) for at least 12 days per month greatly reduces this risk [CSM, 2004a].
- The optimal number of days of progestogen needed is still debated, with some studies concluding that cyclical and continuous progestogens are similarly effective [Pike et al, 1997], while others recommend that continuous combined regimens may be needed to minimize the risk of endometrial cancer [Weiderpass et al, 1999b].
- The daily dosages of progestogens used in combined HRT products (both monthly cyclical products and continuous products) are considered to provide adequate endometrial protection. See *Which dose?* for further information.
- There is conflicting evidence regarding the endometrial safety of 3-monthly cyclical HRT. Some data suggest that the risk of endometrial hyperplasia and endometrial cancer is higher with a quarterly progestogen regimen than with monthly progestogen regimens [Pukkala et al, 2001; Lethaby et al, 2004]. Other data suggest that there is little increased risk of hyperplasia [Erkkola et al, 2004].
- The risk of endometrial cancer with tibolone is not known [CSM, 2003a].

Stroke

- Studies have found an increase in the risk of stroke in HRT users [Beral et al, 2002; CSM, 2002; Women's Health Initiative, 2002; Women's Health Initiative, 2004].
- This is mainly due to an increased risk of ischaemic stroke. A woman's baseline risk of stroke also increases with age, and using HRT further increases this risk (see

Table 3: Increased risk of endometrial cancer associated with taking HRT [CSM, 2004a].

Study	Age	Oestrogen-only HRT*		Combined HRT*	
		No. of cases per 1000 *non-HRT users* over 5 years	No. of cases per 1000 women who *used HRT for 5 years* over the same period	No. of cases per 1000 *non-HRT users* over 5 years	No. of cases per 1000 women who *used HRT for 5 years* over the same period
Women's Health Initiative	50–69	3	8 (+/–1)	3	Cannot be estimated**

* The oestrogen only arm used conjugated equine oestrogens alone. The combined HRT arm used conjugated equine oestrogens plus continuous medroxyprogesterone acetate.
** Risk cannot reliably be estimated in combined HRT users. The addition of a progestogen for at least 12 days per month greatly reduces the additional risk of endometrial cancer due to unopposed oestrogen, but the magnitude of the reduction is poorly defined at present.

M

Table 4). Note: most studies examining the risk of stroke were conducted in women aged 60–70 years, whereas most women using HRT in the UK are younger than this (50–59 years) and therefore have a lower absolute risk of stroke.

Venous thromboembolism

- Taking HRT increases the risk of venous thromboembolism (VTE), particularly in the first year of use [Miller et al, 2002]. Note: the baseline risk of VTE in non-HRT users increases with age, and using HRT further adds to this risk.
- The risk should be assessed in individual women — a personal history of venous thromboembolism is the single biggest risk factor for a future episode [Rees and Purdie, 2002]. Further details on the decision to offer HRT to women with a personal or family history of venous thromboembolism can be found in *HRT use in women with comorbidity*.

Other risks

- **There is a possible increase in the risk of coronary heart disease (CHD) in the first year of combined HRT use.** Oestrogen-only HRT does not seem to increase or decrease the risk of CHD.
- **Ovarian cancer:** there is a small increased risk of ovarian cancer in women who have had a hysterectomy with long-term use of oestrogen-only HRT (about 1 extra case per 1000 women using oestrogen-only HRT for 5 years between the ages of 50 and 69 years). The risks of ovarian cancer with combined HRT (oestrogen plus progestogen) are unclear [CSM, 2004a].
- Oestrogen- and progestogen-related adverse effects such as bloating, breast tenderness, and withdrawal bleeds in women receiving cyclical therapy may be regarded as 'risks' by some women.

M

Unproven benefits

- It has also been suggested that HRT use may be associated with reduced tooth loss, reduced incidence of age-related macular degeneration and cataracts, reduced incidence of dementia, improved faecal incontinence, improved wound healing, and improved balance. There is currently insufficient evidence to either support or refute these hypotheses. The risks of prescribing HRT for any of these problems are likely to outweigh the hypothetical benefits.

HRT for women with a premature menopause

- **HRT may be used in younger women who have experienced a premature menopause up to the age of 50 years, for preventing osteoporosis** and treating menopausal symptoms [CSM, 2003c].
- **This includes women who have had a hysterectomy with oophorectomy,** women with primary ovarian failure, and other causes of premature menopause. Note: menopausal symptoms can be particularly severe after surgical menopause.
- The use of HRT by women with premature menopause probably increases the risk of breast cancer to that of women who do not have a premature menopause [RCPE, 2003].
- **After the age of 50 years** (the time of natural menopause), therapy for osteoporosis should be reviewed and HRT considered a second-line choice [CSM, 2003c]. For guidance on the treatment of established osteoporosis see the PRODIGY guidance *Osteoporosis — treatment*.

Is there a place for HRT in long-term disease prevention?

Osteoporosis

- **HRT is no longer recommended as a first-line therapy for the prevention or treatment of osteoporosis in women aged over 50 years.** Although HRT is effective in preventing osteoporosis, the Committee on Safety of Medicines (CSM) recently advised that the balance of risks and benefits is such that HRT should no longer be considered as a first-line therapy for preventing osteoporosis in postmenopausal women. Tibolone should also be considered as a second-line option for osteoporosis prevention [CSM, 2003c].
- **The benefit of fracture prevention for most women is outweighed by the overall risks of long-term HRT use** [RCPE, 2003].
- **HRT remains an option if** other osteoporosis therapies are contraindicated, not tolerated, or if there is evidence of a lack of response to other therapies [CSM, 2003c]. These women should be made aware of the increased incidence of some conditions with long-term HRT use. In particular, long-term use (>5 years) of combined HRT (used by women with a uterus) has a significantly increased risk of breast cancer. Conversely long-term use of oestrogen-only HRT (only suitable for women with a hysterectomy) has a much smaller increased risk of breast cancer. The risk of stroke and venous thromboembolism (with either type of HRT) seems greatest in the first years of use.
- **If women require both treatment of menopausal symptoms and prevention of osteoporosis, HRT is a reasonable option** [RCPE, 2003]. However, length of treatment should be guided by menopausal symptoms, and the minimum effective dose should be used to control menopausal symptoms. Once treatment of menopausal symptoms is no longer required, therapy for preventing osteoporosis should be reviewed and HRT considered as a second-line choice.
- **For advice about preventing osteoporosis in women with premature menopause** see *HRT for women with a premature menopause.*

Cardiovascular disease

- **HRT should not be prescribed for either primary or secondary prevention of coronary heart disease or stroke**

Table 4: Cardiovascular risks associated with HRT: results from the Women's Health Initiative study [CSM, 2004a].

Condition	Age	Oestrogen-only arm*		Combined HRT arm*	
		No. of cases per 1000 *non-HRT users* over 5 years	No. of cases per 1000 women who *used HRT for 5 years* over the same period	No. of cases per 1000 *non-HRT users* over 5 years	No. of cases per 1000 women who *used HRT for 5 years* over the same period
Stroke	50–59	8	10 (+/–2)	3	4 (+/–1)
	60–69	15	21 (+/-4)	11	15 (+/–3)
VTE	50–59	6.5	7.5 (+/–1)	3	7 (+/–2)
	60–69	11.5	15.5 (+/–4)	8	17 (+/–5)

* The oestrogen-only arm used conjugated equine oestrogens alone. The combined HRT arm used conjugated equine oestrogens plus continuous medroxyprogesterone acetate.

[CSM, 2004a]. Although observational studies indicated that HRT might prevent CHD [Grodstein et al, 2000], this finding has not been supported by findings from randomized controlled trials [Grady et al, 2002; Manson et al, 2003].
- The arm of the Women's Health Initiative (WHI) study using combined HRT (conjugated equine oestrogens with medroxyprogesterone acetate) showed a possible increase in the risk of coronary heart disease (CHD) in the first year of HRT use, and no evidence for benefit thereafter. This was demonstrated both in women with pre-existing CHD, and in women without a history of CHD. The oestrogen-only arm of this study has now been terminated due to an increased risk of stroke. However, oestrogen-only HRT neither increased nor decreased the risk of CHD [Women's Health Initiative, 2004].
- Although other forms of HRT have been less widely studied, data from a small study using estradiol-only HRT for secondary prevention also found that it neither increased nor decreased the risk of further cardiac events [The ESPRIT team, 2002].
- The effects of tibolone on cardiovascular disease mortality are unknown.

Alzheimer's disease

- **HRT should not be prescribed for the prevention or treatment of Alzheimer's disease** [CSM, 2004a].
- Observational studies suggested that the risk of Alzheimer's is reduced, or its onset delayed, in women on HRT. In contrast, the WHI trial demonstrated no reduction in the risk of Alzheimer's, and an increase in all-case dementia in women using HRT. Some experts suggest that this apparent conflict may be because the WHI data were from an older age group of women (average age 63 years), and that the 'window' for Alzheimer's disease prevention is in a much younger age group [Panay, 2004].

What are the options for managing the long-term health implications of the menopause?

- **Osteoporosis prevention:** lifestyle measures to prevent osteoporosis should be encouraged, including a good calcium intake (aim for a dietary intake of 1000 mg calcium daily); exercise (particularly balance and strength training); smoking cessation; and avoidance of excessive alcohol. See the patient information leaflets for further information.
- **Osteoporosis treatment:** treatment options for established osteoporosis, i.e. the presence of two or more vertebral fractures, or for people with risk factors for osteoporosis and a low bone mineral density (T-score of –2.5 or less), include lifestyle measures in conjunction with a bisphosphonate, raloxifene, or calcitonin. For guidance on the treatment of established osteoporosis see the PRODIGY guidance *Osteoporosis — treatment*.
- **Cardiovascular disease:** coronary heart disease (CHD) is a leading cause of death in women in the UK. All women should be aware of lifestyle changes to reduce their future risk of coronary heart disease and stroke (e.g. stopping smoking, aerobic exercise, balanced diet, weight control, and moderate alcohol consumption). Consider calculating 10-year CHD risk in women with hypertension, diabetes mellitus, or a family history of premature myocardial infarction or stroke. For further information see the PRODIGY guidance *Coronary heart disease risk — identification and management*, or the patient information leaflets.

HRT and contraception

- **Perimenopausal women are not infertile and may still get pregnant if contraception is not used.**
- **HRT preparations do not suppress ovulation and do not provide contraceptive cover.** Prescriptions and detailed advice on contraception can be found in the PRODIGY *Contraception* guidance.
- **Follicle-stimulating hormone (FSH) levels are of only limited value as indicators of fertility** as they fluctuate markedly during the perimenopause:
  - Even if FSH levels are in the postmenopausal range (over 30 iu/litre), this does not reliably indicate infertility. (A second level is usually taken 4–8 weeks later to confirm the result.)
  - In addition, HRT or combined oral contraception (COC) suppresses FSH levels. FSH levels should therefore only be checked 6–8 weeks after stopping HRT or the COC. Progestogen-only contraception does not affect FSH levels and so does not need to be stopped for FSH testing [Rees and Purdie, 2002; Beksinska et al, 2003].
- **It is generally accepted that contraception should be continued for** 1 year after the last menstrual period for women over 50 years old, or for 2 years after the last menstrual period for women under the age of 50 years [DTB, 1996; Pitkin, 2000; Rees and Purdie, 2002].
- The same advice applies for women who have FSH levels in the postmenopausal range, i.e. continue contraception for 1 year for women over 50 years old, and for 2 years for women under 50 years old.
- However, many women commence HRT, or are using hormonal contraception or a contraceptive method that renders them amenorrhoeic, prior to the menopause. This makes it difficult to know when the menopause has occurred and for how long contraception is necessary. Women often do not want to stop HRT for 6–8 weeks in order to check FSH levels. In this instance it is usually easiest to recommend that women continue using contraception until the age of 55 years, when sterility can be assumed [Gebbie, 2003].
- **Contraception for perimenopausal women taking HRT:** barrier methods of contraception, an intra-uterine device, or the levonorgestrel-releasing intra-uterine system are all suitable.
- **Perimenopausal women and COC:** women taking COC do not need to have HRT added. COC is only suitable for women over 35 years if they are non-smokers; without a family history of ischaemic heart disease in a first-degree relative; without a personal history of hyperlipidaemia, diabetes, hypertension; and are not obese.
- **Perimenopausal women and the progestogen-only contraceptive pill:** the progestogen-only pill (POP) is suitable throughout the menopause. Its use in combination with HRT has not been well evaluated, and it is unclear whether adding HRT may interfere with the contraceptive effect of the POP [Pitkin, 2000].

HRT use in women with comorbidity

Breast cancer

- **GPs should obtain specialist advice before prescribing HRT for women who have had breast cancer.**
- The Committee on Safety on Medicines has recently advised that HRT remains contraindicated in women who have had breast cancer. The limited available evidence is conflicting. Observational studies suggest that HRT use is not associated with an increased risk of recurrence in this group [Kenemans and Bosman, 2003; RCPE, 2003]. However a recent randomized study

reported an increased risk of recurrence [Holmberg and Anderson, 2004].

- Troublesome symptoms of oestrogen deficiency are common in women receiving treatment for breast cancer. HRT has been given with tamoxifen but should be avoided in women taking aromatase inhibitors (e.g. anastrazole) [RCPE, 2003].
- A range of non-hormonal treatments may be appropriate; see *What are the options for managing menopausal symptoms?* Note: some herbs commonly used for menopausal symptoms (e.g. red clover, black cohosh, ginseng) have estrogenic properties and should also be avoided.

Endometrial cancer

- **Advice from a specialist should be sought.**
- Management usually depends on the stage of the cancer; treatment with HRT is usually limited to women with stage I disease, although women with stage II disease are occasionally treated [Mueck and Seeger, 2003].
- In stage I endometrial cancer, specialists may advise that oestrogens can sometimes be used. Progestogens (in opposition to oestrogen or alone) may also be used.

Thromboembolic disease (personal or family history)

- **Women with a personal history of venous thromboembolism (VTE), with or without an underlying thrombophilia, should be referred to a specialist in thrombophilia.** Such women should avoid using oral HRT (in view of the relatively high risk of recurrent VTE) unless it is taken with anticoagulation therapy. Transdermal therapy may be better in this situation [Scarabin et al, 2003], but specialist advice should be sought [RCOG, 2004].
- Women over 50 years with a personal history of VTE within the previous year should be screened for malignancy and connective tissue disorders [RCOG, 2004].
- **Where a thrombophilic defect has been identified in a woman with a family history but no personal history of VTE, specialist advice for the individual is advisable.**
  - In general, women with antithrombin defects, or combinations of other clotting defects, should avoid HRT, unless it is taken with anticoagulation therapy (these women should be managed via specialist centres) [RCOG, 2004].
  - There is not enough evidence to recommend that women with other clotting defects completely avoid HRT. However, HRT should be avoided in the presence of multiple risk factors for VTE in these women (e.g. varicose veins, obesity). Seek advice from a specialist in thrombophilia [RCOG, 2004].

Other conditions

- **Migraine is not a contraindication to HRT.** Migraine often improves after natural menopause (although it often worsens after surgical menopause). There is no evidence that the risk of stroke is affected by the use of HRT in women with migraine, with or without aura [Bousser et al, 2000]. Some women find that HRT exacerbates migraine, and this can be caused by the oestrogen or the progestogen. See *Managing the adverse effects of HRT.*
- **Hypertension is not a contraindication to HRT.** There is no evidence that HRT elevates blood pressure or has an adverse effect in women with hypertension [Rees and Purdie, 2002].
- **Coronary heart disease (CHD):** HRT may increase the risk of CHD in women with or without a history of CHD, particularly in the first year of use. In general, HRT should not be started in women with active CHD, and consideration should be given to stopping HRT in any woman who has experienced a cardiovascular event. However, for some women with severe menopausal symptoms, the benefits of symptom relief may outweigh the possible increase in CHD events. HRT should not be prescribed for CHD prevention.
- **Diabetes:** use of HRT appears to increase the risk of CHD in women with diabetes [Lokkegaard et al, 2003]. If HRT is used, the transdermal route may be preferred because it has less impact on raised triglyceride levels than oral HRT.
- **Gallbladder disease, mild liver disease, and previous liver disease:** if HRT is to be used, a non-oral route of oestrogen therapy (usually transdermal) is preferred. Specialist advice should be sought, particularly for all cases of liver disease [Rees and Purdie, 2002].
- **Endometriosis:** there is no good evidence on which to base recommendations for using HRT, and specialist advice is usually recommended. Although HRT can theoretically reactivate the disease, this risk appears to be small [Rees and Purdie, 2002]. If the woman has had an oophorectomy as part of the treatment for severe endometriosis, some specialists avoid oestrogen alone for the first 6 months, others use progestogen alone, a continuous combined regimen, or tibolone.
- **Fibroids:** women should be advised that HRT may enlarge fibroids, causing heavy or painful withdrawal bleeds. Regular ultrasound examinations are recommended, initially at 6-monthly intervals, and annually thereafter if there is no marked increase in size [Rees and Purdie, 2002].
- **Asthma:** HRT does not worsen pre-existing asthma. However there seems to be a small increased risk of newly diagnosed asthma in women taking HRT [Barr et al, 2004].

Starting HRT

- **The decision to use HRT should be discussed with each woman on an individual basis,** taking into consideration her history, risk factors, and personal preferences [CSM, 2002].
- Ideally all perimenopausal women should be given the opportunity to discuss the menopause, and the potential role of HRT, alternatives to HRT, and lifestyle changes in their future lives.

Assessment of the woman prior to starting HRT

History taking and contraindication checking

- **Assess menopausal state:** stage of menopause (pre-, peri-, postmenopausal) and the time of the last menstrual period; bleeding pattern; presence or absence of acute menopausal symptoms; premature menopause (i.e. before age of 40 years); surgical menopause (bilateral oophorectomy); or chemotherapy- or radiation-induced menopause.
- **Check for contraindications in current or past medical history.** The following are all contraindications to starting HRT: hormone-dependent malignancy (e.g. endometrial cancer, current or past breast cancer); active or recent arterial thromboembolic disease (e.g. angina or myocardial infarction); venous thromboembolic disease; pulmonary embolism; current pregnancy; severe active liver disease; undiagnosed breast mass, and uninvestigated abnormal vaginal bleeding. See *HRT use in women with comorbidity.*
- **Check for conditions which may require treatment modification or specialist advice:** diabetes, arterial/thromboembolic disease, endometrial hyperplasia, endometriosis, fibroids, liver disease, or gallstones; see *HRT use in women with comorbidity.* Check for

coronary heart disease (CHD); HRT should not be prescribed for prevention of CHD.

- **Current contraception:** in perimenopausal woman taking the combined oral contraceptive pill, HRT should not be added. If they are taking the progestogen-only pill (POP), it is unclear whether adding HRT may interfere with the contraceptive effect of the POP. HRT does not provide contraceptive levels of hormones. For further advice on contraception during the perimenopause see the *HRT and contraception* section above.
- **Ask about family history** of cardiovascular disease, osteoporosis, venous thromboembolism, breast cancer, bowel cancer, and ovarian cancer.
- **Check risk factors for CHD:** consider calculating 10-year CHD risk in women with hypertension, diabetes mellitus, or a family history of premature myocardial infarction or stroke. Other risk factors for cardiovascular disease include cigarette smoking, sedentary lifestyle, and obesity.
- **Check risk factors for osteoporosis:** family history of osteoporosis; age over 60 years; early menopause; thin underweight build; oriental or Caucasian origin; sedentary lifestyle; smoking; prolonged corticosteroid use (3 months or more); excessive alcohol intake; low calcium intake; low vitamin D levels (lack of sunlight, malabsorption disorders, low dietary intake). A previous fragility fracture carries a high risk of further osteoporotic fractures.

[Rees and Purdie, 2002]

Examination

- **Body mass index and blood pressure** should be recorded [Rees and Purdie, 2002].
- **Breast examination should be carried out if indicated** by personal or family history. All women should be advised about breast awareness and be encouraged to participate in the national breast screening programme as appropriate for their age. Mammography has higher sensitivity and specificity than clinical examination [Working Group on Breast and Pelvic Examination, 2001].
- **Pelvic examination should be carried out if indicated** by personal history. All women should be encouraged to participate in the national cervical cancer screening programme as appropriate for their age [Working Group on Breast and Pelvic Examination, 2001].

Investigations

- **No investigations are routinely indicated before starting HRT.**
- **Investigations should be carried out if indicated. Consider:**
  - **Serial FSH** levels if premature menopause is suspected.
  - **Thrombophilia screening in** women with a personal or family history of venous thromboembolism [RCOG, 2004].
  - **Endometrial assessment in** the following situations: sudden change in menstrual pattern, intermenstrual bleeding, postcoital bleeding, or a postmenopausal bleed [Korhonen et al, 1997; Rees and Purdie, 2002].
  - **Mammography** if a woman is at high risk of breast cancer [Rees and Purdie, 2002].

Which hormones, which regimen, which route, which dose?

- This section provides information to help choose a suitable type of product for a woman who wishes to take systemic HRT, and has no contraindications to its use.
- **For women in whom hormones are contraindicated, or who do not wish to take oestrogen or progestogen,** see *What are the options for managing menopausal symptoms?*
- **For women with or without a uterus with urogenital symptoms** who require local treatment only, see *Urogenital symptoms.*

Which hormones?

- **Women without a uterus: oestrogen-only products are suitable.** Most products contain either estradiol or conjugated oestrogen, and may be considered as 'natural'.
- **Women with a uterus: oestrogen plus progestogen is recommended** for endometrial protection (combined HRT).
  - For most women contemplating use of HRT for menopausal symptoms, the small increased risk of breast cancer with short-term use of combined HRT, and the minimal risk of endometrial hyperplasia and cancer, will be outweighed by the benefits of symptom relief.
  - Oestrogen-only HRT has a lower risk of breast cancer than combined HRT, but a higher risk of endometrial cancer. For a few women this may be a more acceptable risk–benefit profile, and oestrogen-only HRT may be prescribed provided the woman is aware of, and willing to accept, these increased risks [CSM, 2003d]. However, we suggest that specialist advice is sought if this is being considered: bleeding and endometrial hyperplasia is more common with oestrogen-only HRT, and all episodes of vaginal bleeding will require investigation. In the PEPI trial, 62% of those taking 0.625 mg conjugated equine oestrogens alone had some form of hyperplasia at 3 years compared with 1.6% of those taking placebo. Conversely, endometrial hyperplasia rates were similar to those with placebo for women given oestrogen with a progestogen [Writing Group for the PEPI Trial, 1996].
- **Choice of progestogen:** women vary in their tolerance to progestogens. The less androgenic 17-hydroxyprogesterone derivatives (medroxyprogesterone, dydrogesterone) are sometimes better tolerated than the more androgenic 19-nortestosterone derivatives (norethisterone, levonorgestrel).
  - Combined HRT tablets contain medroxyprogesterone or dydrogesterone (less androgenic), or norethisterone or levonorgestrel (more androgenic).
  - Combined HRT patches only contain norethisterone or levonorgestrel (more androgenic). There are currently no patches containing less androgenic progestogens.
  - The levonorgestrel-releasing intra-uterine system is an alternative route of delivery of progestogen to protect the endometrium. Since levonorgestrel is delivered locally to the uterus, a much lower daily dose is used, which also results in low systemic levels of levonorgestrel.
- **Tibolone is an alternative to combined HRT for postmenopausal women.** (It is a synthetic oral steroid with mixed oestrogenic, progestogenic, and androgenic actions.)
- **Androgen** (testosterone) implants may be used to improve libido, but are not always successful as other factors may account for the low sex drive [Rees and Purdie, 2002]. They have mainly been shown to be of benefit in women with surgical menopause. Specialist advice should be sought as a wide range of doses, with potentially serious adverse effects, are quoted in the literature [ICSI, 2003].

Which regimen?

- **Oestrogen-only HRT is usually taken continuously.**
- **Combined HRT** is available as cyclical or continuous regimens. It is only suitable for women with an intact uterus:
  - **Perimenopausal: monthly cyclical regimens** with oestrogen given daily plus progestogen given at the end of the cycle are usually recommended. They produce a predictable withdrawal bleed, whereas continuous regimens often cause unpredictable bleeding in this group. A 3-monthly cyclical regimen is also available, but is generally reserved for women who suffer from progestogen-related adverse effects, as the endometrial protective effect of 3-monthly progestogens is less well studied.
  - **Postmenopausal: monthly cyclical regimens** can be taken by postmenopausal women, and will produce a predictable withdrawal bleed. The 3-monthly cyclical regimen should be reseved as an option for women who suffer from progestogen-related adverse effects. **Continuous combined regimens** are also suitable for postmenopausal women (i.e. at least 12 months since the last menstrual period). They induce endometrial atrophy and so do not produce a withdrawal bleed, although irregular bleeding or spotting can occur in the first 4–6 months of treatment. Bleeding should be investigated if it persists beyond 6 months, if it becomes heavier rather than less, or it if occurs after amenorrhoea. **Tibolone** is an alternative no-bleed regimen for postmenopausal women.
- **Adherence to combined HRT:** it is preferable for the oestrogen and progestogen to be in combined form, because the adverse effects of the progestogen may lead to poor compliance if this component is given separately. If oestrogen and progestogen are given separately, an explanation about the endometrial protective effect of progestogens is important to ensure compliance.

M

Which route?

Oral HRT (oestrogen with or without progestogen)

- **Oral products are usually the cheapest form of HRT.** Tablets are available as oestrogen alone, or oestrogen combined with progestogen (cyclical or continuous combined).
- Oestrogen is given as estradiol, conjugated oestrogen, or estriol. Oral oestrogen undergoes first-pass metabolism in the liver, so the level of oestrogen in the body varies from individual to individual.
- **The oral route should be avoided in women taking hepatic enzyme-inducing drugs.**
- Oral oestrogens are more likely to cause nausea than other forms of oestrogen.
- Progestogens (for women with a uterus) are either included in the oestrogen tablet, or given as an additional tablet.

Transdermal HRT (oestrogen with or without progestogen)

- Oestrogen-only products (given as estradiol) are available as patches or gels. Combined HRT (cyclical or continuous combined oestrogen plus progestogen) is only available as patches. Note: the progestogen is either combined into the patch, or given separately as a tablet.
- Hormone levels delivered by patch are more constant than if given orally: oestrogen is absorbed directly through the skin into the systemic circulation, bypassing the liver.
- **Some patches come in four strengths of oestrogen, allowing titration to the optimal dose.**
- Patches are usually placed on the buttocks. Skin reactions are more common with reservoir patches (Estraderm TTS®, Estracombi®), but most are now matrix patches [Rees and Purdie, 2002].
- Some patches may not stick well to different skin types. Some companies produce placebo patches that women can try out.

Intranasal (oestrogen only)

- While most HRT products are designed to deliver continuous oestrogen levels, intranasal HRT has a unique pulse-like pharmacokinetic profile. It is currently a black triangle drug.
- Estradiol-intranasal 300 micrograms daily seems to have similar efficacy and tolerability to oral estradiol 2 mg daily and transdermal estradiol 50 micrograms daily. Nasal symptoms (itching, rhinorrhea, sneezing, nosebleeds) and mastalgia were the most commonly reported adverse effects. However, a blocked or streaming nose does not affect efficacy [Dooley et al, 2001].

Implants (oestrogen only)

- Estradiol implants can be inserted subcutaneously under local anaesthetic.
- Implants release estradiol over many months so the woman does not have to remember to take medication. However, they can scar the skin and cannot be easily removed.
- **Implants may cause tachyphylaxis,** where menopausal symptoms such as hot flushes may recur even when the implant is releasing adequate levels of estradiol [Garnett et al, 1990]. There are also concerns that implants may remain effective for many years.
- Checking that plasma estradiol levels have returned to within the normal range (less than 1000 pmol/L) before inserting a new implant is helpful, especially if symptoms have returned more quickly than usual. This will prevent implantation of more oestrogen when oestrogen levels are still high but flushing symptoms have returned due to tachyphylaxis.

Intra-uterine system (progestogen)

- **The levonorgestrel-releasing intra-uterine system is an alternative route for giving a progestogen** for endometrial protection from the oestrogen [Rees and Purdie, 2002].
- It can provide contraception in perimenopausal women.
- It is the only way that a 'no-bleed' regimen can be achieved in a perimenopausal woman, and can help with idiopathic menorrhagia.

Vaginal oestrogens

- **Low-dose vaginal estradiol or estriol is used for local treatment of urogenital symptoms.** Systemic absorption is very low so they do not relieve other menopausal symptoms such as hot flushes. Estriol is available as vaginal creams, while estradiol is available as vaginal tablets, or the Estring® vaginal ring.
- The Committee on Safety of Medicines has recently advised that [CSM, 2003b]:
  - Topical oestrogens should be used in the lowest effective amount to minimize systemic absorption, i.e. after 2–3 weeks initial therapy, reduce the application frequency of pessaries and creams to twice-weekly.
  - Treatment should be interrupted at least annually to reassess the need for continued treatment.
  - If breakthrough bleeding or spotting appears at any time on therapy, this should be investigated possibly with endometrial biopsy to exclude endometrial malignancy.
- Available studies have found no significant association between the use of low-potency vaginal oestrogens and the relative risk of endometrial cancer [Weiderpass et al, 1999a; Simunic et al, 2003]. Expert consensus is that addition of a progestogen is not necessary for endometrial protection.

- **Topical conjugated equine oestrogens are best avoided** in women with an intact uterus, as higher systemic absorption may potentially result in endometrial stimulation. If used on a long-term basis, an oral progestogen should be taken for 12–14 days of each month for endometrial protection [BNF 48, 2004].
- **The Menoring 50® vaginal ring has sufficient systemic absorption to treat vasomotor symptoms** such as hot flushes and sweats, and urogential symptoms. It is an oestrogen-only product, so should only be used by women who have had a hysterectomy unless a progestogen is given separately for endometrial protection.

Which dose?

Oestrogen dose

- **The lowest dose of oestrogen that controls symptoms should be used.** In general, older women may be less tolerant of oestrogen and need to start (and are usually maintained) on a lower dose (e.g. oral estradiol 1 mg, or transdermal estradiol 25–50 micrograms). Younger women may require higher doses to remain symptom-free [Rees and Purdie, 2002].
- For those women who need symptomatic treatment and also wish to use HRT to prevent osteoporosis during this time, the lowest dose that controls menopausal symptoms should still be used. Once treatment of menopausal symptoms is no longer required, therapy for preventing osteoporosis should be reviewed and HRT considered as a second-line choice.
- Note: the 'standard' bone-conserving doses of oestrogen were considered to be estradiol 2 mg, conjugated equine estrogens 0.625 mg, and transdermal 50 microgram patches. However, there is limited evidence that half these doses also conserve bone mass [British Menopause Society, 2003].

Progestogen dose

- Although the optimal number of days of progestogen is still debated, it is generally accepted that continuous progestogen therapy, or cyclical therapy for the last 12–14 days of a 28-day cycle, provide adequate endometrial protection [Pike et al, 1997; CSM, 2004a].
- The daily dosages of progestogens used in combined HRT products are considered to provide adequate endometrial protection. See Table 5 for further information.
- **Progestogen type or dosages may need to be altered if adverse effects are a problem.** See *Managing the adverse effects of HRT*.
- Levonorgestrel can be delivered directly to the uterus via the levonorgestrel intra-uterine system.

Tibolone dose

- The standard dose is 2.5 mg daily.

Managing the adverse effects of HRT

- **Adverse effects account for almost 35% of HRT discontinuations.** There are no good quality clinical trials on management of adverse effects. The following recommendations are based on consensus [Rees and Purdie, 2002].

Weight gain

- **Meta-analysis has shown no effect of HRT on weight,** indicating that these regimens do not cause extra weight gain in addition to that normally gained at menopause [Norman et al, 2004].

Bleeding

- **Bleeding should always be carefully assessed,** and further investigation or referral should be organized as appropriate.

Table 5: Accepted endometrial protection doses of progestogen.

Progestogen type and route	Accepted endometrial protection dosage
Cyclical preparations	
Norethisterone oral	1 mg for last 12–14 days of 28-day cycle
Norethisterone patch	170–250 micrograms for last 14 days of a 28-day cycle
Levonorgestrel oral	75–250 micrograms for last 12 days of 28-day cycle
Levonorgestrel patch	10 micrograms for last 14 days of 28-day cycle
Norgestrel oral	150–500 micrograms for last 12 days of 28-day cycle
Medroxyprogesterone acetate oral	10 mg for last 14 days of 28-day cycle 20 mg for last 14 days of 3-month cycle
Dydrogesterone oral	10–20 mg for last 14 days of 28-day cycle
Continuous regimens	
Norethisterone oral	0.5–1 mg
Norethisterone patch	170 micrograms
Levonorgestrel patch	7 micrograms
Medroxyprogesterone acetate oral	2.5–5 mg
Dydrogesterone	5 mg

- **Often bleeding problems may be product-related,** and a change to the HRT regimen may be needed. See the *product-related bleeding* sections below for suggested approaches. Also consider stopping therapy to see whether the bleeding is product-related.
- **Investigation to exclude pathology is needed if there is:**
  - A change in the pattern of withdrawal bleeds and breakthrough bleeding that persists for more than 3 months on monthly cyclical regimens.
  - Bleeding that persists beyond 6 months, and bleeding that starts in women previously amenorrhoeic receiving continuous combined regimens.
  - Persistent or unexplained postmenopausal bleeding after stopping HRT for 6 weeks. (Referral guidelines for suspected cancer recommend urgent referral to a team specialising in the management of gynaecological cancer, depending on local arrangements [NICE, 2005].)

Product-related bleeding on monthly cyclical/sequential regimens

- **Monthly cyclical regimens should produce regular predictable bleeds** starting towards or soon after the end of the progestogen phase.
- Unpredictable or unacceptable bleeding may be due to non-adherence to therapy, drug interactions, or gastrointestinal upset (or malignancy if not already excluded).
- **Bleeding problems may be improved by altering the progestogen part of the regimen:**
  - **Heavy or prolonged bleeding:** increase the duration or dosage of the progestogen or change the type of progestogen. Idiopathic menorrhagia may be helped by using the levonorgestrel-releasing intra-uterine system combined with an oestrogen delivered either orally or transdermally.
  - **Bleeding early in the progestogen phase:** increase dosage or change the type of progestogen.
  - **Painful bleeding:** change the type of progestogen.
  - **Irregular bleeding:** change regimen or increase the dosage of progestogen.
  - **No bleeding whilst taking a cyclical regimen** reflects an atrophic endometrium and occurs in 5% of women. Pregnancy needs to be excluded in perimenopausal

women. Check compliance if the progestogen component is taken separately.
  - **If these treatments do not help,** pelvic pathology must be excluded.

Bleeding on continuous combined HRT or during long-cycle HRT regimens

- **Irregular breakthrough bleeding or spotting** is common in the first 3–6 months of therapy, but bleeding beyond 6 months needs further investigation.
- Note: continuous combined regimens are only suitable for postmenopausal women (i.e. at least 12 months since the last menstrual period). Long-cycle regimens are most suitable for women with scant natural menstruation.

Oestrogen-related adverse effects

- **Oestrogen-related adverse effects tend to occur continuously or randomly** through the cycle. They include fluid retention, bloating, breast tenderness/enlargement, nausea, headaches, leg cramps, and dyspepsia.
- **Encourage the woman to persist with therapy for about 3 months** to await resolution, as most adverse effects resolve with increased duration of use.
  - **Leg cramps** can improve with lifestyle changes including exercise and regular stretching of the calf muscles.
  - **Nausea/gastric upset** may be helped by adjusting the timing of the oestrogen dosage or taking with food.
  - **Breast tenderness** may be alleviated by a low-fat, high-carbohydrate diet [Bundred, 2003]. Gamolenic acid (evening primrose oil) is no longer available as a licensed medicinal product because of lack of efficacy.
  - **Migraine** triggered by fluctuating oestrogen levels may respond to transdermal therapy as this produces more stable oestrogen levels.
- **For persistent adverse effects consider either:**
  - Reducing the dosage first or
  - **Changing the oestrogen type** (e.g. swap between the two main forms of oestrogen, that is, estradiol and conjugated oestrogens) or
  - **Changing the route** of delivery (e.g. tablets may cause nausea, but patches generally do not).

M

Progestogen-related adverse effects (other than bleeding)

- **Progestogen-related adverse effects tend to occur in a cyclical pattern** during the progestogen phase of cyclical HRT. They include fluid retention, breast tenderness, headaches/migraine, mood swings, depression, acne, lower abdominal pain, and backache. Bleeding adverse effects are covered in *Bleeding* above.
- **Encourage the woman to persist with therapy for about 3 months** to await possible resolution of adverse effects.
- **For persistent or troublesome symptoms** consider the following options (note that many of these are the opposite of what may be needed to give better bleeding control):
  - **Reducing the duration:** progestogens can be taken for 12–14 days of each monthly sequential regimen, so swapping from a 14-day to a 12-day product may provide benefit.
  - **Reducing the dosage of progestogen** if not already on the lowest dosage (but not below the recommended levels for endometrial protection — dosages are preparation-dependent).
  - **Changing the progestogen type** (e.g. changing from more androgenic ones, such as norethisterone and norgestrel, to less androgenic ones, such as medroxyprogesterone or dydrogesterone).
  - **Changing the route of progestogen,** for example from oral to transdermal, vaginal, or intra-uterine progestogen. (This may be most beneficial when the woman is nauseous receiving oral HRT.) If the oestrogen is to be delivered by a different route to the progestogen, it is easy for the woman to intentionally miss out the progestogen if it is causing unpleasant adverse effects. The woman must, therefore, fully understand that the progestogen is being given to provide endometrial protection.
  - **Reducing the frequency** of progestogen dosing. This can be achieved by switching to a long-cycle regimen administering progestogen for 14 days every 3 months (but only suitable for postmenopausal women or those with scanty periods).
  - **Changing to continuous combined therapy** often reduces progestogenic adverse effects with established use (as these products contain lower dosages of progestogen), but is only suitable for postmenopausal women.

Monitoring and follow-up of women receiving HRT

- **If new HRT has been started, 3-month follow-up is recommended.** This allows adequate time for adverse effects to settle. Subsequent follow-up should be tailored to the individual woman, for example 6-monthly or annual [Rees and Purdie, 2002].
- **All women should be reviewed at least annually,** as the risks and benefits of HRT for each individual woman will alter with time, and need to be discussed on an annual basis [RCPE, 2003].
- **Blood pressure monitoring is not routinely needed** but opportunistic screening is useful. Women with pre-existing hypertension should be followed up according to the PRODIGY *Hypertension* guidance.
- **Breast examination should be carried out if indicated** by personal or family history. All women should be advised about breast awareness and be encouraged to participate in the national breast screening programme as appropriate for their age. Mammography has higher sensitivity and specificity than clinical examination [Working Group on Breast and Pelvic Examination, 2001].
- **Pelvic examination should be carried out if indicated** by personal history. All women should be encouraged to participate in the national cervical cancer screening programme as appropriate for their age [Working Group on Breast and Pelvic Examination, 2001].
- **Adverse effects should be managed at follow-up,** and are covered in *Managing the adverse effects of HRT* above.

Changing HRT

- Adverse effects may necessitate a change in dose, hormone type, or route, and are covered in *Managing the adverse effects of HRT*.
- Some women may wish to change from a cyclical regimen to a continuous combined regimen once they are postmenopausal. In practice, a postmenopausal state (which can be only be declared after 12 months of spontaneous amenorrhoea) is difficult to assess in women who started HRT in the perimenopause. However, it has been estimated that by the age of 54 years, 80% of women are postmenopausal. It is also likely that a woman who has experienced 6 months' amenorrhoea or had an elevated FSH level in her mid 40s is postmenopausal after taking several years of monthly sequential HRT [Rees and Purdie, 2002].
- Women taking HRT who undergo a hysterectomy no longer need to take combined regimens and can change to an oestrogen-only product.

Stopping HRT

- **All women should be reviewed annually** as the risks and benefits of HRT will alter with time [RCPE, 2003].
- Although menopausal symptoms usually resolve within 2–5 years, some women experience symptoms for many years [RCPE, 2003].
- **HRT can be withdrawn once the woman is no longer bothered by symptoms.**
  - **In practice,** if a woman is symptom-free on HRT, a trial withdrawal can be undertaken after 1–2 years of therapy. Women should be advised that symptoms sometimes recur once HRT is stopped.
  - If a woman has already taken HRT for 5 years, it is also worth undertaking a trial withdrawal.
- Many women do not notice any symptoms even with abrupt cessation of HRT, while others may experience a recurrence of hot flushes and sweats. In older women, sleep disorders, rather than hot flushes may be the major manifestation of renewed menopausal symptoms [ICSI, 2003].
- **Many experts suggest that HRT should be gradually reduced rather than stopped abruptly.** Some suggested strategies are listed below [Mansour, Personal Communication, 2004]:
  - **Oestrogen-only tablets:** reduce to a 1 mg tablet for 1–2 months, then use 1 mg on alternate days for a further 1–2 months.
  - **Oestrogen-only patches:** reduce the dose gradually to 25 micrograms daily (e.g. stepping the dose down a patch strength each month). Half a matrix-type patch (12.5 micrograms daily) can be used for a further 1–2 months.
  - **Cyclical combined HRT tablets:** reduce to a cyclical HRT pack containing 1 mg estradiol for 1–2 months. Alternate-day dosing can then be used for the next 1–2 months: taking alternate tablets from the calendar pack will ensure that the woman still receives oestrogen combined with a progestogen for part of the cycle.
  - **Cyclical combined HRT patches:** reduce the dose as for oestrogen-only patches, but ensure that the woman still uses the oestrogen-only patches for 2 weeks of the cycle followed by the combined patches for a further 2 weeks, to ensure endometrial protection.
  - **Continuous combined HRT tablets or patches:** reduce the dose gradually every 1–2 months to the lowest strength tablet or patch. Then one tablet is taken on alternate days (or half a patch is used daily) for a further 1–2 months.
- **Asses risk factors for osteoporosis and discuss alternatives** for preventing or treating osteoporosis (including diet and lifestyle advice) at this time. See the *patient information leaflets*, or the PRODIGY guidance *Osteoporosis — treatment* for further information.
- **If symptoms are severe after HRT is stopped, or persist for several months after stopping, the woman may** wish to restart HRT after reassessment and counselling. Often a lower dose of HRT can be used (e.g. estradiol 1 mg) if HRT is restarted.
- **Women with premature menopause** usually take HRT up to the age of 50 years. HRT is usually withdrawn at this time.
- Some women (with either premature or 'natural' menopause) may wish to continue with HRT to prevent osteoporosis (although they should be made aware of alternative options for the prevention and treatment of osteoporosis, and that bone loss will begin as soon as HRT is stopped).
- **Women who choose to take HRT for more than 5 years should be counselled about the long-term risks** [RCPE, 2003].

References

NHS staff in England can link, free of charge, from references to full text journals by clicking on [Full text] on the PRODIGY website.

1. American Association of Clinical Endocrinologists (1999) *AACE American Association of Clinical Endocrinologists medical guidelines for clinical practice for management of menopause.* American Association of Clinical Endocrinologists. www.aace.com [Accessed: 14/08/2003].
2. Barr, R.G., Wentowski, C.C., Grodstein, F. et al (2004) Prospective study of postmenopausal hormone use and newly diagnosed asthma and chronic obstructive pulmonary disease. *Archives of Internal Medicine* **164**(4), 379–386. [Full text]
3. Barton, D., La Vasseur, B., Loprinzi, C. et al (2002) Venlafaxine for the control of hot flashes: results of a longitudinal continuation study. *Oncology Nursing Forum* **29**(1), 33–40.
4. Beksinska, M.E., Smit, J.A., Kleinschmidt, I. et al (2003) Detection of raised FSH levels among older women using depomedroxyprogesterone acetate and norethisterone enanthate. *Contraception* **68**(5), 339–343.
5. Beral, V., Banks, E. and Reeves, G. (2002) Evidence from randomized trials on the long-term effects of hormone replacement therapy. *Lancet* **360**(9337), 942–944. [Full text]
6. BNF 48 (2004) *British National Formulary.* 48th edn. London: British Medical Association and Royal Pharmaceutical Society of Great Britain.
7. Bousser, M.G., Conard, J., Kittner, S. et al (2000) Recommendations on the risk of ischaemic stroke associated with use of combined oral contraceptives and hormone replacement therapy in women with migraine. The International Headache Society Task Force on Combined Oral Contraceptives & Hormone Replacement Therapy. *Cephalalgia* **20**(3), 155–156.
8. British Menopause Society (2003) *Managing the menopause. British Menopause Society Council consensus statement on hormone replacement therapy.* The British Menopause Society. www.the-bms.org [Accessed: 13/10/2003].
9. Bundred, N. (2003) Breast pain. *Clinical Evidence* **10**(Dec), 2034–2043.
10. Cardozo, L., Bachmann, G., McClish, D. et al (1998) Meta-analysis of estrogen therapy in the management of urogenital atrophy in postmenopausal women: second report of the Hormones and Urogenital Therapy Committee. *Obstetrics & Gynecology* **92**(4 Pt 2), 722–727.
11. Collaborative Group on Hormonal Factors in Breast Cancer (1997) Breast cancer and hormone replacement therapy: a collaborative reanalysis of data from 51 epidemiological studies of 52 705 women with breast cancer and 108 411 women without breast cancer. *Lancet* **350**(9084), 1047–1059. [Full text]
12. CSM (2002) Safety update on long-term HRT. *Current Problems in Pharmacovigilance* **28**(Oct), 11–12.
13. CSM (2003a) HRT: update on the risk of breast cancer and long-term safety. *Current Problems in Pharmacovigilance* **29**(9), 1–3.
14. CSM (2003b) Topical and vaginal oestrogens: endometrial safety. *Current Problems in Pharmacovigilance* **29**(9), 3.
15. CSM (2003c) *Further advice on safety of HRT: risk/benefit unfavourable for first-line use in prevention of osteoporosis.* CEM/CMO/2003/19. Committee on Safety of Medicines. www.mca.gov.uk/aboutagency/

M

regframework/csm/csmhome.htm [Accessed: 09/01/2004].
16. CSM (2003d) *Million Women Study.* Committee on Safety of Medicines. www.mca.gov.uk/aboutagency/regframework/csm/csmhome.htm [Accessed: 24/05/2004].
17. CSM (2003e) Kava-kava and hepatotoxicity. *Current Problems in Pharmacovigilance* 29(Sep), 8.
18. CSM (2004a) Review of the evidence regarding long-term safety of HRT. *Current Problems in Pharmacovigilance* 30(Oct), 4–7.
19. CSM (2004b) Black cohosh (cimicifuga racemosa) and hepatotoxicity. *Current Problems in Pharmacovigilance* 30(Oct), 10.
20. Dooley, M., Spencer, C.M. and Ormrod, D. (2001) Estradiol-intranasal: a review of its use in the management of menopause. *Drugs* **61**(15), 2243–2262.
21. DTB (1996) Hormone replacement therapy. *Drug & Therapeutics Bulletin* **34**(11), 81–84.
22. Erkkola, R., Kumento, U., Lehmuskoski, S. et al (2004) No increased risk of endometrial hyperplasia with fixed long-cycle oestrogen-progestogen therapy after 5 years. *Journal of the British Menopause Society* **10**(1), 9–13.
23. Ernst, E. (2001) *Desktop guide to complementary and alternative medicine.* London: Mosby.
24. Garnett, T., Studd, J.W., Henderson, A. et al (1990) Hormone implants and tachyphylaxis. *British Journal of Obstetrics & Gynaecology* **97**(10), 917–921.
25. Gebbie, A. (2003) Contraception in the perimenopause. *Journal of the British Menopause Society* **9**(3), 123–128.
26. Grady, D., Herrington, D., Bittner, V. et al (2002) Cardiovascular disease outcomes during 6.8 years of hormone therapy. Heart and Estrogen/Progestin Replacement Study Follow-up (HERSII). *Journal of the American Medical Association* **288**(1), 49–57. [Full text]
27. Grodstein, F., Manson, J.E., Colditz, G.A. et al (2000) A prospective, observational study of postmenopausal hormone therapy and primary prevention of cardiovascular disease. *Annals of Internal Medicine* **133**(12), 933–941.
28. Holmberg, L. and Anderson, H. (2004) HABITS (hormonal replacement therapy after breast cancer – is it safe?), a randomized comparison: trial stopped. *Lancet* **363**(9407), 453–455. [Full text]
29. Huntley, A.L. and Ernst, E. (2003) A systematic review of herbal medicinal products for the treatment of menopausal symptoms. *Menopause* **10**(5), 465–476.
30. ICSI (2003) *Menopause and hormone therapy (HT): collaborative decision-making and management.* Healthcare Guideline: fifth edition. Institute for Clinical Systems Improvement. www.icsi.org [Accessed: 23/01/2004]. [Full text]
31. Kenemans, P. and Bosman, A. (2003) Breast cancer and post-menopausal hormone therapy. *Best Practice & Research Clinical Endocrinology & Metabolism* **17**(1), 123–137.
32. Korhonen, M.O., Symons, J.P., Hyde, B.M. et al (1997) Histologic classification and pathologic findings for endometrial biopsy specimens obtained from 2964 perimenopausal and postmenopausal women undergoing screening for continuous hormones as replacement therapy (CHART 2 study). *American Journal of Obstetrics & Gynecology* **176**(2), 377–380.
33. Kronenberg, F. and Fugh-Berman, A. (2002) Complementary and alternative medicine for menopausal symptoms: a review of randomized, controlled trials. *Annals of Internal Medicine* **137**(10), 805–813. [Full text]
34. Lethaby, A., Farquhar, C., Sarkis, A. et al (2004) *Hormone replacement therapy in postmenopausal women: endometrial hyperplasia and irregular bleeding (Cochrane Review).* The Cochrane Library. Issue 1. Chichester, UK: John Wiley & Sons, Ltd.
35. Lokkegaard, E., Pedersen, A.T., Heitmann, B.L. et al (2003) Relation between hormone replacement therapy and ischaemic heart disease in women: prospective observational study. *British Medical Journal* **326**(7386), 426–430. [Full text]
36. MacLennan, A., Lester, S. and Moore, V. (2004) *Oral oestrogen replacement therapy versus placebo for hot flashes (Cochrane Review).* The Cochrane Library. Issue 1. Chichester, UK: John Wiley & Sons, Ltd.
37. Manson, J.E., Hsia, J., Johnson, K.C. et al (2003) Estrogen plus progestin and the risk of coronary heart disease. *New England Journal of Medicine* **349**(6), 523–534. [Full text]
38. Mansour, D. (2004) *Personal communication. Coming off HRT.* Consultant in Community Gynaecology and Reproductive Health Care, Newcastle upon Tyne.
39. McKinlay, S.M., Brambilla, D.J. and Posner, J.G. (1992) The normal menopause transition. *Maturitas* **14**(2), 103–115.
40. Michaelsson, K., Baron, J.A., Farahmand, B.Y. et al (1998) Hormone replacement therapy and risk of hip fracture: population based case-control study. *British Medical Journal* **316**(7148), 1858–1863. [Full text]
41. Miller, J., Chan, B.K. and Nelson, H.D. (2002) Postmenopausal estrogen replacement and risk for venous thromboembolism: a systematic review and meta-analysis for the U.S. Preventive Services Task Force. *Annals of Internal Medicine* **136**(9), 680–690. [erratum appears in: Ann Intern Med (2003) 138(4), 360.].
42. Million Women Study Collaborators (2003) Breast cancer and hormone-replacement therapy in the Million Women Study. *Lancet* **362**(9382), 419–427. [Full text]
43. Modelska, K. and Cummings, S. (2002) Tibolone for postmenopausal women: systematic review of randomized trials. *Journal of Clinical Endocrinology & Metabolism* **87**(1), 16–23.
44. Moehrer, B., Hextall, A. and Jackson, S. (2004) *Oestrogens for urinary incontinence in women (Cochrane Review).* The Cochrane Library. Issue 1. Chichester, UK: John Wiley & Sons, Ltd.
45. Mueck, A.O. and Seeger, H. (2003) Hormone therapy after endometrial cancer. *Journal of the British Menopause Society* **9**(4), 161–166.
46. NICE (2005) *Referral guidelines for suspected cancer – quick reference guide.* Clinical guideline 27. National Institute for Health and Clinical Excellence. www.nice.org.uk [Accessed: 01/07/2005].
47. Norman, R.J., Flight, I.H.K. and Rees, M.C.P. (2004) *Oestrogen and progestogen hormone replacement therapy for peri-menopausal and post-menopausal women: weight and body fat distribution (Cochrane Review).* The Cochrane Library. Issue 1. Chichester, UK: John Wiley & Sons, Ltd.
48. Panay, N. (2004) Hormone replacement therapy: the way forward. *Journal of Family Planning and Reproductive Health Care* **30**(1), 21–24.
49. Pike, M.C., Peters, R.K., Cozen, W. et al (1997) Estrogen-progestin replacement therapy and endometrial cancer. *Journal of the National Cancer Institute* **89**(15), 1110–1116. [Full text]
50. Pitkin, J. (2000) Contraception and the menopause. *Maturitas* **34**(Suppl 1), S29-S36.
51. Pukkala, E., Tulenheimo-Solfvast, A. and Leminen, A. (2001) Incidence of cancer among women using long versus monthly cycle hormonal replacement therapy, Finland 1994–1997. *Cancer Causes & Control* **12**(2), 111–115. [Full text]

M

52. RCOG (2004) *Hormone replacement therapy and venous thromboembolism.* Guideline 19. Royal College of Obstetricians and Gynaecologists. www.rcog.org.uk [Accessed: 24/05/2004].
53. RCPE (2003) *Consensus conference on hormone replacement therapy, October 2003. Final consensus statement.* Royal College of Physicians of Edinburgh. www.rcpe.ac.uk [Accessed: 13/10/2003].
54. Rees, M. and Purdie, D.W (Eds.) (2002) *Management of the menopause: the handbook of the British Menopause Society.* 3rd edn. London: BMS Publications Ltd.
55. Robinson, D. and Cardozo, L. (2003) Urogenital effects of hormone therapy. *Best Practice & Research Clinical Endocrinology & Metabolism* 17(1), 91–104.
56. Scarabin, P.Y., Oger, E., Plu-Bureau, G. and the EStrogen and THromboEmbolism Risk (ESTHER) study group (2003) Differential association of oral and transdermal oestrogen-replacement therapy with venous thromboembolism risk. *Lancet* **362**(9382), 428–432. [Full text]
57. Simunic, V., Banovic, I., Ciglar, S. et al (2003) Local estrogen treatment in patients with urogenital symptoms. *International Journal of Gynaecology & Obstetrics* **82**(2), 187–197.
58. Stearns, V., Beebe, K.L., Lyengar, M. and Dube, E. (2003) Paroxetine controlled release in the treatment of menopausal hot flashes: a randomized controlled trial. *Journal of the American Medical Association* **289**(21), 2827–2834. [Full text]
59. The ESPRIT team (2002) Oestrogen therapy for prevention of reinfarction in postmenopausal women: a randomised placebo controlled trial. *Lancet* **360**(9350), 2001–2008. [Full text]
60. Weiderpass, E., Baron, J.A. and Adami, H.O. (1999a) Low-potency oestrogen and risk of endometrial cancer: a case-control study. *Lancet* **353**(9167), 1824–1828. [Full text]
61. Weiderpass, E., Adami, H.O., Baron, J.A. et al (1999b) Risk of endometrial cancer following estrogen replacement with and without progestins. *Journal of the National Cancer Institute* **91**(13), 1131–1137. [Full text]
62. Women's Health Initiative (2002) Risks and benefits of estrogen plus progestin in healthy postmenopausal women. Principal results from the Women's Health Initiative randomized controlled trial. *Journal of the American Medical Association* **288**(3), 321–333. [Full text]
63. Women's Health Initiative (2004) Effects of conjugated equine estrogen in postmenopausal women with hysterectomy: the Women's Health Initiative randomized controlled trial. *Journal of the American Medical Association* **291**(14), 1701–1712. [Full text]
64. Working Group on Breast and Pelvic Examination (2001) *Breast and pelvic examination in women taking hormone replacement therapy – working group report.* London: Medicines Control Agency.
65. Writing Group for the PEPI Trial (1996) Effects of hormone replacement therapy on endometrial histology in postmenopausal women. The Postmenopausal Estrogen/Progestin Interventions (PEPI) Trial. *Journal of the American Medical Association* **275**(5), 370–375. [Full text]

M

PRODIGY GUIDANCE

Menorrhagia

Last revised in July 2005
www.prodigy.nhs.uk/guidance.asp?gt=Menorrhagia

Applies to women over the age of 12 years

This guidance is based on guidelines published in 1998 by the Royal College of Obstetricians and Gynaecologists (RCOG), *The initial management of menorrhagia: evidence-based clinical guideline no. 1.* This guidance also incorporates the recommendations of the Faculty of Family Planning and Reproductive Health Care (FFPRHC) guidelines, *The Levonorgestrel-releasing intra-uterine system (LNG-IUS) in contraception and reproductive health* (April 2004) and *First Prescription of Combined Oral Contraception* (October 2003). The guidance covers the medical management of menorrhagia.

This guidance does not cover the management of intermenstrual or irregular bleeding, postcoital bleeding, postmenopausal bleeding, or menopausal symptoms. Detailed information about contraceptives that are recommended for the treatment of menorrhagia is available in the PRODIGY guidance on *Contraception.*

There is separate PRODIGY guidance for *Amenorrhoea, Anaemia — iron deficiency, Contraception, Dysmenorrhoea, Endometriosis, Infertility,* and *Menopause.*

Goals

- To reduce or stop excessive menstrual bleeding
- To prevent or correct iron-deficiency anaemia
- To refer women who may benefit from surgical treatments

Contents

Scenarios

- Menorrhagia p.1214
- Copper IUD in situ p.1217

Extended Information, p. 1220

Which scenario?

- **Menorrhagia:** covers the management of menorrhagia in women who do not have a copper intra-uterine device *in situ.*
- **Copper IUD *in situ*:** covers the management of menorrhagia in women who have a copper intra-uterine device (IUD).

Menorrhagia

Which therapy?

- **Consider an underlying gynaecological disorder** (e.g. pelvic inflammatory disease, endometriosis, endometrial carcinoma) **or systemic disease** (e.g. hypothyroidism, coagulation disorder) and manage appropriately.
- **Check a full blood count** and treat anaemia if present.
- **Tranexamic acid** is generally the treatment of first choice (reduces blood loss by 50%).
- **Ibuprofen, mefenamic acid, or naproxen** are alternative choices. Nonsteroidal anti-inflammatory drugs (NSAIDs) reduce blood loss by 20–50%.
- **Tranexamic acid and an NSAID** may be prescribed concurrently in women with heavy bleeding and associated dysmenorrhoea. The addition of an NSAID may be necessary, as tranexamic acid will offer no pain relief and can be prescribed for only up to 4 days.
- **Consider hormonal contraceptives, particularly if contraception is required:**
  - The levonorgestrel intra-uterine system (LNG-IUS) (reduces blood loss by 90%, with 20% of women amenorrhoeic after 1 year).
  - Combined oral contraceptive (COC) (reduces blood loss by 40%).
  - Depot medroxyprogesterone acetate (DMPA) injection (most women become amenorrhoeic).
- **If menorrhagia is associated with dysmenorrhoea,** consider NSAIDs, COCs, the LNG-IUS, or DMPA intramuscular injection, depending on the need for contraception.
- **Use high-dose (30 mg)** norethisterone daily for exceptionally heavy bleeding until bleeding stops; then reduce the dose by 5 mg a day, and then stop. Bleeding will occur when the progesterone is stopped completely.

Practical prescribing points

For further information see the *Medicines Compendium* (www.medicines.org.uk) or the *British National Formulary* (www.bnf.org).

- **Tranexamic acid:** avoid in thromboembolic disease. May cause nausea, vomiting, or diarrhoea, which will reverse with dose reduction. Colour vision disturbance is rare, but discontinue the treatment if it occurs.
- **Standard NSAIDs:** increased risk of gastrointestinal haemorrhage. Avoid if there is a history of peptic ulceration. May worsen asthma, hypertension, renal impairment, and cardiac failure.
- **The World Health Organization (WHO) has published medical eligibility criteria** for different contraceptives. The criteria are labelled with one of the following classes:
  - **Category 4:** there are unacceptable health risks.
  - **Category 3:** the risks usually outweigh the advantages.
  - **Category 2:** presence of these medical problems requires careful follow-up. If two or more of these problems coexist, the risk/benefit balance moves towards category 3.
  - **Category 1:** many women will have no factor in their medical history that gives concern about any increased individual risks for them with progestogen-only pills.
- **For a full list of the WHO criteria,** see www.who.int/reproductive-health/publications/mec/index.htm.
- **None of the contraceptive methods in this scenario protects against sexually transmitted infections (STI) or human immunodeficiency virus (HIV).** If there is a risk of STI/HIV, the correct and ongoing use of condoms is recommended, either alone or with another method of contraception. Male latex condoms offer considerable protection against STI/HIV.
- **Combined oral contraceptive pill:**

- Non-life-threatening adverse effects include:
  - Breakthrough bleeding
  - Breast tenderness
  - Acne
  - Mood changes
- There is a small increased absolute risk of:
  - Venous thromboembolism
  - Myocardial infarction (in smokers only)
  - Stroke
  - Breast cancer
  - Cervical cancer
  - Primary liver cancer
- **Levonorgestrel-intra-uterine system (LNG-IUS):**
  - Prophylactic antibiotics are not recommended for routine insertion of the LNG-IUS. However, women with previous endocarditis, or with a prosthetic heart valve, require intravenous antibiotic prophylaxis to prevent bacterial endocarditis during LNG-IUS insertion or removal.
  - Adverse effects of the LNG-IUS include:
    - Heavy and irregular bleeding (which usually improves after the first 3 months)
    - Breast tenderness, headaches and acne (usually transient)
    - Uterine or cervical perforation (rare)
    - Displacement or expulsion
- **Medroxyprogesterone (DMPA) acetate injection:**
  - Adverse effects of DMPA include:
    - Menstrual irregularities
    - Potential delayed return of fertility
    - Reduction in bone mineral density (it is unclear whether there is an increased risk of osteoporosis and fractures in later life)

Follow-up advice

- **Tranexamic acid or a nonsteroidal anti-inflammatory drug (NSAID):**
  - Review at 3 months to assess response to treatment.
  - If control of menorrhagia is adequate and there are no adverse effects, treatment can be continued.
  - If control of menorrhagia is inadequate, consider using the other drug concurrently while awaiting referral.
  - If there are unacceptable adverse effects, consider changing to the other drug (i.e. tranexamic acid or an NSAID) while awaiting referral.
- **When using the combined oral contraceptive pill:**
  - Review after 3 months.
  - If control of menorrhagia is adequate and there are no adverse effects, treatment can continue with the appropriate monitoring. For more information, see the PRODIGY guidance on *Contraception.*
  - If control of menorrhagia is inadequate, consider adding an NSAID, and refer.
- **When using the levonorgestrel intra-uterine system or depot medroxyprogesterone acetate injection:**
  - Review after 6 months.
  - If control of menorrhagia is adequate and there are no adverse effects, treatment can continue with the appropriate monitoring. For more information, see the PRODIGY guidance on *Contraception.*
  - If the flow is still unacceptable, refer.

Should I refer or investigate?

Refer?

Persistent symptoms or failed medical treatment

Consider referral if:

- Despite 3 months of drug treatment, the heavy bleeding persists and is interfering with the quality of life. Failure is best based upon the woman's own assessment.
- The woman wishes to explore the possibility of surgical intervention rather than persist with drug treatment.
- The woman has severe anaemia that has failed to respond to treatment.

Risk factors for endometrial cancer

- Referral for endometrial biopsy, before medical treatment is started, should be considered if risk factors for endometrial cancer are present (e.g. tamoxifen, unopposed oestrogens, polycystic ovary syndrome, obesity).

Worrying symptoms

- Early referral should be considered if there are other symptoms of underlying pathology, e.g.
  - Irregular bleeding
  - Sudden change in blood loss
  - Intermenstrual bleeding
  - Dyspareunia
  - Pelvic pain
  - Premenstrual pain
- Referral guidelines for suspected cancer published by the National Institute for Health and Clinical Excellence (NICE) recommend that urgent referral is considered for women with persistent intermenstrual bleeding and negative pelvic examination.

Worrying findings on examination

- Referral guidelines for suspected cancer published by NICE recommends that women with a palpable abdominal or pelvic mass on examination that is not obviously uterine fibroids, or not of gastrointestinal or urological origin, should be referred urgently for an ultrasound scan.
  - If the scan is suggestive of cancer refer urgently to a team specialising in the management of gynaecological cancer, depending on local arrangements.
  - If urgent ultrasound is not available, refer urgently.
- Referral should also be considered if the uterus is enlarged to greater than 10 weeks gestation size, or if there is considerable pelvic tenderness.
- Refer urgently women with clinical features of cancer of the cervix, vagina or vulva.

NICE referral advice

- The National Institute for Clinical Excellence in Referral advice: *A guide to appropriate referral from general to specialist services* [NICE, 2001] gives advice for menorrhagia. The referral advice is meant to encourage local health communities to discuss referral issues and enable local referral guidelines and protocols to be produced (for further information, see www.nice.org.uk).
- For detailed advice on cancer referral, see the National Institute for Clinical Excellence referral guidelines for suspected cancer (www.nice.org.uk).

Investigate?

- **Full blood count** to exclude anaemia.
- **Abdominal and pelvic examination, and opportunistic cervical smear if due,** to exclude pelvic pathology.
- **The following tests are not routinely indicated:**

M

- Tests for bleeding disorders should only be performed if there are suggestive features present in the history or on examination.
- **Pelvic ultrasound examination** is not required in the initial menorrhagia assessment, other than to evaluate pelvic disorders discovered during clinical examination.
- **Swabs** need to be taken only if clinically indicated (e.g. vaginal discharge).

Patient information leaflets

The following PILs are available at www.prodigy.nhs.uk

- Anaemia Due to Iron Deficiency
- Biopsy
- Blood Test - Blood Count and Smear
- Blood Test - General
- Hysterectomy
- Laparoscopy and Laparoscopic Surgery
- Periods and Some Period Problems
- Periods - Heavy Periods (Menorrhagia)
- Women's Health
- Women's Health Concern

Shared decision making

Options to treat heavy periods include the following.

- **Tranexamic acid** reduces blood loss by almost half in most cases. You take these tablets for a few days each month during periods. It works by interfering with a blood-clotting chemical. (It does not ease period pain.)
- **Anti-inflammatory medicines** reduce the blood loss by up to half (20–50%) in most cases. They also ease period pain. You take these for a few days before and during each period.
- **The combined oral contraceptive pill** reduces blood loss by about a third in most women — sometimes more. It often reduces period pain, too.
- **The levonorgestrel intra-uterine system** is similar to an intra-uterine device. It is inserted into the uterus and slowly releases a progestogen hormone. Bleeding becomes light in most women and stops altogether in about 1 in 5 women. It also eases period pain. One device lasts 5 years. It is also a good long-term contraceptive.
- **The contraceptive injection** often reduces heavy periods, too. Periods may become irregular at first. Up to half of women on the contraceptive injection have no periods after a year.
- **Surgery** to remove the uterus (hysterectomy) or to strip the lining of the uterus (endometrial ablation) is an option if the non-surgical treatments do not work so well.

Drug rationale

Drugs not included

- **Etamsylate** at currently recommended doses is not an effective treatment for menorrhagia [RCOG, 1998]. It does not relieve dysmenorrhoea.
- **Nonsteroidal anti-inflammatory drugs (NSAIDs) other than ibuprofen, mefenamic acid, and naproxen** are not included as none are licensed for the treatment of menorrhagia, except for mefenamic acid. Also, most NSAIDs are also not licensed for dysmenorrhoea; of those that are, there is either a lack of trial data to support their use in dysmenorrhoea, or they are known to be associated with a higher risk of gastrointestinal toxicity [Zhang and Li Wan Po, 1998; Hernández-Diaz and Garcia-Rodriguez, 2001; CSM, 2002; BNF 47, 2004].
- **Cyclo-oxygenase (COX)-2 selective NSAIDs** are not included. There is no trial data to support their use in menorrhagia and they are not licensed for this indication. They may be considered for women with a high risk of NSAID-related complications [BNF 47, 2004].

Drugs included

- **Tranexamic acid**, an antifibrinolytic, is an effective treatment for menorrhagia [RCOG, 1998]. It reduces menstrual blood loss by 40–50% [Lethaby et al, 2004c].
- **Ibuprofen, mefenamic acid, and naproxen** are the preferred, standard NSAID options included. Mefenamic acid is the only NSAID licensed for the treatment of menorrhagia, but all of these drugs reduce blood loss in dysmenorrhoea, and are licensed for its treatment. Ibuprofen may be the preferred first choice because of its more favourable risk-benefit ratio [Zhang and Li Wan Po, 1998; Hernández-Diaz and Garcia-Rodriguez, 2001; CSM, 2002; BNF 47, 2004].
- **The levonorgestrel intra-uterine system (LNG-IUS)** is an effective treatment for menorrhagia [RCOG, 1998] and also relieves dysmenorrhoea. It is now licensed for both contraception and the treatment of menorrhagia. The LNG-IUS is particularly useful if the COC is contraindicated and long-term contraception is required, as it can be left in place for up to 5 years [ABPI Medicines Compendium, 2001]. Prescriptions are offered only for women aged 18 years or more, because the trial evidence is for this age group.
- **Combined oral contraceptives (COCs)** can be used to reduce menstrual blood loss [RCOG, 1998]. They may also relieve dysmenorrhoea, but data on efficacy data are limited [Proctor et al, 2003]. There is no evidence to guide COC choice in treating menorrhagia [RCOG, 1998].
  - **Careful consideration should be made of** safety, adverse effects, potential drug interactions, individual preference, and cost [FFPRHC Clinical Effectiveness Unit, 2003].
  - **Monophasic** COCs containing 30–35 micrograms ethinylestradiol and low-dose progestogen (levonorgestrel 150 micrograms or norethisterone 500 micrograms) are included.
- **Medroxyprogesterone acetate (DMPA)** depot injection (Depo-Provera) results in more than half the users becoming amenorrhoeic with continued use. Although no trial data are available for its use in menorrhagia, it should be considered in women who also require contraception [RCOG, 1998]. It may be an option for women who require contraception but are unable or unwilling to use the COC or the LNG-IUS method.
- For detailed prescribing advice, see the PRODIGY guidance on *Contraception*.

Prescriptions

Tranexamic acid

Tranexamic acid 1g three times a day during periods

- Age from 12 years onwards
- Tranexamic acid 500mg tablets. Take two tablets three times a day for up to 4 days after your period has begun. (If very heavy bleeding, increase to two tablets four times a day.); supply 42 tablets; NHS Cost £9.54.

NSAIDs

Ibuprofen 400mg three times a day during periods

- Age from 12 years onwards
- Ibuprofen 400mg tablets. Take one tablet three times a day during your period; supply 24 tablets; NHS Cost £0.71; OTC Cost £1.26.

Mefenamic acid 500mg three times a day during periods

- Age from 12 years onwards
- Mefenamic acid 500mg tablets. Take one tablet three times a day during your period; supply 28 tablets; NHS Cost £2.54.

Naproxen 250mg every 6 to 8 hours during periods

- Age from 12 years onwards
- Naproxen 250mg tablets. Take one or two tablets initially, then take one tablet every 6 to 8 hours during your period. Maximum of 5 tablets in 24 hours; supply 28 tablets; NHS Cost £1.57.

Progestogen-releasing intra-uterine system

Levonorgestrel 20mcg/24hours intra-uterine system

- Age from 18 years onwards
- Levonorgestrel 20mcg/24hrs IUS. For insertion into the uterine cavity; supply 1 device; NHS Cost £98.18.

COC containing levonorgestrel or norethisterone

Microgynon 30 (levonorgestrel 150micrograms)

- Age from 12 years onwards
- Microgynon 30 tablets. Take one tablet once a day for 21 days. Start the next packet after a 7-day break. See package insert for full instructions; supply 63 tablets; NHS Cost £2.82.

Ovranette (levonorgestrel 150micrograms)

- Age from 12 years onwards
- Ovranette tablets. Take one tablet once a day for 21 days. Start the next packet after a 7-day break. See package insert for full instructions; supply 63 tablets; NHS Cost £2.46.

Brevinor (norethisterone 500microcgrams)

- Age from 12 years onwards
- Brevinor tablets. Take one tablet once a day for 21 days. Start the next packet after a 7-day break. See package insert for full instructions; supply 63 tablets; NHS Cost £1.99.

Ovysmen (norethisterone 500micrograms)

- Age from 12 years onwards
- Ovysmen tablets. Take one tablet once a day for 21 days. Start the next packet after a 7-day break. See package insert for full instructions; supply 63 tablets; NHS Cost £1.70.

Progestogen depot injection

Medroxyprogesterone acetate 150mg injection

- Age from 12 years onwards
- Medroxyprogest. ac. 150mg/ml. Give 150mg (1ml) by deep intramuscular injection; supply 1 1ml prefilled syringe; NHS Cost £5.01.

Copper IUD in situ

Which therapy?

- **Copper intra-uterine devices (IUDs)** increase menstrual blood loss by about 50%, particularly during the first few cycles after insertion.
- **Ask about:**
  - Menstrual cycle
  - Blood loss (e.g. clots)
  - Postcoital or intermenstrual bleeding
  - Systemic disease (e.g. hypothyroidism, coagulation disorders)
  - Contraceptive use
  - History of sexually transmitted infection or pelvic inflammatory disease
- **Look for signs** of underlying disease (e.g. hypothyroidism, coagulation disorders) and manage appropriately.
- **An abdominal and pelvic examination** is recommended. Check for coil threads.
- **A full blood count should be obtained to check for anaemia;** treat if it is present.
- Consider the following options:
  - **Tranexamic acid** is the treatment of first choice.
  - A nonsteroidal anti-inflammatory drug (NSAID) is an alternative option.
  - **Tranexamic acid and an NSAID** may be prescribed concurrently in women with heavy bleeding and associated dysmenorrhoea. The addition of an NSAID may be necessary because tranexamic acid will offer no pain relief and can be prescribed for only up to 4 days.
- **Alternatively, consider changing to** the levonorgestrel intra-uterine system (LNG-IUS), which is effective at reducing menstrual loss and also relieves dysmenorrhoea.
- If the woman wishes the IUD to be removed and to use alternative contraception, consider:
  - Combined oral contraceptives (COCs).
  - Depot medroxyprogesterone acetate (DMPA) injection — but there are no trial data on its use in menorrhagia, and unpredictable, irregular spotting and bleeding may occur in the first few months.
- For information on combined oral contraceptives, the progestogen-only intra-uterine system, or other long acting progestogen formulations, see the PRODIGY guidance on *Contraception*.

M

Practical prescribing points

For further information see the *Medicines Compendium* (www.medicines.org.uk) or the *British National Formulary* (www.bnf.org).

- **Tranexamic acid:** avoid in thromboembolic disease. May cause nausea, vomiting, or diarrhoea, which will reverse with dose reduction. Colour vision disturbance is rare, but discontinue treatment if it is experienced.
- **Standard NSAIDs:** there is an increased risk of gastrointestinal haemorrhage. Avoid if there is a history of peptic ulceration. They may worsen asthma, hypertension, renal impairment, and cardiac failure.
- **The World Health Organization (WHO) has published medical eligibility criteria** for different contraceptives. The criteria are labelled with one of the following classes:
  - **Category 4:** there are unacceptable health risks.
  - **Category 3:** the risks usually outweigh the advantages.
  - **Category 2:** presence of these medical problems require careful follow-up. If two or more of these problems coexist, the risk/benefit balance moves towards category 3.
  - **Category 1:** many women will have no factor in their medical history that gives concern about any increased individual risks for them with progestogen-only pills.
- **For a full list of the WHO criteria,** see www.who.int/reproductive-health/publications/mec/index.htm.
- **None of the contraceptive methods in this scenario protects against sexually transmitted infections (STI) or human immunodeficiency virus (HIV).** If there is a risk of STI/HIV, the correct and ongoing use of condoms is recommended, either alone or with another method of

contraception. Male latex condoms offer considerable protection against STI/HIV.

- **Combined oral contraceptive pill:**
  - Non-life-threatening adverse effects include:
    - Breakthrough bleeding
    - Breast tenderness
    - Acne
    - Mood changes
  - There is a small increased absolute risk of:
    - Venous thromboembolism
    - Myocardial infarction (in smokers only)
    - Stroke
    - Breast cancer
    - Cervical cancer
    - Primary liver cancer
- **Levonorgestrel-intra-uterine system (LNG-IUS):**
  - Prophylactic antibiotics are not recommended for routine insertion of the LNG-IUS. However, women with previous endocarditis, or with a prosthetic heart valve, require intravenous antibiotic prophylaxis to prevent bacterial endocarditis during LNG-IUS insertion or removal.
  - Adverse effects of the LNG-IUS include:
    - Heavy and irregular bleeding (which usually improves after the first 3 months)
    - Breast tenderness, headaches and acne (usually transient)
    - Uterine or cervical perforation (rare)
    - Displacement or expulsion
- **Medroxyprogesterone (DMPA) acetate injection:**
  - Adverse effects of DMPA include:
    - Menstrual irregularities
    - Potential delayed return of fertility
    - Reduction in bone mineral density (it is unclear whether there is an increased risk of osteoporosis and fractures in later life)

M

Follow-up advice

- **Tranexamic acid or nonsteroidal anti-inflammatory drugs (NSAIDs):**
  - Review at 3 months to assess response to treatment.
  - If control of menorrhagia is adequate and there are no adverse effects, treatment can be continued.
  - If control of menorrhagia is inadequate, remove the IUD, suggest alternative contraception, and arrange a review after a further 3 months.
- **When using a combined oral contraceptive pill:**
  - Review after 3 months.
  - If control of menorrhagia is adequate and there are no adverse effects, treatment can continue with the appropriate monitoring. For more information, see the PRODIGY guidance on *Contraception*.
  - If control of menorrhagia is inadequate, consider addition of an NSAID and refer.
- **When using the levonorgestrel intra-uterine system, or depot medroxyprogesterone acetate injection:**
  - Review after 6 months.
  - If control of menorrhagia is adequate and there are no adverse effects, treatment can continue with the appropriate monitoring. For more information, see the PRODIGY guidance on *Contraception*.
  - If flow is still unacceptable, refer. Alternative contraception may be used while the woman is waiting for an appointment.

Should I refer or investigate?

Refer?

Persistent symptoms or failed medical treatment

Consider referral if:

- Despite 3 months of drug treatment and removal of the copper IUD, the heavy bleeding persists and is interfering with the quality of life. Failure is best based upon the woman's own assessment.
- The woman wishes to explore the possibility of surgical intervention rather than persist with drug treatment.
- The woman has severe anaemia that has failed to respond to treatment.

Risk factors for endometrial cancer

- Referral for endometrial biopsy, before medical treatment is started, should be considered if risk factors for endometrial cancer are present (e.g. tamoxifen, unopposed oestrogens, polycystic ovary syndrome, obesity).

Worrying symptoms

- Early referral should be considered if there are other symptoms of underlying pathology, e.g.
  - Irregular bleeding
  - Sudden change in blood loss
  - Intermenstrual bleeding
  - Dyspareunia
  - Pelvic pain
  - Premenstrual pain
- Referral guidelines for suspected cancer published by the National Institute for Health and Clinical Excellence (NICE) recommend that urgent referral is considered for women with persistent intermenstrual bleeding and negative pelvic examination.

Worrying findings on examination

- Referral guidelines for suspected cancer published by NICE recommends that women with a palpable abdominal or pelvic mass on examination that is not obviously uterine fibroids, or not of gastrointestinal or urological origin, should be referred urgently for an ultrasound scan.
  - If the scan is suggestive of cancer refer urgently to a team specialising in the management of gynaecological cancer, depending on local arrangements.
  - If urgent ultrasound is not available, refer urgently.
- Referral should also be considered if the uterus is enlarged to greater than 10 weeks gestation size, or if there is considerable pelvic tenderness.
- Refer urgently women with clinical features of cancer of the cervix, vagina or vulva.

NICE referral advice

- The National Institute for Clinical Excellence in Referral advice: *A guide to appropriate referral from general to specialist services* [NICE, 2001] gives advice for menorrhagia. The referral advice is meant to encourage local health communities to discuss referral issues and enable local referral guidelines and protocols to be produced (for further information, see www.nice.org.uk).
- For detailed advice on cancer referral, see the National Institute for Clinical Excellence referral guidelines for suspected cancer (www.nice.org.uk).

Investigate?

- **Full blood count** to exclude anaemia.
- **Abdominal and pelvic examination, and opportunistic cervical smear if due,** to exclude pelvic pathology.

- **The following tests are not routinely indicated:**
    - Tests for bleeding disorders should be performed only if there are suggestive features present in the history or on examination.
    - Pelvic ultrasound examination is not required in the initial menorrhagia assessment other than to evaluate pelvic disorders discovered during clinical examination.
    - Swabs need to be taken only if clinically indicated (e.g. vaginal discharge).

Patient information leaflets

The following PILs are available at www.prodigy.nhs.uk

- Anaemia Due to Iron Deficiency
- Biopsy
- Blood Test - Blood Count and Smear
- Blood Test - General
- Hysterectomy
- Laparoscopy and Laparoscopic Surgery
- Periods and Some Period Problems
- Periods - Heavy Periods (Menorrhagia)
- Women's Health
- Women's Health Concern

Shared decision making

The following treatment options are for women with heavy periods who have a copper IUD (intra-uterine device).

- **Waiting to see how it goes** is one option. Periods often become heavier when the IUD is first inserted, but may settle after a few months.
- **Tranexamic acid** reduces blood loss by almost half in most cases. You take these tablets for a few days each month during periods. It works by interfering with a blood-clotting chemical. (It does not ease period pain.)
- **Anti-inflammatory medicines** reduce the blood loss by up to half (20–50%) in most cases. They also ease period pain. You take these for a few days before and during each period.
- **The levonorgestrel intra-uterine system** can replace your current IUD for contraception. It is similar to an IUD but it also contains a progestogen hormone that is slowly released. Bleeding becomes very light in most women and stops altogether in about 1 in 5 women. It also eases period pain. One device lasts 5 years.
- **Removing the IUD and choosing a different method of contraception** is another option.

Drug rationale

Drugs not included

- **Nonsteroidal anti-inflammatory drugs (NSAIDs) other than ibuprofen, mefenamic acid, and naproxen** are not included as none are licensed for the treatment of menorrhagia, except for mefenamic acid. Also, most NSAIDs are also not licensed for dysmenorrhoea; of those that are, there is either a lack of trial data to support their use in dysmenorrhoea, or they are known to be associated with a higher risk of gastrointestinal toxicity [Zhang and Li Wan Po, 1998; Hernández-Diaz and Garcia-Rodriguez, 2001; CSM, 2002; BNF 47, 2004].
- **Etamsylate** has been studied in women with copper IUDs and there is some evidence that it may achieve small reductions in menstrual blood loss, but this is unlikely to be clinically significant [RCOG, 1998].
- **Cyclo-oxygenase (COX)-2 selective NSAIDs** are not included. There are no trial data to support their use in menorrhagia and they are not licensed for this indication. They may be considered for women with a high risk of NSAID-related complications [BNF 47, 2004].

Drugs included

- Only tranexamic acid and NSAIDs have been shown in clinical trials to be effective in the treatment of menorrhagia in women with copper intra-uterine devices (IUDs) [RCOG, 1998].
- **Tranexamic acid,** an antifibrinolytic, is an effective treatment for menorrhagia [RCOG, 1998]. It reduces menstrual blood loss by 40–50% [Lethaby et al, 2004c]. There is evidence that it is similarly effective in women with copper intra-uterine devices (IUDs) who have menorrhagia [RCOG, 1998].
- **Ibuprofen, mefenamic acid, and naproxen** are the preferred, standard NSAID options included. Mefenamic acid is the only NSAID licensed for the treatment of menorrhagia, but all of these drugs reduce blood loss in dysmenorrhoea, and are licensed for its treatment. Ibuprofen may be the preferred first choice because of its more favourable risk-benefit ratio [Zhang and Li Wan Po, 1998; Hernández-Diaz and Garcia-Rodriguez, 2001; CSM, 2002; BNF 47, 2004].
- **The levonorgestrel intra-uterine system** (LNG-IUS) is an alternative intra-uterine preparation that is effective for the treatment for menorrhagia [RCOG, 1998], and it also relieves dysmenorrhoea. It is now licensed for both contraception and the treatment of menorrhagia. If the woman prefers to continue with an IUD for long-term contraception, then changing to the LNG-IUS is an option, as it can be left in place for up to 5 years [ABPI Medicines Compendium, 2001].
- **Combined oral contraceptives** (COCs) can be used to reduce menstrual blood loss [RCOG, 1998]. They may also relieve dysmenorrhoea, but data on efficacy data are limited [Proctor et al, 2003]. There is no evidence to guide COC choice in treating menorrhagia [RCOG, 1998].
    - Careful consideration should be made of safety; adverse effects, potential drug interactions, individual preference, and cost [FFPRHC Clinical Effectiveness Unit, 2003].
    - **Monophasic COCs containing 30–35 micrograms ethinylestradiol and low-dose progestogen** (levonorgestrel 150 micrograms or norethisterone 500 micrograms) are therefore included.
- **Medroxyprogesterone acetate (DMPA) depot injection** (Depo-Provera) results in more than half the users becoming amenorrhoeic with continued use. Although there are no trial data available for its use in menorrhagia, it should be considered in women with menorrhagia who also require contraception [RCOG, 1998]. It may be an option for women who require contraception but who are unable or unwilling to use the COC or the LNG-IUS methods.
- For detailed prescribing advice, see the PRODIGY guidance on *Contraception*.

Prescriptions

Tranexamic acid

Tranexamic acid 1g three times a day during periods

- Age from 12 years onwards
- Tranexamic acid 500mg tablets. Take two tablets three times a day for up to 4 days after your period has begun. (If very heavy bleeding, increase to two tablets four times a day.); supply 12 tablets; NHS Cost £9.54.

M

NSAIDs

Ibuprofen 400mg three times a day during periods
- Age from 12 years onwards
- Ibuprofen 400mg tablets. Take one tablet three times a day during your period; supply 24 tablets; NHS Cost £0.71; OTC Cost £1.26.

Mefenamic acid 500mg three times a day during periods
- Age from 12 years onwards
- Mefenamic acid 500mg tablets. Take one tablet three times a day during your period; supply 28 tablets; NHS Cost £2.54.

Naproxen 250mg every 6 to 8 hours during periods
- Age from 12 years onwards
- Naproxen 250mg tablets. Take one or two tablets initially, then take one tablet every 6 to 8 hours during your period. Maximum of 5 tablets in 24 hours; supply 28 tablets; NHS Cost £1.57.

Progestogen-releasing intra-uterine system

Levonorgestrel 20mcg/24hours intra-uterine system
- Age from 18 years onwards
- Levonorgestrel 20mcg/24hrs IUS. For insertion into the uterine cavity; supply 1 device; NHS Cost £98.18.

COC containing levonorgestrel or norethisterone

Microgynon 30 (levonorgestrel 150micrograms)
- Age from 12 years onwards
- Microgynon 30 tablets. Take one tablet once a day for 21 days. Start the next packet after a 7-day break. See package insert for full instructions; supply 63 tablets; NHS Cost £2.82.

Ovranette (levonorgestrel 150micrograms)
- Age from 12 years onwards
- Ovranette tablets. Take one tablet once a day for 21 days. Start the next packet after a 7-day break. See package insert for full instructions; supply 63 tablets; NHS Cost £2.46.

Brevinor (norethisterone 500microcgrams)
- Age from 12 years onwards
- Brevinor tablets. Take one tablet once a day for 21 days. Start the next packet after a 7-day break. See package insert for full instructions; supply 63 tablets; NHS Cost £1.99.

Ovysmen (norethisterone 500micrograms)
- Age from 12 years onwards
- Ovysmen tablets. Take one tablet once a day for 21 days. Start the next packet after a 7-day break. See package insert for full instructions; supply 63 tablets; NHS Cost £1.70.

Progestogen depot injection

Medroxyprogesterone acetate 150mg injection
- Age from 12 years onwards
- Medroxyprogest. ac. 150mg/ml. Give 150mg (1ml) by deep intramuscular injection; supply 1 1ml prefilled syringe; NHS Cost £5.01.

Extended Information

Background information

- What is it? p.1220
- How common is it? p.1220
- How do I assess a woman presenting with heavy periods? p.1220
- What else might it be? p.1221
- Complications and prognosis p.1222

What is it?

- **Menorrhagia is excessive (heavy) cyclical menstrual bleeding over several cycles.**
  - In research, it is usually defined as an objectively measured blood loss of 80 ml or more per period (the average blood loss is 30–40 ml and 90% of women have losses less than 80 ml).
  - In practice, it is defined by the woman's subjective assessment of blood loss [NICE, 2001].
- **The perceived severity of menstrual blood loss correlates poorly with objective measurements.** Many women who seek help for heavy periods do not have greater than average losses. In one study, 26% of those with losses below 60 ml considered their periods heavy, while 40% of those with losses greater than 80 ml considered their periods to be light or moderate [NHS CRD, 1995].
- **Dysfunctional uterine bleeding is the term used when there is no obvious cause of menorrhagia.** Dysfunctional uterine bleeding occurs in 40–60% of women with excessive menstrual bleeding [Hickey et al, 2001]. In about 20% of cases (particularly at the extremes of reproductive life) dysfunctional uterine bleeding is anovulatory.
- **Other possible causes of menorrhagia include:**
  - Local pathology (e.g. fibroids, carcinoma, or infection).
  - Systemic disease (e.g. hypothyroidism or haematological disorders).
  - Iatrogenic causes (e.g. intra-uterine devices or sterilization).

[NHS CRD, 1995; New Zealand National Health Committee, 1998; RCOG, 1998; Duckitt and McCully, 2003]

How common is it?

- About a third of women describe their periods as heavy.
- One in 20 women aged 30–49 years consult their GP each year for heavy periods.
- Menstrual disorders are the second most common gynaecological condition resulting in hospital referral, and account for 12% of all gynaecological referrals.
- One in five 60-year-old women will have had a hysterectomy, with menorrhagia as the main presenting problem in at least half of these instances.

[NHS CRD, 1995; RCOG, 1998; Duckitt and McCully, 2003]

How do I assess a woman presenting with heavy periods?

History

- **Menstrual cycle details** — length of cycle, the number of days of menstruation, and the length of time that periods were considered to be heavy.
- **Blood loss:**
  - **A general impression may be gained** by ascertaining how many pads or tampons the woman is using and at what frequency they are changed. This is highly subjective, and in practice menorrhagia is usually diagnosed from reported symptoms.
  - **The pictorial blood-loss assessment chart** is an alternative option to support diagnosis. It scores the degree to which each sanitary protection item is soiled with blood (as well as the presence of clots) and correlates reasonably well with objectively measured menstrual blood loss [RCOG, 1999]. The woman herself usually completes the chart; see the *Patient Information Leaflet* for access to a copy of the chart.
- **Current contraceptive use.**

- **Symptoms suggestive of underlying pathology** (e.g. pelvic inflammatory disease, endometriosis, endometrial carcinoma):
  - Postcoital bleeding
  - Intermenstrual bleeding
  - Dyspareunia
  - Dysmenorrhoea
  - Pelvic pain
- **Possible underlying systemic disease, such as:**
  - Thyroid disease
  - Coagulation disorders
- **The desire for a family** in a woman of childbearing age should be assessed, as this might help direct the treatment strategy adopted.

[Campbell and Monga, 2000]

Examination

- Looking for signs of underlying disease:
  - **Endocrine disease:** hirsutism, striae, thyroid enlargement or nodularity, or changes in skin pigment
  - **Coagulopathy:** bruises or petechiae
- **Abdominal examination**
- **Pelvic examination**
  - **Vulval examination** for evidence of external bleeding and signs of local infection.
  - **Speculum examination of vagina and cervix,** and vaginal and cervical swabs if clinically indicated.
  - **Bimanual palpation** to look for uterine or adnexal enlargement or tenderness.
- **Consider opportunistic cervical screening.**

[Campbell and Monga, 2000; Oehler and Rees, 2003]

Investigations in primary care

- **A full blood count should be obtained** in all women complaining of menorrhagia (B) [RCOG, 1998]. The presence of iron-deficiency anaemia is a strong indicator of excessive menstrual bleeding. For further information on the investigation and management of iron-deficiency anaemia, see the PRODIGY guidance *Anaemia — iron deficiency*.
- **Other blood tests** are not routinely indicated [RCOG, 1998].
- **Thyroid function tests** are not necessary unless the woman has symptoms or signs of hypothyroidism (C) [RCOG, 1998]. For more information, see the PRODIGY guidance on *Hypothyroidism*.
- **Other endocrine investigations** are of no value (B) [RCOG, 1998].
- **Tests for bleeding disorders** should be performed only if there are suggestive features present in the history or on examination (C) [RCOG, 1999]. A bleeding disorder should be particularly suspected if there is a history of menorrhagia since menarche, or a history of excessive bleeding after tooth extraction, operations, and childbirth. Investigations should be arranged in conjunction with the local haematology department, as many of the appropriate tests are not routine.

Investigations in secondary care

- **Transvaginal ultrasound scanning** is now a recommended, routine, first-line investigation to select women in need of further investigation (B) [Tsuda et al, 1997; RCOG, 1999].
  - It is a non-invasive, pain-free procedure that is particularly useful in detecting intra-uterine abnormalities (e.g. polyps and submucous fibroids).
  - Although the procedure measures endometrial thickness, the relationship between endometrial thickness and endometrial disease is not established in premenopausal women.

[Dijkhuizen et al, 1996; Vercellini et al, 1997; Vilos et al, 2001; Oehler and Rees, 2003]

- **To make a diagnosis of, or exclude, malignancy and premalignancy, it is necessary to obtain an endometrial biopsy for histological examination.**
  - The two most common methods of endometrial biopsy are the Pipelle sample and the Vatra curette. These do not require a general anaesthetic.
  - The detection rates for endometrial carcinoma using the Pipelle device were found by one metanalysis to be 99.6% in postmenopausal and 91% in premenopausal women [Dijkhuizen et al, 2000].
  - However, endometrial biopsy is insensitive in diagnosing benign causes of menorrhagia (e.g. polyps and fibroids).
  - A woman aged under 40 years with no risk factors and in whom symptoms resolve may not need an endometrial biopsy.
- **Endometrial biopsy should be considered in the following women:**
  - All women aged >40 years with abnormal bleeding.
  - Younger women with risk factors, including for endometrial cancer:
    - Nulliparity (pregnancy confers protection from endometrial carcinoma by interrupting the continued stimulation of the endometrium by oestrogen)
    - Family history of endometrial or colonic cancer (particularly hereditary nonpolyposis colorectal syndrome)
    - Abnormal smear
    - Obesity
    - Polycystic ovary syndrome
    - Tamoxifen therapy
    - Unopposed oestrogen therapy
  - Younger women in whom abnormal bleeding does not resolve with medical treatment

[Rose, 1996; Farquar et al, 1999; Balen, 2001; Oehler and Rees, 2003]

- **Hysteroscopy** allows direct visualisation of the uterine cavity and the opportunity to take an endometrial biopsy (A) [RCOG, 1999].
  - It is a superior method for the detection of endometrial polyps and submucous fibroids, which can be missed by endometrial biopsy, ultrasonography, or 'blind' curettage [Oehler and Rees, 2003].
  - It is indicated if there is persistent abnormal bleeding or a previous history of an endometrial polyp or fibroid [Rees, Personal Communication, 2004].
  - It can be performed as an outpatient procedure without anaesthetic or as a formal theatre procedure.
- **Dilatation and curettage** (D&C) has been considered the 'gold standard' investigation in the past, but it is essentially a blind procedure and can miss lesions such as polyps, submucous fibroids, hyperplasia, and carcinoma in more than 50% of cases [Oehler and Rees, 2003].
  - D&C does not give additional diagnostic information over and above a hysteroscopy with endometrial biopsy (B) [RCOG, 1999].
  - D&C requires a general anaesthetic and is associated with complications, including perforation (0.6–1.3%), haemorrhage (0.4%), and infection (0.3–0.5%) of cases.

What else might it be?

There is no obvious underlying cause of menorrhagia in 40–60% of women. Conditions that may present as excessive menstrual bleeding include:

- **Uterine and ovarian pathology:**
  - Endometrial hyperplasia or carcinoma
  - Endometriosis and adenomyosis

- Endometrial polyps
- Fibroids
- Polycystic ovary disease (causing anovulatory menorrhagia)
- Uterine infection (e.g. chlamydia)
- Uterine vascular malformations
- **Systemic pathology:**
  - Bleeding disorders (e.g. Von Willebrand's disease)
  - Hypothyroidism
  - Liver or renal disease
  - Obesity
- **Iatrogenic causes:**
  - Anticoagulant treatment
  - Chemotherapy
  - Intra-uterine contraceptive device (blood loss may be increased by 40–50% over 6–12 months compared with pre-insertion values) [RCOG, 1998]
  - Sterilization

[NHS CRD, 1995; Shah and Grainger, 1996; Kadir et al, 1998]

Complications and prognosis

- **Reduced quality of life and depression** may result from the adverse effect of menorrhagia on social and professional lifestyle.
- **Iron-deficiency anaemia** occurs in about two-thirds of women with objective menorrhagia (i.e. 80 ml or more blood loss with each menstruation) [RCOG, 1999].

Management issues

- Overview of treatment p.1222
- What medical treatments are available to manage menorrhagia? p.1222
- What surgical treatments are available to manage menorrhagia? p.1225
- When should I refer? p.1226
- Medicines management p.1226

Overview of treatment

- **Reassurance, counselling, and the development of coping strategies** are an important part of management. In one study, a third of women opted not to have any medical treatment after explanation and reassurance about menorrhagia, and a year later 70% of them were content with that choice [RCOG, 1998].
- **Anaemia should be corrected,** usually with oral iron supplements. For further information on the investigation and management of iron-deficiency anaemia, see the PRODIGY guidance *Anaemia — iron deficiency*.
- **There are limited trial data to support clinical decision-making in the treatment of menorrhagia.** Of those trials that have been conducted, sample sizes were often small, length of follow-up was short, and there have been few direct comparisons of the commonly used drugs. In addition, there is considerable variation in treatment doses used, trial inclusion criteria, adverse effect reporting, and baseline measurements.
- **Medical treatments for menorrhagia do not cure the problem, but aim to improve the symptoms** and the quality of life. Symptoms often recur once treatment is stopped.
- **Choice of medical treatment** should be based on the:
  - Presence of other symptoms (e.g. dysmenorrhoea)
  - Need for contraception
  - Adverse-effect profile of the treatment
  - Woman's preference
- **Recommended initial medical treatments** [RCOG, 1998] are:
  - Tranexamic acid
  - Nonsteroidal anti-inflammatory drugs (NSAIDs)
  - The levonorgestrel intra-uterine system (LNG-IUS)
  - Combined oral contraceptives (COCs)
- **High-dose oral progestogen** is sometimes used to stop exceptionally heavy bleeding (flooding); see the *Progestogens (high-dose oral)* section.
- **There is no published evidence on whether combining different treatments for menorrhagia is beneficial** (e.g. tranexamic acid with an NSAID).
- **Surgical intervention is extremely effective in treating menorrhagia.** However, a trial of medical treatment may suffice, and is usually appropriate before considering surgery (either endometrial destruction or hysterectomy) [NHS CRD, 1995; RCOG, 1998].
- **Dilatation and curettage (D&C)** is not an effective treatment [RCOG, 1999; DTB, 2000].

What medical treatments are available to manage menorrhagia?

Tranexamic acid

- **Tranexamic acid is an effective treatment** for reducing heavy menstrual blood loss (A) [RCOG, 1998].
- **It is a plasminogen-activator inhibitor.** Plasminogen activators are a group of enzymes that cause fibrinolysis (dissolution of clots). An increase in the level of plasminogen activators is found in the endometrium of women with heavy menstrual bleeding compared with those having normal menstrual loss [Lethaby et al, 2004c].
- **Tranexamic acid has been found to reduce blood loss by** 40–50% (Table 1) [Lethaby et al, 2004c].
- **Tranexamic acid** is taken only during menstruation and is therefore suitable for women trying to conceive [RCOG, 1998]. It is effective in reducing heavy menstrual blood loss in women with intra-uterine devices (A) [RCOG, 1998].
- **Tranexamic acid compared with other interventions:**
  - **NSAIDs, luteal phase oral progestogens, and etamsylate** — comparative studies show tranexamic acid to be more effective than these agents in reducing menstrual blood loss [Lethaby et al, 2004c; Bonnar and Sheppard, 1996]. However, objective improvement in menstrual blood loss is poorly correlated with perceived improvement by those being treated.
  - **Endometrial resection** — one randomized controlled trial found tranexamic acid to be less effective than this technique in reducing blood loss at 4 months and 2 years, and adverse effects (leg cramps and nausea) were greater with tranexamic acid.
  - **Adverse events** did not seem to be more frequent with tranexamic acid than with NSAIDs, etamsylate, or oral luteal-phase progestogens. It is not possible to comment on the risk of thromboembolic events, as no trial has recorded thromboembolic events as an outcome measurement [Lethaby et al, 2004c].

Nonsteroidal anti-inflammatory drugs

- **Nonsteroidal anti-inflammatory drugs (NSAIDs) are an effective treatment** for reducing heavy menstrual blood loss (**A**) [RCOG, 1998].
- **NSAIDS are thought to act by reducing uterine prostaglandin levels,** which are elevated in women with excessive menstrual bleeding.
- **NSAIDs reduce menstrual blood loss by 20–50%** (Table 1) [RCOG, 1998] and they may also relieve associated dysmenorrhoea [Zhang and Li Wan Po, 1998; Proctor and Farquar, 2003].
- Although mefenamic acid has been studied the most, it is likely that other non-selective NSAIDs are just as effective [Lethaby et al, 2004d].
- **An NSAID** is taken only during menstruation and is therefore suitable for women trying to conceive [RCOG, 1998]. NSAIDs are effective in reducing heavy menstrual blood loss in women with intra-uterine devices (**A**) [RCOG, 1998].
- **NSAIDs compared with other treatments:**
  - **Tranexamic acid or danazol** — have both been found to be more effective than NSAIDs in reducing menstrual blood loss [Lethaby et al, 2004d].
  - **Oral progestogens, combined oral contraceptives, or the levonorgestrel intra-uterine system** — no statistically significant differences were found between NSAIDs and these other treatments [Lethaby et al, 2004d; Lethaby et al, 2004a].
  - **Adverse effects** are less likely than with danazol or etamsylate. In trials using mefenamic acid, in those who discontinued treatment the reason reported was a lack of efficacy [Lethaby et al, 2004d].

Should tranexamic acid be combined with an NSAID?

- Although there is no published evidence to support simultaneous use of NSAIDs and tranexamic acid, they are commonly prescribed together in clinical practice. This seems a pragmatic approach in women with heavy bleeding, because tranexamic acid can only be used for up to 4 days. Where there is associated dysmenorrhoea, the addition of an NSAID may be necessary, as tranexamic acid will offer no pain relief.

Combined oral contraceptives

- **Blood loss and menstrual pain** may be reduced with combined oral contraceptive (COC) use (**C**) [FFPRHC Clinical Effectiveness Unit, 2003].
- COCs are thought to reduce blood loss (Table 1) by inducing regular shedding of a thinner endometrium.
- **It is accepted practice to use COCs as the first choice for women who also require contraception.** However, there is a lack of trial evidence [Duckitt and McCully, 2003] to support this recommendation — a single trial suggested benefit, but evidence is limited as the numbers were small (n = 6) [Iyer et al, 2003].
- COC use may also have the benefit of reducing associated dysmenorrhoea.
- **A COC containing 30–35 micrograms of oestrogen plus a low dose of either levonorgestrel or norethisterone** is a suitable preferred choice of pill.
- **COC compared with other interventions:**
  - Most trial data are old, and there are few studies that have evaluated the efficacy of COCs with less than 50 micrograms ethinyloestradiol.
  - **Mefenamic acid, naproxen, or low-dose danazol** — a reduction in menstrual blood loss has been found to be as effective with COCs as with these agents, but this finding was based on only one small trial (that met the inclusion criteria in a Cochrane review) [Iyer et al, 2003].
  - Note: there is no published information available about the use of the transdermal combination contraceptive patch for the treatment of menorrhagia.
- Tranexamic acid should preferably not be used with a combined oral contraceptive pill because of the potential increased risk of venous thromboembolism.

Progestogen-only intra-uterine system

- **The levonorgestrel intra-uterine system (LNG-IUS) can be used as a first-line option** to treat menorrhagia (**A**) [FFPRHC Clinical Effectiveness Unit, 2004]. It is effective even in the presence of fibroids (**C**), although it is not generally recommended if fibroids are distorting the uterine cavity (**C**) [FFPRHC Clinical Effectiveness Unit, 2004].
- It suppresses endometrial proliferation and results in reduced menstrual blood loss and a shorter duration of menstrual bleeding [RCOG, 1998].
- The LNG-IUS can reduce menstrual blood loss by over 90% (Table 1) (**A**).
- **LNG-IUS compared with other interventions:**
  - There are no good quality randomized controlled trials comparing the LNG-IUS to either placebo or other commonly used medical therapies for menorrhagia. Trials are generally small and need to be interpreted with caution [Coulter et al, 1995; RCOG, 1998; Lethaby et al, 2004b].
  - **Flurbiprofen or tranexamic acid** — the reduction in mean menstrual blood loss at 12 months with LNG-IUS (96%) was significantly greater than with either flurbiprofen (215) or tranexamic acid (44%) [Roy and Bhattacharya, 2004].
  - **Cyclical norethisterone** — the LNG-IUS has been found to be more effective, although the difference was not statistically significant. However, over three times as many women were willing to continue with the LNG-IUS method than were willing to continue in the norethisterone group [Roy and Bhattacharya, 2004].
  - **Surgery** (hysterectomy, endometrial ablation) is more effective than the LNG-IUS in treating menorrhagia at 1 year (**A**) [FFPRHC Clinical Effectiveness Unit, 2004]. The woman's satisfaction and quality of life seem similar after LNG-IUS or surgical treatment of menorrhagia (**A**).
    - **Transcervical resection of the endometrium (TCRE)** — results in a larger mean reduction in menstrual blood loss, and amenorrhoea is more likely [RCOG, 1998; Lethaby et al, 2004b]. However, the LNG-IUS is as effective as conservative surgery (resection and ablation) in the management of menorrhagia *after* the first year (**A**) [FFPRHC Clinical Effectiveness Unit, 2004].
  - **Hysterectomy** — a recent study found that 42% of women initially treated with LNG-IUS eventually underwent hysterectomy. However, at 5-year follow-up there was no significant difference in either health outcomes or overall satisfaction between women who were treated with LNG-IUS as their initial treatment and those who underwent hysterectomy. Hysterectomy was associated with more complications [Hurskainen et al, 2004].
- **Advantages** — relief of dysmenorrhoea, effective contraception, and long-term control of menorrhagia after insertion [RCOG, 1998; Duckitt and McCully, 2003].
- **Disadvantages** — intermenstrual bleeding and breast tenderness in the first few months after insertion. Expulsion of the device may also occur (rates within 12 months were 3.3–5.9%) [Lethaby et al, 2004b].

- **Irregular bleeding on LNG-IUS** can last for 6–12 months [Rees, Personal Communication, 2004]:
  - Refer at 6 months if bleeding is not improving or is getting worse.
  - If flooding, remove the LNG-IUS, as mechanical presence may be a cause.

Progestogens (high-dose oral)

- **Oral progestogens at large doses** are sometimes used to stop exceptionally heavy bleeding (flooding). Although there are no trial data, expert opinion suggests a regimen of norethisterone 30 mg daily until bleeding stops. The dose is then reduced by 5 mg a day and then stopped. Bleeding will occur when the progesterone is stopped completely [Rees, Personal Communication, 2004].

Danazol

- **Danazol is poorly tolerated and should in general be used only after specialist advice** [RCOG, 1998].
- **It works in several ways:** it inhibits pituitary gonadotrophins, causes endometrial suppression, and inhibits ovulation.
- **Danazol reduces excessive menstrual bleeding by up to 80%** [RCOG, 1999], but the degree of blood loss seems to be dose-dependent.
- **Danazol compared with other interventions:**
  - **Danazol seems to be a more effective treatment for heavy menstrual bleeding** than are oral progestogens, NSAIDs and the COC, although trials were under-powered and confidence intervals were wide [Beaumont et al, 2004].
  - There are insufficient data available that compare danazol with other interventions [Roy and Bhattacharya, 2004].

M

Progestogens — oral

- **Oral progestogens have been used cyclically in two different treatment protocols:**
  - A short course during the luteal phase (day 15 or 19 to day 26 of the cycle).
  - A longer course, lasting 21 days from day 5 of each cycle.
- **Short-course, low-dose, luteal-phase oral administration of norethisterone is not an effective treatment** for menorrhagia (**A**) [RCOG, 1998]. Luteal-phase oral progestogens have not been studied in placebo-controlled trials, but comparative studies indicate that they are inferior to other medical treatments. A systematic review concluded that they offer no advantage in women with ovulatory cycles [Lethaby et al, 2004a].
- **Longer oral progestogen regimens** may have a role in the short-term treatment of menorrhagia. There have been reports that 21-day courses of progestogens have reduced menstrual blood loss by 30–90%. However, progestogens are poorly tolerated, and in one study only 22% of women were willing to continue treatment [RCOG, 1998; Duckitt and McCully, 2003; Lethaby et al, 2004a].
- Several reviews have highlighted the lack of good trial data and the likely poor efficacy of commonly used regimes [RCOG, 1998; Duckitt and McCully, 2003; Lethaby et al, 2004a].
- **Oral progestogens compared with other interventions:**
  - **Short-course luteal-phase progestogen** (from day 15 or 19 to day 26) therapy compared with:
    - Tranexamic acid, danazol, and LNG-IUS: these were more effective in reducing menorrhagia.
    - NSAIDs: no significant differences were found in menstrual blood loss [Lethaby et al, 2004a].
  - **Longer oral progestogen regimens** — one randomised controlled trial found no significant difference between norethisterone and the LNG-IUS method. However, women tolerated the LNG-IUS method better.
  - **Adverse effects** — the number of adverse effects associated with luteal-phase norethisterone is similar to the number of those caused by mefenamic acid and tranexamic acid, and fewer than those associated with danazol [BNF 47, 2004; Lethaby et al, 2004a].

Progestogens long-acting — injection or implant

- **Continued use of long-acting progestogens renders most women amenorrhoeic, and therefore could be considered** for use in menorrhagia (**C**) [RCOG, 1998]. However, they are not licensed for this indication. A long-acting progestogen formulation may be an option for women who require contraception but who are unable or unwilling to use the COC pill or the LNG-IUS.
- **Intramuscular depot medroxyprogesterone acetate (DMPA)** is commonly used for contraception in a dose of 150 mg every 12 weeks. It may cause unpredictable, irregular spotting and bleeding in the first few months of use, and may cause heavy bleeding in 1–2% of women. However, after using it for a year, about 50% of women are amenorrhoeic (Table 1) [RCOG, 1998; Roy and Bhattacharya, 2004]. DMPA has the added benefit of reducing dysmenorrhoea.
- Unless required for contraceptive purposes, this represents unlicensed use of DMPA; and although there is no published evidence, it may be a pragmatic option to consider when other strategies have failed [Rees, Personal Communication, 2004].
- **The subdermal progestogen-only contraceptive implant** is also a long-acting formulation. There is no published evidence and this option is not recommended, as there is less experience with its use and there are sometimes problems with removal.

Etamsylate

- **Etamsylate, at currently recommended doses, is not an effective treatment** for menorrhagia (Table 1) (**A**) [RCOG, 1998].
- **Etamsylate** is thought to reduce capillary bleeding by correcting abnormal platelet function.
- There is some evidence that it may achieve menstrual blood loss reductions of about 13% compared with baseline, but this is unlikely to be clinically significant [RCOG, 1998; Duckitt and McCully, 2003].
- **Etamsylate compared with mefenamic acid or traxenamic acid** — one small randomized controlled trial (81 women) compared the three methods and found etamsylate to be significantly less effective in reducing mean menstrual blood loss [Bonnar and Sheppard, 1996].

Gonadotrophin-releasing hormone analogues

- **Gonadotrophin-releasing hormone analogues may be used in the following circumstances under specialist advice** [RCOG, 1998]. Their licence [ABPI Medicines Compendium, 2003b] covers use in:
  - Endometrial thinning before endometrial ablation or resection.
  - Temporary relief of heavy bleeding of fibroids before surgery.
- Gonadotrophin-releasing hormone (GnRH) analogues initially stimulate pituitary secretion of gonadotrophins and then rapidly inhibit secretion due to pituitary down-regulation. This results in anovulation, markedly reduced oestrogen levels, and amenorrhoea.

- The limited evidence available indicates that these analogues are effective in reducing menstrual blood loss in women with menorrhagia (Table 1).
- **They cannot be used long-term** because of rapid bone demineralization associated with oestrogen withdrawal [Oehler and Rees, 2003], although this is reversible when their use is discontinued.
- **They are poorly tolerated** because of adverse effects from low oestrogen level, particularly hot flushes and vaginal dryness [Oehler and Rees, 2003].
- **Adverse effects may be minimized by 'add-back therapy'** (the concomitant use of cyclical oestrogen/progestogen hormone replacement therapy), which influences GnRH analogues without affecting the control of the dysfunctional uterine bleeding [Oehler and Rees, 2003].

Efficacy of medical treatments for menorrhagia

Table 1 shows the efficacy of drug treatments for women with menorrhagia.

What surgical treatments are available to manage menorrhagia?

Hysterectomy

- **About 20% of women in the UK have had a hysterectomy** by the age of 60 years. About 40% are for dysfunctional uterine bleeding, with no gynaecological pathology [Maresh et al, 2002].
- **Operative complications** (e.g. respiratory/cardiac complications, visceral damage, major haemorrhage) occur in one in 30 women and tend to be more common with laparoscopic techniques [Maresh et al, 2002].
- **Post-operative complications** (e.g. sepsis, urinary tract infection, wound haematoma) occur in 1 in 10 women [Garside et al, 2004].
- **Urinary incontinence** — women should be counselled that in the long term there may be an increased risk of developing urinary incontinence [Brown et al, 2000].
- **Quality of life and sexuality** — available evidence shows that hysterectomy improves the quality of life in most cases and does not adversely affect sexuality [Farrell and Kieser, 2000].

Table 1: Efficacy of drug treatments for women with menorrhagia.

Treatment	Reduction of menstrual blood loss*
Nonsteroidal anti-inflammatory drugs	20–50%
Tranexamic acid	47–54%
Combined oral contraceptive pill	43%
Levonorgestrel intra-uterine system	74–97%
Danazol	50–80%
Oral progestogens for 21 days	30–90%
Long-acting progestogen	50–66% of women with menorrhagia experience amenorrhoea between 1–2 years of use
Etamsylate	Possibly 13% — not clinically significant
Gonadotrophin-releasing hormone analogues	>90%

*Note: these data need to be interpreted with caution, as trial data are limited. The table is based on data from different sources [Roy and Bhattacharya, 2004; Duckitt and McCully, 2003].

Endometrial ablation

- All methods of endometrial ablation aim to destroy the endometrium. The process involves removing the full thickness of the endometrium together with the superficial myometrium, and the basal glands thought to be the focus of endometrial growth [Garside et al, 2004].
- **Endometrial ablation is contraindicated in the following circumstances:**
  - Future pregnancy is desired — advise women that endometrial ablation is contraindicated if they have not completed their family.
  - Uterine malignancy or its precursors are present.
  - Acute pelvic infection is present.
- **First-generation techniques** require direct visualisation of the endometrium using a hysteroscope and rely heavily on the skill of the gynaecologist. A general anaesthetic is almost always used [Garside et al, 2004]. Endometrial thinning agents (e.g. danazol, gonadotrophin-releasing hormone analogue) are often used before ablation [Sowter et al, 2004; Garside et al, 2004; Duckitt and McCully, 2003].
  - **Rollerball technique:** a current is passed through a rollerball electrode, which is moved across the surface of the endometrium, thereby destroying the tissue [Garside et al, 2004].
  - **Transcervical resection of the endometrium** (**TCRE**): a cutting loop is used to remove the endometrial lining. Small fibroids (of roughly 2 cm diameter) may also be removed.
  - **Laser ablation** uses bursts of laser-generated energy transmitted through a flexible quartz fibre. It is not commonly used in the UK [Lumsden and McGavigan, 1997; Robins, 2001; Garside et al, 2004;].
- **Second-generation techniques:** these techniques do not require direct visualization of the uterine cavity, and their success is much less dependent on the skill of the surgeon than with first-generation techniques [Garside et al, 2004]. Either general or local anaesthesia is suitable for second-generation techniques [Garside et al, 2004].
  - **Microwave endometrial ablation** (**MEA**) uses high-frequency microwaves to destroy the endometrium. The whole procedure takes 2–3 minutes. A watery vaginal discharge for about 3 weeks is usual. MEA is contraindicated if there are fibroids distorting the uterine cavity or if there has been previous uterine surgery. Oral and vaginal thinning agents may be given before the operation [Garside et al, 2004].
  - **Thermal balloon endometrial ablation** (**TBEA**) relies on the transfer of heat from hot liquid within a balloon that is inserted into the uterine cavity. The lining sloughs off over the next 7–10 days. It cannot be used in women with large or irregular uterine cavities. The endometrium may be thinned with curettage immediately before the operation [Garside et al, 2004].

M

Hysterectomy and endometrial destruction techniques

- **If drug therapy is not effective,** endometrial ablation techniques or hysterectomy should be considered [Garside et al, 2004].
- **Endometrial destruction techniques** should be offered to women with heavy menstrual bleeding as an alternative to hysterectomy. Discuss the possibility that further surgery may be necessary [Lethaby et al, 2004e].

What points should be considered when choosing between hysterectomy and endometrial destruction?

- Effectiveness:
  - Hysterectomy cures menorrhagia.

  - Endometrial destruction is effective in most women at reducing menstrual blood loss.
- However, with endometrial destruction, at 12-month follow-up 13% of women have no change in the severity of their bleeding loss, and within 4 years 38% of women require repeat surgery [Lethaby et al, 2004e]. A Cochrane review concluded that endometrial destruction costs the NHS less than hysterectomy does, but the cost gap narrows with prolonged follow-up, owing to the need for some women to be treated again.
- **The need for contraception:**
  - Is removed after a hysterectomy.
  - Is still required in premenopausal women who have undergone endometrial destruction, as pregnancies have been reported.
- **Risks of endometrial cancer and cervical cancer** are removed after a total hysterectomy.
- **Length of time before a return to normal activities:**
  - The length of stay in hospital for a hysterectomy is commonly 5 days (median and mode) and full recovery may take 4–6 weeks [Maresh et al, 2002; Garside et al, 2004].
  - Endometrial ablation techniques are often done as day cases, and a return to normal activities is usually possible within 3–4 days [Garside et al, 2004].
- **Satisfaction rates** are higher in the first year or two in women with hysterectomy than is the case with endometrial destruction, but by 3 to 4 years there is no difference. Studies looking at quality of life have found no convincing difference.

[NHS CRD, 1995; DTB, 2000; Duckitt and McCully, 2003; Lethaby et al, 2004e]

When should I refer?

M

- **Evidence about the diagnostic value of symptoms and signs of gynaecological cancer presenting in primary care is limited** [NICE, 2005]. The following is a summary of important recommendations from the National Institute of Health and Clinical Excellence and the Royal College of Obstetricians and Gynaecologists (RCOG) relevant to a woman presenting with gynaecological symptoms in primary care.
- **If there are worrying symptoms of underlying pathology** (e.g. irregular bleeding, sudden change in blood loss, intermenstrual bleeding, postcoital bleeding, dyspareunia, pelvic pain, or premenstrual pain), the RCOG recommends considering referral. In most cases PRODIGY would recommend early referral.
- Referral guidelines for suspected cancer published by the National Institute for Health and Clinical Excellence (NICE) recommend that [NICE, 2005]:
  - Women with clinical features of cancer of the cervix should be referred urgently.
  - Urgent referral is considered for women with persistent intermenstrual bleeding and negative pelvic examination.
  - Women with a palpable abdominal or pelvic mass on examination that is not obviously uterine fibroids, or not of gastrointestinal or urological origin should be referred urgently for an ultrasound scan.
    - If the scan is suggestive of cancer refer urgently to a team specialising in the management of gynaecological cancer, depending on local arrangements.
    - If urgent ultrasound is not available refer urgently.
- The RCOG recommends that referral should be considered if there is: a pelvic mass, a uterus enlarged to greater than 10 weeks gestation size, or significant pelvic tenderness (C) [RCOG, 1998].
- **If there are risk factors for endometrial cancer,** the RCOG recommends that, before medical treatment is started, referral for endometrial biopsy should be considered. Risk factors include nulliparity, *any* family history of endometrial or colonic cancer, tamoxifen, unopposed oestrogens, polycystic ovary syndrome, and obesity [Oehler and Rees, 2003].
- NICE in *Referral advice: A guide to appropriate referral from general to specialist services* [NICE, 2001] gives the advice in Table 2 for menorrhagia. The referral advice is meant to encourage local health communities to discuss referral issues and enable local referral guidelines and protocols to be produced (for further information, see www.nice.org.uk).

Medicines management

General information

- Some of the medical treatment options for menorrhagia may also be used as methods of contraception. The World Health Organization (WHO) has published medical eligibility criteria for different contraceptives. The criteria are labelled with one of the following classes:
  - **Category 4:** there are unacceptable health risks.
  - **Category 3:** the risks usually outweigh the advantages.
  - **Category 2:** presence of these medical problems requires careful follow-up. If two or more of these problems coexist, the risk/benefit balance moves towards category 3.
  - **Category 1:** many women will have no factor in their medical history that gives concern about any increased individual risk for them with progestogen-only pills.
- **Categories 3 and 4:** alternative contraceptive methods should be recommended and the potential risk of COCs should be explained to women with any of these conditions.
- **For a full list of the WHO medical eligibility criteria,** see www.who.int/reproductive-health/publications/mec/index.htm.
- For more information on combined oral contraceptives, the levonorgestrel intra-uterine system, or other long acting progestogen formulations, see the PRODIGY guidance on *Contraception.*

Nonsteroidal anti-inflammatory drugs

- **The Committee on Safety of Medicines (CSM)** advises that all nonsteroidal anti-inflammatory drugs (NSAIDs) are associated with serious gastrointestinal toxicity. All non-selective NSAIDs are contraindicated in someone with a history of peptic ulceration.

Table 2: Referral advice for women with menorrhagia.

When referral to a specialist service is appropriate	Referral timing
There is a suspicion of underlying cancer.	***
The woman also has persistent intermenstrual or postcoital bleeding.	**
Despite 3 months of drug treatment, the heavy bleeding persists and is interfering with the quality of life. Failure is best based upon the woman's own assessment.	*
The woman wishes to explore the possibility of surgical intervention rather than persist with drug treatment.	*
The woman has severe anaemia that has failed to respond to treatment.	^

Arrangements should be made so that the woman:
*** is seen urgently (a maximum wait of 2 weeks is recommended, but this should be agreed locally).
** is seen soon (maximum waiting time to be agreed locally).
* has a routine appointment (maximum waiting time to be agreed locally).
^ is seen within an appropriate time depending on his or her clinical circumstances (discretionary).

- The CSM also warns that any degree of worsening of asthma may be related to the ingestion of NSAIDs, either prescribed or bought over the counter.
- **Only one NSAID should be used at a time;** in particular, the combination of an NSAID with low-dose aspirin substantially increases gastrointestinal risk [CSM, 2003].
- Always use the lowest dose that controls symptoms.

Tranexamic acid

- **Tranexamic acid is well tolerated,** with no significant increase in reported adverse events compared with placebo or other treatments [Lethaby et al, 2004c]. It is needed only for the duration of the menses and therefore is preferable to long-term daily medication.
- **Thromboembolic disease** — traxenamic acid is contraindicated here, but long-term studies in Sweden have shown that the rate of incidence of thrombosis with the use of tranexamic acid is comparable to that in the general population [Oehler and Rees, 2003].
- **Gastrointestinal adverse effects** are experienced by about 15% of users; the adverse effects will reverse when the dose is reduced [ABPI Medicines Compendium, 2003a].
- **Colour-vision disturbance** is rare, but a user who experiences it should discontinue treatment [ABPI Medicines Compendium, 2003a].

Depot medroxyprogesterone acetate

- **Reduction in bone mineral density** (BMD) has been reported in women who use Depot medroxyprogesterone acetate (DMPA) but the risk of osteoporosis and fractures in later life remains unclear.
- There is some evidence that BMD starts to recover when DMPA is discontinued; the extent of recovery is probably related to the duration of exposure.
  - One study has found that after 30 months women who discontinued DMPA had a bone density similar to that of non-users [Scholes et al, 2002].
- The effect of BMD reduction may be more important in adolescents in whom the usual process of bone mineral accretion may be reversed.
- **The Committee on Safety of Medicines (CSM) therefore advises** that:
  - In adolescents, DMPA may be used (as first-line contraception) but *only* after other methods have been discussed and considered to be unsuitable or unacceptable.
  - In women of all ages, careful re-evaluation of the risks and benefits of treatment should be carried out in women who wish to continue use for more than 2 years.
  - In women with significant lifestyle and/or medical risk factors for osteoporosis, other methods (of contraception) should be considered.
- **For all users of DMPA, a calcium-rich diet and regular weight-bearing exercise are recommended** in order to reduce any increased risk of fracture, and no smoking is recommended.

[CSM, 2004]

References

NHS staff in England can link, free of charge, from references to full text journals by clicking on [Full text] on the PRODIGY website.

1. ABPI Medicines Compendium (2001) *Summary of product characteristics for Mirena*. Electronic Medicines Compendium. Datapharm Communications Ltd. www.emc.medicines.org.uk [Accessed: 19/04/2004].
2. ABPI Medicines Compendium (2003a) *Summary of product characteristics for Cyklokapron tablets*. Electronic Medicines Compendium. Datapharm Communications Ltd.. www.emc medicines.org.uk [Accessed: 24/06/2004].
3. ABPI Medicines Compendium (2003b) *Summary of product characteristics for Zoladex*. Electronic Medicines Compendium. Datapharm Communications Ltd. www.emc.medicines.org.uk [Accessed: 25/06/2004].
4. Balen, A. (2001) Polycystic ovary syndrome and cancer. *Human Reproduction Update* 7(6), 522–525. [Full text]
5. Beaumont, H., Augood, C., Duckitt, K. and Lethaby, A. (2004) *Danazol for heavy menstrual bleeding (Cochrane Review)*. The Cochrane Library. Issue 2. Chichester, UK: John Wiley & Sons, Ltd.
6. BNF 47 (2004) *British National Formulary*. 47th edn. London: British Medical Association and Royal Pharmaceutical Society of Great Britain.
7. Bonnar, J. and Sheppard, B.L. (1996) Treatment of menorrhagia during menstruation: randomised controlled trial of ethamsylate, mefenamic acid, and tranexamic acid. *British Medical Journal* **313**(7057), 579–582. [Full text]
8. Brown, J.S., Sawaya, G., Thom, D.H. and Grady, D. (2000) Hysterectomy and urinary incontinence: a systematic review. *Lancet* **356**(9229), 535–539. [Full text]
9. Campbell, S. and Monga, A. (Eds.) (2000) Disorders of the menstrual cycle. In: *Gynaecology by ten teachers*. 17th edn. London: Arnold.
10. Coulter, A., Kelland, J., Peto, V. and Rees, M.C. (1995) Treating menorrhagia in primary care. An overview of drug trials and a survey of prescribing practice. *International Journal of Technology Assessment in Health Care* **11**(3), 456–471.
11. CSM (2002) Non-steroidal anti-inflammatory drugs (NSAIDs) and gastrointestinal (GI) safety. *Current Problems in Pharmacovigilance* **28**(Apr), 5.
12. CSM (2003) Reminder: gastrointestinal toxicity and NSAIDs. *Current Problems in Pharmacovigilance* **29**(Sept), 8–9.
13. CSM (2004) *Updated prescribing advice on the effect of depo-provera contraception on bones*. Committee on Safety of Medicines. http://medicines.mhra.gov.uk [Accessed: 14/02/2005].
14. Dijkhuizen, F.P., Brolmann, H.A., Potters, A.E. et al (1996) The accuracy of transvaginal ultrasonography in the diagnosis of endometrial abnormalities. *Obstetrics & Gynecology* **87**(3), 345–349.
15. Dijkhuizen, F.P.H.L.J., Mol, B.W.J., Bromann, H.A.M. and Heintz, A.P.M. (2000) The accuracy of endometrial sampling in the diagnosis of patients with endometrial carcinoma and hyperplasia. *Cancer* **89**(8), 1765–1772.
16. DTB (2000) Which operation for menorrhagia? *Drug & Therapeutics Bulletin* **38**(10), 77–80.
17. Duckitt, K. and McCully, K. (2003) Menorrhagia. *Clinical Evidence* **10**(Dec), 2151–2169.
18. Farquar, C.M., Lethaby, A., Sowter, M. et al (1999) An evaluation of risk factors for endometrial hyperplasia in premenopausal women with abnormal menstrual bleeding. *American Journal of Obstetrics & Gynecology* **181**(3), 525–529.
19. Farrell, S.A. and Kieser, K. (2000) Sexuality after hysterectomy. *Obstetrics & Gynecology* **95**(6:Pt 2), 1045–1051.
20. FFPRHC Clinical Effectiveness Unit (2003) FFPRHC guidance: first prescription of combined oral contraception. *Journal of Family Planning and Reproductive Health Care* **29**(4), 209–223.
21. FFPRHC Clinical Effectiveness Unit (2004) *FFPRHC guidance (April 2004): the levonorgestrel-releasing*

M

intrauterine system (LNG-IUS) in contraception and reproductive health. Faculty of Family Planning and Reproductive Health Care. www.ffprhc.org.uk [Accessed: 07/05/2004].
22. Garside, G., Stein, K., Wyatt, K. et al (2004) The effectiveness and cost-effectiveness of microwave and thermal balloon endometrials abalation for heavy menstrual bleeding: a systematic review and economic modelling. *Health Technology Assessment* 8(3), 1–22.
23. Hernández-Diaz, S. and Garcia-Rodriguez, L.A. (2001) Epidemiologic assessment of the safety of conventional nonsteroidal anti-inflammatory drugs. *American Journal of Medicine* **110**(3A), 20S-27S.
24. Hickey, M., Higham, J. and Fraser, I.S. (2001) *Progestogens versus oestrogens and progestogens for irregular uterine bleeding associated with anovulation (Cochrane Review).* The Cochrane Library. Issue 1. Oxford: Update Software.
25. Hurskainen, R., Teperi, J., Rissanen, P. et al (2004) Clinical outcomes and costs with the levonorgestrel-releasing intrauterine system or hysterectomy for treatment of menorrhagia: randomized trial 5-year follow-up. *Journal of the American Medical Association* **291**(12), 1456–1463. [Full text]
26. Iyer, V., Farquhar, C. and Jepson, R. (2003) *Oral contraceptive pills for heavy menstrual bleeding (Cochrane Review).* The Cochrane Library. Issue 4. Oxford: Update Software.
27. Kadir, R.A., Economides, D.L., Sabin, C.A. et al (1998) Frequency of inherited bleeding disorders in women with menorrhagia. *Lancet* **351**(9101), 485–489. [Full text]
28. Lethaby, A., Irvine, G. and Cameron, I. (2004a) *Cyclical progestogens for heavy menstrual bleeding (Cochrane Review).* The Cochrane Library. Issue 2. Chichester, UK: John Wiley & Sons, Ltd.
29. Lethaby, A.E., Cooke, I. and Rees, M. (2004b) *Progesterone/progestogen releasing intrauterine systems versus either placebo or any other medication for heavy menstrual bleeding (Cochrane Review).* The Cochrane Library. Issue 2. Chichester: John Wiley & Sons, Ltd.
30. Lethaby, A., Farquhar, C. and Cooke, I. (2004c) *Antifibrinolytics for heavy menstrual bleeding (Cochrane Review).* The Cochrane Library. Issue 4. Chichester, UK: John Wiley & Sons, Ltd.
31. Lethaby, A., Augood, C. and Duckitt, K. (2004d) *Nonsteroidal anti-inflammatory drugs for heavy menstrual bleeding (Cochrane Review).* The Cochrane Library. Issue 2. Chichester, UK: John Wiley & Sons, Ltd.
32. Lethaby, A., Shepperd, S., Cooke, I. and Farquhar, C. (2004e) *Endometrial resection and ablation versus hysterectomy for heavy menstrual bleeding (Cochrane Review).* The Cochrane Library. Issue 2. Chichester, UK: John Wiley & Sons, Ltd.
33. Lumsden, M.A. and McGavigan, J. (1997) Menstruation and menstrual disorder. In: Shaw, R.W., Soutter, W.P., Stanton, S.L. et al (Eds.) *Gynaecology.* 2nd edn. Edinburgh: Churchill Livingstone. 459–476.
34. Maresh, M.J., Metcalfe, M.A., McPherson, K. et al (2002) The VALUE national hysterectomy study: description of the patients and their surgery. *BJOG: an International Journal of Obstetrics & Gynaecology* **109**(3), 302–312.
35. New Zealand National Health Committee (1998) *Guidelines for the management of heavy menstrual bleeding.* New Zealand National Health Committee. www.nzgg.org.nz [Accessed: 17/04/2001]. [Full text]
36. NHS CRD (1995) Management of menorrhagia. *Effective Health Care Bulletin* **1**(9), 1–15.
37. NICE (2001) *Referral advice – a guide to appropriate referral from general to specialist services.* National Institute for Clinical Excellence. www.nice.org.uk [Accessed: 11/08/2002].
38. NICE (2005) *Referral guidelines for suspected cancer – quick reference guide.* Clinical guideline 27. National Institute for Health and Clinical Excellence. www.nice.org.uk [Accessed: 01/07/2005].
39. Oehler, M.K. and Rees, M.C. (2003) Menorrhagia: an update. *Acta Obstetricia et Gynecologica Scandinavica* **82**(5), 405–422.
40. Proctor, M. and Farquar, C. (2003) Dysmenorrhoea. *Clinical Evidence* **10**(Dec), 2058–2078.
41. Proctor, M.L., Roberts, H. and Farquhar, C.M. (2003) *Combined oral contraceptive pill (OCP) as treatment for primary dysmenorrhoea (Cochrane Review).* The Cochrane Library. Issue 4. Oxford: Update Software.
42. RCOG (1998) *The initial management of menorrhagia Evidence-based clinical guidelines no. 1.* London: Royal College of Obstetricians & Gynaecologists.
43. RCOG (1999) *The management of menorrhagia in secondary care.* Evidence-based clinical guidelines No. 5. Royal College of Obstetricians & Gynaecologists. www.rcog.org.uk [Accessed: 15/06/2004]. [Full text]
44. Rees, M. (2004) *Personal communication.* Reader in reproductive medicine; honorary consultant in Medical Gynaecology, Women's Centre: John Radcliffe Hospital, Oxford.
45. Robins, J.C. (2001) Therapies for the treatment of abnormal uterine bleeding. *Current Women's Health Reports* **1**(3), 196–201.
46. Rose, P.G. (1996) Endometrial carcinoma. *New England Journal of Medicine* **335**(9), 640–649.
47. Roy, S.N. and Bhattacharya, S. (2004) Benefits and risks of pharmacological agents used for the treatment of menorrhagia. *Drug Safety* **27**(2), 75–90.
48. Scholes, D., Lacroix, A.Z., Ichikawa, L.E. et al (2002) Injectable hormone contraception and bone density: results from a prospective study. *Epidemiology* **13**(5), 581–587.
49. Shah, A.A. and Grainger, D.A. (1996) *Contemporary concepts in managing menorrhagia.* Medscape. www.medscape.com [Accessed: 30/05/2001].
50. Sowter, M.C., Lethaby, A. and Singla, A.A. (2004) *Pre operative endometrial thinning agents before endometrial destruction for heavy menstrual bleeding (Cochrane Review).* The Cochrane Library. Issue 2. Chichester, UK: John Wiley & Sons, Ltd.
51. Tsuda, H., Kawabata, M., Yamamoto, K. et al (1997) Prospective study to compare endometrial cytology and transvaginal ultrasonography for identification of endometrial malignancies. *Gynecologic Oncology* **65**(3), 383–386.
52. Vercellini, P., Cortesi, I., Oldani, S. et al (1997) The role of transvaginal ultrasonography and outpatient diagnostic hysteroscopy in the evaluation of patients with menorrhagia. *Human Reproduction* **12**(8), 1768–1771.
53. Vilos, G.A., Lefebvre, G. and Graves, G.R. (2001) Guidelines for the managment of abnormal uterine bleeding. *SOGC Clinical Practice Guidelines* **106**(August), 1–6.
54. Zhang, W.Y. and Li Wan Po, A. (1998) Efficacy of minor analgesics in primary dysmenorrhoea: a systematic review. *British Journal of Obstetrics & Gynaecology* **105**(7), 780–789.

Evidence grading

The evidence grading used in this guidance represents that used by the Royal College of Obstetricians and Gynaecologists and the Faculty of Family Planning and Reproductive Health Care Clinical Effectiveness Unit in the development of their different guidance. The scheme is similar to that used by other guideline-development organizations. The definitions of the grades of recommendation are:

Grade A	Evidence is based on randomized controlled trials
Grade B	Evidence is based on other robust experimental or observational studies
Grade C	Evidence is limited, but the advice relies on expert opinion and has the endorsement of respected authorities

M

PRODIGY GUIDANCE

Migraine

Last revised in July 2005
www.prodigy.nhs.uk/guidance.asp?gt=Migraine

Applies to people over the age of 16 years

This guidance covers the management of migraine in adults.

This guidance does not cover the management of migraine in children.

There is separate PRODIGY guidance for *Headache* and *Trigeminal neuralgia*.

Goals

- To relieve the symptoms of an acute attack of migraine
- To reduce the frequency and severity of migraine attacks
- To identify possible trigger factors

Contents

Scenarios

- Acute treatment first-line (standard analgesia/anti-emetic) p.1230
- Acute treatment second-line (triptans) p.1232
- Migraine prophylaxis (excluding menstrual migraine) p.1235
- Menstrual migraine prophylaxis p.1236
- Pregnancy and breastfeeding p.1238

Extended Information, p. 1240

M

Which scenario?

- **Acute treatment first-line:** covers the management of a person presenting for the first time with migraine, or a review of successful first-line treatment.
- **Acute treatment second-line:** covers the management of migraine with triptans when first-line treatment is unsuccessful.
- **Migraine prophylaxis (excluding menstrual migraine):** covers the management of a person with frequent episodes of migraine.
- **Menstrual migraine prophylaxis:** covers the management of a woman with frequent episodes of menstrual migraine.
- **Pregnancy and breastfeeding:** covers the management of migraine (acute treatment and prophylaxis) whilst pregnant or breastfeeding.

Acute treatment first-line (standard analgesia/anti-emetic)

Which therapy?

- **Identify trigger factors,** and avoid them if possible. Consider using a migraine diary (one is included in the attached *Patient Information Leaflets*).
- **Analgesia:**
  - **Aspirin, paracetamol, or ibuprofen** are effective and should be started early in the attack.
  - **Nonsteroidal anti-inflammatory drugs (NSAIDs)** such as diclofenac, naproxen, and tolfenamic acid are alternatives.
- **Addition of an anti-emetic** may reduce nausea and vomiting and increase the absorption of analgesics given at the same time.
  - **Domperidone** has fewer adverse effects than metoclopramide, but the evidence for it is less substantial than for metoclopramide. Domperidone is available as a suppository if vomiting is a problem.
  - **Metoclopramide** is effective but can cause extrapyramidal adverse events (especially in younger people). It should be avoided in pregnant or breastfeeding women.
- **Soluble preparations are preferred** as they act more quickly.
- **Combination products** may be particularly useful for people who wish to carry medication with them for early use. *Migramax*® and *Paramax*® are available as dispersible granules. These are the only dispersible forms of metoclopramide available.
- **Avoid products containing opioids.**

Practical prescribing points

For further information please see the *Medicines Compendium* (www.medicines.org.uk) or the *British National Formulary* (www.bnf.org).

- **NSAIDs** may cause gastrointestinal irritation and occasionally gastrointestinal haemorrhage. Do not give if there is a history of peptic ulceration. NSAIDs may worsen asthma, hypertension, renal impairment, or heart failure.
- **Metoclopramide** should not be given to children or young adults because of the increased risk of extrapyramidal adverse effects.

Follow-up advice

- If symptoms do not respond to first-line treatment, or the treatment is poorly tolerated, consider prescribing a triptan (see *Acute treatment second-line* scenario).
- If symptoms respond to first-line treatment but are severe, or occur more than twice per month, consider prophylaxis (see *Migraine prophylaxis* scenario).

Should I refer or investigate?

Refer?

- If there is any uncertainty in the diagnosis, referral to a neurologist should be considered.

Investigate?

- Investigations are not usually required but, if undertaken, reveal no abnormalities. There are no diagnostic tests for migraine.

Patient information leaflets

The following PILs are available at www.prodigy.nhs.uk

- Anti-inflammatory Painkillers
- Migraine
- Migraine Action Association
- Migraine - Medicines to Treat Attacks

- Migraine - The Pill and Migraine
- Migraine - Triggers and Diary
- Migraine Trust

Shared decision making

- Does anything trigger your migraine? A migraine diary may help.
- **Paracetamol, aspirin, or ibuprofen** often ease migraine attacks. Take the full dose as early as possible after symptoms start. Repeat after 4 hours if needed.
- **Anti-inflammatory painkillers** such as diclofenac, naproxen, or tolfenamic acid are alternatives.
- **Anti-sickness tablets** such as metoclopramide or domperidone may help if you feel sick or vomit during a migraine.
- Soluble tablets tend to be best as they are absorbed quickly.
- Some medicines also come as suppositories if vomiting is a problem.
- Some tablets combine a painkiller and an anti-sickness medicine. These may be useful, but the dose of each constituent may not suit everyone or be strong enough.

Drug rationale

Drugs not included

- **Anti-emetics, except domperidone and metoclopramide,** are not included as they do not speed gastric emptying, and have not been shown to enhance the efficacy of analgesics given at the same time.
- **Ergotamine** is not included due to its high risk of adverse effects.
- **Nonsteroidal anti-inflammatory drugs (NSAIDs)** that are not licensed for the treatment of acute migraine are not included. Although flurbiprofen is licensed for the treatment of migraine, it has been less widely studied than the other NSAIDs offered for the acute treatment of migraine, and is therefore not included.
- **Opioids** (as single or combination products) should be avoided. In addition to their usual adverse effects, they increase the risk of medication overuse headache.
- **Triptans** are not recommended as first-line treatment. They are included in the scenario *Acute treatment second-line*.

[DTB, 1998; Micromedex, 2001; BASH, 2004; BNF 48, 2004]

Drugs included

- **Aspirin or paracetamol** are suitable first choices for acute treatment of migraine. Soluble forms are preferred as these are absorbed faster. Paracetamol suppositories are included if oral ingestion is not possible because of vomiting.
- **Domperidone or metoclopramide** may be given at the same time as analgesia. Anti-emetics speed gastric emptying, relieve nausea, and may enhance the efficacy of the co-administered analgesic. Metoclopramide should be avoided in children and young adults, as extrapyramidal adverse effects are more common in these age groups. Domperidone is also available as a suppository.
- **NSAIDs** (ibuprofen, diclofenac potassium, naproxen sodium, and tolfenamic acid) are alternative licensed choices for the acute treatment of migraine. Although not specifically licensed for migraine, diclofenac sodium tablets and naproxen tablets are also commonly used. Ibuprofen is available as dispersible granules, and tolfenamic acid is available as a soluble tablet. Diclofenac sodium is available as a suppository.
- **Combination products** (containing aspirin or paracetamol plus an anti-emetic) are an alternative to separate prescriptions. They may be useful for people who wish to carry medication with them, for early use, but are more expensive to prescribe than the separate constituents.

[DTB, 1998; BASH, 2004; BNF 48, 2004]

Prescriptions

1st-line analgesia

Soluble aspirin: 600mg when required, max 4 times a day
- Age from 16 years onwards
- Aspirin 300mg dispersible tabs. Take two tablets every 4 to 6 hours when required for pain relief. Maximum of 4 doses 24 hours; supply 100 tablets; NHS Cost £1.62; OTC Cost £2.00.

Soluble aspirin: 900mg when required, max 4 times a day
- Age from 16 years onwards
- Aspirin 300mg dispersible tabs. Take three tablets every 4 to 6 hours when required for pain relief. Maximum of 4 doses 24 hours; supply 100 tablets; NHS Cost £1.62; OTC Cost £2.00.

Aspirin tablets: 600mg when required, max 4 times a day
- Age from 16 years onwards
- Aspirin 300mg tablets. Take two tablets every 4 to 6 hours when required for pain relief. Maximum of 4 doses 24 hours; supply 64 tablets; NHS Cost £0.62; OTC Cost £2.00.

Aspirin tablets: 900mg when required, max 4 times a day
- Age from 16 years onwards
- Aspirin 300mg tablets. Take three tablets every 4 to 6 hours when required for pain relief. Maximum of 4 doses 24 hours; supply 96 tablets; NHS Cost £0.93; OTC Cost £2.00.

Ibuprofen tablets: 400mg when required, max 3 times a day
- Age from 16 years onwards
- Ibuprofen 400mg tablets. Take one tablet three times a day when required for pain relief. Do not exceed the stated dose; supply 84 tablets; NHS Cost £2.74; OTC Cost £4.40.

Soluble paracetamol: 1g when required, max 4 times a day
- Age from 16 years onwards
- Paracetamol 500mg soluble tabs. Take two tablets every 4 to 6 hours when required for pain relief. Maximum of 8 tablets in 24 hours; supply 60 tablets; NHS Cost £5.43; OTC Cost £5.00.

Paracetamol tablets: 1g when required, max 4 times a day
- Age from 16 years onwards
- Paracetamol 500mg tablets. Take two tablets every 4 to 6 hours when required for pain relief. Maximum of 8 tablets in 24 hours; supply 100 tablets; NHS Cost £1.06; OTC Cost £1.35.

Paracetamol suppository: 1g when required, max 4 times a day
- Age from 16 years onwards
- Paracetamol 500mg suppositories. Insert one to two suppositories into the rectum every 4 to 6 hours when required for pain relief. Maximum of 8 suppositories in 24 hours; supply 20 suppositories; NHS Cost £19.80; OTC Cost £34.00.

M

Anti-emetics

Metoclopramide tabs: 10mg when required, max 3 times a day
- Age from 20 years onwards
- Metoclopramide 10mg tablets. Take one tablet when required for relief of sickness. Maximum of 3 tablets in 24 hours; supply 28 tablets; NHS Cost £1.32.

Domperidone tabs: 10-20mg when required, max 4 times a day
- Age from 16 years onwards
- Domperidone 10mg tablets. Take one to two tablets every 4 to 8 hours when required for relief of sickness. Maximum of 8 tablets in 24 hours; supply 30 tablets; NHS Cost £2.11.

Domperidone suppository: 30-60mg when required,max 120mg/day
- Age from 16 years onwards
- Domperidone 30mg suppositories. Insert one to two suppositories into the rectum every 4 to 8 hours when required for relief of sickness. Maximum of 4 suppositories in 24 hours; supply 20 suppositories; NHS Cost £5.30.

Other NSAIDs

Ibuprofen tablets: 600mg when required, max 3 times a day
- Age from 16 years onwards
- Ibuprofen 600mg tablets. Take one tablet at onset of migraine attack. Maximum of 3 tablets in 24 hours; supply 24 tablets; NHS Cost £1.34.

Soluble ibuprofen: 600mg when required, max 3 times a day
- Age from 16 years onwards
- Ibuprofen 600mg eff granules. Take the contents of one sachet (dissolved in water) at onset of migraine attack. Maximum of 3 sachets in 24 hours; supply 20 sachets; NHS Cost £6.80.

Diclofenac potassium: 50mg when required, max 4 times a day
- Age from 16 years onwards
- Diclofenac potassium 50mg tabs. Take one tablet at onset of migraine attack. Maximum of 4 tablets in 24 hours; supply 28 tablets; NHS Cost £7.03.

Diclofenac sodium: 50mg when required, max 3 times a day
- Age from 16 years onwards
- Diclofenac 50mg e/c tablets. Take one tablet at onset of migraine attack. Maximum of 3 tablets in 24 hours; supply 21 tablets; NHS Cost £0.48.

Diclofenac suppository: 50mg when required, max 3 in 24hours
- Age from 16 years onwards
- Diclofenac 50mg suppositories. Insert one suppository into the rectum when required for pain relief. Maximum of 3 suppositories in 24 hours; supply 10 suppositories; NHS Cost £2.07.

Naproxen sodium: 825mg when required, max 1375mg in 24 hours
- Age from 16 years onwards
- Naproxen sodium 275mg tablets. Take three tablets at onset of migraine attack. Maximum of 5 tablets in 24 hours; supply 60 tablets; NHS Cost £7.54.

Naproxen tablets: 500mg when required, max twice a day
- Age from 16 years onwards
- Naproxen 500mg tablets. Take one tablet at onset of migraine attack. Maximum of 2 tablets in 24 hours; supply 28 tablets; NHS Cost £2.45.

Tolfenamic acid: 200mg when required, max twice a day
- Age from 16 years onwards
- Tolfenamic acid 200mg tablets. Take one tablet at onset of migraine attack. Maximum of 2 tablets in 24 hours; supply 10 tablets; NHS Cost £15.00.

Combination products

Paracetamol 500mg + domperidone 10mg tablets (Domperamol)
- Age from 16 years onwards
- Paracetamol+domp 500/10mg tabs. Take two tablets at onset of migraine attack. Repeat up to every 4 hours if necessary. Maximum of 8 tablets in 24 hours; supply 16 tablets; NHS Cost £7.00.

Aspirin 900mg + metoclopramide 10mg sachets (Migramax)
- Age from 20 years onwards
- Aspirin+metoclop 900/10mg sachets. Take the contents of one sachet (dissolved in water) at onset of migraine attack. Repeat after 2 hours if necessary. Maximum of 3 sachets in 24 hours; supply 6 sachets; NHS Cost £7.00.

Paracetamol 500mg + metoclopramide 5mg tablets (Paramax)
- Age from 20 years onwards
- Paracet+metoclop 500/5mg tabs. Take two tablets at onset of migraine attack. Repeat after 4 hours if necessary. Maximum of 6 tablets in 24 hours; supply 42 tablets; NHS Cost £6.69.

Paracetamol 500mg + metoclopramide 5mg sachets (Paramax)
- Age from 20 years onwards
- Paracet+metoclop 500/5mg powder. Take the contents of two sachets (dissolved in water) at onset of migraine attack. Repeat after 4 hours if necessary. Max of 6 sachets in 24 hours; supply 42 sachets; NHS Cost £8.69.

Acute treatment second-line (triptans)

Which therapy?

- **If migraine attacks are unresponsive to adequate doses of analgesic and anti-emetic, consider replacing them with a triptan.**
- **Advise the person to use the triptan as soon as possible after the onset of *headache*;** triptans should not be not taken during the aura.
- **Prescribe a standard dose of oral triptan.** These are sumatriptan 50 mg, zolmitriptan 2.5 mg, rizatriptan 10 mg, naratriptan 2.5 mg, almotriptan 12.5 mg, eletriptan 40 mg, and frovatriptan 2.5 mg:
  - **If the initial choice is ineffective:** eletriptan 40 mg (80 mg if necessary), rizatriptan 10 mg, sumatriptan 100 mg, or zolmitriptan 5 mg (second dose can be taken if first is ineffective) may be more effective. There may be more adverse effects.
  - **If the initial dose is poorly tolerated:** almotriptan 12.5 mg, naratriptan 2.5 mg, rizatriptan 5 mg, eletriptan 20 mg, or frovatriptan 2.5 mg may cause less adverse effects and retain efficacy.
- **Other formulations may be useful:**
  - **Orodispersible tablets and wafers** may be useful if swallowing is a problem.
  - **Nasal sprays** give quicker relief (zolmitriptan nasal spray is also useful if vomiting is present).
  - **Subcutaneous injection** (sumatriptan) gives the most rapid relief and is useful if vomiting is present.
- **If relapse of pain occurs,** one or more additional dose (depending on drug) can be taken in 24 h.

Combine triptans with standard analgesia and anti-emetics if necessary.

Practical prescribing points

For further information please see the *Medicines Compendium* (www.medicines.org.uk) or the *British National Formulary* (www.bnf.org).

'Triptan sensations' include a warm–hot sensation, tightness, tingling, flushing, and feelings of heaviness or pressure in areas such as the face, limbs, and occasionally the chest.

- If the person is forewarned of these symptoms they may cause less distress should they occur.
- Discontinue and review if there are particularly intense sensations or chest pain.

Triptans should not be taken by the following people:

- People with uncontrolled hypertension
- People with coronary heart disease or cerebrovascular disease
- People with coronary vasospasm (including Prinzmetal's angina)
- People with risk factors for coronary heart disease or cerebrovascular disease

Sumatriptan may cause drowsiness, and driving or other skilled tasks should be avoided if this occurs [BNF 48, 2004]. Note: this is likely to be a class effect and the same caution applies to other triptans.

Reduce the dose of rizatriptan to 5 mg if the person is taking propranolol, as propranolol may increase the plasma concentration of rizatriptan.

Follow-up advice

Follow up at around 1 month depending on frequency and severity of attacks, in order to assess the effect of treatment.

If symptoms do not respond, refer to a neurologist.

If symptoms respond to treatment but are severe or occur more than twice per month, consider prophylaxis (see *Prophylaxis* scenario).

Should I refer or investigate?

Refer?

If second-line treatment of acute symptoms fails, or diagnosis of migraine is not certain, referral to a neurologist is required.

Investigate?

Investigations are not usually required but, if undertaken, show no abnormalities. There are no diagnostic tests for migraine.

Patient information leaflets

The following PILs are available at www.prodigy.nhs.uk

Migraine
Migraine Action Association
Migraine - Medicines to Treat Attacks
Migraine - The Pill and Migraine
Migraine - Triggers and Diary
Migraine Trust

Shared decision making

Sumatriptan is a commonly used triptan medicine used to treat migraine. It is not a painkiller but works in a different way. Take a dose as soon as the headache starts.

- **Almotriptan, eletriptan, naratriptan, rizatriptan, zolmitriptan, and frovatriptan** are alternative triptans used to treat migraine.
- If one triptan does not work, a different one may do. You can try one for several migraines, but if it does not seem to help, come back to discuss trying another.
- Read the packet leaflet and take exactly as instructed. For example:
  - Do not take a second dose if the first has no effect (apart from zolmitriptan).
  - You can take a second dose after 2 hours (4 hours for naratriptan) if the first one helped but the headache returns.
- If vomiting back tablets is a problem when you have a migraine:
  - Sumatriptan also comes as a nasal spray and as an injection.
  - Rizatriptan and zolmitriptan are available as a wafer or tablet that disperses in the mouth and can be swallowed with saliva.
- Side effects from triptans are usually mild and soon pass. The most common include unsteadiness, dizziness, feeling sick, and 'heavy sensations' in parts of your body.
- Some people cannot take triptans. (For example, some people with heart disease.)

Drug rationale

Drugs not included

- **Standard first-line analgesia and anti-emetics** are offered in the scenario *Acute treatment first-line (standard analgesia/anti-emetic)*. They may be combined with triptans if use of triptans alone is ineffective.

Drugs included

- **Sumatriptan** is available as standard and as rapidly dispersing tablets (50 and 100 mg), nasal spray (10–20 mg), and subcutaneous injection (6 mg). Sumatriptan is the most well established triptan.
  - The usual oral dose is 50 mg, although if ineffective this may be increased to 100 mg, at the possible risk of increased adverse effects.
  - Nasal sprays and subcutaneous injections are useful if a rapid response is required; in addition, the injection is useful if the person is vomiting.
- **Zolmitriptan** is available as 2.5 mg tablets, orodispersible tablets, and nasal spray (5 mg). It has very similar efficacy and adverse effect profile to sumatriptan.
  - The usual oral dose is 2.5 mg, but this can be repeated even if the first tablet was not effective.
  - Orodispersible tablets may be preferred by some people who find swallowing difficult.
  - Zolmitriptan nasal spray is useful if rapid relief of pain is required or the person is vomiting.
- **Rizatriptan** is available as tablets (5 or 10 mg) or orodispersible wafers (10 mg). The higher dose is more effective than sumatriptan 100 mg and has a more sustained action. The lower dose is similar in terms of efficacy and adverse effects.
- **Naratriptan** 2.5 mg tablets are less effective in relieving pain than sumatriptan 100 mg, but may result in less relapses and have less associated adverse effects.
- **Almotriptan** 12.5 mg tablets give similar pain relief to sumatriptan 100 mg, but have a more sustained action and are associated with less adverse effects. Currently it is a black triangle drug, but it may be recommended as the first-line triptan when more data become available.
- **Eletriptan** is available in 20 and 40 mg tablets. It exhibits a clear dose–response relationship; the higher doses (40 and 80 mg) have greater efficacy than sumatriptan

M

100 mg but more adverse effects, the lower dose (20 mg) is not as effective but may be better tolerated.
- **Frovatriptan** is the most recent addition to the triptan family. It is not as effective as sumatriptan 100 mg, but has less adverse effects and may be useful when relapse is a problem.

[Oldman et al, 2002]

Prescriptions

1st line: standard dose triptan tablets

Sumatriptan 50mg when required, max 300mg in 24 hours
- Age from 18 years onwards
- Sumatriptan 50mg tablets. Take one tablet at onset of migraine attack. Maximum of 6 tablets in 24 hours; supply 6 tablets; NHS Cost £27.62.

Almotriptan 12.5mg when required, max 25mg in 24 hours
- Age from 18 years onwards
- Almotriptan 12.5mg tablets. Take one tablet at onset of migraine attack. Maximum of 2 tablets in 24 hours; supply 6 tablets; NHS Cost £18.14.

Eletriptan 40mg when required, max 80mg in 24 hours
- Age from 18 years onwards
- Eletriptan 40mg tablets. Take one tablet at onset of migraine attack. Maximum of 2 tablets in 24 hours; supply 6 tablets; NHS Cost £22.50.

Naratriptan 2.5mg when required, max 5mg in 24 hours
- Age from 18 years onwards
- Naratriptan 2.5mg tablets. Take one tablet at onset of migraine attack. Maximum of 2 tablets in 24 hours; supply 6 tablets; NHS Cost £24.00.

Rizatriptan 10mg when required (if not taking propranolol)
- Age from 18 years onwards
- Rizatriptan 10mg tablets. Take one tablet at onset of migraine attack. Maximum of 2 tablets in 24 hours; supply 6 tablets; NHS Cost £26.74.

Rizatriptan 5mg when required (if taking propranolol)
- Age from 18 years onwards
- Rizatriptan 5mg tablets. Take one tablet at onset of migraine attack. Maximum of 2 tablets in 24 hours; supply 6 tablets; NHS Cost £26.74.

Zolmitriptan 2.5mg when required, max 10mg in 24 hours
- Age from 18 years onwards
- Zolmitriptan 2.5mg tablets. Take one tablet at onset of migraine attack. Maximum of 4 tablets in 24 hours; supply 6 tablets; NHS Cost £24.00.

Frovatriptan 2.5mg when required, max 5 mg in 24 hours
- Age from 18 years onwards
- Frovatriptan 2.5mg tablets. Take one tablet at onset of migraine attack. Maximum of 2 tablets in 24 hours; supply 6 tablets; NHS Cost £17.70.

Triptans: 1st-line dose ineffective

Eletriptan 40mg when required, max 80mg in 24 hours
- Age from 18 years onwards
- Eletriptan 40mg tablets. Take one tablet at onset of migraine attack. Maximum of 2 tablets in 24 hours; supply 6 tablets; NHS Cost £22.50.

Eletriptan 80mg when required, max 80mg in 24 hours
- Age from 18 years onwards
- Eletriptan 40mg tablets. Take two tablets at onset of migraine attack. Do not take more than 2 tablets in 24 hours; supply 12 tablets; NHS Cost £45.00.

Rizatriptan 10mg when required (if not taking propranolol
- Age from 18 years onwards
- Rizatriptan 10mg tablets. Take one tablet at onset of migraine attack. Maximum of 2 tablets in 24 hours; supply 6 tablets; NHS Cost £26.74.

Sumatriptan 100mg when required, max 300mg in 24 hours
- Age from 18 years onwards
- Sumatriptan 100mg tablets. Take one tablet at onset of migraine attack. Maximum of 3 tablets in 24 hours; supply 6 tablets; NHS Cost £44.64.

Zolmitriptan 5mg when required, max 10mg in 24 hours
- Age from 18 years onwards
- Zolmitriptan 2.5mg tablets. Take two tablets at onset of migraine attack. Maximum of 4 tablets in 24 hours; supply 12 tablets; NHS Cost £48.00.

Triptans: 1st-line dose poorly tolerated

Almotriptan 12.5mg when required, max 25mg in 24 hour
- Age from 18 years onwards
- Almotriptan 12.5mg tablets. Take one tablet at onset of migraine attack. Maximum of 2 tablets in 24 hours; supply 6 tablets; NHS Cost £18.14.

Naratriptan 2.5mg when required, max 5mg in 24 hours
- Age from 18 years onwards
- Naratriptan 2.5mg tablets. Take one tablet at onset of migraine attack. Maximum of 2 tablets in 24 hours; supply 6 tablets; NHS Cost £24.00.

Rizatriptan 5mg when required, maximum 10mg in 24 hours
- Age from 18 years onwards
- Rizatriptan 5mg tablets. Take one tablet at onset of migraine attack. Maximum of 2 tablets in 24 hours; supply 6 tablets; NHS Cost £26.74.

Eletriptan 20mg when required, max 40mg in 24 hours
- Age from 18 years onwards
- Eletriptan 20mg tablets. Take one tablet at onset of migraine attack. Maximum of 2 tablets in 24 hours; supply 6 tablets; NHS Cost £22.50.

Frovatriptan 2.5mg when required, max 5 mg in 24 hours
- Age from 18 years onwards
- Frovatriptan 2.5mg tablets. Take one tablet at onset of migraine attack. Maximum of 2 tablets in 24 hours; supply 6 tablets; NHS Cost £17.70.

Alternative formulations: oro-dispersible triptan tablets

Rizatriptan wafers: 10mg if required (not if on propranolol
- Age from 18 years onwards
- Rizatriptan 10mg wafers. Place one wafer on the tongue at onset of migraine. Allow to dissolve before swallowing it. Maximum of 2 wafers in 24 hours; supply 6 wafers; NHS Cost £26.74.

Zolmitriptan oro-dispersible tablets: 2.5mg when required
- Age from 18 years onwards
- Zolmitriptan 2.5mg disp tabs. Place one tablet on the tongue at onset of migraine. Allow to dissolve before swallowing it. Maximum of 4 tablets in 24 hours; supply 6 tablets; NHS Cost £24.00.

Alternative formulations: nasal or subcutaneous triptans

Sumatriptan nasal spray: 10mg if required, max twice a day
- Age from 16 to 17 years
- Sumatriptan 10mg nasal spray. Spray once into ONE nostril at onset of migraine; supply 2 nasal spray; NHS Cost £12.28.

Sumatriptan nasal spray: 20mg if required, max twice a day
- Age from 18 years onwards
- Sumatriptan 10mg nasal spray. Spray once or twice into ONE nostril at onset of migraine; supply 2 nasal spray; NHS Cost £12.28.

Zolmitriptan nasal spray: 5mg if required, max twice a day
- Age from 18 years onwards
- Zolmitriptan 5mg nasal spray. Spray once or twice into ONE nostril at onset of migraine; supply 6 spray; NHS Cost £40.50.

Sumatriptan s/c injection: 6mg if required, max twice a day
- Age from 18 years onwards
- Sumatriptan 6mg/0.5ml inj. Inject the contents of one syringe (6mg) subcutaneously at onset of migraine. Maximum of 2 doses (12mg) in 24 hours; supply 2 pre-filled syringes; NHS Cost £44.19.

Migraine prophylaxis (excluding menstrual migraine)

Which therapy?

- **Prophylaxis should be considered for people with:**
  - Use of acute treatment on more than 2 days per week on a regular basis
  - More than two attacks per month that produce disability lasting 3 or more days
  - Less frequent but severe or prolonged attacks
  - Contraindications to, or ineffectiveness of, acute treatments
- **Acute treatments are still required;** the severity and frequency of attacks are only *reduced* by prophylaxis.
- **Recommended treatment for prophylaxis:**
  - Beta-blockers — atenolol, metoprolol, propranolol, or timolol (first-line)
  - Amitriptyline (alternative first-line if contraindications)
  - Sodium valproate (second-line)
- Start prophylaxis in the low dose range, and titrate upwards gradually.
- **Prophylaxis may need to be tried for 3–4 weeks before efficacy is achieved.**
- **Monitor the effect of treatment by asking the person to continue a migraine diary.**
- **Relaxation techniques, stress reduction, and coping strategies** may help when stress or anxiety exist.

Practical prescribing points

For further information please see the *Medicines Compendium* (www.medicines.org.uk) or the *British National Formulary* (www.bnf.org).

- **Beta-blockers are contraindicated** in people who suffer from asthma, chronic obstructive pulmonary disease, heart block, peripheral vascular disease, or unstable heart failure.
- **Amitriptyline is contraindicated** in people with ischaemic heart disease (particularly following a recent myocardial infarct), arrhythmias, or epilepsy. Amitriptyline may cause drowsiness: if affected, patients are advised not to drive or perform skilled tasks.
- **Sodium valproate is contraindicated** in women of childbearing age and people with active liver disease.

Follow-up advice

- Follow-up should be tailored to the individual:
  - Prophylaxis may need to be tried for 3–4 weeks before efficacy is achieved.
  - Prophylactic drugs that are effective should be used for 4–6 months, and then withdrawn over 2–3 weeks to establish whether they are still required.

Should I refer or investigate?

Refer?

- If prophylactic treatment fails, if frequency or severity of headache is increasing, or diagnosis of migraine is not certain, referral to a neurologist is required.

Investigate?

- Investigations are not usually required but, if undertaken, reveal no abnormalities. There are no diagnostic tests for migraine.

Patient information leaflets

The following PILs are available at www.prodigy.nhs.uk
- Migraine
- Migraine Action Association
- Migraine - Drugs to Prevent Attacks
- Migraine - Triggers and Diary
- Migraine Trust

Shared decision making

- **Beta-blockers such as propranolol, metoprolol, or atenolol** are the most commonly used medicines to prevent migraine attacks.
  - A low dose may work but it can be increased if necessary.
  - Some people cannot take beta blockers (such as some people with asthma).
- **Amitriptyline** is an alternative. It is an antidepressant but has an anti-migraine action separate from its antidepressant effect.
  - A low dose is started and increased if necessary.
  - It may cause a dry mouth.
- **Sodium valproate** is another alternative. It is an antiepileptic but has an anti-migraine action separate from its antiepileptic effect.
- Various other medicines are sometimes used when all else fails.
- Some points about medicines to prevent migraine:
  - You need to take the medicine every day.
  - They are unlikely to stop migraine attacks completely. However, the number and severity of attacks are often much reduced.
  - It may take 1–3 months for maximum benefit. So, do persevere.
- It is common to take one of these medicines for 4–6 months. After this you can stop it to see if it is still needed.
- You can still take painkillers or a triptan for migraine attacks if they occur.
- It is worth trying a different medicine if the first one does not work.

Drug rationale

Drugs not included

- **Anti-epileptics other than sodium valproate** as there is only limited evidence for their efficacy in migraine prophylaxis [Snow et al, 2002; Pappagallo, 2003].
- **Angiotensin-II receptor antagonists** as there is evidence of efficacy in the prevention of headache, but the types of headache prevented are not known [Etminan et al, 2002].

M

- **Beta-blockers other than propranolol, metoprolol, timolol, and atenolol** are not included. Beta-blockers with partial agonist activity are ineffective for migraine prophylaxis. Other beta-blockers have not been shown to be more effective than those offered, and are more expensive. Modified-release preparations are more expensive and are therefore not offered.
- **Clonidine** as it is no more effective than placebo and may aggravate depression and cause insomnia.
- **Feverfew** as there is no evidence of efficacy [Pittler and Ernst, 2004].
- **Methysergide** as it is associated with retroperitoneal and retropleural fibrosis [Snow et al, 2002].
- **Pizotifen** as evidence for its effectiveness is poor, and it is associated with unwanted adverse effects which limit its use [MeReC, 2002; Snow et al, 2002].
- **Selective serotonin reuptake inhibitors** as evidence is inconclusive for their efficacy in migraine.
- **Verapamil** as evidence is limited for its efficacy in migraine [Snow et al, 2002].

[BASH, 2004; BNF 48, 2004; Young et al, 2004]

Drugs included

- **Beta-blockers** are recommended as first-line prophylaxis unless contraindicated. Propranolol, metoprolol, and timolol are licensed for prevention of migraine; atenolol is not licensed but is commonly used [BASH, 2004; BNF 48, 2004].
- **Amitriptyline** (unlicensed) may be more useful when migraine coexists with tension-type headache or medication overuse headache, when there is associated depression, or when insomnia is a problem.
- **Sodium valproate** (unlicensed) has good evidence of efficacy. There is extensive experience of its use in migraine prophylaxis.

[BASH, 2004; BNF 48, 2004]

M

Prescriptions

Beta-blockers: propranolol or metoprolol (1st line)

Propranolol tablets: 40mg twice a day (usual start dose)
- Age from 16 years onwards
- Propranolol 40mg tablets. Take one tablet twice a day; supply 56 tablets; NHS Cost £2.50.

Propranolol tablets: 40mg three times a day
- Age from 16 years onwards
- Propranolol 40mg tablets. Take one tablet three times a day; supply 84 tablets; NHS Cost £3.75.

Propranolol tablets: 80mg twice a day
- Age from 16 years onwards
- Propranolol 80mg tablets. Take one tablet twice a day; supply 56 tablets; NHS Cost £1.45.

Metoprolol tablets: 50mg twice a day (usual start dose)
- Age from 16 years onwards
- Metoprolol 50mg tablets. Take one tablet twice a day; supply 56 tablets; NHS Cost £2.41.

Metoprolol tablets: 100mg twice a day
- Age from 16 years onwards
- Metoprolol 100mg tablets. Take one tablet twice a day; supply 56 tablets; NHS Cost £3.84.

Beta-blockers: atenolol or timolol (1st line)

Atenolol tablets: 50mg once a day (usual start dose)
- Age from 16 years onwards
- Atenolol 50mg tablets. Take one tablet once a day; supply 28 tablets; NHS Cost £1.02.

Atenolol tablets: 100mg once a day
- Age from 16 years onwards
- Atenolol 100mg tablets. Take one tablet once a day; supply 28 tablets; NHS Cost £0.67.

Timolol tablets: 10mg once a day (usual start dose)
- Age from 16 years onwards
- Timolol 10mg tablets. Take one tablet once a day; supply 30 tablets; NHS Cost £2.08.

Timolol tablets: 20mg once a day
- Age from 16 years onwards
- Timolol 10mg tablets. Take two tablets once a day; supply 60 tablets; NHS Cost £4.16.

Amitriptyline (1st line)

Amitriptyline: initial titration from 10mg to 40mg at night
- Age from 16 years onwards
- Amitriptyline 10mg tablets. Take 1 tab at night for 7 nights, then 2 tabs at night for 7 nights, then 3 tabs at night for 7 nights, then 4 tabs at night for 7 nights; supply 70 tablets; NHS Cost £2.50.

Amitriptyline tablets: 50mg at night
- Age from 16 years onwards
- Amitriptyline 50mg tablets. Take one tablet at night; supply 28 tablets; NHS Cost £1.60.

Amitriptyline tablets: 75mg at night
- Age from 16 years onwards
- Amitriptyline 25mg tablets. Take three tablets at night; supply 84 tablets; NHS Cost £5.13.

Sodium valproate (2nd line)

Valproate e/c tablets: 200mg twice a day (usual start dose)
- Age from 16 years onwards
- Sod valproate 200mg e/c tabs. Take one tablet twice a day; supply 56 tablets; NHS Cost £4.03.

Valproate e/c tablets: 400mg twice a day
- Age from 16 years onwards
- Sod valproate 200mg e/c tabs. Take two tablets twice a day; supply 112 tablets; NHS Cost £8.06.

Valproate e/c tablets: 600mg twice a day
- Age from 16 years onwards
- Sod valproate 200mg e/c tabs. Take three tablets twice a day; supply 168 tablets; NHS Cost £12.10.

Valproate e/c tablets: 800mg twice a day
- Age from 16 years onwards
- Sod valproate 200mg e/c tabs. Take four tablets twice a day; supply 224 tablets; NHS Cost £16.13.

Valproate e/c tablets: 1g twice a day
- Age from 16 years onwards
- Sod valproate 500mg e/c tabs. Take two tablets twice a day; supply 112 tablets; NHS Cost £20.07.

Menstrual migraine prophylaxis

Which therapy?

- **Acute treatment** of menstrual migraine is as in scenarios *Acute treatment first-line* and *Acute treatment second-line*.
- **Prophylaxis** for menstrual migraine, however, is different from prophylaxis of migraine associated with other trigger factors.
  - **Consider using peri-menstrual prophylaxis with a nonsteroidal anti-inflammatory drug (NSAID):**
    - Start the NSAID at the onset of menstruation and continue until the last day of bleeding.
    - Mefenamic acid or naproxen are suitable choices.
  - **Also consider oestrogen supplements:**

- Start transdermal oestradiol patches 100 micrograms 3 days before the onset of menses and continue for 7 days.
- If this is effective but poorly tolerated, consider a 50 microgram patch.
- Estradiol gel 1.5 mg is another alternative.

- **If migraine without aura occurs during the pill-free interval** in a cycle of combined oral contraceptives (COCs) consider:
  - Alternative contraception methods if the COC is now contraindicated.
  - Changing to a pill with a lower dose of the same progestogen.
  - Changing to a pill with the lowest available dose of a different progestogen.
  - Tri-cycling: take the pill continuously for three packets (9 weeks) followed by a 7 day pill-free interval, so that the number of menstrual bleeds is reduced.
  - Oestrogen supplements:
    - Start transdermal oestradiol patches 100 micrograms 3 days before the onset of menses and continue for 7 days.
    - If this is effective but poorly tolerated, consider a 50 microgram patch.
    - Estradiol gel 1.5 mg is another alternative.
- **If migraine with aura occurs, the COC must be stopped,** and other methods of contraception used.

Practical prescribing points

For further information please see the *Medicines Compendium* (www.medicines.org.uk) or the *British National Formulary* (www.bnf.org).

Nonsteroidal anti-inflammatory drugs

- **NSAIDs** may cause gastrointestinal irritation and occasionally gastrointestinal haemorrhage. Do not give if there is a history of peptic ulceration. NSAIDs may worsen asthma, hypertension, renal impairment, or heart failure.

Oestrogen replacement

- **Transdermal oestradiol:**
  - Advise women that patches should be stuck on the buttocks (never on the breasts).
  - Patch adhesiveness varies on different skin types.
- **Managing oestrogen-related adverse effects:**
  - Oestrogens can cause breast tenderness, leg cramps, bloating, and headaches, but these are often transient.
  - Options include reducing the dose or changing to estradiol gel 1.5 mg.
- **Avoid use of oestrogen replacement, or use with caution, in the following women:**
  - **Coronary heart disease or stroke:** do not start oestrogen replacement.
  - **Diabetes:** transdermal oestrogen may have less impact on lipids. Advise women that the risk of coronary heart disease seems higher in women with diabetes who take oestrogen replacement.
  - **Fibroids:** oestrogen replacement can be taken, but it may cause heavy or painful periods.
  - **Strong family history of breast cancer, or a personal history of benign breast disease:** avoid oestrogen replacement if possible, or monitor closely.
- **Seek specialist advice for women with** breast cancer, endometrial cancer, undiagnosed vaginal bleeding, liver disease, endometriosis, or a personal or family history of venous thromboembolic disease.

Follow-up advice

- Review every 3 months.
- Consider suspending treatments once attacks have been eliminated or reduced to 1 per month for at least 2 months.

Should I refer or investigate?

Refer?

- If prophylactic treatment fails, if frequency or severity of headache is increasing, or diagnosis of migraine is not certain, referral to a neurologist is required.

Investigate?

- Investigations are not usually required but, if undertaken, reveal no abnormalities. There are no diagnostic tests for migraine.

Patient information leaflets

The following PILs are available at www.prodigy.nhs.uk

- Migraine
- Migraine Action Association
- Migraine - Periods and Migraine
- Migraine - Triggers and Diary
- Migraine Trust

Shared decision making

- Migraines related to periods can be treated in the usual way (painkillers, triptans, etc).
- Options to help prevent period-related migraines include the following.
- **A short course of an anti-inflammatory painkiller each month, such as mefanamic acid or naproxen.** Start as soon as the period starts. Take until the last day of bleeding.
- **Oestrogen supplements** just before and during a period.
  - Oestrogen skin patches are sometimes used for 7 days. Start 3 days before the expected first day of your period.
  - An oestrogen gel used for the 7 days is an alternative.
- Some women who take 'the pill' get migraines with their period in the pill-free interval between pill packets.
  - If the migraines are with aura you should not take the pill at all.
  - If the migraines are without aura, options to prevent the migraines are:
    - Changing to a pill with less progestogen.
    - Tri-cycling — taking the pill continuously for three packets without any breaks, followed by a 7-day pill-free interval. By doing this you will have less withdrawal bleeds per year, and therefore fewer migraines.
    - Oestrogen supplements during the pill-free intervals.
    - A change to a different method of contraception.

Drug rationale

Drugs not included

- Drugs used for the prophylaxis of non-menstrual migraine (beta-blockers, amitriptyline, pizotifen) are not included, as they are not effective for the prophylaxis of menstrual migraine.
- Other oestrogen-only hormone replacement therapy products are not included. Different strength patches have not been studied for use as prophylaxis in menstrual migraine. Tablets are not suitable because

systemic oestrogen levels fluctuate more widely than with transdermal preparations. Once-weekly transdermal preparations that contain the same dose of oestrogen are not included, although they are an alternative if an individual woman would prefer a weekly patch.

Drugs included

- **Mefenamic acid and naproxen** are effective as peri-menstrual prophylaxis.
- **Oestrogen supplements** are effective as peri-menstrual prophylaxis:
  - **Twice-weekly transdermal 100 microgram oestradiol patches** can be used three days before a period and for seven days afterwards. If 100 microgram patches are effective but poorly tolerated, 50 microgram patches may be tried.
  - **Estradiol gel** is an effective alternative, and may produce higher and more stable levels of oestrogen.

[BASH, 2004; BNF 48, 2004]

Prescriptions

NSAIDs

Mefenamic acid tablets: 500mg three times a day

- Age from 16 years onwards
- Mefenamic acid 500mg tablets. Take one tablet three times a day during your period; supply 28 tablets; NHS Cost £2.88.

Naproxen tablets: 250mg twice a day

- Age from 16 years onwards
- Naproxen 250mg tablets. Take one tablet twice a day during your period; supply 28 tablets; NHS Cost £1.34.

Naproxen tablets: 500mg twice a day

- Age from 16 years onwards
- Naproxen 500mg tablets. Take one tablet twice a day during your period; supply 28 tablets; NHS Cost £2.45.

Estradiol supplements

Estraderm MX 100microgram patches

- Age from 16 years onwards
- Estraderm MX 100 patches. Start using the patches 3 days before your period starts and continue using them for 7 days; supply 24 patches; NHS Cost £18.94.

Evorel 100microgram patches

- Age from 16 years onwards
- Evorel 100 patches. Start using the patches 3 days before your period starts and continue using them for 7 days; supply 24 patches; NHS Cost £11.52.

Oestrogel (estradiol 0.06% gel) 1.5mg per dose

- Age from 16 years onwards
- Oestrogel 0.06% gel. Start using the gel 3 days before your period starts and continue using it for 7 days; supply 240 grams; NHS Cost £23.85.

Estraderm MX 50microgram patches (low dose)

- Age from 16 years onwards
- Estraderm MX 50 patches. Start using the patches 3 days before your period starts and continue using them for 7 days; supply 24 patches; NHS Cost £15.65.

Evorel 50microgram patches (low dose)

- Age from 16 years onwards
- Evorel 50 patches. Start using the patches 3 days before your period starts and continue using them for 7 days; supply 24 patches; NHS Cost £10.45.

Pregnancy and breastfeeding

Which therapy?

- **Migraine frequently improves during pregnancy,** although post-partum it usually returns to the original pattern.
- Identify and avoid potential trigger factors.
- Consider non-drug therapies, such as relaxation therapy to avoid drug therapy.
- **Where medication is required for acute attacks:**
  - **Paracetamol** is the drug of choice during pregnancy and breastfeeding.
  - **Ibuprofen** (or aspirin) may be used, but should be avoided after 30 weeks of pregnancy. Aspirin should not be used when breastfeeding.
  - **Cyclizine and promethazine** are the anti-emetics of choice when pregnant. Metoclopramide and prochlorperazine are best reserved for second-line treatment as there are fewer data available on their safety in pregnancy. They are all probably safe to use when breastfeeding. Note: prochlorperazine is available as a suppository, which may be useful if nausea and vomiting are preventing drug ingestion.
  - **Triptans should be avoided** during pregnancy as only limited information is available on their safety. Almotriptan, eletriptan, frovatriptan, rizatriptan, sumatriptan, and zolmitriptan are all excreted in breast milk. Breastfeeding should be avoided for 24 hours after taking these drugs. There is no information available on the safety of naratriptan in breastfeeding mothers.
- **Migraine prophylactic drugs should be avoided.** If prophylaxis must be used, propranolol or amitriptyline could be considered.

Practical prescribing points

For further information please see the *Medicines Compendium* (www.medicines.org.uk) or the *British National Formulary* (www.bnf.org).

Aspirin and NSAIDs

- **Ibuprofen and aspirin** may cause gastrointestinal irritation and occasionally gastrointestinal haemorrhage Do not give if there is a history of peptic ulceration. The may worsen asthma, hypertension, renal impairment, or heart failure.
- **Avoid use of ibuprofen and aspirin in late pregnancy** (3 weeks) due to the risk of premature closure of the ductu arteriosus. Aspirin should be avoided in early pregnancy or conceiving women due to its effect on fetal implantation.

Anti-emetics

- **Cyclizine, promethazine, and prochlorperazine** may cause drowsiness. The degree of sedation will vary between individuals and will depend on the dose given, but, if affected, the woman should avoid driving or performing skilled tasks. Anticholinergic adverse effects may also occur (e.g. blurred vision and dry mouth).
- **Promethazine** should be not be used in the 2 weeks before delivery because of the risk of irritability and excitement in the neonate.
- **Prochlorperazine suppositories** should not be used in the 2 weeks before the expected birth of the child because o the risk of prolonged labour and irritability and excitement in the neonate.

Follow-up advice

Follow-up should be tailored to the individual woman's needs.

Should I refer or investigate?

Refer?

Consider referral if acute attacks are poorly controlled, or if prophylaxis is being considered.

Investigate?

Investigations are not usually required but, if undertaken, reveal no abnormalities. There are no diagnostic tests for migraine.

Patient information leaflets

The following PILs are available at www.prodigy.nhs.uk
Migraine
Migraine Action Association
Migraine - Triggers and Diary
Migraine Trust

Shared decision making

Migraine attacks often become less frequent during pregnancy.
If you have migraines when you are pregnant or when breastfeeding:

- Try to identify and avoid possible trigger factors.
- **Paracetamol** is safe during pregnancy and breastfeeding.
- **Ibuprofen or aspirin** are alternatives but should not be taken after 30 weeks of pregnancy. Aspirin should not be taken when breastfeeding.
- If feeling sick or vomiting is a problem with your migraines:
  - **Cyclizine or promethazine** are the medicines commonly used.
  - **Metoclopramide or prochlorperazine** are sometimes used but there are fewer data available on their safety in pregnancy. They are probably safe to use when breastfeeding.
  - **Prochlorperazine suppositories** may be used if vomiting is making it difficult for you to swallow tablets or solutions.

Triptan medicines should not be used during pregnancy. Also, you should not breastfeed for 24 hours after taking a triptan medicine.
It is best not to take medicines to prevent migraine during pregnancy. If one is needed, propranolol or amitriptyline is probably the safest.

Drug rationale

Drugs not included

Analgesia other than paracetamol, ibuprofen, and aspirin are not included as limited safety data are available.
Anti-emetics other than cyclizine, promethazine, and prochlorperazine are not included as limited safety data are available.
Triptans are not included for use when pregnant or breastfeeding as limited safety data are available.

Drugs included

Paracetamol is the analgesic of choice during pregnancy and breastfeeding.

- **Ibuprofen or aspirin** are second line analgesics, but should be avoided after 30 weeks of pregnancy. Aspirin should not be used when breastfeeding.
- **Cyclizine and promethazine** are the anti-emetics of choice during pregnancy.
- **Prochlorperazine** is a second-line anti-emetic during pregnancy. It is included as it is available as a suppository, which may be useful if nausea and vomiting prevent drug ingestion.

[BASH, 2004; BNF 48, 2004; McElhatton, Personal Communication, 2005]

Prescriptions

1st line: paracetamol

Soluble paracetamol: 1g when required, max 4 times a day

- Age from 16 years onwards
- Paracetamol 500mg soluble tabs. Take two tablets every 4 to 6 hours when required for pain relief. Maximum of 8 tablets in 24 hours; supply 60 tablets; NHS Cost £5.43; OTC Cost £7.00.

Paracetamol tablets: 1g when required, max 4 times a day

- Age from 16 years onwards
- Paracetamol 500mg tablets. Take two tablets every 4 to 6 hours when required for pain relief. Maximum of 8 tablets in 24 hours; supply 100 tablets; NHS Cost £1.06; OTC Cost £1.35.

Paracetamol suppository: 1g when required, max 4 times a day

- Age from 16 years onwards
- Paracetamol 500mg suppositories. Insert one to two suppositories into the rectum every 4 to 6 hours when required for pain relief. Maximum of 8 suppositories in 24 hours; supply 20 suppositories; NHS Cost £19.80; OTC Cost £34.00.

2nd line: ibuprofen or aspirin (NOT if 30+ weeks)

Ibuprofen tablets: 400mg when required, max 3 times a day

- Age from 16 years onwards
- Ibuprofen 400mg tablets. Take one tablet three times a day when required for pain relief. Do not exceed the stated dose; supply 84 tablets; NHS Cost £2.74; OTC Cost £4.40.

Soluble aspirin: 600mg when required, max 4 times a day

- Age from 16 years onwards
- Aspirin 300mg dispersible tabs. Take two tablets every 4 to 6 hours when required for pain relief. Maximum of 4 doses 24 hours; supply 100 tablets; NHS Cost £1.62; OTC Cost £2.00.

Soluble aspirin: 900mg when required, max 4 times a day

- Age from 16 years onwards
- Aspirin 300mg dispersible tabs. Take three tablets every 4 to 6 hours when required for pain relief. Maximum of 4 doses 24 hours; supply 100 tablets; NHS Cost £1.62; OTC Cost £2.00.

Aspirin tablets: 600mg when required, max 4 times a day

- Age from 16 years onwards
- Aspirin 300mg tablets. Take two tablets every 4 to 6 hours when required for pain relief. Maximum of 4 doses 24 hours; supply 64 tablets; NHS Cost £0.62; OTC Cost £2.00.

Aspirin tablets: 900mg when required, max 4 times a day

- Age from 16 years onwards
- Aspirin 300mg tablets. Take three tablets every 4 to 6 hours when required for pain relief. Maximum of 4

doses 24 hours; supply 96 tablets; NHS Cost £0.93; OTC Cost £2.00.

Oral anti-emetics: promethazine and cyclizine

Promethazine hydrochloride 10mg tablets

- Age from 12 to 60 years
- Promethazine HCl 10mg tablets. Take one to two tablets when required for relief of sickness. Maximum of 4 tablets in 24 hours; supply 56 tablets; NHS Cost £1.71.

Promethazine hydrochloride 25mg tablets

- Age from 12 to 60 years
- Promethazine HCl 25mg tablets. Take one tablet when required for relief of sickness. Maximum of 2 tablets in 24 hours; supply 56 tablets; NHS Cost £2.55.

Promethazine teoclate 25mg tablets

- Age from 12 to 60 years
- Promethazine Teoclat 25mg tabs. Take one tablet when required for relief of sickness. Maximum of 4 tablets in 24 hours; supply 28 tablets; NHS Cost £3.13; OTC Cost £5.49.

Cyclizine 50mg tablets

- Age from 12 to 60 years
- Cyclizine 50mg tablets. Take one tablet when required for relief of sickness. Maximum of 3 tablets in 24 hours; supply 56 tablets; NHS Cost £3.46.

Rectal anti-emetics: prochlorperazine suppositories

Prochlorperazine 5mg suppositories

- Age from 16 years onwards
- Prochlorperazine 5mg suppositories. Insert one suppository into the rectum when required for relief of sickness. Maximum of 3 suppositories in 24 hours; supply 10 suppositories; NHS Cost £9.02.

Extended Information

Background information

- What is it? p.1240
- What are the predisposing and trigger factors? p.1240
- How common is it? p.1240
- How do I know my patient has it? p.1240
- What else might it be? p.1242
- Complications and prognosis p.1242

What is it?

- Migraine is a primary episodic headache disorder. It is characterized by various combinations of neurological, gastrointestinal, and autonomic changes. There are many different types of migraine; the most common (described in *How do I know my patient has it?*) are:
  - Migraine with aura — previously called classic migraine
  - Migraine without aura — previously called common migraine
- In 2004 The International Headache Society published the second edition of *The International Classification of Headache Disorders*. An abridged version of this classifies other types of migraine as:
  - Childhood periodic syndromes that are commonly a precursor of migraine (e.g. cyclical vomiting, abdominal migraine)
  - Retinal migraine
  - Complications of migraine (e.g. chronic migraine, status migrainosus, migrainous infarction, migraine-triggered seizure)
  - Probable migraine

[Silberstein et al, 2002; Headache Classification Subcommittee of the International Headache Society, 2004]

What are the predisposing and trigger factors?

- Predisposing factors are important as their treatment may reduce migraine frequency. Predisposing factors include:
  - Depression and anxiety
  - Head or neck trauma
  - Hormonal changes — menstruation and menopause
  - Stress (and relaxation after periods of stress)
- Trigger factors that precipitate attacks may be identified, but only in the minority of sufferers. Dietary triggers affect about 20% of people. Most attacks have no obvious trigger, and some triggers that are identified are unavoidable. Trigger factors include:
  - Bright lights
  - Certain foods (e.g. certain alcoholic drinks, cheese, citrus fruits, chocolate)
  - Extremes of weather (e.g. very hot or cold, strong winds)
  - Long-distance travel
  - Loud noise
  - Missing meals
  - Strenuous unaccustomed exercise
  - Too much or too little sleep

[Directorate of Information and Clinical Effectiveness, 2002; BASH, 2004]

How common is it?

- **The lifetime prevalence of migraine** is 25% in women, and 8% in men [Rasmussen et al, 1991].
- **The one-year prevalence of migraine** is 15% in women, and 6% in men [Silberstein et al, 2002].
- Migraine begins earlier in men than in women, and migraine with aura begins earlier than migraine without aura. Early age of onset in studies may represent the reporting of childhood periodic syndromes (e.g. cyclical vomiting, abdominal migraine) that are commonly a precursor of migraine:
  - In males, the incidence of migraine with aura peaks at 5 years of age, and the incidence of migraine without aura peaks between 10 and 11 years of age. New cases of migraine are uncommon in men in their twenties.
  - In females, the incidence of migraine with aura peaks between 12 and 13 years of age, and the incidence of migraine without aura peaks between 14 and 17 years of age [Mannix, 2001; Silberstein et al, 2002].
- In a practice of 2000 people there are likely to be 5 newly diagnosed cases of migraine each year, and 40 consultations for existing migraine [MeReC, 1997].

How do I know my patient has it?

Overview

- **Migraine is diagnosed by the history.**
- **Examination** yields normal findings after an attack.
- **Investigations** are not usually required but, if undertaken, reveal no abnormalities. There are no diagnostic tests for migraine.
- **There may be a family history of migraine:**
  - Approximately 50–60% of people with migraine have a parent who also has migraine.
  - Up to 80% of people with migraine have at least one first-degree relative who also has migraine [Silberstein et al, 2002].
- **A migraine attack can be divided into four phases: premonitory, aura, headache, and headache resolution.**

Most people with migraine experience more than one phase, but there is no single phase that must be present for migraine to be diagnosed.

- **The premonitory phase** occurs in 20–60% of people with migraine, and occurs hours to days before the onset of the headache. Some people report a poorly characterized feeling that a migraine is coming. Common features of this phase are depression, tiredness, difficulty concentrating, irritability, stiff neck, and food cravings. Although many different features have been described, they are often consistent in an individual.
- **The aura phase** occurs in 25% of people with migraine. It develops over 5–20 minutes, and usually lasts less than 60 minutes. It is a complex of focal neurological symptoms that precedes, accompanies, or, rarely, follows an attack. Headache usually develops within 60 minutes of the end of the aura, but it may be delayed or even absent. Auras may be visual, sensory, motor, or aphasic. The features of auras are described in *Migraine with aura*.
- **The headache phase** occurs in the majority of people with migraine. The features of migraine headache are described in *Migraine without aura*.
- **The resolution phase** occurs as the headache gradually fades. The individual may feel tired, irritable, and depressed, and may have difficulty concentrating.

Migraine without aura (common migraine)

- **Diagnosis** requires at least five attacks, all fulfilling the following criteria:
  - The headache lasts 4–72 hours (untreated or unsuccessfully treated).
  - The headache has at least two of the following characteristics:
    - Unilateral location
    - Pulsating quality
    - Moderate or severe pain intensity
    - Aggravation by, or causing avoidance of, routine physical activity
  - During the headache at least one of the following is present:
    - Nausea and/or vomiting
    - Photophobia and phonophobia
  - The attack is not attributable to another disorder.
- The headache is usually frontotemporal. It is usually unilateral, but may be bilateral at the onset, or may start unilaterally and become generalized.
- The onset of the headache is usually gradual, peaking after 2–12 hours, then gradually subsiding.
- Attacks often begin in the morning, possibly waking the person from sleep, but may begin at any time of day or night.
- The frequency of attacks is extremely variable:
  - Some people may have several attacks a week.
  - Others may go for years between attacks.
- Other features that may occur during an attack include anorexia, blurred vision, impaired concentration, nasal stuffiness, hunger, tenesmus, diarrhoea, abdominal pain, polyuria, pallor, sweating, and sensations of heat or cold.
- Examination during an attack may reveal localized oedema of the scalp, face, or under the eyes; scalp tenderness; prominence of temporal blood vessels; or neck stiffness and tenderness.

Migraine with aura (classical migraine)

- **Diagnosis** requires at least two attacks, both fulfilling the following criteria:
  - The aura has at least one of the following characteristics (but no motor weakness):
    - Fully reversible visual symptoms (e.g. flickering lights, spots, or lines; or loss of vision)
    - Fully reversible sensory symptoms (e.g. paraesthesiae, numbness)
  - The aura, in addition, has at least two of the following features:
    - The visual symptoms are homonymous (affect both visual fields on the same side), or the sensory symptoms are unilateral.
    - At least one symptom develops gradually over more than 5 minutes, or different symptoms occur in succession over more than 5 minutes.
    - Each symptom lasts 5–60 minutes.
  - The headache begins during the aura, or follows the aura within 60 minutes. For details of the headache see *Migraine without aura*.
  - The attack is not attributable to another disorder.
- Visual auras are the most common type of aura. They may move across the visual field, and may cross the midline. Examples of visual aura are:
  - Fortification spectra, which are often 'C'-shaped.
  - Scotoma.
  - Objects may rotate, oscillate, or 'boil'.
  - Simple flashes, specks, and shimmerings.
- Paraesthesiae are the second most common type of aura. Numbness usually starts in the hand, migrates up the arm, then involves the face, lips, and tongue. The leg is sometimes involved. Numbness may follow the paraesthesia. Sensory auras rarely occur alone, and usually follow visual auras.
- Speech disturbances are the third most common type of aura. These are usually dysphasia, but are often hard to categorize.
- Most people who have migraine with aura also have episodes of migraine without aura.

[Silberstein et al, 2002; Headache Classification Subcommittee of the International Headache Society, 2004]

Migraine in children

- Migraine frequently begins during childhood. Childhood periodic syndromes (e.g. cyclical vomiting, abdominal migraine) are thought by many specialists to be a precursor of migraine.
- Features of migraine in childhood are generally the same as in adults, the child being completely well between attacks. Common differences include:
  - The headache is often bilateral, or is felt in the middle of the head.
  - Attacks may be shorter, lasting 1–72 hours.
- Depending on the age of the child, and hence the history given, some features may have to be inferred from the child's behaviour (e.g. covering the eyes or ears, closing the curtains, wanting to lie in a quiet darkened room).

Menstrual migraine

- Menstrual migraine occurs within 1–2 days of the start of menses, and at no other time. Evidence suggests that oestrogen withdrawal triggers migraine in some women.
- Menstrual-associated migraine occurs within the menses and at other times of the menstrual cycle.
- Only 14% of women with migraine suffer from menstrual migraine, but up to 60% suffer from menstrual-associated migraine.
- Migraine diaries can accurately differentiate menstrual migraine from menstrual-associated migraine. This is important since the preventative treatment of menstrual migraine is different from that of menstrual-associated migraine.

[DTB, 2004]

What else might it be?

- When an aura is present, migraine diagnosis is usually relatively easy from the history. The causes of headache that are sometimes difficult to distinguish from migraine without aura are:
  - Episodic tension-type headache (this is more common in people with migraine).
  - Medication overuse headache.
- It is important to remember that people may suffer from more than one type of headache. A separate history must be taken for each type.

Complications and prognosis

Complications

- **Migraine is associated with an increased risk of depression, manic depression, anxiety disorder, and panic disorder** [Silberstein et al, 2002].
- **Status migrainosus** — a debilitating migraine that lasts for more than 72 hours [Headache Classification Subcommittee of the International Headache Society, 2004].
- **Migrainous infarction** — a cerebral infarction occurring during the course of a typical attack of migraine with aura. The aura lasts longer than 60 minutes, and neuroimaging shows ischaemic infarction [Headache Classification Subcommittee of the International Headache Society, 2004].
- **Migraine is associated with increased risk of ischaemic (but not haemorrhagic) stroke.** A meta-analysis of 14 studies showed that the relative risk of ischaemic stroke was 2.16 (confidence interval 1.89 to 2.48). The meta-analysis also showed that users of oral contraceptives had an approximately eight-fold increase in the risk of ischaemic stroke compared with women not taking oral contraceptives [Etminan et al, 2005].

M

Prognosis

- Many people who suffer from migraine find that their attacks cease during adulthood. This is, however, unpredictable, with a minority continuing to suffer attacks into old age.

Management issues

- Overview of management of migraine p.1242
- Managing trigger factors p.1242
- First-line treatment p.1242
- Using triptans p.1243
- Drug treatment for the prevention of attacks p.1245
- Non-drug therapies p.1246
- Management of menstrual migraine p.1246
- Management of women taking combined hormonal contraceptives p.1246
- Management during pregnancy and breastfeeding p.1247
- Management of women taking hormone replacement therapy p.1247
- Medicines management p.1248
- Supporting evidence p.1249

Overview of management of migraine

- **Identify trigger factors,** and avoid them if possible.
- **Treat in a stepwise manner** until symptoms are controlled:
  - First-line treatment is oral analgesia, with or without anti-emetics.
  - If oral analgesia and anti-emetics are poorly tolerated, consider using parenteral administration.
  - If first-line treatments are ineffective, treat with triptans.
  - Consider using combination therapy if triptans alone are ineffective.
- **Consider using prophylactic treatment** if attacks are frequent and troublesome.
- **Women** who are pregnant or breastfeeding, are using the combined oral contraceptive pill, or are receiving hormone replacement treatment may require special management.

Managing trigger factors

How do I identify predisposing trigger factors?

- **Consider using a diary:** the possibility that migraine is being caused or exacerbated by trigger factors can be explored using a migraine diary [BASH, 2004]:
  - The individual can be given a list of potential triggers and asked to record them each day, regardless of whether they have a migraine or not.
  - It is recommended that the diary is not reviewed until there have been at least five attacks, when there may be a clear association between triggers and occurrence of attacks.
- **Identifying triggers is not always possible.** Often there is no obvious cause, or there are multiple triggers which may have to combine and overcome a 'threshold' to precipitate an attack. Too much effort in identifying triggers can cause introspection and be counterproductive [BASH, 2004].

How do I manage trigger factors?

- **Give simple, practical advice** on avoidance where possible, and be aware of the limitations of avoidance of triggers. For example, enforced lifestyle changes and consequent reduction in quality of life may not be offset by improvement in migraine in some instances [BASH, 2004].
- **Known trigger factors can sometimes be reduced** by changes in lifestyle, specific exercises, or relaxation techniques, or by drug therapy. Table 1 lists the most common triggers and their possible management.

[BASH, 2004]

First-line treatment

How should I treat an attack of migraine first-line?

- **Start acute treatment early in the attack.** This is beneficial because gastric stasis during the migraine attack reduces drug absorption.
- **Standard analgesics are suitable first choices for the acute treatment of migraine.** The evidence for their use in migraine is limited, but this is probably due to the fact that there have been few high-quality randomized controlled trials (RCTs) rather than that they are ineffective. Soluble forms are preferred as these are absorbed faster. The following are good choices (although there may be contraindications) [BASH, 2004]:
  - **Aspirin** 600–900 mg

Table 1: Trigger factors for migraine and their management (adapted from BASH guidelines).

Trigger factor	Management strategy
Anxiety and emotion: many migraines occur during relaxation following periods of stress (often at weekends or holidays).	Stress is difficult to avoid. Relaxation, stress reduction, and coping strategies may help when there is specific stress or anxiety present. Yoga and meditation may also help. See *Non-drug therapies*.
Change in habits: sleep patterns (missing sleep, lying in), eating times (missing meals), long-distance travel (jet lag).	Try to revert back to usual habits. However, be aware that the cause of altered sleep or eating patterns (stress or relaxation) may be the true trigger.
Specific food types: these are rarely (less than 20%) implicated in the causation of migraine. Suspect food as a trigger if migraine occurs within 6 hours of ingestion, the effect is reasonably reproducible, and withdrawal leads to improvement.	Exclude suspected food from diet for several weeks to see if improvement occurs. If several foods are suspected, consult a dietitian to avoid malnutrition. There is no reason for a blanket exclusion of cheese, chocolate, or other supposed high-risk foods.
Bright lights and noise	These can induce stress and are best avoided.
Strenuous exercise: especially if the person is unaccustomed to it.	Avoid particularly energetic sessions. However, good physical fitness can lower the incidence of migraines and should be encouraged.
Menstruation can precipitate migraine in some women.	Migraine related to menstruation can be more difficult to treat than migraine related to other factors and is discussed in Management of menstrual migraine.

- **Paracetamol** 1000 mg (may be less effective)
- **Nonsteroidal anti-inflammatory drugs (NSAIDs)** may be used for acute treatment of migraine. The following are specifically licensed for use in migraine [BNF 48, 2004]:
  - **Ibuprofen** 400 mg tablets: 1.2–1.6 g per day in 3–4 divided doses. Ibuprofen is available as an effervescent powder to aid administration in nauseous people.
  - **Diclofenac potassium** tablets (25 or 50 mg), although diclofenac sodium is also commonly used (off-licence use).
  - **Naproxen sodium** tablets (275 mg), although naproxen is commonly used, including generic formulations.
  - **Tolfenamic acid** tablets (200 mg).
- **Codeine and other opioid drugs, or combinations containing these, should be avoided.** Enquire about the person's use of over-the-counter products containing codeine (very common), and advise on their avoidance.

When should I use anti-emetics?

- **Prokinetic anti-emetics are particularly useful in treating migraine associated with nausea and vomiting.** As well as their anti-emetic effect, they increase gastric emptying, and consequently increase the absorption of oral analgesics. Evidence suggests that anti-emetics are an effective migraine treatment when used alone, but they are usually combined with standard analgesics or triptans in the treatment of acute attacks, when they are believed to exhibit a synergistic effect [DTB, 1998; BASH, 2004]:
  - **Domperidone** 20 mg tablets: the evidence for domperidone is less substantial than for metoclopramide but it has fewer adverse effects.
  - **Metoclopramide** 10 mg tablets are effective but can cause extrapyramidal adverse events (especially in younger people). It should be avoided in pregnant or breastfeeding women.
- **Combination products** (containing aspirin or paracetamol plus an anti-emetic) are an alternative to separate prescriptions. They may be particularly useful for people who wish to carry medication with them for early use. Note: *Migramax*® (lysine acetylsalicylate 1620 mg plus metoclopramide 10 mg per sachet) and *Paramax*® (paracetamol 500 mg plus metoclopramide 5 mg per sachet) are available as dispersible granules. These are the only dispersible forms of metoclopramide available [BNF 48, 2004].

When should I use rectal analgesia and anti-emetics?

- **Rectal analgesia** is indicated if a person is vomiting and consequently oral analgesics are not being adequately absorbed [BASH, 2004]:
  - **Diclofenac suppositories** (100 mg) share the same gastrointestinal adverse effects as oral NSAIDs.
  - **Domperidone suppositories** (30 mg) can be used to reduce nausea and vomiting.

Why should I avoid codeine and other opioids?

- **Opioids should be avoided** during a migraine attack for the following reasons [BASH, 2004]:
  - They have no proven pain relieving effect in migraine.
  - They have adverse effects. In particular they have an emetic effect (increase nausea and vomiting), which can exacerbate existing problems. They reduce gastric motility, which can decrease the uptake of other drugs.
  - They have an addictive potential and are implicated in medication overuse headache.

Using triptans

When should I prescribe a triptan?

- **Triptans should be considered if first-line treatment has proved ineffective or is poorly tolerated:**
  - Three attacks when pain relief was not achieved with standard analgesia is a suggested, although arbitrary, guide to when a triptan should be considered [BASH, 2004].
  - Check the person has no contraindications before prescribing.

Which triptans are available?

- **Triptans** work by selectively stimulating 5-hydroxytriptamine 1 ($5HT_1$) receptors in the brain. They have largely replaced ergotamine, which has a poor bioavailability (best administered rectally), has a worse adverse effect profile, and is more likely to be overused or misused [Goadsby et al, 2002].
- Sumatriptan was the first triptan to become licensed in the early 1990s [DTB, 1992]; zolmitriptan, naratriptan, rizatriptan, eletriptan, almotriptan, and, most recently, frovatriptan have since become available [BNF 48, 2004].

Which triptan should I use?

- **Triptans are *not* equivalent to each other;** they each have individual characteristics which make them each suitable for different individuals at different times [BASH, 2004]:
- **Triptans vary in their effectiveness and in their tolerability.** In general (although not always), triptans with greater efficacy also have the greater potential for adverse effects.
  - **Treatment should be individualized** for each person. There is a high degree of variability in individual

M

response to specific triptans. If a particular triptan is not effective in an individual, another can be tried which may be effective. Similarly, if a triptan is poorly tolerated it can be switched.
  - **Triptans have similar safety profiles:** there is no evidence that any particular triptan is safer to use than another.
- **The triptans available in the United Kingdom are listed in Table 2,** as well as a summary of their relative benefits and disadvantages. There is now substantial evidence from randomized controlled trials (RCTs) for the relative efficacy and tolerability of each triptan (see Supporting Evidence).

[BASH, 2004]

The following guide is suggested when first prescribing triptans:

- **Prescribe a standard dose of oral triptan.** These are sumatriptan 50 mg, zolmitriptan 2.5 mg, rizatriptan 10 mg, naratriptan 2.5 mg, almotriptan 12.5 mg, eletriptan 40 mg, and frovatriptan 2.5 mg:
  - Sumatriptan is the longest established triptan with the most clinical experience attached to it [DTB, 1992]. The higher dose of sumatriptan (100 mg) has been used most extensively as a comparator drug in clinical trials, but offers little advantage over 50 mg for most people [Ferrari et al, 2002].
- **If the initial choice of triptan and dose proves ineffective,** there are a range of options that can be tried [Ferrari et al, 2002; BASH, 2004; Cutrer et al, 2004]:
  - **Sumatriptan 100 mg** may prove more effective than the 50 mg dose, but is also associated with more adverse effects.
  - **Zolmitriptan 2.5 mg** is as effective as sumatriptan 100 g and well tolerated. If an initial dose is ineffective a second dose can be tried.
  - **Rizatriptan 10 mg** is more effective than sumatriptan 100 mg and provides better sustained pain relief.
  - **Eletriptan 40 mg** is more effective than sumatriptan 100 mg. If this is well tolerated but is not fully effective, the 80 mg dose may be beneficial and also provides greater sustained pain relief. Eletriptan is currently undergoing post-marketing surveillance (black triangle).
  - **Different formulations** may also be considered if a rapid response is required or triptan effectiveness is limited by nausea and vomiting.
  - **Additional use of an anti-emetic** (such as domperidone or metoclopramide) may be useful if nausea and vomiting are present and affecting triptan effectiveness.
- **If the initial choice is effective but poorly tolerated,** the following options should be considered [Ferrari et al, 2002; BASH, 2004]:
  - **Almotriptan 12.5 mg** is at least as effective at relieving pain as sumatriptan 100 mg, and more effective at giving sustained pain relief. It also has fewer associated adverse effects, and is less expensive. It may be a good choice for first-line treatment, but is currently undergoing post-marketing surveillance (black triangle), after which its place in migraine treatment may be better appreciated.
  - **Naratriptan 2.5 mg** is less effective than sumatriptan 100 mg but has significantly less adverse effects and may be better tolerated.
  - **Frovatriptan 2.5 mg** is less effective than sumatriptan 100 mg, but has less adverse effects. It is currently undergoing post-marketing surveillance (black triangle).
  - **Lower doses of other triptans,** such as rizatriptan 5 mg or eletriptan 20 mg, may still be effective but might be better tolerated. These are off-label uses.

Which formulation should I use?

- **Standard oral tablets are acceptable for most people with migraine.** Other oral formulations may be useful in some individuals [BNF 48, 2004]:
  - **Sumatriptan** is available in a rapidly dispersing tablet, *RADIS*®, although the advantages of this formulation are unclear.
  - **Zolmitriptan and rizatriptan** are available as orodispersible tablets and wafers (*Rapimelt*® and *MELT*® respectively). These preparations may be useful for people who have nausea and vomiting and are finding swallowing difficult.
- **Sumatriptan and zolmitriptan are available as nasal sprays** which act rapidly and may be preferred by some people [BASH, 2004]:
  - **Sumatriptan nasal spray is the only formulation licensed in the adolescent age range** (12–17 years). It is safe and effective in this age group [Major et al, 2003].
  - **Zolmitriptan nasal spray is useful in people with nausea and vomiting,** as it is partially absorbed through the nasal mucosa. However, sumatriptan nasal spray requires ingestion and is not especially useful if vomiting is a problem.
- **Sumatriptan is presently the only triptan available as a subcutaneous injection.** It provides rapid relief of migraine [The Sumatriptan Auto-Injector Study Group, 1991], but is more expensive and people may be unwilling to use an injection.

Table 2: Comparison of triptans.

Triptan	Strength and formulation	Comment
Sumatriptan	50 and 100 mg tablets (rapidly dispersing tablets also available). 6 mg subcutaneous injection. 10 mg intranasal spray	Sumatriptan is the longest established and most extensively studied triptan available. It is the only triptan available as a subcutaneous injection.
Zolmitriptan	2.5 mg tablets and orodispersible tablets. 5 mg nasal spray*	Zolmitriptan has similar efficacy and adverse effects to sumatriptan. Dose can be repeated if the first dose is ineffective. The nasal spray is useful if vomiting is a problem.
Rizatriptan	5 and 10 mg tablets, and 10 mg orodispersible wafers	Rizatriptan is more effective and has a more sustained effect than sumatriptan.
Naratriptan	2.5 mg tablets	Naratriptan has a slower onset of action and is less effective than sumatriptan, but has fewer adverse effects.
Almotriptan*	12.5 mg tablets	Almotriptan is as effective as sumatriptan, has a longer sustained response, and has fewer adverse effects.
Eletriptan*	20 and 40 mg tablets	Eletriptan is more effective than sumatriptan, and at higher doses has a more sustained effect. There may be more adverse effects.
Frovatriptan*	2.5 mg tablets	Frovatriptan is the most recently marketed triptan, and is most useful in people who suffer from relapse during an attack.

* Currently undergoing post-marketing surveillance (black triangle).

M

What should I do if my patient suffers a relapse immediately following triptan use?

The main limitation of triptan use is relapse; 20–50% of people taking a triptan experience a relapse of migraine over a 48 h period [BASH, 2004]:

- **Repeat doses of triptans can be given if the first dose worked** (see *Medicines Management*). This strategy is effective but can lead to repeated rebound attacks and medication overuse headache. Standard analgesia may be more appropriate if there is concern that this may be a problem.
- **Consider using naratriptan, eletriptan, or frovatriptan** for people who consistently suffer from relapse, as these may have lower relapse rates.
- **Diclofenac or tolfenamic acid** can be used pre-emptively if relapse is anticipated.

What should I do if triptans are ineffective or migraines are very frequent?

If migraines fail to respond to two or more different triptans, particularly more effective drugs like eletriptan, then consider the following:

- **Review the diagnosis:** is there another possible cause of headache?
- **Review patient compliance:** are the drugs being used correctly?

If migraine is confirmed and triptans are being used correctly (see Medicines Management), consider combining triptans with standard analgesia with or without anti-emetics. Note: there is little formal evidence for this practice [BASH, 2004].

If triptans are used successfully, but migraines are very frequent, consider using prophylactic drug treatment.

Drug treatment for the prevention of attacks

When should I consider using drug prophylaxis?

There are no definitive guidelines on when an individual should be offered preventive drugs for migraine. Treatment should be given on an individual basis according to patient preference, particularly as many prophylactic drugs have adverse effects [MeReC, 2002].

Preventive treatment is most commonly offered when there is over-frequent use of acute treatments, particularly triptans [BASH, 2004]:

- **Use of medication on more than 2 days per week** on a regular basis carries a clear risk of medication overuse headache. Drug prevention should definitely be considered.
- **Use of medication on more than one day per week** on a regular basis requires enquiry on how the drugs are being used and a review of diagnosis.

Other situations where preventive drugs should be considered include [Snow et al, 2002]:

- Two or more attacks per month that produce disability lasting 3 or more days.
- Standard analgesia and triptans either contraindicated or ineffective.
- Migraine is of an uncommon type, such as hemiplegic migraine, or migraine with prolonged aura, or there is migrainous infarction.

Which drug should I use for prophylaxis?

A large number of drugs have been suggested for the prevention of migraine. The following drugs are relatively safe and effective, and are licensed for the prevention of migraine or are commonly used for this purpose.

Beta-blockers

- **Beta-blockers are first-line drugs** in the absence of contraindications. Theoretically, the ideal beta-blocker for use in migraine should be hydrophilic and cardioselective (properties that are associated with less adverse effects) and should have no intrinsic sympathomimetic activity (partial agonists have been found to be ineffective) [Snow et al, 2002]. Propranolol, metoprolol, and timolol are licensed for prevention of migraine; atenolol is not licensed but is commonly used [BASH, 2004; BNF 48, 2004].
  - **Propranolol** has the best evidence to support its use, and has no sympathomimetic activity. However, it is not cardioselective, and usually requires two or three doses a day.
  - **Metoprolol** has partial cardioselectivity and no sympathomimetic properties; it is taken twice a day.
  - **Timolol** has the advantage that it requires only once-daily dosing, which may improve compliance.
  - **Atenolol,** although not specifically licensed for migraine prophylaxis, is a good choice. It is cardioselective, has no intrinsic sympathomimetic activity, and is hydrophilic.
- Beta-blockers are especially useful when the person has coexisting anxiety or hypertension.

Amitriptyline

- **Amitriptyline is a first-line drug.** It has been shown to be effective in preventing migraines, although it is not licensed for this purpose. It is especially useful in the following instances [BASH, 2004]:
  - The person also suffers from tension-type headache, medication overuse headache, or another chronic pain condition.
  - The person suffers from insomnia.
  - The person suffers from depression. Migraine sufferers who are *not* depressed should be reassured that the drug is intended for the prevention of migraine, otherwise they may be reluctant to comply with treatment.
- Due to its sedative properties, amitriptyline is best given 1–2 hours before bedtime.
- There is no formal evidence regarding the efficacy of other tricyclic antidepressants [Snow et al, 2002].

Sodium valproate

- **Sodium valproate is a second-line drug.** There is some evidence for its efficacy, although it is not licensed for this purpose. There is now extensive experience of its use in migraine prevention [BASH, 2004].

Which drug should I not use for prophylaxis?

- A large number of drugs have been suggested for the prevention of migraine. Some of these have limited evidence regarding their effectiveness or have potentially serious adverse effects, and are therefore not recommended by PRODIGY for first-line treatment in primary care. They may, however, be recommended as prophylaxis by a specialist, and include:
  - Other antiepileptic drugs
    - Gabapentin — only limited evidence for moderate efficacy [Snow et al, 2002]
    - Lamotrigine — insufficient evidence of efficacy [Pappagallo, 2003]
    - Levetiracetam — insufficient evidence of efficacy [Pappagallo, 2003]
    - Topiramate — insufficient evidence of efficacy [Pappagallo, 2003]
  - Angiotensin-II receptor antagonists — there is evidence of efficacy in the prevention of headache, but the types of headache prevented are not known [Etminan et al, 2002].

M

- Clonidine — this is no more effective than placebo, and may aggravate depression and cause insomnia [BNF 48, 2004].
- Methysergide — evidence is limited, but it is considered to be the best prophylactic agent. Its use is reserved for secondary care initiation due to its association with retroperitoneal and retropleural fibrosis [Snow et al, 2002].
- Pizotifen — evidence for its effectiveness is poor, and it is associated with unwanted adverse effects which limit its use [MeReC, 2002; Snow et al, 2002].
- Selective serotonin reuptake inhibitors — evidence is inconclusive for their efficacy in migraine.
- Verapamil — evidence is limited for its efficacy in migraine [Snow et al, 2002].

[BASH, 2004; Young et al, 2004]

Non-drug therapies

What advice can I give my patient during an attack?

- Many people find it helpful to lie down in a darkened, quiet room during an acute attack. Sleep may also be of benefit if this is possible. Although induction of sleep with hypnotics (such as temazepam or zolpidem) has been suggested [BASH, 2004], this should used as a last resort due to the adverse effects and addictive potential of these drugs.

What non-drug therapies are useful to prevent attacks of migraine?

- **Relaxation techniques, stress reduction, and coping strategies** are first-line treatments when stress or anxiety exist, or they can be used as adjuvant treatment for other people. People often find relaxation tapes, yoga, or meditation to be of benefit [BASH, 2004].
- **Feverfew** is a herbal remedy reputed to prevent migraine attacks. However, there is little evidence to support this assertion [Pittler and Ernst, 2004]. In addition, there are issues with quality control and concerns over its long-term safety. It is not recommended.
- **Complementary medicines and practices** have limited value [BASH, 2004]:
  - **Acupuncture and biofeedback** techniques may be of some use but more evidence is required to demonstrate this conclusively.
  - **Spinal manipulation techniques** may be of marginal benefit but more research is required to verify this [Bronfort et al, 2004].
  - **Homeopathy, reflexology, and various 'devices'** that purport to prevent migraines: there is little evidence to support the use of these. Any benefit is likely to be due to the placebo effect.

Management of menstrual migraine

- **The acute treatment** of menstrual migraine should remain the same as for migraine associated with other triggering factors.
- **Prophylaxis** for menstrual migraine, however, is different from prophylaxis for migraine in other cases, and should be tried for a minimum of three cycles before it is judged ineffective.
  - **Consider using peri-menstrual prophylaxis with a nonsteroidal anti-inflammatory drug (NSAID):**
    - Start the NSAID at the onset of menstruation and continue until the last day of bleeding.
    - Mefenamic acid or naproxen are suitable choices.
  - **Oestrogen supplements may also be considered:**
    - Transdermal oestradiol patches 100 micrograms may be started 3 days before the onset of menses and continued for 7 days.
    - If this is effective but poorly tolerated, a 50 microgram patch can be considered.
    - Estradiol gel 1.5 mg is an alternative.
    - Note: provided that the woman is menstruating regularly, additional progestogen for endometrial protection is not required.
- **If migraine without aura occurs during the pill-free interval** in a cycle of combined oral contraceptives (COCs) consider:
  - Alternative contraception methods if the COC is now contraindicated (see below).
  - Changing to a pill with a lower dose of the same progestogen; migraine during the pill-free interval may be more common with high-progestogen contraceptives.
  - Changing to a pill with the lowest available dose of a different progestogen.
  - Tri-cycling: take the pill continuously for three packets (9 weeks) followed by a 7-day pill-free interval, so that the number of menstrual bleeds is reduced.
  - Oestrogen supplements:
    - Transdermal oestradiol patches 100 micrograms may be started 3 days before the onset of menses and continued for 7 days.
    - If this is effective but poorly tolerated, a 50 microgram patch can be considered.
    - Estradiol gel 1.5 mg is an alternative.
- **If migraine with aura occurs, the COC must be stopped,** and other methods of contraception used. See the PRODIGY guidance on *Contraception* for details of other methods.

[Boyle, 1999; BASH, 2004]

Management of women taking combined hormonal contraceptives

Both migraine and the use of combined hormonal contraceptives (both oral drugs and patches) are independent risk factors for ischaemic stroke, although the risk is still very low in otherwise healthy young women.

Which women should avoid using CHCs?

- **Contraindications to the use of combined hormonal contraceptives (CHCs) in women with migraine are based on limited evidence and expert opinion.** The following recommendations are intended to enable most women with migraine to use CHCs safely with minimal risk of ischaemic stroke while protecting those at risk [MacGregor, 2000]. The following women should avoid using CHCs:
  - All women with migraine with aura.
    - However, some people with migraine without aura occasionally suffer from an episode of migraine with aura. This situation is not an absolute contraindication to the use of CHCs, and clinical judgement should be used on the frequency of aura when deciding on the use of CHCs.
  - Women with migraine without aura when there is a history of more than one additional risk factor for stroke (although certain products can be considered, see below). These factors include age 35 years or over, diabetes mellitus, close family history of arterial disease in those under 45 years of age, hyperlipidaemia, hypertension, obesity, and smoking. For more details see the WHO Medical Eligibility Criteria for low dose oral contraceptives www.who.int/reproductive-health/publications/mec/3_cocs.pdf and for combined injectables, rings and patches www.who.int/reproductive-health/publications/mec/3_cocs.pdf.

- Women with migraine without aura in whom the frequency of attacks is increasing.
- Women being treated with ergot derivatives.

What should I do if migraine with aura develops in a woman already taking CHCs?

Note: the woman should be forewarned to seek medical attention if she experiences symptoms consistent with an aura while she is taking CHCs.

- If an aura occurs for the first time while a woman is using CHCs:
  - The contraceptive should be stopped immediately.
  - Emergency contraception should be used if necessary.
  - Alternative contraception should be used from then onwards.

What alternative contraception should I prescribe?

- For women with migraine without aura, with only one additional risk factor for ischaemic stroke, a combined oral contraceptive containing a low-dose oestrogen (e.g. 30 micrograms) can be considered. There is no evidence available on which to base any recommendation regarding the most suitable progestogen for women with a history of migraine who wish to use a CHC [DTB, 2000].
- Suitable alternative methods of contraception for women with a history of migraine with aura include progestogen-only contraceptives, intra-uterine devices or systems, and barrier methods.
- See the PRODIGY guidance *Contraception* for further information on contraceptive choice.

[BASH, 2004]

Management during pregnancy and breastfeeding

- **Migraine frequently improves during pregnancy,** although it usually returns to the original pattern after birth of the child.
- Identify and manage potential trigger factors.
- Non-drug therapies, such as relaxation therapy, may be considered in order to avoid drug therapy.
- **Where medication is required for acute attacks:**
  - **Paracetamol** is the drug of choice during pregnancy and breastfeeding.
  - **Ibuprofen or aspirin** may be used, but, because of the risk of premature closure of the ductus arteriosus, should be avoided after 30 weeks of pregnancy. Aspirin should not be used in early pregnancy or in women conceiving (due to implantation complications), or when breastfeeding (due to the potential risk of Reye's syndrome).
  - **Cyclizine and promethazine** have been widely used in pregnancy; although not prokinetic, they are the anti-emetics of choice when pregnant. Metoclopramide and prochlorperazine are best reserved for second-line treatment as there are fewer data available on their safety in pregnancy [McElhatton, Personal Communication, 2005]. They are all probably safe to use when breastfeeding. Note: prochlorperazine is available as a suppository, which may be useful if nausea and vomiting are preventing drug ingestion.
  - **Triptans should be avoided** during pregnancy as there is only limited information available on their safety. Almotriptan, eletriptan, frovatriptan, rizatriptan, sumatriptan, and zolmitriptan are all excreted in breast milk. Breastfeeding should be avoided for 24 hours after taking these drugs. There is no information available on the safety of naratriptan in breastfeeding mothers.
- **Migraine prophylactic drugs should be avoided.** If prophylaxis must be used, propranolol or amitriptyline could be considered.
- For further information on the use of drugs in pregnancy, contact the National Teratology Information Service (0191 232 1525). For further information on the use of drugs when breastfeeding, contact the UK Drugs in Lactation Advisory Service (0116 255 5779 or 0121 311 1974). Information is also available on their website: www.ukmicentral.nhs.uk/drugpreg/guide.htm.

[National Teratology Information Service, 1997; Aube, 1999; Trent Drug Information Service, 2001; BASH, 2004; BNF 48, 2004]

Management of women taking hormone replacement therapy

After the menopause, about two-thirds of women experience less migraine. However, about two-thirds of women experience worsening migraine after surgical menopause.

Should a woman with migraine be prescribed HRT?

- **Hormone replacement therapy (HRT) is not specifically contraindicated in women with migraine.** There is no evidence that the risk of stroke is affected by the use of HRT in women with migraine, with or without aura [Bousser et al, 2000]. However, both the oestrogen and progestogen component of HRT may exacerbate migraine:
  - **Migraine associated with oestrogens** may respond to a change in the type of oestrogen, to a reduction of the dose, or to the use of transdermal oestrogen.
  - **If migraine is associated with oestrogen withdrawal,** consider using a continuous preparation instead of a cyclic preparation. Patches provide more stable oestrogen levels than tablets. Note: continuous combined HRT is only appropriate for women in whom at least 12 months have passed since the last menstrual period (this reduces the risk of irregular bleeding when starting HRT).
  - **Migraine associated with cyclic progestogens** (which occurs during the progestogen phase) may respond to a change in the type of progestogen, or to the use of transdermal rather than oral progestogen. The number of days of progestogen in the cycle can be reduced, but it must be given for a minimum of 12 days to protect the endometrium [CSM, 2004]. The levonorgestrel-releasing intra-uterine device (Mirena) may also be considered, although this is not licensed as an adjunct to oestrogen replacement therapy.

[Silberstein and de Lignieres, 2000]

- See the PRODIGY guidance *Menopause* for more information on the benefits and risks of HRT.

What should I do if a woman suffers a migraine attack for the first time while taking HRT?

- Migraine occurring for the first time in a middle-aged woman is unusual:
  - Stop the HRT.
  - Investigate for any possible cause.
  - Consider referral to a neurologist.
- If an aura develops for the first time in a woman who previously suffered from migraine *without* aura consider:
  - Reducing the dose of oestrogen.
  - Stopping the HRT if a further episode of aura develops in spite of reducing the dose of oestrogen.

M

Medicines management

Standard analgesics and NSAIDs

Paracetamol and aspirin (and other salicylates) are recommended as standard analgesia; ibuprofen, diclofenac, naproxen, and tolfenamic acid are nonsteroidal anti-inflammatory drugs (NSAIDs) licensed for acute attacks of migraine.

Who should avoid taking NSAIDs?

A full discussion on the contraindications, adverse effects, monitoring issues, and interactions of NSAIDs is beyond the scope of this guidance. For further information, see the separate PRODIGY guidance on *Nonsteroidal anti-inflammatory drugs (NSAIDs)*.

- Consider patient comorbidity when prescribing nonsteroidal anti-inflammatory drugs (NSAIDs).
- NSAIDs commonly cause gastrointestinal adverse effects. Do not give without gastroprotection if there is a history of peptic ulceration.
- NSAIDs can worsen asthma, hypertension, renal impairment, and heart failure.
- For information on using NSAIDs for migraine during pregnancy and breastfeeding, see the section *Management during pregnancy and breastfeeding*.

Anti-emetic drugs

Who should avoid taking an anti-emetic drug?

- **Metoclopramide** should be avoided in young people (age 20 years and less): extrapyramidal adverse effects are more common in this age group.
- **Domperidone** should be avoided by pregnant women and breastfeeding mothers [BNF 48, 2004].

M

Triptans

When should my patient take a dose of triptan?

- **Triptans should not be taken too early** in an attack of migraine, unlike standard analgesia. Evidence suggests that the first dose should be taken when the pain is beginning to develop (i.e. is mild), but not before this stage (e.g. during the aura stage) [BASH, 2004].
- **After the initial dose is taken:**
  - **If the triptan successfully relieves pain,** but there is relapse (as occurs in 20–50% of people), a dose of triptan can be repeated within 2–4 hours. A maximum of two doses of almotriptan, eletriptan, naratriptan, and rizatriptan can be taken in 24 hours. Three doses (maximum 300 mg) of sumatriptan can be taken in 24 hours, whereas four doses of zolmitriptan (maximum 10 mg) can be taken in 24 hours.
  - **If the triptan is ineffective,** a further dose is unlikely to be effective and should not be taken. The exception to this is zolmitriptan, where an additional dose can be tried after 2 h even if the first was unsuccessful.

[BASH, 2004; BNF 48, 2004]

Who should avoid taking triptans?

- Triptans should not be taken by the following people:
  - People with uncontrolled hypertension
  - People with coronary heart disease or cerebrovascular disease
  - People with coronary vasospasm (including Prinzmetal's angina)
  - People with risk factors for coronary heart disease or cerebrovascular disease
- Children under 12 years of age should avoid taking triptans, as there have been no studies to confirm efficacy or safety.
- In addition, each triptan may have specific cautions and contraindications. See the *British National Formulary* (www.bnf.org) for details.

[BASH, 2004; BNF 48, 2004]

What are the adverse effects associated with triptans?

- **Triptans are safe** in the absence of contraindications. Triptans can cause constriction of coronary vessels, and there are theoretical concerns that this may increase the likelihood of myocardial infarction, but extensive experience with these drugs, especially sumatriptan, hav shown this is very rare [Goadsby et al, 2002].
- **'Triptan sensations'** include a warm-hot sensation, tightness, tingling, flushing, and feelings of heaviness or pressure in areas such as the face and limbs, and occasionally the chest:
  - 'Triptan sensations' in the chest can mimic angina pectoris and cause considerable alarm. However, when patients are forewarned about these feelings, they rarely cause problems [Goadsby et al, 2002].
  - **Discontinue** if there are intense chest pains or sensations, as this could be due to coronary vasoconstriction or anaphylaxis [BNF 48, 2004].
- **Other adverse effects** are generally mild and self-limitin for all triptans. They include nausea, dizziness, somnolence, and dry mouth [Fox, 2000].
- **Sumatriptan can cause drowsiness.** If this occurs, skilled tasks such as driving should be avoided [BNF 48, 2004] Note that this is likely to be a class effect, and the same caution should be applied to other triptans.

Drugs for the prevention of migraine

Are acute drugs still necessary?

- Prophylactic treatment should be used in addition to acute treatment; the frequency of migraine attacks is usually only reduced by preventive treatment, not stopped entirely [BASH, 2004].

What dose should be taken?

- Most drugs are started in the low dose range, and titrated gradually upwards in order to avoid adverse effects which may cause the patient to stop using the drug [BASH, 2004].
  - This may lead to a delay in efficacy of the drug.
  - Explain to the patient that beneficial effects may be delayed and patience is required.

How long should prophylactic drugs be used for?

- Prophylactic drugs require time to become effective; it is suggested that, provided there are no unacceptable adverse effects, they should be used for at least 3–4 weeks while efficacy is achieved [BASH, 2004]:
  - In practice the patient will decide when to stop taking preventive medication.
- Preventive drugs are often effective over the relatively short term, but there is generally poor evidence on the long-term benefits of prophylaxis [Linde and Rossnagel, 2004]:
  - If prophylactic drugs are successful in reducing the frequency of migraines, they should be continued for at least 4–6 months.
- If at the end of this period the patient decides to cease medication, drugs should be tapered down over a period of 2–3 weeks.

Who should always avoid taking prophylactic drugs?

- **Beta-blockers** should be avoided in:
  - A person with asthma, or with chronic obstructive airways disease that has an asthmatic component, as they can precipitate bronchospasm that is unresponsive to beta$_2$-agonists.
  - A person with second-degree or third-degree heart block.
- **Amitriptyline** should be avoided in:

- A person with a recent myocardial infarct.
- A person with arrhythmias.

Sodium valproate should be avoided in:

- A woman of childbearing age, due to the markedly increased risk of neural tube defects associated with sodium valproate.
- A person with active liver disease.

[BNF 48, 2004]

When should I prescribe prophylactic drugs with extra caution?

Beta-blockers should be used with caution in:

- A person with unstable heart failure, as they can worsen the heart failure; this should be stabilized before initiation of a beta-blocker.
- A person with peripheral vascular disease.
- A person with diabetes, as they can slightly raise the blood glucose levels and the response to hypoglycaemia may be delayed or symptoms of hypoglycaemia may not occur in the usual way. Avoid beta-blockers in someone who experiences frequent hypoglycaemia.

Amitriptyline should be used with caution in:

- A person with ischaemic heart disease.
- A person with epilepsy.

[BNF 48, 2004]

What are the adverse effects of prophylactic drugs?

Beta-blockers can cause sleep disturbance or nightmares; these are more likely with a lipid-soluble beta-blocker (e.g. propranolol) as this crosses the blood–brain barrier more easily [BNF 48, 2004].

- A recent review highlighted that there is no significant increased risk of depressive symptoms while taking beta-blockers, and only a small increase in the risk of fatigue (18 per 1000 patients, 95% CI 5 to 30) or sexual dysfunction (5 per 1000 patients, 95% CI 2 to 8) [Ko et al, 2002].

Amitriptyline most commonly causes antimuscarinic adverse effects (e.g. dry mouth, sedation, blurred vision, constipation, and urinary retention). Postural hypotension, arrhythmias, or weight gain may also occur [Eccles et al, 1999; Taylor et al, 2001].

- Amitriptyline is also associated with hyponatraemia [CSM, 2000; Taylor et al, 2001]. This should be considered in any person taking amitriptyline who develops drowsiness, confusion, nausea, muscle cramps, or seizures. Risk factors include a history of hyponatraemia, extreme old age, diuretics, diabetes mellitus, hypertension, reduced renal function, and chronic obstructive pulmonary disease.
- It is generally accepted that many people become tolerant to the adverse effects of amitriptyline with continued use, but there is little published evidence to support this.

Before initiating therapy with sodium valproate (and also before surgery), blood cell count, bleeding time, and coagulation tests should be performed to establish that there is no undue potential for bleeding complications. Sodium valproate inhibits platelet aggregation, leading to prolongation of bleeding time and frequently to thrombocytopenia [DTB, 1994].

Sodium valproate may cause liver damage, and therefore monitoring of liver function is important, mainly in those with metabolic, degenerative, or developmental conditions [BNF 48, 2004]. In these people:

- Discontinue treatment if there is an abnormally prolonged prothrombin time.
- Avoid concomitant use of salicylates as they are metabolized via the same metabolic pathway.

Adverse effects of sodium valproate include [Mattson et al, 1992; DTB, 1994; Richens et al, 1994]:

- Weight gain (12%), usually after at least 3 months' treatment, partly due to increased appetite.
- Tremor, at higher doses (5%).
- Transient hair loss (2.9%); regrowth may be curly.
- Menstrual irregularities may occur in adolescent girls (common).
- Pancreatitis (rare).

Supporting evidence

What evidence is there to support the use of first-line treatment in an acute attack?

Analgesics and nonsteroidal anti-inflammatory drugs

- There have been no systematic reviews or meta-analyses conducted on the effectiveness of standard analgesia or nonsteroidal anti-inflammatory drugs (NSAIDs) in acute attacks of migraine. However, they are known to be effective in practice and this has been confirmed by several randomized controlled studies (RCTs) which have shown superiority of the following commonly used drugs to placebo [Snow et al, 2002; Wenzel et al, 2003; Morillo, 2004]:
    - Aspirin and other salicylates.
    - NSAIDs, including ibuprofen, diclofenac, naproxen, and tolfenamic acid.
- In contrast, there is little evidence to suggest that paracetamol *alone* is beneficial [BASH, 2004].
- There have been few trials comparing standard analgesia and NSAIDs alone to other commonly used anti-migraine drugs. Most comparative studies that have been performed have been small, of variable methodological quality, and have generally not conclusively proven additional benefits of these specific drugs compared to other drugs [Pfaffenrath and Scherzer, 1995].

M

Anti-emetic drugs

- Anti-emetic drugs such as metoclopramide and domperidone are known to be effective agents in reducing nausea and vomiting, an important and troublesome symptom of migraine. However, there is strong evidence that their use can also reduce the severity of headache, both when used alone or with an accompanying analgesic:
    - The best evidence consists of a meta-analysis of parenteral metoclopramide used alone or with analgesia. Pooled results obtained from 13 trials (655 adult patients) suggested that metoclopramide was more effective than placebo in reducing migraine pain, and as effective as standard drug alone [Colman et al, 2004].
    - An RCT found that domperidone and paracetamol combined reduced the duration of a migraine attack more than paracetamol alone [MacGregor et al, 1993].
    - An RCT found lysine acetylsalicylate (equivalent to 900 mg of aspirin) and metoclopramide (10 mg) taken together were as effective in reducing pain as oral sumatriptan (100 mg), but were better tolerated, had the additional benefit of treating symptoms of nausea and vomiting, and were less expensive [Tfelt-Hansen et al, 1995].

Triptans

How effective are triptans?

- **Triptans have been extensively studied,** and have been conclusively demonstrated in a large number of RCTs to be more effective than placebo in treating many aspects of migraine [Ferrari et al, 2002]. The usual endpoints studied which have shown the superiority of triptans over placebo include the following:

Table 3: Comparative properties of the triptans, compared to sumatriptan 100 mg (adapted from Ferrari et al, 2002).

Triptan and dose	Initial 2 h relief	Sustained relief	Consistency*	Tolerability
Sumatriptan 50 mg	=	=	=/–	=
Zolmitriptan 2.5 mg	=	=	=	=
Zolmitriptan 5 mg	=	=	=	=
Naratriptan 2.5 mg	–	–	–	++
Rizatriptan 5 mg	=	=	=	=
Rizatriptan 10 mg	+	+	++	=
Eletriptan 20 mg	–	–	–	=
Eletriptan 40 mg	=/+	+	=	–
Eletriptan 80 mg	++	+	=	–
Almotriptan 12.5 mg	=	+	+	++

= No difference when compared to sumatriptan 100 mg; + superior to sumatriptan 100 mg; – inferior to sumatriptan 100 mg
* (Intra-individual) consistency refers to how well an individual responds to the drug over the course of several acute attacks.

- **Response rate:** proportion of people who have a reduction in pain (from moderate or severe to mild or none) after 2–4 hours.
- **Pain-free rate:** proportion of people who feel no pain after 2–4 hours.
- **Recurrence of headache (relapse) rate:** the proportion of people who experience a return of (moderate or severe) pain in the following 22 hours (use of additional analgesics not considered).
- **Sustained pain-free rate:** the proportion of people who do *not* experience a recurrence of (moderate or severe) pain in the following 22 hours (use of additional analgesic not permitted).

- **There is a strong placebo response in people with migraine.** The average placebo responses have been calculated as 29% for headache response rate, 8% for pain-free rate, and 6% for sustained pain-free rate. Despite these high rates, all the triptans have been shown to be significantly superior to placebo [Ferrari et al, 2002].
  - **Consistent lack of response to triptans is rare,** and a great majority of people with migraine will have a response in at least one of three triptan-treated attacks [Ferrari et al, 2002].

What evidence is there for adverse effects of triptans?

- **There is a high adverse effect rate with placebo:** 27% of people report an adverse effect without taking an active substance. However, the adverse effect rate of triptans has been found to be significantly greater than this in most, but not all, triptans (naratriptan, almotriptan, and low-dose eletriptan being exceptions) [Ferrari et al, 2002].

How do triptans compare with each other?

- The best evidence comparing the relative attributes of each triptan to date comes from a systematic review and meta-analysis encompassing 53 RCTs and 24,089 individuals [Ferrari et al, 2002]. Results from this study were comparable to those of other similar reviews and meta-analyses conducted using the equivalent data [Goadsby et al, 2002; Oldman et al, 2002; Cutrer et al, 2004]:
  - The review analysed two types of study: comparisons of individual triptans with placebo, and direct 'head-to-head' drug comparisons.
  - Sumatriptan (100 mg) was the most widely studied drug. When triptan efficacy and tolerability were compared, this was used as the reference drug.
  - Comparisons with placebo and 'head-to-head' studies showed a high level of concordance, adding weight to the overall results.
- Although all the triptans were superior to placebo, there were notable differences in the properties of individual triptans. In general, some of the newer triptans (notably rizatriptan, eletriptan, and almotriptan) were more effective than sumatriptan 100 mg. Depending on the outcome measured, these drugs were 10–38% more effective than sumatriptan. In some cases, though, this was offset by a worse adverse effect profile [Ferrari et al 2002].
- Table 3 lists the comparative properties of the triptans presently available in the United Kingdom. The most recent addition, frovatriptan, is not included as there ar limited data published available for it [Ferrari et al, 2002].

Is there evidence to support the combined use of anti-emetics or analgesics with triptans?

- The use of triptans combined with anti-emetics for people who have previously not responded to triptans is recommended by guidelines [BASH, 2004]. However, there is currently little evidence to guide this practice. One very small RCT (16 individuals) found that sumatriptan (50 mg) combined with metoclopramide (10 mg) gave superior pain relief to sumatriptan alone [Schulman and Dermott, 2003].
- There is no good evidence that triptans should be combined with standard analgesics or nonsteroidal anti inflammatory drugs (NSAIDs), although this practice may be recommended if triptan use alone proves ineffective [BASH, 2004].

Drugs for the prevention of migraine

How effective are beta-blockers in preventing migraine?

- **Propranolol** has been studied in a systematic review of 58 RCTs (5072 individuals). Although the methodological quality of the majority of the studies wa poor (possibly because many were undertaken in the 1970s), there is clear evidence of the efficacy of propranolol in the prevention of migraine [Linde and Rossnagel, 2004].
- The evidence for other beta-blockers is more limited, bu studies have shown efficacy of atenolol, metoprolol, an timolol [Snow et al, 2002].

How effective is amitriptyline in preventing migraine?

- Amitriptyline has been shown to be efficacious in the prevention of migraine. The greatest evidence was for dosages of 30–150 mg daily [Snow et al, 2002].

How effective is sodium valproate in preventing migraine

- Studies of anti-epileptics in the prevention of migraine have generally included small numbers of participants. Sodium valproate has been studied in two RCTs (63 individuals), and showed a significant reduction in migraine frequency compared to placebo. Divalproex sodium (a combination of sodium valproate and valpro acid not available in the UK) has also shown clear efficacy in migraine prevention [Chronicle and Mulleners, 2004].

References

NHS staff in England can link, free of charge, from references to full text journals by clicking on [Full text] on the PRODIGY website.

1. Aube, M. (1999) Migraine in pregnancy. *Neurology* **53**(4 Suppl 1), S26-S28.
2. BASH (2004) *Guidelines for all doctors in the diagnosis and management of migraine and tension-type headache.* British Association for the Study of Headache. www.bash.org.uk [Accessed: 21/09/2004].
3. BNF 48 (2004) *British National Formulary.* 48th edn. London: British Medical Association and Royal Pharmaceutical Society of Great Britain.
4. Bousser, M.G., Conard, J., Kittner, S. et al (2000) Recommendations on the risk of ischaemic stroke associated with use of combined oral contraceptives and hormone replacement therapy in women with migraine. The International Headache Society Task Force on Combined Oral Contraceptives & Hormone Replacement Therapy. *Cephalalgia* **20**(3), 155–156.
5. Boyle, C.A. (1999) Management of menstrual migraine. *Neurology* **53**(4 Suppl 1), S14-S18.
6. Bronfort, G., Nilsson, N., Haas, M. et al (2004) *Non-invasive physical treatments for chronic/recurrent headache (Cochrane Review).* The Cochrane Library. Issue 3. Chichester, UK: John Wiley & Sons, Ltd. www.nelh.nhs.uk/cochrane.asp [Accessed: 02/02/2005]. [Full text]
7. Chronicle, E. and Mulleners, W. (2004) *Anticonvulsant drugs for migraine prophylaxis (Cochrane Review).* The Cochrane Library. Issue 3. Chichester, UK: John Wiley & Sons, Ltd. www.nelh.nhs.uk/cochrane.asp [Accessed: 02/02/2005]. [Full text]
8. Colman, I., Brown, M.D., Innes, G.D. et al (2004) Parenteral metoclopramide for acute migraine: meta-analysis of randomised controlled trials. *British Medical Journal* **329**(7479), 1369–1373.
9. CSM (2000) Selective serotonin reuptake inhibitors (SSRI's). *Current Problems in Pharmacovigilance* **26**(Sep), 11–12.
10. CSM (2004) Review of the evidence regarding long-term safety of HRT. *Current Problems in Pharmacovigilance* **30**(Oct), 4–7.
11. Cutrer, F.M., Goadsby, P.J., Ferrari, M.D. et al (2004) Priorities for triptan treatment attributes and the implications for selecting an oral triptan for acute migraine: a study of US primary care physicians (the TRIPSTAR project). *Clinical Therapeutics* **26**(9), 1533–1545.
12. Directorate of Information and Clinical Effectiveness (2002) *Topic of the month: migraine.* Issue 12. Directorate of Information and Clinical Effectiveness. www.show.scot.nhs.uk [Accessed: 21/09/2004].
13. DTB (1992) Sumatriptan: a new approach to migraine. *Drug & Therapeutics Bulletin* **30**(22), 85–87.
14. DTB (1994) Drug treatment of epilepsy. *Drug & Therapeutics Bulletin* **32**(6), 45–48. [Full text]
15. DTB (1998) Managing migraine. *Drug & Therapeutics Bulletin* **36**(6), 41–44. [Full text]
16. DTB (2000) Oral contraceptives and cardiovascular risk. *Drug & Therapeutics Bulletin* **38**(1), 1–5. [Full text]
17. DTB (2004) Managing migraine in children. *Drug & Therapeutics Bulletin* **42**(4), 25–28. [Full text]
18. Eccles, M., Freemantle, N. and Mason, J. (1999) North of England evidence-based guideline development project: summary version of guidelines for the choice of antidepressants for depression in primary care. *Family Practice* **16**(2), 103–111. [Full text]
19. Etminan, M., Levine, M.A., Tomlinson, G. and Rochon, P.A. (2002) Efficacy of angiotensin II receptor antagonists in preventing headache: a systematic overview and meta-analysis. *American Journal of Medicine* **112**(8), 642–646.
20. Etminan, M., Takkouche, B., Isorna, F.C. and Samii, A. (2005) Risk of ischaemic stroke in people with migraine: systematic review and meta-analysis of observational studies. *British Medical Journal* **330**(7482), 63.
21. Ferrari, M.D., Goadsby, P.J., Roon, K.I. and Lipton, R.B. (2002) Triptans (serotonin, 5-HT1B/1D agonists) in migraine: detailed results and methods of a meta-analysis of 53 trials. *Cephalalgia* **22**(8), 633–658.
22. Fox, A.W. (2000) Comparative tolerability of oral 5-HT1B/1D agonists. *Headache* **40**(7), 521–527.
23. Goadsby, P.J., Lipton, R.B. and Ferrari, M.D. (2002) Migraine – current understanding and treatment. *New England Journal of Medicine* **346**(4), 257–270. [Full text]
24. Headache Classification Subcommittee of the International Headache Society (2004) The international classification of headache disorders. 2nd edition. *Cephalalgia* **24**(Suppl 1), 1–150.
25. Ko, D.T., Hebert, P.R., Coffey, C.S. et al (2002) Beta-blocker therapy and symptoms of depression, fatigue and sexual dysfunction. *Journal of the American Medical Association* **288**(3), 351–352. [Full text]
26. Linde, K. and Rossnagel, K. (2004) *Propranolol for migraine prophylaxis (Cochrane Review).* The Cochrane Library. Issue 3. Chichester, UK: John Wiley & Sons, Ltd. www.nelh.nhs.uk/cochrane.asp [Accessed: 02/02/2005]. [Full text]
27. MacGregor, A. (2000) Migraine associated with menstruation. *Functional Neurology* **15**(Suppl 3), 143–153.
28. MacGregor, E.A., Wilkinson, M. and Bancroft, K. (1993) Domperidone plus paracetamol in the treatment of migraine. *Cephalalgia* **13**(2), 124–127.
29. Major, P.W., Grubisa, H.S. and Thie, N.M. (2003) Triptans for treatment of acute pediatric migraine: a systematic literature review. *Pediatric Neurology* **29**(5), 425–429.
30. Mannix, L.K. (2001) Epidemiology and impact of primary headache disorders. *Medical Clinics of North America* **85**(4), 887–895.
31. Mattson, R.H., Cramer, J.A. and Collins, J.F. (1992) A comparison of valproate with carbamazepine for the treatment of complex partial seizures and secondarily generalized tonic-clonic seizures in adults. *New England Journal of Medicine* **327**(11), 765–771.
32. McElhatton, P. (2005) *Personal communication. Concerning which antiemetics are safest to use when pregnant.* Consultant Teratologist, Wolfson Unit: University of Newcastle.
33. MeReC (1997) Acute treatment of migraine: new products. *MeReC Bulletin* **8**(10), 37–40.
34. MeReC (2002) The management of migraine. *MeReC Bulletin* **13**(2), 5–8.
35. Micromedex (2001) MICROMEDEX [CD-ROM]. Volume 110, fourth quarter, 2001. Thomson Healthcare.
36. Morillo, L.E. (2004) *Migraine headache.* Clincial Evidence. Volume 11. www.clinicalevidence.com [Accessed: 02/02/2005].
37. National Teratology Information Service (1997) *Migraine in pregnancy.* NHS Northern and Yorkshire: Regional Drug and Therapeutics Centre.
38. Oldman, A.D., Smith, L.A., McQuay, H.J. and Moore, R.A. (2002) Pharmacological treatments for acute

migraine: quantitative systematic review. *Pain* **97**(3), 247–257.
39. Pappagallo, M. (2003) Newer antiepileptic drugs: possible uses in the treatment of neuropathic pain and migraine. *Clinical Therapeutics* **25**(10), 2506–2538.
40. Pfaffenrath, V. and Scherzer, S. (1995) Analgesics and NSAIDs in the treatment of the acute migraine attack. *Cephalalgia* **15**(Suppl 15), 14–20.
41. Pittler, M.H. and Ernst, E. (2004) *Feverfew for preventing migraine (Cochrane Review)*. The Cochrane Library. Issue 3. Chichester, UK: John Wiley & Sons, Ltd. www.nelh.nhs.uk/cochrane.asp [Accessed: 02/02/2005]. [Full text]
42. Rasmussen, B.K., Jensen, R., Schroll, M. and Olesen, J. (1991) Epidemiology of headache in a general population – a prevalence study. *Journal of Clinical Epidemiology* **44**(11), 1147–1157.
43. Richens, A., Davidson, D.L., Cartlidge, N.E. and Easter, D.J. (1994) A multicentre comparative trial of sodium valproate and carbamazepine in adult onset epilepsy. *Journal of Neurology, Neurosurgery & Psychiatry* **57**(6), 682–687.
44. Schulman, E.A. and Dermott, K.F. (2003) Sumatriptan plus metoclopramide in triptan-nonresponsive migraineurs. *Headache* **43**(7), 729–733.
45. Silberstein, S.D. and de Lignieres, B. (2000) Migraine, menopause and hormonal replacement therapy. *Cephalalgia* **20**(3), 214–221.
46. Silberstein, S.D., Lipton, R.B. and Goadsby, P.J. (2002) *Headache in clinical practice*. 2nd edn. London: Martin Dunitz.
47. Snow, V., Weiss, K., Wall, E.M. et al (2002) Pharmacologic management of acute attacks of migraine and prevention of migraine headache. *Annals of Internal Medicine* **137**(10), 840–849. [Full text]
48. Taylor, D., McConnell, H., Duncan-McConnell, D. and Kerwin, R. (Eds.) (2001) *The Bethlem & Maudsley NHS Trust: 2001 Maudsley prescribing guidelines*. 6th edn. London: Martin Dunitz.
49. Tfelt-Hansen, P., Henry, P., Mulder, L.J. et al (1995) The effectiveness of combined oral lysine acetylsalicylate and metoclopramide compared with oral sumatriptan for migraine. *Lancet* **346**(8980), 923–926. [Full text]
50. The Sumatriptan Auto-Injector Study Group (1991) Self-treatment of acute migraine with subcutaneous sumatriptan using an auto-injector device. *European Neurology* **31**(5), 323–331.
51. Trent Drug Information Service (2001) *Drugs in breast milk-quick reference guide*. UKMiCentral. www.ukmicentral.nhs.uk [Accessed: 10/12/2001].
52. Wenzel, R.G., Sarvis, C.A. and Krause, M.L. (2003) Over-the-counter drugs for acute migraine attacks: literature review and recommendations. *Pharmacotherapy* **23**(4), 494–505.
53. Young, W.B., Siow, H.C. and Silberstein, S.D. (2004) Anticonvulsants in migraine. *Current Pain & Headache Reports* **8**(3), 244–255.

PRODIGY GUIDANCE

Molluscum contagiosum

Last revised in July 2003
www.prodigy.nhs.uk/guidance.asp?gt=Molluscum contagiosum

Applies to people of all ages

This guidance covers the management of molluscum contagiosum.

This guidance does not cover the management of other viral skin infections (e.g. viral warts).

There is separate PRODIGY guidance for *Warts and verrucae.*

Goals

- To offer appropriate reassurance and management until natural resolution occurs.
- To identify and refer individuals who may be immunocompromised.

Contents

Scenarios

- Molluscum contagiosum p.1253

Extended Information, p. 1253

Molluscum contagiosum

Which therapy?

- **Molluscum contagiosum usually does not require active treatment.**
- If treatment is appropriate because of cosmetic reasons or discomfort, see *Management issues* for options available.
- No exclusion from school, work, or swimming pools is necessary.

Follow-up advice

- Follow-up is not usually necessary.

Should I refer or investigate?

Refer?

- **Urgently refer:**
  - **Anyone who is HIV-positive with extensive lesions to an HIV specialist,** as extensive molluscum contagiosum is a marker that the person may be severely immunocompromised.
  - **People with periocular lesions and red eyes to an ophthalmologist,** as molluscum contagiosum around the eye can cause a toxic conjunctivitis.
- **Consider referring adults with anogenital molluscum contagiosum to the genito-urinary medicine (GUM)** clinic for screening for sexually transmitted infections.
- **If uncertain of diagnosis,** refer to a dermatologist.

Investigate?

- **Consider the possibility of immunocompromise in all persons with extensive lesions.** Investigate and refer appropriately.
- **Consider HIV testing in adults with facial lesions.**

Patient information leaflets

The following PILs are available at www.prodigy.nhs.uk

- Molluscum Contagiosum

Shared decision making

- **Molluscum contagiosum usually clears without treatment within 18 months.** Therefore it is usually best to leave the lesions alone.
- **Some people want treatment for cosmetic reasons.** The best options are 'squeezing', 'freezing', or 'scraping'.
- Other treatments such as acid or silver nitrate are sometimes used, but success is not guaranteed. Also:
  - These treatments can be painful.
  - Some treatments have a risk of burning the surrounding skin.
  - All treatments have a small risk of scarring the skin.
- **Children with mollusca can mix normally with others** and should not be barred from swimming.

Drug rationale

- No prescriptions are included, as lesions usually resolve without treatment.

Extended Information

Background information

- What is it? p.1253
- How common is it? p.1254
- How do I know my patient has it? p.1254
- What else might it be? p.1254
- Complications and prognosis p.1254

What is it?

- **Molluscum contagiosum is a benign viral skin infection.**
- **It is caused by a large pox virus** that replicates in the cytoplasm of infected epidermal cells and induces hyperplasia [Scholz et al, 1989; Janniger and Schwartz, 1993].
- **There are three types of the virus:** MCV1, MCV2, and MCV3 [Porter et al, 1989; Porter and Archard, 1992]. Type 1 is the most common. There is no relationship between virus type and anatomical distribution in the majority of infections [Porter et al, 1989; Scholz et al, 1989].
- **Transmission** is by direct contact, including sexual contact with infected persons or with contaminated objects; or by autoinoculation [Postlethwaite et al, 1967; Porteous, 1979; Janniger and Schwartz, 1993; PHLS, 2003]. Swimming pools, and sharing a bath sponge or bath towel, are associated with an increased

M

risk of transmission [Postlethwaite et al, 1967; Choong and Roberts, 1999].

- **The incubation period is not reliably known, but is between 2 weeks and 6 months** [Lewis et al, 1997; PHLS, 2003].
- **Individuals are thought to be infectious as long as they have lesions** [PHLS, 2003].

How common is it?

- **The incidence of molluscum contagiosum is not precisely known.** A Scottish study found it to be more common in boys than in girls, with peak incidence between 10–12 years of age. It was rare under the age of 1 year. This study also indicated that spread within households was unusual, but expert opinion is that molluscum in siblings is common in practice [Postlethwaite et al, 1967].
- **A later incidence-peak in young adults** (25–29 years of age) may be due to sexual transmission [Oriel, 1987].
- **There is a higher incidence in people who are immunocompromised.** In HIV-infected people, prevalence is high and rates of 5–18% have been reported [Goodman et al, 1987; Coldiron and Bergstresser, 1989; Schwartz and Myskowski, 1992].

How do I know my patient has it?

- **Diagnosis is based on the characteristic clinical appearance of the lesion.** See www.dermis.net/index_e.htm.
- **The typical appearance of lesions** is of shining pearly-white, hemispherical, and often umbilicated papules in which lies a white curd-like core that can be expressed when the lesion is mature. This consists of viral material and is infectious. The lesions are usually grouped in one or two areas, but may be widely disseminated. Occasionally a previously smaller white molluscum lesion may present acutely as a tender red or black lesion [Lowy, 1999].
- **Most people have fewer than 20 lesions,** although some have several hundred. Plaques consisting of many small lesions occur rarely [Lynch and Minkin, 1968]. More widespread disease may occur in people who are immunocompromised, either by disease or by drugs [Rosenberg and Yusk, 1970; Hellier, 1971]. Multiple lesions may occur in people with atopic eczema.
- **The lesions begin as minute papules and grow up to 3–6 mm,** although rarely they may be as large as 3 cm [Lowy, 1999].
- **Distribution is influenced by how the infection is caught and the type of clothing worn** [Sterling and Kurtz, 1998; Choong and Roberts, 1999]. In children the lesions can affect any site. Adults with sexually transmitted molluscum contagiosum, but who are otherwise healthy, usually have lesions in the anogenital region [Sterling and Kurtz, 1998].
- **In uncomplicated molluscum contagiosum, the person is not systemically unwell.**
- **In at least 10% of people with molluscum contagiosum, particularly people with atopy, a patchy eczema,** often quite irritable, develops around one or more of the lesions a month or more after their onset [DeOreo et al, 1956].
- Rarely, molluscum contagiosum can present as undiagnosed lid lesions, chronic follicular conjunctivitis, and superficial punctate keratitis [Charteris et al, 1995].
- It is very unusual for diagnostic clarification to be needed. Light microscopy of the core of the lesion shows molluscoid bodies. Alternatively, the core of lesions can be sent for examination by electron microscopy, under which typical poxvirus-like particles will be seen [Scott, 2001]. However, electron microscopy is expensive and not readily available. If diagnostic testing is appropriate, consider seeking specialist advice from the local laboratory service.

What else might it be?

Differential diagnosis of multiple lesions includes:

- **Warts**
- **Lichen planus** — an inflammatory pruritic disease characterized by distinctive, usually purplish papules.
- **Milia** — white keratinous cysts on the face, most frequent around the eyes.
- **Syringomata** — small pale papules, usually around the eyes.

Solitary molluscum may be difficult to diagnose. It may be best to refer for diagnosis, particularly in the older age group. They may resemble:

- **Pyogenic granuloma** — small, usually solitary, sessile or pedunculated, raspberry-like, friable granulation tissue. They occur most often in children.
- **Keratoacanthoma** (solitary type) — a rapidly growing papule that develops into a skin-coloured nodule with a smooth crater and a central keratin plug.
- **Basal cell carcinoma** — a tumour composed of a small waxy semi-translucent nodule forming around a central depression that may be ulcerated, crusted, or bleeding.
- **Intradermal naevus (mole)** — a papule, which varies in colour from normal skin colour to brown or black.
- **Sebaceous gland hyperplasia** — single or multiple yellowish papules on the face, more common in people who are chronically immunocompromised.
- **Spitz nevus** (epithelial nevus) — a smooth-surfaced, raised, round, slightly scaly, and firm papule with a pink yellow-brown, brownish-red, or purplish-red colour.

[Arnold et al, 1990]

Complications and prognosis

Complications

- **Scarring can be a result of over-treatment.**
- **Bacterial super-infection can occur,** especially in those with atopic eczema or impaired immune function [Lowy 1999].
- **Conjunctivitis and keratitis** may complicate lesions around the eyelid [Lowy, 1999].

Prognosis

- **Experts suggest that molluscum contagiosum usually resolves spontaneously within 18 months,** although it has been reported to resolve after only 6–9 months. Some people may have lesions for 3–4 years [Lewis et al 1997; Sterling and Kurtz, 1998]. Individual lesions may last a few months.
- **Scarring is unusual if left untreated.** Scarring is more likely on areas of adipose tissue such as the thighs, and i the lesions have become inflamed or scabbed.
- **Recurrence is possible** [Ginsburg, 1986].

Management issues

- First-line management p.1255
- Second-line management p.1255
- Treatments that are not generally recommended in primary care p.1255
- Anogenital lesions p.1255
- Eczema and molluscum contagiosum p.1255
- Inflamed molluscum contagiosum p.1255
- Periocular molluscum contagiosum p.1255
- HIV and molluscum contagiosum p.1256

First-line management

- **Treatment is unnecessary in most cases.** Molluscum contagiosum is a benign condition, and spontaneous resolution is likely within 18 months. Treatment, however, can be painful and may cause scarring.
- **Allowing spontaneous resolution is particularly important in children,** for whom freezing or curettage may be painful or frightening. Nevertheless, extensive molluscum contagiosum on visible sites can also be upsetting.
- **No exclusion from school, work, or swimming pools is necessary** [PHLS, 2003], although common-sense measures such as avoiding sharing sponges and towels may reduce transmission.
- **Referral or investigation is rarely necessary.** It may be appropriate if the diagnosis is uncertain or the presentation unusual.
- **In adults presenting with extensive lesions or with facial lesions, consider HIV testing** [Scott, 2001].

Second-line management

- **As lesions usually spontaneously regress, treatment should be offered for cosmetic reasons only** [Scott, 2001], or if the lesions are causing discomfort.
- **There is a lack of good-quality evidence for all of the treatments of molluscum contagiosum.** If treatment is thought to be appropriate, there are a number of options, which are outlined below. The decision to treat molluscum contagiosum, and which treatment to use, should be made on an individual basis.
- **Simple trauma:**
  - **Squeezing** the lesions is generally a task delegated to parents. A few lesions can be done at a time after a bath, when the lesions are softer. The lesion can be squeezed with fingernails (ideally rubber or latex gloves should be worn to avoid spreading the virus) or with a pair of forceps.
  - **Evisceration** of the lesion can be done with an orange stick.
- **Cryotherapy and diathermy** are commonly used, but there is a lack of trial evidence regarding either their efficacy or their safety. Expert opinion advises that a few lesions can usually be treated by cryotherapy, especially in older children, without anaesthesia. If diathermy is used, local anaesthesia is recommended. It is useful for treating a clustered group of lesions that can be anaesthetized using a single application of a topical anaesthetic.

Treatments that are not generally recommended in primary care

The following treatments are not generally recommended in primary care, but may be useful under the direction of a specialist.

- **Phenol ablation:** in a small study, children were treated either by piercing the lesions with an orange stick impregnated with phenol or by physical expression of the lesion with gloved fingers. Both methods caused scarring, but there was considerably more scarring in the phenol group one month after treatment [Weller et al, 1999].
- **Curettage:** although there are no studies assessing this treatment, it is often advocated as a treatment in children when used with lidocaine/prilocaine to prevent pain [de Waard-van der Spek et al, 1990].
- **Silver nitrate paste:** an open study showed a cure rate of 90% following a single treatment after one month. No one had any scarring resulting from this treatment [Niizeki and Hashimoto, 1999]. In practice, it is rarely used, as silver nitrate blackens the skin and can cause silver tattooing if there is a break in the skin.
- **Podophyllotoxin (0.5%):** evidence from a small randomized controlled trial suggests this is effective in sexually transmitted infections [Syed et al, 1994]. However, podophyllotoxin is best initiated by a specialist. It is usually reserved for men, as a limited number of case reports have indicated that its use in pregnancy may be associated with adverse fetal effects [National Teratology Information Service, 1997].
- **Imiquimod:** there is interest in the use of topical immune modifiers such as imiquimod, but as yet this is not a licensed indication.
- Other treatments not recommended owing to lack of evidence of effectiveness or significant adverse effects include nitric oxide [Ormerod et al, 1999]; iodine solution and salicylic acid paste [Ohkuma, 1990]; homeopathy [Manchanda et al, 1997]; intralesional interferon [Nelson et al, 1995]; and potassium hydroxide [Romiti et al, 1999].

Anogenital lesions

- **Sexual transmission of molluscum contagiosum to a child should *only* be suspected if there is other evidence of sexual abuse,** because lesions are seen quite commonly on the genital, perineal, and surrounding skin in children [Highet, 1992].
- **In adults with anogenital lesions,** screening for other sexually transmitted infections is recommended [Scott, 2001].

Eczema and molluscum contagiosum

- **Widespread molluscum contagiosum is more usually seen in children with atopic eczema.** This may be because of altered immunity (related to eczema); treatment with topical steroids; or spread through autoinnoculation either as a result of scratching or by widespread application of emollients.
- **It is often appropriate to treat eczema,** despite concerns that emollients and steroids may contribute to the development of widespread molluscum contagiosum. Use the lowest strength topical steroid to give disease control, and where possible avoid applying the steroid to the immediate vicinity of the molluscum contagiosum lesions.
- **Development of small patches of eczema around individual lesions indicates an immune response** and a likelihood that the lesions may resolve in the near future. This does not usually require treatment.

Inflamed molluscum contagiosum

- **It is common for individual lesions to become inflamed** and it can be difficult to distinguish between infection, trauma, and immunological rejection.
- **Antibiotic treatment is recommended if there is evidence of infection** (e.g. pus).

Periocular molluscum contagiosum

- **Traditionally, advice has been to actively treat children with molluscum contagiosum around the eyes,** as it can cause a toxic conjunctivitis. A retrospective study showed that conjunctivitis associated with periocular molluscum contagiosum rarely if ever causes any permanent structural damage. The indications to treat asymptomatic periocular molluscum contagiosum are therefore not clearly defined [Margo and Katz, 1983], and on current evidence treatment is not recommended by PRODIGY. If the child develops red eyes, consider the possibility of a toxic conjunctivitis and referral to an ophthalmologist.

HIV and molluscum contagiosum

- **Molluscum contagiosum can present in unusual locations, with multiple lesions** in people with HIV. Lesions are common on the face, neck, and scalp [Ficarra and Gaglioti, 1989; Petersen and Gerstoft, 1992; Schwartz and Myskowski, 1992].Molluscum contagiosum may also present atypically with giant lesions [Schwartz and Myskowski, 1992], or mimic other cutaneous diseases (e.g. cutaneous cryptococcus), and biopsy may be needed for diagnostic reasons [Rico and Penneys, 1985].
- **Molluscum contagiosum should be recognized as a sign that the person may be severely immunocompromised, and the person should be referred urgently for specialist assessment.** The severity of the infection varies inversely with the CD4 count [Schwartz and Myskowski, 1992; Stockley, 1999].
- **In severe immunodeficiency,** molluscum contagiosum is usually progressive and resistant to treatment [Schwartz and Myskowski, 1992; Gottlieb and Myskowski, 1994].
- It has been observed that widely disseminated molluscum contagiosum improves with anti-retroviral therapy as the CD4 count improves [Calista et al, 1999].

References

NHS staff in England can link, free of charge, from references to full text journals by clicking on [Full text] on the PRODIGY website.

1. Arnold, H., Odam, R.B. and James, W.D. (Eds.) (1990) *Andrews' diseases of the skin: clinical dermatology*. 8th edn. Philadelphia: Saunders and Co.
2. Calista, D., Boschini, A. and Landi, G. (1999) Resolution of disseminated molluscum contagiosum with highly active anti-retroviral therapy (HAART) in patients with AIDS. *European Journal of Dermatology* 9(3), 211–213.
3. Charteris, D.G., Bonshek, R.E. and Tullo, A.B. (1995) Ophthalmic molluscum contagiosum: clinical and immunopathological features. *British Journal of Ophthalmology* **79**(5), 476–481.
4. Choong, K.Y. and Roberts, L.J. (1999) Molluscum contagiosum, swimming and bathing: a clinical analysis. *Australasian Journal of Dermatology* **40**(2), 89–92.
5. Coldiron, B.M. and Bergstresser, P.R. (1989) Prevalence and clinical spectrum of skin disease in patients infected with human immunodeficiency virus. *Archives of Dermatology* **125**(3), 357–361.
6. DeOreo, G.A., Johnson, H.H. and Binkley, G.W (1956) An eczematous reaction associated with molluscum contagiosum. *Archives of Dermatology* **74**(4), 344–348.
7. de Waard-van der Spek, F.B, Oranje, A.P., Lillieborg, S. et al (1990) Treatment of molluscum contagiosum using a lidocaine/prilocaine cream (EMLA) for analgesia. *Journal of the American Academy of Dermatology* **23**(4), 1–8.
8. Ficarra, G. and Gaglioti, D. (1989) Facial molluscum contagiosum in HIV-infected patients. *International Journal of Oral & Maxillofacial Surgery* **18**(4), 200–201.
9. Ginsburg, C.M. (1986) Management of selected skin and soft tissue infections. *Pediatric Infectious Disease* 5(6), 735–740.
10. Goodman, D.S., Teplitz, E.D., Wishner, A. et al (1987) Prevalence of cutaneous disease in patients with acquired immunodeficiency syndrome (AIDS) or AIDS-related complex. *Journal of the American Academy of Dermatology* **17**(2 Pt 1), 210–220.
11. Gottlieb, S.L. and Myskowski, P.L. (1994) Molluscum contagiosum. *International Journal of Dermatology* 33(7), 453–461.
12. Hellier, F.F. (1971) Profuse mollusca contagiosa of the face induced by corticosteroids. *British Journal of Dermatology* 85(4), 398.
13. Highet, A.S. (1992) Molluscum contagiosum. *Archives of Disease in Childhood* **67**(10), 1248–1249.
14. Janniger, C.K. and Schwartz, R.A. (1993) Molluscum contagiosum in children. *Cutis* **52**(4), 194–196.
15. Lewis, E.J., Lam, M. and Crutchfield, C.E., III (1997) An update on molluscum contagiosum. *Cutis* **60**(1), 29–34.
16. Lowy, D.R. (1999) Molluscum contagiosum. In: Freedberg, I.M., Eisen, A.Z., Wolff, K. et al (Eds.) *Fitzpatrick's dermatology in general medicine*. 5th edn. London: McGraw-Hill. 2478–2481.
17. Lynch, P.J. and Minkin, W. (1968) Molluscum contagiosum of the adult. Probable venereal transmission. *Archives of Dermatology* **98**(2), 141–143.
18. Manchanda, R.K, , Bahl, R., Atey, R. and Mehan, N. (1997) Double blind placebo controlled clinical trials of homoeopathic medicines in warts and molluscum contagiosum. *Central Council For Research in Homoeopathy Quarterly Bulletin* 19(3&4), 25–29.
19. Margo, C. and Katz, N.N. (1983) Management of periocular molluscum contagiosum in children. *Journal of Pediatric Ophthalmology & Strabismus* **20**(1), 19–21.
20. National Teratology Information Service (1997) *Podophyllin exposure in pregnancy*. NHS Northern and Yorkshire: Regional Drug and Therapeutics Centre.
21. Nelson, M.R., Chard, S. and Barton, S.E. (1995) Intralesional interferon for the treatment of recalcitrant molluscum contagiosum in HIV antibody positive individuals – a preliminary report. *International Journal of STD & AIDS* **6**(5), 351–352.
22. Niizeki, K. and Hashimoto, K. (1999) Treatment of molluscum contagiosum with silver nitrate paste. *Pediatric Dermatology* **16**(5), 395–397.
23. Ohkuma, M. (1990) Molluscum contagiosum treated with iodine solution and salicylic acid plaster. *International Journal of Dermatology* **29**(6), 443–445.
24. Oriel, J.D. (1987) The increase in molluscum contagiosum. *British Medical Journal* **294**(6564), 74.
25. Ormerod, A.D., White, M.I., Shah, S.A. and Benjamin, N. (1999) Molluscum contagiosum effectively treated with a topical acidified nitrite, nitric oxide liberating cream. *British Journal of Dermatology* **141**(6), 1051–1053.
26. Petersen, C.S. and Gerstoft, J. (1992) Molluscum contagiosum in HIV-infected patients. *Dermatology* **184**(1), 19–21.
27. PHLS (2003) *Guidelines on the management of communicable diseases in schools and nurseries: Molluscum contagiosum*. Public Health Laboratory Service. www.phls.co.uk [Accessed: 25/09/2002].
28. Porteous, I.B. (1979) Molluscum Contagiosum. *British Medical Journal* **1**(6167), 898.
29. Porter, C.D. and Archard, L.C. (1992) Characterisation by restriction mapping of three subtypes of molluscum contagiosum virus. *Journal of Medical Virology* **38**(1), 1–6.
30. Porter, C.D., Blake, N.W., Archard, L.C. et al (1989) Molluscum contagiosum virus types in genital and non genital lesions. *British Journal of Dermatology* **120**(1), 37–41.
31. Postlethwaite, R., Watt, J.A., Hawley, T.G. et al (1967 Features of molluscum contagiosum in the north-east

of Scotland and in Fijian village settlements. *Journal of Hygiene* **65**(3), 281–291.

32. Rico, M.J. and Penneys, N.S. (1985) Cutaneous cryptococcosis resembling molluscum contagiosum in a patient with AIDS. *Archives of Dermatology* **121**(7), 901–902.
33. Romiti, R., Ribeiro, A.P., Grinblat, B.M. et al (1999) Treatment of molluscum contagiosum with potassium hydroxide: a clinical approach in 35 children. *Pediatric Dermatology* **16**(3), 228–231.
34. Rosenberg, E.W. and Yusk, J.W. (1970) Molluscum contagiosum. Eruption following treatment with prednisone and methotrexate. *Archives of Dermatology* **101**(4), 439–441.
35. Scholz, J., Rosen-Wolff, A., Bugert, J. et al (1989) Epidemiology of molluscum contagiosum using genetic analysis of the viral DNA. *Journal of Medical Virology* **27**(2), 87–90.
36. Schwartz, J.J. and Myskowski, P.L. (1992) Molluscum contagiosum in patients with human immunodeficiency virus infection. A review of twenty-seven patients. *Journal of the American Academy of Dermatology* **27**(4), 583–588.
37. Scott, G (2001) *2001 national guideline for the management of molluscum contagiosum.* Association for Genitourinary Medicine and the Medical Society for the Study of Venereal Diseases. www.bashh.org [Accessed: 22/04/2005].
38. Sterling, J.C. and Kurtz, J.B. (1998) Viral Infections. In: Champion, R.H., Burton, J.L., Burns, D.A and Breathnach, S.M. (Eds.) *Textbook of dermatology*. 6th edn. Oxford: Blackwell Science. 995–1096.
39. Stockley, I.H. (Ed.) (1999) *Drug interactions.* 5th edn. London: The Pharmaceutical Press.
40. Syed, T.A., Lundin, S. and Ahmad, M. (1994) Topical 0.3% and 0.5% podophyllotoxin cream for self-treatment of molluscum contagiosum in males. A placebo-controlled, double-blind study. *Dermatology* **189**(1), 65–68.
41. Weller, R., O'Callaghan, C.J., MacSween, R.M. and White, M.I. (1999) Scarring in Molluscum contagiosum: comparison of physical expression and phenol ablation. *British Medical Journal* **319**(7224), 1540. [Full text]

M

PRODIGY GUIDANCE

Monitoring people on disease-modifying drugs (DMARDs)

Last revised in July 2005
www.prodigy.nhs.uk/guidance.asp?gt=Monitoring people on DMARDs

Applies to people over the age of 1 month

This guidance covers the monitoring of people on disease-modifying drugs (DMARDs) for rheumatoid arthritis, ankylosing spondylitis, or other inflammatory arthritis.

This guidance does not cover the diagnosis or management of inflammatory arthritis. There is separate PRODIGY guidance for *Ankylosing spondylitis* and *Rheumatoid arthritis*.
This guidance will be updated when the British Society for Rheumatology (BSR) publish their review of the BSR guidelines on monitoring DMARDs (planned for 2004–2005) [Kennedy, 2005].

Extended Information

Management issues

- Principles of monitoring people taking disease-modifying drugs (DMARDs) p.1258
- How do I monitor for myelosuppression in someone treated with a DMARD? p.1258
- How do I monitor for renal and urinary tract toxicity in someone treated with a DMARD? p.1260
- How do I monitor for hepatotoxicity in someone treated with a DMARD? p.1260
- How do I manage someone exposed to the varicella-zoster virus (chickenpox or shingles)? p.1260
- How do I monitor someone treated with anakinra? p.1260
- How do I monitor someone treated with azathioprine? p.1260
- How do I monitor someone treated with ciclosporin? p.1261
- How do I monitor someone treated with cyclophosphamide? p.1261
- How do I monitor someone treated with intramuscular gold (sodium aurothiomalate)? p.1262
- How do I monitor someone treated with hydroxychloroquine? p.1262
- How do I monitor someone treated with leflunomide? p.1263
- How do I monitor someone treated with methotrexate? p.1263
- How do I monitor someone treated with penicillamine? p.1264
- How do I monitor someone treated with sulfasalazine? p.1264
- How do I monitor someone treated with TNF-alpha inhibitors: etanercept, infliximab, adalimumab? p.1265

Principles of monitoring people taking disease-modifying drugs (DMARDs)

- Clear guidelines should be agreed between the GP and the local rheumatology department *before* the GP agrees to accept any form of shared responsibility for monitoring.
- Because adverse effects of DMARDs often require immediate decisions about admission or changing therapy, the shared-care arrangement should provide telephone contact details for someone with whom such issues can be discussed.
- Trends are as important as levels of test results. For each laboratory test, absolute thresholds for action are given. However, a fully informed decision must also take into account trends and previous patterns.
- Monitoring is more frequent when a DMARD is commenced, when the dose is increased, or when toxicity occurs.
- Toxicity may be controlled with a dose reduction, cessation, or co-prescription of an antidote.
- If in doubt, refer to each drug's Summary of Product Characteristics, or contact the local rheumatology department.

[BSR, Personal Communication, 2004].

How do I monitor for myelosuppression in someone treated with a DMARD?

Myelosuppression results in anaemia, leucocytopenia, neutropenia, or thrombocytopenia.

- **Monitoring for anaemia**
  - If the full blood count (FBC) is tested regularly, anaemia should be detected before it becomes symptomatic. Clinical symptoms and signs of anaemia such as increased fatigue, decreased effort tolerance, and pallor should nevertheless be sought.
  - Symptomatic anaemia requires prompt treatment with an urgency appropriate to the severity of symptoms. As anaemia is common in people with rheumatoid arthritis (RA), the cause of anaemia should not be ascribed to myelosuppression without further evidence such as leucocytopenia or thrombocytopenia.
- **Monitoring for leucocytopenia and neutropenia**
  - Immunosuppressive disease-modifying drugs (DMARDs) can cause leucocytopenia and neutropenia, with increased susceptibility to infection.
  - Clinical monitoring includes questions about exposure to infections (particularly chickenpox), fever, and presence of respiratory symptoms, and in the

M

Table 1: Summary of recommendations for monitoring for adverse effects from DMARDs.

DMARD	Major toxicity	Parameters to follow	
		History, examination	**Laboratory tests**
Adalimumab	Myelosuppression Demyelinating disease Overwhelming sepsis	Mouth ulcers Fever, chills Bruising, pallor Signs of MS	FBC, LFTs, U&Es Monthly
Anakinra	Pneumonia, neutropenia Overwhelming sepsis	Respiratory signs and symptoms	FBC Monthlyx3 months; then 3-monthly
Azathioprine	Myelosuppression Overwhelming sepsis	Fever, bruising, pallor	FBC Every 2 weeks until dose stable; then every 1–3 months
Ciclosporin	Renal toxicity Anaemia Hypertension Photosensitivity Overwhelming sepsis	Peripheral oedema Mouth ulcer, rash Blood pressure	FBC, U&Es Every 2 weeks until dose stable; then monthly
Cyclophosphamide	Myelosuppression Haemorrhagic cystitis Overwhelming sepsis	Fever, bruising, pallor	FBC, U&Es, LFTs, urine dipstick At least twice a week
Etanercept	Myelosuppression Demyelinating disease Overwhelming sepsis	Mouth ulcers Fever, chills Bruising, pallor Signs of MS	FBC, LFTs, U&Es Monthly
Gold, intramuscular (sodium aurothiomalate)	Myelosuppression Renal toxicity Rash, photosensitivity	Fever, bruising, pallor Mouth ulcer, rash Hyperpigmentation	FBC, U&Es, urine dipstick Every 2 weeks until stable; then before each injection
Hydroxychloroquine	Retinopathy	Visual acuity Annual screen	—
Leflunomide	Hypertension Myelosuppression Hepatotoxicity Overwhelming sepsis	Mouth ulcer, rash Blood pressure	FBC, LFTs 2–4 weekly for the first 6 months; then every 8 weeks
Infliximab	Myelosuppression Demyelinating disease CCF	Mouth ulcers Fever, chills Bruising, pallor Signs of MS, CCF	FBC, LFTs, U&Es Before each infusion
Methotrexate	Myelosuppression Hepatotoxicity Overwhelming sepsis Pneumonitis	Fever, bruising, pallor Mouth ulcer Respiratory signs and symptoms	FBC, U&Es, LFTs, urine dipstick Weekly until dose stable; then every 1–3 months
Penicillamine	Renal toxicity Myelosuppression Myasthenia	Mouth ulcers Fever or chills Muscle weakness	FBC, urine dipstick Weekly until dose stable; then every 1–3 months
Sulfasalazine	Myelosuppression Macrocytosis Hypersensitivity	Mouth ulcers Fever, chills Bruising, pallor	FBC, LFTs Every 1–2 weeks for 2 months; then 3-monthly for a year; then 6-monthly

Abbreviations
MS, multiple sclerosis; FBC, full blood count; LFTs, liver function tests; U&Es, urea and electrolytes; CCF, congestive cardiac failure

examination a search for signs of infection, particularly pneumonitis.

- The FBC test is used to monitor for low white-cell counts:
  - **Leucopenia:** white cell count (WCC) less than 4x10⁹/l, lymphocyte count less than 0.5x10⁹/l.
  - **Neutropenia:** neutrophil count less than 2.0x10⁹/l.
- **Monitoring for thrombocytopenia**
  - Clinically evident thrombocytopenia should be rare if the FBC is tested regularly. Nevertheless, the history and examination should seek evidence of easy bruising and bleeding (including gastrointestinal bleeding).
  - The FBC test is used to monitor for low platelet counts:
    - **Thrombocytopenia:** platelet count less than 150x10⁹/l.
  - Thrombocytopenia that manifests clinically or on the FBC should be managed by stopping the appropriate DMARD and immediately consulting the rheumatology service.

[American College of Rheumatology, 1996; Hamilton et al, 2004; O'Dell, 2004; BNF 49, 2005]

M

How do I monitor for renal and urinary tract toxicity in someone treated with a DMARD?

- Renal function is monitored to ensure that impaired renal function is detected as soon as possible in order to prevent:
  - Continuing toxicity causing further renal damage
  - Levels of drugs that are renally excreted rising to toxic levels
- Assessment of renal function usually includes measurement of blood pressure and dipstick urinalysis for urine protein and blood.
- Serum creatinine is often the only laboratory test that is required for regular monitoring of renal function. Other tests include 'urea and electrolytes' (i.e. serum urea, creatinine, sodium, potassium), 24-hour excretion of protein, and creatinine clearance.
- Dipstick urinalysis to test for urine protein is used when proteinuria is a clinically significant toxicity.

[American College of Rheumatology, 1996; Hamilton et al, 2004; O'Dell, 2004; BNF 49, 2005]

How do I monitor for hepatotoxicity in someone treated with a DMARD?

- An aminotransferase, i.e. alanine aminotransferase (ALT) or aspartate aminotransferase (AST), is used to monitor for hepatotoxicity. Several other tests are included in the standard suite of liver function tests (LFTs), e.g. albumin, alkaline phosphatase (ALP), bilirubins, and gamma glutamyltransferase (GGT), but they may be of little additional benefit.
- Levels of aminotransferases can vary considerably, making interpretation of raised levels difficult. In the absence of other adverse features, no change to therapy is warranted unless levels exceed 2–3 times the upper limit of the normal range.

[American College of Rheumatology, 1996]

How do I manage someone exposed to the varicella-zoster virus (chickenpox or shingles)?

- No action is required for individuals exposed to the varicella-zoster virus who are known to be immune or who are not immunosuppressed.
- **Exposure to chickenpox in an immunosuppressed person not immunized by prior infection or vaccination warrants passive immunization with varicella-zoster immune globulin (VZIG) if the contact risk is appreciable.** Consult immediately with the secondary-care rheumatology service or a public health physician.
- **Appreciable exposure to varicella-zoster virus is regarded as contact with:**
  - An individual with chickenpox or disseminated zoster between 48 hours before the onset of the rash and until cropping has ceased and all lesions are crusted.
  - Someone with exposed lesions (e.g. ophthalmic zoster).
  - An immunosuppressed person with localised zoster on any part of the body from the day of onset of rash until crusting.
- The risk of acquiring infection from an immunocompetent individual with a non-exposed zoster lesion (e.g. thoracolumbar) is remote.
- **The following should be used as a guide to the type of exposure:**
  - Contact in the same room (e.g. in a house or classroom or a hospital bay with 2–4 beds) for an appreciable period (15 minutes or more).
  - Face-to-face contact, for example while having a conversation.
- **Immunosuppression is regarded as clinically relevant in:**
  - People taking 40 mg prednisolone per day for more than one week in the previous 3 months. *Note: for corticosteroids, the dose that can cause immunosuppression is hard to define, and specialist advice is recommended.*
  - People on lower doses of steroids given in combination with other immunosuppressants.
  - People taking DMARDs that can cause myelosuppression (i.e. adalimumab, anakinra, azathioprine, ciclosporin, cyclophosphamide, etanercept, gold, infliximab, leflunomide, methotrexate, penicillamine, sulfasalazine).

[HPA, 2004]

How do I monitor someone treated with anakinra?

Follow local protocols, where available. Advice on the selection and frequency of tests and thresholds for action given here may differ from local recommendations. See *Principles of monitoring people taking DMARDs* above.

- **Monitoring during treatment**
  - **History and examination**
    - Fever, respiratory symptoms and signs
  - **Laboratory tests** monthly for 3 months, then every 3 months
    - Full blood count (FBC)
- **Toxic effects and recommended management**
  - **Myelosuppression:**
    - **Leucopenia** (i.e. white cell count [WCC] less than $4x10^9$/l, lymphocytes less than $0.5x10^9$/l or **neutropenia** with neutrophils less than $2.0x10^9$/l), or **thrombocytopenia** (i.e. less than $150x10^9$/l): stop anakinra and consult rheumatology service immediately.
    - **Falling trend** (WCC or platelet count falling over three consecutive tests): seek specialist advice immediately, even if counts are within the normal range.
  - **Mouth ulcers:**
    - If severe, stop anakinra and immediately consult rheumatology service.
    - Check FBC.
    - Follow local stomatitis/oral mucositis protocol (e.g. benzydamine mouthwash).
  - **Infection:**
    - **Bacterial infection requiring antibiotics:** consult rheumatology service about withdrawing anakinra temporarily.
    - **Chickenpox/shingles exposure.** No action is required for individuals exposed to the varicella-zoster virus who are known to be immune or who are not immunosuppressed. Exposure to chickenpox in an immunosuppressed person not immunized by prior infection or vaccination warrants passive immunization with varicella-zoster immune globulin (VZIG) if the contact risk is appreciable. See *How do I manage someone exposed to the varicella-zoster virus (chickenpox or shingles)?*

[American College of Rheumatology, 1996; Hamilton et al, 2004; O'Dell, 2004; BNF 49, 2005]

How do I monitor someone treated with azathioprine?

Follow local protocols, where available. Advice on the selection and frequency of tests and thresholds for action given here may differ from local recommendations. See *Principles of monitoring people taking DMARDs* above.

M

- **Risk of cancer:** long-term use of azathioprine slightly increases the risk of certain types of treatable cancer.
- **Monitoring during treatment:**
  - **History and examination:**
    - Fever, bruising, pallor
  - **Laboratory tests** every 2 weeks until on stable dose, then every 1–3 months:
    - Full blood count (FBC)
    - Alanine aminotransferase (ALT) or aspartate aminotransferase (AST)
- **Toxic effects and recommended management:**
  - **Myelosuppression:**
    - **Leucopenia** (i.e. white cell count [WCC] less than $4x10^9/l$, lymphocytes less than $0.5x10^9/l$ or **neutropenia** with neutrophils less than $2.0x10^9/l$), or **thrombocytopenia** (i.e. less than $150x10^9/l$): stop azathioprine and consult rheumatology service immediately.
    - **Falling trend** (WCC or platelet count falling over three consecutive tests): consult rheumatology service, even if counts are within the normal range.
  - **Hepatotoxicity:**
    - **Jaundice** or **abnormal liver function tests** (i.e. AST/ALT greater than twice upper limit of normal): stop azathioprine and consult rheumatology service immediately.
  - **Mouth ulcers:**
    - Reduce dose, unless severe, in which case stop azathioprine and consult rheumatology service immediately.
    - Follow local stomatitis/mucositis protocol (e.g. benzydamine mouthwash).
  - **Nausea, vomiting, diarrhoea:**
    - If symptoms remain intolerable, stop azathioprine and consult rheumatology service immediately.
  - **Infection:**
    - **Bacterial infection requiring antibiotics:** consult rheumatology service about temporarily withdrawing azathioprine.
    - **Chickenpox/shingles exposure.** No action is required for individuals exposed to the varicella-zoster virus who are known to be immune or who are not immunosuppressed. Exposure to chickenpox in an immunosuppressed person not immunized by prior infection or vaccination warrants passive immunization with varicella-zoster immune globulin (VZIG) if the contact risk is appreciable. See *How do I manage someone exposed to the varicella-zoster virus (chickenpox or shingles)?*
  - **Fever/flu-like illness:**
    - In early stages of treatment, suspect an unusual hypersensitivity reaction (especially if accompanied by abnormal blood tests): stop azathioprine and consult rheumatology service immediately.

[American College of Rheumatology, 1996; Hamilton et al, 2004; O'Dell, 2004; BNF 49, 2005]

How do I monitor someone treated with ciclosporin?

Note: drug interactions are common. Nonsteroidal anti-inflammatory drugs (NSAIDs), antibiotics, anti-epileptics, and anti-arrhythmics all have appreciable interactions with ciclosporin.

Follow local protocols, where available. Advice on the selection and frequency of tests and thresholds for action given here may differ from local recommendations. See *Principles of monitoring people taking DMARDs* above.

- **Monitoring during treatment**
  - **History and examination:**
    - Oedema, blood pressure
  - **Laboratory tests:** monitor every 2 weeks for 3 months, then every 4 weeks — monitor more frequently if the dose of ciclosporin is increased or concomitant NSAIDs are introduced or the NSAID dose is increased.
    - Full blood count
    - Creatinine
- **Toxic effects and recommended management:**
  - **Creatinine:**
    - **Rising to greater than 30% above baseline on more than one occasion:** decrease dose by 25% and consider consulting rheumatology service.
    - **Rising to greater than 50% above baseline:** decrease dose by 50% and consult rheumatology service immediately.
    - **Failure to return to normal levels within 1 month after dose reduction:** discontinue ciclosporin and consult rheumatology service.
  - **Hypertension:** treat with standard anti-hypertensive therapy (but check for interactions before prescribing); if hypertension cannot be controlled by anti-hypertensive drugs, refer for specialist management.
  - **Hepatotoxicity:**
    - **Aminotransferase greater than 3 times upper limit of normal:** stop ciclosporin and consult rheumatology service immediately.
  - **Myelosuppression:**
    - **Leucopenia** (i.e. white cell count [WCC] less than $4x10^9/l$, lymphocytes less than $0.5x10^9/l$ or **neutropenia** with neutrophils less than $2.0x10^9/l$) or **thrombocytopenia** (i.e. less than $150x10^9/l$): stop ciclosporin and consult rheumatology service immediately.
    - **Falling trend** (rapid fall, or WCC or platelet count falling over three consecutive tests): seek specialist advice, even if counts are still within the normal range.
  - **Infection:**
    - **Bacterial infection requiring antibiotics:** consult rheumatology service about withdrawing ciclosporin temporarily.
    - **Chickenpox/shingles exposure.** No action is required for individuals exposed to the varicella-zoster virus who are known to be immune or who are not immunosuppressed. Exposure to chickenpox in an immunosuppressed person not immunized by prior infection or vaccination warrants passive immunization with varicella-zoster immune globulin (VZIG) if the contact risk is appreciable. See *How do I manage someone exposed to the varicella-zoster virus (chickenpox or shingles)?*

[American College of Rheumatology, 1996; Hamilton et al, 2004; O'Dell, 2004; BNF 49, 2005]

How do I monitor someone treated with cyclophosphamide?

Cyclophosphamide is usually given intravenously in hospital. Oral therapy does not require hospitalization and may occasionally need to be monitored in primary care. Follow local protocols, where available. Advice on the selection and frequency of tests and thresholds for action given here may differ from local recommendations. See *Principles of monitoring people taking DMARDs* above.

- **Monitoring during treatment:**
  - **History and examination:**
    - Fever, bruising, pallor
  - **Laboratory tests:** frequency of monitoring depends on the dose and route of administration, and will usually be at least twice a week.
    - Full blood count

M

        - Alanine aminotransferase (ALT) or aspartate aminotransferase (AST)
        - Creatinine
        - Urine dipstick test for blood
- **Toxic effects and recommended management:**
    - **Myelosuppression:**
        - **Leucopenia** — on oral cyclophosphamide — (i.e. white cell count [WCC] less than 4x10⁹/l, lymphocytes less than 0.5x10⁹/l or **neutropenia** with neutrophils less than 2.0x10⁹/l) or **thrombocytopenia** (i.e. less than 150x10⁹/l): stop cyclophosphamide and consult rheumatology service immediately.
        - **Falling trend** (WCC or platelet count falling over three consecutive tests): seek specialist advice, even if counts are still within the normal range.
        - **Co-trimoxazole** prophylaxis for *Pneumocystis carinii* should be considered for someone who has clinically significant leucopenia, or who requires high-dose steroids in addition to cyclophosphamide.
    - **Haemorrhagic cystitis:**
        - **Blood on urine dipstick test or haematuria:** consult rheumatology service.
    - **Infection:**
        - **Bacterial infection requiring antibiotics:** consult rheumatology service about withdrawing cyclophosphamide temporarily.
        - **Chickenpox/shingles exposure.** No action is required for individuals exposed to the varicella-zoster virus who are known to be immune or who are not immunosuppressed. Exposure to chickenpox in an immunosuppressed person not immunized by prior infection or vaccination warrants passive immunization with varicella-zoster immune globulin (VZIG) if the contact risk is appreciable. See *How do I manage someone exposed to the varicella-zoster virus (chickenpox or shingles)?*

[American College of Rheumatology, 1996; Hamilton et al, 2004; O'Dell, 2004; BNF 49, 2005]

M

How do I monitor someone treated with intramuscular gold (sodium aurothiomalate)?

Gold is effective, but is the most poorly tolerated of all the DMARDs.

Follow local protocols, where available. Advice on the selection and frequency of tests and thresholds for action given here may differ from local recommendations. See *Principles of monitoring people taking DMARDs* above.

- **Monitoring during treatment:**
    - **History and examination:**
        - Rash, mouth ulcers, fever, bruising, pallor
    - **Laboratory tests** (every 2 weeks until stable, then do tests with every injection; check results of previous blood tests before injection):
        - Full blood count (FBC)
        - Creatinine
        - Urine dipstick test for protein
- **Toxic effects and recommended management:**
    - **Proteinuria:**
        - **Trace protein:** ignore.
        - **Protein '+' or more:** withhold treatment; check urine for evidence of infection; quantify proteinuria in 24-hour collection; if protein greater than 0.5 g per 24 hours, stop treatment and consult rheumatology service immediately.
    - **Myelosuppression:**
        - **Leucopenia** — on oral cyclophosphamide — (i.e. white cell count [WCC] less than 4x10⁹/l, lymphocytes less than 0.5x10⁹/l or **neutropenia** with neutrophils less than 2.0x10⁹/l) or **thrombocytopenia** (i.e. less than 150x10⁹/l): stop gold and consult rheumatology service immediately.
        - **Falling trend** (WCC or platelet count falling over three consecutive tests): seek specialist advice, even if counts are still within the normal range.
    - **Skin rash:**
        - If symptoms are poorly tolerated, stop treatment and consult rheumatology service; else miss a dose.
        - Consider topical corticosteroids.
        - If symptoms resolve, resume treatment at a lower dose; otherwise consult rheumatology service.
    - **Eosinophilia** greater than 7%:
        - May indicate hypersensitivity; stop treatment and consult rheumatology service.
    - **Mouth ulcers:**
        - Follow local protocol for stomatitis/mucositis.
        - Check FBC.
        - Withhold treatment until results of FBC are available.
        - If FBC normal: increase interval between injections, or reduce dose.
        - If FBC abnormal or no response to decreased dose, stop treatment and consult rheumatology service.
    - **Abnormal bruising, sore throat:**
        - Withhold treatment until new FBC test results are available to guide management.
    - **Vasomotor instability:**
        - This occurs more commonly in people who are also using angiotensin-converting enzyme (ACE) inhibitors; it tends to occur in the early stages of therapy.
        - Reduce dose; position the person lying down before giving the injection.
    - **Infection:**
        - **Bacterial infection requiring antibiotics:** consult rheumatology service about withdrawing gold temporarily.
        - **Increased frequency of infections:** check immunoglobulins; if low, stop gold and consult rheumatology service.
        - **Chickenpox/shingles exposure.** No action is required for individuals exposed to the varicella-zoster virus who are known to be immune or who are not immunosuppressed. Exposure to chickenpox in an immunosuppressed person not immunized by prior infection or vaccination warrants passive immunization with varicella-zoster immune globulin (VZIG) if the contact risk is appreciable. See *How do I manage someone exposed to the varicella-zoster virus (chickenpox or shingles)?*

[American College of Rheumatology, 1996; Hamilton et al, 2004; O'Dell, 2004; BNF 49, 2005]

How do I monitor someone treated with hydroxychloroquine?

Hydroxychloroquine is the best-tolerated disease-modifying drug (DMARD), but is the least effective. Retinopathy is the main adverse effect, but this occurs rarely if daily doses are kept below 6.5 mg hydroxychloroquine per kg of lean body mass per day [BNF 49, 2005]. The Royal College of Ophthalmologists has advised that a screening protocol for hydroxychloroquine should be negotiated with local ophthalmologists.

Follow local protocols, where available. Advice on the selection and frequency of tests and thresholds for action given here may differ from local recommendations. See *Principles of monitoring people taking DMARDs* above.

- **Monitoring during treatment:**
    - **History and examination:**
        - Ask the person about visual symptoms.

- **Annual visual screening:** monitor visual acuity using the standard Royal College of Ophthalmology test types.
- **Toxic effects and recommended management:**
  - **Retinopathy:**
    - If visual acuity changes or vision becomes blurred, refer to ophthalmologist.
    - Consider specialist consultation after 5 years on hydroxychloroquine.
  - **Nausea:**
    - Uncommon; usually self-limiting.

[American College of Rheumatology, 1996; Hamilton et al, 2004; O'Dell, 2004; BNF 49, 2005]

How do I monitor someone treated with leflunomide?

Leflunomide is eliminated slowly. Thus, if toxicity develops and leflunomide needs to be stopped, "washout" measures must be taken.

Follow local protocols, where available. Advice on the selection and frequency of tests and thresholds for action given here may differ from local recommendations. See *Principles of monitoring people taking DMARDs* above.

- **Monitoring during treatment:**
  - **History and examination:**
    - Weight loss, diarrhoea
    - Blood pressure, every 2 weeks for the first 6 months, then every 8 weeks
  - **Laboratory tests** every 2–4 weeks for the first 6 months, then every 8 weeks:
    - Full blood count (FBC)
    - Alanine aminotransferase (ALT) or aspartate aminotransferase (AST)
- **Toxic effects and recommended management:**
  - **Myelosuppression:**
    - **Leucopenia** — on oral cyclophosphamide — (i.e. white cell count [WCC] less than $4x10^9/l$, lymphocytes less than $0.5x10^9/l$ or **neutropenia** neutrophils less than $2.0x10^9/l$) or **thrombocytopenia** (i.e. less than $150x10^9/l$): stop leflunomide and consult rheumatology service immediately.
    - **Falling trend** (WCC or platelet count falling over three consecutive tests): seek specialist advice, even if counts are still within the normal range.
    - **Bruising, sore throat, and mouth ulcers:** withhold leflunomide until FBC results are available to guide management.
  - **Diarrhoea:**
    - Occurs in up to 20% of cases.
    - Usually self-limiting.
    - If treatment with leflunomide does need to be stopped, consult rheumatology service.
  - **Abnormal aminotransferase tests:**
    - **Markedly abnormal (greater than twice upper limit of normal) or rapidly deteriorating:** stop leflunomide, start a washout procedure (see below), and consult rheumatology service immediately.
    - **Mildly abnormal (not more than twice upper limit of normal):** withhold treatment and repeat tests in 2 weeks.
    - **Persistently abnormal:** stop leflunomide, start a washout procedure, consult rheumatology service.
    - **Results return to normal:** recommence treatment and repeat AST/ALT after 2 weeks.
  - **Infection:**
    - **Bacterial infection requiring antibiotics:** consult rheumatology service about withdrawing leflunomide temporarily.
    - **Chickenpox/shingles exposure.** No action is required for individuals exposed to the varicella-zoster virus who are known to be immune or who are not immunosuppressed. Exposure to chickenpox in an immunosuppressed person not immunized by prior infection or vaccination warrants passive immunization with varicella-zoster immune globulin (VZIG) if the contact risk is appreciable. See *How do I manage someone exposed to the varicella-zoster virus (chickenpox or shingles)?*
- **Washout procedure:**
  - Prescribe:
    - Either **colestyramine** 8 g, three times daily for 11 days, or
    - **Activated charcoal** 50 g, four times daily for 11 days.
  - Consult product literature for full details.
  - Consult rheumatology service.

[American College of Rheumatology, 1996; Hamilton et al, 2004; O'Dell, 2004; BNF 49, 2005]

How do I monitor someone treated with methotrexate?

Follow local protocols, where available. Advice on the selection and frequency of tests and thresholds for action given here may differ from local recommendations. See *Principles of monitoring people taking DMARDs* above.

- **Advise the person that this drug must only be taken once a week for rheumatoid arthritis (RA)** [National Patient Safety Agency, 2004].
- **People taking methotrexate should also take folic acid 5 mg weekly,** as this reduces mucosal and gastrointestinal adverse effects [Ortiz et al, 1999]. Folic acid can also lower homocysteine levels raised by methotrexate (associated with pro-thrombotic action). Folic acid should be started 2 days before starting methotrexate. Note: it does not reduce the efficacy of methotrexate.
- **Monitoring during treatment:**
  - **History and examination:**
    - Symptoms and signs of infection
    - Cough (new onset), shortness of breath
    - Nausea, mouth ulcers
  - **Laboratory tests:** repeat weekly until dose stable; thereafter repeat every 2–3 months (Committee on Safety of Medicines advice). Check test results before methotrexate dose:
    - Full blood count (FBC)
    - Creatinine
    - Alanine aminotransferase (ALT) or aspartate aminotransferase (AST)
- **Toxic effects and recommended management:**
  - **Myelosuppression:**
    - **Leucopenia** (i.e. white cell count [WCC] less than $4x10^9/l$, lymphocytes less than $0.5x10^9/l$ or **neutropenia** with neutrophils less than $2.0x10^9/l$) or **thrombocytopenia** (i.e. less than $150x10^9/l$): stop methotrexate; consult rheumatology service immediately.
    - **Falling trend** (WCC or platelet count falling over three consecutive tests): stop treatment and seek specialist advice, even if counts are still within the normal range.
    - **Bruising, sore throat:** check FBC; withhold methotrexate until FBC results are available to guide management.
  - **Mouth ulcers or oral mucositis (and normal FBC):**
    - Increase folic acid to 10 mg weekly.
    - If severe, stop methotrexate and consult rheumatology service immediately.
    - Start local protocol for stomatitis/mucositis, e.g. benzydamine mouthwash.
  - **Abnormal liver function tests or jaundice:**

M

  - Stop methotrexate and assess clinical state.
  - If there is clinical evidence of liver toxicity or AST/ALT is profoundly abnormal (i.e. greater than 2–3 times upper limit of normal), consult rheumatology service immediately.
  - Otherwise repeat AST/ALT test in 2 weeks.
  - If the liver function tests do not return to normal or there is clinical suspicion of liver toxicity, consult rheumatology service immediately.
  - Otherwise, restart treatment.
- **Pulmonary symptoms or signs of infection:**
  - Treat suspected bacterial infection with an antibiotic.
  - Pneumonitis or severe infection suspected: consult rheumatology service immediately.
- **Increase in size or number of rheumatoid nodules:**
  - No action required.
- **Infection:**
  - **Bacterial infection requiring antibiotics:** consult rheumatology service about withdrawing methotrexate temporarily.
  - **Chickenpox/shingles exposure.** No action is required for individuals exposed to the varicella-zoster virus who are known to be immune or who are not immunosuppressed. Exposure to chickenpox in an immunosuppressed person not immunized by prior infection or vaccination warrants passive immunization with varicella-zoster immune globulin (VZIG) if the contact risk is appreciable. See *How do I manage someone exposed to the varicella-zoster virus (chickenpox or shingles)?*

[American College of Rheumatology, 1996; Hamilton et al, 2004; O'Dell, 2004; BNF 49, 2005]

M

How do I monitor someone treated with penicillamine?

Follow local protocols, where available. Advice on the selection and frequency of tests and thresholds for action given here may differ from local recommendations. See *Principles of monitoring people taking DMARDs* above.

- **Monitoring during treatment:**
  - **History and examination:**
    - Weakness, fatigue, rash, oedema
  - **Laboratory tests** every 1–2 weeks until on a stable dose; then monthly:
    - Full blood count (FBC)
    - Urine dipstick test for protein and blood
- **Toxic effects and recommended management:**
  - **Myelosuppression:**
    - **Leucopenia** (i.e. white cell count [WCC] less than $4x10^9$/l, lymphocytes less than $0.5x10^9$/l or **neutropenia** with neutrophils less than $2.0x10^9$/l) or **thrombocytopenia** (i.e. less than $150x10^9$/l): stop penicillamine and consult rheumatology service immediately.
    - **Falling trend** (WCC or platelet count falling over three consecutive tests): seek specialist advice, even if counts are still within the normal range.
    - **Bruising, sore throat:** check FBC; withhold methotrexate until FBC results are available to guide management.
  - **Mouth ulcers:**
    - Start stomatitis/mucositis protocol.
    - Withhold penicillamine until resolved; restart at lower dose.
    - Stop penicillamine and consult rheumatology service if symptoms remain intolerable.
  - **Proteinuria with/without oedema:**
    - Check mid-stream urine for evidence of infection.
    - If no urinary tract infection, stop treatment, quantify proteinuria with 24-hour urine collection, and consult rheumatology service immediately.
  - **Haematuria:**
    - Trace: ignore.
    - '+' or more; repeat urine dipstick test and consult rheumatology service if persistent.
  - **Rash, macular–papular, early (1–2 months):**
    - Withhold penicillamine until rash clears; restart at lower dose.
  - **Rash, raised scaly circumscribed plaques, late (6–18 months):**
    - Stop and consult rheumatology service.
  - **Myasthenia:**
    - If unexplained weakness and/or fatigue occur, stop treatment and consult rheumatology service immediately.
  - **Loss of taste:**
    - Continue treatment.
  - **Infection:**
    - **Bacterial infection requiring antibiotics:** consult rheumatology service about withdrawing penicillamine temporarily.
    - **Chickenpox/shingles exposure.** No action is required for individuals exposed to the varicella-zoster virus who are known to be immune or who are not immunosuppressed. Exposure to chickenpox in an immunosuppressed person not immunized by prior infection or vaccination warrants passive immunization with varicella-zoster immune globulin (VZIG) if the contact risk is appreciable. See *How do I manage someone exposed to the varicella-zoster virus (chickenpox or shingles)?*

[American College of Rheumatology, 1996; Hamilton et al, 2004; O'Dell, 2004; BNF 49, 2005]

How do I monitor someone treated with sulfasalazine?

Follow local protocols, where available. Advice on the selection and frequency of tests and thresholds for action given here may differ from local recommendations. See *Principles of monitoring people taking DMARDs* above.

- **Monitoring during treatment:**
  - **History and examination:**
    - Fever, bruising, purpura, pallor
  - **Laboratory tests:**
    - Full blood count (FBC) weekly for the first 4 weeks, fortnightly for 2 months, thereafter every 3 months
    - Alanine aminotransferase (ALT) or aspartate aminotransferase (AST) monthly for the first 3 months
- **Toxic effects and recommended management:**
  - **Myelosuppression:**
    - **Leucopenia** (i.e. white cell count [WCC] less than $4x10^9$/l, lymphocytes less than $0.5x10^9$/l or **neutropenia** with neutrophils less than $2.0x10^9$/l) or **thrombocytopenia** (i.e. less than $150x10^9$/l): stop sulfasalazine and consult rheumatology service immediately.
    - **Falling trend** (WCC or platelet count falling over three consecutive tests): seek specialist advice, even if counts are still within the normal range.
    - **Bruising, sore throat:** withhold treatment until FBC results are available to guide management.
  - **Macrocytosis (mean cell volume greater than 105 fl):**
    - Check red-cell folate and serum B_{12} levels.
    - If low, treat accordingly; otherwise no action is required.
  - **Rash:**
    - Withhold treatment with sulfasalazine until rash settles.

  - Consider lower dose when restarting treatment.
- **Mouth ulcers:**
  - Start stomatitis/mucositis protocol.
  - Stop sulfasalazine: discuss with rheumatology service.
- **Nausea, dyspepsia:**
  - Switch to enteric-coated (EC) preparation of sulfasalazine (if person is not already taking it).
  - Reduce dose; when symptoms resolve, increase slowly.
  - Prescribe an anti-emetic such as prochlorperazine.
  - If dyspepsia persists, consider arranging endoscopy.
- **Fever/flu-like illness**
  - Uncommonly, a hypersensitivity reaction can occur in the first month; it is often accompanied by abnormal blood tests.
  - Stop treatment with sulfasalazine; consult rheumatology service immediately.
- **Headache/mood change**
  - Consider decreasing dose of sulfasalazine.
- **Infection:**
  - **Bacterial infection requiring antibiotics:** consult rheumatology service about withdrawing sulfasalazine temporarily.
  - **Chickenpox/shingles exposure.** No action is required for individuals exposed to the varicella-zoster virus who are known to be immune or who are not immunosuppressed. Exposure to chickenpox in an immunosuppressed person not immunized by prior infection or vaccination warrants passive immunization with varicella-zoster immune globulin (VZIG) if the contact risk is appreciable. See *How do I manage someone exposed to the varicella-zoster virus (chickenpox or shingles)?*

[American College of Rheumatology, 1996; Hamilton et al, 2004; O'Dell, 2004; BNF 49, 2005]

How do I monitor someone treated with TNF-alpha inhibitors: etanercept, infliximab, adalimumab?

Follow local protocols, where available. Advice on the selection and frequency of tests and thresholds for action given here may differ from local recommendations. See *Principles of monitoring people taking DMARDs* above.

- **Monitoring during treatment:**
  - **History and examination:**
    - Symptoms and signs of infection
    - Symptoms and signs of congestive heart failure
    - Symptoms and signs of demyelinating disease
  - **Chest X-ray:**
    - Repeat chest X-ray after 6 months of treatment to screen for tuberculosis
  - **Laboratory tests:** etanercept and adalimumab — monthly; infliximab — before each infusion.
    - Full blood count (FBC)
    - Alanine aminotransferase (ALT) or aspartate aminotransferase (AST)
    - Creatinine
- **Toxic effects and recommended management:**
  - **Infection:**
    - Discontinue anti-TNF-alpha treatment until infection has resolved.
    - Discuss with rheumatology service immediately.
  - **Myelosuppression:**
    - **Leucopenia** (i.e. white cell count [WCC] less than $4x10^9$/l, lymphocytes less than $0.5x10^9$/l or **neutropenia** with neutrophils less than $2.0x10^9$/l) or **thrombocytopenia** (i.e. less than $150x10^9$/l): stop treatment and consult rheumatology service immediately.
    - **Falling trend** (WCC or platelet count falling over three consecutive tests): seek specialist advice, even if counts are still within the normal range.
    - **Bruising, sore throat:** check FBC; withhold treatment until FBC results are available to guide management.
  - **Hepatotoxicity:**
    - **Jaundice, or abnormal or deteriorating ALT/AST:** immediately stop therapy and discuss management with rheumatology service.
  - **Infection:**
    - **Mild infection (e.g. common cold):** continue treatment with increased vigilance.
    - **Moderate or severe infection:** stop treatment; treat promptly with antibiotics; discuss immediately with rheumatology service.
    - **Tuberculosis suspected:** stop treatment and immediately discuss with rheumatology service.
    - **Chickenpox/shingles exposure.** No action is required for individuals exposed to the varicella-zoster virus who are known to be immune or who are not immunosuppressed. Exposure to chickenpox in an immunosuppressed person not immunized by prior infection or vaccination warrants passive immunization with varicella-zoster immune globulin (VZIG) if the contact risk is appreciable. See *How do I manage someone exposed to the varicella-zoster virus (chickenpox or shingles)?*
  - **Symptoms of heart failure while taking infliximab:**
    - Stop treatment.
    - Immediately discuss with rheumatology service.
  - **Malignancy:**
    - Stop treatment.
    - Immediately discuss with rheumatology service.
  - **Headache:**
    - Symptomatic treatment — it is normally mild and self-limiting.
  - **Injection-site reaction:**
    - Symptomatic treatment — it is normally mild and self-limiting.

[American College of Rheumatology, 1996]

M

References

NHS staff in England can link, free of charge, from references to full text journals by clicking on [Full text] on the PRODIGY website.

1. American College of Rheumatology (1996) Guidelines for monitoring drug therapy in rheumatoid arthritis. *Arthritis & Rheumatism* 39(5), 723–731.
2. BNF 49 (2005) *British National Formulary.* 49th edn. London: British Medical Association and Royal Pharmaceutical Society of Great Britain.
3. BSR (2004) *Personal communication. Principles of monitoring people taking DMARDs.* British Society for Rheumatology: London.
4. Hamilton, J., Heycock, C. and Kelly, C. (2004) *Rheumatology service: protocols for disease modifying drugs.* Gateshead Health NHS Trust, UK. www.gatesheadhealth.nhs.uk/rheumatology/drugs.html [Accessed: 06/07/2005]. [Full text]
5. HPA (2004) *Immunoglobulin handbook: indications and dosage for normal and specific immunoglobulin preparations issued by the HPA.* Health Protection Agency. www.hpa.org.uk [Accessed: 27/09/2004]. [Full text]
6. Kennedy, T.D. (2005) The BSR Standards Guidelines and Audit Working Group (SGAWG). *Rheumatology* 44(3), 269–270.
7. National Patient Safety Agency (2004) *Methotrexate – patient briefing.* Patient safety alert 03. National Patient

Safety Agency. www.npsa.nhs.uk [Accessed: 06/07/2005].
8. O'Dell, J.R. (2004) Therapeutic strategies for rheumatoid arthritis. *New England Journal of Medicine* 350(25), 2591–2602. [Full text]
9. Ortiz, Z., Shea, B., Suarez-Almazor, M. et al (1999) *Folic acid and folinic acid for reducing side effects in patients receiving methotrexate for rheumatoid arthritis (Cochrane Review)*. The Cochrane Library. Issue 4. Chichester, UK: John Wiley & Sons, Ltd. www.nelh.nhs.uk/cochrane.asp [Accessed: 07/07/2005]. [Full text]

M

PRODIGY GUIDANCE

Nappy rash

Last revised in February 2004
www.prodigy.nhs.uk/guidance.asp?gt=Nappy rash

Applies to children under the age of 6 years

This guidance covers the management of nappy rash in children.

This guidance does not cover the management of nappy rash in older people.

There is separate PRODIGY guidance for *Eczema — atopic*, *Dermatitis — contact*, and *Seborrhoeic dermatitis*.

Goals

- Resolution of established nappy rash.
- Avoidance of the recurrence of nappy rash.

Contents

Scenarios
- Nappy rash p.1267

Extended Information, p. 1269

Nappy rash

Which therapy?

- **As soon as nappy rash develops:**
  - Increase the frequency of nappy changing and skin cleansing.
  - Liberally apply a barrier cream after every change.
  - Let the child spend as long as possible without a nappy on.
- **If these measures do not control the nappy rash:**
  - Apply a topical imidazole (clotrimazole, econazole, ketoconazole, miconazole, sulconazole) or nystatin.
  - This therapy is often combined with 0.5% or 1% hydrocortisone to reduce the associated inflammation.
- **If treatment fails:**
  - Review treatment compliance with the parent.
  - Continue with topical anticandidal therapy (with or without hydrocortisone).
  - Consider changing from an imidazole to nystatin (or vice versa).
- **If the nappy rash still fails to improve:**
  - Treat with flucloxacillin (or erythromycin if allergic to penicillin).

Practical prescribing points

For further information please see the *Medicines Compendium* (www.medicines.org.uk) or the *British National Formulary* (www.bnf.org).

- **Zinc and castor oil ointment** contains pharmaceutical-grade arachis (peanut) oil. This is highly refined, and therefore the peanut oil should have been removed. As a precaution, however the Committee on the Safety of Medicines advises that people with a known allergy to peanuts or soya (possible cross-sensitivity) should not use medicines containing peanut oil.
- **Topical preparations containing hydrocortisone** should be spread thinly on the affected area. Their duration of use should be limited to the licensed recommendation, in order to reduce the likelihood of adverse effects.
- **Topical nystatin** can stain clothing yellow, which may affect compliance.
- **Occasional hypersensitivity reactions** are listed for many of the topical products. Suspect such a reaction if the rash is getting worse or is failing to heal.
- **Flucloxacillin:** the Committee on Safety of Medicines has advised that cholestatic jaundice may occur up to several weeks after treatment with flucloxacillin has been stopped. Administration for more than two weeks is a risk factor.
- **Erythromycin:** use with caution in children with hepatic and renal impairment, and prolongation of the QT interval. Erythromycin may increase the level of certain drugs (e.g. theophylline, carbamazepine).

Should I refer or investigate?

Refer?

- Referral to a dermatologist should be considered if the nappy rash does not respond. Owing to the wide spectrum of manifestations of nappy rash, the differential diagnosis includes most other dermatological problems of childhood.

N

Patient information leaflets

The following PILs are available at www.prodigy.nhs.uk

- Antifungal Medicines
- Nappy Rash

Shared decision making

- **To help prevent and clear nappy rash:**
  - Leave the nappy off as much as possible.
  - Change the nappy often.
  - Wash the baby's bottom with water only.
  - Dry by patting, not by rubbing, with a towel.
  - Don't use powders such as talcum powder.
  - Use liberal amounts of barrier cream or ointment at the first sign of redness.
  - Don't use tight fitting plastic pants over nappies.
- **An anti-thrush cream or ointment** will usually clear a persistent nappy rash.
- **An anti-thrush cream with a mild steroid** is sometimes used to reduce inflammation caused by the infection.
- Apply creams or ointments sparingly after each nappy change, and before using any barrier cream.
- **An antibiotic medicine** is occasionally needed for an infected rash.

Drug rationale

Drugs not included

- **Zinc cream and zinc ointment** may be difficult to source (causing unnecessary delay in treatment) and expensive.

- **Salicylic acid and undecenoate preparations** are considered less suitable for prescribing in fungal skin infections.
- **Products containing a corticosteroid alone** are not recommended. An undiagnosed fungal or secondary bacterial infection may be present, which could be exacerbated by their use.
- **Topical antibacterial products** that do not contain an anticandial component are not recommended, as they are not effective in treating candidal infections.
- **Topical terbinafine** is not licensed for use in children.

Drugs included

- **Barrier preparations** are offered to provide a protective layer between the skin and urine/faeces. We could find no evidence of any difference in efficacy between the different preparations, so we offer the five cheapest proprietary products.
- **Topical imidazole preparations (clotrimazole, econazole, ketoconazole, miconazole, and sulconazole)** are recommended, as they are effective against *Candida albicans*. There is little evidence of difference between these preparations, and they are all licensed to treat candidal skin infections in people of all ages. Product selection will depend on prescriber/user preference.
- **Topical nystatin preparations** are also effective against *C albicans*. They are licensed for use in all ages.
- **Topical combination products containing hydrocortisone 0.5% or 1% plus an anticandidal** (an imidazole or nystatin) are recommended as an option to reduce accompanying inflammation. They should not be used for more than a week unless otherwise directed, in order to try to avoid any adverse effects.
- **Ointment *and* cream** formulations of active anticandidals are included. Creams are emulsions of oil and water; they tend to be well absorbed into the skin. Ointments are greasy preparations that are insoluble in water, are more occlusive than creams and, unlike creams, do not contain preservatives. There is no evidence to support the use of one preparation over another, and the parent's preference will often govern choice.
- **Flucloxacillin** is offered in case the nappy rash does not improve with barrier preparations and anticandidal medication.
- **Erythromycin** is offered for children allergic to penicillin.

Prescriptions

Barrier preparations

Zinc and castor oil ointment BP (contains arachis oil)
- Age under 6 years
- Zinc and castor oil ointment. Apply to the affected area after each nappy change; supply 100 grams; NHS Cost £0.58; OTC Cost £1.02.

Conotrane cream
- Age under 6 years
- Conotrane cream. Apply to the affected area after each nappy change; supply 100 grams; NHS Cost £0.80; OTC Cost £1.41.

Drapolene cream
- Age under 6 years
- Drapolene cream. Apply to the affected area after each nappy change; supply 100 grams; NHS Cost £1.37; OTC Cost £2.29.

Sudocrem cream
- Age under 6 years
- Sudocrem cream. Apply to the affected area after each nappy change; supply 125 grams; NHS Cost £1.56; OTC Cost £2.60.

Vasogen cream
- Age under 6 years
- Vasogen cream. Apply to the affected area after each nappy change; supply 100 grams; NHS Cost £1.36; OTC Cost £2.35.

Anticandidal-only preparations

Clotrimazole 1% cream
- Age under 6 years
- Clotrimazole 1% cream. Apply to the affected area 2 to 3 times a day. Continue for at least 2 weeks after the affected area has healed; supply 20 grams; NHS Cost £1.77; OTC Cost £2.14.

Econazole 1% cream
- Age under 6 years
- Econazole 1% cream. Apply to the affected area twice a day. Continue for at least 2 weeks the affected area has healed; supply 30 grams; NHS Cost £2.75; OTC Cost £4.85.

Ketoconazole 2% cream
- Age under 6 years
- Ketoconazole 2% cream. Apply to the affected area twice a day. Continue for at least 2 weeks the affected area has healed; supply 30 grams; NHS Cost £3.81.

Miconazole 2% cream
- Age under 6 years
- Miconazole 2% cream. Apply to the affected area twice a day. Continue for 10 days after the affected area has healed; supply 30 grams; NHS Cost £2.07; OTC Cost £3.65.

Sulconazole 1% cream
- Age under 6 years
- Sulconazole 1% cream. Apply to the affected area twice a day. Continue for at least 2 weeks the affected area has healed; supply 30 grams; NHS Cost £3.00; OTC Cost £5.29.

Nystatin 100,000units/g cream
- Age under 6 years
- Nystatin 100,000units/g cream. Apply to the affected area 2 to 4 times a day. Continue for 7 days after the affected area has healed; supply 30 grams; NHS Cost £2.18.

Nystatin 100,000units/g ointment
- Age under 6 years
- Nystatin 100,000units/g ointment. Apply to the affected area 2 to 4 times a day. Continue for 7 days after the affected area has healed; supply 30 grams; NHS Cost £1.75.

Anticandidal + hydrocortisone preparations

Clotrimazole 1% + hydrocortisone 1% cream
- Age under 6 years
- Hydrocortisone+clotrimaz cream. Apply thinly to the affected area once or twice a day. Use for a maximum of 7 days unless otherwise directed; supply 30 grams; NHS Cost £2.38.

Miconazole 2% + hydrocortisone 1% cream
- Age under 6 years
- Hydrocortisone+miconazole cream. Apply thinly to the affected area once or twice a day. Use for a maximum of 7 days unless otherwise directed; supply 30 grams; NHS Cost £2.24.

Miconazole 2% + hydrocortisone 1% ointment
- Age under 6 years
- Hydrocortisone+miconazole ointment. Apply thinly to the affected area once or twice a day. Use for a maximum of 7 days unless otherwise directed; supply 30 grams; NHS Cost £2.25.

Econazole 1% + hydrocortisone 1% cream

- Age under 6 years
- Hydrocortisone+econazole cream. Apply thinly to the affected area twice a day. Use for a maximum of 5 days unless otherwise directed; supply 30 grams; NHS Cost £2.25.

Nystatin + chlorhexidine + hydrocortisone 0.5% cream

- Age under 6 years
- Nystaform-HC 0.5% cream. Apply thinly to the affected area twice a day. Use for a maximum of 7 days unless otherwise directed; supply 30 grams; NHS Cost £2.66.

Nystatin + chlorhexidine + hydrocortisone 1% ointment

- Age under 6 years
- Nystaform-HC 1% ointment. Apply thinly to the affected area twice a day. Use for a maximum of 7 days unless otherwise directed; supply 30 grams; NHS Cost £2.66.

Timodine cream (contains nystatin + hydrocortisone 0.5%)

- Age under 6 years
- Timodine cream. Apply thinly to the affected area twice a day. Use for a maximum of 7 days unless otherwise directed; supply 30 grams; NHS Cost £2.38.

Flucloxacillin (if indicated) for 5 days

Flucloxacillin syrup: 62.5mg four times a day

- Age from 1 month to 23 months
- Flucloxacillin 125mg/5ml syrup. Take 2.5ml four times a day for 5 days; supply 100 ml; NHS Cost £3.23.

Flucloxacillin syrup: 125mg four times a day

- Age from 2 to 4 years
- Flucloxacillin 125mg/5ml syrup. Take one 5ml spoonful four times a day for 5 days; supply 100 ml; NHS Cost £3.23.

Flucloxacillin syrup: 250mg four times a day

- Age from 5 to 6 years
- Flucloxacillin 250mg/5ml syrup. Take one 5ml spoonful four times a day for 5 days; supply 100 ml; NHS Cost £6.97.

Penicillin allergy: erythromycin (if indicated) for 5 days

Erythromycin s/f suspension: 125mg four times a day

- Age from 1 month to 23 months
- Erythromycin 125mg/5ml sf susp. Take one 5ml spoonful four times a day for 5 days; supply 100 ml; NHS Cost £1.14.

Erythromycin s/f suspension: 250mg four times a day

- Age from 2 to 6 years
- Erythromycin 250mg/5ml sf susp. Take one 5ml spoonful four times a day for 5 days; supply 100 ml; NHS Cost £1.97.

Extended Information

Background information

- What is it? p.1269
- What are the causative factors of nappy rash? p.1269
- How common is it? p.1270
- What else might it be? p.1270
- Complications and prognosis p.1270

What is it?

- **Nappy rash is a dermatitis confined to the area covered by the nappy.**
- **Nappy rash is not one distinct diagnosis, but is a multifactorial problem.** Attempts have been made to classify it into a set of discrete entities, including:
  - Primary irritant contact nappy rash
  - Allergic contact nappy rash
  - Candidal nappy rash
  - Intertrigo
  - Seborrhoeic dermatitis
  - Atopic dermatitis
  - Psoriasis
- **In practice, however, a case of nappy rash may have features of many (or even all) of the above.** It is therefore more useful to adopt a pragmatic approach, and to consider each case of nappy rash as part of a spectrum that contains all of the above diagnoses.

What are the causative factors of nappy rash?

- **Frequency of changing nappies** is one of the most important factors. Prompt changing of wet or dirty nappies is the ideal. Neonates urinate more than 20 times daily; by the age of 1 year this has reduced to 7 times daily. The ideal of changing the nappy immediately it has become wet or dirty is rarely feasible.
- **The type of nappy** available has changed over recent years. Technological advances have led to the development of absorbent gelling materials as the core of disposable nappies. This material can hold many times its own weight of fluid, and reduces the time that urine is in contact with the skin compared with traditional cotton nappies [Odio and Friedlander, 2000].
- **Contact with faeces** is the greatest irritant factor on the skin. Diarrhoea causes more extensive and prolonged contact, and also increases hydration of the skin. It is not known which factors in faeces are responsible; suggestions include increased pH, faecal proteases, faecal lipases, and *Candida albicans*.
- ***C albicans*** is now agreed to be the most important (and possibly the only) causative microorganism. Many other organisms may be grown on culture from an area of nappy rash, including *Staphylococcus aureus, Escherichia coli, Pseudomonas, Streptococcus, Proteus,* and *Enterococcus,* but their role is uncertain. Some studies have suggested a link between oral thrush and nappy rash, but others have refuted this. Broad-spectrum oral antibiotic therapy has been shown to lead to nappy rash caused by *C albicans* [Dixon et al, 1969; Honig et al, 1988; Hoppe, 1997; Ferrazzini et al, 2003].
- **Contact with urine** may contribute to the development of nappy rash. The cause is thought to be the increasing hydration of the skin, or ammonia production by urea-splitting enzymes.
- **Increased hydration of the nappy area** contributes by leading to the development of macerated skin, which in itself compromises the normal barrier properties of the epidermis. Increased hydration may be due to contact with faeces or urine, nappies that prevent evaporation of moisture from the skin, or contact with urea. Increased hydration also makes the skin more susceptible to trauma from friction.
- **Skin trauma from friction** may be between nappy and skin, or from skin-to-skin contact.
- **Raised temperature in the nappy area** may occur where nappies prevent evaporation of moisture from the skin. The increased temperature may promote vasodilation, leading to inflammation.
- **Chemical irritants,** including deodorants, preservatives, creams, and oils, may cause epidermal damage in some children.

N

- **Allergy** to components of the nappy is theoretically possible, but in practice is rare.

[Berg, 1988; Harper et al, 2000]

How common is it?

- Nappy rash does not exist in underdeveloped countries where nappies are not worn.
- In developed countries, figures vary widely, owing to a lack of diagnostic criteria. It could be argued that all infants will, at some stage, develop some degree of nappy rash.

What else might it be?

- Owing to the wide range of contributory factors and presentations, the differential diagnosis of nappy rash could include most other dermatological problems of childhood.

Complications and prognosis

Complications

- Secondary bacterial infection of nappy rash may occur; this is usually by staphylococcal and streptococcal species. Due to the nature of the area concerned, a large variety of bacteria (mainly faecal flora) have been isolated from skin swabs, making their interpretation difficult [McNulty, Personal Communication, 2004].

Management issues

- Prevention of nappy rash p.1270
- Treatment of nappy rash p.1270

Prevention of nappy rash

- **Prevention** consists of minimizing contact between skin in the nappy area and faeces and urine. Prompt changing of wet or dirty nappies is the ideal. However, changing the nappy immediately it has become wet or dirty is rarely feasible.
- **Disposable nappies** that are currently available contain absorbent gelling material (AGM) as their core. This material can hold many times its own weight of fluid, and reduces the time that urine is in contact with the skin compared with traditional cotton nappies. Studies comparing AGM disposables with traditional cotton nappies have shown reductions in the severity and frequency of nappy rash in children who used AGM disposables [Harper et al, 2000; Odio and Friedlander, 2000].
- **Disposable wipes** when first developed contained alcohol, and were thought to contribute to skin irritation. Those that are currently available do not contain alcohol, and have been shown not to contribute to the development of nappy rash [Odio and Friedlander, 2000].

Treatment of nappy rash

- In spite of careful attention to preventive measures, most (if not all) children will develop nappy rash at some time. Indeed there are some children who seem particularly susceptible no matter how frequently they are changed; it is therefore important not to give the impression that nappy rash is due to poor levels of care.
- **General measures to be taken as soon as nappy rash develops include:**
  - Increasing the frequency of nappy changing and cleansing the skin.
  - Application of a barrier cream (e.g. zinc and castor oil) after every change.
  - Letting the child spend as long as possible without a nappy on, lying on a soft absorbent sheet that is changed as soon as it is wet (disposable sheets are readily available).
- **Topical anticandidal therapy** (an imidazole [clotrimazole, econazole, ketoconazole, miconazole, sulconazole] or nystatin) should be applied, as *Candida albicans* is isolated from most children with nappy rash. This therapy is often combined with 0.5% or 1% hydrocortisone to reduce the associated inflammation. Most trials are old, of small size, and methodologically flawed; three questions remain unanswered, for which we cannot offer guidance, and personal preference and experience are likely to influence prescribing:
  - Which is the best topical anticandidal therapy?
  - Should topical anticandidal therapy be combined with a mild corticosteroid?
  - Do creams or ointments work better?
- **If the nappy rash does not improve rapidly with the above management:**
  - The most likely causative factors are still a combination of *C albicans* and physical irritants (faeces and urine) [McNulty, Personal Communication, 2004].
  - Review treatment compliance with the parent.
  - Continue with the general measures outlined above in combination with topical anticandidal therapy (with or without a mild corticosteroid) [McNulty, Personal Communication, 2004].
  - Even though candidal resistance is not thought to be a problem in this situation, many health professionals would consider changing from an imidazole to nystatin (or vice versa) due to the possibility of infection with a less susceptible organism [Johnson, Personal Communication, 2004].
- **If the nappy rash still fails to improve:**
  - Secondary infection with staphylococcal or streptococcal species must be considered.
  - This diagnosis should be made on clinical grounds only, as skin swabs of this area are very difficult to interpret (due to contamination with faecal flora).
  - Treat with flucloxacillin (or erythromycin if allergic to penicillin) [McNulty, Personal Communication, 2004].

[Hoppe, 1997; Harper et al, 2000]

References

1. Berg, R.W. (1988) Etiology and pathophysiology of diaper dermatitis. *Advances in Dermatology* 3, 75–98.
2. Dixon, P.N., Warin, R.P. and English, M.P. (1969) Role of candida albicans infection in napkin rashes. *British Medical Journal* 2(648), 23–27.
3. Ferrazzini, G., Kaiser, R.R., Hirsig Cheng, S.K. et al (2003) Microbiological aspects of diaper dermatitis. *Dermatology* 206(2), 136–141.
4. Harper, J., Oranje, A. and Prose, N. (Eds.) (2000) Napkin dermatitis. In: *Textbook of pediatric dermatology*. Oxford: Blackwell Science. 139–157.
5. Honig, P.J., Gribetz, B., Leyden, J.J. et al (1988) Amoxicillin and diaper dermatitis. *Journal of the American Academy of Dermatology* 19(2 Pt 1), 275–279.
6. Hoppe, J.E. (1997) Treatment of oropharyngeal candidiasis and candidal diaper dermatitis in neonates and infants: review and reappraisal. *Pediatric Infectious Disease Journal* 16(9), 885–894.
7. Johnson, E. (2004) *Personal communication.* Health Protection Agency: London.

8. McNulty, C. (2004) *Personal communication.* Medical Microbiologist, HPA Primary Care Unit: Gloucestershire Royal Hospital, Gloucester.

9. Odio, M. and Friedlander, S.F. (2000) Diaper dermatitis and advances in diaper technology. *Current Opinion in Pediatrics* 12(4), 342–346.

N

PRODIGY GUIDANCE

Nausea and vomiting in pregnancy

Last revised in July 2005
www.prodigy.nhs.uk/guidance.asp?gt=Nausea/vomiting in pregnancy

Applies to women from the age of 12 to 60 years

This guidance covers the management of nausea and vomiting in pregnancy in primary care.

This guidance does not cover other causes of nausea and vomiting (obstetric and non-obstetric) or dyspepsia during pregnancy.

There is separate PRODIGY guidance for *Hyperthyroidism* and *Gastroenteritis*. The management of dyspepsia in pregnancy is covered in *Dyspepsia — Pregnancy-associated.*

Goals

- To reassure
- To reduce nausea and vomiting
- To reduce time off work and other lifestyle disruptions caused by symptoms

Contents

Scenarios
- Nausea and vomiting in pregnancy p.1272

Extended Information, p. 1273

Nausea and vomiting in pregnancy

Which therapy?

N

- **Reassure:**
  - Nausea and vomiting is a normal part of pregnancy.
  - Symptoms are most common and troublesome in early pregnancy, and resolve in most women by 16 weeks.
- **Offer dietary and lifestyle advice:**
  - Eat small, frequent meals, high in carbohydrate and low in fat.
  - Eat plain (or ginger) biscuits about 20 minutes before getting up.
  - Drinking little and often rather than large amounts may help to prevent vomiting.
  - Avoid food and smells that trigger symptoms.
  - Try to get plenty of rest as tiredness can make nausea worse.
- Drug treatment is indicated if symptoms are persistent, severe and prevent daily activities. Note: no drug is licensed for the treatment of nausea and vomiting in pregnancy.
  - **Promethazine is recommended first-line treatment:**
    - Promethazine hydrochloride is available in two strengths (10 mg and 25 mg) and allows dosing flexibility.
    - Promethazine teoclate is only available as a 25 mg tablet.
  - Cyclizine is an alternative first-line treatment.
  - **Regular doses** to achieve adequate blood concentrations of the drug may be helpful.

Practical prescribing points

For further information, please see the *Medicines Compendium* (www.medicines.org.uk) or the *British National Formulary* (www.bnf.org). For more information about the use of drugs in pregnancy, contact the National Teratology Information Service (tel: 0191 232 1525).

Adverse effects

- **Both promethazine and cyclizine cause drowsiness.** The degree of sedation will vary between individuals and will depend on the dose given. Anticholinergic adverse effects may also occur (e.g. blurred vision and dry mouth).

Cautions in pregnancy

- **No drug is licensed** for the treatment of nausea and vomiting in pregnancy.
- **There is no convincing evidence** to suggest that therapeutic doses of promethazine and cyclizine are associated with an increased risk of congenital abnormalities above the background rate for the population.
- **Promethazine may interfere with pregnancy testing** (urine) to produce false-positive and false-negative results.
- **Promethazine should be discontinued at least 2 weeks before delivery** because of the risk of irritability and excitement in the neonate.

Should I refer or investigate?

Refer?

- **Urgent admission is necessary for intravenous fluid, electrolyte and vitamin replacement if the following are suspected:**
  - Dehydration
  - Acidosis secondary to ketosis
  - Electrolyte imbalance
  - Nutritional deficiency
  - Any suspicion of Wernicke's encephalopathy
  - Severe, uncontrolled symptoms leading to concern about the well-being of mother or fetus

Investigate?

- **Investigations are only indicated** where there is concern regarding risk to the health of the mother or fetus or both.
- **In severe cases:**
  - **Urea and electrolytes and calcium** may reveal dehydration, renal impairment, and metabolic disturbances (e.g. acidosis).
  - **Liver function tests** may be abnormal.
  - **Urinalysis** may show marked ketonuria.
  - **Thyroid function tests** may reveal a high free thyroxine (T_4) level or low thyroid-stimulating hormone (TSH) level, or both. High free tri-iodothyronine (T_3) is much less common.

Patient information leaflets

The following PILs are available at www.prodigy.nhs.uk

- Pregnancy and Sickness and Vomiting

Shared decision making

- About 3 in 4 pregnant women feel sick or vomit during early pregnancy. Symptoms go by week 16 in most cases.
- Vomiting does not affect your baby unless you become very ill (which is rare).
- **No treatment is needed in most cases.** Things that may help include:
  - **Eating small but frequent meals.** Foods high in carbohydrate are best such as bread, crackers, etc. Eating a plain (or ginger) biscuit about 20 minutes before getting up is said by some women to help.
  - **Having lots to drink** to avoid dehydration. Drinking little and often rather than large amounts may help to prevent vomiting.
  - **Avoiding triggers.** (Some women find a 'trigger', such as a particular smell or stress, sets off their sickness.)
- **Anti-sickness medication such as promethazine or cyclizine** is an option if symptoms are severe or not settling. Many women have used these medicines, and there is no evidence that they harm a developing baby.

Drug rationale

Drugs not included

- **Prochlorperazine and metoclopramide** are recommended as second-line treatment. There are fewer studies on these drugs than on promethazine and cyclizine. Extrapyramidal reactions sometimes occur, particularly in young women [National Teratology Information Service, 1999b; National Teratology Information Service, 1999c].
- **Antihistamine anti-emetics other than promethazine and cyclizine** have not been studied extensively in human pregnancy and their long-term safety record is less clear.
- **Pyridoxine (vitamin B_6)** may reduce the severity of nausea but has no significant effect on vomiting [Sahakian et al, 1991; Vutyavanich et al, 1995]. It is not offered because of uncertainty about its effectiveness and the optimal dose. Pyridoxine, however, is less likely to cause adverse effects than antihistamine anti-emetics [Jewell and Young, 2003].

Drugs included

Note: no drug is licensed for the treatment of nausea and vomiting in pregnancy.

- **Promethazine** is the preferred first-line treatment if drug therapy is necessary [National Teratology Information Service, 2002]. It is available as the hydrochloride or teoclate salt. The hydrochloride salt is offered as a regular night-time dose. It is available as 10 mg tablets, which can be titrated for optimum effect. Up to 25 mg can be taken as one dose, and this can be repeated in the morning if necessary. Promethazine teoclate is only available as a 25 mg tablet, which restricts dosing flexibility.
- **Cyclizine** is also offered as an alternative first-line treatment [National Teratology Information Service, 1999a].

Prescriptions

1st line: non-drug management

Advice only: nausea and vomiting in pregnancy

- Age from 12 to 60 years
- Eating small but frequent meals. Foods high in carbohydrate are best such as bread, crackers, etc. Eating a plain (or ginger) biscuit about 20 minutes before getting up is said by some women to help. Have lots to drink to avoid dehydration. Drinking little and often rather than large amounts may help to prevent vomiting. Avoid triggers. (Some women find a 'trigger' sets off their sickness such as a particular smell or stress.)

2nd line: promethazine

Promethazine hydrochloride 10mg to 20mg at night

- Age from 12 to 60 years
- Promethazine HCl 10mg tablets. Take one to two tablets at night to prevent sickness. (The dose may be repeated the next morning if necessary.); supply 56 tablets; NHS Cost £1.71.

Promethazine hydrochloride 25mg at night

- Age from 12 to 60 years
- Promethazine HCl 25mg tablets. Take one tablet at night to prevent sickness. (The dose may be repeated the next morning if necessary.); supply 56 tablets; NHS Cost £2.55.

Promethazine teoclate 25mg at night

- Age from 12 to 60 years
- Promethazine Teoclat 25mg tabs. Take one tablet at night to prevent sickness. (The dose may be repeated the next morning if necessary.); supply 56 tablets; NHS Cost £6.26.

2nd line: cyclizine

Cyclizine 50mg up to three times a day

- Age from 12 to 60 years
- Cyclizine 50mg tablets. Take one tablet up to three times a day, to prevent sickness; supply 56 tablets; NHS Cost £3.45.

Extended Information

Background information

- What is it? p.1273
- How common is it? p.1274
- How do I know my patient has it? p.1274
- What other causes of nausea and vomiting in pregnancy are there? p.1275
- Complications and prognosis p.1275

What is it?

- **Nausea and vomiting are common symptoms** experienced by most women in the early stages of pregnancy.
- **Although often referred to as 'morning sickness', nausea and vomiting can occur at all times of the day.** About 2%–4% of women experience symptoms only in the morning and 80%–95% of women experience symptoms throughout the day.
- **A spectrum of severity exists,** from mild nausea to rare life-threatening symptoms.
  - **Most cases are regarded as mild,** but the effect on pregnant women's sense of well-being and daily activities has probably been underestimated.

N

  - **Hyperemesis gravidarum is the most severe form** of nausea and vomiting in pregnancy and is defined as persistent nausea and vomiting leading to dehydration, ketonuria, electrolyte imbalance and weight loss greater than 5% of pre-pregnancy weight.
- **The pathophysiology** is poorly understood and is likely to be multifactorial. Theories of the cause include:
  - **Hormonal:**
    - Human chorionic gonadotrophin (hCG) levels peak during the first trimester, and are higher in some conditions associated with nausea and vomiting in pregnancy (hydatidiform mole and multiple gestation) [Davis, 2004]. However, no consistent correlation has been found between the severity of nausea and vomiting, and hCG levels.
    - High oestrogen levels are related to increased incidence of nausea and vomiting in pregnancy [ACOG, 2004; Davis, 2004].
  - **Gastrointestinal dysmotility** results in delayed gastric emptying and lower oesophageal sphincter pressure.
  - **Autonomic nervous system disturbance** is related to the physiological changes in pregnancy in blood volume, temperature, heart rate, and vascular resistance.
  - **Nutritional deficiency:** deficiencies of vitamin B_6 have been noted in pregnant women [Czeizel et al, 1992] and vitamin B_6 use during pregnancy is associated with some improvement in nausea severity [Jewell and Young, 2003].
  - **Psychological factors:** some women experience ambivalence or rejection of the pregnancy, particularly if the pregnancy is unplanned [Davis, 2004]. Another theory is that pregnant women may be transforming psychological distress into physical symptoms [Buckwalter and Simpson, 2002].
  - **Hepatic abnormalities:** abnormalities of liver function tests are common in women with hyperemesis gravidarum; however, it is possible that these are secondary to the condition.
  - **Lipid metabolism:** a slow adaptation of the liver to the increased levels of hormones in pregnancy may cause hyperemesis gravidarum and result in differences in serum lipid and lipoproteins.
  - ***Helicobacter pylori* infection** has been found to be significantly associated with hyperemesis gravidarum [Kocak et al, 1999; Shirin et al, 2004]. Five case reports have reported an improvement in symptoms following either erythromycin therapy or a combination of antibiotics and proton pump inhibitor or H_2 receptor antagonist [Kuscu and Koyuncu, 2002].
  - **Hyperthyroxinaemia** (high thyroxine levels) may be associated with hyperemesis gravidarum. It is postulated that hCG, which shares a common alpha subunit with thyroid-stimulating hormone, acts as a thyroid stimulator. This usually resolves spontaneously as pregnancy progresses, in parallel with the hyperemesis gravidarum [DTB, 1995].
- **Nausea and vomiting in pregnancy may have a functional role.**
  - One theory is that an *increased sensitivity* to smell is a natural protective measure, making women more aware of potentially noxious agents in the environment.
  - Another hypothesis is that maintaining low levels of insulin in the first trimester of pregnancy is vital to early placental development [Huxley, 2000]. Human chorionic gonadotrophin (hCG) has been shown to activate the thyroid, stimulating the production and release of thyroxine, a stimulator of placental growth. Insulin has been reported to inhibit hCG production in the first trimester and therefore hinder placental growth.

[Kuscu and Koyuncu, 2002; Jewell and Young, 2003; ACOG, 2004; Davis, 2004]

How common is it?

- **Nausea in pregnancy is reported in 50%–80% of pregnant women;** 52% of pregnant women experience symptoms of both nausea and vomiting during early pregnancy, and 28% experience nausea only.
- **Hyperemesis gravidarum** affects between 0.3% and 2% of all pregnant women.
- **Increased incidence** of nausea and vomiting is associated with:
  - Multiple pregnancies
  - Mother or sister with nausea and vomiting in pregnancy
  - Previous pregnancy with nausea and vomiting
  - Hydatidiform mole
  - Nulliparity
  - Unplanned pregnancy
  - Female gender of the fetus
  - Non-smoking
  - Low socio-economic status
  - Younger maternal age
  - Dependent personality trait
  - Obesity
  - Stress
- **Reduced incidence** is noted in smokers and in women who subsequently experience miscarriage.
- Low body mass index has recently been linked to high incidence of nausea and vomiting in pregnancy in one small observational study of 41 women [Ben Aroya et al, 2005].

[Abell and Riely, 1992; ACOG, 2004; Davis, 2004]

How do I know my patient has it?

Clinical features

- **Symptoms commonly start 4–7 weeks after the last menstrual period and cease by 12 weeks in 60% of affected women.** About 9% of affected women have symptoms that persist beyond 16 weeks and may persist until 22 weeks of gestation [Lagiou et al, 2003; Davis, 2004].
- **Symptoms are often episodic and can occur at any time during the day** [Gadsby et al, 1993].
- **Typical symptoms** include nausea, vomiting, fatigue, anorexia and weight loss (<5% of pre-pregnancy bodyweight).
- **Features of hyperemesis gravidarum** include dehydration, ketosis, weight loss (greater than 5%), postural hypotension, tachycardia and even collapse (as a result of dehydration and electrolyte imbalance).

Investigations

- **Investigations are only required where there is concern regarding risk to the health of the mother or fetus.**
  - Urinalysis may show ketonuria
  - Serum electrolytes, urea, and creatinine may be abnormal
  - Liver function tests may be abnormal
  - Thyroid function tests may reveal a high free thyroxine (T_4) level (hyperthyroxinaemia) or a low thyroid-stimulating hormone (TSH) level, or both, in up to 50% of women with hyperemesis gravidarum [Kuscu and Koyuncu, 2002]. High free tri-iodothyronine (T_3) is much less common.
- Multiple pregnancy and hydatidiform mole should be excluded when hyperemesis gravidarum is diagnosed [Philip, 2003].

What other causes of nausea and vomiting in pregnancy are there?

Other causes should be considered if nausea and vomiting occurs for the first time after 9 weeks of gestation or if fever and abdominal pain (other than from retching) are present. These include:

- Gastrointestinal (e.g. infection, appendicitis, gastritis, cholecystitis, peptic ulceration, hepatitis, pancreatitis)
- Genito-urinary (e.g. urinary tract infection, uraemia, ovarian torsion, kidney stones, degenerating uterine leiomyoma)
- Ear, nose and throat (e.g. labyrinthitis, Meniere's disease, motion sickness)
- Metabolic (e.g. hypercalcaemia, Addison's disease, porphyria, diabetic ketoacidosis)
- Psychological (e.g. eating disorders)
- Neurological (e.g. vestibular lesions, migraines, tumours of the central nervous system)
- Pregnancy-related (e.g. acute fatty liver of pregnancy, pre-eclampsia)
- Drug toxicity or intolerance (e.g. morphine, digoxin, iron)

In women with hyperemesis gravidarum and hyperthyroxinaemia:

- If symptoms are severe or persist into the second trimester, a diagnosis of Graves' disease should be considered [DTB, 1995].
- Goitre is not found with nausea and vomiting in pregnancy and if present may indicate primary thyroid disease.

[ACOG, 2004; Davis, 2004]

Complications and prognosis

Complications

Most cases of nausea and vomiting in pregnancy are self-limiting, and settle without complication as pregnancy progresses.

Sleep disturbances may lead to increased fatigue and irritability [Davis, 2004].

Time off work is needed by 35% of working women, who spend a mean of 62 hours away from their paid work as a result of the symptoms of nausea and vomiting [Gadsby et al, 1993].

In more severe cases, hospitalization is required because dehydration, weight loss, electrolyte disturbance, and nutritional deficiency can occur. Parenteral nutrition may also be necessary if the woman continues to lose weight.

Hyperemesis gravidarum may lead to serious complications, including:

- Wernicke's encephalopathy (due to a deficiency of vitamin B_1/thiamine) which may lead to maternal death or permanent neurological disability
- Central pontine myelinolysis (an uncommon condition associated with rapid correction of severe hyponatremia)
- Spontaneous oesophageal rupture
- Transient hyperthyroxinaemia (elevated free thyroxine [T_4] and suppressed thyroid-stimulating hormone [TSH]) which may not be associated with any clinical manifestations
- Depression secondary to hyperemesis gravidarum, which may develop in up to 60% of women, with some women electing to terminate their pregnancy

[Kuscu and Koyuncu, 2002; ACOG, 2004; Davis, 2004]

Prognosis

The effects on the fetus depend on the severity of the maternal symptoms. Overall, nausea and vomiting of pregnancy is associated with favourable pregnancy outcomes.

- There is a decreased risk of miscarriage and a lower incidence of perinatal death, and preterm birth [Weigel and Weigel, 1989].
- With severe symptoms (abnormal electrolytes and weight loss) there may be an increased risk of low birth weight [Nelson-Piercy, 1997].
- No difference in the incidence of congenital malformations [Depue et al, 1987] was found between infants born to pregnant women who vomited and to those who did not.

[ACOG, 2004; Davis, 2004]

- **Hyperemesis gravidarum has not been associated with adverse pregnancy outcomes.**
  - Studies have shown no increased incidence in adverse pregnancy outcomes in women with hyperemesis gravidarum, compared with pregnant women without hyperemesis gravidarum.
  - There is a higher incidence of low birth weight among infants born to women with hyperemesis gravidarum.
  - Gestational age, preterm delivery, APGAR scores, perinatal mortality and fetal malformations did not differ.

[Tsang et al, 1996; Kuscu and Koyuncu, 2002; ACOG, 2004; Davis, 2004]

Management issues

- Overview p.1275
- What first-line measures should I recommend? p.1275
- What should I do if symptoms are severe despite first-line measures? p.1276
- Which drugs can be used to treat nausea and vomiting in pregnancy in primary care? p.1276
- When should I refer? p.1276
- Are vitamins an effective treatment? p.1276
- Are alternative and complementary therapies effective? p.1277
- Medicines management p.1278

N

Overview

- **Consider and rule out other causes of nausea and vomiting, both pregnancy-related and unrelated to pregnancy** (see *What other causes of nausea and vomiting in pregnancy are there?*), even if the diagnosis of nausea and vomiting in pregnancy seems straightforward.
- Offer reassurance and support.
- Suggest dietary and lifestyle changes that may alleviate symptoms.
- Consider drug treatment or hospitalization if symptoms are persistent, severe, and prevent daily activities.

What first-line measures should I recommend?

- Reassure the woman that this is a normal part of pregnancy and that pregnancy outcomes are generally better for women who suffer from nausea and vomiting in early pregnancy.
- Support from family and friends is regarded as helpful.
- Advise rest as tiredness can make nausea worse.
- Advise drinking little and often rather than in large amounts, as this may help to prevent vomiting.
- Although there is no research-based evidence, it is common practice to recommend:

- Small, frequent meals high in carbohydrate and low in fat
- Eating cold meals rather than hot meals, which may prevent any smell-related nausea, as cold food does not seem to give off as much smell as hot food
- Eating plain (or ginger) biscuits about 20 minutes before getting up
- Glucose tablets to possibly help prevent blood sugar levels from dropping (low blood sugar levels may cause nausea)
- Avoiding any foods or smells that trigger symptoms
- Avoiding drinking cold, tart, or sweet beverages
- Avoiding caffeine and alcohol, to prevent dehydration

[National Teratology Information Service, 1999a; SOGC, 2002; Davis, 2004]

What should I do if symptoms are severe despite first-line measures?

- When symptoms are persistent, severe, and prevent daily activities, drug treatment should be considered.
- Women with raised urine ketone levels should be started on drug treatment.

[Broussard and Richter, 1998; Kuscu and Koyuncu, 2002]

Which drugs can be used to treat nausea and vomiting in pregnancy in primary care?

No drug is licensed for the treatment of nausea and vomiting of pregnancy in the UK.

Antihistamine anti-emetics — promethazine and cyclizine

- **Promethazine and cyclizine are recommended first-line treatment.** They have been widely used in pregnancy, and have not been associated with an increased risk of congenital malformations in infants born to mothers exposed to these drugs during pregnancy [Mazzotta and Magee, 2000; Kallen, 2002].
- Promethazine is preferred as it is the most studied [National Teratology Information Service, 2002].
  - One systematic review demonstrated no increased risk of major malformations following the use of promethazine in pregnancy (n = 1006) [Magee et al, 2002]. The authors pooled the data for all phenothiazines (including promethazine) and showed no association between phenothiazine use and the risk of malformations (RR 1.00, 95% CI 0.84 to 1.18).
  - Drug exposure during pregnancy was identified from the Swedish Birth Registry and included 678 women taking promethazine only and 309 women taking cyclizine only [Kallen, 2002]. The rate of congenital malformations for promethazine was 3.14% and for cyclizine it was 3.17%, which did not differ from that seen in the general population (3.16%).

Prochlorperazine

- Prochlorperazine is regarded as a second-line treatment because there are fewer safety data available compared with promethazine and cyclizine [National Teratology Information Service, 1999a].
  - One review demonstrated no increased risk of major malformations following the use of prochlorperazine in pregnancy (n = 1018) [Magee et al, 2002]. The authors pooled the data for all phenothiazines (including prochlorperazine) and showed no association between phenothiazine use and the risk of malformations (RR = 1.00, 95% CI 0.84 to 1.18).

Metoclopramide

- Metoclopramide is considered safe for use in pregnancy and is also recommended as a second-line treatment for nausea and vomiting in pregnancy [National Teratology Information Service, 1999a].
  - No major difference in the risk of congenital malformations (OR = 1.11, 95% CI 0.6 to 2.1) was found in a retrospective study of 309 women taking metoclopramide during pregnancy [Sorensen et al, 2000]. The incidences of low birth weight infants (OR = 1.79, 95% CI 0.8 to 3.9) or preterm delivery (OR = 1.02, 95% CI 0.6 to 1.7) were not significantly different.
  - Two prospective studies, one including 126 women and the second including 175 women, showed no increase in malformation rate in infants born to women taking metoclopramide during the first trimester of pregnancy [Berkovitch et al, 2000; Berkovitch et al, 2002]. Both studies were carried out by the same authors and the women were recruited via teratology information services, and their pregnancies followed up prospectively. No information regarding the effectiveness of metoclopramide was reported.

Domperidone

- **Domperidone is not recommended** to treat nausea and vomiting of pregnancy as there are no published observational or trial data of its use in pregnancy [Magee et al, 2002].

When should I refer?

- **Women with hyperemesis gravidarum should be referred** for parenteral fluid and electrolyte replacement, together with vitamin supplementation. Nutritional support (enteral or parenteral) is needed in women who have intractable symptoms and weight loss despite appropriate therapy.
- Women with raised urine ketone levels, despite drug treatment, should be referred to secondary care.

Are vitamins an effective treatment?

Multivitamins

- **Multivitamins before and during pregnancy are not recommended.**
- Although multivitamins have been successful in alleviating symptoms in some women, it is difficult to know which ingredient is responsible and there is little good quality evidence of their effectiveness and safety during pregnancy.
- Taking multivitamins around the time of conception and during pregnancy may reduce the incidence or severity, or both of symptoms of nausea and vomiting in pregnancy.
  - A randomized placebo-controlled trial of 1000 women investigated the effect of multivitamin supplementation on nausea and vomiting in pregnancy [Czeizel et al, 1992]. Women taking a multivitamin and mineral supplement (Ro 15-9473, ELEVIT prenatal®) for at least 1 month before conception and during the first trimester of pregnancy, showed a lower incidence in nausea and vomiting of severity that would prompt medical advice or treatment.
  - A prospective observational study found that women taking multivitamins at the time of conception and during pregnancy were less likely to have episodes of vomiting (40%) than those who did not take multivitamins (59%) [Emelianova et al, 2001].

Pyridoxine

- **Pyridoxine is not routinely recommended.**
- Although pyridoxine has been successful in alleviating symptoms in some women and is less likely to cause adverse effects (e.g. drowsiness) than antihistamine anti-

N

emetics [Jewell and Young, 2003], there is still uncertainty concerning effectiveness and the optimal dosage, which prevents a recommendation in this guidance for its use.

A Cochrane review showed pyridoxine was effective at reducing nausea but there was no evidence of its effectiveness for vomiting [Jewell and Young, 2003]. The effect on nausea may be dose-related. Of the two studies included, the study investigating the higher dose showed greater effect.

- One randomized controlled trial (RCT) showed a significant decrease in nausea in 169 women treated with 30 mg pyridoxine daily compared with those given placebo (p = 0.001). There was a non-significant trend in the number of vomiting episodes in the treated group (P = 0.06) [Vutyavanich et al, 1995].
- The other RCT reported improvement in nausea scores in 59 women with severe symptoms who were treated with 75 mg pyridoxine daily (p <0.01), but not in those with mild to moderate nausea. A significant reduction in vomiting for all patients (p <0.005) was also shown [Sahakian et al, 1991]. This study had a small sample size and evaluated only 3 days of treatment. Neither trial reported fetal outcome.

No increase in malformation rate was found in a prospective observational study [Czeizel et al, 2004]. Information from a congenital malformation registry in Hungary did not find any difference in pyridoxine use between mothers of infants born with malformations compared with controls.

Note: high-dose pyridoxine supplements taken over a prolonged time have been reported to cause peripheral neuropathy. Pharmacists have been advised by The Royal Pharmaceutical Society of Great Britain to consider how to advise patients wishing to purchase high-dose preparations (i.e. over 10 mg daily).

re alternative and complementary ierapies effective?

3inger

Although ginger root may be an effective treatment for nausea and vomiting of pregnancy, it cannot be recommended in this guidance:

- The active ingredient is unknown and the composition may vary widely.
- There is insufficient good quality evidence of its effectiveness and safety.

Ginger has been shown to reduce nausea and vomiting in pregnancy although the dose and form of ginger varied greatly across randomized controlled trials (RCTs):

- A significant decrease in nausea and vomiting was reported in 27 women in hospital for severe hyperemesis gravidarum who took 250 mg ginger compared with women who took 250 mg lactose [Fischer-Rasmussen et al, 1991].
- Ginger was effective for relieving the severity of mild and moderate nausea and vomiting in pregnancy [Vutyavanich et al, 2001].
- Ginger (350 mg) was therapeutically equivalent to pyridoxine (25 mg) in improving nausea, dry retching and vomiting in 291 women [Smith et al, 2004]. No complications of pregnancy or adverse effects were reported following the use of ginger in pregnancy.
- Some benefit was reported following use of 125 mg ginger extract in 120 women, compared with placebo (soya bean oil) [Willetts et al, 2003].

The limited data on this issue indicate that ginger is safe for use in pregnancy:

- Three RCTs (481 women in total) showed that the rate of birth defects in the children of women taking ginger in pregnancy was similar to that in the general population [Vutyavanich et al, 2001; Willetts et al, 2003; Smith et al, 2004].
- One prospective observational study showed no increased incidence of adverse outcomes in 187 pregnant women using ginger compared with women not taking ginger during pregnancy [Portnoi et al, 2003]. There were no statistically significant differences between the two groups in terms of live births, infants with congenital malformations, spontaneous abortions, stillbirths, therapeutic abortions, birth weight or gestational age.

Acupuncture, acupressure, and acustimulation

- A recent Cochrane review reported limited evidence of benefit of either acupuncture or acupressure for treating nausea and vomiting in pregnancy [Jewell and Young, 2003].
- **Acupressure may give relief to women** and would seem to produce little risk of adverse effect. Acupressure wristbands have the advantage of being inexpensive and available without a visit to the doctor or midwife.
- **The acupuncture point** most frequently used in traditional Chinese medicine for anti-emetic action is point 6 (P6) on the pericardium channel. This point is on the forearm, about three fingerbreadths proximal to the distal wrist crease, between the tendons of the flexor carpi radialis and palmaris longus muscles, about 1 cm deep.
- **Acupressure involves** the application of pressure at the P6 acupuncture point. It does not require needles, and can be applied using commercially available elastic bands holding a plastic disc that fit around the wrist.
- **Acustimulation** involves the application of a mild electrical current to the P6 point.
- **Acupuncture is not recommended** for the treatment of nausea and vomiting of pregnancy.
  - Two RCTs of 55 women [Knight et al, 2001] and 593 women [Smith et al, 2002] have shown that acupuncture is no more effective than placebo (sham acupuncture) for treating nausea of pregnancy.
  - However, these two studies showed that both acupuncture and sham acupuncture produced notable decreases in nausea, possibly as a result of the opportunity for women to discuss and have their symptoms recognized by professionals.
- **Clinical trials on the use of acupressure have produced inconsistent findings.**
  - A Cochrane systematic review showed that P6 acupressure has beneficial effects for nausea and vomiting in pregnancy, and that this is comparable to that obtained by drugs [Jewell and Young, 2003].
  - However, data from one of the largest RCTs was not in a form that could be included in the systematic review, and this trial showed no benefit from acupressure [Jewell and Young, 2003].
- **Acustimulation is not recommended** for the treatment of nausea and vomiting of pregnancy.
  - Two RCTs found nerve stimulation bands effective in reducing nausea and vomiting in pregnancy [Evans et al, 1993; Rosen et al, 2003].
  - An RCT of 187 women, showed acustimulation was effective at reducing nausea and vomiting and promoting weight gain [Rosen et al, 2003]. Nerve stimulation therapy, provided by a small battery-powered device, was randomly allocated to 95 women, and 92 women used a sham device. The average improvement in total experience (frequency of nausea, vomiting and retching, and degree of distress) over the 21-day period was 6.5 (95% CL 5.3 to 7.7) in

N

the nerve stimulation group and 4.7 (95% CI 3.7 to 5.6) in the placebo group.
- A small randomized placebo crossover study comparing an active sensory afferent stimulation (SAS) unit and an inactive placebo unit, showed symptom improvement in 20 women when the SAS unit was worn and in 10 when the placebo device was worn [Evans et al, 1993]. The placebo bands were identical in size and shape to the active bands but did not deliver an electrical stimulus.

Hypnosis, hypnotherapy, psychotherapy, and behaviour modification

- No randomized trials investigating these treatments have been published. Two case series carried out in 1946 and 1957 described successful treatment of severe forms of nausea and vomiting in pregnancy through hypnosis [Mazzotta and Magee, 2000].

Herbal remedies

- Herbal remedies for nausea and vomiting in pregnancy, such as red raspberry and wild yam, are available over the counter, but have not been studied formally.
- Many herbal treatments have pharmacological effects on the body, and women should be advised that there is no evidence of either efficacy or safety of these remedies.

Homeopathic treatment

- No trials have been published regarding the use of homeopathy to treat nausea and vomiting of pregnancy.

Medicines management

How should drug treatment be prescribed?

- In severe cases the intravenous or rectal route may be considered initially, where available, and changed to the oral route when the symptoms begin to subside.
- **Promethazine** is available as the hydrochloride or teoclate salt.
  - The hydrochloride salt is offered as a regular night-time dose. It is available as 10 mg tablets, which can be titrated for optimal effect. Up to 25 mg can be taken as one dose, and this can be repeated in the morning if necessary.
  - Promethazine teoclate is only available as a 25 mg tablet, which restricts dosing flexibility.
- **Cyclizine** is available as the hydrochloride salt at a dose of 50 mg taken up to three times daily.
- **Prochlorperazine** can be used in nausea and vomiting in pregnancy, for prevention (5–10 mg, two or three times daily) and treatment (20 mg immediately, followed, if necessary, by 10 mg 2 hours later).
- **Metoclopramide** is given at a dose of 10 mg three times daily.

[BNF 49, 2005]

What are the adverse effects of drug treatment?

Promethazine and cyclizine

- **No increased risks of congenital abnormalities,** above the background rate for the population, have been reported when these drugs have been used in therapeutic doses [Seto et al, 1997].
- **There is a risk of neonatal withdrawal symptoms;** promethazine should therefore be stopped 2 weeks before delivery. However, the drug is very rarely required in late pregnancy.
- **Drowsiness** is a significant adverse effect with promethazine, although reported to a lesser extent with cyclizine, and it may diminish after a few days of treatment.
- **Other adverse effects** include headache, psychomotor impairment, and antimuscarinic effects such as urinary retention, dry mouth, blurred vision, and gastrointestinal disturbances.

Prochlorperazine

- **No increased risk of congenital abnormalities** above the background rate for the population has been reported when prochlorperazine has been used in therapeutic doses [National Teratology Information Service, 1999b].
- **There is a risk of neonatal withdrawal symptoms** following chronic use of prochlorperazine, especially in the third trimester [National Teratology Information Service, 1999b].
- **Extrapyramidal symptoms** are the most significant adverse effects reported with prochlorperazine use, although these are particularly reported with depot preparations.
- **Drowsiness and antimuscarinic symptoms** (such as dry mouth, constipation, difficulty with micturition, and blurred vision) are also reported.

Metoclopramide

- **No increased risk of congenital abnormalities** following first-trimester exposure to metoclopramide was found, compared with controls [Berkovitch et al, 2002].
- **Extrapyramidal symptoms** (particularly in young women), hyperprolactinaemia, and occasionally tardive dyskinesia on prolonged administration have been reported.
- Drowsiness, restlessness, diarrhoea, depression, neuroleptic malignant syndrome, rashes, pruritus, and oedema have also been reported.

Domperidone

- Adverse effects include extrapyramidal symptoms and rashes.

[National Teratology Information Service, 1999a; Manx Pharma, 2001; Kallen, 2002; Diav-Citrin et al, 2003; Jewell and Young, 2003; BNF 49, 2005]

References

NHS staff in England can link, free of charge, from references to full text journals by clicking on [Full text] on the PRODIGY website.

1. Abell, T.L. and Riely, C.A. (1992) Hyperemesis gravidarum. *Gastroenterology Clinics of North America* **21**(4), 835–849.
2. ACOG (2004) ACOG practice bulletin number 52: nausea and vomiting of pregnancy. *Obstetrics & Gynecology* **103**(4), 803–813.
3. Ben Aroya, Z., Lurie, S., Segal, D. et al (2005) Association of nausea and vomiting in pregnancy with lower body mass index. *European Journal of Obstetrics, Gynecology, & Reproductive Biology* **118**(2), 196–198.
4. Berkovitch, M., Elbirt, D., Addis, A. et al (2000) Fetal effects of metoclopramide therapy for nausea and vomiting of pregnancy. *New England Journal of Medicine* **343**(6), 445–446. [Full text]
5. Berkovitch, M., Mazzota, P., Greenberg, R. et al (2002) Metoclopramide for nausea and vomiting of pregnancy: a prospective multicenter international study. *American Journal of Perinatology* **19**(6), 311–316.
6. BNF 49 (2005) *British National Formulary.* 49th edn. London: British Medical Association and Royal Pharmaceutical Society of Great Britain.
7. Broussard, C.N. and Richter, J.E. (1998) Nausea and vomiting of pregnancy. *Gastroenterology Clinics of North America* **27**(1), 123–151.
8. Buckwalter, J.G. and Simpson, S.W. (2002) Psychological factors in the etiology and treatment of

N

severe nausea and vomiting in pregnancy. *American Journal of Obstetrics & Gynecology* **186**(5), S210-S214.

9. Czeizel, A.E., Dudas, I., Fritz, G. et al (1992) The effect of periconceptional multivitamin-mineral supplementation on vertigo, nausea and vomiting in the first trimester of pregnancy. *Archives of Gynecology & Obstetrics* **251**(4), 181–185.

0. Czeizel, A.E., Puho, E., Banhidy, F. and Acs, N. (2004) Oral pyridoxine during pregnancy: potential protective effect for cardiovascular malformations. *Drugs in R & D* 5(5), 259–269.

1. Davis, M. (2004) Nausea and vomiting of pregnancy: an evidence-based review. *Journal of Perinatal and Neonatal Nursing* **18**(4), 312–328.

2. Depue, R.H., Bernstein, L., Ross, R.K. et al (1987) Hyperemesis gravidarum in relation to estradiol levels, pregnancy outcome, and other maternal factors: a seroepidemiologic study. *American Journal of Obstetrics & Gynecology* **156**(5), 1137–1141.

3. Diav-Citrin, O., Shechtman, S., Aharonovich, A. et al (2003) Pregnancy outcome after gestational exposure to loratadine or antihistamines: a prospective controlled cohort study. *Journal of Allergy & Clinical Immunology* **111**(6), 1239–1243.

4. DTB (1995) The practical management of thyroid disease in pregnancy. *Drug & Therapeutics Bulletin* **33**(Oct), 75–77. [Full text]

5. Emelianova, S., Mazzotta, P., Einarson, A. and Koren, G. (2001) *Prevalence and severity of nausea and vomiting of pregnancy and effect of vitamin supplementation*. Nausea and Vomiting of Pregnancy. www.nvp-volumes.org [Accessed: 01/04/2005].

6. Evans, A.T., Samuels, S.N., Marshall, C. et al (1993) Suppression of pregnancy-induced nausea and vomiting with sensory afferent stimulation. *Journal of Reproductive Medicine* **38**(8), 603–606.

7. Fischer-Rasmussen, W., Kjaer, S.K., Dahl, C. and Asping, U. (1991) Ginger treatment of hyperemesis gravidarum. *European Journal of Obstetrics, Gynecology, & Reproductive Biology* **38**(1), 19–24.

8. Gadsby, R., Barnie-Adshead, A.M. and Jagger, C. (1993) A prospective study of nausea and vomiting during pregnancy. *British Journal of General Practice* **43**(371), 245–248.

9. Huxley, R.R. (2000) Nausea and vomiting in early pregnancy: its role in placental development. *Obstetrics & Gynecology* **95**(5), 779–782.

0. Jewell, D. and Young, G. (2003) *Interventions for nausea and vomiting in early pregnancy (Cochrane Review)*. The Cochrane Library. Issue 4. Chichester, UK: John Wiley & Sons, Ltd. www.nelh.nhs.uk/cochrane.asp [Accessed: 04/03/2005]. [Full text]

1. Kallen, B. (2002) Use of antihistamine drugs in early pregnancy and delivery outcome. *Journal of Maternal-Fetal & Neonatal Medicine* **11**(3), 146–152.

2. Knight, B., Mudge, C., Openshaw, S. et al (2001) Effect of acupuncture on nausea of pregnancy: a randomized, controlled trial. *Obstetrics & Gynecology* **97**(2), 184–188.

3. Kocak, I., Akcan, Y., Ustun, C. et al (1999) Helicobacter pylori seropositivity in patients with hyperemesis gravidarum. *International Journal of Gynaecology & Obstetrics* **66**(3), 251–254.

4. Kuscu, N.K. and Koyuncu, F. (2002) Hyperemesis gravidarum: current concepts and management. *Postgraduate Medical Journal* **78**(916), 76–79. [Full text]

5. Lagiou, P., Tamimi, R., Mucci, L.A. et al (2003) Nausea and vomiting in pregnancy in relation to prolactin, estrogens, and progesterone: a prospective study. *Obstetrics & Gynecology* **101**(4), 639–644.

26. Magee, L.A., Mazzotta, P. and Koren, G. (2002) Evidence-based view of safety and effectiveness of pharmacologic therapy for nausea and vomiting of pregnancy (NVP). *American Journal of Obstetrics & Gynecology* **186**(5 Suppl Understanding), S256-S261.

27. Manx Pharma (2001) *AvomineT tablets 25mg*. Warwickshire: Manx Pharma.

28. Mazzotta, P. and Magee, L.A. (2000) A risk-benefit assessment of pharmacological and nonpharmacological treatments for nausea and vomiting of pregnancy. *Drugs* **59**(4), 781–800.

29. National Teratology Information Service (1999a) *Nausea and vomiting in pregnancy*. NHS Northern and Yorkshire: Regional Drug and Therapeutics Centre.

30. National Teratology Information Service (1999b) *Prochlorperazine use in pregnancy*. NHS Northern and Yorkshire: Regional Drug and Therapeutics Centre.

31. National Teratology Information Service (1999c) *Metoclopramide use in pregnancy*. NHS Northern and Yorkshire: Regional Drug and Therapeutics Centre.

32. National Teratology Information Service (2002) *Promethazine exposure during pregnancy*. NHS Northern and Yorkshire: Regional Drug and Therapeutics Centre.

33. Nelson-Piercy, C. (1997) Hyperemesis gravidarum. *Current Opinion in Obstetrics & Gynaecology* **7**(2), 98–103.

34. Philip, B. (2003) Hyperemesis gravidarum: literature review. *Wisconsin Medical Journal* **102**(3), 46–51.

35. Portnoi, G., Chng, L., Karimi-Tabesh, L. et al (2003) Prospective comparative study of the safety and effectiveness of ginger for the treatment of nausea and vomiting in pregnancy. *American Journal of Obstetrics and Gynecology* **189**(5), 1374–1377.

36. Rosen, T., de Veciana, M., Miller, H.S. et al (2003) A randomized controlled trial of nerve stimulation for relief of nausea and vomiting in pregnancy. *Obstetrics & Gynecology* **102**(1), 129–135.

37. Sahakian, V., Rouse, D., Sipes, S. et al (1991) Vitamin B6 is effective therapy for nausea and vomiting of pregnancy: a randomized, double-blind placebo-controlled study. *Obstetrics & Gynecology* **78**(1), 33–36.

38. Seto, A., Einarson, T. and Koren, G. (1997) Pregnancy outcome following first trimester exposure to antihistamines: meta-analysis. *American Journal of Perinatology* **14**(3), 119–124.

39. Shirin, H., Sadan, O., Shevah, O. et al (2004) Positive serology for Helicobacter pylori and vomiting in the pregnancy. *Archives of Gynecology & Obstetrics* **270**(1), 10–14.

40. Smith, C., Crowther, C. and Beilby, J. (2002) Acupuncture to treat nausea and vomiting in early pregnancy: a randomized controlled trial. *Birth* **29**(1), 1–9.

41. Smith, C., Crowther, C., Willson, K. et al (2004) A randomized controlled trial of ginger to treat nausea and vomiting in pregnancy. *Obstetrics & Gynecology* **103**(4), 639–645.

42. SOGC (2002) *The management of nausea and vomiting of pregnancy*. Clinical Practice Guideline. Society of Obstetricians and Gynaecologists of Canada. www.sogc.org/SOGCnet/sogc_docs/common/guide/pdfs/ps120.pdf [Accessed: 22/02/2005].

43. Sorensen, H.T., Nielsen, G.L., Christensen, K. et al (2000) Birth outcome following maternal use of metoclopramide. The Euromap study group. *British Journal of Clinical Pharmacology* **49**(3), 264–268.

44. Tsang, I.S., Katz, V.L. and Wells, S.D. (1996) Maternal and fetal outcomes in hyperemesis gravidarum.

International Journal of Gynaecology & Obstetrics 55(3), 231–235.

45. Vutyavanich, T., Wongtra-ngan, S. and Ruangsri, R. (1995) Pyridoxine for nausea and vomiting of pregnancy: a randomized, double-blind, placebo-controlled trial. *American Journal of Obstetrics & Gynecology* **173**(3 Pt 1), 881–884.
46. Vutyavanich, T., Kraisarin, T. and Ruangsri, R. (2001) Ginger for nausea and vomiting in pregnancy: randomized, double-masked, placebo-controlled trial. *Obstetrics & Gynecology* **97**(4), 577–582.
47. Weigel, R.M. and Weigel, M.M. (1989) Nausea and vomiting of early pregnancy and pregnancy outcome. A meta-analytical review. *British Journal of Obstetrics & Gynaecology* **96**(11), 1312–1318.
48. Willetts, K.E., Ekangaki, A. and Eden, J.A. (2003) Effect of a ginger extract on pregnancy-induced nausea: a randomised controlled trial. *Australian & New Zealand Journal of Obstetrics & Gynaecology* **43**(2), 139–144.

N

PRODIGY GUIDANCE

Neck pain

Last revised in July 2005
www.prodigy.nhs.uk/guidance.asp?gt=Neck pain

Applies to people over the age of 10 years

This guidance covers the primary care management of acute or chronic simple neck pain. Simple neck pain includes non-specific neck pain (with no discernable cause), torticollis, and pain after a whiplash incident without complications such as cord compression and vertebral fracture.

This guidance does not cover the management of conditions which can cause neck pain, for example ankylosing spondylitis; rheumatoid arthritis; degenerative conditions such as osteoarthritis; fibromyalgia; neurological conditions; neoplasms; infections; headache associated with neck disorders; cervical dislocation or fracture; acute spasmodic torticollis (cervical dystonia); or myofascial pain (pain with or without autonomic phenomena referred from active trigger points). Also, this guidance does not cover the management of neck pain when this is due to, or aggravated by, the person's work.

There is separate PRODIGY guidance for *Ankylosing spondylitis, Headache, Osteoarthritis, Osteoporosis — treatment, Rheumatoid arthritis,* and *Polymyalgia rheumatica.*

Goals

- To recognize possible serious specific causes of pain in the neck — 'red flags'
- To recognize psycho-social barriers to recovery — 'yellow flags'
- To recognize disability caused by simple neck pain
- To relieve pain
- To improve ability to function and alleviate disability
- To prevent recurrence and the development of chronicity

Contents

Scenarios

- Simple neck pain, acute or chronic p.1281
- Radiculopathy due to cervical spondylosis or disc herniation p.1285
- Whiplash injury without cervical fracture or subluxation p.1288
- Acute torticollis p.1292

Extended Information, p. 1294

Which scenario?

Simple neck pain, acute or chronic: covers the management of acute and chronic neck pain without signs of other conditions.

Radiculopathy due to cervical spondylosis or disc herniation: covers the management of neck pain with signs of nerve root compression from cervical spondylosis or disc herniation.

Whiplash injury without cervical fracture or subluxation: covers the initial and chronic management of neck sprain when the mechanism of injury is known to be hyperextension/flexion/rotation and there are no signs of another pathology.

Acute torticollis: covers the management of acute torticollis in an adult.

Simple neck pain, acute or chronic

Which therapy?

Rule out (or manage) any 'red flags' — see *Should I refer or investigate?*

Identify and manage any comorbidity and risk factors.

- **Provide reassurance and information.**
- **Drug therapy:**
  - **Analgesia** is effective for short-term symptomatic relief. Choice of analgesia depends on the severity and chronicity of pain, personal preferences, tolerability and risk of adverse effects. Options, in increasing order of effectiveness and risk of adverse effects, include:
    - **Analgesics available over the counter and taken as required** — will be sufficient for many people
    - **Paracetamol taken regularly**
    - **Ibuprofen taken regularly**
    - **Two of: paracetamol, ibuprofen, and codeine phosphate** (separate prescriptions; doses titrated to meet the person's needs).
  - **Diazepam** for 3–7 days may be useful for people with severe muscle spasm.
  - **Amitriptyline** for 1 month may be tried for people with chronic pain.
  - **Gabapentin** may be tried if amitriptyline is ineffective or contraindicated.
- **Physiotherapy, mobilization, manipulation:**
  - Active physiotherapy, mobilization, and manipulation may provide short-term relief in people with chronic neck pain.
  - Early mobilization is important. If employed, neck supports should be used for as short a time as possible, i.e. 2–4 days, and under supervision.

Practical prescribing points

For further information, see the *Medicines Compendium* (www.medicines.org.uk) or the *British National Formulary* (www.bnf.org).

Nonsteroidal anti-inflammatory drugs (NSAIDs)

- **Only one NSAID should be prescribed at a time.**
- **NSAIDs may worsen asthma, hypertension, renal impairment, or heart failure.**
- Do not give ibuprofen, diclofenac, or naproxen without gastroprotection if there is a history of peptic ulceration.
- **Pregnancy and breastfeeding:** use paracetamol if possible. If an NSAID is essential, ibuprofen may be used during breastfeeding and before 30 weeks of pregnancy.
- **People with cardiovascular disease:** ibuprofen may reduce the cardiovascular protective effect of low-dose aspirin

N

- **In people with risk factors for gastrointestinal NSAID complications:**
  - Use paracetamol (with or without codeine) instead of a NSAID if possible.
  - Or, use gastroprotection (a PPI or full-dose misoprostol) combined with a standard NSAID.
- **Risk factors for gastrointestinal NSAID complications include:**
  - Age of 65 years and over.
  - Previous history of gastroduodenal ulcer, gastrointestinal (GI) bleeding, or gastroduodenal perforation.
  - Concomitant use of medications that are known to increase the likelihood of upper-GI adverse events, e.g. anticoagulants, aspirin (even a low dose), and corticosteroids.
  - Presence of serious comorbidity, such as cardiovascular disease, renal or hepatic impairment, diabetes, or hypertension.
  - Requirement for prolonged duration of NSAID use.
  - Use of maximum recommended doses of NSAIDs.

Codeine

- Codeine may cause nausea, vomiting, constipation, and drowsiness. A regular laxative is often needed when it is used long-term.

Diazepam

- Diazepam has strong sedative effects. People should be warned not to drive while taking the drug or for a full day after stopping drug treatment. In addition, people should be warned that the effects of alcohol may be exaggerated whilst taking this medication.
- Diazepam has a high potential for tolerance and dependence. It should only be used in people with severe spasm, and in short courses of 3–7 days.
- Avoid use in pregnancy and breastfeeding.

N

Amitriptyline

- Amitriptyline may cause drowsiness: if this occurs advise the person to avoid driving or performing skilled tasks where there is the potential for harm.
- Abrupt withdrawal may be a problem with tricyclic antidepressants.
- Avoid use in people with who have had a myocardial infarction, people with arrhythmias, or women in the third trimester of pregnancy.

Gabapentin

- Sudden withdrawal of gabapentin may cause anxiety, insomnia, nausea, pain, and sweating: it should be tapered off over the course of at least 1 week.
- Reduce the dose of gabapentin in renal impairment. See the *Medicines Compendium* (www.medicines.org.uk) for dosage information.

Misoprostol

- Diarrhoea and abdominal pain are common. Advise women of childbearing age to use adequate contraception, since misoprostol increases the risk of miscarriage.

Should I refer or investigate?

Refer?

- **Refer (with urgency appropriate to the situation)** if **'red flags' are present:**
  - **Myelopathy (compression of the spinal cord)**
    - Insidious progression
    - Gait disturbance; clumsy or weak hands; loss of sexual/bladder/bowel function
    - Lhermitte's sign (shooting electric-like sensations on extending or moving neck)
    - Upper motor neurone signs in the lower limbs (Babinski's sign — up-going plantar reflex, hyperreflexia, clonus, spasticity)
    - Lower motor neurone signs in the upper limbs (atrophy, hyporeflexia)
  - **Malignancy, infection, inflammation**
    - Fever
    - Unexplained loss of weight
    - History of inflammatory arthritis
    - History of malignancy, drug abuse, AIDS, or other infection
    - Immunosuppression
    - Pain that is increasing, unremitting and/or disturbs sleep
    - Lymphadenopathy
  - **Severe trauma/skeletal injury**
    - History of trauma
    - Previous neck surgery
    - Osteoporosis
    - Increasing and/or unremitting pain
  - **Vascular insufficiency**
    - Dizziness and blackouts (restriction of vertebral artery) on movement, especially upward gaze
    - Dizziness, drop attacks
- **Refer** if pain becomes intractable or if complications arise.

Investigate?

- Uncomplicated neck pain does not require imaging studies or other special investigations: the condition is likely to be temporary and benign.
- Full blood count, erythrocyte sedimentation rate or C-reactive protein, liver enzymes, and imaging may be indicated to rule out other possible causes of neck pain.

Patient information leaflets

The following PILs are available at www.prodigy.nhs.uk

- Anti-inflammatory Painkillers
- Neck Pain

Shared decision making

- **Most bouts of neck pain ease** within a few weeks or so.
  - As far as possible, carry on with normal activities. Yo[u] are less likely to develop persistent neck pain if you keep your neck active rather than rest it a lot in a collar.
  - Try to keep a good posture. Sit upright and walk 'like a model'.
  - You should not drive until you can easily move your neck round.
  - Use a pillow that supports the hollow of the neck and supports a comfortable position of the head. Find a comfortable position before going to sleep. Using two pillows may not be helpful.
- **Paracetamol** is commonly used for pain. The normal adult dosage is two 500 mg tablets, four times a day.
- **An anti-inflammatory painkiller** may be an option.
  - Bleeding from the stomach is the most serious possibl[e] side-effect. Stop the medicine and see a doctor if you develop stomach symptoms.
  - Some people with asthma, high blood pressure, kidne[y] failure, or heart failure may not be able to take anti-inflammatories.
- **Codeine** is a painkiller that is stronger than paracetamo[l]. It may be used in combination with paracetamol or an

anti-inflammatory. Possible side-effects include constipation and drowsiness.

- **A muscle relaxant** such as diazepam is sometimes used for a few days if the neck muscles are tense and make the pain worse. Possible side-effects include drowsiness.
- **Amitriptyline** is sometimes used if pain becomes persistent.

Drug rationale

Drugs not included

- **Analgesics other than paracetamol and codeine taken separately,** are not recommended:
  - **Strong opioids** (e.g. morphine, pethidine) should be avoided because of the risk of dependence if they are used inappropriately.
  - **Weak opioids, other than codeine,** have either not been shown to be more effective than codeine (when used in combination with paracetamol), or are more expensive.
  - **Low-dose weak opioids with paracetamol** (combination products), e.g. co-codamol 8/500 mg. There is no evidence that these offer any clinical benefit over paracetamol alone and they are likely to lead to opioid adverse effects [MeReC, 1993; De Craen et al, 1996; Moore and McQuay, 1997].
  - **High-dose weak opioids with paracetamol** (combination products), e.g. co-codamol 30/500 mg, do not allow titration to the most effective and safe analgesic dose to match individual requirements.
  - **Co-proxamol** (dextropropoxyphene 32.5 mg/ paracetamol 325 mg) has been withdrawn by the Committee on Safety of Medicines due to its unfavourable risk/benefit ratio; it is associated with an unacceptable risk of overdose [CSM, 2005a].
- **Standard nonsteroidal anti-inflammatory drugs (NSAIDs), other than ibuprofen, diclofenac, and naproxen,** are not generally recommended, as they have a worse balance between their efficacy and adverse-effect profile than these three recommended drugs [CSM, 1994; Hernández-Diaz et al, 2000; BNF 49, 2005].
- **Cyclo-oxygenase-2 (COX-2) selective inhibitors** are not recommended. After the withdrawal of rofecoxib from the market (the only selective inhibitor licensed for acute pain), there are growing concerns that COX-2 selective inhibitors may cause serious cardiovascular events. Following a European-wide review of the data, the Committee on Safety of Medicines (CSM) has recently advised that [CSM, 2005b]:
  - The evidence suggests that coxibs, as a class, may cause an increased risk of thrombotic events (e.g. myocardial infarction and stroke) compared with placebo and some NSAIDs.
  - The risk may increase with dose and duration of exposure.
- **Strong opioids** (e.g. morphine, pethidine) should be avoided, owing to the risk of dependence if they are used inappropriately. They are usually reserved for moderate to severe pain of a visceral origin [BNF 49, 2005].
- **Pregabalin** has a similar mechanism of action to gabapentin, and is licensed for the treatment of neuropathic pain [BNF 49, 2005]. However, it is currently undergoing post-marketing surveillance (black triangle), and should reserved for use under specialist supervision.
- **Gastroprotective agents** are sometimes needed, but not all are recommended:
  - **H_2-receptor antagonists (H_2RAs).** At standard doses, H_2RAs reduce the risk of duodenal ulceration, and there is some evidence that double doses reduce the risk of gastric ulceration [Rostom et al, 2002]. However, no H_2RAs are currently licensed for the prevention of gastric ulceration induced by NSAIDs [BNF 49, 2005], which is more common than duodenal ulceration.
  - **Rabeprazole** is not included as it is not specifically licensed for the prevention of NSAID-induced gastrointestinal ulcers [BNF 49, 2005].
  - **Fixed-dose combinations of standard NSAIDs with misoprostol.** The optimum dose of misoprostol (i.e. 800 micrograms daily) cannot be reached using these preparations. In particular, only 400 micrograms daily of misoprostol is given with the higher doses of NSAID in these preparations.

Drugs included

Standard analgesics and nonsteroidal anti-inflammatory drugs (NSAIDs)

- **Paracetamol** is a good first-line choice for pain relief, and is not associated with gastrointestinal toxicity [SIGN, 2000].
- **Codeine (in combination with paracetamol):** higher-dose codeine is included for use with regular paracetamol for additional pain relief. Codeine 60 mg plus paracetamol has been shown to provide more pain relief than either codeine 60 mg alone or paracetamol 1000 mg alone [Moore et al, 1997]. Codeine should be prescribed separately to paracetamol to allow flexibility of dosing and titration of analgesic effect.
  - Note: codeine can also be combined with an NSAID, or paracetamol can be combined with an NSAID, but there is less evidence to support this.
- **Standard NSAIDS: ibuprofen, diclofenac, and naproxen** have a good balance of efficacy against adverse effect profile [CSM, 1994; Henry et al, 1996; Hernández-Diaz and Rodriguez, 2000]. Standard doses are offered as these are generally accepted to be sufficient for anti-inflammatory prophylaxis, although data are lacking.

N

Muscle relaxants

- **Diazepam** is recommended as a muscle relaxant, as it has been shown to effectively reduce acute neck pain. However, adverse effects are common, and there is a risk of dependency even after 1 week of treatment. Courses of 3–7 days should be used only in people with severe spasm [Clinical Standards Advisory Group, 1994; Waddell et al, 1999].

Gastroprotective agents

- **Proton pump inhibitors (PPIs): lansoprazole, omeprazole, esomeprazole, and pantoprazole** are licensed for the prevention of gastroduodenal ulceration induced by NSAIDs [BNF 49, 2005]. PPIs reduce the risk of endoscopic ulcers, but there are no data on prevention of ulcer complications [Rostom et al, 2002]. However, they are generally considered to be the preferred choice for gastroprotection, as they are better tolerated than misoprostol.
- **Misoprostol** is licensed for the prevention of gastroduodenal ulceration induced by NSAIDs [BNF 49, 2005]. It reduces the risk of endoscopically proven ulcers and has also been shown to reduce the risk of ulcer complications [Rostom et al, 2002]. It is less well tolerated than PPIs owing to gastrointestinal adverse effects, particularly diarrhoea.

Drugs for chronic pain

Note: although commonly used, amitriptyline and gabapentin are not licensed for the treatment of chronic pain.

- **Amitriptyline** is a tricyclic antidepressant widely used for various causes of chronic pain [McQuay and Moore, 1997]. At present there is uncertainty about the benefit of tricyclic antidepressants in chronic neck pain, but an initial 1-month trial of therapy may be worth considering in people in whom standard analgesia and/or NSAIDs have proved ineffective.
- **Gabapentin** can be considered if amitriptyline has proved ineffective or is contraindicated, although there is little trial evidence at present to verify its efficacy. The exact dose of gabapentin that is required to alleviate chronic neck pain is not known, but the full 'antiepileptic dose' is probably necessary.

Prescriptions

Paracetamol or codeine

Paracetamol tablets: 1g up to four times a day
- Age from 16 years onwards
- Paracetamol 500mg tablets. Take two tablets every 4 to 6 hours when required for pain relief. Maximum of 8 tablets in 24 hours; supply 200 tablets; NHS Cost £2.12; OTC Cost £3.75.

Codeine tablets: 30mg to 60mg up to four times a day
- Age from 16 years onwards
- Codeine 30mg tablets. Take one to two tablets every 4 to 6 hours when required for pain relief. Maximum of 8 tablets in 24 hours; supply 60 tablets; NHS Cost £4.58.

Paracetamol 500mg tablets + codeine 30mg tablets
- Age from 16 years onwards
- Paracetamol 500mg tablets. Take two tablets every 4 to 6 hours when required for pain relief. Maximum of 8 tablets in 24 hours; supply 200 tablets; NHS Cost £2.12; OTC Cost £3.75.
- Codeine 30mg tablets. Take one to two tablets every 4 to 6 hours when required for pain relief. Maximum of 8 tablets in 24 hours; supply 60 tablets; NHS Cost £4.58.

N

Standard NSAIDs: ibuprofen, naproxen and diclofenac

Ibuprofen tablets: 400mg three times a day
- Age from 16 years onwards
- Ibuprofen 400mg tablets. Take one tablet three times a day; supply 84 tablets; NHS Cost £2.74; OTC Cost £4.83.

Ibuprofen tablets: 400mg four times a day
- Age from 16 years onwards
- Ibuprofen 400mg tablets. Take one tablet four times a day; supply 112 tablets; NHS Cost £3.65; OTC Cost £6.44.

Ibuprofen tablets: 600mg three times a day
- Age from 16 years onwards
- Ibuprofen 600mg tablets. Take one tablet three times a day; supply 84 tablets; NHS Cost £2.81.

Ibuprofen tablets: 800mg three times a day
- Age from 16 years onwards
- Ibuprofen 400mg tablets. Take two tablets three times a day; supply 168 tablets; NHS Cost £4.58.

Diclofenac sodium e/c tablets: 25mg three times a day
- Age from 16 years onwards
- Diclofenac 25mg e/c tablets. Take one tablet three times a day; supply 84 tablets; NHS Cost £1.72.

Diclofenac sodium e/c tablets: 50mg three times a day
- Age from 16 years onwards
- Diclofenac 50mg e/c tablets. Take one tablet three times a day; supply 84 tablets; NHS Cost £1.45.

Naproxen tablets: 250mg twice a day
- Age from 16 years onwards
- Naproxen 250mg tablets. Take one tablet twice a day; supply 56 tablets; NHS Cost £2.68.

Naproxen tablets: 500mg twice a day
- Age from 16 years onwards
- Naproxen 500mg tablets. Take one tablet twice a day; supply 56 tablets; NHS Cost £4.90.

GI protection: use ONLY with a standard NSAID

Omeprazole capsules: 20mg once a day
- Age from 16 years onwards
- Omeprazole 20mg capsules. Take one capsule once a day; supply 28 capsules; NHS Cost £12.75.

Omeprazole tablets: 20mg once a day
- Age from 16 years onwards
- Omeprazole 20mg tablets. Take one tablet once a day; supply 28 tablets; NHS Cost £12.75.

Lansoprazole capsules: 15mg each morning
- Age from 16 years onwards
- Lansoprazole 15mg capsules. Take one capsule each morning (on an empty stomach); supply 28 capsules; NHS Cost £12.92.

Lansoprazole capsules: 30mg each morning
- Age from 16 years onwards
- Lansoprazole 30mg capsules. Take one capsule each morning (on an empty stomach); supply 28 capsules; NHS Cost £23.63.

Pantoprazole e/c tablets: 20mg once a day
- Age from 16 years onwards
- Pantoprazole 20mg e/c tablets. Take one tablet once a day; supply 28 tablets; NHS Cost £12.31.

Esomeprazole tablets: 20mg once a day
- Age from 16 years onwards
- Esomeprazole 20mg tablets. Take one tablet once a day; supply 28 tablets; NHS Cost £18.50.

Lansoprazole orodispersible tablets: 15mg each morning
- Age from 16 years onwards
- Lansoprazole 15mg orodisp tabs. Take one tablet each morning (on an empty stomach); supply 28 tablets; NHS Cost £10.86.

Lansoprazole orodispersible tablets: 30mg each morning
- Age from 16 years onwards
- Lansoprazole 30mg orodisp tabs. Take one tablet each morning (on an empty stomach); supply 28 tablets; NHS Cost £21.38.

Misoprostol tablets: 200micrograms four times a day
- Age from 16 years onwards
- Misoprostol 200microgram tabs. Take one tablet four times a day; supply 120 tablets; NHS Cost £18.72.

Muscle relaxant (diazepam): 1-week supply

Diazepam tablets: 2mg to 4mg three times a day
- Age from 16 years onwards
- Diazepam 2mg tablets. Take one to two tablets three times a day; supply 28 tablets; NHS Cost £1.14.

Amitriptyline (1st line) or gabapentin (2nd line)

Amitriptyline tablets: 10mg at night
- Age from 16 years onwards
- Amitriptyline 10mg tablets. Take one tablet at night; supply 28 tablets; NHS Cost £1.00.

Amitriptyline tablets: 25mg at night
- Age from 16 years onwards
- Amitriptyline 25mg tablets. Take one tablet at night; supply 28 tablets; NHS Cost £1.71.

Gabapentin: titrate up to 300mg three times a day

- Age from 18 years onwards
- Gabapentin 100mg capsules. Take one capsule three times a day for 3 days, then take two capsules three times a day for 3 days, then start taking the gabapentin 300mg capsules; supply 27 capsules; NHS Cost £6.92.
- Gabapentin 300mg capsules. Start, once the course of gabapentin 100mg capsules is complete. Take one capsule three times a day; supply 84 capsules; NHS Cost £48.20.

Radiculopathy due to cervical spondylosis or disc herniation

Which therapy?

- **Rule out (or manage) any 'red flags' — see *Should I refer or investigate?***
- **Identify and manage any comorbidity and risk factors.**
- **Provide reassurance and information.**
- **Drug therapy:**
  - **Analgesia** is effective for short-term symptomatic relief. Choice of analgesia depends on the severity and chronicity of pain, personal preferences, tolerability and risk of adverse effects. Options, in increasing order of effectiveness and risk of adverse effects, include:
    - **Analgesics available over the counter and taken as required** — will be sufficient for many people
    - **Paracetamol taken regularly**
    - **Ibuprofen taken regularly**
    - **Two of: paracetamol, ibuprofen, and codeine phosphate** (separate prescriptions; doses titrated to meet the person's needs).
  - **Diazepam** for 3–7 days may be useful for people with severe muscle spasm.
  - **Amitriptyline** for 1 month may be tried for people with chronic pain.
  - **Gabapentin** may be tried if amitriptyline is ineffective or contraindicated.
- **Physiotherapy, mobilization, manipulation**
  - Early mobilization is important: If employed, neck supports should be used for as short a time as possible, i.e. 2–4 days, and under supervision.
  - There is insufficient evidence to recommend manual therapies such as manipulation.

Practical prescribing points

For further information see the *Medicines Compendium* (www.medicines.org.uk) or the *British National Formulary* (www.bnf.org).

Nonsteroidal anti-inflammatory drugs (NSAIDs)

- **Only one NSAID should be prescribed at a time.**
- **NSAIDs may worsen asthma, hypertension, renal impairment, or heart failure.**
- Do not give ibuprofen, diclofenac, or naproxen without gastroprotection if there is a history of peptic ulceration.
- **Pregnancy and breastfeeding:** use paracetamol if possible. If an NSAID is essential, ibuprofen may be used during breastfeeding and before 30 weeks of pregnancy.
- **People with cardiovascular disease:** ibuprofen may reduce the cardiovascular protective effect of low-dose aspirin.
- **In people with risk factors for gastrointestinal NSAID complications:**
  - Use paracetamol (with or without codeine) instead of a NSAID if possible.
  - Or, use gastroprotection (a PPI or full-dose misoprostol) combined with a standard NSAID.
- **Risk factors for gastrointestinal NSAID complications include:**
  - Age of 65 years and over.
  - Previous history of gastroduodenal ulcer, gastrointestinal (GI) bleeding, or gastroduodenal perforation.
  - Concomitant use of medications that are known to increase the likelihood of upper-GI adverse events, e.g. anticoagulants, aspirin (even a low dose), and corticosteroids.
  - Presence of serious comorbidity, such as cardiovascular disease, renal or hepatic impairment, diabetes, or hypertension.
  - Requirement for prolonged duration of NSAID use.
  - Use of maximum recommended doses of NSAIDs.

Codeine

- Codeine may cause nausea, vomiting, constipation, and drowsiness. A regular laxative is often needed when it is used long-term.

Diazepam

- Diazepam has strong sedative effects. People should be warned not to drive while taking the drug or for a full day after stopping drug treatment. In addition, people should be warned that the effects of alcohol may be exaggerated whilst taking this medication.
- Diazepam has a high potential for tolerance and dependence. It should only be used in people with severe spasm, and in short courses of 3–7 days.
- Avoid use in pregnancy and breastfeeding.

Amitriptyline

- Amitriptyline may cause drowsiness: if this occurs advise the person to avoid driving or performing skilled tasks where there is the potential for harm.
- Abrupt withdrawal may be a problem with tricyclic antidepressants.
- Avoid use in people with who have had a myocardial infarction, people with arrhythmias, or women in the third trimester of pregnancy.

Gabapentin

- Sudden withdrawal of gabapentin may cause anxiety, insomnia, nausea, pain, and sweating: it should be tapered off over the course of at least 1 week.
- Reduce the dose of gabapentin in renal impairment. See the *Medicines Compendium* (www.medicines.org.uk) for dosage information.

Misoprostol

- Diarrhoea and abdominal pain are common. Advise women of childbearing age to use adequate contraception, since misoprostol increases the risk of miscarriage.

Follow-up advice

- Follow-up and reassess in about 1–4 weeks, depending on the severity of the condition

Should I refer or investigate?

Refer?

- **Refer (with urgency appropriate to the situation) if 'red flags' are present:**
  - **Myelopathy (compression of the spinal cord)**

- Insidious progression
- Gait disturbance; clumsy or weak hands; loss of sexual/bladder/bowel function
- Lhermitte's sign (shooting electric-like sensations on extending or moving neck)
- Upper motor neurone signs in the lower limbs (Babinski's sign — up-going plantar reflex, hyperreflexia, clonus, spasticity)
- Lower motor neurone signs in the upper limbs (atrophy, hyporeflexia)
- **Malignancy, infection, inflammation**
  - Fever
  - Unexplained loss of weight
  - History of inflammatory arthritis
  - History of malignancy, drug abuse, AIDS, or other infection
  - Immunosuppression
  - Pain that is increasing, unremitting and/or disturbs sleep
  - Lymphadenopathy
- **Severe trauma/skeletal injury**
  - History of trauma
  - Previous neck surgery
  - Osteoporosis
  - Increasing and/or unremitting pain
- **Vascular insufficiency**
  - Dizziness and blackouts (restriction of vertebral artery) on movement, especially upward gaze
  - Dizziness, drop attacks
- **Refer** if pain becomes intractable or if complications arise.

Investigate?

- Neck pain with radiculopathy and no 'red flag' features usually does not require imaging studies or other special investigations: the condition is likely to be self limited.
- Full blood count, erythrocyte sedimentation rate or C-reactive protein, liver enzymes, and imaging may be indicated to rule out other possible causes of neck pain.
- X-rays of the cervical spine may show cervical spondylosis/osteoarthritis. Interpretation is difficult because degenerative features are almost universal over the age of 35 years.
- Magnetic resonance imaging (MRI) (or less preferably, computerized tomography [CT] scan) shows disc herniation and spondylosis and would document nerve root compression. MRI is usually only done for pre-operative planning.

Patient information leaflets

The following PILs are available at www.prodigy.nhs.uk

- Anti-inflammatory Painkillers
- Neck Pain

Shared decision making

- **Most bouts of neck pain ease** within a few weeks or so.
  - As far as possible, carry on with normal activities. You are less likely to develop persistent neck pain if you keep your neck active rather than rest it a lot in a collar.
  - Try to keep a good posture. Sit upright and walk 'like a model'.
  - You should not drive until you can easily move your neck round.
  - Use a pillow that supports the hollow of the neck and supports a comfortable position of the head. Find a comfortable position before going to sleep. Using two pillows may not be helpful.
- **Paracetamol** is commonly used for pain. The normal adult dosage is two 500 mg tablets, four times a day.
- **An anti-inflammatory painkiller** may be an option.
  - Bleeding from the stomach is the most serious possible side-effect. Stop the medicine and see a doctor if you develop stomach symptoms.
  - Some people with asthma, high blood pressure, kidney failure, or heart failure may not be able to take anti-inflammatories.
- **Codeine** is a painkiller that is stronger than paracetamol. It may be used in combination with paracetamol or an anti-inflammatory. Possible side-effects include constipation and drowsiness.
- **A muscle relaxant** such as diazepam is sometimes used for a few days if the neck muscles are tense and make the pain worse. Possible side-effects include drowsiness.
- **Amitriptyline** is sometimes used if pain becomes persistent.
- Tell your doctor if symptoms in your arms (such as pins and needles or numbness) become worse.

Drug rationale

Drugs not included

- **Analgesics other than paracetamol and codeine taken separately,** are not recommended:
  - **Strong opioids** (e.g. morphine, pethidine) should be avoided because of the risk of dependence if they are used inappropriately.
  - **Weak opioids,** other than codeine, have either not been shown to be more effective than codeine (when used in combination with paracetamol), or are more expensive.
  - **Low-dose weak opioids with paracetamol** (combination products), e.g. co-codamol 8/500 mg. There is no evidence that these offer any clinical benefit over paracetamol alone and they are likely to lead to opioid adverse effects [MeReC, 1993; De Craen et al, 1996; Moore and McQuay, 1997].
  - **High-dose weak opioids with paracetamol** (combination products), e.g. co-codamol 30/500 mg, do not allow titration to the most effective and safe analgesic dose to match individual requirements.
  - **Co-proxamol** (dextropropoxyphene 32.5 mg/ paracetamol 325 mg) has been withdrawn by the Committee on Safety of Medicines due to its unfavourable risk/benefit ratio; it is associated with an unacceptable risk of overdose [CSM, 2005a].
- **Standard nonsteroidal anti-inflammatory drugs (NSAIDs), other than ibuprofen, diclofenac, and naproxen,** are not generally recommended, as they have a worse balance between their efficacy and adverse-effect profile than these three recommended drugs [CSM, 1994; Hernández-Diaz et al, 2000; BNF 49, 2005].
- **Cyclo-oxygenase-2 (COX-2) selective inhibitors** are not recommended. After the withdrawal of rofecoxib from the market (the only selective inhibitor licensed for acute pain), there are growing concerns that COX-2 selective inhibitors may cause serious cardiovascular events. Following a European-wide review of the data, the Committee on Safety of Medicines (CSM) has recently advised that [CSM, 2005b]:
  - The evidence suggests that coxibs, as a class, may cause an increased risk of thrombotic events (e.g. myocardial infarction and stroke) compared with placebo and some NSAIDs.
  - The risk may increase with dose and duration of exposure.
- **Strong opioids** (e.g. morphine, pethidine) should be avoided, owing to the risk of dependence if they are used

inappropriately. They are usually reserved for moderate to severe pain of a visceral origin [BNF 49, 2005].

- **Pregabalin** has a similar mechanism of action to gabapentin, and is licensed for the treatment of neuropathic pain [BNF 49, 2005]. However, it is currently undergoing post-marketing surveillance (black triangle), and should reserved for use under specialist supervision.
- **Gastroprotective agents** are sometimes needed, but not all are recommended:
  - **H_2-receptor antagonists (H_2RAs).** At standard doses, H_2RAs reduce the risk of duodenal ulceration, and there is some evidence that double doses reduce the risk of gastric ulceration [Rostom et al, 2002]. However, no H_2RAs are currently licensed for the prevention of gastric ulceration induced by NSAIDs [BNF 49, 2005], which is more common than duodenal ulceration.
  - **Rabeprazole** is not included as it is not specifically licensed for the prevention of NSAID-induced gastrointestinal ulcers [BNF 49, 2005].
  - **Fixed-dose combinations of standard NSAIDs with misoprostol.** The optimum dose of misoprostol (i.e. 800 micrograms daily) cannot be reached using these preparations. In particular, only 400 micrograms daily of misoprostol is given with the higher doses of NSAID in these preparations.

Drugs included

Standard analgesics and nonsteroidal anti-inflammatory drugs (NSAIDs)

- **Paracetamol** is a good first-line choice for pain relief, and is not associated with gastrointestinal toxicity [SIGN, 2000].
- **Codeine (in combination with paracetamol):** higher-dose codeine is included for use with regular paracetamol for additional pain relief. Codeine 60 mg plus paracetamol has been shown to provide more pain relief than either codeine 60 mg alone or paracetamol 1000 mg alone [Moore et al, 1997]. Codeine should be prescribed separately to paracetamol to allow flexibility of dosing and titration of analgesic effect.
  - Note: codeine can also be combined with an NSAID, or paracetamol can be combined with an NSAID, but there is less evidence to support this.
- **Standard NSAIDS: ibuprofen, diclofenac, and naproxen** have a good balance of efficacy against adverse-effect profile [CSM, 1994; Henry et al, 1996; Hernández-Diaz and Rodriguez, 2000]. Standard doses are offered as these are generally accepted to be sufficient for anti-inflammatory prophylaxis, although data are lacking.

Muscle relaxants

- **Diazepam** is recommended as a muscle relaxant, as it has been shown to effectively reduce acute neck pain. However, adverse effects are common, and there is a risk of dependency even after 1 week of treatment. Courses of 3–7 days should be used only in people with severe spasm [Clinical Standards Advisory Group, 1994; Waddell et al, 1999].

Gastroprotective agents

- **Proton pump inhibitors (PPIs): lansoprazole, omeprazole, esomeprazole and pantoprazole** are licensed for the prevention of gastroduodenal ulceration induced by NSAIDs [BNF 49, 2005]. PPIs reduce the risk of endoscopic ulcers, but there are no data on prevention of ulcer complications [Rostom et al, 2002]. However, they are generally considered to be the preferred choice for gastroprotection, as they are better tolerated than misoprostol.
- **Misoprostol** is licensed for the prevention of gastroduodenal ulceration induced by NSAIDs [BNF 49, 2005]. It reduces the risk of endoscopically proven ulcers and has also been shown to reduce the risk of ulcer complications [Rostom et al, 2002]. It is less well tolerated than PPIs owing to gastrointestinal adverse effects, particularly diarrhoea.

Drugs for chronic pain

Note: although commonly used, amitriptyline and gabapentin are not licensed for the treatment of chronic pain.

- **Amitriptyline** is a tricyclic antidepressant widely used for various causes of chronic pain [McQuay and Moore, 1997]. At present there is uncertainty about the benefit of tricyclic antidepressants in chronic neck pain, but an initial 1-month trial of therapy may be worth considering in people in whom standard analgesia and/or NSAIDs have proved ineffective.
- **Gabapentin** can be considered if amitriptyline has proved ineffective or is contraindicated, although there is little trial evidence at present to verify its efficacy. The exact dose of gabapentin that is required to alleviate chronic neck pain is not known, but the full 'antiepileptic dose' is probably necessary.

Prescriptions

Paracetamol or codeine

Paracetamol tablets: 1g up to four times a day

- Age from 16 years onwards
- Paracetamol 500mg tablets. Take two tablets every 4 to 6 hours when required for pain relief. Maximum of 8 tablets in 24 hours; supply 200 tablets; NHS Cost £2.12; OTC Cost £3.75.

Codeine tablets: 30 mg to 60mg up to four times a day

- Age from 16 years onwards
- Codeine 30mg tablets. Take one to two tablets every 4 to 6 hours when required for pain relief. Maximum of 8 tablets in 24 hours; supply 60 tablets; NHS Cost £4.58.

Paracetamol 500mg tablets + codeine 30mg tablets

- Age from 16 years onwards
- Paracetamol 500mg tablets. Take two tablets every 4 to 6 hours when required for pain relief. Maximum of 8 tablets in 24 hours; supply 200 tablets; NHS Cost £2.12; OTC Cost £3.75.
- Codeine 30mg tablets. Take one to two tablets every 4 to 6 hours when required for pain relief. Maximum of 8 tablets in 24 hours; supply 60 tablets; NHS Cost £4.58.

Standard NSAIDs: ibuprofen, naproxen and diclofenac

Ibuprofen tablets: 400mg three times a day

- Age from 16 years onwards
- Ibuprofen 400mg tablets. Take one tablet three times a day; supply 84 tablets; NHS Cost £2.74; OTC Cost £4.83.

Ibuprofen tablets: 400mg four times a day

- Age from 16 years onwards
- Ibuprofen 400mg tablets. Take one tablet four times a day; supply 112 tablets; NHS Cost £3.65; OTC Cost £6.44.

Ibuprofen tablets: 600mg three times a day

- Age from 16 years onwards
- Ibuprofen 600mg tablets. Take one tablet three times a day; supply 84 tablets; NHS Cost £2.81.

Ibuprofen tablets: 800mg three times a day
- Age from 16 years onwards
- Ibuprofen 400mg tablets. Take two tablets three times a day; supply 168 tablets; NHS Cost £4.58.

Diclofenac sodium e/c tablets: 25mg three times a day
- Age from 16 years onwards
- Diclofenac 25mg e/c tablets. Take one tablet three times a day; supply 84 tablets; NHS Cost £1.72.

Diclofenac sodium e/c tablets: 50mg three times a day
- Age from 16 years onwards
- Diclofenac 50mg e/c tablets. Take one tablet three times a day; supply 84 tablets; NHS Cost £1.45.

Naproxen tablets: 250mg twice a day
- Age from 16 years onwards
- Naproxen 250mg tablets. Take one tablet twice a day; supply 56 tablets; NHS Cost £2.68.

Naproxen tablets: 500mg twice a day
- Age from 16 years onwards
- Naproxen 500mg tablets. Take one tablet twice a day; supply 56 tablets; NHS Cost £4.90.

GI protection: use ONLY with a standard NSAID

Omeprazole capsules: 20mg once a day
- Age from 16 years onwards
- Omeprazole 20mg capsules. Take one capsule once a day; supply 28 capsules; NHS Cost £12.75.

Omeprazole tablets: 20mg once a day
- Age from 16 years onwards
- Omeprazole 20mg tablets. Take one tablet once a day; supply 28 tablets; NHS Cost £12.75.

Lansoprazole capsules: 15mg each morning
- Age from 16 years onwards
- Lansoprazole 15mg capsules. Take one capsule each morning (on an empty stomach); supply 28 capsules; NHS Cost £12.92.

Lansoprazole capsules: 30mg each morning
- Age from 16 years onwards
- Lansoprazole 30mg capsules. Take one capsule each morning (on an empty stomach); supply 28 capsules; NHS Cost £23.63.

Pantoprazole e/c tablets: 20mg once a day
- Age from 16 years onwards
- Pantoprazole 20mg e/c tablets. Take one tablet once a day; supply 28 tablets; NHS Cost £12.31.

Esomeprazole tablets: 20mg once a day
- Age from 16 years onwards
- Esomeprazole 20mg tablets. Take one tablet once a day; supply 28 tablets; NHS Cost £18.50.

Lansoprazole orodispersible tablets: 15mg each morning
- Age from 16 years onwards
- Lansoprazole 15mg orodisp tabs. Take one tablet each morning (on an empty stomach); supply 28 tablets; NHS Cost £10.86.

Lansoprazole orodispersible tablets: 30mg each morning
- Age from 16 years onwards
- Lansoprazole 30mg orodisp tabs. Take one tablet each morning (on an empty stomach); supply 28 tablets; NHS Cost £21.38.

Misoprostol tablets: 200micrograms four times a day
- Age from 16 years onwards
- Misoprostol 200microgram tabs. Take one tablet four times a day; supply 120 tablets; NHS Cost £18.72.

Muscle relaxant (diazepam): 1-week supply

Diazepam tablets: 2mg to 4mg three times a day
- Age from 16 years onwards
- Diazepam 2mg tablets. Take one to two tablets three times a day; supply 28 tablets; NHS Cost £1.14.

Amitriptyline (1st line) or gabapentin (2nd line)

Amitriptyline tablets: 10mg at night
- Age from 16 years onwards
- Amitriptyline 10mg tablets. Take one tablet at night; supply 28 tablets; NHS Cost £1.00.

Amitriptyline tablets: 25mg at night
- Age from 16 years onwards
- Amitriptyline 25mg tablets. Take one tablet at night; supply 28 tablets; NHS Cost £1.71.

Gabapentin: titrate up to 300mg three times a day
- Age from 18 years onwards
- Gabapentin 100mg capsules. Take one capsule three times a day for 3 days, then take two capsules three times a day for 3 days, then start taking the gabapentin 300mg capsules; supply 27 capsules; NHS Cost £6.92.
- Gabapentin 300mg capsules. Start, once the course of gabapentin 100mg capsules is complete. Take one capsule three times a day; supply 84 capsules; NHS Cost £48.20.

Whiplash injury without cervical fracture or subluxation

Which therapy?

- **Rule out (or manage) any 'red flags'** — see *Should I refer or investigate?*
- **Identify and manage any comorbidity and psychosocial risk factors.**
- **Provide reassurance and information.**
- **Drug therapy:**
  - **Analgesia** is effective for short-term symptomatic relief. Choice of analgesia depends on the severity and chronicity of pain, personal preferences, tolerability and risk of adverse effects. Options, in increasing order of effectiveness and risk of adverse effects, include:
    - **Analgesics available over the counter and taken as required** — will be sufficient for many people
    - **Paracetamol taken regularly**
    - **Ibuprofen taken regularly**
    - **Two of: paracetamol, ibuprofen, and codeine phosphate** (separate prescriptions; doses titrated to meet the person's needs).
  - **Diazepam** for 3–7 days may be useful for people with severe muscle spasm.
  - **Amitriptyline** for 1 month may be tried for people with chronic pain.
  - **Gabapentin** may be tried if amitriptyline is ineffective or contraindicated.
- **Physiotherapy, mobilization, manipulation**
  - Active physiotherapy, mobilization, and manipulation may provide short-term relief in people with chronic neck pain.
  - Early mobilization is important. If employed, neck supports should be used for as short a time as possible, i.e. 2–4 days, and under supervision.

Practical prescribing points

For further information see the *Medicines Compendium* (www.medicines.org.uk) or the *British National Formulary* (www.bnf.org).

Nonsteroidal anti-inflammatory drugs (NSAIDs)

- **Only one NSAID should be prescribed at a time.**
- **NSAIDs may worsen asthma, hypertension, renal impairment, or heart failure.**

- Do not give ibuprofen, diclofenac, or naproxen without gastroprotection if there is a history of peptic ulceration.
- **Pregnancy and breastfeeding:** use paracetamol if possible. If an NSAID is essential, ibuprofen may be used during breastfeeding and before 30 weeks of pregnancy.
- **People with cardiovascular disease:** ibuprofen may reduce the cardiovascular protective effect of low-dose aspirin.
- **In people with risk factors for gastrointestinal NSAID complications:**
  - Use paracetamol (with or without codeine) instead of a NSAID if possible.
  - Or, use gastroprotection (a PPI or full-dose misoprostol) combined with a standard NSAID.
- **Risk factors for gastrointestinal NSAID complications include:**
  - Age of 65 years and over.
  - Previous history of gastroduodenal ulcer, gastrointestinal (GI) bleeding, or gastroduodenal perforation.
  - Concomitant use of medications that are known to increase the likelihood of upper-GI adverse events, e.g. anticoagulants, aspirin (even a low dose), and corticosteroids.
  - Presence of serious comorbidity, such as cardiovascular disease, renal or hepatic impairment, diabetes, or hypertension.
  - Requirement for prolonged duration of NSAID use.
  - Use of maximum recommended doses of NSAIDs.

Codeine

- Codeine may cause nausea, vomiting, constipation, and drowsiness. A regular laxative is often needed when it is used long-term.

Diazepam

- Diazepam has strong sedative effects. People should be warned not to drive while taking the drug or for a full day after stopping drug treatment. In addition, people should be warned that the effects of alcohol may be exaggerated whilst taking this medication.
- Diazepam has a high potential for tolerance and dependence. It should only be used in people with severe spasm, and in short courses of 3–7 days.
- Avoid use in pregnancy and breastfeeding.

Amitriptyline

- Amitriptyline may cause drowsiness: if this occurs advise the person to avoid driving or performing skilled tasks where there is the potential for harm.
- Abrupt withdrawal may be a problem with tricyclic antidepressants.
- Avoid use in people with who have had a myocardial infarction, people with arrhythmias, or women in the third trimester of pregnancy.

Gabapentin

- Sudden withdrawal of gabapentin may cause anxiety, insomnia, nausea, pain, and sweating: it should be tapered off over the course of at least 1 week.
- Reduce the dose of gabapentin in renal impairment. See the *Medicines Compendium* (www.medicines.org.uk) for dosage information.

Misoprostol

- Diarrhoea and abdominal pain are common. Advise women of childbearing age to use adequate contraception, since misoprostol increases the risk of miscarriage.

Follow-up advice

- Chronic whiplash symptoms are sometimes associated with unresolved issues of litigation or compensation. This stress may need management in its own right.
- Chronic whiplash symptoms may coexist with anxiety and depression which may need management in their own right.

Should I refer or investigate?

Refer?

- **Immediate admission is required for myelopathy** (spinal cord compression).
- **Prompt referral** is required if there is severe trauma/skeletal injury or radiculopathy.
- **Referral** is advised if pain becomes intractable or if anxiety/depression are not responding to management.

Investigate?

- X-rays of the cervical spine (anterior-posterior, lateral, flexion, extension, odontoid process) may be indicated to rule out fractures and subluxation and always required if there are any neurological symptoms or signs.
- Full blood count, erythrocyte sedimentation rate or C-reactive protein, liver enzymes, and imaging may be indicated to rule out other possible causes of neck pain.

Patient information leaflets

The following PILs are available at www.prodigy.nhs.uk

- Anti-inflammatory Painkillers
- Whiplash Neck Sprains

Shared decision making

- **Neck pain** is common after a whiplash injury. It usually eases over a week or so. It lasts longer in some cases.
  - As far as possible, carry on with normal activities. You are less likely to develop persistent neck pain if you keep your neck active rather than rest it a lot in a collar.
  - You should not drive until you can easily move your neck round.
  - Use a pillow that supports the hollow of the neck and supports a comfortable position of the head. Find a comfortable position before going to sleep. Using two pillows may not be helpful.
- **Paracetamol** is commonly used for pain. The normal adult dosage is two 500 mg tablets, four times a day.
- **An anti-inflammatory painkiller** may be an option.
  - Bleeding from the stomach is the most serious possible side-effect. Stop the medicine and see a doctor if you develop stomach symptoms.
  - Some people with asthma, high blood pressure, kidney failure, or heart failure may not be able to take anti-inflammatories.
- **Codeine** is a painkiller that is stronger than paracetamol. It may be used in combination with paracetamol or an anti-inflammatory. Possible side-effects include constipation and drowsiness.
- **A muscle relaxant** such as diazepam is sometimes used for a few days if the neck muscles are tense and make the pain worse. Possible side-effects include drowsiness.
- **Amitriptyline** is sometimes used if pain becomes persistent.
- **Tell your doctor if** you develop symptoms in your arms or legs such as pins and needles or numbness.

Drug rationale

Drugs not included

- **Analgesics other than paracetamol and codeine taken separately,** are not recommended:
  - **Strong opioids** (e.g. morphine, pethidine) should be avoided because of the risk of dependence if they are used inappropriately.
  - **Weak opioids,** other than codeine, have either not been shown to be more effective than codeine (when used in combination with paracetamol), or are more expensive.
  - **Low-dose weak opioids with paracetamol** (combination products), e.g. co-codamol 8/500 mg. There is no evidence that these offer any clinical benefit over paracetamol alone and they are likely to lead to opioid adverse effects [MeReC, 1993; De Craen et al, 1996; Moore and McQuay, 1997].
  - **High-dose weak opioids with paracetamol** (combination products), e.g. co-codamol 30/500 mg, do not allow titration to the most effective and safe analgesic dose to match individual requirements.
  - **Co-proxamol** (dextropropoxyphene 32.5 mg/ paracetamol 325 mg) has been withdrawn by the Committee on Safety of Medicines due to its unfavourable risk/benefit ratio; it is associated with an unacceptable risk of overdose [CSM, 2005a].
- **Standard nonsteroidal anti-inflammatory drugs (NSAIDs), other than ibuprofen, diclofenac, and naproxen,** are not generally recommended, as they have a worse balance between their efficacy and adverse-effect profile than these three recommended drugs [CSM, 1994; Hernández-Diaz et al, 2000; BNF 49, 2005].
- **Cyclo-oxygenase-2 (COX-2) selective inhibitors** are not recommended. After the withdrawal of rofecoxib from the market (the only selective inhibitor licensed for acute pain), there are growing concerns that COX-2 selective inhibitors may cause serious cardiovascular events. Following a European-wide review of the data, the Committee on Safety of Medicines (CSM) has recently advised that [CSM, 2005b]:
  - The evidence suggests that coxibs, as a class, may cause an increased risk of thrombotic events (e.g. myocardial infarction and stroke) compared with placebo and some NSAIDs.
  - The risk may increase with dose and duration of exposure.
- **Strong opioids** (e.g. morphine, pethidine) should be avoided, owing to the risk of dependence if they are used inappropriately. They are usually reserved for moderate to severe pain of a visceral origin [BNF 49, 2005].
- **Pregabalin** has a similar mechanism of action to gabapentin, and is licensed for the treatment of neuropathic pain [BNF 49, 2005]. However, it is currently undergoing post-marketing surveillance (black triangle), and should reserved for use under specialist supervision.
- **Gastroprotective agents** are sometimes needed, but not all are recommended:
  - **H_2-receptor antagonists (H_2RAs).** At standard doses, H_2RAs reduce the risk of duodenal ulceration, and there is some evidence that double doses reduce the risk of gastric ulceration [Rostom et al, 2002]. However, no H_2RAs are currently licensed for the prevention of gastric ulceration induced by NSAIDs [BNF 49, 2005], which is more common than duodenal ulceration.
  - **Rabeprazole** is not included as it is not specifically licensed for the prevention of NSAID-induced gastrointestinal ulcers [BNF 49, 2005].
  - **Fixed-dose combinations of standard NSAIDs with misoprostol:** The optimum dose of misoprostol (i.e. 800 micrograms daily) cannot be reached using these preparations. In particular, only 400 micrograms daily of misoprostol is given with the higher doses of NSAID in these preparations.

Drugs included

Standard analgesics and nonsteroidal anti-inflammatory drugs (NSAIDs)

- **Paracetamol** is a good first-line choice for pain relief, and is not associated with gastrointestinal toxicity [SIGN, 2000].
- **Codeine (in combination with paracetamol):** higher-dose codeine is included for use with regular paracetamol for additional pain relief. Codeine 60 mg plus paracetamol has been shown to provide more pain relief than either codeine 60 mg alone or paracetamol 1000 mg alone [Moore et al, 1997]. Codeine should be prescribed separately to paracetamol to allow flexibility of dosing and titration of analgesic effect.
  - Note: codeine can also be combined with an NSAID, or paracetamol can be combined with an NSAID, but there is less evidence to support this.
- **Standard NSAIDS: ibuprofen, diclofenac, and naproxen** have a good balance of efficacy against adverse-effect profile [CSM, 1994; Henry et al, 1996; Hernández-Diaz and Rodriguez, 2000]. Standard doses are offered as these are generally accepted to be sufficient for anti-inflammatory prophylaxis, although data are lacking.

Muscle relaxants

- **Diazepam** is recommended as a muscle relaxant, as it has been shown to effectively reduce acute neck pain. However, adverse effects such as are common, and there is a risk of dependency even after one week of treatment. Courses of 3–7 days should be used only in people with severe spasm [Clinical Standards Advisory Group, 1994; Waddell et al, 1999].

Gastroprotective agents

- **Proton pump inhibitors (PPIs): lansoprazole, omeprazole, esomeprazole and pantoprazole** are licensed for the prevention of gastroduodenal ulceration induced by NSAIDs [BNF 49, 2005]. PPIs reduce the risk of endoscopic ulcers, but there are no data on prevention of ulcer complications [Rostom et al, 2002]. However, they are generally considered to be the preferred choice for gastroprotection, as they are better tolerated than misoprostol.
- **Misoprostol** is licensed for the prevention of gastroduodenal ulceration induced by NSAIDs [BNF 49, 2005]. It reduces the risk of endoscopically proven ulcers and has also been shown to reduce the risk of ulcer complications [Rostom et al, 2002]. It is less well tolerated than PPIs owing to gastrointestinal adverse effects, particularly diarrhoea.

Drugs for chronic pain

Note: although commonly used, amitriptyline and gabapentin are not licensed for the treatment of chronic pain.

- **Amitriptyline** is a tricyclic antidepressant widely used for various causes of chronic pain [McQuay and Moore, 1997]. At present there is uncertainty about the benefit of tricyclic antidepressants in chronic neck pain, but an initial 1-month trial of therapy may be worth considering in people in whom standard analgesia and/or NSAIDs has proved ineffective.

Gabapentin can be considered if amitriptyline has proved ineffective or is contraindicated, although there is little trial evidence at present to verify its efficacy. The exact dose of gabapentin that is required to alleviate chronic neck pain is not known, but the full 'antiepileptic dose' is probably necessary.

Prescriptions

Paracetamol or codeine

Paracetamol tablets: 1g up to four times a day
- Age from 16 years onwards
- Paracetamol 500mg tablets. Take two tablets every 4 to 6 hours when required for pain relief. Maximum of 8 tablets in 24 hours; supply 200 tablets; NHS Cost £2.12; OTC Cost £3.75.

Codeine tablets: 30mg to 60mg up to four times a day
- Age from 16 years onwards
- Codeine 30mg tablets. Take one to two tablets every 4 to 6 hours when required for pain relief. Maximum of 8 tablets in 24 hours; supply 60 tablets; NHS Cost £4.58.

Paracetamol 500mg tablets + codeine 30mg tablets
- Age from 16 years onwards
- Paracetamol 500mg tablets. Take two tablets every 4 to 6 hours when required for pain relief. Maximum of 8 tablets in 24 hours; supply 200 tablets; NHS Cost £2.12; OTC Cost £3.75.
- Codeine 30mg tablets. Take one to two tablets every 4 to 6 hours when required for pain relief. Maximum of 8 tablets in 24 hours; supply 60 tablets; NHS Cost £4.58.

Standard NSAIDs: ibuprofen, naproxen and diclofenac

Ibuprofen tablets: 400mg three times a day
- Age from 16 years onwards
- Ibuprofen 400mg tablets. Take one tablet three times a day; supply 84 tablets; NHS Cost £2.74; OTC Cost £4.83.

Ibuprofen tablets: 400mg four times a day
- Age from 16 years onwards
- Ibuprofen 400mg tablets. Take one tablet four times a day; supply 112 tablets; NHS Cost £3.65; OTC Cost £6.44.

Ibuprofen tablets: 600mg three times a day
- Age from 16 years onwards
- Ibuprofen 600mg tablets. Take one tablet three times a day; supply 84 tablets; NHS Cost £2.81.

Ibuprofen tablets: 800mg three times a day
- Age from 16 years onwards
- Ibuprofen 400mg tablets. Take two tablets three times a day; supply 168 tablets; NHS Cost £4.58.

Diclofenac sodium e/c tablets: 25mg three times a day
- Age from 16 years onwards
- Diclofenac 25mg e/c tablets. Take one tablet three times a day; supply 84 tablets; NHS Cost £1.72.

Diclofenac sodium e/c tablets: 50mg three times a day
- Age from 16 years onwards
- Diclofenac 50mg e/c tablets. Take one tablet three times a day; supply 84 tablets; NHS Cost £1.45.

Naproxen tablets: 250mg twice a day
- Age from 16 years onwards
- Naproxen 250mg tablets. Take one tablet twice a day; supply 56 tablets; NHS Cost £2.68.

Naproxen tablets: 500mg twice a day
- Age from 16 years onwards
- Naproxen 500mg tablets. Take one tablet twice a day; supply 56 tablets; NHS Cost £4.90.

GI protection: use ONLY with a standard NSAID

Omeprazole capsules: 20mg once a day
- Age from 16 years onwards
- Omeprazole 20mg capsules. Take one capsule once a day; supply 28 capsules; NHS Cost £12.75.

Omeprazole tablets: 20mg once a day
- Age from 16 years onwards
- Omeprazole 20mg tablets. Take one tablet once a day; supply 28 tablets; NHS Cost £12.75.

Lansoprazole capsules: 15mg each morning
- Age from 16 years onwards
- Lansoprazole 15mg capsules. Take one capsule each morning (on an empty stomach); supply 28 capsules; NHS Cost £12.92.

Lansoprazole capsules: 30mg each morning
- Age from 16 years onwards
- Lansoprazole 30mg capsules. Take one capsule each morning (on an empty stomach); supply 28 capsules; NHS Cost £23.63.

Pantoprazole e/c tablets: 20mg once a day
- Age from 16 years onwards
- Pantoprazole 20mg e/c tablets. Take one tablet once a day; supply 28 tablets; NHS Cost £12.31.

Esomeprazole tablets: 20mg once a day
- Age from 16 years onwards
- Esomeprazole 20mg tablets. Take one tablet once a day; supply 28 tablets; NHS Cost £18.50.

Lansoprazole orodispersible tablets: 15mg each morning
- Age from 16 years onwards
- Lansoprazole 15mg orodisp tabs. Take one tablet each morning (on an empty stomach); supply 28 tablets; NHS Cost £10.86.

Lansoprazole orodispersible tablets: 30mg each morning
- Age from 16 years onwards
- Lansoprazole 30mg orodisp tabs. Take one tablet each morning (on an empty stomach); supply 28 tablets; NHS Cost £21.38.

Misoprostol tablets: 200micrograms four times a day
- Age from 16 years onwards
- Misoprostol 200microgram tabs. Take one tablet four times a day; supply 120 tablets; NHS Cost £18.72.

Muscle relaxant (diazepam): 1-week supply

Diazepam tablets: 2mg to 4mg three times a day
- Age from 16 years onwards
- Diazepam 2mg tablets. Take one to two tablets three times a day; supply 28 tablets; NHS Cost £1.14.

Amitriptyline (1st line) or gabapentin (2nd line)

Amitriptyline tablets: 10mg at night
- Age from 16 years onwards
- Amitriptyline 10mg tablets. Take one tablet at night; supply 28 tablets; NHS Cost £1.00.

Amitriptyline tablets: 25mg at night
- Age from 16 years onwards
- Amitriptyline 25mg tablets. Take one tablet at night; supply 28 tablets; NHS Cost £1.71.

Gabapentin: titrate up to 300mg three times a day
- Age from 18 years onwards
- Gabapentin 100mg capsules. Take one capsule three times a day for 3 days, then take two capsules three times a day for 3 days, then start taking the gabapentin 300mg capsules; supply 27 capsules; NHS Cost £6.92.
- Gabapentin 300mg capsules. Start, once the course of gabapentin 100mg capsules is complete. Take one capsule three times a day; supply 84 capsules; NHS Cost £48.20.

Acute torticollis

Which therapy?

- **Rule out (or manage) any 'red flags' — see *Should I refer or investigate?***
- **Provide reassurance and information.**
- **Drug therapy:**
  - **Analgesia** is effective for short-term symptomatic relief. Choice of analgesia depends on the severity and chronicity of pain, personal preferences, tolerability and risk of adverse effects. Options, in increasing order of effectiveness and risk of adverse effects, include:
    - **Analgesics available over the counter and taken as required** — will be sufficient for many people
    - **Paracetamol taken regularly**
    - **Ibuprofen taken regularly**
    - **Two of: paracetamol, ibuprofen, and codeine phosphate** (separate prescriptions; doses titrated to meet the person's needs).
  - **Diazepam** for 3–7 days may be useful for people with severe muscle spasm.
- **Physiotherapy, mobilization, manipulation:**
  - Early mobilization is important. If employed, neck supports should be used for as short a time as possible, i.e. 2–4 days, and under supervision.

Practical prescribing points

For further information see the *Medicines Compendium* (www.medicines.org.uk) or the *British National Formulary* (www.bnf.org).

Nonsteroidal anti-inflammatory drugs (NSAIDs)

- **Only one NSAID should be prescribed at a time.**
- **NSAIDs may worsen asthma, hypertension, renal impairment, or heart failure.**
- Do not give ibuprofen, diclofenac, or naproxen without gastroprotection if there is a history of peptic ulceration.
- **Pregnancy and breastfeeding:** use paracetamol if possible. If an NSAID is essential, ibuprofen may be used during breastfeeding and before 30 weeks of pregnancy.
- **People with cardiovascular disease:** ibuprofen may reduce the cardiovascular protective effect of low-dose aspirin.
- **In people with risk factors for gastrointestinal NSAID complications:**
  - Use paracetamol (with or without codeine) instead of a NSAID if possible.
  - Or, use gastroprotection (a PPI or full-dose misoprostol) combined with a standard NSAID.
- **Risk factors for gastrointestinal NSAID complications include:**
  - Age of 65 years and over.
  - Previous history of gastroduodenal ulcer, gastrointestinal (GI) bleeding, or gastroduodenal perforation.
  - Concomitant use of medications that are known to increase the likelihood of upper-GI adverse events, e.g. anticoagulants, aspirin (even a low dose), and corticosteroids.
  - Presence of serious comorbidity, such as cardiovascular disease, renal or hepatic impairment, diabetes, or hypertension.
  - Requirement for prolonged duration of NSAID use.
  - Use of maximum recommended doses of NSAIDs.

Codeine

- Codeine may cause nausea, vomiting, constipation, and drowsiness. A regular laxative is often needed when it is used long-term.

Diazepam

- Diazepam has strong sedative effects. People should be warned not to drive while taking the drug or for a full day after stopping drug treatment. In addition, people should be warned that the effects of alcohol may be exaggerated whilst taking this medication.
- Diazepam has a high potential for tolerance and dependence. It should only be used in people with severe spasm, and in short courses of 3–7 days.
- Avoid use in pregnancy and breastfeeding.

Misoprostol

- Diarrhoea and abdominal pain are common. Advise women of childbearing age to use adequate contraception, since misoprostol increases the risk of miscarriage.

Should I refer or investigate?

Refer?

- **Referral is recommended for:**
  - Persistent torticollis
  - Cervical dystonia
  - Ocular imbalance

Patient information leaflets

The following PILs are available at www.prodigy.nhs.uk

- Neck Pain

Shared decision making

- **Acute torticollis** (wry neck) is usually is due to a minor injury or poor posture while sleeping. It usually eases over a few days, often without treatment.
  - As far as possible, carry on with normal activities. You are less likely to develop persistent neck pain if you keep your neck active rather than rest it a lot in a collar.
  - You should not drive until you can easily move your neck round.
  - Use a pillow that supports the hollow of the neck and supports a comfortable position of the head. Find a comfortable position before going to sleep. Using two pillows may not be helpful.
- **Paracetamol** is commonly used for pain. The normal adult dosage is two 500 mg tablets, four times a day.
- **An anti-inflammatory painkiller** may be an option.
  - Bleeding from the stomach is the most serious possible side-effect. Stop the medicine and see a doctor if you develop stomach symptoms.
  - Some people with asthma, high blood pressure, kidney failure, or heart failure may not be able to take anti-inflammatories.
- **Codeine** is a painkiller that is stronger than paracetamol It may be used in combination with paracetamol or an anti-inflammatory. Possible side-effects include constipation and drowsiness.
- **A muscle relaxant** such as diazepam is sometimes used for a few days if the neck muscles are tense and make the pain worse. Possible side-effects include drowsiness.
- **Chronic** (persistent) torticollis is rare and may need referral for special treatment.

N

Drug rationale

Drugs not included

Analgesics other than paracetamol and codeine taken separately, are not recommended:

- **Strong opioids** (e.g. morphine, pethidine) should be avoided because of the risk of dependence if they are used inappropriately.
- **Weak opioids,** other than codeine, have either not been shown to be more effective than codeine (when used in combination with paracetamol), or are more expensive.
- **Low-dose weak opioids with paracetamol** (combination products), e.g. co-codamol 8/500 mg. There is no evidence that these offer any clinical benefit over paracetamol alone and they are likely to lead to opioid adverse effects [MeReC, 1993; De Craen et al, 1996; Moore and McQuay, 1997].
- **High-dose weak opioids with paracetamol** (combination products), e.g. co-codamol 30/500 mg, do not allow titration to the most effective and safe analgesic dose to match individual requirements.
- **Co-proxamol** (dextropropoxyphene 32.5 mg/ paracetamol 325 mg) has been withdrawn by the Committee on Safety of Medicines due to its unfavourable risk/benefit ratio; it is associated with an unacceptable risk of overdose [CSM, 2005a].

Standard nonsteroidal anti-inflammatory drugs (NSAIDs), other than ibuprofen, diclofenac, and naproxen, are not generally recommended, as they have a worse balance between their efficacy and adverse-effect profile than these three recommended drugs [CSM, 1994; Hernández-Diaz et al, 2000; BNF 49, 2005].

Cyclo-oxygenase-2 (COX-2) selective inhibitors are not recommended. After the withdrawal of rofecoxib from the market (the only selective inhibitor licensed for acute pain), there are growing concerns that COX-2 selective inhibitors may cause serious cardiovascular events. Following a European-wide review of the data, the Committee on Safety of Medicines (CSM) has recently advised that [CSM, 2005b]:

- The evidence suggests that coxibs, as a class, may cause an increased risk of thrombotic events (e.g. myocardial infarction and stroke) compared with placebo and some NSAIDs.
- The risk may increase with dose and duration of exposure.

Strong opioids (e.g. morphine, pethidine) should be avoided, owing to the risk of dependence if they are used inappropriately. They are usually reserved for moderate to severe pain of a visceral origin [BNF 49, 2005].

Gastroprotective agents are sometimes needed, but not all are recommended:

- **H_2-receptor antagonists (H_2RAs).** At standard doses, H_2RAs reduce the risk of duodenal ulceration, and there is some evidence that double doses reduce the risk of gastric ulceration [Rostom et al, 2002]. However, no H_2RAs are currently licensed for the prevention of gastric ulceration induced by NSAIDs [BNF 49, 2005], which is more common than duodenal ulceration.
- **Rabeprazole** is not included as it is not specifically licensed for the prevention of NSAID-induced gastrointestinal ulcers [BNF 49, 2005].
- **Fixed-dose combinations of standard NSAIDs with misoprostol:** The optimum dose of misoprostol (i.e. 800 micrograms daily) cannot be reached using these preparations. In particular, only 400 micrograms daily of misoprostol is given with the higher doses of NSAID in these preparations.

Drugs included

Standard analgesics and nonsteroidal anti-inflammatory drugs (NSAIDs)

- **Paracetamol** is a good first-line choice for pain relief, and is not associated with gastrointestinal toxicity [SIGN, 2000].
- **Codeine (in combination with paracetamol):** higher-dose codeine is included for use with regular paracetamol for additional pain relief. Codeine 60 mg plus paracetamol has been shown to provide more pain relief than either codeine 60 mg alone or paracetamol 1000 mg alone [Moore et al, 1997]. Codeine should be prescribed separately to paracetamol to allow flexibility of dosing and titration of analgesic effect.
  - Note: codeine can also be combined with an NSAID, or paracetamol can be combined with an NSAID, but there is less evidence to support this.
- **Standard NSAIDS: ibuprofen, diclofenac, and naproxen** have a good balance of efficacy against adverse effect profile [CSM, 1994; Henry et al, 1996; Hernández-Diaz and Rodriguez, 2000]. Standard doses are offered as these are generally accepted to be sufficient for anti-inflammatory prophylaxis, although data are lacking.

Muscle relaxants

- **Diazepam** is recommended as a muscle relaxant, as it has been shown to effectively reduce acute neck pain. However, adverse effects such as are common, and there is a risk of dependency even after 1 week of treatment. Courses of 3–7 days should be used only in people with severe spasm [Clinical Standards Advisory Group, 1994; Waddell et al, 1999].

Gastroprotective agents

- **Proton pump inhibitors (PPIs): lansoprazole, omeprazole, esomeprazole, and pantoprazole** are licensed for the prevention of gastroduodenal ulceration induced by NSAIDs [BNF 49, 2005]. PPIs reduce the risk of endoscopic ulcers, but there are no data on prevention of ulcer complications [Rostom et al, 2002]. However, they are generally considered to be the preferred choice for gastroprotection, as they are better tolerated than misoprostol.
- **Misoprostol** is licensed for the prevention of gastroduodenal ulceration induced by NSAIDs [BNF 49, 2005]. It reduces the risk of endoscopically proven ulcers and has also been shown to reduce the risk of ulcer complications [Rostom et al, 2002]. It is less well tolerated than PPIs owing to gastrointestinal adverse effects, particularly diarrhoea.

Prescriptions

Paracetamol or codeine

Paracetamol tablets: 1g up to four times a day

- Age from 16 years onwards
- Paracetamol 500mg tablets. Take two tablets every 4 to 6 hours when required for pain relief. Maximum of 8 tablets in 24 hours; supply 200 tablets; NHS Cost £2.12; OTC Cost £3.75.

Codeine tablets: 30mg to 60mg up to four times a day

- Age from 16 years onwards
- Codeine 30mg tablets. Take one to two tablets every 4 to 6 hours when required for pain relief. Maximum of 8 tablets in 24 hours; supply 60 tablets; NHS Cost £4.58.

Paracetamol 500mg tablets + codeine 30mg tablets
- Age from 16 years onwards
- Paracetamol 500mg tablets. Take two tablets every 4 to 6 hours when required for pain relief. Maximum of 8 tablets in 24 hours; supply 200 tablets; NHS Cost £2.12; OTC Cost £3.75.
- Codeine 30mg tablets. Take one to two tablets every 4 to 6 hours when required for pain relief. Maximum of 8 tablets in 24 hours; supply 60 tablets; NHS Cost £4.58.

Standard NSAIDs: ibuprofen, naproxen and diclofenac

Ibuprofen tablets: 400mg three times a day
- Age from 16 years onwards
- Ibuprofen 400mg tablets. Take one tablet three times a day; supply 84 tablets; NHS Cost £2.74; OTC Cost £4.83.

Ibuprofen tablets: 400mg four times a day
- Age from 16 years onwards
- Ibuprofen 400mg tablets. Take one tablet four times a day; supply 112 tablets; NHS Cost £3.65; OTC Cost £6.44.

Ibuprofen tablets: 600mg three times a day
- Age from 16 years onwards
- Ibuprofen 600mg tablets. Take one tablet three times a day; supply 84 tablets; NHS Cost £2.81.

Ibuprofen tablets: 800mg three times a day
- Age from 16 years onwards
- Ibuprofen 400mg tablets. Take two tablets three times a day; supply 168 tablets; NHS Cost £4.58.

Diclofenac sodium e/c tablets: 25mg three times a day
- Age from 16 years onwards
- Diclofenac 25mg e/c tablets. Take one tablet three times a day; supply 84 tablets; NHS Cost £1.72.

Diclofenac sodium e/c tablets: 50mg three times a day
- Age from 16 years onwards
- Diclofenac 50mg e/c tablets. Take one tablet three times a day; supply 84 tablets; NHS Cost £1.45.

Naproxen tablets: 250mg twice a day
- Age from 16 years onwards
- Naproxen 250mg tablets. Take one tablet twice a day; supply 56 tablets; NHS Cost £2.68.

Naproxen tablets: 500mg twice a day
- Age from 16 years onwards
- Naproxen 500mg tablets. Take one tablet twice a day; supply 56 tablets; NHS Cost £4.90.

GI protection: use ONLY with a standard NSAID

Omeprazole capsules: 20mg once a day
- Age from 16 years onwards
- Omeprazole 20mg capsules. Take one capsule once a day; supply 28 capsules; NHS Cost £12.75.

Omeprazole tablets: 20mg once a day
- Age from 16 years onwards
- Omeprazole 20mg tablets. Take one tablet once a day; supply 28 tablets; NHS Cost £12.75.

Lansoprazole capsules: 15mg each morning
- Age from 16 years onwards
- Lansoprazole 15mg capsules. Take one capsule each morning (on an empty stomach); supply 28 capsules; NHS Cost £12.92.

Lansoprazole capsules: 30mg each morning
- Age from 16 years onwards
- Lansoprazole 30mg capsules. Take one capsule each morning (on an empty stomach); supply 28 capsules; NHS Cost £23.63.

Pantoprazole e/c tablets: 20mg once a day
- Age from 16 years onwards
- Pantoprazole 20mg e/c tablets. Take one tablet once a day; supply 28 tablets; NHS Cost £12.31.

Esomeprazole tablets: 20mg once a day
- Age from 16 years onwards
- Esomeprazole 20mg tablets. Take one tablet once a day; supply 28 tablets; NHS Cost £18.50.

Lansoprazole orodispersible tablets: 15mg each morning
- Age from 16 years onwards
- Lansoprazole 15mg orodisp tabs. Take one tablet each morning (on an empty stomach); supply 28 tablets; NHS Cost £10.86.

Lansoprazole orodispersible tablets: 30mg each morning
- Age from 16 years onwards
- Lansoprazole 30mg orodisp tabs. Take one tablet each morning (on an empty stomach); supply 28 tablets; NHS Cost £21.38.

Misoprostol tablets: 200micrograms four times a day
- Age from 16 years onwards
- Misoprostol 200microgram tabs. Take one tablet four times a day; supply 120 tablets; NHS Cost £18.72.

Muscle relaxant (diazepam): 1-week supply

Diazepam tablets: 2mg to 4mg three times a day
- Age from 16 years onwards
- Diazepam 2mg tablets. Take one to two tablets three times a day; supply 28 tablets; NHS Cost £1.14.

Extended Information

Background information

- What is it? p.1294
- How common is neck pain? p.1295
- How do I know my patient has simple neck pain? p.129
- How do I know my patient has whiplash associated disorder? p.1296
- How do I know my patient has cervical radiculopathy? p.1296
- What else might it be? p.1296
- Complications and prognosis p.1297

What is it?

Simple neck pain

- **Simple (or non-specific) neck pain** is neck pain with no specific underlying disease causing the pain. Simple neck pain includes pain after a whiplash accident, pain due to minor muscle strains, and pain from acute torticollis. Fo the purposes of this guidance, simple neck pain also includes pain from cervical radiculopathy.
- Simple neck pain is mechanical in nature: it changes in severity with posture and movement, and it changes ove time.

[Barry and Jenner, 1995]

Whiplash-associated disorder

- **Whiplash-associated disorder** is the neck pain and other symptoms that follow sudden or excessive hyperextension/flexion/rotation of the neck. For the purposes of this guidance whiplash-associated disorder excludes complications such as cord compression, nerve root damage, cervical subluxation, and vertebral fracture. (Definitions of whiplash-associated disorder vary and some do include the complications of damage to nerve, joint, and bone.)

- The most common event associated with whiplash associated disorder is a rear-impact or side-impact motor vehicle collision.
- Suggestions that psychosocial factors and cultural play a causative role are controversial but supported by a variety of epidemiological studies [Livingston, 2000].

Acute torticollis

Torticollis means a twisted neck. Acute torticollis is thought to be due to minor local musculoskeletal irritation causing pain and spasm in neck muscles. Barry and Jenner, 1995; Epidemiological Study of Dystonia in Europe Collaborative Group., 2000]

Cervical radiculopathy

Cervical radiculopathy is compression or injury to a nerve root in the cervical spine. The most common causes of cervical radiculopathy are cervical disc herniation and entrapment in the root canal.

Cervical disc herniation occurs when the nucleus pulposus bulges or breaks through the annulus of the intervertebral disc. Posterior herniation causes symptoms by compressing the cord or a nerve root, or by stretching the posterior longitudinal ligament or posterior annulus.

Cervical disc herniation occurs most frequently at the levels of C4/5, C5/6, and C6/7. The clinical consequences of cervical nerve root compression are summarized in Table 1.

Classification of neck pain

Neck pain can be classified as acute (within 4 weeks), subacute (4–12 weeks), and chronic (more than 12 weeks) neck pain.

Neck pain can also be classified according to clinical features: neck pain associated or not associated with whiplash injury; with or without radiculopathy; or with or without torticollis.

However, many studies of neck pain do not distinguish between acute, subacute and chronic neck pain, or between neck pain after a whiplash-associated disorder and other simple neck pain.

The justification commonly made for not making these distinctions is that the causes of simple neck pain are often unclear and seem to be multifactorial, and treatments are similar — no classification has been shown to reliably identify subgroups of people who respond in clinically important different ways to particular interventions.

Nevertheless, it may be important to distinguish subgroups, particularly whiplash-associated disorders, from other simple neck pain conditions so that treatment can be directed appropriately at all the associated symptoms and consequences.

Binder, 2004; Childs et al, 2004; Ferrari et al, 2005]

How common is neck pain?

Findings from epidemiological studies of neck pain vary considerably, as does the methodological quality of the studies. For example, results that rely on responses to questionnaires are likely to overestimate prevalence and incidence rates. Despite the methodological problems there is clear evidence that neck pain is among the most common problems managed in primary care and that it places a heavy burden on individuals, health care services, and employers.

Simple neck pain: incidence, prevalence, and health services usage

A survey of people registered with three general practices in north-west England found that, of adults aged 45–75 years, about 25% of women and 20% of men reported current neck pain [Urwin et al, 1998].

- A questionnaire survey of 10,000 adults in Norway found that 34% of responders had experienced neck pain in the previous year [Bovim et al, 1994].
- A prospective cohort study of adults in Saskatchewan found that:
  - Annual cumulative incidence of neck pain was 15% (age and sex standardized)
  - Women were more likely than men to develop neck pain (incidence rate ratio 1.67). [Cote et al, 2004]
- In a survey of Dutch general practice, GPs were consulted for complaints of the neck or upper extremity 147 times per 1000 registered persons [Bot et al, 2005].
- In the UK about 15% of referrals to a physiotherapy service by general practitioners were for neck problems [Hackett et al, 1987].

Whiplash-associated disorder: incidence and prevalence

The incidence of chronic symptoms after whiplash-associated disorder varies between cultures and countries.

- In Canada more than 50% of accident victims report chronic pain [Ferrari and Russell, 1999].
- A survey of 210 victims of rear-impact collisions in Lithuania found the maximum duration of neck pain to be 17 days and headache 20 days [Obelieniene et al, 1999].
- In a study in the USA of university hospital employees, only 9% of physicians suffering a rear-impact collision had whiplash symptoms but 33% of non-physicians reported symptoms [Virani et al, 2001].
- A Swedish survey found that 30% of respondents with chronic neck pain reported previous injury to the neck [Guez et al, 2003].

Synthesizing the evidence and drawing conclusions from it is difficult because of methodological differences between studies, for example in case definition and case selection: some studies looked at people presenting for treatment, while others looked at reported motor vehicle accidents.

Acute torticollis: incidence

- Acute torticollis is common [Barry and Jenner, 1995]. We were unable to find accurate data on incidence rates.

How do I know my patient has simple neck pain?

- Rule out the presence of conditions that can cause neck pain, particularly those that can be dangerous. '*Red flags*' for possible serious pathology indicate the presence of most disorders that require urgent attention.
- Assess the typical features of simple neck pain:
  - Neck pain is acute or chronic, of abrupt or insidious onset.
  - The pain is poorly localized.
  - Pain may radiate to the base of the skull, the upper arms, upper trunk, face, and/or scalp.
  - Muscle stiffness and spasm are common.
- Confirm the presence or absence of cervical radiculopathy, whiplash-associated disorder, and acute torticollis.

What are the 'red flags' for simple neck pain?

'Red flags' are clinical features that indicate an increased risk of specific conditions that can present with neck pain, and which require urgent attention.

- **Malignancy, infection, inflammation**
  - Fever
  - Unexplained loss of weight
  - History of inflammatory arthritis

- History of malignancy, drug abuse, AIDS, or other infection
  - Immunosuppression
  - Pain that is increasing, unremitting and/or disturbs sleep
  - Lymphadenopathy
- **Myelopathy (compression of the spinal cord)**
  - Insidious progression
  - Gait disturbance; clumsy or weak hands; loss of sexual/bladder/bowel function
  - Lhermitte's sign (shooting electric-like sensations on extending or moving neck)
  - Upper motor neurone signs in the lower limbs (Babinski's sign — up-going plantar reflex, hyperreflexia, clonus, spasticity)
  - Lower motor neurone signs in the upper limbs (atrophy, hyporeflexia)
- **Severe trauma/skeletal injury — rarely present in primary care**
  - History of trauma
  - Previous neck surgery
  - Osteoporosis
  - Increasing and/or unremitting pain
- **Vascular insufficiency**
  - Dizziness and blackouts (restriction of vertebral artery) on movement, especially upward gaze
  - Dizziness, drop attacks

How do I know my patient has whiplash associated disorder?

- **Confirm a history of** sudden or excessive neck extension, flexion, or rotation.
- **Rule out** possible serious pathology such as fracture or subluxation of cervical vertebra.
  - Imaging is indicated in someone with neck pain and a history of a traumatic whiplash incident if they have one or more of the following features:
    - Midline cervical tenderness
    - Focal neurological deficit
    - Altered alertness
    - Intoxication
    - Painful, distracting injury [Royal College of Radiologists, 2003]
  - If imaging is indicated, consider consulting with the radiology department to choose the mode of imaging, e.g. plain X-ray, computerized tomography (CT), or magnetic resonance imaging (MRI).
  - The Royal College of Radiologists guidelines are similar to the Canadian C-spine rule, which has been shown to have sufficient sensitivity and specificity to decide who needs radiographical imaging of the neck [Bandiera et al, 2003; Stiell et al, 2003].
- **If the onset of symptoms is delayed:**
  - Exclude other serious pathology as for simple neck pain — see *Red flags* above for details.
  - Assess the presence of psychosocial risk factors.
- **Assess symptoms of whiplash-associated disorder:**
  - Disabling neck pain with or without referral to shoulder or arm
  - Muscular spasm
  - Point tenderness
  - Decreased range of movement
  - Posterior cervical sympathetic syndrome including headaches, facial formication (sensation of ants crawling over the face)
- **Assess presence of** associated stress, anxiety and/or depression.

[Albert et al, 2003]

How do I know my patient has cervical radiculopathy?

The features of cervical radiculopathy (nerve root compression) are:

- Onset is usually insidious but may be abrupt.
- Neck pain radiates to an upper limb. Usually unilateral but may be bilateral. Pain may be severe enough to wake the person at night.
- Upper limb weakness, paraesthesia, dermatomal sensory deficit, changes to reflexes. Table 1 below details the features of the common cervical radiculopathies.

[Kriss and Kriss, 2000]

What else might it be?

The differential diagnosis of simple neck pain includes:

- Fibromyalgia
- Problems in adjacent structures such as the shoulder
- Headache
- Malignancy involving structures in the neck
- Infections involving structures in the neck
- Inflammatory conditions such as rheumatoid arthritis
- Severe trauma/skeletal injury
- Vascular insufficiency
- Myelopathy (compression of the spinal cord)

[Barry and Jenner, 1995]

The differential diagnosis of acute torticollis includes:

- Acute disc prolapse — the most common cause of severe secondary torticollis
- Drug reactions, e.g. antipsychotic drugs, metoclopramide
- Tonsillitis
- Cervical lymphadenopathy due to infection or malignancy
- Vertebral infection
- Cervical spine injury
- Ocular disorders
- Cervical dystonia (wryneck, spasmodic torticollis). Cervical dystonia is a focal dystonia with painful spasm of neck muscles. It is rare and chronic.

[Barry and Jenner, 1995; Nakashima et al, 1995; Epidemiological Study of Dystonia in Europe Collaborative Group., 2000]

Table 1: Neurological features associated with cervical radiculopathy.

Nerve root	Muscle weakness	Reflex changes	Sensory changes
C5	Shoulder abduction and flexion Elbow flexion	Biceps	Lateral arm
C6	Elbow flexion Wrist extension	Biceps Supinator	Lateral forearm Thumb Index finger
C7	Elbow flexion Wrist flexion Finger extension	Triceps	Middle finger
C8	Finger flexion	None	Medial side lower forearm Ring and little finger
T1	Finger abduction and adduction	None	Medial side upper forearm Lower arm

omplications and prognosis

omplications

Development of chronicity and disability [Gun et al, 2005]

rognosis

imple neck pain

lthough acute simple neck pain tends to resolve over a w weeks it can progress into a chronic disabling ndition with a course marked by periods of remission d exacerbation.

A study in south Manchester of the prognosis for neck pain in adults found that:

- Neck pain persisted at 12 months in about 50%
- Increased risk of persistent neck pain was associated with age 45–59 years, co-existing low back pain, and with cycling [Hill et al, 2004]

A cross-sectional questionnaire-based study in Norway found that 14% of responders reported neck pain that lasted for more than 6 months [Bovim et al, 1994].

A prospective cohort study of adults in Saskatchewan found that [Cote et al, 2004]:

- The annual rate of resolution of new neck pain was 37%, with a further 33% of people reporting improvement.
- Of those people with neck pain at baseline, 37% reported persistent problems and 10% reported an aggravation within a year, and 23% reported a recurrent episode.
- Women were more likely than men to suffer from persistent neck problems and less likely to experience resolution (incidence rate ratios = 1.19, 0.75).

A Swedish study of people treated with physiotherapy or chiropractic for low back pain or neck pain found that about 50% reported pain and disability at the 5-year follow-up [Enthoven et al, 2004].

A study in Dutch general practice found that older age and concomitant low back pain are the best, but weak, predictors for a less favourable prognosis for neck pain. Other, weaker, predictors were previous trauma, a long duration of neck pain, stable neck pain during the 2 weeks prior to baseline measurement, and previous neck pain. [Hoving et al, 2004]

hiplash-associated disorder

The prognosis for whiplash injury is usually favourable. However, some people have diverse, prolonged, and disabling symptoms.

Reported rates of recovery from whiplash associated disorder vary considerably, possibly because of social and cultural factors [Ferrari and Russell, 1999; Obelieniene et al, 1999; Virani et al, 2001; McClune et al, 2002].

High initial pain intensity is an important predictor for delayed functional recovery for people with whiplash injury.

Factors such as age, sex, and compensation do not seem to be of prognostic value [Suissa, 2003].

- A cohort study in Quebec of 2,627 people who had a whiplash injury without associated injuries found that [Suissa, 2003]:
  - The median recovery time was 32 days.
  - 12% of participants had not recovered after 6 months.
  - Several factors were found to be independently associated with a slower recovery from whiplash: mode of accident; having dependents; not being employed full time; female sex; older age; neck pain on palpation; muscle pain; pain or numbness radiating from neck to arms, hands or shoulders; and headache.
  - Median recovery times varied from 17–123 days for people classified with the Quebec classification of signs and symptoms [Hartling et al, 2001], indicating that it might be useful to target early interventions at people with a poor prognosis.
- A Swedish case-control study of 121 people with neck pain after a motor vehicle accident found that, 17 years after the accident, neck pain was reported in 55% of the exposed group and 29% of the control group (who were matched for age and sex) [Bunketorp et al, 2005].
- Some people develop chronic neck pain many months after a whiplash incident. However, only 7% of people who are asymptomatic 3 months after an accident will have symptoms after 2 years. About 85% of people who are symptomatic 3 months after an accident will still be symptomatic after 2 years [Gargan and Bannister, 1994].
- A systematic review of prognostic factors for whiplash-associated disorder (search date up to April 2002) found 50 papers reporting on 29 cohorts. No statistical pooling was able to be performed because of the heterogeneity of participant selection, type of prognostic factors and outcome measures. [Scholten-Peeters et al, 2003]
  - **A factor strongly predictive** of an adverse prognosis is high initial pain intensity (strong evidence)
  - **Factors with limited prognostic value** for functional recovery are physical (e.g. restricted range of motion, high number of complaints), psychosocial (previous psychological problems), neuropsychosocial factors (nervousness), crash related (e.g. accident on highway), and treatment-related factors (need to resume physiotherapy).
  - **Factors not predictive of prognosis** are older age, female gender, high acute psychological response, angular deformity of the neck, rear-end collision, and compensation (strong evidence).

[Kivioja et al, 2004]

Cervical radiculopathy

- The prognosis for cervical radiculopathy is favourable: symptoms resolve in most people without surgical treatment.
- No prognostic or risk factors have been firmly established.

[Wainner and Gill, 2000; Vallee et al, 2001]

Management issues

- Overview of the management of simple neck pain p.1298
- How do I manage simple neck pain? p.1298
- Medicines management p.1299
- Supporting evidence p.1300

Overview of the management of simple neck pain

Rule out (or manage) rare but potentially dangerous conditions which can cause neck pain.
- Confirm absence of 'red flags'.
- If there has been a recent whiplash incident, exclude fracture and dislocation of cervical vertebra.

Identify and manage any comorbidity and risk factors.
Provide reassurance and information.

Drug therapy:
- Analgesics provide short-term pain relief. Prescribe according to the level of pain, personal preferences, and the presence of any cautions or contraindications:
  - Non-prescription analgesics, taken when required
  - Paracetamol or a nonsteroidal anti-inflammatory drug (NSAID), taken at regular intervals
  - Dual therapy with two of either paracetamol, a NSAID, or codeine phosphate
- Diazepam for 3–7 days may be used for people with severe muscle spasm.
- A trial of amitriptyline or gabapentin for 1 month may be helpful for people with chronic pain.

Physical and manual treatments:
- Consider referral for physiotherapy or manual treatment if locally available.

Invasive treatments:
- Surgery and other invasive treatments are rarely indicated. Referral for assessment for invasive treatment could be considered for people with chronic pain and/or nerve root symptoms that is poorly controlled.

How do I manage simple neck pain?

N

This section covers the management of uncomplicated neck pain with or without symptoms of nerve root compression, including torticollis and whiplash-associated neck pain without serious neurologic deficit.

Potentially dangerous conditions which can cause neck pain

- Confirm the absence of 'red flags'. 'Red flags' for possible serious pathology indicate the presence of most disorders that require urgent attention and are listed in the section *How do I know my patient has simple neck pain?*.
- If there has been a recent whiplash incident, exclude fracture and dislocation of cervical vertebra. The indications for radiographic imaging are discussed in the section *How do I know my patient has whiplash-associated disorder?*.

Assessment of neck pain and any disability due to neck pain

- Assess and document severity of neck pain and any disability due to neck pain.
- Consider using a standardized scale for neck pain and disability due to neck pain [Pietrobon et al, 2002].

Comorbidity in chronic neck pain

- In people with chronic neck pain, identify and manage any comorbidity such as other pain syndromes, and psychological problems.
  - Comorbidity is common in people suffering from chronic neck or back pain [Cote et al, 2001; Carroll et al, 2004].
  - At least one other comorbid condition is reported by most people (87%) with chronic spinal pain. Comorbid conditions included other chronic pain conditions (69%), chronic physical conditions (55%) mental disorders (35%), anxiety disorders, and mood disorders.
  - Common conditions not significantly associated with chronic spinal pain were diabetes, heart disease, cancer, and drug abuse.

[Von Korff et al, 2005]

Risk factors for developing neck pain

- Identify and manage risk factors for developing neck pain.
  - Awkward neck postures, neck flexion, arm force, arm posture, duration of sitting, twisting or bending of the trunk, hand-arm vibration, and some workplace designs are associated with neck pain [Ariens et al, 2000; Ariens et al, 2001; York University, 2003].

Psychosocial factors that may indicate increased risk of chronicity and disability

- Identify and address psychosocial factors that may indicate increased risk for chronicity and disability.
  - Identify and address any excessive concerns about the neck pain, unrealistic expectations of treatment, disabling sickness behaviour, and problems with compensation, work, family, moods and emotions.
  - The concept of 'yellow flags', psychosocial factors associated with an increased risk of chronicity and disability, was developed for managing low back pain [NZGG, 2004]. It has been suggested that a similar approach would be useful in managing neck pain [Albert et al, 2003].

Reassurance and information

- **Provide reassurance and information**
  - Acute simple neck pain may require mild analgesia, and usually takes a few days to recover.
  - Early mobilization and return to a normal active lifestyle will improve the outcomes.
    - Evidence of benefit from mobilization comes from several systematic reviews and subsequent randomized controlled trials, but is limited by methodological weaknesses. Little information is available on harms, although early mobilization physiotherapy may be poorly tolerated.
  - Poor posture should be corrected if it is thought to precipitate or aggravate the neck pain.
  - Driving may be inadvisable if the range of motion of the neck is restricted.
  - A firm pillow may provide comfort at night.
    - The pillow should provide lateral support and support the hollow of the neck.
    - A position of comfort should be found before trying to go to sleep.
    - Using two pillows may force the head into a stressed position.
  - Neck supports, if used, should be used for as short a time as possible, i.e. 2–4 days, and under supervision e.g. by a physiotherapist, to ensure that mobilization commenced as soon as possible.

Drug therapy

- Analgesics can provide short-term pain relief. Prescribe according to the level of pain, personal preferences, and the presence of any cautions or contraindications. Options include:
  - Paracetamol, taken when required (usually tried first) or
  - A nonsteroidal anti-inflammatory drug (NSAID), taken at regular intervals, or

- Dual therapy with two of either paracetamol, a NSAID, or codeine phosphate.
- Diazepam for 3–7 days may be used for people with severe muscle spasm.
  - Consider using diazepam if paracetamol or a NSAID, on their own or combined, prove ineffective in the early treatment of acute neck pain.
  - A short course of diazepam is recommended because the risk of developing benzodiazepine dependency is high.
- A trial of amitriptyline for 1 month may be helpful for people with pain unresponsive to 'full dose' analgesics and persisting for 4–6 weeks.
- A trial of gabapentin for 1 month may be helpful for people with chronic pain, if amitriptyline has proved ineffective or is contraindicated.

Evidence of benefits and harms from the use of drug treatments for simple neck pain mostly comes from extrapolation from the use of the drugs in other painful musculoskeletal conditions. There are few randomized controlled trials specifically testing drug treatments for neck pain.

Physical and manual treatment

- Consider referral to a physiotherapist, or chiropractor or osteopath if available.
  - Physiotherapy may assist in achieving early mobilization and return to usual activities.
  - Active physiotherapy, mobilization, manipulation, and exercise may provide short-term relief in people with chronic neck pain.

Invasive treatments

- Surgery and other invasive treatments are rarely indicated.
- Referral for assessment for invasive treatment could be considered for people with chronic pain and/or nerve root symptoms that is poorly controlled.
- Invasive treatments include percutaneous radiofrequency neurotomy and cervical epidural analgesia.

Medicines management

- Analgesia
- Nonsteroidal anti-inflammatory drugs
- Muscle relaxants
- Drugs for management of chronic pain

Analgesia

Paracetamol

- Paracetamol is safe and effective for the treatment of mild to moderate pain when used correctly, and is well tolerated at the recommended daily dose.
- It is more likely to be effective for neck pain when used regularly rather than 'as required'.

Codeine

- Codeine may be added to paracetamol if more pain relief is required. Note: codeine can also be combined with an NSAID, or paracetamol can be combined with an NSAID, but there is less evidence to support this.
- Paracetamol and codeine should be prescribed separately so they can be individually titrated; combination products such as co-codamol are not recommended.
- Codeine may cause nausea, vomiting, constipation, and drowsiness. A regular laxative is often needed when it is used long-term.

Nonsteroidal anti-inflammatory drugs

A full discussion on the contraindications, adverse effects, monitoring issues, and interactions of nonsteroidal anti-inflammatory drugs (NSAIDs) is beyond the scope of this guidance. For further information, see the separate PRODIGY guidance on *Nonsteroidal anti-inflammatory drugs (NSAIDs)*.

- Long-term use of NSAIDs is not required and is not appropriate for neck pain.
- Consider comorbidity when prescribing nonsteroidal anti-inflammatory drugs (NSAIDs).
  - NSAIDs commonly cause gastrointestinal adverse effects, and can worsen asthma, hypertension, renal impairment, and heart failure.
  - There is a small increased risk of cardiovascular events with coxibs (which seems highest in people who already have cardiovascular disease).
- For people with neck pain and NSAID-induced dyspepsia or at high risk of gastrointestinal adverse events, we recommend the following options:
  - Use paracetamol (with or without codeine) instead of a NSAID if possible, or
  - Use a gastroprotective agent with a standard NSAID [NICE, 2001].
- For advice on the management of dyspepsia due to NSAIDs, see the separate PRODIGY guidance on *Dyspepsia — symptoms (uninvestigated by endoscopy)* and *Dyspepsia — proven DU, GU, or NSAID-associated ulcer*.

Which nonsteroidal anti-inflammatory drug should I use?

- **There is a lack of good evidence to support the use of one NSAID over another in the treatment of neck pain.** Consequently ibuprofen, diclofenac, and naproxen are recommended on the basis of the balances between their general efficacy and adverse-effect profile, which are more favourable than for other NSAIDs [CSM, 1994; Hernández-Diaz et al, 2000; BNF 49, 2005]:
  - **Ibuprofen** is probably the least toxic NSAID. Doses of up to 2.4 grams per day may be necessary for acute pain.
  - **Diclofenac** is an alternative to ibuprofen with greater efficacy but more risk of adverse effects. The standard dosage for acute pain relief is 50 mg taken three times a day.
  - **Naproxen** has similar efficacy and risk of adverse effects as diclofenac. Up to 1 gram a day in two divided doses can be prescribed if necessary.
- **Cyclo-oxygenase-2 (COX-2) selective inhibitors are not recommended.** After the withdrawal of rofecoxib from the market (the only selective inhibitor licensed for acute pain), there are growing concerns that COX-2 selective inhibitors may cause serious cardiovascular events. Following a European-wide review of the data, the Committee on Safety of Medicines (CSM) has recently advised that [CSM, 2005b]:
  - The evidence suggests that coxibs, as a class, may cause an increased risk of thrombotic events (e.g. myocardial infarction and stroke) compared with placebo and some NSAIDs.
  - The risk may increase with dose and duration of exposure.

Muscle relaxants

- Several muscle relaxants have been studied for neck pain. Diazepam is usually the preferred choice.
- Expert opinion is that diazepam is primarily a sedative in this situation and helps to relieve muscle tension. There is no evidence that muscle spasm in terms of any neurophysiological phenomenon is a component of simple neck pain [Pickin, Personal Communication, 2005].

What dose of diazepam should I use?

- Suggested treatment regimens are 2–4 mg three times a day for 3–7 days.

What are the adverse effects of diazepam?

- Diazepam has strong sedative effects. People should be warned not to drive while taking the drug or for a full day after stopping drug treatment. In addition, people should be warned that the effects of alcohol may be exaggerated whilst taking this medication.
- Diazepam, like all the benzodiazepines, has a high potential for tolerance and dependence. In addition to avoiding extended use of the drug, it should be avoided in people with a history of drug or alcohol abuse, and in pregnant or breastfeeding women.

Drugs for management of chronic pain

Various antidepressant and anticonvulsant drugs have been suggested for use in people with chronic neck pain. In practice, amitriptyline (tricyclic antidepressant) and gabapentin (anticonvulsant) are most commonly used, although there is limited evidence for the use of these drugs in neck pain and neither is specifically licensed for it.

What dose of amitriptyline should I use?

- Reassure the person that the drug is not for psychiatric purposes, and prescribe low dose amitriptyline on the basis of a 1-month trial. Reassess drug efficacy and adverse effects after this period [BNF 49, 2005]:
  - An initial dose of 10 or 25 mg at night should be used.
  - After reassessment, the dose can be titrated up (in weekly increments) to 75 mg per day; higher doses should only be initiated by a specialist. For many people, however, the effective dose is between 25 mg and 75 mg at night.

What are the adverse effects of amitriptyline?

- Most of the adverse effects of amitriptyline are dose related and are not likely to present a clinically important problem at lower doses:
  - Antimuscarinic adverse effects such as dry mouth, sedation, blurred vision, constipation, and urinary retention are most common.
  - Postural hypotension (especially in the elderly), arrhythmias or weight gain may also occur.
- People should be warned about the risk of sedation and warned not to drive if they are affected [BNF 49, 2005].

Who should avoid taking amitriptyline?

- Amitriptyline should be avoided in people who have had a recent myocardial infarction or have existing cardiac arrhythmias.
- Amitriptyline is dangerous in overdose and should not be prescribed to people who are considered at risk from suicide.

What dose of gabapentin should I use?

- There is little evidence on what dose of gabapentin is required to alleviate chronic neck pain, but the full 'antiepileptic dose' is probably necessary:
  - Titrate slowly from 100 mg three times a day to 300 mg three times a day over 7 days. (Note: this is slower than suggested in the summary of product characteristics.)
  - The effective dose is between 900 mg per day and 1800 mg per day (licensed) for many people.
  - Specialist advice should be sought if higher doses are required.

What are the adverse effects of gabapentin?

- Common adverse effects of gabapentin include drowsiness, dizziness, ataxia, and fatigue.
- Sudden withdrawal of gabapentin may cause anxiety, insomnia, nausea, pain and sweating: it should be tapered off over the course of at least 1 week [BNF 49, 2005].
- The clearance of gabapentin is markedly reduced in renal impairment. The total daily dose should not exceed 1200 mg in those with mild renal impairment (common in the elderly). For further information on dosing in renal impairment, see the summary of product characteristics (www.medicines.org.uk).

Supporting evidence

The following sections summarize the evidence for non-invasive treatments for simple neck pain; acute whiplash-associated disorder; chronic whiplash-associated disorder; and neck pain with cervical radiculopathy as found by a *Clinical Evidence* review [Binder, 2004].

In general, levels of evidence are low, effect sizes are moderate, and treatment goals (e.g. comfort, control, cure, rehabilitation, and risk avoidance) are often unclear. The tables show that, although there are many trials of many interventions, and many reviews of treatment, it is difficult to give a clear overview of the evidence without being misleading. There are several reasons for this difficulty:

- **Lack of agreement on what the evidence means**
  - A critical appraisal of reviews of treatments for neck pain showed that there is a high level of disagreement between reviews [Hoving et al, 2001]. Complete concordance between reviews was present in only 4 of 14 interventions for which there were at least 2 reviews, i.e. for 10 interventions there were reviews that came to different conclusions. The authors did not analyze the causes for the lack of agreement.
- **Publication bias**
  - The critical appraisal of reviews found no review that concluded any treatment was ineffective. The authors took this as prima facie evidence of publication bias arising from negative trials not being published [Hoving et al, 2001]. However, it could also be at least partly due to authors of reviews finding it difficult to conclude that a treatment is ineffective, possibly justifiably [Jones et al, 1996].
- **Even systematic review with high quality scores do not guarantee freedom from bias and error**
  - High quality systematic reviews may overlook important clinical details in the papers reviewed, thereby diminishing their validity [Hopayian, 2001].
  - One systematic review of treatments of neck pain had a high quality score, yet showed evidence of bias introduced by favouring positive results for inclusion in the review. The quality score covers bias introduced by selection of publications, but it does not cover bias arising from partial selection by reviewers of results from individual studies. (The quality score also does not cover selection bias introduced by investigators preferring 'interesting' results rather than pre-specified outcomes [Chan et al, 2004]. This bias will be eliminated only when trials prospectively enter their methods and objectives in a public register [Abbasi, 2004].)
- **Simple neck pain is a heterogeneous condition,** and studies of treatments have various criteria for inclusion and this may obscure important differences in efficacy between treatments as tested in individual studies. The justifications for distinguishing or not distinguishing types of neck pain are discussed above in the *Classification of neck pain* section.
- **Interventions are grouped for review in broad categories** and this may obscure important differences in efficacy between treatments as tested in individual studies. Examples include multi-modal therapies, manipulation, and exercise. In addition, non-drug treatments for neck pain are often not described in enough detail that would be sufficient for the trial to be replicated independently.
- **Treatment goals, outcomes measured and effect sizes** are not always detailed in overviews. One explanation for this is that to do so would make the text difficult to read (and onerous to draft).

What is the evidence for treatments of simple neck pain?

Evidence found by a *Clinical Evidence* synoptic review for non-invasive treatments for simple neck pain is summarized below [Binder, 2004].

Treatments with evidence of benefit

- **Manual treatments** (mobilization and manipulation)
  - Weak evidence of moderate clinical benefit; four systematic reviews and four subsequent randomized controlled trials (RCTs), mainly studying people with chronic neck pain.
- **Some physical treatments** (active physiotherapy, exercise, pulsed electromagnetic field treatment)
  - Systematic reviews have found some evidence of benefit for active physiotherapy and exercise programmes.
  - One RCT provided limited evidence (from subgroup analysis) that pulsed electromagnetic field treatment reduced pain compared with no treatment.
  - A recent RCT with 288 participants concluded that usual physiotherapy may be only marginally better than a brief physiotherapy intervention for neck pain [Klaber Moffett et al, 2005].

Treatments with insufficient evidence to assess effectiveness

- **Drug treatments** (analgesics, nonsteroidal anti-inflammatory drugs (NSAIDs), antidepressants, muscle relaxants)
  - The synoptic review found insufficient evidence on the effects of drugs used to treat neck pain. However, the goals of treatment were not clear. This matters because on the one hand it would reasonable to extrapolate the well known evidence from trials of these drugs for pain relief in other painful somatic conditions. And, on the other hand it would not be reasonable to extrapolate evidence from trials in other conditions if the goals of treatment were to hasten resolution of neck pain.
- **Multidisciplinary (multimodal) treatment**
  - One systematic review of one RCT and two subsequent RCTs provide inadequate evidence on the effects of multidisciplinary (multimodal) treatment.
- **Some physical treatments** (heat, cold, traction, biofeedback, spray and stretch, acupuncture, laser)
  - Several systematic reviews found insufficient evidence to assess the effectiveness of heat, cold, traction, biofeedback, spray and stretch, acupuncture, and laser therapies.
- **Soft collars and special pillows**
  - No systematic reviews or reliable RCTs were found.

Treatments with evidence of lack of benefit

- **Patient education**
  - The synoptic review found two published RCTs of chronic pain and one RCT reported in a thesis and concluded that the evidence showed that patient education provided no benefit.

What is the evidence for treatments of acute whiplash-associated disorder?

Evidence found by a *Clinical Evidence* synoptic review for acute whiplash-associated disorder is summarized below [Binder, 2004].

Treatments with evidence of benefit

- **Early mobilization**
  - One systematic review and two subsequent RCTs provide limited evidence that pain was more effectively reduced by early mobilization than by immobilization or rest plus a collar.
- **Early return to normal activity**
  - One systematic review, which found one RCT, provides limited evidence that advice on early return to normal activities plus anti-inflammatories led to fewer symptoms after 6 months, but had no effect on length of sick-leave or neck range of motion.
- **Electrotherapy**
  - One systematic review, which found one RCT, provides limited evidence that active pulsing electromagnetic field treatment significantly reduced pain compared with sham treatment after 4 weeks, but not after 3 months
- **Multimodal therapy**
  - One systematic review, which found one RCT with 60 participants, compared multimodal treatment (postural training, psychological support, eye fixation exercises, and manual treatment) with physical treatment (electrical, sonic, ultrasound, and transcutaneous electrical nerve stimulation). The group receiving multimodal therapy on average returned to work significantly sooner, and had significantly reduced pain by the end of treatment and after 1 and 6 months.

Treatments with insufficient evidence to assess effectiveness

- **Drug treatments** (analgesics, NSAIDs, antidepressants, muscle relaxants)
  - One Cochrane systematic review found no RCTs of drug treatments specifically for whiplash-associated disorder.
- **Home exercise programmes**
  - One systematic review, which found one RCT, provides limited evidence that instructions to perform an isometric exercise three times a day added no benefit to a regular exercise regime.
  - Summary of evidence on treatments for acute whiplash-associated disorder

N

What is the evidence for treatments of chronic whiplash-associated disorder?

Evidence found by a *Clinical Evidence* synoptic review for chronic whiplash-associated disorder is summarized below [Binder, 2004].

Treatments with evidence of benefit

- **Percutaneous radiofrequency neurotomy**
- Limited supporting evidence is provided by one systematic review, which found one RCT with 24 participants that compared neurotomy with sham treatment. It found that the proportion of people who were free from pain was significantly increased after 27 weeks (58% *cf* 8%), and that the median time for pain to return to at least 50% of baseline levels was significantly increased (263 days *cf* 8 days).

Treatments with insufficient evidence to assess effectiveness

- **Multimodal therapy** (physiotherapy plus cognitive behavioural therapy)
- Limited evidence is provided by one RCT (33 participants), which compared physiotherapy with multimodal treatment (physiotherapy combined with cognitive behavioural therapy. The trial found that significantly more people treated with multimodal therapy were satisfied with pain control at the end of treatment and their ability to perform activities at 3 months. There were no significant differences for disability, pain, or range of movement at the end of treatment or at 3 months.
- **Physiotherapy**
  - See multimodal treatment above.

What is the evidence for treatments of neck pain with radiculopathy?

Evidence found by a *Clinical Evidence* synoptic review for neck pain with radiculopathy is summarized below [Binder, 2004].

Treatments with insufficient evidence to assess effectiveness

- **Drug treatments** (analgesics, NSAIDs, antidepressants, muscle relaxants)
  - One Cochrane systematic review found no RCTs of drug treatments specifically for whiplash-associated disorder.
- **Surgery**
  - Limited evidence is provided by one systematic review, which found one RCT with 81 people who had had severe radicular symptoms for at least 3 months. Surgery was compared with conservative treatment (physiotherapy or immobilisation in a neck collar). There was no significant difference between treatments in symptoms after 1 year.

What is the evidence for acupuncture for chronic neck pain?

- One small, open, uncontrolled trial of acupuncture concluded that it may have some benefit in the short-term treatment of chronic neck pain [Blossfeldt, 2004].

References

NHS staff in England can link, free of charge, from references to full text journals by clicking on [Full text] on the PRODIGY website.

1. Abbasi, K. (2004) Compulsory registration of clinical trials. *British Medical Journal* 329(7467), 637–638.
2. Albert, E., Francis, H. and Elkerton, A. (2003) Whiplash: still a pain in the neck. *Australian Family Physician* 32(3), 152–157.
3. Ariens, G.A., van Mechelen, W., Bongers, P.M. et al (2000) Physical risk factors for neck pain. *Scandinavian Journal of Work, Environment & Health* 26(1), 7–19.
4. Ariens, G.A., Bongers, P.M., Douwes, M. et al (2001) Are neck flexion, neck rotation, and sitting at work risk factors for neck pain? Results of a prospective cohort study. *Occupational & Environmental Medicine* 58(3), 200–207. [Full text]
5. Bandiera, G., Stiell, I.G., Wells, G.A. et al (2003) The Canadian C-spine rule performs better than unstructured physician judgment. *Annals of Emergency Medicine,* 42(3), 395–402.
6. Barry, M. and Jenner, J.R. (1995) Pain in neck, shoulder, and arm. *British Medical Journal* 310(6973), 183–186. [Full text]
7. Binder, A. (2004) *Neck pain.* Clinical Evidence. Volume 11. www.clinicalevidence.com [Accessed: 02/05/2005].
8. Blossfeldt, P. (2004) Acupuncture for chronic neck pain – a cohort study in an NHS pain clinic. *Acupuncture in Medicine* 22(3), 146–151.
9. BNF 49 (2005) *British National Formulary.* 49th edn. London: British Medical Association and Royal Pharmaceutical Society of Great Britain.
10. Bot, S.D., van der Waal, J.M., Terwee, C.B. et al (2005) Incidence and prevalence of complaints of the neck and upper extremity in general practice. *Annals of the Rheumatic Diseases* 64(1), 118–123.
11. Bovim, G., Schrader, H. and Sand, T. (1994) Neck pain in the general population. *Spine* 19(12), 1307–1309.
12. Bunketorp, L., Stener-Victorin, E. and Carlsson, J. (2005) Neck pain and disability following motor vehicle accidents-a cohort study. *European Spine Journal* 14(1), 84–89.
13. Carroll, L.J., Cassidy, J.D. and Cote, P. (2004) Depression as a risk factor for onset of an episode of troublesome neck and low back pain. *Pain* 107(1–2), 134–139.
14. Chan, A.W., Hrobjartsson, A., Haahr, M.T. et al (2004) Empirical evidence for selective reporting of outcomes in randomized trials: comparison of protocols to published articles. *Journal of the American Medical Association* 291(20), 2457–2465. [Full text]
15. Childs, J.D., Fritz, J.M., Piva, S.R. and Whitman, J.M. (2004) Proposal of a classification system for patients with neck pain. *Journal of Orthopaedic & Sports Physical Therapy* 34(11), 686–700.
16. Clinical Standards Advisory Group (1994) *Report on back pain.* London: HMSO.
17. Cote, P., Cassidy, J.D. and Carroll, L. (2001) The treatment of neck and low back pain: who seeks care? Who goes where? *Medical Care* 39(9), 956–967.
18. Cote, P., Cassidy, J.D., Carroll, L.J. and Kristman, V. (2004) The annual incidence and course of neck pain in the general population: a population-based cohort study. *Pain* 112(3), 267–273.
19. CSM (1994) Relative safety of oral non-aspirin NSAIDs. *Current Problems in Pharmacovigilance* 20(Aug), 9–11.
20. CSM (2005a) *Withdrawal of co-proxamol products and interim updated prescribing information.* Committee on Safety of Medicines. www.mca.gov.uk [Accessed: 24/03/2005].
21. CSM (2005b) *Updated advice on the safety of selective cox-2 inhibitors.* Committee on Safety of Medicines. http://medicines.mhra.gov.uk [Accessed: 30/03/2005].
22. De Craen, A.J., Di Giulio, G., Lampe-Schoenmaeckers, J.E. et al (1996) Analgesic efficacy and safety of paracetamol-codeine combinations versus paracetamol alone: a systematic review. *British Medical Journal* 313(7053), 321–325. [Full text]
23. Enthoven, P., Skargen, E. and Oberg, B. (2004) Clinical course in patients seeking primary care for back or neck pain: a prospective 5-year follow-up of outcome and health care consumption with subgroup analysis. *Spine* 29(21), 2458–2465.
24. Epidemiological Study of Dystonia in Europe Collaborative Group. (2000) A prevalence study of primary dystonia in eight European countries. *Journal of Neurology* 247(10), 787–792.
25. Ferrari, R. and Russell, A.J. (1999) Epidemiology of whiplash: an international dilemma. *Annals of the Rheumatic Diseases* 58(1), 1–5. [Full text]
26. Ferrari, R, Russell, A.S., Carroll, L.J. and Cassidy, J.D. (2005) A re-examination of the Whiplash-Associated Disorders (WAD) as a systemic illness. *Annals of the Rheumatic Diseases*(on-line first),
27. Gargan, M.F. and Bannister, G.C. (1994) The rate of recovery following whiplash injury. *European Spine Journal* 3(3), 162–164.
28. Guez, M., Hildingsson, C., Stegmayr, B. and Toolanen, G. (2003) Chronic neck pain of traumatic and non-traumatic origin: a population-based study. *Acta Orthopaedica Scandinavica* 74(5), 576–579.
29. Gun, R.T., Osti, O.L., O'Riordan, A. et al (2005) Risk factors for prolonged disability after whiplash associated disorder: a prospective study. *Spine* 30(4), 386–391.
30. Hackett, G.I., Hudson, M.F., Wylie, J.B. et al (1987) Evaluation of the efficacy and acceptability to patients of a physiotherapist working in a health centre. *British Medical Journal Clinical Research Edition* 294(6563), 24–26.

N

31. Hartling, L., Brison, R.J., Ardern, C. and Pickett, W. (2001) Prognostic value of the Quebec classification of whiplash-associated disorders. *Spine* **26**(1), 36–41.
32. Henry, D., Lim, L.L., Garcia-Rodriguez, L.A. et al (1996) Variability in risk of gastrointestinal complications with individual non-steroidal anti-inflammatory drugs: results of a collaborative meta-analysis. *British Medical Journal* **312**(7046), 1563–1566. [Full text]
33. Hernández-Diaz, S. and Rodriguez, L.A. (2000) Association between nonsteroidal anti-inflammatory drugs and upper gastrointestinal tract bleeding/ perforation: an overview of epidemiologic studies published in the 1990s. *Archives of Internal Medicine* **160**(14), 2093–2099. [Full text]
34. Hernández-Diaz, S., Werler, M.M., Walker, A.M. and Mitchell, A.A. (2000) Folic acid antagonists during pregnancy and the risk of birth defects. *New England Journal of Medicine* **343**(22), 1608–1614. [Full text]
35. Hill, J., Lewis, M., Papageorgiou, A.C. et al (2004) Predicting persistent neck pain: a 1-year follow-up of a population cohort. *Spine* **29**(15), 1648–1654.
36. Hopayian, K. (2001) The need for caution in interpreting high quality systematic reviews. *British Medical Journal* **323**(7314), 681–684. [Full text]
37. Hoving, J.L., Gross, A.R., Gasner, D. et al (2001) A critical appraisal of review articles on the effectiveness of conservative treatment for neck pain. *Spine* **26**(2), 196–205.
38. Hoving, J.L., O'Leary, E.F., Niere, K.R. et al (2003) Validity of the neck disability index, Northwick Park neck pain questionnaire, and problem elicitation technique for measuring disability associated with whiplash-associated disorders. *Pain* **102**(3), 273–281.
39. Hoving, J.L., de Vet, H.C.W., Twisk, J.W.R. et al (2004) Prognostic factors for neck pain in general practice. *Pain* **110**(3), 639–645.
40. Jones, B., Jarvis, P., Lewis, J.A. and Ebbutt, A.F. (1996) Trials to assess equivalence: the importance of rigorous methods. *British Medical Journal* **313**(7048), 36–39. [Full text]
41. Kivioja, J., Sjalin, M. and Lindgren, U. (2004) Psychiatric morbidity in patients with chronic whiplash-associated disorder. *Spine* **29**(11), 1235–1239.
42. Klaber Moffett, J.A., Jackson, D.A., Richmond, S. et al (2005) Randomised trial of a brief physiotherapy intervention compared with usual physiotherapy for neck pain patients: outcomes and patients' preference. *British Medical Journal* **330**(7482), 75.
43. Kriss, T.C. and Kriss, V.M. (2000) Neck pain. Primary care work-up of acute and chronic symptoms. *Geriatrics* **55**(1), 47–48. [Full text]
44. Livingston, M. (2000) Whiplash injury: why are we achieving so little? *Journal of the Royal Society of Medicine* **93**(10), 526–529.
45. McClune, T., Burton, A.K. and Waddell, G. (2002) Whiplash associated disorders: a review of the literature to guide patient information and advice. *Emergency Medicine Journal* **19**(6), 499–506.
46. McQuay, H.J. and Moore, R.A. (1997) Antidepressants and chronic pain. *British Medical Journal* **314**(7083), 763–764. [Full text]
47. MeReC (1993) Combination analgesics. *MeReC Bulletin* **4**(12), 45–48.
48. Moore, R.A. and McQuay, H.J. (1997) Single-patient data meta-analysis of 3453 postoperative patients: oral tramadol versus placebo, codeine and combination analgesics. *Pain* **69**(3), 287–294.
49. Moore, A., Collins, S., Carroll, D. and McQuay, H. (1997) Paracetamol with and without codeine in acute pain: a quantitative systematic review. *Pain* **70**(2–3), 193–201.
50. Myles, P.S., Troedel, S., Boquest, M. and Reeves, M. (1999) The pain visual analog scale: is it linear or nonlinear? *Anesthesia & Analgesia* **89**(6), 1517–1520.
51. Nakashima, K., Kusumi, M., Inoue, Y. and Takahashi, K. (1995) Prevalence of focal dystonias in the western area of Tottori Prefecture in Japan. *Movement Disorders* **10**(4), 440–443.
52. NICE (2001) *Guidance on the use of cyclo-oxygenase (Cox) II selective inhibitors, celecoxib, rofecoxib, meloxicam and etodolac for osteoarthritis and rheumatoid arthritis*. Technology appraisal no. 27. National Institute for Health and Clinical Excellence. www.nice.org.uk [Accessed: 16/10/2003].
53. NZGG (2004) *New Zealand acute low back pain guide*. New Zealand Guidelines Group. www.nzgg.org.nz [Accessed: 30/03/2005].
54. Obelieniene, D., Schrader, H., Bovim, G. et al (1999) Pain after whiplash: a prospective controlled inception cohort study. *Journal of Neurology, Neurosurgery & Psychiatry* **66**(3), 279–283. [Full text]
55. Pickin, M. (2005) *Personal communication. The use of diazepam in neck pain*. Consultant orthopaedic physician, Doncaster Royal Infirmary: Doncaster.
56. Pietrobon, R., Coeytaux, R.R., Carey, T.S. et al (2002) Standard scales for measurement of functional outcome for cervical pain or dysfunction: a systematic review. *Spine* **27**(5), 515–522.
57. Rostom, A., Wells, G., Tugwell, P. et al (2002) *Prevention of NSAID-induced gastroduodenal ulcers (Cochrane Review)*. The Cochrane Library. Issue 4. Chichester, UK: John Wiley & Sons, Ltd. www.nelh.nhs.uk/cochrane.asp [Accessed: 04/04/ 2005]. [Full text]
58. Royal College of Radiologists (2003) *Making the best use of a department of clinical radiology*. 5th edn. London: Royal College of Radiologists.
59. Scholten-Peeters, G.G.M., Verhagen, A.P., Bekkering, G.E. et al (2003) Prognostic factors of whiplash-associated disorders: a systematic review of prospective cohort studies. *Pain* **104**(1–2), 303–322.
60. SIGN (2000) *Management of early rheumatoid arthritis*. Report no. 48. Scottish Intercollegiate Guidelines Network. www.sign.ac.uk [Accessed: 01/ 04/2002].
61. Stiell, I.G., Clement, C.M., McKnight, R.D. et al (2003) The Canadian C-spine rule versus the NEXUS low-risk criteria in patients with trauma. *New England Journal of Medicine* **349**(26), 2510–2518. [Full text]
62. Suissa, S. (2003) Risk factors of poor prognosis after whiplash injury. *Pain Research & Management* **8**(2), 69–75.
63. Urwin, M., Symmons, D., Allison, T. et al (1998) Estimating the burden of musculoskeletal disorders in the community: the comparative prevalence of symptoms at different anatomical sites, and the relation to social deprivation. *Annals of the Rheumatic Diseases* **57**(11), 649–655. [Full text]
64. Vallee, J.N., Feydy, A., Carlier, R.Y. et al (2001) Chronic cervical radiculopathy: lateral-approach periradicular corticosteroid injection. *Radiology* **218**(3), 886–892.
65. Virani, S.N., Ferrari, R. and Russell, A.S. (2001) Physician resistance to the late whiplash syndrome. *Journal of Rheumatology* **28**(9), 2096–2099.
66. Von Korff, M., Crane, P., Lane, M. et al (2005) Chronic spinal pain and physical-mental comorbidity in the United States: results from the national comorbidity survey replication. *Pain* **113**(3), 331–339.

67. Waddell, G., McIntosh, A., Hutchinson, A. et al (1999) *Low back pain evidence review*. London: Royal College of General Practitioners.
68. Wainner, R.S. and Gill, H. (2000) Diagnosis and nonoperative management of cervical radiculopathy. *Journal of Orthopaedic & Sports Physical Therapy* 30(12), 728–744.
69. York University (2003) *Neck pain and office work*. York University. www.yorku.ca/dohs/ergonomics/neck.htm [Accessed: 30/03/2005].

N

PRODIGY GUIDANCE

Nonsteroidal anti-inflammatory drugs (NSAIDs)

Last revised in July 2005
www.prodigy.nhs.uk/guidance.asp?gt=NSAIDs

Applies to people over the age of 12 years

This guidance outlines the factors that need to be considered in the initial selection and maintenance of prescribing a nonsteroidal anti-inflammatory drug (NSAID). The document also compares and contrasts the profiles of standard NSAIDs with the newer cyclo-oxygenase (COX)-2 selective NSAIDs.
Note: the role of NSAIDs should be considered in the wider context of pain management. Long-term use of NSAIDs should ideally be avoided unless an ongoing anti-inflammatory effect is required and this is clinically apparent from NSAID use.

Extended Information

Management issues

- What types of nonsteroidal anti-inflammatory drugs are there? p.1305
- Gastrointestinal adverse effects and NSAIDs p.1305
- Cardiovascular disease and NSAIDs p.1307
- Withdrawal of rofecoxib and suspension of valdecoxib p.1308
- Prescribing an NSAID p.1309

What types of nonsteroidal anti-inflammatory drugs are there?

- **Nonsteroidal anti-inflammatory drugs (NSAIDs) act by inhibiting cyclo-oxygenase (COX) pathways.** There are at least two isoforms of cyclo-oxygenase:
  - COX-1 produces prostaglandins that help to maintain gastric mucosal integrity.
  - COX-2 produces prostaglandins that mediate pain and inflammation.
- The anti-inflammatory effect of NSAIDs is considered to be due to inhibition of COX-2.
- **Aspirin** is now mainly used in low-dose form, for prophylaxis against myocardial infarction (MI), and is therefore often referred to separately from NSAIDs. Low-dose aspirin is a potent and irreversible inhibitor of COX-1, and also has some COX-2 activity.
- **NSAIDs can be classified according to their relative effects on COX-1 and COX-2,** and a variety of formulations (e.g. tablets, suppositories, and topical preparations) are available.
- **Standard NSAIDs** represent the older NSAIDs that inhibit both COX-1 and COX-2. They were not developed to be pathway-selective, although in practice they do differ in pathway selectivity [Warner et al, 1999].
- **COX-2 selective NSAIDS** are difficult to classify because different assay techniques have found a wide variation in reported COX-2 selectivity. The National Institute for Clinical Excellence (NICE) identifies etodolac, meloxicam, and the coxibs (celecoxib, etoricoxib, rofecoxib [withdrawn], and valdecoxib [suspended]) as being COX-2 selective inhibitors [NICE, 2003].
  - Coxibs therefore refer to the COX-2 selective agents that have been most recently developed.

Gastrointestinal adverse effects and NSAIDs

What is the risk of a gastrointestinal adverse effect for someone taking an NSAID?

- It is estimated that a serious gastrointestinal (GI) complication (e.g. perforated ulcer, haematemesis, or gastric outlet obstruction) occurs in 13 out of every 1000 people with rheumatoid arthritis (RA) who take NSAIDs for a year [SIGN, 2000].
- **NSAID use is associated with an increased risk of GI bleeding** in people not considered to be at high risk. This is about a fivefold increased risk for people taking NSAIDs for musculoskeletal pain [North of England Dyspepsia Guideline Development Group, 2004].

How do the gastrointestinal adverse effects of NSAIDs compare?

Gastrointestinal adverse effects are a particular concern with NSAIDs and the risk is generally dose-dependent.

Standard NSAIDs

- **Standard NSAIDs** vary in their risk of causing serious GI adverse effects. The Committee on Safety of Medicines (CSM) created three categories of NSAID risk [CSM, 1994] and has since confirmed that they still apply, after reassessment with further evidence [CSM, 2002]. Other researchers have reported similar findings [Henry et al, 1996]. The three categories of risk are:
  - Lowest risk: ibuprofen (but serious and fatal GI adverse effects have still been reported).
  - Intermediate risk: diclofenac, naproxen, ketoprofen, piroxicam, and indometacin.
  - Highest risk: azapropazone.

COX-2 selective NSAIDs

- **COX-2 selective NSAIDs in theory should be associated with a lower risk of GI adverse events.** However, the CSM has confirmed that COX-2 selective NSAIDs have also been associated with serious and fatal GI adverse reactions [CSM, 2003].
- Trial data have found that the risk of GI adverse effects seems to be reduced with increasing COX-2 selectivity [Bombardier et al, 2000; Silverstein et al, 2000; Laine et al, 2003]. However, there has been much debate and critique concerning these trials in the medical literature [Juni et al, 2002].
- **A systematic review found celecoxib to have statistically significant improvement in GI safety and tolerability** compared with diclofenac, naproxen, and ibuprofen [Deeks et al, 2002]. Others have analysed the data and concluded that there is no evidence that in the long term celecoxib is more beneficial than diclofenac in avoiding severe GI complications [Juni et al, 2003].

N

- **The European Committee for Proprietary Medicinal Products has recently reviewed the GI safety of coxibs** and concluded that:
  - The overall benefit/risk profile of these agents is favourable.
  - No statistically significant and consistent gastrointestinal benefit has been shown in comparison with standard NSAIDs.
- Celecoxib was compared with diclofenac plus omeprazole in a prospective randomized controlled trial of 287 people who had a negative test for *Helicobacter pylori* and had healed ulcers that had bled. The probability of recurrent bleeding did not differ significantly between the two groups at 6 months, being 4.9% and 6.4% respectively [Chan et al, 2002b].

Etodolac and meloxicam

- **There are insufficient data of medium- to long-term duration** to know whether or not etodolac or meloxicam are associated with a possible increased risk of gastrointestinal events. Note: an absence of evidence does not equate to evidence that there is no risk of adverse events.
- The available controlled clinical trials are not of sufficient duration to enable adequate interpretation about the gastrointestinal safety of etodolac or meloxicam. There is a lack of comparative data to compare their gastrointestinal safety to other standard or COX-2 selective NSAIDs.
- Two primary-care prescription-event monitoring studies comparing the rate of GI adverse effects of meloxicam with celecoxib and rofecoxib found that these coxibs were found to be less likely to cause upper-GI events. However, these results have to be interpreted with caution, because primary-care prescription-event monitoring studies have many limitations [Pharmaceutical Journal, 2002; Layton et al, 2003].

N

Aspirin

- **Aspirin use is also associated with adverse GI effects.**
- A meta-analysis involving over 66,000 people found that the risk of GI bleeding for those taking long-term, low-dose aspirin was double the risk of those who did not take aspirin [Derry and Loke, 2000].
- Enteric-coated and buffered formulations of aspirin do not seem to reduce the risk of major upper-GI bleeding [Kelly et al, 1996].
- There is a twofold increased risk of GI bleeding in people taking low-dose aspirin for secondary prevention of cardiovascular disease who are not considered to be at high risk of GI complications [North of England Dyspepsia Guideline Development Group, 2004].

Who is at risk of developing serious NSAID-induced gastrointestinal adverse effects?

- **People at high risk of developing serious NSAID-induced GI adverse events** have one or more of the following risk factors [NICE, 2001]:
  - Age of 65 years and over.
  - Previous history of gastroduodenal ulcer, GI bleeding, or gastroduodenal perforation.
  - Concomitant use of medications that are known to increase the likelihood of upper-GI adverse events (e.g. anticoagulants, aspirin [even low-dose], and corticosteroids).
  - Presence of serious comorbidity, such as cardiovascular disease, renal or hepatic impairment, diabetes, or hypertension.
  - Requirement for a prolonged duration of NSAID use.
  - Use of the maximum recommended doses of NSAIDs.
- **Additional risk factors** for developing NSAID-induced GI adverse events have also been identified, including:
  - The presence of *Helicobacter pylori* infection — try to eradicate it [Chan et al, 2002a].
  - Excessive alcohol use.
  - Heavy smoking.

How can I lower the chances of adverse gastrointestinal effects?

In general

- **Use paracetamol with or without codeine** instead of an NSAID.
- **Use only one NSAID at a time;** in particular, concomitant use of an NSAID with low-dose aspirin substantially increases GI risk and should be avoided where possible [CSM, 2003]. Note: low-dose aspirin use is always the priority over use of an NSAID.
- **Always use the lowest NSAID dosage compatible with symptom relief** [SIGN, 2000].

In someone at high risk of peptic ulceration or bleeding

- **Options to minimize adverse GI events in someone at high risk for whom NSAID continuation is necessary include:**
  - A gastroprotective agent with a standard NSAID.
  - A COX-2 selective NSAID alone. Note: coxibs are not preferred with low-dose aspirin.

[NICE, 2004]

What gastroprotective agents are available and are they effective?

- **Proton-pump inhibitors (PPIs) are generally considered to be the preferred choice for gastroprotection;** they are effective and well tolerated.
  - PPIs reduce the risk of endoscopic gastric ulcers by 63% and the risk of duodenal ulcers by 81% [Rostom et al, 2004].
- **Misoprostol at low dose is less effective than proton PPIs at reducing the incidence of endoscopically detected lesions, and has greater adverse effects** [NICE, 2004].
  - Misoprostol reduces the risk of endoscopic gastric ulcers by 75% and the risk of duodenal ulcers by 78% in people taking an NSAID [Rostom et al, 2004].
  - Studied dosages have ranged from 400 to 800 micrograms daily. The 800-microgram daily dosage is associated with the lowest risk of *gastric* ulceration. There is no statistical difference between the higher and lower daily dosage for risk of *duodenal* ulcer.
  - One large study found that misoprostol 800 micrograms daily reduced the risk of NSAID-induced ulcer complications by 40% [Silverstein et al, 1995].
  - Misoprostol is poorly tolerated because of its GI adverse effects, particularly diarrhoea.
- **H_2-receptor antagonists (H_2RAs) at standard dosages reduce the risk of duodenal ulceration, and there is evidence that double dosages reduce the risk of gastric ulceration** [Rostom et al, 2004]. Note: no H_2RAs are currently licensed for the prevention of NSAID-induced gastric ulceration, and gastric ulcers are more commonly caused by NSAIDs.
  - H_2RAs at standard dosages (equivalent to ranitidine 150 mg twice-daily) reduce the risk of endoscopic duodenal ulcers by 64%, but do not reduce the risk of gastric ulceration [Rostom et al, 2004].
  - There is some evidence that double dosages of H_2RAs may reduce the risk of gastric ulceration; pooled results from three trials (298 people) found a statistically significant 56% reduction in risk, although the confidence interval was wide [Rostom et al, 2004].
  - There are no data regarding the effectiveness of H_2RAs at reducing ulcer complications.

- A recently published systematic review [Hooper et al, 2004] has reported that:
  - **PPIs,** compared with placebo, may reduce the risk of symptomatic ulcers (RR 0.09, 95% CI 0.02 to 0.47).
  - **Misoprostol,** compared with placebo, reduces the risk of serious gastrointestinal complications (0.57, 95% CI 0.36 to 0.91) and symptomatic ulcers (0.36, 95% CI 0.20 to 0.67).
  - **H_2RAs** show no evidence of effectiveness for any primary outcomes; more data are needed.
- **Only misoprostol, omeprazole, lansoprazole, pantoprazole, and esomeprazole are currently licensed** for both prophylaxis and healing of NSAID-associated gastric and duodenal ulcer disease [BNF 48, 2004].

How should I manage someone taking an NSAID who experiences adverse gastrointestinal effects?

- For people taking an NSAID who are experiencing dyspepsia symptoms, see the PRODIGY guidance *Dyspepsia — symptoms (uninvestigated by endoscopy).*
- For people who have a proven NSAID-associated peptic ulcer, see the PRODIGY guidance *Dyspepsia — proven DU, GU, or NSAID-associated ulcer.*

Cardiovascular disease and NSAIDs

Do COX-2 selective NSAIDs increase the risk of cardiovascular disease?

- Rofecoxib has been withdrawn in the UK because of concerns raised about its cardiovascular safety. See *What led to the withdrawal of rofecoxib?* for further information.
- In the Celecoxib Long-term Arthritis Safety Study (CLASS; n = 8059 patients) there was no statistically significant difference in cardiovascular event rates between individuals in the celecoxib and standard NSAID groups [Silverstein et al, 2000].
- However, most people in the CLASS trial had osteoarthritis and were not considered to be at as high a risk of cardiovascular disease. In contrast, the Vioxx Gastrointestinal Outcomes Research Study (VIGOR) investigated the effect of rofecoxib in people with RA, and this population is now recognised at being strongly associated with a risk of cardiovascular disease [van Doornum et al, 2002].
- Following a European-wide review of the data, the Committee on Safety of Medicines (CSM) has recently advised that [CSM, 2005]:
  - The evidence suggests that coxibs, as a class, may cause an increased risk of thrombotic events (e.g. myocardial infarction and stroke) compared with placebo and some NSAIDs.
  - The risk may increase with dose and duration of exposure.
- It is not possible to quantify the risk precisely, but it is considered unlikely to exceed one extra serious thrombotic event per 100 patient years, over the rate for no treatment [CSM, 2005].
- The increased risk seems to be higher in those who already have cardiovascular disease, therefore [CSM, 2005; EMEA, 2005]:
  - Coxibs are contraindicated in people with established ischaemic heart disease, cerebrovascular disease, peripheral arterial disease, and in people with moderate or severe heart failure.
  - In people with risk factors for heart disease (e.g. diabetes, hypertension, hyperlipidaemia, obesity, smoking) the balance of gastrointestinal and cardiovascular risk should be considered before prescribing a coxib.
  - People requiring low dose aspirin should generally not be prescribed a coxib because gastrointestinal benefit has not been clearly demonstrated in this group.
- For both etodolac and meloxicam, there are insufficient data of medium- to long-term duration to know whether or not they are associated with a possible increased risk of cardiovascular events. Note: an absence of evidence does not equate to evidence that there is no risk of adverse events.

Do standard NSAIDs affect the risk of cardiovascular disease?

- **There is no convincing evidence from epidemiological studies that standard NSAIDs protect against cardiovascular events** [Nurmohamed et al, 2002].
  - A prospective population-based cohort study of about 165,000 postmenopausal women found that the long-term use of standard NSAIDs was not associated with a protective effect against the risk of a first MI [Garcia Rodriguez et al, 2000].
  - The same researchers also conducted a case-control study of 4,975 people with a history of an MI matched to 20,000 randomly sampled controls and found no evidence to support a protective effect of NSAIDs (including ibuprofen) against further MI [Garcia Rodriguez et al, 2004].
  - In contrast, a case-control study involving 1,055 people who had a first nonfatal MI suggested that NSAID use seems to reduce the risk of MI in people *not* taking prophylactic aspirin, but does not seem to provide any extra protection to aspirin users [Kimmel et al, 2004].
- **A recent UK case-control study suggested that standard NSAIDs may increase the risk of myocardial infarction** [Hippisley-Cox and Coupland, 2005].
  - Ibuprofen and diclofenac seemed to have a higher increased risk than naproxen.
  - However, the usage of naproxen in this study was much smaller, making it hard to truly compare the relative risks.
- **The European Medicines Agency (EMEA) is currently reviewing the cardiovascular safety of standard NSAIDs** [EMEA, 2005; MHRA, 2005b].
  - The new study [Hippisley-Cox and Coupland, 2005] is being reviewed along with other evidence on this issue (some studies have *not* shown an increased risk of myocardial infarction with standard NSAIDs).
  - Further advice will be issued by the EMEA once the review has concluded.

Does ibuprofen reduce the cardioprotective effect of low-dose aspirin?

- There is concern that ibuprofen may reduce the cardioprotective effect of low-dose aspirin in people with cardiovascular disease by antagonizing the irreversible platelet inhibition induced by aspirin [British Heart Foundation, 2002; NHS CRD, 2003].
- Studies looking at concomitant use of various NSAIDs with aspirin suggest [Catella-Lawson et al, 2001; MacDonald and Wei, 2003]:
  - The risk of an interaction between ibuprofen and aspirin may be more likely when ibuprofen is taken regularly [Catella-Lawson et al, 2001; Kimmel et al, 2004].
  - The frequency of NSAID use may be an important factor [Kurth et al, 2003].
- In contrast, other studies have found *no increase* in risk of death among ibuprofen and aspirin users compared with aspirin users only [Curtis et al, 2003; Garcia Rodriguez et al, 2004; Patel and Goldberg, 2004; Hippisley-Cox and Coupland, 2005].

- Although the interaction of ibuprofen with aspirin is potentially clinically important, the current level of evidence is not sufficient to make clear recommendations for or against the use of concomitant ibuprofen for people requiring prophylactic low-dose aspirin. Therefore:
  - **It would seem prudent to avoid concomitant low-dose aspirin with regular ibuprofen in people with cardiovascular disease risk factors,** including diabetes, hyperlipidaemia, and obesity.
  - Ibuprofen used occasionally is considered to pose less of a risk than regular ibuprofen for people also taking low-dose aspirin.

How should someone taking low-dose aspirin and an NSAID be managed?

- **There is at present no convincing evidence that a COX-2 selective NSAID offers a statistically significant reduction in the risk of GI events for people taking low-dose aspirin compared with a standard NSAID** [Nurmohamed et al, 2002].
  - In people taking aspirin, incidence rates of upper-GI complications were not significantly different when celecoxib was compared with other NSAIDs [Silverstein et al, 2000]. However, this study was not powered to investigate this specific outcome.
  - Sub-group analysis of data in a systematic review found a statistically significant reduction in the incidence of ulcers detected by *endoscopy* in those taking celecoxib and aspirin compared with standard NSAIDs and aspirin [Deeks et al, 2002].
  - A double-blind RCT over 12 weeks found that the risk of ulcers was not significantly less when rofecoxib combined with aspirin was compared with ibuprofen alone [Laine et al, 2004]. Rofecoxib 25 mg together with low-dose aspirin resulted in an increased rate of endoscopic ulceration compared with low-dose aspirin use alone.
- **Coxibs are *not* preferred to other NSAIDs for someone taking aspirin for prevention of cardiovascular events,** because:
  - There is a small increased risk of cardiovascular disease with coxibs, which seems to be higher in those who already have cardiovascular disease [ADRAC, 2003; CSM, 2005].
  - The advantage of a lower risk of GI adverse events is reduced when COX-2 selective agents are prescribed with low-dose aspirin [Laine et al, 2004].
  - There is no convincing evidence that a COX-2 selective agent compared with a standard NSAID offers statistically significant benefit [Nurmohamed et al, 2002].
- **If a person is at high risk of NSAID-induced GI adverse effects** and requires concomitant use of low-dose aspirin prophylaxis and an NSAID:
  - Do not stop the aspirin.
  - Re-consider the use of a paracetamol with or without codeine.
  - If an NSAID is considered necessary, a cautious approach is to prescribe an NSAID with less COX-2 selectivity (e.g. naproxen — but not ibuprofen) together with a gastroprotective agent.
    - **It would seem prudent to avoid concomitant use of aspirin with ibuprofen** until conclusive evidence becomes available to prove otherwise, as there remains uncertainty about whether ibuprofen can negate the effect of aspirin.

N

How should someone who has hypertension and who is taking an NSAID be managed?

- Someone with hypertension should be monitored regularly if an NSAID is considered necessary, as these drugs may be associated with worsening of hypertension and oedema [Wolfe et al, 2004].
- Consider switching from a coxib to a standard NSAID (with a gastroprotective agent if there is a history of peptic ulceration) if hypertension is difficult to control *and* an NSAID is necessary [Wolfe et al, 2004].
- In addition, etoricoxib should not be started in people with uncontrolled hypertension, and careful blood pressure monitoring is advised [CSM, 2005]. (Etoricoxib may be associated with more frequent and severe effects on blood pressure than other coxibs and NSAIDs, particularly at high doses.)

Withdrawal of rofecoxib and suspension of valdecoxib

What led to the withdrawal of rofecoxib?

- Evidence has recently emerged of a possible increase in the risk of cardiovascular events with rofecoxib use [CSM, 2004].
  - This has resulted in the manufacturer's voluntary worldwide withdrawal of the drug.
  - The Committee on Safety of Medicines (CSM) and the Medicines and Healthcare products Regulatory Agency (MHRA) have confirmed that rofecoxib will no longer be available in the UK because of its cardiovascular safety.
- The Vioxx Gastrointestinal Outcomes Research (VIGOR) study, a large (8076 patients), multicentre, randomized controlled trial (RCT), found that the relative risk of developing a confirmed thrombotic cardiovascular event with rofecoxib compared with naproxen was 2.38 (95% CI 1.39 to 4.00, $p = 0.002$) [Bombardier et al, 2000].
- A retrospective cohort study assessed the occurrence of serious coronary heart disease (CHD) in about 175,000 people on different NSAIDs and compared this with the occurrence in over 200,000 non-users of NSAIDs. The study found that dosages of rofecoxib greater than 25 mg were associated with a higher risk of CHD than were dosages of 25 mg or less, and found no increased risk of CHD among users of other NSAIDs, including celecoxib [Ray et al, 2002].
- A matched case-control study of 54,475 people aged 65 years or older found that rofecoxib was associated with an increased risk of acute MI when compared with celecoxib and not using an NSAID. Rofecoxib doses greater than 25 mg were associated with a higher risk than were lower doses, but this risk was elevated in the first 90 days of use only [Solomon et al, 2004].
- A multicentre, randomized, placebo-controlled, double-blind trial showed an increased risk of confirmed serious thrombotic events (including MI and stroke) with rofecoxib compared with placebo, after 18 months use [CSM, 2004]. The absolute event rates were about:
  - 3 per 400 person-years for placebo
  - 6 per 400 person-years for rofecoxib

What led to the suspension of valdecoxib

- Compared with other coxib COX-2 inhibitors, valdecoxib is associated with a higher rate of serious, potentially fatal, skin reactions including Stevens-Johnson Syndrome (SJS) and toxic epidermal necrolysis (TEN).
- Following increasing concerns about the risk of serious skin reactions (in addition to the established class

evidence of cardiovascular disease), the manufacturer's have made a voluntary suspension of the sales and marketing of valdecoxib in Europe and the US. MHRA, 2005a]

Prescribing an NSAID

What should I be aware of when initiating treatment?

- **Comorbidity** needs to be considered when prescribing NSAIDs. See *When should NSAIDs be avoided?*
- **Prescribe with caution in someone with underlying GI disease or risk factors for cardiovascular disease** [EMEA, 2004; CSM, 2005].
- **Assess the cardiovascular risk profile** [ADRAC, 2003] of someone before prescribing an NSAID — if the person has risk factors for heart disease (e.g. diabetes, hypertension, hyperlipidaemia, obesity, smoking), a coxib may be a *less preferred* option compared with a standard NSAID.
- **Assess the presence of high-risk factors for serious NSAID-induced GI adverse events.** Check for over-the-counter use of aspirin and ibuprofen, and warn against *regular* use of this specific combination together. See *How are gastrointestinal adverse effect minimized?* for more information.
- **Certain populations (e.g. the elderly and people with renal, hepatic, or cardiac impairment) are at increased risk of the serious consequences of adverse events.** If an NSAID is considered necessary and initiated, keep the dose as low as possible.
- **In someone with a history of chronic or allergic skin conditions,** a standard NSAID may be preferred to a coxib, as coxibs have rarely been reported to be associated with an increased risk of serious skin reactions [EMEA, 2004]. The majority of cases seem to occur in the first month of use [EMEA, 2005].
- Note: little is still known about the long-term effects and safety of COX-2 selective NSAIDs.

Which NSAID is recommended in which clinical situation?

Table 1 summarizes the PRODIGY recommendations for the NSAID to use in specific clinical situations. These recommendations may change as data from trials in progress are published.

When should NSAIDs be avoided?

- **Allergy to NSAIDs.** Do not prescribe NSAIDs for anyone who has previously experienced bronchospasm, angioedema, urticaria, rhinitis, or a severe skin reaction after administration of aspirin or other NSAIDs.
- **Peptic ulceration or gastrointestinal bleeding.**
  - **Standard NSAIDs** (as well as etodolac and meloxicam) are contraindicated in someone with previous or active peptic ulceration or gastrointestinal (GI) bleeding. However, standard NSAIDs given with gastroprotection may be used in someone with a past history of peptic ulceration or GI bleeding.
  - **Coxibs** are contraindicated in people with active peptic ulceration or GI bleeding.
- **People who are at high risk of developing GI toxicity** should avoid using an NSAID if possible, or they should be closely monitored if an NSAID is considered essential. See *Who is at risk of developing serious NSAID-induced gastrointestinal adverse effects?*
- **Coxibs are also contraindicated in:**
  - Established ischaemic heart disease, cerebrovascular disease, or peripheral arterial disease. (Small increased risk of thrombotic events.)
  - Moderate or severe heart failure

Table 1: Which NSAID in which clinical situation?

At high risk of NSAID-induced GI adverse effect**	Needs aspirin for anti-platelet use	Cardiovascular disease present	Preferred management options
No	No	No	Ibuprofen, diclofenac, or naproxen.
Yes	No	No	Ibuprofen, diclofenac, or naproxen with a gastroprotective agent. Use of celecoxib is an alternative option*.
No	Yes	Yes	Naproxen or diclofenac.
Yes	Yes	Yes	Naproxen or diclofenac with a gastroprotective agent. Note: concomitant use of aspirin with regular ibuprofen is currently best avoided.
No	No	Yes	Ibuprofen, naproxen, or diclofenac.
Yes	No	Yes	Ibuprofen, naproxen, or diclofenac with a gastroprotective agent.

** **People at high risk of developing serious NSAID-induced GI adverse events include those:**
Aged 65 years and over.
With a previous history of gastroduodenal ulcer, GI bleeding, or gastroduodenal perforation.
Using medications concomitantly that are known to increase the likelihood of upper-GI adverse events (e.g. anticoagulants, aspirin — even a low dose— and corticosteroids).
With serious comorbidity, such as cardiovascular disease, renal or hepatic impairment, diabetes, or hypertension.
Who require a prolonged duration of NSAID use.
Who use the maximum recommended doses of NSAIDs.
* COX-2 selective NSAIDs drug prescriptions other than for celecoxib are not included in PRODIGY. Rofecoxib and valdecoxib have recently been withdrawn from the UK market. Etoricoxib is a black-triangle drug that remains under the surveillance of the Committee on Safety of Medicines. It is licensed for use in acute gout and is included in PRODIGY as a second-line option for this. There are no head-to-head controlled trials of etoricoxib with other COX-2 selective NSAIDs and it does not seem to offer any clinical advantage over other drugs included for other musculoskeletal conditions. Parecoxib is also a black-triangle drug licensed for short-term postoperative pain relief, and is only available as an injection. For etodolac and meloxicam, there are insufficient follow-up data of medium- to long-term duration upon which to base recommendations.

- **NSAIDs may worsen asthma, hypertension, renal impairment, or heart failure.**
  - **Asthma:** the Committee on the Safety of Medicines warns that any degree of worsening of asthma may be related to the ingestion of NSAIDs. Someone with asthma should be advised to stop an NSAID if it precipitates an asthma attack.
  - **Hypertension:** monitor blood pressure regularly if an NSAID is considered necessary.
  - **Renal impairment or heart failure:** NSAID prostaglandin inhibition may cause renal function to deteriorate, and there is a risk of oedema (particularly in elderly people). Monitor renal function regularly if an NSAID is considered essential.
- **People requiring low dose aspirin** should generally not be prescribed a coxib because gastrointestinal benefit has not been clearly demonstrated in this group.

Can NSAIDs be used by pregnant or breastfeeding women?

- **Where possible, paracetamol is preferred to an NSAID during pregnancy and breastfeeding.** Experience suggests that paracetamol can be used at any time during pregnancy [NTIS, 2004].
- **During pregnancy, if an NSAID is essential,** ibuprofen is recommended as the NSAID of choice [NTIS, 2004]:
  - The available data do not indicate that exposure to ibuprofen before 30 weeks of pregnancy is associated

N

with an increased risk of malformations or spontaneous abortions [NTIS, 2004].
- In the last trimester (week 30 onwards) chronic NSAID use or high doses should generally be avoided because of the risk of causing premature closure of the ducuts ateriosis, or decreasing amniotic fluid. If treatment with an NSAID is unavoidable, they can be used under specialist supervision, and fetal circulation should be monitored once or twice a week by Doppler ultrasonography [Reuvers, 2001; NTIS, 2004].
- For further information on using NSAIDs during pregnancy, telephone the National Teratology Information Service on 0191 232 1525.

- **During breastfeeding, if an NSAID is essential,** ibuprofen is recommended as the NSAID of choice [Trent Drug Information Services, 2005]:
  - Levels of NSAIDs in milk are generally low as NSAIDs are weak acids and extensively bound to plasma proteins. Short-acting agents and those without active metabolites are preferred, especially in neonates.
  - Levels of ibuprofen in breast milk are negligible.
  - Levels of diclofenac in breast milk are low.
  - Avoid naproxen if possible. It has a longer half-life and a single case of prolonged bleeding time, haemorrhage and acute anaemia has been reported in a neonate whose mother was taking naproxen.
  - There are no data on the use of coxibs during breastfeeding.
  - For further information on using NSAIDs during breastfeeding, see the UK Drugs in Lactation Service website, or telephone 0121 311 1974.

What monitoring is recommended?

- **Consider switching the NSAID for someone who does not respond.** A person who does not respond to one NSAID (at an inflammatory dose) may respond to another. (There is a strong element of individual response to NSAID treatment.) Note: when changing from one NSAID to another, be aware that NSAIDs vary in their risk of causing GI adverse effects.
- **In someone with renal, cardiac, or hepatic impairment,** renal function should be monitored (before and during drug therapy).
  - If there is clinical deterioration, consider discontinuing the NSAID.
  - Both standard NSAIDs and COX-2 selective NSAIDs have been found to be associated with worsening renal function (sodium retention and mild peripheral oedema) [Zhao et al, 2001].
- **Monitor someone with hypertension and/or a history of ischaemic heart disease** — consider discontinuation of the NSAID if there is clinical deterioration in the condition.
- **The risk of adverse effects is dose-related** — review after a dose increase, and consider other therapeutic options if there is no increase in efficacy.
- **Coxibs have been associated with an increased risk of serious skin reactions** [EMEA, 2004]. Consider discontinuing the coxib if there is clinical deterioration; a standard NSAID may be more appropriate.
- **Ask for GI symptoms** in elderly people (especially in the first few weeks), in those taking low-dose aspirin, and in people with a history of GI disease.
- For clinically important drug interactions to monitor, see the section *Which potentially hazardous interactions should be avoided or monitored carefully?*

Which potentially hazardous interactions should be avoided or monitored carefully?

Interactions particularly relevant to primary care include:

- **Selective serotonin reuptake inhibitors (SSRIs) or venlafaxine** — there is an increased risk of bleeding with NSAID use. Note: this has recently been upgraded to a potentially hazardous interaction [BNF 48, 2004]. A study linking hospital-episode data with prescribing data has showed that upper-GI bleeding episodes were considerably increased when SSRIs were combined with NSAIDs or low-dose aspirin [Dalton et al, 2003].
- **Antibiotics (quinolones only)** — there is a possible increased risk of convulsions with NSAID use.
- **Anticoagulants** — there is a possible enhanced anticoagulant effect with NSAID use. If NSAID is still necessary, closely monitor the international normalised ratio (INR) when initiating or changing the dose.
- **Ciclosporin** — there is an increased risk of nephrotoxicity with NSAID use, and serum potassium levels need monitoring. Halve the dose of diclofenac where this is used. Monitor more frequently when NSAIDs are introduced or the dose of NSAIDs is increased. See the separate PRODIGY guidance *Monitoring people on disease-modifying drugs (DMARDs)* for further information.
- **Diuretics** — there is an increased risk of nephrotoxicity and antagonism of the diuretic effect with NSAID use. With potassium-sparing diuretics, NSAIDs possibly increase the risk of hyperkalaemia. Serum potassium levels therefore need monitoring.
- **Lithium** — azapropazone, diclofenac, ibuprofen, indometacin, mefenamic acid, naproxen, parecoxib, piroxicam, and valdecoxib are known to reduce the excretion of lithium (increased risk of toxicity), but all NSAIDs probably have the same effect. Closely monitor lithium levels when an NSAID is introduced or withdrawn.
- **Methotrexate** — excretion is reduced (increased risk of toxicity) with diclofenac, ibuprofen, indometacin, ketoprofen, meloxicam, and naproxen, and the likelihood is that most NSAIDs will probably have this effect on methotrexate. Consider monitoring more frequently when NSAIDs are introduced or the dose of NSAIDs is increased. See the separate PRODIGY guidance *Monitoring people on disease-modifying drugs (DMARDs)* for further information.
- **Phenytoin** — the effects are possibly enhanced, so avoid concomitant use with an NSAID if possible.
- **Sulphonylureas** — the effects are possibly enhanced with NSAID use, so blood glucose needs monitoring.

References

NHS staff in England can link, free of charge, from references to full text journals by clicking on [Full text] on the PRODIGY website.

1. ADRAC (2003) Rofecoxib, celecoxib, and cardiovascular risk. *Australian Adverse Drug Reactions Bulletin* **22**(5), 1.
2. BNF 48 (2004) *British National Formulary.* 48th edn. London: British Medical Association and Royal Pharmaceutical Society of Great Britain.
3. Bombardier, C., Laine, L., Reicin, A. et al (2000) Comparison of upper gastrointestinal toxicity of rofecoxib and naproxen in patients with rheumatoid arthritis. *New England Journal of Medicine* **343**(21), 1520–1528. [Full text]
4. British Heart Foundation (2002) *Aspirin and ibuprofen.* Factfile 11/2002. British Heart Foundation. www.bhf.org.uk [Accessed: 01/12/2002].

5. Catella-Lawson, F., Reilly, M.P., Kapoor, S.C. et al (2001) Cyclooxygenase inhibitors and the antiplatelet effects of aspirin. *New England Journal of Medicine* **345**(25), 1809–1817. [Full text]
6. Chan, F.K., To, K.F., Wu, J.C. et al (2002a) Eradication of Helicobacter pylori and risk of peptic ulcers in patients starting long-term treatment with non-steroidal anti-inflammatory drugs: a randomised trial. *Lancet* **359**(9300), 9–13. [Full text]
7. Chan, F.K.L., Hung, L.C.T., Suen, B.Y. et al (2002b) Celecoxib versus diclofenac and omeprazole in reducing the risk of recurrent ulcer bleeding in patients with arthritis. *New England Journal of Medicine* **347**(26), 2104–2110. [Full text]
8. CSM (1994) Relative safety of oral non-aspirin NSAIDs. *Current Problems in Pharmacovigilance* **20**(Aug), 9–11.
9. CSM (2002) Non-steroidal anti-inflammatory drugs (NSAIDs) and gastrointestinal (GI) safety. *Current Problems in Pharmacovigilance* **28**(Apr), 5.
10. CSM (2003) Reminder: gastrointestinal toxicity and NSAIDs. *Current Problems in Pharmacovigilance* **29**(Sept), 8–9.
11. CSM (2004) *Immediate withdrawal of rofecoxib (vioxx/vioxxacute).* Committee on Safety of Medicines. www.mca.gov.uk/ourwork/monitorsafequalmed/safetymessages/vioxx.pdf [Accessed: 21/10/2004].
12. CSM (2005) *Updated advice on the safety of selective cox-2 inhibitors.* Committee on Safety of Medicines. http://medicines.mhra.gov.uk [Accessed: 30/03/2005].
13. Curtis, J.P., Wang, Y., Portnay, E.L. et al (2003) Aspirin, ibuprofen, and mortality after myocardial infarction: retrospective cohort study. *British Medical Journal* **327**(7427), 1322–1333. [Full text]
14. Dalton, S.O., Johansen, C., Mellemkjaer, L. et al (2003) Use of selective serotonin reuptake inhibitors and risk of upper gastrointestinal tract bleeding: a population-based cohort study. *Archives of Internal Medicine* **163**(1), 59–64. [Full text]
15. Deeks, J.J., Smith, L.A. and Bradley, M.D. (2002) Efficacy, tolerability, and upper gastrointestinal safety of celecoxib for treatment of osteoarthritis and rheumatoid arthritis: systematic review of randomised controlled trials. *British Medical Journal* **325**(7365), 619–627. [Full text]
16. Derry, S. and Loke, Y.K. (2000) Risk of gastrointestinal haemorrhage with long term use of aspirin: meta-analysis. *British Medical Journal* **321**(7270), 1183–1187. [Full text]
17. EMEA (2004) *Committee for proprietary medicinal products (CPMP) opinion following an article 31 referral: for all medicinal products containing celecoxib, etoricoxib, parecoxib, rofecoxib or valdecoxib.* Evaluation of Medicines for Human Use: EMEA/CPMP/1747/04A. The European Agency for the Evaluation of Medicinal Products. www.emea.eu.int [Accessed: 18/08/2004].
18. EMEA (2005) *Press release: European Medicines Agency concludes action on COX-2 inhibitors.* EMEA/207766/2005. European Medicines Agency. www.emea.eu.int [Accessed: 05/07/2005].
19. Garcia Rodriguez, L.A., Varas, C. and Patrono, C. (2000) Differential effects of aspirin and non-aspirin nonsteroidal antiinflammatory drugs in the primary prevention of myocardial infarction in postmenopausal women. *Epidemiology* **11**(4), 382–387.
20. Garcia Rodriguez, L.A.M., Varas-Lorenzo, C., Maguire, A. and Gonzalez-Perez, A. (2004) Nonsteroidal antiinflammatory drugs and the risk of myocardial infarction in the general population. *Circulation* **109**(24), 3000–3006.
21. Henry, D., Lim, L.L., Garcia-Rodriguez, L.A. et al (1996) Variability in risk of gastrointestinal complications with individual non-steroidal anti-inflammatory drugs: results of a collaborative meta-analysis. *British Medical Journal* **312**(7046), 1563–1566. [Full text]
22. Hippisley-Cox, J. and Coupland, C. (2005) Risk of myocardial infarction in patients taking cyclo-oxygenase-2 inhibitors or conventional non-steroidal anti-inflammatory drugs: population based nested case-control analysis. *British Medical Journal* **330**(7504), 1366–1372.
23. Hooper, L., Brown, T.J., Elliott, R. et al (2004) The effectiveness of five strategies for the prevention of gastrointestinal toxicity induced by non-steroidal anti-inflammatory drugs: systematic review. *British Medical Journal* **329**(7472), 948–957.
24. Juni, P., Rutjes, A.W. and Dieppe, P.A. (2002) Are selective COX 2 inhibitors superior to traditional non steroidal anti-inflammatory drugs? *British Medical Journal* **324**(7349), 1287–1288. [erratum appears in: BMJ (2002) 324(7353), 1538]. [Full text]
25. Juni, P., Sterchi, R. and Dieppe, P. (2003) Systematic review of celecoxib for osteoarthritis and rheumatoid arthritis. Problems compromise review's validity. *British Medical Journal* **326**(7384), 334. [Full text]
26. Kelly, J.P., Kaufman, D.W., Jurgelon, J.M. et al (1996) Risk of aspirin-associated major upper-gastrointestinal bleeding with enteric-coated or buffered product. *Lancet* **348**(9039), 1413–1416. [Full text]
27. Kimmel, S.E., Berlin, J.A., Reilly, M. et al (2004) The effects of nonselective non-aspirin non-steroidal anti-inflammatory medications on the risk of nonfatal myocardial infarction and their interaction with aspirin. *Journal of the American College of Cardiology* **43**(6), 985–990.
28. Kurth, T., Glynn, R.J., Walker, A.M. et al (2003) Inhibition of clinical benefits of aspirin on first myocardial infarction by nonsteroidal antiinflammatory drugs. *Circulation* **108**(10), 1191–1195.
29. Laine, L., Connors, L.G., Reicin, A. et al (2003) Serious lower gastrointestinal clinical events with nonselective NSAID or coxib use. *Gastroenterology* **124**(2), 288–292.
30. Laine, L., Maller, E.S., Yu, C. et al (2004) Ulcer formation with low-dose enteric-coated aspirin and the effect of COX-2 selective inhibition: a double-blind trial. *Gastroenterology* **127**(2), 395–402.
31. Layton, D., Hughes, K., Harris, S. and Shakir, S.A. (2003) Comparison of the incidence rates of selected gastrointestinal events reported for patients prescribed celecoxib and meloxicam in general practice in England using prescription-event monitoring (PEM) data. *Rheumatology* **42**(11), 1332–1341. [Full text]
32. MacDonald, T.M. and Wei, L. (2003) Effect of ibuprofen on cardioprotective effect of aspirin. *Lancet* **361**(9357), 573–574. [Full text]
33. MHRA (2005a) *Voluntary suspension of valdecoxib (bextra) by Pfizer Ltd.* Medicines and Healthcare products Regulatory Agency. www.mca.gov.uk/aboutagency/regframework/csm/csmhome.htm [Accessed: 25/04/2005].
34. MHRA (2005b) *Non steroidal anti inflammatory drugs.* Press statement 10th June 2005. Medicines and Healthcare products Regulatory Agency. www.mca.gov.uk/aboutagency/regframework/csm/csmhome.htm [Accessed: 13/07/2005].
35. NHS CRD (2003) *Ibuprofen may reduce the protective benefits of aspirin on cardiovascular disease.* Hitting the Headlines Archive. National Electronic Library for

Health. www.nelh.nhs.uk/hth/ibuprofen.asp [Accessed: 15/07/2005].
36. NICE (2001) *Guidance on the use of cyclo-oxygenase (Cox) II selective inhibitors, celecoxib, rofecoxib, meloxicam and etodolac for osteoarthritis and rheumatoid arthritis*. Technology appraisal no. 27. National Institute for Health and Clinical Excellence. www.nice.org.uk [Accessed: 16/10/2003].
37. NICE (2003) *Final scope: Cox-II inhibitors for the treatment of osteoarthritis and rheumatoid arthritis*. Technology appraisal – In progress. National Institute for Clinical Excellence. www.nice.org.uk [Accessed: 25/08/2004].
38. NICE (2004) *Dyspepsia: management of dyspepsia in adults in primary care: NICE guideline*. Clinical guideline 17. National Institute for Clinical Excellence. www.nice.org.uk [Accessed: 27/08/2004].
39. North of England Dyspepsia Guideline Development Group (2004) *Dyspepsia: managing dyspepsia in adults in primary care: full guideline*. Centre for Health Services Research. www.nice.org.uk [Accessed: 27/08/2004].
40. NTIS (2004) *Use of ibuprofen in pregnancy*. Regional Drug and Therapeutics Service, Newcastle upon Tyne: National Teratology Information Service.
41. Nurmohamed, N.T., van Halm, V.P. and Dijkmans, B.A.C. (2002) Cardiovascular risk profile of antirheumatic agents in patients with osteoarthritis and rheumatoid arthritis. *Drugs* **62**(11), 1599–1609.
42. Patel, T.N. and Goldberg, K.C. (2004) Use of aspirin and ibuprofen compared with aspirin alone and the risk of myocardial infarction. *Archives of Internal Medicine* **164**(8), 852–856. [Full text]
43. Pharmaceutical Journal (2002) Incidence of GI events differs among COX-2s. *Pharmaceutical Journal* **269**(7214), 309.
44. Ray, W.A., Stein, C.M., Daugherty, J.R. et al (2002) COX-2 selective non-steroidal anti-inflammatory drugs and risk of serious coronary heart disease. *Lancet* **360**(9339), 1071–1073. [Full text]
45. Reuvers, M. (2001) Analgesics and antiphlogistics. In: Schaefer, C. (Ed.) *Drugs during pregnancy and lactation*. London: Elsevier. 21–22.
46. Rostom, A., Dube, C., Wells, G. et al (2004) *Prevention of NSAID-induced gastroduodenal ulcers (Cochrane Review)*. The Cochrane Library. Issue 2. Chichester, UK: John Wiley & Sons, Ltd. [Full text]
47. SIGN (2000) *Management of early rheumatoid arthritis*. Report no. 48. Scottish Intercollegiate Guidelines Network. www.sign.ac.uk [Accessed: 01/04/2002].
48. Silverstein, F.E., Graham, D.Y., Senior, J.R. et al (1995) Misoprostol reduces serious gastrointestinal complications in patients with rheumatoid arthritis receiving nonsteroidal anti-inflammatory drugs. A randomized, double-blind, placebo-controlled trial. *Annals of Internal Medicine* **123**(4), 241–249.
49. Silverstein, F.E., Faich, G., Goldstein, J.L. et al (2000) Gastrointestinal toxicity with celecoxib vs nonsteroida anti-inflammatory drugs for osteoarthritis and rheumatoid arthritis: The CLASS Study: a randomized controlled trial. *Journal of the American Medical Association* **284**(10), 1247–1255. [Full text]
50. Solomon, D.H., Schneeweiss, S., Glynn, R.J. et al (2004) Relationship between selective cyclooxygenase-2 inhibitors and acute myocardial infarction in older adults. *Circulation* **109**(17), 2068–2073.
51. Trent Drug Information Services (2005) *Non-steroidal anti-inflammatories*. UK Drugs in Lactation Advisory Service. www.ukmicentral.nhs.uk/drugpreg/nonsteroidalantiinflammatories.asp [Accessed: 13/07/2005].
52. van Doornum, S., McColl, G. and Wicks, I.P. (2002) Accelerated atherosclerosis: an extraarticular feature o rheumatoid arthritis? *Arthritis & Rheumatism* **46**(4), 862–873.
53. Warner, T.D., Giuliano, F., Vojnovic, I. et al (1999) Nonsteroid drug selectivities for cyclo-oxygenase-1 rather than cyclo-oxygenase-2 are associated with human gastrointestinal toxicity: a full in vitro analysis. *Proceedings of the National Academy of Sciences of the United States of America* **96**(13), 7563–7568.
54. Wolfe, F., Zhao, S. and Pettitt, D. (2004) Blood pressure destabilization and edema among 8538 users of celecoxib, rofecoxib, and nonselective nonsteroidal antiinflammatory drugs (NSAID) and nonusers of NSAID receiving ordinary clinical care. *Journal of Rheumatology* **31**(6), 1143–1151.
55. Zhao, S.Z., Reynolds, M.W., Lejkowith, J. et al (2001 A comparison of renal-related adverse drug reactions between rofecoxib and celecoxib, based on the World Health Organization/Uppsala Monitoring Centre safety database. *Clinical Therapeutics* **23**(9), 1478–1491.

PRODIGY GUIDANCE

Obesity

Last revised in July 2002
At the time of print this topic was being updated. The newly revised guidance will be issued on to the website in 2006.
www.prodigy.nhs.uk/guidance.asp?gt=Obesity

Applies to people over the age of 16 years

This guidance is for the management of overweight (BMI greater than 25) or obese (BMI greater than 30) adult men and non-pregnant women.

This guidance does not cover obesity in children, eating disorders, underweight, or the primary prevention of obesity. It does not cover the maintenance of weight loss in detail.

There is separate PRODIGY guidance for *Angina, Hyperlipidaemia, Hypertension, Osteoarthritis,* and *Stopping smoking.*

Goals

The main priority is weight management with risk factor reduction, rather than major weight loss.
The goal is modest sustainable weight loss, e.g. 5–10 kg loss in 3 months.
Ideally, the eventual BMI should be less than 25, but a modest amount of weight loss is the most important goal.

Contents

Scenarios

- BMI 25–26.9 p.1313
- BMI 27–29.9 no comorbidities p.1314
- BMI 27–29.9 plus comorbidities p.1316
- BMI 30 or more p.1318

Extended Information, p. 1320

Which scenario?

BMI 25–26.9: covers the management of overweight people with a BMI in this range. The scenario does not differentiate between people with and without comorbidities because they do not affect the weight management recommendations at these BMIs.
BMI 27–29.9 no comorbidities: covers the management of overweight people with a BMI in this range who do not have relevant comorbidities (i.e. do not have hypertension, hyperlipidaemia, or Type 2 diabetes).
BMI 27–29.9 plus comorbidities: covers the management of overweight people with a BMI in this range who have relevant comorbidities (hypertension, hyperlipidaemia, Type 2 diabetes).
BMI 30 or more: covers the management of obese people with a BMI in this range.

BMI 25–26.9

Which therapy?

Assess motivation to change, and if not motivated advise individual to return when they are ready to alter their lifestyle.
Review drugs that may be aggravating weight problem, e.g. tricyclic antidepressants, sulphonylureas, corticosteroids, valproate.
Manage any additional risk factors and pre-existing conditions, e.g. smoking, hypertension, hyperlipidaemia, diabetes.

- **A 3-month programme of weight reduction should aim for a 5–10 kg weight loss over 3 months or 0.5 kg per** week (combining diet, exercise, and behavioural strategies):
  - Give advice on the importance of weight restraint.
  - **Give advice on a healthy diet** — e.g. calories 1200–1600 kcal per day, moderate fat intake, more fruit and vegetables.
  - **Give advice on physical activity** — e.g. increase walking, housework activities, stair climbing; decrease amount of time sat down; build up exercise programme that person enjoys.
  - **Behaviour therapy as an adjunct** to diet and physical activity may increase weight loss, e.g. cognitive therapies, food diaries and reducing triggers of inappropriate eating, relaxation techniques, mood management.
  - **Provide written advice** (non-drug prescriptions or Patient Information Leaflets).
- **Consider enrolling the person into an organized local weight management programme** (at the general practice, local dietetic department, slimming organization, or self-help group).
- Drug therapy is not recommended at BMIs between 25 and 26.9.

Follow-up advice

- Regular review (e.g. every 2 weeks) is essential for people on an intensive weight management programme. Weight loss of 0.5 kg per week should be aimed for.
- After a 3-month period of weight loss, a 3-month period of weight maintenance should be instigated.

Should I refer or investigate?

Refer?

- **Consider referral to an organized local weight management programme** run at:
  - The general practice (usually by a practice nurse), or
  - The local dietetic department, or
  - A commercial slimming organization , or
  - A self-help group

Investigate?

- Urinalysis for glycosuria — if positive do fasting blood glucose
- Thyroid function tests (see PRODIGY *Hypothyroidism* guidance)
- Serum lipids (see PRODIGY *Hyperlipidaemia* guidance)

Patient information leaflets

The following PILs are available at www.prodigy.nhs.uk

- British Nutrition Foundation
- Exercise - A Summary
- Exercise for Health
- Healthy Eating
- Healthy Eating - A Summary
- Healthy Lifestyle - Five Choices
- Medicines - Name Changes of Medicines
- Obesity and Overweight
- Obesity and Overweight - A Summary
- Orlistat - Help With Weight Loss
- Sibutramine - Help With Weight Loss
- TOAST - The Obesity Awareness and Solutions Trust
- Weight Reduction - A Summary
- Weight Reduction - How to Lose Weight

Shared decision making

- You are classed as overweight (but not obese).
- Health risks increase the more overweight you become.
- If you lose 5–10 kg, you will greatly reduce your increased health risks.
- For some people, it is more realistic to keep to your present weight, but to take action to prevent further weight gain.
- **A healthy diet** is the key to losing weight, or to preventing further weight gain.
- **Exercise** will also help you to lose weight. If you are not used to exercise, try starting with a brisk walk for 30–60 minutes each day.

Drug rationale

Drugs not included

- **Orlistat** may have a place in the management of overweight people with BMI of 28 or more and associated comorbidities, or those with a BMI of 30 or more, but should only be used in the setting of a well-organized weight management program. The licensed criteria for starting and continuing treatment should be adhered to [NICE, 2001a].
- **Sibutramine** may have a place in the management of overweight people with BMI of 27 or more and associated comorbidities, or those with a BMI of 30 or more. Again, it should only be used in the setting of a well-organized weight management program. The licensed criteria for starting and continuing treatment should be adhered to [NICE, 2001b].
- **Methylcellulose** is claimed to reduce food intake by producing feelings of satiety, but we have found no evidence from randomised controlled trials to show that it is effective in producing weight loss.
- **Phentermine, dexfenfluramine, and fenfluramine** are not offered due to reports of pulmonary hypertension and valvular heart disease [CSM, 2000].
- **Other drugs** such as diuretics or levothyroxine (thyroxine) should not be used for achieving weight loss.

Drugs included

- No drugs are recommended for people with a BMI between 25 and 26.9 kg/m^2.

Prescriptions

Non-drug management

Weight management advice

- Age from 16 years onwards
- Losing weight – The first steps: Follow this plan to lose weight over the next 3 months. 1. Aim for 5-10 kg weight loss over the 3 months, or 0.5 kg per week. But be realistic, if this seems too difficult, aim for a smaller weight loss, as even small amounts of weight loss bring health benefits. 2. A healthy balanced diet should be followed e.g. 1200-1600 kcal per day, moderate fat intake, more fruit and vegetables. 3. Increase the amour of daily routine activities you do e.g. walking, housework activities and stair climbing. Decrease the amount of time you spend sitting down. Build up an exercise programme that you enjoy e.g. swimming, walking, aerobics, cycling. 4. Contact a local slimming club if you think it will suit you. 5. If you smoke, quitting will bring great health benefits. 6. If you have hypertension, hyperlipidaemia or diabetes, the doctor can discuss it with you. 7. Make sure you tell others about your plans to lose weight, as the support of other can help you to stay motivated. Check in with your practice nurse, slimming club, weight management clini or other support group regularly.

Diet advice

- Age from 16 years onwards
- Tips for a 'less fat diet' from the Food Standards Agency Fat contains twice as many calories as starch or protein of the same weight. Beware of invisible fats in biscuits, cakes, chocolate, pastry, and savory snacks. Read the labels. Trim fat from meat and poultry. Opt for lower fa milk, dairy products and spreads. Choose to bake or gri food rather than frying it (e.g. use oven chips instead of fried potatoes). Eat more fruit and vegetables. Fill up on bread, cereals and potatoes. Choose low-fat snack food to suit your taste.

Physical activity advice

- Age from 16 years onwards
- Tips on physical activity for achieving weight loss: 1. Increase the amount of daily routine activity, such as shopping, walking, housework and gardening. 2. Decrease the amount of time you are inactive, for example, do not sit down for more than 30 minutes at a time. 3. Build up slowly towards 30 minutes-per-day of moderate intensity exercise (moderate intensity means breathing slightly more than normal, but still being comfortable enough to talk at the same time). Consider extending some exercise sessions to 45 minutes, to encourage the use of body fat. 4. The most effective activities for achieving weight loss are 'aerobic' activitie that involve large muscle groups such as the buttocks and leg muscles. Activities include walking, swimming and cycling. 5. Consider weight-bearing exercises (wher your bodyweight is lifted or moved along) such as walking or climbing stairs, as these help to conserve muscle mass and maintain strength and resting metabol weight. 6. Choose physical activities that you enjoy, as this will help you stick to them.

BMI 27–29.9 no comorbidities

Which therapy?

- **Assess motivation to change,** and if not motivated advis individual to return when they are ready to alter their lifestyle.

- **Review drugs that may be aggravating weight problem,** e.g. tricyclic antidepressants, sulphonylureas, corticosteroids, valproate.
- **Manage any additional risk factors** e.g. smoking, hypertension, hyperlipidaemia, diabetes.
- **A 3-month programme of weight reduction should aim for a 5–10 kg weight loss over 3 months or 0.5 kg per week** (combining diet, exercise, and behavioural strategies):
  - Give advice on the importance of weight restraint.
  - **Give advice on a healthy diet** — e.g. calories 1200–1600 kcal per day, moderate fat intake, more fruit and vegetables.
  - **Give advice on physical activity** — e.g. increase walking, housework activities, stair climbing; decrease amount of time sat down; build up exercise programme that person enjoys.
  - **Behaviour therapy as an adjunct** to diet and physical activity may increase weight loss, e.g. cognitive therapies, food diaries and reducing triggers of inappropriate eating, relaxation techniques, mood management.
  - **Provide written advice** (non-drug prescriptions or Patient Information Leaflets).
- **Consider enrolling the person into an organized local weight management programme** (at the general practice, local dietetic department, slimming organization, or self-help group).
- Drug therapy is not recommended at BMIs between 27 and 29.9 in the absence of comorbidities.

Follow-up advice

- Regular review (e.g. every 2 weeks) is essential for people on an intensive weight management programme. Weight loss of 0.5 kg per week should be aimed for.
- After a 3-month period of weight loss, a 3-month period of weight maintenance should be instigated.

Should I refer or investigate?

Refer?

- **Consider referral to an organized local weight management programme** run at:
  - The general practice (usually by a practice nurse), or
  - The local dietetic department, or
  - A commercial slimming organization , or
  - A self-help group.

Investigate?

- Urinalysis for glycosuria — if positive do fasting blood glucose
- Thyroid function tests (see PRODIGY *Hypothyroidism* guidance)
- Serum lipids (see PRODIGY *Hyperlipidaemia* guidance)

Patient information leaflets

The following PILs are available at www.prodigy.nhs.uk

- British Nutrition Foundation
- Exercise - A Summary
- Exercise for Health
- Healthy Eating
- Healthy Eating - A Summary
- Healthy Lifestyle - Five Choices
- Medicines - Name Changes of Medicines
- Obesity and Overweight
- Obesity and Overweight - A Summary
- Orlistat - Help With Weight Loss
- Sibutramine - Help With Weight Loss
- TOAST - The Obesity Awareness and Solutions Trust
- Weight Reduction - A Summary
- Weight Reduction - How to Lose Weight

Shared decision making

- You are classed as overweight (but not obese).
- Health risks increase the more overweight you become.
- If you lose 5–10 kg you will greatly reduce your increased health risks.
- For some people it is more realistic to keep to your present weight, but to take action to prevent further weight gain.
- **A healthy diet** is the key to losing weight, or to preventing further weight gain.
- **Exercise** will also help you to lose weight. If you are not used to exercise, try starting with a brisk walk for 30–60 minutes each day.

Drug rationale

Drugs not included

- **Orlistat** may have a place in the management of overweight people with a BMI of 28 or more and associated comorbidities, or those with a BMI of 30 or more, but should only be used in the setting of a well-organized weight management program. The licensed criteria for starting and continuing treatment should be adhered to [NICE, 2001a].
- **Sibutramine** may have a place in the management of overweight people with a BMI of 27 or more and associated comorbidities, or those with a BMI of 30 or more. Again, it should only be used in the setting of a well-organized weight management program. The licensed criteria for starting and continuing treatment should be adhered to [NICE, 2001b].
- **Methylcellulose** is claimed to reduce food intake by producing feelings of satiety, but we have found no evidence from randomised controlled trials to show that it is effective in producing weight loss.
- **Phentermine, dexfenfluramine, and fenfluramine** are not offered due to reports of pulmonary hypertension and valvular heart disease [CSM, 2000].
- **Other drugs** such as diuretics or levothyroxine (thyroxine) should not be used for achieving weight loss.

Drugs included

- No drugs are recommended for people with a BMI between 27 and 29.9 kg/m^2 in the absence of comorbidities (e.g. hypertension, hyperlipidaemia, Type 2 diabetes).

Prescriptions

Non-drug management

Weight management advice

- Age from 16 years onwards
- Losing weight – The first steps: Follow this plan to lose weight over the next 3 months. 1. Aim for 5-10 kg weight loss over the 3 months, or 0.5 kg per week. But be realistic, if this seems too difficult, aim for a smaller weight loss, as even small amounts of weight loss bring health benefits. 2. A healthy balanced diet should be followed e.g. 1200-1600 kcal per day, moderate fat intake, more fruit and vegetables. 3. Increase the amount of daily routine activities you do e.g. walking, housework activities and stair climbing. Decrease the amount of time you spend sitting down. Build up an exercise programme that you enjoy e.g. swimming,

walking, aerobics, cycling. 4. Contact a local slimming club if you think it will suit you. 5. If you smoke, quitting will bring great health benefits. 6. If you have hypertension, hyperlipidaemia or diabetes, the doctor can discuss it with you. 7. Make sure you tell others about your plans to lose weight, as the support of others can help you to stay motivated. Check in with your practice nurse, slimming club, weight management clinic or other support group regularly.

Diet advice

- Age from 16 years onwards
- Tips for a 'less fat diet' from the Food Standards Agency: Fat contains twice as many calories as starch or protein of the same weight. Beware of invisible fats in biscuits, cakes, chocolate, pastry, and savory snacks. Read the labels. Trim fat from meat and poultry. Opt for lower fat milk, dairy products and spreads. Choose to bake or grill food rather than frying it (e.g. use oven chips instead of fried potatoes). Eat more fruit and vegetables. Fill up on bread, cereals and potatoes. Choose low-fat snack food to suit your taste.

Physical activity advice

- Age from 16 years onwards
- Tips on physical activity for achieving weight loss: 1. Increase the amount of daily routine activity, such as shopping, walking, housework and gardening. 2. Decrease the amount of time you are inactive, for example, do not sit down for more than 30 minutes at a time. 3. Build up slowly towards 30 minutes-per-day of moderate intensity exercise (moderate intensity means breathing slightly more than normal, but still being comfortable enough to talk at the same time). Consider extending some exercise sessions to 45 minutes, to encourage the use of body fat. 4. The most effective activities for achieving weight loss are 'aerobic' activities that involve large muscle groups such as the buttocks and leg muscles. Activities include walking, swimming and cycling. 5. Consider weight-bearing exercises (where your bodyweight is lifted or moved along) such as walking or climbing stairs, as these help to conserve muscle mass and maintain strength and resting metabolic weight. 6. Choose physical activities that you enjoy, as this will help you stick to them.

BMI 27–29.9 plus comorbidities

Which therapy?

- **Assess motivation to change,** and if not motivated advise individual to return when they are ready to alter their lifestyle.
- **Review drugs that may be aggravating weight problem,** e.g. tricyclic antidepressants, sulphonylureas, corticosteroids, valproate.
- **Manage any additional risk factors or pre-existing conditions,** e.g. smoking, hypertension, hyperlipidaemia, diabetes, coronary heart disease.
- **A 3-month programme of weight reduction should aim for a 5–10 kg weight loss over 3 months or 0.5 kg per week** (combining diet, exercise, and behavioural strategies):
  - Give advice on the importance of weight restraint.
  - **Give advice on a healthy diet** — e.g. calories 1200–1600 kcal per day, moderate fat intake, more fruit and vegetables.
  - **Give advice on physical activity** — e.g. increase walking, housework activities, stair climbing; decrease amount of time sat down; build up exercise programme that person enjoys.
  - **Behaviour therapy as an adjunct** to diet and physical activity may increase weight loss, e.g. food diaries and reducing triggers of inappropriate eating.
  - **Provide written advice** (non-drug prescriptions or Patient Information Leaflets).
- **Consider enrolling the person into an organized local weight management programme** (at the general practice, local dietetic department, slimming organization, or self-help group).
- **Drug treatment should be only added if strict criteria (or locally agreed guidance) are met:**
  - *Orlistat*: BMI >28, plus comorbidities such as Type 2 diabetes, hypertension, or high total cholesterol. Patient is aged 18–75 years.
  - *Sibutramine*: BMI >27, plus comorbidities such as Type 2 diabetes or dyslipidaemia. Patient has previously had difficulty achieving or maintaining >5% weight loss over 3 months and is aged 18–65 years (see *Prescribing points* for contraindications).

Practical prescribing points

For further information please see the *Medicines Compendium* (www.medicines.org.uk) or the *British National Formulary* (www.bnf.org).

Orlistat

- **GI adverse effects** (e.g. fatty stools, urgency, oily spotting, and sometimes faecal incontinence) usually reduce with time. These can be reduced by limiting fat intake.

Sibutramine

- **Blood pressure** and **pulse** are raised by sibutramine use in some people. See *Follow up* for advice on monitoring.
- **Sibutramine is contraindicated** in people whose blood pressure is uncontrolled or is greater than 145/90 mmHg, or in those with a history of coronary heart disease, congestive heart failure, peripheral vascular disease, arrhythmias, or cerebrovascular disease.

Follow-up advice

General

- Regular review (e.g. every 2 weeks) is essential for people on an intensive weight management programme. Weight loss of 0.5 kg per week should be aimed for.
- After a 3-month period of weight loss, a 3-month period of weight maintenance should be instigated.
- People taking orlistat and sibutramine should be reviewed as follows.

Orlistat

- Review at least once a month [RCP, 1998].
- **In order to continue on treatment** there must be evidence of:
  - At least 5% of initial bodyweight lost at 3 months
  - At least 10% of initial bodyweight lost at 6 months
- Consider checking levels of fat-soluble vitamins (A, D, E, K, and beta-carotene) if the person is *not* eating a balanced diet.

Sibutramine

- Review every 2 weeks for the first 3 months, once a month for the next 3 months, then every 3 months thereafter.
- **In order to continue on treatment** there must be evidence of:

- A 2 kg weight loss at 4 weeks (see below if this is not achieved by 10 mg sibutramine daily)
- At least 5% of initial bodyweight lost at 3 months
- Improved glycaemic control in people with diabetes, and improved lipid profiles in people with dyslipidaemia, should be associated with the weight loss.

- Stop treatment if the person regains 3 kg or more of previously achieved weight loss.
- **If 2 kg weight loss at 4 weeks is *not* achieved,** the dose can be increased to 15 mg daily, provided that sibutramine 10 mg daily was well tolerated. However, if there is not a 2 kg weight loss after 4 weeks at 15 mg daily, treatment with sibutramine must be discontinued.
- **Check BP and pulse** every 2 weeks for the first 3 months, every month for the next 3 months, and then 3 monthly thereafter. **Discontinue treatment if** on two consecutive visits:
  - BP rises above 145/90 mmHg
  - BP rises by >10 mmHg from baseline
  - Resting pulse rate rises by >10 bpm
- Treatment should not continue beyond 12 months.

Should I refer or investigate?

Refer?

- **Consider referral to an organized local weight management programme** run at:
  - The general practice (usually by a practice nurse), or
  - The local dietetic department, or
  - A commercial slimming organization , or
  - A self-help group.

Investigate?

- Urinalysis for glycosuria — if positive do fasting blood glucose
- Thyroid function tests (see PRODIGY *Hypothyroidism* guidance)
- Serum lipids (see PRODIGY *Hyperlipidaemia* guidance)

Patient information leaflets

The following PILs are available at www.prodigy.nhs.uk

- British Nutrition Foundation
- Exercise - A Summary
- Exercise for Health
- Healthy Eating
- Healthy Eating - A Summary
- Healthy Lifestyle - Five Choices
- Medicines - Name Changes of Medicines
- Obesity and Overweight
- Obesity and Overweight - A Summary
- Orlistat - Help With Weight Loss
- Sibutramine - Help With Weight Loss
- TOAST - The Obesity Awareness and Solutions Trust
- Weight Reduction - A Summary
- Weight Reduction - How to Lose Weight

Shared decision making

- If you lose 5–10 kg you will greatly reduce your increased health risks.
- **A healthy diet** is the key to losing weight, or to preventing further weight gain.
- **Exercise** will also help you to lose weight. If you are not used to exercise, try starting with a brisk walk for 30–60 minutes each day.
- **Medication** is not usually advised, but may be helpful for some people.
- **Orlistat** works by preventing some fat from being absorbed from the gut.
  - Once you start orlistat, it should be stopped if you have not lost at least 5% of your weight after 12 weeks.
  - Side effects may occur due to extra fat remaining in the gut. These include: wind, urgency to get to the toilet, fatty or oily faeces (motions), mild diarrhoea, and sometimes faecal incontinence. The less fat that you eat, the less chance of side effects.
- **Sibutramine** works by decreasing your appetite.
  - It is only given if you have had real difficulty in losing weight over three months.
  - Once you start sibutramine, it should be stopped if you have not lost at least 2 kg after 4 weeks of treatment.
  - Sibutramine is not suitable for everyone. For example, if you have high blood pressure or heart disease.
  - Side effects include a raised blood pressure, so your blood pressure must be monitored.

Drug rationale

Drugs not included

- **Methylcellulose** is claimed to reduce food intake by producing feelings of satiety, but we have found no evidence from randomised controlled trials to show that it is effective in producing weight loss.
- **Phentermine, dexfenfluramine, and fenfluramine** are not offered due to reports of pulmonary hypertension and valvular heart disease [CSM, 2000].
- **Other drugs** such as diuretics or levothyroxine (thyroxine) should not be used for achieving weight loss.

Drugs included

- **Orlistat** may have a place in the management of overweight people with a BMI of 28 or more and associated comorbidities, but should only be used in the setting of a well-organized weight management program. The licensed criteria for starting and continuing treatment should be adhered to [NICE, 2001a].
- **Sibutramine** may have a place in the management of overweight people with a BMI of 27 or more and associated comorbidities. Again, it should only be used in the setting of a well-organized weight management program. The licensed criteria for starting and continuing treatment should be adhered to [NICE, 2001b].

Prescriptions

Non-drug management

Weight management advice

- Age from 16 years onwards
- Losing weight – The first steps: Follow this plan to lose weight over the next 3 months. 1. Aim for 5-10 kg weight loss over the 3 months, or 0.5 kg per week. But be realistic, if this seems too difficult, aim for a smaller weight loss, as even small amounts of weight loss bring health benefits. 2. A healthy balanced diet should be followed e.g. 1200-1600 kcal per day, moderate fat intake, more fruit and vegetables. 3. Increase the amount of daily routine activities you do e.g. walking, housework activities and stair climbing. Decrease the amount of time you spend sitting down. Build up an exercise programme that you enjoy e.g. swimming, walking, aerobics, cycling. 4. Contact a local slimming club if you think it will suit you. 5. If you smoke, quitting will bring great health benefits. 6. If you have

hypertension, hyperlipidaemia or diabetes, the doctor can discuss it with you. 7. Make sure you tell others about your plans to lose weight, as the support of others can help you to stay motivated. Check in with your practice nurse, slimming club, weight management clinic or other support group regularly.

Diet advice

- Age from 16 years onwards
- Tips for a 'less fat diet' from the Food Standards Agency: Fat contains twice as many calories as starch or protein of the same weight. Beware of invisible fats in biscuits, cakes, chocolate, pastry, and savory snacks. Read the labels. Trim fat from meat and poultry. Opt for lower fat milk, dairy products and spreads. Choose to bake or grill food rather than frying it (e.g. use oven chips instead of fried potatoes). Eat more fruit and vegetables. Fill up on bread, cereals and potatoes. Choose low-fat snack food to suit your taste.

Physical activity advice

- Age from 16 years onwards
- Tips on physical activity for achieving weight loss: 1. Increase the amount of daily routine activity, such as shopping, walking, housework and gardening. 2. Decrease the amount of time you are inactive, for example, do not sit down for more than 30 minutes at a time. 3. Build up slowly towards 30 minutes-per-day of moderate intensity exercise (moderate intensity means breathing slightly more than normal, but still being comfortable enough to talk at the same time). Consider extending some exercise sessions to 45 minutes, to encourage the use of body fat. 4. The most effective activities for achieving weight loss are 'aerobic' activities that involve large muscle groups such as the buttocks and leg muscles. Activities include walking, swimming and cycling. 5. Consider weight-bearing exercises (where your bodyweight is lifted or moved along) such as walking or climbing stairs, as these help to conserve muscle mass and maintain strength and resting metabolic weight. 6. Choose physical activities that you enjoy, as this will help you stick to them.

Orlistat (BMI >28 + comorbidity)

Orlistat 120mg with each meal (three times a day)

- Age from 18 to 75 years
- Orlistat 120mg capsules. Take one capsule with each main meal. Maximum of 3 capsules in 24 hours. (Take each capsule just before, during, or up to 1 hour after a main meal.); supply 84 capsules; NHS Cost £41.16.

Sibutramine (BMI >27 + comorbidity)

Sibutramine 10mg each morning

- Age from 18 to 65 years
- Sibutramine 10mg capsules. Take one capsule each morning; supply 28 capsules; NHS Cost £35.00.

Sibutramine 15mg once a day: if no response to 10mg at 4 wks

- Age from 18 to 65 years
- Sibutramine 15mg capsules. Take one capsule each morning; supply 28 capsules; NHS Cost £39.09.

BMI 30 or more

Which therapy?

- **Assess motivation to change,** and if not motivated advise individual to return when they are ready to alter their lifestyle.
- **Review drugs that may be aggravating weight problem,** e.g. tricyclic antidepressants, sulphonylureas, corticosteroids, valproate.
- **Manage any additional risk factors or pre-existing conditions,** e.g. smoking, hypertension, hyperlipidaemi diabetes, coronary heart disease.
- **A 3-month programme of weight reduction should aim for a 5–10 kg weight loss over 3 months or 0.5 kg per week** (combining diet, exercise, and behavioural strategies):
  - Give advice on the importance of weight restraint.
  - **Give advice on a healthy diet** — e.g. calories 1200–1600 kcal per day, moderate fat intake, more fruit and vegetables.
  - **Give advice on physical activity** — e.g. increase walking, housework activities, stair climbing; decreas amount of time sat down; build up exercise programme that person enjoys.
  - **Behaviour therapy as an adjunct** to diet and physical activity may increase weight loss, e.g. food diaries an reducing triggers of inappropriate eating.
  - **Provide written advice** (non-drug prescriptions or Patient Information Leaflets).
- **Consider enrolling the person into an organized local weight management programme** (at the general practic local dietetic department, slimming organization, or sel help group).
- **Drug treatment should be only added if strict criteria (o locally agreed guidance) are met:**
  - *Orlistat*: If BMI 30 or more, patient must be aged 18–75 years.
  - *Sibutramine*: If BMI 30 or more, patient must have had difficulty achieving or maintaining >5% weight loss over a 3 month period, and be aged 18–65 years (see *Prescribing points* for contraindications).

Practical prescribing points

For further information please see the *Medicines Compendium* (www.medicines.org.uk) or the *British National Formulary* (www.bnf.org).

Orlistat

- **GI adverse effects** (e.g. fatty stools, urgency, oily spotting, and sometimes faecal incontinence) usually reduce with time. These can often be reduced by limitin fat intake.

Sibutramine

- **Blood pressure** and **pulse** are raised by sibutramine use in some people. See *Follow up* for advice on monitoring
- **Sibutramine is contraindicated** in people whose blood pressure is uncontrolled or greater than 145/90 mmHg, or in those with a history of coronary heart disease, congestive heart failure, peripheral vascular disease, arrhythmias, or cerebrovascular disease.

Follow-up advice

- Regular review (e.g. every 2 weeks) is essential for peop on an intensive weight management programme. Weigh loss of 0.5 kg per week should be aimed for.
- After a 3-month period of weight loss, a 3-month perio of weight maintenance should be instigated.
- People taking orlistat and sibutramine should be reviewed as follows.

Orlistat

- Review at least once a month [RCP, 1998].
- **In order to continue on treatment** there must be evidenc of:
  - At least 5% of initial bodyweight lost at 3 months
  - At least 10% of initial bodyweight lost at 6 months

Consider checking levels of fat-soluble vitamins (A, D, E, K, and beta-carotene) if the person is *not* eating a balanced diet.

Sibutramine

Review every 2 weeks for the first 3 months, once a month for the next 3 months, then every 3 months thereafter.

In order to continue on treatment there must be evidence of:

- A 2 kg weight loss at 4 weeks (see below if this is not achieved by 10 mg sibutramine daily)
- At least 5% of initial bodyweight lost at 3 months
- Improved glycaemic control in people with diabetes, and improved lipid profiles in people with dyslipidaemia, should be associated with the weight loss.

Stop treatment if the person regains 3 kg or more of previously achieved weight loss.

If 2 kg weight loss at 4 weeks is *not* achieved, the dose can be increased to 15 mg daily, provided that sibutramine 10 mg daily was well tolerated. However, if there is not a 2 kg weight loss after 4 weeks at 15 mg daily, treatment with sibutramine must be discontinued.

Check BP and pulse every 2 weeks for the first 3 months, every month for the next 3 months, and then 3 monthly thereafter. **Discontinue treatment if** on two consecutive visits:

- BP rises above 145/90 mmHg
- BP rises by >10 mmHg from baseline
- Resting pulse rate rises by >10 bpm

Treatment should not continue beyond 12 months.

Should I refer or investigate?

Refer?

If BMI is 40 or more then specialist referral should be strongly considered.

Consider referral to an organized local weight management programme run at:

- The general practice (usually by a practice nurse), or
- The local dietetic department, or
- A commercial slimming organization , or
- A self-help group.

Investigate?

Urinalysis for glycosuria — if positive do fasting blood glucose

Thyroid function tests (see PRODIGY *Hypothyroidism* guidance)

Serum lipids (see PRODIGY *Hyperlipidaemia* guidance)

Patient information leaflets

The following PILs are available at www.prodigy.nhs.uk

British Nutrition Foundation
Exercise - A Summary
Exercise for Health
Healthy Eating
Healthy Eating - A Summary
Healthy Lifestyle - Five Choices
Medicines - Name Changes of Medicines
Obesity and Overweight
Obesity and Overweight - A Summary
Orlistat - Help With Weight Loss
Sibutramine - Help With Weight Loss
TOAST - The Obesity Awareness and Solutions Trust
Weight Reduction - A Summary
Weight Reduction - How to Lose Weight

Shared decision making

- If you lose 5–10 kg you will greatly reduce your increased health risks.
- **A healthy diet** is the key to losing weight, or to preventing further weight gain.
- **Exercise** will also help you to lose weight. If you are not used to exercise, try starting with a brisk walk for 30–60 minutes each day.
- **Medication** is not usually advised, but may be helpful for some people.
- **Orlistat** works by preventing some fat from being absorbed from the gut.
  - Once you start orlistat, it should be stopped if you have not lost at least 5% of your weight after 12 weeks.
  - Side effects may occur due to extra fat remaining in the gut. These include: wind, urgency to get to the toilet, fatty or oily faeces (motions), mild diarrhoea, and sometimes faecal incontinence. The less fat that you eat, the less chance of side effects.
- **Sibutramine** works by decreasing your appetite.
  - It is only given if you have had real difficulty in losing weight over three months.
  - Once you start sibutramine, it should be stopped if you have not lost at least 2 kg after 4 weeks of treatment.
  - Sibutramine is not suitable for everyone. For example, if you have high blood pressure or heart disease.
  - Side effects include a raised blood pressure, so your blood pressure must be monitored.

Drug rationale

Drugs not included

- **Methylcellulose** is claimed to reduce food intake by producing feelings of satiety, but we have found no evidence from randomised controlled trials to show that it is effective in producing weight loss.
- **Phentermine, dexfenfluramine, and fenfluramine** are not offered due to reports of pulmonary hypertension and valvular heart disease [CSM, 2000].
- **Other drugs** such as diuretics or levothyroxine (thyroxine) should not be used for achieving weight loss.

Drugs included

- **Orlistat** may have a place in the management of overweight people with a BMI of 30 or more, but should only be used in the setting of a well-organized weight management program. The licensed criteria for starting and continuing treatment should be adhered to [NICE, 2001a].
- **Sibutramine** may have a place in the management of overweight people with a BMI of 30 or more. Again, it should only be used in the setting of a well-organized weight management program. The licensed criteria for starting and continuing treatment should be adhered to [NICE, 2001b].

Prescriptions

Non-drug management

Weight management advice

- Age from 16 years onwards
- Losing weight – The first steps: Follow this plan to lose weight over the next 3 months. 1. Aim for 5-10 kg weight loss over the 3 months, or 0.5 kg per week. But be realistic, if this seems too difficult, aim for a smaller weight loss, as even small amounts of weight loss bring

O

health benefits. 2. A healthy balanced diet should be followed e.g. 1200-1600 kcal per day, moderate fat intake, more fruit and vegetables. 3. Increase the amount of daily routine activities you do e.g. walking, housework activities and stair climbing. Decrease the amount of time you spend sitting down. Build up an exercise programme that you enjoy e.g. swimming, walking, aerobics, cycling. 4. Contact a local slimming club if you think it will suit you. 5. If you smoke, quitting will bring great health benefits. 6. If you have hypertension, hyperlipidaemia or diabetes, the doctor can discuss it with you. 7. Make sure you tell others about your plans to lose weight, as the support of others can help you to stay motivated. Check in with your practice nurse, slimming club, weight management clinic or other support group regularly.

Diet advice

- Age from 16 years onwards
- Tips for a 'less fat diet' from the Food Standards Agency: Fat contains twice as many calories as starch or protein of the same weight. Beware of invisible fats in biscuits, cakes, chocolate, pastry, and savory snacks. Read the labels. Trim fat from meat and poultry. Opt for lower fat milk, dairy products and spreads. Choose to bake or grill food rather than frying it (e.g. use oven chips instead of fried potatoes). Eat more fruit and vegetables. Fill up on bread, cereals and potatoes. Choose low-fat snack food to suit your taste.

Physical activity advice

- Age from 16 years onwards
- Tips on physical activity for achieving weight loss: 1. Increase the amount of daily routine activity, such as shopping, walking, housework and gardening. 2. Decrease the amount of time you are inactive, for example, do not sit down for more than 30 minutes at a time. 3. Build up slowly towards 30 minutes-per-day of moderate intensity exercise (moderate intensity means breathing slightly more than normal, but still being comfortable enough to talk at the same time). Consider extending some exercise sessions to 45 minutes, to encourage the use of body fat. 4. The most effective activities for achieving weight loss are 'aerobic' activities that involve large muscle groups such as the buttocks and leg muscles. Activities include walking, swimming and cycling. 5. Consider weight-bearing exercises (where your bodyweight is lifted or moved along) such as walking or climbing stairs, as these help to conserve muscle mass and maintain strength and resting metabolic weight. 6. Choose physical activities that you enjoy, as this will help you stick to them.

Orlistat (BMI > 30)

Orlistat 120mg with each meal (three times a day)

- Age from 18 to 75 years
- Orlistat 120mg capsules. Take one capsule with each main meal. Maximum of 3 capsules in 24 hours. (Take each capsule just before, during, or up to 1 hour after a main meal.); supply 84 capsules; NHS Cost £41.16.

Sibutramine (BMI > 30)

Sibutramine 10mg each morning

- Age from 18 to 65 years
- Sibutramine 10mg capsules. Take one capsule each morning; supply 28 capsules; NHS Cost £35.00.

Sibutramine 15mg once a day: if no response to 10mg at 4 wks

- Age from 18 to 65 years
- Sibutramine 15mg capsules. Take one capsule each morning; supply 28 capsules; NHS Cost £39.09.

Extended Information

Background information

- What is it? p.1320
- How common is it? p.1320
- How do I know my patient has it? p.1321
- What else might it be? p.1321
- Complications and prognosis p.1321

What is it?

- Obesity and overweight are the result of an excess accumulation of fat. Table 2 gives the widely used World Health Organisation's classification of bodyweight. The classification is based on the body mass index (BMI). [WHO, 2000].
- **The BMI has some limitations** because it is an indirect measurement of body fat. Although BMI values are the same for both sexes and all ages, they may not correspond to the same degree of fatness in different populations, e.g. in some communities a BMI of 18.5 may not be underweight [WHO, 2000]. BMI does not take into account body frame and the proportion of lean mass, which means that some individuals are not accounted for, e.g. athletes with well-developed muscles will have spuriously high BMIs [NHS CRD, 1997a; National Task Force on the Prevention and Treatment of Obesity, 2000]. Despite these limitations, BMI is the accepted measure in the UK.
- **Waist circumference** is an alternative indirect measurement of body fat that reflects the intra-abdominal fat mass, which is strongly correlated with coronary heart disease risk, diabetes, hyperlipidaemia, and hypertension [National Institutes of Health, 1998; RCP, 1998; WHO, 2000; National Audit Office, 2001]. It is measured halfway between the superior iliac crest and the rib cage in the mid-axillary line. The values in the table below are suggested cut off points for populations, but there is significant individual variability in the amount of visceral fat at a given waist circumference. Most people with an 'at risk' waist circumference are also in an overweight or obese BMI category, thus in most individuals BMI alone is an adequate indicator for treatment [National Task Force on the Prevention and Treatment of Obesity, 2000].

How common is it?

The National Audit Office reported the following figures and trends in 2001:

- In England in 1998, 21% of women were obese (BMI over 30) and 19% of men were obese.
- In England in 1998, 32% of women were overweight (BMI between 25 and 30), and 46% of men were overweight.
- The prevalence of obesity in England has almost tripled since 1980, and will increase further on present trends.
- Obesity in the population increases with age.
- Women gain excess weight more readily than men, perhaps for metabolic reasons relating to their lower lean body mass.

Table 1: Association of waist circumference with risks of CHD and diabetes.

	Waist circumference: *Increased risk of CHD, diabetes*	Waist circumference: *Substantial risk of CHD, diabetes*
Men	94 cm (37 inches) or more	102 cm (40 inches) or more
Women	80 cm (32 inches) or more	88 cm (35 inches) or more

People in lower socio-economic groups have an increased risk of obesity.
There is a higher prevalence of obesity some ethnic groups, in particular black Caribbean and Pakistani women. Adults from the Indian subcontinent are especially prone to abdominal fat deposition, are very susceptible to glucose intolerance and diabetes, and are more prone to coronary heart disease than Caucasians. National Audit Office, 2001]

How do I know my patient has it?

Table 2 gives the widely used World Health Organisation's classification of bodyweight. The classification is based on the body mass index (BMI). [WHO, 2000].

What else might it be?

Pregnancy
Fluid overload: heart failure, nephrotic syndrome, ascites
Medication adverse effect, e.g. tricyclic antidepressant, sulphonylureas, corticosteroids, valproate
Endocrine problem (rarely): hypothyroidism, Cushing's disease
Excessive muscular development (as seen in trained athletes) increases the BMI.

Complications and prognosis

Mortality rates progressively increase above a BMI of 24. In the Framingham Heart Study, the risk of death within a 26-year period increased by 1% for each extra pound (0.45 kg) gain in weight between the ages 30–42 years, and by 2% between the ages 50–62 years [RCP, 1998].
Morbidity risks increase steadily from BMI 25–30 and increase more rapidly at higher BMIs.
The risk of coronary heart disease is doubled if the BMI is greater than 25 and nearly quadrupled if it is 29 or more [Wilding, 1997].
The risk of developing diabetes is 40 times greater if the BMI is greater than 35 [Wilding, 1997].
Complications of excess weight are:
Increased blood pressure
Hyperlipidaemia and a low HDL cholesterol
Type 2 diabetes
Stroke
Coronary heart disease (related to increased lipids and hypertension)
Gallstones, especially in women, and non-alcoholic steatohepatitis
Weight-related musculoskeletal disorders and arthritis (especially weight-bearing joints)
Cancers: postmenopausal breast, endometrial, ovarian, gallbladder, prostate, and colon cancers
Breathlessness, respiratory disease, sleep apnoea
Menstrual abnormalities and hirsutism
Pregnancy complications: increased risk of neural tube defects, perinatal mortality, hypertension, toxaemia, gestational diabetes, preterm labour, Caesarean section, and hospitalisation
Stress incontinence (urinary)

Table 2: WHO classification of weight

Weight class	BMI = wt(kg)/ht(m)^2
Underweight	below 18.5 kg/m^2
Normal	between 18.5 kg/m^2 and 24.9 kg/m^2
Overweight	between 25kg/m^2 and 29.9kg/m^2
Obese	between 30kg/m^2 and 39.9kg/m^2
Morbidly obese	over 40 kg/m^2

- **Psychological:** social isolation, low self-esteem, depression, binge eating, night eating, and reduced employment prospects
- **Disability,** which may lead to early retirement on reduced income

[Wilding, 1997; National Task Force on the Prevention and Treatment of Obesity, 2000; National Audit Office, 2001]

Management issues

- General issues p.1321
- Benefits of weight loss p.1321
- Who to treat p.1321
- Weight management programmes and national initiatives p.1322
- Main components of treatment, targets and timetables for weight loss p.1322
- Dietary changes p.1322
- Physical activity p.1322
- Psychological and behavioural approaches p.1323
- Anti-obesity drugs p.1323
- Surgery p.1323

General issues

- **Many factors interact to cause weight gain,** including behavioural, physiological, genetic, medical, therapeutic, and psychological factors.
- **The main contributory factors are an increasingly sedentary lifestyle with increased energy intake** (mainly as dietary fat). This is compounded by increased eating outside the home, a tendency to eat "little and often", and eating at times when energy expenditure is likely to be low (e.g. late in the evening) [Prentice and Jebb, 1995; NHS CRD, 1997a].
- **Small discrepancies between daily intake and energy output can cause progressive, substantial weight gain.** A daily excess of 100 kcal (equivalent to a small chocolate bar) will lead to a 4 kg weight gain in a year [Wilding, 1997].
- **Spontaneous weight loss is unusual once weight gain has occurred.** When food intake is reduced, metabolic rate falls and desire to eat increases, making weight reduction difficult.
- **Smoking** is a major cardiovascular risk factor, and the benefits of quitting usually outweigh the benefits of weight reduction. Up to 80% of people who quit smoking gain weight, and fear of this is a major barrier to smoking cessation [National Institutes of Health, 1998]. All smokers, regardless of their weight, should quit smoking. However, active efforts to help prevent weight gain are necessary (see PRODIGY *Stopping Smoking* guidance).

Benefits of weight loss

- Weight loss in obese and overweight people has been shown to produce a variety of health benefits. Even a moderate weight loss of 5–10 kg can result in substantial health gains.
- A 10 kg weight loss in a person with an initial weight of 100 kg with comorbidities would be expected to have the following effects [RCP, 1998; Davis et al, 2000]:

Who to treat

- People should be prioritized for weight management programmes in order to make best use of available resources.
- The people at greatest risk are those with a BMI of 30 or more; then those with a BMI of 25–29.9 if other risk factors are present such as adverse family history,

Table 3: Benefits of weight loss.

Condition	Health benefit
Mortality	20–25% fall in overall mortality 30–40% fall in diabetes-related deaths 40–50% fall in obesity-related cancer deaths
Blood pressure	10 mmHg fall in diastolic and systolic pressures
Diabetes	Up to a 50% fall in fasting blood glucose Reduces risk of developing diabetes by over 50%
Lipids	Fall of 10% total cholesterol, 15% LDL, and 30% triglycerides Increase of 8% HDL

smoking, hypertension, hyperlipidaemia, or current disease (diabetes, coronary heart disease).
- People who are motivated are most likely to lose weight successfully, e.g. those showing positive preparation to change their lifestyle, or those already taking action. People who are not motivated should be advised of the benefits of weight loss, and encouraged to return in the future when they feel ready to try to lose weight.

Weight management programmes and national initiatives

- **Weight management involves** helping overweight individuals to lose weight, to maintain any weight loss achieved, and to manage interacting risk factors (smoking, physical inactivity, inappropriate diets).
- **A local strategy** for weight management is desirable, and should be derived from national strategies. Obesity is recognised as a national priority in the UK through Saving Lives, Our Healthier Nation, and the National Service Frameworks for coronary heart disease and diabetes. Locally, Health Improvement and Modernization Programmes (HIMPs) set specific policies and targets.
- **Weight management programmes** can be offered by the primary care team, the local dietetic department, a commercial slimming group, or self-help group. It can be difficult to advise the individual on which group to attend as none have been formally evaluated — getting the practice nurse to look into these may be useful.
- If a weight management programme is set up within a general practice, it is vital to identify the practice staff responsible for weight management and to ensure adequate training.

Main components of treatment, targets and timetables for weight loss

- **Diet, increased physical activity, and behaviour change** are the three main components that constitute the effective management of obesity. **Drug treatment** may also be needed in some people [SIGN, 1996; RCP, 1998; National Obesity Forum, 2000].
- **Clear and realistic goals** for risk factor and weight reduction are more likely to be achieved — modest weight reductions can bring substantial health benefits.
- **A three-month structured weight loss programme** (including diet, exercise, and behavioural advice) aiming for 5–10 kg weight loss (0.5 kg/week), or 5–10% reduction from initial bodyweight will usually achieve the target weight loss [Miller et al, 1997]. This level of weight loss has also been shown to improve hypertension, glucose control, hyperlipidaemia, depression, and self-esteem [Wadden, 1998].
- **Regular review** is necessary (possibly by telephone), e.g. every 2 weeks.
- **A three-month weight maintenance period** is then advised, as clinical trials show that most people are unable to continue losing weight for longer than 12–16 weeks. Further weight reduction targets may then be renegotiated with the individual.
- **Most people gain some weight in the months or years after their weight loss period. To maintain weight loss, permanent lifestyle changes are needed.** If 10 kg of weight is lost, a permanent change of about 300 kcal/day less intake or 300 kcal/day extra physical activity is required to maintain this.
- Long-term support is necessary to help prevent weight regain, although it is not known how often people need to be seen [National Institutes of Health, 1998].
- **Referral to a specialist centre** should be considered for people with BMIs which remain greater than 35. However, localities vary enormously in their access to specialist services.

Dietary changes

- **A reduction in calorific intake** of about 600 kcal/day or a total daily intake of 1200–1600 kcal, will usually achieve the target weight loss [NHS CRD, 1997a; National Obesity Forum, 2000].
- **A reduction of fat in the diet** is an effective way to achieve weight loss in many people, with or without a reduction in total calories [Glenny et al, 1997; NHS CRD, 1997b; Astrup et al, 2000]. Lowering saturated fat intake will lead to a reduction in cholesterol and the risk of cardiovascular disease, whether or not weight is also lost [Thorogood et al, 2001]. Mediterranean diets that contain moderate fat levels are an alternative to low fat diets [McManus et al, 2001]. The Food Standards Agency 'Tips for a less fat diet' are included in the appropriate scenarios of this guidance.
- Very low calorie diets can induce rapid weight loss over a 3-month period, but long-term weight maintenance is poor and such diets should normally be reserved for use at specialist centres.
- The Committee on Medical Aspects of Food and Nutrition Policy recommends that any dietary change should include an increase in fruit and vegetables to at least 5 portions a day. An increased intake of potatoes and bread acts as a substitute for reduced fat levels.
- The provision of meal plans and grocery lists may help increase the amount of weight lost [NHS CRD, 1997a; NHS CRD, 1997b].
- Recommendations on dietary changes are available from a wide range of sources. A dietician will be able to offer appropriate advice to overweight or obese people.
- The amount of weight loss can be increased if dietary change is combined with increased physical activity and behavioural approaches.

Physical activity

- **Increased physical activity can lead to weight loss.**
- **Physical activity (and subsequent fitness) have many other benefits,** such as reduction in blood pressure, improved functional capacity, and improved insulin sensitivity, regardless of the amount of weight lost [Miller, 2001].
- **Moderate exercise during day-to-day living** (e.g. walking and stair climbing) will help weight loss, and may be as effective as a structured exercise programme [Anderson et al, 1999; Dunn et al, 1999]. Even light exercise such as callisthenics or stretching exercises may aid weight loss [NHS CRD, 1997a].
- **Low intensity aerobic exercise** promotes a greater fat oxidation (fat-burning) than high intensity exercise [Miller, 2001].
- **Intense exercise** uses up more calories (e.g. running), but obese and overweight people should build up exercise gradually towards more aerobic activities.

- Supervised exercise sessions, or exercising in a social setting with support of others, may result in more weight loss than providing exercise education [NHS CRD, 1997a].
- Drop-out rates for exercise programmes are reported as 50% in 6 months and 70% within a year.
- Specific recommendations for physical activity for people who are obese are available from a variety of sources e.g. [Fox, 1999] and are included in the appropriate scenarios of this guidance.

Psychological and behavioural approaches

- There is little reliable evidence that behavioural treatments by themselves are effective in achieving weight loss. However, behavioural treatments combined with a diet and exercise programme may aid weight loss [NHS CRD, 1997a; Thorogood et al, 2001].
- Cognitive behaviour programmes may include self-monitoring (e.g. keeping a food diary), stimulus control (developing strategies to reduce triggers of inappropriate eating), and relaxation techniques.
- Other approaches include healthy eating advice, setting behavioural goals, mood management, managing work and family, avoiding self-defeating thinking, and improving body image [Chambers and Wakley, 2002].

Anti-obesity drugs

- **There is currently a very limited role for anti-obesity drugs.** The use of drugs is governed by strict criteria which should be met before the person receives the medication.
- **The two products available in the UK are orlistat and sibutramine.**
- **Orlistat** is a pancreatic lipase inhibitor that inhibits triglyceride digestion and reduces fat absorption by approximately 30%.
- **Sibutramine** is a centrally-acting serotonin and noradrenaline reuptake inhibitor, which is thought to promote satiety and stimulate energy expenditure.
- Both orlistat and sibutramine have been shown to promote weight loss when combined with other treatments such as a reduced calorie diet [NICE, 2001a; NICE, 2001b]. Although continued use has been shown to reduce weight gain, once the drugs are stopped, weight gain is usually seen [Sjöström et al, 1998; Davidson et al, 1999; Hauptman et al, 2000; James et al, 2000].
- Sibutramine's use is limited in some people by its unwanted effects and contraindications in several conditions that may accompany obesity (see table). Orlistat's use may be limited by its gastrointestinal adverse effects.
- Combination therapy with orlistat and sibutramine is not recommended, and has not been demonstrated to increase weight loss [Wadden et al, 2000; NICE, 2001b].
- **The criteria for prescribing and monitoring orlistat or sibutramine** are given in the Table below [DTB, 1998; NICE, 2001a; NICE, 2001b; ABPI Medicines Compendium, 2002a; ABPI Medicines Compendium, 2002b]:
- **Phentermine, dexfenfluramine,** and **fenfluramine** have been withdrawn following reports of pulmonary hypertension and valvular heart disease [CSM, 2000].

Surgery

- **Gastric plication or bypass** is the most clinically effective and possibly cost-effective methods of reducing weight in severe, morbid obesity [NHS CRD, 1997a; National Institutes of Health, 1998].
- Surgery should only be performed in specialist centres.

Table 4: Criteria for prescribing orlistat and sibutramine.

	Orlistat	Sibutramine
Indication for initiation of drug	BMI >=30 or BMI >=28 + significant comorbidity (e.g. Type 2 diabetes or hypertension or high total cholesterol)	Patient has difficulty achieving or maintaining > 5% weight loss within 3 months *and* BMI >=30 or BMI >=27 + significant comorbidity (e.g. Type 2 diabetes or dyslipidaemia)
Contraindications to initiation that may be commonly found in obese patients		Contraindicated if blood pressure is uncontrolled or greater than 145/90 mmHg or in coronary heart disease, congestive heart failure, peripheral vascular disease, arrhythmias, or cerebrovascular disease.
Recommended ages for use	18–75 years	18–65 years
Concomitant therapies that must be given	Advice, support, and counselling on diet, physical activity, and behavioural strategies	Advice, support, and counselling on diet, physical activity, and behavioural strategies
Monitoring use	At least 5% of initial bodyweight at 3 months	A 2 kg weight loss at 4 weeks
Weight loss required to continue treatment	At least 10% of initial bodyweight at 6 months	At least 5% of initial bodyweight beyond 3 months
Monitoring adverse effects	GI adverse effects (e.g. fatty stools, urgency, oily spotting, and sometimes faecal incontinence) are common, but usually reduce with time. These can often be reduced by limiting fat intake. Vitamin supplements are not usually necessary. Only consider checking levels of fat-soluble vitamins (A, D, E, K, and beta-carotene) if the patient is not eating a balanced diet.	Raised BP is a common adverse effect. Check BP and pulse every 2 weeks for the first 3 months, every month for the next 3 months, and then 3 monthly thereafter. Discontinue treatment if at 2 consecutive visits: BP rises above 145/90 mmHg BP rises by >10 mmHg from baseline Resting pulse rate rises by >10 bpm
Length of treatment	No maximum duration of treatment.	Maximum of 12 months.

References

NHS staff in England can link, free of charge, from references to full text journals by clicking on [Full text] on the PRODIGY website.

1. ABPI Medicines Compendium (2002a) *Summary of product characteristics for Xenecal.* Electronic Medicines Compendium. Datapharm Communications Ltd. www.emc.medicines.org.uk [Accessed: 2/02/13].
2. ABPI Medicines Compendium (2002b) *Summary of product characteristics for Reductil.* Electronic Medicines Compendium. Datapharm Communications Ltd. www.emc.medicines.org.uk [Accessed: 2/04/10].

O

3. Anderson, R.E., Wadden, T.A., Bartlett, S.J. et al (1999) Effects of lifestyle activity vs structured aerobic exercise in obese women: a randomised trial. *Journal of the American Medical Association* **281**(4), 335–340. [Full text]
4. Astrup, A., Grunwald, G.K., Melanson, E.L. et al (2000) The role of low-fat diets in body weight control: a meta-analysis of ad libitum dietary intervention studies. *International Journal of Obesity* **24**(12), 1545–1552.
5. Chambers, R. and Wakley, G. (Eds.) (2002) *Obesity and overweight matters in primary care.* Oxford: Radcliffe Medical Press.
6. CSM (2000) Current position of anorectic agents/ appetite suppressants. *Current Problems in Pharmacovigilance* **26**(Sep), 12.
7. Davidson, M.H., Hauptman, J., Di Girolamo, M. et al (1999) Weight control and risk factor reduction in obese subjects treated for 2 years with orlistat. *Journal of the American Medical Association* **281**(3), 235–242. [Full text]
8. Davis, A.M., Giles, A. and Rona, R. (2000) *Tackling obesity: a toolbox for local partnership action.* London: Royal Colleges of Physicians.
9. DTB (1998) Why and how should adults lose weight? *Drug & Therapeutics Bulletin* **36**(12), 89–95.
10. Dunn, A.L., Marcus, B.H., Kampert, J.B. et al (1999) Comparison of lifestyle and structured interventions to increase physical activity and cardiorespiratory fitness: a randomised trial. *Journal of the American Medical Association* **281**(4), 327–334. [Full text]
11. Fox, K. (1999) Treatment of obesity III. Physical activity and exercise. In: British Nutrition Foundation (Ed.) *Obesity: report of the British Nutrition Foundation Task Force.* Oxford: Blackwell Science.
12. Glenny, A-M., O'Meara, S., Melville, A. et al (1997) The treatment and prevention of obesity: a systematic review of the literature. *International Journal of Obesity* **21**(9), 715–737.
13. Hauptman, J., Lucas, C., Boldrin, M.N. et al (2000) Orlistat in the long-term treatment of obesity in primary care settings. *Archives of Family Medicine* **9**(2), 160–167. [Full text]
14. James, W.P., Astrup, A., Finer, N. et al (2000) Effect of sibutramine on weight maintenance after weight loss: a randomised trial. STORM Study Group. Sibutramine Trial of Obesity Reduction and Maintenance. *Lancet* **356**(9248), 2119–2125. [Full text]
15. McManus, K., Antinoro, L. and Sacks, F. (2001) A randomized controlled trial of a moderate-fat, low-energy diet compared with a low fat, low-energy diet for weight loss in overweight adults. *International Journal of Obesity* **25**(10), 1503–1511.
16. Miller, W.C. (2001) Effective diet and exercise treatments for overweight and recommendations for intervention. *Sports Medicine* **31**(10), 717–724.
17. Miller, W.C., Koceja, D.M. and Hamilton, E.J. (1997) A meta-analysis of the past 25 years of weight loss research using diet, exercise or diet plus exercise intervention. *International Journal of Obesity & Related Metabolic Disorders* **21**(10), 941–947.
18. National Audit Office (2001) *Tackling obesity in England.* HC 220. London: National Audit Office.
19. National Institutes of Health (1998) Clinical guidelines on the identification, evaluation, and treatment of overweight and obesity in adults. *Obesity Research* **6**(Suppl 2), 51S-209S.
20. National Obesity Forum (2000) *Guidelines on management of adult obesity and overweight in primary care.* Nottingham: National Obesity Forum.
21. National Task Force on the Prevention and Treatment of Obesity (2000) Overweight, obesity, and health risk. *Archives of Internal Medicine* **160**(7), 898–904. [Full text]
22. NHS CRD (1997a) The prevention and treatment of obesity. *Effective Health Care Bulletin* **3**(2), 1–12.
23. NHS CRD (1997b) *A systematic review of the interventions for the prevention and treatment of obesity, and the maintenance of weight loss.* CRD Report No.10. York: National Health Service Centre for Reviews and Dissemination.
24. NICE (2001a) *Guidance on the use of orlistat for the treatment of obesity in adults.* Technology appraisal no. 22. National Institute for Clinical Excellence. www.nice.org.uk [Accessed: 3/02/24].
25. NICE (2001b) *Guidance on the use of sibutramine for the treatment of obesity in adults.* Technology appraisal no. 31. National Institute for Clinical Excellence. www.nice.org.uk [Accessed: 3/02/24].
26. Prentice, A.M. and Jebb, S.A. (1995) Obesity in Britain: gluttony or sloth? *British Medical Journal* **311**(7002), 437–439. [Full text]
27. RCP (1998) *Clinical management of overweight and obese patients: with particular reference to the use of drugs.* London: Royal College of Physicians of London
28. SIGN (1996) *Obesity in Scotland: integrating prevention and weight management74.* Report no. 8. Scottish Intercollegiate Guidelines Network. www.sign.ac.uk [Accessed: 3/10/06].
29. Sjöström, L., Rissanen, A., Andersen, T. et al (1998) Randomised placebo-controlled trial of orlistat for weight loss and prevention of weight regain in obese patients. *Lancet* **352**(9123), 167–172. [Full text]
30. Thorogood, M., Hillsdon, M. and Summerbell, C. (2001) Changing behaviour. *Clinical Evidence* **6**, 31–49.
31. Wadden, T.A. (1998) New goals of obesity treatment: a healthier weight and other ideals. *Primary Care Psychiatry* **5**, 45–54.
32. Wadden, T.A., Berkowitz, R.I., Womble, L.G. et al (2000) Effects of Sibutramine plus Orlistat in obese women following 1 year of treatment by Sibutramine alone: a placebo-controlled trial. *Obesity Research* **8**(6), 431–437.
33. WHO (2000) *Obesity: preventing and managing the global epidemic.* WHO Technical Report Series – 894. Geneva: World Health Organisation.
34. Wilding, J. (1997) Obesity treatment. *British Medical Journal* **315**(7114), 997–1000. [Full text]

PRODIGY GUIDANCE

Opioid dependence

Last revised in February 2004
www.prodigy.nhs.uk/guidance.asp?gt=Opioid dependence

Applies to people over the age of 16 years

This guidance is based on the Department of Health publication *Drug misuse and dependence — guidelines on clinical management* (1999) and the Royal College of General Practitioners publication *Guidance for the use of buprenorphine for the treatment of opioid dependence in primary care (2003).*

This guidance covers the management of opioid dependence in adults.

This guidance does not cover the management of drug dependency in neonates or in those aged under 16 years, the management of other drug misuse (e.g. cocaine), or the prevention of drug dependence.

There is separate PRODIGY guidance for *Alcohol — problem drinking* and *Hypnotic or anxiolytic dependence.*

Goals

- To help a person with opioid dependency to remain healthy
- To reduce the harm associated with illicit drug misuse
- To reduce the dangers associated with sharing needles (hepatitis A, B, and C; HIV; other blood-borne infections)
- To help a person with opioid dependency to try to achieve a drug free life
- If abstinence is not possible, to establish the person on maintenance treatment at a sufficient dose to prevent or avoid withdrawal effects, reduce illicit drug misuse, and reduce the chance of future episodes of drug misuse
- To reduce the adverse social consequences associated with illegal drug misuse (e.g. unemployment, marital problems, criminal activity, diversion of prescribed drugs onto the illegal market)

DH et al, 1999]

Contents

Scenarios

- Initial assessment and management to determine treatment p.1325
- Initiation and stabilization of a substitute drug p.1326
- Maintenance on a substitute drug p.1328
- Planned detoxification leading to abstinence p.1330
- Acute withdrawal syndrome p.1331
- Collapse due to opioid overdose p.1333
- Unknown patient–new patient/temporary resident/ out of hours p.1334
- Changing substitute treatment p.1335

Extended Information, p. 1337

Which scenario?

- **Initial assessment and management to determine treatment:** covers the initial assessment of a drug user that is required before treatment can be started.
- **Initiation and stabilization of a substitute drug:** covers the initiation and dose titration of methadone or buprenorphine treatment for the first time.
- **Maintenance on a substitute drug:** covers the long-term use of methadone for those who are unable to achieve abstinence. The scenario also covers the place of buprenorphine, the legal requirements for a patient taking methadone and/or buprenorphine out of the country for self-administration, and pain control in a person on maintenance therapy.
- **Planned detoxification leading to abstinence:** covers the management of opioid dependence with methadone after stabilization, where gradual reduction of the use of methadone is appropriate.
- **Acute withdrawal syndrome:** covers the symptomatic management of acute withdrawal syndrome using non-opioid treatment.
- **Collapse due to opioid overdose:** covers the emergency management of opioid overdose.
- **Unknown patient–new patient/temporary resident/out of hours:** covers the management of a new patient/ temporary resident/unknown patient.
- **Changing substitute treatment:** covers initiation and stabilization when switching from one substitute drug to another.

Initial assessment and management to determine treatment

Which therapy?

- **Enquire** about what precipitated the consultation and the person's expectations.
- **Take a history to determine:**
  - The type of drug misused, route, dosage, and for how long it has been used
  - Degree of dependence
  - Motivation to stop or change pattern of drug misuse, and attitude towards maintenance therapy.
  - At-risk behaviour
  - Hepatitis A, B or C, and HIV status — if known
  - Psychiatric history
  - Forensic history
  - Social history
  - Past contact with treatment services
  - What precipitated the relapse (if relapsed)
- **Examine for:**
  - **Evidence of drug misuse** (e.g. needle tracks, signs of drug intoxication or withdrawal).
  - **The presence of complications** (e.g. poor nutrition, anaemia, skin abscess, thrombophlebitis, viral hepatitis, HIV, chest infection, tuberculosis).
- **Assess mental health.**
- **Refer to or liaise with a community drug team or specialist service.**
- **Discuss harm reduction** — access to sterile needles and syringe; testing for HIV/hepatitis A, B, or C; safe sex; hepatitis A and B immunization.
- Depending upon expertise:
  - Consider whether substitution therapy is appropriate:

O

- How does the person wish to change, and will substitution therapy encourage this?
- Is the person taking drugs regularly? (Daily use is a strong indicator of dependence.)
- Is there convincing evidence of dependence?
- **Discuss the options for substitution therapy** (i.e. detoxification or maintenance). Always find out what the user wants, and check this against what you are able and willing to offer.
- Discuss the importance of shared care.
- **Agree on a management plan** based on either drug or non-drug treatment, or both.
- Arrange a urine screen to confirm opioid use.

Follow-up advice

- Arrange a follow-up appointment within a few days to:
  - Establish how they are coping
  - Establish how they now view the decisions made at this consultation and their goals
  - Review the results of blood and urine tests (see *Should I refer or investigate?*)
  - Establish if they have received appointments/contact from referral agencies

Should I refer or investigate?

Refer?

- **Assess the most appropriate level of expertise required** to manage the person, and refer or liaise appropriately.
- **Pregnant women should be referred urgently.**

Investigate?

Arrange a urine drug screen.

- **Try to ensure that the urine belongs to this person** (Note: a fresh sample should be warm).
- **Results should be interpreted in the light of clinical findings, as false negatives and false positives can occur.** False positives can be caused by the use of quinolones or loperamide. Note also that many over-the-counter medicines contain opioids (for example, codeine). Negative results can occur despite the presence of buprenorphine or tramadol, as these drugs do not test as opioid-positive on urine tests.
- **At least one positive urine test** (and preferably two) for opioids should usually be obtained before starting substitute treatment.
- **A negative result brings into doubt whether the person is currently dependent on drugs.** Reassess at an appropriate time to observe withdrawal symptoms, and repeat the urine test.

Investigations to exclude complications.

- **Consider investigations to exclude complications.** Choice of investigations is guided by clinical judgement, but would usually include:
  - Full blood count (to exclude anaemia, signs of infection)
  - Electrolytes (to assess renal function)
  - Liver function tests (to possibly identify hepatitis)
  - Tests for hepatitis A, B or C, and HIV (a pre-test discussion covering the main points is important before testing)

Patient information leaflets

The following PILs are available at www.prodigy.nhs.uk

- Addaction
- ADFAM
- Cognitive Behaviour Therapy (CBT)
- Methadone Replacement for Heroin
- National Drugs Helpline

Shared decision making

- **If you have been injecting drugs such as heroin, we** usually advise:
  - A blood test, which includes testing for HIV, and hepatitis A, B and C
  - A urine test to check for drugs in your urine
  - Immunization against hepatitis B
- **Do you know about the dangers of using shared needles, syringes, etc?**
- **We do not prescribe opioid drugs until** you have been assessed, and we have the result of the urine test.
- **After assessment, an option is to replace your drug-taking with prescribed oral methadone (or buprenorphine).**
  - Many people stay on methadone long-term (maintenance). But it is much better than injecting street drugs.
  - Some people gradually reduce the dose and come off it (detox).
- **If you decide to take methadone (or buprenorphine), we need to agree:**
  - The goals and basis of treatment
  - That you will keep appointments
  - That lost scripts or medication will not be replaced

Drug rationale

- There are no prescriptions offered in this scenario.

Initiation and stabilization of a substitute drug

Which therapy?

General points

- **Most GPs will initiate treatment after consultation with a community drug team or specialist service.**
- **Consider a written agreement with the person.** A suggested format is available as a Patient Information Leaflet.
- **Methadone in its liquid form is the drug of choice** (note: methadone linctus is not licensed for opioid dependence).
- **Buprenorphine is an alternative option,** especially for people who have *moderate* opioid dependence and have:
  - A preference for the 'clear head' response often reported with buprenorphine, in contrast to the 'clouding' sometimes associated with methadone or heroin use
  - Previously had problems with using heroin 'on top' of maintenance methadone treatment, and who may benefit from using buprenorphine because it reduces the subjective effects in combination with heroin
  - Experienced unwanted effects or difficulties with methadone in the past

Initiating treatment and stabilization with methadone

- **Careful induction is necessary,** as the first 2 weeks of treatment is associated with a greater risk of overdose mortality. Note: not giving enough can also cause problems. Self-reported habits may be misleading.
- **The usual initial daily dose is methadone 10–30 mg.** If tolerance is low or uncertain, 10 to 20 mg is more appropriate; doses less than 20 mg in opioid-naïve persons are relatively safe.

O

- **If a low starting dose of methadone is used,** further small doses can be given under supervision after a few hours (depending on the severity of the withdrawal symptoms) if there is no evidence of excess sedation, this may be more appropriately done by experienced GPs.
- **Increase the dose gradually, but not too slowly, until signs of withdrawal have disappeared.**
  - Incremental dose increases over the first 7 days should be no more than 5 to 10 mg on one day, and a total weekly increase should not exceed 30 mg above the first day's dose.
  - Subsequent increases should not exceed 10 mg per week up to a total of between 60 and 120 mg (it is recommended to obtain specialist advice for higher doses).
- **Stabilization is usually complete by the end of the sixth week, but it may take longer.**

Initiating treatment and stabilization with buprenorphine

- **Withdrawal symptoms may be precipitated** by the partial antagonist properties of buprenorphine.
- **To avoid withdrawal when switching from heroin, delay the first dose of buprenorphine until at least 8 hours after the last dose of heroin,** and ask the person to wait as long as possible until they are experiencing features of opioid withdrawal.
- **The usual recommended starting dose is 4 mg.**
- Rapidly titrate dose according to clinical response.
- Daily increases of 4 mg a day are possible, up to a maximum of 32 mg daily. The most commonly effective dose is 12–24 mg. During dose titration, the person should be reviewed frequently.

Practical prescribing points

For further information, please see the *Medicines Compendium* (www.medicines.org.uk) or the *British National Formulary* (www.bnf.org).

Methadone and buprenorphine

- **Methadone should always be prescribed in its liquid form** to minimize illicit use (note: methadone linctus is not licensed for opioid dependence). If not supervised, sugar-free methadone may have a greater potential for abuse in terms of being injected.
- **Take-home doses should not be prescribed** if the person shows a continued and unstable, or unauthorized, pattern of drug misuse, or has housing problems and cannot keep methadone safely.
- **Buprenorphine should be prescribed as Subutex® (buprenorphine),** as it is the only licensed product containing buprenorphine for the management of drug dependence.

Clinical drug interactions to be aware of include the following:

Clinical drug interactions to be aware of include the following:

- **Methadone may interact with other drugs — these may be clinically important:**
  - **Rifampicin** accelerates the metabolism of methadone (i.e. reduced effect) and this may precipitate withdrawal symptoms.
  - **Anti-epileptics** (carbamazepine and phenytoin) may also accelerate the metabolism of methadone and precipitate withdrawal symptoms.
  - **Antivirals:** methadone possibly increases plasma concentration of zidovudine. Plasma concentration of methadone is reduced by efavirenz, ritonavir, and possibly by abacavir and nevirapine.
  - **Additive central nervous system depression with alcohol and benzodiazepines.**

Legal and practical information for prescribing opioid-substitute controlled-drug prescriptions

Legal and practical information for prescribing opioid-substitute controlled-drug prescriptions

- **For one-off prescriptions,** a standard FP10 form can be used.
- **For instalment dispensing of methadone or buprenorphine,** GPs are required to use a blue FP10MDA1000 form.
- **Legally a pharmacist cannot dispense methadone or buprenorphine without the following information,** written in the prescriber's own handwriting (unless exempt) in ink, or otherwise so as to be indelible:
  - The person's name and address
  - The form and strength of the preparation (sugar-free has to be written if required)
  - The total quantity of the preparation or the number of dose units, in both words AND figures
  - The dose
  - The signature of the prescriber who has written the prescription
  - The date of signing by the prescriber who has written the prescription
  - The prescriber's address specified on the prescription
- **State the date when it is intended that the first instalment should start.**
- **Specify the interval** (e.g. daily dispensing) and the amount required or instalment dispensing on the prescription.
- **If the prescriber wants supervised consumption in the pharmacy,** specify 'supervised consumption' on the prescription if a local scheme is in place.
- **If extra quantities need to be prescribed on any day** (e.g. two doses on a Saturday because the pharmacy is closed on Sunday), this needs to be specified on the prescription. Once specified, the prescription cannot be dispensed on alternative dates.
- **Do not prescribe more than 14 days' supply** on either a blue FP10MDA1000 form or a standard FP10.
- **A prescription is valid for 13 weeks** from the date stated thereon.
- **A prescription that was posted to the pharmacy but that has not arrived cannot legally be dispensed,** even at the verbal request of the prescriber.
- **Other prescription items cannot be written on the same form.**

Follow-up advice

- **Review the person daily during the first few days** in order to titrate the dose against withdrawal symptoms and for assessment.
- **When treating people long-term, review every 3 months** (or more frequently according to clinical judgement) to reassess the goals of treatment and observe the effect of maintenance.
- **Review the results of blood and urine tests** as appropriate (see *Should I refer or investigate?*).
- **Random urine testing** may encourage compliance.

Should I refer or investigate?

Refer?

- **Do not prescribe in isolation,** but liaise with other professionals who will be able to help with factors contributing to an individual's drug misuse.

Investigate?

Arrange a urine drug screen.

- **At least one positive urine test (and preferably two) for opioids should usually be obtained before starting substitute treatment.** Try to ensure that the urine belongs to the person in question (note: a fresh sample should be warm).
- **Results should be interpreted in the light of clinical findings, as false negatives and false positives can occur.** False positives can be caused by the use of quinolones or loperamide. Note also that many over-the-counter medicines contain opioids (for example, codeine). Negative results can occur despite the presence of buprenorphine or tramadol, as these drugs do not test as opioid-positive on urine tests.
- **A negative result brings into doubt whether the person is currently dependent on drugs.** Re-assess in terms of withdrawal symptoms, and repeat the urine test. Substitute treatment should not be prescribed unless the prescriber is experienced enough to be certain that the person is currently suffering from withdrawal symptoms.

Investigations to exclude complications.

- **Consider investigations to exclude complications.** Choice of investigations is guided by clinical judgement, but would usually include:
  - Full blood count (to exclude anaemia, signs of infection)
  - Electrolytes (to assess renal function)
  - Liver function tests (to possibly identify hepatitis)
  - Tests for hepatitis A, B, or C, and HIV (a pre-test discussion covering the main points is important before testing)

O

Patient information leaflets

The following PILs are available at www.prodigy.nhs.uk

- Addaction
- ADFAM
- Cognitive Behaviour Therapy (CBT)
- Methadone Replacement for Heroin
- National Drugs Helpline

Shared decision making

- **Methadone** (or buprenorphine) can replace heroin that you currently use.
- **If you decide on this, we need to agree:**
  - The goals and basis of treatment
  - That you will keep appointments
  - That lost scripts or medication will not be replaced
- **The aim is to prevent withdrawal symptoms.**
- **The dose may need to be increased in steps over a few weeks,** depending if you get any withdrawal symptoms. But note:
  - Methadone takes 2–4 hours to reach peak effect.
  - Methadone accumulates in your body. So you will feel a greater effect of the drug over days, even without increasing the dose.
  - It may take a few weeks to get to the correct dose that prevents all withdrawal symptoms.
- **You should not take any street drugs or much alcohol.** Try to accept that you may have some withdrawal symptoms until the correct dose is found.
- **Once on a regular dose of methadone:**
  - Many people stay on methadone long-term (maintenance).
  - Some people gradually reduce the dose and come off it (detox). However, it may take months or years before you are ready to consider this.
- **Have you been offered blood tests** for HIV, and hepatitis A, B and C?
- Have you been offered hepatitis B immunization?
- **You are more likely to succeed in staying off street drugs if you have regular support** from a local drug community team (or similar).

Drug rationale

- There are no prescriptions offered in this scenario. For the legal and practical information for prescribing opioid-substitute controlled-drug prescriptions, see *Prescribing points*.

Maintenance on a substitute drug

Which therapy?

- **Advice from a specialist** is important, as is following local protocols on maintenance. Ideally, there should be shared care with the drug dependence team or a specialist.
- **Check that harm-reduction issues** have been covered (see scenario *Initial assessment and management to determine treatment*).
- **Consider a written agreement with the person.** A suggested format is available as a Patient Information Leaflet.
- **Methadone is the drug of choice,** and should always be prescribed in its liquid form (note: methadone linctus is not licensed for opioid dependence).
- **Buprenorphine** may sometimes be used in a person with moderate opioid dependence.
- **It may take many months or even years before a reduction in prescribed drugs can be considered.**

Maintenance treatment with methadone

- **After initiating and stabilising the dosage,** it is considered that the greatest benefit in retaining people in treatment and avoiding illicit opioid use is when people are maintained on a daily dosage of methadone 60–120 mg, but this must be determined for each person.
- **If tolerance is particularly high,** doses above 120 mg may occasionally be necessary. Plasma methadone monitoring may help determine whether the dosage is adequate. This would usually involve specialist assessment or advice. Particular care is needed if high doses are used and there is associated alcohol or benzodiazepine dependence.

Maintenance treatment with buprenorphine

- The daily dosage of buprenorphine can range from 8–32 mg, but the usual dose range is 12–24 mg.
- Buprenorphine should be prescribed for daily use — the effectiveness of alternate-day prescribing is unclear, and such a prescription should be carried out only after consultation with a specialist.

Missed doses

- **It is not unusual for a drug misuser to present claiming to have missed several doses of methadone.** Phoning the pharmacy can check the validity of this. Often the drug

misuser claims to have used street drugs, but this can never be verified or the purity known.
- **If more than 2 days have been missed,** then tolerance may have been lost, especially in those in the lower range of maintenance doses. Reinitiate therapy starting at a low dose.
- **If 1 or 2 days missed, give usual dose.**

Practical prescribing points

For further information, please see the *Medicines Compendium* (www.medicines.org.uk) or the *British National Formulary* (www.bnf.org).

Methadone and buprenorphine

- **'Take home' doses should not be prescribed** if the person shows a continued and unstable, or unauthorized, pattern of drug misuse.
- **If the person has been entrusted with taking the substitute drug unsupervised,** then this can be picked up daily, or every two or three days, but no more than one week's supply should be dispensed at one time.
- **Information on travelling abroad** while taking substitute therapy is covered in the *Management issues* section of this guidance.

Clinical drug interactions to be aware of include the following:

Clinical drug interactions to be aware of include the following:

- **Methadone may interact with other drugs — these may be clinically important:**
  - **Rifampicin** accelerates the metabolism of methadone (i.e. reduced effect) and this may precipitate withdrawal symptoms.
  - **Anti-epileptics** (carbamazepine and phenytoin) may also accelerate the metabolism of methadone and precipitate withdrawal symptoms.
  - **Antivirals:** methadone possibly increases plasma concentration of zidovudine. Plasma concentration of methadone is reduced by efavirenz, ritonavir, and possibly by abacavir and nevirapine.
  - **Additive central nervous system depression with alcohol and benzodiazepines.**

Legal and practical information for prescribing opioid-substitute controlled-drug prescriptions

Legal and practical information for prescribing opioid-substitute controlled-drug prescriptions

- **For one-off prescriptions,** a standard FP10 form can be used.
- **For instalment dispensing of methadone or buprenorphine,** GPs are required to use a blue FP10MDA1000 form.
- **Legally a pharmacist cannot dispense methadone or buprenorphine unless the following information is written in the prescriber's own handwriting in ink** (or otherwise so as to be indelible):
  - The person's name and address
  - The form and strength of the preparation (sugar-free has to be written if required)
  - The total quantity of the preparation or the number of dose units, in both words AND figures
  - The dose
  - The signature of the prescriber who has written the prescription
  - The date of signing by the prescriber who has written the prescription
  - The prescriber's address specified on the prescription
- **State the date when it is intended that the first instalment should start.**
- **Specify the interval** (e.g. daily dispensing) and the amount required or instalment dispensing on the prescription.
- **If the prescriber wants supervised consumption in the pharmacy,** specify 'supervised consumption' on the prescription if a local scheme is in place.
- **If extra quantities need to be prescribed on any day** (e.g. two doses on a Saturday because the pharmacy is closed on Sunday), this needs to be specified on the prescription. Once specified, the prescription cannot be dispensed on alternative dates.
- **Do not prescribe more than 14 days' supply** on either a blue FP10MDA1000 form or a standard FP10.
- **A prescription is valid for 13 weeks from the date stated thereon.**
- **A prescription that was posted to the pharmacy but that has not arrived cannot legally be dispensed,** even at the verbal request of the prescriber.
- **Other prescription items cannot be written on the same form.**

Follow-up advice

- **Review the results of blood and urine tests** as appropriate (see *Should I refer or investigate?*).
- **People should keep appointments with the shared-care team and the practice.**
- **Review at regular intervals,** initially fortnightly and then, if stable, at least monthly. A thorough review every 3 months should include achievements and goal setting.

Should I refer or investigate?

Refer?

- **Do not prescribe in isolation,** but liaise with other professionals who will be able to help with factors contributing to an individual's drug misuse.

Investigate?

- **Random urine analysis** for opioids is useful in identifying how treatment is progressing, but it should be remembered that buprenorphine cannot be detected in routine urine tests.
- **Consider investigations to exclude complications.** Choice of investigations is guided by clinical judgement, but would usually include:
  - Full blood count (to exclude anaemia, signs of infection)
  - Electrolytes (to assess renal function)
  - Liver function tests (to possibly identify hepatitis)
  - Tests for hepatitis A, B, or C, and HIV (a pre-test discussion covering the main points is important before testing.)

Patient information leaflets

The following PILs are available at www.prodigy.nhs.uk

- Addaction
- ADFAM
- Cognitive Behaviour Therapy (CBT)
- Methadone Replacement for Heroin
- National Drugs Helpline

Shared decision making

- **Taking prescribed methadone** (or buprenorphine) is far safer than injecting street drugs.
- **Have you been offered blood tests** for HIV, and hepatitis A, B and C?
- **Have you been offered hepatitis B immunization?**
- **Once on a regular dose of methadone:**
  - Many people stay on methadone long-term (maintenance).
  - Some people gradually reduce the dose and come off it (detox). However, it may take months or years before you are ready to consider this.
- **Note: lost scripts or medication will not be replaced.**
- **You are more likely to succeed in staying off heroin if you have regular support** from a local drug community team (or similar).

Drug rationale

- There are no prescriptions offered in this scenario. For the legal and practical information for prescribing opioid-substitute controlled-drug prescriptions, see *Prescribing points*.

Planned detoxification leading to abstinence

Which therapy?

The drug user should have previously been assessed (see scenario *Initial assessment and management to determine treatment*) and stabilized on substitute drug treatment (see scenario *Initiation and stabilization of a substitute drug*).

- **Consider drug detoxification *only* if the person is motivated to withdraw from opioids.** Note: despite requesting detoxification, many people are more suitable for maintenance treatment and should be returned to maintenance if necessary.
- **It is important that clear aims and the ways in which these will be carried out have been agreed.** Some doctors may choose to have a written agreement with the person. A suggested format is available as a Patient Information Leaflet.
- **Discuss the importance of continued shared care.**
- **Methadone – there is more experience in the use of methadone for detoxification.**
- **Buprenorphine is an alternative for people with moderate opioid dependence.** It is particularly suitable for those who:
  - Have a preference for the 'clear head' response often reported with buprenorphine in contrast to the 'clouding' sometimes associated with methadone or heroin use
  - Have experienced unwanted effects or difficulties with methadone
  - Are considering naltrexone treatment (requires specialist initiation) after detoxification
- **Consider buprenorphine for detoxification once methadone reduction has reached 30 mg/day.**

Methadone detoxification

Note: the user should have been stabilized on a methadone maintenance programme and have abstained completely from heroin.

- **Reduce the daily dosage of methadone, *usually* by 5–10 mg every week or fortnight.** Note: dose reductions can occur at any time interval and will generally be dictated by the needs of the user
- **Reduction should be more gradual as the daily dose of methadone decreases.** Note: be aware that too slow a reduction rate may result in the person slipping between detoxification and methadone maintenance.

Buprenorphine detoxification

Note: the user should have been stabilized on a buprenorphine maintenance programme and have abstained completely from heroin.

- **A schedule for detoxification** using buprenorphine is suggested in Table 1.
- **Different rates of detoxification may be necessary according to the person's preference.**
- **Most people will not experience significant withdrawal discomfort until they have reduced to low doses** of buprenorphine or after they have stopped.

Table 1: Proposed schedule for detoxification using buprenorphine.

Daily buprenorphine dose	Reduction rate
Above 16 mg	4 mg every 1–2 weeks
8–16 mg	2–4 mg every 1–2 weeks
2–8 mg	2 mg every week or fortnight
Below 2 mg	0.4 – 0.8 mg every week or fortnight

Switching from methadone to buprenorphine for detoxification

Note: the methadone should be reduced to 30 mg a day, or less, before commencing buprenorphine.

- **Withdrawal symptoms may be precipitated** by the partial agonist properties of buprenorphine.
- **To avoid withdrawal when switching from methadone, delay the first dose of buprenorphine until the person is experiencing features of opioid withdrawal** (at least 24–36 hours after the last methadone dose).
- Starting doses of buprenorphine when switching from methadone are suggested in Table 2.

Table 2: Proposed starting doses for switching from methadone to buprenorphine.

Last methadone dose	Buprenorphine day 1	Buprenorphine day 2	Buprenorphine day 3 onwards
>30 mg	Not recommended in primary care		
20–30 mg	4 mg	6–8 mg	Daily increases of 4 mg a day are possible, up to a maximum of 32 mg a day
10–20 mg	4 mg	4–6 mg	
<10 mg	2 mg	2–6 mg	

Practical prescribing points

For further information, please see the *Medicines Compendium* (www.medicines.org.uk) or the *British National Formulary* (www.bnf.org).

Methadone and buprenorphine

- **Methadone should always be prescribed in its liquid form** to minimize illicit use (note: methadone linctus is not licensed for opioid dependence). If not supervised, sugar-free methadone may have a greater potential for abuse in terms of being injected.
- **Buprenorphine should be prescribed as Subutex® (buprenorphine),** as it is the only licensed product containing buprenorphine for the management of drug dependence.

Clinical drug interactions to be aware of include the following:

Clinical drug interactions to be aware of include the following:

- **Methadone may interact with other drugs — these may be clinically important:**
  - **Rifampicin** accelerates the metabolism of methadone (i.e. reduced effect) and this may precipitate withdrawal symptoms.
  - **Anti-epileptics** (carbamazepine and phenytoin) may also accelerate the metabolism of methadone and precipitate withdrawal symptoms.
  - **Antivirals:** methadone possibly increases plasma concentration of zidovudine. Plasma concentration of methadone is reduced by efavirenz, ritonavir, and possibly by abacavir and nevirapine.
  - **Additive central nervous system depression with alcohol and benzodiazepines.**

Legal and practical information for prescribing opioid substitute controlled drug prescriptions

Legal and practical information for prescribing opioid substitute controlled drug prescriptions

- **For one-off prescriptions,** a standard FP10 form can be used.
- **For instalment dispensing of methadone and buprenorphine,** GPs are required to use a blue FP10MDA1000 form.
- **Legally a pharmacist cannot dispense methadone or buprenorphine unless the following information is written in the prescriber's own handwriting in ink** (or otherwise so as to be indelible):
  - The person's name and address
  - The form and strength of the preparation (sugar-free has to be written if required)
  - The total quantity of the preparation or the number of dose units in both words AND figures
  - The dose
  - The signature of the prescriber who has written the prescription
  - The date of signing by the prescriber who has written the prescription
  - The prescriber's address specified on the prescription
- **State the date when it is intended that the first instalment should start.**
- **Specify the interval** (e.g. daily dispensing) and the amount required or instalment dispensing on the prescription.
- **If the prescriber wants supervised consumption in the pharmacy,** specify 'supervised consumption' on the prescription if a local scheme is in place.
- **If extra quantities need to be prescribed on any day** (e.g. two doses on a Saturday because the pharmacy is closed on Sunday), this needs to be specified on the prescription. Once specified, the prescription cannot be dispensed on alternative dates.
- **Do not prescribe more than 14 days' supply** on either a blue FP10MDA1000 form or a standard FP10.
- **A prescription is valid for 13 weeks from the date stated thereon.**
- **A prescription that was posted to the pharmacy but that has not arrived cannot legally be dispensed,** even at the verbal request of the prescriber.
- **Other prescription items cannot be written on the same form.**

Follow-up advice

- **Review at intervals,** determined by the speed of withdrawal and the supportive care available from the shared-care team.
- **Review, according to clinical judgement and the person's wishes, once a person is off opioids** to address any outstanding or new problems. A follow-up appointment at 3 months is advisable.
- **Advise that relapse is common** and that it is in the person's own interests to seek help as soon as possible.
- **If lofexidine has been prescribed,** blood pressure will require regular monitoring in accordance with local protocols.

Should I refer or investigate?

Investigate?

- **Random urine analysis** for opioids is useful in identifying relapse, but it should be remembered that buprenorphine cannot be detected in routine urine tests.
- **Consider investigations to exclude complications.** Choice of investigations is guided by clinical judgement, but would usually include:
  - Full blood count (to exclude anaemia, signs of infection)
  - Electrolytes (to assess renal function)
  - Liver function tests (to possibly identify hepatitis)
  - Tests for hepatitis A, B, or C, and HIV (a pre-test discussion covering the main points is important before testing)

Patient information leaflets

The following PILs are available at www.prodigy.nhs.uk

- Cognitive Behaviour Therapy (CBT)
- Methadone Replacement for Heroin

O

Shared decision making

- **Taking prescribed methadone** (or buprenorphine) is far safer than injecting street drugs.
- **Once you are on a regular dose of methadone, and free of heroin,** you may want to gradually reduce the dose. The aim is to eventually stop methadone completely.
- **The timescale varies from case to case.** It can take from a few weeks to several months.
- Typically, the dose of methadone is reduced by 5–10 mg every 1–2 weeks.
- **If reducing or stopping methadone does not work out,** you can go back to your previous maintenance dose.

Drug rationale

- There are no prescriptions offered in this scenario. For the legal and practical information for prescribing opioid-substitute controlled-drug prescriptions, see *Prescribing points*.

Acute withdrawal syndrome

Which therapy?

- **A doctor may feel pressurized to prescribe opioids in order to prevent withdrawal symptoms, but it is considered good practice NOT to do so.**
- **Offer referral** to the local drug service for support and to discuss management options.
- **Relieve symptoms and provide support.**

- **Diarrhoea:** loperamide is effective in reducing stool frequency and increasing stool consistency.
- **Nausea and vomiting:** domperidone or metoclopramide speed gastric emptying and relieve nausea.
- **General aches and pains or high temperature:** a short course of analgesia is effective for symptomatic relief.
  - **Paracetamol** is preferred
  - **Ibuprofen** is an alternative, in the absence of contraindications
- **Lofexidine** is licensed for the management of symptoms of opioid withdrawal. We recommend that it is prescribed only by practitioners with knowledge of lofexidine or following advice from specialist practitioners.

Practical prescribing points

For further information, please see the *Medicines Compendium* (www.medicines.org.uk) or the *British National Formulary* (www.bnf.org).

Loperamide

- **Note that when screening urine to detect opioid use, loperamide can cause false positive results.**

Metoclopramide

- **Metoclopramide** should only be used in young adults where there is severe intractable vomiting of known cause. Metoclopramide may cause extrapyramidal adverse effects, and there is an increased risk of this occurring in the younger population.

Nonsteroidal anti-inflammatory drugs

- **Ibuprofen,** as with other nonsteroidal anti-inflammatory drugs (NSAIDs), may worsen or precipitate gastrointestinal haemorrhage, asthma, hypertension, renal impairment, or cardiac failure. Avoid if there is a history of peptic ulcers.
- **NSAIDs should be taken in the lowest effective dose possible,** after food.
- **Consider gastroprotection in the following circumstances:**
  - Age 65 and over.
  - Previous clinical history of gastroduodenal ulcer, gastrointestinal (GI) bleeding, or gastroduodenal perforation.
  - Concomitant use of medications that are known to increase the likelihood of upper GI adverse events (e.g. corticosteroids and anticoagulants).
  - Presence of serious comorbidity, such as cardiovascular disease, renal or hepatic impairment, diabetes, and hypertension.
  - Requirement for the prolonged use of maximum recommended dosage of standard NSAIDs.
- **Carefully weigh up the risks** in people with cardiovascular morbidity, cerebrovascular disease, or a history of depression. Use in pregnancy only if the benefit outweighs the harm.

Follow-up advice

- **Arrange a follow-up appointment** with the person for a full initial assessment, if not done at this time.
- **If full assessment has been done, then arrange an appointment within a few days** to establish:
  - How they are coping
  - How they feel about the decisions made at this consultation and their goals
  - A review of the results of blood and urine tests (see *Should I refer or investigate?*)
  - If they have received appointments/contact from referral agencies
- **Even when treating people long-term, a 3-monthly review is appropriate** (or more frequently according to clinical judgement) to observe the effect of maintenance treatment and reassess the goals and targets of treatment.
- **If lofexidine has been prescribed,** blood pressure will require regular monitoring, but in accordance with local protocols.

Should I refer or investigate?

Refer?

- **Advice from a specialist should usually be sought when prescribing maintenance treatment,** unless local arrangements for GP initiation have been made.

Investigate?

- **Consider investigations to exclude complications.** Choice of investigations is guided by clinical judgement, but would usually include:
  - Full blood count (to exclude anaemia, signs of infection)
  - Electrolytes (to assess renal function)
  - Liver function tests (to possibly identify hepatitis)
  - Tests for hepatitis A, B, or C, and HIV (a pre-test discussion covering the main points is important before testing)

Patient information leaflets

The following PILs are available at www.prodigy.nhs.uk

- Cognitive Behaviour Therapy (CBT)
- Methadone Replacement for Heroin

Shared decision making

- **We do not prescribe opioid drugs in the short term.**
- **If you like, we can refer you for assessment of your drug situation** (with a view to replacement with methadone if appropriate). This may take time to arrange.
- **To help ease some of the withdrawal symptoms in the short term:**
  - **Loperamide** should help if you have diarrhoea.
  - **Domperidone** should help if you have sickness.
  - **Paracetamol** or **ibuprofen** should help if you have headaches, pains, or fever.
  - **Lofexidine** is sometimes prescribed by specialists for 7–10 days, and helps to ease various withdrawal symptoms.

Drug rationale

Drugs not included

- **Antidiarrhoeal** agents (other than loperamide) are not included. Many of these preparations are either opioids or combination products containing opioids. They have adverse effects on the central nervous system and have the potential for abuse.
- **Anti-emetics, other than domperidone and metoclopramide,** are not included, as they do not speed gastric emptying.
- **Aspirin** is not included because of its extensive adverse effect profile.
- **Nonsteroidal anti-inflammatory drugs (NSAIDs) other than ibuprofen, diclofenac, and naproxen that are** associated with a higher risk of gastrointestinal adverse events or that are not licensed for general

musculoskeletal pain and inflammation are not included [CSM, 1994; Henry et al, 1996; Hernández-Diaz and Rodriguez, 2000]. Suppositories are not offered, as they do not improve efficacy or safety, and are generally less acceptable to people [Tramer et al, 1998].
- **NSAID modified-release and topical preparations** are not included. Improvement in efficacy has not been demonstrated, and they are relatively expensive.
- **Cyclo-oxygenase (COX)-2 selective NSAIDs** (celecoxib, etodolac, and meloxicam) should only be used for specific circumstances [NICE, 2001]. They are not licensed for use in general musculoskeletal pain and inflammation.
- **Codeine, combination opioid products, and strong opioids** are not offered. Non-opioid agents should be considered as first- or second-line treatment of mild to moderate symptomatic pain relief.
- **Lofexidine** is most commonly used in specialist centres. We therefore recommend that it is prescribed only by practitioners with knowledge of lofexidine or following advice from specialist practitioners.

Drugs included

- **Loperamide** may be a useful adjunct for symptom control in some adults, but it should not be used routinely and it has a low incidence of adverse effects on the central nervous system.
- **Anti-emetics: domperidone and metoclopramide** relieve nausea and speed gastric emptying. If analgesia is required at the same time, these agents may enhance the efficacy of the co-administered analgesic. Domperidone is also available as a suppository.
- **Paracetamol** is an effective and safe analgesic and antipyretic agent for most people.
- **Standard nonsteroidal anti-inflammatory drugs (NSAIDs): ibuprofen, diclofenac, and naproxen** have a good balance of efficacy against adverse effect profile. Ibuprofen is associated with the lowest risk of gastrointestinal adverse effects and should be tried first before diclofenac and naproxen, which are associated with intermediate risk [CSM, 1994; Garcia and Jick, 1994; Henry et al, 1996; Eccles et al, 1998; Hernández-Diaz and Rodriguez, 2000].

Prescriptions

Loperamide

Loperamide: 4mg now, then 2mg after stool. Max 16mg/24hours
- Age from 16 years onwards
- Loperamide 2mg capsules. Take TWO capsules initially, then take ONE capsule after each loose stool for up to 5 days. Maximum of 8 capsules in 24 hours; supply 30 capsules; NHS Cost £1.95; OTC Cost £3.44.

Anti-emetics

Metoclopramide tabs: 10mg when required, max 3 times a day
- Age from 20 years onwards
- Metoclopramide 10mg tablets. Take one tablet when required for relief of sickness. Maximum of 3 tablets in 24 hours; supply 28 tablets; NHS Cost £0.86.

Domperidone tabs: 10-20mg when required, max 4 times a day
- Age from 16 years onwards
- Domperidone 10mg tablets. Take one to two tablets every 4 to 8 hours when required for relief of sickness. Maximum of 8 tablets in 24 hours; supply 30 tablets; NHS Cost £2.50.

Domperidone suppository: 30-60mg when required, max 120mg/day
- Age from 16 years onwards
- Domperidone 30mg suppositories. Insert one to two suppositories into the rectum every 4 to 8 hours when required for relief of sickness. Maximum of 4 suppositories in 24 hours; supply 20 suppositories; NHS Cost £5.30.

1st-line analgesia/antipyretic: use when required

Paracetamol tablets: 1g up to four times a day
- Age from 16 years onwards
- Paracetamol 500mg tablets. Take two tablets every 4 to 6 hours when required for relief of pain or high temperature. Maximum of 8 tablets in 24 hours; supply 50 tablets; NHS Cost £0.67; OTC Cost £1.18.

Ibuprofen tablets: 400mg three times a day
- Age from 16 years onwards
- Ibuprofen 400mg tablets. Take one tablet three times a day when required for relief of pain or high temperature. Do not exceed the stated dose; supply 24 tablets; NHS Cost £0.70; OTC Cost £1.25.

Other NSAIDs: use when required

Ibuprofen tablets: 400mg four times a day
- Age from 16 years onwards
- Ibuprofen 400mg tablets. Take one tablet four times a day when required for pain relief. Do not exceed the stated dose; supply 24 tablets; NHS Cost £0.70; OTC Cost £1.25.

Ibuprofen tablets: 600mg three times a day
- Age from 16 years onwards
- Ibuprofen 600mg tablets. Take one tablet three times a day when required for pain relief. Do not exceed the stated dose; supply 21 tablets; NHS Cost £0.96.

Ibuprofen tablets: 800mg three times a day
- Age from 16 years onwards
- Ibuprofen 400mg tablets. Take two tablets three times a day when required for pain relief. Do not exceed the stated dose; supply 48 tablets; NHS Cost £1.40.

Diclofenac sodium e/c tablets: 50mg three times a day
- Age from 16 years onwards
- Diclofenac 50mg e/c tablets. Take one tablet three times a day when required for pain relief. Do not exceed the stated dose; supply 21 tablets; NHS Cost £0.94.

Diclofenac sodium e/c tablets: 50mg twice a day
- Age from 16 years onwards
- Diclofenac 50mg e/c tablets. Take one tablet twice a day when required for pain relief. Do not exceed the stated dose; supply 14 tablets; NHS Cost £0.63.

Naproxen tablets: 250mg twice a day
- Age from 16 years onwards
- Naproxen 250mg tablets. Take one tablet twice a day when required for pain relief. Do not exceed the stated dose; supply 14 tablets; NHS Cost £0.80.

Naproxen tablets: 500mg twice a day
- Age from 16 years onwards
- Naproxen 500mg tablets. Take one tablet twice a day when required for pain relief. Do not exceed the stated dose; supply 14 tablets; NHS Cost £1.54.

Collapse due to opioid overdose

Which therapy?

- **Call an ambulance and check for any immediate risks such as discarded used needles.**
- **Institute routine emergency procedures — airway, breathing, and circulatory support.**

- **Naloxone is the antidote for opioid overdose.** Give naloxone 0.8–2 mg intravenously repeated every 2 to 3 minutes up to a maximum of 10 mg if respiratory function does not improve. If still no response to treatment, question the diagnosis and consider other causes of collapse.
- **However, it is estimated that most overdoses will respond to naloxone 400–800 micrograms (i.e. 1–2 ampoules).**
- **If unable to administer intravenously, give the naloxone via the intramuscular or the subcutaneous route.** A slower response can be expected.
- **To reverse the effects of buprenorphine,** 10–30 times the usual dose of naloxone may be needed.
- **If respiratory function does not improve with naloxone,** then question diagnosis and consider other causes of collapse.
- **Admit the person to hospital.**

Practical prescribing points

For further information, please see the *Medicines Compendium* (www.medicines.org.uk) or the *British National Formulary* (www.bnf.org).

Follow-up advice

- **The person should stay in hospital until medical staff judge that discharge is safe.**
- **Arrange a follow-up appointment** for either initial assessment or ongoing assessment as appropriate.
- **A more thorough review every 3 months** (or more frequently according to clinical judgement) should include achievements and clarification of goals and targets set. The potential goal of abstinence can always be reconsidered at these reviews.

Should I refer or investigate?

O

Refer?

- **Admit the person to hospital,** as the effect of methadone overdose can persist for up to 72 hours and therefore needs hospital admission for observation. Intoxication is not in itself sufficient grounds for compulsory admission under the Mental Health Act.

Patient information leaflets

The following PILs are available at www.prodigy.nhs.uk

- Methadone Replacement for Heroin

Shared decision making

Drug rationale

- There are no prescriptions offered in this scenario.

Unknown patient — new patient/temporary resident/out of hours

Which therapy?

General

- **No opioids should be given, unless the patient's continued consumption of substitution medication can be confirmed** (e.g. consumption is supervised regularly by a local scheme with no missed doses).
- **It may be possible to verify the person's story.** Potential sources of information are:
  - Past or current GP.
  - Community pharmacist, who may be able to confirm when the last dose was taken and advise on the suitability of prescribing further substitution therapy.
  - Prison medical officer, if the person has recently been released from prison.
- **Fully assess before deciding on the appropriateness of prescribing substitution therapy** (see scenario *Initial assessment and management to determine treatment*). Explain that opioid drugs will not be supplied except under a shared-care scheme with local drug dependency services (where this exists).
- **If the request for a prescription of substitution therapy is from a temporary resident** who will be returning home within a short time, it may be more appropriate for them to see their own GP.
- **For the management of acute withdrawal symptoms,** see scenario *Acute withdrawal syndrome*. Symptomatic treatment with non-opioid drugs is generally the appropriate action.

Unknown person requesting a replacement prescription out of hours

- **A doctor may feel pressurized to prescribe opioids in order to prevent withdrawal symptoms, but it is considered good practice not to do so.**
- **Explain that the person's own GP is responsible for prescribing,** and that there will be an agreement in place with that GP regarding prescriptions. Loss of a prescription is the person's own responsibility.
- **If methadone is prescribed, this may make it difficult to manage further out-of-hours contacts.** Many co-operatives or groups of GPs who share an on-call rota have a policy of no prescriptions of opioids.
- **Symptomatic treatment with non-opioid drugs for withdrawal symptoms** may be appropriate (see scenario *Acute withdrawal syndrome*).

Practical prescribing points

For further information, please see the *Medicines Compendium* (www.medicines.org.uk) or the *British National Formulary* (www.bnf.org).

Follow-up advice

- **Advise the person to contact their own GP if appropriate.**
- **If the person is a new patient, arrange a follow-up appointment within a few days for initial assessment.** If this needs to be done, see *Initial assessment* scenario.
- **If the person is already established on methadone,** then arrange a follow-up appointment within a few days to:
  - Establish how they are coping
  - Establish how they feel about the decisions made at this consultation and their goals
  - Review the results of blood and urine tests (see *Should I refer or investigate?*) as appropriate
  - Establish if they have received appointments/contact from referral agencies if referred
- **Review at regular intervals,** initially fortnightly and then if stable, at least monthly.
- **Even when treating people long-term, a 3-monthly review is appropriate** (or more frequently according to clinical judgement) to observe the effect of maintenance treatment and reassess the goals and targets of treatment.

Should I refer or investigate?

Refer?

- **Stress the importance of referral/shared care and refer to the most appropriate level of expertise** required to manage the person, and refer/liaise appropriately (i.e. shared care, specialist care, or other forms of psychosocial care). See *Initial assessment* scenario, *Maintenance* scenario, or *Planned detoxification* scenario as appropriate.
- **Liaison with a pharmacist is important** in order to agree arrangements for supervision of opioid substitute treatment.
- **Pregnant women should be referred urgently** to a specialist in obstetrics and drug misuse.

nvestigate?

- **Consider investigations to exclude complications.** Choice of investigations is guided by clinical judgement, but would usually include:
  - Full blood count (to exclude anaemia, signs of infection)
  - Electrolytes (to assess renal function)
  - Liver function tests (to possibly identify hepatitis)
  - Tests for hepatitis A, B, or C, and HIV (a pre-test discussion covering the main points is important before testing)

Patient information leaflets

The following PILs are available at www.prodigy.nhs.uk

- Methadone Replacement for Heroin

Shared decision making

- We do not prescribe opioid drugs unless we can confirm that you are on a planned shared-care scheme (where available) and you are under continuous supervision by a community pharmacist.

Drug rationale

- There are no prescriptions offered in this scenario. Should a prescription be necessary, refer to the appropriate scenario.

Changing substitute treatment

Which therapy?

Switching from buprenorphine to methadone

Methadone may be more suitable than buprenorphine for people who have:

- An inadequate treatment response on buprenorphine
- Intolerable adverse effects
- Lack of availability of buprenorphine after moving to a new area
- Recurrent pain requiring opioid analgesics (because of the antagonistic properties of buprenorphine)

Start methadone 24 hours after the last dose of buprenorphine.

Starting doses of methadone when switching from buprenorphine are suggested in Table 3.

Table 3: Proposed starting doses for switching from buprenorphine to methadone.

Buprenorphine dose	Methadone dose
>8 mg	40 mg
4 mg	20 mg
2 mg	10 mg

- **Titrate dose according to response.**

Switching from methadone to buprenorphine

- **Buprenorphine may be more suitable for people who:**
  - Have a preference for the 'clear head' response often reported with buprenorphine, in contrast to the 'clouding' sometimes associated with methadone or heroin use.
  - Have had problems with using heroin 'on top' of maintenance methadone treatment, and who may benefit from using buprenorphine because it reduces the subjective effects in combination with heroin.
  - Take 30 mg of methadone or less a day, or who can reduce to that level.
  - Experienced unwanted effects or difficulties with methadone.
- **Withdrawal symptoms may be precipitated** by the partial agonist properties of buprenorphine.
- **To avoid withdrawal when switching from methadone, delay the first dose of buprenorphine until the person is experiencing features of opioid withdrawal** (at least 24–36 hours after last methadone dose).
- **Starting doses of buprenorphine** when switching from methadone are suggested in Table 9.

Practical prescribing points

For further information, please see the *Medicines Compendium* (www.medicines.org.uk) or the *British National Formulary* (www.bnf.org).

Methadone and buprenorphine

- **Methadone should always be prescribed in its liquid form** to minimize illicit use (note: methadone linctus is not licensed for opioid dependence). If not supervised, sugar-free methadone may have a greater potential for abuse in terms of being injected.
- **Take-home doses should not be prescribed** if the person shows a continued and unstable, or unauthorized, pattern of drug misuse, or has housing problems and cannot keep methadone safely.
- **Buprenorphine should be prescribed as Subutex® (buprenorphine),** as it is the only licensed product containing buprenorphine for the management of drug dependence.

Table 4: Proposed starting doses for switching from methadone to buprenorphine.

Last methadone dose	Buprenorphine day 1	Buprenorphine day 2	Buprenorphine day 3 onwards
>30 mg	Not recommended in primary care		
20–30 mg	4 mg	6–8 mg	Daily increases of 4 mg a day are possible, up to a maximum of 32 mg a day
10–20 mg	4 mg	4–6 mg	
<10 mg	2 mg	2–6 mg	

O

Clinical drug interactions to be aware of include the following:

Clinical drug interactions to be aware of include the following:

- Methadone may interact with other drugs — these may be clinically important:
  - **Rifampicin** accelerates the metabolism of methadone (i.e. reduced effect) and this may precipitate withdrawal symptoms.
  - **Anti-epileptics** (carbamazepine and phenytoin) may also accelerate the metabolism of methadone and precipitate withdrawal symptoms.
  - **Antivirals:** methadone possibly increases plasma concentration of zidovudine. Plasma concentration of methadone is reduced by efavirenz, ritonavir, and possibly by abacavir and nevirapine.
  - **Additive central nervous system depression with alcohol and benzodiazepines.**

Legal and practical information for prescribing opioid-substitute controlled-drug prescriptions

Legal and practical information for prescribing opioid-substitute controlled-drug prescriptions

- **For one-off prescriptions,** a standard FP10 form can be used.
- **For instalment dispensing of methadone or buprenorphine,** GPs are required to use a blue FP10MDA1000 form.
- **Legally a pharmacist cannot dispense methadone or buprenorphine without the following information,** written in the prescriber's own handwriting (unless exempt) in ink, or otherwise so as to be indelible:
  - The person's name and address
  - The form and strength of the preparation (sugar-free has to be written if required)
  - The total quantity of the preparation or the number of dose units, in both words AND figures
  - The dose
  - The signature of the prescriber who has written the prescription
  - The date of signing by the prescriber who has written the prescription
  - The prescriber's address specified on the prescription
- **State the date when it is intended that the first instalment should start.**
- **Specify the interval** (e.g. daily dispensing) and the amount required or instalment dispensing on the prescription.
- **If the prescriber wants supervised consumption in the pharmacy,** specify 'supervised consumption' on the prescription if a local scheme is in place.
- **If extra quantities need to be prescribed on any day** (e.g. two doses on a Saturday because the pharmacy is closed on Sunday), this needs to be specified on the prescription. Once specified, the prescription cannot be dispensed on alternative dates.
- **Do not prescribe more than 14 days' supply** on either a blue FP10MDA1000 form or a standard FP10.
- **A prescription is valid for 13 weeks** from the date stated thereon.
- **A prescription that was posted to the pharmacy but that has not arrived cannot legally be dispensed,** even at the verbal request of the prescriber.
- **Other prescription items cannot be written on the same form.**

O

Follow-up advice

- **Review the results of blood and urine tests** as appropriate (see *Should I refer or investigate?*).
- **People should keep appointments with the shared-care team and the practice.**
- **Review at regular intervals,** initially fortnightly and then, if stable, at least monthly. A thorough review every 3 months should include achievements and goal setting.

Should I refer or investigate?

Refer?

- **Do not prescribe in isolation,** but liaise with other professionals who will be able to help with factors contributing to an individual's drug misuse.

Investigate?

- **Random urine analysis** for opioids is useful in identifying relapse, but it should be remembered that buprenorphine cannot be detected in routine urine tests.
- **Consider investigations to exclude complications.** Choice of investigations is guided by clinical judgement, but would usually include:
  - Full blood count (to exclude anaemia, signs of infection)
  - Electrolytes (to assess renal function)
  - Liver function tests (to possibly identify hepatitis)
  - Tests for hepatitis A, B, or C, and HIV (a pre-test discussion covering the main points is important before testing)

Patient information leaflets

The following PILs are available at www.prodigy.nhs.uk

- Cognitive Behaviour Therapy (CBT)

Shared decision making

- **When switching from buprenorphine to methadone:**
  - Start methadone 24 hours after the last dose of buprenorphine.
  - The dose may need to be increased in steps over a few weeks, depending if you get any withdrawal symptoms. But note, methadone:
    - Takes 2–4 hours to reach peak effect.
    - Accumulates in your body. So you will feel a greater effect of the drug over days, even without increasing the dose.
- **When switching from methadone to buprenorphine:**
  - Start the first dose of buprenorphine when you first start to get 'withdrawal' symptoms. This is at least 24–36 hours after your last dose of methadone.
  - The dose may need to be increased in steps over a few weeks, depending on whether you get any withdrawal symptoms.
- **Have you been offered blood tests** for HIV, and hepatitis A, B and C?
- **Have you been offered hepatitis B immunization?**
- **Note: lost scripts or medication will not be replaced.**
- **You are more likely to succeed in staying off street drugs if you have regular support** from a local drug community team (or similar).

Drug rationale

- There are no prescriptions offered in this scenario. For the legal and practical information for prescribing opioid-substitute controlled-drug prescriptions, see *Prescribing points*.

Extended Information

Background information

- What is it? p.1337
- How common is it? p.1337
- How do I know my patient has it? p.1337
- Complications and prognosis p.1337

What is it?

- **An opioid is** either a natural derivative of opium; or a synthetic substance with agonist, partial agonist, or mixed agonist and antagonist activity at opioid receptors. An opiate is either a natural derivative or a semi-synthetic constituent of opium.
- **The World Health Organization states that a definite diagnosis of drug dependence** (including opioid dependence) should only be made if three or more of the following have been present together at some time during the previous year:
  - A strong desire to take the substance
  - Difficulty in controlling use
  - A physiological withdrawal state
  - Tolerance
  - Neglect of alternative pleasures and interests
  - Persistence of use despite harm to oneself and others

[WHO, 2001]

- **All opioids have dependence potential, to varying degrees** [Swadi et al, 1990]. Heroin (diamorphine) has the greatest potential for dependency, especially when injected [DH et al, 1999].
- **The US National Institute of Health states that opioid dependence should be viewed as a chronic relapsing disorder** and treated using a medical model: 'For decades opiate addiction has been viewed as a problem of motivation, willpower, or strength of character. Through careful study of its natural history and through research at the genetic, molecular, neuronal, and epidemiological levels, it has been proven that opiate addiction is a medical disorder characterized by predictable signs and symptoms' [National Institutes of Health, 1997].
- **Other arguments for classifying opioid dependence as a medical disorder** include the following:
  - The signs, and symptoms in people who are opioid dependent are consistent across varying cultural, ethnic, and socio-economic backgrounds.
  - There is a strong tendency to relapse after long periods of abstinence.
  - Craving for opioids results in continued use even where there is an expressed and demonstrated strong motivation to stop, and where powerful social adverse consequences to continued use are present.
  - Continuous exposure to opioids causes pathophysiological changes in the brain.

How common is it?

- **In the UK,** it is estimated that there are a quarter of a million opioid dependent drug users with approximately 160,000 in treatment at some point in the course of a year.
- Data from the Regional Drug Misuse Databases reported 33,200 drug misusers presenting for treatment in the 6 months ending March 2001. Of those, 38% were aged 30 years or over, 50% were in their twenties, and 13% were aged under 20 years.
- **Many people dependent on opioids are likely to be polydrug users** — two-thirds (67%) presenting for treatment reported heroin as their main drug of misuse, followed by cannabis (9%), methadone (8%), cocaine (7%), and amphetamines (3%).
- **The male to female ratio of those presenting for treatment is 3:1.**

[DH, 2002a]

How do I know my patient has it?

People may present in a variety of ways:

- **An active request for help with drug dependency** (e.g. motivated to change behaviour, or a crisis has developed).
- **As a result of an impending court case.**
- **Disclosure of drug misuse** while consulting with another medical problem.
- **With clinical features of opioid intoxication or withdrawal** (see *Symptoms and signs of opioid withdrawal*).

Drug misuse may be suspected by:

History

- **Medical history:** complications of drug use (e.g. abscess; thrombophlebitis; recurrent chest infections; hepatitis A, B or C infection; HIV infection).
- **Psychiatric history:** overdoses, depression, psychosis (not specifically an indicator of opioid misuse but may be linked to polydrug use).
- **Forensic history:** past custodial sentences, probation, community service.
- **Social history:** family problems, unemployment, accommodation issues, financial problems.

Examination

- **Physical examination:** e.g. poor nutrition, dental caries, other signs of neglect, needle tracks, skin abscess, signs of drug intoxication or withdrawal (see *Symptoms and signs of opioid withdrawal*).
- **Mental health assessment:** abnormal general behaviour , disorders of mood (particularly anxiety or low mood), delusions or hallucinations, confusion.

Investigations

- **Analysis of urine for drug screen:** opioids can be detected in the urine for up to 2–4 days (up to 7–9 days for methadone). Be aware that false positive and negative results can occur (for further information, see *Initial assessment*).

Complications and prognosis

Complications

- **Death**
  - Mortality in heroin addicts is nearly 12 times greater than in the general population [Oppenheimer et al, 1994].
  - One study found that injecting drug misusers were 22 times more likely to die than people of the same age who did not misuse drugs [Frischer et al, 1997].
  - A marked increase in deaths related to opioids (studied 1985 to 1995) has been found among those aged 15 to 19 years [Roberts et al, 1997].
  - In 2001 there were 749 deaths in England and Wales involving methadone, heroin, or morphine [Office for National Statistics, 2003].
- **Overdose**
- **Infection** (e.g. septicaemia, abscesses, and blood-borne viruses)
- **Deep-vein thrombosis**
- **Risk of prescribed drugs getting into the wrong hands** — for example, the person may sell prescribed drugs to purchase illicit drugs, thereby perpetuating controlled drug misuse and contributing towards an illicit market.

O

Prognosis

- **If psychosocial interventions are used in addition to a substitute treatment, then evidence suggests that long-term prognosis is improved.**
- **Detoxification regimens have high relapse rates.** They are improved when linked to long-term psychosocial support, and are unlikely to succeed if done without the patient's consent.
- **Failure to identify and address non-compliance at an early stage** can result in loss of motivation and drive, for both the patient and the clinician.

[DH et al, 1999]

Management issues

- General issues p.1338
- Initial assessment p.1338
- Initiation and stabilization of treatment p.1339
- Maintenance p.1340
- Improving compliance with initiation and maintenance of treatment p.1341
- Changing substitute treatment p.1341
- Prescribing when doses of substitute drug have been missed p.1342
- Detoxification p.1342
- Writing prescriptions for substitute therapy p.1343
- Relapse p.1343
- Acute withdrawal syndrome p.1343
- Management of the emergency situation — collapse due to opioid overdose p.1344
- Management of the unknown patient p.1345
- Pregnancy p.1345
- Reporting drug misuse p.1346
- Issues concerning driving ability p.1346
- Management of pain in a person on substitute drug maintenance treatment p.1346
- Travelling abroad p.1346
- Deciding on practice policy p.1347

General issues

- **Drug misuse is common, and GPs have an important role in the assessment and decision concerning whether to treat or refer,** even if they do not wish to be directly involved in either initiation or maintenance of treatment.
- **A multidisciplinary approach to the management of people with opioid dependence is essential.** Most localities will have a clearly defined drug dependency service with a readily accessible entry point. Many areas have community drug teams that implement treatment plans, monitor treatment, provide counselling, and promote needle exchange and other harm-reduction activities.
- **GPs should not prescribe in isolation and should never feel pressurized to prescribe;** an appropriate assessment is required first. Many GPs refer to the local drug dependency service for initiation of treatment, but are willing to prescribe and supervise maintenance therapy.
- **GPs should know which local community pharmacies provide substitute drug dispensing and supervision services.**
- **Voluntary counselling services** may be available in some areas, and can be particularly useful while people are waiting for assessment by local specialist services.
- **People may be encouraged to engage in treatment by strong external influences** (e.g. family, employment, or the criminal justice system), which can help to improve outcomes [Leshner, 1999].

Initial assessment

History and examination

- **Explore the person's past history and current situation.** Table 1 outlines the key features of the history. It may not be possible to cover all these areas adequately during a single consultation.
- **Always find out what the user wants and whether he or she wishes to choose detoxification or maintenance.**
- **Examine the person,** in order to:
  - **Confirm evidence of drug misuse** (e.g. needle tracks, signs of drug intoxication or withdrawal, see *Symptoms and signs of opioid withdrawal*)
  - **Check for the presence of complications** (e.g. poor nutrition, signs of anaemia, skin abscess, thrombophlebitis, viral hepatitis, HIV, chest infection, tuberculosis)
  - **Assess mental health** (e.g. general behaviour, depression, risk of self-harm, delusions or hallucinations, confusional states)

Investigations to exclude complications

- **Choice of investigations is guided by clinical judgement, but would usually include:**
  - Full blood count (to exclude anaemia, signs of infection)
  - Electrolytes (to assess renal function)
  - Liver function tests (to identify hepatitis, if present)
  - Tests for infection — i.e. hepatitis A, B, and C; HIV (with informed consent)

Confirmation of opioid use

Urine drug screen

- **Opioids persist in the urine** for up to 2–4 days (up to 7–9 days for methadone).

Table 5: History and examination.

History	Specific information
Degree of dependence: past and current	Age of starting, types, frequency, route, and spend on drugs; overdoses, periods of abstinence, symptoms when unable to obtain the drug
Motivation	To stop or change pattern of drug misuse; attitude towards maintenance therapy
At-risk behaviour	Supply of needles and syringes; sharing habits; knowledge of how to inject safely; correct disposal of used equipment; cleaning of equipment; knowledge of HIV/hepatitis A, B, and C; issues of transmission and advice on safer sex
Medical history	Complications of drug use (e.g. abscess; thrombosis; chest infections; hepatitis A, B, and C; HIV status if known), last menstrual period, last smear
Psychiatric history	Psychiatric admissions or outpatient attendance; overdoses (accidental and deliberate), depression, or psychosis
Forensic history	Past custodial sentences, probation, community service, outstanding charges
Social history	Family (especially children), employment, accommodation, financial situation; drug and alcohol use in partner and other family members; impact of drug misuse on other aspects of the person's life; social supports available
Past contact with treatment services	Previous efforts to reduce or stop taking drugs; past contact with treatment and rehabilitation, social, medical, and community services

When arranging a urine drug screen, try to ensure that the urine belongs to the person in question (Note: a fresh sample should be warm).

Results should be interpreted in the light of clinical findings, as false negatives and false positives can occur. False positives can be caused by the use of quinolones [Baden et al, 2001] or loperamide. Negative results can occur despite the presence of buprenorphine or tramadol, as these drugs do not test as opioid-positive on urine tests.

Note also that many over-the-counter medicines contain opioids (for example, codeine).

At least one positive urine test (and preferably two) for opioids should usually be obtained before starting substitute treatment.

A negative result brings into doubt whether the person is currently dependent on drugs. Reassess at an appropriate time to be able to observe withdrawal symptoms, and repeat the urine test. Substitute treatment should not be prescribed unless the prescriber is experienced enough to be certain that the person is currently suffering from withdrawal symptoms.

Other tests

Other tests to confirm opioid use are rarely used in practice.

Hair analysis can give information about drug use over several weeks or months. This is sometimes considered in specific situations such as child protection cases.

Saliva tests provide only a preliminary result, but are currently used by some clinicians as a diagnostic test. Such a test is easier than analysing urine, more acceptable for those involved, and produces quicker results; but currently it must be purchased by practices.

'Point of care' urine tests (for example, reagent strips) are available and can be ordered.

Harm reduction

Advise on harm reduction. Make sure that the person has access to clean needles and syringes etc. Give advice on safer sex, the risks of overdose, the dangers of sharing dirty water, blood-borne viruses, and hepatitis A and B vaccination.

Management plan

Consider whether substitution therapy is appropriate.

- How does the person wish to change, and will substitution therapy encourage this?
- Is the person taking opioids regularly? (Daily use is a strong indicator of dependence.)
- Is there convincing evidence of dependence?

Discuss the options for substitution therapy — detoxification or maintenance. Always find out what the user wants and check this against what you are able or willing to offer.

Discuss the importance of shared care.

Agree on a management plan based on either drug or non-drug treatment, or both.

Initiation and stabilization of treatment

General points

Most GPs will initiate treatment only after consultation with a community drug team or specialist service. Those who choose to initiate prescriptions should:

- Have had some training in the management of drug dependence.
- Carry out appropriate assessments (history and examination to confirm dependence and analysis of urine).
- Start substitution at low doses to avoid overdose.
- Titrate dose carefully according to a local protocol, or see Department of Health clinical guidelines to ensure safety but also to avoid sub-optimal doses.
- Have a structure of shared care.
- Use a dispensing pharmacist who is willing to give daily doses under observed supervision.

- **Confirm the person's wishes to choose detoxification or maintenance.**
- **Some doctors may choose to have a written agreement with the person.** It is important to agree clear aims and the ways in which these will be carried out. A suggested format is available as a Patient Information Leaflet.
- **Before prescribing,** it is advisable that the person fully understands that replacement prescriptions or medication can only be given under the most exceptional circumstances and will normally be refused.
- **Supervised consumption is an important part of substitution treatment** [DH et al, 1999].

Which drug?

Methadone

- **Oral methadone mixture is usually the drug of choice for substitution therapy,** because it is long acting, easy to titrate, less likely to be diverted or injected, and backed by evidence of efficacy. Methadone substitution, at appropriate doses, is cost effective in reducing injecting behaviour, illicit opioid use, and criminal activity [DH et al, 1999].
- **Methadone should always be prescribed in its liquid form to minimize illicit use** (note: methadone 'linctus' is not licensed for opioid dependence). Other formulations exist [Strang et al, 1996] but [Strang et al, 2000]:
  - **Injectable methadone is not advisable** except under specialist supervision.
  - **Methadone tablets are not licensed for the treatment of opioid dependence,** and they can be crushed and inappropriately injected. They should only be prescribed under specialist supervision.

Buprenorphine

- **Buprenorphine may be a useful alternative to methadone,** and is licensed for the treatment of opioid dependence.
- **Buprenorphine is an effective intervention** for use in the maintenance treatment of heroin dependence, but it is not more effective than methadone at adequate dosages [Mattick et al, 2003].
- **It also has some disadvantages** including that it can be injected and so is liable to abuse, and it can precipitate withdrawal symptoms in those recently having used opioids; so it is important to understand its clinical use.
- **Buprenorphine may be the preferred option** with people who have:
  - A preference for the 'clear head' response often reported with buprenorphine, in contrast to the 'clouding' sometimes associated with methadone or heroin use.
  - Previously had problems with using heroin 'on top' of maintenance methadone treatment and who may benefit from using buprenorphine, because it reduces the subjective effects in combination with heroin.
  - Experienced unwanted effects or difficulties with methadone in the past.
- **The only licensed product containing buprenorphine for the management of drug dependence is marketed under the brand name 'Subutex® sublingual tablets'.** Another product containing buprenorphine, 'Temgesic', is not licensed for the management of opioid dependence, does not contain the correct patient information leaflet, and should not be used for this purpose.

- **Buprenorphine supervision in the pharmacy may be difficult,** as a sublingual tablet will usually take 5–10 minutes to dissolve.
- **Supervision is most important in the first 2–3 minutes,** during which time the tablets will have started to dissolve, and their value for diversion (i.e. street price) will decrease.

Initiation and stabilization of methadone

- **Careful induction is necessary,** as the first 2 weeks of treatment is associated with a greater risk of overdose mortality. Note: not giving enough can also cause problems. Self-reported habits by people may be misleading: many may be unaware of how much they have been taking.
- **The usual recommended initial dose of methadone is 10–30 mg/day.** Care is needed if starting a dose greater than 30 mg/day, because of the risk of overdose. If tolerance is low or uncertain, then starting methadone at 10–20 mg/day is more appropriate. After a few hours small additional doses can be given if in withdrawal, this may be more appropriately done by experienced GPs. Incremental dose increases should be given to those who may need higher doses. However, too rapid a dose increase may mean that a fatal dose is reached [Humeniuk et al, 2000].
- **The necessary dose of methadone should be determined by titration.** Titrate against withdrawal symptoms.
- **In order for the dose to be titrated against withdrawal symptoms,** it is advisable for the person to attend daily during the first few days. People should be warned about the possibility of withdrawal.
- **When increasing the dose** [DH et al, 1999]:
  - Over the first week, the incremental increase for any one day should be no more than methadone 5–10 mg.
  - The total increase over the first week should be no more than 30 mg above the starting dose.
  - Subsequent increases should not exceed 10 mg per week, until a usual maintenance dose of between 60 and 120 mg/day is reached.
- Larger doses are sometimes needed, but should be given only after consultation with a specialist.
- It may take several weeks to reach the correct maintenance dose.

Initiation and stabilization of buprenorphine

- **Withdrawal symptoms may be precipitated by the partial agonist properties of buprenorphine.**
- **The withdrawal symptoms typically occur 1–3 hours after the initial dose of buprenorphine,** peaking in severity after the first 3–6 hours, and generally subsiding thereafter.
- **To avoid withdrawal when switching from heroin:**
  - Delay the first dose of buprenorphine until at least 8 hours after the last dose of heroin, and ask the person to wait as long as possible until they are experiencing features of opioid withdrawal.
  - The usual recommended starting dose is 4 mg (as opposed to the usual 200–400 microgram dose used in non-addicts for pain relief).
  - Rapidly titrate dose according to clinical response over the next few days.
  - Daily increases of up to 4 mg a day are possible up to a maximum of 32 mg daily.
  - The most commonly effective dose is 12–24 mg.
  - During dose titration, the person should be reviewed frequently.
- **To avoid withdrawal when switching from methadone:**
  - Before commencing buprenorphine, the methadone should be reduced to 30 mg/day or less (see Table 2). This can be done by reducing the dose by 5 mg every 1–2 weeks until this goal is reached.
  - Delay the first dose of buprenorphine until the person is experiencing symptoms of opioid withdrawal (this typically means at least 24–36 hours after the last methadone dose). Increasing the time interval between the last dose of methadone and the first dose of buprenorphine reduces the incidence and severity of precipitated withdrawal.
- **If withdrawal symptoms on switching to buprenorphine are severe,** symptomatic treatment such as lofexidine (e.g. 400–600 micrograms every 8 hours) can be given, but no more buprenorphine should be prescribed until withdrawal symptoms have settled [RCGP, 2003]. It is recommended that lofexidine should only be used by prescribers with knowledge of lofexidine or following advice from specialist practitioners.
- **Buprenorphine should be prescribed for daily use** — the effectiveness of alternate-day prescribing is unclear, and such a prescription should be carried out only after consultation with a specialist.

[RCGP, 2003]

- **Rapid titration is essential** to prevent dropout and to achieve the stabilization dose — people can usually be stabilized within 1–2 weeks.

Maintenance

General points

- **Maintenance is a cost-effective approach to harm reduction, but should be part of a broader programme c social and psychological support.** Becoming stabilized o a substitute drug offers the opportunity to discover and address those issues that have led to drug misuse.
- **Evidence suggests that reducing barriers to entry to maintenance treatment:**
  - Increases participation in maintenance treatment
  - Improves retention in treatment
  - Improves outcomes when people remain in treatment
- **In the past, entry to maintenance treatment has been made difficult** because of practitioners' fears of either creating iatrogenic dependence or unnecessarily prolonging dependence [Bell et al, 1994].
- **Methadone maintenance treatment (MMT) offers substantial benefits over no treatment.** Specific benefits are [Bell and Zador, 2000; Marsch, 1998]:
  - Less use of illicit opioids
  - Reduced risk of death and disease
  - Reduced involvement in crime
  - An improvement in well-being
- **Research suggests a linear relationship between *time* spent in MMT and reductions of heroin use and crime i the long term.** People who leave treatment prematurely are at high risk of relapsing to heroin use [Ward et al, 1999].
- **A recent placebo-controlled trial,** involving 40 drug misusers, assessed the 1-year efficacy of maintenance buprenorphine [Kakko et al, 2003]. Both the placebo

Table 6: Proposed starting doses for switching from methadone to buprenorphine.

Last methadone dose	Buprenorphine day 1	Buprenorphine day 2	Buprenorphine day 3 onwards
>30 mg	Not recommended in primary care		
20–30 mg	4 mg	6–8 mg	Daily increases of 4 mg a day are possible up to a maximum of 32 m a day
10–20 mg	4 mg	4–6 mg	
<10 mg	2 mg	2–6 mg	

and treatment groups received intensive psychosocial treatment. Of the 20 participants who received buprenorphine, 15 were still on treatment after a year, in contrast to none of the 20 people in the placebo group. Buprenorphine was found to be safe and effective.

Prescribing methadone maintenance treatment

Support from a specialist service is important, as is following local protocols on maintenance.

People maintained on methadone 60–120 mg/day are more likely to remain in a treatment programme and avoid the use of illicit opioids. Lower or higher doses may be appropriate in some individuals [Strain et al, 1993; Strain et al, 1999; Johnson et al, 2000] although methadone doses less than 60 mg/day generally seems to be inadequate [Faggiano et al, 2003].

There should be a low threshold for increasing the dose, if the person is continuing to use illicit opioids and there is evidence of motivation to stop this illicit use.

If tolerance is high, doses above 120 mg/day occasionally may be necessary (but specialist assessment or advice is recommended).

It is important to warn people about the dangers of associated alcohol or benzodiazepine use.

Review at regular intervals, initially fortnightly and then if stable, at least monthly. A thorough review every 3 months should include achievements and goal setting.

Prescribing buprenorphine maintenance treatment

The daily dosage of buprenorphine can range from 8–32 mg, and the usual dose range is from 12–24 mg; but lower doses may be adequate in some people.

There should be a low threshold for increasing the dose, if the person is continuing to use illicit opioids and there is evidence of motivation to stop this illicit use.

Buprenorphine should be prescribed for daily use — the effectiveness of alternate-day prescribing is unclear, and such a prescription should be carried out only after consultation with a specialist.

People should only be given buprenorphine if they have normal liver function tests (LFTs). If they have co-existing liver disease but normal LFTs, they should be monitored periodically throughout treatment.

Improving compliance with initiation and maintenance of treatment

Assessment during treatment

The ideal would be for either the GP or the shared-care worker to see the person daily for the first few days, while titration is being undertaken. However, this may not be possible for the busy GP. After stabilization, a full review every 3 months is essential.

Encourage feedback from the community pharmacist and other professionals who may be seeing the drug misuser more frequently. This needs to be carefully balanced with issues of patient confidentiality and should be discussed with the patient to ensure consent..

Look for signs of withdrawal that would suggest that the dose is not sufficient. Continued illegal drug misuse may occur if the dose of the substitute drug is too low. Unless there are signs of intoxication, consider increasing the dose by small increments of methadone or buprenorphine until the signs of withdrawal have disappeared and misuse of illegal drugs reduces or ceases.

Analysis of urine may encourage compliance, particularly in people taking methadone maintenance treatment who have been entrusted with non-supervised consumption. It should be noted that buprenorphine is not detectable in routine urine tests for opioids.

Supervised consumption

- **Supervised consumption of the substitute drug by an appropriate healthcare professional** (usually a community pharmacist if a local scheme is in place) provides the best guarantee that the drug is being taken as directed by the prescriber, and is also associated with a better clinical outcome (as well as reduced diversion).
- **Supervised consumption is particularly useful for the first 3–6 months** and can be re-introduced periodically, or when there is concern about a change in the patient.
- **Non-supervised consumption should be considered when stability has been achieved.** In general, people starting substitute medication should be required to take their daily dose under direct supervision of a professional (usually a community pharmacist) for at least 3 months and any change should be made after discussing the advantages and disadvantages for the patient.
- **If a person restarts substitute medication after a break, or receives a considerable increase in the dose,** daily dispensing with supervised consumption should then be restarted.
- **These arrangements should only be relaxed when the prescriber can be satisfied that compliance will be maintained.** Such relaxation can be seen as an important component of rehabilitation and the re-establishment of acceptable, responsible behaviour.
- **If a person on non-supervised consumption uses opioids on top of the prescribed drugs or other drugs** such as alcohol or benzodiazepines that increase the risk of overdose, then supervised consumption should be reinstated until an appropriate degree of stability has been achieved.

[DH et al, 1999]

Changing substitute treatment

Buprenorphine to methadone

- **Some people may need to transfer from buprenorphine to methadone** because of:
  - An inadequate treatment response
  - Intolerable adverse effects
  - Needing other opioids for pain control
  - Moving to an area where buprenorphine is not used
- **If a patient is stable on buprenorphine,** methadone can be commenced 24 hours after the last dose, at an initial daily dose of up to 40 mg [RCGP, 2003].
- **Table 7 gives guidance, but methadone should be titrated according to the person's response,** taking into account the residual partial antagonist action of buprenorphine, which may last for several days [RCGP, 2003].

Methadone to buprenorphine

- **Some people may need to transfer from methadone to buprenorphine.** Buprenorphine may be more suitable for people who:
  - Have a preference for the 'clear head' response often reported with buprenorphine in contrast to the

Table 7: Proposed starting doses for switching from buprenorphine to methadone.

Buprenorphine dose	Methadone dose
>8 mg	40 mg
4 mg	20 mg
2 mg	10 mg

O

'clouding' sometimes associated with methadone or heroin use.
  - Have previously had problems with using heroin 'on top' of maintenance methadone treatment, and who may benefit from using buprenorphine because it reduces the subjective effects in combination with heroin.
  - Take 30 mg of methadone or less a day, or can reduce to that level.
  - Have experienced unwanted effects or difficulties with methadone in the past.
- For people on 30 mg or less of methadone daily, see *Initiation and stabilization of buprenorphine.*

Prescribing when doses of substitute drug have been missed

- **If a person misses a daily dosage, it must not be replaced.** The next dose should be taken at the usual time on the following day.
- **If the person missed one day's dose or two in succession, the usual dose should be given.**
- **If more than 2 days of methadone have been missed** (i.e. three or more consecutive doses), tolerance may have been lost (especially for those in the lower range of maintenance doses). Re-initiate treatment starting at a low dose [Gilvarry, Personal Communication, 2002].
- **If more than 2 days of buprenorphine have been missed** (i.e. three or more consecutive days) tolerance will have been lost and treatment should be initiated at a low dose and titrated up to an appropriate maintenance dose [Ford, Personal Communication, 2003].
- **If a person has used street drugs in the intervening period,** the dose must be re-titrated.

Detoxification

General points

- **After a person has been stabilized on a substitute drug and has made other changes in lifestyle, at the patient's request it may be appropriate to consider a formal drug detoxification regimen.**
- **A regimen is only likely to be successful if both the person and the doctor agree that detoxification is desirable.** Little clinical improvement can be expected if carried out against the person's wishes, and if the person is not going to comply it is best to continue with the existing stable regimen. However, it is important that the issue is actively explored (particularly for example with those with shorter duration of dependence).
- **The treatment outcome may be influenced by** the availability of support services (e.g. counselling), the extent and quality of non-drug services, and information provision [Green and Gossop, 1988; Amato et al, 2003].
- **The National Treatment Outcome Research Study (NTORS) suggests** that people tend to do better on methadone maintenance treatment (MMT) rather than detoxification [Gossop et al, 2001].
- **If detoxification is requested, it is imperative to discuss** goals, a starting date, and the extra support needed (e.g. what sort of support will enable them to get through the programme and prevent relapse).
- **It is important that there is a clear distinction between maintenance and detoxification** so that the person does not slip between the two.
- **Never reduce dosage without discussion and agreement with the person.**
- **Slow reduction of methadone without consent is completely ineffective** and should not be done. If a person does not wish to reduce, then continue at an adequate maintenance dose for as long as necessary [Ford, Personal Communication, 2003].
- **Detoxification should be planned and continued at a pace judged appropriate by the drug misuser,** after clinical assessment and jointly agreed treatment goals have been set.
- **Most individuals are mildly anxious about withdrawal symptoms.** However, about a third of people on MMT report a phobic-like fear of detoxification [Milby et al, 1986].
- **Many people who request detoxification do so for a number of reasons:**
  - That is what the doctor wishes to hear.
  - There is no alternative.
  - They have reached a point when they think the advantages of stopping the drug outweigh the advantages of continuing, and see stopping opioids as the only possibility.
  - They do not understand the value of maintenance treatment.
- **If they decide to try detoxification, inform them about the risks of overdose** due to loss of tolerance, or due to subsequent de-stabilisation and polydrug use, and be prepared to return to maintenance treatment if appropriate [Ford, Personal Communication, 2003].
- **Many people will relapse** — heroin addiction is a chroni relapsing disorder [O'Brien and McLellan, 1996].

Which drug?

- **Most detoxification regimens will be initiated by a specialist or the shared-care support team,** but this depends on the locality.
- **Methadone, buprenorphine, and lofexidine** are all licensed for initiation in primary care.
- **Buprenorphine and methadone both have the advantage over lofexidine** of also being suitable for maintenance treatment if the person is unable to complete withdrawal.
- **Buprenorphine is much more expensive that methadone** and the cost of a year's maintenance treatment at equivalent dosage is currently over five times the cost of methadone.

Methadone

- **This is the standard treatment as there is more experience with using methadone, and currently there is no clear evidence that other drugs are more effective.** At the latter stage of detoxification with methadone symptomatic treatments may be helpful. Further researc is needed to evaluate the most effective way of tapering doses.

Buprenorphine

- **Buprenorphine has mixed agonist and antagonist properties,** which potentially makes it a good agent for the management of opioid withdrawal. Effectiveness compared with methadone requires further investigatio [Ling et al, 1996; Strain et al, 1996; Gowing et al, 2002
- **Buprenorphine is an alternative option for:**
  - Those stabilized on methadone (but not whilst the dose is above 30 mg)
  - Those who choose detoxification rather than methadone maintenance
  - Those considering naltrexone treatment after detoxification (as this can be initiated earlier than wit methadone)

Lofexidine

- **Lofexidine is an alpha-adrenergic agonist** and is licensed for the management of symptoms of opioid withdrawal. Studies comparing lofexidine with methadone-based detoxification regimens have found similar efficacy.
- **Detoxification with lofexidine is often carried out in specialist centres, but in some localities is done by GPs.**

O

We recommend that it should be prescribed only by practitioners with knowledge of lofexidine, or following advice from specialist practitioners.

- **People taking lofexidine need to have their blood pressure monitored,** although possible hypotensive adverse effects are less marked than with clonidine [Gowing et al, 2000].

Naltrexone

Naltrexone is an opioid antagonist and therefore blocks the effects of opioids. It can be given orally as an aid to prevent relapse, but is only licensed for initiation in a drug addiction centre by a suitably qualified physician [ABPI Medicines Compendium, 2002]. Despite the clear rationale for its use, oral naltrexone has only limited evidence for its efficacy (particularly in the context of a package of care including additional psychosocial support) [Prunty, Personal Communication, 2004].

Naltrexone is not licensed for detoxification. However, some services, particularly in the private sector, may induct people on to naltrexone treatment using rapid assisted withdrawal techniques (using heavy sedation or anaesthesia). In these cases the people or services involved may request on-going maintenance prescribing of naltrexone at short notice. The value of naltrexone in ultra-rapid detoxification procedures remains controversial [Gossop and Strang, 1997].

Dihydrocodeine (not recommended)

Dihydrocodeine is not licensed for the treatment of drug dependence, and there is a lack of trial data to support its use. It is associated with problems of abuse on the street. [DH et al, 1999].

Although in practice it is sometimes prescribed to aid withdrawal in people using illicit dihydrocodeine, it is not a recommended treatment.

Prescribing methadone for detoxification

The duration of detoxification regimens can be as short as 7–21 days, or may take months or even years. Withdrawal limited to 30 days is too rapid for many people, resulting in them being prematurely withdrawn and consequently resuming heroin use.

Methadone doses can be reduced at any time interval (e.g. daily, alternate days, weekly). As the daily dose of methadone decreases, smaller reductions in dosage should be made to avoid precipitating withdrawals and relapse [DH et al, 1999]. Note: be aware that too slow a reduction rate may result in the person slipping between detoxification and methadone maintenance.

It may be necessary to hold the stage of detoxification steady at a given dose over a few days, to decrease the person's anxiety and increase their sense of control.

Prescribing buprenorphine for detoxification

Buprenorphine has mixed agonist and antagonist properties, which potentially makes it a good agent for the management of opioid withdrawal. Effectiveness compared to methadone requires further investigation [Ling et al, 1996; Strain et al, 1996; Gowing et al, 2002].

Before starting buprenorphine in people who are taking methadone, the dose of methadone should be reduced to at most 30 mg/day in order to prevent precipitating withdrawal symptoms. This can be done by reducing the dose of methadone by 5 mg every 1–2 weeks until 30 mg or less has been reached. See *Initiation and stabilization of buprenorphine.*

For dose details in using buprenorphine for detoxification, see Table 8.

Different rates of detoxification may be necessary according to patient preferences.

Table 8: Proposed schedule for detoxification using buprenorphine.

Daily buprenorphine dose	Reduction rate
Above 16 mg	4 mg every 1–2 weeks
8–16 mg	2–4 mg every 1–2 weeks
2–8 mg	2 mg every week or fortnight
Below 2 mg	0.4–0.8 mg every week or fortnight

- **Most people will not experience considerable withdrawal discomfort until they have reduced to low doses of buprenorphine or after they have stopped.**
- **Transferring from buprenorphine to naltrexone after detoxification** should only be done by a specialist.

Writing prescriptions for substitute therapy

Table 9 provides information on writing prescriptions for substitute prescribing of methadone and buprenorphine

Relapse

Prevention after abstinence

- **Withdrawal and detoxification regimes have a high failure rate unless linked to long-term rehabilitation** [DH et al, 1999]. Continuation of supportive counselling both during detoxification and after cessation of methadone reduces the risk of relapse [McAuliffe, 1990; Amato et al, 2003].
- **Naltrexone is the only drug currently licensed for prevention of relapse after abstinence.** It is an opioid antagonist and therefore blocks the euphoric effects of opioids.
- **Naltrexone should be initiated and reviewed only by specialists** with a working knowledge of the appropriate regimens and required monitoring.
- **There is insufficient evidence to support the routine use of naltrexone to help people stay off heroin,** but it may be helpful for some people who are highly motivated [Kirchmayer et al, 2002; MeReC, 2002].
- **If a person requests further naltrexone prescriptions** after having been discharged from specialist care, then the GP should seek further specialist support.

Management of relapse after abstinence

- **Opioid dependence is a chronic relapsing disorder,** and cravings and relapses are common.
- The clinician should establish what precipitated the relapse, what prompted the person to consult, and what the person's expectations and goals are.
- **Consider restarting substitution therapy.** This may be best carried out in consultation with the local drug dependency service.
- **Separate sections in this guidance deal with the following situations:**
  - *Initial assessment*
  - *Initiation and stabilization of treatment*
  - *Acute withdrawal syndrome*

Acute withdrawal syndrome

General points

- **Drug users may present in acute withdrawal and need symptomatic relief.** A range of non-opioid treatments can be taken to reduce the physical effects of withdrawal.
- **A doctor may be pressurized to prescribe opioids in an unplanned manner in order to abolish withdrawal symptoms, but it is considered good practice not to do so.**

O

Table 9: Writing of prescriptions for substitute prescribing of methadone and buprenorphine.

Issue	Comments
Legal requirements for writing prescriptions	Unless exempt, all prescriptions must be hand-written with the following: The patient's name and address The form and strength of the preparation The dose The total quantity of the preparation or the number of dose units in both words AND figures The signature of the prescriber who has written the prescription The date of signing by the prescriber who has written the prescription
Handwriting exemption	GPs who prescribe controlled drugs regularly for drug misusers may apply to the Home Office fo handwriting exemption.
Other practical points when writing blue instalment prescriptions forms (FP10MDA1000)	Instalments can only be authorized for up to 14 days. State the intended date on which the first instalment should start. Specify the dispensing instructions (e.g. daily dispensing) and the amount to be dispensed on the instalment prescription form. If the prescriber wants supervised consumption in the pharmacy, specify 'supervised consumption' on the prescription if a local scheme is in place. If extra quantities need to be prescribed on any day because the pharmacy is closed on a Sunday or Bank Holiday, then the doctor should specify the actual days and quantities to be supplied fo those days. Once specified, the prescription cannot be dispensed on alternative dates. A prescription for a controlled drug is valid for 13 weeks from the date stated thereon. The Home Office has expressed a view that a dose of 'as directed' or 'when required' is not acceptable, but 'one to be taken as directed/when required' is acceptable. Where possible, always issue a prescription directly to the drug misuser. A prescription that was posted to the pharmacy but has not arrived cannot be dispensed, even at the verbal request of the prescriber. Other prescription items cannot be written on the same form.

- **Detoxification with lofexidine is an option in this situation.** Such detoxification is often carried out in specialist centres, but in some localities is done by GPs. We recommend that lofexidine be prescribed only by practitioners with knowledge of it or following advice from specialist practitioners.
- **Heroin withdrawal symptoms reach their peak 36–72 hours** after the last dose of heroin. Symptoms will have subsided substantially after 5 days.
- **Methadone withdrawal symptoms typically reach their peak 4–6 days** after the last dose of methadone. Symptoms do not substantially subside for 10–12 days. There may be variations in the time for withdrawal symptoms to reach their peak, depending on the dose.

O

Symptoms and signs of opioid withdrawal

- Sweating
- Lacrimation and rhinorrhoea
- Yawning
- Feeling hot and cold
- Anorexia and abdominal cramps
- Nausea, vomiting, and diarrhoea
- Tremor
- Insomnia and restlessness
- Generalized aches and pains
- Tachycardia, hypertension
- Gooseflesh
- Dilated pupils
- Increased bowel sounds

Acute symptoms are often followed by protracted fatigue, insomnia, and craving for opioids.
[DH et al, 1999]

Symptomatic treatments

Diarrhoea

- **Anti-motility drugs** reduce stool frequency and increase stool consistency.

Nausea and vomiting

- **Anti-emetics** speed gastric emptying and relieve nausea.

General aches and pains (e.g. headache, muscular pain or high temperature

- **Paracetamol** relieves pain and high temperature.
- **Ibuprofen or other nonsteroidal anti-inflammatory drug (NSAIDs)** are an alternative, in the absence of contraindications.

[DH et al, 1999]

Anxiety/agitation

- **Benzodiazepines** can be useful if used short-term [Ford, Personal Communication, 2003] but care should be taken not to extend prescribing beyond a short period. The patient should be warned of the increased risk of an overdose if benzodiazepines are taken with opioid and/or with alcohol.

Other symptoms

- Other symptoms (e.g. stomach cramps, muscle cramps, bone pain, sleeplessness, and agitation) should be managed symptomatically with the appropriate therapy

Management of the emergency situation — collapse due to opioid overdose

General points

- **People may inadvertently take an overdose** because of:
  - Varying purity of illicit supplies.
  - Reduction in tolerance after a period of abstinence (e.g. release from prison, discharge from rehabilitatio or hospital and recently having stopped naltrexone use).
  - Mixing drugs (particularly injecting benzodiazepine c cocaine), perhaps including alcohol.
  - Leakage from poorly wrapped drugs that have been ingested (body stuffers and packers).
  - Accidentally taking other methadone-containing preparations — diversion of methadone linctus is related to an increasing number of deaths among dru users.
- **Be aware of other causes of coma or collapse** (e.g. hypoglycaemia, head injury), particularly if there is no history available from a witness.
- **Call an ambulance and check for any immediate risks (such as discarded used needles).**

- **Institute routine emergency lifesaving procedures** (i.e. airway, breathing, and circulatory support).
- **Naloxone is the antidote for opioid overdose.** The Department of Health clinical guidelines recommend naloxone 0.8–2 mg intravenously, repeated every 2 to 3 minutes up to a maximum of 10 mg if respiratory function does not improve. If the person does not respond to this, question the diagnosis and consider other causes of collapse. Intramuscular or subcutaneous administration may be necessary if dosing by the intravenous rout is not feasible [ABPI Medicines Compendium, 2003].
- **However, it is estimated that most overdoses will respond to 400–800 micrograms naloxone (i.e. 1–2 ampoules)** [Heyworth, Personal Communication, 2002].
- **GPs should make a decision on how many ampoules to carry in their emergency bag, based on their local circumstances and ambulance services.**
- **Buprenorphine is not easily displaced by the opioid antagonist naloxone,** and therefore 10–30 times the usual dose of naloxone may be needed to reverse the effects of buprenorphine.
- **Admit the person to hospital.** Naloxone's duration of action is shorter than that of many opioids, and therefore close monitoring with repeated administration of naloxone may be necessary.

[DH et al, 1999]

Management of the unknown patient

New patient or temporary resident requesting a continuation or replacement prescription for substitution therapy

- **No opioids should be given, unless the person's continued consumption of substitution medication can be confirmed** (e.g. consumption is supervised regularly with no missed doses).
- **Potential sources of information** include:
  - Past or current GP.
  - Current pharmacist, who may be able to confirm when the last dose was taken and advise on the suitability of prescribing further substitution therapy.
  - Prison medical officer, if the person has recently been released from prison.
- **A new patient will need a full assessment** before a decision can be made on the appropriateness of prescribing substitution therapy (see *Initial Assessment*).
- Explain that opioid drugs will not be supplied except under a shared-care scheme with local drug dependency services (where available).
- **If the request for a prescription of substitution therapy is from a temporary resident who will be returning home within a short time,** it will be more appropriate for the person to see his or her own GP.
- **If there are acute withdrawal symptoms,** see *Acute withdrawal syndrome*. Symptomatic treatment with non-opioid drugs is generally the appropriate action.

Unknown patient requesting a replacement prescription out of hours

- **GPs should not prescribe in isolation. Methadone should also not be prescribed in emergency situations.**
- **Explain that the person's own GP is responsible for prescribing,** and that there will be an agreement in place with that GP regarding prescriptions. Loss of a prescription is the person's own responsibility.
- **If methadone is prescribed, this may make it difficult to manage further out-of-hours contacts.** Many co-operatives or groups of GPs who share an on-call rota have a policy of no prescriptions of opioids [DH et al, 1999].
- **Symptomatic treatment with non-opioid drugs for withdrawal symptoms** may be appropriate (see *Acute withdrawal syndrome*).

Pregnancy

General points

- **An increased incidence of intra-uterine growth retardation and pre-term delivery** contributes to an increased rate of low birth weight and perinatal mortality. These outcomes are also affected by factors such as socio-economic deprivation and smoking [DH et al, 1999].
- **Refer a pregnant woman who is opioid dependent** to an obstetrician specializing in drug misuse (depending on local expertise) and to the local drug dependency service.
- **Encourage the woman to use healthcare services.** In particular, emphasize and reinforce the importance of regular attendance for antenatal care.
- **Testing for HIV and hepatitis B is now routinely offered to all pregnant women.** The antenatal setting provides an opportunity for offering hepatitis C testing to injecting women at increased risk [Moran, Personal Communication, 2002].
- **Try to involve the woman's partner where appropriate.**
- **It is important for all relevant healthcare and social care professionals to work together,** as there may be child protection issues.

Treatment issues

- **Methadone has been used safely for many years.** Follow-up studies suggest that the long-term outcomes in women who enter methadone treatment programmes during pregnancy are better in terms of their pregnancy, childbirth, and infant development, irrespective of continuing drug use [DH et al, 1999].
- **Methadone maintenance treatment seems to be the best option** for ensuring continuity of care during pregnancy and afterwards [Finnegan, 1991]. Low-dose treatment is preferred, aiming for a dose that minimizes withdrawal in both mother and fetus. Higher doses may be required if illicit opioid use persists or the person relapses. It is important to choose the right dose that the mother is happy with and that protects the child.
- **Pregnancy is often a time of potential change:** some women may request detoxification, and this option should be fully explored.
- **Neonatal opioid withdrawal is common;** it is more likely to occur and to be severe the higher the dose of opioid taken by the mother. Symptoms typically develop within 48 hours of birth for heroin-dependent neonates, and within 7 days for methadone-dependent neonates [Wills, 2000]. Occasionally, methadone withdrawal may take 2 weeks or more to manifest.
- **Not all babies suspected of being drug dependent have been found to require pharmacological treatment.** Recent data from the Northern and Yorkshire region recorded that 139 from 365 of live births received treatment for withdrawal symptoms [Northern & Yorkshire Public Health Observatory, 2002].
- **Breastfeeding should be encouraged even if the mother continues to use drugs.** Exceptions [DH, 2002b] are women who are:
  - HIV positive
  - Hepatitis C positive
  - Using high-dose benzodiazepines
- **Although hepatitis C has been isolated from breast milk, the role of breastfeeding in mother-to-infant transmission is unclear** and several studies have recorded

O

no significant difference in transmission rates between breastfed infants and bottle-fed infants [DH, 2002b].

- **It is recommended that mothers should breastfeed immediately before an opioid dose is taken** to avoid peak concentrations of opioid in milk [Wills, 2000].

Reporting drug misuse

- **Doctors are expected to report cases of drug misusers presenting for treatment to their regional centres in England or to their national drug treatment monitoring system in Scotland and Wales.**
- **A report should be made when a person first presents with a drug problem or re-presents after a gap of 6 months or more (with recent introduction of new requirements to provide data on progress for those in treatment).** Report all types of problem drug misuse (e.g. opioids, benzodiazepines, central nervous system stimulants).
- **The Regional Drug Misuse Database is sufficiently anonymized** so that it cannot be used as a check on multiple prescribing for drug misusers.
- **Contact details** for the regional centres of the National Drugs Treatment Monitoring System (since April 2003 under the auspices of the National Treatment Agency) are available in the British National Formulary, in the section *Guidance on prescribing: controlled drugs and drug dependence* (www.bnf.org).

Issues concerning driving ability

- **Persistent use of or dependency on heroin, morphine, buprenorphine, or methadone will lead to refusal or revocation of a driving licence** [DVLA, 2003]. A licence will be considered only if the person has been free of drug use for at least 1 year for Group 1 entitlement, and at least 3 years for Group 2 entitlement.
- **An exception may be made for an individual complying fully with a consultant-supervised methadone maintenance programme.**
  - Group 1 entitlement may be granted subject to annual medical review and favourable assessment. People on an oral buprenorphine programme may be considered, applying the same criteria.
  - Group 2 entitlement may be granted once a minimum 3-year period of stability on the maintenance programme has been established. People on an oral buprenorphine maintenance programme that is supervised by a consultant may be considered, applying the same criteria [DVLA, Personal Communication, 2003].
- For more information regarding opioid and other drug misuse, see: www.dvla.gov.uk/at_a_glance/ch5_drugandalcohol.htm.
- **A person who is opioid-dependent or who is persistently using opioids should be told of the need to inform the DVLA.** Some individuals may refuse to do this, and in certain circumstances confidentiality may need to be overridden. Whether the GP should breach confidence and inform the DVLA without the person's consent is a complex ethical issue. GPs may need to consult their defence union.
- **The General Medical Council's position on reporting relevant medical conditions to the DVLA is as follows:** 'The doctor should explain to the patient that they have a legal duty to inform the DVLA. If the patient refuses to accept the diagnosis of the effect of the condition, you can suggest that the patient seeks a second opinion. You should advise the patient not to drive until the second opinion has been obtained. If the patient continues to drive, you should make every reasonable effort to persuade them to stop. This may involve telling their next of kin. If you do not manage to persuade a patient to stop driving, or you are given or find evidence that a patient is continuing to drive contrary to advice, you should disclose relevant medical information immediately in confidence to the medical advisor at the DVLA. Before giving information to the DVLA you should inform the patient of your decision to do so. Once the DVLA has been informed, you should also write to the patient to confirm that a disclosure had beer made.'

Management of pain in a person on substitute drug maintenance treatment

- People on substitute drug maintenance treatment experience as much pain associated with illness, injury, or surgery as other people do (and may be more sensitive). People on substitute opioids still need appropriate treatment for pain.

Severe acute pain

- **If the person is in acute severe pain, it may be appropriate to give morphine sulphate or a derivative** before transfer to hospital. Avoid opioids with both agonist and antagonist properties (e.g. buprenorphine, pentazocine, and nalbuphine), particularly for people taking methadone maintenance treatment, as withdrawa may be precipitated.
- **It is usually necessary to give a dose that is at least the dose that would be given to a person not on substitute drug maintenance treatment.** It is not possible to predict how much of an extra dose will be required.

Chronic pain

- **Use non-opioid treatments wherever appropriate,** for example, paracetamol, nonsteroidal anti-inflammatory drugs, tricyclic antidepressants, anticonvulsants, corticosteroids, and local anaesthetics. Beware of drug interactions (e.g. if either phenytoin or carbamazepine are added for neuropathic pain).
- **Continue the usual daily dose of the substitute drug.** Titrate dose of additional opioid to required dose.
- **Consider referral to a pain clinic if the person continues to have pain that is difficult to manage** [Scimeca et al, 2000].

Travelling abroad

Aim

- To prescribe the appropriate dose and amount of methadone that will cover the time spent abroad.

Home Office licence requirements

- **For total amounts less than methadone 500 mg and Subutex® (buprenorphine) 140 mg,** the Home Office advises that travellers should carry a 'To whom it may concern' letter from the prescriber, indicating that they are in possession of the drug for legitimate medical purposes.
- **For amounts over methadone 500 mg and Subutex® (buprenorphine) 140 mg or more, a Home Office expor licence is required.** Note that where buprenorphine is being used for analgesia, a Home Office licence is required for Temgesic (buprenorphine) 24 mg or more.
- To obtain the export licence, the prescriber must write t the Home Office, Drugs Branch, 312 Horseferry House, Dean Ryle Street, London SW1 2AW. The following must be stated:
  - The name and current address of the person
  - The strength, form, and quantity of the drug
  - The daily rate prescribed
  - The person's dates of travel to and from the UK

- **Anyone applying for a Home Office export licence should allow at least 10 working days** (assuming all the information is contained in the letter from the prescriber) for the processing of the application.
- **There is no legislation about the maximum amounts that individuals may travel with,** and the Home Office advises that each case is treated on its merits. Further details may be obtained from the Home Office by telephoning 0207 273 3806.
- **The export licence is to take the drug out of the UK and bring any surplus back.** It does not mean that the holder of the licence has the right to take the drug into the country to be visited. Therefore, it is important that the user checks with the embassy or consulate before departure, to establish that the country or countries to be visited will allow the drug user entry with the controlled drugs for medical use. Many people carry documentation about their treatment, to confirm the status of their medication.
- For more information, please see the notes on 'Controlled drugs and drug dependence' within the 'Guidance on prescribing' section of the *British National Formulary* (www.bnf.org).

Deciding on practice policy

- **The care for people who have problems with drug misuse needs to be managed by the whole primary healthcare team.**
- **All people, including drug misusers, may occasionally present with demands,** and previously agreed procedures and processes should be in place, to cover the most difficult scenarios.
- **Ideally, all the practice staff should be involved in developing these.** A useful setting might be a lunchtime meeting with all the staff, facilitated by someone from the local drug service.
- **In a survey investigating the training needs of primary care team members** in contact with substance misusers, the most popular topic for training was handling aggression [Sherratt and Jones, 2003]. Up to 80% of respondents had experienced aggressive behaviour. A meeting for the whole practice team was thought to be the best forum for training.

Points to consider

Note: the following points apply to all people, not only to drug misusers.

- Has the whole team decided on a common policy?
- Are prescription pads kept safe?
- What procedures are in place when hazards exist (e.g. consulting alone in a late evening surgery or a Saturday surgery)?
- What procedures are in place regarding a potentially difficult home visit?
- What is the 'bottom line' for removal of someone from the practice list?
- Do all staff feel able to report fears or difficult situations? Whom should they approach?
- How and where should incidents be recorded?
- In which situations should the police be called?
- Should the practice staff have training on handling aggression and violence?

In the practice policy it is important to have a process for dealing with the following situations if they should arise:

- Requests for lost prescriptions or medication?
- Requests for medication early?
- Another drug user or unknown person coming to collect the person's prescription?
- The drug misuser attending appointments with groups of friends?
- A person arriving either later or without an appointment?
- Threatening behaviour or shouting at nurses, receptionists, doctors, and others?
- Physical violence?

The Department of Health advises:

- **If a member of staff is working alone, reception staff should check with the staff member if an appointment overruns.** Staff should notify reception of anticipated delays.
- **Avoid seeing a person alone who has been aggressive or threatening to staff,** or who is judged by reception staff to be clearly upset or angry while waiting. If this is not possible, ask reception staff to make periodic checks. It is advisable to carry out predictably difficult consultations in an open area or with someone else present.
- **If it is necessary to see the person alone:**
  - **Keep a clear exit route** by positioning yourself nearest to the door.
  - Hide potential weapons (e.g. sharps).
  - **Have a means of requesting help,** such as assistance, alarms, or mobile phones.
  - **Be consistent** (e.g. where receptionists are expected to be firm in their application of the policy, they must be supported by more senior staff).
  - **If the behaviour is clearly unmanageable, it becomes a criminal matter.** This should be made clear to the person. If they refuse to co-operate, the police should be called to remove them. Where theft or clearly witnessed unacceptable behaviour or injury has taken place, the practice should consider pressing criminal charges.
  - **Yielding to demands is often not helpful,** and can undermine the patient's expectation of a firm decision. The message of a firm course of action soon gets communicated to other drug misusers, making recurrence of unacceptable behaviour much less likely.

[DH et al, 1999]

O

Useful contacts

- Department of Health drug dependency web site: www.doh.gov.uk/drugs
- National Drugs Helpline: provides free and confidential advice, including information on local services. Telephone 0800 776600
- Also see Annex 19 (References and Contact Numbers) in the Department of Health 'Orange Book', *Drug Misuse and Dependence — Guidelines on Clinical Management* [DH et al, 1999]

References

NHS staff in England can link, free of charge, from references to full text journals by clicking on [Full text] on the PRODIGY website.

1. ABPI Medicines Compendium (2002) *Summary of product characteristics for Nalorex.* Electronic Medicines Compendium. Datapharm Communications Ltd. www.emc.medicines.org.uk [Accessed: 04/09/2003].
2. ABPI Medicines Compendium (2003) *Summary of product characteristics for Narcan injection 400 mcg/ml.* Electronic Medicines Compendium. Datapharm Communications Ltd.. www.emc.medicines.org.uk [Accessed: 27/01/2004].
3. Amato, L., Davoli, M., Ferri, M. and Ali, R. (2003) *Methadone at tapered doses for the management of*

opioid withdrawal (Cochrane Review). The Cochrane Library. Issue 3. Oxford: Update Software.
4. Baden, L.R., Horowitz, G., Jacoby, H. and Eliopoulos, G.M. (2001) Quinolones and false-positive urine screening for opiates by immunoassay technology. *Journal of the American Medical Association* **286**(24), 3115–3119. [Full text]
5. Bell, J. and Zador, D. (2000) A risk-benefit analysis of methadone maintenance treatment. *Drug Safety* **22**(3), 179–190.
6. Bell, J., Caplehorn, J.R. and McNeil, D.R. (1994) The effect of intake procedures on performance in methadone maintenance. *Addiction* **89**(4), 463–471.
7. CSM (1994) Relative safety of oral non-aspirin NSAIDs. *Current Problems in Pharmacovigilance* **20**(Aug), 9–11.
8. DH (2002a) *Statistics from the regional drug misuse database for 6 months ending March 2001*. Department of Health. www.dh.gov.uk [Accessed: 16/10/2003].
9. DH (2002b) *Hepatitis C strategy for England*. Department of Health. www.dh.gov.uk [Accessed: 30/04/2004]. [Full text]
10. DH, Scottish Office DH, Welsh Office and DH and Social Services of NI (1999) *Drug misuse and dependence – guidelines on clinical management*. Department of Health. www.dh.gov.uk [Accessed: 27/04/2004]. [Full text]
11. DVLA (2003) *At a glance guide to current medical standards of fitness to drive. Drug and alcohol misuse and dependency*. Drivers Medical Group, Driver and Vehicle Licensing Authority. www.dvla.gov.uk [Accessed: 29/01/2004].
12. DVLA (2003) *Personal communication*. Driving and Vehicle Licensing Agency: Swansea.
13. Eccles, M., Freemantle, N. and Mason, J. (1998) North of England evidence based guideline development project: summary guideline for non-steroidal anti-inflammatory drugs versus basic analgesia in treating the pain of degenerative arthritis. *British Medical Journal* **317**(7157), 526–530. [Full text]
14. Faggiano, F., Vigna-Taglianti, F., Versino, E. and Lemma, P. (2003) *Methadone maintenance at different dosages for opioid dependence (Cochrane Review)*. The Cochrane Library. Issue 3. Oxford: Update Software.
15. Finnegan, L.P. (1991) Treatment Issues for opioid-dependent women during the perinatal period. *Journal of Psychoactive Drugs* **23**(2), 191–201.
16. Ford, C. (2003) *Personal communication*. Royal College of General Practitioners: London.
17. Frischer, M., Goldberg, D., Rahman, M. and Berney, L. (1997) Mortality and survival among a cohort of drug injectors in Glasgow, 1982–1994. *Addiction* **92**(4), 419–427. [Full text]
18. Garcia, R.L. and Jick, H. (1994) Risk of upper gastrointestinal bleeding and perforation associated with individual non-steroidal anti-inflammatory drugs. *Lancet* **343**(8900), 769–772. [Full text]
19. Gilvarry, E. (2002) *Personal communication*. Northern Regional Drug and Alcohol Services: Newcastle upon Tyne.
20. Gossop, M. and Strang, J. (1997) Rapid anaesthetic-antagonist detoxification of heroin addicts: What origins, evidence base and clinical justification? *British Journal of Intensive Care* **7**(2), 66–69.
21. Gossop, M., Marsden, J., Stewart, D. and Treacy, S. (2001) Outcomes after methadone maintenance and methadone reduction treatments: two-year follow-up results from the National Treatment Outcome Research Study. *Drug & Alcohol Dependence* **62**(3), 255–264.
22. Gowing, L., Farrell, M., Ali, R. and White, J. (2000) *Alpha 2 adrenergic agonists for the management of opioid withdrawal (Cochrane Review)*. The Cochrane Library. Issue 3. Oxford: Update Software.
23. Gowing, L., Ali, R. and White, J. (2002) *Buprenorphone for the management of opioid withdrawal (Cochrane Review)*. The Cochrane Library. Issue 3. Oxford: Update Software.
24. Green, L. and Gossop, M. (1988) Effects of information on the opiate withdrawal syndrome. *British Journal of Addiction* **83**(3), 305–309.
25. Henry, D., Lim, L.L., Garcia-Rodriguez, L.A. et al (1996) Variability in risk of gastrointestinal complications with individual non-steroidal anti-inflammatory drugs: results of a collaborative meta-analysis. *British Medical Journal* **312**(7046), 1563–1566. [Full text]
26. Hernández-Diaz, S. and Rodriguez, L.A. (2000) Association between nonsteroidal anti-inflammatory drugs and upper gastrointestinal tract bleeding/perforation: an overview of epidemiologic studies published in the 1990s. *Archives of Internal Medicine* **160**(14), 2093–2099. [Full text]
27. Heyworth, J. (2002) *Personal communication*. British Association for Accident and Emergency Medicine: Royal College of Surgeons of England, London.
28. Humeniuk, R., Ali, R., White, J. et al (2000) *Proceedings of expert workshop on the induction and stabilisation of patients onto methadone*. Monograph 39. Australian Department of Health and Ageing. www.health.gov.au [Accessed: 24/01/2003].
29. Johnson, R.E., Chutape, M.A., Strain, E.C. et al (2000) A comparison of levomethadyl acetate, buprenorphine, and methadone for opioid dependence. *New England Journal of Medicine* **343**(18), 1290–1297. [Full text]
30. Kakko, J, Svanborg, K.D., Kreek, M.J. and Heilig, M. (2003) 1-year retention and social function after buprenorphine-assisted relapse prevention treatment for heroin dependence in Sweden: a randomised, placebo-controlled trial. *Lancet* **361**(9358), 662–668. [Full text]
31. Kirchmayer, U., Davoli, M. and Verster, A. (2002) *Naltrexone maintenace treatment for opioid dependence*. The Cochrane Library. Issue 3. Oxford: Update Software.
32. Leshner, A.I. (1999) Science-based views of drug addiction and its treatment. *Journal of the American Medical Association* **282**(14), 1314–1316. [Full text]
33. Ling, W., Wesson, D.R., Charuvastra, C. and Klett, C.J. (1996) A controlled trial comparing buprenorphine and methadone maintenance in opioid dependence. *Archives of General Psychiatry* **53**(5), 401–407.
34. Marsch, L.A. (1998) The efficacy of methadone maintenance interventions in reducing illicit opiate use, HIV risk behavior and criminality: a meta-analysis. *Addiction* **93**(4), 515–532. [Full text]
35. Mattick, R.P., Kimber, J., Breen, C. and Davoli, M. (2003) *Buprenorphine maintenance versus placebo or methadone maintenance for opioid dependence (Cochrance Review)*. The Cochrane Library. Issue 3. Oxford: Update Software.
36. McAuliffe, W.E. (1990) A randomized controlled trial of recovery training and self-help for opioid addicts in New England and Hong Kong. *Journal of Psychoactive Drugs* **22**(2), 197–209.
37. MeReC (2002) The management of opioid dependence. *MeReC Bulletin* **12**(4), 13–16.
38. Milby, J.B., Gurwitch, R.H., Wiebe, D.J. et al (1986) Prevalence and diagnostic reliability of methadone maintenance detoxification fear. *American Journal of Psychiatry* **143**(6), 739–743.

39. Moran, P. (2002) *Personal communication.* Consultant Obstetrician and Gynaecologist, Royal Victoria Infirmary: Newcastle upon Tyne.
40. National Institutes of Health (1997) *Effective medical treatment of heroin addiction.* NIH Consensus Statements: 108. US Department of Health and Human Services. www.nih.gov [Accessed: 29/01/2003].
41. NICE (2001) *Guidance on the use of cyclo-oxygenase (Cox) II selective inhibitors, celecoxib, rofecoxib, meloxicam and etodolac for osteoarthritis and rheumatoid arthritis.* Technology appraisal no. 27. National Institute for Health and Clinical Excellence. www.nice.org.uk [Accessed: 16/10/2003].
42. Northern & Yorkshire Public Health Observatory (2002) *Drug misuse in pregnancy in the Northern and Yorkshire region.* Occasional paper no. 6. Northern & Yorkshire Public Health Observatory. www.nypho.org.uk [Accessed: 27/02/2003].
43. O'Brien, C.P. and McLellan, A.T. (1996) Myths about the treatment of addiction. *Lancet* **347**(8996), 237–240. [Full text]
44. Office for National Statistics (2003) Deaths related to drug poisoning: results for England and Wales, 1997–2001. *Health Statistics Quarterly* **17**(Spring), 65–71.
45. Oppenheimer, E., Tobutt, C., Taylor, C. and Andrew, T. (1994) Death and survival in a cohort of heroin addicts from London clinics: a 22-year follow-up study. *Addiction* **89**(10), 1299–1308.
46. Prunty, M. (2004) *Personal communication.* Senior Medical Officer, Substance Misuse Team, Department of Health: London.
47. RCGP (2003) *Guidance for the use of buprenorphine for the treatment of opioid dependence in primary care.* London: Royal College of General Practitioners.
48. Roberts, I., Barker, M. and Li, L. (1997) Analysis of trends in deaths from accidental drug poisoning in teenagers, 1985–95. *British Medical Journal* **315**(7103), 289. [Full text]
49. Scimeca, M.M., Savage, S.R., Portenoy, R. and Lowinson, J. (2000) Treatment of pain in methadone-maintained patients. *The Mount Sinai Journal of Medicine* **67**(5 & 6), 412–422.
50. Sherratt, M. and Jones, K. (2003) Training needs of local primary health care teams dealing with drug abusers – a survey in Tyneside. *Drugs: Education, prevention and policy* **10**(1), 87–94.
51. Strain, E.C., Stitzer, M.L., Liebson, I.A. and Bigelow, G.E. (1993) Dose-response effects of methadone in the treatment of opioid dependence. *Annals of Internal Medicine* **119**(1), 23–27.
52. Strain, E.C., Stitzer, M.L., Liebson, I.A. and Bigelow, G.E. (1996) Buprenorphine versus methadone in the treatment of opiod dependence: self reports, urinalysis, and the addiction severity index. *Journal of Clinical Psychopharmacology* **16**(1), 58–67.
53. Strain, E.C., Bigelow, G.E., Liebson, I.A. and Stitzer, M.L. (1999) Moderate- vs high-dose methadone in the treatment of opioid dependence: a randomized trial. *Journal of the American Medical Association* **281**(11), 1000–1005. [Full text]
54. Strang, J., Sheridan, J. and Barber, N. (1996) Prescribing injectable and oral methadone to opiate addicts: results from the 1995 national postal survey of community pharmacies in England and Wales. *British Medical Journal* **313**(7052), 270–272. [Full text]
55. Strang, J., Marsden, J., Cummins, M. et al (2000) Randomized trial of supervised injectable versus oral methadone maintenance: report of feasibility and 6-month outcome. *Addiction* **95**(11), 1631–1635. [Full text]
56. Swadi, H., Wells, B. and Power, R. (1990) Addicts. *British Medical Journal* **300**(6735), 1313–1313.
57. Tramer, M.R., Williams, J.E., Carroll, D. et al (1998) Comparing analgesic efficacy of non-steroidal anti-inflammatory drugs given by different routes in acute and chronic pain: a qualitative systematic review. *Acta Anaesthesiologica Scandinavica* **42**(1), 71–79.
58. Ward, J., Hall, W. and Mattick, R.P. (1999) Role of maintenance treatment in opioid dependence. *Lancet* **353**(9148), 221–226. [Full text]
59. WHO (2001) *Mental health: new understanding, new hope.* The world health report 2001. World Health Organisation. www.who.int/whr2001/2001/main/en/chapter3/003d3.htm [Accessed: 21/01/2003].
60. Wills, S. (2000) Street drugs. In: Lee, A., Inch, S., Finnigan, D. et al (Eds.) *Therapeutics in pregnancy and lactation.* Oxon: Radcliffe Medical Press Ltd. 227–246.

PRODIGY GUIDANCE

Osteoarthritis

Last revised in July 2005
www.prodigy.nhs.uk/guidance.asp?gt=Osteoarthritis

Applies to people over the age of 16 years

This guidance covers osteoarthritis.

This guidance does not cover rheumatoid arthritis or psoriatic arthropathy.
There is separate PRODIGY guidance for *Ankylosing spondylitis, Back pain — lower, Dyspepsia — proven DU or GU, Dyspepsia — symptoms, Gout, Neck pain, Nonsteroidal anti-inflammatory drugs (NSAIDs)*, and *Rheumatoid arthritis.*

Goals

- Reduce pain and stiffness
- Maintain or improve joint mobility
- Limit the progression of joint damage
- Reduce functional disability
- Avoid or reduce the use of drugs where possible

Contents

Scenarios
- Osteoarthritis — knee joint p.1350
- Osteoarthritis — hip joint p.1354
- Osteoarthritis — any other joint p.1357
- Acutely painful prosthetic joint p.1361

Extended Information, p. 1364

Which scenario?

- **Osteoarthritis — knee joint:** covers the management of knee OA.
- **Osteoarthritis — hip joint:** covers the management of hip OA.
- **Osteoarthritis — any joint:** covers the management of OA affecting any other joint.
- **Acutely painful prosthetic joint:** covers the differential diagnosis, initial management, and indications for referral of an acutely painful prosthetic joint.

O

Osteoarthritis — knee joint

Which therapy?

- **Consider non-drug treatment for all people with knee osteoarthritis (OA) at all stages:**
  - Braces and orthoses
  - Patellar taping of the knee
  - The use of a cane in the contralateral hand
  - Exercise therapy
  - Weight loss if BMI >28
- The use of a TENS machine or acupuncture might provide symptomatic relief but more studies are needed to clarify the specific benefit in OA.
- **If analgesia is required:**
  - Paracetamol (with codeine where needed) is the drug of first choice — it may be more effective if taken regularly.
  - Oral NSAIDs may be required if adequate analgesia is not obtained with paracetamol.
  - Topical NSAIDs may be used:
    - For an acute flare-up
    - As an alternative to oral NSAIDs if gastroprotection is needed
  - Topical capsaicin may be tried if other options have failed.
- **Intra-articular corticosteroid injection** provides short-term relief from a flare-up.
- **Glucosamine** can be tried for mild knee OA if analgesia has failed or the person is intolerant of NSAIDs. It can be purchased from various retail outlets.
- **Referral to an orthopaedic surgeon** should be considered if pain has not responded to therapy, and there is progressive limitation of function.

Practical prescribing points

For further information, please see the *Medicines Compendium* (www.medicines.org.uk) or the *British National Formulary* (www.bnf.org).

Nonsteroidal anti-inflammatory drugs (NSAIDs)

- **Only one NSAID should be prescribed at a time.**
- **NSAIDs may worsen asthma, hypertension, renal impairment, or heart failure.**
- Do not give ibuprofen, diclofenac, or naproxen without gastroprotection if there is a history of peptic ulceration.
- Do not give celecoxib if there is active peptic ulceration.
- **Pregnancy and breastfeeding:** use paracetamol if possible. If an NSAID is essential, ibuprofen may be used during breastfeeding and before 30 weeks of pregnancy.
- **People with cardiovascular disease:**
  - Ibuprofen may reduce the cardiovascular protective effect of low-dose aspirin.
  - Do not give celecoxib to people with established ischaemic heart disease, cerebrovascular disease, peripheral arterial disease, or moderate or severe heart failure due to the small increased risk of thrombotic events.
  - Do not use celecoxib with low-dose aspirin. (Gastrointestinal protective effects of celecoxib are reduced.)
- **In people with risk factors for gastrointestinal NSAID complications:**
  - Use paracetamol (with or without codeine) instead of a NSAID if possible.
  - Or, use gastroprotection (a PPI or full-dose misoprostol) combined with a standard NSAID.
  - Or, consider switching to celecoxib alone (COX-2 selective).
  - Or, consider using a topical nonsteroidal anti-inflammatory drug.
- **Risk factors for gastrointestinal NSAID complications include:**
  - Age of 65 years and over.
  - Previous history of gastroduodenal ulcer, gastrointestinal (GI) bleeding, or gastroduodenal perforation.

- Concomitant use of medications that are known to increase the likelihood of upper-GI adverse events, e.g. anticoagulants, aspirin (even a low dose), and corticosteroids.
- Presence of serious comorbidity, such as cardiovascular disease, renal or hepatic impairment, diabetes, or hypertension.
- Requirement for prolonged duration of NSAID use.
- Use of maximum recommended doses of NSAIDs.

Misoprostol

- Diarrhoea and abdominal pain are common. Advise women of child-bearing age to use adequate contraception, because misoprostol increases the risk of miscarriage.

Codeine phosphate

- Codeine may cause nausea, vomiting, constipation, and drowsiness. People may need regular laxatives if long-term use of codeine is necessary.

Intra-articular corticosteroids

- In general, triamcinolone or methylprednisolone for injection of large joints (e.g. knee).
- Atrophy of subcutaneous tissues and local skin depigmentation may occur from periarticular leakage of corticosteroid.
  - The risk of local-tissue atrophy and depigmentation occurs from subcutaneous or shallow injections as well as from small-joint injections (e.g. tennis elbow, de Quervain's tenosynovitis and shallow intramuscular injections).
  - The risk is greatest if large or repeated doses of a long-acting, potent corticosteroid are given.
- Lidocaine should be used to provide local anaesthesia.

Capsaicin

- Warn people that they may feel an intense burning sensation after application. This effect diminishes with continued use.

Follow-up advice

- The person's requirements for analgesia should be reviewed regularly, at least 6-monthly.

Should I refer or investigate?

Refer?

- **Physiotherapy:**
  - Exercise therapy, or if it is difficult to motivate the person
  - Patellar taping
  - TENS machine
  - Acupuncture
- **Occupational therapy:**
  - If aids or modifications in the home are required
- **Orthotics:**
  - Braces and orthoses
  - Provision of a cane
- **Rheumatologist:**
  - If there is doubt over the diagnosis, or the person requires injections that cannot be performed in primary care
- **Orthopaedic surgeon:**
  - If there is persistent pain that has not responded to medical therapy, and the person has progressive limitation in activities of daily living

Investigate?

- All blood tests are normal in osteoarthritis.
- X-rays may help to confirm the diagnosis, and to exclude other forms of arthritis.

Patient information leaflets

The following PILs are available at www.prodigy.nhs.uk

- Anti-inflammatory Painkillers
- Arthritis Care
- Arthritis Research Campaign - ARC
- Osteoarthritis
- Paracetamol

Shared decision making

- **Non-drug treatments** which may help to ease symptoms of osteoarthritis of the knee include:
  - **Exercise** if possible. General exercise such as swimming is ideal, but any exercise is better than none. Exercises to strengthen the quadriceps may also help.
  - **Losing weight** if you are very overweight or obese
  - **A walking stick** held in the opposite hand
  - **Shoe insoles and/or a knee brace**
  - **Pulling the kneecap slightly inwards** with a special tape
  - **TENS machine**
  - **Acupuncture**
- **Paracetamol** is commonly used for pain. The normal adult dosage is two 500 mg tablets, four times a day.
- **An anti-inflammatory painkiller** tablet or gel may be an option.
  - Bleeding from the stomach is the most serious possible side-effect. Stop the medicine and see a doctor if you develop stomach symptoms.
  - Some people with asthma, high blood pressure, kidney failure, or heart failure may not be able to take anti-inflammatories.
- **Codeine** is a painkiller that is stronger than paracetamol. It may be used in combination with paracetamol or an anti-inflammatory. Possible side-effects include constipation and drowsiness.
- **A steroid injection** into a joint is an option if the joint is badly inflamed.
- **Glucosamine** food supplements may also help to ease pain.
- **Joint replacement surgery** is an option for badly affected joints. Most people with osteoarthritis do not become bad enough to need surgery.

Drug rationale

Drugs not included

Analgesia

- **Standard oral nonsteroidal anti-inflammatory drugs (NSAIDs), other than ibuprofen, diclofenac, and naproxen,** are not included, as they are associated with a higher risk of gastrointestinal (GI) adverse events or are not licensed for osteoarthritis (OA) [CSM, 1994; Henry et al, 1996; Hernández-Diaz and Rodriguez, 2000; CSM, 2002]. Suppositories are not offered, as they do not improve efficacy or safety, and are generally less acceptable to people [Tramer et al, 1998].
- **Cyclo-oxygenase-2 (COX-2) selective NSAIDs, other than celecoxib,** are not included. COX-2 inhibitors have shown an increased risk of thrombotic adverse cardiovascular reactions, such as heart attacks and strokes [EMEA, 2005].

- Etoricoxib is licensed for osteoarthritis and there is some trial data to support its use. It is currently under the surveillance of the Committee on Safety of Medicines and in view of the ongoing uncertainty about the long terms thrombotic risks associated with COX-2 inhibitors it seems prudent to reconsider once its 'black-triangle' status has been lifted.
- Parecoxib is a 'black-triangle' drug that is currently licensed for the short-term treatment of postoperative pain only.
- Etodolac and meloxicam — for both these drugs there are insufficient data of medium- to long-term duration to know whether or not they are associated with a possible increased risk of gastrointestinal or cardiovascular events, they are therefore not recommended because of the lack of follow-up data available.

- **Modified-release NSAIDs:** improvement in efficacy and reduction in adverse events have not been shown and they are also relatively expensive. They may be worth trying in someone with prominent morning stiffness despite use of standard NSAID preparations.
- **Topical diclofenac solution** is not included: it is licensed for the localized treatment of osteoarthritic pain in superficial joints, including the knee. There is no evidence to suggest that it is any more effective than other topical NSAIDs available and it is considerably more expensive.
- **Rubefacients:** no randomized controlled trials (RCTs) have compared a topical rubefacient with another active treatment and there is therefore little evidence to support their efficacy in osteoarthritis [Mason et al, 2004c; Bandolier, 2005].
- **Chondroitin** is not offered. It is a food supplement and is not licensed for the treatment of OA. There are insufficient trial data of its use in people with knee OA.
- **Hyaluronic acid (HA)** intra-articular injection is not offered. It may be a further option for those who have not responded to intra-articular corticosteroids or those who cannot tolerate corticosteroids, or in people waiting for total knee replacement. However, this treatment option is not likely to be given in primary care and there is still much controversy about its use [Espallargues and Pons, 2003].
- **Strong opioids** (e.g. morphine, pethidine) should be avoided because of the risk of dependence if used inappropriately.
- **Weak opioids other than codeine** have not shown greater efficiency than higher doses of codeine combined with paracetamol or are more expensive.
- **Low-dose weak opioids with paracetamol** (e.g. co-codamol 8/500, co-dydramol 10/500): there is no evidence that these offer any clinical benefit over paracetamol alone and they are likely to lead to opioid adverse effects [MeReC, 1993; De Craen et al, 1996].

Gastroprotection

- **Proton-pump inhibitors (PPIs): rabeprazole** is not currently licensed for preventing NSAID-induced complications [BNF 49, 2005].
- **H_2-receptor antagonists (H_2RAs):** double doses of H_2-receptor antagonists are effective at reducing the risk of endoscopic gastric and duodenal ulcers but this is an off-licence use [Rostom et al, 2002]. Standard doses only reduce the risk of endoscopic duodenal ulcers. H_2RAs are therefore not included [BNF 49, 2005].
- **Fixed-dose combinations of standard NSAIDs with misoprostol:** the optimum dosage of misoprostol (i.e. 800 micrograms daily) cannot be reached using these preparations. In particular, only 400 micrograms daily of misoprostol is given with the higher dosages of NSAID in these preparations.
- **Low-dose misoprostol:** lower doses (e.g. 400 micrograms per day) are less effective than PPIs at reducing the incidence of endoscopic lesions, and have greater adverse effects [NICE, 2004]. (Diarrhoea and abdominal pain are common.)
- **Glucosamine** is not included but it can be purchased from various retail outlets — 1500 mg daily might provide modest symptom relief for OA of the knee [Richy et al, 2003]. It is not a licensed medicine in the UK, and although it can be prescribed, the relative purity and glucosamine content in different preparations obtained from different manufacturers may vary as manufacturers are not bound by statutory monitoring or good manufacturing requirements [DTB, 2002].

Drugs included

Analgesia

- **Paracetamol** is the analgesic drug of first choice in people of all age groups. It works well for some people, especially where mild symptoms of osteoarthritis (OA) are present.
- **Codeine (in combination with paracetamol):** higher-dosage codeine is included for use with regular paracetamol for additional pain relief. Codeine 60 mg plus paracetamol has been shown to provide more pain relief than either codeine 60 mg alone or paracetamol 1000 mg alone [Moore et al, 1997]. Codeine should be prescribed separately from paracetamol to allow flexibility of dosing and titration of analgesic effect.
- **Standard nonsteroidal anti-inflammatory drugs (NSAIDs): ibuprofen, diclofenac, and naproxen** have a good balance of efficacy against adverse-effect profile [CSM, 1994; Henry et al, 1996; Hernández-Diaz and Rodriguez, 2000]. Naproxen has a long half-life and can be given twice-daily; it may be particularly useful for someone with morning stiffness.
- **Topical NSAIDs: diclofenac, felbinac, ibuprofen, ketoprofen and piroxicam are available as topical formulations.** Topical NSAIDs have been found to be no more effective than oral NSAIDs [Mason et al, 2004b] but a short course could be considered if an NSAID is required and someone is at high risk of peptic ulceration or bleeding with an oral NSAID, therefore needing gastroprotection.
- **Cyclo-oxygenase-2 (COX-2) selective NSAIDs: celecoxib** is licensed for use in OA and is an option for use in people at high risk of NSAID-induced GI complications [NICE, 2001a].
- **Intra-articular corticosteroids:** triamcinolone acetonide or methylprednisolone is available for intra-articular injection of the knee joint. Intra-articular corticosteroid injection, by an appropriately skilled person, will often give rapid relief of severe symptoms [Ravaud et al, 1999]. Lidocaine (lignocaine) is available for local anaesthesia.
- **Capsaicin 0.025% cream** is included and it is licensed for use in symptomatic relief of osteoarthritis. The few published trials available only assessed treatment response at four weeks and although it only has moderate to poor efficacy in the treatment of chronic musculoskeletal pain, it may be useful as an adjunct or alone for a people who are either unresponsive or intolerant of other treatments [Mason et al, 2004d].

Gastroprotection

- **Proton-pump inhibitors (PPIs): esomeprazole, lansoprazole, omeprazole, and pantoprazole** are generally the preferred choice for gastroprotection and

are licensed for this use. They are effective and well tolerated; they reduce the risk of endoscopic gastric ulcers by 63% and the risk of duodenal ulcers by 81% [Rostom et al, 2002]. However there is a lack of data on prevention of ulcer complications.
- **Full-dose misoprostol** (200 micrograms four times a day) is licensed for prevention of NSAID-induced gastroduodenal ulceration [BNF 49, 2005]. It is effective for the treatment and prophylaxis of NSAID-associated ulcers, but it is not always well tolerated [Hawkey et al, 1998; Rostom et al, 2002].

Prescriptions

Analgesia

Paracetamol tablets: 1g up to four times a day
- Age from 16 years onwards
- Paracetamol 500mg tablets. Take two tablets every 4 to 6 hours when required for pain relief. Maximum of 8 tablets in 24 hours; supply 200 tablets; NHS Cost £3.06.

Add on if required: codeine 30-60mg up to four times a day
- Age from 16 years onwards
- Codeine 30mg tablets. Take one to two tablets every 4 to 6 hours when required for pain relief. Maximum of 8 tablets in 24 hours; supply 56 tablets; NHS Cost £3.34.

Paracetamol 500mg tablets + codeine 30mg tablets
- Age from 16 years onwards
- Paracetamol 500mg tablets. Take two tablets every 4 to 6 hours when required for pain relief. Maximum of 8 tablets in 24 hours; supply 200 tablets; NHS Cost £3.06.
- Codeine 30mg tablets. Take one to two tablets every 4 to 6 hours when required for pain relief. Maximum of 8 tablets in 24 hours; supply 56 tablets; NHS Cost £3.34.

NSAIDs: standard and COX-2

Ibuprofen tablets: 400mg three times a day
- Age from 16 years onwards
- Ibuprofen 400mg tablets. Take one tablet three times a day; supply 84 tablets; NHS Cost £2.66; OTC Cost £4.69.

Ibuprofen tablets: 600mg three times a day
- Age from 16 years onwards
- Ibuprofen 600mg tablets. Take one tablet three times a day; supply 84 tablets; NHS Cost £4.10.

Ibuprofen tablets: 800mg three times a day
- Age from 16 years onwards
- Ibuprofen 400mg tablets. Take two tablets three times a day; supply 168 tablets; NHS Cost £5.32.

Diclofenac sodium e/c tablets: 25mg three times a day
- Age from 16 years onwards
- Diclofenac 25mg e/c tablets. Take one tablet three times a day; supply 84 tablets; NHS Cost £1.52.

Diclofenac sodium e/c tablets: 50mg three times a day
- Age from 16 years onwards
- Diclofenac 50mg e/c tablets. Take one tablet three times a day; supply 84 tablets; NHS Cost £2.14.

Naproxen tablets: 250mg twice a day
- Age from 16 years onwards
- Naproxen 250mg tablets. Take one tablet twice a day; supply 56 tablets; NHS Cost £3.14.

Naproxen tablets: 500mg twice a day
- Age from 16 years onwards
- Naproxen 500mg tablets. Take one tablet twice a day; supply 56 tablets; NHS Cost £4.90.

Celecoxib capsules: 100mg twice a day (COX-2 selective)
- Age from 16 years onwards
- Celecoxib 100mg capsules. Take one capsule twice a day; supply 60 capsules; NHS Cost £21.55.

Celecoxib capsules: 200mg twice a day (COX-2 selective)
- Age from 16 years onwards
- Celecoxib 200mg capsules. Take one capsule twice a day; supply 60 capsules; NHS Cost £43.10.

GI protection: use ONLY with a standard NSAID

Omeprazole capsules: 20mg once a day
- Age from 16 years onwards
- Omeprazole 20mg capsules. Take one capsule once a day; supply 28 capsules; NHS Cost £12.75.

Omeprazole tablets: 20mg once a day
- Age from 16 years onwards
- Omeprazole 20mg tablets. Take one tablet once a day; supply 28 tablets; NHS Cost £12.75.

Lansoprazole capsules: 15mg each morning
- Age from 16 years onwards
- Lansoprazole 15mg capsules. Take one capsule each morning (on an empty stomach); supply 28 capsules; NHS Cost £12.92.

Lansoprazole capsules: 30mg each morning
- Age from 16 years onwards
- Lansoprazole 30mg capsules. Take one capsule each morning (on an empty stomach); supply 28 capsules; NHS Cost £23.63.

Pantoprazole e/c tablets: 20mg once a day
- Age from 16 years onwards
- Pantoprazole 20mg e/c tablets. Take one tablet once a day; supply 28 tablets; NHS Cost £12.31.

Esomeprazole tablets: 20mg once a day
- Age from 16 years onwards
- Esomeprazole 20mg tablets. Take one tablet once a day; supply 28 tablets; NHS Cost £18.50.

Lansoprazole orodispersible tablets: 15mg each morning
- Age from 16 years onwards
- Lansoprazole 15mg orodisp tabs. Take one tablet each morning (on an empty stomach); supply 28 tablets; NHS Cost £10.86.

Lansoprazole orodispersible tablets: 30mg each morning
- Age from 16 years onwards
- Lansoprazole 30mg orodisp tabs. Take one tablet each morning (on an empty stomach); supply 28 tablets; NHS Cost £21.38.

Misoprostol tablets: 200micrograms four times a day
- Age from 16 years onwards
- Misoprostol 200microgram tabs. Take one tablet four times a day; supply 120 tablets; NHS Cost £18.72.

Topical NSAIDs and capsaicin cream

Diclofenac 1% gel
- Age from 16 years onwards
- Diclofenac 1% gel. Apply 2 to 2.5 cm (1 inch) to the affected area 3 to 4 times a day for up to 2 weeks; supply 100 grams; NHS Cost £7.00.

Felbinac 3% gel
- Age from 16 years onwards
- Felbinac 3% gel. Apply 2.5cm (1 inch) to the affected area 2 to 4 times a day for up to 2 weeks; supply 100 grams; NHS Cost £7.00.

Felbinac 3.17% foam
- Age from 16 years onwards
- Felbinac 3.17% foam. Apply 2.5cm (1 inch) to the affected area 2 to 4 times a day for up to 2 weeks; supply 100 grams; NHS Cost £7.00.

Ibuprofen 5% cream

- Age from 16 years onwards
- Ibuprofen 5% cream. Apply 4 to 10cm (1.5 to 4 inches) to the affected area 3 to 4 times a day for up to 2 weeks; supply 100 grams; NHS Cost £6.21; OTC Cost £10.95.

Ibuprofen 5% gel

- Age from 16 years onwards
- Ibuprofen 5% gel. Apply 4 to 10cm (1.5 to 4 inches) to the affected joint 3 to 4 times a day for up to 2 weeks; supply 100 grams; NHS Cost £5.31; OTC Cost £7.97.

Ibuprofen 5% mousse

- Age from 16 years onwards
- Ibuprofen 5% mousse. Shake the container and then apply 1 to 2g (1 to 2 golf-ball sized amounts of mousse in the hand) to the affected area 3 to 4 times a day for 2 weeks; supply 125 grams; NHS Cost £6.12; OTC Cost £10.79.

Ketoprofen 2.5% gel

- Age from 16 years onwards
- Ketoprofen 2.5% gel. Apply 4 to 7cm (2 to 3 inches) to the affected area 2 to 4 times a day for up to 10 days; supply 100 grams; NHS Cost £5.89.

Piroxicam 0.5% gel

- Age from 16 years onwards
- Piroxicam 0.5% topical gel. Apply 3cm (about 1 and 1/4 inches) to the affected area 3 to 4 times a day for up to 2 weeks; supply 112 grams; NHS Cost £5.63.

Capsaicin 0.025% cream

- Age from 16 years onwards
- Capsaicin 0.025% cream. Apply a small amount of cream (pea size) to the affected area four times a day; supply 45 grams; NHS Cost £15.04.

Intra-articular corticosteroids

Medium joint: methylprednisolone 40mg/ml + lidocaine 1%

- Age from 16 years onwards
- Depo-Medrone+lidocaine 40/10mg. Inject into medium joint: 0.25ml (10mg) to 1ml (40mg), according to joint size; supply 1 1ml vial; NHS Cost £3.28.

Large joint: methylprednisolone 80mg/2ml + lidocaine 1%

- Age from 16 years onwards
- Depo-Medrone+lidocaine 80/20mg. Inject into large joint: 0.5ml (20mg) to 2ml (80mg), according to joint size; supply 1 2ml vial; NHS Cost £5.88.

Large joint: triamcinolone acetonide 40mg/ml+ lidocaine1%

- Age from 16 years onwards
- Triamcinolone acet 40mg/ml inj. Inject into large joint: 0.25ml (10mg) to 1ml (40mg), according to joint size; supply 1 1ml vial; NHS Cost £1.70.
- Lidocaine 1% injection (2ml). For local anaesthetic injection; supply 1 2ml ampoule; NHS Cost £0.22.

Osteoarthritis — hip joint

Which therapy?

- **Consider non-drug treatment for all people with hip osteoarthritis (OA) at all stages:**
  - The use of a cane in the contralateral hand
  - Exercise therapy
  - Weight loss if BMI >28
- The use of a TENS machine or acupuncture might provide symptomatic relief but more studies are needed to clarify the specific benefit in OA.
- **If analgesia is required:**
  - Paracetamol (with codeine where needed) is the drug of first choice — it may be more effective if taken regularly.
  - Oral NSAIDs may be required if adequate analgesia is not obtained with paracetamol.
  - Topical capsaicin may be tried if other options have failed.
- **Referral to an orthopaedic surgeon** should be considered if pain has not responded to therapy, and there is progressive limitation of function.

Practical prescribing points

For further information, please see the *Medicines Compendium* (www.medicines.org.uk) or the *British National Formulary* (www.bnf.org).

Nonsteroidal anti-inflammatory drugs (NSAIDs)

- **Only one NSAID should be prescribed at a time.**
- **NSAIDs may worsen asthma, hypertension, renal impairment, or heart failure.**
- Do not give ibuprofen, diclofenac, or naproxen without gastroprotection if there is a history of peptic ulceration.
- Do not give celecoxib if there is active peptic ulceration.
- **Pregnancy and breastfeeding:** use paracetamol if possible. If an NSAID is essential, ibuprofen may be used during breastfeeding and before 30 weeks of pregnancy.
- **People with cardiovascular disease:**
  - Ibuprofen may reduce the cardiovascular protective effect of low-dose aspirin.
  - Do not give celecoxib to people with established ischaemic heart disease, cerebrovascular disease, peripheral arterial disease, or moderate or severe heart failure due to the small increased risk of thrombotic events.
  - Do not use celecoxib with low-dose aspirin. (Gastrointestinal protective effects of celecoxib are reduced.)
- **In people with risk factors for gastrointestinal NSAID complications:**
  - Use paracetamol (with or without codeine) instead of a NSAID if possible.
  - Or, use gastroprotection (a PPI or full-dose misoprostol) combined with a standard NSAID.
  - Or, consider switching to celecoxib alone (COX-2 selective).
- **Risk factors for gastrointestinal NSAID complications include:**
  - Age of 65 years and over.
  - Previous history of gastroduodenal ulcer, gastrointestinal (GI) bleeding, or gastroduodenal perforation.
  - Concomitant use of medications that are known to increase the likelihood of upper-GI adverse events, e.g. anticoagulants, aspirin (even a low dose), and corticosteroids.
  - Presence of serious comorbidity, such as cardiovascular disease, renal or hepatic impairment, diabetes, or hypertension.
  - Requirement for prolonged duration of NSAID use.
  - Use of maximum recommended doses of NSAIDs.

Misoprostol

- Diarrhoea and abdominal pain are common. Advise women of child-bearing age to use adequate contraception, because misoprostol increases the risk of miscarriage.

Codeine phosphate

Codeine may cause nausea, vomiting, constipation, and drowsiness. People may need regular laxatives if long-term use of codeine is necessary.

Capsaicin

Warn people that they may feel an intense burning sensation after application. This effect diminishes with continued use.

Follow-up advice

The person's requirements for analgesia should be reviewed regularly, at least 6-monthly.

Should I refer or investigate?

Refer?

Physiotherapy:
- Exercise therapy
- TENS machine
- Acupuncture

Occupational therapy:
- If aids or modifications in the home are required

Orthotics:
- Provision of a cane

Rheumatologist:
- If there is doubt over the diagnosis, or the person requires a corticosteroid injection (cannot be performed in primary care)

Orthopaedic surgeon:
- If there is persistent pain that has not responded to medical therapy, and the person has progressive limitation in activities of daily living

Investigate?

All blood tests are normal in osteoarthritis.
X-rays may help to confirm the diagnosis, and to exclude other forms of arthritis.

Patient information leaflets

The following PILs are available at www.prodigy.nhs.uk
Anti-inflammatory Painkillers
Arthritis Care
Arthritis Research Campaign - ARC
Osteoarthritis
Paracetamol

Shared decision making

Non-drug treatments which may help to ease symptoms of osteoarthritis of the hip include:
- **Exercise** if possible. Swimming is ideal, but any exercise is better than none.
- **Losing weight** if you are very overweight or obese
- **A walking stick** held in the opposite hand
- **TENS machine**
- **Acupuncture**

Paracetamol is commonly used for pain. The normal adult dosage is two 500 mg tablets, four times a day.
An anti-inflammatory painkiller tablet or gel may be an option.
- Bleeding from the stomach is the most serious possible side-effect. Stop the medicine and see a doctor if you develop stomach symptoms.
- Some people with asthma, high blood pressure, kidney failure, or heart failure may not be able to take anti-inflammatories.
- **Codeine** is a painkiller that is stronger than paracetamol. It may be used in combination with paracetamol or an anti-inflammatory. Possible side-effects include constipation and drowsiness.
- **Joint replacement surgery** is an option for badly affected joints. Most people with osteoarthritis do not become bad enough to need surgery.

Drug rationale

Drugs not included

Analgesia

- **Standard oral nonsteroidal anti-inflammatory drugs (NSAIDs), other than ibuprofen, diclofenac, and naproxen,** are not included, as they are associated with a higher risk of gastrointestinal (GI) adverse events or are not licensed for osteoarthritis (OA) [CSM, 1994; Henry et al, 1996; Hernández-Diaz and Rodriguez, 2000; CSM, 2002]. Suppositories are not offered, as they do not improve efficacy or safety, and are generally less acceptable to people [Tramer et al, 1998].
- **Cyclo-oxygenase-2 (COX-2) selective NSAIDs, other than celecoxib,** are not included. There is concern about the use of these drugs precipitated by the withdrawal of rofecoxib and international regulatory authorities are currently reviewing the cardiovascular safety and cardio-renal events for all coxib NSAIDs [EMEA, 2004].
  - Etoricoxib is licensed for osteoarthritis and there is some trial data to support its use. It is currently under the surveillance of the Committee on Safety of Medicines and in view of the ongoing uncertainty about the long terms thrombotic risks associated with COX-2 inhibitors it seems prudent to reconsider once its 'black-triangle' status has been lifted.
  - Parecoxib is a 'black-triangle' drug that is currently licensed for the short-term treatment of postoperative pain.
  - Etodolac and meloxicam — for both these drugs there are insufficient data of medium- to long-term duration to know whether or not they are associated with a possible increased risk of gastrointestinal or cardiovascular events, they are therefore not recommended because of the lack of follow-up data available.
- **Modified-release NSAIDs:** improvement in efficacy and reduction in adverse events have not been shown and they are also relatively expensive. They may be worth trying in someone with prominent morning stiffness despite use of standard NSAID preparations.
- **Rubefacients:** no randomized controlled trials (RCTs) have compared a topical rubefacient with another active treatment and there is therefore little evidence to support their efficacy in osteoarthritis [Mason et al, 2004c; Bandolier, 2005].
- **Topical NSAIDs** are not offered in this scenario. They may have a role in people who experience acute flare-ups of OA of the fingers, knees and toes but there is no evidence to support their role in OA of the hip.
- **Glucosamine** is not offered. Trial data only support a role in knee OA. It is not a licensed medicine in the UK, and the relative purity and glucosamine content in different preparations obtained from different manufacturers may vary as manufacturers are not bound by statutory monitoring or good manufacturing requirements [DTB, 2002].
- **Chondroitin** is not offered. It is a food supplement and is not licensed for the treatment of OA. There are insufficient trial data of its use in people with OA.

- **Intra-articular corticosteroids** are not offered as they cannot be injected without ultrasound or X-ray guidance and therefore are not used in OA of the hip in primary care.
- **Hyaluronic acid (HA)** intra-articular injection is not offered. It may be a further option for those who have not responded to intra-articular corticosteroids or those who cannot tolerate corticosteroids, or in people waiting for total knee replacement. However, this treatment option is not likely to be given in primary care and there is still much controversy about its use [Espallargues and Pons, 2003].
- **Strong opioids** (e.g. morphine, pethidine) should be avoided because of the risk of dependence if used inappropriately.
- **Weak opioids other than codeine** have not shown greater efficiency than higher doses of codeine combined with paracetamol or are more expensive.
- **Low-dose weak opioids with paracetamol** (e.g. co-codamol 8/500, co-dydramol 10/500): there is no evidence that these offer any clinical benefit over paracetamol alone and they are likely to lead to opioid adverse effects [MeReC, 1993; De Craen et al, 1996].
- **Co-proxamol** has been withdrawn due to the undesirable profile of the dextropropoxyphene component.

Gastroprotection

- **Proton-pump inhibitors (PPIs): rabeprazole** is not currently licensed for preventing NSAID-induced complications [BNF 49, 2005].
- **H_2-receptor antagonists (H_2RAs):** double doses of H_2-receptor antagonists are effective at reducing the risk of endoscopic gastric and duodenal ulcers but this is an off-licence use [Rostom et al, 2002]. Standard doses only reduce the risk of endoscopic duodenal ulcers. H_2RAs are therefore not included [BNF 49, 2005].
- **Fixed-dose combinations of standard NSAIDs with misoprostol:** the optimum dosage of misoprostol (i.e. 800 micrograms daily) cannot be reached using these preparations. In particular, only 400 micrograms daily of misoprostol is given with the higher dosages of NSAID in these preparations.
- **Low-dose misoprostol:** lower doses (e.g. 400 micrograms per day) are less effective than PPIs at reducing the incidence of endoscopic lesions, and have greater adverse effects [NICE, 2004]. (Diarrhoea and abdominal pain are common.)

Drugs included

Analgesia

- **Paracetamol** is the analgesic drug of first choice in people of all age groups. It works well for some people, especially where mild symptoms of osteoarthritis (OA) are present.
- **Codeine (in combination with paracetamol):** higher-dosage codeine is included for use with regular paracetamol for additional pain relief. Codeine 60 mg plus paracetamol has been shown to provide more pain relief than either codeine 60 mg alone or paracetamol 1000 mg alone [Moore et al, 1997]. Codeine should be prescribed separately from paracetamol to allow flexibility of dosing and titration of analgesic effect.
  - **Standard nonsteroidal anti-inflammatory drugs (NSAIDs): ibuprofen, diclofenac, and naproxen** have a good balance of efficacy against adverse-effect profile [CSM, 1994; Henry et al, 1996; Hernández-Diaz and Rodriguez, 2000]. Naproxen has a long half-life and can be given twice-daily; it may be particularly useful for someone with morning stiffness.
- **Cyclo-oxygenase-2 (COX-2) selective NSAIDs: celecoxi** is licensed for use in OA and is an option for use in people at high risk of NSAID-induced GI complications [NICE, 2001a].
- **Intra-articular corticosteroids:** triamcinolone acetonide, methylprednisolone, hydrocortisone acetate, dexamethasone sodium phosphate, and prednisolone acetate are all available for intra-articular injection. The vary in their potency and duration of effect. Intra-articular corticosteroid injection, by an appropriately skilled person, will often give rapid relief of severe symptoms [Ravaud et al, 1999]. Lidocaine (lignocaine) available for local anaesthesia.
- **Capsaicin 0.025% cream** is included and it is licensed fc use in symptomatic relief of osteoarthritis. The few published trials available only assessed treatment response at four weeks and although it only has moderate to poor efficacy in the treatment of chronic musculoskeletal pain, it may be useful as an adjunct or alone for a people who are either unresponsive or intolerant of other treatments [Mason et al, 2004d].

Gastroprotection

- **Proton-pump inhibitors (PPIs): esomeprazole, lansoprazole, omeprazole and pantoprazole** are general the preferred choice for gastroprotection and are license for this use. They are effective and well tolerated; they reduce the risk of endoscopic gastric ulcers by 63% and the risk of duodenal ulcers by 81% [Rostom et al, 2002 However there is a lack of data on prevention of ulcer complications.
- **Full-dose misoprostol** (200 micrograms four times a day is licensed for prevention of NSAID-induced gastroduodenal ulceration [BNF 49, 2005]. It is effectiv for the treatment and prophylaxis of NSAID-associated ulcers, but it is not always well tolerated [Hawkey et al, 1998; Rostom et al, 2002].

Prescriptions

Analgesia

Paracetamol tablets: 1g up to four times a day

- Age from 16 years onwards
- Paracetamol 500mg tablets. Take two tablets every 4 to 6 hours when required for pain relief. Maximum of 8 tablets in 24 hours; supply 200 tablets; NHS Cost £3.0

Add on if required: codeine 30-60mg up to four times a day

- Age from 16 years onwards
- Codeine 30mg tablets. Take one to two tablets every 4 6 hours when required for pain relief. Maximum of 8 tablets in 24 hours; supply 56 tablets; NHS Cost £3.34.

Paracetamol 500mg tablets + codeine 30mg tablets

- Age from 16 years onwards
- Paracetamol 500mg tablets. Take two tablets every 4 to 6 hours when required for pain relief. Maximum of 8 tablets in 24 hours; supply 200 tablets; NHS Cost £3.0
- Codeine 30mg tablets. Take one to two tablets every 4 6 hours when required for pain relief. Maximum of 8 tablets in 24 hours; supply 56 tablets; NHS Cost £3.34.

NSAIDs: standard and COX-2

Ibuprofen tablets: 400mg three times a day

- Age from 16 years onwards
- Ibuprofen 400mg tablets. Take one tablet three times a day; supply 84 tablets; NHS Cost £2.66; OTC Cost £4.69.

uprofen tablets: 600mg three times a day
- Age from 16 years onwards
- Ibuprofen 600mg tablets. Take one tablet three times a day; supply 84 tablets; NHS Cost £4.10.

uprofen tablets: 800mg three times a day
- Age from 16 years onwards
- Ibuprofen 400mg tablets. Take two tablets three times a day; supply 168 tablets; NHS Cost £5.32.

clofenac sodium e/c tablets: 25mg three times a day
- Age from 16 years onwards
- Diclofenac 25mg e/c tablets. Take one tablet three times a day; supply 84 tablets; NHS Cost £1.52.

clofenac sodium e/c tablets: 50mg three times a day
- Age from 16 years onwards
- Diclofenac 50mg e/c tablets. Take one tablet three times a day; supply 84 tablets; NHS Cost £2.14.

aproxen tablets: 250mg twice a day
- Age from 16 years onwards
- Naproxen 250mg tablets. Take one tablet twice a day; supply 56 tablets; NHS Cost £3.14.

aproxen tablets: 500mg twice a day
- Age from 16 years onwards
- Naproxen 500mg tablets. Take one tablet twice a day; supply 56 tablets; NHS Cost £4.90.

elecoxib capsules: 100mg twice a day (COX-2 lective)
- Age from 16 years onwards
- Celecoxib 100mg capsules. Take one capsule twice a day; supply 60 capsules; NHS Cost £21.55.

elecoxib capsules: 200mg twice a day (COX-2 lective)
- Age from 16 years onwards
- Celecoxib 200mg capsules. Take one capsule twice a day; supply 60 capsules; NHS Cost £43.10.

il protection: use ONLY with a standard NSAID

neprazole capsules: 20mg once a day
- Age from 16 years onwards
- Omeprazole 20mg capsules. Take one capsule once a day; supply 28 capsules; NHS Cost £12.75.

neprazole tablets: 20mg once a day
- Age from 16 years onwards
- Omeprazole 20mg tablets. Take one tablet once a day; supply 28 tablets; NHS Cost £12.75.

nsoprazole capsules: 15mg each morning
- Age from 16 years onwards
- Lansoprazole 15mg capsules. Take one capsule each morning (on an empty stomach); supply 28 capsules; NHS Cost £12.92.

nsoprazole capsules: 30mg each morning
- Age from 16 years onwards
- Lansoprazole 30mg capsules. Take one capsule each morning (on an empty stomach); supply 28 capsules; NHS Cost £23.63.

ntoprazole e/c tablets: 20mg once a day
- Age from 16 years onwards
- Pantoprazole 20mg e/c tablets. Take one tablet once a day; supply 28 tablets; NHS Cost £12.31.

someprazole tablets: 20mg once a day
- Age from 16 years onwards
- Esomeprazole 20mg tablets. Take one tablet once a day; supply 28 tablets; NHS Cost £18.50.

nsoprazole orodispersible tablets: 15mg each morning
- Age from 16 years onwards
- Lansoprazole 15mg orodisp tabs. Take one tablet each morning (on an empty stomach); supply 28 tablets; NHS Cost £10.86.

Lansoprazole orodispersible tablets: 30mg each morning
- Age from 16 years onwards
- Lansoprazole 30mg orodisp tabs. Take one tablet each morning (on an empty stomach); supply 28 tablets; NHS Cost £21.38.

Misoprostol tablets: 200micrograms four times a day
- Age from 16 years onwards
- Misoprostol 200microgram tabs. Take one tablet four times a day; supply 120 tablets; NHS Cost £18.72.

Topical capsaicin cream

Capsaicin 0.025% cream
- Age from 16 years onwards
- Capsaicin 0.025% cream. Apply a small amount of cream (pea size) to the affected area four times a day; supply 45 grams; NHS Cost £15.04.

Osteoarthritis — any other joint

Which therapy?

- **Consider non-drug treatment for all people with osteoarthritis (OA) of any other joint at all stages:**
  - Exercise therapy
  - Weight loss if BMI >28 — for OA of the ankle or foot
- The use of a TENS machine or acupuncture might provide symptomatic relief but more studies are needed to clarify the specific benefit in OA.
- **If analgesia is required:**
  - Paracetamol (with codeine where needed) is the drug of first choice — it may be more effective if taken regularly.
  - Oral NSAIDs may be required if adequate analgesia is not obtained with paracetamol
  - Topical NSAIDs may be used:
    - For an acute flare-up
    - As an alternative to oral NSAIDs if gastroprotection is needed
  - Topical capsaicin may be tried if other options have failed.
- **Intra-articular corticosteroid injection** provides short-term relief from a flare-up.
- **Referral to an orthopaedic surgeon** should be considered if pain has not responded to therapy, and there is progressive limitation of function.

Practical prescribing points

For further information, please see the *Medicines Compendium* (www.medicines.org.uk) or the *British National Formulary* (www.bnf.org).

Nonsteroidal anti-inflammatory drugs (NSAIDs)

- **Only one NSAID should be prescribed at a time.**
- **NSAIDs may worsen asthma, hypertension, renal impairment, or heart failure.**
- Do not give ibuprofen, diclofenac, or naproxen without gastroprotection if there is a history of peptic ulceration.
- Do not give celecoxib if there is active peptic ulceration.
- **Pregnancy and breastfeeding:** use paracetamol if possible. If an NSAID is essential, ibuprofen may be used during breastfeeding and before 30 weeks of pregnancy.
- **People with cardiovascular disease:**
  - Ibuprofen may reduce the cardiovascular protective effect of low-dose aspirin.
  - Do not give celecoxib to people with established ischaemic heart disease, cerebrovascular disease, peripheral arterial disease, or moderate or severe heart

O

- failure due to the small increased risk of thrombotic events.
  - Do not use celecoxib with low-dose aspirin. (Gastrointestinal protective effects of celecoxib are reduced.)
- **In people with risk factors for gastrointestinal NSAID complications:**
  - Use paracetamol (with or without codeine) instead of a NSAID if possible.
  - Or, use gastroprotection (a PPI or full-dose misoprostol) combined with a standard NSAID.
  - Or, consider switching to celecoxib alone (COX-2 selective).
  - Or, consider using a topical nonsteroidal anti-inflammatory drug.
- **Risk factors for gastrointestinal NSAID complications include:**
  - Age of 65 years and over.
  - Previous history of gastroduodenal ulcer, gastrointestinal (GI) bleeding, or gastroduodenal perforation.
  - Concomitant use of medications that are known to increase the likelihood of upper-GI adverse events, e.g. anticoagulants, aspirin (even a low dose), and corticosteroids.
  - Presence of serious comorbidity, such as cardiovascular disease, renal or hepatic impairment, diabetes, or hypertension.
  - Requirement for prolonged duration of NSAID use.
  - Use of maximum recommended doses of NSAIDs.

Misoprostol

- Diarrhoea and abdominal pain are common. Advise women of child-bearing age to use adequate contraception, because misoprostol increases the risk of miscarriage.

Codeine phosphate

- Codeine may cause nausea, vomiting, constipation, and drowsiness. People may need regular laxatives if long-term use of codeine is necessary.

Intra-articular corticosteroids

- In general, hydrocortisone, prednisolone, or dexamethasone are recommended for injection of small joints (e.g. hand).
- Atrophy of subcutaneous tissues and local skin depigmentation may occur from periarticular leakage of corticosteroid.
  - The risk of local-tissue atrophy and depigmentation occurs from subcutaneous or shallow injections as well as from small-joint injections (e.g. tennis elbow, de Quervain's tenosynovitis and shallow intramuscular injections).
  - The risk is greatest if large or repeated doses of a long-acting, potent corticosteroid are given.
- Lidocaine should be used to provide local anaesthesia.

Capsaicin

- Warn people that they may feel an intense burning sensation after application. This effect diminishes with continued use.

Follow-up advice

- The person's requirements for analgesia should be reviewed regularly, at least 6-monthly.

Should I refer or investigate?

Refer?

- **Physiotherapy:**
  - Exercise therapy
  - TENS machine
  - Acupuncture
- **Occupational therapy:**
  - If aids or modifications in the home are required
- **Rheumatologist:**
  - If there is doubt over the diagnosis, or the person requires injections that cannot be performed in primary care.
- **Orthopaedic surgeon:**
  - If there is persistent pain that has not responded to medical therapy, and the person has progressive limitation in activities of daily living.

Investigate?

- All blood tests are normal in osteoarthritis.
- X-rays may help to confirm the diagnosis, and to exclud other forms of arthritis.

Patient information leaflets

The following PILs are available at www.prodigy.nhs.uk

- Anti-inflammatory Painkillers
- Arthritis Care
- Arthritis Research Campaign - ARC
- Osteoarthritis
- Paracetamol

Shared decision making

- **Non-drug treatments** which may help to ease symptoms of osteoarthritis include:
  - **Exercise** if possible. Swimming is ideal, but any exercise is better than none.
  - **Losing weight** if you are very overweight or obese an a foot or leg joint is affected
  - **TENS machine**
  - **Acupuncture**
- **Paracetamol** is commonly used for pain. The normal adult dosage is two 500 mg tablets, four times a day.
- **An anti-inflammatory painkiller** tablet or gel may be an option.
  - Bleeding from the stomach is the most serious possib side-effect. Stop the medicine and see a doctor if you develop stomach symptoms.
  - Some people with asthma, high blood pressure, kidne failure, or heart failure may not be able to take anti-inflammatories.
- **Codeine** is a painkiller that is stronger than paracetamo It may be used in combination with paracetamol or an anti-inflammatory. Possible side-effects include constipation and drowsiness.
- **A steroid injection** into a joint is an option if the joint is badly inflamed.
- **Joint replacement surgery** is an option for badly affecte joints. Most people with osteoarthritis do not become bad enough to need surgery.

Drug rationale

Drugs not included

Analgesia

- **Standard oral nonsteroidal anti-inflammatory drugs (NSAIDs), other than ibuprofen, diclofenac, and**

naproxen, are not included, as they are associated with a higher risk of gastrointestinal (GI) adverse events or are not licensed for osteoarthritis (OA) [CSM, 1994; Henry et al, 1996; Hernández-Diaz and Rodriguez, 2000; CSM, 2002]. Suppositories are not offered, as they do not improve efficacy or safety, and are generally less acceptable to people [Tramer et al, 1998].

Cyclo-oxygenase-2 (COX-2) selective NSAIDs, other than celecoxib, are not included. There is concern about the use of these drugs precipitated by the withdrawal of rofecoxib and international regulatory authorities are currently reviewing the cardiovascular safety and cardio-renal events for all coxib NSAIDs [EMEA, 2004].

- Etoricoxib is licensed for osteoarthritis and there is some trial data to support its use. It is currently under the surveillance of the Committee on Safety of Medicines and in view of the ongoing uncertainty about the long terms thrombotic risks associated with COX-2 inhibitors it seems prudent to reconsider once its 'black-triangle' status has been lifted.
- Parecoxib is a 'black-triangle' drug that is currently licensed for the short-term treatment of postoperative pain.
- Etodolac and meloxicam — for both these drugs there are insufficient data of medium- to long-term duration to know whether or not they are associated with a possible increased risk of gastrointestinal or cardiovascular events, they are therefore not recommended because of the lack of follow-up data available.

Modified-release NSAIDs: improvement in efficacy and reduction in adverse events have not been shown and they are also relatively expensive. They may be worth trying in someone with prominent morning stiffness despite use of standard NSAID preparations.

Topical diclofenac solution is not included: it is licensed for the localized treatment of osteoarthritic pain in superficial joints, including the knee. There is no evidence to suggest that it is any more effective than other topical NSAIDs available and it is considerably more expensive.

Rubefacients: no randomized controlled trials (RCTs) have compared a topical rubefacient with another active treatment and there is therefore little evidence to support their efficacy in osteoarthritis [Mason et al, 2004c; Bandolier, 2005].

Glucosamine is not offered. Trial data only support a role in knee OA. It is not a licensed medicine in the UK, and the relative purity and glucosamine content in different preparations obtained from different manufacturers may vary as manufacturers are not bound by statutory monitoring or good manufacturing requirements [DTB, 2002].

Chondroitin is not offered. It is a food supplement and is not licensed for the treatment of OA. There are insufficient trial data of its use in people with OA.

Hyaluronic acid (HA) intra-articular injection is not offered. It may be a further option for those who have not responded to intra-articular corticosteroids or those who cannot tolerate corticosteroids, or in people waiting for total knee replacement. However, this treatment option is not likely to be given in primary care and there is still much controversy about its use [Espallargues and Pons, 2003].

Strong opioids (e.g. morphine, pethidine) should be avoided because of the risk of dependence if used inappropriately.

Weak opioids other than codeine have not shown greater efficiency than higher doses of codeine combined with paracetamol or are more expensive.

Low-dose weak opioids with paracetamol (e.g. co-codamol 8/500, co-dydramol 10/500): there is no evidence that these offer any clinical benefit over paracetamol alone and they are likely to lead to opioid adverse effects [MeReC, 1993; De Craen et al, 1996].

- **Co-proxamol** has been withdrawn due to the undesirable profile of the dextropropoxyphene component.

Gastroprotection

- **Proton-pump inhibitors (PPIs): rabeprazole** is not currently licensed for preventing NSAID-induced complications [BNF 49, 2005].
- **H_2-receptor antagonists (H_2RAs):** double doses of H_2-receptor antagonists are effective at reducing the risk of endoscopic gastric and duodenal ulcers but this is an off-licence use [Rostom et al, 2002]. Standard doses only reduce the risk of endoscopic duodenal ulcers. H_2RAs are therefore not included [BNF 49, 2005].
- **Fixed-dose combinations of standard NSAIDs with misoprostol:** the optimum dosage of misoprostol (i.e. 800 micrograms daily) cannot be reached using these preparations. In particular, only 400 micrograms daily of misoprostol is given with the higher dosages of NSAID in these preparations.
- **Low-dose misoprostol:** lower doses (e.g. 400 micrograms per day) are less effective than PPIs at reducing the incidence of endoscopic lesions, and have greater adverse effects [NICE, 2004]. (Diarrhoea and abdominal pain are common.)

Drugs included

Analgesia

- **Paracetamol** is the analgesic drug of first choice in people of all age groups. It works well for some people, especially where mild symptoms of osteoarthritis (OA) are present.
- **Codeine (in combination with paracetamol):** higher-dosage codeine is included for use with regular paracetamol for additional pain relief. Codeine 60 mg plus paracetamol has been shown to provide more pain relief than either codeine 60 mg alone or paracetamol 1000 mg alone [Moore et al, 1997]. Codeine should be prescribed separately from paracetamol to allow flexibility of dosing and titration of analgesic effect.
  - **Standard nonsteroidal anti-inflammatory drugs (NSAIDs): ibuprofen, diclofenac, and naproxen** have a good balance of efficacy against adverse-effect profile [CSM, 1994; Henry et al, 1996; Hernández-Diaz and Rodriguez, 2000]. Naproxen has a long half-life and can be given twice-daily; it may be particularly useful for someone with morning stiffness.
- **Topical NSAIDs: diclofenac, felbinac, ibuprofen, ketoprofen and piroxicam are available as topical formulations.** Topical NSAIDs have been found to be no more effective than oral NSAIDs [Mason et al, 2004b] but a short course could be considered if an NSAID is required and someone is at high risk of peptic ulceration or bleeding with an oral NSAID, therefore needing gastroprotection.
- **Cyclo-oxygenase-2 (COX-2) selective NSAIDs: celecoxib** is licensed for use in OA and is an option for use in people at high risk of NSAID-induced GI complications [NICE, 2001a].
- **Intra-articular corticosteroids:** hydrocortisone, prednisolone, or dexamethasone is available for injection of small joints (e.g. hand). Methylprednisolone is also available for medium sized joints. Intra-articular corticosteroid injection, by an appropriately skilled person, will often give rapid relief of severe symptoms [Ravaud et al, 1999]. Lidocaine (lignocaine) is available for local anaesthesia.

- **Capsaicin 0.025% cream** is included and it is licensed for use in symptomatic relief of osteoarthritis. The few published trials available only assessed treatment response at four weeks and although it only has moderate to poor efficacy in the treatment of chronic musculoskeletal pain, it may be useful as an adjunct or alone for a people who are either unresponsive or intolerant of other treatments [Mason et al, 2004d].

Gastroprotection

- **Proton-pump inhibitors (PPIs): esomeprazole, lansoprazole, omeprazole, and pantoprazole** are generally the preferred choice for gastroprotection and are licensed for this use. They are effective and well tolerated; they reduce the risk of endoscopic gastric ulcers by 63% and the risk of duodenal ulcers by 81% [Rostom et al, 2002]. However there is a lack of data on prevention of ulcer complications.
- **Full-dose misoprostol** (200 micrograms four times a day) is licensed for prevention of NSAID-induced gastroduodenal ulceration [BNF 49, 2005]. It is effective for the treatment and prophylaxis of NSAID-associated ulcers, but it is not always well tolerated [Hawkey et al, 1998; Rostom et al, 2002].

Prescriptions

Analgesia

Paracetamol tablets: 1g up to four times a day
- Age from 16 years onwards
- Paracetamol 500mg tablets. Take two tablets every 4 to 6 hours when required for pain relief. Maximum of 8 tablets in 24 hours; supply 200 tablets; NHS Cost £3.06.

Add on if required: codeine 30-60mg up to four times a day
- Age from 16 years onwards
- Codeine 30mg tablets. Take one to two tablets every 4 to 6 hours when required for pain relief. Maximum of 8 tablets in 24 hours; supply 56 tablets; NHS Cost £4.58.

Paracetamol 500mg tablets + codeine 30mg tablets
- Age from 16 years onwards
- Paracetamol 500mg tablets. Take two tablets every 4 to 6 hours when required for pain relief. Maximum of 8 tablets in 24 hours; supply 200 tablets; NHS Cost £3.06.
- Codeine 30mg tablets. Take one to two tablets every 4 to 6 hours when required for pain relief. Maximum of 8 tablets in 24 hours; supply 56 tablets; NHS Cost £4.58.

NSAIDs: standard and COX-2

Ibuprofen tablets: 400mg three times a day
- Age from 16 years onwards
- Ibuprofen 400mg tablets. Take one tablet three times a day; supply 84 tablets; NHS Cost £2.66; OTC Cost £4.69.

Ibuprofen tablets: 600mg three times a day
- Age from 16 years onwards
- Ibuprofen 600mg tablets. Take one tablet three times a day; supply 84 tablets; NHS Cost £4.10.

Ibuprofen tablets: 800mg three times a day
- Age from 16 years onwards
- Ibuprofen 400mg tablets. Take two tablets three times a day; supply 168 tablets; NHS Cost £5.32.

Diclofenac sodium e/c tablets: 25mg three times a day
- Age from 16 years onwards
- Diclofenac 25mg e/c tablets. Take one tablet three times a day; supply 84 tablets; NHS Cost £1.52.

Diclofenac sodium e/c tablets: 50mg three times a day
- Age from 16 years onwards
- Diclofenac 50mg e/c tablets. Take one tablet three time a day; supply 84 tablets; NHS Cost £2.14.

Naproxen tablets: 250mg twice a day
- Age from 16 years onwards
- Naproxen 250mg tablets. Take one tablet twice a day; supply 56 tablets; NHS Cost £3.14.

Naproxen tablets: 500mg twice a day
- Age from 16 years onwards
- Naproxen 500mg tablets. Take one tablet twice a day; supply 56 tablets; NHS Cost £4.90.

Celecoxib capsules: 100mg twice a day (COX-2 selective)
- Age from 16 years onwards
- Celecoxib 100mg capsules. Take one capsule twice a day; supply 60 capsules; NHS Cost £21.55.

Celecoxib capsules: 200mg twice a day (COX-2 selective)
- Age from 16 years onwards
- Celecoxib 200mg capsules. Take one capsule twice a day; supply 60 capsules; NHS Cost £43.10.

GI protection: use ONLY with a standard NSAID

Omeprazole capsules: 20mg once a day
- Age from 16 years onwards
- Omeprazole 20mg capsules. Take one capsule once a day; supply 28 capsules; NHS Cost £12.75.

Omeprazole tablets: 20mg once a day
- Age from 16 years onwards
- Omeprazole 20mg tablets. Take one tablet once a day; supply 28 tablets; NHS Cost £12.75.

Lansoprazole capsules: 15mg each morning
- Age from 16 years onwards
- Lansoprazole 15mg capsules. Take one capsule each morning (on an empty stomach); supply 28 capsules; NHS Cost £12.92.

Lansoprazole capsules: 30mg each morning
- Age from 16 years onwards
- Lansoprazole 30mg capsules. Take one capsule each morning (on an empty stomach); supply 28 capsules; NHS Cost £23.63.

Pantoprazole e/c tablets: 20mg once a day
- Age from 16 years onwards
- Pantoprazole 20mg e/c tablets. Take one tablet once a day; supply 28 tablets; NHS Cost £12.31.

Esomeprazole tablets: 20mg once a day
- Age from 16 years onwards
- Esomeprazole 20mg tablets. Take one tablet once a da supply 28 tablets; NHS Cost £18.50.

Lansoprazole orodispersible tablets: 15mg each mornir
- Age from 16 years onwards
- Lansoprazole 15mg orodisp tabs. Take one tablet each morning (on an empty stomach); supply 28 tablets; NHS Cost £10.86.

Lansoprazole orodispersible tablets: 30mg each mornir
- Age from 16 years onwards
- Lansoprazole 30mg orodisp tabs. Take one tablet each morning (on an empty stomach); supply 28 tablets; NHS Cost £21.38.

Misoprostol tablets: 200micrograms four times a day
- Age from 16 years onwards
- Misoprostol 200microgram tabs. Take one tablet four times a day; supply 120 tablets; NHS Cost £18.72.

0

Topical NSAIDs and capsaicin cream

iclofenac 1% gel

Age from 16 years onwards

Diclofenac 1% gel. Apply 2 to 2.5 cm (1 inch) to the affected area 3 to 4 times a day for up to 2 weeks; supply 100 grams; NHS Cost £7.00.

elbinac 3% gel

Age from 16 years onwards

Felbinac 3% gel. Apply 2.5cm (1 inch) to the affected area 2 to 4 times a day for up to 2 weeks; supply 100 grams; NHS Cost £7.00.

elbinac 3.17% foam

Age from 16 years onwards

Felbinac 3.17% foam. Apply 2.5cm (1 inch) to the affected area 2 to 4 times a day for up to 2 weeks; supply 100 grams; NHS Cost £7.00.

uprofen 5% cream

Age from 16 years onwards

Ibuprofen 5% cream. Apply 4 to 10cm (1.5 to 4 inches) to the affected area 3 to 4 times a day for up to 2 weeks; supply 100 grams; NHS Cost £6.21; OTC Cost £10.95.

uprofen 5% gel

Age from 16 years onwards

Ibuprofen 5% gel. Apply 4 to 10cm (1.5 to 4 inches) to the affected joint 3 to 4 times a day for up to 2 weeks; supply 100 grams; NHS Cost £5.31; OTC Cost £7.97.

uprofen 5% mousse

Age from 16 years onwards

Ibuprofen 5% mousse. Shake the container and then apply 1 to 2g (1 to 2 golf-ball sized amounts of mousse in the hand) to the affected area 3 to 4 times a day for 2 weeks; supply 125 grams; NHS Cost £6.12; OTC Cost £10.79.

etoprofen 2.5% gel

Age from 16 years onwards

Ketoprofen 2.5% gel. Apply 4 to 7cm (2 to 3 inches) to the affected area 2 to 4 times a day for up to 10 days; supply 100 grams; NHS Cost £5.89.

roxicam 0.5% gel

Age from 16 years onwards

Piroxicam 0.5% topical gel. Apply 3cm (about 1 and 1/4 inches) to the affected area 3 to 4 times a day for up to 2 weeks; supply 112 grams; NHS Cost £6.01.

apsaicin 0.025% cream

Age from 16 years onwards

Capsaicin 0.025% cream. Apply a small amount of cream (pea size) to the affected area four times a day; supply 45 grams; NHS Cost £15.04.

ntra-articular corticosteroids

nall joint: dexamethasone sod phos 5mg/ml + ocaine1%

Age from 16 years onwards

Dexamethasone sod phos 5mg/ml. Inject into small joint: 0.16ml (0.8mg) to 0.2ml (1mg), according to joint size; supply 1 1ml ampoule; NHS Cost £0.83.

Lidocaine 1% injection (2ml). For local anaesthetic injection; supply 1 2ml ampoule; NHS Cost £0.22.

nall joint: hydrocortisone acetate 25mg/ml+ lidocaine %

Age from 16 years onwards

Hydrocortisone 25mg/ml inj. Inject into small joint: 0.2ml (5mg) to 0.5ml (12.5mg), according to joint size; supply 1 1ml vial; NHS Cost £4.77.

Lidocaine 1% injection (2ml). For local anaesthetic injection; supply 1 2ml ampoule; NHS Cost £0.22.

Small joint: prednisolone acetate 25mg/ml + lidocaine 1%

- Age from 16 years onwards
- Prednisolone acet 25mg/ml inj. Inject into small joint: 0.2ml (5mg) to 0.4ml (10mg), according to joint size; supply 1 1ml ampoule; NHS Cost £4.77.
- Lidocaine 1% injection (2ml). For local anaesthetic injection; supply 1 2ml ampoule; NHS Cost £0.22.

Medium joint: methylprednisolone 40mg/ml + lidocaine 1%

- Age from 16 years onwards
- Depo-Medrone+lidocaine 40/10mg. Inject into medium joint: 0.25ml (10mg) to 1ml (40mg), according to joint size; supply 1 1ml vial; NHS Cost £3.28.

Acutely painful prosthetic joint

Which therapy?

- **Consider the following possibilities, and manage according to findings:**
  - **If pain is acute or onset is recent:**
    - Septic arthritis
    - Fracture
    - Loosening
    - Soft-tissue trauma
    - Referred pain (spine, proximal joint)
  - **If chronic pain predates the replacement:**
    - Referred pain (spine, proximal joint)
- **Prescribe symptomatic treatment:**
  - Paracetamol (with codeine where needed) is the drug of first choice — it may be more effective if taken regularly.
  - Oral nonsteroidal anti-inflammatory drugs (NSAIDs) may be required if adequate analgesia is not obtained with paracetamol.
- **Never inject a prosthetic joint.**
- Consider physiotherapy and occupational therapy.

Practical prescribing points

For further information see the *Medicines Compendium* (www.medicines.org.uk) or the *British National Formulary* (www.bnf.org).

Nonsteroidal anti-inflammatory drugs (NSAIDs)

- **Only one NSAID should be prescribed at a time.**
- **NSAIDs may worsen asthma, hypertension, renal impairment, or heart failure.**
- Do not give ibuprofen, diclofenac, or naproxen without gastroprotection if there is a history of peptic ulceration.
- Do not give celecoxib if there is active peptic ulceration.
- **Pregnancy and breastfeeding:** use paracetamol if possible. If an NSAID is essential, ibuprofen may be used during breastfeeding and before 30 weeks of pregnancy.
- **People with cardiovascular disease:**
  - Ibuprofen may reduce the cardiovascular protective effect of low-dose aspirin.
  - Do not give celecoxib to people with established ischaemic heart disease, cerebrovascular disease, peripheral arterial disease, or moderate or severe heart failure due to the small increased risk of thrombotic events.
  - Do not use celecoxib with low-dose aspirin. (Gastrointestinal protective effects of celecoxib are reduced.)
- **In people with risk factors for gastrointestinal NSAID complications:**
  - Use paracetamol (with or without codeine) instead of a NSAID if possible.

- Or, use gastroprotection (a PPI or full-dose misoprostol) combined with a standard NSAID.
- Or, consider switching to celecoxib alone (COX-2 selective).

- **Risk factors for gastrointestinal NSAID complications include:**
  - Age of 65 years and over.
  - Previous history of gastroduodenal ulcer, gastrointestinal (GI) bleeding, or gastroduodenal perforation.
  - Concomitant use of medications that are known to increase the likelihood of upper-GI adverse events, e.g. anticoagulants, aspirin (even a low dose), and corticosteroids.
  - Presence of serious comorbidity, such as cardiovascular disease, renal or hepatic impairment, diabetes, or hypertension.
  - Requirement for prolonged duration of NSAID use.
  - Use of maximum recommended doses of NSAIDs.

Misoprostol

- Diarrhoea and abdominal pain are common. Advise women of child-bearing age to use adequate contraception, because misoprostol increases the risk of miscarriage.

Codeine phosphate

- Codeine may cause nausea, vomiting, constipation, and drowsiness. People may need regular laxatives if long-term use of codeine is necessary.

Follow-up advice

- Advise the person to seek medical advice if any of the following occur:
  - Worsening pain, swelling, and joint redness
  - Systemic upset (fever, sweats, shivers)
  - Deteriorating mobility
- **Ask people taking nonsteroidal anti-inflammatory drugs (NSAIDs) if they have experienced gastrointestinal (GI) symptoms** — especially elderly people in the first few weeks, those taking low-dose aspirin, and people with a history of GI disease.
- NSAIDs should be reduced and if possible withdrawn once the exacerbation settles.

Should I refer or investigate?

Refer?

- **Emergency admission is necessary if septic arthritis is suspected.** This may present with pain, swelling, and inflammation of a single joint. The joint may feel hot and may be tender with limited movement. Systemic upset is common, with fever, shivers, and sweats. Septic arthritis may involve multiple joints (e.g. in someone with immunosuppression) and can be a trigger for a polyarticular flare of osteoarthritis.
- Atypical presentations may occur (e.g. lesser signs) in someone taking corticosteroids, or who is immunosuppressed, or who is elderly.
- If mechanical failure or loosening is suspected, refer promptly.

Investigate?

- A normal C-reactive protein (CRP) or erythrocyte sedimentation rate (ESR) and white-cell count would reassure that the cause of symptoms is purely mechanical.
  - However, CRP and ESR may be normal in immunosuppressed people with septic arthritis, especially early in the course of the infection.
- Radiography may reveal loosening, fracture, or mechanical failure (e.g. protrusion, broken wires).

Patient information leaflets

The following PILs are available at www.prodigy.nhs.uk

- Anti-inflammatory Painkillers
- Arthritis Care
- Arthritis Research Campaign - ARC
- Osteoarthritis
- Paracetamol

Shared decision making

- Sometimes symptoms flare up over an artificial joint.
- **Paracetamol** is commonly used for pain. The normal adult dosage is two 500 mg tablets, four times a day.
- **An anti-inflammatory painkiller** tablet or gel may be an option.
  - Bleeding from the stomach is the most serious possibl side-effect. Stop the medicine and see a doctor if you develop stomach symptoms.
  - Some people with asthma, high blood pressure, kidne failure, or heart failure may not be able to take anti-inflammatories.
- **Codeine** is a painkiller that is stronger than paracetamc It may be used in combination with paracetamol or an anti-inflammatory. Possible side-effects include constipation and drowsiness.
- **Physiotherapy** is sometimes a useful option.
- If your doctor feels that the replacement joint has failed or loosened, or the bone has fractured, further investigation will be required.
- Rarely, a hot, red, swollen artificial joint is due to infection. This requires urgent referral to an orthopaed surgeon.

Drug rationale

Drugs not included

Analgesia

- **Standard oral nonsteroidal anti-inflammatory drugs (NSAIDs), other than ibuprofen, diclofenac, and naproxen,** are not included, as they are associated with higher risk of gastrointestinal (GI) adverse events or are not licensed for osteoarthritis (OA) [CSM, 1994; Henry et al, 1996; Hernández-Diaz and Rodriguez, 2000; CSM, 2002]. Suppositories are not offered, as they do not improve efficacy or safety, and are generally less acceptable to people [Tramer et al, 1998].
- **Cyclo-oxygenase-2 (COX-2) selective NSAIDs, other than celecoxib,** are not included. There is concern abou the use of these drugs precipitated by the withdrawal of rofecoxib and international regulatory authorities are currently reviewing the cardiovascular safety and cardi renal events for all coxib NSAIDs [EMEA, 2004].
  - Etoricoxib is licensed for osteoarthritis and there is some trial data to support its use. It is currently unde the surveillance of the Committee on Safety of Medicines and in view of the ongoing uncertainty about the long terms thrombotic risks associated wit COX-2 inhibitors it seems prudent to reconsider onc its 'black-triangle' status has been lifted.
  - Parecoxib is a 'black-triangle' drug that is currently licensed for the short-term treatment of postoperativ pain.

- Etodolac and meloxicam — for both these drugs there are insufficient data of medium- to long-term duration to know whether or not they are associated with a possible increased risk of gastrointestinal or cardiovascular events, they are therefore not recommended because of the lack of follow-up data available.
- **Modified-release NSAIDs:** improvement in efficacy and reduction in adverse events have not been shown and they are also relatively expensive.
- **Rubefacients:** no randomized controlled trials (RCTs) have compared a topical rubefacient with another active treatment and there is therefore little evidence to support their efficacy in osteoarthritis [Mason et al, 2004c; Bandolier, 2005].
- **Topical NSAIDs** are not offered in this scenario as their use is inappropriate in people with prosthetic joints.
- **Topical capsaicin** is not offered in this scenario as their use is inappropriate in people with prosthetic joints.
- **Glucosamine** is not offered. It is not a licensed medicine in the UK, and the relative purity and glucosamine content in different preparations obtained from different manufacturers may vary as manufacturers are not bound by statutory monitoring or good manufacturing requirements [DTB, 2002].
- **Chondroitin** is not offered. It is a food supplement and is not licensed for the treatment of OA. There are insufficient trial data of its use in people with OA.
- **Strong opioids** (e.g. morphine, pethidine) should be avoided, owing to the risk of dependence if used inappropriately.
- **Weak opioids other than codeine** have not shown greater efficiency than higher dosages of codeine combined with paracetamol or are more expensive.
- **Intra-articular corticosteroids:** are not offered as prosthetic joints should not be injected.
- **Hyaluronic acid (HA)** intra-articular injection is not offered as prosthetic joints should not be injected.

Gastroprotection

- **Proton-pump inhibitors (PPIs): rabeprazole** is not currently licensed for preventing NSAID induced complications [BNF 49, 2005].
- **H_2-receptor antagonists (H_2RAs):** double doses of H_2-receptor antagonists are effective at reducing the risk of endoscopic gastric and duodenal ulcers but this is an off-licence use [Rostom et al, 2002]. Standard doses only reduce the risk of endoscopic duodenal ulcers. H_2RAs are therefore not included [BNF 49, 2005].
- **Fixed-dosage combinations of standard NSAIDs with misoprostol:** the optimum dosage of misoprostol (i.e. 800 micrograms daily) cannot be reached using these preparations. In particular, only 400 micrograms daily of misoprostol is given with the higher dosages of NSAID in these preparations.
- **Low-dose misoprostol:** lower doses (e.g. 400 micrograms per day) are less effective than PPIs at reducing the incidence of endoscopic lesions, and have greater adverse effects [NICE, 2004]. (Diarrhoea and abdominal pain are common.)

Drugs included

Analgesia

- **Paracetamol** is a good, preferred choice for pain relief and is not associated with gastrointestinal (GI) toxicity [SIGN, 2000].
- **Codeine (in combination with paracetamol):** higher-dosage codeine is included for use with regular paracetamol for additional pain relief. Codeine 60 mg plus paracetamol has been shown to provide more pain relief than either codeine 60 mg alone or paracetamol 1000 mg alone [Moore et al, 1997]. Codeine should be prescribed separately from paracetamol to allow flexibility of dosing and titration of analgesic effect.
- **Standard nonsteroidal anti-inflammatory drugs (NSAIDs): ibuprofen, diclofenac, and naproxen** have a good balance of efficacy against adverse-effect profile [CSM, 1994; Henry et al, 1996; Hernández-Diaz and Rodriguez, 2000]. Naproxen has a long half-life and can be given twice-daily; it may be particularly useful for someone with morning stiffness.
- **Cyclo-oxygenase-2 (COX-2) selective NSAIDs: celecoxib** is licensed for use in osteoarthritis (OA) and is an option for use in people at high risk of NSAID-induced GI complications [NICE, 2001a].

Gastroprotection

- **Proton-pump inhibitors (PPIs): lansoprazole, omeprazole, and pantoprazole** are licensed for prevention of NSAID-induced gastroduodenal ulceration [BNF 49, 2005]. PPIs reduce the risk of endoscopic ulcers, but there is a lack of data on prevention of ulcer complications [Rostom et al, 2002]. However, they are generally considered to be the preferred choice for gastroprotection, as they are well-tolerated compared with misoprostol.
- **Full-dose misoprostol** (200 micrograms four times a day) is licensed for prevention of NSAID-induced gastroduodenal ulceration [BNF 49, 2005]. It is effective for the treatment and prophylaxis of NSAID-associated ulcers, but it is not always well tolerated [Hawkey et al, 1998; Rostom et al, 2002].

Prescriptions

Analgesia

Paracetamol tablets: 1g up to four times a day

- Age from 16 years onwards
- Paracetamol 500mg tablets. Take two tablets every 4 to 6 hours when required for pain relief. Maximum of 8 tablets in 24 hours; supply 200 tablets; NHS Cost £3.06.

Add on if required: codeine 30-60mg up to four times a day

- Age from 16 years onwards
- Codeine 30mg tablets. Take one to two tablets every 4 to 6 hours when required for pain relief. Maximum of 8 tablets in 24 hours; supply 56 tablets; NHS Cost £4.58.

Paracetamol 500mg tablets + codeine 30mg tablets

- Age from 16 years onwards
- Paracetamol 500mg tablets. Take two tablets every 4 to 6 hours when required for pain relief. Maximum of 8 tablets in 24 hours; supply 200 tablets; NHS Cost £3.06.
- Codeine 30mg tablets. Take one to two tablets every 4 to 6 hours when required for pain relief. Maximum of 8 tablets in 24 hours; supply 56 tablets; NHS Cost £4.58.

NSAIDs: standard and COX-2

Ibuprofen tablets: 400mg three times a day

- Age from 16 years onwards
- Ibuprofen 400mg tablets. Take one tablet three times a day; supply 84 tablets; NHS Cost £2.66; OTC Cost £4.69.

Ibuprofen tablets: 600mg three times a day

- Age from 16 years onwards
- Ibuprofen 600mg tablets. Take one tablet three times a day; supply 84 tablets; NHS Cost £4.10.

Ibuprofen tablets: 800mg three times a day
- Age from 16 years onwards
- Ibuprofen 400mg tablets. Take two tablets three times a day; supply 168 tablets; NHS Cost £5.32.

Diclofenac sodium e/c tablets: 25mg three times a day
- Age from 16 years onwards
- Diclofenac 25mg e/c tablets. Take one tablet three times a day; supply 84 tablets; NHS Cost £1.52.

Diclofenac sodium e/c tablets: 50mg three times a day
- Age from 16 years onwards
- Diclofenac 50mg e/c tablets. Take one tablet three times a day; supply 84 tablets; NHS Cost £2.14.

Naproxen tablets: 250mg twice a day
- Age from 16 years onwards
- Naproxen 250mg tablets. Take one tablet twice a day; supply 56 tablets; NHS Cost £3.14.

Naproxen tablets: 500mg twice a day
- Age from 16 years onwards
- Naproxen 500mg tablets. Take one tablet twice a day; supply 56 tablets; NHS Cost £4.90.

Celecoxib capsules: 100mg twice a day (COX-2 selective)
- Age from 16 years onwards
- Celecoxib 100mg capsules. Take one capsule twice a day; supply 60 capsules; NHS Cost £21.55.

Celecoxib capsules: 200mg twice a day (COX-2 selective)
- Age from 16 years onwards
- Celecoxib 200mg capsules. Take one capsule twice a day; supply 60 capsules; NHS Cost £43.10.

GI protection: use ONLY with a standard NSAID

Omeprazole capsules: 20mg once a day
- Age from 16 years onwards
- Omeprazole 20mg capsules. Take one capsule once a day; supply 28 capsules; NHS Cost £12.75.

Omeprazole tablets: 20mg once a day
- Age from 16 years onwards
- Omeprazole 20mg tablets. Take one tablet once a day; supply 28 tablets; NHS Cost £12.75.

Lansoprazole capsules: 15mg each morning
- Age from 16 years onwards
- Lansoprazole 15mg capsules. Take one capsule each morning (on an empty stomach); supply 28 capsules; NHS Cost £12.92.

Lansoprazole capsules: 30mg each morning
- Age from 16 years onwards
- Lansoprazole 30mg capsules. Take one capsule each morning (on an empty stomach); supply 28 capsules; NHS Cost £23.63.

Pantoprazole e/c tablets: 20mg once a day
- Age from 16 years onwards
- Pantoprazole 20mg e/c tablets. Take one tablet once a day; supply 28 tablets; NHS Cost £12.31.

Esomeprazole tablets: 20mg once a day
- Age from 16 years onwards
- Esomeprazole 20mg tablets. Take one tablet once a day; supply 28 tablets; NHS Cost £18.50.

Lansoprazole orodispersible tablets: 15mg each morning
- Age from 16 years onwards
- Lansoprazole 15mg orodisp tabs. Take one tablet each morning (on an empty stomach); supply 28 tablets; NHS Cost £10.86.

Lansoprazole orodispersible tablets: 30mg each morning
- Age from 16 years onwards
- Lansoprazole 30mg orodisp tabs. Take one tablet each morning (on an empty stomach); supply 28 tablets; NHS Cost £21.38.

Misoprostol tablets: 200micrograms four times a day
- Age from 16 years onwards
- Misoprostol 200microgram tabs. Take one tablet four times a day; supply 120 tablets; NHS Cost £18.72.

Extended Information

Background information

- What is osteoarthritis? p.1364
- What are the risk factors for developing osteoarthritis? p.1364
- How common is osteoarthritis? p.1365
- How do I know my patient has osteoarthritis? p.1365
- What else might it be? p.1365
- Complications and prognosis p.1366

What is osteoarthritis?

- Osteoarthritis (OA) is a disorder of synovial joints characterized by [Jordan et al, 2003; Scott et al, 2004]:
  - Focal areas of damage to the articular cartilage
  - Remodelling of underlying bone
  - Mild synovitis
- Although OA may affect any synovial joint, the most commonly affected are hands, knees, hips, neck, and low back. Less commonly affected joints are shoulders, elbows, wrists, ankles, and feet.

What are the risk factors for developing osteoarthritis?

- The risk factors for developing osteoarthritis (OA) vary between affected joints, and include:
  - Increasing age
  - Obesity
    - Associated with the development of knee OA, with an odds ratio of 9 for women, and 4.5 for men
    - Associated with the development of hip OA, with an odds ratio of 2 [Lievense et al, 2002]
  - Sex — hand and knee OA is more common in women
  - Genetic factors — in a study of twins, genetic factors have been suggested in at least 50% of cases of women with OA in the hands and knees, and in a smaller percentage in OA of other joints [Spector, 1996]
  - Trauma — intra-articular fracture is accepted as a cause of OA, but there is a lack of good evidence to support this. Also joint injury leading to instability e.g. cruciate ligament tear in the knee and lateral ligament to the ankle can lead to premature OA
  - Occupational
    - Hip OA is more common in farmers
    - Knee OA is more common in miners and elite athletes
    - Elbow OA is more common in people who work with pneumatic drills
  - Recreational — there is evidence of an association between hip OA and sporting activities [Lievense et al, 2003]
  - Malalignment — abnormalities of joint contour are linked with hip and knee OA, e.g. Perthes' disease, slipped upper femoral epiphysis, congenital dislocation of the hip
  - Ethnic origin — hip OA is more common in white Europeans than in black people or Asians [Lievense et al, 2002]
  - Increased bone density

[Doherty et al, 1998; Brion and Kalunian, 2003]

How common is osteoarthritis?

- **Osteoarthritis (OA) is the most common form of arthritis.**
- Prevalence studies of OA have used different diagnostic criteria:
  - Post-mortem studies show that most people over the age of 65 years have OA in at least one joint [Doherty et al, 1998].
  - X-ray studies show that at least 50% of people over the age of 65 years have evidence of OA [Doherty et al, 1998]. However, only 30% of people with X-ray evidence of OA have pain at the relevant site [ICSI, 2004].
  - Symptomatic OA (pain with X-ray changes) is found in 6% of people over the age of 30 years [Brion and Kalunian, 2003].
- Symptomatic knee OA affects about 12% of people over the age of 65 years [Brouwer et al, 2005]. It is about twice as common as hip OA in this age group.

How do I know my patient has osteoarthritis?

Symptoms

- **The onset is usually insidious.**
- **The principal symptoms are pain and stiffness.**
  - **Pain** can be transient, and may even be absent in spite of severe joint damage. Pain worsens with joint use, and is usually best at the start of the day and after rest, and is usually worst at the end of the day. Pain at rest, however, may occur with severe osteoarthritis (OA).
    - The pain of knee OA is felt in and around the knee. It is typically worsened by weight-bearing or stairs. It is usually bilateral.
    - The pain of hip OA is felt in the groin and anterior or lateral thigh.
  - **Stiffness** is usually short-lived (up to 30 minutes duration), and is known as 'gelling'. It typically occurs in the morning, or after prolonged rest.
- Systemic symptoms are absent in OA.

Signs

- Bony enlargement and deformity (due to osteophytes):
  - Heberden's nodes (distal interphalangeal [DIP] joints)
  - Bouchard's nodes (proximal interphalangeal [PIP] joints)
  - First carpometacarpal (CMC) joint has a 'squared appearance'
- Crepitus
- Instability
- Joint line tenderness
- Muscle weakness and wasting
- Pain on stressing the joint
- Reduced range of movement
- Synovitis may be present (warmth, effusion, synovial thickening), but is usually mild; if severe, an alternative diagnosis should be considered

Investigations

- **The diagnosis of OA is principally clinical,** based on the history and examination, but X-rays are required to diagnose knee and hip OA. Investigations may have a role in excluding other diagnoses.
- **Blood tests** are normal in OA.
- **X-rays** may show one or more of the following signs of osteoarthritis:
  - Joint space narrowing
  - Osteophytes
  - Sclerosis
  - Cysts
- Other features of OA that may be shown by X-ray include:
  - Subluxation and deformity
  - Loose bodies
  - Effusion
- Many people with radiographic features of OA have no symptoms.

[Doherty et al, 1998]

Diagnostic criteria

- The American College of Rheumatology has produced diagnostic criteria for OA of the knee, hip, and hand.
  - Knee OA requires the presence of knee pain and X-ray findings of osteophytes and at least 1 of the following 3 items:
    - Age >50 years
    - Morning stiffness <30 minutes in duration
    - Crepitus on motion [Hochberg et al, 1995a]
  - Hip OA requires the presence of hip pain and at least 2 of the following 3 items:
    - Normal erythrocyte sedimentation rate (ESR)
    - X-ray findings of femoral or acetabular osteophytes
    - X-ray findings of joint space narrowing [Hochberg et al, 1995b]
  - Hand OA requires the presence of hand pain, aching, or stiffness, and 3 or 4 of the following items:
    - Hard tissue enlargement of 2 or more of 10 specific joints (2nd and 3rd DIP, 2nd and 3rd PIP, and 1st CMC joints of both hands)
    - Hard tissue enlargement of 2 or more DIP joints
    - Fewer than 3 swollen metacarpophalangeal (MCP) joints
    - Deformity of at least 1 of 10 specific joints (2nd and 3rd DIP, 2nd and 3rd PIP, and 1st CMC joints of both hands) [Altman et al, 1990]

What else might it be?

Most other causes of arthritis usually cause more obvious inflammation and synovitis as follows:

Knee osteoarthritis (OA)

- Anserine bursitis — pain over the upper medial proximal tibia
- Infrapatellar bursitis
- Prepatellar bursitis
- Pain from the hip and spine can be referred to the knee

Hip OA

- Trochanteric bursitis — pain posterolaterally in the area of the greater trochanter, may extend down the lateral thigh
- Piriformis syndrome
- Pain from the knee and spine can be referred to the hip

OA of any joint

- Pseudogout (calcium pyrophosphate deposition) — typically affects knees, wrists, shoulders, and metacarpophalangeal joints and may coexist with OA
- Psoriatic arthritis
- Septic arthritis — usually a monoarthritis, but may be polyarticular if gonococcal, or if the person is immunocompromised
- Tuberculous arthritis — affects all ages, and may present atypically
- Viral arthritis — e.g. parvovirus, rubella, hepatitis B
- Reactive arthritis — e.g. Reiter's syndrome, streptococcal, campylobacter, salmonella, chlamydia
- Rheumatoid arthritis
- Polyarticular gout
- Seronegative spondyloarthropathy — e.g. ankylosing spondylitis, inflammatory bowel disease

- Connective tissue disease — e.g. systemic lupus erythematosus, scleroderma
- Medical conditions presenting with arthropathy — e.g. sarcoidosis, thyroid disease, infective endocarditis, haemochromatosis, diabetic cheiroarthropathy, paraneoplastic syndromes, multiple myeloma
- Referred pain

Complications and prognosis

Complications

- Reduced mobility
- Difficulties with activities of daily living
- Employment difficulties

Prognosis

- Most people with osteoarthritis (OA) do not become severely disabled.
- The prognosis of OA is poorly understood.
  - Knee OA seems to have the worst prognosis, with most cases deteriorating in long-term studies (more than 10 years).
  - Long-term studies of people with hip OA show that deterioration is not inevitable, with some people improving over 10-year follow-up.
  - Prognosis for hand OA seems best; symptoms and function change little over long-term follow-up.

[Doherty et al, 1998]

Management issues

- Overview p.1366
- Analgesia recommendations summary p.1366
- How does paracetamol compare with NSAIDs in symptomatic pain relief for OA? p.1366
- When should I prescribe a COX-2 selective inhibitor? p.1367
- What evidence supports the use of topical NSAIDs? p.1367
- What is the role of intra-articular injections in OA? p.1367
- Osteoarthritis of the knee p.1367
- Osteoarthritis of the hip p.1371
- Osteoarthritis of any other joint p.1372
- Medicines management p.1372

Overview

- The management of osteoarthritis (OA) should begin with non-drug interventions including:
  - Exercise
  - Weight loss
- Where non-drug treatments are insufficient alone, additional drug treatment options consists of:
  - Analgesia
    - Paracetamol (with or without codeine)
    - Oral nonsteroidal anti-inflammatory drugs
    - Topical nonsteroidal anti-inflammatory drugs
    - Topical capsaicin
    - Topical rubefacients
  - Intra-articular corticosteroid injection
  - Intra-articular hyaluronic acid
  - Glucosamine
  - Chondroitin
  - Surgery

- Pharmacological management of OA is limited to short-term symptomatic relief of pain and stiffness but does not alter disease progression.
- The considerations of the use of analgesia apply to OA of any joint. The section describing analgesia therefore refers to all joints.
- Other treatments, however, apply differently, and are therefore described in sections headed:
  - Osteoarthritis of the knee
  - Osteoarthritis of the hip
  - Osteoarthritis of any other joint

Analgesia recommendations summary

- **Paracetamol remains the drug of first choice** in all age groups. It works well for many people, especially where mild symptoms of osteoarthritis (OA) are present.
- **Paracetamol (with codeine where needed)** should be used in place of nonsteroidal anti-inflammatory drugs (NSAIDs) if possible.
- **NSAIDs may be the best option in people with moderate to severe pain.**
  - Ibuprofen is recommended as the first choice for an NSAID as it has the lowest risk of adverse effects [CSM, 1994; Henry et al, 1996; CSM, 2002].
  - Long-term NSAID use should be avoided without appropriate monitoring and re-evaluation of the clinical need.
  - See the separate supporting PRODIGY guidance on *Nonsteroidal anti-inflammatory drugs (NSAIDs)* for further information on NSAIDs.
- **Topical NSAIDs may have a role in people who experience acute flare-ups of OA of the knees, fingers, and toes.**
  - The evidence supports that benefit is obtained in the first couple of weeks and after that there is limited evidence of benefit [Lin et al, 2004].
  - A topical NSAID is safer than a systemic form and could also be considered as an alternative to an oral NSAID when gastroprotection is needed.
- **Topical rubefacients** are not routinely recommended as there is only limited trial data of their use specifically in OA and trial data is further limited by small size, inadequate design and validity [Mason et al, 2004c; Bandolier, 2005]. There might be a high placebo response due to massage of the affected area.
- **Topical capsaicin** may be tried when consideration of all other options is exhausted.

How does paracetamol compare with NSAIDs in symptomatic pain relief for OA?

- Pooled data from trials indicate that nonsteroidal anti-inflammatory drugs (NSAIDs) have a greater effect of in the symptomatic relief of people with osteoarthritis (OA) compared with paracetamol. However, the increased risk of adverse events with NSAIDs coupled with the limited clinical significance of their greater effect means paracetamol is still the preferred first choice here.
- A Cochrane review has compared paracetamol compared with NSAIDs for treating OA [Towheed et al, 2003]. In the five comparator-controlled randomized controlled trials (RCTs) included in the review:
  - NSAIDs were superior to paracetamol for improving knee and hip pain in OA (with moderate to severe pain levels), as well as global assessment.
  - Both drugs had similar efficacy in terms of improvements in physical functional status.
- Other Cochrane reviews of analgesia and non-aspirin NSAIDs in OA of the hip [Towheed et al, 1997] and knee [Watson et al, 1997] reported a lack of

standardization of outcome assessments in trials and found distinguishing between equivalent trial doses of NSAIDs was difficult.
  - With knee OA the recommendation was to base NSAID selection on safety, patient acceptability, and cost.
- Three recent systematic meta-analyses have reviewed whether paracetamol reduces pain in people with OA, and compared RCTs of paracetamol and NSAIDs. Inclusion criteria varied but the outcomes were all similar:
  - The first review [Zhang et al, 2004] found paracetamol was slightly more effective than placebo but less effective than NSAIDs.
  - The second review [Wegman et al, 2004] found NSAIDs were slightly better than paracetamol for reducing OA-related general pain or pain at rest.
  - The third review [Lee et al, 2004] found NSAIDs were significantly superior in reducing rest and walking pain compared with paracetamol for symptomatic OA.
- A further meta-analysis estimated the analgesic efficacy of NSAIDs only, in OA of the knee [Bjordal et al, 2004]. NSAIDs reduced short-term pain slightly better than placebo, but their long-term use was not supported by this analysis in view of their potential serious adverse effects.
- **Overall meaningful evidence-based comparisons between paracetamol and placebo, and paracetamol and NSAIDs are not possible** as there are so few trials available of adequate duration, size, validity, and quality.

When should I prescribe a COX-2 selective inhibitor?

- **The National Institute of Clinical Excellence** (NICE) **recommends that cyclo-oxygenase-2 (COX-2) selective nonsteroidal anti-inflammatory drugs (NSAIDs) should not be used routinely for people with osteoarthritis** (OA) [NICE, 2001a].
- COX-2 selective inhibitors should only be considered in preference to standard NSAIDs in people who are at high risk of serious gastrointestinal (GI) adverse events.
- There is no robust evidence to justify the simultaneous prescription of gastroprotective agents with COX-2 selective NSAIDs as a means of further reducing potential GI events.
- For further information, see the separate supporting PRODIGY guidance on *Nonsteroidal anti-inflammatory drugs (NSAIDs)*.

What evidence supports the use of topical NSAIDs?

- Topical nonsteroidal anti-inflammatory drugs (NSAIDs) can provide some pain relief and they are associated with fewer adverse effects than oral NSAIDs. However, they have been found to be no more effective than oral NSAIDs [Mason et al, 2004b; Bandolier, 2005].
- In people with osteoarthritis (OA), a systematic review found that topical NSAIDs were better than placebo in reducing pain and improving function over a fortnight [Lin et al, 2004].
  - No evidence was found of superior efficacy to placebo after this time period and no evidence exists to support the long-term use of topical NSAIDs in people with OA [Lin et al, 2004].
- A systematic review has found that topical NSAIDs were effective and safe in treating in people with chronic musculoskeletal pain for 2 weeks [Mason et al, 2004a].
  - Limitations included the short duration of the trials and that no single preparation could be shown to be better than another.
- Trial data directly comparing the same NSAID in topical and oral forms are still limited. Recently one trial has compared 12 weeks' use of the oral form of diclofenac with a topical solution form in people with OA [Tugwell et al, 2004]. Pain, stiffness, physical functioning, and patient global assessment outcome measures were similar for both forms. The adverse-effect profile of the oral form was less favourable than the topical form.
- More quality comparative trial data are needed of different topical NSAID use in people with OA to determine which may be more effective than others [Cooper and Jordan, 2004].

What is the role of intra-articular injections in OA?

- Corticosteroids and hyaluronic acid (and derivatives) are available for people with osteoarthritis (OA) of the knee where alternative options have failed either because of a lack of efficacy or adverse effects (toxicity).
  - Intra-articular corticosteroids should be tried for short-term control of marked pain, or a flare-up.
  - Hyaluronic acid may be considered as a further option for those who have not responded to other medical options including intra-articular corticosteroids but it is unlikely to be given in primary care and there is still much controversy about its use.
- Hyaluronic acid intra-articular injection is believed to supplement the natural hyaluronic acid in the synovial fluid in the joint space to return the elasticity and viscosity of the synovial fluid to normal but there is limited evidence to support this theory.
- For more information see: *What evidence supports intra-articular corticosteroid injection use in knee OA?* and *What evidence supports the use of intra-articular hyaluronic acid injections for knee OA?*
- There have been experiments with the intra-articular injection of a variety of other substances. However there is limited evidence to support the use of any of them [Uthman et al, 2003].

Osteoarthritis of the knee

Which non-drug treatments are recommended for OA of the knee?

- **Braces and orthoses (shoe insoles) are recommended for osteoarthritis (OA) of the knee.** They have been the subject of a recent Cochrane systematic review [Brouwer et al, 2005].
  - The use of a valgus knee brace was shown to improve pain, stiffness, and physical function at 6 months compared to a neoprene sleeve. The use of a neoprene sleeve was shown to improve pain, stiffness, and physical function at 6 months compared to placebo.
  - The use of both neutrally and laterally wedged insoles was shown to improve pain and stiffness at 6 months. The use of laterally wedged insoles was shown to reduce intake of nonsteroidal anti-inflammatory drugs (NSAIDs) compared to the use of neutrally wedged insoles.
  - The use of a strapped insole was shown to improve pain compared to a laterally wedged insole. The use of both types of insole was shown to improve function.
  - The use of a sock-type insole was shown not to improve pain.
  - Braces and insoles were well tolerated. The use of strapped insoles was shown to be associated with pain elsewhere (low back, sole of foot, back of knee); this pain, however, did not stop any people from continuing to use the insoles.

O

- **Patellar taping of the knee is recommended for OA of the knee.** It has only been studied in small randomized controlled trials (RCTs), with methodological weaknesses, but seems to be a simple, efficacious effective method of pain relief treatment that is free from clinically important adverse effects [Hinman et al, 2003b; Hinman et al, 2003a; Scott et al, 2004].
- **The use of a cane (in the hand contralateral to the affected knee) is recommended for knee OA.** This reduces the forces through the joint, and has been associated with improved pain and function [Hochberg et al, 1995a]. Referral to a physiotherapist is suggested to ensure provision of the correct type of cane, of the correct height, for the individual.
- **Exercise therapy is recommended for knee OA, irrespective of age.** A Cochrane systematic review (of 2562 people) concluded that it reduces pain and improves physical function [Fransen et al, 2001]. There were insufficient data to recommend the type of exercise, or the optimum frequency. A separate Cochrane systematic review (of only 39 people) studied the intensity of exercise, and concluded that high- and low-intensity exercise seemed to be equally effective [Brosseau et al, 2003].
- **Weight loss is recommended for obese people (BMI >28) with knee OA.** In one study of 80 people, weight loss of 10% improved overall function score by 28% [Christensen et al, 2005]. In another study of 316 people which looked at the effects of weight loss and exercise, the combination of weight loss and exercise led to greater improvements in function and pain than either weight loss or exercise alone [Messier et al, 2004].
- **The use of transcutaneous electrical nerve stimulation (TENS) is recommended for knee OA.** A Cochrane systematic review (of 294 people) concluded that TENS and acupuncture-like TENS significantly improved pain and stiffness compared to placebo [Osiri et al, 2000].
- **The use of acupuncture might help provide symptomatic relief with knee OA.** Acupuncture for OA has been the subject of several systematic reviews:
    - Most studies show a benefit for acupuncture compared to no treatment in OA.
    - They all acknowledge the presence of methodological problems, especially associated with the use of sham acupuncture as placebo, in studies of acupuncture.
    - Further studies are underway to help clarify the specific effects of acupuncture in OA [AHRQ, 2003].
- **The use of avocado-soybean unsaponifiables (ASU) may be effective for knee OA.** A Cochrane systematic review (of 327 people with knee or hip OA) concluded that there is convincing evidence for the use of ASU in OA [Little et al, 2000].
- **Referral to a physiotherapist and an occupational therapist should be considered for knee OA.** Although not supported by studies, referral should be considered on an individual basis as physical treatments and provision of appliances may be of benefit.

What analgesia is recommended for OA of the knee?

See analgesia recommendations summary where non-drug treatment options alone are adequate.

What evidence supports intra-articular corticosteroid injection use in knee OA?

- **The use of intra-articular corticosteroids is recommended as an option for short-term relief of pain and functional impairment with inflammatory flare-ups of knee OA.**
- Currently no evidence supports the promotion of disease progression by corticosteroid injections [Arroll and Goodyear-Smith, 2004].
- Two systematic reviews confirm the short-term moderate efficacy of corticosteroid injection in terms of improving pain outcomes [Bandolier, 2004]. There are limitations to these reviews though including that:
    - The outcome of symptom improvement is not always clearly defined.
    - Different corticosteroids used at different doses are used.
    - Each study and the total number of studies was small.
- The first review identified five studies (312 participants) of long-acting corticosteroid use compared with placebo. Intra-articular corticosteroid use was found to significantly (both statistically and clinically) reduce knee pain 1 week after injection [Godwin and Dawes, 2004]. The beneficial effect may last for three to 4 weeks, but no evidence was found to support any longer-term benefit.
- The second review identified 10 studies (546 participants) [Godwin and Dawes, 2004]. It included any corticosteroid formulation (therefore all the five studies from the previous review) and the search history was more recent. Corticosteroid dose varied between 6 mg and 80 mg prednisone equivalent, though most were between 25 and 50 mg equivalent. Seven of the 10 trials showed improvement with use of corticosteroid injection.
    - Meta-analysis pooling of six studies (five using long acting corticosteroid injections) showed symptom improvement (not always clearly defined) up to 2 weeks after intervention occurred in 74% patients given corticosteroid and 45% given placebo. For every four people treated there was one extra responder (NNT = 4).
    - The pooled results of two high quality studies also showed slight longer term benefit at 16–24 weeks in OA symptoms for 44% people using corticosteroid compared with 21% using placebo. For every five people treated there was one extra responder (NNT = 5). However this result is inconclusive as the effect may be dose dependent.
    - Five studies that used a visual analogue scale showed improvement in pain up to 2 weeks after corticosteroid injections compared with placebo.
    - A dose of triamcinolone 20 mg (equivalent to prednisone 25 mg) seems to be efficacious for pain control at 2 weeks.
    - A dose equivalent to prednisone 50 mg may be needed to show benefit at 16-24 weeks.
- Although they are effective and provide immediate benefits to people, long-term outcomes show little difference from other treatments, such as physiotherapy.

What evidence supports the use of intra-articular hyaluronic acid injections for knee OA?

- **Hyaluronic acid (HA) may have a place in the short-term relief of pain and functional impairment of people with mild to moderate knee OA who cannot tolerate corticosteroids, or in people waiting for total knee replacement.**
- However, this treatment option is not likely to be given in primary care and there is still much controversy. Also there are several hyaluronic acid derivatives which differ in molecular weight and they cannot be assumed to have similar efficacy.
- There is little evidence on the long-term benefits and safety of HA [Espallargues and Pons, 2003].
- Hyaluronic acid use for knee OA has been associated with controversial efficacy and three recent systematic reviews have been published that found trials were often

small with clinical heterogeneity regarding type of preparation, dose, outcome(s) measured and study duration (6 weeks to 1 year), and most were company sponsored

- **The first review** included 22 trials with 2949 participants [Lo et al, 2003]. Only three studies had a statistically significant effect size — two used the 6,000 kD high molecular weight (MW) preparation but one study just had 30 participants. A third trial with the low MW preparation reported a similar effect to placebo. The pooled effect size was 0.3 (95% CI 0.2 to 0.5), indicating a small effect.
- **The second review** used different inclusion exclusion criteria and evaluated 13 trials (all of which were included in the first review) and five case series [Aggarwal and Sempowski, 2004]. Overall similar findings were reported to the previous review. In addition, injection site pain and swelling were reported in 2–23% of injections, and back pain and gastrointestinal adverse events were also cited. The review found that:
  - Viscosupplementation with high MW hyaluronic acid was an effective treatment for people with knee OA who have ongoing pain or are unable to tolerate conservative treatment or joint replacement.
  - The effects of HA seemed to begin after 4–12 weeks and last up to a year. This contrasts with corticosteroid injections that act more quickly but lose effectiveness after 3 months i.e. hyaluronic acid seems to have a slower onset of action but the effect seems to last longer.
  - Corticosteroids might be more effective for joint effusion or other acute inflammation.
  - Intra-articular corticosteroids and HA might be good for combination therapy.
- **A third review** assessed 20 randomized controlled trials (RCTs) (16 were included in the meta-analysis by Lo) that compared the therapeutic effect of HA on OA of the knee [Wang et al, 2004]. The analysis found significant improvements in pain and functional outcomes. Despite the significant between-study heterogeneity in the estimates of the efficacy of HA, the authors concluded that their analysis confirmed the therapeutic efficacy and safety of intra-articular injection of HA for the symptomatic treatment of OA of the knee (in terms of pain and functional outcomes with few adverse events.
  - With regard to pain with activities the pooled mean difference for the percentage of pain intensity improvement was 7.9% (95% CI 4.1 to 11.7). After adjusting this for the baseline pain intensity, the improvement was 13.4% (95% CI 5.5 to 21.3). Finally the pooled mean difference for the peak improvement in pain intensity was 9.9% (95% CI 4.8 to 15.0).
  - People over 65 years of age and those with the most advanced radiographic stage of OA were less likely to benefit from hyaluronic acid.
- **Hyaluronic acid** — three to five injections into the knee at weekly interval have been shown to provide pain relief and functional improvements for up to 6 months [Huskisson and Donnelly, 1999; Miltner et al, 2002].

What evidence supports the use of glucosamine for knee OA?

- **Glucosamine hydrochloride/sulphate 1500 mg daily is an option for people with mild knee OA** [DTB, 2002] **where analgesia has either failed, or in people who are NSAID intolerant.**
  - There is little published evidence in its use for OA at other sites.
- Although glucosamine may be prescribed generically on the NHS, it is a food supplement and not a licensed medicine in the UK. Therefore, the manufacturers are not bound by statutory monitoring or good manufacturing requirements and the relative purity and glucosamine content in different preparations obtained from different manufacturers may vary [DTB, 2002].
- The effect of glucosamine on cartilage loss as part of the disease process is not clear but radiological findings provide some evidence that glucosamine may slow disease progression. However, there are concerns about the validity of available tools as markers of disease progression [DTB, 2002].
- A Cochrane review of pooled data from seven placebo-controlled trials (657 people) found glucosamine provided a clinically significant treatment benefit. Glucosamine was also found to have a clinical effect at least equivalent to ibuprofen 400 mg three times a day or piroxicam 20 mg a day [Towheed et al, 2000].
  - 12 of 13 RCTs compared glucosamine to placebo found glucosamine superior in relieving pain or improving function.
- A systematic review of placebo-controlled trials also has found both glucosamine (and chondroitin) offered a moderate treatment benefit in terms of pain relief and functional improvement in people with knee OA [McAlindon et al, 2000]. Limitations include the varying quality of RCTs and a likely publication bias possibly exaggerating the benefits.
- A more recent systematic review of 15 double blind RCTs of glucosamine and chondroitin in knee OA, reported significant short-term symptomatic benefits [Richy et al, 2003]. Glucosamine doses were mainly 1500 mg daily — trial duration was 6–8 weeks to 3 years. Chondroitin doses were 800 to 2000 mg daily — trial duration 3 months to 1 year.
  - The combination improved continuous outcome measures using pain, mobility, and other functional outcome assessment tools.
  - Glucosamine also significantly reduced joint-space narrowing.
  - The results suggest that the long-term administration of daily oral glucosamine sulphate at the minimal dosage of 1500 mg during a minimal period of 3 years slows the degenerative process of the joint cartilage.
  - In all trials rescue medications (e.g. NSAIDs) were allowed. However, the combination of glucosamine or chondroitin and NSAIDs at lower cumulative doses then alone showed better efficacy on pain reduction than placebo and NSAIDs.
  - The relative risk of being a responder (defined by the authors on the basis of global assessment) when allocated to glucosamine or chondroitin or placebo was 1.6 (95% CI 1.38 to 1.82). Responders were therefore more frequent with glucosamine and chondroitin and the authors calculated that for every five people treated there was one additional responder (NNT = 5) with an absolute risk increase of 20% (95% CI 15 to 26).
- Glucosamine has been found to be well tolerated [Towheed et al, 2000], although its long-term safety has not been established. Also, the shellfish-derived formulation might cause allergic reactions in susceptible people.
  - There has been anecdotal evidence that glucosamine may potentiate the effect of warfarin, therefore close monitoring is needed when therapy is initiated or modified during concomitant treatment [Micromedex, 2005].

What is the role of chondroitin in knee OA?

- **Chondroitin is not recommended for use in people with knee OA.** Chondroitin is not licensed for the treatment of OA and there are insufficient trial data of its use in people with OA.
- Chondroitin sulphate is found in cartilage and is available as an animal-derived food supplement.
- A systematic review of chondroitin use in OA of the hip or knee has found it to be effective in reducing pain and improving function in seven RCTs (702 participants) over 3 months or more [Bandolier, 2000]. Doses ranged from 800–1200 mg a day and all comparisons were with placebo.
- Evidence is limited on the effectiveness of chondroitin include the small number of trials, small study sample sizes, type of chondroitin preparation and difficulty in quantifying the doses taken.
- Chondroitin has been taken with glucosamine and the combination has been found to be beneficial in mild to moderate disease (only) compared with placebo but the role of chondroitin (if any) it is not apparent. For more information, see *What evidence supports the use of glucosamine for knee OA?*
- Chondroitin has no reported clinically important adverse effects.

What is the role of magnetic bracelets in knee OA?

- A recent trial involved 194 people with OA of the hip or knee randomised to wearing a standard strength static bipolar magnetic bracelet, a weak magnetic bracelet, or a non-magnetic (dummy) bracelet for 12 weeks [Harlow et al, 2004]. Based on Western Ontario and McMaster Universities OA lower limb pain scale, the researchers concluded that magnetic bracelets decreased pain symptoms but were uncertain of an explanation as to why. Limitations included:
  - Lack of description regarding the severity of OA in participants, participant duration of symptoms prior to the study, and use of analgesia during the trial.
  - That despite randomization and blinding of study participants, many correctly guessed which group they had been assigned to.
- **Larger clinical trials are needed before magnetic bracelet therapy can be proven and therefore clinically recommended.** Future trials should include laboratory markers of local inflammation in addition to subjective pain assessment. Also the range of products available on the market may vary in quality and therefore there is controversy regarding which product represents the gold standard for use in trials.

O

Surgery

When should I refer my patient with OA of the knee to an orthopaedic surgeon?

- Most people with OA of the knee are managed in primary care.
- A person with severe symptomatic knee OA who has pain that has not responded to medical therapy, and who has progressive limitation in activities of daily living, should be referred to an orthopaedic surgeon [Hochberg et al, 1995a; American College of Rheumatology, 2000].
- The general consensus among orthopaedic surgeons on indications for surgery (obtained from a postal survey) were:
  - Severe daily pain, and
  - X-ray evidence of joint space narrowing [Jordan et al, 2003]
- Night-time pain in people may well be a clinical marker of severe OA.
- The National Institute for Clinical Excellence in *Referral advice: a guide to appropriate referral from general to specialist services* [NICE, 2001b] advises the following for osteoarthritis of the knee (see Table 1). The referral advice is meant to encourage local health communities to discuss referral issues and enable local referral guidelines and protocols to be produced (for further information see **www.nice.org.uk**):

Which surgical treatments are available for OA of the knee?

- **Total knee replacement (TKR)** is a well-established treatment for moderate to severe knee OA. Systematic reviews have found that TKR is effective in relieving pain and improving function [Scott et al, 2004]. Long-term results are comparable to those for total hip replacement (THR). Survival rates of the prosthesis for TKR are 84–98% at 15 years [Gidwani and Fairbank, 2004].
  - The European League Against Rheumatism concludes that TKR is a safe and effective treatment in improving quality of life, as well as reducing pain and improving function in people with knee OA. However, there are no RCTs comparing TKR with non-surgical interventions [Jordan et al, 2003].
  - The American College of Rheumatology concludes that TKR provides marked pain relief and functional improvement in most people with knee OA [American College of Rheumatology, 2000].
- **Osteotomy** may provide pain relief for some people with knee OA who are not yet candidates for TKR, particularly those who are young and active [American College of Rheumatology, 2000; AAOS, 2003]. Osteotomy may delay the need for TKR by 5–10 years, and may allow a return to sport (something not advised after TKR) [Gidwani and Fairbank, 2004].
- **Fusion of the knee** may be considered in young, active people with knee OA, particularly when associated with severe instability [AAOS, 2003].
- **Arthroscopic debridement** may be considered for knee OA with mechanical symptoms (painful locking or catching), particularly in young people, if:
  - There is no gross malalignment or instability, and
  - There is some articular cartilage remaining, and
  - Symptoms are well localized [AAOS, 2003; Gidwani and Fairbank, 2004]
- **In people with isolated patellofemoral OA** (up to one tenth of people with knee OA):
  - The role of patellofemoral arthroplasty and patellectomy is not well defined, and indications are limited

Table 1: Referral advice for people with osteoarthritis of the knee.

****	There is evidence of infection in the joint.
***	There is evidence of acute inflammation caused by, for example, haemarthrosis, gout, or pseudogout.
**	Giving way is a problem despite therapy.
**	Symptoms rapidly deteriorate and are causing severe disability.
*	The symptoms impair quality of life. Referral should be based on an explicit scoring system that should be developed locally in a partnership involving patients together with healthcare professionals in primary and secondary care. Referral criteria should take into account the extent to which the condition is causing pain, disability, sleeplessness, loss of independence, inability to undertake normal activities, reduced functional capacity, or psychiatric illness.

Key to referral timings
Arrangements should be made so that the person:
**** is seen immediately (within a day)
*** is seen urgently (maximum wait of 2 weeks recommended but to be agreed locally)
** is seen soon (maximum waiting time to be agreed locally)
* has a routine appointment (maximum waiting time to be agreed locally)

Tibial tubercle elevation has variable results and a significant complication rate [AAOS, 2003; Gidwani and Fairbank, 2004].

Osteoarthritis of the hip

Which non-drug treatments are recommended for osteoarthritis (OA) of the hip?

Exercise therapy is recommended for hip OA. The evidence base for this recommendation is less than for knee OA, as exercise therapy has only been studied in about 100 people with hip OA. There were insufficient data to recommend the type of exercise, or the optimum frequency [Fransen et al, 2001]. It is, however, generally accepted that exercise is beneficial for people with hip OA [Scott et al, 2004; Zhang et al, 2005; Roddy et al, 2005].

Weight loss is recommended for obese people (BMI >28) with hip OA. There is limited evidence to support this recommendation, but it is generally accepted that reduction of adverse mechanical forces across a joint affected by OA is beneficial [Zhang et al, 2005].

The use of a cane (in the hand contralateral to the affected hip) is recommended for hip OA. This reduces the forces through the joint, and has been associated with improved pain and function [Hochberg et al, 1995b]. Referral to a physiotherapist is suggested to ensure provision of the correct type and height of cane for the individual.

The use of acupuncture might help provide symptomatic relief with hip OA. Acupuncture for OA has been the subject of several systematic reviews:

- Most studies show a benefit for acupuncture compared to no treatment in OA.
- They all acknowledge the presence of methodological problems, especially associated with the use of sham acupuncture as placebo, in studies of acupuncture.
- Further studies are underway to help clarify the specific effects of acupuncture in OA [AHRQ, 2003].

The use of avocado-soybean unsaponifiables (ASU) may be effective for hip OA. A Cochrane systematic review (of 327 people with knee or hip OA) concluded that there is convincing evidence for the use of ASU in OA [Little et al, 2000].

Referral to a physiotherapist and an occupational therapist should be considered for hip OA. Although not supported by studies, referral should be considered on an individual basis as physical treatments and provision of appliances may be of benefit.

The use of transcutaneous electrical nerve stimulation (TENS) might be effective for hip OA. Although not supported by evidence, the likelihood of harm is small, and a trial of a TENS machine might provide benefit.

What analgesia is recommended for OA of the hip?

See analgesia recommendations summary where non-drug treatment options alone are adequate.

Is intra-articular corticosteroid injection recommended for hip OA?

The use of intra-articular corticosteroids is not recommended for hip OA in primary care:

- Injection of a hip joint requires ultrasound or X-ray guidance, and is therefore not feasible in primary care.
- Trials of intra-articular corticosteroid injection for hip OA are small in number (we could only find one RCT). There is therefore limited evidence for the efficacy of this treatment [Zhang et al, 2005].

What is the role of chondroitin in hip OA?

- **Chondroitin is not recommended for use in people with hip OA.** Chondroitin is not licensed for the treatment of OA and there are insufficient trial data of its use in people with OA.
- Chondroitin sulphate is found in cartilage and is available as an animal-derived food supplement.
- A systematic review of chondroitin use in OA of the hip or knee has found it to be effective in reducing pain and improving function in seven randomized controlled trials (RCTs) (702 participants) over 3 months or more [Bandolier, 2000]. Doses ranged from 800–1200 mg a day and all comparisons were with placebo.
- Limitations of the body of evidence on the effectiveness of chondroitin include the small number of trials, small study sample sizes, type of chondroitin preparation and difficulty in quantifying the doses taken.
- Chondroitin has been taken with glucosamine and the combination has been found to be beneficial in mild to moderate disease (only) compared with placebo but the role of chondroitin (if any) it is not apparent. For more information, see *What evidence supports the use of glucosamine for knee OA?*
- Chondroitin has no reported clinically important adverse effects.

Surgery

When should I refer my patient with OA of the hip to an orthopaedic surgeon?

- Most people with OA of the hip are managed in primary care.
- A person with severe symptomatic hip OA who has pain that has not responded to medical therapy, and who has progressive limitation in activities of daily living, should be referred to an orthopaedic surgeon [Hochberg et al, 1995b; American College of Rheumatology, 2000].
- The general consensus among orthopaedic surgeons on indications for surgery (obtained from a postal survey) were:
  - Severe daily pain, and
  - X-ray evidence of joint space narrowing [Jordan et al, 2003]
- Night-time pain in people may well be a clinical marker of severe OA.
- The National Institute for Clinical Excellence in *Referral advice: a guide to appropriate referral from general to specialist services* [NICE, 2001b] advises the following for OA of the hip (see Table 2). The referral advice is meant to encourage local health communities to discuss referral issues and enable local referral guidelines and protocols to be produced (for further information see **www.nice.org.uk**).

Table 2: Referral advice for people with osteoarthritis of the hip.

****	There is evidence of infection in the joint
***	Symptoms rapidly deteriorate and are causing severe disability
*	The symptoms impair quality of life. Referral should be based on an explicit scoring system that should be developed locally in a partnership involving patients together with healthcare professionals in primary and secondary care. Referral criteria should take into account the extent to which the condition is causing pain, disability, sleeplessness, loss of independence, inability to undertake normal activities, reduced functional capacity, or psychiatric illness.

Key to referral timings
Arrangements should be made so that the person:
**** is seen immediately (within a day)
*** is seen urgently (maximum wait of 2 weeks recommended but to be agreed locally)
** is seen soon (maximum waiting time to be agreed locally)
* has a routine appointment (maximum waiting time to be agreed locally)

O

Which surgical treatments are available for OA of the hip?

- **Total hip replacement** (THR) is a well-established treatment for moderate to severe hip OA. Systematic reviews have found that THR is effective in relieving pain and improving function for at least 10 years [Scott et al, 2004].
  - The European League Against Rheumatism concludes that THR is effective in hip OA in improving pain and function [Zhang et al, 2005].
  - The American College of Rheumatology concludes that THR provides marked pain relief and functional improvement in most people with hip OA [American College of Rheumatology, 2000].
- **Osteotomy** may provide pain relief for some people with hip OA who are not yet candidates for THR, particularly those who are young and active [American College of Rheumatology, 2000; Zhang et al, 2005].

What is the role of magnetic bracelets in OA of the hip?

See What is the role of magnetic bracelets in knee OA?

Osteoarthritis of any other joint

Which non-drug treatments are recommended for OA of any other joint?

- **Weight loss is recommended for obese people (BMI >28) with OA of the ankle or foot.** There is limited evidence to support this recommendation, but it is generally accepted that reduction of adverse mechanical forces across a joint affected by OA is beneficial [Zhang et al, 2005].
- **The use of acupuncture might help provide symptomatic relief with OA of any other joint.** Acupuncture for OA has been the subject of several systematic reviews:
  - Most studies show a benefit for acupuncture compared to no treatment in OA.
  - They all acknowledge the presence of methodological problems, especially associated with the use of sham acupuncture as placebo, in studies of acupuncture.
  - Further studies are underway to help clarify the specific effects of acupuncture in OA [AHRQ, 2003].
- **Exercise therapy should be considered for OA of any other joint.** There is no evidence base for this recommendation. It is, however, accepted that exercise therapy may benefit some people with OA of any other joint [American College of Rheumatology, 2000]. Consider referral to a physiotherapist on an individual basis.
- **Referral to a physiotherapist and an occupational therapist should be considered for OA of any joint.** Although not supported by studies, referral should be considered on an individual basis as physical treatments and provision of appliances may be of benefit.
- **The use of transcutaneous electrical nerve stimulation (TENS) might be effective for OA of any other joint.** Although not supported by evidence, the likelihood of harm is small, and a trial of a TENS machine might provide benefit.

What analgesia is recommended for OA of any other joint?

See analgesia recommendations summary where non-drug treatment options alone are adequate.

Is intra-articular corticosteroid injection recommended for OA of any other joint?

- **The use of intra-articular corticosteroids may be considered for OA of any other joint.** The evidence for their use in any joint other than the knee is limited. However, it may improve pain and swelling of an individual joint (e.g. shoulder, hand joints).

Surgery

When should I refer my patient with OA of any other joint to an orthopaedic surgeon?

- Most people with OA are managed in primary care.
- A person with severe symptomatic OA who has pain tha has not responded to medical therapy, and who has progressive limitation in activities of daily living, should be referred to an orthopaedic surgeon.
- Night-time pain in people may well be a clinical marker of severe OA.

Which surgical treatments are available for OA of any other joint?

- There are many different surgical options available. Replacement can be considered for shoulders, elbows, and hand joints. The decision of which surgical treatment is based on the individual joint and the characteristics of the person affected.

Medicines management

Paracetamol

- **Paracetamol** is safe and effective for the treatment of mild to moderate pain when used correctly, and is well tolerated at the recommended daily dose.
- It is more likely to be effective for osteoarthritis when used regularly rather than 'as required'.
- When paracetamol is used correctly, it is generally safer for use in the long-term compared with nonsteroidal anti-inflammatory drugs (NSAIDs). It has been found to have a similar safety profile to that of placebo [Zhang et al, 2004] and most trial data report participant discontinuation due to adverse effects to be notably greater with NSAIDs than paracetamol.

Codeine

- **Codeine** may be added to paracetamol if more pain relie is required.
- Paracetamol and codeine should be prescribed separatel so they can be individually titrated; combination products such as co-codamol are not recommended.
- Codeine may cause nausea, vomiting, constipation, and drowsiness. A regular laxative is often needed when it is used long-term.

Nonsteroidal anti-inflammatory drugs

A full discussion on the contraindications, adverse effects, monitoring issues, and interactions of NSAIDs is beyond the scope of this guidance. For further information, see the separate PRODIGY guidance on *Nonsteroidal anti-inflammatory drugs (NSAIDs)*.

- Consider comorbidity when prescribing NSAIDs.
  - NSAIDs commonly cause gastrointestinal adverse effects, and can worsen asthma, hypertension, renal impairment, and heart failure.
  - There is a small increased risk of cardiovascular event with coxibs (which seems highest in people who already have cardiovascular disease).
- For people with osteoarthritis at high risk of gastrointestinal adverse events, we recommend the following options:
  - Use paracetamol (with or without codeine) instead of an NSAID if possible or
  - Use a gastroprotective agent with a standard NSAID [NICE, 2001a] or
  - Use a cyclo-oxygenase-2 (COX-2) selective NSAID alone [NICE, 2001a] or

- Consider using a topical NSAID alone for acute flare-ups of the fingers, knees, and toes.

For advice on the management of dyspepsia due to NSAIDs, see the separate PRODIGY guidance on *Dyspepsia — symptoms (uninvestigated by endoscopy)* and *Dyspepsia — proven DU, GU, or NSAID-associated ulcer*.

opical NSAIDs

Topical NSAIDs have the advantage of a better gastrointestinal adverse-effect profile than oral NSAIDs [Heyneman et al, 2000]. However local adverse effects have been reported [Mason et al, 2004b].

Intra-articular corticosteroids

low should they be given?

Intra-articular corticosteroids can be used to treat an acute flare up in knee joints only. They should only be given by health care professionals with experience of giving intra-articular injections [DTB, 1995].

Vhich corticosteroid injection should I use?

Specific corticosteroids are recommended for different joints according to their size. Atrophy of subcutaneous tissues and local skin depigmentation may occur from periarticular leakage of corticosteroid. The risk is greatest if large or repeated doses of a long-acting, potent corticosteroid are given:

- **Smaller joints:** hydrocortisone, dexamethasone, or prednisolone are recommended.
- **Larger joints:** triamcinolone or methylprednisolone are recommended.

Vhen should I avoid injecting a joint?

void injecting:

Prosthetic joints

When there is any possibility of sepsis

Joints within 3 months of a previous injection

ject with caution if:

The person is taking anticoagulants

Vhat clinically important adverse effects should I be ware of?

People report the procedure to be painful or very painful about 20% of the time.

Adverse effects from intra-articular injections of corticosteroids are rare.

- **The most serious complication is septic arthritis,** with an incidence of 1/17,000 to 1/50,000 after injection [DTB, 1995].
- **Concern about joint damage after repeated corticosteroid injections** is controversial; despite the large number of people treated with intra-articular corticosteroids, case reports that suggest such damage are rare [DTB, 1995].
- **Atrophy of subcutaneous tissues and local skin depigmentation** may occur from periarticular leakage of corticosteroid.
  - The risk of local tissue atrophy and depigmentation occurs from subcutaneous or shallow injections as well as from small-joint injections (e.g. tennis elbow, de Quervain's tenosynovitis, and shallow intramuscular injections).
  - The risk is greatest if large or repeated doses of a long-acting, potent corticosteroid are given.
- In general, hydrocortisone, dexamethasone, or prednisolone are recommended for injection of small joints, and triamcinolone or methylprednisolone for injection of large joints.

References

IHS staff in England can link, free of charge, from eferences to full text journals by clicking on [Full text] on ie PRODIGY website.

1. AAOS (2003) *AAOS clinical guideline on osteoarthritis of the knee (phase II)*. American Academy of Orthopaedic Surgeons. www.aaos.org [Accessed: 18/11/2004].
2. Aggarwal, A. and Sempowski, I.P. (2004) Hyaluronic acid injections for knee osteoarthritis. Systematic review of the literature. *Canadian Family Physician* 50(Feb), 249–256.
3. AHRQ (2003) *Acupuncture for osteoarthritis.* Technology Assessment. Agency for Healthcare Research and Quality. www.cms.hhs.gov/coverage/download/id84.pdf [Accessed: 10/11/2004].
4. Altman, R., Alarcon, G., Appelrouth, D. et al (1990) The American College of Rheumatology criteria for the classification and reporting of osteoarthritis of the hand. *Arthritis & Rheumatism* 33(11), 1601–1610.
5. American College of Rheumatology (2000) *Recommendations for the medical management of osteoarthritis of the hip and knee.* American College of Rheumatology Subcommittee on Osteoarthritis Guidelines. www.rheumatology.org [Accessed: 09/11/2004]. [Full text]
6. Arroll, B. and Goodyear-Smith, F. (2004) Corticosteroid injections for osteoarthritis of the knee: meta-analysis. *British Medical Journal* 328(7444), 869–873.
7. Bandolier (2000) *Chondroitin sulphate for osteoarthritis.* Bandolier. www.jr2.ox.ac.uk/bandolier/booth/Arthritis/CSOA.html [Accessed: 05/11/2004]. [Full text]
8. Bandolier (2004) *Steroid injections for OA knee.* Bandolier. www.jr2.ox.ac.uk/bandolier/band123/b123-3.html [Accessed: 09/06/2004].
9. Bandolier (2005) *Topical analgesics: a review of reviews and a bit of perspective.* Bandolier Extra. www.jr2.ox.ac.uk/bandolier/Extraforbando/Topextra3.pdf [Accessed: 10/03/2005].
10. Bjordal, J.M., Ljunggren, A.E., Klovning, A. and Slordal, L. (2004) Non-steroidal anti-inflammatory drugs, including cyclo-oxygenase-2 inhibitors, in osteoarthritic knee pain: meta-analysis of randomised placebo controlled trials. *British Medical Journal* 329(7478), 1317–1322.
11. BNF 49 (2005) *British National Formulary.* 49th edn. London: British Medical Association and Royal Pharmaceutical Society of Great Britain.
12. Brion, P.H. and Kalunian, K.C. (2003) Osteoarthritis. In: Warrell, D.A., Cox, T.M., Firth, J.D. and Benz, E.J.Jr (Eds.) *Oxford textbook of medicine.* 4th edn. Oxford: Oxford University Press. Section 18.8.
13. Brosseau, L., MacLeay, L., Robinson, V. et al (2003) *Intensity of exercise for the treatment of osteoarthritis (Cochrane Review).* The Cochrane Library. Issue 2. Chichester, UK: John Wiley & Sons, Ltd. www.nelh.nhs.uk/cochrane.asp [Accessed: 04/04/2005]. [Full text]
14. Brouwer, R.W., Jakma, T.S.C., Verhagen, A.P. et al (2005) *Braces and orthoses for treating osteoarthritis of the knee (Cochrane Review).* The Cochrane Library. Issue 1. Chichester, UK: John Wiley & Sons, Ltd. www.nelh.nhs.uk/cochrane.asp [Accessed: 04/04/2005]. [Full text]
15. Christensen, R., Astrup, A. and Bliddal, H. (2005) Weight loss: the treatment of choice for knee osteoarthritis? A randomized trial. *Osteoarthritis & Cartilage* 13(1), 20–27.
16. Cooper, C. and Jordan, K.M. (2004) Topical NSAIDs in osteoarthritis. *British Medical Journal* 329(7461), 304–305.
17. CSM (1994) Relative safety of oral non-aspirin NSAIDs. *Current Problems in Pharmacovigilance* 20(Aug), 9–11.

18. CSM (2002) Non-steroidal anti-inflammatory drugs (NSAIDs) and gastrointestinal (GI) safety. *Current Problems in Pharmacovigilance* 28(Apr), 5.
19. De Craen, A.J., Di Giulio, G., Lampe-Schoenmaeckers, J.E. et al (1996) Analgesic efficacy and safety of paracetamol-codeine combinations versus paracetamol alone: a systematic review. *British Medical Journal* **313**(7053), 321–325. [Full text]
20. Doherty, M., Jones, A. and Cawston, T.E. (1998) Osteoarthritis. In: Maddison, P.J., Isenberg, D.A., Woo, P. and Glass, D.N. (Eds.) *Oxford textbook of rheumatology*. 2nd edn. Oxford: Oxford University Press. 1515–1553.
21. DTB (1995) Articular and periarticular corticosteroid injections. *Drug & Therapeutics Bulletin* **33**(9), 67–70. [Full text]
22. DTB (2002) Is glucosamine worth taking for osteoarthritis? *Drug & Therapeutics Bulletin* **40**(11), 81–83. [Full text]
23. EMEA (2004) *Press release: EMEA to review COX-2 inhibitors*. EMEA/117908/2004. European Medicines Agency. www.emea.eu.int [Accessed: 28/01/2005].
24. EMEA (2005) *Press release: European Medicines Agency concludes action on COX-2 inhibitors*. EMEA/207766/2005. European Medicines Agency. www.emea.eu.int [Accessed: 05/07/2005].
25. Espallargues, M. and Pons, J.M. (2003) Efficacy and safety of viscosupplementation with Hylan G-F 20 for the treatment of knee osteoarthritis: a systematic review. *International Journal of Technology Assessment in Health Care* **19**(1), 41–56.
26. Fransen, M., McConnell, S. and Bell, M. (2001) *Exercise for osteoarthritis of the hip or knee (Cochrane Review)*. The Cochrane Library. Issue 2. Chichester, UK: John Wiley & Sons, Ltd. www.nelh.nhs.uk/cochrane.asp [Accessed: 04/04/2005]. [Full text]
27. Gidwani, S. and Fairbank, A. (2004) The orthopaedic approach to managing osteoarthritis of the knee. *British Medical Journal* **329**(7476), 1220–1224.
28. Godwin, M. and Dawes, M. (2004) Intra-articular steroid injections for painful knees. Systematic review with meta-analysis. *Canadian Family Physician* **50**(Feb), 241–248.
29. Harlow, T., Greaves, C., White, A. et al (2004) Randomised controlled triala of magnetic bracelets for relieving pain in osteoarthritis of the hip and knee. *British Medical Journal* **329**(7480), 1450–1454.
30. Hawkey, C.J., Karrasch, J.A., Szczepanski, L. et al (1998) Omeprazole compared with misoprostol for ulcers associated with nonsterodial antiinflammatory drugs. *New England Journal of Medicine* **338**(11), 727–734. [Full text]
31. Henry, D., Lim, L.L., Garcia-Rodriguez, L.A. et al (1996) Variability in risk of gastrointestinal complications with individual non-steroidal anti-inflammatory drugs: results of a collaborative meta-analysis. *British Medical Journal* **312**(7046), 1563–1566. [Full text]
32. Hernández-Diaz, S. and Rodriguez, L.A. (2000) Association between nonsteroidal anti-inflammatory drugs and upper gastrointestinal tract bleeding/ perforation: an overview of epidemiologic studies published in the 1990s. *Archives of Internal Medicine* **160**(14), 2093–2099. [Full text]
33. Heyneman, C.A., Lawless-Liday, C. and Wall, G.C. (2000) Oral versus topical NSAIDs in rheumatic diseases: a comparison. *Drugs* **60**(3), 555–574.
34. Hinman, R.S., Crossley, K.M., McConnell, J. and Bennell, K.L. (2003a) Efficacy of knee tape in the management of osteoarthritis of the knee: blinded randomised controlled trial. *British Medical Journal* **327**(7407), 135–138. [Full text]
35. Hinman, R.S., Bennell, K.L., Crossley, K.M. and McConnell, J. (2003b) Immediate effects of adhesive tape on pain and disability in individuals with knee osteoarthritis. *Rheumatology* **42**(7), 865–869. [Full text]
36. Hochberg, M.C., Altman, R.D., Brandt, K.D. et al (1995a) Guidelines for the medical management of osteoarthritis. Part II. Osteoarthritis of the knee. American College of Rheumatology. *Arthritis & Rheumatism* 38(11), 1541–1546.
37. Hochberg, M.C., Altman, R.D., Brandt, K.D. et al (1995b) Guidelines for the medical management of osteoarthritis. Part I. Osteoarthritis of the hip. American College of Rheumatology. *Arthritis & Rheumatism* 38(11), 1535–1540.
38. Huskisson, E.C. and Donnelly, S. (1999) Hyaluronic acid in the treatment of osteoarthritis of the knee. *Rheumatology* **38**(7), 602–607. [Full text]
39. ICSI (2004) *Diagnosis and treatment of adult degenerative joint disease of the knee*. Health Care Guideline. Institute for Clinical Systems Improvement. www.icsi.org [Accessed: 03/12/2004]. [Full text]
40. Jordan, K.M., Arden, N.K., Doherty, M. et al (2003) EULAR Recommendations 2003: an evidence based approach to the management of knee osteoarthritis: report of a Task Force of the Standing Committee for International Clinical Studies Including Therapeutic Trials (ESCISIT). *Annals of the Rheumatic Diseases* **62**(12), 1145–1155. [Full text]
41. Lee, C., Straus, W.L., Balshaw, R. et al (2004) A comparison of the efficacy and safety of nonsteroidal antiinflammatory agents versus acetaminophen in the treatment of osteoarthritis: a meta-analysis. *Arthritis & Rheumatism* **51**(5), 746–754.
42. Lievense, A.M., Bierma-Zeinstra, S.M., Verhagen, A.P. et al (2002) Influence of obesity on the development of osteoarthritis of the hip: a systematic review. *Rheumatology* **41**(10), 1155–1162. [Full text]
43. Lievense, A.M., Bierma-Zeinstra, S.M., Verhagen, A.P. et al (2003) Influence of sporting activities on the development of osteoarthritis of the hip: a systematic review. *Arthritis & Rheumatism* **49**(2), 228–236.
44. Lin, J., Zhang, W., Jones, A. and Doherty, M. (2004) Efficacy of topical non-steroidal anti-inflammatory drugs in the treatment of osteoarthritis: meta-analysis of randomised controlled trials. *British Medical Journa[l]* **329**(7461), 324–326.
45. Little, C.V., Parsons, T. and Logan, S. (2000) *Herbal therapy for treating osteoarthritis (Cochrane Review)*. The Cochrane Library. Issue 4. Chichester, UK: John Wiley & Sons, Ltd. www.nelh.nhs.uk/cochrane.asp [Accessed: 04/04/2005]. [Full text]
46. Lo, G., LaValley, M., McAlindon, T. and Felson, D.T. (2003) Intra-articular hyaluronic acid in treatment of knee osteoarthritis: a meta-analysis. *Journal of the American Medical Association* **290**(23), 3115–3121. [Full text]
47. Mason, L., Moore, R.A., Edwards, J.E. et al (2004a) Topical NSAIDs for chronic musculoskeletal pain: systematic review and meta-analysis. *BMC Musculoskeletal Disorders* 5(1), 28.
48. Mason, L., Moore, R.A., Edwards, J.E. et al (2004b) Topical NSAIDs for acute pain: a meta-analysis. *BMC Family Practice* 5(1), 10.
49. Mason, L., Moore, R.A., Edwards, J.E. et al (2004c) Systematic review of efficacy of topical rubefacients containing salicylates for the treatment of acute and chronic pain. *British Medical Journal* **328**(7446), 995–998.
50. Mason, L., Moore, R.A., Derry, S. et al (2004d) Systematic review of topical capsaicin for the treatmen[t]

of chronic pain. *British Medical Journal* **328**(7446), 991–995.

51. McAlindon, T.E., LaValley, M., Gulin, J.P. and Felson, D.T. (2000) Glucosamine and chrondroitin for treatment of osteoarthritis: a systematic quality assessment and meta-analysis. *Journal of the American Medical Association* **283**(11), 1469–1475. [Full text]
52. MeReC (1993) Combination analgesics. *MeReC Bulletin* **4**(12), 45–48.
53. Messier, S.P., Loeser, R.F., Miller, G.D. et al (2004) Exercise and dietary weight loss in overweight and obese older adults with knee osteoarthritis: the Arthritis, Diet, and Activity Promotion Trial. *Arthritis & Rheumatism* **50**(5), 1501–1510.
54. Micromedex (2005) MICROMEDEX [CD-ROM]. (volume 124, second quarter 2005). Thomson Healthcare.
55. Miltner, O., Schneider, U., Siebert, C.H. et al (2002) Efficacy of intraarticular hyaluronic acid in patients with osteoarthritis – a prospective clinical trial. *Osteoarthritis & Cartilage* **10**(9), 680–686.
56. Moore, A., Collins, S., Carroll, D. and McQuay, H. (1997) Paracetamol with and without codeine in acute pain: a quantitative systematic review. *Pain* **70**(2–3), 193–201.
57. NICE (2001a) *Guidance on the use of cyclo-oxygenase (Cox) II selective inhibitors, celecoxib, rofecoxib, meloxicam and etodolac for osteoarthritis and rheumatoid arthritis.* Technology appraisal no. 27. National Institute for Health and Clinical Excellence. www.nice.org.uk [Accessed: 16/10/2003].
58. NICE (2001b) *Referral advice – a guide to appropriate referral from general to specialist services.* National Institute for Clinical Excellence. www.nice.org.uk [Accessed: 11/08/2002].
59. NICE (2004) *Dyspepsia: management of dyspepsia in adults in primary care: NICE guideline.* Clinical guideline 17. National Institute for Clinical Excellence. www.nice.org.uk [Accessed: 27/08/2004].
60. Osiri, M., Welch, V., Brosseau, L. et al (2000) *Transcutaneous electrical nerve stimulation for knee osteoarthritis (Cochrane Review).* The Cochrane Library. Issue 4. Chichester, UK: John Wiley & Sons, Ltd. www.nelh.nhs.uk/cochrane.asp [Accessed: 04/04/2005]. [Full text]
61. Ravaud, P., Moulinier, L., Giraudeau, B. et al (1999) Effects of joint lavage and steroid injection in patients with osteoarthritis of the knee: results of a multicenter, randomized, controlled trial. *Arthritis & Rheumatism* **42**(3), 475–482.
62. Richy, F., Bruyere, O., Ethgen, O. et al (2003) Structural and symptomatic efficacy of glucosamine and chondroitin in knee osteoarthritis: a comprehensive meta-analysis. *Archives of Internal Medicine* **163**(13), 1514–1522. [Full text]
63. Roddy, E., Zhang, W., Doherty, M. et al (2005) Evidence-based recommendations for the role of exercise in the management of osteoarthritis of the hip or knee – the MOVE consensus. *Rheumatology* **44**(1), 67–73. [Full text]
64. Rostom, A., Wells, G., Tugwell, P. et al (2002) *Prevention of NSAID-induced gastroduodenal ulcers (Cochrane Review).* The Cochrane Library. Issue 4. Chichester, UK: John Wiley & Sons, Ltd. www.nelh.nhs.uk/cochrane.asp [Accessed: 04/04/2005]. [Full text]
65. Scott, D., Smith, C., Lohmander, S. and Chard, J. (2004) *Osteoarthritis.* Clinical Evidence. Volume 11. www.clinicalevidence.com [Accessed: 31/03/2005].
66. SIGN (2000) *Management of early rheumatoid arthritis.* Report no. 48. Scottish Intercollegiate Guidelines Network. www.sign.ac.uk [Accessed: 01/04/2002].
67. Spector, T.D. (1996) Genetic influences on osteoarthritis in women: a twin study. *British Medical Journal* **312**(7036), 940–943. [Full text]
68. Towheed, T., Shea, B., Wells, G. and Hochberg, M. (1997) *Analgesia and non-aspirin, non-steroidal anti-inflammatory drugs for osteoarthritis of the hip (Cochrane Review).* The Cochrane Library. Issue 4. Chichester, UK: John Wiley & Sons, Ltd. www.nelh.nhs.uk/cochrane.asp [Accessed: 30/03/2005]. [Full text]
69. Towheed, T.E., Anastassiades, T.P., Shea, B. et al (2000) *Glucosamine therapy for treating osteoarthritis (Cochrane Review).* The Cochrane Library. Issue 2. Chichester, UK: John Wiley & Sons, Ltd. www.nelh.nhs.uk/cochrane.asp [Accessed: 30/03/2005]. [Full text]
70. Towheed, T.E., Judd, M.J., Hochberg, M.C. and Wells, G. (2003) *Acetaminophen for osteoarthritis (Cochrane Review).* The Cochrane Library. Issue 1. Chichester, UK: John Wiley & Sons, Ltd. www.nelh.nhs.uk/cochrane.asp [Accessed: 30/03/2005]. [Full text]
71. Tramer, M.R., Williams, J.E., Carroll, D. et al (1998) Comparing analgesic efficacy of non-steroidal anti-inflammatory drugs given by different routes in acute and chronic pain: a qualitative systematic review. *Acta Anaesthesiologica Scandinavica* **42**(1), 71–79.
72. Tugwell, P.S., Wells, G.A. and Shainhouse, J.Z. (2004) Equivalence study of a topical diclofenac solution (pennsaid(r)) compared with oral diclofenac in symptomatic treatment of osteoarthritis of the knee: a randomized controlled trial. *Journal of Rheumatology* **31**(10), 2002–2012.
73. Uthman, I., Raynauld, J.P. and Haraoui, B. (2003) Intra-articular therapy in osteoarthritis. *Postgraduate Medical Journal* **79**(934), 449–453. [Full text]
74. Wang, C.T., Lin, J., Chang, C.J. et al (2004) Therapeutic effects of hyaluronic acid on osteoarthritis of the knee. A meta-analysis of randomized controlled trials. *Journal of Bone & Joint Surgery – American Volume* **86-A**(3), 538–545. [Full text]
75. Watson, M.C., Brookes, S.T., Kirwan, J.R. and Faulkner, A. (1997) *Non-aspirin, non-steroidal anti-inflammatory drugs for treating osteoarthritis of the knee (Cochrane Review).* The Cochrane Library. Issue 1. Chichester, UK: John Wiley & Sons, Ltd. www.nelh.nhs.uk/cochrane.asp [Accessed: 30/03/2005]. [Full text]
76. Wegman, A., van der Windt, D., van Tulder, M. et al (2004) Nonsteroidal antiinflammatory drugs or acetaminophen for osteoarthritis of the hip or knee? A systematic review of evidence and guidelines. *Journal of Rheumatology* **31**(2), 344–354.
77. Zhang, W., Jones, A. and Doherty, M. (2004) Does paracetamol (acetaminophen) reduce the pain of osteoarthritis? A meta-analysis of randomised controlled trials. *Annals of the Rheumatic Diseases* **63**(8), 901–907.
78. Zhang, W., Doherty, M., Arden, N. et al (2005) EULAR evidence based recommendations for the management of hip osteoarthritis – report of a task force of the EULAR standing committee for international clinical studies including therapeutics (ESCISIT). *Annals of the Rheumatic Diseases* **64**(5), 669–681.

PRODIGY GUIDANCE

Osteoporosis — treatment

Last revised in October 2003

At the time of print this topic was being updated. The newly revised guidance will be issued on to the website in 2006.

www.prodigy.nhs.uk/guidance.asp?gt=Osteoporosis- treatment

Applies to people over the age of 16 years

This guidance is based on the Scottish Intercollegiate Guidelines Network (SIGN) Guideline *Management of Osteoporosis* (2003) and the Royal College of Physicians guideline *Glucocorticoid-induced Osteoporosis* (2003).

This guidance covers the identification and treatment of osteoporosis in postmenopausal women, elderly women, and men. It includes advice on assessing and managing the risk of falls and covers the prevention and treatment of glucocorticoid-induced osteoporosis.

This guidance does not cover prevention of osteoporosis (other than glucocorticoid-induced osteoporosis); or the treatment of osteoporosis in children, or premenopausal women.

There is separate PRODIGY guidance on the *Menopause*.

Goals

- Treatment of confirmed osteoporosis.
- Prevention of falls in people at risk of falling.
- Prevention of osteoporosis in people taking corticosteroids.
- Reduced number of fractures, particularly fractured femur [DH, 2003].
- Reduced number of deaths following fractured femur [DH, 2003].

Contents

Scenarios

- Who needs a bone mineral density scan? p.1376
- Who needs a falls assessment? p.1377
- Postmenopausal women with osteoporosis p.1377
- Elderly women with osteoporosis p.1379
- Men with osteoporosis p.1381
- Prevention and treatment of steroid-induced osteoporosis p.1382

Extended Information, p. 1384

O

Which scenario?

Note: younger men and premenopausal women usually require specialist investigation and treatment.

- **Who needs a bone mineral density scan?** Advice on targeting bone mineral density scans at those at highest risk of osteoporotic fracture.
- **Who needs a falls assessment?** Advice on the initial assessment of the risk of falling, and who to refer for further assessment.
- **Postmenopausal women with osteoporosis:** covers the management of postmenopausal women with confirmed osteoporosis.
- **Elderly women with osteoporosis:** covers the management of elderly women with confirmed osteoporosis.
- **Men with osteoporosis:** covers the management of men with confirmed osteoporosis.
- **Prevention and treatment of steroid-induced osteoporosis:** covers the prevention and treat of corticosteroid-induced osteoporosis in adult men and women.

Who needs a bone mineral density scan?

Which therapy?

- **Bone mineral density (BMD) scanning is not needed for people with two or more vertebral fractures.** They are a very high risk of further fractures, and should be offered treatment (provided that other causes of vertebral fracture have been excluded).
- **Others at high risk of osteoporotic fracture should be targeted for BMD scanning:**
  - X-ray evidence of osteopenia or vertebral deformity
  - Decrease in height
  - Previous low impact/fragility fracture
  - Long-term oral steroid treatment (3 months or more)
  - Menopause <45 years
  - History of amenorrhoea for >1 year
  - Primary hypogonadism
  - Chronic disorders associated with osteoporosis e.g. rheumatoid arthritis
  - Hyperthyroidism
  - Maternal family history of hip fracture
  - Body mass index <19
  - Quantitative ultrasound of the calcaneum, or peripheral dual energy X-ray absorptiometry (DEXA of the wrist or heel, suggesting osteoporosis
- **BMD should be measured by axial DEXA at two sites,** preferably the anteroposterior spine and hip.
- **People with a T-score of –2.5 or less should be offered treatment for osteoporosis.**

Practical prescribing points

For further information please see the *Medicines Compendium* (www.medicines.org.uk) or the *British National Formulary* (www.bnf.org).

Follow-up advice

Offer treatment to:

- Those with two or more vertebral fractures. Bone mineral density measurement is not required to confirm the diagnosis in these people.
- People with risk factors for osteoporosis and a T-score of –2.5 or less.

Exclude secondary causes of osteoporosis by:

- Full blood count (FBC) and erythrocyte sedimentation rate (ESR). (If the ESR is raised then serum and urine electrophoresis are indicated to exclude multiple myeloma.)

Bone, liver, and renal biochemistry: to exclude osteomalacia, other metabolic causes of osteoporosis, and renal osteodystrophy.

Oestradiol: to exclude hypogonadism in women

Testosterone: to exclude hypogonadism in men

Thyroid function tests: to exclude hyperthyroidism

'atient information leaflets

he following PILs are available at www.prodigy.nhs.uk

Calculate your calcium - SIGN

DEXA Scan

Menopause and HRT

National Osteoporosis Society

Osteoporosis

;hared decision making

You are at risk of developing osteoporosis (fragile bones which are more easy to break).

You should have a scan to check the thickness of your bones. If you have osteoporosis then medication can help to strengthen the bones.

The following also help to prevent, or slow down, 'bone thinning':

- A diet that includes at least 1000 mg calcium each day and plenty of vitamin D. For example, 1000 mg calcium is in:
  - A pint of milk, *plus*
  - 60 g (2 oz) hard cheese such as Cheddar or Edam, or one pot of yoghurt (125 g), or 60 g of sardines.
- Regular weight-bearing exercise such as brisk walking, jogging, dancing, etc.
- Stopping smoking if you smoke.
- Cutting down the amount of alcohol if you drink a lot.

)rug rationale

There are no prescriptions offered.

Who needs a falls assessment?

Vhich therapy?

Regularly ask elderly people whether they fall (e.g. annually).

A falls assessment is needed if:

- They have difficulty getting up from a chair without using their arms and walking a few paces
- They present following a fall, or have recurrent falls

Refer to a specialist falls service for a falls assessment where possible, as multiple risk factors require thorough assessment.

For further information on the assessment and management of the risk of falling, see *Managing the risk of falls.*

'ollow-up advice

Those at increased risk of falls should be offered multiple interventions to modify risks. This is often co-ordinated by the specialist falls service and should include:

- Assessment and correction of vision, if possible
- Correction of postural hypotension or other underlying medical conditions
- Review of medication to stop inappropriate medication
- Occupational therapy to identify and correct hazards in the home
- Repairs and improvements to the home
- Rehabilitation including physiotherapy to improve confidence after falls
- Weight-bearing exercise (focusing on strength and flexibility) and balance training
- Use of hip protectors (from hospital or community services: these are not available on FP10)

Patient information leaflets

The following PILs are available at www.prodigy.nhs.uk

- DEXA Scan
- National Osteoporosis Society
- Osteoporosis

Shared decision making

Drug rationale

- There are no prescriptions offered.

Postmenopausal women with osteoporosis

Which therapy?

- **Give lifestyle advice** on good calcium intake, exercise, stopping smoking, and alcohol.
- **Offer treatment to:**
  - Women with two or more vertebral fractures (dual energy X-ray absorptiometry [DEXA] scan not required)
  - Women with risk factors for osteoporosis and a T score of –2.5 or less
- **First-line treatment:** use alendronate, or risedronate (fracture reduction at spine and hip).
- **Second-line treatment:** consider raloxifene, intranasal calcitonin (salmon), or cyclical etidronate (fracture reduction at spine). Consider using hormone replacement therapy (off-licence use) if the benefits of treatment outweigh the risks (for prescriptions see the separate PRODIGY guidance on *Menopause*).
- **Use calcium + vitamin D as an adjunct to treatment if dietary intake is low.**
- If vitamin D deficiency is suspected, or the person is housebound, or in a residential or nursing home: give calcium 1.2 g + 800 iu vitamin D daily.

Factors affecting choice of treatment

- **Oesophageal stricture or achalasia:** if a bisphosphonate is required, use cyclical etidronate or risedronate (but monitor closely for adverse effects). Do not use alendronate.
- **Current or recent history of other upper gastrointestinal disorders:** if a bisphosphonate is required, use risedronate or cyclical etidronate. Avoid alendronate.
- **Venous thrombosis (past or at risk of):** avoid raloxifene.
- **Endometrial cancer, unexplained vaginal bleeding, or breast cancer:** do not use raloxifene.
- For information on the risks and benefits of hormone replacement therapy (HRT), see the separate PRODIGY guidance on *Menopause.*

Practical prescribing points

For further information please see the *Medicines Compendium* (www.medicines.org.uk) or the *British National Formulary* (www.bnf.org).

Bisphosphonates

- Bisphosphonates should be taken with a full glass of water whilst sitting upright or standing (not lying down), and the person should remain upright for at least 30 minutes afterwards.
- Ask people taking alendronate to report any symptoms suggesting oesophageal irritation, e.g. dysphagia, new or worsening heartburn, pain on swallowing, or retrosternal pain.
- Alendronate or risedronate should be taken at least 30 minutes before breakfast or any other medicines, especially calcium supplements or antacids.
- Etidronate should be taken 2 hours before and 2 hours after meals, or medicines containing calcium, aluminium, magnesium, or iron.

Other treatments

- **Raloxifene** does not relieve vasomotor symptoms, and may worsen them in some women.
- **Intranasal calcitonin** commonly causes nasal irritation, e.g. rhinitis, epistaxis. If mild ulceration of nasal mucosa occurs, discontinue treatment until healed.

Should I refer or investigate?

Refer?

- When there is evidence of continued bone loss on treatment, e.g. vertebral or peripheral fractures, loss of height.

Investigate?

Exclude secondary causes of osteoporosis by:

- Full blood count (FBC) and erythrocyte sedimentation rate (ESR). (If the ESR is raised then serum and urine electrophoresis are indicated to exclude multiple myeloma.)
- Bone, liver, and renal biochemistry: to exclude osteomalacia, other metabolic causes of osteoporosis, and renal osteodystrophy.
- Thyroid function tests: to exclude hyperthyroidism.

O

Patient information leaflets

The following PILs are available at www.prodigy.nhs.uk

- Calculate your calcium - SIGN
- DEXA Scan
- Menopause and HRT
- National Osteoporosis Society
- Osteoporosis

Shared decision making

- You have osteoporosis.
- **Medication** can increase bone strength and reduce the risk of fractures. Options include:
  - **Alendronate** or **risedronate.** These are the most commonly used.
    - Swallow the tablets whole with a glass of water on an empty stomach (30 minutes before breakfast).
    - Do not lie down for at least 30 minutes after taking (as they may irritate the gullet).
    - Report any symptoms of heartburn or difficulty swallowing to a doctor.
  - **Etidronate** is an alternative. You take this each day for 14 days followed by 76 days of a calcium tablet. You then repeat this 90-day cycle. When you take etidronate:
    - You may feel a little sickly.
    - Do not eat for 2 hours before and 2 hours after taking the tablet, to make sure it is absorbed.
  - **Raloxifene** or **calcitonin** nasal spray are less commonl used alternatives.
  - **Calcium and vitamin D supplements** are also often advised (unless you take in at least 1000 mg of calciu every day in your diet).
- The following also help to prevent or slow down 'bone thinning':
  - Regular weight-bearing exercise such as brisk walkin jogging, dancing, etc.
  - Stopping smoking if you smoke.
  - Cutting down the amount of alcohol if you drink a lo

Drug rationale

Drugs not included

- **Calcitriol** has been shown to reduce bone loss in postmenopausal women, but studies have had variable results.
- **Calcium supplementation alone** may reduce the rate of bone loss in postmenopausal women with osteoporosis and reduce the risk of vertebral fracture. Observational data suggests some effect on non-vertebral and hip fracture risk. It is less effective than other agents, and is not generally recommended other than in conjunction with other bone-protective agents [Royal College of Physicians of London, 1999]. In addition, many people over the age of 65 years require vitamin D supplementation to ensure an adequate vitamin D intak [SIGN, 2003].
- **Hormone replacement therapy** (HRT) is likely to reduc fracture risk in women with known low bone mineral density [SIGN, 2003], but this is an off-licence use. However, the risks and benefits of HRT are complex, and should be discussed with each woman before treatment is started. For information on the risks and benefits of HRT, see the separate PRODIGY guidance on *Menopause*.

Drugs included

- **Bisphosphonates: alendronate and risedronate are recommended as first-line treatments.** Both alendronate 10 mg daily, and risedronate 5 mg daily have been shown to prevent bone loss and reduce the risk of osteoporotic fracture at all major sites [Black et al, 199 Cummings et al, 1998]. Alendronate and risedronate ar both also available as once a week preparations.
- **Bisphosphonates: cyclical etidronate** reduces the risk of vertebral fracture, and may reduce hip fracture [Cranne et al, 2001]. It is most conveniently taken as Didronel PMO, a 90-day treatment pack containing disodium etidronate and Cacit tablets.
- **Raloxifene** prevents bone loss in the lumbar spine and proximal femur. A significant reduction in the risk of vertebral, but not hip, fracture has been shown [Ettinge et al, 1999]. Raloxifene should be considered if a bisphosphonate is inappropriate or not tolerated.
- **Intranasal calcitonin** reduced the incidence of radiographic vertebral fractures in one study. It has not been shown to have any effect on non-vertebral fractur [Chesnut et al, 2000]. It is more expensive than other therapies for osteoporosis.
- **Calcium and vitamin D supplements** are included as an adjunct to treatment for those who have, or are likely t have a low dietary intake of calcium and vitamin D. Th cheapest tablets providing at least 500 mg elemental calcium plus 400 iu vitamin D per tablet are included.

Prescriptions

Adjunct to treatment: lifestyle measures

Advice note: diet and lifestyle measures
- Age from 16 years onwards
- You can help to keep your bones healthy by: eating foods that are high in calcium; doing exercise such as walking; stopping smoking; avoid excessive alcohol. Aim to have a pint of milk a day, plus one pot of yoghurt or about 2 oz of hard cheese. If you find it difficult to eat enough calcium in your diet, your doctor can prescribe a calcium supplement for you.

1st-line treatment: alendronate or risedronate

Alendronate 10mg each morning
- Age from 16 years onwards
- Alendronate 10mg tablets. Take one tablet each morning; supply 28 tablets; NHS Cost £23.12.

Alendronate 70mg once a WEEK
- Age from 16 years onwards
- Alendronate 70mg tablets. Take one tablet once a WEEK (on the same day each week); supply 4 tablets; NHS Cost £23.12.

Risedronate 5mg each morning
- Age from 16 years onwards
- Risedronate 5mg tablets. Take one tablet each morning; supply 28 tablets; NHS Cost £21.83.

Risedronate 35mg once a WEEK
- Age from 16 years onwards
- Risedronate 35mg tablets. Take one tablet once a WEEK (on the same day each week); supply 4 tablets; NHS Cost £21.83.

2nd-line treatment options

Didronel PMO pack: one tablet once a day
- Age from 16 years onwards
- Didronel PMO tablets. Take one tablet once a day. See package insert for full instructions; supply 1 pack; NHS Cost £40.20.

Raloxifene 60mg once a day
- Age from 50 years onwards
- Raloxifene hydrochloride 60mg. Take one tablet once a day; supply 28 tablets; NHS Cost £21.74.

Intranasal calcitonin (salmon) 200iu once a day
- Age from 16 years onwards
- Calcitonin 200 iu/spray. Spray once into ONE nostril once a day; supply 4 ml; NHS Cost £41.00.

Consider using HRT if benefits outweigh risks
- Age from 16 years onwards
- Consider HRT if the woman also has menopausal symptoms that need treatment. See PRODIGY Menopause guidance for HRT prescriptions, and further information on the risks and benefits of HRT.

Adjunct to treatment: calcium + vitamin D

Elemental calcium 600mg + vitamin D 400iu per day
- Age from 16 years onwards
- Adcal-D3 tablets. Chew one tablet once a day; supply 28 tablets; NHS Cost £2.10.

Elemental calcium 1.2g + vitamin D 800iu per day
- Age from 16 years onwards
- Adcal-D3 tablets. Chew one tablet twice a day; supply 56 tablets; NHS Cost £4.20.

Elderly women with osteoporosis

Which therapy?

- **Assess the risk of falls** (see scenario *Who needs a falls assessment?* for further information).
- **Give lifestyle advice** on exercise, stopping smoking, and alcohol.
- **Offer treatment for osteoporosis to:**
  - Women with two or more vertebral fractures (dual energy X-ray absorptiometry [DEXA] scan not required)
  - Women with risk factors for osteoporosis and a T score of −2.5 or less
- **First-line treatment:** use alendronate or risedronate (fracture reduction at spine and hip).
- **Second-line treatment:** use calcium 1.2 g + vitamin D 800 iu as a sole treatment if aged 80+ years, frail or housebound (fracture reduction at hip), or consider cyclical etidronate or raloxifene (fracture reduction at spine).
- **Use calcium + vitamin D as an adjunct to bisphosphonates or raloxifene if dietary intake is low.**
- If vitamin D deficiency is suspected, give calcium 1.2 g + 800 iu vitamin D daily.
- Note: also give calcium 1.2 g + vitamin D 800 iu to prevent fractures, even in those without osteoporosis, particularly if housebound, frail, or in a residential or nursing home.

Factors affecting choice of treatment

- **Oesophageal stricture or achalasia:** if a bisphosphonate is required, use cyclical etidronate or risedronate (but monitor closely for adverse effects). Do not use alendronate.
- **Current or recent history of other upper gastrointestinal disorders:** if a bisphosphonate is required, use risedronate or cyclical etidronate. Avoid alendronate.
- **Venous thrombosis (past or at risk of):** avoid raloxifene.
- **Endometrial cancer, unexplained vaginal bleeding, or breast cancer:** do not use raloxifene.

O

Practical prescribing points

For further information please see the *Medicines Compendium* (www.medicines.org.uk) or the *British National Formulary* (www.bnf.org).

Bisphosphonates

- Bisphosphonates should be taken with a full glass of water whilst sitting upright or standing (not lying down), and the person should remain upright for at least 30 minutes afterwards.
- Ask people taking alendronate to report any symptoms suggesting oesophageal irritation, e.g. dysphagia, new or worsening heartburn, pain on swallowing, or retrosternal pain.
- Alendronate or risedronate should be taken at least 30 minutes before breakfast or any other medicines, especially calcium supplements or antacids.
- Etidronate should be taken 2 hours before and 2 hours after meals, or medicines containing calcium, aluminium, magnesium, or iron.

Should I refer or investigate?

Refer?

- When there is evidence of continued bone loss on treatment, e.g. vertebral or peripheral fractures, loss of height.

Investigate?

Exclude secondary causes of osteoporosis by:

- Full blood count (FBC) and erythrocyte sedimentation rate (ESR). (If the ESR is raised then serum and urine electrophoresis is indicated to exclude multiple myeloma.)
- Bone, liver, and renal biochemistry: to exclude osteomalacia, other metabolic causes of osteoporosis, and renal osteodystrophy.
- Thyroid function tests: to exclude hyperthyroidism.

Patient information leaflets

The following PILs are available at www.prodigy.nhs.uk

- Calculate your calcium - SIGN
- DEXA Scan
- Menopause and HRT
- National Osteoporosis Society
- Osteoporosis

Shared decision making

- You have osteoporosis.
- **Calcium and vitamin D supplements** help to increase bone strength and reduce the chance of fractures.
- **Medication** may also be advised to strengthen the bones. Options include:
  - **Alendronate** or **risedronate.** These are the most commonly used.
    - Swallow the tablets whole with a glass of water on an empty stomach (30 minutes before breakfast).
    - Do not lie down for at least 30 minutes after taking (as they may irritate the gullet).
    - Report any symptoms of heartburn or difficulty swallowing to a doctor.
  - **Etidronate** is an alternative. You take this each day for 14 days followed by 76 days of a calcium tablet. You then repeat this 90-day cycle. When you take etidronate:
    - You may feel a little sickly.
    - Do not eat for 2 hours before and 2 hours after taking the tablet, to make sure it is absorbed.
  - **Raloxifene** is another alternative.

O

Drug rationale

Drugs not included

- **Calcium supplementation alone** may reduce the rate of bone loss in postmenopausal women with osteoporosis and reduce the risk of vertebral fracture. Observational data suggests some effect on non-vertebral and hip fracture risk. It is less effective than other agents, and is not generally recommended other than in conjunction with other bone-protective agents [Royal College of Physicians of London, 1999]. In addition, many people over the age of 65 years require vitamin D supplementation to ensure an adequate vitamin D intake [SIGN, 2003].
- **Calcitriol** has been shown to reduce bone loss in postmenopausal women, but studies have had variable results. Again, there is a lack of data for older women.
- **Hormone replacement therapy (HRT):** the monthly withdrawal bleeds and oestrogenic/progestagenic adverse effects would make this difficult to tolerate in women over the age of 75 years. The risks and benefits of HRT are complex, and should be discussed with each woman before treatment is started. Note that HRT is not licensed for the treatment of osteoporosis. For information on the risks and benefits of HRT, see the separate PRODIGY guidance on *Menopause*.
- **Intranasal calcitonin** reduced the incidence of radiographic vertebral fractures in one study. It has not been shown to have any effect on non-vertebral fractures [Chesnut et al, 2000]. However, there is a lack of data about older women.

Drugs included

- **Calcium and vitamin D supplements** are included as an adjunct to treatment for those who have, or are likely to have a low dietary intake of calcium and vitamin D. A dose of 1 g elemental calcium and 800 iu vitamin D may also be given for the prevention or treatment of osteoporosis in the frail, elderly (age 80+), and housebound [Chapuy et al, 1994]. The cheapest tablets providing at least 500 mg elemental calcium plus 400 iu vitamin D per tablet are included.
- **Bisphosphonates: alendronate and risedronate** are included. Both alendronate 10 mg daily, and risedronate 5 mg daily have been shown to prevent bone loss and reduce the risk of osteoporotic fracture at all major sites [Black et al, 1996; Cummings et al, 1998]. Alendronate and risedronate are both also available as once-a-week preparations.
- **Bisphosphonates: cyclical etidronate** reduces the risk of vertebral fracture, and may reduce hip fracture [Cranney et al, 2001]. It is most conveniently taken as Didronel PMO, a 90-day treatment pack containing disodium etidronate and Cacit tablets.
- **Raloxifene:** experience is limited in elderly women. The average age of study participants was 66 years, although women up to the age of 80 years were recruited [Ettinger et al, 1999]. Raloxifene should therefore only be considered in elderly women with confirmed osteoporosis in whom a bisphosphonate is contraindicated or not tolerated.

Prescriptions

Adjunct to treatment: lifestyle measures

Advice note: diet and lifestyle measures

- Age from 16 years onwards
- You can help to keep your bones healthy by: eating foods that are high in calcium; doing exercise such as walking; stopping smoking; avoid excessive alcohol. Aim to have a pint of milk a day, plus one pot of yoghurt or about 2 oz of hard cheese. If you find it difficult to eat enough calcium in your diet, your doctor can prescribe a calcium supplement for you.

1st-line treatment: alendronate or risedronate

Alendronate 10mg each morning

- Age from 65 years onwards
- Alendronate 10mg tablets. Take one tablet each morning; supply 28 tablets; NHS Cost £23.12.

Alendronate 70mg once a WEEK

- Age from 65 years onwards
- Alendronate 70mg tablets. Take one tablet once a WEEK (on the same day each week); supply 4 tablets; NHS Cost £23.12.

Risedronate 5mg each morning

- Age from 65 years onwards
- Risedronate 5mg tablets. Take one tablet each morning; supply 28 tablets; NHS Cost £21.83.

Risedronate 35mg once a WEEK

- Age from 65 years onwards
- Risedronate 35mg tablets. Take one tablet once a WEEK (on the same day each week); supply 4 tablets; NHS Cost £21.83.

2nd-line treatment options

Elemental calcium 1.2g + vitamin D 800iu per day
- Age from 65 years onwards
- Adcal-D3 tablets. Chew one tablet twice a day; supply 56 tablets; NHS Cost £4.20.

Didronel PMO pack: one tablet once a day
- Age from 65 years onwards
- Didronel PMO tablets. Take one tablet once a day. See package insert for full instructions; supply 1 pack; NHS Cost £40.20.

Raloxifene 60mg once a day
- Age from 65 years onwards
- Raloxifene hydrochloride 60mg. Take one tablet once a day; supply 28 tablets; NHS Cost £21.74.

Adjunct to bisphosphonates/raloxifene: calcium + vitamin D

Elemental calcium 600mg + vitamin D 400iu per day
- Age from 65 years onwards
- Adcal-D3 tablets. Chew one tablet once a day; supply 28 tablets; NHS Cost £2.10.

Elemental calcium 1.2g + vitamin D 800iu per day
- Age from 65 years onwards
- Adcal-D3 tablets. Chew one tablet twice a day; supply 56 tablets; NHS Cost £4.20.

Prevention of osteoporosis in frail/housebound/ elderly women

Elemental calcium 1.2g + vitamin D 800iu per day
- Age from 65 years onwards
- Adcal-D3 tablets. Chew one tablet twice a day; supply 56 tablets; NHS Cost £4.20.

Men with osteoporosis

Which therapy?

- **Consider referring all men with osteoporosis** for specialist assessment.
- Exclude secondary causes of osteoporosis.
- **Assess the risk of falls** (see scenario *Who needs a falls assessment?* for further information).
- **Give lifestyle advice** on good calcium intake, exercise, stopping smoking, and alcohol.
- **Offer treatment for osteoporosis to:**
  - Men with two or more vertebral fractures (dual energy X-ray absorptiometry [DEXA] scan not required)
  - Men with risk factors for osteoporosis and a T score of −2.5 or less

Treat with alendronate and give calcium + vitamin D if dietary intake is low. Seek specialist advice for other treatment options if alendronate is contraindicated or not tolerated.

Or, use calcium 1.2 g + 800 iu vitamin D as a sole therapy in the frail, elderly (aged 80+ years), or housebound.

Note: also give calcium 1.2 g + vitamin D 800 iu to prevent fractures in elderly men even without osteoporosis, particularly if housebound, frail, or in a residential or nursing home.

Factors affecting choice of treatment

Oesophageal stricture or achalasia: do not use alendronate.

Current or recent history of other upper gastrointestinal disorders: avoid alendronate.

Practical prescribing points

For further information please see the *Medicines Compendium* (www.medicines.org.uk) or the *British National Formulary* (www.bnf.org).

- Bisphosphonates should be taken with a full glass of water whilst sitting upright or standing (not lying down), and the person should remain upright for at least 30 minutes afterwards.
- Ask people taking alendronate to report any symptoms suggesting oesophageal irritation, e.g. dysphagia, new or worsening heartburn, pain on swallowing, or retrosternal pain.
- Alendronate should be taken at least 30 minutes before breakfast or any other medicines, especially calcium supplements or antacids.

Should I refer or investigate?

Refer?

- When there is evidence of continued bone loss on treatment, e.g. vertebral or peripheral fractures, loss of height.

Investigate?

- **All men with osteoporosis should be investigated for hypogonadism.**
- **Exclude secondary causes of osteoporosis** by performing the following investigations:
  - Testosterone: to exclude hypogonadism
  - Full blood count (FBC) and erythrocyte sedimentation rate (ESR). (If ESR is raised then serum and urine electrophoresis is indicated to exclude multiple myeloma.)
  - Bone, liver, and renal biochemistry: to exclude osteomalacia, other metabolic causes of osteoporosis, and renal osteodystrophy
  - Thyroid function tests: to exclude hyperthyroidism

Patient information leaflets

The following PILs are available at www.prodigy.nhs.uk
- Calculate your calcium - SIGN
- DEXA Scan
- National Osteoporosis Society
- Osteoporosis

Shared decision making

- You have osteoporosis.
- **Alendronate tablets** help to increase bone strength and reduce the risk of fractures.
  - Swallow these tablets whole with a glass of water on an empty stomach (30 minutes before breakfast).
  - Do not lie down for at least 30 minutes after taking (as they may irritate the gullet).
  - Report any symptoms of heartburn or difficulty swallowing to a doctor.
- **Calcium and vitamin D supplements** are also commonly advised (unless you take in at least 1000 mg of calcium every day in your diet).
- The following also help to prevent, or slow down 'bone thinning':
  - Taking regular weight-bearing exercise such as brisk walking, jogging, dancing, etc.
  - Stopping smoking if you smoke.
  - Cutting down the amount of alcohol if you drink a lot.

Drug rationale

Drugs not included

- **Bisphosphonates: risedronate and cyclical etidronate** have not been studied in men with osteoporosis, although there are some data on their use in men with glucocorticoid-induced osteoporosis.
- **Calcium supplementation alone** may reduce the rate of bone loss in postmenopausal women with osteoporosis and reduce the risk of vertebral fracture. Observational data suggests some effect on non-vertebral and hip fracture risk. It is less effective than other agents, and is not generally recommended other than in conjunction with other bone-protective agents [Royal College of Physicians of London, 1999]. In addition, many people over the age of 65 years require vitamin D supplementation to ensure an adequate vitamin D intake [SIGN, 2003].
- **Hormone replacement therapy (testosterone)** has not been studied in men with osteoporosis. There is no convincing data of efficacy in changing bone mineral density (BMD) in eugonadal men, although testosterone in hypogonadal men may increase spinal BMD [SIGN, 2003].
- **Other available treatments for osteoporosis** are not included because they have not been prospectively studied in men (intranasal calcitionin or calcitriol) or are not suitable for men (raloxifene).

Drugs included

- **Bisphosphonates: alendronate** is the only antiresorptive drug to have been studied in men with osteoporosis. It has been found to reduce morphometric vertebral fractures and decreases in vertebral height [Orwoll et al, 2000].
- **Calcium and vitamin D supplements** are included as an adjunct to treatment for those who have, or are likely to have a low dietary intake of calcium and vitamin D. A dose of 1 g elemental calcium and 800 iu vitamin D may also be given for the prevention or treatment of osteoporosis in the frail, elderly (age 80+), and housebound [Chapuy et al, 1994]. The cheapest tablets providing at least 500 mg elemental calcium plus 400 iu vitamin D per tablet are included.

Prescriptions

Adjunct to treatment: lifestyle measures

Advice note: diet and lifestyle measures

- Age from 16 years onwards
- You can help to keep your bones healthy by: eating foods that are high in calcium; doing exercise such as walking; stopping smoking; avoid excessive alcohol. Aim to have a pint of milk a day, plus one pot of yoghurt or about 2 oz of hard cheese. If you find it difficult to eat enough calcium in your diet, your doctor can prescribe a calcium supplement for you.

1st-line treatment: alendronate

Alendronate 10mg each morning

- Age from 16 years onwards
- Alendronate 10mg tablets. Take one tablet each morning; supply 28 tablets; NHS Cost £23.12.

Alendronate 70mg once a WEEK

- Age from 16 years onwards
- Alendronate 70mg tablets. Take one tablet once a WEEK (on the same day each week); supply 4 tablets; NHS Cost £23.12.

2nd-line treatment option for frail/elderly/housebound men

Elemental calcium 1.2g + vitamin D 800iu per day

- Age from 16 years onwards
- Adcal-D3 tablets. Chew one tablet twice a day; supply 56 tablets; NHS Cost £4.20.

Adjunct to alendronate: calcium + vitamin D

Elemental calcium 600mg + vitamin D 400iu per day

- Age from 16 years onwards
- Adcal-D3 tablets. Chew one tablet once a day; supply 2 tablets; NHS Cost £2.10.

Elemental calcium 1.2g + vitamin D 800iu per day

- Age from 16 years onwards
- Adcal-D3 tablets. Chew one tablet twice a day; supply 56 tablets; NHS Cost £4.20.

Prevention of osteoporosis in frail/housebound/elderly men

Elemental calcium 1.2g + vitamin D 800iu per day

- Age from 16 years onwards
- Adcal-D3 tablets. Chew one tablet twice a day; supply 56 tablets; NHS Cost £4.20.

Prevention and treatment of steroid-induced osteoporosis

Which therapy?

Osteoporosis prophylaxis for people on oral steroids

- **People starting or currently on any dose of *oral* steroids for more than 3 months should be given osteoporosis prophylaxis if they:**
  - Are aged over 65 years
  - Had a previous fragility fracture (i.e. occurring after age 40 years on minimal trauma)
- **In other individuals, measure bone mineral density usin dual energy X-ray absorptiometry (DEXA) to assess fracture risk.** Consider treatment if T score –1.5 or lower.
- **Give lifestyle advice** on good calcium intake, exercise, stopping smoking, and alcohol.
- **First-line therapy:** use alendronate, risedronate, or cyclical etidronate.
- Use calcium + vitamin D as an adjunct to bisphosphonates if dietary intake is low.
- **Second-line therapy:** consider alfacalcidol or calcitriol, especially for women of childbearing age in whom bisphosphonates should be used with extreme caution.
- Hormone replacement therapy can also be considered i postmenopausal women if the benefits of treatment outweigh the risks. See the separate PRODIGY guidanc on *Menopause*.

Factors affecting choice of treatment

- **Pregnancy or breastfeeding:** do not use bisphosphonate Consider alfacalcidol or calcitriol, but high doses have caused hypercalcaemia in infants during breastfeeding.
- **Oesophageal stricture or achalasia:** if a bisphosphonate is required, use cyclical etidronate or risedronate (but monitor closely for adverse effects). Do not use alendronate.
- **Current or recent history of other upper gastrointestina disorders:** if a bisphosphonate is required, use risedronate, or cyclical etidronate. Avoid alendronate.

Practical prescribing points

For further information please see the *Medicines Compendium* (www.medicines.org.uk) or the *British National Formulary* (www.bnf.org).

Bisphosphonates

Bisphosphonates should be taken with a full glass of water while sitting upright or standing (but not lying down), and the person should remain upright for at least 30 minutes afterwards.
Ask people taking alendronate to report any symptoms suggesting oesophageal irritation, e.g. dysphagia, new or worsening heartburn, pain on swallowing, or retrosternal pain.
Take alendronate or risedronate at least 30 minutes before breakfast or any other medicines, especially calcium supplements or antacids.
Etidronate should be taken 2 hours before and 2 hours after meals, or medicines containing calcium, aluminium, magnesium, or iron.

Alfacalcidol and calcitriol

May cause hypercalcaemia. Monitor serum calcium and creatinine levels.

Follow-up advice

Alfacalcidol: check serum calcium and creatinine levels after 1 week, and then monthly to exclude hypercalcaemia.
Calcitriol: check serum calcium and creatinine levels at 4 weeks, 3 months, 6 months, and then at 6-monthly intervals to exclude hypercalcaemia.

Should I refer or investigate?

Refer?

Premenopausal women who are hypogonadal, and hypogonadal men.
When there is evidence of continued bone loss on treatment, e.g. vertebral or peripheral fractures, loss of height.

Investigate?

All men and premenopausal women (if periods are irregular or absent) should be investigated for hypogonadism.
Exclude secondary causes of osteoporosis by performing the following investigations:

- Oestradiol: to exclude hypogonadism in women
- Testosterone: to exclude hypogonadism in men
- Full blood count (FBC) and erythrocyte sedimentation rate (ESR). (If ESR is raised then serum and urine electrophoresis is indicated to exclude multiple myeloma.)
- Bone, liver, and renal biochemistry: to exclude osteomalacia, other metabolic causes of osteoporosis, and renal osteodystrophy.
- Thyroid function tests: to exclude hyperthyroidism.

Patient information leaflets

The following PILs are available at www.prodigy.nhs.uk
Calculate your calcium - SIGN
DEXA Scan
National Osteoporosis Society
Osteoporosis

Shared decision making

- Regular steroid medication may cause bone thinning, and lead to osteoporosis.
- Medication can help increase bone strength and reduce the chance of fractures. Options include:
  - **Alendronate** or **risedronate.** These are the most commonly used.
    - Swallow the tablets whole with a glass of water on an empty stomach (30 minutes before breakfast).
    - Do not lie down for at least 30 minutes after taking (as they may irritate the gullet).
    - Report any symptoms of heartburn or difficulty swallowing to a doctor.
  - **Etidronate** is an alternative. You take this each day for 14 days followed by 76 days of a calcium tablet. You then repeat this 90-day cycle. When you take etidronate:
    - You may feel a little sickly.
    - Do not eat for 2 hours before and 2 hours after taking the tablet, to make sure it is absorbed.
  - **Calcitriol or alfacalcidol** are alternatives, especially for women of childbearing age as you should not take the above medicines if you are pregnant.
  - **Calcium and vitamin D supplements** are also commonly advised (unless you take in at least 1000 mg of calcium every day in your diet).
- The following also help to prevent, or slow down, 'bone thinning':
  - Regular weight-bearing exercise such as brisk walking, jogging, dancing, etc.
  - Stopping smoking if you smoke.
  - Cutting down the amount of alcohol if you drink a lot.

Drug rationale

Drugs not included

- **Intranasal calcitonin** has been studied in glucocorticoid-induced bone loss, but the results are conflicting.
- **Calcium supplements,** as a sole therapy for glucocorticoid-induced osteoporosis are ineffective for preventing bone loss. **They are** not generally recommended other than in conjunction with other bone-protective agents. In addition, many people over the age of 65 years require vitamin D supplementation to ensure an adequate vitamin D intake [SIGN, 2003].
- **Hormone replacement therapy (HRT)** has been found to increase bone mineral density at the spine, but not at the hip, in people taking glucocorticoids. However, the risks and benefits of HRT are complex, and should be discussed with each woman before treatment is started. Note that HRT is not licensed for the prevention or treatment of glucocorticoid-induced osteoporosis. For information on the risks and benefits of HRT, see the separate PRODIGY guidance on *Menopause*.
- **Raloxifene,** a selective oestrogen receptor modulator (SERM), has not been evaluated in corticosteroid-induced bone loss.

[Royal College of Physicians of London, 2002]

Drugs included

- **Bisphosphonates** (alendronate, risedronate, cyclical etidronate): *post hoc* analyses of studies of risedronate and etidronate, and secondary end points in a study of alendronate, found that all these drugs reduced the risk of vertebral fractures in people taking glucocorticoids. However, fracture reduction was not a primary end point in any of these studies. The once-weekly preparations of alendronate and risedronate are also

O

included, but are not licensed for prevention of steroid-induced osteoporosis
- **Vitamin D analogues:** alfacalcidol and calcitriol use (off-licence) have both demonstrated increases in bone mineral density (BMD) at the spine and hip in some studies, although the data is conflicting. However, studies show a consistent increase in BMD at the spine with alfacalcidol use.
- **Calcium and vitamin D supplements** are included as an adjunct to bisphosphonates for people with a low dietary intake of calcium and vitamin D. They should not be used with vitamin D analogues, due to the increased risk of hypercalcaemia. The cheapest tablets providing at least 500 mg elemental calcium + 400 iu vitamin D per tablet are included.

[Royal College of Physicians of London, 2002]

Prescriptions

Adjunct to treatment: lifestyle measures

Advice note: diet and lifestyle measures
- Age from 16 years onwards
- You can help to keep your bones healthy by: eating foods that are high in calcium; doing exercise such as walking; stopping smoking; avoid excessive alcohol. Aim to have a pint of milk a day, plus one pot of yoghurt or about 2 oz of hard cheese. If you find it difficult to eat enough calcium in your diet, your doctor can prescribe a calcium supplement for you.

1st-line treatment: bisphosphonates

Alendronate 10mg each morning
- Age from 16 years onwards
- Alendronate 10mg tablets. Take one tablet each morning; supply 28 tablets; NHS Cost £23.12.

Alendronate 70mg once a WEEK
- Age from 16 years onwards
- Alendronate 70mg tablets. Take one tablet once a WEEK (on the same day each week); supply 4 tablets; NHS Cost £23.12.

Risedronate 5mg once a day
- Age from 16 years onwards
- Risedronate 5mg tablets. Take one tablet once a day; supply 28 tablets; NHS Cost £21.83.

Risedronate 35mg once a WEEK
- Age from 16 years onwards
- Risedronate 35mg tablets. Take one tablet once a WEEK (on the same day each week); supply 4 tablets; NHS Cost £21.83.

Didronel PMO pack: one tablet once a day
- Age from 16 years onwards
- Didronel PMO tablets. Take one tablet once a day. See package insert for full instructions; supply 90 pack; NHS Cost £40.20.

2nd-line treatment: alfacalcidol or calcitriol

Alfacalcidol 1microgram once a day
- Age from 16 years onwards
- Alfacalcidol 1mcg capsules. Take one capsule once a day; supply 30 capsules; NHS Cost £10.02.

Alfacalcidol 500nanograms once a day
- Age from 60 years onwards
- Alfacalcidol 0.5microgram caps. Take one capsule once a day; supply 30 capsules; NHS Cost £6.69.

Calcitriol 250nanograms twice a day
- Age from 16 years onwards
- Calcitriol 250nanogram caps. Take one capsule twice a day; supply 56 capsules; NHS Cost £11.53.

Adjunct to bisphosphonates: calcium + vitamin D

Elemental calcium 600mg + vitamin D 400iu per day
- Age from 16 years onwards
- Adcal-D3 tablets. Chew one tablet once a day; supply 28 tablets; NHS Cost £2.00.

Elemental calcium 1.2g + vitamin D 800iu per day
- Age from 16 years onwards
- Adcal-D3 tablets. Chew one tablet twice a day; supply 56 tablets; NHS Cost £4.00.

Extended Information

Background information

- What is it? p.1384
- How common is it? p.1384
- What are the risk factors for osteoporosis? p.1384
- What are the risk factors for fracture? p.1385
- What are the secondary causes of osteoporosis? p.1385
- How do I know my patient has osteoporosis? p.1385
- What else might it be? p.1385
- Complications and prognosis p.1385

What is it?

- **Osteoporosis is a disease characterized by low bone mass and microarchitectural deterioration of bone tissue,** leading to enhanced bone fragility and a consequent increase in fracture risk.
- The World Health Organization defines osteoporosis on the basis of bone mineral density (BMD).
- BMD is usually reported as a T-score. This is the number of standard deviations by which the individual's BMD differs from the mean peak BMD for young adults of the same gender. For every standard deviation below the mean, the risk of fracture is approximately doubled.
- A T-score of –2.5 or less indicates osteoporosis.
- A T-score of between –1 and –2.5 indicates osteopaenia.
- However, this arbitrary threshold should be used with caution: the proportion of individuals classified as having osteoporosis will vary substantially, depending on the site and method of bone density measurement.
- A Z-score is another measure of BMD. It is the number of standard deviations by which the individual's BMD differs from the mean BMD for people of the same age.

[SIGN, 2003]

How common is it?

- **One in three women and one in 12 men over the age of 50 years will sustain an osteoporotic fracture in their lifetime** [National Osteoporosis Society, 2002].
- On an average GP list of 2000 people there will be 140 women affected by osteoporosis.
- The lifetime risk of osteoporosis in men is approximately half that of women (see also Table 1).
- In the UK, osteoporosis results in over 310,000 fractures each year, with a cost to the NHS of over £1.7 billion [National Osteoporosis Society, 2002].

Table 1: Prevalence of osteoporosis.

	60–69 years	70–79 years	80+ years
Men	6%	14%	24%
Women	14%	37%	61%

What are the risk factors for osteoporosis?

- There are many factors that increase the risk of osteoporosis (Table 2).

- The more risk factors that are present, the greater the risk.

Table 2: Risk factors for osteoporosis.

Strongest risk factors	Other significant risk factors
Female sex	Caucasian or Asian origin
Age >60 years	Early menopause
Family history of osteoporosis	Low BMI (<19)
	Smoking
	Low calcium intake
	Low vitamin D levels (lack of sunlight and/or low dietary intake)
	Sedentary lifestyle
	Long-term (3 months or more) oral corticosteroid use

BMI, body mass index

Alcohol is thought to be a risk factor for low bone mineral density. However, the evidence is inconsistent, as most studies do not include people with excessive alcohol intake.

[SIGN, 2003]

What are the risk factors for fracture?

Osteoporosis is a risk factor for fracture.

People who have suffered one or more fragility fracture are at the highest risk of further fractures. This includes painless vertebral fractures that cause loss of height, or kyphosis.

Falls are one of the biggest risk factors for fracture, and people at high risk of falling are at high risk of sustaining a fracture.

Key risk factors for hip fracture include:

- Previous low-trauma fracture after the age of 50 years
- Maternal history of hip fracture
- Low body mass index (<19)

[DH, 2003]

What are the secondary causes of osteoporosis?

Many clinical conditions, and some drugs are also associated with osteoporosis. The most common secondary causes of osteoporosis are:

- **Endocrine:** thyrotoxicosis, and male hypogonadism.
- **Malabsorption or nutritional:** inflammatory bowel disease, chronic liver disease, coeliac disease, anorexia nervosa, and vitamin D deficiency.
- **Drugs:** long-term corticosteroid use, and Depo-Provera (although the evidence for Depo-Provera is conflicting). Phenytoin, phenobarbitone, and overtreatment with thyroid hormone have also been associated with osteoporosis.
- **Other:** rheumatoid arthritis, myeloma, and renal disease including renal tubular acidosis.

[SIGN, 2003]

How do I know my patient has osteoporosis?

- The following suggest a possible diagnosis of osteoporosis:
  - Previous low impact/fragility fracture
  - Back pain, kyphosis, and loss of height secondary to vertebral crush fracture (after radiological confirmation)
  - Radiological evidence of osteopenia or vertebral deformity, or both
  - Risk factors such as prolonged corticosteroid use; untreated early menopause (younger than 45 years); untreated prolonged amenorrhoea (greater than 1 year but not associated with the menopause); or family history of maternal hip fracture
  - Quantitative ultrasound of the calcaneum, or peripheral dual energy X-ray absorptiometry (DEXA) of the wrist or heel, suggesting osteoporosis
  - Computed axial tomography suggesting osteoporosis
- Bone mineral density (BMD) measurement using DEXA is needed to confirm the diagnosis of osteoporosis in these people before a decision about treatment is made.
- People with two or more vertebral fractures (including painless fractures) are at very high risk of further fractures. Treatment can be started without the need for BMD measurement, provided that underlying destructive disease such as myeloma or infection has been excluded.

[Royal College of Physicians of London, 1999; SIGN, 2003]

What else might it be?

- Osteoarthritis
- Degenerative disc disease
- Osteomalacia
- Skeletal metastases
- Multiple myeloma

Complications and prognosis

Complications

- Fractures (often following falls) can occur at any site, but commonly occur at the spine, wrist, and hip [SIGN, 2003].
- Hip fractures are the most common serious injury related to falls [DH, 2003].
- However, not all osteoporotic fractures are related to falls: only 25% of vertebral fractures are associated with falls [National Osteoporosis Society, 2002].

Prognosis

- Fifty per cent of people with hip fractures lose the ability to live independently [National Osteoporosis Society, 2002].
- Excess mortality after a hip fracture is approximately 20% [National Osteoporosis Society, 2002].
- Men have fewer osteoporotic fractures but greater fracture-associated morbidity and mortality.

Risk of further fractures

- People who have suffered one or more fragility fractures are at increased risk of further fractures. This includes painless vertebral fractures that cause loss of height, or kyphosis.
- Existing vertebral fractures increase the risk of further vertebral fracture at least sevenfold [Ross et al, 1993]. Only half of people with vertebral fractures have pain, but the morbidity in regard to future fracture risk and mortality risk is the same [Ross, 1997].
- Vertebral fractures also increase the 5-year risk of a hip fracture by 13% in both men and women aged 65 years or older [van Staa et al, 2002].

Management issues

- Identifying people at risk of an osteoporotic fracture p.1386
- Managing the risk of falls p.1386
- Who should be offered treatment for osteoporosis? p.1387
- How should I treat osteoporosis? p.1387
- Supporting evidence for drug treatment p.1388
- What is the place of hormone replacement therapy? p.1389
- Is bone mass maintained after drug treatment is stopped? p.1389
- Glucocorticoid-induced osteoporosis p.1389

- Medicines management p.1390

Identifying people at risk of an osteoporotic fracture

- Osteoporosis is a risk factor for fracture.
- Osteoporotic fractures commonly occur at the wrist, spine, and hip.
- **The risk of sustaining a fracture depends both on the strength of the bone and on the likelihood of falls.**
- The assessment and management of the risk of falling is therefore equally important in fracture prevention, particularly for hip and wrist fractures (see the section *Managing the risk of falls*).
- It is not known which combination of risk factors has most effect on the risk of osteoporosis. Current risk scores available for osteoporosis are not of satisfactory quality and have not been validated [SIGN, 2003].
- **Those at highest risk of osteoporotic fracture should be targeted for bone mineral density (BMD) scanning to confirm whether treatment is required** [Royal College of Physicians of London, 1999; DH, 2003].
- The Royal College of Physicians recommends BMD scanning in the following circumstances:
  - Previous low impact/fragility fracture
  - Kyphosis, and loss of height secondary to vertebral crush fracture (after radiological confirmation)
  - X-ray evidence of osteopenia or vertebral deformity
  - Oral steroids for 3 months or more (see *Glucocorticoid-induced osteoporosis*)
  - Premature menopause (<45 years)
  - History of amenorrhoea for more than 1 year
  - Primary hypogonadism
  - Chronic disorders associated with osteoporosis, e.g. rheumatoid arthritis, hyperthyroidism
  - Maternal family history of hip fracture
  - Body mass index < 19
- People in whom quantitative ultrasound of the calcaneum or peripheral dual energy X-ray absorptiometry (DEXA) of the wrist or heel suggest osteoporosis, should also be referred for BMD scanning.
- In areas where DEXA scanning is not available, it is recommended that local guidelines, which will take into account locally available resources, are followed.
- People with two or more vertebral fractures (including painless fractures) are at very high risk of further fractures. Treatment can be started without the need for BMD measurement, provided that underlying destructive disease such as myeloma or infection has been excluded [SIGN, 2003].

BMD scanning

- **BMD should be measured by DEXA at two sites,** preferably the anteroposterior spine and hip [SIGN, 2003].
- Ideally, the annual hip fracture risk should be included in the DEXA bone mineral scan report.
- **A T-score of –2.5 or below indicates osteoporosis.**
- **Note: BMD assessment alone has high specificity but low sensitivity.** The low sensitivity means that in the general population, half of all osteoporotic fractures will occur in women, who are said not to have osteoporosis. Therefore, a case-finding strategy for individuals with strong risk factors for osteoporosis is recommended.

Methods of scanning that are not recommended

- Quantitative computed tomography can be used to measure BMD, but is costly, not widely available, and the radiation dose is relatively high.
- Plain X-rays should not be used for the diagnosis or exclusion of osteoporosis. When plain films are interpreted as 'severe osteopenia' it is appropriate to suggest referral for DEXA.
- Peripheral techniques (e.g. DEXA at the forearm or heel, or quantitative ultrasound) are often inappropriately used as screening methods for diagnosis or monitoring due to their portability and modest cost.
  - Forearm or heel DEXA scanning shows only a moderate correlation with axial bone mineral density and therefore is not appropriate for making treatment decisions or monitoring response to treatment.
  - The precision of quantitative ultrasound is generally poor, and changes at the heel may not reflect changes at the spine or hip. It is therefore not recommended fo investigating or monitoring people suspected of being at risk of osteoporosis, or to justify initiating treatment.
- Biochemical markers have no role in the diagnosis of osteoporosis or in the selection of patients for BMD measurements.

[SIGN, 2003]

Monitoring BMD

- **Repeat measurements should only be performed if they influence treatment.** There is insufficient evidence to determine whether repeating BMD 2 years after starting treatment is useful [SIGN, 2003].
- If repeat measurements are thought to be useful, take them using DEXA at the same sites as the original scan, e.g. the spine and hip.

Managing the risk of falls

- **Falls are one of the biggest risk factors for fracture,** and assessment and management of the risk of falling is as important as treating osteoporosis.
- **The tendency to fall increases with age:** risk factors for falling tend to increase in prevalence with age, leading to more frequent falls.
- **All elderly people should have their risk of falls assessed regularly** (including those without osteoporosis).

Assessing the risk of falls

- It is important to ask people whether they fall, as many older people who fall do not seek medical advice.
- People who can get up from a chair without using their arms, walk several paces and return with no difficulty or unsteadiness (i.e. the 'Get Up and Go' test), are at low risk of falling.
- **People who have difficulty with the 'Get Up and Go' test have to stop walking while talking, present following a fall, or who have recurrent falls, need a falls assessment.**
- Falls assessments should be comprehensive, and often require multidisciplinary input. They are generally best carried out by a specialist falls service.
- **A falls assessment should include:**
  - A history of circumstances around any previous fall
  - A review of drug therapy: polypharmacy, hypnotics, sedatives, diuretics, antihypertensives
  - Assessment of vision
  - An examination of gait and balance, including abnormalities due to foot problems or arthritis, and those due to motor disorders such as Parkinson's disease or stroke
  - An examination of basic neurological function, including mental status (impaired cognition or depression), muscle strength, lower extremity peripheral nerves, proprioception, and reflexes
  - Assessment of basic cardiovascular status including blood pressure (particularly to exclude postural hypotension), heart rate, and rhythm
  - Assessment of environmental risk factors, e.g. poor lighting particularly on the stairs, loose carpets or rugs, badly fitting footwear or clothing, lack of safety

equipment such as grab rails, steep stairs, slippery floors, or inaccessible lights or windows

[Lundin-Olsson et al, 1997; American Geriatrics Society, 2001; DH, 2003]

Measures to reduce the risk of falls and damage from falling

Those at increased risk should be offered multiple interventions aimed at reducing the identified individual and environmental risks [SIGN, 2002; DH, 2003]. This is often co-ordinated by the specialist falls service and should include:

- **Modification of identified hazards or risk factors:**
  - Assessment and correction of vision, if possible
  - Correction of postural hypotension or other underlying medical conditions
  - Medication review and discontinuation of inappropriate medication
  - Occupational therapy to identify and correct hazards in the home
  - Repairs and improvements to the home.
- **Rehabilitation including physiotherapy to improve confidence after falls.**
- **Weight-bearing exercise (focusing on strength and flexibility) and balance training.**
- **Use of hip protectors.** Hip protectors may be helpful in people at high risk of hip fracture (e.g. older people in long-term care or in a supported home environment) and are unlikely to be harmful. **Although a meta-analysis found that** hip protectors reduce the risk of a hip fracture following a fall [Parker et al, 2003], a more recent randomized controlled trial involving 561 high risk patients found that they were not effective in preventing hip fractures [van Schoor et al, 2003]. Compliance is a problem because they are bulky and uncomfortable, but this can be improved by education [Meyer et al, 2003]. They are not available on prescription but may be provided by a hospital department.

Who should be offered treatment for osteoporosis?

- **Those at highest risk of osteoporotic fracture should be targeted for treatment** [SIGN, 2003].
- Assessment of bone mineral density (BMD) by axial dual energy X-ray absorptiometry (DEXA) is a prerequisite for targeting treatment in the vast majority of cases [SIGN, 2003]. However, because BMD alone has low sensitivity for predicting fractures, DEXA scans should be targeted at people with existing risk factors for osteoporosis. See *Identifying people at risk of an osteoporotic fracture* for further information.
- People with two or more vertebral fractures (including painless fractures) are considered to be at such high risk of further fracture that treatment can be started without the need for BMD measurement [SIGN, 2003].
- **Offer treatment to those with confirmed osteoporosis:**
  - People with two or more vertebral fractures (DEXA scan not required)
  - People with risk factors for osteoporosis and a T-score of –2.5 or less
- People with a T-score of between – 1 and –2.5 (osteopenia) should be offered lifestyle advice (see *Lifestyle interventions*). Drug treatment should only be considered for those with a previous fracture [Royal College of Physicians of London, 2002].

How should I treat osteoporosis?

- **Assess and manage risk of falls, particularly in the elderly.** Antiresorptive treatments only strengthen bone: drug treatment will not prevent fractures in those people who are at high risk of fracture because of their risk of falls.
- **Offer lifestyle advice in conjunction with drug therapy to treat osteoporosis.**
- Consider referring all men to a specialist centre for investigation of underlying causes and advice on further management [Royal College of Physicians and the Bone and Tooth Society of Great Britain, 2000].
- Exclude secondary causes and other destructive disease (e.g. multiple myeloma, metastases) before starting treatment. Secondary causes of osteoporosis are common in men. (For further information on secondary causes, see *What are the risk factors for osteoporosis?*)

Lifestyle interventions

- Bone loss is influenced by a number of lifestyle factors [Royal College of Physicians of London, 1999; SIGN, 2003]. The following should be encouraged:
  - **A good calcium intake** (aim for a dietary intake of 1000 mg calcium daily)
  - **Exercise** (including low-impact weight-bearing exercise such as walking, and high-intensity strength training that targets the muscle groups around the hip, spine, and wrists)
  - **Smoking cessation** (see separate PRODIGY guidance *Smoking Cessation*)
  - **Avoidance of excessive alcohol** (see separate PRODIGY guidance *Alcohol: problem drinking*)
- **Dietary calcium** is as effective as calcium in tablet form at maintaining calcium levels [SIGN, 2003], and a systematic review suggests that 1000 mg of dietary calcium per day leads to a 24% reduction in hip fractures [Cumming et al, 1997].
- An average daily intake of 1000 mg calcium can most easily be obtained from 1 pint of milk with either 60 g (2 oz) hard cheese such as Cheddar or Edam, or one pot of yoghurt (125 g), or 60 g of sardines.
- White bread and calcium-fortified soya milk are also good sources of calcium. Butter, cream, and soft cheeses are poor sources. For more detailed information on the calcium content of different foods, see the Patient Information Leaflet *Calculate your calcium* (reproduced with permission of the Scottish Intercollegiate Guidelines Network [SIGN]).
- **Vitamin D** is also important. Levels are maintained through both dietary intake and exposure to sunlight. Everyone over 65 years of age should aim to take 400 iu daily of vitamin D. For most people this can only be achieved by using a supplement. All people in residential and nursing homes (and those who are housebound) should be prescribed calcium with vitamin D to help prevent osteoporosis and future fracture [DH, 2003].
- **Exercise programmes** should be tailored to the individual's needs; begin at a low level that is comfortable, and progress as fitness and strength levels improve [SIGN, 2003]. Balance and gait training should be incorporated for people at risk of falls (see *Managing the risk of falls*).
- Moderate levels of activity, including walking, have been found to be associated with a substantially lower risk of hip fracture in postmenopausal women [Feskanich et al, 2002].

Which drug treatment should I use?

First-line treatment

- **Use alendronate or risedronate.** (Note: risedronate is not recommended as a first-line treatment of osteoporosis in men as there are few data on its use in men, and this is an off-licence indication.) Do not give bisphosphonates to people who are unable to adhere to the dosing instructions.

Second-line treatment

- **Postmenopausal women with diagnosed osteoporosis:** consider raloxifene, intranasal calcitonin (salmon), or cyclical etidronate. Consider using hormone replacement therapy if the benefits of treatment outweigh the risks.
- **Elderly women with diagnosed osteoporosis:** consider cyclical etidronate or raloxifene (off-licence use).
- **Calcium 1.2 g + 800 iu vitamin D is also an option for the elderly (age 80+), frail, or housebound** [Chapuy et al, 1994].

Adjunctive treatment with calcium + vitamin D

- **Give calcium supplements + vitamin D as an adjunct to bisphosphoneates or raloxifene if dietary intake is suboptimal** (in the absence of conditions associated with hypercalcaemia).
- The dose of calcium (600 mg to 1.2 g per day) and vitamin D (400–800 iu) will depend on dietary intake. See *Lifestyle interventions* for further information on optimal dietary calcium and vitamin D intake.
- Consider prescribing calcium 1.2 g + 800 iu vitamin D daily to prevent osteoporosis in people who are frail or housebound (e.g. those in residential and nursing homes) [Chapuy et al, 1994].

[SIGN, 2003]

Other treatments

- Although water fluoridation may improve axial bone mineral density, it has no effect on fracture rates [SIGN, 2003].
- Phytoestrogens have been suggested to prevent fractures in people with osteoporosis. Soy isoflavones (such as ipriflavone) are a common source of dietary phytoestrogens. However, the available data are conflicting, and phytoestrogens cannot be recommended as a sole therapy for fracture reduction [SIGN, 2003].
- **Tibolone** is a synthetic steroid that combines oestrogenic and progestogenic activity with weak androgenic activity. It increases bone density in the spine in postmenopausal women comparably to the effects of oestrogens. There are no data regarding fracture prevention [Royal College of Physicians of London, 1999]. Tibolone may only be used in women at least 12 months beyond the menopause.
- Teriparatide is a recombinant protein that is identical to the 34 N-terminal amino acid sequence of endogenous human parathyroid hormone. Unlike other therapies for osteoporosis, which prevent bone resorption, teriparatide stimulates bone formation by direct effects on osteoblasts (bone-forming cells). It has recently been licensed in the UK for the treatment of established osteoporosis in postmenopausal women, at a dose of 20 micrograms by subcutaneous injection once a day. A significant reduction in the incidence of vertebral but not hip fractures has been demonstrated [Crandall, 2002].

O

Supporting evidence for drug treatment

Postmenopausal women

Alendronate

- **The risk of both vertebral and non-vertebral fractures is reduced by alendronate** in postmenopausal women with:
  - Confirmed low bone mineral density (BMD) (T < –2.1) and at least one vertebral fracture [Black et al, 1996]
  - Confirmed low BMD but no previous vertebral fractures [Cummings et al, 1998]
- Although alendronate has not been prospectively studied in women with multiple vertebral fractures, there is no reason to suppose that it would not be effective [SIGN, 2003].
- In women with no previous vertebral fracture, the reduction in fracture risk was only significant for a T-score of less than –2.5; over 4.2 years one vertebral fracture was prevented for every 30 people treated (NNT = 30), and one hip fracture was prevented for every 81 people treated (NNT = 81) [Cummings et al, 1998].
- Alendronate 70 mg once a week is therapeutically equivalent to 10 mg once a day [Greenspan et al, 2002].

Risedronate

- **The risk of both vertebral and non-vertebral fractures is reduced by risedronate** in:
  - Postmenopausal women with multiple vertebral fractures [Harris et al, 1999; Reginster et al, 2000]
  - Women aged 70–79 years with confirmed low BMD (T < –2) and one vertebral fracture [Harris et al, 1999]
- Again, in women with no previous fractures, the risk of hip fracture was reduced for elderly women with a T-score of less than –2.7, but not for those with only clinical risk factors for osteoporosis [McClung et al, 2001].
- Risedronate 35 mg once a week is therapeutically equivalent to 5 mg once a day for the treatment of osteoporosis [Brown et al, 2002].

Other antiresorptive treatments

- **Etidronate, raloxifene, and intranasal calcitonin (salmon) reduce the risk of vertebral fracture only.**
- They do not reduce the risk of non-vertebral fractures [Ettinger et al, 1999; Chesnut et al, 2000; Cranney et al, 2001].

Elderly people

- **Age *per se* should not preclude treatment with antiresorptive therapies** in elderly women with confirmed osteoporosis or multiple vertebral fractures [SIGN, 2003]. Studies of alendronate, etidronate, raloxifene, and risedronate have generally recruited women up to 80-85 years of age.
- **Calcium 1.2 g + 800 iu vitamin D reduced the risk of hip and non-vertebral fracture in frail elderly women** (age 80+) who were housebound, but ambulatory; over 3 years one hip fracture was prevented for every 20 people treated (NNT = 20, for 3 years) [Chapuy et al, 1994]. Although only women were studied, this is also likely to be an effective intervention for frail elderly men.
- Calcium 500 mg + 700 iu vitamin D taken daily in healthy men and women, without osteoporosis, aged over 65 and living in the community, moderately reduced bone loss and reduced the risk of non-vertebral fractures. Over 3 years one non-vertebral fracture was avoided for every 15 individuals treated (NNT = 15, for 3 years), but this should be interpreted with caution as the study was small [Dawson-Hughes et al, 1997].

Men

- It is not known whether men's bones fracture at similar BMD levels to those of women.
- Consider referring all men to a specialist centre for investigation of underlying causes and advice on further management [Royal College of Physicians and the Bone and Tooth Society of Great Britain, 2000].
- Alendronate prevented morphometric vertebral fracture and a decrease in vertebral height in men with a T-score less than –2 and a history of one or more vertebral fractures or one non-vertebral osteoporotic fracture [Orwoll et al, 2000].
- Alendronate is the only licensed biphosphonate for the treatment of osteoporosis in men. If it is not tolerated or is contraindicated, seek specialist advice for further treatment options.
- The efficacy of calcitriol as a treatment for osteoporosis has not been established [SIGN, 2003].
- Testosterone in hypogonadal men may increase spinal BMD but there are no studies with fracture outcomes.

There are no convincing data about efficacy in changing BMD in eugonadal men. No studies have targeted testosterone on the basis of low BMD [SIGN, 2003].

What is the place of hormone replacement therapy?

Does hormone replacement therapy prevent fractures in women with osteoporosis?

- **It is likely that hormone replacement therapy (HRT) reduces fracture risk in women with known low bone mineral density (BMD)** [SIGN, 2003].
- However, there is very little data on the effect of HRT on fracture risk for women with osteoporosis (off-licence use).
- There is more data on the effect of HRT on fracture risk for women with unknown BMD, i.e. in primary prevention of osteoporosis (outside the scope of this guidance).
- A systematic review of studies that collected non-vertebral fracture data, found that HRT reduced the risk of non-vertebral fractures by 27% compared with placebo [Torgerson and Bell-Syer, 2001]. However, the effect was reduced in women aged over 60. Note that this meta-analysis was mainly influenced by two large trials, one of which (the Heart and Estrogen/Progestin Replacement Study, or HERS) produced a negative result [Hulley et al, 2002].
- The recent Women's Health Initiative Study found that HRT reduced the risk of both vertebral and hip fractures [Women's Health Initiative, 2002]. This study was much larger than the HERS study, and recruited 16,608 healthy postmenopausal women aged 50 to 79 years. BMD was unknown at the start of the study, i.e. it concerned primary prevention, and again fracture was a secondary end point.

What are the risks of using HRT?

- **Potential risks of chronic oestrogen use are breast cancer, endometrial cancer, stroke, and venous thromboembolism.** Note: all these conditions occur without using HRT, and a woman's risk of getting any of these conditions depends on her own health, her lifestyle, and her family medical history. To put these risks into perspective, the extra number of cases of each of these conditions associated with HRT is typically smaller than the health risks associated with smoking or being very overweight [CSM, 2002].
- **For a more comprehensive discussion of the risks and benefits of HRT, see the separate PRODIGY *Menopause* guidance.**

Who should be considered for HRT?

- **We suggest that HRT should mainly be considered as one of the range of treatment options for postmenopausal women soon after the menopause** (i.e. for women who also require control of vasomotor symptoms).
- The risks and benefits of HRT are complex, and should be discussed with each woman before a decision to start HRT is made. Note that HRT is not licensed for the treatment of osteoporosis.
- However, the decision to use HRT should also take into consideration a woman's history, risk factors, and personal preferences.

Is bone mass maintained after drug treatment is stopped?

- There is little data on the effect of discontinuing drug treatment, with regard to bone mass or fracture risk.
- A high rate of bone mineral density loss, similar to that seen after the menopause, has been observed after discontinuation of hormone replacement therapy (HRT) [Ascott-Evans et al, 2003]. This is thought to explain epidemiological findings that current HRT use is associated with fracture reduction but previous use is not.
- Conversely, in women who discontinued alendronate after 5 years, bone mass was still maintained at 2 years after stopping treatment [Tonino et al, 2000]. However, it is not known whether bone mass continues to be maintained for more than 2 years after alendronate is stopped.
- We have found no published studies regarding the rate of bone loss after stopping raloxifene or calcitonin at this time.

Glucocorticoid-induced osteoporosis

Glucocorticoids and bone mineral density

Oral glucocorticoids

- **Oral glucocorticoids significantly increase the risk of spine and hip fracture, even at doses of less than 7.5 mg of prednisolone per day** [Royal College of Physicians of London, 2002].
- The rate of bone mineral density (BMD) loss is greatest in the first few months of glucocorticoid use.
- In addition, oral glucocorticoids increase the risk of fracture above the effect of low BMD, i.e. for a given BMD, the risk of fracture is higher in glucocorticoid-induced osteoporosis than in postmenopausal osteoporosis.
- **People starting or currently on oral steroids for more than 3 months should be given osteoporosis prophylaxis if they:**
  - Are aged over 65 years
  - Have a previous fragility fracture (i.e. occurring after the age of 40 years on minimal trauma)
- **In other individuals, measure BMD using dual energy X-ray absorptiometry (DEXA) to assess fracture risk.** Consider treatment if T score is –1.5 or lower.
- Also consider using DEXA to assess BMD in people taking intermittent courses of oral steroids over longer periods of time: there is some evidence that bone loss is related to cumulative doses of corticosteroids.

Inhaled corticosteroids

- **The effect of inhaled glucocorticoids on bone mineral density (BMD) is currently unclear.** Epidemiological studies examining the relationship between inhaled corticosteroids (ICS) and BMD give conflicting results and are difficult to interpret due to confounding factors. However, it is possible that there is a decrease in BMD with long-term use of high dose inhaled glucocorticoids (above 800 micrograms per day of beclometasone or equivalent). The clinical significance of these changes in BMD is not known, as there is a lack of long-term studies.
- General measures to counteract osteoporosis (such as regular exercise, smoking cessation, adequate dietary calcium) are prudent in people who require high doses of ICS for prolonged periods of time.

Which treatment should I use?

- Offer lifestyle advice (to prevent osteoporosis) in conjunction with drug treatment.
- Assess and manage the risk of falls, particularly in the elderly.
- **First-line therapy:** use alendronate, risedronate, or cyclical etidronate.
- **Second-line therapy:** consider alfacalcidol or calcitriol. Hormone replacement therapy (off-licence use) may also

be considered if the benefits of treatment outweigh the risks (oestrogen with or without progestogen for women, or testosterone for men).

Supporting evidence: glucocorticoid-induced osteoporosis

- Fracture was not a primary end point in any studies of glucocorticoid-induced osteoporosis; the evidence for fracture risk reduction is therefore less robust than for some interventions used in postmenopausal women with osteoporosis.
- *Post hoc* analyses of studies of risedronate and etidronate, and analysis of secondary end points in a study of alendronate, found that these drugs all reduced the risk of vertebral fractures in people taking glucocorticoids.
- HRT (including testosterone) has been found to increase BMD at the spine, but not at the hip. A further study using tibolone found an increase in BMD at both the spine and the hip.
- Alfacalcidol or calcitriol use have both demonstrated increases in BMD at the spine and hip in some studies, although the data is conflicting. However, studies show a consistent increase in BMD at the spine with alfacalcidol use.
- Calcitonin (both intranasal and subcutaneous) has been studied in glucocorticoid-induced bone loss, but once again the results are conflicting.
- Calcium as a sole therapy is ineffective for preventing bone loss.
- Calcium with vitamin D has been shown in some studies to prevent bone loss, but the data is inconsistent. It is generally regarded as an adjunct to treatment.
- Raloxifene has not been studied in glucocorticoid-induced osteoporosis.

[Royal College of Physicians of London, 2002]

Medicines management

Bisphosphonates

- Bisphosphonates are very poorly absorbed. Absorption is reduced by food and medicines or supplements containing calcium, aluminium, iron, or magnesium. Failure to take bisphosphonates correctly will reduce their efficacy.
- Gastrointestinal adverse effects such as abdominal pain, dyspepsia, diarrhoea, or constipation, are common. Oesophageal reactions are serious adverse events, but are uncommon.
- There was no difference in upper gastrointestinal adverse events between alendronate and placebo in two large studies, but it should be noted that women with recent peptic ulcer disease or dyspepsia requiring treatment were excluded [Black et al, 1996; Cummings et al, 1998].
- A recent meta-analysis found that risedronate 5 mg daily was not associated with an increased risk of gastrointestinal adverse effects compared with placebo [Taggart et al, 2002]. This analysis included people with active dyspepsia, peptic ulcer disease, oesophagitis, or other oesophageal disorders at study entry.
- Severe oesophageal reactions (oesophagitis, oesophageal ulcers, strictures, and erosions) continue to be reported for alendronate. Oesophageal reactions may be slightly less common with risedronate, but this remains to be confirmed by post-marketing surveillance [DTB, 2001].
- People with delayed oesophageal emptying (e.g. strictures or achalasia) should not take alendronate, and should avoid taking risedronate where possible. Cyclical etidronate is an alternative bisphosphonate for these people [DTB, 2001]. However, etidronate only prevents vertebral fractures; studies have not demonstrated a reduced risk of hip fracture.
- Alendronate should also be avoided in people with active or recent gastrointestinal problems, such as dysphagia, oesophageal disease, gastritis, duodenitis, or ulcers.
- People who develop dysphagia, new or worsening heartburn, pain on swallowing, or retrosternal pain while taking alendronate should be advised to stop taking the tablets and seek medical advice.
- Oesophageal adverse effects can be avoided by taking bisphosphonates with a full glass of water while sitting upright or standing (but not lying down), and by remaining upright for at least 30 minutes afterwards.

Raloxifene

- Unlike hormone replacement therapy (HRT), raloxifene does not relieve vasomotor symptoms, and may increase them.
- Raloxifene has been found to decrease the relative risk of invasive breast cancer by 72%, predominately due to a reduction in oestrogen receptor-positive tumours [Cauley et al, 2001]. To prevent one case of invasive breast cancer, 93 osteoporotic women would need to be treated with raloxifene for 4 years (NNT = 93 for 4 years).
- Raloxifene increases the risk of venous thromboembolism (VTE) by about 2.5-fold, which is similar to the risk increase with HRT [DTB, 1999]. People who have a personal or family history of deep vein thrombosis or pulmonary embolism should not take raloxifene. Raloxifene should also be avoided in people at increased risk of VTE, e.g. with severe varicose veins, obesity, recent surgery or trauma, or prolonged bed rest.
- Raloxifene has not been found to cause endometrial proliferation, and available data suggest that there is no increase in the risk of developing endometrial cancer after 3 years of treatment.
- Although the risks of breast cancer or endometrial cancer seem to be low with raloxifene, it has not been studied in women with active disease. Avoid raloxifene in women with current breast cancer, endometrial cancer, or unexplained uterine bleeding.

Intranasal calcitonin (salmon)

- Local irritation to the nose is very common. Rhinitis, sinusitis, epistaxis, and mild ulceration of the nasal mucosa have been reported. If mild ulceration occurs, discontinue calcitonin until healing occurs.
- Flushing, dizziness, and gastrointestinal adverse effects such as nausea, diarrhoea, and abdominal pain, are also common. Some people report an unpleasant taste.
- Salmon calcitonin is a peptide and allergic reactions have been reported, e.g. generalized skin reactions, flushing, and oedema. A few cases of anaphylactic shock have occurred.

[ABPI Medicines Compendium, 2003]

Alfaclacidol and calcitriol

- Alfacalcidol and calcitriol are vitamin D analogues. Hypercalcaemia and hypercalcuria have occasionally been reported. They are dose-related adverse effects, and tend to occur in people who are at higher risk of hypercalcaemia, e.g. people with renal failure or on regular dialysis.
- Both require regular monitoring to exclude hypercalcaemia. For calcitriol, serum calcium and creatinine levels should be checked at 4 weeks, 3 months 6 months, and every 6 months thereafter. For alfacalcidol, they should be checked after 1 week, and then monthly. Hypercalcaemia should also be excluded if nausea and vomiting develop.

Pregnancy and breastfeeding

- Bisphosphonates should be used with care in women of childbearing age. They should not be used during pregnancy or breastfeeding, as there is a lack of data on their effects on the fetus or infant.
- Alfacalcidol or calcitriol are an option during pregnancy, although they should be used with care. High doses are teratogenic in animals, but therapeutic doses are unlikely to be harmful. Alfacalcidol or calcitriol can be considered for breastfeeding mothers, although high doses have caused hypercalcaemia in infants.

[BNF 45, 2003]

References

NHS staff in England can link, free of charge, from references to full text journals by clicking on [Full text] on the PRODIGY website.

1. ABPI Medicines Compendium (2003) *Summary of product characteristics for Miaclcic nasal spray.* Electronic Medicines Compendium. Datapharm Communications Ltd. www.emc.medicines.org.uk [Accessed: 16/05/2003].
2. American Geriatrics Society (2001) Guideline for the prevention of falls in older persons. American Geriatrics Society, British Geriatrics Society, and American Academy of Orthopaedic Surgeons panel on falls prevention. *Journal of the American Geriatrics Society* **49**(5), 664–672.
3. Ascott-Evans, B.H., Guanabens, N., Kivinen, S. et al (2003) Alendronate prevents loss of bone density associated with discontinuation of hormone replacement therapy: a randomized controlled trial. *Archives of Internal Medicine* **163**(7), 789–794. [Full text]
4. Black, D.M., Cummings, S.R., Karpf, D.B. et al (1996) Randomised trial of effect of alendronate on risk of fracture in women with existing vertebral fractures. *Lancet* **348**(9041), 1535–1541. [Full text]
5. Brown, J.P., Kendler, D.L., McClung, M.R. et al (2002) The efficacy and tolerability of risedronate once a week for the treatment of postmenopausal osteoporosis. *Calcified Tissue International* **71**(2), 103–111.
6. Cauley, J.A., Norton, L., Lippman, M.E. et al (2001) Continued breast cancer risk reduction in postmenopausal women treated with raloxifene: 4-year results from the MORE trial. Multiple outcomes of raloxifene evaluation. *Breast Cancer Research and Treatment* **65**(2), 125–134.
7. Chapuy, M.C., Arlot, M.E., Delmas, P.D. and Meunier, P.J. (1994) Effect of calcium and cholecalciferol treatment for three years on hip fractures in elderly women. *British Medical Journal* **308**(6936), 1081–1082. [Full text]
8. Chesnut, C.H., Silverman, S., Andriano, K. et al (2000) A randomized trial of nasal spray salmon calcitonin in postmenopausal women with established osteoporosis: the prevent recurrence of osteoporotic fractures study. *American Journal of Medicine* **109**(4), 267–276.
9. Crandall, C. (2002) Parathyroid hormone for treatment of osteoporosis. *Archives of Internal Medicine* **162**(20), 2297–2309. [Full text]
10. Cranney, A., Welch, V., Adachi, J.D. et al (2001) *Etidronate for treating and preventing postmenopausal osteoporosis (Cochrane Review)*. The Cochrane Library. Issue 1. Oxford: Update Software. www.nelh.nhs.uk
11. CSM (2002) Safety update on long-term HRT. *Current Problems in Pharmacovigilance* **28**(Oct), 11–12.
12. Cumming, R.G., Cummings, S.R., Nevitt, M.C. et al (1997) Calcium intake and fracture risk: results from the study of osteoporotic fractures. *American Journal of Epidemiology* **145**(10), 926–934.
13. Cummings, S.R., Black, D.M., Thompson, D.E. et al (1998) Effect of alendronate on risk of fracture in women with low bone density but without vertebral fractures: results from the Fracture Intervention Trial. *Journal of the American Medical Association* **280**(24), 2077–2082. [Full text]
14. Dawson-Hughes, B., Harris, S.S., Krall, E.A. and Dallal, G.E. (1997) Effect of calcium and vitamin D supplementation on bone density in men and women 65 years of age or older. *New England Journal of Medicine* **337**(10), 670–676. [Full text]
15. DH (2003) *National service framework for older people – a report of progress and future challenges, 2003.* Department of Health. www.dh.gov.uk [Accessed: 27/04/2004].
16. DTB (1999) Raloxifene to prevent postmenopausal osteoporosis. *Drug & Therapeutics Bulletin* **37**(5), 33–36.
17. DTB (2001) Biphosphonates for osteoporosis. *Drug & Therapeutics Bulletin* **39**(9), 68–72.
18. Ettinger, B., Black, D.M., Mitlak, B.H. et al (1999) Reduction of vertebral fracture risk in postmenopausal women with osteoporosis treated with raloxifene: results from a 3-year randomized clinical trial. Multiple Outcomes of Raloxifene Evaluation (MORE) Investigators. *Journal of the American Medical Association* **282**(7), 637–645. [Full text]
19. Feskanich, D., Willett, W. and Colditz, G. (2002) Walking and leisure-time activity and risk of hip fracture in postmenopausal women. *Journal of the American Medical Association* **288**(18), 2300–2306. [Full text]
20. Greenspan, S.L., Bone, G., III, Schnitzer, T.J. et al (2002) Two-year results of once-weekly administration of alendronate 70 mg for the treatment of postmenopausal osteoporosis. *Journal of Bone and Mineral Research* **17**(11), 1988–1996.
21. Harris, S.T., Watts, N.B., Genant, H.K. et al (1999) Effects of risedronate treatment on vertebral and nonvertebral fractures in women with postmenopausal osteoporosis: a randomized controlled trial. *Journal of the American Medical Association* **282**(14), 1344–1352.
22. Hulley, S., Furberg, C., Barrett-Connor, E. et al (2002) Noncardiovascular disease outcomes during 6.8 years of hormone therapy. Heart and Estrogen/Progestin Replacement Study follow-up (HERSII). *Journal of the American Medical Association* **288**(1), 58–66. [Full text]
23. Lundin-Olsson, L., Nyberg, L. and Gustafson, Y. (1997) "Stops walking when talking" as a predictor of falls in elderly people. *Lancet* **349**(9052), 617. [Full text]
24. McClung, M.R., Geusens, P., Miller, P.D. et al (2001) Effect of risedronate on the risk of hip fracture in elderly women. *New England Journal of Medicine* **344**(5), 333–340. [Full text]
25. Meyer, G., Warnke, A., Bender, R. and Muhlhauser, I. (2003) Effect on hip fractures of increased use of hip protectors in nursing homes: cluster randomised controlled trial. *British Medical Journal* **326**(7380), 76–80. [Full text]
26. National Osteoporosis Society (2002) *Primary care strategy for osteoporosis and falls.* National Osteoporosis Society. www.nos.org.uk [Accessed: 28/04/2003].
27. Orwoll, E., Ettinger, M., Weiss, S. et al (2000) Alendronate for the treatment of osteoporosis in men.

New England Journal of Medicine **343**(9), 604–610. [Full text]

28. Parker, M.J., Gillespie, L.D. and Gillespie, W.J. (2003) *Hip protectors for preventing hip fractures in the elderly.* The Cochrane Library. Issue 2. Oxford: Update Software. www.nelh.nhs.uk
29. Reginster, J., Minne, H.W., Sorensen, O.H. et al (2000) Randomized trial of the effects of risedronate on vertebral fractures in women with established postmenopausal osteoporosis. *Osteoporosis International* **11**(1), 83–91.
30. Ross, P.D. (1997) Clinical consequences of vertebral fractures. *American Journal of Medicine* **103**(suppl. 2A), 30S-42S.
31. Ross, P.D., Genant, H.K., Davis, J.W. et al (1993) Predicting vertebral fracture incidence from prevalent fractures and bone density among non-black, osteoporotic women. *Osteoporosis International* **3**(3), 120–126.
32. Royal College of Physicians and the Bone and Tooth Society of Great Britain (2000) *Osteoporosis: clinical guidelines for prevention and treatment. Update on pharmacological interventions and an algorithm for management.* London: Royal College of Physicians.
33. Royal College of Physicians of London (1999) *Osteoporosis. Clinical guidelines for prevention and treatment.* London: Royal College of Physicians.
34. Royal College of Physicians of London (2002) *Glucocorticoid-induced osteoporosis.* Royal College of Physicians. www.rcplondon.ac.uk [Accessed: 22/04/2003].
35. SIGN (2002) *Prevention and management of hip fracture in older people.* Report no. 56. Scottish Intercollegiate Guidelines Network. www.sign.ac.uk [Accessed: 22/04/2003].
36. SIGN (2003) *Management of osteoporosis.* Report no. 71. Scottish Intercollegiate Guidelines Network. www.sign.ac.uk [Accessed: 22/04/2003].
37. Taggart, H., Bolognese, M.A., Lindsay, R. et al (2002) Upper gastrointestinal tract safety of risedronate: a pooled analysis of 9 clinical trials. *Mayo Clinic Proceedings* **77**(3), 262–270. [Full text]
38. Tonino, R.P., Meunier, P.J., Emkey, R. et al (2000) Skeletal benefits of alendronate: 7-year treatment of postmenopausal osteoporotic women. Phase III Osteoporosis Treatment Study Group. *Journal of Clinical Endocrinology & Metabolism* **85**(9), 3109–3115.
39. Torgerson, D.J. and Bell-Syer, S.E. (2001) Hormone replacement therapy and prevention of nonvertebral fractures: a meta-analysis of randomized trials. *Journal of the American Medical Association* **285**(22), 2891–2897. [Full text]
40. van Schoor, N.M., Smit, J.H., Twisk, J.W.R. et al (2003) Prevention of hip fractures by external hip protectors: a randomized controlled trial. *Journal of the American Medical Association* **289**(15), 1957–1962. [Full text]
41. van Staa, T.P., Leufkens, H.G.M. and Cooper, C. (2002) Does fracture at one site predict later fractures at other sites? A British cohort study. *Osteoporosis International* **13**(8), 624–629.
42. Women's Health Initiative (2002) Risks and benefits of estrogen plus progestin in healthy postmenopausal women. Principal results from the Women's Health Initiative randomized controlled trial. *Journal of the American Medical Association* **288**(3), 321–333. [Full text]

PRODIGY GUIDANCE

Otitis externa

Last revised in July 2004
www.prodigy.nhs.uk/guidance.asp?gt=Otitis externa

Applies to people over the age of 3 months

This guidance covers the management of otitis externa.

This guidance does not cover the management of otitis externa caused by more general skin conditions, such as seborrhoeic dermatitis, acne, psoriasis, atopic dermatitis, dermatophytoses, lupus erythematosus, herpes simplex, and herpes zoster.

There is separate PRODIGY guidance for *Otitis media — acute*, *Glue ear*, and *Earwax*.

Goals

- To settle symptoms
- To cure infection
- To reduce risk of recurrence
- To prevent complications

Contents

Scenarios

- Localized otitis externa (furunculosis) p.1393
- Acute diffuse otitis externa p.1394
- Treatment failure (acute diffuse) p.1397
- Chronic otitis externa p.1400

Extended Information, p. 1402

Which scenario?

- **Localized otitis externa (furunculosis):** covers the management of a pustule or furuncle in the external ear canal.
- **Acute diffuse otitis externa:** covers the management of acute diffuse otitis externa.
- **Treatment failure (acute diffuse):** outlines the management of acute diffuse otitis externa that has failed to respond to treatment.
- **Chronic otitis externa:** outlines the management of chronic otitis externa.

Localized otitis externa (furunculosis)

Which therapy?

- **Symptomatic treatment** with analgesics and application of local heat (e.g. a hot flannel) are often adequate.
- **If symptoms are severe or there is systemic upset,** strong pain relief and treatment with oral antibiotics that cover *Staphylococcus aureus*, such as flucloxacillin (or erythromycin if the person is allergic to penicillin), may be indicated.
- If symptoms do not resolve, urgent specialist opinion should be sought.
- Lancing the furuncle is generally not necessary.

Practical prescribing points

For further information, please see the *Medicines Compendium* (www.medicines.org.uk) or the *British National Formulary* (www.bnf.org).

Should I refer or investigate?

Refer?

Consider referral if:

- Symptoms are not resolving with primary care management.
- Symptoms are severe or there is systemic upset.

Investigate?

- Glucose tests to rule out diabetes mellitus, if furunculosis is a recurrent problem.

Patient information leaflets

The following PILs are available at www.prodigy.nhs.uk

- Otitis Externa - Furuncle

Shared decision making

- You have a small boil in the ear canal.
- Because of its site, the pain may be severe even though the boil is small.
- **The boil is likely to clear without treatment** within a few days.
- **Painkillers** such as paracetamol or ibuprofen, and a hot flannel held against the ear, help to relieve the pain.
- **Antibiotics** may be needed if the boil spreads. Spreading of the boil is unlikely, but come back to see a doctor if symptoms become worse.

Drug rationale

Drugs not included

- **Topical antibiotics/antiseptics** are not generally recommended for furunculosis of the external ear canal.
- **Systemic antibiotics** that are not considered first-line treatments for *S aureus* are excluded.
- **Aspirin** is excluded because of its extensive adverse-effect profile and unsuitability for children under 16 years.

Drugs included

- **Paracetamol** is usually effective for pain relief.
- **Codeine in combination with paracetamol** is offered for more severe pain.
- **Ibuprofen** is included as an alternative to paracetamol.
- **Flucloxacillin (or erythromycin if the person is allergic to penicillin)** are usually both active against *Staphylococcus aureus* and are the preferred treatments.

O

Prescriptions

Analgesia: use when required

Paracetamol s/f susp: 60mg to 120mg up to four times a day
- Age from 3 to 11 months
- Paracetamol 120mg/5ml s/f susp. Take 2.5ml to 5ml every 4 to 6 hours when required for pain relief. Maximum of 4 doses in 24 hours; supply 150 ml; NHS Cost £0.65; OTC Cost £1.15.

Paracetamol s/f susp: 120mg to 240mg up to four times a day
- Age from 12 months to 5 years
- Paracetamol 120mg/5ml s/f susp. Take one to two 5ml spoonfuls every 4 to 6 hours when required for pain relief. Maximum of 4 doses in 24 hours; supply 300 ml; NHS Cost £1.30; OTC Cost £2.30.

Paracetamol s/f susp: 250mg to 500mg up to four times a day
- Age from 6 to 11 years
- Paracetamol 250mg/5ml s/f susp. Take one to two 5ml spoonfuls every 4 to 6 hours when required for pain relief. Maximum of 4 doses in 24 hours; supply 300 ml; NHS Cost £1.59; OTC Cost £2.80.

Paracetamol tablets: 500mg to 1g up to four times a day
- Age from 12 to 15 years
- Paracetamol 500mg tablets. Take one to two tablets every 4 to 6 hours when required for pain relief. Maximum of 8 tablets in 24 hours; supply 50 tablets; NHS Cost £0.38; OTC Cost £0.67.

Paracetamol tablets: 1g up to four times a day
- Age from 16 years onwards
- Paracetamol 500mg tablets. Take two tablets every 4 to 6 hours when required for pain relief. Maximum of 8 tablets in 24 hours; supply 50 tablets; NHS Cost £0.38; OTC Cost £0.67.

O

Codeine 30mg tablets: add on to paracetamol if required
- Age from 16 years onwards
- Codeine 30mg tablets. Take one to two tablets every 4 to 6 hours when required for pain relief. Maximum of 8 tablets in 24 hours; supply 30 tablets; NHS Cost £1.54.

Codeine 30mg tablets + paracetamol 500mg tablets
- Age from 16 years onwards
- Paracetamol 500mg tablets. Take two tablets every 4 to 6 hours when required for pain relief. Maximum of 8 tablets in 24 hours; supply 50 tablets; NHS Cost £0.38.
- Codeine 30mg tablets. Take one to two tablets every 4 to 6 hours when required for pain relief. Maximum of 8 tablets in 24 hours; supply 30 tablets; NHS Cost £1.54.

Ibuprofen s/f susp: 50mg three to four times a day
- Age from 12 months to 2 years
- Ibuprofen 100mg/5ml s/f susp. Take 2.5ml three to four times a day when required for pain relief. Do not exceed the stated dose; supply 100 ml; NHS Cost £1.82; OTC Cost £3.20.

Ibuprofen s/f susp: 100mg three to four times a day
- Age from 3 to 7 years
- Ibuprofen 100mg/5ml s/f susp. Take one 5ml spoonful 3 to 4 times a day when required for pain relief. Do not exceed the stated dose; supply 150 ml; NHS Cost £2.73; OTC Cost £4.81.

Ibuprofen s/f susp: 200mg three to four times a day
- Age from 8 to 11 years
- Ibuprofen 100mg/5ml s/f susp. Take two 5ml spoonfuls 3 to 4 times a day when required for pain relief. Do not exceed the stated dose; supply 300 ml; NHS Cost £5.46; OTC Cost £9.62.

Ibuprofen tablets: 400mg three times a day
- Age from 12 years onwards
- Ibuprofen 400mg tablets. Take one tablet three times a day when required for pain relief. Do not exceed the stated dose; supply 21 tablets; NHS Cost £0.62; OTC Cost £1.09.

Antibiotic for 5 days (not usually indicated)

Flucloxacillin syrup: 62.5mg four times a day
- Age from 3 to 11 months
- Flucloxacillin 125mg/5ml syrup. Take 2.5ml four times a day for 5 days; supply 100 ml; NHS Cost £3.23.

Flucloxacillin syrup: 125mg four times a day
- Age from 12 months to 4 years
- Flucloxacillin 125mg/5ml syrup. Take one 5ml spoonful four times a day for 5 days; supply 100 ml; NHS Cost £3.23.

Flucloxacillin syrup: 250mg four times a day
- Age from 5 to 11 years
- Flucloxacillin 250mg/5ml syrup. Take one 5ml spoonful four times a day for 5 days; supply 100 ml; NHS Cost £6.97.

Flucloxacillin capsules: 250mg four times a day
- Age from 12 years onwards
- Flucloxacillin 250mg capsules. Take one capsule four times a day for 5 days; supply 20 capsules; NHS Cost £2.09.

Flucloxacillin capsules: 500mg four times a day
- Age from 12 years onwards
- Flucloxacillin 500mg capsules. Take one capsule four times a day for 5 days; supply 20 capsules; NHS Cost £3.54.

Erythromycin s/f suspension: 125mg four times a day
- Age from 3 to 23 months
- Erythromycin 125mg/5ml sf susp. Take one 5ml spoonful four times a day for 5 days; supply 100 ml; NHS Cost £1.01.

Erythromycin s/f suspension: 250mg four times a day
- Age from 2 to 11 years
- Erythromycin 250mg/5ml sf susp. Take one 5ml spoonful four times a day for 5 days; supply 100 ml; NHS Cost £1.97.

Erythromycin s/f suspension: 500mg four times a day
- Age from 9 to 11 years
- Erythromycin 500mg/5ml sf susp. Take one 5ml spoonful four times a day for 5 days; supply 100 ml; NHS Cost £3.38.

Erythromycin e/c tablets: 250mg four times a day
- Age from 12 years onwards
- Erythromycin 250mg e/c tablets. Take one tablet four times a day for 5 days; supply 20 tablets; NHS Cost £2.20.

Erythromycin e/c tablets: 500mg four times a day
- Age from 12 years onwards
- Erythromycin 250mg e/c tablets. Take two tablets four times a day for 5 days; supply 40 tablets; NHS Cost £4.40.

Acute diffuse otitis externa

Which therapy?

- **Clear the ear canal** by gentle syringing, dry mopping, or ear suction (if available).
- **Pain relief** with local heat and paracetamol (with or without codeine) or ibuprofen is usually adequate.
- **Bacterial infection suspected:**
  - **First-line treatment** is topical acetic acid, or a combined antibacterial/corticosteroid preparation.

Topical corticosteroid may be used with the acetic acid.

- **Oral antibiotics** are indicated if there is systemic upset or evidence of spreading infection, in which case flucloxacillin (or erythromycin if the person is allergic to penicillin) should be used.
- **Superficial fungal infection suspected:**
  - **First-line treatment** is topical acetic acid alone or with a corticosteroid preparation, or a topical anti-infective combined with a corticosteroid.
- **Contact dermatitis suspected:**
  - **Remove the offending irritant or allergen** (e.g. stop topical medications, switch to hypoallergenic ear moulds for hearing aids, use hypoallergenic ear plugs).
  - Topical steroids may hasten relief.
- **If the ear canal is swollen,** consider inserting a wick, which will allow medication to travel along the length of the ear canal. The wick should be inserted by an appropriately trained person.

Practical prescribing points

For further information, please see the *Medicines Compendium* (www.medicines.org.uk) or the *British National Formulary* (www.bnf.org).

- **Acetic acid 2%** ear drops may cause burning or irritation on application. The person should be warned of this, as it may otherwise affect compliance.
- **Aminoglycosides (neomycin and gentamicin):** the Committee on Safety of Medicines advises that treatment with a topical aminoglycoside antibiotic is contraindicated in those with a tympanic perforation.
- **Fungal superinfection** can occur with prolonged use of antibacterial/corticosteroid combinations. These products should be used for no longer than 7 days.
- **Contact sensitivity** may occur with topically applied **ear drops** and aggravate the condition.

Should I refer or investigate?

Refer?

- **Insertion of a wick** into a tender, swollen ear canal may require referral to a service with the required skills and equipment.
- **Malignant (necrotizing) otitis externa** requires urgent admission.

Investigate?

- **Ear swab** for culture should be reserved for treatment failures or chronic cases.
  - An ear swab is best taken from the medial aspect of the canal under visualization to reduce contamination.
  - Bacterial and fungal stains and cultures should be obtained.
  - Note that reported bacterial susceptibility may not correlate with clinical outcomes because sensitivities are determined for systemic (not topical) administration. However, identifying the organism, and especially distinguishing a fungal from a bacterial infection, can be of therapeutic significance.

Patient information leaflets

The following PILs are available at www.prodigy.nhs.uk

- Otitis Externa

Shared decision making

- **Ear drops** usually clear otitis externa within a week.
  - Most drops contain an antibiotic to clear infection and a steroid to reduce itch and inflammation.
  - Acetic acid ear drops are an alternative. When using ear drops:
    - Lie with the ear upwards.
    - Put in several drops, and lie in this position for 1–2 minutes.
    - Press the cartilage at the front of the ear canal a few times to push the drops deep inside.
- Do not use ear drops that contain steroids or antibiotics for more than 7 days. Come back if symptoms persist.
- **Painkillers** such as paracetamol or ibuprofen, and a hot flannel held against the ear, help to ease the pain.
- **Antibiotic tablets** are sometimes needed if the infection is severe.
- If you need to put cotton wool into the ear to absorb discharge, place it loosely and replace it frequently.
- Do not irritate the ear canal:
  - Try not to scratch inside it.
  - Try to keep it dry and prevent soap or shampoo from getting in.
  - Do not clean or dry it with cotton buds, the corner of a towel, etc.

Drug rationale

Drugs not included

- **Neomycin/dexamethasone/glacial acetic acid (Otomize®), neomycin/triamcinolone (Audicort®), neomycin/hydrocortisone (Neo-Cortef®), framycetin/gramicidin/dexamethasone (Sofradex®) and neomycin/polymyxin B/ hydrocortisone (Otosporin®)** have been excluded because they are more expensive than other equally effective products. There is no good evidence to support greater efficacy.
- **Chloramphenicol** ear drops are excluded because they contain propylene glycol, which can cause hypersensitivity reactions in about 10% of people.
- **Clotrimazole** is not included, as fungal infection is less common and usually can be effectively treated by topical products that have been included.
- **Systemic antibiotics** that are not considered to be first-line treatments against *S aureus* (the most common pathogen) are excluded.
- **Aluminium acetate drops** are as effective as combination products [Hajioff, 2003]. They do not have a product licence and can only be obtained by special order. They are thus seldom a practical option.
- **Aspirin** is excluded because of its extensive adverse-effect profile and unsuitability for children under 16 years.

Drugs included

For infection

- **Acetic acid 2% ear drops** are as effective as combination products, and are particularly useful when a sensitivity reaction is possible. Acetic acid has both antibacterial and antifungal activity [Ruddy and Bickerton, 1992] and the ear drops can be bought over the counter (EarCalm®).
- **Prednisolone/neomycin (Predsol-N®), betamethasone/neomycin (Vista-methasone N® or Betnesol-N®), and flumetasone/clioquinol (Locorten-Vioform®)** ear drops are similarly priced and contain an antibacterial (that is not used systemically) combined with a corticosteroid (to relieve irritation and inflammation). In addition, Locorten-Vioform has both antibacterial and antifungal activity and does not have shared components with any other product if a sensitivity reaction is likely.
- **Gentamicin/hydrocortisone** ear drops are included as an alternative to neomycin-containing products. They do not have any components in common with flumetasone/

O

clioquinol, but there is a possibility of cross-sensitivity with neomycin-containing products.

- **Gentamicin ear drops** are included if there is no accompanying inflammation. They do not have any shared components with flumetasone/clioquinol, but there is a possibility of cross-sensitivity and cross-resistance with neomycin-containing products.
- **Flucloxacillin (and erythromycin if the person is allergic to penicillin)** are both active against *Staphylococcus aureus*.

For inflammation

- **Corticosteroid ear drops are offered for symptomatic relief in acute diffuse otitis externa.** They can be used in conjunction with **acetic acid 2% ear drops** to reduce inflammation when infection is present. They may also be used for an underlying inflammatory skin condition (such as atopic dermatitis or psoriasis).

For analgesia

- **Paracetamol** is usually effective for pain relief.
- **Codeine in combination with paracetamol** is offered for more severe pain.
- **Ibuprofen** is included as an alternative to paracetamol.

Prescriptions

Acetic acid 2% ear spray or flumetasone + clioquinol drops

Acetic acid 2% ear spray
- Age from 3 months onwards
- Acetic acid 2% ear spray. Spray once into the affected ear(s) at least three times a day. Maximum of one spray every 2 to 3 hours. Do not use for more than 7 days; supply 1 spray; NHS Cost £3.80; OTC Cost £6.38.

O

Flumetasone 0.02% + clioquinol 1% ear drops
- Age from 2 years onwards
- Flumetasone + clioquinol drops. Put two to three drops into the affected ear(s) twice a day for 7 to 10 days; supply 8 ml; NHS Cost £0.97.

Ear drops with neomycin/gentamicin

Betamethasone 0.1% + neomycin 0.5% ear drops
- Age from 3 months onwards
- Betamethasone + neomycin drops. Put two to three drops into the affected ear(s) 3 to 4 times a day until symptoms improve, then reduce frequency. Do not use for longer than 7 days; supply 10 ml; NHS Cost £1.84.

Prednisolone 0.5% + neomycin 0.5% ear drops
- Age from 3 months onwards
- Predsol-N ear drops. Put two to three drops into the affected ear(s) 3 to 4 times a day until symptoms improve, then reduce frequency. Do not use for longer than 7 days; supply 10 ml; NHS Cost £1.95.

Hydrocortisone 1% + gentamicin 0.3% ear drops
- Age from 3 months onwards
- Gentisone HC ear drops. Put two to three drops into the affected ear(s) 3 to 4 times a day and at night until symptoms improve, then reduce frequency. Max 7 days; supply 10 ml; NHS Cost £3.97.

Gentamicin 0.3% ear drops
- Age from 3 months onwards
- Gentamicin 0.3% eye drops. Put two to three drops into the affected ear(s) 3 to 4 times a day and at night. Use for a maximum of 7 days; supply 10 ml; NHS Cost £1.79.

Ear drops (steroid) for contact dermatitis

Betamethasone 0.1% ear drops
- Age from 3 months onwards
- Betamethasone 0.1% ear drops. Put two to three drops into the affected ear(s) every 2 to 3 hours until symptoms improve, then reduce frequency. Do not use for longer than 7 days; supply 10 ml; NHS Cost £1.84.

Prednisolone 0.5% ear drops
- Age from 3 months onwards
- Prednisolone 0.5% ear drops. Put two to three drops into the affected ear(s) every 2 to 3 hours until symptoms improve, then reduce frequency. Do not use for longer than 7 days; supply 10 ml; NHS Cost £1.83.

Analgesia: use when required

Paracetamol s/f susp: 60mg to 120mg up to four times a day
- Age from 3 to 11 months
- Paracetamol 120mg/5ml s/f susp. Take 2.5ml to 5ml every 4 to 6 hours when required for pain relief. Maximum of 4 doses in 24 hours; supply 150 ml; NHS Cost £0.65; OTC Cost £1.15.

Paracetamol s/f susp: 120mg to 240mg up to four times a day
- Age from 12 months to 5 years
- Paracetamol 120mg/5ml s/f susp. Take one to two 5ml spoonfuls every 4 to 6 hours when required for pain relief. Maximum of 4 doses in 24 hours; supply 300 ml; NHS Cost £1.30; OTC Cost £2.30.

Paracetamol s/f susp: 250mg to 500mg up to four times a day
- Age from 6 to 11 years
- Paracetamol 250mg/5ml s/f susp. Take one to two 5ml spoonfuls every 4 to 6 hours when required for pain relief. Maximum of 4 doses in 24 hours; supply 300 ml; NHS Cost £1.59; OTC Cost £2.80.

Paracetamol tablets: 500mg to 1g up to four times a day
- Age from 12 to 15 years
- Paracetamol 500mg tablets. Take one to two tablets every 4 to 6 hours when required for pain relief. Maximum of 8 tablets in 24 hours; supply 50 tablets; NHS Cost £0.38; OTC Cost £0.67.

Paracetamol tablets: 1g up to four times a day
- Age from 16 years onwards
- Paracetamol 500mg tablets. Take two tablets every 4 to 6 hours when required for pain relief. Maximum of 8 tablets in 24 hours; supply 50 tablets; NHS Cost £0.38; OTC Cost £0.67.

Codeine 30mg tablets: add on to paracetamol if required
- Age from 16 years onwards
- Codeine 30mg tablets. Take one to two tablets every 4 to 6 hours when required for pain relief. Maximum of 8 tablets in 24 hours; supply 30 tablets; NHS Cost £1.54.

Codeine 30mg tablets + paracetamol 500mg tablets
- Age from 16 years onwards
- Paracetamol 500mg tablets. Take two tablets every 4 to 6 hours when required for pain relief. Maximum of 8 tablets in 24 hours; supply 50 tablets; NHS Cost £0.38.
- Codeine 30mg tablets. Take one to two tablets every 4 to 6 hours when required for pain relief. Maximum of 8 tablets in 24 hours; supply 30 tablets; NHS Cost £1.54.

Ibuprofen s/f susp: 50mg three to four times a day
- Age from 12 months to 2 years
- Ibuprofen 100mg/5ml s/f susp. Take 2.5ml three to four times a day when required for pain relief. Do not exceed the stated dose; supply 100 ml; NHS Cost £1.82; OTC Cost £3.20.

Ibuprofen s/f susp: 100mg three to four times a day
- Age from 3 to 7 years
- Ibuprofen 100mg/5ml s/f susp. Take one 5ml spoonful 3 to 4 times a day when required for pain relief. Do not exceed the stated dose; supply 150 ml; NHS Cost £2.73; OTC Cost £4.81.

Ibuprofen s/f susp: 200mg three to four times a day
- Age from 8 to 11 years
- Ibuprofen 100mg/5ml s/f susp. Take two 5ml spoonfuls 3 to 4 times a day when required for pain relief. Do not exceed the stated dose; supply 300 ml; NHS Cost £5.46; OTC Cost £9.62.

Ibuprofen tablets: 400mg three times a day
- Age from 12 years onwards
- Ibuprofen 400mg tablets. Take one tablet three times a day when required for pain relief. Do not exceed the stated dose; supply 21 tablets; NHS Cost £0.62; OTC Cost £1.09.

Antibiotic for 5 days (not usually indicated)

Flucloxacillin syrup: 62.5mg four times a day
- Age from 3 to 11 months
- Flucloxacillin 125mg/5ml syrup. Take 2.5ml four times a day for 5 days; supply 100 ml; NHS Cost £3.23.

Flucloxacillin syrup: 125mg four times a day
- Age from 12 months to 4 years
- Flucloxacillin 125mg/5ml syrup. Take one 5ml spoonful four times a day for 5 days; supply 100 ml; NHS Cost £3.23.

Flucloxacillin syrup: 250mg four times a day
- Age from 5 to 11 years
- Flucloxacillin 250mg/5ml syrup. Take one 5ml spoonful four times a day for 5 days; supply 100 ml; NHS Cost £6.97.

Flucloxacillin capsules: 250mg four times a day
- Age from 12 years onwards
- Flucloxacillin 250mg capsules. Take one capsule four times a day for 5 days; supply 20 capsules; NHS Cost £2.09.

Flucloxacillin capsules: 500mg four times a day
- Age from 12 years onwards
- Flucloxacillin 500mg capsules. Take one capsule four times a day for 5 days; supply 20 capsules; NHS Cost £3.54.

Erythromycin s/f suspension: 125mg four times a day
- Age from 3 to 23 months
- Erythromycin 125mg/5ml sf susp. Take one 5ml spoonful four times a day for 5 days; supply 100 ml; NHS Cost £1.01.

Erythromycin s/f suspension: 250mg four times a day
- Age from 2 to 11 years
- Erythromycin 250mg/5ml sf susp. Take one 5ml spoonful four times a day for 5 days; supply 100 ml; NHS Cost £1.97.

Erythromycin s/f suspension: 500mg four times a day
- Age from 9 to 11 years
- Erythromycin 500mg/5ml sf susp. Take one 5ml spoonful four times a day for 5 days; supply 100 ml; NHS Cost £3.38.

Erythromycin e/c tablets: 250mg four times a day
- Age from 12 years onwards
- Erythromycin 250mg e/c tablets. Take one tablet four times a day for 5 days; supply 20 tablets; NHS Cost £2.20.

Erythromycin e/c tablets: 500mg four times a day
- Age from 12 years onwards
- Erythromycin 250mg e/c tablets. Take two tablets four times a day for 5 days; supply 40 tablets; NHS Cost £4.40.

Treatment failure (acute diffuse)

Which therapy?

- **Review the diagnosis** and exclude suppurative otitis media, inadequate aural toilet, poor compliance, contact dermatitis, continued trauma (e.g. scratching), excessive exposure to water (e.g. swimming), and underlying skin conditions. Consider resistant infection, fungal superinfection, underlying fungal infection. Consider the possibility of conditions with increased susceptibility to infection (e.g. immunosuppression, diabetes mellitus).
- **Re-emphasize advice to keep the ear dry,** to refrain from blocking off drainage with cotton wool (unless it is put in loosely and replaced frequently), and neither to scratch nor to 'clean' with cotton buds.
- **Ensure ear canal is kept clear** by gentle syringing, dry mopping, or ear suction (if available).
- **Check usage of topical treatments** (frequency and method of application). Manipulating the tragus and pinna a few times while lying down with the affected ear uppermost helps to deliver drops to the deep part of the ear.
- **Consider inserting a wick** (by an appropriately trained person) to allow the drops to travel along the length of the ear canal, especially if the ear canal is swollen. Daily visits to the practice nurse to replace the wick and ensure compliance are generally recommended.
- **If there is suspected contact sensitivity** to topical medication/excipients, use an alternative topical treatment. If symptoms persist, consider referral to a dermatologist for patch testing.
- **If there is systemic upset or evidence of spreading infection,** prescribe oral flucloxacillin (or erythromycin if the person is allergic to penicillin).
- If symptoms persist, consider referral to an ear, nose, and throat service.
- **Continue pain relief if necessary.**

Practical prescribing points

For further information please see the *Medicines Compendium* (www.medicines.org.uk) or the *British National Formulary* (www.bnf.org).

- **Acetic acid 2% ear drops** may cause burning or irritation on application. The person should be warned of this, as it may otherwise affect compliance.
- **Aminoglycosides (neomycin and gentamicin):** the Committee on Safety of Medicines advises that treatment with a topical aminoglycoside antibiotic is contraindicated in those with a tympanic perforation.
- **Fungal superinfection** can occur with prolonged use of antibacterial/corticosteroid combinations. These products should be used for no longer than 7 days.
- **Contact sensitivity** may occur with topically applied ear drops and may aggravate the condition.

Should I refer or investigate?

Refer?

- **Contact sensitivity to constituents:** consider referral for patch testing.
- **Malignant (necrotizing) otitis externa:** requires urgent admission.

Investigate?

- **Ear swab** for culture should be reserved for treatment failures or chronic cases.
    - An ear swab is best taken from the medial aspect of the canal under visualization to reduce contamination.

- Bacterial and fungal stains and cultures should be obtained.
- Note that reported bacterial susceptibility may not correlate with clinical outcomes because sensitivities are determined for systemic (not topical) administration. However, identifying the organism, and especially distinguishing a fungal from a bacterial infection, can be of therapeutic significance.

Patient information leaflets

The following PILs are available at www.prodigy.nhs.uk

- Otitis Externa
- Otitis Externa - Chronic
- Otitis Externa - Furuncle

Shared decision making

- **A change of ear drops may be needed** if an ear infection has not gone.
  - Most drops contain an antibiotic to clear infection and a steroid to reduce itch and inflammation.
  - **Acetic acid ear drops** are an alternative.
  - **Antifungal ear drops** are used if a fungal infection is suspected.
  - **Steroid-only drops** are used if an allergy is suspected.
  - When using drops:
    - Lie with the ear upwards.
    - Put in several drops, and lie in this position for 1–2 minutes.
    - Press the cartilage at the front of the ear canal a few times to push the drops deep inside.
- **The ear may need special cleansing** to clear discharge.
- **A wick** soaked in **ear drops** and placed into the ear is an option that helps to keep the medicine working all the time.
- **Painkillers** such as paracetamol or ibuprofen, and a hot flannel held against the ear, help to ease the pain.
- **Antibiotic tablets** are sometimes needed if the infection is severe.
- If you need to put cotton wool into the ear to absorb discharge, place it loosely and replace it frequently.
- Do not irritate the ear canal:
  - Try not to scratch inside it.
  - Try to keep it dry and prevent soap or shampoo from getting in.
  - Do not clean or dry it with cotton buds, the corner of a towel, etc.

Drug rationale

Drugs not included

- **Neomycin/dexamethasone/glacial acetic acid (Otomize®), neomycin/triamcinolone (Audicort®), neomycin/hydrocortisone (Neo-Cortef®), framycetin/ gramicidin/ dexamethasone (Sofradex®) and neomycin/ polymyxin B/hydrocortisone (Otosporin®)** have been excluded because they are more expensive than other equally effective products. There is no good evidence to support greater efficacy.
- **Systemic antibiotics** that are not considered first-line treatment against *S aureus* (the most common pathogen) are excluded.
- **Chloramphenicol ear drops** are excluded because they contain propylene glycol, which can cause hypersensitivity reactions in about 10% of people.
- **Fluoroquinolone antibiotic ear drops** (ciprofloxacin and ofloxacin) are unlicensed and only available on a named-patient basis. They might be initiated in secondary care for resistant cases of pseudomonal infection.
- **Clotrimazole** is not included, as fungal infection is less common and usually can be effectively treated by topical products that have been included.
- **Aluminium acetate drops** are as effective as combination products [Hajioff, 2003]. They do not have a product licence and can only be obtained by special order. They are thus seldom a practical option.
- **Aspirin** is excluded because of its extensive adverse-effect profile and unsuitability for children under 16 years.

Drugs included

For infection

- **Acetic acid 2% ear drops** are as effective as combination products and are particularly useful when a sensitivity reaction is possible. Acetic acid has both antibacterial and antifungal activity [Ruddy and Bickerton, 1992] and the **ear drops** can be bought over the counter (EarCalm®).
- **Prednisolone/neomycin (Predsol-N®), betamethasone/ neomycin (Vista-methasone N® or Betnesol-N®), and flumetasone/clioquinol (Locorten-Vioform®) ear drops** are all similarly priced and contain an antibacterial (that is not used systemically) combined with a corticosteroid (to relieve irritation and inflammation). In addition, flumetasone/clioquinol has antibacterial and antifungal activity and does not have shared components with any other product if a sensitivity reaction is suspected.
- **Gentamicin/hydrocortisone ear drops** are included as an alternative. They do not have any components in common with flumetasone/clioquinol, but there is a possibility of cross-sensitivity with neomycin-containing products.
- **Gentamicin ear drops** are included if there is no accompanying inflammation. They do not have any shared components with flumetasone/clioquinol, but there is a possibility of cross-sensitivity and cross-resistance with neomycin-containing products.
- **Flucloxacillin (and erythromycin if allergic to penicillin)** are both active against *Staphylococcus aureus*.

For inflammation

- **Corticosteroid ear drops are offered for symptomatic relief in acute diffuse otitis externa.** They can be used in conjunction with **acetic acid 2% ear drops** to reduce inflammation when infection is present. They may also be used for an underlying inflammatory skin condition (such as atopic dermatitis or psoriasis).

For analgesia

- **Paracetamol** is usually effective for pain relief.
- **Codeine in combination with paracetamol** is offered for more severe pain.
- **Ibuprofen** is included as an alternative to paracetamol.

Prescriptions

Acetic acid 2% ear spray or flumetasone + clioquinol drops

Acetic acid 2% ear spray

- Age from 3 months onwards
- Acetic acid 2% ear spray. Spray once into the affected ear(s) at least three times a day. Maximum of one spray every 2 to 3 hours. Do not use for more than 7 days; supply 1 spray; NHS Cost £3.80; OTC Cost £6.38.

Flumetasone 0.02% + clioquinol 1% ear drops
- Age from 2 years onwards
- Flumetasone + clioquinol drops. Put two to three drops into the affected ear(s) twice a day for 7 to 10 days; supply 8 ml; NHS Cost £0.97.

Ear drops with neomycin/gentamicin

Betamethasone 0.1% + neomycin 0.5% ear drops
- Age from 3 months onwards
- Betamethasone + neomycin drops. Put two to three drops into the affected ear(s) 3 to 4 times a day until symptoms improve, then reduce frequency. Do not use for longer than 7 days; supply 10 ml; NHS Cost £1.84.

Prednisolone 0.5% + neomycin 0.5% ear drops
- Age from 3 months onwards
- Predsol-N ear drops. Put two to three drops into the affected ear(s) 3 to 4 times a day until symptoms improve, then reduce frequency. Do not use for longer than 7 days; supply 10 ml; NHS Cost £1.95.

Hydrocortisone 1% + gentamicin 0.3% ear drops
- Age from 3 months onwards
- Gentisone HC ear drops. Put two to three drops into the affected ear(s) 3 to 4 times a day and at night until symptoms improve, then reduce frequency. Max 7 days; supply 10 ml; NHS Cost £3.97.

Gentamicin 0.3% ear drops
- Age from 3 months onwards
- Gentamicin 0.3% eye drops. Put two to three drops into the affected ear(s) 3 to 4 times a day and at night. Use for a maximum of 7 days; supply 10 ml; NHS Cost £1.79.

Ear drops (steroid) for contact dermatitis

Betamethasone 0.1% ear drops
- Age from 3 months onwards
- Betamethasone 0.1% ear drops. Put two to three drops into the affected ear(s) every 2 to 3 hours until symptoms improve, then reduce frequency. Do not use for longer than 7 days; supply 10 ml; NHS Cost £1.84.

Prednisolone 0.5% ear drops
- Age from 3 months onwards
- Prednisolone 0.5% ear drops. Put two to three drops into the affected ear(s) every 2 to 3 hours until symptoms improve, then reduce frequency. Do not use for longer than 7 days; supply 10 ml; NHS Cost £1.83.

Analgesia: use when required

Paracetamol s/f susp: 60mg to 120mg up to four times a day
- Age from 3 to 11 months
- Paracetamol 120mg/5ml s/f susp. Take 2.5ml to 5ml every 4 to 6 hours when required for pain relief. Maximum of 4 doses in 24 hours; supply 150 ml; NHS Cost £0.65; OTC Cost £1.15.

Paracetamol s/f susp: 120mg to 240mg up to four times a day
- Age from 12 months to 5 years
- Paracetamol 120mg/5ml s/f susp. Take one to two 5ml spoonfuls every 4 to 6 hours when required for pain relief. Maximum of 4 doses in 24 hours; supply 300 ml; NHS Cost £1.30; OTC Cost £2.30.

Paracetamol s/f susp: 250mg to 500mg up to four times a day
- Age from 6 to 11 years
- Paracetamol 250mg/5ml s/f susp. Take one to two 5ml spoonfuls every 4 to 6 hours when required for pain relief. Maximum of 4 doses in 24 hours; supply 300 ml; NHS Cost £1.59; OTC Cost £2.80.

Paracetamol tablets: 500mg to 1g up to four times a day
- Age from 12 to 15 years
- Paracetamol 500mg tablets. Take one to two tablets every 4 to 6 hours when required for pain relief. Maximum of 8 tablets in 24 hours; supply 50 tablets; NHS Cost £0.38; OTC Cost £0.67.

Paracetamol tablets: 1g up to four times a day
- Age from 16 years onwards
- Paracetamol 500mg tablets. Take two tablets every 4 to 6 hours when required for pain relief. Maximum of 8 tablets in 24 hours; supply 50 tablets; NHS Cost £0.38; OTC Cost £0.67.

Codeine 30mg tablets: add on to paracetamol if required
- Age from 16 years onwards
- Codeine 30mg tablets. Take one to two tablets every 4 to 6 hours when required for pain relief. Maximum of 8 tablets in 24 hours; supply 30 tablets; NHS Cost £1.54.

Codeine 30mg tablets + paracetamol 500mg tablets
- Age from 16 years onwards
- Codeine 30mg tablets. Take one to two tablets every 4 to 6 hours when required for pain relief. Maximum of 8 tablets in 24 hours; supply 30 tablets; NHS Cost £1.54.
- Paracetamol 500mg tablets. Take two tablets every 4 to 6 hours when required for pain relief. Maximum of 8 tablets in 24 hours; supply 50 tablets; NHS Cost £0.38.

Ibuprofen s/f susp: 50mg three to four times a day
- Age from 12 months to 2 years
- Ibuprofen 100mg/5ml s/f susp. Take 2.5ml three to four times a day when required for pain relief. Do not exceed the stated dose; supply 100 ml; NHS Cost £1.82; OTC Cost £3.20.

Ibuprofen s/f susp: 100mg three to four times a day
- Age from 3 to 7 years
- Ibuprofen 100mg/5ml s/f susp. Take one 5ml spoonful 3 to 4 times a day when required for pain relief. Do not exceed the stated dose; supply 150 ml; NHS Cost £2.73; OTC Cost £4.81.

Ibuprofen s/f susp: 200mg three to four times a day
- Age from 8 to 11 years
- Ibuprofen 100mg/5ml s/f susp. Take two 5ml spoonfuls 3 to 4 times a day when required for pain relief. Do not exceed the stated dose; supply 300 ml; NHS Cost £5.46; OTC Cost £9.62.

Ibuprofen tablets: 400mg three times a day
- Age from 12 years onwards
- Ibuprofen 400mg tablets. Take one tablet three times a day when required for pain relief. Do not exceed the stated dose; supply 21 tablets; NHS Cost £0.62; OTC Cost £1.09.

Antibiotic for 5 days (not usually indicated)

Flucloxacillin syrup: 62.5mg four times a day
- Age from 3 to 11 months
- Flucloxacillin 125mg/5ml syrup. Take 2.5ml four times a day for 5 days; supply 100 ml; NHS Cost £3.23.

Flucloxacillin syrup: 125mg four times a day
- Age from 12 months to 4 years
- Flucloxacillin 125mg/5ml syrup. Take one 5ml spoonful four times a day for 5 days; supply 100 ml; NHS Cost £3.23.

Flucloxacillin syrup: 250mg four times a day
- Age from 5 to 11 years
- Flucloxacillin 250mg/5ml syrup. Take one 5ml spoonful four times a day for 5 days; supply 100 ml; NHS Cost £6.97.

Flucloxacillin capsules: 250mg four times a day
- Age from 12 years onwards
- Flucloxacillin 250mg capsules. Take one capsule four times a day for 5 days; supply 20 capsules; NHS Cost £2.09.

Flucloxacillin capsules: 500mg four times a day
- Age from 12 years onwards
- Flucloxacillin 500mg capsules. Take one capsule four times a day for 5 days; supply 20 capsules; NHS Cost £3.54.

Erythromycin s/f suspension: 125mg four times a day
- Age from 3 to 23 months
- Erythromycin 125mg/5ml sf susp. Take one 5ml spoonful four times a day for 5 days; supply 100 ml; NHS Cost £1.01.

Erythromycin s/f suspension: 250mg four times a day
- Age from 2 to 11 years
- Erythromycin 250mg/5ml sf susp. Take one 5ml spoonful four times a day for 5 days; supply 100 ml; NHS Cost £1.97.

Erythromycin s/f suspension: 500mg four times a day
- Age from 9 to 11 years
- Erythromycin 500mg/5ml sf susp. Take one 5ml spoonful four times a day for 5 days; supply 100 ml; NHS Cost £3.38.

Erythromycin e/c tablets: 250mg four times a day
- Age from 12 years onwards
- Erythromycin 250mg e/c tablets. Take one tablet four times a day for 5 days; supply 20 tablets; NHS Cost £2.20.

Erythromycin e/c tablets: 500mg four times a day
- Age from 12 years onwards
- Erythromycin 250mg e/c tablets. Take two tablets four times a day for 5 days; supply 40 tablets; NHS Cost £4.40.

Chronic otitis externa

Which therapy?

- **Review the diagnosis** and exclude suppurative otitis media, inadequate aural toilet, poor compliance, and continued trauma (e.g. scratching) or excessive exposure to water. Exclude more generalized conditions such as seborrhoeic dermatitis, atopic dermatitis, dermatophytosis, acne, and psoriasis. Consider the possibility of conditions with increased susceptibility to infection (e.g. immunosuppression, diabetes mellitus).
- **Contact sensitivity:** this should be particularly suspected if there is a history of frequent use of preparations containing aminoglycosides (e.g. neomycin). Avoid the offending products. If infection/superinfection has been eliminated, treat with topical corticosteroids. Alternatively, consider referral to a dermatologist for patch testing.
- **Advise the person** to keep the ear dry and to avoid scratching or cleaning the ear canal with cotton buds. If possible, it is best to avoid inserting cotton wool in the ear canal (as this blocks drainage). However, if this is necessary the cotton wool should be put in loosely and changed frequently.
- **Ensure the ear canal is clear** by regular gentle syringing, dry mopping, or ear suction (if available). *This maintenance is crucial to successful resolution.*
- **Continue pain relief if necessary** (but often there is little or no pain).
- **Take a swab of the ear canal** for microscopy and culture to identify possible infection and guide subsequent treatment.
- **If no cause is evident,** prescribe a 7-day course of acetic acid 2% ear drops or aluminium acetate ear drops (which are obtained by special order) together with a corticosteroid ear drop.
- **Bacterial infection:** treat according to sensitivity results. Flumetasone/clioquinol ear drops may be used while waiting for the results. Other options are acetic acid 2% ear drops (available over the counter and also on prescription) or aluminium acetate ear drops (which are obtained by special order). Continue treatment for 3 days after the symptoms have resolved.
- **Superficial fungal infection** with *Candida* or *Aspergillus*, or epidermal infection with dermatophytes may occur with long-term use of antibacterials or topical corticosteroids. These organisms can be difficult to treat. Acetic acid 2% ear drops may be tried first.
- **If dermatophyte infection** is suspected, consider specialist referral to confirm the diagnosis before starting specific antifungal treatment (e.g. with clotrimazole solution). Clotrimazole should be continued for at least 14 days after the infection has cleared.
- **Underlying seborrhoeic dermatitis:** combined antifungal and corticosteroid topical preparations are helpful (e.g. clotrimazole plus hydrocortisone).
- **Manipulating the tragus and pinna** a few times while lying down with the affected ear uppermost helps to deliver drops to the deep part of the ear.
- **Consider inserting a wick** to allow topical treatment to travel along the length of the ear canal, especially if the ear canal is swollen.
- **Consider daily visits to the practice nurse** to replace the wick and ensure compliance.

Practical prescribing points

For further information, please see the *Medicines Compendium* (www.medicines.org.uk) or the *British National Formulary* (www.bnf.org).

- **Acetic acid 2% ear drops** may cause burning or irritation on application. The person should be warned of this, as it may otherwise affect compliance.
- **Aminoglycosides (neomycin and gentamicin):** the Committee on Safety of Medicines advises that treatment with a topical aminoglycoside antibiotic is contraindicated in someone with a tympanic perforation.
- **Fungal superinfection** can occur with prolonged use of antibacterial/corticosteroid combinations. They should be used for no longer than 7 days.
- **Contact sensitivity** may occur with topically applied ear drops and may aggravate the condition.

Follow-up advice

- Review in 1 week to assess response to treatment.

Should I refer or investigate?

Refer?

- **Unresolving otitis externa** despite appropriate first-line treatment.
- **Contact sensitivity suspected:** consider referral for patch testing.
- **Occlusion (full or partial) of external ear canal.**
- **Malignant (necrotizing) otitis externa:** requires urgent admission.

Investigate?

- **Ear swab** for culture, although organisms that are isolated may not play a pathogenic role.

Patient information leaflets

The following PILs are available at www.prodigy.nhs.uk
- Otitis Externa - Chronic

Shared decision making

- **You may need a change of ear drops if the ear infection persists.**
  - Most drops contain an antibiotic to clear infection, and a steroid to reduce itch and inflammation.
  - Acetic acid or aluminium acetate ear drops are an alternative.
  - **Antifungal ear drops** are used if a fungal infection is suspected.
  - **Steroid-only drops** are used if an allergy is suspected.
  - When using drops:
    - Lie with the ear upwards.
    - Put in several drops, and lie in this position for 1–2 minutes.
    - Press the cartilage at the front of the ear canal a few times to push the drops deep inside.
- **The ear may need special cleansing** to clear any discharge.
- **A wick** soaked in ear drops and placed into the ear is an option that helps to keep the medicine working all the time.
- **Painkillers** such as paracetamol or ibuprofen, and a hot flannel held against the ear, help to ease the pain.
- **Antibiotic tablets** are sometimes needed if the infection is severe.
- If you need to put cotton wool into the ear to absorb discharge, place it loosely and replace it frequently.
- Do not irritate the ear canal:
  - Try not to scratch inside it.
  - Try to keep it dry and prevent soap or shampoo from getting in.
  - Do not clean or dry it with cotton buds, the corner of a towel, etc.

Drug rationale

Drugs not included

- **Systemic antibiotics** are not included, because they are not appropriate in this situation.
- **Chloramphenicol ear drops** are excluded because they contain propylene glycol, which can cause hypersensitivity reactions in about 10% of people.
- **Ear drops** containing an aminoglycoside are excluded because they have a high incidence of causing sensitivity reactions, and they may precipitate the chronic situation.
- **Aluminium acetate drops** are as effective as combination products [Hajioff, 2003]. They do not have a product licence and can only be obtained by special order. They are thus seldom a practical option.
- **Combination antifungal/corticosteroid topical preparations** that are not creams containing a mild corticosteroid (1% hydrocortisone) are not included.
- **Analgesia** is not included because chronic otitis externa is not usually painful [Bojrab et al, 1996].

Drugs included

For infection

- **Acetic acid 2% ear drops** are a 'best guess' treatment for use while awaiting the results of swabs. They have antibacterial and antifungal activities and are as effective as combination products. They are particularly useful in the chronic situation after previous frequent treatment with antibacterial/corticosteroid combinations, with risk of contact sensitization. They can also be bought over the counter (EarCalm®).
- **Flumetasone/clioquinol (Locorten-Vioform®) ear drops** are an alternative 'best guess' treatment. They do not contain aminoglycosides, which have a high incidence of contact sensitivity in chronic otitis externa [Ruddy and Bickerton, 1992].
- **Clotrimazole solution** is the only preparation available that specifically treats fungal infection.
- **Combination antifungal/corticosteroid creams** containing a mild steroid (hydrocortisone 1%) with miconazole (Daktacort®), econazole (Econacort®), clotrimazole (Canestan HC®), or clioquinol (Vioform-Hydrocortisone®) are effective treatments for seborrhoeic dermatitis.

For inflammation

- **Corticosteroid ear drops** are offered for short-term symptomatic relief. They can be used in conjunction with **acetic acid 2% ear drops** to reduce inflammation when infection is present. They may also be used for an underlying inflammatory skin condition (such as atopic dermatitis or psoriasis).

Prescriptions

Steroid ear drops

Betamethasone 0.1% ear drops
- Age from 3 months onwards
- Betamethasone 0.1% ear drops. Put two to three drops into the affected ear(s) every 2 to 3 hours until symptoms improve, then reduce frequency. Do not use for longer than 7 days; supply 10 ml; NHS Cost £1.84.

Prednisolone 0.5% ear drops
- Age from 3 months onwards
- Prednisolone 0.5% ear drops. Put two to three drops into the affected ear(s) every 2 to 3 hours until symptoms improve, then reduce frequency. Do not use for longer than 7 days; supply 10 ml; NHS Cost £1.83.

Antifungal ear drops

Acetic acid 2% ear spray
- Age from 3 months onwards
- Acetic acid 2% ear spray. Spray once into the affected ear(s) at least three times a day. Maximum of one spray every 2 to 3 hours. Do not use for more than 7 days; supply 2 spray; NHS Cost £7.60; OTC Cost £12.76.

Flumetasone 0.02% + clioquinol 1% ear drops
- Age from 2 years onwards
- Flumetasone + clioquinol drops. Put two to three drops into the affected ear(s) twice a day for 7 to 10 days; supply 8 ml; NHS Cost £0.97.

Clotrimazole 1% solution
- Age from 3 months onwards
- Clotrimazole 1% solution. Put two to three drops into the affected ear(s) 2 to 3 times a day; supply 20 ml; NHS Cost £2.43; OTC Cost £4.25.

Ribbon gauze for wick
- Age from 3 months onwards
- Ribbon gauze 1.25cm. Use to make a wick; supply 1 roll; NHS Cost £0.71.

Antifungal + steroid cream for seborrhoeic dermatitis

Clotrimazole 1% + hydrocortisone 1% cream
- Age from 3 months onwards
- Hydrocortisone+clotrimaz cream. Apply thinly to the affected area twice a day for 7 days; supply 30 grams; NHS Cost £2.38.

Miconazole 2% + hydrocortisone 1% cream
- Age from 3 months onwards
- Hydrocortisone+miconazole cream. Apply thinly to the affected area twice a day for 7 days; supply 30 grams; NHS Cost £2.24.

O

Econazole 1% + hydrocortisone 1% cream
- Age from 3 months onwards
- Hydrocortisone+econazole cream. Apply thinly to the affected area twice a day for 5 days; supply 30 grams; NHS Cost £2.25.

Clioquinol 1% + hydrocortisone 1% cream
- Age from 2 years onwards
- Vioform-Hydrocortisone cream. Apply thinly to the affected area 1 to 3 times a day for 7 days; supply 30 grams; NHS Cost £1.46.

Non-drug management

Advice only: aural toilet
- Age from 3 months onwards
- To keep the ear canal free of inflammation: Do not scratch or poke the ear canal with fingers, cotton buds, etc. Do not clean the ear canal with cotton buds. They may scratch and irritate and push wax or dirt further in. Try to stop soap or shampoo from getting in. A piece of cotton wool coated in soft white paraffin (e.g. Vaseline) placed in the outer ear may help when showering. Do not use corners of towels or cotton buds to dry any water that does get into the ear canal. This will push things further in. Let it dry naturally. Consider using silicone plugs when swimming to keep water out.

Extended Information

Background information

- What is it? p.1402
- How common is it? p.1402
- How do I know my patient has it? p.1402
- What else might it be? p.1403
- Complications and prognosis p.1403

What is it?

- **Otitis externa includes all the inflammatory conditions of the auricle, external ear canal, or outer surface of the eardrum.** Otitis externa can be localized, or diffuse; can be acute or chronic; and can be caused by infections, allergies, irritants or inflammatory conditions.
- **Localized otitis externa (furunculosis)** is an infected hair follicle in the outer ear canal; *Staphylococcus aureus* is the usual organism [Ruddy and Bickerton, 1992].
- **Acute diffuse otitis externa:**
  - **Bacterial infection,** most commonly *Pseudomonas aeruginosa* or *S aureus*, is the most common cause of acute diffuse otitis externa.
  - **Fungal infection** is much less common, but is more likely after prolonged courses of topical antibacterials and/or corticosteroids.
    - Superficial fungal infection is usually due to *Candida albicans* and occasionally *Aspergillus* species.
    - Dermatophyte infections of the stratum corneum are due to epidermophyton, trichophyton, and microsporum genera.
    - Seborrhoeic dermatitis is a common cause of chronic otitis externa (or may be a background factor in acute otitis externa). Seborrhoeic dermatitis may affect the ears in isolation, or may be associated with one or more of dandruff, eyebrow scaling, blepharitis, or facial redness and scaling. Seborrhoeic dermatitis is an eczematous reaction provoked by commensal yeast (*Pityrosporum* or *Malassezia* species).
  - **Contact dermatitis** is caused by a local irritant or allergen, such as topical medications, hearing aids, or earplugs.
  - **Allergic contact dermatitis** usually has a sudden onset.
  - **Irritant contact dermatitis** tends to have an insidious onset.
  - Factors that may precipitate or underlie otitis externa include ear trauma (scratching, foreign objects in ear, use of cotton buds, ear syringing, hearing aids); excessive moisture, swimming (especially in polluted water); chemicals (hair spray, hair dyes, shampoo, cerumenolytics); and skin conditions (e.g. atopic dermatitis, seborrhoeic dermatitis, psoriasis, acne, dermatophytoses).
  - Sometimes no cause can be identified.

[MERCK, 1999; Brook, 2001; Sander, 2001].
- **Chronic otitis externa** usually occurs as the result of long-term infection of the ear canal lasting from months to years. The low-grade, persistent infection causes thickening of the skin in the ear canal, loss of normal skin structure, and reduced cerumen (earwax) production. Often the ear-canal flora have been modified by prolonged and extensive use of topical antibacterials or corticosteroids, predisposing the ear to secondary fungal infections [Brook, 2001].
- **Malignant (necrotizing) otitis externa** is a life-threatening extension of otitis externa into the bone surrounding the ear canal (i.e. mastoid and temporal bones). This complication is most frequently due to *P aeruginosa* or *S aureus*. [Walshe et al, 2002; Grandis et al, 2004].

How common is it?

- **Acute otitis externa affects up to 10% of the population at some time in their lives,** and a general practitioner can expect to see 16 new cases per year [Raza et al, 1995].
- **Otitis externa** is slightly more common in women than in men, the prevalence peaking in women aged 45–54 years and in men aged 65–74 years [Rowlands et al, 2001].
- **Acute otitis externa is five times more common in swimmers as compared with non-swimmers** [Raza et al, 1995].
- **Acute otitis externa occurs more frequently in hot, humid environments** (e.g. in Mediterranean countries, Australia, and South East Asia), with an incidence 10–20 times higher in the summer than during cooler months [Marcy, 1985].
- **A small number of cases become chronic,** with symptoms persisting for more than 2 months and maybe even for years [Ruddy and Bickerton, 1992].
- **Malignant (necrotizing) otitis externa** is rare, usually affecting people who are immunocompromised or elderly with insulin-dependent diabetes, but can occur at any age and in people who are not immunocompromised [Walshe et al, 2002; Grandis et al, 2004].

How do I know my patient has it?

Acute localized otitis externa (furunculosis)

- **The main symptom is severe ear pain,** disproportionate to the size of the lesion.
- Hearing loss may occur if the ear canal is occluded.
- There may be sudden relief of pain if the furuncle bursts.
- **On examination of the ear canal,** a small red swelling in the ear canal is typical of an early presentation. Sometimes this progresses and the swelling eventually completely occludes the ear canal.
- The person complains of exquisite pain when the tragus or pinna is moved, or when an auriscope is inserted.
- The post-auricular lymph node may also be tender and painful.

[Hirsch, 1992; Bojrab et al, 1996; Brook, 2001; Sander, 2001]

Acute diffuse otitis externa

- **Symptoms include** any combination of ear pain, itch, discharge, or deafness.
- **On examination,** the ear canal or external ear, or both, appear red, swollen, or eczematous, with shedding of the scaly skin. There may be a discharge in the ear canal. The eardrum often looks inflamed and may be difficult to visualize. There is often tenderness on moving the ear or jaw. There may be tender regional lymphadenitis.
- Table 1 lists clinical characteristics that can help distinguish causes of otitis externa.

[Hirsch, 1992; Bojrab et al, 1996; Brook, 2001; Sander, 2001]

Chronic otitis externa

- **Symptoms include** a constant itch in the ear and mild discomfort. Pain, if present, is usually mild.
- **On examination,** there is a lack of cerumen, and dry hypertrophic skin, which varies in thickness but often results in at least partial canal stenosis. Manipulation of the external ear canal and auricle may be painful.
- Table1 lists clinical characteristics that can help distinguish causes of otitis externa.

[Hirsch, 1992]

What is the role of ear swabs in establishing the cause of otitis externa?

- **Ear swabs** should be reserved for treatment failures or chronic cases.
  - An ear swab is best taken from the medial aspect of the canal under visualization to reduce contamination.
  - Bacterial and fungal stains and cultures should be obtained.
  - Reported bacterial susceptibility may not correlate with clinical outcomes because sensitivities are determined for systemic (not topical) administration. However, identifying the organism, and especially distinguishing a fungal from a bacterial infection, can be of therapeutic significance.
  - Swab microbiology can not distinguish infection from contact dermatitis. This is particularly problematic when a fungus is isolated from an ear that has been treated with antibiotics such as neomycin.

[Bluestone et al, 2003; Roland, Personal Communication, 2004]

Clinical characteristics of otitis externa that aid differentiation of causes

- Table 1 is designed to help establish the cause of otitis externa. For each cause of otitis externa, the typical clinical characteristics are listed.

Table 1: Clinical characteristics of otitis externa that aid differentiation of causes of otitis externa.

Cause of otitis externa	Clinical characteristics
Bacterial: localized (furuncle)	Severe ear pain. Localized swelling of ear canal. Mild fever (e.g. =<38°C). Lymphadenopathy (pre-auricular).
Bacterial: acute, diffuse	Pain of variable severity. Generalized swelling of ear canal. Mild fever (e.g. =<38°C). Lymphadenopathy (pre-auricular). Discharge (Acute: scant, white; occasionally thick. Chronic: bloody). Bacterial infection is often secondary.
Bacterial: chronic, diffuse	Cerumen absent. Skin of ear canal dry, hypertrophic, variable swelling and stenosis, may be excoriated with mucopurulent discharge.
Fungal: superficial infection	Acute or subacute onset. Itching. Discomfort. Scaling. Discharge, if present, varies in colour; hyphae may be visible.
Fungal otitis externa: dermatophyte infection	Insidious onset. 'Ringworm': annular lesions, erythematous spreading borders, central clearing. Rarer presentations vary widely; may have erythema, swelling, vesicles, and abscesses.
Bullous otitis externa	Multiple bluish-red haemorrhagic blisters on the eardrum and in the ear canal; often associated with viral infections or infection with *Haemophilus* or *Mycoplasma*.
Contact dermatitis: irritant	Insidious onset. Lichenification.
Contact dermatitis: allergic	Rapid onset. Itching. Erythema. Oedema. Occasionally vesiculation. Exudate.
Seborrhoeic dermatitis	Skin greasy or powdery scaling. More generalized involvement, especially scalp, face, upper trunk.
Atopic dermatitis	Chronic, intense itching associated with allergens or stress. Skin: erythematous, excoriated, lichenified, hyperpigmented. More generalized involvement, especially face and neck.
Malignant (necrotizing) otitis externa	Pain and headache more severe than clinical signs would suggest. Facial nerve palsy. Granulation tissue at bone–cartilage junction of ear canal.

Adapted and augmented from [Sander, 2001]

What else might it be?

- **Foreign body:** suspect particularly in children.
- **Earwax:** may become impacted causing pain and deafness.
- **Otitis media:** causes ear pain, and, if the eardrum perforates, purulent smelly discharge.
- **Cholesteatoma:** eroding epithelial tissue in the middle ear and mastoid, with discharge in the ear canal.
- **Mastoiditis:** consider if the person feels very unwell, or has a high temperature or marked hearing loss, or there is mastoid tenderness or swelling.
- **Neoplasm:** consider if there is a swelling in the ear canal that bleeds easily on contact.
- **Referred pain:** may originate from the sphenoidal sinus, teeth, neck, or throat.
- **Ramsay Hunt syndrome:** a form of herpes zoster affecting the facial nerve, associated with facial paralysis and loss of taste, which can also produce pain in the ear and other areas supplied by the nerve.
- **Barotrauma:** consider this in divers, in people who have recently flown, or if the person has received a blow to the ear.
- **Skin conditions:** seborrhoeic dermatitis, atopic dermatitis, dermatophytosis, psoriasis, acne, herpes simplex, herpes zoster, lupus erythematosus. These may be risk factors, or the underlying cause of otitis externa.

These conditions can usually be differentiated by history (e.g. rapidity of onset, duration, pattern of symptoms) and clinical examination.

[Marcy, 1985; Cohen and Friedman, 1987; Ruddy and Bickerton, 1992]

Complications and prognosis

Complications

- Abscess development
- Spreading cellulitis
- Stenosis of the ear canal causing conductive deafness may complicate chronic otitis externa

Management issues

- Acute localized otitis externa (furunculosis) p.1404
- Acute diffuse otitis externa p.1404
- Chronic otitis externa p.1404
- Special considerations p.1405

Acute localized otitis externa (furunculosis)

- **Symptomatic treatment** with analgesia and application of local heat (e.g. a hot flannel) is often adequate.
- **If symptoms are severe or there is systemic upset,** treatment with oral flucloxacillin (or, if allergic to penicillin, erythromycin) is indicated.
- **Incision and drainage is rarely necessary,** but may be needed to relieve severe pain and swelling.

[Brook, 2001; Sander, 2001]

Acute diffuse otitis externa

General measures

- **Exclude the possibility** of an underlying chronic otitis media before commencing treatment.
- **Effective ear toilet is most important.** Clear the ear canal of all debris and discharge. The presence of infected debris lowers the pH of the ear canal and reduces the activity of aminoglycoside ear drops. Cleaning is most conveniently done by gentle syringing, but can also be done by dry mopping, or by ear suction (if available). Cleaning may be needed several times a week if the debris is heavy.
- **Effective pain relief** can be achieved using paracetamol, which can be combined with codeine when the pain is more severe. Ibuprofen is an effective alternative.
- **Removal of the precipitating antigen or irritant** is the most important measure for contact dermatitis.
- **Periodic use of a topical mild corticosteroid may be necessary** to prevent recurrent acute otitis externa if there is underlying skin disease, such as atopic dermatitis or psoriasis. (For advice on underlying seborrhoeic dermatitis, see *Chronic otitis externa*.)
- **Advise the person to keep the ear dry and to avoid scratching and cleaning the ear canal** with cotton buds. It is best to avoid inserting any kind of plug (e.g. cotton wool, gauze) in the ear canal, because this blocks drainage. However, if this is necessary (e.g. for cosmetic reasons), the plug should be put in loosely and changed frequently. To keep water from entering the ear while washing, plug the ear with cotton wool covered with petroleum jelly. To keep water from entering the ear while swimming, use a tightly fitting cap that covers the ears; ear plugs may traumatize and aggravate inflamed skin in the ear canal.

[Yelland, 1992; Raza et al, 1995; Bojrab et al, 1996; Brook, 2001; Sander, 2001]

When are topical drug treatments recommended?

- **Topical treatment is usually effective, and is recommended unless the person is systemically unwell or there is evidence of spreading infection (cellulitis).**
- **If the ear canal is swollen,** packing with a wick or ribbon gauze soaked in corticosteroid or an astringent allows medication to travel along the length of the ear canal [Pond et al, 2002]. When this is not practical, the person should be advised to introduce the ear drops while lying with the affected ear uppermost and to keep this position for 10 minutes [BNF 47, 2004].
- There is insufficient evidence on relative effectiveness to prefer one treatment to its alternatives [Hajioff, 2003]. Rational choices are thus made on the basis of patient preferences, the risk of adverse effects (e.g. discomfort, superinfection, contact dermatitis, promotion of resistance), availability, cost, and simplicity.
- **Options for topical treatments** include acetic acid alone, acetic acid ear drops plus corticosteroid ear drops, or corticosteroid alone. In the case of infection, anti-infective preparations alone or anti-infective preparations combined with corticosteroid could be used, but acetic acid and/or corticosteroid drops are also effective, because infection is usually secondary.
- **Acetic acid 2% ear drops** are available on prescription and over the counter as Earcalm®. They can be used first-line to treat bacterial and/or fungal disease. Because they are acidic, they can sting inflamed skin, and this could reduce patient compliance [Dohar, 2003]. The risk of contact dermatitis may be lower than with aminoglycosides, and the risk of superinfection may be lower than with corticosteroids. They may be more effective when used together with a corticosteroid preparation [van Balen et al, 2003].
- **Aluminium acetate drops** are effective [Hajioff, 2003], but they do not have a product licence and can only be obtained by special order, which makes them expensive and causes delays. They are thus seldom a practical option.
- **Anti-infective topical treatments** are available in a large number of products. These include antibacterials (aminoglycosides, fluoroquinolones), antifungals, drugs with both anti-bacterial and anti-fungal activity (clioquinol), and various combinations of anti-infectives with a corticosteroid. First choices in this class of treatment include:
    - **For antibacterial cover:** neomycin combined with betamethasone, hydrocortisone, triamcinolone or prednisolone, or gentamicin on its own or combined with hydrocortisone.
    - **For antibacterial and antifungal cover:** clioquinol plus flumetasone.
- Second choices would be fluoroquinolones (concerns about promoting resistance), and preparations with multiple drugs (simpler products are probably equally effective).
- **Treatment with drops containing an antibacterial or corticosteroid should be used for no longer than 7 days,** owing to the risk of secondary fungal infection or possible sensitization of the auricle or external ear canal.
- **Contact sensitivity** may occur with topically applied ear drops, and is most commonly due to antibiotics (especially aminoglycosides, which may all cross-react) and preservatives. Referral for patch testing may be necessary in some cases.

[Raza et al, 1995; Bojrab et al, 1996; Brook, 2001; Sood et al, 2002; BNF 47, 2004]

When are oral antibiotics recommended?

- **Oral antibiotics are indicated if** the person is systemically unwell or there is evidence of spreading infection.
- **Flucloxacillin (or erythromycin if the person is allergic to penicillin)** is preferred, because infection is usually due to *Staphylococcus aureus*.

[Bojrab et al, 1996; BNF 47, 2004]

Chronic otitis externa

- **Chronic otitis externa is usually due to** inadequate aural toilet; continued trauma (e.g. scratching) or exposure to water (swimming); poor adherence to treatment; contact sensitivity to previous topical treatment; fungal superinfection due to excessive use of antibacterial drops; skin disease (e.g. atopic dermatitis, seborrhoeic dermatitis, psoriasis); use of a hearing aid or ear plugs; or underlying anatomical abnormality, such as meatal stenosis.

- **Apply general measures, as for** *Acute diffuse otitis externa*: keep ear canal dry and free of debris and discharge; relieve pain; remove any precipitating antigens or irritants; treat any underlying skin condition such as seborrhoeic dermatitis; advise on ear care and avoidance of aggravating factors.
- **Topical treatments are recommended,** generally as for *Acute diffuse otitis externa.*
- **If sensitivity to a previous topical treatment is suspected,** then choose a different product with no shared or cross-reacting constituents.
- **If no cause is evident,** prescribe a 7-day course of acetic acid 2% ear drops or aluminium acetate ear drops (which are obtained by special order) together with a corticosteroid ear drop.
- **Referral for specialist care** may be necessary, as chronic otitis externa can be difficult to treat.
- **Fungal infection** may occur if topical antibiotics or topical steroids are used long-term. Fungal infections can be difficult to treat, and specialist referral should be considered if this is suspected, or if there is inadequate response to treatment.
  - Superficial fungal infection is caused by *Aspergillus* (80–90% of cases) and *Candida.* Acetic acid 2% or clotrimazole solution for 4 weeks may be tried first to treat superficial fungal infections of the ear canal.
  - Dermatophyte infection is due to *Epidermophyton, Trichophyton,* and *Microsporum* species. These are the moulds that cause tinea capitis, tinea corporis, etc.
  - Seborrhoeic dermatitis causing otitis externa is treated topically with an antifungal combined with a corticosteroid.

[Raza et al, 1995; Bojrab et al, 1996; Brook, 2001; BNF 47, 2004]

Special considerations

- **If the eardrum is perforated,** the Committee on Safety of Medicines (CSM) has issued a reminder that the use of drops containing aminoglycosides (neomycin, framycetin, gentamicin) is contraindicated in view of possible ototoxicity. However, some specialists do use these products cautiously in the presence of a perforation in people with otitis externa where other measures have failed [BNF 47, 2004].
- **Malignant (necrotizing) otitis externa** presents with severe pain, discharge, and an intensely inflamed ear canal, with redness and swelling of the ear and surrounding tissue. There may be a unilateral facial palsy due to infection of the facial nerve. The malignant form may be difficult to differentiate from a severe otitis externa. Admit urgently for confirmation of diagnosis and treatment [Walshe et al, 2002; Grandis et al, 2004].
- **Pseudomonal infection in people who are immunocompromised or have diabetes mellitus** may require treatment with ciprofloxacin (or gentamicin).

[Cohen and Friedman, 1987; Ruddy and Bickerton, 1992]

References

NHS staff in England can link, free of charge, from references to full text journals by clicking on [Full text] on the PRODIGY website.

1. Bluestone, C., Casselbrant, M. and Dohar, J. (2003) *Targeted therapies in otitis media and otitis externa.* Ontario: BC Decker.
2. BNF 47 (2004) *British National Formulary.* 47th edn. London: British Medical Association and Royal Pharmaceutical Society of Great Britain.
3. Bojrab, D.I., Bruderly, T. and Abdulrazzak, Y. (1996) Otitis externa. *Otolaryngologic Clinics of North America* **29**(5), 761–782.
4. Brook, I. (2001) Treatment of otitis externa in children. *Paediatric Drugs* **1**(4), 283–289.
5. Cohen, D. and Friedman, P. (1987) The diagnostic criteria of malignant external otitis. *Journal of Laryngology & Otology* **101**(3), 216–221.
6. Dohar, J.E. (2003) Evolution of management approaches for otitis externa. *Pediatric Infectious Disease Journal* **22**(4), 299–305.
7. Grandis, J.R., Branstetter IV, B.F. and Yu, V.L. (2004) The changing face of malignant (necrotising) external otitis: clinical, radiological, and anatomic correlations. *Lancet Infectious Diseases* **4**(1), 34–39.
8. Hajioff, D. (2003) Otitis externa. *Clinical Evidence* **10**(Dec), 605–611.
9. Hirsch, B.E. (1992) Infections of the external ear. *American Journal of Otolaryngology* **13**(3), 145–155.
10. Marcy, S.M. (1985) Infections of the external ear. *Pediatric Infectious Disease Journal* **4**(2), 192–201.
11. MERCK (1999) Bacterial infections of the skin. In: Beers, M.H. and Berkow, R. (Eds.) *Merck Manual.* New York: Merck Publishing. 793–801.
12. Pond, F., McCarty, D. and O'Leary, S. (2002) Randomized trial on the treatment of oedematous acute otitis externa using ear wicks or ribbon gauze: clinical outcome and cost. *Journal of Laryngology & Otology* **116**(6), 415–419. [Full text]
13. Raza, S.A., Denholm, S.W. and Wong, J.C. (1995) An audit of the management of acute otitis externa in an ENT casualty clinic. *Journal of Laryngology & Otology* **109**(2), 130–133.
14. Roland, P.S. (2004) *Personal communication.* Chief of Pediatric Otology, Children's Medical Center: Dallas.
15. Rowlands, S., Devalia, H., Smith, C. et al (2001) Otitis externa in UK general practice: a survey using the UK General Practice Research Database. *British Journal of General Practice* **51**(468), 533–538.
16. Ruddy, J. and Bickerton, R.C. (1992) Optimum management of the discharging ear. *Drugs* **43**(2), 219–235.
17. Sander, R. (2001) Otitis externa: a practical guide to treatment and prevention. *American Family Physician* **63**(5), 927–936. [Full text]
18. Sood, S., Strachan, D.R., Tsikoudas, A. and Stables, G.I. (2002) Allergic otitis externa. *Clinical Otolaryngology & Allied Sciences* **27**(4), 233–236.
19. van Balen, F.A.M., Smit, W.M., Zuithoff, N.P.A. and Verheij, T.J.M. (2003) Clinical efficacy of three common treatments in acute otitis externa in primary care: randomised controlled trial. *British Medical Journal* **327**(7425), 1201–1205. [Full text]
20. Walshe, P., Cleary, M., McConn, W.R. and Walsh, M. (2002) Malignant otitis externa – a high index of suspicion is still needed for diagnosis. *Irish Medical Journal* **95**(1), 14–16.
21. Yelland, M. (1992) Otitis externa in general practice. *Medical Journal of Australia* **156**(5), 325–326.

PRODIGY GUIDANCE

Otitis media — acute

Last revised in June 2004
www.prodigy.nhs.uk/guidance.asp?gt=Otitis media - acute

Applies to people of all ages

This guidance covers infections of the middle ear. It focuses on the treatment of diagnosed uncomplicated infection, mainly, but not exclusively, in children.

This guidance does not cover glue ear or chronic suppurative conditions. There is a separate PRODIGY guidance for *Glue ear*.

Goals

- To resolve physical signs and symptoms within 7 days
- To prevent complications, recurrence, and chronicity
- To prescribe antibiotics only when appropriate, and to minimize the occurrence of antibiotic-related adverse effects

Contents

Scenarios

- First-line treatment p.1406
- Persistent acute otitis media or treatment failure p.1408

Extended Information, p. 1411

Which scenario?

- **First-line treatment:** covers the treatment of a new episode of otitis media.
- **Persistent acute otitis media or treatment failure:** covers the management of people returning with the same episode (within 2 weeks) of **acute otitis media** (AOM). This includes both people who did not initially receive antibiotics (i.e. persistent AOM) and those who received first-line antibiotics (i.e. treatment failure).

0

First-line treatment

Which therapy?

- **Analgesics should be the mainstay of treatment** for acute otitis media (AOM) in most cases.
  - **Paracetamol** is the preferred treatment for both adults and children.
  - **Ibuprofen** is an alternative to paracetamol.
- **Antibiotics should NOT be routinely prescribed** for uncomplicated AOM.
- **Discuss and reassure the individual or their guardian on the benefits of and drawbacks of using antibiotics for AOM.** The PRODIGY Patient Information Leaflet, *Otitis Media (Ear Infection)*, and Shared Decision Making screens are useful resources for this.
- **A good compromise is to use a 'wait and see' policy** by issuing a prescription to be redeemed after 72 hours (after the *start* of pain) if symptoms have not cleared.
- **Consider using an antibiotic** if the person is a child under 2 years of age, if there is bilateral AOM, or if there are significant systemic symptoms (e.g. temperature >38.5°C, or vomiting):
  - Amoxicillin for 5 days is the antibiotic of choice.
  - If the person has a true allergy to penicillin, the recommended choice is azithromycin for 3 days. Erythromycin or clarithromycin for 5 days are possible alternatives.

Practical prescribing points

For further information please see the *Medicines Compendium* (www.medicines.org.uk) or the *British National Formulary* (www.bnf.org).

Follow-up advice

- **Most people do not require follow-up.**
- **Consider follow-up in the following circumstances:**
  - The person is a young child (<2 years of age).
  - There are systemic symptoms such as high temperature (>38.5°C) or vomiting.
  - There is discharge from the ear. Visualisation of the tympanic membrane can be difficult when there is discharge present. Re-examine after 2 weeks to check the integrity of the membrane.

Should I refer or investigate?

Refer?

- **The National Institute for Clinical Excellence** (NICE) recommends that a child should be referred to an otolaryngologist if there are more than four episodes of acute otitis media in a 6-month period.
- **Consider referral** if there is persisting effusion or impaired hearing after 3 to 6 months (also see the separate PRODIGY guidance for *Glue ear*).
- **Refer urgently** if any of the following is present:
  - Sudden severe hearing loss (except in simple perforation)
  - Sudden dizziness with nystagmus
  - Signs suggesting meningitis
  - Progression to mastoiditis

Patient information leaflets

The following PILs are available at www.prodigy.nhs.uk

- Anti-inflammatory Painkillers
- Ear Infection (Otitis Media)
- Paracetamol
- Temperatures (Fevers) in Children

Shared decision making

- **Most bouts of ear infection clear on their own within a few days.**
- **Painkillers such as paracetamol or ibuprofen** are the main treatment. Use regularly until the pain eases. These will also lower a raised temperature.
- **Antibiotics are not advised in most cases.** They are an option if the infection is severe, or if it does not ease after 2–3 days:
  - **Amoxicillin** is the common antibiotic used for ear infections.

- **Azithromycin, erythromycin, or clarithromycin** are alternatives for people allergic to penicillin.
- **Antibiotics may cause side effects** such as diarrhoea or feeling sick.

Drug rationale

Drugs not included

- **Broad-spectrum penicillins, other than amoxicillin,** are not included, as they have not been studied as extensively as amoxicillin in acute otitis media (AOM), or have not been shown to have any advantage over amoxicillin [Glasziou et al, 2003; Takata et al, 2001].
  - **Ampicillin** has to be taken more frequently than amoxicillin [BNF 45, 2003].
  - **Phenoxymethylpenicillin** is effective against *Streptococcus pneumoniae*, but lacks efficacy against *Haemophilus influenzae* [Celin et al, 1991; Hoppe, 1996].
- **Co-amoxiclav** is usually regarded as a second-line antibiotic in the treatment of AOM. However, it should be considered in place of amoxicillin when resistant beta-lactamase-producing strains are known or thought to be present [BNF 45, 2003; SIGN, 2003].
- **Cephalosporins** are not usually recommended in the first-line treatment of AOM. Their effectiveness in AOM has not been extensively studied, and they are not always practical in primary care, owing to their formulation (that may require parenteral administration). In addition, people who are allergic to penicillin may be cross-sensitive to cephalosporins [DTB, 1996].
- **Co-trimoxazole** should be used only in exceptional circumstances, according to a recommendation from the Committee on Safety of Medicines [BNF 45, 2003].
- **Quinolones** are contraindicated in children under 16 years of age. In addition, they should only be used in adults when the organism sensitivity to them is known, as there are growing concerns about the development of resistance to these drugs in the community [DH and SMAC, 1998].
- **Antihistamines or decongestants** are not recommended for use in AOM, as they are not effective and have adverse effects [Flynn et al, 2003].
- **Aspirin and nonsteroidal anti-inflammatory drugs (NSAIDs), other than ibuprofen,** are excluded because of their relatively extensive adverse-effect profiles. In addition, aspirin should not be used in children under the age of 16 years [CSM, 2002].

Drugs included

- **Paracetamol and ibuprofen** are the mainstays of treatment for most people with acute otitis media (AOM). They are effective and relatively safe antipyretics and analgesics in both children and adults [Bertin et al, 1996].
- **Amoxicillin** is the recommended drug if a course of antibiotics is required. The best available evidence suggests that higher doses of amoxicillin should be used for 5 days:
  - It is effective against most of the organisms involved in AOM and has favourable pharmacokinetics, giving good concentrations in the middle ear.
  - It has been proven effective in clinical trials.
  - It has relatively few adverse effects.

[Alberta Clinical Practice Guidelines Working Group, 2000; Guidelines and Protocols Advisory Committee, 2002; PHLS, 2002; SIGN, 2003].

- **Macrolide antibiotics** are indicated in people who have a true allergy to penicillin or if amoxicillin is otherwise contraindicated:
  - **Azithromycin** is the preferred macrolide. It has superior activity against *Haemophilus influenzae* when compared with erythromycin, and has fewer associated gastrointestinal adverse effects. It is taken once a day for 3 days only, which may improve practical compliance.
  - **Erythromycin** is most commonly used and is inexpensive. However, it has poor activity against *H influenzae*, and often causes gastrointestinal adverse effects such as nausea.
  - **Clarithromycin** may have slightly better activity than erythromycin, and causes fewer gastrointestinal adverse effects. Although it is licensed as a 7-day antibiotic course, a 5-day course is likely to be as effective.

[DTB, 1991; PHLS, 2002; BNF 45, 2003]

Prescriptions

Analgesia: use when required

Paracetamol s/f susp: 60mg to 120mg up to four times a day
- Age from 3 to 11 months
- Paracetamol 120mg/5ml s/f susp. Take 2.5ml to 5ml every 4 to 6 hours when required for pain relief. Maximum of 4 doses in 24 hours; supply 150 ml; NHS Cost £0.63; OTC Cost £1.15.

Paracetamol s/f susp: 120mg to 240mg up to four times a day
- Age from 12 months to 5 years
- Paracetamol 120mg/5ml s/f susp. Take one to two 5ml spoonfuls every 4 to 6 hours when required for pain relief. Maximum of 4 doses in 24 hours; supply 300 ml; NHS Cost £1.26; OTC Cost £2.29.

Paracetamol s/f susp: 250mg to 500mg up to four times a day
- Age from 6 to 11 years
- Paracetamol 250mg/5ml s/f susp. Take one to two 5ml spoonfuls every 4 to 6 hours when required for pain relief. Maximum of 4 doses in 24 hours; supply 300 ml; NHS Cost £1.61; OTC Cost £2.80.

Paracetamol tablets: 500mg to 1g up to four times a day
- Age from 12 to 15 years
- Paracetamol 500mg tablets. Take one to two tablets every 4 to 6 hours when required for pain relief. Maximum of 8 tablets in 24 hours; supply 56 tablets; NHS Cost £0.42; OTC Cost £0.67.

Paracetamol tablets: 1g up to four times a day
- Age from 16 years onwards
- Paracetamol 500mg tablets. Take two tablets every 4 to 6 hours when required for pain relief. Maximum of 8 tablets in 24 hours; supply 56 tablets; NHS Cost £0.42; OTC Cost £0.67.

Ibuprofen s/f susp: 50mg three to four times a day
- Age from 12 months to 2 years
- Ibuprofen 100mg/5ml s/f susp. Take 2.5ml three to four times a day when required for pain relief. Do not exceed the stated dose; supply 100 ml; NHS Cost £1.82; OTC Cost £3.53.

Ibuprofen s/f susp: 100mg three to four times a day
- Age from 3 to 7 years
- Ibuprofen 100mg/5ml s/f susp. Take one 5ml spoonful 3 to 4 times a day when required for pain relief. Do not exceed the stated dose; supply 150 ml; NHS Cost £2.73; OTC Cost £4.81.

Ibuprofen s/f susp: 200mg three to four times a day
- Age from 8 to 11 years
- Ibuprofen 100mg/5ml s/f susp. Take two 5ml spoonfuls 3 to 4 times a day when required for pain relief. Do not

exceed the stated dose; supply 300 ml; NHS Cost £5.46; OTC Cost £9.62.

Ibuprofen tablets: 400mg three times a day
- Age from 12 years onwards
- Ibuprofen 400mg tablets. Take one tablet three times a day when required for pain relief. Do not exceed the stated dose; supply 21 tablets; NHS Cost £0.62; OTC Cost £1.75.

1st-line antibiotic: amoxicillin

Amoxicillin s/f suspension: 125mg three times a day
- Age from 1 month to 23 months
- Amoxicillin 125mg/5ml s/f susp. Take one 5ml spoonful three times a day for 5 days; supply 100 ml; NHS Cost £1.30.

Amoxicillin s/f susp: 250mg three times a day
- Age from 2 to 9 years
- Amoxicillin 250mg/5ml s/f susp. Take one 5ml spoonful three times a day for 5 days; supply 100 ml; NHS Cost £2.25.

Amoxicillin s/f susp: 500mg three times a day
- Age from 10 to 11 years
- Amoxicillin 250mg/5ml s/f susp. Take two 5ml spoonfuls three times a day for 5 days; supply 200 ml; NHS Cost £4.50.

Amoxicillin capsules: 500mg three times a day
- Age from 12 years onwards
- Amoxicillin 500mg capsules. Take one capsule three times a day for 5 days; supply 15 capsules; NHS Cost £1.32.

1st-line in penicillin allergy: azithromycin

Azithromycin suspension: 10mg/kg once a day
- Age from 6 months to 2 years
- Azithromycin 200mg/5ml susp. *WEIGHT REQUIRED* Take 10mg per kg bodyweight ONCE a day for 3 days; supply 15 ml; NHS Cost £5.08.

O

Azithromycin suspension: 200mg once a day
- Age from 3 to 7 years
- Azithromycin 200mg/5ml susp. Take one 5ml spoonful once a day for 3 days; supply 15 ml; NHS Cost £5.08.

Azithromycin suspension: 300mg once a day
- Age from 8 to 11 years
- Azithromycin 200mg/5ml sf susp. Take 7.5ml once a day for 3 days; supply 1 22.5 ml bottle; NHS Cost £7.62.

Azithromycin suspension: 400mg once a day
- Age from 12 to 13 years
- Azithromycin 200mg/5ml susp. Take two 5ml spoonfuls once a day for 3 days; supply 30 ml; NHS Cost £13.80.

Azithromycin capsules: 500mg once a day
- Age from 14 years onwards
- Azithromycin 250mg capsules. Take two capsules once a day for 3 days; supply 6 capsules; NHS Cost £13.42.

2nd-line penicillin allergy: erythromycin or clarithromycin

Erythromycin s/f suspension: 125mg four times a day
- Age from 1 month to 23 months
- Erythromycin 125mg/5ml sf susp. Take one 5ml spoonful four times a day for 5 days; supply 100 ml; NHS Cost £1.12.

Erythromycin s/f suspension: 250mg four times a day
- Age from 2 to 8 years
- Erythromycin 250mg/5ml sf susp. Take one 5ml spoonful four times a day for 5 days; supply 100 ml; NHS Cost £1.97.

Erythromycin s/f suspension: 500mg four times a day
- Age from 9 to 11 years
- Erythromycin 500mg/5ml sf susp. Take one 5ml spoonful four times a day for 5 days; supply 100 ml; NHS Cost £3.38.

Erythromycin e/c tablets: 500mg four times a day
- Age from 12 years onwards
- Erythromycin 250mg e/c tablets. Take two tablets four times a day for 5 days; supply 40 tablets; NHS Cost £4.40.

Clarithromycin suspension: 62.5mg twice a day
- Age from 12 months to 2 years
- Clarithromycin 125mg/5ml susp. Take 2.5ml twice a day for 5 days; supply 70 ml; NHS Cost £6.00.

Clarithromycin suspension: 125mg twice a day
- Age from 3 to 6 years
- Clarithromycin 125mg/5ml susp. Take one 5ml spoonful twice a day for 5 days; supply 70 ml; NHS Cost £6.00.

Clarithromycin suspension: 187.5mg twice a day
- Age from 7 to 9 years
- Clarithromycin 125mg/5ml susp. Take 7.5ml twice a day for 5 days; supply 100 ml; NHS Cost £10.32.

Clarithromycin suspension: 250mg twice a day
- Age from 10 to 11 years
- Clarithromycin 250mg/5ml susp. Take one 5ml spoonful twice a day for 5 days; supply 70 ml; NHS Cost £12.00.

Clarithromycin tablets: 250mg twice a day
- Age from 12 years onwards
- Clarithromycin 250mg tablets. Take one tablet twice a day for 5 days; supply 10 tablets; NHS Cost £8.03.

Persistent acute otitis media or treatment failure

Which therapy?

If an antibiotic has *not* already been prescribed for this episode

- **Consider giving a first-line antibiotic,** especially if the person is a child under 2 years of age, if there is bilateral AOM, or if there are significant systemic symptoms (e.g. temperature >38.5°C, or vomiting):
  - Amoxicillin for 5 days is the antibiotic of choice.
  - If the person has a true allergy to penicillin, azithromycin for 3 days is recommended. Erythromycin or clarithromycin for 5 days are possible alternatives.

If an antibiotic has already been prescribed for this episode (i.e. treatment failure)

- **Co-amoxiclav** is the second-line antibiotic of choice. It is effective against beta-lactamase-positive organisms that may be implicated in resistant AOM.
- **Azithromycin** should be considered if the person was initially prescribed erythromycin, but has encountered adverse effects that have affected compliance.
- **Consult your local microbiologist** if a first-line course of a macrolide was successfully completed (i.e. azithromycin, erythromycin, or clarithromycin). A cephalosporin or trimethoprim may be recommended.

Analgesia

- **Analgesics** should be continued.
  - **Paracetamol** is the preferred treatment for both adults and children.
  - **Ibuprofen** is an alternative to paracetamol.

Practical prescribing points

For further information, please see the *Medicines Compendium* (www.medicines.org.uk) or the *British National Formulary* (www.bnf.org).

- **The Committee on Safety of Medicines** has advised that the incidence of cholestatic jaundice with co-amoxiclav is about six times greater than with amoxicillin alone. Older people (over 65 years) are at greatest risk, and cases in children are rare. The condition is usually self-limiting and very rarely fatal.

Follow-up advice

- **Ask the person to return if second-line antibiotic treatment fails to clear the infection.** In addition, consider follow-up in the following circumstances:
  - The person is a young child (less than 2 years of age).
  - There are systemic symptoms such as high temperature (>38.5°C) or vomiting.
  - There is discharge from the ear. Visualisation of the tympanic membrane can be difficult when there is discharge present. Re-examine after 2 weeks to check the integrity of the membrane.

Should I refer or investigate?

Refer?

- **The National Institute for Clinical Excellence (NICE)** recommends that a child should be referred to an otolaryngologist if there are more than four episodes of acute otitis media (AOM) in a 6-month period.
- **Consider referral** if there is persisting effusion or impaired hearing after 3 to 6 months (also see the separate PRODIGY guidance for *Glue ear*).
- **Refer urgently** if any of the following is present:
  - Sudden severe hearing loss (except in simple perforation)
  - Sudden dizziness with nystagmus
  - Signs suggesting meningitis
  - Progression to mastoiditis

Investigate?

- **Consider sending a swab for culture and microbial sensitivity testing if there is perforation of the tympanic membrane** allowing a sample to be taken. This may be especially useful if first-line antibiotic treatment has failed.

Patient information leaflets

The following PILs are available at www.prodigy.nhs.uk

- Anti-inflammatory Painkillers
- Ear Infection (Otitis Media)
- Paracetamol
- Temperatures (Fevers) in Children

Shared decision making

- **The ear infection is still present.**
- **An antibiotic** is likely to clear the infection.
- **Amoxicillin** is the common antibiotic used for ear infections.
- Alternatives are:
  - **Co-amoxiclav,** if you have already had a course of amoxicillin that has not worked (some bacteria are resistant to some antibiotics.)
  - Azithromycin, erythromycin, or clarithromycin for people allergic to penicillin.
- **Antibiotics may cause side effects** such as diarrhoea or feeling sick.
- **Painkillers such as paracetamol or ibuprofen** are an important treatment *in addition* to antibiotics. Use regularly until the pain eases.

Drug rationale

Drugs not included

- **Broad-spectrum penicillins, other than amoxicillin and co-amoxiclav,** are not included. Either they have not been studied as extensively as amoxicillin in acute otitis media (AOM), or they have not been shown to have any advantage over amoxicillin. Co-amoxiclav is effective as a second-line antibiotic [Takata et al, 2001; Glasziou et al, 2003].
  - **Ampicillin** has to be taken more frequently than amoxicillin [BNF 45, 2003].
  - **Phenoxymethylpenicillin** is effective against *Streptococcus pneumoniae*, but lacks efficacy against *Haemophilus influenzae* [Celin et al, 1991; Hoppe, 1996].
- **Cephalosporins** are not usually recommended in the treatment of AOM without specialist advice or supervision. Their effectiveness in AOM has not been extensively studied, and they are not always practical in primary care, owing to their formulation (that may require parenteral administration). In addition people who are allergic to penicillin may be cross-sensitive to cephalosporins [DTB, 1996].
- **Co-trimoxazole** should be used only in exceptional circumstances, according to a recommendation from the Committee on Safety of Medicines [BNF 45, 2003].
- **Quinolones** are contraindicated in children under 16 years of age. In addition, they should only be used in adults when the organism sensitivity to them is known, as there are growing concerns about the development of resistance to these drugs in the community [DH and SMAC, 1998].
- **Antihistamines or decongestants** are not recommended for use in AOM, as they are not effective and have adverse effects [Flynn et al, 2003].
- **Aspirin and nonsteroidal anti-inflammatory drugs (NSAIDs), other than ibuprofen,** are excluded because of their relatively extensive adverse-effect profiles. In addition, aspirin should not be used in children under the age of 16 years [CSM, 2002].

Drugs included

- **Amoxicillin** is usually considered as the first-line antibiotic for acute otitis media (AOM). The best available evidence suggests that higher doses of amoxicillin should be used for 5 days:
  - It is effective against most of the organisms involved in AOM and has favourable pharmacokinetics, giving good concentrations in the middle ear.
  - It has been proven effective in clinical trials.
  - It has relatively few adverse effects.

[Alberta Clinical Practice Guidelines Working Group, 2000; Guidelines and Protocols Advisory Committee, 2002; PHLS, 2002; SIGN, 2003].

- The recommended dose of amoxicillin in the treatment of AOM varies according to different formularies. It is generally accepted that the dose may be doubled in adults and older children who exhibit symptoms of a severe infection [BNF 45, 2003].
- **Macrolide antibiotics** are first-line antibiotics in people who have a true allergy to penicillin, or for whom amoxicillin is otherwise contraindicated.
  - **Azithromycin** is the preferred macrolide. It has superior activity against *Haemophilus influenzae* when compared with erythromycin, and has fewer

associated gastrointestinal adverse effects. It is taken once a day for 3 days only, which may improve practical compliance.
- **Erythromycin** is most commonly used and is inexpensive. However, it has poor activity against *H influenzae*, and often causes gastrointestinal adverse effects such as nausea.
- **Clarithromycin** may have slightly better activity against *H influenzae* than erythromycin, and causes fewer gastrointestinal adverse effects. Although it is licensed as a 7-day antibiotic course, a 5-day course is likely to be as effective.

[DTB, 1991; PHLS, 2002; BNF 45, 2003].

- **Co-amoxiclav** is indicated as second-line treatment when amoxicillin has failed. It is a combination product consisting of amoxicillin and clavulanic acid.
  - It is effective against beta-lactamase-producing bacteria, including *Moraxella catarrhalis* and resistant strains of *Streptococcus pneumoniae*.
  - Co-amoxiclav is as effective as other beta-lactamase-resistant antibiotics (e.g. third-generation cephalosporins), is taken orally, and is inexpensive.
  - It has relatively few adverse effects.

[Alberta Clinical Practice Guidelines Working Group, 2000; Guidelines and Protocols Advisory Committee, 2002; PHLS, 2002; Easton et al, 2003].

- **Paracetamol and ibuprofen** should be continued if they are giving pain relief. They are effective and relatively safe antipyretics and analgesics in both children and adults [Bertin et al, 1996].

Prescriptions

1st-line antibiotic: amoxicillin

Amoxicillin s/f suspension: 125mg three times a day
- Age from 1 month to 23 months
- Amoxicillin 125mg/5ml s/f susp. Take one 5ml spoonful three times a day for 5 days; supply 100 ml; NHS Cost £1.30.

O

Amoxicillin s/f susp: 250mg three times a day
- Age from 2 to 9 years
- Amoxicillin 250mg/5ml s/f susp. Take one 5ml spoonful three times a day for 5 days; supply 100 ml; NHS Cost £2.25.

Amoxicillin s/f susp: 500mg three times a day
- Age from 10 to 11 years
- Amoxicillin 250mg/5ml s/f susp. Take two 5ml spoonfuls once a day for 5 days; supply 200 ml; NHS Cost £4.50.

Amoxicillin capsules: 500mg three times a day
- Age from 12 years onwards
- Amoxicillin 500mg capsules. Take one capsule three times a day for 5 days; supply 15 capsules; NHS Cost £1.32.

2nd-line treatment: co-amoxiclav

Co-amoxiclav 125/31mg/5ml susp: 0.25ml/kg three times a day
- Age from 1 month to 11 months
- Co-amoxiclav 125/31mg/5ml susp. *WEIGHT REQUIRED* Take 0.25ml per kg bodyweight THREE times a day for 5 days; supply 100 ml; NHS Cost £4.57.

Co-amoxiclav suspension: 125/31mg three times a day
- Age from 12 months to 6 years
- Co-amoxiclav 125/31mg/5ml susp. Take one 5ml spoonful three times a day for 5 days; supply 100 ml; NHS Cost £4.57.

Co-amoxiclav suspension: 250/62mg three times a day
- Age from 7 to 11 years
- Co-amoxiclav 250/62mg/5ml susp. Take one 5ml spoonful three times a day for 5 days; supply 100 ml; NHS Cost £6.42.

Co-amoxiclav tablets: 250/125mg three times a day
- Age from 12 years onwards
- Co-amoxiclav 375mg tablets. Take one tablet three times a day for 5 days; supply 15 tablets; NHS Cost £7.08.

1st-line in penicillin allergy: azithromycin

Azithromycin suspension: 10mg/kg once a day
- Age from 6 months to 2 years
- Azithromycin 200mg/5ml susp. *WEIGHT REQUIRED* Take 10mg per kg bodyweight ONCE a day for 3 days; supply 15 ml; NHS Cost £5.08.

Azithromycin suspension: 200mg once a day
- Age from 3 to 7 years
- Azithromycin 200mg/5ml susp. Take one 5ml spoonful once a day for 3 days; supply 15 ml; NHS Cost £5.08.

Azithromycin suspension: 300mg once a day
- Age from 8 to 11 years
- Azithromycin 200mg/5ml susp. Take 7.5ml once a day for 3 days; supply 22 ml; NHS Cost £7.62.

Azithromycin suspension: 400mg once a day
- Age from 12 to 13 years
- Azithromycin 200mg/5ml susp. Take two 5ml spoonfuls once a day for 3 days; supply 30 ml; NHS Cost £13.80.

Azithromycin capsules: 500mg once a day
- Age from 14 years onwards
- Azithromycin 250mg capsules. Take two capsules once a day for 3 days; supply 6 capsules; NHS Cost £13.43.

2nd-line penicillin allergy: erythromycin or clarithromycin

Erythromycin s/f suspension: 125mg four times a day
- Age from 1 month to 23 months
- Erythromycin 125mg/5ml sf susp. Take one 5ml spoonful four times a day for 5 days; supply 100 ml; NHS Cost £1.12.

Erythromycin s/f suspension: 250mg four times a day
- Age from 2 to 8 years
- Erythromycin 250mg/5ml sf susp. Take one 5ml spoonful four times a day for 5 days; supply 100 ml; NHS Cost £1.97.

Erythromycin s/f suspension: 500mg four times a day
- Age from 9 to 11 years
- Erythromycin 500mg/5ml sf susp. Take one 5ml spoonful four times a day for 5 days; supply 100 ml; NHS Cost £3.38.

Erythromycin e/c tablets: 500mg four times a day
- Age from 12 years onwards
- Erythromycin 250mg e/c tablets. Take two tablets four times a day for 5 days; supply 40 tablets; NHS Cost £4.40.

Clarithromycin suspension: 62.5mg twice a day
- Age from 12 months to 2 years
- Clarithromycin 125mg/5ml susp. Take 2.5ml twice a day for 5 days; supply 70 ml; NHS Cost £6.00.

Clarithromycin suspension: 125mg twice a day
- Age from 3 to 6 years
- Clarithromycin 125mg/5ml susp. Take one 5ml spoonful twice a day for 5 days; supply 70 ml; NHS Cost £6.00.

Clarithromycin suspension: 187.5mg twice a day
- Age from 7 to 9 years
- Clarithromycin 125mg/5ml susp. Take 7.5ml twice a day for 5 days; supply 100 ml; NHS Cost £10.32.

Clarithromycin suspension: 250mg twice a day
- Age from 10 to 11 years
- Clarithromycin 250mg/5ml susp. Take one 5ml spoonful twice a day for 5 days; supply 70 ml; NHS Cost £12.00.

Clarithromycin tablets: 250mg twice a day
- Age from 12 years onwards
- Clarithromycin 250mg tablets. Take one tablet twice a day for 5 days; supply 10 tablets; NHS Cost £8.03.

Analgesia: use when required

Paracetamol s/f susp: 60mg to 120mg up to four times a day
- Age from 3 to 11 months
- Paracetamol 120mg/5ml s/f susp. Take 2.5ml to 5ml every 4 to 6 hours when required for pain relief. Maximum of 4 doses in 24 hours; supply 150 ml; NHS Cost £0.63; OTC Cost £1.15.

Paracetamol s/f susp: 120mg to 240mg up to four times a day
- Age from 12 months to 5 years
- Paracetamol 120mg/5ml s/f susp. Take one to two 5ml spoonfuls every 4 to 6 hours when required for pain relief. Maximum of 4 doses in 24 hours; supply 300 ml; NHS Cost £1.26; OTC Cost £2.29.

Paracetamol s/f susp: 250mg to 500mg up to four times a day
- Age from 6 to 11 years
- Paracetamol 250mg/5ml s/f susp. Take one to two 5ml spoonfuls every 4 to 6 hours when required for pain relief. Maximum of 4 doses in 24 hours; supply 300 ml; NHS Cost £1.61; OTC Cost £2.80.

Paracetamol tablets: 500mg to 1g up to four times a day
- Age from 12 to 15 years
- Paracetamol 500mg tablets. Take one to two tablets every 4 to 6 hours when required for pain relief. Maximum of 8 tablets in 24 hours; supply 56 tablets; NHS Cost £0.42; OTC Cost £0.67.

Paracetamol tablets: 1g up to four times a day
- Age from 16 years onwards
- Paracetamol 500mg tablets. Take two tablets every 4 to 6 hours when required for pain relief. Maximum of 8 tablets in 24 hours; supply 56 tablets; NHS Cost £0.42; OTC Cost £0.67.

Ibuprofen s/f susp: 50mg three to four times a day
- Age from 12 months to 2 years
- Ibuprofen 100mg/5ml s/f susp. Take 2.5ml three to four times a day when required for pain relief. Do not exceed the stated dose; supply 100 ml; NHS Cost £1.82; OTC Cost £3.53.

Ibuprofen s/f susp: 100mg three to four times a day
- Age from 3 to 7 years
- Ibuprofen 100mg/5ml s/f susp. Take one 5ml spoonful 3 to 4 times a day when required for pain relief. Do not exceed the stated dose; supply 150 ml; NHS Cost £2.73; OTC Cost £4.81.

Ibuprofen s/f susp: 200mg three to four times a day
- Age from 8 to 11 years
- Ibuprofen 100mg/5ml s/f susp. Take two 5ml spoonfuls 3 to 4 times a day when required for pain relief. Do not exceed the stated dose; supply 300 ml; NHS Cost £5.46; OTC Cost £9.62.

Ibuprofen tablets: 400mg three times a day
- Age from 12 years onwards
- Ibuprofen 400mg tablets. Take one tablet three times a day when required for pain relief. Do not exceed the stated dose; supply 21 tablets; NHS Cost £0.62; OTC Cost £1.75.

Extended Information

Background information

- What is it? p.1411
- How common is it? p.1411
- How do I know my patient has it? p.1412
- What else might it be? p.1412
- Complications and prognosis p.1412

What is it?

- **There is no universal or exact definition of acute otitis media (AOM)**, although the features of AOM and associated disorders are widely recognized.
  - **Otitis media** is the generic term for all types of inflammation of the middle ear.
  - **Acute otitis media** is usually a short-term inflammation of the middle ear, and is principally characterized by earache that may be severe. It is often preceded by upper respiratory symptoms, including a cough and rhinorrhoea.
  - **Otitis media with effusion** (glue ear) can be defined as chronic inflammation of the middle ear accompanied by accumulation of fluid. It is often asymptomatic, and pain in particular is relatively uncommon.
  - **Recurrent acute otitis media** refers to frequent episodes of the illness within a period of 6 or 12 months. The National Institute for Clinical Excellence (NICE) currently defines this as more than four episodes in 6 months [NICE, 2000].

[SIGN, 2003]

- **The cause of AOM may be of viral or bacterial origin,** although studies have shown that 25% of cases of AOM are not associated with a specific pathogen [Klein, 1995].
- **Viruses** are present in about 25% of people with AOM, and often precede or coexist with a bacterial infection [Klein, 1995].
- **The main bacteria responsible for AOM** have been cultured from middle-ear effusions obtained from needle aspirates.
  - *Streptococcus pneumoniae* is the most common cause, accounting for nearly 40% of infections.
  - *Haemophilus influenzae* is involved in about a quarter of people with AOM. It is more common in younger children.
  - *Moraxella cattarhalis* accounts for about 10% of infections, and is increasing in prevalence. Strains are now usually resistant to amoxicillin.

[Klein, 1995]

O

How common is it?

- **Acute otitis media (AOM)** is one of the most common complaints seen in primary care in the United Kingdom. Estimates vary widely, but at least 25% of children have a minimum of one episode before they are 10 years old. The peak incidence occurs in children aged between 3 and 6 years of age [SIGN, 2003].
- Most North American studies have estimated that the incidence of AOM is even higher, with over two-thirds of children under 3 years of age having had at least one episode, and the peak incidence occurring between 6 and 24 months of age [Klein, 1995]. It has been suggested that AOM is over diagnosed in North America [Alberta Clinical Practice Guidelines Working Group, 2000].
- **AOM is relatively uncommon in adults,** with over 75% of cases occurring in children aged under 10 [SIGN, 2003].

How do I know my patient has it?

What are the risk factors?

- **Young age is the single most important risk factor** for developing acute otitis media (AOM) — it is predominantly a disease of infancy and early childhood.
- **Contact with other children,** such as attendance at a nursery, is the next most significant risk factor. Other risk factors documented are the use of formula milk (rather than breast milk), the use of a dummy, and feeding in a flat, supine position [Alberta Clinical Practice Guidelines Working Group, 2000].

Symptoms

- **Local symptoms are nearly always present in AOM.** Pain is the main symptom, which may present as irritability or crying in younger children, possibly with characteristic ear tugging. Loss of hearing may also occur due to the presence of effusion in the middle ear.
- **Systemic symptoms may be present** depending on the extent or severity of the illness. Fever (temperature over 38.5°C), loss of appetite, nausea and vomiting, and loss of sleep are common symptoms. Tinnitus, voice resonance, and giddiness may also occur.

[Alberta Clinical Practice Guidelines Working Group, 2000; Guidelines and Protocols Advisory Committee, 2002; SIGN, 2003]

Signs

- **Diagnosis of AOM should not be made on a history alone.** The appearance of the eardrum should be examined with the appropriate use of an otoscope.
- **Otoscopic appearances** typical of AOM include:
  - Bulging tympanic membrane with loss of landmarks
  - Changes in membrane colour (typically red or yellow)
  - Perforated tympanic membrane with discharge of pus (which may alleviate symptoms)
- **Pneumato-otoscopy** can help detect differences between a healthy eardrum and one with effusion, and increases the sensitivity of diagnosing AOM. However, at present pneumato-otoscopes are not used routinely in primary care.

[SIGN, 2003]

Acute otitis media or otitis media with effusion?

- **It is important to distinguish between AOM and otitis media with effusion.** Ear discomfort, red tympanic membranes, or fever *alone* are NOT specific diagnostic criteria. The diagnosis of AOM should be made according to combinations of symptoms and signs consistent with the illness [Guidelines and Protocols Advisory Committee, 2002].
- **The diagnostic features of AOM and otitis media with effusion** are summarized in Table 1.

[SIGN, 2003]

Table 1: The diagnostic features of AOM and otitis media with effusion (glue ear), adapted from the Scottish Intercollegiate Guidelines Network (SIGN).

Symptom or sign	Acute otitis media	Otitis media with effusion
Earache, fever, or irritability	Present	Usually absent
Middle ear effusion	Present	Present
Opaque drum	Present	May be absent
Bulging drum	May be present	Usually absent
Impaired drum mobility	Present	Present
Hearing loss	Present	Usually present

What else might it be?

- **Otitis media with effusion** may present with signs or symptoms similar to those of acute otitis media (AOM), such as hearing loss. For the differential diagnosis, see *Acute otitis media or otitis media with effusion?*
- **Otitis externa** (diffuse or furuncular) may cause earache similar to AOM. It is more common in adults and is frequently bilateral.
- **Otitic barotrauma** may cause severe ear pain. It is more likely in people who have recently travelled by aeroplane, scuba dived, or received a blow to the ear.
- **Mastoiditis** may have developed from a previous episode of AOM.
- **A foreign body** may be the cause of ear pain, particularly in children. Impacted earwax may be present in adults.
- **Referred otalgia** should be considered in people who have earache but otherwise do not show the typical symptoms of AOM. The likelihood of referred otalgia increases with age — it is relatively rare in children. The presence of bilateral pain virtually excludes the possibility of referred otalgia. The true nature of the pain may be caused by dysfunction of one of several sites in the head and neck:
  - **Teeth** (e.g. impacted molars, abscess, dental work)
  - **Jaw** (e.g. temperomandibular joint dysfunction)
  - **Cervical spine** (and associated bones, muscles, ligaments, and nerves)
  - **Other less common sites** include the lymph and salivary glands of the neck (especially the parotid gland); the nose and sinuses; the tonsils, tongue, and pharynx; and the meninges.

[Seller, 1996]

Complications and prognosis

- **About 80% of episodes of acute otitis media (AOM) in children will resolve within 3 days without treatment** [Glasziou et al, 2003].
- **Recurrent episodes of AOM** may occur because of treatment failure or reinfection with a new pathogen. [Leibovitz et al, 2003]. Possible long-term consequences include atrophy and scarring of the eardrum; chronic perforation and otorrhoea; cholesteatoma; and chronic or permanent hearing loss.
- **The most important factors involved in recurrent AOM** are young age and attendance at a nursery. Other poor prognostic factors include white race, male gender, multiple previous episodes, history of ear infections in parents or siblings, history of asthma, history of tonsillitis, enlarged adenoids, bottle feeding, and the use of a dummy [Froom et al, 1997].
- **Severe progressive complications of AOM,** such as mastoiditis, labyrinthitis, meningitis, intracranial sepsis, or facial nerve palsy are rare in otherwise healthy children from developed countries [O'Neill and Roberts, 2002]. The most common of these conditions, mastoiditis, has been found to occur in less than 1 in 1000 children with untreated AOM [Takata et al, 2001].
- **Otitis media with effusion** (glue ear) is a very common complication of AOM, to the extent that it may be seen as a natural progression of the disease. Some authors contend that otitis media with effusion and AOM should be considered as part of the same disease continuum [SIGN, 2003]. However, otitis media with effusion should not be diagnosed until the effusion has been present for 3 months or more (see the separate PRODIGY guidance for *Glue ear).*

Management issues

- How effective are antibiotics? p.1413
- Analgesia p.1415

O

- Other therapies p.1415
- Preventative measures p.1415
- Referral advice p.1415

Despite a large number of published studies and clinical trials, there is still no national or international consensus on the best treatment of acute otitis media (AOM). In particular, the use of antibiotics remains contentious. The overwhelming majority of research on AOM has been performed on children, and this guidance reflects this.

How effective are antibiotics?

- **AOM is usually a self-limiting illness.** About 80% of AOM will resolve within 3 days without antibiotic treatment [Froom et al, 1990; Glasziou et al, 2003].
- **A recent updated Cochrane systematic review of AOM** has combined seven high-quality clinical trials with a total of 2202 children from developed countries. It concluded that:
  - Children treated with antibiotics had a 28% relative reduction in pain at 2–7 days.
  - The high rate of spontaneous resolution (80%) meant that the absolute reduction rate was only 6%, with a NNT of about 17.
  - The use of antibiotics did not reduce the incidence of complications, including hearing problems, although the data on long-term complications was limited.
  - Progression to mastoiditis was reported in only one child (from a penicillin-treated group).
  - Antibiotics were associated with increased adverse effects, such as nausea and diarrhoea.

[Glasziou et al, 2003]

- **Another recent systematic review,** including more studies of younger children, has estimated that to avoid clinical failure between 2–7 days the NNT is eight. No particular antibiotic was found to be more effective, but some caused more adverse effects than others. It concluded that the benefits of antibiotics for AOM were modest [Takata et al, 2001].
- **The clinical impact of antibiotic treatment in children under 2 years of age may be greater than in older children,** although it is still modest. A high-quality randomized controlled trial of 240 children aged 6–24 months estimated that the NNT for improved symptomatic outcome after 4 days was between seven and eight [Damoiseaux et al, 2000].
- **The frequency of adverse effects** seen with antibiotics used to treat AOM may be as high as the NNT required to produce a clinical benefit; that is, for every child who benefits from antibiotics, another suffers from adverse effects [NZGG, 1998].

Should I prescribe an antibiotic?

- **Although there is no definitive consensus on the optimum treatment of acute otitis media (AOM) in children,** the available evidence suggests that antibiotic treatment should NOT be offered routinely.
  - The Scottish Intercollegiate Guideline Network (SIGN) concludes that 'children diagnosed with AOM should not routinely be prescribed antibiotics as the initial treatment' [SIGN, 2003].
  - The Public Health Laboratory Service (now part of the Health Protection Agency) points out that many cases of AOM are viral, and poor outcomes (without antibiotics) are unlikely if there are no systemic symptoms [PHLS, 2002].
  - The Specialist Advisory Committee on Antimicrobial Resistance (SACAR), formerly the Standing Medical Advisory Committee (SMAC), concluded that 'antibiotics are probably unnecessary in acute otitis media. Reassurance, time and adequate pain relief are required'. There is concern that over-prescribing of antibiotics contributes to increased bacterial resistance [DH and SMAC, 1998].
- **Parents should be reassured** that the long-term prognosis of AOM is good, and that in most cases the prescribing of antibiotics does not improve on this. Parent-doctor discussions should be encouraged, such as weighing the benefits of antibiotics against their adverse effects (e.g. diarrhoea, nausea, and vomiting), and the contribution to antibiotic resistance in the community [Froom et al, 1990; Del Mar et al, 1997; Majeed and Harris, 1997].
- The PRODIGY Patient Information Leaflet — *Otitis Media (Ear Infection)*, and Shared Decision Making screens are useful resources for reassuring parents and discussing the role of antibiotics in AOM.
- **A 'wait-and-see' approach** may be a good compromise for some people. A prescription for antibiotics can be given on the day of the consultation, but only redeemed if the condition has not resolved after 72 hours. This has been found to be both effective and feasible in two pragmatic studies [Cates, 1999; Little et al, 2001].
- **Although antibiotics should not be routinely prescribed, the following indications may support their selective use:**
  - Child under 2 years of age
  - Bilateral AOM
  - Systemic symptoms, including high temperature (more than 38.5°C) or vomiting
  - Local signs that suggest the infection is severe, such as a particularly bulging or inflamed tympanic membrane

[Alberta Clinical Practice Guidelines Working Group, 2000; Guidelines and Protocols Advisory Committee, 2002; Hendley, 2002; SIGN, 2003].

What is the preferred antibiotic?

- **It is not known what is the best antibiotic to use in acute otitis media (AOM).** The most recent systematic reviews either did not distinguish between different antibiotics [Glasziou et al, 2003] or did not find any to be more effective than another [Takata et al, 2001]. The recommended antibiotics in this guidance are derived from known sensitivity data, current guidelines, and expert opinion and consensus.
- **Amoxicillin is the recommended first-line antibiotic for most people.**
  - Amoxicillin provides coverage against most of the bacteria involved in AOM, including penicillin intermediate *Streptococcus pneumoniae* (bacteria in an intermediate stage of developing full penicillin resistance).
  - It demonstrates favourable pharmacokinetics, with high concentrations forming in the middle ear.
  - It has relatively few adverse effects.
  - Amoxicillin has been proven effective in clinical trials.

[Alberta Clinical Practice Guidelines Working Group, 2000; Guidelines and Protocols Advisory Committee, 2002; PHLS, 2002; SIGN, 2003].

- **The macrolide antibiotics** are recommended if amoxicillin is contraindicated because of a *true* history of allergy to penicillin.
  - **Azithromycin** is the drug of choice in this situation. It is active against all the major organisms involved in acute otitis media, and it is given as a convenient regimen that may increase practical compliance. In addition it is reputed to cause fewer gastrointestinal adverse effects than erythromycin does [DTB, 1991].
  - **Erythromycin** is most commonly used. The Public Health Laboratory Service recommends it as the first-line antibiotic in penicillin-allergic people [PHLS, 2002].

- Erythromycin has poor activity against *Haemophilus influenzae*, which may affect the outcome of treatment.
- Gastrointestinal disturbances (such as nausea) are common with erythromycin and may affect practical compliance.
- **Clarithromycin** is another possible option. Like azithromycin, it is reputed to cause fewer gastrointestinal-related adverse effects [DTB, 1991].

[DTB, 1995; BNF 45, 2003]

- **If symptoms persist past 7 days, or reoccur within 14 days, treatment failure may have occurred.** In this case it may be appropriate to use a second-line antibiotic. Reoccurrence after 14 days is unlikely to be due to the original organism, but suggests infection by a new pathogen [Leibovitz et al, 2003].
- **Co-amoxiclav is the preferred second-line agent** in people who are not allergic to penicillin. Co-amoxiclav is a combination product consisting of amoxicillin and clavulanic acid.
  - It is effective against beta-lactamase-producing bacteria, including *Moraxella catarrhalis* and resistant strains of *S pneumoniae*.
  - Co-amoxiclav is as effective as other beta-lactamase-resistant antibiotics (e.g. third-generation cephalosporins), is taken orally, and is inexpensive.
  - It has relatively few adverse effects.

[Alberta Clinical Practice Guidelines Working Group, 2000; PHLS, 2002; Easton et al, 2003].

- **There is no obvious or preferred second-line agent for people who have a history of allergy to penicillin.** It may be necessary to consult expert advice from a local microbiologist:
  - In people who were intolerant of an initial course of erythromycin (and where compliance was a problem), consider prescribing a course of clarithromycin or azithromycin. These antibiotics are reputed to cause fewer gastrointestinal-related adverse effects [DTB, 1991].
  - Cephalosporins should be used with caution, owing to the possibility of cross-sensitivity with penicillins [DTB, 1996].
  - Quinolones are contraindicated in children under 16 years of age [BNF 45, 2003].
  - Local sensitivity patterns to trimethoprim vary, and co-trimoxazole should be used only in exceptional cases [BNF 45, 2003].
- **The recommended antibiotics for uncomplicated AOM and treatment failure are summarized in Table 2.**

How long should I prescribe an antibiotic for?

- **There is currently no consensus on the optimal length of treatment with antibiotics for acute otitis media (AOM).**
  - The Public Health Laboratory Service (now part of the Health Protection Agency) and the British National Formulary (BNF) both recommend 3–7-day courses of antibiotics [PHLS, 2002; BNF 45, 2003].
  - The Scottish Intercollegiate Guidelines Network (SIGN) advocates a 5-day course of antibiotics [SIGN, 2003].
  - The Specialist Advisory Committee on Antimicrobial Resistance (SACAR), formerly the Standing Medical Advisory Committee (SMAC), recommends that a course of antibiotics for AOM should be limited to 3 days, to minimize the spread of community-acquired resistance [DH and SMAC, 1998].
  - Most North American practice and guidelines suggest longer courses of treatment, typically 10 days, especially for younger children [Paradise, 1997; Alberta Clinical Practice Guidelines Working Group, 2000; Guidelines and Protocols Advisory Committee, 2002].
- A recent updated Cochrane systematic review of 1524 children compared children taking short courses of antibiotics (less than 7 days) with those taking longer courses (more than 7 days).
  - There was a slightly increased risk of persistent signs and symptoms, relapse, or reinfection with the shorter courses of antibiotics in the short term (8–19 days).
  - There was no difference in outcomes in the longer term (over 30 days).
  - The review concluded that 5-day courses of antibiotics are an effective treatment for uncomplicated AOM.

[Kozyrskyj et al, 2000]

- **The available evidence suggests that a 5-day course of antibiotics is usually adequate** for AOM (3 days is the sufficient and licensed dose for azithromycin). The benefits of longer courses may be outweighed by the increased risk of adverse effects and the spread of community-acquired resistance.

What dose of antibiotic should I use?

- Doses of antibiotics used in the treatment of acute otitis media (AOM) vary significantly in clinical trials. PRODIGY uses doses from recognised formularies and product literature in prescriptions wherever possible.
- It is generally recognised that doses of amoxicillin can be doubled in *severe* infections. However, PRODIGY

Table 2: Recommended antibiotics for treatment of AOM.

Indication	History of *true* allergy to penicillin	Preferred antibiotic	Comment
AOM (first-line)	No	Amoxicillin	Amoxicillin has good activity against the most common bacteria involved in AOM, including *Streptococcus pneumoniae* and *Haemophilus influenzae*. It is well tolerated, and no antibiotic has been found to be superior in clinical trials.
	Yes	Azithromycin *or* Erythromycin *or* Clarithromycin	The macrolides are the preferred choice when amoxicillin is contraindicated. However, erythromycin has lower activity against *H influenzae* than azithromycin does, and is particularly associated with gastrointestinal-related adverse effects.
AOM treatment failure (second-line)	No	Co-amoxiclav	Co-amoxiclav is effective against beta-lactamase-producing bacteria and *Moraxella catarrhalis*. It is more effective, less toxic, and less expensive than most cephalosporins.
	Yes	Azithromycin *or* Seek specialist advice	Consider using azithromycin if a previous course of erythromycin has failed because of non-compliance. People who are allergic to amoxicillin may also be allergic to cephalosporins. Quinolones are contraindicated in children under 16 years of age. Local sensitivity patterns to trimethoprim may vary, and co-trimoxazole is recommended only in exceptional circumstances.

recommends the use of higher doses of amoxicillin in all cases of AOM that warrant antibiotic use:

- There is some research that suggests lower doses of amoxicillin may not be effective in eradicating AOM, due to insufficient concentrations of the drug being maintained in the middle ear.
- Sub-therapeutic doses of amoxicillin are more likely to result in the formation of resistant strains of bacteria.

[BNF 45, 2003; Royal College of Paediatrics and Child Health, 2003; Infectious Diseases and Immunization Committee, 2004].

Analgesia

- **For most people, simple analgesia is the mainstay of treatment.** Paracetamol and ibuprofen are adequate analgesics.
- **One trial has compared the efficacies of paracetamol and ibuprofen against placebo** [Bertin et al, 1996]. It concluded that ibuprofen, but not paracetamol, was an effective analgesic in acute otitis media (AOM). However, the study was methodologically flawed, and subsequent recalculation of the results suggests that paracetamol is also effective [SIGN, 2003].
- **Aspirin** should be avoided in children under 16 years of age [CSM, 2002].

Other therapies

- **Treatment of acute otitis media (AOM) with antihistamines or decongestants is not recommended.** A Cochrane systematic review of 2569 cases found:
  - There was no benefit in outcome in people taking antihistamines or decongestants alone.
  - There was an increase in adverse effects associated with these drugs.
  - There was a small improvement in outcome in people taking combined antihistamines and decongestants after 2 weeks. However, the author concluded that this benefit was small, unlikely to be clinically significant, and could have been an artefact due to the trial designs.

[Flynn et al, 2003]

- **Homeopathy is unlikely to be of benefit for AOM.** One randomized controlled trial claimed marginal benefits of homeopathic remedies compared with conventional treatment, but was small and of low methodological quality, with very uneven treatment groups [Friese et al, 1997].
- **Myringotomy alone is not considered to be useful,** nor does it alter outcome in combination with antibiotic therapy. However, individual cases may warrant it if there is severe pain or a high fever, or if complications occur. If performed, the aspirate should be sent for culture [Kaleida et al, 1991; Paradise, 1995].

Preventative measures

- **Acute otitis media (AOM) is a common illness,** and will affect many children at some point in their development. Risk factors that have been implicated in the development of AOM and can, at least in principle, be avoided include:
  - Contact with a large number of other children (e.g. at a nursery)
  - Use of formula milk rather than breast milk
  - Use of a dummy
  - Feeding in a supine, flat position

[Paradise et al, 1994; Froom et al, 1997; Paradise et al, 1997; Alberta Clinical Practice Guidelines Working Group, 2000].

- **The effect of passive smoking** as a contributor to poor outcome of AOM is controversial and likely to be slight [Froom et al, 1997]. However, it has been associated with the development of otitis media with effusion, so parents are recommended to avoid exposing their children to tobacco smoke [SIGN, 2003].
- **Swimming probably does not increase the risk of contracting AOM,** although the evidence for this is limited to small controlled trials [Cohen et al, 1994; Robertson et al, 1997]. In addition, surface swimming with tympanostomy tubes dose not increase the incidence of AOM, and using protection such as swimming caps or ear plugs does not change this risk [Salata and Derkay, 1996; Carbonell and Ruiz-Garcia, 2002].
- **There is no evidence on the effects of either shallow or scuba diving** with tympanostomy tubes, but these activities should probably be avoided.
- **Soap** reduces the surface tension of water, so children with tympanostomy tubes should avoid immersion of the head in soapy water [SIGN, 2003].
- **Long-term prophylaxis of AOM with antibiotics** may reduce the incidence of recurrent AOM, but the evidence for this is inconsistent. In addition, there is insufficient evidence on which antibiotic should be used, for how long, and how many episodes of AOM would be required to justify this approach [O'Neill and Roberts, 2002].
- **Xylitol** syrup or chewing gum has been reported to reduce the incidence of AOM in one randomized controlled trial, but the practicalities of long-term use may make this treatment unfeasible [O'Neill and Roberts, 2002].
- **Pneumococcal conjugate vaccines** may have a limited role in the prevention of AOM, but they are not used routinely in the United Kingdom for this indication [Jacobs, 2002].

Referral advice

- **The National Institute for Clinical Excellence (NICE)** recommends that children with frequent episodes of AOM should be referred to an otolaryngologist. 'Frequent' is currently defined (by expert opinion) as more than four episodes in a period of 6 months [NICE, 2000].
- **Children with persistent problems** with effusion, discharge, or perforation should be referred to an otolaryngologist [SIGN, 2003].
- **Potentially serious complications,** such as mastoiditis or facial nerve paresis, require urgent referral [SIGN, 2003].

O

References

NHS staff in England can link, free of charge, from references to full text journals by clicking on [Full text] on the PRODIGY website.

1. Alberta Clinical Practice Guidelines Working Group (2000) *Guideline for the diagnosis and treatment of acute otitis media in children.* Alberta Medical Association. www.albertadoctors.org [Accessed: 09/11/2000].
2. Bertin, L., Pons, G., d'Athis, P. et al (1996) A randomized, double-blind, multicentre controlled trial of ibuprofen versus acetaminophen and placebo for symptoms of acute otitis media in children. *Fundamental and Clinical Pharmacology* 10(4), 387–392.
3. BNF 45 (2003) *British National Formulary.* 45th edn. London: British Medical Association and Royal Pharmaceutical Society of Great Britain.
4. Carbonell, R. and Ruiz-Garcia, V. (2002) Ventilation tubes after surgery for otitis media with effusion or acute otitis media and swimming. Systematic review

and meta-analysis. *International Journal of Pediatric Otorhinolaryngology* **66**(3), 281–289.
5. Cates, C. (1999) An evidence based approach to reducing antibiotic use in children with acute otitis media: controlled before and after study. *British Medical Journal* **318**(7185), 715. [Full text]
6. Celin, S.E., Bluestone, C.D., Stephenson, J. et al (1991) Bacteriology of acute otitis media in adults. *Journal of the American Medical Association* **266**(16), 2249–2252. [Full text]
7. Cohen, H.A., Kauschansky, A., Ashkenasi, A. et al (1994) Swimming and grommets. *Journal of Family Practice* **38**(1), 30–32.
8. CSM (2002) Aspirin and Reye's syndrome in children up to and including 15 years of age. *Current Problems in Pharmacovigilance* **28**(Apr), 4.
9. Damoiseaux, R.A.M.J., van Balen, F.A.M., Hoes, A.W. et al (2000) Primary care based randomised, double blind trial of amoxicillin versus placebo for acute otitis media in children aged under 2 years. *British Medical Journal* **320**(7231), 350–354. [Full text]
10. Del Mar, C., Glasziou, P. and Hayem, M. (1997) Are antibiotics indicated as initial treatment for children with acute otitis media? A meta-analysis. *British Medical Journal* **314**(7093), 1526–1529. [Full text]
11. DH and SMAC (1998) *The path of least resistance.* Department of Health. www.dh.gov.uk [Accessed: 27/04/2004]. [Full text]
12. DTB (1991) Clarithro- and azithromycin: better erythromycins? *Drug & Therapeutics Bulletin* **29**(26), 101–102.
13. DTB (1995) Management of acute otitis media and glue ear. *Drug & Therapeutics Bulletin* **33**(2), 12–15.
14. DTB (1996) Penicillin allergy. *Drug & Therapeutics Bulletin* **34**(11), 87–88.
15. Easton, J., Noble, S. and Perry, C.M. (2003) Amoxicillin/clavulanic acid: a review of its use in the management of paediatric patients with acute otitis media. *Drugs* **63**(3), 311–340.
16. Flynn, C.A., Griffin, G. and Tudiver, F. (2003) *Decongestants and antihistamines for acute otitis media in children (Cochrane Review).* The Cochrane Library. Issue 2. Oxford: Update Software.
17. Friese, K.H., Kruse, S., Ludtke, R. and Moeller, H. (1997) The homoeopathic treatment of otitis media in children–comparisons with conventional therapy. *International Journal of Clinical Pharmacology and Therapeutics* **35**(7), 296–301.
18. Froom, J., Culpepper, L., Grob, P. et al (1990) Diagnosis and antibiotic treatment of acute otitis media: report from International Primary Care Network. *British Medical Journal* **300**(6724), 582–586.
19. Froom, J., Culpepper, L., Jacobs, M. et al (1997) Antimicrobials for acute otitis media? A review from the International Primary Care Network. *British Medical Journal* **315**(7100), 98–102. [Full text]
20. Glasziou, P.P., Del Mar, C.B., Sanders, S.L. and Hayem, M. (2003) *Antibiotics for acute otitis media in children (Cochrane Review).* The Cochrane Library. Issue 2. Oxford: Update Software.
21. Guidelines and Protocols Advisory Committee (2002) *Acute otitis media (AOM).* British Colombia Medical Association. www.hlth.gov.bc.ca/ [Accessed: 25/04/2003].
22. Hendley, J.O. (2002) Clinical practice. Otitis media. *New England Journal of Medicine* **347**(15), 1169–1174. [Full text]
23. Hoppe, J.E. (1996) Rational prescribing of antibacterials in ambulatory children. *Pharmacoeconomics* **10**(6), 552–574.
24. Infectious Diseases and Immunization Committee (2004) High dose amoxicillin: rationale for use in otitis media treatment failures. *Canadian Journal of Infectitious Diseases* **10**(4),
25. Jacobs, M.R. (2002) Prevention of otitis media: role of pneumococcal conjugate vaccines in reducing incidence and antibiotic resistance. *Journal of Pediatrics* **141**(2), 287–293.
26. Kaleida, P.H., Casselbrant, M.L., Rockette, H.E. et al (1991) Amoxicillin or myringotomy or both for acute otitis media: results of a randomized clinical trial. *Pediatrics* **87**(4), 466–474.
27. Klein, J.O. (1995) Otitis externa, otitis media, mastoiditis. In: Mandell, G.L., Bennett, J.E., Dolin, R. et al (Eds.) *Principles and practice of infectious diseases.* 4th edn. New York: Churchill Livingstone. 579–585.
28. Kozyrskyj, A.L., Hildes-Ripstein, G.E., Longstaffe, S.E. et al (2000) *Short course antibiotics for acute otitis media (Cochrane Review).* The Cochrane Library. Issue 4. Oxford: Update Software.
29. Leibovitz, E., Greenberg, D., Piglansky, L. et al (2003) Recurrent acute otitis media occurring within one month from completion of antibiotic therapy: relationship to the original pathogen. *Pediatric Infectious Disease Journal* **22**(3), 209–216.
30. Little, P., Gould, C., Williamson, I. et al (2001) Pragmatic randomised controlled trial of two prescribing strategies for childhood acute otitis media. *British Medical Journal* **322**(7282), 336–342. [Full text]
31. Majeed, A. and Harris, T. (1997) Acute otitis media in children. *British Medical Journal* **315**(7104), 321–322. [Full text]
32. NICE (2000) *Persistent otitis media with effusion (glue ear) in young children (Referral Practice – version under pilot).* National Institute for Clinical Excellence. www.nice.org.uk [Accessed: 20/10/2003].
33. NZGG (1998) *Acute otitis media. Meta-analysis.* New Zealand Guidelines Group. www.nzgg.org.nz [Accessed: 09/11/2000].
34. O'Neill, P. and Roberts, T. (2002) Acute otitis media. *Clinical Evidence* **9**(Jun), 274–286.
35. Paradise, J.L. (1995) Treatment guidelines for otitis media: the need for breadth and flexibility. *Pediatric Infectious Disease Journal* **14**(5), 429–435.
36. Paradise, J.L. (1997) Short-course antimicrobial treatment for acute otitis media: not best for infants and young children. *Journal of the American Medical Association* **278**(20), 1640–1642. [Full text]
37. Paradise, J.L., Elster, B.A. and Tan, L. (1994) Evidence in infants with cleft palate that breast milk protects against otitis media. *Pediatrics* **94**(6 Pt 1), 853–860.
38. Paradise, J.L., Rockette, H.E., Colborn, D.K. et al (1997) Otitis media in 2253 Pittsburgh-area infants: prevalence and risk factors during the first two years of life. *Pediatrics* **99**(3), 318–333. [Full text]
39. PHLS (2002) *Management of infection guidance for primary care: draft for consultation & local adaptation.* Public Health Laboratory Service. www.hpa.org.uk [Accessed: 01/04/2002].
40. Robertson, L.M., Marino, R.V. and Namjoshi, S. (1997) Does swimming decrease the incidence of otitis media? *Journal of the American Osteopathic Association* **97**(3), 150–152.
41. Royal College of Paediatrics and Child Health (Ed.) (2003) *Medicines for children.* 2nd edn. London: RCPCH.
42. Salata, J.A. and Derkay, C.S. (1996) Water precautions in children with tympanostomy tubes. *Archives of Otolaryngololgy Head and Neck Surgery* **122**(3), 276–280.

43. Seller, R.H. (1996) Earache. In: Seller, R.H. (Ed.) *Differential diagnosis of common complaints*. 3rd edn. London: W. B. Saunders Company. 120–128.
44. SIGN (2003) *Diagnosis and management of childhood otitis media in primary care*. Report No. 66. Scottish Intercollegiate Guidelines Network. www.sign.ac.uk [Accessed: 02/06/2003].
45. Takata, G.S., Chan, L.S., Shekelle, P. et al (2001) Evidence assessment of management of acute otitis media: I. The role of antibiotics in treatment of uncomplicated acute otitis media. *Pediatrics* 108(2), 239–247. [Full text]

O

PRODIGY GUIDANCE

Palliative care — cough

Last revised in February 2004
www.prodigy.nhs.uk/guidance.asp?gt=Palliative care - cough

Applies to people over the age of 16 years

This guidance covers the management of cough in palliative care patients.

This guidance does not cover the management of the non-malignant causes of cough.

There is separate PRODIGY guidance for the management of *Asthma, Chest infections, Chronic obstructive pulmonary disease, Heart failure,* and *Lung cancer — suspected.*
There is also separate PRODIGY guidance for *Palliative care — dyspnoea, Palliative care — malodorous malignant ulcer of skin, Palliative care — nausea/vomiting/malignant bowel obstruction, Palliative care — oral problems, Palliative care — pain,* and *Palliative care — respiratory secretions at the end of life.*

Goals

- To identify the cause of the cough in patients with known malignant disease of the chest
- To alleviate the cough in a manner that most enhances the patient's quality of life

Contents

Scenarios

- Dry cough in palliative care patients p.1418
- Productive cough, including haemoptysis, in palliative care p.1420

Extended Information, p. 1423

Which scenario?

- **Dry cough in palliative care patients:** covers the management of the malignant causes of dry cough in the palliative care patient.
- **Productive cough, including haemoptysis, in palliative care:** covers the management of productive cough in the palliative care patient.

P

Dry cough in palliative care patients

Which therapy?

- **Assess the cause of the cough:**
  - Non-malignant causes of dry cough are managed in the usual way.
  - If dyspnoea is present, see the PRODIGY guidance *Palliative care — dyspnoea.*
- **Use simple measures to soothe dry cough:**
  - Advise the patient to try moist inhalations, or use nebulized saline 0.9%.
  - Simple linctus may be useful for some people.
- **Treat with a cough suppressant:**
  - If opioid-naïve: use pholcodine or codeine linctus; or use morphine solution 2.5 mg every 4 hours and 'as required'.
  - If codeine or pholcodine is ineffective, switch to morphine solution 5–10 mg every 4 hours and 'as required'.
  - If already on regular morphine: use an 'as required' dose to relieve cough initially. If this is effective, increase the dose of regular morphine by 30–50% every 2–3 days until symptoms are controlled, or until adverse effects prevent further dose increases.
- **If irritating dry cough persists:**
  - Consider referral for treatment of underlying cause (e.g. oncological treatment of tumour or draining of pleural effusion).
  - Consider a trial of dexamethasone 8 mg each morning if the presence of a tumour is known to be the cause of an uncontrolled dry cough. This trial can be started whilst awaiting referral for further treatment, or as an alternative to oncological treatment if this is not considered appropriate.

Practical prescribing points

For further information please see the *Medicines Compendium* (www.medicines.org.uk) or the *British National Formulary* (www.bnf.org) or the *Palliative Care Formulary* (www.palliativedrugs.com).

- **There should be no contraindications to the use of opioids or dexamethasone in the palliative-care situation,** provided that they are carefully titrated against symptoms.

Morphine

- **Titrate morphine in the same way as for pain management.**
- **If using 4-hourly morphine:**
  - After 1–2 days, calculate the total dose given over 24 hours, and use this to recalculate the 4-hourly dose. (The new 4-hourly and 'as required' dose is one sixth of the new total daily dose.)
  - Repeat this process every 1–2 days until cough is controlled.
  - Once a stable dose has been reached, this can be converted to once- or twice-daily modified-release morphine if preferred.
- **If already on regular morphine:** if an 'as required' dose relieves cough, increase the regular dose by 30–50% every 2–3 days until symptoms are controlled, or until adverse effects prevent further dose increases.
  - Note: if the dose of regular modified-release morphine is increased, the 'as required' dose also needs to be increased (usually one sixth of the total daily dose).
- **Co-prescribe a regular stimulant laxative with a faecal softener** (e.g. co-danthrusate or co-danthramer) to prevent opioid-induced constipation.
- **Give an anti-emetic** (e.g. haloperidol or metoclopramide) regularly for the first few days to prevent opioid-induced nausea and vomiting. Then use as required.
- **Sedation** is common, but most patients quickly develop tolerance.

Dexamethasone

- **All people taking corticosteroids should carry a Steroid Treatment Card.**

Advise people taking corticosteroids to avoid close contact with people with chickenpox or shingles, and to seek urgent medical advice if they are exposed.
Advise people taking corticosteroids that they should not suddenly stop taking them.
Corticosteroids may worsen diabetic control or heart failure.
Concurrent nonsteroidal anti-inflammatory drugs (NSAIDs) increase the risk of gastrointestinal perforation. Stop NSAIDs or co-prescribe a proton pump inhibitor or misoprostol.
Except in the last hours and days of life, corticosteroids should not be stopped suddenly in patients who:

- Have received dexamethasone 4–6 mg or more per day.
- Have received more than 3 weeks' treatment.
- Have taken a second dose in the evening.
- Are taking a short course within 1 year of stopping long-term corticosteroids.
- Have other possible causes of adrenal suppression.

hould I refer or investigate?

efer?

If dry cough is proving difficult to palliate, consider referral to the local palliative-care team or Macmillan nurses.

nvestigate?

Clinical reassessment should occur with the emergence of any new symptom.
The burden of investigation and treatment should be weighed against the likely benefits of treatment.
A chest X-ray is indicated in most circumstances where a malignant cause for a new cough is suspected.
Other investigations will be determined by clinical findings.

atient information leaflets

he following PILs are available at www.prodigy.nhs.uk
Coping with Breathlessness - Macmillan Cancer Relief
Living with Breathlessness - Macmillan Cancer Relief
Managing Breathlessness - Macmillan Cancer Relief

rug rationale

rugs not included

Compound cough mixtures are not offered, because there is no good evidence for their effectiveness [Schroeder and Fahey, 2002].
Methadone linctus should be avoided, because it has a long duration of action and tends to accumulate [BNF 45, 2003].
Other opioids (except morphine) are not offered, because there is less experience with their use for treating cough in the palliative-care setting.
Corticosteroids other than dexamethasone are not included, because they are less potent than dexamethasone, and have a greater mineralocorticoid effect. These properties make them less suitable for high-dose therapy [Twycross et al, 2002].

rugs included

An advice note for moist inhalations is included.
Nebulized physiological 0.9% saline is an alternative to moist inhalations.
Simple linctus has a high sugar content that simulates the production of saliva and soothes the oropharynx. The effect, however, is short-lived, so there is little point in increasing the dose or trying another compound cough mixture if simple linctus is ineffective [Twycross et al, 2002].

- **Pholcodine or codeine linctus can be used to suppress coughing.** However, the licensed doses (pholcodine 10 mg every 8 hours or codeine 15–30 mg every 6–8 hours) are probably lower than the doses needed to relieve cough [Fuller and Jackson, 1990].
- **Codeine tablets** are also included. Some experts suggest that codeine should be given at a dose of 30–60 mg every 6–8 hours to suppress cough adequately [Regnard and Hockley, 2004]. This dose is offered as tablets because of the large volume of linctus needed to achieve doses of 60 mg.
- **Morphine solution** is an alternative if cough is not suppressed by codeine or pholcodine linctus:
  - **For an opioid-naïve patient,** standard-release oral morphine 10 mg/5 ml solution (a prescription-only medicine) is included for initial dose titration. Note: this should be converted to once- or twice-daily modified-release morphine once dosing requirements are stable.
  - **For someone already taking morphine,** an advice note regarding dose titration of modified-release morphine products is available.
- **Note: prescriptions from PRODIGY are generated by computer, and therefore do not fulfil the handwriting requirements for controlled-drug prescriptions.** Prescriptions for modified-release morphine and standard-release morphine tablets are therefore not provided, although in practice most patients will be maintained on modified-release morphine once dose requirements are stable.
- **Dexamethasone** may help to relieve cough if it is due to the tumour causing irritation of the airways. Treatment should be undertaken on a trial basis, and stopped if it is ineffective or if any initial effect is lost [Hardy et al, 2001]. Note: do not stop treatment suddenly if adrenal suppression is likely, unless it is the end of life. See *Which therapy?* for further information.

Prescriptions

Simple measures

Advice note: moist inhalations

- Age from 16 years onwards
- Inhalations can be soothing for a dry cough. Put hot (but not boiling) water to a bowl, and inhale the vapour as often as needed.

Nebulized 0.9% saline

- Age from 16 years onwards
- Sodium chloride 0.9% injection. Inhale the contents of one ampoule using the nebulizer, when required to relieve coughing; supply 20 injection; NHS Cost £6.52.

Simple linctus

- Age from 16 years onwards
- Simple linctus. Take one 5ml spoonful 3 to 4 times a day, when required to relieve coughing; supply 200 ml; NHS Cost £0.36.

Cough suppressants

Pholcodine linctus

- Age from 16 years onwards
- Pholcodine 5mg/5ml linctus. Take one to two 5ml spoonfuls 3 to 4 times a day, when required to relieve coughing; supply 300 ml; NHS Cost £0.72.

Codeine linctus
- Age from 16 years onwards
- Codeine15mg/5ml linctus. Take one to two 5ml spoonfuls 3 to 4 times a day, when required to relieve coughing; supply 300 ml; NHS Cost £1.20.

Codeine 30mg tablets
- Age from 16 years onwards
- Codeine 30mg tablets. Take one to two tablets 3 to 4 times a day, when required to relieve coughing; supply 56 tablets; NHS Cost £2.00.

Morphine solution: initial titration for opioid-naive people
- Age from 16 years onwards
- Morphine sulphate 10mg/5ml sol. Take 1.25ml regularly every 4 hours, and when required to relieve coughing; supply 100 ml; NHS Cost £2.08.

Morphine sol: initial titration if previously on weak opioid
- Age from 16 years onwards
- Morphine sulphate 10mg/5ml sol. Take 2.5ml to 5ml regularly every 4 hours, and when required to relieve coughing; supply 100 ml; NHS Cost £2.08.

Advice note: dose increases for people already on morphine
- Age from 16 years onwards
- For those already on oral morphine: Increase the dose of regular (analgesic) morphine by 30-50% every 2-3 days until cough is controlled, or adverse effects prevent further dose increases.

Trial of dexamethasone (if tumour is cause of cough)

Dexamethasone 8mg once a day (7-day supply)
- Age from 16 years onwards
- Dexamethasone 2mg tablets. Take four tablets each morning; supply 28 tablets; NHS Cost £3.16.

Productive cough, including haemoptysis, in palliative care

P

Which therapy?

Assess the cause of the productive cough:
- Non-malignant causes of productive cough should be managed in the usual way.
- If new-onset dyspnoea is an associated feature, consider urgent referral for emergency admission.

Decide if the patient is in the terminal phase:
- If not in the terminal phase, treat the underlying cause of the productive cough.
- In the terminal phase, consider using morphine to suppress cough if the patient is becoming distressed by productive cough.

Assess the effectiveness of the cough:
- If loose secretions are not being effectively cleared by cough, consider referral for physiotherapy.
- If tenacious secretions are difficult to clear with coughing:
  - Consider using moist inhalations.
  - Nebulized hypertonic saline is usually effective. Try normal saline if this is not available.
  - Alternatively, an oral mucolytic such as carbocisteine may be worth trying.

Haemoptysis due to malignant disease:
- **Minor haemoptysis** (streaking of sputum):
  - Consider treatment with tranexamic acid to reduce bleeding.
- **Moderate haemoptysis** (clots, frequent small bleeds, or anaemia):
  - Refer urgently for radiotherapy.
  - Treat with tranexamic acid to reduce bleeding whilst awaiting referral for radiotherapy.
- **Life-threatening haemoptysis** (where bleeding or further bleeding may be life-threatening):
  - Arrange emergency admission.
- **Massive life-threatening haemoptysis in the terminal phase:**
  - Massive life-threatening haemoptysis is frightening, and sedation to relieve distress should be given as soo[n] as possible. Give midazolam by slow intravenous injection (approximately 2 mg per minute) and increase as necessary in steps of 1 mg until the patient is settled. Rectal diazepam is an alternative.
  - Soak up blood loss with dark green or red towels (if available). These have less of a visual impact since the[y] look dark rather than red when soaked with blood.
  - Consider parenteral diamorphine to manage any associated dyspnoea.

Chest infection:
- If not in the terminal phase, see PRODIGY guidance *Chest infection*.
- In the terminal phase:
  - The patient may benefit from treatment of a chest infection if large quantities of purulent sputum and associated symptoms are distressing.
  - Consider giving a single intravenous dose of a broad-spectrum antibiotic (e.g. ceftriaxone or cefotaxime). Repeat only if symptoms reoccur.
  - Symptomatic management, such as control of fever, may be more appropriate.

Bronchorrhoea:
- If profuse, consider supportive measures to prevent electrolyte imbalance and dehydration.
- Treatment success is highly variable — seek specialist help.

Practical prescribing points

For further information please see the *Medicines Compendium* (www.medicines.org.uk) or the *British National Formulary* (www.bnf.org) or the *Palliative Care Formulary* (www.palliativedrugs.com).

Morphine

- **Start and titrate morphine in the same way as for pain management.**
- **If opioid-naïve:** use morphine solution 2.5 mg regularly every 4 hours *and* 'as required'.
- **If already on a weak opioid:** switch to morphine solutio[n] 5–10 mg every 4 hours *and* 'as required'.
  - After 1–2 days, calculate the total dose given over 24 hours, and use this to recalculate the 40hourly dose. (The new 'as required' dose is one sixth of the new total daily dose.)
  - Repeat this process every 1–2 days until breathlessne[ss] is controlled.
  - Once a stable dose has been reached, this can be converted to once- or twice-daily modified-release morphine.
- **If already on regular morphine:** use an 'as required' dos[e] to relieve cough (this is one sixth of the total daily dose of regular morphine). If this is effective, increase the do[se] of regular morphine by 30–50% every 2–3 days until symptoms are controlled, or until adverse effects preven[t] further dose increases.
  - Note: if the dose of regular modified-release morphin[e] is increased, the 'as required' dose also needs to be increased (usually one sixth of the total daily dose).
- **Co-prescribe a regular stimulant laxative with a faecal softener** (e.g. co-danthrusate or co-danthramer) to prevent opioid-induced constipation.

Give an anti-emetic (e.g. haloperidol or metoclopramide) regularly for the first few days to prevent opioid-induced nausea and vomiting. Then use as required.
Sedation is common, but most patients quickly develop tolerance.

Mixing drugs in syringe drivers

Always follow local palliative care guidelines or seek advice from local palliative care services or hospital pharmacy drug information services *before* mixing drugs in a syringe driver. The following information is included as a brief guide when these sources of help are unavailable:
Check compatibilities before mixing drugs. See www.palliativedrugs.com, or Table 1 below.
Use water for injection as the diluent when mixing drugs in a syringe driver (except for octreotide and ketamine).
Do not use solutions that are cloudy or have precipitated.
Converting oral morphine to parenteral diamorphine: divide the total daily dose of oral morphine by three to calculate the 24-hour dose of subcutaneous diamorphine.

Should I refer or investigate?

Refer?

If not in the terminal phase, consider arranging emergency admission for any patient:
- Who develops dyspnoea in association with a productive cough.
- After a large haemoptysis.

If not in the terminal phase, consider urgent referral to an oncologist for anyone with a malignant cause of haemoptysis.
For anyone with problematic bronchorrhoea, consider referral to palliative-care team or Macmillan nurses.
Referral to a physiotherapist is indicated if loose secretions are not being effectively cleared from the airway by coughing.

Investigate?

A chest X-ray is indicated in most circumstances where a malignant cause for a new cough is suspected.
- Other investigations will be determined by clinical findings.

Patient information leaflets

The following PILs are available at www.prodigy.nhs.uk
- Coping with Breathlessness - Macmillan Cancer Relief
- Living with Breathlessness - Macmillan Cancer Relief
- Managing Breathlessness - Macmillan Cancer Relief

Drug rationale

Drugs not included

Therapies to aid expectoration

- **Mecysteine** is not included, because we have found no studies evaluating its effect on cough clearance.

Cough suppression

- **Compound cough mixtures** are not offered, because there is no good evidence for their effectiveness [Schroeder and Fahey, 2002].
- **Weak opioids** (e.g. codeine or pholcodine linctus) are not included. Cough suppressants are not used for a productive cough unless the patient is too weak to expectorate properly, i.e. at the end of life. Morphine solution offers more flexibility in this situation because the dose can be titrated upwards against symptoms.
- **Methadone linctus** should be avoided, because it has a long duration of action and tends to accumulate [BNF 45, 2003].
- **Other opioids (except morphine)** are not offered, because there is less experience with their use for treating cough in the palliative care setting.

Minor haemoptysis

- **Etamsylate** is not included, although it is an alternative if tranexamic acid is not tolerated.

Chest infection at the end of life

- **Other intravenous antibiotics (except ceftriaxone and cefotaxime) are not included.** However, they should be

P

Table 1: Compatibility and alternative routes of drugs commonly given by syringe driver.

Drug	Compatibility with diamorphine[1]	Alternative routes/drugs[2]
Cyclizine	Diamorphine any strength + cyclizine 6.7 mg/ml Diamorphine 15 mg/ml + cyclizine 15 mg/ml Diamorphine 20 mg/ml + cyclizine 10 mg/ml	Levomepromazine (methotrimeprazine) as a single subcutaneous (s/c) bedtime dose
Dexamethasone	Compatible at usual concentrations, but mix carefully to prevent precipitation	Dexamethasone as a single s/c morning dose
Glycopyrronium bromide	Compatible at usual concentrations	Hyoscine hydrobromide sublingual tablets or patches
Haloperidol	Diamorphine 20–100 mg/ml + haloperidol 0.75 mg/ml Diamorphine 50 mg/ml + haloperidol 1.5 mg/ml	Haloperidol as a single s/c bedtime dose
Hyoscine butylbromide	Compatible at all usual concentrations	Hyoscine butylbromide as a s/c dose every 4–6 hours
Hyoscine hydrobromide	Compatible at all usual concentrations	Hyoscine hydrobromide sublingual tablets or patches
Levomepromazine (methotrimeprazine)	Compatible at all usual concentrations	Levomepromazine as a single s/c bedtime dose
Metoclopramide	Diamorphine 25 mg/ml + metoclopramide 5 mg/ml	Metoclopramide s/c 8-hourly or rectal domperidone
Midazolam	Compatible at all usual concentrations	Diazepam as a single rectal bedtime dose or levomepromazine as a single s/c bedtime dose

[1] Twycross, R., Wilcock, A., Charlesworth, S., and Dickman, A. (2002) *Palliative care formulary*. Palliativedrugs.com Ltd. www.palliativedrugs.com [Accessed: 30-7-2002].
[2] Regnard, C. and Hockley, J. (2004) *A guide to symptom relief in palliative care*. 5th edn. Oxon: Radcliffe Medical Press.

used if, in the clinician's judgement, they are more suitable for empirical therapy of the suspected pathogen.

Drugs included

Therapies to aid expectoration

- **An advice note for moist inhalations is included.**
- **Nebulized hypertonic 6% saline** (loosens secretions to aid expectoration) is included as an advice-only prescription. It is only available from Specials Manufacturers, and may take a few days to obtain.
- **Nebulized physiological 0.9% saline** has been used, but has not been found to increase cough clearance unless used with physiotherapy [Sutton et al, 1988; Houtmeyers et al, 1999]. However, it may be worth trying if hypertonic saline is not available.
- **Carbocisteine (a mucolytic)** has little evidence to support its use for increasing cough clearance, but may be worth trying when nebulized hypertonic saline is not available, or the patient does not wish to use a nebulizer.

Cough suppression (if appropriate)

- **Morphine solution** can be used to suppress a productive cough if the patient is at the end of life, and the productive cough is causing distress:
  - **For an opioid-naïve patient,** standard-release oral morphine 10 mg/5 ml solution (a prescription-only medicine) is included for initial dose titration. Note: this should be converted to once- or twice-daily modified-release morphine once dosing requirements are stable.
  - **For someone already taking morphine,** an advice note regarding dose titration of modified-release morphine products is available.
- **Note: prescriptions from PRODIGY are generated by computer, and therefore do not fulfil the handwriting requirements for controlled-drug prescriptions.** Prescriptions for modified-release morphine and standard-release morphine tablets are therefore not provided, although in practice most patients will be maintained on modified-release morphine once dose requirements are stable.

P

Minor haemoptysis

- **Tranexamic acid** can be used empirically to reduce bleeding while awaiting radiotherapy, or if haemoptysis is only minor (e.g. sputum streaked with blood). However, there are no well-conducted studies to support its use [Dean and Tuffin, 1997].

Chest infection at the end of life

- **Intravenous ceftriaxone** is included. A single-dose of a broad-spectrum antibiotic can be useful in the terminal phase to reduce distressing symptoms of chest infection, such as purulent sputum or fever. Ceftriaxone has a broad spectrum of activity and only requires once-daily administration. Note: a chest infection in a patient who is not at the end of life should be managed in the usual way.
- **Intravenous cefotaxime** is also included, as it is commonly carried by GPs in their emergency bags.

Terminal-phase standby drug pack

- **A terminal-phase standby drug pack** containing drugs commonly needed at the end of life is included. The pack contains cyclizine, diamorphine, hyoscine hydrobromide, midazolam, and water for injection [Ellershaw and Griffiths, 2003].

Prescriptions

Therapies to aid expectoration

Advice note: moist inhalations

- Age from 16 years onwards
- Inhalations can be soothing for a dry cough. Put hot (bu not boiling) water into a bowl, and inhale the vapour as often as needed. Aromatic liquids like menthol and eucalyptus, or Friars' Balsam can be added if desired. You can buy these from a pharmacy.

Advice note: nebulized hypertonic saline

- Age from 16 years onwards
- This item is only available from Specials Manufactures, and may take a few days to obtain: Sodium chloride 6% ampoules. Inhale the contents of one ampoule using the nebulizer once or twice, a day, when required to loosen sputum. Supply 10 ampoules.

Nebulized 0.9% saline

- Age from 16 years onwards
- Sodium chloride 0.9% injection. Inhale the contents of one ampoule using the nebulizer, when required to relieve coughing; supply 20 injection; NHS Cost £6.52.

Carbocisteine 750mg twice a day

- Age from 16 years onwards
- Carbocisteine 375mg capsules. Take two capsules twice a day; supply 30 capsules; NHS Cost £4.48.

Morphine solution (if cough suppression appropriate)

Morphine solution: initial titration for opioid-naive people

- Age from 16 years onwards
- Morphine sulphate 10mg/5ml sol. Take 1.25ml regularl every 4 hours, and when required to relieve coughing; supply 100 ml; NHS Cost £2.08.

Advice note: dose increases for people already on morphine

- Age from 16 years onwards
- For those already on oral morphine: Increase the dose o regular (analgesic) morphine by 30-50% every 2-3 days until cough is controlled, or adverse effects prevent further dose increases.

Minor/moderate haemoptysis

Tranexamic acid 1g three times a day

- Age from 16 years onwards
- Tranexamic acid 500mg tablets. Take two tablets three times a day; supply 42 tablets; NHS Cost £9.56.

Chest infection in the terminal phase

Single dose: cefotaxime 1g injection

- Age from 16 years onwards
- Cefotaxime 1g injection. For intravenous injection after reconstitution; supply 1 1g vial; NHS Cost £4.50.

Single dose: ceftriaxone 1g injection

- Age from 16 years onwards
- Ceftriaxone 1g injection. For intravenous injection after reconstitution; supply 1 1g vial; NHS Cost £9.00.

Terminal phase standby drug pack

Standby drug pack

- Age from 16 years onwards
- Midazolam 5mg/ml injection. For intravenous or subcutaneous injection as directed; supply 5 2ml ampoules; NHS Cost £4.05.
- Water for injection (5ml). Use as directed; supply 10 5m ampoule; NHS Cost £2.82.

Hyoscine hydrobrom 400mcg/ml. For intravenous or subcutaneous injection as directed; supply 5 1ml ampoules; NHS Cost £13.55.
Instructions for handwriting CD prescription for diamorphine: Patients name and address. Diamorphine 10mg injection. State the dose and dose interval, e.g. 5-10 mg every 4 hours when required. Supply 2 (two) ampoules. Signed and dated.
Cyclizine lactate 50mg/ml inj. For intravenous or subcutaneous injection as directed; supply 5 1ml ampoules; NHS Cost £2.71.

Extended Information

Background information

What is it? p.1423
How common is it? p.1423
How do I know the cause of my patient's cough? p.1423

What is it?

Cough is a defensive reflex that occurs in response to stimulation of irritant receptors within the bronchial tree.
Irritant receptors respond to mechanical and chemical stimuli, and inflammatory and immunological mediators.
Malignant disease may cause mechanical distortion of the airways, stimulating irritant receptors and causing dry cough (e.g. by pleural effusion, pulmonary collapse, or presence of tumour).
Malignant disease may cause an accumulation of material within the airway, mechanically stimulating irritant receptors and causing a productive cough of blood, mucus, or purulent sputum.

How common is it?

Cough in patients with all types of cancer has a prevalence of 33% [Chang et al, 2000].
Moderate to severe cough in patients with all types of cancer has a prevalence of 13% [Chang et al, 2000].
The prevalence of cough in patients with lung cancer is 47–86% [Krech et al, 1992; Muers and Round, 1993; Hopwood et al, 1995].
Moderate to severe cough occurs in 17–48% of patients with lung cancer [Krech et al, 1992; Muers and Round, 1993; Hopwood et al, 1995].

How do I know the cause of my patient's cough?

Cough may have malignant or non-malignant causes; both should be considered.
Cough commonly has more than one cause [Smyrnios et al, 1995; Irwin, 1998].
Non-malignant causes of cough are listed in Table 2.
The clinical features of the malignant causes of cough are given in Table 3.
Cough is commonly associated with dyspnoea. If dyspnoea is the predominant symptom, see the PRODIGY guidance *Palliative care — dyspnoea*.

Primary-care investigations of cough

It is assumed that patients with an established diagnosis of malignancy will have been previously referred and investigated in secondary care.
The burden of investigation and treatment should be weighed against the prognosis, the likely benefit of treatment, and the patient's wishes.

- **The exact investigations requested will depend on the clinical assessment.** In general, the most useful investigations in primary care include:
  - Chest X-ray to assess possible chest disease.
  - Sputum for microbiological examination if infection is suspected.

Management issues

- General issues in palliative care p.1423
- Managing the malignant causes of cough p.1425
- Managing dry cough in palliative care p.1426
- Managing productive cough in palliative care (including haemoptysis) p.1426
- Medicines management p.1427

General issues in palliative care

- **The goal of palliative care is to achieve the best quality of life for the patient and family.** It is most easily achieved when there is a shared awareness of the diagnosis.
- **The truth should be made available to, but not forced upon, the patient and family.**
- **The well-being of a person is multidimensional** and is composed of the fulfilment of their *physical, psychological, social,* and *spiritual needs*. All these aspects need to be considered in the palliative-care situation.
- **A framework** to formalize a high-quality standard of palliative care in the community is being used across the UK — the *Gold Standards Framework*. It has shown outcome benefits such as more patients dying where they chose, fewer crises, and better communication and co-working with specialists [Patchett, 2003; Thomas, 2003]. For details, contact gsf@macmillan.org.uk.

Assessment and management of physical symptoms

- **Symptoms rarely occur in isolation.**
- **Concurrent symptoms may influence each other directly** (e.g. coughing may worsen the pain from spinal metastases).
- **Concurrent symptoms may influence each other indirectly,** so that the onset or deterioration of one symptom may lead to an increased perception of other pre-existing symptoms (e.g. onset of nausea may lead to an increased perception of pain, even though there has been no change in the noxious stimulus).
- **It is important to ask about the presence and severity of individual symptoms.** Do not assume that patient's will volunteer them [Roberts et al, 1993].
- **Doctors tend to underestimate the severity of symptoms,** and this is associated with under-treatment of those symptoms [Roberts et al, 1993].
- **Do not delay treatment.** Patients commonly become 'sensitized' to prolonged symptoms, making these symptoms more difficult to manage.
- **Treatment should be taken regularly,** at intervals that maintain suppression of the symptoms.
- **As symptoms are often multiple and interrelated, a systematic approach to assessment and management is necessary.** The following is suggested:
  - List symptoms, assess their severity, and prioritize them with the patient.
  - Diagnose the cause of symptoms as accurately as possible.
  - Elicit the patient's understanding of the diagnosis.
  - Set goals for treatment with the patient.
  - Negotiate a treatment plan.
  - Review and reassess changing symptoms regularly.

P

Table 2: Common non-malignant causes of cough.

Respiratory	Cardiac	Gastrointestinal	Other
Pulmonary embolism* Upper respiratory tract infections Post-viral cough Post-nasal drip Asthma Chronic obstructive pulmonary disease Smokers' cough Pneumonia Bronchiectasis Fibrosing lung disease Sarcoidosis	Heart failure	Reflux Aspiration	Angiotensin-converting enzyme (ACE) inhibitors Beta-blockers Psychogenic

*Pulmonary embolism in patients with incurable cancer is not uncommon, and the decision to anti-coagulate or not is a difficult one. The benefits and risks of treatment need to be assessed on an individual basis. The trend has been towards treating and maintaining with low-molecular weight heparin.

Assessment of the psychological state

- **Assessment of the psychological state of the patient is essential** and should be repeated at key points during the course of the illness, including:
  - At the time of diagnosis
  - Around treatment episodes
  - As treatments end
  - At the time of a relapse

[NICE, 2003]
- **At around the time of diagnosis, about 50% of patients with cancer experience levels of anxiety and depression** severe enough to adversely affect the quality of their life. This percentage improves over time, but rises again to 50% in patients with advanced disease [NICE, 2003].
- **Psychological distress and physical distress are closely associated** — deterioration in one often leads to deterioration in the other.
- **Understanding and being understood is in itself therapeutic.** The patient's understanding of the course o the illness and treatments available, may help to allay preconceived fears, and is essential if meaningful choice are to be made.
- **The healthcare professional's acknowledgement of problems** and understanding of what they mean to the patient is not only an essential part of the assessment, but may also be therapeutic. In some circumstances, it may be the only thing that can be done.
- **Feelings of loss of control and helplessness** may follow a progressive physical limitation leads to increased

Table 3: Causes of cough associated with malignant disease of the lung.

Diagnosis	Other symptoms	Onset/ progression	Signs	Primary-care investigations	Mechanism
Dry cough					
Pleural effusion	Possible dyspnoea	Insidious onset, possible rapid progression.	Reduced chest wall movements and stony dull percussion note on the affected side	Chest X-ray (CXR) able to show effusion of 300 ml or more	Exudate fro tumour
Partial lung collapse	Possible dyspnoea	Rapid onset	Reduced chest movements and percussion note dull on affected side	CXR may show collapse	Bronchiolar obstruction by tumour
Irritation to airways by tumour	—	Insidious onset and slow progression	May have no signs. If large, may cause localized wheeze or stridor.	CXR may show lesion	Non-obstructive endobronch tumour
Lymphangitis carcinomatosa	Dyspnoea	Insidious onset and slow progression	Few signs, may have basal crepitations.	CXR changes only seen later in illness. Magnetic resonance imaging (MRI) or computerized tomography (CT) scan in secondary care is able to show disease earlier.	Diffuse infiltration c lymphatic drainage, leading to pulmonary congestion.
Productive cough					
Bronchorrhoea	Productive cough — watery mucus	Insidious onset and slow progression	Few signs unless other complications of tumour	CXR may show tumour	Excessive production watery muc by tumour
Consolidation	Productive cough — infected mucus	Rapid onset may progress rapidly	Fever. Reduced chest movements, percussion note dull, breath sounds reduced on affected side.	CXR shows consolidation	Obstructive endobronch tumour predisposing to consolidatio
Haemoptysis	Productive cough — blood	Sudden onset, may be recurrent episodes.	Few signs unless other complications of tumour	CXR may show tumour. Consider further investigation to exclude pulmonary embolism.	Bleeding fro tumour or erosion by tumour

dependence. Where possible, the patient should be given control in all choices affecting care.

ocial needs

Terminal illness impacts on the patient and their family, and may affect how they relate to each other. It is important to recognize this impact and to offer appropriate support and advice when needed.

The social-care needs of the patient need to be identified. These include:

- Emotional support derived from engaging in social activities, companionship, and contact with healthcare professionals.
- Help with personal care.
- Assistance to secure financial support.
- Help inside and outside the home (e.g. with cleaning and shopping).
- Practical aids (e.g. wheelchairs and other equipment).
- Help to care for children and other dependants.

Social care may be provided informally by family and friends, or formally by providers of health and social-care services.

ICE, 2003]

piritual needs

Spiritual need relates to a person's search for meaning within his or her life. Religion is a means of expressing underlying spirituality, but spiritual belief may not always be expressed in a religious way.

The level of support people need may range from an informal sharing of ideas about life, death, and the ultimate purpose of our existence, to the provision of formalized religious ritual.

Death and dying has become a taboo subject in Western society, and consequently people, including healthcare professionals, are often reluctant to address such issues. However, issues such as the place of dying will need to be discussed. It may be that reassurance can be given about specific fears relating to dying if these issues are explored.

ICE, 2003]

eeking help and advice in primary care

The multidimensional nature of problems in palliative care requires a multidisciplinary approach.

Both the GP and district nurse should be involved as early as possible after diagnosis.

After clinical assessment, referral may be necessary for an identified specialist need.

The palliative-care team may include any or all of the following specialities:

- Palliative-care consultant
- Macmillan nurses
- Palliative-care nurse-practitioners
- Physiotherapists
- Occupational therapists
- Social workers
- Spiritual advisers

Where these services are not organized into a team, they may be accessed via referral to the Macmillan nurses.

Marie Curie Cancer Care provides nursing, totally free, to give terminally ill patients the choice of dying at home supported by their families. Their service can be accessed via the district nurse.

ecognising the terminal phase

order to care for dying patients it is essential to diagnose ing. Healthcare professionals are sometimes reluctant to agnose dying, and therefore the appropriate adjustments the terminal phase may not be made.

- **The terminal phase starts** a median of 24 hours before death, varying from hours to several days.
- **Patients in the terminal phase have several common features:**
  - They deteriorate day-by-day or faster because of their underlying condition or because of an irreversible complication of their disease.
  - They express a realization that they are dying.
  - They have reduced cognition, and are drowsy or comatose.
  - They are bed-bound.
  - They take little food or fluid, and have difficulty with oral medication.
  - The breathing pattern alters.
  - They are peripherally cyanosed and cold.

[Morita et al, 1998]

Adjustments in the terminal phase

- **The terminal phase is a time of adjustments for all** [Regnard and Hockley, 2004]:
  - **Stop unnecessary drugs** and continue with other drugs by an appropriate route.
  - **Ensure commonly required medication are available in the house** (e.g. cyclizine, diamorphine, hyoscine hydrobromide, and midazolam), so that there is no delay in treatment of new or developing symptoms. A prescription containing these items is available in the scenario *Productive cough*.
  - **Ensure physical symptoms are well controlled.**
  - **Explore understanding and provide appropriate explanation** of the situation to the patient, family, and other professional carers.
  - **Set realistic goals.**
  - **Ensure that religious and spiritual care** is offered if wanted.
  - **Ensure the environment is appropriate.**
- **The Liverpool Care Pathway for the dying patient** provides a national framework caring for patient in the terminal phase. It integrates professional communication and documentation integrating national guidelines into clinical practice. Further information can be obtained from www.lcp-mariecurie.org.uk.

Managing the malignant causes of cough

- **Cough may have malignant or non-malignant causes —** both should be considered.
- **Non-malignant causes of cough should be managed in the usual way.**
- **Cough commonly has more than one cause** [Smyrnios et al, 1995; Irwin, 1998].

Is dyspnoea a feature of the cough?

- If dyspnoea is present, see the PRODIGY guidance *Palliative care — dyspnoea*.

Should I suppress the cough?

- **In general, treatment to suppress the cough is used when:**
  - The cough is unproductive and not associated with dyspnoea.
  - The decision has been made to keep intervention to a minimum (for example, in a patient with a productive cough in the terminal phase).

Should I treat the underlying cause of the cough?

- **In general, treatment is directed at the underlying cause of the cough when:**
  - The cough is productive.
  - Treatment with cough suppressants has failed to control dry cough.
- The decision to treat the underlying cause of the cough will depend on:

P

- The wishes of the patient.
- The inconvenience and risks of the investigations of the cause.
- The likely benefit of treatments.
- The patient's life expectancy.

Managing dry cough in palliative care

- **Dry cough is usually managed with simple measures and cough suppressants,** unless dyspnoea is a feature (see the PRODIGY guidance *Palliative care — dyspnoea*).
- **If this fails, treatment of the underlying cause can be considered.** Treatment of the underlying cause is usually more involved for the patient, but is potentially more effective.

Simple measures

- **Simple measures such as moist inhalations or nebulized 0.9% saline** involve inspiration of moist air, which is often comforting. These measures also enable the patient to exert some control over treatment. Note: boiling water should not be used for moist inhalations because of the risk of scalding [BNF 45, 2003].
- **Simple linctus** may also be tried. The high sugar content stimulates the production of saliva and soothes the oropharynx. The associated swallowing may also interfere with the cough reflex. However, the effect is short-lived, so there is little point in increasing the dose or trying another compound cough mixture if simple linctus is ineffective [Twycross et al, 2002].

Cough suppressants

- **A weak opioid such as pholcodine or codeine linctus can be used to suppress coughing.** However, the licensed doses (pholcodine 10 mg every 8 hours or codeine 15–30 mg every 6–8 hours) are probably lower than the doses needed to relieve cough [Fuller and Jackson, 1990]. Some experts suggest that codeine should be given at a dose of 30–60 mg four times a day [Regnard and Hockley, 2004]. This dose is probably best given as tablets because of the large volume of linctus needed to achieve doses of 60 mg.
- **Morphine solution is an alternative** if cough is not suppressed by codeine or pholcodine linctus.

What dose of morphine should I use?

- **The initial starting dose will depend on the patient's previous exposure to opioids:**
  - A dose of 2.5 mg regularly every 4 hours, *and* as required, is suitable for an opioid-naïve patient.
  - A dose of 5–10 mg regularly every 4 hours, *and* as required, should be used for patients who have already tried codeine or pholcodine.
- **After 1–2 days,** calculate the total dose given over 24 hours, and use this to recalculate the 4-hourly dose. (The new 4-hourly and 'as required' dose is one sixth of the new total daily dose.) Repeat this process every 1–2 days until the cough is controlled. Once a stable dose has been reached, this can be converted to once- or twice-daily modified-release morphine if preferred.
- **If the patient is already on regular (analgesic) morphine:** use an 'as required' dose of morphine solution to relieve cough. (It is illogical to try a weak opioid such as codeine or pholcodine if the patient is already taking a strong opioid such as morphine.) Note: the 'as required' dose is one sixth of the total daily dose of regular morphine.
- **If an 'as required' dose relieves cough,** either increase the regular daily dose by 30–50% every 2–3 days until symptoms are controlled, or adverse effects prevent further dose increases, or continue to use additional morphine as required. (Note: if the total daily dose is increased, the 'as required' dose will also need to be recalculated.) If an 'as required' dose of morphine does not relieve cough, there is little point continuing to increase the dose.
- **Some patients with cough but no pain** can benefit from bedtime dose of morphine to prevent cough from disturbing sleep.

[Twycross et al, 2002]

What should I do if opioids do not suppress cough adequately?

- **Consider seeking specialist advice if dry cough is still persistent and troublesome,** as there is little evidence to guide symptomatic treatment.
- **Lidocaine** (lignocaine) spray is known to prevent coughing when used during bronchoscopy. There are case reports to suggest that nebulized lidocaine is helpf in suppressing cough arising anywhere down to the larger bronchi [Ahmedzai and Davis, 1997; Udezue, 2001; Doyle et al, 2004], but no formal studies have been conducted. Its place is also limited by the unpleasant taste, the risk of oropharangeal numbness leading to aspiration, the risk of bronchoconstriction, and the short duration of action (10–30 minutes) [Twycross et al, 2002].
- **One small double-blind study found that inhaled sodiu cromoglicate 10 mg four times a day** improved cough within 36–48 hours in patients with cough related to lung cancer [Moroni et al, 1996]. Some authors have suggested that the patient groups may have included those with asthma [Irwin, 1998].
- **Inhaled ipratropium bromide** has also been shown to reduce cough in patients with chronic bronchitis, and i patients with chronic persistent cough after upper respiratory tract infection [Irwin et al, 1993].

Treating the underlying malignant cause of dry cough

- **The presence of a tumour or an effusion may distort th airway,** stimulate irritant receptors, and therefore caus dry cough.
- **Treatments that reduce the tumour size or drain the effusion** will reduce distortion of the airways and tend relieve the cough.
- **Such treatments include** radiotherapy, chemotherapy, aspiration of pleural effusion, and corticosteroids.
- **If the presence of a tumour is known to be the cause of** an uncontrolled dry cough, a trial of dexamethasone c be considered whilst awaiting referral for treatment of the tumour. Alternatively, it may be used if oncologica treatment is not considered appropriate.
  - **There is little evidence to guide the best starting dos of oral dexamethasone.** A starting dose of 8 mg once day is often used; however, some experts suggest tha 6 mg once a day is sufficient for initial doses. If no initial benefit is obtained, consider increasing the do to 10–12 mg per day [Hardy et al, 2001].
  - **If dexamethasone does help to relieve cough, it shou be tapered** to the lowest effective dose that controls symptoms. It should be discontinued if no benefit is obtained, or any initial benefit is lost [Hardy et al, 2001].
  - Corticosteroids should probably be avoided for othe causes of cough, because there is no consensus on whether they are useful.

Managing productive cough in palliative ca (including haemoptysis)

- **In general, treatment should be aimed at the underlyin cause when the cough is productive.** If the cough is ineffective at clearing the airways, physiotherapy or nebulized saline can be helpful (see *Ineffective productive cough*).

Treating the underlying cause of productive cough

Chest infection

- There is separate PRODIGY guidance for the management of chest infection.
- **In patients in the terminal phase, antibiotics will make little difference** to the course of events [Doyle et al, 2004].
- **Symptomatic management, such as control of fever, may be more appropriate** [Doyle et al, 2004].
- **If infected secretions are causing distress** and are not easily managed by other means, then consider giving a single intravenous dose of a broad-spectrum antibiotic, e.g. ceftriaxone (once-daily administration) or cefotaxime (commonly carried by GPs in their emergency bags). Repeat only if symptoms reoccur [Regnard and Hockley, 2004].

Haemoptysis

- **Non-malignant causes of haemoptysis** (e.g. chest infection, pulmonary embolism) should be managed in the usual way.
- **Minor haemoptysis** (streaking of sputum):
  - **Treat empirically with tranexamic acid to reduce bleeding.** One small pilot study found that tranexamic acid 1 g three times a day might be of some benefit [Dean and Tuffin, 1997]. However, there are no well-conducted studies to support its use.
- **Moderate haemoptysis** (clots, frequent small bleeds, or anaemia):
  - Refer urgently for radiotherapy.
  - Successful palliation of haemoptysis with radiotherapy occurs in 74–97% of patients [Detterbeck et al, 2001].
  - **Bronchoscopy** is usually employed to identify the site of bleeding before treatment.
  - Treat with tranexamic acid to reduce bleeding whilst awaiting referral for radiotherapy.
- **Life-threatening haemoptysis** (where bleeding or recurrent bleeding may be life-threatening):
  - Arrange emergency admission.
- **Massive life-threatening haemoptysis in the terminal phase:**
  - **The psychological impact** of a person dying from massive haemoptysis is enormous, and both the family and staff will need support after such an experience [Doyle et al, 2004; Regnard and Hockley, 2004].
  - **Massive life-threatening haemoptysis is frightening, and sedation to relieve distress should be given as soon as possible.** Midazolam is generally used: start with 2 mg by slow intravenous injection (approximately 2 mg per minute) and increase as necessary in steps of 1 mg until the patient is settled. Rectal diazepam is an alternative if midazolam is not available [BNF 45, 2003; Doyle et al, 2004; Regnard and Hockley, 2004].
  - **The blood loss can be soaked up with towels.** Dark green or red towels (if available) are less frightening since they look dark rather than red when soaked with blood [Doyle et al, 2004; Regnard and Hockley, 2004].
  - **Consider parenteral diamorphine to manage any associated dyspnoea** [Doyle et al, 2004].

Bronchorrhoea

- **Patients with bronchorrhoea produce more than 100 ml of watery sputum per day.** Production of up to 9 litres per day has been reported.
- **Supportive measures** to ensure electrolyte balance and prevent dehydration may be required if bronchorrhoea is profuse.
- **Seek specialist advice for treatment options.** Numerous oncological and pharmacological treatments have been tried (e.g. antimuscarinic drugs, nebulized terbutaline, nebulized indometacin, or octreotide), but the individual response is variable [Lembo and Donnelly, 1995; Tamaoki et al, 2000].

Ineffective productive cough

- Respiratory muscle weakness and the presence of tenacious sputum can result in ineffective cough.
- **Clearance of copious secretions can be enhanced by specific physiotherapy** [Irwin, 1998].
- **Thick sputum is difficult to clear with coughing:**
  - **Consider simple measures such as moist inhalations.** Aromatic inhalations (e.g. menthol and eucalyptus inhalation, benzoin tincture) can be used if the patient so prefers. Although the vapour will contain little of the additive, it encourages deliberate inspiration of warm moist air, which is often comforting. Note: boiling water should not be used, because of the risk of scalding [BNF 45, 2003].
  - If these measures are ineffective, or if sputum is particularly thick and tenacious, consider using nebulized hypertonic saline 6% (4 ml nebulized every 12 hours) to loosen sputum — the hypertonicity induces influx of water from the epithelium to the mucus. The cough reflex must be intact so that loosened secretions can be expectorated [Doyle et al, 2004; Regnard and Hockley, 2004]. Hypertonic saline may take a few days to obtain, as it is only available from Specials Manufacturers. Physiological 0.9% saline has not been found to increase cough clearance on its own, but does increase the amount of sputum yielded after chest physiotherapy [Sutton et al, 1988; Houtmeyers et al, 1999].
  - **Alternatively, consider trying carbocisteine (a mucolytic).** Few studies have examined the effect of mucolytics on cough clearance, which is surprising, as they are given to improve the effectiveness of coughing [Houtmeyers et al, 1999]. However there is some evidence that long-term mucolytic treatment can reduce the number of exacerbations in people with chronic obstructive pulmonary disease [Poole and Black, 2001]. Although there is little evidence to support the use of carbocisteine to increase the effectiveness of cough, it may be worth trying, particularly if hypertonic saline is not available.
- For the management of noisy respiratory secretions in the terminal phase, see the PRODIGY guidance *Palliative care — respiratory secretions at the end of life.*

Should I use a cough suppressant?

- **Consider using an opioid** to suppress a productive cough if the decision has been made to keep intervention to a minimum in the terminal phase, and the productive cough is distressing to the patient.

Medicines management

Morphine

- **There should be no contraindications to the use of morphine in palliative care,** provided that it is carefully titrated against symptoms (i.e. pain or dyspnoea) [Twycross et al, 2002].
- **Common adverse effects** of morphine (and other opioids) include nausea and vomiting, drowsiness, unsteadiness, and constipation.
- **Some drowsiness is common** at the start of treatment or after dose increases, but it resolves within a few days for most patients. Persistent sedation can usually be resolved by dose reduction.
- **Nausea** subsides after the first few days in many patients, but can be an ongoing problem for others. An anti-emetic (e.g. haloperidol or metoclopramide) should be

P

taken regularly for the first few days to prevent opioid-induced nausea and vomiting, and then used as required.

- **Constipation** is an ongoing problem, as tolerance does not develop [Twycross et al, 2002]. A stimulant laxative with a faecal softener (e.g. co-danthrusate or co-danthramer) should always be taken regularly to prevent opioid-induced constipation.
- **More occasional adverse effects** of strong opioids include dry mouth, sweating, pruritus, hallucinations, myoclonus, and bronchoconstriction [Twycross et al, 2002].

Dexamethasone

- **Dexamethasone is used in preference to prednisolone** in palliative care because it is a more potent glucocorticoid (2 mg of dexamethasone is approximately equivalent to 15–25 mg of prednisolone) and has an insignificant mineralocorticoid effect (minimal risk of oedema and hypertension). These properties make it particularly suitable for high-dose therapy [Twycross et al, 2002].
- **Since dexamethasone is used empirically when indicated for dyspnoea, it is important to taper** to the minimum effective dose that controls symptoms. It should be discontinued if no benefit is obtained (e.g. after 7–10 days), or if any initial benefit is lost [Hardy et al, 2001].
- **Dexamethasone is generally given as a single dose in the morning** to reduce adrenal suppression and the likelihood of corticosteroid-induced insomnia [Twycross et al, 2002]. However, some patients may still require a benzodiazepine to treat insomnia or agitation.
- **Oral candidiasis is a common problem** in people taking oral corticosteroids. Consider giving prophylactic oral nystatin to prevent this.
- **Dyspepsia and indigestion** are also common. The risk of serious gastrointestinal complications (e.g. peptic ulcer or silent perforation) is markedly increased in patients who are also taking nonsteroidal anti-inflammatory drugs (NSAIDs) [Piper et al, 1991]. Gastrointestinal prophylaxis with a proton pump inhibitor or misoprostol should be considered for someone on concurrent NSAIDs or with a history of peptic ulcer disease. Only use dexamethasone in someone with active peptic ulcer disease if the benefits are likely to outweigh the risks.
- **Diabetic control** may be worsened by corticosteroids.
- **Corticosteroid myopathy** is usually only seen after several months of treatment with dexamethasone at doses of 4 mg per day or more. However, it can occur earlier and with lower doses [Twycross et al, 2002]. It is often distressing, as muscle wasting and weakness cause difficulty with normal activities such as climbing stairs and getting out of chairs [Hardy et al, 2001]. Consider stopping dexamethasone, reducing the dose, or changing to prednisolone. Weakness should improve after 3–4 weeks of stopping or dose reduction [Twycross et al, 2002]. Physiotherapy may be beneficial for some patients.
- **High doses of corticosteroids may occasionally cause psychosis and depression.** Seek specialist advice in this situation.
- **Check history of chickenpox (risk of potentially fatal disseminated chickenpox if non-immune).** Advise all patients on corticosteroids to seek urgent medical attention if they come into contact with someone with chickenpox or shingles [CSM, 1998]. If the patient has been exposed:
  - **A positive history of chickenpox is not a foolproof guide to immunity.** Check varicella-zoster antibody status in *all* patients who are likely to be immunosuppressed. Note: anyone taking dexamethasone 4 mg per day (or more) for more than 1 week in the previous 3 months is likely to be immunosuppressed.
  - Varicella-zoster immunoglobulin should *only* be given to those with negative antibody status (even if the individual has a positive history of chickenpox).
  - **If antibody status results are not likely to be available within 7 days of exposure,** give varicella-zoster immunoglobulin without testing antibody status [PHLS, 2002].
- **Steroid Treatment Cards** should be issued by the GP or pharmacist and their contents discussed.

Stopping dexamethasone

- **Dexamethasone can be stopped abruptly if** it is not relieving symptoms, *and* the patient has received treatment for less than 3 weeks, *and* is unlikely to be at risk of adrenal suppression (see below) [Twycross et al, 2002].
- **Gradual withdrawal is recommended for patients at risk of adrenal suppression** [CSM, 1998], e.g. patients who:
  - Have received dexamethasone 4–6 mg or more per day.
  - Have received more than 3 weeks' treatment.
  - Have taken a second dose in the evening.
  - Are taking a short course within 1 year of stopping long-term corticosteroids.
  - Have other possible causes of adrenal suppression.
- **The dose can be tapered rapidly** (e.g. halving the dose daily) until physiological doses are reached (about dexamethasone 1 mg). Then reduce more slowly to allow the adrenals to recover, e.g. reduce by 500 micrograms every 1–2 weeks.
- **Stopping dexamethasone in the terminal phase lacks expert consensus:**
  - If the oral route is no longer available, dexamethasone can be given as a single slow subcutaneous dose once a day.
  - If treatment is not given, the patient may become agitated and distressed owing to corticosteroid withdrawal. The onset of withdrawal symptoms is highly variable, and depends on the risk of adrenal suppression, the length of time the person lives after the last treatment, and the degree of physical stress. It is highly unlikely within the first 24 hours.
  - The clinician will need to balance the disadvantages of intrusive treatment of a dying person against the risks of not treating.

Tranexamic acid

- **Tranexamic acid promotes clotting by preventing thrombolysis.** It should therefore not be used in patients with active thromboembolic disease, and should be avoided in patients who have had a previous thromboembolic event, or have a family history of thromboembolic disease.
- **Gastrointestinal adverse effects** (nausea, vomiting, and diarrhoea) are common, but usually resolve with dose reduction [BNF 45, 2003].

Non-oral routes of drug delivery

- **Syringe drivers** are used for drug delivery if the patient is unable to take medicines by mouth, (e.g. because of persistent nausea and vomiting, dysphagia, severe weakness, or coma).
- **Use only drugs that are known to be safe and effective by syringe driver.** Use water for injection as the diluent when mixing drugs in a syringe driver (except for ketamine or octreotide).
- **Check the compatibility of drugs before mixing.** There are most data on combinations of two drugs in a syringe driver, although some combinations of three or four drugs are compatible.

P

Table 4: Compatibility and alternative routes of drugs commonly given by syringe driver.

Drug	Compatibility with diamorphine[1]	Alternative routes/drugs[2]
Cyclizine	Diamorphine any strength + cyclizine 6.7 mg/ml Diamorphine 15 mg/ml + cyclizine 15 mg/ml Diamorphine 20 mg/ml + cyclizine 10 mg/ml	Levomepromazine (methotrimeprazine) as a single subcutaneous (s/c) bedtime dose
Dexamethasone	Compatible at usual concentrations, but mix carefully to prevent precipitation	Dexamethasone as a single s/c morning dose
Glycopyrronium bromide	Compatible at usual concentrations	Hyoscine hydrobromide sublingual tablets or patches
Haloperidol	Diamorphine 20–100 mg/ml + haloperidol 0.75 mg/ml Diamorphine 50 mg/ml + haloperidol 1.5 mg/ml	Haloperidol as a single s/c bedtime dose
Hyoscine butylbromide	Compatible at all usual concentrations	Hyoscine butylbromide as a s/c dose every 4–6 hours
Hyoscine hydrobromide	Compatible at all usual concentrations	Hyoscine hydrobromide sublingual tablets or patches
Levomepromazine (methotrimeprazine)	Compatible at all usual concentrations	Levomepromazine as a single s/c bedtime dose
Metoclopramide	Diamorphine 25 mg/ml + metoclopramide 5 mg/ml	Metoclopramide s/c 8-hourly or rectal domperidone
Midazolam	Compatible at all usual concentrations	Diazepam as a single rectal bedtime dose or levomepromazine as a single s/c bedtime dose

1. Twycross, R., Wilcock, A., Charlesworth, S., and Dickman, A. (2002) *Palliative care formulary*. Palliativedrugs.com Ltd. www.palliativedrugs.com [Accessed: 30-7-2002].
2. Regnard, C. and Hockley, J. (2004) *A guide to symptom relief in palliative care*. 5th edn. Oxon: Radcliffe Medical Press.

The compatibility of diamorphine with other drugs commonly used in palliative care is addressed in Table 4. For further information on the compatibility of drugs in syringe drivers, see www.palliativedrugs.com, or seek advice from your local palliative-care team or hospital drug information service.

Do not use solutions that are discoloured or have precipitated.

Some drugs can be given by subcutaneous bolus, or by the rectal, buccal or sublingual route. Such a route could be considered if more than two drugs require administration by a non-oral route, or if the patient does not want a syringe driver.

[Twycross et al, 2002; BNF 45, 2003; Regnard and Hockley, 2004]

Drugs for cough used in syringe drivers

Opioids: diamorphine is the opioid of choice for subcutaneous infusion. Parenteral diamorphine is approximately three times as potent as oral morphine, so the *total* daily dose of oral morphine should be divided by three to obtain the 24-hour dose of diamorphine. For example, if the patient takes oral modified-release morphine 30 mg twice a day (i.e. a total daily dose of 60 mg), start with diamorphine 20 mg over 24 hours via a syringe driver and adjust according to response [BNF 45, 2003].

Dexamethasone: this can be given as a single subcutaneous dose in the morning, or as a 24-hour subcutaneous infusion [Regnard and Hockley, 2004]. The injectable forms use a different salt of dexamethasone from that in oral tablets — 1 mg of oral dexamethasone is equivalent to 1.2 mg dexamethasone phosphate or 1.3 mg dexamethasone sodium phosphate [BNF 45, 2003]. The dose should be adjusted to the nearest volume that can easily be measured.

Drugs commonly used in syringe drivers

Always follow local palliative care guidelines or seek advice from local palliative care services or hospital pharmacy drug information services *before* mixing drugs in a syringe driver.

If you are unable to contact them see www.palliativedrugs.com. Alternatively, Table 4 is included as a brief guide.

References

NHS staff in England can link, free of charge, from references to full text journals by clicking on [Full text] on the PRODIGY website.

1. Ahmedzai, S. and Davis, C. (1997) Nebulised drugs in palliative care. *Thorax* **52**(Suppl 2), 75–77. [Full text]
2. BNF 45 (2003) *British National Formulary*. 45th edn. London: British Medical Association and Royal Pharmaceutical Society of Great Britain.
3. Chang, V.T., Hwang, S.S., Feuerman, M. and Kasimis, B.S. (2000) Symptom and quality of life survey of medical oncology patients at a veterans affairs medical center. *Cancer* **88**(5), 1175–1183.
4. CSM (1998) Withdrawal of systemic corticosteroids. *Current Problems in Pharmacovigilance* **24**(May), 5–10.
5. Dean, A. and Tuffin, P. (1997) Fibrinolytic inhibitors for cancer-associated bleeding problems. *Journal of Pain and Symptom Management* **13**(1), 20–24.
6. Detterbeck, F.C., Jones, D.R. and Morris, D.E. (2001) Palliative treatment of lung cancer. In: Detterbeck, F.C., Rivera, M.P., Socinski, M.A. and Rosenman, J.G. (Eds.) *Diagnosis and treatment of lung cancer – an evidence based guide for the practising clinician*. Philadelphia: WB Saunders. 419–436.
7. Doyle, D., Hanks, G.W.C. and MacDonald, N. (Eds.) (2004) *Oxford textbook of palliative medicine*. 3rd edn. Oxford: Oxford University Press.
8. Ellershaw, J. and Griffiths, C. (2003) *The Liverpool care pathway for the dying patient (LCP)*. Liverpool: Marie Curie Centre Liverpool and The Royal Liverpool & Broadgreen University Hospitals NHS Trust.
9. Fuller, R.W. and Jackson, D.M. (1990) Physiology and treatment of cough. *Thorax* **45**(6), 425–430.
10. Hardy, J.R., Rees, E., Ling, J. et al (2001) A prospective survey of the use of dexamethasone on a palliative care unit. *Palliative Medicine* **15**(1), 3–8.
11. Hopwood, P., Stephens, R.J., Bleehen, N.M. et al (1995) Symptoms at presentation for treatment in patients with lung cancer: implications for the evaluation of palliative treatment. *British Journal of Cancer* **71**(3), 633–636.

12. Houtmeyers, E., Gosselink, R., Gayan-Ramirez, G. and Decramer, M. (1999) Effects of drugs on mucus clearance. *European Respiratory Journal* **14**(2), 452–467.
13. Irwin, R.S. (1998) Managing cough as a defense mechanism and as a symptom. *Chest* **114**(2 Suppl 2), 133–181. [Full text]
14. Irwin, R.S., Curley, F.J. and Bennett, F.M. (1993) Appropriate use of antitussives and protussives: a practical review. *Drugs* **46**(1), 80–91.
15. Krech, R.L., Davis, J., Walsh, D. and Curtis, E.B. (1992) Symptoms of lung cancer. *Palliative Medicine* **6**, 309–315.
16. Lembo, T. and Donnelly, T.J. (1995) A case of pancreatic carcinoma causing massive bronchial fluid production and electrolyte abnormalities. *Chest* **108**(4), 1161–1163.
17. Morita, T., Ichiki, T., Tsunoda, J. et al (1998) A prospective study on the dying process in terminally ill cancer patients. *American Journal of Hospice & Palliative Care* **15**(4), 217–222.
18. Moroni, M., Porta, C., Gualtieri, G. et al (1996) Inhaled sodium cromoglycate to treat cough in advanced lung cancer patients. *British Journal of Cancer* **74**(2), 309–311.
19. Muers, M.F. and Round, C.E. (1993) Palliation of symptoms in non-small cell lung cancer: a study by the Yorkshire Regional Cancer Organisation Thoracic Group. *Thorax* **48**(4), 339–343.
20. NICE (2003) *Guidance on cancer services: improving supportive and palliative care for adults with cancer (draft for first consultation)*. London: National Institute for Clinical Excellence.
21. Patchett, M. (2003) *Gold standards framework interim evaluation report*. Leicester: NHS Modernisation Agency.
22. PHLS (2002) *Immunoglobulin handbook*. Public Health Laboratory Service. www.hpa.org.uk [Accessed: 09/10/2003].
23. Piper, J.M., Ray, W.A., Daugherty, J.R. and Griffin, M.R. (1991) Corticosteroid use and peptic ulcer disease: role of nonsteroidal anti-inflammatory drugs. *Annals of Internal Medicine* **114**(9), 735–740.
24. Poole, P.J. and Black, P.N. (2001) Oral mucolytic drugs for exacerbations of chronic obstructive pulmonary disease: systematic review. *British Medical Journal* **322**(7297), 1271–1276. [Full text]
25. Regnard, C. and Hockley, J. (Eds.) (2004) *A guide to symptom relief in palliative care*. 5th edn. Oxford: Radcliffe Medical Press.
26. Roberts, D.K., Thorne, S.E. and Pearson, C. (1993) The experience of dyspnea in late-stage cancer. Patients' and nurses' perspectives. *Cancer Nursing* **16**(4), 310–320.
27. Schroeder, K. and Fahey, T. (2002) Systematic review of randomised controlled trials of over the counter cough medicines for acute cough in adults. *British Medical Journal* **324**(7333), 329–331. [Full text]
28. Smyrnios, N.A., Irwin, R.S. and Curley, F.J. (1995) Chronic cough with a history of excessive sputum production: the spectrum and frequency of causes, key components of the diagnostic evaluation, and outcome of specific therapy. *Chest* **108**(4), 991–997.
29. Sutton, P.P., Gemmell, H.G., Innes, N. et al (1988) Use of nebulised saline and nebulised terbutaline as an adjunct to chest physiotherapy. *Thorax* **43**(1), 57–60.
30. Tamaoki, J., Kohri, K., Isono, K. and Nagai, A. (2000) Inhaled indomethacin in bronchorrhea in bronchioloalveolar carcinoma: role of cyclooxygenase. *Chest* **117**(4), 1213–1214. [Full text]
31. Thomas, K. (2003) The gold standards framework in community palliative care. *European Journal of Palliative Care* **10**(3), 113–115.
32. Twycross, R., Wilcock, A., Charlesworth, S. and Dickman, A. (2002) *Palliative care formulary*. Palliativedrugs.com Ltd. www.palliativedrugs.com [Accessed: 07/06/2005].
33. Udezue, E. (2001) Lidocaine inhalation for cough suppression. *American Journal of Emergency Medicine* **19**(3), 206–207.

P

PRODIGY GUIDANCE

Palliative care — dyspnoea

Last revised in February 2004
www.prodigy.nhs.uk/guidance.asp?gt=Palliative care - dyspnoea

Applies to people over the age of 16 years

This guidance covers the management of dyspnoea in palliative care.

This guidance does not cover the detailed management of the non-malignant causes of dyspnoea.

There is separate PRODIGY guidance for the management of *Asthma*, *Chest infections*, *Chronic obstructive pulmonary disease*, *Heart failure*, and *Lung cancer — suspected*.
There is also separate PRODIGY guidance for *Palliative care — cough*, *Palliative care — malodorous malignant ulcer of skin*, *Palliative care — nausea/vomiting/malignant bowel obstruction*, *Palliative care — oral problems*, *Palliative care — pain*, and *Palliative care — respiratory secretions at the end of life*.

Goals

To alleviate the distress of dyspnoea in a manner that most enhances the patient's quality of life
To diagnose the cause of the dyspnoea where possible

Contents

Scenarios
- Rapid onset dyspnoea p.1431
- Slow onset dyspnoea p.1431
- Managing dyspnoea in the terminal phase p.1433

Extended Information, p. 1434

Which scenario?

Rapid onset dyspnoea: covers the urgent management of an acutely breathless patient with cancer.
Slow onset dyspnoea: covers the investigation and management of the underlying cause of slow onset dyspnoea in patients with cancer.
Managing dyspnoea in the terminal phase: covers the management of dyspnoea in patients in the terminal phase of their illness (on average this is the last 24 hours of life).

Rapid onset dyspnoea

Which therapy?

Sit the patient upright.
Give oxygen if hypoxia is suspected or proven.
Assess and manage as for any urgent medical situation.
Most patients will require emergency admission to hospital.
Acute dyspnoea is most commonly due to non-malignant causes.
Malignant causes of acute dyspnoea are rare.
- If stridor is present, suspect upper airway obstruction.
- If facial swelling and distended veins of upper body are present, suspect superior vena cava obstruction (SVCO).

If stridor is present or acute SVCO is suspected, give intravenous corticosteroids immediately and arrange emergency admission to hospital.

Practical prescribing points

For further information please see the *Medicines Compendium* (www.medicines.org.uk) or the *British National Formulary* (www.bnf.org) or the *Palliative Care Formulary* (www.palliativedrugs.com).

Patient information leaflets

The following PILs are available at www.prodigy.nhs.uk
- Coping with Breathlessness - Macmillan Cancer Relief
- Living with Breathlessness - Macmillan Cancer Relief
- Managing Breathlessness - Macmillan Cancer Relief
- Relaxation Exercises

Drug rationale

Drugs not included

- Corticosteroids other than dexamethasone and hydrocortisone are not routinely used for emergency treatment in the UK.

Drugs included

- **Intravenous dexamethasone** is commonly used in palliative care because of its high potency and minimal mineralocorticoid effect.
- **Intravenous hydrocortisone** is commonly carried by GPs in their emergency treatment bags.

Prescriptions

IV corticosteroid prescriptions for reimbursement

Hydrocortisone 100mg/2ml injection
- Age from 16 years onwards
- Hydrocortisone 100mg injection. For intravenous injection after reconstitution; supply 2 vials; NHS Cost £2.32.

Dexamethasone sodium phosphate 8mg/2ml injection
- Age from 16 years onwards
- Dexamethasone sod phos 8mg/2ml. For intravenous injection; supply 2 2ml vials; NHS Cost £2.54.

Dexamethasone sodium phosphate 5mg/ml injection
- Age from 16 years onwards
- Dexamethasone sod phos 5mg/ml. For intravenous injection; supply 3 1ml ampoule; NHS Cost £2.49.

Slow onset dyspnoea

Which therapy?

Use simple measures to reduce dyspnoea.
- Sit the patient up.
- Provide cool airflow over the face.
- Give oxygen if the patient is hypoxic.

P

Treat the underlying physical causes.

- Assess the possible underlying physical causes. Causes are commonly multiple and may be malignant or non-malignant.
- Decide whether to treat the underlying physical cause(s). This will depend on:
  - The wishes of the patient.
  - The inconvenience and risks of investigations.
  - The likely benefit of treatment.
  - The life expectancy of the patient.
- Consider a trial of dexamethasone 8 mg daily if dyspnoea is due to pressure on, or infiltration of, structures in the lung (e.g. lung tumour or metastases) or if lymphangitis carcinomatosa is present.
- Consider a trial of continuous or intermittent oxygen therapy if oxygen saturation is below 90%.

Assess and manage the underlying psychological state

- Listen to, understand, and address the patient's fears.
- Teach the controlled breathing technique (see the *Patient information leaflet — Controlled breathing technique)* and distraction techniques to be used during exacerbations of dyspnoea.
- Teach the patient a relaxation technique (see the *Patient information leaflet — Relaxation exercises)* to use regularly to reduce long-term levels of anxiety.
- Drug therapy may be required. Consider:
  - As required lorazepam to relieve panic during episodes of dyspnoea.
  - Treat underlying anxiety or depression in the usual way (e.g. with antidepressants if the patient is depressed).

Reduce the perception of dyspnoea

- Use morphine to reduce the perception of dyspnoea if the underlying physical cause is not going to be treated, or if treatment does not fully relieve symptoms.
  - If opioid-naïve: start with morphine solution 2.5 mg every 4 hours and 'as required'.
  - If already on a weak opioid: switch to morphine solution 5–10 mg every 4 hours and 'as required'.
  - If already on regular morphine: increase the dose by 30–50% every 2–3 days until symptoms are controlled, or adverse effects prevent further dose increases.

P

Practical prescribing points

For further information please see the *Medicines Compendium* (www.medicines.org.uk) or the *British National Formulary* (www.bnf.org) or the *Palliative Care Formulary* (www.palliativedrugs.com).

- There should be no contraindications to the use of morphine, dexamethasone, lorazepam, or oxygen in the palliative-care situation, provided that they are carefully titrated against symptoms.

Morphine

- **Titrate morphine in the same way as for pain management.**
- **If using 4-hourly morphine:**
  - **After 1–2 days,** calculate the total dose given over 24 hours, and use this to recalculate the 4-hourly dose. (The new 4-hourly and 'as required' dose is one sixth of the new total daily dose.)
  - **Repeat this process** every 1–2 days until breathlessness is controlled.
  - **Convert to once- or twice-daily modified-release morphine** once a stable dose has been reached.
- **If already on regular morphine:**
  - **Increase the dose by 30–50% every 2–3 days** until symptoms are controlled, or adverse effects prevent further dose increases.
  - Note: if the dose of regular modified-release morphine is increased, the 'as required' dose also needs to be increased (usually one sixth of the total daily dose).
- **Co-prescribe a regular stimulant laxative with a faecal softener** (e.g. co-danthrusate or co-danthramer) to prevent opioid-induced constipation.
- **Give an anti-emetic** (e.g. haloperidol or metoclopramide) regularly for the first few days to prevent opioid-induced nausea and vomiting. Then use as required.
- **Sedation is common,** but most patients quickly develop tolerance.

Dexamethasone

- **All people taking corticosteroids should carry a Steroid Treatment Card.**
- **Advise people taking corticosteroids to avoid close contact with people with chickenpox or shingles,** and to seek urgent medical advice if they are exposed.
- **Advise people taking corticosteroids that they should not suddenly stop taking them.**
- **Corticosteroids may worsen diabetic control or heart failure.**
- **Concurrent nonsteroidal anti-inflammatory drugs (NSAIDs)** increase the risk of gastrointestinal perforation. Stop NSAIDs or co-prescribe a proton pump inhibitor or misoprostol.
- **Except in the last hours and days of life, corticosteroids should not be stopped suddenly in patients who:**
  - Have received dexamethasone 4–6 mg or more per day.
  - Have received more than 3 weeks' treatment.
  - Have taken a second dose in the evening.
  - Are taking a short course within 1 year of stopping long-term corticosteroids.
  - Have other possible causes of adrenal suppression.

Oxygen therapy

- Clinically important further increases in $PaCO_2$ are unusual in stable hypercapnic chronic obstructive airways disease when the oxygen flow rate is below 3 l/min or when oxygen is given through a 28% controlled oxygen mask.

Should I refer or investigate?

Refer?

- **After clinical assessment, a specialist clinical need may be identified.**
- **If the underlying cause of worsening dyspnoea is due to the malignancy,** always consider arranging early review with an oncologist.
- **If dyspnoea is proving difficult to manage,** consider referral to the palliative-care team or Macmillan nurses.
- **Dyspnoea clinics may be available locally.** The local palliative-care team or Macmillan nurses will be able to advise on this.
- **Controlled breathing techniques** can be taught by physiotherapists, Macmillan nurses, and palliative-care nurse-practitioners.
- **Relaxation techniques** may be taught by occupational therapists, Macmillan nurses, and palliative-care nurse-practitioners.
- **Macmillan nurses may undertake cognitive therapy** for recurrent episodes of anxiety associated with dyspnoea.

Investigate?

- **Chest X-ray and full blood count are advised** if investigations are to be undertaken.

- **Use pulse oximetry** (if available) to check oxygen saturation if oxygen therapy is being considered. A trial of oxygen therapy is worth considering if oxygen saturation is less than 90%.
- **Other investigations in primary care** will depend on clinical findings.

Patient information leaflets

The following PILs are available at www.prodigy.nhs.uk

- Coping with Breathlessness - Macmillan Cancer Relief
- Living with Breathlessness - Macmillan Cancer Relief
- Managing Breathlessness - Macmillan Cancer Relief
- Relaxation Exercises

Shared decision making

Controlled breathing may help to ease shortness of breath in addition to any other treatment:

- **Sit upright.**
- **Control the rate of your breathing** — try to make your breath out twice as long as your breath in.
- **Mainly use your diaphragm (lower chest muscle) to breathe.**
- **Try to relax your shoulders and upper chest muscles when you breathe:**
  - Take the weight off your shoulders by supporting your arms on the side arms of a chair, or on your lap.
  - Gentle massage of your shoulders by a friend or relative may help you to relax.
- **Try not to focus on your breathlessness.** Distract yourself from this by (for example) watching TV or listening to the radio.

Drug rationale

Drugs not included

- **Oxygen cylinders** are not included, because individual requirements are very variable.
- **Corticosteroids other than dexamethasone** are not included, because they are less potent than dexamethasone and have a greater mineralocorticoid effect. These properties make them less suitable for high-dose therapy [Twycross et al, 2002].
- **Opioids other than morphine** are not offered, because there is less experience with their use for treating the sensation of dyspnoea in palliative care.
- **Benzodiazepines other than lorazepam** are not included. Lorazepam tablets can be administered sublingually, leading to a more rapid onset of action.

Drugs included

- **Dexamethasone** can sometimes relieve breathlessness if dyspnoea is due to the tumour causing pressure on structures in the lung. Treatment should be undertaken on a trial basis, and stopped if it is ineffective or if any initial effect is lost [Hardy et al, 2001]. Note: do not stop treatment suddenly if adrenal suppression is likely, unless it is the end of life. See *Which therapy?* for further information.
- **Morphine** is commonly used to reduce the patient's perception of dyspnoea.
  - **For an opioid-naïve patient,** standard-release oral morphine 10 mg/5 ml solution (a prescription-only medicine) is included for initial dose titration. Note: this should be converted to once- or twice-daily modified-release morphine once dosing requirements are stable.
  - **For someone already taking morphine,** an advice note regarding dose titration of modified-release morphine products is available.
  - Note: prescriptions from PRODIGY are generated by computer, and therefore do not fulfil the handwriting requirements for controlled-drug prescriptions. Prescriptions for modified-release morphine and standard-release morphine tablets are therefore not provided, although in practice most patients will be maintained on modified-release morphine once dose requirements are stable.
- **Lorazepam** can be considered for use sublingually to provide rapid relief from anxiety during acute periods of dyspnoea.

Prescriptions

Trial of dexamethasone

Dexamethasone 8mg once a day (7-day supply)

- Age from 16 years onwards
- Dexamethasone 2mg tablets. Take four tablets each morning; supply 28 tablets; NHS Cost £3.16.

Morphine (to reduce the perception of dyspnoea)

Morphine solution: initial titration for opioid-naive people

- Age from 16 years onwards
- Morphine sulphate 10mg/5ml sol. Take 1.25ml regularly every 4 hours, and when required to relieve breathlessness; supply 100 ml; NHS Cost £2.08.

Morphine sol: initial titration if previously on weak opioid

- Age from 16 years onwards
- Morphine sulphate 10mg/5ml sol. Take 2.5ml to 5ml regularly every 4 hours, and when required to relieve breathlessness; supply 100 ml; NHS Cost £2.08.

Advice note: dose increases for patients already on morphine

- Age from 16 years onwards
- For those already on oral morphine: Increase the dose of regular (analgesic) morphine by 30-50% every 2-3 days until breathlessness is controlled, or adverse effects prevent further dose increases.

P

Lorazepam

Lorazepam tablets: 500mcg when required to relieve anxiety

- Age from 16 years onwards
- Lorazepam 1mg tablets. Place half a tablet under the tongue and allow to dissolve, when required to relieve anxiety during episodes of breathlessness. Max 2 doses in 24 hrs; supply 28 tablets; NHS Cost £1.25.

Lorazepam tablets: 1mg when required to relieve anxiety

- Age from 16 years onwards
- Lorazepam 1mg tablets. Place one tablet under the tongue and allow to dissolve, when required to relieve anxiety during episodes of breathlessness. Max 2 doses in 24 hours; supply 28 tablets; NHS Cost £1.00.

Managing dyspnoea in the terminal phase

Which therapy?

- **Confirm the patient is in the terminal phase.** Patients in the terminal phase have several common features:
  - They deteriorate day-by-day or faster because of their underlying condition or because of an irreversible complication of their disease.
  - They express a realization that they are dying.

- They have reduced cognition, and are drowsy or comatose.
- They are bed-bound.
- They take little food or fluid, and have difficulty with oral medication.
- The breathing pattern alters.
- They are peripherally cyanosed and cold.

- **In all patients consider:**
  - Sitting the person up — a common mistake is to nurse a dying, breathless patient flat.
  - Giving oxygen if hypoxia is suspected or proven — avoid face masks if possible, as these impair speech.
  - Providing a cool airflow over the face.
  - Using the controlled breathing technique if clinically appropriate — see the *Patient information leaflet — Controlled breathing technique*.
- **Treat the perception of dyspnoea:** use opioids. (See *Reviewing drugs* below.)
- **Manage anxiety:**
  - If clinically appropriate, consider using distraction techniques.
  - Consider use of benzodiazepines. (See *Reviewing drugs* below.)

Reviewing drugs for dyspnoea in the last hours and days

- **Opioids:** convert to a 24-hour subcutaneous (s/c) infusion of diamorphine. Note: divide the total daily dose of oral morphine by three to calculate the 24-hour dose of subcutaneous diamorphine.
- **Benzodiazepines:** use a 24-hour s/c infusion of midazolam.
- **Dexamethasone:** stopping dexamethasone in the terminal phase lacks expert consensus.
  - The onset of withdrawal symptoms (including agitation and distress) is very variable, but is unlikely within the first 24 hours of stopping.
  - Alternatively, dexamethasone can be given as a single morning s/c bolus. The injectable forms use a different salt of dexamethasone from that in oral tablets — 1 mg oral dexamethasone is equivalent to 1.2 mg dexamethasone phosphate or 1.3 mg dexamethasone sodium phosphate. The dose should be adjusted to the nearest volume that can easily be measured.

P

Practical prescribing points

For further information please see the *Medicines Compendium* (www.medicines.org.uk) or the *British National Formulary* (www.bnf.org) or the *Palliative Care Formulary* (www.palliativedrugs.com).

Mixing drugs in syringe drivers

Always follow local palliative care guidelines or seek advice from local palliative care services or hospital pharmacy drug information services *before* mixing drugs in a syringe driver. The following information is included as a brief guide when these sources of help are unavailable:

- Check compatibilities before mixing drugs. See www.palliativedrugs.com, or Table 1 below.
- Use water for injection as the diluent when mixing drugs in a syringe driver (except for octreotide and ketamine).
- Do not use solutions that are cloudy or have precipitated.

Patient information leaflets

The following PILs are available at www.prodigy.nhs.uk

- Coping with Breathlessness - Macmillan Cancer Relief
- Living with Breathlessness - Macmillan Cancer Relief
- Managing Breathlessness - Macmillan Cancer Relief
- Relaxation Exercises

Drug rationale

Drugs included

- **A terminal-phase stand-by drug pack** containing drugs commonly needed at the end of life is included. The pack contains cyclizine, diamorphine, hyoscine hydrobromide midazolam, and water for injection [Ellershaw and Griffiths, 2003].

Prescriptions

Terminal phase standby drug pack

Standby drug pack

- Age from 16 years onwards
- Cyclizine lactate 50mg/ml inj. For intravenous or subcutaneous injection as directed; supply 5 1ml ampoules; NHS Cost £2.71.
- Hyoscine hydrobrom 400mcg/ml. For intravenous or subcutaneous injection as directed; supply 5 1ml ampoules; NHS Cost £13.55.
- Instructions for handwriting CD prescription for diamorphine: Patients name and address. Diamorphine 10mg injection. State the dose and dose interval, e.g. 5-10 mg every 4 hours when required. Supply 2 (two) ampoules. Signed and dated.
- Midazolam 5mg/ml injection. For intravenous or subcutaneous injection as directed; supply 5 2ml ampoules; NHS Cost £4.05.
- Water for injection (5ml). Use as directed; supply 10 5ml ampoule; NHS Cost £2.82.

Extended Information

Background information

- What is dyspnoea? p.1434
- How common is dyspnoea in palliative care? p.1434
- How do I diagnose the cause of my patient's dyspnoea? p.1434

What is dyspnoea?

- Dyspnoea is the subjective sensation of difficulty in breathing.
- It relates poorly to objective measurements of lung function.
- Anxiety is often a major component of dyspnoea.

How common is dyspnoea in palliative care?

- Dyspnoea has a prevalence of 50% in people with any type of cancer.
- The prevalence increases in people with pre-existing lung disease, people with lung cancer, and as the point of death approaches.
- Dyspnoea is moderate to severe in more than 28% of terminally ill cancer patients.

[Reuben and Mor, 1986]

How do I diagnose the cause of my patient's dyspnoea?

General points in diagnosing the cause of dyspnoea

- It is useful to consider whether the dyspnoea is of acute or gradual onset.

'able 1: Compatibility and alternative routes of drugs commonly given by syringe driver.

rug	Compatibility with diamorphine[1]	Alternative routes/drugs[2]
yclizine	Diamorphine any strength + cyclizine 6.7 mg/ml Diamorphine 15 mg/ml + cyclizine 15 mg/ml Diamorphine 20 mg/ml + cyclizine 10 mg/ml	Levomepromazine (methotrimeprazine) as a single subcutaneous (s/c) bedtime dose
examethasone	Compatible at usual concentrations, but mix carefully to prevent precipitation	Dexamethasone as a single s/c morning dose
lycopyrronium :omide	Compatible at usual concentrations	Hyoscine hydrobromide sublingual tablets or patches
aloperidol	Diamorphine 20–100 mg/ml + haloperidol 0.75 mg/ml Diamorphine 50 mg/ml + haloperidol 1.5 mg/ml	Haloperidol as a single s/c bedtime dose
yoscine ıtylbromide	Compatible at all usual concentrations	Hyoscine butylbromide as a s/c dose every 4–6 hours
yoscine ydrobromide	Compatible at all usual concentrations	Hyoscine hydrobromide sublingual tablets or patches
evomepromazine nethotrimeprazine)	Compatible at all usual concentrations	Levomepromazine as a single s/c bedtime dose
etoclopramide	Diamorphine 25 mg/ml + metoclopramide 5 mg/ml	Metoclopramide s/c 8-hourly or rectal domperidone
idazolam	Compatible at all usual concentrations	Diazepam as a single rectal bedtime dose or levomepromazine as a single s/c bedtime dose

Twycross, R., Wilcock, A., Charlesworth, S., and Dickman, A. (2002) *Palliative care formulary*. Palliativedrugs.com Ltd. www.palliativedrugs.com [Accessed: 30-7-)02].
Regnard, C. and Hockley, J. (2004) *A guide to symptom relief in palliative care*. 5th ed. Oxon: Radcliffe Medical Press.

Acute dyspnoea is most commonly due to non-malignant causes (see Table 1). Acute dyspnoea due to a malignant cause is rare, and when it occurs is usually due to acute superior vena cava obstruction or upper airway obstruction (see Table 2).

Gradually worsening dyspnoea often has more than one cause in someone with cancer; malignant and non-malignant causes should be considered [Dudgeon and Lertzman, 1998]. The diagnostic pointers to a malignant cause of dyspnoea are outlined in Table 2. Further investigation, in either primary or secondary care, is often required to diagnose the cause(s) of the dyspnoea accurately.

'rimary-care investigation of dyspnoea

In the non acute situation, investigations into the cause of the dyspnoea may be ordered. The exact investigations will depend on the clinical assessment. The most useful investigations to consider in all patients with non-acute dyspnoea in primary care include:

- **Chest X-ray** (CXR) to assess lung disease and heart failure.
- **Spirometry** to assess possible undiagnosed chronic obstructive pulmonary disease (COPD).
- **Electrocardiogram** to exclude arrhythmia.
- **Full blood count** to exclude anaemia.
- **Pulse oximetry** (if available) to assess hypoxia.

Common non-malignant causes of dyspnoea

'he common non-malignant causes of dyspnoea in alliative care patients are outlined in Table 2.

Clinical features of the malignant causes of dyspnoea

'able 3 outlines the clinical features of the malignant ıuses of dyspnoea in palliative care patients.

Malignant causes of dyspnoea — further information

Upper airway obstruction can be due to an intraluminal tumour, or to extrinsic compression by the tumour or lymph nodes. The dyspnoea is associated with wheeze and stridor, and is commonly misdiagnosed as chronic obstructive pulmonary disease (COPD) or asthma. Dyspnoea is distinguished from COPD and asthma by its relentless progress without fluctuation. *At any time, the narrowed segment of airway may become oedematous, leading to complete obstruction of the airway.* Lung cancer accounts for most intraluminal lesions.

- **Acute superior vena cava obstruction** occurs when the superior vena cava becomes compressed or invaded by tumour. This obstruction often leads to secondary thrombosis. If this situation develops acutely, there is no time for effective collateral circulation to develop, and venous return to the heart is impaired. *The patient becomes acutely breathless,* as well as developing facial swelling, moderate venous distension, and symptoms and signs of raised intracranial pressure.
- **Chronic superior vena cava obstruction** occurs when an effective collateral circulation develops, maintaining venous return to the heart. ***The patient is not breathless,*** and does not have symptoms and signs of raised intracranial pressure, but usually has markedly distended veins of the upper torso and arms. No intervention is required. About 75% of all cases of superior vena cava obstruction are caused by lung cancer. Lymphoma accounts for 15%, and other cancers for the remaining 10%.
- **Bronchial obstruction** by tumour may lead to loss of lung volume by causing collapse, or by predisposing to consolidation distal to the tumour.
- **Pleural effusion** is a potent cause of dyspnoea, particularly if it occurs rapidly. Clinically, it is detectable when there is at least 500 ml of fluid present. Pleural effusion is most commonly seen with lung cancer, but also occurs with lymphomas, and metastatic cancers of breast, gut, and other solid tumours.

Table 2: Common non-malignant causes of dyspnoea.

Pulmonary	Cardiac	Other
Chest infection	Heart failure	Pain
Asthma/COPD**	Angina	Anxiety
Pulmonary embolism*	Myocardial infarction	Anaemia
Pneumothorax	Arrhythmia	Diabetic ketoacidosis

* Pulmonary embolism in patients with incurable cancer is not uncommon, and the decision to anti-coagulate or not is a difficult one. The benefits and risks of treatment need to be assessed on an individual basis. The trend has been towards treating and maintaining with low-molecular-weight heparin.
** Undiagnosed and therefore untreated COPD is commonly present in patients with bronchial carcinoma. COPD is strongly associated with dyspnoea, and many of these patients benefit from simple bronchodilator therapy [Congleton and Muers, 1995].

Table 3: Clinical features of the malignant causes of dyspnoea.

Additional symptoms	Signs	Onset/progression	Investigations	Diagnosis
Dry cough	Stridor, wheeze	Relentless progression, no fluctuations. *May rapidly progress to complete occlusion of airway.*	Refer urgently for investigation and management in secondary care	Acute upper airway obstruction
Headache on lying flat	Facial swelling and moderate dilation of the veins of the face, upper limbs, and torso.	*Rapid onset and progression of dyspnoea*	Refer urgently for investigation and management in secondary care	Acute superior vena cava obstruction
Cough (productive if consolidation present)	Reduced chest movements, percussion note dull, breath sounds reduced on affected side.	Gradual onset. Deterioration in dyspnoea over period of days.	CXR shows collapse/ consolidation. Consider referral for bronchoscopy.	Bronchial obstruction causing lung collapse/ consolidation
Dry cough	Reduced chest-wall movements and stony dull percussion note on affected side	Insidious onset. Slow progressive deterioration over days to weeks.	CXR able to show effusion of 300 ml or more	Pleural effusion
Dry cough	Pulse fast, low volume. Pulsus paradoxus proportional to severity of tamponade. Raised jugular venous pressure, muffled heart sounds.	Insidious onset. Progressive deterioration over days to weeks.	CXR may show globular cardiac outline. Low-voltage electrocardiogram. Echocardiography is definitive investigation in secondary care.	Pericardial effusion
Dry cough	Few may have basal crepitations	Insidious onset, but relentless progression.	CXR changes only seen later in illness. Magnetic resonance imaging (MRI) or computerized tomography (CT) scan in secondary care able to show disease earlier.	Lymphangitis carcinomatosa

- **Pericardial effusion** occurs when a tumour invades or irritates the surface of the pericardium. The resultant effusion may lead to cardiac tamponade by restricting ventricular filling and hence reducing stroke volume. A compensatory increase in heart rate occurs in response to the reduced stroke volume. The pulse is therefore low-volume and fast. Lung cancer, breast cancer, and lymphoma are the most common cancers causing pericardial effusion.
- **Lymphangitis carcinomatosa** is caused by diffuse infiltration of lymphatic vessels by malignant disease. This obstructs pulmonary lymphatic drainage and leads to pulmonary congestion. Lymphangitis carcinomatosa is a difficult diagnosis to make, and is probably under-recognized. It most commonly occurs in people with lung cancer, but may also originate from metastatic cancers, particularly of breast, gut, and prostate.

Management issues

- General issues in palliative care p.1436
- General management of dyspnoea p.1438
- Treating the underlying physical cause of dyspnoea p.1438
- Treating the underlying psychological state p.1439
- Treating the perception of dyspnoea p.1440
- Seeking help and advice in the management of dyspnoea p.1440
- Medicines management p.1440

General issues in palliative care

- **The goal of palliative care is to achieve the best quality of life for the patient and family.** It is most easily achieved when there is a shared awareness of the diagnosis.
- **The truth should be made available to, but not forced upon, the patient and family.**
- **The well-being of a person is multidimensional** and is composed of the fulfilment of their *physical, psychological, social,* and *spiritual needs.* All these aspects need to be considered in the palliative care situation.
- **A framework to formalize a high-quality standard of palliative care** in the community is being used across the UK — the *Gold Standards Framework.* It has shown outcome benefits such as more patients dying where the[y] chose, fewer crises, and better communication and co-working with specialists [Patchett, 2003; Thomas, 2003]. For details, contact gsf@macmillan.org.uk.

Assessment and management of physical symptoms

- **Symptoms rarely occur in isolation.**
- **Concurrent symptoms may influence each other directly** (e.g. coughing may worsen the pain from spinal metastases).
- **Concurrent symptoms may influence each other indirectly,** so that the onset or deterioration of one symptom may lead to an increased perception of other pre-existing symptoms (e.g. onset of nausea may lead to an increased perception of pain even though there has been no change in the noxious stimulus).
- **It is important to ask about the presence and severity of individual symptoms.** Do not assume patient's will volunteer them [Roberts et al, 1993].
- **Doctors tend to underestimate the severity of symptoms** and this is associated with under-treatment of those symptoms [Roberts et al, 1993].

Do not delay treatment. Patients commonly become 'sensitized' to prolonged symptoms, making these symptoms more difficult to manage.

Treatment should be taken regularly, at intervals that maintain suppression of the symptoms.

As symptoms are often multiple and inter-related, a systematic approach to assessment and management is necessary. The following is suggested:

- List symptoms, assess their severity, and prioritize them with the patient.
- Diagnose the cause of symptoms as accurately as possible.
- Elicit the patient's understanding of the diagnosis.
- Set goals for treatment with the patient.
- Negotiate a treatment plan.
- Review and reassess changing symptoms regularly.

Assessment of the psychological state

Assessment of the psychological state of the patient is essential and should be repeated at key points during the course of the illness, including [NICE, 2003]:

- At the time of diagnosis
- Around treatment episodes
- As treatments end
- At the time of a relapse

At around the time of diagnosis, about 50% of people with cancer experience levels of anxiety and depression severe enough to adversely affect the quality of their life. This percentage improves over time but rises again to 50% in patients with advanced disease [NICE, 2003].

Psychological distress and physical distress are closely associated — deterioration in one often leads to deterioration in the other.

Understanding and being understood is in itself therapeutic. The patient's understanding of the course of the illness and treatments available, may help to allay preconceived fears, and is essential if meaningful choices are to be made.

The healthcare professional's acknowledgement of problems and understanding of what they mean to the patient is not only an essential part of the assessment, but may also be therapeutic. In some circumstances, it may be the only thing that can be done.

Feelings of loss of control and helplessness may follow as progressive physical limitation leads to increased dependence. Where possible, the patient should be given control in all choices affecting care.

Social needs

Terminal illness impacts on the patient and their family, and may affect how they relate to each other. It is important to recognize this impact and to offer appropriate support and advice when needed.

The social-care needs of the patient need to be identified. These include:

- Emotional support derived from engaging in social activities, companionship, and contact with healthcare professionals.
- Help with personal care.
- Assistance to secure financial support.
- Help inside and outside the home (e.g. with cleaning and shopping).
- Practical aids (e.g. wheelchairs and other equipment).
- Help to care for children and other dependants.

Social care may be provided informally by family and friends, or formally by providers of health and social care services.

[NICE, 2003]

Spiritual needs

- **Spiritual need relates to a person's search for meaning within their life.** Religion is a means of expressing underlying spirituality, but spiritual belief may not always be expressed in a religious way.
- **The level of support people need may range** from an informal sharing of ideas about life, death, and the ultimate purpose of our existence, to the provision of formalized religious ritual.
- **Death and dying has become a taboo subject in Western society,** and consequently people, including healthcare professionals, are often reluctant to address such issues. However, issues such as the place of dying will need to be discussed. It may be that reassurance can be given about specific fears relating to dying if these issues are explored.

[NICE, 2003]

Seeking help and advice in primary care

- **The multidimensional nature of problems in palliative care requires a multidisciplinary approach.**
- **Both the GP and district nurse should be involved** as early as possible after diagnosis.
- **After clinical assessment, referral may be necessary** for an identified specialist need.
- **The palliative care team** may include any or all of the following specialities:
  - Palliative care consultant
  - Macmillan nurses
  - Palliative care nurse-practitioners
  - Physiotherapists
  - Occupational therapists
  - Social workers
  - Spiritual advisers
- **Where these services are not organized into a team,** they may be accessed via referral to the Macmillan nurses.
- **Marie Curie Cancer Care** provides nursing, totally free, to give terminally ill people the choice of dying at home supported by their families. Their service can be accessed via the district nurse.

Recognising the terminal phase

P

In order to care for dying patients it is essential to diagnose dying. Healthcare professionals are sometimes reluctant to diagnose dying, and therefore the appropriate adjustments in the terminal phase may not be made.

- **The terminal phase** starts a median of 24 hours before death, varying from hours to several days.
- **Patients in the terminal phase have several common features:**
  - They deteriorate day-by-day or faster because of their underlying condition or because of an irreversible complication of their disease.
  - They express a realization that they are dying.
  - They have reduced cognition, and are drowsy or comatose.
  - They are bed-bound.
  - They take little food or fluid, and have difficulty with oral medication.
  - The breathing pattern alters.
  - They are peripherally cyanosed and cold.

[Morita et al, 1998]

Adjustments in the terminal phase

- The terminal phase is a time of adjustments for all [Regnard and Hockley, 2004]:
  - **Stop unnecessary drugs** and continue with other drugs by an appropriate route.
  - **Ensure commonly required medications are available in the house** (e.g. cyclizine, diamorphine, hyoscine

hydrobromide, and midazolam) so that there is no delay in treatment of new or developing symptoms.
- **Ensure physical symptoms are well controlled.**
- **Explore understanding and provide appropriate explanation** of the situation to the patient, family, and other professional carers.
- **Set realistic goals.**
- **Ensure that religious and spiritual care** is offered if wanted.
- **Ensure the environment is appropriate.**

- **The Liverpool Care Pathway** for the dying patient provides a national framework caring for patients in the terminal phase. It integrates professional communication and documentation integrating national guidelines into clinical practice. Further information can be obtained from www.lcp-mariecurie.org.uk.

General management of dyspnoea

Measures to reduce dyspnoea in all patients

- **Simple measures to reduce dyspnoea:**
  - Sit the patient up, as this increases vital capacity and reduces abdominal splinting.
  - Arrange cool airflow over the patient's face with a fan or by opening a window.
  - Give oxygen if hypoxia is confirmed or suspected (up to 40% of dyspnoeic patients with cancer are hypoxic) [Dudgeon and Lertzman, 1998].
- **Controlled breathing technique:** during episodes of dyspnoea, breathing is often too fast and shallow, poorly co-ordinated, and consequently inefficient. The controlled breathing technique counteracts these tendencies [Corner, 1995]. The principles of it are:
  - Sit upright.
  - Control the breathing rate.
  - Use the lower-chest breathing technique.
  - Relax the shoulders and upper chest. Massage by a carer from behind can help this, and provides psychological support.
  - This technique will need to be taught to the patient before an acute episode of dyspnoea.
  - See the Patient information leaflet — Controlled breathing technique for further information.
- **Manage anxiety if it is present.**

Managing an episode of acute dyspnoea

- **Acute dyspnoea is most commonly due to non-malignant causes.** If a non-malignant cause is present, this should be managed in the usual way. Most patients will require emergency admission to hospital.
- **Acute dyspnoea due to a malignant cause is rare, and when it occurs is usually due to acute superior vena cava obstruction or upper airway obstruction.** If either diagnosis is suspected, administer dexamethasone sodium phosphate 15–16 mg [Regnard and Hockley, 2004] or hydrocortisone 100–200 mg as a slow intravenous injection over 2 minutes, and arrange immediate admission to hospital.
- The actions listed in *Simple measures to reduce dyspnoea* should also be used to help calm the patient.

Managing recurrent exacerbations of chronic dyspnoea

- **Malignant disease often reduces the respiratory reserve,** so that even a modest challenge may leave the patient breathless. The patient therefore suffers recurrent exacerbations of dyspnoea.
- **Dyspnoea is made up of three components:** the *underlying physical cause*, the *underlying psychological state* of the patient and how these factors combine to produce the *perception of dyspnoea*.
  - The management of dyspnoea will require treatment of some or all of these components.
  - Managing the underlying physical cause is usually more involved for the patient but also potentially mor beneficial in terms of symptom control and prognosis.
  - The underlying psychological state should be assessed in all patients. It may have a profound effect on the perception of any symptom. Anxiety is particularly associated with dyspnoea. In some cases, anxiety or panic may be the sole cause of dyspnoea.
  - Modifying the perception of dyspnoea is most useful when management of the underlying physical cause is either not fully effective or not desirable. This is most commonly achieved using opioids.

Treating the underlying physical cause of dyspnoea

Should I treat the underlying cause of dyspnoea?

- **Accurate diagnosis of the cause** of the dyspnoea is required if the underlying cause is to be treated.
- **Multiple causes of dyspnoea are often present.** These may be malignant and/or non-malignant causes (see Table 1 and Table 2), and should generally be treated concurrently [Dudgeon and Lertzman, 1998].
- **Further investigation,** in either primary or secondary care, may be required to diagnose each cause of dyspnoea.
- **The process of deciding on how to proceed should be made, where possible, with both the patient and the family.** It will depend on:
  - The wishes of the patient.
  - The inconvenience and risks of investigations.
  - The likely benefit of treatments.
  - The life expectancy of the patient.

Treatment options

- Dyspnoea is often due to several causes, and these shoul generally be treated concurrently [Dudgeon and Lertzman, 1998].
- The non-malignant causes of dyspnoea should be managed in the usual way. Undiagnosed chronic obstructive pulmonary disease has been found to be strongly associated with breathlessness in patients with bronchogenic carcinoma. These patients may,therefore, benefit from simple bronchodilator therapy [Congleton and Muers, 1995].
- The treatment options for malignant causes of dyspnoea are given in Table 4.

Primary-care treatment of physical causes of malignant dyspnoea

Treatments available in primary care include corticosteroids and oxygen therapy.

Corticosteroids

- **Corticosteroids are commonly used,** although there are no controlled studies to support their use. They may reduce breathlessness by reducing inflammation around the tumour, or, in the case of corticosteroid responsive neoplasms, by shrinkage of the tumour mass itself.
- **High-dose dexamethasone** is used empirically if the tumour is causing stridor or acute superior vena cava obstruction [Doyle et al, 2004]. See *Managing an episoc of acute dyspnoea.*
- **If prognosis allows, patients with tumours causing dyspnoea** due to pressure on surrounding structures should be referred for specific treatments to relieve the pressure (e.g. radiotherapy, chemotherapy, hormonal therapy, or stenting). A trial of dexamethasone can be

able 4: Treatments of underlying physical causes of alignant dyspnoea.

iagnosis	Possible treatments of underlying cause	Urgent management required?
pper airway bstruction	Corticosteroids* Debulking of intraluminal lesions using endobronchial therapies Stenting of extrinsic compression Radiotherapy	*Yes* — if diagnosis suspected, give intravenous corticosteroids and arrange emergency admission to hospital.
cute uperior vena ava bstruction	Corticosteroids* Radiotherapy Chemotherapy for sensitive tumours Stenting of superior vena cava Thrombolysis	*Yes* — if diagnosis suspected, give intravenous corticosteroids and arrange emergency admission to hospital.
ericardial ffusion	Aspiration	If evidence of tamponade
leural fusion	Aspiration*, if recurrent consider pleurodesis.	Possibly
ronchial bstruction ausing lung ollapse	Corticosteroids* Radiotherapy Chemotherapy Endobronchial therapies	Possibly
ymphangitis arcinomatosa	Corticosteroids* Chemotherapy for sensitive tumours	Not usually

Possible primary-care treatments

given while awaiting treatment, or if prognosis does not support referral.

Lymphangitis carcinomatosa is also an indication for a trial of oral dexamethasone; there are anecdotal reports of a transient subjective improvement [Bruce et al, 1996].

There is little evidence to guide the best starting dose of oral dexamethasone. A starting dose of 8 mg once a day is often used, though some experts suggest that 6 mg once a day is sufficient for initial doses. If no initial benefit is obtained, consider increasing the dose to 10–12 mg per day [Hardy et al, 2001].

If dexamethasone does help to relieve breathlessness, it should be tapered to the lowest effective dose that controls symptoms. It should be discontinued if no benefit is obtained, or if any initial benefit is lost [Hardy et al, 2001].

Oxygen therapy

Oxygen therapy has some disadvantages to the patient:

- It severely limits mobility both inside and outside the house.
- Patients often become psychologically dependent on oxygen, and being deprived of it for even a short period may provoke acute anxiety and hence dyspnoea.

It is uncertain whether oxygen is better than air for relieving dyspnoea in patients with advanced cancer. However, it seems reasonable to prescribe oxygen to cancer patients with dyspnoea whose oxygen saturation levels are below 90% [Doyle et al, 2004].

Not all breathless patients are hypoxaemic, and not all hypoxaemic patients benefit from oxygen therapy. A simple trial of oxygen is often the best guide to therapy [Booth and Wade, 2003], particularly when pulse oximetry is not available. Oxygen should not be prescribed if no benefit is seen.

Secondary care management of the physical causes of dyspnoea

- **Where prognosis allows, all patients should be considered for referral to consider disease-modifying treatments.** Advances in chemotherapy, radiotherapy, and the development of endobronchial therapies have led to their increased use in advanced cancers in recent years.
- **Endobronchial therapies** allow the application of anti-tumour treatment directly to the site of the disease. They currently include local radiotherapy, laser treatments, cryotherapy, and stents.
- **Hormonal therapies** may be used for sensitive cancers (most commonly testicular, prostatic, and breast cancers).
- **Aspiration of a pleural effusion** can be highly effective at relieving dyspnoea, and should be considered even in later stages of the illness. The recurrence rate at 1 month after pleural aspiration alone is close to 100% [Antunes et al, 2003]. Where prognosis allows, recurrent effusions should be considered for pleurodesis.

Treating the underlying psychological state

- **The most common problems likely to be encountered are anxiety and depression.**
- **Anxiety is particularly strongly associated with dyspnoea.** In some cases, anxiety or panic can be the sole cause of dyspnoea.
- **Listen empathetically** and understand the fears of the patient.
- **Informing the patient of the likely course of the illness** will often alleviate many unknown fears.
- When asked, patients most commonly express the fear that they will choke or stop breathing and die during an acute episode of dyspnoea.
- **Inform the patient about available treatments,** how to access them, and how best to use them.

Immediate management of acute anxiety associated with dyspnoea

- **Whatever the trigger to dyspnoea, anxiety will tend to make breathing less efficient** by making it too fast, too shallow, and poorly co-ordinated.
- Use *simple measures to reduce dyspnoea*, and advise the patient to learn the *controlled breathing technique* to counteract these problems.
- **Teaching the patient these techniques** provides them and their carers a tool for dealing with episodes of dyspnoea. The confidence this gives tends to reduce anxiety during acute episodes and therefore reduces the length and severity of the episodes.
- **During an acute exacerbation of dyspnoea, try to distract the person** from focusing on their dyspnoea (for example, by suggesting watching TV or listening to music).
- **Benzodiazepines** can be used empirically to treat acute anxiety. Lorazepam 0.5–1 mg orally is often used — the aim is to promote relaxation, not necessarily to sedate the patient [Regnard and Hockley, 2004]. The sublingual route may be particularly useful if a rapid onset of action is needed (e.g. in respiratory panic attacks).

Long-term management of recurrent episodes of anxiety associated with dyspnoea

- **Identify and address psychological and physical triggers** to dyspnoeic episodes.
- **Regular use of relaxation techniques** such as aromatherapy, massage, and relaxation exercises can reduce levels of anxiety, and may avoid the need for drug

P

treatment [Regnard and Hockley, 2004]. See the *Patient information leaflet — Relaxation exercises* for further information.

- **Cognitive therapy** may help with recurrent episodes of anxiety associated with dyspnoea.
- **Some people will need regular drug treatment to manage anxiety effectively.** Options include benzodiazepines (e.g. lorazepam or diazepam) and selective serotonin-reuptake inhibitors or tricyclic antidepressants (particularly for people with panic attacks).

Treating the perception of dyspnoea

- **Dyspnoea of any cause can be managed by modifying the patient's perception of dyspnoea.** Opioids are the most commonly used drugs for this purpose. Opioids can be started in any patient distressed with dyspnoea from any cause. They should not be withheld in patients awaiting referral or other treatments.
- **Opioids can reduce the demand for ventilation without significant respiratory depression.** Even with significant pulmonary disease, carbon dioxide retention is unusual.
- There are few published studies of opioids to relieve dyspnoea, and most only involved a small number of patients [Doyle et al, 2004].
- **Oral and subcutaneous morphine** seem to be useful in relieving dyspnoea [Jennings et al, 2002]. A recent study of low-dose modified-release morphine also found that morphine relieved refractory dyspnoea [Abernethy et al, 2003].
- **Oral dihydrocodeine** has also been reported to be useful in relieving dyspnoea in patients with chronic obstructive pulmonary disease, but has not been studied in patients with advanced cancer [Doyle et al, 2004].
- **Controlled studies have not shown any significant benefit of nebulized morphine compared with control groups,** despite initial reports of success in uncontrolled studies [Jennings et al, 2002]. Opioids can induce histamine release, so bronchospasm is a potential, but uncommon, adverse effect.

What dose of morphine should I use?

- **The initial starting dose will depend on the patients' previous exposure to opioids:**
  - In an opioid-naïve patient, start with oral morphine 2.5 mg regularly every 4 hours, *and* as required.
  - A dose of 5–10 mg regularly every 4 hours, *and* as required, should be used for patients who have previously been taking a weak opioid, e.g. codeine.
- **After 1–2 days,** calculate the total dose given over 24 hours, and use this to recalculate the 4-hourly dose. (The new 4-hourly and 'as required' dose is one sixth of the new total daily dose.) Repeat this process every 1–2 days until breathlessness is controlled. Once a stable dose has been reached, this can be converted to once or twice-daily modified-release morphine [Twycross et al, 2002].
- **If the patient is already on regular (analgesic) morphine:** increase the dose of regular morphine by 30–50% every 2–3 days until symptoms are controlled, or adverse effects prevent further dose increases [Twycross et al, 2002].

Seeking help and advice in the management of dyspnoea

- **After clinical assessment, a defined specialist need may be identified.**
- **If the underlying cause of worsening dyspnoea is due to the malignancy,** always consider arranging early review with an oncologist.
- **If dyspnoea is proving difficult to manage,** consider referral to the palliative-care team or Macmillan nurses
- **There may be dyspnoea clinics available locally** that wi teach controlled breathing and relaxation techniques. The local palliative-care team or Macmillan nurses will be able to advice on this.
- **If such clinics are not available, there may be healthcar professionals available** who are able to teach these techniques (e.g. Macmillan nurses, palliative-care nurse practitioners, physiotherapists, or occupational therapists).
- **Macmillan nurses and palliative-care nurse-practitione may undertake cognitive therapy** for recurrent episodes of anxiety associated with dyspnoea.
- **Consider seeking dietary advice in patients who are losing weight and becoming progressively dyspnoeic.**
  - Decreased exercise capacity relates to weight loss in patients with chronic obstructive pulmonary disease, and nutritional support is effective at reversing weigh loss and improving exercise capacity [European Respiratory Society, 2003].
  - There no studies demonstrating a relationship betwe dyspnoea and weight loss in patients with cancer, although it would seem sensible that one exists.

Medicines management

Morphine

- **There should be no contraindications to the use of morphine in palliative care,** provided that it is carefully titrated against symptoms (i.e. pain or dyspnoea) [Twycross et al, 2002].
- **Common adverse effects** of morphine (and other opioids) include nausea and vomiting, drowsiness, unsteadiness, and constipation.
- **Some drowsiness is common** at the start of treatment o after dose increases, but it resolves within a few days fo most patients. Persistent sedation can usually be resolve by dose reduction.
- **Nausea** subsides after the first few days in many patien but can be an ongoing problem for others. An anti-emetic (e.g. haloperidol or metoclopramide) should be taken regularly for the first few days to prevent opioid-induced nausea and vomiting, and then used as require
- **Constipation** is an ongoing problem, as tolerance does not develop [Twycross et al, 2002]. A stimulant laxativ with a faecal softener should always be taken regularly (e.g. co-danthrusate or co-danthramer) to prevent opioid-induced constipation.
- **More occasional adverse effects** of strong opioids inclu dry mouth, sweating, pruritus, hallucinations, myoclonus, and bronchoconstriction [Twycross et al, 2002].

Oxygen therapy

- **Nasal cannulae are preferred to a mask,** as they do not impair speech, or eating and drinking [Regnard and Hockley, 2004].
- **Patients with hypercapnia (carbon dioxide retention)** a dependent on some hypoxia to stimulate their respiration. Clinically important further increases in $PaCO_2$ are unusual in stable hypercapnia when the oxygen flow rate is below 3 l/min or when oxygen is given through a 28% controlled oxygen mask [Royal College of Physicians, 1999].
- Patients on oxygen therapy must not smoke, because of the fire hazard.

orazepam

- **In general, there are no absolute contraindications to using lorazepam in advanced cancer** [Regnard and Hockley, 2004].
- **Common adverse effects** include drowsiness, light-headedness, confusion, ataxia, and paradoxical agitation [Regnard and Hockley, 2004].
- **Lorazepam is preferred to diazepam for treating acute attacks of anxiety** because it can be given sublingually for a rapid onset of action, has a shorter duration of action, and tends to cause less sedation.
- **Note: although the duration of action is shorter than that of diazepam, it is long enough that a dose should only be taken once or twice in 24 hours.**

examethasone

- **Dexamethasone is used in preference to prednisolone in palliative care** because it is a more potent glucocorticoid (2 mg of dexamethasone is approximately equivalent to 15–25 mg of prednisolone) and has an insignificant mineralocorticoid effect (minimal risk of oedema and hypertension). These properties make it particularly suitable for high-dose therapy [Twycross et al, 2002].
- **Since dexamethasone is used empirically when indicated for dyspnoea, it is important to taper** to the minimum effective dose that controls symptoms. It should be discontinued if no benefit is obtained (e.g. after 7–10 days), or if any initial benefit is lost [Hardy et al, 2001].
- **Dexamethasone is generally given as a single dose in the morning** to reduce adrenal suppression and the likelihood of corticosteroid-induced insomnia [Twycross et al, 2002]. However, some patients may still require a benzodiazepine to treat insomnia or agitation.
- **Oral candidiasis** is a common problem in people taking oral corticosteroids. Consider giving prophylactic oral nystatin to prevent this.
- **Dyspepsia and indigestion** are also common. The risk of serious gastrointestinal complications (e.g. peptic ulcer or silent perforation) is markedly increased in patients who are also taking nonsteroidal anti-inflammatory drugs (NSAIDs) [Piper et al, 1991]. Gastrointestinal prophylaxis with a proton pump inhibitor or misoprostol should be considered for people on concurrent NSAIDs or with a history of peptic ulcer disease. Only use dexamethasone in people with active peptic ulcer disease if the benefits are likely to outweigh the risks.
- **Diabetic control may be worsened by corticosteroids.**
- **Corticosteroid myopathy** is usually only seen after several months of treatment with dexamethasone at doses of 4 mg per day or more. However, it can occur earlier and with lower doses [Twycross et al, 2002]. It is often distressing, as muscle wasting and weakness cause difficulty with normal activities such as climbing stairs and getting out of chairs [Hardy et al, 2001]. Although rare, the respiratory muscles can be affected [Gallagher, 1994], which could exacerbate dyspnoea. If myopathy occurs, consider stopping dexamethasone, reducing the dose, or changing to prednisolone. Weakness should improve after 3–4 weeks of stopping or dose reduction [Twycross et al, 2002]. Physiotherapy may be beneficial for some patients.
- **High doses of corticosteroids may occasionally cause psychosis and depression.** Seek specialist advice in this situation.
- **Check history of chickenpox** (risk of potentially fatal disseminated chickenpox if non-immune). Advise all patients on corticosteroids to seek urgent medical attention if they come into contact with someone with chickenpox or shingles [CSM, 1998]. If the patient has been exposed:
  - **A positive history of chickenpox is not a foolproof guide to immunity.** Check varicella-zoster antibody status in *all* patients who are likely to be immunosuppressed. Note: any patient taking dexamethasone 4 mg per day (or more) for more than 1 week in the previous 3 months is likely to be immunosuppressed.
  - Varicella-zoster immunoglobulin should *only* be given to those with negative antibody status (even if the if the individual has a positive history of chickenpox).
  - **If antibody status results are not likely to be available within 7 days of exposure,** give varicella-zoster immunoglobulin without testing antibody status [PHLS, 2002].
- **Steroid Treatment Cards** should be issued by the GP or pharmacist and their contents discussed.

Stopping dexamethasone

- **Dexamethasone can be stopped abruptly if** it is not relieving symptoms *and* the patient has received treatment for less than 3 weeks, *and* they are unlikely to be at risk of adrenal suppression (see below) [Twycross et al, 2002].
- **Gradual withdrawal is recommended for patients at risk of adrenal suppression** [CSM, 1998], e.g. patients who:
  - Have received dexamethasone 4–6 mg or more per day.
  - Have received more than 3 weeks' treatment.
  - Have taken a second dose in the evening.
  - Are taking a short course within 1 year of stopping long-term corticosteroids.
  - Have other possible causes of adrenal suppression.
- **The dose can be tapered rapidly** (e.g. halving the dose daily) until physiological doses are reached (about dexamethasone 1 mg). Then reduce more slowly to allow the adrenals to recover, e.g. reduce by 500 micrograms every 1–2 weeks.
- **Stopping dexamethasone in the terminal phase lacks expert consensus:**
  - If the oral route is no longer available, dexamethasone can be given as a single slow subcutaneous dose once a day.
  - If treatment is not given, then patients may become agitated and distressed owing to corticosteroid withdrawal. The onset of withdrawal symptoms is highly variable, depending on the risk of adrenal suppression, the length of time the person lives after the last treatment, and the degree of physical stress. It is highly unlikely within the first 24 hours.
  - The clinician will need to balance the disadvantages of intrusive treatment of a dying person against the risks of not treating.

Non-oral routes of drug delivery

- **Syringe drivers** are used for drug delivery if the patient is unable to take medicines by mouth (e.g. because of persistent nausea and vomiting, dysphagia, severe weakness, or coma).
- **Use only drugs that are known to be safe and effective by the subcutaneous route.** Use water for injection as the diluent when mixing drugs in a syringe driver (except for ketamine or octreotide).
- **Check the compatibility of drugs before mixing.** There are most data on combinations of two drugs in a syringe driver, although some combinations of three or four drugs are compatible.
- **The compatibility of diamorphine with other drugs** commonly used in palliative care is addressed in Table 5. For further information on the compatibility of drugs in syringe drivers, see www.palliativedrugs.com, or seek

P

advice from your local palliative-care team or hospital drug information service.

- **Do not use solutions that are discoloured or have precipitated.**
- **Some drugs can be given by subcutaneous bolus, or by the rectal, buccal, or sublingual route.** Such a route could be considered if more than two drugs require administration by a non-oral route, or if the patient does not want a syringe driver.

[Twycross et al, 2002; BNF 45, 2003; Regnard and Hockley, 2004]

Drugs for dyspnoea used in syringe drivers

- **Opioids:** diamorphine is the opioid of choice for subcutaneous infusion. Parenteral diamorphine is approximately three times as potent as oral morphine, so the *total* daily dose of oral morphine should be divided by three to obtain the 24-hour dose of diamorphine. For example, if the patient takes oral modified-release morphine 30 mg twice a day (i.e. a total daily dose of 60 mg per day), start with diamorphine 20 mg over 24 hours via a syringe driver, and adjust according to response [BNF 45, 2003].
- **Dexamethasone:** this can be given as a single subcutaneous dose in the morning, or as a 24-hour subcutaneous infusion [Regnard and Hockley, 2004]. The injectable forms use a different salt of dexamethasone from that in oral tablets — 1 mg of oral dexamethasone is equivalent to 1.2 mg dexamethasone phosphate or 1.3 mg dexamethasone sodium phosphate [BNF 45, 2003]. The dose should be adjusted to the nearest volume that can easily be measured.
- **Anxiolytics:** midazolam is the anxiolytic of choice for subcutaneous infusion. A suggested initial infusion rate is 20–30 mg over 24 hours [BNF 45, 2003]. Diazepam is contraindicated because of severe injection-site reactions, but can be given as a single rectal dose at bedtime. Lorazepam tablets can be given sublingually.

Drugs commonly used in syringe drivers

- **Always** follow local palliative care guidelines or seek advice from local palliative care services or hospital pharmacy drug information services *before* mixing drugs in a syringe driver.
- If you are unable to contact them see www.palliativedrugs.com. Alternatively, Table 4 is included as a brief guide.

References

NHS staff in England can link, free of charge, from references to full text journals by clicking on [Full text] o the PRODIGY website.

1. Abernethy, A.P., Currow, D.C., Frith, P. et al (2003) Randomised, double blind, placebo controlled crossover trial of sustained release morphine for the management of refractory dyspnoea. *British Medical Journal* 327(7414), 523–528. [Full text]
2. Antunes, G., Neville, E., Duffy, J. and Ali, N. (2003) BTS guidelines for the management of malignant pleural effusions. *Thorax* 58(Suppl 2), 29–38.
3. BNF 45 (2003) *British National Formulary*. 45th edn London: British Medical Association and Royal Pharmaceutical Society of Great Britain.
4. Booth, S. and Wade, R. (2003) Oxygen or air for palliation of breathlessness in advanced cancer. *Journ of the Royal Society of Medicine* 96(5), 215–218.
5. Bruce, D.M., Heys, S.D. and Eremin, O. (1996) Lymphangitis carcinomatosa: a literature review. *Journal of the Royal College of Surgeons of Edinbur* **41**(1), 7–13.
6. Congleton, J. and Muers, M.F. (1995) The incidence airflow obstruction in bronchial carcinoma, its relati to breathlessness, and response to bronchodilator therapy. *Respiratory Medicine* 89(4), 291–296.
7. Corner, J. (1995) *Coping with shortness of breath*. London: The Institute of Cancer Research.
8. CSM (1998) Withdrawal of systemic corticosteroids. *Current Problems in Pharmacovigilance* 24(May), 5–10.
9. Doyle, D., Hanks, G.W.C. and MacDonald, N. (Eds. (2004) *Oxford textbook of palliative medicine*. 3rd edn. Oxford: Oxford University Press.
10. Dudgeon, D.J. and Lertzman, M. (1998) Dyspnea in the advanced cancer patient. *Journal of Pain and Symptom Management* 16(4), 212–219.
11. Ellershaw, J. and Griffiths, C. (2003) *The Liverpool care pathway for the dying patient (LCP)*. Liverpool: Marie Curie Centre Liverpool and The Royal Liverpool & Broadgreen University Hospitals NHS Trust.
12. European Respiratory Society (2003) *Nutrition and metabolism in chronic respiratory disease*. Monogra

Table 5: Compatibility and alternative routes of drugs commonly given by syringe driver.

Drug	Compatibility with diamorphine[1]	Alternative routes/drugs[2]
Cyclizine	Diamorphine any strength + cyclizine 6.7 mg/ml Diamorphine 15 mg/ml + cyclizine 15 mg/ml Diamorphine 20 mg/ml + cyclizine 10 mg/ml	Levomepromazine (methotrimeprazine) as a single subcutaneo (s/c) bedtime dose
Dexamethasone	Compatible at usual concentrations, but mix carefully to prevent precipitation	Dexamethasone as a single s/c morning dose
Glycopyrronium bromide	Compatible at usual concentrations	Hyoscine hydrobromide sublingual tablets or patches
Haloperidol	Diamorphine 20–100 mg/ml + haloperidol 0.75 mg/ml Diamorphine 50 mg/ml + haloperidol 1.5 mg/ml	Haloperidol as a single s/c bedtime dose
Hyoscine butylbromide	Compatible at all usual concentrations	Hyoscine butylbromide as a s/c dose every 4–6 hours
Hyoscine hydrobromide	Compatible at all usual concentrations	Hyoscine hydrobromide sublingual tablets or patches
Levomepromazine (methotrimeprazine)	Compatible at all usual concentrations	Levomepromazine as a single s/c bedtime dose
Metoclopramide	Diamorphine 25 mg/ml + metoclopramide 5 mg/ml	Metoclopramide s/c 8-hourly or rectal domperidone
Midazolam	Compatible at all usual concentrations	Diazepam as a single rectal bedtime dose or levomepromazine a single s/c bedtime dose

1. Twycross, R., Wilcock, A., Charlesworth, S., and Dickman, A. (2002) *Palliative care formulary*. Palliativedrugs.com Ltd. www.palliativedrugs.com [Accessed: 30-7-2002].
2. Regnard, C. and Hockley, J. (2004) *A guide to symptom relief in palliative care*. 5th ed. Oxon: Radcliffe Medical Press.

24. Sheffield: European Respiratory Society Journals Ltd. www.ersnet.org [Accessed: 26/01/2004].

13. Gallagher, C.G. (1994) Respiratory steroid myopathy. *American Journal of Respiratory & Critical Care Medicine* **150**(1), 4–6.
14. Hardy, J.R., Rees, E., Ling, J. et al (2001) A prospective survey of the use of dexamethasone on a palliative care unit. *Palliative Medicine* **15**(1), 3–8.
15. Jennings, A.L., Davies, A.N., Higgins, J.P. et al (2002) A systematic review of the use of opioids in the management of dyspnoea. *Thorax* **57**(11), 939–944. [Full text]
16. Morita, T., Ichiki, T., Tsunoda, J. et al (1998) A prospective study on the dying process in terminally ill cancer patients. *American Journal of Hospice & Palliative Care* **15**(4), 217–222.
17. NICE (2003) *Guidance on cancer services: improving supportive and palliative care for adults with cancer (draft for first consultation).* London: National Institute for Clinical Excellence.
18. Patchett, M. (2003) *Gold standards framework interim evaluation report.* Leicester: NHS Modernisation Agency.
19. PHLS (2002) *Immunoglobulin handbook.* Public Health Laboratory Service. www.hpa.org.uk [Accessed: 09/10/2003].
20. Piper, J.M., Ray, W.A., Daugherty, J.R. and Griffin, M.R. (1991) Corticosteroid use and peptic ulcer disease: role of nonsteroidal anti-inflammatory drugs. *Annals of Internal Medicine* **114**(9), 735–740.
21. Regnard, C. and Hockley, J. (Eds.) (2004) *A guide to symptom relief in palliative care.* 5th edn. Oxford: Radcliffe Medical Press.
22. Reuben, D.B. and Mor, V. (1986) Dyspnea in terminally ill cancer patients. *Chest* **89**(2), 234–236.
23. Roberts, D.K., Thorne, S.E. and Pearson, C. (1993) The experience of dyspnea in late-stage cancer. Patients' and nurses' perspectives. *Cancer Nursing* **16**(4), 310–320.
24. Royal College of Physicians (1999) *Domiciliary oxygen therapy services: clinical guidelines and advice for prescribers.* London: Royal College of Physicians.
25. Thomas, K. (2003) The gold standards framework in community palliative care. *European Journal of Palliative Care* **10**(3), 113–115.
26. Twycross, R., Wilcock, A., Charlesworth, S. and Dickman, A. (2002) *Palliative care formulary.* Palliativedrugs.com Ltd. www.palliativedrugs.com [Accessed: 07/06/2005].

PRODIGY GUIDANCE

Palliative care — malodorous malignant ulcer of the skin

Last revised in December 2002
www.prodigy.nhs.uk/guidance.asp?gt=Palliative - malignant ulcer

Applies to people over the age of 14 years

This guidance mainly covers the management of the malodour of malignant ulcers on the skin. There is limited background information on the management of exudate, bleeding, and pain.

This guidance does not cover the treatment of the cancer itself. It is assumed that patients have been assessed for local control of the tumour by radiotherapy, chemotherapy, hormonal treatment, or surgery.

There is separate PRODIGY guidance for *Palliative care — cough*, *Palliative care — dyspnoea*, *Palliative care — nausea/vomiting/malignant bowel obstruction*, *Palliative care — oral problems*, *Palliative care — pain* and *Palliative care — respiratory secretions at the end of life.*

Goals

- To control exudate
- To control offensive odour
- To reduce psychological distress and social isolation
- To improve patient and carer quality of life

Contents

Scenarios
- Malodorous ulcer p.1444

Extended Information, p. 1445

Malodorous ulcer

Which therapy?

Although prescriptions are only offered for oral and topical metronidazole, other management options should also be considered for controlling malodour.

- **Ensure adequate cleansing of the ulcer.** If the ulcer is dirty (surface slough or debris), irrigate with physiological saline or tap water warmed to at least room temperature (the ideal temperature is 37°C, but this may be difficult to achieve in practice). Cleansing may be most easily achieved by the patient having a shower.
- **Control exudate.** Dressings suitable for ulcers producing large amounts of exudate include alginate, fibrous hydrocolloid, and foam dressings. Choice of dressing will be determined by the location and depth of the ulcer, familiarity with the different products, and local availability or local wound care policies.
- **Consider use of an activated charcoal dressing,** usually as a secondary dressing, which may help to contain the odour. Charcoal dressings are ineffective once wet and may require frequent changing.
- **Oral metronidazole** reduces levels of the anaerobic bacteria that cause malodour and is usually very effective at reducing odour.
  - **Treatment may need to be continued over the long term,** as the smell usually returns once metronidazole is stopped. There is no evidence of reduced effectiveness with prolonged use, and it is usually well tolerated.
  - **Alcohol and metronidazole.** It is generally recommended that alcohol should be avoided while taking oral metronidazole (Manufacturer's Summary of Product Characteristics), but a recent study has suggested that adverse reactions to this combination are uncommon. Inform patients that vomiting may occasionally occur if alcohol is taken with metronidazole. If this occurs, alcohol should be avoided or a switch to topical metronidazole considered.
- **Topical metronidazole** is an effective but much more expensive alternative. This is applied once or twice a day and covered with a dressing.
- **Taking oral and topical metronidazole together is not recommended:** there is no published research on whether this is more effective than either treatment used alone.

Additional points

- **If the ulcer is bleeding heavily,** apply pressure to the area and then apply an alginate dressing (these have haemostatic properties). If heavy bleeding continues, seek urgent advice from your local palliative care service.
- **Ensure adequate pain control during dressing changes:** prior administration of an analgesic may be helpful. This usually requires use of a quick-acting strong opioid (instant-release tablets or solutions of morphine), taken 30–60 minutes prior to the dressing change. A suitable starting dose of oral morphine is usually 5 mg, but smaller doses should be considered in patients who are elderly or have renal impairment. If the patient is already taking regular opioids, a booster dose equivalent to one-sixth of the 24-hour dosage (i.e. the same as the 4-hourly dose of opioid) can be taken. For patients with swallowing difficulties, or where a more rapid effect is desired, subcutaneous administration (given at an appropriate dose) could be considered. Entonox (nitrous oxide and oxygen mixture) may be useful if the patient can comply, but is not usually available in the community.

Practical prescribing points

For further information please see the *Medicines Compendium* (www.medicines.org.uk) or the *British National Formulary* (www.bnf.org).

Should I refer or investigate?

Refer?

- **If there are ongoing difficulties with primary care management,** consult with the local palliative care service.

If the ulcer is bleeding heavily and is not responding to locally applied pressure and alginate dressings, seek urgent advice from your local palliative care service.

Patient information leaflets

The following PILs are available at www.prodigy.nhs.uk
- Cancerbacup
- Macmillan Cancer Relief
- Malignant Skin Ulcers
- Marie Curie Cancer Care

Shared decision making

- Cleansing is usually best with plenty of warm tap water. A shower may be easiest for some people.
- **A dressing** is chosen according to how moist the ulcer is, and how much discharge needs to be absorbed.
- Special charcoal dressings may be used to reduce any unpleasant smell. However, these may need to be changed often as they do not work well if they become moist.
- **Metronidazole tablets** may also be prescribed to reduce any smell. This antibiotic kills the bacteria which cause the smell. You can take it as long as necessary. Vomiting may occasionally occur if alcohol is taken with metronidazole. If this occurs, avoid alcohol and inform your doctor or nurse, as an alternative treatment may be possible.
- **Metronidazole ointment** is sometimes used instead of tablets.
- **Strong painkillers,** taken half-an-hour or so before changing the dressing, can ease or prevent pain.
- Other treatments may be advised, depending on the exact cause of the ulcer, for example, surgery, radiotherapy, chemotherapy, etc.

Drug rationale

Drugs not included

Dressings are not included. Choice of dressing should be guided by local wound care policies. Other issues to consider are the location and depth of the ulcer, the amount of exudate, the need for control of odour, and familiarity with the different products.

Activated charcoal dressings should be used as an adjunct to appropriate dressings for the individual wound.

Drugs included

Both oral and topical metronidazole have been shown to reduce malodour, although there are no studies comparing both formulations. Treatment with preparations licensed for topical use is markedly more expensive than oral metronidazole.

Treatment may need to be prolonged, as the odour usually returns on stopping treatment.

[Twycross et al, 2002]

Prescriptions

Acute treatment: oral metronidazole for 14 days

Metronidazole tablets: 400mg three times a day
- Age from 14 years onwards
- Metronidazole 400mg tablets. Take one tablet three times a day for 14 days; supply 42 tablets; NHS Cost £3.09.

Frail or debilitated: metronidazole 400mg tabs twice a day
- Age from 14 years onwards
- Metronidazole 400mg tablets. Take one tablet twice a day for 14 days; supply 28 tablets; NHS Cost £2.06.

Acute treatment: topical metronidazole for 14 days

Metronidazole 0.75% gel: apply liberally once or twice a day
- Age from 14 years onwards
- Metronidazole 0.75% gel (30g). Apply liberally to the ulcer once or twice a day; supply 7 30-gram tubes; NHS Cost £55.23.

Metronidazole 0.8% gel: apply liberally once or twice a day
- Age from 14 years onwards
- Metronidazole 0.8% gel. Apply liberally to the ulcer once or twice a day; supply 7 30-gram tubes; NHS Cost £58.52.

Maintenance: low-dose metronidazole for recurrent malodour

Metronidazole tablets: 200mg twice a day
- Age from 14 years onwards
- Metronidazole 200mg tablets. Take one tablet twice a day; supply 56 tablets; NHS Cost £1.12.

Metronidazole 0.75% gel: apply liberally once a day
- Age from 14 years onwards
- Metronidazole 0.75% gel (30g). Apply liberally to the ulcer once a day; supply 7 30-gram tubes; NHS Cost £55.23.

Metronidazole 0.8% gel: apply liberally once a day
- Age from 14 years onwards
- Metronidazole 0.8% gel. Apply liberally to the ulcer once a day; supply 7 30-gram tubes; NHS Cost £58.52.

Extended Information

Background information

- What is it? p.1445
- How common is it? p.1445
- Complications and prognosis p.1446

What is it?

- **Malignant ulcers** are caused by malignant infiltration of the skin by a primary tumour or a metastasis to the skin. These lesions can grow rapidly, and commonly present with both ulcerative and fungating (nodular) features. They may be complicated by sinus or fistula formation [Collier, 2000].
- **Malodour is a common problem.** The blood supply to parts of the tumour is often impaired, resulting in areas of hypoxic or necrotic tissue. These areas become infected with anaerobic bacteria, which release malodorous volatile fatty acids as a metabolic by-product.
- **Excessive exudate** is also a common problem.

How common is it?

- **There is no reliable information on how many people are treated for malignant ulcers.** A total of 114 respondents to a questionnaire survey of practitioners working mainly in radiotherapy and oncology units reported seeing 295 malignant ulcers in the previous month [Thomas, 1992].
- **The most common locations of malignant ulcers** in this study were: breast (62%), head and face (24%), groin and genitals (3%), back (3%), and other areas (8%).

P

Complications and prognosis

Complications

- **Psychological distress** is common. Patients often become depressed, anxious, embarrassed and ashamed. They may have difficulties with body image and sexuality. The appearance and smell of the wound is a constant reminder of their disease.
- **Social withdrawal** may occur due to embarrassment about the unpleasant smell.
- **Exudate** may soil or stain clothing, and require frequent dressing changes.
- **Bleeding** may also cause staining. Bleeding can be profuse and difficult to control.
- **Pain** is common, due to infiltration or compression of nerves and surrounding tissues [Naylor, 2002].

Prognosis

- **Prognosis is generally poor,** as the presence of a malignant ulcer usually indicates advanced disease. However, in some cases certain primary tumours, such as malignant melanoma and breast cancer, may be cured with appropriate treatment [Mortimer, 1998].
- **Malignant ulcers usually fail to heal,** but considerable benefit can be obtained by appropriate nursing care of the wound. Palliative radiotherapy, chemotherapy, hormonal treatment, or surgery may be beneficial in some cases.

Management issues

- General points p.1446
- Is the ulcer dirty? p.1446
- Is discharge excessive? p.1446
- Is the ulcer smelly? p.1446
- Is the ulcer bleeding? p.1447
- Is pain present? p.1447

General points

- **This guidance focuses particularly on the management of the malodour commonly associated with malignant ulcers.** There has been little research into how best to manage malignant ulcers, and most management is based on recommended good practice.
- **Management of a malignant ulcer requires a comprehensive assessment of the patient.** Suggested areas to cover are outlined in Table 1.
- **Psychosocial problems** are common and should be addressed.
- **Wound dressings** are used to improve cosmetic appearance, reduce discomfort, protect the area, control exudate, control odour, and control bleeding. Choice of dressing will be determined by the location and depth of the ulcer, the amount of exudate, the need for control of odour, familiarity with the different products, and local availability or local wound care policies.
- **Antimicrobial treatment** (oral or topical) is used to control malodour (see *Is the ulcer smelly?*).
- **Local control of the tumour** by radiotherapy, chemotherapy, hormonal treatment, or surgery should have been considered.
- Assessment of a patient with a malodorous malignant ulcer is outlined in Table 1.

Table 1: Assessment of a patient with a malignant ulcer.

Area to assess	Comments
History of the ulcer	For example: for how long it has been presen previous treatments received, and their effectiveness. In particular, ensure that local control of the tumour by chemotherapy, hormonal treatment, radiotherapy, or surger has been considered.
Physical properties of the ulcer	The location, diameter, depth, and colour of the malignant ulcer. The presence of odour, exudate, and bleeding.
Signs of infection	For example, purulent discharge, surroundin cellulitis.
Factors which may exacerbate the condition	For example, previous radiotherapy, poor nutrition, drug treatments, disease progression.
Pain associated with the ulcer	Effective control of pain is essential, includin during dressing changes.
Psychosocial impact	Patients with malignant ulcers may be depressed, anxious, and socially withdrawn. They often have problems with altered body image, sexuality, embarrassment, and shame The unpleasant smell may be particularly distressing, and may be bad enough to cause gagging or even vomiting.
Home situation	In particular, the level of home support available to the patient.

Adapted from Miller, 1998

Is the ulcer dirty?

- **Cleansing (removal of surface slough and debris) is best carried out by irrigating with physiological saline or ordinary tap water** [CREST, 1998; Miller, 1998]. Cleansing may be most easily achieved by the patient having a shower. Use of swabs can be painful and traumatic, and should be avoided.
- **Saline and water used for cleansing should be warmed t at least room temperature** [CREST, 1998]. The ideal temperature is 37°C, but this may be difficult to achieve in practice. Cold solutions impair cellular repair [CREST, 1998].
- **Topical antiseptic solutions are not recommended.** Mos antiseptics are rapidly inactivated by body fluids, and therefore their cleansing action is mainly mechanical [Miller, 1998]. Some may have toxic effects on tissues [CREST, 1998].
- **Chemical or surgical debridement is not recommended.** In particular, surgical debridement is likely to lead to bleeding [Naylor, 2002]. Autolytic debridement is promoted by use of dressings that provide a moist wound environment, which encourages natural wound healing. Such dressings include hydrocolloids, hydrogel polysaccharide beads or paste, foam dressings, and alginate dressings [NICE, 2001].

Is discharge excessive?

- **Malignant ulcers usually produce moderate to high leve of exudate.** This can cause problems with odour, staining, and maceration of surrounding skin.
- **Dressings vary in their ability to absorb exudate.**
- **Dressings suitable for ulcers producing large amounts o exudate** include alginate, fibrous hydrocolloid, and foa dressings [CREST, 1998].
- **Where exudate level is low, dressings that have a low absorbency should be used,** so as not to dry out the wound (e.g. low-absorbency hydrocolloids, hydrogels, low-adherence absorbent dressings) [Naylor, 2002].

Is the ulcer smelly?

- **Malodour can have a devastating effect on the patient's and the carers' quality of life.** It is caused by the presen of anaerobic bacteria, which produce volatile malodorous fatty acids.
- **The subjective reporting of smell by the patient and carers should guide treatment.** Health care professiona may become desensitized to the odour, as a result of

repeated exposure to other wounds with similar symptoms [Collier, 2000].

Management of odour involves effective wound cleansing and control of exudate (see above), use of odour-absorbing activated charcoal dressings, and use of topical or systemic metronidazole [Regnard et al, 1997; Miller, 1998; Back, 2001; Naylor, 2002].

Perfumes are usually unhelpful, as their particular smell commonly becomes associated with the unpleasant odour [Regnard et al, 1997].

Activated charcoal dressings

Activated charcoal dressings may help to contain offensive odours. They are usually used as a secondary dressing, but some can be applied directly to the wound surface as a primary dressing.

There are no clinical studies comparing the effectiveness of the various products in controlling odour. Although laboratory studies suggest that activated charcoal dressings may differ in their effectiveness [Thomas et al, 1998], it is difficult to extrapolate laboratory results to the clinical setting.

The odour-absorbing property of activated charcoal is reduced once the charcoal becomes wet with exudate [CREST, 1998]. Once malodour is noticed, the dressing should be changed. Frequent dressing changes may be required to maintain effective control of odour.

Oral metronidazole

Metronidazole is an antimicrobial that is active against anaerobic organisms. It reduces the malodour associated with malignant ulcers.

Clinical studies of oral metronidazole have been small and methodologically poor, but have shown marked reductions in odour [Sparrow et al, 1980; Ashford et al, 1984]. This is consistent with clinical experience.

Treatment may need to be continued over the long term, as the odour usually returns when treatment is stopped.

There is no evidence of reduced effectiveness of metronidazole with prolonged or repeated use.

Resistance to metronidazole by the odour-producing anaerobes is unlikely to develop [UK Medicines Information, 2002].

Alcohol and metronidazole. It is generally recommended that alcohol should be avoided while taking oral metronidazole (Manufacturer's Summary of Product Characteristics), but a recent study has suggested that adverse reactions to this combination are uncommon [Visapaa et al, 2002]. Patients should be informed that vomiting may occasionally occur if alcohol is taken with metronidazole. If this occurs, alcohol should be avoided or a switch to topical metronidazole considered.

Topical metronidazole

Studies of the use of topical metronidazole have found marked reductions in odour [Newman et al, 1989; Bower et al, 1992; Finlay et al, 1996; Kuge et al, 1996]. These studies have been small and methodologically poor, but their findings are consistent with numerous case reports and clinical experience.

There are no studies comparing oral with topical metronidazole.

Treatment with preparations licensed for topical use is markedly more expensive than oral metronidazole.

Is the ulcer bleeding?

Trauma during dressing changes should be minimized. If the wound needs cleansing, it should be gently irrigated (see *Is the ulcer dirty?*). Low-adherence dressings that maintain a moist environment between the dressing and the ulcer should be used.

- **If the ulcer is bleeding,** an alginate dressing may help as these promote local clotting [CREST, 1998; Regnard and Tempest, 1998].
- **Topical adrenaline is not recommended:** it may cause ischaemic necrosis due to local vasoconstriction, and it should be used only under medical supervision [Naylor, 2002].

Is pain present?

- A full discussion of pain management is beyond the scope of this guidance.
- Pain control should follow the World Health Organization (WHO) guidelines for the control of cancer pain.
- **Before dressing changes, administration of an analgesic may be helpful.** This usually requires use of a quick-acting strong opioid (instant-release tablets or solutions of morphine), taken 30–60 minutes prior to the dressing change. A suitable starting dose of oral morphine is usually 5 mg, but smaller doses should be considered in patients who are elderly or have renal impairment. If the patient is already taking regular opioids, a booster dose equivalent to one-sixth of the 24-hour dosage (i.e. the same as the 4-hourly dose of opioid) can be taken [Hanks and Cherny, 1998; Regnard and Tempest, 1998]. For patients with swallowing difficulties, or where a more rapid effect is desired, subcutaneous administration (given at an appropriate dose) could be considered. Entonox (nitrous oxide and oxygen mixture) may be useful if the patient is able to use it properly, but it is not usually available in the community.

References

NHS staff in England can link, free of charge, from references to full text journals by clicking on [Full text] on the PRODIGY website.

1. Ashford, R., Plant, G., Maher, J. and Teare, L. (1984) Double-blind trial of metronidazole in malodorous ulcerating tumours. *Lancet* **1**(8388), 1232–1233.
2. Back, I (Ed.) (2001) *Palliative medicine handbook*. 3rd edn. Cardiff: BPM Books.
3. Bower, M., Stein, R., Evans, T.R.J. et al (1992) A double-blind study of the efficacy of metronidazole gel in the treatment of malodorous fungating tumours. *European Journal of Cancer* **28A**(4/5), 888–889.
4. Collier, M. (2000) Management of patients with fungating wounds. *Nursing Standard* **15**(11), 46–52. [Full text]
5. CREST (1998) *Guidelines on the general principles of caring for patients with wounds*. http://www.crestni.org.uk/publications/wounds.pdf [Accessed: 31/07/2002].
6. Finlay, I.G., Bowszyc, J., Ramlau, C. and Gwiezdzinski, Z. (1996) The effect of topical 0.75% metronidazole gel on malodorous cutaneous ulcers. *Journal of Pain and Symptom Management* **11**(3), 158–162.
7. Hanks, G. and Cherny, N. (1998) Opioid analgesic therapy. In: Doyle, D., Hanks, G.W.C., MacDonald, N. et al (Eds.) *Oxford textbook of palliative medicine*. 2nd edn. Oxford: Oxford University Press. 331–355.
8. Kuge, S., Tokuda, Y., Ohta, M. et al (1996) Use of metronidazole gel to control malodor in advanced and recurrent breast cancer. *Japanese Journal of Clinical Oncology* **26**(4), 207–210.
9. Miller, C. (1998) Skin problems in palliative care: nursing aspects. In: Doyle, D., Hanks, G.W.C., MacDonald, N. et al (Eds.) *Oxford Textbook of Palliative Medicine*. 2nd edn. Oxford: Oxford University Press. 642–656.

P

10. Mortimer, P.S. (1998) Skin problems in palliative care: medical aspects. In: Doyle, D., Hanks, G.W.C., MacDonald, N. et al (Eds.) *Oxford Textbook of Palliative Medicine*. 2nd edn. Oxford: Oxford University Press. 617–627.
11. Naylor, W. (2002) *Part 1: symptom control in the management of fungating wounds.* World Wide Wounds. www.worldwidewounds.com [Accessed: 31/07/2002].
12. Newman, V., Allwood, M. and Oakes, R.A. (1989) The use of metronidazole gel to control the smell of malodorous lesions. *Palliative Medicine* 3, 303–305.
13. NICE (2001) *Guidance on the use of debriding agents and specialist wound care clinics for difficult to heal surgical wounds.* Technology appraisal no. 24. National Institute for Clinical Excellence. www.nice.org.uk [Accessed: 31/07/2002].
14. Regnard, C. and Tempest, S. (Eds.) (1998) *A guide to symptom relief in advanced disease.* 4th edn. Hale: Hochland & Hochland Ltd.
15. Regnard, C., Allport, S. and Stephenson, L. (1997) ABC of palliative care: mouth care, skin care, and lymphoedema. *British Medical Journal* **315**(7114), 1002–1005. [Full text]
16. Sparrow, G., Minton, M., Rubens, R.D. et al (1980) Metronidazole in smelly tumours. *Lancet* **1**(8179), 1185.
17. Thomas, S. (1992) *Current practices in the management of fungating lesions and radiation-damaged skin.* Bridgend: Surgical Materials Testing Laboratory.
18. Thomas, S., Fisher, B., Fram, P. and Waring, M. (1998) *Odour absorbing dressings: a comparative laboratory study.* World Wide Wounds. www.worldwidewounds.com [Accessed: 31/07/2002].
19. Twycross, R., Wilcock, A., Charlesworth, S. and Dickman, A. (2002) *Palliative care formulary.* Palliativedrugs.com Ltd. www.palliativedrugs.com [Accessed: 07/06/2005].
20. UK Medicines Information (2002) *Will long-term metronidazole for malodorous wounds cause resistance and therefore reduced efficiency?* UK Medicines Information. www.ukmi.nhs.uk [Accessed: 30/07/2002].
21. Visapaa, J.P., Tillonen, J.S., Kaihovaara, P.S. and Salaspuro, M.P. (2002) Lack of disulfiram-like reaction with metronidazole and ethanol. *Annals of Pharmacotherapy* **36**(6), 971–974.

PRODIGY GUIDANCE

Palliative care — nausea/vomiting/ malignant bowel obstruction

Last revised in February 2005
www.prodigy.nhs.uk/guidance.asp?gt=Palliative care - nausea/vomit

Applies to people over the age of 16 years

This guidance covers the management of nausea and vomiting in palliative care patients.

There is separate PRODIGY guidance for *Palliative care — cough, Palliative care — dyspnoea, Palliative care — malodorous malignant ulcer of skin, Palliative care — oral problems, Palliative care — pain and Palliative care — respiratory secretions at the end of life,*

This guidance does not cover the management of nausea and vomiting due to cytotoxic chemotherapy.

Goals

To alleviate the symptoms of nausea and vomiting in a manner that most enhances the quality of life of the patient

Contents

Scenarios

- Starting treatment for nausea and vomiting p.1449
- Persistent nausea and vomiting on first-line therapy p.1452
- Malignant bowel obstruction (MBO) p.1454
- Managing nausea and vomiting in the terminal phase p.1457

Extended Information, p. 1459

Which scenario?

Starting treatment for nausea and vomiting: covers the initial management of palliative care patients who have nausea and vomiting.
Persistent nausea and vomiting on first-line therapy: covers the management of palliative care patients who have not responded to first-line treatment of nausea and vomiting.
Malignant bowel obstruction (MBO): covers the management of palliative care patients who have inoperable bowel obstruction caused by tumour.
Managing nausea and vomiting in the terminal phase: covers the management of palliative care patients in the days or hours before death. To recognise the terminal phase see the section *Recognising the terminal phase*.

Starting treatment for nausea and vomiting

Which therapy?

Assess the cause of nausea, retching, and vomiting and correct reversible causes.
Start a first-line anti-emetic appropriate to the suspected cause of nausea and vomiting.

- **Raised intracranial pressure:** start high-dose dexamethasone 16 mg oral, then reduce the dose to the lowest dose that controls symptoms, 4–6 mg daily if possible. Stop therapy if there is no demonstrable benefit. Consider referral for radiotherapy.
- **Abdominal and pelvic tumour inducing nausea and vomiting:** if tumour is causing malignant bowel obstruction see scenario *Malignant bowel obstruction*. Start cyclizine and review effectiveness within 24 hours.
- **Gastric stasis:** start a prokinetic, metoclopramide oral or parenteral, domperidone oral or rectal.
- **Opioid-induced nausea and vomiting:** start haloperidol or metoclopramide when initiating or increasing the dose of opioids.
- **Movement-related nausea and vomiting:** start cyclizine (oral or parenteral).
- **Nausea and vomiting of multiple or uncertain origin:** offer levomepromazine, a broad-spectrum anti-emetic. Where the cause is uncertain, always consider seeking specialist advice.

- **Manage complications of prolonged nausea and vomiting.** Consider:
  - Hydration and electrolyte balance
  - Psychological and functional impact

Practical prescribing points

For further information please see the *Medicines Compendium* (www.medicines.org.uk) or the *British National Formulary* (www.bnf.org) or the *Palliative Care Formulary* (www.palliativedrugs.com).

Dexamethasone

- **All people taking corticosteroids should carry a Steroid Treatment Card.**
- **Advise people taking corticosteroids to avoid close contact with people with chickenpox or shingles,** and to seek urgent medical advice if they are exposed.
- **Advise people taking corticosteroids that they should not suddenly stop taking them.**
- **Corticosteroids may worsen diabetic control or heart failure.**
- **Concurrent nonsteroidal anti-inflammatory drugs (NSAIDs)** increase the risk of gastrointestinal perforation. Stop NSAIDs or co-prescribe a proton pump inhibitor or misoprostol.
- **Corticosteroids should not be stopped suddenly in patients who:**
  - Have received dexamethasone 4–6 mg or more per day for more than 3 weeks.
  - Are taking a short course within 1 year of stopping long-term corticosteroids.
  - Have other possible causes of adrenal suppression.

Metoclopramide

- **Metoclopramide can induce acute dystonic reactions** involving facial and skeletal muscle spasms and oculogyric crises. These are more common in young

P

adults. Injection of procyclidine 5–10 mg intravenously or intramuscularly will abort a dystonic attack.

Mixing drugs in syringe drivers

Always follow local palliative care guidelines or seek advice from local palliative care services or hospital pharmacy drug information services *before* mixing drugs in a syringe driver. The following information is included as a brief guide when these sources of help are unavailable:

- Check compatibilities before mixing drugs. See www.palliativedrugs.com, or Table 1 below.
- Use water for injection as the diluent when mixing drugs in a syringe driver (except for octreotide and ketamine).
- Do not use solutions that are cloudy or have precipitated.

Follow-up advice

- **Review response to treatment.** The frequency of review will depend on the clinical state of the patient at the time of the presentation and on the response to treatment.
- **If response to treatment is unexpectedly poor, reconsider the diagnosis.**
- **If nausea and vomiting improves but persists** on first-line therapy after 24–48 hours, see scenario *Persistent nausea and vomiting on first-line therapy*.

Should I refer or investigate?

Refer?

- Consider referring all patients with nausea and vomiting presenting with:
  - Hypercalcaemia
  - Tense ascites
  - A treatable malignant cause

Table 1: Compatibility of first-line drugs for nausea and vomiting in a syringe driver.

Drug	Compatibility with diamorphine[1]	Alternative routes/ drugs[2]
Cyclizine	Diamorphine any strength + cyclizine 6.7 mg/ml Diamorphine 15 mg/ml + cyclizine 15 mg/ml Diamorphine 20 mg/ml + cyclizine 10 mg/ml	Levomepromazine as a single subcutaneous (s/c) bedtime dose
Dexamethasone	Compatible at usual concentrations, but mix carefully to prevent precipitation	Dexamethasone as a single s/c morning dose
Haloperidol	Diamorphine 20–100 mg/ ml + haloperidol 0.75 mg/ ml Diamorphine 50 mg/ml + haloperidol 1.5 mg/ml	Haloperidol as a single bedtime dose
Hyoscine hydrobromide	Compatible at all usual concentrations	Hyoscine hydrobromide sublingual tablets or patches
Levomepromazine	Compatible at all usual concentrations	Levomepromazine as a single s/c bedtime dose
Metoclopramide	Diamorphine 25 mg/ml + metoclopramide 5 mg/ml	Metoclopramide 8-hourly or rectal domperidone

1. Twycross, R., Wilcock, A., Charlesworth, S., and Dickman, A. (2002) *Palliative care formulary*. Palliativedrugs.com Ltd. www.palliativedrugs.com [Accessed: 30-7-2002].
2. Regnard, C. and Hockley, J. (Eds.) (2004a) *A guide to symptom relief in palliative care*. 5th edn. Oxford: Radcliffe Medical Press.

Investigate?

- Investigations will be determined by clinical suspicion, the prognosis, and wishes of the patient.

Shared decision making

- If the patient is vomiting, make available a large bowel, tissues, and water.
- Some people find the smell of food, and particularly cooking, can precipitate symptoms and should be avoided where possible. If the patient is at home and cooking their own meals, it is often helpful for someone else to take this over.
- Taking food and fluid is one of the most basic requirements of life. It is a natural instinct of carers to encourage someone who is ill to eat and drink. However undue pressure may lead to anxiety regarding eating, which can be counterproductive.
- Select foods that the patients can enjoy or tolerate rather than being overly concerned with healthy eating. Generally, carbohydrate meals that are easily digested, and sour flavours such as citrus-flavoured foods and drinks, are most easily tolerated.
- Small, regular meals or snacks are more likely to be well tolerated.

Drug rationale

Drugs not included

- **Corticosteroids other than dexamethasone** are not included, because they have a greater mineralocorticoid effect, increasing the risk of fluid retention, e.g. cerebral oedema, which make them less suitable for high-dose therapy [Twycross et al, 2002].
- **Cinnarizine, meclozine, promethazine, and alimemazine** (trimeprazine) increase sedation and offer no advantage over cyclizine in the management of nausea and vomiting in palliative care. Cinnarizine may have a role as a vestibular sedative for persistent symptoms due to movement-related nausea.
- **Combination of cyclizine with opioid products:** cyclizine is not the drug of choice in opioid-induced nausea. An anti-emetic is usually necessary only for the first 4 or 5 days when initiating an opioid. Combined preparations may lead to unnecessary anti-emetic therapy and associated adverse effects with long-term use.
- **Ondansetron, tropisetron, granisetron, and dolasetron** are not included. These are rarely indicated in the palliative care setting. Their use is limited to chemotherapy- and radiotherapy-induced nausea.
- **Phenothiazines other than haloperidol:** phenothiazines, e.g. thioridazine, have differing antimuscarinic activity, which may be marked. Chlorpromazine and prochlorperazine offer no advantage over non-sedative haloperidol.
- **Glycopyrronium bromide and hyoscine butylbromide** have antimuscarinic effects and where possible they should not be used concurrently with prokinetic drugs. They are useful for the management of nausea and vomiting associated with malignant bowel obstruction.
- **Nabilone** is a synthetic cannabinoid with anti-emetic properties. It may be useful for nausea and vomiting caused by cytotoxic chemotherapy that is unresponsive to conventional anti-emetics, but its use should be directed by specialist care.

Drugs included

Dexamethasone has very high glucocorticoid activity in conjunction with insignificant mineralocorticoid activity. Dexamethasone also has a long duration of action. A starting dose of dexamethasone 16 mg daily is offered along with prescriptions for dose titration.
Cyclizine is useful for nausea and vomiting due to mechanical bowel obstruction, raised intracranial pressure, and motion sickness.
Haloperidol is useful for most chemical and metabolic causes of vomiting, e.g. hypercalcaemia, renal failure. Once-daily administration may be an advantage.
Levomepromazine is usually reserved for second-line therapy but may be useful for nausea and vomiting of unknown or multiple causes. Sodium chloride 0.9% for injection is offered as diluent before intravenous administration.
Metoclopramide and domperidone have prokinetic action and are used for nausea and vomiting associated with gastritis, gastric stasis, and functional bowel obstruction.

Prescriptions

Cyclizine (oral or parenteral)

Cyclizine tablets: 50mg up to three times a day
- Age from 16 years onwards
- Cyclizine 50mg tablets. Take one tablet up to three times a day when required for sickness; supply 21 tablets; NHS Cost £1.30.

Cyclizine sc injection: 50mg up to three times a day
- Age from 16 years onwards
- Cyclizine lactate 50mg/ml inj. FOR SUBCUTANEOUS INJECTION. Give 1ml (50mg) up to three times a day when required; supply 10 1ml ampoules; NHS Cost £7.04.

Cyclizine im or iv injection: 50mg up to three times a day
- Age from 16 years onwards
- Cyclizine lactate 50mg/ml inj. FOR INTRAMUSCULAR OR INTRAVENOUS INJECTION. Give 1ml (50mg) up to three times a day when required; supply 10 1ml ampoules; NHS Cost £7.04.

Cyclizine subcutaneous infusion: 150mg over 24 hours
- Age from 16 years onwards
- Cyclizine lactate 50mg/ml inj. FOR CONTINUOUS SUBCUTANEOUS INFUSION. Give up to 3ml (150mg) over 24 hours via a syringe driver when required for sickness; supply 10 1ml ampoules; NHS Cost £7.04.

Metoclopramide or domperidone (oral or parenteral or rectal)

Metoclopramide tablets: 10mg up to three times a day
- Age from 16 years onwards
- Metoclopramide 10mg tablets. Take one tablet up to three times a day when required for sickness; supply 21 tablets; NHS Cost £0.62.

Metoclopramide sc injection: 10mg up to 3 times a day
- Age from 16 years onwards
- Metoclopramide 10mg/2ml inj. FOR SUBCUTANEOUS INJECTION. Give 2ml (10mg) up to three times a day when required for sickness; supply 6 2ml ampoules; NHS Cost £1.56.

Metoclopramide im or iv injection: 10mg up to 3 times a day
- Age from 16 years onwards
- Metoclopramide 10mg/2ml inj. FOR INTRAMUSCULAR OR SLOW INTRAVENOUS INJECTION. Give 2ml (10mg) up to three times a day when required for sickness; supply 6 2ml ampoules; NHS Cost £1.56.

Metoclopramide subcutaneous infusion: 20-60mg over 24 hours
- Age from 16 years onwards
- Metoclopramide 5mg/ml 20ml inj. FOR CONTINUOUS SUBCUTANEOUS INFUSION. Give 4ml (20mg) to 12ml (60mg) over 24 hours via a syringe driver when required for sickness; supply 5 20ml ampoules; NHS Cost £13.34.

Domperidone tablets: 10mg to 20mg up to four times a day
- Age from 16 years onwards
- Domperidone 10mg tablets. Take one to two tablets every 4 to 8 hours when required for relief of sickness. Maximum of 8 tablets in 24 hours; supply 30 tablets; NHS Cost £2.51.

Domperidone suppositories: 30mg to 60mg when required
- Age from 16 years onwards
- Domperidone 30mg suppositories. Insert one to two suppositories into the rectum every 4 to 8 hours when required for relief of sickness. Maximum of 4 suppositories in 24 hours; supply 20 suppositories; NHS Cost £5.30.

Dexamethasone (oral)

Start dexamethasone tablets: 16mg each morning
- Age from 16 years onwards
- Dexamethasone 2mg tablets. Take eight tablets each morning for sickness; supply 56 tablets; NHS Cost £6.16.

Step down: dexamethasone 12mg each morning
- Age from 16 years onwards
- Dexamethasone 2mg tablets. Take six tablets each morning for sickness; supply 42 tablets; NHS Cost £4.62.

Step down: dexamethasone 8mg each morning
- Age from 16 years onwards
- Dexamethasone 2mg tablets. Take four tablets each morning for sickness; supply 28 tablets; NHS Cost £3.08.

Step down: dexamethasone 6mg each morning
- Age from 16 years onwards
- Dexamethasone 2mg tablets. Take three tablets each morning for sickness; supply 21 tablets; NHS Cost £2.31.

Step down: dexamethasone 4mg each morning
- Age from 16 years onwards
- Dexamethasone 2mg tablets. Take two tablets each morning for sickness; supply 14 tablets; NHS Cost £1.54.

Haloperidol (oral or parenteral)

Haloperidol tablets: 1.5mg at night
- Age from 16 years onwards
- Haloperidol 1.5mg tablets. Take one tablet at night when required for sickness; supply 5 tablets; NHS Cost £0.30.

Haloperidol subcutaneous injection: 1mg to 2.5mg once a day
- Age from 16 years onwards
- Haloperidol 5mg/ml injection. FOR SUBCUTANEOUS INJECTION. Give 0.2ml (1mg) to 0.5ml (2.5mg) by subcutaneous injection once a day when required for sickness; supply 5 1ml ampoules; NHS Cost £2.65.

Haloperidol im injection: 1mg to 2mg once a day
- Age from 16 years onwards
- Haloperidol 5mg/ml injection. FOR INTRAMUSCULAR INJECTION. Give 0.2ml (1mg) to 0.4ml (2mg) by intramuscular injection once a day when required for sickness; supply 5 1ml ampoules; NHS Cost £2.65.

Haloperidol subcutaneous infusion: 2.5mg-10mg over 24 hours
- Age from 16 years onwards
- Haloperidol 5mg/ml injection. FOR CONTINUOUS SUBCUTANEOUS INFUSION. Give 0.5ml (2.5mg) to 2ml (10mg) over 24 hours via a syringe driver when required for sickness; supply 10 1ml ampoules; NHS Cost £5.90.

Levomepromazine (oral or parenteral)

Levomepromazine tablets: 6.25mg to 12.5mg at night
- Age from 16 years onwards
- Levomepromazine 25mg tablets. Take a quarter to a half of a tablet at night when required for sickness; supply 7 tablets; NHS Cost £1.65.

Levomepromazine sc injection: 6.25mg to 12.5mg once a day
- Age from 16 years onwards
- Levomepromazine 25mg/ml inj. FOR SUBCUTANEOUS INJECTION. Give 0.25ml (6.25mg) to 0.5ml (12.5mg) once a day when required for sickness; supply 3 1ml ampoules; NHS Cost £6.38.

Levomepromazine im injection: 6.25mg to 12.5mg once a day
- Age from 16 years onwards
- Levomepromazine 25mg/ml inj. FOR INTRAMUSCULAR INJECTION. Give 0.25ml (6.25mg) to 0.5ml (12.5mg) once a day when required for sickness; supply 3 1ml ampoules; NHS Cost £6.38.

Levomepromazine iv injection: 6.25mg to 12.5mg once a day
- Age from 16 years onwards
- Levomepromazine 25mg/ml inj. Give 0.25ml (6.25mg) to 0.5ml (12.5mg) by iv injection once a day when required. Mix with an equal volume of sodium chloride before administration; supply 3 1ml ampoules; NHS Cost £6.38.
- Sodium chloride 0.9% injection. Mix with equal volume of levomepromazine injection before intravenous administration; supply 3 injection; NHS Cost £0.21.

P

Persistent nausea and vomiting on first-line therapy

Which therapy?

- **Add in or switch to a second-line therapy** if nausea, retching and vomiting persists 24-48 hours after starting a first-line anti-emetic. Choose an anti-emetic appropriate for the suspected cause of nausea and vomiting.
  - **Raised intracranial pressure: add cyclizine or** levomepromazine to dexamethasone. Levomepromazine is preferred if sedation is required.
  - **Abdominal and pelvic tumour:** add dexamethasone to cyclizine if short-term relief of obstruction is appropriate.
  - **Gastric stasis:** if prokinetics are ineffective, ensure the prokinetic is being given by a non-oral route and consider increasing the dose. Consider adding therapies that reduce gastric secretions. Ranitidine will reduce the volume of secretions and their acidity. Octreotide may be useful in resistant cases.
  - **Chemically or metabolically induced:** substitute levomepromazine.
- **Reconsider diagnosis** if symptoms persist.
- **Manage complications** of prolonged nausea and vomiting.
- **Seek specialist help** if symptoms remain difficult to control.

Practical prescribing points

For further information please see the *Medicines Compendium* (www.medicines.org.uk) or the *British National Formulary* (www.bnf.org) or the *Palliative Care Formulary* (www.palliativedrugs.com).

Dexamethasone

- **All people taking corticosteroids should carry a Steroid Treatment Card.**
- **Advise people taking corticosteroids to avoid close contact with people with chickenpox or shingles,** and to seek urgent medical advice if they are exposed.
- **Advise people taking corticosteroids that they should no[t] suddenly stop taking them.**
- **Corticosteroids may worsen diabetic control or heart failure.**
- **Concurrent nonsteroidal anti-inflammatory drugs** (NSAIDs) increase the risk of gastrointestinal perforation. Stop NSAIDs or co-prescribe a proton pump inhibitor or misoprostol.
- **Corticosteroids should not be stopped suddenly in patients who:**
  - Have received dexamethasone 4–6 mg or more per day for more than 3 weeks.
  - Are taking a short course within 1 year of stopping long-term corticosteroids.
  - Have other possible causes of adrenal suppression.

Mixing drugs in syringe drivers

Always follow local palliative care guidelines or seek advice from local palliative care services or hospital pharmacy drug information services *before* mixing drugs i[n] a syringe driver. The following information is included as [a] brief guide when these sources of help are unavailable:
- Check compatibilities before mixing drugs. See www.palliativedrugs.com, or Table 2 below.
- Use water for injection as the diluent when mixing drug[s] in a syringe driver (except for octreotide and ketamine).
- Do not use solutions that are cloudy or have precipitated.
- **Use sodium chloride as the diluent** for octreotide when used in a syringe driver.

Should I refer or investigate?

Refer?

- Consider referring all patients with nausea and vomiting presenting with:
  - Hypercalcaemia
  - Tense ascites
  - A treatable malignant cause
- Consider seeking specialist help if symptoms are proving difficult to manage.

Investigate?

- Investigations will depend on clinical suspicion, prognosis, and wishes of the patient.

Table 2: Compatibility of drugs for nausea and vomiting in a syringe driver.

Drug	Compatibility with diamorphine[1]	Alternative routes/ drugs[2]
Cyclizine	Diamorphine any strength + cyclizine 6.7 mg/ml Diamorphine 15 mg/ml + cyclizine 15 mg/ml Diamorphine 20 mg/ml + cyclizine 10 mg/ml	Levomepromazine (methotrimeprazine) as a single subcutaneous (s/c) bedtime dose
Dexamethasone	Compatible at usual concentrations, but mix carefully to prevent precipitation	Dexamethasone as a single s/c morning dose
Glycopyrronium bromide	Compatible at usual concentrations	Hyoscine hydrobromide sublingual tablets or patches
Haloperidol	Diamorphine 20–100 mg/ml + haloperidol 0.75 mg/ml Diamorphine 50 mg/ml + haloperidol 1.5 mg/ml	Haloperidol as a single s/c bedtime dose
Hyoscine butylbromide	Compatible at all usual concentrations	Hyoscine butylbromide as a s/c dose every 4–6 hours
Hyoscine hydrobromide	Compatible at all usual concentrations	Hyoscine hydrobromide sublingual tablets or patches
Levomepromazine	Compatible at all usual concentrations	Levomepromazine as a single s/c bedtime dose
Metoclopramide	Diamorphine 25 mg/ml + metoclopramide 5 mg/ml	Metoclopramide s/c 8-hourly or rectal domperidone

1. Twycross, R., Wilcock, A., Charlesworth, S., and Dickman, A. (2002) *Palliative care formulary*. Palliativedrugs.com Ltd. www.palliativedrugs.com [Accessed: 30-?-2002].
2. Regnard, C. and Hockley, J. (Eds.) (2004a) *A guide to symptom relief in palliative care*. 5th edn. Oxford: Radcliffe Medical Press.

Shared decision making

- If the patient is vomiting, make available a large bowel, tissues, and water.
- Some people find the smell of food, and particularly cooking, can precipitate symptoms and should be avoided where possible. If the patient is at home and cooking their own meals, it is often helpful for someone else to take this over.
- Taking food and fluid is one of the most basic requirements of life. It is a natural instinct of carers to encourage someone who is ill to eat and drink. However, undue pressure may lead to anxiety regarding eating, which can be counterproductive.
- Select foods that the patients can enjoy or tolerate rather than being overly concerned with healthy eating. Generally, carbohydrate meals that are easily digested, and sour flavours such as citrus-flavoured foods and drinks, are most easily tolerated.
- Small, regular meals or snacks are more likely to be well tolerated.

Drug rationale

Drugs not included

- **Prokinetics: metoclopramide and domperidone** are used for nausea and vomiting associated with gastritis, gastric stasis, and functional bowel obstruction.
- **Corticosteroids other than dexamethasone** are not included, because they have a greater mineralocorticoid effect, increasing the risk of fluid retention, e.g. cerebral oedema, which make them less suitable for high-dose therapy [Twycross et al, 2002].
- **Cinnarizine, meclozine, promethazine, and alimemazine** (trimeprazine) increase sedation and offer no advantage over cyclizine in the management of nausea and vomiting in palliative care. Cinnarizine may have a role as a vestibular sedative for persistent symptoms due to movement-related nausea.
- **Hyoscine butylbromide and glycopyrronium bromide** have antimuscarinic effects. They are useful for the management of nausea and vomiting associated with malignant bowel obstruction.
- **Combination cyclizine with opioid products:** an anti-emetic is usually necessary only for the first 4 or 5 days when initiating an opioid. Combined preparations may lead to unnecessary anti-emetic therapy and associated adverse effects with long-term use.
- **Ondansetron, tropisetron, granisetron and dolasetron** are not included. These are rarely indicated in the palliative care setting. Their use is limited to chemotherapy and radiotherapy induced nausea.
- **Nabilone** is a synthetic cannabinoid with anti-emetic properties. It may be useful for nausea and vomiting caused by cytotoxic chemotherapy that is unresponsive to conventional anti-emetics but its use should be directed by specialist care.

Drugs included

- **Dexamethasone** has very high glucocorticoid activity in conjunction with insignificant mineralocorticoid activity. Dexamethasone also has a long duration of action. A starting dose of dexamethasone 16 mg daily is offered along with prescriptions for dose titration. Subcutaneous dexamethasone is offered as an alternative to oral administration.
- **Cyclizine** is useful for nausea and vomiting due to mechanical bowel obstruction, raised intracranial pressure, and motion sickness.
- **Levomepromazine** is usually reserved for second-line therapy but may be useful for nausea and vomiting of unknown or multiple causes. Dexamethasone may be used as an adjunct.
- **Ranitidine** is offered for a trial of add-on therapy, to reduce gastric secretions in gastric stasis due to functional bowel obstruction that is unresponsive to prokinetics.
- **Octreotide** is offered for add-on therapy, to reduce gastric secretions in gastric stasis unresponsive to prokinetics.

P

Prescriptions

Cyclizine (oral or parenteral)

Cyclizine tablets: 50mg up to three times a day

- Age from 16 years onwards
- Cyclizine 50mg tablets. Take one tablet up to three times a day when required for sickness; supply 21 tablets; NHS Cost £1.30.

Cyclizine sc injection: 50mg up to three times a day

- Age from 16 years onwards
- Cyclizine lactate 50mg/ml inj. FOR SUBCUTANEOUS INJECTION. Give 1ml (50mg) up to three times a day when required; supply 10 1ml ampoules; NHS Cost £7.04.

Cyclizine im or iv injection: 50mg up to 3 times a day

- Age from 16 years onwards
- Cyclizine lactate 50mg/ml inj. FOR INTRAMUSCULAR OR INTRAVENOUS INJECTION. Give 1ml (50mg) up

to three times a day when required; supply 10 1ml ampoules; NHS Cost £7.04.

Cyclizine subcutaneous infusion: 150mg over 24 hours
- Age from 16 years onwards
- Cyclizine lactate 50mg/ml inj. FOR CONTINUOUS SUBCUTANEOUS INFUSION. Give up to 3ml (150mg) over 24 hours via a syringe driver when required for sickness; supply 10 1ml ampoules; NHS Cost £7.04.

Levomepromazine (oral or parenteral)

Levomepromazine tablets: 6.25-12.5mg at night
- Age from 16 years onwards
- Levomepromazine 25mg tablets. Take a quarter to a half of a tablet at night when required for sickness; supply 7 tablets; NHS Cost £1.65.

Levomepromazine sc injection: 6.25mg to 12.5mg once a day
- Age from 16 years onwards
- Levomepromazine 25mg/ml inj. FOR SUBCUTANEOUS INJECTION. Give 0.25ml (6.25mg) to 0.5ml (12.5mg) once a day when required for sickness; supply 3 1ml ampoules; NHS Cost £6.58.

Levomepromazine im injection: 6.25mg to 12.5mg once a day
- Age from 16 years onwards
- Levomepromazine 25mg/ml inj. FOR INTRAMUSCULAR INJECTION. Give 0.25ml (6.25mg) to 0.5ml (12.5mg) once a day when required for sickness; supply 3 1ml ampoules; NHS Cost £6.58.

Levomepromazine iv injection: 6.25mg to 12.5mg once a day
- Age from 16 years onwards
- Levomepromazine 25mg/ml inj. Give 0.25ml (6.25mg) to 0.5ml (12.5mg) by iv injection once a day when required. Mix with an equal volume of sodium chloride before administration; supply 3 1ml ampoules; NHS Cost £6.58.
- Sodium chloride 0.9% injection. Mix with equal volume of levomepromazine injection before intravenous administration; supply 3 injection; NHS Cost £0.19.

P

Dexamethasone (oral or parenteral)

Start dexamethasone tablets: 16mg each morning
- Age from 16 years onwards
- Dexamethasone 2mg tablets. Take eight tablets each morning for sickness; supply 56 tablets; NHS Cost £6.16.

Step down: dexamethasone 12mg each morning
- Age from 16 years onwards
- Dexamethasone 2mg tablets. Take six tablets each morning for sickness; supply 42 tablets; NHS Cost £4.62.

Step down: dexamethasone 8mg each morning
- Age from 16 years onwards
- Dexamethasone 2mg tablets. Take four tablets each morning for sickness; supply 28 tablets; NHS Cost £3.08.

Step down: dexamethasone 6mg each morning
- Age from 16 years onwards
- Dexamethasone 2mg tablets. Take three tablets each morning for sickness; supply 21 tablets; NHS Cost £2.31.

Step down: dexamethasone 4mg each morning
- Age from 16 years onwards
- Dexamethasone 2mg tablets. Take two tablets each morning for sickness; supply 14 tablets; NHS Cost £1.54.

Start dexamethasone im injection: 16mg to 24mg once a day
- Age from 16 years onwards
- Dexamethasone sod phos 8mg/2ml. FOR INTRAMUSCULAR INJECTION. Give 4ml (16mg) once a day for sickness. Increase to 6ml (24mg) once a day if necessary; supply 3 2ml vials; NHS Cost £5.94.

Octreotide (subcutaneous)

Octreotide sc infusion: 250-500micrograms over 24 hours
- Age from 16 years onwards
- Octreotide 500 micrograms/ml. FOR CONTINUOUS SUBCUTANEOUS INFUSION. Give 250mcg (0.5ml) to 500mcg (1ml) over 24 hours via a syringe driver to reduce gastric secretions; supply 1 1ml ampoule; NHS Cost £32.75.

Octreotide sc inj: 50-200micrograms up to three times a day
- Age from 16 years onwards
- Octreotide 100microgram/ml inj. FOR SUBCUTANEOUS INJECTION. Give 50mcg (0.5ml) once or twice a day to reduce gastric secretions. Increase as needed to max 200mcg three times a day; supply 5 1ml ampoules; NHS Cost £32.67.

Ranitidine (intramuscular)

Ranitidine im injection: 50mg up to four times a day
- Age from 16 years onwards
- Ranitidine 50mg/2ml injection. FOR INTRAMUSCULAR INJECTION. Give 2ml (50mg) every six to eight hours when required to reduce gastric secretions; supply 3 2ml ampoules; NHS Cost £1.92.

Malignant bowel obstruction (MBO)

Which therapy?

A specialist should evaluate and plan the management of patients presenting with malignant bowel obstruction (MBO). Some patients with MBO may be adequately managed in the community.

Nausea and vomiting due to functional or partial bowel obstruction

- If the patient does not have colic and continues to pass flatus, start a prokinetic anti-emetic, metoclopramide.
- Stop metoclopramide and treat as complete obstruction if colic develops.

Nausea and vomiting due to complete bowel obstruction

- **Treat nausea with cyclizine.** If nausea persists, consider changing to levomepromazine or haloperidol as a once-daily dose at bedtime. Vomiting usually settles once nausea is controlled.
- **Treat large-volume vomiting with an antisecretory:**
  - If due to gastric outflow obstruction with rapid dehydration, insert nasogastric tube and start intravenous hydration. Use ranitidine to reduce volume of gastric secretions.
  - If complete distal obstruction, start either hyoscine butylbromide or octreotide. If colic is present hyoscine will reduce secretions and treat colic but its full antisecretory effect is only achieved after 3 days. Use octreotide when a rapid or more profound effect on intestinal secretions is required.

- **Refer for a venting gastrostomy** if there is an ongoing need for a nasogastric tube.
- **Consider parenteral hydration** with 1000–1500 ml of fluid subcutaneously to reduce the intensity of nausea in a dehydrated patient.
- **Consider referral** for stent emplacement to overcome obstruction or consider starting corticosteroids.

Managing pain in MBO

- **For patients on a strong opioid** and who have both continuous and colicky pain:
  - Titrate opioid upwards until their continuous pain is relieved.
  - If colic persists, add in hyoscine butylbromide.
- **For patients not on a strong opioid** who have both continuous and colicky pain, expert opinion differs when it comes to starting treatment:
  - Start with a strong opioid and add in hyoscine butylbromide if colic persists.
  - Start with hyoscine butylbromide and add in a strong opioid if continuous pain persists.
  - Start antisecretory and a strong opioid together.
  - Start treatment based on clinical judgement.

Practical prescribing points

For further information please see the *Medicines Compendium* (www.medicines.org.uk) or the *British National Formulary* (www.bnf.org) or the *Palliative Care Formulary* (www.palliativedrugs.com).

Only parenteral routes of drugs are offered. A parenteral route is recommended initially for at least 48 hours, as there is likely to be reduced absorption following oral administration.

Metoclopramide

- **Metoclopramide:** there is an increased risk of extrapyramidal adverse effects in young adults.

Mixing drugs in syringe drivers

Always follow local palliative care guidelines or seek advice from local palliative care services or hospital pharmacy drug information services *before* mixing drugs in a syringe driver. The following information is included as a brief guide when these sources of help are unavailable:

- Check compatibilities before mixing drugs. See www.palliativedrugs.com, or Table 3.
- Use water for injection as the diluent when mixing drugs in a syringe driver (except for octreotide and ketamine).
- Do not use solutions that are cloudy or have precipitated.
- **Use sodium chloride as the diluent** for octreotide in a syringe driver.

Follow-up advice

- **Nasogastric tubes:** remove as soon as effective therapeutic control of nausea and vomiting has been established.
- Patients with malignant bowel obstruction will require regular review, the frequency of which will be dependent on their symptom control.

Should I refer or investigate?

Refer?

- Consider referral or seeking specialist advice for all patients with an established diagnosis of malignant bowel obstruction.

Table 3: Compatibility of drugs used for malignant bowel obstruction in a syringe driver.

Drug	Compatibility with diamorphine[1]	Alternative routes/ drugs[2]
Cyclizine	Diamorphine any strength + cyclizine 6.7 mg/ml Diamorphine 15 mg/ml + cyclizine 15 mg/ml Diamorphine 20 mg/ml + cyclizine 10 mg/ml	Levomepromazine (methotrimeprazine) as a single subcutaneous (s/c) bedtime dose
Dexamethasone	Compatible at usual concentrations, but mix carefully to prevent precipitation	Dexamethasone as a single s/c morning dose
Glycopyrronium bromide	Compatible at usual concentrations	Hyoscine hydrobromide sublingual tablets or patches
Haloperidol	Diamorphine 20–100 mg/ml + haloperidol 0.75 mg/ml Diamorphine 50 mg/ml + haloperidol 1.5 mg/ml	Haloperidol as a single s/c bedtime dose
Hyoscine butylbromide	Compatible at all usual concentrations	Hyoscine butylbromide as an s/c dose every 4–6 hours
Hyoscine hydrobromide	Compatible at all usual concentrations	Hyoscine hydrobromide sublingual tablets or patches
Levomepromazine	Compatible at all usual concentrations	Levomepromazine as a single s/c bedtime dose
Metoclopramide	Diamorphine 25 mg/ml + metoclopramide 5 mg/ml	Metoclopramide s/c 8-hourly or rectal domperidone

1. Twycross, R., Wilcock, A., Charlesworth, S., and Dickman, A. (2002) *Palliative care formulary*. Palliativedrugs.com Ltd. www.palliativedrugs.com [Accessed: 30-7-2002].
2. Regnard, C. and Hockley, J. (Eds.) (2004a) *A guide to symptom relief in palliative care*. 5th edn. Oxford: Radcliffe Medical Press.

Investigate?

- Further radiological investigations should be considered to confirm the diagnosis of malignant bowel obstruction and to exclude constipation.

Drug rationale

Drugs not included

- **Hyoscine hydrobromide** is useful as an antisecretory agent in malignant bowel obstruction but causes sedation.
- **Corticosteroids other than dexamethasone** are not included, because they have a greater mineralocorticoid effect, increasing the risk of fluid retention, e.g. cerebral oedema, which make them less suitable for high-dose therapy [Twycross et al, 2002].
- **Cinnarizine, meclozine, promethazine, and alimemazine** (trimeprazine) increase sedation and offer no advantage over cyclizine in the management of nausea and vomiting in palliative care.
- **Combination of cyclizine with opioid products:** an anti-emetic is usually necessary only for the first 4 or 5 days when initiating an opioid. Combined preparations may lead to unnecessary anti-emetic therapy and associated adverse effects with long-term use. Cyclizine is not the first-choice anti-emetic for opioid-induced nausea and vomiting.
- **Tropisetron, ondansetron, granisetron, and dolasetron** are not included. The role of somatostatin analogues in

P

the relief of nausea and vomiting due to malignant bowel obstruction is not clear.

- **Phenothiazines other than haloperidol and levomepromazine:** phenothiazines, e.g. thioridazine, have differing antimuscarinic activity, which may be marked. Chlorpromazine and prochlorperazine offer no advantage over non-sedative haloperidol.
- **Nabilone** is a synthetic cannabinoid with anti-emetic properties. It may be useful for nausea and vomiting, caused by cytotoxic chemotherapy, that is unresponsive to conventional anti-emetics, but its use should be directed by specialist care.
- **Glycopyrronium bromide** is an alternative antisecretory drug to hyoscine butylbromide. Compared to hyoscine butylbromide, the onset of action of glycopyrronium bromide is slower. It has lesser cardiac effects because of a reduced affinity for muscarinic type 2 receptors.

Drugs included

- **Metoclopramide:** parenteral metoclopramide is the drug of choice in patients with mainly functional bowel obstruction but is not recommended in complete mechanical bowel obstruction.
- **Cyclizine** is useful for nausea and vomiting due to mechanical bowel obstruction and associated motion sickness.
- **Haloperidol** is useful for most metabolic causes of vomiting such as an increase in circulating toxins due to bowel obstruction. Levomepromazine is usually reserved for second-line therapy but may be useful.
- **Dexamethasone** may be useful as an adjunct to reduce peritumour and perineuronal oedema.
- **Octreotide** is offered as a potent antisecretory agent. If using in a syringe driver, mix with sodium chloride 0.9% for injection.
- **Hyoscine butylbromide** is an antisecretory drug that is also a useful antispasmodic. The full antisecretory effect may not be achieved for 3 days.
- **Ranitidine** is offered to reduce gastric secretions in malignant bowel obstruction.

P

Prescriptions

Prokinetic: metoclopramide

Metoclopramide sc injection: 10mg up to three times a day

- Age from 16 years onwards
- Metoclopramide 10mg/2ml inj. FOR SUBCUTANEOUS INJECTION. Give 2ml (10mg) up to three times a day when required for sickness; supply 6 2ml ampoules; NHS Cost £1.56.

Metoclopramide im/iv injection: 10mg up to three times a day

- Age from 16 years onwards
- Metoclopramide 10mg/2ml inj. FOR INTRAMUSCULAR OR SLOW INTRAVENOUS INJECTION. Give 2ml (10mg) up to three times a day when required for sickness; supply 6 2ml ampoules; NHS Cost £1.56.

Metoclopramide subcutaneous infusion: 20-60mg over 24 hours

- Age from 16 years onwards
- Metoclopramide 5mg/ml 20ml inj. FOR CONTINUOUS SUBCUTANEOUS INFUSION. Give 4ml (20mg) to 12ml (60mg) over 24 hours via a syringe driver when required for sickness; supply 10 20ml ampoules; NHS Cost £26.68.

Complete MBO: cyclizine

Cyclizine sc injection: 50mg up to three times a day

- Age from 16 years onwards
- Cyclizine lactate 50mg/ml inj. FOR SUBCUTANEOUS INJECTION. Give 1ml (50mg) up to three times a day when required; supply 10 1ml ampoules; NHS Cost £7.04.

Cyclizine im or iv injection: 50mg up to 3 times a day

- Age from 16 years onwards
- Cyclizine lactate 50mg/ml inj. FOR INTRAMUSCULAR OR INTRAVENOUS INJECTION. Give 1ml (50mg) up to three times a day when required; supply 10 1ml ampoules; NHS Cost £7.04.

Cyclizine subcutaneous infusion: 150mg over 24 hours

- Age from 16 years onwards
- Cyclizine lactate 50mg/ml inj. FOR CONTINUOUS SUBCUTANEOUS INFUSION. Give up to 3ml (150mg) over 24 hours via a syringe driver when required for sickness; supply 10 1ml ampoules; NHS Cost £7.04.

Levomepromazine or haloperidol

Levomepromazine sc injection: 6.25mg to 12.5mg once a day

- Age from 16 years onwards
- Levomepromazine 25mg/ml inj. FOR SUBCUTANEOUS INJECTION. Give 0.25ml (6.25mg) to 0.5ml (12.5mg) once a day when required for sickness; supply 3 1ml ampoules; NHS Cost £6.58.

Levomepromazine im injection: 6.25mg to 12.5mg once a day

- Age from 16 years onwards
- Levomepromazine 25mg/ml inj. FOR INTRAMUSCULAR INJECTION. Give 0.25ml (6.25mg) to 0.5ml (12.5mg) once a day when required for sickness; supply 3 1ml ampoules; NHS Cost £6.58.

Levomepromazine iv injection: 6.25mg to 12.5mg once a day

- Age from 16 years onwards
- Levomepromazine 25mg/ml inj. Give 0.25ml (6.25mg) to 0.5ml (12.5mg) by iv injection once a day when required. Mix with an equal volume of sodium chloride before administration; supply 3 1ml ampoules; NHS Cost £6.58.
- Sodium chloride 0.9% injection. Mix with equal volume of levomepromazine injection before intravenous administration; supply 3 injection; NHS Cost £0.19.

Haloperidol subcutaneous injection: 1mg to 2.5mg once a day

- Age from 16 years onwards
- Haloperidol 5mg/ml injection. FOR SUBCUTANEOUS INJECTION. Give 0.2ml (1mg) to 0.5ml (2.5mg) by subcutaneous injection once a day when required for sickness; supply 5 1ml ampoules; NHS Cost £2.65.

Haloperidol im injection: 1mg to 2mg once a day

- Age from 16 years onwards
- Haloperidol 5mg/ml injection. FOR INTRAMUSCULAR INJECTION. Give 0.2ml (1mg) to 0.4ml (2mg) by intramuscular injection once a day when required for sickness; supply 5 1ml ampoules; NHS Cost £2.65.

Haloperidol subcutaneous infusion: 2.5-10mg over 24 hours

- Age from 16 years onwards
- Haloperidol 5mg/ml injection. FOR CONTINUOUS SUBCUTANEOUS INFUSION. Give 0.5ml (2.5mg) to 2ml (10mg) over 24 hours via a syringe driver when required for sickness; supply 10 1ml ampoules; NHS Cost £5.90.

Antisecretory: hyoscine butylbromide/ranitidine/ octreotide

Ranitidine im injection: 50mg up to four times a day

Age from 16 years onwards
Ranitidine 50mg/2ml injection. FOR INTRAMUSCULAR INJECTION. Give 2ml (50mg) every six to eight hours when required to reduce gastric secretions; supply 3 2ml ampoules; NHS Cost £1.92.

Hyoscine butylbromide sc inj: 10-20mg up to 3 times a day

Age from 16 years onwards
Hyoscine butylbromide 20mg/ml. FOR SUBCUTANEOUS INJECTION. Give 0.5ml (10mg) to 1ml (20mg) up to three times a day when required to reduce gastric secretions or colic; supply 10 1ml ampoules; NHS Cost £2.03.

Hyoscine butylbromide im/iv inj: 10-20mg up to 3 times a day

Age from 16 years onwards
Hyoscine butylbromide 20mg/ml. FOR INTRAMUSCULAR OR INTRAVENOUS INJECTION. Inject 0.5ml (10mg) to 1ml (20mg) three times a day when required to reduce gastric secretions or colic; supply 10 1ml ampoules; NHS Cost £2.03.

Hyoscine butylbromide sc infusion: 30-120mg over 24 hours

Age from 16 years onwards
Hyoscine butylbromide 20mg/ml. FOR CONTINUOUS SUBCUTANEOUS INFUSION. Give 1.5ml (30mg) to 6ml (120mg) over 24 hours via a syringe driver when required to reduce gastric secretions; supply 10 1ml ampoules; NHS Cost £2.03.

Octreotide sc infusion: 250-500micrograms over 24 hours

Age from 16 years onwards
Octreotide 500 micrograms/ml. FOR CONTINUOUS SUBCUTANEOUS INFUSION. Give 250mcg (0.5ml) to 500mcg (1ml) over 24 hours via a syringe driver to reduce gastric secretions; supply 1 1ml ampoule; NHS Cost £32.75.

Octreotide sc inj: 50-200micrograms up to three times a day

Age from 16 years onwards
Octreotide 100microgram/ml inj. FOR SUBCUTANEOUS INJECTION. Give 50mcg (0.5ml) once or twice a day to reduce gastric secretions. Increase as needed to max 200mcg three times a day; supply 5 1ml ampoules; NHS Cost £32.67.

Dexamethasone

Start dexamethasone im injection: 16mg to 24mg once a day

Age from 16 years onwards
Dexamethasone sod phos 8mg/2ml. FOR INTRAMUSCULAR INJECTION. Give 4ml (16mg) once a day for sickness. Increase to 6ml (24mg) once a day if necessary; supply 3 2ml vials; NHS Cost £5.94.

Managing nausea and vomiting in the terminal phase

Which therapy?

Confirm the patient is in the terminal phase. Patients in the terminal phase have several common features:

- Deteriorating day-by-day or faster because of their underlying condition, or because of an irreversible complication of their disease.
- Patient expresses a realisation that they are dying.
- Reduced cognition, drowsy or comatose.
- Bed-bound.
- Taking little food or fluid and having difficulty with oral medication.
- Altered breathing pattern.
- Peripherally cyanosed and cold.

- **Adjustments in the terminal phase**
  - Stop unnecessary drugs; continue with other drugs by an appropriate route.
  - Ensure commonly required medications are available in the house (e.g. cyclizine, diamorphine, hyoscine hydrobromide, and midazolam in parenteral formulations) so that there is no delay in treatment of new or developing symptoms.
  - Ensure that parenteral equipment is available: syringes, butterfly needles, dressings.
  - Ensure physical symptoms are well controlled.
  - Explore understanding and provide appropriate explanation of the situation to the patient, family, and other professional carers.
  - Set realistic goals.
  - Ensure that religious and spiritual care is offered if wanted.
  - Ensure the environment is appropriate.
  - Ensure the out-of-hours/deputising service knows the plan for care at home to avoid a crisis admission.
- **Consider using the Liverpool Care Pathway.**

Reviewing drugs for nausea and vomiting in the last hours and days

- **Levomepromazine** may be useful for uncontrolled nausea, because of its broad-spectrum effect.
- **Metoclopramide** dose may be titrated up to a dose of 60 mg/24 hours by continuous subcutaneous infusion.
- **Dexamethasone:** stopping of dexamethasone in the terminal phase lacks expert consensus.
  - The onset of withdrawal symptoms (including agitation and distress) is very variable, but is unlikely within the first 24 hours of stopping.
  - Alternatively, dexamethasone can be given as a single morning subcutaneous bolus. Oral dexamethasone 1 mg is equivalent to 1.2 mg dexamethasone phosphate or 1.3 mg dexamethasone sodium phosphate. Adjust the dose to the nearest volume that can easily be measured.

Practical prescribing points

For further information please see the *Medicines Compendium* (www.medicines.org.uk) or the *British National Formulary* (www.bnf.org) or the *Palliative Care Formulary* (www.palliativedrugs.com).

Mixing drugs in syringe drivers

Always follow local palliative care guidelines or seek advice from local palliative care services or hospital pharmacy drug information services *before* mixing drugs in a syringe driver. The following information is included as a brief guide when these sources of help are unavailable:

- Check compatibilities before mixing drugs. See www.palliativedrugs.com, or Table 4.
- Use water for injection as the diluent when mixing drugs in a syringe driver (except for octreotide and ketamine).
- Do not use solutions that are cloudy or have precipitated.

P

Table 4: Compatibility of drugs used in the terminal phase in a syringe driver.

Drug	Compatibility with diamorphine[1]	Alternative routes/drugs[2]
Cyclizine	Diamorphine any strength + cyclizine 6.7 mg/ml Diamorphine 15 mg/ml + cyclizine 15 mg/ml Diamorphine 20 mg/ml + cyclizine 10 mg/ml	Levomepromazine (methotrimeprazine) as a single subcutaneous (s/c) bedtime dose
Dexamethasone	Compatible at usual concentrations, but mix carefully to prevent precipitation	Dexamethasone as a single s/c morning dose
Glycopyrronium bromide	Compatible at usual concentrations	Hyoscine hydrobromide sublingual tablets or patches
Haloperidol	Diamorphine 20–100 mg/ml + haloperidol 0.75 mg/ml Diamorphine 50 mg/ml + haloperidol 1.5 mg/ml	Haloperidol as a single s/c bedtime dose
Hyoscine butylbromide	Compatible at all usual concentrations	Hyoscine butylbromide as a s/c dose every 4–6 hours
Hyoscine hydrobromide	Compatible at all usual concentrations	Hyoscine hydrobromide sublingual tablets or patches
Levomepromazine (methotrimeprazine)	Compatible at all usual concentrations	Levomepromazine as a single s/c bedtime dose
Metoclopramide	Diamorphine 25 mg/ml + metoclopramide 5 mg/ml	Metoclopramide s/c 8-hourly or rectal domperidone

1. Twycross, R., Wilcock, A., Charlesworth, S., and Dickman, A. (2002) *Palliative care formulary*. Palliativedrugs.com Ltd. www.palliativedrugs.com [Accessed: 30-7-2002].
2. Regnard, C. and Hockley, J. (Eds.) (2004a) *A guide to symptom relief in palliative care*. 5th edn. Oxford: Radcliffe Medical Press.

Should I refer or investigate?

Refer?

- Consider seeking specialist help if symptoms are proving difficult to manage.

Investigate?

- Investigations will rarely be indicated in patients in the terminal phase.

Drug rationale

Drugs included

- **A terminal-phase stand-by drug pack** containing drugs commonly needed at the end of life is included. The pack contains cyclizine, diamorphine, hyoscine hydrobromide, midazolam, and water for injection [Ellershaw and Griffiths, 2003].
- **Metoclopramide** dose may be titrated up to a dose of 60 mg/24 hours by continuous subcutaneous infusion.
- **Levomepromazine** may be useful for uncontrolled nausea due to a broad-spectrum of effect.

P

Prescriptions

Terminal phase standby drug pack

Standby drug pack

- Age from 16 years onwards
- Hyoscine hydrobrom 400mcg/ml. For intravenous or subcutaneous injection as directed; supply 5 1ml ampoules; NHS Cost £13.55.
- Midazolam 5mg/ml injection. For intravenous or subcutaneous injection as directed; supply 5 2ml ampoules; NHS Cost £4.05.
- Water for injection (5ml). Use as directed; supply 10 5ml ampoule; NHS Cost £2.82.
- Instructions for handwriting CD prescription for diamorphine: Patients name and address. Diamorphine 10mg injection. State the dose and dose interval, e.g. 5-10 mg every 4 hours when required. Supply 2 (two) ampoules. Signed and dated.
- Cyclizine lactate 50mg/ml inj. For intravenous or subcutaneous injection as directed; supply 5 1ml ampoules; NHS Cost £2.71.

Levomepromazine (parenteral)

Levomepromazine sc injection: 6.25mg to 12.5mg once a day

- Age from 16 years onwards
- Levomepromazine 25mg/ml inj. FOR SUBCUTANEOUS INJECTION. Give 0.25ml (6.25mg) to 0.5ml (12.5mg) once a day when required for sickness; supply 3 1ml ampoules; NHS Cost £6.58.

Levomepromazine im injection: 6.25mg to 12.5mg once a day

- Age from 16 years onwards
- Levomepromazine 25mg/ml inj. FOR INTRAMUSCULAR INJECTION. Give 0.25ml (6.25mg) to 0.5ml (12.5mg) once a day when required for sickness; supply 3 1ml ampoules; NHS Cost £6.58.

Levomepromazine iv injection: 6.25mg to 12.5mg once a day

- Age from 16 years onwards
- Levomepromazine 25mg/ml inj. Give 0.25ml (6.25mg) to 0.5ml (12.5mg) by iv injection once a day when required. Mix with an equal volume of sodium chloride before administration; supply 3 1ml ampoules; NHS Cost £6.58.
- Sodium chloride 0.9% injection. Mix with equal volume of levomepromazine injection before intravenous administration; supply 3 injection; NHS Cost £0.19.

Metoclopramide (parenteral)

Metoclopramide sc injection: 10mg up to three times a day

- Age from 16 years onwards
- Metoclopramide 10mg/2ml inj. FOR SUBCUTANEOUS INJECTION. Give 2ml (10mg) up to three times a day when required for sickness; supply 6 2ml ampoules; NHS Cost £1.56.

Metoclopramide im/iv injection: 10mg up to three times a day

- Age from 16 years onwards
- Metoclopramide 10mg/2ml inj. FOR INTRAMUSCULAR OR SLOW INTRAVENOUS INJECTION. Give 2ml (10mg) up to three times a day when required for sickness; supply 6 2ml ampoules; NHS Cost £1.56.

Metoclopramide subcutaneous infusion: 20-60mg over 24 hours

- Age from 16 years onwards
- Metoclopramide 5mg/ml 20ml inj. FOR CONTINUOUS SUBCUTANEOUS INFUSION. Give 4ml (20mg) to 12ml (60mg) over 24 hours via a syringe driver when required for sickness; supply 10 20ml ampoules; NHS Cost £26.68.

Dexamethasone (parenteral)

Start dexamethasone im injection: 16 to 24mg once a day

- Age from 16 years onwards
- Dexamethasone sod phos 8mg/2ml. FOR INTRAMUSCULAR INJECTION. Give 4ml (16mg) once a day for sickness. Increase to 6ml (24mg) once a day if necessary; supply 3 2ml vials; NHS Cost £5.00.

Extended Information

Background information

- What is palliative care? p.1459
- How common is it? p.1459
- What triggers nausea and vomiting? p.1459
- What are the causes of nausea and vomiting? p.1459
- How is nausea and vomiting assessed in palliative care patients? p.1459
- What else might it be? p.1460

What is palliative care?

- **Palliative care is the total care of patients who do not respond to curative treatment** with a goal of achieving the best quality of life for patients and their families.

How common is it?

- **Nausea has a prevalence of 20–30% in all patients with advanced cancer,** and this rises to 70% in the last week of life [Fainsinger et al, 1991; Grond et al, 1994; Vainio et al, 1996].
- **Vomiting has a prevalence of 20% of all patients with** cancer [Grond et al, 1994]. The prevalence of nausea and vomiting is highest in advanced gynaecological cancers (42%) and advanced stomach cancer (36%) [Vainio et al, 1996].
- **Malignant bowel obstruction occurs in about 3% of patients with advanced cancer** but is reported to occur in 5–42% of patients with advanced ovarian cancer and 4–24% of patients with advanced colorectal cancer [Ripamonti et al, 2001].
- **Opioid-induced nausea, retching and vomiting:** about 30% of patients who receive morphine feel nauseated during the first week of treatment.

What triggers nausea and vomiting?

- Nausea, retching and vomiting are brought about by a complex reflex that is initiated and controlled by the 'vomiting centre' (VC) in the brainstem. Nausea usually precedes retching, that in turn may precede vomiting. Nausea and vomiting are produced by the same stimuli, and represent a progressive response to an increasing stimulus.
- The VC receives and processes inputs from a number of pathways in the brain and gut most of which are excitatory. The principal receptors, their locations and the stimuli that produce excitation of these pathways are presented in Table 5.
- Blocking receptors in these different pathways forms the pharmacological basis for the treatment of nausea and vomiting.
- The VC receives inputs from an area of the brain where there is no blood–brain barrier called the chemoreceptor trigger zone (CTZ). Receptors in the CTZ are therefore exposed to chemicals and metabolites in the blood.

What are the causes of nausea and vomiting?

There are many causes of nausea and vomiting in patients with cancer. These can be grouped into seven syndromes according to the mechanism leading to nausea and vomiting, the receptors involved, their clinical features and their treatment. Table 6 lists the most common syndromes and their causes.

How is nausea and vomiting assessed in palliative care patients?

Diagnosing the cause of nausea and vomiting

An accurate diagnosis of the cause of nausea and vomiting is required for selection of the most effective therapy. Enquire about the symptoms of nausea and of vomiting as separate complaints (precipitating and relieving factors, onset, timescale, volume of vomits, and character of vomited material). Treatment may be directed at removing the underlying cause, inhibiting the pathways that lead to nausea and vomiting, or both.

- The clinical features of common syndromes of nausea and vomiting in cancer are summarized in Table 7. These will be elicited by taking a full history and clinical examination including a neurological examination. The

P

Table 5: The principal pathways producing nausea and vomiting.

Location	Stimulus	Receptor
Vomiting centre (VC)	Excitatory stimulus from the CTZ, vestibular system and autonomic afferents from the gut and viscera and from higher centres within the brain.	Histamine (H_1) Acetylcholine (Ach_m) 5-Hydroxytryptamine 2 ($5\text{-}HT_2$)
Chemoreceptor trigger zone (CTZ)	Drugs, toxins, metabolites	Dopamine (D_2) $5\text{-}HT_3$
Cerebral cortex	Anxiety	Multiple receptors in cortex
	Raised intracranial pressure	Meningeal mechanoreceptors
Vestibular system	Movement, disease of ear	H_1 Ach_m
Gut and serosal surfaces in viscera	Drugs, radiotherapy and bacterial exotoxins.	$5\text{-}HT_3$ in gut only
	Mechanical distortion	H_1 Ach_m

Table 6: Common syndromes of nausea and vomiting.

Syndrome	Causes	Mechanism leading to nausea and vomiting
Meningeal irritation or stretch	Intracranial tumour causing raised intracranial pressure Meningeal infiltration by tumour Skull metastases	Not known, possibly meningeal mechanoreceptors
Abdominal and pelvic tumour	Mesenteric metastases Liver metastases Ureteric obstruction Retroperitoneal cancer	Stretching of mechanoreceptors
Malignant bowel obstruction	*Mechanical obstruction* — intrinsic or extrinsic by tumour *Functional obstruction* — intestinal motility disorders caused by malignant involvement of blood supply, bowel muscle or nerves. Paraneoplastic neuropathy	Stretching of mechanoreceptors
Gastric stasis	Opioids and anticholinergic drugs Mechanical resistance to emptying: ascites, hepatomegaly, peptic ulcer, gastritis, tumour Autonomic failure*	Gastric mechanoreceptors
Chemically/ metabolically induced	Drugs — opioids, anti-epileptics, cytotoxics, antibiotics, digoxin. Metabolic — e.g. hypercalcaemia† Toxins — e.g. bacterial exotoxins, tumour necrosis	Chemoreceptors in the chemoreceptor trigger zone
Movement-related nausea and vomiting	Abdominal tumours	Accentuates stretch of mechanoreceptors by tumour
	Opioids	Increased vestibular sensitivity
	Disease affecting vestibular system	Disturbed vestibular function
Anxiety-induced	Anxiety about diagnosis, treatment, meaning of symptoms, family Anticipatory emesis with cytotoxics	Not known: multiple receptors in cerebral cortex

*Autonomic failure (gastroparesis): autonomic failure resulting in gastroparesis is a paraneoplastic phenomenon that is common in patients with advanced malignancies.
†Hypercalcaemia: symptoms are insidious and mimic the symptoms seen in the dying patient, so that hypercalcaemia is often missed or undertreated. Drowsiness, nausea, vomiting, confusion, constipation and thirst may occur, but drowsiness alone is common. Polyuria is also common but is difficult to detect from the history alone. Patients who were well 1–2 weeks previously and have deteriorated unexpectedly may be hypercalcaemic and should have their blood biochemistry checked [Regnard and Hockley, 2004b].

neurological examination should include examination of the optic fundi to exclude raised intracranial pressure.

- **Blood biochemistry** should be obtained to exclude:
  - Hypercalcaemia
  - Electrolyte imbalance and dehydration
  - Renal failure
- **The extent of the underlying malignancy** may be suspected on clinical grounds and is usually defined with imaging or other investigations. Typically, investigations will have been obtained at the time of the initial diagnosis of the malignancy. However, if there has been significant progression of the malignancy, it may be appropriate to consider further imaging or other investigations to redefine the extent of the disease and ascertain whether the malignancy is implicated as a cause of nausea and vomiting.

Assessing the complications of prolonged nausea and vomiting

- **Assess hydration and electrolyte balance** in patients who are vomiting or taking little fluid.
- **Assess the functional impact** of the symptom, considering the effect on activities of daily living and on the family.
- **Assess anxiety and depression** at the initial assessment, and subsequently if symptoms prove difficult to manage.

What else might it be?

- **Regurgitation** due to dysphagia produces unaltered food or drink vomited within minutes of ingestion that test negative to acid with litmus paper. It occurs when there is difficulty in transferring food and drink from the mouth to the stomach.
- **Dysphagia** is seen in 12–23% of patients with cancer and is seen much more commonly in patients with neurological disease [Regnard and Hockley, 2004c].
- **Constipation** may produce symptoms of bowel obstruction and should be excluded.

Management issues

- Steps in managing nausea and vomiting p.1460
- Managing food and fluid p.1461
- Correcting reversible causes of nausea and vomiting p.1461
- Starting treatment with first-line anti-emetic drugs p.1462
- Persistent nausea and vomiting on first-line therapy p.1463
- Summary of anti-emetic therapy p.1464
- Seeking help and advice in primary care p.1464
- Recognising the terminal phase p.1464
- Medicines management p.1464

Steps in managing nausea and vomiting

- **Diagnose the cause of the nausea and vomiting.** Nausea and vomiting may have more than one cause. Different causes may require separate treatments.
- **Correct reversible causes.**
- **Select a first-line anti-emetic** depending on the clinical picture and knowledge of the receptors involved.

Table 7: Clinical features of the nausea and vomiting syndromes.

Syndrome	Clinical features may include
Meningeal irritation or stretch	Headache and nausea on lying flat, papilloedema and focal neurological signs. A computed tomography (CT) scan/ magnetic resonance imaging (MRI) scan will confirm the diagnosis.
Abdominal and pelvic tumour	Tumours within the abdomen and pelvis may cause nausea, vomiting, or both by stretching mechanoreceptors in the serosal layer of the gut, mesentery, ureters, or liver, and may also cause pain poorly localized to those structures with or without radiation. Radiological investigations will usually be required to confirm the diagnosis.
Malignant bowel obstruction	Obstruction usually develops slowly and often remains partial and this is reflected in the presentation of the symptoms. *Abdominal pain* is continuous and present in 90% with superimposed colic in 75%. *Abdominal distension* may be absent in high obstruction or if bowel is stuck down by omental spread. *Vomiting* generally develops early and in large amounts in high obstruction and later in large bowel obstruction. Consider investigations to confirm the diagnosis and exclude constipation.
Gastric stasis	Epigastric pain, fullness, early satiety, flatulence, acid reflux, hiccup, and large-volume vomit often with little preceding nausea. Vomiting relieves all symptoms.
Chemically/ metabolically induced	If due to drugs, there may be a temporal association with starting the drug. If due to hypercalcaemia, nausea and vomiting may be associated with drowsiness (present as the sole symptom in 50%) and confusion. Polyuria and nocturia are often present but rarely noticed by the patient once dehydration intervenes. Diagnosis is confirmed by blood biochemistry. If due to food poisoning there may be associated diarrhoea, colicky abdominal pain, and symptoms and signs of infection.
Movement-related nausea and vomiting	Vomiting made worse with movement: features of abdominal tumour or recent commencement or increase in opioid, or vestibular disease.
Anxiety-induced	This is usually a diagnosis by exclusion; symptoms are generally preceded by symptoms and signs of psychological tension.

- **Manage complications** of prolonged nausea and vomiting.
- **Review** and reconsider the diagnosis if response to treatment is unexpectedly poor.
- **Add in or switch to a second-line anti-emetic** if nausea and vomiting improves but persists after 24–48 hours.
- **Review** and reconsider the diagnosis if symptoms persist.
- **Seek specialist help** if symptoms remain poorly controlled.

Managing food and fluid

- Dehydration can worsen nausea and vomiting, and correcting this may help control symptoms [Ripamonti et al, 2000].
- Some people find the smell of food, and particularly cooking, can precipitate symptoms and should be avoided where possible. If the patient is at home and cooking their own meals, it is often helpful for someone else to take this over.
- Taking food and fluid is one of the most basic requirements of life. It is a natural instinct of carers to encourage someone who is ill to eat and drink. However, undue pressure may lead to anxiety regarding eating, which can be counterproductive.
- Select foods that the patients can enjoy or tolerate rather than being overly concerned with healthy eating. Generally, carbohydrate meals that are easily digested, and sour flavours such as citrus-flavoured foods and drinks, are most easily tolerated.
- Small, regular meals or snacks are more likely to be well tolerated.

Correcting reversible causes of nausea and vomiting

Nausea and vomiting caused directly by the tumour

- **Radiotherapy is an effective palliative treatment for cerebral metastases.** Symptomatic improvement occurs in around 80% of selected patients with a complete response in 35–55%. There is usually little acute toxicity associated with treatment, although whole-brain radiotherapy for multiple metastases is complicated by unavoidable complete alopecia [Borgelt et al, 1980]. However, cranial irradiation can itself cause nausea and if the prognosis is short, it would be better to treat with dexamethasone to reduce intracranial irritation or pressure.
- **Corticosteroids can reduce the size of a tumour** by reducing peritumoural oedema and in steroid-responsive tumours, by reducing the size of the tumour itself. In addition, corticosteroids also have a pharmacological effect on the receptors involved in vomiting. They may improve nausea and vomiting caused by cerebral, abdominal, and pelvic tumours.
  - **Dexamethasone** has very high glucocorticoid activity in conjunction with insignificant mineralocorticoid activity. This makes it particularly suitable for high-dose therapy in conditions where fluid retention would be a disadvantage, e.g. cerebral oedema. Dexamethasone also has a long duration of action.
- **Surgical management of malignant bowel obstruction** may be appropriate if caused by mechanical obstruction, when the patient's prognosis allows. Resection, bypassing, or stenting of the restriction may be used and where this possibility exists, referral to secondary care should be made for further assessment.

Other reversible causes

- **Hypercalcaemia:** management includes rehydration and appropriate use of bisphosphonates. Patients who are hypercalcaemic will often deteriorate in a manner that is easily misinterpreted as terminal decline. Their prognosis is difficult to determine on clinical grounds therefore all hypercalcaemic patients should be admitted for further treatment in secondary care.
- **Gastric irritation or ulceration:** stop nonsteroidal anti-inflammatory drugs or other drugs that may cause gastrointestinal problems. Offer gastroprotection or healing doses of proton pump inhibitors, histamine H_2-receptor antagonists or misoprostol.
- **Infection:** treat with antibiotics as appropriate.
- **Constipation:** rule out obstruction and manage with rectal measures and laxatives.
- **Tense ascites:** aspiration of ascites will require admission to secondary care.
- **Anxiety:** explanation and reassurance, anxiolytics and other drug therapies if appropriate.

P

Starting treatment with first-line anti-emetic drugs

General points

- **Select a first-line anti-emetic** based upon the presenting clinical syndrome and knowledge of the receptors involved.
- **Start regular treatment using a non-oral route for first 48 hours.** Gastric emptying is delayed in the presence of nausea, slowing drug absorption. Once symptoms have settled treatment can be changed to the oral route.
- **Review response to treatment.** The aim is to treat nausea and reduce the frequency of vomiting. It may not be possible to stop the vomiting altogether, but patients often state that it is the nausea that is the most distressing of the two.

Raised intracranial pressure

- **Consider referral for radiotherapy** for all patients with raised intracranial pressure due to tumour.
- **Corticosteroids:** headache, nausea, and vomiting due to raised intracranial pressure often respond to a high dose of dexamethasone 16 mg daily for 4 to 5 days, subsequently reduced to 4–6 mg daily if possible. Where there is no demonstrable benefit, dexamethasone should be discontinued.

Abdominal and pelvic tumour

- **Cyclizine** blocks histamine H_1 and acetylcholine receptors in the vomiting centre that receive inputs from mechanoreceptors in the abdominal and pelvic viscera. Cyclizine 25–50 mg, as oral tablets or subcutaneous injection, is a good first-line anti-emetic for nausea and vomiting caused by abdominal and pelvic tumour including when movement accentuates these symptoms.

Inoperable malignant bowel obstruction

A specialist should evaluate and plan the management of patients presenting with malignant bowel obstruction (MBO). Some patients with MBO may be adequately managed in the community.

P

Vomiting due to functional or partial bowel obstruction

- **In partial bowel obstruction** it is important to preserve bowel motility while still preventing colic.
  - Stop osmotic and stimulant laxatives.
  - Docusate has minimal stimulant effect on the bowel and should be titrated to produce a comfortable stool without colic.
  - Advise avoidance of high-fibre foods and taking food and fluids more frequently in small quantities.
- **If the patient does not have colic and continues to pass flatus, start a prokinetic anti-emetic.**
- **Stop prokinetic and treat as complete obstruction if colic develops.**

Nausea and vomiting due to complete bowel obstruction

- **Treat nausea with cyclizine.** If nausea persists, consider changing to levomepromazine as a once-daily dose at bedtime. Vomiting usually settles once nausea is controlled.
- **Treat large-volume vomiting with an antisecretory:**
  - **If due to gastric outflow obstruction** with rapid dehydration, insert nasogastric tube and start intravenous hydration. Use ranitidine to reduce volume of gastric secretions.
  - **If complete distal obstruction,** start either hyoscine butylbromide or octreotide. If colic is present hyoscine will reduce secretions and treat colic but its full antisecretory effect is only achieved after 3 days. Use octreotide when a rapid or more profound effect on intestinal secretions is required.
- **Nasogastric tubes may be used** to drain intestinal secretions and reduce vomiting. However, they are unpleasant for the patient and are generally reserved for persistent symptoms that do not respond to drug therapy. As soon as effective therapeutic control of nausea and vomiting has been established, they should be removed. They are most useful in patients with complete gastric outflow obstructions or patients with faeculant vomiting due to complete distal bowel obstruction.
- **Refer for a venting gastrostomy** if there is an ongoing need for a nasogastric tube.
- **Consider referral** for stent emplacement to overcome obstruction, or consider starting corticosteroids.
- **Consider parenteral hydration** with 1000–1500 ml of fluid to reduce the intensity of nausea in a dehydrated patient. This can be given subcutaneously at home.
- **Most patients will require a parenteral route of drug administration** for at least 48 hours even if vomiting has settled, as gastric motility is likely to be decreased, reducing drug absorption.

Managing pain in MBO

- Treat colic, when it occurs alone, with hyoscine. Treat continuous pain, where it occurs alone, with standard analgesics in the WHO analgesic ladder. However, more commonly both types of pain occur together.
- **Continuous abdominal pain is present in 90% and colic in 75% of patients with MBO.** Antispasmodics such as hyoscine butylbromide relieve colic. Strong opioids relieve continuous pain and may relieve colic. Antispasmodics relieve colicky pain but may also relieve continuous pain when this is caused by smooth muscle spasm.
- **For patients on a strong opioid** and who have both continuous and colicky pain:
  - Titrate opioid upwards until their continuous pain is relieved.
  - If *colic* persists, add in hyoscine butylbromide.
- **For patients who are not on a strong opioid** who have both continuous and colicky pain, expert opinion differs when it comes to starting treatment:
  - Start with a strong opioid and add in hyoscine butylbromide if colic persists.
  - Start with hyoscine butylbromide and add in a strong opioid if continuous pain persists.
  - Start an antisecretory plus a strong opioid if both type of pain are present.
  - Start treatment based on clinical judgement.

[Ripamonti et al, 2001]

Anti-emetic drugs for MBO

- **Parenteral metoclopramide is the drug of choice** in patients with mainly functional or partial obstruction who do not have colic and who continue to pass flatus. I is not recommended for patients who have complete MBO, where a stimulatory effect may cause or worsen colicky abdominal pain.
- **Haloperidol is a specific dopamine D_2-receptor antagonist** that has a profound inhibitory effect on the chemoreceptor trigger zone. The mode of action may relate to blocking the effect of 'toxins' absorbed from th obstructed bowel. It is effective in relieving nausea due t MBO, in relatively small doses, e.g. 2.5 mg haloperidol once at bedtime by subcutaneous injection.
- **Cyclizine exerts a central anti-emetic effect in the vomiting centre** and may be useful if there is complete obstruction when the distended bowel behind the obstruction triggers stimulation of the vomiting centre through vagal afferents.

- **Levomepromazine** is a useful second-line anti-emetic which can be given as a single, bedtime dose, and has actions at both the chemoreceptor trigger zone and the vomiting centre.

Antisecretory drugs for MBO

- **Hyoscine butylbromide is an antispasmodic and antisecretory drug,** and this combination may be particularly useful in treating colic and vomiting when they occur together with MBO. However, its full antisecretory effect may take up to 3 days to develop. It does not cross the blood–brain barrier and so does not cause drowsiness or have a central anti-emetic action.
- **Octreotide** inhibits gastrointestinal motility, gastric, pancreatic, and small-bowel secretions and increases water and electrolyte absorption. When a more rapid or more profound. reduction in gastrointestinal secretions is desired, octreotide should be considered as the first choice drug [Mercadante et al, 2000].
- **Glycopyrronium bromide is an alternative** and may be effective in some patients who fail to respond to hyoscine butylbromide.

Gastric stasis

- **Prokinetics, metoclopramide and domperidone,** block dopamine D_2-receptors in the gut and improve gastric emptying. Metoclopramide has a direct excitatory effect in the gut, which is an advantage over domperidone particularly for patients with functional bowel obstruction.
- **Metoclopramide may be given as a 10 mg oral dose four times a day or as a** 40–60 mg/24 hours continuous subcutaneous infusion.
- **Domperidone** has a long plasma half-life; a starting oral dose of 20 mg twice a day may be increased if necessary to a 30 mg oral dose, or a 90 mg rectal dose every 8 hours.
- **Do not give prokinetics concurrently with drugs with antimuscarinic activity (e.g. cyclizine, hyoscine).** Antimuscarinic drugs competitively block the action of prokinetics.

Chemically or metabolically induced nausea and vomiting

- **Haloperidol is effective for opioid-induced or metabolically induced nausea and vomiting:** it has a profound inhibitory effect on the chemoreceptor trigger zone. Once-a-day dosing with 1.5–2.5 mg haloperidol orally or by subcutaneous administration is usually sufficient.
- **A prophylactic prokinetic, metoclopramide or domperidone,** may be useful during initiation and titration of morphine.
- A systematic review published in 1999 identified droperidol as the most widely studied anti-emetic with a proven benefit in the prophylaxis of analgesic-induced nausea and vomiting [Tramer and Walder, 1999]. Droperidol is no longer available in the United Kingdom [BNF 47, 2004].
- **Prevention and management of nausea and vomiting due to cytotoxic drugs** will primarily be the responsibility of the specialist prescribing those drugs. When possible, it is recommended that if problems arise in the community then specialist advice should be sought.

Movement-related nausea and vomiting

Vestibular disturbance

- **Motion sickness** and diseases of the inner ear are commonly associated with movement-associated nausea and vomiting.
- **Cyclizine 25–50 mg every 8 hours is a useful first-line therapy:** cyclizine blocks histamine H_1 and acetylcholine receptors in the vomiting centre.
- **Hyoscine hydrobromide,** 300 microgram orally or subcutaneously or 1000 microgram/24 hours transdermally, is an alternative.

Abdominal and pelvic tumour

- Symptoms may be accentuated by movement — see *Abdominal and pelvic tumour* above for management.

Anxiety-related nausea and vomiting

- Exclude other causes before making a diagnosis of anxiety-induced nausea and vomiting. Manage anxiety independently, appropriately to the patient's prognosis.
- **Avoid diazepam:** it has a long plasma half-life and marked individual variation in metabolism, and the effects of a constant dose may vary greatly. Concurrent administration with other sedative drugs including strong opioids, old age, debilitation, or hepatic impairment may lead to excessive sedation.

Nausea and vomiting of multiple or uncertain origin

- **Where possible identify the cause of the nausea and vomiting** and select the most appropriate therapy; where there is uncertainty consider seeking specialist advice. There may be times, such as at the end of life when the effects of drugs, dehydration and advanced disease may occur together to cause nausea and vomiting and when further investigation is not considered appropriate. Under such circumstances the selection of a broad-spectrum anti-emetic may be the most practical choice.
- **Levomepromazine blocks 5-hydroxytriptamine ($5\text{-}HT_2$), histamine H_1, dopamine D_2 and acetylcholine (Ach_m) receptors.** It therefore acts on the vestibular system, the chemoreceptor trigger zone and the vomiting centre and is the most broad-spectrum anti-emetic available. Levomepromazine has a broader spectrum of receptor affinity than other phenothiazines and is a better first-line therapy for vomiting of unknown or multiple causes.

Persistent nausea and vomiting on first-line therapy

- **Add in or switch to a second-line therapy** if nausea, retching and vomiting persists 24–48 hours after starting a first-line anti-emetic.
- **Review and reconsider the diagnosis if symptoms persist** with the second-line therapy.
- **Consider seeking specialist help** if symptoms remain difficult to control.

Choose a second-line anti-emetic appropriate for the suspected cause of nausea and vomiting.

- **Raised intracranial pressure: consider adding either cyclizine** 25–50 mg three times a day or levomepromazine once a day to dexamethasone. Levomepromazine may be of benefit, using a single bedtime doses of 2.5–5 mg subcutaneously or a 12.5 mg oral dose. Higher doses may cause significant adverse effects.
- **Abdominal and pelvic tumour:** the addition of dexamethasone to cyclizine may improve control by reducing the size of the tumour. In addition the pharmacological action of dexamethasone inhibits receptors in the vomiting pathways.
- **Gastric stasis:** if prokinetics are ineffective consider adding therapies that reduce gastric secretions. Ranitidine reduces both the volume and acidity of gastric secretions, both of which are useful in controlling symptoms of gastric stasis. Where a more profound

effect of reducing gastric secretions is required, octreotide can be considered.

- **Chemically or metabolically induced:** substitute levomepromazine for haloperidol if symptoms persist. When cytotoxic drugs cause persistent vomiting, seek advice from an oncologist.
- **Movement-related nausea and vomiting:** seek specialist advice and consider the use of an alternative sedative antihistamine such as cinnarizine.
- **Nausea and vomiting of multiple or uncertain origin:** dexamethasone may be used as an adjuvant to levomepromazine but when the cause is uncertain, always consider seeking specialist help.

Summary of anti-emetic therapy

- See Table 8 for a summary of anti-emetic therapy.

Seeking help and advice in primary care

- **The multidimensional nature of problems in palliative care requires a multidisciplinary approach.**
- Both the GP and district nurse should be involved as early as possible after diagnosis.
- After clinical assessment, referral may be necessary for an identified specialist need.
- The palliative care team may include any or all of the following specialities:
  - Palliative care consultant
  - Macmillan nurses
  - Palliative care nurse-practitioners
  - Physiotherapists
  - Occupational therapists
  - Social workers
  - Psychologists
  - Spiritual advisers
- **Where these services are not organized into a team,** they may be accessed via referral to the Macmillan nurses.
- **Marie Curie Cancer Care** provides nursing, free to the patient, to give terminally ill people the choice of dying at home supported by their families. Their service can be accessed via the district nurse.

P

Recognising the terminal phase

In order to care for dying patients it is essential to diagnose dying. Healthcare professionals are sometimes reluctant to diagnose dying, and therefore the appropriate adjustments in the terminal phase may not be made.

- **The terminal phase** starts a median of 24 hours before death, varying from hours to several days.
- **Patients in the terminal phase have several common features:**
  - They deteriorate day-by-day or faster because of their underlying condition or because of an irreversible complication of their disease.
  - They may express a realization that they are dying.
  - They have reduced cognition, and are drowsy or comatose.
  - They are bed-bound.
  - They take little food or fluid, and have difficulty with oral medication.
  - The breathing pattern alters.
  - They are peripherally cyanosed and cold.

[Morita et al, 1998]

Adjustments in the terminal phase

- The terminal phase is a time of adjustments for all [Regnard and Hockley, 2004a]:
  - Stop unnecessary drugs and continue with other drugs by an appropriate route.
  - Ensure commonly required medications are available in the house (e.g. cyclizine, diamorphine, hyoscine hydrobromide, and midazolam), so that there is no delay in treatment of new or developing symptoms.
  - Ensure physical symptoms are well controlled.
  - Explore understanding and provide appropriate explanation of the situation to the patient, family, and other professional carers.
  - Set realistic goals.
  - Ensure that religious and spiritual care is offered if wanted.
  - Ensure the environment is appropriate.
- **The Liverpool Care Pathway** for the dying patient provides a national framework for caring for patients in the terminal phase. It facilitates multidisciplinary communication and documentation, integrating national guidelines into clinical practice. Further information can be obtained from www.lcp-mariecurie.org.uk.

Medicines management

Anti-emetics vary in their affinities for the receptors involved in the syndromes of nausea and vomiting (see Table 9).

[Twycross and Back, 1998]

Prokinetics

- **Metoclopramide** is generally given orally up to three times a day but may be given as a subcutaneous injection or infusion.
- **Metoclopramide can induce acute dystonic reactions** involving facial and skeletal muscle spasms and oculogyric crises. These are more common in the young (particularly girls and young women), generally occur

Table 8: Summary of anti-emetic therapy.

Syndrome	Receptor/site	First-line therapy	Second-line therapy
Meningeal irritation or stretch	Direct stimulation of cerebral histamine H_1 receptors Meningeal mechanoreceptors	Dexamethasone Radiotherapy	Add cyclizine or levomepromazine
Abdominal and pelvic tumour	Vomiting centre: H_1 and acetylcholine (Ach_m) receptors	Cyclizine	Add dexamethasone
Gastric stasis	Usually mechanical vomiting triggered by stretch	Metoclopramide or domperidone	Reduce gastric secretions: ranitidine or octreotide
Chemically induced or metabolically induced	Chemoreceptor trigger zone: D_2	If starting opioids — metoclopramide or haloperidol	Add dexamethasone or substitute with levomepromazine
		Other drugs and metabolic causes — haloperidol	
Movement-related nausea and vomiting	Vomiting centre: H_1 and Ach_m Vestibular system: H_1 and Ach_m	Cyclizine	Hyoscine hydrobromide (transdermal patch is an alternative route of administration)

Table 9: Anti-emetics: receptor site affinities.

Anti-emetic	Dopamine D_2 antagonist	Histamine H_1 antagonist	Acetylcholine antagonist	5-HT_2 antagonist	5-HT_3 antagonist	5-HT_4 agonist
Metoclopramide	++	–	–	–	+*	++
Domperidone	++	–	–	–	–	–
Ondansetron	–	–	–	–	+++	–
Cyclizine	–	++	++	–	–	–
Hyoscine	–	–	+++	–	–	–
Haloperidol	+++	–	–	–	–	–
Levomepromazine	++	+++	–	+++	–	–

— none or insignificant; + slight; ++ moderate; +++ marked
*Metoclopramide in higher doses ≥100 mg, demonstrates 5-HT_3-receptor antagonism

within a few days of starting treatment, and subside within 24 hours of stopping the drug. Injection of procyclidine, 5–10 mg intravenously or intramuscularly, will abort a dystonic attack.

- **Domperidone** is less likely to cause central adverse effects such as sedation and dystonic reactions.
- **Do not give prokinetics concurrently with drugs with antimuscarinic activity (e.g. cyclizine, hyoscine)** as antimuscarinic drugs competitively block the action of prokinetics.

Phenothiazines/antipsychotics

- **Haloperidol** has many active metabolites, and plasma concentrations vary considerably after oral administration; it is not possible to relate clinical response to plasma haloperidol concentrations. Once-daily oral dosing is usually effective and adverse effects such as dystonias, dyskinesia and akathisia are unusual at the low doses used for the palliation of nausea and vomiting.
- **Levomepromazine** is usually given once a day but some people may benefit from dividing the daily dose to twice or three times a day. Dose-dependent postural hypotension, and antimuscarinic adverse effects of dry mouth, sedation, and blurred vision have been reported, but doses of less than 12.5 mg levomepromazine daily do not usually cause problems.
- **Chlorpromazine and prochlorperazine** are less receptor-specific than haloperidol or cyclizine.

Dexamethasone

- Dexamethasone is generally given as a single dose in the morning but may be combined with diamorphine in a syringe driver when appropriate. If possible, oral or subcutaneous dexamethasone should be taken no later than 1600 hours to avoid nocturnal restlessness.
- All patients need regular mouth care as oral candidiasis is a common problem in people taking oral corticosteroids.
- Dyspepsia and indigestion are also common. The risk of serious gastrointestinal complications (e.g. peptic ulcer or silent perforation) is markedly increased in patients who are also taking nonsteroidal anti-inflammatory drugs (NSAIDs) [Piper et al, 1991]. Gastrointestinal prophylaxis with a proton pump inhibitor or misoprostol should be considered for people on concurrent NSAIDs or with a history of peptic ulcer disease. Only use dexamethasone in people with active peptic ulcer disease if the benefits are likely to outweigh the risks.
- Diabetic control may be worsened by corticosteroids.
- Corticosteroid myopathy is usually only seen after several months of treatment with dexamethasone at doses of 4 mg per day or more. However it can occur earlier and with lower doses [Twycross et al, 2002]. It is often distressing as muscle wasting and weakness cause difficulty with normal activities such as climbing stairs and getting out of chairs [Hardy et al, 2001]. Although rare, the respiratory muscles can be affected [Gallagher, 1994], which could exacerbate dyspnoea. If myopathy occurs, consider stopping dexamethasone, reducing the dose, or changing to prednisolone. Weakness should improve after 3–4 weeks of stopping or dose reduction [Twycross et al, 2002]. Physiotherapy may be beneficial for some patients.
- High doses of corticosteroids may occasionally cause psychosis and depression. Seek specialist advice in this situation.
- **Check history of chickenpox** (risk of potentially fatal disseminated chickenpox if non-immune). Advise all patients on corticosteroids to seek urgent medical attention if they come into contact with someone with chickenpox or shingles [CSM, 1998]. If the patient has been exposed:
  - A positive history of chickenpox is not a foolproof guide to immunity. Check varicella-zoster antibody status in *all* patients who are likely to be immunosuppressed. Note: any patient taking dexamethasone 4 mg per day (or more) for more than 1 week in the previous 3 months is likely to be immunosuppressed.
  - Varicella-zoster immunoglobulin should *only* be given to those with negative antibody status (even if the if the individual has a positive history of chickenpox).
  - If antibody status results are not likely to be available within 7 days of exposure, give varicella-zoster immunoglobulin without testing antibody status [HPA, 2004].
- **Steroid Treatment Cards** should be issued by the GP or pharmacist and their contents discussed.

Stopping dexamethasone

- Dexamethasone can be stopped abruptly if it is not relieving symptoms, *and* the patient has received treatment for less than 3 weeks, *and* they are unlikely to be at risk of adrenal suppression (see below) [CSM, 1998; Twycross et al, 2002].
- Gradual withdrawal is recommended for patients at risk of adrenal suppression, e.g. patients who:
  - Have received dexamethasone 4–6 mg or more per day for more than 3 weeks.
  - Are taking a short course within 1 year of stopping long-term corticosteroids.
  - Have other possible causes of adrenal suppression.
- The dose can be tapered rapidly (e.g. halving the dose daily) until physiological doses are reached (about 1 mg dexamethasone). Then reduce more slowly to allow the adrenals to recover, e.g. reduce by 500 micrograms every 1–2 weeks.
- Stopping dexamethasone in the terminal phase lacks expert consensus:

P

- If the oral route is no longer available, dexamethasone can be given as a single slow subcutaneous dose once a day.
- If treatment is not given then patients may become agitated and distressed due to corticosteroid withdrawal. The onset of withdrawal symptoms is highly variable, depending on their risk of adrenal suppression, the length of time they live after their last treatment, and their degree of physical stress; it is highly unlikely within the first 24 hours.
- The clinician will need to balance the disadvantages of intrusive treatment of a dying person against the risks of not treating.

Antihistamines: cyclizine

- Drowsiness and antimuscarinic adverse effects are common; there may be dry mouth and, rarely, blurred vision.
- Subcutaneous administration may cause skin irritation at the injection site in some patients.

Antisecretory agents

Antimuscarinics

- **Hyoscine butylbromide must not be confused with hyoscine hydrobromide** which is used in lower doses.
- Unlike hyoscine hydrobromide, hyoscine butylbromide does not cross the blood–brain barrier and so does not cause drowsiness or have a central anti-emetic action. Despite a plasma half-life of several hours, the duration of the antisecretory effect is only about 1 hour for hyoscine butylbromide; however, particularly after repeat injections and in moribund patients, duration of effect of up to 9 hours has been observed.
- **Glycopyrronium bromide:** compared with hyoscine butylbromide, the onset of action of glycopyrronium bromide is slower. It has lesser cardiac effects because of a reduced affinity for muscarinic type 2 receptors. At standard dose glycopyrronium bromide does not change ocular pressures or pupil size but it can precipitate narrow-angle glaucoma. It is excreted by the kidneys, and lower doses are effective in patients with renal impairment.
- Antimuscarinics should be avoided in paralytic ileus and, as they relax the lower oesophageal sphincter, they should also be avoided in patients with symptomatic acid reflux. Glaucoma may be precipitated in those at risk, particularly the elderly.

Octreotide

- Octreotide is generally given as a bolus subcutaneous injection or by continuous subcutaneous infusion. The intravenous route may be used when a rapid effect is required.
- Octreotide decreases insulin requirements in Type 1 diabetes mellitus; however, in Type 2 diabetes, octreotide suppresses both insulin and glucagon release, leaving plasma glucose concentrations either unchanged or slightly elevated.

Non-oral routes of drug delivery

- **Syringe drivers** are used for drug delivery if the patient is unable to take medicines by mouth, (e.g. because of persistent nausea and vomiting, dysphagia, severe weakness, or coma).
- **Use only drugs that are known to be safe and effective by the subcutaneous route.** These include metoclopramide, haloperidol, cyclizine, hyoscine butylbromide, and levomepromazine.
- **Use water for injection as the diluent** when mixing drugs in a syringe driver (except for octreotide).
- **Use sodium chloride as the diluent for octreotide** and consider a second syringe driver if octreotide is to be co-administered with other drugs.
- **Check the compatibility of drugs before mixing.** Most data concern combinations of two drugs in a syringe driver, although some combinations of three or four drugs are compatible.
- **The compatibility of diamorphine with other drugs commonly used in palliative care** is addressed in Table 6. For further information on the compatibility of drugs in syringe drivers, see www.palliativedrugs.com, or seek advice from your local palliative care team or hospital drug information service.
- **Do not use solutions that are discoloured or have precipitated.**
- **Some drugs can be given by subcutaneous bolus, or by the rectal, buccal, or sublingual route.** Such routes could be considered if more than two drugs require administration by a non-oral route, or if the patient does not want a syringe driver.

[Twycross et al, 2002; BNF 47, 2004; Regnard and Hockley, 2004a]

Drugs for nausea used in syringe drivers

- **Always** follow local palliative care guidelines or seek advice from local palliative care services or hospital pharmacy drug information services *before* mixing drugs in a syringe driver.
- If you are unable to contact them see www.palliativedrugs.com. Alternatively, Table 10 is included as a brief guide.
- **Metoclopramide** is given in a subcutaneous infusion dose of 30–60 mg/24 hours. Metoclopramide may cause localized skin reactions.
- **Haloperidol** is given in a subcutaneous infusion dose of 2.5–5 mg/24 hours, but single bedtime doses are often effective. Mixtures of haloperidol and diamorphine are liable to precipitate after 24 hours if haloperidol concentration is above 2 mg/ml.
- **Levomepromazine** is given in a subcutaneous infusion dose of no more than 25 mg/24 hours, but single bedtime subcutaneous doses of 5–10 mg are often effective and have fewer side effects. In higher doses, sedation occurs in about 50% of patients and with subcutaneous administration there may be local irritation.
- **Cyclizine** is given in a subcutaneous infusion dose of 150 mg/24 hours. However, solutions of cyclizine may precipitate at concentrations above 10 mg/ml, in the presence of physiological saline, or as the concentration of diamorphine relative to cyclizine increases. Precipitation can be immediate or delayed. Local irritation may result.
- **Octreotide** can be used by subcutaneous infusion, in a dose of 300–600 micrograms/24 hours, to reduce intestinal secretions and vomiting. Do not use water for injection as diluent as precipitation may occur.
- **Dexamethasone may be combined with diamorphine; ensure precipitation does not occur when preparing.** The injectable forms use a different salt of dexamethasone from that in oral tablets — 1 mg of oral dexamethasone is equivalent to 1.2 mg dexamethasone phosphate or 1.3 mg dexamethasone sodium phosphate. The dose should be adjusted to the nearest volume that can easily be measured.
- **Hyoscine butylbromide** is given in a subcutaneous infusion dose of 20–60 mg/24 hours.
- **Glycopyrronium bromide** 0.6–1.2 mg/24 hours may also be used.

[BNF 47, 2004]

Table 10: Compatibilities and alternative routes of drugs commonly given by syringe driver.

Drug	Compatibility with diamorphine[1]	Alternative routes/ drugs[2]
Cyclizine	Diamorphine any strength + cyclizine 6.7 mg/ml Diamorphine 15 mg/ml + cyclizine 15 mg/ml Diamorphine 20 mg/ml + cyclizine 10 mg/ml	Levomepromazine (methotrimeprazine) as a single subcutaneous (s/c) bedtime dose
Dexamethasone	Compatible at usual concentrations, but mix carefully to prevent precipitation	Dexamethasone as a single s/c morning dose
Glycopyrronium bromide	Compatible at usual concentrations	Hyoscine hydrobromide sublingual tablets or patches
Haloperidol	Diamorphine 20–100 mg/ml + haloperidol 0.75 mg/ml Diamorphine 50 mg/ml + haloperidol 1.5 mg/ml	Haloperidol as a single s/c bedtime dose
Hyoscine butylbromide	Compatible at all usual concentrations	Hyoscine butylbromide as a s/c dose every 4–6 hours
Hyoscine hydrobromide	Compatible at all usual concentrations	Hyoscine hydrobromide sublingual tablets or patches
Levomepromazine	Compatible at all usual concentrations	Levomepromazine as a single s/c bedtime dose
Metoclopramide	Diamorphine 25 mg/ml + metoclopramide 5 mg/ml	Metoclopramide s/c 8-hourly or rectal domperidone

1. Twycross, R., Wilcock, A., Charlesworth, S., and Dickman, A. (2002) *Palliative care formulary*. Palliativedrugs.com Ltd. www.palliativedrugs.com [Accessed: 30-7-2002].
2. Regnard, C. and Hockley, J. (Eds.) (2004a) *A guide to symptom relief in palliative care*. 5th edn. Oxford: Radcliffe Medical Press.

References

1. BNF 47 (2004) *British National Formulary*. 47th edn. London: British Medical Association and Royal Pharmaceutical Society of Great Britain.
2. Borgelt, B., Gelber, R., Kramer, S. et al (1980) The palliation of brain metastases: final results of the first two studies by the Radiation Therapy Oncology Group. *International Journal of Radiation Oncology, Biology, Physics* **6**(1), 1–9.
3. CSM (1998) Withdrawal of systemic corticosteroids. *Current Problems in Pharmacovigilance* **24**(May), 5–10.
4. Ellershaw, J. and Griffiths, C. (2003) *The Liverpool care pathway for the dying patient (LCP)*. Liverpool: Marie Curie Centre Liverpool and The Royal Liverpool & Broadgreen University Hospitals NHS Trust.
5. Fainsinger, R., Miller, M., Bruera, E. et al (1991) Symptom control during the last week of life on a palliative care unit. *Journal of Palliative Care* **7**(1), 5–11.
6. Gallagher, C.G. (1994) Respiratory steroid myopathy. *American Journal of Respiratory & Critical Care Medicine* **150**(1), 4–6.
7. Grond, S., Zech, D., Diefenbach, C. and Bischoff, A. (1994) Prevalence and pattern of symptoms in patients with cancer pain: a prospective evaluation of 1635 cancer patients referred to a pain clinic. *Journal of Pain and Symptom Management* **9**(6), 372–382.
8. Hardy, J.R., Rees, E., Ling, J. et al (2001) A prospective survey of the use of dexamethasone on a palliative care unit. *Palliative Medicine* **15**(1), 3–8.
9. HPA (2004) *Immunoglobulin handbook: indications and dosage for normal and specific immunoglobulin preparations issued by the HPA*. Health Protection Agency. www.hpa.org.uk [Accessed: 27/09/2004]. [Full text]
10. Mercadante, S., Ripamonti, C., Casuccio, A. et al (2000) Comparison of octreotide and hyoscine butylbromide in controlling gastrointestinal symptoms due to malignant inoperable bowel obstruction. *Supportive Care in Cancer* **8**(3), 188–191.
11. Morita, T., Ichiki, T., Tsunoda, J. et al (1998) A prospective study on the dying process in terminally ill cancer patients. *American Journal of Hospice & Palliative Care* **15**(4), 217–222.
12. Piper, J.M., Ray, W.A., Daugherty, J.R. and Griffin, M.R. (1991) Corticosteroid use and peptic ulcer disease: role of nonsteroidal anti-inflammatory drugs. *Annals of Internal Medicine* **114**(9), 735–740.
13. Regnard, C. and Hockley, J. (Eds.) (2004a) *A guide to symptom relief in palliative care*. 5th edn. Oxford: Radcliffe Medical Press.
14. Regnard, C. and Hockley, J. (Eds.) (2004b) Emergencies. In: *A guide to symptom relief in palliative care*. 5th edn. Oxford: Radcliffe Medical Press. 206–208.
15. Regnard, C. and Hockley, J. (Eds.) (2004c) Dysphagia. In: *A guide to symptom relief in palliative care*. 5th edn. Oxford: Radcliffe Medical Press. 91–95.
16. Ripamonti, C., Mercadante, S., Groff, L. et al (2000) Role of octreotide, scopolamine butylbromide, and hydration in symptom control of patients with inoperable bowel obstruction and nasogastric tubes: a prospective randomized trial. *Journal of Pain and Symptom Management* **19**(1), 23–34.
17. Ripamonti, C., Twycross, R., Baines, M. et al (2001) Clinical-practice recommendations for the management of bowel obstruction in patients with end-stage cancer. *Supportive Care in Cancer* **9**(4), 223–233.
18. Tramer, M.R. and Walder, B. (1999) Efficacy and adverse effects of prophylactic antiemetics during patient-controlled analgesia therapy: a quantitative systematic review. *Anesthesia & Analgesia* **88**(6), 1354–1361.
19. Twycross, R. and Back, I. (1998) Nausea and vomiting in advanced cancer. *European Journal of Palliative Care* **5**(2), 39–44.
20. Twycross, R., Wilcock, A., Charlesworth, S. and Dickman, A. (2002) *Palliative care formulary*. Palliativedrugs.com Ltd. www.palliativedrugs.com [Accessed: 07/06/2005].
21. Vainio, A., Auvinen, A., Ahmedzai, S. et al (1996) Prevalence of symptoms among patients with advanced cancer: an international collaborative study. *Journal of Pain and Symptom Management* **12**(1), 3–10.

P

PRODIGY GUIDANCE

Palliative care — oral problems

Last revised in June 2004
www.prodigy.nhs.uk/guidance.asp?gt=Palliative care - oral problem

Applies to people over the age of 16 years

This guidance covers the management of dry mouth, oral *Candida* infection, oral *Herpes simplex* infection, mouth ulcers, and regular mouth care in palliative care patients.

This guidance does not cover the management of oral tumours.

There is separate guidance for *Palliative care — cough, Palliative care — dyspnoea, Palliative care — malodorous malignant ulcer of skin, Palliative care — nausea/vomiting/malignant bowel obstruction, Palliative care — pain and Palliative care — respiratory secretions at the end of life.*

Goals

- To alleviate symptoms in a manner that most enhances quality of life

Contents

Scenarios

- Dry mouth p.1468
- Oral Candida infection p.1469
- Mouth ulcers p.1470

Extended Information, p. 1472

Which scenario?

- **Dry mouth:** covers the management of patients with dry mouth.
- **Oral *Candida* infection:** covers the management of patients with *Candida* infection of the mouth (oral thrush).
- **Mouth ulcers:** covers the management of patients with aphthous ulcers, oral herpes simplex infection, chemotherapy- or radiotherapy-induced mucositis, neutropaenic ulcers, and malodour from malignant tumours in the oral cavity.

P

Dry mouth

Which therapy?

- **Manage any underlying causes of dry mouth:**
  - **Drugs** (e.g. morphine, diuretics, tricyclic antidepressants): reduce the dose or change to another drug.
  - **Dehydration:** simple measures (see below) can relieve symptoms. Rehydration helps only a small number of patients.
  - **Anxiety:** manage in the usual way, depending on prognosis.
- **Advise all patients to use simple measures to relieve dry mouth, such as:**
  - Frequent sips or sprays of cold water.
  - Suck ice cubes, or eat partly frozen melon or pineapple chunks.
  - Avoid acidic drinks (e.g. orange juice).
  - Use petroleum jelly to prevent sore, cracked lips.
- **If simple measures are inadequate,** consider using artificial saliva containing mucin (AS Saliva Orthana®) or lactoperoxidase (Biotene Oralbalance® and BioXtra®).
- **Chewing sugar-free gum is also useful.**
- **Consider using pilocarpine 5 mg three times a day for difficult cases:**
  - Most people with drug-induced dry mouth respond after the first dose.
  - It can take 4–12 weeks before a response is seen in radiotherapy-induced dry mouth.
- **Acupuncture may be useful for resistant cases.**
- **Advise all patients and carers that routine mouth care is also important.** See *Management issues* for further information.

Practical prescribing points

For further information please see the *Medicines Compendium* (www.medicines.org.uk) or the *British National Formulary* (www.bnf.org).

- **Asthma, chronic obstructive pulmonary disease, bradycardia, bowel obstruction, glaucoma:** do not use pilocarpine.
- Advise patients taking pilocarpine that sweating is a common adverse effect.

Follow-up advice

- Consider follow-up on an individual basis, depending on the severity of dry mouth, and the stage of the person's illness.
- Patients with dry mouth are at increased risk of infection. Regular examination of the oral cavity will highlight any new problems promptly.

Patient information leaflets

The following PILs are available at www.prodigy.nhs.uk

- Cancerbacup
- Cancer Research UK
- Dry Mouth
- Macmillan Cancer Relief

Shared decision making

- **There are several things you can do to help** relieve a dry mouth:
  - Take frequent sips or sprays of cold water.
  - Suck ice cubes, or eat partly frozen melon or pineapple chunks.
  - Avoid acidic drinks (e.g. orange juice) as these are more drying in the long run.
  - Use petroleum jelly to prevent sore, cracked lips.
- **An artificial saliva spray** helps some people.
- **Pilocarpine tablets** may also be used to increase the amount of saliva produced.
- **Acupuncture** also helps some people.

Drug rationale

Drugs not included

- **Carmellose-based artificial saliva products** (e.g. Luborant and Saliveze) are not included. Many patients find no additional benefit with carmellose-based preparations compared with frequent tea, coffee, milk, or fruit juice [Vissink et al, 1983]. Glandsone is not included because it is acidic, so long-term use may damage teeth.
- **Saliva-stimulants containing malic acid** (e.g. Salivix pastilles and SST tablets) are not included. Long-term use can cause demineralization of teeth [Miller and Kearney, 2001].

Drugs included

- **An advice prescription** offering advice on non-drug management of dry mouth is included.
- **Artificial saliva containing mucin or lactoperoxidase** may offer more symptomatic relief than artificial saliva containing carmellose [Vissink et al, 1983; Epstein et al, 1999]. However the duration of action of mucin products is still only 10–15 minutes. (Duration of action was not reported in the lactoperoxidase study [Epstein et al, 1999].) AS Saliva Orthana® is the only mucin-containing product available in the UK. Biotene Oralbalance® and BioXtra® both contain lactoperoxidase. (They are all borderline substances, so the prescription must be endorsed 'ACBS'.)
- **Pilocarpine** is more effective than artificial saliva [Davies et al, 1998], and is useful for more difficult cases.

Prescriptions

Non-drug management

Advice note: simple measures to relieve dry mouth

- Age from 16 years onwards
- There are several things you can do to help relieve a dry mouth. Take frequent sips or sprays of cold water. Suck ice cubes, or eat partly frozen melon or pineapple chunks. Avoid acidic drinks (e.g. orange juice) as these are more drying in the long run. Use petroleum jelly to prevent sore, cracked lips.

Advice note: routine mouth care

- Age from 16 years onwards
- Brush your teeth twice a day with a soft toothbrush and fluoride toothpaste. After meals and before bed, rinse the mouth with water or saline solution, and gently clean the tongue and sides of the mouth using a soft toothbrush. (If using a toothbrush to clean your mouth makes it bleed, ask your doctor to provide you with soft foam sticks instead.) If you have a very dry mouth, mouth ulcers, or a mouth infection, rinse and clean the mouth every 2 hours. This helps your mouth heal and helps to prevent further problems.

Artificial saliva

AS Saliva Orthana

- Age from 16 years onwards
- AS Saliva Orthana spray. Spray into the mouth when required to relieve dry mouth; supply 50 ml; NHS Cost £4.25.

Biotene Oralbalance

- Age from 16 years onwards
- Biotene Oralbalance. Apply to the gums and tongue when required to relieve dry mouth; supply 50 grams; NHS Cost £4.10.

BioXtra

- Age from 16 years onwards
- BioXtra oral gel. Apply to the inside of the mouth when required to relieve dry mouth; supply 40 ml; NHS Cost £2.25.

Pilocarpine

Pilocarpine 5mg three times a day

- Age from 16 years onwards
- Pilocarpine 5mg tablets. Take one tablet three times a day (to relieve dry mouth); supply 84 tablets; NHS Cost £51.43.

Oral Candida infection

Which therapy?

- **Treat any predisposing factors in conjunction with specific anticandidal therapy:**
  - **Manage dry mouth** (see the scenario Dry mouth for further information).
  - **Diabetes mellitus** control should be optimized.
  - **Review oral corticosteroid therapy** (oral, inhaled, and topical).
  - **Denture hygiene** should be optimized.
- **Use topical nystatin, amphotericin, or miconazole.**
- **Consider oral fluconazole or itraconazole** if infection is severe or widespread, topical anticandidals are not tolerated, or there is no response to treatment.
- **Advise all patients and carers that routine mouth care is also important.** See *Management issues* for further information.

Practical prescribing points

For further information please see the *Medicines Compendium* (www.medicines.org.uk) or the *British National Formulary* (www.bnf.org).

- **Advise patients to hold topical anticandidals in the mouth for as long as possible** before swallowing.
- **Nystatin is inactivated by chlorhexidine mouthwash.** Do not use them at the same time.
- **Do not give itraconazole to patients at high risk of heart failure.** Those at highest risk are the elderly, patients taking high doses or receiving longer treatment courses, patients with cardiac disease, and patients taking negative inotropic drugs.
- **Patients on warfarin:** oral fluconazole, oral itraconazole, and *topical* miconazole may enhance the anticoagulant effect of warfarin.

Follow-up advice

- Consider follow-up on an individual basis, depending on the severity of dry mouth and the stage of the person's illness.
- Regular examination of the oral cavity will highlight any new problems promptly.

Patient information leaflets

The following PILs are available at www.prodigy.nhs.uk

- Cancerbacup
- Cancer Research UK
- Macmillan Cancer Relief
- Thrush - Oral

Shared decision making

- **Topical nystatin, amphotericin, or miconazole** will usually clear oral thrush.

P

- With drops, use a dropper to put the liquid onto affected areas.
- With lozenges, suck them as they dissolve in the mouth.
- With gel, smear it onto affected areas (and onto dentures if appropriate).

- **Antithrush tablets** such as **fluconazole** and **itraconazole** are only used in more serious cases.
- **Some bouts of oral thrush can be prevented:**
  - If you have diabetes — is your blood sugar well controlled?
  - If you use steroid inhalers — do you use a spacer? Also, gargle and rinse your mouth after using the inhaler.
  - If you use dentures — remove and soak them overnight in a cleansing solution.
  - If you take medication that causes a dry mouth — take frequent sips of water.

Drug rationale

Drugs not included

- **Systemic candidal treatment other than preparations containing fluconazole or itraconazole** are either not licensed for oral candidiasis, or are only licensed for the treatment of resistant cases.

Drugs included

- **Topical nystatin and amphotericin** are available as suspension or lozenges/pastilles. Neither is absorbed systemically, so it is important that the patient holds them near the lesions for as long as possible before swallowing.
- **Topical miconazole** is also included. However, it is systemically absorbed to an extent that interactions (e.g. with warfarin) may need to be considered.
- **Oral fluconazole and itraconazole** are included for use when topical treatments are not tolerated or there is no response to treatment.

P

Prescriptions

1st line: topical anticandidals

Nystatin 100,000units/ml s/f susp: use 1ml four times a day

- Age from 16 years onwards
- Nystatin 100,000u/ml s/f susp. Using the oral dispenser provided, place 1 ml in the mouth and hold near the affected area(s) four times a day; supply 30 ml; NHS Cost £1.96.

Nystatin pastilles: use one pastille four times day

- Age from 16 years onwards
- Nystatin 100,000unit pastilles. Suck one pastille slowly four times a day; supply 28 pastilles; NHS Cost £3.00.

Amphotericin 100mg/ml s/f susp: use 1ml four times a day

- Age from 16 years onwards
- Amphotericin 100mg/ml susp. Using the oral dispenser provided, place 1 ml in the mouth and hold near the affected area(s) four times a day; supply 12 ml; NHS Cost £2.31.

Amphotericin 10mg lozenges: use one lozenge four times a day

- Age from 16 years onwards
- Amphotericin 10mg lozenges. Allow one lozenge to dissolve slowly in the mouth four times a day; supply 60 lozenge; NHS Cost £3.00.

Miconazole oral gel: use 5ml to 10ml four times a day

- Age from 16 years onwards
- Miconazole 24mg/ml oral gel. Place 5ml to 10ml in the mouth and hold near the affected area(s) four times a day; supply 80 grams; NHS Cost £5.00.

2nd line: oral anticandidals

Fluconazole 50mg once a day for 7 days

- Age from 16 years onwards
- Fluconazole 50mg capsules. Take one capsule once a day for 7 days; supply 7 capsules; NHS Cost £14.51.

Fluconazole 50mg once a day for 14 days

- Age from 16 years onwards
- Fluconazole 50mg capsules. Take one capsule once a day for 14 days; supply 14 capsules; NHS Cost £29.02.

Itraconazole 100mg once a day for 15 days

- Age from 16 years onwards
- Itraconazole 100mg capsules. Take one capsule once a day for 15 days; supply 15 capsules; NHS Cost £15.72.

Severe infection

Fluconazole 100mg once a day for 7 days

- Age from 16 years onwards
- Fluconazole 50mg capsules. Take two capsules once a day for 7 days; supply 14 capsules; NHS Cost £29.02.

Fluconazole 100mg once a day for 14 days

- Age from 16 years onwards
- Fluconazole 50mg capsules. Take two capsules once a day for 14 days; supply 28 capsules; NHS Cost £58.04.

Additional non-drug management

Advice only: routine mouth care

- Age from 16 years onwards
- Brush your teeth twice a day with a soft toothbrush and fluoride toothpaste. After meals and before bed, rinse the mouth with water or saline solution, and gently clean the tongue and sides of the mouth using a soft toothbrush. (If using a toothbrush to clean your mouth makes it bleed, ask your doctor to provide you with soft foam sticks instead.) If you have a very dry mouth, mouth ulcers, or a mouth infection, rinse and clean the mouth every 2 hours. This helps your mouth heal and helps to prevent further problems.

Mouth ulcers

Which therapy

- **Different types of mouth ulcer require different management:**
  - **Aphthous ulcers:** use chlorhexidine mouthwash or topical corticosteroids.
  - **Badly fitting dentures:** seek advice from a dentist.
  - **Oral herpes simplex infection:** use oral aciclovir.
  - **Malodorous malignant ulcer:** use oral metronidazole. Treatment may need to be continued at a low-dose as odour commonly returns when treatment is stopped.
  - **Mucositis:** discuss with the oncology team, as it may limit the patient's ability to tolerate chemotherapy or radiotherapy.
  - **Neutropaenic ulcers:** seek specialist advice if neutropaenia is suspected; recovery of the neutrophil count is essential for healing.
- **Exclude atrophic *Candida* infection** (causes a red, painful mouth without white plaques).
- **Advise all patients (or carers) to use routine mouth care,** to aid healing and prevent secondary bacterial infection.
- **Consider using chlorhexidine mouthwash** to help prevent secondary bacterial infection.
- **Offer topical analgesia if mouth ulcers are painful:**

- **Localized pain:** choline salicylate, benzydamine spray, or lidocaine (lignocaine) ointment or spray can be used, but have a short duration of action.
- **Mechanical protection:** carbenoxolone or carmellose can be used to provide a protective barrier over the ulcer.
- **Diffuse oral pain:** benzydamine mouthwash or diclofenac dispersible tablets (used as a mouthwash) can be used.

- **Use systemic analgesia if topical analgesia does not relieve pain.** See the PRODIGY guidance *Palliative care — pain* for further information.

Practical prescribing points

For further information please see the *Medicines Compendium* (www.medicines.org.uk) or the *British National Formulary* (www.bnf.org).

Treatments

- **Advise patients** to avoid spicy, acidic, or salty foods. Sucking ice cubes can be soothing.
- **Chlorhexidine mouthwash:** this can stain teeth brown when used regularly. The stain is not usually permanent and can be reduced by avoiding drinks that contain tannin (e.g. tea, coffee, red wine), and by brushing teeth before use. (Note: rinse mouth well after brushing as chlorhexidine can be inactivated by the some ingredients in toothpaste.) Chlorhexidine inactivates nystatin. Do not use them at the same time.
- **Alcohol and metronidazole:** adverse reactions to this combination are uncommon. Patients should be informed that vomiting may occasionally occur if alcohol is taken with metronidazole.

Pain relief

- **Benzydamine mouthwash:** numbness and stinging are sometimes a problem. Diluting the mouthwash in an equal volume of water before use reduces stinging.
- **Choline salicylate gel:** excessive use can cause ulceration, particularly in denture wearers.
- **Lidocaine (lignocaine) ointment or spray:** avoid using before meals. Lidocaine can numb the pharynx, leading to aspiration or choking.

Follow-up advice

- Consider follow-up on an individual basis, depending on the severity of dry mouth and the stage of the person's illness.
- Regular examination of the oral cavity will highlight any new problems promptly.

Should I refer or investigate?

Refer?

- **Oral herpes simplex infection:** refer for intravenous administration of aciclovir if pain limits the patient's ability to take oral medication.
- **Mucositis: discuss with the oncology team.** It can be extremely painful, and may limit the patient's ability to tolerate chemotherapy or radiotherapy.
- **Neutropaenic ulcers: seek specialist advice** if neutropaenia is suspected. Recovery of the neutrophil count is essential for healing.

Investigate?

- **Iron, folate, or vitamin B_{12} deficiency:** if prognosis allows, correction of iron, folate, or vitamin B_{12} deficiency may help to prevent aphthous ulcers recurring.

Patient information leaflets

The following PILs are available at www.prodigy.nhs.uk

- Cancerbacup
- Cancer Research UK
- Macmillan Cancer Relief
- Mouth Ulcers (Minor Aphthous Type)

Drug rationale

Drugs not included

- **Oral chlorhexidine preparations other than 0.2% mouthwash** are not included. Chlorhexidine 1% dental gel is more difficult to apply evenly to all areas of the mouth than a mouthwash. We have found no evidence that chlorhexidine 0.12% mouthwash or 2% spray have been evaluated for treating aphthous ulcers.
- **Tetracycline mouthwash** may reduce the duration and severity of ulcers, but causes oral candidiasis and a burning-like sensation of the pharynx [Porter et al, 2000]. Tetracycline capsules are no longer available in the UK, so doxycycline capsules are generally substituted instead; the contents of a 100 mg capsule are dispersed in water and rinsed around the mouth for 2–3 minutes, four times a day [BNF 47, 2004].

Drugs included

- **Chlorhexidine 0.2% mouthwash** is used to treat aphthous ulcers; there is some evidence that it reduces the severity and duration of ulceration [Porter and Scully, 2003]. However, regular use can stain teeth, which is unacceptable to some people.
- **Triamcinolone oral paste or hydrocortisone lozenges** are probably most useful when applied early. There are few studies to support their use but there is some evidence that they reduce the duration of ulcers and hasten pain relief without causing notable local or systemic adverse reactions [Porter and Scully, 2003]. Triamcinolone oral paste may be difficult to apply to some parts of the mouth.
- **Beclometasone spray or betamethasone soluble tablets** are more potent than hydrocortisone lozenges or triamcinolone oral paste, but have an increased risk of systemic adverse effects and oral candidiasis. They are generally reserved for use when ulceration is extensive, or is at a difficult-to-reach site.
- **Oral aciclovir** is commonly used to treat oral herpes simplex infection in oncology and palliative care patients, as they are at higher risk of severe infection than healthy adults [Leflore et al, 2000].
- **Oral metronidazole** is included for managing malodour from malignant oral tumours. Although there are no studies of its use in malignant ulcers in the oral cavity, some small studies in cutaneous malignant ulcers found a marked reduction in odour [Sparrow et al, 1980; Ashford et al, 1984]. Treatment may need to be continued over the long term, as the odour usually returns when treatment is stopped.

Topical analgesia

- **Benzydamine mouthwash or spray** may be useful if the area is more extensive [Regnard and Hockley, 2004]. The spray is more convenient to carry for frequent applications.
- **Choline salicylate gel** can be used if the pain is well localized, but its effect is short-lived [BNF 47, 2004]. Excessive use should be avoided as this can lead to ulceration, particularly if the gel is trapped under dentures.

- **Carbenoxolone and carmellose** are thought to provide a protective barrier over the ulcer site. Carbenoxolone mouthwash may be of some value, but it is relatively expensive compared with other mouthwashes. Carmellose paste can be difficult to apply effectively to some parts of the mouth [BNF 47, 2004].
- **Diclofenac dispersible tablets** can be used as a mouthwash before swallowing. They also have a systemic analgesic effect.
- **Lidocaine (lignocaine) 5% ointment should be reserved for severe pain** (e.g. chemotherapy- or radiotherapy-induced mucositis). Again, the duration of action is relatively short, so it will not provide continuous analgesia throughout the day. Care should also be taken not to anaesthetize the pharynx before meals as this might lead to aspiration or choking.

Prescriptions

Aphthous ulcers

Chlorhexidine mouthwash: rinse with 10ml twice a day
- Age from 16 years onwards
- Chlorhexidine 0.2% mouthwash. Rinse the mouth with 10ml for about 1 minute twice a day; supply 300 ml; NHS Cost £1.93.

Triamcinolone 0.1% oral paste: apply 2 to 4 times a day
- Age from 16 years onwards
- Triamcinolone 0.1% oral paste. Apply a thin layer to the affected area(s) 2 to 4 times a day. Do not rub in; supply 10 grams; NHS Cost £1.27.

Hydrocortisone 2.5mg lozenges: use four times a day
- Age from 16 years onwards
- Hydrocortisone 2.5mg lozenges. Place one lozenge over the affected area and allow it to dissolve slowly, four times a day; supply 40 lozenges; NHS Cost £5.00.

Betamethasone 500mcg soluble tablets: use twice a day
- Age from 16 years onwards
- Betamethasone 500mcg tablets. Dissolve one tablet in water and rinse around the mouth twice a day; supply 28 tablets; NHS Cost £1.15.

Beclometasone 50mcg inhaler: use 2 to 4 times a day
- Age from 16 years onwards
- Beclometasone 50mcg inhaler. Spray one puff into the mouth 2 to 4 times a day; supply 1 200 dose inhaler; NHS Cost £4.30.

Herpes simplex infection

Aciclovir 200mg five times a day for 7 days
- Age from 16 years onwards
- Aciclovir 200mg tablets. Take one tablet five times a day for 7 days; supply 35 tablets; NHS Cost £5.85.

Immunosuppressed:aciclovir 400mg five times a day for 7 days
- Age from 16 years onwards
- Aciclovir 400mg tablets. Take one tablet five times a day for 7 days; supply 35 tablets; NHS Cost £14.10.

Malodorous malignant ulcer

Initial treatment: metronidazole 400mg three times a day
- Age from 16 years onwards
- Metronidazole 400mg tablets. Take one tablet three times a day for 14 days; supply 42 tablets; NHS Cost £3.09.

Initial treatment if frail: metronidazole 400mg twice a day
- Age from 16 years onwards
- Metronidazole 400mg tablets. Take one tablet twice a day for 14 days; supply 28 tablets; NHS Cost £2.06.

Maintenance: metronidazole 200mg twice a day
- Age from 16 years onwards
- Metronidazole 200mg tablets. Take one tablet twice a day; supply 56 tablets; NHS Cost £4.12.

Topical products for localized oral pain

Choline salicylate: use 1/2inch of gel up to 6 times a day
- Age from 16 years onwards
- Choline salicylate oral gel. Gently massage 1/2 inch of gel onto the affected area when required for pain relief. Maximum of 6 applications in 24 hours; supply 15 grams; NHS Cost £1.70.

Benzydamine spray: use 4 to 8 sprays every 3 hours
- Age from 16 years onwards
- Benzydamine 0.15% spray. Spray 4 to 8 times onto the affected area every 3 hours when required for pain relief. Increase to every one and a half hours if required; supply 30 ml; NHS Cost £3.41.

Lidocaine 5% ointment: use when required
- Age from 16 years onwards
- Lidocaine 5% ointment. Apply a small amount of ointment to the affected area when required for pain relief; supply 15 grams; NHS Cost £0.85.

Lidocaine 10% spray: use when required
- Age from 16 years onwards
- Lidocaine 10% spray. Spray one puff into the mouth when required for pain relief; supply 1 50ml spray; NHS Cost £3.13.

Mechanical protection: carmellose paste
- Age from 16 years onwards
- Orabase oral paste. Apply a thin layer to the affected area after meals; supply 30 grams; NHS Cost £1.91.

Topical products for diffuse oral pain

Benzydamine 0.15% mouthwash: rinse with 15ml every 3 hours
- Age from 16 years onwards
- Benzydamine 0.15% mouthwash. Rinse the mouth with 15ml every 3 hours when required for pain relief. Increase to every one and a half hours if required; supply 300 ml; NHS Cost £3.92.

Diclofenac 50mg soluble tablets: use as a mouthwash
- Age from 16 years onwards
- Diclofenac 50mg disp tablets. Dissolve one tablet in water and rinse around the mouth for a few minutes before swallowing; supply 42 tablets; NHS Cost £12.26.

Mechanical protection: carbenoxolone mouthwash
- Age from 16 years onwards
- Bioplex 1% mouthwash granules. Dissolve the contents of one sachet in 30-50ml of warm water. Rinse around the mouth three times a day and at night; supply 48 sachets; NHS Cost £17.42.

Extended Information

Background information

- How common are oral problems in palliative care? p.1472
- How do oral problems present? p.1473
- How do I diagnose the cause of oral problems in palliative care? p.1473

How common are oral problems in palliative care?

- Oral problems reflect the general health of the patient and therefore become increasingly common with advancing illness.

- Oral problems are common, and often predictable, following chemotherapy and head and neck radiotherapy.
- Dry mouth was reported by nearly 90% of patients with advanced cancer in one survey [Oneschuk et al, 2000].
- Oral candidiasis was present in nearly 30% of patients admitted to an oncology ward [Bagg et al, 2003].
- Approximately 40% of chemotherapy patients develop an oral problem related to treatment, and patients with haematological malignancies develop oral problems at two or three times the rate of patients with solid tumours [Doyle et al, 2004]. Nearly all patients who receive radiotherapy to the head or neck develop oral mucositis.

How do oral problems present?

- Oral health requires an intact mucosa, normal production of saliva, and an intact immune system.
- Alteration to any of these may result in an oral problem's developing.
- A large number of underlying causes present with a limited number of symptoms, these being:
  - Dry mouth
  - Painful mouth
  - Excessive salivation
- These symptoms may have a significant impact on the quality of life of the patient by interfering with:
  - Eating and drinking
  - Ability to talk comfortably

How do I diagnose the cause of oral problems in palliative care?

General points

- The cause of most oral problems can usually be diagnosed on clinical features alone, and investigations are rarely required.
- Symptoms commonly have more than one cause. Each cause should be considered for treatment.
- Infection commonly complicates dryness or ulceration of the mucosa.

Oral cavity examination

- Examine the mouth for evidence of:
  - Dryness
  - Ulceration and vesicles
  - Erythema
  - White plaques and membranes

Causes of dry mouth

Table 1 outlines the common causes of dry mouth in palliative care patients.

Causes of mouth pain

Table 2 outlines the clinical features that are useful to diagnose the cause of mouth pain in palliative care patients.

Oral Candida infection

- **Pseudomembranous *Candida* infection** typically presents with oral pain and white plaques on the mucosal surfaces. Plaques are most commonly seen on the buccal mucosa, tongue, and gums; they may also occur on the palate, fauces, uvula, and tonsils. The plaques may coalesce, and may even cover the entire oral cavity. They can be wiped off to reveal a raw, erythematous base that may bleed.
- **Acute atrophic form:** there are no plaques, but there are erythematous areas on the tongue, palate, or buccal mucosa. This form may follow therapy with oral antibiotics or oral corticosteroids.

Table 1: Common causes of dry mouth in palliative care patients.

Underlying cause	Clinical features
Dehydration	Poor fluid intake/ poor urine output Reduced skin turgor
Drugs (e.g. morphine, drugs with antimuscarinic effects)	Reduced salivary production
Mouth breathing	More common with consciousness impaired Nasal obstruction
Radiotherapy of head and neck	Reduced salivary production
Anxiety	Intermittent and associated with psychological symptoms

- **Chronic atrophic form:** denture wearers may develop an area of chronic erythema and oedema under the upper dentures. The mucosal surface under the lower dentures is rarely affected.

Aphthous ulcers

- Although they are common, their cause is unclear. Predisposing factors are thought to include immunodeficiency; local trauma (e.g. caused by excessive tooth brushing); dietary deficiency of iron, folate, vitamin B_{12}, or zinc; stress; and smoking cessation [Scully and Shotts, 2000].

Chemotherapy- or radiotherapy-induced mucositis

- Oral mucositis (inflammation and ulceration of the oral cavity) is a significant problem in patients treated with chemotherapy or radiotherapy.

Other oral problems

Malodorous malignant ulcers

- Malodour is a common problem with oral cancers. The blood supply to parts of the tumour is often impaired, resulting in areas of hypoxic or necrotic tissue. These

Table 2: Diagnosing the common causes of mouth pain.

Cause of pain	Diagnosis	Clinical features
Dry mouth	See Table 1	See Table 1
Ulceration	Herpes simplex	Painful ++ yellowish lesions that are easily removed Preceding crops of vesicles — may also occur on lips Systemic upset common
	Aphthous ulcer*	Ulcers round or oval with yellowish base Not easily removed Less than 5 in number
	Neutropaenic ulcer	Clinical features as above — complicating severe neutropaenia (neutrophil count of less than 100 mm³). most commonly as complication of acute leukaemia
	Mucositis*	Ulceration associated with diffuse erythema and pseudomembrane formation following chemotherapy/radiotherapy
	Local tumour	Ulceration, slough, bleeding, malodour
Erythema	Oral candida*	Localized areas of erythema and associated white plaques that are easily removed
	Mucositis	As above
	Ill-fitting dentures	Localized erythema of surfaces in contact with denture
	Dental abscess	Periodontal erythema may have associated signs of infection

*See information below for further information.

P

areas become infected with anaerobic bacteria, which release malodorous volatile by-products.

Excessive salivation

- Excessive salivation is uncommon but can cause discomfort and embarrassment, as well as irritation of the lips and chin. The problem is exacerbated if the patient also has difficulty swallowing.
- The most frequent causes of excess salivation include oral pain (e.g. from aphthous ulcers), local irritation from badly fitting dentures, or drugs (e.g. lithium, cholinesterase inhibitors, and muscarinic agonists such as pilocarpine) [Doyle et al, 2004].
- Dysphagia may cause problems with excessive salivation because the saliva cannot be removed by swallowing.

Management issues

- Preventing oral problems p.1474
- Treating oral problems p.1474
- Pain control for oral problems p.1476
- Oral care in the terminal phase p.1476

Preventing oral problems

- **Routine mouth examination and care reduces the risk of oral problems developing.**
- People at particular risk of developing oral problems include:
  - People with advanced debilitating disease.
  - People undergoing chemotherapy and radiotherapy [Regnard and Hockley, 2004].

Routine mouth care

- **Brush teeth twice a day** with a soft toothbrush and fluoride-containing toothpaste.
- **Rinse the mouth after meals and at night,** with water or 0.9% sodium chloride [Regnard and Hockley, 2004]. Fresh sodium chloride solution can be made for each rinse by dissolving half a teaspoon of salt in 250 ml fresh water.
- **Remove visible debris** by gently brushing the tongue or mucosal surfaces with a soft toothbrush. (This should be undertaken after meals and at night, or as often as tolerated.) Foam sticks are an alternative if gentle brushing with a soft toothbrush causes pain or bleeding. Chewing pineapple may also help to clean the mouth — pineapple contains ananase, an enzyme which may help to break down mouth debris. (Unsweetened fresh or tinned pineapple can be used.)
- **Dentures** should be removed at night and cleaned with a soft toothbrush and toothpaste. Soak overnight in a denture solution containing sodium hypochlorite, and rinse before use [Milligan et al, 2001]. (Soak metal dentures in chlorhexidine solution.)
- **The frequency of mouth care should be increased if:**
  - There is a high risk of oral problems developing.
  - An oral problem has developed.
- Rinsing with water or saline can be repeated as often as required.
- **Although there is little evidence to guide practice, consider:**
  - Two-hourly care for patients with active oral problems or patients at risk of mucositis.
  - Hourly care for patients with severe oral problems or those at very high risk of developing oral problems (e.g. patients on oxygen therapy, mouth breathers, or unconscious patients) [Krishnasamy, 1995].

Choice of mouthwash

There is little evidence to guide the best choice of mouthwash.

- **We recommend using water or sodium chloride 0.9% solution:** they are widely used, and are soothing, non-traumatic, and *safe to use as frequently as required.* Water can be given warm or cool, depending on individual preference.
- **Chlorhexidine** can be used in patients with, or at risk of, secondary bacterial infection, but should not be used more than twice a day. It contains alcohol which may cause stinging, particularly in patients with inflamed mucosa, e.g. patients with mucositis. Povidone-iodine mouthwash should generally be avoided because high doses of iodine can be absorbed [BNF 47, 2004].
- **Other mouthwashes are used in some centres, but are less suitable for long-term use:**
  - Effervescent ascorbic acid solution is widely used, but citric acid can damage tooth enamel, and high sugar levels can promote fungal growth [Milligan et al, 2001].
  - Sodium bicarbonate 1% mouthwash is used by some, but it has an unpleasant taste, and higher concentrations can irritate the oral mucosa [Milligan et al, 2001].
  - Hydrogen peroxide 1.5% mouthwash is also used because its foaming action helps to remove debris. However many patients find the foaming sensation and its taste unpleasant. Higher concentrations may cause burns, and regular use may promote fungal overgrowth because of its antimicrobial effects [Milligan et al, 2001].
  - Glycerine and lemon mouthwashes should be avoided. They often increase the sensation of dry mouth, probably because of a direct dehydrating effect of glycerine and over-stimulation and exhaustion of the salivary glands by lemon juice [Krishnasamy, 1995].

Treating oral problems

Dry mouth

Where possible, treatment is directed at the underlying cause of dry mouth. If this is not possible or is only partially successful, symptomatic treatment is used.

Treating the underlying cause of dry mouth

- **Drugs** are a common cause of dry mouth. Reduce the dose or change the drug if possible. Morphine is a common, but often overlooked, cause of dry mouth [Doyle et al, 2004]. Other drugs that cause dry mouth include tricyclic antidepressants, antihistamines, antimuscarinic drugs, antiepileptic drugs, antipsychotics, beta-blockers, and diuretics.
- **Dehydration** should be reversed in patients who are not in the terminal phase. For managing dehydration in the terminal phase see *Oral care in the terminal phase.* Simple measures will often relieve symptoms of dry mouth, even if rehydration is not undertaken.
- **Anxiety** can also cause dry mouth. It becomes increasingly common as patients reach the end of life and should be managed in the usual way, depending on prognosis.

Symptomatic management of dry mouth

- **Simple measures should be used by all patients:**
  - Advise patients to take frequent sips or sprays of cold water, or suck ice cubes or boiled sweets. Eating partly frozen melon, pineapple chunks, or chewing sugar-free chewing gum is also soothing.
  - Petroleum jelly can be applied to the lips to prevent drying and cracking.
- **Artificial saliva offers little advantage compared to simple measures for most patients.** The few available studies are of poor quality, but suggest that:
  - Many patients find no additional benefit with carmellose (carboxymethylcellulose)-based

preparations compared with frequent tea, coffee, milk, or fruit juice [Vissink et al, 1983]. In addition, some patients find carmellose-based products feel sticky.
  - Artificial saliva containing mucin or lactoperoxidase may offer more symptomatic relief than artificial saliva containing carmellose [Vissink et al, 1983; Epstein et al, 1999]. However the duration of action of mucin products is still only 10–15 minutes. (Duration of action was not reported in the lactoperoxidase study [Epstein et al, 1999].)
- AS Saliva Orthana® is the only mucin-containing product available in the UK. Biotene Oralbalance® and BioXtra® both contain lactoperoxidase. (They are all borderline substances, so the prescription must be endorsed 'ACBS'.)
- Note: long-term use of acidic products may demineralize tooth enamel. (Glandsone® spray, Salivix® pastilles, and SST® tablets are acidic products.)
- **Consider using an artificial saliva containing mucin or lactoperoxidase when simple measures have been tried, but symptoms remain troublesome.**
- **Sugar-free chewing gum** is as effective as artificial salivas [Davies, 2000].
- **Pilocarpine can be considered for difficult cases:**
  - Most patients with drug-induced dry mouth usually respond to treatment after the first dose [Davies et al, 1998].
  - Only about 50% of patients with radiotherapy-induced dry mouth respond to treatment, and it may take up to 3 months before a response is seen [Davies et al, 1998].
  - Pilocarpine 5 mg three times a day is more effective than artificial saliva, but also has more adverse effects (e.g. sweating, dizziness, rhinitis, urinary frequency, blurred vision).
  - It is a muscarinic agonist, so should not be used by patients with asthma or COPD (reduced airways responsiveness), or in patients with bradycardia, bowel obstruction, or angle-closure glaucoma.
- **Acupuncture** may be a useful alternative to pilocarpine in resistant cases [Johnstone et al, 2001].

Oral *Candida* infection

- **Manage predisposing factors** for oral candida, in conjunction with anticandidal therapy:
  - Dry mouth
  - Poor diabetic control
  - Poor denture hygiene
  - Corticosteroid therapy (oral, inhaled, and topical)
- **First-line therapy — topical anticandidal treatment** (amphotericin, miconazole, and nystatin).
  - Although topical treatments are widely used, there are few studies comparing their use [Pankhurst, 2003].
  - Amphotericin and nystatin are not systemically absorbed, so it is important that they are held in the mouth for as long as possible before swallowing. Avoiding eating or drinking for 30 minutes after each dose also helps to increase contact time with the mucosal surface [Regnard and Hockley, 2004]. Note: nystatin is inactivated by chlorhexidine mouthwashes.
  - Although it is a topical treatment, miconazole is absorbed to an extent that possible interactions (e.g. with warfarin) may need to be considered.
- **Second-line therapy — systemic anticandidal therapy**
  - Systemic treatments are reserved for use cases of widespread or severe infection, or when topical anticandidals are not tolerated, or there is no response to topical treatment. However, there are few studies and most are of small sample size [Pankhurst, 2003].
  - Fluconazole is widely used in the UK.
  - Ketoconazole is less commonly used following the Committee on Safety of Medicines (CSM) advice that it should not be used for superficial fungal infections because of rare reports of liver damage.
  - Itraconazole is an alternative, but is less suitable for people at high risk of heart failure. There have only been rare reports of heart failure, but the risk seems to be higher in the elderly, those with cardiac disease, people taking negative inotropic drugs (e.g. calcium-channel blockers), and people taking high doses or receiving longer treatment courses [CSM, 2001].

Mouth ulcers

Treatment of mouth ulceration aims to:
- **Treat the cause of the ulcer** (see below).
- **Prevent secondary infection:** use regular mouth care. Twice daily chlorhexidine mouthwashes can also be used short-term, but may not be suitable for all patients as the alcohol content can cause stinging.
- **Treat the pain of the ulcer** (see *Pain control for oral problems* below for further information).

Aphthous ulcers

- **The underlying cause cannot be identified** in the majority of cases. Correct any underlying iron, folate, or vitamin B_{12} deficiency if the prognosis allows.
- **Chlorhexidine mouthwash** can be used; there is some evidence that it reduces the duration and severity of aphthous ulcers [Porter and Scully, 2003]. It should not be used for longer than 1 month, and can stain the plaque on teeth brown. It should not be used at the same time as nystatin because it reduces the activity of nystatin [Milligan et al, 2001].
- **Topical steroids** can also be tried (triamcinolone oral paste or hydrocortisone lozenges). Again, there are few studies to support their use, but there is some evidence that they reduce the duration of ulcers and hasten pain relief without causing notable local or systemic adverse reactions [Porter and Scully, 2003]. Beclometasone spray or betamethasone soluble tablets are more potent, but have an increased risk of systemic adverse effects and oral candidiasis. They are generally reserved for use when ulceration is extensive, or is at a difficult-to-reach site.
- Tetracycline mouthwash has been used for severe recurrent aphthous ulceration. Although it may reduce the duration and severity of ulcers, it can cause oral candidiasis and a burning-like sensation of the pharynx [Porter et al, 2000]. Tetracycline capsules are no longer available in the UK, so doxycycline capsules are generally substituted instead; the contents of a 100 mg capsule are dispersed in water and rinsed around the mouth for 2–3 minutes, four times a day [BNF 47, 2004].

Oral herpes simplex infection

- **Specific antiviral treatment with oral aciclovir** 200 mg five times a day for 5 days is recommended. The dose should be increased to 400 mg if the patient is immunosuppressed [Regnard and Hockley, 2004].

Chemotherapy- or radiotherapy-induced mucositis

- Mucositis occurs about 5–7 days after chemotherapy administration, or about 2 weeks after starting radiotherapy (due to the 2-week renewal rate of oral mucosa).
- **There is no specific treatment** for oral mucositis, although many strategies have been tried [Kostler et al, 2001]. However, it is self-limiting and heals within 2–3 weeks of the end of treatment.
- **Pain control and routine mouth care are the most important measures.**
- **Discuss management with the oncology team,** as mucositis may limit the patient's ability to tolerate chemotherapy or radiotherapy.

P

Malodorous malignant ulcers

- Management of malodour involves effective wound cleansing using regular mouth care, and use of systemic metronidazole.
- **Metronidazole** is active against anaerobic organisms. Although there are no studies of its use in malignant ulcers in the oral cavity, some small studies in cutaneous malignant ulcers found a marked reduction in odour [Sparrow et al, 1980; Ashford et al, 1984].
- **Treatment may need to be continued over the long term,** as the odour usually returns when treatment is stopped. There is no evidence of reduced effectiveness of metronidazole with prolonged or repeated use. Resistance to metronidazole by the odour-producing anaerobes is unlikely to develop [UK Medicines Information, 2002].

Neutropaenic ulcers

- **Specialist advice should be sought** if neutropaenia is suspected; recovery of the neutrophil count is essential for healing.

Excessive salivation

- **Excessive salivation is uncommon.** It is most commonly caused by oral pain and drugs (e.g. lithium, cholinesterase inhibitors, and muscarinic agonists such as pilocarpine).
- Managing the underlying cause will resolve excess salivation in most cases. Where this is not possible symptomatic treatment with hyoscine hydrobromide can be considered, but sedation is a common adverse effect.
- There are few data to guide dosage recommendations. Experts suggest trying hyoscine hydrobromide 75–150 micrograms sublingually every 8–12 hours or applying hyoscine hydrobromide 1 mg/72 hour patches [Regnard and Hockley, 2004]. Alternatively, consider using drugs with antimuscarinic side effects if the patient has other comorbidities that warrant their use, e.g. consider amitriptyline if the patient also needs treatment for depression or neuropathic pain [Twycross et al, 2002].

Pain control for oral problems

P

- Treat the underlying cause of oral pain where possible. Where this is not possible, or not fully effective, treat pain symptomatically.
- Oral pain can be treated with topical or systemic therapy.
- Topical treatment is preferred to systemic treatment due to the lower incidence of significant adverse effects. Some drugs have both topical and systemic actions, e.g. dispersible diclofenac.
- Systemic analgesics are used when topical therapies are inadequate at controlling pain.

Topical treatment of oral pain

Localized pain

- **Choline salicylate gel** can be used if the pain is well localized, but its effect is short-lived [BNF 47, 2004]. Excessive use should be avoided as this can lead to ulceration, particularly if the gel is trapped under dentures.
- **Topical local anaesthetics have a definite but limited role** in the management of oral ulceration [Twycross et al, 2002], and should be reserved for severe pain (e.g. chemotherapy- or radiotherapy-induced mucositis). Again, their duration of action is relatively short, so they will not provide continuous analgesia throughout the day. Care should also be taken not to anaesthetize the pharynx before meals as this might lead to aspiration or choking. Lidocaine (lignocaine) 5% ointment or 10% spray is suitable for use.
- **Carmellose** paste is thought to provide a protective barrier over the ulcer site, but there is little evidence for its use. Carmellose paste can be difficult to apply effectively to some parts of the mouth [BNF 47, 2004]. It hardens on contact with saliva to form a protective cover over the ulcer.

Diffuse oral pain

- **Benzydamine mouthwash or spray** (a nonsteroidal anti-inflammatory drug) may be more useful if the area is more extensive. However, the duration of action is still short-lived.
- **Diclofenac dispersible tablets** can be used as a mouthwash, and be rinsed around the mouth before swallowing.
- **Topical morphine can be considered for severe pain.** Morphine sulphate 10 mg/5 ml solution can be used as a mouthwash, but this contains alcohol and may cause stinging [Twycross et al, 2002].
- **Carbenoxolone** is thought to provide a protective barrier over the ulcer site, but there is little evidence for its use.
- **Gelclair** is a novel viscous gel that forms a protective film round the entire oral cavity (mechanical protection). It is available on FP10, but is markedly more expensive than other topical measures for pain relief. In general, Gelclair is reserved for severe pain, for example due to oral mucositis.

Systemic treatment of oral pain

- The choice of systemic analgesia will depend on the severity of pain, and the benefits compared with risks for the individual patient.
- **Mild pain:** nonsteroidal anti-inflammatory drug (NSAID) or paracetamol.
- **Mild to moderate pain:** full dose weak opioid *plus* paracetamol or NSAID.
- **Moderate to severe pain:** morphine *plus* paracetamol or NSAID.
- Oral analgesia is preferred where possible, but if the patient is unable to eat or drink (e.g. mucositis) consider using a 24-hour continuous subcutaneous infusion of diamorphine. See the PRODIGY guidance *Palliative care — pain* for further information on starting and titrating oral morphine.
- **Seek specialist advice if pain is difficult to manage.** Some patients may benefit from short-term treatment with ketamine, while thalidomide has been used in cases of resistant mouth ulceration [Twycross et al, 2002].

Oral care in the terminal phase

- Patients in the last 24–48 hours of life often have difficulty taking food, fluid, or oral medication. Good symptom control may allow the dying person to eat, drink, and talk comfortably.
- The symptoms of dry mouth and thirst are very common in dying patients whether they are dehydrated or not. Reversing dehydration only improves symptoms in a very limited number of patients [Ellershaw et al, 1995].
- Simple measures are used as often as wanted to maintain a moist mouth.
- Frequent mouth care is used as often as necessary to maintain a clean mouth. This can easily be carried out by the family, giving them greater involvement in the care of their dying relative.
- In unconscious patients, or patients who have difficulty swallowing, it is easiest to clean and moisten the mouth gently using foam sticks soaked with water [Milligan et al, 2001].
- Pain should be managed symptomatically, using analgesics via a suitable route. Stop treatment of the underlying cause of pain when the burden of treatment outweighs the benefits.

Recognizing the terminal phase

In order to care for dying patients it is essential to diagnose dying. Healthcare professionals are sometimes reluctant to diagnose dying, and therefore the appropriate adjustments in the terminal phase may not be made.

- **The terminal phase** starts a median of 24 hours before death, varying from hours to several days.
- **Patients in the terminal phase have several common features:**
  - They deteriorate day-by-day or faster because of their underlying condition or because of an irreversible complication of their disease.
  - They express a realization that they are dying.
  - They have reduced cognition, and are drowsy or comatose.
  - They are bed-bound.
  - They take little food or fluid, and have difficulty with oral medication.
  - The breathing pattern alters.
  - They are peripherally cyanosed and cold.

[Morita et al, 1998]

Adjustments in the terminal phase

- The terminal phase is a time of adjustments for all [Regnard and Hockley, 2004]:
  - Stop unnecessary drugs and continue with other drugs by an appropriate route.
  - Ensure commonly required medications are available in the house (e.g. cyclizine, diamorphine, hyoscine hydrobromide, and midazolam) so that there is no delay in treatment of new or developing symptoms.
  - Ensure physical symptoms are well controlled.
- **The Liverpool Care Pathway** for the dying patient provides a national framework caring for patients in the terminal phase. It integrates professional communication and documentation integrating national guidelines into clinical practice. Further information can be obtained from www.lcp-mariecurie.org.uk.

References

NHS staff in England can link, free of charge, from references to full text journals by clicking on [Full text] on the PRODIGY website.

1. Ashford, R., Plant, G., Maher, J. and Teare, L. (1984) Double-blind trial of metronidazole in malodorous ulcerating tumours. *Lancet* **1**(8388), 1232–1233.
2. Bagg, J., Sweeney, M.P., Lewis, M.A.O. et al (2003) High prevalence of non-albicans yeasts and detection of anti-fungal resistance in the oral flora of patients with advanced cancer. *Palliative Medicine* **17**(6), 477–481.
3. BNF 47 (2004) *British National Formulary*. 47th edn. London: British Medical Association and Royal Pharmaceutical Society of Great Britain.
4. CSM (2001) Cardiodepressant effects of itraconazole (Sporanox). *Current Problems in Pharmacovigilance* **27**(Aug), 11–12.
5. Davies, A.N. (2000) A comparison of artificial saliva and chewing gum in the management of xerostomia in patients with advanced cancer. *Palliative Medicine* **14**(3), 197–203.
6. Davies, A.N., Daniels, C., Pugh, R. and Sharma, K. (1998) A comparison of artificial saliva and pilocarpine in the management of xerostomia in patients with advanced cancer. *Palliative Medicine* **12**(2), 105–111.
7. Doyle, D., Hanks, G.W.C. and MacDonald, N. (Eds.) (2004) *Oxford textbook of palliative medicine*. 3rd edn. Oxford: Oxford University Press.
8. Ellershaw, J.E., Sutcliffe, J.M. and Saunders, C.M. (1995) Dehydration and the dying patient. *Journal of Pain and Symptom Management* **10**(3), 192–197
9. Epstein, J.B., Emerton, S., Le, N.D. and Stevenson-Moore, P. (1999) A double-blind crossover trial of Oral Balance gel and Biotene toothpaste versus placebo in patients with xerostomia following radiation therapy. *Oral Oncology* **35**(2), 132–137.
10. Johnstone, P.A., Peng, Y.P., May, B.C. et al (2001) Acupuncture for pilocarpine-resistant xerostomia following radiotherapy for head and neck malignancies. *International Journal of Radiation Oncology, Biology, Physics* **50**(2), 353–357.
11. Kostler, W.J., Hejna, M., Wenzel, C. and Zielinski, C.C. (2001) Oral mucositis complicating chemotherapy and/or radiotherapy: options for prevention and treatment. *CA: A Cancer Journal for Clinicians* **51**(5), 290–315.
12. Krishnasamy, M. (1995) Oral problems in advanced cancer. *European Journal of Cancer Care* **4**(4), 173–177.
13. Leflore, S., Anderson, P.L. and Fletcher, C.V. (2000) A risk-benefit evaluation of aciclovir for the treatment and prophylaxis of herpes simplex virus infections. *Drug Safety* **23**(2), 131–142.
14. Miller, M. and Kearney, N. (2001) Oral care for patients with cancer: a review of the literature. *Cancer Nursing* **24**(4), 241–254.
15. Milligan, S., McGill, M., Sweeney, M.P. and Malarkey, C. (2001) Oral care for people with advanced cancer: an evidence-based protocol. *International Journal of Palliative Nursing* **7**(9), 418–426.
16. Morita, T., Ichiki, T., Tsunoda, J. et al (1998) A prospective study on the dying process in terminally ill cancer patients. *American Journal of Hospice & Palliative Care* **15**(4), 217–222.
17. Oneschuk, D., Hanson, J. and Bruera, E. (2000) A survey of mouth pain and dryness in patients with advanced cancer. *Supportive Care in Cancer* **8**(5), 372–376.
18. Pankhurst, C. (2003) Candidiasis (oropharyngeal). *Clinical Evidence* **10**(Dec), 1623 1639.
19. Porter, S. and Scully, C. (2003) *Aphthous ulcers (recurrent)*. Clinical Evidence. Volume 10. www.clinicalevidence.com [Accessed: 01/06/2004].
20. Porter, S.R., Hegarty, A., Kaliakatsou, F. et al (2000) Recurrent aphthous stomatitis. *Clinics in Dermatology* **18**(5), 569–578.
21. Regnard, C. and Hockley, J. (Eds.) (2004) *A guide to symptom relief in palliative care*. 5th edn. Oxford: Radcliffe Medical Press.
22. Scully, C. and Shotts, R. (2000) ABC of oral health: mouth ulcers and other causes of orofacial soreness and pain. *British Medical Journal* **321**(7254), 162–165. [Full text]
23. Sparrow, G., Minton, M., Rubens, R.D. et al (1980) Metronidazole in smelly tumours. *Lancet* **1**(8179), 1185.
24. Twycross, R., Wilcock, A., Charlesworth, S. and Dickman, A. (2002) *Palliative care formulary*. Palliativedrugs.com Ltd. www.palliativedrugs.com [Accessed: 07/06/2005].
25. UK Medicines Information (2002) *Will long-term metronidazole for malodorous wounds cause resistance and therefore reduced efficiency?* UK Medicines Information. www.ukmi.nhs.uk [Accessed: 30/07/2002].
26. Vissink, A., Gravenmade, E.J., Panders, A.K. et al (1983) A clinical comparison between commercially available mucin- and CMC-containing saliva substitutes. *International Journal of Oral Surgery* **12**(4), 232–238.

PRODIGY GUIDANCE

Palliative care — pain

Last revised in February 2005
www.prodigy.nhs.uk/guidance.asp?gt=Palliative care - pain

Applies to people over the age of 16 years

This guidance covers the assessment and management of people with cancer and pain.

This guidance does not cover the management of pain from non-malignant causes, including pain caused by the investigation and treatment of cancer.

There is separate PRODIGY guidance for *Palliative care — cough, Palliative care — dyspnoea, Palliative care — respiratory secretions at the end of life, Palliative care — malodorous malignant ulcer of skin, Palliative care — oral problems* and *Palliative care — nausea/vomiting/malignant bowel obstruction.*

Goals

- To alleviate pain
- To achieve the best quality of life for the patient and their family

Contents

Scenarios

- Overview of pain management p.1478
- Acute severe pain p.1479
- Treating the symptom of pain p.1480
- Managing neuropathic pain p.1482
- Managing bowel colic p.1484
- Difficult to manage pain p.1485
- Managing pain in the terminal phase p.1485

Extended Information, p. 1486

Which scenario?

- **Overview of pain management:** provides an overview of treating a person with cancer and pain with hyperlinks to the other scenarios and the background document.
- **Acute severe pain:** covers the immediate management of a patient in acute severe pain while awaiting emergency admission.
- **Treating the symptom of pain:** covers the management of chronic pain with standard analgesics in the WHO analgesic ladder.
- **Managing neuropathic pain:** covers the management of neuropathic pain with tricyclic antidepressants or antiepileptic drugs.
- **Managing bowel colic:** covers the approach to managing bowel colic.
- **Difficult to manage pain:** provides information on the management difficult pain problems such as when the patient is on the maximum tolerable dose of strong opioid.
- **Managing pain in the terminal phase:** covers adjustments (therapeutic and other) in the terminal phase.

Overview of pain management

Which therapy?

- **Diagnose the cause and type of pain.**
- **Treat acute severe pain** if present. See scenario *Acute severe pain.*
- **Treat the *underlying* cause of pain** if appropriate:
  - **Non-malignant causes of pain.** These are usually managed by treating the underlying cause.
  - **Treat the underlying malignancy to relieve pain** if appropriate; see Management issues *Is treatment of the underlying cause of pain appropriate?*
- **Treat the *symptom* of pain** with standard analgesics in the WHO analgesic ladder. Even when other treatments are given, relieve pain promptly with analgesics. See scenario *Treating the symptom of pain.*
- **Some types of pain require a specific treatment,** for example:
  - **Neuropathic pain** — see scenario *Managing neuropathic pain.*
  - **Bone pain** — treat with standard analgesics while waiting for treatment of the underlying cause (e.g. radiotherapy).
  - **Bowel colic** — see scenario *Managing bowel colic.*
  - **Myofascial pains** — inject trigger point with local anaesthetic or saline.
  - **Oral pain** — see PRODIGY guidance *Palliative care — oral problems.*
  - **Ureteric colic** — relieve colic using intramuscular diclofenac. Use subcutaneous hyoscine butylbromide if renal function is poor. For persistent pain use a strong opioid.

Practical prescribing points

For further information please see the *Medicines Compendium* (www.medicines.org.uk) or the *British National Formulary* (www.bnf.org) or the *Palliative Care Formulary* (www.palliativedrugs.com).

Follow-up advice

- After starting treatment for pain, early follow-up is essential to assess response to treatment and make necessary adjustments. How soon this occurs will depend on the severity of the pain and clinical judgement.
- Subsequent follow-up will depend on the initial response to treatment.

Should I refer or investigate?

Refer?

- Most patients with acute severe pain will require urgent admission to hospital for further investigation and management unless prognosis excludes this.
- Consider referral for all patients where treatment of the underlying cause of pain is a possibility.
- Refer all patients where pain proves difficult to manage.

Investigate?

- Consider investigating the cause of pain if this cannot be established following initial assessment.
- The burden of investigations must be balanced against the likely benefits to the patient of clearly identifying the cause of the pain.

Patient information leaflets

The following PILs are available at www.prodigy.nhs.uk
- Cancerbacup
- Cancer Research UK
- Macmillan Cancer Relief

Drug rationale

- There are no prescriptions offered in this scenario.

Acute severe pain

Which therapy?

- **Acute severe pain in a person with cancer is a medical emergency.**
- **Treat severe pain immediately:**
  - **If opioid-naïve:** give 5 mg (2.5 mg in elderly) diamorphine by subcutaneous injection.
  - **If already taking a regular opioid:** convert the usual 4-hourly *oral* dose to the equivalent dose of *parenteral* morphine or diamorphine, and give by subcutaneous infection.
  - **For colic:** give hyoscine butylbromide 10–20 mg by subcutaneous injection.
- **Arrange emergency admission to secondary care.** Common causes of acute severe pain include:
  - Spinal cord compression
  - Pathological fractures
  - Bleeding into hepatic metastases
  - Note: non-malignant causes should be managed in the usual way.
- **Give intravenous corticosteroids for suspected spinal cord compression** while awaiting admission.
  - Suspect spinal cord compression in all patients with cancer and back pain, particularly when there is associated radiating pain and motor, sensory, or sphincter disturbance.
  - Give whatever corticosteroid is available, preferably 15 mg dexamethasone intravenously.
- **If emergency admission is not appropriate** (e.g. the likely cause does not need urgent management):
  - **Make a full assessment when severe pain is controlled.**
  - Admission may not be appropriate if a person with spinal cord compression is in the last days of life. Give immediate intravenous corticosteroids and continue with oral dexamethasone 16 mg daily, starting the following day.

Practical prescribing points

For further information please see the *Medicines Compendium* (www.medicines.org.uk) or the *British National Formulary* (www.bnf.org) or the *Palliative Care Formulary* (www.palliativedrugs.com).
- The equivalent subcutaneous dose of morphine is half the oral morphine dose.
- The equivalent subcutaneous dose of diamorphine is a third of the oral morphine dose.
- For example, if the patient is taking oral morphine 30 mg twice a day, divide the total 24-hour dose by 6 to obtain the 4-hourly dose, i.e. 60 mg divided by 6 – 10 mg oral morphine. This is equivalent to 5 mg subcutaneous morphine or 3 mg subcutaneous diamorphine (usually rounded down for convenience to 2.5 mg).

Follow-up advice

- After giving treatment for acute severe pain it is essential to stay with the patient to assess the response to treatment and, if necessary, give further treatment until the pain settles or the person is transferred to hospital.
- If the person is not admitted, early follow-up is essential. How soon this occurs will depend on the severity of the pain and on clinical judgement.

Should I refer or investigate?

Refer?

- Most patients will require urgent admission to hospital for further investigation and management unless prognosis excludes this.

Investigate?

- Once the acute severe pain has been controlled investigations to determine the cause may be required.
- The burden of investigations must be balanced against the likely benefits to the patient of clearly identifying the cause of the pain.

Patient information leaflets

The following PILs are available at www.prodigy.nhs.uk
- Cancerbacup
- Cancer Research UK
- Macmillan Cancer Relief

Drug rationale

Drugs not included

- **Injectable opioids other than diamorphine** are not commonly used for emergency treatment of pain in primary care.
- **Corticosteroids other than dexamethasone and hydrocortisone** are not commonly used for emergency treatment in the UK.

Drugs included

- **Diamorphine** is included for the emergency treatment of acute severe pain.
- **Hyoscine butylbromide** is commonly used to relieve pain from bowel colic.
- **Intravenous dexamethasone** is indicated if spinal cord compression is suspected.
- **Intravenous hydrocortisone** is commonly carried by GPs in their emergency treatment bags, and is an alternative if dexamethasone is unavailable.

Prescriptions

Emergency drugs: prescriptions for reimbursement

Diamorphine 5mg injection
- Age from 16 years onwards
- Instructions for handwriting CD prescription for diamorphine: Patients name and address. Diamorphine 10mg injection. State the dose and dose interval, e.g. 5-10 mg every 4 hours when required. Supply 2 (two) ampoules. Signed and dated.

P

- Water for injection (5ml). Use as directed; supply 2 5ml ampoule; NHS Cost £0.56.

Hyoscine butylbromide 20mg/ml injection

- Age from 16 years onwards
- Hyoscine butylbromide 20mg/ml. For intravenous, intramuscular, or subcutaneous injection; supply 10 1ml ampoules; NHS Cost £2.00.

Dexamethasone sodium phosphate 8mg/2ml injection

- Age from 16 years onwards
- Dexamethasone sod phos 8mg/2ml. For intravenous injection; supply 2 2ml vials; NHS Cost £2.54.

Dexamethasone sodium phosphate 5mg/ml injection

- Age from 16 years onwards
- Dexamethasone sod phos 5mg/ml. For intravenous injection; supply 3 1ml ampoule; NHS Cost £2.49.

Hydrocortisone 100mg injection

- Age from 16 years onwards
- Hydrocortisone 100mg injection. For intravenous injection after reconstitution; supply 2 vials; NHS Cost £2.32.

Treating the symptom of pain

Which therapy?

- **Diagnose** the cause and type of pain
- **Treat the underlying cause** of pain where possible — see Management issues *Is treatment of the underlying cause appropriate?*
- **Treat types of pain** requiring a specific treatment — see Management issues *Which types of pain may need a specific approach?*
- **Treat the symptom of pain using the WHO analgesic ladder.** Even when other treatments are given for pain, pain should always be relieved promptly with analgesics.
  - **All patients with moderate to severe cancer pain should receive a trial of strong opioid** as well as a non-opioid analgesic, regardless of the cause of the pain.
  - **For other patients, start at step 1 of the analgesic ladder** and titrate upwards until the patient is comfortable:
    - **Step 1** — give paracetamol or a NSAID (nonsteroidal anti-inflammatory drug).
    - **Step 2** — give a full dose of weak opioid (e.g. codeine 30–60 mg) *plus* paracetamol or a NSAID.
    - **Step 3** — give morphine *plus* paracetamol or a NSAID.
  - **Review regularly and step treatment up or down the analgesic ladder as necessary.**

Practical prescribing points

For further information please see the *Medicines Compendium* (www.medicines.org.uk) or the *British National Formulary* (www.bnf.org) or the *Palliative Care Formulary* (www.palliativedrugs.com).

Starting and titrating morphine

- **The start dose will vary between patients:**
  - If opioid-naïve: use morphine solution 2.5 mg every 4 hours *and* 'as required'.
  - If already on a weak opioid: switch to morphine solution 5–10 mg every 4 hours *and* 'as required'.
- After 1–2 days, calculate the total dose given over 24 hours, and use this to recalculate the 4-hourly dose. (For example, if the patient has taken a total of 60 mg oral morphine in the last 24 hours: 60 mg divided by 6 = 10 mg oral morphine.) The recalculated dose should now be given every 4 hours *and* as required.
- Repeat this process every 1–2 days until pain is controlled.
- **Once a stable daily dosage of morphine solution has been reached, switch to the same total daily dose of once- or twice-daily m/r morphine.**

Managing common adverse effects

- Co-prescribe a regular stimulant laxative with a faecal softener (e.g. senna + lactulose or co-danthrusate) to prevent opioid-induced constipation.
- Give an anti-emetic (e.g. haloperidol or metoclopramide) regularly for the first few days to prevent opioid-induced nausea and vomiting. Then use as required.
- Sedation is common, but most patients become tolerant within a few days after a dose increase.
- **Driving:** advise patients not to drive if adversely affected, but tolerance to sedative effects usually develops within a week or two of dose stabilization.

NSAIDs

- NSAIDs may worsen asthma, hypertension, renal impairment, or cardiac failure.
- **For people at higher risk of gastrointestinal adverse events with NSAIDs:**
  - Either use paracetamol instead of a NSAID
  - Or use a gastroprotective agent with a standard NSAID (omeprazole, lansoprazole)
  - Or use a COX-2 selective NSAID alone (without gastroprotection)
- **For people with cardiovascular disease:**
  - Avoid celecoxib in people with established ischaemic heart disease, cerebrovascular disease, or moderate or severe heart failure; and in people on aspirin (gastrointestinal safety benefits lost).
  - Avoid ibuprofen — it may reduce the cardiovascular protective effect of low-dose aspirin.

Laxatives

- Stimulant laxatives can cause abdominal cramp — avoid if intestinal obstruction is a possibility.

Follow-up advice

- After starting treatment for pain, early follow-up is essential to assess response to treatment and make necessary adjustments. How soon this occurs will depend on the severity of the pain and clinical judgement.
- Subsequent follow-up will depend on the initial response to treatment.

Should I refer or investigate?

Refer?

- Most patients with acute severe pain will require urgent admission to hospital for further investigation and management unless prognosis excludes this.
- Consider referral of all patients where treatment of the underlying cause of pain is a possibility.
- Refer all patients where pain proves difficult to manage.

Investigate?

- Consider investigating the cause of pain if this cannot be established following initial assessment.
- The burden of investigations must be balanced against the likely benefits to the patient of clearly identifying the cause of the pain.

Patient information leaflets

The following PILs are available at www.prodigy.nhs.uk

- Cancerbacup
- Cancer Research UK
- Macmillan Cancer Relief

Drug rationale

Drugs not included

- **Standard NSAIDs other than ibuprofen, diclofenac, or naproxen** are associated with a higher risk of gastrointestinal adverse events [Henry et al, 1996; Hernández-Diaz and Rodriguez, 2000; CSM, 2003]. Modified-release products are relatively more expensive. Suppositories are an option if the oral route is no longer available.
- **Weak opioids other than codeine** could be used, but there are surprisingly few data on their relative efficacy and adverse effects with chronic use, and many preparations are more expensive than codeine tablets.
- **Low-dose weak opioids with paracetamol** (e.g. co-codamol 8/500, co-dydramol 10/500) are subtherapeutic and should not be used for pain control in patients with cancer [SIGN, 2000].
- **Strong opioids other than morphine** have not, so far, demonstrated advantages that would make them preferable as the first-choice oral opioid for cancer pain [Hanks et al, 2001].
- **Laxatives:** other combinations of a stimulant with a faecal softener can also be achieved using bisacodyl or glycerol with lactulose or docusate sodium.
- **Gastroprotective agents other than omeprazole and lansoprazole** are not included. Other proton pump inhibitors (PPIs) are not licensed for both the prevention and treatment of NSAID-induced ulcers. Although misoprostol is also effective, it is generally accepted that it is less well tolerated than PPIs.
- **COX-2 selective NSAIDs other than celecoxib** are not included. Rofecoxib and valdecoxib have been withdrawn from the market. A recent drug safety study found that the rate of complicated upper gastrointestinal events (perforation/bleeding) was higher with meloxicam than celecoxib [Layton et al, 2003]. Etoricoxib is a black triangle drug, and further data from post-marketing safety surveillance are awaited. Etodolac is less widely used than celecoxib in the UK [DH, 2003].

Drugs included

- **Paracetamol** has minimal adverse effects at the recommended daily dose.
- **Standard NSAIDs: ibuprofen, diclofenac, and naproxen** have a good balance of efficacy against adverse effect profile [Henry et al, 1996; Hernández-Diaz and Rodriguez, 2000; CSM, 2003]. Naproxen has a long half-life; it may be particularly useful for people who suffer pain on waking. NSAIDs are an alternative to paracetamol at all steps of the WHO ladder.
- **Codeine** at higher doses (30–60 mg per dose) is the first-choice weak opioid for mild to moderate cancer pain. It should be used with paracetamol or a NSAID: codeine 60 mg plus paracetamol has been shown to provide more pain relief than either codeine 60 mg alone or paracetamol 1000 mg alone [Moore et al, 1997]. Codeine should be prescribed separately to allow flexibility of dosing and titration of analgesic effect.
- **Morphine** is the first-choice strong opioid for moderate to severe cancer pain for reasons of familiarity, availability, and cost, rather than proven superiority over other strong opioids [Hanks et al, 2001].
- **Anti-emetics: haloperidol and metoclopramide** are included for prevention of nausea and vomiting associated with initiation of morphine.
- **Laxatives:** it is generally accepted that a stimulant laxative in combination with a faecal softener should be taken regularly to prevent opioid-induced constipation. Co-danthramer, co-danthrusate, senna plus docusate sodium, and senna plus lactulose are included.
- **Gastroprotective agents: omeprazole and lansoprazole** are recommended for first-line use for the prevention or treatment of ulcers induced by standard NSAIDs.
- **COX-2 selective NSAIDs: celecoxib** is included for use in people at high risk of NSAID-induced gastrointestinal adverse events. It is an alternative to using a standard NSAID with a gastroprotective agent.

Prescriptions

Step 1: paracetamol or NSAID

Paracetamol 1g up to four times a day

- Age from 16 years onwards
- Paracetamol 500mg tablets. Take two tablets every 4 to 6 hours when required for pain relief. Maximum of 8 tablets in 24 hours; supply 200 tablets; NHS Cost £1.48; OTC Cost £2.61.

Ibuprofen 400mg three times a day

- Age from 16 years onwards
- Ibuprofen 400mg tablets. Take one tablet three times a day; supply 84 tablets; NHS Cost £2.46.

Diclofenac sodium 50mg e/c three times a day

- Age from 16 years onwards
- Diclofenac 50mg e/c tablets. Take one tablet three times a day; supply 84 tablets; NHS Cost £3.55.

Naproxen 250mg to 500mg twice a day

- Age from 16 years onwards
- Naproxen 250mg tablets. Take one to two tablets twice a day; supply 112 tablets; NHS Cost £5.88.

Step 2: codeine PLUS paracetamol or NSAID

Add on: codeine 30-60mg up to four times a day

- Age from 16 years onwards
- Codeine 30mg tablets. Take one to two tablets every 4 to 6 hours when required for pain relief. Maximum of 8 tablets in 24 hours; supply 60 tablets; NHS Cost £2.92.

Paracetamol 1g up to four times a day

- Age from 16 years onwards
- Paracetamol 500mg tablets. Take two tablets every 4 to 6 hours when required for pain relief. Maximum of 8 tablets in 24 hours; supply 200 tablets; NHS Cost £1.48; OTC Cost £2.61.

Ibuprofen 400mg three times a day

- Age from 16 years onwards
- Ibuprofen 400mg tablets. Take one tablet three times a day; supply 84 tablets; NHS Cost £2.46.

Diclofenac sodium 50mg e/c three times a day

- Age from 16 years onwards
- Diclofenac 50mg e/c tablets. Take one tablet three times a day; supply 84 tablets; NHS Cost £3.55.

Naproxen 250mg to 500mg twice a day

- Age from 16 years onwards
- Naproxen 250mg tablets. Take one to two tablets twice a day; supply 112 tablets; NHS Cost £5.88.

Step 3: morphine PLUS paracetamol or NSAID

Morphine solution: initial titration for opioid-naive people

- Age from 16 years onwards
- Morphine sulphate 10mg/5ml sol. Take 1.25ml regularly every 4 hours, and when required to relieve pain; supply 100 ml; NHS Cost £2.08.

Morphine sol: initial titration if previously on weak opioid

- Age from 16 years onwards
- Morphine sulphate 10mg/5ml sol. Take 2.5ml to 5ml regularly every 4 hours, and when required to relieve pain; supply 200 ml; NHS Cost £4.16.

Paracetamol 1g up to four times a day

- Age from 16 years onwards
- Paracetamol 500mg tablets. Take two tablets every 4 to 6 hours when required for pain relief. Maximum of 8 tablets in 24 hours; supply 200 tablets; NHS Cost £1.48; OTC Cost £2.61.

Ibuprofen 400mg three times a day

- Age from 16 years onwards
- Ibuprofen 400mg tablets. Take one tablet three times a day; supply 84 tablets; NHS Cost £2.46.

Diclofenac sodium 50mg e/c three times a day

- Age from 16 years onwards
- Diclofenac 50mg e/c tablets. Take one tablet three times a day; supply 84 tablets; NHS Cost £3.55.

Naproxen 250mg to 500mg twice a day

- Age from 16 years onwards
- Naproxen 250mg tablets. Take one to two tablets twice a day; supply 112 tablets; NHS Cost £5.88.

Alternative NSAID options if high risk of GI adverse effects

Paracetamol 1g up to four times a day

- Age from 16 years onwards
- Paracetamol 500mg tablets. Take two tablets every 4 to 6 hours when required for pain relief. Maximum of 8 tablets in 24 hours; supply 200 tablets; NHS Cost £1.48; OTC Cost £2.61.

Ibuprofen + omeprazole

- Age from 16 years onwards
- Ibuprofen 400mg tablets. Take one tablet three times a day; supply 84 tablets; NHS Cost £2.46.
- Omeprazole 20mg capsules. Take one capsule once a day; supply 28 capsules; NHS Cost £12.75.

Ibuprofen + lansoprazole

- Age from 16 years onwards
- Ibuprofen 400mg tablets. Take one tablet three times a day; supply 84 tablets; NHS Cost £2.46.
- Lansoprazole 30mg capsules. Take one capsule once a day, on an empty stomach; supply 28 capsules; NHS Cost £23.63.

Diclofenac + omeprazole

- Age from 16 years onwards
- Diclofenac 50mg e/c tablets. Take one tablet three times a day; supply 84 tablets; NHS Cost £3.55.
- Omeprazole 20mg capsules. Take one capsule once a day; supply 28 capsules; NHS Cost £12.75.

Diclofenac + lansoprazole

- Age from 16 years onwards
- Diclofenac 50mg e/c tablets. Take one tablet three times a day; supply 84 tablets; NHS Cost £3.55.
- Lansoprazole 30mg capsules. Take one capsule once a day, on an empty stomach; supply 28 capsules; NHS Cost £23.63.

Naproxen + omeprazole

- Age from 16 years onwards
- Naproxen 250mg tablets. Take one to two tablets twice a day; supply 112 tablets; NHS Cost £5.52.
- Omeprazole 20mg capsules. Take one capsule once a day; supply 28 capsules; NHS Cost £12.75.

Naproxen + lansoprazole

- Age from 16 years onwards
- Naproxen 250mg tablets. Take one to two tablets twice a day; supply 112 tablets; NHS Cost £5.52.
- Lansoprazole 30mg capsules. Take one capsule once a day, on an empty stomach; supply 28 capsules; NHS Cost £23.63.

Celecoxib 100mg twice a day

- Age from 16 years onwards
- Celecoxib 100mg capsules. Take one capsule twice a day; supply 60 capsules; NHS Cost £21.55.

Laxatives and antiemetics (for use with morphine)

Co-danthramer 25mg/200mg capsules

- Age from 16 years onwards
- Co-danthramer 25/200mg caps. Take one to two capsules at night; supply 14 capsules; NHS Cost £3.00.

Co-danthrusate 50mg/60mg capsules

- Age from 16 years onwards
- Co-danthrusate 50/60mg caps. Take one to three capsules at night; supply 21 capsules; NHS Cost £4.49.

Senna + lactulose

- Age from 16 years onwards
- Senna 7.5mg tablets. Take two tablets at night; supply 60 tablets; NHS Cost £0.86.
- Lactulose 3.35g/5ml solution. Take three 5ml spoonfuls twice a day; supply 1000 ml; NHS Cost £4.86.

Senna + docusate

- Age from 16 years onwards
- Senna 7.5mg tablets. Take two tablets at night; supply 60 tablets; NHS Cost £0.86.
- Docusate 100mg capsules. Take one capsule three times a day; supply 84 capsules; NHS Cost £6.72.

Haloperidol 1.5mg to 3mg at night

- Age from 16 years onwards
- Haloperidol 1.5mg tablets. Take one to two tablets at night when required for sickness; supply 56 tablets; NHS Cost £3.22.

Metoclopramide 10mg three times a day

- Age from 20 years onwards
- Metoclopramide 10mg tablets. Take one tablet up to three times a day when required for sickness; supply 84 tablets; NHS Cost £2.61.

Managing neuropathic pain

Which therapy?

- **Assess cause and type of pain**
  - Treat underlying cause where appropriate — see Management issues *Is treatment of the underlying cause of pain appropriate?*
  - Decide if pain is predominantly neuropathic or mixed (i.e. neuropathic pain mixed with somatic or visceral pain).
- **If the pain is neuropathic mixed with somatic or visceral pain:**
  - **Start treatment with standard analgesics** in the WHO ladder and titrate upwards until pain is relieved or until the adverse effects of drugs limit further dose increases.
  - **Start either a tricyclic antidepressant (TCA) or an antiepileptic drug (AED)** and continue analgesics if pain with a neuropathic character persists.
    - Suitable first-line TCAs: amitriptyline, imipramine, and nortriptyline.
    - Suitable first-line AEDs: gabapentin and carbamazepine.
  - Titrate the dose of TCA or AED upwards until pain settles or adverse effects limit further dose increases.
- **If the pain is pure or predominantly neuropathic:**
  - **Start either a TCA or AED** depending on the relative contraindications, possible drug interactions, and risk of adverse effects for each individual patient.

- Titrate the dose of TCA or AED upwards until pain settles or adverse effects limits further dose increases.

ractical prescribing points

ɔr further information please see the *Medicines ɔmpendium* (www.medicines.org.uk) or the *British ational Formulary* (www.bnf.org) or the *Palliative Care ɔrmulary* (www.palliativedrugs.com).

actors affecting the choice of TCA or AED

Elderly: consider choosing gabapentin or nortriptyline. The elderly are more sensitive to postural hypotension and antimuscarinic effects of other drugs.
Cardiac disease: use gabapentin, or use nortriptyline with caution. Avoid TCAs or carbamazepine if possible.
Prostatism, narrow-angle glaucoma, urinary retention: use gabapentin.
Epilepsy or risk of seizures: avoid TCAs as they lower the seizure threshold.
Bipolar disorder: caution with TCAs (may precipitate mania).
Renal impairment: reduce the dose of gabapentin. See the *Medicines Compendium* (www.medicines.org.uk) for dosage information.

ollow-up advice

After starting treatment for pain, early follow-up is essential to assess response to treatment and make necessary adjustments. How soon this occurs will depend on the severity of the pain and on clinical judgement.
Subsequent follow-up will depend on the initial response to treatment.

hould I refer or investigate?

efer?

Most patients with acute severe pain will require urgent admission to hospital for further investigation and management unless prognosis excludes this.
Consider referral for all patients where treatment of the underlying cause of pain is a possibility.
Refer all patients where pain proves difficult to manage.

ıvestigate?

Consider investigating the cause of pain if this cannot be established following initial assessment.
The burden of investigations must be balanced against the likely benefits to the patient of clearly identifying the cause of the pain.

'atient information leaflets

he following PILs are available at www.prodigy.nhs.uk
Cancerbacup
Cancer Research UK
Macmillan Cancer Relief

)rug rationale

rugs not included

Tricyclic antidepressants other than amitriptyline, imipramine, and nortriptyline are not included. Maprotiline and desipramine have also been found to be effective, but maprotiline has a high incidence of rash and desipramine is not available in the UK.

- **Sodium valproate** is commonly used in practice, but there are no studies to support its use [Wiffen et al, 2000].
- **Pregabalin** has recently been licensed for neuropathic pain, but it is a black triangle drug and further post-marketing safety data are needed. Dizziness, somnolence, blurred vision, gastrointestinal adverse effects, and weight gain are common adverse effects.

Drugs included

- **Amitriptyline** is the most widely studied and is commonly used for neuropathic pain in the UK [McQuay and Moore, 1997].
- **Imipramine** is a less sedative alternative to amitriptyline.
- **Nortriptyline** is an alternative to amitriptyline for people at increased risk of adverse effects, particularly the elderly [Lussier and Portenoy, 2004].
- **Gabapentin** is effective in several types of neuropathic pain, seems to be well tolerated, and has few drug interactions [Wiffen et al, 2000].
- **Carbamazepine** has traditionally been used for the treatment of neuropathic pain, but has only been studied in trigeminal neuralgia [Wiffen et al, 2000]. It must be titrated very slowly to avoid adverse effects.
- For prescriptions for standard analgesics for use in the WHO ladder, see scenario *Treating the symptom of pain.*

Prescriptions

Start doses of adjuvant analgesics

Amitriptyline: titrate up from 10mg daily until pain settles
- Age from 16 years onwards
- Amitriptyline 10mg tablets. Increase the dose as directed on the right hand side of the prescription until the pain settles; supply 70 tablets; NHS Cost £1.95.

Imipramine: titrate up from 10mg daily until pain settles
- Age from 16 years onwards
- Imipramine 10mg tablets. Increase the dose as directed on the right hand side of the prescription until the pain settles; supply 70 tablets; NHS Cost £2.13.

Nortriptyline: titrate up from 10mg daily until pain settles
- Age from 16 years onwards
- Nortriptyline 10mg tablets. Increase the dose as directed on the right hand side of the prescription until the pain settles; supply 70 tablets; NHS Cost £8.44.

Gabapentin: initial titration from 300mg to 900mg per day
- Age from 18 years onwards
- Gabapentin 100mg capsules. Take one capsule three times a day for 3 days, then take two capsules three times a day for 3 days, then take three capsules three times a day; supply 36 capsules; NHS Cost £8.22.

Carbamazepine:titrate up from 100mg daily until pain settles
- Age from 16 years onwards
- Carbamazepine 100mg tablets. Increase the dose as directed on the right hand side of the prescription until the pain settles; supply 70 tablets; NHS Cost £2.03.

Gabapentin and carbamazepine maintenance doses

Gabapentin 300mg three times a day
- Age from 18 years onwards
- Gabapentin 300mg capsules. Take one capsule three times a day; supply 84 capsules; NHS Cost £44.52.

Gabapentin 400mg three times a day
- Age from 18 years onwards
- Gabapentin 400mg capsules. Take one capsule three times a day; supply 84 capsules; NHS Cost £51.52.

Gabapentin 600mg three times a day
- Age from 18 years onwards
- Gabapentin 600mg tablets. Take one tablet three times a day; supply 84 tablets; NHS Cost £89.04.

Gabapentin 800mg three times a day
- Age from 18 years onwards
- Gabapentin 400mg capsules. Take two capsules three times a day; supply 168 capsules; NHS Cost £103.04.

Carbamazepine 200mg twice a day
- Age from 16 years onwards
- Carbamazepine 200mg tablets. Take one tablet twice a day; supply 56 tablets; NHS Cost £3.34.

Carbamazepine 200mg three times a day
- Age from 16 years onwards
- Carbamazepine 200mg tablets. Take one tablet three times a day; supply 84 tablets; NHS Cost £4.50.

Carbamazepine 200mg four times a day
- Age from 16 years onwards
- Carbamazepine 200mg tablets. Take one tablet four times a day; supply 112 tablets; NHS Cost £6.68.

Amitriptyline maintenance doses

Amitriptyline 25mg at night
- Age from 16 years onwards
- Amitriptyline 25mg tablets. Take one tablet at night; supply 28 tablets; NHS Cost £0.80.

Amitriptyline 50mg at night
- Age from 16 years onwards
- Amitriptyline 50mg tablets. Take one tablet at night; supply 28 tablets; NHS Cost £1.20.

Amitriptyline 75mg at night
- Age from 16 years onwards
- Amitriptyline 25mg tablets. Take three tablets at night; supply 84 tablets; NHS Cost £2.40.

Imipramine maintenance doses

Imipramine 25mg at night
- Age from 16 years onwards
- Imipramine 25mg tablets. Take one tablet at night; supply 28 tablets; NHS Cost £1.01.

Imipramine 50mg at night
- Age from 16 years onwards
- Imipramine 25mg tablets. Take two tablets at night; supply 56 tablets; NHS Cost £2.02.

Imipramine 75mg at night
- Age from 16 years onwards
- Imipramine 25mg tablets. Take three tablets at night; supply 84 tablets; NHS Cost £3.03.

Nortriptyline maintenance doses

Nortriptyline 25mg at night
- Age from 16 years onwards
- Nortriptyline 25mg tablets. Take one tablet at night; supply 28 tablets; NHS Cost £6.87.

Nortriptyline 50mg at night
- Age from 16 years onwards
- Nortriptyline 25mg tablets. Take two tablets at night; supply 56 tablets; NHS Cost £13.73.

Nortriptyline 75mg at night
- Age from 16 years onwards
- Nortriptyline 25mg tablets. Take three tablets at night; supply 84 tablets; NHS Cost £20.60.

Managing bowel colic

Which therapy?

- **Assess** the cause and type of pain.
- **Treat underlying causes** where possible, e.g. constipatic or *operable* malignant bowel obstruction — see PRODIGY guidance *Palliative care — nausea/vomiting malignant bowel obstruction* for further information.
- **If bowel colic is present alone:**
  - Relieve pain with subcutaneous hyoscine butylbromide 10–20 mg up to three times a day (unlicensed route of administration).
- **If there is both colicky and continuous pain**
  - **In patients on a strong opioid:**
    - Titrate opioid upwards until the continuous pain is relieved.
    - If *colic* persists, add in hyoscine butylbromide.
  - **In patients who are *not* on a strong opioid** expert opinion differs when it comes to starting treatment. Start treatment based on clinical judgement:
    - Start a strong opioid and add in hyoscine if colic persists.
    - Start hyoscine butylbromide and add in a strong opioid if continuous pain persists.
    - Start hyoscine butylbromide plus a strong opioid if both types of pain are present.

Practical prescribing points

For further information please see the *Medicines Compendium* (www.medicines.org.uk) or the *British National Formulary* (www.bnf.org) or the *Palliative Care Formulary* (www.palliativedrugs.com).
- Antimuscarinics may exacerbate tachycardia, hypertension, and urinary retention.

Follow-up advice

- After starting treatment for pain, early follow-up is essential to assess response to treatment and make necessary adjustments. How soon this occurs will depend on the severity of the pain and clinical judgement.
- Subsequent follow-up will depend on the initial respons to treatment.

Should I refer or investigate?

Refer?

- Most patients with acute severe pain will require urgent admission to hospital for further investigation and management unless prognosis excludes this.
- Consider referral for all patients where treatment of the underlying cause of pain is a possibility.
- Refer all patients where pain proves difficult to manage

Investigate?

- Consider investigating the cause of pain if this cannot b established following initial assessment.
- The burden of investigations must be balanced against the likely benefits to the patient of clearly identifying th cause of the pain.

Patient information leaflets

The following PILs are available at www.prodigy.nhs.uk
- Cancerbacup
- Cancer Research UK
- Macmillan Cancer Relief

)rug rationale

)rugs not included

Hyoscine hydrobromide is an alternative antispasmodic, but causes sedation.

)rugs included

Hyoscine butylbromide has an antispasmodic action and does not cause sedation.

'rescriptions

Iyoscine butylbromide

yoscine butylbromide injection: 10-20mg up to 3 times a ay

Age from 16 years onwards

Hyoscine butylbromide 20mg/ml. Give 0.5ml (10mg) to 1ml (20mg) up to three times a day by subcutaneous, intramuscular, or intravenous injection; supply 10 1ml ampoules; NHS Cost £2.03.

Difficult to manage pain

Vhich therapy?

'henever pain proves difficult to manage, we strongly commend seeking specialist help from the palliative care am or Macmillan nursing team.

ıin, whatever its cause, will respond to a strong opioid if ;ed at a sufficient dose. However, the adverse effects of rong opioids may limit their maximum effective dose.

'hen pain does not respond well to treatment:

Reconsider the diagnosis:

- Review the history and examination. Consider further investigations if appropriate.
- Does the pain have a non-malignant cause?
- Does the pain have a malignant cause?
- Is the pain caused by treatment?

Reconsider the treatment:

- Is the underlying cause of pain treatable? — see Management issues *Is treatment of the underlying cause appropriate?*
- Would the type of pain (e.g. neuropathic pain) benefit from a specific treatment? — see Management issues *Which types of pain may need a specific approach?*
- Have the adverse effects of strong opioids been optimally managed when they limit further dose increases? — see Medicines management: Standard analgesics *Managing the adverse effects of morphine.*

Consider factors increasing the perception of pain:

- Is there unresolved psychological, social, or spiritual distress?

Consider further treatment in secondary care:

- Is an interventional technique appropriate? See Management issues What should I do if pain is still difficult to manage *Interventional techniques.*
- Would a change in opioid help? See Management issues What should I do if pain is still difficult to manage *Switching strong opioid.*

'ractical prescribing points

or further information please see the *Medicines 'ompendium* (www.medicines.org.uk) or the *British 'ational Formulary* (www.bnf.org) or the *Palliative Care ormulary* (www.palliativedrugs.com).

Follow-up advice

- After starting treatment for pain, early follow-up is essential to assess response to treatment and make necessary adjustments. How soon this occurs will depend on the severity of the pain and clinical judgement.
- Subsequent follow-up will depend on the initial response to treatment.

Should I refer or investigate?

Refer?

- Whenever pain proves difficult to manage, we strongly recommend seeking specialist help from the palliative care team or Macmillan nursing team.
- Most patients with acute severe pain will require urgent admission to hospital for further investigation and management unless prognosis excludes this.
- Consider referral for all patients where treatment of the underlying cause of pain is a possibility.

Investigate?

- Consider investigating the cause of pain if this cannot be established following initial assessment.
- The burden of investigations must be balanced against the likely benefits to the patient of clearly identifying the cause of the pain.

Patient information leaflets

The following PILs are available at www.prodigy.nhs.uk

- Cancerbacup
- Cancer Research UK
- Macmillan Cancer Relief

Drug rationale

- There are no prescriptions offered in this scenario.

Managing pain in the terminal phase

Which therapy?

- **Confirm the patient is in the terminal phase:** patients in the terminal phase have several common features:
  - Deteriorating day-by-day or faster because of their underlying condition, or because of an irreversible complication of their disease
  - Patient expresses a realisation that they are dying
  - Reduced cognition, drowsy or comatose
  - Bed-bound
  - Taking little food or fluid and having difficulty with oral medication
  - Altered breathing pattern
  - Peripherally cyanosed and cold
- **Adjustments in the terminal phase**
  - **Stop unnecessary drugs:** continue with other drugs by an appropriate route.
  - **Ensure commonly required medications are available in the house** (e.g. cyclizine, diamorphine, hyoscine hydrobromide, and midazolam) so that there is no delay in treatment of new or developing symptoms.
  - Ensure physical symptoms are well controlled.
  - Explore understanding and provide appropriate explanation of the situation to the patient, family, and other professional carers.
  - Set realistic goals.

- Ensure that religious and spiritual care is offered if wanted.
- Ensure the environment is appropriate.
- **Consider using The Liverpool Care Pathway for the Dying Patient** (www.lcp-mariecurie.org.uk).

Reviewing drugs for pain in the last hours and days

- **Paracetamol and NSAIDs:** give paracetamol or diclofenac suppositories or switch to a 24-hour subcutaneous infusion of diamorphine (depending on clinical need).
- **Opioids:** convert to a 24-hour subcutaneous infusion of diamorphine. Note: divide the total daily dose of *oral* morphine by three to calculate the 24-hour dose of subcutaneous diamorphine.
- **Benzodiazepines:** use a 24-hour subcutaneous infusion of midazolam.
- **Antidepressants:** stop.
- **Antiepileptic drugs:** stop, use carbamazepine suppositories once a day, or use a 24-hour subcutaneous infusion of midazolam.
- **Dexamethasone:** stopping dexamethasone in the terminal phase lacks expert consensus.
  - The onset of withdrawal symptoms (including agitation and distress) is very variable, but is unlikely within the first 24 hours of stopping.
  - Alternatively, dexamethasone can be given as a single morning subcutaneous bolus. One milligram of oral dexamethasone is equivalent to 1.2 mg dexamethasone phosphate or 1.3 mg dexamethasone sodium phosphate. Adjust the dose to the nearest volume that can easily be measured.

Practical prescribing points

For further information please see the *Medicines Compendium* (www.medicines.org.uk) or the *British National Formulary* (www.bnf.org) or the *Palliative Care Formulary* (www.palliativedrugs.com).

Mixing drugs in syringe drivers

Always follow local palliative care guidelines or seek advice from local palliative care services or hospital pharmacy drug information services *before* mixing drugs in a syringe driver. The following information is included as a brief guide when these sources of help are unavailable:

- Check compatibilities before mixing drugs. See www.palliativedrugs.com, or Table 1 below.
- Use water for injection as the diluent when mixing drugs in a syringe driver (except for octreotide and ketamine).
- Do not use solutions that are cloudy or have precipitated.

Follow-up advice

- Regular review and reassessment of pain are an integral part of ongoing management.

Should I refer or investigate?

- Avoid unnecessary investigations.

Refer?

- Seek help from the palliative care team or Macmillan nurse team if pain is difficult to control.
- Refer to the district nurse to arrange involvement of social services, Marie Curie Cancer Care nursing, and other services to support the patient to remain at home. Some areas provide enhanced care at the end of life, and some palliative care units provide a hospice-at-home service.
- Arrange support for spiritual/religious needs if wanted.

Investigate?

- Avoid unnecessary investigations.

Patient information leaflets

The following PILs are available at www.prodigy.nhs.uk

- Cancerbacup
- Cancer Research UK
- Macmillan Cancer Relief

Drug rationale

Drugs included

- **A terminal phase stand-by drug pack** containing drugs commonly needed at the end of life is included. The pac contains cyclizine, diamorphine, hyoscine hydrobromid midazolam, and water for injection [Ellershaw and Griffiths, 2003].

Prescriptions

Terminal phase standby drug pack

Standby drug pack

- Age from 16 years onwards
- Midazolam 5mg/ml injection. For intravenous or subcutaneous injection as directed; supply 5 2ml ampoules; NHS Cost £4.05.
- Water for injection (5ml). Use as directed; supply 10 5m ampoule; NHS Cost £2.82.
- Hyoscine hydrobrom 400mcg/ml. For intravenous or subcutaneous injection as directed; supply 5 1ml ampoules; NHS Cost £13.55.
- Instructions for handwriting CD prescription for diamorphine: Patients name and address. Diamorphine 10mg injection. State the dose and dose interval, e.g. 5-10 mg every 4 hours when required. Supply 2 (two) ampoules. Signed and dated.
- Cyclizine lactate 50mg/ml inj. For intravenous or subcutaneous injection as directed; supply 5 1ml ampoules; NHS Cost £2.71.

Extended Information

Background information

- What is pain? p.1486
- How common is pain in people with cancer? p.1487
- What are the causes of pain in a person with cancer? p.1487
- How do I assess the causes of pain in a person with cancer? p.1487
- How do I assess the severity and impact of pain? p.1488

What is pain?

- **Pain** is a subjective unpleasant experience that is the product of a physical sensation and the psychological state of the patient.
- **Somatic pain** occurs with activation of nociceptors in cutaneous and musculoskeletal tissues, and in pleural and peritoneal membranes.
- **Visceral pain** occurs with activation of nociceptors in thoracic or abdominal viscera, due to infiltration, compression, or distension of these organs.

able 1: Compatibilities and alternative routes of drugs commonly given by syringe driver.

rug	Compatibility with diamorphine[1]	Alternative routes/drugs[2]
yclizine	Diamorphine any strength + cyclizine 6.7 mg/ml Diamorphine 15 mg/ml + cyclizine 15 mg/ml Diamorphine 20 mg/ml + cyclizine 10 mg/ml	Levomepromazine (methotrimeprazine) as a single subcutaneous (s/c) bedtime dose
examethasone	Compatible at usual concentrations, but mix carefully to prevent precipitation	Dexamethasone as a single s/c morning dose
lycopyrronium ·omide	Compatible at usual concentrations	Hyoscine hydrobromide sublingual tablets or patches
aloperidol	Diamorphine 20–100 mg/ml + haloperidol 0.75 mg/ml Diamorphine 50 mg/ml + haloperidol 1.5 mg/ml	Haloperidol as a single s/c bedtime dose
yoscine ıtylbromide	Compatible at all usual concentrations	Hyoscine butylbromide as a s/c dose every 4–6 hours
yoscine ·drobromide	Compatible at all usual concentrations	Hyoscine hydrobromide sublingual tablets or patches
·vomepromazine ıethotrimeprazine)	Compatible at all usual concentrations	Levomepromazine as a single s/c bedtime dose
letoclopramide	Diamorphine 25 mg/ml + metoclopramide 5 mg/ml	Metoclopramide s/c 8-hourly or rectal domperidone
lidazolam	Compatible at all usual concentrations	Diazepam as a single rectal bedtime dose or levomepromazine as a single s/c bedtime dose

Twycross, R., Wilcock, A., Charlesworth, S., and Dickman, A. (2002) *Palliative care formulary*. Palliativedrugs.com Ltd. www.palliativedrugs.com [Accessed: 20-10-·03].
Regnard, C. and Hockley, J. (2004) *A guide to symptom relief in palliative care*. 5th ed. Oxford: Radcliffe Medical Press.

Neuropathic pain results from injury to the peripheral and/or central nervous system.
Sympathetically maintained pain is thought to follow injury to peripheral nerves or musculoskeletal tissue. An ongoing peripheral injury leads to sensitization of the central nervous system, causing neuropathic-like pain to be felt in the distribution of a sympathetic nerve.

low common is pain in people with cancer?

Pain is experienced by 30–40% of people with cancer undergoing treatment [Foley, 2004].
Pain is experienced by 70–90% of people with advanced cancer [Foley, 2004].
Severe pain is experienced by 66% of people with cancer at some point in their illness [SIGN, 2000].

Vhat are the causes of pain in a person with ancer?

ain commonly has more than one cause in a person with ıncer. These may be malignant, non-malignant, or due to eatment or investigations.

Malignant causes of pain

Pain caused by direct tumour involvement accounts for 62–78% of pain problems [Foley, 1979].
The most common causes are bone tumours (primary and metastatic), tumours invading a hollow viscus, and tumours infiltrating nervous tissue.
Common malignant causes of pain and their clinical features are summarized in Table 2.

Non-malignant causes of pain

Non-malignant causes of pain account for 3–10% of pain problems [Foley, 1979]. These may be unrelated to the malignancy (e.g. pre-existing arthritis) or indirectly caused by the underlying malignancy (e.g. pulmonary embolism, peptic ulceration, constipation, infection, pressure sores).

Pain due to investigations or treatment

Pain due to treatment or investigation accounts for up to 25% of pain problems in patients with cancer [Foley, 1979]. It tends to be acute, closely related in time to the cause, and is usually self-limiting.

- Chemotherapy: pain may be associated with the infusion of chemotherapy. Peripheral neuropathy and severe mucositis can also occur although these take longer to develop.
- Radiotherapy: this can cause inflammation and ulceration of exposed mucous membranes (e.g. the alimentary canal, vagina, and bladder). Myelopathy may occur following radiation of the cervical and thoracic spinal cord; it tends to develop weeks after treatment and may take up to 6 months to resolve.
- Hormonal therapy: tumour flare may occur transiently with initiation of luteinizing hormone releasing hormone (LHRH) therapy in patients with prostate cancer. Tumour flare may also occur following hormonal treatment of breast cancer.

[Foley, 2004]

How do I assess the causes of pain in a person with cancer?

It is important to assess all possible causes of pain, both malignant and non-malignant, by undertaking a comprehensive history and examination, including neurological examination. Aspects of the assessment deserving emphasis are given below.

- **Review the past medical history and medical records** to determine the known site and extent of the malignancy. Pain occurring distant from the previously known sites of malignancy may indicate either a non-malignant cause or secondary spread of the malignancy.
- **The timing of the pain** ***may*** suggest the cause:
  - **Pain that presents insidiously** and progressively worsens suggests a malignant cause for the pain.
  - **Acute onset of pain** should always prompt non-cancer causes to be considered, e.g. pulmonary embolism, myocardial infarction, perforation of a viscus. Cancer-related causes include pathological fracture, bleeding into hepatic metastases, or spinal cord compression.
- **The site and radiation of the pain** indicate the structures that the pain originates from.
- **The character of the pain** indicates the tissue of origin of the pain.

P

Table 2: Common malignant causes of pain.

Tissue affected	Mechanism of pain	Characteristics of pain
Bone	Tumour in bone stretching periosteum	Continuous, dull, poorly localized pain, worsened by weight bearing or by straining the bone.
	Pathological fracture caused by lysis of bone by tumour	Severe pain worsened by the slightest passive movement.
Muscle	Strain	Well-localized sharp pain provoked by palpation and active movement.
	Myofascial pain	Well-localized sharp pain provoked by palpation and active movement. Characterized by trigger points (a hyperirritable spot in skeletal muscle associated with a tight muscle band that may be palpable). Palpation is very painful and may produce referred pain.
Skin	Ulceration	Pain usually well localized to the edge of the ulcer.
Pleura and peritoneum	Infiltration of pleura or peritoneum by tumour	Well-localized sharp pain provoked by inspiration. Non-malignant causes are common (e.g. pulmonary embolism and chest infection).
Visceral pain	Pain from deep structures of chest, abdomen, or pelvis.	Pain poorly localized to the affected viscera and may refer to other sites. May be tender to palpation over affected organ. Non-malignant causes are common. For further information on malignant bowel obstruction see PRODIGY guidance *Palliative care — nausea/vomiting/ malignant bowel obstruction.*
Nerve compression pain	Compression of nerve by tumour or bone	Pain may be continuous (e.g. tumour compression) or intermittent (e.g. skeletal instability), but only investigations will differentiate the cause. Reduced sensation or paraesthesiae are common.
Neuropathic pain	Altered spinal and central neurotransmitter levels caused by nerve damage	Unpleasant sensory change at rest in the distribution of a peripheral nerve or nerve root. Often accompanied by hypersensitivity or allodynia (pain on light touch). Typical pain descriptions are burning, cold, numb, stabbing. Some neuropathic pains involve the sympathetic system and have a vascular distribution accompanied by sympathetic changes (pallor or flushing, sweating or absence of sweating).
Central nervous system	Spinal cord compression	Back pain with radiation occurs early. Motor and sensory signs occur later. Sphincter disturbanc is a late sign.
	Cerebral metastases	Headache on lying flat, vomiting, drowsiness, focal neurological deficit.

- **Somatic pain:** the pain is typically sharp and well localized.
- **Visceral pain:** the pain is poorly localized, often described as deep and squeezing, and may be associated with nausea and vomiting. Visceral pain is often referred to sites that may be remote from the site of the lesion.
- **Neuropathic pain:** the pain is often severe, and has a different quality compared to somatic or visceral pain. It is typically described as a constant, dull, aching pain. Superimposed paroxysms of burning and/or electric shock-like sensations are common.
- **Sympathetically maintained pain:** pain of a neuropathic character is felt in the distribution of sympathetic nerve (these follow blood vessels) and is associated with skin changes caused by either vasoconstriction or vasodilation.

How do I assess the severity and impact of pain?

- **Healthcare professionals tend to underestimate pain** (particularly moderate to severe pain) when compared to the patient's own measure of their pain.
- Underestimating the severity of pain is associated with inadequate treatment of pain [Grossman et al, 1991].
- To assess the response to treatment, it is useful to have some measure of the severity of pain before and after an intervention.
- Assessing when and how pain impacts on a person allows treatment to be tailored to the needs of the patient in order to maintain their lifestyle.
- **The severity and impact of pain is indicated by:**
  - The patient's self-assessment of the severity
  - The impact on a patient's activities
  - The patient's mood

[Abu-Saad and Courtens, 2001]

How should I assess the severity of pain?

- **Ask the patient** whether they have pain, and how bad it is.
- Assessment tools can help to measure the severity of pain, heighten awareness of it, and improve its treatme [Bookbinder et al, 1996].
- A simple verbal rating scale is quick and easy to use an when recorded regularly, allows the response of pain to treatment to be assessed more accurately. This can be done by asking the patient to rate their pain on a scale zero to ten.

How do I assess the impact of pain on a person's activities?

- **Ask if pain restricts:**
  - Self care
  - Housework
  - Shopping
  - Social activities
  - Sleep

Why is it important to assess mood?

- **Depression and anxiety are strongly correlated with pain.**
- Poorly controlled pain is likely to adversely affect a person's mood, and psychological distress is likely to increase the perception of pain [Spiegel et al, 1994].
- **It is important to review the patient's mood regularly:**
  - Grief is a normal, common reaction, and usually resolves without medical intervention.
  - Depression, anxiety, or unresolved grief reactions should be considered for treatment because they caus prolonged, distressing psychological symptoms.
- **Depression is still a treatable condition in people who a terminally ill.** Experts recommend that clinicians have a low threshold for initiating a therapeutic trial of antidepressants when the diagnosis is in question [Block and Snyder, 2000].

ow do I distinguish between grief and depression?

Distinguishing grief from depression can be difficult in people who are terminally ill.

Characteristics that help to distinguish a grief reaction from depression are outlined in Table 3.

lanagement issues

Jeneral principles of managing pain in people with :ancer p.1489

How do I manage acute severe pain? p.1489

Is treatment of the underlying cause of pain appropriate? p.1489

Which types of pain may need a specific approach? p.1490

How should I manage the symptom of pain? p.1491

How should breakthrough pain be managed? p.1492

What should I do if pain is still difficult to manage? p.1492

Seeking help and advice in primary care p.1493

Adjustments in the terminal phase p.1493

Medicines management: standard analgesics p.1493

Medicines management: drugs for neuropathic pain p.1495

Medicines management: non-oral routes of drug delivery p.1496

eneral principles of managing pain in eople with cancer

- **Relieve acute severe pain promptly** prior to a fuller assessment and management.
- **Diagnose the cause and type of pain as accurately as possible.** This is required to plan the most effective treatment.
- **Always *consider* treating the underlying cause of pain.** This may involve a greater burden for the patient but has a greater potential benefit.
- **Some types of pain require a specific approach** (e.g. neuropathic pain, bone pain, myofascial pain). Drugs or treatments that are not directly analgesic are used (e.g. radiotherapy for bone pain) and can help to reduce the amount of standard analgesics needed.
- **Treat pain symptomatically using the WHO analgesic ladder.** Pain should always be relieved promptly and effectively with standard analgesic drugs, even when other treatments are given for pain.
- **Seek specialist help** promptly if pain proves difficult to manage.

ble 3: Depression and grief compared [Block and yder, 2000].

aracteristics of grief	Characteristics of depression
ological symptoms of loss of ep, appetite, and ncentration	Biological symptoms plus psychological symptoms of hopelessness, worthlessness, and guilt
ef is experienced by nearly the terminally ill	Depression is present in up to 50% of the terminally ill
stress relates to a particular s	Distress is usually generalized to all facets of life
ient retains capacity for asure	Patient enjoys nothing
ef comes in waves	Depression is constant and unremitting
ient may express passive h for life to end	Patient may express suicidal ideation
ient able to look forward to ure	Patient has no sense of a positive future
ost patients cope without dical intervention	Medical or psychological intervention is usually necessary

How do I manage acute severe pain?

- **Acute severe pain in a person with cancer should be considered a medical emergency** and will commonly require admission to secondary care.
- **Clinicians should have a low threshold of suspicion for spinal cord compression** in any patient with cancer who presents with back pain, particularly if this is associated with radiating pain.

Immediate treatment of pain (while awaiting admission)

- **For colic:** give hyoscine butylbromide 20 mg by subcutaneous, intramuscular, or intravenous injection.
- **For spinal cord compression:** give a high dose of any available corticosteroid immediately (preferably dexamethasone 15–16 mg intravenously) and arrange emergency admission to secondary care. However, when patients are in the last hours or days of life, transfer to hospital may not be appropriate. In these circumstances corticosteroids should be given immediately and then followed the next day by dexamethasone 16 mg daily orally.
- **For other causes of severe pain:** give a strong opioid.
  - If the patient is opioid-naïve, give diamorphine 5 mg (2.5 mg in elderly patients) as a subcutaneous injection.
  - If the patient is already taking a regular opioid, calculate the 4-hourly dose, and give the equivalent parenteral dose.
  - Note: the equivalent subcutaneous dose of morphine is half the oral dose. The equivalent subcutaneous dose of diamorphine is a third of the oral morphine dose. (For example if the patient is taking oral morphine 30 mg twice a day, divide the total 24-hour dose by 6 to obtain the 4-hourly dose, i.e. 60 mg divided by 6 = 10 mg oral morphine. This is equivalent to 5 mg subcutaneous morphine or 3 mg subcutaneous diamorphine [usually rounded down for convenience to 2.5 mg].)
- If emergency admission is not appropriate (e.g. the likely cause does not need urgent management) reassess the patient fully when severe pain is controlled.

[Regnard and Hockley, 2004a]

Is treatment of the underlying cause of pain appropriate?

- **Pain may have more than one cause,** and causes may be malignant, non-malignant, or due to treatment.
- **Consider treatment for each cause** of pain.
- (Note: pain should always be relieved with standard analgesics using the WHO ladder while the underlying cause of pain is sought or treated.)

Non-malignant causes of pain

- **Treatment of pain due to non-malignant causes can usually be directed at the underlying cause.** It is therefore important that these are identified and treated separately.

Malignant causes of pain

- **It is important to consider treatment of the malignancy to relieve pain.** Progression of the malignancy may result in pain developing or worsening. Treatments that reduce the size or effect of the tumour may reduce pain and the need for analgesia, even in advanced disease.

P

- The burden of treatment *must* always be balanced against the likely benefits to the patient.
- Clinical situations to consider are included in Table 4. This is not an exhaustive list and, where doubt exists, consult a specialist.

[SIGN, 2000; Regnard and Hockley, 2004b]

Which types of pain may need a specific approach?

- **Certain types of pain may benefit from specific treatments,** e.g. neuropathic pain, bone pain, myofascial pain, bowel colic, ureteric colic.
- Specific treatments can be used first line or second line, depending on the type of pain. For example, injecting trigger points is the first-line treatment for myofascial pain.
- Specific treatments for these types of pain can also reduce the need for standard analgesic drugs.

How should I manage neuropathic pain?

- **Neuropathic pain is usually present with other types of pain** (visceral or somatic) as a mixed pain syndrome. It can be difficult to distinguish the contribution of each type of pain to the overall pain picture.
- Somatic and visceral pain usually responds to the use of non-opioids, weak and strong opioid analgesics, but the response of neuropathic pain to these drugs is unpredictable and may be limited.

How do I manage mixed pain?

- **Start treatment with standard analgesics** in the WHO analgesic ladder and titrate upwards until pain is relieved or the adverse effects limit further dose increases.
- Continue with analgesics and start either a tricyclic antidepressant (TCA) or an antiepileptic drug (AED) if pain with a neuropathic character persists.
- Titrate the dose of TCA or AED upwards until pain settles or adverse effects limit further dose increases.
- The use of a TCA or AED, if successful in relieving the pain, may allow the dose of standard analgesics to be reduced. This should be attempted if the patient is pair free but exhibiting opioid adverse effects.

How do I manage predominantly neuropathic pain?

- **Start either a TCA or AED** when pain is purely or predominantly neuropathic in character.
- Titrate the dose until pain settles or adverse effects lim further increases in dose.

Which TCAs or AEDs are suitable for neuropathic pain?

- **There is no measurable difference in the analgesic effec of TCAs or AEDs** in neuropathic pain, or in the overal incidence of adverse effects [SIGN, 2000].
- The choice depends on the relative contraindications, possible drug interactions, and risk of adverse effects fo each individual patient.
    - Tricyclic antidepressants are usually effective at low doses. Amitriptyline is the most widely studied TCA, and is commonly used for neuropathic pain in the UK. Imipramine is a less sedative alternative. Nortriptyline is another alternative; it has a similar adverse effect profile to amitriptyline, but is less likely to cause antimuscarinic adverse effects (including sedation) o postural hypotension.
    - Antiepileptics usually require a full antiepileptic dose to treat neuropathic pain. Gabapentin is effective, ha few drug interactions, and is generally well tolerated although a slower titration than that recommended i the summary of product characteristics is usually required [Wiffen et al, 2000; Twycross et al, 2002]. Carbamazepine is also traditionally used for neuropathic pain. Although sodium valproate is commonly used in practice, there are no studies to support its use [Wiffen et al, 2000]. Pregabalin has recently been licensed for neuropathic pain, but it is black triangle drug and further post-marketing safet data are needed. Dizziness, somnolence, blurred

Table 4: Treating the underlying malignant causes of pain.

Diagnosis	When to consider further treatment	Possible treatments
Local distension due to tumour	When the space occupying effect of the tumour results in pain	Corticosteroids. Other treatments will depend on the type and position of the tumour
Bone metastases	All cases of painful metastatic lesions	Radiotherapy, bisphosphonates, corticosteroids
	All cases of mechanical instability, including pathological fracture, caused by metastases.	Surgical stabilization
Cerebral metastases	When symptoms suggest cerebral metastases	Radiotherapy, corticosteroids
Spinal cord compression	In all patients who are symptomatic or likely to become symptomatic	Depending on clinical factors, radiotherapy, steroids, surgery
Nerve compression	In all cases	Corticosteroids
Malignant bowel obstruction* or ureteric obstruction	In all cases	Surgery, stents, corticosteroids
Hepatic metastases	Capsular pain	Corticosteroids
Breast cancer	Widespread painful bone metastases with a reasonable performance status	Chemotherapy
	Progressive metastatic disease despite prior tamoxifen	Aromatase inhibitors
	Painful widespread bone metastases	Bisphosphonates
Small cell lung cancer	Extensive disease, including cerebral metastases, causing pain	Chemotherapy
Non-small-cell lung cancer	Inoperable locally advanced or metastatic disease	Chemotherapy
Pancreatic cancer	Inoperable locally advanced or metastatic disease	Chemotherapy
Prostate cancer	In all cases of prostate cancer and painful bone metastases	Hormonal therapy
	Widespread painful bony metastases	Radioactive strontium, bisphosphonates
Multiple myeloma	In all cases	Radiotherapy, bisphosphonates

*For further information regarding treatment of malignant bowel obstruction see PRODIGY guidance *Palliative care — nausea/ vomiting/malignant bowel obstruction*

vision, gastrointestinal adverse effects, and weight gain are common adverse effects.
- For further information on using TCAs and AEDs (including suggested titration doses) see section *Medicines management: neuropathic pain.*

How should I manage bone pain?

- All patients with persistent bone pain or an acute exacerbation of bone pain require an X-ray to exclude a fracture.
- The most effective way to relieve pain from bone metastases is to direct treatment at the underlying cause (see Table 4), and this should be considered in all patients.
- Standard analgesia (using the WHO ladder) should always be started whilst awaiting treatment.
- If the patient is in severe pain, or has pain at rest, start at step 3 of the analgesic ladder (i.e. a strong opioid such as morphine *plus* paracetamol or a nonsteroidal anti-inflammatory drug [NSAID]).

How should I manage myofascial pain?

- The underlying cause should be sought and treated where possible. Injecting the trigger point with local anaesthetic or saline will often relieve the pain. For persistent pain, other therapies such as TENS (transcutaneous electrical nerve stimulation) may be considered [Regnard and Hockley, 2004b].

How should I manage muscle spasm?

- Muscle spasm is probably under-diagnosed in people with cancer. Weakened muscles under increased strain (e.g. underlying bony metastases), direct invasion of the muscle by cancer, anxiety, and biochemical abnormalities are some of the causes.
- The underlying cause should be sought and treated where possible.
- Standard analgesics should be used if muscle spasm is part of a mixed pain picture. However, muscle spasm does not respond to strong opioids. Consider additional use of:
  - Non-drug therapies, e.g. positioning, heat, massage
  - Muscle relaxants, e.g. diazepam
  - Injecting associated trigger points, as for myofascial pain
- Note: although there are few studies assessing the effect of diazepam on muscle spasm, it is widely used. A single dose at night should be used (not three times a day dosing) to reduce the impact of common adverse effects such as drowsiness and dizziness.

How should I manage bowel colic?

- Treat underlying causes where possible, e.g. constipation or *operable* malignant bowel obstruction — see PRODIGY guidance *Palliative care — nausea/vomiting/ malignant bowel obstruction* for further information.
- **Relieve acute bowel colic when it occurs alone** with hyoscine butylbromide 10–20 mg up to three times a day.
- **For people on a strong opioid and who have both continuous and colicky pain:**
  - Titrate the opioid upwards until their continuous pain is relieved.
  - If *colic* persists, add in hyoscine butylbromide.
- **For people who are *not* on a strong opioid who have both continuous and colicky pain,** expert opinion differs when it comes to starting treatment. Start treatment based on clinical judgement:
  - Start a strong opioid and add in hyoscine butylbromide if colic persists.
  - Start hyoscine butylbromide and add in a strong opioid if continuous pain persists.
  - Start hyoscine butylbromide plus a strong opioid if both types of pain are present.

[Ripamonti et al, 2001]

How should I manage ureteric colic?

- Consider treating the underlying cause in all patients.
- Give analgesia for acute pain relief. Intramuscular diclofenac is widely used but NSAIDs should be avoided in individuals with poor renal function. Subcutaneous hyoscine butylbromide is a suitable alternative [Regnard and Hockley, 2004b].
- Consider starting a strong opioid or giving a breakthrough dose of an existing opioid if pain is severe.

How should I manage pain due to a skin ulcer?

- Optimize wound care to promote ulcer healing. If the prognosis is too short to allow healing (e.g. day by day deterioration), choose the dressings for comfort [Regnard and Hockley, 2004b].
- Give standard analgesia and titrate according to response.

How should I manage the symptom of pain?

WHO analgesic ladder

The WHO analgesic ladder is a framework for providing symptomatic pain relief. Up to 88% of patients with pain will have their pain adequately managed by implementing the WHO programme for cancer pain relief [SIGN, 2000].

- **Before starting treatment for the symptom of pain,** consider whether treatment of the underlying cause is possible, and would the type of pain benefit from a specific treatment?
- **Relieve the symptom of pain promptly and effectively with standard analgesia** according to the principles of the WHO analgesic ladder, even when other treatments are given for pain.
- **All patients with moderate to severe cancer pain should receive a trial of strong opioid** combined with a non-opioid analgesic, regardless of the cause of the pain (i.e. step 3).
- **For other patients, start at step 1 of the analgesic ladder and titrate upwards** until the patient is comfortable:
  - **Step 1 — give paracetamol or a NSAID** (nonsteroidal anti-inflammatory drug).
  - **Step 2 — give a full dose of weak opioid (e.g. codeine 30–60 mg) *plus* paracetamol or a NSAID.** Codeine should usually be prescribed separately to paracetamol to allow flexibility of dosing and titration of analgesic effect. Note: if a weak opioid (step 2) does not provide adequate pain relief at maximum dose, move to step 3 of the analgesic ladder. Do not change to another weak opioid [SIGN, 2000].
  - **Step 3 — give morphine *plus* paracetamol or a NSAID.** In the UK, diamorphine is preferred if a strong opioid needs to be given by 24-hour subcutaneous infusion, due to its increased solubility compared to morphine.
- For further information on starting and titrating oral morphine, see *Medicines management: standard analgesics.*

Practical issues

- **Give analgesia by mouth** whenever possible.
- **Give analgesia by the clock:** continuous pain needs regular analgesia, so give analgesia at fixed intervals. Always provide 'rescue doses' for breakthrough pain.
- **Tailor analgesia to the individual:**

P

- Link the first and last dose with waking and sleeping times.
- Write out drug regimen in full and check that the patient and family or assistant at home understand it.
- Review the patient regularly to ensure pain does not return and the patient is as alert as possible.
- Step treatment up or down the ladder according to the response.

Which standard analgesics are suitable for the WHO ladder steps?

- **Non-opioids:** the final decision between paracetamol and a NSAID depends on the likely risk of adverse effects compared with benefit for each individual patient. (There are few comparative studies to examine their relative efficacy and adverse effects with chronic use. Most data are from single dose studies [McQuay and Moore, 1997].) If a standard NSAID is needed, PRODIGY recommends ibuprofen, diclofenac, and naproxen because they have a good balance of efficacy against adverse effect profile [CSM, 2003]. If a COX-2 selective NSAID is required, there is most experience with celecoxib. For further information on the risks and benefits of NSAIDs, see PRODIGY guidance *Nonsteroidal anti-inflammatory drugs (NSAIDs)*.
- **Weak opioids:** PRODIGY recommends codeine as a suitable first-line weak opioid. Other weak opioids could be used, but there are surprisingly few data on their relative efficacy and adverse effects with chronic use, and many preparations are more expensive than codeine tablets. Compound analgesics containing subtherapeutic doses of opioids (e.g. codeine 8 mg per tablet or dihydrocodeine 10 mg per tablet) should not be used for pain control in patients with cancer [SIGN, 2000].
- **Strong opioids:** the safety and efficacy of morphine are well established [Zech et al, 1995; Wiffen et al, 2003] and morphine is available as a wide variety of oral formulations, allowing flexibility in dosing regimens. Although other opioids are available, none has so far demonstrated advantages that would make it preferred to morphine as the first-choice oral opioid for cancer pain [Hanks et al, 2001]. For further information on using oral morphine, see section *Medicines management: standard analgesics*.

P

How should breakthrough pain be managed?

- **Additional analgesia for breakthrough pain should always be provided** — despite good pain control with regular analgesia, patients can still experience periods of worsening pain.
  - **For patients on a regular oral or parenteral opioid:** use a 4-hourly dose for breakthrough analgesia. (For example, if the patient is taking oral morphine 30 mg twice a day, divide the total 24-hour dose by 6 to obtain the 4-hourly dose, i.e. 60 mg divided by 6 = 10 mg oral morphine.) If there is no response to a breakthrough dose, it can be repeated after 1 hour.
  - **For patients taking non-opioid analgesics:** give one dose of regular analgesic. This can be repeated after 4 hours if there is no response to the first breakthrough dose, but care should be taken not to exceed the maximum licensed dose of paracetamol or nonsteroidal anti-inflammatory drug used. If the maximum licensed dose is already prescribed, use a full dose of a step 2 analgesic (e.g. codeine 30–60 mg) for breakthrough pain.
  - **Transdermal patches are only suitable for patients with stable pain requirements,** but breakthrough analgesia should still be provided. There are several options for patients taking transdermal fentanyl. See the section *Alternative strong opioids to morphine* for further information.
- **If there is a response to the breakthrough dose:** consider increasing the regular analgesic dose or using a higher step on the *WHO analgesic ladder*.
- **If there is no response after two doses of breakthrough analgesia:** reassess the cause of pain so that therapy can be better targeted at the underlying cause.

What should I do if pain is still difficult to manage?

We strongly recommend seeking specialist help from the palliative care team or Macmillan nursing team if pain remains difficult to manage.

- **If pain does not respond well to treatment consider:**
  - Is the diagnosis of the cause of pain right?
  - Is the treatment right?
    - Is the cause treatable?
    - Does the type of pain require a specific therapy?
  - Are there factors increasing the perception of pain, such as unresolved psychological, social, or spiritual distress?
- Situations where standard analgesic treatments may only have a limited effectiveness include:
  - Neuropathic pain
  - Muscle spasm pain
  - Incident pain (pain on movement or activity), where the dose of drugs required to control the peak pain may be excessive when the pain subsides
- **Additional management options to consider include:**
  - Referral for an interventional technique
  - Referral for a supervised switch of strong opioid

Interventional techniques

- **Consider referral for an interventional technique** when pain is proving difficult to manage with systemic drug therapy.
- **Spinal drug administration:** by introducing opioids and/or local anaesthetic drugs into the epidural or intrathecal space, it is possible to achieve profound analgesia with small doses and few adverse effects. Epidural or intrathecal catheters can be placed percutaneously and the drugs delivered through a small pump or a syringe driver. Intrathecal lines can be kept in place for a year or more.
- **Peripheral nerve blockade:** blockade of peripheral nerves can be used to manage severe pain that is well localized, such as pain from a pathological rib fracture. Blockade can be achieved temporarily using local anaesthetic or long term by destroying neural tissue using a variety of techniques e.g. injecting phenol.
- **Sympathetic nerve blockade:** this can be achieved by using neuroablative techniques, e.g. in the management of abdominal (coeliac plexus block), pelvic (superior hypogastric plexus block), and perineal (ganglion impar block) pain of visceral origin. Coeliac plexus block has been shown to achieve excellent pain relief in 85–90% of patients with upper abdominal and back pain caused by pancreatic cancer [Mercadante, 1993]. With the increased use of tricyclic antidepressants and antiepileptic drugs there has been a reduced reliance on coeliac plexus block.
- Neurosurgical procedures are rarely used, but include cordotomy, midline myelotomy, hypophysectomy, thalamotomy, and cingulotomy.

[Swarm et al, 2004]

Switching strong opioid

A supervised switch of strong opioid may be considered when effective analgesia can only be achieved with doses that produce adverse effects.

Switching opioid should only be carried out under the supervision of an experienced clinician because the effect of switching opioids is variable and unpredictable, and there is a risk of under- or overdosing the patient (depending on individual sensitivity).

The analgesic effect of strong opioids increases as the dose increases. There is no ceiling effect (except with buprenorphine). However, the onset of adverse effects limits the maximum dose of the opioid that can be achieved for an individual patient.

The adverse effects of different opioids may vary for an individual patient. Changing to a different opioid may result in reduced adverse effects, allowing for an increased analgesic dose of opioid.

As morphine metabolites accumulate in renal impairment, switching to an alternative can reduce or remove the adverse effects of these metabolites.

Ianks et al, 2004]

ƽeeking help and advice in primary care

The multidimensional nature of problems in palliative care requires a multidisciplinary approach.

Both the GP and district nurse should be involved as early as possible following diagnosis.

Following clinical assessment, referral may be necessary for an identified specialist need.

The palliative care team may include any or all of the following specialities:

- Palliative medicine consultant
- Macmillan nurses
- Palliative care nurse practitioners
- Physiotherapists
- Occupational therapists
- Social workers
- Spiritual advisers

Where these services are not organized into a team they may be accessed via referral to the Macmillan nurses.

Marie Curie Cancer Care provides nursing, totally free, to give terminally ill people the choice of dying at home supported by their families. Their service can be accessed via the district nurse.

ɩdjustments in the terminal phase

ʀecognizing the terminal phase

ı order to care for dying patients it is essential to diagnose 'ying'. Healthcare professionals are sometimes reluctant ɔ diagnose dying, and therefore the appropriate ʤjustments in the terminal phase may not be made.

The terminal phase starts a median of 24 hours before death, varying from hours to several days.

Patients in the terminal phase have several common features:

- Deteriorating day-by-day or faster because of their underlying condition or because of an irreversible complication of their disease
- Patient expresses a realization that they are dying
- Reduced cognition, drowsy or comatose
- Bed-bound
- Taking little food or fluid and having difficulty with oral medication
- Altered breathing pattern
- Peripherally cyanosed and cold

ʌorita et al, 1998].

Adjustments in the terminal phase

The terminal phase is a time of adjustments for all [Regnard and Hockley, 2004a]:

- Stop unnecessary drugs and continue with other drugs by an appropriate route.
- Ensure commonly required medications are available in the house (e.g. cyclizine, diamorphine, hyoscine hydrobromide, and midazolam) so that there is no delay in treatment of new or developing symptoms.
- Ensure physical symptoms are well controlled.
- Explore understanding and provide appropriate explanation of the situation to the patient, family, and other professional carers.
- Set realistic goals.
- Ensure that religious and spiritual care is offered if wanted.
- Ensure the environment is appropriate.

- The Liverpool Care Pathway for the Dying Patient provides a national framework caring for patients in the terminal phase. It integrates professional communication and documentation integrating national guidelines into clinical practice. Further information can be obtained from www.lcp-mariecurie.org.uk.

Medicines management: standard analgesics

Paracetamol and NSAIDs

- Paracetamol is well tolerated at the recommended daily dose.
- Consider patient comorbidity when prescribing NSAIDs; they commonly cause gastrointestinal adverse effects, and can worsen asthma, hypertension, renal impairment, and heart failure.
- Options to reduce the risk of gastrointestinal adverse events include:
  - Use paracetamol instead of a NSAID.
  - Or, use a gastroprotective agent with a standard NSAID [NICE, 2001].
  - Or, use a COX-2 selective NSAID alone [NICE, 2001]. Note: COX-2 selective inhibitors should not be given with low-dose aspirin as the advantage of a lower risk of gastrointestinal adverse effects is then lost.
- PRODIGY recommends a proton pump inhibitor (e.g. omeprazole or lansoprazole) as first-line gastroprotective agents; it is generally accepted that they are better tolerated than misoprostol.
- For further information on using NSAIDs, see PRODIGY guidance *Nonsteroidal anti-inflammatory drugs (NSAIDs).*

P

Codeine

- Codeine may cause nausea, vomiting, constipation, and drowsiness. A regular laxative is often needed when it is used long-term.
- It should usually be prescribed separately to paracetamol to allow flexibility of dosing and titration of analgesic effect.

Morphine

- There should be no contraindications to the use of morphine in palliative care provided that a suitable start dose is used and it is carefully titrated against pain [Twycross et al, 2002].
- Morphine-6-glucuronide (one of the active metabolites of morphine) accumulates during renal impairment. It is therefore sensible to start with a lower dose in opioid-naïve patients, particularly the elderly or debilitated, who are likely to have a degree of renal impairment. The dose should then be titrated carefully against pain in the usual way.

Starting and titrating oral morphine

- **Immediate-release morphine is recommended while titrating the dose** where possible [SIGN, 2000].

Oramorph® solution and Sevredol® tablets are both immediate-release morphine products.

- **Give morphine regularly every 4 hours** (to maintain constant analgesic levels) *and* as required for breakthrough pain [SIGN, 2000].
  - Extra doses for breakthrough pain can be given as often as required (up to hourly).
  - A double dose given at bedtime may prevent the patient being woken by pain, and avoids the overnight dose [SIGN, 2000; Hanks et al, 2001].
- **The starting dose of oral morphine** will vary between patients:
  - For opioid-naïve patients, the elderly, and those with renal impairment: start with 2.5 mg every 4 hours *and* as required for breakthrough pain.
  - For patients previously on a weak opioid: start with 5–10 mg every 4 hours *and* as required for breakthrough pain.
- **After 24–48 hours,** calculate the total dose given over 24 hours, and use this to recalculate the 4-hourly dose.
  - The new 4-hourly and 'as required' dose is a sixth of the new total daily dose [SIGN, 2000; Hanks et al, 2001].
  - For example, if the patient is taking oral morphine 30 mg twice a day, divide the total 24-hour dose by 6 to obtain the 4-hourly dose, i.e. 60 mg divided by 6 = 10 mg oral morphine.
  - Note: care should be taken when calculating morphine requirements for patients who are pain-free at rest but have pain on movement. If all the analgesia for this incident pain is incorporated into the new morphine dose, the patient is likely to be excessively sedated at rest, or possibly even opioid toxic [SIGN, 2000].
- **Repeat this process every 24 hours** until pain is controlled, or adverse effects prevent further dose increases. (Some patients may need longer than this to become tolerant to drowsiness.)
- **Once a stable dose has been reached,** switch from immediate-release morphine to the same total daily dosage of once- or twice-daily modified-release morphine [Twycross et al, 2002].

Using modified-release morphine

- When changing from immediate-release morphine (i.e. Oramorph® or Sevredol®) to modified-release morphine (e.g. MST®, MXL®), start the modified-release preparation at the same time as the next standard release dose is due, and discontinue regular immediate-release morphine [SIGN, 2000].
  - Modified-release morphine is available as both once-daily products (e.g. MXL® capsules) and twice-daily products (e.g. MST Continus® tablets or suspension, Zomorph® capsules).
  - It would seem sensible to prescribe modified-release morphine by brand. Slight differences in bioavailability between products may compromise pain control and require dose adjustment.
- Continue to prescribe 'as required' morphine for breakthrough pain (use a sixth of the total daily dose). 'As required' morphine can also be given for predictable movement-related pain. Where possible it should be used 30 minutes before movement [SIGN, 2000].
- If further dose titration is needed, increase morphine by 30–50% every 2–3 days until pain is controlled, or adverse effects prevent further dose increases [Twycross et al, 2002].
- Note: it is possible to start and titrate morphine with modified-release products, but they have a slower onset of action (1–2 hours) and later peak levels (4 hours) than standard release preparations. They therefore do not allow rapid titration for patients in severe pain [McQuay and Moore, 1997; SIGN, 2000].

Managing the adverse effects of morphine

- A patient may appear to have symptoms due to the adverse effects of morphine that are in fact caused by th underlying illness. It is important to consider and exclude these first.
  - **Comorbidities** that may mimic opioid-induced advers effects include dehydration, hypercalcaemia, hypoxaemia, sepsis, cerebral metastases, extradural haemorrhage, stroke, renal impairment, and hepatic impairment. Further information on hypercalcaemia can be found in the PRODIGY guidance *Palliative care — nausea/vomiting/malignant bowel obstructio*
  - **Other drugs** can also cause similar adverse effects, e.g benzodiazepines.

Minimizing common adverse effects of morphine

- Careful management of morphine's adverse effects may significantly increase the maximal tolerable dose.
- **Common adverse effects of morphine** (and other opioids) include drowsiness, nausea and vomiting, constipation, and dry mouth.
- **Drowsiness is common at the start of treatment or after dose increases,** but it resolves within a few days for mos patients. Persistent sedation can usually be resolved by dose reduction.
- **Nausea subsides after the first few days in many patient** but can be an ongoing problem for others. An anti-emetic should be taken regularly for 4–5 days to preven opioid-induced nausea and vomiting, and then used as required. Haloperidol 1.5–3 mg at night or metoclopramide 10 mg three times a day is generally effective.
- **Constipation is an ongoing problem as tolerance does not develop** [Twycross et al, 2002]. It is generally accepted that a stimulant laxative with a faecal softener should always be taken regularly (e.g. senna with lactulose; co-danthrusate) to prevent opioid-induced constipation [Sykes, 1996; Fallon and Hanks, 1999]. There is no linear relationship between morphine dose and the level of constipation, so the dose of laxative wi need to be titrated against symptoms.
- **Dry mouth** can be troublesome. Patients should be encouraged to use simple measures such as frequent sip of cool drinks, ice cubes, frozen segments of fruit such a pineapple or melon, or chewing sugar-free gum [O'Nei and Fallon, 1997; SIGN, 2000]. Consider rationalizing any other drugs that also cause dry mouth.
- **Less common adverse effects of strong opioids include** sweating, pruritus, hallucinations, myoclonus, unsteadiness, and bronchoconstriction [Twycross et al, 2002].

Opioid toxicity

- There is wide individual variation in the dose of opioid that causes toxicity.
- Opioid toxicity can present as subtle agitation, seeing shadows at the periphery of the visual field, vivid dreams, nightmares, visual and auditory hallucinations confusion, and myoclonic jerks.
- Agitated confusion may be misinterpreted as uncontrolled pain and further opioids given.
- Opioid toxicity should be managed by reducing the dos ensuring adequate hydration, and treating the agitation confusion with haloperidol 1.5–3 mg orally or subcutaneously [SIGN, 2000]. (This dose can be repeated hourly in the acute situation.)

Alternative strong opioids to morphine

- **Hydromorphone** may be particularly useful where patients have persistent drowsiness and cognitive impairment despite careful dose titration with morphin [de Stoutz et al, 1995].

Oxycodone has a more predictable bioavailability than oral morphine. Modified-release oxycodone has a biphasic release profile, allowing onset of analgesia within an hour, but a 12-hour duration of action.
Hydromorphone or oxycodone may also be considered as an alternative in mild to moderate renal impairment if accumulation of morphine metabolites is thought to be causing adverse effects.
Fentanyl patches are another alternative to oral morphine, provided that analgesic requirements are stable [Hanks et al, 2001]. There is some evidence that fentanyl is associated with less constipation than morphine [Ahmedzai and Brooks, 1997]. Fentanyl patches have similar efficacy to oral morphine in patients with stable analgesic requirements [Ahmedzai and Brooks, 1997] but is less flexible to use: the onset of action is 6–8 hours after a patch is first applied, any dose increase takes 36–48 hours to reach steady state, and it takes over 17 hours for the serum concentration to fall by half once a patch is removed. Hence, it is most suitable for patients with stable analgesic requirements.
Each fentanyl patch should provide analgesia for 3 days.
Increased temperature of the skin can increase the absorption of fentanyl, so patches should not be applied after a bath or shower. Other heat sources to avoid include hot water bottles, electric blankets, and saunas.
If the patient develops a fever, they should be monitored for increased adverse effects [ABPI Medicines Compendium, 2002; MeReC, 2003].

onversion values

Specialist advice is strongly recommended before switching strong opioid. The conversion values are only approximations, and are given for information only. See Table 5.

reakthrough analgesia options for patients taking ntanyl patches

Doses of oral morphine for breakthrough pain are approximately half the fentanyl patch strength, given as immediate-release morphine in milligrams. For example, with fentanyl 50 microgram/hour patches, use morphine 20–30 mg (as Oramorph® or Sevredol®) when required [Twycross et al, 2002].
Oral transmucosal fentanyl lozenges can be used. However the successful dose cannot be predicted, and is not directly related to the daily dosage of regular fentanyl. The effective dose can only, therefore, be found by titration [ABPI Medicines Compendium, 2002].

able 5: Switching from oral morphine to other commonly sed strong opioids.

om	To	Total daily dose of new opioid	Breakthrough pain dose
ral orphine	Subcutaneous diamorphine	Divide the total daily dose of oral morphine by three	Use a sixth of the total daily dose of subcutaneous diamorphine
	Oral hydromorphone	Divide the total daily dose of oral morphine by five	Use a sixth of the total daily dose of oral hydromorphone
	Oral oxycodone	Divide the total daily dose of oral morphine by two	Use a sixth of the total daily dose of oral oxycodone
	Transdermal fentanyl	Seek specialist advice — there are wide variations in the conversion values cited in the literature	See *Breakthrough analgesia options for patients taking fentanyl patches*

lapted from Regnard, C. and Hockley, J. (2003) *A guide to symptom relief in lliative care*. 5th ed. Oxford: Radcliffe Medical Press.

- Alternatively, the equivalent 1-hourly dose can be given by subcutaneous injection, e.g. with fentanyl 25 microgram/hour patches, give fentanyl 25 micrograms by subcutaneous injection.

Medicines management: drugs for neuropathic pain

Starting and titrating adjuvant analgesics for neuropathic pain

- **Start with a low dose and titrate gradually** (e.g. weekly) to reduce the risk of adverse effects. Elderly or frail patients are at particular risk of adverse effects.
- **Amitriptyline, imipramine, or nortriptyline:** start with 10 mg at night (25 mg in younger patients) and titrate weekly until pain is controlled or adverse effects prevent further dose increases. For many patients, the effective dose is between 25 mg and 75 mg at night. At trial of 1–2 weeks' treatment at these doses is usually sufficient to assess response to a tricyclic antidepressant. If pain is not controlled within this dose range, either continue to titrate up to the maximum tolerated dose (do not exceed 150 mg at night), or switch to gabapentin.
- **Gabapentin:** titrate slowly from 100 mg three times a day to 300 mg three times a day over 7 days. (Note: this is slower than suggested in the summary of product characteristics.) The effective dose is between 900 mg per day and 1800 mg per day (licensed) for many patients. However, doses up to 2400 mg or 3600 mg per day (off-licence) were used in many studies.
- **Carbamazepine:** start with a low dose (e.g. 100 mg daily) and titrate by 100–200 mg every 2 weeks. A maintenance dose of 200 mg three or four times a day is commonly used.

Minimizing adverse effects

Amitriptyline, imipramine, and nortriptyline

- Antimuscarinic adverse effects (such as dry mouth, blurred vision, sedation, constipation, nausea, and difficulty with micturition) are common. Tricyclic antidepressants should therefore be avoided in conditions that will be exacerbated by these effects, e.g. angle-closure glaucoma, benign prostatic hypertrophy, or a history of urinary retention. Note: nortriptyline and imipramine are less sedative than amitriptyline.
- Avoid tricyclic antidepressants in patients with cardiovascular disease where possible: they commonly cause postural hypotension, but can also cause tachycardia, ECG changes, and arrhythmias. Note: nortriptyline is less likely to cause postural hypotension.
- All antidepressants should be used with caution in patients with a history of epilepsy as they can lower the seizure threshold. Stop amitriptyline if seizure frequency increases.
- Hyponatraemia is associated with all types of antidepressant [CSM, 2000] but is usually well tolerated. It should be considered if the patient develops drowsiness, confusion, nausea, muscle cramps, or seizures.

Gabapentin

- Common adverse effects include drowsiness, dizziness, ataxia, and fatigue.
- The clearance of gabapentin is markedly reduced in renal impairment. The total daily dose should not exceed 1200 mg in those with mild renal impairment (common in the elderly). For further information on dosing in renal impairment, see the summary of product characteristics (www.medicines.org.uk) or www.palliativedrugs.com.

P

Carbamazepine

- Dose-related adverse effects include dizziness, ataxia (unsteadiness), diplopia, insomnia, nausea, and vomiting. Ataxia may occur from high blood levels of carbamazepine and this may result in falls, especially in elderly people.
- Mild skin rashes (e.g. isolated macular or maculopapular exanthemata) are also common, but usually disappear within a few weeks [ABPI Medicines Compendium, 2003].
- Idiosyncratic adverse effects are rare but serious. They include Stevens-Johnson syndrome, exfoliative dermatitis, and hepatitis [DTB, 1994]. Advise patients to seek advice if a rash or symptoms such as fever, sore throat, mouth ulcers, bruising, or bleeding develop.
- Check full blood count, liver function tests, and serum creatinine if an idiosyncratic reaction is suspected. Routine testing is not helpful.
- Dose adjustment is not generally needed in renal impairment, provided that the dose is titrated slowly against pain [Bunn and Ashley, 1999].
- Avoid carbamazepine in patients with angle-closure glaucoma (mild antimuscarinic action).
- Disturbances in cardiac rhythm have rarely been reported; carbamazepine should not be used in patients with arrhythmias, particularly heart block.
- Hyponatraemia is found in 20% of people receiving carbamazepine [van Amelsvoort et al, 1994] but is usually well tolerated. If the hyponatraemia is problematic, such as in an elderly person, restriction of fluid intake or a slight reduction in the carbamazepine dose usually resolves the issue.
- Carbamazepine induces liver microsomal enzymes and interacts with many drugs.

Medicines management: non-oral routes of drug delivery

- Syringe drivers are used for drug delivery if the patient is unable to take medicines by mouth, e.g. persistent nausea and vomiting, dysphagia, severe weakness, or coma.
- **Always** follow local palliative care guidelines or seek advice from local palliative care services or hospital pharmacy drug information services *before* mixing drugs in a syringe driver.
- The following information is included as a brief guide when these sources of help are unavailable:
  - Only use drugs that are known to be safe and effectiv by the subcutaneous route.
  - Check the compatibilities of drugs before mixing. There is most data on combinations of two drugs in a syringe driver, although some combinations of three four drugs are compatible.
  - If you are unable to contact your local palliative care team or hospital drug information service for compatibility advice, see www.palliativedrugs.com o Table 6 below.
  - Use water for injection as the diluent when mixing drugs in a syringe driver (except for ketamine or octreotide).
  - Do not use solutions that are discoloured or have precipitated.
- Some drugs can be given by subcutaneous bolus, or by the rectal, buccal, oromucosal, sublingual, or transdermal route. This could be considered if more tha two drugs require administration by a non-oral route, o the patient does not want a syringe driver.

[Twycross et al, 2002; BNF 46, 2003; Regnard and Hockley, 2004a].

Drugs for pain used in syringe drivers

- **Opioids:** diamorphine is the opioid of choice for subcutaneous infusion. Parenteral diamorphine is approximately three times as potent as oral morphine, s the *total* daily dosage of oral morphine should be divid by three to obtain the 24-hour dose of diamorphine. Fo example, if the patient takes oral modified-release morphine 30 mg twice a day (i.e. a total daily dose of 60 mg per day), start with diamorphine 20 mg over 24 hours via a syringe driver and adjust according to response [BNF 46, 2003].

Drugs commonly used in syringe drivers

- **Always** follow local palliative care guidelines or seek advice from local palliative care services or hospital pharmacy drug information services *before* mixing dru in a syringe driver.
- If you are unable to contact them see www.palliativedrugs.com. Alternatively, Table 6 is included as a brief guide.

Table 6: Compatibilities and alternative routes of drugs commonly given by syringe driver.

Drug	Compatibility with diamorphine[1]	Alternative routes/drugs[2]
Cyclizine	Diamorphine any strength + cyclizine 6.7 mg/ml Diamorphine 15 mg/ml + cyclizine 15 mg/ml Diamorphine 20 mg/ml + cyclizine 10 mg/ml	Levomepromazine (methotrimeprazine) as a single subcutaneou (s/c) bedtime dose
Dexamethasone	Compatible at usual concentrations, but mix carefully to prevent precipitation	Dexamethasone as a single s/c morning dose
Glycopyrronium bromide	Compatible at usual concentrations	Hyoscine hydrobromide sublingual tablets or patches
Haloperidol	Diamorphine 20–100 mg/ml + haloperidol 0.75 mg/ml Diamorphine 50 mg/ml + haloperidol 1.5 mg/ml	Haloperidol as a single s/c bedtime dose
Hyoscine butylbromide	Compatible at all usual concentrations	Hyoscine butylbromide as a s/c dose every 4–6 hours
Hyoscine hydrobromide	Compatible at all usual concentrations	Hyoscine hydrobromide sublingual tablets or patches
Levomepromazine (methotrimeprazine)	Compatible at all usual concentrations	Levomepromazine as a single s/c bedtime dose
Metoclopramide	Diamorphine 25 mg/ml + metoclopramide 5 mg/ml	Metoclopramide s/c 8-hourly or rectal domperidone
Midazolam	Compatible at all usual concentrations	Diazepam as a single rectal bedtime dose or levomepromazine a a single s/c bedtime dose

1. Twycross, R., Wilcock, A., Charlesworth, S., and Dickman, A. (2002) *Palliative care formulary*. Palliativedrugs.com Ltd. www.palliativedrugs.com [Accessed: 20-10-2003].
2. Regnard, C. and Hockley, J. (2004) *A guide to symptom relief in palliative care*. 5th ed. Oxford: Radcliffe Medical Press.

P

References

NHS staff in England can link, free of charge, from references to full text journals by clicking on [Full text] on the PRODIGY website.

1. ABPI Medicines Compendium (2002) *Summary of product characteristics for Durogesic.* Electronic Medicines Compendium. Datapharm Communications Ltd. www.emc.medicines.org.uk [Accessed: 09/02/2004].
2. ABPI Medicines Compendium (2003) *Summary of product characteristics for Tegretol retard tablets 200mg, 400mg.* Electronic Medicines Compendium. Datapharm Communications Ltd. www.emc.medicines.org.uk [Accessed: 09/02/2004].
3. Abu-Saad, H.H. and Courtens, A. (2001) Pain and symptom management. In: Abu-Saad, H.H. (Ed.) *Evidence-based palliative care: across the life span.* Oxford: Blackwell Science. 63–87.
4. Ahmedzai, S. and Brooks, D. (1997) Transdermal fentanyl versus sustained-release oral morphine in cancer pain: preference, efficacy, and quality of life. *Journal of Pain and Symptom Management* **13**(5), 254–261.
5. Block, S.D. and Snyder, L. (2000) Assessing and managing depression in the terminally ill patient. *Annals of Internal Medicine* **132**(3), 209–218.
6. BNF 46 (2003) *British National Formulary.* 46th edn. London: British Medical Association and Royal Pharmaceutical Society of Great Britain.
7. Bookbinder, M., Coyle, N., Kiss, M. et al (1996) Implementing national standards for cancer pain management: program model and evaluation. *Journal of Pain and Symptom Management* **12**(6), 334–347.
8. Bunn, R. and Ashley, C. (1999) *The renal drug handbook.* Abingdon: Radcliffe Medical Press Ltd.
9. CSM (2000) Selective serotonin reuptake inhibitors (SSRI's). *Current Problems in Pharmacovigilance* **26**(Sep), 11–12.
10. CSM (2003) Reminder: gastrointestinal toxicity and NSAIDs. *Current Problems in Pharmacovigilance* **29**(Sept), 8–9.
11. de Stoutz, N.D., Bruera, E. and Suarez-Almazor, M. (1995) Opioid rotation for toxicity reduction in terminal cancer patients. *Journal of Pain and Symptom Management* **10**(5), 378–384.
12. DH (2003) *Prescription cost analysis: England 2002.* Department of Health. www.dh.gov.uk [Accessed: 10/02/2004]. [Full text]
13. DTB (1994) Drug treatment of epilepsy. *Drug & Therapeutics Bulletin* **32**(6), 45–48. [Full text]
14. Ellershaw, J. and Griffiths, C. (2003) *The Liverpool care pathway for the dying patient (LCP).* Liverpool: Marie Curie Centre Liverpool and The Royal Liverpool & Broadgreen University Hospitals NHS Trust.
15. Fallon, M.T. and Hanks, G.W. (1999) Morphine, constipation and performance status in advanced cancer patients. *Palliative Medicine* **13**(2), 159–160.
16. Foley, K.M. (1979) Pain syndromes in patients with cancer. In: Bonica, J.J. and Ventafridda, V. (Eds.) *International symposium on pain of advanced cancer. Advances in pain research and therapy vol. 2.* New York: Raven Press. 59–76.
17. Foley, K.M. (2004) Acute and chronic cancer pain syndromes. In: Doyle, D., Hanks, G., Cherny, N. and Calman, K. (Eds.) *Oxford textbook of palliative medicine.* 3rd edn. Oxford: Oxford University Press. 298–316.
18. Grossman, S.A., Sheidler, V.R., Swedeen, K. et al (1991) Correlation of patient and caregiver ratings of cancer pain. *Journal of Pain and Symptom Management* **6**(2), 53–57.
19. Hanks, G.W., Conno, F., Cherny, N. et al (2001) Morphine and alternative opioids in cancer pain: the EAPC recommendations. *British Journal of Cancer* **84**(5), 587–593.
20. Hanks, G., Cherny, N.I. and Fallon, M. (2004) Opioid analgesic therapy. In: Doyle, D., Hanks, G., Cherny, N. and Calman, K. (Eds.) *Oxford textbook of palliative medicine.* 3rd edn. Oxford: Oxford University Press. 316–341.
21. Henry, D., Lim, L.L., Garcia-Rodriguez, L.A. et al (1996) Variability in risk of gastrointestinal complications with individual non-steroidal anti-inflammatory drugs: results of a collaborative meta-analysis. *British Medical Journal* **312**(7046), 1563–1566. [Full text]
22. Hernández-Diaz, S. and Rodriguez, L.A. (2000) Association between nonsteroidal anti-inflammatory drugs and upper gastrointestinal tract bleeding/perforation: an overview of epidemiologic studies published in the 1990s. *Archives of Internal Medicine* **160**(14), 2093–2099. [Full text]
23. Layton, D., Hughes, K., Harris, S. and Shakir, S.A. (2003) Comparison of the incidence rates of thromboembolic events reported for patients prescribed celecoxib and meloxicam in general practice in England using Prescription-Event Monitoring (PEM) data. *Rheumatology* **42**(11), 1354–1364. [Full text]
24. Lussier, D. and Portenoy, R.K. (2004) Adjuvant analgesics in pain management. In: Doyle, D., Hanks, G., Cherny, N. and Calman, K. (Eds.) *Oxford textbook of palliative medicine.* 3rd edn. Oxford: Oxford University Press. 349–378.
25. McQuay, H. and Moore, A. (1997) *Bibliography and systematic reviews in cancer pain management.* NCP/ICV/I03. Oxford: NHS National Cancer Research & Development Programme.
26. Mercadante, S. (1993) Celiac plexus block versus analgesics in pancreatic cancer pain. *Pain* **52**(2), 187–192.
27. MeReC (2003) The use of strong opioids in palliative care. *MeReC Briefing* **22**(Jun), 1–8.
28. Moore, A., Collins, S., Carroll, D. and McQuay, H. (1997) Paracetamol with and without codeine in acute pain: a quantitative systematic review. *Pain* **70**(2–3), 193–201.
29. Morita, T., Ichiki, T., Tsunoda, J. et al (1998) A prospective study on the dying process in terminally ill cancer patients. *American Journal of Hospice & Palliative Care* **15**(4), 217–222.
30. NICE (2001) *Guidance on the use of cyclo-oxygenase (Cox) II selective inhibitors, celecoxib, rofecoxib, meloxicam and etodolac for osteoarthritis and rheumatoid arthritis.* Technology appraisal no. 27. National Institute for Health and Clinical Excellence. www.nice.org.uk [Accessed: 16/10/2003].
31. O'Neill, B. and Fallon, M. (1997) ABC of palliative care: principles of palliative care and pain control. *British Medical Journal* **315**(7111), 801–804. [Full text]
32. Regnard, C. and Hockley, J. (Eds.) (2004a) *A guide to symptom relief in palliative care.* 5th edn. Oxford: Radcliffe Medical Press.
33. Regnard, C. and Hockley, J. (2004b) Diagnosing and treating pain. In: *A guide to symptom relief in palliative care.* 5th edn. Oxon: Radcliffe Medical Press Ltd.. 39–44.
34. Ripamonti, C., Twycross, R., Baines, M. et al (2001) Clinical-practice recommendations for the management of bowel obstruction in patients with end-stage cancer. *Supportive Care in Cancer* **9**(4), 223–233.

35. SIGN (2000) *Control of pain in patients with cancer.* Scottish Intercollegiate Guidelines Network. www.sign.ac.uk [Accessed: 20/10/2003].
36. Spiegel, D., Sands, S. and Koopman, C. (1994) Pain and depression in patients with cancer. *Cancer* **74**(9), 2570–2578.
37. Swarm, R.A., Karanikolas, M. and Cousins, M.J. (2004) Anaesthetic techniques for pain control. In: Doyle, D., Hanks, G., Cherny, N. and Calman, K. (Eds.) *Oxford textbook of palliative medicine.* 3rd edn. Oxford: Oxford University Press. 378–396.
38. Sykes, N.P. (1996) A volunteer model for the comparison of laxatives in opioid-related constipation. *Journal of Pain and Symptom Management* **11**(6), 363–369.
39. Twycross, R., Wilcock, A., Charlesworth, S. and Dickman, A. (2002) *Palliative care formulary.* Palliativedrugs.com Ltd. www.palliativedrugs.com [Accessed: 07/06/2005].
40. van Amelsvoort, T., Bakshi, R., Devaux, C.B. and Schwabe, S. (1994) Hyponatremia associated with carbamazepine and oxcarbazepine therapy: a review. *Epilepsia* **35**(1), 181–188.
41. Wiffen, P., McQuay, H., Carroll, D. et al (2000) *Anticonvulsant drugs for acute and chronic pain (Cochrane Review).* The Cochrane Library. Issue 3. Chichester, UK: John Wiley & Sons, Ltd. www.nelh.nhs.uk/cochrane.asp [Accessed: 05/07/2005]. [Full text]
42. Wiffen, P.J., Edwards, J.E., Barden, J. and McQuay, H.J.M. (2003) *Oral morphine for cancer pain (Cochrane Review).* The Cochrane Library. Issue 4. Oxford: Update Software.
43. Zech, D.F.J., Grond, S., Lynch, J. et al (1995) Validation of World Health Organization Guidelines for cancer pain relief: a 10-year prospective study. *Pain* **63**(1), 65–76.

P

PRODIGY GUIDANCE

Palliative care — respiratory secretions at the end of life

Last revised in February 2004
www.prodigy.nhs.uk/guidance.asp?gt=Palliative care - secretions

Applies to people over the age of 16 years

This guidance covers the management of problematic respiratory secretions at the end of life.

This guidance does not cover the management of haemoptysis.

There is separate PRODIGY guidance for the management of *Chest infections.*

There is separate PRODIGY guidance for *Palliative care — cough, Palliative care — dyspnoea, Palliative care — malodorous malignant ulcer of skin, Palliative care — nausea/vomiting/malignant bowel obstruction, Palliative care — oral problems, and Palliative care — pain.*

Goals

To alleviate the distress to the patient caused by accumulated respiratory secretions at the end of life
To alleviate the distress to the family and carers caused by noisy respiratory secretions at the end of life

Contents

Scenarios

- Noisy respiratory secretions at the end of life p.1499

Extended Information, p. 1500

Noisy respiratory secretions at the end of life

Which therapy?

Confirm the patient is in the terminal phase. Patients in the terminal phase have several features in common:

- They deteriorate day-by-day or faster because of their underlying condition.
- They express a realization that they are dying.
- They have reduced cognition, and are drowsy or comatose.
- They are bed-bound.
- They take little food or fluid and have difficulty with oral medication.
- The breathing pattern alters.
- They are peripherally cyanosed and cold.

Explain to the family that noisy respiratory secretions in a person with impaired levels of consciousness are unlikely to be distressing for that person. Such explanation is particularly relevant if treatment fails.

Treat using an antimuscarinic if there is any possibility of distress either to the person or to the family or carers.

- Sedation required: use hyoscine hydrobromide.
- Sedation not required: use hyoscine butylbromide or glycopyrronium bromide.

Consider:

- Repositioning of the patient on one side with upper body elevated.
- Suctioning secretions with a soft catheter.

Practical prescribing points

For further information please see the *Medicines Compendium* (www.medicines.org.uk) or the *British National Formulary* (www.bnf.org) or the *Palliative Care Formulary* (www.palliativedrugs.com).

Antimuscarinic drugs

- Antimuscarinics may exacerbate tachycardia, hypertension, and urinary retention.
- Hyoscine hydrobromide causes paradoxical agitation in some people.

Mixing drugs in syringe drivers

Always follow local palliative care guidelines or seek advice from local palliative care services or hospital pharmacy drug information services *before* mixing drugs in a syringe driver. The following information is included as a brief guide when these sources of help are unavailable:

- Check compatibilities before mixing drugs. See www.palliativedrugs.com, or Table 1.
- Use water for injection as the diluent when mixing drugs in a syringe driver (except for octreotide and ketamine).
- Do not use solutions that are cloudy or have precipitated.
- **Converting oral morphine to parenteral diamorphine:** divide the total daily dose of oral morphine by three to calculate the 24-hour dose of subcutaneous diamorphine.

Patient information leaflets

The following PILs are available at www.prodigy.nhs.uk

- Coping with Breathlessness - Macmillan Cancer Relief
- Living with Breathlessness - Macmillan Cancer Relief
- Managing Breathlessness - Macmillan Cancer Relief

Drug rationale

Drugs not included

- **Hyoscine hydrobromide patches** are not offered. One patch delivers 1 mg over 72 hours (i.e. 0.33 mg per 24 hours), so three or four patches need to be applied to achieve a dose of hyoscine hydrobromide over 24 hours that is similar to a continuous s/c infusion. They are generally tried only if the patient or the family does not wish a syringe driver to be used.

Drugs included

- **Hyoscine hydrobromide injection** is used by many centres. It causes sedation, which may be an advantage for some patients.

P

Table 1: Compatibility and alternative routes of drugs commonly given by syringe driver.

Drug	Compatibility with diamorphine[1]	Alternative routes/drugs[2]
Cyclizine	Diamorphine any strength + cyclizine 6.7 mg/ml Diamorphine 15 mg/ml + cyclizine 15 mg /ml Diamorphine 20 mg/ml + cyclizine 10 mg/ml	Levomepromazine (methotrimeprazine) as a single subcutaneous (s/c) bedtime dose
Dexamethasone	Compatible at usual concentrations, but mix carefully to prevent precipitation	Dexamethasone as a single s/c morning dose
Glycopyrronium bromide	Compatible at usual concentrations	Hyoscine hydrobromide sublingual tablets or patches
Haloperidol	Diamorphine 20–100 mg/ml + haloperidol 0.75 mg/ml Diamorphine 50 mg/ml + haloperidol 1.5 mg/ml	Haloperidol as a single s/c bedtime dose
Hyoscine butylbromide	Compatible at all usual concentrations	Hyoscine butylbromide as a s/c dose every 4–6 hours
Hyoscine hydrobromide	Compatible at all usual concentrations	Hyoscine hydrobromide sublingual tablets or patches
Levomepromazine (methotrimeprazine)	Compatible at all usual concentrations	Levomepromazine as a single s/c bedtime dose
Metoclopramide	Diamorphine 25 mg/ml + metoclopramide 5 mg/ml	Metoclopramide s/c 8-hourly or rectal domperidone
Midazolam	Compatible at all usual concentrations	Diazepam as a single rectal bedtime dose or levomepromazine as a single s/c bedtime dose

1. Twycross, R., Wilcock, A., Charlesworth, S., and Dickman, A. (2002) *Palliative care formulary*. Palliativedrugs.com Ltd. www.palliativedrugs.com [Accessed: 30-7-2002].
2. Regnard, C. and Hockley, J. (2004) *A guide to symptom relief in palliative care*. 5th ed. Oxon: Radcliffe Medical Press.

- **Glycopyrronium bromide injection** is used by some centres. It rarely causes sedation, so is useful when minimal sedation is wanted by the patient or the family.
- **Hyoscine butylbromide** can also be used. It does not cause sedation, but has a short duration of action as a single subcutaneous injection.
- **A terminal-phase stand-by drug pack** containing drugs commonly needed at the end of life is also included. The pack contains cyclizine, diamorphine, hyoscine hydrobromide, midazolam, and water for injection [Ellershaw and Griffiths, 2003].

Prescriptions

Antimuscarinics (to reduce respiratory secretions)

Hyoscine hydrobromide 400mcg/ml injection

- Age from 16 years onwards
- Hyoscine hydrobrom 400mcg/ml. Give 400mcg as a single s/c injection. Review the response after 30mins. If effective, continue using 1.2mg as a continuous 24-hour s/c infusion; supply 10 1ml ampoules; NHS Cost £27.12.

Glycopyrronium bromide 200mcg/ml injection

- Age from 16 years onwards
- Glycopyrronium 200mcg/ml inj. Give 200mcg as a single s/c injection. Review response after 1 hour. If effective, continue using 1.2mg as a continuous 24-hour s/c infusion; supply 20 1ml ampoules; NHS Cost £12.00.

Hyoscine butylbromide 20mg/ml injection

- Age from 16 years onwards
- Hyoscine butylbromide 20mg/ml. Give 20mg as a single s/c injection. Review the response after 30mins. If effective, continue using 60-120mg as a continuous 24-hour s/c infusion; supply 10 1ml ampoules; NHS Cost £2.00.

Terminal phase standby drug pack

Standby drug pack

- Age from 16 years onwards
- Hyoscine hydrobrom 400mcg/ml. For intravenous or subcutaneous injection as directed; supply 5 1ml ampoules; NHS Cost £13.55.
- Midazolam 5mg/ml injection. For intravenous or subcutaneous injection as directed; supply 5 2ml ampoules; NHS Cost £4.05.
- Water for injection (5ml). Use as directed; supply 10 5ml ampoule; NHS Cost £2.82.
- Instructions for handwriting CD prescription for diamorphine: Patients name and address. Diamorphine 10mg injection. State the dose and dose interval, e.g. 5-10 mg every 4 hours when required. Supply 2 (two) ampoules. Signed and dated.
- Cyclizine lactate 50mg/ml inj. For intravenous or subcutaneous injection as directed; supply 5 1ml ampoules; NHS Cost £2.71.

Extended Information

Background information

- What is it? p.1500
- How common is it? p.1500
- How do I know my patient has it? p.1501
- What else might it be? p.1501

What is it?

- Alteration of the normal production and clearance of mucus may result in the retention of secretions in the airway of the dying patient.
  - **Mucus production may increase** in response to inflammation and coughing.
  - **Mucociliary transport may be impaired,** owing to loss of cilia, most commonly from smoking or because of the loss of the fluidity of the mucus associated with dehydration.
  - **The cough reflex may become impaired** with reduced levels of consciousness and with sedative, hypnotic, and opioid drugs in the dying patient.

How common is it?

- Loose airway secretions are a problem in approximately 25% of patients in the last hours, or occasionally days, of life [Wildiers and Menten, 2002].

Loose airway secretions are heard in approximately 50% of dying patients.

How do I know my patient has it?

Audible secretions in airway.
Patient in last hours and days of life (see *Recognising the terminal phase*).
Impaired level of consciousness.
Ineffective or absent cough reflex.

What else might it be?

Problematic airway secretions with intact cough reflex

Airway secretions may be problematic in patients who are not at the end of life. Usually the cough reflex is intact, the problems are chronic (starting well before the terminal phase), and the level of consciousness is not impaired at the outset.
Abnormal secretions may be produced within the respiratory tree (e.g. bronchorrhoea or infection) or outside of it and aspirated into the airway (e.g. via a tracheo-oesophageal fistula).
For further information on treating respiratory secretions causing cough, see the PRODIGY guidance *Palliative care – cough*.

Secretions from inside the respiratory tree

Chest infection is common in patients with advanced cancer, and the decision to treat or not with antibiotics can be a difficult one (see *Is the sputum infected?*).
Bronchorrhoea is rare. It is defined as the production of 100 ml or more per day of watery mucus. Up to 9 litres of mucus production per day has been reported.

- Bronchorrhoea is usually a chronic problem, and most commonly occurs with bronchioalveolar carcinoma (which accounts for 1–2% of lung cancers) but may also arise from pulmonary metastases from other tumours.
- Numerous treatment options have been tried and their effect is often variable. Consider specialist referral.

[Doyle et al, 2004]

Secretions from outside the respiratory tree

Aspiration may be occurring when a patient presents with recurrent episodes of choking, coughing, or pneumonia. Factors predisposing to aspiration in the dying patient include old age, impaired level of consciousness, impaired cough or gag reflex, near-supine feeding position, and structural diseases of the airway and upper gastrointestinal tract. If suspected, consider referral to a speech therapist for videofluoroscopy [Doyle et al, 2004].
Tracheo-oesophageal fistula can form because of malignant disease, and may lead to aspiration. If suspected, referral for further investigation and possible stent emplacement should be considered.

Management issues

Recognising the terminal phase p.1501
Adjustments in the terminal phase p.1501
The distress of respiratory secretions in the terminal phase p.1501
Managing respiratory secretions in the terminal phase p.1501
Medicines management p.1503

Recognising the terminal phase

In order to care for dying patients it is essential to diagnose dying. Healthcare professionals are sometimes reluctant to diagnose dying, and therefore the appropriate adjustments in the terminal phase may not be made.

- **The terminal phase starts a median of 24 hours before death,** varying from hours to several days.
- **Patients in the terminal phase have several common features:**
  - They deteriorate day-by-day or faster because of their underlying condition.
  - They express a realization that they are dying.
  - They have reduced cognition, and are drowsy or comatose.
  - They are bed-bound.
  - They take little food or fluid, and have difficulty with oral medication.
  - The breathing pattern alters.
  - They are peripherally cyanosed and cold.

[Morita et al, 1998]

Adjustments in the terminal phase

- **The terminal phase is a time of adjustments for all** [Regnard and Hockley, 2004]:
  - **Stop unnecessary drugs** and continue with other drugs by an appropriate route.
  - **Ensure commonly required medication is available in the house** (e.g. cyclizine, diamorphine, hyoscine hydrobromide, and midazolam), so that there is no delay in treatment of new or developing symptoms. A prescription is available for these items in the scenario *Noisy respiratory secretions*.
  - **Ensure physical symptoms are well controlled.**
  - **Explore understanding and provide appropriate explanation** of the situation to the patient, family, and other professional carers.
  - **Set realistic goals.**
  - **Ensure that religious and spiritual care** is offered if wanted.
  - **Ensure the environment is appropriate.**
- **The Liverpool Care Pathway for the dying patient** provides a national framework caring for patients in the terminal phase. It integrates professional communication and documentation integrating national guidelines into clinical practice. Further information can be obtained from www.lcp-mariecurie.org.uk.

P

The distress of respiratory secretions in the terminal phase

- **Once a patient's level of consciousness is reduced to such a point that they have no cough reflex, they are unlikely to be aware or distressed by accumulated respiratory secretions.** Explanation of this to the family and carers can help to alleviate concerns that the patient is suffering.
- Despite this, noisy respiratory secretions may distress family and carers. It is therefore seems reasonable to try to control this where possible.

Managing respiratory secretions in the terminal phase

Measures that may be employed in all patients with problematic respiratory secretions

- **Repositioning** of the patient on one side with upper body elevated.
- **Suction with soft catheter.**

[Regnard and Hockley, 2004]

Is the sputum loose and fluid?

- Coughing normally easily clears loose fluid sputum.
- **Sputum usually only accumulates if there is significant impairment of the cough reflex,** and this usually only

occurs with significantly reduced levels of consciousness, e.g. at the end of life.

- **Antimuscarinic drugs, such as hyoscine hydrobromide, are commonly used to reduce retained secretions at the end of life,** and can relieve death rattle in 50–60% of patients [Hughes et al, 2000].
- **Such drugs should not replace non-pharmacological interventions such as repositioning the patient, and gentle suction.**
- **Antimuscarinics should be started promptly,** as they only inhibit new secretions. They do not affect existing secretions. There is also less impact if secretions are due to pulmonary infection or oedema.
- **There is a lack of evidence comparing different antimuscarinic drugs in the clinical setting.** The final choice of antimuscarinic drug and route will depend on the needs of each individual [Bennett et al, 2002]:
  - **Hyoscine hydrobromide** is used by many centres. A single subcutaneous (s/c) dose has a moderate duration of action, and causes sedation.
  - **Hyoscine butylbromide** is cheaper and is commonly carried by GPs in their emergency bags, but has a short duration of action (about an hour as a single s/c dose). This drug does not cross the blood-brain barrier, and so does not cause sedation.
  - **Glycopyrronium bromide** is used by some centres. This drug is not sedating and has a longer duration of action (about 6 hours as a single s/c dose). It crosses the blood-brain barrier only slowly and erratically, so rarely causes sedation.
- **Hyoscine hydrobromide patches are also available.** One patch delivers 1 mg over 72 hours (i.e. 0.33 mg per 24 hours), so three or four patches need to be applied to achieve a dose of hyoscine hydrobromide over 24 hours that is similar to a continuous s/c infusion. They are generally tried only if the patient or the family does not wish a syringe driver to be used.

What dose of antimuscarinic should I use?

- **Hyoscine hydrobromide:** give 400 micrograms as a single s/c injection. Review the response after 30 minutes. If effective, continue, using 1.2 mg as a continuous 24-hour s/c infusion.
- **Glycopyrronium bromide:** give 200 micrograms as a single s/c injection. Review the response after 1 hour (it has a slower onset of action than hyoscine hydrobromide does). If effective, continue using 1.2 mg as a continuous 24-hour s/c infusion.
- **Hyoscine butylbromide:** give 20 mg as a single subcutaneous injection. Review the response after 30 minutes. If effective, continue, using 60–120 mg as a continuous 24-hour s/c infusion.

[Bennett et al, 2002; Twycross et al, 2002]

Is the sputum thick and tenacious?

- **Tenacious sputum may be difficult to clear by coughing.**
- **Dehydration or cystic fibrosis** may render sputum tenacious.
- **If the patient is dehydrated, consider the appropriateness of re-hydration.** The prognosis, the burden of the intervention, and the wishes or the patient and family need to be considered.
- **Consider using hypertonic saline 6%** (4 ml nebulised every 12 hours) to loosen sputum — the hypertonicity induces influx of water from the epithelium to the mucous. **The cough reflex must be intact** so that loosened secretions can be expectorated [Doyle et al, 2004; Regnard and Hockley, 2004]. Note: hypertonic saline may take a few days to obtain, as it is only available from Specials Manufacturers.
- **If the problem persists, seek specialist advice.** Propranolol, carbocisteine, and dornase alfa are used by some specialist centres to loosen tenacious secretions [Regnard and Hockley, 2004].

Is the sputum infected?

- **In patients in the terminal phase, antibiotics will make little difference to the course of events** [Doyle et al, 2004].
- **Symptomatic management** such as control of fever and management of sputum may be more appropriate [Doyle et al, 2004].
- **If infected secretions are causing distress and are not easily managed by other means,** then consider giving a single intravenous dose of a broad-spectrum antibiotic, e.g. ceftriaxone (once-daily administration) or cefotaxime (commonly carried by GPs in their emergency bags). Repeat only if symptoms reoccur [Regnard and Hockley, 2004].

Table 2: Compatibility and alternative routes of drugs commonly given by syringe driver.

Drug	Compatibility with diamorphine[1]	Alternative routes/drugs[2]
Cyclizine	Diamorphine any strength + cyclizine 6.7 mg/ml Diamorphine 15 mg/ml + cyclizine 15 mg/ml Diamorphine 20 mg/ml + cyclizine 10 mg/ml	Levomepromazine (methotrimeprazine) as a single subcutaneous (s/c) bedtime dose
Dexamethasone	Compatible at usual concentrations, but mix carefully to prevent precipitation	Dexamethasone as a single s/c morning dose
Glycopyrronium bromide	Compatible at usual concentrations	Hyoscine hydrobromide sublingual tablets or patches
Haloperidol	Diamorphine 20-100 mg/ml + haloperidol 0.75 mg/ml Diamorphine 50 mg/ml + haloperidol 1.5 mg/ml	Haloperidol as a single s/c bedtime dose
Hyoscine butylbromide	Compatible at all usual concentrations	Hyoscine butylbromide as a s/c dose every 4–6 hours
Hyoscine hydrobromide	Compatible at all usual concentrations	Hyoscine hydrobromide sublingual tablets or patches
Levomepromazine (methotrimeprazine)	Compatible at all usual concentrations	Levomepromazine as a single s/c bedtime dose
Metoclopramide	Diamorphine 25 mg/ml + metoclopramide 5 mg/ml	Metoclopramide s/c 8-hourly or rectal domperidone
Midazolam	Compatible at all usual concentrations	Diazepam as a single rectal bedtime dose or levomepromazine as a single s/c bedtime dose

1. Twycross, R., Wilcock, A., Charlesworth, S., and Dickman, A. (2002) *Palliative care formulary*. Palliativedrugs.com Ltd. www.palliativedrugs.com [Accessed: 30-7-2002].
2. Regnard, C. and Hockley, J. (2004) *A guide to symptom relief in palliative care*. 5th ed. Oxford: Radcliffe Medical Press.

Medicines management

Antimuscarinic drugs

- **There should be no contraindications to the use of antimuscarinics for retained secretions in moribund patients,** provided that they are carefully titrated against symptoms [Twycross et al, 2002].
- Dry mouth, constipation, urinary retention, and blurred vision are common adverse effects, although they may not be an issue in the terminal phase [Bennett et al, 2002].
- Low doses of glycopyrronium bromide (200 micrograms as a single subcutaneous dose) are less likely than hyoscine salts to exacerbate tachycardia or hypertension [Bennett et al, 2002].
- **Hyoscine hydrobromide is usually sedating,** but causes paradoxical agitation in some people.

Non-oral routes of drug delivery

- **Syringe drivers** are used for drug delivery if the patient is unable to take medicines by mouth (e.g. if there is persistent nausea and vomiting, dysphagia, severe weakness, or coma).
- **Use only drugs that are known to be safe and effective by the subcutaneous route.** Use water for injection as the diluent when mixing drugs in a syringe driver (except for ketamine or octreotide).
- **Check the compatibility of drugs before mixing.** There are most data on combinations of two drugs in a syringe driver, although some combinations of three or four drugs are compatible.
- **Do not use solutions that are discoloured or have precipitated.**
- **Some drugs can be given by subcutaneous bolus, or by the rectal, buccal or sublingual route.** Such a route could be considered if more than two drugs require administration by a non-oral route, or if the patient does not want a syringe driver.

[Regnard and Hockley, 2004]

Drugs commonly used in syringe drivers

- **Always** follow local palliative care guidelines or seek advice from local palliative care services or hospital pharmacy drug information services *before* mixing drugs in a syringe driver.
- If you are unable to contact them see www.palliativedrugs.com. Alternatively, Table 2 is included as a brief guide.

References

1. Bennett, M., Lucas, V., Brennan, M. et al (2002) Using anti-muscarinic drugs in the management of death rattle: evidence-based guidelines for palliative care. *Palliative Medicine* **16**(5), 369–374.
2. Doyle, D., Hanks, G.W.C. and MacDonald, N. (Eds.) (2004) *Oxford textbook of palliative medicine.* 3rd edn. Oxford: Oxford University Press.
3. Ellershaw, J. and Griffiths, C. (2003) *The Liverpool care pathway for the dying patient (LCP).* Liverpool: Marie Curie Centre Liverpool and The Royal Liverpool & Broadgreen University Hospitals NHS Trust.
4. Hughes, A., Wilcock, A., Corcoran, R. et al (2000) Audit of three antimuscarinic drugs for managing retained secretions. *Palliative Medicine* **14**(3), 221–222.
5. Morita, T., Ichiki, T., Tsunoda, J. et al (1998) A prospective study on the dying process in terminally ill cancer patients. *American Journal of Hospice & Palliative Care* **15**(4), 217–222.
6. Regnard, C. and Hockley, J. (Eds.) (2004) *A guide to symptom relief in palliative care.* 5th edn. Oxford: Radcliffe Medical Press.
7. Twycross, R., Wilcock, A., Charlesworth, S. and Dickman, A. (2002) *Palliative care formulary.* Palliativedrugs.com Ltd. www.palliativedrugs.com [Accessed: 07/06/2005].
8. Wildiers, H. and Menten, J. (2002) Death rattle: prevalence, prevention and treatment. *Journal of Pain and Symptom Management* **23**(4), 310–317.

P

PRODIGY GUIDANCE

Parkinson's disease

Last revised in April 2005
www.prodigy.nhs.uk/guidance.asp?gt=Parkinson's disease

Applies to people over the age of 16 years

This guidance covers the accurate diagnosis of Parkinson's disease, the differential diagnosis of Parkinsonism, the management of Parkinson's disease, and the management of drug-induced Parkinsonism.

There is separate PRODIGY guidance for the management of *Depression.*

Goals

- To ensure accurate diagnosis
- To provide treatment tailored to the individual's needs
- To relieve symptoms of Parkinson's disease and reduce disability
- To optimize mobility and functional status
- To restore normal level of function for as long as possible
- To minimize adverse effects of medication
- To minimize fluctuation of symptoms throughout the day
- To slow disease progression

Contents

Scenarios

- Diagnosis of Parkinson's disease p.1504
- Drug-induced Parkinsonism p.1504

Extended Information, p. 1506

Which scenario?

- **Diagnosis of Parkinson's disease:** covers the need to refer all people with features suggestive of Parkinson's disease to a specialist.
- **Drug-induced Parkinsonism:** covers the management of Parkinsonism caused by drugs.

P

Diagnosis of Parkinson's disease

Which therapy?

- **It is recommended that all people suspected to have Parkinson's disease are referred to a neurologist, or physician with an interest in Parkinson's disease, before drug treatment is initiated:**
  - An accurate diagnosis is vital to ensure correct treatment.
  - Up to a quarter of people diagnosed with Parkinson's disease do not have it.
  - In early disease there is not usually a need to begin treatment immediately.
  - One of the most difficult decisions is when to start treatment, and with which drug to start.
  - The drug management is becoming increasingly complex with the recent advent of new medication.
  - An average GP's list will have only 2–3 people with Parkinson's disease, making it difficult to acquire sufficient experience of the condition.
- **Ensure that a full drug history has been taken to screen for drug-induced Parkinsonism** (see the scenario *Drug-induced Parkinsonism* below).

Should I refer or investigate?

Refer?

- **It is recommended that all people suspected to have Parkinson's disease are referred to a neurologist, or physician with an interest in Parkinson's disease, before drug treatment is initiated.**
- **Referral to the Parkinson's disease Nurse Specialist** (if locally available) is also recommended.
- **Physiotherapy, speech therapy, occupational therapy, and dietetics** may all have a part to play. Discussion should include consideration of driving ability; the person should also be asked to inform the DVLA and their insurance broker.
- **The Parkinson's Disease Society** is an invaluable source of support and information, for people with Parkinson's disease and primary care teams alike. It can be contacted at:
  - Parkinson's Disease Society, 215 Vauxhall Bridge Road, London, SW1V 1EJ
  - Helpline: 0808 800 0303
  - Web: www.parkinsons.org.uk

Investigate?

- **There are no specific investigations** for Parkinson's disease.
- It may be appropriate to check full blood count, creatinine and electrolytes, thyroid function tests, and liver function tests to help rule out other underlying disease.

Patient information leaflets

The following PILs are available at www.prodigy.nhs.uk

- Parkinson's Disease
- Parkinson's Disease Society
- YAPP&RS - Young Alert Parkinson's Partners and Relatives

Drug rationale

- There are no prescriptions offered in this scenario.

Drug-induced Parkinsonism

Which therapy?

- **Reduce or stop the causative drug.**
- **If it is not possible to reduce or stop the drug,** or if the Parkinsonism is problematic, use an antimuscarinic to improve symptoms. Increase the dose gradually to the level that controls symptoms, then stop after several weeks if possible.
- **Drug-induced Parkinsonism is caused by dopamine-receptor blocking agents,** such as phenothiazines (e.g.

prochlorperazine), butyrophenones (e.g. haloperidol), metoclopramide, and cinnarizine.

Drug-induced Parkinsonism starts within days or weeks of beginning the causative drug; it usually resolves within 3 months of stopping the drug, but in some cases may persist.

The newer atypical antipsychotic agents may have a lower risk of drug-induced Parkinsonism. If it is not possible to stop the causative antipsychotic agent, consideration should be given to switching to one of the atypical antipsychotics.

ractical prescribing points

›r further information please see the *Medicines ɔmpendium* (www.medicines.org.uk) or the *British ational Formulary* (www.bnf.org).

Common adverse effects include dry mouth, constipation, problems with micturition, blurred vision, tachycardia, and confusion.

Advise people that antimuscarinics can affect the performance of skilled tasks, so they should not drive if affected.

Antimuscarinics may worsen tardive dyskinesia.

Elderly: adverse effects are common, especially confusion. Avoid antimuscarinics if possible or titrate the dose slowly.

Prostatic hypertrophy, urinary retention, or glaucoma: avoid antimuscarinics.

hould I refer or investigate?

efer?

All people who still have Parkinsonian symptoms after the offending drug has been withdrawn should be considered for referral to a specialist.

If an atypical antipsychotic is being considered, the person should be referred to a psychiatrist.

atient information leaflets

ıe following PILs are available at www.prodigy.nhs.uk

Medicines - Name Changes of Medicines

Parkinson's Disease

Parkinson's Disease Society

YAPP&RS - Young Alert Parkinson's Partners and Relatives

hared decision making

One of the medicines you are taking may be causing side-effects, such as muscle problems, stiffness, and shaking.

Stopping or changing your medicine may be an option. This may not be possible if you need to carry on with your treatment.

An extra medicine is another option to counteract these side-effects. Three commonly used medicines are trihexyphenidyl (benzhexol), procyclidine, and orphenadrine.

Taking one of these will usually stop or ease the above side-effects.

These extra medicines sometimes cause different side-effects. These include: constipation, a dry mouth, difficulty in passing urine, a fast pulse, and some confusion in older people.

Adjusting the dose may be necessary if side-effects occur.

Drug rationale

Drugs included

- **All antimuscarinics** currently licensed for drug-induced Parkinsonism in the UK are included.
- **Antimuscarinics** (trihexyphenidyl [benzhexol], orphenadrine, and procyclidine) can reduce the symptoms of drug-induced Parkinsonism. No important differences exist between them, although it is possible to titrate more slowly with trihexyphenidyl and orphenadrine than with procyclidine.

Prescriptions

Trihexyphenidyl (benzhexol) (if appropriate)

Start trihexyphenidyl (benzhexol): titrate 1mg to 4mg/day
- Age from 16 years onwards
- Trihexyphenidyl 2mg tablets. Take half a tablet once a day for 3 days, then take half a tablet twice a day for 3 days, then take one tablet twice a day; supply 56 tablets; NHS Cost £2.00.

Trihexyphenidyl (benzhexol) 4mg/day (2mg twice a day)
- Age from 16 years onwards
- Trihexyphenidyl 2mg tablets. Take one tablet twice a day; supply 56 tablets; NHS Cost £2.00.

Trihexyphenidyl (benzhexol) 6mg/day (2mg three times a day)
- Age from 16 years onwards
- Trihexyphenidyl 2mg tablets. Take one tablet three times a day; supply 84 tablets; NHS Cost £3.00.

Trihexyphenidyl (benzhexol) 8mg/day (2mg four times a day)
- Age from 16 years onwards
- Trihexyphenidyl 2mg tablets. Take one tablet four times a day; supply 112 tablets; NHS Cost £4.00.

Trihexyphenidyl (benzhexol) 10mg/day (5mg twice a day)
- Age from 16 years onwards
- Trihexyphenidyl 5mg tablets. Take one tablet twice a day; supply 56 tablets; NHS Cost £2.37.

Trihexyphenidyl (benzhexol) 15mg/day (5mg three times a day)
- Age from 16 years onwards
- Trihexyphenidyl 5mg tablets. Take one tablet three times a day; supply 84 tablets; NHS Cost £3.56.

Max dose: trihexyphenidyl (benzhexol) 5mg four times a day
- Age from 16 years onwards
- Trihexyphenidyl 5mg tablets. Take one tablet four times a day; supply 112 tablets; NHS Cost £4.74.

Orphenadrine (if appropriate)

Usual start dose: orphenadrine 150mg per day (50mg tds)
- Age from 16 years onwards
- Orphenadrine 50mg tablets. Take one tablet three times a day; supply 84 tablets; NHS Cost £4.83.

Low dose: orphenadrine 100mg per day (50mg twice a day)
- Age from 16 years onwards
- Orphenadrine 50mg tablets. Take one tablet twice a day; supply 56 tablets; NHS Cost £3.22.

Orphenadrine 200mg per day (50mg four times a day)
- Age from 16 years onwards
- Orphenadrine 50mg tablets. Take one tablet four times a day; supply 112 tablets; NHS Cost £6.44.

Orphenadrine 300mg per day (100mg three times a day)
- Age from 16 years onwards
- Orphenadrine 50mg tablets. Take two tablets three times a day; supply 168 tablets; NHS Cost £9.66.

Max dose: orphenadrine 400mg/day (100mg four times a day)
- Age from 16 years onwards
- Orphenadrine 50mg tablets. Take two tablets four times a day; supply 224 tablets; NHS Cost £12.88.

Procyclidine (if appropriate)

Start procyclidine: titrate from 7.5mg to 15mg per day
- Age from 16 years onwards
- Procyclidine 5mg tablets. Take half a tablet three times a day for 3 days, then take one tablet three times a day; supply 84 tablets; NHS Cost £6.42.

Procyclidine 15mg per day (5mg three times a day)
- Age from 16 years onwards
- Procyclidine 5mg tablets. Take one tablet three times a day; supply 84 tablets; NHS Cost £6.42.

Max dose: procyclidine 30mg/day (10mg three times a day)
- Age from 16 years onwards
- Procyclidine 5mg tablets. Take two tablets three times a day; supply 168 tablets; NHS Cost £12.84.

Extended Information

Background information

- What is it? p.1506
- How common is it? p.1506
- How do I know my patient has it? p.1506
- What else might it be? p.1507
- Complications and prognosis p.1507

What is it?

- **Parkinson's disease is an age-related, chronic, progressive, neurodegenerative disorder.**
- **Parkinsonism is a clinical syndrome comprising akinesia, rigidity, and tremor.** The core diagnostic feature is bradykinesia. Parkinsonism can be divided into three groups of conditions (for further details see the section *What else might it be?* below):
  - Parkinson's disease
  - Atypical Parkinsonian syndromes and other neurodegenerative disorders
  - Secondary causes
- **Parkinson's disease affects movement, cognitive function, emotion, and autonomic function.**
- **Neuronal degeneration and loss occur** in the nigrostriatal pathway, with subsequent depletion of the neurotransmitter dopamine. Lewy bodies are found in surviving cells.
- The cause of Parkinson's disease is unknown, but is believed to be multifactorial, caused by environmental factors acting on genetically susceptible people as they age [AHRQ, 2003]. Eight monogenic forms of Parkinson's disease have been identified so far, together with a number of genes that may exert a weaker predisposing effect [Healy et al, 2004].

How common is it?

- **Parkinson's disease is the second most common cause of chronic neurological disability in the UK.**
- **The prevalence** of Parkinson's disease has been estimated worldwide at 31–328 per 100,000.
- **Parkinson's disease is predominantly a condition of the elderly,** although it does occur in younger people. It is estimated that 1–2% of people over 65 years of age hav Parkinson's disease, and 8% of cases occur under the a of 40 years.
- The estimated prevalence in nursing home residents is 5–10%; it is estimated that 20% of older people with Parkinson's disease will eventually be institutionalized.

[American Medical Directors Association, 2002; AHRQ, 2003]

How do I know my patient has it?

- **The diagnosis of Parkinson's disease is made on clinica grounds and is often difficult — there is no clinical gold standard diagnostic test.**
  - A study in primary care found that 25% of people being treated for Parkinson's disease had no evidence of Parkinsonian features [Meara et al, 1999].
  - Post-mortem studies have previously shown that the diagnosis of Parkinson's disease made by a neurologist, or a physician with an interest in Parkinson's disease, is wrong in 24% of cases [Rajpu et al, 1991; Hughes et al, 1992].
  - More recent post-mortem studies, however, have shown that the diagnosis of Parkinson's disease mad by a neurologist, or a physician with an interest in Parkinson's disease, has improved. Positive predictiv values for the clinical diagnosis of Parkinson's diseas of 85% [Hughes et al, 2002] and 90% [Hughes et al, 2001] have been reported.
- **An asymmetric onset is usual,** although the features usually become bilateral.
- **Bradykinesia** (slowness of movement), **akinesia** (inabili to move), and **hypokinesia** (reduced amplitude of movements): these are the defining features of Parkinson's disease. They may coexist, and manifest as early fatiguing, reduced amplitude and speed of repeate movements, poor sequencing, and difficulty performin simultaneous motor tasks. Common features are:
  - Poor facial expression
  - Monotonous soft speech
  - Reduced arm-swinging (and hence presentation with frozen shoulder)
  - Reduced walking speed
  - Reduced blinking rate
  - Small handwriting
  - Difficulty with fine motor tasks (e.g. buttons)
  - Weakness and fatigue
  - Difficulty in chewing and eating
- **Rigidity:** this may be either lead-pipe or cog-wheel; the latter occurs when an increase in tone is present with a tremor (which may not be clinically evident). The increase in tone is constant throughout the range of movement and is independent of the speed of moveme The rigidity is more apparent to the clinician than to th patient, who may describe it as 'slowness'.
- **Tremor:** this is present in 75% of people at presentatio and will develop in most as the disease progresses. It usually begins unilaterally, distally, and in the arm. It is most obvious when the affected part is rested and supported. It is usually reduced by movement and slee It is usually increased by stress, anxiety, and fatigue. T most prominent feature is the 'pill-rolling tremor' of th fingers and hands.
- **Gait disturbance:** gait is typically short-paced and shuffling, with a flexed stance, reduced arm-swing, festination, and a tendency to fall. There is poor gait initiation, poor turning, and unsteadiness when turnin
- **Postural instability:** there is impairment of postural reflexes, with a tendency to fall backwards. Falls occur notably late in Parkinson's disease (in contrast to

atypical Parkinsonian syndromes, where they occur early). There may be difficulties turning the body axis, e.g. turning in bed, or getting out of a chair, bed, or car.
- **Cognitive dysfunction:**
  - **Dementia** is found in up to 40% of people with Parkinson's disease. Most, however, show signs of distinct and subtle cognitive dysfunction even early in the disease [Goetz et al, 2002h; Hobson and Meara, 2004].
  - **Depression** affects 40–50% of people with Parkinson's disease. It occurs as a prodrome to the disease in up to 30% of people. It is usually of mild-to-moderate severity. Suicide is rare [Goetz et al, 2002g].
  - **Hallucinations** occur in 30% of people during the first 5 years.
  - It is important to remember that hallucinations, delirium, and dementia may be part of the disease process; however, they may be caused or aggravated by drug treatment.
- **Autonomic dysfunction:** postural hypotension is common, especially in the later stages, and may be exacerbated by drug treatment. Other features include:
  - Urinary symptoms
  - Excess salivation
  - Dysphagia
  - Constipation
  - Sweating
  - Impotence
  - Disturbed temperature regulation
- **Other features commonly found** in people with Parkinson's disease include:
  - Speech disorders (hypokinetic or Parkinsonian dysarthria)
  - Sleep disturbances
  - Olfactory disturbances
  - Seborrhoeic dermatitis

[Olanow et al, 2001; American Medical Directors Association, 2002; AHRQ, 2003]

What else might it be?

The term 'Parkinsonism' describes a clinical syndrome with akinesia as the core feature. Parkinsonism can be divided into three groups of conditions: Parkinson's disease; atypical Parkinsonian syndromes and other neurodegenerative disorders; and secondary causes.

- **Atypical Parkinsonian syndromes and other neurodegenerative disorders:**
  - Progressive supranuclear palsy
  - Multiple system atrophy
  - Corticobasal degeneration
  - Dementia with Lewy bodies
  - Alzheimer's disease
  - Motor neurone disease
- **Secondary causes:**
  - Drug-induced (e.g. antipsychotics)
  - Cerebrovascular disease
  - Infections: viral encephalitis, AIDS-associated, Creutzfeld–Jacob disease
  - Toxicity (e.g. carbon monoxide, manganese, methanol)
  - Head injury (e.g. boxers)
  - Tumours
  - Hydrocephalus
  - Chronic subdural haematoma
- Features that suggest a diagnosis other than Parkinson's disease include:
  - Early dementia or apraxia
  - Early instability and falls
  - Prominent autonomic impairment
  - Oculomotor disturbances
  - Cerebellar signs
  - Rapid progression over several months to a year
- **The management of the above conditions is different to that of Parkinson's disease,** therefore accurate diagnosis is vital.

[American Medical Directors Association, 2002; AHRQ, 2003]

- **Essential tremor is often confused with Parkinson's disease.** Essential tremor is increasingly common with age. It is bilateral and usually symmetric. There may be an autosomal dominant family history. People may be unable to carry cups of tea or pints of beer without spilling them, but retain the ability to do up buttons (the opposite occurs in Parkinson's disease). Essential tremor may respond to alcohol or beta-blockers.
- **Other causes of tremor include:**
  - Drugs, especially antipsychotics
  - Hyperthyroidism
  - Peripheral neuropathy
  - Cerebrovascular disease
  - Alcohol dependency

[Rao et al, 2003]

Complications and prognosis

Complications

- **Complications of Parkinson's disease include** [American Medical Directors Association, 2002]:
  - Infections
  - Aspiration pneumonia
  - Poor nutritional status
  - Pressure ulcers
  - Falls and injuries due to falls
  - Contractures
  - Urinary or faecal incontinence, and faecal impaction
- **Long-term levodopa treatment is associated with adverse motor effects that limit its use:**
  - These are motor fluctuations (on–off phenomena, wearing off, dose failures, and freezing) and dyskinesias.
  - They become more of a problem as the disease progresses and can be disabling.
  - They occur in 50–80% of people who have received levodopa for 5–10 years.
  - They occur in virtually all young-onset patients; therefore, in this group, careful consideration needs to be given to the ideal time for starting levodopa.
  - They are less likely to occur in those whose symptoms begin after the age of 70 years [Olanow et al, 2001; Olanow et al, 2004].

Prognosis

- **Parkinson's disease is slowly progressive,** with a mean duration of 15 years. The severity, however, varies widely; some people may only be slightly disabled 20 years after diagnosis, whereas others may be completely disabled after 10 years [American Medical Directors Association, 2002].
- **The mortality** for elderly people with Parkinson's disease is 2–5 times higher than that in age-matched controls [AHRQ, 2003].

P

Management issues

- Who should manage people with Parkinson's disease? p.1508
- What advice should people with Parkinson's disease be given about driving? p.1508
- Which drug treatments are used by specialists? p.1508
- What is the role of surgical treatments? p.1509
- How do I treat depression in people with Parkinson's disease? p.1509
- How do I treat drug-induced Parkinsonism? p.1509
- Medicines management: Parkinson's disease p.1510
- Medicines management: drug-induced Parkinsonism p.1511

Who should manage people with Parkinson's disease?

- **Misdiagnosis is a common problem.** Up to a quarter of people diagnosed with Parkinson's disease do not have it.
- **It is therefore recommended that all people suspected to have Parkinson's disease are referred to a neurologist, or physician with an interest in Parkinson's disease, before drug treatment is initiated:**
  - An accurate diagnosis is vital to ensure correct treatment.
  - In early disease there is not usually a need to begin treatment immediately.
  - One of the most difficult decisions is when to start treatment, and with which drug to start.
  - The drug management is becoming increasingly complex with the recent advent of new medication.
  - An average GP's list will have only 2–3 people with Parkinson's disease, making it difficult to acquire sufficient experience of the condition.
- The role of Parkinson's disease Nurse Specialists is becoming increasingly important. They have been shown to improve the sense of well-being of people with Parkinson's disease.
- Other members of the multidisciplinary team who are involved in the care of a person with Parkinson's disease include physiotherapists, occupational therapists, speech therapists, and dietitians [American Medical Directors Association, 2002; DTB, 2002].
- **The Parkinson's Disease Society** is an invaluable source of support and information, for people with Parkinson's disease and primary care teams alike. It can be contacted at:
  - Parkinson's Disease Society, 215 Vauxhall Bridge Road, London, SW1V 1EJ
  - Helpline: 0808 800 0303
  - Web: www.parkinsons.org.uk

What advice should people with Parkinson's disease be given about driving?

- **A person who has Parkinson's disease must inform the Driver and Vehicle Licensing Agency (DVLA) and their motor insurance company.** The DVLA states that providing medical assessment confirms that driving is not impaired the person may continue to drive [DVLA, 2004]. Studies on accident rates suggest that people with Parkinson's disease are not more prone to cause road traffic accidents than the rest of the population [Homann et al, 2003].
- **Somnolence may be caused by** levodopa (given as co-beneldopa or co-careldopa) and all dopamine agonists [CSM, 2003]. However, sleep disturbance can also be a feature of Parkinson's disease itself [Homann et al, 2002; Goetz et al, 2002f; Körner et al, 2004].
- People must be informed that daytime sleepiness and sudden onset of sleep can occur with these drugs. Note: sudden onset of sleep without previous sleepiness is rare.
- Anyone who experiences excessive drowsiness or sudden onset of sleep should not drive or operate machinery.

Which drug treatments are used by specialists?

Overview

- There is no cure for Parkinson's disease. The goal of drug treatment is to control the signs and symptoms, while keeping adverse effects to a minimum, for as long as possible.
- People with early Parkinson's disease require different treatment regimens from those with advanced disease:
  - In early Parkinson's disease the goal is to maintain independence for as long as possible, using the least amount of medication possible to achieve this goal. There is no consensus about when treatment should begin, and which drug should be used first.
  - In advanced Parkinson's disease much of the focus is on treating medication-induced complications, e.g. dyskinesias, motor fluctuations, and psychiatric problems.

[AHRQ, 2003]

Which drug treatments do specialists use as monotherapy for early Parkinson's disease?

- **Levodopa (given as co-beneldopa or co-careldopa) is the most effective drug in the treatment of Parkinson's disease.** Virtually all patients respond to it, and treatment is associated with reduced morbidity.
- **There is no consensus about when to initiate treatment with levodopa:**
  - Some experts start levodopa early in the disease to provide maximum benefit.
  - Some experts believe that levodopa is neurotoxic, and that it promotes further neuronal degeneration. These experts prefer to start treatment with other agents, delaying the use of levodopa until symptoms are severe.
  - The main reason to delay initiation of levodopa is to limit its adverse effects, particularly those associated with long-term treatment (motor fluctuations and dyskinesias) [Olanow et al, 2004].
- **Dopamine agonists (e.g. cabergoline, pergolide, pramipexole, ropinirole, apomorphine) have been traditionally used as an adjunct to levodopa** in people who have developed motor complications.
  - **There is now a considerable body of evidence to support their use as preferred treatment** in place of levodopa [Clarke and Guttman, 2002; Goetz et al, 2002f].
  - They provide anti-Parkinsonian benefits with a reduced risk of developing motor complications compared with levodopa. They are, however, less efficacious than levodopa [AHRQ, 2003], and the use of levodopa is eventually required.
  - **There is a growing body of evidence that dopamine agonists may have neuroprotective effects in Parkinson's disease,** but this is not yet proven [Schapira, 2002; Schapira and Olanow, 2003].
  - All dopamine agonists currently available in the UK are licensed for monotherapy and as an adjunct to levodopa except cabergoline (licensed as an adjunct only). Bromocriptine and lisuride are now used less frequently than other dopamine agonists. Note: cabergoline is the only dopamine agonist that is given once a day.

Selegiline (a monoamine-oxidase-B inhibitor) has been shown to have a modest benefit as initial monotherapy in Parkinson's disease [Goetz et al, 2002d]. It improves the symptoms of Parkinson's disease, and delays the need for levodopa compared with placebo [Clarke and Moore, 2004]. It is licensed for monotherapy or as an adjunct to levodopa.

- Early research suggested that selegiline was neuroprotective, delaying the need for levodopa by 9–12 months. However, this is controversial, and further studies have not confirmed that selegiline slows disease progression [Lang and Lozano, 1998; Schapira, 1999; Shoulson et al, 2002].
- One study raised concerns that selegiline may be associated with excess mortality in some people also taking levodopa [Ben-Shlomo et al, 1998]. However a recent systematic review of nine studies found no increase in mortality with selegiline compared to controls [Ives et al, 2004].

[Olanow et al, 2001]

What strategies do specialists use to manage motor fluctuations?

The management of motor fluctuations and dyskinesias can be difficult. Discussion with the Parkinson's disease Nurse Specialist or neurologist, or both, is always advised.

Long-term levodopa treatment is associated with adverse motor effects that limit its use. These are motor fluctuations (on–off phenomena, wearing off, dose failures, and freezing) and dyskinesias (peak-dose dyskinesias, diphasic dyskinesia, and dystonia) [Olanow et al, 2001; Goetz et al, 2002c; Jankovic, 2002].

- Increasing the frequency of administration, whilst keeping the overall dose steady, is a strategy often used to address end-of-dose wearing off. For example, levodopa 600 mg daily is often given as levodopa 100 mg six times a day, rather than as 200 mg three times a day.
- Modified-release (m/r) preparations may be used, in combination with standard preparations, to reduce the severity of nocturnal akinesia. Alternatively, they may be used in the treatment of end-of-dose wearing off. Modified-release preparations are less well absorbed; therefore, a 20–30% higher dose is needed when substituting for conventional tablets. If m/r preparations are used, a standard agent, rather than an m/r preparation, may be used on first wakening to allow the person to dress.
- Dispersible co-beneldopa is also useful on first wakening to allow the person to dress. It may also be used for people with motor fluctuations, particularly on–off phenomena, to switch them back 'on'.

Dopamine agonists (e.g. cabergoline, pergolide, pramipexole, ropinirole, apomorphine) are often used as an adjunct to levodopa in people who have developed motor complications [Olanow et al, 2001; Clarke and Guttman, 2002; Goetz et al, 2002f].

Apomorphine is an injectable potent dopamine agonist. It is used as a rescue agent in advanced disease to treat severe 'off' episodes, where it provides rapid but short-lived benefit. It is given subcutaneously. People who respond well to apomorphine injections, but whose control remains poor and who require frequent injections, may be treated with a continuous subcutaneous infusion, which provides a constant therapeutic effect.

Catechol-O-methyltransferase [COMT] inhibitors (entacapone and tolcapone) have been shown to produce clinical benefits in people with levodopa motor fluctuations, and in those with stable responses to levodopa. They have been shown to reduce off-time, reduce levodopa dose, and modestly improve motor impairment and disability [Deane et al, 2004].

- Tolcapone was suspended by the CSM in November 1998 because serious hepatic reactions occurred unpredictably. However, in April 2004 the suspension was lifted due, in part, to evidence of increased efficacy for tolcapone over entacapone in the control of motor fluctuations in advanced Parkinson's disease.
- Tolcapone is now indicated for people who fail to respond to, or are intolerant of, other COMT inhibitors, but may only be prescribed by specialists in managing Parkinson's disease [CSM, 2004].

- **Amantadine** has a weak and relatively short-lived benefit in early disease, but may be helpful in the management of dyskinesias and motor fluctuations in moderate to advanced illness. Trials, however, have been of poor quality, and there is a lack of evidence for its safety and efficacy [Crosby et al, 2003].

[Olanow et al, 2001]

Other drug treatments

- **Antimuscarinics are now mainly used for treating drug-induced Parkinsonism.**
- **However, they may have beneficial effects on tremor and rigidity** in some people with Parkinson's disease. Antimuscarinics have been shown to be more effective than placebo in improving motor function, either as monotherapy or as an adjunct to other antiparkinsonian therapies [Katzenschlager et al, 2002]. They are useful in reducing excess salivation but have no effect on other features of Parkinson's disease.
- Due to their extensive adverse effect profile some specialists do not recommend them for people aged over 65 years. They are more typically recommended as second-line treatment for younger people who are cognitively intact, and who have resting tremor as their predominant symptom. Even in these people, however, drug-related cognitive dysfunction may occur.

What is the role of surgical treatments?

- In recent years there has been a resurgence of interest in the surgical treatment of advanced Parkinson's disease. This has been due to advances in stereotactic neurosurgical procedures, advances in neuro-imaging, and the development of deep brain stimulation procedures. Deep brain stimulation has the advantage that it does not necessitate making a destructive brain lesion.
- Surgery may be considered for people with intolerable adverse effects from medication, and who are cognitively unimpaired.

[Olanow et al, 2001; Olanow, 2002; AHRQ, 2003; Betchen and Kaplitt, 2003]

How do I treat depression in people with Parkinson's disease?

- There is a lack of good quality evidence on the effectiveness and safety of the use of antidepressants in people with Parkinson's disease [Goetz et al, 2002g; Shabnam et al, 2003].
- It is recommended that depression in people with Parkinson's disease should be treated in the same way as for people without Parkinson's disease, with particular consideration of the adverse effect profiles of different antidepressants [Marsh and Berk, 2003]. See the PRODIGY guidance on *Depression*.

How do I treat drug-induced Parkinsonism?

- **Drug-induced Parkinsonism is caused by dopamine receptor-blocking agents,** such as phenothiazines (e.g.

P

prochlorperazine), butyrophenones (e.g. haloperidol), metoclopramide, and cinnarizine.

- **A high index of suspicion is necessary.** Causative drugs are usually prescribed for psychotic symptoms, but may be used for a wide variety of reasons, such as dizziness (prochlorperazine), gastro-oesophageal reflux (metoclopramide), and Ménière's disease (cinnarizine). They may also be present in combination drugs, for example, for migraine (MigraMax® and Paramax® contain metoclopramide) and for depression (Triptafen® contains perphenazine; Motival® contains fluphenazine).
- **Drug-induced Parkinsonism is typically an akinetic rigid syndrome with no tremor.** Some cases, however, may be indistinguishable from Parkinson's disease, with an asymmetric onset and a resting tremor.
- **The features usually start within 10–30 days of starting treatment.** Cases have, however, been reported within hours of exposure, or after greater delay.
- **Drug-induced Parkinsonism usually resolves within 3 months of drug withdrawal,** but in some cases the features persist.
- **Treatment options are** discontinuation or reduction in dosage of the drug involved. If this is not possible, or if Parkinsonian features are severe, the use of antimuscarinics will reduce symptoms (see *Drug-induced Parkinsonism* scenario); antimuscarinics, however, have no beneficial effect on tardive dyskinesia, and may make it worse. In rare circumstances, levodopa may be necessary.

[Olanow et al, 2001]

Medicines management: Parkinson's disease

How do drugs for Parkinson's disease work?

- **In Parkinson's disease, neuronal degeneration and loss occur** in the nigrostriatal pathway, with subsequent depletion of the neurotransmitter dopamine.
- **Dopamine agonists act directly on post-synaptic dopaminergic receptors,** and do not need to be converted in the brain to active compounds.
- **Levodopa is a precursor of dopamine** and is metabolized centrally and peripherally by dopa-decarboxylase and catechol-O-methyltransferase (COMT). It is routinely given with a dopa-decarboxylase inhibitor (as co-beneldopa or co-careldopa) to prevent its peripheral metabolism to dopamine; this reduces its peripheral adverse effects and increases the amount available to cross the blood–brain barrier.
- **Dopa-decarboxylase inhibitors** (benserazide and carbidopa) are formulated with levodopa — benserazide as co-beneldopa (Madopar®) and carbidopa as co-careldopa (Sinemet®).
- **COMT inhibitors** (entacapone and tolcapone) work by further inhibiting the peripheral metabolism of levodopa, thereby increasing its bioavailability to the brain and prolonging the action of dopamine. Tolcapone also inhibits central COMT metabolism.
- **Monoamine-oxidase-B inhibitors (selegiline) inhibit central dopamine metabolism, thereby increasing nigrostriatal dopamine levels.**
- **Amantadine is an antiviral agent with relatively weak anti-Parkinsonian activity.** Its mechanism of action has not been established.

[American Medical Directors Association, 2002]

Minimizing common adverse effects

- **Levodopa should be started at low doses** and gradually increased, to reduce the risk of acute adverse effects, such as nausea, vomiting, and hypotension. If nausea and vomiting are a problem, they may be eased by the co-prescription of domperidone; this should be prescribed as a short course of 20 mg three times a day, reducing and stopping when the nausea and vomiting abate.
  - The dose of levodopa is titrated over weeks or month The final dose of levodopa is a balance between mobility and dose-limiting adverse effects.
  - The lowest dose of levodopa that provides a satisfactory response should be used. In early disease this is usually 300–400 mg daily in divided doses.
  - If the dose has been increased to 600 mg daily withou any improvement, then the diagnosis of Parkinson's disease must be questioned.
  - When introduced, levodopa should be taken with foo to minimize nausea. Later in the disease, however, it i best given on an empty stomach, as dietary amino acids compete with it for absorption; this may lead to lack of efficacy or a 'no-on' effect.
  - It is helpful if people can keep diary cards so that symptoms can be related to drug or food intake.
- **Dopamine agonists should also be started at low doses.** Acute adverse effects are similar to levodopa and incluc nausea, vomiting, hypotension, and psychiatric symptoms (including hallucinations and hypersexuality They occur at the start of treatment and abate over several days to weeks. The initial dose should therefore be low, titrating the dose gradually to achieve the desire response. The use of domperidone can reduce the acute adverse effects and allow a more rapid titration.
- **The catechol-O-methyltransferase inhitiors are given differently** [Goetz et al, 2002e]. Entacapone must be given with each dose of levodopa/dopa-decarboxylase inhibitor (i.e. each dose of co-beneldopa or co-careldop up to ten times a day. Conversely tolcapone is given three times a day (and does not have to be taken at the same time as a levodopa dose).
  - Because COMT inhibitors enhance availability of levodopa this can lead to increased levodopa-related adverse effects, and the levodopa dose may need to b reduced.
  - Both entacapone and tolcapone can cause diarrhoea, which is sometimes severe enough to warrant discontinuation. Diarrhoea due to tolcapone tends to start several months after therapy is initiated, but no particular time-course has been identified with entacapone.
  - They may also colour the urine and other body fluids orange; people should be warned of this.
- **Amantadine** causes central nervous system adverse effects such as confusion, hallucinations, insomnia, nightmares, depression, and ankle oedema [Goetz et al, 2002b]. Adverse effects are more common in the elderly so therapy should be started at 100 mg daily and only increased to the usual frequency of twice a day after at least a week.
- **Selegiline** is generally well tolerated. Unlike unselective monoamine-oxidase-A and -B inhibitors, it does not interact with tyramine-containing foods (e.g. cheese, Marmite). Infrequently reported adverse effects include nausea, dry mouth, hypotension, and insomnia. Insomnia is less common if the dose is taken in the morning. It is important to start at a low dose (2.5 mg daily) to avoid confusion and agitation, particularly in the elderly. When selegiline is given with levodopa, levodopa adverse effects can be enhanced but can be managed by reducing the levodopa dose.

Which drugs require monitoring?

- **Tolcapone** has rarely caused fulminant hepatic failure. Liver function should be checked before starting treatment with tolcapone and then monitored every 2 weeks for the first year of therapy, every 4 weeks for the next 6 months, and every 8 weeks thereafter [ABPI Medicines Compendium, 2005]. However, liver function monitoring is not always able to predict the development of severe hepatic disease [CSM, 1999], and people using tolcapone should be asked to report any signs or symptoms of liver disease (e.g. yellowing of the skin or eyes).

Entacapone does not seem to cause hepatic problems, and monitoring of liver function tests is not required.

Apomorphine's summary of product characteristics states that people using apomorphine *with* levodopa should have regular haematological monitoring (e.g. every 6 months) to detect rare instances of haemolytic anaemia [ABPI Medicines Compendium, 2003]. There is no need to do this if a person using apomorphine does not use levodopa (even if they are taking other drugs to treat Parkinson's disease) [American Medical Directors Association, 2002; Goetz et al, 2002e].

ledicines management: drug-induced arkinsonism

Antimuscarinics

Adverse effects are common and limit the use of antimuscarinics [Goetz et al, 2002a]. Confusion, hallucinations, and memory impairment are particularly common in the elderly, but may also occur in younger individuals.

Advise people that antimuscarinics can affect the performance of skilled tasks, so they should not drive if affected.

Peripheral adverse effects include dry mouth, urinary retention, constipation, nausea, blurred vision, and tachycardia. Antimuscarinics should therefore not be used in people with angle-closure glaucoma, urinary retention, or prostatic hypertrophy, and should preferably also be avoided in people with cardiovascular disease.

₹eferences

HS staff in England can link, free of charge, from ferences to full text journals by clicking on [Full text] on e PRODIGY website.

ABPI Medicines Compendium (2003) *Summary of product characteristics for APO-go ampoules 10mg/ml.* Electronic Medicines Compendium. Datapharm Communications Ltd. www.emc.medicines.org.uk [Accessed: 08/04/2005].

ABPI Medicines Compendium (2005) *Summary of product characteristics for Tasmar 100mg tablets.* Electronic Medicines Compendium. Datapharm Communications Ltd. www.emc.medicines.org.uk [Accessed: 18/04/2005].

AHRQ (2003) *Diagnosis and treatment of Parkinson's disease: a systematic review of the literature.* Evidence Report/Technology Assessment 57. Agency for Healthcare Research and Quality. www.ahrq.gov/clinic/epcsums/parksum.htm [Accessed: 01/11/2004].

American Medical Directors Association (2002) *Parkinson's disease in the long-term care setting.* Columbia, M.D.: American Medical Directors Association.

Ben-Shlomo, Y., Churchyard, A., Head, J. et al (1998) Investigation by Parkinson's Disease Research Group of United Kingdom into excess mortality seen with combined levodopa and selegiline treatment in patients with early, mild Parkinson's disease: further results of randomised trial and confidential inquiry. *British Medical Journal* **316**(7139), 1191–1196. [Full text]

6. Betchen, S.A. and Kaplitt, M. (2003) Future and current surgical therapies in Parkinson's disease. *Current Opinion in Neurology* **16**(4), 487–493.
7. Clarke, C.E. and Guttman, M. (2002) Dopamine agonist monotherapy in Parkinson's disease. *Lancet* **360**(9347), 1767–1769. [Full text]
8. Clarke, C. and Moore, P. (2004) *Parkinson's disease.* Clinical Evidence. Volume 11. www.clinicalevidence.com [Accessed: 02/02/2005].
9. Crosby, N.J., Deane, K.H.O. and Clarke, C.E. (2003) *Amantadine for dyskinesia in Parkinson's disease (Cochrane Review).* The Cochrane Library. Issue 2. Chichester, UK: John Wiley & Sons, Ltd. www.nelh.nhs.uk/cochrane.asp [Accessed: 02/02/2005].
10. CSM (1999) Withdrawl of tolcapone (Tasmar). *Current Problems in Pharmacovigilance* **25**(Feb), 2.
11. CSM (2003) Dopaminergic drugs and sudden sleep onset. *Current Problems in Pharmacovigilance* **29**(Sept), 9.
12. CSM (2004) Tolcapone (Tasmar): return to market. *Current Problems in Pharmacovigilance* **30**(Oct), 3.
13. Deane, K.H.O., Spieker, S. and Clarke, C.E. (2004) *Catechol-O-methyltranferase inhibitors for levodopa-induced complications in Parkinson's disease (Cochrane Review).* The Cochrane Library. Issue 4. Chichester, UK: John Wiley & Sons, Ltd. www.nelh.nhs.uk/cochrane.asp [Accessed: 02/02/2005].
14. DTB (2002) MS, Parkinson's disease and physiotherapy. *Drug & Therapeutics Bulletin* **40**(5), 38–40. [Full text]
15. DVLA (2004) *At a glance. Guide to the current medical standards of fitness to drive: neurological disorders.* Drivers Medical Group, Driver and Vehicle Licensing Authority. www.dvla.gov.uk/at_a_glance/content.htm [Accessed: 08/11/2004].
16. Goetz, C.G., Koller, W.C., Poewe, W. et al (2002a) Anticholinergic therapies in the treatment of Parkinson's disease. *Movement Disorders* **17**(Suppl. 4), S7-S12.
17. Goetz, C.G., Koller, W.C., Poewe, W. et al (2002b) Amantadine and other antiglutamate agents. *Movement Disorders* **17**(Suppl. 4), S13-S22.
18. Goetz, C.G., Koller, W.C., Poewe, W. et al (2002c) Levodopa. *Movement Disorders* **17**(Suppl. 4), S23-S37.
19. Goetz, C.G., Koller, W.C., Poewe, W. et al (2002d) MAO-B inhibitors for the treatment of Parkinson's disease. *Movement Disorders* **17**(Suppl. 4), S38-S44.
20. Goetz, C.G., Koller, W.C., Poewe, W. et al (2002e) COMT inhibitors. *Movement Disorders* **17**(Suppl. 4), S45-S51.
21. Goetz, C.G., Koller, W.C., Poewe, W. et al (2002f) DA agonists – overview. *Movement Disorders* **17**(Suppl. 4), S52.
22. Goetz, C.G., Koller, W.C., Poewe, W. et al (2002g) Treatment of depression in idiopathic Parkinson's disease. *Movement Disorders* **17**(Suppl. 4), S112-S119.
23. Goetz, C.G., Koller, W.C., Poewe, W. et al (2002h) Drugs to treat dementia and psychosis. *Movement Disorders* **17**(Suppl. 4), S120-S127.
24. Healy, D.G., Abou-Sleiman, P.M. and Wood, N.W. (2004) PINK, PANK, or PARK? A clinicians' guide to familial parkinsonism. *Lancet Neurology* **3**(11), 652–662.
25. Hobson, P. and Meara, J. (2004) Risk and incidence of dementia in a cohort of older subjects with Parkinson's disease in the United Kingdom. *Movement Disorders* **19**(9), 1043–1049.

P

26. Homann, C.N., Wenzel, K., Suppan, K. et al (2002) Sleep attacks in patients taking dopamine agonists: review. *British Medical Journal* **324**(7352), 1483–1487. [Full text]
27. Homann, C.N., Suppan, K., Homann, B. et al (2003) Driving in Parkinson's disease – a health hazard? *Journal of Neurology* **250**(12), 1439–1446. [Full text]
28. Hughes, A.J., Daniel, S.E., Kilford, L. and Lees, A.J. (1992) Accuracy of clinical diagnosis of idiopathic Parkinson's disease: a clinico-pathological study of 100 cases. *Journal of Neurology, Neurosurgery & Psychiatry* **55**(3), 181–184.
29. Hughes, A.J., Daniel, S.E. and Lees, A.J. (2001) Improved accuracy of clinical diagnosis of Lewy body Parkinson's disease. *Neurology* **57**(8), 1497–1499.
30. Hughes, A.J., Daniel, S.E., Ben Shlomo, Y. and Lees, A.J. (2002) The accuracy of diagnosis of parkinsonian syndromes in a specialist movement disorder service. *Brain* **125**(4), 861–870. [Full text]
31. Ives, N.J., Stowe, R.L., Marro, J. et al (2004) Monoamine oxidase type B inhibitors in early Parkinson's disease: meta-analysis of 17 randomised trials involving 3525 patients. *British Medical Journal* **329**(7466), 593–599.
32. Jankovic, J. (2002) Levodopa strengths and weaknesses. *Neurology* **58**(Suppl. 1), S19-S32.
33. Katzenschlager, R., Sampaio, C., Costa, J. and Lees, A. (2002) *Anticholinergics for symptomatic management of Parkinson's disease (Cochrane Review)*. The Cochrane Library. Issue 3. Chichester, UK: John Wiley & Sons, Ltd. www.nelh.nhs.uk/cochrane.asp [Accessed: 02/02/2005]. [Full text]
34. Körner, Y., Meindorfner, C., Möller, J.C. et al (2004) Predictors of sudden onset of sleep in Parkinson's disease. *Movement Disorders* **19**(11), 1298–1305.
35. Lang, A.E. and Lozano, A.M. (1998) Parkinson's disease. Second of two parts. *New England Journal of Medicine* **339**(16), 1130–1143. [Full text]
36. Meara, J., Bhowmick, B.K. and Hobson, P. (1999) Accuracy of diagnosis in patients with presumed Parkinson's disease. *Age & Ageing* **28**(2), 99–102. [Full text]
37. Olanow, C.W. (2002) Surgical therapy for Parkinson's disease. *European Journal of Neurology* **9**(Suppl. 3), 31–39.
38. Olanow, C.W., Watts, R.L. and Koller, W.C. (2001) An algorithm (decision tree) for the management of Parkinson's disease (2001): treatment guidelines. *Neurology* **56**(11 Suppl 5), S1-S88.
39. Olanow, C.W., Agid, Y., Mizuno, Y. et al (2004) Levodopa in the treatment of Parkinson's disease: current controversies. *Movement Disorders* **19**(9), 997–1005.
40. Rajput, A.H., Rozdilsky, B. and Rajput, A. (1991) Accuracy of clinical diagnosis in parkinsonism – a prospective study. *Canadian Journal of Neurological Sciences* **18**(3), 275–278.
41. Rao, G., Fisch, L., Srinivasan, S. et al (2003) Does this patient have parkinson disease? *Journal of the American Medical Association* **289**(3), 347–353. [Full text]
42. Schapira, A.H.V. (1999) Parkinson's disease. *British Medical Journal* **318**(7179), 311–314. [Full text]
43. Schapira, A.H. (2002) Neuroprotection and dopamine agonists. *Neurology* **58**(Suppl. 1), S9-S18.
44. Schapira, A.H. and Olanow, C.W. (2003) Rationale for the use of dopamine agonists as neuroprotective agents in Parkinson's disease. *Annals of Neurology* **53**(Suppl. 3), S149-S159.
45. Shoulson, I., Oakes, D., Fahn, S. et al (2002) Impact of sustained deprenyl (selegiline) in levodopa-treated Parkinson's disease: a randomized placebo-controlled extension of the deprenyl and tocopherol antioxidative therapy of parkinsonism trial. *Annals of Neurology* **51**(5), 604–612.

P

PRODIGY GUIDANCE

Pelvic inflammatory disease

Last revised in April 2003
www.prodigy.nhs.uk/guidance.asp?gt=Pelvic inflammatory disease

Applies to women over the age of 14 years

This guidance covers the management of acute pelvic inflammatory disease (PID).

This guidance does not cover the management of chronic PID or chronic pelvic pain.

There is separate PRODIGY guidance for *Bacterial vaginosis, Candida — female genital, Chlamydia — genital*, and *Trichomoniasis*.

Goals

- To alleviate symptoms
- To prevent complications (e.g. infertility, ectopic pregnancy, and chronic pelvic pain)
- To prevent transmission of infection to sexual partners or neonate
- To prevent reinfection

Contents

Scenarios

- Acute pelvic inflammatory disease p.1513

Extended Information, p. 1515

Acute pelvic inflammatory disease

Which therapy?

Pregnant women with PID

Pregnant women with suspected pelvic inflammatory disease (PID) should be admitted for intravenous antibiotic treatment.

Treatment of PID

If PID is clinically suspected, do not delay antibiotic treatment while waiting for the results of tests.
Treat with broad-spectrum antibiotics to cover *Chlamydia trachomatis, Neisseria gonorrhoeae*, and anerobic infection.
Recommended regimens are:

- Ofloxacin and metronidazole for 14 days
- Initial single intramuscular dose of ceftriaxone, followed by oral doxycycline and metronidazole for 14 days (less convenient for use in primary care, but an option if a quinolone is contraindicated)

If neither of these regimens are suitable, seek advice from a local microbiologist or genito-urinary medicine (GUM) clinic.
Analgesics may be required.
If a woman has an intra-uterine contraceptive device (IUD) ***in situ,*** it is uncertain whether removal is needed. However, most clinicians would remove an IUD if a woman had suspected PID.

Management of sexual partners

Advise sexual abstinence until the infected women and her partner(s) have been treated.
Screen for other sexually transmitted infections (obtain informed consent). Ideally, this should be carried out by a GUM clinic.

- **Partner notification is best carried out by a GUM clinic.** All sexual partners within the previous 6 months (or the most recent sexual partner if there have been no sexual contacts with the previous 6 months) should be notified and offered screening for sexually transmitted infections.
- **Sexual partners should be treated for chlamydial infection even if this is not identified on testing.** Treatment for gonorrhoea only needs to be offered if *N gonorrhoeae* is identified in the women or her partner. Empirical treatment for chlamydia and gonorrhoea should be considered for those partners who are unwilling to be screened.

Practical prescribing points

For further information, please see the *Medicines Compendium* (www.medicines.org.uk) or the *British National Formulary* (www.bnf.org).

- **Ofloxacin:** the Committee on Safety of Medicines advises that quinolones can cause tendon damage, and that treatment should be stopped if pain or inflammation of a tendon occurs. Use with caution in people with epilepsy or who are predisposed to seizures (because of other conditions or medicines they are taking).
- **Doxycycline** can cause oesophageal irritation and, rarely, photosensitivity. Avoid during pregnancy and breastfeeding.
- **Metronidazole:** advise avoidance of alcohol for the duration of treatment and for at least 48 hours afterwards, because of the possibility of a disulfiram-like (Antabuse) reaction.
- **Ibuprofen** causes an increased risk of gastrointestinal haemorrhage. Avoid if there is a history of peptic ulceration. May worsen asthma, hypertension, renal impairment, and cardiac failure.

Follow-up advice

- **Review within 3 days to ensure clinical improvement.** Admit to hospital if there is no substantial improvement.
- **Follow-up at 3–4 weeks is advisable in order to:**
  - **Confirm partner notification.**
  - **Advise on prevention of reinfection.**
  - **Repeat vaginal swabs in women with** continuing symptoms or where reinfection is suspected. (If still infected, consider referral to a genito-urinary medicine clinic to ensure adequate treatment of the women and her partner.)

Should I refer or investigate?

Refer?

- **Admit pregnant women with suspected pelvic inflammatory disease (PID) for intravenous antibiotics.** The antibiotic regimens recommended for the treatment

P

of PID in primary care are not suitable for use during pregnancy and breastfeeding.
- **Consider admission to secondary care in the following situations:**
  - Diagnostic uncertainty (e.g. where appendicitis or ectopic pregnancy cannot be excluded)
  - Severe symptoms or signs
  - Deteriorating clinical condition
  - Clinical failure with oral treatment (i.e. failure to show substantial improvement within 3 days)
  - Inability to tolerate oral treatment (e.g. due to nausea and vomiting)
  - Presence of a tubo-ovarian abscess
  - Pregnancy
  - Immunodeficiency (e.g. taking immunosuppressive therapy)
- **Referral to a genito-urinary medicine clinic** is generally advised for screening for sexually transmitted infections, follow-up, and partner notification. However, not all women or their partners are willing to attend such a clinic and management in primary care may be necessary.

Investigate?

- **Cervical swabs for chlamydia and gonorrhoea are recommended,** as a positive result supports a diagnosis of pelvic inflammatory disease (PID). A negative result does not exclude PID.
  - If uncertain, confirm with the local laboratory the testing methods available, required samples, and how soon these should reach the laboratory.
  - Adequate sample collection is important. When carrying out a cervical swab, the swab should be inserted inside the cervical os and firmly rotated against the endocervix. Swabbing a collection of discharge will result in an inadequate specimen (it is generally recommended that excess cervical secretions be cleaned away prior to taking the swab).
- **An elevated erythrocyte sedimentation rate (ESR) or C-reactive protein level supports a diagnosis of PID.**
- **Other tests to consider are:**
  - **Pregnancy test** (pregnant women with PID require admission, and ectopic pregnancy may be confused with PID)
  - **Urinalysis and urine culture** (to exclude urinary tract infection)

P

Patient information leaflets

The following PILs are available at www.prodigy.nhs.uk
- Laparoscopy and Laparoscopic Surgery
- Pelvic Inflammatory Disease
- Women's Health
- Women's Health Concern

Shared decision making

- **Pelvic inflammatory disease (PID) is an infection of the uterus and Fallopian tubes.**
- It is usually (but not always) caused by a sexually transmitted infection. Chlamydia and gonorrhoea are the most common causes.
- **Ofloxacin plus metronidazole for 14 days will usually clear the infection.** Two antibiotics are needed to make sure all possible bacteria are killed.
- **Do not drink alcohol whilst taking metronidazole and for at least a further 48 hours.** The two together can make you quite ill. Metronidazole may also cause a metallic taste.
- Other antibiotics may be advised if side effects do occur or if you are pregnant.
- **Painkillers may be needed.**
- **Treatment is advised for your sexual partner too,** even if he has no symptoms. Tell any sexual partner in the last 6 months to see a doctor or go to a genito-urinary clinic.
- You are also advised to be tested for other sexually transmitted infections if this has not already been done.
- **Do not have sex until you and your sexual partner have finished treatment.**
- **Condoms help protect against sexually transmitted infections.**

Drug rationale

Drugs not included

- **There are many intravenous antibiotic regimens recommended in the literature for pelvic inflammatory disease (PID).** These come from studies in hospital patients.
- **Doxycycline plus metronidazole** (without the addition of a parenteral cephalosporin) is commonly used in practice but we could find no evidence to support its continued use. In addition, this combination does not adequately cover *Neisseria gonorrhoeae*. Recommendations from the Association of Genitourinary Medicine and the Medical Society for the Study of Venereal Diseases [CEG, 2001a] recommend that treatment of PID should cover *N gonorrhoeae* for the following reasons:
  - Although much of the evidence supporting the use of antibiotics active against *N gonorrhoeae* is from the US, and anecdotally *N gonorrhoeae* is a less common cause of PID in the UK, the only recent UK study found gonococcal infection in 14% of women with PID. There is evidence that the incidence of gonorrhoea is increasing in the UK. In England, Wales and Northern Ireland between 1995 and 2000, diagnoses of gonorrhoea made by genito-urinary medicine clinics more than doubled (10,204 to 20,663) [PHLS et al, 2001].
  - The absence of endocervical gonorrhoea does not exclude gonococcal PID.
  - Although PID presenting in primary care may be less severe than in other settings, there is no published evidence to support the use of less intensive regimens.
- **The regimen of intramuscular cefoxitin 2 g (single dose) with oral probenecid 1 g (single dose) followed by oral doxycycline and metronidazole** is not included because probenecid is only available on a named patient basis in the UK and obtaining it would cause unnecessary delay.
- **Other oral regimens (except those in *Drugs included*)** have not been adequately studied [CEG, 2001a].
- **Nonsteroidal anti-inflammatory drugs (NSAIDs) other than ibuprofen** are not offered because of their less favourable risk–benefit ratio.

Drugs included

Antibiotic treatment

- **Broad-spectrum antibiotic treatment** to cover *Neisseria gonorrhoeae*, *Chlamydia trachomatis*, and anaerobic infection is recommended in guidelines produced by the Association of Genitourinary Medicine and the Medical Society for the Study of Venereal Diseases [CEG, 2001a]. The recommended regimens that are suitable for use in primary care are:
  - Oral ofloxacin 400 mg twice a day plus oral metronidazole 400 mg twice a day, for 14 days.
  - Intramuscular single dose of ceftriaxone 250 mg, followed by oral doxycycline 100 mg twice a day plus oral metronidazole 400 mg twice a day both for

14 days. (This may be less convenient in primary care due to the initial intramuscular injection.)

- **The regimen containing ofloxacin is not offered for those aged under 16 years** because quinolones are contraindicated in growing adolescents (they are associated with the development of arthropathy in weight-bearing joints in young animals).
- **If neither of the two regimens offered is suitable, consult with the local microbiology service or genito-urinary medicine clinic.**

Analgesia

- **Paracetamol** is a safe and effective analgesic and antipyretic that is suitable for most patients.
- **Ibuprofen** is an effective analgesic and antipyretic and has a favourable risk–benefit profile [BNF 44, 2002; CSM, 2002].
- **Codeine** (alone or in combination with regular paracetamol) can be helpful when paracetamol alone is insufficient [De Craen et al, 1996; Moore et al, 2002]. Prescribing it separately offers greater flexibility in dosing and hence pain control.

Prescriptions

Antibiotic treatment for 14 days

Ofloxacin + metronidazole

- Age from 16 years onwards
- Ofloxacin 400mg tablets. Take one tablet twice a day for 14 days; supply 28 tablets; NHS Cost £62.88.
- Metronidazole 400mg tablets. Take one tablet twice a day for 14 days; supply 28 tablets; NHS Cost £1.16.

Ceftriaxone im (stat) + doxycycline + metronidazole

- Age from 14 years onwards
- Ceftriaxone 250mg injection. For intramuscular injection; supply 1 250mg vial; NHS Cost £2.74.
- Doxycycline 100mg capsules. Take one capsule twice a day for 14 days; supply 28 capsules; NHS Cost £5.84.
- Metronidazole 400mg tablets. Take one tablet twice a day for 14 days; supply 28 tablets; NHS Cost £1.16.

Analgesia

Paracetamol tablets: 500mg to 1g up to four times a day

- Age from 14 to 15 years
- Paracetamol 500mg tablets. Take one to two tablets every 4 to 6 hours when required for pain relief. Maximum of 8 tablets in 24 hours; supply 50 tablets; NHS Cost £0.38; OTC Cost £0.67.

Paracetamol tablets: 1g up to four times a day

- Age from 16 years onwards
- Paracetamol 500mg tablets. Take two tablets every 4 to 6 hours when required for pain relief. Maximum of 8 tablets in 24 hours; supply 56 tablets; NHS Cost £0.42; OTC Cost £0.74.

Add on if required: codeine 30-60mg up to four times a day

- Age from 16 years onwards
- Codeine 30mg tablets. Take one to two tablets every 4 to 6 hours when required for pain relief. Maximum of 8 tablets in 24 hours; supply 56 tablets; NHS Cost £2.90.

Ibuprofen tablets: 400mg three to four times a day

- Age from 14 years onwards
- Ibuprofen 400mg tablets. Take one tablet 3 to 4 times a day when required for pain relief; supply 28 tablets; NHS Cost £0.82; OTC Cost £1.44.

Extended Information

Background information

- What is it? p.1515
- How common is it? p.1515
- Risk factors for acquiring pelvic inflammatory disease p.1515
- How do I know my patient has it? p.1515
- What else might it be? p.1516
- Complications and prognosis p.1516

What is it?

- **Pelvic inflammatory disease (PID)** is a general term for infection of the upper genital tract, including the uterus, Fallopian tubes, and ovaries. PID usually results from ascending infection from the cervix [CEG, 2001a].
- **Sexually transmitted infections are a common cause of PID.** A UK study of women with laparoscopically confirmed PID identified chlamydia in 52% of women, gonorrhoea in 14% of women, and infection with both chlamydia and gonorrhoea in nearly 8% of women [Bevan et al, 1995]. More recent data suggests that the incidence of gonorrhoea is increasing and therefore that gonorrhoea may be becoming a more common cause of PID. In England, Wales, and Northern Ireland between 1995 and 2000, diagnoses of gonorrhoea made at genito-urinary clinics more than doubled (10,204 to 20,663) [PHLS et al, 2001].
- **Other organisms implicated in PID include those commonly associated with bacterial vaginosis** (e.g. *Gardnerella vaginosis, Mycoplasma hominis, Mobiluncus species*, and other anaerobes). *Actinomyces* are part of the normal vaginal flora, and are rare causes of PID (even in the presence of an intra-uterine contraceptive device) [Lippes, 1999].
- **Polymicrobial infection is likely to be the main cause of PID.** Primary infection with *Chlamydia trachomatis* or *Neisseria gonorrhoeae* may allow opportunistic infection with other bacteria [Ross, 2002a].There is some evidence that bacterial vaginosis may impair the cervical barrier and increase the likelihood of ascending infection [Walker et al, 1999].

P

How common is it?

- **Incidence** of pelvic inflammatory disease (PID) is unknown because the disease cannot be diagnosed reliably from clinical symptoms and signs [Ross, 2002a].
- **Prevalence** is estimated to be about 2% of women of reproductive age seen in general practice each year; this is likely to be an underestimate, as many cases will be undiagnosed because of absent or atypical symptoms [Simms and Stephenson, 2000].

Risk factors for acquiring pelvic inflammatory disease

- The main risk factors for acquiring pelvic inflammatory disease (PID) are outlined in Table 1.

How do I know my patient has it?

- **No single symptom, sign, or laboratory finding is both sensitive and specific** for the diagnosis of pelvic inflammatory disease (PID). The positive predictive value of a clinical diagnosis of acute PID is 65–90% compared with laparoscopic diagnosis.

Table 1: Risk factors for pelvic inflammatory disease.

Risk factor	Comments
Risk factors for acquiring sexually transmitted infections	For example: young age, new sexual partner, multiple sexual partners, lack of barrier contraception, lower socioeconomic group [Simms and Stephenson, 2000; Ross, 2002b].
Insertion of intra-uterine device (IUD)	Risk is increased in the 3 weeks following insertion of an IUD, particularly in those at risk of sexually transmitted infections. A review of the World Health Organization's IUD clinical trial data found that the overall rate of PID was 1.6 cases per 1000 woman-years of use [Farley et al, 1992]. PID risk was more than six times higher during the 20 days following insertion than during later times. Beyond 20 days, the risk of PID was low and similar to that of women without an IUD.
Termination of pregnancy	Up to 10% of women may develop PID following termination of pregnancy [Sawaya et al, 1996; RCOG, 2002]. Prior to carrying out a termination, screening for and treating any identified lower genital tract infection may reduce the risk of PID.
Cigarette smoking	Smoking may compromise the immune response to infection [Simms and Stephenson, 2000]. However, smoking is also associated with belonging to a lower socioeconomic group, a known risk factor for PID.

Symptoms

- Lower abdominal pain (usually the most prominent symptom)
- Dyspareunia
- Abnormal vaginal bleeding (e.g. menorrhagia, postcoital or intermenstrual bleeding)
- Abnormal vaginal discharge
- Many women with PID will have no symptoms

Signs

- Lower abdominal tenderness (usually bilateral; in severe cases there may be rebound tenderness and guarding)
- Mucopurulent cervical discharge and cervicitis which may be seen on speculum examination
- Cervical motion tenderness and adnexal tenderness on bimanual vaginal examination (a tender adnexal mass is suggestive of a tubo-ovarian abscess)
- Fever greater than 38°C (but present in less than 40% of women with PID)

Investigations

- **Cervical swabs for chlamydia and gonorrhoea are recommended,** as a positive result supports a diagnosis of PID. A negative result does not exclude PID.
  - If uncertain, confirm with the local laboratory the testing methods available, required samples, and how soon these should reach the laboratory.
  - Adequate sample collection is important. When carrying out a cervical swab, the swab should be inserted inside the cervical os and firmly rotated against the endocervix. Swabbing a collection of discharge will result in an inadequate specimen (it is generally recommended that excess cervical secretions be cleaned away prior to taking the swab).
- **An elevated erythrocyte sedimentation rate (ESR) or C-reactive protein level also supports a diagnosis of PID.**
- **Other tests to consider are:**
  - **Pregnancy test** (pregnant women with PID require admission, and ectopic pregnancy may be confused with PID)
  - **Urinalysis and urine culture** (to exclude urinary tract infection)
- **Laparoscopy** with direct visualization of the Fallopian tubes is the best single diagnostic test. This is an invasive procedure and is not routinely used in clinical practice.

[CEG, 2001a; CEG, 2001b; MMWR, 2002; PHLS South West GP Laboratory Use Project Team, 2002; Ross, 2002b]

What else might it be?

- **Other causes of abdominal pain** (e.g. appendicitis, cholecystitis, ectopic pregnancy, endometriosis, irritable bowel syndrome, torsion or rupture of an ovarian cyst, and urinary tract infection)
- **Other causes of postcoital and intermenstrual bleeding** (e.g. breakthrough bleeding while on the combined pill, cervical polyp, cervical carcinoma)
- **Other causes of menorrhagia** (e.g. coagulation disorders, endometrial polyps and carcinoma, fibroids)
- **Other causes of vaginal discharge** (e.g. cervical ectropion, foreign body, irritants such as perfumed soap, physiological discharge, tumours such as cervical carcinoma)
- **Other causes of dyspareunia** (e.g. endometriosis)

Complications and prognosis

Complications

- **Infertility.** The risk of infertility following pelvic inflammatory disease (PID) is related to the number of episodes of PID and their severity. In a study of 1309 women with a history of laparoscopically confirmed PID who were attempting to conceive:
  - 16% of women with a history of PID were not pregnant within a year compared with 2.7% of controls.
  - 10.8% of women with a history of PID had confirmed tubal factor infertility compared with none in the control group.
  - 0.6% of women had tubal factor infertility after an episode of mild PID and 21.4% after an episode of severe PID.
  - Each repeated episode of PID roughly doubled the rate of tubal factor infertility. After one, two, and three or more episodes, the rates were 8%, 19.5%, and 40% respectively [Westrom et al, 1992].
  - The risk of infertility problems is likely to be lower in women treated in primary care for clinically suspected PID.
- **Ectopic pregnancy.** About 10% of women with a history of PID who conceive have an ectopic pregnancy. Ectopic pregnancy is the commonest cause of maternal death in the first trimester, and accounts for 9% of maternal deaths in the UK [DH, 1998b].
- **Chronic pelvic pain** occurs in 24–75% of women with a history of PID [Rowe, 1996]. Women admitted with PID have been found to be 10 times more likely to be subsequently hospitalized for non-specific abdominal pain [Buchan et al, 1993].
- **Perihepatitis (Fitz-Hugh–Curtis syndrome)** is a rare disorder that may complicate PID. It is characterized by adhesions between the liver and peritoneum, causing right upper quadrant pain.
- **Tubo-ovarian abscess is usually** associated with anaerobic infection [Rowe, 1996].

- **Reactive arthritis/Reiter's syndrome** is an inflammatory polyarthropathy that is triggered by exposure to a number of different infections, most commonly genital chlamydial infection. It occurs more commonly in men [Jones, 1995; CEG, 2001b].
- **Complications in pregnancy.** PID is associated with an increase in preterm delivery, and maternal and fetal morbidity. Admission for intravenous antibiotic treatment is recommended [MMWR, 2002].
- **Neonatal complications.** Perinatal transmission of *Chlamydia trachomatis* or *Neisseria gonorrhoeae* can cause ophthalmia neonatorum and subsequent visual loss in the infant if untreated. Chlamydial pneumonitis can also occur [Brocklehurst and Rooney, 2002].

Management issues

- General issues p.1517
- Management of sexual partners p.1517
- Antibiotic treatment p.1517
- Pelvic inflammatory disease (PID) and intra-uterine contraceptive devices p.1517
- Actinomyces and intra-uterine contraceptive devices p.1518
- Referral to secondary care p.1518

General issues

- **Have a low threshold for diagnosing pelvic inflammatory disease (PID).** Many episodes of PID go unrecognized, as women often have absent, mild, or atypical symptoms [MMWR, 2002].
- **Do not delay antibiotic treatment while waiting for the results of tests if PID is clinically suspected** (see *Antibiotic treatment*). It is likely that delayed treatment increases the risk of long-term complications, such as ectopic pregnancy, infertility, and pelvic pain [CEG, 2001a].
- **Negative swabs do not exclude PID** and therefore should not influence the decision to treat [MMWR, 2002].
- **Provide appropriate pain relief.**
- **Give women a detailed explanation of their condition.** In particular, discuss:
  - **The importance of completing the course of antibiotics** to reduce the risk of long-term complications. High rates of non-compliance have been reported in people treated for sexually transmitted infections [Walker et al, 1999].
  - **The need for treatment of sexual partners to prevent reinfection.** Although most infected male partners have no symptoms, infection rates of 53% for *Chlamydia trachomatis* and 41% for *Neisseria gonorrhoeae* have been reported among partners of women with PID [Lawson and Blythe, 1999].

Management of sexual partners

- **Advise sexual abstinence until** both the infected women and her partner(s) have completed a course of treatment [CEG, 2001a]. Discuss safe sexual practices.
- **Consider referral to a genito-urinary medicine (GUM) clinic,** for contact tracing and treatment of sexual partners. However, not all women or their partners are willing to attend such a clinic and management in primary care may be necessary.
  - **Contact tracing of all sexual partners in the previous 6 months is recommended** [CEG, 2001a; CEG, 2001b]. If there have been no sexual contacts within the previous 6 months, the most recent sexual partner should be notified. Partners should be offered health advice and screening for chlamydia and gonorrhoea.
  - **Sexual partners should be treated for chlamydial infection even if this is not identified on testing.** Treatment for gonorrhoea only needs to be offered if *N gonorrhoeae* is identified in the women or her partner. Empirical treatment for chlamydia and gonorrhoea should be considered for those partners who are unwilling to be screened.

Antibiotic treatment

- **Broad-spectrum antibiotic treatment to cover *Chlamydia trachomatis, N gonorrhoeae,*** and anaerobic infection is recommended in guidelines produced by the Association of Genitourinary Medicine and the Medical Society for the Study of Venereal Diseases [CEG, 2001a].
- **The reasons for covering gonococcal infection are:**
  - Although much of the evidence supporting the use of antibiotics active against *N gonorrhoeae* is from the US, and anecdotally *N gonorrhoeae* is a less common cause of PID in the UK, the only recent UK study found gonococcal infection in 14% of women with PID [Bevan et al, 1995]. More recent data suggests that the incidence of gonorrhoea is increasing [PHLS et al, 2001].
  - The absence of endocervical gonorrhoea does not exclude gonococcal PID.
  - Although PID presenting in primary care may be less severe than in other settings, there is no published evidence to support the use of less intensive regimens.
- **Several different antibiotic regimens have been studied and found to offer high cure rates.** Many of these involve intravenous administration of antibiotics, which is more appropriate for hospital-based therapy. Antibiotic regimens suitable for use in primary care are outlined in Table 2 [CEG, 2001a].
- **If the regimens recommended in Table 2 are not suitable,** seek advice from a local microbiologist or GUM specialist.

Pelvic inflammatory disease (PID) and intra-uterine contraceptive devices

- **The Chief Medical Officer's Expert Advisory Group on *Chlamydia trachomatis* recommends that screening for chlamydia should be considered prior to intra-uterine contraceptive device (IUD) insertion [DH, 1998a].** Limited evidence suggests that screening for chlamydia and treating identified infection prior to IUD insertion reduces the risk of PID. However, the prevalence of chlamydia in women receiving IUDs is likely to be low, as most are multiparous and over 25 years. The Family Planning Association states that it is good practice to screen for infection in all women before IUD insertion [Belfield, 1999]. A recent *Drug and Therapeutics Bulletin* recommends that chlamydia testing be offered to women at increased risk of sexually transmitted infections and all sexually active women aged under 25 years [DTB, 2002].
- **Routine prophylactic antibiotics prior to IUD insertion are not recommended.** A Cochrane Review found no significant difference in the incidence of PID whether women were pre-treated with doxycycline 200 mg, azithromycin 500 mg, or placebo (OR 0.89, 95% CI 0.53 to 1.51) [Grimes and Schulz, 2004]. However, the risk of PID following IUD insertion was low in the study populations, and it is difficult to extrapolate these findings to a population with a higher prevalence of sexually transmitted infections.
- **It is uncertain whether a woman with an IUD *in situ* needs to have it removed if she develops PID.** However, most clinicians would remove an IUD if a woman had suspected PID. The Family Planning Association emphasize the importance of immediate treatment of

Table 2: Antibiotic regimens suitable for the primary care treatment of PID.

Antibiotic regimen	Comments
Oral ofloxacin 400 mg twice a day plus oral metronidazole 400 mg twice a day, both for 14 days	Ofloxacin is not recommended as monotherapy; although it is effective against *C trachomatis* and *N gonorrhoeae* it does not cover anaerobic infections [CEG, 2001a]. Ofloxacin monotherapy may have a place in people who are unable to tolerate metronidazole. Two randomized controlled trials compared oral ofloxacin with parenteral cefoxitin and doxycycline and found no difference in cure rates (clinical cure rates about 95% for all treatments) [Ross, 2002b].
Intramuscular ceftriaxone 250 mg immediately followed by oral doxycycline 100 mg twice a day plus oral metronidazole 400 mg twice a day both for 14 days	Less convenient for use in primary care, but an option if a quinolone is contraindicated. Oral cephalosporins have not been evaluated sufficiently to recommend their use [CEG, 2001a].

PID if this is suspected, but make no specific recommendations regarding whether the IUD should be removed [Belfield, 1999]. The Association of Genitourinary Medicine and the Medical Society for the Study of Venereal Diseases state that removal of the IUD may be required if the woman has clinically severe PID [CEG, 2001a].

Actinomyces and intra-uterine contraceptive devices

- *Actinomyces* are bacteria that commonly colonize the vagina and are a rare cause of PID. Laboratories do not routinely culture for *Actinomyces* on receiving vaginal swabs. However, cytologic features seen during examination of a routine cervical smear may suggest the presence of actinomyces-like organisms (ALOs). It is rare for smears to be reported as positive for ALOs; one study found that ALOs were identified in only 107 of 80,000 cervical smears [Family Planning Perspectives, 1982]. The detection of ALOs is more common in women with an IUD. However, the presence of ALOs is not diagnostic of any disease and is poorly predictive of development of disease [Lippes, 1999].
- **If ALOs are identified on cervical smear and the woman has symptoms or signs suggestive of pelvic infection,** the Family Planning Association (FPA) recommends that the IUD be removed and the threads sent for culture [Belfield, 1999]. The woman should receive treatment with an appropriate antibiotic while the results of culture are awaited [Cayley et al, 1998]. Seek advice on choice and duration of treatment from the local microbiology service, GUM department, or gynaecology department. Treatment is normally with a penicillin, tetracycline, or erythromycin for at least 2 weeks.
- **If ALOs are identified on cervical smear and the woman has no symptoms,** the FPA recommends that the woman be counselled regarding the options of either removing the IUD, changing the IUD, or leaving it in place [Belfield, 1999]. It is important to discuss the lack of evidence of harm but that a small increased risk of developing pelvic actinomyces cannot be excluded.
  - **If the IUD is removed,** a new one can be inserted on the same occasion, ensuring ongoing contraception. The removed IUD does not need to be sent for culture. A cervical smear should be repeated in 3 to 6 months to check for the presence of persisting ALOs.
  - **If the IUD is left in place,** adequate follow-up is necessary (e.g. every 6 months). The woman should be warned about symptoms suggesting PID and advised to seek immediate medical advice if these occur. Cervical smears are likely to continue to show the presence of ALOs, and therefore should only be repeated at intervals recommended by the national cervical screening programme.

Referral to secondary care

- **Admission to secondary care (for intravenous antibiotics and/or further investigation) should be considered in the following situations:**
  - Diagnostic uncertainty (e.g. where appendicitis or ectopic pregnancy cannot be excluded)
  - Severe symptoms or signs
  - Deteriorating clinical condition
  - Clinical failure with oral treatment (i.e. failure to show substantial improvement within 3 days)
  - Inability to tolerate oral treatment (e.g. due to nausea and vomiting)
  - Presence of a tubo-ovarian abscess
  - Pregnancy
  - Immunodeficiency (e.g. HIV infection, taking immunosuppressive therapy)

[CEG, 2001a]

References

NHS staff in England can link, free of charge, from references to full text journals by clicking on [Full text] on the PRODIGY website.

1. Belfield, T. (Ed.) (1999) *FPA contraceptive handbook: a guide for family planning and other health professionals.* 3rd edn. London: Family Planning Association.
2. Bevan, C.D., Johal, B.J., Mumtaz, G. et al (1995) Clinical laparoscopic and microbiological findings in acute salpingitis: a report on a United Kingdom cohort. *British Journal of Obstetrics & Gynaecology* **102**(5), 407–414.
3. BNF 44 (2002) *British National Formulary.* 44th edn. London: British Medical Association and Royal Pharmaceutical Society of Great Britain.
4. Brocklehurst, P. and Rooney, G. (2002) *Interventions for treating genital Chlamydia trachomatis infection in pregnancy (Cochrane Review).* The Cochrane Library. Issue 2. Oxford: Update Software.
5. Buchan, H., Vessey, M., Goldacre, M. and Fairweather, J. (1993) Morbidity following pelvic inflammatory disease. *British Journal of Obstetrics & Gynaecology* **100**(6), 558–562.
6. CEG (2001a) *Guidelines for the management of pelvic infection and perihepatitis.* Clinical Effectiveness Group (Association for Genitourinary Medicine and the Medical Society for the Study of Venereal Diseases). www.bashh.org/guidelines/ceguidelines.htm [Accessed: 07/05/2002].
7. CEG (2001b) *Clinical effectiveness guideline for the management of Chlamydia trachomatis genital tract infection.* Clinical Effectiveness Group (Association for Genitourinary Medicine and the Medical Society for the Study of Venereal Diseases). www.bashh.org/guidelines/ceguidelines.htm [Accessed: 07/05/2002].

8. CSM (2002) Non-steroidal anti-inflammatory drugs (NSAIDs) and gastrointestinal (GI) safety. *Current Problems in Pharmacovigilance* **28**(Apr), 5.
9. De Craen, A.J., Di Giulio, G., Lampe-Schoenmaeckers, J.E. et al (1996) Analgesic efficacy and safety of paracetamol-codeine combinations versus paracetamol alone: a systematic review. *British Medical Journal* **313**(7053), 321–325. [Full text]
10. DH (1998a) *Summary and conclusions of CMO's Expert Advisory Group Report on chlamydia trachomatis.* Department of Health. www.dh.gov.uk [Accessed: 26/04/2004]. [Full text]
11. DH (1998b) *Why mothers die: report on confidential enquiries into maternal deaths in the United Kingdom 1994–1996.* Department of Health. [Accessed: 24/05/2002]. [Full text]
12. DTB (2002) Copper IUDs, infection and infertility. *Drug & Therapeutics Bulletin* **40**(9), 67–69.
13. Farley, T.M., Rosenberg, M.J., Rowe, P.J. et al (1992) Intrauterine devices and pelvic inflammatory disease: an international perspective. *Lancet* **339**(8796), 785–788. [Full text]
14. Grimes, D.A. and Schulz, K.F. (2004) *Antibiotic prophylaxis for intrauterine contraceptive device insertion (Cochrane Review).* The Cochrane Library. Issue 1. Chichester, UK: John Wiley & Sons, Ltd.
15. Jones, R.B. (1995) Chlamydia trachomatis (trachoma, perinatal infections, lymphogranuloma venereum, and other genital infections). In: Mandell, G.L., Dolin, R., Bennet, J.E. et al (Eds.) *Principles and practice of infectious diseases.* 4th edn. London: Churchill Livingstone. 1679–1693.
16. Lawson, M.A. and Blythe, M.J. (1999) Pelvic inflammatory disease in adolescents. *Pediatric Clinics of North America* **46**(4), 767–783.
17. Lippes, J. (1999) Pelvic actinomycosis: a review and preliminary look at prevalence. *American Journal of Obstetrics and Gynecology* **180**(2 Pt 1), 265–269.
18. MMWR (2002) Sexually transmitted diseases treatment guidelines 2002. *Morbidity & Mortality Weekly Report* **51**(RR-6),
19. Moore, A., Collins, S., Carroll, D. et al (2002) *Single dose paracetamol (Acetaminophen), with and without codeine, for postoperative pain.* The Cochrane Library. Issue 3. Oxford: Update Software.
20. PHLS, DHSS & PS and Scottish ISD(D)5 Collaborative Group (2001) *Sexually transmitted infections in the UK: new episodes seen at genitourinary medicine clinics, 1995 to 2000.* London: Public Health Laboratory Service.
21. PHLS South West GP Laboratory Use Project Team (2002) *Quick reference guide: diagnosis of chlamydia.* Public Health Laboratory Service. www.phls.org.uk [Accessed: 01/11/2002].
22. RCOG (2002) *The care of women requesting induced abortion.* Royal College of Obstetricians. www.rcog.org.uk [Accessed: 13/12/2002]. [Full text]
23. Ross, J.D.C. (2002a) An update on pelvic inflammatory disease. *Sexually Transmitted Infections* **78**(1), 18–19. [Full text]
24. Ross, J. (2002b) Pelvic inflammatory disease. *Clinical Evidence* **7**(Jun), 1452–1457.
25. Rowe, P.J. (1996) Sequelae of pelvic infection. In: Templeton, A. (Ed.) *The prevention of pelvic infection.* London: Royal College of Obstetricians and Gynaecologists. 14–32.
26. Sawaya, G.F., Grady, D., Kerlikowske, K. and Grimes, D.A. (1996) Antibiotics at the time of induced abortion: the case for universal prophylaxis based on a meta-analysis. *Obstetrics and Gynecology* **87**(5 Pt 2), 884–890.
27. Simms, I. and Stephenson, J.M. (2000) Pelvic inflammatory disease epidemiology: what do we know and what do we need to know. *Sexually Transmitted Infections* **76**(2), 80–87. [Full text]
28. Walker, C.K., Workowski, K.A., Washington, A.E. et al (1999) Anaerobes in pelvic inflammatory disease: implications for the Centers for Disease Control and Prevention's guidelines for treatment of sexually transmitted diseases. *Clinical Infectious Diseases* **28**(Suppl 1), S29-S36.
29. Westrom, L.V., Joesoef, R., Reynolds, G. et al (1992) Pelvic inflammatory disease and fertility: a cohort study of 1, 844 women with laparoscopically verified disease and 657 control women with normal laparoscopic results. *Sexually Transmitted Diseases* **19**(4), 185–192.

PRODIGY GUIDANCE

Poisoning

Last revised in September 2004
www.prodigy.nhs.uk/guidance.asp?gt=Poisoning

Applies to people of all ages

This guidance covers advice on obtaining information about poisoning and when to refer people to hospital.

This guidance does not cover detailed information on how to treat individual cases of poisoning since referral is advised in such circumstances.

There is separate PRODIGY guidance for *Adverse drug reactions*.

Goals

- To take an appropriate course of action in order to minimize the effects of poisoning

Extended Information

Background information

- What is it? p.1520
- How common is it? p.1520

What is it?

- **Poisoning** is the inappropriate exposure to an agent such as a drug, household product, industrial chemical, plant, fungus, or animal derivative.
- **The most common route of poisoning** is by ingestion, but poisoning by inhalation, injection, skin/eye contamination or bites may also occur.
- **Accidental poisoning** may occur as the result of household accidents, therapeutic errors, occupational exposure, and environmental accidents. Errors in drug administration occur most frequently in people who are on multiple medications or taking drugs with a narrow therapeutic index. Poor eyesight and confusion can also lead to accidental poisoning.
- **Intentional poisoning** (i.e. self-harm, abuse and criminal) is often the result of drug overdoses involving easily available over-the-counter medicines (e.g. paracetamol) or prescribed drugs such as antidepressants, anxiolytics, or antipsychotics.

How common is it?

- **In the UK during 2001,** approximately 6% of all deaths due to external causes were due to accidental poisoning or exposure to noxious substances.
- **Nationally, the most frequent calls** to the National Poisons Information Service (NPIS) were for the following:
  - Pharmaceutical agents — 68% (the combination of paracetamol with dextropropoxyphene [co-proxamol] is the most frequent pharmaceutical agent to cause death)
  - Industrial chemicals — 15%
  - Household chemicals — 8%
  - However, these tend to be a poor reflection of the epidemiology of poisoning because only difficult cases are referred.
- **Household accidental poisoning** (with chemicals or pharmaceuticals) accounts for 49% of all accidental poisonings.
- **In total, 36% of all calls to the NPIS** were accidental poisonings involving children under 10 years old. Although the incidence of fatal poisoning in young children is very low, the difficulty in obtaining reliable information can cause a great deal of distress and anxiety to parents, healthcare workers and children, representing a significant workload.

[NPIS, 2001; Office for National Statistics, 2003]

Management issues

- Obtaining information about poisoning p.1520
- General assessment and admission to hospital p.1521

Obtaining information about poisoning

Primary source	**TOXBASE**	**www.spib.axl.co.uk/**
Complicated/ high-risk cases	**National Poisons Information Service**	**Tel: 0870 600 6266**

- **There are six National Poisons Information Service (NPIS) centres** (based in Belfast, Birmingham, Cardiff, Edinburgh, London, and Newcastle) that provide a UK-wide clinical toxicology service for healthcare professionals working in the NHS. The service, provided by specialists in poisons information and consultant medical staff, offers information and advice on the diagnosis, treatment, and management of patients who may have been accidentally or deliberately poisoned. They are contactable day and night.
- **TOXBASE is the primary clinical toxicology database of the NPIS** and is available on the Internet at **spib.axl.co.uk.**
- **TOXBASE should be used by all medical practitioners and other healthcare professionals working in the NHS as the primary source of poisons information.** The Department of Health recommends that local protocols that require a telephone call to the NPIS in all cases of poisoning or overdoses should be replaced with a requirement to access TOXBASE. The details of each enquiry can be printed out from the website to provide clear information and advice which can then be appended to the patient's medical record.
- **It is necessary to register at the TOXBASE site and this should be done as a matter of course. (In the event of difficulty contact 0131 242 1381/1383).**
- **All NPIS centres contribute to and authenticate the content of TOXBASE.** It is continually updated and provides information about routine diagnosis, treatment, and management of people exposed to drugs, household products, and industrial and agricultural chemicals. The level of information it provides will assist with the proper treatment and management of the majority of cases.
- **In cases where there is doubt about degree of risk or about appropriate management,** contact the UK National Poisons Information Service on 0870 600 6266, which directs the caller to the relevant local centre.

P

- **It would be appropriate to contact the NPIS for:**
  - Unfamiliar poisons or where there is insufficient information on TOXBASE
  - Atypical presentations or diagnostic difficulty
  - Life-threatening poisoning
  - Specialist patient groups (e.g. children, pregnant women)
  - Tablet identification
  - Location and use of unfamiliar antidotes
  - Need for specialist medical advice

Other sources of information

- **Advice from appropriately trained accident and emergency and other medical staff** is usually available for most episodes of suspected drug poisoning or drug overdose. It is not usually necessary to use NPIS for simple, uncomplicated, or common poisonings.
- **Tictac** is a computer-aided tablet and capsule identification system. It is available to authorized users including Regional Drug Information Centres and Poisons Information Centres.

[NTIS, 1999; DH, 2003; BNF 47, 2004]

General assessment and admission to hospital

- **Obtain as much relevant information from the poisoned individual or carer as possible.** This should include any details of the type, timing, and amount of poison consumed. Treat this information with caution, however, as it may not be complete or entirely reliable.
- **Treat any reported ingested amounts with extreme caution: they could be an underestimate or overestimate of the true amount.** Additionally, ingestion of lower doses may also require urgent admission since co-medication could increase the likelihood of toxicity. All people who show features of poisoning should generally be admitted to hospital, with an accompanying note detailing the history and any treatment given prior to admission.
- **It is often impossible to identify the poison with any certainty** but since few drugs have a specific antidote, this is often not important. In most people treatment is directed at managing symptoms as they arise.
- **People who have taken poisons with delayed actions should also be admitted,** even if they appear well. Delayed-action poisons include aspirin, iron, paracetamol, tricyclic antidepressants, co-phenotrope (diphenoxylate with atropine, Lomotil brand), and paraquat. This should also be considered when the drug has been formulated as a delayed- or modified-release tablet or capsule.

[BNF 47, 2004]

People with intentional poisoning (i.e. self-harm behaviour)

- **Refer for urgent treatment in an emergency department if there is a significant risk to the individual who has self-harmed.**
- **Treatment for the physical consequences of self-harm should be offered,** regardless of willingness to accept psychosocial assessment or psychiatric treatment.
- **Full information about the treatment options should be provided.** All necessary efforts should be made to ensure that someone who has self-harmed has the opportunity to give, meaningful and informed consent before any and each procedure e.g. taking the person to hospital by ambulance.
- **A preliminary psychosocial assessment should be offered to all people** who have self-harmed at the initial assessment — mental capacity, willingness for further (psychosocial) assessment, level of distress and the possible presence of mental illness.
- **All people who have self-harmed should be assessed for risk** — identification of features known to be associated with risk of further self-harm and/or suicide, and identification of the key psychological characteristics associated with risk, in particular depression, hopelessness and continuing suicidal intent.
- **Following psychosocial assessment offer referral for further treatment and help** depending upon comprehensive psychiatric, psychological and social assessment, including an assessment of risk. This should *not* be based solely on having self-harmed.

[NICE, 2004]

References

1. BNF 47 (2004) *British National Formulary*. 47th edn. London: British Medical Association and Royal Pharmaceutical Society of Great Britain.
2. DH (2003) *National Poisons Information Service*. Department of Health. www.dh.gov.uk [Accessed: 17/11/2003]. [Full text]
3. NICE (2004) *Self harm: the short term physical and psychological management and secondary prevention of self harm in primary and secondary care*. National Institute for Clinical Evidence. www.nice.org.uk [Accessed: 16/08/2004].
4. NPIS (2001) *NPIS combined annual report*. Birmingham: National Poisons Information Service.
5. NTIS (1999) *Management of poisoning*. NHS Northern and Yorkshire: Regional Drug and Therapeutics Centre.
6. Office for National Statistics (2003) *Health statistics quarterly*. The Stationery Office. www.statistics.gov.uk [Accessed: 10/11/2003].

P

PRODIGY GUIDANCE

Polymyalgia rheumatica

Last revised in January 2004

At the time of print this topic was being updated. The newly revised guidance will be issued on to the website in late 2005.

www.prodigy.nhs.uk/guidance.asp?gt=Polymyalgia rheumatica

Applies to people over the age of 40 years

This guidance covers the management of polymyalgia rheumatica (PMR), including the use of osteoporosis prophylaxis in people prescribed long-term corticosteroids. PMR has not been reported in people under the age of 40 years and so only those aged 40 years or over are covered by this guidance.

This guidance does not cover giant-cell (temporal) arteritis in detail, and does not cover rheumatoid arthritis, or polymyositis.

There is separate PRODIGY guidance for *Ankylosing spondylitis, Neck pain, Osteoarthritis,* and *Rheumatoid arthritis.*

Goals

- To control symptoms of polymyalgia rheumatica, e.g. limb girdle stiffness, weakness, pain and tenderness, anorexia, fever, and fatigue
- To preserve mobility, independence, and quality of life
- To minimize complications of associated conditions, e.g. giant-cell (temporal) arteritis
- To minimize the risk of complications of corticosteroid therapy, e.g. osteoporosis, weight gain, hypertension, immunosuppression, peptic ulceration, depression, psychosis, glaucoma, cataract, or skin fragility

Contents

Scenarios

- New PMR without giant cell arteritis – initiation of therapy p.1522
- Follow-up visit with good control p.1523
- Follow-up visit with poor control p.1526

Extended Information, p. 1529

P

Which scenario?

- **New PMR without giant-cell arteritis — initiation of therapy:** covers the management of people when polymyalgia rheumatica (PMR) is initially suspected.
- **Follow-up visit with good control:** covers the management of people reporting no return of symptoms, and inflammatory markers are within normal limits.
- **Follow-up visit with poor control:** covers the management of people reporting return of some or all of the initial symptoms, or inflammatory markers are elevated.

New PMR without giant cell arteritis — initiation of therapy

Which therapy?

- **Oral prednisolone is indicated in all cases.**
- **The optimal starting dose is 15 mg daily for the first month.** The risk of relapse is high with lower doses, and the risk of adverse effects is increased without additional benefit at higher doses. The lowest possible dose should be used to avoid complications of corticosteroid therapy.
- **The median duration of treatment is 2 years.**
- **Giant-cell (temporal) arteritis may occur at any time and urgently requires treatment with 40–60 mg of prednisolone daily and an urgent ophthalmological referral.**

Practical prescribing points

For further information please see the *Medicines Compendium* (www.medicines.org.uk) or the *British National Formulary* (www.bnf.org).

- **Document history of chickenpox** (there is a risk of potentially fatal disseminated chickenpox if the person is non-immune). Advise people taking systemic corticosteroids to avoid close contact with people who have chickenpox or shingles, and to seek urgent medical advice if they are exposed.
- **Corticosteroids may worsen diabetic control or heart failure.**
- **Concurrent nonsteroidal anti-inflammatory drugs (NSAIDs) increase the risk of gastrointestinal perforation.**
- **All people taking steroids should carry a Steroid Treatment Card.**
- **Advise the person not to stop taking prednisolone suddenly** and of the need to increase the dose in the case of intercurrent illness.
- **Advise the person that adverse effects** (such as weight gain and hypertension) may occur.

Follow-up advice

- **Review in 1 week** to assess clinical response. Symptoms should dramatically resolve within 2–4 days.
- **Give osteoporosis prophylaxis to** people aged over 65 years and those with a previous fragility fracture (i.e. occurring after age 40 years on minimal trauma).
- **In other individuals,** measure bone mineral density using dual-energy X-ray absorptiometry (DEXA) to assess fracture risk. Consider treatment if T score is –1.5 or lower.
- **Recheck inflammatory markers** (erythrocyte sedimentation rate [ESR], C-reactive protein [CRP], or plasma viscosity) in 2–6 weeks to assess response to treatment. The ESR returns to normal by 2 weeks in 56% and by 5 weeks in 76%. CRP decreases more rapidly, with 67% normalizing in 2 weeks and 75% in 3 weeks [Andersson et al, 1986]. If they are still elevated after this time, other causes must be excluded, e.g. neoplasm, multiple myeloma, infection, or connective tissue disease.

Should I refer or investigate?

Refer?

- **Referral is not usually necessary.** Indications for referral include:
  - Uncertainty over diagnosis
  - A person at high risk from adverse effects of corticosteroids
  - Symptoms of giant-cell arteritis (urgent referral)
  - Synovitis or suspicion of inflammatory arthritis (see PRODIGY *Rheumatoid arthritis* guidance)

Investigate?

- **Erythrocyte sedimentation rate (ESR) or plasma viscosity:** an ESR over 40 mm per hour occurs in over 75% of cases, but a significant number of people have a normal ESR.
- **Most people with a normal ESR at presentation have a raised level of C-reactive protein (CRP);** therefore if the ESR is normal check the level of CRP.
- **Full blood count:** normocytic normochromic anaemia is common.
- **Thyroid function tests:** to rule out hypothyroidism.
- **Serum electrophoresis:** to rule out multiple myeloma.
- **Creatine kinase:** to rule out polymyositis and statin-induced myositis.
- **Consider serological determination of previous exposure to chickenpox.**
- **Consider chest X-ray** particularly in a smoker: lung carcinoma may present with polymyalgia symptoms.

Shared decision making

- **Steroid tablets** are very effective for treating polymyalgia rheumatica (PMR).
- **The dose is slowly reduced** to the lowest dose that keeps symptoms away.
- **Treatment lasts 2–3 years** but may be longer.
- **Possible side effects of steroids include:**
  - Osteoporosis ('thinning of the bones') — but measures can be taken to protect against this if you have a high risk.
  - Weight gain.
  - Increased chance of infections: in particular, you should see a doctor urgently if you come into contact with chickenpox or shingles and you have not had chickenpox in the past.
  - Increase in blood pressure, so have it checked regularly.
  - High blood sugar, which may mean extra treatment if you have diabetes.
- **Do not stop steroid tablets suddenly.**
- **Some people with polymyalgia also develop inflammation of arteries in their forehead.** See a doctor urgently if you get a one-sided headache, tenderness in your scalp, or an aching in the jaw when you chew.

Drug rationale

Drugs not included

- **Nonsteroidal anti-inflammatory drugs (NSAIDs):** combinations of NSAIDs and prednisolone do not improve symptom control and may potentiate adverse effects.
- **Methotrexate:** specialist advice required.
- **Azathioprine:** specialist advice required.
- **Osteoporosis prophylaxis:** see separate scenarios *Follow-up visit with good control* or *Follow-up visit with poor control*.
- **Corticosteroids (alternative to prednisolone)** are not included. In particular:
  - **Deflazacort** has been found to have similar effects on bone mass to prednisolone in people with polymyalgia rheumatica (PMR), and costs are higher [Cimmino et al, 1994; Krogsgaard et al, 1996].
  - **Intramuscular methylprednisolone** is effective in achieving remission of disease [Dasgupta et al, 1998] but treatment by repeated injection is not first choice in primary care.
  - **Prednisone** has to be metabolized to prednisolone before it is effective.

Drugs included

- **Prednisolone** 15 mg per day is an adequate starting dose for people with pure PMR (i.e. no signs or symptoms of giant-cell arteritis [Li and Dasgupta, 2000]. It should be given as a single morning dose to reduce adverse effects.

Prescriptions

Start dose: prednisolone 15mg each morning

Prednisolone 15mg e/c each morning
- Age from 40 years onwards
- Prednisolone 5mg e/c tablets. Take three tablets each morning; supply 90 tablets; NHS Cost £1.29.

Follow-up visit with good control

Which therapy?

- **Giant-cell (temporal) arteritis may occur at any time and urgently requires treatment with 40–60 mg of prednisolone daily and an urgent ophthalmological referral.**
- **Suggested reduction of prednisolone dose:**
  - **First month:** remain at 15 mg once daily. Risk of relapse is high.
  - **Initial reduction:** reduce by 2.5 mg each fortnight until 10 mg daily, providing symptoms and (less importantly) inflammatory markers remain controlled.
  - Reduce from 10 mg daily by 1 mg of daily dose each 6 weeks until 5–7 mg daily dose, providing symptoms and (less importantly) inflammatory markers remain controlled.
  - **Maintenance dose:** 5–7 mg for 12 months providing symptoms and (less importantly) inflammatory markers remain controlled. Risk of relapse is high.
  - **Final reduction:** reduce by 1 mg of daily dose every 6–8 weeks, providing symptoms and (less importantly) inflammatory markers remain controlled.

Osteoporosis prophylaxis

- **Give osteoporosis prophylaxis** to people aged over 65 years, and those with a previous fragility fracture (i.e. occurring after age 40 years on minimal trauma).
- **In other individuals,** measure bone mineral density (BMD) using DEXA to assess fracture risk. Consider treatment if T score –1.5 or lower.
- **Use a bisphosphonate** (alendronate, risedronate, or cyclical etidronate) and give calcium with vitamin D as an adjunctive treatment.
- If a bisphosphonate is contraindicated or not tolerated, use alfacalcidol or calcitriol.
- Hormone replacement treatment (HRT) may also be considered as a second-line option for postmenopausal women if the benefits of treatment outweigh the risks

(off-licence use). See PRODIGY *Menopause* guidance for further information and prescriptions.

Factors affecting choice of osteoporosis prophylaxis

- **Oesophageal stricture or achalasia:** use cyclical etidronate, alfacalcidol, or calcitriol. Do not use alendronate. If using risedronate, monitor closely for adverse effects.
- **Current or recent history of other upper gastrointestinal disorders:** avoid alendronate.

Practical prescribing points

For further information please see the *Medicines Compendium* (www.medicines.org.uk) or the *British National Formulary* (www.bnf.org).

Corticosteroids

- **Document history of chickenpox** (risk of potentially fatal disseminated chickenpox if non-immune). Advise people taking systemic corticosteroids to avoid close contact with people who have chickenpox or shingles, and to seek urgent medical advice if they are exposed.
- **Corticosteroids may worsen diabetic control or heart failure.**
- **Concurrent nonsteroidal anti-inflammatory drugs (NSAIDs) increase the risk of gastrointestinal perforation.**
- **All people taking steroids should carry a Steroid Treatment Card.**
- **Advise the person not to stop taking prednisolone suddenly** and of the need to increase the dose in the case of intercurrent illness.
- **Advise the person that adverse effects** (such as weight gain and hypertension) may occur.

Bisphosphonates

- Take bisphosphonates with a full glass of water while sitting upright or standing (but not lying down), remaining upright for at least 30 minutes afterwards.
- Ask people taking alendronate to report any symptoms suggesting oesophageal irritation, e.g. dysphagia, new or worsening heartburn, pain on swallowing, or retrosternal pain.
- Take alendronate or risedronate at least 30 minutes before breakfast or any other medicines, especially calcium supplements or antacids.
- Etidronate should be taken 2 hours before and 2 hours after meals, or after medicines containing calcium, aluminium, magnesium, or iron.

Alfacalcidol and calcitriol

- May cause hypercalcaemia. Monitor serum calcium and creatinine levels.

Follow-up advice

- **Regular review is important for two reasons:**
  - To ensure that the person is adequately treated
  - To ensure that dose reduction is performed as rapidly as is safe
- **Review in 1 week** after a change of prednisolone dose to assess clinical response; this may be possible by telephone. Plan the next dose change (see *Which therapy?*).
- **Recheck inflammatory markers** after 2–6 weeks to assess serological response. The erythrocyte sedimentation rate (ESR) and C-reactive protein (CRP) return to normal by 2 weeks. If they are still elevated after this time, other causes must be excluded, e.g. neoplasm, multiple myeloma, infection, or connective tissue disease.

Monitoring drugs used for osteoporosis prophylaxis

- **Alfacalcidol:** check serum calcium and creatinine levels after 1 week, and then monthly to exclude hypercalcaemia.
- **Calcitriol:** check serum calcium and creatinine levels at 4 weeks, 3 months, 6 months and then at 6-monthly intervals to exclude hypercalcaemia.

Should I refer or investigate?

Refer?

- **Referral is not usually necessary.** Indications for referral include:
  - Uncertainty over diagnosis
  - A person at high risk from adverse effects of corticosteroids
  - High corticosteroid dose required to control symptom (more than 10 mg daily at 6 months)
  - Symptoms of giant-cell arteritis (urgent referral)
  - Synovitis or suspicion of inflammatory arthritis (see PRODIGY *Rheumatoid arthritis* guidance)

Investigate?

- Erythrocyte sedimentation rate (ESR) or plasma viscosity (depending on local availability, ESR usually preferred).
- C-reactive protein (CRP) if ESR or plasma viscosity was normal at diagnosis.

Shared decision making

- **Your symptoms of polymyalgia rheumatica (PMR) have eased with steroids.**
- **The dose is now slowly reduced** to the lowest that keeps symptoms away.
- **Possible side effects** of steroids include:
  - Osteoporosis ('thinning of the bones') — but measures can be taken to protect against this if you have a high risk.
  - Weight gain.
  - Increased chance of infections; in particular, you should see a doctor urgently if you come into contact with chickenpox or shingles and you have not had chickenpox in the past.
  - Increase in blood pressure, so have it checked regularly.
  - High blood sugar, which may mean extra treatment if you have diabetes.
- **Do not stop steroid tablets suddenly.**
- **Some people with polymyalgia also develop inflammation of arteries in their forehead.** See a doctor urgently if you get a one-sided headache, tenderness in your scalp, or an aching in the jaw when you chew.

Drug rationale

Drugs not included

Treatment of polymyalgia rheumatica

- **Nonsteroidal anti-inflammatory drugs (NSAIDs):** combinations of NSAIDs and prednisolone do not improve symptom control and may potentiate adverse effects.
- **Methotrexate:** specialist advice required.
- **Azathioprine:** specialist advice required.

Corticosteroids (except prednisolone) are not included. In particular:

- **Deflazacort** has been found to have similar effects on bone mass to prednisolone in people with polymyalgia rheumatica (PMR), and costs are higher [Cimmino et al, 1994; Krogsgaard et al, 1996].
- **Intramuscular methylprednisolone** is effective in achieving remission of disease [Dasgupta et al, 1998].but treatment by repeated injection is not first choice in primary care.
- **Prednisone** has to be metabolized to prednisolone before it is effective.

Osteoporosis prophylaxis

Intranasal calcitonin has been studied in glucocorticoid-induced bone loss, but the results are conflicting.
Calcium supplements as a sole therapy for glucocorticoid-induced osteoporosis are ineffective for preventing bone loss.
Hormone replacement therapy (HRT) should only be considered as a second-line option for preventing osteoporosis [CSM, 2003].It has been found to increase BMD at the spine, but not at the hip in people taking glucocorticoids. However, trisks and benefits of HRT are complex and should be discussed with each woman before treatment is started. Note that HRT is not licensed for the treatment of osteoporosis. For information on the risks and benefits of HRT, see PRODIGY *Menopause* guidance.
Raloxifene, a selective oestrogen receptor modulator (SERM), has not been evaluated in corticosteroid-induced bone loss. [Royal College of Physicians of London, 2002].

Drugs included

Treatment of polymyalgia rheumatica

Prednisolone is included in a range of doses to permit tapering. It should be reduced by 2.5 mg each fortnight until 10 mg per day is reached, providing symptoms remain controlled. Subsequent dose reductions are slower, and the dose is reduced by 1 mg every month [Hazleman, 1998; Li and Dasgupta, 2000]. It should be given as a single morning dose to reduce adverse effects. Both plain and enteric-coated prednisolone are used so that all doses can be achieved without halving tablets.

Osteoporosis prophylaxis

Bisphosphonates (alendronate, risedronate, cyclical etidronate): post-hoc analyses of studies risedronate and etidronate and analysis of secondary end points in a study of alendronate found that they all reduced the risk of vertebral fractures in people taking glucocorticoids. However, fracture reduction was not a primary end point in any of these studies. The once-weekly preparations of alendronate and risedronate are also included, but are not licensed for prevention of steroid-induced osteoporosis.
Vitamin D analogues alfacalcidol and calcitriol have both demonstrated increases in bone mineral density (BMD) at the spine and hip in some studies, although the data are conflicting. However, studies show a consistent increase in BMD at the spine by alfacalcidol.
Calcium and vitamin D have been shown to prevent bone loss in some studies, but the data are inconsistent. They are generally regarded as an adjunct to bisphosphonates. They should not be used with vitamin D analogues, due to the increased risk of hypercalcaemia.
[Royal College of Physicians of London, 2002]

Prescriptions

Prednisolone doses: 15mg to 10mg each morning

Prednisolone 10mg e/c each morning
- Age from 40 years onwards
- Prednisolone 5mg e/c tablets. Take two tablets each morning; supply 60 tablets; NHS Cost £0.86.

Prednisolone 12.5mg e/c each morning
- Age from 40 years onwards
- Prednisolone 5mg e/c tablets. Take two tablets each morning; supply 60 tablets; NHS Cost £0.86.

Prednisolone 15mg e/c each morning
- Age from 40 years onwards
- Prednisolone 5mg e/c tablets. Take three tablets each morning; supply 90 tablets; NHS Cost £1.29.

Prednisolone doses: 9mg to 5mg each morning

Prednisolone 9mg each morning
- Age from 40 years onwards
- Prednisolone 5mg e/c tablets. Take one tablet each morning; supply 28 tablets; NHS Cost £0.29.

Prednisolone 8mg each morning
- Age from 40 years onwards
- Prednisolone 5mg e/c tablets. Take one tablet each morning; supply 28 tablets; NHS Cost £0.29.

Prednisolone 7mg each morning
- Age from 40 years onwards
- Prednisolone 5mg e/c tablets. Take one tablet each morning; supply 28 tablets; NHS Cost £0.29.

Prednisolone 6mg each morning
- Age from 40 years onwards
- Prednisolone 5mg e/c tablets. Take one tablet each morning; supply 28 tablets; NHS Cost £0.29.

Prednisolone 5mg e/c each morning
- Age from 40 years onwards
- Prednisolone 5mg e/c tablets. Take one tablet each morning; supply 30 tablets; NHS Cost £0.43.

Prednisolone doses: 4mg to 1mg each morning

Prednisolone 4mg each morning
- Age from 40 years onwards
- Prednisolone 1mg tablets. Take four tablets each morning; supply 112 tablets; NHS Cost £2.08.

Prednisolone 3mg each morning
- Age from 40 years onwards
- Prednisolone 1mg tablets. Take three tablets each morning; supply 84 tablets; NHS Cost £1.56.

Prednisolone 2mg each morning
- Age from 40 years onwards
- Prednisolone 1mg tablets. Take two tablets each morning; supply 56 tablets; NHS Cost £1.04.

Prednisolone 1mg each morning
- Age from 40 years onwards
- Prednisolone 1mg tablets. Take one tablet each morning; supply 28 tablets; NHS Cost £0.52.

Osteoporosis prophylaxis options

Alendronate 10mg each morning
- Age from 40 years onwards
- Alendronate 10mg tablets. Take one tablet each morning; supply 28 tablets; NHS Cost £23.12.

Alendronate 70mg once a WEEK
- Age from 40 years onwards
- Alendronate 70mg tablets. Take one tablet once a WEEK (on the same day each week); supply 4 tablets; NHS Cost £23.12.

Risedronate 5mg once a day
- Age from 40 years onwards
- Risedronate 5mg tablets. Take one tablet once a day; supply 28 tablets; NHS Cost £21.83.

Risedronate 35mg once a WEEK
- Age from 40 years onwards
- Risedronate 35mg tablets. Take one tablet once a WEEK (on the same day each week); supply 4 tablets; NHS Cost £21.83.

Didronel PMO pack: one tablet once a day
- Age from 40 years onwards
- Didronel PMO tablets. Take one tablet once a day. See package insert for full instructions; supply 90 pack; NHS Cost £40.20.

Alfacalcidol 1microgram once a day
- Age from 40 years onwards
- Alfacalcidol 1mcg capsules. Take one capsule once a day; supply 30 capsules; NHS Cost £10.02.

Alfacalcidol 500nanograms once a day
- Age from 60 years onwards
- Alfacalcidol 0.5microgram caps. Take one capsule once a day; supply 30 capsules; NHS Cost £6.69.

Calcitriol 250nanograms twice a day
- Age from 40 years onwards
- Calcitriol 250nanogram caps. Take one capsule twice a day; supply 56 capsules; NHS Cost £11.53.

Adjunct to bisphosphonates: calcium + vitamin D

Elemental calcium 600mg + vitamin D 400iu per day
- Age from 40 years onwards
- Adcal-D3 tablets. Chew one tablet once a day; supply 28 tablets; NHS Cost £2.10.

Elemental calcium 1.2g + vitamin D 800iu per day
- Age from 40 years onwards
- Adcal-D3 tablets. Chew one tablet twice a day; supply 56 tablets; NHS Cost £4.20.

Follow-up visit with poor control

P

Which therapy?

- **Giant-cell (temporal) arteritis may occur at any time and urgently requires treatment with 40–60 mg of prednisolone daily and an urgent ophthalmological referral.**
- **For poorly controlled polymyalgia rheumatica (PMR),** the prednisolone dose may need to be increased:
  - **Increasing the corticosteroid dose increases the risk of adverse effects.**
  - **If symptoms of PMR are controlled,** but the inflammatory markers are raised, consider other causes of a raised erythrocyte sedimentation rate (ESR), specifically giant-cell arteritis (with symptoms of headache or jaw claudication), neoplasm, multiple myeloma, infection, or connective tissue disease.
  - **Treat the person's symptoms rather than the inflammatory markers.**
  - Initially increase the dose of prednisolone to that dose which previously controlled the symptoms, or increase the dose of prednisolone by 5 mg — whichever is the least.

Osteoporosis prophylaxis

- **Give osteoporosis prophylaxis** to people aged over 65 years and those with a previous fragility fracture (i.e. occurring after age 40 years on minimal trauma).
- **In other individuals,** measure bone mineral density using dual-energy X-ray absorptiometry (DEXA) to assess fracture risk. Consider treatment if T score is –1.5 or lower.
- **Use a bisphosphonate** (alendronate, risedronate, or cyclical etidronate) and give calcium with vitamin D as an adjunctive treatment.
- If a bisphosphonate is contraindicated or not tolerated, use alfacalcidol or calcitriol.
- Hormone replacement therapy (HRT) may also be considered as a second-line therapy for postmenopausal women if the benefits of treatment outweigh the risks (off-licence use). See PRODIGY *Menopause* guidance fc further information and prescriptions.

Factors affecting choice of osteoporosis prophylaxis

- **Oesophageal stricture or achalasia:** use cyclical etidronate, alfacalcidol, or calcitriol. Do not use alendronate. If using risedronate, monitor closely for adverse effects.
- **Current or recent history of other upper gastrointestinal disorders:** avoid alendronate.

Practical prescribing points

For further information please see the *Medicines Compendium* (www.medicines.org.uk) or the *British National Formulary* (www.bnf.org).

Corticosteroids

- **Document history of chickenpox** (risk of potentially fat disseminated chickenpox if non-immune). Advise peopl taking systemic corticosteroids to avoid close contact with people who have chickenpox or shingles, and to seek urgent medical advice if they are exposed.
- **Corticosteroids may worsen diabetic control or heart failure.**
- **Concurrent nonsteroidal anti-inflammatory drugs (NSAIDs) increase the risk of gastrointestinal perforation.**
- **All people taking steroids should carry a Steroid Treatment Card.**
- **Advise the person not to stop prednisolone suddenly an** of the need to increase the dose in the case of intercurrent illness.
- **Advise the person that adverse effects** (such as weight gain and hypertension) may occur.

Bisphosphonates

- Take bisphosphonates with a full glass of water while sitting upright or standing (but not lying down), remaining upright for at least 30 minutes afterwards.
- Ask people taking alendronate to report any symptoms suggesting oesophageal irritation, e.g. dysphagia, new o worsening heartburn, pain on swallowing, or retrosternal pain.
- Take alendronate or risedronate at least 30 minutes before breakfast or any other medicines, especially calcium supplements or antacids.
- Etidronate should be taken 2 hours before and 2 hours after meals, or medicines containing calcium, aluminiu magnesium, or iron.

Alfacalcidol and calcitriol

- May cause hypercalcaemia. Monitor serum calcium an creatinine levels.

Follow-up advice

- **Regular review is important for two reasons:**
  - To ensure that the person is adequately treated

- To ensure that dose reduction is performed as rapidly as is safe.

Review in 1 week after a change of prednisolone dose to assess clinical response; this may be possible by telephone. Plan the next dose change.

Recheck inflammatory markers after 2–6 weeks to assess serological response. The erythrocyte sedimentation rate (ESR) and C-reactive protein (CRP) return to normal by 2 weeks. If they are still elevated after this time, other causes must be excluded, e.g. neoplasm, multiple myeloma, infection, or connective tissue disease.

Monitoring drugs used for osteoporosis prophylaxis

Alfacalcidol: check serum calcium and creatinine levels after 1 week, and then monthly to exclude hypercalcaemia.

Calcitriol: check serum calcium and creatinine levels at 4 weeks, 3 months, 6 months and then at 6-monthly intervals to exclude hypercalcaemia.

Should I refer or investigate?

Refer?

Referral is not usually necessary. Indications for referral include:

- Uncertainty over diagnosis
- A person at high risk from adverse effects of corticosteroids
- High corticosteroid dose required to control symptoms (more than 10 mg daily at 6 months)
- Inability to control symptoms with prednisolone up to 25 mg daily
- Symptoms of giant-cell arteritis (urgent referral)
- Synovitis or suspicion of inflammatory arthritis (see PRODIGY *Rheumatoid arthritis* guidance)

Investigate?

Erythrocyte sedimentation rate (ESR) or plasma viscosity (depending on local availability, ESR usually preferred).

C-reactive protein (CRP) if ESR or plasma viscosity was normal at diagnosis.

Tests for other causes of a raised ESR as clinically indicated. The raised ESR may be due to alternative pathology, e.g. neoplasm, multiple myeloma, infection, connective tissue disease.

Shared decision making

Your symptoms of polymyalgia rheumatica (PMR) are not controlled.

The dose of steroids needs to be increased. Once symptoms improve, the aim is to reduce the dose to the lowest one that keeps symptoms away.

Possible side effects of steroids include:

- Osteoporosis ('thinning of the bones') — but measures can be taken to protect against this if you have a high risk.
- Weight gain.
- Increased chance of infections: in particular, you should see a doctor urgently if you come into contact with chickenpox or shingles and you have not had chickenpox in the past.
- Increase in blood pressure, so have it checked regularly.
- High blood sugar, which may mean extra treatment if you have diabetes.

Do not stop steroid tablets suddenly.

- **Some people with polymyalgia also develop inflammation of arteries in their forehead.** See a doctor urgently if you get a one-sided headache, tenderness in your scalp, or an aching in the jaw when you chew.

Drug rationale

Drugs not included

Treatment of polymyalgia rheumatica

- **Nonsteroidal anti-inflammatory drugs (NSAIDs):** combinations of NSAIDs and prednisolone do not improve symptom control and may potentiate adverse effects.
- **Methotrexate:** specialist advice required.
- **Azathioprine:** specialist advice required.
- **Osteoporosis prophylaxis:** see separate PRODIGY *Osteoporosis* guidance.
- **Corticosteroids (except prednisolone)** are not included. In particular:
  - **Deflazacort** has been found to have similar effects on bone mass to prednisolone in people with polymyalgia rheumatica (PMR), and costs are higher [Cimmino et al, 1994; Krogsgaard et al, 1996].
  - **Intramuscular methylprednisolone** is effective in achieving remission of disease [Dasgupta et al, 1998]but treatment by repeated injection is not first choice in primary care.
  - **Prednisone** has to be metabolized to prednisolone before it is effective.

Osteoporosis prophylaxis

- **Intranasal calcitonin** has been studied in glucocorticoid-induced bone loss, but the results are conflicting.
- **Calcium supplements** as a sole therapy for glucocorticoid-induced osteoporosis are ineffective in preventing bone loss.
- **Hormone replacement therapy (HRT)** should only be considered as a second-line option for preventing osteoporosis [CSM, 2003]. It has been found to increase bone mineral density at the spine, but not at the hip in people taking glucocorticoids. However, the risks and benefits of HRT are complex, and should be discussed with each woman before treatment is started. Note that HRT is not licensed for the treatment of osteoporosis. For information on the risks and benefits of HRT, see PRODIGY *Menopause* guidance.
- **Raloxifene,** a selective oestrogen receptor modulator (SERM), has not been evaluated in corticosteroid-induced bone loss.

[Royal College of Physicians of London, 2002]

Drugs included

Treatment of polymyalgia rheumatica

- **Prednisolone** is included in a range of doses. The dose should be increased if symptoms are not controlled, but reduction should begin again as soon as symptoms (and inflammatory markers) allow. The dose should be reduced by 2.5 mg each fortnight until 10 mg per day is reached, providing symptoms remain controlled. Subsequent dose reductions are slower, and the dose is reduced by 1 mg every month [Hazleman, 1998; Li and Dasgupta, 2000]. It should be given as a single morning dose to reduce adverse effects.
- Both plain and enteric-coated prednisolone are used so that all doses can be achieved without halving tablets.

P

Osteoporosis prophylaxis

- **Bisphosphonates** (alendronate, risedronate, cyclical etidronate): post-hoc analyses of studies risedronate and etidronate and analysis of secondary end points in a study of alendronate found that they all reduced the risk of vertebral fractures in people taking glucocorticoids. However, fracture reduction was not a primary end point in any of these studies. The once-weekly preparations of alendronate and risedronate are also included, but are not licensed for prevention of steroid-induced osteoporosis.
- **Vitamin D analogues** alfacalcidol and calcitriol have both demonstrated increases in bone mineral density (BMD) at the spine and hip in some studies, although the data are conflicting. However, studies show a consistent increase in BMD at the spine with alfacalcidol.
- **Calcium and vitamin D** has been shown to prevent bone loss in some studies, but the data are inconsistent. It is generally regarded as an adjunct to bisphosphonates. It should not be used with vitamin D analogues, due to the increased risk of hypercalcaemia.

[Royal College of Physicians of London, 2002]

Prescriptions

Prednisolone doses: 30mg to 20mg each morning

Prednisolone 30mg e/c each morning
- Age from 40 years onwards
- Prednisolone 5mg e/c tablets. Take six tablets each morning; supply 180 tablets; NHS Cost £2.58.

Prednisolone 27.5mg e/c each morning
- Age from 40 years onwards
- Prednisolone 5mg e/c tablets. Take five tablets each morning; supply 150 tablets; NHS Cost £2.15.

Prednisolone 25mg e/c each morning
- Age from 40 years onwards
- Prednisolone 5mg e/c tablets. Take five tablets each morning; supply 150 tablets; NHS Cost £2.15.

Prednisolone 22.5mg e/c each morning
- Age from 40 years onwards
- Prednisolone 5mg e/c tablets. Take four tablets each morning; supply 120 tablets; NHS Cost £1.72.

Prednisolone 20mg e/c each morning
- Age from 40 years onwards
- Prednisolone 5mg e/c tablets. Take four tablets each morning; supply 120 tablets; NHS Cost £1.72.

Prednisolone doses: 17.5mg to 10mg each morning

Prednisolone 17.5mg e/c each morning
- Age from 40 years onwards
- Prednisolone 5mg e/c tablets. Take three tablets each morning; supply 90 tablets; NHS Cost £1.29.

Prednisolone 15mg e/c each morning
- Age from 40 years onwards
- Prednisolone 5mg e/c tablets. Take three tablets each morning; supply 90 tablets; NHS Cost £1.29.

Prednisolone 12.5mg e/c each morning
- Age from 40 years onwards
- Prednisolone 5mg e/c tablets. Take two tablets each morning; supply 60 tablets; NHS Cost £0.86.

Prednisolone 10mg e/c each morning
- Age from 40 years onwards
- Prednisolone 5mg e/c tablets. Take two tablets each morning; supply 60 tablets; NHS Cost £0.86.

Prednisolone doses: 9mg to 1mg each morning

Prednisolone 9mg each morning
- Age from 40 years onwards
- Prednisolone 5mg e/c tablets. Take one tablet each morning; supply 28 tablets; NHS Cost £0.29.

Prednisolone 8mg each morning
- Age from 40 years onwards
- Prednisolone 5mg e/c tablets. Take one tablet each morning; supply 28 tablets; NHS Cost £0.29.

Prednisolone 7mg each morning
- Age from 40 years onwards
- Prednisolone 5mg e/c tablets. Take one tablet each morning; supply 28 tablets; NHS Cost £0.29.

Prednisolone 6mg each morning
- Age from 40 years onwards
- Prednisolone 5mg e/c tablets. Take one tablet each morning; supply 28 tablets; NHS Cost £0.29.

Prednisolone 5mg e/c each morning
- Age from 40 years onwards
- Prednisolone 5mg e/c tablets. Take one tablet each morning; supply 28 tablets; NHS Cost £0.29.

Prednisolone 4mg each morning
- Age from 40 years onwards
- Prednisolone 1mg tablets. Take four tablets each morning; supply 112 tablets; NHS Cost £2.08.

Prednisolone 3mg each morning
- Age from 40 years onwards
- Prednisolone 1mg tablets. Take three tablets each morning; supply 84 tablets; NHS Cost £1.56.

Prednisolone 2mg each morning
- Age from 40 years onwards
- Prednisolone 1mg tablets. Take two tablets each morning; supply 56 tablets; NHS Cost £1.04.

Prednisolone 1mg each morning
- Age from 40 years onwards
- Prednisolone 1mg tablets. Take one tablet each morning; supply 28 tablets; NHS Cost £0.52.

Osteoporosis prophylaxis options

Alendronate 10mg each morning
- Age from 40 years onwards
- Alendronate 10mg tablets. Take one tablet each morning; supply 28 tablets; NHS Cost £23.12.

Alendronate 70mg once a WEEK
- Age from 40 years onwards
- Alendronate 70mg tablets. Take one tablet once a WEEK (on the same day each week); supply 4 tablets; NHS Cost £23.12.

Risedronate 5mg once a day
- Age from 40 years onwards
- Risedronate 5mg tablets. Take one tablet once a day; supply 28 tablets; NHS Cost £21.83.

Risedronate 35mg once a WEEK
- Age from 40 years onwards
- Risedronate 35mg tablets. Take one tablet once a WEEK (on the same day each week); supply 4 tablets; NHS Cost £21.83.

Didronel PMO pack: one tablet once a day
- Age from 40 years onwards
- Didronel PMO tablets. Take one tablet once a day. See package insert for full instructions; supply 90 pack; NHS Cost £40.20.

Alfacalcidol 1microgram once a day
- Age from 40 years onwards
- Alfacalcidol 1mcg capsules. Take one capsule once a day; supply 30 capsules; NHS Cost £10.02.

lfacalcidol 500nanograms once a day
Age from 60 years onwards
Alfacalcidol 0.5microgram caps. Take one capsule once a day; supply 30 capsules; NHS Cost £6.69.

alcitriol 250nanograms twice a day
Age from 40 years onwards
Calcitriol 250nanogram caps. Take one capsule twice a day; supply 56 capsules; NHS Cost £11.53.

Adjunct to bisphosphonates: calcium + vitamin D

lemental calcium 600mg + vitamin D 400iu per day
Age from 40 years onwards
Adcal-D3 tablets. Chew one tablet once a day; supply 28 tablets; NHS Cost £2.10.

lemental calcium 1.2g + vitamin D 800iu per day
Age from 40 years onwards
Adcal-D3 tablets. Chew one tablet twice a day; supply 56 tablets; NHS Cost £4.20.

Extended Information

Background information

What is it? p.1529
How common is it? p.1529
How do I know my patient has it? p.1529
What else might it be? p.1529
Complications and prognosis p.1529

What is it?

- **Polymyalgia rheumatica (PMR) is an inflammatory soft-tissue condition which is rare under the age of 60.**
- **PMR is characterized by persistent pain and stiffness of the neck, shoulder girdle, and pelvic girdle.**
- The causes of PMR are unknown.
- **Systemic features** are frequently present (see *How do I know my patient has it?*).
- **An association with giant-cell (temporal) arteritis** is found in 6–42% of cases [Bahlas et al, 1998; Labbe and Hardouin, 1998].

How common is it?

- **The incidence of PMR varies between different populations.** It is seven times more common in white people than in black people. It is rare before the age of 60 years. The mean age of onset is 70 years. It is three times more common in women than in men [Labbe and Hardouin, 1998].
- **It is extremely difficult to find UK incidence figures.** The annual incidence in studies from Scandinavia and America was 34–53 per 100,000. The prevalence in an American study was 6 per 100,000 in those aged 50 or over [Labbe and Hardouin, 1998].
- **The epidemiology of giant-cell arteritis bears remarkable similarities to PMR.** Their incidences vary between different populations. They are seven times more common in white people than in black people. They are very rare before the age of 50 years. Their mean age of onset is 70 years. They are three times more common in women than in men. The incidence of giant-cell arteritis in studies from Italy and Denmark was 7–23 per 100,000. Symptoms of PMR are found in 40% of people with giant-cell arteritis [Labbe and Hardouin, 1998].

How do I know my patient has it?

Clinical features

- **There is a characteristic history in over 95% of people** [Bahlas et al, 1998]:
  - Pain and stiffness affect the neck, shoulder girdle, and pelvic girdle.
  - The symptoms are bilateral and symmetrical.
  - Stiffness is usually the predominant symptom, and is particularly severe after rest, especially on waking.
  - Affected muscles are tender.
  - The onset is usually insidious; symptoms may have been present for weeks or months before the diagnosis is made.
  - There is a dramatic response to corticosteroid therapy, usually within 2–4 days.
- **Systemic features affect most people with PMR:**
  - Fever
  - Fatigue
  - Anorexia
  - Weight loss
  - Depression
- **Peripheral musculoskeletal features occur in about 50% of people** [Salvarani et al, 2000; Narvaez et al, 2001]:
  - Inflammatory synovitis and effusions
  - Tenosynovitis
  - Carpal tunnel syndrome
  - Swelling of extremities with pitting oedema

Investigations

- **Inflammatory markers (erythrocyte sedimentation rate [ESR], C-reactive protein [CRP], plasma viscosity) are typically elevated.** The ESR may, however, be normal at presentation and even during a flare of disease activity. At presentation 7–22% of people with PMR have a normal ESR (less than 40 mm per hour). This group of people tend to be younger, the female predominance is less marked, there is a greater diagnostic delay, and there are fewer systemic features. ESR and CRP levels usually correlate well. However, most people with a normal ESR at presentation have a raised level of CRP [Bahlas et al, 1998].
- **A normochromic normocytic anaemia is common.**

Diagnostic criteria

- **Disease criteria for PMR have been proposed.** A person may be regarded as having PMR if three or more of the criteria are present (sensitivity 92%, specificity 80%, likelihood ratio 5) [Bird et al, 1979]:
  - Bilateral shoulder pain or stiffness
  - Onset of illness less than 2 weeks' duration
  - Initial ESR greater than 40 mm per hour
  - Morning stiffness lasting longer than 1 hour
  - Age 65 years or more
  - Depression and/or weight loss
  - Bilateral tenderness in the upper arms

What else might it be?

- Late-onset rheumatoid arthritis (often seronegative for rheumatoid factor)
- Multiple myeloma
- Cervical and lumbar spondylosis
- Bilateral frozen shoulder
- Proximal myopathy, e.g. corticosteroid-induced
- Polymyositis
- Neoplasia, e.g. lung carcinoma
- Hypothyroidism
- Drug-induced myositis due to statins
- Drug-induced PMR-like syndrome due to quinidine

[Hazleman, 1998]

Complications and prognosis

Complications

- **Disability** due to the neck, shoulder girdle, and pelvic girdle symptoms

P

- **Visual loss** from associated giant-cell (temporal) arteritis; giant-cell arteritis occurs in 1–6% of people during treatment for PMR, but visual loss is rare [Bengtsson and Malmvall, 1981; Bahlas et al, 1998]
- **Complications of long-term corticosteroid therapy** (e.g. osteoporosis, weight gain, hypertension, immunosuppression, peptic ulceration, depression, psychosis, glaucoma, cataract, and skin fragility); these occur in 76% of people on long-term treatment [Li and Dasgupta, 2000]
- **Other complications of giant-cell arteritis** (e.g. jaw claudication, hemiparesis, peripheral neuropathy, deafness, depression, and confusion)

[Hazleman, 1998]

Prognosis

- **The response to corticosteroid treatment is rapid and dramatic.** Typically there is complete resolution of symptoms within 2–4 days.
- **The median treatment time is 2 years** [Bahlas et al, 1998]. Some people require therapy for substantially longer, with up to 40% still requiring corticosteroid treatment at 4 years [Ayoub et al, 1985]. Neither severity of symptoms nor elevation of inflammatory markers at onset can predict duration of treatment.
- **Relapse is common** after cessation or reduction of prednisolone treatment, but responds to reintroduction of prednisolone. Relapse is most likely in the first 18 months of treatment and within a year of stopping treatment [Bengtsson and Malmvall, 1981; Behn et al, 1983].
- **PMR is not associated with raised mortality** [Andersson et al, 1986; Gran et al, 2001].

Management issues

- General issues p.1530
- Drug management p.1530
- Giant-cell (temporal) arteritis p.1531

General issues

Erythrocyte sedimentation rate

- **Is it better to use symptoms or erythrocyte sedimentation rate (ESR) for monitoring?** Although in most people the ESR is a reasonable guide to disease activity, it may be normal when the disease is active, and raised when the disease is quiescent. Some authorities advocate the use of the person's symptoms as a more reliable guide to disease activity than the ESR.

Rheumatoid arthritis

- **Seronegative rheumatoid arthritis** in the elderly may be of insidious onset and may be very similar to polymyalgia rheumatica (PMR) at presentation. In one large series 17 out of 142 people who were initially diagnosed as having PMR were subsequently diagnosed as having rheumatoid arthritis. It is important to remember that their symptoms will improve with corticosteroid therapy; this is therefore not a diagnostic test [Bahlas et al, 1998].

Referral

- **Referral** may be necessary in those people whose symptom control requires high maintenance doses of corticosteroid, in those who develop significant adverse corticosteroid effects, and where there is doubt about the diagnosis.

Drug management

General

- **Corticosteroid therapy is indicated in all cases.**
- **Outline of management:**
  - No advantage has been shown for starting doses of prednisolone greater than 15 mg daily, and adverse effects are significantly increased [Li and Dasgupta, 2000].
  - Corticosteroid therapy should be started as soon as th diagnosis of PMR is suspected. A dramatic clinical response would be expected in 2–4 days; inflammatory markers normalize over 2 weeks [Li an Dasgupta, 2000].
  - Corticosteroid doses should be reduced gradually, taking into account the clinical symptoms and the inflammatory markers. The median duration of treatment is approximately 2 years, but treatment ma take much longer [Bahlas et al, 1998]. Relapse is common, occurring in up to 60% of people; it responds rapidly to an increase in corticosteroid dose [Ayoub et al, 1985].
  - There is no agreed protocol for the reduction of the corticosteroid dose; indeed, the requirements of individuals may vary.
- **Giant-cell (temporal) arteritis may occur at any time, ar urgently requires treatment with 40–60 mg of prednisolone daily, and an urgent ophthalmological referral.**

Corticosteroid therapy

- **Adverse effects due to long-term corticosteroid treatme are very common and may be more significant than the complications of PMR itself.** If sustained weight gain is included, 76% of people taking long-term corticosteroids will experience adverse effects. Older ag female sex, and higher cumulative dose increase the risk [Li and Dasgupta, 2000].
- **The risk of corticosteroid-induced osteoporosis** is of particular concern. All people should be considered for prophylaxis against osteoporosis (see *Osteoporosis prophylaxis* below).
- **Document history of chickenpox** (risk of potentially fat disseminated chickenpox if non-immune). Advise peopl taking systemic corticosteroids to avoid close contact with people who have chickenpox or shingles, and to seek urgent medical advice if they are exposed.
- **Steroid Treatment Cards** should be issued by the GP or pharmacist and their contents discussed.
- **Corticosteroid-sparing therapy:** studies of alternative corticosteroid preparations or corticosteroid-sparing drugs are small, and such regimens are not in routine u at present:
  - **Use of alternate-day corticosteroids** to minimize adverse reactions has been proposed. Trials have bee small in size and no advantage has been shown over daily dosing.
  - **Deflazacort** has been suggested to have fewer advers effects than prednisolone, but this is not fully established. It has been found to have similar effects on bone mass to prednisolone in people with PMR, and costs are higher [Krogsgaard et al, 1996].
  - **Intramuscular depot methylprednisolone** at a dose of 120 mg every 3 weeks was compared with oral prednisolone in a small trial, and was found to suppress disease activity of PMR as well as prednisolone. There is however no compelling reasor to recommend this over conventional treatment with oral prednisolone [Dasgupta et al, 1998].

- **Azathioprine** was found in a small, randomized controlled trial to reduce corticosteroid requirement at 12 months from initiation of treatment. Dose reduction was small and no effect was seen before 1 year [De Silva and Hazleman, 1986].

Osteoporosis prophylaxis

- **People starting or currently on *any dose* of oral steroids for more than 3 months should be given osteoporosis prophylaxis if they:**
  - Are aged over 65 years
  - Have a previous fragility fracture (i.e. occurring after age 40 years on minimal trauma)
- **In other individuals, measure bone mineral density using dual-energy X-ray absorptiometry (DEXA) to assess fracture risk.** Consider treatment if T score is –1.5 or lower [Royal College of Physicians of London, 2002].
- **Bisphosphonates (alendronate, risedronate, or cyclical etidronate) are a first-line option for the prevention or treatment of corticosteroid-induced osteoporosis.**
  Calcium with vitamin D can be used as an adjunct to bisphosphonate treatment.
  Post-hoc analyses of studies of risedronate and etidronate, and analysis of secondary end points in a study of alendronate, found that they all reduced the risk of vertebral fractures in people taking glucocorticoids. Note that fracture was not a primary end point in any of these studies [Royal College of Physicians of London, 2002].
  Gastrointestinal adverse effects such as abdominal pain, dyspepsia, diarrhoea, or constipation, are common with bisphosphonates. Oesophageal reactions (oesophagitis, oesophageal ulcers, strictures, and erosions) are uncommon but serious adverse events that continue to be reported with alendronate [DTB, 2001].
  People with delayed oesophageal emptying, e.g. strictures or achalasia, should not take alendronate, and should avoid taking risedronate where possible. Cyclical etidronate is an alternative bisphosphonate for these people [DTB, 2001].
  If a bisphosphonate is contraindicated or not tolerated, consider alfacalcidol, or calcitriol.
  Alfacalcidol and calcitriol are vitamin D analogues. Hypercalcaemia and hypercalciuria have occasionally been reported. Regular monitoring of serum calcium and creatinine is needed.
  Hormone replacement therapy (HRT) should only be considered as a second-line option for for preventing osteoporosis in perimenopausal and postmenopausal women [CSM, 2003] if the benefits of treatment outweigh the risks (off-licence use). See the PRODIGY *Menopause* guidance for further information on the risks and benefits of HRT.
  For further information on the prevention and treatment of corticosteroid-induced osteoporosis, see the PRODIGY *Osteoporosis* guidance.

Giant-cell (temporal) arteritis

- **Giant-cell (temporal) arteritis may occur at any stage. People with PMR should be advised to report unilateral temporal headache or jaw claudication as a matter of urgency.**
- **Treatment of giant-cell arteritis requires urgent treatment with 40–60 mg of oral prednisolone daily.**
- **Giant-cell arteritis is an inflammatory condition that may affect any artery.** The commonest presentation is of temporal arteritis, with headache, inflammation and tenderness of the temporal artery, and visual loss if untreated. Other presentations of giant-cell arteritis include jaw claudication, hemiparesis, peripheral neuropathy, deafness, depression, and confusion [Hazleman, 1998].

References

NHS staff in England can link, free of charge, from references to full text journals by clicking on [Full text] on the PRODIGY website.

1. Andersson, R., Malmvall, B.E. and Bengtsson, B.A. (1986) Long-term survival in giant cell arteritis including temporal arteritis and polymyalgia rheumatica. A follow-up study of 90 patients treated with corticosteroids. *Acta Medica Scandinavica* **220**(4), 361–364.
2. Ayoub, W.T., Franklin, C.M. and Torretti, D. (1985) Polymyalgia rheumatica. Duration of therapy and long-term outcome. *American Journal of Medicine* **79**(3), 309–315.
3. Bahlas, S., Ramos-Remus, C. and Davis, P. (1998) Clinical outcome of 149 patients with polymyalgia rheumatica and giant cell arteritis. *Journal of Rheumatology* **25**(1), 99–104.
4. Behn, A.R., Perera, T. and Myles, A.B. (1983) Polymyalgia rheumatica and corticosteroids: how much for how long? *Annals of the Rheumatic Diseases* **42**(4), 374–378.
5. Bengtsson, B.A. and Malmvall, B.E. (1981) Prognosis of giant cell arteritis including temporal arteritis and polymyalgia rheumatica. A follow-up study on ninety patients treated with corticosteroids. *Acta Medica Scandinavica* **209**(5), 337–345.
6. Bird, H.A., Esselinckx, W., Dixon, A.S. et al (1979) An evaluation of criteria for polymyalgia rheumatica. *Annals of the Rheumatic Diseases* **38**(5), 434–439.
7. Cimmino, M.A., Moggiana, G., Montecucco, C. et al (1994) Long term treatment of polymyalgia rheumatica with deflazacort. *Annals of the Rheumatic Diseases* **53**(5), 331–333.
8. CSM (2003) *Further advice on safety of HRT: risk/ benefit unfavourable for first-line use in prevention of osteoporosis*. CEM/CMO/2003/19. Committee on Safety of Medicines. www.mhra.gov.uk [Accessed: 09/ 01/2004].
9. Dasgupta, B., Dolan, A.L., Panayi, G.S. and Fernandes, L. (1998) An initially double-blind controlled 96 week trial of depot methylprednisolone against oral prednisolone in the treatment of polymyalgia rheumatica. *British Journal of Rheumatology* **37**(2), 189–195.
10. De Silva, M. and Hazleman, B.L. (1986) Azathioprine in giant cell arteritis/polymyalgia rheumatica: a double-blind study. *Annals of the Rheumatic Diseases* **45**(2), 136–138.
11. DTB (2001) Biphosphonates for osteoporosis. *Drug & Therapeutics Bulletin* **39**(9), 68–72.
12. Gran, J.T., Myklebust, G., Wilsgaard, T. and Jacobsen, B.K. (2001) Survival in polymyalgia rheumatica and temporal arteritis: a study of 398 cases and matched population controls. *Rheumatology* **40**(11), 1238–1242. [Full text]
13. Hazleman, B.L. (1998) The vasculitides: polymyalgia rheumatica and giant cell arteritis. In: Klippel, J.H. and Dieppe, P.A. (Eds.) *Rheumatology*. 2nd edn. London: Mosby International. 21.1–21.8.
14. Krogsgaard, M.R., Thamsborg, G. and Lund, B. (1996) Changes in bone mass during low dose corticosteroid treatment in patients with polymyalgia rheumatica: a double blind, prospective comparison between prednisolone and deflazacort. *Annals of the Rheumatic Diseases* **55**(2), 143–146.

15. Labbe, P. and Hardouin, P. (1998) Epidemiology and optimal management of polymyalgia rheumatica. *Drugs & Aging* 13(2), 109–118.
16. Li, C. and Dasgupta, B. (2000) Corticosteroids in polymyalgia rheumatica – a review of different treatment schedules. *Clinical & Experimental Rheumatology* 18(4 Suppl 20), S56-S57.
17. Narvaez, J., Nolla-Sole, J.M., Narvaez, J.A. et al (2001) Musculoskeletal manifestations in polymyalgia rheumatica and temporal arteritis. *Annals of the Rheumatic Diseases* 60(11), 1060–1063. [Full text]
18. Royal College of Physicians of London (2002) *Glucocorticoid-induced osteoporosis*. Royal College of Physicians. www.rcplondon.ac.uk [Accessed: 22/04/2003].
19. Salvarani, C., Cantini, F. and Olivieri, I. (2000) Distal musculoskeletal manifestations in polymyalgia rheumatica. *Clinical & Experimental Rheumatology* 18(4 Suppl 20), S51-S52.

P

PRODIGY GUIDANCE

Preconceptual counselling

Last revised in June 2004
www.prodigy.nhs.uk/guidance.asp?gt=Preconceptual counselling

Applies to women from the age of 16 to 45 years

This guidance covers advice and information for women who are planning a pregnancy.

This guidance does not cover antenatal or postnatal care.

There is separate PRODIGY guidance for some of the specific conditions mentioned in this guidance: *Alcohol—problem drinking, Asthma, Depression, Diabetes, Epilepsy, Hypertension in pregnancy, Hyperthyroidism, Hypothyroidism, Opioid dependence, Schizophrenia, Smoking cessation.*

Goals

- To provide the information a woman and her partner need in order to make informed choices about planning a pregnancy and ensuring the best possible outcome

Contents

Scenarios
- The healthy woman p.1533
- Women with epilepsy p.1534
- Women with chronic conditions p.1536
- Women with mental health issues p.1537
- Ethnic issues p.1538

Extended Information, p. 1540

Which scenario?

- **The healthy woman:** covers general points that should be addressed when counselling all women who are planning a pregnancy. There are a number of *Patient information leaflets* available that will provide useful background information for the woman to take away with her.
- **Women with epilepsy:** covers the main issues that the GP can address in the surgery before referral to a specialist. These are in addition to those issues applicable to healthy women.
- **Women with chronic conditions:** covers the main issues that the GP can address in the surgery before referral to a specialist. The conditions covered are: hypertension, diabetes, renal disease, thyroid disease, asthma, and cardiac disease. These are in addition to those issues applicable to healthy women.
- **Women with mental health issues:** covers the main issues that the GP can address in the surgery before referral to a specialist. The conditions covered are: depression, bipolar affective disorder, and schizophrenia. These are in addition to those issues applicable to healthy women.
- **Ethnic issues:** covers issues that should be considered when the woman and/or her partner are from what is considered in the United Kingdom to be an ethnic or minority background.

The healthy woman

Which therapy?

Check that all women who are planning a pregnancy:

- Are taking folic acid supplements and continue for 12 weeks into the pregnancy.
  - **Prescribe folic acid 400 micrograms daily** to prevent first occurrence of a neural tube defect.
  - **Prescribe folic acid 5 mg daily for any woman who:**
    - Has had a previously affected pregnancy (approximately a 10 times greater risk of neural tube defect compared to women without a previously affected pregnancy);
    - Has a neural tube defect, or whose partner or first-degree relative has a neural tube defect;
    - Has coeliac disease (when dietary intake of folate is likely to be compromised due to inability to digest wheat products);
    - Is taking antiepileptic drugs (see scenario *Women with epilepsy*);
    - Has sickle cell anaemia or thalassaemia (see scenario *Ethnic issues*).
- **Have an up-to-date cervical smear;**
- **Have clearly documented immunity to rubella.** Testing is not required if any of the below apply:
  - At least two previous rubella antibody screening tests have detected antibodies.
  - At least two documented doses of rubella vaccine have been given.
  - One documented dose of vaccine has been followed by a rubella antibody screening test which has detected antibodies.
- **Have hepatitis B immunity, if appropriate** (e.g. health care personnel, parenteral drug abusers, women who change sexual partners frequently).

Review all medication and advise on the use of over-the-counter medication.

If applicable, give advice (or refer, if more appropriate) on the following:

- Stopping smoking
- Reducing alcohol intake
- Healthy eating
- Illicit substance misuse

Practical prescribing points

For further information please see the *Medicines Compendium* (www.medicines.org.uk) or the *British National Formulary* (www.bnf.org).

Should I refer or investigate?

Refer?

- In some cases referral will depend on the wishes of the woman and/or the local resources. In general refer:
  - Women who smoke to a smoking cessation specialist
  - Women who use illicit substances to the community drugs team
  - Women who drink alcohol excessively to the local alcohol advisory service or whichever resources are locally available

P

Investigate?

- **Check rubella status.** This will not need to be checked if the woman has clearly documented immunity to rubella. Testing is not required if any of the below apply:
  - At least two previous rubella antibody screening tests have detected antibodies
  - At least two documented doses of rubella vaccine have been given
  - One documented dose of vaccine has been followed by a rubella antibody screening test which has detected antibodies
- Check hepatitis B status, if appropriate.

Patient information leaflets

The following PILs are available at www.prodigy.nhs.uk

- Pregnancy and Alcohol
- Pregnancy and Caffeine
- Pregnancy and Diet
- Pregnancy and Employment
- Pregnancy and Folic Acid
- Pregnancy and Medication
- Pregnancy and Rubella
- Pregnancy and Smoking
- Pregnancy and Street Drugs
- Pregnancy - Planning to Become Pregnant?
- Pregnancy - Planning to Become Pregnant? - A summary

Shared decision making

- **Things you should do before becoming pregnant:**
  - Take folic acid tablets.
  - Check if you are immune to rubella. Get immunized if not immune.
  - Eat a healthy diet. Include foods rich in iron, calcium, and folic acid.
  - Wash your hands after handling raw meat, or handling cats and kittens.
  - Wear gloves when you are gardening.
- **Things you should avoid:**
  - Too much vitamin A (don't eat liver, liver products, or vitamin A tablets)
  - Too much caffeine (a 'safe' limit is 300 mg a day, equivalent to 3 cups of brewed coffee. It is also in chocolate, cola, and 'energy drinks'.)
  - Listeriosis (don't eat soft cheese, paté, shellfish, raw fish, or unpasteurized milk)
  - Fish which may contain a lot of mercury (shark, marlin, swordfish, or excessive amounts of tuna, see Patient information leaflet)
  - Sheep, lambs, cat faeces, cat litters, which may carry certain infections
  - Peanuts, if you have a personal or family history of eczema, hay fever, or asthma
- **Things you are strongly advised to stop:**
  - Smoking
  - Excess alcohol (have no more than 1–2 drinks, once or twice a week)
  - Street drugs
- **Other things to consider:**
  - Immunization against hepatitis B if you are at increased risk
  - Your medication — including herbal and over-the-counter medicines
  - Your work environment — is it safe?
  - Medical conditions in yourself, or any that run in your family

P

Drug rationale

Drugs not included

- **Vitamin supplements** other than folic acid are not included. In a healthy, well-nourished woman, there is no justification for giving additional vitamin supplements [Campbell, 2001].

Drugs included

- **Folic acid 400 micrograms** daily is recommended in all women who are planning a pregnancy and should be continued for the first 12 weeks of pregnancy. This dose is recommended to prevent first occurrence of a neural tube defect *in women who have no risk factors for the pregnancy being complicated by a neural tube defect* [Wald, 1991].
- **Folic acid 5 mg daily** is recommended for women who are at high risk of having a baby with a neural tube defect [Scottish Obstetric Guidelines Audit Project, 1997]. This should be started preconceptually and continued for the first 12 weeks of pregnancy.
- **Rubella vaccine** is offered in the form of the combined measles, mumps, and rubella vaccine (due to the non-availability of the single rubella vaccine) for women who are sero-negative for rubella [DH, 2003].

Prescriptions

Folic acid 400microgram tablets

Folic acid 400micrograms once a day

- Age from 16 to 45 years
- Folic acid 400microgram tabs. Take one tablet once a day; supply 90 tablets; NHS Cost £2.19; OTC Cost £3.85.

Folic acid 5mg tablets (special cases)

Folic acid 5mg once a day

- Age from 16 to 45 years
- Folic acid 5mg tablets. Take one tablet once a day; supply 90 tablets; NHS Cost £1.34.

Rubella vaccination

Rubella vaccine (as MMR) – NOT if pregnant

- Age from 16 to 45 years
- MMR vaccine. Give 0.5ml by deep subcutaneous or intramuscular injection. Read attached information; supply 1 0.5ml injection; NHS Cost £2.53.

Women with epilepsy

Which therapy

Specific issues relating to a diagnosis of epilepsy:

- **Reassure** the woman that most babies born to women with epilepsy are normal.
- **Prescribe** folic acid 5 mg daily, to be started preconceptually and continued for the first 12 weeks of pregnancy.
- **Advise the woman** that a referral may lead to changes/ reduction in current medication.
- **Ensure effective contraception** while the woman is undergoing *any* changes in medication (including any trial withdrawals of drugs).

General issues to consider in all women:

Check the woman:

- **Has an up-to-date cervical smear.**
- **Has clearly documented immunity to rubella.** Testing is not required if any of the below apply:

- At least two previous rubella antibody screening tests have detected antibodies
- At least two documented doses of rubella vaccine have been given
- One documented dose of vaccine has been followed by a rubella antibody screening test which has detected antibodies
- Has hepatitis B immunity, if appropriate (e.g. health care personnel, parenteral drug abusers, women who change sexual partners frequently).

Review all medication and advise on the use of over-the-counter medication.

If applicable, give advice (or refer, if more appropriate) on the following:

- Stopping smoking
- Reducing alcohol intake
- Healthy eating
- Illicit substance misuse

Practical prescribing points

For further information please see the *Medicines Compendium* (www.medicines.org.uk) or the *British National Formulary* (www.bnf.org).

Should I refer or investigate?

Refer?

- **Refer all women** to a specialist for consideration of a reduction in the number of drugs taken and/or a reduction in individual drug dosage.

Investigate?

- **Check rubella status.** This will not need to be checked if the woman has clearly documented immunity to rubella. Testing is not required if any of the below apply:
  - At least two previous rubella antibody screening tests have detected antibodies
  - At least two documented doses of rubella vaccine have been given
  - One documented dose of vaccine has been followed by a rubella antibody screening test which has detected antibodies
- Check hepatitis B status, if appropriate.

Patient information leaflets

The following PILs are available at www.prodigy.nhs.uk

- Pregnancy and Alcohol
- Pregnancy and Caffeine
- Pregnancy and Diet
- Pregnancy and Employment
- Pregnancy and Folic Acid
- Pregnancy and Medication
- Pregnancy and Rubella
- Pregnancy and Smoking
- Pregnancy and Street Drugs
- Pregnancy - Planning to Become Pregnant?
- Pregnancy - Planning to Become Pregnant? - A summary

Shared decision making

- **Things you should do before becoming pregnant:**
  - If you have epilepsy:
    - You should take 5 mg folic acid tablets each day.
    - It is usual to refer you to a specialist to review your medication.
    - Check if you are immune to rubella. Get immunized if not immune.
    - Eat a healthy diet. Include foods rich in iron, calcium, and folic acid.
    - Wash your hands after handling raw meat, or handling cats and kittens.
    - Wear gloves when you are gardening.
- **Things you should avoid:**
  - Too much vitamin A (don't eat liver, liver products, or vitamin A tablets)
  - Too much caffeine (a 'safe' limit is 300 mg a day, equivalent to 3 cups of brewed coffee. It is also in chocolate, cola, and 'energy drinks'.)
  - Listeriosis (don't eat soft cheese, paté, shellfish, raw fish, or unpasteurized milk)
  - Fish which may contain a lot of mercury (shark, marlin, swordfish, or excess tuna)
  - Sheep, lambs, cat faeces, cat litters, which may carry certain infections
  - Peanuts, if you have a personal or family history of eczema, hay fever, or asthma
- **Things you are strongly advised to stop:**
  - Smoking
  - Excess alcohol (have no more than 1–2 drinks, once or twice a week)
  - Street drugs
- **Other things to consider:**
  - Immunization against hepatitis B if you are at increased risk
  - Your medication — including herbal and over-the-counter medicines
  - Your work environment — is it safe?
  - Medical conditions in yourself, or any that run in your family

Drug rationale

Drugs not included

- **Folic acid 400 micrograms is not included.** This is only recommended for the primary prevention of neural tube defects in women who are at low risk of having an affected baby.
- **Vitamin supplements** other than folic acid are not included. In a healthy, well-nourished woman, there is no justification for giving additional vitamin supplements [Campbell, 2001].

Drugs included

- **Folic acid 5 mg daily** is recommended for *all* women who are taking antiepileptic drugs and planning a pregnancy [Scottish Obstetric Guidelines Audit Project, 1997]. This should be started preconceptually and continued for the first 12 weeks of pregnancy.
- **Rubella vaccine** is offered in the form of the combined measles, mumps, and rubella vaccine (due to the non-availability of the single rubella vaccine) for women who are sero-negative for rubella [DH, 2003].

Prescriptions

Folic acid 5mg tablets

Folic acid 5mg once a day

- Age from 16 to 45 years
- Folic acid 5mg tablets. Take one tablet once a day; supply 90 tablets; NHS Cost £1.34.

P

Rubella vaccination

Rubella vaccine (as MMR) – NOT if pregnant
- Age from 16 to 45 years
- MMR vaccine. Give 0.5ml by deep subcutaneous or intramuscular injection. Read attached information; supply 1 0.5ml injection; NHS Cost £2.53.

Women with chronic conditions

Which therapy

These points are for consideration in addition to those listed in the scenario *The healthy woman.*

Effective contraception is advised in women with any of the following until they have had a consultation with the specialist, if appropriate:

- **Chronic hypertension**
  - **Advise a woman who is taking angiotensin-converting enzyme (ACE) inhibitors or angiotensin-II receptor antagonists inhibitors that she must use effective contraception** until her blood pressure is controlled by other means.
- Diabetes
  - **Advise a woman** taking oral hypoglycaemic medication that on referral she will be switched to an insulin regimen.
  - **Tight glycaemic control** is necessary to reduce the risk of major congenital abnormalities. The glycosylated haemoglobin level should be no more than 1% above the upper limit of normal.
- **Renal disease**
  - **Ensure adequate contraception until the woman has been assessed.**
  - **Women with renal diseases** that tend to progress should be encouraged to complete childbearing whilst renal function is preserved.
  - **Advise women who have had a renal transplant that:**
    - They should wait at least 1.5 years after transplant and only attempt pregnancy once the creatinine is stable at 200 mg/l or less.
    - The specialist may need to change their immunosuppressant medication (tacrolimus and mycophenolate are contraindicated in pregnancy).
- **Thyroid disease**
  - **Hypothyroidism:** ensure optimal control with levothyroxine (thyroxine).
  - **Hyperthyroidism:** refer any woman not already under consultant care and request early review by the consultant during the preconceptual period. Although there is no convincing evidence that antithyroid drugs are teratogenic, there have been some recent concerns that carbimazole may cause fetal abnormalities.
- **Asthma**
  - Unless asthma is severe it should be managed in the surgery.
  - **Reassure the woman that,** unless asthma is very severe, it is unlikely to affect the course or outcome of the pregnancy.
  - **Reassure the woman that inhaled corticosteroids and short-acting beta$_2$-agonists are not teratogenic.**
- Cardiac disease
  - **The risk to the woman and the fetus** depends on the severity of the disease.
  - **Accurate diagnosis and functional assessment** are necessary to predict maternal and fetal risk.

Practical prescribing points

For further information please see the *Medicines Compendium* (www.medicines.org.uk) or the *British National Formulary* (www.bnf.org).

Should I refer or investigate?

Refer?

- Referral to the appropriate specialist is necessary in all women who are planning a pregnancy with the chronic conditions listed in this scenario:
  - Chronic hypertension
  - Diabetes
  - Renal disease
  - Hyperthyroidism
  - Severe asthma
  - Cardiac disease

Investigate?

- **Check rubella status.** This will not need to be checked if the woman has clearly documented immunity to rubella. Testing is not required if any of the below apply:
  - At least two previous rubella antibody screening tests have detected antibodies
  - At least two documented doses of rubella vaccine have been given
  - One documented dose of vaccine has been followed by a rubella antibody screening test which has detected antibodies
- Check hepatitis B status, if appropriate.

Patient information leaflets

The following PILs are available at www.prodigy.nhs.uk
- Pregnancy and Alcohol
- Pregnancy and Caffeine
- Pregnancy and Diet
- Pregnancy and Employment
- Pregnancy and Folic Acid
- Pregnancy and Medication
- Pregnancy and Rubella
- Pregnancy and Smoking
- Pregnancy and Street Drugs
- Pregnancy - Planning to Become Pregnant?
- Pregnancy - Planning to Become Pregnant? - A summary

Shared decision making

- **Before becoming pregnant, if you have a condition** such as high blood pressure, diabetes, kidney disease, heart problems, epilepsy, overactive thyroid, severe asthma, etc., then you may be referred to a specialist for advice about your condition and your medication.
- **Things you should do before becoming pregnant:**
  - Take folic acid tablets.
  - Check if you are immune to rubella. Get immunized if not immune.
  - Eat a healthy diet. Include foods rich in iron, calcium, and folic acid.
  - Wash your hands after handling raw meat, or handling cats and kittens.
  - Wear gloves when you are gardening.
- **Things you should avoid:**
  - Too much vitamin A (don't eat liver, liver products, or vitamin A tablets)
  - Too much caffeine (a 'safe' limit is 300 mg a day, equivalent to 3 cups of brewed coffee. It is also in chocolate, cola, and 'energy drinks'.)
  - Listeriosis (don't eat soft cheese, paté, shellfish, raw fish, or unpasteurized milk)
  - Fish which may contain a lot of mercury (shark, marlin, swordfish, or excess tuna)
  - Sheep, lambs, cat faeces, cat litters, which may carry certain infections

P

- Peanuts, if you have a personal or family history of eczema, hay fever, or asthma
- **Things you are strongly advised to stop:**
  - Smoking
  - Excess alcohol (have no more than 1–2 drinks, once or twice a week)
  - Street drugs
- **Other things to consider:**
  - Immunization against hepatitis B if you are at increased risk
  - Your medication — including herbal and over-the-counter medicines
  - Your work environment — is it safe?
  - Medical conditions in yourself, or any that run in your family

Drug rationale

Drugs not included

Vitamin supplements other than folic acid are not included. In a healthy, well-nourished woman, there is no justification for giving additional vitamin supplements [Campbell, 2001].

Drugs included

Folic acid 400 micrograms daily is recommended in all women who are planning a pregnancy and should be continued for the first 12 weeks of pregnancy. This dose is recommended to prevent first occurrence of a neural tube defect *in women who have no risk factors for the pregnancy being complicated by a neural tube defect* [Wald, 1991].

Folic acid 5 mg daily is recommended for women who are at high risk of having a baby with a neural tube defect and are planning a pregnancy [Scottish Obstetric Guidelines Audit Project, 1997]. This should be started preconceptually and continued for the first 12 weeks of pregnancy.

Rubella vaccine is offered in the form of the combined measles, mumps, and rubella vaccine (due to the non-availability of the single rubella vaccine) for women who are sero-negative for rubella [DH, 2003].

Prescriptions

Folic acid 400microgram tablets

Folic acid 400micrograms once a day

Age from 16 to 45 years

Folic acid 400microgram tabs. Take one tablet once a day; supply 90 tablets; NHS Cost £2.19; OTC Cost £3.85.

Folic acid 5mg tablets

Folic acid 5mg once a day

Age from 16 to 45 years

Folic acid 5mg tablets. Take one tablet once a day; supply 90 tablets; NHS Cost £1.34.

Rubella vaccination

Rubella vaccine (as MMR) – NOT if pregnant

Age from 16 to 45 years

MMR vaccine. Give 0.5ml by deep subcutaneous or intramuscular injection. Read attached information; supply 1 0.5ml injection; NHS Cost £2.53.

Women with mental health issues

Which therapy

These points for consideration are in addition to those listed in the scenario *The healthy woman.*

Effective contraception is advised in women with any of these mental health issues until they have had a consultation with a psychiatrist.

- **Depression**
  - **Reassure** the woman that there is no evidence of increased risk of major malformations or spontaneous abortion following exposure to antidepressants in early or later pregnancy.
  - **There is no indication** to routinely stop tricyclic antidepressants or selective serotonin reuptake inhibitors (SSRIs) in early pregnancy.
- **Bipolar affective disorder**
  - **Prescribe folic acid 5 mg preconceptually** and during the first 12 weeks of pregnancy if antiepileptic drugs are used for stabilizing mood.
  - **Lithium is highly teratogenic** if taken in the first 12 weeks of pregnancy.
- **Schizophrenia**
  - **Advise the woman that adequate contraception is needed** until a full assessment by a psychiatrist has taken place.
  - **Advise the woman that** maintenance therapy may be continued and discuss the relative risk/benefit. This will particularly be the case if she has deteriorated on trial withdrawals of medication in the past. Increased doses may be needed to treat a relapse of the illness in the event of any medication being stopped.

Practical prescribing points

For further information please see the *Medicines Compendium* (www.medicines.org.uk) or the *British National Formulary* (www.bnf.org).

Should I refer or investigate?

Refer?

- Women with any of these mental health issues should be referred to a psychiatrist.

Investigate?

- **Check rubella status.** This will not need to be checked if the woman has clearly documented immunity to rubella. Testing is not required if any of the below apply:
  - At least two previous rubella antibody screening tests have detected antibodies
  - At least two documented doses of rubella vaccine have been given
  - One documented dose of vaccine has been followed by a rubella antibody screening test which has detected antibodies
- Check hepatitis B status, if appropriate.

Patient information leaflets

The following PILs are available at www.prodigy.nhs.uk

- Pregnancy and Alcohol
- Pregnancy and Caffeine
- Pregnancy and Diet
- Pregnancy and Employment
- Pregnancy and Folic Acid
- Pregnancy and Medication

P

- Pregnancy and Rubella
- Pregnancy and Smoking
- Pregnancy and Street Drugs
- Pregnancy - Planning to Become Pregnant?
- Pregnancy - Planning to Become Pregnant? - A summary

Shared decision making

- **Before becoming pregnant,** if you have a mental health condition such as bipolar affective disorder or schizophrenia, then you may be referred to a specialist for advice about your condition and medication.
- **Things you should do before becoming pregnant:**
  - Take folic acid tablets.
  - Check if you are immune to rubella. Get immunized if not immune.
  - Eat a healthy diet. Include foods rich in iron, calcium, and folic acid.
  - Wash your hands after handling raw meat, or handling cats and kittens.
  - Wear gloves when you are gardening.
- **Things you should avoid:**
  - Too much vitamin A (don't eat liver, liver products, or vitamin A tablets)
  - Too much caffeine (a 'safe' limit is 300 mg a day, equivalent to 3 cups of brewed coffee. It is also in chocolate, cola, and 'energy drinks'.)
  - Listeriosis (don't eat soft cheese, paté, shellfish, raw fish, or unpasteurized milk)
  - Fish which may contain a lot of mercury (shark, marlin, swordfish, or excess tuna)
  - Sheep, lambs, cat faeces, cat litters, which may carry certain infections
  - Peanuts, if you have a personal or family history of eczema, hay fever, or asthma
- **Things you are strongly advised to stop:**
  - Smoking
  - Excess alcohol (have no more than 1–2 drinks, once or twice a week).
  - Street drugs
- **Other things to consider:**
  - Immunization against hepatitis B if you are at increased risk
  - Your medication, including herbal and over-the-counter medicines
  - Your work environment — is it safe?
  - Medical conditions in yourself, or any that run in your family

P

Drug rationale

Drugs not included

- **Vitamin supplements** other than folic acid are not included. In a healthy, well-nourished woman, there is no justification for giving additional vitamin supplements [Campbell, 2001].

Drugs included

- **Folic acid 400 micrograms** daily is recommended in all women who are planning a pregnancy and should be continued for the first 12 weeks of pregnancy. This dose is recommended to prevent first occurrence of a neural tube defect *in women who have no risk factors for the pregnancy being complicated by a neural tube defect* [Wald, 1991].
- **Folic acid 5 mg** daily is recommended for all women who are taking antiepileptic drugs, or have a high risk of having a baby with a neural tube defect and are planning a pregnancy [Scottish Obstetric Guidelines Audit Project, 1997]. This should be started preconceptually and continued for the first 12 weeks of pregnancy.
- **Rubella vaccine** is offered in the form of the combined measles, mumps, and rubella vaccine (due to the non-availability of the single rubella vaccine) for women who are sero-negative for rubella [DH, 2003].

Prescriptions

Folic acid 400microgram tablets

Folic acid 400micrograms once a day

- Age from 16 to 45 years
- Folic acid 400microgram tabs. Take one tablet once a day; supply 90 tablets; NHS Cost £2.19; OTC Cost £3.85.

Folic acid 5mg tablets

Folic acid 5mg once a day

- Age from 16 to 45 years
- Folic acid 5mg tablets. Take one tablet once a day; supply 90 tablets; NHS Cost £1.34.

Rubella vaccination

Rubella vaccine (as MMR) – NOT if pregnant

- Age from 16 to 45 years
- MMR vaccine. Give 0.5ml by deep subcutaneous or intramuscular injection. Read attached information; supply 1 0.5ml injection; NHS Cost £2.53.

Ethnic issues

Which therapy

- **Check the woman's rubella status.** Some women will be from countries that do not have an organized immunization programme, and as a result may be susceptible to rubella. They may also be less likely to have *clearly documented* immunity to rubella. Testing is not required if any of the below apply:
  - At least two previous rubella antibody screening tests have detected antibodies
  - At least two documented doses of rubella vaccine have been given
  - One documented dose of vaccine has been followed by a rubella antibody screening test which has detected antibodies
- **Ancestry fully or partially Ashkenazi Jewish:** offer genetic screening for Tay–Sachs disease, Gaucher's disease, and cystic fibrosis.
- **Ancestry from the Mediterranean, Africa, Middle East, Indian subcontinent, South East Asia, Southern China, and the Caribbean:** offer screening for active haemoglobinopathies or the carrier state.
- **Prescribe folic acid 5 mg daily to** women who have a high risk of having a baby with a neural tube defect. A woman is at higher risk if:
  - She has had a previously affected pregnancy (approximately a 10 times greater risk of neural tube defect compared to women without a previously affected pregnancy)
  - She, her partner, or a first-degree relative has a neural tube defect
  - She has coeliac disease (when dietary intake of folate likely to be compromised due to inability to digest wheat products)
  - She is taking antiepileptic drugs (see scenario *Women with epilepsy*).

- **Continue folic acid 5 mg daily** in all women who have sickle cell anaemia (HBS/S), HbH disease, or HbS/C disease.
- **Consider the possibility of hepatitis B (particularly in women from the Far East) and HIV infection (particularly in women from Africa and the Caribbean).** These possibilities should be discussed sensitively with appropriate testing and counselling where necessary.
- **Some women, particularly from parts of Africa and the Middle East,** may have undergone female genital mutilation and may have related anxieties about pregnancy and labour that should be sensitively discussed.

General issues to consider in all women:

- **Check the woman:**
  - Has an up-to-date cervical smear
  - Has hepatitis B immunity, if appropriate (e.g. health care personnel, parenteral drug abusers, women who change sexual partners frequently)
- **Review all medication and advise on the use of over-the-counter medication.**
- **If applicable, give advice (or refer, if more appropriate) on the following:**
  - Stopping smoking
  - Reducing alcohol intake
  - Healthy eating
  - Illicit substance misuse

Practical prescribing points

For further information please see the *Medicines Compendium* (www.medicines.org.uk) or the *British National Formulary* (www.bnf.org).

Follow-up advice

- **Offer a screening blood test** to the partners of women who are either positive for one or more of the haemoglobinopathies or who are carriers.

Should I refer or investigate?

Refer?

- Refer all women with a haemoglobinopathy to a haematologist for assessment.
- Refer or seek advice from either a haematologist or a geneticist regarding women in whom either a haemoglobinopathy trait has been identified or who at high risk of being a carrier. Their partners should be tested too. This will include people either at high risk of carrying, or who have been identified as having a trait, (e.g. beta-thalassaemia, HbE, Hb Lepore, HbC, HbD Punjab, HbO Arab and sickle cell trait [HbA/S]).
- Refer to a geneticist if the woman or her partner are at high risk or are known to be carriers of Tay–Sachs disease, Gaucher's disease, or cystic fibrosis.

Investigate?

- Send a blood test to screen for haemoglobinopathies in people from the Mediterranean, Africa, Middle East, Indian subcontinent, South East Asia, and Southern China.
- Check rubella status in women where there is *any doubt* about whether they are protected.

Patient information leaflets

The following PILs are available at www.prodigy.nhs.uk

- Pregnancy and Alcohol
- Pregnancy and Caffeine
- Pregnancy and Diet
- Pregnancy and Employment
- Pregnancy and Folic Acid
- Pregnancy and Medication
- Pregnancy and Rubella
- Pregnancy and Smoking
- Pregnancy and Street Drugs
- Pregnancy - Planning to Become Pregnant?
- Pregnancy - Planning to Become Pregnant? - A summary

Shared decision making

- **Things you should do before becoming pregnant:**
  - Take folic acid tablets.
  - Check if you are immune to rubella. Get immunized if not immune.
  - Eat a healthy diet. Include foods rich in iron, calcium, and folic acid.
  - Wash your hands after handling raw meat, or handling cats and kittens.
  - Wear gloves when you are gardening.
- **Things you should avoid:**
  - Too much vitamin A (don't eat liver, liver products, or vitamin A tablets)
  - Too much caffeine. (A 'safe' limit is 300 mg a day, equivalent to 3 cups of brewed coffee. It is also in chocolate, cola, and 'energy drinks'.)
  - Listeriosis (don't eat soft cheese, paté, shellfish, raw fish, or unpasteurized milk)
  - Fish which may contain a lot of mercury (shark, marlin, swordfish, or excess tuna)
  - Sheep, lambs, cat faeces, cat litters, which may carry certain infections
  - Peanuts, if you have a personal or family history of eczema, hay fever, or asthma
- **Things you are strongly advised to stop:**
  - Smoking
  - Street drugs
  - Excess alcohol (have no more than 1–2 drinks, once or twice a week)
- **Other things to consider:**
  - Excess alcohol (have no more than 1–2 drinks, once or twice a week)
  - Immunization against hepatitis B if you are at increased risk.
  - Your medication — including herbal and over-the-counter medicines.
  - Your work environment — is it safe?
  - Medical conditions in yourself, that run in your family, or that are common in your ethnic background. For example, you may want:
    - A blood test to screen for haemoglobinopathies if you are from the Mediterranean, Africa, Middle East, Indian subcontinent, South East Asia, Southern China or the Caribbean.
    - Genetic screening and counselling for Tay–Sachs disease, Gaucher's disease and cystic fibrosis if your ancestry is fully or partially Ashkenazi Jewish.

Drug rationale

Drugs not included

- **Vitamin supplements** other than folic acid are not included. In a healthy, well-nourished woman, there is no justification for giving additional vitamin supplements [Campbell, 2001].

Drugs included

- **Folic acid 5 mg should be prescribed** for life to all women who have sickle cell anaemia (HbS/S), HbH

disease, or HbS/C disease. It should also be prescribed for women at high risk of having a baby with a neural tube defect or those taking antiepileptic medication. It should be started preconceptually and continued for the first 12 weeks of the pregnancy.
- **Folic acid 400 micrograms** daily is recommended in all women who are planning a pregnancy and should be continued for the first 12 weeks of pregnancy. This dose is recommended to prevent first occurrence of a neural tube defect [Scottish Obstetric Guidelines Audit Project, 1997].
- **Rubella vaccine** is offered in the form of the combined measles, mumps, and rubella vaccine (due to the non-availability of the single rubella vaccine) for women who are sero-negative for rubella [DH, 2003].

Prescriptions

Folic acid 400microgram tablets

Folic acid 400micrograms once a day
- Age from 16 to 45 years
- Folic acid 400microgram tabs. Take one tablet once a day; supply 90 tablets; NHS Cost £2.19; OTC Cost £3.85.

Folic acid 5mg tablets

Folic acid 5mg once a day
- Age from 16 to 45 years
- Folic acid 5mg tablets. Take one tablet once a day; supply 90 tablets; NHS Cost £1.34.

Rubella vaccination

Rubella vaccine (as MMR) – NOT if pregnant
- Age from 16 to 45 years
- MMR vaccine. Give 0.5ml by deep subcutaneous or intramuscular injection. Read attached information; supply 1 0.5ml injection; NHS Cost £2.53.

Extended Information

P

Background information

What is it?

- **Preconceptual counselling should not be confused with antenatal care.**
- **Preconceptual counselling** has several components:
  - It begins with attitudes and practices that value pregnant women, children, and families and respects the diversity of people's lives and experiences.
  - It incorporates informed choice, thus encouraging women and men to understand health issues that may affect conception and pregnancy.
  - It encourages women and men to prepare actively for pregnancy, and enables them to be as healthy as possible.
  - It attempts to identify couples who are at increased risk of producing babies with a genetic malformation, and provide them with sufficient knowledge to make informed decisions.

[Health Canada, 2000]

Management issues

- How can a woman prepare for pregnancy? p.1540
- Advising women over 35 years old p.1541
- Advising women with chronic conditions p.1542
- Advising women who have had pre-eclampsia or recurrent miscarriage p.1546
- When is genetic screening advised? p.1546
- Advising women who use illicit substances p.1547

How can a woman prepare for pregnancy?

Folic acid

- **Folic acid supplementation during pregnancy reduces the risk of neural tube defect (spina bifida).** A large randomized controlled trial comparing folic acid supplementation with placebo in women at high risk of having a pregnancy affected by a neural tube defect found that folic acid supplementation reduced the risk of neural tube defect by 72% (95% CI 29 to 88) [Wald, 1991].
- **All women who are planning a pregnancy should take folic acid supplements and, once pregnant, continue this for the first 12 weeks of pregnancy.**
- **Women who have not been taking folic acid supplements** and suspect or know that they are pregnant should start taking folic acid at once and continue for 12 weeks into the pregnancy [BNF 47, 2004].
- **Remind all women** to eat a folate-rich diet and advise them how to achieve this (e.g. eating breakfast cereals, bread, and leafy green vegetables).

Folic acid 400 micrograms daily
- **Folic acid 400 micrograms daily** is recommended to prevent the *first* occurrence of a neural tube defect *in women who have no risk factors for the pregnancy being complicated by a neural tube defect*. This should be started during the preconceptual period and continued for the first 12 weeks of the pregnancy.

Folic acid 5 mg daily
- **All women at higher risk** of having a baby with a neural tube defect should take folic acid 5 mg daily preconceptually and for 12 weeks into the pregnancy.
- **A woman is at higher risk** if:
  - She has had a previously affected pregnancy (approximately a ten times greater risk of neural tube defect compared to women without a previously affected pregnancy) [Wald, 1991; Lumley et al, 2003].
  - She, her partner, or a first-degree relative has a neural tube defect.
  - She has coeliac disease (when dietary intake of folate is likely to be compromised due to inability to digest wheat products) [DH, 2000; BNF 47, 2004]
  - She is taking antiepileptic drugs (see section on Epilepsy).
- **Women with sickle cell anaemia** (HbS/S), HbH disease, or HbS/C disease should take 5 mg folic acid daily for life and continue to do so during pregnancy [Taylor, Personal Communication, 2004].

Stopping smoking

- **All women who smoke should quit smoking before becoming pregnant.**
- **Smoking in pregnancy increases the risk** of miscarriage, preterm delivery, reduced birthweight, and perinatal death [Dobson et al, 1998].
- **Quitting before or early in pregnancy is strongly recommended,** but the fetus will benefit from quitting at any stage during the pregnancy.
- **Women who quit before pregnancy are less likely to relapse** [DiClemente et al, 2000; Lumley et al, 2004].
- **Women who smoke and wish to become pregnant** should receive clear, accurate, and specific information on the risks of smoking to themselves and the fetus, and be advised to stop smoking [West et al, 2000].
- **There is a lack of data on the use and relative risks of nicotine replacement therapy (NRT) in pregnancy.** Cigarette smoking, in general, delivers more nicotine

than NRT, and exposes the mother and fetus to many other toxins. NRT is likely to be appreciably safer than continued smoking and theoretically can be justified in pregnant women in whom non-pharmacological interventions have failed [RCP, 1999; Dempsey and Benowitz, 2001].

- **Do not prescribe bupropion during pregnancy, as there is a lack of data available on its safety in pregnancy.** If bupropion is prescribed, the course should be completed before the woman tries for a pregnancy [NICE, 2002].

(For further details see separate PRODIGY guidance on *Smoking Cessation.*)

Reducing alcohol intake

- **Women should be advised** to reduce their alcohol intake if they are planning a pregnancy. Once pregnant, current advice is that light occasional drinking (one or two drinks once or twice a week) is unlikely to harm the fetus [SIGN, 2003b].
- **Heavy drinking** is associated with miscarriage and sometimes has serious effects on the baby's development:
  - Maternal consumption of 15 units/week or more is associated with a reduction in birthweight.
  - Maternal consumption in excess of 20 units/week is associated with intellectual impairment in the child.
  - Fetal alcohol syndrome (brain damage, prenatal and postnatal growth retardation, and facial malformations) is relatively uncommon even amongst heavily drinking pregnant women. It occurs in approximately a third of children born to women who drink about 18 units/day [RCOG, 1999; SIGN, 2003b].
- **Preconceptual counselling** and routine antenatal care provide a useful opportunity to deliver a brief intervention for reducing alcohol consumption. Two studies have looked at brief interventions in the antenatal setting and found that increased intervention (whether this is simply giving the woman a booklet or brief contact with a physician) does prompt women to reduce their alcohol consumption [SIGN, 2003b].
- **It is important to identify women** who are drinking heavily and are likely to continue drinking throughout their pregnancy so that appropriate help and support can be offered.

(For further details see separate PRODIGY guidance on *Alcohol – problem drinking.)*

Up-to-date cervical smear

- **Opportunity should be taken to identify women who need a cervical smear.** Cervical smears are not routinely taken during pregnancy as pregnancy-related inflammatory changes make them difficult to interpret. If an abnormality is detected many interventional treatments cannot be carried out during pregnancy.

Checking rubella status

- **Primary rubella infection can have a devastating effect on the fetus.** Fetal defects include mental handicap, cataract, deafness, cardiac abnormalities, intra-uterine growth retardation, and inflammatory lesions of the brain, liver, lungs, and bone marrow [Donaldson et al, 2003]. Infection in the first 8–10 weeks of pregnancy results in damage in up to 90% of infants. The risk declines to about 10–20% by 16 weeks, and damage is rare after this.
- Check rubella status in all women who are not clearly documented as being immune. Testing is not required if any of below apply:
  - At least two previous rubella antibody screening tests have detected antibodies.
  - At least two documented doses of rubella vaccine have been given.
  - One documented dose of vaccine has been followed by a rubella antibody screening test which has detected antibodies [HPA, 2000].
- **Offer vaccination against rubella to all women who are found not to have antibodies against rubella on preconception screening.** Women should be advised to avoid becoming pregnant for 1 month after receiving rubella-containing vaccine, although extensive studies have failed to identify fetal damage as a consequence of immunizing with rubella vaccine in early pregnancy [Donaldson et al, 2003]. The measles, mumps, and rubella (MMR) combined vaccine is now used for immunization of unprotected women of childbearing age due to the non-availability of single rubella vaccine. The Joint Committee on Vaccination and Immunization recognizes that MMR is a suitable alternative (and it also offers protection against mumps and measles in this group).
- **Immunity against rubella is generally high in the UK** (susceptibility less than 2% in British-born women) due to the national immunization programme.

[Tookey et al, 2002; DH, 2003; Donaldson et al, 2003]

Other immunization status to consider

- **Hepatitis B should be strongly recommended if the woman is considered to be at high risk.** In the UK high risk groups include:
  - Parenteral drug abusers
  - People who change sexual partners frequently
  - Close family contacts of a case of hepatitis B or a carrier of hepatitis B
  - Health-care personnel and other occupational risk groups, e.g. staff at day care or residential centres

[BNF 47, 2004]

Assessing risks from the environment

- This is a complex area involving potential hazards:
  - At work
  - In the home (e.g. pets)
  - Farm animals
- **Advise any woman who thinks that her occupation may pose a risk** to a pregnancy to discuss this with her employer or occupational health department, if available, before becoming pregnant [Chamberlain and Morgan, 2002].
- Information guides for employers and expectant mothers can be downloaded from the Health and Safety Executive website at www.hse.gov.uk.

Review of medication (including over-the-counter drugs)

- **It is important to minimize exposure to all drugs** whenever conception is possible. All non-essential drug treatment should be discouraged, including self-medication with over-the-counter products (See *Patient information leaflets*).
- **Herbal remedies** are unlicensed products and there is little or no information on their safety immediately before or during pregnancy.

Advising women over 35 years old

- **Although it is important to discuss the risks associated with increasing maternal age,** it is also important to emphasize that most pregnancies are uneventful and have a good outcome. In practice, management in pregnancy is not altered except for discussion about prenatal diagnosis of chromosome abnormalities [Wildschut, 1999].

- **The risk of** fetal chromosomal abnormalities, in particular trisomy 21 (Down's syndrome) increases sharply with maternal age. The estimated risk of having a baby with trisomy 21, 18, 13, and sex chromosome aberrations is 6 per 1000 live births at age 35 years; 15 at age 40 years; and 54 at age 45 years [Wildschut, 1999].
- **There is also an increased risk** of miscarriage, twins, fibroids, hypertension, gestational diabetes, labour problems, and perinatal mortality [Wildschut, 1999]. This risk increases with age [Jolly et al, 2000].

Advising women with chronic conditions

Depression

Should I refer?
- **Women with severe depression should be referred to a psychiatrist.**

Are there any risks?
- **A past history of mental health problems during pregnancy is a risk factor for future postnatal depression.** Low social support, poor marital relationships, recent adverse life events, and 'baby blues' are also risk factors [SIGN, 2002].
- **There is no evidence of teratogenicity or adverse pregnancy outcomes following exposure to antidepressants in early or later pregnancy** (see Table 1). There are most safety data on tricyclic antidepressants (TCAs) and the selective serotonin reuptake inhibitors (SSRIs) fluoxetine, citalopram, fluvoxamine, paroxetine, and sertraline [SIGN, 2002].

What can be done to minimize these risks?
- **Assess the risks of stopping TCAs or SSRIs** in relation to the woman's mental state and previous history.

(For further details see separate PRODIGY guidance on *Depression*.)

Bipolar affective disorder

Should I refer?
- **Refer to a psychiatrist,** as management needs careful assessment and mood-stabilizing drugs should be avoided during the first 12 weeks of pregnancy if at all possible [Stowe et al, 2001].

Are there any risks?
- **The risks of major congenital abnormality,** including Ebstein's anomaly, in women treated with lithium during the early stages of pregnancy is 4–12% [Cohen et al, 1994]. (Ebstein's anomaly is a congenital heart defect which includes displacement and deformity of the tricuspid valve [Collier et al, 1997].)
- **The risk of a relapse if lithium is withdrawn should also be discussed with the mother** before pregnancy [SIGN, 2002].

What can be done to minimize these risks?
- **Effective contraception is essential until the woman has been fully assessed.**
- **If lithium is continued,** serum levels will be carefully monitored [SIGN, 2002].
- **A daily dose of folic acid 5 mg** should be prescribed preconceptually and continued until the end of the first 12 weeks if antiepileptic drugs are used as mood stabilizers.

Schizophrenia

Should I refer?
- **Refer all women with schizophrenia who are planning a pregnancy to a psychiatrist for assessment.**

Are there any risks?
- There is conflicting evidence regarding the teratogenic risks of the older antipsychotic drugs and a lack of information regarding the new antipsychotic drugs.

What can be done to minimize these risks?
- **Ensure adequate contraception** until a full assessment by the psychiatrist has taken place.
- **In severe or chronic psychosis,** it may be preferable to continue maintenance therapy, particularly if the woman has deteriorated in the past when medication has been stopped. This is because increased doses may be needed to treat a relapse of the illness in the event of any medication being stopped [Kumar and O'Dowd, 2001].

(For further details see separate PRODIGY guidance on *Schizophrenia*.)

Epilepsy

Should I refer?
- **Refer all women taking antiepileptic drugs to a specialist to consider a reduction in the number of drugs and the total daily dosage** [Scottish Obstetric Guidelines Audit Project, 1997]. The risk of fetal abnormalities increases with the number of different antiepileptic drugs taken. If antiepileptic drug treatment cannot be stopped, try at least to reduce to one antiepileptic drug only [Delgado-Escueta and Janz, 1992].

Are there any risks?
- **Most babies born to women with epilepsy are normal.**
- **Major and minor fetal malformations** are more common in infants exposed to antiepileptic drugs during pregnancy. The risk of major fetal abnormality in any pregnancy is 2% and this increases two- to three-fold if a women is taking a single antiepileptic drug [SIGN, 2003a]. Polytherapy, particularly with certain combinations of drugs, carries a much higher risk (up to 24% in women taking four antiepileptic drugs) [SIGN, 2003a].
- **The risk of teratogenicity** is minimized if treatment is limited to a single drug at the lowest possible dose that protects against seizures [DTB, 1994; Scottish Obstetric Guidelines Audit Project, 1997; BNF 47, 2004].
- **The most common malformations** associated with established antiepileptic drugs are neural tube defects (valproate 3%, carbamazepine 1%), orofacial defects, congenital heart defects, and hypospadias [SIGN, 2003a].
- **Newer antiepileptic drugs:** there is insufficient evidence about the risks associated with the newer drugs (gabapentin, levetiracetam, tiagabine, topiramate, vigabatrin) in pregnancy. Data on lamotrigine have shown a malformation rate of 3% [SIGN, 2003a].
- **The risk of minor defects such as** hypertelorism, epicanthic folds, and digital hypoplasia are also increased with antiepileptic drugs [SIGN, 2003a].

What can be done to minimize these risks?
- **Ensure that all women with epilepsy take folic acid 5 mg once daily while trying to become pregnant and for the first 12 weeks of pregnancy** — this reduces the risk of the fetus having a neural tube defect [Scottish Obstetric Guidelines Audit Project, 1997; CSM, 2003; SIGN, 2003a].
- **Effective contraception is essential to ensure that pregnancies are planned** [Scottish Obstetric Guidelines Audit Project, 1997]. Pregnancy should be avoided when there is any change to the antiepileptic drug or any trial withdrawals of medication.

(For further details see separate PRODIGY guidance on *Epilepsy*.)

Table 1: Summary of drug use in preconception and pregnancy.

Condition	Drug(s)/drug group	Advice
Depression	Tricyclic and related antidepressants	No evidence of teratogenicity with standard doses. Review risk–benefit.
	Selective serotonin reuptake inhibitors (SSRI)	Use only if potential benefit outweighs risk. No teratogenicity reported. Fluoxetine is SSRI of choice.
	Monoamine oxidase inhibitors (e.g. phenelzine, tranylcypromine)	No evidence of harm but manufacturers advise against use.
Bipolar disorder	Lithium	Strong evidence of teratogenicity. Only give if absolutely necessary.
Schizophrenia	Phenothiazines (e.g. chlorpromazine, trifluoperazine)	There is a small increase in fetal abnormalities but benefits may outweigh the risks. Chlorpromazine and trifluoperazine are the treatments of choice. Avoid fluphenazine.
	Butyrophenones (e.g. haloperidol and droperidol)	Haloperidol: probably safe, treatment of choice Droperidol: limited data, avoid
	Thioxanthines (e.g. flupentixol, zuclopenthixol)	Limited data, avoid
	Atypicals (e.g. risperidone, olanazapine, sertindole)	Insufficient information, use is not recommended.
Epilepsy	Sodium valproate	In common with all older antiepileptic drugs, sodium valproate has strong evidence of teratogenicity. The Committee on Safety of Medicines has advised that women of childbearing age should not be started on sodium valproate. The lowest effective dose should be given, in divided doses and if possible as a modified-release preparation. Prescribe folic acid 5 mg as soon contraception is stopped.
	Phenytoin, carbamazepine, and phenobarbital (phenobarbitone)	All have strong evidence of teratogenicity but benefit may outweigh risk. Reduce the number of antiepileptic drugs used. Prescribe folic acid 5 mg as soon contraception is stopped.
	Newer antiepileptics, e.g. gabapentin, vigabatrin, tiagabine, lamotrigine	Insufficient evidence on use in pregnancy. Do not use unless absolutely necessary.
Chronic hypertension	Angiotensin-converting enzyme inhibitors (ACE) and angiotensin-II receptor antagonists	Absolutely contraindicated. ACE inhibitors decrease fetal renal function and urine production which may lead to a decrease in amniotic fluid. There is little experience with angiotensin-II inhibitors but animal studies have shown serious problems that are likely to be due to their effect on the renin–angiotensin–aldosterone system.
	Methyldopa	The antihypertensive of choice in pregnancy.
	Beta blockers	There are most data for labetolol, propranolol, and metoprolol. There is some evidence of risk of intra-uterine growth restriction with atenolol but no evidence of teratogenicity.
	Calcium-channel blockers	No evidence of teratogenic effects. Most experience is with nifedipine.
Hypothyroidism and hyperthyroidism	Carbimazole, propylthiouracil, levothyroxine (thyroxine)	Some evidence of increased risk of malformations with carbimazole. Overtreatment with carbimazole or propylthiouracil increases the risk of fetal goitre and hypothyroidism.
Asthma	Inhaled short-acting beta$_2$-agonists (e.g. salbutamol and terbutaline)	Data suggest that there are no risks to the fetus.
	Inhaled long-acting beta$_2$-agonists (e.g. salmeterol, fenoterol, and eformoterol)	Limited experience with these drugs as yet. Preferably avoid unless control cannot be achieved by other means.
	Inhaled corticosteroids	Studies have provided evidence of good outcome. Most experience with beclometasone and least with fluticasone.
	Oral corticosteroids	Prednisolone is the corticosteroid of choice. Prolonged exposure increases the risk of intra-uterine growth retardation. There is a theoretical risk of adrenal suppression but this usually resolves spontaneously after birth and is rarely clinically important.
	Theophylline, anticholinergic bronchodilators, leukotriene inhibitors	Some studies suggest that theophylline may be associated with fetal harm. There is a low risk of harm with ipratropium. Avoid oxitropium as there is limited experience. Avoid leukotriene inhibitors as there is a lack of data.
	Sodium cromoglicate, nedocromil	No evidence of increased fetal risk.
Diabetes	Metformin, sulphonylureas	No evidence of teratogenicity but metformin may be associated with growth retardation and hyperbilirubinaemia; sulphonylureas may cause hyperinsulinaemia and macrosomia in the fetus. Convert to insulin regimen in preconception period.

[Chaplin, 2000; Gilmour-White, 2000; Parkinson, 2000; Worsley, 2000; Barwell et al, 2002; Diav-Citrin and Ornoy, 2002; National Teratology Information Service, 2002a; National Teratology Information Service, 2002b; Guignon et al, 2003; SIGN, 2003a; BNF 47, 2004;]

Chronic hypertension

Should I refer?

- **Refer all women with hypertension to a specialist for advice on drug manipulation and to organize shared care monitoring** [Working Group on High Blood Pressure in Pregnancy, 2000].

Are there any risks?

- **Chronic hypertension** is associated with an increased risk of pre-eclampsia, placental abruption, and increased neonatal morbidity and mortality [Sibai et al, 1998].
- **Pre-eclampsia complicates 25% of pregnancies with chronic hypertension** and the incidence is higher if there is associated renal insufficiency, presence of hypertension for 4 years or more, and a history of hypertension in

P

Start ACE inhibitor (4-week supply)

Lisinopril 5mg once a day for 2 days, then 10mg once a day
- Age from 16 years onwards
- Lisinopril 5mg tablets. Take one tablet once a day for 2 days and then take two tablets once a day; supply 56 tablets; NHS Cost £15.34.

Ramipril 2.5mg once a day for 7 days, then 5mg once a day
- Age from 55 years onwards
- Ramipril 2.5mg tablets. Take one tablet once a day for 7 days, then take two tablets once a day; supply 49 tablets; NHS Cost £15.02.

Start low-dose ACE inhibitor (2-week supply)

Lisinopril 2.5mg once a day
- Age from 16 years onwards
- Lisinopril 2.5mg tablets. Take one tablet once a day; supply 14 tablets; NHS Cost £3.23.

Ramipril 1.25mg twice a day for 2days then 2.5mg twice a day
- Age from 55 years onwards
- Ramipril 1.25mg tablets. Take one tablet twice a day for 2 days, then take two tablets twice a day; supply 63 tablets; NHS Cost £10.35.

Start statin therapy

Simvastatin 20mg at night
- Age from 16 years onwards
- Simvastatin 20mg tablets. Take one tablet at night; supply 28 tablets; NHS Cost £29.69.

Pravastatin 20mg at night
- Age from 16 years onwards
- Pravastatin 20mg tablets. Take one tablet at night; supply 28 tablets; NHS Cost £29.69.

Atorvastatin 10mg once a day
- Age from 16 years onwards
- Atorvastatin 10mg tablets. Take one tablet once a day; supply 28 tablets; NHS Cost £18.03.

Fluvastatin 20mg at night
- Age from 18 years onwards
- Fluvastatin 20mg capsules. Take one capsule at night; supply 28 capsules; NHS Cost £12.72.

Prior MI and no heart failure — maintenance treatment

Which therapy?

Which drugs?

- **Maintenance dosages** of the drugs recommended for prophylaxis after myocardial infarction (MI) are offered.
- **All people should be offered long-term treatment firstly with a beta-blocker and an antiplatelet drug (aspirin or clopidogrel), and then with a statin and an ACE inhibitor.** This sequencing of initiation reflects the evidence from trials and estimates of cost-effectiveness (**A**).
- Statin treatment should be adjusted to achieve desired cholesterol targets. It is generally accepted that patients with a total serum cholesterol of 5 mmol/l or greater should receive treatment to reduce their cholesterol level. The National Service Framework for Coronary Heart Disease states that total serum cholesterol should be lowered to below 5 mmol/l or by 20–25%, whichever will result in the lower level. Equivalent figures for low-density lipoprotein (LDL) cholesterol are 3 mmol/l or a 30% reduction. If the statin dosages offered are insufficient to reach the agreed target cholesterol, see separate PRODIGY guidance on *Hyperlipidaemia* for more detailed advice.

Practical prescribing points

The information below is not covered within the Nation Institute for Clinical Excellence (NICE) guideline, but ha been added by PRODIGY. For further information see th *Medicines Compendium* (www.medicines.org.uk) or the *British National Formulary* (www.bnf.org).

Aspirin

- **Avoid** in gastrointestinal ulceration, haemophilia and other bleeding disorders, and breastfeeding. Use with caution in impaired renal or hepatic function, asthma, and pregnancy.
- **Concurrent nonsteroidal anti-inflammatory drugs (NSAIDs):** the risk of serious gastrointestinal complications doubles in people who regularly take lo dose aspirin and another NSAID. If possible, stop the second NSAID.
- **If a second NSAID must be continued, avoid ibuprofe** — it may reduce the cardiovascular protective effect o low-dose aspirin. Consider using diclofenac if a seconc NSAID must be used.

Beta-blockers

- **Avoid** in asthma, chronic obstructive pulmonary disea (COPD), or heart block. Caution in peripheral vascula disease.

ACE inhibitors

- **Avoid potassium-sparing diuretics or potassium supplements** in patients on ACE inhibitors (other than spironolactone in patients with heart failure), because the risk of hyperkalaemia.
- **Stop nonsteroidal anti-inflammatory drugs (NSAIDs)** possible) as they reduce the effectiveness of diuretics a increase the risk of renal impairment with ACE inhibitors.

Statins

- **Adverse effects** are usually minor and rarely require cessation of treatment. They include transient headach minor gastrointestinal upset, rashes, dizziness, pruritu fatigue, and insomnia.
- **Rarely,** hepatotoxicity or myopathy may occur.
- **Risk of myositis** is increased by concomitant treatmen with fibrates, ciclosporin, nicotinic acid, or danazol. Simvastatin may slightly potentiate the effects of warfarin; this may be significant in a small number of patients so initial monitoring is advised.

Follow-up advice

Some of the information below has been obtained from National Institute for Clinical Excellence (NICE) guideli Additional information has been added by PRODIGY.

People taking a beta-blocker

- **Increase dosage** to the recommended maintenance dosages offered in this scenario.

People taking a statin

- **Statin treatment should be adjusted to achieve desired cholesterol targets.** The National Service Framework f Coronary Heart Disease states that total serum cholesterol should be lowered to below 5 mmol/l or by previous pregnancies [Working Group on High Blood Pressure in Pregnancy, 2000].

What can be done to minimize these risks?

- **Stop angiotensin-converting enzyme (ACE) inhibitors and angiotensin-II receptor blockers.** ACE inhibitors have been associated with fetal growth restriction, oligohydramnios, neonatal renal failure, and neonatal death [Ramsay et al, 1999; Working Group on High Blood Pressure in Pregnancy, 2000]. On the basis of the experience with ACE inhibitors and data from case studies showing a similar spectrum of toxicity, angiotensin-II receptor antagonists are not recommended for use during pregnancy [National Teratology Information Service, 2002c].
- **Consider changing to an antihypertensive that is considered safer during pregnancy.** The drugs with most safety data are methyldopa, beta-blockers (labetolol, metoprolol, propranolol), and hydralazine. If these drugs are ineffective, a modified-release preparation of nifedipine may be considered as a second-line alternative (Table 1) [National Teratology Information Service, 2002a].
- **The role of antihypertensive medication** in pregnant women with mild-to-moderate hypertension (diastolic pressure 90–109 mmHg) is uncertain. A Cochrane review found that antihypertensive medication reduced the risk of progressing to severe hypertension but did not reduce the incidence of pre-eclampsia or improve perinatal outcomes [Abalos et al, 2002; Magee and Duley, 2002].

(For further details see separate PRODIGY guidance on *Hypertension in pregnancy*.)

Diabetes

Should I refer?

- **Refer to a specialist and, if available, to a diabetic preconceptual counselling clinic.**

Are there any risks?

- **Poor control of diabetes** increases the risks of major congenital abnormality and spontaneous abortion. A normal glycosylated haemoglobin level at the onset of pregnancy appears to reduce this risk [Super et al, 1986].
- There is no evidence that metformin or the sulphonylureas are teratogenic. However, metformin may be associated with growth retardation and hyperbilirubinaemia. Sulphonylureas cross the placenta and may cause hyperinsulinaemia and macrosomia in the fetus (Table 1) [Seymour and Pugh, 2000; American Diabetes Association, 2003].

What can be done to minimize these risks?

- **It is very important to optimize glycaemic control preconceptually,** as the rate of major congenital abnormalities can be reduced if control is good in the first 8 weeks of pregnancy [Diabetes UK, 2000]. Aim for a glycosylated haemoglobin level of not more than 1% above the upper limit of normal. Effective contraception should be used until this target is achieved [American Diabetes Association, 2003].
- **Following hospital review,** in the ideal situation all women should be switched to human insulin. However, in certain cases the specialist may decide that metformin is an acceptable alternative for the preconceptual period.

Renal disease

Should I refer?

- **Women who are planning a pregnancy and have renal disease should be referred to a specialist for assessment.**

Are there any risks?

- **Renal disease during pregnancy is associated with risk** of prematurity, intra-uterine growth retardation, and/or accelerated deterioration in maternal renal function [Jungers and Chauveau, 1997].
- **Mild renal disease does not usually worsen during pregnancy,** but fetal survival may be moderately reduced.
- **Moderate or severe renal disease** may accelerate during pregnancy and jeopardize fetal survival.
- **If there is associated hypertension before conception or in early pregnancy** there is a 10-fold higher relative risk of fetal loss.

What can be done to minimize these risks?

- **Ensure adequate contraception** until the woman has been assessed.
- **Women with renal diseases that tend to progress** should be encouraged to complete childbearing whilst renal function is preserved.
- **Women who have had a renal transplant** should be advised to wait 1.5–2 years after the transplant and only attempt pregnancy if creatinine is stable at 200 mg/l or below. After the first 12 weeks of pregnancy, 92% of infants survive. The specialist may also need to change the immunosuppressant medication (tacrolimus and mycophenolate are contraindicated in pregnancy).

[Working Group on High Blood Pressure in Pregnancy, 2000]

Thyroid disease

Should I refer?

- **Hypothyroidism:** ensure optimum control before pregnancy. There is no need to refer.
- **Hyperthyroidism:** refer women who are not already under consultant care, or inform the specialist responsible for the woman's care if she wishes to conceive.

Are there any risks?

- **Hypothyroidism:** women who become pregnant when they are hypothyroid (i.e. inadequately treated) have a higher incidence of abortion, stillbirth, pre-eclampsia, prematurity, placental abruption, anaemia, post-partum haemorrhage, cardiac dysfunction, and congenital abnormalities [McGregor, 1996]. If inadequately treated, hypothyroidism is associated with anovulation. However, with adequate replacement, ovulation is normal [Chamberlain and Morgan, 2002].
- **Hyperthyroidism:** although there is no convincing evidence that antithyroid drugs are teratogenic, there have been some recent concerns that carbimazole may cause fetal abnormalities. Overtreatment with antithyroid drugs can cause a fetal goitre (Table 1) [McGregor, 1996; Barwell et al, 2002; Diav-Citrin and Ornoy, 2002; Guignon et al, 2003].

What can be done to minimize these risks?

- **Hypothyroidism** should be monitored and adequately treated. Effective contraception should be used until this has been achieved.
- **Hyperthyroidism:** careful monitoring during pregnancy is required. Deferring pregnancy until the course of treatment has been completed may be a better option. If the woman wishes to become pregnant then inform the specialist responsible for her care.

(For further details see separate PRODIGY guidance on *Hyperthyroidism* and *Hypothyroidism*.)

Venous thromboembolism

Should I refer?

- **Seek specialist advice** for women who have a past history of deep vein thrombosis, or pulmonary embolism, or with an abnormal thrombophilia screen.
- **Women on warfarin therapy** who are planning a pregnancy should be referred to a specialist for advice.

Are there any risks?

- **Pulmonary embolism is the leading cause of maternal death** in the UK, accounting for one third of deaths [Bonnar, 2001]. Women with a history of deep vein thrombosis or pulmonary embolism in association with pregnancy, surgery, or the contraceptive pill should be considered especially at risk of recurrence during pregnancy whether or not an underlying thrombophilia has been detected [Bonnar, 2001].
- One retrospective study of women with a history of previous thromboembolism found a recurrence rate of 10.9 per 100 patient-years [Pabinger et al, 2002].
- **Inherited and acquired thrombophilia** not only increase the risk of venous thrombosis in pregnancy but may also be partly responsible for recurrent fetal death and intra-uterine growth retardation [Bonnar, 2001].
- **Heparin use for more than 3 months** is associated with bone demineralization that is reversible. Rarely this may present as fractured vertebrae or ribs [De Swiet, 1999].

What can be done to minimize these risks?

- **Screen all women with a personal history** of venous thromboembolism for both inherited and acquired thrombophilia [Royal College of Obstetricians and Gynaecologists, 2004]. Thromboprophylaxis either in the first trimester or post-partum may be required.
- **Warfarin is teratogenic,** and stopping anticoagulation before the 6th week of gestation may minimize this risk [BNF 47, 2004].
- **Advise all women on warfarin** to contact their GP immediately if they suspect that they may be pregnant.

Asthma

Should I refer?

- **Women with *severe* asthma** should be referred to a chest physician for adequate control and monitoring both preconceptually and during pregnancy.

Are there any risks?

- **There is little evidence** that asthma affects the outcome of pregnancy and no evidence that the clinical course of pregnancy is affected by asthma, except in women with very severe asthma, where there is a risk of intra-uterine growth retardation [De Swiet, 1996].
- **Data suggest that are no risks to the fetus** with inhaled short-acting beta$_2$-agonists and inhaled corticosteroids (see Table 1).

What can be done to minimize these risks?

- **Asthma should be well controlled.**
- **Treatment of asthma requires little modification in pregnancy.** Women who rely on prophylactic treatment should remain on inhaled corticosteroids, with short-acting beta$_2$-agonists as rescue therapy.
- The indications for oral corticosteroids are the same as in the non-pregnant state. Prednisolone is the corticosteroid of choice. Prolonged exposure increases the risk of intra-uterine growth retardation and there is a theoretical risk of adrenal suppression, but this usually spontaneously resolves after birth and is rarely clinically important [Chaplin, 2000].

[De Swiet, 1996]

(For further details see separate PRODIGY guidance on *Asthma*.)

Cardiac disease

Should I refer?

- Refer all women with cardiac disease to a cardiologist for accurate diagnosis and functional assessment so that maternal and fetal risk can be assessed.

Are there any risks?

- **Women with no symptoms or minimal symptoms** have a relatively low risk during pregnancy and the peripartum period.
- **Women with moderate to severe limitations** are at much higher risk and need careful monitoring and, if necessary, intervention.
- **Women who are symptomatic at rest** have high maternal and fetal mortality, and pregnancy is contraindicated.

What can be done to minimize these risks?

- **Ensure that the woman fully understands** any risks and the importance of attending for regular monitoring.
- **Effective contraception** is necessary until the woman has been fully assessed.

[Forfar, 2001]

Sickle cell syndromes

Should I refer?

- **Refer all women** with a sickle cell syndrome to a haematologist for assessment.

Are there any risks?

- **Sickle cell anaemia (HbS/S):** pregnancy may be uneventful, or may be associated with an increased incidence of painful crises. Abortion and preterm loss are more common. Although risks remain higher for women with sickle cell disease, modern obstetric care has reduced both maternal morbidity and mortality and has improved fetal outcome [Letsky, 1996; Letsky, 1999].
- **Sickle cell trait (HbA/S):** women have no problems during pregnancy but care is needed to avoid hypoxia if a general anaesthetic is required.
- **HbS/C disease:** many women have uncomplicated pregnancies, but a severe sickling crisis leading to death can occur in pregnancy or during the puerperium [Letsky, 1999].

What can be done to minimize these risks?

- **Ensure adequate contraception** until the disease status has been fully assessed by a haematologist.
- **Prescribe folic acid 5 mg daily for life to women with HbS/S and HbS/C disease.** Women with the trait can receive folic acid 400 micrograms daily [Taylor, Personal Communication, 2004].
- **Explain that regular monitoring is essential.**
- **Screen the partner** to detect carrier couples (see *When is genetic screening advised?*).

Thalassaemias

Should I refer?

- **Refer all women** with thalassaemia to a haematologist for assessment.
- Seek advice from a haematologist for women in whom a trait has been identified.

Are there any risks?

- **Alpha-thalassaemia trait:** the woman may become anaemic particularly if she is a carrier of two defective genes [Letsky, 1999].
- **3-Alpha-thalassaemia (HbH disease):** the woman will have a chronic haemolytic anaemia and may require transfusion [Letsky, 1999].
- **Beta-thalassaemia major:** pregnancy would be rare in transfusion-dependent homozygotes and is likely to have serious complications [Letsky, 1999].
- **Beta-thalassaemia trait:** if iron stores are depleted, the woman may need oral iron supplements during

P

pregnancy. Before giving iron supplements it is important to confirm with the local haematologist that the woman is truly iron-deficient. A low mean cell volume (which is a feature of beta-thalassaemia) usually does not mean the woman is iron deficient [Letsky, 1999].

- **The homozygous state for alpha-thalassaemia** produces Bart's haemoglobin hydrops syndrome (in which the child is either stillborn or only lives for a short time) and pregnancy is associated with severe, sometimes life-threatening pre-eclampsia. Vaginal deliveries are associated with obstetric complications resulting from the large fetus and bulky placenta, and the generally small stature of the mother (usually of Far Eastern origin) [Letsky, 1999].

What can be done to minimize these risks?

- **Screening should be carried** out to detect carrier couples (see *When is genetic screening advised?*). Haemoglobin electrophoresis will detect beta-thalassaemias, but alpha-thalassaemia can only be confirmed by globin chain synthesis studies or by DNA analysis of nucleated cells [Letsky, 1999; Pagana and Pagana, 2002].
- **All women** should receive folic acid 5 mg daily throughout the pregnancy. Women who have the trait can receive 400 micrograms daily unless they are iron depleted when higher doses of folic acid will be required [Letsky, 1999; Taylor, Personal Communication, 2004].

Advising women who have had pre-eclampsia or recurrent miscarriage

Pre-eclampsia

Are there any risks?

- **Pre-eclampsia** occurs in about 5% of first pregnancies and in about 15% of women with chronic hypertension.
- For women without a history of pre-eclampsia in the first pregnancy, the risk of developing pre-eclampsia falls in subsequent pregnancies. However, the risk of developing pre-eclampsia approaches that of primigravidae if a pregnancy occurs with a different partner.
- The following have also been associated with an increased risk of developing pre-eclampsia:
  - Advanced maternal age (paradoxically, teenage mothers also have a higher risk)
  - Family history of pre-eclampsia
  - Diabetes
  - Obesity
  - Low socioeconomic status
  - Chronic renal disease
  - Idiopathic hypertension
  - Multiple pregnancy or hydatiform mole
  - Systemic lupus erythematosus
  - Rhesus isoimmunization

[Beevers et al, 2000]

Recurrent miscarriage

Should I refer?

- **Refer all women** who have had three consecutive miscarriages to a gynaecologist.

[Khot and Polmear, 2003]

Are there any risks?

- The overall incidence of miscarriage is 12%.
- If the last pregnancy ended normally, the risk of a miscarriage in the next pregnancy is 5%.
- If the last pregnancy ended in a miscarriage, the risk of a miscarriage in the next pregnancy is 19%.

[Regan et al, 1989]

What can be done to minimize these risks?

- **Refer the woman to a gynaecologist** for identification and management of any treatable cause. Causes of recurrent miscarriage include fibroids, incompetent cervix, and antiphospholipid syndrome [Chamberlain and Morgan, 2002].

When is genetic screening advised?

The following people should be offered genetic counselling and screening:

- **Couples who have a personal or family history** of an abnormality that is assumed to be genetic.
- **Couples who have had a fetus or baby** with an abnormality that is assumed to be genetic.

Common types of genetic disorder

- **Autosomal dominant disorders** are manifest in the heterozygous state but can be very variable in their expression.
- **Autosomal recessive disorders are usually manifest only in the homozygous state** and both parents must be carriers before there is a risk of affected offspring. If both parents are carriers the risk is one in four in each pregnancy. In the UK, one in 24 individuals carries the cystic fibrosis gene and the birth incidence for cystic fibrosis is one in 2,400 [Adab et al, 2001] but this varies significantly in different ethnic populations. An unaffected sibling of an affected person has a two in three chance of being a carrier [Farndon and Kilby, 1999]. Most carrier couples opt for prenatal diagnosis [Brock, 1996]. Prenatal diagnosis may require development of a test for a specific couple, so preconceptual investigation is the ideal [Wright, Personal Communication, 2004].
- **X-linked recessive disorders** are manifest in 50% of the sons of a female carrier. Carriers of X-linked recessive disorders can be very difficult to detect, e.g. 30% of carriers of Duchenne's muscular dystrophy have normal biochemical carrier tests [Farndon and Kilby, 1999]. Daughters of affected men will be carriers [Farndon and Kilby, 1999].
- **Chromosomal abnormalities:** balanced chromosomal abnormalities in one partner may cause recurrent miscarriage and multiple congenital abnormalities [Wright, Personal Communication, 2004].

[Farndon and Kilby, 1999]

Consanguineous couples

- Consanguineous couples have an ancestor in common. There is therefore an increased risk that both partners will carry a heterozygous genetic mutation that may produce a recessively inherited disease in their children. The likelihood of this happening depends on the ethnic origin of the couple and the closeness of the relationship.
- Preconceptual and antenatal screening should therefore be offered for diseases found at increased prevalence in the relevant ethnic grouping. Discussion with or referral to a clinical geneticist should be considered [Wright, Personal Communication, 2004].

High-risk ethnic/minority groups who should also be offered genetic screening and counselling

- Certain ethnic or minority groups have a high prevalence of being heterozygous carriers of certain autosomal recessive disorders (see Table 3). Screening is aimed at detecting carriers, thus allowing them to make informed decisions about having children [Motulsky, 1997]. Carrier screening does not detect all carriers [Super, 1993]. Couples in which both partners are carriers have a 25% risk in each pregnancy that their child will be born with a homozygous genetic defect.
- For couples belonging to high-risk ethnic or minority groups, it is recommended that both partners are screened for the relevant autosomal recessive disorder, as

P

able 2: Some common genetic disorders.

enetic disorder	Condition
ominantly inherited sorders	Neurofibromatosis
	Tuberous sclerosis
	Huntington's disease
	Adult polycystic disease
	Marfan's syndrome
	Achondroplasia
ecessively inherited sorders	Cystic fibrosis
	Tay–Sachs disease
	Gaucher's disease
	Sickle cell disease
	Thalassaemia
	Congenital adrenal hyperplasia
	Friedrich's ataxia
	Spinal muscular atrophy
-linked disorders	Duchenne's muscular dystrophy
	Fragile X syndrome
	Haemophilia A and B
	Glucose-6-phosphate dehydrogenase deficiency
nromosome anslocations	Recurrent miscarriage
	Multiple congenital abnormalities

this minimizes raising needless concerns if only one of the partners is a carrier [Wald et al, 2003].

Certain ethnic groups have, on average, an 8% carrier rate of one of the haemoglobinopathies (for a list of these groups, see Table 3). These groups account for approximately 6% of the UK population [Modell et al, 1998].

Cypriots, amongst whom the prevalence of beta-thalassaemia is particularly high, are generally aware of the risks and usually request pre-pregnancy screening [Modell et al, 2000]. In contrast, other communities (e.g. British Pakistanis) are often unaware of their risks [Modell et al, 2000].

Approximately 1 in 8 of the Ashkenazi Jewish population is a carrier of Tay–Sachs disease, Gaucher's disease, or cystic fibrosis [Eng et al, 1997]. There does not need to be a family history for an individual to be a carrier [Sutton, 2002]. Anyone whose ancestry is fully or partially Jewish should be offered carrier testing.

Anonymous testing for Tay–Sachs disease is available in some Jewish communities and the coded results are made available only to the rabbi of the community, who will prevent carrier matches without stigmatizing a family [Super, 1993; Sutton, 2002].

Veatherall, 1996; Hickman et al, 1999; Wildschut, 1999]

able 3: Ethnic groups at risk of autosomal recessive sorders.

opulation/region most affected	Condition
outh East Asia and Southern China	Alpha-thalassaemia and beta-thalassaemia
editerranean, parts of North and 'est Africa, the Middle East, Indian bcontinent	Alpha-thalassaemia, beta-thalassaemia, and sickling disorders
lack Africa and Caribbean	Sickling disorders
shkenazi Jews	Tay–Sachs disease, Gaucher's disease, and cystic fibrosis

Screening for haemoglobinopathies

- It is advisable to consult the local haematologist to find out which tests are preferred locally and which sample bottles to use, as there may be variation between laboratories.
- An initial screening test is sometimes used for sickle cell anaemia and trait (e.g. Sickledex™, Sickle Cell Prep™). Samples that test positive are investigated further, usually by electrophoresis. Sickle cell anaemia and trait, haemoglobin H, haemoglobin C and beta-thalassaemia major and minor can all be detected by electrophoresis [Chamberlain and Morgan, 2002; Pagana and Pagana, 2002].
- A low mean cell volume and low mean cell haemoglobin will identify many carriers of beta-thalassaemia, but people who are heterozygous for both alpha-thalassaemia and beta-thalassaemia may exhibit normal values [Cao et al, 2002].

Advising women who use illicit substances

Should I refer?

- **Refer to the community drugs team.** A multidisciplinary approach to the management of women with opioid and other drug dependence is essential. Most localities will have a clearly defined drug dependency service with a readily accessible entry point. Many areas have community drug teams that implement treatment plans, monitor treatment, provide counselling, and promote needle exchange and other harm-reduction activities.

Are there any risks?

- **Advise all women taking illicit drugs to stop.**
- **Cocaine: this is particularly hazardous and should be stopped before conception.** There is no safe substitute. Cocaine is associated with spontaneous abortion, placental abruption, premature birth, and low birthweight. There is conflicting evidence regarding fetal abnormalities. Studies have described clinical brain damage that appears to have a vascular cause [De Swiet, 1996; DH et al, 1999; Wills, 2000].
- **Opioids:** an increased incidence of intra-uterine growth retardation and preterm delivery contributes to an increased rate of low birthweight and perinatal mortality. These outcomes are also affected by factors such as socio-economic deprivation and smoking [DH et al, 1999].

References

NHS staff in England can link, free of charge, from references to full text journals by clicking on [Full text] on the PRODIGY website.

1. Abalos, E., Duley, L., Steyn, D.W. and Henderson-Smart, D.J. (2002) *Antihypertensive drug therapy for mild to moderate hypertension during pregnancy (Cochrane Review)*. The Cochrane Library. Issue 3. Oxford: Update Software.
2. Adab, N., Jacoby, A., Smith, D. and Chadwick, D. (2001) Additional educational needs in children born to mothers with epilepsy. *Journal of Neurology, Neurosurgery & Psychiatry* 70(1), 15–21. [Full text]
3. American Diabetes Association (2003) Preconception care of women with diabetes. *Diabetes Care* 26(Suppl 1), S91-S93. [Full text]
4. Barwell, J., Fox, G.F., Round, J. and Berg, J. (2002) Choanal atresia: the result of maternal thyrotoxicosis or fetal carbimazole? *American Journal of Medical Genetics* 111(1), 55–56.

5. Beevers, G., Lip, G.Y.H and O'Brien, E. (Eds.) (2000) Hypertension in pregnancy. In: *ABC of hypertension*. 4th edn. London: BMJ Books. 88–93.
6. BNF 47 (2004) *British National Formulary*. 47th edn. London: British Medical Association and Royal Pharmaceutical Society of Great Britain.
7. Bonnar, J. (2001) Venous thrombosis and pulmonary embolism. In: Chamberlain, G. and Steer, P.J. (Eds.) *Turnbull's obstetrics*. 3rd edn. London: Churchill Livingstone. 671–680.
8. Brock, D.J. (1996) Prenatal screening for cystic fibrosis: 5 years' experience reviewed. *Lancet* **347**(8995), 148–150. [Full text]
9. Campbell, D.M. (2001) Nutrition in pregnancy. In: Weatherall, D.J., Ledingham, J.G.G., Warrell, D.A. et al (Eds.) *Oxford textbook of medicine*. 3rd edn. Oxford: Oxford University Press. 1769–1775.
10. Chamberlain, G. and Morgan, M. (Eds.) (2002) *ABC of antenatal care*. 4th edn. London: BMJ Books.
11. Chaplin, S. (2000) Respiratory disorders. In: Lee, A., Inch, S., Finnigan, D. et al (Eds.) *Therapeutics in pregnancy and lactation*. Oxon: Radcliffe Medical Press Ltd. 79–88.
12. Cohen, L.S., Friedman, J.M., Jefferson, J.W. et al (1994) A re-evaluation of risk of in utero exposure to lithium. *Journal of the American Medical Association* **271**(2), 146–150. [Full text]
13. Collier, J.A.B., Longmore, J.M. and Hodgson, H.J. (Eds.) (1997) *Oxford handbook of clinical specialities*. 4th edn. Oxford: Oxford University Press.
14. CSM (2003) Sodium valproate and prescribing in pregnancy. *Current Problems in Pharmacovigilance* **29**(Sept), 6.
15. Delgado-Escueta, A.V. and Janz, D. (1992) Consensus guidelines: preconception counseling, management, and care of the pregnant woman with epilepsy. *Neurology* **42**(Suppl 5), 149–160.
16. Dempsey, D.A. and Benowitz, N.L. (2001) Risks and benefits of nicotine to aid smoking cessation in pregnancy. *Drug Safety* **24**(4), 277–322.
17. De Swiet, M. (1996) Chest diseases in pregnancy. In: Weatherall, D.J., Ledingham, J.G.G., Warrell, D.A. et al (Eds.) *Oxford textbook of medicine*. 3rd edn. Oxford: Oxford University Press. 1744–1747.
18. De Swiet, M. (1999) Thromboembolic disease. In: James, D.K., Steer, P.J., Weiner, C.P. and Gonik, B. (Eds.) *High risk pregnancy: management options*. 2nd edn. London: W.B. Saunders. 901–909.
19. DH (2000) *Folic acid and the prevention of disease*. No. 50. London: Department of Health.
20. DH (2003) *Screening for the infectious diseases in pregnancy*. Department of Health. www.dh.gov.uk [Accessed: 26/04/2004]. [Full text]
21. DH, Scottish Office DH, Welsh Office and DH and Social Services of NI (1999) *Drug misuse and dependence – guidelines on clinical management*. Department of Health. www.dh.gov.uk [Accessed: 27/04/2004]. [Full text]
22. Diabetes UK (2000) *Pregnancy and diabetes: planning your pregnancy*. British Diabetic Association. www.diabetes.org.uk/pregnancy/plan.htm [Accessed: 11/11/2003].
23. Diav-Citrin, O. and Ornoy, A. (2002) Teratogen update: antithyroid drugs-methimazole, carbimazole and propylthiouracil. *Teratology* **65**(1), 38–44.
24. DiClemente, C.C., Dolan-Mullen, P. and Windsor, R.A. (2000) The process of pregnancy smoking cessation: implications for interventions. *Tobacco Control* **9**(Suppl 3), 6–21.
25. Dobson, F., Donald, D., Mowlam, M. and Michael, A. (1998) *Smoking kills: a white paper on tobacco*. London: Department of Health.
26. Donaldson, L., Mullally, S. and Smith, J. (2003) *Protecting women against rubella: switch from rubella vaccine to MMR*. London: Department of Health.
27. DTB (1994) Folic acid to prevent neural tube defects. *Drug & Therapeutics Bulletin* **32**(4), 31–32.
28. Eng, C.M., Schechter, C., Robinowitz, J. et al (1997) Prenatal genetic carrier testing using triple disease screening. *Journal of the American Medical Association* **278**(15), 1265–1272. [Full text]
29. Farndon, P.A. and Kilby, M.D. (1999) Genetics, risks and genetic counseling. In: James, D.K., Steer, P.J., Weiner, C.P. and Gonik, B. (Eds.) *High risk pregnancy management options*. 2nd edn. London: W.B. Saunders. 23–38.
30. Forfar, J.C. (2001) Heart disease in pregnancy. In: Weatherall, D.J., Leadingham, J.G.G., Warrell, D.A. et al (Eds.) *Oxford textbook of medicine*. 3rd edn. Oxford: Oxford University Press. 1735–1740.
31. Gilmour-White, S. (2000) Epilepsy. In: Lee, A., Inch, S., Finnigan, D. et al (Eds.) *Therapeutics in pregnancy and lactation*. Oxon: Radcliffe Medical Press Ltd. 89–99.
32. Guignon, A.M., Mallaret, M.P. and Jouk, P.S. (2003) Carbimazole-related gastroschisis. *Annals of Pharmacotherapy* **37**(6), 829–831.
33. Health Canada (2000) *Family-centred maternity and newborn care: national guidelines*. Ottawa: Minister of Public Works and Government Services. www.hc-sc.gc.ca [Accessed: 02/12/2003].
34. Hickman, M., Modell, B., Greengross, P. et al (1999) Mapping the prevalence of sickle cell and beta thalassaemia in England: estimating and validating ethnic-specific rates. *British Journal of Haematology* **104**(4), 860–867.
35. HPA (2000) *Guidance on the management of, and exposure to, rash illness in pregnancy*. Health Protection Agency. www.hpa.org.uk [Accessed: 13/01/2004].
36. Jolly, M., Sebire, N., Harris, J. et al (2000) The risks associated with pregnancy in women aged 35 years or older. *Human Reproduction* **15**(11), 2433–2437. [Full text]
37. Jungers, P. and Chauveau, D. (1997) Pregnancy in renal disease. *Kidney International* **52**(4), 871–885.
38. Khot, A. and Polmear, A. (Eds.) (2003) Obstetric problems. In: *Practical general practice: guidelines for effective clinical management*. 4th edn. Edinburgh: Butterworth-Heinemann.
39. Kumar, C and O'Dowd, L. (2001) Psychiatric problems in pregnancy and puerperium. In: Chamberlain, G. and Steer, P.J. (Eds.) *Turnbull's obstetrics*. 3rd edn. London: Churchill Livingstone.
40. Letsky, E.A. (1996) Blood disorders in pregnancy. In: Weatherall, D.J., Leadingham, J.G.G., Warrell, D.A. et al (Eds.) *Oxford textbook of medicine*. 3rd edn. Oxford: Oxford University Press. 1758–1766.
41. Letsky, E. (1999) Anemia. In: James, D.K., Steer, P.J., Weiner, C.P. and Gonik, B. (Eds.) *High risk pregnancy management options*. 2nd edn. London: W.B. Saunders. 738–747.
42. Lumley, J., Watson, L., Watson, M. and Bower, C. (2003) *Periconceptional supplementation with folate and/or multivitamins for preventing neural tube defects (Cochrane Review)*. The Cochrane Library. Issue 4. Oxford: Update Software.
43. Lumley, J., Oliver, S., Chamberlain, C. and Oakley, L. (2004) *Interventions for promoting smoking cessation during pregnancy (Cochrane Review)*. The Cochrane Library. Issue 3. Chichester, UK: John Wiley & Sons Ltd. www.nelh.nhs.uk/cochrane.asp [Accessed: 19/07/2005]. [Full text]

P

4. Magee, L.A. and Duley, L. (2002) *Oral beta-blockers for mild to moderate hypertension during pregnancy.* The Cochrane Library. Issue 3. Oxford: Update Software.

5. McGregor, A.M. (1996) Endocrine disease in pregnancy. In: Weatherall, D.J., Ledingham, J.G.G., Warrell, D.A. et al (Eds.) *Oxford textbook of medicine.* 3rd edn. Oxford: Oxford University Press. 1747–1752.

6. Modell, M., Wonke, B., Anionwu, E. et al (1998) A multidisciplinary approach for improving services in primary care: randomised controlled trial of screening for haemoglobin disorders. *British Medical Journal* **317**(7161), 788–791. [Full text]

7. Modell, B., Harris, R., Lane, B. et al (2000) Informed choice in genetic screening for thalassaemia during pregnancy: audit from a national confidential inquiry. *British Medical Journal* **320**(7231), 337–341. [Full text]

8. Motulsky, A.G. (1997) Screening for genetic diseases. *New England Journal of Medicine* **336**(18), 1314–1316. [Full text]

9. National Teratology Information Service (2002a) *Use of nifedipine during pregnancy.* NHS Northern and Yorkshire: Regional Drug and Therapeutics Centre.

0. National Teratology Information Service (2002b) *Use of paroxetine in pregnancy.* NHS Northern and Yorkshire: Regional Drug and Therapeutics Centre.

1. National Teratology Information Service (2002c) *Angiotensin II receptor antagonists exposure during pregnancy.* NHS Northern and Yorkshire: Regional Drug and Therapeutics Centre.

2. NICE (2002) *Guidance on the use of nicotine replacement therapy (NRT) and bupropion for smoking cessation.* Technology appraisal no. 39. National Institute for Clinical Excellence. www.nice.org.uk [Accessed: 18/07/2005].

3. Pabinger, I., Grafenhofer, H., Kyrle, P.A. et al (2002) Temporary increase in the risk for recurrence during pregnancy in women with a history of venous thromboembolism. *Blood* **100**(3), 1060–1062.

4. Pagana, K.D. and Pagana, T.J. (Eds.) (2002) *Mosby's manual of diagnostic and laboratory tests.* 2nd edn. London: Mosby.

5. Parkinson, M. (2000) Hypertension. In: Lee, A., Inch, S., Finnigan, D. et al (Eds.) *Therapeutics in pregnancy and lactation.* Oxon: Radcliffe Medical Press Ltd. 59–69.

6. Ramsay, L.E., Williams, B., Johnston, G. et al (1999) Guidelines for management of hypertension: report of the third working party of the British Hypertension Society. *Journal of Human Hypertension* **13**(9), 569–592.

7. RCOG (1999) *Alcohol consumption in pregnancy.* No. 9. Royal College of Obstetricians and Gynaecologists. www.rcog.org.uk [Accessed: 06/11/2003].

8. RCP (1999) *The management of nicotine addiction.* Royal College of Physicians. www.rcplondon.ac.uk/pubs/books/nicotine/7-management.htm [Accessed: 12/07/2005].

9. Regan, L., Braude, P.R. and Trembath, P.L. (1989) Influence of past reproductive performance on risk of spontaneous abortion. *British Medical Journal* **299**(6698), 541–545.

0. Royal College of Obstetricians and Gynaecologists (2004) *Thromboprophylaxis during pregnancy, labour and after vaginal delivery.* Guideline No. 37. Royal College of Obstetricians and Gynaecologists. www.rcog.org.uk [Accessed: 05/04/2004].

1. Scottish Obstetric Guidelines Audit Project (1997) *The management of pregnancy in women with epilepsy.* Scottish Programme for Clinical Effectiveness in Reproductive Health. www.sign.ac.uk/guidelines/sogap/sogap1.html [Accessed: 10/12/2003].

62. Seymour, H. and Pugh, K. (2000) Endocrine disorders. In: Lee, A., Inch, S., Finnigan, D. et al (Eds.) *Therapeutics in pregnancy and lactation.* Oxon: Radcliffe Medical Press. 149–161.

63. Sibai, B.M., Lindheimer, M., Hauth, J. et al (1998) Risk factors for preeclampsia, abruptio placentae, and adverse neonatal outcomes among women with chronic hypertension. *New England Journal of Medicine* **339**(10), 667–671. [Full text]

64. SIGN (2002) *Postnatal depression and puerperal psychosis.* Guideline no. 60. Scottish Intercollegiate Guidelines Network. www.sign.ac.uk [Accessed: 30/05/2003].

65. SIGN (2003a) *Diagnosis and management of epilepsy in adults.* Report no. 70. Scottish Intercollegiate Guidelines Network. www.sign.ac.uk [Accessed: 30/05/2003].

66. SIGN (2003b) *The management of harmful drinking and alcohol dependence in primary care.* Report no. 74. Scottish Intercollegiate Guidelines Network. www.sign.ac.uk [Accessed: 29/10/2003].

67. Stowe, Z.N., Calhoun, K., Ramsey, C. et al (2001) Mood disorders during pregnancy and lactation: defining issues of exposure and treatment. *CNS Spectrums* **6**(2), 150–166.

68. Super, M. (1993) Who should be offered genetic screening? *Postgraduate Medical Journal* **69**(815), 669–671.

69. Super, M., Hambleton, G. and Elles, R. (1986) Pre-conception counselling for parents who have a child with cystic fibrosis. *Lancet* **2**(8503), 393–394.

70. Sutton, V.R. (2002) Tay-Sachs disease screening and counseling families at risk for metabolic disease. *Obstetrics & Gynecology Clinics of North America* **29**(2), 287–296.

71. Taylor, P. (2004) *Personal communication.* Consultant haematologist, Royal Victoria Infirmary: Newcastle upon Tyne.

72. Tookey, P.A., Cortina-Borja, M. and Peckham, C.S. (2002) Rubella susceptibility among pregnant women in north London, 1996–1999. *Journal of Public Health Medicine* **24**(3), 211–216. [Full text]

73. Wald, N. (1991) Prevention of neural tube defects: results of the medical research council vitamin study. *Lancet* **338**(8760), 131–137. [Full text]

74. Wald, N.J., Morris, J.K., Rodeck, C.H. et al (2003) Cystic fibrosis: selecting the prenatal screening strategy of choice. *Prenatal Diagnosis* **23**(6), 474–483.

75. Weatherall, D.J. (1996) Disorders of the synthesis or function of haemoglobin. In: Weatherall, D.J., Ledingham, J.G.G., Warrell, D.A. et al (Eds.) *Oxford textbook of medicine.* 3rd edn. Oxford: Oxford University Press. 3500–3520.

76. West, R., McNeill, A. and Raw, M. (2000) Smoking cessation guidelines for health professionals: an update. *Thorax* **55**(12), 987–999. [Full text]

77. Wildschut, H.I.J. (1999) Sociodemographic factors: age, parity, social class and ethnicity. In: James, D.K., Steer, P.J., Weiner, C.P. and Gonik, B. (Eds.) *High risk pregnancy: management options.* 2nd edn. London: W.B. Saunders. 39–52.

78. Wills, S. (2000) Street drugs. In: Lee, A., Inch, S., Finnigan, D. et al (Eds.) *Therapeutics in pregnancy and lactation.* Oxon: Radcliffe Medical Press Ltd. 227–246.

79. Working Group on High Blood Pressure in Pregnancy (2000) Report of the national high blood pressure education program working group on high blood pressure in pregnancy. *American Journal of Obstetrics & Gynecology* **183**(1), S1-S22.

80. Worsley, A.J. (2000) Psychiatric disorders. In: Lee, A., Inch, S., Finnigan, D. et al (Eds.) *Therapeutics in pregnancy and lactation.* Oxon: Radcliffe Medical Press Ltd. 101–116.

81. Wright, M. (2004) *Personal communication.* Geneticist, Centre for Life: Newcastle upon Tyne.

P

PRODIGY GUIDANCE

Prior myocardial infarction — prophylactic treatments

Last revised in December 2002
At the time of print this topic was being updated. The newly revised guidance will be issued on to the website in 2006.
www.prodigy.nhs.uk/guidance.asp?gt=Prior MI - prophylactic Rxs

Applies to people over the age of 16 years

This is the PRODIGY implementation of the National Institute for Clinical Excellence (NICE) guideline *Prophylaxis for patients who have experienced a myocardial infarction: drug treatment, cardiac rehabilitation and dietary manipulation* (April 2001). Some additional information has been included — where such information has been added, this is clearly referenced to the source.

This guidance covers the management of people who have a history of myocardial infarction (MI), with or without heart failure.

There is separate PRODIGY guidance on *Angina*, *Atrial fibrillation*, *Heart failure*, *Hyperlipidaemia*, *Hypertension*, *Obesity*, *Supraventricular tachycardia — paroxysmal*, and *Smoking cessation*.

Goals

To reduce the risk of re-infarction and death in people with a prior myocardial infarction (MI)

Contents

Scenarios

- Prior MI and no heart failure — start treatment p.1551
- Prior MI and no heart failure — maintenance treatment p.1554
- Prior MI and heart failure — start treatment (no Beta-blocker) p.1556
- Prior MI and heart failure — maintenance (no Beta-blocker) p.1559
- Prior MI and heart failure — start and continue Beta-blocker p.1562

Extended Information, p. 1564

Which scenario?

Prior MI and no heart failure — start treatment: covers the management of people who have a history of myocardial infarction (MI), *without* heart failure, who should be offered long-term treatment firstly with a beta-blocker and an antiplatelet drug (aspirin or clopidogrel), and then with a statin and an ACE inhibitor.

Prior MI and no heart failure — maintenance treatment: covers the management of people who have a history of myocardial infarction (MI), *without* heart failure, who require long-term maintenance treatment with a beta-blocker and an antiplatelet drug (aspirin or clopidogrel), and then with a statin and an ACE inhibitor.

Prior MI and heart failure — start treatment (no Beta-blocker): covers the management of people who have a history of myocardial infarction (MI), *with* heart failure, who should be offered long-term treatment firstly with a an ACE inhibitor and an antiplatelet drug (aspirin or clopidogrel), and then with a beta-blocker (see separate scenario *Prior MI and heart failure — start and continue Beta-blocker*).

Prior MI and heart failure — maintenance (no Beta-blocker): covers the management of people who have a history of myocardial infarction (MI), *with* heart failure, who require long-term maintenance treatment firstly with a an ACE inhibitor and an antiplatelet drug (aspirin or clopidogrel), and then with a beta-blocker (see separate scenario *Prior MI and heart failure — start and continue Beta-blocker*).

- **Prior MI and heart failure — start and continue Beta-blocker:** covers the initiation and maintenance of Beta-blockers in people who have a history of myocardial infarction (MI), *with* heart failure.

Prior MI and no heart failure — start treatment

Which therapy?

Patients should be offered enrolment in a rehabilitation programme that has a prominent exercise component within it (A).

Which drugs?

- **All patients should be offered long-term treatment firstly with a beta-blocker and an antiplatelet drug (aspirin or clopidogrel), and then with a statin and an ACE inhibitor.** This sequencing of initiation reflects the evidence from trials and estimates of cost-effectiveness (A).
- **The precise lower limit of the level of cholesterol** that should be treated is unclear. It is generally accepted that patients with a total serum cholesterol of 5 mmol/l or greater should receive treatment to reduce their cholesterol level. The National Service Framework for Coronary Heart Disease states that total serum cholesterol should be lowered to below 5 mmol/l or by 20–25%, whichever will result in the lower level. Equivalent figures for LDL cholesterol are 3 mmol/l or a 30% reduction.
- **Calcium-channel blockers, nitrates, and potassium-channel activators have no effect on premature mortality,** making their role the management of symptoms and risk factors (principally hypertension) (A). If these are indicated, advice and prescriptions are offered in separate PRODIGY guidance on *Angina* or *Hypertension*.

When to start drug treatment

- **Beta-blockers, antiplatelet drugs, and ACE inhibitors** should be initiated whilst patients are in hospital, as there is evidence to support benefit following early initiation. If this does not happen then primary care clinicians should initiate them as soon after discharge as possible (**A**).

- **All patients discharged from hospital who are not already taking a statin** should be assessed and have treatment initiated 12 weeks after an MI (**A**). Although there is no evidence of long-term benefit from the use of statins initiated prior to 12 weeks post-infarct, many patients will have been taking statins prior to admission or will have them initiated in hospital.

Practical prescribing points

The information below is not covered within the National Institute for Clinical Excellence (NICE) guideline, but has been added by PRODIGY. For further information see the *Medicines Compendium* (www.medicines.org.uk) or the *British National Formulary* (www.bnf.org).

Aspirin

- **Avoid** in gastrointestinal ulceration, haemophilia and other bleeding disorders, and breastfeeding. Use with caution in impaired renal or hepatic function, asthma, and pregnancy.
- **Concurrent nonsteroidal anti-inflammatory drugs (NSAIDs):** the risk of serious gastrosintestinal complications doubles in people who regularly take low-dose aspirin and another NSAID. If possible, stop the second NSAID.
- **If a second NSAID must be continued, avoid ibuprofen** — it may reduce the cardiovascular protective effect of low-dose aspirin. Consider using diclofenac if a second NSAID must be used.

Beta-blockers

- **Avoid** in asthma, chronic obstructive pulmonary disease (COPD), or heart block. Caution in peripheral vascular disease.

ACE inhibitors

- **The risk of first-dose hypotension or renal impairment is increased in the following patients:**
  - Creatinine >200 micromol/l
  - Urea >12 mmol/l
  - Sodium <130 mmol/l
  - Systolic blood pressure <100 mmHg
  - Diuretic dosage > furosemide (frusemide) 80 mg/d or equivalent
  - Known or suspected renal artery stenosis (e.g. if peripheral vascular disease)
  - Frail elderly
- **Avoid** potassium-sparing diuretics or potassium supplements in patients receiving ACE inhibitors (other than spironolactone in patients with heart failure), because of the risk of hyperkalaemia.
- **Stop nonsteroidal anti-inflammatory drugs (NSAIDs)** (if possible) as they reduce the effectiveness of diuretics and increase the risk of renal impairment with ACE inhibitors.
- **Avoid ACE inhibitors if** there is significant cardiac outflow tract obstruction (e.g. due to aortic stenosis or hypertrophic obstructive cardiomyopathy).

Statins

- **Adverse effects** are usually minor and rarely require cessation of treatment. They include transient headache, minor gastrointestinal upset, rashes, dizziness, pruritus, fatigue, and insomnia.
- **Rarely,** hepatotoxicity or myopathy may occur.
- **Risk of myositis** is increased by concomitant treatment with fibrates, ciclosporin, nicotinic acid, or danazol. Simvastatin may slightly potentiate the effects of warfarin; this may be significant in a small number of patients so initial monitoring is advised.

Follow-up advice

Some of the information below has been obtained from th National Institute for Clinical Excellence (NICE) guidelin Additional information has been added by PRODIGY.

People started on a beta-blocker

- **If tolerated,** increase the dosage of beta-blocker to the maintenance dosages offered in the scenario *Prior MI and no heart failure — maintenance treatment.*

People started on a statin

- **Review about 6 weeks later** to check for adverse effects and check lipids and liver function tests (although risk hepatotoxicity is extremely small).
- **Advise the person** to report any muscular pains immediately. Creatine kinase (CK) level should then be checked. If strong suspicion of myopathy, or if CK level is greater than 10× upper limit normal, then discontinu immediately.

People started on an ACE inhibitor

- **Repeat serum electrolytes** within 1 week of starting an ACE inhibitor and review patient with the results.
- **Check for adverse effects,** such as symptomatic hypotension, renal dysfunction or hyperkalaemia (i.e. a rise in urea to 12 mmol/l, creatinine to 200 micromol/l, or potassium to 5.5 mmol/l). If these occur either stop c reduce the dosage of ACE inhibitor.
- **If tolerated,** increase the dosage of the ACE inhibitor to the maintenance dosages offered in the scenario *Prior M and no heart failure — maintenance treatment.*

Should I refer or investigate?

Investigate?

People being considered for treatment with a statin

- **An initial serum cholesterol measurement** should be taken, both to exclude familial lipid disorders and to identify those people with a serum cholesterol level tha does not need treating. (Following an acute MI, serum total cholesterol and LDL cholesterol decrease. Therefore, if lipids are not measured within 24 hours o an acute MI it is best to check them about 12 weeks later.)
- **PRODIGY recommends** that secondary causes of hyperlipidaemia should be excluded, particularly if tota serum cholesterol is greater than 6.5 mmol/l. Tests should include electrolytes, liver function tests, blood glucose level, and thyroid function tests. Consider alcohol excess as a cause of raised lipids.

People being considered for treatment with an ACE inhibitor

- **Renal function** (urea and electrolytes) should be checke prior to initiation of an ACE inhibitor.

Patient information leaflets

The following PILs are available at www.prodigy.nhs.uk

- Aspirin to Prevent Blood Clots
- British Cardiac Patients Association

British Heart Foundation
Cholesterol
Eat More Fruit and Vegetables
Exercise for Health
Healthy Eating
Heart UK
Myocardial Infarction - Medication Infor
Smoking - Help to Stop with Bupropion
Smoking - Nicotine Replacement Therapy
Smoking - The Facts
Smoking - Tips on Stopping

hared decision making

Four medicines are commonly advised if you have had a heart attack.

Aspirin (low dose) reduces the risk of blood clots forming.

A beta-blocker reduces the workload on the heart.

An ACE inhibitor (angiotensin-converting enzyme inhibitor) has a protective effect on the heart muscle. When you take an ACE inhibitor:

- Lie or sit down for 2–4 hours after the very first dose.
- A low dose is started at first, and gradually increased.
- A blood test is usual before, and about a week after starting.

A statin medicine lowers the cholesterol level. This helps to prevent atheroma which 'clogs up' the arteries. Whilst taking a statin:

- A muscle problem is a rare but serious adverse effect. Tell a doctor if you develop muscle pains.
- A blood test is usual before and about 6 weeks after starting.

You should also reduce any other 'risk factors':

- Exercise regularly (unless your doctor advises not to).
- Do not smoke.
- Lose weight if you are overweight.

rug rationale

ugs not included

Enteric-coated aspirin preparations are not offered, as there is no convincing evidence that these reduce toxicity at a dosage of 75 mg [DTB, 1997].

Dipyridamole is licensed for the secondary prevention of ischaemic stroke and transient ischaemic attacks, but there is no evidence to support its use in prophylaxis after myocardial infarction (MI).

Beta-blockers other than atenolol, propranolol, metoprolol and timolol are either more expensive or not licensed for prophylaxis after MI.

Angiotensin-converting enzyme (ACE) inhibitors other than ramipril and lisinopril are not included as they are not licensed for prophylaxis after MI when there is no evidence of heart failure.

Calcium-channel blockers have no effect on premature mortality after MI and should only be considered for the management of symptoms and risk factors (principally hypertension or angina).

Nitrates have no effect on premature mortality after MI and should only be considered for the management of symptoms.

Nicorandil is licensed in the UK for the prophylaxis and treatment of angina. A recent study of nicorandil in patients with angina (of whom 66% had a previous MI) found a significant reduction in the combined endpoint of coronary heart disease (CHD) death, non-fatal MI, or unplanned hospital admission with cardiac chest pain. However, the study was unable to demonstrate a significant reduction in CHD death or non-fatal MI when analyzed separately, or a significant reduction in the combined outcome of CHD death or non-fatal MI [IONA Study Group, 2002]. The results of this study will be further considered when the National Institute for Clinical Excellence (NICE) update their guidance.

Drugs included

- **Aspirin 75 mg** reduces the risk of subsequent cardiovascular events in people with established cardiovascular disease.
- **Clopidogrel** is offered as an alternative antiplatelet for the small number of people with genuine aspirin intolerance.
- **Beta-blockers** significantly reduce the risk of premature mortality following MI. Most evidence for long-term beta-blocker use comes from studies of propranolol, metoprolol and timolol, which are licensed for prophylaxis after MI. Atenolol has shown a similar effect to the licensed beta-blockers and is widely used.
- **ACE inhibitors** reduce the risk of premature mortality following MI. Lisinopril and ramipril are both licensed for prophylaxis after MI when there is no evidence of heart failure.
- **Statins** reduce the risk of premature mortality following MI. Most evidence comes from trials of pravastatin and simvastatin. Atorvastatin and fluvastatin are alternatives.

Prescriptions

Start antiplatelet therapy

Aspirin 75mg dispersible once a day

- Age from 16 years onwards
- Aspirin 75mg dispersible tabs. Take one tablet once a day; supply 28 tablets; NHS Cost £0.36.

Clopidogrel 75mg once a day – only if intolerant of aspirin

- Age from 16 years onwards
- Clopidogrel 75mg tablets. Take one tablet once a day; supply 28 tablets; NHS Cost £35.31.

P

Start beta-blocker therapy

Atenolol 25mg once a day

- Age from 16 years onwards
- Atenolol 25mg tablets. Take one tablet once a day; supply 28 tablets; NHS Cost £0.72.

Atenolol 50mg once a day

- Age from 16 years onwards
- Atenolol 50mg tablets. Take one tablet once a day; supply 28 tablets; NHS Cost £0.83.

Metoprolol 50mg twice a day

- Age from 16 years onwards
- Metoprolol 50mg tablets. Take one tablet twice a day; supply 56 tablets; NHS Cost £2.32.

Propranolol 40mg x4 a day for 3 days, then 80mg twice a day

- Age from 16 years onwards
- Propranolol 40mg tablets. Take one tablet four times a day for 3 days and then take two tablets twice a day; supply 112 tablets; NHS Cost £2.60.

Timolol 5mg twice a day for 2 days, then 10mg twice a day

- Age from 16 years onwards
- Timolol 10mg tablets. Take half a tablet twice a day for 2 days and then take one tablet twice a day; supply 60 tablets; NHS Cost £4.90.

20–25%, whichever will result in the lower level. Equivalent figures for LDL cholesterol are 3 mmol/l or a 30% reduction.

- **After any increase in statin dosage:**
  - Review about 6 weeks later to check for adverse effects, and check lipids and liver function tests (although risk of hepatotoxicity is extremely small).
  - Advise the person to report any muscular pains immediately. Creatine kinase (CK) level should then be checked. If there is strong suspicion of myopathy, or if CK level is greater than 10× upper limit normal, then discontinue immediately.
  - Titrate dosage to lower serum total cholesterol to desired target.
  - Review yearly thereafter with repeat serum lipid profile. Liver function tests should be checked 6-monthly for the first year following a stable treatment dosage.

People taking an ACE inhibitor

- **Increase dosage to the recommended maintenance dosages offered in this scenario.**
- **After any dosage increase:**
  - Repeat serum electrolytes within 1 week and review patient with the results.
  - Check for adverse effects, such as symptomatic hypotension, renal dysfunction, or hyperkalaemia (i.e. a rise in urea to 12 mmol/l, creatinine to 200 micromol /l, or potassium to 5.5 mmol/l). If these occur either stop or reduce the dosage of ACE inhibitor.
  - Once the patient is receiving a stable dosage, serum electrolytes should be checked at least annually.

Should I refer or investigate?

Investigate?

Some of the information below has been obtained from the NICE guideline. Additional information has been added by PRODIGY.

Patients taking a statin

- **If not already done, check cholesterol level and liver function tests** if 6 weeks or more has elapsed since any increase in statin dosage.
- **Once the patient is receiving a stable dosage,** review yearly with repeat serum lipid profile. Liver function tests should be checked 6-monthly for the first year following a stable treatment dosage.

Patients taking an ACE inhibitor

- **If not already done, check serum electrolytes** if 7 days or more have elapsed since any increase in dosage of ACE inhibitor.
- Once on a stable dosage, serum electrolytes should be checked at least annually.

Patient information leaflets

The following PILs are available at www.prodigy.nhs.uk

- Aspirin to Prevent Blood Clots
- British Cardiac Patients Association
- British Heart Foundation
- Cholesterol
- Eat More Fruit and Vegetables
- Exercise for Health
- Healthy Eating
- Heart UK
- Myocardial Infarction - Medication Infor
- Smoking - Help to Stop with Bupropion
- Smoking - Nicotine Replacement Therapy
- Smoking - The Facts
- Smoking - Tips on Stopping

Shared decision making

- **The doses of the medicines taken following a heart attack** are often increased gradually to a usual maintenance dose.
- **Beta-blockers** reduce the workload on the heart.
- **ACE inhibitors** (angiotensin-converting enzyme inhibitors) have a protective effect on the heart muscle.
- **Statin medicines** lower the cholesterol level. This helps to prevent atheroma which 'clogs up' the arteries.
- **Aspirin** (remains at low dosage) reduces the risk of blood clots forming.
- Blood tests are needed from time to time. These aim to:
  - Detect certain uncommon problems before they become serious.
  - Check that the cholesterol level has reduced to the target level.
- **You should also reduce any other 'risk factors':**
  - Exercise regularly (unless your doctor advises not to).
  - Do not smoke.
  - Lose weight if you are overweight.

Drug rationale

Drugs not included

- **Enteric-coated aspirin** preparations are not offered as there is no convincing evidence that these reduce toxicity at a dose of 75 mg [DTB, 1997].
- **Dipyridamole** is licensed for the secondary prevention of ischaemic stroke and transient ischaemic attacks, but there is no evidence to support its use in prophylaxis after myocardial infarction (MI).
- **Beta-blockers other than atenolol, propranolol, metoprolol and timolol** are either more expensive or not licensed for prophylaxis after MI.
- **Angiotensin-converting enzyme (ACE) inhibitors other than ramipril and lisinopril** are not included as they are not licensed for prophylaxis after MI when there is no evidence of heart failure.
- **Calcium-channel blockers** have no effect on premature mortality after MI and should only be considered for the management of symptoms and risk factors (principally hypertension or angina).
- **Nitrates** have no effect on premature mortality after MI and should only be considered for the management of symptoms.
- **Nicorandil** is licensed in the UK for the prophylaxis and treatment of angina. A recent study of nicorandil in patients with angina (of whom 66% had a previous MI) found a significant reduction in the combined endpoint of coronary heart disease (CHD) death, non-fatal MI, or unplanned hospital admission with cardiac chest pain. However, the study was unable to demonstrate a significant reduction in CHD death or non-fatal MI when analyzed separately, or a significant reduction in the combined outcome of CHD death or non-fatal MI [IONA Study Group, 2002]. The results of this study will be further considered when the National Institute for Clinical Excellence (NICE) update their guidance.

Drugs included

- **Aspirin 75 mg** reduces the risk of subsequent cardiovascular events in people with established cardiovascular disease.
- **Clopidogrel** is offered as an alternative antiplatelet for the small number of people with genuine aspirin intolerance.

- **Beta-blockers** significantly reduce the risk premature mortality following MI. Most evidence for long-term beta-blocker use comes from studies of propranolol, metoprolol and timolol, which are licensed for prophylaxis after MI. Atenolol has shown a similar effect to the licensed beta-blockers and is widely used.
- **ACE inhibitors** reduce the risk of premature mortality following MI. Lisinopril and ramipril are both licensed for prophylaxis after MI when there is no evidence of heart failure.
- **Statins** reduce the risk of premature mortality following MI. Most evidence comes from trials of pravastatin and simvastatin. Atorvastatin and fluvastatin are alternatives.

Prescriptions

Antiplatelet therapy

Aspirin 75mg dispersible once a day
- Age from 16 years onwards
- Aspirin 75mg dispersible tabs. Take one tablet once a day; supply 28 tablets; NHS Cost £0.36.

Clopidogrel 75mg once a day – only if intolerant of aspirin
- Age from 16 years onwards
- Clopidogrel 75mg tablets. Take one tablet once a day; supply 28 tablets; NHS Cost £35.31.

Beta-blocker: maintenance doses

Atenolol 50mg twice a day
- Age from 16 years onwards
- Atenolol 50mg tablets. Take one tablet twice a day; supply 56 tablets; NHS Cost £1.66.

Atenolol 100mg once a day
- Age from 16 years onwards
- Atenolol 100mg tablets. Take one tablet once a day; supply 28 tablets; NHS Cost £1.06.

Metoprolol 100mg twice a day
- Age from 16 years onwards
- Metoprolol 100mg tablets. Take one tablet twice a day; supply 56 tablets; NHS Cost £3.75.

Propranolol 80mg twice a day
- Age from 16 years onwards
- Propranolol 80mg tablets. Take one tablet twice a day; supply 56 tablets; NHS Cost £0.95.

Timolol 10mg twice a day
- Age from 16 years onwards
- Timolol 10mg tablets. Take one tablet twice a day; supply 60 tablets; NHS Cost £4.90.

ACE inhibitor: target maintenance dose

Lisinopril 10mg once a day
- Age from 16 years onwards
- Lisinopril 10mg tablets. Take one tablet once a day; supply 28 tablets; NHS Cost £9.07.

Ramipril 5mg twice a day
- Age from 55 years onwards
- Ramipril 5mg tablets. Take one tablet twice a day; supply 56 tablets; NHS Cost £19.02.

ACE inhibitor: lower maintenance doses

Lisinopril 5mg once a day
- Age from 16 years onwards
- Lisinopril 5mg tablets. Take one tablet once a day; supply 28 tablets; NHS Cost £7.86.

Ramipril 2.5mg twice a day
- Age from 55 years onwards
- Ramipril 2.5mg tablets. Take one tablet twice a day; supply 56 tablets; NHS Cost £15.02.

Statin therapy

Simvastatin 20mg at night
- Age from 16 years onwards
- Simvastatin 20mg tablets. Take one tablet at night; supply 28 tablets; NHS Cost £29.69.

Simvastatin 40mg at night
- Age from 16 years onwards
- Simvastatin 40mg tablets. Take one tablet at night; supply 28 tablets; NHS Cost £29.68.

Pravastatin 20mg at night
- Age from 16 years onwards
- Pravastatin 20mg tablets. Take one tablet at night; supply 28 tablets; NHS Cost £29.69.

Pravastatin 40mg at night
- Age from 16 years onwards
- Pravastatin 40mg tablets. Take one tablet at night; supply 28 tablets; NHS Cost £29.69.

Atorvastatin 10mg once a day
- Age from 16 years onwards
- Atorvastatin 10mg tablets. Take one tablet once a day; supply 28 tablets; NHS Cost £18.03.

Atorvastatin 20mg once a day
- Age from 16 years onwards
- Atorvastatin 20mg tablets. Take one tablet once a day; supply 28 tablets; NHS Cost £30.60.

Fluvastatin 20mg at night
- Age from 18 years onwards
- Fluvastatin 20mg capsules. Take one capsule at night; supply 28 capsules; NHS Cost £12.72.

Fluvastatin 40mg at night
- Age from 18 years onwards
- Fluvastatin 40mg capsules. Take one capsule at night; supply 28 capsules; NHS Cost £12.72.

Prior MI and HF — start treatment (no beta-blocker)

Which therapy?

- **Patients should be offered** enrolment in a rehabilitation programme that has a prominent exercise component within it (A).
- **Patients with prior MI and heart failure** are a relatively ill group of patients and care is required when initiating drug treatment.

Which drugs?

- **All patients should be offered long-term treatment with an ACE inhibitor and then a beta-blocker (A).** Prescriptions for beta-blockers are offered in the separat scenario *Prior MI and heart failure — start and continu Beta-blocker*.
- **In addition, they should be treated with an antiplatelet drug (aspirin or clopidogrel) (A).**
- Patients who have moderate or severe heart failure (New York Heart Association [NYHA] grade 3 or 4) should b treated with spironolactone (A). In patients with mild symptoms of heart failure (NYHA grade 1 or 2) it is unclear whether spironolactone decreases premature mortality. It may represent a reasonable choice of adjuvant symptomatic therapy (D).
- **Patients are likely to continue to need symptomatic treatment with a loop diuretic (D).**
- **As patients with heart failure were almost always excluded from trials** there is no evidence on which to recommend the use of statins in such patients. Statin use will be influenced by clinical and practical considerations, such as whether patients were treated

P

with them prior to developing heart failure (D). Prescriptions for statins are offered in the scenario *Prior MI and no heart failure — start treatment.*

When to start drug treatment

ACE inhibitors and antiplatelet drugs should be initiated whilst patients are in hospital, as there is evidence to support benefit following early initiation. If this does not happen then primary care clinicians should initiate them as soon after discharge as possible (A).

Spironolactone can be initiated at any point. In patients with moderate to severe symptoms of heart failure (NYHA grade 3 or 4), given the time involved in achieving full dosages of beta-blockers, it seems reasonable to consider initiating spironolactone before beta-blockers (D).

Beta-blockers can be initiated at any point. Given the limited experience initiating beta-blockers, it is currently unclear whether this can be done safely in primary care. For those GPs who feel confident at initiating and monitoring beta-blockers in such patients, prescriptions are offered in the scenario *Prior MI and heart failure — start and continue Beta-blocker.*

Practical prescribing points

The information below is not covered within the National Institute for Clinical Excellence (NICE) guideline, but has been added by PRODIGY. For further information see the *Medicines Compendium* (www.medicines.org.uk) or the *British National Formulary* (www.bnf.org).

Aspirin

Avoid in gastrointestinal ulceration, haemophilia and other bleeding disorders, and breastfeeding. Use with caution in impaired renal or hepatic function, asthma, and pregnancy.

Concurrent nonsteroidal anti-inflammatory drugs (NSAIDs): the risk of serious gastrointestinal complications doubles in people who regularly take low-dose aspirin and another NSAID. If possible, stop the second NSAID.

If a second NSAID must be continued, avoid ibuprofen — it may reduce the cardiovascular protective effect of low-dose aspirin. Consider using diclofenac if a second NSAID must be used.

ACE inhibitors

The risk of first-dose hypotension or renal impairment is increased in the following patients:

- Creatinine >200 micromol/l
- Urea >12 mmol/l
- Sodium <130 mmol/l
- Systolic blood pressure <100 mmHg
- Diuretic dosage > furosemide (frusemide) 80 mg/d or equivalent
- Known or suspected renal artery stenosis (e.g. if peripheral vascular disease)
- Frail elderly

Avoid potassium-sparing diuretics (other than spironolactone) or potassium supplements in patients receiving ACE inhibitors because of the risk of hyperkalaemia.

Stop nonsteroidal anti-inflammatory drugs (NSAIDs) (if possible) as they reduce the effectiveness of diuretics and increase the risk of renal impairment with ACE inhibitors.

Avoid ACE inhibitors if there is significant cardiac outflow tract obstruction (e.g. due to aortic stenosis or hypertrophic obstructive cardiomyopathy).

Spironolactone

- **Careful monitoring** for hyperkalaemia and hypovolaemia is required. However, safety data is reassuring; in a large trial of spironolactone 25 mg daily added to ACE inhibitor treatment, the median potassium concentration increased by only 0.3 mmol/l and there was no increased risk of serious hyperkalaemia.

Follow-up advice

Some of the information below has been obtained from the National Institute for Clinical Excellence (NICE) guideline. Additional information has been added by PRODIGY.

People started on an ACE inhibitor

- **Repeat serum electrolytes** within 1 week of starting an ACE inhibitor and review patient with the results.
- **Check for adverse effects,** such as symptomatic hypotension, renal dysfunction, or hyperkalaemia (i.e. a rise in urea to 12 mmol/l, creatinine to 200 micromol /l, or potassium to 5.5 mmol/l). If these occur either stop or reduce the dosage of ACE inhibitor.
- **If tolerated,** increase the dosage of the ACE inhibitor to the maintenance dosages offered in the scenario *Prior MI and heart failure — maintenance treatment.*
- **Cough** is common in heart failure but is also caused by an ACE inhibitor in a small percentage of patients. Cough is not an indication to stop an ACE inhibitor unless it is troublesome.

People started on spironolactone

- **Check serum electrolytes** within 1 week of starting spironolactone, in order to exclude hyperkalaemia. There are no clear recommendations available on how often to check thereafter; it would seem sensible to repeat electrolytes a month later and then annually. It is also worth considering checking electrolytes a week after any change in concomitant medication.

Should I refer or investigate?

P

Investigate?

- **Renal function** (urea and electrolytes) should be checked prior to initiation of an ACE inhibitor or diuretic.

Patient information leaflets

The following PILs are available at www.prodigy.nhs.uk

- Aspirin to Prevent Blood Clots
- British Cardiac Patients Association
- British Heart Foundation
- Cholesterol
- Eat More Fruit and Vegetables
- Exercise for Health
- Healthy Eating
- Heart UK
- Medicines - Name Changes of Medicines
- Myocardial Infarction - Medication Infor
- Smoking - Help to Stop with Bupropion
- Smoking - Nicotine Replacement Therapy
- Smoking - The Facts
- Smoking - Tips on Stopping

Shared decision making

- **The following medicines** are commonly advised if you have had a heart attack.
- **Aspirin** (low dose) reduces the risk of blood clots forming.

- **ACE inhibitors** (angiotensin-converting enzyme inhibitors) have a protective effect on the heart muscle. When you take an ACE inhibitor:
  - Lie or sit down for 2–4 hours after the very first dosage.
  - A low dosage is started at first and gradually increased.
  - A blood test is usual before, and about a week after starting.
- **Diuretics ('water tablets')** are often prescribed if you develop heart failure. They make you pass out extra urine to help clear excess body fluid that builds up.
- **Spironolactone** is also used to treat heart failure if symptoms are more severe. This is a diuretic that has a protective effect on the heart.
  - A blood test is usual about a week after starting spironolactone, and every so often as advised by your doctor.
- **Beta-blockers** ease the workload of the heart.
- **Statin medicines** lower the cholesterol level. This helps to prevent atheroma which 'clogs up' the arteries. Whilst taking a statin:
  - A muscle problem is a rare, but serious adverse effect. Tell a doctor if you develop muscle pains.
  - A blood test is usual before, and about 6 weeks after starting.
- **You should also reduce any other 'risk factors':**
  - Exercise regularly (unless your doctor advises not to).
  - Do not smoke.
  - Lose weight if you are overweight.

Drug rationale

Drugs not included

- **Enteric-coated aspirin** preparations are not offered as there is no convincing evidence that this reduces toxicity at a dose of 75 mg [DTB, 1997].
- **Dipyridamole** is licensed for the secondary prevention of ischaemic stroke and transient ischaemic attacks but there is no evidence to support its use in prophylaxis after myocardial infarction (MI).
- **Beta-blockers** substantially reduce all cause mortality in patients with symptoms of heart failure being treated with angiotensin-converting enzyme (ACE) inhibitors, who have experienced an MI. The BNF recommends hospital supervision for initiation. There may be a group of people for whom GPs (based on their knowledge of the patient's clinical condition) feel able to initiate treatment. Prescriptions for beta-blockers are offered in a separate scenario called *Prior MI and heart failure — start and continue Beta-blocker*.
- **ACE inhibitors other than captopril, enalapril, lisinopril, ramipril and trandolapril** are not offered, as they are not licensed for prophylaxis after MI.
- **Diuretics other than furosemide (frusemide) and bumetanide.** Thiazides are not as effective in heart failure as loop diuretics, especially if renal function is impaired. Combination with a loop diuretic may be valuable but should usually only be initiated under specialist supervision [DTB, 1994]. Torasemide offers no clinical advantage to furosemide or bumetanide and is significantly more expensive.
- **Calcium-channel blockers** have no effect on premature mortality after MI and should only be considered for the management of symptoms and risk factors (principally hypertension).
- **Nitrates** have no effect on premature mortality after MI and should only be considered for the management of symptoms.
- **Nicorandil** is licensed in the UK for the prophylaxis and treatment of angina. A recent study of nicorandil in patients with angina (of whom 66% had a previous MI) found a significant reduction in the combined endpoint of coronary heart disease (CHD) death, non-fatal MI, or unplanned hospital admission with cardiac chest pain. However, the study was unable to demonstrate a significant reduction in CHD death or non-fatal MI when analyzed separately, or a significant reduction in the combined outcome of CHD death or non-fatal MI [IONA Study Group, 2002]. The results of this study will be further considered when the National Institute for Clinical Excellence (NICE) update their guidance.
- **Statins:** there is no evidence on which to recommend statins. Statin use will be influenced by clinical and practical considerations, such as whether patients were treated with them prior to developing heart failure. Prescriptions for statins are offered in the scenario *Prior MI and no heart failure — start treatment*.

Drugs included

- **Aspirin 75 mg** reduces the risk of subsequent cardiovascular events in people with established cardiovascular disease.
- **Clopidogrel** is offered as an alternative antiplatelet for the small number of people with genuine aspirin intolerance.
- **Loop diuretics** are the most effective diuretics for increasing renal sodium excretion and giving symptom relief in heart failure. Furosemide (frusemide) is the most commonly used diuretic in the UK. Bumetanide is an effective alternative to furosemide [DTB, 1994]. Bumetanide is thought to be less ototoxic than furosemide and may be preferred in people receiving other ototoxic medication or with hearing problems [MeReC, 1990].
- **ACE inhibitors** reduce the risk of premature mortality after MI, particularly in those with heart failure. Captopril, enalapril, lisinopril, ramipril and trandolapril are licensed for prophylaxis after MI in patients with heart failure.
- **Spironolactone** reduces the risk of premature mortality in patients with heart failure being treated with ACE inhibitors. In patients with moderate to severe symptoms of heart failure (New York Heart Association [NYHA] grade 3 or 4), given the time involved in achieving full dosages of beta-blockers, it seems reasonable to consider initiating spironolactone before beta-blockers.

Prescriptions

Start antiplatelet therapy

Aspirin 75mg dispersible once a day
- Age from 16 years onwards
- Aspirin 75mg dispersible tabs. Take one tablet once a day; supply 28 tablets; NHS Cost £0.36.

Clopidogrel 75mg once a day – only if intolerant of aspirin
- Age from 16 years onwards
- Clopidogrel 75mg tablets. Take one tablet once a day; supply 28 tablets; NHS Cost £35.31.

Loop diuretics for symptoms/ spironolactone for prophylaxis

Bumetanide 1mg each morning
- Age from 16 years onwards
- Bumetanide 1mg tablets. Take one tablet each morning; supply 14 tablets; NHS Cost £0.91.

Bumetanide 2mg each morning
- Age from 16 years onwards
- Bumetanide 1mg tablets. Take two tablets each morning; supply 28 tablets; NHS Cost £1.81.

Furosemide (frusemide) 40mg each morning
- Age from 16 years onwards
- Furosemide 40mg tablets. Take one tablet each morning; supply 14 tablets; NHS Cost £0.14.

Furosemide (frusemide) 80mg each morning
- Age from 16 years onwards
- Furosemide 40mg tablets. Take two tablets each morning; supply 28 tablets; NHS Cost £0.28.

Spironolactone 25mg once a day
- Age from 16 years onwards
- Spironolactone 25mg tablets. Take one tablet once a day; supply 28 tablets; NHS Cost £2.10.

Start ACE inhibitor: increase dose weekly (4-week supply)

Lisinopril: titrate from 2.5mg to 20mg daily
- Age from 16 years onwards
- Lisinopril 2.5mg tablets. Take one tablet once a day for 7 days, then take two tablets once a day for 7 days. Then, start taking the lisinopril 10mg tablets; supply 21 tablets; NHS Cost £4.76.
- Lisinopril 10mg tablets. Start, once the course of lisinopril 2.5mg tablets is complete. Take one tablet once a day for 7 days, then take two tablets once a day; supply 21 tablets; NHS Cost £7.65.

Enalapril: titrate from 5mg to 20mg per day
- Age from 16 years onwards
- Enalapril 2.5mg tablets. Take one tablet twice a day for 7 days, then take two tablets twice a day for 7 days. Then start taking the enalapril 10mg tablets; supply 42 tablets; NHS Cost £4.55.
- Enalapril 10mg tablets. Start, once the course of enalapril 2.5mg tablets is complete. Take one tablet twice a day; supply 28 tablets; NHS Cost £5.32.

Ramipril: titrate from 1.25mg to 5mg per day
- Age from 16 years onwards
- Ramipril 1.25mg tablets. Take one tablet once a day for 7 days, then take one tablet twice a day for 7 days. Then start taking the ramipril 2.5mg tablets; supply 21 tablets; NHS Cost £3.95.
- Ramipril 2.5mg tablets. Start, once the course of ramipril 1.25mg tablets is complete. Take one tablet twice a day; supply 28 tablets; NHS Cost £9.55.

Trandolapril: titrate from 500mcg to 2mg daily
- Age from 16 years onwards
- Trandolapril 500mcg capsules. Take one capsule once a day for 7 days, then take two capsules once a day for 7 days. Then start taking the trandolapril 2mg capsules; supply 21 capsules; NHS Cost £8.19.
- Trandolapril 2mg capsules. Start, once the course of trandolapril 500microgram capsules is complete. Take one capsule once a day; supply 14 capsules; NHS Cost £5.17.

Start lisinopril, ramipril or enalapril: increase each month

Lisinopril 2.5mg once a day: weeks 1 to 4
- Age from 16 years onwards
- Lisinopril 2.5mg tablets. Take one tablet once a day; supply 28 tablets; NHS Cost £6.26.

Lisinopril 5mg once a day: weeks 5 to 8
- Age from 16 years onwards
- Lisinopril 5mg tablets. Take one tablet once a day; supply 28 tablets; NHS Cost £7.86.

Enalapril 2.5mg once a day: weeks 1 to 4
- Age from 16 years onwards
- Enalapril 2.5mg tablets. Take one tablet once a day; supply 28 tablets; NHS Cost £2.42.

Enalapril 2.5mg twice a day: weeks 5 to 8
- Age from 16 years onwards
- Enalapril 2.5mg tablets. Take one tablet twice a day; supply 56 tablets; NHS Cost £5.22.

Enalapril 5mg twice a day: weeks 9 to 12
- Age from 16 years onwards
- Enalapril 5mg tablets. Take one tablet twice a day; supply 56 tablets; NHS Cost £7.54.

Ramipril 1.25mg once a day: weeks 1 to 4
- Age from 16 years onwards
- Ramipril 1.25mg tablets. Take one tablet once a day; supply 28 tablets; NHS Cost £5.30.

Ramipril 1.25mg twice a day: weeks 5 to 8
- Age from 16 years onwards
- Ramipril 1.25mg tablets. Take one tablet twice a day; supply 56 tablets; NHS Cost £10.60.

Ramipril 2.5mg twice a day: weeks 9 to 12
- Age from 16 years onwards
- Ramipril 2.5mg tablets. Take one tablet twice a day; supply 56 tablets; NHS Cost £19.10.

Start captopril or trandolapril : increase dose each month

Captopril 12.5mg twice a day: weeks 1 to 4
- Age from 16 years onwards
- Captopril 12.5mg tablets. Take one tablet twice a day; supply 56 tablets; NHS Cost £2.29.

Captopril 12.5mg three times a day: weeks 5 to 8
- Age from 16 years onwards
- Captopril 12.5mg tablets. Take one tablet three times a day; supply 84 tablets; NHS Cost £3.39.

Captopril 25mg three times a day: weeks 9 to 12
- Age from 16 years onwards
- Captopril 25mg tablets. Take one tablet three times a day; supply 84 tablets; NHS Cost £4.81.

Trandolapril 500micrograms once a day: weeks 1 to 4
- Age from 16 years onwards
- Trandolapril 500mcg capsules. Take one capsule once a day; supply 28 capsules; NHS Cost £8.18.

Trandolapril 1mg once a day: weeks 5 to 8
- Age from 16 years onwards
- Trandolapril 1mg capsules. Take one capsule once a day; supply 28 capsules; NHS Cost £12.28.

Prior MI and heart failure — maintenance (no beta-blocker)

Which therapy?

- **Maintenance dosages of the drugs recommended for prophylaxis post MI in people with heart failure are offered.** In addition, maintenance prescriptions for loop diuretics are also offered for symptom relief.
- **All patients should be offered long-term treatment with an ACE inhibitor and then a beta-blocker (A).** Prescriptions for beta-blockers are offered in the separate scenario *Prior MI and heart failure — start or continue Beta-blocker.*
- **In addition, they should be treated with an antiplatelet drug (aspirin or clopidogrel) (A).**
- Patients who have moderate or severe heart failure (New York Heart Association [NYHA] grade 3 or 4) should be treated with spironolactone (A). In patients with mild symptoms of heart failure (NYHA grade 1 or 2) it is

unclear whether spironolactone decreases premature mortality. It may represent a reasonable choice of adjuvant symptomatic therapy (D).
- **Patients are likely to continue to need symptomatic treatment with a loop diuretic (D).**

Practical prescribing points

The information below is not covered within the National Institute for Clinical Excellence (NICE) guideline, but has been added by PRODIGY. For further information see the *Medicines Compendium* (www.medicines.org.uk) or the *British National Formulary* (www.bnf.org).

Aspirin

- **Avoid** in gastrointestinal ulceration, haemophilia and other bleeding disorders, and breastfeeding. Use with caution in impaired renal or hepatic function, asthma, and pregnancy.
- **Concurrent nonsteroidal anti-inflammatory drugs (NSAIDs):** the risk of serious gastrointestinal complications doubles in people who regularly take low-dose aspirin and another NSAID. If possible, stop the second NSAID.
- **If a second NSAID must be continued, avoid ibuprofen** — it may reduce the cardiovascular protective effect of low-dose aspirin. Consider using diclofenac if a second NSAID must be used.

ACE inhibitors

- **Avoid** potassium-sparing diuretics (other than spironolactone) or potassium supplements in patients receiving ACE inhibitors because of the risk of hyperkalaemia.
- **Stop nonsteroidal anti-inflammatory drugs (NSAIDs)** (if possible) as they reduce the effectiveness of diuretics and increase the risk of renal impairment with ACE inhibitors.

Spironolactone

- **Careful monitoring** for hyperkalaemia and hypovolaemia is required. However, safety data is reassuring; in a large trial of spironolactone 25 mg daily added to ACE inhibitor treatment, the median potassium concentration increased by only 0.3 mmol/l and there was no increased risk of serious hyperkalaemia.

Follow-up advice

Some of the information below has been obtained from the National Institute for Clinical Excellence (NICE) guideline. Additional information has been added by PRODIGY.

People taking an ACE inhibitor

- **Increase dosage to the recommended maintenance dosages offered in this scenario.**
- **After any dosage increase:**
  - Repeat serum electrolytes within 1 week and review patient with the results.
  - Check for adverse effects, such as symptomatic hypotension, renal dysfunction, or hyperkalaemia (i.e. a rise in urea to 12 mmol/l, creatinine to 200 micromol /l, or potassium to 5.5 mmol/l). If these occur either stop or reduce the dosage of ACE inhibitor.
  - Once the patient is receiving a stable dosage, serum electrolytes should be checked at least annually.

People taking spironolactone

- **There are no clear recommendations** on how often to check serum electrolytes. It would seem sensible to check electrolytes 7 days after starting spironolactone, a mont[h] later, and then annually. It is also worth considering checking electrolytes a week after any change in concomitant medication.

Should I refer or investigate?

Investigate?

Some of the information below has been obtained from th[e] National Institute for Clinical Excellence (NICE) guidelin[e]. Additional information has been added by PRODIGY.

Patients taking an ACE inhibitor

- **If not already done,** check serum electrolytes if 7 days o[r] more have elapsed since any increase in dosage of ACE inhibitor.
- **Once the patient is receiving a stable dosage,** serum electrolytes should be checked at least annually.

Patients taking spironolactone

- **If not already done,** check serum electrolytes if 7 days o[r] more have elapsed since starting spironolactone. There are no clear recommendations on how often to check thereafter, but it would seem sensible to repeat electrolytes a month later and after any change in concomitant medication.

Patient information leaflets

The following PILs are available at www.prodigy.nhs.uk

- Aspirin to Prevent Blood Clots
- British Cardiac Patients Association
- British Heart Foundation
- Cholesterol
- Eat More Fruit and Vegetables
- Exercise for Health
- Healthy Eating
- Heart UK
- Medicines - Name Changes of Medicines
- Myocardial Infarction - Medication Infor
- Smoking - Help to Stop with Bupropion
- Smoking - Nicotine Replacement Therapy
- Smoking - The Facts
- Smoking - Tips on Stopping

Shared decision making

- **The dosages of the medicines taken following a heart attack** are often increased gradually to a usual maintenance dosage.
- **ACE inhibitors** (angiotensin-converting enzyme inhibitors) have a protective effect on the heart muscle.
- **Diuretics ('water tablets')** are often prescribed if you develop heart failure. They make you pass out extra urine to help clear excess body fluid that builds up.
- **Spironolactone** is also used to treat heart failure if symptoms are more severe. This is a diuretic that has a protective effect on the heart.
- **Aspirin** remains at a low dosage. (It reduces the risk of blood clots forming.)
- **Beta-blockers** reduce the workload on the heart.
- **Statin medicines** lower the cholesterol level. This helps prevent atheroma which 'clogs up' the arteries.
- **Blood tests** are needed from time to time, which aim to detect certain uncommon problems before they become serious.
- **You should also reduce any other 'risk factors':**
  - Exercise regularly (unless your doctor advises not to)
  - Do not smoke.
  - Lose weight if you are overweight.

Drug rationale

Drugs not included

- **Enteric-coated aspirin** preparations are not offered as there is no convincing evidence that this reduces toxicity at a dose of 75 mg [DTB, 1997].
- **Dipyridamole** is licensed for the secondary prevention of ischaemic stroke and transient ischaemic attacks but there is no evidence to support its use in prophylaxis after myocardial infarction (MI).
- **Beta-blockers** substantially reduce all cause mortality in patients with symptoms of heart failure being treated with angiotensin-converting enzyme (ACE) inhibitors who have experienced an MI. The BNF recommends hospital supervision for initiation. There may be a group of patients for whom GPs (based on their knowledge of the patient's clinical condition) feel able to initiate treatment. Prescriptions for beta-blockers are offered in the separate scenario *Prior MI and heart failure — start and continue Beta-blocker*.
- **ACE inhibitors other than captopril, enalapril, lisinopril, ramipril and trandolapril** are not offered as they are not licensed for prophylaxis after MI.
- **Diuretics other than furosemide (frusemide) and bumetanide.** Thiazides are not as effective in heart failure as loop diuretics, especially if renal function is impaired. Combination with a loop diuretic may be valuable but should usually only be initiated under specialist supervision [DTB, 1994]. Torasemide offers no clinical advantage to furosemide or bumetanide and is significantly more expensive.
- **Calcium-channel blockers** have no effect on premature mortality after MI and should only be considered for the management of symptoms and risk factors (principally hypertension).
- **Nitrates** have no effect on premature mortality after MI and should only be considered for the management of symptoms.
- **Nicorandil** is licensed in the UK for the prophylaxis and treatment of angina. A recent study of nicorandil in patients with angina (of whom 66% had a previous MI) found a significant reduction in the combined endpoint of coronary heart disease (CHD) death, non-fatal MI, or unplanned hospital admission with cardiac chest pain. However, the study was unable to demonstrate a significant reduction in CHD death or non-fatal MI when analyzed separately, or a significant reduction in the combined outcome of CHD death or non-fatal MI [IONA Study Group, 2002]. The results of this study will be further considered when the National Institute for Clinical Excellence (NICE) update their guidance.
- **Statins:** there is no evidence on which to recommend statins. Statin use will be influenced by clinical and practical considerations, such as whether people were treated with them prior to developing heart failure. Prescriptions for statins are offered in the scenario *Prior MI and no heart failure — start treatment.*

Drugs included

- **Aspirin 75 mg** reduces the risk of subsequent cardiovascular events in people with established cardiovascular disease.
- **Clopidogrel** is offered as an alternative antiplatelet for the small number of people with genuine aspirin intolerance.
- **Loop diuretics** are the most effective diuretics for increasing renal sodium excretion and giving symptom relief in heart failure. Furosemide (frusemide) is the most commonly used diuretic in the UK. Bumetanide is an effective alternative to furosemide [DTB, 1994]. Bumetanide is thought to be less ototoxic than furosemide and may be preferred in people receiving other ototoxic medication or with hearing problems [MeReC, 1990].
- **ACE inhibitors** reduce the risk of premature mortality after MI, particularly in those with heart failure. Captopril, enalapril, lisinopril, ramipril and trandolapril are licensed for prophylaxis after MI in patients with heart failure.
- **Spironolactone** reduces the risk of premature mortality in patients with heart failure being treated with ACE inhibitors. In patients with moderate to severe symptoms of heart failure (New York Heart Association [NYHA] grade 3 or 4), given the time involved in achieving full dosages of beta-blockers, it seems reasonable to consider initiating spironolactone before beta-blockers.

Prescriptions

Antiplatelet therapy

Aspirin 75mg dispersible once a day
- Age from 16 years onwards
- Aspirin 75mg dispersible tabs. Take one tablet once a day; supply 28 tablets; NHS Cost £0.36.

Clopidogrel 75mg once a day – only if intolerant of aspirin
- Age from 16 years onwards
- Clopidogrel 75mg tablets. Take one tablet once a day; supply 28 tablets; NHS Cost £35.31.

Loop diuretic

Bumetanide 1mg each morning
- Age from 16 years onwards
- Bumetanide 1mg tablets. Take one tablet each morning; supply 14 tablets; NHS Cost £0.91.

Bumetanide 2mg each morning
- Age from 16 years onwards
- Bumetanide 1mg tablets. Take two tablets each morning; supply 28 tablets; NHS Cost £1.81.

Furosemide (frusemide) 40mg each morning
- Age from 16 years onwards
- Furosemide 40mg tablets. Take one tablet each morning; supply 14 tablets; NHS Cost £0.14.

Furosemide (frusemide) 80mg each morning
- Age from 16 years onwards
- Furosemide 40mg tablets. Take two tablets each morning; supply 28 tablets; NHS Cost £0.28.

Spironolactone therapy

Spironolactone 25mg once a day
- Age from 16 years onwards
- Spironolactone 25mg tablets. Take one tablet once a day; supply 28 tablets; NHS Cost £2.10.

ACE inhibitor: target maintenance doses

Lisinopril 10mg once a day
- Age from 16 years onwards
- Lisinopril 10mg tablets. Take one tablet once a day; supply 28 tablets; NHS Cost £9.07.

Lisinopril 20mg once a day
- Age from 16 years onwards
- Lisinopril 20mg tablets. Take one tablet once a day; supply 28 tablets; NHS Cost £10.97.

Enalapril 10mg twice a day
- Age from 16 years onwards
- Enalapril 10mg tablets. Take one tablet twice a day; supply 56 tablets; NHS Cost £10.66.

P

Ramipril 5mg twice a day
- Age from 16 years onwards
- Ramipril 5mg tablets. Take one tablet twice a day; supply 56 tablets; NHS Cost £19.02.

Captopril 50mg three times a day
- Age from 16 years onwards
- Captopril 50mg tablets. Take one tablet three times a day; supply 84 tablets; NHS Cost £8.12.

Trandolapril 2mg once a day
- Age from 16 years onwards
- Trandolapril 2mg capsules. Take one capsule once a day; supply 28 capsules; NHS Cost £12.28.

Trandolapril 4mg once a day
- Age from 16 years onwards
- Trandolapril 2mg capsules. Take two capsules once a day; supply 56 capsules; NHS Cost £24.58.

ACE inhibitor: lower maintenance doses

Lisinopril 5mg once a day
- Age from 16 years onwards
- Lisinopril 5mg tablets. Take one tablet once a day; supply 28 tablets; NHS Cost £7.86.

Ramipril 2.5mg twice a day
- Age from 16 years onwards
- Ramipril 2.5mg tablets. Take one tablet twice a day; supply 56 tablets; NHS Cost £15.02.

Enalapril 5mg twice a day
- Age from 16 years onwards
- Enalapril 5mg tablets. Take one tablet twice a day; supply 56 tablets; NHS Cost £7.54.

Captopril 25mg three times a day
- Age from 16 years onwards
- Captopril 25mg tablets. Take one tablet three times a day; supply 84 tablets; NHS Cost £4.82.

Trandolapril 1mg once a day
- Age from 16 years onwards
- Trandolapril 1mg capsules. Take one capsule once a day; supply 28 capsules; NHS Cost £10.34.

P

Prior MI and heart failure — start and continue beta-blocker

Which therapy?

- **Patients should be offered enrolment in a rehabilitation programme** that has a prominent exercise component within it (A).
- **Patients with prior MI and heart failure** are a relatively ill group of patients and care is required when initiating drug treatment.
- **Beta-blockers substantially reduce all cause mortality in patients with heart failure** (A).
- **Prescriptions for the titration and maintenance of beta-blockers are offered** for those GPs who feel confident at initiating and monitoring beta-blockers in patients with heart failure.
- **Given the limited experience initiating beta-blockers,** it is currently unclear whether this can be done safely in primary care. The BNF recommends that beta-blockers should only be started by those experienced in the management of heart failure. It is possible that there is a group of patients with heart failure for whom GPs (based on their knowledge of the patient's clinical condition) may feel able to initiate treatment in primary care. Unfortunately, the characteristics of this patient group are not currently clear. Discussion at a local level may inform appropriate methods of treatment initiation (D).
- **Remember** that patients should also be taking an ACE inhibitor and an antiplatelet drug (aspirin or clopidogrel (A). Patients with moderate to severe symptoms of heart failure (New York Heart Association [NYHA] grade 3 or 4) should also be taking spironolactone (A). Given the time involved in achieving full dosages of beta-blockers, it seems reasonable to consider initiating spironolactone before beta-blockers (D).

Practical prescribing points

The information below is not covered within the National Institute for Clinical Excellence (NICE) guideline, but has been added by PRODIGY. For further information see the *Medicines Compendium* (www.medicines.org.uk) or the *British National Formulary* (www.bnf.org).

- **Avoid** beta-blockers in asthma, chronic obstructive pulmonary disease (COPD), or heart block. Caution in peripheral vascular disease.

Follow-up advice

- **If tolerated,** treatment should be slowly increased, for example at fortnightly intervals, over a period of up to 12 weeks (D). Aim for the maintenance dosages offered in this scenario.
- **The two beta-blockers offered are increased every 2 weeks for the first 6 weeks.** Thereafter there are slight differences in speed of titration to the recommended maintenance dosages, and review dates may need to be adjusted to take this into account.

Should I refer or investigate?

Refer?

- **Specialist referral should be considered if there are no contraindications to beta-blockers but initiation of a beta-blocker within primary care is not possible.** Whilst the BNF recommends hospital supervision, it seems possible that there is a group of patients with heart failure for whom GPs (based on their knowledge of the patient's clinical condition) may feel able to initiate treatment in primary care. Unfortunately, the characteristics of this patient group are not currently clear. Discussion at a local level may inform appropriate methods of treatment initiation (D).

Patient information leaflets

The following PILs are available at www.prodigy.nhs.uk
- Aspirin to Prevent Blood Clots
- British Cardiac Patients Association
- British Heart Foundation
- Cholesterol
- Eat More Fruit and Vegetables
- Exercise for Health
- Healthy Eating
- Heart UK
- Myocardial Infarction - Medication Infor
- Smoking - Help to Stop with Bupropion
- Smoking - Nicotine Replacement Therapy
- Smoking - The Facts
- Smoking - Tips on Stopping

Shared decision making

- **A beta-blocker medicine,** such as bisoprolol or carvedilol, is commonly prescribed if you have heart failure following a heart attack. These medicines reduce the workload on the heart.

- A low dosage is started at first, and then increased every few weeks until a regular dose is reached.
- When a beta-blocker is first started, some people develop side effects (which are often just temporary) such as low blood pressure (you may feel faint or dizzy) or an increase in breathlessness or tiredness.

- **Other medicines** are also commonly advised after a heart attack. These include:
  - **ACE inhibitors** (angiotensin-converting enzyme inhibitors), which have a protective effect on the heart muscle
  - **Statin medicines,** which lower the cholesterol level
  - **Aspirin,** to reduce the risk of blood clots forming
  - **Diuretics ('water tablets'),** to help clear the body of excess fluid
  - **Spironolactone,** which is a diuretic that has a protective effect on the heart
- **You should also reduce any other 'risk factors':**
  - Exercise regularly (unless your doctor advises not to).
  - Do not smoke.
  - Lose weight if you are overweight.

Drug rationale

Drugs not included

- **Beta-blockers, other than bisoprolol or carvedilol,** which are not licensed for use in heart failure.

Drugs included

- **The beta-blockers bisoprolol and carvedilol** are licensed for use in heart failure. Beta-blockers substantially reduce all cause mortality in patients with symptoms of heart failure being treated with angiotensin-converting enzyme (ACE) inhibitors who may or may not have experienced a myocardial infarction (MI). Whilst the BNF recommends hospital supervision, it seems possible that there are a group of patients with heart failure for whom GPs (based on their knowledge of the patient's clinical condition) may feel able to initiate treatment in primary care. Unfortunately, the characteristics of this patient group are not currently clear. Discussion at a local level may inform appropriate methods of treatment initiation.

Prescriptions

Start bisoprolol: titration over 15 weeks

Weeks 1 and 2: bisoprolol 1.25mg each morning
- Age from 16 years onwards
- Bisoprolol 1.25mg tablets. Take one tablet each morning; supply 14 tablets; NHS Cost £2.14.

Weeks 3 and 4: bisoprolol 2.5mg each morning
- Age from 16 years onwards
- Bisoprolol 2.5mg tablets. Take one tablet each morning; supply 14 tablets; NHS Cost £2.14.

Weeks 5 and 6: bisoprolol 3.75mg each morning
- Age from 16 years onwards
- Bisoprolol 3.75mg tablets. Take one tablet each morning; supply 14 tablets; NHS Cost £2.14.

Weeks 7 to 10: bisoprolol 5mg each morning
- Age from 16 years onwards
- Bisoprolol 5mg tablets. Take one tablet each morning; supply 28 tablets; NHS Cost £8.56.

Weeks 11 to 14: bisoprolol 7.5mg each morning
- Age from 16 years onwards
- Bisoprolol 7.5mg tablets. Take one tablet each morning; supply 28 tablets; NHS Cost £9.09.

Week 15 onwards: bisoprolol 10mg each morning
- Age from 16 years onwards
- Bisoprolol 10mg tablets. Take one tablet each morning; supply 28 tablets; NHS Cost £9.61.

Start carvedilol: titration over 7 to 9 weeks

Weeks 1 and 2: carvedilol 3.125mg twice a day
- Age from 16 years onwards
- Carvedilol 3.125mg tablets. Take one tablet twice a day; supply 28 tablets; NHS Cost £8.14.

Weeks 3 and 4: carvedilol 6.25mg twice a day
- Age from 16 years onwards
- Carvedilol 6.25mg tablets. Take one tablet twice a day; supply 28 tablets; NHS Cost £9.04.

Weeks 5 and 6: carvedilol 12.5mg twice a day
- Age from 16 years onwards
- Carvedilol 12.5mg tablets. Take one tablet twice a day; supply 28 tablets; NHS Cost £10.05.

People > 85kg: weeks 7 and 8: carvedilol 25mg twice a day
- Age from 16 years onwards
- Carvedilol 25mg tablets. Take one tablet twice a day; supply 28 tablets; NHS Cost £12.56.

People < 85kg: week 7 onwards: carvedilol 25mg twice a day
- Age from 16 years onwards
- Carvedilol 25mg tablets. Take one tablet twice a day; supply 56 tablets; NHS Cost £25.12.

People > 85kg – week 9 onwards: carvedilol 50mg twice a day
- Age from 16 years onwards
- Carvedilol 25mg tablets. Take two tablets twice a day; supply 112 tablets; NHS Cost £50.24.

Bisoprolol and carvedilol: target maintenance doses

Carvedilol 25mg twice a day
- Age from 16 years onwards
- Carvedilol 25mg tablets. Take one tablet twice a day; supply 56 tablets; NHS Cost £25.12.

People > 85kg: carvedilol 50mg twice a day
- Age from 16 years onwards
- Carvedilol 25mg tablets. Take two tablets twice a day; supply 112 tablets; NHS Cost £50.24.

Bisoprolol 10mg each morning
- Age from 16 years onwards
- Bisoprolol 10mg tablets. Take one tablet each morning; supply 28 tablets; NHS Cost £9.61.

Bisoprolol and carvedilol: lower maintenance doses

Bisoprolol 1.25mg once a day
- Age from 16 years onwards
- Bisoprolol 1.25mg tablets. Take one tablet each morning; supply 28 tablets; NHS Cost £2.14.

Bisoprolol 2.5mg once a day
- Age from 16 years onwards
- Bisoprolol 2.5mg tablets. Take one tablet each morning; supply 28 tablets; NHS Cost £2.14.

Bisoprolol 3.75mg once a day
- Age from 16 years onwards
- Bisoprolol 3.75mg tablets. Take one tablet each morning; supply 28 tablets; NHS Cost £2.14.

Bisoprolol 5mg once a day
- Age from 16 years onwards
- Bisoprolol 5mg tablets. Take one tablet each morning; supply 28 tablets; NHS Cost £8.56.

Bisoprolol 7.5mg once a day
- Age from 16 years onwards
- Bisoprolol 7.5mg tablets. Take one tablet each morning; supply 28 tablets; NHS Cost £9.09.

Carvedilol 3.125mg twice a day
- Age from 16 years onwards
- Carvedilol 3.125mg tablets. Take one tablet twice a day; supply 56 tablets; NHS Cost £16.28.

Carvedilol 6.25mg twice a day
- Age from 16 years onwards
- Carvedilol 6.25mg tablets. Take one tablet twice a day; supply 56 tablets; NHS Cost £18.08.

Carvedilol 12.5mg twice a day
- Age from 16 years onwards
- Carvedilol 12.5mg tablets. Take one tablet twice a day; supply 56 tablets; NHS Cost £20.10.

Extended Information

Background information

- What is it? p.1564
- How common is it? p.1564
- How do I know my patient has had an MI? p.1564
- How do I know my patient has heart failure? p.1564
- Complications and prognosis of MI p.1565

What is it?

- **Myocardial infarction (MI) is the death of a segment of heart muscle,** usually due to interruption of its blood supply following occlusion of a coronary artery with thrombus.
- **Definitions of the diagnosis of an acute MI vary.** Chest pain compatible with infarction is the usual reason for hospital admission, and an MI is diagnosed with the presence of one or more of the following: electrocardiographic changes with development of Q waves, bundle branch block, ST segment elevation or depression over 24 hours, and increased activity of cardiac enzymes or other biochemical tests.

P

How common is it?

- **National mortality and health service data** are unable to differentiate between first or subsequent ischaemic events, making a demographic profile of those who have already experienced a myocardial infarction (MI) problematic.
- **Ischaemic heart disease** may be broadly defined to include MI, angina, coronary atherosclerosis, and heart failure: often these conditions coexist in people.
- **Ischaemic heart disease is the most common cause of death,** accounting for about a quarter of all mortality in England and Wales.
- **In 1994,** there were approximately 300,000 hospital admissions in England for ischaemic heart disease, requiring 2 million bed-days. Ischaemic heart disease accounted for nearly 4% of all NHS admissions.
- **A GP** with a list size of 2000 would expect each year on average 5 deaths, 12 hospitalizations, and to have 50 people making 130 primary care consultations for ischaemic heart disease.

How do I know my patient has had an MI?

- **The diagnosis of myocardial infarction (MI)** may have been reached during a hospital admission or in a general practice setting.
- **For those people in whom the diagnosis of MI was made during a hospital admission,** the hospital discharge summary must mention this diagnosis in unambiguous terms [NICE, 2002].
- Hospital clinicians may have used one of two systems (1 or 2) for determining the diagnosis of MI.
- In the last two decades, MI has been defined by a combination of two or three characteristics: typical symptoms, enzyme rise, and a typical electrocardiogram (ECG) pattern involving the development of Q waves [Joint International Society et al, 1979].
- Recent changes in clinical practice and refinement of the diagnostic tools have required a redefinition of MI [The Joint European Society of Cardiology/American College of Cardiology Committee, 2000]. The following are the current criteria for acute, evolving, or recent MI:
  - Typical rise and gradual fall (troponin) or more rapid rise and fall (CK-MB) of biochemical markers of myocardial necrosis with at least one of the following:
    - Ischaemic symptoms
    - Development of pathologic Q waves on the ECG
    - ECG changes indicative of ischaemia (ST segment elevation or depression)
    - Coronary artery intervention (e.g. coronary angioplasty)
- **If the diagnosis of acute MI is suspected in general practice,** the person must be admitted to a local hospital without delay for further investigations and management [NICE, 2002].
- **There may be individuals with silent MIs who cannot be identified.** It is estimated that 25% of non-fatal infarctions are silent [Kannel and Abbott, 1984].
- **ECG changes in established MI are characterized by the presence of abnormal Q waves.** An abnormal Q wave is a broad (more than 1 mm) and deep (more than 2 mm, or more than 25% of the amplitude of the following R wave) negative deflection that starts the QRS complex. Q waves may occur normally in leads aVR and V1 (and sometimes in lead III) but in other leads are abnormal. Abnormal Q waves are also produced by severe abnormalities such as left bundle branch block, ventricular tachycardia, and the Wolff–Parkinson–White syndrome. Q waves are usually permanent ECG features following full-thickness MI, but do not develop with subendocardial infarctions.

How do I know my patient has heart failure?

- **All people whose records contain a diagnosis of chronic heart failure should have had the diagnosis confirmed by echocardiography** [NICE, 2002].
- As open-access echocardiography becomes more widely available, the number of confirmed diagnoses is likely to increase; this will bring an improvement in the accuracy of the information held.
- A provisional diagnosis of heart failure may be made if there are symptoms and signs of heart failure, supported by an abnormal chest X-ray (see below) [SIGN, 1999].
- **Symptoms include:**
  - Shortness of breath on exertion (sensitivity 66%, specificity 52%)
  - Decreased exercise tolerance (often simply 'fatigue')
  - Paroxysmal nocturnal dyspnoea (sensitivity 33%, specificity 76%)
  - Orthopnoea (sensitivity 21%, specificity 81%)
  - Ankle swelling (sensitivity 23%, specificity 80%)
- **The most specific signs are:**
  - Laterally displaced apex beat
  - Elevated jugular venous pressure
  - Third heart sound
- **Less specific signs include:**
  - Tachycardia
  - Lung crepitations
  - Hepatic engorgement (tender hepatomegaly)

- Peripheral oedema
- Chest X-ray (CXR)
  - Helps to exclude pulmonary causes of dyspnoea.
  - Radiological features of heart failure are pulmonary vascular congestion (upper lobe diversion), pulmonary oedema, effusions, or cardiomegaly.

Complications and prognosis of MI

Complications

- Heart failure
- Fatal and non-fatal arrhythmias
- Valvular dysfunction
- Ventricular aneurysm
- Pericarditis
- Cardiac thromboembolism
- Myocardial rupture
- Cardiogenic shock
- Postinfarction angina
- Psychosocial and socioeconomic complications

[Waters and Jamil, 1999]

Prognosis

- **Epidemiological studies,** following people surviving a first myocardial infarction, have found average mortalities of 5–10% per year in those people aged 50 to 70. This can be compared with an average mortality in the population in this age group of 1% per year.
- **Survival following infarct** does not appear to vary significantly by diagnosis of definite or probable infarction, or by gender, although prognosis worsens with increasing age. Multivariate analyses conducted in these studies identified few important prognostic risk factors. Exceptions are increasing ventricular dysfunction and recurrent MI indicating poorer prognosis, and moderate (compared with occasional) alcohol consumption associated with a better prognosis.

Management issues

- General issues p.1565
- Patients with prior MI who do not have heart failure p.1565
- Patients with prior MI and heart failure p.1566
- Patient with prior MI who have diabetes p.1567

A description of the evidence grading is outlined at the end of the *References* section.

General issues

Rehabilitation

- **Patients should be offered enrolment in a rehabilitation programme** that has a prominent exercise component within it (A). Although many of the trials imposed upper age limits for recruitment, in a service setting it is more appropriate to be guided by functional ability and patient preference (D).
- **There is good evidence** that cardiac rehabilitation that includes an exercise component is associated with a reduction in mortality and major morbidity in patients post myocardial infarction (MI). Overall, cardiac rehabilitation is associated with a 26% reduction in the odds of death (95% CI 11% to 38%). If 1000 patients are treated with cardiac rehabilitation commencing soon after MI and followed up for between 3 months and 5 years, 24 deaths will be avoided (95% CI 3 to 45).

Diet

- Given the nature of the available evidence of the effectiveness of dietary manipulation as a strategy for secondary prophylaxis, it is not possible to recommend specific dietary manipulation (B).

Other risk factors

- **Other cardiovascular risk factors** should be addressed, such as smoking and hypertension [DH, 2000]. The National Service Framework for Coronary Heart Disease recommends that people with established coronary heart disease should receive advice and treatment to maintain blood pressure below 140/85 mmHg.

Patients with prior MI who do not have heart failure

Which drugs?

- **All patients should be offered long-term treatment** firstly with a *beta-blocker* and an *antiplatelet drug* (aspirin or clopidogrel), and then with a *statin* and an *angiotensin-converting enzyme (ACE) inhibitor*. This sequencing of initiation reflects the evidence from trials and estimates of cost-effectiveness (A).
- **The precise lower limit of the level of cholesterol** that should be treated is unclear. Across the statin trials considered, the lower limit of the range of cholesterol values defining entry into the trials varied; one large trial enrolled people with serum cholesterols down to 4 mmol/l. Licence indications currently suggest a lower limit of 4.8 mmol/l or 5.5 mmol/l depending on the drug used (D). It is generally accepted that people with a total serum cholesterol of 5 mmol/l or greater should receive treatment to reduce their cholesterol level [BNF 44, 2002]. The NSF for CHD states that total serum cholesterol should be lowered to below 5 mmol/l or by 20–25%, whichever will result in the lower level. Equivalent figures for low-density lipoprotein (LDL) cholesterol are 3 mmol/l or a 30% reduction [DH, 2000].
- **Beta-blockers and ACE inhibitors** can also be considered for the management of symptoms (e.g. in stable angina) or risk factors (e.g. hypertension) (D).
- **Calcium-channel blockers, nitrates, and potassium-channel activators** have no effect on premature mortality, making their role the management of symptoms and risk factors (principally hypertension) (A). They should therefore only be used in those patients who are intolerant of beta-blockers and ACE inhibitors (D). Given their effect on non-fatal MI, verapamil or diltiazem should then be considered initially (B). Subsequent necessary treatment with other calcium-channel blockers, nitrates, or potassium-channel activators is then appropriate (D).

When to start drug treatment

- **The recommended starting points** for drug treatments are based on the initiation points in the clinical trials.
- ***Beta-blockers, antiplatelet drugs*** **(aspirin), and** ***ACE inhibitors*** should be initiated whilst patients are in hospital, as there is evidence to support benefit following early initiation. If this does not happen then primary care clinicians should initiate them as soon after discharge as possible (A).
- **All patients discharged from hospital who are not already taking a** ***statin*** should be assessed and have treatment initiated 12 weeks after an MI (A). Although there is no evidence of long-term benefit from the use of statins initiated prior to 12 weeks after infarct, many patients will have been taking statins prior to admission or will have them initiated in hospital.

P

Monitoring treatment

- **Patients being considered for treatment with a statin** should have an initial serum cholesterol measurement, both to exclude familial lipid disorders and to identify those patients with a serum cholesterol level that does not need treating. Once these have been excluded, further measurement allows an assessment of response to treatment and informs the assessment of compliance with treatment. The frequency of such monitoring is unclear; however, the National Service Framework for Coronary Heart Disease suggests annually (D).
- **Patients being considered for treatment with ACE inhibitors** should have their renal function checked (urea and electrolytes) prior to initiation and after each significant dosage increase (D).

Continuation of treatment

- **The treatment durations,** for which there is at least one trial that provides direct support, are 3½ years for antiplatelet drugs (aspirin), 4 years for beta-blockers and ACE inhibitors, and 6 years for statins. In the absence of a clear reason to stop treatment, it seems reasonable to continue treatment indefinitely (D).

Supporting evidence

- **Beta-blockers:** reduce the odds of death following MI by 24% (95% CI 17% to 30%) and the odds of non-fatal re-infarction by 24% (95% CI 15% to 33%). Treating 1000 patients for a year will avoid 13 deaths (95% CI 7 to 18) and 8 non-fatal MIs (95% CI 2 to 4).
- **ACE inhibitors:** reduce the odds of death following MI by 17% (95% CI 5% to 27%). Treating 1000 patients with an ACE inhibitor for a year will avoid four deaths (95% CI 1 to 6) and five non-fatal MIs (95% CI 2 to 7).
- Antiplatelet therapy:
  - Reduces the odds of death following MI by 16% (95% CI 2% to 27%). Treating 1000 patients for a year will avoid seven deaths (95% CI 1 to 13) and eight non-fatal MIs (95% CI 5 to 11). In addition, antiplatelet therapy reduces the odds of non-fatal stroke by 41% (95% CI 20% to 56%). Treating 1000 patients for a year will avoid two non-fatal strokes (95% CI 1 to 4). There is no evidence that any alternative antiplatelet agent is more effective than aspirin in this patient group; the majority of evidence comes from trials of aspirin.
  - The absolute excess risk for episodes of major gastrointestinal bleeding is approximately 0.6 per 1000 middle-aged men receiving low-dose aspirin for a year. A higher rate of 2 episodes per 1000 is likely in elderly patients. The estimated annual excess risk of haemorrhagic stroke is 0.2 per 1000 patients treated [Hayden et al, 2002; USPSTF, 2002].
- **Statins:** reduce the odds of death following MI by 24% (95% CI 5% to 40%). Treating 1000 people for a year will avoid 4 deaths (95% CI 2 to 6) and 6 non-fatal MIs (95% CI 2 to 10).
- **Calcium-channel blockers:** have not been shown to reduce all cause mortality following MI. Treatment with a calcium-channel blocker reduces the odds of non-fatal MI by 19% (95% CI 4% to 31%). The evidence is most convincing for verapamil and diltiazem. Treating 1000 patients for a year would avoid 10 non-fatal MIs (95% CI 2 to 19). However, the absence of an effect on mortality in the trials raises questions about the effects of calcium-channel blockers, as some mortality reduction would be expected if they reduced the risk of non-fatal MI.
- **Nitrates:** have been shown not to improve outcome following MI.
- **Nicorandil:** a large study of nicorandil in patients with angina (of whom 66% had a previous MI) found a significant reduction in the combined endpoint of coronary heart disease (CHD) death, non-fatal MI, or unplanned hospital admission with cardiac chest pain. However, the study was unable to demonstrate a significant reduction in CHD death or non-fatal MI when analyzed separately, or a significant reduction in the combined outcome of CHD death or non-fatal MI [IONA Study Group, 2002]. The results of this study will be further considered when the National Institute for Clinical Excellence (NICE) updates its guidance.

Patients with prior MI and heart failure

Which drugs?

- **Patients with prior MI and heart failure** are a relatively ill group and care is required when initiating drug treatment.
- **All patients should be offered long-term treatment with an *ACE inhibitor* and then a *beta-blocker*** (not all beta-blockers have a licence for this indication). In addition, they should be treated with an *antiplatelet drug* (aspirin or clopidogrel). Patients who have moderate or severe heart failure (New York Heart Association [NYHA] grade 3 or 4) should be treated with *spironolactone*. All of these treatments are cost effective (A).
- Patients are likely to continue to need symptomatic treatment with a loop diuretic (D). In patients with mild symptoms of heart failure (NYHA grade 1 or 2) it is unclear whether spironolactone decreases premature mortality. It may represent a reasonable choice of adjuvant symptomatic therapy (D).
- **As patients with heart failure were almost always excluded from trials** there is no evidence on which to recommend the use of statins in such patients. Statin use will be influenced by clinical and practical considerations, such as whether patients were treated with them prior to developing heart failure (D).

When to start drug treatment

- **The recommended starting points** for drug treatments are based on the initiation points in the trials.
- ***ACE inhibitors* and *antiplatelet drugs* (aspirin)** should be initiated whilst patients are in hospital, as there is evidence to support benefit following early initiation. If this does not happen then primary care clinicians should initiate them as soon after discharge as possible (A).
- *Beta-blockers* can be initiated at any point. Treatment should start with low doses and should be slowly increased, for example at fortnightly intervals, over a period of up to 12 weeks (A). Given the limited experience initiating beta-blockers, it is currently unclear whether this can be done safely in primary care. The BNF recommends that beta-blockers should only be started by those experienced in the management of heart failure [BNF 44, 2002]. It is possible that there is a group of patients with heart failure for whom GPs (based on their knowledge of the patient's clinical condition) may feel able to initiate treatment in primary care. Unfortunately, the characteristics of this patient group are not currently clear. Discussion at a local level may inform appropriate methods of treatment initiation (D).
- *Spironolactone* can be initiated at any point. In patients with moderate to severe symptoms of heart failure (NYHA grade 3 or 4), given the time involved in achieving full dosages of beta-blockers, it seems reasonable to consider initiating spironolactone before beta-blockers (D).

Monitoring treatment

- **Patients being considered for treatment with ACE inhibitors** should have their renal function checked prior to initiation and after each significant dosage increase (**D**).
- **Patients being treated with spironolactone** should have their serum potassium monitored (**D**).

Continuation of treatment

- **The treatment durations,** for which there is at least one trial that provides direct support, are 3½ years for ACE inhibitors, 2½ years for beta-blockers, and 2 years for spironolactone. In the absence of a clear reason to stop treatment, it seems reasonable to continue treatment indefinitely (**D**).

Supporting evidence

- **Beta-blockers:** substantially reduce all cause mortality in patients with symptoms of heart failure being treated with ACE inhibitors, who may or may not have had an MI. For many years beta-blockers have been contraindicated in patients who have heart failure. Several large trials have examined the effectiveness of beta-blockers in addition to conventional (ACE inhibitor) treatment in patients with heart failure. Since most patients randomized in these trials were being treated with an ACE inhibitor, the benefits observed for beta-blockers may be considered as additional to those achieved with ACE inhibition. Overall, beta-blockers reduce the odds of death by 35% (95% CI 25% to 45%). Treating 1000 patients with heart failure for a year with beta-blockers will avoid 35 deaths (95% CI 23 to 46). If 1000 patients are treated with both an ACE inhibitor and a beta-blocker, it is estimated that 49 deaths will be avoided (95% CI 38 to 61).
- **ACE inhibitors:** in patients with signs of heart failure who have had a recent MI, ACE inhibitors reduce the odds of death by 26% (95% CI 14% to 38%). Treating 1000 patients with heart failure with ACE inhibitors for a year, commencing soon after the MI, will avoid 18 deaths (95% CI 8 to 28). Long-term treatment with ACE inhibitors is associated with a substantial reduction in all cause mortality in patients with heart failure who may or may not have experienced an MI. Treating 1000 patients for 1 year will avoid about 15 deaths.
- **Spironolactone:** is associated with a decrease in all cause mortality among patients with moderate to severe heart failure treated optimally with ACE inhibitors. The RALES trial (1999) examined the effect of spironolactone 25 mg daily in patients with severe symptoms of heart failure (NYHA grade 3 and 4) [Pitt et al, 1999]. Spironolactone reduced all cause mortality by 11.3%. If 1000 patients were treated for a year, 57 deaths would be avoided (95% CI 26 to 87).
- **Calcium-channel blockers:** do not lead to a statistically significant reduction in mortality in trials in patients with heart failure.

Patient with prior MI who have diabetes

- There is evidence that intensive insulin therapy initiated soon after admission for acute MI reduces mortality (**B**). To achieve the benefits demonstrated in the single trial in this area involves four daily insulin injections, continuing for at least 3 months (**B**).

References

NHS staff in England can link, free of charge, from references to full text journals by clicking on [Full text] on the PRODIGY website.

Some additional information has been included (in particular relating to diagnosis of myocardial infarction) — where such information has been added, this is clearly referenced to the source as outlined below.

1. BNF 44 (2002) *British National Formulary*. 44th edn. London: British Medical Association and Royal Pharmaceutical Society of Great Britain.
2. DH (2000) *National service framework for coronary heart disease*. Department of Health. www.dh.gov.uk [Accessed: 15/07/2005]. [Full text]
3. DTB (1994) Diuretics for heart failure. *Drug & Therapeutics Bulletin* **32**(11), 83–85.
4. DTB (1997) Which prophylactic aspirin? *Drug & Therapeutics Bulletin* **35**(1), 7–8. [Full text]
5. Hayden, M., Pignone, M., Phillips, C. and Mulrow, C. (2002) Aspirin for the primary prevention of cardiovascular events: a summary of the evidence for the U.S. Preventive Services Task Force. *Annals of Internal Medicine* **136**(2), 161–172.
6. IONA Study Group (2002) Effect of nicorandil on coronary events in patients with stable angina: the impact of nicorandil in angina (IONA) randomised trial. *Lancet* **359**(9314), 1269–1275. [Full text]
7. Joint International Society, Federation of Cardiology and WHO (1979) Nomenclature and criteria for diagnosis of ischemic heart disease. Report of the Joint International Society and Federation of Cardiology/World Health Organization task force on standardization of clinical nomenclature. *Circulation* **59**(3), 607–609.
8. Kannel, W.B. and Abbott, R.D. (1984) Incidence and prognosis of unrecognized myocardial infarction: an update on the Framingham study. *New England Journal of Medicine* **311**(18), 1144–1147.
9. MeReC (1990) Diuretics. *MeReC Bulletin* **2**, 1–8.
10. NICE (2002) *Audit of the management of post-MI patients in primary care*. National Institute for Clinical Excellence. www.nice.org.uk [Accessed: 04/11/2002].
11. Pitt, B., Zannad, F., Remme, W.J. et al (1999) The effect of spironolactone on morbidity and mortality in patients with severe heart failure. *New England Journal of Medicine* **341**(10), 709–717. [Full text]
12. SIGN (1999) *Diagnosis and treatment of heart failure due to left ventricular systolic dysfunction*. Report no. 35. Scottish Intercollegiate Guidelines Network. www.sign.ac.uk [Accessed: 26/02/2003].
13. The Joint European Society of Cardiology/American College of Cardiology Committee (2000) Myocardial infarction redefined – a consensus document of the Joint European Society of Cardiology/American College of Cardiology Committee for the Redefinition of Myocardial Infarction. *Journal of the American College of Cardiology* **36**(3), 959–969.
14. USPSTF (2002) Aspirin for the primary prevention of cardiovascular events: recommendation and rationale. U.S. Preventive Services Task Force. *Annals of Internal Medicine* **136**(2), 157–160.
15. Waters, D. and Jamil, G (1999) Complications after myocardial infarction. In: Yusuf, S, Cairns, A.J., Camm, A.J. et al (Eds.) *Evidence based cardiology*. London: BMJ Books. 493–511.

Evidence grading

Strength of recommendations are:
A Directly based on category I evidence (meta-analysis of randomized controlled trials or at least one randomized controlled trial)
B Directly based on category II evidence (at least one controlled study without randomization or one other type of quasi-experimental study) or extrapolated recommendation from category I evidence
C Directly based on category III evidence (non-experimental descriptive studies) or extrapolated recommendation from category I or II evidence
D Directly based on category IV evidence (expert committee reports or opinions and/or clinical experience of respected authorities) or extrapolated recommendation from category I, II or III evidence

P

PRODIGY GUIDANCE

Prostate — benign hyperplasia

Last revised in December 2002
At the time of print this topic was being updated. The newly revised guidance will be issued on to the website in late 2005.
www.prodigy.nhs.uk/guidance.asp?gt=Prostate - benign hyperplasia

Applies to men over the age of 40 years

This guidance covers the management of benign prostatic hyperplasia (BPH).

This guidance does not cover the management of prostate cancer.

There is separate PRODIGY guidance for *Prostatitis*.

Goals

Reduce symptoms and improve quality of life
Prevent complications
Minimize adverse effects of treatment

Contents

Scenarios

- Benign prostatic hyperplasia p.1569

Extended Information, p. 1571

Benign prostatic hyperplasia

Which therapy?

Discuss the natural history of benign prostatic hyperplasia (BPH) so the man can make an informed contribution to treatment decisions.
Watchful waiting may be appropriate for men who feel that their symptoms are tolerable.
An alpha-blocker is the drug of first choice. Symptoms should be improved within several days, with full response after 4 to 6 weeks. However, adverse effects are often prominent.
A 5-alpha reductase inhibitor (e.g. finasteride) is an option for men who experience troublesome adverse effects from an alpha-blocker. However, symptomatic improvements occur slowly and the full effect may take several months.
Surgery is more effective than medical therapy. However, surgery incurs risks of severe and irreversible complications including incontinence. Some men may therefore wish to delay surgery.

Practical prescribing points

For further information please see the *Medicines Compendium* (www.medicines.org.uk) or the *British National Formulary* (www.bnf.org).

Alpha-blockers

Adverse effects predominantly affect the cardiovascular and central nervous systems:

- Cardiovascular adverse effects include orthostatic hypotension, dizziness, palpitations, peripheral oedema, and, rarely, angina.
- Central nervous system adverse effects include weakness, tiredness, headache, and somnolence.

Concurrent antihypertensive medication: care should be taken when initiating an alpha-blocker in these men because there is a risk of excessive hypotension if alpha-blockers are added to existing antihypertensive therapy.

- Avoid in people with a history of orthostatic hypotension and micturition syncope.

5-alpha reductase inhibitor (Finasteride)

- Adverse effects include decreased libido, impotence, and ejaculation disorders.
- Finasteride is excreted in semen. Therefore condoms should be worn if the sexual partner is pregnant or could possibly become pregnant. Women who are pregnant or are likely to become pregnant should also be warned against handling the tablets.

Follow-up advice

- If watchful waiting is undertaken, review every 12 months.
- Monitoring progress is facilitated by the International Prostate Symptom Score (IPSS), which quantifies symptoms. The IPSS questionnaire is available as a patient information leaflet (PIL) that can be printed out.

Should I refer or investigate?

Refer?

- **Referral guidelines for suspected cancer** published by the National Institute for Health and Clinical Excellence (NICE) [NICE, 2005] recommend urgent referral to a team specialising in the management of urological cancer, depending on local arrangements, for people:
  - Of any age with painless macroscopic haematuria.
  - Aged 40 years or older who present with recurrent or persistent urinary tract infection associated with haematuria.
  - Aged 50 years or older who are found to have unexplained microscopic haematuria.
  - With an abdominal mass identified clinically or on imaging that is thought to arise from the urinary tract.
  - Who have macroscopic haematuria and symptoms suggestive of a urinary tract infection *if* infection is not confirmed.
- **Recurrent urinary tract infections** require prompt urology referral.
- **The NHS Prostate Cancer Risk Management Programme** (www.cancerscreening.nhs.uk/) recommends as interim guidance, the following PSA cut-off values for referral:
  - Age 50–59 years — 3.0 nanogram/ml or more
  - Age 60–69 years — 4.0 nanogram/ml or more
  - Age 70 and over — 5.0 nanogram/ml or more
- The National Institute for Clinical Excellence in *Referral advice: a guide to appropriate referral from general to specialist services* [NICE, 2001] advises the following for urinary tract outflow symptoms ('prostatism') in men. The referral advice is meant to encourage local health

P

communities to discuss referral issues and enable local referral guidelines and protocols to be produced (for further information see **www.nice.org.uk**). Most men with urinary tract 'outflow' symptoms can be managed in primary care.

Investigate?

- **Dipstick urinalysis** to check for haematuria, proteinuria, and white cells.
- **Glucose** (urine or blood) to exclude diabetes mellitus.
- **Creatinine** to assess renal function.
- **Urine culture** to exclude urinary tract infection.
- Transrectal ultrasound enables measurement of the size of the prostate. This would be useful if treatment with a 5-alpha reductase inhibitor is being considered, because a response is more likely if the volume of the prostate is at least 40 ml. Transrectal ultrasound, however, would require referral to secondary care.

When to perform prostate specific antigen (PSA) testing?

- **There is no consensus whether men with lower urinary tract symptoms should opt-in or opt-out of PSA testing.**
- PSA testing should only be performed after counselling. Several patient information leaflets (PILs) have been made available for this purpose and can be printed out as required. Patient information on PSA tests can also be obtained from the NHS Prostate Cancer Risk Management Programme (www.cancerscreening.nhs.uk/).
- The International Consultation on BPH suggested that, if active treatment is chosen, the PSA should be assayed before the initiation of therapy if the diagnosis of prostate cancer would make a difference in the management of the man.
- Note: 5-alpha reductase inhibitors decrease markers of prostate activity such as serum PSA levels. Therefore, when using a 5-alpha reductase inhibitor, PSA test results should be doubled, and the doubled figure used for comparison with reference ranges (although there is great variation in individual response).

PSA test practicalities

- **Before having a PSA test the man should NOT have:**
  - An active urinary tract infection.
  - Ejaculated in the previous 48 hours.
  - Exercised vigorously in the last 48 hours.
  - Had a prostate biopsy in the previous 6 weeks.
- **If practical the man should have the PSA test before the digital rectal examination.** If not, it is recommended tha the PSA test be delayed for one week.
- The blood sample should reach the laboratory (and be separated) within 16 hours of taking it.

Table 1: Referral advice for men with urinary tract outflow symptoms.

Timing	Criteria for referral
****	They develop acute urinary retention
****	They have evidence of acute renal failure
***	They have visible haematuria
***	There is suspicion of prostate cancer — based on the finding of a nodular or firm prostate, and/or a raised serum prostate specific antigen (PSA) level
***	They have culture-negative dysuria
***	They develop chronic urinary retention with overflow or night-time incontinence.
**	They have recurrent urinary tract infection
**	They develop microscopic haematuria
^	The symptoms have failed to respond to treatment in primary care and are severe enough to affect quality of life. This is best assessed by the man using a symptom scoring system such as the World Health Organization's International Prostate Symptom Score (IPSS)
^	They have evidence of chronic renal failure or renal damage

Key to referral timings. Arrangements should be made so that the man:

- **** is seen immediately (within 1 day)
- *** is seen urgently (maximum wait of 2 weeks recommended but to be agreed locally)
- ** is seen soon (maximum waiting time to be agreed locally)
- * has a routine appointment (maximum waiting time to be agreed locally)
- ^ is seen within an appropriate time depending on clinical circumstances (discretionary)

Patient information leaflets

The following PILs are available at www.prodigy.nhs.uk

- Biopsy
- Prostate Gland - Benign Enlargement
- Prostate Help Association
- Prostate Research Campaign UK
- Prostate Symptom Score (The International)
- PSA Test for Prostate Cancer - (In-depth 5 Page Summary)

Shared decision making

- About one in three men over the age of 50 have some prostate symptoms.
- **No treatment** is an option if symptoms are mild-to-moderate. Symptoms do not always become worse, and can even improve without treatment in some men.
- **Alpha-blocker medication** often eases symptoms. Severa brands are available. They work by relaxing the muscle in the prostate and the base of the bladder. They usually work within a few days but can take up to 6 weeks for the full effect. Side effects are a problem in some men.
- **Finasteride** is an alternative medicine. It works by 'shrinking' the prostate and works best in men with particularly large prostates. It takes up to 6 months for symptoms to improve. Side effects are uncommon, but i about 3 in 100 men it causes impotence.
- **Herbal remedies** are popular but there is little scientific evidence that they work. They include: saw palmetto, beta sitosterol, rye grass, and *Pygeum africanum* bark extract.
- **Surgery** to remove the prostate is an option if symptoms are severe, or if medication does not help. As with all operations, there are some failures, and complications, such as impotence or incontinence, sometimes occur after the surgery.

Drug rationale

Drugs not included

- **Alfuzosin, doxazosin and terazosin** are not included because they are more expensive than alternatives and there is little evidence of any advantage, in terms of efficacy or adverse effects, over other alpha$_1$-adrenoreceptor antagonists [Barry and Roehrborn, 2001].

Drugs included

- **Prazosin and indoramin** are effective and relatively safe for most men. There is little evidence that any one alpha$_1$-adrenoreceptor antagonist is more effective or better tolerated than another, because there are few comparative studies [Barry and Roehrborn, 2001].
- **Tamsulosin** has an increased selectivity for alpha$_1$-adrenoreceptors. Tamsulosin may be useful in men who

are unable to tolerate the hypotensive effects of less selective $alpha_1$-adrenoreceptor antagonists. However, there is little evidence of clinical advantages; it is more expensive to prescribe than less selective alpha-blockers. **Finasteride** is included for men with a large prostate (weighing more than 40 g) and as an alternative for those who are unable to tolerate the adverse effects of $alpha_1$-adrenoreceptor antagonists.

rescriptions

st choice: alpha-blocker

art prazosin: starter pack (2-week supply)
Age from 40 years onwards
Prazosin starter pack. Follow the instructions given inside this pack; supply 40 tablets; NHS Cost £2.52.

art prazosin: slower titration for elderly (3-week supply)
Age from 40 years onwards
Prazosin 500microgram tablets. Take one tablet at night for 7 nights, then take one tablet twice a day for 7 days, then take two tablets twice a day for 7 days; supply 49 tablets; NHS Cost £1.96.

azosin 2mg twice a day
Age from 40 years onwards
Prazosin 2mg tablets. Take one tablet twice a day; supply 56 tablets; NHS Cost £4.06.

azosin 1mg twice a day
Age from 40 years onwards
Prazosin 1mg tablets. Take one tablet twice a day; supply 56 tablets; NHS Cost £2.82.

doramin 20mg twice a day
Age from 40 years onwards
Indoramin 20mg tablets. Take one tablet twice a day; supply 60 tablets; NHS Cost £12.30.

doramin 20mg at night (elderly people)
Age from 40 years onwards
Indoramin 20mg tablets. Take one tablet at night; supply 30 tablets; NHS Cost £6.15.

lternative IF alpha-blocker not tolerated: amsulosin

msulosin 400micrograms at night
Age from 40 years onwards
Tamsulosin 400microgram caps. Take one capsule at night; supply 30 capsules; NHS Cost £23.90.

lternative for men with large prostate (>40g): nasteride

nasteride 5mg once a day
Age from 40 years onwards
Finasteride 5mg tablets. Take one tablet once a day; supply 28 tablets; NHS Cost £24.90.

xtended Information

ackground information

What is it? p.1571
How common is it? p.1571
How do I know my patient has it? p.1571
What else might it be? p.1572
Complications and prognosis p.1572

hat is it?

Benign prostatic hyperplasia (BPH) is also known as:
- Benign prostatic hypertrophy
- Benign prostatic enlargement
- Benign prostatic obstruction

- **BPH is defined:**
  - **Histologically,** as nodular proliferation of glandular epithelium, stroma and smooth muscle.
  - **Clinically,** as the coexistence of lower urinary tract symptoms (LUTS), bladder outflow obstruction, and benign prostatic enlargement. This is also known as prostatism.
- **Enlargement of the prostate is almost universal in aging men.** The posterior urethra becomes elongated, tortuous and compressed leading to significant chronic obstruction and acute urinary retention in some men. However, symptoms in many men do not worsen, and often improve over time.
- **The pathogenesis of benign prostatic hyperplasia is not well understood.** However possible causes include:
  - Conversion in the prostate of plasma testosterone (from the testes) by 5-alpha reductase to dihydrotestosterone, which promotes prostate growth.
  - Increasing estradiol levels as a result of increasing age. Oestrogens act synergistically with dihydrotestosterone to induce androgen receptors and prostate growth.
  - Activation of alpha-1 adrenoreceptors, which increase bladder neck and prostate smooth muscle tone.

[Barry et al, 1992; Sagalowski and Wilson, 1998; Barry and Roehrborn, 2001]

How common is it?

- Benign prostatic hyperplasia (BPH) affects men over the age of 45 and increases with age.
- Evidence from autopsies suggests that more than 90% of men older than 70 years have BPH.
- The mean age for symptomatic development is about 65 years for American white men and about 60 years for African-American men.

[Sagalowski and Wilson, 1998]

How do I know my patient has it?

Symptoms

- There is no direct relationship between severity of symptoms and size of the prostate. Some men have severe urinary obstruction but minimal enlargement of the prostate, while others have minimal symptoms but very large prostates. Hypertrophy of bladder detrusor muscle may initially compensate for urinary obstruction.
- **Obstructive symptoms include:**
  - Hesitancy in initiating voiding
  - Weak urinary stream, prolonged voiding
  - Post-voiding dribbling
  - Sensation of incomplete emptying
  - Nocturia
  - Overflow incontinence
  - Acute urinary retention
- **Irritative symptoms include:**
  - Dysuria
  - Frequency
  - Urgency
- **Symptoms may be exacerbated by:**
  - Over-the-counter medications (e.g. cold and 'flu remedies, sedating antihistamines), prescribed medications with antimuscarinic effects (e.g. tricyclic antidepressants)
  - Acute ingestion of alcohol
  - Immobility
- The International Prostate Symptom Score (IPSS) allows symptoms to be objectively and reproducibly graded as *mild*, *moderate*, or *severe*. The questionnaire, to be completed by the patient, is available as a patient

information leaflet (PIL) and can be printed out if required.

Signs

- **Digital rectal examination** usually reveals smooth, firm, elastic enlargement of the prostate.

Investigations for benign prostatic hypertrophy

- **Glucose** (blood or urine) to exclude diabetes mellitus.
- **Plasma creatinine** to assess renal function.
- **Urine culture** to exclude urinary tract infection.
- **Serum prostate specific antigen (PSA)** level (for more details see the section, *Prostate specific antigen* below). Men should be counselled prior to testing. Several patient information leaflets (PILs) have been made available for this purpose and can be printed out as required. Patient information on PSA tests can also be obtained from the NHS Prostate Cancer Risk Management Programme (www.cancerscreening.nhs.uk/).
- Investigations by specialist urology services include cystoscopy, urine flow measurements, ultrasound and radiological imaging, and biopsy [Sagalowski and Wilson, 1998; De La Rosette et al, 2001].

[International Consensus Committee, 1993b]

Prostate specific antigen (PSA)

General

- PSA is an enzyme made in the prostate gland and is found in the peripheral circulation in two forms — bound to alpha1-antichymotrypsin and free (non-complexed).
- **PSA is the most sensitive test for detecting early prostate cancer** and can lead to the diagnosis of localised prostate cancer when potentially curative treatment can be offered.
- **PSA values tend to rise with age** and this causes difficulty defining the normal range and knowing when referral and biopsy are indicated.
- **The Prostate Cancer Risk Management Programme** aims to ensure that men who are concerned about the risk of prostate cancer receive clear and balanced information about the advantages and disadvantages of the PSA test and treatment for prostate cancer. Information packs are available at www.cancerscreening.nhs.uk/.

PSA test limitations

- **The PSA test is not diagnostic of prostatic cancer.** Men with an elevated PSA will require a transrectal ultrasound (TRUS) guided prostate biopsy to obtain tissue on which a diagnosis can be made.
- **Conditions such as benign prostatic hyperplasia (BPH), prostatitis and lower urinary tract infection can also cause an elevated PSA.** About two-thirds of men with an elevated PSA do NOT have prostate cancer.
- **Up to 20% of all men with clinically significant prostate cancer will have a normal PSA.**
- PSA testing will lead to the identification of prostate cancers that would not have become clinically evident in the man's lifetime.
- The PSA test cannot differentiate between early-stage aggressive tumours and tumours that are not aggressive.

PSA test practicalities

- **Before having a PSA test the man should *not* have:**
  - An active urinary tract infection
  - Ejaculated in the previous 48 hours
  - Exercised vigorously in the previous 48 hours
  - Had a prostate biopsy in the previous 6 weeks
- **If practical the man should have the PSA test before the digital rectal examination.** If not, it is recommended that the PSA test be delayed for one week.
- The blood sample should reach the laboratory (and be separated) within 16 hours of taking it.

When to perform a PSA test

- **Opportunistic PSA testing is not recommended.**
- There is no good evidence to suggest that the presence lower urinary tract symptoms is predictive of localised prostate cancer.
- **There is no consensus whether men with lower urinary tract symptoms should opt-in or opt-out of PSA testing**
- All men should know they are having a PSA test and be fully counselled of the implications prior to testing.
- The International Consultation on BPH recommends that 'PSA should be tested before "active" treatment of BPH is chosen if the diagnosis of prostate cancer would make a difference in management' [International Consensus Committee, 1993a].

When to refer a raised PSA result

- There is a wide range of practice around the country, with laboratories in some areas using a single cut-off value of 4 nanogram/ml and others providing age-related reference ranges.
- Further work is being done to consider the evidence, with the aim of standardising the test itself and the cut off values used.
- **The NHS Prostate Cancer Risk Management Programme recommends as interim guidance, the following cut-off values for referral:**
  - Age 50–59 years — 3.0 nanogram/ml or more
  - Age 60–69 years — 4.0 nanogram/ml or more
  - Age 70 and over — 5.0 nanogram/ml or more
- A very high PSA value is strongly suggestive of cancer, however the diagnosis is less clear when the PSA is mildly elevated.

[DH, 2002]

What else might it be?

Differential diagnosis includes:

- Adverse effects of drugs causing urine retention such as tricyclic antidepressants, sedating antihistamines, and other antimuscarinics.
- Prostate carcinoma — digital rectal examination may reveal the hard, nodular, and irregular mass typically found with cancer of the prostate; but these features are also found with BPH, focal infarcts, and calculi.
- Urinary tract infection including prostatitis.
- Intra-abdominal mass (e.g. bladder or rectal neoplasm)
- Diabetes mellitus.
- Neurogenic bladder.
- Urethral stricture.

[Sagalowski and Wilson, 1998; De La Rosette et al, 200

Complications and prognosis

Complications

- Acute urine retention — incidence is about 1–2% per year.
- Urinary tract infections including pyelonephritis.
- Chronic urinary retention, hydronephrosis, and renal failure.

Prognosis

- Prognosis of benign prostatic hyperplasia is variable and unpredictable.
- In some men symptoms become progressively worse.
- In others, symptoms remain static or improve over time without treatment.

[Sagalowski and Wilson, 1998; Barry and Roehrborn, 2001; De La Rosette et al, 2001]

lanagement issues

Treatment choices p.1573
ndications for referral p.1574

eatment choices

ndividual preferences should be taken into account vhen making management choices for any condition, ut this is particularly important in benign prostatic yperplasia (BPH):

- The prognosis for symptoms in BPH is variable and unpredictable.
- There are several effective medical and surgical treatments but little evidence of relative harms and benefits.

ffected men need to take into account the impact of heir symptoms and the risks and benefits of each reatment option.

'he suggested stepwise approach to the management of PH is:

- Watchful waiting
- Alpha-blocker
- 5-alpha reductase inhibitor if intolerable adverse effects from alpha-blocker
- Surgical procedure

rry and Roehrborn, 2001; De La Rosette et al, 2001; rray et al, 2001a; Murray et al, 2001b]

atchful waiting

itially, watchful waiting is appropriate for many men ecause, once they are fully informed about the natural istory of benign prostatic hyperplasia, their symptoms ay generate less anxiety and remain tolerable for xtended periods of time.

n one study performed over a period of 3 years, eatment failure occurred in only 17% of men assigned the watchful waiting group compared with treatment ilure in 8% of those assigned to transurethral surgery; lso, only 7% of men in the watchful waiting group equired surgery for treatment failure. (Treatment failure vas defined as any of a number of events, including eath, new symptoms and deterioration in symptoms.)

'he consensus is that watchful waiting is safe for men vith mild-to-moderate symptoms.

Ionitor at least annually by reassessing symptoms, linical examination, and the man's preferences.

asson et al, 1995]

pha-blockers

lpha-blockers are the drug treatment of first choice.

'hey produce small improvements in urinary flow rate nd in the symptom score, which may be maintained for p to 3 years in those who continue to take the drug. here is a lack of published data on effect beyond 3 ears. Symptoms are relieved within a few days, with full ffect by 4–6 weeks. The more severe the symptoms, the reater the absolute reduction in symptom scores.

dverse effects predominantly affect the cardiovascular nd central nervous systems:

- Cardiovascular adverse effects include orthostatic hypotension, dizziness, palpitations, peripheral oedema, and, rarely, angina.
- Central nervous system adverse effects include weakness, tiredness, headache, and somnolence.

or men who have both hypertension and symptomatic enign prostatic hyperplasia, the most appropriate eatment for each individual condition should be used. or example, a man who is coping with his prostatism ould not be offered an alpha-blocker just because he is lso hypertensive. However, if drug treatment for prostatism is to be started, then an alpha-blocker may be preferred.

- **Tamsulosin** may be more selective than other alpha-blockers. Thus, theoretically, it may cause fewer adverse effects such as hypotension. Although there is limited evidence to support this hypothesis, tamsulosin therapy may be considered for men who are unable to tolerate the hypotension caused by other alpha-blockers.

[McConnell, 1994; Coffey, 1998; Suzuki, 1998; Barry and Roehrborn, 2001; De La Rosette et al, 2001]

5-alpha reductase inhibitors (e.g. finasteride)

- Finasteride improves symptoms in benign prostatic hyperplasia, especially in men with prostates weighing more than 40 g (or prostate volume more than 40 ml).
- 5-alpha reductase inhibitors have been advocated as a first-line treatment option for men with larger prostates and those with raised serum prostate specific antigen (PSA) levels.
- The result of PSA measurement should not generally be used to make a decision to prescribe a 5-alpha reductase inhibitor. It has been argued that PSA test results greater than 1.4 nanogram/ml would be an indication for treatment with a 5-alpha reductase inhibitor. Trial evidence of possible benefits of this strategy has not been published and possible benefits are likely to be small — one randomized controlled study, lasting for 4 years, compared finasteride with placebo in men with benign prostatic hyperplasia and found an absolute risk reduction of acute urinary retention of 4% (equivalent to preventing 1 episode of acute urinary retention per year, per hundred men treated for BPH) [McConnell et al, 1998].
- There is limited evidence on the relative efficacy of finasteride compared with alpha-blockers. Two randomized controlled trials of limited quality found that finasteride was less effective in relieving symptoms than the alpha-blockers terazosin and alfuzosin.
- Adverse effects differ from those of alpha-blockers and are milder. Sexual dysfunction such as decreased libido (6%), impotence (8%), and decreased volume of ejaculation (4%), occurs in the first year of treatment. After the first year finasteride and placebo have similar adverse effects.
- It may take several months before there is a noticeable effect on symptoms, but benefits have been reported for up to 6 years after starting treatment.
- PSA test results should be doubled when using a 5-alpha reductase inhibitor as they reduce the serum PSA level by about 50% on average (although there is great variation in individual responses).

[Stoner and The Finasteride Study Group, 1992; Medicines Resource, 1998; Barry and Roehrborn, 2001; De La Rosette et al, 2001;]

Combination therapy: a 5-alpha reductase inhibitor with an alpha-blocker

- Combination therapy with finasteride and an alpha-blocker is more effective than placebo in reducing symptoms. Current limited evidence suggests that combination therapy offers no improvement over an alpha-blocker alone.

[Barry and Roehrborn, 2001]

Herbal preparations

- Popular herbal therapies (phytotherapies) include:
  - Saw palmetto (Serenoa repens) — extracts from fruit of the American dwarf palm
  - Beta sitosterol — plant extracts
  - Rye grass (Secale cereale) — pollen extracts
  - Pygeum africanum — bark extract

- Most studies of herbal preparations suffer from methodological problems such as inadequate outcome measures, no direct comparison with other active treatments, short study periods, non-standard preparations, and little evidence of safety, especially with chronic use.
- Men with milder symptoms may wish to try saw palmetto extract. The evidence for clinical benefit of saw palmetto is limited but better than that for other herbal therapies.

[Ishani et al, 2000; Barry and Roehrborn, 2001; De La Rosette et al, 2001; Wilt et al, 2001a; Wilt et al, 2001b]

Surgical treatments

- **Surgical treatments** are more effective for relieving symptoms, but have higher complication rates compared with drug treatments or watchful waiting.
- A large number of surgical procedures have been developed. The newer procedures tend to be less invasive and have fewer adverse effects than transurethral resection of the prostate (TURP), which has been the standard operation for symptomatic benign prostatic hyperplasia in the UK. However, because the changes in techniques have been rapid and there are few controlled trials, there is little evidence on the relative safety and efficacy of the newer procedures compared with TURP.
- **Surgical procedures include:**
  - Transurethral resection of the prostate (TURP). Complications include retrograde ejaculation (73.4%), impotence (13.6%), urinary incontinence (1%) and death (0.3% mortality at 30 days, 1.7% mortality at 90 days). The average length of stay in hospital is 5 days.
  - Transurethral incision of the prostate (TUIP) is a newer, less invasive technique.
  - Transurethral microwave thermotherapy (TUMT) uses heat generated by a microwave antenna passed through the urethra to coagulate prostate tissue. It can be performed in an outpatient setting.
  - Transurethral needle ablation (TUNA) uses heat generated by radiofrequency energy from two intra-prostatic needles to coagulate the prostate tissue.

Indications for referral

- **The NHS Prostate Cancer Risk Management Programme recommends the following PSA cut-off values for referral:**
  - Age 50–59 years — 3.0 nanogram/ml or more
  - Age 60–69 years — 4.0 nanogram/ml or more
  - Age 70 and over — 5.0 nanogram/ml or more
- The National Institute for Clinical Excellence in *Referral advice: a guide to appropriate referral from general to specialist services* [NICE, 2001] advises the following for urinary tract outflow symptoms ('prostatism') in men. The referral advice is meant to encourage local health communities to discuss referral issues and enable local referral guidelines and protocols to be produced (for further information see **www.nice.org.uk**). Most men with urinary tract 'outflow' symptoms can be managed in primary care. Referral to a specialist is advised if:

Specialist services are in a position to:

- Supplement, where necessary, advice on self-management given in primary care.
- Investigate, establish, or confirm the diagnosis using ultrasound and flow studies, imaging, prostate biopsy, and/or cystoscopy.
- Provide advice on management and undertake medical treatment as necessary.
- Relieve acute urinary retention by catheterization, and then, if appropriate, undertake a trial without a catheter.

Table 2: Referral advice for men with urinary tract outfl symptoms.

Timing	Criteria for referral
****	They develop acute urinary retention
****	They have evidence of acute renal failure
***	They have visible haematuria
***	There is suspicion of prostate cancer — based on the find of a nodular or firm prostate, and/or a raised serum prost specific antigen (PSA) level
***	They have culture-negative dysuria
***	They develop chronic urinary retention with overflow or night-time incontinence.
**	They have recurrent urinary tract infection
**	They develop microscopic haematuria
^	The symptoms have failed to respond to treatment in primary care and are severe enough to affect quality of lif This is best assessed by the man using a symptom scoring system such as the World Health Organization's International Prostate Symptom Score (IPSS)
^	They have evidence of chronic renal failure or renal dama

Key to referral timings. Arrangements should be made so that the man:

- **** is seen immediately (within 1 day)
- *** is seen urgently (maximum wait of 2 weeks recommended but to be agreed locally)
- ** is seen soon (maximum waiting time to be agreed locally)
- * has a routine appointment (maximum waiting time to be agreed locally)
- ^ is seen within an appropriate time depending on clinical circumstances (discretionary)

- Assess the need for, and carry out, minimally invasive surgical interventions.

[McConnell, 1994; NHS CRD, 1995; Medicines Resou 1998; Bandolier, 2001; Barry and Roehrborn, 2001; De Rosette et al, 2001]

References

NHS staff in England can link, free of charge, from references to full text journals by clicking on [Full text] o the PRODIGY website.

1. Bandolier (1995) *Benign prostatic hyperplasia: diagnosis and treatment.* Bandolier. www.jr2.ox.ac. bandolier/band11/b11-3.html [Accessed: 10/01/200
2. Bandolier (2001) *Incision or resection for prostate surgery?* Bandolier. www.jr2.ox.ac.uk/bandolier/ booth/Mens/TUIP.html [Accessed: 28/11/2001].
3. Barry, M.J. and Roehrborn, C.G. (2001) Extracts fr "Clinical Evidence": benign prostatic hyperplasia. *British Medical Journal* 323(7320), 1042–1046. [Fu text]
4. Barry, M.J., Fowler, F.J., Jr., O'Leary, M.P. et al (1992) The American Urological Association sympt index for benign prostatic hyperplasia. The Measurement Committee of the American Urologica Association. *Journal of Urology* **148**(5), 1549–1557
5. Coffey, D.S. (1998) Controversies in the manageme of lower urinary tract symptoms: an overview. *Britis Journal of Urology* **81**(Suppl 1), 1–5.
6. De La Rosette, J.J., Alivizatos, G., Madersbacher, S. al (2001) EAU Guidelines on benign prostatic hyperplasia (BPH). *European Urology* **40**(3), 256–2
7. DH (2002) *Prostate cancer risk management programme: reference booklet.* Department of Healt www.cancerscreening.nhs.uk/prostate/ informationpack.html [Accessed: 01/12/2002].

International Consensus Committee (1993a) The 2nd international conference on benign prostatic hyperplasia 27–30 June, 1993. (Ed.) 553–564.

International Consensus Committee (1993b) The 2nd international conference on benign prostatic hyperplasia 27–30 June, 1993. (Ed.) 276–291.

Ishani, A., MacDonald, R., Nelson, D. et al (2000) Pygeum africanum for the treatment of patients with benign prostatic hyperplasia: a systematic review and quantitative meta-analysis. *American Journal of Medicine* **109**(8), 654–664.

McConnell, J.D. (1994) *Benign prostatic hyperplasia: diagnosis and treatment. Clinical practice guideline.* Rockville, MD: AHCPR.

McConnell, J.D., Bruskewitz, R., Walsh, P. et al (1998) The effect of finasteride on the risk of acute urinary retention and the need for surgical treatment among men with benign prostatic hyperplasia. *New England Journal of Medicine* **338**(9), 557–563. [Full text]

Medicines Resource (1998) Benign prostatic hyperplasia. *Medicines Resource* **49**, 191–194.

Murray, E., Davis, H., Tai, S.S. et al (2001a) Randomised controlled trial of an interactive multimedia decision aid on benign prostatic hypertrophy in primary care. *British Medical Journal* **323**(7311), 493–496. [Full text]

Murray, E., Davis, H., Tai, S.S. et al (2001b) Randomised controlled trial of an interactive multimedia decision aid on hormone replacement therapy in primary. *British Medical Journal* **323**(7311), 490. [Full text]

NHS CRD (1995) Benign prostatic hyperplasia: treatment for lower urinary tract symptoms in older men. *Effective Health Care Bulletin* **2**(2), 2–16.

17. NICE (2001) *Referral advice – a guide to appropriate referral from general to specialist services.* National Institute for Clinical Excellence. www.nice.org.uk [Accessed: 11/08/2002].
18. NICE (2005) *Referral guidelines for suspected cancer – quick reference guide.* Clinical guideline 27. National Institute for Health and Clinical Excellence. www.nice.org.uk [Accessed: 01/07/2005].
19. Sagalowski, A.L. and Wilson, J.D. (1998) Hyperplasia and carcinoma of the prostate. In: Fauci, A.S. and Longo, D. (Eds.) *Harrison's principles of internal medicine.* 14th edn. New York: McGraw-Hill. 1–10.
20. Stoner, E. and The Finasteride Study Group (1992) The clinical effects of 5à-reductase inhibitor, finasteride, on benign prostatic hyperplasia. *Journal of Urology* **147**(5), 1298–1302.
21. Suzuki, H. (1998) Treatment of benign prostatic hyperplasia and hypertension in elderly hypertensive patients. *British Journal of Urology* **81**(1), 51–55.
22. Wasson, J.H., Reda, D.J., Bruskewitz, R.C. et al (1995) A comparison of transurethral surgery with watchful waiting for moderate symptoms of benign prostatic hyperplasia. The Veterans Affairs Cooperative Study Group on transurethral resection of the prostate. *New England Journal of Medicine* 332(2), 75–79.
23. Wilt, T., Ishani, A., Stark, G. et al (2001a) *Serenoa repens for benign prostatic hyperplasia.* The Cochrane Library. Issue 4. Oxford: Update Software. [Accessed: 22/11/2001].
24. Wilt, T., Mac, Donald R., Ishani, A. et al (2001b) *Cernilton for benign prostatic hyperplasia (Cochrane Review).* The Cochrane Library. Issue 4. Chichester, UK: John Wiley & Sons, Ltd. www.nelh.nhs.uk/cochrane.asp [Accessed: 22/11/2001].

P

PRODIGY GUIDANCE

Prostatitis

Last revised in April 2002
At the time of print this topic was being updated. The newly revised guidance will be issued on to the website in late 2005.
www.prodigy.nhs.uk/guidance.asp?gt=Prostatitis

Applies to men over the age of 16 years

This guidance covers the management of acute and chronic bacterial prostatitis, non-bacterial prostatitis, and prostatodynia (chronic pelvic pain syndrome).

This guidance does not cover prostatic abscess or asymptomatic prostatitis.

There is separate PRODIGY guidance for *Prostate — benign hyperplasia, Urinary tract infection (lower) — men*, and *Pyelonephritis — acute.*

Goals

- To reduce symptoms and cure any infection
- To reduce likelihood of complications

Contents

Scenarios

- Acute bacterial prostatitis p.1576
- Chronic bacterial prostatitis p.1578
- Chronic abacterial prostatitis p.1579

Extended Information, p. 1581

Which scenario?

- **Acute bacterial prostatitis:** covers the management of men with acute bacterial prostatitis.
- **Chronic bacterial prostatitis:** covers the management of men with chronic bacterial prostatitis.
- **Chronic abacterial prostatitis:** covers the management of men with chronic abacterial prostatitis (chronic pelvic pain syndrome).

P

Acute bacterial prostatitis

Which therapy?

- **General measures include:**
  - Ample hydration
  - Rest
  - Stool softener
  - Analgesia, e.g. with ibuprofen
- **Empirical antibiotic therapy** should be started immediately after collecting urine for culture.
- Quinolones (e.g. ciprofloxacin, ofloxacin, norfloxacin) produce excellent prostatic penetration and are effective against most urinary organisms.
- Trimethoprim attains high concentrations in prostatic fluid (up to three times serum concentration) and is effective against most urinary pathogens.
- Duration of treatment: expert opinion (mostly reflecting hospital experience) suggests that antibiotics be given for 4 weeks at full dose in order to prevent chronic prostatitis developing.
- Reassess initial antibiotic choice when urine culture results are available.

Practical prescribing points

For further information please see the *Medicines Compendium* (www.medicines.org.uk) or the *British National Formulary* (www.bnf.org).

- **Quinolones** may cause tendon damage (Committee on Safety of Medicines [CSM] advice in BNF). They can induce convulsions in people with epilepsy or in those with conditions that predispose to seizures. People concurrently taking nonsteroidal anti-inflammatory drugs (NSAIDs) may also be susceptible.
- **Trimethoprim** may rarely cause blood dyscrasias and skin disorders.
- **Ibuprofen** use is associated with an increased risk of gastrointestinal haemorrhage. Avoid if there is a histo[ry] of peptic ulceration. May worsen asthma, hypertensio[n,] renal impairment, or cardiac failure.

Follow-up advice

- **When urine culture results are available,** check the sensitivities of organism to the initial antibacterial age[nt] and, if necessary, change the prescription.
- **Reassess** the person after 7–14 days therapy.
- **Continue antibiotics** for a complete course of 4–6 wee[ks]
- **When well,** people should be referred for imaging stu[dies] to exclude a structural cause for their urinary tract infection.

Should I refer or investigate?

Refer?

Referral criteria and purposes are detailed in Table 1:

Investigate?

- **Urine culture and sensitivity** usually identifies the caus[ative] pathogen and identifies the appropriate antibacterial. Repeating culture after completion of treatment helps ensure that infection has resolved.
  - Note: prostatic massage is painful, may lead to bacteraemia and sepsis, and does not significantly a[dd] to information from the urine culture. It should therefore not be performed.
- **Transrectal ultrasound examination** helps to diagnose and localize a suspected prostatic abscess.
- **Investigations for sexually transmitted diseases** (including urethral swab and culture for chlamydia) o[r] referral for investigation by a genito-urinary clinic should be considered, particularly for those men at highest risk (in terms of age and sexual habits).

Patient information leaflets

The following PILs are available at www.prodigy.nhs.u[k]

- Biopsy
- Pelvic Pain Syndrome (Chronic)
- Prostate Help Association

ble 1: Referral criteria for men with acute prostatitis.

teria for referral	Purpose of referral
xic, severely ill able to tolerate oral therapy :eriorating on oral therapy	Admission for parenteral antibiotics
dequate response to ibacterials	Transrectal ultrasound examination or computerized tomography (CT) scan of prostate to look for prostatic abscess which would need surgical drainage
-existing urologic conditions ;. obstruction, indwelling heter) ronic urinary irritative nptoms nunocompromised	Specialist urology management
ıte urinary retention	The bladder should be catheterized by the suprapubic route since insertion of a urethral catheter may damage the prostate
ematuria omplete response to ibacterials	Imaging of urinary tract
ll	Imaging studies to exclude a structural cause for urinary tract infection
statitis associated with ually transmitted disease D)	Genito-urinary medicine service for treatment, screening for other STDs, safe sex counselling, and partner notification

'rostate Research Campaign UK
'rostatitis (Acute Infective)

ıared decision making

- Acute (sudden onset) prostate infection is usually caused by the same bacteria (germs) that cause urine infections.
- **Antibiotics** for 4–6 weeks are needed to treat a prostate nfection.
- **A urine sample** often shows which bacterium is causing he infection and the best antibiotic to use. You may eed to change the antibiotic when the result of the test s back (2–3 days).
- **'aracetamol or ibuprofen** ease pain and fever (high emperature). They are best taken regularly rather than now and then'.
- **.axatives** to keep your stools (faeces) soft may help ease pain if you have hard stools in your rectum (back passage) pressing on your infected prostate.
- **Tests** (X-rays etc.) may be advised when you are well again, to see if you have any problem with your urinary ract.

rug rationale

ugs not included

- **Quinolones: nalidixic acid and levofloxacin:** nalidixic cid has a similar antimicrobial spectrum and adverse ffect profile to the newer quinolones but requires more requent dosing. Levofloxacin has similar effects to other uinolones but remains under the surveillance of the Committee on Safety of Medicines (CSM) black triangle cheme.
- **'enicillin-group agents such as amoxicillin** are unsuitable or therapy without culture results as there is a high ncidence of resistance among urinary tract pathogens. About 50% of urinary tract pathogens are amoxicillin-esistant.
- **Nitrofurantoin** does not achieve high enough tissue concentrations to be effective.
- **First-generation cephalosporins:** the incidence of resistance to the first-generation cephalosporins is increasing in bacteria that cause urinary tract infections. They are thus unsuitable for empirically treating prostatitis. Second-generation agents are not very well absorbed orally and are relatively expensive. Cefotaxime and other third-generation agents are effective. They may be administered to initiate treatment in secondary care.
- **Co-amoxiclav** is best reserved for use as an alternative agent where sensitivities are known. It is unclear how well it penetrates the prostatic tissue.
- **Co-trimoxazole** is restricted by CSM recommendation and should only be used if there is good bacteriological evidence of sensitivity, and sufficient reason to prefer it to other antibiotics.
- **Erythromycin and other macrolides** have poor cover against Gram-negative organisms and are unsuitable as empirical therapy. They may be suitable if the organism is shown to be sensitive, and have been used in chronic prostatitis.
- **Tetracyclines** have no activity against *Pseudomonas aeruginosa* and unreliable activity against coagulase-negative staphylococci, *Escherichia coli*, other Enterobacteriaceae, and enterococci. They are unsuitable for empirical therapy of acute prostatitis, although some of these agents such as doxycycline and minocycline have been used in the chronic condition. They may be suitable for a minority of people if the organism is shown to be sensitive.
- **Laxatives other than docusate and lactulose:** bulk-forming agents are not suitable for acute relief as they take several days to exert an effect; stimulant agents will not soften the stool to ease defecation; co-danthrusate has limited prescribing indications and liquid paraffin is not recommended. Enemas and rectal preparations are not included as they may exacerbate symptoms of pain and discomfort.

Drugs included

- **Quinolones: ciprofloxacin, norfloxacin, and ofloxacin** achieve high prostatic concentrations and are effective against most typical and atypical pathogens and *Pseudomonas aeruginosa*.
- **Trimethoprim** achieves high prostatic concentrations and is effective against many of the pathogens that cause prostatitis. It is safe in most people, inexpensive, and a suitable alternative agent pending culture results if quinolones are inappropriate.
- **Paracetamol:** this is an effective first-line choice for pain relief, especially when taken at regular intervals, rather than 'as required'.
- **Low-dose ibuprofen:** this may be used at an analgesic dosage and should be taken at regular dose intervals.
- **Stool softeners: docusate and lactulose** may be useful for some people to avoid painful defecation. Lactulose may take 1–3 days to exert an effect and must be taken regularly rather than 'as required'.

Prescriptions

1st-line empirical therapy: quinolone antibiotic for 4 weeks

Norfloxacin 400mg twice a day

- Age from 16 years onwards
- Norfloxacin 400mg tablets. Take one tablet twice a day for 28 days; supply 56 tablets; NHS Cost £20.44.

Ciprofloxacin 500mg twice a day

- Age from 16 years onwards
- Ciprofloxacin 500mg tablets. Take one tablet twice a day for 28 days; supply 56 tablets; NHS Cost £79.52.

Ofloxacin 200mg twice a day

- Age from 16 years onwards
- Ofloxacin 200mg tablets. Take one tablet twice a day for 28 days; supply 56 tablets; NHS Cost £57.40.

Alternative 1st-line therapy: trimethoprim for 4 weeks

Trimethoprim 200mg twice a day

- Age from 16 years onwards
- Trimethoprim 200mg tablets. Take one tablet twice a day for 28 days; supply 56 tablets; NHS Cost £2.68.

Analgesia: use when required

Paracetamol 1g up to four times a day

- Age from 16 years onwards
- Paracetamol 500mg tablets. Take two tablets every 4 to 6 hours when required for pain relief. Maximum of 8 tablets in 24 hours; supply 100 tablets; NHS Cost £0.75; OTC Cost £1.50.

Ibuprofen 400mg three times a day

- Age from 16 years onwards
- Ibuprofen 400mg tablets. Take one tablet three times a day when required for pain relief. Do not exceed the stated dose; supply 84 tablets; NHS Cost £2.46.

Stool softeners

Docusate capsules: 100mg to 200mg once or twice a day

- Age from 16 years onwards
- Docusate 100mg capsules. Take one to two capsules once or twice a day when required; supply 30 capsules; NHS Cost £1.75.

Lactulose solution: 15ml twice a day

- Age from 16 years onwards
- Lactulose 3.35g/5ml solution. Take three 5ml spoonfuls twice a day; supply 200 ml; NHS Cost £1.01.

Chronic bacterial prostatitis

Which therapy?

- **General advice to be given to people:** Explain the strategy for treatment and long-term implications for their health. Reinforce explanations with written information, for example the patient information leaflet (PIL) for chronic bacterial prostatitis.
- **Analgesia:**
  - Relieve pain with ibuprofen or paracetamol
- **Antibiotic** treatment should be chosen according to culture sensitivity tests and ability of the antibiotic to penetrate prostatic tissue (which is not acutely inflamed).
  - **First-line therapy** is with a quinolone (e.g. ciprofloxacin, ofloxacin, norfloxacin)
  - Alternatives in the case of intolerance to quinolones include trimethoprim
  - Duration of antibiotic treatment: expert opinion suggests that antibiotics be given for at least 4 weeks
- One small trial suggests that an alpha$_1$-adrenoceptor blocker added to antibiotic therapy may improve symptoms and reduce recurrence of bacterial prostatitis.

Practical prescribing points

For further information please see the *Medicines Compendium* (www.medicines.org.uk) or the *British National Formulary* (www.bnf.org).

- **Quinolones** may cause tendon damage (Committee on Safety of Medicines [CSM] advice in BNF). They can induce convulsions in people with epilepsy or in those with conditions that predispose to seizures. People concurrently taking nonsteroidal anti-inflammatory drugs (NSAIDs) may also be susceptible.
- **Trimethoprim** may rarely cause blood dyscrasias and skin disorders.
- **Ibuprofen** use is associated with an increased risk of gastrointestinal haemorrhage. Avoid if there is a histo of peptic ulceration. May worsen asthma, hypertensio renal impairment, or cardiac failure.

Follow-up advice

- Repeat culture of prostatic urine on completion of antibacterial course to ensure that infection has resolv ('Prostatic urine' is a sample of urine taken after the prostate has been massaged and should contain prost secretions.)

Should I refer or investigate?

Refer?

- **Referral guidelines for suspected cancer** published by t National Institute for Health and Clinical Excellence (NICE) [NICE, 2005] recommend urgent referral to a team specialising in the management of urological cancer, depending on local arrangements, for people:
  - Of any age with painless macroscopic haematuria.
  - Aged 40 years or older who present with recurrent persistent urinary tract infection associated with haematuria.
  - Aged 50 years or older who are found to have unexplained microscopic haematuria.
  - With an abdominal mass identified clinically or on imaging that is thought to arise from the urinary tra
  - Who have macroscopic haematuria and symptoms suggestive of a urinary tract infection *if* infection is confirmed.

Investigate?

- Urine culture and sensitivity after prostatic massage usually identifies the causal pathogen and identifies th appropriate antibacterial.
- Repeating prostatic urine culture after completion of treatment helps to ensure that infection has resolved.

Patient information leaflets

The following PILs are available at www.prodigy.nhs.u

- Biopsy
- Pelvic Pain Syndrome (Chronic)
- Prostate Help Association
- Prostate Research Campaign UK
- Prostatitis (Acute Infective)

Shared decision making

- Chronic (ongoing) prostate infection is usually caused the same bacteria (germs) that cause urine infections. Sexually transmitted infection is sometimes the cause.
- **Antibiotics** for 4–6 weeks are needed to treat a prosta infection.
- **A urine sample** taken after your prostate is massaged often shows which bacterium is causing the infection the best antibiotic to use. You may need to change th antibiotic when the result of the test is back (2–3 days
- **Paracetamol or ibuprofen** ease pain. They are best tak regularly rather than 'now and then'.

Laxatives to keep your stools (faeces) soft may help ease pain if you have hard stools in your rectum (back passage) pressing on your infected prostate.
A repeat urine sample is needed after you finish the course of antibiotics to check that the infection has gone.

)rug rationale

rugs not included

Quinolones: nalidixic acid and levofloxacin: nalidixic acid has a similar antimicrobial spectrum and adverse effect profile to the newer quinolones but requires more frequent dosing. Levofloxacin has similar effects to other quinolones but remains under the surveillance of the Committee on Safety of Medicines (CSM) black triangle scheme.
Penicillin-group agents such as amoxicillin are unsuitable for therapy without culture results as there is a high incidence of resistance among urinary tract pathogens. About 50% of urinary tract pathogens are amoxicillin-resistant.
Nitrofurantoin does not achieve high enough tissue concentrations to be effective.
First-generation cephalosporins: there is an increasing incidence of resistance among bacteria causing urinary tract infection to the first-generation agents, making them an unsuitable choice as an empirical therapy for prostatitis. Second-generation agents are not very well absorbed orally and are relatively expensive. Cefotaxime and other third-generation agents are effective; they may be administered to initiate treatment in secondary care.
Co-amoxiclav is best reserved as an alternative agent where sensitivities are known. It is unclear how well it penetrates the prostatic tissue.
Co-trimoxazole is restricted by CSM recommendation and should only be used if there is good bacteriological evidence of sensitivity and reason to prefer it to another therapy.
Erythromycin and other macrolides have poor cover against Gram-negative organisms and are unsuitable as empirical therapy. They may be suitable if the organism is shown to be sensitive, and have been used in chronic prostatitis.
Tetracyclines have no activity against *Pseudomonas aeruginosa* and unreliable activity against coagulase-negative staphylococci, *Escherichia coli*, other Enterobacteriaceae, and enterococci. They are unsuitable for empirical therapy of acute prostatitis, although some of these agents such as doxycycline and minocycline have been used in the chronic condition. They may be suitable for a minority of people if the organism is shown to be sensitive.
Laxatives other than docusate and lactulose: bulk-forming agents are not suitable for acute relief as they take several days to exert an effect; stimulant agents will not soften the stool to ease defecation; co-danthrusate has limited prescribing indications and liquid paraffin is not recommended. Enemas and rectal preparations are not included as they may exacerbate symptoms of pain and discomfort.
Alpha$_1$-adrenoceptor blockers may relieve symptoms and reduce the rate of recurrence but there is insufficient evidence to recommend them as standard treatment.

rugs included

Quinolones: ciprofloxacin, norfloxacin, and ofloxacin achieve high prostatic concentrations and are effective against most typical and atypical pathogens and *Pseudomonas aeruginosa*.

- **Trimethoprim** achieves high prostatic concentrations and is effective against many of the pathogens that cause prostatitis. It is safe in most people, inexpensive, and a suitable alternative agent pending culture results if quinolones are inappropriate.
- **Paracetamol:** this is an effective first-line choice for pain relief, especially when taken at regular intervals, rather than 'as required'.
- **Low-dose ibuprofen:** this may be used at an analgesic dose and should be taken at regular dose intervals.
- **Stool softeners: docusate and lactulose** may be useful for some people to avoid painful defecation. Lactulose may take 1–3 days to exert an effect and must be taken regularly rather than 'as required'.

Prescriptions

1st-line empirical therapy: quinolone antibiotic for 4 weeks

Norfloxacin 400mg twice a day
- Age from 16 years onwards
- Norfloxacin 400mg tablets. Take one tablet twice a day for 28 days; supply 56 tablets; NHS Cost £20.44.

Ciprofloxacin 500mg twice a day
- Age from 16 years onwards
- Ciprofloxacin 500mg tablets. Take one tablet twice a day for 28 days; supply 56 tablets; NHS Cost £79.52.

Ofloxacin 200mg twice a day
- Age from 16 years onwards
- Ofloxacin 200mg tablets. Take one tablet twice a day for 28 days; supply 56 tablets; NHS Cost £57.40.

Alternative 1st-line therapy: trimethoprim for 4 weeks

Trimethoprim 200mg twice a day
- Age from 16 years onwards
- Trimethoprim 200mg tablets. Take one tablet twice a day for 28 days; supply 56 tablets; NHS Cost £2.68.

Analgesia: use when required

Paracetamol 1g up to four times a day
- Age from 16 years onwards
- Paracetamol 500mg tablets. Take two tablets every 4 to 6 hours when required for pain relief. Maximum of 8 tablets in 24 hours; supply 100 tablets; NHS Cost £0.75; OTC Cost £1.50.

Ibuprofen 400mg three times a day
- Age from 16 years onwards
- Ibuprofen 400mg tablets. Take one tablet three times a day when required for pain relief. Do not exceed the stated dose; supply 84 tablets; NHS Cost £2.46.

Stool softeners

Docusate capsules: 100mg to 200mg once or twice a day
- Age from 16 years onwards
- Docusate 100mg capsules. Take one to two capsules once or twice a day when required; supply 30 capsules; NHS Cost £1.75.

Lactulose solution: 15ml twice a day
- Age from 16 years onwards
- Lactulose 3.35g/5ml solution. Take three 5ml spoonfuls twice a day; supply 200 ml; NHS Cost £1.01.

Chronic abacterial prostatitis

Which therapy?

- **General advice to be given to people:** explain the strategy for treatment and long-term implications for their health.

Reinforce explanations with written information, e.g. the patient information leaflet (PIL) for chronic abacterial prostatitis.

- **No therapy has proven benefit** in chronic pelvic pain syndrome (CPPS). However, the following may be tried:
  - **Analgesia:** a trial of pain relief with a nonsteroidal anti-inflammatory drug (NSAID) or paracetamol is usually warranted.
  - **Trial of antibiotics:** despite negative cultures and absence of evidence of efficacy, most clinicians would initially offer antibiotic treatment as for chronic bacterial prostatitis, i.e. 4 weeks of a quinolone or trimethoprim.
  - Alpha$_1$-adrenoceptor blockers.
- **Popular therapies which require further study** because evidence on effectiveness and harms is lacking include:
  - **Bioflavinoids,** e.g. quercetin
  - **Allopurinol**
  - **Cernilton** (pollen extract)
  - **Prostatic ablation**
  - **Stress management,** e.g. pharmacological anxiolytics, psychological stress management techniques such as biofeedback, and relaxation therapies for the pelvic musculature

Practical prescribing points

For further information, please see the *Medicines Compendium* (www.medicines.org.uk) or the *British National Formulary* (www.bnf.org).

- **Quinolones** may cause tendon damage (Committee on Safety of Medicines [CSM] advice in BNF). They can induce convulsions in people with epilepsy or in those with conditions that predispose to seizures. People concurrently taking nonsteroidal anti-inflammatory drugs (NSAIDs) may also be susceptible.
- **Trimethoprim** may rarely cause blood dyscrasias and skin disorders.
- **Ibuprofen** use is associated with an increased risk of gastrointestinal haemorrhage. Avoid if there is a history of peptic ulceration. May worsen asthma, hypertension, renal impairment, or cardiac failure.
- **Alpha-blockers:** can cause postural hypotension and first-dose hypotension. Alfuzosin should be initiated carefully to patients being treated with antihypertensives. Blood pressure should be monitored regularly, especially at the beginning of treatment. In patients with coronary insufficiency specific anti-anginal therapy should be continued, but if the angina reappears or worsens alfuzosin should be discontinued.

Should I refer or investigate?

Refer?

- **Referral guidelines for suspected cancer** published by the National Institute for Health and Clinical Excellence (NICE) [NICE, 2005] recommend urgent referral to a team specialising in the management of urological cancer, depending on local arrangements, for people:
  - Of any age with painless macroscopic haematuria.
  - Aged 40 years or older who present with recurrent or persistent urinary tract infection associated with haematuria.
  - Aged 50 years or older who are found to have unexplained microscopic haematuria.
  - With an abdominal mass identified clinically or on imaging that is thought to arise from the urinary tract.
  - Who have macroscopic haematuria and symptoms suggestive of a urinary tract infection *if* infection is not confirmed.

Investigate?

- **Urine culture after prostatic massage** distinguishes between chronic abacterial prostatitis and chronic bacterial prostatitis.

Patient information leaflets

The following PILs are available at www.prodigy.nhs.uk

- Biopsy
- Pelvic Pain Syndrome (Chronic)
- Prostate Help Association
- Prostate Research Campaign UK

Shared decision making

- The cause of chronic (ongoing) pelvic pain syndrome is not known. The source of the pain is probably your prostate gland but it is not clear why it is causing pain.
- **Antibiotics** for 4–6 weeks may help even though no bacteria have been found. Unknown bacteria or a 'low-grade' infection that cannot be identified may cause son cases. Antibiotics also have an anti-inflammatory actior that may help.
- **Paracetamol or ibuprofen** ease pain. They are best take regularly rather than 'now and then'.
- **Alpha-blocker medication** may ease pain. Several brand are available. There is only limited evidence that they help but one may be worth a trial for 4 weeks. They ma work by relaxing the muscle in the prostate and base of the bladder.
- **Symptoms tend to come and go.** Referral to a specialist an option if symptoms do not improve.

Drug rationale

Drugs not included

- **Finasteride** has demonstrated a reduction in prostate volume but not pain associated with chronic abacterial prostatitis.
- **Allopurinol** has demonstrated a reduction in urate concentrations in expressed prostatic secretions but it is not clear if this directly relates to symptom relief.
- **Laxatives other than docusate and lactulose:** bulk-forming agents are not suitable for acute relief as they take several days to exert an effect; stimulant agents wi not soften the stool to ease defecation; co-danthrusate has limited prescribing indications and liquid paraffin is not recommended. Enemas and rectal preparations are not included as they may exacerbate symptoms of pain and discomfort.

[Bjerklund Johansen et al, 1998]

Drugs included

- **Paracetamol:** this is an effective first-line choice for pain relief, especially when taken at regular intervals, rather than on an 'as required' basis.
- **Low-dose ibuprofen:** this may be used at an analgesic dose and should be taken at regular dose intervals.
- There is no evidence that antibiotics are effective for chronic pelvic pain syndrome (CPPS) but treatment for month with a quinolone or trimethoprim may sometim be useful.
- **Quinolones (ciprofloxacin, norfloxacin, and ofloxacin)** achieve high prostatic concentrations and are effective against most typical and atypical pathogens and *Pseudomonas aeruginosa*. A trial of antibacterial thera may be appropriate despite negative cultures and absence of evidence of efficacy.

Trimethoprim achieves high prostatic concentrations and is effective against many of the pathogens that cause prostatitis. It is safe in most people, inexpensive, and a suitable alternative agent pending culture results if quinolones are inappropriate.

Alpha$_1$ adrenoceptor blockers: there is insufficient evidence to recommend them as standard treatment, but a trial of therapy for 4 weeks may sometimes be useful.

Stool softeners: docusate and lactulose may be useful for some people to avoid painful defecation. Lactulose may take 1–3 days to exert an effect and must be taken regularly rather than 'as required'.

Prescriptions

Analgesia: use when required

Paracetamol 1g up to four times a day

Age from 16 years onwards

Paracetamol 500mg tablets. Take two tablets every 4 to 6 hours when required for pain relief. Maximum of 8 tablets in 24 hours; supply 100 tablets; NHS Cost £0.75; OTC Cost £1.50.

Ibuprofen 400mg three times a day

Age from 16 years onwards

Ibuprofen 400mg tablets. Take one tablet three times a day when required for pain relief. Do not exceed the stated dose; supply 84 tablets; NHS Cost £2.46.

Stool softeners

Docusate capsules: 100mg to 200mg once or twice a day

Age from 16 years onwards

Docusate 100mg capsules. Take one to two capsules once or twice a day when required; supply 30 capsules; NHS Cost £1.75.

Lactulose solution: 15ml twice a day

Age from 16 years onwards

Lactulose 3.35g/5ml solution. Take three 5ml spoonfuls twice a day; supply 200 ml; NHS Cost £1.01.

Alpha-blocker: trial of therapy

Alfuzosin 2.5mg once a day

Age from 16 years onwards

Alfuzosin 2.5mg tablets. Take one tablet once a day; supply 28 tablets; NHS Cost £8.86.

4-week trial of antibiotic therapy: quinolones

Norfloxacin 400mg twice a day

Age from 16 years onwards

Norfloxacin 400mg tablets. Take one tablet twice a day for 28 days; supply 56 tablets; NHS Cost £20.44.

Ciprofloxacin 500mg twice a day

Age from 16 years onwards

Ciprofloxacin 500mg tablets. Take one tablet twice a day for 28 days; supply 56 tablets; NHS Cost £79.52.

Ofloxacin 200mg twice a day

Age from 16 years onwards

Ofloxacin 200mg tablets. Take one tablet twice a day for 28 days; supply 56 tablets; NHS Cost £57.40.

4-week trial of antibiotic therapy: trimethoprim

Trimethoprim 200mg twice a day

Age from 16 years onwards

Trimethoprim 200mg tablets. Take one tablet twice a day for 28 days; supply 56 tablets; NHS Cost £2.68.

Extended Information

Background information

- What is it? p.1581
- How common is it? p.1582
- How do I know my patient has it? p.1582
- What else might it be? p.1583
- Complications and prognosis p.1583

What is it?

Classification of the prostatitis conditions has changed in recent years. The National Institutes of Health (NIH) consensus statements of 1995 and 1998 designate four categories of prostatitis. These are listed below, with the older terms in parenthesis when different:

- Acute bacterial prostatitis
- Chronic bacterial prostatitis
- Chronic abacterial prostatitis/chronic pelvic pain syndrome:
  - Inflammatory (non-bacterial prostatitis)
  - Non-inflammatory (prostatodynia)
- Asymptomatic inflammatory prostatitis

[McNaughton Collins et al, 2000]

Acute bacterial prostatitis

- **Acute inflammation of the prostate gland** due to bacterial infection with urinary pathogens
- **Pathogens** include (in approximately decreasing order of prevalence):
  - Gram-negative organisms, e.g. *Escherichia coli*, *Proteus* species, *Klebsiella* species, and *Pseudomonas aeruginosa*
  - Enterococci such as *Streptococcus faecalis*
  - *Staphylococcus aureus*
  - Anaerobes such as *Bacteroides* species
- **Acute prostatitis is associated with urinary tract infection.** Occasionally there may be associated epididymitis or urethritis.
- Acute prostatitis may follow urethral instrumentation, trauma, bladder outflow obstruction, or dissemination of infection elsewhere in the body.

[CEG, 2001]

Chronic bacterial prostatitis

- **Chronic or recurrent infection of the prostate for at least 6 months** — but in practice the diagnosis is made earlier.
- Culture of prostatic secretions or urine after prostatic massage reveals pathogens, but urine before prostatic massage yields no pathogens on culture.
- Pathogens are similar to those causing acute bacterial prostatitis:
  - Gram-negative organisms (most common) e.g. *Escherichia coli*, *Klebsiella* species, *Proteus* species, and *Pseudomonas aeruginosa*
  - Enterococci such as *Streptococcus faecalis*
  - Staphylococci, *Trichomonas vaginalis*, *Neisseria gonorrhoeae*, genital viruses, and fungi have been implicated as rare causes
- Organisms whose pathogenicity is debated include *Chlamydia trachomatis*, ureaplasma, mycobacteria, coagulase-negative staphylococci, non-group D streptococci, and diphtheroids.
- The health status impact of chronic bacterial prostatitis is similar to that of myocardial infarction, angina, and Crohn's disease.

[McNaughton Collins et al, 2000; CEG, 2001; McNaughton Collins et al, 2001]

Chronic pelvic pain syndrome (abacterial prostatitis)

- **Pelvic discomfort** for more than 6 months — but in practice the diagnosis is made earlier.
- **Cultures of urine and prostatic fluid grow no pathogens.**
- **Leucocytes present** in expressed prostatic fluid, semen, or urine after prostatic massage.
- **The cause of chronic pelvic pain syndrome (CPPS) is unknown.** Many theories have been propounded, including infection with an organism that has not yet been identified, immune reaction to a persistent antigen from an organism or from a urinary constituent, pelvic sympathetic nervous system dysfunction, interstitial cystitis, prostatic cysts and calculi, and mechanical events causing retention of prostatic fluid.
- The National Institutes of Health (NIH) classification distinguishes between inflammatory and non-inflammatory variants of CPPS if leucocytes are present in or absent from expressed prostatic fluid, semen, or urine after prostatic massage.
- Inflammatory CPPS and non-inflammatory CPPS (prostatodynia) may be variants of the same condition.
- There is no 'gold-standard' diagnostic test for chronic abacterial prostatitis.
- The health status impact of CPPS is similar to that of myocardial infarction, angina, and Crohn's disease.

[McNaughton Collins et al, 2000; CEG, 2001; McNaughton Collins et al, 2001]

Asymptomatic inflammatory prostatitis

- **No symptoms associated** with prostatitis
- **Leucocytes** are found in prostate tissue or secretions (usually discovered during the evaluation of other conditions)

[CEG, 2001]

How common is it?

- Prostatitis affects men of all ages.
- Prostatitis (all types) is the most common genito-urinary disease in men aged 18–50 years and is the third most common urologic diagnosis in men aged over 50 years.
- As many as 50% of men will have at least one episode of prostatitis during their life.
- The relative frequencies of the symptomatic prostatitis conditions are about:
  - 5% bacterial prostatitis (acute is rarer than chronic bacterial prostatitis)
  - 95% abacterial chronic prostatitis
    - 30% non-inflammatory chronic pelvic pain syndrome
    - 65% inflammatory chronic pelvic pain syndrome
- About 6% of autopsies on men reveal histological prostatitis.

[McNaughton Collins et al, 2000]

How do I know my patient has it?

Acute bacterial prostatitis

- **Symptoms:**
  - Sudden onset
  - Fever, rigors, arthralgia, myalgia
  - Dysuria, frequency, urgency, haematuria
  - Severe pain in the prostate, perineal region, rectum, lower back, tenesmus
- **Signs:**
  - Pyrexia, tachycardia
  - Prostate on digital rectal examination is exquisitely tender, swollen, tense or boggy, warm, smooth
  - Inguinal lymphadenopathy
  - Urethral discharge
- **Tests and investigations:**
  - Urine culture usually shows heavy growth with a urinary pathogen.
  - Note: prostatic secretions are *not* obtained for culture because this is painful, may cause bacteraemia, and would not add to information provided by the urine culture.

[CEG, 2001]

Chronic bacterial prostatitis

- **Symptoms:**
  - Present for more than 3 months
  - Relapsing, subacute, variable
  - Chronic pelvic (perineal, testicular, penile, lower abdominal, ejaculatory) pains are the most prominent symptoms
  - Mild urinary irritation (frequency, hesitancy, urgency, dysuria, poor stream)
  - Fatigue, abdominal pain, arthralgia, myalgia, pain at other locations
- **Signs:**
  - Prostate on digital rectal examination may be normal or may be tender or swollen
- **Tests and investigations:**
  - Urine culture — often positive for urinary pathogen
  - Culture of prostatic secretions or urine after prostatic massage — positive for pathogen
  - The research standard for culture (impractical in routine primary care) is:
    - No antibiotics for at least 1 month
    - No ejaculation for at least 2 days
    - Full but not distended bladder
    - No urethritis and no urinary tract infection
    - Careful collection of expressed prostatic secretions and three urine samples (avoiding possibility of contamination from foreskin) to investigate urine in urethra and in bladder before and after prostatic massage
  - Prostate specific antigen (PSA) test is not used to diagnose prostatitis. Because it can be raised in the presence of prostatitis, PSA is not helpful in distinguishing between prostatitis and prostatic cancer.

[Bjerklund Johansen et al, 1998; McNaughton Collins et al, 2000; CEG, 2001]

Chronic abacterial prostatitis (chronic pelvic pain syndrome)

- **Symptoms:**
  - Present for more than 3 months
  - Relapsing, subacute, variable
  - Chronic pelvic (perineal, testicular, penile, lower abdominal, ejaculatory) pains are the most prominent symptoms
  - Mild urinary irritation (frequency, hesitancy, urgency, dysuria, poor stream)
  - Fatigue, abdominal pain, arthralgia, myalgia, pain at other locations
- **Signs:**
  - Prostate is usually normal on digital rectal examination
- **Tests and investigations:**
  - No pathogens found in urine, prostatic secretions, or urine after prostatic massage
  - Leucocytes in urine, prostatic secretions, or urine after prostatic massage distinguish inflammatory from non-inflammatory CPPS
  - There is no 'gold-standard' diagnostic test
  - Prostate specific antigen (PSA) test is not used to diagnose prostatitis. PSA is not helpful in distinguishing between prostatitis and prostatic cancer

because it tends to be raised in the presence of prostatitis

[Bjerklund Johansen et al, 1998; McNaughton Collins et al, 2000; CEG, 2001]

What else might it be?

Sexually transmitted disease
Prostate abscess, diverticulitis, urinary tract infection
Urethritis, epididymo-orchitis, epididymitis
Obstructive calculus in the urinary tract, foreign body
Benign prostatic hypertrophy
Prostate cancer

Complications and prognosis

Acute bacterial prostatitis

Complications

Complications that may arise include:

- Progression to chronic prostatitis — more likely if antibiotics are taken for short periods (i.e. less than 4 weeks)
- Urinary retention secondary to prostatic oedema
- Septicaemia, pyelonephritis, epididymitis, and prostatic abscess — immunocompromised people are most at risk
- Infertility

Prognosis

Cure is likely in most men.

Chronic prostatitis (bacterial and abacterial)

Prognosis

Chronic prostatitis is difficult to manage and tends to relapse over long periods of time.

The prognosis is more favourable in bacterial than in abacterial chronic prostatitis.

[CEG, 2001]

Management issues

Acute bacterial prostatitis p.1583
Chronic bacterial prostatitis p.1583
Chronic abacterial prostatitis, chronic pelvic pain syndrome (CPPS) p.1584

Acute bacterial prostatitis

Diagnosis should be made on urine culture.

Prostatic massage should not be performed as this would be painful, might result in bacteraemia, and would be unlikely to add to information provided by urine culture.

General measures include:

- Ample hydration
- Rest
- Stool softener
- Analgesia

Empirical antibiotic therapy should be started immediately after collecting urine for culture, because acute prostatitis is a serious and severe illness.

The initial antibiotic choice should be reassessed when urine culture results are available.

Acute inflammation allows antibiotics to penetrate into the prostate.

Quinolones produce excellent prostatic penetration and are effective against the majority of urinary organisms.

Trimethoprim attains high concentrations in prostatic fluid (up to three times serum concentration) [Schaeffer, 1990; Meares, 1991] and is effective against most urinary pathogens. Trimethoprim would be first-line oral therapy for people intolerant of or allergic to quinolones.

- Erythromycin and azithromycin attain good concentrations in the prostatic fluid and are effective against Gram-positive organisms. They would only be used for acute prostatitis if indicated by culture, as they are ineffective against the more common Gram-negative organisms.
- Aminoglycosides such as gentamicin would be used intravenously in secondary care in combination with another drug such as a cephalosporin or a quinolone.
- Duration of treatment: there is a lack of trial evidence in primary care on the recommended duration of treatment with antibacterials for acute prostatitis. Expert opinion (mostly reflecting hospital experience) suggests that antibacterials be given for 4 weeks at full dose in order to prevent chronic prostatitis developing.
- Referral criteria and purposes are detailed in Table 2.

[Childs, 1991; Meares, 1991; Leigh, 1993; BNF 41, 2001; CEG, 2001]

Chronic bacterial prostatitis

- **General advice** for people with chronic bacterial prostatitis: the strategy for treatment and long-term implications for their health should be explained and reinforced with written information, e.g. the patient information leaflet (PIL) for chronic bacterial prostatitis.
- **Analgesia:** paracetamol or a nonsteroidal anti-inflammatory drug (NSAID) could be offered for pain relief.
- **Antibiotic** treatment should be chosen according to culture sensitivity tests and ability of the antibiotic to penetrate non-inflamed prostatic tissue.
  - **First-line therapy** is a quinolone for 28 days.
  - Alternatives in the case of intolerance to quinolones include trimethoprim.
  - Duration of antibiotic treatment: existing studies provide limited evidence on duration of treatment since they had small numbers of people, were not controlled, defined chronic bacterial prostatitis in

Table 2: Referral advice for men with acute bacterial prostatitis.

Criteria for referral	Purpose of referral
Toxic, severely ill Unable to tolerate oral therapy Deteriorating on oral therapy	Admission for parenteral antibacterials
Inadequate response to antibacterials	Transrectal ultrasound examination or computerized tomography (CT) scan of prostate to look for prostatic abscess which would need surgical drainage
Pre-existing urologic conditions (e.g. obstruction, indwelling catheter) Chronic urinary irritative symptoms Immunocompromised	Specialist urology management
Acute urinary retention	The bladder should be catheterized by the suprapubic route since insertion of a urethral catheter may damage the prostate
Haematuria Incomplete response to antibacterials	Imaging of urinary tract
All patients when well	Imaging studies to exclude a structural cause for urinary tract infection
Prostatitis associated with sexually transmitted disease (STD)	Genito-urinary medicine service for treatment, screening for other STDs, safe sex counselling, and partner notification

different ways, used various doses for different lengths of time, used different outcomes, and had different periods of follow-up. Expert opinion suggests that antibiotics be given for at least 4 weeks and continued for a further 2–4 weeks if there is improvement.
- One trial (n = 64) suggests that an *alpha₁-adrenoceptor blocker* added to antibiotic therapy improves symptoms and reduces recurrence of bacterial prostatitis [Barbalias et al, 1998]. However, methodological weaknesses in the study and report allow little confidence to be placed in the results.
- **Prostatectomy** has been used when prostatic calculi were thought to be the cause of recurrent infection. Since prostatic calculi are common and the effectiveness of ablative surgery has not been adequately investigated, this cannot be recommended outside a clinical trial.

[Barbalias et al, 1998; Bjerklund Johansen et al, 1998; CEG, 2001; McNaughton Collins et al, 2001; Stern and Schaeffer, 2001]

Chronic abacterial prostatitis, chronic pelvic pain syndrome (CPPS)

- **General advice** for people with chronic abacterial prostatitis: the strategy for treatment and long-term implications for their health should be explained and reinforced with written information, e.g. the PIL for chronic abacterial prostatitis.
- **Analgesia:** a trial of analgesia could be offered for pain relief.
- **Therapies requiring further scientific study:**
- A systematic review found no convincing evidence on harms or efficacy from many of the therapies promoted for CPPS. The review concluded that the routine use of antibiotics and alpha$_1$-adrenoceptor blockers is not supported by existing evidence. Therapies which are being used but which require further evidence include:
  - **Antibiotics:**
    - A systematic review found only one small randomized controlled trial (RCT). Minocycline was compared with diazepam: there was no difference in symptom improvement. Because there is no evidence that diazepam is superior to placebo in treating CPPS, it may be inferred that minocycline has no benefit over placebo.
    - However, despite negative cultures and despite lack of evidence of efficacy, many clinicians would initially manage CPPS the same as chronic bacterial prostatitis, i.e. with antibiotic treatment for 4 weeks.
  - **Alpha$_1$-adrenoceptor blockers:**
    - Alfuzosin was not different from placebo in one RCT.
    - Two trials of phenoxybenzamine/ diphenoxybenzamine found improved CPPS symptoms but orthostatic adverse effects.
    - One RCT compared the use of alpha$_1$-adrenoceptor blockers alone with their use combined with antibiotics. This RCT found a lower rate of symptom recurrence in the group treated with alpha$_1$-adrenoceptor blockers alone.
  - **Bioflavinoids:** a small RCT investigated the bioflavinoid quercetin and found a slight reduction in symptoms after 1 month of treatment.
  - **Allopurinol:** a systematic review found only one RCT and this had several methodological deficiencies. The study reported improved symptoms in men treated with allopurinol.
  - **Anti-inflammatory medication:**
    - Cernilton (pollen extract): two descriptive studies suggest that cernilton is beneficial. One hypothesis is that cernilton has anti-inflammatory effects.
    - Seaprose S together with local prostate hyperthermia was more effective than hyperthermia alone in a small study.
    - Pentosan polysulphate in a small study had minimal benefits and significant adverse effects.
  - **PPC,** an amino acid preparation, has been compared with pollen extract in a study whose results are difficult to interpret.
  - **Prostatic thermotherapy:** it has been hypothesized that heating the prostate could relieve symptoms of CPPS either by accelerating the resolution of inflammation, or by altering afferent nerve fibres responsible for pain.
    - A systematic review found five RCTs, three of which used sham treatments in the control group. Most had methodological problems such as small numbers, short follow-up periods, or unvalidated symptom scoring systems. Overall, thermotherapy seems as though it might be beneficial and it seems that the diverse adverse effects are transient.
  - **Stress management:** pharmacological anxiolytics, psychological stress management techniques such as biofeedback, and relaxation therapies for the pelvic musculature are used. However, evidence of benefits, harms, and costs is not available from rigorous scientific studies.

[Barbalias et al, 1998; Bjerklund Johansen et al, 1998; Shoskes et al, 1999; McNaughton Collins et al, 2000; CEG, 2001; McNaughton Collins, 2001; McNaughton Collins et al, 2001; Stern and Schaeffer, 2001;]

References

NHS staff in England can link, free of charge, from references to full text journals by clicking on [Full text] on the PRODIGY website.

1. Barbalias, G.A., Nikiforidis, G. and Liatsikos, E.N. (1998) Alpha-blockers for the treatment of chronic prostatitis in combination with antibiotics. *Journal of Urology* **159**(3), 883–887.
2. Bjerklund Johansen, T.E., Gruneberg, R.N., Guibert, J et al (1998) The role of antibiotics in the treatment of chronic prostatitis: a consensus statement. *European Urology* **34**(6), 457–466.
3. BNF 41 (2001) *British National Formulary*. 41st edn. London: British Medical Association and Royal Pharmaceutical Society of Great Britain.
4. CEG (2001) *National guideline for the management of prostatitis*. Clinical Effectiveness Group (Association for Genitourinary Medicine and the Medical Society for the Study of Venereal Diseases). www.bashh.org [Accessed: 06/09/2005]. [Full text]
5. Childs, S.J. (1991) Current concepts in the treatment of urinary tract infections and prostatitis. *American Journal of Medicine* **91**(6A), 120S-123S.
6. Leigh, D.A. (1993) Prostatitis – an increasing clinical problem for diagnosis and management. *Journal of Antimicrobial Chemotherapy* **32**(Suppl A), 1–9.
7. McNaughton Collins, M. (2001) *Allopurinol for chronic prostatitis (Cochrane Review)*. The Cochrane Library. Issue 4. Oxford: Update Software.
8. McNaughton Collins, M., MacDonald, R. and Wilt, T.J. (2000) Diagnosis and treatment of chronic abacterial prostatitis: a systematic review. *Annals of Internal Medicine* **133**(5), 367–381.
9. McNaughton Collins, M., Pontari, M.A., O'Leary, M.P. et al (2001) Quality of life is impaired in men with chronic prostatitis: the Chronic Prostatitis Collaborative Research Network. *Journal of General Internal Medicine* **16**(10), 656–662.

0. Meares, E.M., Jr. (1991) Prostatitis. *Medical Clinics of North America* 75(2), 405–424.
1. NICE (2005) *Referral guidelines for suspected cancer – quick reference guide.* Clinical guideline 27. National Institute for Health and Clinical Excellence. www.nice.org.uk [Accessed: 01/07/2005].
2. Schaeffer, A.J. (1990) Diagnosis and treatment of prostatic infections. *Urology* 36(5 Suppl), 13–17.
13. Shoskes, D.A., Zeitlin, S.I., Shahed, A. and Rajfer, J. (1999) Quercetin in men with category III chronic prostatitis: a preliminary prospective, double blind, placebo-controlled trial. *Urology* 54(6), 960–963.
14. Stern, J. and Schaeffer, A. (2001) Chronic prostatitis. *Clinical Evidence* 6(Dec), 660–666.

P

PRODIGY GUIDANCE

Pruritus ani

Last revised in April 2005
www.prodigy.nhs.uk/guidance.asp?gt=Pruritus ani

Applies to people over the age of 1 month

This guidance covers the management of pruritus ani (itching in the perianal area).

This guidance does not cover in detail the management of secondary causes (such as infections, dermatological conditions, systemic conditions, or specific gastrointestinal pathology) of pruritus ani, other than to recommend that any underlying disease be excluded before conservative treatments for itch are started.

There is separate PRODIGY guidance for *Anal fissure, Candida — skin and nails, Dermatitis — contact, Haemorrhoids, Seborrhoeic dermatitis,* and *Threadworm.*

Goals

- To identify and treat secondary causes of pruritus ani
- To relieve the symptoms of pruritus ani
- To prevent the recurrence of pruritus ani

Contents

Scenarios
- Pruritus ani p.1586

Extended Information, p. 1588

Pruritus ani

Which therapy?

- **Exclude secondary causes of perianal itching,** e.g. threadworms and fungal infections; dermatological conditions; specific gastrointestinal disease (e.g. haemorrhoids); local malignancy; or systemic disease (see *What are the secondary causes?*).
- **Advise the person to avoid local irritants,** e.g. soap, perfumes, scented toilet paper, and locally applied topical medications.
- **Emphasize the importance of good perianal hygiene** (see *Patient Information Leaflet*).
- **Suggest measures to help reduce excessive moisture,** which may exacerbate the itch (see *Patient Information Leaflet*).
- **Consider suggesting alterations to the diet** if the person can relate pruritus to certain food or drink.
- **Consider offering symptomatic treatment** while waiting for the above measures to take effect.
  - **Bland protective or soothing ointments** (e.g. bismuth subgallate or zinc oxide) may be useful where there is excoriation.
  - **A short course (5–7 days) of a mild-potency topical corticosteroid** may provide temporary relief of symptoms when inflammation is present.
- **Systemic antihistamines** may be useful at night if sleep disturbance is a major issue.

Practical prescribing points

For further information, please see the *Medicines Compendium* (www.medicines.org.uk) or the *British National Formulary* (www.bnf.org).

- **Avoid long-term use of topical products containing a corticosteroid.** These products can cause skin atrophy and may also exacerbate pruritus in some people, through the development of contact dermatitis.

Follow-up advice

- People who fail to respond after 3 or 4 weeks of conservative treatment should undergo further investigation for secondary causes.

Should I refer or investigate?

Refer?

- In intractable cases, consider referral to a dermatologist, colorectal surgeon, or colorectal specialist nurse.

Investigate?

- People who fail to respond after 3 or 4 weeks of conservative treatment should undergo further investigation for secondary causes.

Patient information leaflets

The following PILs are available at www.prodigy.nhs.uk

- Medicines - Name Changes of Medicines
- Pruritus Ani (Itchy Bottom)
- Threadworms

Shared decision making

Pruritus ani of unknown cause is often helped or cured by the following:

- **Avoid any potential irritants.**
  - Stop using scented soaps, bubble bath, perfume, etc, near the anus.
  - Use plain, non-coloured toilet tissue.
  - Could any foods or medicines be causing the itch?
- **Pay special attention to hygiene around the anus.**
  - Wash the anus after passing faeces. It is best to use water only.
  - When not at home, use a moistened cloth or tissue.
  - Bath or shower daily.
  - Change your underwear daily.
- **Avoid excessive moisture around the anus.**
  - After washing, dry around the anus properly (a hair dryer is best).
  - Do not put on underwear until fully dry.
  - Wear loose cotton underwear (not nylon).
  - If you sweat a lot, put tissue in your underwear to absorb moisture.
- **As much as possible, try not to scratch** (which makes th itch worse).
  - This may be especially difficult when trying to get to sleep.
  - Keep fingernails short to limit damage done by scratching.
  - Consider wearing cotton gloves at night.

- An antihistamine medicine that makes you drowsy may be worth a try at bedtime.
- **In some cases, a doctor may advise:**
  - A bland soothing cream or ointment to use after going to the toilet and at bedtime.
  - A short course of a mild steroid cream if there is inflammation of the anal skin.

Drug rationale

Drugs not included

- **Creams** are less protective to skin because they are water-soluble. They contain preservatives and are therefore more likely to lead to sensitization of the perianal area.
- **Suppositories** are not appropriate, because pruritus ani is not a rectal condition.
- **Any products containing local anaesthetics and topical antihistamines** have not been included, because any relief tends to be short-lived. They may also cause contact sensitization [BNF 48, 2004].
- **Non-sedative antihistamines** have not been shown to be effective in relieving pruritus. Sedative effects may be desirable to help break the itch–scratch cycle at night.
- **Long-acting sedating antihistamines** are not included, so there is no 'hangover' effect.

Drugs included

- **Anusol ointment** is included as a soothing agent for more frequent application. Ointments have fewer additive constituents, especially preservatives, which might sensitize the skin. They are also less readily washed off than creams are.
- **Anusol-HC ointment** is included because it is the only preparation containing hydrocortisone without a local anaesthetic. It is useful in a short course (maximum of 7 days) to help reduce inflammation and itching.
- **Hydrocortisone 1% ointment** is included for short-term use to relieve symptoms in people with inflammation.
- **Hydroxyzine** is specifically licensed for pruritus and is sedating. It is offered as a night-time dose for temporary help with sleeping, to help break the itch–scratch cycle.
- **Chlorphenamine (chlorpheniramine)** is also included because it is inexpensive and is an effective sedating antihistamine of intermediate duration.

Prescriptions

First line: non-drug management

Advice only: good peri-anal hygiene & avoid irritants
- Age from 1 month onwards
- Gently clean the peri-anal area after each bowel movement and at bedtime with water. If you use a mild soap, make sure you wash it off well. Dry the area gently, do not rub hard (try using a hair dryer or patting with a dry pad). When away from home use a damp toilet tissue, and clean gently. Wear cotton underwear. If necessary a cotton tissue placed on the peri-anal area may help absorb moisture. Avoid using perfumes/ powders on the area. If you are using a medicated cream or wipes and itching gets worse stop using the cream immediately. If there are any foods that you think make the itching worse (e.g. tomatoes, spicy foods, dairy products, coffee or beer) try reducing the amount of them you eat. Although it is difficult, try to stop scratching the area. Try wearing cotton gloves at night, so if you itch, you do less damage.

Anusol (bland, soothing)

Anusol ointment
- Age from 12 years onwards
- Anusol ointment. Apply each morning and night, and after a bowel movement; supply 25 grams; NHS Cost £1.88; OTC Cost £3.15.

Topical corticosteroid: short course only

Anusol-HC ointment
- Age from 12 years onwards
- Anusol-HC ointment. Apply each morning and night, and after a bowel movement; supply 30 grams; NHS Cost £2.66.

Hydrocortisone 1% ointment
- Age from 12 years onwards
- Hydrocortisone 1% ointment (15g). Apply each morning and night, and after a bowel movement; supply 15 grams; NHS Cost £0.37.

Sedating antihistamine (for sleep disturbance)

Chlorphenamine (chlorpheniramine) syrup: 1mg at night prn
- Age from 1 month to 11 months
- Chlorphenamine 2mg/5ml syrup. Take 2.5ml at night when required for relief of itching; supply 50 ml; NHS Cost £0.76.

Chlorphenamine (chlorpheniramine) syrup: 1mg at night prn
- Age from 12 to 23 months
- Chlorphenamine 2mg/5ml syrup. Take 2.5ml at night when required for relief of itching; supply 50 ml; NHS Cost £0.76; OTC Cost £1.26.

Chlorphenamine (chlorpheniramine) syrup: 1-2mg at night prn
- Age from 2 to 5 years
- Chlorphenamine 2mg/5ml syrup. Take 2.5ml to 5ml at night when required for relief of itching; supply 100 ml; NHS Cost £1.52; OTC Cost £2.53.

Chlorphenamine (chlorpheniramine) syrup: 2-4mg at night prn
- Age from 6 to 11 years
- Chlorphenamine 2mg/5ml syrup. Take one to two 5ml spoonfuls at night when required for relief of itching; supply 150 ml; NHS Cost £2.28; OTC Cost £4.02.

Chlorphenamine (chlorpheniramine) tablets: 4mg at night prn
- Age from 12 years onwards
- Chlorphenamine 4mg tablets. Take one tablet at night when required for relief of itching; supply 14 tablets; NHS Cost £0.22; OTC Cost £1.40.

Hydroxyzine syrup: 5mg to 15mg at night when required
- Age from 6 months to 6 years
- Hydroxyzine 10mg/5ml syrup. Take 2.5ml to 7.5ml at night when required for relief of itching; supply 100 ml; NHS Cost £0.96.

Hydroxyzine syrup: 15mg to 25mg at night when required
- Age from 7 to 11 years
- Hydroxyzine 10mg/5ml syrup. Take 7.5ml to 12.5ml at night when required for relief of itching; supply 200 ml; NHS Cost £1.91.

Hydroxyzine tablets: 25mg at night when required
- Age from 12 years onwards
- Hydroxyzine 25mg tablets. Take one tablet at night when required for relief of itching; supply 14 tablets; NHS Cost £0.51.

Extended Information

Background information

- What is it? p.1588
- How common is it? p.1588
- How do I know my patient has it? p.1588
- What are the secondary causes? p.1588
- Complications and prognosis p.1588

What is it?

- **Pruritus ani is a symptom** and not a disease.
- **Pruritus ani is defined** as an unpleasant cutaneous sensation that induces the desire to scratch the skin around the anal orifice [Sullivan and Garnjobst, 1978].
- **Pruritus ani may be idiopathic (primary) or secondary to an identified cause** (see *What are the secondary causes?*).

[Stolz et al, 1990]

How common is it?

- Pruritus ani is a common condition affecting up to 5% of the population.
- Pruritus ani is four times more common in men than in women.
- Pruritus ani occurs in all age groups, but is most common in the fourth, fifth, and sixth decades of life.

[Hanno and Murphy, 1987; Vincent, 1999; Chaudhry and Bastawrous, 2003]

How do I know my patient has it?

- **The main symptom is an irresistible urge to scratch the anus.**
  - This urge may occur at any time, but is more common after a bowel movement (especially liquid stools) and at night (particularly just before falling asleep).
  - Itching may be exacerbated by heat, wool, moisture, leaking, soiling, stress, and anxiety.
  - The itching sensation ranges in severity from mild to extremely intense.
- **A detailed history** may reveal problems in keeping the anal area dry; the use of potential irritants, including powders, creams, and soaps; exacerbating dietary factors (in particular tomatoes, citrus fruits, and spicy foods); chronic diarrhoea; and anxiety or stress.
- **On examination,** the appearance of the perianal skin varies depending on the intensity and duration of the symptoms.
  - Initially in mild cases there may only be minimal perianal erythema.
  - In more severe cases the perianal area may be inflamed, with excoriations, cracking, and bleeding.
  - The anal ring may have a shiny appearance in chronic cases.
- **A digital rectal examination should be performed** to look for secondary causes, such as local malignancy.

[Hanno and Murphy, 1987; Vincent, 1999; Chaudhry and Bastawrous, 2003]

P

What are the secondary causes?

To make a diagnosis of idiopathic pruritus ani, secondary causes must be excluded, in particular:

- **Infections:** bacterial (e.g. *Staphylococcus* or *Streptococcus*, erythrasma), fungal (e.g. *Candida*, dermatophyte infections), parasitic (e.g. threadworms, scabies), viral (condyloma acuminata, herpes simplex), or sexually transmitted disease.
- **Gastrointestinal pathology,** e.g. fistula, fissure, haemorrhoids, or sphincter incompetence causing leakage of faecal material.
- **Dermatological conditions,** e.g. psoriasis, contact dermatitis, atopy, lichen sclerosus, seborrhoeic dermatitis, or atopic eczema.
- **Local malignancy,** e.g. Bowen's disease or extramammary Paget's disease.
- **Systemic disease,** e.g. diabetes mellitus, lymphoma, renal failure, iron deficiency anaemia, or hyperthyroidism.
- **Systemic medications,** e.g. colchicine or peppermint oil.
- **Topical medication,** e.g. local anaesthetics, glyceryl trinitrate, or topical corticosteroids.

[Hanno and Murphy, 1987; Chaudhry and Bastawrous, 2003]

Complications and prognosis

Complications

- Persistent scratching can tear the perianal skin, leading to eczematiform dermatitis, lichenification, ulceration, excoriation, and secondary infection.
- Depression may result from severe and persistent symptoms.

[Chaudhry and Bastawrous, 2003]

Prognosis

- Unless a specific cause is diagnosed and treated, pruritus ani may be a chronic condition.
- Most people respond well to management, although many suffer brief relapses.

[Hanno and Murphy, 1987; Mazier, 1994]

Management issues

- How should I assess someone with perianal itching? p.1588
- How should I manage idiopathic pruritus ani? p.1588
- When should I refer someone with pruritus ani? p.1589
- What is the supporting evidence? p.1589

How should I assess someone with perianal itching?

- **Look for secondary causes of pruritus ani.**
  - A careful history and examination is essential to exclude possible secondary causes of pruritus ani (see *How do I know my patient has it?*).
  - Some of the more common causes of pruritus ani are listed in the section *What are the secondary causes?*
  - If a specific secondary cause cannot be identified, idiopathic pruritus ani is diagnosed.
- Management of specific secondary causes of pruritus ani is beyond the scope of this guidance. There are separate PRODIGY guidance for *Anal fissure, Candida — skin and nails, Dermatitis — contact, Haemorrhoids, Seborrhoeic dermatitis,* and *Threadworm.*

How should I manage idiopathic pruritus ani?

- **Avoiding local irritants and maintaining a good level of perianal hygiene** are the cornerstones of managing idiopathic pruritus ani.
- **Dietary manipulation** may be of value if pruritus can be related to certain foods or drinks.
- **Symptomatic treatment** may provide interim relief during initiation of these measures.

What is the role of local irritants?

- **Action to avoid local irritants is often successful** in improving or preventing symptoms of pruritus ani.

- Local irritants include faeces, moisture (e.g. sweat), soap, perfumes, scented or coloured toilet paper, aggressive anal wiping, and locally applied topical medications.

What advice should I give about perianal hygiene?

- **Advise the person regarding the importance of maintaining good perianal hygiene.**
- **Faecal soiling** due to inadequate cleansing is commonly the cause of pruritus ani. Such soiling is more often a problem in people who are obese or hirsute. Good perianal hygiene to prevent soiling is an important part of management.
  - Advise washing gently with water after a bowel movement and at bedtime, and patting dry with a soft towel.
- **Excessive moisture** can contribute to the development of pruritus ani. This is more often a problem in people who are obese or hirsute.
  - Moisture can be reduced by carefully drying the anal area with a hairdryer after washing.
  - A cotton tissue placed on the perianal area may help absorb moisture throughout the day.
  - Cotton underwear should be worn instead of nylon or other synthetic materials.

[Hanno and Murphy, 1987; Chaudhry and Bastawrous, 2003]

- Advice regarding these general measures should be backed up with written information — see the PRODIGY Patient Information Leaflet on *Pruritus Ani (Itchy Bottom)*.

Should dietary manipulation be recommended?

- **If a person can relate pruritus to certain food or drinks, then dietary manipulation may be of value.** Certain foods are commonly cited as being known to exacerbate pruritus ani. These include tomatoes, citrus fruits, spicy foods, nuts, chocolate, dairy products, coffee (including decaffeinated), and excessive amounts of liquids such as beer, wine, and milk.
- **High-fibre diets and fibre supplements** may relieve symptoms in some people by helping to keep the stools soft, formed, and regular.

[Hanno and Murphy, 1987; Chaudhry and Bastawrous, 2003]

What symptomatic treatments should I offer?

- **The application of bland protective or soothing ointments** (e.g. bismuth subgallate or zinc oxide) is often recommended where there is excoriation [Hanno and Murphy, 1987; Chaudhry and Bastawrous, 2003].
- **A short course (5–7 days) of a mildly potent topical corticosteroid** may provide temporary relief of symptoms when inflammation is present [Hanno and Murphy, 1987; Chaudhry and Bastawrous, 2003]. Long-term use of topical corticosteroids should be avoided, as this may lead to contact dermatitis, which will exacerbate the itch.
- There is no evidence that antihistamines help the primary condition of pruritus ani. However, a short course of a sedating oral antihistamine at night may be useful if sleep disturbance due to itching is a problem.

What treatments are not recommended in primary care?

- **Local anaesthetics** are not generally recommended in the symptomatic relief of pruritus ani, as any relief experienced may be short-lived, and there is a risk of contact sensitization associated with their use.
- **Systemic corticosteroids** are not recommended for the symptomatic treatment of pruritus ani. We found no evidence to support their use.
- **Capsaicin:** limited evidence suggests that capsaicin 0.006% ointment may be effective at relieving the symptoms of pruritus ani [Lysy et al, 2003]. However, there is no capsaicin product currently commercially available in the UK at the concentration studied; higher concentrations are associated with an increased risk of perianal burning. Therefore, the use of capsaicin for the treatment of idiopathic pruritus ani in general practice is not recommended.
- **Intradermal methylene blue may be considered in secondary care** for people with severe intractable pruritus ani [Botterill and Sagar, 2002; Mentes et al, 2004]. Its use in primary care is not recommended.
- **Hypnosis** is not recommended for the management of pruritus ani, as there is insufficient evidence to support its use [Rucklidge and Saunders, 1999].

When should I refer someone with pruritus ani?

- **If after 3 or 4 weeks these conservative treatments are unsuccessful,** further investigations are recommended.
- **Referral to a dermatologist, colorectal surgeon, or colorectal specialist nurse may be needed in intractable cases,** to make sure a secondary cause has not been missed.

What is the supporting evidence?

The evidence available for the treatments recommended in the management of pruritus ani is poor. Most recommendations are based on expert opinion.

What is the evidence for good perianal hygiene?

- We found no controlled clinical trials regarding the efficacy of hygiene measures in the treatment of pruritus ani. However, use of such measures is widely accepted and is recommended by experts.

What is the evidence for dietary manipulation?

- Certain foods have been implicated as a cause of pruritus ani. However, we found no evidence from controlled clinical trials that dietary manipulation relieves the symptoms of pruritus ani. This recommendation is a common-sense approach, based on expert opinion.

What is the evidence for the use of systemic antihistamines?

- We found no controlled clinical studies investigating antihistamines in the management of pruritus ani.

What is the evidence for soothing creams or ointments?

- We found no controlled clinical trials regarding the use of soothing creams or ointments in the management of pruritus ani. However, the use of such creams and ointments is widespread and is generally recommended by experts.

What is the evidence for the use of corticosteroids?

- One study of 60 people with idiopathic perianal pruritus found twice-daily perianal cleansing with a liquid cleanser (Protex®) to be as effective as twice-daily application of a topical corticosteroid (methylprednisolone aceponate 0.1%) in controlling pruritus. The quality of this study was poor.

[Oztas et al, 2004]

- In a case study of a woman with intractable pruritus ani refractory to general measures including anal hygiene and topical corticosteroids, injection of methylprednisolone acetate 80 mg into the site of excoriation resulted in relief from pruritus, with no

P

recurrence after one year. Further studies are needed to determine the place in therapy of intralesional corticosteroids.
[Tunuguntla and Sullivan, 2004]

References

NHS staff in England can link, free of charge, from references to full text journals by clicking on [Full text] on the PRODIGY website.

1. BNF 48 (2004) *British National Formulary*. 48th edn. London: British Medical Association and Royal Pharmaceutical Society of Great Britain.
2. Botterill, I.D. and Sagar, P.M. (2002) Intra-dermal methylene blue, hydrocortisone and lignocaine for chronic, intractable pruritus ani. *Colorectal Disease* 4(2), 144–146.
3. Chaudhry, V. and Bastawrous, A. (2003) Idiopathic pruritus ani. *Seminars in Colon & Rectal Surgery* 14(4), 196–202.
4. Hanno, R. and Murphy, P. (1987) Pruritus ani. Classification and management. *Dermatologic Clinics* 5(4), 811–816.
5. Lysy, J., Sistiery-Ittah, M., Israelit, Y. et al (2003) Topical capsaicin: a novel and effective treatment for idiopathic intractable pruritus ani: a randomised, placebo controlled, crossover study. *Gut* 52(9), 1323–1326. [Full text]
6. Mazier, W.P. (1994) Hemorrhoids, fissures, and pruritus ani. *Surgical Clinics of North America* 74(6), 1277–1292.
7. Mentes, B.B., Akin, M., Leventoglu, S. et al (2004) Intradermal methylene blue injection for the treatment of intractable idiopathic pruritus ani: results of 30 cases. *Techniques in Coloproctology* 8(1), 11–14. [Full text]
8. Oztas, M.O., Oztas, P. and Onder, M. (2004) Idiopathic perianal pruritus: washing compared with topical corticosteroids. *Postgraduate Medical Journal* 80(943), 295–297.
9. Rucklidge, J.J. and Saunders, D. (1999) Hypnosis in a case of long-standing idiopathic itch. *Psychosomatic Medicine* 61(3), 355–358.
10. Stolz, E., Vuzevski, V.D. and van der Stek, J. (1990) General perianal skin problems. *Netherlands Journal o Medicine* 37(Suppl 1), S43-S46.
11. Sullivan, E.S. and Garnjobst, W.M. (1978) Symposium on colon and anorectal surgery. Pruritus ani: a practical approach. *Surgical Clinics of North America* 58(3), 505–512.
12. Tunuguntla, A. and Sullivan, M.J. (2004) A new concept for the treatment of intractable pruritus ani. *Southern Medical Journal* 97(7), 710.
13. Vincent, C. (1999) Anorectal pain and irritation: anal fissure, levator syndrome, proctalgia fugax, and pruritus ani. *Primary Care; Clinics in Office Practice* 26(1), 53–68.

P

PRODIGY GUIDANCE

Pruritus vulvae

Last revised in July 2005
www.prodigy.nhs.uk/guidance.asp?gt=Pruritus vulvae

Applies to women over the age of 16 years

This guidance covers the initial management of adult women presenting with the symptom pruritus vulvae. It contains advice on diagnosis and general symptomatic treatment for vulval conditions that present with itching.
It does not contain detailed information on the management of specific causes of pruritus vulvae. It does not cover vulval pain.

There is separate PRODIGY guidance for *Candida — female genital, Trichomoniasis, Bacterial vaginosis, Chlamydia — genital, Candida — skin and nails, Herpes simplex — genital, Threadworm, Pubic lice, Scabies, Urinary tract infection (lower) — women, Pruritus ani,* and *Gynaecological cancer — suspected.*

Goals

- To ensure underlying causes have been identified or excluded
- To relieve discomfort
- To prevent potential complications (e.g. development of malignancy in premalignant conditions)

Contents

Scenarios

- Diagnosing the underlying cause p.1591
- Symptomatic treatment for itch p.1592

Extended Information, p. 1595

Which scenario?

- **Diagnosing the underlying cause:** covers the management of women who present with pruritus vulvae who have not yet had an underlying cause diagnosed. The scenario contains a list of causes that should be considered.
- **Symptomatic treatment for itch:** covers the management of women who require symptomatic treatment for vulval itch, but it does not contain management advice or treatments for the underlying cause.

Diagnosing the underlying cause

Which therapy?

- **The majority of cases of vulval itching will have an identifiable cause.**
- **History:** Ask about the extent of the itching, pain (managed differently), dyspareunia, or other symptoms (e.g. discharge); topical applications already tried; current medication; general health including stress; personal or family history of skin conditions (e.g. psoriasis, eczema) or autoimmune disease (associated with lichen sclerosus); and an obstetric and gynaecological history.
- **Examination:** Always examine the vulva, pubis and perianal area. Examine the vagina and cervix if a genital infection is suspected. Examine other areas of skin on the body (including the oral mucosa) if dermatological disease is suspected.

Consider the following differential diagnoses:

Infections

- **Candida** — pruritus, thick white discharge, erythema, oedema, white plaques, and satellite lesions
- **Trichomoniasis** — often severe pruritus, with thin, frothy and malodorous discharge
- **Bacterial vaginosis** — mild pruritus with thin white discharge
- **Pubic lice** — intense vulval pruritus, possibly with sky-blue spots on trunk and thighs. Lice should be visible.
- **Threadworm** nocturnal vulval and perianal pruritus
- **Scabies** — intense nocturnal pruritus, burrows (also between fingers, axillae and soles of feet)

Dermatological conditions

- **Contact dermatitis (eczema)** — e.g. reaction to proprietary creams, contraceptives, perfumes, soaps and wet wipes.
- **Psoriasis** — well-demarcated border, absence of scale, often with typical lesions elsewhere on body.
- **Seborrhoeic dermatitis (eczema)** — ill-defined border, some scaling, with or without other sites involved (axillae, anterior chest etc.).
- **Lichen simplex** — thickened skin, accentuated skin markings, pale colour.
- **Lichen planus** — erythema or ulceration with intense pruritus, possibly with involvement of other sites, Wickham's striae.
- **Lichen sclerosus** — white, thin, wrinkled, parchment-like, and usually symmetric lesion of the vestibule, clitoris, labia minora, inner aspects of labia majora, and perianal skin.
- **Squamous cell hyperplasia** — inflammation, whitening, increased skin markings, and lichenification are often present.
- **Fox-Fordyce disease** — small dome-shaped papules, with or without axillae involved.
- **Hailey-Hailey disease** — vesicles erupt causing pruritus, with or without involvement of the axillae and sides of the neck.
- **Darier's disease** — warty plaques, may be macerated, malodorous, possibly with involvement of seborrhoeic areas of the trunk, flank and face.
- **Symptomatic dermatographism** — a form of localised urticaria triggered by direct touch.

Neoplasia

- Squamous cell carcinoma and other neoplastic conditions e.g. peri-anal intra-epithelial neoplasia, basal cell carcinoma, melanoma and carcinoma of Bartholin's gland. Suspician should be increased by the presence of ulceration, contact bleeding and thickening.

Other

- **Declining oestrogen levels** — atrophic, pale, dry vulva and vagina. If the vulva is irritated it may show

P

erythema, petechiae, telangiectasia, or fissuring, with or without cessation of menstruation, and hot flushes.
- **Gastrointestinal disease**
- **Urinary incontinence** — makes vulval skin moist and macerated.
- **Pregnancy** — can cause perineal pruritus through vulval engorgement.
- **Any cause of generalized pruritus** — including drug reactions and systemic diseases such as renal or hepatic disease, diabetes, iron deficiency anaemia, other haematological abnormalities, and thyroid dysfunction.
- **Psychological problems** may occasionally present with pruritus vulvae.
- **Idiopathic pruritus vulvae** is uncommon. It is a diagnosis that can only be made when all other possible causes have been excluded.

Follow-up advice

- **Misdiagnosis is possible;** therefore consider reviewing each woman in order to observe the development of any potentially malignant changes within the area of the pruritus.
- **Women who are prescribed topical corticosteroids** should be seen again after approximately 1–2 weeks to assess response.
- **Women with dermatitis, psoriasis, and other skin conditions** should be followed up as clinically required if the disease is mild, but reviewed at approximately one month if the disease is severe (especially if they are using potent corticosteroids).
- **Women with lichen sclerosus** have a small risk (2–5%) of developing squamous cell carcinoma, and should be followed up long-term; either in general practice or by secondary care.
- **Women with vulval or vaginal infections** should be followed up in line with separate PRODIGY guidance. See *Candida — female genital*, *Trichomoniasis*, *Bacterial vaginosis*, *Chlamydia*, *Candida — skin and nails*, *Herpes simplex — genital*, *Threadworm*, *Pubic lice*, and *Scabies*.

P

Should I refer or investigate?

Refer?

- **If there is an unexplained vulval lump or vulval bleeding due to ulceration,** referral guidelines for suspected cancer recommend urgent referral to a team specialising in the management of gynaecological cancer, depending upon local arrangements.
- **If a sexually-transmitted infection is suspected,** refer to a genito-urinary medicine clinic for screening tests and further management.
- **If unsure of a dermatological diagnosis,** refer to dermatologist.
- **If contact allergy is suspected,** referral to a dermatologist for patch testing may be needed.
- **If an underlying cause has not been identified, and symptoms do not respond** to simple advice or a short trial of topical hydrocortisone, refer to secondary care.
- **In difficult cases** referral to a multidisciplinary vulval clinic may be appropriate.

Investigate?

- **If an infection is suspected,** appropriate swabs or cultures should be taken.

Patient information leaflets

The following PILs are available at www.prodigy.nhs.uk
- Antifungal Medicines
- Biopsy
- Pruritus Vulvae (Itchy Vulva)

Shared decision making

- **Finding and treating the cause of your vulval itch should stop the itching.** This may involve treatment with moisturizers (emollients), steroid creams, or an antihistamine.
- **Referral** to a specialist is sometimes necessary.
- **General care of the vulval skin** helps to ease itch, whatever the cause:
  - Wear cotton underwear, and avoid nylon materials.
  - Avoid tight clothes. Let 'fresh air' get to your vulva.
  - Don't use soaps, perfumes, deodorants, bubble bath, etc, on the vulva.
  - Wash the vulva gently once a day. Too much washing can make the itch worse. Use a bland moisturizer as a soap substitute.
  - Dry fully before putting on underwear.
  - Avoid scratching if at all possible. Cut nails short.
  - Don't use condoms that are lubricated with spermicide.
- Tell a doctor if symptoms persist, or if any changes occur to the vulval skin.

Drug rationale

- No drugs are included in this scenario. Where confident of the diagnosis please see the appropriate PRODIGY guidance or refer to a specialist as necessary.

Symptomatic treatment for itch

Which therapy?

- **Reassure and give simple advice** on hygiene and avoidance of irritants to all women.
- **Symptomatic treatment for vulval itching may give some relief, but should not be a substitute for seeking and treating the underlying cause.**
- **Bland emollients** can ease itching caused by almost all vulval disease, and can be used in addition to most other therapies. They should be used liberally as a soap substitute and moisturizer. Choice of preparation will depend on the individual. If topical corticosteroids are being used concomitantly, they may be more effective if applied immediately before emollients.
- Over-the-counter medications may contain irritants.
- **Low potency topical corticosteroids** are effective at alleviating itching, but *must only be given if suitable for the underlying condition* (e.g. dermatitis, psoriasis). Explain that between half and one fingertip unit of corticosteroid cream for one application will suffice. Their effect should be seen within a few days. More potent corticosteroids may be needed for some conditions. A trial of corticosteroids may alleviate the itch if no underlying cause can be found.
- **Where corticosteroids are ineffective, unsuitable, or being used excessively,** increased use of bland emollients may be useful.
- **Sedating antihistamines** help women to cope with vulval itching by causing sedation rather than by any other effect.

Practical prescribing points

For further information, please see the *Medicines Compendium* (www.medicines.org.uk) or the *British National Formulary* (www.bnf.org).

Follow-up advice

- **Misdiagnosis is possible;** therefore consider reviewing each women in order to observe the development of any potentially malignant changes within the area of the pruritus.
- **Women who are prescribed topical corticosteroids** should be seen again after approximately 1–2 weeks to assess response.
- **Women with dermatitis, psoriasis, and other skin conditions** should be followed up as clinically required if the disease is mild, but reviewed at approximately one month if the disease is severe (especially if they are using potent corticosteroids).
- **Women with lichen sclerosus** have a small risk (2–5%) of developing squamous cell carcinoma, and should be followed up long-term; either in general practice or by secondary care.
- **Women with vulval or vaginal infections** should be followed up in line with separate PRODIGY guidance. See *Candida — female genital, Trichomoniasis, Bacterial vaginosis, Chlamydia, Candida — skin and nails, Herpes simplex — genital, Threadworm, Pubic lice*, and *Scabies*.

Should I refer or investigate?

Refer?

- **If there is an unexplained vulval lump or vulval bleeding due to ulceration,** referral guidelines for suspected cancer recommend urgent referral to a team specialising in the management of gynaecological cancer, depending upon local arrangements.
- **If a sexually-transmitted infection is suspected,** refer to a genito-urinary medicine clinic for screening tests and further management.
- **If unsure of a dermatological diagnosis,** refer to dermatologist.
- **If contact allergy is suspected** referral to a dermatologist for patch testing may be needed.
- **If an underlying cause has not been identified, and symptoms do not respond** to simple advice or a short trial of topical hydrocortisone, refer to secondary care.
- **In difficult cases** referral to a multidisciplinary vulval clinic may be appropriate.

Investigate?

- **If an infection is suspected,** appropriate swabs or cultures should be taken.

Patient information leaflets

The following PILs are available at www.prodigy.nhs.uk

- Antifungal Medicines
- Biopsy
- Medicines - Name Changes of Medicines
- Pruritus Vulvae (Itchy Vulva)

Shared decision making

- Sometimes no cause can be found for a vulval itch.
- **General care of the vulval skin** helps to ease itch, whatever the cause:
  - Wear cotton underwear, and avoid nylon materials.
  - Avoid tight clothes. Let 'fresh air' get to your vulva.
  - Don't use soaps, perfumes, deodorants, bubble bath, etc, on the vulva.
  - Wash the vulva gently once a day. Too much washing can make the itch worse. Use a bland moisturiser as a soap substitute.
  - Dry fully before putting on underwear.
  - Avoid scratching if at all possible. Cut nails short.
  - Don't use condoms that are lubricated with spermicide.
- **Moisturizers (emollients),** such as **aqueous cream** or **emulsifying ointment,** may help relieve the itch. Use liberal amounts.
- **A mild steroid cream** such as **hydrocortisone,** is useful. Use a small amount, for 2–3 days only, every now and then. This often settles the itch, and breaks any 'itch scratch cycle'.
- **An antihistamine** at bedtime may help you to sleep at night.
- Tell a doctor if symptoms persist, or if any changes occur to the vulval skin.

Drug rationale

Drugs not included

- **Emollients other than aqueous cream BP and emulsifying ointment BP** are not included. There is no established difference in efficacy and others preparations are more expensive. Emollients with additional excipients should not be used unless bland/simple emollients have been tried first. Aqueous cream BP and emulsifying ointment BP will be acceptable for the majority of women.
- **Bath emollients other than emulsifying ointment BP** are not included. Bath emollients may be useful to provide additional moisturization in some women with widespread dry skin.
- **Combination topical emollient and antiseptic products** are excluded. There is a lack of good quality evidence comparing the efficacy of these products with other agents, and therefore they are not recommended for routine prophylactic use. Antiseptics can also cause skin irritation [DTB, 1998; MeReC, 1998].
- **Topical corticosteroids, except for short-term use of hydrocortisone,** are not included. Use of more potent corticosteroids may lead to adverse effects but they are appropriate for some diagnoses (e.g. lichen sclerosus, lichen planus, severe psoriasis, or dermatitis).
- **Combination topical corticosteroid and anti-infective agents** should not be used unless a diagnosis has been confirmed. Some anti-infective agents may cause sensitization of the skin.
- **First-generation (sedating) oral antihistamines, other than chlorphenamine (chlorpheniramine) and hydroxyzine,** are not offered. Others are either not licensed, are more expensive, or tend to have a longer duration of action that may result in a 'prolonged hangover effect' the next day.
- **Second-generation (non-sedating) oral antihistamines** have no proven efficacy in relieving pruritus.
- **Topical antihistamines** provide only a mild topical antipruritic effect and there is a risk of sensitization of the skin. It is thought that the intact epidermis poorly absorbs the salt form of these drugs.
- **Topical local anaesthetics** are only marginally effective and they can cause skin sensitization. It is thought that the intact epidermis poorly absorbs the salt form of these drugs.
- **Topical doxepin cream** is not included, as there is limited evidence to support its efficacy.
- **Topical oestrogen vaginal preparations** are suitable for atrophic vaginitis. See separate PRODIGY guidance on *Menopause*.

[DTB, 1998; MeReC, 1998; Klein and Clark, 1999; Marek-Thompson and Bond, 2000; BNF 43, 2002; BSSVD, 2002; Edwards et al, 2002]

Drugs included

Underlying causes of pruritus vulvae should be sought and managed appropriately. Use of the following agents may help alleviate the symptoms of pruritus vulvae but will not necessarily treat the underlying condition.

- **Creams** may be easier to spread on the skin, are generally well-absorbed, and may soothe the affected area.
- **Ointments** are greasy preparations and are more occlusive than creams. Generally, the more oily the preparation, the more prolonged the emollient effect.
- **Emollients (aqueous cream BP and emulsifying ointment)** are included. They help relieve pruritus especially where associated with dry and cracked skin and are good first-line choices. The majority of women should find aqueous cream acceptable and where occasionally the preservative present causes sensitization, emulsifying ointment BP may be used. Either formulation can be used when bathing and emulsifying ointment may be used as a bath emollient.
- **Topical hydrocortisone, for use in the short-term,** is included. Use of low potency 0.5% and 1% hydrocortisone cream or ointment can help break the itch–scratch cycle. Hydrocortisone is especially recommended where pruritus is severe enough to cause inflammation [MeReC, 1999].
- **First-generation (sedating) oral antihistamines (chlorphenamine [chlorpheniramine] and hydroxyzine)** are offered as a night-time dose for temporary help with sleeping, to help break the itch-scratch cycle. **Hydroxyzine** is licensed for pruritus. **Chlorphenamine (chlorpheniramine),** although not specifically licensed for pruritus, is inexpensive and widely used.

[DTB, 1998; MeReC, 1998; Klein and Clark, 1999; Marek-Thompson and Bond, 2000; Ridley et al, 2000; BNF 43, 2002; BSSVD, 2002; Edwards et al, 2002]

Prescriptions

Non-drug management

P

Advice only: avoidance of vulval irritants
- Age from 16 years onwards
- Vulval skin is sensitive, and may react to irritants such as soaps. You should avoid all contact of the vulva skin with soap, shampoo, bath salts, bubble bath, perfumes and personal deodorants, wet wipes, textile dyes, sanitary wear, detergents and fabric softeners. Wash the vulva every day, but avoid washing excessively. Aqueous cream BP or emulsifying ointment BP are examples of bland emollients that can be used both as a soap substitute and moisturiser. Either formulation can also be used when bathing. Avoid tight-fitting clothes and materials that irritate, for example, nylon. Wear cotton underwear. Avoid the use of spermicidally-lubricated condoms. Try not to scratch, keep fingernails short, and consider wearing cotton gloves at night to stop scratching in your sleep.

Bland emollients

Aqueous cream BP (100g)
- Age from 16 years onwards
- Aqueous cream BP. Apply to the vulva liberally as a moisturiser 3 to 4 times a day, and after bathing. If the condition is inflammatory, also use as a soap substitute; supply 100 grams; NHS Cost £0.21; OTC Cost £0.48.

Aqueous cream BP (500g)
- Age from 16 years onwards
- Aqueous cream BP. Apply to the vulva liberally as a moisturiser 3 to 4 times a day, and after bathing. If the condition is inflammatory, also use as a soap substitute; supply 500 grams; NHS Cost £1.05; OTC Cost £1.81.

Emulsifying ointment BP (100g)
- Age from 16 years onwards
- Emulsifying ointment BP. Apply to the vulva liberally as a moisturiser 3 to 4 times a day, and after bathing. If the condition is inflammatory, also use as a soap substitute; supply 100 grams; NHS Cost £0.30; OTC Cost £0.53.

Emulsifying ointment BP (500g)
- Age from 16 years onwards
- Emulsifying ointment BP. Apply to the vulva liberally as a moisturiser 3 to 4 times a day, and after bathing. If the condition is inflammatory, also use as a soap substitute; supply 500 grams; NHS Cost £1.51; OTC Cost £2.66.

Advice only: over-the-counter purchase
- Age from 16 years onwards
- Emollient cream and ointment preparations are available to buy from pharmacies and many are cheaper than the NHS prescription charge. The emollient can be applied liberally as a moisturiser 3 or 4 times a day to the vulva and after bathing. If the condition is inflammatory, the preparation can also be used as a soap substitute. Very occasionally people are sensitive to an ingredient in an emollient preparation. If you experience an allergic reaction then STOP applying the cream or ointment and see your doctor or pharmacist. It is best to sample a few emollients and choose the one that suits you best.

Topical corticosteroid – short trial

Hydrocortisone 0.5% cream
- Age from 16 years onwards
- Hydrocortisone 0.5% cream(15g). Apply thinly to the vulva once or twice a day when required for relief of itching. Use for 2 or 3 days, but up to 7 days if necessary supply 15 grams; NHS Cost £0.34.

Hydrocortisone 0.5% ointment
- Age from 16 years onwards
- Hydrocortisone 0.5% ointment (15g). Apply thinly to the vulva once or twice a day when required for relief of itching. Use for 2 or 3 days, but up to 7 days if necessary supply 15 grams; NHS Cost £0.35.

Hydrocortisone 1% cream
- Age from 16 years onwards
- Hydrocortisone 1% cream (15g). Apply thinly to the vulva once or twice a day when required for relief of itching. Use for 2 or 3 days, but up to 7 days if necessary supply 15 grams; NHS Cost £0.35.

Hydrocortisone 1% ointment
- Age from 16 years onwards
- Hydrocortisone 1% ointment (15g). Apply thinly to the vulva once or twice a day when required for relief of itching. Use for 2 or 3 days, but up to 7 days if necessary supply 15 grams; NHS Cost £0.36.

Sedating antihistamines (for sleep disturbance)

Chlorphenamine (chlorpheniramine) 4mg at night prn
- Age from 16 years onwards
- Chlorphenamine 4mg tablets. Take one tablet at night when required for relief of itching; supply 14 tablets; NHS Cost £0.22; OTC Cost £1.40.

Hydroxyzine 25mg at night when required
- Age from 16 years onwards
- Hydroxyzine 25mg tablets. Take one tablet at night when required for relief of itching; supply 14 tablets; NHS Cost £0.51.

Extended Information

Background information

- What is it? p.1595
- How common is it? p.1595
- History and examination of women with vulval itching p.1595
- Underlying causes that may present with itching of the vulva p.1595
- Complications and prognosis p.1596

What is it?

- Pruritus vulvae is itching of the vulva. The term describes a symptom, not a diagnosis.
- In the majority of cases, careful history and examination will find an underlying cause.

How common is it?

- The exact incidence and prevalence is not clear, although it is thought that most women will complain of pruritus vulvae at some time in their lives, and around 10% of women seen by gynaecologists experience symptoms [Jeffcoate and Tindall, 1987; Dambro, 1996].

History and examination of women with vulval itching

An accurate diagnosis depends as much upon detail derived from the woman's history as the clinical examination.

History and symptoms

- **The woman is likely to complain of** constant or intermittent itching of the vulva, which may vary in intensity. Some women find it difficult to differentiate between the symptom of itch and the symptoms of irritation, soreness, rawness and burning.
- **A history should determine:**
  - Whether there is any pain (which would be managed differently), dyspareunia, or other symptoms (e.g. discharge)
  - What topical applications have already been tried
  - Current medication
  - General health including amount of stress
  - Personal or family history of skin conditions (e.g. atopy, psoriasis, eczema) or autoimmune disease (associated with lichen sclerosus)
  - An obstetric and gynaecological history (including a history of genital warts and abnormal cervical smears)
  - Information on any potential allergens or sensitizer such as underclothes, sanitary wear, washing agents for person and clothes

Examination

- **Perform the examination** in a very well lit area with a bright examination lamp. A chaperone or a friend should be present if the woman wishes.
- **The vulva, pubis and perianal area must be examined.**
- **The vagina and cervix** should be examined if certain diseases are suspected e.g. genital infection.
- **Other areas of skin on the body,** including the oral mucosa, should be examined to determine if there is a more widespread skin disorder.

Investigations

- **If an infection is suspected,** appropriate swabs or cultures should be taken to look for conditions such as candida, bacterial vaginosis and streptococcal infections.
- **If a sexually transmitted disease is suspected,** screening tests should be performed, usually at a genito-urinary medicine clinic.
- **If vulval carcinoma is suspected** (i.e. there is an unexplained vulval lump or vulval bleeding due to ulceration) referral guidelines for suspected cancer published by the National Institute for Health and Clinical Excellence (NICE) recommend urgent referral to a team specialising in the management of gynaecological cancer, depending upon local arrangements [NICE, 2005].
- **If the skin looks abnormal but carcinoma is not suspected** consider referral to either a dermatologist or a gynaecologist depending on local expertise and protocol.
- **If a contact allergy is suspected,** referral to a dermatologist for patch testing may be needed.

[Ridley et al, 2000; Edwards et al, 2002]

Underlying causes that may present with itching of the vulva

Many skin disorders can affect the vulva — if the diagnosis is not clear then specialist referral to a dermatologist or a gynaecologist with expertise in managing vulval disease should be considered.

Infections

- **Candida** — pruritus, thick white discharge, erythema, oedema, white plaques, and satellite lesions. Primary candida of the skin is rare — if suspected consider underlying immunodeficiency and diabetes mellitus.
- **Trichomoniasis** — often severe pruritus, with thin, frothy and malodorous discharge
- **Bacterial vaginosis** — mild pruritus with thin white discharge
- **Pubic lice** (*Pediculus pubis*) — intense vulval pruritus, possibly with sky-blue spots on trunk and thighs. Lice may be seen on hair, pubis, trunk, legs, axillae, scalp, eyelashes, and eyebrows.
- **Threadworm** — nocturnal vulval and perianal pruritus
- **Scabies** — intense nocturnal pruritus, burrows (also look between fingers, axillae, and soles of feet)
- **Herpes simplex of the genitalia** — vesicles, ulcers, cutaneous hyperaesthesia, perineal burning with or without severe dysuria, systemic symptoms
- **Urinary tract infections** and vulval vestibulitis that may cause burning

Dermatological conditions

- **Contact dermatitis (eczema)** — e.g. reaction to proprietary creams (especially those containing local anaesthetics), topical antibiotic preparations, barrier contraceptives, perfumes, soaps, wet wipes, textile dyes, detergents, fabric conditioners and sanitary wear.
- **Psoriasis** — well-demarcated border, absence of scale, often with typical lesions elsewhere on the body.
- **Seborrhoeic dermatitis (eczema)** — ill-defined border, some scaling, with or without involvement of other sites (e.g. axillae, anterior chest, scalp etc.).
- **Lichen simplex** — thickened skin, accentuated skin markings, pale colour.
- **Lichen planus** — erythema or ulceration with intense pruritus (possibly with other sites involved), Wickham's striae.
- **Lichen sclerosus** — white, thin, wrinkled skin, parchment-like and usually symmetric lesion of the vestibule, clitoris, labia minora, inner aspects of labia majora and perianal skin. Bleeding into the affected areas produces red or purple purpuric lesions. Scarring and loss of tissue can lead to burying of the clitoris, loss of the labia minora and narrowing of the vulval

P

introitus. Vulval carcinoma develops in 2–5% of women with lichen sclerosus.

- **Squamous cell hyperplasia** — chronic reactive disorder to problems such as chronic fungal vulvitis or allergies. Inflammation, whitening, increased skin markings, and lichenification are often present. It is associated with vulval carcinoma but not considered to be causal; any potential for malignancy relates to the underlying disease.
- **Fox-Fordyce disease** — small dome-shaped papules, with or without involvement of the axillae. This disease is very rare, but intensely itchy and will often present as lichenification (grossly thickened skin with accentuated skin markings).
- **Hailey-Hailey disease** — vesicles erupt causing pruritus, with or without involvement of the axillae and sides of the neck. This disease, which is very rare, is also known as familial benign chronic pemphigus, and is an inherited autosomal dominant condition. It is easily mistaken for intertrigo or dermatitis.
- **Darier's disease** — warty plaques, which may be macerated and malodorous, possibly with the involvement of seborrhoeic areas of the trunk, flank and face. This is also a very rare, autosomal dominant condition, and may be confused with Hailey-Hailey disease.
- **Symptomatic dermatographism** — a form of localised urticaria triggered by direct touch.

Neoplasia

- Malignant neoplasms of the vulva are uncommon.
- **Squamous cell carcinomas** account for 90% of malignant disease of the vulva and often arise from a preexisting disease:
  - **In the elderly,** the background disease is most likely to be lichen sclerosus or lichen planus.
  - **In young women** the most likely malignancy is vulval intraepithelial neoplasia (VIN). This is usually linked to the wart virus.
- **Other neoplastic conditions** include perianal intra-epithelial neoplasia, basal cell carcinoma, melanoma, and carcinoma of Bartholin's gland.

P

Other

- **Declining oestrogen levels in peri- and postmenopausal women,** may contribute to vaginal and vulval changes that result in vulvovaginal itching, dryness, and sometimes burning although the natural aging process may be a key factor in this change. The vulva will look atrophic, pale and dry, and if irritated may show erythema, petechiae, telangiectasia, or fissuring (Note: these signs and symptoms are similar to the features of lichen sclerosus). The vaginal epithelium will be dry, pale, thin and smooth due to the loss of rugae. Cessation of menstruation and other symptoms such as hot flushes may indicate that the cause is the menopause.
- **Gastrointestinal disease** — from prolonged contact of stool with the vulval skin due to faecal incontinence or poor perianal hygiene.
- **Urinary incontinence** — makes vulval skin moist and macerated.
- **Pregnancy** — can cause perineal pruritus through vulval engorgement. Pregnancy is also associtaed with increased vaginal discharge as a result of increased hormone levels and an increased incidence of *Candida*.
- **Any cause of generalized pruritus** — includes drug reactions and systemic diseases such as renal or hepatic disease, diabetes, iron deficiency anaemia, lymphoma, other haematological abnormalities, and thyroid dysfunction.
- **Psychological problems** — may occasionally present as pruritus vulvae.
- **Idiopathic pruritus vulvae** is uncommon. It is a diagnosis that can only be made when all other possible causes have been excluded.

[Goolamali, 1981; Lavery, 1986; Jeffcoate and Tindall, 1987; Phillips, 1992; Sherertz, 1994; Kehoe and Luesley, 1995; Ridley et al, 2000; Margesson, 2001; BSSVD, 2002; Edwards et al, 2002;]

Complications and prognosis

- **If correctly diagnosed,** most underlying causes can be successfully treated.
- **Failure to diagnose serious underlying conditions,** such as neoplasia, can be fatal.
- **Pruritus at night** can result in sleep loss and reduce quality of life [Dambro, 1996].
- **Embarrassment and stigma** may be felt by some women, which could potentially lead to sexual problems and psychiatric morbidity, such as anxiety states and neuroses [Jeffcoate and Tindall, 1987].
- **Topical products** may exacerbate pruritus in some women.

Management issues

- Confirming the diagnosis p.1596
- Treating the underlying cause p.1596
- General advice for all vulval conditions p.1597
- Topical therapy for symptomatic treatment of vulval itch p.1597

Confirming the diagnosis

- **The underlying cause must always be sought** — the majority of cases of vulval itching will have an identifiable cause.
- **Misdiagnosis is possible,** therefore consider reviewing each woman in order to observe the development of any potentially malignant changes within the area of the pruritus.
- **Reassurance and tact** may help to reduce the possible embarrassment and stigma felt by the woman.

Treating the underlying cause

- **Appropriate treatment of the underlying cause** should resolve the pruritus.
- **In addition to treating the underlying cause, some general advice for care of the vulva and symptomatic treatments will be useful for most women** (see sections on *General advice for all vulval conditions* and *Topical therapy for symptomatic treatment of vulval itch*).
- **Infections:** Vulval and vaginal infections are treated with the appropriate antibiotic, antifungal, antiviral, or other agent. See separate PRODIGY guidance on *Candida — female genital*, *Trichomoniasis*, *Bacterial vaginosis*, *Chlamydia*, *Candida — skin and nails*, *Herpes simplex — genital*, *Threadworm*, *Pubic lice*, and *Scabies*.
- **Dermatological conditions:** Dermatologists or gynaecologists with the necessary expertise will be able to give comprehensive advice for the treatment of individuals, but in general terms, the following management is suitable:
  - **Contact dermatitis** should be treated by identifying and removing the irritants (e.g. soaps and deodorants). Corticosteroid treatment is secondary to the avoidance of irritants and protective measures.
  - **Seborrhoeic dermatitis and psoriasis** can usually be treated with careful use of topical corticosteroids (sometimes combined with an antibacterial or anticandidal agent). In psoriasis, avoid dithranol, tar,

and calcipotriol, as they are too irritating to be used on the vulva.
- **Lichen simplex** can be treated with potent corticosteroids to break the itch–scratch cycle (always make sure that any underlying eczema or psoriasis has been ruled out).
- **Lichen sclerosus** and **lichen planus** may respond to short-term regular potent or superpotent topical corticosteroids followed by maintenance of less frequent application. Super potent corticosteroids should not be used unless a diagnosis has been firmly established. Lichen sclerosus is a relatively common condition and benign presentations should be managed by either the GP, a dermatologist or gynaecologist depending upon expertise and local protocol. Malignant presentations are uncommon but where there are concerns, consider urgent referral. Women with lichen sclerosus have a small risk (2–5%) of developing carcinoma, so long-term follow-up is recommended.

- **Cancer:** women with an unexplained vulval lump or with vulval bleeding due to ulceration should be referred urgently to a team specialising in the management of gynaecological cancer, depending upon local arrangements [NICE, 2005].
- **Declining oestrogen levels causing atrophic vaginitis** — for oestrogen therapy see the PRODIGY guidance on *Menopause*.
- **Other medical conditions that may cause generalized pruritus** for which there is separate PRODIGY guidance are *Anaemia — iron deficiency*, *Anaemia — macrocytic*, *Hyperthyroidism*, and *Hypothyroidism*.
- **If no underlying cause is identified,** the itch–scratch cycle may be broken by the application of low-dose topical corticosteroid for a trial period. If the symptoms persist the corticosteroid should be stopped, and referral should be considered.

[Dambro, 1996; Ridley et al, 2000; BSSVD, 2002; Edwards et al, 2002]

General advice for all vulval conditions

- These recommendations are based on expert opinion, because there is little published evidence on general care of the vulva.
- Vulval skin is sensitive, and may react to irritants such as soaps. Women should avoid all contact of the vulval skin with soap, shampoo, bubble bath, perfumes, personal deodorants, wet wipes, textile dyes, detergents, fabric conditioners and sanitary wear.
- Certain types of clothing may make vulval disease (including itching symptoms) worse. Women should avoid tight-fitting garments that may irritate the area.
- People should avoid use of spermicidally-lubricated condoms.
- Women should be given a detailed explanation of their condition with particular emphasis on the long-term implications for the health of themselves and their partner(s). This should be reinforced by giving them clear and accurate written information. (See PRODIGY patient leaflet and The British Society for the Study of Vulval Disease patient information leaflets at www.bssvd.org/leaflets.asp)

[BSSVD, 2002; Edwards et al, 2002]

Topical therapy for symptomatic treatment of vulval itch

- These recommendations are based on expert opinion, because there is little published evidence on symptomatic treatment for pruritus vulvae.
- **Symptomatic treatment for vulval itching may give some relief, but should not be a substitute for seeking and treating the underlying cause.**
- **Emollients** are suitable for easing itching symptoms in almost all types of vulval disease, and can be used in addition to most other therapies:
  - If the vulval condition is inflammatory, emollients should be used liberally as a moisturizer and soap substitute.
  - There is a lack of good quality evidence comparing emollients and choice of preparation will depend on the individual [MeReC, 1998]. There is also wide inter-patient variability in response to particular products.
  - If topical corticosteroids are being used concomitantly, they may be more effective if applied immediately before emollients. Alternatively, if applying the emollient first, wait for 10–20 minutes before applying the topical corticosteroid to ensure the skin is moisturized, and to prevent the corticosteroid being spread to other skin areas [MeReC, 1999].
  - Over-the-counter medications containing emollients may be suitable for individuals, but advice about these should include information on the potential sensitizing and irritating effect of many of the products.
- **Corticosteroids** are effective at alleviating itching in many cases, but must only be given if suitable for the underlying condition (e.g. dermatitis, psoriasis):
  - Do not use super potent topical corticosteroids unless the diagnosis is established as the diagnostic clinical and histological features will be lost.
  - Women may infer from package inserts that the preparation should not be applied to the genital area, so it is important to give them a clear explanation about how to use the corticosteroid (e.g. half a fingertip unit OR up to one fingertip unit for one application will suffice).
  - A trial of corticosteroids may alleviate the itch if no underlying cause can be found. If corticosteroids are ineffective after 1–2 weeks, consider referral to a specialist.
- **Antihistamines:** There is little evidence that antihistamines are effective in treating non-histamine-mediated pruritus [Marek-Thompson and Bond, 2000]. Sedating oral antihistamines help women to cope with vulval itching by causing sedation rather than by any other effect. Non-sedating oral anti-histamines have no proven clinical efficacy in relieving pruritus [Klein and Clark, 1999].

[Ridley et al, 2000]

References

NHS staff in England can link, free of charge, from references to full text journals by clicking on [Full text] on the PRODIGY website.

1. BNF 43 (2002) *British National Formulary*. 43rd edn. London: British Medical Association and Royal Pharmaceutical Society of Great Britain.
2. BSSVD (2002) *Patient leaflets: lichen simplex*. British Society for the Study of Vulval Disease. www.bssvd.org/leaflets.asp [Accessed: 12/07/2005].
3. Dambro, M.R. (Ed.) (1996) *Griffith's 5 minute clinical consult*. Baltimore, USA: Williams and Wilkins.
4. DTB (1998) Antiseptic/emollient combinations. *Drug & Therapeutics Bulletin* 36(11), 84–86.
5. Edwards, S., Handfield-Jones, S. and Gull, S. (2002) National guideline on the management of vulval conditions. *International Journal of STD & AIDS* **13**(6), 411–415.

6. Goolamali, S.K. (1981) Pruritus vulvae. *Clinics in Obstetrics and Gynaecology* 8(1), 227–240.
7. Jeffcoate, N. and Tindall, V.R. (1987) Pruritus vulvae. In: *Jeffcoates's principles of gynaecology*. 5th edn. London: Butterworths. 553–558.
8. Kehoe, S. and Luesley, D. (1995) Pathology and management of vulval pain and pruritus. *Current Opinion in Obstetrics & Gynaecology* 7(1), 16–19.
9. Klein, P.A. and Clark, R.A. (1999) An evidence-based review of the efficacy of antihistamines in relieving pruritus in atopic dermatitis. *Archives of Dermatology* 135(12), 1522–1525. [Full text]
10. Lavery, H.A. (1986) The management of pruritus vulvae. *Practitioner* 230, 167–171.
11. Marek-Thompson, T.A. and Bond, C.A. (2000) Pruritus. In: Koda-Kimble, M.A. and Young, L.Y. (Eds.) *Applied therapeutics: the clinical use of drugs*. 7th edn. Baltimore: Lippincott Wiliams and Wilkins. 1–16.
12. Margesson, L.J. (2001) Vulvovaginal dryness and itching. *Skin Therapy Letter* 6(10), 3–4.
13. MeReC (1998) The use of emollients in dry skin conditions. *MeReC Bulletin* 9(12), 45–48.
14. MeReC (1999) Using topical corticosteroids in general practice. *MeReC Bulletin* 10(6), 21–24.
15. NICE (2005) *Referral guidelines for suspected cancer – quick reference guide.* Clinical guideline 27. National Institute for Health and Clinical Excellence. www.nice.org.uk [Accessed: 01/07/2005].
16. Phillips, W.G. (1992) Pruritus – what to do when the itching won't stop. *Postgraduate Medicine* 92(7), 34–36.
17. Ridley, C.M., Robinson, A.J., Oriel, J.D. and Barker, G.H. (Eds.) (2000) *Vulval disease: a practical guide to diagnosis and management*. London: Arnold.
18. Sherertz, E.F. (1994) Clinical Pearl: symptomatic dermatographism as a cause of genital pruritus. *Journal of the American Academy of Dermatology* 31(6), 1040–1041.

P

PRODIGY GUIDANCE

Pubic lice

Last revised in February 2004
www.prodigy.nhs.uk/guidance.asp?gt=Pubic lice

Applies to people over the age of 6 months

This guidance covers the management of pubic or crab lice infestation (*pediculosis pubis*).

There is separate PRODIGY guidance for the management of *Head lice* and *Scabies*.

Goals

- To eradicate live pubic lice and viable eggs

Contents

Scenarios
- Treatment of pubic lice p.1599

Extended Information, p. 1601

Treatment of pubic lice

Which therapy?

- **Adult lice and/or eggs need to be found to confirm the diagnosis.**
- **Sexual contacts and close family contacts should be examined, and treated if infested.**
- **Give two applications of insecticide, used 7 days apart.**
  - Use malathion 0.5% aqueous liquid, phenothrin 0.5% aqueous liquid, or permethrin 5% dermal cream.
  - Give 100 ml liquid or 30 g cream per application.
  - Advise people to inspect the body 1 week after the final application to check that treatment was successful.
- **If itching is troublesome,** oral sedative antihistamines given at night may be useful for breaking the itch–scratch cycle.
- **Screening for coexisting sexually transmitted infections is recommended.** (Note: people need to give informed consent prior to screening.) Consider referral to a genito-urinary medicine clinic.
- **If treatment failure or reinfestation occurs,** use a different insecticide for the second course of treatment.

Factors affecting choice of treatment

- **Pregnancy and breastfeeding:** use a single application of malathion (in an aqueous base). If this is ineffective, consider a second application after an interval of at least 7 days. Consider chlorphenamine (chlorpheniramine) to relieve itch. Do not use hydroxyzine.
- **Benign prostatic hyperplasia, urinary retention, or glaucoma:** avoid sedating antihistamines.
- **Epilepsy:** avoid antihistamines (which may lower the seizure threshold).

Practical prescribing points

For further information please see the *Medicines Compendium* (www.medicines.org.uk) or the *British National Formulary* (www.bnf.org). For further information regarding pregnancy, contact the National Teratology Information Service (telephone 0191 232 152).

- **Apply treatment to *all* parts of the body below the neck** (not merely the groin and axillae).
  - Apply malathion or phenothrin aqueous liquids for 12 hours or overnight.
  - Apply permethrin 5% dermal cream for 24 hours.
- **Beards and moustaches should be carefully treated, but not usually other areas of the head** unless the hair is widely spaced (e.g. in red hair).
- **Shaving the infested area(s) does not provide protection from reinfestation.**
- **Advise the person that sedative antihistamines cause drowsiness, which may persist the next day.** People should not drive or operate machinery if affected.

Follow-up advice

- **People should be advised to check for the absence of lice 1 week after the second application of treatment,** to confirm that treatment was successful.
- **If treatment failure or reinfestation occurs,** a different insecticide should be used for the second course of treatment.

Should I refer or investigate?

Refer?

- **Consider referral to a genito-urinary medicine clinic** for specialist advice, diagnostic services, and partner notification. Contact-tracing of partners from the previous 3 months should be undertaken.

Investigate?

- **Screening for coexisting sexually transmitted infections is recommended.** (Note: people need to give informed consent prior to screening.)

Patient information leaflets

The following PILs are available at www.prodigy.nhs.uk

- Medicines - Name Changes of Medicines
- Pubic Lice

Shared decision making

- **Pubic lice can affect other parts of the body — not just the pubic area.**
- **Treat the whole body below the neck, plus any beard and moustache, but not the rest of the head.** (Avoid eyes and mouth.) Options include:
  - **Malathion lotion.** Leave it on for 12 hours, then wash it off. An adult needs about 100 ml. A small paintbrush may be helpful in applying it.
  - **Permethrin cream.** Leave it on for 24 hours, then wash it off. The cream is not suitable for pregnant or breastfeeding women, or for children.
- **You need two treatments, seven days apart.**
- Occasionally, some people (e.g. those with red hair) may need to apply treatment to the scalp as well.
- **Antihistamine tablets may help with itch,** which can last for a few days after treatment.

P

- **You do not need to shave affected areas or wash bedding, clothes, etc.**
- **Avoid close bodily contact** until you have finished treatment.
- **All close contacts and sleeping partners should be checked.**

Drug rationale

Drugs not included

Treatment of pubic lice

- **Alcohol-based products** are not included, because they irritate excoriated skin and genitalia.
- **Benzyl benzoate** is licensed for the treatment of pubic lice, but is not included because it causes irritation, especially to the genitals.
- **Carbaryl** should be considered only when resistance to all other insecticides is suspected. Carbaryl is now a prescription-only medicine (because of reports of carcinogenicity in rodents after continuous dosing) [Chief Medical Officer, 1995] and is no longer licensed for treating pubic lice.

Treatment of itch

- **Non-sedative antihistamines** have not been shown to be effective in relieving pruritus. Sedative effects may be desirable to help break the itch–scratch cycle at night.
- **Long-acting sedating antihistamines** are not included, so there is minimal 'hangover' effect.
- **Topical antihistamines** may cause sensitization, are only marginally effective, and are therefore not recommended.
- **Preparations containing calamine** do not offer significant benefit in most people, and are not recommended.

Drugs included

Treatment of pubic lice

- **Aqueous-based products** are preferred because they are less likely to irritate excoriated skin and the genitalia, or to cause wheezing in people with asthma [BNF 45, 2003].
- **Malathion 0.5% aqueous liquid** is licensed for the treatment of pubic lice.
- **Phenothrin 0.5% aqueous liquid** is an alternative, but this is an off-licence use.
- **Permethrin 5% dermal cream** is also licensed for the treatment of pubic lice, but only for adults.

Treatment of itch

- **Hydroxyzine** is specifically licensed for pruritus and is sedating. Hydroxyzine is offered as a night-time dose for temporary help with sleeping, to help break the itch–scratch cycle.
- **Chlorphenamine (chlorpheniramine)** is also included because it is inexpensive, and is an effective sedating antihistamine of intermediate duration.

Prescriptions

Usual treatment options

Aqueous-based liquid: malathion

- Age from 6 months onwards
- Malathion 0.5% aqueous liquid. Apply to the whole body from the neck down. Leave on for 12 hours or overnight. Wash off. Repeat after 7 days; supply 200 ml; NHS Cost £5.28; OTC Cost £9.25.

Aqueous-based liquid: phenothrin

- Age from 6 months onwards
- Phenothrin 0.5% aqueous liquid. Apply to the whole body from the neck down. Leave on for 12 hours or overnight. Wash off. Repeat after 7 days; supply 200 ml; NHS Cost £5.28; OTC Cost £9.25.

Dermal cream: permethrin

- Age from 18 years onwards
- Permethrin 5% dermal cream. Apply to all hairy parts of the body. Leave on for 24 hours. Wash off. Repeat after 7 days; supply 60 grams; NHS Cost £11.04; OTC Cost £19.24.

Pregnancy and breastfeeding

Aqueous-based liquid: malathion

- Age from 12 to 60 years
- Malathion 0.5% aqueous liquid. Apply to the whole body from the neck down. Leave on for 12 hours or overnight. Wash off; supply 100 ml; NHS Cost £4.44.

Sedating antihistamine (for sleep disturbance)

Chlorphenamine (chlorpheniramine) syrup: 1mg at night prn

- Age from 6 to 11 months
- Chlorphenamine 2mg/5ml syrup. Take 2.5ml at night when required for relief of itching; supply 50 ml; NHS Cost £0.72.

Chlorphenamine (chlorpheniramine) syrup: 1mg at night prn

- Age from 12 to 23 months
- Chlorphenamine 2mg/5ml syrup. Take 2.5ml at night when required for relief of itching; supply 50 ml; NHS Cost £0.72; OTC Cost £1.26.

Chlorphenamine (chlorpheniramine) syrup: 1-2mg at night prn

- Age from 2 to 5 years
- Chlorphenamine 2mg/5ml syrup. Take 2.5ml to 5ml at night when required for relief of itching; supply 100 ml; NHS Cost £1.43; OTC Cost £2.53.

Chlorphenamine (chlorpheniramine) syrup: 2-4mg at night prn

- Age from 6 to 11 years
- Chlorphenamine 2mg/5ml syrup. Take one to two 5ml spoonfuls at night when required for relief of itching; supply 100 ml; NHS Cost £1.43; OTC Cost £2.53.

Chlorphenamine (chlorpheniramine) tablets: 4mg at night prn

- Age from 12 years onwards
- Chlorphenamine 4mg tablets. Take one tablet at night when required for relief of itching; supply 14 tablets; NHS Cost £0.22; OTC Cost £1.40.

Hydroxyzine syrup: 5mg to 15mg at night when required

- Age from 6 months to 6 years
- Hydroxyzine 10mg/5ml syrup. Take 2.5ml to 7.5ml at night when required for relief of itching; supply 100 ml; NHS Cost £0.96.

Hydroxyzine syrup: 15mg to 25mg at night when required

- Age from 7 to 11 years
- Hydroxyzine 10mg/5ml syrup. Take 7.5ml to 12.5ml at night when required for relief of itching; supply 200 ml; NHS Cost £1.91.

Hydroxyzine tablets: 25mg at night when required

- Age from 12 years onwards
- Hydroxyzine 25mg tablets. Take one tablet at night when required for relief of itching; supply 14 tablets; NHS Cost £0.51.

Extended Information

Background information

- What is it? p.1601
- How common is it? p.1601
- How do I know my patient has it? p.1601
- How is it transmitted? p.1601
- What else might it be? p.1601

What is it?

- The pubic louse is 'crab' shaped, grey-brown in colour, and about 2 mm in length (smaller than a match-head).
- The female lays eggs (smaller than a pinhead) on the hair shaft, near to the body. The eggs hatch after about 7 days. The empty eggshells (nits) are tightly attached to the hair and cannot be brushed off.

[Ibarra, 1998]

How common is it?

- The exact incidence of pubic lice is unknown, but it is thought to be quite common among young adults.

[Ibarra, 1998]

How do I know my patient has it?

- **Itching is the most common presenting symptom,** and is due to hypersensitivity to feeding lice. Itching is worse at night and may not develop for several weeks.
- **Adult lice and/or eggs need to be found to confirm the diagnosis.**
- **Pubic lice may be found in any coarse hair,** such as moustaches, beards, and axillary hair, as well as pubic hair. Therefore, all hairy parts of the body may need to be examined.
- **The eyebrows and eyelashes can also be affected,** but this generally occurs only in young children.
- **Pubic lice can also be found around the scalp margins.** Lice are most likely to be found when the hair shafts are widely spaced (e.g. in red hair).
- **Blue macules** (maculae caerulae) may be visible at feeding sites.
- **Scatterings of minute dark-brown specks** (louse excreta) are sometimes seen on the skin and underwear.

[Burns, 1998; Ibarra, 1998; Wendel and Rompalo, 2002]

How is it transmitted?

- **Pubic lice are transmitted by close body contact,** which can be from sexual contact or from close family contact (e.g. from an infested beard or chest).
- **Pubic lice are not transmitted via clothing, bed linen, or toilet seats.**

[Ibarra, 1998; Wendel and Rompalo, 2002]

What else might it be?

- **Seborrhoeic scales, small crusts of scratched dermatitis, and hair casts** (which can all be brushed off) may be confused with nits (which stick to the hair like glue).
- **Clothing lice (*Pediculus humanis*) and head lice (*Pediculus capitis*)** are slightly larger than pubic lice. Clothing lice are found only on clothes, not on body hairs. Head lice are found only on the scalp.

Management issues

- General p.1601
- How should I treat pubic lice? p.1601
- How should treatment be applied? p.1601
- Treatment of itch p.1601
- Eyelash infestation p.1601
- Treatment failure p.1601
- Medicines management p.1602

General

- **Sexual contacts and close family contacts should be examined, and treated if infested.**
- **Screening for coexisting sexually transmitted infections is recommended.** (Note: people need to give informed consent prior to screening.)
- Consider referral to a genito-urinary medicine clinic for specialist advice, diagnostic services, and partner notification.
- Contact-tracing of partners from the previous 3 months should be undertaken.

[Scott, 2001]

How should I treat pubic lice?

- **Two applications of insecticide are used 7 days apart.** (The second application of insecticide is used to kill pubic lice emerging from eggs that survived the first application.)
- **Use malathion 0.5% aqueous liquid, permethrin 5% dermal cream, or phenothrin 0.5% aqueous liquid.** Note: permethrin dermal cream is licensed for use only in those over 18 years of age, and phenothrin aqueous liquid is not licensed for the treatment of pubic lice.
- **People should be advised to check for the absence of lice 1 week after treatment is complete,** to ensure that treatment was successful.
- **Shaving the infested area(s) will not provide protection from reinfestation,** because pubic lice need only a minimal length of hair on which to lay eggs.

How should treatment be applied?

- **Treatment should be applied to all parts of the body** (not merely the groin and axillae) [BNF 45, 2003]. Beards and moustaches should be carefully treated, but not usually other areas of the head.
- **Consider treating the scalp if the hair is widely spaced** (e.g. for red hair) [Ibarra, 1998].
- **Aqueous-based liquids should be applied for 12 hours or overnight** (e.g. malathion or phenothrin). Permethrin 5% dermal cream should be applied for 24 hours.

P

Treatment of itch

- **Antihistamines are of little help** in treating pruritus [DTB, 2002].
- **However, it may be useful to give an oral sedative antihistamine at night** for temporary help with sleeping, to break the itch–scratch cycle.

Eyelash infestation

- **Pubic lice can occasionally infest the eyelashes,** but this generally only occurs in young children.
- **Petroleum jelly** can be applied to the lashes and lids twice a day for 10 days [Clinical Effectiveness Group, 1999].
- Aqueous malathion or permethrin 1% cream rinse have also been used, but they are not licensed for this indication. Permethrin 5% dermal cream can cause irritation to the eyes, so it should not be used [Rundle and Hughes, 1993; Ibarra, 1998; Clinical Effectiveness Group, 1999; ABPI Medicines Compendium, 2001; BNF 45, 2003].

Treatment failure

- **Before using another course of treatment, consider whether** treatment failure could be due to inadequate treatment, incorrectly applied treatment, misdiagnosis, or reinfestation (e.g. were all infested contacts treated?).

- **Use a different class of insecticide for the second course of treatment.** This change reduces repeated exposure to the same insecticide, and it is hoped that resistance will emerge more slowly as a result (although resistance of pubic lice to insecticides has not been studied in the UK). Note: permethrin and phenothrin are from the same chemical class (pyrethroids).
- **Carbaryl should be considered only when resistance to all other insecticides is suspected.** There are no longer any carbaryl preparations licensed for the treatment of pubic lice available in the UK, and it is now a prescription-only medicine (licensed for the treatment of head lice) because of reports of carcinogenicity in rodents after continuous dosing [Chief Medical Officer, 1995].

Medicines management

Insecticides

- **Aqueous-based preparations are preferred** (for both adults and children). Alcoholic lotions are not recommended, because they irritate excoriated skin and genitalia, and may cause wheezing in people with asthma.
- **For each application, 100 ml of liquid or 30 g of cream is needed to treat an average-sized adult.**
- Concerns have been raised in the past that topical malathion (an organophosphate) could potentially cause serious systemic adverse effects. However, a recent Committee on Safety of Medicines review concluded there is no evidence to suggest that this is the case [CSM, 2000].
- **Children:** malathion can be used for children aged over 6 months (note: pubic lice infestation is likely to occur only on the eyelashes in children younger than this). Permethrin is only licensed for the treatment of adults aged 18 years or over.

Sedating antihistamines

P

- **Advise people that drowsiness may persist the next day, and that they should not drive or operate machinery if affected.**
- **Antimuscarinic adverse effects** (sedation, dry mouth, urinary retention, blurred vision) are common. Sedating antihistamines should therefore be avoided in someone with prostatic hypertrophy, urinary retention, or glaucoma. Antihistamines may also reduce the seizure threshold, and so should be avoided in someone with epilepsy.

Pregnancy and breastfeeding

- **The National Teratology Information Service currently recommends malathion** because it is poorly absorbed and rapidly eliminated. A single application should be used where possible. If a single dose is ineffective, a second application could be considered after an interval of at least 7 days (telephone 0191 232 1525 for further information) [National Teratology Information Service, 1999].
- **Breastfeeding mothers** should remove the liquid or cream from the nipples before breastfeeding, and reapply treatment afterwards.
- **If treatment of itch is required,** consider chlorphenamine (chlorpheniramine). Avoid hydroxyzine, crotamiton, and topical steroid creams.

References

NHS staff in England can link, free of charge, from references to full text journals by clicking on [Full text] on the PRODIGY website.

1. ABPI Medicines Compendium (2001) *Summary of product characteristics for Lyclear Dermal Cream.* Datapharm Communications Ltd. www.emc.medicines.org.uk [Accessed: 23/08/2003].
2. BNF 45 (2003) *British National Formulary.* 45th edn. London: British Medical Association and Royal Pharmaceutical Society of Great Britain.
3. Burns, D.A. (1998) Diseases caused by arthropods and other noxious animals: *phthiriasis pubis.* In: Champion, R.H., Burton, J.L., Burns, D.A. and Breathnach, S.M. (Eds.) *Textbook of dermatology.* Oxford: Blackwell Science Ltd. 1443–1444.
4. Chief Medical Officer (1995) *New advice to government on use of insecticide as a treatment for lice: experts advise restricted use of carbaryl.* London: Department of Health.
5. Clinical Effectiveness Group (1999) *National guideline for the management of phthirus pubis infestation.* London: Assoication for Genitourinary Medicine and the Medical Society for the Study of Veneral Disease.
6. CSM (2000) Safety of malathion for the treatment of louse and scabies infestation. *Current Problems in Pharmacovigilance* 26(May), 2.
7. DTB (2002) Oral antihistamines for allergic disorders. *Drug & Therapeutics Bulletin* 40(8), 59–62. [Full text]
8. Ibarra, J. (1998) Phthiriasis. In: Figueroa, J., Hall, S., Ibarra, J. et al (Eds.) *Primary health care guide to common UK parasitic diseases.* London: Community Hygiene Concern. 21–24.
9. National Teratology Information Service (1999) *Management of scabies and head lice in pregnancy.* NHS Northern and Yorkshire: Regional Drug and Therapeutics Centre.
10. Rundle, P.A. and Hughes, D.S. (1993) *Phthirus pubis* infestation of the eyelids. *British Journal of Ophthalmology* 77(12), 815–816.
11. Scott, G.R. (2001) European guideline for the management of *pediculosis pubis. International Journal of STD & AIDS* 12(Suppl 3), 62. [Full text]
12. Wendel, K. and Rompalo, A. (2002) Scabies and *pediculosis pubis*: an update of treatment regimens and general review. *Clinical Infectious Diseases* 35(Suppl 2), S146-S151.

PRODIGY GUIDANCE

Pyelonephritis — acute

Last revised in April 2002
At the time of print this topic was being updated. The newly revised guidance will be issued on to the website in late 2005.
www.prodigy.nhs.uk/guidance.asp?gt=Pyelonephritis - acute

Applies to people over the age of 16 years

This guidance covers the management of acute pyelonephritis.
It does not cover complicated pyelonephritis (i.e. pyelonephritis in which there is underlying deficient host response or increased susceptibility to infection); recurrent pyelonephritis; or chronic pyelonephritis.

There is separate PRODIGY guidance for *Prostatitis, Urinary tract infection (lower) — men, Urinary tract infection (lower) — women,* and *Urinary tract infection — children.*

Goals

- To treat infection, reduce symptoms, and prevent complications

Contents

Scenarios

- Acute pyelonephritis p.1603

Extended Information, p. 1604

Acute pyelonephritis

Which therapy?

- **Ensure adequate hydration** to maintain urine output.
- **Treat pain or fever** with paracetamol or ibuprofen according to severity.
- **Antimicrobials** should be started immediately without waiting for culture results.
- **Review culture results and adjust** according to sensitivities and clinical response.
- **If there is no response within 48 hours consider admission to hospital.**

Practical prescribing points

For further information please see the *Medicines Compendium* (www.medicines.org.uk) or the *British National Formulary* (www.bnf.org).

Breastfeeding women

- **Quinolones** are not recommended in breastfeeding women as they can be excreted into breast milk.

Other cautions

- **Quinolones** may cause tendon damage (Committee on Safety of Medicines [CSM] advice in BNF). They can induce convulsions in people with epilepsy or in those with conditions that predispose to seizures. People concurrently taking nonsteroidal anti-inflammatory drugs (NSAIDs) may also be susceptible to seizures.
- **Co-amoxiclav** may rarely cause cholestatic jaundice during or shortly after a course of treatment (CSM advice in BNF). Cholestatic jaundice is more common in men, in people aged over 65 years, and with longer courses of treatment. In people with liver disease, the liver function needs to be monitored. In people with moderate to severe renal impairment, the dose should be reduced.
- **Ibuprofen**, as with other NSAIDs, may worsen or precipitate gastrointestinal haemorrhage, asthma, hypertension, renal impairment, or cardiac failure. Avoid if there is a history of peptic ulcers.

Follow-up advice

- Follow-up is important in order to check that the person has responded to treatment. The timing of follow-up depends on the clinical scenario, but should be sufficiently soon to pick up any possible deterioration in the person.

Should I refer or investigate?

Refer?

Hospital admission is indicated for:

- Acute severe pyelonephritis (suggested by the presence of systemic symptoms other than fever)
- People with severe nausea and vomiting (oral antimicrobials and fluids poorly tolerated)
- Pregnant women
- People with diabetes
- Complicated pyelonephritis, that is, where functional or structural abnormalities are present
- Treatment failure or relapse after a 2-week course of oral therapy — intravenous treatment may be required
- Men who relapse when not taking treatment — may require secondary care investigations

Less urgent referral for investigation is indicated in:

- Repeated episodes of acute pyelonephritis

Investigate?

- **Urine culture and sensitivity testing should be performed in all people.**
- **For complicated pyelonephritis,** imaging of upper urinary tract (usually with intravenous pyelogram or ultrasound) would be performed in secondary care.

Patient information leaflets

The following PILs are available at www.prodigy.nhs.uk

- Kidney Infection (Pyelonephritis)
- Midstream Specimen of Urine (MSU)

Shared decision making

- **Antibiotics** are the main treatment for a kidney infection and should be started straight away.
- **A urine test** is needed. This will find which bacterium is causing the infection and whether the antibiotic needs to be changed.

P

- **Drink plenty** to prevent dehydration.
- **Painkillers** such as paracetamol or ibuprofen ease pain and reduce fever.
- You should improve over the next two or three days with the antibiotic. See a doctor if symptoms become worse.
- **It is important to complete the full course of antibiotics,** as some bacteria may be present for a few days after symptoms have gone.

Drug rationale

Drugs not included

- **Trimethoprim** should not be used for empirical treatment of pyelonephritis without culture results.
- **Penicillin-group agents such as amoxicillin** are unsuitable for empirical therapy without culture results, because about 50% of all urinary pathogen isolates are amoxicillin-resistant.
- **First-generation cephalosporins** are not recommended for empirical therapy because there is an increasing incidence of resistance to these agents.
- **Second-generation cephalosporins** are not as well absorbed orally as first-generation cephalosporins, have a greater incidence of gastrointestinal adverse effects, and are more expensive than the first-generation agents.
- **Third-generation cephalosporins** generally require parenteral administration. Cefotaxime has been recommended as an initial therapy for pyelonephritis but, along with other third-generation agents, would be administered in secondary care for more serious infections.
- **Nitrofurantoin** is not offered because it does not achieve high concentrations in renal tissue.
- **Quinolones other than norfloxacin and ciprofloxacin** should be reserved as second-line agents, or for complicated infections where sensitivities are known, in order to preserve their efficacy and limit the development of resistance. The newer quinolones have a slightly broader spectrum of activity than the older agents but there is no evidence of greater efficacy.
- **Erythromycin and other macrolides** have poor activity against Gram-negative organisms and are unsuitable for empirical treatment.
- **Tetracyclines** are unsuitable for empirical treatment because they have poor Gram-negative activity.
- **Co-trimoxazole** is restricted to certain prescribing indications by Committee on Safety of Medicines (CSM) recommendation and it should only be used if there is good bacteriological evidence of sensitivity and reason to prefer it to another therapy.

[Stamm and Hooton, 1993; Medicines Resource, 1995; MeReC, 1995; De Craen et al, 1996; DTB, 1998; MeReC, 1998; Read, 2000; BNF 42, 2001]

Drugs included

The choice of antibiotic is primarily based on recommendations by the Public Health Laboratory Service (PHLS) for the empirical treatment of acute pyelonephritis. Local advice or protocols should be followed if available, and a local microbiologist consulted. Therapy changes should be guided by results of urine culture and sensitivity tests.

- **Norfloxacin and ciprofloxacin** are effective against most urinary pathogens (only around 5% of pathogens are resistant) and both are licensed for upper urinary tract infections (UTIs). A recent randomized controlled trial (RCT) indicated that a 7-day course of ciprofloxacin is adequate in acute uncomplicated pyelonephritis. Norfloxacin and ciprofloxacin are the least expensive quinolones.
- **Co-amoxiclav** is a suitable alternative for infections caused by bacteria resistant to trimethoprim or other agents. It is effective against up to 90% of urinary pathogens.
- **Paracetamol** is an effective, safe analgesic and antipyretic.
- **Ibuprofen** is a good alternative to paracetamol if there are no contraindications.

[DTB, 1998; Talan et al, 2000; Cooper, 2001; Cooper and Jepson, 2001]

Prescriptions

1st-line antibiotics

Norfloxacin 400mg twice a day for 7 days
- Age from 16 years onwards
- Norfloxacin 400mg tablets. Take one tablet twice a day for 7 days; supply 14 tablets; NHS Cost £4.72.

Ciprofloxacin 500mg twice a day for 7 days
- Age from 16 years onwards
- Ciprofloxacin 500mg tablets. Take one tablet twice a day for 7 days; supply 14 tablets; NHS Cost £19.88.

Co-amoxiclav 500/125mg three times a day for 14 days
- Age from 16 years onwards
- Co-amoxiclav 625mg tablets. Take one tablet three times a day for 14 days; supply 42 tablets; NHS Cost £31.44.

Analgesic/antipyretic: use when required

Paracetamol 1g up to four times a day
- Age from 16 years onwards
- Paracetamol 500mg tablets. Take two tablets every 4 to 6 hours when required for relief of pain or high temperature. Maximum of 8 tablets in 24 hours; supply 50 tablets; NHS Cost £0.38; OTC Cost £0.70.

Ibuprofen 400mg three times a day
- Age from 16 years onwards
- Ibuprofen 400mg tablets. Take one tablet three times a day when required for relief of pain or high temperature. Do not exceed the stated dose; supply 21 tablets; NHS Cost £0.61; OTC Cost £1.08.

Extended Information

Background information

- What is it? p.1604
- How common is it? p.1605
- How do I know my patient has it? p.1605
- What else might it be? p.1605
- Complications and prognosis p.1605

What is it?

- Pyelonephritis is an infection of the upper urinary tract, specifically of the kidney and renal pelvis.
- It may be classified as acute or chronic, and as complicated or uncomplicated:
  - **Acute pyelonephritis** is the result of acute suppuration
  - **Chronic pyelonephritis** or chronic interstitial nephritis is the result of a chronic bacterial infection. (Non-infectious causes of chronic interstitial nephritis are not covered here.)
  - **Uncomplicated pyelonephritis**
    - Infection by a usual pathogen in a person with a normal urinary tract and with normal renal function
  - **Complicated pyelonephritis**

- Abnormal urinary tract, for example calculus, vesicoureteric reflux, obstruction, neurogenic bladder, indwelling catheter
- Abnormal renal function
- Immunocompromised, e.g. neutropaenia, immunosuppressive therapy, diabetes mellitus
- Virulent organism, e.g. urease-producing *Proteus* species

- Bilateral pyelonephritis can cause acute oliguric renal failure.
- *Escherichia coli* is the commonest pathogen (more than 80% of acute pyelonephritis cases). Other organisms include *Enterococcus faecalis*, and *Klebsiella* and *Proteus* species. The infection usually starts in the bladder and ascends to the renal parenchyma. Initially the bacteria replicate within the tubules. By 48 hours damage to the tubular epithelium has started.
- Pyelonephritis may occur following genito-urinary instrumentation.

How common is it?

- The epidemiology of pyelonephritis is poorly documented. In the USA the annual incidence of acute pyelonephritis is 250,000.

[Cooper, 2001]

How do I know my patient has it?

- **Symptoms** of acute pyelonephritis include high fever (39°C or greater), rigors, flank pain (which is usually unilateral and may worsen on micturition), nausea, vomiting, and diarrhoea. Symptoms of cystitis (frequency, dysuria, etc.) may or may not be present. Symptoms develop rapidly over a few hours or a day.
- **Examination** usually finds pyrexia, tachycardia, muscle pain, and tenderness on deep pressure in one or both costovertebral angles or on deep abdominal palpation.
- **Urinalysis and urine culture** usually reveal bacteriuria, pyuria, and haematuria.
- **Silent/subclinical pyelonephritis** may occur. This is more common in:
  - Diabetes
  - Those receiving immunosuppressive treatment
  - Pregnant women with urinary tract infection (UTI)
  - Those with a history of previous UTI before the age of 12 years
  - People who have had three or more UTIs in the past year
  - People with a previous history of pyelonephritis
- There should therefore be a low threshold for culturing the urine in these groups. It is postulated that many people with cystitis that is not cured with standard antibiotic therapy have silent pyelonephritis [Bergeron, 1995].
- **Levels of C-reactive protein** (CRP) tend to be elevated in pyelonephritis but normal with cystitis. However CRP is non-specific for pyelonephritis since it is raised in many other conditions.

What else might it be?

- Renal calculi (which may also coexist with pyelonephritis)
- Other causes of urinary tract obstruction
- Other UTI, for example cystitis
- Acute glomerulonephritis
- Renal infarction, renal vein thrombosis, haemorrhage into a renal tumour or cyst
- Other abdominal pathology (e.g. cholecystitis, empyema, peptic ulcer, appendicitis, pelvic inflammatory disease, basal pneumonia)
- Referred pain from lesion of vertebrae

Complications and prognosis

Complications

- **Reduction in renal function** is a rare complication in adults unless there is underlying obstruction to urinary flow, diabetes, or another predisposing factor.
- **Development of severe infection** can lead to localized renal abscess, papillary necrosis, metastatic infections, septicaemia, disseminated intravascular coagulation, and respiratory distress syndrome.
- **Chronic pyelonephritis** may develop after repeated episodes of acute pyelonephritis. This may lead to impaired renal function and hypertension.

[Bergeron, 1995]

Prognosis

- **The prognosis is good in uncomplicated pyelonephritis.**
- **People with other coexisting conditions** such as renal disease, diabetes mellitus, or immunosuppression may be at greater risk for poor outcomes [Cooper, 2001].
- **Relapse** (recurrence of infection with the same bacteria) up to 4 months after treatment with antibiotic therapy varies between 17% and 18%.
- **Reinfection** (recurrence of infection with a different bacteria) rates vary between 21% and 44% at 4 months.

[Bergeron, 1995]

Management issues

- Principles of treatment of pyelonephritis p.1605
- Treatment of pyelonephritis at home or in hospital? p.1605
- Antimicrobials for pyelonephritis p.1605
- Management of pyelonephritis in pregnancy p.1606

Principles of treatment of pyelonephritis

- There is little evidence on clinical outcomes from studies of pyelonephritis in primary care. Thus recommendations tend to be based on consensus.
- **Men and women** with acute uncomplicated pyelonephritis require the same initial treatment.
- **The organisms** that commonly cause pyelonephritis are Gram-negative bacteria.

P

Treatment of pyelonephritis at home or in hospital?

- **Oral antimicrobials** are safe and effective primary care treatments for pyelonephritis in otherwise healthy people [Cooper, 2001].
- **Intravenous antimicrobials and admission are required in the following circumstances:**
  - Inability to tolerate oral medication
  - Severe illness
  - High risk (e.g. immunocompromised, diabetes)
  - Pregnancy (see below for more information) [Angel et al, 1990]

Antimicrobials for pyelonephritis

- **A quinolone or co-amoxiclav** should be started immediately.
- **If there is no response to treatment** the antibiotic should be changed according to the culture and sensitivity results.
- **Resistance patterns vary** with time and geographical location. Therefore up-to-date information should sought, for example from a local microbiology department.

- **Route of administration:** treatment of mild to moderate disease is with oral antibiotics. Moderate to severe disease should be treated with intravenous antibiotics.
- **Duration of treatment:** 14 days of antibiotic treatment is likely to be as effective as 6 weeks. For acute uncomplicated pyelonephritis in women, ciprofloxacin for 7 days has been shown to be at least as effective as 14 days of trimethoprim–sulfamethoxazole.
- **If there is no response within 48 hours,** consider admission to hospital.

[Stamm and Hooton, 1993; Bergeron, 1995; Cattell, 1997; DTB, 1998; Talan et al, 2000]

Management of pyelonephritis in pregnancy

- **The incidence of pyelonephritis increases in pregnancy.**
- **Because pyelonephritis in pregnancy is associated with risks to mother and child** it is recommended that it be treated in hospital with intravenous antimicrobials. However, a few randomized controlled trials in the USA have provided evidence that uncomplicated pyelonephritis in pregnancy might be safely and effectively treated with oral cephalosporins.
- **Quinolones are contraindicated** at any time during pregnancy since they have caused arthropathy in animal studies.

[Angel et al, 1990; Millar et al, 1995; Wing, 2001]

References

NHS staff in England can link, free of charge, from references to full text journals by clicking on [Full text] on the PRODIGY website.

1. Angel, J.L., O'Brien, W.F., Finan, M.A. et al (1990) Acute pyelonephritis in pregnancy: a prospective study of oral versus intravenous antibiotic therapy. *Obstetrics & Gynecology* **76**(1), 28–32.
2. Bergeron, M.G. (1995) Treatment of pyelonephritis in adults. *Medical Clinics of North America* **79**(3), 619–649.
3. BNF 42 (2001) *British National Formulary*. 42nd edn. London: British Medical Association and Royal Pharmaceutical Society of Great Britain.
4. Cattell, W.R. (1997) Renal disease: II. Urinary tract infection in women. *Journal of the Royal College of Physicians of London* **31**(2), 130–133.
5. Cooper, B. (2001) Pyelonephritis in non-pregnant women. *Clinical Evidence* **5**(Jun), 1332–1337.
6. Cooper, B. and Jepson, R. (2001) Recurrent cystitis in non-pregnant women. *Clinical Evidence* **5**(Jun), 1338–1345.
7. De Craen, A.J., Di Giulio, G., Lampe-Schoenmaeckers, J.E. et al (1996) Analgesic efficacy and safety of paracetamol-codeine combinations versus paracetamol alone: a systematic review. *British Medical Journal* **313**(7053), 321–325. [Full text]
8. DTB (1998) Managing urinary tract infection in women. *Drug & Therapeutics Bulletin* **36**(4), 30–32. [Full text]
9. Medicines Resource (1995) Combination analgesics. *Medicines Resource* **25**, 95–98.
10. MeReC (1995) Urinary tract infection. *MeReC Bulleti* **6**(8),
11. MeReC (1998) Analgesics. *MeReC Bulletin* **34**(12), 12
12. Millar, L.K., Wing, D.A., Paul, R.H. and Grimes, D.A. (1995) Outpatient treatment of pyelonephritis in pregnancy: a randomized controlled trial. *Obstetrics & Gynecology* **86**(4 Pt 1), 560–564.
13. Read, R.C. (2000) Drugs in focus: newer oral fluoroquinolone antibacterials. *Prescribers' Journal* **40**(2), 147–151.
14. Stamm, W.E. and Hooton, T.M. (1993) Management of urinary tract infections in adults. *New England Journal of Medicine* **329**(18), 1328–1334.
15. Talan, D.A., Stamm, W.E., Hooton, T.M. et al (2000) Comparison of ciprofloxacin (7 days) and trimethoprim-sulfamethoxazole (14 days) for acute uncomplicated pyelonephritis in women: a randomized trial. *Journal of the American Medical Association* **283**(12), 1583–1590. [Full text]
16. Wing, D.A. (2001) Pyelonephritis in pregnancy: treatment options for optimal outcomes. *Drugs* **61**(14) 2087–2096.

PRODIGY GUIDANCE

Raynaud's phenomenon

Last revised in December 2002
www.prodigy.nhs.uk/guidance.asp?gt=Raynaud's phenomenon

Applies to people over the age of 14 years

This guidance covers the management of Raynaud's phenomenon.

This guidance does not cover the management of the underlying causes of secondary Raynaud's phenomenon.

Goals

- To alleviate symptoms
- To differentiate between primary and secondary Raynaud's phenomenon

Contents

Scenarios

- Raynaud's phenomenon p.1607

Extended Information, p. 1608

Raynaud's phenomenon

Which therapy?

Non-drug approaches

- **Explanation and reassurance**
- **Keeping warm** (in some cases electrically heated gloves and socks, or portable heat packs, may be useful. These are often available from medical supply shops)
- Smoking cessation
- Stopping vasoconstrictor drugs (e.g. beta-blockers)
- Avoiding use of vibrating tools
- Stress management may benefit some people whose symptoms are precipitated by emotional stress.

Medication

- May only be required during colder weather
- First-choice treatment is nifedipine

Practical prescribing points

For further information please see the *Medicines Compendium* (www.medicines.org.uk) or the *British National Formulary* (www.bnf.org).

Nifedipine should not be given to pregnant women or nursing mothers, or to women capable of child-bearing.

Should I refer or investigate?

Refer?

Consider referring people with suspected secondary Raynaud's phenomenon, for example:

- Male sex
- Onset after 40 years of age
- Abrupt onset with rapid progression
- Unilateral involvement
- Trophic changes such as digital scarring or ulceration
- Symptoms or signs of connective tissue disease (e.g. arthritis or arthralgia, skin rashes or photosensitivity, dry eyes or mouth, muscle weakness or pain, swallowing difficulties, breathlessness, mouth ulcers, alopecia, altered skin texture, calcinosis, or telangiectasia)
- Abnormal investigations — raised erythrocyte sedimentation rate (ESR), abnormal auto-antibody screen

Investigate?

- Routine investigations:
  - Full blood count
  - ESR
  - Auto-antibody screen (in particular, antinuclear antibody)

Patient information leaflets

The following PILs are available at www.prodigy.nhs.uk

- Antibody and Antigen Tests
- Blood Test - Detecting Inflammation
- Blood Test - General
- Medicines - Name Changes of Medicines
- Raynauds and Scleroderma Association
- Raynaud's Phenomenon (Cold Hands)

Shared decision making

- **Raynaud's phenomenon** causes cold, pale, and painful fingers (and/or toes, nose, or earlobes). The small blood vessels are sensitive to cold or emotional stress, and narrow (constrict).
- **If you smoke,** stopping smoking may ease or cure symptoms.
- **Some medicines** have a side-effect of causing Raynaud's; for example, beta-blockers.
- **Keep warm.** Warm gloves, socks, and shoes are essential when out in cool weather. Put gloves on before going into colder areas. Portable heat packs or battery-heated gloves and socks may help.
- **Medication** may be needed in severe cases. It works by opening up the blood vessels. Nifedipine is usually used. Other medicines may be tried if this is not helpful.
- **Stress counselling** may be helpful if symptoms occur when you are emotionally stressed.

Drug rationale

Drugs not included

- **Calcium antagonists other than nifedipine (i.e. amlodipine, felodipine, and isradipine)** have shown some benefit in some small studies. There are conflicting results for nicardipine and nisoldipine [Gjorup et al, 1986; Challenor et al, 1987]. Verapamil and diltiazem are not advised: the dihydropyridines are more likely to be of benefit because of their selectivity for vascular smooth muscle and reduced effects on cardiac function [Block and Sequeira, 2001].
- **Other vasodilators:** alpha-blockers (e.g. moxisylyte [thymoxamine]), naftidrofuryl oxalate, and nicotinic acid derivatives (inositol nicotinate, nicotinyl alcohol)

R

have been used in Raynaud's phenomenon but are of doubtful value.
- **Oxpentifylline** has shown no convincing benefit over placebo in Raynaud's phenomenon.
- **Intravenous iloprost** is a prostaglandin analogue that is available only on a named patient basis. It is used in secondary care for the management of severe Raynaud's phenomenon [Belch and Ho, 1996]. Oral iloprost appears to be less effective [Black et al, 1998; Pope et al, 2002].
- **Losartan,** an angiotensin-II receptor antagonist, showed some benefit in a 15-week randomized controlled open-label trial compared with nifedipine. However, larger trials looking at the long-term use of losartan are needed before its use can be recommended [Dziadzio et al, 1999].
- **Fluoxetine** (a selective serotonin re-uptake inhibitor) has been investigated in a pilot study to counteract the increased release of serotonin by platelets (and hence contributing to the increased vasoconstriction). Results were promising but there is insufficient evidence to recommend it at this time [Coleiro et al, 2001].
- **Cinnarizine** has calcium-channel blocking activity but has little evidence of benefit in Raynaud's phenomenon [BNF 43, 2002].

Drugs included

- **Nifedipine** has been confirmed in a number of studies to decrease the severity and frequency of vasospastic attacks [Landry et al, 1997; Merritt, 1997]. The modified-release preparations, unlike the standard-release capsules, are not specifically licensed for this indication, but may be better tolerated.
- A selection of branded products is included as recommended by the *British National Formulary.* Branded products available in more than one strength have been included in preference to brands offering only 'one-off strengths'. This is to allow titration of clinical effect without any independent variation in absorption characteristics or adverse event profile. This has not been possible for the once-a-day products where all products offering a daily dosage equal to or less than 40 mg are offered.

Prescriptions

R

Standard-release nifedipine three times a day

Nifedipine 5mg three times a day
- Age from 14 years onwards
- Nifedipine 5mg capsules. Take one capsule three times a day; supply 84 capsules; NHS Cost £3.57.

Nifedipine 10mg three times a day
- Age from 14 years onwards
- Nifedipine 10mg capsules. Take one capsule three times a day; supply 84 capsules; NHS Cost £4.47.

Nifedipine 20mg three times a day
- Age from 14 years onwards
- Nifedipine 10mg capsules. Take two capsules three times a day; supply 168 capsules; NHS Cost £8.94.

Nifedipine m/r 10mg twice a day

Adalat Retard 10mg twice a day
- Age from 14 years onwards
- Adalat Retard 10mg m/r tablets. Take one tablet twice a day; supply 56 tablets; NHS Cost £8.50.

Adipine MR 10mg twice a day
- Age from 14 years onwards
- Adipine MR 10mg m/r tablets. Take one tablet twice a day; supply 56 tablets; NHS Cost £6.62.

Cardilate MR 10mg twice a day
- Age from 14 years onwards
- Cardilate MR 10mg m/r tablets. Take one tablet twice a day; supply 56 tablets; NHS Cost £4.97.

Coracten SR 10mg twice a day
- Age from 14 years onwards
- Coracten SR 10mg m/r capsules. Take one capsule twice a day; supply 60 capsules; NHS Cost £6.25.

Tensipine MR 10mg twice a day
- Age from 14 years onwards
- Tensipine MR 10mg m/r tablets. Take one tablet twice a day; supply 56 tablets; NHS Cost £4.65.

Nifedipine m/r 20mg twice a day

Adalat Retard 20mg twice a day
- Age from 14 years onwards
- Adalat Retard 20mg m/r tabs. Take one tablet twice a day; supply 56 tablets; NHS Cost £10.20.

Adipine MR 20mg twice a day
- Age from 14 years onwards
- Adipine MR 20mg m/r tablets. Take one tablet twice a day; supply 56 tablets; NHS Cost £8.26.

Cardilate MR 20mg twice a day
- Age from 14 years onwards
- Cardilate MR 20mg m/r tablets. Take one tablet twice a day; supply 56 tablets; NHS Cost £9.31.

Coracten SR 20mg twice a day
- Age from 14 years onwards
- Coracten SR 20mg m/r capsules. Take one capsule twice a day; supply 60 capsules; NHS Cost £8.67.

Tensipine MR 20mg twice a day
- Age from 14 years onwards
- Tensipine MR 20mg m/r tablets. Take one tablet twice a day; supply 56 tablets; NHS Cost £5.99.

Nifedipine m/r 20mg or 30mg once a day

Adalat LA 20mg once a day
- Age from 14 years onwards
- Adalat LA 20mg m/r tablets. Take one tablet once a day supply 28 tablets; NHS Cost £8.15.

Adalat LA 30mg once a day
- Age from 14 years onwards
- Adalat LA 30mg m/r tablets. Take one tablet once a day supply 28 tablets; NHS Cost £9.89.

Coracten XL 30mg once a day
- Age from 14 years onwards
- Coracten XL 30mg m/r capsules. Take one capsule once a day; supply 28 capsules; NHS Cost £6.73.

Slofedipine XL 30mg once a day
- Age from 14 years onwards
- Slofedipine XL 30mg m/r tabs. Take one tablet once a day; supply 28 tablets; NHS Cost £9.89.

Nifedipine m/r 40mg once a day

Fortipine LA 40mg once a day
- Age from 14 years onwards
- Fortipine LA 40mg m/r tablets. Take one tablet once a day; supply 30 tablets; NHS Cost £8.00.

Extended Information

Background information

- What is it? p.1609
- What are the causes of secondary Raynaud's phenomenon? p.1609
- How common is it? p.1609
- How do I know my patient has it? p.1609
- Complications and prognosis p.1610

What is it?

- **In Raynaud's phenomenon** exposure to cold or emotional stress causes exaggerated vasospasm in the extremities, with pallor followed by cyanosis, and then redness as reperfusion occurs — the classic triphasic white, blue, red colour change. The full triphasic colour change is not, however, essential for the diagnosis. Numbness and tingling are also common symptoms. The phenomenon typically affects the digits but can affect other sites such as the nose, tongue, and ear lobes. People with Raynaud's phenomenon appear to have a generalized increase in vascular reactivity, with an increased incidence of Prinzmetal angina and migraine.
- **Primary Raynaud's phenomenon,** also called Raynaud's disease, occurs in the absence of causes such as connective tissue disease. The cause is unknown, but probably involves a combination of abnormalities in the peripheral sympathetic nervous system, the blood vessel wall, and inflammatory and immune responses.
- **Secondary Raynaud's phenomenon,** also called Raynaud's syndrome, occurs with underlying diseases that affect blood vessels, most commonly connective tissue diseases (e.g. scleroderma).

[Belch and Ho, 1996; Lawlor-Smith and Lawlor-Smith, 1997; Ho and Belch, 1998; Turton et al, 1998]

What are the causes of secondary Raynaud's phenomenon?

About 10% of cases of Raynaud's phenomenon are associated with an underlying condition, most commonly connective tissue disease. In men, the most common cause is probably the use of vibratory tools.

Examples of the more common causes of secondary Raynaud's phenomenon

Connective tissue disorders
- Systemic sclerosis (scleroderma)
- Mixed connective tissue disease
- Systemic lupus erythematosus (SLE)
- Dermatomyositis/polymyositis
- Sjögren's syndrome

Obstructive arterial disorders
- Atherosclerosis, especially thromboangiitis obliterans (Buerger's disease)
- Microemboli
- Thoracic outlet syndrome, especially cervical rib

Occupational
- Vibration white finger
- Cold injury (e.g. in frozen-food packers)
- Vinyl chloride exposure (e.g. in PVC industry)

Drug-induced
- Beta-blockers
- Nicotine
- Ergotamine
- Cytotoxic drugs
- Oestrogen therapy

Blood disorders
- Polycythaemia rubra vera
- Cold agglutinin disease
- Monoclonal gammopathies
- Thrombocytosis

Miscellaneous
- Hypothyroidism
- Anorexia nervosa
- Malignancy (rare)

[Belch and Ho, 1996; Paw et al, 1996; Valeriano, 1997; Waller, 1997; Fraenkel et al, 1998; Turton et al, 1998; Barrett-Connor, 1999]

How common is it?

- **Prevalence is uncertain** owing to differences in diagnostic criteria; overall it is probably about 5–10%, but may affect up to 20–30% of women in the younger age groups. It is uncommon in children.
- **Primary Raynaud's phenomenon** accounts for more than 90% of cases.
- The female:male ratio is 9:1.
- **There is a familial predisposition,** particularly when age of onset is less than 30 years.

[Belch and Ho, 1996; Waller, 1997]

How do I know my patient has it?

History

- **There is a triphasic colour change (white, blue, red) affecting the fingers** or other extremities on exposure to cold or emotional stress, often with paraesthesiae or discomfort. The full sequence of colour change is not, however, essential to the diagnosis.
- **Identify possible underlying causes, such as:**
  - Drugs known to cause vasospasm
  - Conditions known to be associated with Raynaud's phenomenon
  - Occupational causes, such as use of vibrating tools
  - Cold damage from working in freezing conditions
  - Exposure to chemicals, such as vinyl chloride (see section *What are the causes of secondary Raynaud's phenomenon?*)
- **Suspect secondary Raynaud's phenomenon if:**
  - Onset after 40 years of age
  - Abrupt onset with rapid progression
  - Unilateral involvement
  - Male sex
- **Suspect a connective tissue disorder if:**
  - Symptoms such as arthritis or arthralgia
  - Skin rashes or photosensitivity
  - Dry eyes or mouth
  - Muscle weakness or pain
  - Swallowing difficulties
  - Breathlessness
  - Mouth ulcers

Examination

- **Peripheral pulses** to exclude peripheral vascular disease
- **Blood pressure** in both arms, as asymmetry suggests proximal vascular occlusion
- **Neck examination** to detect visible or palpable cervical rib
- **Signs suggesting connective tissue disease,** e.g. alopecia, altered skin texture, calcinosis, or telangiectasia
- **Trophic changes,** such as digital scarring or ulceration, which occur in severe disease

Investigation

- **Primary care investigations** are full blood count, erythrocyte sedimentation rate (ESR), and auto-antibody screen. A raised ESR and abnormal auto-antibody screen (in particular positive antinuclear antibodies) suggest secondary Raynaud's phenomenon. Consider chest X-ray if cervical rib is suspected.
- **Secondary care investigations may include** further serological testing, nail fold capillary microscopy, and cold challenge with finger plethysmography or finger blood pressure measurement.

[Isenberg and Black, 1995; Belch and Ho, 1996]

Complications and prognosis

Complications

- Impaired quality of life
- Digital ischaemia with ulceration and gangrene in severe cases (usually secondary Raynaud's phenomenon)

Prognosis

- **Primary Raynaud's phenomenon:** usually mild symptoms with good long-term outlook. However, may precede the onset of connective tissue disease by many years. One prospective study of people referred to a specialist centre found that 33–83% of people found to be seropositive for rheumatoid factor or antinuclear antibody went on to develop a connective tissue disorder over the next 10 years, compared with only 10% of people who were found to be seronegative.
- **Secondary Raynaud's phenomenon:** usually more severe than primary Raynaud's phenomenon and responds less well to treatment.

[Landry et al, 1996; Landry et al, 1997; Ho and Belch, 1998]

Management issues

- General measures p.1610
- Drug treatment p.1610
- Surgical treatment p.1610

General measures

- **Many people have only minor symptoms,** and non-pharmacological approaches may be adequate:
- **Explanation and reassurance** that lifestyle modification is usually successful in controlling symptoms, and that symptoms do not indicate serious circulation problems
- **Keeping warm** — in some cases electrically heated gloves and socks may be useful
- Smoking cessation
- Consider stopping vasoconstrictor drugs (e.g. beta-blockers)
- Avoiding use of vibrating tools
- Stress management, relaxation, or biofeedback appear to benefit some people.

[Kaufman and All, 1996; Landry et al, 1997; Waller, 1997]

R

Drug treatment

- **Medication should be considered if** symptoms interfere with either social or work lifestyle. People with primary Raynaud's phenomenon usually respond better than those with secondary Raynaud's phenomenon.
- **Numerous different drugs have been tried** — interpretation of studies is difficult owing to varying diagnostic criteria, lack of discrimination between primary and secondary Raynaud's phenomenon, small sample sizes, and frequent reliance on surrogate markers of improvement.

Vasodilators

- **Nifedipine is the first-choice treatment:** it is confirmed in numerous studies to decrease the severity and frequency of vasospastic attacks, and improve objective measures of blood flow following cold exposure in 70–80% of people [Landry et al, 1997; Merritt, 1997].
- **Other calcium antagonists:** amlodipine [La Civita et al, 1993], diltiazem [Kahan et al, 1985; Rhedda et al, 1985], felodipine [Kallenberg et al, 1991], and isradipine [Leppert et al, 1989] also appear to be of benefit on the basis of a number of small studies. There are conflicting results for nicardipine [Kahan et al, 1987; Vayssairat, 1991; Wollersheim and Thien, 1991], and nisoldipine [Gjorup et al, 1986; Challenor et al, 1987].
- **Other vasodilators:** alpha-blockers (e.g. prazosin), naftidrofuryl, and inositol nicotinate are of less certain value and should be reserved for people either intolerant of, or who gain no benefit from, calcium antagonists [Belch and Ho, 1996; Merritt, 1997; Pope et al, 1999]. There is no trial data on the value of add-on treatment for those with inadequate response to a calcium antagonist alone; in this situation a specialist opinion is usually more appropriate in order to clarify the diagnosis.

Other treatments

- **Intravenous iloprost** (a prostaglandin analogue that is available only on a named patient basis) may be of benefit in people with severe Raynaud's phenomenon. It is given over 3–5 days with benefit lasting 6 weeks to 6 months in most people [Belch and Ho, 1996].
- **Oral iloprost** appears to be less effective [Belch et al, 1995; Black et al, 1998].
- **Losartan,** an angiotensin-II receptor antagonist, showed some benefit in a 15-week randomized controlled open-label trial compared with nifedipine. However, larger trials looking at the long-term use of losartan are needed before its use can be recommended [Dziadzio et al, 1999].
- **Fluoxetine** (a selective serotonin re-uptake inhibitor) has been investigated in a pilot study to counteract the increased release of serotonin by platelets (and hence contributing to the increased vasoconstriction). Results were promising but there is insufficient evidence to recommend it at this time [Coleiro et al, 2001].
- **Oral prostaglandin therapies** are still being evaluated, but to date are either ineffective, or are of limited value, and are poorly tolerated owing to vasodilatory effects [Vayssairat, 1996; Black et al, 1998; Ho and Belch, 1998; Wigley et al, 1998].
- **Cinnarizine** has calcium-channel blocking activity but has little evidence of benefit in Raynaud's phenomenon [BNF 43, 2002].
- **Oxpentifylline** alters the characteristics of blood, in particular viscosity, red blood cell deformability, and platelet aggregation [Merritt, 1997]. A number of small studies suggest possible modest benefits.
- **Traditional Chinese acupuncture** was shown to be effective in one small non-blinded randomized controlled trial [Appiah et al, 1997]. A large placebo effect is likely.
- **Evening primrose oil and fish oils** are suggested as being useful in some people but more data is needed on this [Landry et al, 1997].

Surgical treatment

- **Surgery may benefit some people with proximal arterial obstruction** e.g. due to atherosclerosis, emboli, thoracic outlet syndrome, aneurysms, or trauma.
- **Lumbar sympathectomy** may be useful for lower limb disease, but cervical sympathectomy for upper limb disease is usually of limited, transient value, and is rarely carried out [Landry et al, 1997; Ho and Belch, 1998].

References

NHS staff in England can link, free of charge, from references to full text journals by clicking on [Full text] on the PRODIGY website.

1. Appiah, R., Hiller, S., Caspary, L. et al (1997) Treatment of primary Raynaud's syndrome with traditional Chinese acupuncture. *Journal of Internal Medicine* **241**(2), 119–124.

Barrett-Connor, E. (1999) Post menopausal estrogen therapy and selected (less often considered) disease outcomes. *Menopause: the Journal of the American Menopause Society* **6**(1), 14–20.

Belch, J.J. and Ho, M. (1996) Pharmacotherapy of Raynaud's phenomenon. *Drugs* **52**(5), 682–695.

Belch, J.J., Capell, H.A., Cooke, E.D. et al (1995) Oral iloprost for Raymaud's syndrome: a double blind multicentre placebo controlled study. *Annals of Rheumatic Diseases* **54**(3), 197–200.

Black, C.M., Halkier-Sorensen, L., Belch, J.J. et al (1998) Oral iloprost in Raynaud's phenomenon secondary to systemic sclerosis: a multicentre, placebo-controlled, dose-comparison study. *British Journal of Rheumatology* **37**(9), 952–960.

Block, J.A. and Sequeira, W. (2001) Raynaud's phenomenon. *Lancet* **357**(9273), 2042–2048. [Full text]

BNF 43 (2002) *British National Formulary*. 43rd edn. London: British Medical Association and Royal Pharmaceutical Society of Great Britain.

Challenor, V.F., Waller, D.G., Francis, D.A. et al (1987) Nisoldipine in primary Raynaud's phenomenon. *European Journal of Clinical Pharmacology* **33**(1), 27–30.

Coleiro, B., Marshall, S.E., Denton, C.P. et al (2001) Treatment of Raynaud's phenomenon with the selective serotonin reuptake inhibitor fluoxetine. *Rheumatology* **40**(9), 1038–1043. [Full text]

0. Dziadzio, M., Denton, C.P., Smith, R. et al (1999) Losartan therapy for Raynaud's phenomenon and scleroderma: clinical and biochemical findings in a fifteen-week, randomized, parallel-group, controlled trial. *Arthritis & Rheumatism* **42**(12), 2646–2655.

1. Fraenkel, L., Zhang, Y., Chaisson, C.E. et al (1998) The association of estrogen replacement therapy and the Raynaud phenomenon in postmenopausal women. *Annals of Internal Medicine* **129**(3), 208–211.

2. Gjorup, T., Hartling, O.J., Kelbaek, H. and Nielsen, S.L. (1986) Controlled double blind trial of nisoldipine in the treatment of idiopathic Raynaud's phenomenon. *European Journal of Clinical Pharmacology* **31**(4), 387–389.

3. Ho, M. and Belch, J.J. (1998) Raynaud's phenomenon: state of the art 1998. *Scandinavian Journal of Rheumatology* **27**(5), 319–322.

4. Isenberg, D.A. and Black, C. (1995) ABC of rheumatology: Raynaud's phenomenon, scleroderma, and overlap syndromes. *British Medical Journal* **310**(6982), 795–798. [Full text]

5. Kahan, A., Amor, B. and Menkes, C.J. (1985) A randomised double-blind trial of diltiazem in the treatment of Raynaud's phenomenon. *Annals of the Rheumatic Diseases* **44**(1), 30–33.

6. Kahan, A., Amor, B., Menkes, C.J. et al (1987) Nicardipine in the treatment of Raynaud's phenomenon: a randomized double-blind trial. *Angiology* **38**(4), 333–337.

7. Kallenberg, C.G., Wouda, A.A., Meems, L. and Wesseling, H. (1991) Once daily felodipine in patients with primary Raynaud's phenomenon. *European Journal of Clinical Pharmacology* **40**(3), 313–315.

8. Kaufman, M.W. and All, A.C. (1996) Raynaud's disease: patient education as a primary nursing intervention. *Journal of Vascular Nursing* **14**(2), 34–39.

19. La Civita, L., Pitaro, N., Rossi, M. et al (1993) Amlodipine in the treatment of Raynaud's phenomenon. *British Journal of Rheumatology* **32**(6), 524–525.

20. Landry, G.J., Edwards, J.M., McLafferty, R.B. et al (1996) Long-term outcome of Raynaud's syndrome in a prospectively analyzed patient cohort. *Journal of Vascular Surgery* **23**(1), 76–85.

21. Landry, G.J., Edwards, J.M. and Porter, J.M. (1997) Current managment of Raynaud's syndrome. *Advances in Surgery* **30**, 333–347.

22. Lawlor-Smith, L. and Lawlor-Smith, C. (1997) Vasospasm of the nipple–a manifestation of Raynaud's phenomenon: case reports. *British Medical Journal* **314**(7081), 644–645. [Full text]

23. Leppert, J., Jonasson, T., Nilsson, H. and Ringqvist, I. (1989) The effect of isradipine, a new calcium-channel antagonist, in patients with primary Raynaud's phenomenon: a single-blind dose-response study. *Cardiovascular Drugs & Therapy* **3**(3), 397–401.

24. Merritt, W.H. (1997) Comprehensive management of Raynaud's syndrome. *Clinics in Plastic Surgery* **24**(1), 133–159.

25. Paw, P., Dharan, S.M. and Sackier, J.M. (1996) Digital ischemia and occult malignancy. *International Journal of Colorectal Disease* **11**(4), 196–197.

26. Pope, J., Fenlon, D., Thompson, A. et al (1999) *Prazosin for Raynaud's phenomenon in progressive systemic sclerosis (Cochrane Review)*. The Cochrane Library. Issue 3. Oxford: Update Software.

27. Pope, J., Fenlon, D., Thompson, A. et al (2002) *Iloprost and cisaprost for Raynaud's phenomenon in progressive systemic sclerosis (Cochrane Review)*. The Cochrane Library. Issue 2. Oxford: Update Software.

28. Rhedda, A., McCans, J., Willan, A.R. and Ford, P.M. (1985) A double blind placebo controlled crossover randomized trial of diltiazem in Raynaud's phenomenon. *Journal of Rheumatology* **12**(4), 724–727.

29. Turton, E.P., Kent, P.J. and Kester, R.C. (1998) The aetiology of Raynaud's phenomenon. *Cardiovascular Surgery* **6**(5), 431–440.

30. Valeriano, J. (1997) Malignancy and rheumatic disease. *Cancer Control: Journal of the Moffitt Cancer Centre* **4**(3), 236–244.

31. Vayssairat, M. (1991) Controlled multicenter double-blind trial of nicardipine in the treatment of primary Raynaud phenomenon. French Cooperative Multicenter Group for Raynaud Phenomenon, Paris, France. *American Heart Journal* **122**(1 Pt 2), 352–355.

32. Vayssairat, M. (1996) Controlled multicenter double blind trial of an oral analog of prostacyclin in the treatment of primary Raynaud's phenomenon. French Microcirculation Society Multicentre Group for the Study of Vascular Acrosyndromes. *Journal of Rheumatology* **23**(11), 1917–1920.

33. Waller, D. (1997) GP management of Raynaud's phenomenon. *Prescriber* **8**(3), 61–67.

34. Wigley, F.M., Korn, J.H., Csuka, M.E. et al (1998) Oral iloprost treatment in patients with Raynaud's phenomenon secondary to systemic sclerosis: a multicenter, placebo-controlled, double-blind study. *Arthritis & Rheumatism* **41**(4), 670–677.

35. Wollersheim, H. and Thien, T. (1991) Double-blind placebo-controlled crossover study of oral nicardipine in the treatment of Raynaud's phenomenon. *Journal of Cardiovascular Pharmacology* **18**(6), 813–818.

R

PRODIGY GUIDANCE

Renal colic — acute

Last revised in July 2002

At the time of print this topic was being updated. The newly revised guidance will be issued on to the website in late 2005.

www.prodigy.nhs.uk/guidance.asp?gt=Renal colic - acute

Applies to people over the age of 16 years

This guidance covers the symptomatic management of renal colic in primary care. Renal colic is sometimes (and more correctly) called ureteric colic. It is also often loosely termed 'kidney stones'.

This guidance does not cover in detail the prevention of renal tract calculi.

There is separate PRODIGY guidance for *Prostatitis*, *Urethritis — male, Urinary tract infection (lower) — women,* and *Urinary tract infection (lower) — men.*

Goals

- Reduction in symptoms
- Appropriate referral to secondary care
- Prevention of renal damage

Contents

Scenarios

- Acute renal colic in adults p.1612

Extended Information, p. 1614

Acute renal colic in adults

Which therapy?

- **Diclofenac is the first line choice in the relief of acute pain in renal colic:**
  - Intramuscular preparations give fast relief and are recommended initially where there is severe pain.
  - If admission is not indicated or is delayed, depending on the individual situation, it may be appropriate to leave the patient with a supply of oral diclofenac, or diclofenac suppositories, in case of pain recurrence.
- **Opioids such as pethidine, morphine or diamorphine are alternative (or additional) therapies,** according to clinical judgement. Co-administration of an anti-emetic is usually required.
- **If pain is severe and persists beyond 24 hours, urgent admission is necessary as renal function may be compromised by persistent obstruction.**

Practical prescribing points

For further information please see the *Medicines Compendium* (www.medicines.org.uk) or the *British National Formulary* (www.bnf.org).

Diclofenac

- People are at increased risk from nonsteroidal anti-inflammatory drug (NSAID) induced adverse effects if they:
  - Are aged 65 years and over
  - Have a previous clinical history of gastroduodenal ulcer, gastrointestinal bleeding, or gastroduodenal perforation
  - Use other medications concomitantly that are known to increase the likelihood of upper GI adverse events, e.g. corticosteroids and anticoagulants
  - Have serious comorbidity, such as cardiovascular disease, renal or hepatic impairment, diabetes, and hypertension
- NSAIDs may worsen asthma, hypertension, renal impairment, or cardiac failure.

Should I refer or investigate?

Refer?

- **All patients who are not admitted should be referred urgently,** for early investigations (such as intravenous urogram). This is vital in order to exclude or treat complete obstruction, infection and other complications. If it is not possible to arrange this, hospital admission may be required.
- **Admit:**
  - Presence of fever
  - Non-functioning kidney
  - Solitary kidney
  - Failure to control pain
- **Refer:**
  - **Factors limiting provision of analgesia** (for example, duodenal ulcer, bleeding problems etc.), poor social support.
  - **Emergency outpatient referral** may be more appropriate providing that analgesia is effective, there is adequate fluid intake, and there is social support.

Investigate?

- **Urinalysis:**
  - Absence of microscopic or frank haematuria makes diagnosis of ureteric colic unlikely
  - Urine dipstick tests for nitrites and leucocyte esterase can help to identify the likelihood of infection
- **Urine culture** is necessary to exclude infection.
- **Serum urea and electrolytes** can be used to assess renal function, although a normal serum creatinine does not rule out an obstruction.
- **Sieve urine:** in patients who pass a stone after the colic, analysis of the calculus can provide useful information on calculus type, and facilitate preventative therapy.
- **Secondary care investigations:**
  - Plain abdominal films, intravenous urography, or ultrasound, or both, are normally arranged (sometimes as part of the outpatient work-up prior to review by a urologist).
  - In patients unable to retrieve a calculus, other tests can be informative, including: urine examination for crystals; serum calcium, uric acid, bicarbonate and phosphate; 24 hour urine collection for calcium, uric

acid, oxalate, phosphate, magnesium, citrate, and creatinine.

Patient information leaflets

The following PILs are available at www.prodigy.nhs.uk

Intravenous Urography

Kidney Stones

Shared decision making

Renal colic is a severe pain usually caused by a kidney stone stuck in the tube carrying urine from the kidney to the bladder (ureter).

Recurrent stones are common.

Sometimes there is an underlying reason why a stone has formed. If this cause is found, specific advice on diet and fluid consumption can sometimes be given to prevent a recurrence.

However, there is often no apparent reason for the formation of stones.

Drink lots of fluid — it is the main way to help prevent further stones as it keeps the urine dilute.

Unless your doctor advises against this, aim to drink at least 3–3.5 litres a day. Drink more if working or living in a hot environment.

Drink during the day. Also, take a large glass of water at bedtime and during the night if you wake to go to the toilet.

Drug rationale

Drugs not included

Analgesics such as paracetamol, aspirin and ibuprofen are not appropriate for the relief of acute pain associated with renal colic.

Modified-release nonsteroidal anti-inflammatory drugs (NSAIDs) are less effective for acute pain due to their slower onset of action. There is little evidence of greater efficacy or safety over standard treatment and they are more expensive [De Craen et al, 1996; Eccles et al, 1998].

NSAIDs other than diclofenac: ketorolac has been demonstrated to be as effective as diclofenac or pethidine when given intramuscularly for the relief of pain in renal colic; however, it is unlicensed for this use [Sandhu et al, 1994; Cohen et al, 1998]. Other NSAIDs are not included, either because they have not been studied as extensively in the literature for renal colic, or they are not specifically licensed.

Antispasmodics do not appear to be as effective as NSAIDs or opioids in relieving pain, and they are no longer advocated.

Drugs included

Diclofenac has been demonstrated to be effective in the treatment of renal colic. Intramuscular and rectal preparations are recommended for initial relief of pain, while tablets may be more useful for less severe or recurrent spasm, or once vomiting has settled.

Intramuscular opioids have similar efficacy to intramuscular diclofenac in relieving the acute pain of renal colic. Opioids are offered as an alternative to diclofenac for people intolerant to nonsteroidal anti-inflammatory drugs. Co-administration of an anti-emetic is usually required.

Metoclopramide, cyclizine lactate, and prochlorperazine are effective anti-emetic medications licensed for intramuscular use.

Prescriptions

Diclofenac suppositories and intramuscular injection

Diclofenac 75mg intramuscular injection: one ampoule

- Age from 16 years onwards
- Diclofenac 75mg/3ml injection. For deep intramuscular injection into gluteal muscle; supply 1 3ml ampoule; NHS Cost £0.83.

Diclofenac 75mg intramuscular injection: two ampoules

- Age from 16 years onwards
- Diclofenac 75mg/3ml injection. For deep intramuscular injection into gluteal muscle; supply 2 3ml ampoule; NHS Cost £1.66.

Diclofenac suppositories: 100mg when required

- Age from 16 years onwards
- Diclofenac 100mg suppositories. Insert one suppository into the rectum when required for pain relief. Maximum of 1 suppository in 24 hours; supply 10 suppositories; NHS Cost £3.76.

Diclofenac oral tablets

Diclofenac sodium 50mg e/c three times a day

- Age from 16 years onwards
- Diclofenac 50mg e/c tablets. Take one tablet three times a day; supply 15 tablets; NHS Cost £0.91.

Advice note: collecting ureteric stones

Advice only

- Age from 16 years onwards
- To catch a stone, pass urine through gauze, a nylon stocking, or a filter such as a coffee filter. Your doctor can send the stone for analysis to identify the type of stone that has formed.

Opioids for subcutaneous or intramuscular injection

CD Pethidine 25mg to 100mg by sc or im injection

- Age from 18 years onwards
- Pethidine 100mg/2ml injection. Inject 0.25ml (25mg) to 2ml (100mg) by subcutaneous or intramuscular injection; supply 1 2ml ampoule; NHS Cost £0.56.

CD Morphine sulphate 10mg by sc or im injection

- Age from 18 years onwards
- Morphine sulphate 10mg/ml inj. Reconstitute with water for injection and inject 10mg by subcutaneous or intramuscular injection; supply 1 1ml ampoule; NHS Cost £0.72.

CD Diamorphine hydrochloride 5mg by sc or im injection

- Age from 18 years onwards
- Diamorphine 5mg injection. Reconstitute with water for injection and inject 5mg by subcutaneous or intramuscular injection; supply 1 1ml ampoule; NHS Cost £0.23.

Water for injection (5ml) ampoule

- Age from 18 years onwards
- Water for injection (5ml). For reconstitution; supply 1 5ml ampoule; NHS Cost £0.18.

Anti-emetic for intramuscular injection

Metoclopramide 10mg/2ml by intramuscular injection

- Age from 18 years onwards
- Metoclopramide 10mg/2ml inj. Inject 2ml (10mg) by intramuscular injection; supply 1 2ml ampoules; NHS Cost £0.34.

Cyclizine lactate 50mg/ml by intramuscular injection

- Age from 18 years onwards
- Cyclizine lactate 50mg/ml inj. Inject 1ml (50mg) by intramuscular injection; supply 1 1ml ampoules; NHS Cost £0.54.

Prochlorperazine 12.5mg/ml by intramuscular injection

- Age from 18 years onwards
- Prochlorperazine 12.5mg/ml inj. Inject 1ml (12.5mg) by intramuscular injection; supply 1 1ml ampoule; NHS Cost £0.59.

Extended Information

Background information

- What is it? p.1614
- How common is it? p.1614
- How do I know my patient has it? p.1614
- What else might it be? p.1614
- Complications and prognosis p.1614

What is it?

- **Renal colic** is invariably due to renal or ureteric calculi.
- **Symptoms are caused by** renal or ureteric stones forming and passing into the renal collecting system. This causes blockage and stretching of the ureter and produces severe, often colicky pain.
- **In most cases no underlying cause is identified.**
- **Underlying causes and conditions associated with renal calculi include:**
  - Primary metabolic abnormalities, such as hypercalcuria, hyperuricosuria, hypocitrauria, and hyperoxaluria
  - Primary hyperparathyroidism
  - Malignancy, including myeloproliferative disorders
  - Sarcoidosis
  - Prolonged immobilisation
  - Crohn's disease
  - Laxative abuse
  - Jejuno-ileal bypass
  - Renal tubular acidosis (type 1)
  - Gout
  - Recurrent urinary tract infection
- **Types of calculi:**
  - Up to 75% of stones are composed of calcium oxalate.
  - The next commonest, accounting for 10–20%, are formed from struvite (magnesium ammonium phosphate), which are frequently associated with infection.
  - Other types include uric acid (5%), brushite, hydroxyapatite (5%) or cystine (1%).

[Saklayen, 1997; Bihl and Meyers, 2001]

- **Drugs associated** with stone formation include; loop diuretics, antacids, acetazolamide, corticosteroids, theophyllines, aspirin, thiazides, allopurinol, and Vitamins D and C [Bihl and Meyers, 2001].

How common is it?

- Kidney stones are common in industrialised nations; up to 15% of caucasian men and 6% of women will develop one stone, with recurrence in about half these people [Bihl and Meyers, 2001].
- **The incidence** of renal colic is thought to be increasing; higher incidence being associated with economic development, possibly due to an increase in dietary protein and salt.
- **The incidence** of renal colic is highest in middle age.
- **Multiple recurrence** is higher in those with primary hyperparathyroidism, renal tubular acidosis, cystinuria, a combination of different metabolic abnormalities, and those who have recurrence within a short period of time

[Bihl and Meyers, 2001]

How do I know my patient has it?

- **The most predictive features are characteristic acute abdominal pain of short duration (less than 12 hours), loin or renal tenderness, and haematuria on testing** [Eskelinen et al, 1998].
- **There is often a history of precipitating factors** which include; dehydration with reduced urine output, increased protein intake, heavy physical exercise, and us of various drugs (in particular diuretics) [Bihl and Meyers, 2001].

Classical symptoms

- Sudden onset severe loin pain.
- Pain last minutes to hours, occurs in spasms with intervals of no pain or dull ache, and is often eased by curling up – often patients cannot lie still (which helps t differentiate from inflammatory causes, such as peritonitis).
- Radiation of pain to the groin and anterior thigh.
- Nausea or vomiting, or both.
- Often there is a desire to urinate frequently.

[Boyd and Gray, 1996]

Examination

- **Examination** may reveal loin tenderness.
- **Microscopic or frank haematuria** is usually present (absence of haematuria on urinary dipstick analysis makes the diagnosis of ureteric colic unlikely).
- **Fever** suggests either a separate diagnosis of urinary trac infection or coexisting urinary tract infection.

Investigations

Diagnosis is confirmed in secondary care with:

- **Intravenous urography** is currently accepted as the gold standard investigation to confirm the clinical diagnosis during an acute episode.
- **Plain abdominal X-ray** is accepted as a useful and necessary adjunct to aid the early diagnosis of renal coli (up to 90% of renal calculi can be visualised on plain X-ray).
- **Ultrasound** is non-invasive and may be useful in initial evaluation and follow-up.

[Haddad, 1992; Boyd and Gray, 1996]

Other emerging investigations are:

- Helicated tomography, particularly where there is history of allergy to contrast media
- Magnetic resonance urography

[Whitfield, 1999]

What else might it be?

Any other cause of acute abdominal pain should be considered, for example:

- Urinary tract infection
- Cardiac ischaemia
- Bowel ischaemia
- Bowel obstruction
- Hepatic capsulitis
- Musculo-skeletal pain
- Biliary colic

Complications and prognosis

Complications

- **Complete obstruction** of the ureter may complicate rena colic. This decreases urinary filtration; persistence of thi

state for more than 48 hours will result in reduced renal perfusion and gradual, irreversible loss of renal function. **Any persisting obstruction also predisposes the patient to ascending urinary tract infection,** particularly pyelonephritis.
[ICES, 1998]

Prognosis

Most symptomatic upper urinary-tract stones are small (less than 5 mm in diameter), and pass spontaneously [Bihl and Meyers, 2001]. These may occur in normal kidneys.
Prognosis is less good for renal colic caused by larger calculi:

- **Calculi between 5 and 10mm in diameter** pass spontaneously in about 50% of cases
- **Calculi larger than 1cm in diameter** usually require intervention, either electively or urgently, if complete obstruction or infection is present

[ICES, 1998]

Management issues

General issues p.1615
Pain relief p.1615
Referral criteria p.1615
Other interventions: p.1615
Preventing further stones p.1615

General issues

It is important to encourage fluid intake. If this is not possible, because of nausea or vomiting, hospital admission may be required.

Pain relief

If the patient is experiencing an acute spasm of pain, rectal, intramuscular or intravenous routes of administration give fastest relief and are recommended.
If admission is not indicated or is delayed, it may be appropriate to give the patient a supply of oral analgesics or suppositories in case of recurrence of spasm, depending on the individual situation.
Nonsteroidal anti-inflammatory drugs (NSAIDs) are now generally regarded as the drugs of choice for relieving acute renal colic:

- NSAIDs lack the emetic side effects of opioids.
- Diclofenac has the most evidence of efficacy, but there are studies supporting ketorolac as an effective alternative [Sandhu et al, 1994; Cohen et al, 1998]. Ketorolac and other parenteral NSAIDs are unlicensed in acute renal colic.
- NSAIDs have the disadvantage of being contraindicated where there is history of peptic ulceration, gastrointestinal haemorrhage, renal impairment, or heart failure.

Opioids such as morphine, diamorphine or pethidine appear equally as effective as NSAIDs:

- Pethidine has historically been used because it is thought to cause less ureteric spasm than other opioids. It may not be as potent as other morphine preparations and is associated with aggravating renal impairment.
- All opioids have the disadvantage of causing nausea and vomiting and also cause respiratory suppression.
- One option is to use opioids if NSAIDs give inadequate relief of pain.

Referral criteria

Admission or home therapy? The majority of those presenting with acute renal colic recover with pain relief and without need for invasive procedures. In one small study of 58 patients attending a hospital Accident and Emergency department in London, 29 were not admitted but instead received analgesia, and were followed up in outpatients. Only three returned within 48 hours because of persistent pain. None of these patients required subsequent intervention for obstruction or infection [Morris et al, 1995].

- A decision has to be made on urgent admission or referral. Investigations will still be necessary as a matter of urgency.
- Some practitioners may admit all patients with acute renal colic, whilst others use clinical judgement and feel that it is not always necessary to admit otherwise healthy patients with renal colic.

Admission

- Hospital admission provides facilities for administration of intravenous fluids, intensive analgesia, and observation and nursing care.
- **Indication for urgent admission** include:
  - Presence of fever
  - Non-functioning kidney
  - Solitary kidney
  - Failure to control pain
  - Factors limiting analgesia (e.g. duodenal ulcer, bleeding problems etc.)
  - Poor social support
  - Inability to arrange early referral

[Morris et al, 1995]

Home therapy with emergency outpatient referral

- **May be appropriate providing:**
  - The initial pain has been relieved
  - The patient is able to drink increased volumes of fluid
  - There is adequate social support
  - There are no complicating factors
- **All patients should be referred urgently, so that investigations (e.g. intravenous urogram) can be carried out quickly.** This is vital in order to exclude or treat complete obstruction, infection and other complications.
- **The patient should filter urine to capture the stone** with each voiding. This can be done through gauze, a nylon stocking, or filter paper (e.g. a coffee filter). Stone analysis is necessary to confirm the stone type and facilitate specific preventative therapy.

[ICES, 1998]

Other interventions:

Secondary care management of renal calculi include:

- Extracorporeal shock wave lithotripsy (85% of calculi that do not pass spontaneously can be removed in this way)
- Endoscopic lithotomy
- Ureteroscopy
- Percutaneous nephrolithotomy
- Open surgical removal of stones

[ICES, 1998]

Preventing further stones

- **High water intake** has been shown to reduce stone recurrence (in previous stone formers) in controlled trials, and is recommended [Buck, 1997].
- **Other strategies to prevent renal calculi** may include treatment with potassium citrate or advice to drink lemonade in hypocitraturic calcium stone formers. The role of low fat, high fibre and low animal-protein diets is not clear [Buck, 1997].
- **Antibiotics:** There is a case for antibiotics for the small proportion of patients (about 6%) who have recurrent infection-related, or *struvite* stones (magnesium

ammonium stones only produced in the presence of urease-producing bacteria in the urine) [ICES, 1998].

References

NHS staff in England can link, free of charge, from references to full text journals by clicking on [Full text] on the PRODIGY website.

1. Bihl, G. and Meyers, A. (2001) Recurrent renal stone disease – advances in pathogenesis and clinical management. *Lancet* **358**(9282), 651–656. [Full text]
2. Boyd, R. and Gray, A.J. (1996) Role of the plain radiograph and urinalysis in acute ureteric colic. *Journal of Accident & Emergency Medicine* **13**(6), 390–391.
3. Buck, A.C. (1997) The treatment of renal colic and the medical and dietary management of urolithiasis. *Current Opinion in Urology* 7, 226–230.
4. Cohen, E., Hafner, R., Rotenberg, Z. et al (1998) Comparison of ketorolac and diclofenac in the treatment of renal colic. *European Journal of Clinical Pharmacology* **54**(6), 455–458.
5. De Craen, A.J., Di Giulio, G., Lampe-Schoenmaeckers, J.E. et al (1996) Analgesic efficacy and safety of paracetamol-codeine combinations versus paracetamol alone: a systematic review. *British Medical Journal* **313**(7053), 321–325. [Full text]
6. Eccles, M., Freemantle, N. and Mason, J. (1998) Nort of England evidence based guideline development project: summary guideline for non-steroidal anti-inflammatory drugs versus basic analgesia in treating the pain of degenerative arthritis. *British Medical Journal* **317**(7157), 526–530. [Full text]
7. Eskelinen, M., Ikonen, J. and Lipponen, P. (1998) Usefulness of history-taking, physical examination an diagnostic scoring in acute renal colic. *European Urology* **34**(6), 467–473.
8. Haddad, M.C. (1992) Renal colic: diagnosis and outcome. *Radiology* **184**(1), 83–88.
9. ICES (1998) *Caution: stones…. no passing! – kidney stones and renal colic*. Canada: Institute for Clinical Evaluative Sciences.
10. Morris, S.B., Hampson, S.J., Gordon, S.J. et al (1995) Should all patients with ureteric colic be admitted? *Annals of the Royal College of Surgeons of England* **77**(450), 452.
11. Saklayen, M.G. (1997) Medical management of nephrolithiasis. *Medical Clinics of North America* **81**(3), 785–799.
12. Sandhu, D.P., Iacovou, J.W., Fletcher, M.S. et al (199 A comparison of intramuscular ketorolac and pethidir in the alleviation of renal colic. *British Journal of Urology* **74**(6), 690–693.
13. Whitfield, H.N. (1999) The management of ureteric stones. Part I: diagnosis. *BJU International* **84**(8), 911–915.

PRODIGY GUIDANCE

Rheumatoid arthritis

Last revised in July 2005
www.prodigy.nhs.uk/guidance.asp?gt=Rheumatoid arthritis

Applies to people over the age of 16 years

This guidance covers the management in UK general practice of suspected or early rheumatoid arthritis (RA), and the acute deterioration of established RA.
This guidance includes relevant UK guidance from the National Institute for Clinical Excellence (NICE) and the Scottish Intercollegiate Guidelines Network (SIGN).

This guidance does not cover the management of RA provided in UK secondary care. It also does not cover the management of juvenile idiopathic arthritis, secondary osteoarthritis, secondary osteoporosis, or the systemic complications of RA (such as anaemia, pulmonary involvement, or vasculitis).
Although this guidance focuses on the medical management of RA, it must not be forgotten that people with RA need support from a wide range of health and social care professionals to ensure that they can remain as active and independent as possible.
There are separate PRODIGY guidance for *Ankylosing spondylitis, Back pain — lower, Gout, Monitoring people on disease-modifying antirheumatic drugs (DMARDs), Neck pain, Nonsteroidal anti-inflammatory drugs (NSAIDs), Osteoarthritis, Osteoporosis — treatment*, and *Polymyalgia rheumatica.*

Goals

To reduce symptoms (e.g. stiffness, pain, fatigue, depression)
To minimize disease progression and maintain joint function
To preserve quality of life, particularly independence and ability to work
To minimize adverse drug effects
To effectively manage comorbidities (coexisting conditions that are associated with poorer clinical outcomes in rheumatoid arthritis)

Contents

Scenarios

- Management of suspected/early rheumatoid arthritis p.1617
- Monoarticular flare (established disease) p.1621
- Polyarticular flare (established disease) p.1625
- Acutely painful prosthetic joint p.1628

Extended Information, p. 1632

Which scenario?

Management of suspected/early rheumatoid arthritis: covers the initial investigation and management of inflammatory arthritis when the diagnosis of rheumatoid arthritis (RA) has not been confirmed. It also highlights management of early RA. The importance of early referral to a rheumatologist is highlighted.
Monoarticular flare (established disease): covers the management of a flare of one to three joints in a person with established RA. It includes indications for referral.
Polyarticular flare (established disease): covers the management of an exacerbation of RA affecting multiple joints. It includes indications for referral.
Acutely painful prosthetic joint: covers the differential diagnosis, initial management, and indications for referral.

Management of suspected/early rheumatoid arthritis

Which therapy?

- **Rheumatology referral is strongly recommended if symptoms persist for more than 6 weeks** (see *Should I refer or investigate?*). Ideally, people should be seen within 12 weeks of the onset of symptoms.
- **Offer symptomatic treatment** in the meantime:
  - Paracetamol is recommended as the preferred treatment; additional benefit may be gained by adding codeine.
  - Use nonsteroidal ant-inflammatory drugs (NSAIDs) if paracetamol (and codeine) is inadequate:
    - Use only one at a time.
    - Use the lowest dose that relieves symptoms.
    - For which NSAID to use in people at high risk of NSAID-induced gastrointestinal effects; on low-dose aspirin; or who have cardiovascular risk factors, see *Prescribing points* below.
- Manage any existing cardiovascular disease and risk factors for cardiovascular disease.
- Offer smoking cessation advice if appropriate. Smoking is a risk factor for cardiovascular disease and makes rheumatoid arthritis worse.
- **Disease-modifying antirheumatic drugs (DMARDs) should be started *on specialist advice* as soon as possible,** once the diagnosis is confirmed. This is usually done under a shared-care arrangement, with a protocol from the local rheumatology service.
- **While waiting for DMARDs to take effect:**
  - Continue symptomatic treatment.
  - **Consider intra-articular corticosteroids** for localized disease.
  - **Consider systemic corticosteroids** for more generalized disease. Intramuscular corticosteroids may be preferred to oral treatment, as this allows control of dosage and of the duration of treatment.
- **Reduce or stop NSAIDs** if there is a good response to DMARDs.
- **Ensure access to a multidisciplinary team** (in particular, to a specialist rheumatology nurse, occupational therapist, and physiotherapist).
- Consider suggesting enrolment in a self-management course. These are provided by:

R

- Arthritis Care, helpline 0808 800 4050, www.arthritiscare.org.uk
- Expert Patients Programme, tel. 0845 606 6040, www.expertpatients.nhs.uk

Practical prescribing points

For further information see the *Medicines Compendium* (www.medicines.org.uk) or the *British National Formulary* (www.bnf.org).

NSAIDs

- **Only one NSAID should be prescribed at a time.**
- **NSAIDs may worsen asthma, hypertension, renal impairment, or heart failure.**
- Do not give ibuprofen, diclofenac, or naproxen without gastroprotection if there is a history of peptic ulceration.
- Do not give celecoxib if there is active peptic ulceration.
- **People with cardiovascular disease:**
  - Ibuprofen may reduce the cardiovascular protective effect of low-dose aspirin.
  - Do not give celecoxib to people with established ischaemic heart disease, cerebrovascular disease, peripheral arterial disease, or moderate or severe heart failure due to the small increased risk of thrombotic events.
  - Do not use celecoxib with low-dose aspirin. (Gastrointestinal protective effects of celecoxib are reduced.)
- **In people with risk factors for gastrointestinal NSAID complications:**
  - Use paracetamol (with or without codeine) instead of a NSAID if possible.
  - Or, use gastroprotection (a PPI or full-dose misoprostol) combined with a standard NSAID.
  - Or, consider switching to celecoxib alone (COX-2 selective).
- **Risk factors for gastrointestinal NSAID complications include:**
  - Age of 65 years and over.
  - Previous history of gastroduodenal ulcer, gastrointestinal (GI) bleeding, or gastroduodenal perforation.
  - Concomitant use of medications that are known to increase the likelihood of upper-GI adverse events, e.g. anticoagulants, aspirin (even a low dose), and corticosteroids.
  - Presence of serious comorbidity, such as cardiovascular disease, renal or hepatic impairment, diabetes, or hypertension.
  - Requirement for prolonged duration of NSAID use.
  - Use of maximum recommended doses of NSAIDs.

Misoprostol

- Diarrhoea and abdominal pain are common. Advise women of child-bearing age to use adequate contraception, because misoprostol increases the risk of miscarriage.

Codeine phosphate

- Codeine may cause nausea, vomiting, constipation, and drowsiness. People may need regular laxatives if long-term use of codeine is necessary.

Follow-up advice

- **Ask people taking nonsteroidal ant-inflammatory drugs (NSAIDs) if they have experienced gastrointestinal (GI) symptoms** — especially elderly people in the first few weeks, those taking low-dose aspirin, and people with a history of GI disease.
- NSAIDs should be reduced and if possible stopped, if a good response to disease-modifying antirheumatic drug is achieved.

Should I refer or investigate?

Refer?

- **Rheumatology referral is strongly recommended if symptoms persist for more than 6 weeks,** even if there is a response to nonsteroidal ant-inflammatory drugs (NSAIDs). Ideally, the person should be seen within 12 weeks of the onset of symptoms.
- **Referral is to:**
  - Establish the diagnosis.
  - Assess whether corticosteroid therapy (intra-articular, intramuscular, or oral) is necessary.
  - Ensure early use of disease-modifying antirheumatic drugs (DMARDs).
  - Monitor response to treatment and screen for toxicit to DMARDs.
  - Access the multidisciplinary team, including physiotherapy and occupational therapy.
- **Emergency admission is necessary if septic arthritis is suspected.** This typically presents with severe pain, swelling, and inflammation of a single joint. The joint usually feels hot and is extremely tender with limited movement. Systemic upset is common, with fever, shivers, and sweats. Septic arthritis may involve multip joints (e.g. in someone with immunosuppression) and can be a trigger for a polyarticular flare of rheumatoid arthritis (RA).
  - Atypical presentations may occur (e.g. fewer, more subtle signs) in a person taking corticosteroids, or wh is immunosuppressed, or who is elderly.
  - Rarely, septic arthritis occurs after recent joint injection, when the clinical features may be modified by the injected corticosteroid.

Investigate?

- There is no specific diagnostic test for RA.
- **Investigations are to support the clinical diagnosis.** Negative results do not exclude a diagnosis of RA. In particular, the absence or presence of rheumatoid facto does not exclude or confirm the diagnosis.
- **C-reactive protein (CRP) or erythrocyte sedimentation rate (ESR):** these are usually, but not always, elevated in RA.
  - CRP may better reflect acute exacerbations, as it is a better measure of inflammation.
  - ESR may measure general severity better, as it is sensitive to immunoglobulins and rheumatoid factor.
- **Full blood count:** normochromic anaemia, normocytic anaemia, and reactive thrombocytosis are common in active RA.
- **Liver function tests:** mild elevations of alkaline phosphatase and gamma-glutamyltransferase (gamma-GT) are common in active RA.
- **Urinalysis:** microscopic haematuria and/or proteinuria are suggestive of connective-tissue disease.
- **Rheumatoid factor:** this is positive in 60–70% of peopl with RA, and may be positive in other inflammatory diseases and in healthy people.
- **Antinuclear antibodies (ANA):** antinuclear antibodies (ANA) are suggestive of connective-tissue diseases such as systemic lupus erythematosus (SLE). However, ANA are positive in up to 30% of people with RA who are also rheumatoid-factor positive, and may be weakly positive in up to 10% of healthy people.
- **Radiology:** may be normal or show periarticular osteopenia and/or erosions.

R

Other tests that may be helpful:
- **Viral titres** — to exclude viral arthritis (e.g. hepatitis B, rubella).
- **Analysis of serum uric acid or synovial fluid** — to help exclude polyarticular gout.

'atient information leaflets

ıe following PILs are available at www.prodigy.nhs.uk
Antibody and Antigen Tests
Anti-inflammatory Painkillers
Arthritis Care
Arthritis Research Campaign - ARC
Arthroscopy and Arthroscopic Surgery
Blood Test - Detecting Inflammation
Blood Test - General
Rheumatoid Arthritis

hared decision making

Most people with suspected rheumatoid arthritis will be referred to a specialist. In the meantime:
- **Painkillers,** such as **paracetamol** may ease the pain.
- **Codeine** can be added for a short while if paracetamol alone is not sufficient.
- **An anti-inflammatory medicine** may be advised to ease pain and stiffness.
- **Side effects sometimes occur with anti-inflammatory medicines.** Stomach pain and bleeding from the stomach are the most serious. A brand with less risk, or an extra medicine to protect the stomach, may be advised in some people. Stop the medicine and see a doctor if you develop abdominal pains, pass blood or black stools, or vomit blood.

For most people who have a confirmed diagnosis of rheumatoid arthritis:
- **A disease-modifying drug** is usually advised. This eases symptoms but also helps to prevent damage to joints.
  - It can take about 6–12 weeks before you start to feel the benefits and up to 6 months to reach the maximum benefit.
  - The aim of treatment is to get on top of the disease as rapidly as possible, and it may be necessary to increase the dose, or to change to another drug, or to use more than one drug.
  - In the meantime...
  - Carry on with painkillers or anti-inflammatories until symptoms ease.
  - Regular blood tests are needed to detect possible problems as early as possible.
- **Steroids** are sometimes used to ease symptoms while waiting for the disease-modifying drug to work.
- To help to prevent associated conditions such as heart disease, if possible:
  - If you smoke, try to stop.
  - Try to eat healthily.
  - Try to take some regular exercise.

)rug rationale

rugs not included

Disease-modifying antirheumatic drugs (DMARDs): specialist advice is usually required before commencing these [SIGN, 2000].
Corticosteroids: specialist advice is usually required before commencing these.
Standard nonsteroidal anti-inflammatory drugs (NSAIDs) other than ibuprofen, diclofenac, and naproxen that are associated with a higher risk of gastrointestinal (GI) adverse events or that are not licensed for rheumatoid arthritis (RA) [CSM, 1994; Henry et al, 1996; Hernández-Diaz and Rodriguez, 2000; CSM, 2002]. Suppositories are not offered, as they do not improve efficacy or safety, and are generally less acceptable to people [Tramer et al, 1998].
- **COX-2 selective NSAIDs other than celecoxib,** are not included. There is concern in the use of these drugs precipitated by the withdrawal of rofecoxib and international regulatory authorities are currently reviewing the cardiovascular safety and cardio-renal events for all coxib NSAIDs [EMEA, 2004].
  - Etoricoxib and valdecoxib are black-triangle drugs that remain under the surveillance of the Committee on Safety of Medicines. There are no head-to-head controlled trials of these drugs with other COX-2 selective NSAIDs and they do not seem to offer any clinical advantage over other drugs included.
  - Lumiracoxib is a black-triangle drug that is licensed for the symptomatic relief of osteoarthritis.
  - Parecoxib is a black-triangle drug that is currently licensed for the short-term treatment of postoperative pain.
  - Etodolac and meloxicam — for both these drugs there are insufficient data of medium- to long-term duration to know whether or not they are associated with a possible increased risk of gastrointestinal or cardiovascular events, they are therefore not recommended because of the lack of follow-up data available.
- **Modified-release NSAIDs:** improvement in efficacy and reduction in adverse events have not been shown and they are also relatively expensive. They may be worth trying in someone with prominent morning stiffness despite use of standard NSAID preparations.
- **Topical NSAIDs:** there are insufficient trial data to support their use in people with RA.
- **Rubefacients** have limited evidence to support their efficacy. They may have a high placebo response due to massage of the affected area.
- **Strong opioids** (e.g. morphine, pethidine): these should be avoided because of the risk of dependence if used inappropriately.
- **Weak opioids other than codeine** have not shown greater efficiency than higher dosages of codeine combined with paracetamol, or are more expensive.
- **Low-dose weak opioids with paracetamol** (e.g. co-codamol 8/500, co-dydramol 10/500): there is no evidence that these offer any clinical benefit over paracetamol alone and they are likely to lead to opioid adverse effects [MeReC, 1993; De Craen et al, 1996].
- **Co-proxamol** (dextropropoxyphene 32.5 mg / paracetamol 325 mg) is no more effective than paracetamol alone [MeReC, 2000]. Additionally, overdosage with co-proxamol is complicated by respiratory depression and acute heart failure.
- **Proton-pump inhibitors (PPIs): rabeprazole** is not currently licensed for preventing NSAID-induced complications [BNF 48, 2004].
- **H_2-receptor antagonists (H_2RAs):** double doses of H_2-receptor antagonists are effective at reducing the risk of endoscopic gastric and duodenal ulcers but this is an off-licence use [Rostom et al, 2002]. Standard doses only reduce the risk of endoscopic duodenal ulcers. H_2RAs are therefore not included [BNF 48, 2004].
- **Fixed-dose combinations of standard NSAIDs with misoprostol:** the optimum dosage of misoprostol (i.e. 800 micrograms daily) cannot be reached using these preparations. In particular, only 400 micrograms daily of misoprostol is given with the higher dosages of NSAID in these preparations.
- **Low-dose misoprostol:** lower doses (e.g. 400 micrograms per day) are less effective than proton pump inhibitors at reducing the incidence of endoscopic lesions, and have

R

greater adverse effects [NICE, 2004]. (Diarrhoea and abdominal pain are common.)

Drugs included

- **Paracetamol:** this is a good, preferred choice for pain relief and is not associated with gastrointestinal (GI) toxicity [SIGN, 2000].
- **Codeine (in combination with paracetamol):** higher-dosage codeine is included for use with regular paracetamol for additional pain relief. Codeine 60 mg plus paracetamol has been shown to provide more pain relief than either codeine 60 mg alone or paracetamol 1000 mg alone [Moore et al, 1997]. Codeine should be prescribed separately from paracetamol to allow flexibility of dosing and titration of analgesic effect.
- **Standard nonsteroidal anti-inflammatory drugs (NSAIDs): ibuprofen, diclofenac, and naproxen** have a good balance of efficacy against adverse effect profile [CSM, 1994; Henry et al, 1996; Hernández-Diaz and Rodriguez, 2000]. Naproxen has a long half-life and can be given twice-daily; it may be particularly useful for someone with morning stiffness. Regarding concomitant ibuprofen and aspirin use, there is insufficient evidence to make clear recommendations for or against the concomitant use of ibuprofen. However:
  - Low-dose aspirin use is always the priority over use of an NSAID.
  - **It would seem prudent to avoid taking concomitant low-dose aspirin with regular ibuprofen in people with cardiovascular disease risk factors,** including diabetes, hyperlipidaemia, and obesity.
  - Either naproxen or diclofenac may be a better option if an NSAID is required.
  - Ibuprofen used occasionally is considered to pose less of a risk than regular ibuprofen for someone also taking low-dose aspirin.
- **COX-2 selective NSAIDs: celecoxib** is licensed for use in rheumatoid arthritis (RA) and is an option for use in people at high risk of NSAID-induced GI complications [NICE, 2001].
- **Proton-pump inhibitors (PPIs): esomeprazole, lansoprazole, omeprazole and pantoprazole** are generally the preferred choice for gastroprotection and are licensed for this use. They are effective and well tolerated; they reduce the risk of endoscopic gastric ulcers by 63% and the risk of duodenal ulcers by 81% [Rostom et al, 2002]. However there is a lack of data on prevention of ulcer complications.
- **Full-dose misoprostol** (200 micrograms four times a day) is licensed for prevention of NSAID-induced gastroduodenal ulceration [BNF 48, 2004]. It is effective for the treatment and prophylaxis of NSAID-associated ulcers, but it is not always well tolerated [Hawkey et al, 1998; Rostom et al, 2002].

Prescriptions

Analgesia

Paracetamol tablets: 1g up to four times a day

- Age from 16 years onwards
- Paracetamol 500mg tablets. Take two tablets every 4 to 6 hours when required for pain relief. Maximum of 8 tablets in 24 hours; supply 200 tablets; NHS Cost £1.48; OTC Cost £2.61.

Add on if required: codeine 30-60mg up to four times a day

- Age from 16 years onwards
- Codeine 30mg tablets. Take one to two tablets every 4 to 6 hours when required for pain relief. Maximum of 8 tablets in 24 hours; supply 56 tablets; NHS Cost £2.60.

Paracetamol 500mg tablets + codeine 30mg tablets

- Age from 16 years onwards
- Paracetamol 500mg tablets. Take two tablets every 4 to 6 hours when required for pain relief. Maximum of 8 tablets in 24 hours; supply 200 tablets; NHS Cost £1.4 OTC Cost £2.61.
- Codeine 30mg tablets. Take one to two tablets every 4 6 hours when required for pain relief. Maximum of 8 tablets in 24 hours; supply 56 tablets; NHS Cost £2.60

Standard NSAIDs: ibuprofen, naproxen and diclofenac

Ibuprofen tablets: 400mg four times a day

- Age from 16 years onwards
- Ibuprofen 400mg tablets. Take one tablet four times a day; supply 112 tablets; NHS Cost £3.28; OTC Cost £9.40.

Ibuprofen tablets: 600mg three times a day

- Age from 16 years onwards
- Ibuprofen 600mg tablets. Take one tablet three times a day; supply 84 tablets; NHS Cost £3.38.

Ibuprofen tablets: 800mg three times a day

- Age from 16 years onwards
- Ibuprofen 400mg tablets. Take two tablets three times day; supply 168 tablets; NHS Cost £4.92.

Diclofenac sodium e/c tablets: 25mg three times a day

- Age from 16 years onwards
- Diclofenac 25mg e/c tablets. Take one tablet three time a day; supply 84 tablets; NHS Cost £2.30.

Diclofenac sodium e/c tablets: 50mg three times a day

- Age from 16 years onwards
- Diclofenac 50mg e/c tablets. Take one tablet three time a day; supply 84 tablets; NHS Cost £3.55.

Naproxen tablets: 250mg twice a day

- Age from 16 years onwards
- Naproxen 250mg tablets. Take one tablet twice a day; supply 56 tablets; NHS Cost £2.76.

Naproxen tablets: 500mg twice a day

- Age from 16 years onwards
- Naproxen 500mg tablets. Take one tablet twice a day; supply 60 tablets; NHS Cost £3.91.

GI protection: use ONLY with a standard NSAID

Omeprazole capsules: 20mg once a day

- Age from 16 years onwards
- Omeprazole 20mg capsules. Take one capsule once a day; supply 28 capsules; NHS Cost £12.75.

Lansoprazole capsules: 15mg each morning

- Age from 16 years onwards
- Lansoprazole 15mg capsules. Take one capsule each morning (on an empty stomach); supply 28 capsules; NHS Cost £13.89.

Lansoprazole capsules: 30mg each morning

- Age from 16 years onwards
- Lansoprazole 30mg capsules. Take one capsule each morning (on an empty stomach); supply 28 capsules; NHS Cost £25.41.

Pantoprazole e/c tablets: 20mg once a day

- Age from 16 years onwards
- Pantoprazole 20mg e/c tablets. Take one tablet once a day; supply 28 tablets; NHS Cost £12.88.

Esomeprazole tablets: 20mg once a day

- Age from 16 years onwards
- Esomeprazole 20mg tablets. Take one tablet once a day supply 28 tablets; NHS Cost £18.50.

ınsoprazole orodispersible tablets: 15mg each morning
Age from 16 years onwards
Lansoprazole 15mg orodisp tabs. Take one tablet each morning (on an empty stomach); supply 28 tablets; NHS Cost £11.68.

ınsoprazole orodispersible tablets: 30mg each morning
Age from 16 years onwards
Lansoprazole 30mg orodisp tabs. Take one tablet each morning (on an empty stomach); supply 28 tablets; NHS Cost £21.38.

isoprostol tablets: 200micrograms four times a day
Age from 16 years onwards
Misoprostol 200microgram tabs. Take one tablet four times a day; supply 120 tablets; NHS Cost £18.72.

OX-2 NSAID: use ONLY if HIGH risk of NSAID-nduced ulcer

elecoxib capsules: 100mg twice a day
Age from 16 years onwards
Celecoxib 100mg capsules. Take one capsule twice a day; supply 60 capsules; NHS Cost £21.55.

elecoxib capsules: 200mg twice a day
Age from 16 years onwards
Celecoxib 200mg capsules. Take one capsule twice a day; supply 60 capsules; NHS Cost £43.10.

Monoarticular flare (established disease)

Which therapy?

yone with rheumatoid arthritis (RA) should ideally be ting disease-modifying antirheumatic drugs MARDs).

Rule out the possibility of septic arthritis.

Consider a nonsteroidal anti-inflammatory drug (NSAID):
- Use only one at a time.
- Use the lowest dose that relieves symptoms.
- For which NSAID to use in someone at high risk of NSAID-induced gastrointestinal effects; on low dose aspirin; or with cardiovascular risk factors, see *Prescribing points* below.

In addition to an NSAID, consider prescribing:
- Paracetamol — a good, preferred option.
- Codeine — may provide additional benefit.

Consider a topical rubefacient if localised rubbing provides relief.

Consider using corticosteroids:
- Intra-articular corticosteroid injection, by an appropriately skilled person, will often give rapid relief of severe symptoms.
- Systemic corticosteroids may be appropriate if intra-articular injection is not possible.
  - Intramuscular corticosteroid allows control of dosage and duration of therapy and may be preferable to oral treatment.
  - Oral corticosteroids should be withdrawn slowly to avoid rebound flare of symptoms.
- Prescribe osteoporosis prophylaxis for someone taking oral corticosteroids for 3 months or longer. For more information, see the scenario *Steroid-induced osteoporosis* in the guidance on *Osteoporosis treatment.*
- Corticosteroids should generally only be used short-term. Specialist advice should be sought before commencing long-term low-dose oral corticosteroids.

Manage any existing cardiovascular disease and risk factors for cardiovascular disease.

- Offer smoking cessation advice if appropriate. Smoking is a risk factor for cardiovascular disease and makes RA worse.
- Consider physiotherapy and occupational therapy.
- Consider suggesting enrolment in a self-management course. These are provided by:
  - Arthritis Care, helpline 0808 800 4050, www.arthritiscare.org.uk
  - Expert Patients Programme, tel. 0845 606 6040, www.expertpatients.nhs.uk

Practical prescribing points

For further information see the *Medicines Compendium* (www.medicines.org.uk) or the *British National Formulary* (www.bnf.org).

Nonsteroidal anti-inflammatory drugs

- **Only one NSAID should be prescribed at a time.**
- **NSAIDs may worsen asthma, hypertension, renal impairment, or heart failure.**
- Do not give ibuprofen, diclofenac, or naproxen without gastroprotection if there is a history of peptic ulceration.
- Do not give celecoxib if there is active peptic ulceration.
- **People with cardiovascular disease:**
  - Ibuprofen may reduce the cardiovascular protective effect of low-dose aspirin.
  - Do not give celecoxib to people with established ischaemic heart disease, cerebrovascular disease, peripheral arterial disease, or moderate or severe heart failure due to the small increased risk of thrombotic events.
  - Do not use celecoxib with low-dose aspirin. (Gastrointestinal protective effects of celecoxib are reduced.)
- **In people with risk factors for gastrointestinal NSAID complications:**
  - Use paracetamol (with or without codeine) instead of a NSAID if possible.
  - Or, use gastroprotection (a PPI or full-dose misoprostol) combined with a standard NSAID.
  - Or, consider switching to celecoxib alone (COX-2 selective).
- **Risk factors for gastrointestinal NSAID complications include:**
  - Age of 65 years and over.
  - Previous history of gastroduodenal ulcer, gastrointestinal (GI) bleeding, or gastroduodenal perforation.
  - Concomitant use of medications that are known to increase the likelihood of upper-GI adverse events, e.g. anticoagulants, aspirin (even a low dose), and corticosteroids.
  - Presence of serious comorbidity, such as cardiovascular disease, renal or hepatic impairment, diabetes, or hypertension.
  - Requirement for prolonged duration of NSAID use.
  - Use of maximum recommended doses of NSAIDs.

Misoprostol

- Diarrhoea and abdominal pain are common. Advise women of child-bearing age to use adequate contraception, because misoprostol increases the risk of miscarriage.

Codeine phosphate

- Codeine may cause nausea, vomiting, constipation, and drowsiness. People may need regular laxatives if long-term use of codeine is necessary.

Systemic corticosteroids

- **Document history of chickenpox** (there is a risk of potentially fatal disseminated chickenpox if the person is non-immune). Advise people taking systemic corticosteroids to avoid close contact with people who have chickenpox or shingles, and to seek urgent medical advice if they are exposed. Make a note about this advice on the steroid treatment card.
- **Blood pressure monitoring** is recommended for someone on corticosteroids.
- **Corticosteroids may worsen diabetic control or heart failure** — aggressively manage cardiovascular risk factors.

Intra-articular corticosteroids

- In general, hydrocortisone, prednisolone, or dexamethasone is recommended for injection of small joints (e.g. hand), and triamcinolone or methylprednisolone for injection of large joints (e.g. knee).
- Atrophy of subcutaneous tissues and local skin depigmentation may occur from periarticular leakage of corticosteroid.
  - The risk of local-tissue atrophy and depigmentation occurs from subcutaneous or shallow injections as well as from small-joint injections (e.g. tennis elbow, de Quervains tenosynovitis and shallow intramuscular injections).
  - The risk is greatest if large or repeated doses of a long-acting, potent corticosteroid are given.
- Lidocaine should be used to provide local anaesthesia.

Follow-up advice

- **If an intra-articular corticosteroid injection is given,** inform the person that symptoms may worsen for the first 24 hours.
- **Advise the person to seek medical advice** if the joint is getting worse despite treatment (but usually allow 24 hours after an intra-articular corticosteroid injection).
- **Advise the person to seek urgent medical advice** if the joint becomes hot, swollen, and painful, and they develop systemic upset (e.g. fever, shivers, sweats) — this may indicate septic arthritis.
- Advise the person to seek medical advice if multiple joint symptoms develop.
- **Ask people taking nonsteroidal anti-inflammatory drugs (NSAIDs) if they have experienced gastrointestinal (GI) symptoms** — especially elderly people in the first few weeks, those taking low-dose aspirin, and people with a history of GI disease.
- **NSAIDs** should be reduced and if possible withdrawn once the exacerbation settles.

Should I refer or investigate?

Refer?

Consider referral if:

- **Symptoms** do not respond to treatment.
- **Intra-articular injection** is necessary and expertise is not available in the practice.
- This is a further exacerbation of the same joint within a 3-month period.
- The person is not taking disease-modifying antirheumatic drug (DMARD) treatment.
- **There is uncertainty** regarding the diagnosis or management.
- **Emergency admission is necessary if septic arthritis is suspected.** This usually presents with severe pain, swelling, and inflammation of a single joint. The joint usually feels hot and is extremely tender with limited movement. Systemic upset is common, with fever, shivers, and sweats. Septic arthritis may involve multip joints (e.g. in someone with immunosuppression) and can be a trigger for a polyarticular flare of rheumatoid arthritis (RA).
  - Atypical presentations may occur (e.g. lesser signs) ir person taking corticosteroids, or who is immunosuppressed, or who is elderly.
  - Rarely, septic arthritis occurs after recent joint injection, when the clinical features may be modified by the injected corticosteroid.

Investigate?

- Checking C-reactive protein (CRP) or erythrocyte sedimentation rate (ESR) may be useful, as normal values would suggest a non-inflammatory cause for the increase in symptoms.

Patient information leaflets

The following PILs are available at www.prodigy.nhs.uk

- Antibody and Antigen Tests
- Anti-inflammatory Painkillers
- Arthritis Care
- Arthritis Research Campaign - ARC
- Arthroscopy and Arthroscopic Surgery
- Blood Test - Detecting Inflammation
- Blood Test - General
- Medicines - Name Changes of Medicines
- Rheumatoid Arthritis

Shared decision making

- Sometimes one joint flares up with symptoms in people with rheumatoid arthritis.
- **An anti-inflammatory medicine** usually eases pain and reduces inflammation.
  - Side effects sometimes occur with anti-inflammatory medicines. Stomach pain and bleeding from the stomach are the most serious. A brand with less risk, or an extra medicine to protect the stomach, may be advised in some people. *Stop the medicine and see a doctor if you develop abdominal pains, pass blood o black stools, or vomit blood.*
- **Painkillers,** such as paracetamol and/or codeine, may help in addition.
- **Steroid medication** is an alternative to reduce inflammation.
  - **An injection of steroid** into the joint is an option. Th can settle the inflammation for several weeks, but th joint may be more painful for 24 hours after the injection. There is a small risk of joint infection and skin damage.
  - A short course of steroid tablets is an alternative.
  - **A steroid injection into a muscle** that slowly releases into the body is an alternative.
  - Keep taking a disease-modifying medicine if you hav been prescribed one.

Drug rationale

Drugs not included

- **Disease-modifying antirheumatic drugs (DMARDs):** specialist advice is usually required before commencin these [SIGN, 2000].
- **Standard nonsteroidal anti-inflammatory drugs (NSAIDs) other than ibuprofen, diclofenac, and naproxen that are associated with a higher risk of**

R

gastrointestinal (GI) adverse events or that are not licensed for rheumatoid arthritis (RA) [CSM, 1994; Henry et al, 1996; Hernández-Diaz and Rodriguez, 2000; CSM, 2002]. Suppositories are not offered, as they do not improve efficacy or safety, and are generally less acceptable to people [Tramer et al, 1998].

COX-2 selective NSAIDs other than celecoxib, are not included. There is concern in the use of these drugs precipitated by the withdrawal of rofecoxib and international regulatory authorities are currently reviewing the cardiovascular safety and cardio-renal events for all coxib NSAIDs [EMEA, 2004].
- Etoricoxib and valdecoxib are black-triangle drugs that remain under the surveillance of the Committee on Safety of Medicines. There are no head-to-head controlled trials of these drugs with other COX-2 selective NSAIDs and they do not seem to offer any clinical advantage over other drugs included.
- Lumiracoxib is a black-triangle drug that is licensed for the symptomatic relief of osteoarthritis
- Parecoxib is a black-triangle drug that is currently licensed for the short-term treatment of postoperative pain.
- Etodolac and meloxicam — for both these drugs there are insufficient data of medium- to long-term duration to know whether or not they are associated with a possible increased risk of gastrointestinal or cardiovascular events, they are therefore not recommended because of the lack of follow-up data available.

Modified-release NSAIDs: improvement in efficacy and reduction in adverse events have not been shown and they are also relatively expensive. They may be worth trying in someone with prominent morning stiffness despite use of standard NSAID preparations.

Topical NSAIDs: there are insufficient trial data to support their use in people with RA.

Rubefacients have limited evidence to support their efficacy. They may have a high placebo response due to massage of the affected area.

Strong opioids (e.g. morphine, pethidine): these should be avoided because of the risk of dependence if used inappropriately.

Weak opioids other than codeine have not shown greater efficiency than higher doses of codeine combined with paracetamol, or are more expensive.

Low-dose weak opioids with paracetamol (e.g. co-codamol 8/500, co-dydramol 10/500): there is no evidence that these offer any clinical benefit over paracetamol alone and they are likely to lead to opioid adverse effects [MeReC, 1993; De Craen et al, 1996].

Co-proxamol (dextropropoxyphene 32.5 mg / paracetamol 325 mg) is no more effective than paracetamol alone [MeReC, 2000]. Additionally, overdosage with co-proxamol is complicated by respiratory depression and acute heart failure.

Proton-pump inhibitors (PPIs): rabeprazole is not currently licensed for preventing NSAID-induced complications [BNF 48, 2004].

H_2-receptor antagonists (H_2RAs): double doses of H_2-receptor antagonists are effective at reducing the risk of endoscopic gastric and duodenal ulcers but this is an off-licence use [Rostom et al, 2002]. Standard doses only reduce the risk of endoscopic duodenal ulcers. H_2RAs are therefore not included [BNF 48, 2004].

Fixed-dosage combinations of standard NSAIDs with misoprostol: the optimum dosage of misoprostol (i.e. 800 micrograms daily) cannot be reached using these preparations. In particular, only 400 micrograms daily of misoprostol is given with the higher dosages of NSAID in these preparations.

- **Low-dose misoprostol:** lower doses (e.g. 400 micrograms per day) are less effective than proton pump inhibitors at reducing the incidence of endoscopic lesions, and have greater adverse effects [NICE, 2004]. (Diarrhoea and abdominal pain are common.)

Drugs included

- **Paracetamol:** this is a good, preferred choice for pain relief and is not associated with gastrointestinal (GI) toxicity [SIGN, 2000]
- **Codeine (in combination with paracetamol):** higher-dosage codeine is included for use with regular paracetamol for additional pain relief. Codeine 60 mg plus paracetamol has been shown to provide more pain relief than either codeine 60 mg alone or paracetamol 1000 mg alone [Moore et al, 1997]. Codeine should be prescribed separately from paracetamol to allow flexibility of dosing and titration of analgesic effect.
- **Standard nonsteroidal anti-inflammatory drugs (NSAIDs): ibuprofen, diclofenac, and naproxen** have a good balance of efficacy against adverse effect profile [CSM, 1994; Henry et al, 1996; Hernández-Diaz and Rodriguez, 2000]. Naproxen has a long half-life and can be given twice-daily; it may be particularly useful for someone with morning stiffness. Regarding concomitant ibuprofen and aspirin use, there is insufficient evidence to make clear recommendations for or against the concomitant use of ibuprofen. However:
  - Low-dose aspirin use is always the priority over use of an NSAID.
  - **It would seem prudent to avoid taking concomitant low-dose aspirin with regular ibuprofen in people with cardiovascular disease risk factors,** including diabetes, hyperlipidaemia, and obesity.
  - Either naproxen or diclofenac may be a better option if an NSAID is required.
  - Ibuprofen used occasionally is considered to pose less of a risk than regular ibuprofen for someone also taking low-dose aspirin.
- **COX-2 selective NSAIDs: celecoxib** is licensed for use in rheumatoid arthritis (RA) and is an option for use in people at high risk of NSAID-induced GI complications [NICE, 2001].
- **Proton-pump inhibitors (PPIs): esomeprazole, lansoprazole, omeprazole and pantoprazole** are generally the preferred choice for gastroprotection and are licensed for this use. They are effective and well tolerated; they reduce the risk of endoscopic gastric ulcers by 63% and the risk of duodenal ulcers by 81% [Rostom et al, 2002]. However there is a lack of data on prevention of ulcer complications.
- **Full-dose misoprostol** (200 micrograms four times a day) is licensed for prevention of NSAID-induced gastroduodenal ulceration [BNF 48, 2004]. It is effective for the treatment and prophylaxis of NSAID-associated ulcers, but it is not always well tolerated [Hawkey et al, 1998; Rostom et al, 2002].
- **Intra-articular corticosteroids:** triamcinolone acetonide, methylprednisolone, hydrocortisone acetate, dexamethasone sodium phosphate, and prednisolone acetate are all available for intra-articular injection. They vary in their potency and duration of effect. Intra-articular corticosteroid injection, by an appropriately skilled person, will often give rapid relief of severe symptoms. Lidocaine (lignocaine) is available for local anaesthesia.
- **Oral corticosteroids: prednisolone** may be given as a low-dose, short-term course of treatment if intra-articular injection is not possible owing to lack of injection skills.

- **Intramuscular corticosteroids: triamcinolone acetonide and methylprednisolone** are available for intramuscular use. They may be appropriate if intra-articular injection is not possible owing to lack of injection skills. Intramuscular corticosteroid allows control of dosage and the duration of treatment and may be preferable to oral treatment [Green and Emery, 1999; SIGN, 2000].

Prescriptions

Analgesia

Paracetamol tablets: 1g up to four times a day

- Age from 16 years onwards
- Paracetamol 500mg tablets. Take two tablets every 4 to 6 hours when required for pain relief. Maximum of 8 tablets in 24 hours; supply 200 tablets; NHS Cost £1.48; OTC Cost £2.61.

Add on if required: codeine 30-60mg up to four times a day

- Age from 16 years onwards
- Codeine 30mg tablets. Take one to two tablets every 4 to 6 hours when required for pain relief. Maximum of 8 tablets in 24 hours; supply 56 tablets; NHS Cost £2.60.

Paracetamol 500mg tablets + codeine 30mg tablets

- Age from 16 years onwards
- Paracetamol 500mg tablets. Take two tablets every 4 to 6 hours when required for pain relief. Maximum of 8 tablets in 24 hours; supply 200 tablets; NHS Cost £1.48; OTC Cost £2.61.
- Codeine 30mg tablets. Take one to two tablets every 4 to 6 hours when required for pain relief. Maximum of 8 tablets in 24 hours; supply 56 tablets; NHS Cost £2.60.

Standard NSAIDs: ibuprofen, naproxen and diclofenac

Ibuprofen tablets: 400mg four times a day

- Age from 16 years onwards
- Ibuprofen 400mg tablets. Take one tablet four times a day; supply 112 tablets; NHS Cost £3.28; OTC Cost £9.40.

Ibuprofen tablets: 600mg three times a day

- Age from 16 years onwards
- Ibuprofen 600mg tablets. Take one tablet three times a day; supply 84 tablets; NHS Cost £3.38.

Ibuprofen tablets: 800mg three times a day

- Age from 16 years onwards
- Ibuprofen 400mg tablets. Take two tablets three times a day; supply 168 tablets; NHS Cost £4.92.

Diclofenac sodium e/c tablets: 25mg three times a day

- Age from 16 years onwards
- Diclofenac 25mg e/c tablets. Take one tablet three times a day; supply 84 tablets; NHS Cost £2.30.

Diclofenac sodium e/c tablets: 50mg three times a day

- Age from 16 years onwards
- Diclofenac 50mg e/c tablets. Take one tablet three times a day; supply 84 tablets; NHS Cost £3.55.

Naproxen tablets: 250mg twice a day

- Age from 16 years onwards
- Naproxen 250mg tablets. Take one tablet twice a day; supply 56 tablets; NHS Cost £2.76.

Naproxen tablets: 500mg twice a day

- Age from 16 years onwards
- Naproxen 500mg tablets. Take one tablet twice a day; supply 60 tablets; NHS Cost £3.91.

GI protection: use ONLY with a standard NSAID

Omeprazole capsules: 20mg once a day

- Age from 16 years onwards
- Omeprazole 20mg capsules. Take one capsule once a day; supply 28 capsules; NHS Cost £12.75.

Lansoprazole capsules: 15mg each morning

- Age from 16 years onwards
- Lansoprazole 15mg capsules. Take one capsule each morning (on an empty stomach); supply 28 capsules; NHS Cost £13.89.

Lansoprazole capsules: 30mg each morning

- Age from 16 years onwards
- Lansoprazole 30mg capsules. Take one capsule each morning (on an empty stomach); supply 28 capsules; NHS Cost £25.41.

Pantoprazole e/c tablets: 20mg once a day

- Age from 16 years onwards
- Pantoprazole 20mg e/c tablets. Take one tablet once a day; supply 28 tablets; NHS Cost £12.88.

Esomeprazole tablets: 20mg once a day

- Age from 16 years onwards
- Esomeprazole 20mg tablets. Take one tablet once a da supply 28 tablets; NHS Cost £18.50.

Lansoprazole orodispersible tablets: 15mg each mornin

- Age from 16 years onwards
- Lansoprazole 15mg orodisp tabs. Take one tablet each morning (on an empty stomach); supply 28 tablets; NHS Cost £11.68.

Lansoprazole orodispersible tablets: 30mg each mornin

- Age from 16 years onwards
- Lansoprazole 30mg orodisp tabs. Take one tablet each morning (on an empty stomach); supply 28 tablets; NHS Cost £21.38.

Misoprostol tablets: 200micrograms four times a day

- Age from 16 years onwards
- Misoprostol 200microgram tabs. Take one tablet four times a day; supply 120 tablets; NHS Cost £18.72.

COX-2 NSAID: use ONLY if HIGH risk of NSAID-induced ulcer

Celecoxib capsules: 100mg twice a day

- Age from 16 years onwards
- Celecoxib 100mg capsules. Take one capsule twice a day; supply 60 capsules; NHS Cost £21.55.

Celecoxib capsules: 200mg twice a day

- Age from 16 years onwards
- Celecoxib 200mg capsules. Take one capsule twice a day; supply 60 capsules; NHS Cost £43.10.

Corticosteroid (intra-articular, intramuscular, or oral)

Intra-articular dexamethasone sod phos 5mg/ml + lidocaine1%

- Age from 16 years onwards
- Dexamethasone sod phos 5mg/ml. Inject into small joi 0.16ml (0.8mg) to 0.2ml (1mg), according to joint size supply 1 1ml ampoule; NHS Cost £0.83.
- Lidocaine 1% injection (2ml). For local anaesthetic injection; supply 1 2ml ampoule; NHS Cost £0.22.

Intra-articular hydrocortisone acetate 25mg/ml+ lidocair 1%

- Age from 16 years onwards
- Hydrocortisone 25mg/ml inj. Inject into small joint: 0.2ml (5mg) to 0.5ml (12.5mg), according to joint size supply 1 1ml vial; NHS Cost £4.77.
- Lidocaine 1% injection (2ml). For local anaesthetic injection; supply 1 2ml ampoule; NHS Cost £0.22.

tra-articular prednisolone acetate 25mg/ml + lidocaine %

Age from 16 years onwards
Prednisolone acet 25mg/ml inj. Inject into small joint: 0.2ml (5mg) to 0.4ml (10mg), according to joint size; supply 1 1ml ampoule; NHS Cost £4.77.
Lidocaine 1% injection (2ml). For local anaesthetic injection; supply 1 2ml ampoule; NHS Cost £0.22.

tra-articular triamcinolone acetonide 40mg/ml+ locaine1%

Age from 16 years onwards
Triamcinolone acet 40mg/ml inj. Inject into large joint: 0.25ml (10mg) to 1ml (40mg), according to joint size; supply 1 1ml vial; NHS Cost £1.70.
Lidocaine 1% injection (2ml). For local anaesthetic injection; supply 1 2ml ampoule; NHS Cost £0.22.

ra-articular methylprednisolone 40mg/ml + lidocaine %

Age from 16 years onwards
Depo-Medrone+lidocaine 40/10mg. Inject into medium joint: 0.25ml (10mg) to 1ml (40mg), according to joint size; supply 1 1ml vial; NHS Cost £3.28.

ra-articular methylprednisolone 80mg/2ml + lidocaine %

Age from 16 years onwards
Depo-Medrone+lidocaine 80/20mg. Inject into large joint: 0.5ml (20mg) to 2ml (80mg), according to joint size; supply 1 2ml vial; NHS Cost £5.88.

ramuscular triamcinolone acetonide 40mg/ml

Age from 16 years onwards
Triamcinolone ace 40mg/ml inj. For deep intramuscular injection: 1ml (40mg) to 2ml (80mg), into gluteal muscle; supply 2 1ml pre-filled syringe; NHS Cost £4.22.

ramuscular methylprednisolone 40mg/ml

Age from 16 years onwards
Methylprednisolone 40mg/ml inj. For deep intramuscular injection: 1ml (40mg) to 3ml (120mg), into gluteal muscle; supply 3 1ml vial; NHS Cost £8.61.

al prednisolone (reducing dose regimen)

Age from 16 years onwards
Prednisolone 5mg tablets. Take two tablets each morning for 1 week and then take one tablet each morning for 1 week, then start taking the 1mg tablets; supply 21 tablets; NHS Cost £0.51.
Prednisolone 1mg tablets. Take 4 tabs once a day for 2 days, then 3 tabs once a day for 2 days, then 2 tabs once a day for 2 days, then one tab once a day for 4 days then STOP; supply 20 tablets; NHS Cost £0.38.

olyarticular flare (established isease)

Vhich therapy?

yone with rheumatoid arthritis (RA) should ideally be king disease-modifying antirheumatic drugs MARDs).

- **Consider a nonsteroidal anti-inflammatory drug (NSAID).**
  - Use only one at a time.
  - Use the lowest dose that relieves symptoms.
  - For which NSAID to use in someone at high risk of NSAID-induced gastrointestinal effects; on low-dose aspirin; or with cardiovascular risk factors, see *Prescribing points* below.
- **In addition to an NSAID, consider prescribing:**
  - Paracetamol — a good, preferred option.
  - Codeine — may provide additional benefit.
- **Consider systemic corticosteroids, especially if NSAIDs give poor symptom relief.**
  - Corticosteroids should only be used short-term. Specialist advice should be sought before commencing long-term low-dose oral corticosteroids.
  - Intramuscular corticosteroid allows control of dose and duration of treatment and may be preferable to oral treatment.
  - Oral corticosteroids should be withdrawn slowly to avoid rebound flare of symptoms.
  - Osteoporosis prophylaxis is necessary for someone taking oral corticosteroids for 3 months or longer. For more information, see the scenario *Prevention and treatment of steroid-induced osteoporosis* in the PRODIGY guidance on *Osteoporosis treatment.*
- Manage any existing cardiovascular disease and risk factors for cardiovascular disease.
- Offer smoking cessation advice if appropriate. Smoking is a risk factor for cardiovascular disease and makes RA worse.
- Consider physiotherapy and occupational therapy.
- Consider suggesting enrolment in a self-management course. These are provided by:
  - Arthritis Care, helpline 0808 800 4050, www.arthritiscare.org.uk
  - Expert Patients Programme, tel. 0845 606 6040, www.expertpatients.nhs.uk

Practical prescribing points

For further information see the *Medicines Compendium* (www.medicines.org.uk) or the *British National Formulary* (www.bnf.org).

Nonsteroidal anti-inflammatory drugs

- **Only one NSAID should be prescribed at a time.**
- **NSAIDs may worsen asthma, hypertension, renal impairment, or heart failure.**
- Do not give ibuprofen, diclofenac, or naproxen without gastroprotection if there is a history of peptic ulceration.
- Do not give celecoxib if there is active peptic ulceration.
- **People with cardiovascular disease:**
  - Ibuprofen may reduce the cardiovascular protective effect of low-dose aspirin.
  - Do not give celecoxib to people with established ischaemic heart disease, cerebrovascular disease, peripheral arterial disease, or moderate or severe heart failure due to the small increased risk of thrombotic events.
  - Do not use celecoxib with low-dose aspirin. (Gastrointestinal protective effects of celecoxib are reduced.)
- **In people with risk factors for gastrointestinal NSAID complications:**
  - Use paracetamol (with or without codeine) instead of a NSAID if possible.
  - Or, use gastroprotection (a PPI or full-dose misoprostol) combined with a standard NSAID.
  - Or, consider switching to celecoxib alone (COX-2 selective).
- **Risk factors for gastrointestinal NSAID complications include:**
  - Age of 65 years and over.
  - Previous history of gastroduodenal ulcer, gastrointestinal (GI) bleeding, or gastroduodenal perforation.
  - Concomitant use of medications that are known to increase the likelihood of upper-GI adverse events, e.g. anticoagulants, aspirin (even a low dose), and corticosteroids.

R

- Presence of serious comorbidity, such as cardiovascular disease, renal or hepatic impairment, diabetes, or hypertension.
- Requirement for prolonged duration of NSAID use.
- Use of maximum recommended doses of NSAIDs.

Misoprostol

- Diarrhoea and abdominal pain are common. Advise women of child-bearing age to use adequate contraception, because misoprostol increases the risk of miscarriage.

Systemic corticosteroids

- **Document history of chickenpox** (there is a risk of potentially fatal disseminated chickenpox if non-immune). Advise people taking systemic corticosteroids to avoid close contact with people who have chickenpox or shingles, and to seek urgent medical advice if they are exposed. Make a note about this advice on the steroid treatment card.
- Avoid corticosteroids if there is any suspicion of an infectious trigger to the flare.
- **Blood pressure monitoring** is recommended in for someone on corticosteroids.
- **Corticosteroids may worsen diabetic control or heart failure** — aggressively manage cardiovascular risk factors.

Codeine phosphate

- **Codeine** may cause nausea, vomiting, constipation, and drowsiness. People may need regular laxatives if long-term use of codeine is necessary.

Follow-up advice

- **Advise the person to seek medical advice** if the joints are getting worse despite treatment.
- **Advise the person to seek urgent medical advice** if any joint becomes hot, swollen, and painful, and he or she develops systemic upset (e.g. fever, shivers, sweats) — this may indicate septic arthritis.
- **Ask people taking NSAIDs if they have experienced GI symptoms** — especially elderly people in the first few weeks, those taking low-dose aspirin, and people with a history of gastrointestinal disease.
- **Nonsteroidal anti-inflammatory drugs** (**NSAIDs**) should be reduced and if possible withdrawn once the exacerbation settles.

R

Should I refer or investigate?

Refer?

- **Always consider referral or immediate telephonic consultation with the local rheumatology service,** as disease-modifying antirheumatic drug (DMARD) treatment may need adjusting; or if the person is not on a DMARD already, then starting one should be considered.
- **Consider referral if** symptoms do not respond to treatment or if there is uncertainty regarding the diagnosis or management.
- **Emergency admission is necessary if septic arthritis is suspected.** This usually presents with severe pain, swelling, and inflammation of a single joint. The joint usually feels hot and is extremely tender with limited movement. Systemic upset is common, with fever, shivers, and sweats. Septic arthritis may involve multiple joints (e.g. in someone with immunosuppression) and can be a trigger for a polyarticular flare of rheumatoid arthritis (RA).
- Atypical presentations may occur (e.g. lesser signs) in someone taking corticosteroids, or who is immunosuppressed, or who is elderly.
- Rarely, septic arthritis occurs after recent joint injection when the clinical features may be modified by the injected corticosteroid.

Investigate?

- Checking C-reactive protein (CRP) or erythrocyte sedimentation rate (ESR) may be useful, as normal values would suggest a non-inflammatory cause for an apparent increase in symptoms.

Patient information leaflets

The following PILs are available at www.prodigy.nhs.uk

- Antibody and Antigen Tests
- Anti-inflammatory Painkillers
- Arthritis Care
- Arthritis Research Campaign - ARC
- Arthroscopy and Arthroscopic Surgery
- Blood Test - Detecting Inflammation
- Blood Test - General
- Rheumatoid Arthritis

Shared decision making

- Sometimes several joints flare up with symptoms in people with rheumatoid arthritis.
- **An anti-inflammatory medicine** usually eases pain and reduces inflammation.
  - Side effects sometimes occur with anti-inflammatory medicines. Stomach pain and bleeding from the stomach are the most serious. A brand with less risk, or an extra medicine to protect the stomach, may be advised in some people. *Stop the medicine and see a doctor if you develop abdominal pains, pass blood o black stools, or vomit blood.*
- **Painkillers,** such as paracetamol and/or codeine, may help in addition.
- **A short course of steroid tablets** is an alternative optior to reduce inflammation.
- **A steroid injection into a muscle** that slowly releases in the body is an alternative.
- **Keep taking a disease-modifying medicine** if you have been prescribed one.

Drug rationale

Drugs not included

- **Disease-modifying antirheumatic drugs (DMARDs):** specialist advice is usually required before commencing these [SIGN, 2000].
- **Standard nonsteroidal anti-inflammatory drugs (NSAIDs) other than ibuprofen, diclofenac, and naproxen** that are associated with a higher risk of gastrointestinal (GI) adverse events or that are not licensed for rheumatoid arthritis (RA) [CSM, 1994; Henry et al, 1996; Hernández-Diaz and Rodriguez, 2000; CSM, 2002]. Suppositories are not offered, as th do not improve efficacy or safety, and are generally les acceptable to people [Tramer et al, 1998].
- **COX-2 selective NSAIDs other than celecoxib,** are not included. There is concern in the use of these drugs precipitated by the withdrawal of rofecoxib and international regulatory authorities are currently reviewing the cardiovascular safety and cardio-renal events for all coxib NSAIDs [EMEA, 2004].
  - Etoricoxib and valdecoxib are black-triangle drugs that remain under the surveillance of the Committee

on Safety of Medicines. There are no head-to-head controlled trials of these drugs with other COX-2 selective NSAIDs and they do not seem to offer any clinical advantage over other drugs included.
- Lumiracoxib is a black-triangle drug that is licensed for the symptomatic relief of osteoarthritis.
- Parecoxib is a black-triangle drug that is currently licensed for the short-term treatment of postoperative pain.
- Etodolac and meloxicam — for both these drugs there are insufficient data of medium- to long-term duration to know whether or not they are associated with a possible increased risk of gastrointestinal or cardiovascular events, they are therefore not recommended because of the lack of follow-up data available.

Modified-release NSAIDs: improvement in efficacy and reduction in adverse events have not been shown and they are also relatively expensive. They may be worth trying in someone with prominent morning stiffness despite use of standard NSAID preparations.

Topical NSAIDs: there are insufficient trial data to support their use in people with RA, and their use is particularly inappropriate for people with polyarticular presentations.

Rubefacients have limited evidence to support their efficacy. They may have a high placebo response due to massage of the affected area.

Strong opioids (e.g. morphine, pethidine): these should be avoided, owing to the risk of dependence if used inappropriately.

Weak opioids other than codeine have not shown greater efficiency than higher doses of codeine combined with paracetamol, or are more expensive.

Low-dose weak opioids with paracetamol (e.g. co-codamol 8/500, co-dydramol 10/500): there is no evidence that these offer any clinical benefit over paracetamol alone and they are likely to lead to opioid adverse effects [MeReC, 1993; De Craen et al, 1996].

Co-proxamol (dextropropoxyphene 32.5 mg / paracetamol 325 mg) is no more effective than paracetamol alone [MeReC, 2000]. Additionally, overdosage with co-proxamol is complicated by respiratory depression and acute heart failure.

Proton-pump inhibitors (PPIs): rabeprazole is not currently licensed for preventing NSAID-induced complications [BNF 48, 2004].

H_2-receptor antagonists (H_2RAs): at standard dosages, H_2RAs reduce the risk of duodenal ulceration and there is some evidence that double dosages reduce the risk of gastric ulceration [Rostom et al, 2002]. However, no H_2RA is currently licensed for the prevention of NSAID-induced gastric ulceration [BNF 48, 2004].

Fixed-dose combinations of standard NSAIDs with misoprostol: the optimum dosage of misoprostol (i.e. 800 micrograms daily) cannot be reached using these preparations. In particular, only 400 micrograms daily of misoprostol is given with the higher dosages of NSAID in these preparations.

Low-dose misoprostol: lower doses (e.g. 400 micrograms per day) are less effective than proton pump inhibitors at reducing the incidence of endoscopic lesions, and have greater adverse effects [NICE, 2004]. (Diarrhoea and abdominal pain are common.)

Intra-articular corticosteroids: intra-articular corticosteroids are not appropriate for polyarticular presentations.

Drugs included

- **Paracetamol:** this is a good, preferred choice for pain relief and is not associated with GI toxicity [SIGN, 2000].
- **Codeine (in combination with paracetamol):** higher-dosage codeine is included for use with regular paracetamol for additional pain relief. Codeine 60 mg plus paracetamol has been shown to provide more pain relief than either codeine 60 mg alone or paracetamol 1000 mg alone [Moore et al, 1997]. Codeine should be prescribed separately from paracetamol to allow flexibility of dosing and titration of analgesic effect.
- **Standard nonsteroidal anti-inflammatory drugs (NSAIDs): ibuprofen, diclofenac, and naproxen** have a good balance of efficacy against adverse effect profile [CSM, 1994; Henry et al, 1996; Hernández-Diaz and Rodriguez, 2000]. Naproxen has a long half-life and can be given twice-daily; it may be particularly useful for someone with morning stiffness. Regarding concomitant ibuprofen and aspirin use, there is insufficient evidence to make clear recommendations for or against the concomitant use of ibuprofen. However:
  - Low-dose aspirin use is always the priority over use of an NSAID.
  - **It would seem prudent to avoid taking concomitant low-dose aspirin with regular ibuprofen in people with cardiovascular disease risk factors,** including diabetes, hyperlipidaemia, and obesity.
  - Either naproxen or diclofenac may be a better option if an NSAID is required.
  - Ibuprofen used occasionally is considered to pose less of a risk than regular ibuprofen for someone also taking low-dose aspirin.
- **COX-2 selective NSAIDs: celecoxib** is licensed for use in rheumatoid arthritis (RA) and is an option for use in people at high risk of NSAID-induced GI complications [NICE, 2001].
- **Proton-pump inhibitors (PPIs): esomeprazole, lansoprazole, omeprazole and pantoprazole** are generally the preferred choice for gastroprotection and are licensed for this use. They are effective and well tolerated; they reduce the risk of endoscopic gastric ulcers by 63% and the risk of duodenal ulcers by 81% [Rostom et al, 2002]. However there is a lack of data on prevention of ulcer complications.
- **Full-dose misoprostol** (200 micrograms four times a day) is licensed for prevention of NSAID-induced gastroduodenal ulceration [BNF 48, 2004]. It is effective for the treatment and prophylaxis of NSAID-associated ulcers, but it is not always well tolerated [Hawkey et al, 1998; Rostom et al, 2002].
- **Oral corticosteroids:** prednisolone: a low-dosage short-term course may be useful for severe exacerbations, particularly if NSAIDs give inadequate symptom relief.
- **Intramuscular corticosteroids: triamcinolone acetonide and methylprednisolone** are available for intramuscular use. Intramuscular corticosteroids allow control of dosage and duration of treatment and may be preferable to oral treatment [Green and Emery, 1999; SIGN, 2000].

Prescriptions

Analgesia

Paracetamol tablets: 1g up to four times a day

- Age from 16 years onwards
- Paracetamol 500mg tablets. Take two tablets every 4 to 6 hours when required for pain relief. Maximum of 8 tablets in 24 hours; supply 200 tablets; NHS Cost £1.48; OTC Cost £2.61.

Add on if required: codeine 30-60mg up to four times a day
- Age from 16 years onwards
- Codeine 30mg tablets. Take one to two tablets every 4 to 6 hours when required for pain relief. Maximum of 8 tablets in 24 hours; supply 56 tablets; NHS Cost £2.60.

Paracetamol 500mg tablets + codeine 30mg tablets
- Age from 16 years onwards
- Paracetamol 500mg tablets. Take two tablets every 4 to 6 hours when required for pain relief. Maximum of 8 tablets in 24 hours; supply 200 tablets; NHS Cost £1.48; OTC Cost £2.61.
- Codeine 30mg tablets. Take one to two tablets every 4 to 6 hours when required for pain relief. Maximum of 8 tablets in 24 hours; supply 56 tablets; NHS Cost £2.60.

Standard NSAIDs: ibuprofen, naproxen and diclofenac

Ibuprofen tablets: 400mg four times a day
- Age from 16 years onwards
- Ibuprofen 400mg tablets. Take one tablet four times a day; supply 112 tablets; NHS Cost £3.28; OTC Cost £9.40.

Ibuprofen tablets: 600mg three times a day
- Age from 16 years onwards
- Ibuprofen 600mg tablets. Take one tablet three times a day; supply 84 tablets; NHS Cost £3.38.

Ibuprofen tablets: 800mg three times a day
- Age from 16 years onwards
- Ibuprofen 400mg tablets. Take two tablets three times a day; supply 168 tablets; NHS Cost £4.92.

Diclofenac sodium e/c tablets: 25mg three times a day
- Age from 16 years onwards
- Diclofenac 25mg e/c tablets. Take one tablet three times a day; supply 84 tablets; NHS Cost £2.30.

Diclofenac sodium e/c tablets: 50mg three times a day
- Age from 16 years onwards
- Diclofenac 50mg e/c tablets. Take one tablet three times a day; supply 84 tablets; NHS Cost £3.55.

Naproxen tablets: 250mg twice a day
- Age from 16 years onwards
- Naproxen 250mg tablets. Take one tablet twice a day; supply 56 tablets; NHS Cost £2.76.

Naproxen tablets: 500mg twice a day
- Age from 16 years onwards
- Naproxen 500mg tablets. Take one tablet twice a day; supply 60 tablets; NHS Cost £3.91.

GI protection: use ONLY with a standard NSAID

Omeprazole capsules: 20mg once a day
- Age from 16 years onwards
- Omeprazole 20mg capsules. Take one capsule once a day; supply 28 capsules; NHS Cost £12.75.

Lansoprazole capsules: 15mg each morning
- Age from 16 years onwards
- Lansoprazole 15mg capsules. Take one capsule each morning (on an empty stomach); supply 28 capsules; NHS Cost £13.89.

Lansoprazole capsules: 30mg each morning
- Age from 16 years onwards
- Lansoprazole 30mg capsules. Take one capsule each morning (on an empty stomach); supply 28 capsules; NHS Cost £25.41.

Pantoprazole e/c tablets: 20mg once a day
- Age from 16 years onwards
- Pantoprazole 20mg e/c tablets. Take one tablet once a day; supply 28 tablets; NHS Cost £12.88.

Esomeprazole tablets: 20mg once a day
- Age from 16 years onwards
- Esomeprazole 20mg tablets. Take one tablet once a day supply 28 tablets; NHS Cost £18.50.

Lansoprazole orodispersible tablets: 15mg each morning
- Age from 16 years onwards
- Lansoprazole 15mg orodisp tabs. Take one tablet each morning (on an empty stomach); supply 28 tablets; NHS Cost £11.68.

Lansoprazole orodispersible tablets: 30mg each morning
- Age from 16 years onwards
- Lansoprazole 30mg orodisp tabs. Take one tablet each morning (on an empty stomach); supply 28 tablets; NHS Cost £21.38.

Misoprostol tablets: 200micrograms four times a day
- Age from 16 years onwards
- Misoprostol 200microgram tabs. Take one tablet four times a day; supply 120 tablets; NHS Cost £18.72.

COX-2 NSAID: use ONLY if HIGH risk of NSAID-induced ulcer

Celecoxib capsules: 100mg twice a day
- Age from 16 years onwards
- Celecoxib 100mg capsules. Take one capsule twice a day; supply 60 capsules; NHS Cost £21.55.

Celecoxib capsules: 200mg twice a day
- Age from 16 years onwards
- Celecoxib 200mg capsules. Take one capsule twice a day; supply 60 capsules; NHS Cost £43.10.

Corticosteroids (intramuscular and oral)

Intramuscular triamcinolone acetonide 40mg/ml
- Age from 16 years onwards
- Triamcinolone ace 40mg/ml inj. For deep intramuscular injection: 1ml (40mg) to 2ml (80mg), into gluteal muscle; supply 2 1ml pre-filled syringe; NHS Cost £4.2

Intramuscular methylprednisolone 40mg/ml
- Age from 16 years onwards
- Methylprednisolone 40mg/ml inj. For deep intramuscular injection: 1ml (40mg) to 3ml (120mg), into gluteal muscle; supply 3 1ml vial; NHS Cost £8.61

Oral prednisolone (reducing dose)
- Age from 16 years onwards
- Prednisolone 5mg tablets. Take two tablets each morning for 1 week and then take one tablet each morning for 1 week, then start taking the 1mg tablets; supply 21 tablets; NHS Cost £0.51.
- Prednisolone 1mg tablets. Take 4 tabs once a day for 2 days, then 3 tabs once a day for 2 days, then 2 tabs once a day for 2 days, then one tab once a day for 4 days then STOP; supply 20 tablets; NHS Cost £0.38.

Acutely painful prosthetic joint

Which therapy?

- **Consider the following possibilities, and manage according to findings:**
  - **If pain is acute or onset is recent:**
    - Septic arthritis
    - Fracture
    - Loosening
    - Soft-tissue trauma
    - Referred pain (spine, proximal joint)
  - **If chronic pain predates the replacement:**
    - Referred pain (spine, proximal joint)
- **Prescribe symptomatic treatment:**
  - Paracetamol is recommended as a preferred treatment; additional benefit may be gained by adding codeine.

- Use nonsteroidal anti-inflammatory drugs (NSAIDs) if paracetamol (and codeine) is inadequate:
  - Use only one at a time.
  - Use the lowest dose that relieves symptoms.
  - For which NSAID to use in someone at high risk of NSAID-induced gastrointestinal effects; on low-dose aspirin; or with cardiovascular risk factors, see *Prescribing points* below.

Never inject a prosthetic joint.

Manage any existing cardiovascular disease and risk factors for cardiovascular disease.

Offer smoking cessation advice if appropriate. Smoking is a risk factor for cardiovascular disease and makes rheumatoid arthritis worse.

Consider physiotherapy and occupational therapy.

Consider suggesting enrolment in a self-management course. These are provided by:

- Arthritis Care, helpline 0808 800 4050, www.arthritiscare.org.uk
- Expert Patients Programme, tel. 0845 606 6040, www.expertpatients.nhs.uk

Practical prescribing points

For further information see the *Medicines Compendium* (www.medicines.org.uk) or the *British National Formulary* (www.bnf.org).

Nonsteroidal anti-inflammatory drugs

Only one NSAID should be prescribed at a time.

NSAIDs may worsen asthma, hypertension, renal impairment, or heart failure.

Do not give ibuprofen, diclofenac, or naproxen without gastroprotection if there is a history of peptic ulceration.

Do not give celecoxib if there is active peptic ulceration.

People with cardiovascular disease:

- Ibuprofen may reduce the cardiovascular protective effect of low-dose aspirin.
- Do not give celecoxib to people with established ischaemic heart disease, cerebrovascular disease, peripheral arterial disease, or moderate or severe heart failure due to the small increased risk of thrombotic events.
- Do not use celecoxib with low-dose aspirin. (Gastrointestinal protective effects of celecoxib are reduced.)

In people with risk factors for gastrointestinal NSAID complications:

- Use paracetamol (with or without codeine) instead of a NSAID if possible.
- Or, use gastroprotection (a PPI or full-dose misoprostol) combined with a standard NSAID.
- Or, consider switching to celecoxib alone (COX-2 selective).

Risk factors for gastrointestinal NSAID complications include:

- Age of 65 years and over.
- Previous history of gastroduodenal ulcer, gastrointestinal (GI) bleeding, or gastroduodenal perforation.
- Concomitant use of medications that are known to increase the likelihood of upper-GI adverse events, e.g. anticoagulants, aspirin (even a low dose), and corticosteroids.
- Presence of serious comorbidity, such as cardiovascular disease, renal or hepatic impairment, diabetes, or hypertension.
- Requirement for prolonged duration of NSAID use.
- Use of maximum recommended doses of NSAIDs.

Misoprostol

- Diarrhoea and abdominal pain are common. Advise women of child-bearing age to use adequate contraception, because misoprostol increases the risk of miscarriage.

Codeine phosphate

- Codeine may cause nausea, vomiting, constipation, and drowsiness. People may need regular laxatives if long-term use of codeine is necessary.

Follow-up advice

- Advise the person to seek medical advice if any of the following occur:
  - Worsening pain, swelling, and joint redness
  - Systemic upset (fever, sweats, shivers)
  - Deteriorating mobility
- **Ask people taking nonsteroidal anti-inflammatory drugs (NSAIDs) if they have experienced gastrointestinal (GI) symptoms** — especially elderly people in the first few weeks, those taking low-dose aspirin, and people with a history of GI disease.
- NSAIDs should be reduced and if possible withdrawn once the exacerbation settles.

Should I refer or investigate?

Refer?

- **Emergency admission is necessary if septic arthritis is suspected.** This may present with pain, swelling, and inflammation of a single joint. The joint may feel hot and may be tender with limited movement. Systemic upset is common, with fever, shivers, and sweats. Septic arthritis may involve multiple joints (e.g. in someone with immunosuppression) and can be a trigger for a polyarticular flare of rheumatoid arthritis (RA).
- Atypical presentations may occur (e.g. lesser signs) in someone taking corticosteroids, or who is immunosuppressed, or who is elderly.
- If mechanical failure or loosening is suspected, refer promptly.

Investigate?

- A normal C-reactive protein (CRP) or erythrocyte sedimentation rate (ESR) and white-cell count would reassure that the cause of symptoms is purely mechanical.
  - However, CRP and ESR may be normal in immunosuppressed people with septic arthritis, especially early in the course of the infection.
- Radiography may reveal loosening, fracture, or mechanical failure (e.g. protrusion, broken wires).

Patient information leaflets

The following PILs are available at www.prodigy.nhs.uk

- Antibody and Antigen Tests
- Anti-inflammatory Painkillers
- Arthritis Care
- Arthritis Research Campaign - ARC
- Blood Test - Detecting Inflammation
- Blood Test - General
- Rheumatoid Arthritis

Shared decision making

- Sometimes symptoms flare up over an artificial joint.
- **An anti-inflammatory medicine** usually eases pain and reduces inflammation.
  - Side effects sometimes occur with anti-inflammatory medicines. Stomach pain and bleeding from the stomach are the most serious. A brand with less risk, or an extra medicine to protect the stomach, may be advised in some people. *Stop the medicine and see a doctor if you develop abdominal pains, pass blood or black stools, or vomit blood.*
- **Painkillers,** such as paracetamol and/or codeine, may help in addition.
- **Physiotherapy** is sometimes a useful option.
- If your doctor feels that the replacement joint has failed or loosened, or the bone has fractured, further investigation will be required.
- Rarely, a hot, red, swollen artificial joint is due to infection. This requires urgent referral to an orthopaedic surgeon.

Drug rationale

Drugs not included

- **Disease-modifying antirheumatic drugs (DMARDs):** specialist advice is usually required before commencing these [SIGN, 2000].
- **Standard nonsteroidal anti-inflammatory drugs (NSAIDs) other than ibuprofen, diclofenac, and naproxen** that are associated with a higher risk of gastrointestinal (GI) adverse events or that are not licensed for rheumatoid arthritis (RA) [CSM, 1994; Henry et al, 1996; Hernández-Diaz and Rodriguez, 2000; CSM, 2002]. Suppositories are not offered, as they do not improve efficacy or safety, and are generally less acceptable to people [Tramer et al, 1998].
- **COX-2 selective NSAIDs other than celecoxib,** are not included. There is concern in the use of these drugs precipitated by the withdrawal of rofecoxib and international regulatory authorities are currently reviewing the cardiovascular safety and cardio-renal events for all coxib NSAIDs [EMEA, 2004].
  - Etoricoxib and valdecoxib are black-triangle drugs that remain under the surveillance of the Committee on Safety of Medicines. There are no head-to-head controlled trials of these drugs with other COX-2 selective NSAIDs and they do not seem to offer any clinical advantage over other drugs included.
  - Lumiracoxib is a black-triangle drug that is licensed for the symptomatic relief of osteoarthritis.
  - Parecoxib is a black-triangle drug that is currently licensed for the short-term treatment of postoperative pain.
  - Etodolac and meloxicam — for both these drugs there are insufficient data of medium- to long-term duration to know whether or not they are associated with a possible increased risk of gastrointestinal or cardiovascular events, they are therefore not recommended because of the lack of follow-up data available.
- **Modified-release NSAIDs:** improvement in efficacy and reduction in adverse events have not been shown and they are also relatively expensive. They may be worth trying in someone with prominent morning stiffness despite use of standard NSAID preparations.
- **Topical NSAIDs:** there are insufficient trial data to support their use in people with RA.
- **Rubefacients** have limited evidence to support their efficacy. They may have a high placebo response due to massage of the affected area.
- **Strong opioids** (e.g. morphine, pethidine): these should be avoided, owing to the risk of dependence if used inappropriately.
- **Weak opioids other than codeine** have not shown greater efficiency than higher dosages of codeine combined with paracetamol or are more expensive.
- **Low-dose weak opioids with paracetamol** (e.g. co-codamol 8/500, co-dydramol 10/500): there is no evidence that these offer any clinical benefit over paracetamol alone and they are likely to lead to opioid adverse effects [MeReC, 1993; De Craen et al, 1996].
- **Co-proxamol** (dextropropoxyphene 32.5 mg / paracetamol 325 mg) is no more effective than paracetamol alone [MeReC, 2000]. Additionally, overdosage with co-proxamol is complicated by respiratory depression and acute heart failure.
- **Proton-pump inhibitors (PPIs): rabeprazole** is not currently licensed for preventing NSAID-induced complications [BNF 48, 2004].
- **H_2-receptor antagonists (H_2RAs):** double doses of H_2-receptor antagonists are effective at reducing the risk of endoscopic gastric and duodenal ulcers but this is an off licence use [Rostom et al, 2002]. Standard doses only reduce the risk of endoscopic duodenal ulcers. H_2RAs are therefore not included [BNF 48, 2004].
- **Fixed-dosage combinations of standard NSAIDs with misoprostol:** the optimum dosage of misoprostol (i.e. 800 micrograms daily) cannot be reached using these preparations. In particular, only 400 micrograms daily of misoprostol is given with the higher dosages of NSAID in these preparations.
- **Low-dose misoprostol:** lower doses (e.g. 400 micrograms per day) are less effective than proton pump inhibitors at reducing the incidence of endoscopic lesions, and have greater adverse effects [NICE, 2004]. (Diarrhoea and abdominal pain are common.)

Drugs included

- **Paracetamol:** this is a good, preferred choice for pain relief and is not associated with gastrointestinal (GI) toxicity [SIGN, 2000].
- **Codeine (in combination with paracetamol):** higher-dosage codeine is included for use with regular paracetamol for additional pain relief. Codeine 60 mg plus paracetamol has been shown to provide more pain relief than either codeine 60 mg alone or paracetamol 1000 mg alone [Moore et al, 1997]. Codeine should be prescribed separately from paracetamol to allow flexibility of dosing and titration of analgesic effect.
- **Standard nonsteroidal anti-inflammatory drugs (NSAIDs): ibuprofen, diclofenac, and naproxen** have a good balance of efficacy against adverse effect profile [CSM, 1994; Henry et al, 1996; Hernández-Diaz and Rodriguez, 2000]. Naproxen has a long half-life and can be given twice-daily; it may be particularly useful for someone with morning stiffness. Regarding concomitant ibuprofen and aspirin use, there is insufficient evidence to make clear recommendations for or against the concomitant use of ibuprofen. However:
  - Low-dose aspirin use is always the priority over use of an NSAID.
  - **It would seem prudent to avoid taking concomitant low-dose aspirin with regular ibuprofen in people with cardiovascular disease risk factors,** including diabetes, hyperlipidaemia, and obesity.
  - Either naproxen or diclofenac may be a better option if an NSAID is required.

- Ibuprofen used occasionally is considered to pose less of a risk than regular ibuprofen for someone also taking low-dose aspirin.

COX-2 selective NSAIDs: celecoxib is licensed for use in rheumatoid arthritis (RA) and is an option for use in people at high risk of NSAID-induced GI complications [NICE, 2001].

Proton-pump inhibitors (PPIs): lansoprazole, omeprazole, and pantoprazole are licensed for prevention of NSAID-induced gastroduodenal ulceration [BNF 48, 2004]. PPIs reduce the risk of endoscopic ulcers, but there is a lack of data on prevention of ulcer complications [Rostom et al, 2002]. However, they are generally considered to be the preferred choice for gastroprotection, as they are well-tolerated compared with misoprostol.

Full-dose misoprostol (200 micrograms four times a day) is licensed for prevention of NSAID-induced gastroduodenal ulceration [BNF 48, 2004]. It is effective for the treatment and prophylaxis of NSAID-associated ulcers, but it is not always well tolerated [Hawkey et al, 1998; Rostom et al, 2002].

rescriptions

nalgesia

racetamol tablets: 1g up to four times a day
- Age from 16 years onwards
- Paracetamol 500mg tablets. Take two tablets every 4 to 6 hours when required for pain relief. Maximum of 8 tablets in 24 hours; supply 200 tablets; NHS Cost £1.48; OTC Cost £2.61.

d on if required: codeine 30-60mg up to four times a y
- Age from 16 years onwards
- Codeine 30mg tablets. Take one to two tablets every 4 to 6 hours when required for pain relief. Maximum of 8 tablets in 24 hours; supply 56 tablets; NHS Cost £2.60.

racetamol 500mg tablets + codeine 30mg tablets
- Age from 16 years onwards
- Paracetamol 500mg tablets. Take two tablets every 4 to 6 hours when required for pain relief. Maximum of 8 tablets in 24 hours; supply 200 tablets; NHS Cost £1.48; OTC Cost £2.61.
- Codeine 30mg tablets. Take one to two tablets every 4 to 6 hours when required for pain relief. Maximum of 8 tablets in 24 hours; supply 56 tablets; NHS Cost £2.60.

tandard NSAIDs: ibuprofen, naproxen and iclofenac

uprofen tablets: 400mg four times a day
- Age from 16 years onwards
- Ibuprofen 400mg tablets. Take one tablet four times a day; supply 112 tablets; NHS Cost £3.28; OTC Cost £9.40.

uprofen tablets: 600mg three times a day
- Age from 16 years onwards
- Ibuprofen 600mg tablets. Take one tablet three times a day; supply 84 tablets; NHS Cost £3.38.

uprofen tablets: 800mg three times a day
- Age from 16 years onwards
- Ibuprofen 400mg tablets. Take two tablets three times a day; supply 168 tablets; NHS Cost £4.92.

clofenac sodium e/c tablets: 25mg three times a day
- Age from 16 years onwards
- Diclofenac 25mg e/c tablets. Take one tablet three times a day; supply 84 tablets; NHS Cost £2.30.

Diclofenac sodium e/c tablets: 50mg three times a day
- Age from 16 years onwards
- Diclofenac 50mg e/c tablets. Take one tablet three times a day; supply 84 tablets; NHS Cost £3.55.

Naproxen tablets: 250mg twice a day
- Age from 16 years onwards
- Naproxen 250mg tablets. Take one tablet twice a day; supply 56 tablets; NHS Cost £2.76.

Naproxen tablets: 500mg twice a day
- Age from 16 years onwards
- Naproxen 500mg tablets. Take one tablet twice a day; supply 60 tablets; NHS Cost £3.91.

GI protection: use ONLY with a standard NSAID

Omeprazole capsules: 20mg once a day
- Age from 16 years onwards
- Omeprazole 20mg capsules. Take one capsule once a day; supply 28 capsules; NHS Cost £12.75.

Lansoprazole capsules: 15mg each morning
- Age from 16 years onwards
- Lansoprazole 15mg capsules. Take one capsule each morning (on an empty stomach); supply 28 capsules; NHS Cost £13.89.

Lansoprazole capsules: 30mg each morning
- Age from 16 years onwards
- Lansoprazole 30mg capsules. Take one capsule each morning (on an empty stomach); supply 28 capsules; NHS Cost £25.41.

Pantoprazole e/c tablets: 20mg once a day
- Age from 16 years onwards
- Pantoprazole 20mg e/c tablets. Take one tablet once a day; supply 28 tablets; NHS Cost £12.88.

Esomeprazole tablets: 20mg once a day
- Age from 16 years onwards
- Esomeprazole 20mg tablets. Take one tablet once a day; supply 28 tablets; NHS Cost £18.50.

Lansoprazole orodispersible tablets: 15mg each morning
- Age from 16 years onwards
- Lansoprazole 15mg orodisp tabs. Take one tablet each morning (on an empty stomach); supply 28 tablets; NHS Cost £11.68.

Lansoprazole orodispersible tablets: 30mg each morning
- Age from 16 years onwards
- Lansoprazole 30mg orodisp tabs. Take one tablet each morning (on an empty stomach); supply 28 tablets; NHS Cost £21.38.

Misoprostol tablets: 200micrograms four times a day
- Age from 16 years onwards
- Misoprostol 200microgram tabs. Take one tablet four times a day; supply 120 tablets; NHS Cost £18.72.

COX-2 NSAID: use ONLY if HIGH risk of NSAID-induced ulcer

Celecoxib capsules: 100mg twice a day
- Age from 16 years onwards
- Celecoxib 100mg capsules. Take one capsule twice a day; supply 60 capsules; NHS Cost £21.55.

Celecoxib capsules: 200mg twice a day
- Age from 16 years onwards
- Celecoxib 200mg capsules. Take one capsule twice a day; supply 60 capsules; NHS Cost £43.10.

Extended Information

Background information

- What is it? p.1632
- How common is it? p.1632
- How do I know my patient has rheumatoid arthritis? p.1632
- How do I know my patient has a flare of rheumatoid arthritis? p.1632
- What else might it be? p.1633
- Complications and prognosis p.1633

What is it?

- **Rheumatoid arthritis** (RA) is an inflammatory arthritis characterized by symmetrical, mainly small joint involvement; radiological erosions; and the development of deformity with loss of function.
- It is a systemic disease and may be associated with haematological, visceral, and vasculitic abnormalities.
- The cause of RA is unknown, but is likely to be multifactorial and include genetic predisposition.

How common is it?

- Rheumatoid arthritis is the most common inflammatory arthropathy.
- In adults, the incidence of new cases is about 50 per 100,000 population each year.
- Prevalence of established disease is about 1% of the population.
- It is three times more frequent in women.
- Incidence increases with age, with peak onset in the sixth decade.

[Scott et al, 1998; SIGN, 2000]

How do I know my patient has rheumatoid arthritis?

Clinical features of rheumatoid arthritis (RA) on initial presentation:

R

- **RA usually presents** as a gradual-onset, symmetrical arthritis mainly affecting the hands and/or feet. It can present acutely and may also present with large-joint involvement (e.g. the shoulders and knees), or with extra-articular or systemic features.
- **Extra-articular and systemic features** include rheumatoid nodules, tenosynovitis, fever, weight loss, dyspnoea, chest pain (pericarditis), and rash (vasculitis). Systemic features may predominate over joint symptoms and this can make diagnosis difficult.
- **A person with RA will typically describe** pain, stiffness, and swelling of the joints. Symptoms are often worse in the morning and after inactivity. Systemic 'flu-like' symptoms may also occur.
- **Examination will usually show** symmetrical swelling and tenderness of the small joints of the hands and feet (and to a variable extent the larger joints).
- **The American College of Rheumatology (ACR) criteria** for the classification of RA are widely accepted [Arnett et al, 1988; SIGN, 2000]. However, they are mainly used in research and are less useful in routine clinical practice, particularly in early disease. Diagnosis of RA requires four out of seven of the criteria in Table 1.

[American College of Rheumatology, 1987]

Investigations useful in the initial presentation of rheumatoid arthritis:

- **There is no specific diagnostic test for RA.**
- **Investigations are to support the clinical diagnosis.** Negative results do not exclude a diagnosis of RA. In particular, the absence or presence of rheumatoid facto[r] does not exclude or confirm the diagnosis.
- **C-reactive protein (CRP) or erythrocyte sedimentation rate (ESR):** these are usually, but not always, elevated i[n] RA [Wolfe, 1997].
  - CRP may better reflect acute exacerbations, as it is a better measure of inflammation.
  - ESR may measure general severity better, as it is sensitive to immunoglobulins and rheumatoid factor.
- **Full blood count:** normochromic, normocytic anaemia and reactive thrombocytosis are common in active RA.
- **Liver function tests:** mild elevations of alkaline phosphatase and gamma-glutamyltransferase (gamma-GT) are common in active RA.
- **Urinalysis:** microscopic haematuria and/or proteinuria are suggestive of connective tissue disease.
- **Rheumatoid factor:** this is positive in 60–70% of peopl[e] with RA, and may be positive in people with other inflammatory diseases and in healthy people.
- **Antinuclear antibodies (ANA):** ANA are suggestive of connective tissue diseases such as systemic lupus erythematosus (SLE). However, ANA are positive in up to 30% of people with RA who are also rheumatoid-factor positive, and may be weakly positive in up to 10[%] of healthy people.
- **Radiology:** may be normal or show periarticular osteopenia and/or erosions.
- **Other tests that may be helpful:**
  - **Viral titres** — to exclude viral arthritis (e.g. hepatitis, rubella, parvovirus).
  - **Analysis of plasma urate or synovial fluid**— to help exclude polyarticular gout. However, plasma urate levels are often raised in people with RA.

[SIGN, 2000]

How do I know my patient has a flare of rheumatoid arthritis?

Clinical features of a flare of rheumatoid arthritis:

- **Symptoms increase:**
  - Early-morning stiffness
  - Pain
  - Fatigue
  - Joint swelling
- **Signs deteriorate:**
  - Synovitis

Table 1: ACR criteria for the diagnosis of RA.

Diagnostic criteria	
Morning stiffness	Duration >1 hour; lasting >6 weeks
Arthritis of three or more joint areas* observed by a physician	Soft-tissue swelling or effusion lasti[ng] >6 weeks
Arthritis of hand joints	Wrist, metacarpophalangeal joints, or proximal interphalangeal joints lasting >6 weeks
Symmetric arthritis*	At least one area, lasting >6 weeks
Rheumatoid nodules	As observed by a physician
Serum rheumatoid factor	As assessed by a method positive in less than 5% of control people
Radiographic changes	As seen on anteroposterior films of wrists and hands

* Proximal interphalangeal joints, metacarpophalangeal joints, wrist, elbow, kne[e], ankle, metatarsophalangeal joints

- Joint tenderness

Ability to move and function deteriorates.

Laboratory markers of inflammation deteriorate:

- ESR and CRP rise.
- (X-rays are not used to assess a flare, but they might be indicated if a fracture or joint failure is suspected.)

'hat else might it be?

/hat is the differential diagnosis of rheumatoid rthritis on first presentation?

people whose symptoms of arthritis started recently, the ferential diagnosis includes:

Viral arthritis (e.g. parvovirus, rubella, hepatitis B)

Reactive arthritis (e.g. postinfective: throat, gut, sexually acquired)

Seronegative spondyloarthropathy (e.g. psoriatic, ankylosing spondylitis, inflammatory bowel disease)

Connective-tissue disease (e.g. systemic lupus erythematosus, scleroderma)

Polymyalgia rheumatica (particularly if the person is elderly)

Polyarticular gout (e.g. any risk factors or tophi present)

Osteoarthritis (e.g. involvement of proximal and distal nterphalangeal joints, Heberden or Bouchard nodes)

Septic arthritis (particularly if monoarthritis)

Fibromyalgia

Medical conditions presenting with arthropathy (e.g. sarcoidosis, thyroid disease, infective endocarditis, haemochromatosis, diabetic cheiroarthropathy, paraneoplastic syndromes, multiple myeloma)

Lyme disease (*Borrelia burgdorferi*)

GN, 2000]

'hat is the differential diagnosis of a flare of eumatoid arthritis?

ople who have rheumatoid arthritis and present with reased symptoms usually have a flare of their disease. owever, other causes need to be considered. These lude:

Mechanical problems from joint damage and/or secondary osteoarthritis:

- History usually prolonged.
- Pain and decreased function.
- Muscle wasting, instability, crepitus, reduced range of movement, minimal or no synovitis.

Osteoporotic fracture or insufficiency fracture:

- Acute onset of pain and immobility.
- History of trauma, which may be minimal.
- Other risk factors for osteoporosis.

Avascular necrosis:

- On steroids.
- Acute onset of pain.
- Absence of synovitis.

Rheumatoid cervical myelopathy; nerve root compression.

- Long duration of disease and marked destruction of peripheral joints.
- Onset sudden or insidious.
- Weakness, unsteadiness, paraesthesia; pain may be absent.
- Neck pain.
- History of trauma (e.g. whiplash injury, fall).

Comorbid conditions such as anaemia, biochemical upset, infection.

Psychological and social difficulties.

Failure to take medication as prescribed.

Complications and prognosis

Complications

- **Adverse effects on work and social life are common.**
  - Many people with rheumatoid arthritis (RA) have restricted mobility and difficulties with activities of daily living.
  - Depression is common.
  - Inability to work may occur early in the course of RA, especially in someone with a manual occupation.
- **Inflammatory conditions other than those involving joint and tendon.**
  - Vasculitis, vasculitic ulcers
  - Pleurisy/pleural effusions, pulmonary fibrosis
  - Pericarditis
  - Lymphadenopathy
  - Dry-eye syndrome (keratoconjunctivitis sicca)
  - Neuropathy
  - Felty's syndrome (enlarged spleen and low white-cell count); can present with an infection or leg ulcer
  - Amyloidosis (rare)
- **Anaemia**
  - Anaemia is a common problem in people with RA; estimates of the prevalence of mild anaemia range from 33% to 60%.
  - People with RA can have any type (or combination) of anaemia; but of those with anaemia, about 77% will have anaemia of chronic disorders, and about 23% will have iron deficiency anaemia [Wilson et al, 2004].
- **Orthopaedic complications**
  - Carpal tunnel syndrome
  - Tendon rupture (particularly extensors of fingers or thumb)
  - Cervical myelopathy (usually after severe and long-standing RA)
- **Osteoporosis**
- **Infectious complications**
  - RA is associated with an approximate doubling of the risk of infection; pulmonary infection and generalized sepsis are particular risks.
  - Septic arthritis is a rare but serious complication.
- **Cardiovascular disease**

[Mikuls and Saag, 2001]

Prognosis

- **The course of RA is variable and unpredictable.** Some people experience flares and remissions, while others have a progressive course.
- **The long-term severity (disease progression) of RA has tended to be underestimated** by health professionals and the public [Pincus and Callahan, 1993].
- Clinical studies have found that 90% of people with RA still have evidence of the disease, generally with progression, when followed up 3–5 years after diagnosis [Pincus and Callahan, 1993].
- About half of people working at disease onset will be disabled or unable to work within 10 years [Emery and Suarez-Almazor, 2004].
- Life expectancy is shortened [SIGN, 2000].
- **Indicators of poor long-term outcome are:**
  - Many active joints.
  - Involvement of large joints early in the course of the disease.
  - High CRP or ESR at outset.
  - Strongly positive rheumatoid factor.
  - Early radiological erosions.
  - Poorer scores of function at outset.
  - Adverse socio-economic circumstances and lower educational level.

[SIGN, 2000]

- **The prognosis for people with RA is adversely affected by tobacco smoking, drugs taken to treat RA, and comorbidity** [Saag et al, 1997; Wolfe, 2000; Mikuls and Saag, 2001; Criswell et al, 2002; O'Dell, 2004].

Effects of comorbidity on the prognosis

- Several conditions that commonly occur with RA adversely affect outcomes such as disability and death. The most important comorbidities are:
  - Cardiovascular disease.
  - Infection.
  - Malignancy — may in part be related to some disease-modifying antirheumatic drugs (DMARDs) such as methotrexate, azathioprine, or cyclosporin.
  - Gastrointestinal disease.
  - Osteoporosis.
- These comorbidities reinforce each other to affect disability in people with arthritis. Further, the number of comorbidities is an independent risk-factor for premature death in RA [Mikuls and Saag, 2001].
- **Cardiovascular disease accounts for about half of all deaths in RA** [van Doornum et al, 2002]. Risk factors for coronary heart disease can be adversely affected by drugs used to treat RA. For instance:
  - **Hypertension** can be raised by nonsteroidal anti-inflammatory drugs (NSAIDs) and glucocorticoids.
  - **Hyperglycaemia** can be worsened by glucocorticoids.
  - **Hyperlipidaemia** can be worsened by glucocorticoids (but improved by hydroxychloroquine).
  - **Serum homocysteine** can be raised by methotrexate, particularly when sulfasalazine is co-administered. Raised serum levels of homocysteine are associated with prothrombotic action and cardiovascular disease; folic acid can lower homocysteine levels.
    - Methotrexate should be prescribed cautiously in people with RA and ischaemic heart disease, and folate should be taken concomitantly [Whittle and Hughes, 2004].
  - **Platelet aggregation** can be increased by cyclo-oxygenase-2 (COX-2) selective inhibitors.
- **Malignancy:** Lymphoproliferative malignancies (leukaemia, lymphoma, and multiple myeloma) are more common in people with RA and are thought to be due, in part, to the use of DMARDs.
  - RA itself predisposes to lymphoma. However, colorectal cancers and other gastrointestinal malignancies are less common.
  - Azathioprine, ciclosporin, and cyclophosphamide probably predispose to malignancy.
  - Sulfasalazine, hydroxychloroquine, and leflunomide probably do not increase the risk of malignancy.
- **Infection:** Mortality due to infection is increased in people with RA. Particular risks are pulmonary infection and generalized sepsis. Drugs such as corticosteroids and immunosuppressants that are commonly used to treat RA increase the risk of opportunistic and other serious infection.
- **Osteoporosis leading to bone fractures** with pain, disability, and complications of immobility and surgery is a major source of morbidity in people with RA. Long-term glucocorticoid therapy is an important cause of osteoporosis in people with RA; but RA increases the risk of osteoporosis even in the absence of glucocorticoid therapy.
- **Gastrointestinal disease:** morbidity and mortality due to upper-gastrointestinal disease are increased in people with RA. This is mainly due to adverse effects of NSAIDs. (In contrast to the case with other comorbidities, there is no evidence that RA itself causes gastrointestinal problems.)

[Mikuls and Saag, 2001; O'Dell, 2004]

Management issues

- Overview p.1634
- How are symptoms managed and function maintained p.1635
- What is the role of nonsteroidal anti-inflammatory drugs? p.1635
- What is the role of corticosteroids? p.1636
- What is the role of disease-modifying antirheumatic drugs? p.1636
- What other treatments are used? p.1637
- How should complications be managed? p.1637
- Medicines management p.1639

Overview

- **Anyone with inflammatory joint disease lasting more than 6 weeks should be considered for rheumatology referral, and ideally should be seen within 12 weeks of the onset of symptoms** [SIGN, 2000].
- **Paracetamol (with codeine where needed) and nonsteroidal anti-inflammatory drugs (NSAIDs)** provic partial relief of pain and stiffness and are especially useful until a definitive diagnosis of rheumatoid arthrit (RA) has been made.
- **RA should be treated as early as possible with disease-modifying antirheumatic drugs (DMARDs)** to control symptoms and delay disease progression (**B**) [SIGN, 2000].
  - There is evidence that a strategy to provide sustaine tight control of disease activity improves outcomes [Grigor et al, 2004].
- **Complications of RA and its treatment should be detected early and managed promptly** [SIGN, 2000].
- **Cardiovascular disease** and its risk factors, if present, should be actively managed, as it is a leading contribu to mortality in RA [Mikuls and Saag, 2001]. See the PRODIGY guidance on *Coronary heart disease risk — identification and management.*
- **Offer smoking cessation advice to smokers,** as smokin is not only a risk factor for cardiovascular disease but also increases the severity of RA [Saag et al, 1997; Wolfe, 2000; Criswell et al, 2002].
- **Encourage people to undertake simple dynamic exerci** (**B**) [SIGN, 2000]. Other strategies that may also be helpful include resting, suitable footwear, and workin splints.
  - Useful booklets on exercise are published by:
    - Arthritis Care: *Fit For Life* [Arthritis Care, 2002].
    - The Arthritis Research Campaign (ARC): *Exercis And Arthritis* [ARC, 2004].
- **Surgery may have a role when the benefit of drug intervention is limited.** Surgery aims to relieve pain an restore function (e.g. carpal tunnel release, extensor tendon repair, synovectomy, joint fusion, joint replacement, and cervical decompression [Oliver, 2001]).
- **Education about the condition and psychological support** are considered important. A systematic review concluded that patient education had measurable sma short-term effects (on disability, counts of swollen and painful joints, global assessment by the individual, psychological status, and depression) but there was no evidence of long-term benefits [Riemsma et al, 2004].
- **Self-management courses** may reduce health-service utilization, improve health status (i.e. pain, fatigue, anxiety, depression, and positive affect), and improve health behaviours (exercise, cognitive symptom management, diet, and relaxation) [Barlow et al, 200 Courses are provided in the UK by:

- Arthritis Care: helpline 0808 800 4050; Internet www.arthritiscare.org.uk
- The Expert Patients Programme: telephone 0845 606 6040; Internet www.expertpatients.nhs.uk
- The National Rheumatoid Arthritis Society (NRAS) has established an Expert Patient Network to enable people to get telephone support and help locally from others who have the disease. See www.rheumatoid.org.uk/2/nras_support.php.
- **Multidisciplinary team involvement is essential** for the effective holistic management of RA [SIGN, 2000]. This includes the assessment and management of mobility, function (especially with regard to the activities of daily living), mood, and pain.
- **Vaccinations:** many people with RA should be given influenza and pneumococcal vaccines.

How are symptoms managed and function maintained?

- Few people with rheumatoid arthritis (RA) will have their symptoms adequately controlled with paracetamol [SIGN, 2000]. The following drugs are usually required to control inflammation and the pain that it causes, and their management is discussed below:
  - *Nonsteroidal anti-inflammatory drugs*
  - *Corticosteroids*
  - *Disease-modifying antirheumatic drugs*
- **Paracetamol** should be considered for preferred use in pain relief. If necessary, a weak opioid such as codeine phosphate may be added (although this may be less well tolerated).
- **Strong opioid analgesics** (e.g. morphine) are rarely, if ever, indicated for chronic pain in arthritis.
- **How do I assess pain?**
  - Routinely include questions about pain and coping ability in the history.
  - Recording pain objectively can conveniently be done by asking the person to indicate the level of pain on a visual analogue scale.
- **How do I assess function?**
  - Routinely include questions about the person's ability to cope with usual daily activities in the history.
  - Recording function objectively is done with the aid of a questionnaire such as the Health Assessment Questionnaire (HAQ) [Bruce and Fries, 2003], although such instruments may be more appropriate for use in specialist services.
    - There is, however, reasonable evidence that, if a HAQ is completed in primary care, and the measure it generates is greater than 1.5, the person is more likely to receive benefits such as the disability living allowance [Hamilton, Personal Communication, 2004].
  - Important surrogate markers of retained function are:
    - Maintaining an occupation.
    - Not receiving disability benefits.
- **Adjuvant analgesia:**
  - **Antidepressants** may help relieve chronic pain [Fishbain, 2000]. The mechanism of pain relief is not clear, but does not seem to be related to their antidepressant effect. Amitriptyline and imipramine have been studied most.
  - **Anticonvulsants** are widely used for chronic pain, but a systematic review of their use in acute and chronic pain (excluding migraine and headache, but including cancer) concluded that 'surprisingly few trials show analgesic effectiveness' [Wiffen et al, 2001].
  - Although these agents are often prescribed, they are not licensed for use in analgesia.
- **Referral** to other members of the multidisciplinary care team for their help in controlling pain and maintaining function may be appropriate (e.g. for physiotherapy, occupational therapy, counselling, social care, or treatment of depression).
- **Physical treatments:**
  - **Dynamic exercise therapy** has a positive effect on physical capacity. Research on the long-term effect of dynamic exercise therapy on radiological progression and functional ability is needed [Van den Ende et al, 2004].
  - **Transcutaneous electrical nerve stimulation (TENS)** is widely used in pain clinics. However, studies of TENS have reported inconsistent results [Brosseau et al, 2004], and few studies have evaluated its effectiveness on chronic pain [Valsecchi et al, 1991].
  - A systematic review found one small randomized controlled trial of electrical stimulation in people with RA and concluded that further research is required [Pelland et al, 2004].
  - There is no evidence to support the use of therapeutic ultrasound or thermal therapies in the treatment of RA [Casimiro et al, 2004b; Robinson et al, 2004].

What is the role of nonsteroidal anti-inflammatory drugs?

General information

- **Nonsteroidal anti-inflammatory drugs (NSAIDs) relieve symptoms of pain, stiffness, and swelling** in rheumatoid arthritis (RA) but do not modify the course of the disease [SIGN, 2000].
- **Paracetamol (with codeine where needed) should be used in place of NSAIDs if possible,** and DMARDs introduced early to suppress disease activity [SIGN, 2000].
- **Intra-articular corticosteroids may avoid the need for NSAIDs,** particularly if the disease is localized, while waiting for DMARDs to take effect [SIGN, 2000].
- NSAIDs should be reduced and if possible withdrawn when a good response to DMARDs is achieved (**B**) [SIGN, 2000].
- Long-term NSAID use should be avoided without appropriate monitoring and re-evaluation of the clinical need. For further information, see the *NSAIDs Medicines management* section.
- See the separate supporting PRODIGY guidance on *Nonsteroidal anti-inflammatory drugs* for further information on NSAIDs.

COX-2 selective inhibitors

- **NICE does not recommend COX-2 selective inhibitors for routine use in people with RA** [NICE, 2001].
- COX-2 selective inhibitors should be used in preference to standard NSAIDs only in people who are at high risk of serious gastrointestinal (GI) adverse events (which probably includes most people with RA).
- There is no robust evidence to justify the simultaneous prescription of gastroprotective agents with COX-2 selective NSAIDs as a means of further reducing potential GI events.

Topical NSAIDs

- **There are insufficient trial data to support the use (especially long-term) of topical NSAIDs in people with RA.**
- Topical NSAIDs have been compared with placebo, and slight improvements in pain relief found in the short term [Moore et al, 1998; Heyneman et al, 2000; Mason et al, 2004].
- **No study has compared topical with oral NSAIDs in people with RA** (there is good evidence for the effectiveness of oral NSAIDs) [Heyneman et al, 2000].

- GI adverse effects are uncommon with topical NSAIDs [Heyneman et al, 2000].

What is the role of corticosteroids?

Oral and intramuscular corticosteroids

- **Corticosteroids rapidly control pain, stiffness, and swelling in the short term.**
  - A Cochrane systematic review found that low-dose oral corticosteroids, equivalent to 15 mg prednisolone daily or less, were more effective than NSAIDs within the first weeks of treatment [Gotzsche and Johansen, 2004].
  - Corticosteroids may be useful while waiting for DMARDs to take effect ('bridging treatment') or for short-term treatment of acute exacerbations.
  - Intramuscular depot corticosteroid allows control of dosage and duration of therapy and may be preferable to oral treatment [Green and Emery, 1999; SIGN, 2000].
  - Corticosteroids should be withdrawn slowly to avoid a rebound flare of symptoms.
- **Long-term use of corticosteroids**
  - The long-term adverse effects of corticosteroid use are cause for concern, and there is conflicting evidence on the disease-modifying effects of corticosteroids taken long-term (2 years) at low doses (prednisolone 7.0–7.5 mg/day) [Kirwan, 1995; Capell et al, 2004].
  - The risks and benefits of corticosteroids should be balanced on an individual basis against the risks and benefits of NSAIDs and DMARDs in the same person. For example, in a frail elderly person, the risks of long-term low-dose prednisolone are far less than those of NSAIDs and many of the DMARDs.
- **Flare of rheumatoid arthritis (RA) and high-dose oral corticosteroids**
  - Use intra-articular corticosteroids rather than high-dose oral corticosteroids where possible.
  - Consult with the local rheumatology team before starting high-dose oral corticosteroids.
  - An intramuscular injection of a long-acting corticosteroid is a useful alternative to oral corticosteroids when managing an acute flare.
- **Osteoporosis prophylaxis** is necessary for someone taking oral corticosteroids for 3 months or longer. For more information, see the section on *How do I prevent osteoporosis?* and the PRODIGY *Osteoporosis — treatment* guidance.

R

Intra-articular corticosteroids

- **Intra-articular corticosteroid injections are useful for treating localized flares.** Relief is rapid, and the effect can last from a few days to several months, depending on the severity of disease, dosage and preparation used, and accuracy of injection. Synovial fluid aspiration at the time of joint injection reduces relapse rates [SIGN, 2000].
- **Only experts should give intra-articular corticosteroids.** General points are:
  - Never inject a prosthetic joint.
  - Never inject where there is any possibility of sepsis.
  - Do not inject a joint more than three times per year.
  - Consider referral to a specialist for injection if the person is taking an anticoagulant.
- **Adverse effects from intra-articular injections of corticosteroids are rare.**
  - **The most serious complication is septic arthritis,** with an incidence of 1/17,000 to 1/50,000 after injection [DTB, 1995].
  - **Concern about joint damage after repeated corticosteroid injections** is controversial; despite the large number of people treated with intra-articular corticosteroids, case reports that suggest such damage are rare [DTB, 1995].
  - **Atrophy of subcutaneous tissues and local skin depigmentation** may occur from periarticular leakage of corticosteroid.
    - The risk of local tissue atrophy and depigmentation occurs from subcutaneous or shallow injections as well as from small-joint injections (e.g. tennis elbow, de Quervains tenosynovitis, and shallow intramuscular injections).
    - The risk is greatest if large or repeated doses of a long-acting, potent corticosteroid are given.
- In general, hydrocortisone, dexamethasone, or prednisolone is recommended for injection of small joints, and triamcinolone or methylprednisolone for injection of large joints.

What is the role of disease-modifying antirheumatic drugs?

- **Disease-modifying antirheumatic drugs (DMARDs)** should usually be initiated under specialist supervision, and monitoring for toxicity is essential (see *DMARDs Medicines management* for details of monitoring). Shared care arrangements will vary with locality.

What are disease-modifying antirheumatic drugs?

- **DMARDs relieve symptoms and have a beneficial effect on the course of rheumatoid arthritis (RA).** They generally have a slow onset of action; benefit becomes apparent after 6–12 weeks, often earlier. Maximum benefit occurs after 4–6 months.
- **Sulfasalazine, methotrexate, intramuscular gold (sodium aurothiomalate), oral gold (auranofin), penicillamine, hydroxychloroquine, and ciclosporin are traditional DMARDs.**
  - Systematic reviews confirm efficacy in the short to moderate term, with improvements in the number of swollen and tender joints, markers of inflammation, physician and patient global assessment, and functional status [Clark et al, 2004; Emery and Suarez-Almazor, 2004; Suarez-Almazor et al, 2004b; Suarez-Almazor et al, 2004c; Suarez-Almazor et al, 2004d; Suarez-Almazor et al, 2004e; Suarez-Almazor et al, 2004f]
  - There is some evidence that radiological progression i slowed.
  - Long-term benefit is less certain, as most studies have not gone beyond a year.
- **Leflunomide** is a relatively recently introduced DMARD which has been compared against sulfasalazine and methotrexate and is similarly effective [DTB, 2000; Emery and Suarez-Almazor, 2004; Osiri et al, 2004]. It seems to have a more rapid onset of action.
- **Azathioprine, ciclosporin, and cyclophosphamide** also have disease-modifying activity [Emery and Suarez-Almazor, 2004; Suarez-Almazor et al, 2004a; Suarez-Almazor et al, 2004g; Well et al, 2004]. They are usuall reserved for people unresponsive to other DMARDs, owing to the risk of serious adverse effects.
- **Minocycline:** Randomized controlled trials have recently provided evidence for effectiveness in RA [Kloppenburg et al, 1994; Tilley et al, 1995; O'Dell et al, 1997]. However, minocycline is not licensed in the UK for treating RA.
- **Tumour necrosis factor alpha inhibitors:**
  - **Etanercept, infliximab, and adalimumab block the effects of tumour necrosis factor alpha (TNF-alpha),** a mediator of inflammation. Trial data have shown reductions in disease activity and joint inflammation i people with RA who have failed to respond to

DMARDs, but studies with long-term outcome data have yet to be published [SIGN, 2000; DTB, 2001a; NICE, 2002; Emery and Suarez-Almazor, 2004; Keystone et al, 2004; van de Putte et al, 2004].
- **Short-term toxicity is low, but long-term safety is unknown.** There are concerns that continued inhibition of pro-inflammatory molecules may increase the risk of infection and cancer [SIGN, 2000]. Recent reports highlight tuberculosis and congestive heart failure in association with infliximab use [NICE, 2002]. However, raised risks for heart failure and opportunistic infections such as tuberculosis are likely to be class effects of all anti-TNF agents.
- **Etanercept is currently licensed** for use in people with RA not responding adequately to DMARDs. It is given twice-weekly by subcutaneous injection.
- **Infliximab is licensed** for concomitant use with methotrexate in people with RA responding inadequately to DMARDs, including methotrexate. It is given by slow intravenous infusion at 0, 2, and 6 weeks and then every 8 weeks.
- **Adalimumab is licensed** for moderate to severe active arthritis when response to other DMARDs (including methotrexate) has been inadequate. NICE is currently appraising adalimumab and will publish recommendations on its use.

Interleukin-1 inhibitors
- **Anakinra** inhibits the activity of interleukon-1 (IL-1), a mediator of inflammation.
- **Anakinra is not recommended for the treatment of RA,** except in the context of a controlled, long-term clinical study [NICE, 2003a; NICE, 2003b].
- **Anakinra is licensed** for use in combination with methotrexate in people who have had an inadequate response to methotrexate alone. It is given by subcutaneous injection at a dose of 100 mg once daily.

When should disease-modifying antirheumatic drugs be used?

Early DMARD therapy in RA is important to maintain function and reduce later disability (B) [SIGN, 2000].
- When RA begins, there is a limited window of opportunity to prevent joint damage and other long-term consequences of the disease [Lard et al, 2002; Mottonen et al, 2002; Korpela et al, 2004; Nell et al, 2004].
- Thus the aim when starting treatment is to control inflammation as soon as possible, i.e. start DMARDs early (within 4 months ideally), and use DMARDs in combination if necessary to achieve adequate control.

DMARD therapy should be sustained in order to maintain disease suppression (B) [SIGN, 2000].
- Increasingly, a more active approach is being taken to rapidly gain and then maintain tight control of RA [Grigor et al, 2004].

DMARDs should usually be initiated under specialist supervision, and monitoring for toxicity is essential (see *DMARDs Medicines management* for monitoring details). Shared care arrangements will vary with locality.

Which disease-modifying antirheumatic drugs?

Sulfasalazine or methotrexate (B) is the usual first choice for a DMARD [SIGN, 2000].

Ciclosporin and leflunomide are alternatives to sulfasalazine and methotrexate; leflunomide is more expensive than methotrexate and sulfasalazine.

Intramuscular gold is as effective as, but more toxic than, sulfasalazine or methotrexate [SIGN, 2000].
- **Azathioprine and cyclophosphamide** are used for severe or systemic manifestations of rheumatoid disease, such as vasculitis.
- **Hydroxychloroquine and oral gold** are least toxic, but are also probably least effective [Felson et al, 1990; Maetzel et al, 2000; Suarez-Almazor et al, 2004b; Suarez-Almazor et al, 2004c].
- **Penicillamine** is not started now for RA (though people currently on it, with good control and without toxicity, may continue with it in the long term).
- **The new 'biologic agents', i.e. the TNF-alpha inhibitors (etanercept and infliximab) and anakinra,** are generally reserved for people who do not respond adequately to the older DMARDs.
  - The place of etanercept and infliximab in treatment has been defined by recommendations of the British Society for Rheumatology and endorsed by NICE [NICE, 2002].
  - Anakinra is not currently recommended for use in the UK, other than in the context of clinical trials [NICE, 2003b].

What other treatments are used?

- **Statins** — treatment with a statin may be useful as an adjunct to a DMARD as the statin's anti-inflammatory action may reduce disease activity [McCarey et al, 2004]. More research is needed to determine the extent of benefit.
- **Radioisotope intra-articular injection** (i.e. yttrium-90) is occasionally used to try to control localized disease, but a systematic review found two randomized controlled trials and no evidence of benefit from intra-articular yttrium-90 when compared with placebo or triamcinolone hexacetonide [Heuft-Dorenbosch et al, 2000].
- **Omega-3 polyunsaturated fatty acids** in the diet may reduce the number of tender joints and the duration of morning stiffness, but has no effect on disease activity or progression [SIGN, 2000].
  - For any potential benefit for arthritis, large quantities of fish oil or vegetable oil are required — this is expensive, is difficult to take, and is not available on prescription.
  - Taking omega-3 polyunsaturated fatty acids may, however, usefully reduce risk for cardiovascular disease.
- **Herbal therapies** are used by some people. A systematic review concluded that there is limited evidence suggesting that gamma-linolenic acid can benefit people with rheumatoid arthritis (RA), but that further research into this and other herbal therapies is needed [Little and Parsons, 2004].
- **Complementary therapies** are popular with some people with RA but are of unproven value [SIGN, 2000]. These include acupuncture [Casimiro et al, 2004a] and balneotherapy (spa therapy) [Verhagen et al, 2004].

How should complications be managed?

How should infection be prevented and managed?

What immunizations are recommended to prevent infection?
- **Vaccination against flu and pneumococcal disease should be offered to someone with RA who is at increased risk of respiratory infections.** Chest infection is a major cause of morbidity and a contributor to early mortality in people with RA [Mikuls and Saag, 2001]. Sepsis can be rapidly overwhelming.
  - **Influenza vaccine** should be given annually to people who are over the age of 65 years, or are taking immunosuppressive drugs, or are on corticosteroids

R

equivalent to a dose of at least 20 mg prednisolone daily for more than a month [CMO, 2004]. See the PRODIGY guidance on *Influenza*.
  - **Pneumococcal vaccine** should be given to elderly people (by April 2005 the age mark was lowered to 65 years), or people taking immunosuppressive drugs, or those on corticosteroids equivalent to a dose of at least 20 mg prednisolone daily for more than a month [CMO, 2004]. See the PRODIGY guidance on *Immunizations — pneumococcal*.
- The British Society for Rheumatology has published guidelines on vaccination for the person taking immunosuppressants, steroids, or the new biologic therapies [BSR, 2002]:
  - The use of live vaccines is contraindicated unless immunosuppressives are stopped at least 3 months beforehand.
  - If use of live vaccines is necessary, allow at least 2 weeks, but preferably 4 weeks, before starting immunosuppressive therapy.
  - A person who is vaccinated while taking immunosuppressives may not mount the appropriate immune response. Consider repeating 3 months after therapy has ceased if viral titres are low.
  - Consider using immunoglobulins if contact risk is appreciable (e.g. varicella, measles).

How should people with RA be managed if they are exposed to the varicella-zoster virus (chickenpox or shingles)?

- No action is required for individuals exposed to the varicella-zoster virus who are known to be immune or who are not immunosuppressed.
- **Exposure to chickenpox in an immunosuppressed person not immunized by prior infection or vaccination warrants passive immunization with varicella-zoster immune globulin (VZIG) if the contact risk is appreciable.** Consult immediately with the secondary-care rheumatology service or a public health physician.
- **Appreciable exposure to varicella-zoster virus is regarded as contact with:**
  - An individual with chickenpox or disseminated zoster between 48 hours before the onset of the rash and until cropping has ceased and all lesions are crusted.
  - Someone with exposed lesions (e.g. ophthalmic zoster).
  - An immunosuppressed person with localised zoster on any part of the body from the day of onset of rash until crusting.
- The risk of acquiring infection from an immunocompetent individual with a non-exposed zoster lesion (e.g. thoracolumbar) is remote.
- **The following should be used as a guide to the type of exposure:**
  - Contact in the same room (e.g. in a house or classroom or a hospital bay with 2–4 beds) for an appreciable period (15 minutes or more).
  - Face-to-face contact, for example while having a conversation.
- **Immunosuppression is regarded as clinically relevant in:**
  - People taking 40 mg prednisolone per day for more than one week in the previous 3 months. *The dose of corticosteroids that can cause immunosuppression is hard to define, and specialist advice is recommended.*
  - People on lower doses of steroids given in combination with other immunosuppressants.
  - People taking DMARDs that can cause myelosuppression (i.e. adalimumab, anakinra, azathioprine, ciclosporin, cyclophosphamide, etanercept, gold, infliximab, leflunomide, methotrexate, penicillamine, sulfasalazine).

[HPA, 2004]

How should people taking DMARDs or corticosteroids be managed if they have an infection?

- Minor infections such as colds require increased vigilance but rarely warrant other interventions.
- More serious infections that require treatment with an antibiotic usually require immunosuppressive DMARD to be withheld for 1 or 2 weeks.
  - Note that this advice does not apply to leflunomide, as it has a long half-life, and withdrawal for 1–2 weeks will make little difference to concentrations of circulating plasma metabolites.
  - If the person is on corticosteroids, the dose may need to be increased to cover the stress response.
- Admit or immediately consult the rheumatology service or microbiologist if there are signs of chest infection or opportunistic infection. Sepsis can be rapidly overwhelming.

How do I recognise and manage septic arthritis?

- **People with RA are particularly susceptible** to septic arthritis, especially when they are prescribed corticosteroids or other immunosuppressant drugs, if they have a prosthetic joint, or if they have comorbidity (e.g. diabetes) [Keat and McHale, 2000].
- **Septic arthritis typically presents with** severe pain, swelling, and inflammation of a single joint. The joint usually feels hot and is extremely tender with limited movement. Systemic upset is common, with fever, shivers, and sweats. Septic arthritis may involve multiple joints (e.g. in people with immunosuppression or gonococcal septicaemia) and can be a trigger for a polyarticular flare of RA.
  - Atypical presentations may occur (e.g. lesser signs) in people who are taking corticosteroids, are immunosuppressed, or are elderly.
  - Rarely, septic arthritis occurs after recent joint injection, when the clinical features may be modified by the injected corticosteroid.
- **Emergency admission** is required if septic arthritis is suspected, because delayed treatment may result in severe joint damage.

How is carpal tunnel syndrome managed?

- Treatments for carpal tunnel syndrome include resting wrist splint, paracetamol (with codeine where needed), NSAIDs, corticosteroid injection (carpal tunnel itself or the wrist if there is active arthritis), or systemic corticosteroids if there is concomitant polyarticular flare. If symptoms fail to improve appreciably despite control of synovitis, carpal tunnel decompression may be necessary.

How do I recognise and manage cervical myelopathy?

- Cervical myelopathy is a serious complication of severe long-standing RA: anterior atlanto-axial subluxation results in the odontoid process compressing the spinal cord [Naranjo et al, 2004].
- It often has an insidious onset, with deteriorating mobility and upper limb function, peripheral paraesthesia, hyperreflexia, and sphincter disturbance.
- Early referral for surgical decompression and stabilization can prevent deterioration and long-term morbidity.

How do I manage cardiovascular risk factors?

- Because cardiovascular disease is a major contributor to early mortality in RA, preventative measures should be taken:
  - Advise on health and lifestyle, including diet, exercise and smoking cessation.

R

- Hypertension, dyslipidaemia, and diabetes, if present, should be well controlled.
- Methotrexate users should be given folate supplementation (if not already on it) to help reduce the prothrombotic effects.
- Consider using low-dose aspirin and/or a statin as part a risk strategy for preventing cardiovascular disease. For more information, see PRODIGY guidance on *Coronary heart disease risk — identification and management.*

Mikuls and Saag, 2001]

How do I manage anaemia?

Evidence suggests that someone with anaemia is likely to have more severe RA, and that if the anaemia is successfully treated the joint disease is likely to improve [Wilson et al, 2004].

Request iron studies and B_{12} and folate levels to establish the underlying cause — although anaemia of chronic disorder and iron deficiency anaemia (including blood loss due to NSAIDs) are the most likely causes, a deficiency in B_{12} or folates may also be present without an obvious macrocytosis.

Iron deficiency is initially investigated by measuring serum ferritin.

- **A serum ferritin** level of less than 25 micrograms/l indicates iron deficiency. However, a normal or high ferritin level does not exclude iron deficiency, as serum ferritin levels may be raised in RA (ferritin is an acute-phase reactant).
- **A serum transferrin receptor assay** may be used if iron deficiency is suspected but a serum ferritin assay is inconclusive. However, even the transferrin receptor may be misleading in chronic inflammatory disease.
- **A bone marrow aspirate** to assess stores of iron in the marrow is the gold-standard indicator of iron deficiency, and it is not unusual to have to request it.

Medicines management

Paracetamol

Paracetamol is safe and effective for the treatment of mild to moderate pain when used correctly, and is well tolerated at the recommended daily dose.

It is more likely to be effective for rheumatoid arthritis when used regularly rather than 'as required'.

Codeine

Codeine may be added to paracetamol if more pain relief is required.

Paracetamol and codeine should be prescribed separately so they can be individually titrated; combination products such as co-codamol are not recommended.

Codeine may cause nausea, vomiting, constipation, and drowsiness. A regular laxative is often needed when it is used long-term.

Nonsteroidal anti-inflammatory drugs

full discussion on the contraindications, adverse effects, onitoring issues, and interactions of NSAIDs is beyond e scope of this guidance. For further information, see the parate PRODIGY guidance on *Nonsteroidal anti-flammatory drugs (NSAIDs).*

Consider patient comorbidity when prescribing nonsteroidal anti-inflammatory drugs (NSAIDs).

- NSAIDs commonly cause gastrointestinal adverse effects, and can worsen asthma, hypertension, renal impairment, and heart failure.
- There is a small increased risk of cardiovascular events with coxibs (which seems highest in people who already have cardiovascular disease).
- For people with rheumatoid arthritis at high risk of gastrointestinal adverse events, we recommend the following options:
  - Use paracetamol (with or without codeine) instead of a NSAID if possible.
  - Or, use a gastroprotective agent with a standard NSAID [NICE, 2001].
  - Or, use a COX-2 selective NSAID alone [NICE, 2001].
- For advice on the management of dyspepsia due to NSAIDs, see the separate PRODIGY guidance on *Dyspepsia — symptoms (uninvestigated by endoscopy)* and *Dyspepsia — proven DU, GU, or NSAID-associated ulcer.*

Corticosteroids

- **Steroid treatment cards** should be issued by and their contents discussed.
- **Predictable adverse effects of corticosteroids include:**
  - Thinning of the skin
  - Cataracts
  - Osteoporosis
  - Hypertension
  - Hyperlipidaemia
- Prevention and treatment of osteoporosis is discussed in the section *How do I prevent osteoporosis?*
- **Blood pressure monitoring** is recommended in someone on corticosteroids.
- **Aggressively manage cardiovascular risk factors.** For more information, see PRODIGY guidance on *Coronary heart disease risk — identification and management.*
- **Document history of chickenpox** (there is a risk of potentially fatal disseminated chickenpox if the person is not immune). Advise people taking systemic corticosteroids to avoid close contact with people who have chickenpox or shingles, and to seek urgent medical advice if they are exposed. Make a note about this advice on the steroid treatment card.

How do I prevent osteoporosis?

- People starting or currently on *any dose* of oral corticosteroids for more than 3 months should be given osteoporosis prophylaxis if they:
  - Are aged over 65 years.
  - Have a previous fragility fracture (i.e. occurring after age 40 years on minimal trauma).
- **In other individuals, measure bone mineral density using dual-energy X-ray absorptiometry (DEXA) to assess fracture risk.** Consider treatment if T-score is –1.5 or lower [Royal College of Physicians of London, 2002].
- **Bisphosphonates** (alendronate, risedronate, or cyclical etidronate) are a preferred option for the prevention or treatment of corticosteroid-induced osteoporosis.
- **Calcium with vitamin D can be used as an adjunct to bisphosphonate treatment.**
  - Calcium and vitamin D are essential for people who are deficient in vitamin D — vitamin D deficiency is not infrequently found in the chronically ill, homebound person with rheumatoid arthritis (RA).
- Post-hoc analyses of studies of risedronate and etidronate, and analysis of secondary end-points in a study of alendronate, found that they all reduced the risk of vertebral fractures in people taking glucocorticoids. Note that fracture was not a primary end-point in any of these studies [Royal College of Physicians of London, 2002].
- **Gastrointestinal adverse effects** such as abdominal pain, dyspepsia, diarrhoea, or constipation, are common with bisphosphonates. Oesophageal reactions (oesophagitis, oesophageal ulcers, strictures, and erosions) are

uncommon but serious adverse events that continue to be reported with alendronate [DTB, 2001b].

- **People with delayed oesophageal emptying (e.g. strictures or achalasia) should not take alendronate, and should avoid taking risedronate where possible.** Cyclical etidronate is an alternative bisphosphonate for these people [DTB, 2001b].
- **If a bisphosphonate is contraindicated or not tolerated,** consider alfacalcidol, or calcitriol, or strontium ranelate.
- Alfacalcidol and calcitriol are vitamin D analogues. Hypercalcaemia and hypercalciuria have occasionally been reported. Regular monitoring of serum calcium and creatinine is needed.
- Hormone replacement therapy (HRT) should only be considered as a second-line option for preventing osteoporosis in perimenopausal and postmenopausal women [CSM, 2003] if the benefits of treatment outweigh the risks (off-licence use). See the PRODIGY *Menopause* guidance for further information on the risks and benefits of HRT.
- For further information on the prevention and treatment of corticosteroid-induced osteoporosis, see the PRODIGY *Osteoporosis* guidance.

Disease-modifying antirheumatic drugs

- **All the disease-modifying antirheumatic drugs (DMARDs) can have serious toxic effects.**
- Prescriptions for DMARDs are usually initiated by a specialist. Monitoring of DMARDs will often be done in primary care under a shared-care arrangement with a protocol from the local rheumatology service.
- **Follow local protocols for monitoring where available.** Considerable clinical judgement is necessary at times to decide when a symptom, sign, or laboratory test is so abnormal that further measures (e.g. stopping treatment, referring for specialist management) need to be taken.
- Advice on the selection and frequency of tests and thresholds for action are also given the in separate PRODIGY guidance *Monitoring people on disease-modifying drugs (DMARDs)*. Note: the information given in this guideline is intended to complement the guidance that local shared-care arrangements provide on monitoring, and may differ from local recommendations.

References

NHS staff in England can link, free of charge, from references to full text journals by clicking on [Full text] on the PRODIGY website.

1. American College of Rheumatology (1987) *Classification criteria for rheumatoid arthritis*. American College of Rheumatology. www.rheumatology.org [Accessed: 28/06/2004].
2. ARC (2004) *Exercise and arthritis*. Arthritis Research Campaign. www.arc.org.uk/about_arth/infosheets/6253/6253.htm [Accessed: 06/12/2004]. [Full text]
3. ARMA (2004) *Standards of care for people with inflammatory arthritis*. Arthritis and Musculoskeletal Alliance. www.arma.uk.net [Accessed: 06/12/2004].
4. Arnett, F.C., Edworthy, S.M., Bioch, D.A. et al (1988) The American Rheumatism Association 1987 revised criteria for the classification of rheumatoid arthritis. *Arthritis & Rheumatism* **31**(3), 315–323.
5. Arthritis Care (2002) *Fit for life: a guide to safe exercise for people with arthritis*. Arthritis Care. www.arthritiscare.org.uk [Accessed: 06/12/2004].
6. Barlow, J.H., Turner, A.P. and Wright, C.C. (2000) A randomized controlled study of the Arthritis Self-Management Programme in the UK. *Health Education Research* **15**(6), 665–680. [Full text]
7. BNF 48 (2004) *British National Formulary*. 48th edn. London: British Medical Association and Royal Pharmaceutical Society of Great Britain.
8. Brosseau, L., Yonge, K.A., Robinson, V. et al (2004) *Transcutaneous electrical nerve stimulation (TENS) f the treatment of rheumatoid arthritis in the hand (Cochrane Review)*. The Cochrane Library. Issue 2. Chichester, UK: John Wiley & Sons, Ltd. www.nelh.nhs.uk/cochrane.asp [Accessed: 06/12/2004]. [Full text]
9. Bruce, B. and Fries, J.F. (2003) The Stanford Health Assessment Questionnaire: a review of its history, issues, progress, and documentation. *Journal of Rheumatology* **30**(1), 167–178.
10. BSR (2002) *Vaccinations in the immunocompromise person – guidelines for the patient taking immunosuppressants, steroids and the new biologic therapies*. British Society for Rheumatology. www.rheumatology.org.uk [Accessed: 06/12/2004]. [Full text]
11. Capell, H.A., Madhok, R., Hunter, J.A. et al (2004) Lack of radiological and clinical benefit over two year of low dose prednisolone for rheumatoid arthritis: results of a randomised controlled trial. *Annals of the Rheumatic Diseases* **63**(7), 797–803.
12. Casimiro, L., Brosseau, L., Milne, S. et al (2004a) *Acupuncture and electroacupuncture for the treatmen of RA (Cochrane Review)*. The Cochrane Library. Issue 2. Chichester, UK: John Wiley & Sons, Ltd.
13. Casimiro, L., Brosseau, L., Robinson, V. et al (2004b *Therapeutic ultrasound for the treatment of rheumatoid arthritis (Cochrane Review)*. The Cochra Library. Issue 2. Chichester, UK: John Wiley & Sons, Ltd.
14. Clark, P., Tugwell, P., Bennet, K. et al (2004) *Injectable gold for rheumatoid arthritis (Cochrane Review)*. The Cochrane Library. Issue 1. Chichester, UK: John Wiley & Sons, Ltd.
15. CMO (2004) *Update on the influenza and pneumococcal immunisation programmes*. PL/CMO/2004/4. Department of Health. www.dh.gov.uk [Accessed: 11/08/2004]. [Full text]
16. Criswell, L.A., Merlino, L.A., Cerhan, J.R. et al (200 Cigarette smoking and the risk of rheumatoid arthriti among postmenopausal women: results from the Iow Women's Health Study. *American Journal of Medici* **112**(6), 465–471.
17. CSM (1994) Relative safety of oral non-aspirin NSAIDs. *Current Problems in Pharmacovigilance* **20**(Aug), 9–11.
18. CSM (2002) Non-steroidal anti-inflammatory drugs (NSAIDs) and gastrointestinal (GI) safety. *Current Problems in Pharmacovigilance* **28**(Apr), 5.
19. CSM (2003) *Further advice on safety of HRT: risk/benefit unfavourable for first-line use in prevention o osteoporosis*. CEM/CMO/2003/19. Committee on Safety of Medicines. www.mhra.gov.uk [Accessed: 0 01/2004].
20. De Craen, A.J., Di Giulio, G., Lampe-Schoenmaecke J.E. et al (1996) Analgesic efficacy and safety of paracetamol-codeine combinations versus paracetam alone: a systematic review. *British Medical Journal* **313**(7053), 321–325. [Full text]
21. DTB (1995) Articular and periarticular corticosteroi injections. *Drug & Therapeutics Bulletin* **33**(9), 67–7 [Full text]
22. DTB (2000) Leflunomide for rheumatoid arthritis. *Drug & Therapeutics Bulletin* **38**(7), 52–54.
23. DTB (2001a) Etanercept and infliximab for rheumatoid arthritis. *Drug & Therapeutics Bulletin* **39**(7), 49–52. [Full text]

24. DTB (2001b) Biphosphonates for osteoporosis. *Drug & Therapeutics Bulletin* 39(9), 68–72.
25. EMEA (2004) *Press release: EMEA to review COX-2 inhibitors.* EMEA/117908/2004. European Medicines Agency. www.emea.eu.int [Accessed: 28/01/2005].
26. Emery, P. and Suarez-Almazor, M. (2004) *Rheumatoid arthritis (web archive).* Clinical Evidence. BMJ Publishing Group Ltd. www.clinicalevidence.com [Accessed: 19/08/2004].
27. Felson, D.T., Anderson, J.J. and Meenan, R.F. (1990) The comparative efficacy and toxicity of second line agents in rheumatoid arthritis: results of two meta-analyses. *Arthritis & Rheumatism* 33(10), 1449–1461.
28. Fishbain, D. (2000) Evidence-based data on pain relief with antidepressants. *Annals of Medicine* 32(5), 305–316.
29. Gotzsche, P.C. and Johansen, H.K. (2004) *Short-term low-dose corticosteroids vs placebo and nonsteroidal antiinflammatory drugs in rheumatoid arthritis (Cochrane Review).* The Cochrane Library. Issue 2. Chichester, UK: John Wiley & Sons, Ltd.
30. Green, M. and Emery, P. (1999) The GP's role in optimising early rheumatoid arthritis care. *Practical Problems: ARC Reports on Rheumatic Disease* Series 3(18).
31. Grigor, C., Capell, H., Stirling, A. et al (2004) Effect of a treatment strategy of tight control for rheumatoid arthritis (the TICORA study): a single-blind randomised controlled trial. *Lancet* **364**(9430), 263–269. [Full text]
32. Hamilton, J. (2004) *Personal communication.* Consultant Rheumatologist, Queen Elizabeth Hospital: Gateshead, UK.
33. Hawkey, C.J., Karrasch, J.A., Szczepanski, L. et al (1998) Omeprazole compared with misoprostol for ulcers associated with nonsterodial antiinflammatory drugs. *New England Journal of Medicine* **338**(11), 727–734. [Full text]
34. Henry, D., Lim, L.L., Garcia-Rodriguez, L.A. et al (1996) Variability in risk of gastrointestinal complications with individual non-steroidal anti-inflammatory drugs: results of a collaborative meta-analysis. *British Medical Journal* **312**(7046), 1563–1566. [Full text]
35. Hernández-Diaz, S. and Rodriguez, L.A. (2000) Association between nonsteroidal anti-inflammatory drugs and upper gastrointestinal tract bleeding/perforation: an overview of epidemiologic studies published in the 1990s. *Archives of Internal Medicine* **160**(14), 2093–2099. [Full text]
36. Heuft-Dorenbosch, L.L., De Vet, H.C. and van der Linden, S. (2000) Yttrium radiosynoviorthesis in the treatment of knee arthritis in rheumatoid arthritis: a systematic review. *Annals of the Rheumatic Diseases* 59(8), 583–586. [Full text]
37. Heyneman, C.A., Lawless-Liday, C. and Wall, G.C. (2000) Oral versus topical NSAIDs in rheumatic diseases: a comparison. *Drugs* 60(3), 555–574.
38. HPA (2004) *Immunoglobulin handbook: indications and dosage for normal and specific immunoglobulin preparations issued by the HPA.* Health Protection Agency. www.hpa.org.uk [Accessed: 27/09/2004]. [Full text]
39. Keat, A. and McHale, J. (2000) Infection and arthritis. *Topical Reviews: ARC Reports on Rheumatic Disease* Series 3(3).
40. Keystone, E.C., Kavanaugh, A.F., Sharp, J.T. et al (2004) Radiographic, clinical, and functional outcomes of treatment with adalimumab (a human anti-tumor necrosis factor monoclonal antibody) in patients with active rheumatoid arthritis receiving concomitant methotrexate therapy: a randomized, placebo-controlled, 52-week trial. *Arthritis & Rheumatism* 50(5), 1400–1411.
41. Kirwan, J.R. (1995) The effect of glucocorticoids on joint destruction in rheumatoid arthritis. The Arthritis and Rheumatism Council Low-dose Glucocorticoid Study Group. *New England Journal of Medicine* 333(3), 142–146.
42. Kloppenburg, M., Breedveld, F.C., Terwiel, J. et al (1994) Minocycline in active rheumatoid arthritis: a double blind placebo controlled trial. *Arthritis & Rheumatism* 37(5), 629–636.
43. Korpela, M., Laasonen, L., Hannonen, P. et al (2004) Retardation of joint damage in patients with early rheumatoid arthritis by initial aggressive treatment with disease-modifying antirheumatic drugs: five-year experience from the FIN-RACo study. *Arthritis & Rheumatism* 50(7), 2072–2081.
44. Lard, L.R., Boers, M., Verhoeven, A. et al (2002) Early and aggressive treatment of rheumatoid arthritis patients affects the association of HLA class II antigens with progression of joint damage. *Arthritis & Rheumatism* 46(4), 899–905.
45. Little, C. and Parsons, T. (2004) *Herbal therapy for treating rheumatoid arthritis (Cochrane Review).* The Cochrane Library. Issue 2. Chichester, UK: John Wiley & Sons, Ltd.
46. Maetzel, A., Wong, A., Strand, V. et al (2000) Meta-analysis of treatment termination rates among rheumatoid arthritis patients receiving disease-modifying anti-rheumatic drugs. *Rheumatology* 39(9), 975–981. [Full text]
47. Mason, L., Moore, R.A., Edwards, J.E. et al (2004) Topical NSAIDs for chronic musculoskeletal pain: systematic review and meta-analysis. *BMC Musculoskeletal Disorders* 5(1), 28.
48. McCarey, D.W., McInnes, P.I., Madhok, R. et al (2004) Trial of Atorvastatin in Rheumatoid Arthritis (TARA): double-blind, randomised placebo-controlled trial. *Lancet* 363(9426), 2015–2021. [Full text]
49. MeReC (1993) Combination analgesics. *MeReC Bulletin* 4(12), 45–48.
50. MeReC (2000) The use of oral analgesics in primary care. *MeReC Bulletin* 11(1), 1–4.
51. Mikuls, T.R. and Saag, K.G. (2001) Comorbidity in rheumatoid arthritis. *Rheumatic Diseases Clinics of North America* 27(2), 283–303.
52. Moore, A., Collins, S., Carroll, D. and McQuay, H. (1997) Paracetamol with and without codeine in acute pain: a quantitative systematic review. *Pain* 70(2–3), 193–201.
53. Moore, R.A., Tramer, M.R., Carroll, D. et al (1998) Quantitative systematic review of topically applied non-steroidal anti-inflammatory drugs. *British Medical Journal* 316(7128), 333–338. [Full text]
54. Mottonen, T., Hannonen, P., Korpela, M. et al (2002) Delay to institution of therapy and induction of remission using single-drug or combination-disease-modifying antirheumatic drug therapy in early rheumatoid arthritis. *Arthritis & Rheumatism* 46(4), 894–898.
55. Naranjo, A., Carmona, L., Gavrila, D. et al (2004) Prevalence and associated factors of anterior atlantoaxial luxation in a nation-wide sample of rheumatoid arthritis patients. *Clinical & Experimental Rheumatology* 22(4), 427–432.
56. Nell, V.P., Machold, K.P., Eberl, G. et al (2004) Benefit of very early referral and very early therapy with disease-modifying anti-rheumatic drugs in patients with early rheumatoid arthritis. *Rheumatology* 43(7), 906–914. [Full text]
57. NICE (2001) *Guidance on the use of cyclo-oxygenase (Cox) II selective inhibitors, celecoxib, rofecoxib,*

R

meloxicam and etodolac for osteoarthritis and rheumatoid arthritis. Technology appraisal no. 27. National Institute for Health and Clinical Excellence. www.nice.org.uk [Accessed: 16/10/2003].

58. NICE (2002) *Guidance on the use of etanercept and infliximab for the treatment of rheumatoid arthritis*. Technology appraisal no. 36. National Institute for Clinical Excellence. www.nice.org.uk [Accessed: 01/04/2002].
59. NICE (2003a) *Assessment report: the clinical and cost-effectiveness of anakinra for the treatment of rheumatoid arthritis in adults*. National Institute for Clinical Excellence. www.nice.org.uk/page.aspx?o=112019 [Accessed: 15/04/2004].
60. NICE (2003b) *Anakinra for rheumatoid arthritis*. Technology appraisal no. 72. National Institute for Clinical Excellence. www.nice.org.uk [Accessed: 05/04/2004].
61. NICE (2004) *Dyspepsia: management of dyspepsia in adults in primary care: NICE guideline*. Clinical guideline 17. National Institute for Clinical Excellence. www.nice.org.uk [Accessed: 27/08/2004].
62. O'Dell, J.R. (2004) Therapeutic strategies for rheumatoid arthritis. *New England Journal of Medicine* **350**(25), 2591–2602. [Full text]
63. O'Dell, J.R., Haire, C.E., Palmer, W. et al (1997) Treatment of early rheumatoid arthritis with minocycline or placebo: results of a randomized, double-blind, placebo-controlled trial. *Arthritis & Rheumatism* **40**(5), 842–848.
64. Oliver, C.W. (2001) Role of surgery in patients with rheumatoid arthritis. *Practical Problems: ARC Reports on Rheumatic Disease* **Series 3**(12).
65. Osiri, M., Shea, B., Robinson, V. et al (2004) *Leflunomide for treating rheumatoid arthritis (Cochrane Review)*. The Cochrane Library. Issue 2. Chichester, UK: John Wiley & Sons, Ltd.
66. Pelland, L., Brosseau, L., Casimiro, L. et al (2004) *Electrical stimulation for the treatment of rheumatoid arthritis (Cochrane Review)*. The Cochrane Library. Issue 2. Chichester, UK: John Wiley & Sons, Ltd.
67. Pincus, T. and Callahan, L.F. (1993) What is the natural history of rheumatoid arthritis? *Rheumatic Disease Clinics of North America* **19**(1), 123–151.
68. Riemsma, R.P., Kirwan, J.R., Taal, E. and Rasker, J.J. (2004) *Patient education for adults with rheumatoid arthritis (Cochrane Review)*. The Cochrane Library. Issue 2. Chichester, UK: John Wiley & Sons, Ltd.
69. Robinson, V., Brosseau, L., Casimiro, L. et al (2004) *Thermotherapy for treating rheumatoid arthritis (Cochrane Review)*. The Cochrane Library. Issue 2. Chichester, UK: John Wiley & Sons, Ltd.
70. Rostom, A., Wells, G., Tugwell, P. et al (2002) *Prevention of NSAID-induced gastroduodenal ulcers (Cochrane Review)*. The Cochrane Library. Issue 4. Chichester, UK: John Wiley & Sons, Ltd. www.nelh.nhs.uk/cochrane.asp [Accessed: 04/04/2005]. [Full text]
71. Royal College of Physicians of London (2002) *Glucocorticoid-induced osteoporosis*. Royal College of Physicians. www.rcplondon.ac.uk [Accessed: 22/04/2003].
72. Saag, K.G., Cerhan, J.R., Kolluri, S. et al (1997) Cigarette smoking and rheumatoid arthritis severity. *Annals of the Rheumatic Diseases* **56**(8), 463–469.
73. Scott, D.L., Shipley, M., Dawson, A. et al (1998) The clinical management of rheumatoid arthritis and osteoarthritis: strategies for improving clinical effectiveness. *British Journal of Rheumatology* **37**(5), 546–554.
74. SIGN (2000) *Management of early rheumatoid arthritis*. Report no. 48. Scottish Intercollegiate Guidelines Network. www.sign.ac.uk [Accessed: 01/04/2002].
75. Suarez-Almazor, M.E., Belseck, E., Shea, B. et al (2004a) *Cyclophosphamide for treating rheumatoid arthritis (Cochrane Review)*. The Cochrane Library. Issue 2. Chichester, UK: John Wiley & Sons, Ltd.
76. Suarez-Almazor, M.E., Spooner, C.H., Belseck, E. and Shea, B. (2004b) *Auranofin versus placebo in rheumatoid arthritis (Cochrane Review)*. The Cochrane Library. Issue 2. Chichester, UK: John Wiley & Sons, Ltd.
77. Suarez-Almazor, M.E., Belseck, E., Shea, B. et al (2004c) *Antimalarials for treating rheumatoid arthritis (Cochrane Review)*. The Cochrane Library. Issue 2. Chichester, UK: John Wiley & Sons, Ltd.
78. Suarez-Almazor, M.E., Belseck, E., Shea, B. et al (2004d) *Methotrexate for treating rheumatoid arthritis (Cochrane Review)*. The Cochrane Library. Issue 2. Chichester, UK: John Wiley & Sons, Ltd.
79. Suarez-Almazor, M.E., Belseck, E., Shea, B. et al (2004e) *Sulfasalazine for treating rheumatoid arthritis (Cochrane Review)*. The Cochrane Library. Issue 2. Chichester, UK: John Wiley & Sons, Ltd.
80. Suarez-Almazor, M.E., Spooner, C. and Belseck, E. (2004f) *Penicillamine for treating rheumatoid arthritis (Cochrane Review)*. The Cochrane Library. Issue 2. Chichester, UK: John Wiley & Sons, Ltd.
81. Suarez-Almazor, M.E., Spooner, C. and Belseck, E. (2004g) *Azathioprine for treating rheumatoid arthritis (Cochrane Review)*. The Cochrane Library. Issue 2. Chichester, UK: John Wiley & Sons, Ltd.
82. Tilley, B.C., Alarcon, G.S., Heyse, S.P. et al (1995) Minocycline in rheumatoid arthritis. A 48-week, double-blind, placebo-controlled trial. MIRA Trial Group. *Annals of Internal Medicine* **122**(2), 81–89.
83. Tramer, M.R., Williams, J.E., Carroll, D. et al (1998) Comparing analgesic efficacy of non-steroidal anti-inflammatory drugs given by different routes in acute and chronic pain: a qualitative systematic review. *Acta Anaesthesiologica Scandinavica* **42**(1), 71–79.
84. Valsecchi, R., Rossi, A., Bigardi, A. and Pigatto, P.D. (1991) The loss of contact sensitization in man. *Contact Dermatitis* **24**(3), 183–186.
85. van den Ende, C.H.M., Vliet Vlieland, T.P.M., Munneke, M. and Hazes, J.M.W. (2004) *Dynamic exercise therapy for treating rheumatoid arthritis (Cochrane Review)*. The Cochrane Library. Issue 2. Chichester, UK: John Wiley & Sons, Ltd.
86. van de Putte, L.B., Atkins, C., Malaise, M. et al (2004) Efficacy and safety of adalimumab as monotherapy in patients with rheumatoid arthritis for whom previous disease modifying antirheumatic drug treatment has failed. *Annals of the Rheumatic Diseases* **63**(5), 508–516.
87. van Doornum, S., McColl, G. and Wicks, I.P. (2002) Accelerated atherosclerosis: an extraarticular feature of rheumatoid arthritis? *Arthritis & Rheumatism* **46**(4), 862–873.
88. Verhagen, A.P., Bierma-Zeinstra, S.M.A., Cardoso, J.R. et al (2004) *Balneotherapy for rheumatoid arthritis (Cochrane Review)*. The Cochrane Library. Issue 2. Chichester, UK: John Wiley & Sons, Ltd.
89. Well, G., Haguenauer, D., Shea, B. et al (2004) *Cyclosporine for treating rheumatoid arthritis (Cochrane Review)*. The Cochrane Library. Issue 2. Chichester, UK: John Wiley & Sons, Ltd.
90. Whittle, S.L. and Hughes, R.A. (2004) Folate supplementation and methotrexate treatment in rheumatoid arthritis: a review. *Rheumatology* **43**(3), 267–271. [Full text]
91. Wiffen, P., Collins, S., McQuay, H. et al (2001) *Anticonvulsant drugs for acute and chronic pain*

(*Cochrane Review*). The Cochrane Library. Issue 4. Chichester, UK: John Wiley & Sons, Ltd. www.nelh.nhs.uk/cochrane.asp [Accessed: 22/02/2005].

92. Wilson, A., Yu, H.T., Goodnough, L.T. and Nissenson, A.R. (2004) Prevalence and outcomes of anemia in rheumatoid arthritis: a systematic review of the literature. *American Journal of Medicine* **116**(Suppl 7A), 50S-57S.
93. Wolfe, F. (1997) Comparative usefulness of C-reactive protein and erythrocyte sedimentation rate in patients with rheumatoid arthritis. *Journal of Rheumatology* **24**(8), 1477–1485.
94. Wolfe, F. (2000) The effect of smoking on clinical, laboratory, and radiographic status in rheumatoid arthritis. *Journal of Rheumatology* **27**(3), 630–637.

Evidence grading

The definitions of grades of recommendation used in this guidance are from the Scottish Intercollegiate Guidelines Network (SIGN), and are as follows:

A	At least one meta-analysis, systematic review, or RCT rated as 1++, and directly applicable to the target population; or A body of evidence consisting principally of studies rated as 1+, directly applicable to the target population, and demonstrating overall consistency of results
B	A body of evidence including studies rated as 2++, directly applicable to the target population, and demonstrating overall consistency of results; or Extrapolated evidence from studies rated as 1++ or 1+
C	A body of evidence including studies rated as 2+, directly applicable to the target population and demonstrating overall consistency of results; or Extrapolated evidence from studies rated as 2++
D	Evidence level 3 or 4; or Extrapolated evidence from studies rated as 2+

Levels of evidence

1++	High quality meta-analyses, systematic reviews of randomized controlled trials (RCTs), or RCTs with a very low risk of bias
1+	Well-conducted meta-analyses, systematic reviews, or RCTs with a low risk of bias
1–	Meta-analyses, systematic reviews, or RCTs with a high risk of bias
2++	High-quality systematic reviews of case-control or cohort studies High-quality case-control or cohort studies with a low risk of confounding or bias and a high probability that the relationship is causal
2+	Well-conducted case-control or cohort studies with a low risk of confounding or bias and a moderate probability that the relationship is causal
2–	Case-control or cohort studies with a high risk of confounding or bias and a [clinically] significant risk that the relationship is not causal
3	Non-analytic studies (e.g. case reports, case series)
4	Expert opinion

R

PRODIGY GUIDANCE

Rosacea

Last revised in July 2005
www.prodigy.nhs.uk/guidance.asp?gt=Rosacea

Applies to people over the age of 16 years

This guidance covers the diagnosis and management of rosacea in primary care.

This guidance does not cover the secondary-care management of rosacea.

There is separate guidance for *Acne vulgaris, Atopic eczema, Blepharitis, Contact dermatitis,* and *Seborrhoeic dermatitis.*

Goals

- To relieve symptoms and signs of rosacea
- To minimize complications
- To refer appropriately to secondary care

Contents

Scenarios

- Rosacea — without eye involvement p.1644
- Rosacea — with eye involvement p.1646

Extended Information, p. 1648

Which scenario?

- **Rosacea — without eye involvement:** covers the management of people with typical facial symptoms of rosacea, including flushing, erythema, papules or pustules, and telangiectasia. It includes advice on the need to refer people with rhinophyma.
- **Rosacea — with eye involvement:** covers the management of people with eye involvement, including sensation of a foreign body in the eye, burning or stinging of eyes, dryness, itching, light sensitivity, or blurred vision.

Rosacea — without eye involvement

R

Which therapy?

- **In all people with rosacea**
  - Stop use of topical corticosteroids, as these can mimic many of the symptoms and signs of rosacea (reduce gradually by reducing the potency of topical corticosteroid to avoid rebound flare-up of symptoms).
  - Recommend daily application of a high-factor sunscreen (at least factor 15 with UVA and UVB protection).
  - Manage rosacea according to predominant symptoms.
- **In people with prolonged intermittent flushing**
  - Advise avoidance of identified triggers of flushing (see Patient Information Leaflet).
  - Check the person is not taking systemic vasodilators.
- **In people with persistent erythema and telangiectasia**
  - Advise on avoidance of potentially exacerbating factors (e.g. cleansers containing acetone or alcohol, abrasive or exfoliant preparations, oil-based or waterproof make-up).
  - Recommend the use of camouflage creams to help conceal redness.
  - Consider laser therapy for people with prominent telangiectasia.
- **In people with papulopustular rosacea**
  - **With few papules or pustules and mild to moderate persistent erythema, prescribe:**
    - Topical metronidazole first-line (once or twice a day).
    - Topical azelaic acid if the person is intolerant of or not responding to topical metronidazole.
  - **With extensive papules and pustules, prescribe:**
    - Oral tetracycline or oxytetracycline first-line.
    - Oral doxycycline or lymecycline if compliance is a problem.
    - Oral erythromycin in women who are pregnant or breastfeeding, or if tetracyclines are contraindicated or are not tolerated.
  - **Continue treatment for at least 12 weeks.**
    - Relapse commonly occurs within weeks of stopping treatment, and further courses of treatment may be needed.
    - Maintenance treatment may be required in some people (see *Follow up advice*).

Practical prescribing points

For further information please see the *Medicines Compendium* (www.medicines.org.uk) or the *British National Formulary* (www.bnf.org).

Camouflage creams

- The British Red Cross provides cosmetic camouflage clinics free of charge throughout the UK in association with hospital dermatology departments. People who need camouflage creams should initially be referred to the service in order that they can find the most suitable cream, and that they are given proper instructions regarding application. For more information, contact:
  - British Red Cross Beauty Care and Camouflage Service, 9 Grosvenor Crescent, London SW1 7EJ, Tel. 020 7235 5454 www.timewarp.demon.co.uk/redcross.html
  - Local arrangements for referral to the service should be in place.

Topical treatments

- Warn people that there may be some initial skin irritation with topical treatments for rosacea, but that this should settle with continued use of the treatment.
- Application of an emollient may be helpful before the application of other skin products and topical treatments.

Tetracyclines

- Tetracyclines are contraindicated in pregnancy, breastfeeding, and children less than 12 years of age.
- Benign intracranial hypertension is a rare but important adverse effect of tetracycline therapy. If a person taking

tetracycline develops headache and visual disturbances, stop the tetracycline.
- Doxycycline is the tetracycline of choice in people with renal impairment.
- Photosensitivity has been reported with doxycycline. Advise people to avoid exposure to direct sunlight or ultraviolet light.

Erythromycin

- Erythromycin may increase the level of certain drugs (e.g. theophylline, carbamazepine, statins), or potentiate warfarin.

Follow-up advice

- Review at 6 weeks to assess response to treatment. Many people will show some response at this point and should continue treatment for at least another 6 weeks or until papules and pustules have resolved. If there is no response to treatment after 6 weeks, continue for a further 6 weeks, as response is delayed in some people. Consider using a combination of oral and topical treatment if severe.
- Relapse within a few weeks of stopping treatment is common, and further courses of treatment are often required.
- If relapses occur frequently, maintenance treatment may be necessary (usually with a topical treatment). The duration of maintenance treatment is unknown, but 6 months is generally advised, followed by a trial 'off-treatment'.
- Despite maintenance topical treatment, some people will still require repeated courses of systemic treatment.

Should I refer or investigate?

Refer?

- **If symptoms remain unresponsive to treatment after 12–16 weeks:** refer to a dermatologist.
- **If the individual shows evidence of skin thickening (e.g. rhinophyma):** refer to a plastic surgeon.

Investigate?

- Occasionally, skin biopsy is necessary to exclude other diagnoses, such as cutaneous lupus. This is usually carried out by a specialist.

Patient information leaflets

The following PILs are available at www.prodigy.nhs.uk

- Acne Support Group (acne or rosacea)
- Rosacea

Shared decision making

- **Apply sunblock** to your face each day if you have rosacea. Use at least factor 15 with UVA and UVB protection.
- **If you have facial flushing:**
  - **Avoid possible triggers.** The most common ones are: extremes of temperature, alcoholic drinks, strenuous exercise, stress, sunlight, spicy food, hot drinks, vasodilator medicines.
- **If you have persistent facial redness or telangiectasia:**
  - **Avoid things that may make it worse:** for example, cleansers containing acetone or alcohol, abrasive or exfoliant preparations, oil-based or waterproof make-up, perfumed sunblocks or those containing insect repellents.
  - **Camouflage creams** can help to hide redness.
  - **Laser therapy** may be an option for telangiectasia.
- **If you have spots:**
  - **Topical metronidazole** (an antibiotic) will often clear mild spots.
  - **Topical azelaic acid** is an alternative.
  - **Antibiotic tablets (tetracycline** or **erythromycin)** are commonly used if you have more severe spots.
  - A 12-week course of treatment is needed to clear spots. Further courses, or maintenance treatment, are commonly needed, as the spots often return after treatment is stopped.

Drug rationale

Drugs not included

- **Prescriptions for camouflage creams** are not included. It is advised that people who need to use a camouflage cream be initially referred to the British Red Cross Beauty Care and Camouflage Service in order that they can find the most suitable cream, and that they are given proper instructions regarding application.
- **Topical erythromycin, clindamycin, and tetracycline** are not included. Although these seem to be effective in some people, there are no good-quality trial data on the use of these products in rosacea, and they are not licensed for this indication. In addition, people with rosacea often have sensitive skin (especially those individuals with predominant symptoms of flushing and redness) and many of these products are in alcoholic formulations that may exacerbate symptoms of rosacea.
- **Topical retinoids, tretinoin and isotretinoin,** are not included. There are no good-quality trial data on the use of these products in rosacea, and they are not licensed for this indication.
- **Topical benzoyl peroxide** is not included. There are no good-quality trial data on the use of benzoyl peroxide in rosacea, and it is not licensed for this condition.
- **Topical tacrolimus and pimecrolimus** are not included. There are limited trial data to support their use in rosacea, and these products are not licensed for this condition.
- **Oral metronidazole** is not included. Data from one small trial suggest that oral metronidazole is effective in the management of rosacea. but long-term treatment can cause peripheral neuropathy, and careful monitoring is needed if treatment exceeds 10 days. Its use in rosacea should be reserved for resistant cases.
- **Oral minocycline** is not included. Minocycline is not licensed for use in rosacea. Because of the risk of adverse effects with long-term use of minocycline (e.g. hepatotoxicity and systemic lupus erythematosus), other tetracyclines are preferred.
- **Oral isotretinoin** is not included. Isotretinoin has been reported to be effective in the control of rosacea resistant to other treatments, and in the treatment of rhinophyma. However, oral isotretinoin should only be prescribed by, or under the supervision of, a consultant dermatologist [BNF 49, 2005], owing to the possibility of serious adverse effects.

Drugs included

- **Topical metronidazole** is included for use in people with few papules or pustules and mild to moderate persistent erythema. Topical metronidazole is available as a 0.75% gel and as a 0.75% or 1% cream. There is no evidence to favour any particular preparation [McClellan and Noble, 2000]. All available preparations licensed for the treatment of rosacea are included; 0.75% gel and cream are licensed for twice-a-day application and 1% cream is licensed for once-a-day application [BNF 49, 2005].

- **Azelaic acid 20% cream** is included for use in people who are intolerant of or not responding to topical metronidazole. There is evidence of its efficacy in the treatment of rosacea; however, azelaic acid is not licensed in the UK for this indication.
- **Oral tetracyclines** are recommended for people with many or extensive papules and pustules and pronounced persistent erythema.
  - **Tetracycline and oxytetracycline** are recommended first-choice systemic treatments for rosacea. However, the need to take them on an empty stomach may limit compliance.
  - **Doxycycline and lymecycline** are better absorbed than tetracycline and can be taken with food, which reduces gastrointestinal intolerance and potentially improves compliance. Neither doxycycline nor lymecycline is licensed for the treatment of rosacea.
- **Oral erythromycin** is included as an alternative in women who are pregnant or breastfeeding, or if tetracyclines are contraindicated or are not tolerated.
- Lower doses of oral antibiotics than those recommended in the BNF are offered here. This approach reflects the doses used in trials, and minimizes the risk of adverse effects. Also, in rosacea the mechanism of antibiotic action is mainly anti-inflammatory, which can be achieved at lower doses.

Prescriptions

Advice note

Advice only: flushing and erythema

- Age from 16 years onwards
- Your rosacea may be made worse with sunshine. Apply sunblock to your face each day. Use at least factor 15 with UVA and UVB protection. If you have facial flushing try to avoid possible triggers such as extremes of temperature, alcoholic drinks, strenuous exercise, stress, sunlight, spicy food, hot drinks, and vasodilator medicines. If you have persistent facial redness try to avoid things that may make it worse such as cleansers containing acetone or alcohol, abrasive or exfoliant preparations, oil-based or waterproof make-up, perfumed sunblocks or those containing insect repellents.

Topical metronidazole

Metronidazole 0.75% gel: apply twice a day

- Age from 16 years onwards
- Metronidazole 0.75% gel (40g). Apply thinly to the affected area(s) twice a day; supply 40 grams; NHS Cost £15.28.

Metronidazole 0.75% cream: apply twice a day

- Age from 16 years onwards
- Metronidazole 0.75% cream. Apply thinly to the affected area(s) twice a day; supply 40 grams; NHS Cost £15.28.

Metronidazole 1% cream: apply once a day

- Age from 16 years onwards
- Metronidazole 1% cream. Apply thinly to the affected area once a day; supply 30 grams; NHS Cost £19.08.

Topical azelaic acid

Azelaic acid 20% cream: apply twice a day

- Age from 16 years onwards
- Azelaic acid 20% cream. Apply to the affected area(s) twice a day; supply 30 grams; NHS Cost £4.40.

Oral antibiotics

Oxytetracycline tablets: 250mg twice a day

- Age from 16 years onwards
- Oxytetracycline 250mg tablets. Take one tablet twice a day; supply 56 tablets; NHS Cost £2.52.

Tetracycline tablets: 250mg twice a day

- Age from 16 years onwards
- Tetracycline 250mg tablets. Take one tablet twice a day; supply 56 tablets; NHS Cost £3.82.

Doxycycline capsules: 50mg once a day

- Age from 16 years onwards
- Doxycycline hyclate 50mg caps. Take one capsule once a day; supply 28 capsules; NHS Cost £3.47.

Lymecycline capsules: 408mg once a day

- Age from 16 years onwards
- Lymecycline 408mg capsules. Take one capsule once a day; supply 28 capsules; NHS Cost £7.16.

Erythromycin e/c tablets: 250mg twice a day

- Age from 16 years onwards
- Erythromycin 250mg e/c tablets. Take one tablet twice a day; supply 56 tablets; NHS Cost £5.38.

Rosacea — with eye involvement

Which therapy

- **If dryness of the eye is a problem:** consider an ocular lubricant.
- **If there is inflammation of the eyelid,** advise on good eyelid hygiene and the use of warm compresses. See separate PRODIGY guidance on *Blepharitis* for further details.
- **Treat rosacea with eye involvement with an oral antibiotic (which will also treat papulopustular skin disease).**
  - Oral tetracycline and oxytetracycline are recommended first-line.
  - Oral doxycycline or lymecycline may be preferred if compliance is a problem.
  - Oral erythromycin is an alternative in women who are pregnant or breastfeeding, or if tetracyclines are contraindicated or are not tolerated.
- **For all people with rosacea:**
  - Stop use of topical corticosteroids (these can mimic many of the symptoms and signs of rosacea).
  - Recommend daily application of a high-factor sunscreen (at least factor 15 with UVA and UVB protection).
- **For prolonged intermittent flushing:**
  - Advise avoidance of identified triggers of flushing (see Patient Information Leaflet).
  - Check the person is not taking systemic vasodilators.
- **For persistent erythema and telangiectasia:**
  - Advise on avoidance of potentially exacerbating factors (e.g. cleansers containing acetone or alcohol, abrasive or exfoliant preparations, oil-based or waterproof make-up).
  - Recommend the use of camouflage creams to help conceal redness.
  - Consider laser therapy for people with prominent telangiectasia.

Practical prescribing points

For further information please see the *Medicines Compendium* (www.medicines.org.uk) or the *British National Formulary* (www.bnf.org).

Camouflage creams

- The British Red Cross provides cosmetic camouflage clinics free of charge throughout the UK in association with hospital dermatology departments. People who need camouflage creams should initially be referred to the service in order that they can find the most suitable cream, and that they are given proper instructions regarding application. For more information, contact:
  - British Red Cross Beauty Care and Camouflage Service, 9 Grosvenor Crescent, London SW1 7EJ, Tel. 020 7235 5454 www.timewarp.demon.co.uk/redcross.html
  - Local arrangements for referral to the service should be in place.

Tetracyclines

- Tetracyclines are contraindicated in pregnancy, breastfeeding, and children less than 12 years of age.
- Benign intracranial hypertension is a rare but important adverse effect of tetracycline therapy. If a person taking a tetracycline develops headache and visual disturbances, stop the tetracycline.
- Doxycycline is the tetracycline of choice in people with renal impairment.
- Photosensitivity has been reported with doxycycline. Advise people to avoid exposure to direct sunlight or ultraviolet light.

Erythromycin

- Erythromycin may increase the level of certain drugs (e.g. theophylline, carbamazepine, statins), or potentiate warfarin.

Follow-up advice

- Review at 6 weeks to assess response to treatment. Many people will show some response at this point and should continue treatment for at least another 6 weeks or until papules and pustules have resolved. If there is no response to treatment after 6 weeks, continue for a further 6 weeks, as response is delayed in some people.
- Relapse within a few weeks of stopping treatment is common, and further courses of treatment are often required.

Should I refer or investigate?

Refer?

- **Refer to an ophthalmologist if:**
  - Ocular symptoms are resistant or severe.
  - Vision is affected.
  - Keratitis is suspected — refer urgently.
- **If skin symptoms remain unresponsive to treatment after 12–16 weeks:** refer to a dermatologist.
- **If the individual shows evidence of skin thickening (e.g. rhinophyma):** refer to a plastic surgeon.

Patient information leaflets

The following PILs are available at www.prodigy.nhs.uk

- Acne Support Group (acne or rosacea)
- Blepharitis
- Eye Drops - (How to Use)
- Rosacea

Shared decision making

- **Apply sunblock** to your face each day if you have rosacea. Use at least factor 15 with UVA and UVB protection.
- **If you have eye symptoms:**
  - **Artificial tears** can help if dryness is a problem.
  - **Eyelid hygiene** eases eyelid inflammation (a leaflet explains).
  - **A course of antibiotic tablets** will usually settle the symptoms.
  - See a doctor urgently if eye pain or visual problems develop.
- **If you have facial flushing:**
  - **Avoid possible triggers.** The most common ones are: extremes of temperature, alcoholic drinks, strenuous exercise, stress, sunlight, spicy food, hot drinks, vasodilator medicines.
- **If you have persistent facial redness or telangiectasia:**
  - **Avoid things that may make it worse:** for example, cleansers containing acetone or alcohol, abrasive or exfoliant preparations, oil-based or waterproof make-up, perfumed sunblocks or those containing insect repellents.
  - **Camouflage creams** can help to hide redness.
  - **Laser therapy** may be an option for telangiectasia.
- **If you have spots:**
  - **Topical metronidazole** (an antibiotic) will often clear mild spots.
  - Topical azelaic acid is an alternative.
  - **Antibiotic tablets (tetracycline** or **erythromycin)** are commonly used if you have more severe spots.
  - A 12-week course of treatment is needed to clear spots. Further courses, or maintenance treatment, are commonly needed, as the spots often return after treatment is stopped.

Drug rationale

Drugs not included

- **Prescriptions for camouflage creams** are not included. It is advised that people who need to use a camouflage cream be initially referred to the British Red Cross Beauty Care and Camouflage Service in order that they can find the most suitable cream and that they are given proper instructions regarding application.
- **Topical antibiotics and azelaic acid** are not included, as systemic antibiotics should be used first-line in people who have rosacea with eye involvement. Topical metronidazole should not be applied to the eyes.
- **Oral metronidazole** is not included. Data from one small trial suggest that oral metronidazole is effective in the management of rosacea, but long-term treatment can cause peripheral neuropathy, and careful monitoring is needed if treatment exceeds 10 days. Its use in rosacea should be reserved for resistant cases.
- **Oral minocycline** is not included. Minocycline is not licensed for use in rosacea. Because of the risk of adverse effects with long-term use of minocycline (e.g. hepatotoxicity and systemic lupus erythematosus), other tetracyclines are preferred.
- **Oral isotretinoin** is not included. Isotretinoin has been reported to be effective in the control of rosacea resistant to other treatments, and in the treatment of rhinophyma. However, oral isotretinoin should only be prescribed by, or under the supervision of, a consultant dermatologist [BNF 49, 2005], owing to the possibility of serious adverse effects.

Drugs included

- **Artificial tears** may be prescribed to provide symptomatic relief in people with eye involvement. Hypromellose 0.3% is a commonly used artificial tear preparation. It is effective, and remains the cheapest option. A preservative-free, single-dose formulation is recommended for users of soft contact lens, and those people unable to tolerate preservatives.
- **Paraffin eye ointments** (Simple eye ointment, Lacri-Lube, and Lubri-Tears) provide prolonged lubrication. Since they cause temporary blurred vision, they are best used before bedtime [Khaw and Elkington, 1999; BNF 49, 2005].
- **Oral tetracyclines** are recommended for people with eye involvement, with or without other signs and symptoms of rosacea.
  - **Tetracycline and oxytetracycline** are recommended first-choice systemic treatments for rosacea. However, the need to take them on an empty stomach may limit compliance.
  - **Doxycycline and lymecycline** are better absorbed than tetracycline and can be taken with food, which reduces gastrointestinal intolerance and potentially improves compliance. Neither doxycycline nor lymecycline is licensed for the treatment of rosacea.
- **Oral erythromycin** is included as an alternative in women who are pregnant or breastfeeding, or if tetracyclines are contraindicated or are not tolerated.
- Lower doses of oral antibiotics than those recommended in the BNF are offered here. This approach reflects the doses used in trials and minimizes the risk of adverse effects. Also, in rosacea the mechanism of antibiotic action is mainly anti-inflammatory, which can be achieved at lower doses.

Prescriptions

Ocular lubricants

Hypromellose 0.3% eye drops
- Age from 16 years onwards
- Hypromellose 0.3% eye drops. Put one drop into the affected eye(s) when required to lubricate the eye(s); supply 10 ml; NHS Cost £0.75; OTC Cost £1.32.

Hypromellose 0.32% preservative-free drops (single-use)
- Age from 16 years onwards
- Hypromellose 0.32% single-use. Put one drop into the affected eye(s) when required to lubricate the eye(s); supply 60 single doses; NHS Cost £23.76; OTC Cost £32.50.

Simple eye ointment: use at bedtime
- Age from 16 years onwards
- Simple 10% eye ointment. Put a small amount into the affected eye(s) at bedtime; supply 4 grams; NHS Cost £2.68; OTC Cost £4.72.

Lacri-Lube eye ointment: use at bedtime
- Age from 16 years onwards
- Lacri-Lube eye ointment. Put a small amount into the affected eye(s) at bedtime; supply 5 grams; NHS Cost £2.47; OTC Cost £4.35.

Lubri-Tears eye ointment: use at bedtime
- Age from 16 years onwards
- Lubri-Tears eye ointment. Put a small amount into the affected eye(s) at bedtime; supply 5 grams; NHS Cost £2.29; OTC Cost £4.03.

Oral antibiotics

Oxytetracycline tablets: 250mg twice a day
- Age from 16 years onwards
- Oxytetracycline 250mg tablets. Take one tablet twice a day; supply 56 tablets; NHS Cost £2.52.

Tetracycline tablets: 250mg twice a day
- Age from 16 years onwards
- Tetracycline 250mg tablets. Take one tablet twice a day; supply 56 tablets; NHS Cost £3.82.

Doxycycline capsules: 50mg once a day
- Age from 16 years onwards
- Doxycycline hyclate 50mg caps. Take one capsule once a day; supply 28 capsules; NHS Cost £3.47.

Lymecycline capsules: 408mg once a day
- Age from 16 years onwards
- Lymecycline 408mg capsules. Take one capsule once a day; supply 28 capsules; NHS Cost £7.16.

Erythromycin e/c tablets: 250mg twice a day
- Age from 16 years onwards
- Erythromycin 250mg e/c tablets. Take one tablet twice a day; supply 56 tablets; NHS Cost £5.38.

Extended Information

Background information

- What is rosacea? p.1648
- How common is it? p.1649
- How do I know my patient has it? p.1649
- What else might it be? p.1649
- Complications and prognosis p.1649

What is rosacea?

- **Rosacea is a chronic inflammatory skin disease** characterized by one or more of the following: recurrent episodes of facial flushing, persistent redness (erythema), dilated blood vessels (telangiectasia), papules and pustules. These features usually present with a central facial distribution [van Zuuren et al, 2003; Powell, 2005].
- **Thickening and enlargement of the skin (phymatous change) can occur,** sometimes without the other changes of rosacea. A well-recognized presentation is bulbous enlargement of the nose, called rhinophyma.
- **Eye involvement** occurs in more than half of people with rosacea, although symptoms are often mild and it frequently goes undiagnosed.
- **The cause of rosacea is unknown.** It is thought that several factors may be implicated, including abnormalities of small blood vessels, sun damage, and abnormal inflammatory responses [van Zuuren et al, 2003; Berth-Jones, 2004]. Although topical and oral antimicrobials are effective treatments, an infective cause has not been found.
- **Traditionally, rosacea has been described in terms of stages,** ranging from early flushing and redness to the development of papulopustular lesions and then phymatous change. A criticism of this approach is that it implies a progressive disorder, with affected individuals moving through various stages of increasing severity. Although this may be seen in some individuals, many people with rosacea show no evidence of this progression.
- **A more recent approach is to describe rosacea in terms of subtypes** based on which features predominate (see Table 1). Differences in severity may occur within each subtype, and some people will have features of more

R

than one subtype [Wilkin et al, 2002; Bikowski and Goldman, 2004].

How common is it?

- Prevalence of rosacea in the UK is unknown and will vary according to diagnostic criteria.
- A study of Swedish office workers found a prevalence of about 10%. Most had mild symptoms and only 18% were classed as papulopustular [Berg and Lidén, 1989].
- Rosacea mainly affects adults between 30 and 60 years of age, but occasionally occurs in children.
- Women are more commonly affected than men, but rosacea is often less severe in women than in men, and women rarely develop rhinophyma.
- Rosacea is more common in fair-skinned than in dark-skinned people.

[Berth-Jones, 2004; Powell, 2005]

How do I know my patient has it?

- **The diagnosis of rosacea is made on clinical grounds;** there is no diagnostic test.
- **Key features are** prolonged flushing, non-transient erythema, papules and pustules, and telangiectasia with a central facial distribution.
- **Secondary features include** burning or stinging, oedema, dry skin, and skin thickening (phymatous changes) [Crawford et al, 2004].
- **Symptoms of eye involvement** include foreign body sensation, burning or stinging, dryness, itching, sensitivity to light, and blurred vision [van Zuuren et al, 2003]. People may present with recurrent chalazia (meibomian cysts) and styes, chronic staphylococcal lid disease, and chronic blepharoconjunctivitis. Ocular rosacea may precede skin disease, in which case diagnosis can be extremely difficult.
- **Not all features are always present.** In many people a certain set of symptoms predominate (see Table 1).

[Wilkin et al, 2002]

What else might it be?

- **Corticosteroid-induced rosacea** — prolonged use of potent topical corticosteroids on the face can mimic many of the symptoms and signs of rosacea. This may occur in anyone, but is thought to be more likely to occur in people who are prone to rosacea. The use of corticosteroid nasal sprays may also cause this reaction [Berth-Jones, 2004; Crawford et al, 2004].
- **Acne vulgaris** is primarily a disorder of the pilosebaceous unit, with comedones, papules, and pustules. Comedones are absent in rosacea (but may be present if a person has both acne vulgaris and rosacea). Flushing and telangiectasia do not occur with acne vulgaris. Extra-facial rosacea is rare, whilst acne vulgaris commonly affects the back, neck, and trunk. Acne vulgaris usually affects a younger age group.
- **Lupus erythematosus** may present with a facial distribution similar to that of rosacea, but the predominant features are scarring, scaling, and follicular plugging. Systemic symptoms may be present. Occasionally, skin biopsy and lupus serology are needed to make a differential diagnosis [Berth-Jones, 2004].
- **Perioral dermatitis** presents as a persistent erythematous eruption in the perioral area, with microvesicles, papules, and scaling and peeling. It does not respond to topical treatments for rosacea, but responds to oral tetracyclines [Wilkin et al, 2002].
- **Seborrhoeic dermatitis** has a characteristic scaly rash and has a different distribution from that of rosacea (it tends to affect the scalp, ears, eyelids, and nasolabial folds).
- **Nasal sarcoidosis** (lupus pernio) may resemble rhinophyma. Both conditions may cause telangiectasia on the nose, but in sarcoidosis the skin is usually smoother, the nasal septum is often affected (causing nasal obstruction), and there are often features of systemic disease.
- **Pyoderma faciale** is also known as rosacea fulminans, but it is not clear if it is a variant of rosacea or acne vulgaris, or if it is a separate disorder [Berth-Jones, 2004]. It is characterized by a sudden severe eruption of papules, pustules and nodules, along with fluctuating and draining sinuses that may be interconnected [Wilkin et al, 2002]. It often results in severe scarring and is usually treated with systemic corticosteroids.
- **Other causes of flushing** with or without cutaneous features of rosacea include: menopausal flushes, carcinoid syndrome, phaeochromocytoma, polycythaemia vera, mixed connective tissue disease, dermatomyositis, mitral regurgitation, and mastocytosis.

Table 1: Key features of rosacea.

Key features	Rosacea subtype
Prolonged intermittent facial flushing. Persistent central facial redness with or without telangiectasia.	Erythematotelangiectatic
Persistent central facial redness with transient papules or pustules or both.	Papulopustular
Thickening and enlargement of the skin, with irregular surface nodularities. May occur on the nose (rhinophyma), chin, forehead, cheeks, or ears. Large inflammatory nodules may be present.	Phymatous
Sensation of foreign body in the eye, burning or stinging of eyes, dryness, itching, light sensitivity, or blurred vision. The conjunctiva may be reddened, and there may be telangiectasia of the sclera or other parts of the eye. Periorbital oedema may be present.	Ocular

Complications and prognosis

Complications

- **Psychological distress:** as rosacea affects the face, it can cause significant psychological distress, with low self-esteem and avoidance of social contacts. Social stigma may be worsened by the common misconception that facial redness and rhinophyma are due to excessive alcohol consumption [Powell, 2005].
- **Keratitis** is a serious complication of ocular involvement, as it can lead to corneal scarring, corneal perforation, and loss of visual acuity. Keratitis occurs in up to 5% of people with rosacea, usually presenting with severe eye pain, blurred vision, and sensitivity to light. If suspected, refer urgently to an ophthalmologist [Berth-Jones, 2004].
- **Chronic lymphoedema** can affect any part of the face and ears. Features may become coarse (leonine facies). The orbital skin can be affected, resulting in severe eyelid swelling and sometimes ectropion [Berth-Jones, 2004].
- **Rhinophyma:** thickened, reddened, bulbous nasal tissue, with indurations affecting other areas of the face.

Prognosis

- Rosacea has a variable duration and prognosis. It typically runs a chronic course, punctuated by episodes of acute inflammation [Dahl et al, 1998].
- There is currently no cure. Treatment aims to control symptoms, with the expectation that this will help prevent disease progression and long-term complications [Gupta and Chaudhry, 2003]. Although experience suggests that this may be the case, there are no studies to

support this view [Odom, 2004]. Relapse is often prompt when treatment is stopped.

Management issues

- Overview of management p.1650
- What general advice should I give? p.1650
- How should I manage facial flushing? p.1650
- How should I manage persistent erythema and telangiectasia? p.1650
- How should I manage papulopustular rosacea? p.1651
- How should I manage rosacea affecting the eye? p.1651
- When should I refer someone with rosacea? p.1651
- What is the supporting evidence for the treatment of rosacea? p.1651
- Medicines management p.1652

Overview of management

- **Stop the use of topical corticosteroids on the face if the person is using these.**
  - There may be an initial flare-up of symptoms when the topical corticosteroid is stopped. This may be reduced by gradually reducing the potency of topical corticosteroid.
  - Symptoms may take several weeks or months to subside after withdrawal of topical corticosteroid.
- **Manage rosacea according to predominant symptoms.** Treatment may need to be adjusted over time, depending on the person's success with lifestyle management, response to treatments, and the unpredictable course of the disease.
- **Facial flushing:**
  - Advise the person to avoid trigger factors.
  - Check the person is not taking systemic vasodilators.
- **Persistent redness and telangiectasia:**
  - Advise on avoidance of potentially exacerbating factors.
  - Recommend the use of camouflage creams to help conceal redness.
  - Consider laser therapy for someone with prominent telangiectasia.
- **Papulopustular rosacea:**
  - Prescribe topical treatment for someone with few papules or pustules and mild to moderate persistent erythema.
    - Metronidazole is the topical treatment of choice.
    - Azelaic acid may be considered if the person is intolerant of or not responding to topical metronidazole.
  - Prescribe a systemic antibiotic for someone with extensive papules and pustules.
    - A tetracycline is the antibiotic of choice.
    - Erythromycin is an alternative if tetracyclines are contraindicated or are not tolerated.
- **Eye involvement:**
  - Prescribe a systemic antibiotic to control eye symptoms.
  - Treat associated eye conditions (e.g. blepharitis).
  - Advise on good eyelid hygiene.
  - Prescribe ocular lubricants such as artificial tears and paraffin eye ointment if required.
- **Refer if:**
  - Symptoms are unresponsive to treatment.
  - There is evidence of skin thickening (e.g. rhinophyma).
  - Ocular symptoms are severe or resistant to treatment.
  - Vision is affected.
  - Keratitis is suspected.

R

What general advice should I give?

- **Reassure the person** about the benign nature of rosacea and the rarity of progression to rhinophyma (especially in women).
- **Recommend daily application of a high-factor sunscreen** (at least sun-protection factor 15) with protection against ultraviolet A and ultraviolet B light.
  - Formulations with a dimethicone or cyclomethicone base may be less irritating than others.
  - Sunblocking creams containing titanium oxide and zinc oxide are usually well tolerated.
  - Sunscreens are listed as a borderline substance, and may only be prescribed on the NHS for skin protection in photodermatoses.

How should I manage facial flushing?

Facial flushing is often a prominent symptom of rosacea and is difficult to treat.

- **Advise the person to avoid identified triggers.** Some individuals may be able to identify certain factors that trigger skin flushing, and avoidance of these (where practical) may be helpful. Commonly reported triggers include:
  - Extremes of temperature (in particular excessive heat)
  - Strenuous exercise
  - Stressful situations
  - Sunlight
  - Spicy food
  - Alcohol
  - Hot drinks

[Pelle et al, 2004; Powell, 2005]

- **Check that the person is not taking systemic vasodilators,** such as calcium-channel blockers, as these are likely to aggravate flushing.
- **No drug is recommended for the prevention of flushing.** Clonidine and betablockers are sometimes advocated, but they have not been found to be effective in small studies [Pelle et al, 2004].

How should I manage persistent erythema and telangiectasia?

- **Advise on avoidance of potentially exacerbating factors.** People with persistent erythema often have highly sensitive skin and should avoid the use of cleansers containing acetone or alcohol, abrasive or exfoliant preparations, oil-based or waterproof make-up, and perfumed sunscreens or those containing insect repellents.
- **Camouflage creams may be useful to help to conceal redness.**
  - The British Red Cross provides cosmetic camouflage clinics free of charge throughout the UK in association with hospital dermatology departments. It is advisable that people who need camouflage creams are initially referred to this service in order that they can find the most suitable cream, and that they are given proper instructions regarding application. For more information contact:
    - British Red Cross Beauty Care and Camouflage Service, 9 Grosvenor Crescent, London SW1 7EJ, Tel. 020 7235 5454 www.timewarp.demon.co.uk/redcross.html
  - Local arrangements for referral to the service should be in place.
- **Drug treatment is not generally recommended** for people with persistent erythema. There is little evidence that topical or systemic drug therapies reduce erythema and telangiectasia. In addition, topical therapy may irritate the sensitive skin of these people.

- **People with prominent telangiectasia** may benefit from ablation of vessels by laser therapy.

[Berth-Jones, 2004; Powell, 2005]

How should I manage papulopustular rosacea?

- **For people with few papules or pustules and mild to moderate persistent erythema,** topical treatment is recommended.
  - **Topical metronidazole** is the preferred topical treatment. Topical metronidazole is available as a 0.75% gel and as a 0.75% or 1% cream. There is no evidence to favour any particular preparation [McClellan and Noble, 2000], although gel preparations that contain alcohol may be more irritating to the skin.
  - **Topical azelaic acid** may be considered for people who are intolerant of or not responding to topical metronidazole. It may cause a mild burning or stinging sensation when initially applied to the skin. The 20% cream available in the UK is not licensed for the treatment of rosacea.
  - **Some dermatologists also consider the use of other topical antibiotics or topical retinoids.** Although these seem to be effective in some people, there are no good-quality trial data on the use of these products in rosacea, and they are not licensed for this condition.
- **For people with many or extensive papules and pustules and pronounced persistent erythema,** systemic treatment is more likely to be needed.
  - **Oral tetracycline and oxytetracycline** are recommended first-choice systemic treatments for rosacea. However, the need to take them on an empty stomach may limit compliance.
  - **Oral doxycycline and lymecycline** are better absorbed than tetracycline and can be taken with food, which reduces gastrointestinal intolerance and potentially improves compliance. Neither doxycycline nor lymecycline is licensed for the treatment of rosacea.
  - **Oral erythromycin** is an alternative in women who are pregnant or breastfeeding, or if tetracyclines are contraindicated or not tolerated.
  - **Oral metronidazole** is not recommended. Long-term treatment can cause peripheral neuropathy, and careful monitoring is needed if treatment exceeds 10 days [BNF 49, 2005]. Its use in rosacea should be reserved for resistant cases.

[van Zuuren et al, 2003; Frampton and Wagstaff, 2004; Elle et al, 2004; Powell, 2005]

Should I combine oral and topical treatments?

There are no trial data to support the combined use of oral and topical treatments, although this is often done in practice. PRODIGY suggests that combined treatment be considered:

- For people on systemic treatment who have not responded after 6 weeks.
- As initial therapy for people with severe papulopustular rosacea.
- For people who experience a flare up of rosacea while on maintenance topical treatment.

How should I manage rosacea affecting the eye?

- Treat associated eye conditions (e.g. see separate PRODIGY guidance on *Blepharitis*).
- Good eyelid hygiene, warm compresses, and lubricants such as artificial tears and paraffin eye ointment may give some relief [Bikowski and Goldman, 2004].
- Systemic antibiotics are usually required to control eye symptoms.

When should I refer someone with rosacea?

- Refer to a dermatologist if symptoms remain unresponsive to treatment. Treatment options in secondary care include oral isotretinoin and laser treatment.
- People with rhinophyma should be referred to a plastic surgeon. Treatment options include laser treatment, dermabrasion, or corrective electrosurgery. There is also some evidence that topical and systemic retinoid therapy may be beneficial in moderate phymatous disease.
- Refer to an ophthalmologist if:
  - Ocular symptoms are resistant or severe.
  - Vision is affected.
  - Keratitis is suspected — severe eye pain, blurred vision, sensitivity to light.

What is the supporting evidence for the treatment of rosacea?

The quality of studies evaluating treatments for rosacea is generally poor. Most people included in the studies had papulopustular rosacea.

What is the evidence for topical treatments?

- A recent Cochrane systematic review (search date up to March 2002) found evidence for the efficacy of topical metronidazole and azelaic acid cream. Data from the trials of azelaic acid were not pooled, owing to differences in trial design.
  - Pooling data from two trials, 68/90 (76%) people treated with topical metronidazole for 8–9 weeks considered their rosacea to be improved, compared with 32/84 (38%) in the placebo group (OR 5.96, 95% CI 2.95 to 12.06).
  - Using physician assessments, pooled data from three trials found that 90/179 (50%) people treated with topical metronidazole improved, compared with 35/134 (26%) in the placebo group (OR 7.01, 95% CI 3.56 to 13.81).
  - One further study compared once-a-day with twice-a-day application of metronidazole and found similar rates of physician-assessed improvement in both groups.
  - In one study, 62/76 (82%) participants improved with azelaic acid cream, compared with 22/38 (58%) in the placebo group (OR 3.22, 95% CI 1.35 to 7.66).
  - In the other trial (a within-patient study), 16/33 (48%) improved with azelaic cream, compared with only 1/33 (3%) with placebo.

[van Zuuren et al, 2003]

- Further recent trials of topical azelaic acid 15% gel have also found benefit, but this product is not currently available in the UK [Elewski et al, 2003; Thiboutot et al, 2003].
- One further randomized study found that, in people successfully treated with a combination of oral tetracycline and topical metronidazole, continued treatment with topical metronidazole for up to 6 months reduced the rate of relapse compared with placebo (23% compared with 42%; $p < 0.05$) [Dahl et al, 1998].

What is the evidence for systemic antibiotics?

- The Cochrane systematic review found one trial of oxytetracycline and two trials of tetracycline compared with placebo, with study duration ranging from 4–6 weeks. Using physician assessment, pooled data from these trials found that 56/73 (77%) treated with tetracyclines improved, compared with 28/79 (35%)

R

treated with placebo (OR 6.06, 95% CI 2.96 to 12.42) [van Zuuren et al, 2003].

- Only one of these studies addressed ocular rosacea. The authors of the systematic review conclude that oral oxytetracycline seems to be effective for ocular rosacea, although only the opinion of the physician was reported in the study [van Zuuren et al, 2003].
- Other tetracyclines (such as doxycycline and lymecycline) are likely to be similarly effective, although no randomized controlled trials were found.
- The Cochrane review was unable to find good-quality trials confirming the effectiveness of systemic erythromycin in the treatment of rosacea [van Zuuren et al, 2003], but it is used in practice, and experience suggests that it is effective in some people [Berth-Jones, 2004; Pelle et al, 2004; Powell, 2005].
- The Cochrane review found two trials investigating the efficacy of oral metronidazole.
  - In one small trial, oral metronidazole 200 mg twice a day was compared with placebo. Physician assessment was that 10/14 (71%) people treated with oral metronidazole improved, compared with only 2/13 (15%) in the placebo group.
  - The other trial compared oral metronidazole 200 mg twice-daily with tetracycline 250 mg twice a day for 12 weeks. No significant difference was found.

[van Zuuren et al, 2003]

Medicines management

How long should I treat for?

- **Long-term treatment** with topical or oral antibiotics may be required.
- **Initial treatment with topical or systemic treatment is usually for at least 12 weeks.** Improvement is usually gradual and may take 4–6 weeks to become apparent. People who do not respond to treatment after 6 weeks should continue for a further 6 weeks, as response is delayed in some people.
- **Relapse within a few weeks of stopping treatment is common,** and further courses of treatment are often required.
- **If relapses occur frequently, maintenance treatment may be necessary** (usually with a topical treatment) [Dahl et al, 1998]. The duration of maintenance treatment is unknown, but 6 months is generally advised, follow by a trial 'off-treatment'.
- Despite maintenance with topical treatment, some people will still require repeated courses of systemic treatment.

[Bikowski and Goldman, 2004; Pelle et al, 2004; Powell, 2005]

Adverse effects

What adverse effects are associated with topical treatments for rosacea?

- **People with rosacea often have sensitive skin** (especially those individuals with predominant symptoms of flushing and redness) and may find that many topical products cause skin irritation.
- Warn people that there may be some initial skin irritation with topical treatments for rosacea, but that this should settle with continued use of the treatment.
- Application of an emollient may be helpful, especially before application of other skin products and topical treatments.

What adverse effects are associated with oral tetracyclines?

- **Tetracyclines should not be used in pregnancy, during breastfeeding, or in children under 12 years of age,** as they are deposited in the teeth and bones of the unborn or developing child. Women of childbearing age should use effective contraception (note that tetracyclines may cause oral contraceptives to fail during the first few weeks of treatment).
- **With the exception of doxycycline and minocycline, the tetracyclines may exacerbate renal failure** and should not be given to anyone with renal disease.
- **Benign intracranial hypertension** is a rare but important adverse effect of tetracycline therapy. If a person taking tetracycline develops headache and visual disturbances, the tetracycline should be stopped.
- **Photosensitivity** has been associated with the tetracyclines (particularly doxycycline). People should be advised to avoid exposure to direct sunlight or ultraviolet light.

[BNF 49, 2005]

What adverse effects are associated with oral erythromycin?

- **Erythromycin may increase the level of certain drugs** (e.g. theophylline, carbamazepine, statins), or potentiate warfarin.

References

NHS staff in England can link, free of charge, from references to full text journals by clicking on [Full text] on the PRODIGY website.

1. Berg, M. and Lidén, S. (1989) An epidemiological study of rosacea. *Acta Dermato-Venereologica* **69**(5), 419–423.
2. Berth-Jones, J. (2004) Rosacea, perioral dermatitis and similar dermatoses, flushing and flushing syndromes. In: Burns, T., Breathnach, S., Cox, N. and Griffiths, C. (Eds.) *Rook's textbook of dermatology*. 7th edn. Oxford: Blackwell Publishing. 44.1–44.19.
3. Bikowski, J.B. and Goldman, M.P. (2004) Rosacea: where are we now? *Journal of Drugs in Dermatology* 3(3), 251–261.
4. BNF 49 (2005) *British National Formulary*. 49th edn. London: British Medical Association and Royal Pharmaceutical Society of Great Britain.
5. Crawford, G.H., Pelle, M.T. and James, W.D. (2004) Rosacea: I. etiology, pathogenesis, and subtype classification. *Journal of the American Academy of Dermatology* 51(3), 327–341.
6. Dahl, M.V., Katz, I., Krueger, G.G. et al (1998) Topical metronidazole maintains remissions of rosacea. *Archives of Dermatology* **134**(6), 679–683. [Full text]
7. Elewski, B.E., Fleischer, A.B.Jr and Pariser, D.M. (2003) A comparison of 15% azelaic acid gel and 0.75% metronidazole gel in the topical treatment of papulopustular rosacea: results of a randomized trial. *Archives of Dermatology* **139**(11), 1444–1450. [Full text]
8. Frampton, J.E. and Wagstaff, A.J. (2004) Azelaic acid 15% gel: in the treatment of papulopustular rosacea. *American Journal of Clinical Dermatology* 5(1), 57–64.
9. Gupta, A.K. and Chaudhry, M.M. (2003) Evaluating the quality of rosacea studies: implications for the patient and physician. *Dermatology* **207**(2), 173–177. [Full text]
10. Khaw, P.T. and Elkington, A.R. (Eds.) (1999) *ABC of eyes*. 3rd edn. London: BMJ Publishing Group.
11. McClellan, K.J. and Noble, S. (2000) Topical metronidazole. A review of its use in rosacea. *American Journal of Clinical Dermatology* 1(3), 191–199.
12. Odom, R.B. (2004) The subtypes of rosacea: implications for treatment. *Cutis* 73(1 Suppl), 9–14.

3. Pelle, M.T., Crawford, G.H. and James, W.D. (2004) Rosacea: II. Therapy. *Journal of the American Academy of Dermatology* **51**(4), 499–512.
4. Powell, F.C. (2005) Rosacea. *New England Journal of Medicine* **352**(8), 793–803. [Full text]
5. Thiboutot, D., Thieroff-Ekerdt, R. and Graupe, K. (2003) Efficacy and safety of azelaic acid (15%) gel as a new treatment for papulopustular rosacea: results from two vehicle-controlled, randomized phase III studies. *Journal of the American Academy of Dermatology* **48**(6), 836–845.
16. van Zuuren, E.J., Graber, M.A., Hollis, S. et al (2003) *Interventions for rosacea (Cochrane Review)*. The Cochrane Library. Issue 4. Chichester, UK: John Wiley & Sons, Ltd. www.nelh.nhs.uk/cochrane.asp [Accessed: 03/03/2005]. [Full text]
17. Wilkin, J., Dahl, M., Detmar, M. et al (2002) Standard classification of rosacea: report of the National Rosacea Society expert committee on the classification and staging of rosacea. *Journal of the American Academy of Dermatology* **46**(4), 584–587.

R

PRODIGY GUIDANCE

Roundworm

Last revised in February 2004
www.prodigy.nhs.uk/guidance.asp?gt=Roundworm

Applies to people of all ages

This guidance covers the treatment of infestation with the roundworm *Ascaris lumbricoides*.

This guidance does not cover the treatment of tapeworm, hookworm, or other more unusual worm infestation. There is a separate PRODIGY guidance for *Threadworm*.

Goals

- To eradicate *Ascaris* (roundworm) infection and prevent reinfection

Contents

Scenarios

- Roundworm treatment p.1654

Extended Information, p. 1655

Roundworm treatment

Which therapy?

- **Drug therapy and hygiene measures** should be combined to break the cycle of reinfection.
- **Mebendazole is the treatment of choice** in adults and children older than 2 years. The dose is 100 mg twice a day for 3 days.
- **Piperazine combined with senna** (as a powder) is an alternative and is suitable for adults and children older than 3 months. It is given as a single dose.
- **Treatment does not usually require repeating** if there is no evidence of reinfection after 2–3 weeks.
- **For people with epilepsy, neurological disease, or severe renal or hepatic impairment, prescribe mebendazole,** as neurotoxic reactions resulting in convulsions have been reported in people with neurological or renal abnormalities.
- **If intestinal or biliary obstruction is suspected, piperazine is the drug of choice.**
- **During pregnancy,** it is generally recommended that, whenever possible, treatment is delayed until after the birth. There is no risk of infection to the fetus or to the baby during birth. Neither mebendazole nor piperazine is licensed for use during pregnancy.
- **In severe cases of *Ascaris* infection** unresponsive to standard treatment, seek specialist advice.
- For further information contact:
  - Birmingham (Department of Infection and Tropical Disease, Heartlands and Solihull Hospitals) 0121 424 0357
  - Liverpool (School of Tropical Medicine) 0151 708 9393
  - London (University College Hospitals, Hospital for Tropical Diseases) 0207 387 9300
  - Scottish Centre for Infection and Environmental Health 0141 300 1130
  - For registered users of Travax only, http://www.axl.co.uk/scieh

Practical prescribing points

For further information please see the *Medicines Compendium* (www.medicines.org.uk) or the *British National Formulary* (www.bnf.org).

Pregnancy and breastfeeding

- **Mebendazole and piperazine are not recommended for use during pregnancy or breastfeeding,** especially in the first trimester.
- Contact the National Teratology Information Service f more details (telephone 0191 232 1525).

Should I refer or investigate?

Refer?

- Admit cases of intestinal obstruction or biliary tract obstruction.
- Specialist medical expertise may be needed for diagnos
- Seek specialist advice for people resistant to treatment.

Investigate?

- Stool examination for *Ascaris* eggs.
- Sputum examination, if pulmonary symptoms exist, occasionally shows presence of larvae.

Patient information leaflets

The following PILs are available at www.prodigy.nhs.uk

- Roundworms

Shared decision making

- **Mebendazole** is a common treatment for roundworms people aged over 2 years. It comes as a tablet or drink. dose is taken twice a day for 3 days. Do not take it if y are or may be pregnant.
- **Piperazine** with a laxative is an alternative. It can be us in children from 3 months onwards. It comes in a sach and is added to water or milk. A single dose is taken.
- **Mebendazole and piperazine** must be prescribed by a doctor for the treatment of roundworm.
- **In pregnant women,** it is best just to stick to hygiene measures to avoid spreading infection and to treat afte the baby has been born.

Drug rationale

Drugs not included

- **Levamisole** is a very effective drug against *Ascaris* (common roundworm) infection. It acts by paralysing the worms. However, it is not licensed in the UK and i available only on a named-patient basis. Generally, if infestation has not responded to either mebendazole o piperazine, specialist advice should be sought.

rugs included

Mebendazole is active against *Ascaris* (common roundworm) in a 3-day treatment course and can be used in children aged over 2 years.

Piperazine powder combined with senna is active against *Ascaris* when given as a single dose.

rescriptions

lebendazole

ebendazole suspension: 100mg twice a day for 3 days

Age from 2 to 11 years

Mebendazole 100mg/5ml susp. Take one 5ml spoonful twice a day for 3 days; supply 30 ml; NHS Cost £1.77.

ebendazole tablets: 100mg twice a day for 3 days

Age from 12 years onwards

Mebendazole 100mg tablets. Take one tablet twice a day for 3 days; supply 6 tablets; NHS Cost £1.53.

iperazine (avoid in epilepsy or liver disease)

perazine + senna sachets: 2.5ml as a single dose

Age from 3 to 11 months

Piperazine 4g powder. Take one level 2.5ml spoonful of sachet contents in the morning as a single dose; supply 1 dual sachet; NHS Cost £1.25.

perazine + senna sachets: 5ml as a single dose

Age from 12 months to 5 years

Piperazine 4g powder. Take one level 5ml spoonful of sachet contents in the morning as a single dose; supply 1 dual sachet; NHS Cost £1.25.

perazine + senna sachets: one sachet as a single dose

Age from 6 to 11 years

Piperazine 4g powder. Take one sachet in the morning as a single dose; supply 1 dual sachet; NHS Cost £1.25; OTC Cost £2.29.

perazine + senna sachets: one sachet as a single dose

Age from 12 years onwards

Piperazine 4g powder. Take one sachet at bedtime as a single dose; supply 1 dual sachet; NHS Cost £1.25; OTC Cost £2.29.

xtended Information

ackground information

What is it? p.1655
How common is it? p.1655
How do I know my patient has it? p.1655
What else might it be? p.1655
Complications and prognosis p.1655

hat is it?

Ascaris lumbricoides (**common human roundworm**) is a parasitic helminth infection, which occurs worldwide, particularly in moist, warm climates.

The host becomes infected by ingesting contaminated food, soil, or water. Larvae hatch from ingested eggs, nvade the intestinal wall, and are carried via the portal and then systemic circulation to the lungs. The larvae then ascend the bronchial tree to the throat and are swallowed. Upon reaching the small intestine, they develop into adult worms, which live for up to 2 years. From ingestion of eggs to the first passage of ova in the stools in man is 60–70 days.

- **Mature females** may be up to 30 cm long. Their eggs are passed in the stool of the host and can remain viable in soil for several years.

[MERCK, 1999; Cook and Zumla, 2002]

How common is it?

- ***Ascaris* infection is rare in the UK**, and infection is likely to have been contracted abroad.
- **It is estimated that over 1 billion people worldwide are infected with *Ascaris*,** of whom over 250,000 of have associated morbidity, and about 60,000 die annually as a result of infection.
- Risk of infection exists where inadequately treated human sewage is used as fertilizer and/or faecal disposal is inadequate. The disease is highly prevalent in many regions of Africa, China, South East Asia, and Central and South America.

[MERCK, 1999; Cook and Zumla, 2002]

How do I know my patient has it?

- ***Ascaris* infection** may be very difficult to identify; if suspected, it may be best to seek specialist advice.
- **An infected person is likely to have been abroad** within the previous 2–3 months.
- **Symptoms are characterized** by early pulmonary and later gastrointestinal symptoms:
  - **In the early stages** (4–16 days after infection), migration of larval forms may cause pneumonitis (Loffler's syndrome) with fever, cough, sputum, dyspnoea, eosinophilia, and radiological infiltration of the lungs. This stage will usually last 2–3 weeks.
  - **Light intestinal worm infestation is usually asymptomatic.**
  - **Heavy worm infestation** may cause colic and diarrhoea. Occasionally, it may present with serious complications, such as intestinal or biliary tract obstruction.
- **Diagnosis is made by microscopic detection of eggs in the stool.** Very occasionally, in cases of heavy infestation, adult worms are passed in the stool or are vomited. Larvae are sometimes found in the sputum during the pulmonary phase.
- **In larval ascariasis there is a high eosinophilia** but in adult infections there is little or none.

[MERCK, 1999; Cook and Zumla, 2002]

What else might it be?

- **Hookworm,** characterized by abdominal discomfort, peptic ulcer-like pain, and anaemia.
- **Threadworm,** characterized by anal itching and white worms measuring 2–13 mm in length, seen either in the stool or on perianal skin.
- **Systemic symptoms of *Ascaris* infection** can mimic many other systemic illnesses.

Complications and prognosis

- **Adult worms usually cause little pathology if they remain in the small intestine.** Heavy worm infestation may cause colic, vomiting, and diarrhoea. Life-threatening complications may rarely result from intestinal obstruction or biliary tract obstruction.
- **Occasionally ascarids migrate to other locations** such as the liver, lungs, heart, or genito-urinary tract, causing acute symptoms such as appendicitis, biliary disease, cholecystitis, liver abscess, or pancreatitis.
- **Nutritional deficiencies may be caused by heavy infestations.** In the UK there is unlikely to be any adverse effect on nutritional status.
- **Serious allergic reactions to the worms rarely occur.**

[Harman, 1999; Cook and Zumla, 2002]

R

Management issues

- General issues p.1656
- Drug treatment p.1656
- Prophylactic drug treatment p.1656
- Medicines management p.1656

General issues

- **Drug therapy and hygiene measures** should be combined to break the cycle of reinfection.
- **If the person is returning to an area where roundworm is endemic** advise meticulous attention to hygiene and food preparation, including thorough cooking of meat and vegetables. Advice to avoid salads and raw fruit and vegetables is also important.

[CDC, 1999; MERCK, 1999]

Drug treatment

- **Mebendazole is the treatment of choice** in adults and children older than 2 years. It should be given twice a day for 3 days. This does not require repeating if there is no evidence of reinfection.
- **Piperazine** paralyses the worms and is given as a single dose, often combined with senna to help their complete expulsion. Piperazine is recommended if intestinal or biliary obstruction is suspected.
- **Levamisole** is very effective against roundworm. It acts by paralysing the worms. However, it is not licensed in the UK and is available only on a named-patient basis. Generally, if infestation has not responded to either mebendazole or piperazine, specialist advice should be sought.

Prophylactic drug treatment

- Piperazine is licensed for repeated monthly use for up to 3 months if there is continued risk of reinfection, e.g. a source of contamination or frequent travel abroad.

Medicines management

Mebendazole

- Mebendazole is largely unabsorbed and systemic adverse effects are minimal. Transient abdominal pain or diarrhoea occasionally occurs, especially in people with heavy infestations.

[Nathan, 1997; Ibarra, 2001]

Piperazine

- **Gastrointestinal disturbances** including abdominal pain, nausea, vomiting, colic, and diarrhoea are the most common adverse effects in people taking piperazine.
- **Neurotoxic reactions resulting in convulsions** have been reported in people with neurological or renal abnormalities, and piperazine should not be prescribed for people with epilepsy, neurological disease, or severe renal or hepatic impairment.
- Rarely, piperazine causes loss of muscular coordination ('worm wobble').

[Nathan, 1997; Ibarra, 2001]

Pregnancy and breastfeeding

- **Mebendazole and piperazine are best avoided during pregnancy,** especially in the first trimester. Mebendazo is poorly absorbed from the gastrointestinal tract and i unlikely to cause harm to the fetus although toxicity ha been noted in animal studies. There is no evidence that exposure to piperazine during pregnancy is harmful to the fetus, but its use during pregnancy is not recommended, and it should especially be avoided in th first trimester [Nathan, 1997; Lee et al, 2000].
- **Mebendazole and piperazine are not recommended to taken during breastfeeding.** The limited data that exist suggest that only very small amounts of anthelmintics pass into breast milk, and there are no apparent ill-effects in most infants. It is recommended that mothers taking piperazine should avoid breastfeeding for 8 hou following a dose [Nathan, 1997; BNF 45, 2003]. Colic has been reported in some infants following maternal ingestion of senna. If piperazine combined with senna i given to a breastfeeding mother, the infant should be fe just prior to the mother's taking this [Nathan, 1997].
- **Contact the National Teratology Information Service more details** (telephone 0191 232 1525).

References

1. BNF 45 (2003) *British National Formulary.* 45th edn. London: British Medical Association and Royal Pharmaceutical Society of Great Britain.
2. CDC (1999) *Ascariasis.* Centers for Disease Control a Prevention. www.dpd.cdc.gov [Accessed: 22/11/2000]
3. Cook, G.C. and Zumla, A. (Eds.) (2002) *Manson's tropical diseases.* 21st edn. London: W.B. Saunders.
4. Harman, R.J. (Ed.) (1999) *Handbook of pharmacy healthcare: diseases and patient advice.* London: Pharmaceutical Press.
5. Ibarra, J. (2001) Threadworms: a starting point for family hygiene. *British Journal of Community Nursin* 6(8), 414–420.
6. Lee, A., Inch, S. and Finnigan, D. (Eds.) (2000) *Therapeutics in pregnancy and lactation.* Abingdon: Radcliffe Medical Press Ltd.
7. MERCK (1999) *Nematode (roundworm infections).* T Merck Manual of Diagnosis and Therapy. Merck & C www.merck.com/pubs/mmanual/section13/chapter16 161e.htm [Accessed: 01/11/2000].
8. Nathan, A. (1997) Anthelmintics. *Pharmaceutical Journal* 258(6945), 770–771.

PRODIGY GUIDANCE

Scabies

Last revised in February 2004
www.prodigy.nhs.uk/guidance.asp?gt=Scabies

Applies to people of all ages

This guidance covers the management of scabies.

This guidance does not offer advice on the management of crusted scabies or outbreaks of scabies in residential or nursing homes. The local Consultant in Communicable Disease Control should be contacted for advice during outbreaks of scabies in residential or nursing homes.

There is separate PRODIGY guidance for the management of *Head lice* and *Pubic lice*.

Goals

To treat the scabies infestation, and to prevent reinfection

Contents

Scenarios

- First-line treatment p.1657
- Treatment failure p.1659

Extended Information, p. 1662

Which scenario?

First-line treatment: covers the first-line management of scabies and itch.
Treatment failure: covers the management of scabies and itch when first-line treatment has failed.

First-line treatment

Which therapy?

Treat *all* members of the household, close contacts, and sexual contacts simultaneously, even if they are asymptomatic. (The itch does not usually appear until 2–6 weeks after the initial infestation.)

Give written advice on the correct application of treatment (see the *Patient information leaflets*).

Give two applications of treatment, used 7 days apart:

- First-line: permethrin 5% dermal cream.
- Second-line: malathion 0.5% aqueous liquid.
- Give 30 g cream or 100 ml liquid per application for an average-sized adult.
- A single application is usually sufficient for children under 2 years of age.

Clothing, towels, and bedding should be washed after the first application of treatment.

Advise the family that itching can persist for up to 3 weeks after successful treatment.

If itching is troublesome, consider trying one of the following:

- **Crotamiton cream or lotion** has soothing qualities and may relieve itching.
- **Moderate-potency topical corticosteroid creams** can also relieve itch, but avoid if the diagnosis is uncertain, as they may mask signs and symptoms.
- **Oral sedative antihistamines given at night** may be useful for breaking the itch–scratch cycle.

Factors affecting choice of treatment

Pregnancy and breastfeeding: use a single application of malathion (in an aqueous base). If this is ineffective, consider a second application after an interval of at least 7 days. Consider chlorphenamine (chlorpheniramine) to relieve itch. Do not use hydroxyzine, crotamiton, or topical steroids.

- **Broken or excoriated skin:** avoid crotamiton and alcohol-based malathion products.
- **Secondary bacterial infection present:** do not use topical corticosteroid creams.
- **Benign prostatic hyperplasia, urinary retention, or glaucoma:** avoid sedating antihistamines.
- **Epilepsy:** avoid antihistamines (they may lower the seizure threshold).

Practical prescribing points

For further information please see the *Medicines Compendium* (www.medicines.org.uk) or the *British National Formulary* (www.bnf.org). For further information on the use of drugs in pregnancy, contact the National Teratology Information Service (telephone 0191 232 1525).

Acaricides

- **Apply treatment to the whole body including the scalp, neck, face, and ears, and especially between the fingers and toes, and under the nails.**
  - Apply permethrin 5% dermal cream for 8–12 hours or overnight.
  - Apply malathion 0.5% aqueous liquid for 24 hours.
- **Do not apply treatment after a hot bath.** Skin should be cool, clean, and dry.

Treatments for itch

- **Advise people that sedative antihistamines** cause drowsiness, which may persist the next day. People should not drive or operate machinery if affected.
- **Moderate- or mild-potency topical steroids** are rarely associated with adverse effects, especially if used only for short periods. Potential local problems associated with excessive use may include worsening or spread of untreated infection; thinning of the skin; irreversible *striae atrophicae* and telangiectasia; contact dermatitis; or mild depigmentation.

Should I refer or investigate ?

Refer?

- **Seek specialist advice for the management of crusted scabies,** e.g. from the local Consultant in Communicable Disease Control.
- **In outbreaks of scabies in a residential or nursing home,** refer to the local Consultant in Communicable Disease Control for advice.

S

- **Consider referral to a dermatologist if the diagnosis is in doubt,** or after continued treatment failure.
- **Consider referral to a genito-urinary medicine clinic** for specialist advice if scabies has been sexually transmitted and associated sexually transmitted infections are suspected.

Investigate?

- **People with crusted scabies are usually immunocompromised.** Assess, investigate, and refer as appropriate.

Patient information leaflets

The following PILs are available at www.prodigy.nhs.uk

- Medicines - Name Changes of Medicines
- Scabies

Shared decision making

- **An anti-mite cream or lotion** will usually clear scabies:
  - **Permethrin** cream is left on for 8–12 hours and then washed off. The cream is not suitable for pregnant or breastfeeding women. An adult needs about 30 g to apply to the whole body.
  - **Malathion** lotion is an alternative. Leave on for 24 hours then wash off. An adult needs about 100 ml to apply to the whole body. A small paintbrush may be helpful when applying it.
- **Apply to all the body,** including the scalp, face, neck, and ears, between the fingers and toes, under nails, genitals, the whole of the back, etc.
- **If you wash during the treatment time,** re-apply cream or lotion.
- **Treat household members and sleeping partners,** even if they have no symptoms.
- **You need two applications of treatment, 7 days apart.**
- **Wash clothes, sheets, etc, after the first application,** to help prevent spread to others.
- **Avoid close skin contact with others until the infestation has cleared.**
- **Itch often lasts 2–3 weeks after successful treatment.** The itch may be relieved by:
  - **Crotamiton** cream or lotion, or
  - **A steroid cream,** or
  - **An antihistamine medication.**

Drug rationale

S

Drugs not included

Treatment of scabies

- **Alcohol-based malathion products** are not included, because they irritate excoriated skin and genitalia, and may cause wheezing in people with asthma.
- **Benzyl benzoate** is less effective than permethrin or malathion, and is irritant, especially to the face and genitals [BNF 45, 2003].
- **Ivermectin,** as a single oral dose of 200 micrograms/kg, is available only on a named-patient basis as an adjunct to topical treatment for crusted (Norwegian) scabies. The treatment is usually initiated on specialist advice [BNF 45, 2003].
- **Lindane** is no longer available in the UK.

Treatment of itch

- **Non-sedative antihistamines** have not been shown to be effective in relieving pruritus [Klein and Clark, 1999].
- **Long-acting sedating antihistamines** are not included, so there is minimal 'hangover' effect.
- **Topical antihistamines** may cause sensitization, are onl[y] marginally effective, and are therefore not recommended.
- **Preparations containing calamine** do not offer significa[nt] benefit in most people and are not recommended.

Drugs included

Treatment of scabies

- **Permethrin** 5% dermal cream has been the most widely studied, and seems to be more effective than crotamito[n], lindane, or oral ivermectin [Usha and Gopalakrishnan Nair, 2000; Walker and Johnstone, 2003].
- **Malathion** has been studied only in non-controlled tria[ls] so is therefore only recommended as second-line treatment [Hanna et al, 1978; Thianprasit and Schuetzenberger, 1984]. Aqueous-based malathion is preferred because it is less likely to irritate excoriated skin and genitalia, or to cause wheezing in people with asthma.

Treatment of itch

- **Hydroxyzine** is specifically licensed for pruritus and is sedating. Hydroxyzine is offered as night-time dose for temporary help with sleeping, to help break the itch–scratch cycle.
- **Chlorphenamine (chlorpheniramine)** is also included because it is inexpensive, and is an effective sedating antihistamine of intermediate duration.
- **Crotamiton** cream or lotion has soothing qualities, and may help to relieve the itch caused by scabies, although there is no objective proof of its anti-pruritic activity.
- **Clobetasone butyrate** cream (a moderate-potency topi[cal] corticosteroid) is included for the treatment of itch. However, it should be used with caution if a diagnosis [of] scabies is not certain, since it may mask symptoms.

Prescriptions

1st-choice treatment: permethrin

Permethrin 5% dermal cream

- Age from 2 to 23 months
- Permethrin 5% dermal cream. Apply to the whole bod[y] including the scalp, face, neck, and ears. Leave on for 8[–]12 hours or overnight. Wash off; supply 30 grams; NHS Cost £5.52.

Permethrin 5% dermal cream

- Age from 2 to 5 years
- Permethrin 5% dermal cream. Apply to the whole bod[y] including the scalp, face, neck, and ears. Leave on for 8[–]12 hours or overnight. Wash off. Repeat after 7 days; supply 30 grams; NHS Cost £5.52; OTC Cost £9.62.

Permethrin 5% dermal cream

- Age from 6 to 11 years
- Permethrin 5% dermal cream. Apply to the whole bod[y] including the scalp, face, neck, and ears. Leave on for 8[–]12 hours or overnight. Wash off. Repeat after 7 days; supply 30 grams; NHS Cost £5.52; OTC Cost £9.62.

Permethrin 5% dermal cream

- Age from 12 years onwards
- Permethrin 5% dermal cream. Apply to the whole bod[y] including the scalp, face, neck, and ears. Leave on for 8[–]12 hours or overnight. Wash off. Repeat after 7 days; supply 60 grams; NHS Cost £11.04; OTC Cost £19.2[4]

2nd-choice treatment: malathion

Malathion 0.5% aqueous liquid
- Age from 2 to 23 months
- Malathion 0.5% aqueous liquid. Apply to the whole body, including the scalp, face, neck and ears. Leave on for 24 hours. Wash off; supply 100 ml; NHS Cost £3.70.

Malathion 0.5% aqueous liquid
- Age from 2 years onwards
- Malathion 0.5% aqueous liquid. Apply to the whole body, including the scalp, face, neck, and ears. Leave on for 24 hours. Wash off. Repeat after 7 days; supply 200 ml; NHS Cost £4.62; OTC Cost £8.99.

Pregnancy and breastfeeding

Malathion 0.5% aqueous liquid
- Age from 12 to 60 years
- Malathion 0.5% aqueous liquid. Apply to the whole body from the neck down. Leave on for 24 hours. Wash off; supply 100 ml; NHS Cost £3.70.

Topical treatments to relieve itching

Crotamiton 10% cream: apply once a day
- Age from 6 months to 2 years
- Crotamiton 10% cream. Apply to the affected area once a day when required for relief of itching; supply 30 grams; NHS Cost £2.23; OTC Cost £3.49.

Crotamiton 10% cream: apply 2 to 3 times a day
- Age from 3 years onwards
- Crotamiton 10% cream. Apply to the affected area 2 to 3 times a day when required for relief of itching; supply 30 grams; NHS Cost £2.23; OTC Cost £3.39.

Crotamiton 10% lotion: apply once a day
- Age from 6 months to 2 years
- Crotamiton 10% lotion. Apply to the affected area once a day when required for relief of itching; supply 100 ml; NHS Cost £2.80; OTC Cost £4.49.

Crotamiton 10% lotion: apply 2 to 3 times a day
- Age from 3 years onwards
- Crotamiton 10% lotion. Apply to the affected area 2 to 3 times a day when required for relief of itching; supply 100 ml; NHS Cost £2.80; OTC Cost £4.49.

Clobetasone 0.05% cream: apply thinly once or twice a day
- Age from 12 months to 11 years
- Clobetasone butyrate 0.05% cream. Apply thinly to the affected area once or twice a day when required for relief of itching. Use for a maximum of 7-14 days unless otherwise directed; supply 30 grams; NHS Cost £1.76.

Clobetasone 0.05% cream: apply thinly once or twice a day
- Age from 12 years onwards
- Clobetasone butyrate 0.05% cream. Apply thinly to the affected area once or twice a day when required for relief of itching. Use for a maximum of 7-14 days unless otherwise directed; supply 100 grams; NHS Cost £5.16.

Sedating antihistamine (for sleep disturbance)

Chlorphenamine (chlorpheniramine) syrup: 1mg at night prn
- Age from 1 month to 11 months
- Chlorphenamine 2mg/5ml syrup. Take 2.5ml at night when required for relief of itching; supply 50 ml; NHS Cost £0.72.

Chlorphenamine (chlorpheniramine) syrup: 1mg at night prn
- Age from 12 to 23 months
- Chlorphenamine 2mg/5ml syrup. Take 2.5ml at night when required for relief of itching; supply 50 ml; NHS Cost £0.72; OTC Cost £1.26.

Chlorphenamine (chlorpheniramine) syrup: 1-2mg at night prn
- Age from 2 to 5 years
- Chlorphenamine 2mg/5ml syrup. Take 2.5ml to 5ml at night when required for relief of itching; supply 100 ml; NHS Cost £1.43; OTC Cost £2.53.

Chlorphenamine (chlorpheniramine) syrup: 2-4mg at night prn
- Age from 6 to 11 years
- Chlorphenamine 2mg/5ml syrup. Take one to two 5ml spoonfuls at night when required for relief of itching; supply 100 ml; NHS Cost £1.43; OTC Cost £2.53.

Chlorphenamine (chlorpheniramine) tablets: 4mg at night prn
- Age from 12 years onwards
- Chlorphenamine 4mg tablets. Take one tablet at night when required for relief of itching; supply 14 tablets; NHS Cost £0.22; OTC Cost £1.40.

Hydroxyzine syrup: 5mg to 15mg at night when required
- Age from 6 months to 6 years
- Hydroxyzine 10mg/5ml syrup. Take 2.5ml to 7.5ml at night when required for relief of itching; supply 100 ml; NHS Cost £0.96.

Hydroxyzine syrup: 15mg to 25mg at night when required
- Age from 7 to 11 years
- Hydroxyzine 10mg/5ml syrup. Take 7.5ml to 12.5ml at night when required for relief of itching; supply 200 ml; NHS Cost £1.91.

Hydroxyzine tablets: 25mg at night when required
- Age from 12 years onwards
- Hydroxyzine 25mg tablets. Take one tablet at night when required for relief of itching; supply 14 tablets; NHS Cost £0.51.

Treatment failure

Which therapy?

- **Re-examine the person to confirm that the diagnosis of scabies is correct.**
- **Itching commonly persists for up to 3 weeks after *successful* treatment.**
- **Treatment failure is likely if:**
  - The itch still persists at the same or increasing intensity at least 2 weeks after treatment was completed.
  - Treatment was uncoordinated or not applied correctly.
  - New burrows appear at any stage after treatment.
- **Re-treat *all* members of the household, close contacts, and sexual contacts** simultaneously, even if they are asymptomatic. (The itch does not usually appear until 2–6 weeks after the initial infestation.)
- **Give written advice on the correct application of treatment** (see the *Patient information leaflets*).
- **Give two applications of treatment, used 7 days apart.**
  - **If all contacts were treated simultaneously and treatment was applied correctly,** give a course of a *different* acaricide.
  - **If contacts were *not* treated simultaneously or treatment was incorrectly applied,** re-treat with the same acaricide, or use a different acaricide.
  - **Give 30 g cream or 100 ml liquid per application for an average-sized adult.**
  - **A single application is usually sufficient for children under 2 years of age.**
- **Clothing, towels, and bedding should be washed after the first application of treatment.**
- **If itching is troublesome, consider trying one of the following:**

S

- **Crotamiton cream or lotion** has soothing qualities and may relieve itching.
- **Moderate-potency topical corticosteroid creams** can also relieve itch, but avoid if the diagnosis is uncertain as they may mask signs and symptoms.
- **Oral sedative antihistamines given at night** may be useful for breaking the itch–scratch cycle.

Factors affecting choice of treatment

- **Pregnancy and breastfeeding:** use a single application of malathion (in an aqueous base). If this is ineffective, consider a second application after an interval of at least 7 days. Consider chlorphenamine (chlorpheniramine) to relieve itch. Do not use hydroxyzine, crotamiton, or topical steroids.
- **Broken or excoriated skin:** avoid crotamiton and alcohol-based malathion products.
- **Secondary bacterial infection present:** do not use topical corticosteroid creams.
- **Benign prostatic hyperplasia, urinary retention, or glaucoma:** avoid sedating antihistamines.
- **Epilepsy:** avoid antihistamines (they may lower the seizure threshold).

Practical prescribing points

For further information please see the *Medicines Compendium* (www.medicines.org.uk) or the *British National Formulary* (www.bnf.org). For further information on the use of drugs in pregnancy, contact the National Teratology Information Service (telephone 0191 232 1525).

Acaricides

- **Apply treatment to the whole body including the scalp, neck, face, and ears, and especially between the fingers and toes and under the nails.**
  - Apply permethrin 5% dermal cream for 8–12 hours or overnight.
  - Apply malathion 0.5% aqueous liquid for 24 hours.
- **Do not apply treatment after a hot bath.** Skin should be cool, clean, and dry.

Treatments for itch

- **Advise people that sedative antihistamines cause drowsiness,** which may persist the next day. People should not drive or operate machinery if affected.
- **Moderate or mild potency topical steroids** are rarely associated with adverse effects, especially if used only for short periods. Potential local problems associated with excessive use may include worsening or spread of untreated infection; thinning of the skin; irreversible *striae atrophicae* and telangiectasia; contact dermatitis; or mild depigmentation.

Should I refer or investigate ?

Refer?

- **Seek specialist advice for the management of crusted scabies,** e.g. from the local Consultant in Communicable Disease Control.
- **In outbreaks of scabies in a residential or nursing home,** refer to the local Consultant in Communicable Disease Control for advice.
- **Consider referral to a dermatologist if the diagnosis is in doubt,** or if the second course of treatment is also ineffective.
- **Consider referral to a genito-urinary medicine clinic** for specialist advice if scabies has been sexually transmitted and associated sexually transmitted infections are suspected.

Investigate?

- **People with crusted scabies are usually immunocompromised.** Assess, investigate, and refer as appropriate.

Patient information leaflets

The following PILs are available at www.prodigy.nhs.uk

- Medicines - Name Changes of Medicines
- Scabies

Shared decision making

- Your scabies persists. Common reasons for this are:
  - **You may not have left treatment on all your body for the full time.**
  - **A close contact who also has scabies may not have been treated.**
- **Avoid close body contact with others until the infection has cleared.** An anti-mite cream or lotion will usually clear scabies:
  - **Permethrin** cream is left on for 8–12 hours, and then washed off. The cream is not suitable for pregnant or breastfeeding women. An adult needs about 30 g to apply to the whole body.
  - **Malathion** lotion is an alternative. Leave on for 24 hours then wash off. An adult needs about 100 ml to apply to the whole body. A small paintbrush may be helpful when applying it.
- **Apply to all the body,** including the scalp, face, neck, an[d] ears, between the fingers and toes, under nails, genitals, the whole of the back, etc.
- **If you wash during the treatment time, re-apply cream o[r] lotion.**
- **Treat household members and sleeping partners,** even if they have no symptoms.
- **You need two applications of treatment, 7 days apart.**
- **Avoid close skin contact with others until the infection has cleared.**
- **Itch often lasts 2–3 weeks after successful treatment.** Th[e] itch may be relieved by:
  - **Crotamiton** cream or lotion, or
  - **A steroid cream,** or
  - **An antihistamine medication.**

Drug rationale

Drugs not included

Treatment of scabies

- **Alcohol-based malathion products** are not included, because they irritate excoriated skin and genitalia, and may cause wheezing in people with asthma.
- **Benzyl benzoate** is less effective than permethrin or malathion, and is irritant, especially to the face and genitals [BNF 45, 2003].
- **Ivermectin,** as a single oral dose of 200 micrograms/kg, is available only on a named-patient basis as an adjunct to topical treatment for crusted (Norwegian) scabies. The treatment is usually initiated on specialist advice [BNF 45, 2003].
- **Lindane** is no longer available in the UK.

Treatment of itch

- **Non-sedative antihistamines** have not been shown to be effective in relieving pruritus [Klein and Clark, 1999].

S

- **Long-acting sedating antihistamines** are not included, so there is minimal 'hangover' effect.
- **Topical antihistamines** may cause sensitization, are only marginally effective, and are therefore not recommended.
- **Preparations containing calamine** do not offer significant benefit in most people and are not recommended.

Drugs included

Treatment of scabies

- **Permethrin** 5% dermal cream has been the most widely studied, and seems to be more effective than crotamiton, lindane (no longer available in the UK), or oral ivermectin [Usha and Gopalakrishnan Nair, 2000; Walker and Johnstone, 2003;].
- **Malathion** has been studied only in non-controlled trials, so is therefore only recommended as second-line treatment [Hanna et al, 1978; Thianprasit and Schuetzenberger, 1984]. Aqueous-based malathion is preferred because it is less likely to irritate excoriated skin and genitalia, or to cause wheezing in people with asthma.

Treatment of itch

- **Hydroxyzine** is specifically licensed for pruritus and is sedating. Hydroxyzine is offered as night-time dose for temporary help with sleeping, to help break the itch–scratch cycle.
- **Chlorphenamine (chlorpheniramine)** is also included because it is inexpensive, and is an effective sedating antihistamine of intermediate duration.
- **Crotamiton** cream or lotion has soothing qualities, and may help to relieve the itch caused by scabies, although there is no objective proof of its anti-pruritic activity.
- **Clobetasone butyrate** cream (a moderate-potency topical corticosteroid) is included for the treatment of itch. However, it should be used with caution if a diagnosis of scabies is not certain, since it may mask symptoms.

Prescriptions

Permethrin 5% dermal cream

Permethrin 5% dermal cream
- Age from 2 to 23 months
- Permethrin 5% dermal cream. Apply to the whole body, including the scalp, face, neck, and ears. Leave on for 8-12 hours or overnight. Wash off; supply 30 grams; NHS Cost £5.52.

Permethrin 5% dermal cream
- Age from 2 to 5 years
- Permethrin 5% dermal cream. Apply to the whole body, including the scalp, face, neck, and ears. Leave on for 8-12 hours or overnight. Wash off. Repeat after 7 days; supply 30 grams; NHS Cost £5.52; OTC Cost £9.62.

Permethrin 5% dermal cream
- Age from 6 to 11 years
- Permethrin 5% dermal cream. Apply to the whole body, including the scalp, face, neck, and ears. Leave on for 8-12 hours or overnight. Wash off. Repeat after 7 days; supply 30 grams; NHS Cost £5.52; OTC Cost £9.62.

Permethrin 5% dermal cream
- Age from 12 years onwards
- Permethrin 5% dermal cream. Apply to the whole body, including the scalp, face, neck, and ears. Leave on for 8-12 hours or overnight. Wash off. Repeat after 7 days; supply 60 grams; NHS Cost £11.04; OTC Cost £19.24.

Malathion 0.5% aqueous liquid

Malathion 0.5% aqueous liquid
- Age from 2 to 23 months
- Malathion 0.5% aqueous liquid. Apply to the whole body, including the scalp, face, neck and ears. Leave on for 24 hours. Wash off; supply 100 ml; NHS Cost £3.70.

Malathion 0.5% aqueous liquid
- Age from 2 years onwards
- Malathion 0.5% aqueous liquid. Apply to the whole body, including the scalp, face, neck, and ears. Leave on for 24 hours. Wash off. Repeat after 7 days; supply 200 ml; NHS Cost £4.62; OTC Cost £8.99.

Pregnancy and breastfeeding

Malathion 0.5% aqueous liquid
- Age from 12 to 60 years
- Malathion 0.5% aqueous liquid. Apply to the whole body from the neck down. Leave on for 24 hours. Wash off; supply 100 ml; NHS Cost £3.70.

Topical treatments to relieve itching

Crotamiton 10% cream: apply once a day
- Age from 6 months to 2 years
- Crotamiton 10% cream. Apply to the affected area once a day when required for relief of itching; supply 30 grams; NHS Cost £2.23; OTC Cost £3.49.

Crotamiton 10% cream: apply 2 to 3 times a day
- Age from 3 years onwards
- Crotamiton 10% cream. Apply to the affected area 2 to 3 times a day when required for relief of itching; supply 30 grams; NHS Cost £2.23; OTC Cost £3.49.

Crotamiton 10% lotion: apply once a day
- Age from 6 months to 2 years
- Crotamiton 10% lotion. Apply to the affected area once a day when required for relief of itching; supply 100 ml; NHS Cost £2.80; OTC Cost £4.49.

Crotamiton 10% lotion: apply 2 to 3 times a day
- Age from 3 years onwards
- Crotamiton 10% lotion. Apply to the affected area 2 to 3 times a day when required for relief of itching; supply 100 ml; NHS Cost £2.80; OTC Cost £4.49.

Clobetasone 0.05% cream: apply thinly once or twice a day
- Age from 12 months to 11 years
- Clobetasone butyrate 0.05% cream. Apply thinly to the affected area once or twice a day when required for relief of itching. Use for a maximum of 7-14 days unless otherwise directed; supply 30 grams; NHS Cost £1.76.

Clobetasone 0.05% cream: apply thinly once or twice a day
- Age from 12 years onwards
- Clobetasone butyrate 0.05% cream. Apply thinly to the affected area once or twice a day when required for relief of itching. Use for a maximum of 7-14 days unless otherwise directed; supply 100 grams; NHS Cost £5.16.

Sedating antihistamine (for sleep disturbance)

Chlorphenamine (chlorpheniramine) syrup: 1mg at night prn
- Age from 1 month to 11 months
- Chlorphenamine 2mg/5ml syrup. Take 2.5ml at night when required for relief of itching; supply 50 ml; NHS Cost £0.72.

Chlorphenamine (chlorpheniramine) syrup: 1mg at night prn
- Age from 12 to 23 months
- Chlorphenamine 2mg/5ml syrup. Take 2.5ml at night when required for relief of itching; supply 50 ml; NHS Cost £0.72; OTC Cost £1.26.

Chlorphenamine (chlorpheniramine) syrup: 1-2mg at night prn

- Age from 2 to 5 years
- Chlorphenamine 2mg/5ml syrup. Take 2.5ml to 5ml at night when required for relief of itching; supply 100 ml; NHS Cost £1.43; OTC Cost £2.53.

Chlorphenamine (chlorpheniramine) syrup: 2-4mg at night prn

- Age from 6 to 11 years
- Chlorphenamine 2mg/5ml syrup. Take one to two 5ml spoonfuls at night when required for relief of itching; supply 100 ml; NHS Cost £1.43; OTC Cost £2.53.

Chlorphenamine (chlorpheniramine) tablets: 4mg at night prn

- Age from 12 years onwards
- Chlorphenamine 4mg tablets. Take one tablet at night when required for relief of itching; supply 14 tablets; NHS Cost £0.22; OTC Cost £1.40.

Hydroxyzine syrup: 5mg to 15mg at night when required

- Age from 6 months to 6 years
- Hydroxyzine 10mg/5ml syrup. Take 2.5ml to 7.5ml at night when required for relief of itching; supply 100 ml; NHS Cost £0.96.

Hydroxyzine syrup: 15mg to 25mg at night when required

- Age from 7 to 11 years
- Hydroxyzine 10mg/5ml syrup. Take 7.5ml to 12.5ml at night when required for relief of itching; supply 200 ml; NHS Cost £1.91.

Hydroxyzine tablets: 25mg at night when required

- Age from 12 years onwards
- Hydroxyzine 25mg tablets. Take one tablet at night when required for relief of itching; supply 14 tablets; NHS Cost £0.51.

Extended Information

Background information

- What is it? p.1662
- How common is it? p.1662
- How do I know my patient has scabies? p.1662
- Does my patient have crusted scabies? p.1662
- How is scabies transmitted? p.1662
- What else might it be? p.1663
- Complications and prognosis p.1663

What is it?

- The parasite *Sarcoptes scabiei* is a skin mite that is about 0.35 mm long.
- The female mite tunnels into the epidermis, and deposits eggs along the burrow.
- The larvae hatch in a few days and create new burrows (moulting pockets) where they remain until maturity.
- Development from egg to adult takes about 10–15 days, and mites die after 4–6 weeks.

[Figueroa, 1998; DTB, 2002b]

How common is it?

- **Scabies has a cyclical rise in incidence roughly** every 20 years in the UK.
- **Reported cases have begun to rise in the UK since 1991,** often presenting as outbreaks in schools, and residential or nursing homes.
- Scabies is more prevalent in urban than rural areas, and in winter than in summer.
- Scabies is more prevalent in children and young adults, but all ages can be affected.

[Downs et al, 1999]

How do I know my patient has scabies?

- The main symptoms of scabies are caused by an immune response to the mites and their saliva or faeces.
- **Itching, particularly at night, is the most common presenting symptom.** Itching is most intense when the person is in bed. It usually develops 2–6 weeks after initial infestation, and coincides with the appearance of a rash. However, symptoms reappear within a few hours if the person is re-infested (owing to prior sensitization to the mite and its saliva and faeces).
- **The accompanying rash is symmetrical.** The rash is usually made up of small, red papules, but vesicles or a nodular reaction may also be seen. The rash is usually most obvious on the inside of the thighs, the axillae, the periumbilical region, the buttocks, and the genitals. See www.dermis.net/index_e.htm.
- **Burrows can be difficult to identify,** as they are easily distorted or destroyed by scratching. They are most commonly found on the finger webs, wrists, and elbows, and appear as fine, wavy, greyish, dark or silvery lines 2–15 mm long with a minute spec (the mite) at the closed end. They may also be found on the ankles, feet, genitals (in males), and nipples.
- **The burrow ink test can help to identify burrows:** rub the underside of a cartridge pen on a suspected papule, and then wipe off with an alcohol pad to remove the surface ink for the lesion. If a burrow is present, the ink will track down the mite burrow, forming a characteristic dark, zigzag line running across and away from the papule.
- **Note: in infants, young children, the elderly, and the immunocompromised, mites can also infect the face, neck, scalp, and ears.** Those who have experienced treatment failure may also have mites in these areas.
- **Scabies is usually diagnosed from the history and clinical findings.** However, misdiagnosis is common because of its similarity to other pruritic skin disorders. If other family members are affected by a similar rash, this increases the likelihood of scabies. The diagnosis can be confirmed by microscopic examination of skin scrapings taken from a burrow for mites, eggs, or faeces.

[Figueroa, 1998; Roberts, 2000; Scott, 2001; Chouela et al, 2002]

Does my patient have crusted scabies?

- **Crusted (hyperkeratotic or Norwegian) scabies** is a different clinical manifestation of scabies that occurs in people with an impaired immune response.
- **Hyperkeratotic, crusted lesions are usually seen on the hands, feet, nails, scalp, and ears.**
- **Crusted scabies may not cause itching,** or may occasionally mimic eczema or psoriasis.
- **Crusted scabies is highly contagious.** An immunocompetent individual carries only about 12 female scabies mites; however, an immunocompromised host can have thousands to millions of mites.
- **Outbreaks of scabies in institutions** can often be traced to one index case of crusted scabies.

[Roberts, 2000; Chouela et al, 2002]

How is scabies transmitted?

- **Classical scabies is transmitted only via direct skin contact.** Transmission may be from close family contact (e.g. prolonged hand-holding) or during sexual contact.
- **Crusted (Norwegian) scabies can also be transmitted via bedding, towels, clothes, and upholstery,** owing to the large numbers of mites on an infested individual.

[Figueroa, 1998; Roberts, 2000]

What else might it be?

- Animal scabies, pubic lice, or body lice.
- Insect bites.
- Other dermatological conditions, including atopic eczema, contact dermatitis, lichen planus, or dermatitis herpetiformis.

Complications and prognosis

Complications

- Secondary infection
- Eczematous eruptions
- Infestation of other contacts

Prognosis

- Scabies persists indefinitely unless treated.
- Itching persists for up to 3 weeks after successful treatment.

[Roberts, 2000]

Management issues

- General points p.1663
- How should I treat scabies? p.1663
- How should treatment be applied? p.1663
- Supporting evidence for scabies treatments (acaricides) p.1663
- Treatment of itch p.1663
- Do children with scabies need to be kept off school? p.1664
- Treatment failure p.1664
- Medicines management p.1664

General points

- **If there is a history of risk behaviour for sexually transmitted infections** (STIs), consider screening for coexisting STIs. (Note: people need to give informed consent prior to screening.)
  - Consider referral to a genito-urinary medicine clinic for specialist advice, diagnostic services, and partner notification.
  - Contact tracing of partners from the previous 3 months should be undertaken.

[Scott, 2001]

How should I treat scabies?

- **Treat *all* members of the household, close contacts, and sexual contacts simultaneously.** Include contacts who are asymptomatic: scabies is highly infectious and there is a latent period before symptoms develop. Encourage the family not to delay treatment. It is important that all contacts apply treatment on the same day to minimize the chances of reinfestation from an untreated contact.
- **Two applications of treatment are used 7 days apart:**
  - First-line: use a course of permethrin 5% dermal cream.
  - Second-line: use a course of malathion 0.5% aqueous liquid.
- **Clothes, towels, and bed linen** should be machine-washed (at 50°C or above) after the first application of treatment, to prevent reinfestation and transmission to others. Items that cannot be washed can be kept in plastic bags for at least 72 hours to contain the mites until they die [Scott, 2001].
- **Outbreaks of scabies in a residential or nursing home** should be referred to a Consultant in Communicable Disease Control. All residents, staff, and their families are treated simultaneously on an agreed treatment date.

[Figueroa, 1998; Roberts, 2000; BNF 45, 2003]

How should treatment be applied?

- **Apply treatment to the whole body, including the scalp, neck, face, and ears,** and especially between the fingers and toes and under the nails. (Note: this is different from the package information, which only recommends application from the neck down for most healthy adults.)
- **Treatment should not be applied after a hot bath,** since this increases systemic absorption and removes the drug from its treatment site.
- If the hands are washed, the liquid or cream must be reapplied.

[Figueroa, 1998; Roberts, 2000; Scott, 2001]

Supporting evidence for scabies treatments (acaricides)

Recommended treatments

- There are few published randomized controlled trials of acaricides.
- **Permethrin 5% dermal cream is recommended as first-line treatment.** This treatment has been the most widely studied. One systematic review found that it seems to be more effective than crotamiton or lindane (lindane is no longer available in the UK) [Walker and Johnstone, 2003]. A subsequent study found that a single application of permethrin had a higher cure-rate at 14 days (97.8%) than a single dose of ivermectin (70%) [Usha and Gopalakrishnan Nair, 2000].
- **Malathion 0.5% aqueous liquid is recommended as second-line treatment.** Malathion has only been studied in non-controlled trials. These found that a single application of malathion 0.5% left on the skin for 24–48 hours cured 70–80% of people by 2–4 weeks [Hanna et al, 1978; Thianprasit and Schuetzenberger, 1984].

Other treatments

- **Crotamiton 10% cream or lotion is less effective than permethrin** [Walker and Johnstone, 2003], and is rarely used in the UK for treating scabies because of its poor efficacy [DTB, 2002b]. However, it may help to relieve the itch caused by scabies. See *Treatment of itch* below.
- **Benzyl benzoate 25% emulsion is less effective than malathion or permethrin** [BNF 45, 2003]. The emulsion can irritate the skin, eyes, and mucosal surfaces [DTB, 2002b].
- **Oral ivermectin** (as a single oral dose of 200 micrograms/kg) is available on a named-patient basis as an adjunct to topical treatment for crusted (Norwegian) scabies [BNF 45, 2003]. This treatment is usually initiated on specialist advice.
- **Ivermectin** given as two doses 1 week apart was more effective than a single dose in one study (95% cure rate compared with 70% cure rate after 2 weeks) [Usha and Gopalakrishnan Nair, 2000].

Treatment of itch

- **Antihistamines are of little help in treating pruritus** [Klein and Clark, 1999; DTB, 2002a].
- However, it may be useful to give a sedative oral antihistamine at night for temporary help with sleeping, to break the itch–scratch cycle.
- **Crotamiton cream or lotion has soothing qualities** and may help to relieve the itch caused by scabies, although there is no objective proof of its anti-pruritic activity.
- **Mild- or moderate-potency topical corticosteroid creams** can also be used. Avoid corticosteroid creams if the diagnosis is not certain, as they may mask signs and

S

symptoms of scabies and other skin conditions, making diagnosis more difficult.

- **If creams for itching need to be applied during the application time of the acaricide,** allow the acaricide to disappear into the skin or dry, before the cream or lotion for itch is applied.

Do children with scabies need to be kept off school?

- **The risk of transmission of scabies is low in schools,** although outbreaks do sometimes occur.
- **Children can return to school after the first application of treatment has been completed.** (Note: all family members and close contacts must be treated simultaneously, even if asymptomatic, to avoid treatment failure.)

[Health Protection Agency, 2003]

Treatment failure

- **Itching commonly persists for up to 3 weeks after successful treatment** [Roberts, 2000]. See the section *Treatment of itch* for advice about relieving itch.
- **Re-examine the person** to confirm that the diagnosis is scabies.
- **Treatment failure is likely if:**
  - The itch still persists at least 2 weeks after treatment was completed (particularly if it persists at the same intensity or is increasing in intensity).
  - Treatment was uncoordinated or not applied correctly.
  - New burrows appear at any stage after treatment.
- **If all contacts were treated simultaneously and treatment was applied correctly,** give a course of a *different* acaricide.
- **If contacts were *not* treated simultaneously or treatment was incorrectly applied,** either re-treat with the same acaricide, or use a different acaricide.
- **Ensure that *all* members of the household,** close contacts, and sexual contacts are identified and re-treated simultaneously.
- **Everyone should ideally be provided with written advice explaining the correct application method.** See the *Patient information leaflets* for further information.
- **Secondary bacterial infections** should be treated with antibiotics if significant.

Medicines management

Acaricides

- **Ensure that the correct permethrin preparation is prescribed** — use of permethrin 1% cream rinse (indicated for head lice) has been associated with treatment failure [Cox, 2000].
- **About 30 g of cream or 100 ml of liquid is needed to treat an average-sized adult for each application.**
- **Aqueous-based preparations of malathion are preferred,** since alcoholic preparations cause irritation of excoriated skin and genitalia [BNF 45, 2003].
- **Children under 2 years of age** can be treated only under medical supervision: permethrin cannot be purchased over the counter (OTC) for children aged 2 months to 2 years, while malathion is unavailable OTC for children under 6 months. A single application is usually effective [Roberts, 2000]. Note: scabies is rare in children under 2 months of age. Seek specialist advice (e.g. from a Paediatric Dermatologist) if treatment will be needed for this age group.

Treatments for itch

- **Sedating antihistamines:** antimuscarinic adverse effects (sedation, dry mouth, urinary retention, blurred vision) are common. Sedating antihistamines should therefore be avoided in someone with prostatic hypertrophy, urinary retention, or glaucoma. Advise people that drowsiness may persist the next day, and that they should not drive or operate machinery if affected. Antihistamines may also reduce the seizure threshold, and so should be avoided in someone with epilepsy.
- **Mild- or moderate- potency topical steroids:** adverse effects are uncommon, especially if steroids are used only for short periods. Potential local problems associated with excessive use may include worsening or spread of untreated infection; thinning of the skin; irreversible *striae atrophicae* and telangiectasia; contact dermatitis; or mild depigmentation.

Pregnancy and breastfeeding

- **The National Teratology Information Service currently recommends malathion** because it is poorly absorbed and rapidly eliminated [National Teratology Information Service, 1999]. A single application should be used where possible. (Telephone 0191 232 1525 for further information.)
- **Breastfeeding mothers** should remove the liquid or cream from the nipples before breastfeeding, and reapply treatment afterwards.
- **If itching is troublesome,** consider using chlorphenamine (chlorpheniramine) to break the itch–scratch cycle at night. Avoid hydroxyzine, crotamiton, and topical corticosteroid creams.

References

NHS staff in England can link, free of charge, from references to full text journals by clicking on [Full text] on the PRODIGY website.

1. BNF 45 (2003) *British National Formulary*. 45th edn. London: British Medical Association and Royal Pharmaceutical Society of Great Britain.
2. Chouela, E., Abeldano A., Pellerano, G. and Hernandez, M.I. (2002) Diagnosis and treatment of scabies: a practical guide. *American Journal of Clinical Dermatology* 3(1), 9–18.
3. Cox, N.H. (2000) Permethrin treatment in scabies infestation: importance of the correct formulation. *British Medical Journal* 320(7226), 37–38. [Full text]
4. Downs, A.M.R., Harvey, I. and Kennedy, C.T.C. (1999) The epidemiology of head lice and scabies in the UK. *Epidemiology and Infection* 122(3), 471–477.
5. DTB (2002a) Oral antihistamines for allergic disorders. *Drug & Therapeutics Bulletin* 40(8), 59–62. [Full text]
6. DTB (2002b) The management of scabies. *Drug & Therapeutics Bulletin* 40(6), 43–46.
7. Figueroa, J. (1998) Scabies. In: Figueroa, J., Hall, S., Ibarra, J. et al (Eds.) *Primary health care guide to common UK parasitic diseases*. London: Community Hygiene Concern. 25–35.
8. Hanna, N.F., Clay, J.C. and Harris, J.R. (1978) Sarcoptes scabiei infestation treated with malathion liquid. *British Journal of Venereal Diseases* 54(5), 354.
9. Health Protection Agency (2003) *Guidelines on the management of communicable diseases in schools and nurseries: scabies*. Health Protection Agency. www.hpa.org.uk [Accessed: 23/09/2003].
10. Klein, P.A. and Clark, R.A. (1999) An evidence-based review of the efficacy of antihistamines in relieving pruritus in atopic dermatitis. *Archives of Dermatology* 135(12), 1522–1525. [Full text]

11. National Teratology Information Service (1999) *Management of scabies and head lice in pregnancy.* NHS Northern and Yorkshire: Regional Drug and Therapeutics Centre.
12. Roberts, D.T. (Ed.) (2000) *Lice and scabies: a health professional's guide to epidemiology and treatment.* London: Public Health Laboratory Service.
13. Scott, G.R. (2001) European guideline for the management of scabies. *International Journal of STD & AIDS* **12**(suppl 3), 58–61. [Full text]
14. Thianprasit, M. and Schuetzenberger, R. (1984) Prioderm lotion in the treatment of scabies. *Southeast Asian Journal of Tropical Medicine and Public Health* **15**(1), 119–121.
15. Usha, V. and Gopalakrishnan Nair, T.V. (2000) A comparative study of oral ivermectin and topical permethrin cream in the treatment of scabies. *Journal of the American Academy of Dermatology* **42**(2 Pt 1), 236–240.
16. Walker, G.J.A. and Johnstone, P.W. (2003) *Interventions for treating scabies (Cochrane Review).* The Cochrane Library. Issue 3. Oxford: Update Software.

S

PRODIGY GUIDANCE

Schizophrenia

Last revised in July 2004
www.prodigy.nhs.uk/guidance.asp?gt=Schizophrenia

Applies to people over the age of 18 years

This guidance is based on the National Institute for Clinical Excellence (NICE) guideline, *Schizophrenia: full national clinical guideline and core interventions in primary and secondary care* (December 2002). It also takes into account the full guideline document produced by the National Collaborating Centre for Mental Health (2003).

This guidance covers the primary care management of schizophrenia in adults, where the onset of schizophrenia occurred before the age of 60 years. It includes starting doses of oral atypical antipsychotic drugs, and discusses the management of the adverse effects of antipsychotic drugs.

This guidance does not cover childhood-onset schizophrenia; very-late-onset schizophrenia (over 60 years of age); or schizophrenia with coexisting learning disabilities, substance misuse, or significant physical or sensory difficulties.

Goals

- Early referral of people presenting with symptoms suggestive of schizophrenia
- Early referral of people experiencing an acute episode of schizophrenia
- Identification and recording of all people with schizophrenia on a case register in primary care, to facilitate clinical audit
- Treatment with only one antipsychotic at a time
- Regular monitoring of the physical health of all people with schizophrenia by primary care

[NICE, 2002a]

Contents

Scenarios
- First acute episode of schizophrenia p.1666
- Monitoring treatment and physical health p.1668
- Managing common adverse effects p.1669
- Relapse: acute episode p.1670

Extended Information, p. 1671

Which scenario?

- **First acute episode of schizophrenia:** covers referral advice for people with suspected schizophrenia. If the individual is unlikely to be assessed by specialist mental health services for a few weeks, atypical antipsychotics are recommended as preferred treatment. Advice on choice of atypical antipsychotic is included, along with prescriptions for starting doses of atypical antipsychotics.
- **Monitoring treatment and physical health:** covers advice on physical health checks and monitoring adverse effects of drug treatment.
- **Managing common adverse effects:** covers the management of common adverse effects of drugs.
- **Relapse: acute episode:** covers referral advice for people in relapse/crisis.

S

First acute episode of schizophrenia

Which therapy?

- **All people with suspected or newly diagnosed schizophrenia should be referred urgently** to secondary mental health services for assessment and development of a care plan.
  - Refer to early intervention services, if they are available.
  - Otherwise, refer to the community mental health care team for assessment.
- **People who are at high risk of harm to self or others should be assessed within 24 hours.**
- **If crises occur out of hours,** contact the local crisis resolution team, crisis helpline, duty psychiatrist, duty social worker, or police.
- **GPs should have a high level of suspicion for schizophrenia.** If the history given by the family is suggestive of schizophrenia, discuss potential cases with the community mental health care team, even if it has not been possible to see the individual.
- **Consider starting an *atypical* antipsychotic** if there are acute symptoms of schizophrenia, but the person is unlikely to be assessed by specialist mental health services for a few weeks.
  - Discuss treatment with specialist mental health services before it is started (if possible).
  - Wherever possible, the person should make an informed choice.
  - If the person is unable to make a preference known, a atypical should be prescribed.

Factors affecting choice of atypical antipsychotic

- **Cardiovascular disease:** consider amisulpride. Avoid quetiapine, risperidone, and zotepine in ischaemic heart disease, and avoid olanzapine and risperidone in hypertension and atrial fibrillation. Avoid co-prescribing drugs that also prolong the QT interval (increased risk of arrhythmias). Risk of arrhythmias is also increased in the elderly, and in the presence of low serum potassium, calcium, or magnesium levels.
- **History of stroke or transient ischaemic attacks:** avoid risperidone and olanzapine.
- **Epilepsy:** use low starting doses and increase the dose slowly. Avoid amisulpride.
- **Diabetes mellitus:** avoid olanzapine, risperidone, and possibly quetiapine.
- **Angle-closure glaucoma or prostatic hypertrophy:** avoid olanzapine.

Practical prescribing points

For further information please see the *Medicines Compendium* (www.medicines.org.uk) or the *British National Formulary* (www.bnf.org).

- **Elderly:** higher risk of postural hypotension, extrapyramidal symptoms, and antimuscarinic effects, especially when starting therapy. Start with a lower dose and titrate slowly.

- **Driving:** the person with scizophrenia must stop driving and inform the Driving and Vehicle Licensing Agency. Consider breaking patient confidentiality if the person will not stop driving (e.g. because of lack of insight).
- **Alcohol:** advise people with schizophrenia to avoid alcohol, as it increases adverse effects of drugs (for example, sedation).

Follow-up advice

- People presenting with an acute episode of schizophrenia should be followed up urgently by specialist mental health services.

Should I refer or investigate?

Refer?

- **Anyone with suspected or newly diagnosed schizophrenia should be referred urgently** to secondary mental health services for assessment and development of a care plan.
- **Refer to early intervention services,** if they are available.
- **If the person is acutely disturbed or at high risk,** refer to crisis-resolution/home-treatment teams, acute day hospitals, or in-patient services. (Note: availability of services will vary locally.)

Patient information leaflets

The following PILs are available at www.prodigy.nhs.uk

- Medicines - Name Changes of Medicines
- Schizophrenia
- Schizophrenia Association of GB

Shared decision making

- Your symptoms indicate that you may have schizophrenia.
- It is usual to be referred to a specialist in mental health.
- You are likely to be advised to take medication to relieve the symptoms. Usually one of the following is prescribed: amisulpride, olanzapine, quetiapine, or risperidone.

Drug rationale

Drugs not included

- **Typical antipsychotics** are not included, as they are not recommended by the National Institute for Clinical Excellence (NICE) as preferred choice of treatment when therapy is being initiated by a GP [NICE, 2002a].
- **Clozapine** is indicated only for treatment-resistant schizophrenia. It can be started only by specialist mental health services. Intensive full blood count monitoring is required because of the rare but extremely serious risk of agranulocytosis [BNF 44, 2002].
- **Sertindole** is restricted to use by people enrolled in clinical trials, following reports of arrhythmias and sudden cardiac death [EMEA, 2002].
- **Zotepine** is not included. In people at risk of arrhythmias, it requires an electrocardiogram before treatment and at every dose increase [BNF 44, 2002]. This is unlikely to be practical in the primary care setting.

Drugs included

- **The atypical antipsychotics amisulpride, olanzapine, quetiapine, and risperidone are included.**
- NICE recommends that where there are acute symptoms of schizophrenia, the GP should consider starting an *atypical* antipsychotic drug at the earliest opportunity This can be before the person sees the psychiatrist; but, wherever possible, it should be started only following discussion with a psychiatrist, and referral should be a matter of urgency [NICE, 2002a].
- **Where more than one atypical antipsychotic is appropriate, the drug with the lowest cost per day should be prescribed** [NICE, 2002b]. Amisulpride and risperidone are the least expensive at initiation doses, and at average maintenance doses [Taylor et al, 2003].
- Consider a lower starting dose of olanzapine (5 mg once a day) in people with more than one 'risk factor' for slow olanzapine metabolism, to reduce the risk of adverse effects (for example, for a female non-smoker).

Prescriptions

Start atypical while awaiting referral (1-week supply)

Amisulpride 200mg twice a day

- Age from 18 years onwards
- Amisulpride 200mg tablets. Take one tablet twice a day; supply 14 tablets; NHS Cost £14.32.

Olanzapine 5mg once a day (low dose)

- Age from 18 years onwards
- Olanzapine 5mg tablets. Take one tablet once a day; supply 7 tablets; NHS Cost £12.20.

Olanzapine 10mg once a day

- Age from 18 years onwards
- Olanzapine 10mg tablets. Take one tablet once a day; supply 7 tablets; NHS Cost £19.86.

Quetiapine: titrate from 25mg to 150mg twice a day in 4 days

- Age from 18 years onwards
- Quetiapine 25mg tablets. Take 1 tab twice a day on day 1, take 2 tabs twice a day on day 2, take 4 tabs twice a day on day 3. Start taking the quetiapine 150mg tabs on day 4; supply 14 tablets; NHS Cost £6.58.
- Quetiapine 150mg tablets. Start, once the quetiapine 25mg tablets are finished. Take one tablet twice a day; supply 8 tablets; NHS Cost £15.08.

Risperidone: 2mg once a day for 1 day, then 4mg once a day

- Age from 18 years onwards
- Risperidone 2mg tablets. Take one tablet once a day for 1 day, then take two tablets once a day; supply 13 tablets; NHS Cost £14.88.

S

Continue atypical while awaiting referral (2-week supply)

Amisulpride 200mg twice a day

- Age from 18 years onwards
- Amisulpride 200mg tablets. Take one tablet twice a day; supply 30 tablets; NHS Cost £33.69.

Olanzapine 5mg once a day (low dose)

- Age from 18 years onwards
- Olanzapine 5mg tablets. Take one tablet once a day; supply 14 tablets; NHS Cost £24.39.

Olanzapine 10mg once a day

- Age from 18 years onwards
- Olanzapine 10mg tablets. Take one tablet once a day; supply 14 tablets; NHS Cost £39.73.

Quetiapine 150mg twice a day

- Age from 18 years onwards
- Quetiapine 150mg tablets. Take one tablet twice a day; supply 30 tablets; NHS Cost £56.55.

Quetiapine 200mg twice a day

- Age from 18 years onwards
- Quetiapine 200mg tablets. Take one tablet twice a day; supply 30 tablets; NHS Cost £56.55.

Risperidone 4mg once a day

- Age from 18 years onwards
- Risperidone 4mg tablets. Take one tablet once a day; supply 14 tablets; NHS Cost £31.11.

Monitoring treatment and physical health

Which therapy?

Monitoring physical health

- **Check physical health annually** (owing to the high risk of coronary heart disease [CHD]).
- **Check blood pressure.** If raised, treat hypertension, and also screen for diabetes and hyperlipidaemia.
- **Calculate 10-year risk of CHD.** If 10-year risk of CHD is >30%, or the person already has CHD:
  - Offer low-dose aspirin.
  - Screen for hyperlipidaemia (if not already done) and treat if present.
- **Check urine/blood glucose** (to exclude diabetes).
- **Offer advice about smoking cessation, healthy diet, and exercise.** Advice should be personalized and achievable.

Monitoring adverse effects of drug treatment

- **Ask about adverse effects** (for example extrapyramidal symptoms, tardive dyskinesia, sexual dysfunction).
- **Monitor weight,** particularly if taking olanzapine.
- **Consider using Liverpool University Neuroleptic Side Effects Rating Scale (LUNSERS)** to assess severity of adverse effects. This is available as a Patient Information Leaflet or from http://www.symplexsoftware.com/lunsers.asp (Before using LUNSERS the authors require that you register your usage.)
- **Check electrocardiogram if taking a drug or dose with a higher risk of QT prolongation,** e.g. sertindole, thioridazine, zotepine, high-dose haloperidol (>20 mg per day), or a dose of any antipsychotic that is above the *British National Formulary* upper limit.
- **Ask about alcohol and illicit drug use.** People with suspected substance-misuse problems should be re-referred to specialist mental health services.

S

Practical prescribing points

For further information please see the *Medicines Compendium* (www.medicines.org.uk) or the *British National Formulary* (www.bnf.org).

If neuroleptic malignant syndrome suspected:

- Stop treatment and refer urgently to Accident and Emergency. Inform care co-ordinator.
- Symptoms include hyperthermia, muscle rigidity, autonomic instability, and fluctuating consciousness.

Follow-up advice

- Check blood pressure and calculate coronary heart disease risk annually in all people with schizophrenia.

Should I refer or investigate?

Refer?

- **The decision to re-refer a person with schizophrenia should take account of the person's view, and, where** appropriate, the carer's. Issues of confidentiality should be respected when involving carers.
- **Consider referral if:**
  - They are at increased risk of harm to themselves or others (referral should be urgent)
  - They are showing symptoms of relapse (some people have very specific 'relapse signatures', and these should be documented in the care plan)
  - They are not responding well to treatment
  - They are not taking their treatment, or you suspect this
  - You suspect they are misusing alcohol or drugs
  - The features of the episode differ from those of previous episodes
  - They require a second opinion
  - They have just joined the practice (for formal assessment and development of a care plan)
  - You feel that you cannot meet the individual's needs
  - The family or carer is not coping

Investigate?

- **Check blood pressure and urine/blood glucose annually.**
- **People with raised blood pressure:** screen for hyperlipidaemia.
- **People taking olanzapine:** monitor weight.

Patient information leaflets

The following PILs are available at www.prodigy.nhs.uk

- Medicines - Name Changes of Medicines
- Schizophrenia
- Schizophrenia Association of GB

Shared decision making

- **Do you have any symptoms that may be side effects to your medication?** In particular:
  - Feeling drowsy
  - Abnormal movements of your lips, tongue, face, legs, or arms
  - Dry mouth
  - Constipation
  - Flushing
  - Agitation or difficulty sleeping
  - Restless legs or feeling generally restless
  - Sexual problems
  - Weight gain
- **If you take olanzapine or quetiapine,** you will need a blood test every so often.
- **Do you smoke?** If so, have you considered stopping?
- **Do you take much exercise?** Regular exercise helps to prevent heart disease. Even a brisk 30-minute walk each day is good.
- **Do you eat a healthy diet?** If not, would you like some advice on foods?
- **Are you taking any illegal drugs or much alcohol?**

Drug rationale

- No prescriptions are offered in this scenario.

Managing common adverse effects

Which therapy?

REFERRAL IS RECOMMENDED WHERE SWITCHING DRUGS IS REQUIRED.

Extrapyramidal symptoms

Dystonia or Parkinsonism: co-prescribe an antimuscarinic drug (e.g. procyclidine). Withdraw antimuscarinic 2–3 months after symptoms have improved.
Akathisia: reduce the dose, or use propranolol or metoprolol (unless contraindicated).
Alternatively, switch to a drug that is less likely to cause extrapyramidal symptoms (e.g. clozapine, amisulpride, quetiapine, olanzapine, or low-dose risperidone [<6 mg per day]).

Factors affecting choice of treatment for extrapyramidal symptoms

Angle-closure glaucoma or benign prostatic hypertrophy: do not use antimuscarinics.
Asthma or a history of bronchospasm: do not use beta-blockers (Committee on Safety of Medicines warning).
Heart failure or severe peripheral vascular disease: do not use propranolol or metoprolol.
Diabetes: use metoprolol (cardioselective), not propranolol for akathisia. Avoid beta-blockers in people who experience frequent hypoglycaemia. Advise people that beta-blockers may slightly raise their blood glucose levels, and that their response to hypoglycaemia may be delayed or symptoms of hypoglycaemia may not occur in the usual way.

Tardive dyskinesia

Consider withdrawing antimuscarinic drugs; this sometimes improves tardive dyskinesia (TD).
Consider reducing the dose of antipsychotic.
Consider referring for switching to clozapine (or possibly olanzapine or quetiapine).

Other adverse effects

Sedation: lower the dose, or consider switching to amisulpride, risperidone, sulpiride, or haloperidol.
Weight gain: offer practical advice and support on healthy eating and exercise. Amisulpride, haloperidol, or trifluoperazine are least likely to affect weight, but weight gain can still occur.
Hyperprolactinaemia: consider switching to olanzapine or quetiapine.
Postural hypotension: tolerance usually develops. Use low doses, and increase slowly.
Antimuscarinic effects: common with most antipsychotics, but tolerance often develops.
Photosensitivity: common with chlorpromazine and phenothiazines. Advise people to avoid strong sunlight, and to use a sunscreen (some high-factor sunscreens are available on FP10).

Practical prescribing points

For further information please see the *Medicines Compendium* (www.medicines.org.uk) or the *British National Formulary* (www.bnf.org).
Alcohol: advise the person to avoid alcohol, as it increases adverse effects of drugs (e.g. sedation).
If neuroleptic malignant syndrome suspected:

- Stop treatment and refer urgently to Accident and Emergency. Inform care co-ordinator.
- Symptoms include hyperthermia, muscle rigidity, autonomic instability, and fluctuating consciousness.

Should I refer or investigate?

Refer?

The decision to re-refer a person with schizophrenia should take account of the person's view, and, where appropriate, the carer's. Issues of confidentiality should be respected when involving carers.

- **Consider referral if:**
  - They are at increased risk of harm to themselves or others (referral should be urgent)
  - They are showing symptoms of relapse (some people have very specific 'relapse signatures', and these should be documented in the care plan)
  - They are not responding well to treatment
  - They are not taking their treatment, or you suspect this
  - You suspect they are misusing alcohol or drugs
  - The features of the episode differ from those of previous episodes
  - They require a second opinion
  - They have just joined the practice (for formal assessment and development of a care plan)
  - You feel that you cannot meet the individual's needs
  - The family or carer is not coping

Patient information leaflets

The following PILs are available at www.prodigy.nhs.uk

- Medicines - Name Changes of Medicines
- Schizophrenia
- Schizophrenia Association of GB

Shared decision making

- **Do you have any symptoms that may be side effects to your medication?** In particular:
  - Feeling drowsy
  - Abnormal movements of your lips, tongue, face, legs, or arms
  - Dry mouth
  - Constipation
  - Flushing
  - Agitation or difficulty sleeping
  - Restless legs or feeling generally restless
  - Sexual problems
  - Weight gain
- **If you take olanzapine or quetiapine,** you will need a blood test every so often.
- **Do you smoke?** If so, have you considered stopping?
- **Do you take much exercise?** Regular exercise helps to prevent heart disease. Even a brisk 30-minute walk each day is good.
- **Do you eat a healthy diet?** If not, would you like some advice on foods?
- **Are you taking any illegal drugs or much alcohol?**

Drug rationale

Drugs not included

- **Antimuscarinic drugs other than procyclidine** (biperiden, trihexyphenidyl [benzhexol], and orphenadrine) are not widely used in the UK. In addition, orphenadrine appears to be more toxic in overdose than do other antimuscarinic drugs [Bazire, 2001].

S

- **Beta-blockers other than propranolol and metoprolol:** betaxolol has shown some benefit in treating akathisia [Holloman and Marder, 1997]. However, it is less widely used in the UK than propranolol or metoprolol.

Drugs included

- **Antimuscarinic drugs: procyclidine** is offered at standard dose to relieve dystonia or Parkinsonism.
- **Antimuscarinic drugs should be withdrawn 2–3 months after symptoms resolve,** as their adverse effects increase cognitive deficit.
- **Beta-blockers: propranolol or metoprolol** (if not contraindicated) are included as options for controlling akathisia [Holloman and Marder, 1997].
- **An advice note with brief advice on healthy eating and exercise** is also included, to assist people suffering from weight gain. More detailed advice can be found in the Patient Information Leaflets.

Prescriptions

Dystonia or parkinsonism: procyclidine

Procyclidine 5mg three times a day
- Age from 18 years onwards
- Procyclidine 5mg tablets. Take one tablet three times a day; supply 84 tablets; NHS Cost £4.95.

Akathisia: propranolol or metoprolol

Propranolol 10mg three times a day
- Age from 18 years onwards
- Propranolol 10mg tablets. Take one tablet three times a day; supply 84 tablets; NHS Cost £3.75.

Propranolol 20mg three times a day
- Age from 18 years onwards
- Propranolol 10mg tablets. Take two tablets three times a day; supply 168 tablets; NHS Cost £7.50.

Metoprolol 50mg twice a day
- Age from 18 years onwards
- Metoprolol 50mg tablets. Take one tablet twice a day; supply 56 tablets; NHS Cost £1.83.

Metoprolol 50mg three times a day
- Age from 18 years onwards
- Metoprolol 50mg tablets. Take one tablet three times a day; supply 84 tablets; NHS Cost £4.71.

Advice note: preventing weight gain

Advice only: healthy eating and exercise
- Age from 16 years onwards
- Exercise and a healthy diet can help with weight loss, and also helps to prevent heart disease. Exercise does not have to be sport. Taking the stairs instead of the lift, and walking instead of using the bus or car are both easy ways to increase the amount of exercise you do. For a healthier diet, try to eat: MORE vegetables, fruit, cereals, wholegrain bread, poultry, fish, rice, skimmed or semi-skimmed milk, grilled food, lean meat, pasta etc. LESS fatty meats, fatty cheeses, full cream milk, fried food, lard, etc. If you do fry, choose a vegetable oil such as sunflower or rapeseed. Use low fat spreads. Add less salt to food, and avoid foods that are very salty. Avoid fizzy drinks as these contain a lot of sugar.

Relapse — acute episode

Which therapy?

- **Details of the action to take in relapse should be in the person's care plan.**
- If it is not in the care plan, refer to the community mental health care team.
- **If a crisis occurs out of hours,** contact the local crisis resolution team, crisis helpline, duty psychiatrist, duty social worker, or police.
- **People who are at high risk of self-harm or harm to others should be assessed within 24 hours.**

Practical prescribing points

For further information please see the *Medicines Compendium* (www.medicines.org.uk) or the *British National Formulary* (www.bnf.org).

- **If an antipsychotic is needed before the person is likely t see specialist mental health services (SMHS), consider:**
  - Increasing the dose of the current antipsychotic (provided the increase is still within *British National Formulary* limits).
  - Changing to a different antipsychotic. Consider an atypical antipsychotic for a person who has relapsed on a typical antipsychotic drug.
  - Restarting a drug that has previously been successful.
- **Where possible, discuss with SMHS before undertaking any changes to treatment.** In particular, do NOT stop antipsychotic drugs abruptly. Seek advice from SMHS on cross-tapering antipsychotic drugs.
- **Driving:** the person must stop driving and inform the Driving and Vehicle Licensing Agency. Consider breaking patient confidentiality if the person will not stop driving (e.g. because of lack of insight).
- **Alcohol:** advise the person to avoid alcohol, as it increases the adverse effects of drugs (e.g. sedation).

Follow-up advice

- People presenting with an acute episode of schizophren should be followed up urgently by specialist mental health services.

Should I refer or investigate?

Refer?

- **Details of the action to take in relapse should be in the person's care plan.**
- If it is not in the care plan, refer to the community mental health care team.
- **If a crisis occurs out of hours,** contact the local crisis resolution team, crisis helpline, duty psychiatrist, duty social worker, or police.
- **People who are high risk of self-harm or harm to others should be assessed within 24 hours.**

Patient information leaflets

The following PILs are available at www.prodigy.nhs.uk
- Medicines - Name Changes of Medicines
- Schizophrenia
- Schizophrenia Association of GB

Shared decision making

- Your symptoms are bad at present.
- It is usual to be referred to a specialist in mental health.
- Altering medication may be an option while you are waiting to see a specialist.

Drug rationale

- Changes to treatment should be discussed with speciali mental health services before being undertaken.
- No prescriptions are offered in this scenario.

S

Extended Information

Background information

What is schizophrenia? p.1671
What is the course of schizophrenia? p.1671
How common is it? p.1671
What are the risk factors for developing schizophrenia? p.1671
How do I know my patient has it? p.1672
What are positive and negative symptoms? p.1672
What else might it be? p.1673
Complications and prognosis p.1673

What is schizophrenia?

Schizophrenia is a severe mental illness of unknown cause that is characterized by the presence of hallucinations, delusions, disordered thought, and problems with feelings, behaviour, motivation, and speech.

Every individual's experience of schizophrenia is different.

Affected individuals often present acutely with delusions and hallucinations, and occasionally disturbances of thought, such as paranoia and thought insertion (these are often referred to as positive symptoms) [American Psychiatric Association, 2000].

Acute episodes are usually followed by a more chronic illness where the person has a lack of interest in social interactions, reduced motivation, reduced emotions, and reduced speech (often referred to as negative symptoms) [Stefan et al, 2002].

Schizophrenia is often preceded by a long prodromal period with a range of ill-defined, insidious, and non-specific symptoms that result in a gradual deterioration in personal functioning. Symptoms could include peculiar or uncharacteristic behaviour, poor communication, unusual ideation, social withdrawal, poor personal hygiene, and reduced interest and motivation [National Collaborating Centre for Mental Health, 2003].

Many people can present to primary care with these types of symptoms, but most do not go on to develop schizophrenia.

Of the minority who do develop schizophrenia, some will develop 'attenuated' positive symptoms first (e.g. mild thought disorders, ideas of reference, suspiciousness, odd beliefs, and perceptual distortion). Attenuated positive symptoms are milder than those seen in established schizophrenia [National Collaborating Centre for Mental Health, 2003].

What is the course of schizophrenia?

Many people with schizophrenia will have long periods of good functioning, with occasional relapses.

The biggest decline in function occurs in the first 5–10 years of illness: generally there are several exacerbations of positive symptoms, followed by a more stable phase. (For a detailed description of positive symptoms, see *What are positive and negative symptoms?*)

About two-thirds of people experience an episodic pattern of schizophrenia. The number of episodes and extent of recovery between episodes can vary. For example, a person may have:

- Only one episode of illness, followed by complete recovery
- Occasional episodes of illness, with periods of complete recovery in between
- Occasional episodes of illness, but never recover fully in between

- **About a third of people experience a more continuous illness,** where they are never free of symptoms, although the severity of symptoms fluctuates over time.

[Mason et al, 1996; Stefan et al, 2002]

How common is it?

- **About 1% of the population experience at least one acute episode of schizophrenia at some time during their lives.**
- **The incidence of new cases** of schizophrenia is 1–2 per 10,000 population per year.
- **Men and women are at equal risk** of developing schizophrenia, although affected men tend to develop schizophrenia 3–4 years earlier than do affected women.
- **The peak age of onset** is in the late teens and early twenties for men, and in the later twenties for women. Women have a second peak in incidence in their late forties.

[Jablensky et al, 1992; Stefan et al, 2002]

What are the risk factors for developing schizophrenia?

- **Schizophrenia does not have one single cause.** It is thought to be triggered by a combination of both genetic and environmental factors.
- **The most important risk factor for schizophrenia is having an affected relative.**
- **As only about half of all monozygotic twins of an individual with schizophrenia also develop schizophrenia, other factors must also have a role in triggering schizophrenia.**
- **A 'stress-vulnerability' model has been proposed** to explain why there seem to be so many different triggers of schizophrenia, and so many different rates of relapse and remission among people with schizophrenia [National Collaborating Centre for Mental Health, 2003]:
  - People with a genetic vulnerability to schizophrenia only develop it in the presence of other environmental stressors.
  - If vulnerability is great, only low levels of environmental stress are needed to trigger schizophrenia.
  - Conversely, if vulnerability is low, a high level of environmental stress can be experienced before schizophrenia is triggered.

Table 1: Lifetime risk of schizophrenia in the relatives of people with schizophrenia.

Relationship to person with schizophrenia	Lifetime risk of developing schizophrenia (%)
Child of one affected parent	13
Child of two affected parents	46
Monozygotic twin	48
Dizygotic twin	13
Sibling	10
Sibling, and also has one affected parent	17
Parent	6
Uncle/aunt/nephew/niece	3
Grandchild	4
Unrelated	1

S

Early environmental risk factors

- People who present with schizophrenia before the age of 25 years are twice as likely to have had complications at birth than is the case in the general population.
- Schizophrenia is more common among those born in the late winter and early spring.
- Children who later go on to develop schizophrenia show early motor, language, and cognitive abnormalities compared with their peers or siblings. However, only a small number of all the children with developmental abnormalities will later develop schizophrenia.

Later environmental risk factors

- Heavy cannabis consumers are six times more likely to develop schizophrenia than are non-users.
- Many other drugs of abuse, such as amphetamines, cocaine, ketamine, and lysergic acid diethylamide (LSD), can induce an acute schizophrenia-like illness.
- Adverse life events can also contribute to schizophrenia (although to a smaller extent than in depression). Unlike in depression, all kinds of life events appear to be important, not just those involving loss.
- People who have migrated to the UK from other countries show an increased rate of schizophrenia compared with both the population that they have left, and the general UK population. For example, the incidence of schizophrenia is 2–3 times higher in Afro-Caribbean people who have migrated to the UK. The impact of the new environment, social isolation, and alienation are probably the crucial factors that trigger schizophrenia in vulnerable individuals.

[Stefan et al, 2002]

How do I know my patient has it?

- **Many different mental illnesses have overlapping symptoms,** and it can be difficult to tell the conditions apart.
- **Reaching a diagnosis can be difficult,** and it takes time to be sure that the individual's symptoms truly indicate schizophrenia.
- **Diagnosis depends on establishing the presence and time course of certain characteristic features.** The DSM-IV (Diagnostic and Statistical Manual of Mental Disorders, 4th Edition) and ICD-10 (International Classification of Diseases — WHO) criteria are often used in the UK to aid diagnosis [WHO, 1992; American Psychiatric Association, 2000].
- Note: for further information on delusions, hallucinations, thought disorders, and negative symptoms, see *What are positive and negative symptoms?*

[Andreasen et al, 2000; Liddle, 2002; Rethink, 2003b]

What are positive and negative symptoms?

Positive symptoms

- Positive symptoms reflect the presence of an abnormal mental process.
- Hallucinations, delusions, and thought disorders are positive symptoms.

Hallucinations

- **Hallucinations are false perceptions** that occur in the absence of a real external stimulus [Stefan et al, 2002]. However, they are *perceived* to be real by the person with schizophrenia.
- **Many people with schizophrenia experience auditory hallucinations.** Voices are the most common. These can be muttering voices or clear conversations.
- Some people experience voices that provide a running commentary on their actions, argue about the person, or repeat the person's thoughts. Others hear whistling, or machinery sounds.
- Hearing voices is a real experience, and may be due to a disorder of inner speech (thinking in words). Positron emission tomography (PET) studies have asked people with schizophrenia who have auditory hallucinations to imagine someone else speaking. These people were foun to have less activity in the areas of the brain concerned with the monitoring of inner speech than is the case wit people with schizophrenia who do not have auditory hallucinations [McGuire et al, 1995].
- **Visual, smell, taste, or tactile hallucinations can also occur.** Note: visual hallucinations occur in about 10% o people with schizophrenia, but organic disorders shoul be excluded. Olfactory hallucinations are more commo in temporal lobe epilepsy than in schizophrenia.

Delusions

- **A delusion is a fixed, false, personal belief** held with absolute conviction despite evidence to the contrary [Stefan et al, 2002].
- Some people have delusions that do not seem to be connected with any previous events or experiences (primary delusions). For instance, 'I woke up and knew that my daughter was the spawn of Satan and should d so that my son could be the new Messiah.'
- Others have delusions that relate to their hallucinations (secondary delusions) and try to make sense of what th are experiencing. For instance, 'voices' may be thought to come from the television, or they could be thought to be magic, or given a religious explanation.
- **Delusions can take many forms:** persecutory, controllin telepathic, grandiose, religious, science-fiction, paranormal, or somatic.
- Some people have delusions about infidelity (their partner is always being unfaithful); doubles (a person known to them — often their spouse — has been

Table 2: Comparison of the DSM-IV and ICD-10 operational diagnostic criteria for schizophrenia.

	DSM-IV	ICD-10
Characteristic symptoms (1 required)	Bizarre delusions (primary or secondary delusions) Voices commenting or conversing	Thought echo/insertion/ withdrawal/ broadcasti Delusions of control, delusional perception Voices commenting or discussing; or coming from a part of the body Persistent impossible delusions
OR **less specific symptoms** (2 required)	Other delusions Other hallucinations Disorganized speech Grossly disorganized or catatonic behaviour Negative symptoms	Other persistent hallucinations Thought-form disorder Catatonia Negative symptoms Significant personality change
AND social/ occupational dysfunction	One or more major areas of dysfunction (work, occupation, interpersonal)	—
AND duration of symptoms	Overt symptoms for 1 month (unless treated) *and* prodromal or residual features for at least 6 months	Overt symptoms for 1 month (most of the time
Exclusions	Dominant mood symptoms Schizo-affective disorder Physiological effects of substance use Organic cause of symptoms	Dominant mood symptoms Schizo-affective disorde Drug intoxication or withdrawal Overt brain disease

replaced by someone else); or infatuation (another person is in love with them).

Disorders of thought possession

Thought insertion is the belief that the thoughts in a person's head are not the person's own, and that they are being put there by an outside agency.

Thought withdrawal occurs when someone believes that thoughts are being removed from the person's mind by an outside agency.

Thought broadcasting occurs when the person believes that thoughts are being 'read' or 'heard' by others.

Thought blocking involves a sudden interruption of the train of thought before it is completed, leaving a blank. The person suddenly stops talking and cannot recall what he or she has been saying.

Other thought disorders

Thought echo is the term used to describe when the person hears his or her own thoughts as if they were being spoken aloud.

Disordered forms of thought can make speech incoherent, and it may not seem to follow a logical sequence.

'Knight's-move thinking' occurs when the person moves from one train of thought to another that has no apparent connection to the first.

Some people may invent new words (neologisms), repeat a single word or phrase out of context (verbal stereotypy), or use ordinary words with a different, special meaning (metonyms) [Stefan et al, 2002].

Negative symptoms

Negative symptoms reflect the reduction or absence of a mental function that is normally present.

They are much less dramatic than positive symptoms, but tend to be more persistent, and are harder to treat.

They are the most important cause of long-term disability.

People with negative symptoms may:

- Talk less spontaneously (poverty of speech)
- Express and/or experience less emotion (flattening of affect)
- Have less energy, drive, and interest (avolition-apathy)
- Become less able to concentrate (attentional impairment)
- Become indifferent to social contact (anhedonia-asociality)
- Be happy to stay up all night and sleep all day
- Have abnormal body language

Over half of all people with schizophrenia have a significant degree of negative symptoms, although it can be difficult to tell whether these are primary symptoms, or secondary to florid positive symptoms, or adverse effects of medication.

Often families only realize with hindsight that their relative's behaviour has been changing subtly over a period. Recognizing these changes can be particularly difficult if the illness develops during the teenage years when it is quite normal for changes in behaviour to occur.

Secondary symptoms

It is important to remember that the secondary symptoms accompanying schizophrenia, such as depression and demoralization, may in themselves be disabling.

Concurrent depression increases the risk of suicide in people with schizophrenia [Tandon and Jibson, 2003].

The reaction of the family members and friends will also have some impact, if through misunderstanding they think that their relative is fantasizing, seeking attention, or simply lying.

[Andreasen et al, 2000; Stefan et al, 2002; Rethink, 2003c]

What else might it be?

Other functional disorders

- Schizo-affective disorder: this occurs where both schizophrenia and affective symptoms (depression or mania) develop *together*, even if the symptoms of schizophrenia would be severe enough on their own to warrant a diagnosis of schizophrenia.
- Schizotypal disorder: people present with eccentric behaviour, unusual thinking, and disturbed affect, features that resemble those seen in schizophrenia, although no definite and characteristic symptoms of schizophrenia have occurred at any stage.
- Dual diagnosis: people present with both symptoms of schizophrenia and a drug or alcohol misuse problem.
- Persistent delusional disorders
- Acute and transient psychotic disorders
- Depression with psychotic symptoms
- Mania

Organic disorders

- Misuse of alcohol or illicit drugs, such as amphetamines, cocaine, ketamine, and lysergic acid diethylamide (LSD)
- Epilepsy, particularly temporal lobe epilepsy
- Stroke
- Early dementia
- Brain tumour
- Brain damage, following head injury or surgery
- Endocrine causes (e.g. Cushing's disease, rarely thyroid disorders)
- Central nervous system infections (e.g. encephalitis, meningitis, neurosyphilis)

[WHO, 1992; Stefan et al, 2002; Rethink, 2003b]

Complications and prognosis

Complications

Social disability

- **Negative symptoms are often the major cause of social disability for people with schizophrenia.**
- A recent UK survey found that nearly two-thirds of adults with schizophrenia had difficulty in at least one activity of daily living [Foster et al, 1996]. Half of all adults were unable to work, and only 19% of people surveyed were in employment.
- **Negative symptoms can also lead to difficulty with education,** which can contribute to difficulties with employment.
- **People may also have problems with relationships,** as their communication skills are impaired by their negative symptoms.

Substance misuse

- **Between 9–35% of people with schizophrenia in the UK misuse alcohol or drugs** [Menezes et al, 1996; Stefan et al, 2002].
- **Helping these people is extremely difficult,** as most interventions give little benefit while people are using psychomimetic drugs. In addition these people often default from treatment programmes, or do not adhere to their treatment, owing to their chaotic lifestyle.

Excess mortality

- **Schizophrenia is associated with a high mortality.**
- **About 30% of people with schizophrenia attempt suicide at least once,** and 1 in 10 people with schizophrenia successfully commit suicide.

- The risk is higher in males and in people under 45 years of age, although all people with schizophrenia are at higher risk of suicide. Other factors that increase this risk include depression, feelings of hopelessness, unemployment, and recent hospital discharge [American Psychiatric Association, 2000].
- **People with schizophrenia die on average 10 years earlier than the general population,** but suicide accounts for only 10% of deaths.
- Cardiovascular disease and/or diabetes are responsible for many of these excess deaths.
- Between 60–90% of people with schizophrenia smoke. This is 2–3 times higher than the smoking rate in the general population.
- Cardiovascular disease is more common in people with schizophrenia than would be expected in the general population. This is likely to be due largely to the poor lifestyle of many people with schizophrenia: smoking, obesity, and a poor diet are common [Brown et al, 1999].
- Type 2 diabetes is also more common in people with schizophrenia. Drug treatment with antipsychotics may also increase this risk, although a causal relationship has not been firmly established. Both typical and atypical antipsychotic drugs have been associated with an increased risk of diabetes, but the risk seems to be highest with clozapine and olanzapine [Sernyak et al, 2002; Lean and Pajonk, 2003].

Prognosis

- **About 20% of people who are admitted to hospital for their first episode of schizophrenia do not have another acute episode,** and about 25% have no further admissions [Mason et al, 1996].
- **About 50% of people with schizophrenia treated in standard services will relapse** and require re-admission within the first two years of their illness [Mason et al, 1996].
- **Another 30% of people experience a more continuous illness,** where they are never free of symptoms, although the severity of symptoms changes over time.
- **Around 20% of people remain completely resistant to drug treatment,** including clozapine.

Factors associated with a poor prognosis

- Early or insidious onset of schizophrenia
- Male gender
- Negative symptoms
- Family history of schizophrenia
- Alcohol or drug misuse
- Low IQ, low social class, or social isolation
- Significant past psychiatric history

Most people experience active psychotic symptoms for 1–2 years before obtaining treatment. Longer periods of untreated symptoms are associated with a lower likelihood of remission, so early identification and referral is important.

[Barnes and Pant, 2002; Stefan et al, 2002; Rethink, 2003a]

Management issues

- Role of the Primary Health Care Team p.1674
- Specialist mental health services p.1674
- Managing the different stages of schizophrenia p.1675
- Treatments used by specialist mental health services p.1677
- Medicines management p.1679

Role of the Primary Health Care Team

- **Early identification and rapid referral of people experiencing an acute episode of schizophrenia.** For mos people, the level of distress, anxiety, and subjective confusion they experience, especially during first episodes, leads to difficulty in accessing services [NICE, 2002a].
- Monitoring the physical health of people with schizophrenia.
- Monitoring the adverse effects of antipsychotic drugs.
- Monitoring the mental health of people with schizophrenia so that they are rapidly re-referred to mental health services if they experience further acute episodes.
- Around 25% of people with schizophrenia receive all or most of their psychiatric care from their GP [Kendrick e al, 1995]. Therefore, many interventions discussed in th guidance as being the responsibility of specialist mental health services will be the responsibility of the GP.

Working in partnership with people with schizophrenia

- **Take time to build a supportive and empathic relationship with the people themselves and their carers.** This should be regarded as an essential element of the routine care offered [NICE, 2002a].
- Avoid using clinical language.
- **Schizophrenia may affect a person's ability to make judgements,** to recognize that they are ill, to comprehen clearly what professionals might say to them, and to make informed decisions about their treatment and care
- **It is important to give adequate time for discussion and to provide written information,** so that the person can give meaningful and properly informed consent before treatment is initiated.

Working in partnership with carers

- **The families of people with schizophrenia often play an essential part in the treatment and care of their relative,** and with the right support and help can positively contribute to promoting recovery [NICE, 2002a].
- Good-quality information about schizophrenia and its treatment should be available to the people themselves and their families.
- **Carers should be provided with information about loca family or carer support programmes.** These are often ru by local branches of charities such as Mind (www.mind.org), and Re-think (www.rethink.org). Some local specialist mental health services may also have carer support groups. However, not all areas have carer support programmes yet.
- **Carers should also have their needs assessed** [DH, 1999 This is often arranged by specialist mental health services, as they are best placed to provide support, and a carer may not necessarily have the same GP as the person with schizophrenia does. However, all carers are entitled to an assessment by social services, irrespective of whether the person is being treated by specialist mental health services or by their GP.

Specialist mental health services

- **Co-ordinated care is delivered using the care programm approach (CPA).** The CPA is a holistic approach that aims to assess, treat, and support people with schizophrenia in the community, rather than during an in-patient stay. It is based on four principles [DH, 2002b]:
  - **Assessment** (including an assessment of risk to self an others).
  - **Allocation of a care co-ordinator** (or 'key worker').

- **Development of a care plan.** This should include all the arrangements for follow-up, responsibility for physical health checks, and the arrangements for social group activities and physical activities. It may also include advance directives covering the action to be taken in the event of specific circumstances (e.g. relapse).
- **Review.**

***Multidisciplinary* teams deliver this care** (e.g. community mental health teams, early intervention teams, assertive outreach teams, and crisis resolution/home treatment teams). These teams specialize in more intensive and comprehensive treatment to enable many people who would previously have been treated as in-patients to be treated in the community.

However, many people with schizophrenia have complex health and social care needs that cannot all be met by one team. 'Enhanced' CPA is used to co-ordinate care between all the different agencies involved.

The care co-ordinator is the main mechanism of managing and integrating an individual's care between all specialist mental health services, social services, and primary care (GPP). The care co-ordinator is often a nurse, but can also be the social worker, or occupational therapist.

What do the different mental health teams do?

Note: not all of these services are available in every Strategic Health Authority.

- **Community mental health teams (CMHT)** provide the core of local specialist mental health services, and offer assessment, treatment, and social care to adults with mental health problems in the community. They operate from a mental health resource centre that is based away from the main hospital site, in order to be easily accessible to clients.
- **In many areas, the CMHT is the gateway to the more specialized teams** (such as assertive outreach teams, etc) [DH, 2002a]. People are referred to the CMHT for an initial assessment, and then placed with the team that best suits their needs. Early intervention teams (where they exist) can often be accessed directly by the GP. Some areas have direct access to all their specialist mental health teams, but this is a less widespread strategy for organizing services.
- **In-patient care** is the most widely available option for people who need rapid assessment and stabilization during an acute episode. This includes people who need compulsory care under the Mental Health Act because they are so severely ill that they cannot make a decision about treatment, or because they refuse any type of treatment.
- **Crisis resolution/home treatment teams** enable people to be treated at home (instead of as in-patients) for an acute episode of schizophrenia. They can also be used to augment the services provided by early intervention services and assertive outreach teams (C) [NICE, 2002a]. They are the only specialist mental health team that is available to help with crises that occur outside normal office hours.
- **Acute day hospital** is another alternative to in-patient care, and also facilitates early discharge from in-patient care [NICE, 2002a].
- **Assertive outreach teams** (also known as assertive community treatment): this service delivers intensive treatment and rehabilitation in community settings for the severely mentally ill. They provide rapid help in crises. Staff will visit people at home, act as an advocate, and liaise with other services such as the GP or social services. People using this service often need help to find housing, secure an adequate income, and sustain basic daily living (e.g. shopping, cooking, and washing) [DH, 1999]. The teams are better at keeping in touch than ordinary services are, and are useful for people who have a history of poor engagement with services, leading to frequent relapse and/or social breakdown (B) [NICE, 2002a]. They should provide care for homeless people with schizophrenia.
- **Early intervention teams** are not yet available in many areas. They provide early identification and treatment of people aged between 14 and 35 years who have the first symptoms of schizophrenia. Early intervention teams are intended to provide the optimum mix of specialist pharmacological, psychological, social, occupational, and educational interventions at the earliest opportunity [DH, 1999].

Managing the different stages of schizophrenia

Acute episode of schizophrenia

First episode of schizophrenia

- **Early treatment of schizophrenia is associated with a better prognosis.**
- The GP is likely to be the first point of contact for someone who may be developing schizophrenia for the first time.
- **Anyone with suspected, or newly diagnosed, schizophrenia should be referred urgently to specialist mental health services for assessment and development of a care plan** [NICE, 2002a].
- Part of the urgent assessment should include an early assessment by a consultant psychiatrist, if there is a presumed diagnosis of schizophrenia [NICE, 2002a].
- Sometimes, because of the distress, anxiety, and confusion caused by the illness, the person will refuse all requests by the family to see the GP.
- **If the history given by the family is suggestive of schizophrenia, every effort should be made to assess the person.**
- If the person is unwilling to come to the surgery (generally because of a lack of insight into the illness), then a home visit should be attempted.
- Depending on the circumstances, the home visit could be by the GP, or by the GP and a consultant psychiatrist.
- If the person refuses a home visit, but the history suggests schizophrenia, a referral for assessment should be made to the Community Mental Health Team.
- **GPs should have a high level of suspicion for schizophrenia.** Schizophrenia is often (but not always) preceded by a long prodromal period with a range of ill-defined, insidious, and non-specific symptoms that result in a gradual deterioration in personal functioning.
- Many people present to primary care with non-specific symptoms such as peculiar or uncharacteristic behaviour, poor communication, unusual ideation, social withdrawal, poor personal hygiene, or reduced interest and motivation. Most do not go on to develop schizophrenia. Nevertheless, people presenting with these types of symptoms should be monitored in primary care [National Collaborating Centre for Mental Health, 2003].
- Of the minority that do develop schizophrenia, some will develop 'attenuated' positive symptoms first, for example mild thought disorders, ideas of reference, suspiciousness, odd beliefs, and perceptual distortion. Attenuated positive symptoms are milder than those seen in established schizophrenia [National Collaborating Centre for Mental Health, 2003].
- **People with possible attenuated positive symptoms should be referred to specialist mental health services for assessment.**

S

- Consider starting an *atypical* antipsychotic if there are acute symptoms of schizophrenia, but the person is unlikely to be assessed by specialist mental health services for a few weeks [NICE, 2002a]. Where possible, treatment should be discussed with specialist mental health services before it is started.

Referral to specialist mental health services

- **The action to be taken when crisis occurs should be documented in the care plan of anyone with established schizophrenia** [DH, 2002a]. The care co-ordinator should be informed, and will generally liaise with the relevant specialist mental health team to provide rapid assessment and treatment.
- **If this is the first episode of schizophrenia that the person has experienced, or if the action in the event of crisis is not documented in the care plan, contact the community mental health team (CMHT).** They will assess the individual, and refer them on to the team that knows the individual best, or that best suits the current need:
  - First episode of schizophrenia: eventually the person will be managed by early intervention services (EIS). However, EIS are not yet available in most areas.
  - Acutely disturbed, at risk, and needs high level of support: managed by the crisis resolution/home treatment team (if this service is available) or by the in-patient unit.
  - Not acutely disturbed and at less risk: managed by the CMHT or assertive outreach team.
  - Specialist community-based teams unavailable, or unable to meet the needs of the person, or compulsory treatment needed under the Mental Health Act: refer to in-patient unit.
  - Acute Day Hospital services are an alternative to acute admission to in-patient services in some areas.
- **Availability of services varies within regions.** Specialist teams such as crisis resolution/home treatment teams or early intervention services are not currently available in all strategic health authorities.
- People who have positive symptoms but are not at high risk should be assessed routinely. Routine assessments should be made within a week if possible, but no longer than 4 weeks after referral [DH, 2002a].
- **If a crisis occurs out of hours,** contact the local crisis resolution team, crisis helpline, duty psychiatrist, or duty social worker. Consider contacting the police if there is a risk of self-harm or injury to others, or if the person is causing a civil disturbance.

People at high risk of harm to self or others

S

- **Someone who is at high risk of self-harm or of harm to others needs urgent assessment,** within a maximum of 24 hours. Local arrangements for urgent assessment vary. In some areas, the person would be admitted directly to in-patient services by the GP. In other areas, the community mental health team is the single point of access for all referrals. They notify the appropriate team for the initial assessment (e.g. the crisis resolution/home treatment team or in-patient services).
- **In potentially violent situations, it is important to try to de-escalate the situation.** The police have specific training in talking people down, and should be called if there is an imminent risk of harm occurring.
- **GPs should not use rapid tranquillization.**
  - Rapid tranquillization is *extremely* traumatic, and is likely to severely damage the relationship between the individual and the GP.
  - There are also significant medical risks involved, such as loss of consciousness instead of sedation, or over-sedation with loss of alertness.
  - Resuscitation equipment and drugs, including flumazenil, must be available and easily accessible if rapid tranquillization is used. This is very unlikely to be the case in primary care.
  - Tranquillization using oral lorazepam (e.g. 1 mg) is an option, provided that the person is willing to accept oral medication.

Use of the Mental Health Act

- Many people with a serious mental illness will enter specialist mental health services voluntarily for assessment and treatment.
- **The Mental Health Act is used only when detainment in hospital is considered necessary for the health and safety of the person with schizophrenia, or for the protection of others.**
- A GP is most often involved in the use of section 2, which allows someone to be detained in hospital for *assessment* for up to 28 days. A GP can also be involved in the use of section 3, which allows someone to be detained in hospital for *treatment*.
- Sections 2 and 3 require an application to be made based on two medical recommendations — often these are from the consultant psychiatrist and the GP. The GP's opinion is as important as that of the psychiatrist, as the GP will often know the person best, and be familiar with what is 'normal' for that person.
- Section 4 is rarely used, but allows someone to be detained in hospital for *emergency assessment*. It is based on the recommendation of only one doctor, often the GP. Section 4 is used only in extremely urgent situations (e.g. emergency admission is needed because of a very high risk of suicide or harm to others).
- Some GPs (although not many) are 'section 12 approved'. This means that they can provide a psychiatric opinion in their own right.

[Andreasen et al, 2000]

Early post-acute period

- **Most people will be managed by specialist mental health services during this period.**
- The health and social care needs of people with schizophrenia should be assessed comprehensively (by specialist mental health services). The assessment should cover medical, social, psychological, economic, occupational, physical, and cultural issues (**GPP**) [NICE, 2002a].
- **Each person with schizophrenia should have a care plan and a named care co-ordinator (key worker).** A copy of the care plan should be sent to the GP.
- **Plans for recovery** should include psychological treatments and medication advice (see *Treatments used by specialist mental health services*).
- **The social needs of the individual should be addressed.** People may need direct practical help with a range of basic needs, such as obtaining benefits, shopping, help with keeping appointments, etc. Others may benefit from being taught these basic skills. Some people may need advocacy with other agencies (for example landlords and employers) [DH, 2002a].
- **People should be encouraged to seek work where possible.** They may need practical help with filling in application forms or accompaniment to job interviews [DH, 2002a]. Some areas have supported employment programmes that help to place people with schizophrenia in employment [National Collaborating Centre for Mental Health, 2003]. Educational opportunities are also important. They can provide extra skills and provide a structure to the day [DH, 2002a].

Recovery phase

- **Care should be co-ordinated between the different agencies involved** (e.g. social workers, specialist mental health team, and GP). Each person with schizophrenia who is referred to specialist mental health services should have a named care co-ordinator responsible for this.

- **The risk of relapse after an acute episode is high.** Relapse occurs in around 80% of untreated people with schizophrenia. Antipsychotics are therefore continued for 1–2 years from the start of recovery, as maintenance therapy significantly reduces the relapse rate.
- **People with schizophrenia should have their mental *and* physical health reviewed regularly** [NICE, 2002a].
- GPs are best placed to monitor the *physical health* of people with schizophrenia.
- Primary care professionals should also monitor the *mental health* of a person with schizophrenia, so that people can be referred *before* crises arise, wherever possible. This is particularly important when individuals are no longer being regularly reviewed by specialist mental health services.
- The frequency of checks should be a joint decision by the person and the clinician. The agreed frequency should be recorded in the person's notes **(GPP)** [NICE, 2002a].
- **We suggest that people should have their physical health and mental health reviewed at least annually.** Mental health will often need to be reviewed more frequently, depending on the stability of symptoms. Physical health checks should be undertaken at least annually, as people with schizophrenia have a higher risk of coronary heart disease than is found in the general population. Smoking, obesity, and a poor diet are common.
- Specialist mental health services should undertake regular and full assessment of the mental health of the users of their services. If a person with schizophrenia does not want physical health to be monitored by the GP, specialist mental health services should be informed, and they should take on this role [NICE, 2002a].

Physical health checks for people with schizophrenia

- **Monitor increased risk of cardiovascular disease.**
- People with established cardiovascular disease should receive secondary prevention measures.
- All other people with schizophrenia should have their 10-year coronary heart disease risk calculated annually (primary prevention).
- All people with schizophrenia should have their blood pressure (BP) measured regularly (primary prevention), and treated as necessary.
- People who are found to have high BP should be screened for hyperlipidaemia, and treated as necessary.
- **Consider routine urine/blood-glucose screen for diabetes.**
- **Offer advice and encouragement about smoking cessation, a healthy diet, and exercise.** Obesity is common, and can be due to a combination of a poor lifestyle and weight gain caused by antipsychotic drugs. A healthy diet and exercise is often the only way to reduce drug-induced weight gain. Advice should be personalized and achievable.
- **Ask about adverse effects of drug treatment.**
  - Include extrapyramidal symptoms and tardive dyskinesia.
  - Include common adverse effects such as sexual dysfunction and lethargy.
  - Consider routine weight monitoring, particularly for drugs that are known to cause weight gain (e.g. olanzapine).
  - Check an electrocardiogram (ECG) if the person is taking a drug or dose with a higher risk of QT prolongation (e.g. sertindole, thioridazine, zotepine, high-dose haloperidol [more than 20 mg per day]) or a dose of any antipsychotic that is above the *British National Formulary* upper limit.
- **Ask about alcohol or illicit drug use.** People with suspected substance-misuse problems should be re-referred to specialist mental health services.

[BNF 44, 2002; NICE, 2002a; Taylor, 2003]

When should re-referral be considered?

- **The decision to re-refer a person with schizophrenia should take account of the person's view,** and, where appropriate, the carer's. Issues of confidentiality should be respected when involving carers.
- **People should be referred back to specialist mental health services if:**
  - They are at increased risk of harm to themselves or others (referral should be urgent)
  - They are showing symptoms of relapse (some people have very specific 'relapse signatures', and these should be documented in the care plan)
  - They are not responding well to treatment
  - They are not taking their treatment, or you suspect this
  - You suspect they are misusing alcohol or drugs
  - The features of the episode differ from those of previous episodes
  - They require a second opinion
  - They have just joined the practice (for formal assessment and development of a care plan)
  - The GP feels unable to meet the individual's needs
  - The family or carer is not coping

[DH, 2002a; NICE, 2002a; NHS Modernisation Agency, 2003]

Driving

- **Driving must stop during any acute psychotic episode,** and the Driver and Vehicle Licensing Agency (DVLA) must be notified. The General Medical Council guidelines advise breaking patient confidentiality and informing the DVLA if the person is unable to appreciate that driving during psychosis is unsafe (i.e. because of lack of insight into their illness), or if the person refuses to stop driving.
- **Re-licensing for an ordinary driving licence is considered when** the person has remained well and stable for at least 3 months, and is free from adverse effects of medication that impair driving. The person must also be compliant with treatment — drivers with psychiatric illnesses are often safer when well and on regular medication than when they are ill. People who have continuing symptoms, or limited insight, can still be considered for relicensing provided that their symptoms do not make them unfit to drive (e.g. poor concentration, or memory impairment).
- Antipsychotic drugs can cause sedation, poor concentration, and extrapyramidal symptoms, which can all potentially impair driving. Careful assessment is therefore needed to determine whether adverse effects of medication will impair driving. This is usually undertaken by specialist mental health services.
- A holder of a licence for heavy goods vehicles or passenger-carrying vehicles will be considered for re-licensing only after remaining well and stable for a minimum of 3 years.
- People should inform their motor vehicle insurance company of the diagnosis.

[DVLA, 2000; NHS direct, 2003]

Treatments used by specialist mental health services

Psychological interventions

Note: not all psychological interventions are currently available in every strategic health authority.

S

- **Psychological treatments are an essential part of the treatment options** for relapse prevention and for symptom reduction. There is most evidence for cognitive behavioural therapy (CBT), and for family interventions (A) [NICE, 2002a].
- **CBT should be offered to people with schizophrenia who are experiencing persistent psychotic symptoms (A).** It should also be considered as a treatment option to assist in the development of insight (B), and to manage poor treatment adherence (C) [NICE, 2002a].
- CBT depends upon an effective therapeutic alliance between the clinician and the affected person.
- CBT encourages people to establish links between their thoughts, feelings, or actions with respect to current or past symptoms, and then re-evaluate their perceptions, beliefs, or reasoning related to the target symptom [National Collaborating Centre for Mental Health, 2003].
- **Family interventions** should be available for families who are living with people with schizophrenia, or who are in close contact with them (A) [NICE, 2002a].
- A high level of 'expressed emotion' within a family has been shown to be an effective predictor of relapse in schizophrenia. This might be the case, for example, in families that are excessively critical, hostile, or over-involved towards the person with schizophrenia.
- These sessions can improve symptoms and reduce the chance of another acute episode. They are also helpful for people who are at risk of a crisis occurring, or who have persisting symptoms.
- Family intervention sessions generally involve the person with schizophrenia as well as the family. They use psycho-educational interventions, or problem-solving/crisis-management work. This aims to help families cope with their relative's illness more effectively, reduce levels of distress, improve the way the family communicates, and provide support and education for the family [National Collaborating Centre for Mental Health, 2003].
- **Counselling and supportive psychotherapy are not recommended** unless CBT is not available locally. However, the individual's preferences should always be taken into account (C) [NICE, 2002a].

Pharmacological interventions

- **Antipsychotic drugs** are used to control acute episodes of schizophrenia, and to prevent relapse. Drugs are also necessary for psychological treatments to be effective.
- **They are only *one* part of a comprehensive package of care** that aims to keep a person stable enough to live as normal a life as possible.
- **Antipsychotics are most effective at controlling positive symptoms** (e.g. hallucinations and delusions). They are generally less effective at controlling negative symptoms. The atypical antipsychotics may be slightly more successful at treating secondary negative symptoms, but they have little effect on primary negative symptoms [Stefan et al, 2002]. Low-dose amisulpride (50–300 mg per day) has been shown to reduce negative symptoms when compared to placebo [BNF 44, 2002]. However, a different study found no difference between low-dose amisulpride and low-dose haloperidol in negative symptom improvement.
- **The final choice of antipsychotic should be a joint decision between the clinician and the individual.** Atypical antipsychotic drugs should be considered in the choice of first-line treatments for schizophrenia. The final choice will depend on the balance of the benefits of a drug and its adverse effect profile. This should be discussed fully with the individual [NICE, 2002b].
- **Doses at the lower end of the standard dose range should be used when starting treatment,** and the minimum effective dose should be used [NICE, 2002a].
- Continuous dosing should be used. Intermittent dosage maintenance strategies should be avoided, because of the increased risk of symptoms worsening or relapse. They should only be considered for people who refuse maintenance treatment, or who have some other contraindication to continuous dosing such as adverse-effect sensitivity (C) [NICE, 2002a].
- If a typical antipsychotic is used for an acute episode, the dose should be within the range of 300–1000 mg chlorpromazine equivalent per day for a minimum of 6 weeks [NICE, 2002a]. There is no benefit in using loading doses, rapid dose escalation, or very high maintenance doses [National Collaborating Centre for Mental Health, 2003].
- **The person should be treated with only one antipsychotic drug at a time,** apart from during short periods to cover changeover (C) [NICE, 2002a].
- **A person who does not improve after 6–8 weeks of a therapeutic dose should be switched to another antipsychotic.** Consider using olanzapine or risperidone, if not previously tried. (They have been shown to benefit some people with treatment-resistant schizophrenia, but there is less evidence of improvement than with clozapine [National Collaborating Centre for Mental Health, 2003].)
- Adjunctive treatments (e.g. lithium, carbamazepine, sodium valproate, and lamotrigine) may also be used by specialist mental health services to augment the action of antipsychotic drugs. Their use was outside the scope of the current National Institute for Clinical Excellence (NICE) guideline, but it is anticipated that they will be reviewed by NICE in the future.
- **If non-adherence is the reason for treatment failure,** consider using a depot preparation. If non-adherence is due to intolerable adverse effects, switch to another oral preparation with a different adverse-effect profile.
- **If there is evidence of treatment-resistant schizophrenia, clozapine should be started as soon as possible:** a person who does not respond to a second antipsychotic after a further 6–8 weeks of treatment should be switched to clozapine [NICE, 2002b].

Maintenance treatment

- **Antipsychotics are generally continued for 1 to 2 years to prevent further relapses,** but this should be discussed with the individual (GPP) [NICE, 2002a].
- About 20% of people with schizophrenia will experience only one episode of schizophrenia in their lifetime. A similar percentage will still experience relapse despite maintenance treatment. It is not possible to identify these people, other than over time. Therefore antipsychotic maintenance treatment should be considered for anyone diagnosed with schizophrenia [National Collaborating Centre for Mental Health, 2003].
- **Withdrawal from antipsychotic medication should be undertaken gradually,** whilst regularly monitoring signs and symptoms for evidence of potential relapse (GPP) [NICE, 2002a].
- **Following withdrawal from antipsychotic medication, people should be monitored regularly** for signs and symptoms of potential relapse for at least 2 years, as the rate of relapse following treatment withdrawal is high.

Types of antipsychotic drugs

- **The typical antipsychotics** exert their therapeutic action by blocking dopamine receptors (D2). Typical antipsychotics include chlorpromazine, thioridazine, and trifluoperazine (phenothiazines); haloperidol (butyrophenone); flupentixol and zuclopenthixol (thioxanthenes); and sulpiride. These are established drugs that have a long safety record, but extrapyramidal effects, hyperprolactinaemia, sedation, and tardive dyskinesia are common.

- **The atypical antipsychotics** are structurally diverse, with different adverse-effect profiles. They include amisulpride, clozapine, olanzapine, quetiapine, risperidone, sertindole, and zotepine. While many atypicals block both serotonin receptors and dopamine receptors, this is not the case with them all (e.g. amisulpride blocks only dopamine receptors). The term 'atypical' is now broadly used to mean the newer antipsychotics. Atypical antipsychotics are thought to have a lower potential risk of extrapyramidal symptoms than typicals have.

Medicines management

Who should start treatment for a first episode of schizophrenia?

- **Generally, antipsychotics are started only by specialist mental health services,** after an initial assessment.
- **However, if it is the person's first acute episode of schizophrenia but the person is unlikely to be assessed urgently by specialist mental health services,** consider starting an *atypical* antipsychotic if there are acute symptoms of schizophrenia [NICE, 2002a]. For example, a person with florid psychotic symptoms but who is not at imminent risk of self-harm, or of causing harm to others, will often be give a routine appointment. Such a person will usually be seen within a few weeks of referral [DH, 2002a].
- **Where possible, treatment should be discussed with specialist mental health services before it is started.**
- **Discuss the use of antipsychotic drugs with the person, and decide *jointly* which to use.** It is important to give adequate time for discussion, and to provide written information, so that the person with schizophrenia can give meaningful and properly informed consent before treatment is initiated [NICE, 2002a].
- **If the person is at risk of suicide or there is a risk of violence to others, refer urgently (or as an emergency) to specialist mental health services.**

Choice of oral atypical antipsychotic for a first episode (if initiation is appropriate in primary care)

Note: this section does not include clozapine and sertindole, as they can be started only by specialist mental health services.

- **Atypical antipsychotics, at the lower end of the dose range, are the preferred treatments** for a person experiencing a first episode of schizophrenia. This is because of the presumed lower potential risk of extrapyramidal symptoms [NICE, 2002b].
- **Cerebrovascular disease:** where possible, avoid starting risperidone and olanzapine in people with a history of stroke or transient ischaemic attack. Consideration should also be given to other risk factors for stroke such as hypertension, diabetes, current smoking, and atrial fibrillation [CSM, 2004]. Studies are ongoing to confirm whether there is an increased risk of cerebrovascular disease with other atypical antipsychotics.
- **Cardiovascular disease: people with angina or a previous myocardial infarction (MI)** should avoid zotepine, risperidone, and quetiapine. These drugs reduce blood pressure, resulting in a reflex tachycardia that may exacerbate angina. (Phenothiazines also have this effect.) Olanzapine may be a safer alternative in someone with angina, or with a previous MI, as it rarely causes hypotension [Taylor et al, 2003].
- **Cardiovascular disease: arrhythmias.** Most antipsychotic drugs have the potential to affect the QT interval. Arrhythmias are more likely to occur in the presence of hypokalaemia, hypocalcaemia, or hypomagnesaemia; or with concomitant administration of other drugs that also prolong the QT interval, or reduce the clearance of antipsychotics. Amisulpride is probably safe in people with arrhythmias. Zotepine (and sertindole) should not be used. Phenothiazines, higher doses of haloperidol (more than 20 mg per day), and doses above the *British National Formulary* upper limit should also be avoided [Taylor, 2003]. Risperidone and olanzapine should also be avoided in people with atrial fibrillation because of concerns about an increased risk of stroke [CSM, 2004].
- **Epilepsy:** all antipsychotic drugs can lower the seizure threshold. The incidence of seizures was low in clinical trials of olanzapine, risperidone, and quetiapine. Whichever antipsychotic is chosen, it is still prudent to use a low starting dose, and to increase the dose slowly in someone with epilepsy. Additional risk factors for seizures are head injury, previous seizure history, concomitant drugs that reduce the seizure threshold, and withdrawal from central depressants (for example alcohol, benzodiazepines, barbiturates etc).
- **Diabetes:** the incidence of Type 2 diabetes is more common in people with schizophrenia than in the general population. Drug treatment with antipsychotics may increase this risk, although a causal relationship has not been firmly established. Both typical and atypical antipsychotic drugs have been associated with an increased risk of diabetes, but the risk seems to be highest with clozapine and olanzapine [Sernyak et al, 2002; Lean and Pajonk, 2003].
- **Angle-closure glaucoma, prostatic hypertrophy, or urinary retention:** most atypical antipsychotics cause antimuscarinic adverse effects. Tolerability may be slightly improved with amisulpride [Stanniland and Taylor, 2000]. Avoid zotepine and olanzapine.
- **Non-smokers:** olanzapine is metabolized more slowly by non-smokers, women, and the elderly. Consider a lower starting dose of olanzapine (5 mg once a day) in people with more than one 'risk factor' for slow metabolism to reduce the risk of adverse effects, for example a female and a non-smoker.
- **Elderly people:** elderly people are at higher risk of postural hypotension, extrapyramidal symptoms, and antimuscarinic effects, especially when starting therapy. Start with a lower dose, and titrate slowly [Taylor et al, 2003].

Adverse effects of antipsychotics

- Antipsychotics cause a wide range of adverse effects including sedation, weight gain, hyperprolactinaemia, and sexual dysfunction, as well as extrapyramidal symptoms (movement disorders) such as Parkinsonism, akathisia (lower-limb restlessness), and dystonia (abnormal movements of the face and body).
- **Tardive dyskinesia (TD)** is a late-onset movement disorder that can occur with prolonged use of antipsychotics. It is characterized by rhythmical, involuntary movements; usually lip smacking and tongue rotating, although it can affect the limbs and trunk. It may be irreversible, and can sometimes worsen on treatment withdrawal.
- **Around 20% of people treated with typical antipsychotics eventually experience TD.** (The incidence is roughly 5% each year.) The emergence of extrapyramidal symptoms is a strong risk factor for later TD [Casey, 1997]. Older people are at higher risk, even with short-term treatment with antipsychotics [Jeste et al, 1999].

Differences between drugs

- **Typical antipsychotics** can potentially cause any of the adverse effects listed above, as well as antimuscarinic

S

Table 3: Adverse effect profiles of a selection of antipsychotic drugs

	EPS	Weight Gain	Hyper-prolactinaemia	Sedation	Anti-muscarinic effects	Tardive dyskinesia	Blood dyscrasia
Chlorpromazine	++	++	+++	+++	+++	+++	+
Haloperidol	+++	++	+++	+	+	+++	+
Clozapine	–	+++	–	+++	+++	–	+++
Olanzapine	+/-	+++	+	++	+	?	–
Quetiapine	–	++	–	++	+	?	+
Risperidone	+	++	+++	+	–	+?	–
Sertindole	–	++	–	–	–	?	–
Zotepine	++	++	+	++	++	?	+
Amisulpride	+	++	+++	–	–	+?	–

Key: +++ high; ++ moderate; + low; – very low/zero; ? data not available.
EPS = extrapyramidal symptoms
Table reproduced from Andreasen et al, 2000

symptoms (e.g. dry mouth, blurred vision, urinary retention, constipation, and cutaneous flushing). They can also cause postural hypotension; photosensitivity; reduced seizure threshold; QT prolongation; and occasionally corneal and lens opacities, and purplish pigmentation of the skin, cornea, conjunctiva, and retina.

- Although they all tend to cause these adverse effects, the intensity varies between the different types of typical antipsychotic drugs [BNF 44, 2002]:
  - Group 1 phenothiazines (chlorpromazine): pronounced sedative effects but moderate antimuscarinic and extrapyramidal effects.
  - Group 2 phenothiazines (thioridazine): moderate sedative effects, marked antimuscarinic effects, and fewer extrapyramidal symptoms (EPS) than groups 1 and 3.
  - Group 3 phenothiazines (fluphenazine, trifluoperazine): fewer sedative and antimuscarinic effects, but more EPS than groups 1 and 2.
  - Butyrophenones (haloperidol): similar to group 3 phenothiazines.
  - Flupentixol, sulpiride, and zuclopenthixol: similar to group 3 phenothiazines.
- **Atypical antipsychotics** have more diverse adverse-effect profiles. They cause fewer extrapyramidal effects than do typical antipsychotics, but their overall tolerability is similar [Geddes et al, 2000]. It is hoped that the lower rate of EPS will translate into a lower rate of tardive dyskinesia (TD). However, there is very little long-term trial data available on comparative rates of TD between atypicals, or between typical and atypical drugs [NICE, 2002b]. In addition, a recent meta-analysis suggested that the rate of EPS might not be significantly different between atypical antipsychotics and chlorpromazine, if chlorpromazine was used at doses of less than 600 mg per day [Leucht et al, 2003].
- Weight gain has emerged as a significant and troublesome adverse effect with atypical antipsychotics. The risk of weight gain varies with individual drugs [Taylor et al, 2003]:
  - High risk: clozapine and olanzapine
  - Moderate/high risk: zotepine and thioridazine
  - Moderate risk: risperidone, quetiapine, and chlorpromazine
  - Low risk: amisulpride, haloperidol, and trifluoperazine
- Type 2 diabetes has been linked to clozapine and olanzapine.
- QT prolongation has emerged as a problem with zotepine and sertindole.
- Hyperprolactinaemia is less common with most atypical antipsychotics, but it can still be a problem with risperidone, amisulpride, and zotepine.
- Insomnia, anxiety, and agitation are also common with amisulpride, risperidone, and zotepine.
- Sedation is common with clozapine, olanzapine, quetiapine, and zotepine.
- A three-fold increase in the risk of stroke has been observed in studies of risperidone and olanzapine in elderly people with dementia [CSM, 2004]. Although no similar data are available on younger people with schizophrenia, it would seem prudent to avoid starting risperidone and olanzapine in any person with a history of stroke or transient ischaemic attack or with risk factors for stroke such as hypertension, diabetes, smoking, and atrial fibrillation. However, if they are already well controlled on risperidone and olanzapine the decision is less clear, and specialist advice should be sought before treatment is switched or gradually withdrawn [RCGP, 2004].

Table 3 highlights the differences in the incidence and intensity of adverse effects between selected antipsychotics.

Adverse effects rating scales

- Although tardive dyskinesia is a severe social handicap, about 80% of people remain free from it. Sexual dysfunction, sedation, and weight gain are often the adverse effects that people with schizophrenia find the most distressing [Day et al, 1998] and adverse effects are a common cause of non-compliance with treatment.
- **The Liverpool University Neuroleptic Side Effect Rating Scale (LUNSERS) can be used to assess the severity of adverse effects,** and takes only 5–20 minutes to complete. No specialist training is needed to use it, and people with schizophrenia can often complete it without supervision [Day et al, 1995].
- It is often most practical to obtain a baseline LUNSERS score once psychotic symptoms have settled.
- **A copy of LUNSERS can be found** in the PRODIGY patient-information leaflets. Important: before using LUNSERS the authors require that you register your usage at http://www.symplexsoftware.com/lunsers.asp. Alternatively write to Symplex Information Solutions Ltd, 25 Bentley Road, Liverpool, L8 0SZ briefly stating the purpose for which you intend to use the scale.
- A computerised autoscore version of LUNSERS and different language versions of LUNSERS are also available from http://www.symplexsoftware.com/lunsers.asp.

Switching antipsychotics

- **Switching antipsychotics needs to be done with care, and we recommend that people be referred to specialist mental health services if a switch is needed.**
- **Antipsychotics should not be stopped suddenly,** as this can precipitate relapse, or cause withdrawal reactions such as cholinergic rebound (e.g. nausea, restlessness,

S

anxiety, insomnia, etc) or withdrawal dyskinesias (e.g. extrapyramidal symptoms, or rebound akathisia) [Bazire, 2001].

The dose of the original antipsychotic should be tapered down slowly (generally over at least 8 weeks), while the new drug is slowly increased. The dose of any antimuscarinic drugs will also need to be stopped slowly.

There is a lack of agreement about equivalent doses of antipsychotic drugs [Bazire, 2001]. The *British National Formulary* gives approximate equivalent doses of some antipsychotics, but the equivalent doses of several atypical antipsychotics are not yet known.

Iinimizing common adverse effects

Iany people with schizophrenia are on the enhanced care :ogramme approach (CPA), and the community mental ealth team will often deal with the management of lverse effects. However, 25% of people with hizophrenia are still managed mainly by their GP Kendrick et al, 1995], and minimizing adverse effects is an nportant aspect of care. (Note: a person who may benefit om switching drugs should be referred to specialist ental health services.)

he information below regarding switching drugs is based oon the Maudsley 2001 Prescribing Guidelines [Taylor et , 2003].

Weight gain is common with all antipsychotics, but may be particularly severe with clozapine and olanzapine. The social stigma associated with being 'fat' adds to the stigma experienced by people with schizophrenia, and is a common reason for non-compliance. Most weight gain seems to occur in the first 6–9 months of treatment and then generally reaches a plateau. Good advice and support on healthy eating and exercise is the most effective way to reduce weight gain. Alternatively, consider switching to a drug that is less likely to cause weight gain, for example amisulpride, haloperidol, or trifluoperazine.

Sedation is common with many antipsychotics (both typical and atypical). Lowering the dose may help. If sedation is still a problem, consider a switch to a less sedating drug such as amisulpride, risperidone, sulpiride or haloperidol. The person should also be advised to avoid alcohol, as this potentiates sedation.

Postural hypotension can also be a problem with some drugs, particularly chlorpromazine and other phenothiazines, clozapine, quetiapine, and risperidone. It is generally dose-related. Tolerance often develops, but people with postural hypotension should be monitored carefully, as some people will still need a change in medication [Stanniland and Taylor, 2000].

Antimuscarinic adverse effects (e.g. dry mouth, blurred vision, urinary retention, constipation, and cutaneous flushing) are common with most antipsychotics, but tolerance often develops [Stanniland and Taylor, 2000].

Photosensitivity is common with chlorpromazine and other typical antipsychotics. Proper use of sunscreen will prevent sunburn in affected people. Some high-factor sun-blocks (sun protection factor 20 or above) are available on FP10.

Extrapyramidal symptoms (EPS): dystonia and Parkinsonism can be alleviated by antimuscarinic drugs such as procyclidine. Antimuscarinic drugs should be withdrawn 2–3 months after symptoms resolve, as their adverse effects increase cognitive deficit. Akathisia can be relieved by reducing the dose of the antipsychotic or by co-prescribing propranolol or metoprolol [Holloman and Marder, 1997]. Alternatively, a drug that is less likely to cause EPS can be used (for example clozapine, olanzapine, or quetiapine). Low-dose risperidone (less than 6 mg per day) is also an option, but higher doses offer little or no advantage [Bazire, 2001].

- **Hyperprolactinaemia** causes amenorrhoea, reduced fertility, galactorrhoea, sexual dysfunction, gynaecomastia, and has an increased risk of osteoporosis. Unfortunately, it seems that typical antipsychotics cause hyperprolactinaemia at doses substantially lower than those needed for therapeutic efficacy, so dose reduction is not always effective. Consider switching to quetiapine, olanzapine, or clozapine.
- **QT interval prolongation** is the most widely reported cardiac conduction defect caused by all antipsychotics. It increases the risk of torsade-de-pointes, a potentially fatal arrhythmia. Most antipsychotics have been associated with QT prolongation. Avoid co-prescribing other drugs that are known to prolong the QT interval (e.g. tricyclic antidepressants).
- **Tardive dyskinesia (TD):** the emergence of EPS is a strong risk factor for later TD. Withdrawal of antimuscarinic drugs can sometimes improve TD, and consider reducing the dose of antipsychotic. Switching to clozapine can slowly help to improve TD. Olanzapine and quetiapine are possible alternatives to clozapine.
- **Neuroleptic malignant syndrome** is a very rare, idiosyncratic, but life-threatening adverse effect that can occur with any antipsychotic. Symptoms include hyperthermia, muscle rigidity, autonomic instability, and fluctuating consciousness. The untreated mortality rate is 20%, so urgent medical treatment is needed.

[Bazire, 2001; BNF 44, 2002; Stefan et al, 2002; Taylor et al, 2003]

When should depot injections be considered?

- Consider depot injections if non-adherence is a problem, or if it is the individual's preference.
- **Switching antipsychotics needs to be done with care, and we recommend that people be referred to specialist mental health services if a switch in dose form is needed.**
- If depot medication is prescribed, give a test dose first — any adverse effects of a depot injection are long-lived. A small test dose is essential to avoid severe, prolonged adverse effects [Taylor et al, 2003].
- If the test dose is successful, begin treatment with the lowest therapeutic dose, and administer at the longest licensed interval.
- Shorter intervals do not improve efficacy, and injections are painful. Since plasma levels of antipsychotics continue to fall (slowly) for a few days after the next injection, people are at most risk of clinical deterioration *after* an injection. In studies, relapse only seemed to occur 3–6 months after withdrawing depot treatment, which is about the time needed to clear steady-state depot drug levels from the blood [Taylor et al, 2003].
- After starting depot therapy, plasma levels take several weeks to reach steady state. Doses should not, therefore, be increased for at least one month (and preferably longer) after treatment begins [Taylor et al, 2003].
- **Risperidone depot injection is also now available.** It has a shorter maximum licensed interval than other depot injections, and must be given every 2 weeks. A test dose is not required. Orthostatic hypotension can occur, particularly after the start of treatment. Note: risperidone depot injection must be stored in a fridge.

Should people on typical antipsychotics be changed to atypicals?

- **If a person with schizophrenia is satisfied with the drug being used, there is no need to change treatment** [NICE, 2002a].

Table 4: Standard doses and dose intervals for depot antipsychotic drugs. Note: lower test doses and start doses are often needed in the elderly: see *British National Formulary* for further details [BNF 44, 2002].

Depot injection	Test dose	Dose interval before standard dose given	Standard start dose	Longest licensed interval
Flupentixol	20 mg	7 days	20–40 mg	4 weeks
Fluphenazine	12.5 mg	4–7 days	12.5–25 mg	5 weeks
Haloperidol	25 mg*	4 weeks	50 mg	4 weeks
Pipotiazine	25 mg	4–7 days	25–50 mg	4 weeks
Zuclopenthixol	100 mg	7 days	200 mg	4 weeks

* Test dose not stated by manufacturer [Taylor et al, 2003]

- **Atypical antipsychotics should be considered for people taking typical antipsychotics who:**
  - Are experiencing unacceptable adverse effects, despite adequate symptom control
  - Have now relapsed, and did not previously get adequate symptom control from typical antipsychotics, or experienced unacceptable adverse effects
- The decision as to what are unacceptable adverse effects should be taken following discussion between the person with schizophrenia and the clinician responsible for treatment (for example the consultant psychiatrist) [NICE, 2002a].

References

NHS staff in England can link, free of charge, from references to full text journals by clicking on [Full text] on the PRODIGY website.

1. American Psychiatric Association (Ed.) (2000) *Diagnostic and statistical manual of mental disorders: DSM-IV-TR*. 4th edn. Washington, DC: American Psychiatric Association.
2. Andreasen, N.C., Lopez, I., Jose, J. and Gelder, M.G. (Eds.) (2000) *New Oxford textbook of psychiatry*. Oxford: Oxford University Press.
3. Barnes, T.R.E. and Pant, A. (2002) Long-term course and outcome of schizophrenia. *Psychiatry* **1**(9), 34–36.
4. Bazire, S. (Ed.) (2001) *The psychotropic drug directory*. 3rd edn. London: Lilly.
5. BNF 44 (2002) *British National Formulary*. 44th edn. London: British Medical Association and Royal Pharmaceutical Society of Great Britain.
6. Brown, S., Birtwistle, J., Rose, L. and Thompson, C. (1999) The unhealthy lifestyle of people with schizophrenia. *Psychological Medicine* **29**(3), 697–701.
7. Casey, D.E. (1997) The relationship of pharmacology to side effects. *Journal of Clinical Psychiatry* **58**(Suppl 10), 55–62.
8. CSM (2004) *Atypical antipsychotic drugs and stroke*. Committee on Safety of Medicines. www.mhra.gov.uk [Accessed: 30/04/2004].
9. Day, J.C., Wood, G., Dewey, M. and Bentall, R.P. (1995) A self-rating scale for measuring neuroleptic side-effects. Validation in a group of schizophrenic patients. *British Journal of Psychiatry* **166**(5), 650–653.
10. Day, J.C., Kinderman, P. and Bentall, R. (1998) A comparison of patients' and prescribers' beliefs about neuroleptic side-effects: prevalence, distress and causation. *Acta Psychiatrica Scandinavica* **97**(1), 93–97.
11. DH (1999) *National service framework for mental health*. Department of Health. www.dh.gov.uk [Accessed: 26/04/2004]. [Full text]
12. DH (2002a) *Mental health policy implementation guide. Community mental health teams*. Department of Health. www.dh.gov.uk [Accessed: 26/04/2004]. [Full text]
13. DH (2002b) *Effective care co-ordination in mental health services. Modernising the care programme approach – a policy booklet*. Department of Health. www.dh.gov.uk [Accessed: 26/04/2004]. [Full text]
14. DVLA (2000) *At a glance guide to current medical standards of fitness to drive. Psychiatric disorders*. Drivers Medical Group, Driver and Vehicle Licensing Authority. www.dvla.gov.uk/at_a_glance/content.htm [Accessed: 27/04/2001].
15. EMEA (2002) *Committee for proprietary medicinal products opinion following an article 36 referral. Sertindole*. The European Agency for the Evaluation of Medicinal Products. www.emea.eu.int/ [Accessed: 17/04/2003].
16. Foster, K., Meltzer, H. and Gill, B. (1996) *Adults with a psychotic disorder living in the community. OPCS surveys of psychiatric morbidity in Great Britain*. Report no. 8. London: HMSO.
17. Geddes, J., Freemantle, N., Harrison, P. and Bebbington, P. (2000) Atypical antipsychotics in the treatment of schizophrenia: systematic overview and meta-regression analysis. *British Medical Journal* **321**(7273), 1371–1376. [Full text]
18. Holloman, L.C. and Marder, S.R. (1997) Management of acute extrapyramidal effects induced by antipsychotic drugs. *American Journal of Health-System Pharmacy* **54**(21), 2461–2477.
19. Jablensky, A., Sartorius, N., Ernberg, G. et al (1992) Schizophrenia: manifestations, incidence and course in different cultures. A World Health Organization ten-country study. *Psychological Medicine* **20**(Monograph supplement), 1–97.
20. Jeste, D.V., Lacro, J.P., Palmer, B. et al (1999) Incidence of tardive dyskinesia in early stages of low-dose treatment with typical neuroleptics in older patients. *American Journal of Psychiatry* **156**(2), 309–311. [Full text]
21. Kendrick, T., Burns, T. and Freeling, P. (1995) Randomised controlled trial of teaching general practioners to carry out structured assessments of their long term mentally ill patients. *British Medical Journal* **311**(6997), 93–98. [Full text]
22. Lean, M.E. and Pajonk, F.G. (2003) Patients on atypical antipsychotic drugs: another high-risk group for type 2 diabetes. *Diabetes Care* **26**(5), 1597–1605. [Full text]
23. Leucht, S., Wahlbeck, K., Hamann, J. and Kissling, W. (2003) New generation antipsychotics versus low-potency conventional antipsychotics: a systematic review and meta-analysis. *Lancet* **361**(9369), 1581–1589. [Full text]
24. Liddle, P.F. (2002) Quantitative measurement of symptoms in schizophrenia. *Psychiatry* **1**(9), 8–10.
25. Mason, P., Harrison, G., Glazebrook, C. et al (1996) The course of schizophrenia over 13 years. A report from the International Study of Schizophrenia (ISoS) coordinated by the World Health Organization. *British Journal of Psychiatry* **169**(5), 580–586.

S

6. McGuire, P.K., Silbersweig, D.A., Wright, I. et al (1995) Abnormal monitoring of inner speech: a physiological basis for auditory hallucinations. *Lancet* **346**(8975), 596–600. [Full text]

7. Menezes, P.R.P., Johnson, S., Thornicroft, G. et al (1996) Drug and alcohol problems among individuals with severe mental illnesses in south London. *British Journal of Psychiatry* **168**(5), 612–619.

8. National Collaborating Centre for Mental Health (2003) *Schizophrenia: the treatment and management of schizophrenia in primary and secondary care.* National Clinical Practice Guideline no. 1. London: National Collaborating Centre for Mental Health.

9. NHS direct (2003) *Schizophrenia – legal issues. Mental illness and driving.* http://cebmh.warne.ox.ac.uk/cebmh/elmh/schizophrenia/legal/driving.html [Accessed: 17/04/2003].

0. NHS Modernisation Agency (2003) *Project to facilitate implementation of NICE schizophrenia guidelines.* London: NHS Modernisation Agency.

1. NICE (2002a) *Schizophrenia: core interventions in the treatment and management of schizophrenia in primary and secondary care.* Clinical guideline no. 1. National Institute for Clinical Excellence. www.nice.org.uk [Accessed: 16/04/2003].

2. NICE (2002b) *Guidance on the use of newer (atypical) antipsychotic drugs for the treatment of schizophrenia.* Technology appraisal no. 43. National Institute for Clinical Excellence. www.nice.org.uk [Accessed: 13/05/2003].

3. RCGP (2004) *Guidance for the management of behavioural and psychiatric symptoms in dementia and the treatment of psychosis in people with a history of stroke/TIA.* Royal College of General Practitioners. www.rcgp.org.uk/corporate/position/drugs.asp [Accessed: 30/04/2004].

4. Rethink (2003a) *Antipsychotic medications.* Rethink. www.rethink.org/information [Accessed: 16/04/2003].

5. Rethink (2003b) *How is a diagnosis reached?* Rethink. www.rethink.org/information [Accessed: 16/04/2003].

6. Rethink (2003c) *What is schizophrenia?* Rethink. www.rethink.org/information [Accessed: 16/04/2003].

7. Sernyak, M.J., Leslie, D.L., Alarcon, R.D. et al (2002) Association of diabetes mellitus with use of atypical neuroleptics in the treatment of schizophrenia. *American Journal of Psychiatry* **159**(4), 561–566. [Full text]

38. Stanniland, C. and Taylor, D. (2000) Tolerability of atypical antipsychotics. *Drug Safety* **22**(3), 195–214.

39. Stefan, M., Travis, M. and Murray, R.M. (Eds.) (2002) *An atlas of schizophrenia.* London: Parthenon Publishing.

40. Tandon, R. and Jibson, M.D. (2003) Suicidal behaviour in schizophrenia: diagnosis, neurobiology, and treatment implications. *Current Opinion in Psychiatry* **16**(2), 193–197.

41. Taylor, D.M. (2003) Antipsychotics and QT prolongation. *Acta Psychiatrica Scandinavica* **107**(2), 85–95.

42. Taylor, D., Paton, C. and Kerwin, R. (Eds.) (2003) *The South London and Maudsley NHS Trust: 2003 Maudsley prescribing guidelines.* 7th edn. London: Martin Dunitz.

43. WHO (Ed.) (1992) *The ICD-10 classification of mental and behavioural disorders. Clinical descriptions and diagnostic guidelines.* Geneva: World Health Organization.

Evidence grading

Evidence grading is from the National Institute of Clinical Excellence guideline, *Schizophrenia: full national clinical guideline and core interventions in primary and secondary care*, December 2002. The definitions of grades of recommendation used in this guideline are as follows:

A At least one randomized controlled trial as part of a body of literature of overall good quality and consistency addressing the specific recommendation without extrapolation.

B Well-conducted clinical studies but no randomized clinical trials on the topic of recommendation, or with extrapolation from evidence obtained from randomized trials of meta-analysis.

C Expert committee reports or opinions and/or clinical experiences of respected authorities. This grading indicates that directly applicable clinical studies of good quality are absent, or with extrapolation from higher levels of evidence.

GPP Good practice point. Recommended good practice based on the clinical experience of the guideline development group.

S

PRODIGY GUIDANCE

Seborrhoeic dermatitis

Last revised in November 2004
www.prodigy.nhs.uk/guidance.asp?gt=Seborrhoeic dermatitis

Applies to people of all ages

This guidance covers the assessment and management of seborrhoeic dermatitis in adults and infants in primary care.

This guidance does not cover in detail the management of secondary bacterial infection. For guidance on this, see separate PRODIGY guidance on *Impetigo*.

There is separate PRODIGY guidance on *Eczema — atopic* and *Nappy rash*.

Goals

- To settle acute exacerbations of seborrhoeic dermatitis
- To reduce the frequency of exacerbations

Contents

Scenarios

- Seborrhoeic dermatitis of the scalp and beard p.1684
- Seborrhoeic dermatitis of the face and body p.1686
- Seborrhoeic dermatitis — infants p.1687

Extended Information, p. 1688

Which scenario?

- **Seborrhoeic dermatitis of the scalp and beard:** covers the management and prophylaxis of seborrhoeic dermatitis of the scalp and beard.
- **Seborrhoeic dermatitis of the face and body:** covers the management and prophylaxis of seborrhoeic dermatitis affecting the face and body, and provides advice on referral of people with widespread disease.
- **Seborrhoeic dermatitis — infants:** covers the management of seborrhoeic dermatitis of the scalp (cradle cap) in infants. Seborrhoeic dermatitis of the nappy area can be found in PRODIGY guidance on *Nappy rash*.

Seborrhoeic dermatitis of the scalp and beard

S

Which therapy?

Seborrhoeic dermatitis is extremely rare between infancy and puberty. Reconsider the diagnosis in anyone in this age group presenting with symptoms of seborrhoeic dermatitis.

- **Mild:** recommend anti-dandruff shampoos containing zinc pyrithione or coal tar preparations, which are widely available for general sale. Ask about general sales or over-the-counter products that may have already been tried.
- **Moderate to severe:** use an antifungal shampoo until symptoms resolve.
  - Ketoconazole 2% shampoo twice a week is the preferred treatment.
  - Selenium sulphide 2.5% shampoo twice a week for 2 weeks then once a week is an alternative, although it may be less well tolerated.
  - Products containing coal tar in combination with an antifungal (e.g. Polytar AF) may be useful.
- **Use a topical corticosteroid scalp application in addition to an antifungal** if there is more severe erythema, itching, and flaking. This should be discontinued within 14 days or as soon as improvement has reached a level acceptab[le] to the person.
- **Removal of adherent crusts or scales:** this may be done by
  - Applying warm mineral or olive oil to the scalp for several hours, then washing with a detergent or coal tar shampoo.
  - Overnight application of a keratolytic preparation.
- **Once symptoms are under control,** the frequency of shampooing with medicated shampoos may be stopped or reduced.
- **If recurrence of symptoms is a problem:** use an antifungal shampoo (e.g. ketoconazole 2%) once a wee[k] or on alternate weeks to maintain remission.

Practical prescribing points

For further information please see the *Medicines Compendium* (www.medicines.org.uk) or the *British National Formulary* (www.bnf.org).

Antifungal shampoos

- Medicated shampoos may dry the hair. If this is a problem, advise the person to use a moisturizing shampoo.
- Polytar preparations contain arachis (peanut) oil. The CSM has recently advised that, although the risk of an allergic reaction is low, people known to be allergic to peanuts or soya should not use medicines containing peanut oil [CSM, 2003].

Topical corticosteroids

- Advise the person to use topical corticosteroids sparingly, and for the shortest amount of time necessar[y].

Follow-up advice

- Follow-up will depend on response to treatment. In mo[st] cases, a well-informed person will be able to manage th[e] condition well with only an occasional medication review by the healthcare professional.

Should I refer or investigate?

Refer?

- Consider specialist referral when there is diagnostic uncertainty, when the disease is widespread, or if it is refractory to topical therapy.

Investigate?

- Investigate people with widespread disease (scalp, face, and body) for HIV infection.

atient information leaflets

ie following PILs are available at www.prodigy.nhs.uk
Eczema - Fingertip Units for Topical Steroids
Seborrhoeic Dermatitis of Adults
Skin Care Campaign

hared decision making

An anti-dandruff shampoo that contains zinc pyrithione or coal tar may clear symptoms in mild cases of seborrhoeic dermatitis.

An antifungal shampoo will normally clear more severe scalp symptoms. It kills the yeast germ that triggers the condition. For example:

- Ketoconazole 2% shampoo twice a week for 2–4 weeks, or
- Selenium sulphide 2.5% shampoo twice a week for 2 weeks, then once a week until symptoms have cleared.

Leave the shampoo on for about 5 minutes before rinsing off.

Thick crusts or scales on the scalp can be removed before using an antifungal shampoo by:

- Applying warm mineral or olive oil to the scalp for several hours, then washing with a detergent or coal tar shampoo, or
- Applying a 'scale-lifting' lotion (keratolytic) overnight.

A steroid scalp lotion may be advised for a short time in severe cases.

Symptoms often recur after treatment.

- Each episode can be treated as above, or
- An antifungal shampoo used once every 1–2 weeks will often prevent recurrences.

rug rationale

rugs not included

Imidazole antifungals (other than ketoconazole) are not as effective as ketoconazole at eliminating *Malassezia* yeasts [Faergemann, 1984] and are not available as shampoos or suitable scalp preparations.

Oral imidazole antifungals are not included in this scenario, as they should be reserved for people with widespread or resistant disease.

Corticosteroids (other than betamethasone, clobetasol propionate, hydrocortisone butyrate, and mometasone furoate) are not available as scalp preparations. Clobetasol propionate is a very potent corticosteroid and is not offered, as it confers a greater risk of adverse effects.

Povidone iodine shampoo is not included as we found no good evidence of its efficacy in seborrhoeic dermatitis.

rugs included

Anti-dandruff shampoos containing zinc pyrithione and shampoos containing coal tar and coal tar extracts may be effective in mild seborrhoeic dermatitis. An over-the-counter advice note is included for people who have not already tried these.

Ketoconazole 2% shampoo is the preferred antifungal shampoo for the treatment and prophylaxis of seborrhoeic dermatitis of the scalp.

Selenium sulphide 2.5% shampoo is an alternative to ketoconazole in the treatment of seborrhoeic dermatitis of the scalp, but is less well tolerated than ketoconazole.

Coal tar plus antifungal (Polytar AF) is included, as it has both keratolytic and antifungal properties.

Corticosteroid scalp applications are recommended in addition to an antifungal when more rapid resolution of symptoms is required. Betamethasone valerate 0.1%, hydrocortisone butyrate 0.1%, and mometasone furoate 0.1% are potent corticosteroids available as scalp applications.

- **Cocois scalp ointment (coal tar solution 12% + salicylic acid 2% + precipitated sulphur 4%)** is recommended as a keratolytic to remove more severe scaling.

Prescriptions

Antifungal shampoo (treatment)

OTC purchase advice: anti-dandruff shampoo

- Age from 12 months onwards
- An anti-dandruff shampoo that contains zinc pyrithione or coal tar may clear symptoms in mild cases of seborrhoeic dermatitis. These are widely available for you to buy – ask your pharmacist if you are not sure which one is best for you.

Ketoconazole 2% shampoo: use twice a WEEK

- Age from 12 months onwards
- Ketoconazole 2% shampoo. Apply to the affected area twice a WEEK for 2 to 4 weeks until symptoms have cleared; supply 120 ml; NHS Cost £4.64; OTC Cost £8.75.

Selenium sulphide 2.5% shampoo: use twice a WEEK

- Age from 5 years onwards
- Selenium sulphide 2.5% shampoo. Apply to the affected area twice a WEEK for 2 weeks, then once a WEEK for 2 weeks; supply 100 ml; NHS Cost £1.96; OTC Cost £3.45.

Coal tar + zinc pyrithione 1% shampoo: use 2-3 times a WEEK

- Age from 12 months onwards
- Polytar AF shampoo. Apply to the affected area 2 to 3 times a WEEK for at least 3 weeks, until symptoms have cleared; supply 150 ml; NHS Cost £4.40; OTC Cost £7.76.

Topical corticosteroid: add-on to antifungal (if severe)

Betamethasone 0.1% scalp application: use twice a day

- Age from 12 months onwards
- Betamethasone 0.1% scalp application. Apply thinly to dry hair in the morning and at night. As your symptoms improve, this can be reduced; supply 100 ml; NHS Cost £4.22.

Mometasone 0.1% scalp application: use once a day

- Age from 12 months onwards
- Mometasone 0.1% lotion. Apply a few drops to the affected area once a day. Massage in thoroughly until the lotion disappears; supply 60 ml; NHS Cost £9.76.

Hydrocortisone butyrate 0.1% scalp application: twice a day

- Age from 12 months onwards
- Hydrocortisone butyr scalp lotion. Apply thinly to dry hair in the morning and at night. As your symptoms improve, this can be reduced; supply 100 ml; NHS Cost £10.49.

Topical corticosteroid + antifungal (if severe)

Ketoconazole shampoo + betamethasone scalp application

- Age from 12 months onwards
- Ketoconazole 2% shampoo. Apply to the affected area twice a WEEK for 2 to 4 weeks until symptoms have cleared; supply 120 ml; NHS Cost £4.64; OTC Cost £8.75.
- Betamethasone 0.1% scalp application. Apply thinly to dry hair in the morning and at night. As your symptoms

improve, this can be reduced; supply 100 ml; NHS Cost £4.22.

Ketoconazole shampoo + mometasone scalp application

- Age from 12 months onwards
- Ketoconazole 2% shampoo. Apply to the affected area twice a WEEK for 2 to 4 weeks until symptoms have cleared; supply 120 ml; NHS Cost £4.64; OTC Cost £8.75.
- Mometasone 0.1% lotion. Apply a few drops to the affected area once a day. Massage in thoroughly until the lotion disappears; supply 60 ml; NHS Cost £9.76.

Selenium shampoo + betamethasone scalp application

- Age from 5 years onwards
- Selenium sulphide 2.5% shampoo. Apply to the affected area twice a WEEK for 2 weeks, then once a WEEK for 2 weeks; supply 100 ml; NHS Cost £1.96; OTC Cost £3.45.
- Betamethasone 0.1% scalp application. Apply thinly to dry hair in the morning and at night. As your symptoms improve, this can be reduced; supply 100 ml; NHS Cost £4.22.

Selenium shampoo + mometasone scalp application

- Age from 5 years onwards
- Selenium sulphide 2.5% shampoo. Apply to the affected area twice a WEEK for 2 weeks, then once a WEEK for 2 weeks; supply 100 ml; NHS Cost £1.96; OTC Cost £3.45.
- Mometasone 0.1% lotion. Apply a few drops to the affected area once a day. Massage in thoroughly until the lotion disappears; supply 60 ml; NHS Cost £9.76.

Keratolytic (to remove scaling)

Cocois scalp ointment

- Age from 6 years onwards
- Cocois scalp ointment (100g). Apply to the scalp once a day for 3 to 7 days until symptoms improve. Then apply once a week when required to remove scaling; supply 100 grams; NHS Cost £12.30; OTC Cost £21.68.

Antifungal shampoo: (prophylaxis)

Ketoconazole 2% shampoo: use once every 1 to 2 WEEKS

- Age from 12 months onwards
- Ketoconazole 2% shampoo. Apply to the affected area once every 1 to 2 WEEKS when needed to control dandruff. Leave for 3 to 5 minutes before rinsing; supply 120 ml; NHS Cost £4.64; OTC Cost £8.75.

S

Selenium sulphide 2.5% shampoo: use as needed

- Age from 5 years onwards
- Selenium sulphide 2.5% shampoo. Apply to the affected area when needed to control dandruff. Do not use more than twice a WEEK; supply 100 ml; NHS Cost £1.96; OTC Cost £3.45.

Seborrhoeic dermatitis of the face and body

Which therapy

Note: seborrhoeic dermatitis is extremely rare between infancy and puberty. Reconsider the diagnosis in anyone in this age group presenting with symptoms of seborrhoeic dermatitis.

- **Start a topical imidazole cream.**
  - Ketoconazole 2% cream is the imidazole of choice
- **Prescribe a mild potency topical corticosteroid in addition to the imidazole** when a more rapid initial improvement is required.
- **Discontinue the topical corticosteroid** within 14 days o as soon as improvement has reached a level acceptable the person.
- **Continue with the imidazole** until complete resolution has occurred.
- **Treat clinically apparent secondary bacterial infection** with oral antibiotics.
- **Recommend daily washing with soap and water** to remove the lipid that is the substrate for the yeast.
- **Consider using prophylactic imidazole cream when relapses are frequent.** Start by applying it once a day or alternate days, and increase or reduce the frequency depending on response.
- **If seborrhoeic dermatitis is widespread or resistant to topical treatment consider:**
  - Is the diagnosis correct?
  - Is the person HIV positive?

Practical prescribing points

For further information please see the *Medicines Compendium* (www.medicines.org.uk) or the *British National Formulary* (www.bnf.org).

- Dermatological hypersensitivity reactions have occasionally been reported in people who have used prolonged treatment with potent topical corticosteroid before the application of ketoconazole. Consider the possibility of contact dermatitis and referral to a dermatologist for patch testing in anyone who does no respond to treatment.

Topical corticosteroids

- Do not apply topical steroids to the eyelids.

Follow-up advice

- Follow-up will depend on response to treatment. In mc cases, a well-informed person will be able to manage th condition well with only an occasional medication review by the healthcare professional.

Should I refer or investigate?

Refer?

- Consider specialist referral when there is diagnostic uncertainty, when the disease is widespread, or if it is r responding to topical therapy. Seek specialist advice regarding appropriate treatment whilst the person is waiting for review.

Investigate?

- Investigate people with widespread disease for HIV infection.

Patient information leaflets

The following PILs are available at www.prodigy.nhs.uk

- Eczema - Fingertip Units for Topical Steroids
- Seborrhoeic Dermatitis of Adults
- Skin Care Campaign

Shared decision making

- **An antifungal cream** will normally clear the rash of seborrhoeic dermatitis within 2–4 weeks. It kills the yeast germ that triggers the condition.
- **A mild steroid cream** may also be advised for a week o so if the skin is badly inflamed. Steroid creams dampen inflammation that reduces the redness and itch.
- **Symptoms often recur after treatment.**

- Each episode can be treated as above, or
- If recurrences are frequent, you may be advised to use an antifungal cream once or twice a week to keep the condition from recurring.
- Also, daily washing with soap and water helps to remove the greasy sebum from the body. This helps to keep the number of yeast germs to a minimum.

)rug rationale

rugs not included

Topical imidazoles, other than ketoconazole, are not included, as there is no evidence to support their use in the treatment of seborrhoeic dermatitis of the face and body.
Topical terbinafine is not included, as there is only weak evidence of its efficacy in the treatment of seborrhoeic dermatitis of the face and body.
Topical metronidazole is not included, as there is conflicting evidence of its efficacy in seborrhoeic dermatitis. It is not licensed for this indication.
Oral imidazoles antifungals are not included in this scenario, as they should be reserved for people with widespread or resistant disease.
Topical corticosteroids, other than hydrocortisone 1% cream, are not recommended for use on the face. More potent steroids carry the risk of increased adverse effects.
Combination products of a topical corticosteroid + a topical antifungal are not included, as this treatment does not allow for stopping the corticosteroid while maintaining the topical antifungal.

rugs included

Ketoconazole 2% cream is the topical imidazole of choice in the treatment of seborrhoeic dermatitis of the face and body. Its efficacy is supported by a number of trials [McGrath and Murphy, 1991].
Hydrocortisone 1% cream is recommended in addition to ketaconazole when more rapid resolution of symptoms is required. Cream is usually preferred to ointment for use on the face.

rescriptions

opical antifungal (treatment)

etoconazole 2% cream: use once or twice a day

- Age from 12 months onwards
- Ketoconazole 2% cream. Apply to the affected area(s) once or twice a day. Continue for a few days after the affected area has healed; supply 30 grams; NHS Cost £3.81.

opical corticosteroid: add-on to antifungal (if evere)

drocortisone 1% cream: apply thinly once or twice a y

- Age from 12 months onwards
- Hydrocortisone 1% cream (30g). Apply thinly to the affected area(s) once or twice a day; supply 30 grams; NHS Cost £0.72.

opical antifungal + corticosteroid

etoconazole 2% + hydrocortisone 1% cream

- Age from 12 months onwards
- Ketoconazole 2% cream. Apply to the affected area(s) in the morning. Continue for a few days after the affected area has healed; supply 30 grams; NHS Cost £3.81.
- Hydrocortisone 1% cream (30g). Apply thinly to the affected area(s) in the evening. Do not use for longer than 14 days; supply 30 grams; NHS Cost £0.72.

Topical antifungal (prophylaxis)

Ketoconazole 2% cream: apply once or twice a week

- Age from 12 months onwards
- Ketoconazole 2% cream. Apply to the affected area(s) once or twice a WEEK; supply 30 grams; NHS Cost £3.81.

Seborrhoeic dermatitis — infants

Which therapy

Scalp (cradle cap)

- **Reassure the parents** of the non-serious and self-limiting nature of the condition.
- **Start with simple measures to remove scales:**
  - Wash the scalp daily with baby shampoo and loosen the scales with soft brushing.
  - Alternatively, soften the scales with baby oil, followed by gentle brushing to loosen the scales. Then wash off with baby shampoo.
- **Consider treating with topical 2% ketoconazole shampoo or cream** if not improving or if deteriorating.

Nappy rash

- See PRODIGY guidance on *Nappy rash*.

Practical prescribing points

For further information please see the *Medicines Compendium* (www.medicines.org.uk) or the *British National Formulary* (www.bnf.org).

- Ketoconazole shampoo may dry the hair. If this is a problem, advise the parent to use a baby shampoo.

Follow-up advice

- Follow-up will depend on response.

Should I refer or investigate?

Refer?

- **Urgent admission is required for all cases of suspected Leiner's disease.**
  - Leiner's disease is a complication of seborrhoeic dermatitis in infants. There is usually a sudden confluence of lesions leading to a universal scaling redness of the skin. The baby is severely ill with anaemia, diarrhoea, and vomiting. Secondary bacterial infection is common.

Patient information leaflets

The following PILs are available at www.prodigy.nhs.uk

- Eczema - Fingertip Units for Topical Steroids
- Seborrhoeic Dermatitis in Babies (Cradle Cap)
- Skin Care Campaign

Shared decision making

- **Treatment is not usually needed for cradle cap and seborrhoeic dermatitis of babies,** as the condition:
  - Is usually mild.
  - Is not serious.
  - Does not usually cause any discomfort to the baby.

S

- Usually goes before the baby is eight months old, and often sooner.
- **The appearance of the scalp can be improved** by:
  - Daily washing of the scalp with a baby shampoo, followed by gentle brushing with a soft brush to loosen the scales.
  - Alternatively, softening the scales with baby oil first, followed by gentle brushing, then washing with baby shampoo.
- In more severe cases, an antifungal cream such as ketoconazole 2% cream will usually clear the rash.

Drug rationale

Drugs not included

- **Topical corticosteroids** are not recommended in infantile seborrhoeic dermatitis. The risk of adverse effects of even mild topical corticosteroids is significantly higher in infants, and in most cases is not justified for treating an infant who is not distressed by this self-limiting condition.
- **Imidazole antifungals,** other than ketoconazole, are not recommended, as there is no evidence to support their use in infantile seborrhoeic dermatitis.

Drugs included

- Washing the scalp with baby shampoo, or softening scales with baby oil followed by gentle brushing, will help to remove scales. An advice note is provided to explain to parents how this can be done.
- **Ketoconazole** is recommended if treatment is considered necessary when the condition is not improving or is deteriorating. Shampoo and cream are both offered.

Prescriptions

Advice note: removing the scales

Advice note

- Age under 11 months
- Treatment is not usually needed as the condition is usually mild and does not cause discomfort to the baby. The appearance of the scalp can be improved by regular washing with a baby shampoo followed by gentle brushing with a soft brush to loosen scales. Alternatively, soften the scales with baby oil or olive oil first, followed by gentle brushing, then wash off with baby shampoo.

Antifungal shampoo

Ketoconazole 2% shampoo: use twice a WEEK

- Age under 11 months
- Ketoconazole 2% shampoo. Apply to the affected area twice a WEEK for 2 to 4 weeks until symptoms have cleared; supply 120 ml; NHS Cost £4.64.

Antifungal cream

Ketoconazole 2% cream: apply once or twice a day

- Age under 11 months
- Ketoconazole 2% cream. Apply to the affected area(s) once or twice a day. Continue for a few days after the affected area has healed; supply 30 grams; NHS Cost £3.81.

Extended Information

Background information

- What is it? p.1688
- How common is it? p.1688
- How do I know my patient has it? p.1688
- What else might it be? p.1689
- Complications and prognosis p.1689

What is it?

- Seborrhoeic dermatitis is a chronic relapsing condition that has a distinctive appearance and distribution. The lesions of seborrhoeic dermatitis are sharply marginate covered with greasy-looking scales, and distributed in areas with a rich supply of sebaceous glands, namely th scalp, face, and upper trunk.
- The yeast *Malassezia sp.* (previously known as *Pityrosporum ovale*) plays an important role in the development of seborrhoeic dermatitis. A direct toxic effect or an immunological reaction to the yeast has be suggested, but the exact mechanism remains unknown Malassezia yeasts are present in large numbers in the sebaceous regions of all adults.
- In people with seborrhoeic dermatitis, the condition is improved by removing the yeasts with antifungal drugs [McGrath and Murphy, 1991].

How common is it?

- Seborrhoeic dermatitis is a common disorder.
- It has a prevalence of 3–5% in adults aged between 18–40 years [Johnson and Roberts, 1977].
- There is a further peak incidence in babies under the ag of 8 months, after which it spontaneously resolves.
- Seborrhoeic dermatitis is more common in:
  - Men than in women.
  - People with HIV (prevalence of 36–83%).
  - People with an underlying neurological illness, such Parkinson's disease [Gupta and Bluhm, 2004].

How do I know my patient has it?

The clinical features of seborrhoeic dermatitis differ in adults, in infants, and in people with HIV infection, but a improve with treatments that eliminate Malassezia yeasts Seborrhoeic dermatitis is extremely rare between infancy and puberty.

Classical seborrhoeic dermatitis

- In adults, seborrhoeic dermatitis usually presents with history of a chronic, relapsing, inflammatory skin problem, most commonly in people of age 18–40 years
- Classical seborrhoeic dermatitis appears as a papular eruption that is characteristically red with greasy-look scales.
- It is distributed in any or all of the following areas: the scalp, nasolabial folds, external ears, eyebrows and eyelashes, the presternal areas of the chest, and on the back between the shoulders.
- The clinical features of the scalp may vary markedly from predominantly scaling (dandruff) to a predominantly red and sore scalp. Dandruff is usually the earliest manifestation of classical seborrhoeic dermatitis.

Infantile seborrhoeic dermatitis

- Seborrhoeic dermatitis in infants typically occurs withi the first 6 months of life and resolves spontaneously by 8 months of age. It most commonly presents at around 3 months of age but cases have been reported in young infants [Gupta and Bluhm, 2004].
- Infants most commonly present with 'cradle cap', characterised by greasy, yellow, scaly patches over the scalp. In some cases a thick scaly layer may cover the whole scalp. Over time the scales may become flaky an rub off easily. The condition is usually not itchy and in

most cases the baby does not seem troubled by symptoms.

Other areas may be involved, including eyebrows, paranasal areas and flexural sites [Yates et al, 1983].

Seborrhoeic dermatitis in infants may also be a cause of nappy rash. For further information. see PRODIGY guidance on *Nappy rash*.

Seborrhoeic dermatitis in people who are HIV-positive

Seborrhoeic dermatitis in people who are HIV-positive has the same appearance as in adults, but is often uncharacteristically widespread and rapid in onset. The severity often corresponds with the degree of immunocompromise [Gupta and Bluhm, 2004].

The possibility of HIV infection should always be considered in anyone with severe, widespread seborrhoeic dermatitis.

What else might it be?

The differential diagnosis varies according to site:

Scalp

- Psoriasis
- Atopic eczema
- Infective dermatitis complicating pediculosis

Ear canal

- Psoriasis
- Contact dermatitis, both allergic and irritant

Face

- Rosacea
- Contact dermatitis
- Psoriasis
- Impetigo

Eye lids

- Atopic dermatitis
- Psoriasis

Chest and back

- Pityriasis rosea
- Pityriasis versicolor

[Plewig and Jansen, 1999]

Complications and prognosis

Complications

Psychosocial impact: chronic visible disease may affect a person's self esteem.

Secondary bacterial infection with *Staphylococcus aureus* may occur, with typical impetigo with increased redness, oozing, and crusting.

Leiner's disease is a complication of seborrhoeic dermatitis in infants. There is usually a sudden confluence of lesions leading to a universal scaling redness of the skin. The child is severely ill with anaemia, diarrhoea, and vomiting. Secondary bacterial infection is common [Plewig and Jansen, 1999].

Prognosis

Infantile seborrhoeic dermatitis: spontaneous resolution may occur within a few weeks or it may persist for several months, but in most cases resolves by 8 months of age.

Adult seborrhoeic dermatitis: usually lasts for years to decades, with periods of improvement in warmer seasons and periods of exacerbation in colder months.

[Plewig and Jansen, 1999]

Management issues

Principles of management p.1689

How should I manage seborrhoeic dermatitis of the scalp and beard? p.1689

- How should I manage seborrhoeic dermatitis of the face and body? p.1690
- How should I manage widespread seborrhoeic dermatitis? p.1691
- How should I manage infantile seborrhoeic dermatitis? p.1691
- Medicines management p.1691

Principles of management

Patient education

- Explain that treatment cannot cure seborrhoeic dermatitis but can control it.
- Seborrhoeic dermatitis may be associated with a significant degree of anxiety regarding its cause and cosmetic appearance.
- Good patient education enables people to be in control of their condition and relieve anxieties associated with it.
- Alcoholic solutions such as tinctures and hair tonics usually aggravate the inflammatory state and should be avoided [Plewig and Jansen, 1999].
- Soap and shaving cream may be irritating when applied to affected skin, and can be avoided by using emollients or emollient soap substitutes.

Treating the acute phase

- **Antifungal treatments remove the Malassezia yeasts, and this is followed by improvement in the inflamed lesions.** Relapse after antifungal treatment is common, but is delayed until re-colonisation has occurred.
- **Topical corticosteroids reduce the inflammation of the lesions.** Inflammation settles initially more quickly with corticosteroids than with antifungals, but the outcome after 4 weeks of treatment is similar. However, the numbers of Malassezia yeasts are not reduced with corticosteroids, and early relapse after treatment stops is common if treatment is not combined with an antifungal [Faergemann, 1986].
- **Topical antifungal and corticosteroid treatments are commonly combined** to achieve a more rapid initial improvement and a prolonged time to relapse.
- **Keratolytics** are used to remove scales from the scalp that are unsightly, and which, when dense, may reduce the effectiveness of other topical treatments.
- **Oral antifungal drugs** are recommended when the condition is widespread or resistant to topical treatment.
- **Oral antibiotics** are recommended for clinically apparent secondary infection, see PRODIGY guidance on *Impetigo* for more information.

Maintaining remission

- **Relapse after treatment of the acute phase is common.** Prophylactic antifungal treatment has been shown to reduce rates of relapse of seborrhoeic dermatitis of the scalp. Some experts also recommend prophylactic treatment of the face and body when this occurs frequently.

How should I manage seborrhoeic dermatitis of the scalp and beard?

Mild seborrhoeic dermatitis

- **Dandruff associated with mild seborrhoeic dermatitis of the scalp** can be treated by shampooing daily or every other day with 'antidandruff shampoos' containing zinc pyrithione [McGrath and Murphy, 1991]. These are widely available for general sale.
- Shampoos containing coal tar extracts are also widely available and may be useful for the treatment of mild

scalp disease. We could find no published evidence to support their use over antifungal preparations for the treatment of seborrhoeic dermatitis. Many people find them unpleasant to use.

Moderate to severe seborrhoeic dermatitis

- **Ketoconazole 2% shampoo is the treatment of choice.**
  - In a multicentre study in 575 people with moderate to severe seborrhoeic dermatitis and dandruff of the scalp, ketoconazole 2% shampoo twice a week produced an excellent response in 55% of people after 2 weeks and 88% after 4 weeks [Peter and Richarz-Barthauer, 1995].
  - In another non-blinded, randomized trial, a significantly greater improvement in total dandruff severity score was seen after 4 weeks treatment with ketoconazole 2% shampoo than with zinc pyrithione 1% shampoo (73% compared with 67%; $p < 0.02$). The recurrence rate was also significantly lower after ketoconazole treatment than after zinc pyrithione treatment (39% compared with 51%; $p < 0.03$) [Pierard-Franchimont et al, 2002].
- **Selenium sulphide may be used as an alternative** to ketoconazole in people with moderate to severe seborrhoeic dermatitis of the scalp. However, it seems to be less well tolerated than ketoconazole.
  - The use of selenium sulphide 2.5% shampoo has been shown to improve dandruff, folliculitis, pain, and dryness [Fredriksson, 1985].
  - Selenium sulphide 2.5% shampoo has shown efficacy similar to that of ketoconazole 2% shampoo in terms of reducing adherent dandruff and irritation in people with moderate to severe seborrhoeic dermatitis of the scalp [Danby et al, 1993].
  - Selenium sulphide is less well tolerated than ketoconazole, with adverse effects including pruritis or burning of the scalp, lightening or leaching of the hair colour, and orange staining of the scalp [Danby et al, 1993].
- **Use a topical corticosteroid scalp application in addition to an antifungal treatment if there is more severe erythema, itching, and flaking.** This should be discontinued within 14 days or as soon as improvement has reached a level acceptable to the person.
  - In a double-blind, randomized study comparing the efficacy of mometasone furoate 0.1% solution once a day with ketoconazole 2% shampoo twice a week, after 2 weeks there was significantly greater improvement in symptom scores (pruritis, scaling, and erythema) with mometasone than with ketoconazole. After 4 weeks the treatment effects were similar, with the only difference being less scaling in the mometasone group [Hersle et al, 1996]. There was no follow-up to determine rates of relapse once treatment was discontinued.
  - One small study has compared an imidazole antifungal (miconazole 2%) plus hydrocortisone 1%, with miconazole 2% and hydrocortisone 1% separately. After 3 weeks of treatment there were no significant differences between treatments in the observed cure rates (68–91%), although there were significantly larger reductions in the numbers of yeasts in the combination and miconazole groups ($p < 0.01$) [Faergemann, 1986].
- **Adherent crusts or scales should be removed before antifungal treatment.** Many ways of doing this have been suggested in the literature, although none is supported by good-quality evidence. These include:
  - Applying warm mineral or olive oil to the scalp for several hours, then washing with a detergent or coal tar shampoo [Johnson and Nunley, 2000].
  - Overnight application of a keratolytic preparation [Plewig and Jansen, 1999] or coal tar–keratolytic preparation [Johnson and Nunley, 2000].
  - Products containing coal tar in combination with an antifungal (e.g. Polytar AF) may be useful [Davies et al, 1999].

Maintaining remission

- **Once symptoms are under control,** the frequency of shampooing with medicated shampoos may be reduced or stopped [Johnson and Nunley, 2000].
- **If relapse is a problem,** prophylaxis with an antifungal shampoo once a week or once every other week is effective at reducing the rate of relapse [Peter and Richarz-Barthauer, 1995].
- **Topical corticosteroids are not appropriate for long-ter[m] use,** and their use in preventing relapse is not recommended.

How should I manage seborrhoeic dermatiti[s] of the face and body?

Treating the acute phase

- **A topical antifungal should be considered in all people with seborrhoeic dermatitis, and continued until complete resolution has been achieved. Ketoconazole 2% cream is the preferred topical antifungal.**
- The efficacy, tolerability, and safety of 2% ketoconazo[le] cream has been established in a number of trials examining the treatment of seborrhoeic dermatitis of th[e] face and body [McGrath and Murphy, 1991].
  - The superiority of ketoconazole over other imidazole[s] at reducing the Malassezia yeasts has been shown bo[th] *in vitro* and *in vivo* [Faergemann, 1984].
  - Although other imidazoles have been shown to be effective in treating the scalp, we could find no trials examining their efficacy on the face and body.
  - Miconazole is widely prescribed, particularly as a combined product with 1% hydrocortisone.
  - The efficacy of topical metronidazole in the treatmen[t] of seborrhoeic dermatitis has yet to be established. Reports regarding its efficacy from two randomized controlled trials are conflicting.
- **The addition of a mild corticosteroid to an antifungal treatment** seems to settle inflammation more quickly bu[t] not to increase the resolution rate of the condition. Prolonged use of a corticosteroid beyond 2 weeks is unlikely to have any additional benefit.
  - Evidence for this comes from a study comparing the rates of improvement of seborrhoeic dermatitis of th[e] scalp when treated with ketoconazole alone compare[d] with mometasone furoate alone [Hersle et al, 1996]. No similar study for treatments relating to the face and body could be found.
  - The possible increased early rate of improvement wit[h] topical corticosteroids needs to be balanced against their potential for adverse effects, particularly in people requiring treatment for frequent relapses.
  - Topical corticosteroids should be discontinued as so[on] as improvement has reached a level acceptable to the person.
- **The time to relapse after treatment with corticosteroids alone is shorter than with an antifungal alone** [Faergemann, 1986]. Therefore, in general, the use of a topical corticosteroid alone is not recommended.
- **Treatment of seborrhoeic dermatitis around the eye requires special consideration.**
  - Ketoconazole cream is a convenient treatment for the eyelids when they are involved. If irritation to the eye occurs with treatment, discontinue the treatment and examine the eyes. Daily hygiene measures using cotto[n]

S

buds moistened with baby shampoo has been shown to be an equally effective treatment, although less convenient [Nelson et al, 1990].
- Topical corticosteroids used on the eyelids may increase intra-ocular pressure, particularly in people over the age of 35 years, and less commonly induce cataract.

Maintaining remission

- **Prophylactic antifungal treatment is recommended by some specialists when relapses are frequent.**
  - Studies support the prophylactic use of antifungal treatments to reduce the relapse rates of seborrhoeic dermatitis in the scalp [Peter and Richarz-Barthauer, 1995].
  - Although no similar studies have been carried out examining prophylactic treatment of the face and body, use of these treatments seems logical and is supported by some specialists.
- **The safe long-term use of topical ketoconazole cream and shampoo is supported by several studies** examining skin absorption, local irritancy, and contact sensitivity [McGrath and Murphy, 1991].
- There is no evidence to guide the frequency of application of prophylactic topical antifungal treatments. Applying treatment once a day on alternate days is a suggested starting point; treatment can then be adjusted according to response.
- **Daily washing with soap and water** is widely recommended, because removal of lipid removes the substrate for the yeast.

How should I manage widespread seborrhoeic dermatitis?

- **Severe widespread disease is uncommon.** When it occurs, consider:
  - Is the diagnosis of seborrhoeic dermatitis correct?
  - Does the person have HIV infection?
- **Oral treatment** with imidazole antifungals (e.g. itraconazole or ketoconazole) may be more effective and more convenient to use than topical treatment when seborrhoeic dermatitis is widespread. People with widespread seborrhoeic dermatitis should be referred to a dermatologist for specialist assessment and management. Seek specialist advice regarding appropriate treatment whilst the person is waiting for review.

How should I manage infantile seborrhoeic dermatitis?

Cradle cap

- **Reassure the parents** that infantile seborrhoeic dermatitis is not a serious condition, does not usually trouble the infant, and will spontaneously resolve within weeks to months.
- **Simple measures are all that are required in most cases.** Regular washing of the scalp with a baby shampoo followed by gentle brushing with a soft brush will loosen scales and improve the condition. Alternatively, soften the scales with baby oil first, followed by gentle brushing, then wash off with baby shampoo. Where this does not achieve softening, a greasy emollient or soap substitute such as emulsifying ointment can be used, which helps to remove the scale more easily.
- **Ketoconazole 2% cream once a day has been shown to be effective.** In an open study of 19 infants, 80% were almost clear after 10 days of treatment [Taieb et al, 1990]. Studies of percutaneous absorption in seven infants showed minimal plasma levels despite the large surface area of topical application [Levron and Taieb, 1991].
- **Avoid topical corticosteroids.** The risk of adverse effects of even mild topical corticosteroids is significantly higher in infants because of the high ratio of surface area to weight, and in most cases this treatment is not justified for treating an infant who is not distressed by this self-limiting condition.

Nappy rash

- See PRODIGY guidance on *Nappy rash*.

Medicines management

Antifungal treatments

- Ketoconazole shampoo should be applied to wet hair, massaged into the scalp and left on for 3–5 minutes before rinsing off.
- Ketoconazole is generally well tolerated. Occasionally the shampoo can dry the hair, and a moisturising shampoo (e.g. baby shampoo or non-medicated shampoo) can be used afterwards or in between applications to prevent desiccation of the hair [Johnson and Nunley, 2000].

Products containing arachis (peanut) oil

- Polytar products contain arachis (peanut) oil extract of coal tar. The Committee on Safety of Medicines (CSM) has recently advised that, although the risk of an allergic reaction is low, people known to be allergic to peanuts or soya should not use medicines containing peanut oil [CSM, 2003].

Topical corticosteroids

- **Do not use topical corticosteroids where there is uncertainty about the diagnosis** — they are contraindicated in ulcerative conditions and rosacea.
- **Adverse effects of topical corticosteroids include:** skin atrophy, especially on thin skin areas such as the face or flexures; exacerbation of skin infection; contact dermatitis; acne at the site of application; and pituitary-adrenal-axis suppression.
- **The risk of adverse effects increases** with the potency of the topical corticosteroid, duration of use, and area of application (e.g. face, flexures). Mild and moderate potency topical corticosteroids used for short periods of time are rarely associated with adverse effects.
- **How much topical corticosteroid should be applied?** As a practical guide, the quantity of topical corticosteroid to apply is often expressed in terms of fingertip units (FTUs).
  - One FTU is roughly equivalent to the amount of cream or ointment that can be squeezed from a tube with a standard nozzle onto an adult index finger from the tip of the finger to the first crease.
  - FTUs should be used together with body charts that show the number of FTUs required to cover each area of a child's or adult's body.
  - As a rough guide, one FTU of topical corticosteroid is sufficient to treat a skin area about twice that of the flat of the hand with the fingers together.

[MeReC, 1999]
- **The duration of corticosteroids** should be kept to a minimum in order to reduce the risk of adverse effects. Improvement should be seen within 3–7 days of starting topical corticosteroids. If the condition does not improve after this time, reassess the diagnosis. In seborrhoeic dermatitis, topical corticosteroids do not usually need to be used for more than 2 weeks. Topical corticosteroids should not be used to maintain remission.

[MeReC, 1999]

- Dermatological hypersensitivity reactions have occasionally been reported in people who have used prolonged treatment with potent topical corticosteroids before the application of ketoconazole. Consider the possibility of contact dermatitis and referral to a dermatologist for patch testing in anyone who does not respond to treatment.

References

NHS staff in England can link, free of charge, from references to full text journals by clicking on [Full text] on the PRODIGY website.

1. CSM (2003) Medicines containing peanut (arachis) oil. *Current Problems in Pharmacovigilance* **29**(Sept), 5.
2. Danby, F.W., Maddin, W.S., Margesson, L.J. and Rosenthal, D. (1993) A randomized, double-blind, placebo-controlled trial of ketoconazole 2% shampoo versus selenium sulfide 2.5% shampoo in the treatment of moderate to severe dandruff. *Journal of the American Academy of Dermatology* **29**(6), 1008–1012.
3. Davies, D.B., Boorman, G.C. and Shuttleworth, D. (1999) Comparative efficacy of shampoos containing coal tar (4.0% w/w; Tarmed(TM)), coal tar (4.0% w/w) plus ciclopirox olamine (1.0% w/w; Tarmed(TM) AF) and ketoconazole (2.0% w/w; Nizoral(TM)) for the treatment of dandruff/seborrhoeic dermatitis. *Journal of Dermatological Treatment* **10**(3), 177–183.
4. Faergemann, J. (1984) In vitro and in vivo activities of ketoconazole and itraconazole against Pityrosporum orbiculare. *Antimicrobial Agents & Chemotherapy* **26**(5), 773–774.
5. Faergemann, J. (1986) Seborrhoeic dermatitis and Pityrosporum orbiculare: treatment of seborrhoeic dermatitis of the scalp with miconazole-hydrocortisone (Daktacort), miconazole and hydrocortisone. *British Journal of Dermatology* **114**(6), 695–700.
6. Fredriksson, T. (1985) Controlled comparison of Clinitar shampoo and Selsun shampoo in the treatment of seborrhoeic dermatitis of the scalp. *British Journal of Clinical Practice* **39**(1), 25–28.
7. Gupta, A.K. and Bluhm, R. (2004) Seborrhoeic dermatitis. *Journal of the European Academy of Dermatology & Venereology* **18**(1), 13–26.
8. Hersle, K., Mobacken, H. and Nordin, P. (1996) Mometasone furoate solution 0.1% compared with ketoconazole shampoo 2% for seborrhoeic dermatitis of the scalp. *Current Therapeutic Research, Clinical & Experimental* 57(7), 516–522.
9. Johnson, B.A. and Nunley, J.R. (2000) Treatment of seborrhoeic dermatitis. *American Family Physician* **61**(9), 2703–2710. [Full text]
10. Johnson, M-L.T and Roberts, J (1977) *Prevalence of dermatological diseases among persons 1–74 years of age: United States.* Advance data report No. 4. Washington DC: U.S. Department of Health, Education, and Welfare.
11. Levron, J.C. and Taieb, A. (1991) Percutaneous absorption of ketoconazole in infant after topical application of Ketoderm(TM). *Therapie* **46**(1), 29–31.
12. McGrath, J. and Murphy, G.M. (1991) The control of seborrhoeic dermatitis and dandruff by antipityrosporal drugs. *Drugs* **41**(2), 178–184.
13. MeReC (1999) Using topical corticosteroids in general practice. *MeReC Bulletin* **10**(6), 21–24.
14. Nelson, M.E., Midgley, G. and Blatchford, N.R. (1990) Ketoconazole in the treatment of blepharitis. *Eye* **4**(Pt 1), 151–159.
15. Peter, R.U. and Richarz-Barthauer, U. (1995) Successful treatment and prophylaxis of scalp seborrhoeic dermatitis and dandruff with 2% ketoconazole shampoo: results of a multicentre, double-blind, placebo-controlled trial. *British Journal of Dermatology* **132**(3), 441–445.
16. Pierard-Franchimont, C., Goffin, V., Decroix, J. and Pierard, G.E. (2002) A multicenter randomized trial of ketoconazole 2% and zinc pyrithione 1% shampoos in severe dandruff and seborrhoeic dermatitis. *Skin Pharmacology & Applied Skin Physiology* **15**(6), 434–441.
17. Plewig, G. and Jansen, T. (1999) Seborrhoeic dermatitis. In: Freedberg, I.M., Eisen, A.Z., Wolff, K. et al (Eds.) *Fitzpatrick's dematology in general practice* 5th edn. London: McGraw – Hill. 1482–1489.
18. Taieb, A., Legrain, V., Palmier, C. et al (1990) Topical ketoconazole for infantile seborrhoeic dermatitis. *Dermatologica* **181**(1), 26–32.
19. Yates, V.M., Kerr, R.E., Frier, K. et al (1983) Early diagnosis of infantile seborrhoeic dermatitis and atopic dermatitis–total and specific IgE levels. *British Journal of Dermatology* **108**(6), 639–645.

PRODIGY GUIDANCE

Shingles and postherpetic neuralgia

Last revised in July 2005
www.prodigy.nhs.uk/guidance.asp?gt=Shingles/postherpetic pain

Applies to people over the age of 12 months

This guidance covers the management of shingles (herpes zoster) and postherpetic neuralgia.

There is separate PRODIGY guidance on *Chickenpox*, *Herpes simplex — oral* (cold sores and gingivostomatitis), *Herpes simplex — ocular*, *Herpes simplex — genital*, and *Trigeminal neuralgia*.

Goals

- To relieve the symptoms of shingles
- To minimize the risk of progression to postherpetic neuralgia
- To reduce symptoms and aid early recovery from postherpetic neuralgia

Contents

Scenarios

- Shingles — children p.1693
- Shingles — adults p.1695
- Postherpetic neuralgia — first line p.1697
- Postherpetic neuralgia — treatment failure p.1700

Extended Information, p. 1703

Which scenario?

- **Shingles — children:** covers the management of children with shingles.
- **Shingles — adults:** covers the management of adults with shingles, including those who are at high risk of severe disease and progression to postherpetic neuralgia (e.g. people with ophthalmic shingles; or people who are immunocompromised).
- **Postherpetic neuralgia — first line:** covers the management of people with postherpetic neuralgia who have not yet started with specific treatment for this. There is no widely agreed definition of postherpetic neuralgia. PRODIGY recommend that, for practical purposes, people should be considered to have postherpetic neuralgia if pain persists after the shingles rash has healed.
- **Postherpetic neuralgia — treatment failure:** covers the management of people who did not respond to treatment in scenario *Postherpetic neuralgia — first-line*.

Shingles — children

Which therapy?

- **Seek immediate specialist advice if the child is immunocompromised, or has an extensive rash, or is systemically unwell.**
- **For immunocompetent children, reassure that shingles is usually mild especially in young children.** Most children do not have acute neuropathic pain.
- **Treat symptomatically.**
  - **If analgesia is required** paracetamol or ibuprofen is recommended.
  - **If the rash is itchy:**
    - Oily calamine lotion may be soothing.
    - Consider a sedative antihistamine at night to break the itch-scratch cycle if the itch is severe and is disturbing sleep.
- Oral antivirals are not generally recommended for immunocompetent children. Consider if the child has atopic eczema, ophthalmic involvement, or Ramsay Hunt Syndrome or if they have contact with very young infants, immunocompromised individuals or pregnant women. Note: antivirals are not licensed in children. Seek specialist advice.
- **Give advice about keeping the rash clean and covered with a non-adherent dressing.**
  - This prevents transmission and may help to reduce any pain caused by contact with clothing.
  - Skin hygiene is important for preventing secondary bacterial infection.
- **Advise that the child is infectious until the lesions crust.**

Practical prescribing points

For further information see the *Medicines Compendium* (www.medicines.org.uk) or the *British National Formulary* (www.bnf.org).

Sedating antihistamines

- **Urinary retention:** avoid sedating antihistamines.
- **Epilepsy or risk of seizures:** avoid sedating antihistamines as they lower the seizure threshold.

Follow-up advice

- **Advise the parents to return for review if:**
  - The lesions become infected
  - They become systemically unwell
  - The rash becomes disseminated
  - Pain persists for more than a few days and is not controlled by the analgesia prescribed.

Should I refer or investigate?

Refer?

- **Seek immediate specialist advice if the child is immunocompromised.**
- **Admission is required** if severe complications develop, such as dissemination or encephalitis.

Investigate?

- Investigation is usually not necessary if a child is usually well, has a clear history of chickenpox, (or if the child's mother had chickenpox during pregnancy), and the shingles is mild.
- Investigate children for immunodeficiency if they have:
  - Recurrent shingles (two episodes or more)
  - Risk factors for immunocompromise
  - Severe, extensive or disseminated shingles or systemic symptoms

Patient information leaflets

The following PILs are available at www.prodigy.nhs.uk

- Herpes Viruses Association
- Medicines - Name Changes of Medicines
- Shingles
- Shingles Support Society

Shared decision making

- Shingles is caused by the same virus that causes chickenpox. The rash usually lasts 2–4 weeks. Shingles pain is not usually bad in children.
- **Paracetamol or ibuprofen** may help if the pain is troublesome.
- **Oily calamine lotion** may help to ease itch.
- **An antihistamine** at bedtime may help with sleep if itch is a problem.
- Keep the rash clean, cover with a non-adherent dressing, and wear loose cotton clothes over it. This helps to:
  - Prevent passing on the virus
  - Reduce pain caused by contact with clothing
  - Prevent secondary infection
- To reduce the risk of passing on the virus to people who are not immune to chickenpox, until the rash has crusted:
  - Do not let your child share towels with other people, or go swimming, or do contact sports.
  - If possible, try to keep the child away from babies, people with a poor immune system, and pregnant women.
- Antiviral medicine is not usually prescribed to children who are otherwise healthy as severe shingles and complications in healthy children are rare. It may be advised if the child:
  - Has a poor immune system
  - Has atopic eczema
  - Has shingles of the eye or inner ear
  - Is in contact with young babies, people with a poor immune system, or pregnant women

Drug rationale

Drugs not included

- **Oral antivirals:** PRODIGY does not recommend using antivirals in *healthy* children with shingles because none of the oral antivirals are licensed for use in this age group for acute shingles, and we found no published evidence examining efficacy of antivirals in children with shingles. Seek immediate specialist advice for children who are immunosuppressed.
- **Topical corticosteroids** should *not* be used during the acute phase of shingles, although they could be considered if the itch persists once the rash has healed.

Drugs included

- **Paracetamol** is often adequate for relief of shingles pain.
- **Oily calamine lotion** may be soothing if the rash is itchy.
- **Hydroxyzine** is specifically licensed for pruritus and is sedating. Hydroxyzine is offered as a night-time dose for temporary help with sleeping, to help break the itch-scratch cycle.
- **Chlorphenamine** (**chlorpheniramine**) is also included because it is inexpensive, and is an effective sedating antihistamine of intermediate duration.

Prescriptions

Analgesia: use when required

Paracetamol s/f susp: 120mg to 240mg up to four times a day

- Age from 12 months to 5 years
- Paracetamol 120mg/5ml s/f susp. Take one to two 5ml spoonfuls every 4 to 6 hours when required for pain relief. Maximum of 4 doses in 24 hours; supply 300 ml; NHS Cost £1.30; OTC Cost £2.28.

Paracetamol s/f susp: 250mg to 500mg up to four times a day

- Age from 6 to 11 years
- Paracetamol 250mg/5ml s/f susp. Take one to two 5ml spoonfuls every 4 to 6 hours when required for pain relief. Maximum of 4 doses in 24 hours; supply 300 ml; NHS Cost £1.70; OTC Cost £2.99.

Paracetamol tablets: 500mg to 1g up to four times a day

- Age from 12 to 15 years
- Paracetamol 500mg tablets. Take one to two tablets every 4 to 6 hours when required for pain relief. Maximum of 8 tablets in 24 hours; supply 100 tablets; NHS Cost £0.75; OTC Cost £1.32.

Itch: oily calamine or sedating antihistamine

Calamine oily lotion: apply when required to relieve itching

- Age from 12 months to 15 years
- Calamine oily lotion. Apply to the affected area(s) when required to relieve itching; supply 200 ml; NHS Cost £1.58; OTC Cost £2.78.

Chlorphenamine (chlorpheniramine) syrup: 1mg at night prn

- Age from 12 to 23 months
- Chlorphenamine 2mg/5ml syrup. Take 2.5ml at night when required for relief of itching; supply 50 ml; NHS Cost £0.72; OTC Cost £1.26.

Chlorphenamine (chlorpheniramine) syrup: 1-2mg at nigh prn

- Age from 2 to 5 years
- Chlorphenamine 2mg/5ml syrup. Take 2.5ml to 5ml at night when required for relief of itching; supply 100 ml; NHS Cost £1.43; OTC Cost £2.53.

Chlorphenamine (chlorpheniramine) syrup: 2-4mg at nigh prn

- Age from 6 to 11 years
- Chlorphenamine 2mg/5ml syrup. Take one to two 5ml spoonfuls at night when required for relief of itching; supply 100 ml; NHS Cost £1.43; OTC Cost £2.53.

Chlorphenamine (chlorpheniramine) tablets: 4mg at night prn

- Age from 12 to 15 years
- Chlorphenamine 4mg tablets. Take one tablet at night when required for relief of itching; supply 14 tablets; NHS Cost £0.22; OTC Cost £1.40.

Hydroxyzine syrup: 5mg to 15mg at night when required

- Age from 12 months to 6 years
- Hydroxyzine 10mg/5ml syrup. Take 2.5ml to 7.5ml at night when required for relief of itching; supply 100 ml; NHS Cost £0.96.

Hydroxyzine syrup: 15mg to 25mg at night when required

- Age from 7 to 11 years
- Hydroxyzine 10mg/5ml syrup. Take 7.5ml to 12.5ml at night when required for relief of itching; supply 200 ml; NHS Cost £1.91.

Hydroxyzine tablets: 25mg at night when required

- Age from 12 to 15 years
- Hydroxyzine 25mg tablets. Take one tablet at night when required for relief of itching; supply 14 tablets; NHS Cost £0.51.

Shingles — adults

Which therapy?

- Antivirals will provide the most benefit to people who have a higher risk of severe acute disease, complications, or progression to postherpetic neuralgia.
- **Antivirals are recommended for adults aged 50 years and over.**
- **Antivirals are recommended for adults of any age who:**
  - Present with severe acute pain or extensive rash
  - Have ophthalmic involvement
  - Are immunocompromised. (Oral antivirals are suitable if shingles is localized and uncomplicated. People with severe immunosuppression require admission.)
  - Have Ramsay Hunt Syndrome
  - Have atopic eczema
  - Have contact with very young infants, immunocompromised people, or pregnant women.
- **Antivirals are also recommended for** adults under the age of 50 years who do not fall into these categories, to help reduce the severity or duration of the rash.
- **Antivirals should be started within 72 hours of the rash onset.**
  - Aciclovir is much less expensive than other antivirals, but is taken five times a day.
  - If compliance is an issue: consider valaciclovir (taken three times a day) or famciclovir (taken once a day or three times a day).
- **Advise people:**
  - **To keep the rash clean and covered** with a non-adherent dressing. (This prevents transmission and may help to reduce pain caused by contact with clothing.)
  - Skin hygiene is important for preventing secondary bacterial infection.
  - **That they should not share towels with other people,** or go swimming, or do contact sports until the lesions have crusted.
- **Analgesia** should be started at the 'step' most appropriate to the person's level of pain:
  - Ice packs may provide short-term pain relief.
  - **Paracetamol alone or with full-dose codeine is often adequate.**
  - **Adjuvant analgesia** with a tricyclic antidepressant or an antiepileptic drug may also be required.
- **If the rash is itchy:**
  - **Oily calamine lotion** may be soothing.
  - Consider a sedative antihistamine at night to break the itch-scratch cycle if the itch is severe and is disturbing sleep.

Practical prescribing points

For further information see the *Medicines Compendium* (www.medicines.org.uk) or the *British National Formulary* (www.bnf.org).

- **Driving:** all people taking drugs with a sedative action (e.g. opioids, tricyclic antidepressants [TCAs], antiepileptic drugs [AEDs]) should be advised not to drive if adversely affected, particularly during the first month of starting or increasing the dose (tolerance develops within a week or two of stabilizing the dose).

Antivirals

- **Renal impairment:** the dose should be reduced in renal impairment.

Factors affecting the choice of TCA or AED

- **Cardiac disease:** use gabapentin, or use nortriptyline with caution. Avoid TCAs or carbamazepine if possible.
- **Prostatism, narrow-angle glaucoma, urinary retention:** use gabapentin.
- **Epilepsy or risk of seizures:** avoid TCAs as they lower the seizure threshold.
- **Bipolar disorder:** caution with TCAs (may precipitate mania).
- **Renal impairment:** reduce the dose of gabapentin. See the *Medicines Compendium* (www.medicines.org.uk) for dosage information.

Sedating antihistamines

- **Prostatism, narrow-angle glaucoma, urinary retention:** avoid sedating antihistamines.
- **Epilepsy or risk of seizures:** avoid sedating antihistamines as they lower the seizure threshold.

Follow-up advice

- **Advise the person to return for review if:**
  - Pain persists for more than a few days and is not controlled by the analgesia prescribed
  - The lesions become infected
  - They become systemically unwell
  - The rash becomes disseminated
- Pain persisting for more than 30 days suggests the possibility of subacute herpetic neuralgia pain persisting for more than 120 days suggests the possibility of postherpetic neuralgia. Management of this is outlined in the scenario *Postherpetic neuralgia — first-line*.

Should I refer or investigate?

Refer?

- **It is advisable to seek specialist advice with people who are immunocompromised.** People with severe immunosuppression may require admission for intravenous aciclovir, as they are at high risk of disseminated zoster and complications.
- **Ophthalmic shingles requires urgent ophthalmological referral if a red eye or other sign of ocular involvement develops.**
- **Admission is required if severe complications develop,** such as dissemination or encephalitis.

Investigate?

- If immunodeficiency is suspected (e.g. recurrent attacks of shingles in a person who is not already known to be immunocompromised), immunological tests should be done (discuss with local haematologist).

Patient information leaflets

The following PILs are available at www.prodigy.nhs.uk

- Herpes Viruses Association
- Medicines - Name Changes of Medicines
- Shingles
- Shingles - Post Herpetic Neuralgia
- Shingles Support Society

S

Shared decision making

- Shingles is caused by the same virus that causes chickenpox. The rash and pain usually last 2–4 weeks.
- **Paracetamol alone, or combined with codeine,** may ease the pain. Stronger painkillers are sometimes needed.
- **An antiviral medicine** is often prescribed, but usually only if it can be started within 72 hours of the rash appearing. In some severe cases, it can be started later. It helps to reduce the severity of shingles and to reduce the risk of pain persisting after the rash has gone.
- **An antidepressant or anticonvulsant medicine** may help if the pain is bad. This is not to treat depression or epilepsy. They are good at easing nerve pains such as the pain of shingles.
- **Ice packs** or wet dressings over the rash may ease discomfort.
- **Oily calamine lotion** may help to ease itch.
- Keep the rash clean, cover with a non-adherent dressing, and wear loose cotton clothes over it. This helps to:
  - Prevent passing on the virus.
  - Reduce pain caused by contact with clothing.
  - Prevent secondary infection.
- To reduce the risk of passing on the virus to people who are not immune to chickenpox:
  - Do not share towels with other people, or go swimming, or do contact sports until the rash has crusted.
  - Avoid babies, people with a poor immune system, and pregnant women.
- If you still have pain after the rash clears, come back to see a doctor.

Drug rationale

Drugs not included

- **Oral antivirals: famciclovir 500 mg three times a day** is not offered. It is licensed at this dosage for the treatment of people who are immunocompromised, but alternative less expensive regimens are available for this purpose.
- **Topical idoxuridine** (an antiviral agent) is rarely used. The evidence to support its use is very poor and it is difficult to determine whether it speeds healing or reduces pain in acute shingles compared to placebo [Wareham, 2004].
- **Systemic corticosteroids** are not included. Although they may speed healing of shingles, it is generally felt that the potential for harm is greater than the potential benefits. There is no evidence that they reduce the risk of postherpetic neuralgia [Alper and Lewis, 2000; Wareham, 2004].
- **Oral NSAIDs (nonsteroidal anti-inflammatory drugs)** are an alternative to paracetamol, but expert consensus suggests that they are of little benefit in the treatment of postherpetic neuralgia [BSSI, 1995; Kanazi et al, 2000; International Herpes Management Forum, 2002].
- **Weak opioids other than codeine** could be used, but there are surprisingly few data on their relative efficacy and adverse effects with chronic use, and many preparations are more expensive than codeine tablets. Tramadol should not be given with tricyclic antidepressants because of the increased risk of CNS toxicity. Products that contain a fixed-dose combination of paracetamol plus a weak opioid do not allow titration to the most effective and safe analgesic dose to match the person's requirements.
- **Low-dose weak opioids with paracetamol** (e.g. co-codamol 8/500 mg, co-dydramol 10/500 mg) have not been shown to offer any clinical benefit over paracetamol alone but are likely to lead to opioid adverse effects [MeReC, 2000].
- **Strong opioids** are best reserved for use in specialist pain clinics, as there is a high risk of chronic usage. The response of neuropathic pain to these drugs is thought to vary widely between individuals.
- **Tricyclic antidepressants other than amitriptyline, imipramine, and nortriptyline** are not included. Maprotiline and desipramine have also been found to be effective for neuropathic pain, but maprotiline has a high incidence of rash and desipramine is not available in the UK.
- **Sodium valproate** is commonly used in practice, but there are no studies to support its use [Wiffen et al, 2000].
- **Pregabalin** has recently been licensed for neuropathic pain, but it is a 'black triangle' drug and further post-marketing safety data are needed. Dizziness, somnolence, blurred vision, gastrointestinal adverse effects, and weight gain are common adverse effects.
- **Topical corticosteroids** should *not* be used during the acute phase of shingles, although they could be considered if the itch persists once the rash has healed.

Drugs included

- **Oral antivirals: aciclovir, famciclovir, or valaciclovir** are recommended for all people who are at high risk of severe shingles or the development of postherpetic neuralgia.
- **Paracetamol with or without codeine** is often adequate for relief of shingles pain.
- **An adjuvant analgesic** may be needed if additional pain relief to paracetamol and codeine is required:
  - **Amitriptyline** is the most widely studied and is commonly used for neuropathic pain in the UK [Collins et al, 2000]. There is also limited evidence that early treatment with amitriptyline may reduce the incidence of postherpetic neuralgia in people with shingles aged 60 years or more [Bowsher, 1997].
  - **Imipramine** is a less sedative alternative to amitriptyline [Collins et al, 2000].
  - **Nortriptyline** is an alternative to amitriptyline for people at increased risk of adverse effects, particularly the elderly [Watson et al, 1998].
  - **Gabapentin** is effective in several types of neuropathic pain, seems to be well tolerated, and has few drug interactions [Wiffen et al, 2000].
  - **Carbamazepine** has not been specifically studied in the treatment of postherpetic neuralgia. However, there are trial data showing efficacy against other types of neuropathic pain (e.g. trigeminal neuralgia and diabetic neuropathy) and it is widely used for the treatment of postherpetic neuralgia.
- **Oily calamine lotion** may be soothing if the rash is itchy.
- **Hydroxyzine** is specifically licensed for pruritus and is sedating. Hydroxyzine is offered as a night-time dose for temporary help with sleeping, to help break the itch-scratch cycle.
- **Chlorphenamine (chlorpheniramine)** is also included because it is inexpensive, and is an effective sedating antihistamine of intermediate duration.

Prescriptions

Antivirals for 7 days

Aciclovir 800mg five times a day

- Age from 16 years onwards
- Aciclovir 800mg disp tablets. Take one tablet five times a day for 7 days; supply 35 tablets; NHS Cost £20.71.

S

alaciclovir 1g three times a day
- Age from 16 years onwards
- Valaciclovir 500mg tablets. Take two tablets three times a day for 7 days; supply 42 tablets; NHS Cost £91.61.

amciclovir 250mg three times a day
- Age from 16 years onwards
- Famciclovir 250mg tablets. Take one tablet three times a day for 7 days; supply 21 tablets; NHS Cost £129.89.

amciclovir 750mg once a day
- Age from 16 years onwards
- Famciclovir 750mg tablets. Take one tablet once a day for 7 days; supply 7 tablets; NHS Cost £123.99.

Antivirals in immunocompromise (discuss with specialist)

ciclovir 800mg five times a day
- Age from 16 years onwards
- Aciclovir 800mg disp tablets. Take one tablet five times a day for 7 days; supply 35 tablets; NHS Cost £20.71.

alaciclovir 1g three times a day
- Age from 16 years onwards
- Valaciclovir 500mg tablets. Take two tablets three times a day for 7 days; supply 42 tablets; NHS Cost £91.61.

Analgesia: use when required

aracetamol 1g up to four times a day
- Age from 16 years onwards
- Paracetamol 500mg tablets. Take two tablets every 4 to 6 hours when required for pain relief. Maximum of 8 tablets in 24 hours; supply 100 tablets; NHS Cost £0.75; OTC Cost £1.32.

dd on if required: codeine 30-60mg up to four times a ay
- Age from 16 years onwards
- Codeine 30mg tablets. Take one to two tablets every 4 to 6 hours when required for pain relief. Maximum of 8 tablets in 24 hours; supply 56 tablets; NHS Cost £2.90.

aracetamol 500mg tablets + codeine 30mg tablets
- Age from 16 years onwards
- Paracetamol 500mg tablets. Take two tablets every 4 to 6 hours when required for pain relief. Maximum of 8 tablets in 24 hours; supply 100 tablets; NHS Cost £0.75; OTC Cost £1.32.
- Codeine 30mg tablets. Take one to two tablets every 4 to 6 hours when required for pain relief. Maximum of 8 tablets in 24 hours; supply 56 tablets; NHS Cost £2.90.

Start doses of adjuvant analgesics

mitriptyline: titrate up from 10mg daily until pain settles
- Age from 16 years onwards
- Amitriptyline 10mg tablets. Increase the dose as directed on the right hand side of the prescription until the pain settles; supply 70 tablets; NHS Cost £1.95.

mitriptyline: titrate up from 25mg daily until pain settles
- Age from 16 to 59 years
- Amitriptyline 25mg tablets. Take one tablet at night for 7 days, then take as instructed (see the right hand side of the prescription); supply 63 tablets; NHS Cost £1.82.

ipramine: titrate up from 10mg daily until pain settles
- Age from 16 years onwards
- Imipramine 10mg tablets. Increase the dose as directed on the right hand side of the prescription until the pain settles; supply 70 tablets; NHS Cost £2.13.

ipramine: titrate up from 25mg daily until pain settles
- Age from 16 to 59 years
- Imipramine 25mg tablets. Take one tablet at night for 7 days, then take as instructed (see the right hand side of the prescription); supply 63 tablets; NHS Cost £2.27.

Nortriptyline: titrate up from 10mg daily until pain settles
- Age from 16 years onwards
- Nortriptyline 10mg tablets. Increase the dose as directed on the right hand side of the prescription until the pain settles; supply 70 tablets; NHS Cost £8.44.

Nortriptyline: titrate up from 25mg daily until pain settles
- Age from 16 to 59 years
- Nortriptyline 25mg tablets. Take one tablet at night for 7 days, then take as instructed (see the right hand side of the prescription); supply 63 tablets; NHS Cost £15.45.

Gabapentin: initial titration from 300mg to 900mg per day
- Age from 18 years onwards
- Gabapentin 100mg capsules. Take one capsule three times a day for 3 days, then take two capsules three times a day for 3 days, then take three capsules three times a day; supply 36 capsules; NHS Cost £8.22.

Carbamazepine:titrate up from 100mg daily until pain settles
- Age from 16 years onwards
- Carbamazepine 100mg tablets. Increase the dose as directed on the right hand side of the prescription until the pain settles; supply 70 tablets; NHS Cost £2.03.

Itch: oily calamine or sedating antihistamine

Calamine oily lotion: apply when required to relieve itching
- Age from 16 years onwards
- Calamine oily lotion. Apply to the affected area(s) when required to relieve itching; supply 200 ml; NHS Cost £1.58; OTC Cost £2.78.

Chlorphenamine (chlorpheniramine) tablets: 4mg at night prn
- Age from 16 years onwards
- Chlorphenamine 4mg tablets. Take one tablet at night when required for relief of itching; supply 14 tablets; NHS Cost £0.22; OTC Cost £1.40.

Hydroxyzine tablets: 25mg at night when required
- Age from 16 years onwards
- Hydroxyzine 25mg tablets. Take one tablet at night when required for relief of itching; supply 14 tablets; NHS Cost £0.51.

Postherpetic neuralgia — first line

Which therapy?

- **Reassure that postherpetic neuralgia is usually a self-limiting condition** (but unfortunately in some people it can be prolonged or even persist indefinitely).
- **If skin hypersensitivity (allodynia) is a problem:** a protective layer over the skin may be helpful (e.g. clingfilm or a vapour-permeable dressing). Natural-fibre clothing is preferable to artificial fibres.
- **Cold pack application may provide short-term relief of pain.**
- **Paracetamol alone or with codeine** may be effective in people with mild to moderate pain.
- **Offer a tricyclic antidepressant (TCA) or an antiepileptic drug (AED):**
  - The choice depends on relative contraindications, possible drug interactions, and risk of adverse effects for each individual person.
    - Amitriptyline, imipramine, and nortriptyline are suitable first-line TCAs.
    - Gabapentin and carbamazepine are suitable first-line AEDs.
  - Advise people that these medicines are being used for pain, not for depression or for epilepsy.

- **Start with a low dose of TCA or AED and titrate slowly upwards** until pain settles or adverse effects limit further dose increases:
  - For a TCA, start with a dose of 10 mg at night (25 mg in young, fit people) and titrate by 10–25 mg every week. A dose between 25 mg and 75 mg at night is often effective, although up to 150 mg per day can be used if tolerated.
  - For gabapentin, titrate from 100 mg three times a day to 300 mg three times a day over 7 days. A dose between 900 mg and 1800 mg per day is commonly needed, although up to 3600 mg per day (off-licence) can be used.
  - For carbamazepine, start with 100 mg daily and titrate by 100–200 mg every 2 weeks. A dose of 200 mg three or four times a day is commonly needed, although a maximum of 1600 mg per day can be used.
- **Topical capsaicin 0.075% is an alternative** if TCAs and AEDs are contraindicated or not tolerated.

Practical prescribing points

For further information see the *Medicines Compendium* (www.medicines.org.uk) or the *British National Formulary* (www.bnf.org).

- **Driving:** all people taking drugs with a sedative action (e.g. opioids, tricyclic antidepressants [TCAs], antiepileptic drugs [AEDs]) should be advised not to drive if adversely affected, particularly during the first month of starting or increasing the dose (tolerance develops within a week or two of stabilizing the dose).

Factors affecting the choice of TCA or AED

- **Cardiac disease:** use gabapentin, or use nortriptyline with caution. Avoid TCAs or carbamazepine if possible.
- **Prostatism, narrow-angle glaucoma, urinary retention:** use gabapentin.
- **Epilepsy or risk of seizures:** avoid TCAs as they lower the seizure threshold.
- **Bipolar disorder:** caution with TCAs (may precipitate mania).
- **Renal impairment:** reduce the dose of gabapentin. See the *Medicines Compendium* (www.medicines.org.uk) for dosage information.

Carbamazepine

- **Always check for potential drug interactions:** carbamazepine induces liver microsomal enzymes and interacts with many drugs, e.g. oral contraception.
- **Warn people about adverse effects:** diplopia, headache, nausea, and vomiting are common after a dose increase but usually settle in a few days.
- **Advise people to report the following symptoms immediately:** fever, sore throat, mouth ulcers, or bruising.
- **If an idiosyncratic reaction is suspected:** check full blood count, liver function tests, and serum creatinine. Routine testing is not helpful.

Capsaicin

- Warn people that they may feel an intense burning sensation after application. This effect diminishes with continued use.

Follow-up advice

- **Review regularly** to ensure treatment is tolerated and pain control is achieved.
- **Continue treatment at the effective dose for 1 month after the pain has disappeared,** then gradually reduce the dose.
- **Restart treatment (or increase the dose) if pain recurs.**
- **If treatment is poorly tolerated or is ineffective** then additional or alternative treatment for neuropathic pain should be tried (see scenario *Postherpetic neuralgia — treatment failure*).

Should I refer or investigate?

Refer?

- **If pain relief is inadequate, despite treatment with a tricyclic antidepressant or an antiepileptic drug,** referral to a pain clinic should be considered. While waiting for the person to be seen, an alternative treatment may be considered (see scenario *Postherpetic neuralgia — treatment failure*).

Patient information leaflets

The following PILs are available at www.prodigy.nhs.uk

- Herpes Viruses Association
- Medicines - Name Changes of Medicines
- Shingles
- Shingles - Post Herpetic Neuralgia
- Shingles Support Society

Shared decision making

- In some cases of shingles, the pain persists for several weeks after the rash has gone. Sometimes the pain lasts months or longer.
- **Ice packs, or layers of clingfilm,** placed over the painful area may ease the discomfort.
- **Soft cotton clothing** is the most comfortable.
- **Paracetamol alone, or combined with codeine,** may help.
- **An antidepressant or an anticonvulsant medicine often helps.** They are not used here to treat depression or epilepsy. They are good at easing nerve pains.
  - A low dose is used at first, and the dose gradually increased if needed.
  - It usually eases the pain within a few days, but it may take 2–3 weeks.
  - It can take several weeks before you get maximum benefit.
  - Take it for a further three months after the pain has gone or eased.
- **Capsaicin cream** is sometimes used if the above medicines do not help or cannot be used. It can cause an intense burning feeling when it is applied.

Drug rationale

Drugs not included

- **Oral NSAIDs** (nonsteroidal anti-inflammatory drugs) a[illegible] an alternative to paracetamol, but expert consensus suggests that they are of little benefit in the treatment of acute shingles pain [BSSI, 1995; Kanazi et al, 2000; International Herpes Management Forum, 2002].
- **Weak opioids other than codeine** could be used, but there are surprisingly few data on their relative efficacy and adverse effects with chronic use, and many preparations are more expensive than codeine tablets. Tramadol should not be given with tricyclic antidepressants because of the increased risk of CNS toxicity. Products that contain a fixed-dose combination of paracetamol plus a weak opioid do not allow titratic to the most effective and safe analgesic dose to match tl person's requirements.
- **Low-dose weak opioids with paracetamol** (e.g. co-codamol 8/500 mg, co-dydramol 10/500 mg) have not

S

been shown to offer any clinical benefit over paracetamol alone but are likely to lead to opioid adverse effects [MeReC, 2000].

Strong opioids are best reserved for use in specialist pain clinics, as there is a high risk of chronic usage. The response of neuropathic pain to these drugs is thought to vary widely between individuals.

Tricyclic antidepressants other than amitriptyline, imipramine, and nortriptyline are not included. Maprotiline and desipramine have also been found to be effective, but maprotiline has a high incidence of rash and desipramine is not available in the UK.

Sodium valproate is commonly used in practice, but there are no studies to support its use [Wiffen et al, 2000].

Pregabalin has recently been licensed for neuropathic pain, but it is a 'black triangle' drug and further post-marketing safety data are needed. Dizziness, somnolence, blurred vision, gastrointestinal adverse effects, and weight gain are common adverse effects.

Capsaicin 0.025% cream has not been shown to provide significantly more pain relief than placebo [Wareham, 2004] and is not licensed for the treatment of postherpetic neuralgia.

Topical lidocaine (lignocaine) 5% patches are not currently available in the UK. There is limited evidence of short-term relief of postherpetic neuralgia [Wareham, 2004].

rugs included

Paracetamol alone or with codeine may be effective in people with mild to moderate pain.

Amitriptyline is the most widely studied tricyclic antidepressant and is commonly used for neuropathic pain in the UK [Collins et al, 2000].

Imipramine is a less sedative alternative to amitriptyline [Collins et al, 2000].

Nortriptyline is an alternative to amitriptyline for people at increased risk of adverse effects, particularly the elderly [Watson et al, 1998].

Gabapentin is effective in several types of neuropathic pain, seems to be well tolerated, and has few drug interactions [Wiffen et al, 2000].

Carbamazepine has not been specifically studied in the treatment of postherpetic neuralgia. However, there are trial data showing efficacy against other types of neuropathic pain (e.g. trigeminal neuralgia and diabetic neuropathy) and it is widely used for the treatment of postherpetic neuralgia.

Capsaicin 0.075% cream is an alternative tricyclic antidepressants and antiepileptic drugs are contraindicated or not tolerated. People should be warned about the intense burning sensation after application, although this effect diminishes with continued use. Some people may not be able to tolerate its use for this reason.

rescriptions

nalgesia: use when required

aracetamol 1g up to four times a day

- Age from 16 years onwards
- Paracetamol 500mg tablets. Take two tablets every 4 to 6 hours when required for pain relief. Maximum of 8 tablets in 24 hours; supply 100 tablets; NHS Cost £0.75; OTC Cost £1.32.

Add on if required: codeine 30-60mg up to four times a day

- Age from 16 years onwards
- Codeine 30mg tablets. Take one to two tablets every 4 to 6 hours when required for pain relief. Maximum of 8 tablets in 24 hours; supply 56 tablets; NHS Cost £2.90.

Paracetamol 500mg tablets + codeine 30mg tablets

- Age from 16 years onwards
- Paracetamol 500mg tablets. Take two tablets every 4 to 6 hours when required for pain relief. Maximum of 8 tablets in 24 hours; supply 100 tablets; NHS Cost £0.75; OTC Cost £1.32.
- Codeine 30mg tablets. Take one to two tablets every 4 to 6 hours when required for pain relief. Maximum of 8 tablets in 24 hours; supply 56 tablets; NHS Cost £2.90.

Start doses of oral adjuvant analgesics

Amitriptyline: titrate up from 10mg daily until pain settles

- Age from 16 years onwards
- Amitriptyline 10mg tablets. Increase the dose as directed on the right hand side of the prescription until the pain settles; supply 70 tablets; NHS Cost £1.95.

Amitriptyline: titrate up from 25mg daily until pain settles

- Age from 16 to 59 years
- Amitriptyline 25mg tablets. Take one tablet at night for 7 days, then take as instructed (see the right hand side of the prescription); supply 63 tablets; NHS Cost £1.82.

Imipramine: titrate up from 10mg daily until pain settles

- Age from 16 years onwards
- Imipramine 10mg tablets. Increase the dose as directed on the right hand side of the prescription until the pain settles; supply 70 tablets; NHS Cost £2.13.

Imipramine: titrate up from 25mg daily until pain settles

- Age from 16 to 59 years
- Imipramine 25mg tablets. Take one tablet at night for 7 days, then take as instructed (see the right hand side of the prescription); supply 63 tablets; NHS Cost £2.27.

Nortriptyline: titrate up from 10mg daily until pain settles

- Age from 16 years onwards
- Nortriptyline 10mg tablets. Increase the dose as directed on the right hand side of the prescription until the pain settles; supply 70 tablets; NHS Cost £8.44.

Nortriptyline: titrate up from 25mg daily until pain settles

- Age from 16 to 59 years
- Nortriptyline 25mg tablets. Take one tablet at night for 7 days, then take as instructed (see the right hand side of the prescription); supply 63 tablets; NHS Cost £15.45.

Gabapentin: initial titration from 300mg to 900mg per day

- Age from 18 years onwards
- Gabapentin 100mg capsules. Take one capsule three times a day for 3 days, then take two capsules three times a day for 3 days, then take three capsules three times a day; supply 36 capsules; NHS Cost £8.22.

Carbamazepine:titrate up from 100mg daily until pain settles

- Age from 16 years onwards
- Carbamazepine 100mg tablets. Increase the dose as directed on the right hand side of the prescription until the pain settles; supply 70 tablets; NHS Cost £2.03.

Maintenance doses: amitriptyline, imipramine, nortriptyline

Amitriptyline 25mg at night

- Age from 16 years onwards
- Amitriptyline 25mg tablets. Take one tablet at night; supply 28 tablets; NHS Cost £0.80.

Amitriptyline 50mg at night
- Age from 16 years onwards
- Amitriptyline 50mg tablets. Take one tablet at night; supply 28 tablets; NHS Cost £1.20.

Amitriptyline 75mg at night
- Age from 16 years onwards
- Amitriptyline 25mg tablets. Take three tablets at night; supply 84 tablets; NHS Cost £2.40.

Imipramine 25mg at night
- Age from 16 years onwards
- Imipramine 25mg tablets. Take one tablet at night; supply 28 tablets; NHS Cost £1.01.

Imipramine 50mg at night
- Age from 16 years onwards
- Imipramine 25mg tablets. Take two tablets at night; supply 56 tablets; NHS Cost £2.02.

Imipramine 75mg at night
- Age from 16 years onwards
- Imipramine 25mg tablets. Take three tablets at night; supply 84 tablets; NHS Cost £3.03.

Nortriptyline 25mg at night
- Age from 16 years onwards
- Nortriptyline 25mg tablets. Take one tablet at night; supply 28 tablets; NHS Cost £6.87.

Nortriptyline 50mg at night
- Age from 16 years onwards
- Nortriptyline 25mg tablets. Take two tablets at night; supply 56 tablets; NHS Cost £13.73.

Nortriptyline 75mg at night
- Age from 16 years onwards
- Nortriptyline 25mg tablets. Take three tablets at night; supply 84 tablets; NHS Cost £20.60.

Maintenance doses: gabapentin and carbamazepine

Gabapentin 300mg three times a day
- Age from 18 years onwards
- Gabapentin 300mg capsules. Take one capsule three times a day; supply 84 capsules; NHS Cost £44.52.

Gabapentin 400mg three times a day
- Age from 18 years onwards
- Gabapentin 400mg capsules. Take one capsule three times a day; supply 84 capsules; NHS Cost £51.52.

Gabapentin 600mg three times a day
- Age from 18 years onwards
- Gabapentin 600mg tablets. Take one tablet three times a day; supply 84 tablets; NHS Cost £89.04.

Gabapentin 800mg three times a day
- Age from 18 years onwards
- Gabapentin 800mg tablets. Take one tablet three times a day; supply 84 tablets; NHS Cost £103.03.

Carbamazepine 200mg twice a day
- Age from 16 years onwards
- Carbamazepine 200mg tablets. Take one tablet twice a day; supply 56 tablets; NHS Cost £3.34.

Carbamazepine 200mg three times a day
- Age from 16 years onwards
- Carbamazepine 200mg tablets. Take one tablet three times a day; supply 84 tablets; NHS Cost £4.50.

Carbamazepine 200mg four times a day
- Age from 16 years onwards
- Carbamazepine 200mg tablets. Take one tablet four times a day; supply 112 tablets; NHS Cost £6.68.

Capsaicin cream

Capsaicin 0.075% cream
- Age from 16 years onwards
- Capsaicin 0.075% cream. Apply a small amount of cream to the affected area three to four times a day; supply 45 grams; NHS Cost £15.04.

Postherpetic neuralgia — treatment failure

Which therapy?

- **Referral to a pain clinic** should be considered if pain relief is inadequate despite treatment with an adequate dose of a tricyclic antidepressant (TCA) or an antiepileptic drug (AED).
  - For a TCA, a dose between 25 mg and 75 mg at nigh is often effective, although up to 150 mg per day can be used if tolerated.
  - For gabapentin, a dose between 900 mg and 1800 m per day is usually effective, although up to 3600 mg per day (off-licence) can be used.
  - For carbamazepine, a dose of 200 mg three or four times a day is commonly used.
- **While waiting for the person to be seen,** an alternative treatment may be considered:
  - **Consider switching treatment,** e.g. switch from a TC to an AED or topical capsaicin (e.g. if there was no response to the first-line drug, or if it is poorly tolerated).
  - **Consider using add-on treatment,** e.g. give a TCA in combination with an AED or topical capsaicin.
- **Psychosocial and behavioural approaches** should be considered (e.g. pain-coping strategies, management of co-existing depression).

Practical prescribing points

For further information see the *Medicines Compendium* (www.medicines.org.uk) or the *British National Formula* (www.bnf.org).

Capsaicin

- Warn people that they may feel an intense burning sensation after application. This effect diminishes with continued use.

Factors affecting the choice of tricyclic antidepressant or antiepileptic drug

- **Cardiac disease:** use gabapentin, or use nortriptyline with caution. Avoid tricyclic antidepressants (TCAs) or carbamazepine if possible.
- **Prostatism, narrow-angle glaucoma, urinary retention:** use gabapentin.
- **Epilepsy or risk of seizures:** avoid TCAs as they lower the seizure threshold.
- **Bipolar disorder:** caution with TCAs (may precipitate mania).
- **Renal impairment:** reduce the dose of gabapentin. See the *Medicines Compendium* (www.medicines.org.uk) f dosage information.

Carbamazepine

- **Always check for potential drug interactions:** carbamazepine induces liver microsomal enzymes and interacts with many drugs, e.g. oral contraception.
- **Warn people about adverse effects:** diplopia, headache nausea, and vomiting are common after a dose increase but usually settle in a few days.
- **Advise people to report the following symptoms immediately:** fever, sore throat, mouth ulcers, or bruising.
- **If an idiosyncratic reaction is suspected:** check full bloo count, liver function tests, and serum creatinine. Routi testing is not helpful.

ollow-up advice

- ₹eview regularly to ensure treatment is tolerated and ›ain control is achieved.
- ;ontinue treatment at the effective dose for least month after the pain has disappeared, then gradually educe the dose.
- ₹estart treatment (or increase the dose) if pain recurs.

ıould I refer or investigate?

›fer?

- ;onsider early referral to a pain clinic if pain relief is ıadequate despite treatment with an adequate dose of a ricyclic antidepressant. While waiting for the person to ›e seen, an alternative treatment may be considered.
- ₹efer to a pain clinic if pain control is inadequate despite ıanagement in general practice.

ıtient information leaflets

: following PILs are available at www.prodigy.nhs.uk
- Ierpes Viruses Association
- Aedicines - Name Changes of Medicines
- hingles
- hingles - Post Herpetic Neuralgia
- hingles Support Society

ıared decision making

- 'our pain after shingles is still troublesome despite reatment.
- f you have taken the maximum dose of your current reatment then treatment options include:
  - If you are taking an antidepressant, then a switch to an anticonvulsant medicine may work.
  - If you are taking an anticonvulsant medicine, then a switch to an antidepressant medicine may work.
  - Some people take a combination of an antidepressant and an anticonvulsant.
  - Capsaicin cream is sometimes used if the above medicines do not help. It can cause an intense burning feeling when it is applied.
- ₹eferral to a pain clinic is an option if the above do not elp.

rug rationale

ugs not included

- 'aracetamol alone or with codeine may be effective in eople with mild to moderate pain. Prescriptions can be ɔund in the scenario *Postherpetic neuralgia — first-line.*
-)ral NSAIDs (nonsteroidal anti-inflammatory drugs) are n alternative to paracetamol, but expert consensus ıggests that they are of little benefit in the treatment of cute shingles pain [BSSI, 1995; Kanazi et al, 2000; ıternational Herpes Management Forum, 2002].
- Veak opioids other than codeine could be used, but here are surprisingly few data on their relative efficacy nd adverse effects with chronic use, and many reparations are more expensive than codeine tablets. 'ramadol should not be given with tricyclic ntidepressants because of the increased risk of CNS ɔxicity. Products that contain a fixed-dose combination f paracetamol plus a weak opioid do not allow titration ɔ the most effective and safe analgesic dose to match the erson's requirements.
- .ow-dose weak opioids with paracetamol (e.g. co-odamol 8/500 mg, co-dydramol 10/500 mg) have not een shown to offer any clinical benefit over paracetamol alone but are likely to lead to opioid adverse effects [MeReC, 2000].
- **Strong opioids** are best reserved for use in specialist pain clinics, as there is a high risk of chronic usage. The response of neuropathic pain to these drugs is thought to vary widely between individuals.
- **Tricyclic antidepressants other than amitriptyline, imipramine, and nortriptyline** are not included. Maprotiline and desipramine have also been found to be effective, but maprotiline has a high incidence of rash and desipramine is not available in the UK.
- **Sodium valproate** is commonly used in practice, but there are no studies to support its use [Wiffen et al, 2000].
- **Pregabalin** has recently been licensed for neuropathic pain, but it is a 'black triangle' drug and further post-marketing safety data are needed. Dizziness, somnolence, blurred vision, gastrointestinal adverse effects and weight gain are common adverse effects.
- **Capsaicin 0.025% cream** has not been shown to provide significantly more pain relief than placebo [Wareham, 2004] and is not licensed for the treatment of postherpetic neuralgia.
- **Topical lidocaine (lignocaine) 5% patches** are not currently available in the UK. There is limited evidence of short-term relief of postherpetic neuralgia [Wareham, 2004].

Drugs included

- **Amitriptyline** is the most widely studied tricyclic antidepressant and is commonly used for neuropathic pain in the UK [Collins et al, 2000].
- **Imipramine** is a less sedative alternative to amitriptyline [Collins et al, 2000].
- **Nortriptyline** is an alternative to amitriptyline for people at increased risk of adverse effects, particularly the elderly [Watson et al, 1998].
- **Gabapentin** is effective in several types of neuropathic pain, seems to be well tolerated, and has few drug interactions [Wiffen et al, 2000].
- **Carbamazepine** has not been specifically studied in the treatment of postherpetic neuralgia. However, there are trial data showing efficacy against other types of neuropathic pain (e.g. trigeminal neuralgia and diabetic neuropathy) and it is widely used for the treatment of postherpetic neuralgia.
- **Capsaicin 0.075% cream** is an alternative if tricyclic antidepressants and antiepileptic drugs are contraindicated or not tolerated. People should be warned about the intense burning sensation after application, although this effect diminishes with continued use. Some people may not be able to tolerate its use for this reason.

Prescriptions

Start doses of oral adjuvant analgesics

Amitriptyline: titrate up from 10mg daily until pain settles
- Age from 16 years onwards
- Amitriptyline 10mg tablets. Increase the dose as directed on the right hand side of the prescription until the pain settles; supply 70 tablets; NHS Cost £1.95.

Amitriptyline: titrate up from 25mg daily until pain settles
- Age from 16 to 59 years
- Amitriptyline 25mg tablets. Take one tablet at night for 7 days, then take as instructed (see the right hand side of the prescription); supply 63 tablets; NHS Cost £1.82.

S

Imipramine: titrate up from 10mg daily until pain settles
- Age from 16 years onwards
- Imipramine 10mg tablets. Increase the dose as directed on the right hand side of the prescription until the pain settles; supply 70 tablets; NHS Cost £2.13.

Imipramine: titrate up from 25mg daily until pain settles
- Age from 16 to 59 years
- Imipramine 25mg tablets. Take one tablet at night for 7 days, then take as instructed (see the right hand side of the prescription); supply 63 tablets; NHS Cost £2.27.

Nortriptyline: titrate up from 10mg daily until pain settles
- Age from 16 years onwards
- Nortriptyline 10mg tablets. Increase the dose as directed on the right hand side of the prescription until the pain settles; supply 70 tablets; NHS Cost £8.44.

Nortriptyline: titrate up from 25mg daily until pain settles
- Age from 16 to 59 years
- Nortriptyline 25mg tablets. Take one tablet at night for 7 days, then take as instructed (see the right hand side of the prescription); supply 63 tablets; NHS Cost £15.45.

Gabapentin: initial titration from 300mg to 900mg per day
- Age from 18 years onwards
- Gabapentin 100mg capsules. Take one capsule three times a day for 3 days, then take two capsules three times a day for 3 days, then take three capsules three times a day; supply 36 capsules; NHS Cost £8.22.

Carbamazepine:titrate up from 100mg daily until pain settles
- Age from 16 years onwards
- Carbamazepine 100mg tablets. Increase the dose as directed on the right hand side of the prescription until the pain settles; supply 70 tablets; NHS Cost £2.03.

Maintenance doses: TCAs 25mg to 75mg at night

Amitriptyline 25mg at night
- Age from 16 years onwards
- Amitriptyline 25mg tablets. Take one tablet at night; supply 28 tablets; NHS Cost £0.80.

Amitriptyline 50mg at night
- Age from 16 years onwards
- Amitriptyline 50mg tablets. Take one tablet at night; supply 28 tablets; NHS Cost £1.20.

Amitriptyline 75mg at night
- Age from 16 years onwards
- Amitriptyline 25mg tablets. Take three tablets at night; supply 84 tablets; NHS Cost £2.40.

Imipramine 25mg at night
- Age from 16 years onwards
- Imipramine 25mg tablets. Take one tablet at night; supply 28 tablets; NHS Cost £1.01.

Imipramine 50mg at night
- Age from 16 years onwards
- Imipramine 25mg tablets. Take two tablets at night; supply 56 tablets; NHS Cost £2.02.

Imipramine 75mg at night
- Age from 16 years onwards
- Imipramine 25mg tablets. Take three tablets at night; supply 84 tablets; NHS Cost £3.03.

Nortriptyline 25mg at night
- Age from 16 years onwards
- Nortriptyline 25mg tablets. Take one tablet at night; supply 28 tablets; NHS Cost £6.87.

Nortriptyline 50mg at night
- Age from 16 years onwards
- Nortriptyline 25mg tablets. Take two tablets at night; supply 56 tablets; NHS Cost £13.73.

Nortriptyline 75mg at night
- Age from 16 years onwards
- Nortriptyline 25mg tablets. Take three tablets at nigh supply 84 tablets; NHS Cost £20.60.

Maintenance doses: TCAs 100mg to 150mg at nigh

Amitriptyline 100mg at night
- Age from 16 years onwards
- Amitriptyline 50mg tablets. Take two tablets at night; supply 56 tablets; NHS Cost £1.40.

Amitriptyline 125mg at night
- Age from 16 years onwards
- Amitriptyline 25mg tablets. Take one tablet at night; supply 28 tablets; NHS Cost £0.80.
- Amitriptyline 50mg tablets. Take two tablets at night; supply 56 tablets; NHS Cost £2.40.

Amitriptyline 150mg at night
- Age from 16 years onwards
- Amitriptyline 50mg tablets. Take three tablets at nigh supply 84 tablets; NHS Cost £3.60.

Imipramine 100mg at night
- Age from 16 years onwards
- Imipramine 25mg tablets. Take four tablets at night; supply 112 tablets; NHS Cost £4.04.

Imipramine 125mg at night
- Age from 16 years onwards
- Imipramine 25mg tablets. Take five tablets at night; supply 140 tablets; NHS Cost £5.05.

Imipramine 150mg at night
- Age from 16 years onwards
- Imipramine 25mg tablets. Take six tablets at night; supply 168 tablets; NHS Cost £6.06.

Nortriptyline 100mg at night
- Age from 16 years onwards
- Nortriptyline 25mg tablets. Take four tablets at night supply 56 tablets; NHS Cost £27.46.

Nortriptyline 125mg at night
- Age from 16 years onwards
- Nortriptyline 25mg tablets. Take five tablets at night; supply 140 tablets; NHS Cost £34.33.

Nortriptyline 150mg at night
- Age from 16 years onwards
- Nortriptyline 25mg tablets. Take six tablets at night; supply 168 tablets; NHS Cost £41.19.

Maintenance doses: gabapentin and carbamazepi

Gabapentin 300mg three times a day
- Age from 18 years onwards
- Gabapentin 300mg capsules. Take one capsule three times a day; supply 84 capsules; NHS Cost £44.52.

Gabapentin 400mg three times a day
- Age from 18 years onwards
- Gabapentin 400mg capsules. Take one capsule three times a day; supply 84 capsules; NHS Cost £51.52.

Gabapentin 600mg three times a day
- Age from 18 years onwards
- Gabapentin 600mg tablets. Take one tablet three tim day; supply 84 tablets; NHS Cost £89.04.

Gabapentin 800mg three times a day
- Age from 18 years onwards
- Gabapentin 800mg tablets. Take one tablet three tim day; supply 84 tablets; NHS Cost £103.03.

Gabapentin 1200mg three times a day
- Age from 18 years onwards
- Gabapentin 600mg tablets. Take two tablets three tin a day; supply 168 tablets; NHS Cost £178.08.

rbamazepine 200mg twice a day
\ge from 16 years onwards
Carbamazepine 200mg tablets. Take one tablet twice a day; supply 56 tablets; NHS Cost £3.34.

rbamazepine 200mg three times a day
\ge from 16 years onwards
Carbamazepine 200mg tablets. Take one tablet three times a day; supply 84 tablets; NHS Cost £4.50.

rbamazepine 200mg four times a day
\ge from 16 years onwards
Carbamazepine 200mg tablets. Take one tablet four times a day; supply 112 tablets; NHS Cost £6.68.

apsaicin cream

psaicin 0.075% cream
\ge from 16 years onwards
Capsaicin 0.075% cream. Apply a small amount of cream to the affected area three to four times a day; supply 45 grams; NHS Cost £15.04.

xtended Information

ackground information

What is it? p.1703
How common is it? p.1703
What are the risk factors for developing post herpetic neuralgia? p.1703
How do I know my patient has it? p.1704
What else might it be? p.1704
Complications and prognosis p.1704

hat is it?

hingles (herpes zoster) is an acute infection caused by reactivation of latent varicella-zoster virus. After primary chickenpox infection, the virus lies dormant in the dorsal root ganglia of the spinal cord. When reactivated, it travels along the sensory nerve to affect one or more dermatomes, causing the characteristic shingles rash. Reactivation of the virus probably occurs after a decrease in cell-mediated immunity (e.g. with increasing age, HIV infection, illness).

Postherpetic neuralgia is pain that persists after resolution of shingles. Various definitions have been used from pain persisting after the shingles rash heals to pain persisting for more than 6 months after the onset or healing of the rash. It has been classified as:

- **Acute herpetic neuralgia.** Pain occurring during the first 30 days after the onset of the rash.
- **Subacute herpetic neuralgia.** Pain that lasts 30-120 days after the onset of the rash.
- **Postherpetic neuralgia.** Pain that persist for more than 120 days after the onset of the rash.

[Dworkin and Portenoy, 1994]

ow common is it?

hingles

- **An annual incidence of just over 3/1000** was estimated in a retrospective UK study of people who had attended their GP with a diagnosis of shingles. In people younger than 50 years, the incidence was less than 2/1000. In people aged 50–79 years this rose to 7/1000, and in people aged 80 years or older to 11/1000 [Hope-Simpson, 1975].
- **National morbidity statistics from general practice for the years 1991–1992 showed an annual GP consultation** rate of 49 per 10,000 people on a GP list [McCormick et al, 1995].
- **Ophthalmic zoster** affecting the first division of the trigeminal nerve occurs in 20% of people with herpes zoster and the eye will be affected in 50–90% of cases [BSSI, 1995; International Herpes Management Forum, 2002].
- **The lifetime risk of shingles is 20%.** The risk of a second attack is less than 5% [Cunningham and Dworkin, 2000].
- **The incidence in HIV positive people** is 15–25 times greater than the rate in the general population [International Herpes Management Forum, 2002].
- **Healthy children rarely develop shingles** but it is more common in children who are immunosuppressed. The incidence in children under 10 years is estimated at 0.74 cases per 1000 children per year. It has also been reported in some children aged less than 2 years who contracted chickenpox during their first year of life or whose mother contracted chickenpox during pregnancy [Arvin, 2002; International Herpes Management Forum, 2002; Kurlan et al, 2004].

Postherpetic neuralgia

- Overall, pain persisting for over 1 month complicated shingles in 14% of people, in a UK retrospective general practice-based study of 321 people with shingles. Pain persisting for more than 1 month was rare in people younger than 50 years (3–4% in those aged 30–49 years) but occurred in 7% of people with shingles aged 50–59 years, 21% of people aged 60–69 years and in 34% of people older than 80 years [Hope-Simpson, 1975].
- A general practice-based study in Iceland followed 421 people with a first episode of shingles [Helgason et al, 2000]. Only 4% of these were treated with antiviral drugs. Overall, 7% of people had pain 3 months after the start of the shingles rash and 3% at 12 months.
  - In people younger than 60 years, 2% had pain at 3 months (which was mild in all cases) and 0.6% at 12 months.
  - In people 60 years and older, 20% had pain at 3 months (or 7% for pain of moderate to severe severity) and 9% at 12 months (with no cases of severe pain).

What are the risk factors for developing post herpetic neuralgia?

- **Older age** is most strongly associated with the risk of developing postherpetic neuralgia. People aged 50 years or older were almost 15 times more likely to have pain 30 days after developing the rash and 27 times more likely to have pain 60 days after developing the rash relative to people aged less than 50 years. The prevalence of pain after 30 days rose by 9% and at 60 days by 12% with each 1-year increment of age [Choo et al, 1997; Jung et al, 2004].
- **Prodromal symptoms** are associated with a higher prevalence of pain when measured 1, 2 and 4 months after the onset of the rash [Choo et al, 1997; Jung et al, 2004]
- **Greater rash severity** has also been associated with the development of postherpetic neuralgia [Jung et al, 2004]. Another study found that people with more than 21 lesions who also had moderate, severe or incapacitating pain were more likely to have pain both at 1 month and 6 months after the appearance of the rash [Whitley et al, 1999].
- **Greater sensory dysfunction in the affected dermatome, female sex, and fever** greater than 38°C have also been

S

identified as risk factors for postherpetic neuralgia [Dworkin and Portenoy, 1996; Jung et al, 2004].

- The development of postherpetic neuralgia was not appreciably influenced by the involvement of the trigeminal dermatome, the total number of affected dermatomes and the presence of affected non-adjacent dermatomes [Jung et al, 2004].

How do I know my patient has it?

Prodromal phase of shingles

- **Paraesthesia and pain over the affected dermatome** may occur between 2–3 days, but occasionally a week or more, prior to the onset of the shingles rash [International Herpes Management Forum, 2002].
- **The pain varies** from a superficial itching, tingling, or burning discomfort to a severe, deep, boring pain or a sharp, stabbing, lancinating pain. It may be constant or intermittent [Wallace and Oxman, 1997].

Acute shingles

Adults

- **Erythematous, maculopapular lesions evolve into a vesicular rash.**
- **New lesions continue to form** over 3–5 days, with pustulation over 4–6 days and scabbing over 7–10 days. Healing occurs over 2–4 weeks and often leads to scarring or permanent changes in pigmentation. In the elderly the course is often more prolonged with vesicles continuing to develop for several days (median time to loss of vesicles is 7 days) and full crusting may not occur until more than 10 days after the onset of the rash [Gnann and Whitley, 2002; International Herpes Management Forum, 2002].
- **The extent of the rash varies,** but it is partially or completely confined to one or occasionally two and rarely more adjacent dermatomes. Although the presence of a few skin lesions outside this area is not unusual in immunocompetent people, simultaneous involvement of multiple non-adjacent dermatomes virtually never occurs [Gnann and Whitley, 2002; Sterling, 2004].
- **The rash is almost always unilateral.** The thoracic dermatomes are most commonly involved, particularly T5 and T6. The ophthalmic branch of the trigeminal nerve is the second most common site [International Herpes Management Forum, 2002].
- **Pain over the affected area** is the most common complaint. The pain can be constant or intermittent and has been described as stabbing, tender, itchy or hot [International Herpes Management Forum, 2002].
- **Mild systemic illness** may occur (e.g. low-grade pyrexia, malaise).

Ophthalmic shingles

- Shingles affecting the first division of the trigeminal nerve presents with unilateral pain and lesions on the forehead, periocular area and nose [Gnann and Whitley, 2002].

Children

- **Prodromal pain is almost non-existent in childhood** [Nikkels and Pierard, 2002].
- **In healthy children the rash is usually mild and unaccompanied by acute neuropathic pain.** Among older children localized pain, hyperesthesia, and pruritus may be prominent symptoms. New lesion formation is brief and healing is complete by 1–2 weeks [Arvin, 2002].

Immunocompromised

- **Herpes zoster in the immunocompromised person often follows a similar course to that in the normal population** although a more severe and prolonged disease is frequently observed and life-threatening complications may develop (see section *Complications and prognosis*) [Nikkels and Pierard, 2002].
- **There are no clear risk factors for identifying people who will progress to widespread cutaneous dissemination and/or to systemic disease** [Nikkels and Pierard, 2002].
- **Herpes zoster infection may present atypically** with a large rash area, or run a protracted course with a small number of lesions that develop into verrucous or crusted nodules [International Herpes Management Forum, 2002; Sterling, 2004].

Postherpetic neuralgia

- **Pain is typically localized to the dermatome that was affected by the shingles rash.** It may be a steady burning aching pain; a paroxysmal, jabbing pain; or a combination of both. Pain may be triggered by usually innocuous stimuli (allodynia), such as clothing moving against the skin. There may be associated impairment of the sensation of touch (hypoaesthesia).
- In some people postherpetic itch can be distressing. The prevalence of disabling postherpetic itch is unknown [Oaklander et al, 2003].
- Note: postherpetic neuralgia is not described in children [Arvin, 2002].

What else might it be?

Differential diagnosis for the rash of shingles includes:

- Bacterial impetigo
- Herpes simplex
- Eczema herpeticum (caused by herpes simplex)
- Coxsackie virus (e.g. hand, foot, and mouth disease)
- Pemphigoid and other blistering conditions
- Insect bites

Differential diagnosis for the pain of shingles or postherpetic neuralgia includes:

- Pathology in underlying bone, muscle, or viscera (e.g. trauma, fracture, inflammation, infection, neoplasm)
- Vertebral pathology (e.g. prolapsed intervertebral disc, crush fractures, neoplasm)
- Diabetic mononeuritis
- Cardiac ischaemia
- Pleurisy
- Tabes dorsalis (a form of neurosyphilis)

Complications and prognosis

Complications

Common complications of shingles

- **Postherpetic neuralgia** (the most common complication
- **Ophthalmic zoster** can lead to ocular complications in 50–90% of people. They include conjunctivitis, scleritis, ocular motor palsies, epithelial keratitis, stromal infiltrates, anterior uveitis and acute retinal necrosis [Gnann and Whitley, 2002; International Herpes Management Forum, 2002].
- **Motor zoster** occurs in 5–10% of people with zoster and increases with age. Motor involvement may occur after myelitis or due to infection of motor roots. It is more common after cervical or lumbosacral zoster. Depending on the segment involved this can lead to a monoparesis affecting the upper or lower limb or to diaphragmatic palsy (with involvement of C5/6). The prognosis is generally good [Tenser, 2001; Sissons, 2003].
- **Bacterial superinfection** occurred in 2.3% of cases in one study [Galil et al, 1997].

Rare complications of shingles

- **Ramsay Hunt syndrome** describes unilateral facial palsy associated with pain and herpetic blisters in the external auditory meatus due to involvement of the geniculate ganglion. Other symptoms include loss of taste in the anterior two-thirds of the tongue, vertigo, tinnitus and deafness. Recovery from facial nerve paralysis is less likely than in Bell's palsy and full recovery only occurs in about 20% of untreated cases [Whitley, 1995; Thomas, 2003; Sterling, 2004].

Delayed contralateral hemiplegia may occur several weeks (average 7 weeks) after zoster (typically trigeminal or upper cervical zoster) [Tenser, 2001]. The mortality rate is 20–25% and there is a high probability or permanent neurological sequelae among survivors. Involvement of the first division of the trigeminal nerve is thought to be caused by direct invasion of cerebral arteries by the virus, resulting in inflammation of the internal carotid artery or one of its branches on the same side as the rash [International Herpes Management Forum, 2002].

Autonomic zoster due to myelitis or cauda equina involvement may result in a neurogenic bladder and acute retention of urine which may be accompanied by haemorrhagic cystitis due to vesicles on the bladder wall. Intestinal ileus and obstruction may occur [Tenser, 2001; Sissons, 2003].

Encephalitis. Cerebral involvement may occur in people with spinal cord involvement or with disseminated infection. Typical symptoms include headache, meningism, fever, impaired consciousness and seizures. The time interval from onset of skin lesions to symptoms of encephalitis is usually about 9 days but may be as long as 6 weeks. Recovery has generally been reported to be good although mortality rates of up to 33% have been described [Tenser, 2001; Sissons, 2003].

Disseminated zoster is more common in people who are immunocompromised; it can be life-threatening.

omplications in the immunocompromised

There is an increased probability of cutaneous and visceral dissemination in a person who is immunocompromised (e.g. pneumonitis, encephalitis, hepatitis) and these may be severe and life-threatening [International Herpes Management Forum, 2002].

Abdominal herpes zoster is a rare serious manifestation of herpes zoster that presents with severe unexplained abdominal pain that may precede the appearance of the cutaneous rash by hours or days. The mortality rate is high [International Herpes Management Forum, 2002].

Purpura fulminans (tissue loss may be extensive) has been reported in people with HIV [Bunker and Gotch, 2004].

omplications of postherpetic neuralgia

Disruption of sleep and work, with impaired quality of life

Depression and anxiety

rognosis

ognosis of shingles

In an acute attack of shingles the rash usually heals within 2–4 weeks and often results in scarring or permanent changes in pigmentation [Gnann and Whitley, 2002].

It is unusual for an immunocompetent person to develop shingles more than once (less than 5% have recurrence) [International Herpes Management Forum, 2002].

The risk of recurrence in people infected with HIV is 12–14% in the year after the first episode of shingles [International Herpes Management Forum, 2002].

ognosis of postherpetic neuralgia

Postherpetic neuralgia is usually a self-limiting condition; however, in some people it can be prolonged or even persist indefinitely.

About 20% of people over the age of 50 years report pain 6 months after the onset of the rash [Johnson and Dworkin, 2003].

- **About 2% of people had pain for more than 5 years after an episode of shingles** according to a UK general practice-based study [Hope-Simpson, 1975]. In a general practice-based study in Iceland, just over 3% of people had pain 12 months after a first episode of shingles, and less than 2% of people had pain after 6 years. In this latter study 4% of people had received antiviral treatment, but most of these had received sub-therapeutic doses [Helgason et al, 2000].

Management issues

- Shingles (acute herpes zoster) p.1705
- Postherpetic neuralgia p.1708
- Medicines management p.1709

Shingles (acute herpes zoster)

What advice should I give about the rash?

- **Skin hygiene** is important for preventing secondary bacterial infection.
- **A non-adherent dressing is suitable** to cover the rash when it is blistered and raw and may help to reduce pain caused by contact with clothing.
- **Oily calamine lotion** may be helpful if the rash is itchy. A sedative antihistamine given at night may be helpful to break the itch-scratch cycle if the itch is severe and disturbing sleep. Topical corticosteroids should *not* be used during the acute phase of shingles, although they could be considered if the itch persists once the rash has healed [Ormerod, Personal Communication, 2005].

Are people with shingles infectious?

- People with shingles are infectious until the lesions crust. Varicella-zoster virus can be transmitted to non immune individuals, resulting in chickenpox (not shingles) [BSSI, 1995]. In particular, pregnant women, neonates, and people who are immunocompromised or who are taking systemic corticosteroids should avoid contact with people who have shingles [HPA, 2004]. For further information see *How should I manage non-immune contacts of someone with shingles?*
- **If lesions are covered, transmission is unlikely** as the virus is usually transmitted by direct contact with vesicles.
- **People with shingles should not share towels with other people,** go swimming or do contact sports e.g. rugby [Sterling, Personal Communication, 2005].
- **People may return to work** once lesions have dried up or earlier if they keep the rash covered and do not have significant pain or feel unwell [BSSI, 1995].

How should I manage pain?

- **Physical measures such as wet dressings and ice packs** may provide short-term relief of symptoms [BSSI, 1995; Wallace and Oxman, 1997; Gross et al, 2003].
- **Effective pain relief is vital.** Acute shingles pain can vary from a mild discomfort to a severe debilitating pain.
- **Systemic analgesia should be offered, based on the** World Health Organization (WHO) three-step analgesic ladder [WHO, 2003]:
  - **Step 1** — give paracetamol
  - **Step 2** — give a full dose of a weak opioid (e.g. codeine 30–60 mg) combined with paracetamol.
  - **Step 3** — give morphine combined with paracetamol.
- A therapeutic trial of morphine should be considered in someone who is in severe pain, but it should be stopped if no benefit is gained after adequate dose titration. (Strong opioids are usually reserved for use in specialist

pain clinics as there is a high risk of chronic usage in this situation.)

- Although oral NSAIDs (nonsteroidal anti-inflammatory drugs) are an alternative to paracetamol, expert consensus suggests that they are of little benefit in the treatment of acute shingles pain [BSSI, 1995; Kanazi et al, 2000; International Herpes Management Forum, 2002].
- **An adjuvant analgesic can be started at any step** if neuropathic pain persists. A low-dose tricyclic antidepressant or an antiepileptic drug is commonly used. See *Medicines management* for further information on dosage and titration schedules.
- Automatic treatment with a tricyclic antidepressant for acute shingles in people aged over 60 years is no longer recommended. Tricyclic antidepressants have clinically significant adverse effects and the results of the only study to examine whether this strategy could prevent postherpetic neuralgia showed only borderline statistical significance [Bowsher, 1997].

Who should receive antiviral drugs?

- Antiviral drugs will provide the most benefit to people who have a higher risk of severe acute disease, complications, or progression to postherpetic neuralgia [BSSI, 1995; Gnann and Whitley, 2002; International Herpes Management Forum, 2002].
- **Antivirals are recommended for adults aged 50 years and over.**
- **Antiviral drugs are recommended in adults of any age who:**
  - Present with severe acute pain or extensive rash
  - Have ophthalmic involvement
  - Are immunocompromised
  - Have Ramsay Hunt Syndrome
  - Have atopic eczema
  - Have contact with very young infants, immunocompromised individuals, or pregnant women
- **Adults under the age of 50 years:** expert opinion is divided as to whether antivirals should routinely be offered to people under the age of 50 years who are not in the categories above.
  - The incidence of post herpetic neuralgia is low in people under the age of 50 years [Hope-Simpson, 1975], so antivirals will only have minimal impact on reducing the risk of progession to postherpetic neuralgia in this age group.
  - However, the rash may not have fully developed at the time of presentation. Antivirals *may* therefore provide benefit for those people who would otherwise have gone on to develop a severe or extensive rash.
  - Until more evidence becomes available, PRODIGY recommends offering antivirals to all adults under the age of 50 years, after discussing these issues with each individual.
- **Children:** healthy children rarely develop shingles, and it is usually mild, especially in young children. However, it is more common in children who are immunosuppressed.
  - PRODIGY does not recommend using antivirals in *healthy* children with shingles because none of the oral antivirals are licensed for use in this age group for acute shingles, and we found no published evidence examining efficacy of antivirals in children with shingles.
  - Consider using antivirals if the child has atopic eczema, ophthalmic involvement, or Ramsay Hunt Syndrome or if they have contact with very young infants, immunocompromised individuals or pregnant women. Seek specialist advice.
  - Seek immediate specialist advice for children who ar[e] immunosuppressed.

When should antivirals be started?

- **Only start antiviral treatment (if indicated) in people who present within 72 hours of the onset of rash.** However, because of the higher risk of complications, would seem sensible to give a course of antiviral treatment to a person presenting for the first time after 72 hours of the onset of the rash if they:
  - Have ophthalmic involvement
  - Are immunosuppressed
  - Are elderly
  - Have Ramsay Hunt syndrome
  - Have a severe, extensive rash, or are not coping well with their illness
- Oral antiviral drugs are not routinely indicated in healthy younger adults with shingles who present after 72 hours, as they are unlikely to have severe symptoms and are at very low risk of developing postherpetic neuralgia [Helgason et al, 2000].

[BSSI, 1995; Gnann and Whitley, 2002; International Herpes Management Forum, 2002]

How should I manage shingles of the ophthalmic nerve?

- **Shingles affecting the ophthalmic division of the trigeminal nerve may involve the eye** (particularly if th[e] rash is present towards the tip of the nose), with a high risk of ocular complications.
- **Oral antiviral treatment,** started within 1 week (preferably within 72 hours) of the appearance of the rash, is therefore recommended for all people with ophthalmic shingles [International Herpes Managemen[t] Forum, 2002].
- If there is a red eye or other signs of ocular involvemen[t] an urgent ophthalmological opinion must be obtained [BSSI, 1995; International Herpes Management Forum, 2002]. Note: ocular complications may affect almost a[ll] structures of the eye, including the orbit, conjunctiva, cornea, retina, and optic nerve.

How should I manage immunocompromised people?

How should I treat shingles in an immunocompromised person?

- **If the shingles is localized and uncomplicated,** oral antivirals may be used provided the person is closely monitored to detect signs of cutaneous, central nervou[s] system, and visceral dissemination necessitating immediate treatment with intravenous therapy [Nikke[ls] and Pierard, 2002].
- **Advise the person to seek immediate medical advice** if the rash extends beyond the original area/dermatome [or] adjacent dermatome, or new lesions develop or if fever headache, neurological or respiratory symptoms occur
- **People with severe immunosuppression** (e.g. those wit[h] cancers, bone marrow transplants, organ transplants) should be admitted for treatment with intravenous aciclovir because they are at the highest risk of complications and disseminated herpes zoster [International Herpes Management Forum, 2002].
- An immunocompromised child who develops cutaneo[us] lesions beyond the area of the primary or adjacent dermatomes should be considered to have a viraemia and at risk of visceral dissemination, and be referred immediately [Arvin, 2002].

Who is regarded as clinically immunosuppressed?

- Adults taking 40 mg prednisolone per day for more th[an] one week in the previous 3 months or children who ha[ve] taken systemic corticosteroids within the past 3 month[s] equivalent to prednisolone 2 mg/kg per day for at least

S

1 week, or 1 mg/kg per day for 1 month. Note: for corticosteroids, the dose that can cause immunosuppression is hard to define, and specialist advice is recommended.
People on lower doses of steroids given in combination with other immunosuppressants.
People taking DMARDs (disease-modifying antirheumatic drugs) that can cause myelosuppression (i.e. adalimumab, anakinra, azathioprine, ciclosporin, cyclophosphamide, etanercept, gold, infliximab, leflunomide, methotrexate, penicillamine, sulfasalazine).
People being treated with chemotherapy or generalized radiotherapy, or who have received this within the past 6 months.
People who have received an organ transplant and are currently on immunosuppressive treatment.
People who have received a bone marrow transplant and who are still considered to be immunosuppressed, including those with graft versus host disease.
People with impaired cell immunity (e.g. severe combined immune deficiency syndromes, di George syndrome).
People with symptomatic HIV infection or asymptomatic people with low CD4 counts.
HPA, 2004]

How should I manage non-immune contacts of someone with shingles?

Over 90% of adults will be immune to varicella-zoster virus; however, immigrants from tropical countries are frequently non-immune.
No action is required for individuals exposed to the varicella-zoster virus who are known to be immune (i.e. past history of chickenpox) or who are not immunosuppressed.
Exposure to shingles in the following individuals warrants passive immunization with varicella-zoster immune globulin (VZIG) if the contact risk is significant. (Consult immediately with the secondary-care, or a public health physician):

- An immunosuppressed person not immunized by prior infection or vaccination.
- Pregnant women who are antibody negative for varicella-zoster.
- Neonates

Significant exposure to varicella-zoster virus is regarded as contact with:

- An individual with disseminated zoster between 48 hours before the onset of the rash and until cropping has ceased and all lesions are crusted.
- Someone with exposed lesions (e.g. ophthalmic zoster).
- An immunosuppressed person with localized zoster on any part of the body from the day of onset of rash until crusting.

The risk of acquiring infection from an immunocompetent individual with a non-exposed zoster lesion (e.g. thoracolumbar) is remote.
Significant exposure to varicella-zoster is defined by the Health Protection Agency as:

- Contact in the same room for an appreciable period (15 minutes or more).
- Face-to-face contact, for example while having a conversation.

HPA, 2004]

When should I investigate a child presenting with shingles to rule out immunodeficiency?

If a child is usually well, has a clear history of chickenpox and the shingles is mild routine investigation is usually not necessary. Children born to women who had chickenpox during pregnancy may also have an episode of shingles in the first two years of life.

- It is advisable to investigate children for immunodeficiency if they have:
  - Recurrent shingles (two episodes or more)
  - Risk factors for immunocompromise
  - Severe, extensive or disseminated shingles or systemic symptoms

What is the supporting evidence for oral antiviral drugs?

Healthy adults

- Oral antiviral drugs, when started within 72 hours of onset of the shingles rash, reduce the duration of shingles rash and associated pain [DTB, 1998; International Herpes Management Forum, 2002; Wareham, 2004]. They also reduce the duration of postherpetic neuralgia (PHN), although it is less clear whether they also reduce the incidence of PHN. No randomized controlled trials have evaluated the efficacy of antivirals if started more than 72 hours after the onset of the rash.
- A systematic review of five small studies using aciclovir 800 mg three times a day for 7–10 days suggested that aciclovir reduced the incidence of pain at 1–3 months compared to placebo. However, the studies were too heterogeneous to permit meta-analysis of the data [Alper and Lewis, 2000].
- Evidence from one large randomized controlled trial comparing valaciclovir 1 g three times a day with aciclovir 800 mg five times a day for 7 days suggests that valaciclovir may be slightly more effective at resolving pain [Beutner et al, 1995]. Valaciclovir resolved pain 1–2 weeks faster compared to aciclovir. Postherpetic neuralgia (pain persisting for more than 30 days) occurred in 57% of the aciclovir group and 50% of the valaciclovir group. Pain persisting for 6 months was found in 25.7% of the aciclovir group and 18.6% of the valaciclovir group.
- A study comparing famciclovir 500 mg three times a day, famciclovir 750 mg three times a day and placebo for 7 days found that famciclovir did not affect the incidence of PHN. However, in the 44% of people who developed PHN (pain lasting for more than 30 days), PHN in people aged over 50 years resolved after a median of 2 months on famciclovir compared to a median of 5.5 months for those taking placebo [Tyring et al, 1995]. Note: these doses are higher than the licensed doses for healthy adults in the UK.
- A further dose-ranging study found that famciclovir 250 mg three times a day and famciclovir 750 mg once a day for 7 days (both licensed doses in the UK) were as effective as aciclovir 800 mg five times a day for 7 days for reducing the duration of the shingles rash and associated pain [Shafran et al, 2004]. However, this study was not designed to assess the effect of treatment on PHN.
- Valaciclovir 1 g three times a day has been compared with famciclovir 500 mg three times a day, with no difference found for duration of the rash and association pain, or for the duration of PHN [Tyring et al, 2000]. Proportions of people with pain were 64% in the valaciclovir and 62% in the famciclovir group at 1 month;, 32% in the valaciclovir and 34% in the famciclovir group at 3 months;, and 19% in both groups at 6 months.

Ophthalmic shingles

- There are only limited data on the efficacy of oral antivirals in ophthalmic shingles. Some studies suggest that antivirals reduce early complications (e.g. conjunctivitis) while others suggest that antivirals reduce the incidence of persistent complications (e.g. keratitis, uveitis) [BSSI, 1995; International Herpes Management Forum, 2002].

Immunocompromised adults

- There are only limited data on the efficacy of oral antivirals in immunocompromised people.
- A double-blind study compared famciclovir 500 mg three times a day with aciclovir 800 mg five times a day for 10 days for acute herpes zoster in people who had received chemotherapy, an organ transplant, or a bone marrow transplant [Tyring et al, 2001]. There were no statistically significant differences between each group for the time to crusting or for the time to loss of acute pain. However, the number who developed disseminated zoster was low in both groups: 3% (2 people) in the famciclovir group and 8% (6 people) in the aciclovir group.
- Valaciclovir has not been studied in immunocompromised people, however it is a prodrug of aciclovir, and is probably at least as effective as aciclovir therapy in this group [International Herpes Management Forum, 2002].

What treatments are not recommended?

- **Systemic corticosteroids** offer only short-term benefit and are not recommended. There is some evidence that high-dose corticosteroids added to antiviral drugs may speed healing of shingles [Wareham, 2004]. There is no evidence that they reduce the risk of postherpetic neuralgia [Wareham, 2004]. It is generally felt that any slight benefit is outweighed by the potential for harm.
- **Topical idoxuridine** (an antiviral agent) is rarely used. The evidence to support its use is poor and it is difficult to determine whether it speeds healing or reduces pain in acute shingles compared to placebo [Wareham, 2004].

Postherpetic neuralgia

PRODIGY recommends that, for practical purposes, people should be considered to have postherpetic neuralgia if pain persists after the shingles rash has healed.

What physical measures help to reduce pain?

- **Measures to reduce stimulation of the skin may be beneficial,** as skin hypersensitivity (allodynia) is common.
- Natural fibre clothing is preferable to artificial fibres.
- A protective layer over the skin may be helpful. Suitable options include a non-adherent dressing, a vapour-permeable dressing, or clingfilm [Kanazi et al, 2000].
- **Cold pack application may provide short-term relief of pain** [Kanazi et al, 2000].

S

Which drugs are recommended for first-line treatment?

- **Analgesic drugs may be helpful.**
- Paracetamol alone or in combination with full-dose codeine (30–60 mg) is commonly prescribed and seems to be effective in people with mild to moderate pain [BSSI, 1995; International Herpes Management Forum, 2002].
- Expert consensus suggests that oral NSAIDs (nonsteroidal anti-inflammatory drugs) seem to be of little benefit for postherpetic neuralgia [BSSI, 1995; Kanazi et al, 2000; International Herpes Management Forum, 2002].
- **A tricyclic antidepressant (TCA) or an antiepileptic drug (AED) is usually necessary to manage neuropathic pain.**
    - A systematic review considering the effects of TCAs and AEDs in both postherpetic neuralgia and diabetic neuropathy suggests that there is no measurable difference between their analgesic effects in neuropathic pain, or in the overall incidence of advers effects [Collins et al, 2000].
    - The choice depends on the relative contraindications, possible drug interactions, and risk of adverse effects for each individual person.
    - Suitable TCAs include amitriptyline, imipramine, and nortriptyline (all off-licence use).
    - Suitable AEDs include gabapentin (licensed) and carbamazepine (off-licence).
- For further information on using TCAs and AEDs (including suggested titration schedules) see section *Medicines management*.
- **Topical capsaicin 0.075% is an alternative** if TCAs and AEDs are contraindicated or not tolerated. People shou be warned about the intense burning sensation after application, although this effect diminishes with continued use. Some people may not be able to tolerate its use for this reason.

What should I use for second-line treatment?

- **If the response to first-line treatment is inadequate,** then referral to a pain clinic for specialist management is strongly recommended. While awaiting referral, the following options may be considered:
    - **Consider switching** to a drug with a different mechanism of action, e.g. switch from a tricyclic antidepressant (TCA) to an antiepilpetic (AED) or topical capsaicin (e.g. if there was no response to the first-line drug, or if it is poorly tolerated).
    - **Consider adding** a drug with a different mechanism o action in combination with the original drug, e.g. giv a TCA in combination with an AED or topical capsaicin.
- Consider a trial of a strong opioid, e.g. morphine, only there is very severe pain plus a lack of response to standard analgesia. However, strong opioids are best reserved for use in specialist pain clinics, as there is a high risk of chronic usage.
    - There is only limited evidence for the efficacy of opio analgesics in postherpetic neuralgia [Wareham, 2004 In general, the response of neuropathic pain to these drugs is thought to vary widely between individuals.
    - A therapeutic trial of a strong opioid should be considered in someone who is in severe pain, but it should be stopped if no benefit is gained after adequa dose titration.
- **Psychological distress is common.** Many people become depressed and may require specific management of this (see PRODIGY *Depression* guidance). Psychological services (e.g. based at pain clinics) may be able to help people develop pain-coping strategies.

How long should treatment for postherpetic neuralgia be continued?

- **Treatment should be continued at full dose for 1 month after the pain has disappeared,** then gradually tailed off [Ormerod, Personal Communication, 2005].
- Treatment should be restarted (or the dose increased) if pain recurs.

How should I manage postherpetic itch?

- A sedative antihistamine given at night may be helpful t break the itch-scratch cycle if the itch is severe and disturbing sleep.
- Topical corticosteroids should *not* be used during the acute phase of shingles, although they could be considered if the itch persists once the rash has healed [Ormerod, Personal Communication, 2005].

What is the supporting evidence for the treatment of postherpetic neuralgia?

Tricyclic antidepressants

- **Tricyclic antidepressants (TCAs) are effective at relieving the pain of postherpetic neuralgia** [DTB, 2000; Kanazi et al, 2000; Wareham, 2004]. A systematic review considering the effects of TCAs in both postherpetic neuralgia and diabetic neuropathy found that for every three people treated, one extra person experienced at least a 50% improvement in pain relief (NNT = 2.9, 95% CI 2.4 to 3.7) [Collins et al, 2000].
- **Amitriptyline** is the most widely studied TCA, and is commonly used for neuropathic pain in the UK [Collins et al, 2000].
- **Imipramine** is a less sedative alternative. It has been studied in diabetic neuropathy but has not been specifically studied in postherpetic neuralgia [Collins et al, 2000].
- **Nortriptyline** is another alternative and has been studied in postherpetic neuralgia [Watson et al, 1998]. It has a similar adverse-effect profile to amitriptyline, but is less likely to cause antimuscarinic adverse effects (including sedation) or postural hypotension [Watson et al, 1998].

Antiepileptic drugs

- **Antiepileptic drugs (AEDs) are effective at relieving the pain of postherpetic neuralgia** [DTB, 2000;Kanazi et al, 2000; Wareham, 2004]. A systematic review considering the effects of AEDs in both postherpetic neuralgia and diabetic neuropathy found that for every three people treated, one extra person experienced at least a 50% improvement on pain relief (NNT = 2.9, 95% CI 2.4 to 3.7) [Collins et al, 2000].
- **Gabapentin** is effective, has few drug interactions, and is generally well tolerated, although a slower titration than that recommended in the summary of product characteristics is usually required [Wiffen et al, 2000].
    - It has been studied in two double-blind randomized placebo-controlled trials. A study of 229 people with postherpetic neuralgia (PHN) found that gabapentin reduced pain by nearly a third [Rowbotham et al, 1998]. However, the dose of gabapentin was titrated up to 3.6 g/day, which is twice the maximum licensed dose in neuropathic pain.
    - In a more recent study of 334 people with PHN, doses of 1.8 g/day or 2.4 g/day were used; about 30% of people treated with either dose of gabapentin had a 50% or greater reduction in mean pain score, compared with just over 10% of people treated with placebo [Rice and Maton, 2001].
- **Carbamazepine** has not been specifically studied in the treatment of PHN. However, there are trial data showing efficacy against other types of neuropathic pain (e.g. trigeminal neuralgia and diabetic neuropathy) and it is widely used for the treatment of postherpetic neuralgia.
- **The following antiepileptic drugs are not recommended for first-line use in primary care:**
    - **Pregabalin** has recently been licensed for neuropathic pain, but further post-marketing safety data are needed. One study reported that 30% of people taking pregabalin 300 mg per day had a 50% or greater reduction in mean pain score, compared with just over 10% of people treated with placebo [Sabatowski et al, 2004]. A second study reported that 50% of people taking pregabalin 600 mg per day had a 50% or greater reduction in mean pain score, compared with 20% of people treated with placebo [Dworkin et al, 2003]. Its adverse-effect profile does not seem to offer any particular advantage over gabapentin: dizziness, somnolence, blurred vision, gastrointestinal adverse effects, and weight gain are common.
    - **Sodium valproate** is commonly used in practice, and is anecdotally reported as being effective, there are no studies to support its use [Wiffen et al, 2000].
    - **Phenytoin** has been less well studied than carbamazepine, but also seems to be effective against neuropathic pain. However, it is usually poorly tolerated so is therefore less preferred.

Topical capsaicin

- Capsaicin is thought to inhibit neurotransmission by causing depletion of substance P in peripheral nerve fibres.
- **Capsaicin 0.075% cream** was found to have some benefit compared to placebo in two trials in people with severe, refractory PHN [Bernstein et al, 1989; Watson et al, 1993]. However, the results are difficult to interpret, as blinding of the trial was impossible due to the burning sensation that follows application of capsaicin. This may lead to an overestimate of effect.
- A further small study of 31 people found no significant difference in pain between people using capsaicin 0.025% cream and placebo [Wareham, 2004].

Topical anaesthesia

- Topical **lidocaine** (lignocaine) 5% patches may provide short-term pain relief in postherpetic neuralgia, but the evidence for their efficacy is poor. Three double-blind randomized controlled trials have been published, but they were very small studies, and one study only recruited people who had responded to lidocaine [Wareham, 2004].
- Systemic absorption is minimal, so lidocaine patches could have a place if TCAs or AEDs are contraindicated or not tolerated. However, they are not currently available in the UK.

What treatments are not recommended?

- **Oral antiviral drugs** have no effect on established postherpetic neuralgia [Acosta and Balfour, 2001].
- **Transcutaneous electrical nerve stimulation (TENS)** is of doubtful benefit [Kanazi et al, 2000].
- **Acupuncture** seems to provide little benefit [Kanazi et al, 2000].

Medicines management

Which antiviral drug should I use for acute shingles?

- The choice of antiviral depends on the balance for an individual between cost and ease of compliance.
- **Aciclovir is least expensive but is taken five times daily.**
- If compliance is an issue, consider valaciclovir (taken three times a day) or famciclovir (taken once a day or three times a day). Both are markedly more expensive than aciclovir.
- Note: the dose of famciclovir licensed for use in the UK (250 mg three times a day or 750 mg once a day) is half the dose that was most widely studied in clinical trials (500 mg three times a day).
- In immunocompromised adults the standard dose of oral aciclovir (800 mg five times a day) and oral valaciclovir (1 g three times a day) can be used. If famciclovir is used, the dose must be doubled to 500 mg three times a day [International Herpes Management Forum, 2002].
- **All antiviral drugs should be given for a 7-day course.**
- The dose of antiviral drugs should be reduced in renal impairment [Ashley and Currie, 2004]:
    - Aciclovir should be reduced to a dose of 400–800 mg three times a day in moderate renal impairment, and twice a day in severe renal impairment.
    - Famciclovir should be reduced to a dose of 250 mg twice a day in mild renal impairment, 250 mg once a

day in moderate renal impairment, and 250 mg once a day in severe renal impairment.
  - Valaciclovir should be reduced to a dose of 1 g every 12–24 hours in moderate renal impairment and 500 mg to 1 g once a day in severe renal impairment.

What are the adverse effects of antiviral drugs?

- Oral antivirals are generally well tolerated. Gastrointestinal adverse effects (e.g. nausea, vomiting, diarrhoea, and abdominal pain) and skin rashes (including photosensitivity and urticaria) are the most common adverse effects.

How should I use tricyclic antidepressants for neuropathic pain?

Which dose should I use?

- **Start with a low dose and titrate gradually** (e.g. weekly) to reduce the risk of adverse effects. Elderly or frail people are at particular risk of adverse effects.
- **Amitriptyline, imipramine, or nortriptyline:** start with 25 mg at night (10 mg in the elderly or frail) and titrate weekly until pain is controlled or adverse effects prevent further dose increases. For many people, the effective dose is between 25 mg and 75 mg at night. A trial of 1–2 weeks' treatment at these doses is usually sufficient to assess response to a tricyclic antidepressant. If pain is not controlled within this dose range, either continue to titrate up to the maximum tolerated dose (do not exceed 150 mg at night), or switch to gabapentin.

How should I minimize adverse effects?

- Antimuscarinic adverse effects (such as dry mouth, blurred vision, sedation, constipation, nausea, and difficulty with micturition) are common. Tricyclic antidepressants should therefore be avoided in conditions that will be exacerbated by these effects, e.g. angle-closure glaucoma, benign prostatic hypertrophy, or a history of urinary retention. Note*:* nortriptyline and imipramine are less sedative than amitriptyline.
- Avoid tricyclic antidepressants in people with cardiovascular disease where possible: they commonly cause postural hypotension, but can also cause tachycardia, ECG changes, and arrhythmias. Note: nortriptyline is less likely to cause postural hypotension.
- All antidepressants should be used with caution in people with a history of epilepsy as they can lower the seizure threshold. Stop amitriptyline if seizure frequency increases.
- Hyponatraemia is associated with all types of antidepressant [CSM, 2000] but is usually well tolerated. It should be considered if the person develops drowsiness, confusion, nausea, muscle cramps, or seizures.

S

How should I use antiepileptic drugs for neuropathic pain?

Which dose should I use?

- The full 'antiepileptic dose' is usually needed to control neuropathic pain.
- **Gabapentin:** titrate slowly from 100 mg three times a day to 300 mg three times a day over 7 days. (Note: this is slower than suggested in the summary of product characteristics.) The effective dose is between 900 mg per day and 1800 mg per day (licensed) for many people. However, doses up to 2400 mg or 3600 mg per day (off-licence) were used in many studies.
- **Carbamazepine:** start with a low dose (e.g. 100 mg daily) and titrate by 100–200 mg every 2 weeks. A maintenance dose of 200 mg three or four times a day is commonly used.

How should I minimize adverse effects of gabapentin?

- Common adverse effects of gabapentin include drowsiness, dizziness, ataxia, and fatigue.
- The clearance of gabapentin is markedly reduced in renal impairment. The total daily dose should not exceed 1200 mg in those with mild renal impairment (common in the elderly). For further information on dosing in renal impairment, see the summary of product characteristics (www.medicines.org.uk).

How should I minimize adverse effects of carbamazepine?

- Dose-related adverse effects include dizziness, ataxia (unsteadiness), diplopia, insomnia, nausea, and vomiting. Ataxia may occur from high blood levels of carbamazepine and this may result in falls, especially in elderly people.
- Mild skin rashes (e.g. isolated macular or maculopapular exanthemata) are also common, but usually disappear within a few weeks [ABPI Medicines Compendium, 2003].
- Idiosyncratic adverse effects are rare but serious. They include decreased platelets or white blood cells, Stevens-Johnson syndrome, exfoliative dermatitis, and hepatitis [DTB, 1994]. Advise people to seek advice if a rash or symptoms such as fever, sore throat, mouth ulcers, bruising, or bleeding develop.
- Check full blood count, liver function tests, and serum creatinine if an idiosyncratic reaction is suspected. Routine testing is not helpful.
- Dose adjustment is not generally needed in renal impairment, provided that the dose is titrated slowly against pain [Ashley and Currie, 2004].
- Avoid carbamazepine in people with angle-closure glaucoma (mild antimuscarinic action).
- Disturbances in cardiac rhythm have rarely been reported; carbamazepine should not be used in people with arrhythmias, particularly atrio-ventricular block.
- Hyponatraemia is found in 20% of people receiving carbamazepine [van Amelsvoort et al, 1994] but is usually well tolerated. If the hyponatraemia is problematic, such as in an elderly person, restriction of fluid intake or a slight reduction in the carbamazepine dose usually resolves the issue.
- Always check for potential drug interactions: carbamazepine induces liver microsomal enzymes and interacts with many drugs.

How should I advise people to use capsaicin cream?

- Capsaicin cream should be applied 3–4 times a day. Hands should be washed immediately after use.
- People should be warned that they may feel an intense burning sensation after application, particularly if too much cream is used, or if it is used less than 3–4 times a day, or if it applied just after taking a hot bath or shower. This effect diminishes with continued use.
- Capsaicin cream should not be applied to broken or inflamed skin. It is therefore not suitable for use during acute shingles.

How should I use sedating antihistamines to manage itch?

- A sedative antihistamine (e.g. chlorphenamine [chlorpheniramine] or hydroxyzine at night may be considered to break the itch-scratch cycle if the itch is severe and is disturbing sleep).
- Antimuscarinic adverse effects (sedation, dry mouth, urinary retention, blurred vision) are common. Sedating antihistamines should therefore be avoided in someone with prostatic hypertrophy, urinary retention, or glaucoma.

- Advise people that drowsiness may persist the next day, and that they should not drive or operate machinery if affected.
- Antihistamines may also reduce the seizure threshold, and so should be avoided in someone with epilepsy.

References

NHS staff in England can link, free of charge, from references to full text journals by clicking on [Full text] on the PRODIGY website.

1. ABPI Medicines Compendium (2003) *Summary of product characteristics for Tegretol retard tablets 200mg, 400mg*. Electronic Medicines Compendium. Datapharm Communications Ltd. www.emc.medicines.org.uk [Accessed: 09/02/2004].
2. Acosta, E.P. and Balfour, H.H., Jr. (2001) Acyclovir for treatment of postherpetic neuralgia: efficacy and pharmacokinetics. *Antimicrobial Agents and Chemotherapy* **45**(10), 2771–2774.
3. Alper, B.S. and Lewis, P.R. (2000) Does treatment of acute herpes zoster prevent or shorten postherpetic neuralgia? *Journal of Family Practice* **49**(3), 255–264.
4. Arvin, A.M. (2002) Antiviral therapy for varicella and herpes zoster. *Seminars in Pediatric Infectious Diseases* **13**(1), 12–21.
5. Ashley, C. and Currie, A. (Eds.) (2004) *The renal drug handbook*. 2nd edn. Abingdon, UK: Radcliffe Medical Press Ltd.
6. Bernstein, J.E., Korman, N.J., Bickers, D.R. et al (1989) Topical capsaicin treatment of chronic postherpetic neuralgia. *Journal of the American Academy of Dermatology* **21**(2 Pt 1), 265–270.
7. Beutner, K.R., Friedman, D.J., Forszpaniak, C. et al (1995) Valaciclovir compared with acyclovir for improved therapy for herpes zoster in immunocompetent adults. *Antimicrobial Agents and Chemotherapy* **39**(7), 1546–1553.
8. Bowsher, D. (1997) The effects of pre-emptive treatment of postherpetic neuralgia with amitriptyline. *Journal of Pain and Symptom Management* **13**(6), 327–331.
9. BSSI (1995) Guidelines for the management of shingles. British Society for the Study of Infection (BSSI) Working Party. *Journal of Infection* **30**(3), 193–200.
10. Bunker, C.B. and Gotch, F. (2004) AIDS and the skin. In: Burns, T., Breathnach, S., Cox, N. and Griffiths, C. (Eds.) *Rook's textbook of dermatology*. 7th edn. Oxford: Blackwell Science. 26.25–26.28.
11. Choo, P.W., Galil, K., Donahue, J.G. et al (1997) Risk factors for postherpetic neuralgia. *Archives of Internal Medicine* **157**(11), 1217–1224. [Full text]
12. Collins, S.L., Moore, R.A., McQuay, H.J. and Wiffen, P. (2000) Antidepressants and anticonvulsants for diabetic neuropathy and postherpetic neuralgia: a quantitative systematic review. *Journal of Pain and Symptom Management* **20**(6), 449–458.
13. CSM (2000) Selective serotonin reuptake inhibitors (SSRI's). *Current Problems in Pharmacovigilance* **26**(Sep), 11–12.
14. Cunningham, Anthony L. and Dworkin, Robert H. (2000) The management of post-herpetic neuralgia. *British Medical Journal* **321**(7264), 778–779. [Full text]
15. DTB (1994) Drug treatment of epilepsy. *Drug & Therapeutics Bulletin* **32**(6), 45–48. [Full text]
16. DTB (1998) Update on drugs for herpes zoster and genital herpes. *Drug & Therapeutics Bulletin* **36**(10), 77–79. [Full text]
17. DTB (2000) Drug treatment of neuropathic pain. *Drug & Therapeutics Bulletin* **38**(12), 89–93. [Full text]
18. Dworkin, R.H. and Portenoy, R.K. (1994) Proposed classification of herpes zoster pain. *Lancet* **343**(8913), 1648. [Full text]
19. Dworkin, R.H. and Portenoy, R.K. (1996) Pain and its persistence in herpes zoster. *Pain* **67**(2–3), 241–251.
20. Dworkin, R.H., Corbin, A.E., Young, J.P., Jr. et al (2003) Pregabalin for the treatment of postherpetic neuralgia: a randomized, placebo-controlled trial. *Neurology* **60**(8), 1274–1283.
21. Galil, K., Choo, P.W., Donahue, J.G. and Platt, R. (1997) The sequelae of herpes zoster. *Archives of Internal Medicine* **157**(11), 1209–1213. [Full text]
22. Gnann, J.W. and Whitley, R.J. (2002) Herpes zoster. *New England Journal of Medicine* **347**(5), 340–346. [Full text]
23. Gross, G., Schofer, H., Wassilew, S. et al (2003) Herpes zoster guideline of the German Dermatology Society (DDG). *Journal of Clinical Virology* **26**(3), 277–289; discussion 291–3.
24. Helgason, S., Petursson, G., Gudmundsson, S. and Sigurdsson, J.A. (2000) Prevalence of postherpetic neuralgia after a first episode of herpes zoster: prospective study with long term follow up. *British Medical Journal* **321**(7264), 1–4. [Full text]
25. Hope-Simpson, R.E. (1975) Postherpetic neuralgia. *Journal of the Royal College of General Practitioners* **25**(157), 571–575.
26. HPA (2004) *Immunoglobulin handbook: indications and dosage for normal and specific immunoglobulin preparations issued by the HPA*. Health Protection Agency. www.hpa.org.uk [Accessed: 27/09/2004]. [Full text]
27. International Herpes Management Forum (2002) *Improving the management of varicella, herpes zoster and zoster-associated pain*. International Herpes Management Forum. www.ihmf.org/guidelines/summary11.asp [Accessed: 18/05/2004].
28. Johnson, R.W. and Dworkin, R.H. (2003) Treatment of herpes zoster and postherpetic neuralgia. *British Medical Journal* **326**(7392), 748–750. [Full text]
29. Jung, B.F., Johnson, R.W., Griffin, D.R. and Dworkin, R.H. (2004) Risk factors for postherpetic neuralgia in patients with herpes zoster. *Neurology* **62**(9), 1545–1551.
30. Kanazi, G.E., Johnson, R.W. and Dworkin, R.H. (2000) Treatment of postherpetic neuralgia: an update. *Drugs* **59**(5), 1113–1126.
31. Kurlan, J.G., Connelly, B.L. and Lucky, A.W. (2004) Herpes zoster in the first year of life following postnatal exposure to varicella-zoster virus: four case reports and a review of infantile herpes zoster. *Archives of Dermatology* **140**(10), 1268–1272. [Full text]
32. McCormick, A., Fleming, D. and Charlton, J. (1995) *Morbidity statistics from general practice. Fourth national study 1991–1992*. Office of Population Censuses and Surveys. www.statistics.gov.uk [Accessed: 03/05/2005].
33. MeReC (2000) The use of oral analgesics in primary care. *MeReC Bulletin* **11**(1), 1–4.
34. Nikkels, A.F. and Pierard, G.E. (2002) Oral antivirals revisited in the treatment of herpes zoster: what do they accomplish? *American Journal of Clinical Dermatology* **3**(9), 591–598.
35. Oaklander, A.L., Bowsher, D., Galer, B. et al (2003) Herpes zoster itch: preliminary epidemiologic data. *Journal of Pain* **4**(6), 338–343.
36. Ormerod, A.D. (2005) *Personal communication. General advice on management of shingles and postherpetic neuralgia.* Consultant Dermatologist, British Association of Dermatology: London.

37. Rice, A.S.C. and Maton, S. (2001) Gabapentin in postherpetic neuralgia: a randomised, double blind, placebo controlled study. *Pain* **94**(2), 215–224.
38. Rowbotham, M., Harden, N., Stacey, B. et al (1998) Gabapentin for the treatment of postherpetic neuralgia: a randomized controlled trial. *Journal of the American Medical Association* **280**(21), 1837–1842. [Full text]
39. Sabatowski, R., Galvez, R., Cherry, D.A. et al (2004) Pregabalin reduces pain and improves sleep and mood disturbances in patients with post-herpetic neuralgia: results of a randomised, placebo-controlled clinical trial. *Pain* **109**(1–2), 26–35.
40. Shafran, S.D., Tyring, S.K., Ashton, R. et al (2004) Once, twice, or three times daily famciclovir compared with aciclovir for the oral treatment of herpes zoster in immunocompetent adults: a randomized, multicenter, double-blind clinical trial. *Journal of Clinical Virology* **29**(4), 248–253.
41. Sissons, J.G.P. (2003) Herpesviruses (excluding Epstein-Barr virus). In: Warrell, D.A., Cox, T.M., Firth, J.D. and Benz, E.J.Jr (Eds.) *Oxford textbook of medicine*. 4th edn. Oxford: Oxford University Press. Section 7.10.2.
42. Sterling, J.C. (2004) Virus infections. In: Burns, T., Breathnach, S., Cox, N. and Griffiths, C. (Eds.) *Rook's textbook of dermatology*. 7th edn. Oxford: Blackwell Science. 25.15–25.37.
43. Sterling, J.C. (2005) *Personal communication. Prevention of shingles infection.* Consultant Dermatologist, Addenbrooke's Hospital: Cambridge.
44. Tenser, R.B. (2001) Herpes zoster infection and postherpatic neuralgia. *Current Neurology and Neuroscience Reports* **1**(6), 526–532.
45. Thomas, P.K. (2003) Disorders of cranial nerves. In: Warrell, D.A., Cox, T.M., Firth, J.D. and Benz, E.J.Jr (Eds.) *Oxford textbook of medicine*. 4th edn. Oxford: Oxford University Press. Section 24.13.15.
46. Tyring, S., Barbarash, R.A., Nahlik, J.E. et al (1995) Famciclovir for the treatment of acute herpes zoster: effects on acute disease and postherpetic neuralgia. A randomized, double-blind, placebo-controlled trial. Collaborative Famciclovir Herpes Zoster Study Group. *Annals of Internal Medicine* **123**(2), 89–96.
47. Tyring, S.K., Beutner, K.R., Tucker, B.A. et al (2000) Antiviral therapy for herpes zoster: randomized, controlled clinical trial of valacyclovir and famciclovir therapy in immunocompetent patients 50 years and older. *Archives of Family Medicine* **9**(9), 863–869.
48. Tyring, S., Belanger, R., Bezwoda, W. et al (2001) A randomized, double-blind trial of famciclovir versus acyclovir for the treatment of localized dermatomal herpes zoster in immunocompromised patients. *Cancer Investigation* **19**(1), 13–22.
49. van Amelsvoort, T., Bakshi, R., Devaux, C.B. and Schwabe, S. (1994) Hyponatremia associated with carbamazepine and oxcarbazepine therapy: a review. *Epilepsia* **35**(1), 181–188.
50. Wallace, M.S. and Oxman, M.N. (1997) Acute herpes zoster and postherpetic neuralgia. *Anesthesiology Clinics of North America* **15**(2), 371–405.
51. Wareham, D. (2004) *Postherpatic neuralgia.* Clinical Evidence. Volume 12. www.clinicalevidence.com [Accessed: 09/02/2005].
52. Watson, C.P.N., Tyler, K.L., Bickers, D.R. et al (1993) A randomized vehicle-controlled trial of topical capsaicin in the treatment of postherpetic neuralgia. *Clinical Therapeutics* **15**(3), 510–526.
53. Watson, C.P., Vernich, L., Chipman, M. and Reed, K. (1998) Nortriptyline versus amitriptyline in postherpetic neuralgia: a randomized trial. *Neurology* **51**(4), 1166–1171.
54. Whitley, R.J. (1995) Varicella-zoster virus. In: Mandell, G.L., Bennett, J.E., Dolin, R. et al (Eds.) *Mandell, Douglas and Bennett's principles and practice of infectious diseases.* 4th edn. New York: Churchill Livingstone. 1345–1351.
55. Whitley, R.J., Weiss, H.L. and Soong, S.J. (1999) Herpes zoster: risk categories for persistent pain. *Journal of Infectious Diseases* **179**(1), 9–15. [Full text]
56. WHO (2003) *WHO's pain ladder.* World Health Organisation. www.who.int/cancer/palliative/painladder/en [Accessed: 05/07/2005].
57. Wiffen, P., McQuay, H., Carroll, D. et al (2000) *Anticonvulsant drugs for acute and chronic pain (Cochrane Review).* The Cochrane Library. Issue 3. Chichester, UK: John Wiley & Sons, Ltd. www.nelh.nhs.uk/cochrane.asp [Accessed: 05/07/2005]. [Full text]

PRODIGY GUIDANCE

Sinusitis

Last revised in July 2002

At the time of print this topic was being updated. The newly revised guidance will be issued on to the website in 2006.

www.prodigy.nhs.uk/guidance.asp?gt=Sinusitis

Applies to people over the age of 3 years

This guidance covers the management of acute sinusitis and gives advice on when to refer for persistent symptoms. Sinusitis is also known as rhinosinusitis.

This guidance does not cover the management of coryza (common cold) or other causes of facial pain.

There is separate PRODIGY guidance for *Allergic rhinitis, Headache, Migraine, and Trigeminal neuralgia.*

Goals

To relieve symptoms of sinusitis

To reduce duration of symptoms

To prevent complications

Contents

Scenarios

- Acute sinusitis in adults p.1713
- Acute sinusitis in children under 16 p.1716
- Persisting or frequently recurring sinusitis p.1718

Extended Information, p. 1719

Which scenario?

Acute sinusitis in adults: covers the management of acute sinusitis in adults older than 16 years.

Acute sinusitis in children: covers the management of acute sinusitis in children aged 3–16 years.

Persisting or frequently recurring sinusitis: covers management of sinusitis when symptoms have lasted longer than 3 months, or where there have been three to four significant episodes in the last year.

Acute sinusitis in adults

Which therapy?

Follow local guidelines. Consider modifying therapy according to local bacterial resistance patterns.

Diagnosis of bacterial acute sinusitis

Diagnosis is commonly based on overall clinical impression, but use of predictive symptoms of significant bacterial infection may help to target antimicrobials most appropriately — for example combinations of the following:

- General malaise
- Pyrexia greater than 38.5°C
- A second phase in the illness ('double sickening')
- Facial pain and tenderness (predominantly on one side)
- Reduced sense of smell (hyposmia)
- A headache that is worse on leaning forwards
- Purulent nasal discharge (more than 7 days)
- Presence of pus in the nasal cavity
- Maxillary toothache or pain on chewing
- Erythrocyte sedimentation rate greater than 10 mm/hour

Symptomatic treatment

- Symptom relief may be the only treatment required, as 70% will get better in a few days with or without antimicrobials.
  - Paracetamol is effective for relieving pain and high temperature.
  - Ibuprofen is an alternative.
  - If paracetamol alone is insufficient, codeine can be added.
  - They are usually needed only for a few days.

Antibiotics

- **Reserve antibiotics for those with severe or persistent symptoms of at least 7 days' duration.**
- **Amoxicillin** is the **first-line** choice if an antibiotic is considered to be necessary.
- **In patients with penicillin allergy,** other choices of first-line antibiotics are:
  - Erythromycin
  - Oxytetracycline
  - Doxycycline
- **Second-line therapy:** if first-line antibiotic treatment is not effective, then try one of the following beta-lactamase resistant antibiotics:
  - Co-amoxiclav
  - Ciprofloxacin
- **Duration of antibiotic treatment: 7 days** is recommended for acute sinusitis, which falls within the treatment duration recommended by the Public Health Laboratory Service and the *British National Formulary.*
- **3-day courses** of antibiotic treatment may be an alternative approach.

Other therapies

- **Steam inhalation** may give symptomatic relief to some people but it is not recommended for routine use, and there is a risk of scalding.
- **Decongestants (oral and intranasal)** are of dubious value and should not be used for more than 7 days.
- **Topical corticosteroids** as an adjuvant to antibiotic treatment may be of some benefit but their precise role remains uncertain.

Practical prescribing points

For further information please see the *Medicines Compendium* (www.medicines.org.uk) or the *British National Formulary* (www.bnf.org).

- **Ibuprofen:** as with other nonsteroidal anti-inflammatory drugs, ibuprofen may worsen or precipitate gastrointestinal haemorrhage, asthma, hypertension, renal impairment or cardiac failure. Avoid if there is a history of peptic ulcers and in pregnant women.

S

- **Amoxicillin:** use with caution in renal impairment.
- **Erythromycin:** use with caution in hepatic and renal impairment, prolongation of the QT interval, and breastfeeding. Erythromycin may increase the level of certain drugs (e.g. theophylline, carbamazepine), or potentiate warfarin.
- **Tetracyclines:** contraindicated in pregnancy, breastfeeding, porphyria, children aged under 12 years and renal failure (except doxycycline and minocycline). Use with caution in hepatic impairment. They may cause photosensitivity reactions (avoid exposure to sunlight or sun lamps).
- **Co-amoxiclav:** use with caution in renal or hepatic impairment, breastfeeding and during pregnancy. The Committee on the Safety of Medicines advises that cholestatic jaundice may occur and is more likely in men, in people aged over 65 years, and with longer courses of treatment.
- **Quinolones:** the Committee on the Safety of Medicines advises that at the first sign of pain or inflammation, people taking quinolones should discontinue the treatment and rest the affected limb until tendon symptoms have resolved. Use with caution in epilepsy or other conditions that predispose to seizures, glucose 6-phosphate dehydrogenase deficiency, myasthenia gravis, renal impairment, hepatic impairment, pregnancy, breastfeeding, children and adolescents. Quinolones may induce convulsions in people with or without a history of convulsions.

Should I refer or investigate?

Refer?

- Consider referral in people that have a history of recurrent troublesome attacks or where symptoms are very severe with systemic upset and/or signs of facial swelling or cellulitis.

Investigate?

- Radiology is not routinely indicated. If considered it may be better to leave this to specialists, following referral.

Patient information leaflets

The following PILs are available at www.prodigy.nhs.uk

- Antibiotics - Why No Antibiotic?
- Sinusitis (Acute)

S

Shared decision making

- Sinusitis (infected sinus) is common, and often follows a cold.
- **No treatment** is a popular option. Most cases are due to a virus infection, and it usually goes away on its own.
- **Paracetamol** will usually ease the pain.
- **Ibuprofen** is an alternative.
- **Codeine** can be added if paracetamol alone is not sufficient.
- **Decongestants and steam inhalations** are often used, but their value is debatable. They may ease symptoms and help to drain the sinuses. You should not used decongestant drops or sprays for more than 7 days as a 'rebound' blockage of the nose may occur.
- **Antibiotics** may be advised if the sinusitis is severe, or lasts longer than 7 days.
- **Nasal nicotine spray should be avoided** as it may cause rhinitis and associated symptoms. People who require nicotine replacement therapy should try an alternative method until sinusitis is resolved.

Drug rationale

Drugs not included

- **Fixed-dose formulations of low-strength weak opioids with paracetamol** (e.g. co-codamol 8/500, co-codaprin and co-dydramol) do not offer any clinical benefit over paracetamol alone and are likely to lead to opioid adverse effects [DTB, 1998; MeReC, 2000; BNF 43, 2002].
- **Fixed-dose formulations of high-strength weak opioids with paracetamol** (e.g. co-codamol 30/500) do not allo titration of the most effective and safe analgesic dose to match the person's requirements.
- **Analgesics other than paracetamol, ibuprofen and codeine (in combination with paracetamol)** are not appropriate to be used routinely for first-line symptomatic relief as they may cause more adverse effects and are more expensive.
- **Penicillins other than amoxicillin** are not offered for firs line use, as evidence indicates that amoxicillin is as effective as more expensive agents [De Ferranti et al, 1998; Brook et al, 2000].
- **Macrolides other than erythromycin** are not included. Clarithromycin and azithromycin are both active agains *Haemophilus influenzae* and may be considered when erythromycin is not tolerated.
- **Tetracyclines other than oxytetracycline and doxycycli** are not included. The spectrum of activity of all the tetracyclines is very similar, therefore no further tetracyclines have been included [Finch, 1997].
- **First-generation cephalosporins** are not offered. They a not effective against beta-lactamase-producing strains such as *H influenzae* and there is little evidence to support their use in acute bacterial sinusitis.
- **Second- and third-generation cephalosporins** have reduced activity against *Streptococcus pneumoniae*. They are generally expensive, not well absorbed orally and gastrointestinal adverse effects are commonly experienced with their use.
- **Trimethoprim** is not included as an option for adults in treating acute bacterial sinusitis, as there is a wider choice of antimicrobials available with superior activity against the more common pathogens.
- **Penicillins other than co-amoxiclav are not offered for use as second line,** as there is little evidence of superior efficacy against beta-lactamase-producing resistant strains (*H influenzae* and *Moraxella catarrhalis)*.
- **Quinolones other than ciprofloxacin** are not included. They should be reserved for complicated infections where sensitivities are known in order to preserve their efficacy and limit the development of resistance [DH an SMAC, 1998]. The newer quinolones have a slightly broader spectrum of activity than the older agents but there is no evidence of greater efficacy.
- **Metronidazole** is effective against beta-lactamase-producing anaerobes but, as these infections tend to be associated primarily with dental sepsis and after dental surgery, they are not offered.
- **Co-trimoxazole** is restricted to certain indications by th Committee on Safety of Medicines and should only be used if there is evidence of bacterial sensitivity.
- **Intranasal corticosteroids** are not offered, as their potential benefit in acute sinusitis remains inconclusive.
- **Oral and intranasal decongestants** are not included as there is limited evidence to support their benefit in acut sinusitis.
- **Antihistamines** are not included. First-generation antihistamines should be avoided in acute bacterial sinusitis because of their tendency to cause excessive dryness with thickening of secretions and crusting whic

can aggravate sinusitis. Second-generation antihistamines may have a role in chronic bacterial sinusitis where a clear allergic component is demonstrated.

Drugs included

- **Paracetamol** is an effective and safe analgesic and antipyretic agent for most people.
- **Ibuprofen** is an effective alternative to paracetamol if there are no contraindications.
- **Codeine (in combination with paracetamol):** higher dose codeine is included for use for up to a few days with regular paracetamol for additional pain relief. Codeine 60 mg plus paracetamol has been shown to provide more pain relief than either codeine 60 mg alone or paracetamol 1000 mg alone [Medicines Resource, 1995; De Craen et al, 1996; Moore et al, 1997; Shuttleworth and Harrad, 2000].
- For all antimicrobials, a 7-day course is given in line with Public Health Laboratory Service and *British National Formulary* recommendations.
- **Amoxicillin** is active against some *Haemophilus influenzae* strains and the majority of *Streptococcus pneumoniae* (some of the most common pathogens found in bacterial sinusitis) [Sokol, 2001].
- **Erythromycin** is offered for penicillin-allergic patients. It is particularly active against *S pneumoniae and Moraxella catarrhalis* although it has low activity against *H influenzae.*
- **Doxycycline** is included as it has a broad spectrum of activity against respiratory pathogens (it covers most typical and atypical pathogens) and can be given once a day [Finch, 1997].
- **Oxytetracycline** has a similar spectrum of activity to doxycycline but must be taken four times a day [Finch, 1997].
- **Co-amoxiclav** is included as an option for second-line treatment when there is no response to the initial antibacterial. It is particularly effective against beta-lactamase-producing organisms.
- **Ciprofloxacin** is recommended as an alternative second-line agent, if there is no response.

BNF 43, 2002; PHLS, 2002]

Prescriptions

Analgesia/antipyretics: use when required

Paracetamol tablets: 1g up to four times a day
- Age from 16 years onwards
- Paracetamol 500mg tablets. Take two tablets every 4 to 6 hours when required for relief of pain or high temperature. Maximum of 8 tablets in 24 hours; supply 50 tablets; NHS Cost £0.70; OTC Cost £1.32.

Codeine 30mg tablets: add on to paracetamol if required
- Age from 16 years onwards
- Codeine 30mg tablets. Take one to two tablets every 4 to 6 hours when required for pain relief. Maximum of 8 tablets in 24 hours; supply 30 tablets; NHS Cost £1.44.

Paracetamol 500mg tablets + codeine 30mg tablets
- Age from 16 years onwards
- Paracetamol 500mg tablets. Take two tablets every 4 to 6 hours when required for pain relief. Maximum of 8 tablets in 24 hours; supply 50 tablets; NHS Cost £0.38; OTC Cost £1.32.
- Codeine 30mg tablets. Take one to two tablets every 4 to 6 hours when required for pain relief. Maximum of 8 tablets in 24 hours; supply 30 tablets; NHS Cost £1.44.

Ibuprofen tablets: 400mg three times a day
- Age from 16 years onwards
- Ibuprofen 400mg tablets. Take one tablet three times a day when required for relief of pain or high temperature. Do not exceed the stated dose; supply 24 tablets; NHS Cost £0.70; OTC Cost £1.25.

1st-line antibiotics: amoxicillin for 7 days

Amoxicillin capsules: 250mg three times a day
- Age from 16 years onwards
- Amoxicillin 250mg capsules. Take one capsule three times a day for 7 days; supply 21 capsules; NHS Cost £1.25.

Amoxicillin capsules: 500mg three times a day
- Age from 16 years onwards
- Amoxicillin 500mg capsules. Take one capsule three times a day for 7 days; supply 21 capsules; NHS Cost £1.84.

1st-line antibiotics: penicillin allergy (7 days)

Oxytetracycline tablets: 250mg four times a day
- Age from 16 years onwards
- Oxytetracycline 250mg tablets. Take one tablet four times a day for 7 days; supply 28 tablets; NHS Cost £0.81.

Erythromycin e/c tablets: 500mg twice a day
- Age from 16 years onwards
- Erythromycin 250mg e/c tablets. Take two tablets twice a day for 7 days; supply 14 tablets; NHS Cost £1.54.

Doxycycline capsules: 100mg once a day
- Age from 16 years onwards
- Doxycycline 100mg capsules. Take TWO capsules now and then take ONE capsule once a day for the next 6 days; supply 8 capsules; NHS Cost £2.49.

Erythromycin e/c tablets: 250mg four times a day
- Age from 16 years onwards
- Erythromycin 250mg e/c tablets. Take one tablet four times a day for 7 days; supply 28 tablets; NHS Cost £3.08.

Treatment failure: 2nd-line antibiotics for 7 days

Co-amoxiclav tablets: 250/125mg three times a day
- Age from 16 years onwards
- Co-amoxiclav 375mg tablets. Take one tablet three times a day for 7 days; supply 21 tablets; NHS Cost £9.73.

Co-amoxiclav tablets: 500/125mg three times a day
- Age from 16 years onwards
- Co-amoxiclav 625mg tablets. Take one tablet three times a day for 7 days; supply 21 tablets; NHS Cost £15.72.

Ciprofloxacin tablets: 500mg twice a day
- Age from 16 years onwards
- Ciprofloxacin 500mg tablets. Take one tablet twice a day for 7 days; supply 14 tablets; NHS Cost £19.88.

Ciprofloxacin tablets: 250mg twice a day
- Age from 16 years onwards
- Ciprofloxacin 250mg tablets. Take one tablet twice a day for 7 days; supply 14 tablets; NHS Cost £10.50.

Acute sinusitis in children under 16

Which therapy?

Diagnosis

- **Sinusitis can be difficult to define in children.** The sinuses grow and develop during childhood and adolescence.
- Children frequently have viral upper respiratory infections and these can run into one another giving the impression of prolonged rhinitis/rhinosinusitis.
- **Allergic rhinitis is common in children and should also be considered as a cause.**
- **Diagnosis is commonly based on overall clinical impression,** but use of predictive symptoms of significant bacterial infection may help to target antimicrobials most appropriately; for example, a combination of the following, *in older children*:
  - General malaise
  - Pyrexia greater than 38.5°C
  - A second phase in the illness ('double sickening')
  - Facial pain and tenderness (predominantly on one side)
  - Reduced sense of smell (hyposmia)
  - A headache that is worse on leaning forwards
  - Purulent nasal discharge (more than 7 days)
  - Presence of pus in the nasal cavity
  - Maxillary toothache or pain on chewing
  - Erythrocyte sedimentation rate greater than 10 mm/hour
- **Facial pain and headache are rare in younger children** where other symptoms such as snoring, mouth breathing, cough, feeding difficulty and hyponasal speech, may point to the diagnosis.

Symptomatic treatment

- Symptom relief may be the only treatment required, as 80% will get better in a few days with or without antimicrobials.
  - Paracetamol is effective to relieve pain and high temperature
  - Ibuprofen is an alternative
  - If paracetamol alone is insufficient, codeine can be added
  - They are usually needed only for a few days

S

Antimicrobials

- Reserve antibiotics for those with severe *or* persistent symptoms of at least 10–14 days' duration. Spontaneous resolution is common.
- **If an antibiotic is thought to be necessary then first-line choices are amoxicillin or erythromycin** (if penicillin allergic) for 7 days.
- **Second-line:** if first-line antibiotic treatment is not effective, then try a beta-lactamase-resistant antibiotic, such as co-amoxiclav.
- **Trimethoprim** is an alternative for children who are allergic to penicillin although its activity may not be as good as erythromycin.
- **Duration of antibiotic treatment: 7 days** is recommended for acute sinusitis, which falls within the treatment duration recommended by the Public Health Laboratory Service and *British National Formulary*.
- **3-day courses** of antibiotic treatment may be an alternative approach.

Other therapies

- **Decongestants (oral and intranasal)** are of dubious value They should not be used for more than 7 days.
- **Topical corticosteroids** as an adjuvant to antibiotic treatment may be of some benefit but their precise role remains uncertain.
- **Steam inhalation** may give symptomatic relief to some children but it is not recommended for routine use and there is a risk of scalding.

Practical prescribing points

For further information please see the *Medicines Compendium* (www.medicines.org.uk) or the *British National Formulary* (www.bnf.org).

- **Ibuprofen:** as with other nonsteroidal anti-inflammatory drugs, ibuprofen may worsen or precipitate gastrointestinal haemorrhage, asthma, hypertension, renal impairment or cardiac failure. Avoid if there is a history of peptic ulcers.
- **Amoxicillin:** use with caution in renal impairment.
- **Erythromycin:** use with caution in hepatic and renal impairment and prolongation of the QT interval. Erythromycin may increase the level of certain drugs (e.g. theophylline, carbamazepine, warfarin).
- **Trimethoprim** may rarely cause blood dyscrasias and skin disorders. In moderate renal impairment the dose of trimethoprim should be reduced, and in very severe renal impairment the drug should be avoided.
- **Co-amoxiclav:** use with caution in renal or hepatic impairment. The Committee on Safety of Medicines advises that cholestatic jaundice may occur and is more likely in males, and with longer courses of treatment.

Should I refer or investigate?

Refer?

- Consider referral if patient has a history of recurrent troublesome attacks or symptoms are very severe with systemic upset and/or signs of facial swelling or cellulitis.

Investigate?

- Radiology is not routinely indicated. If considered it may be better to leave this to specialists, following referral.

Patient information leaflets

The following PILs are available at www.prodigy.nhs.uk

- Antibiotics - Why No Antibiotic?
- Sinusitis (Acute)

Shared decision making

- Sinusitis (infected sinus) is common, and often follows a cold.
- **No treatment** is a popular option. Most cases are due to a virus infection, and it usually goes away on its own.
- **Paracetamol** will usually ease the pain.
- **Ibuprofen** is an alternative.
- **Decongestants and steam inhalations** are often used, but their value is debatable. They may ease symptoms and help to drain the sinuses. You should not used decongestant drops or sprays for more than 7 days as a 'rebound' blockage of the nose may occur.
- **Antibiotics** may be advised if the sinusitis is severe, or lasts longer than 10 days.

Drug rationale

Drugs not included

Fixed-dose formulations of low-strength weak opioids with paracetamol (e.g. co-codamol 8/500, co-codaprin and co-dydramol) do not offer any clinical benefit over paracetamol alone and are likely to lead to opioid adverse effects [DTB, 1998; MeReC, 2000; BNF 43, 2002].

Fixed-dose formulations of high-strength weak opioids with paracetamol (e.g. co-codamol 30/500) do not allow titration of the most effective and safe analgesic dose to match the person's requirements.

Analgesics other than paracetamol, ibuprofen and codeine (in combination with paracetamol) are not appropriate to be used routinely for first-line symptomatic relief as they may cause more adverse effects and are more expensive.

Penicillins other than amoxicillin are not offered for first-line use, as evidence indicates that amoxicillin is as effective as other more expensive agents [De Ferranti et al, 1998; Brook et al, 2000].

Macrolides other than erythromycin are not included. Clarithromycin and azithromycin are both active against *Haemophilus influenzae* and may be considered when erythromycin is not tolerated.

Tetracyclines should be avoided in children younger than 12 years of age because they cause discolouration and malformation of the teeth [BNF 43, 2002]. They are licensed for use in people 12 years and over but development of teeth may still be taking place between 12–16 years of age. Therefore, as there are alternative antibiotics available for use in penicillin-allergic patients, tetracyclines are not offered.

First-generation cephalosporins are not offered. They are not effective against beta-lactamase-producing strains such as *H influenzae* and there is little evidence to support their use in acute bacterial sinusitis.

Second- and third-generation cephalosporins have reduced activity against *Streptococcus pneumoniae*. They are generally expensive, not well absorbed orally and gastrointestinal adverse effects are commonly experienced with their use.

Penicillins other than co-amoxiclav are not offered for use as second line, as there is little evidence of superior efficacy against beta-lactamase-producing resistant strains (*H influenzae* and *Moraxella catarrhalis)*.

Quinolones are not recommended in children and growing adolescents because arthropathy has occurred in studies in young animals. However, quinolones are sometimes initiated in secondary care.

Metronidazole is effective against beta-lactamase-producing anaerobes but, as these infections tend to be associated primarily with dental sepsis or after dental surgery, they are not offered.

Co-trimoxazole is restricted to certain indications by the Committee on Safety of Medicines (CSM) and should only be used if there is evidence of bacterial sensitivity.

Intranasal corticosteroids are not offered, as their potential benefit in acute sinusitis remains inconclusive.

Oral and intranasal decongestants are not included as there is limited evidence to support their benefit in acute sinusitis.

Antihistamines are not included. First-generation antihistamines should be avoided in acute bacterial sinusitis because of their tendency to cause excessive dryness with thickening of secretions and crusting which can aggravate sinusitis. Second-generation antihistamines may have a role in chronic bacterial sinusitis where a clear allergic component is demonstrated.

Drugs included

- **Paracetamol** is an effective and safe analgesic and antipyretic agent for most people.
- **Ibuprofen** is an effective alternative to paracetamol if there are no contraindications.
- For all antimicrobials, a 7-day course is given in line with Public Health Laboratory Service and *British National Formulary* recommendations.
- **Amoxicillin** is active against some *Haemophilus influenzae* strains and the majority of *Streptococcus pneumoniae* (some of the most common pathogens found in bacterial sinusitis) [Sokol, 2001].
- **Erythromycin** is offered for penicillin-allergic people. It is particularly active against *S pneumoniae and Moraxella catarrhalis* although it has low activity against *H influenzae.*
- **Trimethoprim** is an alternative for penicillin-allergic patients although its activity may not be as good as erythromycin.
- **Co-amoxiclav** is included as an option for second-line treatment when there is no response to the initial antibiotic. It is particularly effective against beta-lactamase-producing organisms.

[BNF 43, 2002; PHLS, 2002]

Prescriptions

Analgesia/antipyretics: use when required

Paracetamol s/f susp: 120mg to 240mg up to four times a day
- Age from 3 to 5 years
- Paracetamol 120mg/5ml s/f susp. Take one to two 5ml spoonfuls every 4 to 6 hours when required for relief of pain or high temperature. Maximum of 4 doses in 24 hours; supply 300 ml; NHS Cost £1.24; OTC Cost £2.18.

Paracetamol s/f susp: 250mg to 500mg up to four times a day
- Age from 6 to 11 years
- Paracetamol 250mg/5ml s/f susp. Take one to two 5ml spoonfuls every 4 to 6 hours when required for relief of pain or high temperature. Maximum of 4 doses in 24 hours; supply 300 ml; NHS Cost £1.53; OTC Cost £2.70.

Paracetamol tablets: 500mg to 1g up to four times a day
- Age from 12 to 15 years
- Paracetamol 500mg tablets. Take one to two tablets every 4 to 6 hours when required for relief of pain or high temperature. Maximum of 8 tablets in 24 hours; supply 50 tablets; NHS Cost £0.38; OTC Cost £0.66.

Ibuprofen s/f susp: 100mg three to four times a day
- Age from 3 to 7 years
- Ibuprofen 100mg/5ml s/f susp. Take one 5ml spoonful 3 to 4 times a day when required for relief of pain or high temperature. Do not exceed the stated dose; supply 150 ml; NHS Cost £2.73; OTC Cost £4.81.

Ibuprofen s/f susp: 200mg three to four times a day
- Age from 8 to 11 years
- Ibuprofen 100mg/5ml s/f susp. Take two 5ml spoonfuls 3 to 4 times a day when required for relief of pain or high temperature. Do not exceed the stated dose; supply 300 ml; NHS Cost £5.46; OTC Cost £9.62.

Ibuprofen tablets: 400mg three times a day
- Age from 12 to 15 years
- Ibuprofen 400mg tablets. Take one tablet three times a day when required for relief of pain or high temperature.

Do not exceed the stated dose; supply 24 tablets; NHS Cost £0.70; OTC Cost £1.75.

1st-line antibiotics: amoxicillin for 7 days

Amoxicillin s/f suspension: 125mg three times a day
- Age from 3 to 9 years
- Amoxicillin 125mg/5ml s/f susp. Take one 5ml spoonful three times a day for 7 days; supply 100 ml; NHS Cost £1.29.

Amoxicillin s/f suspension: 250mg three times a day
- Age from 10 to 11 years
- Amoxicillin 250mg/5ml s/f susp. Take one 5ml spoonful three times a day for 7 days; supply 100 ml; NHS Cost £2.25.

Amoxicillin capsules: 250mg three times a day
- Age from 12 to 15 years
- Amoxicillin 250mg capsules. Take one capsule three times a day for 7 days; supply 21 capsules; NHS Cost £1.25.

Amoxicillin capsules: 500mg three times a day
- Age from 12 to 15 years
- Amoxicillin 500mg capsules. Take one capsule three times a day for 7 days; supply 21 capsules; NHS Cost £1.84.

1st-line antibiotics: penicillin allergy (7 days)

Erythromycin s/f suspension: 250mg four times a day
- Age from 3 to 11 years
- Erythromycin 250mg/5ml sf susp. Take one 5ml spoonful four times a day for 7 days; supply 140 ml; NHS Cost £2.88.

Erythromycin s/f suspension: 500mg four times a day
- Age from 9 to 11 years
- Erythromycin 500mg/5ml sf susp. Take one 5ml spoonful four times a day for 7 days; supply 140 ml; NHS Cost £6.56.

Erythromycin e/c tablets: 500mg twice a day
- Age from 12 to 15 years
- Erythromycin 250mg e/c tablets. Take two tablets twice a day for 7 days; supply 28 tablets; NHS Cost £1.54.

Erythromycin e/c tablets: 250mg four times a day
- Age from 12 to 15 years
- Erythromycin 250mg e/c tablets. Take one tablet four times a day for 7 days; supply 28 tablets; NHS Cost £3.08.

S

Trimethoprim s/f suspension: 50mg twice a day
- Age from 3 to 5 years
- Trimethoprim 50mg/5ml s/f susp. Take one 5ml spoonful twice a day for 7 days; supply 70 ml; NHS Cost £1.24.

Trimethoprim s/f suspension: 100mg twice a day
- Age from 6 to 11 years
- Trimethoprim 50mg/5ml s/f susp. Take two 5ml spoonfuls twice a day for 7 days; supply 140 ml; NHS Cost £2.48.

Trimethoprim tablets: 200mg twice a day
- Age from 12 to 15 years
- Trimethoprim 200mg tablets. Take one tablet twice a day for 7 days; supply 14 tablets; NHS Cost £0.67.

Treatment failure: 2nd-line antibiotics for 7 days

Co-amoxiclav suspension: 125/31mg three times a day
- Age from 3 to 5 years
- Co-amoxiclav 125/31mg/5ml susp. Take one 5ml spoonful three times a day for 7 days; supply 100 ml; NHS Cost £4.57.

Co-amoxiclav suspension: 250/62mg three times a day
- Age from 6 to 11 years
- Co-amoxiclav 250/62mg/5ml susp. Take one 5ml spoonful three times a day for 7 days; supply 100 ml; NHS Cost £6.42.

Co-amoxiclav tablets: 250/125mg three times a day
- Age from 12 to 15 years
- Co-amoxiclav 375mg tablets. Take one tablet three times a day for 7 days; supply 21 tablets; NHS Cost £4.25.

Co-amoxiclav tablets: 500/125mg three times a day
- Age from 12 to 15 years
- Co-amoxiclav 625mg tablets. Take one tablet three times a day for 7 days; supply 21 tablets; NHS Cost £15.72.

Persisting or frequently recurring sinusitis

Which therapy?

- **Persistent or chronic sinusitis** is defined as symptoms of sinusitis continuing for 3 months or more, or where there are 3–4 significant episodes of sinusitis in 1 year.
- **There is an overlap with other clinical entities** such as allergic rhinitis, polyps, and anatomical abnormalities such as deviated nasal septum.
- **Dental infections** may sometimes be the cause.
- **The value of antimicrobials is uncertain,** but they are frequently tried, for persistent or relapsing symptoms.
- **Referral for investigation** and specialist treatment is usually indicated, unless there is a clear alternative diagnosis; for example allergic rhinitis or polyps, where trial of intranasal corticosteroids may sometimes be appropriate.
- **Intranasal corticosteroids, antihistamines, and antimicrobials** may all be recommended by specialists, depending on the suspected cause. They may also be used prior to surgery as adjunctive therapy.

Practical prescribing points

For further information please see the *Medicines Compendium* (www.medicines.org.uk) or the *British National Formulary* (www.bnf.org).

- **Ibuprofen:** as with other nonsteroidal anti-inflammatory drugs, ibuprofen may worsen or precipitate gastrointestinal haemorrhage, asthma, hypertension, renal impairment or cardiac failure. Avoid if there is a history of peptic ulcers and in pregnant women.

Should I refer or investigate?

Refer?

- Referral should be considered.

Investigate?

- Radiology is not usually indicated, except guided by specialists.

Patient information leaflets

The following PILs are available at www.prodigy.nhs.uk
- Antibiotics - Why No Antibiotic?
- Sinusitis (Acute)

Shared decision making

An infected sinus may not clear in some people, and it becomes 'chronic' or keeps coming back.
Paracetamol will usually ease the pain.
Ibuprofen is an alternative.
Codeine can be added if paracetamol alone is not sufficient.
Antibiotics may help, but improving the drainage of the sinuses may be more important.
Referral to investigate and consider surgical drainage, or other options, is usually recommended for persistent or chronic sinusitis.

Drug rationale

Drugs not included

Fixed-dose formulations of low-strength weak opioids with paracetamol (e.g. co-codamol 8/500, co-codaprin and co-dydramol) do not offer any clinical benefit over paracetamol alone and are likely to lead to opioid adverse effects [DTB, 1998; MeReC, 2000; BNF 43, 2002].
Fixed-dose formulations of high-strength weak opioids with paracetamol (e.g. co-codamol 30/500) do not allow titration of the most effective and safe analgesic dose to match the person's requirements.
Analgesics other than paracetamol, ibuprofen, and codeine (in combination with paracetamol) are not appropriate to be used routinely for first-line symptomatic relief as they may cause more adverse effects and are more expensive.

Drugs included

Paracetamol is an effective and safe analgesic and antipyretic agent for most people.
Ibuprofen is an effective alternative to paracetamol if there are no contraindications.
Codeine (in combination with paracetamol): higher dose codeine is included for use for up to a few days with regular paracetamol for additional pain relief. Codeine 60 mg plus paracetamol has been shown to provide more pain relief than either codeine 60 mg alone or paracetamol 1000 mg alone [Medicines Resource, 1995; De Craen et al, 1996; Moore et al, 1997].

Prescriptions

Analgesia/antipyretics: use when required

Paracetamol s/f susp: 120mg to 240mg up to four times a day
- Age from 3 to 5 years
- Paracetamol 120mg/5ml s/f susp. Take one to two 5ml spoonfuls every 4 to 6 hours when required for relief of pain or high temperature. Maximum of 4 doses in 24 hours; supply 300 ml; NHS Cost £1.24; OTC Cost £2.18.

Paracetamol s/f susp: 250mg to 500mg up to four times a day
- Age from 6 to 11 years
- Paracetamol 250mg/5ml s/f susp. Take one to two 5ml spoonfuls every 4 to 6 hours when required for relief of pain or high temperature. Maximum of 4 doses in 24 hours; supply 300 ml; NHS Cost £1.53; OTC Cost £2.70.

Paracetamol tablets: 500mg to 1g up to four times a day
- Age from 12 to 15 years
- Paracetamol 500mg tablets. Take one to two tablets every 4 to 6 hours when required for relief of pain or high temperature. Maximum of 8 tablets in 24 hours; supply 50 tablets; NHS Cost £0.38; OTC Cost £0.66.

Paracetamol tablets: 1g up to four times a day
- Age from 16 years onwards
- Paracetamol 500mg tablets. Take two tablets every 4 to 6 hours when required for relief of pain or high temperature. Maximum of 8 tablets in 24 hours; supply 50 tablets; NHS Cost £0.70; OTC Cost £1.32.

Paracetamol 500mg tablets + codeine 30mg tablets
- Age from 16 years onwards
- Paracetamol 500mg tablets. Take two tablets every 4 to 6 hours when required for pain relief. Maximum of 8 tablets in 24 hours; supply 50 tablets; NHS Cost £0.38; OTC Cost £1.32.
- Codeine 30mg tablets. Take one to two tablets every 4 to 6 hours when required for pain relief. Maximum of 8 tablets in 24 hours; supply 42 tablets; NHS Cost £2.13.

Codeine 30mg tablets: add on to paracetamol if required
- Age from 16 years onwards
- Codeine 30mg tablets. Take one to two tablets every 4 to 6 hours when required for pain relief. Maximum of 8 tablets in 24 hours; supply 42 tablets; NHS Cost £2.13.

Ibuprofen s/f susp: 100mg three to four times a day
- Age from 3 to 7 years
- Ibuprofen 100mg/5ml s/f susp. Take one 5ml spoonful 3 to 4 times a day when required for relief of pain or high temperature. Do not exceed the stated dose; supply 150 ml; NHS Cost £2.73; OTC Cost £4.81.

Ibuprofen s/f susp: 200mg three to four times a day
- Age from 8 to 11 years
- Ibuprofen 100mg/5ml s/f susp. Take two 5ml spoonfuls 3 to 4 times a day when required for relief of pain or high temperature. Do not exceed the stated dose; supply 300 ml; NHS Cost £5.46; OTC Cost £9.62.

Ibuprofen tablets: 400mg three times a day
- Age from 12 years onwards
- Ibuprofen 400mg tablets. Take one tablet three times a day when required for relief of pain or high temperature. Do not exceed the stated dose; supply 24 tablets; NHS Cost £0.70; OTC Cost £1.75.

Extended Information

Background information

- What is it? p.1719
- How common is it? p.1720
- How do I know my patient has bacterial sinusitis? p.1720
- What else might it be? p.1720
- Complications and prognosis? p.1721

What is it?

Definitions and pathology

- **Sinusitis is defined as infection of one or more of the paranasal sinuses.** Historically, the term has been used to describe what is perceived to be a bacterial infection. The sinuses are air spaces located in the facial bones, including the cheek bones (maxillary), the bones of the forehead (frontal) and the deeper parts of the skull near the eye sockets (ethmoid and sphenoid). The maxillary sinuses are most commonly affected.
- **Acute sinusitis** is defined as lasting for **up to 4 weeks** [Brook et al, 2000; Snow et al, 2001].
- **Subacute or relapsing sinusitis** is defined as symptoms persisting or recurring after **4 weeks but for less than 3 months.**

S

- **Persistent or *chronic* sinusitis** is diagnosed if the disease persists for **more than 3 months.** People who have more than **three or four significant episodes annually** or who repeatedly fail to respond to medical treatment are also considered to have chronic disease.

Pathophysiology

- Symptoms of sinusitis are an inherent part of the common cold syndrome and viruses are the commonest cause of acute sinusitis-like symptoms. Mucosal swelling of the sinus openings causes discomfort and impedes drainage, with a sense of congestion. Viruses that cause sinusitis include rhinovirus, influenza virus, and parainfluenza virus [Poole, 1999].
- **Obstruction of sinus drainage** and retention of secretions are the primary events in secondary bacterial sinus infection.
- **Acute sinusitis** caused by bacterial infection should not be suspected unless symptoms are severe or have persisted **longer than one week in adults** and **10–14 days in children.** Worsening of symptoms may be a useful pointer to secondary bacterial infection [Lindbaek et al, 1996a].
- Sinuses are developing and growing in children and adolescents, and the exact pathophysiology of infection is poorly defined [Brook et al, 2000].
- **Persistent or chronic sinusitis** overlaps with other clinical entities such as allergic rhinitis, and anatomical abnormalities, including deviation of the nasal septum and polyps. The pathology may show chronic inflammation with eosinophilia and damage to mucosa. Dental sepsis may also be a cause in up to 10% of cases, where anaerobic infections are common. Failure of mucociliary transport, obstruction of sinus openings, mucous hypersecretion, and chronic infection may all be part of chronic sinusitis. If investigation reveals such causes, treatment can be directed accordingly, for example, surgery on polyps [Evans, 1998].

Bacteria

- A recent primary care study in the USA looked at the prevalence of organisms obtained from nasal swabs in acute sinusitis [Sokol, 2001]. *Moraxella catarrhalis* accounted for 29%, *Haemophilus influenzae* for 22%, *Staphylococcus aureus* for 18% and *Streptococcus pneumoniae* for 11%. A number of surveys from other countries show similar organisms, although most data relates to chronic sinusitis and hospital-obtained samples. There appear to be no equivalent data from primary care in the UK, but similar findings might be expected from knowledge of pathogens in other respiratory infections.

How common is it?

- Acute sinusitis-like symptoms are one of the most common respiratory disorders treated in general practice [Birmingham Research Unit, 2002].
- About 0.5%–2% of common colds are complicated by an acute bacterial infection of the sinuses [Hickner et al, 2001].
- There is evidence of over diagnosis of acute sinusitis in primary care, with only 60% of diagnoses confirmed on computed tomography (CT) scanning in one study [Lindbaek et al, 1996a].
- Many cases settle without recourse to definitive investigation.

How do I know my patient has bacterial sinusitis?

Differentiating viral sinusitis from acute bacterial sinusitis is usually difficult, as viral infection usually precedes bacterial sinusitis. The following are pointers to separatin these causes:

Symptoms and signs

- **Duration of symptoms** — symptoms lasting longer than 7 days in adults and 10–14 days in children may be a pointer to bacterial infection [Brook et al, 2000; Gangel 2002].
- **Deterioration in symptoms** after apparent improvement may also be a useful diagnostic feature (so-called 'doub sickening') [Lindbaek et al, 1996a].
- It has been suggested that at least three of the following helped to predict which people might have signs of sinusitis on subsequent CT investigation [Lindbaek et a 1996a]:
  - Two phases in illness history ('double sickening')
  - Purulent nasal discharge (more than 7 days)
  - Presence of pus in the nasal cavity
  - Erythrocyte sedimentation rate greater than 10 mm/hour
- There is no information on how these correlate with response to treatment. Also many people with CT diagnosis improve without antimicrobials [Lindbaek et al, 1996b].
- The **overall clinical impression** may be a more accurate diagnostic predictor than any single diagnostic feature [Brook et al, 2000].
- **Combinations** of the following clinical indicators may enhance predictability:
  - Facial pain and tenderness (predominantly on one side)
  - Painful mastication (especially maxillary toothache)
  - Reduced sense of smell (hyposmia).
  - A headache that is worse on leaning forwards
  - Pyrexia (greater than 38.5°C)
  - General malaise
- Some of these symptoms, such as facial pain and headache, are rare in younger children where other symptoms such as snoring, mouth breathing, cough, feeding difficulty and hyponasal speech, may be associated with the diagnosis [Brook et al, 2000].

Investigations

- **Radiological or invasive investigations are uncommon i general practice.**
- **The Royal College of Radiologists Guidelines** advise th **sinus X-rays** are not indicated routinely and CT scanni is more rewarding [Royal College of Radiologists, 199 These guidelines state that the finding of mucosal thickening is non-specific, as it may occur in asymptomatic people.
- **CT scanning** provides greater definition of the sinus cavity and is more sensitive than plain X-rays for detecting sinusitis. **The Royal College of Radiologists guidelines** advise that CT scanning should be considere when maximal medical treatment has failed, complications arise, or malignancy is suspected [Royal College of Radiologists, 1998].
- **Sinus puncture with culture of aspirate** is regarded as th diagnostic reference standard but it is not a practical routine procedure [Hickner et al, 2001].

What else might it be?

- **Viral rhinosinusitis:** in particular, children frequently have viral upper respiratory infections and these can ru into one another giving the impression of prolonged rhinitis/rhinosinusitis [Brook et al, 2000].

- **Seasonal allergic rhinitis** (hay fever).
- **Perennial allergic rhinitis following** recent exposure to allergen. This includes drugs such as angiotensin-converting enzyme inhibitors and nonsteroidal anti-inflammatory drugs (including aspirin).
- **Other causes of facial pain or headache:**
  - Tension headache
  - Mandibular joint dysfunction
  - Atypical migraine
  - Trigeminal neuralgia

Complications and prognosis?

- Mucocoeles or mucopyocoeles are rare complications. These are chronic cystic lesions of the sinuses, most commonly in the frontal and anterior ethmoid sinuses. Frontal headaches, proptosis and diplopia secondary to downward and outward displacement of the eyeball are the most usual initial complaints.
- Other rare complications include:
  - Periorbital infection
  - Meningitis
  - Epidural abscess, subdural empyema, cerebral abscess
  - Venous sinus thrombosis
- These can arise from direct extension, septic thromboembolism and haematogenous spread.

Management issues

- Antibiotics p.1721
- Decongestants p.1722
- Intranasal corticosteroids p.1722
- Steam inhalation p.1722
- Following referral p.1722

Antibiotics

Adults

In adults reserve antimicrobials for those with severe symptoms, or persistent symptoms of at least 7 days' duration. Most people with acute sinusitis will settle spontaneously and there is little evidence that antimicrobials improve outcome in general practice. Very few studies have looked at people who present in general practice with sinusitis-like symptoms. Two studies, which sought to remedy this lack of evidence, both concluded that antimicrobials did not improve the clinical course of the illness.

- In one study 192 people with specific symptoms (pain on bending forward, purulent nasal discharge, predominantly unilateral face pain, toothache or pain when chewing) were randomized to doxycycline or to placebo for 10 days. There was no difference in recovery rates: 85% reported improvement at 10 days [Stalman et al, 1997].
- In the other study people were included if they had X-ray confirmation of maxillary sinusitis. A total of 214 people were randomized to amoxicillin (750 mg three times daily), or placebo for 7 days; 83% had resolved within 2 weeks on amoxicillin, and 77% on placebo. Adverse effects were more common in people taking amoxicillin than placebo (28% compared with 9%). During the 1-year follow-up, recurrence rates were similar [van Buchem et al, 1997].

A Cochrane review of the use of antimicrobials for acute sinusitis, last substantially updated in 1999, analyzed 32 trials involving hospital referred people with sinusitis, which had been confirmed radiologically or by aspiration [Williams et al, 2003]. This review concluded that current evidence is limited but supports the use of penicillin or amoxicillin for 7–14 days for these people. The review acknowledges problems with applying these results to general practice.

- In another meta-analysis of six studies comparing antimicrobials against placebo in the treatment of acute sinusitis it was concluded that antimicrobials decrease the incidence of clinical failures by half (risk ratio 0.54) [De Ferranti et al, 1998]. It was noted, however, that almost 70% of people who had taken placebo showed spontaneous resolution or improvement of symptoms. The study also indicated that amoxicillin and folate inhibitors were just as clinically effective as more expensive antimicrobials. There was considerable variation in diagnostic criteria for acute sinusitis, with the trials applying the most rigid methods — radiological or computed tomography (CT) evidence of sinusitis — demonstrating clear benefit. Those using less stringent criteria showed little or no benefit.
- There is no evidence that antimicrobials reduce complication rates or progression to chronic sinusitis.

Children

- **In children (up to age 16)** antimicrobials should be avoided in treating symptoms of nasal discharge or suspected sinusitis because symptoms of acute sinusitis will settle spontaneously in most of them [American Academy of Pediatrics, 2001; Gangel, 2002]. Consider treatment only when symptoms are severe or have been present for 10–14 days:
- **There is very little evidence that antimicrobials are effective in children** and many infections are viral, resolving within 7 days.
- **A recent USA study** compared amoxicillin, co-amoxiclav and placebo in 188 children aged 1 to 12 years, with persistent symptoms of acute sinusitis for 10–28 days [Garbutt et al, 2001]. No difference was found in resolution of symptoms at day 14; 80% were better with or without treatment.
- **A Cochrane review** of the treatment of persistent nasal discharge [Morris, 2002] (last substantially updated in 2000) identified five small studies involving 401 children treated either for nasal discharge of 10 days or longer, or radiographically confirmed sinusitis. It concluded that 10 days' treatment with antimicrobials might reduce persistence. The effect was small: six children would need to be treated for one to improve.

Antibiotic recommendation

- Amoxicillin or erythromycin, or alternatively oxytetracycline or doxycycline are recommended as first-line treatment if antimicrobials are considered desirable:
  - **Amoxicillin** is a suitable first-line antibiotic. Newer antibiotics have no clinical advantage over amoxicillin or folate inhibitors (co-trimoxazole) [De Ferranti et al, 1998; Williams et al, 2003].
  - **Erythromycin** is suitable for people allergic to penicillin [BNF 43, 2002].
  - **Oxytetracycline and doxycycline** are also suitable first-line agents in adults [PHLS, 2002].
  - **Trimethoprim** is offered in children as an alternative option for people allergic to penicillin although its activity may not be as good as erythromycin.
- The beta-lactamase-resistant antimicrobials co-amoxiclav or ciprofloxacin are recommended as second-line treatment, where response has been poor, as beta-lactamase-producing organisms are a likely reason for treatment failure [PHLS, 2002].

Duration of treatment

- This guidance recommends 7-day antibiotic courses.
- Most evidence relates to trials of 7 or 10 days' treatment and traditionally general practitioners in the UK have used 7-day courses for acute sinusitis [De Ferranti et al, 1998]. If antimicrobials are used rarely, and reserved for more severe cases, this seems an appropriate duration.
- The problems with comparisons of course length are that, in the context of marginal benefits, the trials are rarely powered or large enough to enable proper comparisons of equivalent efficacy. Most evidence relates to co-trimoxazole and it may not be appropriate to generalize to other antimicrobials.
- The Standing Medical Advisory Committee (SMAC) Sub-Group on antimicrobial resistance suggested that 3 days might be as effective as traditional 7 or 10 days' treatment. This decision was based on one trial of 80 people randomized to co-trimoxazole for 3 or 10 days [Williams et al, 1995]. Therefore 3-day treatment may be considered an alternative strategy.

Decongestants

- **This guidance does not recommend intranasal or oral decongestants.**
- Although there are no published good quality placebo-controlled trials of decongestants, these medications are often used in the treatment of both acute and chronic sinusitis, often following over-the-counter purchase.
- They are of dubious value and, for the intranasal preparations, use beyond 7 days can result in severe rebound symptoms (rhinitis medicamentosa).
- If used, intranasal decongestants should not be continued beyond 7 days [BNF 43, 2002].

Intranasal corticosteroids

- **The use of intranasal corticosteroids is controversial in acute sinusitis.**
- There is some evidence from recent studies that intranasal corticosteroids may be of some benefit when added to antimicrobials in acute sinusitis [Meltzer et al, 2000; Dolor et al, 2001]. However, their added benefit remains inconclusive as all the people included in the studies had varying histories of chronic or recurrent sinusitis.
- Intranasal corticosteroids may be indicated in cases of chronic sinusitis where there is suspicion or evidence of an allergic cause [Evans, 1998].

S

Steam inhalation

- **Steam inhalation is not recommended for routine use. Benefit from steam inhalation is uncertain and there may be danger of scalding.**

Following referral

- A variety of medical treatments may be indicated, according to cause. Further antimicrobials, intranasal corticosteroids and antihistamines may be tried. These may also be used prior to surgery as 'adjunctive' treatment.
- **Surgery** may be indicated to improve drainage and ventilation of the involved sinuses and to remove diseased mucosa in chronic infections of the sinuses, or to treat polyps. Increasingly such operations are carried out using endoscopic techniques [Evans, 1998].
- Surgical drainage may also be used in severe acute sinusitis.

References

NHS staff in England can link, free of charge, from references to full text journals by clicking on [Full text] on the PRODIGY website.

1. American Academy of Pediatrics (2001) Clinical practice guideline: management of sinusitis. *Pediatrics* **108**(3), 798–808. [Full text]
2. Birmingham Research Unit (2002) *Weekly return service: weekly morbidity statistics form general practices.* Birmingham Research Unit, Royal College of General Practitioners. www.rcgp-bru.demon.co.uk/respiratory.htm [Accessed: 05/04/2002].
3. BNF 43 (2002) *British National Formulary.* 43rd edn. London: British Medical Association and Royal Pharmaceutical Society of Great Britain.
4. Brook, I., Gooch, W.M., III, Jenkins, S.G. et al (2000) Medical management of acute bacterial sinusitis. Recommendations of a clinical advisory committee on pediatric and adult sinusitis. *Annals of Otology, Rhinology, & Laryngology – Supplement* **182**, 2–20.
5. De Craen, A.J., Di Giulio, G., Lampe-Schoenmaeckers, J.E. et al (1996) Analgesic efficacy and safety of paracetamol-codeine combinations versus paracetamol alone: a systematic review. *British Medical Journal* **313**(7053), 321–325. [Full text]
6. De Ferranti, S.D., Ioannidis, J.P., Lau, J. et al (1998) Are amoxycilling and folate inhibitors as effective as other antibiotics for acute sinusitis? A meta-analysis. *British Medical Journal* **317**(7159), 632–637. [Full text]
7. DH and SMAC (1998) *The path of least resistance.* Department of Health. www.dh.gov.uk [Accessed: 27/04/2004]. [Full text]
8. Dolor, R.J., Witsell, D.L., Hellkamp, A.S. et al (2001) Comparison of cefuroxime with or without intranasal fluticasone for the treatment of rhinosinusitis: The CAFFS trial: A randomized controlled trial. *Journal of the American Medical Association* **286**(24), 3097–3105.
9. DTB (1998) Co-proxamol or paracetamol for acute pain? *Drug & Therapeutics Bulletin* **36**(10), 80. [Full text]
10. Evans, K.L. (1998) Recognition and management of sinusitis. *Drugs* **56**(1), 59–71.
11. Finch, R.G (1997) Tetracyclines. In: O'Grady, F, Lambert, H.P, Finch, R.G and Greenwood, D (Eds.) *Antibiotic and chemotherapy: anti-infective agents and their use in therapy.* 7th edn. Edinburgh: Churchill Livingstone. 469–484.
12. Gangel, E.K. (2002) *Practice guidelines. AAP issues recommendations for the management of sinusitis in children.* American Family Physician. www.aafp.org/afp/20020315/practice.html [Accessed: 05/04/2002].
13. Garbutt, J.M., Goldstein, M., Gellman, E. et al (2001) A randomized, placebo-controlled trial of antimicrobial treatment for children with clinically diagnosed acute sinusitis. *Pediatrics* **107**(4), 619–625.
14. Hickner, J.M., Bartlett, J.G., Besser, R.E. et al (2001) Principles of appropriate antibiotic use for acute rhinosinusitis in adults: background. *Annals of Internal Medicine* **134**(6), 498–505.
15. Lindbaek, M., Hjortdahl, P. and Johnsen, U.L-H. (1996a) Use of symptoms and signs, and blood tests to diagnose acute sinus infections in primary care: comparison with computed tomography. *Family Medicine* **28**(3), 183–188.
16. Lindbaek, M., Hjortdahl, P. and Johnsen, U.L. (1996b) Randomised, double blind, placebo controlled trial of penicillin V and amoxycillin in treatment of acute sinu

infections in adults. *British Medical Journal* **313**(7053), 325–329. [Full text]

17. Medicines Resource (1995) Combination analgesics. *Medicines Resource* **25**, 95–98.
18. Meltzer, E.O., Charous, B.L., Busse, W.W. et al (2000) Added relief in the treatment of acute recurrent sinusitis with adjunctive mometasone furoate nasal spray. The Nasonex Sinusitis Group. *Journal of Allergy & Clinical Immunology* **106**(4), 630–637.
19. MeReC (2000) The use of oral analgesics in primary care. *MeReC Bulletin* **11**(1), 1–4.
20. Moore, A., Collins, S., Carroll, D. and McQuay, H. (1997) Paracetamol with and without codeine in acute pain: a quantitative systematic review. *Pain* **70**(2–3), 193–201.
21. Morris, P. (2002) *Antibiotics for persistent nasal discharge [rhinosinusitis] in children*. The Cochrane Library. Issue 4. Chichester, UK: John Wiley & Sons, Ltd. www.nelh.nhs.uk/cochrane.asp [Accessed: 21/06/2005].
22. PHLS (2002) *Management of infection guidance for primary care: draft for consultation & local adaptation*. Public Health Laboratory Service. www.hpa.org.uk [Accessed: 01/04/2002].
23. Poole, M.D. (1999) A focus on acute sinusitis in adults: changes in disease management. *American Journal of Medicine* **106**(5A), 38S-47S.
24. Royal College of Radiologists (Ed.) (1998) *Making the best use of a department of clinical radiology: guidelines for doctors*. 4th edn. London: Royal College of Radiologists.
25. Shuttleworth, G. and Harrad, R. (2000) Management of acute eyelid conditions. *Practitioner* **244**(1607), 138–143.
26. Snow, V., Mottur-Pilson, C., Hickner, J.M. et al (2001) Principles of appropriate antibiotic use for acute sinusitis in adults. *Annals of Internal Medicine* **134**(6), 495–497.
27. Sokol, W. (2001) Epidemiology of sinusitis in the primary care setting: results from the 1999–2000 respiratory surveillance program. *American Journal of Medicine* **111**(9 Suppl. 1), 19S-24S.
28. Stalman, W., van Essen, G.A., van der Graaf, Y. and De Melker, R.A. (1997) The end of antibiotic treatment in adults with acute sinusitis-like complaints in general practice? A placebo-controlled double-blind randomized doxycycline trial. *British Journal of General Practice* **47**(425), 794–799.
29. van Buchem, F.L., Knottnerus, J.A., Schrijnemaekers, V.J. and Peeters, M.F. (1997) Primary-care-based randomised placebo-controlled trial of antibiotic treatment in acute maxillary sinusitis. *Lancet* **349**(9053), 683–687. [Full text]
30. Williams, J.W., Jr., Holleman, D.R., Jr., Samsa, G.P. and Simel, D.L. (1995) Randomized controlled trial of 3 vs 10 days of trimethoprim/sulfamethoxazole for acute maxillary sinusitis. *Journal of the American Medical Association* **273**(13), 1015–1021.
31. Williams, J.W., Aguilar, C., Makela, M. et al (2003) *Antibiotics for acute maxillary sinusitis (Cochrane Review)*. The Cochrane Library. Issue 2. Chichester, UK: John Wiley & Sons, Ltd. www.nelh.nhs.uk/cochrane.asp [Accessed: 01/09/2005]. [Full text]

PRODIGY GUIDANCE

Smoking cessation

Last revised in July 2002
At the time of print this topic was being updated. The newly revised guidance will be issued on to the website in 2006.
www.prodigy.nhs.uk/guidance.asp?gt=Smoking cessation

Applies to people of all ages

This guidance covers advice on smoking cessation, use of nicotine replacement therapy and bupropion. The guidance is primarily concerned with cigarette smoking, and is based on evidence regarding cigarette smoking, but may be extrapolated to include cigar and pipe smoking.

This guidance does not cover education or prevention of smoking in non-smokers.

Goals

- Identify smokers and motivate to stop smoking
- Reduce likelihood of relapse
- Reduce amount of tobacco smoked in those who are unable to quit

Contents

Scenarios

- Smoking cessation p.1724

Extended Information, p. 1727

Smoking cessation

Which therapy?

- **The five As of smoking cessation are:**
  - Ask about smoking (and record)
  - Advise smokers to stop
  - Assess willingness to quit
  - Assist the smoker to stop
  - Arrange follow-up and refer to local smoking cessation services as appropriate
- **If the smoker is wanting to quit** set a quit date, emphasize complete abstinence as the goal, identify and suggest strategies to avoid trigger situations, encourage the development of support for quitting from family and friends, suggest find a partner to quit with, consider nicotine replacement therapy (NRT) or bupropion.
- **NRT or bupropion are recommended for smokers who have expressed a desire to quit smoking.** Combining NRT and bupropion is not recommended.
- **NRT or bupropion should normally only be prescribed as part of a structured smoking cessation programme,** in which the smoker sets a target date to quit. To decide which to use and in which order, consider:
  - Intention and motivation to quit, and likelihood of compliance
  - The availability of counselling or support
  - Previous usage of smoking cessation aids
  - Contraindications and potential for adverse effects
  - Personal preferences of the smoker
- **Ideally, the initial prescription of NRT or bupropion** should be sufficient to last only until 2 weeks after the target quit date. Normally, this will be after 2 weeks of NRT, and 3–4 weeks for bupropion.
- **Second prescriptions** should be given only to people who have demonstrated that their quit attempt is continuing on re-assessment.
- **NRT** is available as nicotine skin patches, chewing-gum, lozenges, sublingual tablets, inhalators or nasal spray. There is insufficient evidence to recommend one *form* of NRT over another. Nicotine 4 mg gum may be more effective than 2 mg gum in heavy smokers (20 cigarettes or more per day). High-dose patches may be more effective in *highly* dependent smokers.
  - Start NRT after stopping smoking. Maintain NRT for 8 to 12 weeks with gradual withdrawal over this period according to the manufacturer's instructions. Treatment may be stopped abruptly if necessary.
- If possible, show people examples of different forms of NRT during the consultation.
- The administration of NRT products is described below.
- **Bupropion** is an alternative to NRT and has similar quit rates. Start while still smoking and set target quit date 7–14 days after starting treatment. Treat for 7–9 weeks.
- Provide the free QUITLINE telephone number 0800 002200.

Practical prescribing points

For further information please see the *Medicines Compendium* (www.medicines.org.uk) or the *British National Formulary* (www.bnf.org). Contact the National Teratology Information Service (tel. 0191 232 1525) for more information on NRT and bupropion in pregnancy.

NRT

- **Contraindications to NRT include:**
  - People who have recently had a myocardial infarction or cerebrovascular accident
  - Life-threatening cardiac arrhythmias
  - Severe or worsening angina pectoris
  - Temporomandibular joint disease (only for gum)
- It is recommended that smokers who are under the age of 18 years, who are pregnant or breastfeeding, or who have certain conditions (cardiovascular disease, hyperthyroidism, diabetes mellitus, severe renal or hepatic impairment and peptic ulcer) are advised to use an NRT only after careful consideration of risks and benefits and after discussion with a healthcare professional.
- Nicotine gum may cause hiccoughs, gastrointestinal disturbance and jaw pain.
- Nicotine nasal spray should be used with caution in people with a history of chronic nasal disorders.
- Patches may cause skin irritation.

Administration of patches

Nicorette

- Use 15 mg/16 hours patch daily for 8 weeks, then
  - Use 10 mg/16 hours patch daily for 2 weeks, then
  - Use 5 mg/16 hours patch daily for 2 weeks
- Review treatment if abstinence not achieved in 3 months

S

Nicotinell

- More than 20 cigarettes per day:
  - Use 21 mg/24 hours (30 cm^2) patch daily for 3 to 4 weeks, then
  - Use 14 mg/24 hours (20 cm^2) patch daily for 3 to 4 weeks, then
  - Use 7 mg/24 hours (10 cm^2) patch daily for 3 to 4 weeks
- Less than 20 cigarettes:
  - Use 14 mg/24 hours (20 cm^2) patch daily for 3 to 4 weeks, then
  - Use 7 mg/24 hours (10 cm^2) patch daily for 3 to 4 weeks
- Review treatment if abstinence not achieved in 3 months

NiQuitin CQ

- If person smokes more than 10 cigarettes per day:
  - Use 21 mg/24 hours patch daily for 6 weeks, then
  - Use 14 mg/24 hours patch daily for 2 weeks, then
  - Use 7 mg/24 hours patch daily for 2 weeks
- If person smokes less than 10 cigarettes per day:
  - Use 14 mg patch for 6 weeks, then
  - Use 7 mg patch for 2 weeks
- Review treatment if abstinence not achieved in 10 weeks

Administration of nasal spray

- Apply one spray to each nostril as required daily for 8 weeks, up to a maximum of twice an hour for 16 hours (or 64 sprays in 24 hours), then reduce gradually over the next 4 weeks (reduce the dose by half at the end of 2 weeks and stop by the end of the next 2 weeks)
- Review treatment if abstinence not achieved in 3 months

Administration of inhalator

- Inhale when there is an urge to smoke
- Initially use 6 to 12 cartridges daily for up to 8 weeks, then
  - Reduce by half at end of 2 weeks
  - Stop after a further 2 weeks
- Review treatment if abstinence not achieved in 3 months

Administration of gum

- Chew one piece of gum slowly for approximately 30 minutes when urge to smoke occurs
- In people smoking more than 20 cigarettes per day, or needing more than 15 pieces of 2 mg gum per day, use the 4 mg gum
- Maximum of 15 pieces of gum in 24 hours
- Withdraw gradually over 3 months
- When daily use is 1–2 pieces of gum, use should be stopped

Administration of lozenge

A suggested schedule is:

- During weeks 1 to 6 suck one lozenge every 1 to 2 hours when urge to smoke occurs. (It is recommended that a minimum of 9 lozenges daily are taken.)
- During weeks 7 to 9 suck one lozenge every 2 to 4 hours.
- During weeks 10 to 12 suck one lozenge every 4 to 8 hours.
- Withdraw gradually over 3 months. Do not use for longer than 6 months.

Administration of sublingual tablet

- If less than 20 cigarettes smoked daily:
  - Use one tablet sublingually each hour.
  - Consider increasing to two tablets each hour if person fails to stop smoking or has significant withdrawal symptoms.
  - Continue for at least 3 months and then gradually reduce. Do not use for longer than 6 months.
- If more than 20 cigarettes smoked daily:
  - Use two tablets sublingually each hour.
  - Continue for at least 3 months and then gradually reduce. Do not use for longer than 6 months.
- In both cases stop treatment when daily consumption reaches one or two tablets.

Bupropion

- **Bupropion is associated** with a dose-related risk of seizure.
- **Bupropion is contraindicated** in patients with a current seizure disorder or any history of seizures; with current or previous diagnosis of bulimia or anorexia nervosa; with a known central nervous system tumour; those experiencing abrupt withdrawal from alcohol or benzodiazepines; and in severe hepatic cirrhosis.
- **Bupropion should not be prescribed** in people with other risk factors for seizures unless there is compelling clinical justification for which the potential benefit outweighs the increased risk of seizure. Such risk factors include concomitant use of any drug known to lower the seizure threshold (including antipsychotics, antidepressants, some antimalarials such as mefloquine, theophylline, systemic corticosteroids, tramadol, quinolones and sedating antihistamines), alcohol abuse, a history of head trauma, diabetes treated with hypoglycaemics or insulin and use of stimulants or anorectic products. In such people a lower dose of 150 mg daily throughout the entire treatment period should be considered.
- **Bupropion should be discontinued** in individuals who have experienced a seizure while taking it.
- **Bupropion is not recommended** for smokers under the age of 18 years, as its safety and efficacy have not been evaluated for this group.
- **Bupropion should not be used** in women who are pregnant or breastfeeding.
- **Bupropion should be used with caution** in elderly people and in people with hepatic impairment or renal insufficiency. The recommended dose is 150 mg daily in these people.
- **Adverse effects are similar to those typical of antidepressants,** namely dry mouth, gastrointestinal disturbances, impaired concentration, dizziness.
- **Drug–drug interactions** occur with bupropion and levodopa, monoamine oxidase inhibitors, drugs known to affect the CY2B6 isoenzyme (e.g. orphenadrine, cyclophosphamide, ifosfamide), inducers of metabolism (e.g. carbamazepine, phenytoin); inhibitors of metabolism (e.g. valproate).

Follow-up advice

For nicotine replacement therapy (NRT)

- **Arrange a follow-up visit within 2 weeks** and subsequent visits after that — if possible.
- **If stopped smoking:**
  - Congratulate
  - Enquire about relapses
  - Reinforce the importance of permanent cessation
  - Continue nicotine replacement therapy (NRT) for 8–12 weeks
- **If continuing to smoke:**
  - Explore the circumstances for the relapse
  - Encourage the person to make another quit attempt in the future (e.g. in 2–3 months' time)
  - Discontinue NRT

For bupropion

- Follow up should be normally be part of a structured smoking cessation programme.

Should I refer or investigate?

Refer?

- **Consider referral to a specialist smoking cessation** service, especially if a smoker has made repeated attempts to stop and failed, and/or experienced severe withdrawal, and/or requested more intensive help. If the contact details of the local service are unavailable QUITLINE (telephone 0800 002200) will provide information.

Patient information leaflets

The following PILs are available at www.prodigy.nhs.uk

- ASH - Action on Smoking and Health
- NHS Smoking Helpline
- Quit (help to stop smoking)
- Smokeline
- Smoking - A Summary
- Smoking - Help to Stop with Bupropion
- Smoking - Nicotine Replacement Therapy
- Smoking - The Facts
- Smoking - Tips on Stopping

Shared decision making

- Smokers have much more ill health than non-smokers. For many smokers, years of ill health are followed by an early death. Half of all smokers will be killed by their habit.
- 7 in 10 smokers want to quit. Motivation is the key factor in being able to quit.
- **Support and advice** on quitting will help. If supportive friends, family or nurse are not available, why not try QUITLINE: 0800 002200
- Tips on quitting include: set a date to stop and stick to it. Get rid of cigarettes, ashtrays, lighters, etc. Anticipate problems such as social gatherings, cravings and an increase in appetite. Give up with someone else for mutual support.
- **Nicotine substitutes** such as gum, sprays, inhalators, sublingual tablets, lozenges or patches may help if withdrawal symptoms are troublesome. Using a nicotine substitute roughly doubles the chance of successfully quitting smoking in people who are motivated to stop.
- **Bupropion** is a drug that may also help smokers who want to quit.

S

Drug rationale

Drugs included

- **Nicotine replacement therapy** (NRT) is effective in helping patients stop [Silagy et al, 1998; NICE, 2002b]. There is currently insufficient evidence to conclude that one form of NRT is more effective than another [NICE, 2002a]. All NRT products now prescribable on the National Health Service have been included.
- **Bupropion** is an effective aid to smoking cessation and approximately doubles the number of people not smoking after 1 year compared with placebo. It is most effective when given in conjunction with motivational support [Regional Drug and Therapeutics Centre, 2000; ABPI Medicines Compendium, 2002; NICE, 2002a].

Prescriptions

Nicotine patches: standard dose

Nicotinell '30' patch 21mg/24 hours

- Age from 18 years onwards
- Nicotinell TTS 30cm patches. Apply one patch each morning and leave on for 24 hours. Reapply a new patch the next morning; supply 14 patches; NHS Cost £19.94; OTC Cost £34.98.

NiQuitin CQ patch 21mg/24 hours

- Age from 18 years onwards
- NiQuitin CQ 21mg patches. Apply one patch each morning and leave on for 24 hours. Reapply a new patch the next morning; supply 14 patches; NHS Cost £18.79; OTC Cost £32.95.

Nicotine patch 21mg/24 hours

- Age from 18 years onwards
- Nicotine 21mg patches. Apply one patch each morning and leave on for 24 hours. Reapply a new patch the next morning; supply 14 patches; NHS Cost £19.94; OTC Cost £34.98.

Nicotine patch 15mg/16 hours

- Age from 18 years onwards
- Nicotine 15mg patches. Apply one patch each morning and remove about 16 hours later before going to bed. Reapply a new patch the next morning; supply 14 patches; NHS Cost £18.14; OTC Cost £31.98.

Nicotine patches: low dose

Nicotinell '20' patch 14mg/24 hours

- Age from 18 years onwards
- Nicotinell TTS 20cm patches. Apply one patch each morning and leave on for 24 hours. Reapply a new patch the next morning; supply 14 patches; NHS Cost £18.80; OTC Cost £34.98.

Nicotinell '10' patch 7mg/24 hours

- Age from 18 years onwards
- Nicotinell TTS 10cm patches. Apply one patch each morning and leave on for 24 hours. Reapply a new patch the next morning; supply 14 patches; NHS Cost £18.22; OTC Cost £31.98.

NiQuitin CQ patch 14mg/24 hours

- Age from 18 years onwards
- NiQuitin CQ 14mg patches. Apply one patch each morning and leave on for 24 hours. Reapply a new patch the next morning; supply 14 patches; NHS Cost £19.94; OTC Cost £34.98.

NiQuitin CQ patch 7mg/24 hours

- Age from 18 years onwards
- NiQuitin CQ 7mg patches. Apply one patch each morning and leave on for 24 hours. Reapply a new patch the next morning; supply 14 patches; NHS Cost £19.94; OTC Cost £34.98.

Nicotine patch 14mg/24 hours

- Age from 18 years onwards
- Nicotine 14mg patches. Apply one patch each morning and leave on for 24 hours. Reapply a new patch the next morning; supply 14 patches; NHS Cost £19.94; OTC Cost £34.98.

Nicotine patch 7mg/24 hours

- Age from 18 years onwards
- Nicotine 7mg patches. Apply one patch each morning and leave on for 24 hours. Reapply a new patch the next morning; supply 14 patches; NHS Cost £18.14; OTC Cost £34.98.

Nicotine patch 10mg/16 hours
- Age from 18 years onwards
- Nicotine 10mg patches. Apply one patch each morning and remove about 16 hours later before going to bed. Reapply a new patch the next morning; supply 14 patches; NHS Cost £18.14; OTC Cost £31.98.

Nicotine patch 5mg/16 hours
- Age from 18 years onwards
- Nicotine 5mg patches. Apply one patch each morning and remove about 16 hours later before going to bed. Reapply a new patch the next morning; supply 14 patches; NHS Cost £18.14; OTC Cost £31.98.

Nicotine gum and lozenges

Nicotine 2mg gum
- Age from 18 years onwards
- Nicotine 2mg chewing gum. Chew one piece of gum slowly for approximately 30 minutes when you have the urge to smoke. Maximum of 15 pieces in 24 hours; supply 105 pieces; NHS Cost £8.89; OTC Cost £15.59.

Nicotine 4mg gum
- Age from 18 years onwards
- Nicotine 4mg chewing gum. Chew one piece of gum slowly for approximately 30 minutes when you have the urge to smoke. Maximum of 15 pieces in 24 hours; supply 105 pieces; NHS Cost £10.83; OTC Cost £18.99.

Nicotine 1mg lozenges
- Age from 18 years onwards
- Nicotine 1mg lozenges. Suck one lozenge slowly every 1 to 2 hours when you have the urge to smoke. Maximum of 25 lozenges in 24 hours; supply 96 lozenges; NHS Cost £9.12; OTC Cost £15.99.

Nicotine 2mg lozenges
- Age from 18 years onwards
- Nicotine 2mg lozenges. Suck one lozenge slowly when you have the urge to smoke. Maximum of 15 lozenges in 24 hours; supply 96 lozenges; NHS Cost £9.12; OTC Cost £15.99.

Nicotine 4mg lozenges
- Age from 18 years onwards
- Nicotine 4mg lozenges. Suck one lozenge slowly when you have the urge to smoke. Maximum of 15 lozenges in 24 hours; supply 96 lozenges; NHS Cost £9.12; OTC Cost £15.99.

Nicotine spray, tablets, and inhalator

Nicotine 500microgram nasal spray
- Age from 18 years onwards
- Nicotine 10mg/ml nasal spray. Spray once into each nostril when you have the urge to smoke, up to twice an hour for 16 hours. Maximum of 64 sprays in 24 hours; supply 1 spray; NHS Cost £10.99; OTC Cost £19.25.

Nicotine 2mg sublingual tablets
- Age from 18 years onwards
- Nicotine 2mg s/l tablets. Place one to two tablets under the tongue every hour. Maximum of 40 tablets in 24 hours; supply 105 tablets; NHS Cost £9.84; OTC Cost £17.25.

Nicotine inhalator refill (10mg/cartridge)
- Age from 18 years onwards
- Nicotine 10mg inhalator. Inhale spray when you have the urge to smoke. Maximum of 12 cartridges in 24 hours; supply 42 cartridges; NHS Cost £11.37; OTC Cost £19.95.

Nicotine inhalator starter pack (10mg/cartridge)
- Age from 18 years onwards
- Nicotine inhalator starter pack. Inhale spray when you have the urge to smoke. Maximum of 12 cartridges in 24 hours; supply 1 pack; NHS Cost £3.39; OTC Cost £5.95.
- Nicotine 10mg inhalator. Inhale spray when you have the urge to smoke. Maximum of 12 cartridges in 24 hours; supply 42 cartridges; NHS Cost £11.37; OTC Cost £19.95.

Bupropion

Start bupropion m/r: titrate from 150mg to 300mg per day
- Age from 18 to 65 years
- Bupropion 150mg m/r tablets. Take one tablet once a day for 6 days, then take one tablet twice a day (leaving an interval of at least 8 hours between doses); supply 60 tablets; NHS Cost £42.85.

Usual maintenance dose: bupropion m/r 150mg twice a day
- Age from 18 to 65 years
- Bupropion 150mg m/r tablets. Take one tablet twice a day, leaving an interval of at least 8 hours between doses; supply 60 tablets; NHS Cost £42.85.

>65 years: bupropion m/r 150mg once a day
- Age from 65 years onwards
- Bupropion 150mg m/r tablets. Take one tablet once a day; supply 60 tablets; NHS Cost £42.85.

Caution needed: bupropion m/r 150mg once a day
- Age from 18 to 65 years
- Bupropion 150mg m/r tablets. Take one tablet once a day; supply 60 tablets; NHS Cost £42.85.

Extended Information

Background information

- What are the physiological effects of smoking? p.1727
- How common is smoking? p.1728
- What are the factors associated with smoking? p.1728
- What are the problems associated with smoking? p.1728
- What are the benefits of stopping smoking? p.1728
- How many people successfully stop smoking? p.1729

What are the physiological effects of smoking?

- **Acute exposure to nicotine activates nicotinic cholinergic receptors** in the brain and causes the release of neurotransmitters including dopamine, noradrenaline, acetylcholine, vasopressin, serotonin and beta-endorphin. Nicotinic cholinergic receptors in the adrenal medulla are also activated leading to the release of adrenaline and beta-endorphin.
- **Behavioural effects:** When cigarette smoke is inhaled, nicotine is rapidly absorbed and reaches the brain. After a short period of abstinence, the dependant smoker may experience short-term focusing of attention, hunger suppression, and elevated mood with smoking a cigarette.
- **Cardiovascular effects of smoking** include:
  - Acute increase in blood pressure, heart rate and cardiac output thereby increasing myocardial work and oxygen demand
  - Reduction in the oxygen-carrying capacity of haemoglobin as a consequence of binding by carbon monoxide
  - Increased blood viscosity
  - Alterations in the lipid profile, with an increase in very low-density lipoprotein and low-density lipoprotein, and a decrease in high-density lipoprotein cholesterol. This probably contibutes to the increased the risk of cardiovascular disease experienced by smokers.

S

- **Tolerance** to some of the behavioural and sympathomimetic effects of nicotine occurs over time and when it is stopped abruptly withdrawal symptoms can occur. Withdrawal symptoms include restlessness, inability to concentrate, irritability, headaches, night-time wakening, dizziness, constipation, increased appetite and nicotine craving. Withdrawal symptoms tend to reach a maximum within 24 hours after cessation and decline in intensity over 2–4 weeks.
- Cigarette smoke contains over 4000 different chemicals, including over 50 known carcinogens and metabolic poisons. Although strongly addictive, nicotine is not the primary cause of the adverse effects of tobacco smoke.

[NHS CRD, 1998; RCP, 1999; NICE, 2002a; NICE, 2002b]

How common is smoking?

- **In 1998, 27% of adults aged 16 and over smoked cigarettes in England** — 28% of men and 26% of women.
- **Since 1978 the prevalence of cigarette smoking among adults has dropped substantially** (from 40%), although this decline has levelled out since the 1990s.
- The prevalence of cigarette smoking is higher for people in manual than non-manual socio-economic groups (32% compared with 21%, in 1998).
- Smoking rates are highest in the 20–24 year age group (39% of women and 42% of men in this age band smoke) and are lowest amongst men and women aged 60 years and over (16% for both men and women).
- **During pregnancy 28% of women smoke** and only 33% of women smokers give up during pregnancy.
- **The prevalence of regular smoking among young people aged 11–15 years was 10% in 2000 and 2001.** The prevalence has remained stable between 9 and 11% since 1998. Girls are more likely to be regular smokers (11%) than boys (8%). Prevalence of smoking increases sharply with age — about 1% of young people aged 11 years old smoke regularly compared with 22% of 15 year olds.

[Dobson et al, 1998; RCP, 1999; DH, 2000]

What are the factors associated with smoking?

- **Risk factors and determinants of smoking include:**
  - **Price, advertising and promotion of cigarettes**
  - **Social and economic deprivation:** Smoking behaviour is strongly related to socio-economic status and cessation rates have doubled in the most advantaged groups, but have remained almost unchanged over the past two decades in the most disadvantaged sectors of society.

[DH, 1998]

- **Risk factors associated with smoking in children aged 11–15 years include:**
  - **Low educational achievement:** Of children who plan to take the General Certificate of Secondary Education examinations, those expected to pass less than five subjects are more than twice as likely to be smokers (26%) compared with those with higher expectations (10%).
  - **Living with parents who smoke:** Children are almost three times more likely to smoke if they live with two parents who both smoke compared with children whose parents do not smoke.
  - **Having siblings who smoke:** Children who have at least one sibling who smokes are four times more likely to smoke (26%) than those with no siblings who smoke (6%).
  - **Low socio-economic status**
  - **Having friends who smoke**
  - **Having teachers who smoke**

[RCP, 1999]

What are the problems associated with smoking?

Consequences for the individual

- **Tobacco smoking is the greatest preventable cause of illness and premature death in the UK.**
- **Half of all smokers die prematurely of a smoking-related disease.** This represents about 120,000 deaths each year.
- The decrease in life expectancy for regular smokers, under the age of 35 years who do not subsequently quit, has been estimated to be about 8 years.
- **The younger people start smoking, the more likely they are to smoke for longer and to die early from smoking.** Someone who starts smoking aged 15 is three times more likely to die of cancer due to smoking than someone who starts in their mid-20s.
- **Smoking is a major aetiological factor for lung cancer, cardiovascular disease, peripheral vascular disease and chronic obstructive pulmonary disease.** It causes other respiratory disease; reduced sperm count and impotence in men; premature menopause and infertility in women; tooth disease; and adds to the risk associated with taking the oral contraceptive pill.
- Smoking causes 84% of deaths from lung cancer, and 83% of deaths from chronic obstructive lung disease, including bronchitis.
- Smoking causes approximately 3 out of 10 cancer deaths. As well as lung cancer, smoking can cause death by cancer of the mouth, larynx, oesophagus, bladder, kidney, stomach and pancreas.
- Smoking causes one out of every seven deaths from heart disease.

Smoking in pregnancy increases the risk of:

- Miscarriage
- Preterm delivery
- Reduced birthweight
- Perinatal death

Parental smoking is associated with an increased rate of:

- Sudden infant death syndrome
- Asthma and respiratory disease
- Middle ear disease
- Hospital admission — 17,000 children under 5 years old in England and Wales are admitted because of parental smoking each year

Environmental tobacco smoke (passive smoking)

- Is a cause of lung cancer in non-smokers and, in those with long-term exposure, the increased risk is in the order of 20-30%;
- Contributes to deaths from heart disease;
- May worsen asthma. People with asthma are more prone to attacks in smoky atmospheres;
- May cause eye, nose and throat irritation.

[DH, 1998; Dobson et al, 1998]

What are the benefits of stopping smoking?

- **Stopping smoking has major health benefits.**
- Smokers who quit before the age of about 35 years have a life expectancy only slightly less than those who have never smoked.
- Smokers who stop before the age of 50 years decrease the risk of dying from smoking-related diseases by 50%.
- Stopping smoking for 1 year reduces the excess risk of dying from a myocardial infarction or stroke by 50%.

- The risk of developing lung cancer is reduced by 20–90% — depending on the number of years of abstinence.
- The risk of developing oral cancer is reduced by 50% after stopping smoking for 3–5 years and, after stopping smoking for 10 years, is the same as that of a person who has never smoked.
- Stopping smoking normalizes the decline in lung function found in people with chronic obstructive airways disease.
- Stopping smoking before or during pregnancy reduces the risk of preterm birth and low birthweight [Lumley et al, 2002].

[NICE, 2002b]

How many people successfully stop smoking?

- In 1998, 69% of smokers in England wanted to give up smoking.
- It is estimated that about 4 million smokers a year attempt to quit but that only 3–6% of these (1–2% of all smokers) succeed.
- About half of those setting a quit date through the smoking cessation services in the Health Action Zones have successfully quit by the 4-week follow-up. The majority had received nicotine replacement therapy or bupropion.

[DH, 2002; NICE, 2002a]

Management issues

- Brief advice p.1729
- Behavioural support p.1729
- Self-help interventions p.1730
- NRT p.1730
- Bupropion p.1731
- Nicotine replacement therapy or bupropion? p.1732
- Use of a combination of NRT and bupropion p.1732
- Summary of effectiveness of interventions to help people stop smoking p.1732
- Interventions that are not recommended p.1732
- Guidance on the use of NRT and bupropion for smoking cessation issued by the National Institute for Clinical Excellence p.1733
- Pregnancy p.1733
- Children and young people p.1733
- Weight gain p.1733

Brief advice

Effectiveness

Brief advice (up to 5 minutes) from a general practitioner given to smokers to encourage them to make an attempt to quit is effective in promoting smoking cessation. As a direct consequence of general practitioner advice, about 40% of smokers will make some attempt to quit, but only 1–3% (more than controls) will stop smoking for at least 6 months. From a meta-analysis of 16 trials investigating the effectiveness of brief advice (lasting less than 20 minutes and with up to one follow-up visit) the odds ratio for smoking cessation with brief advice was 1.69 (95% CI 1.45 to 1.98) compared with no advice. Brief advice is probably effective as a result of *triggering* an attempt to quit rather than increasing the chances of success of an attempt to quit.

Although the overall efficacy of brief advice is small, if sufficient numbers of general practitioners offer advice, the reduction in rates of smoking in the general population could be substantial.

- There is insufficient evidence to say whether similar *opportunistic* advice from other health care professionals as part of their general duties is effective.
- Brief advice is more effective for light smokers (less than 10 cigarettes per day).
- The effectiveness of brief advice appears to be similar in people with established disease compared with smokers in an unselected population.

[RCP, 1999; West et al, 2000; Silagy and Stead, 2002]

Essential features of brief advice

- **The essential features** of brief opportunistic smoking cessation advice in primary care are to:
  - **Ask** about and record smoking status, keeping the record up-to-date.
  - **Advise** smokers of the benefits of stopping in a personalized, clear and supportive way, relating this to individual concerns and any health problems where possible.
  - **Assess** motivation to stop — and reinforce if possible.
  - **Assist** smokers to stop: this should include assistance in setting a quit date; identification of and strategies to avoid trigger situations; encouragement to develop support for quitting from family and friends; and consideration of using either nicotine replacement therapy or bupropion.
  - **Arrange** follow-up or review when next seen. Alternatively refer to local smoking cessation services as appropriate.

[British Heart Foundation, 2001; Anderson et al, 2002]

- **Advice should be clear, strong and personalized** for example, 'I need you to know that the most important thing you can do to protect your health now and in the future is to stop smoking.' and 'You have already had one heart attack.' [Anderson et al, 2002]. It is important to consider the patient's views and their reactions to advice, in order to avoid damaging the clinician–patient relationship [Butler et al, 1998].
- Assessing the degree of dependence may be added by questionnaires such as the Fagerström Test for Nicotine Dependence [Heatherton et al, 1991].
- **Relapse** is a normal part of the quitting process, and occurs on average 3–4 times. If a smoker has made repeated attempts to stop and failed, or has experienced severe withdrawal, or has requested more intensive help, then referral to a specialist smoking cessation service should be considered.

The stage of change model may be helpful in assessing the individual's motivation to quit and providing appropriate advice and therapy.

[NZGG, 1999; Anderson et al, 2002]

- **Recognized barriers to providing brief advice to all smokers in general practice** include the demoralizing effect of low success rates, concerns about straining the clinician–patient relationship with insistent advice, other pressing priorities during the consultation, and the shortage of time [RCP, 1999].

Behavioural support

- **Intensive anti-smoking advice** has been defined as an intervention that lasts 20 minutes or more at the initial consultation, involves the use of additional materials other than a leaflet or includes more than one follow-up visit. Intensive advice is only marginally more effective than brief advice (OR 1.44, 95% CI 1.23 to 1.68) and is resource intensive. It is therefore best reserved for smokers who are motivated to quit rather than employed as a routine intervention for all smokers [Silagy and Stead, 2002].
- Behavioural support encompasses a range of methods including focused counselling and advice, coping skills

Table 1: Stage of change model.

Stage	Key identifier	Appropriate therapy
Precontemplation	Does not want to quit smoking	Advise of the value of stopping and the health risks of continuing.
Contemplation	Wants to quit but not in the next month	Identify barriers to quitting, review prior quit attempts to find successes, discuss pros and cons of continued smoking, advise on the help available and encourage to set a quit date.
Action	Wants to quit within next month or has quit for less than a month	Refer to smoking cessation clinic or plan quitting e.g. set a quit date, emphasise complete abstinence as the goal, identify and avoid trigger situations, encourage the development of support for quitting from family and friends, find a partner to quit with, consider nicotine replacement therapy (NRT) or bupropion
Maintenance	Has quit for at least a month	Congratulate, enquire about relapses, reinforce the importance of permanent cessation, continue NRT
Relapse	Previously quit but now smoking on a daily basis	Explore the circumstances for the relapse, assess current stage, encourage to set another quit date, reaffirm person's ability to quit

training, and group support. Little is known about the active ingredient of behavioural support so it is difficult to provide recommendations regarding the content of behavioural support programmes.

- **Behavioural support and advice from a clinic run by smoking cessation specialists is effective in helping smokers quit.** In smokers motivated to quit, a programme of support involving multiple contacts for a period of 4 weeks or more, given by specialists employed and trained for the purpose, approximately doubles success rates even in smokers not using nicotine replacement or bupropion. In patients using these medications success rates are quadrupled compared with unaided quit attempts [West et al, 2000].
- **Behavioural support provided by nurses specifically employed to provide smoking cessation advice is effective** whereas behavioural support as part of their normal duties has not yet been shown to be effective [West et al, 2000].
- **Behavioural support in conjunction with nicotine replacement therapy** provided by pharmacists has also been shown to be effective [West et al, 2000].
- There is insufficient data to know whether providing behavioural support to smokers in groups is more or less effective than providing it individually [West et al, 2000].

Self-help interventions

- **Providing written self-help materials alone (i.e. without brief advice) has been shown to result in 1% of smokers stopping smoking who would not have otherwise done so.**
- Giving self-help materials in addition to brief advice or NRT has been shown not to improve outcome.
- Self-help material that is tailored to an individual smoker may be more effective than generic material.
- Providing telephone counselling in addition to self-help materials appears to increase quit rates.

[Lancaster and Stead, 2002]

NRT

- **NRT aims to replace the nicotine in cigarettes with another form of delivery.** It provides a background level of nicotine and alleviates the short-term difficulties smokers experience when trying to stop smoking by reducing craving and withdrawal symptoms. Forms of NRT currently available are gum (2 mg and 4 mg), transdermal patch (16 and 24 hour in varying doses), inhalator, nasal spray, sublingual tablet and lozenge. Most studies investigating NRT have been performed using either the gum or the patch. There is little evidence regarding the use of NRT for people who smoke less than 10 cigarettes per day.

Effectiveness

- **NRT doubles the rate of smoking cessation** *in those who are motivated to quit*, compared with no treatment or placebo. From a meta-analysis of trials investigating the effectiveness of NRT (97 randomized controlled trials, involving 39,000 smokers), the odds ratio of smoking cessation *at 6 months* after commencing treatment with NRT compared with control was 1.74 (95% CI 1.64 to 1.86). The odds ratio of smoking cessation *at 12 months* after commencing treatment with NRT compared with control (72 randomized controlled trials, involving 29,000 smokers) was 1.69 (95% CI 1.57 to 1.82). In terms of percentages, these trials showed that on average about 10% of people did not smoke for the 12 months following placebo therapy, and about 17% did not smoke following NRT [NICE, 2002b].
- **There is currently insufficient evidence to conclude that one form of NRT is more effective than another** [NICE, 2002b]. Meta-analyses and analyses of the different NRT products taken separately, using 12-month data, showed estimated odds ratios of 1.66 for gum; 1.76 for patches; 2.27 for nasal spray; 2.08 for inhaled nicotine; and 1.73 for nicotine sublingual tablet [Silagy et al, 1998].
- **The effectiveness of NRT is probably independent of the intensity of additional support provided.** However, no definite conclusion can be made as the evidence stems from indirect comparison of trials. All the trials investigating NRT have included brief advice as a minimum and are not representative of the contact and monitoring in a typical over-the-counter setting [West et al, 2000].
- **Short-term therapy with NRT is effective,** but there is insufficient evidence to reach a firm conclusion regarding the relative effectiveness of different durations of therapy [NICE, 2002b].
- **Combining the patch with other forms of NRT that allow as-required dosing may be more effective than the patch alone,** and appears to be as safe. This could be due to the resulting increased dose of NRT and requires further research. Use of combination therapy may be considered for people who were unsuccessful in quitting using a single type of NRT [NICE, 2002b]. Note: combined therapy is not yet licensed [Silagy et al, 1998].
- **Dose of NRT:** Heavy smokers (20 cigarettes or more per day) can benefit from the higher dose of NRT *gum* (4 mg nicotine gum rather than 2 mg gum) [Silagy et al, 1998; NICE, 2002b]. Comparison of the effectiveness of low-dose and high-dose NRT *patches* was equivocal although there was borderline evidence that high-dose patches were more effective than low-dose patches for heavy smokers (greater than 30 cigarettes per day) [Silagy et al, 1998; NICE, 2002b].

S

- Fixed-schedule NRT is probably as effective as as-required dosing [NICE, 2002b].
- There is no evidence of benefit for gradually weaning people off NRT compared to stopping abruptly [Silagy et al, 1998; NICE, 2002b].
- The 16-hour NRT patches are as effective as the 24-hour patches [Silagy et al, 1998; NICE, 2002b].
- **There is only limited published data regarding the effectiveness of NRT in specific subgroups of smokers** (people with lung disease or cardiovascular disease). The effectiveness of NRT in people with lung disease was comparable to that in the general smoking population. There is insufficient evidence to confirm whether NRT is effective in smokers with cardiovascular disease [NICE, 2002b] but it does not appear to lead to an increased risk of adverse cardiovascular events [Silagy et al, 1998].

Availability

- NRT is available to smokers aged over 18 years of age, and to those under 18 years on the recommendation of a medical practitioner [NICE, 2002a].
- Since April 2001 general practitioners are able to prescribe the full range of NRT products on the National Health Service.
- Since May 2001 NRT has been included in the Nurse Prescribers' Formulary.
- All NRT products are available to buy from pharmacies.
- Certain NRT products (low-strength patches and gums) are available for *general sale* (i.e. from supermarkets and other retail outlets).

Use of NRT

- **Ideally NRT should be used in conjunction with brief advice or behavioural support in a smoking cessation strategy.**
- **An adequate dose of NRT should be started once the person has stopped smoking.**
- **Dose of NRT may depend on the number of cigarettes smoked per day** [NICE, 2002a].
- **Duration of NRT is usually up to 8–12 weeks** (varies depending on which form of NRT is used). Use should normally be restricted to the licensed duration of the form of NRT used [NICE, 2002a].
- **Treatment may be stopped abruptly or tapered gradually.** Most NRT products advise use of the full dose for 8-12 weeks followed by a gradual reduction in dose over 4 weeks. However, abruptly stopping NRT does not appear to reduce its effectiveness.
- **Smokers with certain conditions** (cardiovascular disease, hyperthyroidism, diabetes mellitus, severe renal or hepatic impairment and peptic ulcer) are advised to use NRT only after careful consideration of risks and benefits and after discussion with a healthcare professional. Similar advice applies to women who are pregnant or breastfeeding. When giving such advice to people in these groups who have been unable to quit smoking without using a cessation aid, health-care professionals should take into account the significant harm associated with continuing to smoke and that it can be expected that NRT will deliver less nicotine (and none of the other potentially disease-causing agents) than would be obtained from cigarettes [NICE, 2002a].
- **NRT should be discontinued if the user abandons the quit attempt** [NICE, 2002a].
- **The most common adverse effects are localized reactions** (for example, skin irritation with patches, irritation of the nose, throat and eyes with nasal spray), but minor sleep disturbances occur commonly. These adverse effects are unlikely to lead to discontinuation of therapy [NICE, 2002a].

Bupropion

- **Bupropion is an atypical antidepressant licensed in the UK for use as an aid to smoking cessation in conjunction with behavioural support.** It is a relatively weak but selective inhibitor of the neuronal re-uptake of dopamine and noradrenaline. Although the exact mechanism by which it aids smoking cessation is unclear, it is presumed to work directly on the brain pathways involved in addiction and withdrawal. Evidence for effectiveness of bupropion is limited to medium to heavy smokers (15 or more cigarettes per day) receiving behavioural support.

[NICE, 2002a]

Effectiveness

- **Bupropion in conjunction with behavioural support is effective in helping smokers quit** and approximately doubles the rate of smoking cessation. From a meta-analysis of 10 randomized controlled trials involving 3,800 smokers, the odds ratio for smoking cessation with bupropion compared with placebo was 2.16 (95% CI 1.51 to 3.10). This result combines data for smoking cessation at 6 months and 12 months and, in all but one study, measures continuous abstinence. The odds ratio for smoking cessation at 12 months with bupropion (3,100 smokers) was 2.05 (95% CI 1.45 to 2.91) compared with placebo. In terms of percentages these trials showed that about 9% did not smoke for the 12 months following placebo therapy, and about 19% did not smoke following bupropion therapy.
- **There is only limited published data regarding the effectiveness of bupropion in specific subgroups of smokers** (people with pulmonary disease, cardiovascular disease, or those who had failed to quit at least once before they used bupropion). The effectiveness of bupropion in these groups was generally comparable to that in the general smoking population.
- The efficacy of bupropion appears to be independent of its antidepressant effect and bupropion is of benefit to people with no history of depression.

[Hughes et al, 2002; NICE, 2002a; NICE, 2002b]

Availability

- Bupropion is a prescription-only medicine that is available on the National Health Service as a sustained-release preparation.

Use of bupropion

- **Bupropion should normally only be used as part of a structured smoking cessation programme.**
- **Recommended treatment** consists of 150 mg for 6 days increasing to 150 mg twice daily, at least 8 hours apart, for a total of 7 to 9 weeks.
- **Patients are advised to stop smoking** 7–14 days after starting bupropion.

[Regional Drug and Therapeutics Centre, 2000; ABPI Medicines Compendium, 2002]

Bupropion and seizures

- Bupropion is associated with a dose-related risk of seizure (1 in 1000 at the standard dose of 300 mg per day).
- The Committee on Safety of Medicines reminds prescribers that bupropion:
  - Is contraindicated in people with a current seizure disorder or any history of seizures, with current or previous diagnosis of bulimia or anorexia nervosa, with a known central nervous system tumour, and those experiencing abrupt withdrawal from alcohol or benzodiazepines.

S

- Should not be prescribed in people with other risk factors for seizures unless there is compelling clinical justification for which the potential benefit outweighs the increased risk of seizure. Such risk factors include concomitant use of any drug known to lower the seizure threshold (including antipsychotics, antidepressants, some antimalarials such as mefloquine, theophylline, systemic steroids, tramadol, quinolones and sedating antihistamines), alcohol abuse, a history of head trauma, diabetes treated with hypoglycaemics or insulin and use of stimulants or anorectic products. In such people a lower dose of 150 mg daily throughout the entire treatment period should be considered.
- Bupropion should be discontinued in individuals who have experienced a seizure while taking it.

[CSM, 2002]

Nicotine replacement therapy or bupropion?

- There is limited evidence to suggest that bupropion may be more effective than nicotine replacement therapy (NRT). Further trials are required before any firm conclusion can be made.
- There have been only two studies comparing the effectiveness of bupropion with NRT. The first, a double blind, double dummy, randomized placebo controlled trial, compared bupropion with an NRT patch, and with a combination of bupropion plus NRT patch. The odds ratio for smoking cessation (continuous abstinence) at 12 months with bupropion compared to NRT patch was 2.07 (95% CI 1.22 to 3.53), and for bupropion plus patch compared to bupropion it was 1.28 (95% CI 0.82 to 1.99). In the second study, an open-label, non-placebo, randomized controlled trial, bupropion 300 mg/day was compared at 12 months (point abstinence) with NRT gum (4 mg). In this unpublished study, there was no significant difference between the treatment groups in quit rates.

[Silagy et al, 1998; NICE, 2002a; NICE, 2002b]

Use of a combination of NRT and bupropion

- Data from a single published study suggests that bupropion in combination with nicotine patches may be more effective than bupropion alone, but it is important to note that this difference was not statistically significant [Jorenby et al, 1999].
- There is currently insufficient evidence to recommended use of NRT and bupropion in combination [NICE, 2002a].

S

Summary of effectiveness of interventions to help people stop smoking

Table 2: Summary of effectiveness of interventions to help people stop smoking.

Intervention	Estimate of effectiveness at 6 months Odds ratio (95% CI)	Amount of evidence
Brief advice from a doctor	1.69 (1.45 to 1.98) for quitting after brief advice compared with no advice (or usual care)	16 trials
Intensive advice from a doctor	1.44 (1.23 to 1.68) for quitting after intensive advice compared with brief advice Trend to larger effect of intensive advice compared to control but there was heterogeneity between trials	14 trials 5 trials
Nicotine replacement therapy	1.74 (1.64 to 1.86) for quitting after NRT compared to placebo or no treatment	97 trials
Bupropion	2.16 (1.51 to 3.10) for quitting after bupropion compared to placebo 2.07 (1.33 to 3.53) for quitting with bupropion compared to NRT patch	10 trials 1 trial

Interventions that are not recommended

- **Exercise** cannot be currently recommended as a specific aid to smoking cessation as there is inconclusive evidence that exercise programmes are effective in helping smokers quit [Ussher et al, 2002].
- **Acupuncture** does not appear to be an effective intervention to aid smoking cessation [White et al, 2002].
- **Hypnosis** also lacks sufficient evidence of efficacy [Abbot et al, 2002].
- **Aversive smoking** involves puffing cigarettes every few seconds for several minutes while concentrating on the unpleasant feelings. There is no conclusive evidence that rapid smoking aversion therapy is effective but the quality of the trial data is poor [Hajek and Stead, 2002].
- **Clonidine** is an alpha$_2$-noradrenergic agonist that suppresses sympathetic activity. It appears to be effective at helping smoking cessation but is associated with adverse effects (dry mouth, dizziness, drowsiness) and high discontinuation rates [RCP, 1999].
- **Antidepressants other than bupropion:** Nortriptyline has been shown to double quit rates but is not licensed in the UK as an aid to smoking cessation. Studies investigating the effectiveness of fluoxetine, paroxetine and venlafaxine for smoking cessation detected no long-term benefit [Hughes et al, 2002].
- **Lobeline,** a partial nicotinic agonist derived from the leaves of an Indian tobacco plant has not been shown to help smoking cessation in long-term trials [Stead and Hughes, 2002].
- **Opioid antagonists** may reduce the reinforcing properties of nicotine that are mediated by the release of various neurotransmitters, including beta endorphin, in the brain. There is insufficient evidence to know whether opioid antagonists are effective for stopping smoking in the long term [David et al, 2002].
- **Silver acetate** interacts with cigarette smoke to produce an aversive metallic taste. Studies have indicated a lack of efficacy for this treatment [RCP, 1999].
- **Mecamylamine,** a nicotine antagonist, is not effective at aiding smoking cessation [RCP, 1999].

Guidance on the use of NRT and bupropion for smoking cessation issued by the National Institute for Clinical Excellence

- NRT and bupropion are recommended for smokers who have expressed a desire to quit smoking.
- NRT or bupropion should normally only be prescribed as part of an abstinent-contingent treatment, in which the smoker makes a commitment to stop smoking on or before a particular date (target stop date). Smokers should be offered advice and encouragement to aid their attempt to quit. Ideally, initial prescription of NRT or bupropion should be sufficient to last only until 2 weeks after the target stop date. Normally, this will be after 2 weeks of NRT therapy, and 3–4 weeks for bupropion, to allow for the different methods of administration and mode of action. Second prescriptions should be given only to people who have demonstrated that their quit attempt is continuing on reassessment.
- It is recommended that smokers who are under the age of 18 years, who are pregnant or breastfeeding, or who have unstable cardiovascular disorders, should discuss the use of NRT with a relevant healthcare professional before it is prescribed.
- Bupropion is not recommended for smokers under the age of 18 years, as its safety and efficacy have not been evaluated for this group. Women who are pregnant or breastfeeding should not use bupropion.
- If a smoker's attempt to quit is unsuccessful with treatment using either NRT or bupropion, the National Health Service should normally fund no further attempts within 6 months. However, if external factors interfered with an individual's initial attempt to stop smoking, it may be reasonable to try again sooner.
- There is currently insufficient evidence to recommend the use of an NRT and bupropion in combination.
  In deciding which of the available therapies to use and in which order they should be prescribed, practitioners should take into account:
  - Intention and motivation to quit, and likelihood of compliance
  - The availability of counselling or support
  - Previous usage of smoking cessation aids
  - Contraindications and potential for adverse effects
  - Personal preferences of the smoker

[NICE, 2002a]

Pregnancy

Smoking in pregnancy has an adverse impact through a number of mechanisms. Nicotine through its vasoconstrictive properties reduces placental blood flow and may cause fetal hypoxia. Animal studies indicate that nicotine may also have adverse effects on fetal brain development. Carbon monoxide binds to haemoglobin and can reduce the amount of oxygen transferred from maternal to fetal blood. Numerous other components of cigarette smoke are cellular toxins.

Approximately 25% of women smokers quit prior to becoming pregnant or very soon after they learn they are and about a quarter of these will begin smoking again during the pregnancy. Over 70% of women who quit as soon as they learn they are pregnant return to smoking by 6 months after the birth. In contrast women who quit prior to pregnancy are less likely to relapse. Advice to prevent relapse during pregnancy and in the post-partum period should be considered [DiClemente et al, 2000; Lumley et al, 2002].

Quitting early in pregnancy is strongly recommended, but the fetus will benefit from quitting at any stage during the pregnancy.

- **Pregnant smokers should receive clear, accurate, and specific information on the risks of smoking** to the fetus and themselves and be advised to stop smoking [West et al, 2000].
- **Counselling from a smoking cessation specialist together with supporting written materials is effective in helping pregnant smokers to quit,** if they are motivated to do so. Smoking cessation programmes in pregnancy appear to reduce smoking (OR 0.53, 95% CI 0.47 to 0.60), the risk of a low birth weight (OR 0.8, 95% CI 0.67 to 0.95) and preterm birth (OR 0.83, 95% CI 0.69 to 0.99) [Lumley et al, 2002].
- **There is a lack of data on the use and relative risks of NRT in pregnancy.** Cigarette smoking, in general, delivers more nicotine than NRT, and exposes the mother and fetus to many other toxins. NRT is likely to be appreciably safer than continued smoking and theoretically can be justified in pregnant women in whom non-pharmacological interventions have failed. Intermittent dose regimes (gum, spray, inhalator) are preferred to minimize fetal exposure to nicotine [RCP, 1999; Dempsey and Benowitz, 2001].
- **Bupropion should be avoided in pregnancy** (and whilst breastfeeding), as no information on safety is available [NICE, 2002a]. No adverse effects on fetal development were observed during animal studies [Covey et al, 2000].

Children and young people

- Over 80% of smokers take up smoking during their teenage years, and as the rate of smoking in young people is increasing this will eventually be reflected in the adult smoking rates [NHS CRD, 1999].
- Programmes to prevent children and young people from taking up smoking are usually targeted at 11–17 year olds, however targeting younger children (4–8 years) before attitudes towards smoking are established and before experimentation with cigarettes, may be more effective [NHS CRD, 1999].
- There is a lack of evidence regarding the effectiveness of interventions to aid smoking cessation in this age group. NRT is not licensed for people under the age of 18 years but may be considered in young people who are experiencing difficulty quitting, where the risks of NRT are considered to be less than the risks associated with continued smoking [NICE, 2002a]. Bupropion is not recommended for smokers under the age of 18 years [NICE, 2002a].

Weight gain

- Concerns over weight may be a risk factor for adolescents to start smoking, may influence continued smoking, and may prevent smokers to attempt to quit.
- **Most smokers gain weight when they stop smoking** probably due to both increased caloric intake and reduced metabolic rate due to the abstinence of nicotine.
- **Weight gain is on average 3 to 5 kg.** However, the average weight of smokers is 3–5 kg less than the average weight of non-smokers, and people who stop smoking gain weight to the average weight of non-smokers. Most of this weight gain occurs in the first few months following quitting.
- **Large weight gains occur in 10–15% of people who quit.** Women and heavy smokers are particularly at risk.
- **Nicotine *gum*** has been shown to delay, but not prevent, weight gain [Nordstrom et al, 1999]. Other forms of NRT do not have this effect and it is possible that the gum acts as an oral substitution for food.
- Bupropion also reduced weight gain in subjects who stopped smoking [Hurt et al, 1997; Jorenby et al, 1999], but this effect did not last after the drug was stopped.

[Rigotti, 1999]

S

References

NHS staff in England can link, free of charge, from references to full text journals by clicking on [Full text] on the PRODIGY website.

1. Abbot, N.C., Stead, L.F., White, A.R. and Barnes, J. (2002) *Hypnotherapy for smoking cessation (Cochrane Review)*. The Cochrane Library. Issue 2. Oxford: Update Software.
2. ABPI Medicines Compendium (2002) *Summary of product characteristics for Zyban*. Electronic Medicines Compendium. Datapharm Communications Ltd. www.emc.medicines.org.uk [Accessed: 09/05/2002].
3. Anderson, J.E., Jorenby, D.E., Scott, W.J. and Fiore, M.C. (2002) Treating tobacco use and dependence: an evidence-based clinical practice guideline for tobacco cessation. *Chest* **121**(3), 932–941. [Full text]
4. British Heart Foundation (2001) *Stopping smoking: evidence-based guidance*. eGuidelines. Vol. 08. http://www.eguidelines.co.uk/eguidelinesmain/guidelines/summaries/general/bhf_stopping_smoking.htm [Accessed: 06/03/2002].
5. Butler, C.C., Pill, R. and Stott, N.C. (1998) Qualitative study of patients' perceptions of doctors' advice to quit smoking: implications for opportunistic health promotion. *British Medical Journal* **316**(7148), 1878–1881. [Full text]
6. Covey, L.S., Sullivan, M.A., Johnston, J.A. et al (2000) Advances in non-nicotine pharmacotherapy for smoking cessation. *Drugs* **59**(1), 17–31.
7. CSM (2002) Zyban [bupropion (amfebutamone)] – safety reminder. *Current Problems in Pharmacovigilance* **27**, 5–5.
8. David, S., Lancaster, T. and Stead, L.F. (2002) *Opioid antagonists for smoking cessation (Cochrane Review)*. The Cochrane Library. Issue 2. Oxford: Update Software. www.nelh.nhs.uk/cochrane.asp [Accessed: 29/07/2005].
9. Dempsey, D.A. and Benowitz, N.L. (2001) Risks and benefits of nicotine to aid smoking cessation in pregnancy. *Drug Safety* **24**(4), 277–322.
10. DH (1998) *Report of the scientific committee on tobacco and health*. London: Department of Health.
11. DH (2000) *Smoking, drinking & drug use among young people in England in 2000*. Department of Health. www.dh.gov.uk [Accessed: 29/04/2004]. [Full text]
12. DH (2002) *Statistics on smoking cessation services in health authorities: England, April to September 2001*. Department of Health. www.dh.gov.uk [Accessed: 29/04/2004]. [Full text]
13. DiClemente, C.C., Dolan-Mullen, P. and Windsor, R.A. (2000) The process of pregnancy smoking cessation: implications for interventions. *Tobacco Control* **9**(Suppl 3), 6–21.
14. Dobson, F., Donald, D., Mowlam, M. and Michael, A. (1998) *Smoking kills: a white paper on tobacco*. London: Department of Health.
15. Hajek, P. and Stead, L.F. (2002) *Aversive smoking for smoking cessation (Cochrane Review)*. The Cochrane Library. Issue 2. Oxford: Update Software.
16. Heatherton, T.F., Kozlowski, L.T., Frecker, R.C. and Fagerstrom, K.O. (1991) The Fagerstrom Test for Nicotine Dependence: a revision of the Fagerstrom Tolerance Questionnaire. *British Journal of Addiction* **86**(9), 1119–1127.
17. Hughes, J.R., Stead, L.F. and Lancaster, T. (2002) *Antidepressants for smoking cessation (Cochrane Review)*. The Cochrane Library. Issue 1. Oxford: Update Software.
18. Hurt, R.D., Sachs, D.P.L., Glover, E.D. et al (1997) A comparison of sustained-release bupropion and placebo for smoking cessation. *New England Journal of Medicine* **337**(17), 1195–1202. [Full text]
19. Jorenby, D.E., Leischow, S.J., Nides, M.A. et al (1999) A controlled trial of sustained-release bupropion, a nicotine patch, or both for smoking cessation. *New England Journal of Medicine* **340**(9), 685–691 [erratum appears in: NEJM (1999) 341(8), 610–611]. [Full text]
20. Lancaster, T. and Stead, L.F. (2002) *Self-help interventions for smoking cessation (Cochrane Review)*. The Cochrane Library. Issue 3. Chichester, UK: John Wiley & Sons, Ltd. www.nelh.nhs.uk/cochrane.asp [Accessed: 19/07/2005]. [Full text]
21. Lumley, J., Oliver, S. and Waters, E. (2002) *Interventions for promoting smoking cessation during pregnancy (Cochrane Review)*. The Cochrane Library. Issue 1. Oxford: Update Software.
22. NHS CRD (1998) Smoking cessation: what the health service can do. *Effectiveness Matters* **3**(1),
23. NHS CRD (1999) Preventing the uptake of smoking in young people. *Effective Health Care Bulletin* **5**(5), 1–12.
24. NICE (2002a) *Guidance on the use of nicotine replacement therapy (NRT) and bupropion for smoking cessation*. Technology appraisal no. 39. National Institute for Clinical Excellence. www.nice.org.uk [Accessed: 18/07/2005].
25. NICE (2002b) *A rapid and systematic review of the clinical and cost effectiveness of bupropion SR and nicotine replacement therapy (NRT) for smoking cessation*. Technology appraisal no. 39. National Institute for Clinical Excellenece. www.nice.org.uk/ [Accessed: 19/07/2005].
26. Nordstrom, B.L., Kinnunen, T., Utman, C.H. and Garvey, A.J. (1999) Long-term effects of nicotine gum on weight gain after smoking cessation. *Nicotine & Tobacco Research* **1**(3), 259–268.
27. NZGG (1999) *Guidelines for smoking cessation*. New Zealand: New Zealand Guidelines Group.
28. RCP (1999) *The management of nicotine addiction*. Royal College of Physicians. www.rcplondon.ac.uk/pubs/books/nicotine/7-management.htm [Accessed: 12/07/2005].
29. Regional Drug and Therapeutics Centre (2000) Bupropion SR. *New Drug Evaluation*(42), 1–2.
30. Rigotti, N.A. (1999) Treatment options for the weight-conscious smoker. *Archives of Internal Medicine* **159**(11), 1169–1171. [Full text]
31. Silagy, C. and Stead, L.F. (2002) *Physician advice for smoking cessation (Cochrane Review)*. The Cochrane Library. Issue 1. Oxford: Update Software.
32. Silagy, C., Mant, D., Fowler, G. and Lancaster, T. (1998) *Nicotine replacement therapy for smoking cessation*. The Cochrane Library. Issue 3. Oxford: Update Software.
33. Stead, L.F. and Hughes, J.R. (2002) *Lobeline for smoking cessation (Cochrane Review)*. The Cochrane Library. Issue 2. Oxford: Update Software.
34. Ussher, M.H., West, R., Taylor, A.H. and McEwen, A. (2002) *Exercise interventions for smoking cessation (Cochrane Review)*. The Cochrane Library. Issue 1. Oxford: Update Software.
35. West, R., McNeill, A. and Raw, M. (2000) Smoking cessation guidelines for health professionals: an update. *Thorax* **55**(12), 987–999. [Full text]
36. White, A.R., Rampes, H. and Ernst, E. (2002) *Acupuncture for smoking cessation (Cochrane Review)*. The Cochrane Library. Issue 1. Oxford: Update Software. www.nelh.nhs.uk/cochrane.asp [Accessed: 29/07/2005].

S

PRODIGY GUIDANCE

Sore throat — acute

Last revised in November 2004
www.prodigy.nhs.uk/guidance.asp?gt=Sore throat - acute

Applies to people of all ages

This guidance covers the management of acute sore throat due to pharyngitis, laryngitis, or tonsillitis.

This guidance does not cover the management of chronic sore throat or hoarseness.

Goals

- To alleviate symptoms
- To avoid complications

Contents

Scenarios

- Sore throat – acute p.1735

Extended Information, p. 1738

Sore throat — acute

Which therapy?

Sore throat (pharyngitis, tonsillitis, laryngitis) is a self-limiting condition.
Explanation, reassurance, and advice on symptomatic treatment are usually adequate.
Pain relief with paracetamol or ibuprofen will help.
Gargles are reported to help some people, but there is inadequate evidence on which to base any recommendations for their use.
Antibiotics are not indicated for most people with sore throat.
The National Institute for Clinical Excellence recommends antibiotics in the following situations:

- Features of marked systemic upset secondary to the acute sore throat
- Unilateral peritonsillitis
- A history of rheumatic fever
- An increased risk from acute infection (such as a child with diabetes mellitus or immunodeficiency)

If an antibiotic is indicated, phenoxymethylpenicillin or erythromycin (if the person is allergic to penicillin) is preferred.

Practical prescribing points

For further information, please see the *Medicines Compendium* (www.medicines.org.uk) or the *British National Formulary* (www.bnf.org).
The Committee on Safety of Medicines (CSM) advises that all nonsteroidal anti-inflammatory drugs (NSAIDs) are associated with serious gastrointestinal toxicity. The risk is greatest in the elderly. All non-selective NSAIDs (such as ibuprofen) are contraindicated in people with a history of peptic ulceration. The CSM also warns that any degree of worsening of asthma may be related to the ingestion of NSAIDs either prescribed or over-the-counter.
Paracetamol (and increasingly, ibuprofen) are present in many over-the-counter cold remedies. People who are also self-medicating must take care to avoid accidental overdosage.
Erythromycin: use with caution in people with hepatic and renal impairment, those with prolongation of the QT interval, and women who are breastfeeding. Erythromycin may increase the level of certain drugs (e.g. theophylline, carbamazepine, statins), or potentiate warfarin.

Should I refer or investigate?

Refer?

- The National Institute for Clinical Excellence, in *Referral advice: a guide to appropriate referral from general to specialist services*, advises the following for recurrent episodes of acute sore throat in children aged up to 15 years. The referral advice is meant to encourage local health communities to discuss referral issues and enable local referral guidelines and protocols to be produced (for further information, see www.nice.org.uk).
- Almost all children with recurrent sore throat can be managed in primary care. However, children should be referred to a specialist service in the circumstances shown in Table 1.

Investigate?

- Throat swabs cannot differentiate between infection and carriage, they have poor sensitivity, and there is usually delay in getting the result; they are therefore usually of little value.
- Consider a monospot blood test if glandular fever (infectious mononucleosis) is suspected. It is reasonable to delay this until the sore throat has persisted longer than 10 days.

Table 1: Referral advice for children aged up to 15 years with recurrent episodes of acute sore throat.

Referral timing	Reason for referral
****	They have, or are suspected of having, a quinsy
****	The swelling is causing acute upper airways obstruction
****	The swelling is interfering with swallowing, causing dehydration and marked systemic upset
**	They have a history of sleep apnoea, daytime somnolence, and failure to thrive
*	They have had five or more episodes of acute sore throat in the preceding 12 months, documented by the parent or clinician, and these episodes have been severe enough to disrupt the child's normal behaviour or day-to-day activity
*	They have guttate psoriasis, which is exacerbated by recurrent tonsillitis
^	There is suspicion of a serious underlying disorder such as leukaemia

Key to referral timings: arrangements should be made so that the person:
**** is seen immediately (within a day)
*** is seen urgently (maximum wait of 2 weeks recommended, but to be agreed locally)
** is seen soon (maximum waiting time to be agreed locally)
* has a routine appointment (maximum waiting time to be agreed locally)
^ is seen within an appropriate time depending on his or her clinical circumstances (discretionary)

S

Patient information leaflets

The following PILs are available at www.prodigy.nhs.uk

- Antibiotics - Why No Antibiotic?
- Anti-inflammatory Painkillers
- Laryngitis
- Sore Throat
- Tonsillitis

Shared decision making

- Most bouts of sore throat and tonsillitis are due to a virus infection. The immune system usually clears the infection within a few days.
- **Paracetamol** or **ibuprofen** can ease the pain. A regular full dose is better than 'now and then' to ease pain until symptoms go.
- Gargles, sprays, and lozenges that you can buy from the pharmacist may soothe the throat. They do not shorten the length of the illness.
- Antibiotics are not usually advised, apart from in certain circumstances such as for severe infections or for someone with a poor immune system.

Drug rationale

Drugs not included

- **Aspirin and nonsteroidal anti-inflammatory drugs (NSAIDs)**, other than ibuprofen, are excluded because of their relatively extensive adverse-effect profiles. In addition, aspirin should not be used in children under the age of 16 years because of the risk of Reye's syndrome [CSM, 2002].
- **Weak opioids:** there is little evidence to suggest that combining paracetamol with a weak opioid offers any additional advantage, and adverse effects are more likely [SIGN, 1999].
- **Antibiotics other than phenoxymethylpenicillin and erythromycin** are no more effective in most people and are more expensive [DTB, 1995]. Alternative antibiotics are mainly of a broad-spectrum nature, which increases the risk of complications and resistance. In particular, ampicillin and amoxicillin virtually always cause maculopapular rashes in people with glandular fever, and should therefore not be used for 'blind' treatment of a sore throat (people who develop rashes may mistakenly be labelled as penicillin-allergic).
- **Gargles and sprays** have been poorly researched and no specific recommendations can be made. Anecdotally, gargling with salt water or aspirin is reported to relieve pain in some people. One small study showed that benzydamine as a gargle for sore throat resulted in significantly greater relief of pain and dysphagia at 24 hours than did placebo, but this requires confirmation [SIGN, 1999].

S

Drugs included

- **Paracetamol and ibuprofen** are effective antipyretics and analgesics in children and adults.
- **Phenoxymethylpenicillin, and erythromycin (for those with penicillin allergy):** 10-day treatment has been used in most studies and is recommended in order to eradicate possible streptococcus infection [DTB, 1995; SIGN, 1999]. However, shorter courses may be appropriate, as there is no good correlation between microbiological and clinical cure for relief of symptoms. The Health Protection Agency recommends either twice- or four-times-daily dosing, lasting 7–10 days for penicillin and 5–10 days for erythromycin [HPA, 2003]. As it is difficult to recommend any one particular regimen, PRODIGY offers twice- or four-times-daily dosing for 7 or 10 days.

Prescriptions

Analgesia: use when required

Paracetamol s/f susp: 60mg to 120mg up to four times a day

- Age from 3 to 11 months
- Paracetamol 120mg/5ml s/f susp. Take 2.5ml to 5ml every 4 to 6 hours when required for pain relief. Maximum of 4 doses in 24 hours; supply 150 ml; NHS Cost £0.65; OTC Cost £1.15.

Paracetamol s/f susp: 120mg to 240mg up to four times a day

- Age from 12 months to 5 years
- Paracetamol 120mg/5ml s/f susp. Take one to two 5ml spoonfuls every 4 to 6 hours when required for pain relief. Maximum of 4 doses in 24 hours; supply 300 ml; NHS Cost £1.30; OTC Cost £2.29.

Paracetamol s/f susp: 250mg to 500mg up to four times a day

- Age from 6 to 11 years
- Paracetamol 250mg/5ml s/f susp. Take one to two 5ml spoonfuls every 4 to 6 hours when required for pain relief. Maximum of 4 doses in 24 hours; supply 300 ml; NHS Cost £2.20; OTC Cost £3.87.

Paracetamol tablets: 500mg to 1g up to four times a day

- Age from 12 to 15 years
- Paracetamol 500mg tablets. Take one to two tablets every 4 to 6 hours when required for pain relief. Maximum of 8 tablets in 24 hours; supply 56 tablets; NHS Cost £0.42; OTC Cost £0.67.

Paracetamol tablets: 1g up to four times a day

- Age from 16 years onwards
- Paracetamol 500mg tablets. Take two tablets every 4 to 6 hours when required for pain relief. Maximum of 8 tablets in 24 hours; supply 56 tablets; NHS Cost £0.42; OTC Cost £0.67.

Paracetamol soluble tabs: 500mg to 1g up to four times a day

- Age from 12 to 15 years
- Paracetamol 500mg soluble tabs. Take one to two tablets every 4 to 6 hours when required for pain relief. Maximum of 8 tablets in 24 hours; supply 60 tablets; NHS Cost £2.82; OTC Cost £4.97.

Paracetamol soluble tabs: 500mg to 1g up to four times a day

- Age from 16 years onwards
- Paracetamol 500mg soluble tabs. Take two tablets every 4 to 6 hours when required for pain relief. Maximum of 8 tablets in 24 hours; supply 60 tablets; NHS Cost £2.82; OTC Cost £4.97.

Ibuprofen s/f susp: 50mg three to four times a day

- Age from 12 months to 2 years
- Ibuprofen 100mg/5ml s/f susp. Take 2.5ml three to four times a day when required for pain relief. Do not exceed the stated dose; supply 100 ml; NHS Cost £1.82; OTC Cost £3.21.

Ibuprofen s/f susp: 100mg three to four times a day

- Age from 3 to 7 years
- Ibuprofen 100mg/5ml s/f susp. Take one 5ml spoonful 3 to 4 times a day when required for pain relief. Do not exceed the stated dose; supply 150 ml; NHS Cost £2.73; OTC Cost £4.81.

Ibuprofen s/f susp: 200mg three to four times a day

- Age from 8 to 11 years
- Ibuprofen 100mg/5ml s/f susp. Take two 5ml spoonfuls 3 to 4 times a day when required for pain relief. Do not

exceed the stated dose; supply 300 ml; NHS Cost £5.46; OTC Cost £9.62.

Ibuprofen tablets: 400mg three times a day
- Age from 12 years onwards
- Ibuprofen 400mg tablets. Take one tablet three times a day when required for pain relief. Do not exceed the stated dose; supply 24 tablets; NHS Cost £0.70; OTC Cost £1.24.

Penicillin V for 7 days (rarely appropriate)

Penicillin V solution: 125mg twice a day
- Age from 1 month to 11 months
- Penicillin V 125mg/5ml sol. Take one 5ml spoonful twice a day for 7 days; supply 100 ml; NHS Cost £1.66.

Penicillin V solution: 250mg twice a day
- Age from 12 months to 5 years
- Penicillin V 250mg/5ml sol. Take one 5ml spoonful twice a day for 7 days; supply 100 ml; NHS Cost £2.29.

Penicillin V solution: 500mg twice a day
- Age from 6 to 11 years
- Penicillin V 250mg/5ml sol. Take two 5ml spoonfuls twice a day for 7 days; supply 200 ml; NHS Cost £4.58.

Penicillin V tablets: 1g twice a day
- Age from 12 years onwards
- Penicillin V 250mg tablets. Take four tablets twice a day for 7 days; supply 56 tablets; NHS Cost £3.56.

Penicillin V solution: 62.5mg four times a day
- Age from 1 month to 11 months
- Penicillin V 125mg/5ml sol. Take 2.5ml four times a day for 7 days; supply 100 ml; NHS Cost £1.66.

Penicillin V solution: 125mg four times a day
- Age from 12 months to 5 years
- Penicillin V 125mg/5ml sol. Take one 5ml spoonful four times a day for 7 days; supply 200 ml; NHS Cost £3.32.

Penicillin V solution: 250mg four times a day
- Age from 6 to 11 years
- Penicillin V 250mg/5ml sol. Take one 5ml spoonful four times a day for 7 days; supply 200 ml; NHS Cost £4.58.

Penicillin V tablets: 500mg four times a day
- Age from 12 years onwards
- Penicillin V 250mg tablets. Take two tablets four times a day for 7 days; supply 56 tablets; NHS Cost £3.56.

Penicillin V for 10 days (rarely appropriate)

Penicillin V solution: 125mg twice a day
- Age from 1 month to 11 months
- Penicillin V 125mg/5ml sol. Take one 5ml spoonful twice a day for 10 days; supply 100 ml; NHS Cost £1.66.

Penicillin V solution: 250mg twice a day
- Age from 12 months to 5 years
- Penicillin V 250mg/5ml sol. Take one 5ml spoonful twice a day for 10 days; supply 100 ml; NHS Cost £2.29.

Penicillin V solution: 500mg twice a day
- Age from 6 to 11 years
- Penicillin V 250mg/5ml sol. Take two 5ml spoonfuls twice a day for 10 days; supply 200 ml; NHS Cost £4.58.

Penicillin V tablets: 1g twice a day
- Age from 12 years onwards
- Penicillin V 250mg tablets. Take four tablets twice a day for 10 days; supply 80 tablets; NHS Cost £5.09.

Penicillin V solution: 62.5mg four times a day
- Age from 1 month to 11 months
- Penicillin V 125mg/5ml sol. Take 2.5ml four times a day for 10 days; supply 100 ml; NHS Cost £1.66.

Penicillin V solution: 125mg four times a day
- Age from 12 months to 5 years
- Penicillin V 125mg/5ml sol. Take one 5ml spoonful four times a day for 10 days; supply 200 ml; NHS Cost £3.32.

Penicillin V solution: 250mg four times a day
- Age from 6 to 11 years
- Penicillin V 250mg/5ml sol. Take one 5ml spoonful four times a day for 10 days; supply 200 ml; NHS Cost £4.58.

Penicillin V tablets: 500mg four times a day
- Age from 12 years onwards
- Penicillin V 250mg tablets. Take two tablets four times a day for 10 days; supply 80 tablets; NHS Cost £5.09.

Erythromycin for 7 days (rarely appropriate)

Erythromycin s/f suspension: 250mg twice a day
- Age from 1 month to 23 months
- Erythromycin 250mg/5ml sf susp. Take one 5ml spoonful twice a day for 7 days; supply 100 ml; NHS Cost £1.90.

Erythromycin s/f suspension: 500mg twice a day
- Age from 2 to 8 years
- Erythromycin 500mg/5ml sf susp. Take one 5ml spoonful twice a day for 7 days; supply 100 ml; NHS Cost £3.22.

Erythromycin s/f suspension: 1g twice a day
- Age from 9 to 11 years
- Erythromycin 500mg/5ml sf susp. Take two 5ml spoonfuls twice a day for 7 days; supply 200 ml; NHS Cost £6.44.

Erythromycin tablets: 1g twice a day
- Age from 12 years onwards
- Erythromycin 250mg e/c tablets. Take four tablets twice a day for 7 days; supply 56 tablets; NHS Cost £6.16.

Erythromycin s/f suspension: 125mg four times a day
- Age from 1 month to 23 months
- Erythromycin 125mg/5ml sf susp. Take one 5ml spoonful four times a day for 7 days; supply 200 ml; NHS Cost £2.22.

Erythromycin s/f suspension: 250mg four times a day
- Age from 2 to 8 years
- Erythromycin 250mg/5ml sf susp. Take one 5ml spoonful four times a day for 7 days; supply 200 ml; NHS Cost £3.80.

Erythromycin s/f suspension: 500mg four times a day
- Age from 9 to 11 years
- Erythromycin 500mg/5ml sf susp. Take one 5ml spoonful four times a day for 7 days; supply 200 ml; NHS Cost £6.44.

Erythromycin e/c tablets: 500mg four times a day
- Age from 12 years onwards
- Erythromycin 250mg e/c tablets. Take two tablets four times a day for 7 days; supply 56 tablets; NHS Cost £6.16.

Erythromycin for 10 days (rarely appropriate)

Erythromycin s/f suspension: 250mg twice a day
- Age from 1 month to 23 months
- Erythromycin 250mg/5ml sf susp. Take one 5ml spoonful twice a day for 10 days; supply 100 ml; NHS Cost £1.90.

Erythromycin s/f suspension: 500mg twice a day
- Age from 2 to 8 years
- Erythromycin 500mg/5ml sf susp. Take one 5ml spoonful twice a day for 10 days; supply 100 ml; NHS Cost £3.22.

Erythromycin s/f suspension: 1g twice a day
- Age from 9 to 11 years
- Erythromycin 500mg/5ml sf susp. Take two 5ml spoonfuls twice a day for 10 days; supply 200 ml; NHS Cost £6.44.

Erythromycin e/c tablets: 1g twice a day
- Age from 12 years onwards
- Erythromycin 250mg e/c tablets. Take four tablets twice a day for 10 days; supply 80 tablets; NHS Cost £8.80.

Erythromycin s/f suspension: 125mg four times a day
- Age from 1 month to 23 months
- Erythromycin 125mg/5ml sf susp. Take one 5ml spoonful four times a day for 10 days; supply 200 ml; NHS Cost £2.22.

Erythromycin s/f suspension: 250mg four times a day
- Age from 2 to 8 years
- Erythromycin 250mg/5ml sf susp. Take one 5ml spoonful four times a day for 10 days; supply 200 ml; NHS Cost £3.80.

Erythromycin s/f suspension: 500mg four times a day
- Age from 9 to 11 years
- Erythromycin 500mg/5ml sf susp. Take one 5ml spoonful four times a day for 10 days; supply 200 ml; NHS Cost £6.44.

Erythromycin e/c tablets: 500mg four times a day
- Age from 12 years onwards
- Erythromycin 250mg e/c tablets. Take two tablets four times a day for 10 days; supply 80 tablets; NHS Cost £8.80.

Extended Information

Background information

- What is it? p.1738
- How common is it? p.1738
- How do I know my patient has it? p.1738
- What else might it be? p.1738
- Complications and prognosis p.1738

What is it?

- **Sore throat is usually due to a viral infection,** often as part of an upper respiratory tract infection or flu-like illness [DTB, 1995].
- **Group A beta-haemolytic streptococcus (GABHS),** also known as *Streptococcus pyogenes*, is the most common bacterial cause of sore throat. GABHS can be isolated from up to 30% of people presenting with sore throat [DTB, 1995]. However, figures for asymptomatic carriage range from 6% to 40% [Little and Williamson, 1996].
- **Definitions:**
  - **Pharyngitis** is the term used if there is predominantly inflammation of the oropharynx but not of the tonsils.
  - **Tonsillitis** is the term used if there is inflammation of the tonsils.
  - **Laryngitis** is the term used if there are few visible signs of infection but the person complains of soreness lower down the throat, often with a hoarse voice.
- The clinical distinction between tonsillitis and pharyngitis is unclear in the literature. The condition is therefore referred to as 'sore throat'.

How common is it?

- **A GP with 2000 patients will see around 120 cases of acute throat infection every year** [MeReC, 1999]. However, most people with sore throat do not attend their GP: one UK study found that only 1 in 18 episodes of sore throat led to a GP consultation [SIGN, 1999].
- **Acute throat infections most commonly occur in children** aged 5–10 years and in young adults aged 15–25 years [MeReC, 1999].
- **Asymptomatic carriage of group A beta-haemolytic streptococcus is common,** with rates of 6–40% [Little and Williamson, 1996]. Carriers have low infectivity and are not at risk of developing complications.

How do I know my patient has it?

Symptoms

- Symptoms are usually sore throat, pain on swallowing, fever, headache, malaise, and hoarseness if there is laryngeal involvement (laryngitis).

Signs

- **Signs are commonly redness of the pharynx and tonsils, presence of exudate, enlarged tonsils, and swollen tender neck glands.** However, examination of the throat should not be attempted in people with breathing difficulty or stridor, as epiglottitis may be present (urgent admission indicated) [SIGN, 1999].
- **Clinical examination should not be relied upon to differentiate between viral and bacterial sore throat (B).** Streptococcal infection is likely, however, if a scarlet-fever rash is present (red punctate skin eruption that has a sandpaper-like texture and is prominent in skin creases; usually begins on the chest and spreads to the abdomen and extremities; a flushed face with circumoral pallor; and a 'strawberry tongue').

Investigations

- **Throat swabs should not be carried out routinely in sore throat (B).** Throat swabs cannot differentiate between infection and carriage, they have poor sensitivity, results take up to 48 hours to be reported, and the test is relatively expensive [Little and Williamson, 1996; MeReC, 1999; SIGN, 1999]. The results of throat swabs vary according to technique, culture site, and culture conditions [Cooper et al, 2001]. However, swabs may be useful in high-risk groups, to guide choice of treatment if treatment failure occurs (see the section on antibiotics in *Management issues*).
- **Rapid antigen tests should not be carried out routinely in sore throat (B).** Rapid antigen tests detect the presence of group A streptococcal antigen on a throat swab and produce results within a few minutes. However, they have poor sensitivity and make little impact on prescribing decisions [SIGN, 1999; Cooper et al, 2001].

What else might it be?

- **Infectious mononucleosis** (glandular fever)
- **Epiglottitis** (requires urgent admission)
- **Thyroiditis**
- **Gonococcal pharyngitis** (rare)
- **Diphtheria** (very rare in the UK)
- **Neutropaenia** (ensure the person is not on medication known to cause immunosuppression)

Complications and prognosis

Complications

- Otitis media
- Sinusitis
- Peritonsillar abscess (quinsy)
- Cervical adenitis
- Scarlet fever
- Streptococcal toxic shock syndrome (rare)

S

Non-suppurative complications (these are both rare in developed countries, but are still a problem in developing countries):

- Rheumatic fever
- Post-streptococcal glomerulonephritis

[McKerrow, 2003; Del Mar et al, 2004]

Prognosis

Sore throat is a self-limiting condition. Symptoms resolve within 3 days in 40% of people and within 1 week in 85% of people, irrespective of whether or not the sore throat is due to a streptococcal infection [Del Mar et al, 2004].

Management issues

General issues p.1739
What pain relief should be advised for a person with a sore throat? p.1739
When should an antibiotic be prescribed for a person with a sore throat? p.1739
When should tonsillectomy be considered for a person with recurrent sore throat? p.1739
What are the indications for referral of a person with sore throat to a specialist? p.1740

General issues

Sore throat is a self-limiting condition. Symptoms resolve within 3 days in 40% of people and within 1 week in 85% of people, irrespective of whether or not the sore throat is due to a streptococcal infection [Del Mar et al, 2004].

Explanation, reassurance, and advice on symptomatic treatment is frequently all that is necessary when a person consults with a sore throat, as only a third of people want or expect an antibiotic [Butler et al, 1998]. Presentation with sore throat may be part of a wider agenda [SIGN, 1999].

Prescription of an antibiotic increases re-attendance rates for further episodes of sore throat [Little et al, 1997]. There is also the risk of adverse effects, and there is concern that indiscriminate prescribing increases bacterial resistance in the community [DH and SMAC, 1998].

What pain relief should be advised for a person with a sore throat?

Paracetamol or ibuprofen is the analgesic drug of choice in sore throat. A systematic review found that paracetamol or nonsteroidal anti-inflammatory drugs reduce the pain of sore throat compared with placebo [Del Mar and Glasziou, 2003].

Gargles have been poorly researched and no specific recommendations can be made regarding their use. Anecdotally, gargling with salt water or aspirin is reported to relieve pain in some people. One small study found that benzydamine as a gargle for sore throat resulted in significantly greater relief of pain and dysphagia at 24 hours than did placebo, but this requires confirmation [SIGN, 1999].

When should an antibiotic be prescribed for a person with a sore throat?

Antibiotics should not be used for symptomatic relief in sore throat (A). A Cochrane systematic review found that the absolute benefit of antibiotics was modest. The maximum benefit was seen by day 3 of treatment, with an average reduction in illness time of 1 day. The overall reduction in illness time was 16 hours for the first week. The effectiveness of antibiotics was greater in those with throat swabs positive for *Streptococcus*. For every four people with confirmed streptococcal throat infection given antibiotics, one extra person had their symptoms resolved by day 3 compared with those taking placebo (NNT = 4). Without treatment, however, symptoms had disappeared within 3 days in 40% of people and by 1 week in 85% of people, irrespective of whether they were streptococcal-positive or not. The effect of antibiotics on symptom severity was uncertain [Del Mar et al, 2004].

- **The prevention of suppurative complications is not a specific indication for antibiotic therapy in sore throat (C).** Antibiotics reduce the risk of developing sinusitis, otitis media, and peritonsillar abscess (quinsy). However, the absolute risk of developing complications is low, and little actual benefit is gained from antibiotics. It is estimated that to prevent one case of acute otitis media about 200 people need to be given antibiotics [Del Mar et al, 2004].
- **Sore throat should not be treated with antibiotics specifically to prevent the development of rheumatic fever or acute glomerulonephritis (B).** Studies undertaken between 1951 and 1961 (when the incidence of rheumatic fever was much higher than it is today) showed that antibiotics decreased the risk of rheumatic fever by about 70%. More recent studies, however, have not shown any benefit from antibiotic use [DTB, 1995; Little and Williamson, 1996; SIGN, 1999; Del Mar et al, 2004]. Antibiotics have not been shown to reduce the risk of post-streptococcal glomerulonephritis.
- **The National Institute for Clinical Excellence recommends antibiotics for the following situations** [NICE, 2001]:
  - Features of marked systemic upset secondary to the acute sore throat.
  - Unilateral peritonsillitis.
  - A history of rheumatic fever.
  - An increased risk from acute infection (such as a child with diabetes mellitus or immunodeficiency).
- **Antibiotics may prevent cross-infection with group A beta-haemolytic streptococcus in closed institutions (such as barracks or boarding schools) but should not be used routinely to prevent cross-infection in the general community (B).**
- **If an antibiotic is indicated, phenoxymethylpenicillin or erythromycin (if the person is allergic to penicillin) is preferred** [Cooper et al, 2001; HPA, 2003;]
- [Schaad, 2004]. Note that ampicillin and amoxicillin almost always cause maculopapular rashes in people with glandular fever, and should therefore not be used for 'blind' treatment of a sore throat — people who develop rashes may mistakenly be labelled as penicillin-allergic.
- A 10-day course of antibiotic has been used in most studies, and is recommended to eradicate possible streptococcal infection [DTB, 1995; SIGN, 1999]. Shorter courses may be appropriate, however, as there is no good correlation between microbiological and clinical cure for relief of symptoms. The Health Protection Agency recommends either twice- or four-times-daily dosing, lasting 7–10 days for penicillin and 5–10 days for erythromycin [HPA, 2003].

When should tonsillectomy be considered for a person with recurrent sore throat?

- **Tonsillectomy** is occasionally recommended for recurrent attacks of tonsillitis. The quality of the evidence is poor (and no study has been performed in adults), but it suggests that surgery may be beneficial in selected cases [Burton et al, 2004].

- **Surgery should be considered only if the person meets all of the following criteria (C):**
  - Sore throats are due to tonsillitis.
  - The person has five or more episodes of sore throat per year.
  - Symptoms have been occurring for at least a year.
  - The episodes of sore throat are disabling and prevent normal functioning.
- This is consistent with referral advice from the National Institute for Clinical Excellence [NICE, 2001].

What are the indications for referral of a person with sore throat to a specialist?

- The National Institute for Clinical Excellence, in *Referral advice: a guide to appropriate referral from general to specialist services* [NICE, 2001], advises the following for recurrent episodes of acute sore throat in children aged up to 15 years. The referral advice is meant to encourage local health communities to discuss referral issues and enable local referral guidelines and protocols to be produced (for further information, see www.nice.org.uk).
- Almost all children with recurrent sore throat can be managed in primary care. However, children should be referred to a specialist service in the circumstances shown in Table 2, with the referral timings shown.

Table 2: Referral advice for children aged up to 15 years with recurrent episodes of acute sore throat.

Referral timing	Reason for referral
****	They have, or are suspected of having, a quinsy
****	The swelling is causing acute upper airways obstruction
****	The swelling is interfering with swallowing, causing dehydration and marked systemic upset
**	They have a history of sleep apnoea, daytime somnolence, and failure to thrive
*	They have had five or more episodes of acute sore throat in the preceding 12 months, documented by the parent or clinician, and these episodes have been severe enough to disrupt the child's normal behaviour or day-to-day activity
*	They have guttate psoriasis, which is exacerbated by recurrent tonsillitis
^	There is suspicion of a serious underlying disorder such as leukaemia

Key to referral timings: arrangements should be made so that the person:
**** is seen immediately (within a day)
*** is seen urgently (maximum wait of 2 weeks recommended, but to be agreed locally)
** is seen soon (maximum waiting time to be agreed locally)
* has a routine appointment (maximum waiting time to be agreed locally)
^ is seen within an appropriate time depending on his or her clinical circumstances (discretionary)

S

References

NHS staff in England can link, free of charge, from references to full text journals by clicking on [Full text] on the PRODIGY website.

1. Burton, M.J., Towler, B. and Glasziou, P. (2004) *Tonsillectomy versus non-surgical treatment for chronic/recurrent acute tonsillitis (Cochrane Review).* The Cochrane Library. Issue 1. Chichester, UK: John Wiley & Sons, Ltd.
2. Butler, C.C., Rollnick, S., Pill, R. et al (1998) Understanding the culture of prescribing: qualitative study of general practitioners' and patients' perceptions of antibiotics for sore throats. *British Medical Journal* 317(7159), 637–642. [Full text]
3. Cooper, R.J., Hoffman, J.R., Bartlett, J.G. et al (2001) Principles of appropriate antibiotic use for acute pharyngitis in adults: background. *Annals of Internal Medicine* 134(6), 509–517.
4. CSM (2002) Aspirin and Reye's syndrome in children up to and including 15 years of age. *Current Problems in Pharmacovigilance* 28(Apr), 4.
5. Del Mar, C. and Glasziou, P. (2003) Upper respiratory tract infection. *Clinical Evidence* 10(Dec), 1747–175
6. Del Mar, C.B., Glasziou, P.P. and Spinks, A.B. (2004 *Antibiotics for sore throat (Cochrane Review).* The Cochrane Library. Issue 2. Chichester, UK: John Wile & Sons, Ltd.
7. DH and SMAC (1998) *The path of least resistance.* Department of Health. www.dh.gov.uk [Accessed: 27 04/2004]. [Full text]
8. DTB (1995) Diagnosis and treatment of streptococca sore throat. *Drug & Therapeutics Bulletin* 33(2), 9–1
9. HPA (2003) *Management of infection guidance for primary care: for consultation and local adaptation.* Health Protection Agency. www.hpa.org.uk [Accesse 26/02/2004]. [Full text]
10. Little, P. and Williamson, I. (1996) Sore throat management in general practice. *Family Practice* 13(3 317–321.
11. Little, P., Gould, C., Williamson, I. et al (1997) Reattendance and complications in a randomised tria of prescribing strategies for sore throat: the medicalising effect of prescribing antibiotics. *British Medical Journal* 315(7104), 350–352. [Full text]
12. McKerrow, W. (2003) Tonsillitis. *Clinical Evidence* 10(Dec), 644–648.
13. MeReC (1999) Managing sore throats. *MeReC Bulletin* 10(11), 41–44.
14. NICE (2001) *Referral advice – a guide to appropriate referral from general to specialist services.* National Institute for Clinical Excellence. www.nice.org.uk [Accessed: 11/08/2002].
15. Schaad, U.B. (2004) Acute streptococcal tonsillopharyngitis: a review of clinical efficacy and bacteriological eradication. *Journal of International Medical Research* 32(1), 1–13.
16. SIGN (1999) *Management of sore throat and indications for tonsillectomy: a national clinical guideline.* Report No. 34. Scottish Intercollegiate Guidelines Network. www.sign.ac.uk [Accessed: 14/ 06/2004].

:vidence grading

/idence grading is from the Scottish Intercollegiate uideline Network (SIGN) guideline on *Management of re throat and indications for tonsillectomy* (1999). The idence grading is as follows:

rength of evidence

— Evidence obtained from meta-analysis of randomized ntrolled trials.

— Evidence obtained from at least one randomized ntrolled trial.

a — Evidence obtained from at least one well-designed ntrolled study without randomization.

o — Evidence obtained from at least one other type of ell-designed quasi-experimental study.

[— Evidence obtained from well-designed non- :perimental descriptive studies, such as comparative udies, correlation studies, and case studies.

IV — Evidence from expert committee reports or opinions and/or clinical experiences of respected authorities.

Strength of recommendation

A — Requires at least one randomized controlled trial as part of a body of literature of overall good quality and consistency addressing the specific recommendation. (Evidence levels Ia, Ib)

B — Requires the availability of well- conducted clinical studies but no randomized clinical trials on the topic of recommendation.
(Evidence levels IIa, IIb, III)

C — Requires evidence obtained from expert committee reports or opinions and /or clinical experiences of respected authorities. Indicates an absence of directly applicable clinical studies of good quality.
(Evidence level IV)

S

PRODIGY GUIDANCE

Sprains and strains

Last revised in July 2005
www.prodigy.nhs.uk/guidance.asp?gt=Sprains and strains

Applies to people over the age of 5 years

This guidance covers the immediate management of the common acute sprains and strains. A brief overview of prevention strategies is given.

This guidance does not cover the management of completely ruptured tendons or ligaments, or soft-tissue problems that are chronic or recurrent, or problems associated with a strain or sprain such as fracture or dislocation. It also does not cover the management of back strains.

There is separate PRODIGY guidance for cervical and lumbar strains covered in *Neck pain* and *Back pain — lower*. This version of the guidance has limited details on the evidence to support the recommendations. The version that includes a detailed review of the evidence is available on request from prodigy-enquiries@schin.ncl.ac.uk.

Goals

- To ease pain, reduce swelling, and allow the person to return to pre-injury level of joint function in the shortest possible time
- To minimize the need for drug therapy
- To promptly refer people who need special assessment or treatment

Contents

Sprains and strains

Which therapy?

- **Severe sprain or strain (e.g. suspected complete rupture)**
  - Refer immediately.
- **Mild to moderate sprain or strain**
  - Advise rest, ice, compression, and elevation ('RICE') for the first 24–48 hours, then start active mobilization.
    - **Rest** for up to 2 days, then start active movement; movement should be within the limits of pain.
    - **Ice:** for 10–30 minutes, not directly to skin (avoid cold injury). A bag of frozen peas is ideal; allow adequate time for warming between applications. Repeat as often as desired (e.g. every 2 hours).
    - **Compression** with an elastic bandage provides comfort and support without constricting nerves or blood flow. A compression bandage may be helpful well beyond the period of acute swelling.
    - **Elevation** minimizes swelling.
  - **Early mobilization**
    - Advise the person to exercise into the range of discomfort, aiming to improve the range of movement a little every day.
    - **Sprained ankle:** advise that balance is likely to be affected and that, once the pain has settled, practising balancing on the injured leg, with the eyes shut, is useful.
- **Options for the management of symptomatic relief include:**
  - **Paracetamol** — the preferred option for pain relief.
  - **An NSAID** — the preferred option if rapid return to work or sport is important.
  - **Paracetamol combined with an NSAID** — an option if either drug alone does not provide adequate pain relief.
  - **Paracetamol combined with codeine** — if paracetamol alone is insufficient.
  - **Elasticated tubular bandage** — may be preferred if firm compression is needed.
    - Other products marketed as providing additional comfort, support, and compression may be preferr[ed] by the person, but are not available on an F10 prescription.
- **Domestic violence**
  - Be alert to the possibility of domestic violence.
  - If suspected, see the victim alone so that the relevant history, examination, and consultation can be done i[n] a supportive manner.

Practical prescribing points

For further information, please see the *Medicines Compendium* (www.medicines.org.uk) or the *British National Formulary* (www.bnf.org).

Nonsteroidal anti-inflammatory drugs

- **Only one NSAID should be prescribed at a time.**
- **NSAIDs may worsen asthma, hypertension, renal impairment, or heart failure.**
- Do not give oral ibuprofen, diclofenac, or naproxen without gastroprotection if there is a history of peptic ulceration.
- **Pregnancy and breastfeeding:** use paracetamol if possible. If an NSAID is essential, ibuprofen may be us[ed] during breastfeeding and before 30 weeks of pregnancy.
- **People with cardiovascular disease:** ibuprofen may reduce the cardiovascular protective effect of low-dose aspirin.
- **In people with risk factors for gastrointestinal NSAID complications:**
  - Use paracetamol (with or without codeine) instead of a NSAID if possible.
  - Or, use gastroprotection (a PPI or full-dose misoprostol) combined with a standard NSAID.
  - Or, consider using a topical nonsteroidal anti-inflammatory drug.
- **Risk factors for gastrointestinal NSAID complications include:**
  - Age of 65 years and over.
  - Previous history of gastroduodenal ulcer, gastrointestinal (GI) bleeding, or gastroduodenal perforation.
  - Concomitant use of medications that are known to increase the likelihood of upper-GI adverse events, e.g. anticoagulants, aspirin (even a low dose), and corticosteroids.
  - Presence of serious comorbidity, such as cardiovascular disease, renal or hepatic impairment, diabetes, or hypertension.

S

- Requirement for prolonged duration of NSAID use.
- Use of maximum recommended doses of NSAIDs.

odeine

Codeine may cause nausea, vomiting, and drowsiness. Constipation is also another common adverse effect, although, with short-term use, there may not be a need for additional laxative use.

lisoprostol

Diarrhoea and abdominal pain are common. Advise women of childbearing age to use adequate contraception, since misoprostol increases the risk of miscarriage.

ollow-up advice

Follow up people with moderately severe sprains and strains when the swelling has largely gone (after about 7–10 days) to assess if referral for further treatment is indicated.

hould I refer or investigate?

efer?

eferral criteria vary according to local service provision. llow local guidelines where these exist; otherwise nsider the following criteria.

Red flags indicate a need for immediate referral:

- Unexplained deformity or swelling
- Significant weakness not due to pain
- Fever, chills, malaise
- Unexplained neurological deficit (sensory or motor)
- Pulmonary or vascular compromise
- Suspected malignancy or bleeding diathesis

Physiotherapy

- Severe injuries requiring intensive/prolonged rehabilitation
- Major soft-tissue swelling
- Functional deficit
- Where GP feels specific expertise will accelerate recovery

Orthopaedic specialist

- Severe sprain with joint laxity (i.e. probable complete rupture of joint ligament)
- Severe muscle strain (i.e. probable complete rupture of muscle)
- Fracture (definite or suspected)
- Swelling of a joint persisting more than 10 days — may have intra-articular pathology
- A sprain or strain that seriously impedes ability to function at work or competitive sport
- Recurrent sprains or strains

Sports medicine specialist

- For people involved in professional or competitive sport
- If diagnosis in doubt
- Slow progress of recovery or rehabilitation
- Deteriorating symptoms
- To discuss appropriate imaging

Domestic violence.

- People subjected to domestic violence should be referred to the appropriate service(s) with an urgency appropriate to the situation.

nvestigate?

If a fracture is suspected, an X-ray is indicated.
Use the Ottawa ankle and knee rules to help decide if the likelihood of a fracture in the ankle or knee is high enough to order X-rays.

- **Ottawa ankle rules:**
  - **An ankle X-ray series** is indicated for someone with an ankle injury and either:
    - Bone tenderness at the posterior edge or tip of either the lateral or medial malleolus, *or*
    - Inability to bear weight both immediately after the injury, and for at least four steps when examined
  - **A foot X-ray series** is indicated for someone with an ankle injury and pain in the midfoot and any of the following:
    - Bone tenderness at the base of the fifth metatarsal
    - Bone tenderness at the navicular
    - Inability to bear weight, both immediately and when examined
- **Ottawa knee rules:**
  - **A knee X-ray series** is indicated for people with a knee injury and any of the following:
    - Age 55 or older
    - Isolated tenderness of patella (no bone tenderness of knee other than patella)
    - Tenderness of head of fibula
    - Inability to flex to 90 degrees
    - Inability to bear weight both immediately and in the emergency department for four steps

Patient information leaflets

The following PILs are available at www.prodigy.nhs.uk

- Anti-inflammatory Painkillers
- Sprains

Shared decision making

- A sprain is an injury to a ligament. It heals usually within 1 to 6 weeks, but complete healing may take several months.
- **Painkillers** taken regularly, such as paracetamol, will usually ease the pain.
- **Additional painkillers,** such as codeine, may be needed if pain is severe.
- **An anti-inflammatory medicine,** such as ibuprofen, may be useful for 1–2 weeks. It helps ease pain and reduce inflammation if taken regularly.
- Adverse effects sometimes occur with anti-inflammatory medicines. Stomach pain and bleeding from the stomach are the most serious. Some people with asthma, high blood pressure, kidney failure, or heart failure may not be able to take anti-inflammatory medication.
- **Remember RICE,** straight after a sprain to reduce inflammation and swelling:
  - **Rest** the joint for 2 days. Then gradually get it moving and as active as possible.
  - **Ice:** press it on for 10–30 minutes as soon as possible after injury. Wrap ice cubes in a plastic bag to make an ice pack. A bag of frozen peas is an alternative. (Do not put ice directly next to skin, as it may cause an 'ice-burn'.)
  - **Compression:** an elastic bandage is useful for 2 days.
  - **Elevation:** rest a swollen ankle or knee at or above hip level as much as possible. A swollen hand or wrist can be elevated in a sling.
- **Physiotherapy** is an option if symptoms do not improve quickly.

Drug rationale

Drugs not included

- **Standard nonsteroidal anti-inflammatory drugs (NSAIDs) other than ibuprofen, diclofenac and naproxen** are excluded, because they are associated with a higher risk of gastrointestinal adverse events [CSM, 1994; Henry et al, 1996; CSM, 2002].

- **Cyclo-oxygenase (COX)-2 inhibitors:** they are not included, although they may have a role in people at increased risk of adverse gastrointestinal events. They are not specifically licensed for use in sprains or strains, and international regulatory authorities are currently reviewing the cardiovascular safety and cardio-renal events for all coxib NSAIDs [EMEA, 2004], precipitated by the withdrawal of rofecoxib.
- **Rubefacients:** no randomized controlled trials (RCTs) have compared a topical rubefacient with another active treatment and there is therefore little evidence to support their efficacy in soft-tissue injuries [Mason et al, 2004b].
- **Weak opioids other than codeine** have either not been shown to be more effective than higher-dose codeine, or are more expensive.
- **Modified-release NSAIDs** are relatively expensive, and there is no evidence that they show an improvement in efficacy or safety over standard NSAID treatment.
- **Strong opioid analgesics** are unsuitable. It is unlikely that the pain of a simple sprain will not be controlled by other measures, and inappropriate use of these drugs may risk dependence [BNF 48, 2004].
- **Low-dose weak opioids with paracetamol (combination products)** — e.g. co-codamol 8/500 and co-dydramol 10/500 — do not allow flexible titration of analgesic effect. There is no evidence that these offer any clinical benefit over paracetamol alone. They have sub-therapeutic doses of opioid, but may cause opioid adverse effects (e.g. constipation) [MeReC, 2000; BNF 48, 2004].
- **High-dose weak opioids with paracetamol (combination products)** — e.g. co-codamol 30/500 — should only be used when the need for analgesia has been carefully titrated, and the combined product exactly matches the person's requirements [De Craen et al, 1996; MeReC, 2000].
- **Co-proxamol** (dextropropoxyphene 32.5 mg/paracetamol 325 mg) has been shown to be no more effective as an analgesic than paracetamol alone. In addition, overdosage with co-proxamol is complicated by respiratory depression and acute heart failure [Medicines Resource, 1995; DTB, 1998; MeReC, 2000].
- **Light support compression bandages** such as crepe bandages are used to provide support for mild sprains and joints, but they have unproven benefit and people may not find them easy to use.

Drugs included

S

- **Paracetamol** is an effective and preferred analgesia if used regularly. It is generally well tolerated (but is dangerous in overdose) and is inexpensive whether prescribed or purchased over the counter. Regular analgesia is preferable to 'as required'.
- **Standard nonsteroidal anti-inflammatory drugs (NSAIDS): ibuprofen, diclofenac, and naproxen** have a good balance of efficacy against adverse effect profile [CSM, 1994; Henry et al, 1996; CSM, 2002].
  - Consider prescribing an NSAID for someone who needs to return as soon as possible to full function at work or competitive sport, as the NSAID may hasten the healing process.
  - NSAIDs must be taken regularly for optimal analgesic and anti-inflammatory effect.
  - Ibuprofen is recommended as first choice, as it has the lowest risk of adverse effects.
  - Naproxen and diclofenac have intermediate risk and should be considered if ibuprofen is ineffective.
  - NSAIDs can be combined with paracetamol if required.
- **Codeine (in combination with regular paracetamol)** car be helpful when paracetamol alone is insufficient [De Craen et al, 1996]. Paracetamol and codeine should be prescribed as two separate medicines and the doses of each drug individually titrated to the person's needs.
- **Topical NSAIDs: diclofenac, felbinac, ibuprofen, ketoprofen, and piroxicam are available as topical formulations.** Topical NSAIDs have been found to be n more effective than oral NSAIDs [Mason et al, 2004a], but a short course could be considered if an NSAID is required and someone is at high risk of peptic ulceratio or bleeding with an oral NSAID, and therefore needs gastroprotection.
- **Elasticated tubular compression bandages** are convenie for people to use and are popular. Elasticated tubular bandaging may be more convenient for people to use. A range of different-sized bandages available on the NHS are included, and can also be purchased over the counter.
- **Proton pump inhibitors (PPIs): esomeprazole, lansoprazole, omeprazole, and pantoprazole** are license for prevention of NSAID-induced gastroduodenal ulceration [BNF 48, 2004]. PPIs reduce the risk of endoscopic ulcers, but there is a lack of data on prevention of ulcer complications [Rostom et al, 2002] However, they are generally considered to be the preferred choice for gastroprotection, as they are well tolerated compared with misoprostol.
- **Misoprostol** (a prostaglandin analogue): this is licensed for prevention of NSAID-induced gastroduodenal ulceration [BNF 48, 2004]. It reduces the risk of endoscopic ulcers and has also been shown to reduce th risk of ulcer complications [Rostom et al, 2002; North England Dyspepsia Guideline Development Group, 2004]. It is less well tolerated than PPIs because of GI adverse effects, particularly diarrhoea.

Prescriptions

Paracetamol or codeine

Paracetamol s/f susp: 120mg to 240mg up to four times a day

- Age from 5 to 5 years
- Paracetamol 120mg/5ml s/f susp. Take one to two 5ml spoonfuls every 4 to 6 hours when required for pain relief. Maximum of 4 doses in 24 hours; supply 300 ml NHS Cost £1.30; OTC Cost £2.29.

Paracetamol s/f susp: 250mg to 500mg up to four times day

- Age from 6 to 11 years
- Paracetamol 250mg/5ml s/f susp. Take one to two 5ml spoonfuls every 4 to 6 hours when required for pain relief. Maximum of 4 doses in 24 hours; supply 300 ml NHS Cost £1.70; OTC Cost £3.00.

Paracetamol tablets: 500mg to 1g up to four times a day

- Age from 12 to 15 years
- Paracetamol 500mg tablets. Take one to two tablets every 4 to 6 hours when required for pain relief. Maximum of 8 tablets in 24 hours; supply 50 tablets; NHS Cost £0.37; OTC Cost £0.66.

Paracetamol tablets: 1g up to four times a day

- Age from 16 years onwards
- Paracetamol 500mg tablets. Take two tablets every 4 to 6 hours when required for pain relief. Maximum of 8 tablets in 24 hours; supply 100 tablets; NHS Cost £0.7 OTC Cost £1.31.

d on if required: codeine 30-60mg up to four times a y

- Age from 16 years onwards
- Codeine 30mg tablets. Take one to two tablets every 4 to 6 hours when required for pain relief. Maximum of 8 tablets in 24 hours; supply 30 tablets; NHS Cost £1.45.

racetamol 500mg tablets + codeine 30mg tablets

- Age from 16 years onwards
- Paracetamol 500mg tablets. Take two tablets every 4 to 6 hours when required for pain relief. Maximum of 8 tablets in 24 hours; supply 100 tablets; NHS Cost £0.74; OTC Cost £1.31.
- Codeine 30mg tablets. Take one to two tablets every 4 to 6 hours when required for pain relief. Maximum of 8 tablets in 24 hours; supply 30 tablets; NHS Cost £1.45.

SAIDs

uprofen s/f susp: 100mg three to four times a day

- Age from 5 to 7 years
- Ibuprofen 100mg/5ml s/f susp. Take one 5ml spoonful 3 to 4 times a day when required for pain relief. Do not exceed the stated dose; supply 150 ml; NHS Cost £2.73; OTC Cost £4.81.

uprofen s/f susp: 200mg three to four times a day

- Age from 8 to 11 years
- Ibuprofen 100mg/5ml s/f susp. Take two 5ml spoonfuls 3 to 4 times a day when required for pain relief. Do not exceed the stated dose; supply 300 ml; NHS Cost £5.62; OTC Cost £9.91.

uprofen tablets: 400mg three times a day

- Age from 12 years onwards
- Ibuprofen 400mg tablets. Take one tablet three times a day; supply 42 tablets; NHS Cost £1.23; OTC Cost £2.17.

clofenac sodium e/c tablets: 50mg three times a day

- Age from 16 years onwards
- Diclofenac 50mg e/c tablets. Take one tablet three times a day; supply 42 tablets; NHS Cost £1.78.

proxen tablets: 500mg twice a day

- Age from 16 years onwards
- Naproxen 500mg tablets. Take one tablet twice a day; supply 28 tablets; NHS Cost £1.83.

I protection: ONLY if at high risk of NSAID-duced ulcer

neprazole capsules: 20mg once a day

- Age from 16 years onwards
- Omeprazole 20mg capsules. Take one capsule once a day; supply 14 capsules; NHS Cost £6.38.

neprazole tablets: 20mg once a day

- Age from 16 years onwards
- Omeprazole 20mg tablets. Take one tablet once a day; supply 14 tablets; NHS Cost £6.38.

nsoprazole capsules: 15mg each morning

- Age from 16 years onwards
- Lansoprazole 15mg capsules. Take one capsule each morning (on an empty stomach); supply 14 capsules; NHS Cost £6.46.

nsoprazole capsules: 30mg each morning

- Age from 16 years onwards
- Lansoprazole 30mg capsules. Take one capsule each morning (on an empty stomach); supply 14 capsules; NHS Cost £11.82.

ntoprazole e/c tablets: 20mg once a day

- Age from 16 years onwards
- Pantoprazole 20mg e/c tablets. Take one tablet once a day; supply 14 tablets; NHS Cost £6.16.

Esomeprazole tablets: 20mg once a day

- Age from 16 years onwards
- Esomeprazole 20mg tablets. Take one tablet once a day; supply 14 tablets; NHS Cost £9.25.

Lansoprazole orodispersible tablets: 15mg each morning

- Age from 16 years onwards
- Lansoprazole 15mg orodisp tabs. Take one tablet each morning (on an empty stomach); supply 14 tablets; NHS Cost £5.43.

Lansoprazole orodispersible tablets: 30mg each morning

- Age from 16 years onwards
- Lansoprazole 30mg orodisp tabs. Take one tablet each morning (on an empty stomach); supply 14 tablets; NHS Cost £9.94.

Misoprostol tablets: 200micrograms four times a day

- Age from 16 years onwards
- Misoprostol 200microgram tabs. Take one tablet four times a day; supply 60 tablets; NHS Cost £10.03.

Topical NSAIDs

Diclofenac 1% gel

- Age from 12 years onwards
- Diclofenac 1% gel. Apply 2 to 2.5 cm (1 inch) to the affected area 3 to 4 times a day for up to 2 weeks; supply 100 grams; NHS Cost £7.00.

Felbinac 3% gel

- Age from 12 years onwards
- Felbinac 3% gel. Apply 2.5cm (1 inch) to the affected area 2 to 4 times a day for up to 2 weeks; supply 100 grams; NHS Cost £7.00.

Felbinac 3.17% foam

- Age from 12 years onwards
- Felbinac 3.17% foam. Apply 2.5cm (1 inch) to the affected area 2 to 4 times a day for up to 2 weeks; supply 100 grams; NHS Cost £7.00.

Ibuprofen 5% cream

- Age from 12 years onwards
- Ibuprofen 5% cream. Apply 4 to 10cm (1.5 to 4 inches) to the affected area 3 to 4 times a day for up to 2 weeks; supply 100 grams; NHS Cost £6.21; OTC Cost £10.95.

Ibuprofen 5% gel

- Age from 12 years onwards
- Ibuprofen 5% gel. Apply 4 to 10cm (1.5 to 4 inches) to the affected joint 3 to 4 times a day for up to 2 weeks; supply 100 grams; NHS Cost £5.31; OTC Cost £7.97.

Ibuprofen 5% mousse

- Age from 12 years onwards
- Ibuprofen 5% mousse. Shake the container and then apply 1 to 2g (1 to 2 golf-ball sized amounts of mousse in the hand) to the affected area 3 to 4 times a day for 2 weeks; supply 125 grams; NHS Cost £6.12; OTC Cost £10.79.

Ketoprofen 2.5% gel

- Age from 12 years onwards
- Ketoprofen 2.5% gel. Apply 4 to 7cm (2 to 3 inches) to the affected area 2 to 4 times a day for up to 10 days; supply 100 grams; NHS Cost £5.89.

Piroxicam 0.5% gel

- Age from 12 years onwards
- Piroxicam 0.5% topical gel. Apply 3cm (about 1 and 1/4 inches) to the affected area 3 to 4 times a day for up to 2 weeks; supply 112 grams; NHS Cost £6.01.

Elasticated tubular bandages

Elasticated tubular bandage: size C (6.75cm x 1m)

- Age from 5 years onwards
- Elasticat tubular bandage C 1m. Use as directed; supply 1 1m bandage; NHS Cost £1.09; OTC Cost £1.92.

Elasticated tubular bandage: size D (7.5cm x 1m)
- Age from 5 years onwards
- Elasticat tubular bandage D 1m. Use as directed; supply 1 1m bandage; NHS Cost £1.09; OTC Cost £1.92.

Elasticated tubular bandage: size E (8.75cm x 1m)
- Age from 5 years onwards
- Elasticat tubular bandage E 1m. Use as directed; supply 1 1m bandage; NHS Cost £1.14; OTC Cost £1.94.

Elasticated tubular bandage: size F (10cm x 1m)
- Age from 5 years onwards
- Elasticat tubular bandage F 1m. Use as directed; supply 1 1m bandage; NHS Cost £1.14; OTC Cost £1.94.

Elasticated tubular bandage: size G (12cm x 1m)
- Age from 5 years onwards
- Elasticat tubular bandage G 1m. Use as directed; supply 1 1m bandage; NHS Cost £1.40; OTC Cost £2.30.

Extended Information

Background information

- What is it? p.1746
- How common is it? p.1746
- How do I assess someone with a sprain or strain? p.1747
- What else might it be? p.1748
- Complications and prognosis p.1748

What is it?

Sprains and strains are soft-tissue injuries of ligaments and muscles.

What is a sprain?

A sprain is an injury to a ligament.

- The degree of the sprain is graded according to the extent of damage to, and integrity of, the ligament.
- **American Medical Association classification of sprains:**
  - **Grade 1 sprain:** no gross damage to collagen fibres; therefore no laxity is present.
  - **Grade 2 sprain:** partial tear of ligament; some degree of laxity, but without discontinuity of the ligament.
  - **Grade 3 sprain:** complete tear of ligament; abnormal joint laxity, and no discernible end-point to this laxity.
- Classification of sprains, although widely quoted, can be hard to apply in practice, particularly in the first few days when pain, swelling, and muscle tension make clinical examination difficult [Dutch College of General Practitioners, 2000]. This guidance thus uses the terms 'severe' and 'mild to moderate' to classify sprains that, on examination in primary care, are likely to involve complete or incomplete ligamentous rupture.
- Table 1 outlines the ligaments that are injured in sprains of commonly affected joints.

What is a strain?

A strain is an injury to a muscle.

- A muscle strain (or 'pull') is a stretching or tearing of muscle fibres. Most muscle strains happen for one of two reasons: either the muscle has been stretched beyond its limits or it has been forced to contract too strongly. Muscle strains are graded depending on the severity of muscle fibre damage [Jarvinen et al, 2000]:
  - **Grade 1 strain.** This is a mild strain; only a few muscle fibres are stretched or torn. Although the injured muscle is tender and painful, it has normal strength.

Table 1: Ligaments injured in sprains of commonly affected joints.

Sprain	Ligament
Ankle sprain	Lateral ligaments of the ankle: • Anterior talofibular ligament — usually involved • Fibulocalcaneal ligament — sometimes involved • Posterior talofibular ligament — rarely involved
High ankle sprain	The ligament that joins the distal tibia and fibula (the syndesmosis)
Knee sprain	Anterior cruciate ligament (most common) Posterior cruciate ligament Medial collateral ligament Lateral collateral ligament (least common)
Thumb	Ulnar collateral ligament

  - **Grade 2 strain.** This is a moderate strain, with a greater number of injured fibres and more severe muscle pain and tenderness. There is also mild swelling, noticeable loss of strength, and sometimes bruise.
  - **Grade 3 strain.** This strain tears the muscle all the w through, sometimes producing a 'pop' sensation as t muscle rips into two separate pieces or shears away from its tendon.
- Classification of strains can be hard to apply in practic when pain, swelling, and muscle tension make clinical examination difficult. This guidance thus uses the term 'severe' and 'mild to moderate' to classify strains that, examination in primary care, are likely to involve complete or incomplete muscle rupture.

[Garrick and Webb, 1999; Schenck, 1999]

How common is it?

Ankle sprains

- **Ankle sprains are the most common form of soft-tissu injury treated in primary care.** About 50% of ankle sprains occur while participating in sport [Dutch Colle of General Practitioners, 2000].
- The annual incidence rate of people in England presenting to Accident and Emergency (A&E) departments with a sprained ankle is about 6 per 100C About 14% of these were classed as severe [Bridgman al, 2003].
- More than three-quarters of ankle injuries are spraine ankles [Dutch College of General Practitioners, 2000].
- The proportion of sprained ankles with ruptured ligaments varied from 10% to 20% in Dutch casualty departments [Dutch College of General Practitioners, 2000].

Strains

- **Muscle strains are the most common injury sustained i sport,** accounting for up to 55% of such injuries. They are especially common in sports that require sprinting jumping [Jarvinen et al, 2000].
- The muscles most commonly strained are the hamstrir rectus femoris, gastrocnemius, and adductor longus (groin) muscles [Garrett, 1996].

ow do I assess someone with a sprain or train?

Ask about:

The time, circumstances, and kind of trauma experienced, including its force and direction.
Onset and development of symptoms such as pain, swelling, bruising, loss of function, heat, a sense of instability — instability can indicate a significant sprain.
Experiencing a pop or snap at the time of the injury — can signify a ruptured ligament or fractured bone.
Any predisposing or aggravating conditions such as epilepsy, anti-coagulant treatment, haemophilia.
Previous episodes, their management, and outcomes.
Domestic violence — if this is a possibility (for further information see the section on *Domestic violence*).

Look for:

Asymmetry, deformity, or wasting — compare the affected limb with the other.

- A strain with complete rupture usually produces a sharp break in the normal outline of the muscle, with a 'dent' under the skin where the ripped pieces of muscle have come apart.

Signs of heat over the site of the injury, and, with time, spreading to adjoining areas
Tenderness localized to the site of the damaged ligament or muscle
Swelling and bruising:

- The amount of swelling and bruising depends partly on severity and partly on the time since the injury, as it can take up to 24 hours for the full extent of bruising to become apparent.
- Muscle strain often results in a large haematoma.
  - Intramuscular haematoma: bleeding is contained within the muscle sheath, resulting in pain and localized swelling.
  - Extramuscular haematoma: bleeding spreads through the intermuscular spaces; pain is less than that due to a intramuscular haematoma, and swelling is more diffuse.

Loss of function — initially worsens over the first few days as swelling increases

- Range of movement, active and passive
- Instability in affected joints — check all directions of movement for laxity
- Complete loss of muscle function — suggests a severe strain with complete rupture

Absence of:

- Bone tenderness
- Deformity, swelling, or asymmetry not due to the presenting sprain or strain
- Neurological deficit, sensory or motor

epeating the physical examination a few days later, when e pain and swelling have subsided, can be helpful in certaining the presence of a ruptured ligament [Dutch ollege of General Practitioners, 2000].

Ankle sprain:

- Rupture of the lateral ligament complex should be considered if there is:
  - Pain during palpation of the anterior side of the lateral malleolus, *and*
  - Visible bruising *or* laxity on pulling heel forward

nvestigate

X-rays — arrange only if a fracture needing specific treatment is suspected or needs to be excluded.
he 'Ottawa ankle rules' and 'Ottawa knee rules' are idely used to guide the decision on whether or not to rder X-rays of an injured ankle or knee.

- **Ottawa ankle rules**
  - **An ankle X-ray series** is indicated for someone with an ankle injury and either:
    - Bone tenderness at the posterior edge or tip of either the lateral or medial malleolus, *or*
    - Inability to bear weight both immediately after the injury and for four steps when examined
  - **A foot X-ray series** is indicated for someone with an ankle injury, pain in the midfoot, and any of the following:
    - Bone tenderness at the base of the fifth metatarsal
    - Bone tenderness of the navicular (palpate the 'N spot' on the dorsum of the foot, about 3–4 cm distal and anterior to the medial malleolus, in line with the great toe)
    - Inability to bear weight, both immediately and when examined
  - **Tips for accurate usage of the ankle rules:**
    - When assessing a person with ankle injury, the clinician has to decide whether to order an ankle series, a foot series, or both.
    - Begin by palpating away from tender areas. For example, the proximal fibula and the forefoot, are usually non-painful.
    - Next, assess swollen areas, such as over the anterior talofibular ligament.
    - Finally, palpate the posterior edge of the distal 6 cm of the fibula and the posterior edge of the distal medial malleolus. If the person has no bone tenderness, then assess ability to bear weight. Ask the person to stand up and attempt to take four steps, transferring weight twice onto each foot. If they can transfer weight they are regarded as being able to bear weight even if they limp.
  - Evidence for the Ottawa ankle rules is reviewed below.
- **Ottawa knee rules**
  - **A knee X-ray series** is indicated for people with a substantial knee injury and any of the following:
    - Age 55 years or older
    - Isolated tenderness of patella (no bone tenderness of knee other than patella)
    - Tenderness of head of fibula
    - Inability to flex to 90 degrees
    - Inability to bear weight, both immediately and in the emergency department, for four steps
  - **Tips for accurate usage of Ottawa knee rules:**
    - Tenderness of the patella only counts if it is the only area of the bone tenderness in the knee
    - Inability to bear weight means the person is unable to transfer weight twice onto each leg, regardless of limping
  - Evidence for the Ottawa knee rules is reviewed below.

[Ottawa Health Research Institute, 1999a; Ottawa Health Research Institute, 1999b; Schenck, 1999]

Domestic violence

- **Be alert to the possibility of domestic violence.** Markers for undisclosed domestic violence include:
  - Delay in presenting
  - Frequent appointments for vague complaints; missed appointments
  - Attempts to conceal injuries, or to minimize the extent of injuries
  - Excessive fear, anxiety, depression, distress
  - History of psychiatric illness or alcohol/drug dependency
  - Person is always accompanied by partner; person is passive or afraid of partner; partner is aggressive, overly-dominant
  - History of loss of consciousness

  - Injuries inconsistent with the explanation; injuries to the face, hands, or abdomen; multiple injuries; fractures
  - Pregnancy
- If domestic violence is suspected, see the victim alone so that the relevant history, examination, and consultation can be done in as supportive a manner as possible.
- It is not easy to ask (or to be asked) about domestic violence. Helpful guidance on recognizing and managing domestic violence can be found in the Department of Health's guideline: Domestic violence: A resource manual for health care professionals [DH, 2000].

What else might it be?

- **Fracture** — bone tenderness, inability to bear weight
- **Tendon rupture** — palpable gap in course of tendon, loss of function
- **Cartilage injury** (e.g. torn meniscus in knee) — catching, locking
- **Acute arthritis** (e.g. osteoarthritis, rheumatoid arthritis) — minimal trauma, signs of arthritis
- **Nerve injury** — loss of motor and/or sensory function
- **Osteomyelitis, bone tumour** — subacute onset, atypical presentation
- **Referred pain** from other structures supplied by the same nerve root
- **Tendinitis** — tendon swollen, tender, crepitus
- **Bleeding diathesis** — minimal trauma, large haemarthrosis

Complications and prognosis

Complications

- Prolonged symptoms
- Loss of range of movement in affected joint
- Delayed return to normal level of activity
- Reduced power in the surrounding muscles with consequent muscle wasting

[Schenck, 1999]

Prognosis

There are few published data on the prognosis for sprains and strains in general.

Prognosis for a sprained ankle

- **The ultimate prognosis for a sprained ankle is good,** whatever the severity of the sprain. The time to full recovery, however, depends on the severity of the injury. [Dutch College of General Practitioners, 2000]
  - People with a mild sprain usually resume normal activities within 1–2 weeks
  - Among people with a severe ankle sprain (grade 3) who have had early mobilization:
    - Over 50% return to work in less than 3 weeks, and 90% within 6 weeks.
    - From 60% to 90% return to sport at the same level as before the injury within 12 weeks.
    - From 20% to 40% have residual complaints such as pain, stiffness, swelling, and a feeling of instability, although these do not appreciably impair function.

Management issues

- How do I manage an acute sprain or strain? p.1748
- Medicines management p.1749
- What is the supporting evidence? p.1750
- What evidence supports treatments of sprains and strains? p.1750
- What is the evidence to support diagnostic strategies? p.1752
- What evidence supports strategies to prevent sprains and strains? p.1752

How do I manage an acute sprain or strain?

The evidence to support the following recommendations is summarized in the section *What is the supporting evidence?* A version of this document containing more detailed reviews of the evidence is available on request from prodigy-enquiries@schin.ncl.ac.uk.

Overview of management of acute sprains and strains

- Assess the cause, circumstances and extent of injury.
- Refer if necessary for emergency or specialized treatment.
- Initiate short-term treatment with RICE (Rest, Ice, Compression, Elevation).
- If pain needs additional measures, treat with analgesics.
- If rapid return to work or competitive sport is important, consider using an oral nonsteroidal anti-inflammatory drug (NSAID) for anti-inflammatory effect and analgesia.
- Advise early mobilization, typically starting after 2 days' rest.
- Advise on prognosis — recovery to usual function at work and sport depends on the site and severity of the injury, as well as on levels of activity. For example, with a severe sprained ankle it can take a few weeks to be able to return to work, but several months before fully active participation in sport is possible.
- Follow up people with a severe sprain or strain when the swelling has largely subsided (after about 7–10 days) to assess if referral for further treatment is indicated.

Who needs referral?

'Red flags' for major trauma or serious underlying condition

- People who have any of the 'red flags' in the following list need immediate referral [New Zealand Guidelines Group, 2003]:
  - Unexplained deformity or swelling
  - Appreciable weakness not due to pain
  - Fever, chills, malaise
  - Unexplained neurological deficit (sensory or motor)
  - Pulmonary or vascular compromise
  - Suspected malignancy or bleeding diathesis
- People subjected to domestic violence should be referred with an urgency appropriate to the situation.
  - Markers for undisclosed domestic violence are detailed below.

Criteria for referral of sprains and strains

Consider referring people as follows (according to local service provision):

- **Physiotherapy**
  - Severe injuries requiring intensive/prolonged rehabilitation
  - Major soft-tissue swelling

S

- Functional deficit
- Where GP feels specific expertise will accelerate recovery

Orthopaedic specialist

- Joint laxity (i.e. sprain with complete rupture of joint capsule)
- Severe strain with complete rupture of muscle
- Fracture (definite or suspected)
- Swelling of a joint persisting more than 10 days — may have intra-articular pathology
- A sprain or strain that seriously impedes ability to function at work or competitive sport
- Recurrent sprains or strains

Sports medicine specialist

- For people involved in professional or competitive sport
- If diagnosis in doubt
- Slow progress of recovery or rehabilitation
- Deteriorating symptoms
- To discuss appropriate imaging

ow do I initiate treatment for an acute sprain or train?

RICE: Rest, Ice, Compression, and Elevation should be started as soon as possible

- **Rest** avoids pain from movement.
  - Stabilize, protect, and rest the affected part (e.g. with an elasticated bandage) for up to 48 hours after injury, depending on pain. Complete immobilization (e.g. by a cast) is not indicated for sprains and strains treated in primary care.
- **Ice** (i.e. cryotherapy) reduces pain.
  - Immerse the affected part in ice water for up to 10 minutes, or apply a malleable ice-pack (e.g. bag of frozen peas) for 10–30 minutes. Take care to avoid cold injury, and allow the affected part to warm up before repeating the procedure. Repeat as frequently as desired for 48 hours, e.g. every 2 hours while awake.
- **Compression** provides comfort by limiting movement, and may restrict development of swelling.
  - Apply compression (e.g. with an elasticated bandage), taking care not to constrict blood flow — if tissues distal to the compression become blue or painful, the compression should be loosened and reapplied with less tension.
  - Compression must be used with caution if peripheral arterial disease is present or suspected (e.g. in elderly persons or people with diabetes).
- **Elevation** helps to control swelling.
  - Elevate the injured part above the level of the heart, if practical.

Analgesia should be prescribed if pain control is needed — see next section for details.

'hich analgesic should I prescribe?

Paracetamol taken regularly is effective for pain relief and is the first choice in minor injuries.

NSAIDs also provide effective pain relief, but the risk of adverse effects is greater than with paracetamol.

- NSAIDs may reduce the time sprains and strains take to heal.
- Consider prescribing an NSAID for people who need to return as soon as possible to full function at work or competitive sport.
- Ibuprofen is recommended as the first choice for an NSAID, as it has the lowest risk of adverse effects [CSM, 1994; Henry et al, 1996; CSM, 2002].
- Consider giving gastroprotection (a proton pump inhibitor or misoprostol) to people at high risk of NSAID gastrointestinal adverse effects.
  - A topical NSAID is seldom indicated. A systematic review identified only three small RCTs comparing topical with oral NSAIDs and found topical NSAIDs to be no more effective than oral NSAIDs [Mason et al, 2004a]. However they have a better gastrointestinal adverse effect profile in comparison with oral NSAIDs, although local adverse effects, such as rash have been reported [Mason et al, 2004a].
- **Paracetamol combined with codeine phosphate** should be considered if paracetamol alone provides insufficient analgesia.
  - Paracetamol and codeine should be prescribed as two separate medicines and the doses of each drug individually titrated to the person's needs.
- **Paracetamol may also be combined with an NSAID** if either drug alone does not provide adequate pain relief.
- **Combining an NSAID with codeine phosphate** may be a further option worth considering. However, the greatest body of evidence is for codeine combined with paracetamol.

What subsequent treatment is advised?

- **Early mobilization.** The most important component of rehabilitation is early mobilization. Movement should be within the constraints imposed by pain. Advise the person to exercise into the range of discomfort, and to aim to improve the range of movement a little every day.
- **Stop compression.** There is little benefit after 48 hours from the use of crepe or support bandages.
- **Ultrasound, short-wave diathermy, infrared lamps, and manipulation:** these and other physical treatments are used by physiotherapists for treating sprains and strains. Referral to a chartered physiotherapist may therefore be indicated.

Is there evidence to support the use of rubefacients, ultrasound, homeopathic arnica, and oral hydrolytic enzymes?

There is no good evidence to support the use of rubefacients, ultrasound, homeopathic arnica, or oral hydrolytic enzymes in treating acute soft-tissue injuries.

What advice can I give about preventing sprains and strains?

Strategies to prevent sprains and strains are mostly based on expert opinion, as there is little good evidence from randomized controlled trials.

- **Stretching** may be beneficial. There is insufficient evidence either to endorse or to discontinue the commonly recommended practice of stretching before and/or after exercise.
- **Warm-up** may be beneficial. There is insufficient evidence either to endorse or to discontinue the commonly recommended practice of warming up before and/or after exercise.
- **Pre-season strength and endurance training** may be beneficial.
- **External ankle supports** can reduce the risk of recurrent ankle sprains.
- **Various bracing systems, boot cleat designs, and ski-boot binding systems** have been proposed for preventing **knee injuries.** However, there is no good evidence to support any of these technologies.

Medicines management

Paracetamol and codeine

- **Paracetamol** is the preferred analgesic. It is most effective if used regularly rather than 'as required'. It is safe and effective for the treatment of mild to moderate pain when used correctly, and is well tolerated at the recommended daily dose.

- **Codeine** (in combination with regular paracetamol) can be helpful when paracetamol alone is insufficient [De Craen et al, 1996].
  - Paracetamol and codeine should be prescribed separately so they can be individually titrated; combination products such as co-codamol are not recommended.
  - Codeine may cause nausea, vomiting, and drowsiness. Constipation is also another common adverse effect, although, with short-term use, there may not be a need for additional laxative use.

Nonsteroidal anti-inflammatory drugs

A full discussion on the contraindications, adverse effects, monitoring issues, and interactions of NSAIDs is beyond the scope of this guidance. For further information, see the separate PRODIGY guidance on *Nonsteroidal anti-inflammatory drugs (NSAIDs)*.

- Consider patient comorbidity when prescribing nonsteroidal anti-inflammatory drugs (NSAIDs).
- NSAIDs commonly cause gastrointestinal adverse effects, and can worsen asthma, hypertension, renal impairment, and heart failure.
- For people at high risk of gastrointestinal adverse events, we recommend the following options:
  - Use paracetamol (with or without codeine) instead of a NSAID if possible.
  - Or, use a gastroprotective agent with a standard NSAID [NICE, 2001].
  - Or, consider using a topical NSAID.
- For advice on the management of dyspepsia due to NSAIDs, see the separate PRODIGY guidance on *Dyspepsia — symptoms (uninvestigated by endoscopy)* and *Dyspepsia — proven DU, GU, or NSAID-associated ulcer*.

Compression bandages

- Crepe, cotton crepe and cotton, polyamide, and elastane bandaging all provide support without exerting undue pressure.
- Elasticated tubular bandaging may be more convenient for people to use. This can be prescribed for NHS patients and also may be purchased over the counter.
- A range of other products are marketed as providing additional comfort, support, and compression. These are not available on an F10 prescription, but can be bought over the counter, and are often recommended by sports medicine specialists.

S

What is the supporting evidence?

The evidence to support the recommendations in this guidance is summarized below. A version of this document containing more detailed reviews of the evidence is available on request from prodigy-enquiries@schin.ncl.ac.uk.

What evidence supports treatments of sprains and strains?

Abbreviations

The abbreviations listed below are used in the following sections on supporting evidence:

CI	95% confidence interval
OR	Odds ratio
RCT	Randomized controlled trial
RR	Relative risk
WMD	Weighted mean difference

Introduction

Evidence to support treatments of sprains and strains comes from relatively few randomized controlled trials (RCTs), most of which are for treatments of ankle sprains in adults. However, this evidence can often be applied to the management of other sprains and strains.

Evidence for RICE (Rest, Ice, Compression, Elevation)

RICE (Rest, Ice, Compression, Elevation) is standard first aid treatment for sprains and strains. Not many would doubt the common sense on which RICE is based, or the comfort that it provides. However, few high-quality RCTs have studied the various ways in which RICE is implemented, or its efficacy in terms of return to full function at work and sport.

Evidence for rest, immobilization, functional treatment, and surgery

- A systematic review assessed the evidence from RCTs published between 1966 and 2002 of treating acute limb injuries with rest or mobilization [Nash et al, 2004].
  - The authors concluded that there is no benefit for immobilization after acute upper or lower limb injuries in adults.
- **One Cochrane systematic review assessed methods of immobilization** for the acute sprained ankle, and compared immobilization with functional treatment methods. Functional treatments involve early mobilisation and the use of an external support (e.g. tape and/or elastic bandage or orthotic support), combined with co-ordination training. [Kerkhoffs et al, 2002a]
  - Twenty-one trials involving 2184 participants were included in the analyses
  - The review concluded that: 'functional treatment appears to be the favourable strategy for treating acute ankle sprains when compared with immobilization. However, these results should be interpreted with caution, as most of the differences are not statistically significant after exclusion of the low-quality trials. Many trials were poorly reported and there was variety amongst the functional treatments evaluated.'
- **A Cochrane systematic review compared different functional treatments** for ankle sprains [Kerkhoffs et al, 2002b].
  - Nine trials involving 892 participants were included in the analysis.
  - The review concluded that:
    - **Lace-up ankle support** seems to be effective in reducing swelling in the short term, compared with semi-rigid ankle support, elastic bandage, and tape.
    - **The use of an elastic bandage has fewer complications than taping,** but seems to be associated with a slower return to work and sport, and more reported instability than with a semi-rigid ankle support.
    - Definitive conclusions are hampered by the variety of treatments used, and the inconsistency of reported follow-up times.
- **A Cochrane systematic review compared surgical and conservative treatments** for acute ankle sprains [Kerkhoffs et al, 2002c].
  - The review found 17 RCTs with a total of 1950 subjects, and concluded that there is insufficient evidence to determine the relative efficacies of surgical and conservative treatments of acute ankle sprains.

Evidence for ice, cryotherapy

- One systematic review found 22 RCTs of cryotherapy for treating soft-tissue injuries due to trauma or surgery [Bleakley et al, 2004; Hubbard and Denegar, 2004]
- The authors concluded that:

- Cryotherapy seems to be effective in reducing pain.
- There is limited evidence that cryotherapy has only minimal benefit in terms of reducing swelling and restoring function.

idence for compression

We found no systematic review of trials of compression used to treat soft-tissue injuries. We therefore conducted a rapid review: Medline was searched (1966 to October 2004) for RCTs in which compression was used to treat acute soft tissue injuries.

- **Immediate external compression.** One study investigated immediate external compression in the management of an acute muscle injury. The authors concluded that the application of a maximum compression bandage within 5 minutes of a traumatic muscle injury did not significantly reduce the size of the haematoma nor significantly shorten the time to complete subjective recovery, compared with no immediate treatment. [Thorsson et al, 1997]
- **Elasticated tubular bandage.** One randomized controlled trial investigated the effectiveness of double Tubigrip in grade 2 and 3 ankle sprains [Lewis and Atkinson, 2002]. Subjects were all given analgesia and rehabilitation advice; half were randomly chosen to be given a double Tubigrip bandage in addition. The study found no statistically significant difference between the two groups in the time to recovery.
- **Quality of compression bandage.** One study compared the effectiveness of two different qualities of compression bandage and found no significant effect on pain, swelling, or tenderness [Andersson et al, 1983].
- **Layer bandage compared with elastic adhesive tape bandage.** One study compared different methods of compression for acute ankle sprains. No statistically significant difference was observed between the differently bandaged groups with regard to clinical findings and foot volume. However, elastic adhesive tape bandage caused significantly more complications, mainly excessive compression, irritation of the skin, or rash [Viljakka and Rokkanen, 1983].

idence for elevation

We found no systematic review of trials of elevation used to treat soft-tissue injuries. We therefore conducted a rapid review. Medline was searched (1966 to October 2004) for RCTs in which elevation was used to treat acute soft-tissue injuries. No trial was found.

vidence for NSAIDs used to treat acute sprains nd strains

s common practice to use NSAIDs as adjunctive atment to RICE in the acute management of sprains and ains [Weiler, 1992; Schenck, 1999]. The efficacy of SAIDs used as analgesics is well-known from studies in her conditions, and the evidence is not reviewed here. owever, we sought practical answers in the literature for o clinical questions related to the management of sprains d strains:

- Does the use of NSAIDs speed recovery from sprains and strains?
- Is there a role for topical NSAIDs in treating pain due to acute sprains and strains?

ese two questions are addressed in the following tions.

es the use of NSAIDs speed recovery from sprains and ains?

It has been suggested that the anti-inflammatory properties of NSAIDs improve healing of soft tissues and thus hasten return to full function at work and sport. The rationale is that inflammation after an acute injury is harmful and that its control will speed healing [Weiler, 1992; Schenck, 1999].

- However, other plausible hypotheses are that:
  - Inflammation due to trauma aids healing, and that interfering with this process is harmful.
  - NSAIDs do not effectively control inflammation due to trauma.
  - Inflammation due to trauma resolves in a few days, so anti-inflammatory treatment could have only a marginal effect.
- We found a comprehensive review (but no systematic review) of evidence on the use of NSAIDs in soft-tissue injuries [Weiler, 1992].
- The review summarised the results of 11 double blind, placebo controlled RCTs. All studies looked at short-term (7–14 days) outcomes. The review concluded that:
  - **There is no evidence that NSAIDs delay the healing process when given soon after an injury.**
  - **Modest benefits were seen in 7 of 11 studies.**
- On searching Medline, 1996 through to October 2004 we found a further 12 RCTs of NSAIDs in which at least one outcome reflected a possible anti-inflammatory affect. The conclusions from this rapid review are that:
  - There is limited evidence of effectiveness in terms of return to functionality when NSAIDs are used to treat sprains and strains — the quality of reporting and methodology is variable and the results are not entirely consistent.
  - The size of any anti-inflammatory effect is likely to be moderate (i.e. a difference of about 1–3 days in returning to usual activities).

Is there a role for topical NSAIDs in treating pain due to acute sprains and strains?

To address the question, we searched for evidence that topical NSAIDs, when used for in soft-tissue injuries, have (i) an anti-inflammatory effect, (ii) a clinically useful analgesic effect, and (iii) an analgesic effect at least equivalent to that of oral NSAIDs.

- **What is the evidence for anti-inflammatory benefit from topical NSAIDs used to treat soft-tissue injuries?**
  - We found no review or clinical trial of topical NSAIDs used in soft-tissue injuries for anti-inflammatory benefit.
- **What is the evidence for analgesic benefit from topical NSAIDs?**
  - A systematic review found 26 RCTs of topical NSAIDs and concluded that they provide effective, safe analgesia in acute pain due to strains, sprains, and sports injuries [Mason et al, 2004a].
- **What is the evidence for topical NSAIDs providing analgesia comparable to that from oral NSAIDs?**
  - A systematic review compared the efficacy of topical and oral NSAIDs for acute pain due to soft-tissue injuries [Mason et al, 2004a].
    - The review found three trials comparing a topical NSAID with an oral NSAID, but only two trials directly compared the same topical and oral NSAID.
    - Overall rates of treatment success were similar for topical (57%) and oral (62%) NSAIDs with no statistically significant benefit (relative benefit 0.9; CI 0.8 to 1.1).

Evidence for rubefacients used to treat acute sprains and strains

- We found no systematic reviews or controlled trials of rubefacients used to treat acute sprains and strains.
- We found one systematic review (search date March 2003) of evidence for efficacy of topical rubefacients containing salicylates for the treatment of acute and chronic pain [Mason et al, 2004b].

S

- The review concluded that treatments with salicylate rubefacients were significantly better than placebo in controlling pain.
- Adverse events were rare, with no significant difference between treatment and control groups.

Evidence for ultrasound used to treat acute sprains and strains

Ultrasound is used in the treatment of a wide variety of musculoskeletal disorders.

- A Cochrane systematic review evaluated the effects of ultrasound therapy in the treatment of acute ankle sprains [van der Windt et al, 2002]. The review found 5 trials involving 572 patients suitable for analysis:
- The review concluded that:
  - The results do not support the use of ultrasound in the treatment of ankle sprains
  - The magnitude of most reported treatment effects seemed to be small, and may be of limited clinical importance

Evidence for homeopathic arnica used to treat acute sprains and strains

Arnica is used in two kinds of preparation to treat soft-tissue injuries: homeopathic and herbal. We found no clinical trial of herbal arnica (arnica oil). However, trials of homeopathic arnica have been published.

- A review of trials of homeopathic arnica used to treat acute soft-tissue injuries found that most trials were methodologically weak, and concluded that there is no good evidence of benefit [Ernst and Pittler, 1998].

Evidence for oral hydrolytic enzymes used to treat acute sprains and strains

- An RCT with 8 treatment arms compared the effectiveness and safety of treating acute ankle sprains with the enzymes rutoside, bromelain, and trypsin in all possible combinations, and placebo [Kerkhoffs et al, 2004]. The authors concluded that:
  - The triple combination was not found superior to the three two-drug combinations, the three single substances, or placebo for treatment of people with acute unilateral sprain of the lateral ankle joint.
  - However, subgroup analysis (of questionable validity) found that people treated without the support of a brace showed evidence of superiority of the triple enzyme combination over placebo.

What is the evidence to support diagnostic strategies?

Evidence for the Ottawa ankle rules

The set of Ottawa ankle rules is a decision-aid to help avoid unnecessary X-rays by assessing the likelihood of a fracture of the ankle or mid-foot on the basis of clinical evidence.

- A systematic review summarized the evidence to support the accuracy of the Ottawa ankle rules and conducted a meta-analysis on 27 studies involving 15,581 people [Bachmann et al, 2003].
  - The review concluded that evidence supports the Ottawa ankle rules as an accurate instrument for excluding fractures of the ankle and mid-foot. The instrument has a sensitivity of almost 100% and a modest specificity, and its use should reduce the number of unnecessary radiographs by 30–40%.

Evidence for the Ottawa knee rules

The set of Ottawa knee rules is a decision-aid to help avo unnecessary X-rays by assessing the likelihood of a knee fracture on the basis of clinical evidence.

- A systematic review assessed the evidence to support tl use of decision rules for deciding when to use plain X-rays of the knee [Jackson et al, 2003].
  - The review found five decision rules and recommend that the Ottawa knee rules be used to decide when t obtain plain films for suspected knee fracture.
  - The review also concluded that a careful physical examination should be sufficient to decide whether t refer people with potential meniscal and ligament injuries.
- Another systematic review summarized the evidence to support the accuracy of the Ottawa knee rules and conducted a meta-analysis on 6 studies involving 4249 adults [Bachmann et al, 2004].
  - In the pooled analysis the sensitivity was 98.5% (CI 93.2% to 100%).
  - The review concluded that a negative result on an Ottawa knee rule test accurately excluded knee fractures after acute knee injury.

What evidence supports strategies to prevent sprains and strains?

Evidence for risk factors for injury during sport an recreation

- A systematic review examined the published evidence from 117 articles on the effectiveness of current injury prevention strategies in sport and recreational activitie and assessed the applicability of the evidence to childre and youth [MacKay et al, 2004].
  - The review found that 'surprisingly few' well-design and controlled studies investigated strategies to prevent injuries, and that an even smaller number evaluated strategies to reduce injury in children and youth.
  - Most of the reviewed studies were of engineering-based interventions involving modification of the environment or protective equipment. However, this class of intervention often does not ensure injury reduction unless it is combined with educational/promotional activities and/or policy/legislation requiring use.
  - The review did not discuss specific interventions, as i main purpose was to highlight the paucity of eviden
- A systematic review found 45 studies that identified ris factors and potential prevention strategies which coulc be used to modify risk factors for injury in children an adolescents while participating in sport [Emery, 2003]
  - There were problems with study design, internal validity, and generalizability.
  - However, the review concluded that there is some evidence that potentially modifiable risk factors, including poor endurance, lack of preseason trainin and some psychosocial factors, are important risk factors for injury in sport for children and adolescen

Evidence for prevention of injury in football

- A systematic review sought evidence on the effectivene of current injury-prevention strategies in football [Olse et al, 2004].
  - The review found one study of a complex set of interventions to prevent dehydration, and three stud of strategies to prevent injury.
    - One strategy was strength-training out of season. The other two were complex strategies that includ specific education and supervised training.

- The review concluded that some of the strategies look promising, but that they lack adequate evaluation and require further research, particularly in younger players.

Evidence for stretching to prevent injury in sport

We found one systematic review of stretching (before or after exercise) to prevent injuries in competitive or recreational athletes [Thacker et al, 2004]. The review found 6 controlled studies and could pool the results from 5 studies for a meta-analysis. The review concluded that:

- Stretching was not significantly associated with a reduction in total injuries
- There is insufficient evidence either to endorse or to discontinue the practice of stretching

Evidence for prevention of ankle injuries in sport

A Cochrane systematic review assessed the effects of interventions used to prevent ankle sprains in physically active individuals from adolescence to middle age [Handoll et al, 2001].

The review found 14 randomized trials with 8279 participants:

- Twelve trials involved active, predominantly young, adults participating in organised, generally high-risk, activities
- Two trials involved injured patients who had been active in sports before their injury

Prophylactic interventions included:

- External ankle support in the form of a semi-rigid orthosis
- Air-cast brace
- High top shoes
- Ankle disk training
- Taping
- Muscle stretching
- Boot inserts
- Health education programmes
- Controlled rehabilitation

Results and conclusions:

- **External ankle support**
  - The number of ankle sprains was significantly lower.
  - This reduction in number of ankle sprains was greater for those with a previous history of ankle sprain.
  - The severity of ankle sprains was not changed.
  - The incidence of other leg injuries was not altered.
- **Ankle disk training exercises:** there was limited evidence for reduction in ankle sprain for those with previous ankle sprains.
- **'High-top' shoes:** a protective effect remains to be established.
- **Other interventions:** problems with data-reporting limited interpretation.

Evidence for prevention of knee injuries in sport

A systematic review of the evidence for effectiveness of prevention strategies found 13 reports that compared alternative methods to prevent knee injury [Thacker et al, 2003].

- **Bracing.** Five studies addressed the effectiveness of bracing in football players; these studies showed no consistent evidence of benefit.
- **Cleat design.** Two studies comparing alternative cleat designs were difficult to interpret because of inadequate reporting of methodology.
- **Ski-boot/binding system.** A controlled study testing the effects of adjustments in the ski-boot/binding system was difficult to interpret because of inadequate reporting of methodology.
- **Conditioning and training.** Six studies addressed the impact of conditioning and training. There were serious flaws in study design, control of bias, and statistical methods; the median quality scores ranged from 11 to 56 (out of 100). Nevertheless, the authors concluded that there is encouraging evidence for the prevention of knee injuries from structured training programmes that emphasize neuromuscular and proprioceptive training.

References

NHS staff in England can link, free of charge, from references to full text journals by clicking on [Full text] on the PRODIGY website.

Note: all users can access the full texts of DH papers without an Athens password.

1. Andersson, S., Fredin, H., Lindberg, H. et al (1983) Ibuprofen and compression bandage in the treatment of ankle sprains. *Acta Orthopaedica Scandinavica* **54**(2), 322–325.
2. Bachmann, L.M., Kolb, E., Koller, M.T. et al (2003) Accuracy of Ottawa ankle rules to exclude fractures of the ankle and mid-foot: systematic review. *British Medical Journal* 326(7386), 417–419. [Full text]
3. Bachmann, L.M., Haberzeth, S., Steurer, J. and ter Riet, G. (2004) The accuracy of the Ottawa knee rule to rule out knee fractures: a systematic review. *Annals of Internal Medicine* **140**(2), 121–124. [Full text]
4. Bleakley, C., McDonough, S. and MacAuley, D. (2004) The use of ice in the treatment of acute soft-tissue injury: a systematic review of randomized controlled trials. *American Journal of Sports Medicine* **32**(1), 251–261.
5. BNF 48 (2004) *British National Formulary*. 48th edn. London: British Medical Association and Royal Pharmaceutical Society of Great Britain.
6. Bridgman, S.A., Clement, D., Downing, A. et al (2003) Population based epidemiology of ankle sprains attending accident and emergency units in the West Midlands of England, and a survey of UK practice for severe ankle sprains. *Emergency Medicine Journal* **20**(6), 508–510. [Full text]
7. CSM (1994) Relative safety of oral non-aspirin NSAIDs. *Current Problems in Pharmacovigilance* **20**(Aug), 9–11.
8. CSM (2002) Non-steroidal anti-inflammatory drugs (NSAIDs) and gastrointestinal (GI) safety. *Current Problems in Pharmacovigilance* **28**(Apr), 5.
9. De Craen, A.J., Di Giulio, G., Lampe-Schoenmaeckers, J.E. et al (1996) Analgesic efficacy and safety of paracetamol-codeine combinations versus paracetamol alone: a systematic review. *British Medical Journal* **313**(7053), 321–325. [Full text]
10. DH (2000) *Domestic violence: a resource manual for health care professionals*. Department of Health. www.dh.gov.uk [Accessed: 26/11/2004]. [Full text]
11. DTB (1998) Co-proxamol or paracetamol for acute pain? *Drug & Therapeutics Bulletin* **36**(10), 80. [Full text]
12. Dutch College of General Practitioners (2000) *NHG practice guideline: ankle sprains*. http://nhg.artsennet.nl/upload/104/guidelines2/E04.htm [Accessed: 25/11/2004]. [Full text]
13. EMEA (2004) *Press release: EMEA to review COX-2 inhibitors*. EMEA/117908/2004. European Medicines Agency. www.emea.eu.int [Accessed: 28/01/2005].
14. Emery, C.A. (2003) Risk factors for injury in child and adolescent sport: a systematic review of the literature. *Clinical Journal of Sport Medicine* **13**(4), 256–268.

15. Ernst, E. and Pittler, M.H. (1998) Efficacy of homeopathic arnica: a systematic review of placebo-controlled clinical trials. *Archives of Surgery* **133**(11), 1187–1190. [Full text]
16. Garrett, W.E., Jr. (1996) Muscle strain injuries. *American Journal of Sports Medicine* **24**(6 Suppl), S2-S8.
17. Garrick, J.G. and Webb, D.R. (Eds.) (1999) *Sports injuries. Diagnosis and management.* 2nd edn. Oxford: W.B. Saunders Company.
18. Handoll, H.H., Rowe, B.H., Quinn, K.M. and de Bie, R. (2001) *Interventions for preventing ankle ligament injuries (Cochrane Review).* The Cochrane Library. Issue 2. Chichester, UK: John Wiley & Sons, Ltd. www.nelh.nhs.uk/cochrane.asp [Accessed: 22/04/2005]. [Full text]
19. Henry, D., Lim, L.L., Garcia-Rodriguez, L.A. et al (1996) Variability in risk of gastrointestinal complications with individual non-steroidal anti-inflammatory drugs: results of a collaborative meta-analysis. *British Medical Journal* **312**(7046), 1563–1566. [Full text]
20. Hubbard, T.J. and Denegar, C.R. (2004) Does cryotherapy improve outcomes with soft tissue injury? *Journal of Athletic Training* **39**(3), 278–279. [Full text]
21. Jackson, J.L., O'Malley, P.G. and Kroenke, K. (2003) Evaluation of acute knee pain in primary care. *Annals of Internal Medicine* **139**(7), 575–588. [Full text]
22. Jarvinen, T.A., Kaariainen, M., Jarvinen, M. and Kalimo, H. (2000) Muscle strain injuries. *Current Opinion in Rheumatology* **12**(2), 155–161.
23. Kerkhoffs, G.M., Rowe, B.H., Assendelft, W.J. et al (2002a) *Immobilisation and functional treatment for acute lateral ankle ligament injuries in adults (Cochrane Review).* The Cochrane Library. Issue 3. Chichester, UK: John Wiley & Sons, Ltd. www.nelh.nhs.uk/cochrane.asp [Accessed: 22/04/2005]. [Full text]
24. Kerkhoffs, G.M., Struijs, P.A., Marti, R.K. et al (2002b) *Different functional treatment strategies for acute lateral ankle ligament injuries in adults (Cochrane Review).* The Cochrane Library. Issue 3. Chichester, UK: John Wiley & Sons, Ltd. www.nelh.nhs.uk/cochrane.asp [Accessed: 22/04/2005]. [Full text]
25. Kerkhoffs, G.M., Handoll, H.H., de Bie, R. et al (2002c) *Surgical versus conservative treatment for acute injuries of the lateral ligament complex of the ankle in adults (Cochrane Review).* The Cochrane Library. Issue 2. Chichester, UK: John Wiley & Sons, Ltd. www.nelh.nhs.uk/cochrane.asp [Accessed: 22/04/2005]. [Full text]
26. Kerkhoffs, G.M., Struijs, P.A., De Wit, C. et al (2004) A double blind, randomised, parallel group study on the efficacy and safety of treating acute lateral ankle sprain with oral hydrolytic enzymes. *British Journal of Sports Medicine* **38**(4), 431–435.
27. Lewis, D. and Atkinson, P. (2002) Effectiveness of double Tubigrip in grade 1 and 2 ankle sprains. *Emergency Medicine Journal* **19**(1), 90–91.
28. MacKay, M., Scanlan, A., Olsen, L. et al (2004) Looking for the evidence: a systematic review of prevention strategies addressing sport and recreational injury among children and youth. *Journal of Science & Medicine in Sport* **7**(1), 58–73.
29. Mason, L., Moore, R.A., Edwards, J.E. et al (2004a) Topical NSAIDs for acute pain: a meta-analysis. *BMC Family Practice* **5**(1), 10.
30. Mason, L., Moore, R.A., Edwards, J.E. et al (2004b) Systematic review of efficacy of topical rubefacients containing salicylates for the treatment of acute and chronic pain. *British Medical Journal* **328**(7446), 995–998.
31. Medicines Resource (1995) Combination analgesics. *Medicines Resource* **25**, 95–98.
32. MeReC (2000) The use of oral analgesics in primary care. *MeReC Bulletin* **11**(1), 1–4.
33. Nash, C.E., Mickan, S.M., Del Mar, C.B. and Glasziou, P.P. (2004) Resting injured limbs delays recovery: a systematic review. *Journal of Family Practice* **53**(9), 706–712.
34. New Zealand Guidelines Group (2003) *The diagnosis and management of soft tissue knee injuries: internal derangements. Best practice evidence-based guideline* New Zealand Guidelines Group. www.nzgg.org.nz [Accessed: 20/12/2004].
35. NICE (2001) *Guidance on the use of cyclo-oxygenase (Cox) II selective inhibitors, celecoxib, rofecoxib, meloxicam and etodolac for osteoarthritis and rheumatoid arthritis.* Technology appraisal no. 27. National Institute for Health and Clinical Excellence. www.nice.org.uk [Accessed: 16/10/2003].
36. North of England Dyspepsia Guideline Development Group (2004) *Dyspepsia: managing dyspepsia in adults in primary care: full guideline.* Centre for Health Services Research. www.nice.org.uk [Accessed: 27/08/2004].
37. Olsen, L., Scanlan, A., MacKay, M. et al (2004) Strategies for prevention of soccer related injuries: a systematic review. *British Journal of Sports Medicine* **38**(1), 89–94.
38. Ottawa Health Research Institute (1999a) *Ottawa Ankle Rules for ankle injury radiography.* Ottawa Health Research Institute. www.ohri.ca [Accessed: 25/11/2004]. [Full text]
39. Ottawa Health Research Institute (1999b) *Ottawa Knee Rule for knee injury radiography.* Ottawa Health Research Institute. www.ohri.ca [Accessed: 25/11/2004]. [Full text]
40. Rostom, A., Wells, G., Tugwell, P. et al (2002) *Prevention of NSAID-induced gastroduodenal ulcers (Cochrane Review).* The Cochrane Library. Issue 4. Chichester, UK: John Wiley & Sons, Ltd. www.nelh.nhs.uk/cochrane.asp [Accessed: 04/04/2005]. [Full text]
41. Schenck, R.C. (1999) *Athletic training and sports medicine.* 3rd edn. Rosemont, IL: American Academy of Orthopaedic Surgeons.
42. Struijs, P. and Kerkhoffs, G. (2004) *Ankle sprain.* Clinical Evidence. Volume 11. www.clinicalevidence.com [Accessed: 25/11/2004].
43. Thacker, S.B., Stroup, D.F., Branche, C.M. et al (200[illegible] Prevention of knee injuries in sports. A systematic review of the literature. *Journal of Sports Medicine & Physical Fitness* **43**(2), 165–179. [Full text]
44. Thorsson, O., Lilja, B., Nilsson, P. and Westlin, N. (1997) Immediate external compression in the management of an acute muscle injury. *Scandinavian Journal of Medicine & Science in Sports* **7**(3), 182–190.
45. van der Windt, D.A., van der Heijden, G.J., Van Den Berg, S.G. et al (2002) *Ultrasound therapy for acute ankle sprains (Cochrane Review).* The Cochrane Library. Issue 1. Chichester, UK: John Wiley & Sons, Ltd. www.nelh.nhs.uk/cochrane.asp [Accessed: 22/04/2005]. [Full text]
46. Viljakka, T. and Rokkanen, P. (1983) The treatment ankle sprain by bandaging and antiphlogistic drugs. *Annales Chirurgiae et Gynaecologiae* **72**(2), 66–70.
47. Weiler, J.M. (1992) Medical modifiers of sports injur[illegible] The use of nonsteroidal anti-inflammatory drugs (NSAIDs) in sports soft-tissue injury. *Clinics in Sports Medicine* **11**(3), 625–644.

S

PRODIGY GUIDANCE

Supraventricular tachycardia — paroxysmal

Last revised in July 2005
www.prodigy.nhs.uk/guidance.asp?gt=SVT - paroxysmal

Applies to people of all ages

This guidance covers the initial management of a person presenting with suspected supraventricular tachycardia (other than atrial fibrillation or flutter) in primary care.
This guidance is based upon the *American College of Cardiology/American Heart Association/European Society of Cardiology Guidelines for the Management of Patients With Supraventricular Arrhythmias*, published in October 2003.

This guidance does not cover the treatment or prevention of supraventricular tachycardia, or the management of atrial fibrillation or atrial flutter.

There is separate PRODIGY guidance for the management of *Atrial fibrillation.*

Goals

To refer all people with a history suggestive of supraventricular tachycardia (SVT) to a cardiologist
To admit all people presenting with an episode of suspected SVT

Contents

Scenarios

- Supraventricular tachycardia (initial presentation) p.1755

Extended Information, p. 1756

Supraventricular tachycardia (initial presentation)

Which therapy?

If suspected SVT is present:

- Admit to hospital immediately.
- Treatment must only be undertaken in hospital, as full ECG monitoring and resuscitation facilities are needed.
- If possible, and as long as it does not delay admission, take an ECG to aid diagnosis in case the episode terminates before the person reaches hospital.
- **Vagal manoeuvres** (e.g. Valsalva, carotid massage, facial immersion in cold water) may terminate an episode of SVT.
- **Intravenous drug treatment** is required if vagal manoeuvres fail:
  - **Intravenous adenosine** is the treatment of choice except for people with severe asthma.
  - **Intravenous verapamil** is recommended if adenosine is contraindicated (e.g. in somebody with severe asthma).
- **DC cardioversion** is the most effective and rapid treatment if the person is haemodynamically unstable.

If there is a history suggestive of paroxysmal SVT:

- Refer to a cardiologist.

Should I refer or investigate?

Refer?

- **A person presenting with suspected or definite SVT:** admit for termination of the arrhythmia.
- **A person presenting with a history suggestive of paroxysmal SVT:** refer for a cardiology outpatient appointment.

Investigate?

- ECG taken during an episode of tachycardia:
  - Shows a ventricular rate of 140–250 per minute.
  - Usually shows a regular narrow-complex tachycardia.
  - Sometimes, however, a broad-complex tachycardia may occur due to bundle branch block or due to an accessory pathway. SVT with a broad-complex tachycardia can be confused with an episode of ventricular tachycardia.
- An ECG taken whilst in sinus rhythm is usually normal, but may show evidence of pre-excitation due to accessory pathways (e.g. short PR interval, delta wave [slurring of the initial deflection of the QRS complex]), prolonged QT interval, or evidence of underlying heart disease.

Patient information leaflets

The following PILs are available at www.prodigy.nhs.uk

- British Heart Foundation
- How the Heart Works
- Supraventricular Tachycardia (SVT)

Shared decision making

- You have a tachycardia which means an abnormal fast heart rate.
- It usually needs hospital referral for tests and treatment.
- Most causes of tachycardia can be treated effectively

Drug rationale

- No prescriptions are offered. Treatment must only be undertaken in hospital, as full ECG monitoring and resuscitation facilities are needed.
- If preventative treatment is required, it is not appropriate to initiate therapy without specialist assessment.

Extended Information

Background information

- What is it? p.1756
- How common is it? p.1756
- How do I know my patient has it? p.1756
- What else might it be? p.1756
- Complications and prognosis p.1756

What is it?

- **Supraventricular tachycardia (SVT) is a disorder of cardiac rhythm.** SVT is due to abnormalities of impulse conduction (re-entrant tachycardias) or disorders of impulse initiation (automatic tachycardias). SVT can be classified as the following types.
  - Re-entrant tachycardias:
    - Atrioventricular nodal reciprocating tachycardia (AVNRT) — due to the presence of two functionally and anatomically distinct conducting pathways in the atrioventricular (AV) node. One of these is fast-conducting, the other slow-conducting. During an episode of SVT one of these acts as the antegrade limb of a re-entrant circuit, while the other acts as the retrograde limb. AVNRT is the most common form of SVT.
    - Atrioventricular reciprocating tachycardia (AVRT) — due to the presence of accessory pathways that connect the atria and ventricles, but that lie outside the AV node. Accessory pathways may be capable of antegrade or retrograde conduction, or both. Wolff–Parkinson–White syndrome is the most well-known type of AVRT.
  - Automatic tachycardias:
    - Focal junctional tachycardia — due to abnormally rapid discharges from the junctional region. This type of SVT originates from the AV node or bundle of His. This type is also known as automatic or paroxysmal junctional tachycardia.
    - Focal atrial tachycardia — due to regular atrial activation from atrial areas with centrifugal spread. Neither the sinus nor the AV node plays a role in the initiation or continuation of this type of SVT.
- Re-entrant tachycardia is the most common type. SVT is usually due to AVNRT or AVRT.
- SVT usually occurs in younger people in the absence of heart disease.
- SVT is usually paroxysmal (occurs in between episodes of sinus rhythm). Episodes may occur regularly or very infrequently (sometimes years apart), and may only last for a few minutes or for several months [Ganz and Friedman, 1995].

[Blomstrum-Lundquist et al, 2003]

S

How common is it?

- Accurate figures of incidence and prevalence are difficult to find, as studies of arrhythmias have not discriminated between SVT, atrial fibrillation, and atrial flutter.
- The prevalence of paroxysmal SVT in a sample of medical records (of the general population) in the USA has been estimated as 2.25 per 1000 people.
- In the same study the incidence was estimated as 35 per 100,000 person-years.

[Blomstrum-Lundquist et al, 2003]

How do I know my patient has it?

History

- Paroxysmal SVT occurs in all age groups, and may be associated with minimal symptoms, or may present wit[h] syncope. Symptoms vary with the ventricular rate and duration of the SVT. Symptoms are more likely in thos[e] with underlying heart disease, and include:
  - Palpitations — abrupt in onset and termination
  - Fatigue
  - Lightheadedness
  - Chest discomfort
  - Angina
  - Dyspnoea
  - Polyuria — due to release of atrial natriuretic peptid[e]
  - Presyncope
  - Syncope — occurs in 15% of people, usually just aft[er] the initiation, or due to a prolonged pause just after abrupt termination of the SVT
- There may be a history of recurrent episodes with features suggestive of SVT.

Examination

- During an episode of SVT the pulse rate is 140–250 pe[r] minute.

Investigations

- The diagnosis of SVT is made by analysis of an ECG taken during an episode of tachycardia.
  - This usually shows a regular narrow-complex tachycardia.
  - Sometimes, however, a broad-complex tachycardia may occur due to bundle branch block or due to an accessory pathway. SVT with a broad-complex tachycardia can be confused with an episode of ventricular tachycardia.
- An ECG taken whilst in sinus rhythm is usually normal but may show evidence of pre-excitation due to accessory pathways (e.g. short PR interval, delta wave [slurring of the initial deflection of the QRS complex]), prolonged QT interval, or evidence of underlying heart disease.

[Blomstrum-Lundquist et al, 2003]

What else might it be?

- **Sinus tachycardia,** e.g. due to anxiety, infection, medication, panic attack, thyrotoxicosis. The heart rat[e] rarely exceeds 150 except during exercise. The tachycardia accelerates and terminates gradually.
- **Ventricular tachycardia** may be confused with a fast broad-complex supraventricular tachycardia.
- **Drug adverse effects,** e.g. with amiodarone, digoxin, theophylline.

[Blomstrum-Lundquist et al, 2003]

Complications and prognosis

Complications

- Haemodynamic collapse can occur. This is more likely [in] people with underlying heart disease who are unable to tolerate increases in heart rate.
- SVT that persists for weeks or months may lead to a tachycardia-mediated cardiomyopathy.

[Blomstrum-Lundquist et al, 2003]

Management issues

How do I manage someone with a history suggestive of paroxysmal SVT? p.1757
How do I manage someone presenting with an episode of suspected SVT? p.1757
What is recommended to treat an episode of SVT? p.1757
Which treatments are recommended to prevent further episodes of SVT? p.1757
Can my patient drive after an episode of SVT? p.1757

How do I manage someone with a history suggestive of paroxysmal SVT?

A correct diagnosis must be obtained in all cases and the underlying mechanism clarified. This requires referral to a cardiologist [Zimetbaum and Josephson, 1998].

Secondary care investigations may include 24-hour ECG monitoring, event recorders (cardio-memo), exercise tolerance testing, transoesophageal atrial recordings, and electrophysiological studies [Blomstrum-Lundquist et al, 2003].

How do I manage someone presenting with an episode of suspected SVT?

Immediate admission is recommended, as treatment must only be undertaken in hospital.

Whenever possible, an ECG should be taken during an episode of suspected SVT; this will aid diagnosis if the episode has terminated before the person reaches hospital. However, recording the ECG must not delay the hospital admission; i.e. if practical it is advised to obtain an ECG while waiting for the ambulance to arrive.

[Blomstrum-Lundquist et al, 2003]

What is recommended to treat an episode of SVT?

Treatment must only be undertaken in hospital, as full ECG monitoring and resuscitation facilities are needed.

Vagal manoeuvres (e.g. Valsalva, carotid massage, facial immersion in cold water) may terminate an episode of SVT.

Intravenous drug treatment is required if vagal manoeuvres fail:

- **Intravenous adenosine** is the treatment of choice except for people with severe asthma. Adenosine has a rapid onset and short half-life. It blocks conduction through the AV node.
- **Intravenous verapamil,** although effective, is rarely used now. It has a more prolonged action than adenosine on blocking AV node conduction, and there is a risk of prolonged depression of ventricular function, especially if the person is taking a beta-blocker. It still has a place if adenosine is contraindicated (e.g. in somebody with severe asthma) [Chun and Sung, 1995; Ganz and Friedman, 1995].

DC cardioversion is the most effective and rapid treatment if the person is haemodynamically unstable.

[Blomstrum-Lundquist et al, 2003]

Which treatments are recommended to prevent further episodes of SVT?

Long-term preventative treatment is not required in all people. The frequency and severity of the episodes of SVT need to be balanced against the risks of long-term therapy.

- The choice of maintenance therapy depends on the underlying type of SVT.
- **Anti-arrhythmic drug therapy** is used in many people to prevent further episodes. The choice of which drug (from which anti-arrhythmic class) for the different types of SVT is beyond the scope of this guidance. All anti-arrhythmic drugs have adverse effects, and, as they need to be taken long-term, it is important to consider referral for consideration of radiofrequency catheter ablation.
- **Radiofrequency catheter ablation** is associated with a high success rate and low complication rate for people with SVT. Radiofrequency catheter ablation is indicated in the following situations:
  - As first-line therapy as a curative option.
  - If the SVT is refractory to anti-arrhythmic drug therapy.
  - If the person is intolerant of anti-arrhythmic drug therapy.
  - If anti-arrhythmic drug therapy is contraindicated.

[Noorani et al, 2002; Blomstrum-Lundquist et al, 2003]

Can my patient drive after an episode of SVT?

- The Driver and Vehicle Licensing Agency (DVLA) states the following apply after an arrhythmia:
  - Driving must cease if the arrhythmia has caused or is likely to cause incapacity.
  - Driving may be permitted when the underlying cause has been identified and controlled for at least 4 weeks.
  - DVLA need not be notified unless there are distracting/disabling symptoms.

References

NHS staff in England can link, free of charge, from references to full text journals by clicking on [Full text] on the PRODIGY website.

1. Blomstrum-Lundquist, C., Scheinmann, M.M., Aliot, E.M. et al (2003) *ACC/AHA/ESC guidelines for the management of patients with supraventricular arrhythmias. A report of the American College of Cardiology/American Heart Association Task Force and the European Society of Cardiology Committee for Practice Guidelines (Writing Committee to Develop Guidelines for the Management of Patients With Supraventricular Arrhythmias)*. American College of Cardiology. www.acc.org/clinical/guidelines/arrhythmias/update_index.htm [Accessed: 10/03/2005].
2. Chun, H.M. and Sung, R.J. (1995) Supraventricular tachyarrhythmias. Pharmacologic versus nonpharmacologic approaches. *Medical Clinics of North America* 79(5), 1121–1134.
3. Ganz, L.I. and Friedman, P.L. (1995) Supraventricular tachycardia. *New England Journal of Medicine* **332**(3), 162–173.
4. Noorani, H.Z., Yee, R., Marshall, D. et al (2002) *Radiofrequency catheter ablation for cardiac arrhythmias: a clinical and economic review.* Technology report no. 25. Canadian Coordinating Office for Health Technology Assessment. www.ccohta.ca [Accessed: 15/03/2005].
5. Zimetbaum, P. and Josephson, M.E. (1998) Evaluation of patients with palpitations. *New England Journal of Medicine* 338(19), 1369–1373. [Full text]

PRODIGY GUIDANCE

Threadworm

Last revised in March 2004
www.prodigy.nhs.uk/guidance.asp?gt=Threadworm

Applies to people of all ages

This guidance covers the treatment of threadworm infection (*Enterobius vermicularis*).

This guidance does not cover the treatment of tapeworm, hookworm, or more unusual worm infections.

There is separate PRODIGY guidance for the treatment of *Roundworm*, and *Pruritus ani*.

Goals

- To eradicate threadworm infection and prevent reinfection

Contents

Scenarios

- Drug treatment p.1758
- Non-drug treatment p.1759

Extended Information, p. 1760

Which scenario?

- **Drug treatment:** covers the management of threadworms.
- **Non-drug treatment:** covers hygiene measures when drug treatment is contraindicated or undesirable, for example during pregnancy or breastfeeding, or in children less than 3 months.

Drug treatment

Which therapy?

- **All household members should be treated simultaneously.**
- **Mebendazole is the treatment of choice** in adults and children older than 2 years. It is given as a single dose, which often needs to be repeated after 2–3 weeks if reinfection occurs.
- **Piperazine combined with senna** (as a powder) is an alternative and is licensed for adults and children older than 3 months. It is given as a single dose, repeated after 14 days.
- **For people with epilepsy, neurological disease, or severe renal or hepatic impairment,** prescribe mebendazole, as neurotoxic reactions to piperazine resulting in convulsions have been reported in people with neurological or renal abnormalities.
- **Environmental and personal hygiene measures are an integral part of drug treatment** and should be used by all members of the household for 2 weeks following drug treatment (see patient information leaflet). At the same time as drug treatment is initiated, people should be advised to:
  - Wear close-fitting underpants or knickers at night.
  - Have a bath or shower, wash around the anus each morning, immediately on rising.
  - Change and wash underwear, nightwear, and (if possible) bed linen and towels each day (avoid shaking them as this also spreads eggs). Avoid the use of 'communal' towels.
  - Keep fingernails short.
  - Wash hands and scrub under the nails first thing in the morning, after using the toilet or changing nappies, and before eating or preparing food.
  - Put toothbrushes in a closed cupboard, and rinse them well before use.
- **Daily disinfection of bathroom surfaces and vacuuming of carpets is advisable,** as eggs can survive for up to 2 weeks on clothing, bedding, or other objects.
- **It is not necessary to exclude children from school once treatment has been started.**
- **In cases of treatment failure or reinfection,** hygiene methods need to be re-emphasized and re-treatment will be necessary.

Practical prescribing points

For further information please see the *Medicines Compendium* (www.medicines.org.uk) or the *British National Formulary* (www.bnf.org).

Pregnancy and breastfeeding

- **Mebendazole and piperazine are not recommended for use during pregnancy or breastfeeding,** especially in the first trimester. Hygiene methods alone are preferred (see scenario *Non-drug treatment*).
- Contact the National Teratology Information Service for more details (telephone 0191 232 1525).

Follow-up advice

- Reinfection is common, and a second course of treatment after 14 days is often required.

Patient information leaflets

The following PILs are available at www.prodigy.nhs.uk

- Threadworms

Shared decision making

- Medication *and* hygiene measures are the treatment for threadworms.
- **All household members should be treated at the same time.**
- **Medication** is available at pharmacies or on prescription.
  - **Mebendazole** is commonly used for those over 2 years. A single dose is usually sufficient. A second dose after 2 weeks is sometimes needed.
  - **Piperazine** with a laxative is an alternative for those over 3 months. You take two doses 14 days apart. (Piperazine is not to be taken if you have epilepsy or liver disease.)
- **Hygiene measures.** Threadworms lay eggs around the anus. Eggs can get under fingernails and then back into the mouth to cause further infection. So, for 14 days after the first dose of medication, all household members should:

- Wear underpants or knickers at night.
- Keep fingernails short.
- Wash hands and scrub nails each morning. Wash hands before meals or snacks, before preparing food, and after going to the toilet or changing nappies.
- Every morning have a bath, or wash around the anus, to get rid of any eggs laid overnight. You must do this straight away after getting up from bed.
- Change and wash underwear, nightwear, bed linen, and towels (if possible) each day. Do not share towels.

Also, vacuum all carpets and clean bathroom surfaces daily for 14 days.

Drug rationale

Drugs included

Mebendazole and piperazine are both active against threadworm infection.

Mebendazole is recommended as the treatment of choice in people over 2 years of age. It acts by killing the worms. Mebendazole is licensed to be given as a single dose. In cases of reinfection, a second tablet may be taken after 2 weeks.

Piperazine paralyses the worms, which are expelled by peristalsis. Piperazine combined with senna, as *Pripsen* sachets, may be given to infants older than 3 months. A second dose is required after 2 weeks.

[BNF 45, 2003]

Prescriptions

Mebendazole

Mebendazole suspension: 100mg single dose

Age from 2 to 11 years

Mebendazole 100mg/5ml susp. Take one 5ml spoonful as a single dose. Repeat after 2 weeks if infection persists; supply 10 ml; NHS Cost £0.60.

Mebendazole tablets: 100mg single dose

Age from 12 years onwards

Mebendazole 100mg tablets. Take one tablet as a single dose. Repeat in 2 weeks if infection persists; supply 2 tablets; NHS Cost £0.51; OTC Cost £4.00.

Piperazine (avoid in epilepsy or liver disease)

Piperazine+senna: 2.5ml as a single dose. Repeat in 2 weeks

Age from 3 to 11 months

Piperazine 4g powder. Take one level 2.5ml spoonful of sachet contents in the morning as a single dose. Repeat after 2 weeks; supply 1 dual sachet; NHS Cost £1.25; OTC Cost £2.29.

Piperazine+senna: 5ml as a single dose. Repeat in 2 weeks

Age from 12 months to 5 years

Piperazine 4g powder. Take one level 5ml spoonful of sachet contents in the morning as a single dose. Repeat after 2 weeks; supply 1 dual sachet; NHS Cost £1.25; OTC Cost £2.29.

Piperazine+senna: 1 sachet as a single dose. Repeat in 2 wk

Age from 6 to 11 years

Piperazine 4g powder. Take one sachet in the morning as a single dose. Repeat after 2 weeks; supply 1 dual sachet; NHS Cost £1.25; OTC Cost £2.29.

Piperazine+senna: 1 sachet as a single dose. Repeat in 2 wks

- Age from 12 years onwards
- Piperazine 4g powder. Take one sachet at bedtime as a single dose. Repeat after 2 weeks; supply 1 dual sachet; NHS Cost £1.25; OTC Cost £2.29.

Non-drug treatment

Which therapy?

- **Threadworm infection can be treated solely by meticulous attention to hygiene for 6 weeks.** The worms in the intestine will die within this time, and, if no eggs are swallowed, no new worms will replace them. Hygiene measures alone may be considered when drug treatment is not wanted or is not recommended (e.g. during pregnancy, or in children less than 2 years with contraindications to piperazine).
- **Hygiene measures require every member of the household to do the following:**
  - Wear close-fitting underpants or knickers at night.
  - Have a bath or shower, wash around the anus each morning, immediately on rising.
  - Change and wash underwear, nightwear, and (if possible) bed linen and towels each day (avoid shaking them as this also spreads eggs). Avoid the use of 'communal' towels.
  - Keep fingernails short.
  - Wash hands and scrub under the nails first thing in the morning, after using the toilet or changing nappies, and before eating or preparing food.
  - Put toothbrushes in a closed cupboard, and rinse them well before use.
- **Daily disinfection of bathroom surfaces and vacuuming of carpets is advisable,** as eggs can survive for up to 2 weeks on clothing, bedding, or other objects.

Patient information leaflets

The following PILs are available at www.prodigy.nhs.uk

- Threadworms

Shared decision making

- You can clear threadworms without using medicines by strict hygiene measures for 6 weeks.
- The worms in your gut will die within 6 weeks, and if you do not swallow any eggs in this time, no new worms will hatch to replace them.
- For 6 weeks, all household members need to:
  - Wear underpants or knickers at night.
  - Keep fingernails short.
  - Wash hands and scrub nails each morning. Wash hands before meals or snacks, before preparing food, and after going to the toilet or changing nappies.
  - Every morning have a bath, or wash around the anus, to get rid of any eggs laid overnight. You must do this straight away after getting up from bed.
  - Change and wash underwear, nightwear, bed linen, and towels (if possible) each day. Do not share towels.
- Also, vacuum all carpets and clean bathroom surfaces daily for 6 weeks.

Drug rationale

- There are no prescriptions offered in this scenario.

Extended Information

Background information

- What is it? p.1760
- How common is it? p.1760
- How do I know my patient has it? p.1760
- What else might it be? p.1760
- Complications and prognosis p.1760

What is it?

- **Threadworm or pinworm** (*Enterobius vermicularis*) is a small, white, thread-like worm between 2 and 13 mm long, which lives in the upper part of the colon. Infection is limited to humans; threadworms are not transferable to or from animals.
- **Female threadworms produce large numbers of tiny eggs, which are not visible to the naked eye.** The female lays these eggs outside the anus, or, in girls, around the vagina and urethra. Eggs are usually laid at night when the host is asleep; inactivity promotes movement of the female to the anus. The female secretes the eggs, together with irritant mucus, which causes intense itching and promotes scratching by the host. Reinfection occurs when eggs are ingested from contaminated hands.
- **Adult threadworms** live for up to 6 weeks. For fresh worms to develop, eggs must be swallowed and exposed to the action of digestive juices in the upper intestinal tract.
- **Infection or reinfection can occur** by directly swallowing, or by inhaling and then swallowing, the eggs [Ibarra, 2001]. Occasionally retroinfection occurs where the eggs hatch on the mucosa and the larvae migrate back up the rectum [Cook and Zumla, 2002].
- Following ingestion of the eggs, the larvae hatch in the small intestine and establish themselves in the colon, reaching maturity in approximately 2 weeks.

[CDC, 2002; Cook and Zumla, 2002; BNF 45, 2003]

How common is it?

- **Threadworm** is the most common helminth infection in the UK.
- **In a general practice of 10,000 patients,** about 40 consultations a year are due to threadworm [McCormick et al, 1995]. However, it is likely that many more people seek over-the-counter treatment. In addition, asymptomatic infection is common.
- **Threadworms are much more common in school or pre-school children than adults,** because of their inattention to good personal hygiene and close contact with other children. Threadworms often affect family groups or institutions, especially if conditions are crowded [CDC, 2002; Cook and Zumla, 2002].

How do I know my patient has it?

- **Threadworm infection is frequently asymptomatic.**
- **Intense itching** in the perianal region may occur, especially during the night. This may lead to loss of sleep and irritability. Occasionally, invasion of the female genital tract may cause perivaginal itching. Girls presenting before puberty with vaginal discharge, urinary tract infection, or uncharacteristic bedwetting should be checked for threadworm.
- **Diagnosis is confirmed if threadworms are seen in the perianal area or, more rarely, in the stool.** Threadworms look like 'small threads of slowly-moving white cotton', but may be very difficult to see. They are usually best seen at night or when the person is resting.
- **If the diagnosis is uncertain, the adhesive tape test for eggs may be useful.** Transparent wide hypo-allergenic adhesive tape is applied to the perianal skin first thing in the morning, before wiping or bathing. The tape is then placed on a slide or put in a specimen container for later examination under a microscope (either by the GP or the local laboratory).
- **Stool examination** is much less reliable. Eggs are present on the faeces of no more than 5% of infected individuals [Cook and Zumla, 2002].

[Prescribing Nurse Bulletin, 1999; CDC, 2002]

What else might it be?

- **Perianal itching in adults** may be due to irritation by deodorants, tight nylon underclothes, haemorrhoids, or perianal eczema.
- **Other worm infections** are much less common in the UK. Human roundworms may occasionally be passed in the stool (adult worms are approximately 30 cm long). Tapeworm infection often only becomes evident when segments are passed in the stool — these are called proglottids and are ribbon-like, approximately 5 cm long, and (unlike threadworms) do not move.

Complications and prognosis

- **Reinfection is common.**
- **Scratching** of the perianal skin may make it inflamed and broken, with a risk of secondary infection.
- **Persistent or particularly heavy cases** of infestation can cause loss of appetite, weight loss, insomnia, enuresis, and irritability.
- **Ectopic lesions:** occasionally worms are found in the female genital organs, and more rarely in the ears and nose. Rarely worms invade the abdominal cavity, causing granulomas of the liver, ovary, kidney, spleen, and lung. Chronic pelvic peritonitis and ileocolitis have been described [Cook and Zumla, 2002].

Management issues

- Non-drug treatments p.1760
- Drug treatments p.1761
- Do children with threadworms need to be kept off school? p.1761
- Medicines management p.1761

Non-drug treatments

- **Threadworm infection can be treated solely by meticulous attention to hygiene for 6 weeks.** The worm in the intestine will die within this time, and if no eggs are swallowed, no new worms will replace them. Hygiene measures alone may be considered when drug treatment is not wanted or is not recommended (e.g. during pregnancy).
- **Hygiene measures require every member of the household to do the following:**
  - Wear close-fitting underpants or knickers at night.
  - Have a bath or shower, wash around the anus each morning, immediately on rising.
  - Change and wash underwear, nightwear, and (if possible) bed linen and towels each day (avoid shaking them as this also spreads eggs). Avoid the use of 'communal' towels.
  - Keep fingernails short.
  - Wash hands and scrub under the nails first thing in the morning, after using the toilet or changing nappies, and before eating or preparing food.
  - Put toothbrushes in a closed cupboard, and rinse them well before use.

Eggs can be removed by daily damp dusting of surfaces and washing the cloth frequently in hot water. Good ventilation and reduced humidity both help to reduce the viability of eggs [HPA, Personal Communication, 2003]. Daily vacuuming of all carpets is advisable, as eggs can survive for up to 2 weeks on clothing, bedding, or other objects [Prescribing Nurse Bulletin, 1999; CDC, 2002].

ug treatments

Hygiene measures are important for the 2 weeks following drug treatment (see the above section *Non-drug treatments*). Drug treatment has no effect on threadworm eggs, which may remain viable for up to 2 weeks. To avoid reinfection it is essential to clear the living environment of viable worm eggs on the day that drug treatment is started. An initial cleaning blitz in bedrooms and bathrooms followed by continued routine good hygiene would seem a sensible approach.

All family members should be treated simultaneously unless contraindicated; asymptomatic infection is common, and person-to-person transmission is possible through handling of contaminated food, clothing, and bed linen [Prescribing Nurse Bulletin, 1999].

Mebendazole is the treatment of choice in adults and children older than 2 years. It is usually given as a single oral dose, but often needs to be repeated after 2–3 weeks if reinfection occurs. Mebendazole acts by inhibiting the uptake of glucose by the worms, causing immobilization and death [Lee et al, 2000].

Piperazine combined with senna (as a powder) is an alternative and is licensed for adults and children older than 3 months. It is given as a single dose, repeated after 14 days. Piperazine blocks the neurotransmitter acetylcholine in the worm, leading to paralysis, and senna helps to expel the worms from the intestine by its laxative effect.

o children with threadworms need to be pt off school?

It is not necessary to exclude children with threadworms from school [HPA, Personal Communication, 2003]. Schools and nurseries should be encouraged to promote hygiene measures.

edicines management

ebendazole

Mebendazole is largely unabsorbed and systemic adverse effects are minimal. Transient abdominal pain or diarrhoea occasionally occur, especially in people with heavy infestations.

athan, 1997; Ibarra, 2001]

iperazine

Gastrointestinal disturbances including nausea, vomiting, colic, and diarrhoea are the most common adverse effects in people taking piperazine.

Neurotoxic reactions resulting in convulsions have been reported in people with neurological or renal abnormalities, and piperazine should not be prescribed for people with epilepsy, neurological disease, or severe renal or hepatic impairment.

Rarely, piperazine causes loss of muscular coordination ('worm wobble').

athan, 1997; Ibarra, 2001]

Pregnancy and breastfeeding

- **During pregnancy,** hygiene methods alone are preferred. Mebendazole and piperazine are best avoided during pregnancy, especially in the first trimester. Mebendazole is poorly absorbed from the gastrointestinal tract and is unlikely to cause harm to the fetus although toxicity has been noted in animal studies. There is no evidence that exposure to piperazine during pregnancy is harmful to the fetus, but its use during pregnancy is not recommended, and it should especially be avoided in the first trimester.

[Nathan, 1997; Lee et al, 2000]

- **During breastfeeding,** hygiene methods are also preferred. However, the limited data that exist suggest that only very small amounts of anthelmintics pass into breast milk, and there are no apparent ill-effects in most infants. It is recommended that mothers taking piperazine should avoid breastfeeding for 8 hours following a dose [Nathan, 1997; BNF 45, 2003]. Colic has been reported in some infants following maternal ingestion of senna. If piperazine combined with senna is given to a breastfeeding mother, the infant should be fed just prior to the mother's taking this [Nathan, 1997].
- **Contact the National Teratology Information Service for more details** (telephone 0191 232 1525).

Children less than 3 months

- **For children less than 3 months old,** hygiene methods alone are preferred. Neither of the drugs available for the treatment of threadworm in the UK is licensed for use in children less than 3 months old.
- **Advise cleansing the bottom gently but thoroughly at nappy changes,** and changing the nappy at least every 3 hours to prevent any return through the anus of worms hatching in the nappy [Ibarra, 2001].

References

1. BNF 45 (2003) *British National Formulary.* 45th edn. London: British Medical Association and Royal Pharmaceutical Society of Great Britain.
2. CDC (2002) *Enterobiasis.* Centers for Disease Control and Prevention. www.dpd.cdc.gov/ [Accessed: 22/11/2000].
3. Cook, G.C. and Zumla, A. (Eds.) (2002) *Manson's tropical diseases.* 21st edn. London: W.B. Saunders.
4. HPA (2003) *Personal communication.* Health Protection Agency: London.
5. Ibarra, J. (2001) Threadworms: a starting point for family hygiene. *British Journal of Community Nursing* 6(8), 414–420.
6. Lee, A., Inch, S. and Finnigan, D. (Eds.) (2000) *Therapeutics in pregnancy and lactation.* Abingdon: Radcliffe Medical Press Ltd.
7. McCormick, A., Fleming, D. and Charlton, J. (1995) *Morbidity statistics from general practice. Fourth national study 1991–1992.* Office of Population Censuses and Surveys. www.statistics.gov.uk [Accessed: 03/05/2005].
8. Nathan, A. (1997) Anthelmintics. *Pharmaceutical Journal* 258(6945), 770–771.
9. Prescribing Nurse Bulletin (1999) Threadworms. *Prescribing Nurse Bulletin* 1(3), 11–12.

PRODIGY GUIDANCE

Thrombophlebitis

Last revised in July 2005
At the time of print this topic was being updated. The newly revised guidance will be issued on to the website in 2006.
www.prodigy.nhs.uk/guidance.asp?gt=Thrombophlebitis

Applies to people over the age of 16 years

This guidance covers the management of superficial thrombophlebitis.

This guidance does not cover deep venous thrombosis.

There is separate PRODIGY guidance for the management of *Deep vein thrombosis*.

The target audience for this guidance is healthcare professionals working within the NHS in England, and providing first contact or primary health care. *Patient information leaflets* (PILs) are intended to be printed and given to people with this condition, whilst the *Shared decision making* sections are designed to provide a focus for discussion during the consultation about the treatment options.

Goals

- To alleviate symptoms
- To avoid complications

Contents

Scenarios

- Superficial thrombophlebitis p.1762

Extended Information, p. 1764

Superficial thrombophlebitis

Which therapy?

- **Oral nonsteroidal anti-inflammatory drugs** (NSAIDs) reduce inflammation and pain.
- **Paracetamol** is an alternative analgesic for patients intolerant of NSAIDs.
- **Compression stockings** may help to alleviate pain and reduce the chance of further thrombosis in superficial thrombophlebitis of the lower limbs.
- **Leg elevation** is thought to improve venous blood flow and reduce swelling. Bed rest is not generally advised and patients should be encouraged to keep mobile. Local heat may help.
- **Antibiotics** are not indicated in aseptic superficial thrombophlebitis.

T

Practical prescribing points

For further information please see the *Medicines Compendium* (www.medicines.org.uk) or the *British National Formulary* (www.bnf.org).

Pregnancy

- NSAIDs should ideally be avoided, especially in the later stages of pregnancy, due to the risk of oligohydramnios and premature closure of the ductus arteriosus.
- Telephone the National Teratology Information Service for further information (0191 2321525)

Compression stockings

- Adequate arterial circulation should be ensured by Doppler assessment before compression stockings are prescribed.

Follow-up advice

- The patient should be warned that superficial thrombophlebitis can progress into the deep veins and that any change in symptoms warrants immediate evaluation.

Should I refer or investigate?

Refer?

- **Admit or arrange urgent hospital assessment if suspect deep venous thrombosis (DVT). Particularly suspect th if:**
  - Past history of DVT
  - The thrombosis reaches the proximal part of the lon saphenous vein in the thigh
  - History of hereditary thrombophilia
  - Underlying cancer
  - Bilateral involvement
  - Recent bed rest or immobilisation
- **Admit or arrange urgent hospital assessment if chest pa or dyspnoea are present** as this may indicate progressio to pulmonary embolus.
- **Consider admission if suspected septic thrombophlebit** (rare and more likely if recent intravenous cannulation or intravenous drug abuser).

Investigate?

- Diagnosis may require radiological investigation to exclude deep vein thrombosis. Consider urgent referra for investigation to exclude deep vein thrombosis (DV if any of the above risk factors are present.
- Migratory thrombophlebitis may be an indication for a more detailed evaluation of the gastrointestinal tract in search of malignant lesion, and a more extensive work up for antithrombin III, protein C or protein S abnormalities.
- Recurrent thrombophlebitis with no obvious explanat requires further investigation.

Patient information leaflets

The following PILs are available at www.prodigy.nhs.uk

- Phlebitis

Shared decision making

- Thrombophlebitis usually goes within 2–6 weeks.
- Not taking any treatment is an option if symptoms are mild.

Keep on with normal activities as much as possible.
A hot flannel placed over the vein may ease the pain.
Keep an affected leg raised when you rest.
Support stockings may ease discomfort, particularly if you have varicose veins.
Paracetamol will often ease the pain.
Anti-inflammatory painkillers, such as ibuprofen, are an alternative.
Occasionally the vein becomes infected, or a blood clot may extend to a deep vein, or a rare condition causes the inflammation. Tell a doctor if:

- Symptoms become worse.
- Inflammation spreads up the inner part of your thigh towards your groin.
- Your whole leg swells.
- Large parts of your leg become warm.
- You develop any new breathing problems, or get chest pains.
- You have recurring bouts of thrombophlebitis.

Drug rationale

Drugs not included

Anticoagulants are not usually indicated for superficial thrombophlebitis. If deep vein thrombosis is suspected, arrange for urgent referral.
Antithrombotic (antiplatelet) agents: because superficial thrombophlebitis is primarily due to inflammation and fibrin clot, antiplatelet agents have little value.
Antibacterials: there is no role for antibacterial therapy in aseptic superficial thrombophlebitis. If septic superficial thrombophlebitis is suspected then admission for antibiotic treatment is advised.
Topical nonsteroidal anti-inflammatory drugs (NSAIDs): these are excluded because there are no good quality trials that compare the efficacy of either topical NSAIDs with the same NSAID given orally, or with paracetamol [Moore et al, 1998; Heyneman et al, 2000; Gotzsche, 2001].
NSAIDs (other than ibuprofen, diclofenac and naproxen) that are associated with a higher risk of gastrointestinal adverse events or that are not licensed for general musculoskeletal pain and inflammation [CSM, 1994; Henry et al, 1996; Hernández-Diaz and Rodriguez, 2000].
NSAID modified-release preparations: improvement in efficacy and reduction in adverse events have not been demonstrated [Eccles et al, 1998]. Modified-release formulations are also relatively expensive.
Cyclo-oxygenase (COX)-2 selective NSAIDs (celecoxib, etodolac, meloxicam, and etoricoxib) should only be used for specific circumstances [NICE, 2001].
Co-proxamol (dextropropoxyphene 32.5 mg/ paracetamol 325 mg) has not been shown to be more effective as an analgesic than paracetamol alone. A significant disadvantage of co-proxamol is that overdosage is complicated by respiratory depression and acute heart failure [Medicines Resource, 1995; DTB, 1998; MeReC, 2000].
Topical heparinoid preparations: There are few controlled trials with topical heparinoid preparations and patient numbers are generally small [Mehta et al, 1977; O'Herlihy, 1980; Bergqvist et al, 1990; Annoni et al, 1991].
Class I graduated support hosiery (14–17 mmHg at ankle): There is insufficient evidence to support the use of low-level compression in the management of thrombophlebitis.

- **Class III graduated support hosiery (25–35 mmHg at ankle):** Better levels of compliance are achieved with a Class II garment [O'Hare, 1997].

Drugs included

- **Standard NSAIDs: ibuprofen, diclofenac, and naproxen** have a good balance of efficacy against adverse effect profile. Ibuprofen is associated with the lowest risk of gastrointestinal adverse effects and should be tried first before diclofenac and naproxen, which are associated with intermediate risk [CSM, 1994; Garcia and Jick, 1994; Henry et al, 1996; Bandolier, 1996; Eccles et al, 1998; Hernández-Diaz and Rodriguez, 2000].
- **Paracetamol:** This is an effective first-line choice for pain relief, especially when taken at regular intervals, rather than on an as required basis.
- **Class II graduated support hosiery (18–24 mmHg at ankle):** Class II graduated support stockings may help relieve pain and reduce the incidence of further thrombosis in superficial thrombophlebitis of the lower limbs. Compression hosiery is *not* appropriate where there is evidence of significant arterial disease.

Prescriptions

NSAID

Ibuprofen 400mg three times a day

- Age from 16 years onwards
- Ibuprofen 400mg tablets. Take one tablet three times a day; supply 48 tablets; NHS Cost £1.23; OTC Cost £2.17.

Ibuprofen 400mg four times a day

- Age from 16 years onwards
- Ibuprofen 400mg tablets. Take one tablet four times a day; supply 48 tablets; NHS Cost £1.23; OTC Cost £2.17.

Diclofenac sodium 25mg e/c three times a day

- Age from 16 years onwards
- Diclofenac 25mg e/c tablets. Take one tablet three times a day; supply 42 tablets; NHS Cost £2.30.

Diclofenac sodium 50mg e/c twice a day

- Age from 16 years onwards
- Diclofenac 50mg e/c tablets. Take one tablet twice a day; supply 28 tablets; NHS Cost £1.64.

Diclofenac sodium 50mg e/c three times a day

- Age from 16 years onwards
- Diclofenac 50mg e/c tablets. Take one tablet three times a day; supply 42 tablets; NHS Cost £2.45.

Naproxen 250mg twice a day

- Age from 16 years onwards
- Naproxen 250mg tablets. Take one tablet twice a day; supply 28 tablets; NHS Cost £2.76.

Naproxen 500mg twice a day

- Age from 16 years onwards
- Naproxen 500mg tablets. Take one tablet twice a day; supply 28 tablets; NHS Cost £3.70.

Paracetamol (intolerant of NSAID)

Paracetamol 1g up to four times a day

- Age from 16 years onwards
- Paracetamol 500mg tablets. Take two tablets every 4 to 6 hours when required for pain relief. Maximum of 8 tablets in 24 hours; supply 100 tablets; NHS Cost £0.56; OTC Cost £1.50.

Class II compression stockings

Knee-length stockings

- Age from 16 years onwards
- Class II knee-length stocking. One pair of circular knit, knee length class II compression stockings to be measured and fitted in the pharmacy; supply 2 single stockings; NHS Cost £8.32.

Thigh-length stockings with suspender belt

- Age from 16 years onwards
- Class II thigh-length stocking. One pair of circular knit, thigh length class II compression stockings to be measured and fitted in the pharmacy; supply 2 single stockings; NHS Cost £9.26.
- Suspender belt SP13. Use as directed; supply 2 belts; NHS Cost £8.30.

Thigh-length stockings with trouser suspenders

- Age from 16 years onwards
- Class II thigh-length stocking. One pair of circular knit, thigh length class II compression stockings to be measured and fitted in the pharmacy; supply 2 single stockings; NHS Cost £9.26.
- Trouser suspenders. Use as directed; supply 4 trouser suspenders; NHS Cost £2.16.

Extended Information

Background information

- What is it? p.1764
- How common is it? p.1764
- How do I know my patient has it? p.1764
- What else might it be? p.1764
- Complications and prognosis p.1764

What is it?

- **Superficial thrombophlebitis,** commonly known as 'phlebitis', is an inflammatory condition of the superficial veins, usually the long saphenous vein of the legs and its tributaries, with thrombus of a vein under the skin.
- **Superficial thrombophlebitis is most often associated** with one of the components of the Virchow triad, i.e. intimal damage (as a result of trauma, infection or inflammation), stasis, or changes in coaguable status [Johnson, 2001].
- **Thrombophlebitis frequently occurs in varicose veins,** commonly due to minor trauma or stasis. In upper limb veins, drug abuse, intravenous cannulas, and catheters are common causes [Messmore et al, 1991; Belcaro et al, 1999].
- **The risk of developing superficial thrombophlebitis is increased in** conditions known to increase thrombotic tendency, such as underlying malignancy, pregnancy, or use of oral oestrogen containing contraception [Samlaska and James, 1990b; DePalma and Johnson, 2000]; the risk of lower-oestrogen doses has not been well defined [Johnson, 2001]. Hereditary pro-thrombotic conditions (hereditary thrombophilia) can also present with recurrent superficial thrombophlebitis [Samlaska and James, 1990a; Hanson et al, 1998].
- **Rare conditions** such as Behcet's disease, Buerger's disease, and Mondor's disease also frequently present with superficial thrombophlebitis [Samlaska and James, 1990b].
- **Septic (suppurative) thrombophlebitis** is a more serious, even lethal, complication of intravenous cannulation and intravenous drug abuse and is frequently associated with septicaemia. Rarely, it may be secondary to a primary infectious disease (mainly syphilis and psittacosis) [Samlaska and James, 1990b].

How common is it?

- **There are few estimates of prevalence.** In the U.S., prevalence has been reported to be 125,000 cases a year the true prevalence is probably higher, with many unreported cases [Wasserman et al, 1997; Blumenberg e al, 1998; Murgia et al, 1999].
- **It is more common** in females, people above 60 years of age, people with varicose veins, the obese, and cigarette smokers [Johnson, 2001].
- **Among people with varicose veins the incidence of thrombophlebitis** is reported to range from 14.6 to 50% [Agus et al, 1993].

How do I know my patient has it?

- **Swelling, redness, pain and tenderness along the course of the vein** are the typical presentation.
- The thrombosed veins feel like cords (knots) or a chain of nodules along the course of the vein.
- Fever, lymphangitis, and signs of systemic upset (especially if septic) may also be present.
- **Superficial thrombophlebitis frequently occurs at the sit of an intravenous infusion** either as a result of the drugs being given or due to the intraluminal catheter or cannula itself. Redness and pain, while the infusion is being given, signal its presence.However, thrombosis may manifest as a small lump days or weeks after the infusion has been removed and may take months to completely resolve.
- **Consider septic thrombophlebitis** if recent intravenous cannulation or intravenous drug abuse.

[Bendick et al, 1995; Wasserman et al, 1997; Johnson, 2001]

What else might it be?

- Cellulitis
- Deep vein thrombosis (DVT)
- Tendonitis
- Soft tissue trauma
- Cutaneous polyarteritis nodosa
- Sarcoid
- Erythema nodosum
- Lymphangitis
- Neuritis
- Ruptured medial head of gastrocnemius

[Samlaska and James, 1990b; Wasserman et al, 1997; Belcaro et al, 1999; Johnson, 2001]

Complications and prognosis

Complications

Aseptic thrombophlebitis

- **Superficial thrombophlebitis is usually a benign self-limiting disease.** However, it has been associated with extension into the deep venous system and pulmonary embolism.
- **Deep venous thrombosis (DVT).** The frequency of deep venous involvement (detected by duplex ultrasound scanning) in studies of highly selected patients with superficial thrombophlebitis referred for vascular investigation, ranges from 9–44% [Bounameaux and Reber-Wasem, 1997]. However, the true incidence is likely to be much lower and the risk of deep venous thrombosis with superficial thrombophlebitis in genera practice is unclear.
- **Progression to the deep venous system should be considered** if the thrombosis involves the proximal part of the long saphenous vein in the thigh (but may extenc

from the short saphenous vein or thigh and calf perforators), or if other risk factors are present, e.g. past history of DVT, hereditary thrombophilia, cancer, bilateral involvement, or recent bed rest/immobilisation [Lutter et al, 1991].

Other risk factors which may be associated with a greater likelihood of DVT includes: age greater than 60 years, male sex, and systemic infection [Lutter et al, 1991].

Pulmonary embolism (PE) (rarely). When thrombophlebitis progresses into the deep venous system, it may lead to PE (reported in 10–20% cases) [Lutter et al, 1991; Bendick et al, 1995; Blumenberg et al, 1998; Murgia et al, 1999; Verlato et al, 1999]. Very rarely the thrombus may undergo embolization to the lungs with no obvious deep venous involvement [Kesteven and Robinson, 2001].

ptic thrombophlebitis

Systemic sepsis, septicaemia

Septic pulmonary emboli

Abscess formation

Pneumonia

rognosis

eptic

Duration of symptoms is variable. In uncomplicated cases, patients should be told to expect the symptoms to persist for 2 to 6 weeks (or longer in some cases).

Prognosis depends on development of DVT and early detection of complications.

Death from superficial thrombophlebitis without complications is very rare. However, if it extends into the deep venous system, it can be the source of PE.

ptic

Mortality can be high if untreated.

ndick et al, 1995; Bounameaux and Reber-Wasem, 97; Blumenberg et al, 1998]

Ianagement issues

General issues p.1765

Treatments p.1765

Complications p.1765

eneral issues

Before treatment is started, associated deep vein thrombosis (DVT) should be excluded. The frequency of deep venous involvement (detected by duplex ultrasound scanning) in highly selected patients with superficial thrombophlebitis referred for vascular investigation ranges from 9–44%. The true incidence is likely to be much lower and the risk of deep venous thrombosis with superficial thrombophlebitis in general practice is unclear.

The possibility of DVT and referral to exclude it should be considered if other risk factors are present, for example; past history of DVT, involvement of the proximal part of the long saphenous vein in the thigh, hereditary thrombophilia, cancer, bilateral involvement, or immobilisation.

tter et al, 1991; Jorgensen et al, 1993; Bendick et al, 95; Campbell, 1996; Bounameaux and Reber-Wasem, 97; Blumenberg et al, 1998]

eatments

Uncomplicated superficial thrombophlebitis is usually treated symptomatically with heat, simple analgesia, nonsteroidal anti-inflammatory drugs (NSAIDs), and compression stockings [Wakefield, 1994], although there is a lack of data on how effective these treatments are.

- **Treatment should continue** until symptoms have completely subsided (usually 2–6 weeks to subside but the thrombosed vein may be palpable and tender for months).
- **Patients should be encouraged to** use the affected arm/leg and continue their usual daily activities. Leg elevation is thought to improve venous blood flow and to reduce swelling. Bed rest is not generally advised and patients should be encouraged to keep mobile.
- **More severe thrombophlebitis,** as indicated by the degree of pain and redness and the extent of abnormality, should be treated by bed rest with elevation of the extremity and application of massive, hot, wet compresses [Messmore et al, 1991; Johnson, 2001].

Complications

- **Septic thrombophlebitis may require admission for antibiotic therapy.**
- **A hereditary thrombophilia** should be suspected if there is a family history of thrombosis, or if superficial thrombophlebitis is recurrent, or occurs at an early age [Samlaska and James, 1990a].
- **An underlying malignancy** should be considered in all cases of recurrent or migratory superficial thrombophlebitis [Samlaska and James, 1990b; Blumenberg et al, 1998].

References

NHS staff in England can link, free of charge, from references to full text journals by clicking on [Full text] on the PRODIGY website.

1. Agus, G.B., De Angelis, R., Mondani, P. and Moia, R. (1993) Double-blind comparison of nimesulide and diclofenac in the treatment of superficial thrombophlebitis with telethermographic assessment. *Drugs* **46**(Suppl 1), 200–203.
2. Annoni, F., De Stefano, A., Pabisch, S. et al (1991) Efficacy and safety of topical treatment with heparan sulfate in superficial phlebitis. A double-blind placebo-controlled trial. *Acta Therapeutica* **17**(3), 263–272.
3. Bandolier (1996) *GI complications and NSAIDs.* Bandolier 25. www.jr2.ox.ac.uk/bandolier/band25/b25-1.html [Accessed: 01/09/2005].
4. Belcaro, G., Nicolaides, A.N., Errichi, B.M. et al (1999) Superficial thrombophlebitis of the legs: a randomized, controlled, follow-up study. *Angiology* **50**(7), 523–529. [Full text]
5. Bendick, P.J., Ryan, R., Alpers, M. et al (1995) Clinical significance of superficial thrombophlebitis. *Journal of Vascular Technology* **19**(2), 57–61.
6. Bergqvist, D., Brunkwall, J., Jensen, N. and Persson, N.H. (1990) Treatment of superficial thrombophlebitis. A comparative trial between placebo, Hirudoid cream and piroxicam gel. *Annales Chirurgiae et Gynaecologiae* **79**(2), 92–96.
7. Blumenberg, R.M., Barton, E., Gelfand, M.L. et al (1998) Occult deep venous thrombosis complicating superficial thrombophlebitis. *Journal of Vascular Surgery* **27**(2), 338–343.
8. Bounameaux, H. and Reber-Wasem, M.A. (1997) Superficial thrombophlebitis and deep vein thrombosis. A controversial association. *Archives of Internal Medicine* **157**(16), 1822–1824. [Full text]
9. Campbell, B. (1996) Thrombosis, phlebitis, and varicose veins. *British Medical Journal* **312**(7025), 198–199. [Full text]

10. CSM (1994) Relative safety of oral non-aspirin NSAIDs. *Current Problems in Pharmacovigilance* **20**(Aug), 9–11.
11. DePalma, R.G. and Johnson, G. (2000) Superficial thrombophlebitis: diagnosis and management. In: Rutherford, R.B. (Ed.) *Vascular Surgery*. 5th edn. London: W.B.Saunders Company. 1979–1981.
12. DTB (1998) Co-proxamol or paracetamol for acute pain? *Drug & Therapeutics Bulletin* **36**(10), 80. [Full text]
13. Eccles, M., Freemantle, N. and Mason, J. (1998) North of England evidence based guideline development project: summary guideline for non-steroidal anti-inflammatory drugs versus basic analgesia in treating the pain of degenerative arthritis. *British Medical Journal* **317**(7157), 526–530. [Full text]
14. Garcia, R.L. and Jick, H. (1994) Risk of upper gastrointestinal bleeding and perforation associated with individual non-steroidal anti-inflammatory drugs. *Lancet* **343**(8900), 769–772. [Full text]
15. Gotzsche, P.C. (2001) Non-steroidal anti-inflammatory drugs. *Clinical Evidence* **5**(Jun), 800–807.
16. Hanson, J.N., Ascher, E., De Pippo, P. et al (1998) Saphenous vein thrombophlebitis (SVT): a deceptively benign disease. *Journal of Vascular Surgery* **27**(4), 677–680.
17. Henry, D., Lim, L.L., Garcia-Rodriguez, L.A. et al (1996) Variability in risk of gastrointestinal complications with individual non-steroidal anti-inflammatory drugs: results of a collaborative meta-analysis. *British Medical Journal* **312**(7046), 1563–1566. [Full text]
18. Hernández-Diaz, S. and Rodriguez, L.A. (2000) Association between nonsteroidal anti-inflammatory drugs and upper gastrointestinal tract bleeding/perforation: an overview of epidemiologic studies published in the 1990s. *Archives of Internal Medicine* **160**(14), 2093–2099. [Full text]
19. Heyneman, C.A., Lawless-Liday, C. and Wall, G.C. (2000) Oral versus topical NSAIDs in rheumatic diseases: a comparison. *Drugs* **60**(3), 555–574.
20. Johnson, G. (2001) *Superficial thrombophlebitis*. eMedicine Journal. Vol 2, No.8. www.emedicine.com/MED/topic3201.htm [Accessed: 14/11/2001].
21. Jorgensen, J.O., Hanel, K.C., Morgan, A.M. and Hunt, J.M. (1993) The incidence of deep venous thrombosis in patients with superficial thrombophlebitis of the lower limbs. *Journal of Vascular Surgery* **18**(1), 70–73.
22. Kesteven, P. and Robinson, B. (2001) Superficial thrombophlebitis followed by pulmonary embolism. *Journal of the Royal Society of Medicine* **94**(4), 186–187.
23. Lutter, K.S., Kerr, T.M., Roedersheimer, L.R. et al (1991) Superficial thrombophlebitis diagnosed by duplex scanning. *Surgery* **110**(1), 42–46.
24. Medicines Resource (1995) Combination analgesics. *Medicines Resource* **25**, 95–98.
25. Mehta, P.P., Sagar, S. and Kakkar, V.V. (1977) Treatment of superficial thrombophlebitis: a randomized, double-blind trial of heparinoid cream. *British Medical Journal* 3(5984), 614–616.
26. MeReC (2000) The use of oral analgesics in primary care. *MeReC Bulletin* **11**(1), 1–4.
27. Messmore, H.L., Bishop, M. and Wehrmacher, W.H. (1991) Acute venous thrombosis. Therapeutic choices for superficial and deep veins. *Postgraduate Medicine* **89**(7), 73–77.
28. Moore, R.A., Tramer, M.R., Carroll, D. et al (1998) Quantitative systematic review of topically applied non-steroidal anti-inflammatory drugs. *British Medic Journal* **316**(7128), 333–338. [Full text]
29. Murgia, A.P., Cisno, C., Pansini, G.C. et al (1999) Surgical management of ascending saphenous thrombophlebitis. *International Angiology* **18**(4), 343–347. [Full text]
30. NICE (2001) *Guidance on the use of cyclo-oxygenas (Cox) II selective inhibitors, celecoxib, rofecoxib, meloxicam and etodolac for osteoarthritis and rheumatoid arthritis*. Technology appraisal no. 27. National Institute for Health and Clinical Excellence www.nice.org.uk [Accessed: 16/10/2003].
31. O'Hare, L. (1997) Scholl compression hosiery in the management of venous disorders. *British Journal of Nursing* **6**(7), 391–394.
32. O'Herlihy, C. (1980) Heparinoid cream in pregnancy–associated superficial thrombophlebitis. *Practitioner* **224**(1349), 1202–1203.
33. Samlaska, C.P. and James, W.D. (1990a) Superficial thrombophlebitis: I. Primary hypercoagulable states. *Journal of the American Academy of Dermatology* **22**(6 Pt 1), 975–989. [erratum appears in J Am Acad Dermatol (1990) 23(3 Pt 1), 472].
34. Samlaska, C.P. and James, W.D. (1990b) Superficial thrombophlebitis: II. Secondary hypercoagulable stat *Journal of the American Academy of Dermatology* **23**(1), 1–18.
35. Verlato, F., Zucchetta, P., Prandoni, P. et al (1999) A unexpectedly high rate of pulmonary embolism in patients with superficial thrombophlebitis of the thig *Journal of Vascular Surgery* **30**(6), 1113–1115.
36. Wakefield, T.W. (1994) Venous disorders. *Problems General Surgery* **11**(3), 497–510.
37. Wasserman, D., Bonner, K., Devereaux, C. et al (199 Duplex surveillance of superficial thrombophlebitis. *Vascular & Endovascular Surgery* **31**(4), 427–431.

T

PRODIGY GUIDANCE

Transient ischaemic attack — not in atrial fibrillation

Last revised in February 2004

At the time of print this topic was being updated. The newly revised guidance will be issued on to the website in 2006.

www.prodigy.nhs.uk/guidance.asp?gt=TIA - not in AF

Applies to people over the age of 16 years

This guidance covers the management of transient ischaemic attack (TIA) in people who are in sinus rhythm.

This guidance does not cover the management of TIA in people who are in atrial fibrillation (AF), or the management of acute or completed stroke.

There is separate PRODIGY guidance for the management of *Atrial fibrillation*, within which the management of TIA in a person with AF is covered.

Goals

To reduce the risk of subsequent episodes of transient ischaemic attack or of stroke
To reduce the risk of other vascular disease
To arrange urgent specialist assessment

Contents

Scenarios

- TIA – in a person tolerant of aspirin – not in AF p.1767
- TIA – in a person intolerant of aspirin – not in AF p.1768

Extended Information, p. 1769

Which scenario?

TIA — in a person tolerant of aspirin — not in AF: covers the management of TIA in a person who can tolerate aspirin and who is not in atrial fibrillation.

TIA — in a person intolerant of aspirin — not in AF: covers the management of TIA in a person who cannot tolerate aspirin and who is not in atrial fibrillation.

TIA — in a person tolerant of aspirin — not in AF

Which therapy?

Consider referral for urgent assessment (e.g. a fast-track transient ischaemic attack (TIA) assessment clinic); arrangements may vary depending on the local situation. **Treatment should not be delayed while waiting for this assessment.**

Aspirin is preferred treatment.

The combination of aspirin with modified-release dipyridamole could be considered for people who have further TIAs while taking aspirin.

Other modifiable risk factors must be dealt with (i.e. smoking, hypertension, atrial fibrillation, hyperlipidaemia, diabetes mellitus, excessive alcohol consumption, and physical inactivity).

Practical prescribing points

For further information please see the *Medicines Compendium* (www.medicines.org.uk) or the *British National Formulary* (www.bnf.org).

Low-dosage aspirin

- **Avoid** in gastrointestinal ulceration, haemophilia and other bleeding disorders.
- **Concurrent nonsteroidal anti-inflammatory drugs (NSAIDs):** the risk of serious gastrointestinal complications doubles in people who regularly take low-dose aspirin and another NSAID. If possible, stop the second NSAID.
- **If a second NSAID must be continued, avoid ibuprofen** — it may reduce the cardiovascular protective effect of low-dose aspirin. Consider using diclofenac if a second NSAID must be used.
- **Asthma:** aspirin can induce bronchospasm in people who are hypersensitive to aspirin, but this is rare.

Dipyridamole

- **It acts as a potent vasodilator and may therefore lead to clinical deterioration** in people with severe coronary artery disease, including unstable angina, recent myocardial infarction, and heart failure.
- **Diarrhoea and headache** have been reported as being the reason why some people have stopped dipyridamole.
- **Other adverse effects** such as nausea, dyspepsia, and gastric pain have been reported. People may also develop hot flushes, hypotension, and dizziness.

Should I refer or investigate?

Refer?

- Consider referral for urgent assessment (e.g. a fast track TIA assessment clinic) to confirm the diagnosis and ensure optimal management.

Investigate?

- Initial primary care investigations include full blood count, erythrocyte sedimentation rate, serum electrolytes, serum lipid levels, blood glucose, and electrocardiogram.
- Further investigations may be carried out in secondary care, including carotid duplex ultrasound (and subsequent angiography in those identified as having possibly greater than 70% stenosis of the carotid artery), echocardiography, and cranial computed tomography or magnetic resonance imaging.

Patient information leaflets

The following PILs are available at www.prodigy.nhs.uk

- Aspirin to Prevent Blood Clots
- Blood Test - Detecting Inflammation
- Blood Test - General
- Chest Heart & Stroke Scotland
- Stroke Association
- Transient Ischaemic Attack (TIA)

Shared decision making

- A transient ischaemic attack (TIA) occurs when a tiny 'flake' of clotted blood temporarily blocks the blood flow to a part of the brain.
- **Aspirin** is the usual treatment. A low dose taken each day reduces the risk of blood clots forming and causing a further TIA or stroke.
- **Dipyridamole** may be added if you have a further TIA while taking aspirin.
- Reducing risk factors is important. You should stop smoking and take regular exercise. Your blood pressure and blood cholesterol level need to be checked, and lowered if the results are high.
- **Referral** to a specialist is common after a TIA. This is to clarify the diagnosis. Some people with TIA also have very narrowed arteries leading to the brain, and surgery may then be an option.

Drug rationale

Drugs not included

- **Enteric-coated** aspirin is not usually required because the difference in gastrointestinal toxicity at 75 mg between plain and enteric-coated tablets is minimal [DTB, 1997].
- **Clopidogrel** is licensed for the secondary prevention of stroke, and may be marginally more effective than aspirin, but more data is needed [Medicines Resource, 1998; Hankey et al, 1999]. It is also very expensive. Clopidogrel could be considered in people who are intolerant of aspirin.
- **Dipyridamole alone** is not included because the evidence of efficacy as an antiplatelet agent is not as great as for aspirin. The standard-release product is not licensed for transient ischaemic attack (TIA).
- **Warfarin and other anticoagulants** are not advised for the secondary prevention of stroke in people with TIA, unless atrial fibrillation coexists.

Drugs included

- **Aspirin 75 mg** has a favourable risk:benefit ratio for the secondary prevention of stroke and TIA. The 75 mg dose is as effective as higher doses of aspirin [Eccles et al, 1998; Medicines Resource, 1998; Antithrombotic Trialists' Collaboration, 2002].
- **The combination of aspirin with modified-release dipyridamole.** Dipyridamole is licensed for the secondary prevention of TIA, and its use in addition to aspirin could be considered for people who continue to have TIAs despite aspirin use, although there is no consensus on this issue [Rodgers, 1998; Albers et al, 1999]. There is no evidence to support any one dosage or combination. The European Stroke Prevention Study 2 used a combined daily dose of aspirin 50 mg and dipyridamole modified-release 400 mg.

T

Prescriptions

Aspirin

Aspirin 75mg dispersible once a day

- Age from 16 years onwards
- Aspirin 75mg dispersible tabs. Take one tablet once a day; supply 28 tablets; NHS Cost £0.36; OTC Cost £0.63.

Aspirin + dipyridamole

Separate bottles: aspirin 75mg + dipyridamole 400mg p[er] day

- Age from 16 years onwards
- Aspirin 75mg dispersible tabs. Take one tablet once a day; supply 28 tablets; NHS Cost £0.36; OTC Cost £0.63.
- Dipyridamole 200mg m/r caps. Take one capsule twic[e] day; supply 60 capsules; NHS Cost £9.75.

Combined capsules: aspirin 50mg + dipyridamole 400m[g] per day

- Age from 16 years onwards
- Dipyrid+Asp 200mg/25mg m/r cap. Take one capsule twice a day; supply 60 capsules; NHS Cost £9.75.

TIA — in a person intolerant of aspirin — not in AF

Which therapy?

- **Consider referral for urgent assessment** (e.g. a fast-trac[k] transient ischaemia attack (TIA) assessment clinic); arrangements may vary depending on the local situati[on]
- **Treatment should not be delayed while waiting for thi[s] assessment.**
- **Clopidogrel is an alternative to aspirin for those peopl[e] who are hypersensitive to aspirin.**
- **Modified-release dipyridamole is an alternative for tho[se] people who are intolerant of aspirin** and clopidogrel (e[.g.] due to gastrointestinal adverse effects). It is the preferr[ed] option where aspirin and clopidogrel are contraindica[ted] (e.g.in people with active bleeding such as gastric and duodenal ulcer, or intracranial haemorrhage).
- **Other modifiable risk factors must be dealt with** (i.e. smoking, hypertension, atrial fibrillation, hyperlipidaemia, diabetes mellitus, excessive alcohol consumption, and physical inactivity).

Practical prescribing points

For further information please see the *Medicines Compendium* (www.medicines.org.uk) or the *British National Formulary* (www.bnf.org).

Clopidogrel

- **Adverse effects** that have been reported as being fairly common include: bleeding, indigestion, nausea, vomiting, headache, dizziness, vertigo, paraesthesia, rashes, and diarrhoea.
- **Carefully monitor people** for any signs (purpura, bruising and haematoma) of internal or external bleeding during the first few weeks of treatment.

Dipyridamole

- **Acts as a potent vasodilator and may therefore lead to clinical deterioration** in people with severe coronary artery disease, including unstable angina, recent myocardial infarction, and heart failure.

Adverse effects tend to occur early after initiating treatment and may disappear with continued treatment. Diarrhoea and headache have been reported as causing some people to stop treatment.

Other adverse effects include: nausea, dyspepsia and gastric pain. People may also develop hot flushes, hypotension, and dizziness.

Should I refer or investigate?

Refer?

Consider referral for urgent assessment (e.g. a fast-track TIA assessment clinic) to confirm the diagnosis and ensure optimal management.

Investigate?

Initial primary care investigations include full blood count, erythrocyte sedimentation rate, serum electrolytes, serum lipid levels, blood glucose, and electrocardiogram.

Further investigations may be carried out in secondary care, including carotid duplex ultrasound (and subsequent angiography in those identified as having possibly greater than 70% stenosis of the carotid artery), echocardiography, and cranial computed tomography or magnetic resonance imaging.

Patient information leaflets

The following PILs are available at www.prodigy.nhs.uk

Blood Test - Detecting Inflammation
Blood Test - General
Chest Heart & Stroke Scotland
Stroke Association
Transient Ischaemic Attack (TIA)

Shared decision making

A transient ischaemic attack (TIA) occurs when a tiny 'flake' of clotted blood temporarily blocks the blood flow to a part of the brain.

Treatment aims to reduce the risk of blood clots forming and causing a further TIA or stroke. Aspirin is the usual treatment but some people cannot take aspirin.

Clopidogrel is an alternative. Most people have no problems with taking this. Side effects sometimes occur and include: abdominal discomfort, feeling sick, vomiting, diarrhoea, constipation, and bleeding from the gut.

Dipyridamole is another alternative. Most people have no problems with taking this. Side effects sometimes occur and include: abdominal discomfort, feeling sick, vomiting, diarrhoea, constipation, headaches, and hot flushes.

Reducing risk factors is important. You should stop smoking and take regular exercise. Your blood pressure and blood cholesterol level need to be checked, and lowered if the results are high.

Referral to a specialist is common after a TIA. This is to clarify the diagnosis. Some people with TIAs also have very narrowed arteries leading to the brain, and surgery may then be an option.

Drug rationale

Drugs not included

Aspirin or aspirin-containing combinations are not included.

- **Warfarin and other anticoagulants** are not advised for the secondary prevention of stroke in people with TIA, unless atrial fibrillation coexists.

Drugs included

- **Clopidogrel** is licensed for the secondary prevention of stroke, and may be moderately more effective than aspirin, but more data are needed [Medicines Resource, 1998; Hankey et al, 1999]. It is also very expensive.
- **Modified-release dipyridamole** is included for those people who cannot tolerate clopidogrel. It is proposed as second-line to clopidogrel, as dipyridamole has not been shown to have any effect on the risk of myocardial infarction or vascular death in people who have had a TIA [Diener et al, 1996].

Prescriptions

Clopidogrel or dipyridamole

Clopidogrel 75mg once a day

- Age from 18 years onwards
- Clopidogrel 75mg tablets. Take one tablet once a day; supply 28 tablets; NHS Cost £35.31.

Dipyridamole 200mg m/r twice a day

- Age from 16 years onwards
- Dipyridamole 200mg m/r caps. Take one capsule twice a day; supply 60 capsules; NHS Cost £9.00.

Extended Information

Background information

- What is it? p.1769
- How common is it? p.1769
- How do I know my patient has it? p.1770
- What else might it be? p.1770
- Complications and prognosis p.1770

What is it?

- **A transient ischaemic attack (TIA) is defined as** the sudden onset of a focal cerebral or retinal deficit that recovers within 24 hours. After adequate investigation it is presumed to be due to thromboembolic vascular disease. The majority of episodes last less than 30 minutes [Warlow and Davenport, 1996; Rodgers, 1998].
- **The source of the thromboembolism** is most commonly the carotid arteries, the heart (particularly in people with atrial fibrillation), the aorta, or the vertebrobasilar arteries.
- **Haemodynamic TIAs occur rarely.** They are caused by hypotensive episodes (e.g. drug-induced), or arrhythmias. Their management depends on the cause, and is not discussed here.

How common is it?

- **The incidence of transient ischaemic attack (TIA)** is 0.42 per 1000 population [Rodgers, 1998].
- **A general practitioner with a list size of 2000 people** will see five new people with a TIA or a stroke each year [Eccles et al, 1998].
- About 15% of people who suffer their first ever stroke have had preceding TIAs [Warlow and Davenport, 1996].

T

How do I know my patient has it?

History

- **The history is of the sudden onset of a focal cerebral or retinal deficit that recovers within 24 hours.** It usually lasts no longer than 30 minutes. If the deficit lasts longer than 24 hours it is defined as a stroke.
- **Ischaemia in the carotid territory occurs in 80% of cases.** This may cause weakness or sensory symptoms affecting an arm, leg, or one side of the face. It may also cause monocular visual loss (amaurosis fugax), dysphasia, or dysarthria.
- **Ischaemia in the vertebrobasilar territory occurs in 20% of cases.** This may cause a hemiparesis, hemisensory symptoms, homonymous hemianopia, bilateral blindness, diplopia, vertigo, vomiting, dysarthria, dysphagia, or ataxia.
- **Global symptoms by themselves are rarely due to TIA** (e.g. unsteadiness, dizziness, syncope).

[Rothwell and Warlow, 1997; DTB, 1998]

Examination

- **Examination is usually normal,** unless neurological signs are still present, but may provide evidence of risk factors (e.g. hypertension, carotid bruits, or atrial fibrillation). Bruits are an unreliable guide to the presence or severity of carotid stenosis; severe stenosis may cause no bruit.

What else might it be?

There are many differential diagnoses of transient ischaemic attack (TIA), which include:

- Migrainous aura
- Retinal or vitreous haemorrhage
- Giant cell arteritis
- Focal epileptic seizure
- Intracranial lesion (e.g. tumour, subdural haematoma)
- Multiple sclerosis
- Labyrinthine disorders
- Peripheral nerve lesions
- Transient global amnesia
- Psychological disorders (including hyperventilation)
- Metabolic disturbance (e.g. hypoglycaemia)

[Warlow and Davenport, 1996; SIGN, 1997a]

Complications and prognosis

Prognosis

Subsequent stroke

- The risk of stroke in the first month after a transient ischaemic attack (TIA) is 5%.
- The risk of stroke in the first year after a TIA is 10%.
- The annual risk during the next 4 years is 7% (seven times the risk of the normal population) [Warlow and Davenport, 1996; SIGN, 1997b; DTB, 1998].
- The risk is greater with frequent TIAs, cerebral rather than ocular events, and severe carotid stenosis [Warlow and Davenport, 1996; Rodgers, 1998].

Other atheromatous event

- The annual risk of myocardial infarction after a TIA is about 2–3%, and 35% of people who have had a TIA will eventually die of cardiac disease.
- The combined risk of stroke, myocardial infarction, or vascular death is about 9% per year [Warlow and Davenport, 1996; Rodgers, 1998].

T

Management issues

- General issues p.1770
- Antiplatelet treatment p.1770
- Anticoagulation p.1771
- Other drug treatments p.1771
- Surgery p.1771
- Medicines management p.1771

General issues

- **People with a suspected transient ischaemic attack (TIA require urgent assessment** because there is a significant risk of subsequent stroke; this risk is 5% in the first month after a TIA [Warlow and Davenport, 1996; SIGN, 1997a; Rodgers, 1998]. Local arrangements for this vary, although many districts now have fast-track assessment clinics.
- **Other modifiable risk factors must be dealt with** (i.e. smoking, hypertension, atrial fibrillation, hyperlipidaemia, diabetes mellitus, excessive alcohol consumption, and physical inactivity) [SIGN, 1997a; Albers et al, 1999]. Numerous trials have consistently shown a reduction in risk of stroke with control of thes conditions, but few of these involved people with TIA [Albers et al, 1999].
- **Hypertension** is the single most important modifiable risk factor, with 26% of strokes attributable to raised blood pressure [Medicines Resource, 1998] (see PRODIC guidance on *Hypertension*).
- **Hyperlipidaemia** should be managed in line with secondary prevention recommendations because people with TIA have a high risk of coronary heart disease (see PRODIGY guidance on *Hyperlipidaemia*). Trials of lipid-lowering therapy in people with TIA have not yet been published, but are currently under way. There is eviden that lipid-lowering therapy reduces the risk of stroke, b the data is derived from trials of primary and secondary prevention of coronary heart disease [SIGN, 1997a; Medicines Resource, 1998; Albers et al, 1999].

Antiplatelet treatment

- **Aspirin is preferred therapy for the secondary preventic of TIA/stroke.** It inhibits platelet aggregation by inhibiting platelet cyclooxygenase and thromboxane A production. It reduces the 3-year risk of subsequent stroke, myocardial infarction, or vascular death in people with TIA by 22% (equivalent to treating 100 people with TIA for 3 years to prevent four major vascular events) [Antiplatelet Trialists Collaboration, 1994; Hankey et al, 1999]. Medium-dose aspirin (75–325 mg) compares favourably with high-dose aspirin (500–1500 mg) [Albers et al, 1999; Hankey et a 1999; Antithrombotic Trialists' Collaboration, 2002]. dose of 75 mg is effective, and is recommended in preference to higher doses, and should be continued lor term in at-risk people [SIGN, 1997a; Eccles et al, 1998 Clinical Evidence, 2001; Antithrombotic Trialists' Collaboration, 2002]. There is some suggestion that ev lower doses of aspirin are effective, but less data exists for doses below 75 mg [Clinical Evidence, 2001; Antithrombotic Trialists' Collaboration, 2002].
- **Clopidogrel is licensed for the secondary prevention of vascular events in people with established atheroscler disease.** Clopidogrel belongs to the group known as the thienopyridines and acts by inhibiting platelet aggregation by irreversibly modifying the platelet adenosine diphosphate receptor [DTB, 1999]. It was compared with aspirin 325 mg daily in a large trial of people with established atherosclerotic disease (but not TIA). Clopidogrel had a slightly greater efficacy than aspirin in reducing the combined end-point of myocardial infarction, stroke, and vascular death in people with atherosclerotic disease; the absolute benefi however, was small (0.5% absolute annual risk

reduction). Gastrointestinal adverse-effects occurred less frequently in the clopidogrel group (however, people with aspirin hypersensitivity were excluded) [CAPRIE Steering Committee, 1996; Albers et al, 1999; Hankey et al, 1999]. **The current recommendation is still to use aspirin as preferred therapy** for the secondary prevention of stroke and TIA [SIGN, 1997a; DTB, 1998; Eccles et al, 1998; Antithrombotic Trialists' Collaboration, 2002]. Clopidogrel could be considered for people who are intolerant of aspirin, although there is no consensus on this issue [Albers et al, 1999].

Dipyridamole inhibits phosphodiesterase, resulting in increased antiplatelet levels of cyclic adenosine monophosphate and inhibition of thromboxane A2. Evidence from the European Stroke Prevention Study 2 (which enrolled 6602 people with TIA or stroke) showed dipyridamole (400 mg modified-release daily) to be as effective at preventing stroke as very-low-dose aspirin (50 mg daily), with a 16% reduction in risk with dipyridamole and an 18% reduction with aspirin compared with placebo. However, this study showed dipyridamole to have no effect on the risk of myocardial infarction or vascular death [Diener et al, 1996]. There is still insufficient trial data comparing dipyridamole (as a single agent) with other antiplatelet agents to recommend its preferred use in TIA [Antithrombotic Trialists' Collaboration, 2002]. Modified-release dipyridamole could be considered for people who are intolerant of aspirin, although there is no consensus on this issue.

The combination of modified-release dipyridamole with aspirin is an option, however. Until recently there was little evidence of any benefit from dipyridamole, given alone or in combination with aspirin [The American Canadian Co-operative Study Group, 1985; Antiplatelet Trialists Collaboration, 1994]. In the European Stroke Prevention Study 2, the combination of dipyridamole with aspirin was more effective than either drug given alone at reducing the risk of stroke, with a 37% reduction in risk compared with placebo. The combination, however, did not significantly reduce the combined risk of stroke or death, or the risk of myocardial infarction, compared with either aspirin or dipyridamole alone [Diener et al, 1996]. **The current recommendation is still to use aspirin as preferred therapy** for the secondary prevention of stroke [SIGN, 1997a; DTB, 1998; Eccles et al, 1998; Antithrombotic Trialists' Collaboration, 2002]. The combination of aspirin with modified-release dipyridamole could be considered for people who continue to have TIAs despite aspirin use, although there is no consensus on this issue [Rodgers, 1998; Albers et al, 1999].

Computed tomographic examination is not necessary before starting treatment in people with TIA [Eccles et al, 1998].

nticoagulation

Warfarin is much more effective than aspirin for the secondary prevention of stroke in people with atrial fibrillation who have had a TIA [Albers et al, 1999; Koudstaal, 2002]. Warfarin is not recommended for the secondary prevention of stroke in people in sinus rhythm who have had a TIA [Rothwell and Warlow, 1997; SPIRIT, 1997; Rodgers, 1998] (see the scenario *Deciding antithrombotic treatment* in the PRODIGY guidance on *Atrial fibrillation* for details of warfarin treatment).

ther drug treatments

The use of hormone replacement therapy in women with a history of TIA has not been evaluated. Trials are currently in progress.

Surgery

- **Carotid endarterectomy** in a person with severe symptomatic carotid stenosis (more than 70% stenosis) who has had a TIA reduces the risk of disabling stroke or death by 48% [SIGN, 1997b; DTB, 1998; Albers et al, 1999; Cina et al, 2001]. In trials of carotid endarterectomy in people with TIA the perioperative risk of disabling stroke or death was less than 5% [SIGN, 1997b; Rodgers, 1998]. The number of people with severe stenosis who needed to be operated on to prevent one disabling stroke or death over 2–6 years follow-up (number needed to treat) was 15; the number needed to be operated on to cause one disabling stroke or death (number needed to harm) was 45 [Cina et al, 2001].
- **Carotid angioplasty** has not been adequately assessed in people with a history of TIA [SIGN, 1997b; Clinical Evidence, 2001]. The CAVATAS trial showed that angioplasty was as effective at preventing stroke over 3 years as carotid endarterectomy, with similar major risks; confidence intervals, however, were wide [CAVATAS, 2001].

Medicines management

Aspirin

- Dispersible aspirin 75 mg daily is recommended.
- Lower doses of aspirin are as effective as higher doses at preventing ischaemic vascular events [Antithrombotic Trialists' Collaboration, 2002]. The risk of bleeding with aspirin has not been clearly demonstrated to be dose-dependent, therefore caution is needed irrespective which dose of aspirin is chosen [He et al, 1998; Derry and Loke, 2000; Pignone et al, 2002].
- There is no evidence that different formulations of aspirin differ in their risk of causing gastrointestinal bleeding [Derry and Loke, 2000]. Dispersible aspirin is the cheapest formulation available.
- **Aspirin** often causes dyspepsia. Increasing doses of aspirin are associated with greater risks of gastrointestinal toxicity (e.g. ulceration, bleeding, and perforation).

Clopidogrel

- **The current standard initiation and maintenance dose is 75 mg daily.** It is recommended for use in people aged 18 years and over.
- **Clopidogrel is contraindicated in people:**
  - With active bleeding such as gastric and duodenal ulcer or intracranial haemorrhage.
  - For the first few days after myocardial infarction and for 7 days after ischaemic stroke.
- **Avoid concomitant use with warfarin** as the intensity of bleeds may be increased.
- **Consider the benefit against the risk in people more susceptible to bleeding,** and monitor carefully where the decision is taken to prescribe clopidogrel in such people, for example:
  - Those taking nonsteroidal anti-inflammatory drugs.
  - Those who are due surgery.
- **Adverse effects** that have been reported as being fairly common, see Table 1, these include: bleeding, indigestion, nausea, vomiting, headache, dizziness, vertigo, paraesthesia, rashes and diarrhoea.
- **Carefully monitor people** for any signs (purpura, bruising and haematoma) of internal or external bleeding during the first few weeks of treatment.

Dipyridamole

- Dipyridamole modified-release 200 mg twice a day is recommended.

T

- **Avoid** where possible in people with severe coronary artery disease, including unstable angina, recent myocardial infarction and heart failure, as dipyridamole acts as a potent vasodilator and may therefore lead to clinical deterioration.
- **Only the modified-release preparation is licensed for stroke and TIA prevention** and concordance is likely to be better with this regimen.
- The combination product of aspirin plus dipyridamole (Asasantin Retard) provides only 50 mg daily of aspirin, which has been less studied than the usual recommended dose of 75 mg daily.
- **Adverse effects** tend to occur early after initiating treatment and may disappear with continued treatment. Diarrhoea and headache have been reported as causing some people to stop treatment.
- **Other adverse effects** such as nausea, dyspepsia and gastric pain have been reported. People may also develop hot flushes, hypotension and dizziness.

What are the indications for switching from aspirin to clopidogrel?

- There are few indications for switching from aspirin to clopidogrel.
- **The main indication is aspirin hypersensitivity** (e.g. rash or bronchospasm). The Committee on Safety of Medicines (CSM) advises that aspirin may worsen asthma in up to 5% of people with asthma. Cross-sensitivity between aspirin and clopidogrel has not been reported.
- **The incidence of gastrointestinal adverse effects is similar for aspirin and clopidogrel** (see Table 1). If a person develops dyspepsia while taking aspirin, switching to clopidogrel may not improve the dyspeptic symptoms. The presence of dyspepsia, however is not a good guide to severity of adverse effects: many people who experience perforations do not have prior aspirin-induced dyspepsia.

[CAPRIE Steering Committee, 1996; Albers et al, 1999; Hankey et al, 1999]

What common drug interactions should I look out for?

- **Antiplatelet drugs should usually not be co-prescribed with warfarin or other anticoagulants,** due to an increased risk of bleeding.
- **Aspirin should ideally not be co-prescribed with other nonsteroidal anti-inflammatory drugs** (NSAIDs), due to an increased risk of gastrointestinal bleeding. If an NSAID is continued, this should only be after carefully considering the risks and benefits.
- **If co-prescribing of aspirin and an NSAID is thought to be necessary, ibuprofen is probably best avoided** as it may reduce the cardioprotective effect of aspirin. A recent retrospective study found that people with cardiovascular disease who took ibuprofen as well as low-dose aspirin had a higher risk of all-cause mortality than those who only took low-dose aspirin (adjusted hazard ratio 1.93, 95% CI 1.3 to 2.87) [MacDonald an Wei, 2003]. There was no difference in mortality for people taking diclofenac plus low-dose aspirin, or another NSAID plus low-dose aspirin. The results of thi study should be viewed with caution as it was not able t control for confounding factors, and only small number of people were taking ibuprofen or diclofenac (303). However, until more evidence becomes available, it would seem prudent to follow the advice of the British Heart Foundation and avoid ibuprofen in people taking low-dose aspirin [British Heart Foundation, 2002].
- **Aspirin should ideally be avoided in people taking methotrexate,** as it reduces the excretion of methotrexa and may increase risk of toxicity.

Table 1: The incidences of gastrointestinal adverse reactions from the CAPRIE study are given below, as percentages of the total exposed.

	Clopidogrel (n = 9599)	Aspirin (n = 9586)
Any GI event (e.g. abdominal pain, dyspepsia, diarrhoea, nausea)	27.1	29.8
Resulting in early permanent discontinuation	3.2	4.0
Clinically severe	3.0	3.6
Diarrhoea	4.5	3.4
Peptic, gastric, duodenal ulcers	0.7	1.2

References

NHS staff in England can link, free of charge, from references to full text journals by clicking on [Full text] on the PRODIGY website.

1. Albers, G.W., Hart, R.G., Lutsep, H.L. et al (1999) AHA scientific statement. Supplement to the guideline for the management of transient ischemic attacks: a statement from the Ad Hoc Committee on guidelines for the management of transient ischemic attacks, Stroke Council, American Heart Association. *Stroke* 30(11), 2502–2511. [Full text]
2. Antiplatelet Trialists Collaboration (1994) Collaborative overview of randomised trials of antiplatelet therapy–I: Prevention of death, myocardia infarction, and stroke by prolonged antiplatelet thera in various categories of patients. *British Medical Journal* 308(6921), 81–106. [Full text]
3. Antithrombotic Trialists' Collaboration (2002) Collaborative meta-analysis of randomised trials of antiplatelet therapy for the prevention of death, myocardial infarction and death in high risk patients. *British Medical Journal* 324(7329), 71–86. [Full text]
4. British Heart Foundation (2002) *Aspirin and ibuprofen.* Factfile 11/2002. British Heart Foundation www.bhf.org.uk [Accessed: 01/12/2002].
5. CAPRIE Steering Committee (1996) A randomised, blinded, trial of clopidogrel versus aspirin in patients a risk of ischaemic events (CAPRIE). *Lancet* 348(9038) 1329–1339. [Full text]
6. CAVATAS (2001) Endovascular versus surgical treatment in patients with carotid stenosis in the Carotid and Vertebral Artery Transluminal Angioplasty Study (CAVATAS): a randomised trial. *Lancet* 357(9270), 1729–1737. [Full text]
7. Cina, C.S., Clase, C.M. and Haynes, R.B. (2001) *Carotid endarterectomy for symptomatic carotid stenosis (Cochrane Review).* The Cochrane Library. Issue 4. Oxford: Update Software.
8. Clinical Evidence (2001) Stroke prevention. *Clinical Evidence* 5(Jun), 140–157.
9. Derry, S. and Loke, Y.K. (2000) Risk of gastrointestinal haemorrhage with long term use of aspirin: meta-analysis. *British Medical Journal* 321(7270), 1183–1187. [Full text]
10. Diener, H.C., Cunha, L., Forbes, C. et al (1996) European Stroke Prevention Study: 2. Dipyridamole and acetylsalicylic acid in the secondary prevention of stroke. *Journal of the Neurological Sciences* 143(1–2) 1–13.
11. DTB (1997) Which prophylactic aspirin? *Drug & Therapeutics Bulletin* 35(1), 7–8. [Full text]
12. DTB (1998) Managing carotid stenosis. *Drug & Therapeutics Bulletin* 36(2), 9–12.

3. DTB (1999) Clopidogrel and ticlopidine–improvements on aspirin? *Drug & Therapeutics Bulletin* **37**(8), 59–61.
4. Eccles, M., Freemantle, N. and Mason, J. (1998) North of England evidence based guideline development project: guideline on the use of aspirin as secondary prophylaxis for vascular disease in primary care. North of England Aspirin Guideline Development Group. *British Medical Journal* **316**(7140), 1303–1309. [Full text]
5. Hankey, G.J., Sudlow, C.L. and Dunbabin, D.W. (1999) *Thienopyridine derivatives (ticlopidine, clopidogrel) versus aspirin for preventing stroke and other serious vascular events in high vascular risk patients (Cochrane Review).* The Cochrane Library. Issue 4. Chichester, UK: John Wiley & Sons, Ltd. www.nelh.nhs.uk/cochrane.asp [Accessed: 19/07/2005].
6. He, J., Whelton, P.K., Vu, B. and Klag, M.J. (1998) Aspirin and risk of hemorrhagic stroke: a meta-analysis of randomized controlled trials. *Journal of the American Medical Association* **280**(22), 1930–1935. [Full text]
7. Koudstaal, P. (2002) *Anticoagulants versus antiplatelet therapy for preventing stroke in patients with nonrheumatic atrial fibrillation and a history of stroke or transient ischaemic attacks (Cochrane Review).* The Cochrane Library. Issue 4. Oxford:Update Software.
8. MacDonald, T.M. and Wei, L. (2003) Effect of ibuprofen on cardioprotective effect of aspirin. *Lancet* **361**(9357), 573–574. [Full text]
19. Medicines Resource (1998) Stroke prevention. *Medicines Resource* **51**(Nov), 199–202.
20. Pignone, M, Rihal, C. and Bazian Ltd. (2002) Secondary prevention of ischaemic cardiac events. *Clinical Evidence* **9**(Jun), 166–205.
21. Rodgers, H. (1998) Features and treatment of transient ischaemic attacks. *Prescriber* **9**(24), 31–36.
22. Rothwell, P.M. and Warlow, C.P. (1997) Management of transient ischaemic attacks: from clinical trials to individual patients. In: Farthing, M.J.G. (Ed.) *Horizons in Medicine No. 8.* London: Royal College of Physicians. 315–332.
23. SIGN (1997a) *Management of patients with stroke. Part 1: assessment, investigation, immediate management and secondary prevention.* Report No. 13. Edinburgh: Scottish Intercollegiate Guidelines Network.
24. SIGN (1997b) *Management of patients with stroke. Part 2: management of carotid stendosis and carotid endarterectomy.* Report No. 14. Edinburgh: Scottish Intercollegiate Guidelines Network.
25. SPIRIT (1997) A randomized trial of anticoagulants versus aspirin after cerebral ischemia of presumed arterial origin. The Stroke Prevention in Reversible Ischemia Trial (SPIRIT) study group. *Annals of Neurology* **42**(6), 857–865.
26. The American Canadian Co-operative Study Group (1985) Persantin aspirin trial in cerebral ischemia part 2: endpoint results. *Stroke* **16**(3), 406–415.
27. Warlow, C.P. and Davenport, R.J. (1996) The management of transient ischaemic attacks. *Prescribers' Journal* **36**(1), 1–8.

T

PRODIGY GUIDANCE

Trichomoniasis

Last revised in July 2002
www.prodigy.nhs.uk/guidance.asp?gt=Trichomoniasis

Applies to people over the age of 12 years

This guidance covers the management of *Trichomonas vaginalis* infection in women and men.

There is separate PRODIGY guidance for *Bacterial vaginosis*, *Candida — female genital*, *Chlamydia — genital*, *Pelvic inflammatory disease*, and *Pruritus vulvae*.

Goals

- To cure infection and prevent recurrence
- To reduce risk of complications, such as preterm delivery in infected pregnant women

Contents

Scenarios
- New Presentation p.1774
- Treatment failure p.1775

Extended Information, p. 1776

Which scenario?

- **New presentation:** covers the management of trichomoniasis in men and women who present for the first time.
- **Treatment failure:** covers the management of trichomoniasis in men and women who do not respond to initial management.

New Presentation

Which therapy?

- **Screen for co-existing sexually transmitted infections** in both men and women. Consider referral to a genito-urinary medicine clinic for specialist advice, diagnostic services, and partner notification.
- **Treat sexual partners simultaneously** and advise sexual abstinence until treatment is completed.
- **Oral metronidazole is the recommended treatment.** Options are:
  - 400 mg twice daily for 7 days.
  - Two grams as a single dose (but not during pregnancy or breastfeeding) — compliance may be better but failure rate may be higher, especially if partners are not treated concurrently.

T

Practical prescribing points

For further information see the *Medicines Compendium* (www.medicines.org.uk) or the *British National Formulary* (www.bnf.org).

- **Metronidazole and alcohol:** advise avoidance of alcohol for the duration of treatment and for at least 48 hours afterwards, because of the possibility of a disulfiram-like (antabuse) reaction.
- **Metronidazole and pregnancy:** There is no evidence of teratogenicity from the use of metronidazole in women during the first trimester of pregnancy. However, single large doses should be avoided.
- **Metronidazole and breastfeeding:** Women should be encouraged to continue breastfeeding while taking metronidazole. Small amounts of metronidazole may enter breast milk and affect its taste, but feeding problems are unusual. The single 2-gram dose of metronidazole should be avoided during breastfeeding.

Follow-up advice

- Tests of cure should be carried out if the person remains symptomatic following treatment, or if symptoms recur (see scenario *Treatment failure*).

Should I refer or investigate?

Refer?

- Referral to a genito-urinary medicine clinic is appropriate if the diagnosis is uncertain, or contact tracing and screening for coexisting sexually transmitted infections are not possible in primary care.
- Seek advice from a local obstetrician or genito-urinary medicine specialist if uncertain regarding management during pregnancy. Alternatively contact the National Teratology Information Service for latest information regarding the safety of metronidazole during pregnancy (telephone 0191 232 1525).

Investigate?

Screening for coexisting sexually transmitted infections is recommended in both men and women (ensure informed consent is obtained).

In women, infection with *Trichomonas vaginalis* should be confirmed by:

- Culture of vaginal fluid, using the appropriate media (will diagnose up to 95% of infected women).
- Direct observation of a wet smear from the posterior fornix (will diagnose 40–80% of infected women). This requires appropriate skills and facilities (e.g. use of a light microscope).
- Cervical cytology may detect *T vaginalis* as an incidental finding, with a sensitivity of 60–80% but a false positive rate of 30%; therefore diagnosis should be confirmed by culture or direct observation of vaginal secretions.

In men, infection should be confirmed by:

- Urethral culture or culture of first-void urine (will diagnose 60–80% of infected men).
- Sampling both sites will increase the diagnostic rate.

Patient information leaflets

The following PILs are available at www.prodigy.nhs.uk

- Trichomonas Infection

Shared decision making

- Trichomonas causes a genital infection passed on by sexual contact.
- Metronidazole (or similar antibiotic) usually clears the infection quickly.

- Your sexual partner should be treated at the same time. This prevents infection recurring as Trichomonas can be present without symptoms, particularly in men.
- Do not drink alcohol whilst taking metronidazole and for 48 hours after stopping the drug. The two together can make you quite ill.
- Metronidazole may give a short-term metallic taste.
- Do not have sex until treatment is over and symptoms have gone.
- Tell your doctor if you are pregnant, as treatment may be different.
- Return to see a doctor if symptoms do not clear.
- Testing for other sexually transmitted infections may be recommended.

Drug rationale

Drugs not included

Tinidazole is a 5-nitroimidazole with a similar action to metronidazole. However, it has no proven additional benefits over metronidazole, has been less extensively studied, and is more expensive. It is not recommended as a first-choice treatment in the Clinical Effectiveness Group or Public Health laboratory Service guidelines [CEG, 2001; PHLS, 2002].

Other antibiotics are not as effective in the treatment of trichomoniasis as those of the 5-nitroimidazole group.

Topical intravaginal metronidazole has not been shown to be useful in the treatment of trichomoniasis. It is thought to ineffective due to the spread of the infection from the vagina to other adjacent areas, such as the urethra [Forna and Gulmezoglu, 2002]. Therefore, oral dosing is strongly recommended.

Other topical treatments, such as clotrimazole and Aci-Jel (acetic acid jelly) may provide temporary relief of symptoms for women reluctant to take systemic medication (e.g. pregnant women). However, persistence of infection is highly likely in women opting for this treatment.

Drugs included

Oral metronidazole has proven efficacy against most strains of *Trichomonas vaginalis*, with a cure rate of 95% [CEG, 2001]. It has a long safety record and is usually well tolerated. It is also inexpensive.

There are two recommended regimens of oral metronidazole. The preferred treatment is a twice-daily dose of 400 mg metronidazole for 5 or 7 days. Alternatively, the drug can be given as a single 2-gram dose. This may improve patient compliance, but there is some evidence of an increased rate of treatment failure using this regimen [CEG, 2001; Forna and Gulmezoglu, 2002].

It is very important to treat a sexual partner concurrently to avoid reinfection [CEG, 2001].

Pregnancy and breastfeeding

Oral metronidazole is the preferred treatment for trichomoniasis in all stages of pregnancy. The published data shows no evidence of a teratogenic effect using this drug. However, due to theoretical safety concerns, single, high doses are not recommended. Pregnant women should be reassured of the drug's safety if necessary [CEG, 2001; National Teratology Information Service, 1999].

Metronidazole passes into breast milk, but at concentrations unlikely to affect the infant. As a precaution, the single high-dose regimen should be avoided. Metronidazole may affect breast milk taste, but this does not usually lead to feeding problems. Mothers should be encouraged to continue breastfeeding wherever possible [CEG, 2001].

Prescriptions

Oral metronidazole

Metronidazole 400mg twice a day for 7 days

- Age from 12 years onwards
- Metronidazole 400mg tablets. Take one tablet twice a day for 7 days; supply 14 tablets; NHS Cost £1.03.

Metronidazole 400mg twice a day for 5 days

- Age from 12 years onwards
- Metronidazole 400mg tablets. Take one tablet twice a day for 5 days; supply 10 tablets; NHS Cost £0.73.

Metronidazole single 2g dose – NOT pregnancy/breastfeeding

- Age from 12 years onwards
- Metronidazole 400mg tablets. Take five tablets together as one dose; supply 5 tablets; NHS Cost £0.37.

Pregnancy: oral metronidazole for 7 days

Metronidazole 400mg twice a day for 7 days

- Age from 12 years onwards
- Metronidazole 400mg tablets. Take one tablet twice a day for 7 days; supply 14 tablets; NHS Cost £1.03.

Treatment failure

Which therapy?

- **If there is failure to respond to treatment:**
  - Check compliance.
  - Ensure the person has not been vomiting.
  - Consider possibility of reinfection.
  - Check partners have been treated.
- **A repeat course of oral metronidazole is often effective.**
- **If infection persists,** consider a high vaginal swab or treat empirically with erythromycin or amoxicillin to reduce beta-haemolytic streptococci, before retreating with metronidazole. Some organisms present in the vagina may interact and reduce the effectiveness of metronidazole.
- **If infection still persists, advice from a genito-urinary medicine clinic should be sought.** A number of treatments have been reported as being successful, including combining oral metronidazole with rectal or vaginal metronidazole, use of high-dose intravenous metronidazole, use of high-dose oral and intravaginal tinidazole, and use of nonoxynol, acetarsol, or paromomycin sulphate pessaries.

T

Practical prescribing points

For further information see the *Medicines Compendium* (www.medicines.org.uk) or the *British National Formulary* (www.bnf.org).

- **Metronidazole and alcohol:** advise avoidance of alcohol for the duration of treatment and for at least 48 hours afterwards, because of the possibility of a disulfiram-like (antabuse) reaction.
- **Metronidazole and pregnancy:** There is no evidence of teratogenicity from the use of metronidazole in women during the first trimester of pregnancy. However, single large doses should be avoided.
- **Metronidazole and breastfeeding:** Women should be encouraged to continue breastfeeding while taking metronidazole. Small amounts of metronidazole may enter breast milk and affect its taste, but feeding

problems are unusual. The single 2-gram dose of metronidazole should be avoided during breastfeeding.

Follow-up advice

- Tests of cure should be carried out if the person remains symptomatic following treatment, or if symptoms recur.

Should I refer or investigate?

Refer?

- Referral to a genito-urinary medicine clinic is appropriate if the diagnosis is uncertain, or contact tracing and screening for coexisting sexually transmitted infections are not possible in primary care.
- Seek advice from a local obstetrician or genitor-urinary medicine specialist if uncertain regarding management during pregnancy. Alternatively contact the National Teratology Information Service for latest information regarding the safety of metronidazole during pregnancy (telephone 0191 232 1525).

Investigate?

Confirm persistence of infection in *women* by using one of the following:

- Culture of vaginal fluid, using the appropriate media (will diagnose up to 95% of infected women).
- Direct observation of a wet smear from the posterior fornix (will diagnose 40–80% of infected women). This requires appropriate skills and facilities (e.g. use of a light microscope).

Confirm persistence of infection in *men* by using one of the following:

- Urethral culture or culture of first-void urine (will diagnose 60–80% of infected men).
- Sampling both sites will increase the diagnostic rate.

Patient information leaflets

The following PILs are available at www.prodigy.nhs.uk

- Trichomonas Infection

Shared decision making

- Some possible reasons why Trichomonas infections do not clear are:
  - If the antibiotic medicine was vomited.
  - If the course of medicine was not taken correctly.
  - The infection has recurred due to a sexual partner not being treated.
- Metronidazole for a further course will usually clear the infection.
- Do not drink alcohol whilst taking metronidazole and for 48 hours after stopping the drug. The two together can make you quite ill.
- Metronidazole may give a short-term metallic taste.
- Do not have sex until treatment is over and symptoms have gone.
- Tell your doctor if you are pregnant, as the treatment may be different.
- Return if symptoms still do not clear. A different treatment may be needed.

Drug rationale

Drugs not included

- **Tinidazole** is a 5-nitroimidazole with a similar action to metronidazole. Its role in the treatment of recurrent trichomoniasis is unclear, and species resistant to metronidazole are likely to be cross-resistant to tinidazole. It is not recommended for the treatment of trichomoniasis by the Clinical Effectiveness Group or Public Health Laboratory Service guidelines [CEG, 2001 PHLS, 2002]. It may have a role in persistent failure to respond to metronidazole, but a specialist should be consulted for advice first.
- **Topical treatments** of metronidazole or other drugs are of little benefit in the treatment of recurrent trichomoniasis [Forna and Gulmezoglu, 2002].

Drugs included

- **Oral metronidazole** is usually very effective at treating trichomoniasis, with a cure rate of about 95%. Treatment failure is usually due to factors other than drug resistance (see *Which Therapy?*). A further treatment of oral metronidazole is usually sufficient to cure the condition [CEG, 2001].
- Oral metronidazole is available either as a twice-daily 400 mg dose for 7 days, or as a single 2-gram dose. Whilst compliance may be improved with the latter, there is evidence that suggests the longer course of antibiotics is more effective [CEG, 2001; Forna and Gulmezoglu, 2002].

Pregnancy and breastfeeding

- **Oral metronidazole** is the preferred treatment for trichomoniasis in all stages of pregnancy. The published data shows no evidence of a teratogenic effect using this drug. However, due to theoretical safety concerns, single, high doses are not recommended. Pregnant women should be reassured of the drug's safety if necessary [National Teratology Information Service, 1999; CEG, 2001].
- Metronidazole passes into breast milk, but at concentrations unlikely to affect the infant. As a precaution, the single high dose regimen should be avoided. Metronidazole may affect breast milk taste, but this does not usually lead to feeding problems. Mothers should be encouraged to continue breastfeeding wherever possible [CEG, 2001].

Prescriptions

Repeat metronidazole

Metronidazole 400mg twice a day for 7 days

- Age from 12 years onwards
- Metronidazole 400mg tablets. Take one tablet twice a day for 7 days; supply 14 tablets; NHS Cost £1.03.

Metronidazole single 2g dose – NOT pregnancy/ breastfeeding

- Age from 12 years onwards
- Metronidazole 400mg tablets. Take five tablets together as one dose; supply 5 tablets; NHS Cost £0.37.

Extended Information

Background information

- What is it? p.1777
- How common is it? p.1777
- How do I know my patient has it? p.1777
- What else might it be? p.1777
- Complications and prognosis p.1777

T

What is it?

Trichomonas vaginalis is a flagellated protozoan.
In women, this can cause infection in the vagina, urethra, and paraurethral glands. Urethral infection is present in 90% of cases, although the urinary tract is the sole site of infection in less than 5% of cases.
In men, infection is usually of the urethra.
The infection is almost exclusively sexually transmitted.
[CEG, 2001]

How common is it?

In 1997, genito-urinary medicine clinics in the UK reported over 5,600 cases of trichomoniasis in women and 250 cases in men [Hughes et al, 1998].
Prevalence is highest in those aged 20–45 years [Petrin et al, 1998].
Trichomonas vaginalis is identified in 30–40 % of male sexual partners of infected women [Sobel, 1997].

How do I know my patient has it?

Women

Symptoms
Symptoms may not be present in 10–50% of infected women.
The commonest symptoms include vaginal discharge, vulval itching, dysuria, or offensive odour. Occasionally, women may present with lower abdominal discomfort.

Signs
No abnormalities are found in 5–15% of women.
Vaginal discharge is present in up to 70% of infected women. This varies in consistency from thin and scanty to profuse and thick. The classical frothy, yellow-green discharge occurs in 10–30% of women.
Vulvitis and vaginitis are frequently present.
Approximately 2% of infected women have a strawberry appearance of the cervix on visual examination (higher rates are found on colposcopic examination).

Investigations
Culture of vaginal fluid, using appropriate media, will diagnose up to 95% of infected women.
Direct observation of a wet smear from the posterior fornix will diagnose 40–80% of infected women. This requires appropriate skills and facilities (e.g. use of a light microscope).
Cervical cytology may detect *Trichomonas vaginalis* as an incidental finding, with a sensitivity of 60–80% but a false positive rate of 30%; therefore diagnosis should be confirmed by culture or direct observation of vaginal secretions.

Men

Symptoms
Symptoms are absent in 15–50% of infected men (who usually present as sexual partners of infected women).
The commonest presentation is urethral discharge or dysuria, or both. Other symptoms include urethral irritation and frequency of micturition. Rarely, there may be a copious purulent urethral discharge, or complications such as balanoposthitis or prostatitis.

Signs
Examination is often normal, even in the presence of symptoms suggesting urethritis.
Urethral discharge is present in 50–60% of men (usually only small or moderate amounts).

Investigations
Urethral culture or culture of first-void urine will diagnose 60–80% of infected men. Sampling both sites will increase the diagnostic rate.

- Direct observation by wet mount or staining will only diagnose about 30% of infected men.

[CEG, 2001]

What else might it be?

Other infection that may result in vaginal discharge include:
- Bacterial vaginosis
- Candida
- Chlamydia
- Gonococci
- Herpes virus

Irritants that may result in vaginal discharge include:
- Spermicides, perfumed soaps and washing powders; frequent douching; tight nonabsorbent underwear.
- There is little evidence to know to what extent these irritants cause discharge.

Other cause of vaginal discharge include:
- Normal physiological variation in discharge throughout the menstrual cycle.
- Discharge secondary to tumours of the vulva, vagina, cervix, or uterine lining.
- Normal physiological increases in discharge during pregnancy, although there should be no irritation, pruritis, or malodour.
- Postmenopausal vaginal discharge due to atrophic vaginitis (but consider neoplasia in this group).
- Vaginal discharge following surgery of the vagina or uterus — may last up to 6 weeks.
- Foreign body.
- Cervical ectropion.

Other infections that may result in penile discharge include:
- Chlamydia
- Gonococci

[Plummer and Walters, 1993]

Complications and prognosis

Complications

- **In pregnancy,** *Trichomonas vaginalis* infection is associated with preterm delivery and low birth weight [CEG, 2001]. It is unclear whether treatment of trichomoniasis reduces the risk of complications during pregnancy [Klebanoff et al, 2001; Gulmezoglu, 2002].
- **In men,** trichomoniasis can rarely cause balanoposthitis, epididymitis, and prostatitis.

Prognosis

- There is a spontaneous cure rate of 20–25% at 6-weeks follow-up in women [Forna and Gulmezoglu, 2002].
- Antibiotic treatment cures 95% of infected women at 6-weeks follow-up [Forna and Gulmezoglu, 2002].

T

Management issues

- General issues p.1777
- Drug treatment p.1778
- Pregnancy and breastfeeding p.1778
- Alternative therapies p.1778

General issues

- **Sexual partners** should be treated simultaneously, and sexual abstinence advised until treatment is completed [CEG, 2001].
- **Screening for coexisting sexually transmitted infections** is recommended in both men and women [CEG, 2001].
- **Consider referral** to a genito-urinary medicine clinic for specialist advice, diagnostic services, and partner notification.

Drug treatment

First-line treatment

- **Oral antibiotic treatment is recommended,** due to the high incidence of infection of the urethra and paraurethral glands. A Cochrane systematic review identified only two trials of intravaginal compared with oral treatment — oral treatment was more effective [Forna and Gulmezoglu, 2002].
- **Oral metronidazole** achieves cure rates of up to 95% [CEG, 2001; Forna and Gulmezoglu, 2002].
- **Recommended regimens** are metronidazole 400 mg twice daily for 5–7 days or metronidazole 2 grams orally as a single dose [CEG, 2001; PHLS, 2002]. Single-dose treatment may improve compliance and is less expensive, but there is some evidence that failure rate is higher, especially if partners are not treated concurrently [CEG, 2001; Forna and Gulmezoglu, 2002].

Treatment failure

- **If symptoms persist,** check compliance, ensure the person has not been vomiting, exclude possibility of reinfection, and verify partners have been treated [CEG, 2001].
- **A repeat course of oral metronidazole is often effective** in people who fail to respond to the first course of treatment [CEG, 2001].
- **If infection persists,** consider a high vaginal swab or treat empirically with erythromycin or amoxicillin to reduce beta-haemolytic streptococci, before retreating with metronidazole [CEG, 2001]. Some organisms present in the vagina may interact and reduce the effectiveness of metronidazole.
- **If infection still persists,** it is likely that the strain of organism involved can exist under aerobic conditions. In this situation there is no effective recommended treatment and advice from a genito-urinary medicine clinic should be sought. A number of treatments have been reported as being successful, including combining oral metronidazole with rectal or vaginal metronidazole, use of high-dose intravenous metronidazole, use of high-dose oral and intravaginal tinidazole, and use of nonoxynol, acetarsol, or paromomycin sulphate pessaries [CEG, 2001].

Pregnancy and breastfeeding

- **In pregnancy,** *Trichomonas vaginalis* infection is associated with preterm delivery and low birth weight [CEG, 2001].
- **It is uncertain whether treatment of infection reduces the risk of complications.** A Cochrane systematic review identified one placebo-controlled trial of single-dose metronidazole in low-risk symptomatic and asymptomatic women, which failed to show any difference in mean birth weight, gestational age, or incidence of low birth weight [Gulmezoglu, 2002]. A recent placebo-controlled trial that was not included in the Cochrane review also failed to find any benefit. This trial treated asymptomatic pregnant women with two 2-gram doses of metronidazole given 48 hours apart. Only 10% of women had a history of preterm delivery.
- **Treatment is usually recommended for pregnant women who are symptomatic.** Symptoms are usually unpleasant and spontaneous resolution of infection only occurs in 20–25% of women [Forna and Gulmezoglu, 2002].
- **The recommended treatment during pregnancy is oral metronidazole** 400 mg twice daily for 5–7 days. Systematic reviews have concluded that there is no evidence of teratogenicity from the use of metronidazol in women during the first trimester of pregnancy [National Teratology Information Service, 1999; CEG, 2001]. However, single high-dose metronidazole should be avoided, both during pregnancy and while breastfeeding [CEG, 2001].
- **Local treatments,** such as clotrimazole pessaries, are sometimes used in early pregnancy for symptom relief (a different use from their role as an antifungal), but systemic treatments will ultimately be needed to eradicate the infection [CEG, 2001].

Alternative therapies

- **Studies of live yoghurt** or *Lactobacillus acidophilus* are not beneficial in the treatment of trichomoniasis [Bandolier, 1999].

References

NHS staff in England can link, free of charge, from references to full text journals by clicking on [Full text] on the PRODIGY website.

1. Bandolier (1999) *Yoghurt and vaginal infections.* Bandolier. www.jr2.ox.ac.uk/bandolier/band60/b60-3.html [Accessed: 12/02/2002].
2. CEG (2001) *National guidelines on the management Trichomoniasis vaginalis.* Clinical Effectiveness Grou (Association of Genitourinary Medicine and the Medical Society for the Study of Venereal Diseases). www.bashh.org [Accessed: 22/04/2005].
3. Forna, F. and Gulmezoglu, A.M. (2002) *Intervention for treating trichomoniasis in women (Cochrane Review).* The Cochrane Library. Issue 1. Oxford: Update Software.
4. Gulmezoglu, A.M. (2002) *Interventions for trichomoniasis in pregnancy (Cochrane Review).* The Cochrane Library. Issue 1. Oxford: Update Software.
5. Hughes, G., Simms, I., Rogers, P.A. et al (1998) New cases seen at genitourinary medicine clinics: England 1997. *Communicable Disease Report* 8(Suppl 7), S1-S12.
6. Klebanoff, M.A., Carey, J.C., Hauth, J.C. et al (2001 Failure of metronidazole to prevent preterm delivery among pregnant women with asymptomatic Trichomonas vaginalis infection. *New England Journ of Medicine* **345**(7), 487–493. [Full text]
7. National Teratology Information Service (1999) *Metronidazole in pregnancy.* NHS Northern and Yorkshire: Regional Drug and Therapeutics Centre.
8. Petrin, D., Delgaty, K., Bhatt, R. and Garber, G. (199 Clinical and microbiological aspects of trichomonas vaginalis. *Clinical Microbiology Reviews* **11**(2), 300–317.
9. PHLS (2002) *Management of infection guidance for primary care: draft for consultation & local adaptation.* Public Health Laboratory Service. www.hpa.org.uk [Accessed: 01/04/2002].
10. Plummer, D.C. and Walters, W.A. (1993) Female genital tract discharge. *Baillieres Clinical Obstetrics & Gynaecology* 7(1), 139–159.
11. Sobel, J.D. (1997) Vaginitis. *New England Journal of Medicine* **337**(26), 1896–1903. [Full text]

PRODIGY GUIDANCE

Trigeminal neuralgia

Last revised in July 2005
www.prodigy.nhs.uk/guidance.asp?gt=Trigeminal neuralgia

Applies to people over the age of 40 years

This guidance covers the management of trigeminal neuralgia.

This guidance does not cover the management of other causes of facial pain.

There is separate PRODIGY guidance for *Headache*, *Migraine*, *Palliative care — pain*, and *Shingles and postherpetic neuralgia*.

Goals

- To reduce the severity, duration, and frequency of attacks of trigeminal neuralgia

Contents

Scenarios

- Trigeminal neuralgia p.1779

Extended Information, p. 1781

Trigeminal neuralgia

Which therapy?

- **Give carbamazepine for first-line treatment.**
- **Gabapentin is an alternative for first-line treatment *if*** carbamazepine is contraindicated or not tolerated.
- **Aim to control the pain until remission occurs.** Note: drug treatment does not prevent future attacks or alter the disease process.
  - **Start with a low dose** and titrate slowly upwards until pain settles or adverse effects limit further dose increases:
    - For carbamazepine, start with 100 mg daily and titrate by 100–200 mg every 1–2 weeks. A dose of 200 mg three or four times a day is commonly needed, although a maximum of 1600 mg per day can be used.
    - For gabapentin, titrate from 100 mg three times a day to 300 mg three times a day over 7 days. A dose between 900 mg and 1800 mg per day is commonly needed, although up to 3600 mg per day (off-licence) can be used.
  - **A pain diary is useful** to assess the frequency of attacks and the response to treatment.
- **When the pain is in remission,** reduce the dose of carbamazepine (or gabapentin) and gradually withdraw it if the person remains pain-free.
- **If pain recurs,** re-start or increase the dose of carbamazepine (or gabapentin).
- **If first-line drug treatment cannot be tolerated, or is ineffective:**
  - Refer for neurosurgery.
  - A switch of drug therapy may be needed while referral is awaited. Seek specialist advice if this is being considered. Options include gabapentin or a tricyclic antidepressant, or seek advice from a pain clinic.

Practical prescribing points

For further information please see the *Medicines Compendium* (www.medicines.org.uk) or the *British National Formulary* (www.bnf.org).

- **Driving:** all people taking drugs with a sedative action (e.g. carbamazepine, gabapentin) should be advised not to drive if adversely affected, particularly during the first month of starting or increasing the dose (tolerance develops within a week or two of stabilizing the dose).

Carbamazepine

- **Always check for potential drug interactions:** carbamazepine induces liver microsomal enzymes and interacts with many drugs (e.g. oral contraceptives).
- **Warn people about adverse effects:** diplopia, headache, nausea, and vomiting are common after a dose increase but usually settle in a few days.
- **Advise people to report the following symptoms immediately:** fever, sore throat, mouth ulcers, or bruising.
- **If an idiosyncratic reaction is suspected:** check full blood count, liver function tests, and serum creatinine. Routine testing is not helpful.

Gabapentin

- **Reduce the dose of gabapentin in renal impairment.** See the *Medicines compendium* (www.medicines.org.uk) for dosage information.

Follow-up advice

- **Follow up the person regularly** to assess the response to treatment. A pain diary is particularly useful to aid titration of dose.
- **If an idiosyncratic reaction to carbamazepine is suspected:** check full blood count, liver function tests, and serum creatinine. Routine testing is not helpful.

Should I refer or investigate?

Refer?

- If there is no response to first-line treatment after the maximum tolerated dose is reached, or if it is not tolerated:
  - Refer to a neurosurgeon.
  - Consider seeking advice from a pain clinic on pain management while awaiting the neurosurgical opinion.

Investigate?

- Investigations are not necessary in primary care. The diagnosis is made on the history alone.
- MRI may be undertaken after neurosurgical referral. It provides information about the presence or absence of tortuous or aberrant blood vessels in contact with the trigeminal nerve root.

Patient information leaflets

The following PILs are available at www.prodigy.nhs.uk

- Trigeminal Neuralgia
- Trigeminal Neuralgia Association UK
- Trigeminal Neuralgia Self Help Group

Shared decision making

- **Carbamazepine** is the usual treatment for trigeminal neuralgia. It works by quieting nerve impulses. About 9 in 10 people obtain relief within 48 hours of starting this.
  - A low dose is started at first, and built up if required.
  - Once the pains have gone, continue carbamazepine for a further month, and then gradually reduce and stop it.
  - Side-effects such as dizziness or drowsiness may occur.
- Bouts of pains typically recur from time to time. Restart carbamazepine as soon as a new bout of pains starts.
- **Other medicines** such as **gabapentin** and **amitriptyline** may be used if carbamazepine does not help or it causes bad side-effects. A combination of two medicines is sometimes needed.
- **Surgery** to release the pressure on the trigeminal nerve is an option if medication does not help. There is a good chance of cure with surgery.

Drug rationale

Drugs not included

- **Antiepileptic drugs other than carbamazepine and gabapentin** are not included, because there is currently little evidence to support their use specifically for the treatment of trigeminal neuralgia.
- **Tricyclic antidepressants** have been shown to be effective in other types of neuropathic pain [Collins et al, 2000]. However, there is no study of their efficacy in trigeminal neuralgia, so they are therefore not recommended for first-line use.
- **Baclofen** has been investigated in only one small controlled trial (n = 10), in which the method of randomization was unclear [Fromm et al, 1984].
- **Conventional analgesics** are not included. They are not generally thought to be helpful in trigeminal neuralgia, and there is no evidence of their efficacy in this condition.

T

Drugs included

- **Carbamazepine** is recommended for first-line treatment of trigeminal neuralgia. A systematic review of anticonvulsants for pain control found three small studies comparing carbamazepine with placebo in trigeminal neuralgia. Meta-analysis found that carbamazepine had an NNT of 2.5 (95% CI 2.0 to 3.4) for trigeminal neuralgia [Wiffen et al, 2001]. It is also specifically licensed for this indication [Zakrzewska, 1990; Zakrzewska and Patsalos, 1992].
- **Gabapentin** is reserved for use if carbamazepine is contraindicated or not tolerated. It has been shown to be effective in the treatment of other types of neuropathic pain [Collins et al, 2000]. However, there is no randomized controlled trial on its efficacy in trigeminal neuralgia. One small, retrospective case series of people with treatment-resistant trigeminal neuralgia found that gabapentin provided some degree of pain relief in about half the people studied [Cheshire, 2002].

Prescriptions

1st line: start carbamazepine

Carbamazepine: titrate up by 100mg each fortnight

- Age from 40 years onwards
- Carbamazepine 100mg tablets. Take one tablet once a day for 14 days, then increase the dose as instructed (see the right hand side of the prescription) until the pain settles; supply 140 tablets; NHS Cost £4.06.

Carbamazepine: titrate up by 100mg each week

- Age from 40 years onwards
- Carbamazepine 100mg tablets. Take one tablet once a day for 7 days, then increase the dose as instructed (see the right hand side of the prescription) until the pain settles; supply 70 tablets; NHS Cost £2.03.

Alternative: start gabapentin

Gabapentin: initial titration from 300mg to 900mg per day

- Age from 40 years onwards
- Gabapentin 100mg capsules. Take one capsule three times a day for 3 days, then take two capsules three times a day for 3 days, then take three capsules three times a day; supply 36 capsules; NHS Cost £8.22.

Maintenance doses: standard-release carbamazepine

Carbamazepine 300mg daily (100mg three times a day)

- Age from 40 years onwards
- Carbamazepine 100mg tablets. Take one tablet three times a day; supply 84 tablets; NHS Cost £2.43.

Carbamazepine 400mg daily (100mg four times a day)

- Age from 40 years onwards
- Carbamazepine 100mg tablets. Take one tablet four times a day; supply 112 tablets; NHS Cost £3.24.

Carbamazepine 600mg daily (200mg three times a day)

- Age from 40 years onwards
- Carbamazepine 200mg tablets. Take one tablet three times a day; supply 84 tablets; NHS Cost £4.50.

Carbamazepine 800mg daily (200mg four times a day)

- Age from 40 years onwards
- Carbamazepine 200mg tablets. Take one tablet four times a day; supply 112 tablets; NHS Cost £6.48.

Maintenance doses: gabapentin

Gabapentin 300mg three times a day

- Age from 40 years onwards
- Gabapentin 300mg capsules. Take one capsule three times a day; supply 84 capsules; NHS Cost £44.52.

Gabapentin 400mg three times a day

- Age from 40 years onwards
- Gabapentin 400mg capsules. Take one capsule three times a day; supply 84 capsules; NHS Cost £51.52.

Gabapentin 600mg three times a day

- Age from 40 years onwards
- Gabapentin 600mg tablets. Take one tablet three times a day; supply 84 tablets; NHS Cost £89.04.

Gabapentin 800mg three times a day

- Age from 40 years onwards
- Gabapentin 800mg tablets. Take one tablet three times a day; supply 84 tablets; NHS Cost £103.03.

Extended Information

Background information

- What is it? p.1781
- How common is it? p.1781
- How do I know my patient has it? p.1781
- What else might it be? p.1781
- Complications and prognosis p.1782

What is it?

- Trigeminal neuralgia is defined by the International Headache Society as:
  - A unilateral disorder characterised by brief electric shock-like pains, abrupt in onset and termination, limited to one or more divisions of the trigeminal nerve.
  - The pain is commonly evoked by light touch, including washing, shaving, smoking, talking, and brushing the teeth (trigger factors), and frequently occurs spontaneously.
  - Small areas in the nasolabial fold or chin may be particularly susceptible to the precipitation of pain (trigger areas).
  - The pains usually remit for variable periods.
- The different divisions of the trigeminal nerve are affected in the following proportion of people [Katusic et al, 1990]:
  - Maxillary — 66%
  - Mandibular — 49%
  - Ophthalmic — 16%
  - Both maxillary and mandibular — 19%
  - All three divisions — 1%
- In many people trigeminal neuralgia is thought to be caused by compression of the trigeminal nerve root by tortuous or aberrant blood vessels. In some people the cause is unknown.

[Headache Classification Subcommittee of the International Headache Society, 2004]

How common is it?

- The annual incidence of trigeminal neuralgia is 4.7 per 100,000.
- It is more common in women (5.9 per 100,000) than in men (3.4 per 100,000).
- The incidence increases with age. The median age of presentation is 67 years, with a range of 24–93 years. It is rare before the age of 40 years.

[Katusic et al, 1990; Zakrzewska and Lopez, 2004]

How do I know my patient has it?

The diagnosis of trigeminal neuralgia is made on the history alone.

History

- There are paroxysmal attacks of pain lasting from a fraction of a second to several minutes, affecting one or more divisions of the trigeminal nerve.
- The pain has at least one of the following characteristics:
  - Intense, sharp, superficial, or stabbing
  - Precipitated from trigger areas or by trigger factors
- In an affected person the pain has the same characteristics in different attacks.
- The pain never crosses to the opposite side, but occurs bilaterally in 3% of people. If it is bilateral, a central cause (e.g. multiple sclerosis) should be considered [Katusic et al, 1990].
- The frequency of the paroxysms can vary from several hundred a day to long periods of remission that can last for years [Zakrzewska and Lopez, 2004].
- The paroxysm of pain often causes a spasm of the facial muscles on the affected side. This is known as tic doloureux.
- Between paroxysms the person is usually asymptomatic. In some people with longstanding trigeminal neuralgia, however, a dull, burning background pain may persist.
- In some people a paroxysm may be triggered by atypical triggers, for example:
  - Stimulus outside the usual trigger areas (touch of any other area of skin)
  - Bright lights
  - Loud noises
  - Tastes

[Headache Classification Subcommittee of the International Headache Society, 2004]

Examination

- Neurological examination is normal.

Investigations

- MRI provides information about the presence or absence of tortuous or aberrant blood vessels in contact with the trigeminal nerve root [Zakrzewska, 2002]. It will also exclude a diagnosis of tumours or multiple sclerosis.

What else might it be?

- **Dental disease** (e.g. apical periodontitis, pulpal pain) can cause paroxysmal as well as continuous pain. However, the overall features should readily distinguish this from trigeminal neuralgia.
- **Atypical facial pain** causes a dull nagging or throbbing ache in the maxillary and cheek areas, which can extend to affect the whole side of the head and the neck. It may be bilateral. It may be intermittent or continuous. There is often a long history of the pain.
- **Cluster headache** occurs in paroxysms, but the characteristic features readily distinguish this from trigeminal neuralgia.
  - Cluster headache is unilateral and is felt in or around the eye or temple.
  - Each attack lasts 15–180 minutes, and may occur from once every other day to eight times daily.
  - Attacks occur in clusters lasting for weeks or months, separated by remission periods lasting months or years.
  - The pain is severe and is associated with ipsilateral conjunctival injection, lacrimation, nasal congestion, rhinorrhoea, forehead and facial sweating, miosis, ptosis, and eyelid oedema.
  - The character of the pain is burning, boring, or piercing.
- **Multiple sclerosis** (MS) causes trigeminal neuralgia in 4% of affected people, although it is rarely a presenting feature. If a young person presents with trigeminal neuralgia, multiple sclerosis should be considered as the possible underlying cause, particularly if it is bilateral.
- **Postherpetic neuralgia** is readily distinguished by a history of shingles in the distribution of the pain. It most commonly affects the ophthalmic division of the trigeminal nerve, the division least commonly affected by trigeminal neuralgia.
- **Other cranial neuralgias** (e.g. glossopharyngeal, nervus intermedius, superior laryngeal, nasociliary, supraorbital, occipital) can all cause pain that is of similar character to, but in a different site from, trigeminal neuralgia.
- **Primary tumours of the trigeminal nerve, arteriovenous malformations, or compression of the nerve** (e.g. by a

tumour or aneurysm) can rarely cause features of trigeminal neuralgia. They more commonly cause continuous pain or numbness, and usually there are abnormal clinical signs (but these can appear later).

[Hilton-Jones, 2001; Zakrzewska, 2002; Headache Classification Subcommittee of the International Headache Society, 2004]

Complications and prognosis

Complications

- Depression and anxiety may occur because of chronic pain.
- Poor oral hygiene and weight loss may occur as a result of avoiding stimulation of trigger points.

Prognosis

- We could find no study describing the natural history of trigeminal neuralgia, but recurrences and variable periods of remission are typical.
- Most people are initially managed medically, and a proportion subsequently undergo surgery.

[Katusic et al, 1990; Zakrzewska and Lopez, 2004]

Management issues

- What is first-line treatment? p.1782
- How should I manage treatment failure? p.1782
- What is the supporting evidence for drug treatment? p.1782
- What is the supporting evidence for neurosurgery? p.1783
- Medicines management p.1783

What is first-line treatment?

- **Carbamazepine is recommended** for first-line treatment [Zakrzewska and Lopez, 2004].
- **The aim is to control the pain until remission occurs.**
  - The full 'antiepileptic dose' is usually required to control neuropathic pain, but it should be titrated slowly to reduce adverse effects.
  - Although trigeminal neuralgia is usually responsive to carbamazepine for the first few years of treatment, longer-term efficacy does not tend to be maintained in most people [Taylor et al, 1981]. It is not known whether this is due to tolerance to drug treatment or to progression of disease severity.
  - Drug treatment does not prevent future attacks or alter the disease process [Zakrzewska and Patsalos, 2002].
- **Gabapentin is an alternative *if* carbamazepine** is contraindicated or not tolerated. Although there are no randomized controlled trials in trigeminal neuralgia, gabapentin has been shown to be effective in other types of neuropathic pain [Collins et al, 2000]. It is generally well tolerated, has few drug interactions, and can be titrated faster than carbamazepine to the minimum effective dose.
- For further information on using carbamazepine and gabapentin (including dose titration) see *Medicines management*.

How should I manage treatment failure?

- **Consider neurosurgical referral** for those people who someone who is unable to tolerate the adverse effects of carbamazepine, or for whom carbamazepine is ineffective after 4 weeks at the maximum tolerated dose.
  - There is no consensus on the optimal timing of neurosurgery. Some specialists advise drug treatment until it fails to give pain relief, but others advise early surgery.
  - **Microvascular decompression** is the most commonly used procedure. It seems to provide the best rates of long-term complete pain relief and preservation of facial sensation, but is a major neurosurgical procedure [Elias and Burchiel, 2002]. It is the preferred option for younger people [International RadioSurgery Association, 2003; Lopez et al, 2004].
  - **Radiofrequency thermocoagulation** is an alternative that can be used for less medically fit people or for those who do not want to undergo a neurosurgical operation, but causes trigeminal nerve sensory loss [Lopez et al, 2004].
  - **Other procedures** that may be offered (depending on local expertise) include: glycerol rhizolysis, gamma knife sterotactic radiosurgery, and balloon compression of the ganglion [Lopez et al, 2004].
- **Drug treatments providing an alternative to carbamazepine should be considered if** carbamazepine cannot be tolerated or is ineffective while awaiting referral for neurosurgery, or if neurosurgery is declined. Antiepileptic drugs (AEDs) or tricyclic antidepressants (TCAs) are widely used to manage neuropathic pain.
  - The choice depends on the relative contraindications, possible drug interactions, and risk of adverse effects for each individual.
  - Suitable AEDs for second-line use in primary care include gabapentin (licensed for neuropathic pain) and oxcarbazepine (off-licence).
  - Suitable TCAs include amitriptyline, imipramine, and nortriptyline (all off-licence use).
- **Referral to a neurologist or specialist pain clinic** should be considered if drug treatments cannot be tolerated or are ineffective while awaiting referral for neurosurgery, or if neurosurgery is declined. Combination AED treatment may be used in this situation (e.g. carbamazepine with gabapentin, or carbamazepine with lamotrigine) but this should be undertaken only on specialist advice.

What is the supporting evidence for drug treatment?

Carbamazepine

- Although carbamazepine is widely accepted as the first-line treatment for trigeminal neuralgia, there are few studies examining its efficacy for this condition.
- A systematic review of anticonvulsants for pain control found three small studies comparing carbamazepine with placebo in trigeminal neuralgia. Meta-analysis found that carbamazepine had an NNT of 2.5 (95% CI 2.0 to 3.4) for trigeminal neuralgia [Wiffen et al, 2001]. The largest study in this analysis (n = 144) found that, using doses in the range of 400–800 mg per day for two-week treatment periods, the mean fall in maximum pain intensity was 58% with carbamazepine compared with 26% on placebo [Wiffen et al, 2001].
- The long-term effects of carbamazepine have been assessed only in open trials. One report of 143 people with trigeminal neuralgia followed for 16 years found that carbamazepine was initially successful in 69%; however, after 5–16 years only 22% were still gaining benefit from carbamazepine monotherapy [Taylor et al, 1981].

Second-line drug treatments

- Antiepileptic drugs and tricyclic antidepressants have been widely studied in other types of neuropathic pain. However, there are few studies examining their efficacy specifically in trigeminal neuralgia, and most of these studies are small.

Gabapentin has been shown to be effective in diabetic neuropathy and postherpetic neuralgia, and is licensed for neuropathic pain [Collins et al, 2000]. However, there is no randomized controlled trial on its efficacy in trigeminal neuralgia. One small, retrospective case series of people with treatment-resistant trigeminal neuralgia found that gabapentin provided some degree of pain relief in about half the people studied [Cheshire, 2002].

Tricyclic antidepressants (off-licence use) have been shown to be effective in the treatment of neuropathic pain generally [Collins et al, 2000]. However, there is no study of their efficacy specifically in trigeminal neuralgia. Amitriptyline has been widely studied in other types of neuropathic pain. Imipramine was found to be effective in a study of diabetic neuropathy, and nortriptyline was effective in one study of postherpetic neuralgia [Collins et al, 2000].

Oxcarbazepine is used by some specialists. This is, however, an unlicensed indication, and open-label trials of its use in trigeminal neuralgia have been small [Zakrzewska and Patsalos, 2002; Zakrzewska and Lopez, 2004].

The following drugs are not currently recommended for second line use in primary care:

- **Phenytoin** is licensed for second-line therapy in trigeminal neuralgia. However, it is usually poorly tolerated, so is therefore less preferred. There is no randomized controlled trial of its use specifically for trigeminal neuralgia [Zakrzewska and Lopez, 2004].
- **Pregabalin** has recently been licensed for neuropathic pain, but further post-marketing safety data are needed. Its adverse effect profile does not seem to offer any particular advantage over carbamazepine: dizziness, somnolence, blurred vision, gastrointestinal adverse effects, and weight gain are common.
- **Lamotrigine, sodium valproate, and topiramate** do not have studies of sufficient quality in trigeminal neuralgia [Zakrzewska and Lopez, 2004] or other types of neuropathic pain [Collins et al, 2000; Wiffen et al, 2001] to make recommendations about their use.
- **Baclofen** has been investigated in only one small controlled trial (n = 10), in which the method of randomization was unclear [Fromm et al, 1984]. In addition, four participants were using an existing drug treatment for trigeminal neuralgia.

Acupuncture is sometimes used for neuropathic pain. There is a lack of published literature on its use in trigeminal neuralgia [Zakrzewska and Lopez, 2004].

What is the supporting evidence for neurosurgery?

Microvascular decompression: the supporting evidence for microvascular decompression is based mostly on case studies, as there is no high-quality, randomized controlled trial.

- Initial success rates are 96%. Pain control after a single treatment is 64% at 10 years. Mortality rate of the procedure is 0.5%. The postoperative rate of facial numbness is 3–29% [International RadioSurgery Association, 2003].
- A review of 284 people treated by microvascular decompression showed that 74% believed that they should have undergone surgery earlier, and that 89% were satisfied with the outcome [Zakrzewska et al, 2003].

There is no high-quality comparison of the different types of neurosurgery [Zakrzewska, 2004; Zakrzewska and Lopez, 2004]. A recent systematic review of ablative neurosurgical techniques concluded that [Lopez et al, 2004]:

- Pain control after a single treatment seems to be about 60% after 3 years for radiofrequency lesioning, and about 55% after 3 years for glycerol rhizolysis or stereotactic radiosurgery. Pain control after a single treatment with balloon compression was found to be 69% after 3 years in one study, but more studies are needed to confirm this.
- Postoperative trigeminal nerve sensory loss affects virtually all people treated with radiofrequency lesioning or balloon compression if the procedure has been performed correctly. Permanent sensory loss can substantially affect the quality of life of some people.
- Sensory loss affected about 50% of people treated with glycerol rhizolysis, and less than 20% of those treated with stereotactic radiosurgery.

Medicines management

Which dose should I use?

- **A pain diary** helps to assess the frequency of attacks and the response to treatment, enabling the dose of medication to be titrated [Zakrzewska, 1990].
- **Carbamazepine: start with a low dose** (e.g. 100 mg daily) and titrate by 100–200 mg every 1–2 weeks (depending on tolerability). The full 'antiepileptic dose' is usually needed to control neuropathic pain. A maintenance dose of 200 mg three or four times a day is commonly used, but in some people doses of 1600 mg may be needed.
- **Gabapentin:** titrate slowly from 100 mg three times a day to 300 mg three times a day over 7 days. (Note: this is slower than suggested in the summary of product characteristics.) The licensed dose for neuropathic pain is between 900 mg per day and 1800 mg per day. However, doses up to 2400 mg or 3600 mg per day (off-licence) were used in many studies of diabetic neuropathy and postherpetic neuralgia.
- **Once the pain is in remission,** the dosage should be reduced to the lowest possible maintenance level. At periodic intervals, the need to continue treatment should be assessed by reducing the dose of carbamazepine (or gabapentin), and gradually withdrawing it if the person remains pain-free.
- **Measuring carbamazepine serum levels is not helpful** unless toxicity is suspected. The correlation between dosage and plasma levels, clinical efficacy, and tolerability is tenuous and there is no consensus on the optimum therapeutic range in trigeminal neuralgia. The dose should be titrated clinically against pain and adverse effects.

What are the adverse effects of carbamazepine, and can I avoid them?

- Dose-related adverse effects include dizziness, ataxia, diplopia, insomnia, nausea, and vomiting. Ataxia may occur from high blood levels of carbamazepine and this may result in falls, especially in elderly people.
- Mild skin rashes (e.g. isolated macular or maculopapular exanthemata) are also common, but usually disappear within a few weeks [ABPI Medicines Compendium, 2003].
- Idiosyncratic adverse effects are rare but serious. They include decreased platelets or white blood cells, Stevens–Johnson syndrome, exfoliative dermatitis, and hepatitis [DTB, 1994]. Advise the person to seek advice if a rash or symptoms such as fever, sore throat, mouth ulcers, bruising, or bleeding develop.
- Check full blood count, liver function tests, and serum creatinine if an idiosyncratic reaction is suspected. Routine testing is not helpful.

- Dose adjustment is not generally needed in renal impairment if the dose is titrated slowly against pain [Bunn and Ashley, 1999].
- Avoid carbamazepine in people with angle-closure glaucoma (mild antimuscarinic action).
- Disturbances in cardiac rhythm have rarely been reported; carbamazepine should not be used in people with arrhythmias, particularly atrio-ventricular block.
- Hyponatraemia is found in 20% of people receiving carbamazepine [van Amelsvoort et al, 1994] but is usually well tolerated. If the hyponatraemia is problematic, such as in an elderly person, restriction of fluid intake or a slight reduction in the carbamazepine dose usually resolves the issue.
- Always check for potential drug interactions: carbamazepine induces liver microsomal enzymes and interacts with many drugs.

What are the adverse effects of gabapentin?

- Common adverse effects of gabapentin include drowsiness, dizziness, ataxia, and fatigue.
- The clearance of gabapentin is markedly reduced in renal impairment. The total daily dose should not exceed 1200 mg in someone with mild renal impairment (common in elderly people). For further information on dosing in renal impairment, see the summary of product characteristics (www.medicines.org.uk).

References

NHS staff in England can link, free of charge, from references to full text journals by clicking on [Full text] on the PRODIGY website.

1. ABPI Medicines Compendium (2003) *Summary of product characteristics for Tegretol retard tablets 200mg, 400mg.* Electronic Medicines Compendium. Datapharm Communications Ltd. www.emc.medicines.org.uk [Accessed: 09/02/2004].
2. Bunn, R. and Ashley, C. (1999) *The renal drug handbook.* Abingdon: Radcliffe Medical Press Ltd.
3. Cheshire, W.P. (2002) Defining the role for gabapentin in the treatment of trigeminal neuralgia: a retrospective study. *Journal of Pain* 3(2), 137–142.
4. Collins, S.L., Moore, R.A., McQuay, H.J. and Wiffen, P. (2000) Antidepressants and anticonvulsants for diabetic neuropathy and postherpetic neuralgia: a quantitative systematic review. *Journal of Pain and Symptom Management* 20(6), 449–458.
5. DTB (1994) Drug treatment of epilepsy. *Drug & Therapeutics Bulletin* 32(6), 45–48. [Full text]
6. Fromm, G.H., Terrence, C.F. and Chattha, A.S. (1984) Baclofen in the treatment of trigeminal neuralgia: double-blind study and long-term follow-up. *Annals of Neurology* 15(3), 240–244.
7. Headache Classification Subcommittee of the International Headache Society (2004) The international classification of headache disorders. 2nd edition. *Cephalalgia* 24(Suppl 1), 1–150.
8. Hilton-Jones, D. (2001) Lower cranial nerves and dysphagia. In: Donaghy, M. (Ed.) *Brain's Diseases of the Nervous System.* 11th edn. Oxford: Oxford University Press. 320–321.
9. International RadioSurgery Association (2003) *Stereotactic radiosurgery for patients with failed medical management.* Radiosurgery practice guideline report #1–03. International RadioSurgery Association. www.irsa.org [Accessed: 03/03/2005].
10. Katusic, S., Beard, C.M., Bergstralh, E. and Kurland, L.T. (1990) Incidence and clinical features of trigeminal neuralgia, Rochester, Minnesota, 1945–1984. *Annals of Neurology* 27(1), 89–95.
11. Lopez, B.C., Hamlyn, P.J. and Zakrzewska, J.M. (2004) Systematic review of ablative neurosurgical techniques for the treatment of trigeminal neuralgia. *Neurosurgery* 54(4), 973–983.
12. Taylor, J.C., Brauer, S. and Espir, M.L. (1981) Long-term treatment of trigeminal neuralgia with carbamazepine. *Postgraduate Medical Journal* 57(663) 16–18.
13. van Amelsvoort, T., Bakshi, R., Devaux, C.B. and Schwabe, S. (1994) Hyponatremia associated with carbamazepine and oxcarbazepine therapy: a review. *Epilepsia* 35(1), 181–188.
14. Wiffen, P., Collins, S., McQuay, H. et al (2001) *Anticonvulsant drugs for acute and chronic pain (Cochrane Review).* The Cochrane Library. Issue 4. Chichester, UK: John Wiley & Sons, Ltd. www.nelh.nhs.uk/cochrane.asp [Accessed: 22/02/2005].
15. Zakrzewska, J.M. (1990) Medical management of trigeminal neuralgia. *British Dental Journal* 168(10), 399–401.
16. Zakrzewska, J.M. (2002) Diagnosis and differential diagnosis of trigeminal neuralgia. *Clinical Journal of Pain* 18(1), 14–21.
17. Zakrzewska, J.M. (2004) Trigeminal neuralgia and facial pain. *Seminars in Pain Medicine* 2(2), 76–84.
18. Zakrzewska, J.M. and Lopez, B.C. (2004) *Trigeminal neuralgia.* Clinical Evidence. Volume 12. www.clinicalevidence.com [Accessed: 25/02/2005].
19. Zakrzewska, J.M. and Patsalos, P.N. (1992) Drugs used in the management of trigeminal neuralgia. *Oral Surgery, Oral Medicine, Oral Pathology* 74(4), 439–450.
20. Zakrzewska, J.M. and Patsalos, P.N. (2002) Long-terr cohort study comparing medical (oxcarbazepine) and surgical management of intractable trigeminal neuralgia. *Pain* 95(3), 259–266.
21. Zakrzewska, J., Lopez, B., Kim, S. and Coakham, H. (2003) Microvascular decompression for trigeminal neuralgia – the patient's perspective. *Cephalalgia* 23(7 737.

T

PRODIGY GUIDANCE

Urethritis — male

Last revised in April 2003
www.prodigy.nhs.uk/guidance.asp?gt=Urethritis - male

Applies to men over the age of 14 years

This guidance covers the management of suspected urethritis, urethral discharge, gonococcal urethritis, non-gonococcal urethritis including chlamydial urethritis, and persistent urethritis in men.

This guidance does not cover the management of the non-infectious causes of acute urethritis.

There is separate PRODIGY guidance for *Prostatitis, Pyelonephritis — acute, Trichomoniasis,* and *Urinary tract infection (lower) — men.*

Goals

- Alleviation of symptoms
- Prevention of complications (e.g. epididymitis, sexually acquired reactive arthritis, and Reiter's syndrome)
- Prevention of reinfection
- Prevention of transmission to uninfected sexual partners
- Treatment of infected sexual partners

Contents

Scenarios

- Suspected urethritis/urethral discharge/first presentation p.1785
- Gonococcal urethritis p.1786
- Non-gonococcal urethritis p.1788
- Persistent/recurrent urethritis p.1789

Extended Information, p. 1789

Which scenario?

- **Suspected urethritis/urethral discharge/first presentation:** covers the initial management of men with symptoms of urethritis or urethral discharge.
- **Gonococcal urethritis:** covers management when gonorrhoea has been confirmed as the cause of the urethritis, either by Gram-stained urethral smear or by culture.
- **Non-gonococcal urethritis:** covers management when urethritis has been confirmed and gonococcal infection excluded; includes the management of chlamydial urethritis.
- **Persistent/recurrent urethritis:** covers management of persistent or recurrent symptoms after an episode of acute non-gonococcal urethritis.

Suspected urethritis/urethral discharge/first presentation

Which therapy?

- **Referral to a genito-urinary medicine (GUM) clinic is strongly recommended in all cases of suspected urethritis** for diagnosis, sensitivity testing, counselling, and contact tracing.
- **For men unwilling or unable to attend a GUM clinic,** try to confirm the diagnosis and establish the cause of urethritis BEFORE starting treatment. See *Should I refer or investigate?*
- **If it is strongly suspected that the man will not attend for follow-up,** treat empirically with one of the following:
  - **Ofloxacin,** 400 mg once a day (or 200 mg twice a day) for 7 days.
  - **Ceftriaxone** 250 mg OR **cefotaxime** 500 mg as a single intramuscular dose, **followed by a 7-day course of doxycycline.**
- **If it is known or suspected that the urethritis has been contracted abroad** (especially Southeast Asia), consider treatment with a cephalosporin and doxycycline.

Practical prescribing points

For further information, please see the *Medicines Compendium* (www.medicines.org.uk) or the *British National Formulary* (www.bnf.org).

- **Quinolones** may cause tendon damage (Committee on Safety of Medicines advice); stop treatment if pain or inflammation of a tendon occurs. They can induce convulsions in someone with epilepsy or with a condition that predisposes to seizures. Someone concurrently taking nonsteroidal anti-inflammatory drugs (NSAIDs) may also be susceptible. The risks and benefits of prescribing a quinolone should be considered on an individual basis for any such person.
- **Doxycycline** can cause oesophageal irritation and, rarely, photosensitivity.

Should I refer or investigate?

Refer?

- **Refer to the genito-urinary medicine (GUM) clinic** if the facilities to investigate and manage urethral discharge/suspected urethritis are unavailable in primary care.
- Not all men will be willing to attend a GUM clinic, and a general practice management strategy for this group may be required.

Investigate?

- **Gram-stained urethral smear and/or Gram-stained preparation from a first-pass urine sample:** the presence of five or more polymorphonuclear leucocytes per high-power (x1000) microscopic field (urethral smear) or 10 or more polymorphonuclear leucocytes per high-power microscopic field (first-pass urine sample) is diagnostic of urethritis. Either test can be used; each test will identify cases missed by the other. The presence of Gram-negative, intracellular diplococci on a urethral smear is diagnostic of gonorrhoea.
- **A urethral swab for culture of gonorrhoea should be performed in all cases,** even if diplococci are seen on microscopy. An appropriate transport medium must be used (Amies' with activated charcoal) and prompt transport to the laboratory (within 24 hours) is important.
- **Test for Chlamydia,** either by a urethral swab or through a first-pass urine sample, depending on the local laboratory.

- **Analysis of a mid-stream urine specimen** should be performed for leucocytes, nitrites, protein, and blood, with positive specimens sent for microscopy and culture.
- **Test for *Trichomonas vaginalis*** (urethral swab for culture or wet mount) if a sexual contact is known to have had trichomoniasis.

Patient information leaflets

The following PILs are available at www.prodigy.nhs.uk
- Gonorrhoea in Men
- Urethral Stricture
- Urethritis and Urethral Discharge in Men
- Urethritis - Non Gonococcal

Shared decision making

- **You may have an inflammation of the urethra (urethritis).**
- This is usually, but not always, caused by a sexually transmitted infection.
- **Tests are advised** to check if there is infection and to find out the cause if it is present.
- These tests are usually carried out in a genito-urinary medicine clinic.
- **Antibiotics** will usually clear most infections. The best antibiotic to use depends on the cause of the infection.
- **Your sexual partner should be tested and treated too,** even if your partner has no symptoms.
- **Do not have sex until the tests and treatment are completed in you and your sexual partner.**
- Condoms help to protect against sexually transmitted infections.

Drug rationale

Drugs not included

- There is growing concern about bacterial resistance to many of the drugs used in the treatment of urethritis, particularly when it is due to *Neisseria gonorrhoeae*. As a result, most (but not all) macrolides, tetracyclines, cephalosporins, and penicillins are inappropriate for empirical treatments.

[Moran, 2002]

Drugs included

- There are currently no controlled clinical trials comparing the efficacies of combined treatment for *Neisseria gonorrhoeae* and *Chlamydia trachomatis*. The drugs offered here are based on the best current practice, according to theory and expert opinion.
- **Ofloxacin** given as a single 400-mg dose once a day, or a divided 200-mg dose twice a day, for 7 days, is usually effective against both *Neisseria gonorrhoeae* and *Chlamydia trachomatis*. However, there is growing resistance of *Neisseria gonorrhoeae* to quinolones, especially in Southeast Asia.
- **The cephalosporins,** ceftriaxone (250 mg) and cefotaxime (500 mg), given as a single intramuscular dose, are both highly effective against *Neisseria gonorrhoeae*, including quinolone-resistant strains. **Doxycycline** 100 mg twice a day for 7 days is effective against *Chlamydia trachomatis*. Thus the two regimens combined should provide adequate cover for urethritis. Although these regimens are not as convenient as ofloxacin, they should be considered when bacterial resistance is suspected or there is a contraindication to quinolones.

[CEG, 2001c; CEG, 2001b; Moran, 2002]

Prescriptions

Ofloxacin

Ofloxacin tablets: 400mg once a day for 7 days
- Age from 16 years onwards
- Ofloxacin 400mg tablets. Take one tablet once a day for 7 days; supply 7 tablets; NHS Cost £15.01.

Ofloxacin tablets: 200mg twice a day for 7 days
- Age from 16 years onwards
- Ofloxacin 200mg tablets. Take one tablet twice a day for 7 days; supply 14 tablets; NHS Cost £15.11.

Intramuscular cephalosporin and oral doxycycline

Ceftriaxone (intramuscular) + doxycycline
- Age from 14 years onwards
- Ceftriaxone 250mg injection. For deep intramuscular injection; supply 1 250mg vial; NHS Cost £2.74.
- Doxycycline 100mg capsules. Take one capsule twice a day for 7 days; supply 14 capsules; NHS Cost £2.92.

Cefotaxime (intramuscular) + doxycycline
- Age from 14 years onwards
- Cefotaxime 500mg injection. For deep intramuscular injection; supply 1 500mg vial; NHS Cost £2.41.
- Doxycycline 100mg capsules. Take one capsule twice a day for 7 days; supply 14 capsules; NHS Cost £2.92.

Gonococcal urethritis

Which therapy?

- **Ideally, men who are identified as having gonococcal urethritis should be managed in a genito-urinary medicine clinic.**
- **When managed in primary care treat according to local patterns of antibiotic sensitivity:**
  - **Ciprofloxacin or ofloxacin** as single oral doses are recommended treatments.
  - **Ceftriaxone or cefotaxime** given as a single intramuscular dose is an effective treatment and recommended in cases where there is proven or suspected resistance to quinolones, or where quinolones are contraindicated.
- **Information about gonorrhoea should be given** with particular reference to the long-term health implications to the man and his partner(s) (e.g. epididymitis, pelvic inflammatory disease, and infertility).
- **Screen for co-existent sexually transmitted infections.** Consider prescribing antibiotic treatment that is also effective against *Chlamydia*.
- **Sexual partners** should be notified, offered screening for sexually transmitted diseases, and treated even if they do not have proven gonococcal infection.
- **Advise the man to abstain from sexual intercourse** until he and his partner(s) have completed treatment and follow-up.
- **Advise on safe sex** (e.g. use of condoms).

Practical prescribing points

For further information, please see the *Medicines Compendium* (www.medicines.org.uk) or the *British National Formulary* (www.bnf.org).
- **Quinolones** may cause tendon damage (Committee on Safety of Medicines advice); stop treatment if pain or inflammation of a tendon occurs. They can induce convulsions in someone with epilepsy or with a condition that predisposes to seizures. Someone concurrently taking nonsteroidal anti-inflammatory drugs (NSAIDs) may also be susceptible. The risks and

U

enefits of prescribing a quinolone should be considered n an individual basis for such a person.

ollow-up advice

ollow-up at least 72 hours after completing treatment is ecommended to ensure:

- Partner notification
- Compliance with treatment
- Resolution of symptoms
- Successful treatment with a test of cure (urethral smear and culture)

ould I refer or investigate?

fer?

eferral to the genito-urinary medicine clinic is strongly ecommended.

estigate?

creen for other sexually transmitted infections, articularly *Chlamydia*. Informed consent is required rior to screening.

tient information leaflets

: following PILs are available at www.prodigy.nhs.uk
ionorrhoea in Men
rethral Stricture
rethritis and Urethral Discharge in Men
Jrethritis - Non Gonococcal

ared decision making

'ou have an infection of the urethra (urethritis) due to onorrhoea.
'his is a sexually transmitted infection.
:iprofloxacin or ofloxacin are the common treatments.
single large dose of one of these antibiotics clears most onorrhoeal infections.
'ell your doctor if you are allergic to any antibiotic.
'ests are usual after treatment to check that the infection as gone.
'our sexual partner should be tested and treated too, ven if your partner has no symptoms.
)o not have sex until the tests and treatment are ompleted in you and your sexual partner.
:ondoms help to protect against sexually transmitted ıfections.

rug rationale

ugs not included

)ral cephalosporins are not recommended in this uidance:

- **Single-dose cefixime** is an effective treatment, although not specifically licensed for the treatment of gonorrhoea. Although equally effective alternatives exist, it is current practice in UK genito-urinary medicine clinics to reserve the third-generation cephalosporins, including cefixime, for individuals in whom quinolones or penicillins are contraindicated or ineffective. This policy aims to reduce selection pressure for the development of microbial resistance to these cephalosporins [Korting and Kollmann, 1994; Moran and Levine, 1995; Bignell, 1996].
- **Oral cefuroxime and cefalexin** are licensed for this indication, but they are not sufficiently effective to be recommended [Moran and Levine, 1995].

- **Quinolones, other than ciprofloxacin or ofloxacin,** have not been studied as extensively in the treatment of gonorrhoeal infection, and are not recommended by the Clinical Effectiveness Group (CEG) guidelines [Korting and Kollmann, 1994; Moran and Levine, 1995; Bignell, 1996].
- **Macrolides** are not suitable for the treatment of gonorrhoea. High-dose azithromycin (2 g) has been shown to be effective against *Neisseria gonorrhoeae*, but is associated with a higher frequency of gastrointestinal upset, and it is not recommended by UK National Guidelines [CEG, 2001b]. The lower 1-g dose of azithromycin is not sufficiently effective. (Note: azithromycin 1 g is recommended for the treatment of chlamydial infection; see *Non-gonococcal urethritis* scenario.)
- **Tetracyclines** are less effective than the antibiotics included, and resistance to them is increasing. Tetracyclines remain effective antibiotics for treating urethritis caused by chlamydial infection (see *Non-gonococcal urethritis* scenario.) [Echols et al, 1994].
- **Co-trimoxazole:** the Committee on the Safety of Medicines does not recommend the use of co-trimoxazole for the treatment of gonorrhoea [BNF 44, 2002].
- **A single dose regimen of ampicillin or amoxicillin, taken with probenecid,** is effective in areas where the regional prevalence of *Neisseria gonorrhoeae* is less than 5% [MMWR, 2002; CEG, 2001b]. However, unless this information is available, this regimen is not recommended for routine use [Bignell, 1996; BNF 44, 2002]. In addition, probenecid is now only available on a named-patient basis in the UK, and dispensing this drug would cause unnecessary delay.
- **Spectinomycin** is highly effective in the treatment of uncomplicated gonorrhoea, but is not commercially available in the UK.

Drugs included

- **Single doses of ofloxacin (400 mg) and ciprofloxacin (500 mg)** have both been shown to be effective [Korting and Kollmann, 1994; Moran and Levine, 1995]. A dose of 250 mg ciprofloxacin has been used [Echols et al, 1994], but concerns have been raised about the effectiveness of this dose [Moran, 1996]. The 500-mg dose is advocated to delay the development of resistance [Bignell, 1996; CEG, 2001b].
- **A single dose of intramuscular ceftriaxone (250 mg) or cefotaxime (500 mg)** is recommended as an alternative treatment when quinolones are contraindicated, or where there is involvement of a known or suspected quinolone-resistant strain of gonorrhoea (e.g. contracted in Southeast Asia). Although less convenient than oral quinolones, ceftriaxone and cefotaxime are both highly effective against most strains of *Neisseria gonorrhoeae* [CEG, 2001b].

U

Prescriptions

Quinolones

Ciprofloxacin tablet: 500mg single dose

- Age from 16 years onwards
- Ciprofloxacin 500mg tablets. Take one tablet as a single dose; supply 1 tablets; NHS Cost £1.42.

Ofloxacin tablet: 400mg single dose

- Age from 16 years onwards
- Ofloxacin 400mg tablets. Take one tablet as a single dose; supply 1 tablets; NHS Cost £2.04.

Cephalosporins intramuscular injection

Ceftriaxone intramuscular injection: 250mg single dose
- Age from 14 years onwards
- Ceftriaxone 250mg injection. For deep intramuscular injection; supply 1 250mg vial; NHS Cost £2.74.

Cefotaxime intramuscular injection: 500mg single dose
- Age from 14 years onwards
- Cefotaxime 500mg injection. For deep intramuscular injection; supply 1 500mg vial; NHS Cost £2.41.

Non-gonococcal urethritis

Which therapy?

- **Ideally, men with non-gonococcal urethritis (NGU) should be managed by a genito-urinary medicine clinic.**
- **When managed in primary care:**
  - **Doxycycline or single-dose azithromycin** are first-choice options.
  - **Ofloxacin or erythromycin** is recommended if doxycycline and azithromycin are unsuitable.
- **Information about NGU** should be given with particular reference to the long-term health implications for the man and his partner(s) (e.g. epididymitis, pelvic inflammatory disease, and infertility).
- **Screen for co-existent sexually transmitted diseases.** Note: these men need to give informed consent prior to screening.
- **Sexual partners** should be notified, offered screening for sexually transmitted diseases, and treated for genital chlamydia, even in the absence of proven infection.
- **Advise the man to abstain from sexual intercourse** until the man and his partner(s) have completed treatment.
- **Advise on safe sex** (e.g. use of condoms).

Practical prescribing points

For further information, please see the *Medicines Compendium* (www.medicines.org.uk) or the *British National Formulary* (www.bnf.org).
- **Doxycycline** can cause oesophageal irritation and, rarely, photosensitivity.
- **Quinolones** may cause tendon damage (Committee on Safety of Medicines advice); stop treatment if pain or inflammation of a tendon occurs. They can induce convulsions in someone with epilepsy or with a condition that predisposes to seizures. Someone concurrently taking nonsteroidal anti-inflammatory drugs (NSAIDs) may also be susceptible. The risks and benefits of prescribing a quinolone should be considered on an individual basis for such a person.

U

Follow-up advice

- **Follow-up 2 weeks** after initiating treatment is recommended to:
  - Confirm partner notification
  - Assess effectiveness of, and compliance with treatment
  - Repeat Gram-stained urethral smear and/or first-pass urine specimen as a test for cure

Should I refer or investigate?

Refer?

- Referral to a genito-urinary medicine clinic for partner notification and contact tracing is strongly recommended.

Investigate?

- Screening for other sexually transmitted diseases is recommended.

Patient information leaflets

The following PILs are available at www.prodigy.nhs.u
- Gonorrhoea in Men
- Urethral Stricture
- Urethritis and Urethral Discharge in Men
- Urethritis - Non Gonococcal

Shared decision making

- **You have a non-gonococcal infection of the urethra** (sometimes called NGU or NSU).
- This is usually, but not always, caused by a sexually transmitted infection.
- **Doxycycline or azithromycin** are the usual antibiotics used. These will clear most episodes of NGU.
- **Ofloxacin** is an alternative, depending on various circumstances.
- **Tell your doctor if you are allergic to any antibiotic.**
- Tests are usual after treatment to check that the infec has gone.
- **Your sexual partner should be tested and treated too, even if your partner has no symptoms.**
- **Do not have sex until the tests and treatment are completed in you and your sexual partner.**
- Condoms help to protect against sexually transmitted infections.

Drug rationale

Drugs not included

- Treatment for non-gonococcal urethritis (NGU) shou be effective against the bacteria *Chlamydia trachoma* ideally effecting microbiological cure in 95% of cases. Other micro-organisms involved in NGU are usually sensitive to drugs effective against chlamydia [CEG, 2001c].
- **Penicillins and cephalosporins** have no role in the management of chlamydial infection in men.
- **Clarithromycin** has not been as well studied as erythromycin or azithromycin. It is not licensed for th treatment of genital chlamydial infection [CEG, 2001
- **Tetracyclines** other than doxycycline are not offered. Although they are effective, they are not offered for th following reasons [SIGN, 2000; Low and Cowan, 20(CEG, 2001d]:
  - **Tetracycline and oxytetracycline** need to be taken f times a day, and compliance may be a problem [SIG 2000].
  - **Deteclo** is taken twice a day and is probably as effective as doxycycline, but contains demeclocycli which is more likely to cause photosensitivity than i doxycycline [BNF 44, 2002].
  - **Lymecycline and minocycline** require a longer cour of treatment. Minocycline has more adverse effects than other tetracyclines [BNF 44, 2002].
- **Quinolones,** other than ofloxacin, are either not as effective or have not been as extensively studied in the treatment of chlamydia [SIGN, 2000; CEG, 2001d].
- **Clindamycin** has been studied in a small number of tri and seems to be effective. It is not offered, as there is l data on its effectiveness compared with established treatments, and it is licensed only for serious anaerobi infections and Gram-positive infections [BNF 44, 200

'ugs included

)oxycycline is an effective and established treatment for JGU and genital chlamydial infection. It is taken at a losage of 100 mg twice a day for 7 days [SIGN, 2000; ;EG, 2001c; CEG, 2001d; Low and Cowan, 2001].

\zithromycin as a single 1-g dose is an effective and stablished treatment for chlamydia. It is more expensive han doxycycline, but the single-dose regimen may nprove compliance [SIGN, 2000; CEG, 2001d; CEG, :001c].

)floxacin has similar efficacy to that of azithromycin or loxycycline, but is more expensive. It is an alternative if ioxycycline or azithromycin are contraindicated.)floxacin is taken as either a single dose of 400 mg once day, or a divided dosage of 200 mg twice a day, for ' days. Both regimens appear to be equally effective CEG, 2001c]. Ofloxacin is not offered for those aged nder 16 years, as it is contraindicated in growing dolescents (quinolones are associated with the evelopment of arthropathy in weight-bearing joints in 'oung animals).

:rythromycin is recommended as an alternative if other lrugs are not suitable. It is taken as a 500-mg dose, twice day, for 14 days. The relatively long course may affect atient compliance, particularly in those with erratic ealth-care seeking behaviour [CEG, 2001c].

'rescriptions

;t-line treatment

xycycline capsules: 100mg twice a day for 7 days

\ge from 14 years onwards

)oxycycline 100mg capsules. Take one capsule twice a lay for 7 days; supply 14 capsules; NHS Cost £2.92.

ithromycin 250mg capsules: 1g single dose

\ge from 14 years onwards

\zithromycin 250mg capsules. Take four capsules as a ingle dose; supply 4 capsules; NHS Cost £8.95.

ternative treatment

oxacin tablets: 400mg once a day for 7 days

\ge from 16 years onwards

)floxacin 400mg tablets. Take one tablet once a day; upply 7 tablets; NHS Cost £15.49.

oxacin tablets: 200mg twice a day for 7 days

\ge from 16 years onwards

)floxacin 200mg tablets. Take one tablet twice a day; upply 14 tablets; NHS Cost £15.79.

/thromycin e/c tablets: 500mg twice a day for 14 days

\ge from 14 years onwards

:rythromycin 250mg e/c tablets. Take two tablets twice day for 14 days; supply 56 tablets; NHS Cost £6.16.

'ersistent/recurrent urethritis

/hich therapy?

'ersistent/recurrent urethritis can be difficult to manage; eferral to a genito-urinary medicine (GUM) clinic is trongly recommended.

:onsider reasons for the treatment failure:

:heck compliance with the initial treatment. If the man lid not complete the course, consider re-prescribing the ntibiotics.

f adverse effects were a problem, consider giving a uitable alternative course of antibiotics.

:xclude the possibility of reinfection from an untreated or new sexual partner.

- **If the man has completed the course of antibiotics AND has not been exposed to reinfection, refer to GUM clinic or get advice from a specialist.**

Should I refer or investigate?

Refer?

- **Referral to a genito-urinary medicine clinic** is strongly recommended.
- Consider urological referral, particularly if the man has urinary flow symptoms.

Investigate?

- **Use a urethral smear and/or a preparation from a first-pass urine sample.** The presence of five or more polymorphonuclear leucocytes per high-power (x1000) microscopic field (urethral smear), or 10 or more polymorphonuclear leucocytes per high-power microscopic field (first-pass urine sample) is diagnostic of urethritis.
- **Test for *Trichomonas vaginalis*** (wet mount or culture).
- **Rule out reinfection,** either by history or by investigations (urethral swab and/or a Gram-stained urethral smear for gonorrhoea, and a urethral swab or first-pass urine sample for *Chlamydia*).

Patient information leaflets

The following PILs are available at www.prodigy.nhs.uk

- Gonorrhoea in Men
- Urethral Stricture
- Urethritis and Urethral Discharge in Men
- Urethritis - Non Gonococcal

Shared decision making

- As your symptoms have not gone, it is likely that you still have inflammation of the urethra. Some things to check are:
  - Did you take the full course of treatment?
  - Was your sexual partner tested and treated too?
  - Did you have sex before the tests and treatment were finished?
  - Have you had sex with a new partner?

Drug rationale

- **There are no prescriptions offered as there is no good evidence on how to treat this complicated condition.** Erythromycin combined with metronidazole is recommended by national guidelines, but the effectiveness of this regimen is unproven and should not be initiated without expert advice.

Extended Information

Background information

- What is it? p.1789
- How common is it? p.1790
- How do I know my patient has it? p.1790
- What else might it be? p.1791
- Complications and prognosis p.1791

What is it?

- **Urethritis** is inflammation of the urethra. It is primarily a sexually acquired disease.
- Urethritis is classified as:

- Gonococcal urethritis
- Non-gonococcal urethritis
- Persistent or recurrent non-gonococcal urethritis
- Post-gonococcal urethritis

- **Gonococcal urethritis** is caused by *Neisseria gonorrhoeae*, and is commonly referred to as uncomplicated gonorrhoea.
- **Non-gonococcal urethritis** (NGU) is caused by a variety of organisms other than *Neisseria gonorrhoeae*:
  - *Chlamydia trachomatis* is the most frequent cause of NGU, accounting for 30–50% of cases.
  - *Ureaplasma urealyticum* and *Mycoplasma genitalium* each account for 10–20% of cases. The prevalence of *Trichomonas vaginalis* varies widely, between 1% and 17%.
  - Rare causes include *Neisseria meningitidis*, herpes simplex virus, *Candida* species, bacterial urinary tract infection, urethral stricture, foreign bodies, and trauma (e.g. urethral catheterization or instrumentation).
  - No identifiable cause can be found in 20–30% of cases.
  - NGU has also been associated with bacterial vaginosis in the partner.

[CEG, 2001c]

- **Persistent or recurrent NGU** occurs in 20–60% of men treated for NGU:
  - The aetiology of persistent or recurrent NGU is probably multifactorial; usually, no organism is identified. Possible causes include infection with tetracycline-resistant *Ureaplasma urealyticum*; infection with organisms not isolated by usual methods; or an autoimmune or allergic condition.
  - Persistence of NGU due to chlamydial infection is rare — provided the man and his partner(s) have complied with treatment [Wong et al, 1988; Hooton et al, 1990].
- **Post-gonococcal urethritis** is usually due to NGU being present but not identified at the time of treatment for gonorrhoea. *Chlamydia trachomatis* is identified in about 50% of affected men [McCormack and Rein, 1995].

How common is it?

- **The prevalence of urethritis in men in the community is unknown.** One study suggested that, on average each year, a general practitioner will see one man with a urethral discharge [Ross and Champion, 1998].
- **Cases of gonococcal and non-gonococcal urethritis (NGU) reported by genito-urinary medicine (GUM) clinics are increasing in number.**
- The reported incidence of gonorrhoea fell in the late 1980s and early 1990s, probably because of increased awareness of safe sexual practices owing to the emergence of HIV. Since then, however, diagnoses of gonorrhoea have risen considerably. This trend is continuing, with a 7% increase between 2000 and 2001. Gonorrhoea is the second most common bacterial sexually transmitted disease in England, Wales, and Northern Ireland, with 22,697 infections diagnosed in GUM clinics in 2001 [PHLS, 2002b].
- **High-risk groups for gonorrhoea include young men, homosexual and bisexual men, and black men.** It occurs more commonly in urban areas, especially London [PHLS, 2002b].
- **The incidence of *Chlamydia trachomatis*, the main causative agent of NGU, is also increasing.** There were 30,763 GUM-diagnosed cases of genital chlamydial infections in men in 2001, up 9% on the previous year [PHLS, 2002a]. Infection with *Chlamydia trachomatis* is more common in heterosexual than in homosexual me [McCormack and Rein, 1995].

How do I know my patient has it?

Symptoms

- **Urethral discharge:** may be profuse or scanty. It is present in 80% of men with gonococcal urethritis and significant proportion of men with asymptomatic non-gonococcal urethritis. Not all men with a urethral discharge will be aware of it.
- **Dysuria:** in sexually active young men, dysuria is more commonly due to urethritis than to other urinary tract infections. Dysuria is present in 50% of men with gonococcal urethritis.
- **Penile irritation.**
- **No symptoms:** urethritis is asymptomatic in 5–10% o affected men.

[Carter et al, 1998; CEG, 2001b; CEG, 2001c]

Signs

- **Urethral discharge** may be clear, mucopurulent, or frankly purulent. It is sometimes apparent only on urethral massage. Most men with gonococcal urethrit have a frankly purulent discharge at some stage, wher most of those with non-gonococcal urethritis have a clear or mucopurulent discharge [McCormack and Re 1995].
- **Epididymal tenderness/swelling and balanitis** are rare, and usually associated with *Neisseria gonorrhoeae*.
- **Haematuria and bloody discharge** are uncommon in urethritis, particularly if it is painless. Haematuria should be investigated if it persists after urethritis has been cured.
- **Examination may be normal.**

[CEG, 2001b; CEG, 2001c]

Investigations

- Investigation of suspected urethritis or urethral discha is usually performed in a genito-urinary medicine clini where on-site microscopy and expertise is available.
- The main investigations appropriate in diagnosing the cause of urethritis are listed in Table 1.

[CEG, 2001b; CEG, 2001c]

Table 1: Summary of investigations for urethritis in a ma

Investigation	Specimen	Indication	To diagnos
Microscopy	Urethral swab; first-pass urine	All	Urethritis; Gonorrhoe
Culture for *Neisseria gonorrhoeae*	Urethral swab If indicated by sexual activity: swabs of throat, rectum	All	Gonorrhoe
Antigen detection for *Neisseria gonorrhoeae*	Swab of urethra; first-pass urine If indicated by sexual activity: swabs of throat, rectum	Asymptomatic Delayed transportation of specimen	Gonorrhoe
Test for *Chlamydia trachomatis*	Urethral smear; first-pass urine	All	Chlamydial infection
Microscopy/ culture for *Trichomonas vaginalis*	Urethral smear; first-pass urine	Persistent/ recurrent urethritis or contact	Trichomoni
Dipstick urinalysis	Mid-stream urine	All	Other urina tract infecti
Naked-eye examination	First-pass urine	Rapid check	Mucoid strands sugg urethritis

ecimen collection

'irst-pass urine specimens should be collected 4 hours fter the previous voiding, because the urine stream ransiently eliminates most of the evidence of nflammation. (The optimum time is not known; 4 hours s conventionally considered adequate.)

Jrethral swab: intra-urethral material is collected with a mm plastic hoop or, with the likelihood of more iscomfort, a cotton-tipped swab.

:G, 2001b; CEG, 2001c]

'estigations for diagnosis of urethritis

Jrethritis is confirmed by the detection of olymorphonuclear leucocytes (PMNLs) in the anterior rethra, by Gram-staining specimens of a urethral swab r first-pass urine. More cases will be detected if both ests are done.

)iagnostic criteria for urethritis are:

- **Urethral smear:** more than 5 PMNLs per high-power field (average of 5)
- **First-pass urine:** more than 10 PMNLs per high-power field (average of 5)

Jaked-eye examination of first-pass urine specimens nay show 'threads' or mucoid strands. Their presence orrelates well with urethritis; however, a normal ppearance does not exclude the diagnosis.

positive leucocyte esterase test on a first-pass urine pecimen is indicative of urethritis; but this is not ensitive enough to be a rapid diagnostic test.

:G, 2001b]

'estigations for diagnosis of gonorrhoea

Aicroscopy may show Gram-negative diplococci within MNLs, thus enabling rapid diagnosis.

Culture and sensitivity testing for *Neisseria gonorrhoeae* hould be done in every case of urethritis. Swab the rethra and, if indicated by sexual activity, also the hroat and rectum. Use an appropriate swab and ransport medium, such as a "mini-tip" swab with Amies nedium gel and activated charcoal. Swabs should be ent promptly to the laboratory (within 24 hours) — therwise the sensitivity of the test is markedly ecreased.

:G, 2001b; CEG, 2001c]

'estigations for diagnosis of chlamydial infection

***Chlamydia trachomatis* should be sought.** There are a ariety of laboratory tests in use, and general ractitioners are advised to confirm the testing methods vailable locally. (See separate PRODIGY guidance *Chlamydia — genital* for further details on laboratory iagnosis.)

'he most useful tests are antigen detection and nucleic cid amplification techniques. The preferred samples for oth are first-voided urine, rather than urethral swabs which can be painful).

:G, 2001b; CEG, 2001c; CEG, 2001d]

'estigations for diagnosis of trichomoniasis

test for *Trichomonas vaginalis* is indicated if a sexual ontact has trichomoniasis, or if urethritis is persistent or ecurrent.

Jrethral culture or culture of first-void urine will iagnose 60–80% of infected men. Sampling both pecimens will increase the diagnostic rate. (See separate RODIGY guidance *Trichomoniasis* for further details on aboratory diagnosis.)

:G, 2001b; CEG, 2001c; CEG, 2001a]

'estigations for diagnosis of other urinary tract ections and conditions

Dipstick urinalysis of a mid-stream urine specimen hould be performed, to test for leucocyte esterase, itrites, protein, and blood. Specimens with positive esults should be sent for microscopy and culture, to dentify other urinary tract conditions such as cystitis or pyelonephritis. (See separate PRODIGY guidance *Urinary tract infection (lower) — men* for further details on laboratory diagnosis.)

[CEG, 2001b; CEG, 2001c]

What else might it be?

- **Physiological discharge:** small amounts of clear or mucoid discharge may be apparent with sexual excitement. However, it is not possible to differentiate this on appearance alone from a discharge secondary to inflammatory urethritis.
- **Sub-preputial infection** (e.g. candidiasis).
- **Other urinary tract infections** (e.g. cystitis, epididymitis, prostatitis).
- **Malignancy:** urethritis is an extremely rare presentation of malignancy.

[Adler, 1995]

Complications and prognosis

Complications

- **Transmission:** infection of female partners leading to pelvic inflammatory disease (PID) is known to occur with *Neisseria gonorrhoeae* and *Chlamydia trachomatis*. It is suspected that other organisms causing NGU may also be transmitted and cause PID. The complications of PID include infertility, ectopic pregnancy, and chronic pelvic pain. However, female partners of men with persistent/recurrent urethritis do not appear to be at increased risk of pelvic inflammatory disease [CEG, 2001b; CEG, 2001c].
- **Epididymo-orchitis** is rare, and is commonly due to *Chlamydia trachomatis* or *Neisseria gonorrhoeae* [MMWR, 2002].
- **Gonorrhoea** spreads to the prostate in not more than 1% of cases. Even less frequently, haematogenous dissemination causes skin lesions, arthralgia, arthritis, and tenosynovitis [CEG, 2001b].
- **Sexually acquired reactive arthritis** is a sterile inflammation of synovial membrane, tendons, and fascia, triggered by a sexually transmitted infection. It occurs in 0.8–4% of lower genital tract infections. Susceptibility is increased by possession of the HLA-B27 gene [CEG, 2001c].
- **Reiter's syndrome:** this refers to the triad of urethritis, reactive arthritis, and conjunctivitis, with or without cutaneous or mucous membrane lesions [CEG, 2001c].
- **Whether chlamydial infection or gonorrhoea cause male infertility is currently unclear** [Ness et al, 1997].

Prognosis

- **Natural history:** symptoms of infectious urethritis usually resolve without treatment.
  - **Acute non-gonococcal urethritis** (NGU) if untreated will resolve in up to 30% of men within 2 weeks and in up to 70% after 6 months [McCormack and Rein, 1995].
  - **Acute gonococcal urethritis** if untreated will become asymptomatic in about 95% of men within 6 months. Many of these asymptomatic men remain infected and probably infectious [McCormack and Rein, 1995].

Management issues

- General issues regarding the management of acute urethritis p.1792
- Gonococcal urethritis p.1792
- Non-gonococcal urethritis p.1792
- Empirical treatment of men who are unlikely or unable to attend follow-up p.1793
- Persistent/recurrent urethritis p.1793

U

General issues regarding the management of acute urethritis

- **Referral to a genito-urinary medicine (GUM) clinic is strongly recommended if urethritis is suspected,** particularly if the facilities and expertise to make an accurate diagnosis (e.g. microscopy) are unavailable in primary care. However, some men will be unwilling to attend GUM clinics, and a general practice management strategy for this group may be required.
- **Make an accurate diagnosis:** confirm the presence of urethritis by demonstrating polymorphonuclear leucocytes in a urethral smear and/or first-pass urine specimen, and test for gonorrhoea and *Chlamydia trachomatis* (see *How do I know my patient has it?*).
- **Give verbal and printed advice and information** about:
  - Urethritis: including the long-term health implications for the man and his partner(s)
  - Safe sexual practices: for example, use of condoms
  - Sexual abstinence: until treatment has been completed by the man and his partner(s)
- **If the expertise is available, screen for co-existent sexually transmitted diseases** because of the increased risk of co-infections. Informed consent should be obtained prior to screening.
- **Notify sexual partners,** offer them screening for sexually transmitted diseases, arrange treatment even if they do not have proven infection, and advise on safe sexual practices.
- **Commence treatment once a diagnosis is made.** Immediate empirical treatment of symptoms is recommended only for men who are at high risk of infection, and who are unlikely to return for follow-up or attend a GUM clinic. Treatment in these circumstances should be effective against both *Chlamydia trachomatis* and gonorrhoea.

[CEG, 2001b; CEG, 2001c]

Gonococcal urethritis

- **Ideally, men identified as having gonococcal urethritis should be managed by a GUM clinic.** The following recommendations apply to men who are unwilling or unable to attend a GUM clinic.
- **Indications for therapy:**
  - Positive rapid diagnostic test (e.g. microscopy)
  - Positive culture for *N gonorrhoeae*
  - Epidemiological grounds: a recent sexual partner has confirmed gonococcal infection
  - Empirical grounds: clinically at high risk for infection and unlikely to attend future appointments
- **Trace sexual partners and contacts:**
  - Symptomatic men — all partners of the previous 2 weeks
  - Asymptomatic men — all partners of the previous 3 months
- **Follow up** at least 72 hours after completion of antibiotic treatment to:
  - Assess the symptom relief.
  - Assess compliance with treatment.
  - Confirm partner notification.
  - Reinforce health education.
  - Repeat microscopy and culture of a Gram-stained urethral smear and/or first-pass urine specimen as a routine test of cure.
- **Antibiotic resistance:**
  - Ideally, local antibiotic resistance patterns should influence the choice of treatment of *Neisseria gonorrhoeae*. The regimen should be chosen so that infection would be eliminated in at least 95% of cases in the local community.
  - The prevalence of penicillinase-producing strains is less than 5% in the UK, but it is much greater abroa[d]. Gonorrhoeal infection contracted abroad should be presumed to be resistant to penicillin and tetracycli[ne] and possibly resistant to quinolones.
  - The prevalence of quinolone-resistant strains is less than 2% in the UK, but this is rising rapidly in som[e] countries, particularly in Southeast Asia and the Pacific regions, including California [McCormack a[nd] Rein, 1995].

[CEG, 2001b]

Antibiotic regimens for gonococcal urethritis

- **Consider local antibiotic resistance patterns** and follo[w] local guidelines if these exist.
- First-choice therapeutic options are:
  - **Ciprofloxacin 500 mg, single oral dose**
  - **Ofloxacin 400 mg, single oral dose**
- If resistance or intolerance to quinolones is likely (e.g. imported infection), consult the local GUM clinic or public health laboratory for the most appropriate treatment regimen. Alternatively, consider either of th[e] following:
  - **Ceftriaxone 250 mg, single-dose intramuscular injection**
  - **Cefotaxime 500 mg, single-dose intramuscular injection**
- Single-dose ampicillin or amoxicillin with probenecid no longer a practical option, because probenecid is available only on a named-patient basis.
- Single-dose cefixime is an effective treatment for gonorrhoea, but it is not licensed for this condition. Although equally effective alternatives exist, it is curr[ent] practice in UK GUM clinics to reserve cefixime for individuals in whom quinolones are contraindicated o[r] ineffective. This policy aims to reduce selection pressu[re] for the development of microbial resistance to these cephalosporins.
- Single-dose azithromycin 1 g has cure rates of less tha[n] 95%. Single-dose azithromycin 2 g is more effective, b[ut] has a high incidence of gastrointestinal adverse effects. Neither is therefore recommended.

[CEG, 2001b]

Non-gonococcal urethritis

- **Ideally, men identified as having non-gonococcal urethritis (NGU) should be managed in a GUM clinic**. The following recommendations apply to men who ar[e] unwilling or unable to attend a GUM clinic.
- **Treatment for NGU is indicated if, on follow-up, *Neisseria gonorrhoeae* has not been detected,** regardle[ss] of the identification of other organisms.
- **Trace sexual partners and contacts:**
  - Symptomatic men — all partners of the previous 4 weeks
  - Asymptomatic men — all partners of the previous 6 months
- **Follow up 2 weeks after initiating treatment to:**
  - Assess the symptom relief.
  - Assess compliance with treatment.
  - Confirm partner notification.
  - Reinforce health education.
  - Repeat microscopy and culture of a Gram-stained urethral smear and/or first-pass urine specimen ON[LY] IF symptoms or signs of urethritis persist.
- **Antibiotic regimens effective against *Chlamydia trachomatis* are generally also effective in other causes [of] NGU.**

U

tibiotic regimens for NGU

- **onsider local antibiotic resistance patterns** and follow ›cal guidelines if these exist.
- lternatively, first-choice therapeutic options are:
  - **Doxycycline 100 mg twice a day for 7 days.**
  - **Azithromycin 1 g orally in a single dose:** as effective as doxycycline, more expensive, but may be preferred when compliance is anticipated to be poor.
- tetracyclines and azithromycin are poorly tolerated, ›nsult the local GUM clinic or public health laboratory ›r the most appropriate treatment regimen.
- lternatively, consider:
  - **Ofloxacin 200 mg twice a day (or 400 mg once a day) for 7 days.** The ofloxacin regimen is more expensive than the doxycycline and azithromycin regimens and has no advantage with regard to efficacy or convenience.
  - **Erythromycin 500 mg twice a day for 14 days.** This regimen is less convenient than the alternatives, but may be appropriate for some patients.

G, 2001c]

›pirical treatment of men who are unlikely ›nable to attend follow-up

› some cases it may be anticipated that men are unlikely › attend a follow-up appointment because either they ›hibit erratic health-care seeking behaviour, or they are ›nable to attend (e.g. they are travelling). In these ›rcumstances it may be appropriate to treat the ›ethritis empirically, covering both gonococcal ›ethritis and *Chlamydia trachomatis*.

tibiotic regimens for the empirical treatment of ›diagnosed urethritis

- **onsider local antibiotic resistance patterns** and follow ›cal guidelines if these exist.
- lternatively, the first-choice therapeutic option is:
  - **Ofloxacin 200 mg twice a day (or 400 mg once a day) for 7 days:** ofloxacin is effective against both *Neisseria gonorrhoeae* and *Chlamydia trachomatis*.
- **resistance to quinolone antibiotics is likely to be a ›roblem** (e.g. urethritis contracted from abroad), or if ›inolones are contraindicated, consider the use of ›mbination antibiotics to treat both *Neisseria ›norrhoeae* and *Chlamydia trachomatis*:
  - **Ceftriaxone 250 mg** by intramuscular injection (single dose), followed by
  - **Doxycycline 100 mg** twice a day for 7 days
  - **Cefotaxime 500 mg** by intramuscular injection (single dose), followed by
  - **Doxycycline 100 mg** twice a day for 7 days
- **ual treatment for gonorrhoea and genital chlamydia ›ith two antibiotics** is based on theory and expert ›inion rather than on evidence-based clinical trials. ›owever, its use in the treatment of undiagnosed ›norrhoea-like urethritis is recognised, and has become ›ore routine over the past 10 years [Moran, 2002].

›rsistent/recurrent urethritis

- **here is no consensus** on the diagnostic criteria or ›anagement of this complex condition [CEG, 2001c].
- **›eferral to a GUM clinic is strongly recommended.**
- **›or those men who do not wish, or are unable, to attend ›e GUM clinic:**
  - **Check compliance** with initial treatment. If the man did not complete the antibiotic course, consider re-prescribing it, or an alternative regimen if adverse effects were a problem.
  - **Consider reinfection** from an untreated or new sexual partner.
  - **Symptoms alone are not a sufficient basis for re-treatment** (i.e. there should be signs of urethritis or laboratory confirmation of inflammation/infection) [MMWR, 2002].
  - **A course of erythromycin and metronidazole** to treat tetracycline-resistant *Ureaplasma urealyticum* infection or *Trichomonas vaginalis* infection may benefit some men, because these infections cause some cases of persistent or recurrent urethritis [MMWR, 2002].
  - If symptoms continue despite a second course of treatment, referral to or advice from a GUM clinic is necessary.

[CEG, 2001c]

References

1. Adler, M. (Ed.) (1995) *ABC of sexually transmitted diseases*. 3rd edn. London: BMJ Publishing.
2. Bignell, C. (1996) Antibiotic treatment of gonorrhoea–clinical evidence for choice. *Genitourinary Medicine* **72**(5), 315–320.
3. BNF 44 (2002) *British National Formulary*. 44th edn. London: British Medical Association and Royal Pharmaceutical Society of Great Britain.
4. Carter, Y., Moss, C. and Weyman, A. (Eds.) (1998) *RCGP Handbook of Sexual Health in Primary Care*. London: Royal College of General Practitioners.
5. CEG (2001a) *National guidelines on the management of Trichomoniasis vaginalis*. Clinical Effectiveness Group (Association of Genitourinary Medicine and the Medical Society for the Study of Venereal Diseases). www.bashh.org [Accessed: 22/04/2005].
6. CEG (2001b) *National guideline on the management of gonorrhoea in adults*. Clinical Effectiveness Group (Association for Genitourinary Medicine and the Medical Society for the Study of Venereal Diseases). www.bashh.org [Accessed: 22/04/2005].
7. CEG (2001c) *National guideline on the management of non-gonococcal urethritis*. Clinical Effectiveness Group (Association for Genitourinary Medicine and the Medical Society for the Study of Venereal Diseases). www.bashh.org [Accessed: 22/04/2005].
8. CEG (2001d) *Clinical effectiveness guideline for the management of Chlamydia trachomatis genital tract infection*. Clinical Effectiveness Group (Association for Genitourinary Medicine and the Medical Society for the Study of Venereal Diseases). www.bashh.org/guidelines/ceguidelines.htm [Accessed: 07/05/2002].
9. Echols, R.M., Heyd, A., O'Keeffe, B.J. and Schacht, P. (1994) Single-dose ciprofloxacin for the treatment of uncomplicated gonorrhea: a worldwide summary. *Sexually Transmitted Diseases* **21**(6), 345–352.
10. Hooton, T.M., Wong, E.S., Barnes, R.C. et al (1990) Erythromycin for persistent or recurrent nongonococcal urethritis. A randomized, placebo-controlled trial. *Annals of Internal Medicine* **113**(1), 21–26.
11. Korting, H.C. and Kollmann, M. (1994) Effective single dose treatment of uncomplicated gonorrhoea. *International Journal of STD & AIDS* **5**(4), 239–243.
12. Low, N. and Cowan, F. (2001) Genital chlamydial infection. *Clinical Evidence* **6**(Dec), 1216–1222.
13. McCormack, W.M. and Rein, M.F. (1995) Urethritis. In: Mandell, G.L., Douglas, R.G., Bennett, J.E. et al (Eds.) *Mandell, Douglas and Bennett's Principles and Practice of Infectious Diseases*. 4th edn. New York: Churchill Livingstone. 1063–1072.
14. MMWR (2002) Sexually transmitted diseases treatment guidelines 2002. *Morbidity & Mortality Weekly Report* **51**(RR-6),

15. Moran, J.S. (1996) Ciprofloxacin for gonorrhea–250 mg or 500 mg? *Sexually Transmitted Diseases* 23(2), 165–167.
16. Moran, J (2002) Gonorrhoea. *Clinical Evidence* 8(Dec.), 1633–1641.
17. Moran, J.S. and Levine, W.C. (1995) Drugs of choice for the treatment of uncomplicated gonococcal infections. *Clinical Infectious Diseases* 20(Suppl 1), S47-S65.
18. Ness, R.B., Markovic, N., Carlson, C.L. and Coughlin, M.T. (1997) Do men become infertile after having sexually transmitted urethritis? An epidemiologic examination. *Fertility & Sterility* 68(2), 205–213.
19. PHLS (2002a) *New episodes of selected diagnoses by age and sex: England, Wales and Northern Ireland 1995–2000: genital chlamydia (uncomplicated).* Public Health Laboratory Service. www.hpa.org.uk [Accessed: 01/07/2002].
20. PHLS (2002b) *Gonorrhoea: epidemiological data.* Public Health Laboratory Service. www.phls.org.uk [Accessed: 15/12/2002].
21. Ross, J.D.C. and Champion, J (1998) How are men with urethral discharge managed in general practice *International Journal of STD & AIDS* 9, 192–195.
22. SIGN (2000) *Management of genital chlamydia trachomatis infection.* Report no. 42. Scottish Intercollegiate Guidelines Network. www.sign.ac.uk [Accessed: 08/05/2002].
23. Wong, E.S., Hooton, T.M., Hill, C.C. et al (1988) Clinical and microbiological features of persistent o recurrent nongonococcal urethritis in men. *Journal Infectious Diseases* 158(5), 1098–1101.

U

PRODIGY GUIDANCE

Urinary tract infection (lower) — men

Last revised in July 2005
www.prodigy.nhs.uk/guidance.asp?gt=UTI (lower) - men

Applies to men over the age of 12 years

This guidance deals with the management of cystitis in men, as well as urinary tract infection (UTI) in men with long-term urethral catheters.

This guidance does not deal with the treatment of prostatitis and urethritis (although they are technically lower urinary tract infections), or infection of the upper urinary tract.

There is separate PRODIGY guidance for *Pyelonephritis — acute, Prostatitis*, and *Urethritis — male.*

Goals

Prompt recognition of UTI
Accurate diagnosis, appropriate therapy, safe avoidance of unnecessary antibiotics
Symptom relief
Eradication of infection
Prevention of recurrence and complications
Detection and management of predisposing and associated conditions

Contents

Scenarios

- Acute cystitis in men p.1795
- Treatment failure in acute cystitis p.1797
- Prophylaxis for recurrent cystitis in men p.1799
- Cystitis in elderly men p.1800
- UTI in men with chronic indwelling urinary catheters p.1802

Extended Information, p. 1804

Which scenario?

Acute cystitis in men: covers the management of uncomplicated cystitis (UTI) in men, but excludes *Prostatitis* and *Urethritis – male* for which there is separate PRODIGY guidance.
Treatment failure in acute cystitis: covers the management of lower UTIs in men who have failed to respond to treatment.
Prophylaxis for recurrent cystitis in men: covers the management of lower UTIs that recur two or more times a year in otherwise healthy men.
Cystitis in elderly men: covers the management of lower UTIs in elderly men.
UTI in men with chronic indwelling urinary catheters: covers the management of lower UTIs in men with chronic indwelling urinary catheters.

Acute cystitis in men

Which therapy?

Follow local guidelines. Consider modifying therapy according to local bacterial resistance patterns.

- **Send urine sample for culture and sensitivity.**
- Exclude or manage possible risk factors and associated conditions:
  - Prostatic enlargement
  - Previous urinary tract surgery
  - Abnormalities of urinary tract function
  - Immunocompromise
  - Anal intercourse
- **If symptoms are severe:**
  - Admit to hospital (may be pyelonephritis; will need parenteral therapy).
- **Otherwise, treat with a preferred antibiotic for 7 days.** Options include:
  - Trimethoprim
  - Nitrofurantoin
  - Cefalexin
- **Offer analgesic and antipyretic (paracetamol or ibuprofen).**
- Review choice of antibiotic when urine culture results are ready.
- Consider referral for specialist assessment when recovered from acute infection.

Practical prescribing points

For further information see the *Medicines Compendium* (www.medicines.org.uk) or the *British National Formulary* (www.bnf.org).

- **Trimethoprim** may rarely cause blood dyscrasias and skin disorders. In moderate renal impairment the dose of trimethoprim should be reduced, and in very severe renal impairment this drug should be avoided.
- **Nitrofurantoin** is contraindicated in people with renal impairment: there is a risk of peripheral neuropathy, and urine concentrations would be inadequate for effective treatment. It should not be used in people who are known to be G6PD deficient. It may cause nausea and vomiting.
- **Cefalexin** in high dosages may cause diarrhoea and, rarely, pseudomembranous colitis.
- **Ibuprofen,** as with other NSAIDs, may worsen or precipitate gastrointestinal haemorrhage, asthma, hypertension, renal impairment, or cardiac failure. Avoid if there is a history of peptic ulcer.

Follow-up advice

- Review according to the clinical situation (e.g. at around 48 hours) to ensure the man is responding to treatment, and to check the results of the urine culture.

Should I refer or investigate?

Refer?

- Referral for assessment is not routinely indicated.
- **Referral for assessment may be indicated for men who have:**
  - Features of urinary obstruction (e.g. in older men, enlarged prostate).
  - Failed to respond to appropriate antibiotic therapy.

- More than two episodes of urinary tract infection (UTI) a year.
- A history of pyelonephritis, calculi, or previous genito-urinary tract surgery.

- **Referral guidelines for suspected cancer** published by the National Institute for Health and Clinical Excellence (NICE) [NICE, 2005] recommend urgent referral to a team specialising in the management of urological cancer, depending on local arrangements, for people:
  - Of any age with painless macroscopic haematuria.
  - Aged 40 years or older who present with recurrent or persistent urinary tract infection associated with haematuria.
  - Aged 50 years or older who are found to have unexplained microscopic haematuria.
  - With an abdominal mass identified clinically or on imaging that is thought to arise from the urinary tract.
  - Who have macroscopic haematuria and symptoms suggestive of a urinary tract infection *if* infection is not confirmed.

Investigate?

- **Culture the urine whenever UTI is suspected in a man.**
- **Urine dipstick tests:**
  - Urine dipstick tests are useful to guide initial therapy.
  - If either nitrite or leucocyte esterase tests are positive, diagnose and treat the UTI.
  - If nitrite and leucocyte esterase are both negative, consider treating symptomatically and review decision when the urine culture result is available.
- **Urine microscopy,** if available, is a quick and accurate near-patient screening test.
- **Special investigations** are not routinely indicated.
- **Referral for imaging or functional tests** may be indicated for men who have:
  - Features of urinary obstruction (e.g. in older men, enlarged prostate)
  - Failed to respond to appropriate antibiotic therapy
  - Frequent recurrences (e.g. more than two a year)
  - Persistent haematuria
  - A history of pyelonephritis, calculi, or previous genito-urinary tract surgery
- Screening for sexually transmitted disease may be indicated in sexually active men.

Patient information leaflets

The following PILs are available at www.prodigy.nhs.uk

- Cystoscopy
- Intravenous Urography
- Kidney Infection (Pyelonephritis)
- Midstream Specimen of Urine (MSU)
- Urine Infection In Men

U

Shared decision making

- An antibiotic for 7 days is recognized treatment for men with cystitis.
- If a urine culture test is done, telephone for the results in 3 days' time. Ask if it is necessary to change the treatment.
- Paracetamol or ibuprofen will help with pain or discomfort.
- See a doctor if symptoms are not gone or nearly gone after 3 days.
- Consult a doctor if cystitis becomes a recurring problem.
- Drink plenty of fluid is traditional advice to 'flush out the bladder', but its effect is unproven, and the increased urine flow may be uncomfortable.

Drug rationale

Drugs not included

- **Penicillins such as amoxicillin** are unsuitable for empirical therapy because about 50% of all urinary pathogen isolates are amoxicillin resistant.
- **First-generation cephalosporins other than cefalexin** have similar antibiotic sensitivities and adverse effect profiles, and are more expensive.
- **Second-generation cephalosporins** are not so well absorbed orally as first-generation cephalosporins; they have a greater incidence of gastrointestinal adverse effects, and are more expensive than the first-generation agents.
- **Third-generation cephalosporins** generally require parenteral administration, and are reserved for use in secondary care for serious infections.
- **Co-amoxiclav** should be reserved for use when preferred therapy has failed, or for complicated UTI when sensitivities are known.
- **Quinolones** should be reserved as second-line agents, or for complicated infections where sensitivities are known in order to preserve their efficacy and limit the development of resistance.
- **Pivmecillinam** should be reserved for use when preferred therapy has failed, or for complicated UTI when sensitivities are known.
- **Co-trimoxazole** is restricted to certain indications by the Committee on Safety of Medicines (CSM) and should be used only if there is evidence of bacterial sensitivity.
- **Urine alkalinizing agents** are not included as there is some evidence that they do not relieve the symptoms of cystitis [Brumfitt et al, 1990].

[DTB, 1998]

Drugs included

- For all antibiotics, a 7-day course is given in line with Public Health Laboratory Service and MeReC recommendations.
- **Trimethoprim** is the agent of choice for empirical therapy in uncomplicated UTI; it is effective, safe, and inexpensive. It should not be used if the man has a history of recurrent infections resistant to this agent, or has recently taken trimethoprim.
- **Nitrofurantoin** is a useful alternative agent, effective against most urinary pathogens. For most people the standard tablet formulation should be adequate. The macrocrystalline capsules may be better tolerated if nausea is troublesome; they are offered as an alternative. The twice-daily modified-release formulation is also better tolerated and is offered as an alternative when concordance may be a problem.
- **Cefalexin** is a first-generation cephalosporin that is effective against most urinary pathogens.
- **Paracetamol** is an effective and safe analgesic and antipyretic agent.
- **Ibuprofen** is an effective alternative to paracetamol if there are no contraindications.

[MeReC, 1995; DTB, 1998; BNF 42, 2001; PHLS, 2001]

Prescriptions

1st-line antibiotics for 7 days

Trimethoprim tablets: 200mg twice a day

- Age from 16 years onwards
- Trimethoprim 200mg tablets. Take one tablet twice a day for 7 days; supply 14 tablets; NHS Cost £0.67.

trofurantoin tablets: 50mg four times a day
Age from 16 years onwards
Nitrofurantoin 50mg tablets. Take one tablet four times a day for 7 days; supply 28 tablets; NHS Cost £2.47.

trofurantoin capsules: 50mg four times a day
Age from 16 years onwards
Nitrofurantoin 50mg capsules. Take one capsule four times a day for 7 days; supply 28 capsules; NHS Cost £2.85.

trofurantoin m/r capsules: 100mg twice a day
Age from 16 years onwards
Nitrofurantoin 100mg m/r caps. Take one capsule twice a day for 7 days; supply 14 capsules; NHS Cost £4.89.

falexin tablets: 500mg twice a day
Age from 16 years onwards
Cefalexin 500mg tablets. Take one tablet twice a day for 7 days; supply 14 tablets; NHS Cost £2.44.

nalgesic/antipyretic: use when required

racetamol tablets: 1g up to four times a day
Age from 16 years onwards
Paracetamol 500mg tablets. Take two tablets every 4 to 6 hours when required for relief of pain or high temperature. Maximum of 8 tablets in 24 hours; supply 50 tablets; NHS Cost £0.67; OTC Cost £1.18.

uprofen tablets: 400mg three times a day
Age from 16 years onwards
Ibuprofen 400mg tablets. Take one tablet three times a day when required for relief of pain or high temperature. Do not exceed the stated dose; supply 20 tablets; NHS Cost £0.58; OTC Cost £1.03.

Treatment failure in acute cystitis

Which therapy?

llow local guidelines. Consider modifying therapy cording to local bacterial resistance patterns.

Exclude or manage associated factors and conditions:

- Prostatitis
- Enlarged prostate (in older men)
- Previous urinary tract surgery
- Abnormalities of the urinary tract
- Immunocompromise
- Anal intercourse

If symptoms are severe:

- Consider admission to hospital (may be pyelonephritis).

If symptoms are moderate:

- Culture the urine and immediately change to a different antibiotic.
- If on trimethoprim or cefalexin: change to nitrofurantoin, co-amoxiclav or a quinolone.
- If on nitrofurantoin: change to co-amoxiclav or quinolone.

If symptoms are mild:

- Culture the urine and use the results of the sensitivity tests to guide the choice of antibiotics. If practical, delay taking the specimen until all antibiotics have been excreted. For trimethoprim the delay should be 7 days.
- Offer paracetamol or ibuprofen to relieve pain and high temperature.

ractical prescribing points

r further information see the *Medicines Compendium* ww.medicines.org.uk) or the *British National Formulary* ww.bnf.org).

- **Trimethoprim** may rarely cause blood dyscrasias and skin disorders. In moderate renal impairment the dose of trimethoprim should be reduced, and in very severe renal impairment this drug should be avoided.
- **Nitrofurantoin** is contraindicated in people with renal impairment: there is a risk of peripheral neuropathy, and urine concentrations would be inadequate for effective treatment. It should not be used in people who are known to be G6PD deficient. It may cause nausea and vomiting.
- **Cefalexin** in high dosages may cause diarrhoea and, rarely, pseudomembranous colitis.
- **Ibuprofen,** as with other NSAIDs, may worsen or precipitate gastrointestinal haemorrhage, asthma, hypertension, renal impairment, or cardiac failure. Avoid if there is a history of peptic ulcer.
- **Quinolones** may cause tendon damage (Committee on Safety of Medicines advice in BNF). They can induce convulsions in people with epilepsy or in those with conditions that predispose to seizures; people concurrently taking nonsteroidal anti-inflammatory drugs may also be susceptible.

Follow-up advice

- Review according to the clinical situation (e.g. at around 48 hours) to ensure the man is responding to treatment, and to check the results of the urine culture.

Should I refer or investigate?

Refer?

- **Referral guidelines for suspected cancer** published by the National Institute for Health and Clinical Excellence (NICE) [NICE, 2005] recommend urgent referral to a team specialising in the management of urological cancer, depending on local arrangements, for people:
  - Of any age with painless macroscopic haematuria.
  - Aged 40 years or older who present with recurrent or persistent urinary tract infection associated with haematuria.
  - Aged 50 years or older who are found to have unexplained microscopic haematuria.
  - With an abdominal mass identified clinically or on imaging that is thought to arise from the urinary tract.
  - Who have macroscopic haematuria and symptoms suggestive of a urinary tract infection *if* infection is not confirmed.
- **Referral for assessment should be considered in the following circumstances:**
  - Recurrent, or unexplained cystitis
  - Relapse or failure to respond to treatment

Investigate?

- **Urine culture should be obtained whenever treatment has failed.** The sample should be taken with care to avoid contamination, placed in a preservative-containing bottle, or refrigerated and cultured as soon as possible. If practical, delay collecting the specimen until all antibiotics have been excreted. For trimethoprim, the delay should be at least 7 days.
- Testing for chlamydial infection and other sexually transmitted diseases may be appropriate in sexually active men.

Patient information leaflets

The following PILs are available at www.prodigy.nhs.uk

- Cystoscopy
- Intravenous Urography

- Kidney Infection (Pyelonephritis)
- Midstream Specimen of Urine (MSU)
- Urine Infection In Men

Shared decision making

- Cystitis sometimes does not clear with an antibiotic. This may be because the germ is 'resistant' to the antibiotic (or in some cases, because the cystitis has not been caused by an infection). A urine test is needed to see whether a germ is present, and which germ it is.
- If a urine culture test is done, telephone for the results in 3 days' time. Ask if it is necessary to change the treatment.
- A second antibiotic will usually work. It is best to wait until the urine result is back to see which germ is present and which antibiotic kills it.
- Paracetamol or ibuprofen will help with pain or discomfort.
- Consult a doctor if the cystitis still does not clear or becomes a recurring problem.
- Drinking plenty of fluid is traditional advice to 'flush out the bladder', but this is unproven and the increased urine flow may be uncomfortable.

Drug rationale

Drugs not included

- **Penicillins such as amoxicillin** are unsuitable for empirical therapy because about 50% of all urinary pathogen isolates are amoxicillin resistant.
- **First-generation cephalosporins other than cefalexin** have similar antibiotic sensitivities and adverse effect profiles, and are more expensive.
- **Second-generation cephalosporins** are not so well absorbed orally as first-generation cephalosporins; they have a greater incidence of gastrointestinal adverse effects, and are more expensive than the first-generation agents.
- **Third-generation cephalosporins** generally require parenteral administration, and are reserved for use in secondary care for serious infections.
- **Quinolones other than norfloxacin and ciprofloxacin** should be reserved as second-line agents, or for complicated infections when sensitivities are known, in order to preserve their efficacy and limit the development of resistance. The newer quinolones have a slightly broader spectrum of activity than the older agents but there is no evidence of greater efficacy. (Ciprofloxacin in the 100 mg strength is not offered for men.)
- **Co-trimoxazole** is restricted to certain indications by the Committee on Safety of Medicines (CSM) and should be used only if there is evidence of bacterial sensitivity.
- **Urine alkalinizing agents** are not included as there is some evidence that they do not relieve the symptoms of cystitis [Brumfitt et al, 1990].

[DTB, 1998]

U

Drugs included

- For all antibiotics, **a 7-day course** is given in line with Public Health Laboratory Service and MeReC recommendations.
- **Trimethoprim** is effective against most urinary tract pathogens, safe, and inexpensive. It should not be used if the man has a history of recurrent infections resistant to this agent, or has recently taken trimethoprim.
- **Nitrofurantoin** is a useful alternative agent, effective against most urinary pathogens. For most people the standard tablet formulation should be adequate. The macrocrystalline capsules may be better tolerated if nausea is troublesome; they are offered as an alternativ[e]. The twice-daily modified-release formulation is also better tolerated, and is offered as an alternative when concordance may be a problem.
- **Cefalexin** is a first-generation cephalosporin effective against most urinary pathogens.
- **Co-amoxiclav** is a suitable second-line alternative for infections caused by bacteria resistant to trimethoprim or other agents. It is effective against up to 90% of urinary pathogens.
- **Norfloxacin and ciprofloxacin** are recommended as second-line agents. They are effective against most urinary pathogens (only about 5% of pathogens are resistant), and are currently the least expensive of the available quinolones.
- **Pivmecillinam** is highly active against many Gram-negative pathogens, and is an appropriate second-line agent when bacteria are resistant to trimethoprim or other agents.
- **Paracetamol** is an effective and safe analgesic and antipyretic agent.
- **Ibuprofen** is an effective alternative to paracetamol if there are no contraindications.

[MeReC, 1995; DTB, 1998; PHLS, 2001]

Prescriptions

1st-line antibiotics for 7 days

Trimethoprim tablets: 200mg twice a day
- Age from 16 years onwards
- Trimethoprim 200mg tablets. Take one tablet twice a day for 7 days; supply 14 tablets; NHS Cost £0.67.

Nitrofurantoin tablets: 50mg four times a day
- Age from 16 years onwards
- Nitrofurantoin 50mg tablets. Take one tablet four time[s] a day for 7 days; supply 28 tablets; NHS Cost £2.47.

Nitrofurantoin capsules: 50mg four times a day
- Age from 16 years onwards
- Nitrofurantoin 50mg capsules. Take one capsule four times a day for 7 days; supply 28 capsules; NHS Cost £2.85.

Nitrofurantoin m/r capsules: 100mg twice a day
- Age from 16 years onwards
- Nitrofurantoin 100mg m/r caps. Take one capsule twic[e] a day for 7 days; supply 14 capsules; NHS Cost £4.89.

Cefalexin tablets: 500mg twice a day
- Age from 16 years onwards
- Cefalexin 500mg tablets. Take one tablet twice a day f[or] 7 days; supply 14 tablets; NHS Cost £2.44.

2nd-line antibiotics for 7 days

Co-amoxiclav tablets: 250/125mg three times a day
- Age from 16 years onwards
- Co-amoxiclav 375mg tablets. Take one tablet three times a day for 7 days; supply 21 tablets; NHS Cost £9.73.

Ciprofloxacin tablets: 250mg tablets twice a day
- Age from 16 years onwards
- Ciprofloxacin 250mg tablets. Take one tablet twice a day for 7 days; supply 14 tablets; NHS Cost £10.50.

Norfloxacin tablets: 400mg twice a day
- Age from 16 years onwards
- Norfloxacin 400mg tablets. Take one tablet twice a da[y] for 7 days; supply 14 tablets; NHS Cost £4.72.

Pivmecillinam tablets: 200mg three times a day
- Age from 16 years onwards
- Pivmecillinam 200mg tablets. Take TWO tablets now and then take ONE tablet three times a day for 7 days; supply 22 tablets; NHS Cost £9.90.

nalgesic/antipyretic: use when required

racetamol tablets: 1g up to four times a day

Age from 16 years onwards

Paracetamol 500mg tablets. Take two tablets every 4 to 6 hours when required for relief of pain or high temperature. Maximum of 8 tablets in 24 hours; supply 50 tablets; NHS Cost £0.67; OTC Cost £1.18.

uprofen tablets: 400mg three times a day

Age from 16 years onwards

Ibuprofen 400mg tablets. Take one tablet three times a day when required for relief of pain or high temperature. Do not exceed the stated dose; supply 20 tablets; NHS Cost £0.58; OTC Cost £1.03.

'rophylaxis for recurrent cystitis n men

Vhich therapy?

llow local guidelines. Consider modifying therapy cording to local bacterial resistance patterns.

Exclude or manage possible risk factors and associated conditions:

- Prostatitis
- Bladder carcinoma
- Incomplete bladder emptying (e.g. prostatism, neurogenic bladder)
- Previous urinary tract surgery
- Abnormalities of the urinary tract
- Calculi
- Immunocompromise
- Anal intercourse

Refer men who have recurrent cystitis (more than two episodes in a year) for specialist assessment.

While waiting for specialist assessment, manage the acute episode of cystitis with a 7-day course of preferred antibiotic.

ractical prescribing points

r further information see the *Medicines Compendium* ww.medicines.org.uk) or the *British National Formulary* ww.bnf.org).

Trimethoprim may rarely cause blood dyscrasias and skin disorders. In moderate renal impairment the dose of trimethoprim should be reduced, and in very severe renal impairment this drug should be avoided.

Nitrofurantoin is contraindicated in people with renal impairment: there is a risk of peripheral neuropathy, and urine concentrations would be inadequate for effective treatment. It should not be used in people who are known to be G6PD deficient. It may cause nausea and vomiting.

Cefalexin in high dosages may cause diarrhoea and, rarely, pseudomembranous colitis.

Ibuprofen, as with other NSAIDs, may worsen or precipitate gastrointestinal haemorrhage, asthma, hypertension, renal impairment, or cardiac failure. Avoid if there is a history of peptic ulcer.

hould I refer or investigate?

efer?

Men who have more than two urinary tract infections (UTIs) in a year.

Referral guidelines for suspected cancer published by the National Institute for Health and Clinical Excellence (NICE) [NICE, 2005] recommend urgent referral to a team specialising in the management of urological cancer, depending on local arrangements, for people:

- Of any age with painless macroscopic haematuria.
- Aged 40 years or older who present with recurrent or persistent urinary tract infection associated with haematuria.
- Aged 50 years or older who are found to have unexplained microscopic haematuria.
- With an abdominal mass identified clinically or on imaging that is thought to arise from the urinary tract.
- Who have macroscopic haematuria and symptoms suggestive of a urinary tract infection *if* infection is not confirmed.

Patient information leaflets

The following PILs are available at www.prodigy.nhs.uk

- Cystoscopy
- Intravenous Urography
- Kidney Infection (Pyelonephritis)
- Midstream Specimen of Urine (MSU)
- Urine Infection In Men

Shared decision making

- Some men tend to have recurrent bouts of cystitis. A prostate problem is sometimes the cause, but usually the reason for recurring cystitis is not clear.
- Specialist assessment is sometimes needed.
- If a urine culture test is done, the results will be ready in 2 or 3 days. Telephone to ask if it is necessary to change the antibiotic.
- Cranberry juice is a popular remedy for preventing urinary infection in women. There is no evidence that it prevents urinary infection in men.

Drug rationale

Drugs not included

- **Penicillins such as amoxicillin** are unsuitable for empirical therapy because about 50% of urinary pathogens are amoxicillin resistant.
- **First-generation cephalosporins other than cefalexin** have similar antibiotic sensitivities and adverse effect profiles, and are more expensive.
- **Second-generation cephalosporins** are not so well absorbed orally as first-generation cephalosporins; they have a greater incidence of gastrointestinal adverse effects, and are more expensive than the first-generation agents.
- **Third-generation cephalosporins** generally require parenteral administration, and are reserved for use in secondary care for serious infections.
- **Co-amoxiclav** should be reserved for use when preferred therapy has failed, or for complicated UTI when sensitivities are known.
- **Quinolones** should be reserved as second-line agents, or for complicated infections when sensitivities are known, in order to preserve their efficacy and limit the development of resistance.
- **Pivmecillinam** should be reserved for use when preferred therapy has failed, or for complicated UTI when sensitivities are known.
- **Co-trimoxazole** is restricted to certain indications by the Committee on Safety of Medicines (CSM), and should be used only if there is evidence of bacterial sensitivity.
- **Methenamine hippurate** does not have enough evidence to support its routine use in the prevention of recurrent UTI [Lee et al, 2002].

- **Urine alkalinizing agents** are not included as there is some evidence that they do not relieve the symptoms of cystitis [Brumfitt et al, 1990].

[MeReC, 1995; DTB, 1998; Read, 2000; BNF 42, 2001; Cooper and Jepson, 2001]

Drugs included

- For recurrent infections, a 7-day antibiotic course is offered to treat the acute episode of cystitis (in line with Public Health Laboratory Service recommendations).
- **Trimethoprim** is the agent of choice for empirical therapy and is effective, safe, and inexpensive. It should not be used if the man has a history of recurrent infections resistant to this agent, or has recently taken trimethoprim.
- **Nitrofurantoin** is a useful alternative agent, effective against most urinary pathogens. For most people the standard tablet formulation should be adequate. The macrocrystalline capsules may be better tolerated if nausea is troublesome; they are offered as an alternative. The twice-daily modified-release formulation is also better tolerated, and is offered as an alternative when concordance may be a problem.
- **Cefalexin** is a first-generation cephalosporin effective against most urinary pathogens.
- **Paracetamol** is an effective and safe analgesic and antipyretic agent.
- **Ibuprofen** is an effective alternative to paracetamol if there are no contraindications.

[MeReC, 1995; DTB, 1998; Read, 2000; BNF 42, 2001; Cooper and Jepson, 2001; Gould et al, 2001; PHLS, 2001]

Prescriptions

1st-line antibiotics for 7 days

Trimethoprim tablets: 200mg twice a day
- Age from 16 years onwards
- Trimethoprim 200mg tablets. Take one tablet twice a day for 7 days; supply 14 tablets; NHS Cost £0.67.

Nitrofurantoin tablets: 50mg four times a day
- Age from 16 years onwards
- Nitrofurantoin 50mg tablets. Take one tablet four times a day for 7 days; supply 28 tablets; NHS Cost £2.47.

Nitrofurantoin capsules: 50mg four times a day
- Age from 16 years onwards
- Nitrofurantoin 50mg capsules. Take one capsule four times a day for 7 days; supply 28 capsules; NHS Cost £2.85.

Nitrofurantoin m/r capsules: 100mg twice a day
- Age from 16 years onwards
- Nitrofurantoin 100mg m/r caps. Take one capsule twice a day for 7 days; supply 14 capsules; NHS Cost £4.89.

Cefalexin tablets: 500mg twice a day
- Age from 16 years onwards
- Cefalexin 500mg tablets. Take one tablet twice a day for 7 days; supply 14 tablets; NHS Cost £2.44.

Cystitis in elderly men

Which therapy?

Follow local guidelines. Consider modifying therapy according to local bacterial resistance patterns.

Asymptomatic bacteriuria

- Asymptomatic bacteriuria in elderly men should be neither investigated nor treated.
- **In elderly men, symptoms of urinary tract infection (UTI) may be atypical (e.g. incontinence, disorientatio**

Cystitis (symptomatic bacteriuria)

- **Exclude or manage associated conditions and risk factors** (if present):
  - Prostatitis
  - Prostatism
  - Incomplete bladder emptying (e.g. chronic indwellin urethral catheter)
  - Previous urinary tract surgery
  - Abnormalities of urinary tract function
  - Immunocompromise
- **If symptoms are severe:**
  - Admit to hospital (may be pyelonephritis; will need parenteral therapy).
- **Otherwise, treat with a preferred antibiotic for 7 days.** Options include:
  - Trimethoprim
  - Nitrofurantoin
  - Cefalexin
- **Offer analgesic and antipyretic (paracetamol or ibuprofen).**
- Review choice of antibiotic when urine culture results are ready.

Practical prescribing points

For further information see the *Medicines Compendium* (www.medicines.org.uk) or the *British National Formula* (www.bnf.org).

- **Trimethoprim** may rarely cause blood dyscrasias and skin disorders. In moderate renal impairment the dose trimethoprim should be reduced, and in very severe ren impairment this drug should be avoided.
- **Nitrofurantoin** is contraindicated in people with renal impairment: there is a risk of peripheral neuropathy, a urine concentrations would be inadequate for effective treatment. It should not be used in people who are known to be G6PD deficient. It may cause nausea and vomiting.
- **Cefalexin** in high dosages may cause diarrhoea and, rarely, pseudomembranous colitis.
- **Ibuprofen,** as with other NSAIDs, may worsen or precipitate gastrointestinal haemorrhage, asthma, hypertension, renal impairment, or cardiac failure. Av if there is a history of peptic ulcer.

Follow-up advice

- Review according to the clinical situation (e.g. at arour 48 hours) to ensure the man is responding to treatment and to check the results of the urine culture.

Should I refer or investigate?

Refer?

- **Referral for assessment is not routinely indicated.**
- **Referral for assessment may be indicated for men who have:**
  - Features of urinary obstruction (e.g. enlarged prosta
  - Failed to respond to appropriate antibiotic therapy
  - More than two episodes of urinary tract infection (UTI) a year
  - A history of pyelonephritis, calculi, or previous genit urinary tract surgery
- **Referral guidelines for suspected cancer** published by t National Institute for Health and Clinical Excellence (NICE) [NICE, 2005] recommend urgent referral to a

team specialising in the management of urological cancer, depending on local arrangements, for people:

- Of any age with painless macroscopic haematuria.
- Aged 40 years or older who present with recurrent or persistent urinary tract infection associated with haematuria.
- Aged 50 years or older who are found to have unexplained microscopic haematuria.
- With an abdominal mass identified clinically or on imaging that is thought to arise from the urinary tract.
- Who have macroscopic haematuria and symptoms suggestive of a urinary tract infection *if* infection is not confirmed.

ıvestigate?

Asymptomatic bacteriuria

Asymptomatic bacteriuria in elderly men should not be investigated or treated.
In elderly people, symptoms of UTI may be atypical (e.g. incontinence, disorientation).

;ystitis (symptomatic bacteriuria)

Referral for imaging or functional tests may be indicated for men who have:

- Features of urinary obstruction (e.g. in older men, enlarged prostate)
- Failed to respond to appropriate antibiotic therapy
- Frequent recurrences (e.g. more than two a year)
- Persistent haematuria
- A history of pyelonephritis, calculi, or previous genito-urinary tract surgery.

'atient information leaflets

he following PILs are available at www.prodigy.nhs.uk
Cystoscopy
Intravenous Urography
Kidney Infection (Pyelonephritis)
Midstream Specimen of Urine (MSU)
Urine Infection In Men

hared decision making

An antibiotic for 7 days is the recognized treatment for men with cystitis.
If a urine culture test is done, telephone for the results in 2 or 3 days' time. Ask if it is necessary to change the treatment.
Paracetamol or ibuprofen will help with pain or discomfort.
See a doctor if the symptoms are not gone or nearly gone after 3 days.
Consult a doctor if cystitis becomes a recurring problem.
Drinking plenty of fluid is traditional advice to 'flush out the bladder', but it is unproven and the increased urine flow may be uncomfortable.

)rug rationale

'rugs not included

First-generation cephalosporins other than cefalexin have similar antibiotic sensitivities and adverse effect profiles, and are more expensive.
Second-generation cephalosporins are not so well absorbed orally as first-generation cephalosporins; they have a greater incidence of gastrointestinal adverse effects, and are more expensive than the first-generation agents.

- **Third-generation cephalosporins** generally require parenteral administration, and are reserved for use in secondary care for serious infections.
- **Co-amoxiclav** should be reserved for use when preferred therapy has failed, or for complicated UTI when sensitivities are known.
- **Quinolones** should be reserved as second-line agents, or for complicated infections when sensitivities are known, in order to preserve their efficacy, and limit the development of resistance.
- **Pivmecillinam** should be reserved for use when preferred therapy has failed, or for complicated UTI when sensitivities are known.
- **Co-trimoxazole** is restricted to certain indications by the Committee on Safety of Medicines (CSM), and should be used only if there is evidence of bacterial sensitivity.
- **Urine alkalinizing agents** are not included as there is some evidence that they do not relieve the symptoms of cystitis [Brumfitt et al, 1990].

[DTB, 1998]

Drugs included

- For all antibiotics, a 7-day course is given in line with Public Health Laboratory Service and MeReC recommendations.
- **Trimethoprim** is the agent of choice for empirical therapy in uncomplicated UTI, and is an effective, safe, and inexpensive treatment. It should not be used if the man has a history of recurrent infections resistant to this agent, or has recently taken trimethoprim.
- **Nitrofurantoin** is useful alternative agent, effective against most urinary pathogens. For most people the standard tablet formulation should be adequate. The macrocrystalline capsules may be better tolerated if nausea is troublesome; they are offered as an alternative. The twice-daily modified-release formulation is also better tolerated, and offered as an alternative when concordance may be a problem.
- **Cefalexin** is a first-generation cephalosporin effective against most urinary pathogens.
- **Amoxicillin** should be used only if the organism is known to be sensitive, because there is a high incidence of bacterial resistance.
- **Paracetamol** is an effective and safe analgesic and antipyretic agent.
- **Ibuprofen** is an effective alternative to paracetamol if there are no contraindications.

[MeReC, 1995; DTB, 1998; PHLS, 2001]

Prescriptions

1st-line antibiotics for 7 days

Trimethoprim tablets: 200mg twice a day

- Age from 60 years onwards
- Trimethoprim 200mg tablets. Take one tablet twice a day for 7 days; supply 14 tablets; NHS Cost £0.67.

Nitrofurantoin tablets: 50mg four times a day

- Age from 60 years onwards
- Nitrofurantoin 50mg tablets. Take one tablet four times a day for 7 days; supply 28 tablets; NHS Cost £2.47.

Nitrofurantoin capsules: 50mg four times a day

- Age from 60 years onwards
- Nitrofurantoin 50mg capsules. Take one capsule four times a day for 7 days; supply 28 capsules; NHS Cost £2.85.

Nitrofurantoin m/r capsules: 100mg twice a day

- Age from 60 years onwards
- Nitrofurantoin 100mg m/r caps. Take one capsule twice a day for 7 days; supply 14 capsules; NHS Cost £4.89.

Cefalexin tablets: 500mg twice a day

- Age from 16 years onwards
- Cefalexin 500mg tablets. Take one tablet twice a day for 7 days; supply 14 tablets; NHS Cost £2.44.

Analgesic/antipyretic: use when required

Paracetamol tablets: 1g up to four times a day

- Age from 60 years onwards
- Paracetamol 500mg tablets. Take two tablets every 4 to 6 hours when required for relief of pain or high temperature. Maximum of 8 tablets in 24 hours; supply 50 tablets; NHS Cost £0.67; OTC Cost £1.18.

Ibuprofen tablets: 400mg three times a day

- Age from 60 years onwards
- Ibuprofen 400mg tablets. Take one tablet three times a day when required for relief of pain or high temperature. Do not exceed the stated dose; supply 20 tablets; NHS Cost £0.58; OTC Cost £1.03.

UTI in men with chronic indwelling urinary catheters

Which therapy?

Follow local guidelines. Consider modifying therapy according to local bacterial resistance patterns.

Asymptomatic bacteriuria in a man with a long-term indwelling urinary catheter

- Asymptomatic bacteriuria in a man with a long-term indwelling urinary catheter needs neither investigation nor treatment.

Symptomatic urinary tract infection in a man with a long-term indwelling urinary catheter

- Exclude or manage possible risk factors and associated conditions:
  - Incomplete bladder emptying
  - Poor perineal/periurethral/catheter hygiene
  - Encrusted catheter.
- **If symptoms are severe:**
  - Admit to hospital (may be pyelonephritis; will need parenteral therapy).
- **Otherwise:**
  - Culture urine before commencing antibiotics.
  - If practical, withhold antibiotics until the result of urine culture is available.
  - Treat with a preferred antibiotic for 7 days. Choices are:
    - Trimethoprim
    - Nitrofurantoin
    - Cefalexin
  - Review choice of antibiotic with progress and culture results.
  - Consider replacing the catheter if it has not been changed for some time.
  - Encourage fluid intake to promote urine flow.
  - Offer paracetamol or ibuprofen to treat pain and high temperature.
- **Preventive measures:**
  - Recommend intermittent catheterization (rather than indwelling catheter) if care circumstances permit.
  - Consider regular replacement of the catheter if infections recur frequently.

Practical prescribing points

For further information see the *Medicines Compendium* (www.medicines.org.uk) or the *British National Formulary* (www.bnf.org).

- **Trimethoprim** may rarely cause blood dyscrasias and skin disorders. In moderate renal impairment the dose of trimethoprim should be reduced; and in very severe renal impairment this drug should be avoided.
- **Nitrofurantoin** is contraindicated in people with renal impairment: there is a risk of peripheral neuropathy, and urine concentrations would be inadequate for effective treatment. It should not be used in people who are known to be G6PD deficient. It may cause nausea and vomiting.
- **Cefalexin** in high dosages may cause diarrhoea and, rarely, pseudomembranous colitis.
- **Ibuprofen,** as with other NSAIDs, may worsen or precipitate gastrointestinal haemorrhage, asthma, hypertension, renal impairment, or cardiac failure. Avoid if there is a history of peptic ulcer.
- **Quinolones** may cause tendon damage (Committee on Safety of Medicines advice in BNF). They can induce convulsions in people with epilepsy or in those with conditions that predispose to seizures; people concurrently taking nonsteroidal anti-inflammatory drugs may also be susceptible.

Follow-up advice

- Review according to the clinical situation (e.g. at around 48 hours) to ensure the man is responding to treatment, and to check the results of the urine culture.

Should I refer or investigate?

Refer?

- **Referral for assessment is not routinely indicated.**
- Referral for assessment may be indicated when there is recurrent or unexplained cystitis, relapse, or failure to respond to treatment.
- **Referral guidelines for suspected cancer** published by the National Institute for Health and Clinical Excellence (NICE) [NICE, 2005] recommend urgent referral to a team specialising in the management of urological cancer, depending on local arrangements, for people:
  - Of any age with painless macroscopic haematuria.
  - Aged 40 years or older who present with recurrent or persistent urinary tract infection associated with haematuria.
  - Aged 50 years or older who are found to have unexplained microscopic haematuria.
  - With an abdominal mass identified clinically or on imaging that is thought to arise from the urinary tract.
  - Who have macroscopic haematuria and symptoms suggestive of a urinary tract infection *if* infection is not confirmed.

Investigate?

Asymptomatic bacteriuria

- Asymptomatic bacteriuria in people with chronic indwelling urethral catheters should be neither investigated nor treated.

Cystitis (i.e. symptomatic bacteriuria)

- **Urine culture** should be performed when:
  - The man is symptomatic and cystitis is suspected
  - Treatment has failed
  - Symptoms recur

U

Urine dipstick tests or microscopy may be used to guide therapy until culture results are available.

Patient information leaflets

The following PILs are available at www.prodigy.nhs.uk
Kidney Infection (Pyelonephritis)
Urine Infection In Men

Shared decision making

An antibiotic for 7 days is the recognized treatment.
Telephone in 2 or 3 days' time for the results of the urine culture. Ask if it is necessary to change the treatment.
See a doctor if the symptoms are not gone or nearly gone after 3 days.
Paracetamol or ibuprofen will help with pain or discomfort.

Drug rationale

Drugs not included

Penicillin-group agents such as amoxicillin are unsuitable for empirical therapy because about 50% of urinary pathogens are amoxicillin resistant. (If culture reveals the organism to be sensitive, then amoxicillin would be appropriate.)
First-generation cephalosporins other than cefalexin have similar antibiotic sensitivities and adverse effect profiles, and are more expensive.
Second-generation cephalosporins are not so well absorbed orally as first-generation cephalosporins; they have a greater incidence of gastrointestinal adverse effects, and are more expensive than the first-generation agents.
Quinolones other than norfloxacin and ciprofloxacin should be reserved as second-line agents, or for complicated infections when sensitivities are known, in order to preserve their efficacy and limit the development of resistance. The newer quinolones have a slightly broader spectrum of activity than the older agents, but there is no evidence of greater efficacy. The 100 mg strength of ciprofloxacin is not offered.
Co-trimoxazole is restricted to certain indications by the Committee on Safety of Medicines (CSM), and should be used only if there is evidence of bacterial sensitivity.
Prophylactic systemic antibiotics, topical antibiotic ointments, and instillation of antibiotics into the bladder are not recommended for people with long-term catheters.
Urine alkalinizing agents are not included as there is some evidence that they do not relieve the symptoms of cystitis [Brumfitt et al, 1990].
[DTB, 1998; AHCPR, 1999]

Drugs included

For all antibiotics, a 7-day course is given in line with Public Health Laboratory Service and MeReC recommendations.
Trimethoprim is the agent of choice for empirical therapy in uncomplicated UTI; it is effective, safe, and inexpensive. It should not be used if the man has a history of recurrent infections resistant to this agent, or has recently taken trimethoprim.
Nitrofurantoin is useful alternative agent, effective against most urinary pathogens. For most people the standard tablet formulation should be adequate. The macrocrystalline capsules are additionally offered because intolerable adverse effects may occur (e.g. nausea). The twice-daily modified-release formulation is also better tolerated, and is offered as an alternative when concordance may be a problem.

- **Cefalexin** is a first-generation cephalosporin effective against most urinary pathogens.
- **Co-amoxiclav** is a suitable second-line alternative for infections caused by bacteria resistant to trimethoprim or other agents. It is effective against up to 90% of urinary pathogens.
- **Norfloxacin and ciprofloxacin** are recommended as second-line agents. They are effective against most urinary pathogens (only around 5% of pathogens are resistant), and are currently the least expensive of the quinolones available.
- **Pivmecillinam** is highly active against many Gram-negative pathogens, and is an appropriate second-line agent when bacteria are resistant to trimethoprim or other agents.
- **Paracetamol** is an effective and safe analgesic and antipyretic agent.
- **Ibuprofen** is an effective alternative to paracetamol if there are no contraindications.

[MeReC, 1995; Bailey, 1996; DTB, 1998; AHCPR, 1999; PHLS, 2001]

Prescriptions

1st-line antibiotics for 7 days

Trimethoprim tablets: 200mg twice a day
- Age from 12 years onwards
- Trimethoprim 200mg tablets. Take one tablet twice a day for 7 days; supply 14 tablets; NHS Cost £0.67.

Nitrofurantoin tablets: 50mg four times a day
- Age from 12 years onwards
- Nitrofurantoin 50mg tablets. Take one tablet four times a day for 7 days; supply 28 tablets; NHS Cost £2.47.

Nitrofurantoin capsules: 50mg four times a day
- Age from 12 years onwards
- Nitrofurantoin 50mg capsules. Take one capsule four times a day for 7 days; supply 28 capsules; NHS Cost £2.85.

Nitrofurantoin m/r capsules: 100mg twice a day
- Age from 12 years onwards
- Nitrofurantoin 100mg m/r caps. Take one capsule twice a day for 7 days; supply 14 capsules; NHS Cost £4.89.

Cefalexin tablets: 500mg twice a day
- Age from 12 years onwards
- Cefalexin 500mg tablets. Take one tablet twice a day for 7 days; supply 14 tablets; NHS Cost £2.44.

2nd-line antibiotics for 7 days

Co-amoxiclav tablets: 500/125mg three times a day
- Age from 12 years onwards
- Co-amoxiclav 625mg tablets. Take one tablet three times a day for 7 days; supply 21 tablets; NHS Cost £15.72.

Ciprofloxacin tablets: 500mg twice a day
- Age from 16 years onwards
- Ciprofloxacin 500mg tablets. Take one tablet twice a day for 7 days; supply 14 tablets; NHS Cost £19.88.

Norfloxacin tablets: 400mg twice a day
- Age from 16 years onwards
- Norfloxacin 400mg tablets. Take one tablet twice a day for 7 days; supply 14 tablets; NHS Cost £4.72.

Pivmecillinam tablets: 400mg three times a day
- Age from 12 years onwards
- Pivmecillinam 200mg tablets. Take two tablets three times a day for 7 days; supply 42 tablets; NHS Cost £18.72.

Analgesic/antipyretic: use when required

Paracetamol tablets: 500mg to 1g up to four times a day

- Age from 12 to 15 years
- Paracetamol 500mg tablets. Take one to two tablets every 4 to 6 hours when required for relief of pain or high temperature. Maximum of 8 tablets in 24 hours; supply 32 tablets; NHS Cost £0.43; OTC Cost £0.75.

Paracetamol tablets: 1g up to four times a day

- Age from 16 years onwards
- Paracetamol 500mg tablets. Take two tablets every 4 to 6 hours when required for relief of pain or high temperature. Maximum of 8 tablets in 24 hours; supply 50 tablets; NHS Cost £0.67; OTC Cost £1.18.

Ibuprofen tablets: 400mg three times a day

- Age from 12 years onwards
- Ibuprofen 400mg tablets. Take one tablet three times a day when required for relief of pain or high temperature. Do not exceed the stated dose; supply 20 tablets; NHS Cost £0.58; OTC Cost £1.03.

Extended Information

Background information

- What is it? p.1804
- How common is it? p.1804
- Risk factors for urinary tract infection p.1804
- How do I know my patient has it? p.1804
- What else might it be? p.1805
- Complications and prognosis p.1806

What is it?

- **Bacteriuria** is the presence of bacteria in the urine.
- **Urinary tract infection (UTI)** is the presence of pathogenic micro-organisms in the urine, urethra, bladder, kidney, or prostate. Infection is usually caused by bacteria from the gastrointestinal tract.
- **Common organisms** causing UTI include:
  - *Escherichia coli*
  - *Staphylococcus saprophyticus*
  - *Proteus mirabilis* (its motility and adherence to uroepithelium facilitate movement up the urinary tract and invasive infection; urease production promotes stone formation)
- **Less common organisms** causing UTI include:
  - *Proteus vulgaris*, *Klebsiella* species, *Enterobacter* species, *Citrobacter* species, *Serratia marcescens*, *Acinetobacter* species, *Pseudomonas* species, and *Staphylococcus aureus*
  - *Candida albicans* infection is rarely found in the community, but it is common in hospital patients with risk factors such as indwelling catheters, immunosuppression, diabetes mellitus, and antibiotic treatment.
- **Lower urinary tract infection** is infection of the urethra and bladder (i.e. urethritis, prostatitis, and cystitis).
- **The pragmatic criterion for diagnosing urinary tract infection** (and that used by the Public Health Laboratory Service) is detection of more than 10^5 organisms per millilitre of suitably collected urine. Urine cultures that grow multiple organisms usually indicate contamination or multiple urinary calculi. If the urine is collected under sterile conditions (e.g. suprapubic aspiration, or 'in-and-out' catheterization) colony counts as low as 10^2 to 10^4 per millilitre may indicate infection.
- **Recurrent UTI** is repeated episodes of lower UTI. There is no consensus on the threshold number of infections at which specific interventions should be taken for recurrence.
- **Relapse** is a repeat UTI with the same strain of organism (which suggests failure to eradicate the pathogen). In practice, because routine laboratory testing does not include typing to identify the strain, a UTI is considered to be a relapse if a repeat infection occurs within a short period (e.g. 2 weeks).
- **Reinfection** is a repeat UTI with a different strain or species of organism.
- **Asymptomatic bacteriuria** is the presence of bacteriuria, but without symptoms. It is commonly found when there is long-term catheterization.
- **Uncomplicated UTI** is infection by a usual pathogen in a person with a normal urinary tract, and with normal renal function.
- **Complicated UTI includes:**
  - Virulent organism (e.g. *S aureus*)
  - Abnormal urinary tract (e.g. calculus, vesico-ureteric reflux, reflux nephropathy, neurogenic bladder, indwelling catheter, urinary obstruction such as prostate enlargement)
  - Impaired host defences (e.g. diabetes mellitus, immunosuppressive therapy)
  - Impaired renal function.

[Brumfitt et al, 1998; Stamm, 1998]

How common is it?

- Urinary tract infection (UTI) is rare in men between 20 and 50 years old; and is considerably less common in men than in women, except in the first year of life and in elderly people.
- In both men and women the incidences of asymptomatic bacteriuria and UTI increase substantially with advancing age, coexisting illnesses, and institutional care.
- The annual incidence of UTI in men is shown in Table 1

Table 1: Annual incidence of UTI in men.

Age group (years)	Incidence (approximate %)
20–60	<1
60–70	3
>80	>=10

[McMurdo and Gillespie, 2000; Wallach, 2001]

Risk factors for urinary tract infection

- **Most urinary tract infections (UTIs) are not associated with any risk factor. However, the following risk factors need to be excluded or managed, especially in recurrent UTI:**
  - Abnormalities of urinary tract function (e.g. indwelling catheter, neurogenic bladder, vesico-ureteric reflux, anatomical abnormalities)
  - Incomplete bladder emptying (e.g. obstruction in men with prostatic enlargement, chronic indwelling catheter)
  - Previous urinary tract surgery
  - Immunocompromise
  - Anal intercourse

How do I know my patient has it?

The spectrum of illness in urinary tract infection ranges from asymptomatic bacteriuria to life-threatening systemic illness.

Typical presentation of lower urinary tract infection

- **Symptoms:** dysuria, frequency, urgency, nocturia, haematuria, suprapubic discomfort

- **Signs:** suprapubic tenderness; cloudy or foul smelling urine

Atypical presentations of lower urinary tract infection

- Urinary tract infection in elderly people may present with non-specific features such as secondary incontinence, confusion, anorexia, high temperature, or shock.
- High temperature (>38.5°C) is more characteristic of pyelonephritis than of cystitis.

Investigations

Collection, storage, and transport of urine samples

- Careful collection, storage, and transport of urine samples minimizes contamination and deterioration.
- Usually, a clean-catch, mid-stream urine (MSU) can be collected from a man with little difficulty, and is adequate for diagnosis.
- Procedure for a man to provide a clean-catch MSU:
  - Discard the first portion of urine and catch the middle portion — a wide-mouthed gallipot or disposable funnel is helpful.
  - Uncircumcised men probably do *not* need to take particular care (e.g. withdraw prepuce and clean glans penis) [Lipsky et al, 1984].
- Occasionally it may be necessary to obtain a suprapubic aspirate or use 'in-and-out' catheterization. Referral to secondary care services would then be warranted.
- **Containers:** urine should be transferred to a specimen bottle within 30 minutes of collection. The bottle should be filled if it contains boric acid because the preservative is bactericidal at high concentrations.
- **Storage:** urine should be refrigerated at 4°C while awaiting processing. Urine that has been stored at 4°C for 48 hours would be suitable for culture, but not for microscopy, because most cells would have disintegrated.
- **Contamination** of the urine specimen is suggested by the presence of one or both of:
  - Bacteria but no leucocytes (except in immunocompromised men)
  - Multiple organisms cultured
- Laboratory reports usually mention the possibility of contamination if there are suspicious features, but criteria for reporting vary between laboratories.

Urine culture

- Urine should be cultured whenever urinary tract infection is suspected in a man (even if dipstick tests are negative).
- The urine specimen should, if possible, be collected before antibiotics are taken or changed.
- False-negative culture results are sometimes due to boric acid (stabilizer in the specimen bottle), or to antibiotics that are excreted in the urine.

Urine dipstick

- Recommendations for use of urine dipstick tests in men:
- The dipstick test helps to confirm clinical impressions:
  - If either nitrite or leucocyte esterase (LE) dipstick tests are positive, diagnose urinary tract infection (UTI).
  - If both nitrite and LE dipstick tests are negative, exclude UTI.
- Always culture the urine to support decisions made on dipstick test results.
- Urine dipstick tests are not suitable for screening for UTI in asymptomatic men.

- Urine dipstick tests are the most widely used near-patient test for UTI.
- We found no studies of urine dipstick tests for UTI in men.
- Dipstick tests cannot be relied on to exclude or confirm a diagnosis of UTI. Urine culture provides the definitive diagnosis, and guides antibiotic therapy. Several studies document the limitations of urine dipstick tests. See [Lammers et al, 2001] and [Hurlbut and Littenberg, 1991] for comprehensive discussions and references to the literature.
- **Nitrite test**
  - Most urinary pathogens reduce nitrate to nitrite.
  - **A positive test is suggestive of bacteriuria.**
  - **A negative test does not rule out UTI** because some pathogens do not produce nitrate reductase, and frequent urination (which is common in cystitis) gives the enzyme less time to act.
- **Leucocyte esterase test**
  - LE is a marker for leucocytes, but the LE test is less sensitive than microscopy.
  - **A positive LE test indicates pyuria, and therefore suggests UTI,** but leucocytes can contaminate the specimen, so a positive test does not make a diagnosis of UTI certain.
  - **A negative LE test does not rule out the diagnosis of UTI** because the test is insensitive, and pyuria is not always found in UTI.
- **Blood and protein**
  - Blood and protein are sometimes found in the urine when there is a UTI, but neither their presence nor their absence helps to make the diagnosis.
- **Combinations of tests**
  - Combining results from nitrite, LE, blood, and protein tests increases sensitivity, but decreases specificity. With the combination that gives maximum sensitivity the over-treatment rate would be about 50%, while the under-treatment rate would still be more than 10%.

[Hurlbut and Littenberg, 1991; Lammers et al, 2001]

Urine microscopy

- Microscopy of urine is a quick and reliable near-patient test for urinary tract infection (UTI).
- UTI is likely if bacteria and leucocytes are seen in the urine.
- Minimal processing is required because the urine is neither centrifuged nor stained.
- Moderate investment in equipment, training, and organization is required.
- Some general practices in the UK offer urine microscopy during a consultation.

Imaging and functional tests

- Special investigations are not routinely indicated.
- Referral for imaging or functional tests may be indicated for men who have:
  - Features of urinary obstruction (e.g. enlarged prostate)
  - Failed to respond to appropriate antibiotic therapy
  - Frequent episodes of urinary tract infection (e.g. more than two in a year)
  - Persistent haematuria
  - History of pyelonephritis, calculi, or previous genito-urinary tract surgery.

[MeReC, 1992; MeReC, 1995; DTB, 1997; DTB, 1998; Lifshitz and Kramer, 2000]

What else might it be?

Conditions associated with or predisposing to lower urinary tract infection

- Prostatic enlargement (common in older men)
- Prostatitis (common with recurrent UTI)

- Abnormal urinary tract: including anatomical changes, calculi, tumours
- Impaired host defences
- Impaired renal function

[Bailey, 1996]

Conditions with presentations similar to lower urinary tract infection

- **Prostatitis:** 'flu-like symptoms; swollen, tender prostate
- **Pyelonephritis:** high temperature, rigors, loin pain/ tenderness, severe illness with prostration, vomiting, oliguric renal failure
- **Urethritis:** *Chlamydia trachomatis* (pyuria without bacteriuria), *Neisseria gonorrhoeae*, herpes simplex virus, or other sexually transmitted disease
- **Drug-induced cystitis** (e.g. cyclophosphamide, allopurinol, danazol, tiaprofenic acid and possibly other NSAIDs)

[Bailey, 1996]

Complications and prognosis

Complications

- Ascending infection can occur, leading to pyelonephritis, renal failure and sepsis.

Management issues

- Acute cystitis in men p.1806
- Recurrent cystitis p.1807
- Cystitis in elderly men p.1807
- Urinary tract infections in men with chronic indwelling urinary catheters p.1808

Acute cystitis in men

Overview of management of urinary tract infection in men

- Send urine sample for culture and sensitivity.
- Treat with a preferred antibiotic for 7 days. Options include:
  - Trimethoprim
  - Nitrofurantoin
  - Cefalexin.
- Review choice of antibiotic when urine culture results are ready.
- Offer an analgesic and an antipyretic.
- Consider referral for specialist assessment when recovered from acute infection if:
  - Features of urinary obstruction (e.g. enlarged prostate)
  - Failure to respond to appropriate antibiotic therapy
  - Frequent episodes of urinary tract infection (e.g. more than two in a year)
  - Persistent haematuria
  - History of pyelonephritis, calculi, or previous genito-urinary tract surgery

Local guidelines and bacterial resistance patterns may require changes to the above recommendations.

Investigations

- Culture the urine if a urinary tract infection is suspected in a man.
- Exclude chlamydia infection in a sexually active man with urinary symptoms, especially if he has sterile pyuria.

The policy of routine referral (e.g. for imaging studies or cystoscopy) after urinary tract infections in otherwise healthy men is controversial, and is not supported by evidence [Stamm and Hooton, 1993; Dawson and Whitfield, 1996].

Investigations are discussed in more detail in the *Background* section.

Antibiotics

- **Adhere to local policies (if available) and be guided by local patterns of bacterial resistance.**
- Cystitis in men should be treated with the same antibiotics as used for cystitis in women.
- The preferred antibiotics are:
  - Trimethoprim
  - Nitrofurantoin
  - Cefalexin.
- The length of therapy is 7 days (rather than the 3-day course that is used for women).
- Studies on bacterial sensitivities can be difficult to extrapolate to general practice because:
  - Study populations from hospitals and from general practice tend to have higher proportions of complicated cases and treatment failures.
  - Uncomplicated urinary tract infection (UTI) generally resolves within a few days, even if no specific treatment is given.
  - Drugs commonly used in UTI are excreted in higher concentrations in the urine than are used in laboratory testing. This explains, in part, why bacterial resistance in the laboratory is not always associated with treatment failure.
  - Patterns of antibiotic resistance vary widely when different centres are compared.

[Wise and Andrews, 1998; Baerheim, 2001; Priest et al, 2001; Tran et al, 2001]

Trimethoprim

- Rates of resistance of *Escherichia coli* to trimethoprim have recently been reported as rising to between 20% and 40%, but the study populations were different from those served by primary care in the UK, where true resistance in acute uncomplicated UTI is probably 10–20% [McNulty, Personal Communication, 2002].
- Trimethoprim is still an effective preferred treatment for uncomplicated UTI in UK general practice, and most infections respond clinically.

[Baerheim, 2001; Manges et al, 2001; Stamm, 2001; Steinke et al, 2001]

Nitrofurantoin

- Nitrofurantoin is at least as effective as trimethoprim, but it is more expensive and frequently causes nausea and vomiting.
- Approximately 10% of the bacteria responsible for UTI in UK general practice are resistant to nitrofurantoin [McNulty, Personal Communication, 2002].
- Nitrofurantoin is ineffective against *Proteus mirabilis.*
- Macrocrystalline nitrofurantoin is promoted as having fewer adverse effects than other formulations [Kalowski et al, 1974], but the published studies were done when the recommended length of treatment was 2 weeks and the recommended dose was 100 mg four times a day. Thus, adverse effects were more likely to occur and less likely to be well tolerated than with current shorter courses of lower doses.
- Modified-release preparations are taken twice a day and may be more convenient.

Cefalexin

- Cefalexin is at least as effective as trimethoprim, but it is more expensive, and, because of its broad anti-bacterial spectrum, it is more likely to disrupt gut flora [Leigh et al, 1970; Parfitt, 1999].

- Approximately 10% of the bacteria responsible for UTIs seen in UK general practice are resistant to cefalexin [McNulty, Personal Communication, 2002].
- Although treatment failure with cefalexin has been reported to be as high as 30% [DTB, 1998], recent urine culture data from the northeast of England showed that 96% of *E coli* isolates and 90% of all other isolates are sensitive to cefalexin [Pedler, Personal Communication, 2002].

Other antibiotics

- **Amoxicillin** is unsuitable as an empirical treatment because 50% of urinary pathogens are resistant to it. However, it may be used if the organism is known to be sensitive.
- **Co-amoxiclav** is appropriate for second-line treatment (e.g. for trimethoprim resistance). Resistance in uncomplicated UTI is less than 5% [McNulty, Personal Communication, 2002]. It is more expensive than trimethoprim, nitrofurantoin, and cefalexin, and it has some undesirable adverse drug reactions.
- **Quinolones** (e.g. ciprofloxacin and norfloxacin) are appropriate for second-line treatment (e.g. for trimethoprim resistance). Resistance in uncomplicated UTI is less than 5% [McNulty, Personal Communication, 2002].
- **Pivmecillinam** may be prescribed for second-line treatment (e.g. for trimethoprim resistance). It is highly active against many Gram-negative pathogens, including *E coli*.

[MeReC, 1995; DTB, 1998; Read, 2000; Baerheim, 2001]

Analgesia and antipyrexia

- Paracetamol or ibuprofen relieve pain and high temperature.

Other treatments

- **Urine alkalinizing agents,** such as potassium citrate, sodium citrate, and sodium bicarbonate, are popular remedies for urinary symptoms in women. However, there is evidence that casts doubt on their efficacy [Brumfitt et al, 1990]. We could find no trials of urine alkalinizing agents taken by men with urinary symptoms.
- **Increasing fluid intake** is common advice (for women), but is controversial and unproven. Theoretically, it could help to 'wash out' the bladder, but it would distress people with dysuria (which can be excruciating).
- **Cranberry juice** has not been shown to be of benefit in acute urinary tract infection, although there is some evidence of effectiveness in preventing recurrent cystitis in women.

[Dawson and Whitfield, 1996; Jepson et al, 2000]

Recurrent cystitis

Recurrent cystitis in men

- Culture urine.
- Treat each episode as for acute cystitis: an antibiotic for 7 days.
- Exclude or confirm and manage possible underlying causes, for example:
  - Prostatitis
  - Calculi
  - Prostatic enlargement
  - Bladder carcinoma
  - Vesico-ureteric reflux
- Refer for assessment if more than two episodes of urinary tract infection (UTI) in a year.

[Nicolle and Ronald, 1998]

Relapse of infection (i.e. infection with the same strain of organism)

- Relapse implies failure of treatment.
- True relapse is difficult to prove because the pathogens identified on urine culture must be typed to show that they are identical. Typing is not routinely done, so relapse is assumed when infection recurs within a short period (e.g. 2 weeks).

Risk factors and associated conditions

- Prostatitis
- Enlarged prostate (in older men)
- Calculi
- Urinary tract anatomical anomalies (e.g. papillary necrosis, vesico-ureteric reflux)
- Previous urinary tract surgery
- Immunocompromise
- Anal intercourse

[Fihn et al, 1985; Fihn et al, 1998]

Investigations

- Chlamydial infection should be ruled out in sexually active men.
- Limited evidence suggests that routine investigation (e.g. with excretory urography, cystoscopy, or ultrasound) is not likely to be beneficial. Subgroups that could benefit from specialized investigations have not been defined.

[Cooper and Jepson, 2001]

Treatment of recurrent cystitis in men

- Recurrent cystitis in a man is likely to be secondary to an associated condition such as prostatitis, prostatic hyperplasia, calculi in the genito-urinary tract, or vesico-ureteric reflux.
- The acute infection should be managed as an uncomplicated UTI:
  - Culture urine
  - Preferred antibiotic for 7 days; choices are:
    - Trimethoprim
    - Nitrofurantoin
    - Cefalexin.

Referral

- Refer for assessment men who have more than two UTIs in a year.

Cystitis in elderly men

Asymptomatic bacteriuria

- Asymptomatic bacteriuria or pyuria in elderly men should not be investigated or treated [McMurdo and Gillespie, 2000].

Presentation

- Cystitis in elderly men may present with non-specific features such as secondary incontinence, confusion, anorexia, high temperature, or shock.
- Recurrent cystitis in elderly men may be due to prostatic enlargement and/or prostatitis.

Management

- Give a preferred antibiotic for 7 days (e.g. trimethoprim, nitrofurantoin, or cefalexin).
- Cystoscopy is occasionally indicated when urinary tract abnormalities are suspected.

[Nicolle et al, 1994; Ouslander et al, 1996; Lutters and Vogt, 2000]

Urinary tract infections in men with chronic indwelling urinary catheters

Background

- All people with indwelling catheters will have bacteriuria at some stage.
- Urine culture is indicated only in those who become symptomatic.
- Solid surfaces (e.g. catheter, stone) in the urinary tract tend to be covered soon after their introduction by a biofilm of microbes embedded in an organic polymer matrix primarily produced by the microbes. Antibiotics may fail to eradicate bacteria sequestered in the biofilm.
- **Asymptomatic bacteriuria should not be treated.**

Prevention

- Intermittent urethral catheterization rarely results in symptomatic lower urinary tract infection (UTI). Therefore, if care circumstances permit, use intermittent catheterization rather than an indwelling catheter.
- High fluid intake promotes urine flow, and tends to prevent symptomatic infection.
- A systematic review failed to find evidence of benefit for continuous prophylactic antibiotics in people with neurogenic bladder caused by spinal cord dysfunction [Morton et al, 2002].
- Consider routine, regular replacement of the catheter if there are frequent recurrent UTIs.

Treatment

- Consider replacing the catheter (especially if it is blocked or has been *in situ* for some time).
- Treat with:
  - A preferred antibiotic for 7 days (as for acute uncomplicated UTI)
  - An analgesic/antipyretic

[Stamm and Hooton, 1993; Reid et al, 1998; AHCPR, 1999; Raz et al, 2000; Nicolle, 2001; Biering-Sorensen, 2002]

References

NHS staff in England can link, free of charge, from references to full text journals by clicking on [Full text] on the PRODIGY website.

1. AHCPR (1999) *Prevention and management of urinary tract infections in paralyzed persons.* Evidence report/ technology assessment: no. 6. Rockville, MD: Agency for Health Care Policy and Research.
2. Baerheim, A. (2001) Empirical treatment of uncomplicated cystitis. *British Medical Journal* **323**(7323), 1197–1198. [Full text]
3. Bailey, R.R. (1996) Urinary tract infection. In: Weatherall, D.J., Ledingham, J.G.G., Warrell, D.A. et al (Eds.) *Oxford Textbook of Medicine.* 3rd edn. Oxford: Oxford University Press. Section 20.8.1.
4. Biering-Sorensen, F. (2002) Urinary tract infection in individuals with spinal cord lesion. *Current Opinion in Urology* **12**(1), 45–49.
5. BNF 42 (2001) *British National Formulary.* 42nd edn. London: British Medical Association and Royal Pharmaceutical Society of Great Britain.
6. Brumfitt, W., Hamilton-Miller, J .M., Cooper, J. and Raeburn, A. (1990) Relationship of urinary pH to symptoms of 'cystitis'. *Postgraduate Medical Journal* **66**(779), 727–729.
7. Brumfitt, W., Hamilton-Miller, J. and Bailey, R.R. (Eds.) (1998) *Urinary tract infections.* London: Chapman & Hall Medical.
8. Cooper, B. and Jepson, R. (2001) Recurrent cystitis in non-pregnant women. *Clinical Evidence* 5(Jun), 1338–1345.
9. Dawson, C. and Whitfield, H. (1996) ABC of urology: urinary incontinence and urinary infection. *British Medical Journal* **312**(7036), 961–964. [Full text]
10. DTB (1997) The management of urinary tract infection in children. *Drug & Therapeutics Bulletin* **35**(9), 65–69.
11. DTB (1998) Managing urinary tract infection in women. *Drug & Therapeutics Bulletin* **36**(4), 30–32. [Full text]
12. Fihn, S.D., Latham, R.H., Roberts, P. et al (1985) Association between diaphragm use and urinary tract infection. *Journal of the American Medical Association* **254**(2), 240–245.
13. Fihn, S.D., Boyko, E.J., Chen, C.L. et al (1998) Use of spermicide-coated condoms and other risk factors for urinary tract infection caused by Staphylococcus saprophyticus. *Archives of Internal Medicine* **158**(3), 281–287. [Full text]
14. Gould, K., Orr, K. and Bint, A. (2001) *GP antimicrobial prescribing guidelines.* Newcastle upon Tyne: Newcastle and North Tyneside NHS Health Authority.
15. Hurlbut, T.A. and Littenberg, B. (1991) The diagnostic accuracy of rapid dipstick tests to predict urinary tract infection. *American Journal of Clinical Pathology* **96**(5), 582–588.
16. Jepson, R.G., Mihaljevic, L. and Craig, J. (2000) *Cranberries for treating urinary infections (Cochrane Review).* The Cochrane Library. Issue 2. Oxford: Update Software.
17. Kalowski, S., Radford, N. and Kincaid-Smith, P. (1974) Crystalline and macrocrystalline nitrofurantoin in the treatment of urinary-tract infection. *New England Journal of Medicine* **290**(7), 385–387.
18. Lammers, R.L., Gibson, S., Kovacs, D. et al (2001) Comparison of test characteristics of urine dipstick and urinalysis at various test cutoff points. *Annals of Emergency Medicine* **38**(5), 505–512.
19. Lee, B., Bhuta, T., Craig, J. and Simpson, J. (2002) *Methenamine hippurate for preventing urinary tract infections (Cochrane Review).* The Cochrane Library. Issue 1. Oxford: Update Software.
20. Leigh, D.A., Faiers, M.C. and Brumfitt, W. (1970) Laboratory and clinical studies with cephalexin. *Postgraduate Medical Journal* **Suppl**, 69–74.
21. Lifshitz, E. and Kramer, L. (2000) Outpatient urine culture: does collection technique matter? *Archives of Internal Medicine* **160**(16), 2537–2540. [Full text]
22. Lipsky, B.A., Inui, T.S., Plorde, J.J. and Berger, R.E. (1984) Is the clean-catch midstream void procedure necessary for obtaining urine culture specimens from men? *American Journal of Medicine* **76**(2), 257–262.
23. Lutters, M. and Vogt, N. (2000) What's the basis for treating infections your way? Quality assessment of review articles on the treatment of urinary and respiratory tract infections in older people. *Journal of the American Geriatrics Society* **48**(11), 1454–1461.
24. Manges, A.R., Johnson, J.R., Foxman, B. et al (2001) Widespread distribution of urinary tract infections caused by a multidrug-resistant Escherichia coli clonal group. *New England Journal of Medicine* **345**(14), 1007–1013. [Full text]
25. McMurdo, M.E. and Gillespie, N.D. (2000) Urinary tract infection in old age: over-diagnosed and over-treated. *Age & Ageing* **29**(4), 297–298. [Full text]
26. McNulty, C. (2002) *Personal communication.* Medical Microbiologist, HPA Primary Care Unit: Gloucestershire Royal Hospital, Gloucester.

27. MeReC (1992) Urinary tract infections in children. *MeReC Bulletin* 3(11), 41–44.
28. MeReC (1995) Urinary tract infection. *MeReC Bulletin* 6(8),
29. Morton, S.C., Shekelle, P.G., Adams, J.L. et al (2002) Antimicrobial prophylaxis for urinary tract infection in persons with spinal cord dysfunction. *Archives of Physical Medicine & Rehabilitation* 83(1), 129–138.
30. NICE (2005) *Referral guidelines for suspected cancer – quick reference guide.* Clinical guideline 27. National Institute for Health and Clinical Excellence. www.nice.org.uk [Accessed: 01/07/2005].
31. Nicolle, L.E. (2001) The chronic indwelling catheter and urinary infection in long-term-care facility residents. *Infection Control and Hospital Epidemiology* 22(5), 316–321. [Full text]
32. Nicolle, L.E. and Ronald, A.R. (1998) Recurrent urinary infection and its prevention. In: Brumfitt, W., Hamilton-Miller, J., Bailey, R.R. et al (Eds.) *Urinary tract infections.* London: Chapman & Hall Medical. 293–301.
33. Nicolle, L.E., Louie, T.J., Dubois, J. et al (1994) Treatment of complicated urinary tract infections with lomefloxacin compared with that with trimethoprim-sulfamethoxazole. *Antimicrobial Agents & Chemotherapy* 38(6), 1368–1373.
34. Ouslander, J.G., Schapira, M., Schnelle, J.F. and Fingold, S. (1996) Pyuria among chronically incontinent but otherwise asymptomatic nursing home residents. *Journal of the American Geriatrics Society* 44(4), 420–423.
35. Parfitt, K. (Ed.) (1999) *Martindale.* 32nd edn. London: Pharmaceutical Press.
36. Pedler, S. (2002) *Personal communication.* Consultant Microbiologist, Royal Victoria Infirmary: Newcastle upon Tyne.
37. PHLS (2001) *Management of infection: guidance for primary care.* Public Health Laboratory Service. www.hpa.org.uk [Accessed: 03/02/2002].
38. Priest, P., Yudkin, P., McNulty, C. and Mant, D. (2001) Antibacterial prescribing and antibacterial resistance in English general practice: cross sectional study. *British Medical Journal* 323(7320), 1037–1041. [Full text]
39. Raz, R., Schiller, D. and Nicolle, L.E. (2000) Chronic indwelling catheter replacement before antimicrobial therapy for symptomatic urinary tract infection. *Journal of Urology* 164(4), 1254–1258.
40. Read, R.C. (2000) Drugs in focus: newer oral fluoroquinolone antibacterials. *Prescribers' Journal* 40(2), 147–151.
41. Reid, G., van der Mei, H.C. and Busscher, H.J. (1998) Microbial biofilms and urinary tract infections. In: Brumfitt, W., Hamilton-Miller, J., Bailey, R.R. et al (Eds.) *Urinary tract infections.* London: Chapman & Hall Medical. 111–116.
42. Stamm, W.E. (1998) Urinary tract infections and pyelonephritis. In: *Harrison's Principles of Internal Medicine.* New York: McGraw-Hill.
43. Stamm, W.E. (2001) An epidemic of urinary tract infections? *New England Journal of Medicine* 345(14), 1055–1057. [Full text]
44. Stamm, W.E. and Hooton, T.M. (1993) Management of urinary tract infections in adults. *New England Journal of Medicine* 329(18), 1328–1334.
45. Steinke, D.T., Seaton, R.A., Phillips, G. et al (2001) Prior trimethoprim use and trimethoprim-resistant urinary tract infection: a nested case-control study with multivariate analysis for other risk factors. *Journal of Antimicrobial Chemotherapy* 47(6), 781–787. [Full text]
46. Tran, D., Muchant, D.G. and Aronoff, S.C. (2001) Short-course versus conventional length antimicrobial therapy for uncomplicated lower urinary tract infections in children: a meta-analysis of 1279 patients. *Journal of Pediatrics* 139(1), 93–99.
47. Wallach, F.R. (2001) Infectious disease. Update on treatment of pneumonia, influenza, and urinary tract infections. *Geriatrics* 56(9), 43–47.
48. Wise, R. and Andrews, J.M. (1998) Local surveillance of antimicrobial resistance. Synercid Resistance Surveillance Group. *Lancet* 352(9128), 657–658. [Full text]

U

PRODIGY GUIDANCE

Urinary tract infection (lower) — women

Last revised in July 2005
www.prodigy.nhs.uk/guidance.asp?gt=UTI (lower) - women

Applies to women over the age of 14 years

This guidance covers the management of healthy, elderly, and pregnant women with cystitis and asymptomatic bacteriuria. It also covers recurrent cystitis, urethral syndrome, and urinary tract infection (UTI) with a long-term catheter in-situ.

This guidance does not cover the treatment of upper urinary tract infections, UTI in women with an abnormal urinary tract, or UTI in women with impaired renal function. It also does not cover the management of UTI in girls under 14 years old.

There is separate PRODIGY guidance for *Pyelonephritis — acute, Urinary tract infection — children, Urinary tract infection (lower) — men* and *Renal colic — acute.*

Goals

- Prompt recognition of urinary tract infection (UTI)
- Accurate diagnosis, appropriate treatment, avoidance of unnecessary antibiotics
- Symptom relief
- Eradication of infection
- Prevention of recurrence and complications
- Detection and management of predisposing and associated conditions

Contents

Scenarios

- Cystitis in otherwise healthy women who are not pregnant p.1810
- Acute cystitis treatment failure p.1812
- Recurrent cystitis in non-pregnant women p.1814
- Cystitis and asymptomatic bacteriuria in pregnancy p.1816
- Cystitis and asymptomatic bacteriuria in elderly women p.1818
- UTI in women with indwelling urinary catheters p.1819
- Urethral syndrome p.1821

Extended Information, p. 1822

Which scenario?

- **Cystitis in otherwise healthy women who are not pregnant:** covers the management of uncomplicated acute lower urinary tract infection (UTI) in women.
- **Uncomplicated cystitis — treatment failure:** covers the management of cystitis in women who have failed to respond to treatment.
- **Recurrent cystitis in non-pregnant women:** covers the management of cystitis that recurs three or more times a year in otherwise healthy women.
- **Cystitis and asymptomatic bacteriuria in pregnancy:** covers the management of bacteriuria and cystitis in pregnant women.
- **Cystitis and asymptomatic bacteriuria in elderly women:** covers the management of cystitis in elderly women.
- **UTI in women with indwelling urinary catheters:** covers the management of cystitis in women with chronic indwelling urinary catheters.
- **Urethral syndrome:** covers the management of urethral syndrome in women.

U

Cystitis in otherwise healthy women who are not pregnant

Which therapy?

The following apply to otherwise healthy women, who are not pregnant, with a suspected lower urinary tract infection.

- **If symptoms are mild,** consider omitting urine tests and treating symptomatically.
- **If symptoms are troublesome, dipstick the urine to guid therapy:**
  - If nitrite and leucocyte esterase are both negative — UTI unlikely, treat symptomatically with paracetamo or ibuprofen.
  - If nitrite or leucocyte esterase are positive — UTI likely, treat with either trimethoprim, nitrofurantoin, or cefalexin for 3 days. Alternatively treat according t local guidelines.
- Microscopy is an alternative near-patient test. If bacteri and leucocytes are seen, UTI is likely and treatment is recommended as above.
- Advice to encourage fluid intake is of unproven benefit and may aggravate distress from dysuria.

Practical prescribing points

For further information see the *Medicines Compendium* (www.medicines.org.uk) or the *British National Formular* (www.bnf.org).

Breastfeeding

- **Nitrofurantoin** is not recommended if the infant is glucose-6-phosphate dehydrogenase (G6PD)-deficient.

Other cautions

- **Nitrofurantoin** should not be used in people known to b G6PD-deficient.
- **Ibuprofen,** as with other nonsteroidal anti-inflammator drugs (NSAIDs), may worsen or precipitate gastrointestinal haemorrhage, asthma, hypertension, renal impairment, or cardiac failure. Avoid if there is a history of peptic ulcers.

Follow-up advice

- Follow-up is recommended if symptoms have not resolved after 3 days.

Should I refer or investigate?

Refer?

- **Referral for investigation** should be considered for women with recurrent UTI, or who persistently fail to respond to treatment.
- **Referral guidelines for suspected cancer** published by the National Institute for Health and Clinical Excellence (NICE) [NICE, 2005] recommend urgent referral to a team specialising in the management of urological cancer, depending on local arrangements, for people:
  - Of any age with painless macroscopic haematuria.
  - Aged 40 years or older who present with recurrent or persistent urinary tract infection associated with haematuria.
  - Aged 50 years or older who are found to have unexplained microscopic haematuria.
  - With an abdominal mass identified clinically or on imaging that is thought to arise from the urinary tract.
  - Who have macroscopic haematuria and symptoms suggestive of a urinary tract infection *if* infection is not confirmed.

Investigate?

- **Urine dipstick — interpretation of results:**
  - Positive for nitrite:
    - Diagnose and treat as cystitis.
  - Positive for leucocytes, negative for nitrite:
    - Diagnose and treat as cystitis.
    - Consider urethral syndrome.
  - Negative for nitrites, leucocytes, haemoglobin, protein:
    - Diagnose and manage as urethral syndrome.
  - Positive for haemoglobin and/or protein, negative for leucocytes and nitrites:
    - Cystitis is unlikely; culture urine to detect those women who do have a UTI.
    - Consider other differential diagnosis including renal disease and malignancy.
- **Urine microscopy,** if available, is a quick and accurate near-patient screening test. If bacteria and leucocytes are seen, UTI is likely.
- **Urine culture** is indicated when:
  - Cystitis is suspected, but the dipstick is negative for nitrites and leucocytes.
  - Treatment has failed.
  - Symptoms recur.
- **Investigations for sexually transmitted diseases** should be considered in sexually active women (e.g. chlamydia screen).

Patient information leaflets

The following PILs are available at www.prodigy.nhs.uk

- Cystitis in Women
- Kidney Infection (Pyelonephritis)
- Midstream Specimen of Urine (MSU)

Shared decision making

- **An option for non pregnant women is to take no treatment at all:** about half of women with cystitis will be free of symptoms within 3 days even if they take no treatment.
- **An antibiotic for 3 days** is a recognised treatment for women with cystitis.
- If a urine culture test is done, telephone for the results in 3 days time. Ask if it is necessary to change the treatment.
- **Paracetamol or ibuprofen** will help with pain or discomfort.
- **Potassium citrate or other similar products are often taken to reduce the symptoms of 'burning urine'.** Their benefit is not proven.
- Drink plenty of fluid to 'flush out the bladder' is common advice. But it is unproven and passing urine more often may be unpleasant.
- **If symptoms have not gone or nearly gone after 3 days,** see a doctor.
- **If cystitis becomes a recurring problem,** consult a doctor.

Drug rationale

Drugs not included

- **Penicillins such as amoxicillin** are unsuitable for therapy unless culture results indicate that the bacterium is sensitive. Around 50% of urinary pathogens are amoxicillin-resistant.
- **First-generation cephalosporins other than cefalexin** have similar antibiotic sensitivities and adverse effect profiles, and are more expensive.
- **Second-generation cephalosporins** are not as well absorbed orally as first generation cephalosporins, have a greater incidence of gastrointestinal adverse effects, and are more expensive than the first-generation agents.
- **Third-generation cephalosporins** generally require parenteral administration and are reserved for use in secondary care for serious infections.
- **Co-amoxiclav, quinolones, and pivmecillinam** should be reserved for second-line treatment, in order to limit the development of resistance and to preserve their efficacy.
- **Urine alkalinizing agents** are of unproven benefit and there is some evidence that they do not relieve the symptoms of cystitis [Brumfitt et al, 1990].

[MeReC, 1995; DTB, 1998; Read, 2000; BNF 42, 2001; Gould et al, 2001; PHLS, 2001]

Drugs included

- For all antibiotics, a 3-day course is given in line with national guidelines [DH and SMAC, 1998; PHLS, 2001].
- **Trimethoprim** is the antibiotic of choice for empirical treatment in uncomplicated urinary tract infection (UTI). It is effective, safe, and inexpensive. It should not be used if the patient has a history of recurrent infections resistant to this drug, or has recently taken trimethoprim.
- **Nitrofurantoin** is a useful alternative antibiotic, effective against most urinary pathogens. For most people the standard tablet formulation is suitable. The macrocrystalline capsules and the twice-daily modified-release formulation may be better tolerated if nausea is troublesome, and are offered as alternatives.
- **Cefalexin** is a first-generation cephalosporin effective against most urinary pathogens.
- **Paracetamol** is an effective and safe analgesic and antipyretic.
- **Ibuprofen** is an effective alternative to paracetamol if there are no contraindications.

[MeReC, 1995; DTB, 1998; Read, 2000; BNF 42, 2001; Gould et al, 2001; PHLS, 2001]

Prescriptions

1st-line antibiotics for 3 days

Trimethoprim tablets: 200mg twice a day

- Age from 14 to 75 years
- Trimethoprim 200mg tablets. Take one tablet twice a day for 3 days; supply 6 tablets; NHS Cost £0.29.

U

Nitrofurantoin tablets: 50mg four times a day

- Age from 14 to 75 years
- Nitrofurantoin 50mg tablets. Take one tablet four times a day for 3 days; supply 12 tablets; NHS Cost £1.06.

Nitrofurantoin capsules: 50mg four times a day

- Age from 14 to 75 years
- Nitrofurantoin 50mg capsules. Take one capsule four times a day for 3 days; supply 12 capsules; NHS Cost £1.22.

Nitrofurantoin m/r capsules: 100mg twice a day

- Age from 14 to 75 years
- Nitrofurantoin 100mg m/r caps. Take one capsule twice a day for 3 days; supply 6 capsules; NHS Cost £2.10.

Cefalexin tablets: 500mg twice a day

- Age from 14 to 75 years
- Cefalexin 500mg tablets. Take one tablet twice a day for 3 days; supply 6 tablets; NHS Cost £1.05.

Analgesic/antipyretic: use when required

Paracetamol tablets: 500mg to 1g up to four times a day

- Age from 14 to 15 years
- Paracetamol 500mg tablets. Take one to two tablets every 4 to 6 hours when required for relief of pain or high temperature. Maximum of 8 tablets in 24 hours; supply 32 tablets; NHS Cost £0.43; OTC Cost £0.75.

Paracetamol tablets: 1g up to four times a day

- Age from 16 to 75 years
- Paracetamol 500mg tablets. Take two tablets every 4 to 6 hours when required for relief of pain or high temperature. Maximum of 8 tablets in 24 hours; supply 32 tablets; NHS Cost £0.43; OTC Cost £0.75.

Ibuprofen tablets: 400mg three times a day

- Age from 14 to 75 years
- Ibuprofen 400mg tablets. Take one tablet three times a day when required for relief of pain or high temperature. Do not exceed the stated dose; supply 12 tablets; NHS Cost £0.35; OTC Cost £0.62.

Advice note

Advice only: over-the-counter purchase

- Age from 14 to 75 years
- You have cystitis. This is an inflammation of the bladder. The burning and stinging sensation when passing water may be aggravated by acid urine. Preparations that aim to neutralise the acidity (urinary alkalinizing preparations) are popular, but it is not known if they are effective. These alkalinizing preparations are not suitable in people with certain conditions such as high blood pressure or heart disease, or if you are taking some other medications. Paracetamol or ibuprofen may help relieve symptoms. If your symptoms do not go away after 3 days consult your doctor. You should see your doctor, midwife or nurse if you think you have cystitis and are pregnant.

U

Acute cystitis treatment failure

Which therapy?

The following apply to otherwise healthy women, who are not pregnant, with a suspected lower urinary tract infection that has failed to respond to first-line treatment.

- **If symptoms are mild,** send a sample for urine culture and wait for sensitivity results to guide choice of treatment.
- **If symptoms are particularly troublesome,** send a urine sample for culture and change to a different first-line antibiotic (trimethoprim, nitrofurantoin, cefalexin). Alternatively a second-line antibiotic (i.e. co-amoxiclav, or a quinolone, or pivmecillinam) may be used. Follow local guidelines if different antibiotics are recommended.
- **Paracetamol or ibuprofen** can be used for symptomatic treatment.
- Advice to encourage fluid intake is of unproven benefit and may aggravate distress from dysuria.

Practical prescribing points

For further information see the *Medicines Compendium* (www.medicines.org.uk) or the *British National Formulary* (www.bnf.org).

Breastfeeding

- **Nitrofurantoin** is not recommended if the infant is glucose-6-phosphate dehydrogenase (G6PD)-deficient.
- **Quinolones** are not recommended as they can be excreted into breast milk and studies in young animals have found a possible association with arthropathy.

Other cautions

- **Nitrofurantoin** should not be used in people who are known to be G6PD-deficient.
- **Ibuprofen,** as with other nonsteroidal anti-inflammatory drugs (NSAIDs), may worsen or precipitate gastrointestinal haemorrhage, asthma, hypertension, renal impairment, or cardiac failure. Avoid if there is a history of peptic ulcers.
- **Quinolones** may cause tendon damage (Committee on Safety of Medicines advice); stop treatment if pain or inflammation of a tendon occurs. They can induce convulsions in people with epilepsy or in those with conditions that predispose to seizures. People concurrently taking NSAIDs may also be susceptible. The risks and benefits of prescribing a quinolone should be considered on an individual basis for these people.

Follow-up advice

- Review with culture results to ensure that treatment is appropriate.
- Consider reviewing by telephone.

Should I refer or investigate?

Refer?

- **Referral for investigation** should be considered for women with recurrent UTI, or who persistently fail to respond to treatment.
- **Referral guidelines for suspected cancer** published by the National Institute for Health and Clinical Excellence (NICE) [NICE, 2005] recommend urgent referral to a team specialising in the management of urological cancer, depending on local arrangements, for people:
  - Of any age with painless macroscopic haematuria.
  - Aged 40 years or older who present with recurrent or persistent urinary tract infection associated with haematuria.
  - Aged 50 years or older who are found o have unexplained microscopic haematuria.
  - With an abdominal mass identified clinically or on imaging that is thought to arise from the urinary tract.
  - Who have macroscopic haematuria and symptoms suggestive of a urinary tract infection *if* infection is not confirmed.

Investigate?

- **Urine culture** should be obtained whenever treatment has failed. The sample taken for culture should be taken with care to avoid contamination, placed in a

preservative containing bottle or refrigerated, and cultured as soon as possible.
Consider testing for chlamydia and other sexually transmitted diseases in sexually active women.

Patient information leaflets

The following PILs are available at www.prodigy.nhs.uk
Cystitis in Women
Cystoscopy
Intravenous Urography
Kidney Infection (Pyelonephritis)
Midstream Specimen of Urine (MSU)

Shared decision making

Cystitis sometimes does not clear with an antibiotic. This may be because the germ is 'resistant' to the antibiotic (or in some cases, because the cystitis has not been caused by an infection). A urine test is needed to see whether a germ is present, and which germ it is.
If a urine culture test is done, telephone for the results in 3 days' time. Ask if it is necessary to change the treatment.
A second antibiotic will usually work. It is best to wait until the urine result is back to see which germ is present and which antibiotic kills it.
Paracetamol or ibuprofen will help with pain or discomfort.
Potassium citrate or other similar products are often taken to reduce the symptoms of 'burning urine'. Their benefit is not proven.
Drink plenty of fluid to 'flush out the bladder' is common advice. But it is unproven and passing urine more often may be unpleasant.
Consult a doctor if cystitis still does not clear, or becomes a recurring problem.

Drug rationale

Drugs not included

Penicillins such as amoxicillin are unsuitable for empirical therapy because about 50% of all urinary pathogen isolates are amoxicillin-resistant.
First-generation cephalosporins other than cefalexin have similar antibiotic sensitivities and adverse effect profiles, and are more expensive.
Second-generation cephalosporins are not as well absorbed orally as first-generation cephalosporins, have a greater incidence of gastrointestinal adverse effects, and are more expensive than the first-generation agents.
Third-generation cephalosporins generally require parenteral administration, and are reserved for use in secondary care for serious infections.
Quinolones (other than norfloxacin and ciprofloxacin) are not offered. They should be reserved for complicated infections where sensitivities are known, in order to preserve their efficacy and limit the development of resistance. The newer quinolones have a slightly broader spectrum of activity than the older drugs but there is no evidence of greater efficacy.
Urine alkalinizing agents are of unproven benefit and there is some evidence that they do not relieve the symptoms of cystitis [Brumfitt et al, 1990].
[MeReC, 1995; DTB, 1998; Read, 2000; BNF 42, 2001]

Drugs included

For all antibiotics, a 3-day course is given in line with national guidelines [DH and SMAC, 1998; PHLS, 2001].

- **Trimethoprim** is effective against most urinary tract pathogens, and safe and inexpensive. It should not be used if the patient has recently taken trimethoprim, or has a history of recurrent infections resistant to this drug.
- **Nitrofurantoin** is a useful alternative antibiotic, effective against most urinary pathogens. For most people the standard tablet formulation is suitable. The macrocrystalline capsules and the twice-daily modified-release formulation may be better tolerated if nausea is troublesome, and are offered as alternatives.
- **Cefalexin** is a first-generation cephalosporin effective against most urinary pathogens.
- **Co-amoxiclav** is a suitable second-line alternative. It is effective against up to 90% of urinary pathogens.
- **Norfloxacin and ciprofloxacin** are recommended as second-line antibiotics. They are effective against most urinary pathogens (only around 5% of pathogens are resistant) and are currently the least expensive of the quinolones available.
- **Pivmecillinam** is highly active against many Gram-negative pathogens and is an appropriate second-line treatment.
- **Paracetamol** is an effective and safe analgesic and antipyretic.
- **Ibuprofen** is an effective alternative to paracetamol if there are no contraindications.

[MeReC, 1995; DTB, 1998; Read, 2000; BNF 42, 2001; Gould et al, 2001; PHLS, 2001]

Prescriptions

1st-line antibiotics for 3 days

Trimethoprim tablets: 200mg twice a day
- Age from 14 to 75 years
- Trimethoprim 200mg tablets. Take one tablet twice a day for 3 days; supply 6 tablets; NHS Cost £0.29.

Nitrofurantoin tablets: 50mg four times a day
- Age from 14 to 75 years
- Nitrofurantoin 50mg tablets. Take one tablet four times a day for 3 days; supply 12 tablets; NHS Cost £1.06.

Nitrofurantoin capsules: 50mg four times a day
- Age from 14 to 75 years
- Nitrofurantoin 50mg capsules. Take one capsule four times a day for 3 days; supply 12 capsules; NHS Cost £1.22.

Nitrofurantoin m/r capsules: 100mg twice a day
- Age from 14 to 75 years
- Nitrofurantoin 100mg m/r caps. Take one capsule twice a day for 3 days; supply 6 capsules; NHS Cost £2.10.

Cefalexin tablets: 500mg twice a day
- Age from 14 to 75 years
- Cefalexin 500mg tablets. Take one tablet twice a day for 3 days; supply 6 tablets; NHS Cost £1.05.

U

2nd-line antibiotics for 3 days (IF needed)

Co-amoxiclav tablets: 250/125mg three times a day
- Age from 14 to 75 years
- Co-amoxiclav 375mg tablets. Take one tablet three times a day for 3 days; supply 9 tablets; NHS Cost £4.25.

Ciprofloxacin tablets: 100mg twice a day
- Age from 16 to 75 years
- Ciprofloxacin 100mg tablets. Take one tablet twice a day for 3 days; supply 6 tablets; NHS Cost £2.80.

Norfloxacin tablets: 400mg twice a day
- Age from 16 to 75 years
- Norfloxacin 400mg tablets. Take one tablet twice a day for 3 days; supply 6 tablets; NHS Cost £2.03.

Pivmecillinam tablets: 200mg three times a day
- Age from 14 to 75 years
- Pivmecillinam 200mg tablets. Take TWO tablets now and then take ONE tablet three times a day for 3 days; supply 10 tablets; NHS Cost £4.50.

Analgesic/antipyretic: use when required

Paracetamol tablets: 500mg to 1g up to four times a day
- Age from 14 to 15 years
- Paracetamol 500mg tablets. Take one to two tablets every 4 to 6 hours when required for relief of pain or high temperature. Maximum of 8 tablets in 24 hours; supply 32 tablets; NHS Cost £0.43; OTC Cost £0.75.

Paracetamol tablets: 1g up to four times a day
- Age from 16 to 75 years
- Paracetamol 500mg tablets. Take two tablets every 4 to 6 hours when required for relief of pain or high temperature. Maximum of 8 tablets in 24 hours; supply 32 tablets; NHS Cost £0.43; OTC Cost £0.75.

Ibuprofen tablets: 400mg three times a day
- Age from 14 to 75 years
- Ibuprofen 400mg tablets. Take one tablet three times a day when required for relief of pain or high temperature. Do not exceed the stated dose; supply 12 tablets; NHS Cost £0.35; OTC Cost £0.62.

Recurrent cystitis in non-pregnant women

Which therapy?

- **Consider an underlying cause** and manage if appropriate. Refer if serious pathology is a concern.
  - Sexual intercourse
  - Female diaphragm or spermicide-coated condoms
  - Atrophic urethritis and vaginitis (in postmenopausal women)
  - Incomplete bladder emptying
  - Previous urinary tract surgery
  - Abnormalities of the urinary tract e.g. carcinoma of the bladder, calculus, vesicoureteric reflux
  - Constipation
  - Immunocompromise
- **Consider prophylaxis if more than three UTIs per year.**
- **If recurrent cystitis is related to sexual intercourse consider:**
  - Changing to another form of contraception if either the female diaphragm or spermicides are being used.
  - Lubrication — it may improve symptoms by minimizing trauma.
  - Voiding the bladder after coitus.
  - A single dose of trimethoprim, nitrofurantoin or cefalexin taken less than 2 hours after sex.
- **If recurrent cystitis is not related to sexual intercourse consider:**
  - Continuous low-dose antibiotic therapy
    - Taken nightly or 3 nights a week depending on individual preferences.
  - Self-treatment of new episodes
    - When symptoms recur the woman is advised to send a urine specimen for culture, and start treatment ideally when a UTI is confirmed.
  - Cranberry juice (limited evidence of efficacy)
- **If infection occurs while taking prophylactic antibiotics:**
  - Send urine for culture.
  - Treat the acute infection with an antibiotic to which the organism is sensitive.
  - Restart prophylaxis with an antibiotic that is active against the infecting organism.

Practical prescribing points

For further information see the *Medicines Compendium* (www.medicines.org.uk) or the *British National Formular* (www.bnf.org).

Breastfeeding

- **Nitrofurantoin** is not recommended for use in breastfeeding if the infant is glucose-6-phosphate dehydrogenase (G6PD)-deficient.
- **Trimethoprim** is safe if used for a short period, but there is no information about its long-term use in breastfeeding.

Other cautions

- **Nitrofurantoin** should not be used in people who are known to be G6PD-deficient.
- **Ibuprofen**, as with other nonsteroidal anti-inflammatory drugs (NSAIDs), may worsen or precipitate gastrointestinal haemorrhage, asthma, hypertension, renal impairment, or cardiac failure. Avoid if there is a history of peptic ulcers.

Follow-up advice

- If prophylactic antibiotics are prescribed, follow up after 6 months (or sooner).

Should I refer or investigate?

Refer?

- **Women who continue to experience symptoms despite prophylactic treatment,** should be referred.
- **Referral guidelines for suspected cancer** published by the National Institute for Health and Clinical Excellence (NICE) [NICE, 2005] recommend urgent referral to a team specialising in the management of urological cancer, depending on local arrangements, for people:
  - Of any age with painless macroscopic haematuria.
  - Aged 40 years or older who present with recurrent or persistent urinary tract infection associated with haematuria.
  - Aged 50 years or older who are found o have unexplained microscopic haematuria.
  - With an abdominal mass identified clinically or on imaging that is thought to arise from the urinary tract
  - Who have macroscopic haematuria and symptoms suggestive of a urinary tract infection *if* infection is not confirmed.

Investigate?

- **Urine culture** is needed to confirm a microbial cause for at least one episode of urinary tract infection (UTI) prior to commencing prophylactic treatment. Urine culture and sensitivity tests are helpful to manage breakthrough infections.
- **Urinary tract imaging** is rarely indicated.
- **Cystoscopy** is rarely indicated.

Patient information leaflets

The following PILs are available at www.prodigy.nhs.uk
- Cystitis - Recurrent Infections in Women
- Cystoscopy
- Intravenous Urography
- Kidney Infection (Pyelonephritis)
- Midstream Specimen of Urine (MSU)

Shared decision making

Some women tend to have recurrent bouts of cystitis. A kidney or bladder problem is sometimes the cause but usually the reason for recurring cystitis is not clear.
Some women tend to get cystitis after having sex. In these circumstances the chance of cystitis can be reduced by:

- Changing the method of contraception if either spermicides or a diaphragm are used
- Going to the toilet and fully emptying the bladder after sex
- Lubrication, possibly, if the symptoms are due to irritation
- Taking a single dose of an antibiotic after sex

Antibiotic prevention is an option in other circumstances.

- This means taking a low dose of an antibiotic every day (or sometimes three times a week)
- It is best to take the antibiotic at bedtime
- It is usual to take a course for 3–6 months and then to review the situation
- A change of antibiotic may be needed if cystitis recurs

Cranberry juice

- Only one of several studies provides good evidence that cranberry juice can help prevent recurrent cystitis. There is no scientific evidence that assesses the form of the supplementation or the dose and frequency. However, it might be worth trying cranberry juice.

If a urine culture test is done, telephone for the results in 2 or 3 days. Ask if it is necessary to change the antibiotic.

Drug rationale

Drugs not included

Penicillins such as amoxicillin are unsuitable for empirical therapy because about 50% of all urinary pathogen isolates are amoxicillin-resistant.
First-generation cephalosporins other than cefalexin have similar antibiotic sensitivities and adverse effect profiles, and are more expensive.
Second-generation cephalosporins are not as well absorbed orally as first-generation cephalosporins, have a greater incidence of gastrointestinal adverse effects, and are more expensive than the first-generation agents.
Third-generation cephalosporins generally require parenteral administration, and are reserved for use in secondary care for serious infections.
Co-amoxiclav, quinolones, and pivmecillinam should be reserved for second-line treatment, in order to limit the development of resistance and to preserve their efficacy.
Urine alkalinizing agents are of unproven benefit and there is some evidence that they do not relieve the symptoms of cystitis [Brumfitt et al, 1990].
[MeReC, 1995; DTB, 1998; Read, 2000; BNF 42, 2001]

Drugs included

For recurrent cystitis *not* associated with sexual intercourse, treatment options include continuous low-dose antibiotic therapy taken nightly or 3 nights a week depending on individual preferences. There is also the option of a standby 7-day antibiotic course for self-treatment of a new episode.
For recurrent cystitis associated with sexual intercourse, prescriptions for a single dose of an antibiotic taken less than 2 hours after sex are offered.
Trimethoprim is effective against most urinary tract pathogens, and safe and inexpensive. It should not be used if the patient has recently taken trimethoprim, or has a history of recurrent infections resistant to this drug.

- **Nitrofurantoin** is a useful alternative antibiotic, effective against most urinary pathogens. For most people the standard tablet formulation is suitable. The macrocrystalline capsules and the twice-daily modified-release formulation may be better tolerated if nausea is troublesome, and are offered as alternatives.
- **Cefalexin** is a first-generation cephalosporin effective against most urinary pathogens. For prophylaxis, the licensed 125 mg dose is only available as a suspension (with a shelf-life of 10 days) and may be impractical for management in many people; therefore the unlicensed 250 mg capsule formulation is recommended instead.
- **Paracetamol** is an effective and safe analgesic and antipyretic agent.
- **Ibuprofen** is an effective alternative to paracetamol if there are no contraindications.

[MeReC, 1995; DTB, 1998; Read, 2000; BNF 42, 2001; Cooper and Jepson, 2001; Gould et al, 2001; PHLS, 2001]

Prescriptions

Nightly prophylaxis

Trimethoprim tablets: 100mg at night

- Age from 14 years onwards
- Trimethoprim 100mg tablets. Take one tablet at night; supply 30 tablets; NHS Cost £0.72.

Nitrofurantoin tablets: 50mg at night

- Age from 14 years onwards
- Nitrofurantoin 50mg tablets. Take one tablet at night; supply 28 tablets; NHS Cost £2.47.

Nitrofurantoin capsules: 50mg at night

- Age from 14 years onwards
- Nitrofurantoin 50mg capsules. Take one capsule at night; supply 30 capsules; NHS Cost £3.05.

Nitrofurantoin capsules: 100mg at night

- Age from 14 years onwards
- Nitrofurantoin 100mg capsules. Take one capsule at night; supply 30 capsules; NHS Cost £5.76.

Cefalexin capsules: 250mg at night

- Age from 14 years onwards
- Cefalexin 250mg capsules. Take one capsule at night; supply 28 capsules; NHS Cost £2.61.

Thrice-weekly prophylaxis

Trimethoprim tablets: 100mg on 3 nights each week

- Age from 14 years onwards
- Trimethoprim 100mg tablets. Take one tablet on 3 nights each week; supply 12 tablets; NHS Cost £0.28.

Nitrofurantoin tablets: 50mg on 3 nights each week

- Age from 14 years onwards
- Nitrofurantoin 50mg tablets. Take one tablet on 3 nights each week; supply 12 tablets; NHS Cost £1.05.

Nitrofurantoin capsules: 50mg on 3 nights each week

- Age from 14 years onwards
- Nitrofurantoin 50mg capsules. Take one capsule on 3 nights each week; supply 12 capsules; NHS Cost £1.22.

Nitrofurantoin capsules: 100mg on 3 nights each week

- Age from 14 years onwards
- Nitrofurantoin 100mg capsules. Take one capsule on 3 nights each week; supply 12 capsules; NHS Cost £2.30.

Cefalexin capsules: 250mg on 3 nights each week

- Age from 14 years onwards
- Cefalexin 250mg capsules. Take one capsule on 3 nights each week; supply 12 capsules; NHS Cost £1.12.

Standby antibiotics (7-day course)

Trimethoprim tablets: 200mg twice a day
- Age from 14 years onwards
- Trimethoprim 200mg tablets. Take one tablet twice a day for 7 days; supply 14 tablets; NHS Cost £0.67.

Nitrofurantoin tablets: 50mg four times a day
- Age from 14 years onwards
- Nitrofurantoin 50mg tablets. Take one tablet four times a day for 7 days; supply 28 tablets; NHS Cost £2.47.

Nitrofurantoin capsules: 50mg four times a day
- Age from 14 years onwards
- Nitrofurantoin 50mg capsules. Take one capsule four times a day for 7 days; supply 28 capsules; NHS Cost £2.85.

Nitrofurantoin m/r capsules: 100mg twice a day
- Age from 14 years onwards
- Nitrofurantoin 100mg m/r caps. Take one capsule twice a day for 7 days; supply 14 capsules; NHS Cost £4.89.

Cefalexin tablets: 500mg twice a day
- Age from 14 years onwards
- Cefalexin 500mg tablets. Take one tablet twice a day for 7 days; supply 14 tablets; NHS Cost £2.44.

Postcoital antibiotics (1-month supply)

Nitrofurantoin tablets: 50mg after intercourse
- Age from 14 years onwards
- Nitrofurantoin 50mg tablets. Take one tablet after intercourse as directed; supply 28 tablets; NHS Cost £2.47.

Trimethoprim tablets: 100mg after intercourse
- Age from 14 years onwards
- Trimethoprim 100mg tablets. Take one tablet after intercourse as directed; supply 28 tablets; NHS Cost £0.67.

Nitrofurantoin capsules: 50mg after intercourse
- Age from 14 years onwards
- Nitrofurantoin 50mg capsules. Take one capsule after intercourse as directed; supply 30 capsules; NHS Cost £3.05.

Nitrofurantoin capsules: 100mg after intercourse
- Age from 14 years onwards
- Nitrofurantoin 100mg capsules. Take one capsule after intercourse as directed; supply 30 capsules; NHS Cost £5.76.

Cefalexin capsules: 250mg after intercourse
- Age from 14 years onwards
- Cefalexin 250mg capsules. Take one capsule after intercourse as directed; supply 28 capsules; NHS Cost £2.61.

U

Cystitis and asymptomatic bacteriuria in pregnancy

Which therapy?

Treat asymptomatic bacteriuria and acute cystitis in pregnancy with antibiotics.

Asymptomatic bacteriuria

- **Treat for 7 days with an antibiotic according to results of sensitivity tests.**
- Amoxicillin, trimethoprim, nitrofurantoin, and cefalexin are suitable for use in pregnancy.

Acute cystitis

- **Send urine for culture before commencing antibiotics.**
- **If the clinical diagnosis is uncertain, dipstick the urine to guide the decision to treat while culture results are awaited:**
  - If nitrite and leucocyte esterase are both negative — UTI is unlikely, await results of urine culture.
  - If nitrite or leucocyte esterase are positive — UTI is likely, treat with an antibiotic.
- Urine microscopy is a reliable, alternative, near-patient test. UTI is likely if bacteria and leucocytes are seen.
- **If the diagnosis of cystitis is likely, treat with trimethoprim, or nitrofurantoin, or cefalexin while waiting for the culture and sensitivity report.**
- **Check the result of the urine culture.** Treat for 7 days with an antibiotic that the pathogen is reported to be sensitive to. Amoxicillin, trimethoprim, nitrofurantoin, and cefalexin are suitable for use in pregnancy.
- **Paracetamol** can be used to treat symptoms.
- Advice to encourage fluid intake is of unproven benefit and may aggravate distress from dysuria.

Practical prescribing points

For further information see the *Medicines Compendium* (www.medicines.org.uk) or *the British National Formulary* (www.bnf.org).

- **Trimethoprim** is a folate antagonist and its use should be avoided in women with known folate deficiency, or taking folate antagonists (e.g. antiepileptics, proguanil) unless a folate supplement is taken.
- **Nitrofurantoin** should not be prescribed if the mother is glucose-6-phosphate dehydrogenase (G6PD)-deficient. It can otherwise be used during pregnancy, but should not be taken near term as it can cause haemolysis in a G6PD deficient infant.

Follow-up advice

- **Review according to the clinical situation,** for example, at around 72 hours, to ensure the individual is responding to treatment and to check the results of the urine culture.
- **Repeat the urine culture 1–2 weeks after an antibiotic course** has been completed.
- **After an initial infection, urine should be cultured monthly throughout pregnancy.** Monitoring for bacteriuria should be done in conjunction with the hospital-based antenatal care services.

Should I refer or investigate?

Refer?

- Admit if there is systemic illness, or pyelonephritis is suspected.
- Refer if Group B streptococcus is isolated: the individual may need prophylactic antibiotics during labour.
- Refer if urine culture is still positive 1–2 weeks after treatment.
- Refer if urinary tract infection (UTI) recurs in pregnancy: obtain specialist advice with regard to prophylactic antibiotics.

Investigate?

- Culture urine before starting antibiotics. Empirical treatment may need to be modified in the light of the results.

- Samples taken for culture should be taken mid-stream, placed in a preservative-containing bottle or refrigerated, and cultured as soon as possible.

Patient information leaflets

The following PILs are available at www.prodigy.nhs.uk

- Kidney Infection (Pyelonephritis)
- Urine Infection in Pregnancy

Shared decision making

- **An antibiotic for 7 days** is the usual treatment for pregnant women with cystitis.
- **Usually a urine culture test will be done. Telephone or see your nurse, midwife, or doctor for the results after 3 days.** Ask if it is necessary to change the antibiotic treatment.
- Drink plenty of fluid to 'flush out the bladder' is common advice, but it is unproven and passing urine more often may be unpleasant.
- **Paracetamol** will help with pain or discomfort. (Ibuprofen is best avoided during pregnancy).
- **A urine test 1 week after the antibiotic treatment is finished** is important to check that the infection has gone. Regular urine checks throughout pregnancy are usual.

Drug rationale

Drugs not included

- **Quinolones** are not recommended in any trimester because of safety concerns.
- **Co-amoxiclav** is not generally recommended for use during pregnancy, as there is insufficient data on the safety of clavulanic acid [National Teratology Information Service, Personal Communication, 2001]. It should only be used if thought to be essential.
- **First-generation cephalosporins other than cefalexin** have similar antibiotic sensitivities and adverse effect profiles, and are more expensive.
- **Second-generation cephalosporins** are not as well absorbed orally as first-generation cephalosporins, have a greater incidence of gastrointestinal adverse effects, and are more expensive than the first-generation agents.
- **Third-generation cephalosporins** generally require parenteral administration and are reserved for use in secondary care for serious infections.
- **Pivmecillinam** is not known to be teratogenic, but it is not recommended in pregnancy because of insufficient safety data.
- **Urine alkalinizing agents** are of unproven benefit and there is some evidence that they do not relieve the symptoms of cystitis [Brumfitt et al, 1990]. Sodium citrate should be avoided in pregnancy because of the high sodium content.
- **Nonsteroidal anti-inflammatory drugs (NSAIDs), including ibuprofen,** are best avoided during pregnancy.

[MeReC, 1995; DTB, 1998; Read, 2000; BNF 42, 2001]

Drugs included

- **Paracetamol** is an effective and safe analgesic and antipyretic.
- **Amoxicillin is recommended only if the organism is known to be sensitive,** due to a high incidence of resistance. Penicillins are not associated with any increased risk to the fetus.
- **Cefalexin** is a first-generation cephalosporin. It is not associated with any increased risk to the fetus and is effective against most urinary pathogens.
- **Trimethoprim** can be used during pregnancy except in women with a known folate deficiency, or who are taking folate antagonists (unless a folate supplement is taken) [Cattell, 1997; National Teratology Information Service, Personal Communication, 2001]. It should not be used if the woman has recently taken trimethoprim, or has a history of recurrent infections resistant to this drug.
- **Nitrofurantoin** is effective against most urinary-tract infections. It should not be prescribed if the mother is glucose-6-phosphate dehydrogenase (G6PD)-deficient. Nitrofurantoin can otherwise be used in pregnancy, but may cause haemolysis in a G6PD-deficient infant if used close to term. For most people the standard tablet formulation is suitable. The macrocrystalline capsules and the twice-daily modified-release formulation may be better tolerated if nausea is troublesome, and are offered as alternatives.

[MeReC, 1995; DTB, 1998; Read, 2000; BNF 42, 2001; Gould et al, 2001; PHLS, 2001]

Prescriptions

1st-line antibiotics for 7 days

Cefalexin tablets: 500mg twice a day

- Age from 14 to 59 years
- Cefalexin 500mg tablets. Take one tablet twice a day for 7 days; supply 14 tablets; NHS Cost £2.44.

Amoxicillin capsules: 250mg three times a day (IF sensitive)

- Age from 14 to 59 years
- Amoxicillin 250mg capsules. Take one capsule three times a day for 7 days; supply 21 capsules; NHS Cost £1.25.

Nitrofurantoin tabs: 50mg four times a day (NOT near term)

- Age from 14 to 59 years
- Nitrofurantoin 50mg tablets. Take one tablet four times a day for 7 days; supply 28 tablets; NHS Cost £2.47.

Nitrofurantoin caps: 50mg four times a day (NOT near term)

- Age from 14 to 59 years
- Nitrofurantoin 50mg capsules. Take one capsule four times a day for 7 days; supply 28 capsules; NHS Cost £2.85.

Nitrofurantoin m/r caps: 100mg twice a day (NOT near term)

- Age from 14 to 59 years
- Nitrofurantoin 100mg m/r caps. Take one capsule twice a day for 7 days; supply 14 capsules; NHS Cost £4.89.

Trimethoprim tablets: 200mg twice a day

- Age from 14 to 59 years
- Trimethoprim 200mg tablets. Take one tablet twice a day for 7 days; supply 14 tablets; NHS Cost £0.67.

Analgesic/antipyretic: use when required

Paracetamol tablets: 500mg to 1g up to four times a day

- Age from 14 to 15 years
- Paracetamol 500mg tablets. Take one to two tablets every 4 to 6 hours when required for relief of pain or high temperature. Maximum of 8 tablets in 24 hours; supply 32 tablets; NHS Cost £0.43; OTC Cost £0.75.

Paracetamol tablets: 1g up to four times a day

- Age from 16 to 59 years
- Paracetamol 500mg tablets. Take two tablets every 4 to 6 hours when required for relief of pain or high temperature. Maximum of 8 tablets in 24 hours; supply 50 tablets; NHS Cost £0.67; OTC Cost £1.18.

U

Cystitis and asymptomatic bacteriuria in elderly women

Which therapy?

Asymptomatic bacteriuria

- Asymptomatic bacteriuria in elderly women should not be investigated or treated.

Cystitis

Note: elderly women may present with atypical symptoms e.g. incontinence and disorientation.

- **Send urine for culture** before commencing antibiotics.
- **Dipstick test the urine** to guide the decision to treat while culture results are awaited:
  - If either nitrite or leucocyte esterase are negative — UTI unlikely, await culture result.
  - If nitrite and leucocyte esterase are both positive — UTI likely, treat with an antibiotic.
- Urine microscopy is a reliable, alternative, near-patient test. UTI is likely if bacteria and leucocytes are seen.
- **If a diagnosis of cystitis is likely, prescribe trimethoprim, nitrofurantoin, or cefalexin** while waiting for the culture and sensitivity report. Alternatively treat according to local guidelines.
- **Check the results of the urine culture.** Treat for 7 days with an antibiotic that the pathogen is reported to be sensitive to.
- Advice to encourage fluid intake is of unproven benefit and may aggravate distress from dysuria.

Recurrent cystitis

- Consider topical oestrogens in postmenopausal women as recurrent cystitis may be due to atrophic vaginitis.

Practical prescribing points

For further information see the *Medicines Compendium* (www.medicines.org.uk) or the *British National Formulary* (www.bnf.org).

- **Trimethoprim:** in moderate renal impairment the dose of trimethoprim should be reduced, and in very severe renal impairment the drug should be avoided.
- **Nitrofurantoin** is contraindicated in people with renal impairment. There is a risk of peripheral neuropathy, and urine concentrations would be inadequate for effective treatment. It should not be used in people who are glucose-6-phosphate dehydrogenase (G6PD)-deficient.
- **Ibuprofen,** as with other nonsteroidal anti-inflammatory drugs (NSAIDs), may worsen or precipitate gastrointestinal haemorrhage, asthma, hypertension, renal impairment, or cardiac failure. Avoid if there is a history of peptic ulcers.

Follow-up advice

- **Review** according to the clinical situation. Follow-up is recommended if symptoms have not resolved after 7 days.
- **Check the results of the urine culture** and ensure treatment is appropriate.

Should I refer or investigate?

Refer?

- **Referral for investigation** should be considered for women with recurrent UTI, or who persistently fail to respond to treatment.
- **Referral guidelines for suspected cancer** published by the National Institute for Health and Clinical Excellence (NICE) [NICE, 2005] recommend urgent referral to a team specialising in the management of urological cancer, depending on local arrangements, for people:
  - Of any age with painless macroscopic haematuria.
  - Aged 40 years or older who present with recurrent or persistent urinary tract infection associated with haematuria.
  - Aged 50 years or older who are found o have unexplained microscopic haematuria.
  - With an abdominal mass identified clinically or on imaging that is thought to arise from the urinary tract
  - Who have macroscopic haematuria and symptoms suggestive of a urinary tract infection *if* infection is no confirmed.

Investigate?

Since asymptomatic bacteriuria does not need to be treated, urine needs to be tested only in symptomatic patients.

- **Urine dipstick — interpretation of results in the symptomatic patient.**
  - Positive for nitrites:
    - Diagnose and treat as UTI.
  - Positive for leucocytes, negative for nitrites:
    - Diagnose and treat as UTI.
    - Consider urethral syndrome.
  - Negative for nitrites, leucocytes, haemoglobin, protein:
    - Consider urethral syndrome.
  - Negative for leucocytes and nitrites, positive for haemoglobin and/or protein:
    - Cystitis is unlikely; culture urine to detect those women who do have a urinary tract infection.
    - Consider other differential diagnosis including rena disease and malignancy.
- **Urine microscopy,** if available, is a quick and accurate near-patient screening test. UTI is likely if bacteria and leucocytes are seen.
- **Urine culture is appropriate when:**
  - The individual is symptomatic and cystitis is suspected.
  - Treatment has failed.
  - Symptoms recur.
- **Collection and processing**
  - Ideally, samples for culture should be taken mid-stream. This may be difficult, but try to obtain as clea a urine specimen as possible.
  - Place in a preservative-containing bottle or refrigerate and culture as soon as possible.

Patient information leaflets

The following PILs are available at www.prodigy.nhs.uk

- Cystitis in Women
- Cystitis - Recurrent Infections in Women
- Cystoscopy
- Intravenous Urography
- Kidney Infection (Pyelonephritis)
- Midstream Specimen of Urine (MSU)

U

Shared decision making

An antibiotic for 7 days is the recognised treatment for older people with cystitis.
If a urine culture test is done, telephone for the results in 3 days' time. Ask if it is necessary to change the treatment.
If symptoms are not gone or nearly gone after 7 days, see a doctor.
Drink plenty of fluid to 'flush out the bladder' is common advice. But it is unproven and passing more urine may be unpleasant.
Potassium citrate or other similar products are often used to reduce the symptoms of 'burning urine'. Their benefit is unproven.
Paracetamol or ibuprofen will help with pain or discomfort.
If cystitis becomes a recurring problem, consult a doctor.

Drug rationale

Drugs not included

Penicillins such as amoxicillin are unsuitable for therapy unless culture results indicate that the bacterium is sensitive. Around 50% of urinary pathogens are amoxicillin-resistant.
First-generation cephalosporins other than cefalexin have similar antibiotic sensitivities and adverse effect profiles, and are more expensive.
Second-generation cephalosporins are not as well absorbed orally as first-generation cephalosporins, have a greater incidence of gastrointestinal adverse effects, and are more expensive than the first-generation agents.
Third-generation cephalosporins generally require parenteral administration and are reserved for use in secondary care for serious infections.
Co-amoxiclav, quinolones, and pivmecillinam should be reserved for use as second-line treatment, or for complicated infections where sensitivities are known, in order to limit the development of resistance and preserve their efficacy.
Urine alkalinizing agents are of unproven benefit and there is some evidence that they do not relieve the symptoms of cystitis [Brumfitt et al, 1990].
[MeReC, 1995; DTB, 1998; Read, 2000; BNF 42, 2001]

Drugs included

For all antibiotics, a 7-day course is given in line with national guidelines [DH and SMAC, 1998; PHLS, 2001].
Trimethoprim is the antibiotic of choice for empirical treatment in uncomplicated urinary tract infection (UTI). It is effective, safe, and inexpensive. It should not be used if the patient has recently taken trimethoprim, or has a history of recurrent infections resistant to this drug.
Nitrofurantoin is a useful alternative treatment, effective against most urinary pathogens. For most people the standard tablet formulation is suitable. The macrocrystalline capsules and the twice-daily modified-release formulation may be better tolerated if nausea is troublesome, and are offered as alternatives.
Cefalexin is a first-generation cephalosporin that is effective against most urinary pathogens.
Paracetamol is an effective and safe analgesic and antipyretic.
Ibuprofen is an effective alternative to paracetamol if there are no contraindications.
[MeReC, 1995; DTB, 1998; Read, 2000; BNF 42, 2001; Gould et al, 2001; PHLS, 2001]

Prescriptions

1st-line antibiotics for 7 days

Trimethoprim tablets: 200mg twice a day
- Age from 60 years onwards
- Trimethoprim 200mg tablets. Take one tablet twice a day for 7 days; supply 14 tablets; NHS Cost £0.67.

Nitrofurantoin tablets: 50mg four times a day
- Age from 60 years onwards
- Nitrofurantoin 50mg tablets. Take one tablet four times a day for 7 days; supply 28 tablets; NHS Cost £2.47.

Nitrofurantoin capsules: 50mg four times a day
- Age from 60 years onwards
- Nitrofurantoin 50mg capsules. Take one capsule four times a day for 7 days; supply 28 capsules; NHS Cost £2.85.

Nitrofurantoin m/r capsules: 100mg twice a day
- Age from 60 years onwards
- Nitrofurantoin 100mg m/r caps. Take one capsule twice a day for 7 days; supply 14 capsules; NHS Cost £4.89.

Cefalexin tablets: 500mg twice a day
- Age from 60 years onwards
- Cefalexin 500mg tablets. Take one tablet twice a day for 7 days; supply 14 tablets; NHS Cost £2.44.

Analgesic/antipyretic: use when required

Paracetamol tablets: 1g up to four times a day
- Age from 60 years onwards
- Paracetamol 500mg tablets. Take two tablets every 4 to 6 hours when required for relief of pain or high temperature. Maximum of 8 tablets in 24 hours; supply 50 tablets; NHS Cost £0.67; OTC Cost £1.18.

Ibuprofen tablets: 400mg three times a day
- Age from 60 years onwards
- Ibuprofen 400mg tablets. Take one tablet three times a day when required for relief of pain or high temperature. Do not exceed the stated dose; supply 20 tablets; NHS Cost £0.58; OTC Cost £1.03.

UTI in women with indwelling urinary catheters

Which therapy?

Asymptomatic bacteriuria

- Asymptomatic bacteriuria in women with a long-term indwelling urinary catheter does not need to be treated.

Symptomatic UTI

- **Send urine for culture** before commencing antibiotics.
- **Dipstick test the urine** to guide the decision to treat while culture results are awaited:
  - If nitrite or leucocyte esterase are both negative — UTI unlikely, await culture result.
  - If either nitrite or leucocyte esterase are positive — UTI likely, treat with an antibiotic.
- Urine microscopy is a reliable, alternative, near-patient test. UTI is likely if bacteria and leucocytes are seen.
- **If a diagnosis of UTI is likely, prescribe trimethoprim, nitrofurantoin, or cefalexin** while waiting for the culture and sensitivity report. Alternatively treat according to local guidelines.
- **Check the results of the urine culture.** Treat for 7 days with an antibiotic that the pathogen is reported to be sensitive to.

U

- **Relieve pain and high temperature with paracetamol or ibuprofen.**
- Encourage fluid intake to promote urine flow.
- **Catheter management:**
  - Consider replacing the catheter if it has not been changed for some time.
  - Consider intermittent catheterization (rather than indwelling catheter) if care circumstances permit.
  - Consider replacing the catheter regularly if recurrent urinary tract infections (UTIs) are a problem.

Practical prescribing points

For further information see the *Medicines Compendium* (www.medicines.org.uk) or *the British National Formulary* (www.bnf.org).

- **Trimethoprim:** in moderate renal impairment the dose of trimethoprim should be reduced, and in very severe renal impairment the drug should be avoided.
- **Nitrofurantoin** is contraindicated in people with renal impairment. There is a risk of peripheral neuropathy, and urine concentrations would be inadequate for effective treatment. It should not be used in people who are glucose-6-phosphate dehydrogenase (G6PD)-deficient.
- **Ibuprofen,** as with other nonsteroidal anti-inflammatory drugs (NSAIDs), may worsen or precipitate gastrointestinal haemorrhage, asthma, hypertension, renal impairment, or cardiac failure. Avoid if there is a history of peptic ulcers.
- **Quinolones** may cause tendon damage (Committee on Safety of Medicines advice); stop treatment if pain or inflammation of a tendon occurs. They can induce convulsions in people with epilepsy or in those with conditions that predispose to seizures. People concurrently taking NSAIDs may also be susceptible. The risks and benefits of prescribing a quinolone should be considered on an individual basis for these people.

Follow-up advice

- **Review** according to the clinical situation. Follow-up is recommended if symptoms have not resolved after 7 days.
- **Check the results of the urine culture** and ensure treatment is appropriate.

Should I refer or investigate?

Refer?

- **Referral for investigation** should be considered for women with recurrent UTI, or who persistently fail to respond to treatment.
- **Referral guidelines for suspected cancer** published by the National Institute for Health and Clinical Excellence (NICE) [NICE, 2005] recommend urgent referral to a team specialising in the management of urological cancer, depending on local arrangements, for people:
  - Of any age with painless macroscopic haematuria.
  - Aged 40 years or older who present with recurrent or persistent urinary tract infection associated with haematuria.
  - Aged 50 years or older who are found o have unexplained microscopic haematuria.
  - With an abdominal mass identified clinically or on imaging that is thought to arise from the urinary tract.
  - Who have macroscopic haematuria and symptoms suggestive of a urinary tract infection *if* infection is not confirmed.

Investigate?

Since asymptomatic bacteriuria does not need to be treate in women with a long-term indwelling catheter, urine need to be tested only in symptomatic patients.

- **Urine dipstick — interpretation of results in the symptomatic patient.**
  - Positive for nitrites:
    - Diagnose and treat as UTI.
  - Positive for leucocytes, negative for nitrites:
    - Diagnose and treat as UTI.
    - Consider urethral syndrome.
  - Negative for nitrites, leucocytes, haemoglobin, protein:
    - Consider urethral syndrome.
  - Negative for leucocytes and nitrites, positive for haemoglobin and/or protein:
    - Cystitis is unlikely; culture urine to detect those women who do have a urinary tract infection.
    - Consider other differential diagnosis including rena disease and malignancy.
- **Urine microscopy,** if available, is a quick and accurate near-patient screening test. UTI is likely if bacteria and leucocytes are seen.
- **Urine culture is appropriate when:**
  - The individual is symptomatic and cystitis is suspected.
  - Treatment has failed.
  - Symptoms recur.
- **Collection and processing:**
  - Place in a preservative-containing bottle or refrigerat and culture as soon as possible.

Patient information leaflets

The following PILs are available at www.prodigy.nhs.uk

- Cystitis in Women
- Kidney Infection (Pyelonephritis)

Shared decision making

- **An antibiotic for 7 days** is the recognised treatment.
- **Telephone in 2 or 3 days' time** for the results of the urir culture. Ask if it is necessary to change the treatment.
- **If symptoms are not gone or nearly gone after 7 days, s** a doctor.
- **Paracetamol or ibuprofen** will help with pain or discomfort.

Drug rationale

Drugs not included

- **Penicillins such as amoxicillin** are unsuitable for therap unless culture results indicate that the bacterium is sensitive. Around 50% of urinary pathogens are amoxicillin-resistant. (If culture reveals the organism to be sensitive then amoxicillin would be appropriate.)
- **First-generation cephalosporins other than cefalexin** have similar antibiotic sensitivities and adverse effect profiles, and are more expensive.
- **Second-generation cephalosporins** are not as well absorbed orally as first-generation cephalosporins, have a greater incidence of gastrointestinal adverse effects, and are more expensive than the first-generation agents
- **Third-generation cephalosporins** generally require parenteral administration and are reserved for use in secondary care for serious infections.
- **Quinolones (other than norfloxacin and ciprofloxacin)** are not offered. They should be reserved for complicate infections where sensitivities are known, in order to preserve their efficacy and limit the development of

resistance. The newer quinolones have a slightly broader spectrum of activity than the older drugs but there is no evidence of greater efficacy.
Prophylactic systemic antibiotics, topical antibiotic ointments, and instillation of antibiotics into the bladder are not recommended for people with long-term catheters.
[MeReC, 1995; DTB, 1998; Read, 2000; BNF 42, 2001]

Drugs included

For all antibiotics, a 7-day course is given in line with national guidelines [DH and SMAC, 1998; PHLS, 2001].
Trimethoprim is effective against most urinary tract pathogens, and safe and inexpensive. It should not be used if the patient has recently taken trimethoprim, or has a history of recurrent infections resistant to this drug.
Nitrofurantoin is a useful alternative antibiotic, effective against most urinary pathogens. For most people the standard tablet formulation is suitable. The macrocrystalline capsules and the twice-daily modified-release formulation may be better tolerated if nausea is troublesome, and are offered as alternatives.
Cefalexin is a first-generation cephalosporin effective against most urinary pathogens.
Co-amoxiclav is a suitable second-line alternative. It is effective against up to 90% of urinary pathogens.
Norfloxacin and ciprofloxacin are recommended as second-line antibiotics. They are effective against most urinary pathogens (only around 5% of pathogens are resistant) and are currently the least expensive of the quinolones available.
Pivmecillinam is highly active against many Gram-negative pathogens and is an appropriate second-line treatment.
Paracetamol is an effective and safe analgesic and antipyretic.
Ibuprofen is an effective alternative to paracetamol if there are no contraindications.
[MeReC, 1995; DTB, 1998; Read, 2000; BNF 42, 2001; Gould et al, 2001; PHLS, 2001]

Prescriptions

1st-line antibiotics for 7 days

Trimethoprim tablets: 200mg twice a day
- Age from 14 years onwards
- Trimethoprim 200mg tablets. Take one tablet twice a day for 7 days; supply 14 tablets; NHS Cost £0.67.

Nitrofurantoin tablets: 50mg four times a day
- Age from 14 years onwards
- Nitrofurantoin 50mg tablets. Take one tablet four times a day for 7 days; supply 28 tablets; NHS Cost £2.47.

Nitrofurantoin capsules: 50mg four times a day
- Age from 14 years onwards
- Nitrofurantoin 50mg capsules. Take one capsule four times a day for 7 days; supply 28 capsules; NHS Cost £2.85.

Nitrofurantoin m/r capsules: 100mg twice a day
- Age from 14 years onwards
- Nitrofurantoin 100mg m/r caps. Take one capsule twice a day for 7 days; supply 14 capsules; NHS Cost £4.89.

Cefalexin tablets: 500mg twice a day
- Age from 14 years onwards
- Cefalexin 500mg tablets. Take one tablet twice a day for 7 days; supply 14 tablets; NHS Cost £2.44.

2nd-line antibiotics for 7 days

Co-amoxiclav tablets: 500/125mg three times a day
- Age from 14 years onwards
- Co-amoxiclav 625mg tablets. Take one tablet three times a day for 7 days; supply 21 tablets; NHS Cost £15.72.

Ciprofloxacin tablets: 500mg twice a day
- Age from 16 years onwards
- Ciprofloxacin 500mg tablets. Take one tablet twice a day for 7 days; supply 14 tablets; NHS Cost £19.88.

Norfloxacin tablets: 400mg twice a day
- Age from 16 years onwards
- Norfloxacin 400mg tablets. Take one tablet twice a day for 7 days; supply 14 tablets; NHS Cost £4.72.

Pivmecillinam tablets: 400mg three times a day
- Age from 14 years onwards
- Pivmecillinam 200mg tablets. Take two tablets three times a day for 7 days; supply 42 tablets; NHS Cost £18.72.

Analgesic/antipyretic: use when required

Paracetamol tablets: 500mg to 1g up to four times a day
- Age from 14 to 15 years
- Paracetamol 500mg tablets. Take one to two tablets every 4 to 6 hours when required for relief of pain or high temperature. Maximum of 8 tablets in 24 hours; supply 32 tablets; NHS Cost £0.43; OTC Cost £0.75.

Paracetamol tablets: 1g up to four times a day
- Age from 16 years onwards
- Paracetamol 500mg tablets. Take two tablets every 4 to 6 hours when required for relief of pain or high temperature. Maximum of 8 tablets in 24 hours; supply 50 tablets; NHS Cost £0.67; OTC Cost £1.18.

Ibuprofen tablets: 400mg three times a day
- Age from 14 years onwards
- Ibuprofen 400mg tablets. Take one tablet three times a day when required for relief of pain or high temperature. Do not exceed the stated dose; supply 20 tablets; NHS Cost £0.58; OTC Cost £1.03.

Urethral syndrome

Which therapy?

Acute urethral syndrome

- Dipstick the urine to rule out infection. If symptoms do not resolve or recur frequently, culture the urine.
- Explanation and reassurance may be all that is required.
- An analgesic may alleviate dysuria.
- Antibiotics are not recommended.

Chronic urethral syndrome (more than three episodes per year)

- Rule out occult infection by sending a urine sample for culture and treating empirically with a 3-day course of an antibiotic (as for acute cystitis).
- Consider psychological conditions (although these are rare).
- Acupuncture, diazepam, and surgical interventions (e.g. urethral dilation, urethrotomy) are not recommended.

Practical prescribing points

For further information see the *Medicines Compendium* (www.medicines.org.uk) or the *British National Formulary* (www.bnf.org).

Breastfeeding

- **Nitrofurantoin** is not recommended if the infant is glucose-6-phosphate dehydrogenase (G6PD)-deficient.

Other cautions

- **Nitrofurantoin** should not be used in people who are known to be G6PD-deficient.
- **Ibuprofen,** as with other nonsteroidal anti-inflammatory drugs (NSAIDs), may worsen or precipitate gastrointestinal haemorrhage, asthma, hypertension, renal impairment, or cardiac failure. Avoid if there is a history of peptic ulcers.

Should I refer or investigate?

Refer?

- Consider referral for urological assessment when symptoms remain intolerable despite appropriate management.

Investigate?

- Rule out infection by means of microscopy or a urine dipstick in the first instance, and with urine culture if symptoms do not resolve within 3 days or if they frequently recur.

Patient information leaflets

The following PILs are available at www.prodigy.nhs.uk

- Cystitis in Women

Shared decision making

- **Antibiotics** do not work for urethral syndrome.
- **If a urine culture is done, telephone in 2 or 3 days' time** for the results. Ask if it is necessary to change the treatment.
- **If symptoms are not gone or nearly gone after 3 days,** see a doctor.
- **Potassium citrate** or other similar products are often taken to reduce the symptoms of 'burning urine'. Their benefit is not proven.
- **Paracetamol or ibuprofen** will help with pain or discomfort.

Drug rationale

U

Drugs not included

- **Antibiotics** are not recommended for the treatment of acute urethral syndrome. An empirical 3-day course of an antibiotic (as for acute cystitis) may be appropriate for women with chronic urethral syndrome, to rule out occult infection [Brumfitt et al, 1998].
- **Urine alkalinizing agents** are of unproven benefit and there is some evidence that they do not relieve the symptoms of cystitis [Brumfitt et al, 1990].

Drugs included

- **Paracetamol** is an effective and safe analgesic agent.
- **Ibuprofen** is an effective alternative to paracetamol if there are no contraindications.

Prescriptions

Analgesic/antipyretic: use when required

Paracetamol tablets: 500mg to 1g up to four times a day

- Age from 14 to 15 years
- Paracetamol 500mg tablets. Take one to two tablets every 4 to 6 hours when required for relief of pain or high temperature. Maximum of 8 tablets in 24 hours; supply 32 tablets; NHS Cost £0.43; OTC Cost £0.75.

Paracetamol tablets: 1g up to four times a day

- Age from 16 years onwards
- Paracetamol 500mg tablets. Take two tablets every 4 to 6 hours when required for relief of pain or high temperature. Maximum of 8 tablets in 24 hours; supply 50 tablets; NHS Cost £0.67; OTC Cost £1.18.

Ibuprofen tablets: 400mg three times a day

- Age from 14 years onwards
- Ibuprofen 400mg tablets. Take one tablet three times a day when required for relief of pain or high temperature. Do not exceed the stated dose; supply 20 tablets; NHS Cost £0.58; OTC Cost £1.03.

Extended Information

Background information

- What is it? p.1822
- How common is it? p.1823
- What are the risk factors? p.1823
- How do I know my patient has it? p.1823
- What else might it be? p.1824
- Complications and prognosis p.1825

What is it?

Urinary tract infection

- **Urinary tract infection** (UTI) is defined as the occurrenc of pathogenic micro-organisms in the urine, urethra, bladder, or kidney. Lower UTI refers to urethritis and/o cystitis.
- Infection is usually caused by bacteria from the gastrointestinal tract. Organisms that cause UTI are outlined in Table 1.
- ***Candida albicans*** **infection is rarely found in the community,** but is common in hospital patients with ris factors such as indwelling catheters, immunosuppression, diabetes mellitus, and antibiotic treatment.
- **The usual criterion for diagnosing urinary tract infectio** (and that used by the Public Health Laboratory Service [PHLS]) is detection of more than 10^5 organisms per ml of suitably collected urine. If the urine is collected unde sterile conditions (e.g. suprapubic aspiration, or 'in-and

Table 1: Organisms responsible for UTI.

Common organisms	Less common organisms
Escherichia coli	*Proteus vulgaris*
Staphylococcus saprophyticus	*Klebsiella* species
Proteus mirabilis	*Enterobacter* species
—	*Citrobacter* species
—	*Serratia marcescens*
—	*Acinetobacter* and *Pseudomonas* species
—	*Candida albicans*

out' catheterization), counts as low as 10^2 to 10^4 organisms per ml may indicate infection.
- **Recurrent UTI** is defined as repeated episodes of infection. There is no consensus on the threshold number of infections at which specific interventions should be taken to prevent recurrence. Expert opinion ranges from as few as two to as many as six episodes per year. The recommendation in this guidance is three or more episodes per year of acute UTI.
- **Relapse** is defined as a repeat UTI with the same strain of organism, and suggests treatment failure. In practice, because routine laboratory testing does not include typing to identify the strain, a UTI is considered to be a relapse if a repeat infection occurs within 2 weeks.
- **Asymptomatic bacteriuria** is the presence of bacteriuria with no symptoms.
- **Uncomplicated UTI** is infection by a typical pathogen in a person with a normal urinary tract and with normal renal function.
- **Complicated UTI may involve:**
  - Virulent organism, e.g. *Staphylococcus aureus*.
  - Abnormal urinary tract, e.g. calculus, vesicoureteric reflux, reflux nephropathy, neurogenic bladder, indwelling catheter, urinary obstruction.
  - Impaired host defences e.g. pregnancy, diabetes mellitus, immunosuppressive therapy.
  - Impaired renal function.

Acute urethral syndrome

Acute urethral syndrome is characterized by dysuria, frequency, and urgency, with no significant bacteriuria. Synonyms include: abacterial cystitis, frequency and dysuria syndrome, non-urethral syndrome, acute dysuria–pyuria syndrome, irritable urethral syndrome, and acute dysuria syndrome.
[Brumfitt et al, 1998; Stamm, 1998]

The aetiology of the urethral syndrome is unknown, and there is debate about whether it is a discrete entity. Pathogenic roles have been postulated for:
- Bacteria found in low concentrations.
- Fastidious organisms (such as *Ureaplasma urealyticum*).
- Genital pathogens (such as *Chlamydia trachomatis*, *Neisseria gonorrhoeae*, Herpes simplex virus).
- Vaginal infections with *Trichomonas vaginalis* and *Candida albicans*.
- Infestation with pinworm/threadworm.
- Irritants (such as deodorants, bubble baths, and detergents).
- Atrophic urethritis (in postmenopausal women).

How common is it?

- **Urinary tract infection** (UTI) is the commonest bacterial infection managed in general practice, and is the reason for between 1% and 3% of all GP consultations [MeReC, 1995].
- **About 5% of women each year** present to their GP with frequency and dysuria.
- **Up to 50% of women, during their lifetime,** will suffer from a symptomatic UTI [MeReC, 1995; DTB, 1998]
- **Among pregnant women, 1–2%** develop acute bacterial cystitis [Cunningham and Lucas, 1994].
- **Up to 20% of non-pregnant women who have cystitis will experience a recurrence.** About 90% of recurrences are due to reinfection and about 10% to relapse [Cooper and Jepson, 2001; Lawrenson and Logie, 2001].
- **Elderly people show an increased incidence:** in both men and women the incidences of asymptomatic bacteriuria and UTI increase substantially with advancing age, coexisting illnesses, and institutional care [McMurdo and Gillespie, 2000; Wallach, 2001].
- **Urethral syndrome:** about 50% of women who present with urinary symptoms do not have bacteriuria [Brumfitt et al, 1998].
- **Annual incidence of urinary tract infection in women** is summarized in Table 2.

Table 2: Annual incidence of urinary tract infection.

Age group (years)	Incidence (approximate)
Sexually active young women	3%
Women over 60	7%
Women over 70	8%
Women over 80	20%

What are the risk factors?

Most lower urinary tract infections are not associated with any risk factor. The following risk factors should be considered in women with recurrent cystitis:
- **Sexual intercourse:** common risk factor for young women.
- **Atrophic urethritis and vaginitis** (in postmenopausal women).
- **Abnormalities of urinary tract function** (e.g. indwelling catheter, neuropathic bladder, vesicoureteric reflux, outflow obstruction, anatomical abnormalities).
- **Incomplete bladder emptying** (e.g. dysfunctional urination, chronic indwelling catheter).
- **Female diaphragm, spermicide-coated condoms** [Fihn et al, 1985; Fihn et al, 1998]
- **Previous urinary tract surgery.**
- **Immunocompromise.**

How do I know my patient has it?

Cystitis

Clinical features

- The spectrum of illness in lower urinary tract infection (UTI) ranges from asymptomatic bacteriuria to life-threatening systemic illness.
- **Typical features** of cystitis include:
  - Symptoms of dysuria, frequency, urgency, nocturia, haematuria, and suprapubic discomfort.
  - Signs of suprapubic tenderness, and cloudy or foul smelling urine.
- **Atypical presentations** of cystitis may occur in the elderly and include secondary incontinence, confusion, anorexia, high temperature, or shock.
- **High temperature** (more than 38.5°C) is more characteristic of pyelonephritis than of cystitis.

Investigations

Urine dipstick

Urine dipstick tests should be used as follows:
- In otherwise healthy women with urinary symptoms:
  - If either nitrite or leucocyte esterase (LE) dipstick tests are positive, diagnose UTI
  - If both nitrite and LE dipstick tests are negative, exclude UTI
- Culture the urine if it is important to make an accurate diagnosis or to select an effective antibiotic (as in pregnancy, treatment failure, immunocompromise).
- Urine dipstick tests are not suitable for screening for UTI in asymptomatic women.
- Urine dipstick tests are the most widely used near-patient test for UTI.
- Samples for testing should be obtained by the 'clean-catch, mid-stream urine' method.
- **Dipstick tests cannot be relied on to definitely exclude or confirm a diagnosis of UTI.** Urine culture provides the definitive diagnosis and guides antibiotic therapy. Several studies document the limitations of urine dipstick tests.

U

See [Lammers et al, 2001] and [Hurlbut and Littenberg, 1991] for comprehensive discussions and references to the literature.

- **Nitrite test**
  - Most urinary pathogens reduce nitrate to nitrite.
  - A positive test indicates bacteriuria and therefore suggests UTI.
  - A negative test does not rule out UTI because some pathogens do not produce nitrate reductase, and frequent urination (common in cystitis) reduces the time available for the enzyme to act.
- **Leucocyte esterase (LE) test**
  - Leucocyte esterase is a marker for leucocytes.
  - A positive LE test indicates pyuria and therefore suggests UTI. Because leucocytes can contaminate the specimen, a positive test does not make a diagnosis of UTI certain.
  - A negative LE test does not rule out the diagnosis of UTI, since the test is insensitive, and pyuria is not always found in UTI.
- **Blood and protein**
  - Blood and protein are sometimes found in the urine when there is a UTI, but their presence or absence does not help in making the diagnosis.
  - Haematuria is common in uncomplicated cystitis, and resolves with treatment.
- **Combinations of tests**
  - Combining results from nitrite, LE, blood, and protein tests increases sensitivity but decreases specificity.

[Hurlbut and Littenberg, 1991; Lammers et al, 2001]

Urine microscopy

- Microscopy of urine is a quick and reliable near-patient test for UTI.
- **UTI is likely if bacteria and leucocytes are seen in the urine.**
- Minimal processing is required as the urine is neither centrifuged nor stained.
- Moderate investment in equipment, training, and organization is required.
- Some general practices offer urine microscopy during the consultation.

Urine culture

- **Urine culture is indicated for:**
  - Pregnant women:
    - At the first antenatal visit to screen for asymptomatic bacteriuria.
    - After treatment of bacteriuria (screen monthly).
    - If symptoms of UTI are present.
  - Elderly people with clinical signs of infection.
  - Recurrent cystitis.
  - Treatment failure (antibiotic resistance is more common).
  - People who are immunocompromised or have diabetes if they have features of a UTI.
  - People who have a long-term indwelling catheter and features of a UTI.
  - People with an abnormal genito-urinary tract and features of UTI.
- **Urine culture is not indicated when cystitis is suspected in an otherwise healthy woman.**
- Careful collection, storage, and transport of urine samples minimizes contamination and deterioration.
- The sample should, if possible, be collected before antibiotics are taken or changed.
- **A clean-catch mid-stream urine sample (MSU) is generally recommended** [Walter and Knopp, 1989]. A description of how to collect an MSU is available in a Patient Information Leaflet (PIL) that can be printed out.
- Providing an MSU may be impractical in women who are pregnant, obese, physically handicapped, or frail.
- There is some evidence that MSU collection may not meaningfully reduce contamination and may not be necessary in practice [Belmin et al, 1993; Lifshitz and Kramer, 2000].
- **Containers:** urine should be transferred within 30 minutes of collection to a specimen bottle. The bottle should be filled to the line if it contains boric acid, as the preservative is bactericidal at high concentrations.
- **Storage:** urine should be refrigerated at 4° Celsius while waiting to be processed. Urine that has been stored at 4° Celsius for 48 hours is suitable for culture but not for microscopy, as most cells would have disintegrated.
- **Interpretation of results:**
  - Infection is indicated by more than 10^5 organisms per ml of suitably collected urine.
  - Contamination is suggested by the presence of one or more of the following:
    - Bacteria but no leucocytes (except in immunocompromised people).
    - Multiple organisms cultured.
    - Blood, if the woman is menstruating.
- The possibility of contamination is usually mentioned in the culture report, but reporting criteria vary between laboratories.
- **False-negative culture results** are sometimes due to inadequate filling of a specimen bottle containing boric acid (as the preservative is bactericidal at high concentrations) or antibiotics excreted in the urine.

Imaging and functional tests

- Special investigations are not routinely indicated in women who have a UTI.
- Referral for imaging or functional tests is indicated for women who have:
  - Persistently failed to respond to appropriate antibiotic therapy.
  - Frequent episodes of UTI, i.e. more than three a year.
  - Haematuria.
  - History of pyelonephritis, calculi, or previous genito-urinary tract surgery.

[Watson and Duerden, 1977; Jewkes et al, 1990; Ahmad et al, 1991; MeReC, 1995; DTB, 1998; Stamm, 1998; Sanderson, 1998; Lifshitz and Kramer, 2000; Lammers et al, 2001]

Urethral syndrome

- Acute urethral syndrome presents with dysuria, frequency, and urgency.
- Pyuria may be present or absent.
- Urine culture is negative.

[Brumfitt et al, 1998]

What else might it be?

Conditions with presentations similar to those of bacterial cystitis include:

- **Urethral syndrome:** dysuria, frequency and urgency, no significant bacteriuria.
- **Pyelonephritis:** high temperature, rigors, loin pain/ tenderness, severe illness with prostration, vomiting, oliguric renal failure.
- **Atrophic vaginitis/urethritis:** in postmenopausal women.
- **Urethritis, vaginitis, cervicitis:** *Chlamydia trachomatis* (pyuria without bacteriuria), *Neisseria gonorrhoeae*, Herpes simplex virus, or other sexually transmitted disease.
- **Drug-induced cystitis** (e.g. with cyclophosphamide, allopurinol, danazol, tiaprofenic acid and possibly other nonsteroidal anti-inflammatory drugs [NSAIDs]).
- **Pinworms/threadworms.**

Complications and prognosis

Complications

- Ascending infection can occur, leading to pyelonephritis, renal failure, and sepsis.
- Recurrent infection occurs in up to 20% of young women with acute cystitis [Stamm and Hooton, 1993].
- Asymptomatic bacteriuria in pregnancy, if untreated, develops into pyelonephritis in up to 40% of women.
- Untreated asymptomatic bacteriuria in pregnancy has also been implicated in pre-term delivery and low birthweight [Gilstrap and Whalley, 1998].
- The urethral syndrome can be resistant to therapy [Smaill, 2001].

Prognosis

- Most episodes of untreated, acute uncomplicated cystitis resolve in about 3 days.
- Acute uncomplicated cystitis responds rapidly to appropriate antibiotic treatment.
- Symptoms of urethral syndrome usually resolve over 3 days, but may recur frequently.

Management issues

Principles of treatment of urinary tract infection p.1825
Uncomplicated cystitis p.1826
Recurrent cystitis p.1826
Cystitis/asymptomatic bacteriuria in pregnancy p.1827
Cystitis/asymptomatic bacteriuria in elderly women p.1828
Urinary tract infections in women with chronic indwelling urinary catheters p.1828
Urethral syndrome p.1828

Principles of treatment of urinary tract infection

Symptomatic treatment

- Offer paracetamol or ibuprofen to relieve pain and high temperature. (This should not be needed for more than 1 to 2 days.) Note: a temperature of more than 38.5°C is more characteristic of pyelonephritis.
- Urine-alkalinizing agents, such as potassium citrate, sodium citrate, and sodium bicarbonate are popular remedies for urinary symptoms in women. However, there is evidence to doubt their efficacy [Brumfitt et al, 1990].

Antibiotic treatment

- Adhere to local policies (if available) and be guided by local patterns of bacterial resistance.
- Population studies on bacterial sensitivities can be difficult to apply to usual clinical settings:
  - Urine samples from hospitals and from general practice are likely to be preferentially selected from complicated cases and treatment failures.
  - Uncomplicated urinary tract infection (UTI) generally resolves within a few days, even if no specific treatment is given.
  - Drugs commonly used in UTI are excreted in higher concentrations in the urine than are used in laboratory testing. This explains, in part, why bacterial resistance is not always associated with treatment failure.
  - Patterns of antibiotic resistance vary widely when different centres are compared.

[Wise and Andrews, 1998; Priest et al, 2001; Tran et al, 2001]

Trimethoprim

- Rates of resistance of *Escherichia coli* to trimethoprim have been reported as 20–40%. However, the populations studied were different from those seen in primary care, where true resistance in acute uncomplicated UTI is probably 10–20% [McNulty, Personal Communication, 2002].
- Trimethoprim is still an effective first-choice treatment for uncomplicated UTI in general practice.

[Baerheim, 2001; Manges et al, 2001; Stamm, 2001; Steinke et al, 2001]

Nitrofurantoin

- Nitrofurantoin is at least as effective as trimethoprim, but is more expensive and can cause nausea and vomiting.
- Approximately 10% of bacteria responsible for UTI in general practice are resistant to nitrofurantoin [McNulty, Personal Communication, 2002].
- Nitrofurantoin is ineffective against *Proteus mirabilis*.
- Macrocrystalline nitrofurantoin is promoted as having fewer adverse effects than other formulations [Kalowski et al, 1974]. However, the published studies compared macrocrystalline with other formulations of nitrofurantoin, when the recommended length of treatment was 2 weeks and the recommended dose was 100 mg four times a day. Adverse effects were more likely to occur than with lower dose, short-course treatment that is now recommended.
- Modified-release preparations are taken twice a day and may be more convenient.

Cefalexin

- Cefalexin is at least as effective as trimethoprim but is more expensive. It is a broad-spectrum antibiotic and is therefore more likely to cause diarrhoea and vaginal thrush [Leigh et al, 1970; Parfitt, 1999].
- Approximately 10% of bacteria responsible for UTI in general practice are resistant to cefalexin [McNulty, Personal Communication, 2002].
- Although treatment failure with cefalexin has been reported to be as high as 30% [DTB, 1998], more recent urine culture data from the north-east of England found that 96% of *E coli* isolates and 90% for all other isolates are sensitive to cefalexin [Pedler, Personal Communication, 2002].

Other antibiotics

- **Amoxicillin** is unsuitable as an empirical treatment because 50% of urinary pathogens are resistant. However, it may be used if the organism is known to be sensitive.
- **Co-amoxiclav** is appropriate for second-line treatment, e.g. for trimethoprim resistance. Resistance in uncomplicated UTI is less than 5% [McNulty, Personal Communication, 2002]. It is more expensive than trimethoprim, nitrofurantoin, and cefalexin and it has some undesirable adverse drug reactions.
- **Quinolones** (e.g. ciprofloxacin and norfloxacin) are appropriate for second-line treatment. Resistance in uncomplicated UTI is less than 5% [McNulty, Personal Communication, 2002].
- **Pivmecillinam** is appropriate for second-line treatment. It is highly active against many Gram-negative pathogens including *E coli*.

[MeReC, 1995; DTB, 1998; Baerheim, 2001]

Length of antibiotic treatment for uncomplicated cystitis

For otherwise healthy women with cystitis who are not pregnant:

- Single-dose therapy results in lower cure rates and more recurrences than longer courses.
- 3 days of antibiotic treatment is as likely to be as effective as 5 or 7 days.

U

Table 3: Management of symptoms of acute cystitis.*

Step 1. History and examination suggest uncomplicated lower urinary tract infection (UTI):			
If symptoms are mild: Omit urine tests and treat symptomatically for UTI or Urethral syndrome as in step 3		*If diagnosis is certain:* Omit dipstick test and manage as in step 3	
Step 2. Dipstick test on clean-catch mid-stream urine:			
nitrite + leucocyte esterase +/– protein +/– blood +/–	nitrite – leucocyte esterase + protein +/– blood +/–	nitrite – leucocyte esterase – protein – blood –	nitrite – leucocyte esterase – protein + and/or blood +
Step 3. Diagnose and manage:	**Step 3. Diagnose and manage:**	**Step 3. Diagnose and manage:**	**Step 3. Diagnose and manage:**
UTI	**UTI or Urethral syndrome**	**Urethral syndrome**	**Other diagnosis**
Culture urine only if: — Diagnosis in doubt — Need to guide Rx — Risk factors (e.g. diabetes, immuno-compromise)	Review: — Symptoms, — Urine collection method Culture urine	Reassure	Document menstrual status Culture urine to confirm diagnosis
If symptoms not mild: Rx first-line antibiotic	*If symptoms not mild:* Rx first-line antibiotic	—	Workup and manage according to differential diagnosis
Symptomatic Rx: Analgesic/antipyretic *If no response/relapse:* Culture urine: for definitive diagnosis and to guide Rx	*Symptomatic Rx:* Analgesic/antipyretic *If no response/relapse:* Culture urine: for definitive diagnosis and to guide Rx	*Symptomatic Rx:* Analgesic/antipyretic *If no response/relapse:* Culture urine: for definitive diagnosis and to guide Rx	*Criteria for urgent referral*** Painless macroscopic haematuria Painless microscopic haematuria, 50 years or older Haematuria associated with recurrent or persistent UTI, 40 years or older Macroscopic haematuria and symptoms suggestive of a urinary tract infection *if* infection is not confirmed

* Adapted from a protocol drafted by the Public Health Laboratory Service (PHLS) [McNulty, Personal Communication, 2002]
** Criteria for referral for suspected cancer are from *Referral guidelines for suspected cancer* published by the National Institute for Health and Clinical Excellence (NICE) [NICE, 2005]

- The longer the course of treatment the more bacterial resistance is promoted.

Blind antibiotic therapy for bacterial cystitis

- Some economic analysts have suggested that dipstick and other tests should not be used for women with typical symptoms of cystitis, and that empirical antibiotic treatment should be prescribed [Fenwick et al, 2000; Niewoehner et al, 2005].
- We do not recommend this strategy because: (a) the theoretical analyses have not been tested in practice, and (b) the risk of promoting resistance to antibiotics has not been adequately taken into account [McIsaac et al, 2002].

[Gossius and Vorland, 1984; Leibovici and Wysenbeek, 1991a; Leibovici and Wysenbeek, 1991b; MeReC, 1995]

U

Other treatments

- **Increasing fluid intake** is common advice but is controversial and unproven. Theoretically it might help to 'wash out' the bladder but it can distress people with dysuria. Other unproven measures include advice 'not to hold on' and to 'void after intercourse'.
- **Cranberry juice** has not been shown to be of benefit in the treatment of acute urinary tract infection (although there is limited evidence of benefit in preventing recurrent UTIs).

[Dawson and Whitfield, 1996; Jepson et al, 2000]

Uncomplicated cystitis

A protocol for the management of symptoms of acute cystitis in otherwise healthy women who are not pregnant is outlined in Table 3.

Recurrent cystitis

Recommended management of otherwise healthy women with recurrent cystitis who are not pregnant is outlined in Table 4.

Evidence from the UK General Practice Research Database

A study of urinary tract infection (UTI) in young women using the UK General Practice Research Database [Lawrenson and Logie, 2001] found the following:

- 14% of patients were prescribed a second antibiotic within 28 days.
- Use of a second antibiotic was more common in older women, pregnancy, or diabetes.
- People prescribed amoxicillin were more likely to receiv a second course of antibiotics than those given trimethoprim.
- No statistically significant or clinically important difference between the failure rates of trimethoprim, nitrofurantoin, norfloxacin, ciprofloxacin, or the cephalosporins.
- Courses of 3 days were as effective as those of 5 or 7 days.

Relapse of infection

- To prove relapse, the pathogens identified on urine culture must be typed to show that they are identical. Since typing is not routinely carried out, relapse is assumed when infection recurs with a short period, e.g. 2 weeks.

ble 4: Management of recurrent cystitis.

atment of each episode of cystitis should take into account:
Clinical presentation (mild, moderate, severe illness) Past history of urinary tract infection (important to exclude or manage risk factors) Recent antibiotic therapy (bacterial resistance is more probable) Presumed or documented infecting organism (choice of antibiotic)
lapse (failure to eradicate the organism)
Consider underlying source of infection or urological abnormality Culture urine to ensure appropriate antibiotic treatment is given Treat with an antibiotic for 3 days Refer if persistent failure to eradicate the infection
nfection
Treat each new episode with an antibiotic for 7 days Consider prophylaxis if 3 or more episodes per year: • If unrelated to sexual intercourse: continuous antibiotic prophylaxis; or patient-initiated antibiotic therapy for new episodes; or consider a trial of cranberry juice If related to sexual intercourse: single-dose postcoital antibiotic prophylaxis

Limited evidence suggests that routine investigation (e.g. with excretory urography, cystoscopy, or ultrasound) is not likely to be beneficial [Cooper and Jepson, 2001].

If treatment fails to eradicate the initial organism:
- Ensure that the organism grown on culture is sensitive to the antibiotic prescribed.
- Confirm that the antibiotic treatment has been taken.
- Assess for possible serious underlying causes e.g. stones, papillary necrosis, vesicoureteric reflux.

Persistent failure to eradicate the infection is an indication for referral.

amm and Hooton, 1993; Cattell, 1997]

rophylaxis for recurrent cystitis NOT related to exual intercourse

The threshold for starting prophylactic treatment is controversial, with experts advocating as few as two or as many as six episodes of UTI per year [Brumfitt et al, 1998; Cooper and Jepson, 2001].

Medium-term continuous antibiotic prophylaxis:
- A review found evidence from seven randomized controlled trials that medium-term continuous antibiotic prophylaxis (most commonly with trimethoprim, nitrofurantoin, a cephalosporin, or a quinolone) can reduce the likelihood of further attacks of cystitis [Cooper and Jepson, 2001].
- This option is appropriate when there is no relation of recurrent symptoms to sexual intercourse. There is little evidence of difference between nightly or 3 times a week regimens. Individual preferences and response should be taken into account when choosing the dose frequency, and 6 months of treatment before re-assessment would be reasonable [Nicolle and Ronald, 1998].

Long-term continuous antibiotic prophylaxis:
- A small cohort study found no significant adverse effects from long-term prophylaxis (up to 5 years) although there was an increase in bacteria resistant to co-trimoxazole [Cooper and Jepson, 2001].

Self-treatment
- This option is appropriate for a woman who has three or more episodes of lower UTI per year.
- Limited evidence supports the efficacy of self-treatment [Stamm and Hooton, 1993; Cooper and Jepson, 2001; Gupta et al, 2001]. The woman is given a prescription so that she can initiate treatment on recurrence of symptoms, or preferably when a UTI is confirmed by urine culture.

- **Cranberry juice**
  - A systematic review found a few small trials with insufficient evidence to recommend the use of cranberry juice for preventing UTIs in women [Jepson et al, 1998]. Subsequently, one small randomized controlled trial of cranberry–lingon berry juice extract found an absolute risk reduction of 20% for recurrence of UTI (n = 50 per group; NNT = 5) [Kontiokari et al, 2001].

Prophylaxis for recurrent cystitis related to sexual intercourse

- **Miscellaneous**
  - Consider change of contraceptive method if female diaphragm or spermicide is being used.
  - Voiding after intercourse may help to prevent infection.
  - In some cases, symptoms may be due to trauma rather than infection. These people may find a lubricant helpful.
- **Postcoital antibiotic prophylaxis**
  - Consider if more than three UTIs per year.
  - Four randomized controlled trials found significant reductions in rates of urinary tract infection when an antibiotic (nitrofurantoin, a quinolone, trimethoprim, or co-trimoxazole) was taken less than 2 hours after sexual intercourse.
  - This option is appropriate when recurrent cystitis is related to intercourse and risk factors have been managed.

[Cooper and Jepson, 2001]

Infection occurring while taking prophylactic antibiotics

- Infection occurring while taking prophylactic antibiotics indicates resistance to the prophylactic agent. Urine culture should be carried out to ensure treatment with a drug to which the organism is sensitive.
- After eradication of the acute infection consider restarting prophylaxis with an antibiotic active against the responsible organism.
- Specialist advice should be sought if prophylaxis fails repeatedly.

Cystitis/asymptomatic bacteriuria in pregnancy

Asymptomatic bacteriuria in pregnancy

- For women who are pregnant, a urine sample should be cultured to screen for bacteriuria.
- **Treatment of asymptomatic bacteriuria reduces the risk of pyelonephritis, pre-term delivery, and low birthweight.** A Cochrane review found that treatment reduces the incidence of pyelonephritis (NNT = 7, CI 6–9). It also found some evidence that treatment reduces the incidence of pre-term delivery and low birthweight [Smaill, 2001].
- A Cochrane review found insufficient evidence to assess the effects of different durations of treatment for asymptomatic bacteriuria in pregnancy [Villar et al, 2001].
- After treatment of asymptomatic bacteriuria, women should have a urine culture monthly throughout pregnancy [Gilstrap and Whalley, 1998].

women whose initial screening urine culture is negative have a less than 1% risk of subsequent urinary tract infection during pregnancy [Gilstrap and Whalley, 1998].

Antibiotics for cystitis/asymptomatic bacteriuria in pregnancy

- A Cochrane review found evidence that antibiotic treatment effectively cures urinary tract infection (UTI) in pregnancy, but concluded that there is insufficient evidence to prefer any of the antibiotics that are safe in pregnancy [Vazquez and Villar, 2001].
- **Cephalosporins** are recommended in pregnancy because of their long-term safety record and efficacy.
- **Penicillins:** these are associated with a high incidence of bacterial resistance and should not be used without laboratory confirmation of sensitivity.
- **Nitrofurantoin** should not be prescribed if the mother is glucose-6-phosphate dehydrogenase (G6PD)-deficient. It can otherwise be used during pregnancy, but should not be taken near term as it can cause haemolysis in a G6PD-deficient infant.
- **Trimethoprim** can also be used to treat acute infections during pregnancy [Cattell, 1997; National Teratology Information Service, Personal Communication, 2001]. It is a folate antagonist and should be avoided in women with known folate deficiency or on another folate antagonist unless they are taking folate supplementation.
- **Quinolones** are not recommended for use during any trimester because arthropathy has been seen in animal studies.
- **Co-amoxiclav** is not recommended for use during pregnancy, as there is insufficient data on the safety of clavulanic acid [National Teratology Information Service, Personal Communication, 2001].
- **Pivmecillinam** is not recommended for use during pregnancy, as there is insufficient usage data.
- Local microbiology departments are able to provide help if there is difficulty in selecting an appropriate antibiotic.

Duration of treatment of cystitis in pregnancy

- A 7-day course of an antibiotic is recommended: a Cochrane review found insufficient evidence to favour a shorter regime [Vazquez and Villar, 2001].

Relapse and recurrence of cystitis in pregnancy

- If cultures remain positive after 7 days of treatment, or if symptoms return, seek specialist advice. Prophylactic treatment with nitrofurantoin for the remainder of the pregnancy is usually recommended, although it should be stopped before term.

Cystitis/asymptomatic bacteriuria in elderly women

U

Evidence base

- Studies on treatment of urinary tract infection (UTI) in the elderly are in general of poor quality [Lutters and Vogt, 2000].

Presentation

- Cystitis in elderly women may present with non-specific features such as secondary incontinence, confusion, anorexia, high temperature, or shock.

Asymptomatic bacteriuria

- Asymptomatic bacteriuria or pyuria in the elderly does not need to be investigated or treated, as there is evidence that treatment does not improve outcome [McMurdo and Gillespie, 2000].

Symptomatic bacteriuria (cystitis)

- Cystitis in an elderly woman should be treated with antibiotics for 7 days, but otherwise follow the princip of treatment of UTI in younger women.
- Cystoscopy is occasionally indicated when urinary trac abnormalities are suspected.
- Recurrent symptomatic cystitis in elderly women may due to atrophic vaginitis.
  - Topical or oral oestrogens promote the growth of *Lactobacillus* species by returning vaginal epithelial cells to the premenopausal state that may protect against infection.
  - Oestrogen therapy may also increase urethral pressu and improve incontinence.
  - A systematic review found evidence from a small number of small trials to support the use of topical oestrogens in preventing recurrent UTIs in postmenopausal women [Cardozo et al, 2001].

Urinary tract infections in women with chronic indwelling urinary catheters

Background

- All people with indwelling urinary catheters will have bacteriuria at some stage.
- Urine culture is indicated only in symptomatic patients
- Solid surfaces (e.g. catheter, stone) in the urinary tract tend to be covered soon after their introduction by a biofilm of microbes embedded in an organic polymer matrix primarily produced by the microbes. Antibiotic may fail to eradicate bacteria sequestered in the biofilm
- A systematic review failed to find evidence of benefit fo continuous prophylactic antibiotics in people with neurogenic bladder caused by spinal cord dysfunction [Morton et al, 2002].

Prevention

- Intermittent urethral catheterization rarely results in symptomatic lower urinary tract infection. Therefore, i possible, use intermittent catheterization rather than a indwelling catheter.
- High fluid intake promotes urine flow and tends to prevent symptomatic infection.
- Consider routine, regular replacement of the catheter i there are frequent recurrent UTIs. We could find no evidence on which to base a recommendation about th frequency of replacement.

Management

- Asymptomatic bacteriuria does not need to be treated with antibiotics.
- Measures for treating symptomatic infection include:
  - Catheter replacement (especially if it is blocked or ha been *in situ* for some time).
  - Analgesics/antipyretics.
  - A first-line antibiotic for 7 days.

[Stamm and Hooton, 1993; Reid et al, 1998; AHCPR, 1999; Raz et al, 2000; Nicolle, 2001; Biering-Sorensen, 2002]

Urethral syndrome

Symptoms of the urethral syndrome are similar to those i acute cystitis, but urine tests show no pathogenic bacteria

Acute urethral syndrome

- Use a urine dipstick in the first instance to rule out infection. If symptoms do not resolve within 3 days or i they frequently recur, then send urine for culture.
- Explanation and reassurance may be all that is require

Analgesics help relieve dysuria.
rumfitt et al, 1998]

hronic urethral syndrome (more than three pisodes per year)

Rule out infection by checking a urine culture and empirical treatment with a 3-day course of an antibiotic (as for acute cystitis).
Consider underlying psychological conditions (although these are rare).
Surgical interventions have not been shown to improve symptoms.
Less invasive treatments that have been tried include acupuncture and diazepam, but there is insufficient evidence to recommend their use.
Referral for urological assessment may be indicated when symptoms remain intolerable despite the above measures.
rumfitt et al, 1998]

eferences

IS staff in England can link, free of charge, from erences to full text journals by clicking on [Full text] on PRODIGY website.

AHCPR (1999) *Prevention and management of urinary tract infections in paralyzed persons.* Evidence report/ technology assessment: no. 6. Rockville, MD: Agency for Health Care Policy and Research.

Ahmad, T., Vickers, D., Campbell, S. et al (1991) Urine collection from disposable nappies. *Lancet* 338(8768), 674–676. [Full text]

Baerheim, A. (2001) Empirical treatment of uncomplicated cystitis. *British Medical Journal* 323(7323), 1197–1198. [Full text]

Belmin, J., Hervias, Y., Avellano, E. et al (1993) Reliability of sampling urine from disposable diapers in elderly incontinent women. *Journal of the American Geriatrics Society* 41(11), 1182–1186.

Biering-Sorensen, F. (2002) Urinary tract infection in individuals with spinal cord lesion. *Current Opinion in Urology* 12(1), 45–49.

BNF 42 (2001) *British National Formulary.* 42nd edn. London: British Medical Association and Royal Pharmaceutical Society of Great Britain.

Brumfitt, W., Hamilton-Miller, J .M., Cooper, J. and Raeburn, A. (1990) Relationship of urinary pH to symptoms of 'cystitis'. *Postgraduate Medical Journal* 66(779), 727–729.

Brumfitt, W., Hamilton-Miller, J. and Bailey, R.R. (Eds.) (1998) *Urinary tract infections.* London: Chapman & Hall Medical.

Cardozo, L., Lose, G., McClish, D. et al (2001) A systematic review of estrogens for recurrent urinary tract infections: third report of the hormones and urogenital therapy (HUT) committee. *International Urogynecology Journal and Pelvic Floor Dysfunction* 12(1), 15–20.

. Cattell, W.R. (1997) Renal disease: II. Urinary tract infection in women. *Journal of the Royal College of Physicians of London* 31(2), 130–133.

. Cooper, B. and Jepson, R. (2001) Recurrent cystitis in non-pregnant women. *Clinical Evidence* 5(Jun), 1338–1345.

. Cunningham, F.G. and Lucas, M.J. (1994) Urinary tract infections complicating pregnancy. *Baillieres Clinical Obstetrics & Gynaecology* 8(2), 353–373.

. Dawson, C. and Whitfield, H. (1996) ABC of urology: urinary incontinence and urinary infection. *British Medical Journal* 312(7036), 961–964. [Full text]

14. DH and SMAC (1998) *The path of least resistance.* Department of Health. www.dh.gov.uk [Accessed: 27/ 04/2004]. [Full text]

15. DTB (1998) Managing urinary tract infection in women. *Drug & Therapeutics Bulletin* 36(4), 30–32. [Full text]

16. Fenwick, E.A.L., Briggs, A.H. and Hawke, C.I. (2000) Management of urinary tract infection in general practice: a cost-effectiveness analysis. *British Journal of General Practice* 50(457), 635–639.

17. Fihn, S.D., Latham, R.H., Roberts, P. et al (1985) Association between diaphragm use and urinary tract infection. *Journal of the American Medical Association* 254(2), 240–245.

18. Fihn, S.D., Boyko, E.J., Chen, C.L. et al (1998) Use of spermicide-coated condoms and other risk factors for urinary tract infection caused by Staphylococcus saprophyticus. *Archives of Internal Medicine* 158(3), 281–287. [Full text]

19. Gilstrap, L.C. and Whalley, P.J. (1998) Asymptomatic bacteriuria during pregnancy. In: Brumfitt, W., Hamilton-Miller, J., Bailey, R.R. et al (Eds.) *Urinary tract infections.* London: Chapman & Hall Medical. 199–209.

20. Gossius, G. and Vorland, L. (1984) A randomised comparison of single-dose vs. three-day and ten-day therapy with trimethoprim-sulfamethoxazole for acute cystitis in women. *Scandinavian Journal of Infectious Diseases* 16(4), 373–379.

21. Gould, K., Orr, K. and Bint, A. (2001) *GP antimicrobial prescribing guidelines.* Newcastle upon Tyne: Newcastle and North Tyneside NHS Health Authority.

22. Gupta, K., Hooton, T.M., Roberts, P.L. and Stamm, W.E. (2001) Patient-initiated treatment of uncomplicated recurrent urinary tract infections in young women. *Annals of Internal Medicine* 135(1), 9–16.

23. Hurlbut, T.A. and Littenberg, B. (1991) The diagnostic accuracy of rapid dipstick tests to predict urinary tract infection. *American Journal of Clinical Pathology* 96(5), 582–588.

24. Jepson, R.G., Mihaljevic, L. and Craig, J. (1998) *Cranberries for the prevention of urinary tract infections (Cochrane Review).* The Cochrane Library. Issue 4. Oxford: Update Software.

25. Jepson, R.G., Mihaljevic, L. and Craig, J. (2000) *Cranberries for treating urinary infections (Cochrane Review).* The Cochrane Library. Issue 2. Oxford: Update Software.

26. Jewkes, F.E., McMaster, D.J., Napier, W.A. et al (1990) Home collection of urine specimens–boric acid bottles or Dipslides? *Archives of Disease in Childhood* 65(3), 286–289.

27. Kalowski, S., Radford, N. and Kincaid-Smith, P. (1974) Crystalline and macrocrystalline nitrofurantoin in the treatment of urinary-tract infection. *New England Journal of Medicine* 290(7), 385–387.

28. Kontiokari, T., Sundqvist, K., Nuutinen, M. et al (2001) Randomised trial of cranberry-lingonberry juice and Lactobacillus GG drink for the prevention of urinary tract infections in women. *British Medical Journal* 322(7302), 1571. [Full text]

29. Lammers, R.L., Gibson, S., Kovacs, D. et al (2001) Comparison of test characteristics of urine dipstick and urinalysis at various test cutoff points. *Annals of Emergency Medicine* 38(5), 505–512.

30. Lawrenson, R.A. and Logie, J.W. (2001) Antibiotic failure in the treatment of urinary tract infections in young women. *Journal of Antimicrobial Chemotherapy* 48(6), 895–901. [Full text]

31. Leibovici, L. and Wysenbeek, A.J. (1991a) Single-dose treatment of urinary tract infections with and without antibody-coated bacteria: a metaanalysis of controlled trials. *Journal of Infectious Diseases* **163**(4), 928–929.
32. Leibovici, L. and Wysenbeek, A.J. (1991b) Single-dose antibiotic treatment for symptomatic urinary tract infections in women: a meta-analysis of randomized trials. *Quarterly Journal of Medicine* **78**(285), 43–57.
33. Leigh, D.A., Faiers, M.C. and Brumfitt, W. (1970) Laboratory and clinical studies with cephalexin. *Postgraduate Medical Journal* **Suppl**, 69–74.
34. Lifshitz, E. and Kramer, L. (2000) Outpatient urine culture: does collection technique matter? *Archives of Internal Medicine* **160**(16), 2537–2540. [Full text]
35. Lutters, M. and Vogt, N. (2000) What's the basis for treating infections your way? Quality assessment of review articles on the treatment of urinary and respiratory tract infections in older people. *Journal of the American Geriatrics Society* **48**(11), 1454–1461.
36. Manges, A.R., Johnson, J.R., Foxman, B. et al (2001) Widespread distribution of urinary tract infections caused by a multidrug-resistant Escherichia coli clonal group. *New England Journal of Medicine* **345**(14), 1007–1013. [Full text]
37. McIsaac, W.J., Low, D.E., Biringer, A. et al (2002) The impact of empirical management of acute cystitis on unnecessary antibiotic use. *Archives of Internal Medicine* **162**(5), 600–605. [Full text]
38. McMurdo, M.E. and Gillespie, N.D. (2000) Urinary tract infection in old age: over-diagnosed and over-treated. *Age & Ageing* **29**(4), 297–298. [Full text]
39. McNulty, C. (2002) *Personal communication.* Medical Microbiologist, HPA Primary Care Unit: Gloucestershire Royal Hospital, Gloucester.
40. MeReC (1995) Urinary tract infection. *MeReC Bulletin* **6**(8),
41. Morton, S.C., Shekelle, P.G., Adams, J.L. et al (2002) Antimicrobial prophylaxis for urinary tract infection in persons with spinal cord dysfunction. *Archives of Physical Medicine & Rehabilitation* **83**(1), 129–138.
42. National Teratology Information Service (2001) *Personal communication.* NHS Northern and Yorkshire Regional Drug and Therapeutics Centre: Wolfson Unit, Claremont Place, Newcastle upon Tyne.
43. NICE (2005) *Referral guidelines for suspected cancer – quick reference guide.* Clinical guideline 27. National Institute for Health and Clinical Excellence. www.nice.org.uk [Accessed: 01/07/2005].
44. Nicolle, L.E. (2001) The chronic indwelling catheter and urinary infection in long-term-care facility residents. *Infection Control and Hospital Epidemiology* **22**(5), 316–321. [Full text]
45. Nicolle, L.E. and Ronald, A.R. (1998) Recurrent urinary infection and its prevention. In: Brumfitt, W., Hamilton-Miller, J., Bailey, R.R. et al (Eds.) *Urinary tract infections.* London: Chapman & Hall Medical. 293–301.
46. Niewoehner, D.E., Rice, K., Cote, C. et al (2005) Prevention of Exacerbations of Chronic Obstructive Pulmonary Disease with Tiotropium, a Once-Daily Inhaled Anticholinergic Bronchodilator: A Randomized Trial. *Annals of Internal Medicine* **143**(5), 317–326.
47. Parfitt, K. (Ed.) (1999) *Martindale.* 32nd edn. London: Pharmaceutical Press.
48. Pedler, S. (2002) *Personal communication.* Consultant Microbiologist, Royal Victoria Infirmary: Newcastle upon Tyne.
49. PHLS (2001) *Management of infection: guidance for primary care.* Public Health Laboratory Service. www.hpa.org.uk [Accessed: 03/02/2002].
50. Priest, P., Yudkin, P., McNulty, C. and Mant, D. (2001) Antibacterial prescribing and antibacterial resistance in English general practice: cross sectional study. *British Medical Journal* **323**(7320), 1037–104 [Full text]
51. Raz, R., Schiller, D. and Nicolle, L.E. (2000) Chroni indwelling catheter replacement before antimicrobia therapy for symptomatic urinary tract infection. *Journal of Urology* **164**(4), 1254–1258.
52. Read, R.C. (2000) Drugs in focus: newer oral fluoroquinolone antibacterials. *Prescribers' Journal* **40**(2), 147–151.
53. Reid, G., van der Mei, H.C. and Busscher, H.J. (199 Microbial biofilms and urinary tract infections. In: Brumfitt, W., Hamilton-Miller, J., Bailey, R.R. et al (Eds.) *Urinary tract infections.* London: Chapman & Hall Medical. 111–116.
54. Sanderson, P.J. (1998) Laboratory methods. In: Brumfitt, W., Hamilton-Miller, J., Bailey, R.R. et al (Eds.) *Urinary tract infections.* London: Chapman & Hall Medical.
55. Smaill, F. (2001) *Antibiotics for asymptomatic bacteriuria in pregnancy (Cochrane Review).* The Cochrane Library. Issue 1. Oxford: Update Software
56. Stamm, W.E. (1998) Urinary tract infections and pyelonephritis. In: *Harrison's Principles of Internal Medicine.* New York: McGraw-Hill.
57. Stamm, W.E. (2001) An epidemic of urinary tract infections? *New England Journal of Medicine* **345**(1 1055–1057. [Full text]
58. Stamm, W.E. and Hooton, T.M. (1993) Managemen of urinary tract infections in adults. *New England Journal of Medicine* **329**(18), 1328–1334.
59. Steinke, D.T., Seaton, R.A., Phillips, G. et al (2001) Prior trimethoprim use and trimethoprim-resistant urinary tract infection: a nested case-control study w multivariate analysis for other risk factors. *Journal o Antimicrobial Chemotherapy* **47**(6), 781–787. [Full text]
60. Tran, D., Muchant, D.G. and Aronoff, S.C. (2001) Short-course versus conventional length antimicrobi therapy for uncomplicated lower urinary tract infections in children: a meta-analysis of 1279 patien *Journal of Pediatrics* **139**(1), 93–99.
61. Vazquez, J.C. and Villar, J. (2001) *Treatments for symptomatic urinary tract infections during pregnan (Cochrane Review).* The Cochrane Library. Issue 3. Oxford: Update Software.
62. Villar, J., Ba'aqeel, H., Piaggio, G. et al (2001) WHO antenatal care randomised trial for the evaluation of new model of routine antenatal care. *Lancet* **357**(9268), 1551–1564. [Full text]
63. Wallach, F.R. (2001) Infectious disease. Update on treatment of pneumonia, influenza, and urinary tract infections. *Geriatrics* **56**(9), 43–47.
64. Walter, F.G. and Knopp, R.K. (1989) Urine samplin in ambulatory women: midstream clean-catch versus catheterization. *Annals of Emergency Medicine* **18**(2 166–172.
65. Watson, P.G. and Duerden, B.I. (1977) Laboratory assessment of physical and chemical methods of preserving urine specimens. *Journal of Clinical Pathology* **30**(6), 532–536.
66. Wise, R. and Andrews, J.M. (1998) Local surveillanc of antimicrobial resistance. Synercid Resistance Surveillance Group. *Lancet* **352**(9128), 657–658. [Fu text]

U

PRODIGY GUIDANCE

Urinary tract infection — children

Last revised in April 2002
www.prodigy.nhs.uk/guidance.asp?gt=UTI - children

Applies to children under the age of 15 years

This guidance covers the management of children with urinary tract infection (UTI) undifferentiated with respect to location (i.e. upper or lower urinary tract).

This guidance does not cover the management of UTI in adults.

There is separate PRODIGY guidance for *Pyelonephritis — acute, UTI (lower) — women*, and *UTI (lower) — men.*

Goals

Prompt recognition of UTI, especially in babies and young children in whom presenting features are non-specific
Accurate diagnosis, appropriate therapy
Symptom relief
Eradication of infection
Prevention of recurrence and complications
Detection and management of predisposing and associated conditions

Contents

Scenarios

- Urinary tract infections in children p.1831
- Prophylactic antibiotic therapy p.1834

Extended Information, p. 1835

Which scenario?

Urinary tract infections in children: covers the management of children (under 16 years old) with UTI (undifferentiated with respect to lower or upper tract involvement).
Prophylactic antibiotic therapy: covers management when prophylactic antibiotic therapy is to be prescribed. This will usually be as an interim measure when waiting for dimercaptosuccinic acid scan results or when waiting for specialist assessment of the need for long-term prophylaxis for recurrent UTI.

Urinary tract infections in children

Which therapy?

Follow local guidelines. Consider modifying therapy according to local bacterial resistance patterns.
Rule out or manage associated conditions, such as urinary tract obstruction, constipation, vulval irritation, threadworms, and incomplete bladder emptying.
Culture urine (before starting antibiotic therapy).
Start a 7-day course of a preferred antibiotic (without waiting for the culture results).
- Preferred antibiotics:
  - Trimethoprim
  - Nitrofurantoin
  - Cefalexin

Review choice of antibiotic with progress and results of culture.
Treat pain and high temperature with paracetamol or ibuprofen.

- Advise parents/caregivers about possible recurrence of urinary tract infections:
  - Repeated urinary tract infections (UTIs) need prompt recognition and early treatment.
- Children awaiting a dimercaptosuccinic acid (DMSA) scan should receive prophylactic low-dose antibiotics.

Breakthrough infections in children on prophylactic antibiotic therapy
- Treat as for an acute UTI, but choose an antibiotic different from the prophylactic agent.
- Consider non-compliance if the offending organism is susceptible to the agent used for prophylaxis.

Practical prescribing points

For further information see the *Medicines Compendium* (www.medicines.org.uk) or the *British National Formulary* (www.bnf.org).
- **Trimethoprim** may rarely cause blood dyscrasias and skin disorders. In moderate renal impairment, the dose of trimethoprim should be reduced; and in very severe renal impairment the drug should be avoided.
- **Nitrofurantoin** is contraindicated in children with renal impairment. There is a risk of peripheral neuropathy, and urine concentrations would be inadequate for effective treatment. It should not be used in children who are known to be G6PD (glucose-6-phosphate dehydrogenase) deficient.
- **Cefalexin** in high dosages may cause diarrhoea and, rarely, pseudomembranous colitis.
- **Ibuprofen** (and other NSAIDs) may worsen asthma in children.

Follow-up advice

- Review according to the clinical situation (e.g. at around 48 hours) to ensure that the child is responding to treatment, and to reassess the choice of antibiotic in the light of the urine culture result.
- Repeat urine culture at least 24 hours after completing the course of antibiotics to ensure that infection has been eradicated.
- Children with recurrent UTIs or abnormalities of the urinary tract should be started on low-dose prophylactic antibiotics, and referred for specialist assessment and management.
- Children who have abnormal imaging studies should have follow-up plans developed in conjunction with secondary care services.

Should I refer or investigate?

Refer?

- **Follow local referral guidelines if these exist.**
- **Admit:**

- Children with sepsis, or dehydration, or vomiting and an inability to tolerate oral fluids and medication.
- Neonates and infants (unless the child is relatively well, a confident diagnosis has been made, and management is within the competence of the general practice and parents).
- The younger the child, the lower the threshold is for admission.
- **Refer urgently to a paediatric surgeon or urologist:**
  - When there is evidence of urinary outflow obstruction or stone.
- **Refer promptly when:**
  - The diagnosis of uncomplicated UTI is in doubt.
  - The child has an anatomical abnormality of the urinary tract.
  - The child has recently undergone instrumentation of the urinary tract.
  - It is necessary to arrange imaging of the urinary tract to rule out obstructions (including calculi), anatomical defects, and dysfunctional bladder emptying.
  - Imaging of urinary tract is abnormal.
  - The child is under 5 years of age.
  - There is failure to respond to therapy.
  - There have been repeated UTIs (two or more episodes).
- If indicated, organize ultrasonography of the genito-urinary tract (including residual post-voiding volume) to be performed before specialist assessment.

Investigate?

Follow local investigation guidelines if these exist.
The *Background* and *Management issues* sections give detailed guidance on investigations.

Urine culture

- **Indications:**
  - All children with signs or symptoms suggestive of UTI, irrespective of dipstick test results (e.g. dysuria, frequency)
  - Any infant with a high temperature but no clinically definite source of infection (e.g. a red eardrum in a crying child does not rule out the need for a urine culture)
  - Secondary enuresis
  - Haematuria, hypertension
  - Children of any age with recurrent or persistent fever, general ill health, unexplained abdominal pain or vomiting
  - Neonates with prolonged jaundice
  - Neonates and young infants who fail to thrive or who are feeding poorly
- **Repeat urine culture** at least 24 hours after completing the course of antibiotics to ensure that infection has been eradicated.

U

Urine dipstick tests

- Urine dipstick tests are the most widely used near-patient test for UTI.
- **Dipstick tests cannot be relied on to exclude or to confirm a diagnosis of UTI in a child.**
  - When UTI is probable (symptoms and signs of UTI):
    - A positive nitrite or leucocyte esterase (LE) test confirms UTI.
    - Negative tests do not exclude UTI.
  - When UTI is unlikely (asymptomatic):
    - A positive nitrite or LE test does not confirm UTI.
    - Negative tests do not exclude UTI.
- **Culture the urine to guide any management decision made using dipstick tests.**

Urine microscopy

- **Urine microscopy, if available, is a quick and accurate near patient screening test.**

Imaging of the urinary tract

Follow local guidelines if available; otherwise, arrange investigations as given in Table 1.

Table 1: Investigations to be arranged after UTI diagnose

Investigation	Indications	To look for	When
Ultrasound of the kidneys, ureters and bladder, including post-voiding residual urine volume	All children with UTI (except older girls with typical uncomplicated cystitis)	Obstructions (including calculi and urethral valves), anatomical defects, post-voiding volume, etc.	As soon as convenient an if possible, before speciali review
DMSA scan	Children aged under 5 years of age with first UTI Abnormal ultrasound All children with recurrent UTIs	Renal scarring	At least 3 months after t acute episode (allow transie lesions to resolve)
Cystogram	Infants aged under 1 year Abnormal DMSA scan Abnormal ultrasound (e.g. mega-ureter)	Vesicoureteric reflux	After urine ha been sterilized

Patient information leaflets

The following PILs are available at www.prodigy.nhs.uk

- Intravenous Urography
- Kidney Infection (Pyelonephritis)
- Midstream Specimen of Urine (MSU)
- Urine Infection in Young Children

Shared decision making

- **An antibiotic** taken for 7 days is the usual treatment fo children with a urinary infection.
- It may be necessary to admit very young or ill children hospital.
- Referral to a specialist is usual. This is to check for any problems of the kidney or bladder. These are uncommon, but it is best that they should be checked out.
- **Plenty of fluids** should be given to the child.
- **Paracetamol or ibuprofen** will help to ease pain or a hig temperature.
- If a urine culture test is done, the results will be ready i 2 or 3 days. Telephone to check the result of the test an ask for advice.
- **A daily low dose of antibiotic** is usual for young childre once the infection is cleared until tests are complete. Th prevents further infections until it is known that there i no bladder or kidney problem.

Drug rationale

Drugs not included

- **Penicillins such as amoxicillin** are unsuitable for therap unless the culture results indicate that the bacterium is sensitive. Around 50% of urinary pathogens are amoxicillin resistant.

First-generation cephalosporins other than cefalexin have similar antibiotic sensitivities, similar adverse effects, and are more expensive.
Second-generation cephalosporins are not so well absorbed orally as first-generation cephalosporins; they have a greater incidence of gastrointestinal adverse effects, and are more expensive than the first-generation agents.
Third-generation cephalosporins generally require parenteral administration and are reserved for use in secondary care for serious infections.
Co-amoxiclav should be reserved for use when preferred therapy has failed, or when sensitivity results indicate it is appropriate.
Quinolones are not recommended in children and growing adolescents because arthropathy has occurred in studies in young animals. However, quinolones are sometimes initiated in secondary care. **Nalidixic acid** is the only quinolone licensed for use in children for urinary tract infection; it carries the same risk of arthropathy as the other quinolones. Most microbiology laboratories would not routinely screen for sensitivity to this agent.
Co-trimoxazole is restricted to certain indications by the Committee on Safety of Medicines (CSM), and should be used only if there is evidence of bacterial sensitivity.
Urine alkalinizing agents are not included as there is some evidence that do not relieve the symptoms of cystitis [Brumfitt et al, 1990].
[Royal College of Paediatrics and Child Health, 1999; BNF 42, 2001]

Drugs included

A 7-day course of all agents for children is recommended — this is in line with Public Health Laboratory Service, *Drug & Therapeutics Bulletin*, and *MeReC Bulletin* advice.
Trimethoprim is effective against most urinary pathogens and is suitable for use in children. It should not be used for an acute infection if the child has had infections that were resistant to this agent, or has recently taken trimethoprim.
Nitrofurantoin is effective against most urinary pathogens. Nitrofurantoin 25 mg per 5 ml suspension has recently been licensed in the UK. Tablets are suitable for older children. The macrocrystalline capsules, which may be better tolerated if nausea is troublesome, are offered as an alternative. The modified-release formulation is not licensed for use in children under 12 years of age, but it is an option for 12–16-year-olds.
Cefalexin is a first-generation cephalosporin effective against most urinary pathogens, and is suitable for use in children.
Paracetamol is an effective and safe analgesic and antipyretic agent.
Ibuprofen is an effective alternative to paracetamol if there are no contraindications.
[DTB, 1997; Royal College of Paediatrics and Child Health, 1999; BNF 42, 2001; PHLS, 2001]

Prescriptions

First-line antibiotics for 7 days

Trimethoprim s/f suspension: 4mg/kg twice a day
- Age from 2 to 5 months
- Trimethoprim 50mg/5ml s/f susp. *WEIGHT REQUIRED* Take 4mg per kg bodyweight TWICE a day for 7 days; supply 70 ml; NHS Cost £1.24.

Trimethoprim s/f suspension: 50mg twice a day
- Age from 6 months to 5 years
- Trimethoprim 50mg/5ml s/f susp. Take one 5ml spoonful twice a day for 7 days; supply 70 ml; NHS Cost £1.24.

Trimethoprim s/f suspension: 100mg twice a day
- Age from 6 to 11 years
- Trimethoprim 50mg/5ml s/f susp. Take two 5ml spoonfuls twice a day for 7 days; supply 140 ml; NHS Cost £2.48.

Trimethoprim tablets: 200mg twice a day
- Age from 12 to 15 years
- Trimethoprim 200mg tablets. Take one tablet twice a day for 7 days; supply 14 tablets; NHS Cost £0.67.

Nitrofurantoin s/f suspension: 750mcg/kg four times a day
- Age from 3 months to 9 years
- Nitrofurantoin 25mg/5ml sf susp. *WEIGHT REQUIRED* Take 750micrograms per kg bodyweight FOUR times a day for 7 days; supply 200 ml; NHS Cost £65.00.

Nitrofurantoin tablets: 50mg four times a day
- Age from 10 to 15 years
- Nitrofurantoin 50mg tablets. Take one tablet four times a day for 7 days; supply 28 tablets; NHS Cost £2.47.

Nitrofurantoin capsules: 50mg four times a day
- Age from 10 to 15 years
- Nitrofurantoin 50mg capsules. Take one capsule four times a day for 7 days; supply 28 capsules; NHS Cost £2.85.

Nitrofurantoin m/r capsules: 100mg twice a day
- Age from 12 to 15 years
- Nitrofurantoin 100mg m/r caps. Take one capsule twice a day for 7 days; supply 14 capsules; NHS Cost £4.89.

Cefalexin mixture:12.5mg/kg twice a day
- Age from 3 to 11 months
- Cefalexin 125mg/5ml mixture. *WEIGHT REQUIRED* Take 12.5mg per kg bodyweight TWICE a day for 7 days; supply 100 ml; NHS Cost £1.33.

Cefalexin mixture: 125mg three times a day
- Age from 12 months to 5 years
- Cefalexin 125mg/5ml mixture. Take one 5ml spoonful three times a day for 7 days; supply 100 ml; NHS Cost £1.33.

Cefalexin mixture: 250mg three times a day
- Age from 6 to 11 years
- Cefalexin 250mg/5ml mixture. Take one 5ml spoonful three times a day for 7 days; supply 100 ml; NHS Cost £2.32.

Cefalexin tablets: 500mg twice a day
- Age from 12 to 15 years
- Cefalexin 500mg tablets. Take one tablet twice a day for 7 days; supply 14 tablets; NHS Cost £2.44.

Analgesia/antipyretics: use when required

Paracetamol s/f susp: 60mg to 120mg up to four times a day
- Age from 3 to 11 months
- Paracetamol 120mg/5ml s/f susp. Take 2.5ml to 5ml every 4 to 6 hours when required for relief of pain or high temperature. Maximum of 4 doses in 24 hours; supply 150 ml; NHS Cost £0.65; OTC Cost £1.15.

Paracetamol s/f susp: 120mg to 240mg up to four times a day
- Age from 12 months to 5 years
- Paracetamol 120mg/5ml s/f susp. Take one to two 5ml spoonfuls every 4 to 6 hours when required for relief of pain or high temperature. Maximum of 4 doses in 24 hours; supply 300 ml; NHS Cost £1.24; OTC Cost £2.18.

Paracetamol s/f susp: 250mg to 500mg up to four times a day

- Age from 6 to 11 years
- Paracetamol 250mg/5ml s/f susp. Take one to two 5ml spoonfuls every 4 to 6 hours when required for relief of pain or high temperature. Maximum of 4 doses in 24 hours; supply 300 ml; NHS Cost £1.53; OTC Cost £2.70.

Paracetamol tablets: 500mg to 1g up to four times a day

- Age from 12 to 15 years
- Paracetamol 500mg tablets. Take one to two tablets every 4 to 6 hours when required for relief of pain or high temperature. Maximum of 8 tablets in 24 hours; supply 50 tablets; NHS Cost £0.38; OTC Cost £0.66.

Ibuprofen s/f susp: 50mg three to four times a day

- Age from 12 months to 2 years
- Ibuprofen 100mg/5ml s/f susp. Take 2.5ml three to four times a day when required for relief of pain or high temperature. Do not exceed the stated dose; supply 100 ml; NHS Cost £2.00; OTC Cost £3.53.

Ibuprofen s/f susp: 100mg three to four times a day

- Age from 3 to 7 years
- Ibuprofen 100mg/5ml s/f susp. Take one 5ml spoonful 3 to 4 times a day when required for relief of pain or high temperature. Do not exceed the stated dose; supply 150 ml; NHS Cost £2.73; OTC Cost £4.81.

Ibuprofen s/f susp: 200mg three to four times a day

- Age from 8 to 11 years
- Ibuprofen 100mg/5ml s/f susp. Take two 5ml spoonfuls 3 to 4 times a day when required for relief of pain or high temperature. Do not exceed the stated dose; supply 300 ml; NHS Cost £5.46; OTC Cost £9.62.

Ibuprofen tablets: 400mg three times a day

- Age from 12 to 15 years
- Ibuprofen 400mg tablets. Take one tablet three times a day when required for relief of pain or high temperature. Do not exceed the stated dose; supply 24 tablets; NHS Cost £0.70; OTC Cost £1.75.

Prophylactic antibiotic therapy

Which therapy?

Follow local guidelines. Consider modifying therapy according to local bacterial resistance patterns.

- **Treat with prophylactic antibiotics while waiting for:**
  - Dimercaptosuccinic acid scan results
  - Referral appointment for assessment for possible long-term prophylaxis
- **Consider long-term prophylactic antibiotics if urinary tract infection (UTI) occurs more than once within a year.**
  - Check that predisposing conditions such as voiding dysfunction and constipation have been eliminated.
  - Refer for assessment before commencing long-term prophylactic antibiotics.
  - Start interim antibiotic prophylaxis while waiting for appointment.
- **Antibiotic prophylaxis**
  - Trimethoprim or nitrofurantoin are recommended for children under 12 years of age.
  - Tell parents/carers that it is important to adhere to the prescribed treatment because it is intended to prevent UTIs and renal complications.
- **Breakthrough infections**
  - Treat as for an acute UTI with a different antibiotic.
  - Consider non-compliance if the offending organism is susceptible to the agent used for prophylaxis.
- **Elimination**
  - Advise parents/carers to encourage regular eliminatic habits. 'Holding on' should be discouraged; this mak it more likely that the bowel and bladder are completely emptied.

Practical prescribing points

For further information see the *Medicines Compendium* (www.medicines.org.uk) or the *British National Formula* (www.bnf.org).

Follow local guidelines. Consider modifying therapy according to local bacterial resistance patterns.

- **Trimethoprim** may rarely cause blood dyscrasias and skin disorders. In moderate renal impairment, the dose of trimethoprim should be reduced; in very severe renal impairment the drug should be avoided.
- **Nitrofurantoin** is contraindicated in children with renal impairment. There is a risk of peripheral neuropathy, and urine concentrations would be inadequate for effective treatment. It should not be used in children wh are known to be G6PD (glucose-6-phosphate dehydrogenase) deficient.
- **Cefalexin** in high dosages may cause diarrhoea and, rarely, pseudomembranous colitis.

Should I refer or investigate?

Refer?

Follow local referral guidelines if these exist.

- Start prophylactic antibiotics and refer for assessment.
- Children under 4 years of age who have had two episodes of UTI would usually have long-term prophylactic antibiotics started in secondary care.

Investigate?

Follow local investigation guidelines if these exist.

- **Urine should be cultured for every episode of UTI.**
- Arrange ultrasonography of kidneys, ureters and bladd (including before and after micturition). If practical, thi should be done before referral.
- Other investigations are not routinely performed and would usually require referral.

Patient information leaflets

The following PILs are available at www.prodigy.nhs.uk

- Kidney Infection (Pyelonephritis)
- Midstream Specimen of Urine (MSU)
- Urine Infection in Young Children

Shared decision making

- **An antibiotic** is advised after a urinary infection in a child. This is to prevent further infections while awaitir tests.
- **Long-term antibiotic treatment** is advised if:
  - Two or more urinary infections occur in a young chi or
  - Tests show that there is an abnormality of the kidney or bladder.
- The aim is to limit the number of urinary infections anc to limit the damage done to the kidneys and bladder.

Drug rationale

Drugs not included

- **Antibiotics that are not licensed for prophylactic use in children under 12 years of age are not included.**

Jrine alkalinizing agents are not included as there is some evidence that do not relieve the symptoms of cystitis [Brumfitt et al, 1990].
oyal College of Paediatrics and Child Health, 1999; BNF , 2001]

ugs included

Trimethoprim is effective against most urinary pathogens. It is licensed for use in children more than 6 weeks old. It should not be used for an acute infection if the child has had infections resistant to this agent, or if the child has recently taken trimethoprim.
Nitrofurantoin is effective against most urinary pathogens. Nitrofurantoin 25 mg per 5 ml suspension has recently been licensed in the UK for use in children from 3 months of age. The tablet form is suitable for older children. The macrocrystalline capsules are an option when nausea is troublesome.
Cefalexin is licensed for prophylactic use in children over the age of 12 years.
TB, 1997; Royal College of Paediatrics and Child alth, 1999; BNF 42, 2001; PHLS, 2001; Williams et al, 01a]

rescriptions

terim or long-term antibiotic prophylaxis

methoprim s/f suspension: 2mg/kg at night
- Age from 2 to 5 months
- Trimethoprim 50mg/5ml s/f susp. *WEIGHT REQUIRED* Take 2mg per kg bodyweight at night; supply 100 ml; NHS Cost £1.77.

methoprim s/f suspension: 25mg at night
- Age from 6 months to 5 years
- Trimethoprim 50mg/5ml s/f susp. Take 2.5ml at night; supply 100 ml; NHS Cost £1.77.

methoprim s/f suspension: 50mg at night
- Age from 6 to 11 years
- Trimethoprim 50mg/5ml s/f susp. Take one 5ml spoonful at night; supply 150 ml; NHS Cost £2.66.

methoprim tablets: 100mg at night
- Age from 12 to 15 years
- Trimethoprim 100mg tablets. Take one tablet at night; supply 28 tablets; NHS Cost £0.67.

trofurantoin s/f suspension: 1mg/kg at night
- Age from 3 months to 9 years
- Nitrofurantoin 25mg/5ml sf susp. *WEIGHT REQUIRED* Take 1mg per kg bodyweight at night; supply 300 ml; NHS Cost £65.00.

trofurantoin tablets: 50mg at night
- Age from 10 to 15 years
- Nitrofurantoin 50mg tablets. Take one tablet at night; supply 28 tablets; NHS Cost £2.47.

trofurantoin capsules: 50mg at night
- Age from 10 to 15 years
- Nitrofurantoin 50mg capsules. Take one capsule at night; supply 30 capsules; NHS Cost £3.05.

trofurantoin capsules: 100mg at night
- Age from 10 to 15 years
- Nitrofurantoin 100mg capsules. Take one capsule at night; supply 30 capsules; NHS Cost £5.76.

efalexin mixture: 125mg at night
- Age from 12 to 15 years
- Cefalexin 125mg/5ml mixture. Take one 5ml spoonful at night; supply 200 ml; NHS Cost £2.66.

Cefalexin capsules: 250mg at night
- Age from 12 to 15 years
- Cefalexin 250mg capsules. Take one capsule at night; supply 28 capsules; NHS Cost £2.61.

Extended Information

Background information

- What is it? p.1835
- How common is it? p.1836
- Risk factors for urinary tract infection p.1836
- How do I know my patient has it? p.1836
- What else might it be? p.1838
- Complications and prognosis p.1838

What is it?

- **Bacteriuria** is the presence of bacteria in the urine.
- **Asymptomatic bacteriuria** is bacteriuria without symptoms.
- **Urinary tract infection (UTI)** comprises symptoms of infection together with the presence of pathogenic micro-organisms in the urine, urethra, bladder, or kidney. UTI is usually caused by bacteria from the gastrointestinal tract.
  - **Common organisms** causing UTI include:
    - *Escherichia coli*
    - *Staphylococcus saprophyticus*
    - *Proteus mirabilis* (its motility and adherence to uroepithelium facilitate movement up the urinary tract and invasive infection; urease production promotes stone formation)
  - **Less common organisms** causing UTI include:
    - *Proteus vulgaris*, *Klebsiella* species, *Enterobacter* species, *Citrobacter* species, *Serratia marcescens*, *Acinetobacter* species, *Pseudomonas* species, and *Staphylococcus aureus*
    - *Candida albicans* infection is rarely found in the community but it is common in hospital patients who have risk factors such as indwelling catheters, immunosuppression, diabetes mellitus, or antibiotic treatment
- **Undifferentiated UTI:** it is sometimes difficult to distinguish clinically between infections of the upper urinary tract and those of the lower tract. This is especially true in young children and the term 'UTI' is often used (as in this guidance) to refer to undifferentiated UTI.
- **The pragmatic criterion for diagnosing urinary tract infection** (and that used by the Public Health Laboratory Service) is detection of more than 10^5 organisms per millilitre of suitably collected urine. Urine cultures that grow multiple organisms usually indicate contamination or multiple urinary calculi. If the urine is collected under sterile conditions (e.g. suprapubic aspiration, or 'in-and-out' catheterization) colony counts as low as 10^2 to 10^4 per millilitre may indicate infection [Buys et al, 1994].
- **Recurrent UTI** is repeated episodes of UTI.
- **Relapse** is recurrent UTI with the same strain of organism (which suggests failure to eradicate the pathogen). In practice, because routine laboratory testing does not include typing to identify the strain, a UTI is considered to be a relapse if infection occurs within a short period (e.g. 2 weeks).
- **Reinfection** is recurrent UTI with a different strain or species of organism.
- **Uncomplicated UTI** is infection by a usual pathogen in a child with a normal urinary tract and with normal kidney function.
- **Complicated UTI is:**

U

- Virulent organism (e.g. *S aureus*)
- Abnormal urinary tract (e.g. calculus, vesicoureteric reflux, reflux nephropathy, neurogenic bladder, indwelling catheter, urinary obstruction)
- Impaired host defences (e.g. diabetes mellitus, immunosuppressive therapy)
- Impaired renal function

- **A renal scar** is a focal lesion in the kidney, detected best by a dimercaptosuccinic acid (DMSA) radionuclide scan. Extensive renal scarring in children may eventually lead to hypertension, pregnancy-induced hypertension, and chronic renal failure.
- **Vesicoureteric reflux** is reflux from the bladder up the ureter.

[Bailey, 1996; Brumfitt et al, 1998; Stamm, 1998; Cooper and Jepson, 2001; Lambert and Coulthard, 2002]

How common is it?

- Urinary tract infections (UTIs) are among the most common bacterial childhood infections and are responsible for about 5% of febrile bacterial illnesses in children under 2 years of age [Hoberman et al, 1993; Verrier-Jones K. et al, 2001].
- The criteria for selecting infants for urine testing vary, as do standards for urine collection and testing. There is thus variation in apparent rates of UTI [Deshpande and Jones, 2001; Roberts, 2002].
- Table 2 shows the cumulative incidence of UTI in children.

Risk factors for urinary tract infection

- **Most urinary tract infections (UTIs) are not associated with any risk factor. However, the following risk factors should be excluded or managed, especially if UTI recurs:**
  - Abnormalities of urinary tract function (e.g. outflow obstruction (such as posterior urethral valves in boys), anatomical abnormalities, indwelling catheter, neuropathic bladder)
  - Incomplete bladder emptying (e.g. dysfunctional urination)
  - Constipation (especially in younger children)
  - Previous urinary tract surgery
  - Immunocompromise

How do I know my patient has it?

Presentation of urinary tract infection in children

- The spectrum of illness extends from minor symptoms to life-threatening systemic illness.
- Fever may be mild or absent. Some authorities interpret high temperature (>38.5°C) to indicate pyelonephritis, but proof of upper urinary tract infection (UTI) requires imaging to demonstrate new lesions in renal tissue.
- The younger the child, the more diverse and less specific are the symptoms and signs of UTI:
  - **Neonate**
    - Fever
    - Prolonged jaundice
    - Poor feeding, failure to thrive
    - Severe systemic illness
  - **Infant**
    - Fever
    - Poor feeding, vomiting, diarrhoea
  - **Child**
    - Fever
    - Dysuria, frequency, urgency, nocturia, haematuria, cloudy or foul-smelling urine, suprapubic discomf or tenderness
    - Secondary incontinence

Investigations

Collection, storage, and transport of urine samples

- Careful collection, storage, and transport of urine samples minimizes contamination and deterioration.
- **In older children,** a clean-catch mid-stream urine samp can be collected with little difficulty, and is adequate fc diagnosis [Walter and Knopp, 1989].
- **In infants,** urine can conveniently be collected from an absorbent pad in the nappy [Vernon et al, 1994]. Alternatively, the clean-catch method or an adhesive b can be used. Occasionally in infants it may be necessar to obtain a suprapubic aspirate or use 'in-and-out' catheterization. Referral to secondary care would then be warranted.
- **In toddlers,** a potty is convenient. The potty should be cleaned with detergent and hot water (bleach should n be used because it may inhibit culture of bacteria) [Ree et al, 1996].
- **In girls,** the perineum should be wiped from front to back with a gauze swab moistened with water (antiseptics should be avoided because they may inhibi bacterial culture; cotton wool swabs should not be use because fibres may be confused under the microscope with casts) [Brumfitt et al, 1998]. A wide-mouthed gallipot or disposable funnel facilitates collecting a mid stream urine specimen from girls. Girls who are menstruating must take particular care to avoid contamination (e.g. by holding the labia apart while providing a clean-catch mid-stream urine specimen).
- **Containers:** urine should be transferred within 30 minutes of collection to a specimen bottle. The bottle should be filled if it contains boric acid because this preservative is bactericidal at high concentrations.
- **Storage:** urine should be refrigerated at 4°C while awaiting processing. Urine that has been stored at 4°C for 48 hours is suitable for culture, but not for microscopy because most cells would have disintegrate
- **False-negative culture** results are sometimes due to bori acid (stabilizer in the specimen bottle) or antibiotics tha are excreted in the urine.
- **Contamination** of the urine specimen is suggested by tl presence of one or more of the following:
  - Bacteria but no leucocytes (except in immunocompromised people)
  - Multiple organisms cultured
  - Blood, if the specimen is from a menstruating girl
- Laboratory reports usually mention the possibility of contamination if there are suspicious features but reporting criteria vary between laboratories.

[Verrier-Jones K. et al, 2001; Lambert and Coulthard, 2002]

Urine culture

- **Urine should be cultured whenever urinary tract infection (UTI) is suspected in a child.** This provides a definitive diagnosis and guides future therapy.
- **Indications for urine culture:**

Table 2: Cumulative incidence of UTI in children.

Age (years)	Boys (%)	Girls (%)	Region	Reference
2	2.2	2.1	Sweden	[Jakobsson et al, 1999]
7	2.8	8.2	Northern England	[Coulthard et al, 1997]
16	3.6	11.3	Northern England	[Coulthard et al, 1997]

- Before commencing antibiotics for a urinary tract infection
- Child of any age with:
  - Fever but no clinical source of infection
  - General ill health, unexplained abdominal pain, or vomiting
  - Dysuria, frequency
  - Secondary enuresis, haematuria, or hypertension
- Neonate, infant with
  - Fever
  - Prolonged jaundice
  - Failure to thrive

The urine specimen should, if possible, be collected before antibiotics are taken or changed.

If there is a family history of recurrent UTIs or vesicoureteric reflux, the threshold for deciding to culture the urine should be lowered.

ear-patient tests

The ideal near-patient test would cheaply, quickly, and accurately confirm or exclude urinary tract infection.

A large meta-analysis showed that microscopy (i.e. determination of bacterial count and leucocyte count) performs considerably better than other tests. However, combinations of dipstick tests (e.g. leucocyte esterase (LE) together with nitrite) could not be definitively assessed because there were too few data [Huicho et al, 2002].

'rine dipstick tests

ummary of recommendations for use of urine dipstick ests in children:

- Urine dipstick tests can be used to guide initial management:
  - If either the nitrite or the LE dipstick test is positive, diagnose urinary tract infection (UTI)
  - If both nitrite and LE dipstick tests are negative, exclude UTI in older children who are otherwise healthy
- **Culture the urine whatever the dipstick test results**

Urine dipstick tests are the most widely used near-patient test for UTI.

For UTIs in children the most useful dipstick tests are leucocyte esterase (LE) and nitrite.

Dipstick tests cannot be relied on to exclude or to confirm a diagnosis of UTI in a child. No combination of dipstick tests (i.e. nitrite, LE, protein, blood) can avoid clinically important rates of over-treatment and under-treatment (i.e. false positives and false negatives).

Urine should therefore always be cultured in order to provide the definitive diagnosis and guide antibiotic therapy.

The limitations of urine dipstick tests are discussed in [Lammers et al, 2001]. The predictive values given below are derived from data published in the meta-analysis of [Huicho et al, 2002].

Nitrite test

- Most urinary pathogens reduce nitrate to nitrite.
- However, children with UTI urinate frequently and bacterial enzymes may not have sufficient time to produce nitrites.
- **When UTI is clinically probable** (suggestive symptoms and signs):
  - **A positive nitrite test confirms UTI** (predictive value approaches 100%)
  - A negative test in not useful (predictive value is less than 80%)
- **When UTI is clinically unlikely** (no suggestive symptoms or signs):
  - A positive nitrite test is not useful (predictive value is less than 40%)
  - **A negative test excludes UTI** (predictive value approaches 100%)
- **LE test**
  - LE is a marker for leucocytes, but the LE test is less sensitive than microscopy.
  - Leucocytes in stored urine lyse over several hours and would not be visible under the microscope, although LE may still be detectable. Leucocytes from vaginitis or other sources can contaminate the urine.
  - **When UTI is clinically probable:**
    - **A positive LE test suggests UTI** (predictive value about 80%).
    - A negative test does not exclude UTI (predictive value less than 95%).
  - **When UTI is clinically unlikely:**
    - A positive LE test does not confirm UTI (predictive value less than 40%.); the LE test is thus not suitable for screening.
    - **A negative test excludes UTI** (predictive value approaches 100%).
- **Blood and protein**
  - Blood and protein are sometimes found in the urine when there is a UTI but neither their presence nor their absence help in making a diagnosis.

[Lammers et al, 2001; Huicho et al, 2002; Lambert and Coulthard, 2002]

Urine microscopy

- Microscopy of urine is a quick and reliable near-patient test for UTI.
- Detection of bacteria with the microscope is the best single test for UTI in children [Huicho et al, 2002].
- Minimal processing is required because the urine is neither centrifuged nor stained.
- Moderate investment in equipment, training and organization is required [Lambert and Coulthard, 2002].
- Some general practices in the UK offer urine microscopy during a consultation.

Imaging investigations for children with urinary tract infection

- Imaging investigations are seldom needed in the *diagnosis* of urinary tract infection in children.
- However, a number of imaging investigations are performed to discover risk factors such as anatomical abnormalities, obstructions, and vesicoureteric reflux.

Aims of imaging

- To identify for appropriate management:
  - Obstructions and structural abnormalities of the urinary tract
  - Renal 'scars' (from pyelonephritis)
  - Abnormal bladder emptying
  - Vesicoureteric reflux
- The younger the child, the greater is the risk of future renal damage. Hence younger children are investigated more intensively.

Imaging modalities

- **Ultrasonography** is used to visualize the structure of the urinary tract. Anatomical features such as a dilated ureter are well shown on ultrasonography.
- **Dimercaptosuccinic acid (DMSA) tagged with a radionuclide** is used to image the kidneys and urinary tract. This demonstrates renal function. Focal areas of decreased activity in the kidney associated with urinary tract infection are assumed to be due to infection and are called 'scars', although initially they are due to swelling and inflammation.
- **Cystography** is used to visualize the bladder and the flow of urine. vesicoureteric reflux is best demonstrated with cystography. Traditionally, cystography has required the urethra to be catheterized to instil contrast material into the bladder, and then to obtain images during

micturition (i.e. a micturating cystourethrogram [MCUG]). Indirect radionuclide cystography does not require the bladder to be catheterized. The debate over the relative merits of the various tests is outside the scope of this guidance, and the non-specific term 'cystogram' is used under the assumption that local imaging services will decide on the appropriate method to use when children are referred. Radionuclide cystography involves exposure to radiation about two orders of magnitude greater than that with a routine chest radiograph. Radiation exposure with a traditional MCUG is greater still.

Imaging policy issues

Debate on imaging policies to follow treatment of a urinary tract infection involves a number of issues:

- Urinary tract infection (UTI) in the presence of vesicoureteric reflux (VUR) may lead to renal damage, with the long-term complications of hypertension, pregnancy-induced hypertension, and chronic renal failure.
- The role of VUR is controversial because reports have shown that renal damage may occur with UTI in the absence of VUR. Furthermore, a significant proportion of children with VUR and a proven UTI do not develop renal scarring. Yet, the VUR is likely to be more severe in those children with a UTI, renal damage, and VUR. This suggests that, in the presence of UTI and VUR, other factors are required to cause the renal damage [Jakobsson et al, 1994; Gordon, 1995; Rushton, 1997; Lambert and Coulthard, 2002].
- Imaging is used as a screening tool with the aim of detecting children who are at risk of progressive renal damage that could be prevented, but:
  - Evaluation of the potential benefits of different imaging protocols is hampered by a lack of evidence [Dick and Feldman, 1996].
  - A systematic review found little evidence to support the benefit of long-term antibiotics in preventing recurrent UTIs [Le Saux et al, 2000].
  - There is no direct evidence to show that long-term antibiotics prevent the consequences of renal damage, such as hypertension, pregnancy-induced hypertension, and chronic renal failure.
  - Surgical treatment of VUR has been shown to offer no greater benefit than medical treatment [Piepsz et al, 1998].
- The management of acute UTI in children has not been systematic in the past. Thus, greater opportunities for health gain could lie in improving the detection and treatment of acute UTI in children, rather than in improving the detection and management of VUR [van der Voort et al, 1997; Verrier-Jones K. et al, 2001].

[Royal College of Physicians of London, 1991; Dick and Feldman, 1996; Larcombe, 1999; Deshpande and Jones, 2001; Kraus, 2001; Lambert and Coulthard, 2002; Roberts, 2002]

U

Recommendations for imaging investigations following a first uncomplicated proven urinary tract infection

In the absence of local policies or clinical trials, a simple and moderately selective approach is recommended:

- **Ultrasound** of the kidneys, ureters and bladder (consensus)
  - For all children
  - As soon as convenient
- **Dimercaptosuccinic acid (DMSA)** scan (debate on age range)
  - For all children under 5 years of age, and those with abnormal ultrasonography
  - At least 2 months after the episode (to allow transient lesions to resolve)
  - Low-dose antibiotic prophylaxis while waiting for scan
- **Cystogram** (debates on age range and modality)
  - For infants aged under 1 year
  - For children whose ultrasonographic result suggests vesicoureteric reflux (e.g. mega-ureter), or whose DMSA scan is abnormal
  - Perform only after urine has been sterilized
  - Local availability and expertise determine which modality to employ for cystography

What else might it be?

- **Conditions with presentations similar to lower urinary tract infection (UTI):**
  - Vulval irritation from soap, bubble baths, poor hygiene
  - Threadworms
- **Conditions associated with or predisposing to lower UTIs:**
  - Constipation
  - Abnormal urinary tract
  - Impaired host defences
  - Impaired renal function
  - Sexual abuse

[Bailey, 1996; Lambert and Coulthard, 2002]

Complications and prognosis

Complications of urinary tract infection

- In neonates and young infants, urinary tract infection (UTI) can be associated with life-threatening sepsis.
- UTIs in babies and young children can remain undetected for long periods of time. This causes considerable avoidable morbidity from the UTI itself ar from damage to the kidneys [Lambert and Coulthard, 2002].

Prognosis after urinary tract infection

Recurrent urinary tract infection in children

- Urinary tract infection (UTI) recurs at least once in abo 20% of boys and 30% of girls, and more than once in about 4% of boys and 8% of girls [Jodal, 1987].
- Some children with recurrent UTIs eventually develop hypertension, pregnancy-induced hypertension, or chronic renal failure [Verrier-Jones K. et al, 2001].
- The greatest risk of progressive renal damage is in children with severe vesicoureteric reflux (VUR) and recurrent UTI.
- Delay in starting treatment for repeated episodes of UT seems to be the main preventable risk factor for permanent renal damage [Dick and Feldman, 1996; va der Voort et al, 1997; Deshpande and Jones, 2001].
- Systematic reviews have found few trials of antibiotic prophylaxis for UTI. Because the studies had methodological weaknesses, they provide limited evidence of benefit and harms [Le Saux et al, 2000; Williams et al, 2001b].
- We could find no trials that used hypertension, pregnancy-induced hypertension, or chronic renal failu as outcomes to evaluate antibiotic prophylaxis of UTI i children.
- Low-dose chronic prophylactic antibiotic therapy has two indications: recurrent UTI and VUR.
- We would suggest that, in UK primary care, prophylac antibiotics would be initiated:
  - To cover the period while waiting for imaging investigations, and
  - To cover the period while waiting for specialist assessment.

esicoureteric reflux

The natural history of vesicoureteric reflux (VUR) and its sequelae are known imprecisely. Findings from different centres differ for a number of reasons, including:

- Cystography is performed infrequently because it is invasive.
- Long-term sequelae have a low prevalence — thus researchers need to follow large numbers of children over many years.
- Criteria for selecting children for cystography and dimercaptosuccinic acid (DMSA) scanning often are not well defined, are inconsistently applied, or are poorly reported — thus systematic reviews are difficult or impossible.

[errick et al, 1995a; Merrick et al, 1995b; Bailey and)lleston, 1997; Wennerstrom et al, 2000b; Wennerstrom al, 2000c]

VUR is found in about 1% of normal infants [Jacobson et al, 1999].

A systematic review found an indistinct association between VUR and renal scarring [Gordon, Personal Communication, 2002].

Table 3 shows the association of VUR with scarring (demonstrated by DMSA scan) in the same kidney.

Swedish studies have shown that children who have had a urinary tract infection (UTI) and renal scarring have a low risk of developing decreased glomerular filtration rate and hypertension. The low risk is attributed to the efficient detection of UTI in children and prevention of recurrent infections [Wennerstrom et al, 1998; Wennerstrom et al, 2000a; Wennerstrom et al, 2000b].

VUR resolves over several years. The more severe the reflux, the longer it takes to resolve. A Swedish study found the time for 50% of affected children to be reflux free was 2.5 years for those with grade I reflux and 8 years for those with grades III–V (reflux in girls took longer to resolve than in boys, but this differed from other studies) [Wennerstrom et al, 1998].

Studies in New Zealand concluded that infancy and early childhood are the critical periods for renal damage to occur, that damage is confined to kidneys that are subjected to severe degrees of reflux, that lesser degrees of reflux were not associated with renal damage, and that a spontaneous lessening of the severity of reflux occurred with increasing age [Bailey and Rolleston, 1997].

Children with a family history of VUR are 20–50 times more likely to have VUR themselves than the normal population [Zerin et al, 1993]. One report suggests that it may not be necessary to screen asymptomatic siblings for VUR because reflux in this group seems to be less severe, resolves more quickly, and is not associated with renal damage [Parekh et al, 2002]. The decision whether to or not to screen asymptomatic siblings should be made in consultation with the family and secondary care services.

Management issues

General issues p.1839
Symptomatic treatment p.1839
Antibiotic treatment p.1839
Length of antibiotic treatment for acute urinary tract infection in children p.1840
Other treatments p.1840
Admission criteria p.1840
Referral criteria p.1840
Follow-up p.1840
Management of recurrent urinary tract infection in children p.1840

Table 3: Association of VUR with scarring.

	VUR absent (%)	VUR present (%)	Total
Scar absent	50	10	60
Scar present	25	15	40
Total	75	25	100

General issues

- For many important management decisions in urinary tract infection (UTI), little or no convincing evidence is available, and recommendations have to be made on the basis of 'best practice' and expert opinion.
- UTIs affect many young children, are more difficult to diagnose in the younger the child, cause acute illness and symptoms, and may have long-term sequelae: hypertension, pregnancy-induced hypertension, and chronic renal failure.
- Prompt diagnosis and rapid treatment with antibiotics will reverse acute changes and may limit future complications.

[Dick and Feldman, 1996; Gorelick and Shaw, 1999; Larcombe, 1999; Lambert and Coulthard, 2002]

Symptomatic treatment

- Paracetamol or ibuprofen relieves pain and high temperature.
- Urine alkalinizing agents, such as potassium citrate, sodium citrate, and sodium bicarbonate, are popular remedies for urinary symptoms in women. However, there is evidence to doubt their efficacy in adults [Brumfitt et al, 1990] and no evidence to support their use in children.

Antibiotic treatment

- Adhere to local policies (if available) and be guided by local patterns of bacterial resistance.
- An antibiotic should be commenced immediately and be adjusted if necessary when the results of the urine culture are available.
- Population studies on bacterial sensitivities can be difficult to apply because:
  - Urine samples from hospitals and from general practice are likely to include few children, and to be preferentially selected from complicated cases and treatment failures.
  - Uncomplicated urinary tract infection (UTI) in adults generally resolves within a few days, even if no specific treatment is given.
  - Drugs commonly used in UTI are excreted in higher concentrations in the urine than are used in laboratory testing. This is one of the reasons why laboratory reports of resistance are not always associated with treatment failure.
  - Patterns of antibiotic resistance vary widely when different centres are compared.

[Wise and Andrews, 1998; Baerheim, 2001; Priest et al, 2001; Tran et al, 2001]

- **Trimethoprim**
  - Rates of resistance of *Escherichia coli* to trimethoprim have recently been reported as rising to between 20% and 40%, but the study populations were different from those served by primary care in the UK, where true resistance in acute uncomplicated UTI is probably 10–20% [McNulty, Personal Communication, 2002].
  - Trimethoprim is still an effective preferred treatment of uncomplicated UTI in UK general practice, and most infections respond clinically.

[Baerheim, 2001; Manges et al, 2001; Stamm, 2001; Steinke et al, 2001]

U

- **Nitrofurantoin**
  - Nitrofurantoin is at least as effective as trimethoprim, but it is more expensive and frequently causes nausea and vomiting.
  - Approximately 10% of the bacteria responsible for UTI in UK general practice are resistant to nitrofurantoin [McNulty, Personal Communication, 2002].
  - Nitrofurantoin is ineffective against *Proteus mirabilis.*
  - Macrocrystalline nitrofurantoin is promoted as having fewer adverse effects than other formulations [Kalowski et al, 1974], but the published studies were done when the recommended length of treatment was 2 weeks and the recommended dose was 100 mg four times a day. Thus, adverse effects were more likely to occur and less likely to be well tolerated than with current shorter courses of lower doses.
  - Modified-release preparations are taken twice a day and may be more convenient.
- **Cefalexin**
  - Cefalexin is at least as effective as trimethoprim, but it is more expensive, and, because of its broad antibacterial spectrum, it is more likely to disrupt gut flora or, in girls, to cause vaginal thrush [Leigh et al, 1970; Parfitt, 1999].
  - Approximately 10% of the bacteria responsible for UTIs seen in UK general practice are resistant to cefalexin [McNulty, Personal Communication, 2002].
  - Although treatment failure with cefalexin has been reported to be as high as 30% [DTB, 1998], recent urine culture data from the northeast of England showed that 96% of *E coli* isolates and 90% of all other isolates are sensitive to cefalexin [Pedler, Personal Communication, 2002].
- **Amoxicillin** is unsuitable as an empirical treatment because 50% of urinary pathogens are resistant to it. However, it may be used if the organism is known to be sensitive.
- **Co-amoxiclav** is appropriate for second-line treatment (e.g. for trimethoprim resistance). Resistance in uncomplicated UTI is less than 5% [McNulty, Personal Communication, 2002]. It is more expensive than trimethoprim, nitrofurantoin, and cefalexin; and it has some undesirable adverse drug reactions.
- **Quinolones** are best avoided in children because they have caused arthropathy in animal studies.
- **Pivmecillinam** may be prescribed for second-line treatment (e.g. for trimethoprim resistance), but dosage titration in children may be difficult because only 200 mg tablets are currently available in the UK. It is highly active against many Gram-negative pathogens, including *E coli.*

[MeReC, 1995; DTB, 1998; Baerheim, 2001]

Length of antibiotic treatment for acute urinary tract infection in children

- A 7-day course of antibiotics is recommended for acute infection.
- Longer courses (>10 days) are no more effective and are more likely to increase resistance, and, with broad-spectrum antibiotics, alter the natural flora in the vagina and bowel, causing candidiasis and diarrhoea.
- The use of courses shorter than 3 days is controversial. It has been suggested that short courses increase recurrence rates. Limited evidence suggests that courses of 3 or 5 days are safe and effective.
- Interim prophylaxis with an antibiotic should be given if a dimercaptosuccinic acid scan has been arranged. Details are in the scenario *Prophylactic antibiotics.*

- Long-term antibiotics to prevent recurrent urinary tract infection would usually be initiated in secondary care. Little good evidence of benefit is available.

[Gossius and Vorland, 1984; Leibovici and Wysenbeek, 1991a; Leibovici and Wysenbeek, 1991b; MeReC, 1995; Tran et al, 2001; Abrahamsson et al, 2002]

Other treatments

- **Increasing fluid intake** is common advice for cystitis, bu it is controversial and its beneficial effects are unproven. Theoretically it could help to 'wash out' the bladder, b it would distress people with dysuria (which can be excruciating).
- **Cranberry juice:** a systematic review failed to find evidence of benefit when cranberries were used to treat acute urinary tract infection.

[Dawson and Whitfield, 1996; Jepson et al, 2000]

Admission criteria

- **Young age:** the younger the child, the lower the threshold for admission. Neonates and young infants will almost always require admission to hospital for investigation and treatment.
- **'Toxic', dehydrated, unlikely to tolerate oral fluids:** admit for intravenous fluids and parenteral antibiotics.
- **Suspected obstruction or stone:** admit for urgent review by a paediatric surgeon or urologist.

[Lambert and Coulthard, 2002]

Referral criteria

- **Refer urgently to a paediatric surgeon or urologist whe**
  - There is evidence of urinary outflow obstruction or stone
  - The child has recently undergone instrumentation of the urinary tract
- **Refer promptly when:**
  - Diagnosis of uncomplicated urinary tract infection (UTI) is in doubt
  - The child is known to have an anatomical abnormali of the urinary tract
  - It is necessary to arrange imaging of the urinary tract to rule out obstructions (including calculi), anatomic defects, and dysfunctional bladder emptying
  - The child is under 5 years of age
  - There is a failure to respond to appropriate therapy
  - There is repeated UTI (two or more episodes within 1 year)

Follow-up

- Parents, caregivers, and older children must be taught t recognize the features of UTI, and to seek medical attention without delay, should this recur.
- Young children with recurrent UTI should be given prophylactic antibiotics, and referred for secondary car
- Children who have abnormal imaging studies should have a plan for future care, developed in conjunction with secondary care services. They require long-term monitoring of blood pressure and renal function.

[Lambert and Coulthard, 2002]

Management of recurrent urinary tract infection in children

- Neither the possible benefits (prevention of urinary trac infection (UTI), prevention of renal damage) nor the risks (adverse effects, bacterial resistance) of prophylactic antibiotics have been adequately evaluate Systematic reviews have found few randomized trails; a were of low quality [Le Saux et al, 2000; Williams et al 2001a].

'he optimum duration of prophylactic treatment has not ›een established, and published guidelines differ in their ecommendations [Le Saux et al, 2000; Larcombe, .001].

'or long-term treatment, nitrofurantoin may be more ffective than trimethoprim, but it has more adverse ffects [Williams et al, 2001a].

Aethenamine hippurate should not be used for ›rophylaxis because there is not enough supporting vidence [Lee et al, 2002].

Cranberry juice has limited evidence to support its use in vomen with recurrent UTIs [Jepson et al, 1998; Kontiokari et al, 2001]. Its efficacy and safety have not ›een studied in children.

Recommendations

Follow local polices when they are available.

Otherwise:

- Treat each episode of acute uncomplicated UTI the same as a first episode.

If a second episode occurs within a year:

- Check for predisposing conditions such as anatomical abnormalities of the urinary tract, voiding dysfunction, and constipation; ensure that the bladder and the bowel are emptied regularly.
- Start prophylactic antibiotic therapy.
- Refer for assessment and possible long-term prophylactic antibiotics.
- Advise parents/carers on the importance of adhering to treatment regimens.

eferences

IS staff in England can link, free of charge, from erences to full text journals by clicking on [Full text] on PRODIGY website.

Abrahamsson, K., Hansson, S., Larsson, P. and Jodal, U. (2002) Antibiotic treatment for five days is effective in children with acute cystitis. *Acta Paediatrica* **91**(1), 55–58.

Baerheim, A. (2001) Empirical treatment of uncomplicated cystitis. *British Medical Journal* **323**(7323), 1197–1198. [Full text]

Bailey, R.R. (1996) Urinary tract infection. In: Weatherall, D.J., Ledingham, J.G.G., Warrell, D.A. et al (Eds.) *Oxford Textbook of Medicine*. 3rd edn. Oxford: Oxford University Press. Section 20.8.1.

Bailey, R.R. and Rolleston, G.L. (1997) Vesicoureteric reflux and reflux nephropathy: the Christchurch contribution. *New Zealand Medical Journal* **110**(1048), 266–269.

BNF 42 (2001) *British National Formulary*. 42nd edn. London: British Medical Association and Royal Pharmaceutical Society of Great Britain.

Brumfitt, W., Hamilton-Miller, J .M., Cooper, J. and Raeburn, A. (1990) Relationship of urinary pH to symptoms of 'cystitis'. *Postgraduate Medical Journal* **66**(779), 727–729.

Brumfitt, W., Hamilton-Miller, J. and Bailey, R.R. (Eds.) (1998) *Urinary tract infections*. London: Chapman & Hall Medical.

Buys, H., Pead, L., Hallett, R. and Maskell, R. (1994) Suprapubic aspiration under ultrasound guidance in children with fever of undiagnosed cause. *British Medical Journal* **308**(6930), 690–692. [Full text]

Cooper, B. and Jepson, R. (2001) Recurrent cystitis in non-pregnant women. *Clinical Evidence* **5**(Jun), 1338–1345.

Coulthard, M.G., Lambert, H.J. and Keir, M.J. (1997) Occurrence of renal scars in children after their first referral for urinary tract infection. *British Medical Journal* **315**(7113), 918–919.

11. Dawson, C. and Whitfield, H. (1996) ABC of urology: urinary incontinence and urinary infection. *British Medical Journal* **312**(7036), 961–964. [Full text]
12. Deshpande, P.V. and Jones, K.V. (2001) An audit of RCP guidelines on DMSA scanning after urinary tract infection. *Archives of Disease in Childhood* **84**(4), 324–327. [Full text]
13. Dick, P.T. and Feldman, W. (1996) Routine diagnostic imaging for childhood urinary tract infections: a systematic overview. *Journal of Pediatrics* **128**(1), 15–22.
14. DTB (1997) The management of urinary tract infection in children. *Drug & Therapeutics Bulletin* **35**(9), 65–69.
15. DTB (1998) Managing urinary tract infection in women. *Drug & Therapeutics Bulletin* **36**(4), 30–32. [Full text]
16. Gordon, I. (1995) Vesico-ureteric reflux, urinary-tract infection, and renal damage in children. *Lancet* **346**(8973), 489–490. [Full text]
17. Gordon, I. (2002) *Personal communication. Data submitted for publication*. Great Ormond Street Hospital NHS Trust: London.
18. Gorelick, M.H. and Shaw, K.N. (1999) Screening tests for urinary tract infection in children: a meta-analysis. *Pediatrics* **104**(5), e54.
19. Gossius, G. and Vorland, L. (1984) A randomised comparison of single-dose vs. three-day and ten-day therapy with trimethoprim-sulfamethoxazole for acute cystitis in women. *Scandinavian Journal of Infectious Diseases* **16**(4), 373–379.
20. Hoberman, A., Chao, H.P., Keller, D.M. et al (1993) Prevalence of urinary tract infection in febrile infants. *Journal of Pediatrics* **123**(1), 17–23.
21. Huicho, L., Campos Sanchez, M. and Alamo, C. (2002) Metaanalysis of urine screening tests for determining the risk of urinary tract infection in children. *Pediatric Infectious Disease Journal* **21**(1), 1–11.
22. Jacobson, S.H., Hansson, S. and Jakobsson, B. (1999) Vesico-ureteric reflux: occurrence and long-term risks. *Acta Paediatrica Supplement* **88**(431), 22–30.
23. Jakobsson, B., Berg, U. and Svensson, L. (1994) Renal scarring after acute pyelonephritis. *Archives of Disease in Childhood* **70**(2), 111–115.
24. Jakobsson, B., Esbjorner, E. and Hansson, S. (1999) Minimum incidence and diagnostic rate of first urinary tract infection. *Pediatrics* **104**(2 Pt 1), 222–226. [Full text]
25. Jepson, R.G., Mihaljevic, L. and Craig, J. (1998) *Cranberries for the prevention of urinary tract infections (Cochrane Review)*. The Cochrane Library. Issue 4. Oxford: Update Software.
26. Jepson, R.G., Mihaljevic, L. and Craig, J. (2000) *Cranberries for treating urinary infections (Cochrane Review)*. The Cochrane Library. Issue 2. Oxford: Update Software.
27. Jodal, U. (1987) The natural history of bacteriuria in childhood. *Infectious Disease Clinics of North America* **1**(4), 713–729.
28. Kalowski, S., Radford, N. and Kincaid-Smith, P. (1974) Crystalline and macrocrystalline nitrofurantoin in the treatment of urinary-tract infection. *New England Journal of Medicine* **290**(7), 385–387.
29. Kontiokari, T., Sundqvist, K., Nuutinen, M. et al (2001) Randomised trial of cranberry-lingonberry juice and Lactobacillus GG drink for the prevention of urinary tract infections in women. *British Medical Journal* **322**(7302), 1571. [Full text]
30. Kraus, S.J. (2001) Genitourinary imaging in children. *Pediatric Clinics of North America* **48**(6), 1381–1424.

U

31. Lambert, H.J. and Coulthard, M.G. (2002) The child with urinary tract infection. In: Webb, N. and Postlethwaite, R. (Eds.) *Clinical paediatric nephrology*. 3rd edn. Oxford: Oxford University Press.
32. Lammers, R.L., Gibson, S., Kovacs, D. et al (2001) Comparison of test characteristics of urine dipstick and urinalysis at various test cutoff points. *Annals of Emergency Medicine* **38**(5), 505–512.
33. Larcombe, J. (1999) Urinary tract infection in children. *British Medical Journal* **319**(7218), 1173–1175. [Full text]
34. Larcombe, J. (2001) Urinary tract infection in children. *Clinical Evidence* **6**(Dec), 320–329.
35. Lee, B., Bhuta, T., Craig, J. and Simpson, J. (2002) *Methenamine hippurate for preventing urinary tract infections (Cochrane Review)*. The Cochrane Library. Issue 1. Oxford: Update Software.
36. Leibovici, L. and Wysenbeek, A.J. (1991a) Single-dose treatment of urinary tract infections with and without antibody-coated bacteria: a metaanalysis of controlled trials. *Journal of Infectious Diseases* **163**(4), 928–929.
37. Leibovici, L. and Wysenbeek, A.J. (1991b) Single-dose antibiotic treatment for symptomatic urinary tract infections in women: a meta-analysis of randomized trials. *Quarterly Journal of Medicine* **78**(285), 43–57.
38. Leigh, D.A., Faiers, M.C. and Brumfitt, W. (1970) Laboratory and clinical studies with cephalexin. *Postgraduate Medical Journal* **Suppl**, 69–74.
39. Le Saux, N., Pham, B. and Moher, D. (2000) Evaluating the benefits of antimicrobial prophylaxis to prevent urinary tract infections in children: a systematic review. *Canadian Medical Association Journal* **163**(5), 523–529. [Full text]
40. Manges, A.R., Johnson, J.R., Foxman, B. et al (2001) Widespread distribution of urinary tract infections caused by a multidrug-resistant Escherichia coli clonal group. *New England Journal of Medicine* **345**(14), 1007–1013. [Full text]
41. McNulty, C. (2002) *Personal communication*. Medical Microbiologist, HPA Primary Care Unit: Gloucestershire Royal Hospital, Gloucester.
42. MeReC (1995) Urinary tract infection. *MeReC Bulletin* **6**(8),
43. Merrick, M.V., Notghi, A., Chalmers, N. et al (1995a) Long-term follow up to determine the prognostic value of imaging after urinary tract infections. Part 2: scarring. *Archives of Disease in Childhood* **72**(5), 393–396.
44. Merrick, M.V., Notghi, A., Chalmers, N. et al (1995b) Long-term follow up to determine the prognostic value of imaging after urinary tract infections. Part 1: reflux. *Archives of Disease in Childhood* **72**(5), 388–392.
45. Parekh, D.J., Pope, J.C., Adams, M.C. and Brock, J.W., III (2002) Outcome of sibling vesicoureteral reflux. *Journal of Urology* **167**(1), 283–284.
46. Parfitt, K. (Ed.) (1999) *Martindale*. 32nd edn. London: Pharmaceutical Press.
47. Pedler, S. (2002) *Personal communication*. Consultant Microbiologist, Royal Victoria Infirmary: Newcastle upon Tyne.
48. PHLS (2001) *Management of infection: guidance for primary care*. Public Health Laboratory Service. www.hpa.org.uk [Accessed: 03/02/2002].
49. Piepsz, A., Tamminen-Mobius, T., Reiners, C. et al (1998) Five-year study of medical or surgical treatment in children with severe vesico-ureteral reflux dimercaptosuccinic acid findings. International Reflux Study Group in Europe. *European Journal of Pediatrics* **157**(9), 753–758.
50. Priest, P., Yudkin, P., McNulty, C. and Mant, D. (2001) Antibacterial prescribing and antibacterial resistance in English general practice: cross sectional study. *British Medical Journal* **323**(7320), 1037–104 [Full text]
51. Rees, J.C., Vernon, S., Pedler, S.J. and Coulthard, M (1996) Collection of urine from washed-up potties. *Lancet* **348**(9021), 197.
52. Roberts, K.B. (2002) Urinary tract infections in your febrile infants: is selective testing acceptable? *Archiv of Pediatrics & Adolescent Medicine* **156**(1), 6–7. [F text]
53. Royal College of Paediatrics and Child Health (Ed.) (1999) *Medicines for children*. London: RCPCH Publications.
54. Royal College of Physicians of London (1991) Guidelines for the management of acute urinary trac infection in childhood. Report of a Working Group the Research Unit, Royal College of Physicians. *Jour of the Royal College of Physicians of London* **25**(1), 36–42.
55. Rushton, H.G. (1997) The evaluation of acute pyelonephritis and renal scarring with technetium 99 dimercaptosuccinic acid renal scintigraphy: evolving concepts and future directions. *Pediatric Nephrology* **11**(1), 108–120.
56. Stamm, W.E. (1998) Urinary tract infections and pyelonephritis. In: *Harrison's Principles of Internal Medicine*. New York: McGraw-Hill.
57. Stamm, W.E. (2001) An epidemic of urinary tract infections? *New England Journal of Medicine* **345**(1 1055–1057. [Full text]
58. Steinke, D.T., Seaton, R.A., Phillips, G. et al (2001) Prior trimethoprim use and trimethoprim-resistant urinary tract infection: a nested case-control study w multivariate analysis for other risk factors. *Journal c Antimicrobial Chemotherapy* **47**(6), 781–787. [Full text]
59. Tran, D., Muchant, D.G. and Aronoff, S.C. (2001) Short-course versus conventional length antimicrobi therapy for uncomplicated lower urinary tract infections in children: a meta-analysis of 1279 patier *Journal of Pediatrics* **139**(1), 93–99.
60. van der Voort, Edwards, A., Roberts, R. and Verrier Jones K. (1997) The struggle to diagnose UTI in children under two in primary care. *Family Practice* **14**(1), 44–48.
61. Vernon, S., Redfearn, A., Pedler, S.J. et al (1994) Uri collection on sanitary towels. *Lancet* **344**(8922), 61
62. Verrier-Jones K., Hockley, B., Scrivener, R. and Pollack, J.I. (2001) *Diagnosis and management of urinary tract infections in children under two years: assessment of practice against published guidelines*. Royal College of Paediatrics and Child Health. www.rcpch.ac.uk [Accessed: 17/06/2001].
63. Walter, F.G. and Knopp, R.K. (1989) Urine samplin in ambulatory women: midstream clean-catch versus catheterization. *Annals of Emergency Medicine* **18**(2 166–172.
64. Wennerstrom, M., Hansson, S., Jodal, U. and Stokland, E. (1998) Disappearance of vesicoureteral reflux in children. *Archives of Pediatrics & Adolesce Medicine* **152**(9), 879–883. [Full text]
65. Wennerstrom, M., Hansson, S., Hedner, T. et al (2000a) Ambulatory blood pressure 16–26 years aft the first urinary tract infection in childhood. *Journal Hypertension* **18**(4), 485–491.
66. Wennerstrom, M., Hansson, S., Jodal, U. et al (2000 Renal function 16 to 26 years after the first urinary tract infection in childhood. *Archives of Pediatrics & Adolescent Medicine* **154**(4), 339–345. [Full text]
67. Wennerstrom, M., Hansson, S., Jodal, U. and Stokland, E. (2000c) Primary and acquired renal scarring in boys and girls with urinary tract infection *Journal of Pediatrics* **136**(1), 30–34.

U

. Williams, G., Lee, A. and Craig, J. (2001a) Antibiotics for the prevention of urinary tract infection in children: a systematic review of randomized controlled trials. *Journal of Pediatrics* **138**(6), 868–874.

. Williams, G., Lee, A. and Craig, J. (2001b) *Long-term antibiotics for preventing recurrent urinary tract infection in children (Cochrane Review)*. The Cochrane Library. Issue 1. Oxford: Update Software.

70. Wise, R. and Andrews, J.M. (1998) Local surveillance of antimicrobial resistance. Synercid Resistance Surveillance Group. *Lancet* **352**(9128), 657–658. [Full text]

71. Zerin, J.M., Ritchey, M.L. and Chang, A.C. (1993) Incidental vesicoureteral reflux in neonates with antenatally detected hydronephrosis and other renal abnormalities. *Radiology* **187**(1), 157–160.

PRODIGY GUIDANCE

Urticaria and angio-oedema

Last revised in June 2004
www.prodigy.nhs.uk/guidance.asp?gt=Urticaria

Applies to people over the age of 1 month

This guidance covers the management of urticaria and angio-oedema.

This guidance does not cover the management of anaphylaxis, acute drug reactions, or urticaria and angio-oedema in pregnancy.

There is separate PRODIGY guidance for *Insect bites and stings* that covers the management of anaphylaxis.

Goals

- To diagnose the type of urticaria
- To determine the cause of urticaria where possible
- To relieve the symptoms of urticaria and angio-oedema

Contents

Scenarios

- Acute urticaria with or without angio-oedema p.1844
- Chronic urticaria with or without angio-oedema p.1846
- Angio-oedema without urticaria p.1847
- Treatment failure p.1848

Extended Information, p. 1850

Which scenario?

- **Acute urticaria with or without angio-oedema:** covers the management of people who have had urticaria, with or without angio-oedema, for less than 6 weeks.
- **Chronic urticaria with or without angio-oedema:** covers the management of people who have had urticaria, with or without angio-oedema, for more than 6 weeks.
- **Angio-oedema without urticaria:** covers the management and referral of people who have angio-oedema without urticaria.
- **Treatment failure:** covers further treatment options for people in whom first-choice treatment with an oral antihistamine has not worked.

Acute urticaria with or without angio-oedema

Which therapy?

- **If there is airways involvement** (tongue swelling, wheeze, or breathlessness) treat as anaphylaxis.
- **Advise the person** that if they develop any tongue swelling, wheezing, or breathlessness they should seek urgent medical advice (dial 999).
- **Enquire about any obvious precipitant** including:
  - Foods
  - Insect bites or stings
  - Medication
  - Physical triggers
  - Recent infection
- **Treat with a non-sedating oral antihistamine.** Note: assess previous treatments used, including over-the-counter preparations and their effects, and the person's expectations.
- **If night-time symptoms are a problem** consider using a sedating oral antihistamine.
- **A short course of oral prednisolone** may hasten resolution of symptoms if severe.

Practical prescribing points

For further information please see the *Medicines Compendium* (www.medicines.org.uk) or the *British National Formulary* (www.bnf.org).

- **Sedating antihistamines** cause sedation in 10–50% people, which can persist into the next day.
- **Most non-sedating antihistamines have the potential t cause sedation,** especially at higher doses. Advise peop taking non-sedating antihistamines that these drugs ma cause sedation, and that the sedative effects are enhanc when combined with alcohol.
- The non-sedating antihistamines cetirizine and loratadine and most sedating antihistamines, can be bought over the counter.

Follow-up advice

- Follow-up is generally not necessary unless symptoms persist.

Should I refer or investigate?

Refer?

- Referral is rarely necessary in acute urticaria.
- Consider referral to an immunologist if:
  - Urticaria is thought to be due to a peanut or latex allergy (for confirmation).
  - There has been angio-oedema with airway involvement.
  - There has been angio-oedema without urticaria.

Investigate?

- Investigations are rarely necessary in acute urticaria.
- Consider radioallergosorbent (RAST) testing if the history suggests a peanut or latex allergy, or other foo allergy. Contact your local laboratory for further detai

Patient information leaflets

The following PILs are available at www.prodigy.nhs.uk

- Urticaria - Acute
- Urticaria - Physical

Shared decision making

- **For acute urticaria, often no treatment is needed** as the rash commonly goes within 24–48 hours.
- A cool bath or shower may ease the itch.
- **Antihistamine tablets** can ease symptoms.
  - Modern brands such as **cetirizine, fexofenadine,** and **loratadine** usually work well and are unlikely to cau

side effects. They sometimes cause drowsiness — particularly if you drink alcohol.
Older brands such as chlorphenamine (chlorpheniramine) and **hydroxyzine** often make you drowsy — but this effect may be welcome at bedtime if the itch is troublesome.

f you can identify a 'trigger' such as a food, then it vould be sensible to avoid it in the future.

short course of steroids is sometimes prescribed in evere cases.

rug rationale

ugs not included

Jon-sedating antihistamines other than cetirizine, exofenadine, and loratadine are not offered as first hoice. Desloratadine (a metabolite of loratadine) and evocetirizine (an isomer of cetirizine) are more recently narketed products that are still under close post-narketing surveillance. Mizolastine has been implicated n causing an abnormal prolongation of the QT interval nd is not recommended first-line. Acrivastine is not ecommended as it has a short half-life and needs to be aken three times a day.

opical antipruritics are not recommended. Oral ntihistamines are the mainstay of treatment in acute rticaria, and there is no evidence to support the use of opical antipruritics.

opical antihistamines are not included as they are only narginally effective and may occasionally cause ensitization [BNF 46, 2003].

ugs included

Jon-sedating antihistamines are considered the mainstay f treatment in acute urticaria. Cetirizine, fexofenadine, nd loratadine are recommended as they all have a good afety profile and a once-a-day dosing schedule.

edating antihistamines are not commonly used in acute rticaria owing to their adverse effects (in particular edation). They may be useful when night-time ymptoms are a problem. Chlorphenamine chlorpheniramine) and hydroxyzine are offered in this ituation, as they have a good history of efficacy and afety.

)ral prednisolone: a short course of oral prednisolone nay hasten resolution of symptoms. A 3-day course of lain prednisolone is offered for people over 12 years of ge.

escriptions

al antihistamine: non-sedating

xofenadine tablets: 30mg once a day
- ge from 6 to 11 years
- exofenadine 30mg tablets. Take one tablet once a day; upply 7 tablets; NHS Cost £0.65.

xofenadine tablets: 180mg once a day
- ge from 12 years onwards
- exofenadine 180mg tablets. Take one tablet once a day; upply 7 tablets; NHS Cost £2.25.

irizine 5mg/5ml s/f solution: 2.5mg twice a day
- ge from 2 to 5 years
- etirizine 5mg/5ml s/f sol. Take 2.5ml twice a day; upply 50 ml; NHS Cost £2.63; OTC Cost £5.99.

irizine 5mg/5ml s/f solution: 5mg once a day
- ge from 2 to 5 years
- etirizine 5mg/5ml s/f sol. Take one 5ml spoonful once a ay; supply 50 ml; NHS Cost £2.63; OTC Cost £5.99.

Cetirizine 5mg/5ml s/f solution: 5mg twice a day
- Age from 6 to 11 years
- Cetirizine 5mg/5ml s/f sol. Take one 5ml spoonful twice a day; supply 100 ml; NHS Cost £5.25; OTC Cost £8.78.

Cetirizine 5mg/5ml s/f solution: 10mg once a day
- Age from 6 to 11 years
- Cetirizine 5mg/5ml s/f sol. Take two 5ml spoonfuls once a day; supply 100 ml; NHS Cost £5.25; OTC Cost £8.78.

Cetirizine tablets: 10mg once a day
- Age from 12 years onwards
- Cetirizine 10mg tablets. Take one tablet once a day; supply 7 tablets; NHS Cost £1.58; OTC Cost £4.45.

Loratadine 5mg/5ml syrup: 5mg once a day
- Age from 2 to 5 years
- Loratadine 5mg/5ml syrup. Take one 5ml spoonful once a day; supply 50 ml; NHS Cost £1.43; OTC Cost £4.99.

Loratadine 5mg/5ml syrup: 10mg once a day
- Age from 6 to 11 years
- Loratadine 5mg/5ml syrup. Take two 5ml spoonfuls once a day; supply 100 ml; NHS Cost £2.85; OTC Cost £4.99.

Loratadine tablets: 10mg once a day
- Age from 12 years onwards
- Loratadine 10mg tablets. Take one tablet once a day; supply 7 tablets; NHS Cost £1.42; OTC Cost £4.45.

Oral antihistamine: sedating (at night)

Chlorphenamine (chlorpheniramine) syrup: 1mg at night prn
- Age from 12 to 23 months
- Chlorphenamine 2mg/5ml syrup. Take 2.5ml at night when required for relief of itching; supply 50 ml; NHS Cost £0.76; OTC Cost £1.27.

Chlorphenamine (chlorpheniramine) syrup: 1-2mg at night prn
- Age from 2 to 5 years
- Chlorphenamine 2mg/5ml syrup. Take 2.5ml to 5ml at night when required for relief of itching; supply 50 ml; NHS Cost £0.76; OTC Cost £1.27.

Chlorphenamine (chlorpheniramine) syrup: 2-4mg at night prn
- Age from 6 to 11 years
- Chlorphenamine 2mg/5ml syrup. Take one to two 5ml spoonfuls at night when required for relief of itching; supply 100 ml; NHS Cost £1.43; OTC Cost £2.53.

Chlorphenamine (chlorpheniramine) tablets: 4mg at night prn
- Age from 12 years onwards
- Chlorphenamine 4mg tablets. Take one tablet at night when required for relief of itching; supply 7 tablets; NHS Cost £0.11; OTC Cost £0.74.

Hydroxyzine syrup: 5mg to 15mg at night when required
- Age from 6 months to 6 years
- Hydroxyzine 10mg/5ml syrup. Take 2.5ml to 7.5ml at night when required for relief of itching; supply 100 ml; NHS Cost £0.96.

Hydroxyzine syrup: 15mg to 25mg at night when required
- Age from 7 to 11 years
- Hydroxyzine 10mg/5ml syrup. Take 7.5ml to 12.5ml at night when required for relief of itching; supply 100 ml; NHS Cost £0.96.

Hydroxyzine tablets: 25mg at night when required
- Age from 12 years onwards
- Hydroxyzine 25mg tablets. Take one tablet at night when required for relief of itching; supply 7 tablets; NHS Cost £0.31.

Oral prednisolone for 3 days (if severe)

Prednisolone tablets: 50mg once a day for 3 days
- Age from 12 years onwards
- Prednisolone 25mg tablets. Take two tablets once a day for 3 days; supply 6 tablets; NHS Cost £1.02.

Chronic urticaria with or without angio-oedema

Which therapy?

- **If there is airways involvement** (tongue swelling, wheeze, or breathlessness) treat as anaphylaxis.
- **Advise the person** that if they develop any tongue swelling, wheezing, or breathlessness, they should seek urgent medical advice (dial 999).
- **Take a history** including:
  - Family history
  - Foods
  - Medication
  - Physical triggers
  - Systemic symptoms or airway involvement
- **Treat with a non-sedating antihistamine.** Note: assess previous treatments used, including over-the-counter preparations and their effects, and the person's expectations.
- **If night-time symptoms are predominant and problematic,** consider using a sedating oral antihistamine instead.
- **The addition of a sedating histamine at night** to a non-sedating antihistamine during the day may be helpful in people who are unable to sleep owing to night-time symptoms.

Practical prescribing points

For further information please see the *Medicines Compendium* (www.medicines.org.uk) or the *British National Formulary* (www.bnf.org).

- **Sedating antihistamines** cause sedation in 10–50% people, which can persist into the next day.
- **Most non-sedating antihistamines have the potential to cause sedation,** especially at higher doses. Advise people taking non-sedating antihistamines that these drugs may cause sedation, and that the sedative effects are enhanced when combined with alcohol.
- The non-sedating antihistamines cetirizine and loratadine and most sedating antihistamines can be bought over the counter.

Follow-up advice

- Follow-up is rarely necessary if symptoms are responsive to antihistamines.
- A 2-week trial of one antihistamine is generally reasonable before trying a different antihistamine.

Should I refer or investigate?

Refer?

- Referral is not usually necessary in chronic urticaria.
- Consider referral to a dermatologist if:
  - Symptoms are severe and not responsive to antihistamines.
  - Vasculitic urticaria is suspected (weals fixed in same site for more than 24 hours, more painful than pruritic, weals may leave skin markings when they resolve.
  - The condition remains unresponsive to antihistamir and persists over 6 weeks.
- Consider referral to an immunologist if:
  - There has been angio-oedema affecting the airway.
  - There has been angio-oedema without urticaria.

Investigate?

- Investigations are rarely necessary in chronic urticaria but may be considered if symptoms are more severe o resistant.
- Simple initial screening tests include:
  - Full blood count, to look for eosinophilia of parasit infection.
  - Erythrocyte sedimentation rate, which may be raise in vasculitic urticaria.
- Other investigations should be guided by the history (stool sample if the person has spent time in the tropics
- Thyroid function tests, including thyroid autoantibod may be helpful to identify existing or potential thyroi disease.

Patient information leaflets

The following PILs are available at www.prodigy.nhs.ul
- Urticaria - Chronic
- Urticaria - Physical

Shared decision making

- **Antihistamine tablets** are the main treatment for chro urticaria.
  - Modern brands such as **cetirizine, fexofenadine,** an **loratadine** usually work well and are unlikely to cau side effects. They sometimes cause drowsiness — particularly if you drink alcohol.
  - Older brands such as chlorphenamine (chlorpheniramine) and **hydroxyzine** often make yo drowsy — but this effect may be welcome at bedtim itch is troublesome.
  - Some people take a modern brand during the day a an older 'sedating' brand at bedtime.
  - Some people take antihistamines 'as required' when symptoms flare up. Some people take them regularl to prevent the rash appearing.
- **No 'trigger' is found in most cases** and investigations often unhelpful.
- **Symptoms may 'come and go'** — sometimes for years
- **Avoid things that may make symptoms worse,** such as
  - Tight clothes (tight belts, tight-fitting shoes, etc.).
  - Heat. Keep cool; in particular, keep the bedroom co at night. A tepid bath or shower may help just befo bedtime.
  - Alcohol, hot baths, strong sunlight, undue emotion.
  - Some medicines. For example, aspirin, anti-inflammatory painkillers, codeine, ACE inhibitors.

Drug rationale

Drugs not included

- **Non-sedating antihistamines other than cetirizine, fexofenadine and loratadine** are not offered as first choice. Desloratadine (a metabolite of loratadine) and levocetirizine (an isomer of cetirizine) are more recen marketed products that are still under close post-marketing surveillance. Mizolastine has been implica in causing an abnormal prolongation of the QT interv and is not recommended first-line. Acrivastine is not recommended as it has a short half-life and needs to b taken three times a day.

U

Topical antihistamines are not included as they are only
marginally effective and may occasionally cause
ensitization [BNF 46, 2003].
.ong-term oral corticosteroids are not recommended for
general use in chronic urticaria.

ugs included

Non-sedating antihistamines are the treatment of choice n chronic urticaria. Cetirizine, fexofenadine, and oratadine are recommended as they all have a good afety profile and a once-a-day dosing schedule.
Sedating antihistamines may be useful when night-time edation is required, or in addition to non-sedating ntihistamines if night-time symptoms are troublesome. Chlorphenamine (chlorpheniramine) and hydroxyzine re offered as they have a good history of efficacy and afety.

'escriptions

ral antihistamine: non-sedating

:ofenadine tablets: 30mg once a day

- Age from 6 to 11 years
- 'exofenadine 30mg tablets. Take one tablet once a day; upply 30 tablets; NHS Cost £5.55.

:ofenadine tablets: 180mg once a day

- Age from 12 years onwards
- 'exofenadine 180mg tablets. Take one tablet once a day; upply 30 tablets; NHS Cost £9.63.

irizine 5mg/5ml s/f solution: 2.5mg twice a day

- Age from 2 to 5 years
- Cetirizine 5mg/5ml s/f sol. Take 2.5ml twice a day; upply 150 ml; NHS Cost £7.88; OTC Cost £13.16.

irizine 5mg/5ml s/f solution: 5mg once a day

- Age from 2 to 5 years
- Cetirizine 5mg/5ml s/f sol. Take one 5ml spoonful once a day; supply 150 ml; NHS Cost £7.88; OTC Cost £13.16.

irizine 5mg/5ml s/f solution: 5mg twice a day

- Age from 6 to 11 years
- Cetirizine 5mg/5ml s/f sol. Take one 5ml spoonful twice a day; supply 300 ml; NHS Cost £15.76; OTC Cost £26.32.

irizine 5mg/5ml s/f solution: 10mg once a day

- Age from 6 to 11 years
- Cetirizine 5mg/5ml s/f sol. Take two 5ml spoonfuls once a day; supply 300 ml; NHS Cost £15.76; OTC Cost £26.32.

irizine tablets: 10mg once a day

- Age from 12 years onwards
- Cetirizine 10mg tablets. Take one tablet once a day; upply 30 tablets; NHS Cost £7.14; OTC Cost £14.95.

atadine 5mg/5ml syrup: 5mg once a day

- Age from 2 to 5 years
- Loratadine 5mg/5ml syrup. Take one 5ml spoonful once a day; supply 150 ml; NHS Cost £4.28; OTC Cost £7.49.

atadine 5mg/5ml syrup: 10mg once a day

- Age from 6 to 11 years
- Loratadine 5mg/5ml syrup. Take two 5ml spoonfuls once a day; supply 300 ml; NHS Cost £8.55; OTC Cost £14.97.

atadine tablets: 10mg once a day

- Age from 12 years onwards
- Loratadine 10mg tablets. Take one tablet once a day; upply 30 tablets; NHS Cost £6.32; OTC Cost £12.84.

Oral antihistamine: sedating (at night)

Chlorphenamine (chlorpheniramine) syrup: 1mg at night prn

- Age from 12 to 23 months
- Chlorphenamine 2mg/5ml syrup. Take 2.5ml at night when required for relief of itching; supply 100 ml; NHS Cost £1.52; OTC Cost £2.68.

Chlorphenamine (chlorpheniramine) syrup: 1-2mg at night prn

- Age from 2 to 5 years
- Chlorphenamine 2mg/5ml syrup. Take 2.5ml to 5ml at night when required for relief of itching; supply 150 ml; NHS Cost £2.28; OTC Cost £4.02.

Chlorphenamine (chlorpheniramine) syrup: 2-4mg at night prn

- Age from 6 to 11 years
- Chlorphenamine 2mg/5ml syrup. Take one to two 5ml spoonfuls at night when required for relief of itching; supply 300 ml; NHS Cost £4.56; OTC Cost £8.04.

Chlorphenamine (chlorpheniramine) tablets: 4mg at night prn

- Age from 12 years onwards
- Chlorphenamine 4mg tablets. Take one tablet at night when required for relief of itching; supply 28 tablets; NHS Cost £0.43; OTC Cost £0.76.

Hydroxyzine syrup: 5mg to 15mg at night when required

- Age from 6 months to 6 years
- Hydroxyzine 10mg/5ml syrup. Take 2.5ml to 7.5ml at night when required for relief of itching; supply 200 ml; NHS Cost £1.91.

Hydroxyzine syrup: 15mg to 25mg at night when required

- Age from 7 to 11 years
- Hydroxyzine 10mg/5ml syrup. Take 7.5ml to 12.5ml at night when required for relief of itching; supply 300 ml; NHS Cost £2.87.

Hydroxyzine tablets: 25mg at night when required

- Age from 12 years onwards
- Hydroxyzine 25mg tablets. Take one tablet at night when required for relief of itching; supply 28 tablets; NHS Cost £1.22.

Angio-oedema without urticaria

Which therapy?

- **If there is airways involvement** (tongue swelling, wheeze, or breathlessness) treat as anaphylaxis.
- **Advise the person** that if they develop any tongue swelling, wheezing, or breathlessness they should seek urgent medical advice (dial 999).
- **Otherwise enquire about possible causes:**
  - Insect bites
  - Medications
  - Occupational exposure
  - Physical stimulants
  - Family history of angio-oedema
  - Associated symptoms e.g. abdominal pain
- **Treat with a non-sedating antihistamine.**
- **If symptoms lead to suspicion of C1 esterase inhibitor deficiency,** e.g. family history or episodic abdominal pain and regional swelling following trauma such as dental work, refer to an immunologist.
- **If C1 esterase deficiencies are suspected** advise the person to avoid dental or surgical procedures until further investigations are carried out.

U

Practical prescribing points

For further information please see the *Medicines Compendium* (www.medicines.org.uk) or the *British National Formulary* (www.bnf.org).

- **Most non-sedating antihistamines have the potential to cause sedation,** especially at higher doses. Advise people taking non-sedating antihistamines that these drugs may cause sedation, and that the sedative effects are enhanced when combined with alcohol.

Should I refer or investigate?

Refer?

- Refer to an immunologist if C1 esterase inhibitor deficiency is suspected.

Investigate?

- Measure C4 levels in people with chronic angio-oedema without urticaria and no obvious precipitating factor.

Patient information leaflets

The following PILs are available at www.prodigy.nhs.uk

- Biopsy
- Urticaria - Acute

Shared decision making

- **Antihistamine tablets** are the main treatment for angio-oedema.
  - Modern antihistamines such as **cetirizine, fexofenadine**, and **loratadine** usually work well and are unlikely to cause side effects.
  - They sometimes cause drowsiness — particularly if you drink alcohol.
- **If you can identify a 'trigger'** such as a food, then it would be sensible to avoid it in the future.
  - No 'trigger' is found in most cases.
  - A medicine is sometimes a trigger. For example, aspirin, anti-inflammatory painkillers, codeine, ACE inhibitors.
  - A rare cause is a hereditary condition. Do you have a family history of angio-oedema?
- **Symptoms may 'come and go'** — sometimes for years.
- **Get medical help immediately if your breathing is ever affected.**

Drug rationale

Drugs not included

- **Non-sedating antihistamines other than cetirizine, fexofenadine, and loratadine** are not offered as first choice. Desloratadine (a metabolite of loratadine) and levocetirizine (an isomer of cetirizine) are more recently marketed products that are still under close post-marketing surveillance. Mizolastine has been implicated in causing an abnormal prolongation of the QT interval and is not recommended first line. Acrivastine is not recommended as it has a short half-life and needs to be taken three times a day.
- **Sedating antihistamines** are less preferred in the treatment of angio-oedema without urticaria, because of adverse effects.
- **Oral steroids** are not recommended for the treatment of angio-oedema without urticaria.

Drugs included

- **Non-sedating antihistamines** are the first-line treatme of choice in angio-oedema where there is no suspicion anaphylaxis or C1 esterase inhibitor deficiency. Cetirizine, fexofenadine, and loratadine are recommended as they all have a good safety profile an once-a-day dosing schedule.

Prescriptions

Oral antihistamine: non-sedating

Fexofenadine tablets: 30mg once a day
- Age from 6 to 11 years
- Fexofenadine 30mg tablets. Take one tablet once a da supply 30 tablets; NHS Cost £5.55.

Fexofenadine tablets: 180mg once a day
- Age from 12 years onwards
- Fexofenadine 180mg tablets. Take one tablet once a d supply 30 tablets; NHS Cost £9.63.

Cetirizine 5mg/5ml s/f solution: 2.5mg twice a day
- Age from 2 to 5 years
- Cetirizine 5mg/5ml s/f sol. Take 2.5ml twice a day; supply 150 ml; NHS Cost £7.88; OTC Cost £13.16.

Cetirizine 5mg/5ml s/f solution: 5mg once a day
- Age from 2 to 5 years
- Cetirizine 5mg/5ml s/f sol. Take one 5ml spoonful on day; supply 150 ml; NHS Cost £7.88; OTC Cost £13.16.

Cetirizine 5mg/5ml s/f solution: 5mg twice a day
- Age from 6 to 11 years
- Cetirizine 5mg/5ml s/f sol. Take one 5ml spoonful tw a day; supply 300 ml; NHS Cost £15.76; OTC Cost £26.32.

Cetirizine 5mg/5ml s/f solution: 10mg once a day
- Age from 6 to 11 years
- Cetirizine 5mg/5ml s/f sol. Take two 5ml spoonfuls or a day; supply 300 ml; NHS Cost £15.76; OTC Cost £26.32.

Cetirizine tablets: 10mg once a day
- Age from 12 years onwards
- Cetirizine 10mg tablets. Take one tablet once a day; supply 30 tablets; NHS Cost £7.14; OTC Cost £14.9

Loratadine 5mg/5ml syrup: 5mg once a day
- Age from 2 to 5 years
- Loratadine 5mg/5ml syrup. Take one 5ml spoonful o a day; supply 150 ml; NHS Cost £4.28; OTC Cost £7.49.

Loratadine 5mg/5ml syrup: 10mg once a day
- Age from 6 to 11 years
- Loratadine 5mg/5ml syrup. Take two 5ml spoonfuls once a day; supply 300 ml; NHS Cost £8.55; OTC Cost £14.97.

Loratadine tablets: 10mg once a day
- Age from 12 years onwards
- Loratadine 10mg tablets. Take one tablet once a day; supply 30 tablets; NHS Cost £6.32; OTC Cost £12.8

Treatment failure

Which therapy?

- Reassess the history, including possible precipitating factors.
- Check that the person is avoiding aggravating factors that may precipitate or worsen symptoms, such as str overheating, and tight clothing.

Check that the person is avoiding medications such as aspirin, NSAIDs, codeine, ACE inhibitors, and angiotensin-II receptor antagonists.
There is often variation in responsiveness to antihistamines:
- An initial suitable trial period of one antihistamine may be 2 weeks.
- If there has been no response after 2 weeks try an alternative antihistamine.
- If symptoms are mainly nocturnal, adding a sedating antihistamine at night may be helpful.

ractical prescribing points

r further information please see the *Medicines ompendium* (www.medicines.org.uk) or the *British tional Formulary* (www.bnf.org).

Sedating antihistamines cause sedation in 10–50% people, which can persist into the next day.

Most non-sedating antihistamines have the potential to cause sedation, especially at higher doses. Advise people taking non-sedating antihistamines that they may cause sedation, and that the sedative effects are enhanced when combined with alcohol.

Mizolastine has the potential to prolong the QT interval in some people and is contraindicated in people with significant cardiac disease, symptomatic arrhythmias, or those taking anti-arrhythmic drugs.

The non-sedating antihistamines cetirizine and loratadine and most sedating antihistamines can be bought over the counter.

hould I refer or investigate?

efer?

Consider referral if:
- Symptoms are severe and not responsive to antihistamines.
- Symptoms have persisted over 6 weeks.

vestigate?

Investigations are rarely necessary in chronic urticaria but may be considered if symptoms are more severe or resistant.

Simple initial screening tests include:
- Full blood count, to look for eosinophilia of parasite infection.
- Erythrocyte sedimentation rate, which may be raised in vasculitic urticaria.
- Thyroid function tests and thyroid autoantibodies.

Other investigations should be guided by the history (e.g. stool sample if the person has spent time in the tropics).

atient information leaflets

e following PILs are available at www.prodigy.nhs.uk
- Urticaria - Acute
- Urticaria - Chronic
- Urticaria - Physical

nared decision making

Antihistamine tablets are the main treatment for chronic urticaria.
- Modern brands such as **cetirizine, fexofenadine,** and **loratadine** usually work well and are unlikely to cause side effects. They sometimes cause drowsiness — particularly if you drink alcohol.
- Older brands such as chlorphenamine (chlorpheniramine) and **hydroxyzine** often make you drowsy — but this effect may be welcome at bedtime if the itch is troublesome.
- Some people take a modern brand during the day and an older 'sedating' brand at bedtime.
- Some people respond to one antihistamine better than another. If one has not helped much, a different one may suit better.
- Some people take antihistamines 'as required' when symptoms flare up. Some people take them regularly to prevent the rash appearing.

- **Avoid things which may make symptoms worse,** such as:
  - Tight clothes (tight belts, tight-fitting shoes, etc.).
  - Heat. Keep cool; in particular, keep the bedroom cool at night.
  - Alcohol, hot baths, strong sunlight, undue emotion.
  - Some medicines. For example, aspirin, anti-inflammatory painkillers, codeine, ACE inhibitors.

Drug rationale

Drugs not included

- **Non-sedating antihistamines other than cetirizine, fexofenadine, loratadine,** and mizolastine are not offered. Desloratadine (a metabolite of loratadine) and levocetirizine (an isomer of cetirizine) are more recently marketed products that are still under close post-marketing surveillance. Acrivastine is not recommended as it has a short half-life and needs to be taken three times a day.
- **Sedating antihistamines** other than chlorphenamine (chlorpheniramine) and hydroxyzine are not offered as they are generally more expensive and less frequently used.

Drugs included

- **Non-sedating antihistamines:** individual response to antihistamines may vary. If an individual has not responded to one antihistamine after 2 weeks, it is reasonable to try another. Cetirizine, fexofenadine, and loratadine are recommended as they all have a good safety profile and a once-a-day dosing schedule. Mizolastine has been implicated in causing an abnormal prolongation of the QT interval and is not recommended first line. However, there are good trial data emerging in support of its efficacy, and it may be considered in someone with no contraindications who has not responded to other antihistamines.
- **Sedating antihistamines** may be useful when night-time sedation is required. Chlorphenamine (chlorpheniramine) and hydroxyzine are offered as they have a good history of efficacy and safety.

Prescriptions

Oral antihistamine: non-sedating

Fexofenadine tablets: 30mg once a day
- Age from 6 to 11 years
- Fexofenadine 30mg tablets. Take one tablet once a day; supply 30 tablets; NHS Cost £5.55.

Fexofenadine tablets: 180mg once a day
- Age from 12 years onwards
- Fexofenadine 180mg tablets. Take one tablet once a day; supply 30 tablets; NHS Cost £9.63.

Cetirizine 5mg/5ml s/f solution: 2.5mg twice a day
- Age from 2 to 5 years
- Cetirizine 5mg/5ml s/f sol. Take 2.5ml twice a day; supply 150 ml; NHS Cost £7.88; OTC Cost £13.16.

Cetirizine 5mg/5ml s/f solution: 5mg once a day
- Age from 2 to 5 years
- Cetirizine 5mg/5ml s/f sol. Take one 5ml spoonful once a day; supply 150 ml; NHS Cost £7.88; OTC Cost £13.16.

Cetirizine 5mg/5ml s/f solution: 5mg twice a day
- Age from 6 to 11 years
- Cetirizine 5mg/5ml s/f sol. Take one 5ml spoonful twice a day; supply 300 ml; NHS Cost £15.76; OTC Cost £26.32.

Cetirizine 5mg/5ml s/f solution: 10mg once a day
- Age from 6 to 11 years
- Cetirizine 5mg/5ml s/f sol. Take two 5ml spoonfuls once a day; supply 300 ml; NHS Cost £15.76; OTC Cost £26.32.

Cetirizine tablets: 10mg once a day
- Age from 12 years onwards
- Cetirizine 10mg tablets. Take one tablet once a day; supply 30 tablets; NHS Cost £7.14; OTC Cost £14.95.

Loratadine 5mg/5ml syrup: 5mg once a day
- Age from 2 to 5 years
- Loratadine 5mg/5ml syrup. Take one 5ml spoonful once a day; supply 150 ml; NHS Cost £4.28; OTC Cost £7.49.

Loratadine 5mg/5ml syrup: 10mg once a day
- Age from 6 to 11 years
- Loratadine 5mg/5ml syrup. Take two 5ml spoonfuls once a day; supply 300 ml; NHS Cost £8.55; OTC Cost £14.97.

Loratadine tablets: 10mg once a day
- Age from 12 years onwards
- Loratadine 10mg tablets. Take one tablet once a day; supply 30 tablets; NHS Cost £6.32; OTC Cost £12.84.

Mizolastine 10mg tablets: once a day (not if heart disease)
- Age from 12 years onwards
- Mizolastine 10mg tablets. Take one tablet once a day; supply 30 tablets; NHS Cost £6.20.

Oral antihistamine: sedating (at night)

Chlorphenamine (chlorpheniramine) syrup: 1mg at night prn
- Age from 12 to 23 months
- Chlorphenamine 2mg/5ml syrup. Take 2.5ml at night when required for relief of itching; supply 50 ml; NHS Cost £0.72; OTC Cost £1.26.

Chlorphenamine (chlorpheniramine) syrup: 1-2mg at night prn
- Age from 2 to 5 years
- Chlorphenamine 2mg/5ml syrup. Take 2.5ml to 5ml at night when required for relief of itching; supply 100 ml; NHS Cost £1.43; OTC Cost £2.53.

U

Chlorphenamine (chlorpheniramine) syrup: 2-4mg at night prn
- Age from 6 to 11 years
- Chlorphenamine 2mg/5ml syrup. Take one to two 5ml spoonfuls at night when required for relief of itching; supply 100 ml; NHS Cost £1.43; OTC Cost £2.53.

Chlorphenamine (chlorpheniramine) tablets: 4mg at night prn
- Age from 12 years onwards
- Chlorphenamine 4mg tablets. Take one tablet at night when required for relief of itching; supply 14 tablets; NHS Cost £0.22; OTC Cost £1.40.

Hydroxyzine syrup: 5mg to 15mg at night when required
- Age from 6 months to 6 years
- Hydroxyzine 10mg/5ml syrup. Take 2.5ml to 7.5ml at night when required for relief of itching; supply 100 ml; NHS Cost £0.96.

Hydroxyzine syrup: 15mg to 25mg at night when require
- Age from 7 to 11 years
- Hydroxyzine 10mg/5ml syrup. Take 7.5ml to 12.5ml a night when required for relief of itching; supply 200 ml NHS Cost £1.91.

Hydroxyzine tablets: 25mg at night when required
- Age from 12 years onwards
- Hydroxyzine 25mg tablets. Take one tablet at night when required for relief of itching; supply 14 tablets; NHS Cost £0.51.

Oral antihistamine: sedating (during the day)

Chlorphenamine (chlorpheniramine) syrup: 1mg twice a day
- Age from 12 to 23 months
- Chlorphenamine 2mg/5ml syrup. Take 2.5ml twice a day; supply 100 ml; NHS Cost £1.53; OTC Cost £2.6

Chlorphenamine (chlorpheniramine): 1-2mg three times day
- Age from 2 to 5 years
- Chlorphenamine 2mg/5ml syrup. Take 2.5ml to 5ml three times a day; supply 300 ml; NHS Cost £4.58; OTC Cost £7.98.

Chlorphenamine (chlorpheniramine): 2-4mg three times day
- Age from 6 to 11 years
- Chlorphenamine 2mg/5ml syrup. Take one to two 5ml spoonfuls three times a day; supply 450 ml; NHS Cost £6.87; OTC Cost £11.97.

Chlorphenamine (chlorpheniramine) tab: 4mg three time a day
- Age from 12 years onwards
- Chlorphenamine 4mg tablets. Take one tablet three times a day; supply 42 tablets; NHS Cost £0.66; OTC Cost £4.20.

Extended Information

Background information

- What is it? p.1850
- What causes it? p.1851
- How common is it? p.1851
- How do I know my patient has it? p.1851
- What else might it be? p.1852
- Complications and prognosis p.1852

What is it?

- **Urticaria is itchy, superficial swelling of the skin due to plasma leakage from small blood vessels.**
- The mechanism is a local vasodilation and increase in capillary permeability, with plasma leakage and activation of mast cells causing mediator release, predominantly histamine [Kobza-Black and Champion 1998].
- **Angio-oedema is a deeper form of urticaria,** with swelling deeper in the dermis, subcutaneous, and submucosal tissues. This can occur anywhere on the body, most often the eyelids, lips, and genitalia. It may also affect the tongue and pharynx, e.g. when it is a feature of anaphylaxis [Kobza-Black and Champion, 1998]. Angioneurotic oedema is a disused term that is synonymous with angio-oedema.
- **Urticaria is usually classified as acute or chronic.**
  - **Urticaria is acute** when symptoms have been present for less than 6 weeks.
  - **Urticaria is chronic** if symptoms are present daily or episodically for more than 6 weeks.

- Traditionally in chronic urticaria without an identifiable cause, the term 'chronic idiopathic urticaria' was used. It is now recognized that at least a third of these cases have an autoimmune basis and the remainder are, as yet, unexplained. Therefore the use and intended meaning of the term 'idiopathic' now varies and often just 'chronic urticaria' is used [Kobza-Black and Champion, 1998].

Classification is also based on clinical grounds. There is no consensus on the exact categories, and there is often overlap. The categories are ordinary, physical, contact, or vasculitic urticaria:

- **Ordinary urticaria** is a term used if physical, contact, and vasculitic urticarias have been excluded.
- **Physical urticaria** is reproducible with certain physical stimuli. This may be heat or cold, solar, aquagenic, or vibratory. In dermographism, stroking the skin causes urticaria. If urticaria follows a brief increase in body core temperature it is termed 'cholinergic'. Delayed pressure urticaria may be present in up to 37% of chronic ordinary urticaria [Kobza-Black and Champion, 1998].
- **Contact urticaria** follows a biological or chemical skin contact.
- **Vasculitic urticaria** is a histopathological diagnosis; it is considered a chronic immune-complex urticaria.

People may have two or more types of urticaria occurring simultaneously.

[Wanderer et al, 2000]

What causes it?

Acute urticaria

Acute urticaria may have a clear cause, such as:

- **A preceding upper respiratory tract infection.**
- **Insect bites or stings.**
- **Drugs** — acute urticarial reactions from drugs are common. Some drugs, e.g. penicillins, are well-recognized causes of urticaria; others, e.g. aspirin, nonsteroidal anti-inflammatory drugs (NSAIDs), and codeine, can also exacerbate urticaria. Angiotensin-converting enzyme (ACE) inhibitors and angiotensin-II receptor antagonists (AIIRAs) can provoke angio-oedema, usually without associated urticaria, and may exacerbate urticaria.
- **A physical trigger** or contact exposure.
- **Certain foods** or food additives.

[Kobza-Black and Champion, 1998; Wanderer et al, 2000]

Chronic urticaria

In chronic urticaria it is often more difficult to identify a cause [Grattan et al, 2001].

- **Dietary pseudoallergens** such as salicylates, azo dyes, and food preservatives are often overestimated to be a cause of urticaria.
- **Drugs** are rarely a cause of chronic urticaria; however, drugs such as aspirin and NSAIDs may exacerbate chronic urticaria.
- **Parasite infection** is a rare cause, but may be relevant if a person has had exposure to parasites in the tropics [Wanderer et al, 2000].
- **There is a higher prevalence of thyroid autoantibodies** in people with urticaria than in population controls. This is probably just an association, and reflects the understanding that about a third of chronic urticaria is thought to be autoimmune [Leznoff and Sussman, 1989].
- **Autoimmune disorders and chronic inflammatory conditions** have rarely been identified as a cause of urticaria.
- There is little evidence to support an association with occult infections such as dental abscess and gastrointestinal candidiasis [Grattan et al, 2001]. Hepatitis viral infections have been identified as a possible cause for urticaria, mainly in southern Europe [Zuberbier, 2003].
- There is no association between urticaria and malignancy [Lindelof et al, 1990].
- **Urticaria in childhood has the same causative factors as in adults,** except in infants under 6 months where there is a higher incidence of allergy to cows' milk [Kobza-Black and Champion, 1998].

Angio-oedema without urticaria

- **Angio-oedema without urticaria can occur with physical triggers** such as pressure, cold, or exercise, e.g. pressure from walking may cause angio-oedema of the feet. It can also occur with occupational exposure, such as on the hands following use of latex gloves. ACE inhibitors and AIIRAs are also known to precipitate angio-oedema [Wanderer et al, 2000].
- **Angio-oedema without urticaria may rarely be due to a hereditary C1 esterase inhibitor deficiency** (hereditary angio-oedema). People with lymphoproliferative disorders and some connective tissue disorders may also acquire a C1 esterase inhibitor deficiency that presents with angio-oedema alone [Kozel et al, 1998].

How common is it?

- **Approximately 15% of the population** experience urticaria at some time in their lives [Humphreys and Hunter, 1998].
- **Estimates of prevalence vary** from 1 per 1000 people to 5 per 1000 people [Kobza-Black and Champion, 1998; Kozel et al, 1998].
- **Acute urticaria is more common in people with atopy** [Zuberbier, 2003].
- **Urticaria is more common in women.** Chronic urticaria is reported to be more common in adults, and acute urticaria more common in children.
- **Angio-oedema occurs concurrently in around half of people with urticaria.**
- **Hereditary angio-oedema is a rare condition,** accounting for about 0.5% of cases of urticaria seen by dermatologists [Kobza-Black and Champion, 1998].

How do I know my patient has it?

Signs and symptoms

- **Urticaria** presents as characteristic red, itchy raised weals or hives that blanche with pressure. Not all features of urticaria (erythema, itch, and swelling) are present in every case.
  - Weals may be well circumscribed or coalesce, and can occur anywhere on the body.
  - Individual weals last for less than 24 hours and the person remains systemically well.
  - Pruritus is the most common associated symptom.
- **Angio-oedema** appears as a less well-defined swelling. It is often more painful than pruritic and lasts longer than urticaria, taking up to 72 hours to resolve [Grattan et al, 2001]. Angio-oedema tends to affect the eyes, lips, and genitalia. It may also affect the tongue and pharynx [Kobza-Black and Champion, 1998].
- **Vasculitic urticaria** should be considered if weals last more than 24 hours in a fixed position, or if they are painful or purpuric, or leave pigmentation when they resolve [Wanderer et al, 2000].
- Diagnosis of urticaria and angio-oedema can be helped by illustrations. These can be found indexed under 'patient information' on the New Zealand

Dermatological Society website at www.dermnetnz.org, or in the dermatology online atlas at www.dermis.net/index_e.htm.

How do I assess a person with urticaria and angio-oedema?

A detailed history should be taken in acute and chronic urticaria. In acute urticaria in particular, a clear precipitant may be identifiable. History should include:

- Current or previous medications, including over-the-counter preparations.
- Relationship to food pseudoallergens such as salicylates, azo dyes, and food preservatives, which can be associated with urticaria. Food diaries may be helpful, although food reactions are often overestimated to be the cause of urticaria.
- Relationship to physical triggers.
- Foreign travel or recent viral infections.
- Possible insect bites or stings (see PRODIGY guidance Insect bites and stings).
- Family history of urticaria.
- Timing in relation to menstruation.
- Occupational exposure.
- General health-screening questions to exclude systemic disease such as thyroid disease; and enquire about airway involvement in angio-oedema.

[Wanderer et al, 2000]

A general physical examination may be appropriate, as guided by the history, e.g. examination of the thyroid gland, or chest auscultation for wheeze.

- Physical urticarias can be tested for with provocation tests; dermographism may be elicited by firmly stroking the skin.

Which investigations or prognostic tests are appropriate in urticaria and angio-oedema?

- **In most cases of self-limiting acute urticaria no investigations are needed.**
- **Radioallergosorbent (RAST) testing** may be helpful in moderate to severe acute urticaria, if an environmental trigger such as latex, nuts, or fish is suspected [Wanderer et al, 2000]. If you are considering a RAST test, contact your local laboratory for further details.
- In the majority of chronic mild urticaria no investigations are required unless indicated by other factors in the history.
- **Further investigations may be considered** if symptoms are more problematic. Studies have shown that detailed history taking with limited laboratory investigations (full blood count, erythrocyte sedimentation rate) is just as effective as extensive laboratory screening in identifying possible causes of urticaria [Kozel et al, 1998].
- **Possible screening tests for chronic urticaria include:**
  - Full blood count — eosinophilia may indicate parasite infection.
  - Erythrocyte sedimentation rate — may be raised in vasculitic urticaria.
  - Omission of suspected drugs.
  - If time has been spent in the tropics, a stool sample to check for parasites [Wanderer et al, 2000].
- **Thyroid function tests, including thyroid autoantibodies,** may be helpful in identifying existing or potential thyroid disease. Occasionally, appropriate treatment for an occult thyroid disorder may help the urticaria, but usually it has no influence [Leznoff and Sussman, 1989; Kobza-Black and Champion, 1998].
- **The presence of angio-oedema without weals is an indication for checking complement levels** to identify hereditary or acquired C1 esterase inhibitor deficiencies. Serum C4 is an appropriate initial screening test, as this is reduced and rarely returns to normal even between episodes of angio-oedema. If positive, further C1 esterase inhibitor assays can be checked [Kobza-Black and Champion, 1998]. Contact your local laboratory for advice.

What else might it be?

- **Erythema multiforme minor** may resemble urticaria, but the lesions remain fixed and target lesions may be seen. There is often a prodrome with fever, malaise and arthralgia.
- **Urticaria pigmentosa,** a form of mastocytosis, presents with hyperpigmented pruritic macules and papules.
- **Bullous pemphigoid and dermatitis herpetiformis** are autoimmune bullous disorders. Early in both diseases the lesions may be pruritic and urticarial.
- **Allergic contact dermatitis** can cause itchy, swollen eyelids; but unlike in urticaria and angio-oedema, there may be peeling of the skin.
- Conditions that mimic angio-oedema are extensive, e.g. superior vena cava obstruction, parotid gland obstruction, myxoedema.
- **Chronic pruritus** may be confused for urticaria if it is unclear whether a person has experienced weals, especially if symptoms occur only at night.

[Wanderer et al, 2000]

- **Polymorphic eruption of pregnancy (PEP),** also known as pruritic urticarial papules and plaques of pregnancy (PUPPP), is the most common rash in pregnancy. It normally occurs in a first pregnancy during the third trimester; intensely itchy urticarial papules and plaques develop, often starting in the stretch marks of a distended abdomen [Pierson, 2001; Fewell, 2003].

Complications and prognosis

Complications

- **Loss of sleep and energy, social isolation, and difficulty with aspects of daily living** can lead to severe disability [Greaves and Sabroe, 1998].
- **Urticaria is not normally accompanied by systemic reactions** although physical urticarias may very rarely progress to anaphylaxis. Urticaria is commonly seen in anaphylaxis.
- **Angio-oedema can cause life-threatening laryngeal obstruction** if it affects the upper respiratory tract.
- People with a C1 esterase inhibitor deficiency are more prone to airways obstruction with angio-oedema [Wanderer et al, 2000].

Prognosis

- **Acute urticaria is usually self-limiting.**
- **Chronic urticaria tends to remit and relapse** and may be triggered by inter-current infection, stress, drugs, and menstruation [Wanderer et al, 2000].
- After 3 years 50% of people with chronic urticaria alone will still have symptoms [Greaves and Sabroe, 1998]. After 5 years, 50% of people with chronic urticaria and angio-oedema will still be symptomatic [Grattan et al, 2001].

Management issues

- General issues p.1853
- Acute Urticaria p.1853
- Chronic Urticaria p.1853
- Angio-oedema p.1854
- When should I refer someone with urticaria? p.1854
- Medicines Management p.1854

General issues

- **If possible, identify and avoid the causative stimulus** (see *What causes it?* in Background information).
- **Aggravating factors** such as stress, overheating, and tight clothing may precipitate or worsen urticaria and should be avoided where possible.
- **Where practical, advise the person to avoid drugs such as aspirin and codeine,** which can aggravate urticaria. If aspirin is known to be a cause of urticaria, other nonsteroidal anti-inflammatory drugs (NSAIDs) should be used with caution.
    - **Urticaria is not a contraindication to aspirin** and the benefits of treatment for many individuals will outweigh the possible exacerbating effects on urticaria. Aspirin-aggravated urticaria is thought to be a dose-dependent reaction and is greater when urticaria is in the active phase.
    - **Angiotensin-converting enzyme (ACE) inhibitors and angiotensin-II receptor antagonists can exacerbate urticaria** and should be used with caution in people with angio-oedema or urticaria.

Acute Urticaria

General issues

- **Acute urticaria is generally self-limiting** and in mild cases drug treatment may not be necessary.

Antihistamines (H1-receptor antagonists)

- **H1 antihistamines are considered the first choice of drug treatment,** because histamine is one of the primary mediators of urticaria.
- Although most trial evidence is for chronic idiopathic urticaria, there is consensus that oral antihistamines are the mainstay of treatment for acute urticaria [Wanderer et al, 2000; Grattan et al, 2001].
- **Non-sedating antihistamines are usually preferred,** as they are less likely to cause sedation, and they also exhibit anti-inflammatory effects [Zuberbier, 2003].
- **Sedating antihistamines are no longer commonly used** owing to concerns about reduced cognitive function, although some people tolerate them well. They may be useful when non-sedating antihistamines have not been effective [Grattan et al, 2001] or if symptoms are troublesome at night.

Oral corticosteroids

- **A short course of oral prednisolone** may shorten the duration of acute urticaria [Zuberbier et al, 1996]. This may be considered if symptoms are severe, although it is not often necessary.

Chronic Urticaria

Topical antipruritics

- A topical antipruritic such as 1% menthol in aqueous cream may be soothing [Greaves and Sabroe, 1998; Grattan et al, 2001].

Antihistamines (H1-receptor antagonists)

- **Management aims to alleviate symptoms,** and for most people H1 antihistamines are the mainstay of treatment.
- **Non-sedating antihistamines are usually preferred** over sedating antihistamines. Non-sedating antihistamines such as loratadine, fexofenadine, cetirizine, and mizolastine have been shown to alleviate pruritus and decrease the incidence of weals in people with chronic urticaria [DTB, 2002]. Desloratadine (a metabolite of loratadine) and levocetirizine (an isomer of cetirizine) are also licensed for the treatment of chronic idiopathic urticaria.
- **There is no strong evidence that one antihistamine is more effective than any other.** Individual response to a particular antihistamine is variable. If the first choice of antihistamine is ineffective, an alternative should be offered [Grattan et al, 2001]. A suitable trial period of one drug may be 2 weeks.
- **Sedating antihistamines are useful** when non-sedating antihistamines have not worked or if night-time sedation would be beneficial. The addition of a sedating antihistamine at night to a non-sedating antihistamine during the day may be helpful in people who are unable to sleep because of their symptoms [Grattan et al, 2001], and is generally considered safe.
- **The timing of dosage may be important,** e.g. if symptoms are predominant during the night [Grattan et al, 2001].
- Many expert authorities commonly prescribe antihistamines at doses above the manufacturers' licensed recommended dose; however, this is likely to increase the risk of adverse effects [Grattan et al, 2001].

Corticosteroids

- **Long-term oral corticosteroids are not recommended** for use in chronic urticaria. They may be used under specialist supervision and for vasculitic urticaria [Grattan et al, 2001].
- **Short courses may be used to control 'flare-up'** in severe urticaria [Greaves and Sabroe, 1998; Kobza-Black and Champion, 1998].
- **The use of topical corticosteroids is not recommended in chronic urticaria** [Grattan et al, 2001]. In one small study in highly selected people, the application of a potent topical corticosteroid (clobetasol propionate) followed by plastic occlusion resulted in only a short-term improvement of symptoms [Ellingsen and Thestrup-Pedersen, 1996].

Other interventions

Numerous other interventions have been used. Much of the supporting evidence for these comes from secondary care settings and we do not generally recommend their use in primary care.

- **H_2-receptor antagonists:** if optimal doses of H1 antihistamines do not provide adequate control, there is evidence from randomized controlled trials that the addition of an H_2-receptor antagonist (e.g. cimetidine or ranitidine) may have some additional benefit in reducing symptoms of pruritus and the number and duration of weals [Paul and Bodeker, 1986; Bleehen et al, 1987].
- **Diets and food avoidance** remain controversial. A non-controlled trial of a strict pseudoallergen diet in hospital inpatients led to remission in 73% of participants within 2 weeks, but only 19% of these responded to pseudoallergen provocation testing [Zachariae et al, 1969].
- **Thyroxine** may have a benefit if thyroid autoantibodies are positive, even if the person is euthyroid. In one non-randomized trial, thyroid replacement therapy in people with severe urticaria who were hypothyroid, euthyroid with raised thyroid-stimulating hormone, or had thyroid autoantibodies did improve symptoms or lead to remission in a small number of people, although this was not a significant result [Leznoff and Sussman, 1989].
- ***Helicobacter pylori* eradication:** a systematic review of 10 small studies of people with chronic urticaria found that eradication of *H pylori* was associated with an increased remission rate of urticaria, compared with people in whom *H pylori* was not eradicated (OR 2.9, 95% CI 1.4 to 8.6) [Federman et al, 2003].

- **Leukotriene-receptor antagonists** have not been proven to be beneficial in chronic urticaria [Reimers et al, 2002]. There is emerging evidence that they may be beneficial in combination with an antihistamine [Erbagci, 2002; Bagenstose et al, 2004] but this needs to be confirmed.
- **Doxepin** has H1-blocking activity and has been found to be effective in reducing pruritus and urticarial lesions in small randomized controlled trials, but adverse effects were commonly observed [Goldsobel et al, 1986].
- **Nifedipine** has not been found to improve symptoms of urticaria convincingly [Liu et al, 1990]. One study of only seven people did support its use as an adjunct to antihistamines [Bressler et al, 1989].
- **Immunosuppressants** such as ciclosporin, plasmapheresis, and intravenous immunoglobulin can be beneficial in people with severe resistant autoimmune urticaria [Grattan et al, 2000].
- **Relaxation therapy and hypnosis:** stress is often felt to be a factor in urticaria. In one small non-randomized study, relaxation therapy and hypnosis improved self-reported symptoms but not the number of observed weals [Shertzer and Lookingbill, 1987].
- **Phototherapy** has not been proven to be of benefit in ordinary chronic urticaria, but has been used in mastocytosis [Olafsson et al, 1986].

Angio-oedema

- **Treatment of angio-oedema is essentially the same as that of chronic urticaria** unless there is airway involvement.
- **If there is evidence of airway involvement, manage as anaphylaxis.** See PRODIGY guidance *Insect bites and stings* for the management of anaphylaxis. Note: angio-oedema may occur as part of anaphylaxis.
- **People who have experienced laryngeal angio-oedema, or recurrent angio-oedema as a manifestation of anaphylaxis,** should be referred to an immunology clinic, where they may be provided with an adrenaline syringe for use in future episodes.
- **Angio-oedema caused by C1 esterase inhibitor deficiency can be severe or life-threatening.** Prophylactic use of a synthetic androgen (e.g. danazol) or an antifibrinolytic (e.g. tranexamic acid) for frequent episodes, or before elective dentistry or surgery, may be helpful [Wanderer et al, 2000].

When should I refer someone with urticaria?

- **If there is airway involvement with wheeze,** treatment for anaphylaxis should be commenced and the person admitted immediately.
- **If acute urticaria is thought to be due to a peanut or latex allergy,** refer to an immunologist.
- **When urticaria is severe or persists** beyond 6 weeks with no response to antihistamines, refer to a dermatologist.
- **If urticarial vasculitis is suspected** or there are associated systemic symptoms of the urticaria, refer to a dermatologist.
- **When there has been angio-oedema affecting the airway,** or angio-oedema without weals, refer to immunology where available, or dermatology.

[Greaves and Sabroe, 1998]

Medicines Management

Antihistamines

Sedation

- **Sedating antihistamines** (e.g. chlorphenamine [chlorpheniramine] and hydroxyzine) cause sedation in 10–50% people, which can persist into the next day.
- **Most non-sedating antihistamines (e.g. cetirizine, loratadine, or fexofenadine) have the potential to cause sedation,** especially at higher doses. In clinical trials, 2–23% of people taking non-sedating antihistamines complained of sedation (compared with 0–11% on placebo).
    - People taking non-sedating antihistamines should be warned that these drugs may cause sedation, and that the sedative effects are enhanced when combined with alcohol.
    - Fexofenadine is generally considered to have minimal affect on performance and is recommended for use by people involved in skilled activities [Mohler et al, 2002].
- Sedation due to non-sedating antihistamines is less impairing on daily activities, e.g. performance at school, than that due to sedating antihistamines.

[DTB, 2002]

Cardiotoxicity

- **An arrythmogenic effect occurs with some antihistamines,** resulting from abnormal prolongation of the QT interval. The antihistamines implicated in this include alimemazine (trimeprazine), hydroxyzine, mizolastine, and promethazine.
- Cardiological studies suggest that acrivastine, cetirizine, desloratadine, fexofenadine, and levocetirizine are not likely to produce adverse arrythmogenic effects.
- **Toxic cardiac effects are more likely with higher doses** (especially doses greater than the licensed doses) and when drug metabolism is impaired, e.g. by inhibition of cytochrome P450 by drugs such as erythromycin or ketoconazole, or grapefruit juice.
- **Potentially fatal ventricular arrhythmias have occurred with terfenadine** and it is no longer widely used.

[DTB, 2002]

Dosing in renal and hepatic disease

- **In people with severe liver disease,** sedating antihistamines and mizolastine (a non-sedating antihistamine) should be avoided as their sedative effects may precipitate coma.
- **In people with moderate renal failure,** hydroxyzine should be started at low doses, e.g. 25 mg at night, increasing the frequency to 2–3 times a day if necessary; the dose of cetirizine should be halved.

[BNF 46, 2003]

Use in pregnancy

- **The safety of oral antihistamines in pregnancy has not been established and where possible oral antihistamines should be avoided,** especially during the first trimester. Available evidence, however, does not suggest that antihistamines (sedating or non-sedating) are associated with a high risk of teratogenic effects.
- **If antihistamines are necessary to control chronic urticaria, sedating antihistamines are preferred** over non-sedating, as there is more experience of their use during pregnancy. Chlorphenamine (chlorpheniramine) is the antihistamine of choice in this situation.

[Lee et al, 2000; DTB, 2002]

References

NHS staff in England can link, free of charge, from references to full text journals by clicking on [Full text] on the PRODIGY website.

1. Bagenstose, S.E., Levin, L. and Bernstein, J.A. (2004) The addition of zafirlukast to cetirizine improves the treatment of chronic urticaria in patients with positive autologous serum skin test results. *Journal of Allergy & Clinical Immunology* 113(1), 134–140.
2. Bleehen, S.S., Thomas, S.E., Greaves, M.W. et al (1987) Cimetidine and chlorpheniramine in the

U

treatment of chronic idiopathic urticaria: a multi-centre randomized double-blind study. *British Journal of Dermatology* **117**(1), 81–88.

3. BNF 46 (2003) *British National Formulary*. 46th edn. London: British Medical Association and Royal Pharmaceutical Society of Great Britain.
4. Bressler, R.B., Sowell, K. and Huston, D.P. (1989) Therapy of chronic idiopathic urticaria with nifedipine: demonstration of beneficial effect in a double-blinded, placebo-controlled, crossover trial. *Journal of Allergy & Clinical Immunology* **83**(4), 756–763.
5. DTB (2002) Oral antihistamines for allergic disorders. *Drug & Therapeutics Bulletin* **40**(8), 59–62. [Full text]
6. Ellingsen, A.R. and Thestrup-Pedersen, K. (1996) Treatment of chronic idiopathic urticaria with topical steroids. An open trial. *Acta Dermato-Venereologica* **76**(1), 43–44.
7. Erbagci, Z. (2002) The leukotriene receptor antagonist montelukast in the treatment of chronic idiopathic urticaria: a single-blind, placebo-controlled, crossover clinical study. *Journal of Allergy & Clinical Immunology* **110**(3), 484–488.
8. Federman, D.G., Kirsner, R.S., Moriarty, J.P. and Concato, J. (2003) The effect of antibiotic therapy for patients infected with Helicobacter pylori who have chronic urticaria. *Journal of the American Academy of Dermatology* **49**(5), 861–4.
9. Fewell, H. (2003) *Pruritic urticarial papules and plaques of pregnancy – PUPPP*. About.com. http://dermatology.about.com/cs/pregnancy/a/puppp.htm [Accessed: 19/11/2003].
10. Goldsobel, A.B., Rohr, A.S., Siegel, S.C. et al (1986) Efficacy of doxepin in the treatment of chronic idiopathic urticaria. *Journal of Allergy & Clinical Immunology* **78**(5 Pt. 1), 867–873.
11. Grattan, C.E., O'Donnell, B.F., Francis, D.M. et al (2000) Randomized double-blind study of cyclosporin in chronic 'idiopathic' urticaria. *British Journal of Dermatology* **143**(2), 365–372.
12. Grattan, C., Powell, S., Humphreys, F. and British Association of Dermatologists (2001) Management and diagnostic guidelines for urticaria and angio-oedema. *British Journal of Dermatology* **144**(4), 708–714.
13. Greaves, M.W. and Sabroe, R.A. (1998) ABC of allergies. Allergy and the skin. I-urticaria. *British Medical Journal* **316**(7138), 1147–1150. [Full text]
14. Humphreys, F. and Hunter, J.A. (1998) The characteristics of urticaria in 390 patients. *British Journal of Dermatology* **138**(4), 635–638.
15. Kobza-Black, A. and Champion, R.H. (1998) Urticaria. In: Champion, R.H., Burton, J.L., Breathnach, S.M. and Burns, D.A (Eds.) *Textbook of dermatology*. 6th edn. Oxford: Blackwell Science.
16. Kozel, M.M., Mekkes, J.R., Bossuyt, P.M. and Bos, J.D. (1998) The effectiveness of a history-based diagnostic approach in chronic urticaria and angioedema. *Archives of Dermatology* **134**(12), 1575–1580. [Full text]
17. Lee, A., Inch, S. and Finnigan, D. (Eds.) (2000) *Therapeutics in pregnancy and lactation*. Abingdon: Radcliffe Medical Press Ltd.
18. Leznoff, A. and Sussman, G.L. (1989) Syndrome of idiopathic chronic urticaria and angioedema with thyroid autoimmunity: a study of 90 patients. *Journal of Allergy & Clinical Immunology* **84**(1), 66–71.
19. Lindelof, B., Sigurgeirsson, B., Wahlgren, C.F. and Eklund, G. (1990) Chronic urticaria and cancer: an epidemiological study of 1155 patients. *British Journal of Dermatology* **123**(4), 453–456.
20. Liu, H.-N., Pan, L.-M., Hwang, S.-C. and Chu, T.-L. (1990) Nifedipine for the treatment of chronic urticaria: a double-blind cross-over study. *Journal of Dermatological Treatment* **1**(4), 187–189.
21. Mohler, S.R., Nicholson, A., Harvey, P. et al (2002) The use of antihistamines in safety-critical jobs: a meeting report. *Current Medical Research and Opinion* **18**(6), 332–337. [Full text]
22. Olafsson, J.H., Larko, O. and Roupe, G. (1986) Treatment of chronic urticaria with PUVA or UVA plus placebo: a double-blind study. *Archives of Dermatological Research* **278**(3), 228–231.
23. Paul, E. and Bodeker, R.H. (1986) Treatment of chronic urticaria with terfenadine and ranitidine. A randomized double-blind study in 45 patients. *European Journal of Clinical Pharmacology* **31**(3), 277–280.
24. Pierson, J.C. (2001) *Pruritic urticarial papules and plaques of pregnancy*. eMedicine. www.emedicine.com/derm/topic351.htm [Accessed: 19/11/2003].
25. Reimers, A., Pichler, C., Helbling, A. et al (2002) Zafirlukast has no beneficial effects in the treatment of chronic urticaria. *Clinical & Experimental Allergy* **32**(12), 1763–1768.
26. Shertzer, C.L. and Lookingbill, D.P. (1987) Effects of relaxation therapy and hypnotizability in chronic urticaria. *Archives of Dermatology* **123**(7), 913–916.
27. Wanderer, A.A., Bernstein, I.L., Goodman, D.L. et al (2000) The diagnosis and management of urticaria: a practice parameter. *Annals of Allergy, Asthma, & Immunology* **85**(6 suppl 2), 521–544. [Full text]
28. Zachariae, H., Niordson, A.M. and Henningsen, S.J. (1969) Indomethacin in urticaria and histamine induced wealing. A double-blind evaluation. *Acta Dermato-Venereologica* **49**(1), 49–54.
29. Zuberbier, T. (2003) Urticaria. *Allergy* **58**(12), 1224–1234.
30. Zuberbier, T., Ifflander, J., Semmler, C. and Henz, B.M. (1996) Acute urticaria: clinical aspects and therapeutic responsiveness. *Acta Dermato-Venereologica* **76**(4), 295–297.

PRODIGY GUIDANCE

Warts and verrucae

Last revised in July 2003
www.prodigy.nhs.uk/guidance.asp?gt=Warts and verrucae

Applies to people of all ages

This guidance covers the management of cutaneous warts.

This guidance does not cover the management of anogenital warts, mucosal warts, and other viral skin infections.

There is separate PRODIGY guidance for *Molluscum contagiosum*.

Goals

- To offer adequate reassurance until natural resolution occurs
- To eliminate warts if treatment is appropriate with minimal adverse effects

Contents

Scenarios
- Warts and verrucae p.1856

Extended Information, p. 1857

Warts and verrucae

Which therapy?

- A policy of no treatment is generally recommended.
- Consider treatment if the warts are causing embarrassment or are painful.
- **Topical salicylic acid** is recommended if treatment is appropriate. Topical salicylic acid is not suitable for application to the face, anogenital region, or large areas.
- **Cryotherapy** is often used when topical treatments have failed. Little evidence exists regarding its efficacy, and at its best it is equal in efficacy to topical salicylic acid.
- **Children with plantar warts should not be barred from swimming.** Some swimming pools and schools insist the warts are covered with plastic socks or waterproof plasters.

Practical prescribing points

For further information please see the *Medicines Compendium* (www.medicines.org.uk) or the *British National Formulary* (www.bnf.org).

Topical salicylic acid

- **Treatment may need to be used for 12 weeks or longer.**
- **Before applying treatment, soak the wart** in the bath or shower for five minutes to soften the skin.
- **Debride the wart/verruca surface** gently with a nail file or foot file once a week (or more often if necessary) to remove hard skin.
- **Occlusion,** for example with a plaster, can improve the clearance of warts.

Follow-up advice

- Follow-up is not usually necessary.

Should I refer or investigate?

Refer?

- People with recalcitrant or multiple warts: referral to a dermatologist may be warranted
- Immunosuppressed patients with multiple warts
- Where there is doubt about the diagnosis

Patient information leaflets

The following PILs are available at www.prodigy.nhs.uk

- Warts and Verrucas

Shared decision making

- **Warts and verrucas usually clear without treatment.** You have about a 50/50 chance that they will go within a year. Most go eventually.
- If you prefer treatment, salicylic acid will usually clear warts.
  - Apply each day. It takes up to 3 months or more to clear warts.
  - Rub off the dead tissue from the top of the wart with a nail file or similar once or twice a week.
  - It is best to soak the wart in water for 5 minutes before applying the salicylic acid.
  - You should not apply it to the face.
  - Try not to get the salicylic acid on the surrounding skin.
  - Treatment may work more quickly if you cover the wart with a plaster after applying the salicylic acid each day.
- **Freezing the warts** with liquid nitrogen is an alternative. It is about as effective as acid, but may be painful.
- Children with verrucas should not be barred from swimming.

Drug rationale

Drugs not included

- **Topical formaldehyde:** formaldehyde soaks may be useful in combination with salicylic acid for the treatment of mosaic warts. There is no proprietary product available, but it can be obtained from a specials manufacturer.
- **Topical glutaraldehyde:** glutaraldehyde soaks are an alternative to formaldehyde soaks for the treatment of mosaic warts. However, glutaraldehyde stains the skin brown.
- **Topical silver nitrate:** one small randomized controlled trial showed some evidence of benefit of silver nitrate over placebo. Occasionally pigmented scars develop after silver nitrate use [Yazar and Bazaran, 1994].

Drugs included

Although most studies of topical treatments for cutaneous warts are of poor quality, a recent meta-analysis found that the best available evidence was for treatments containing salicylic acid [Gibbs et al, 2003].
Collodion-based salicylic acid products (Cuplex gel, Duofilm paint, Salatac gel, Salactol paint) form a film over the wart, so often a plaster is not needed to keep the active treatment on the wart area. Occasionally, some people can develop an allergy to the collodion [BNF 49, 2005].
Polyacrylic-based salicylic acid solution (Occlusal solution) also forms a film over the wart.
Salicylic acid 50% ointment does not form a film over the wart. A plaster must be used to keep the ointment in place.
Occlusion has been shown to improve clearance rates of plantar warts [Veien et al, 1991; Focht et al, 2002].

Prescriptions

Advice only: OTC purchase and application

Advice note: over-the counter purchase and application
- Age from 1 month onwards
- You have a wart or a verruca. You can buy preparations from a pharmacist to treat warts and verrucas. Wart/verruca treatment should be applied once a day. It may need to be used for up to 3 months to be effective. Before applying the treatment to the wart or verruca, soak the affected area in warm water to soften the skin (e.g. for 5–10 minutes). Avoid applying the treatment to the skin surrounding the wart/verruca. Wipe off excess paint or gel with a tissue, or apply Vaseline to the surrounding area to protect it, or use a specially designed plaster. Rub the wart/verruca surface gently with a nail file or foot file once a week to remove hard skin.

11% and 12% salicylic acid gel (collodion based)

Salicylic acid 11% gel (Cuplex)
- Age from 1 month onwards
- Cuplex gel. Apply to the wart or verruca twice a day; supply 5 grams; NHS Cost £2.23; OTC Cost £3.49.

Salicylic acid 12% gel (Salatac)
- Age from 1 month onwards
- Salatac gel. Apply to the wart or verruca once a day; supply 8 grams; NHS Cost £3.36; OTC Cost £5.26.

Salicylic acid 12% gel (Bazuka)
- Age from 1 month onwards
- Bazuka gel. Apply to the wart or verruca once a day; supply 5 grams; NHS Cost £3.08; OTC Cost £4.95.

16.7% salicylic acid paint (collodion based)

Salicylic acid 16.7% paint (Duofilm)
- Age from 1 month onwards
- Duofilm paint. Apply to the wart or verruca once a day; supply 15 ml; NHS Cost £1.95; OTC Cost £3.43.

Salicylic acid 16.7% paint (Salactol)
- Age from 1 month onwards
- Salactol. Apply to the wart or verruca once a day; supply 10 ml; NHS Cost £1.95; OTC Cost £3.43.

26% salicylic acid topical solution or gel

Salicylic acid 26% solution (Occlusal)
- Age from 1 month onwards
- Occlusal 26% topical solution. Apply to the wart or verruca once a day; supply 10 ml; NHS Cost £2.98; OTC Cost £5.25.

Salicylic acid 26% gel (Bazuka)
- Age from 1 month onwards
- Bazuka 26% extra strength gel. Apply to the wart or verruca once a day; supply 5 grams; NHS Cost £3.57; OTC Cost £5.75.

50% salicylic acid ointment + plasters (verrucae only)

Salicylic acid 50% ointment (Verrugon)
- Age from 1 month onwards
- Verrugon 50% ointment. Apply to the wart or verruca once a day; supply 6 grams; NHS Cost £2.61; OTC Cost £4.25.

Extended Information

Background information

- What are they? p.1857
- How common are they? p.1857
- How do I know my patient has warts? p.1858
- How are warts caught and spread? p.1858
- What else might it be? p.1858
- Complications and prognosis p.1859

What are they?

- **Warts are benign growths of the skin or mucous membranes** caused by infection with the human papilloma virus (HPV), of which there are more than 80 genotypes.
- **Generally, each type has an affinity for a particular tissue and site of the body.** However, it is possible for some virus types to infect more than one site [Cobb, 1990].
- **Many types of HPV have an affinity for skin** and produce common warts (verruca vulgaris), plane/flat warts (verruca plana), and plantar or foot warts (verruca plantaris). Anogenital warts are caused by several types of HPV that have an affinity for mucous membranes and anogenital skin.

How common are they?

- **Cutaneous warts of the skin can occur at any age** [Lowy and Androphy, 1999], but the incidence peaks at 12–16 years [Cobb, 1990] and declines after 20 years of age [Sterling and Kurtz, 1998].
- **Cutaneous warts are common, but there is little information about incidence and prevalence.** The incidence has been estimated to be 10% in children and young adults [Sterling and Kurtz, 1998]. A study of school children found that 4% of 11-year-olds had warts, but that by the age of 16 years 93% of these children no longer had warts [Williams et al, 1993].
- **A UK study of 1000 children with warts** found that 70% had common warts, 24% plantar warts, 3.5% plane warts, 2% filiform warts, and 0.5% anogenital warts [Sterling and Kurtz, 1998].
- **People with decreased cellular immunity are particularly susceptible to human papilloma virus (HPV) infection** — for example, those on long-term immunosuppressive therapy; or those who have had organ transplants; or those who have AIDS, lymphomas, leukaemias, or Hodgkin's disease. They also tend to have numerous warts that are resistant to treatment [Cobb, 1990; Ordoukhanian and Lane, 1997].
- **Occupational handlers of meat, fish, and poultry have a high incidence of warts on the hands,** where the skin is in prolonged contact with animal flesh [Sterling and Kurtz, 1998].

How do I know my patient has warts?

The diagnosis is made from the characteristic clinical appearance.

Common warts

- **Common warts are rough, scaly, pink or skin-coloured papules with a papillomatous rough surface.** They can be found on any surface, and are usually less than a centimetre in diameter but are occasionally larger.
- **They occur commonly as single or grouped papules** on the hands, fingers, elbows, and feet, but can occur anywhere on the body. In children under 12 years they are common on the knees [Sterling and Kurtz, 1998; Lowy and Androphy, 1999].
- **Periungual warts may be associated with nail biting** [Sterling and Kurtz, 1998].

Filiform warts

- **Filiform warts are hyperkeratotic lesions consisting of small finger-like keratotic projections** [Allen and Siegfried, 2001].
- **They tend to be distributed irregularly,** are often clustered, and commonly occur in the beard area in males [Sterling and Kurtz, 1998].

Plantar warts

- **Plantar warts (commonly called verrucae) first appear as small, shining, sago-grain-like papules,** which soon assume the typical appearance of sharply defined, rounded lesions, with a rough keratotic surface surrounded by a smooth collar of thickened skin. They vary from a millimetre to many centimetres in diameter.
- **They usually occur beneath pressure points** (e.g. the heel or metatarsal head). In older girls and women they occur predominantly on the forefoot [Sterling and Kurtz, 1998].
- **Punctuate black dots** (due to thrombosed capillaries) can be seen after the outer keratinous surface is shaved away. Warts may be painful on pressure, especially if they are sited over a pressure point [Ordoukhanian and Lane, 1997].

Palmar warts

- **Palmar warts are thick, hyperkeratotic lesions** that may be painful on pressure [Lowy and Androphy, 1999].

Mosaic warts

- **Mosaic warts are coalescent plaques of plantar or occasionally palmar warts** [Lowy and Androphy, 1999]. They are often not as painful on pressure as isolated plantar warts are.

Plane/flat warts

- **Plane/flat warts are small (1–5 mm), slightly elevated, smooth, flat-topped lesions with minimal scale.** They are round or polygonal in shape and are usually skin-coloured, light brown, or greyish-yellow, but may be pigmented.
- The number of lesions can vary from one to hundreds.
- They are found most frequently on the hands, face, and legs.
- Contiguous warts may coalesce.
- A linear arrangement in scratch marks due to inoculation is a characteristic feature.
- **Children and young adults are most commonly affected.** However, plane warts also occur in adults, especially in the male beard area.
- Regression is often heralded by inflammation of the lesion, causing itch and erythema.

Butchers' warts

- **Butchers' warts are often larger that common warts and occur on the hands of occupational handlers of meat, poultry, and fish** [Lowy and Androphy, 1999]. Butchers warts are rare.
- **They are usually multiple** [Sterling and Kurtz, 1998] and look like plentiful, normal hand warts.

Epidermodysplasia verruciformis

- **Epidermodysplasia verruciformis is a rare autosomal recessive condition** in which individuals are susceptible to cutaneous human papilloma virus (HPV) infection.
- It usually presents in childhood with widespread warts that persist despite treatment.
- **Lesions occurring on the face and neck are indistinguishable from plane warts.** Lesions on the trunk and limbs tend to be larger, scaly, macular lesions showing depigmentation or varying degrees of brown pigmentation. Thicker plaques are dull pink to violet in colour.
- Typical common warts are often present too.

How are warts caught and spread?

- **Warts of the skin can be transmitted** from person to person by direct contact, indirectly from contaminated surfaces, and from one body location to another in the same person by auto-inoculation [PHLS, 2002]. The virus can be present in the skin before or after obvious clinical infection.
- **The incubation period probably varies from 1 to 24 months** following infection with human papilloma virus (HPV) [PHLS, 2002]. The virus can be present in the skin before or after obvious clinical infection.
- **The risk of a person with cutaneous warts transmitting the infection to others is thought to be low.** Infection is more likely to occur if the skin is macerated and in contact with roughened surfaces (e.g. at swimming pools and communal washing areas) [Johnson, 1995; Sterling et al, 2001].
- **The infectious period is presumed to be as long as the wart is present** [PHLS, 2002].
- **Skin trauma,** including mild abrasions or maceration, greatly predisposes to inoculation of the virus [Sterling and Kurtz, 1998].
- **Common hand warts may spread widely** round the nails, lips, and surrounding skin in those who bite their nails, or to periungual skin in those who suck their fingers [Sterling and Kurtz, 1998].
- **Auto-inoculation** accounts for the local spread of warts and the appearance of apposed lesions on adjacent digits [Cobb, 1990].
- **Shaving of the face or legs** can cause plane/flat warts to spread [Sterling and Kurtz, 1998].

What else might it be?

Differential diagnosis of common warts

- **Seborrhoeic keratosis** — common, superficial, benign, brown or black, greasy plaques [Ankrett and Williams, 1999].
- **Solar keratosis** (actinic keratosis) — scaly lesion on skin exposed to sunlight [Ankrett and Williams, 1999].
- **Pigmented naevus** (mole).
- **Skin tag** — small flesh-coloured or dark brown sessile and pedunculated papillomata predominantly on the neck [Arnold et al, 1990].
- **Squamous cell carcinoma** — a malignant epithelial tumour, usually occurring in sun-exposed areas. It begins as a small, slightly raised, warty, grey or brownish, hyperkeratotic lesion and may metastasise.

- **Molluscum contagiosum** — white umbilicated papules, often with a central depression [Arnold et al, 1990].

Differential diagnosis of plane/flat warts

- **Lichen planus** — an inflammatory pruritic disease of the skin and mucous membranes distinguished by purplish, flat-topped papules.

Differential diagnosis of plantar warts

- **Corns** — circumscribed, horny thickenings on the dorsum of toes and soles [Arnold et al, 1990], usually with a central glassy 'seed'.

Complications and prognosis

Complications

- **Malignant change is extremely rare** [Sterling and Kurtz, 1998]. It may need to be considered in older patients, immunosuppressed patients or subungual lesions.

Prognosis

- **There have been few studies on the natural history of warts, but one study found that two-thirds disappeared within two years,** and large warts were more likely than smaller ones to disappear [Massing and Epstein, 1963].
- A single wart may persist unchanged for months or years, or alternatively large numbers may develop rapidly or after an interval [Sterling and Kurtz, 1998].
- **The average duration of plantar warts (commonly called verrucae) in children** is probably less than one year, and 30–50% disappear over a 6-month period. In older children and adults, a longer duration is not uncommon, and they may persist for several years [Sterling and Kurtz, 1998].
- **Butchers' warts** recur after successful treatment in 50% of people [Sterling and Kurtz, 1998].
- **Warts may be impossible to eradicate in immunocompromised people** [Lowy and Androphy, 1999].

Management issues

General issues p.1859
Recommended treatments for use in primary care p.1859
Medicines management: topical salicylic acid p.1860
Other pharmacological and alternative treatments p.1860

General issues

- **A policy of no treatment is generally recommended.** Cutaneous warts are benign, and in immunocompetent people usually resolve spontaneously in months or years as natural immunity is gained. However:
- **Warts are often unsightly,** and many people request treatment for cosmetic reasons. There is considerable social stigma associated with visible warts.
- Plantar and periungual warts can be painful.
- Many people will have tried over-the-counter treatments before seeking advice.
- **Children with plantar warts should not be barred from swimming.** Some swimming-pool attendants or schools have their own regulations and insist on covering the plantar wart with plastic verruca socks or waterproof plasters. Care is needed at swimming pools, gymnasiums, and changing rooms [PHLS, 2002].
- **The main problem with plantar warts is the pain on walking and pressure.** Chiropody has an important role. Pain can frequently be relieved by paring or rubbing down the wart regularly, and may be all that is required for symptom relief. This can be the most important part of treatment for plantar warts.
- **Topical wart treatments should not be used on the face,** because of the risk of severe irritation and possible scarring.
- **Referral to a dermatologist** for someone with recalcitrant or multiple warts may be warranted. Many areas will have locally agreed guidelines or policies on whether patients with warts should be referred.

Recommended treatments for use in primary care

Salicylic acid

- **Although most studies of topical treatments for cutaneous warts are of poor quality, a recent Cochrane review** found that topical treatments containing salicylic acid compared to placebo are effective and safe — NNT = 4, odds ratio 3.9 (95% CI 2.4 to 6.4) [Gibbs et al, 2003].
- **Minor skin irritation occurs occasionally but there are no major adverse effects** [Gibbs et al, 2002].
- Topical salicylic acid is not suitable for application to the face, anogenital region, or large areas [BNF 49, 2005].

Cryotherapy

- **Cryotherapy is often used as a second-line treatment** when topical salicylic acid has failed, but there is no clear evidence to support this approach. Little evidence exists for the efficacy of cryotherapy. At best, it may be only of equal efficacy to topical salicylic acid (OR 1.15, 95% CI 0.7 to 1.8). [Bigby et al, 2002; Gibbs et al, 2002].
- A Cochrane review compared trials of aggressive cryotherapy with gentle cryotherapy and found that aggressive was more effective (OR 3.7, 95% CI 1.5 to 9.4). There were insufficient data on adverse effects, but the impression was that pain and blistering were more frequent with aggressive cryotherapy [Gibbs et al, 2003]. The criteria for distinguishing aggressive from gentle cryotherapy have never been properly defined [Bigby et al, 2002].
- **Risks of cryotherapy** include pain, blistering, pigmentary disturbance, scarring, damage to nail growth (periungual warts), and rarely damage to deeper structures (nerve, tendon).

Combination treatment with salicylic acid and cryotherapy

- Although there is no good evidence, common sense dictates that using salicylic acid between cryotherapy treatments may be useful. Salicylic acid thins the wart, which improves cosmesis (hands) or function (foot) and may reduce the insulating effect of keratin against cold when the next cryotherapy is performed, therefore improving response.

Duct tape

- **One small randomized controlled trial found that occlusion with duct tape was at least as effective as cryotherapy.** Warts were occluded for a mean of 6.5 days and the duct tape removed for 12 hours before being reapplied [Focht et al, 2002].
- **Duct tape may be a useful option:** it is a painless, inexpensive treatment that GPs may wish to try. However, there is a lack of standardisation of treatment, and it is not known whether or not occlusion with other types of tape or plasters would be equally effective. There is a lack of data on possible adverse effects.

Ethylene glycol

- **Products containing ethylene glycol** (e.g. Wartner) are also available for the treatment of warts. However, we have found no evidence of their efficacy or safety.

Treatment of mosaic warts

- **Mosaic warts can be difficult to treat.** If salicylic acid is applied, smaller warts may be missed if application is circumspect; and if applied more liberally, normal skin may become macerated. Some experts recommend the use of formaldehyde soak, but this is not available as a proprietary product and has to be obtained from a specials manufacturer. Common sense suggests that it is best to combine the two treatments — a formaldehyde soak to the affected zones to get rid of tiny lesions, and salicylic acid to the thicker area within it.
- **Glutaraldehyde** is an alternative soak, but stains the skin brown.

Medicines management: topical salicylic acid

- Topical salicylic acid should be applied daily for a number of weeks.
- Treatment may need to be continued for 12 weeks or more to clear warts.
- There is no available evidence to guide the best choice of salicylic acid product.
- **The warts should be soaked in a bath or shower for five minutes before applying salicylic acid.** Debride the wart/verruca surface gently with a nail file or foot file once a week (or more often if necessary) to remove hard skin. (Note: some products require more frequent debridement, e.g. 2–3 times a week.)
- **Collodion-based salicylic acid products** (Cuplex gel, Duofilm paint, Salatac gel, Salactol paint) form a film over the wart, so often a plaster is not needed to keep the active treatment on the wart area. Occasionally, some people can develop an allergy to the collodion [BNF 49, 2005].
- **Polyacrylic-based salicylic acid solution** (Occlusal solution) also forms a film over the wart.
- **Salicylic acid 50% ointment** does not form a film over the wart. A plaster must be used to keep the ointment in place, and care is needed to protect the surrounding skin from the ointment. (This can be achieved using a corn pad to protect the surrounding skin, or by applying Vaseline or white soft paraffin to the surrounding skin before treatment is applied.)
- **Occlusion has been shown to improve clearance rates of plantar warts.** One open study found that treatment with a collodion-based salicylic acid gel plus occlusion was more effective at clearing plantar warts than was salicylic acid gel alone [Veien et al, 1991]. A more recent randomized controlled trial found that occlusion with duct tape was more effective for the treatment of common warts than was cryotherapy [Focht et al, 2002].
- **In profoundly immunosuppressed individuals,** such as transplant recipients, warts are usually impossible to cure, and the emphasis should be on symptomatic relief.

Other pharmacological and alternative treatments

- Table 1 outlines the pharmacological and physical treatments other than salicylic acid and cryotherapy that may be used to treat warts and verrucae, and table 2 outlines complimentary therapies that are available.

[Hirose et al, 1994; Bigby et al, 2002; Gibbs et al, 2002; Gibbs et al, 2003]

W

able 1: Pharmacological and physical treatments other than salicylic acid and cryotherapy (many are not suitable for use primary care).

'eatment	Type and number of studies	Study findings	Comment
eomycin — intralesional [Rossi et al, 1981; unkvad et al, 1983; Bunney et al, 1984; ayes and O'Keefe, 1986; Perez et al, 1992]	5 randomized controlled trials (RCTs)	Conflicting evidence regarding benefit	Uncertain benefit, but it works in some. Also significant handling and side effect (vasospasm) risks
arbon dioxide laser	No RCTs		
metidine [Bauman et al, 1996; Yilmaz et 1996; Karabulut et al, 1997; Rogers et al, 99]	4 RCTs	No significant difference between cimetidine and placebo or local treatments	Small studies Limited evidence High doses needed. May cause gastrointestinal upset.
metidine plus levamisole [Parsad et al, 99]	1 RCT	Evidence of significant benefit	Limited evidence Not licensed in the UK
ntact immunotherapy with nitrochlorobenzene (DNCB) 'ilson, 1983; Rosado-Cancino et al, 1989] NCB is not suitable for use now, but phencyprone was used in one small study uckley et al, 1999]	2 small RCTs 1 small open trial	Some evidence of efficacy	Small studies Limited evidence of benefit. Best confined to specialist centres in view of possible major local irritation and blistering for the patient and for staff handling the agent.
orouracil unney, 1973; Hursthouse, 1975; Schmidt d Jacobsen, 1981; Artese et al, 1994]	3 RCTS 1 open trial	Some evidence of efficacy	Trials generally of poor quality Risk of toxicity. Evidence of similar effectiveness to other topical treatments
rmaldehyde nderson, 1963]	One controlled trial (not randomized)	No significant difference compared with placebo	Insignificant benefit
utaraldehyde lirose et al, 1994]	No RCT One small, non placebo, non controlled trial	Insufficient data	Insufficient data
osine pranobex enton et al, 1991]	One RCT	No significant difference compared with placebo	Small study Limited evidence of no benefit
terferon alpha systemic	No RCTs	No data	No data
erferon alpha — intralesional azin et al, 1982; Berman et al, 1986; nce et al, 1986; Varnavides et al, 1997]	4 RCTs	Pooled data from 3 trials showed no benefit over placebo	Poor quality trials. Limited evidence of no benefit Significant systemic adverse effects with higher doses
vamisole orales-Caballero et al, 1978; Saul et al, 80; Amer et al, 1991]	Two RCTs One controlled clinical trial that was not randomized	The RCTs found no significant difference compared with placebo. The controlled trial showed evidence of benefit	Small studies. Insufficient evidence of benefit Not licensed
otodynamic treatment eien et al, 1977; Stahl et al, 1979; Stender al, 1999; Stender et al, 2000; Fabbrocini et 2001]	5 RCTs	Generally showed benefit	Limited evidence of benefit. Trials differed considerably in quality and methodology
dophyllin	No RCTs		
dophyllotoxin	No RCTs		
lsed dye laser obson et al, 2000]	One RCT	Similar benefit to treatment with cryotherapy or canthradin	Limited evidence of benefit
ver nitrate azar and Bazaran, 1994]	One RCT	Evidence of benefit compared with placebo	Limited evidence of benefit. No adverse effects reported in this trial. Can tattoo the skin black because of silver salts.
rgical procedures — curettage and cision	No RCTs		

W

Table 2: Complementary therapies.

Treatment	Type and number of studies	Study findings	Comment
Distant healing [Harkness et al, 2000]	One RCT	No significant difference compared with placebo	Evidence of no benefit. Note: the end point in this trial was the number of warts that disappeared, rather than total clearance.
Homeopathy [Labrecque et al, 1992; Kainz et al, 1996]	2 RCTs	No significant difference compared with placebo	Evidence of no benefit.
Hypnotic suggestion 1 RCT [Spanos et al, 1990] 2 RCTS [Spanos et al, 1988]	3 RCTs (two reported in same article)	Limited evidence of benefit for clearance of one wart	Small studies. Lack of evidence of benefit for total wart clearance.

References

NHS staff in England can link, free of charge, from references to full text journals by clicking on [Full text] on the PRODIGY website.

Note: all users can access the full texts of DH papers without an Athens password.

1. Allen, A.L. and Siegfried, E.C. (2001) Management of warts and molluscum in adolescents. *Adolescent Medicine State of the Art Reviews* **12**(2), 229–242. [Full text]
2. Amer, M., Tosson, Z., Soliman, A. et al (1991) Verrucae treated by levamisole. *International Journal of Dermatology* **30**(10), 738–740.
3. Anderson, I. (1963) The treatment of plantar warts. *British Journal of Dermatology* **75**(1), 29–32.
4. Ankrett, V.O. and Williams, I. (Eds.) (1999) *Quick reference atlas of dermatology*. Tunbridge Wells: M.S.L.
5. Arnold, H., Odam, R.B. and James, W.D. (Eds.) (1990) *Andrews' diseases of the skin: clinical dermatology*. 8th edn. Philadelphia: Saunders and Co.
6. Artese, O., Cazzato, C., Cucchiarelli, S. et al (1994) Controlled study: medical therapy (5-fluouracil, salicylic acid) vs physical therapy (DTC) of warts. *Dermatologic Clinics* **14**(1), 55–59.
7. Bauman, C., Francis, J.S., Vanderhooft, S. and Sybert, V.P. (1996) Cimetidine therapy for multiple viral warts in children. *Journal of the American Academy of Dermatology* **35**(2 Pt 1), 271–272.
8. Benton, E.C., Nolan, M.W., Kemmett, D. and Cubie, H.A. (1991) Trial of inosine pranobex in the management of cutaneous viral warts. *Journal of Dermatological Treatment* **1**, 295–297.
9. Berman, B., Davis-Reed, L., Silverstein, L. et al (1986) Treatment of verrucae vulgaris with alpha 2 interferon. *Journal of Infectious Diseases* **154**(2), 328–330.
10. Bigby, M., Gibbs, S., Harvey, I. and Sterling, J. (2002) Non-genital warts. *Clinical Evidence* **Volume 8**, 1731–1744.
11. BNF 49 (2005) *British National Formulary*. 49th edn. London: British Medical Association and Royal Pharmaceutical Society of Great Britain.
12. Buckley, D.A., Keane, F.M., Munn, S.E. et al (1999) Recalcitrant viral warts treated by diphencyprone immunotherapy. *British Journal of Dermatology* **141**(2), 292–296.
13. Bunney, M.H. (1973) The treatment of plantar warts with 5-fluorouracil. *British Journal of Dermatology* **89**(1), 96–97.
14. Bunney, M.H., Nolan, M.W., Buxton, P.K. et al (198 The treatment of resistant warts with intralesional bleomycin: a controlled clinical trial. *British Journal c Dermatology* **111**(2), 197–207.
15. Cobb, M.W. (1990) Human papillomavirus infection *Journal of the American Academy of Dermatology* **22**(4), 547–566.
16. Fabbrocini, G., Di Costanzo, M.P., Riccardo, A.M. e al (2001) Photodynamic therapy with topical delta-aminolaevulinic acid for the treatment of plantar war *Journal of Photochemistry & Photobiology. B – Biology* **61**(1–2), 30–34.
17. Focht, D.R., Spicer, C. and Fairchok, M.P. (2002) Th efficacy of duct tape vs cryotherapy in the treatment c verruca vulgaris (the common wart). *Archives of Pediatrics & Adolescent Medicine* **156**(10), 971–974 [Full text]
18. Gibbs, S., Harvey, I., Sterling, J. et al (2002) Local treatments for cutaneous warts: systematic review. *British Medical Journal* **325**(7362), 461–468. [Full text]
19. Gibbs, S., Harvey, I., Sterling, J.C. and Stark, R. (200 *Local treatments for cutaneous warts (Cochrane Review)*. The Cochrane Library. Issue 3. Chichester, UK: John Wiley & Sons, Ltd. www.nelh.nhs.uk/cochrane.asp [Accessed: 07/07/2005].
20. Harkness, E.F., Abbot, N.C. and Ernst, E. (2000) A randomized trial of distant healing for skin warts. *American Journal of Medicine* **108**(6), 448–452.
21. Hayes, M.E. and O'Keefe, E.J. (1986) Reduced dose bleomycin in the treatment of recalcitrant warts. *Journal of the American Academy of Dermatology* **15**(5 Pt 1), 1002–1006.
22. Hirose, R., Hori, M., Shukuwa, T. et al (1994) Topic treatment of resistant warts with glutaraldehyde. *Journal of Dermatology* **21**(4), 248–253.
23. Hursthouse, M.W. (1975) A controlled trial on the u of topical 5-fluorouracil on viral warts. *British Journ of Dermatology* **92**(1), 93–96.
24. Kainz, J.T., Kozel, G., Haidvogl, M. and Smolle, J. (1996) Homoeopathic versus placebo therapy of children with warts on the hands: a randomized, double-blind clinical trial. *Dermatology* **193**(4), 318–320.

25. Karabulut, A.A., Sahin, S. and Eksioglu, M. (1997) Is cimetidine effective for nongenital warts: a double-blind, placebo-controlled study. *Archives of Dermatology* **133**(4), 533–534.
26. Labrecque, M., Audet, D., Latulippe, L.G. and Drouin, J. (1992) Homeopathic treatment of plantar warts. *Canadian Medical Association Journal* **146**(10), 1749–1753.
27. Lowy, D.R. and Androphy, E.A. (1999) Warts. In: Fradberg, I.M., Eisen, A.Z., Wolff, K. et al (Eds.) *Fitzpatrick's dermatology in general medicine*. 5th edn. New York: McGraw-Hill.
28. Massing, A.M. and Epstein, W.L. (1963) Natural history of warts. *Archives of Dermatology* **87**, 306–310.
29. Morales-Caballero, H.G., Ruiz, M.R. and Tamayo, L. (1978) Levamisole in the treatment of warts (double blind study). *Dermatologia* **22**, 20–25.
30. Munkvad, M., Genner, J., Staberg, B. and Kongsholm, H. (1983) Locally injected bleomycin in the treatment of warts. *Dermatologica* **167**(2), 86–89.
31. Ordoukhanian, E. and Lane, A.T. (1997) Warts and molluscum contagiosum: beware of treatments worse than the disease. *Postgraduate Medicine* **101**(2), 223–226.
32. Parsad, D., Saini, R. and Negi, K.S. (1999) Comparison of combination of cimetidine and levamisole with cimetidine alone in the treatment of recalcitrant warts. *Australasian Journal of Dermatology* **40**(2), 93–95.
33. Pazin, G.J., Ho, M., Haverkos, H.W. et al (1982) Effects of interferon-alpha on human warts. *Journal of Interferon Research* **2**(2), 235–243.
34. Perez, A.R., Weiss, E. and Piquero, M.J. (1992) Hypertonic saline solution vs intralesional bleomycin in the treatment of common warts. *Dermatologia Venezolana* **30**, 176–178.
35. PHLS (2002) *Guidelines on the management of communicable diseases in schools and nurseries: warts and verrucas*. Public Health Laboratory Service. www.phls.co.uk [Accessed: 25/09/2002].
36. Robson, K.J., Cunningham, N.M., Kruzan, K.L. et al (2000) Pulsed-dye laser versus conventional therapy in the treatment of warts: a prospective randomized trial. *Journal of the American Academy of Dermatology* **43**(2 Pt 1), 275–280.
37. Rogers, C.J., Gibney, M.D., Siegfried, E.C. et al (1999) Cimetidine therapy for recalcitrant warts in adults: is it any better than placebo? *Journal of the American Academy of Dermatology* **41**(1), 123–127.
38. Rosado-Cancino, M.A., Ruiz-Maldonado, R., Tamayo, L. and Laterza, A.M. (1989) Treatment of multiple and stubborn warts in children with 1-chloro-2, 4-dinitrobenzene (DNCB) and placebo. *Dermatoligia Revista Mexicana* **33**(4), 245–252.
39. Rossi, E., Soto, J.H., Battan, J. and Villalba, L. (1981) Intralesional bleomycin in verruca vulgaris. Double-blind study. *Dermatoligia Revista Mexicana* **25**, 158–165.
40. Saul, A., Sanz, R. and Gomez, M. (1980) Treatment of multiple viral warts with levamisole. *International Journal of Dermatology* **19**(6), 342–343.
41. Schmidt, H. and Jacobsen, F.K. (1981) Double-blind randomized clinical study on treatment of warts with fluouracil-containing topical preparation. *Zeitschrift fur Hautkrankheiten* **56**(1), 41–43.
42. Spanos, N.P., Stenstrom, R.J. and Johnston, J.C. (1988) Hypnosis, placebo, and suggestion in the treatment of warts. *Psychosomatic Medicine* **50**(3), 245–260.
43. Spanos, N.P., Williams, V. and Gwynn, M.I. (1990) Effects of hypnotic, placebo, and salicylic acid treatments on wart regression. *Psychosomatic Medicine* **52**(1), 109–114.
44. Stahl, D., Veien, N.K. and Wulf, H.C. (1979) Photodynamic inactivation of virus warts: a controlled clinical trial. *Clinical & Experimental Dermatology* **4**(1), 81–85.
45. Stender, I.M., Lock-Andersen, J. and Wulf, H.C. (1999) Recalcitrant hand and foot warts successfully treated with photodynamic therapy with topical 5-aminolaevulinic acid: a pilot study. *Clinical & Experimental Dermatology* **24**(3), 154–159.
46. Stender, I.M., Na, R., Fogh, H. et al (2000) Photodynamic therapy with 5-aminolaevulinic acid or placebo for recalcitrant foot and hand warts: randomised double-blind trial. *Lancet* **355**(9208), 963–966. [Full text]
47. Sterling, J.C. and Kurtz, J.B. (1998) Viral Infections. In: Champion, R.H., Burton, J.L., Burns, D.A and Breathnach, S.M. (Eds.) *Textbook of dermatology*. 6th edn. Oxford: Blackwell Science. 995–1096.
48. Vance, J.C., Bart, B.J., Hansen, R.C. et al (1986) Intralesional recombinant alpha-2 interferon for the treatment of patients with condyloma acuminatum or verruca plantaris. *Archives of Dermatology* **122**(3), 272–277.
49. Varnavides, C.K., Henderson, C.A. and Cuncliffe, W.J. (1997) Intralesional interferon: ineffective in common viral warts. *Journal of Dermatological Treatment* **8**, 169–172.
50. Veien, N.K., Genner, J., Brodthagen, H. and Wettermark, G. (1977) Photodynamic inactivation of verrucae vulgares II. *Acta Dermato-Venereologica* **57**(5), 445–447.
51. Veien, N.K., Madsen, S.M., Avrach, W. et al (1991) The treatment of plantar warts with a keratolytic agent and occlusion. *Journal of Dermatological Treatment* **2**(2), 59–61.
52. Williams, H.C., Pottier, A. and Strachan, D. (1993) The descriptive epidemiology of warts in British schoolchildren. *British Journal of Dermatology* **128**(5), 504–511.
53. Wilson, P. (1983) Immunotherapy v cryotherapy for hand warts: a controlled trial. *Scottish Medical Journal* **28**(2), 191.
54. Yazar, S and Bazaran, E. (1994) Efficacy of silver nitrate pencils in the treatment of common warts. *Journal of Dermatology* **21**(5), 329–333.
55. Yilmaz, E., Alpsoy, E. and Basaran, E. (1996) Cimetidine therapy for warts: a placebo-controlled, double-blind study. *Journal of the American Academy of Dermatology* **34**(6), 1005–1007.

W

A

Acne vulgaris 1

What is it? 10
How common is it? 10
How do I know my patient has it? 10
What else might it be? 11

Anti-androgens 14
Antibiotic resistance 11
Antibiotics, oral 11, 13
Other 14
Antibiotics, topical 13
Assessing people with acne 11
Azelaic acid 13
Benzoyl peroxide 12
In combination with topical antibiotics 14
Combination therapy 14
Complications and prognosis 11
Erythromycin 14
General issues 11
Isotretinoin, oral 15
Referral 12
Retinoids, topical 13
In combination with topical antibiotics 15
Tetracyclines 13
Therapy, topical 11
In combination with oral antibiotics 15
Topical retinoids in combination with benzoyl peroxide 15
Treatment, duration of 12
Treatment options 12
Other topical agents 13
Trimethoprim 14
Zinc in combination with topical antibiotics 14

Acupuncture

in Back pain – lower 204
in Nausea and vomiting in pregnancy 1277
in Neck pain 1302

Adverse drug reactions 17

What is it? 17
How common is it? 17
What should alert me to the possibility of an adverse drug reaction? 17
How do I establish causality? 17
What about defective medicines? 19
What happens to the information? 19
How do I make a report? 18
What should be reported? 18
Newer products 18
Established products 18
Who can report? 18

Additional reporting 20
Adverse reactions, preventing 19
Complications and prognosis 18
Special problems 19

Alcohol

see Alcohol – problem drinking
in Breast cancer – managing women with a family history 252
in Coronary heart disease risk – identification and management 464
in Gout 867
in Infertility 1081
in Preconceptual counselling 1541

Alcohol – problem drinking 21

What is it? 25
How common is it? 25
How do I know my patient has a drink problem? 26
How do I know if there is dependence on alcohol? 26
How do I assess the degree of alcohol dependence? 26
When is pharmacological detoxification appropriate? 29
What should I prescribe for pharmacological detoxification? 29
What is the recommended regimen for detoxification with chlordiazepoxide? 30
When should I recommend vitamin B supplements? 30
When should acamprosate be started? 31
How long should I continue treatment for? 32
How should I prescribe benzodiazepines in the elderly? 32
How should I prescribe benzodiazepines in people with hepatic impairment? 32

Abstinence, maintaining 31
Maintaining contact 31
Other interventions 31
Pharmacological interventions 31
Psychosocial interventions 31
Acamprosate 31
Alcohol, reducing intake 28
Alcohol, unit of 25
Alcohol dependence 25
Alcohol Use Disorders Identification Test 26
Benzodiazepines 32
Binge drinking 25
Clinical presentations where the role of alcohol should be considered 27
Social 27
Occupational 27
Psychiatric 27
Physical 27
Complications 27
Detoxification 29
Community *vs* inpatient 29
Pharmacological 29
Practical issues 29
Supportive care 29
Disulfiram 31
Driving licence implications 28
General issues 28
Harmful drinking 25
Hazardous drinking 25
Medicines management 31
Minimal interventions 28
Naltrexone 31
Presentation 26
Prognosis 28
Sensible drinking 25
during pregnancy 25
Thiamine, parenteral (Pabrinex®) 32
Treatments, brief 28
Treatments, intensive 29
Vitamin B supplements in chronic deficiency 30
Vitamin B supplements during detoxification 30

Allergic rhinitis 34

What is it? 48
How is it classified? 48
How common is it? 48
How do I know my patient has it? 48
What are the triggers? 48
What else might it be? 49
Are complementary therapies effective? 54
How should I manage allergic rhinitis in pregnancy? 53
How should I manage related eye symptoms? 53
What drug treatments should I use first-line? 50

When should I use oral antihistamines? 51
Which oral antihistamine should I use? 51
What is the evidence for oral antihistamines? 51
When should I use intranasal antihistamines? 51
Which intranasal antihistamine should I use? 51
What is the evidence for intranasal antihistamines? 51
When should I use oral corticosteroids? 53
When should I use intranasal corticosteroids? 52
Which intranasal corticosteroid should I use? 52
What is the evidence for intranasal corticosteroids? 51
What alternative or add-on drugs are useful? 52
Is allergen avoidance effective? 50
What practical advice can be given on allergen avoidance? 50
When is surgery of benefit? 53
When should immunotherapy (desensitization) be used? 53

Allergen avoidance 50
Antihistamines, intranasal 51
Antihistamines, oral 51, 54
Complications 49
Corticosteroids, intranasal 51, 55
Decongestants, intranasal 52
Decongestants, oral 52
Drug treatment, adverse effects of 54
    Decongestants 55
    Oral corticosteroids 55
Drug treatment, practical issues of 54
Drug treatment, in children 55
Drug treatment, in pregnant women 55
    Oral drugs 55
    Topical drugs 55
Examination 49
History 48
Investigations 49
Ipratropium bromide, intranasal 52
Leukotriene antagonists 53
Management, overview of 50
Medicines management 54
Prognosis 49
Sodium cromoglicate, intranasal 52

Alpha-blockers

in Anal fissure 85
in Diabetes Type 1 and 2 – hypertension 543, 551, 552
in Hypertension 978, 996, 997
in Prostate – benign hyperplasia 1569, 1573

Amenorrhoea 58

What is it? 59
How common is it? 60
What are the more common causes seen in general practice? 60
What can cause primary amenorrhoea? 59
How do I assess my patient with primary amenorrhoea? 61
What can cause secondary amenorrhoea? 60
How do I assess my patient with secondary amenorrhoea? 62
How do I interpret the laboratory findings? 62

Cardiovascular disease, prevention of 64
Complications and prognosis 62
Constitutional delay 60
Definitions 59
Endometrial hyperplasia, prevention of 64
Examination 61, 62
Exercise-associated amenorrhoea 61
General 63
History 61, 62
Hyperprolactinaemia 61
Infertility, management of 63
Investigations 61, 62
Osteoporosis, prevention of 64
Polycystic ovary syndrome 60
'Post-pill' amenorrhoea 61
    Management of 64
Premature ovarian failure 61
Primary, common causes of 60
Progestogen-associated amenorrhoea 61
Secondary, common causes of 60
Secondary to use of depot medroxyprogesterone acetate, management of 64
Turner's syndrome 60
Weight-related amenorrhoea 61

Anaemia – iron deficiency 66

What is it? 68
How common is it? 68
How do I know my patient has it? 69
Which symptoms may be present? 69
Which signs may be present? 69
Which investigations are useful in the diagnosis of iron deficiency anaemia? 69
How are these investigations affected by pregnancy? 69
How do I diagnose the cause of iron deficiency anaemia? 70
What else might it be? 69
How do I treat iron deficiency anaemia? 70
How do I treat iron deficiency anaemia during pregnancy? 70

Complications 69
    specific to pregnancy 69
Medicines management 71

Anaemia – macrocytic 72

What is it? 74
How common is vitamin B_{12} deficiency? 74
How common is folate deficiency? 74
How do I know my patient has it? 74
Which symptoms may be present? 74
Which signs may be present? 74
What else might it be? 75
How do I treat vitamin B_{12} deficiency? 76
How do I treat folate deficiency? 76
Which issues of folate deficiency are particular to pregnancy? 76

Complications 75
General issues 75
Investigations 74
Prognosis 75

Anal fissure 77

What is it? 81
What causes it? 81
How common is it? 82
How do I know my patient has it? 82
What else might it be? 82
How should I manage acute anal fissures in adults? 82
How do I manage children with anal fissure in primary care? 84
How do I manage chronic anal fissures in adults? 83
How do I manage recurrent anal fissures? 84
What is the evidence for the use of glyceryl trinitrate in adults? 83
What is the evidence for the use of glyceryl trinitrate in children? 84
What new drug treatments may be effective for the treatment of chronic anal fissures? 85
What treatments are available in secondary care? 84

Alpha-adrenoreceptor blockers 85
Botulinum toxin 85

Calcium-channel blockers 85
Complications 82
Management, overview of 82
Muscarinic agonists 85
Nitrates other than GTN, topical 85
Prognosis 82
Signs 82
Surgical treatments 84
Symptoms 82

Analgesia

in Ankylosing spondylitis 124
in Back pain – lower 203
in Chlamydia – genital 323
in Dental abscess 479
in Dysmenorrhoea 619
in Endometriosis 736, 743
in Gout 848, 851
in Haemorrhoids 871
in Influenza 1086
in Insect bites and stings 1101
in Migraine 1230, 1243
in Neck pain 1299
in Osteoarthritis 1351, 1352, 1355, 1356, 1358, 1359, 1362, 1363, 1366, 1368, 1371, 1372
in Otitis externa 1396, 1398
in Otitis media – acute 1408, 1415
in Palliative care – oral problems 1471
in Palliative care – pain 1495
in Pelvic inflammatory disease 1515
in Urinary tract infection (lower) – men 1807

Angina 87

What is it? 102
How common is it? 102
How do I know my patient has it? 103
What else might it be? 103
How might angina affect the person's lifestyle? 104

Antiplatelet drugs 106
Beta-blockers 107
Calcium-channel blockers 107
Cardiovascular risk, estimation of 104
Chest pain, cardiac causes of 103
Chest pain, non-cardiac causes of 103
Coexisting disease, management of 105
Complications 103
Diagnosis and investigations 104
Dual therapy 106
Examination 103
History 103
HRT in the management of angina 107
Lifestyle interventions 105
Medicines management 106
Nitrates 107
Potassium-channel activators 107
Prognosis 103
Referral to a cardiologist 104
Risk factors, managing 105
Surgical treatment 107
Symptoms, immediate relief of 106
Symptoms, long-term prevention of 106
    Supporting evidence 106
Therapeutic interventions 105

Ankylosing spondylitis 109

What is it? 119
How common is it? 120
How do I know my patient has it? 120
What else might it be? 121
How do I manage ankylosing spondylitis? 122
Which nonsteroidal anti-inflammatory drug should I use? 123
Which injectable corticosteroid should I use? 124
How should intra-articular corticosteroids be administered? 124
When should I avoid injecting a joint? 124

Analgesia 124
Clinical features 120
Codeine 124
Complications, common 121
Complications, less common 121
Corticosteroids for injection, long-acting 123
Corticosteroids, intra-articular 124
Drug treatment 122
    New and specialized treatments 123
Management, non-drug 122
Management, overview of 122
Medicines management 123
Methotrexate 123
New York criteria, modified 121
Nonsteroidal anti-inflammatory drugs 122, 123
Paracetamol 124
Prognosis 121
Quality of life 121
Socio economic impact 121
Sulfasalazine 123
Surgery 123
TNF-alpha blocking agents 123

Anorexia nervosa

see Eating disorders

Antibiotics

in Acne vulgaris 11, 13, 14, 15
in Bites – human and animal 216, 220
in Blepharitis 225
in Boils, carbuncles, paronychia, & staphylococcal whitlow 244
in Chest infections 292, 305, 306
in Chlamydia – genital 323
in Chronic obstructive pulmonary disease 334, 344
in Conjunctivitis – infective 368, 371
in Corneal superficial injury 450
in Dental abscess 480
in Dermatitis – contact 507, 509
in Dyspepsia – proven DU, GU, or NSAID-associated ulcer 648
in Dyspepsia – proven non-ulcer dyspepsia 675, 676
in Dyspepsia – symptoms (uninvestigated by endoscopy) 698
in Eczema – atopic 732
in Gastroenteritis 802, 805, 807, 810, 813, 815, 818, 825
in Impetigo 1074
in Lacerations 1130, 1133, 1141
in Otitis externa 1404
in Otitis media – acute 1408, 1413, 1414
in Pelvic inflammatory disease 1514, 1517
in Rosacea 1651
in Sinusitis 1713, 1721
in Sore throat – acute 1739
in Urethritis – male 1792, 1793
in Urinary tract infection (lower) – men 1806, 1807
in Urinary tract infection (lower) – women 1825, 1826, 1827, 1828
in Urinary tract infection – children 1834, 1839, 1840

Antihistamines

in Allergic rhinitis 51, 54
in Chickenpox 317
in Conjunctivitis – allergic 366
in Insect bites and stings 1099, 1101, 1107

in Nausea and vomiting in pregnancy 1276
in Palliative care – nausea/vomiting/malignant bowel obstruction 1466
in Pruritus ani 1589
in Pubic lice 1602
in Shingles and postherpetic neuralgia 1693, 1695, 1710
in Urticaria and angio-oedema 1853, 1854

Antiplatelets

see Aspirin
in Angina 106
in Atrial fibrillation 185
in Diabetes Type 1 and 2 – hypertension 552
in Hypertension 997
in Transient ischaemic attack – not in atrial fibrillation 1770

Aphthous ulcer 126

What is it? 128
What causes it? 128
How common is it? 128
How do I know my patient has it? 128
What else might it be? 128
How should I treat aphthous ulcers? 129
Which factors might precipitate aphthous ulcers? 129
- Complications 129
- General issues 129
- Prognosis 129
- Specialist treatments 130

Aspirin

in Angina 88
in Atrial fibrillation 176, 185, 186
in Coronary heart disease risk – identification and management 453, 455, 456, 464
in Diabetes Type 1 and 2 – hypertension 545, 551
in Diabetes Type 2 – lipid management 587
in Gout 865
in Hypertension 981, 992
in Migraine 1238
in Nonsteroidal anti-inflammatory drugs (NSAIDs) 1306, 1307, 1308
in Prior myocardial infarction – prophylactic treatments 1552, 1554, 1557, 1560
in Transient ischaemic attack – not in atrial fibrillation 1767, 1768, 1771, 1772

Asthma 131

What is asthma? 152
How common is asthma? 153
How do I know my patient has asthma? 153
What else might it be? 153
What are the principles of managing asthma? 154
How can asthma be prevented? 154
What interventions other than drugs are used in managing asthma? 154
Does allergen avoidance help? 154
Is it advisable to stop smoking? 154
How do I help people to stop smoking? 155
What is the role of patient education and self-management? 155
How do I set up a structured asthma programme and action plan? 155
What drugs should be used to manage chronic asthma? 155
What is the stepwise approach to the management of chronic asthma? 156
What else do I need to know about managing asthma? 158
How should I review and monitor someone with asthma? 158
Is there a standard way to structure and record the clinical review? 158
Should I prescribe a peak flow meter to be used at home? 159
When should I refer someone with asthma? 159
How do I manage exercise-induced asthma? 159
How do I manage occupational asthma? 159
How do I manage asthma during pregnancy and breastfeeding? 160
How do I manage someone with an acute exacerbation asthma? 160
What delivery system should I recommend for inhaled drugs? 162
What factors influence the choice of inhaler device? 162
What inhaler devices are suitable for adults? 162
What inhaler devices are suitable for children aged 5–15 years? 162
What inhaler devices are suitable for children under 5 years? 162
What spacer device for pressurized metered-dose inhale and when? 162
When should a breath-actuated device be recommended? 163
When is a nebulizer recommended? 163
Which pressurized metered-dose inhalers are available a HFA products? 164
How do I transfer someone from CFC pMDI to HFA pMDI? 165
- Adverse reactions to HFA pMDIs, reporting 165
- Complementary and alternative medicine 158
- Chlorofluorocarbon-free inhaler devices 164
- Complications 154
- Differential diagnosis of asthma in older children and adults 153
- Differential diagnosis of asthma in younger children and infants 153
- Indications for referral of older children and adults with possible asthma 159
- Indications for referral of younger children with possible asthma 159
- Inhaled corticosteroids: safety issues 163
  - ICS in adults 164
  - ICS in children 164
- Interventions for which asthma alone is not an indication 158
- Interventions which may be beneficial in specific circumstances 158
- Leukotriene receptor antagonists 164
- Management of chronic asthma, stepwise approach to 156
  - Step 1: as-required reliever therapy 156
  - Step 2: introduction of regular preventer therapy 156
  - Step 3: add-on therapy 157
  - Step 4: trials of dual treatment with add-on drugs 157
  - Step 5: continuous or frequent oral corticosteroids 158
- Medication issues for elite athletes 165
- Medicines management 163
- Recommendations, key SIGN/BTS 154, 155
- Stepping down treatment 163
- Theophylline 164

Atrial fibrillation 168

What is it? 180
What causes atrial fibrillation? 180
How common is it? 180
How do I know my patient has it? 180
What else might it be? 180
Rate control or rhythm control? 183

Who should receive antithrombotic prophylaxis? 184
What is the role of the GP in managing atrial fibrillation? 181
Amiodarone 183
Antiplatelet agents, other 185
Antithrombotic treatment 184
Medicines management 185
Aspirin 186
risk of major adverse effects with 185
Beta-blockers 182
Cardioversion 183
indications for attempted 183
Complications 180
Diagnosis and investigation 181
Digoxin 182
Paroxysmal 183
Prognosis 181
Rate control 181
Drugs used for 182
Rhythm control 182
Stroke, prevention, supporting evidence for 185
Stroke, risk of 181
Verapamil 182
Warfarin 185
risk of major bleeding with 185

B

Back pain – lower 188
What is simple low back pain? 196
What are the origins of low back pain? 196
What are the risk factors for low back pain? 196
How common is low back pain? 197
How often does low back pain occur? 197
How common is disability due to simple low back pain? 197
What is the impact of low back pain on the health services? 197
Adults 197
Children 197
How common are serious causes of low back pain? 197
How do I know my patient has simple low back pain? 197
What else might it be? 198
How do I manage acute low back pain? 199
What do I do if significant low back pain remains after 4–6 weeks? 200
How can low back pain be prevented? 202
What dose of diazepam should I use? 202
What are the adverse effects of diazepam? 202
What dose of amitriptyline should I use? 202
What are the adverse effects of amitriptyline? 203
Who should avoid taking amitriptyline? 203
What dose of gabapentin should I use? 203
What are the adverse effects of gabapentin? 203
What is the supporting evidence for analgesia? 203
Which nonsteroidal anti-inflammatory drug should I use? 203
What is the evidence for physiotherapy? 203
What is the evidence for exercise? 204
What is the evidence for spinal manipulation therapy? 204
What is the evidence for acupuncture? 204
Amitriptyline 202
Codeine 202
Complications 198
Definitions and classifications 196
Disability, definition and distinction from pain 196
Disability, due to low back pain in adults 197
Disability, due to low back pain in children 197
Disability and work loss 199
Distress and disability and psychosocial risk factors 201
Drugs for management of chronic pain 203
Drug treatment 200
Supporting evidence for 203
Evidence, additional supporting 203
Follow up and reassessment 200
Gabapentin 203
Interventions, assessments of 202
Interventions not recommended for the treatment of low back pain 202
Low back pain with a specific cause 198
Medicines management 202
Muscle relaxants 202
Nonsteroidal anti-inflammatory drugs 202
Occupational health issues – work and back pain 201
Occurrence of, in adults 197
Occurrence of, in children 197
Pain from an adjacent structure 198
Pain management 201
Paracetamol 202
Prognosis for acute low back pain 198
Prognosis for chronic disability due to low back pain 198
Radicular pain, management of persistent 201
Red flags indicating serious pathology 199
For spine fracture 199
For cancer or infection 199
For cauda equina syndrome 199
Risk factors for acute simple low back pain in adults 196
Risk factors for acute simple low back pain in children 196
Risk factors for developing chronic low back pain 196
Yellow flags 196
Risk factors, psycho-social ('yellow flags') 199
Treatment and support 199

Bacterial vaginosis 207
What is it? 208
How common is it? 208
How do I know my patient has it? 208
What else might it be? 209
Breastfeeding 210
Complications 209
General issues 209
Investigations 209
Pregnancy 210
Termination of 210
Prognosis 209
Signs 209
Symptoms 208
Treatments, drug 209
Treatments, non-drug 209
Vaginal discharge, irritants that may result in 209
Vaginal discharge, other causes 209
Vaginal discharge, other infections that may result in 209

Balanitis 211
What is it? 213
How common is it? 214
How do I know my patient has it? 214
What else might it be? 214
Circumcision 214
General issues 214
Prognosis 214
Treatment issues 214

Bedwetting

see Enuresis – nocturnal

Benzodiazepines

in Alcohol – problem drinking 21, 32
in Hypnotic or anxiolytic dependence 1019, 1020
in Insomnia 1118

Beta2-agonists

in Asthma 131, 132, 135, 138, 141, 145, 148, 149
in Chest infections 292
in Chronic obstructive pulmonary disease 330, 334, 342, 345

Beta-blockers

in Angina 88, 91, 99, 107
in Atrial fibrillation 168, 173, 178, 182
in Diabetes Type 1 and 2 – hypertension 532, 540, 550, 552
in Heart failure 901, 910, 912
in Hypertension 963, 966, 971, 991, 993, 994
in Hyperthyroidism 1007, 1010
in Migraine 1245, 1250
in Prior myocardial infarction – prophylactic treatments 1552, 1554

Bites – human and animal 216

What is it? 219
How common is it? 219
What else might it be? 219

Antibiotic prophylaxis 220
Complications 219
Hepatitis B, hepatitis C, and HIV 221
Infection, treatment of established 220
Management, initial 219
Rabies prophylaxis 221
Tetanus prophylaxis 221
Wound closure 220

Blepharitis 223

What is it? 230
How common is it? 231
How do I know my patient has it? 231
How do I determine the cause of blepharitis? 231
What else might it be? 232
How should eyelid hygiene be performed? 233
How should infection be treated? 233
How should I treat meibomian gland dysfunction that is not adequately managed with eyelid hygiene? 233
What information should I give people with blepharitis? 232
When should tear replacement be used? 233
When should topical corticosteroids be used? 233
When should I refer? 234

Complications 231
Investigations 231
Management, overview of 232
Prognosis 231
Signs 231
Symptoms 231

Blood pressure, high

see Hypertension

Boils, carbuncles, paronychia, & staphylococcal whitlow 235

What is it? 241
How common is it? 241
How do I know my patient has it? 242
What else might it be? 242
How do I minimize staphylococcal carriage? 244
Which antibiotic should I prescribe, and for how long? 244
Who should I swab for carriage of Staphylococcus aureus? 243

Boil 242
Boils and carbuncles 242, 243
Carbuncle 242
Causative organisms 241
Complications 242
Definition 241
Folliculitis 243
Furunculosis, recurrent 243
exclude underlying causes 243
Furunculosis and carbuncles 243
Paronychia 242
Acute 242
Prognosis 243
Risk factors and predisposing conditions 242
Staphylococcal deep folliculitis 243
Staphylococcal folliculitis 242
Staphylococcal paronychia 243
Staphylococcal superficial folliculitis 243
Staphylococcal whitlow 242, 243

BPH

see Prostate – benign hyperplasia

Breast cancer – managing women with a family history 245

How common is breast cancer? 249
What is known about the genetic risk factors? 249
What are the risk categories? 249
How does family history affect the risk of developing breast cancer? 249
When and how do I make an initial assessment? 250
How is family defined? 250
How is genetic testing carried out? 254
What advice can I give regarding risk? 252
When should I refer to secondary care or to a specialist genetic service? 251
Women up to the age of 39 years 251
Women aged 40–49 years 251
Women aged 50 years and over 252
What is likely to happen in secondary care? 253
Women who should be referred to a specialist geneti[c] service 253
Women classified as moderate risk 254
What is likely to happen in tertiary care? 254
What should I do with those I don't refer? 253
Who should have mammographic surveillance? 254
Efficacy and risks 254

Alcohol consumption 252
Breastfeeding 252
Follow-up 253
General issues 250
Hormonal contraceptives 252
Hormone replacement therapy 253
Physical activity 253
Reassurance 252
Referral to a specialist genetics service 251, 252
Referral to secondary care, considering 251, 252
Reproductive factors 253
Risk reduction 253
Smoking 253
Surgery, risk-reducing 254
Weight 253

Breastfeeding

in Asthma 160
in Bacterial vaginosis 210

in Breast cancer – managing women with a family history 252
in Chickenpox 316
in Chlamydia – genital 320, 327
in Colic – infantile 353
in Contraception 401, 428
in Depression 500
in Epilepsy 778
in Hyperthyroidism 1010
in Hypothyroidism 1026
in Irritable bowel syndrome 1123
in Migraine 1238, 1247
in Nonsteroidal anti-inflammatory drugs (NSAIDs) 1309
in Osteoporosis – treatment 1391
in Pubic lice 1602
in Pyelonephritis – acute 1603
in Roundworm 1654, 1656
in Scabies 1664
in Threadworm 1758, 1761
in Trichomoniasis 1775, 1776, 1778
in Urinary tract infection (lower) – women 1822

Bronchitis

see Chest infections
see Chronic obstructive pulmonary disease

Bulimia

see Eating disorders

Burns and scalds 256

What is it? 259
How common is it? 259
How do I assess a burn? 260
What else might it be? 259
Who should I refer? 260

Burn, depth of 260
Burn, extent of 260
Complications 259
First aid 259
Minor, management of 260
Sunburn, management of 261
Tetanus prophylaxis 261

C

Calcium-channel blockers

in Anal fissure 85
in Angina 93, 95, 107
in Diabetes Type 1 and 2 – hypertension 532, 541, 550, 552
in Hypertension 963, 966, 967, 975, 995, 996

Candida – female genital 263

What is it? 271
What are the precipitating factors? 272
How common is it? 271
How do I know my patient has it? 272
What else might it be? 272
Infections 272
Non-infective causes 272

Classification of thrush 271
Complications 273
Drug treatments 273
Other 274
General issues 273
Imidazoles, topical 273
Infection, management of complicated 274
Other complicated infections 275
Infection, management of uncomplicated 274
Infections, non-albicans 275
Investigations 272
Management, self 276
Microbiological cause of thrush 271
Prognosis 273
Prophylactic measures 276
Signs 272
Symptoms 272
Treatment failure 274
Triazoles, oral 273
Vulvovaginal candidiasis, in pregnancy 275
Vulvovaginal candidiasis, recurrent 274
Vulvovaginal candidiasis, severe 275

Candida – oral 278

What is it? 280
How common is it? 280
How do I know my patient has it? 280
What else might it be? 280

Anticandidal therapy 280
Complications and prognosis 280
General issues 280
Signs 280
Symptoms 280

Candida – skin and nails 282

What is it? 285
How common is it? 286
How do I know my patient has it? 286
What else might it be? 286

Candidal paronychia 286
Candidal nail infection 287
Candidal onychomycosis 286
Candidal paronychia 287
Candidal paronychia/onychomycosis 286
Complications and prognosis 286
Cutaneous candidiasis 286, 287
General measures 287

Cardiac impairment

see Heart failure

Cerumen

see Earwax

Cervical spondylosis

see Neck pain

CHD risk

see Coronary heart disease risk – identification and management

Chest infections 288

What is it? 302
How common is it? 303
How do I know my patient has it? 303
What else might it be? 304
Should I use an antibiotic? 305
Which antibiotic? 306
Non-antibiotic treatments? 306
Treat at home or admit? 306
What are the usual pathogens? 303

Antibiotics, general issues 305
Antibiotics, resistance 305
Bronchitis, acute 303, 304, 305, 306
Complications and prognosis 304
COPD, exacerbation of 303, 304, 305, 306
General issues 303
Investigations in primary care 304
Patient advice 305

Pneumonia, community-acquired 303, 304, 305, 306
Symptom relief 305

Chickenpox 309

What is it? 313
How common is it? 314
How do I know my patient has it? 314
What else might it be? 314
Can chickenpox be prevented in healthy adults and children? 315
Can chickenpox be prevented in immunocompromised people? 317
How should I treat chickenpox in healthy adults and children? 315
How should I treat chickenpox in immunocompromised people? 316
Supporting evidence for antiviral treatment 316
How should I treat chickenpox in pregnant women? 315
Which immunocompromised people need post-exposure prophylaxis? 317
Which pregnant women need post-exposure prophylaxis? 316

Aciclovir 317
Antihistamines, sedating 317
Breastfeeding 316
Complications and prognosis 314
In children 314
In adults 314
In pregnancy 314
In neonates 314
In immunocompromised people 315
General issues 315
Healthy adults and children 315
Ibuprofen 317
Immunocompromised individuals 316
Medicines management 317
Neonates 316
Pregnancy 315
Prodrome 314
Rash 314

Chlamydia – genital 319

What is it? 324
How common is it? 324
How do I know my patient has it? 324
What else might it be? 325

Complications 325
Infection, general issues on the management of confirmed 326
Infection, treatment of uncomplicated (lower genital tract) 326
Investigations 325
Pelvic inflammatory disease, treatment of, with tests positive for chlamydia 327
Pregnancy and breastfeeding 327
Uncomplicated (lower genital tract) infection 327
Pelvic inflammatory disease 327
Prognosis 325
Screening 326
Signs 324
Symptoms 324

Chronic obstructive pulmonary disease 329

What is it? 339
How common is it? 339
How do I know my patient has it? 339
What else might it be? 340
Which pressurized metered-dose inhalers are available as HFA products? 347
How do I transfer someone from CFC pMDI to HFA pMDI? 347

Alpha$_1$-antitrypsin, serum 340
Anticholinergics, long-acting 343
Anticholinergics, short-acting 342
Anticholinergics, short- and long-acting 346
Beta$_2$-agonists, long-acting 342
Beta$_2$-agonists, short-acting 342
Beta$_2$-agonists: short- and long-acting 345
Body mass index 340
Bronchopulmonary hygiene therapy 345
Combination therapy 343
Compliance 341
Complications and prognosis 340
Corticosteroids, inhaled 343, 346
Corticosteroids, oral 343, 346
Counselling and compliance issues 345
Exacerbation of 344
Antibiotics 344
Non-antibiotic treatments 344
Treat at home or admit 345
Examination 340
Full blood count 340
History 340
Immunization 345
Inhaled treatment, delivery systems for 341
Inhaler devices, chlorofluorocarbon-free 347
Inhalers 341
Fixed-dose combination 347
Investigations 340
Medicines management 345
Mucolytic therapy 345
Nebulizers 342
Nebulizer solutions 347
Oxygen therapy 343
Prevention 341
Radiology 340
Rehabilitation, pulmonary 345
Spacer devices 347
Spacers 341
Spirometry 340
And reversibility testing 341
Stable 342
Theophylline in 343
Theophyllines 346
Therapy not recommended 345
Therapy steps, currently recommended 342

COAD

see Chronic obstructive pulmonary disease

Cold sore

see Herpes simplex – oral

Colic – infantile 350

What is it? 352
How common is it? 352
How do I know my patient has it? 352
What else might it be? 352
How do I manage infantile colic? 352
What infant milk formulas are available on NHS prescription? And, how do they differ? 354
What is the supporting evidence? 353
Behavioural interventions 354
Drug treatments 353
Excluding dairy products from the diet of breastfeeding mothers 353
Miscellaneous treatments 354
Using hypoallergenic infant milk formulas to eliminate cows' milk proteins from the baby's diet 353
Using lactase to reduce the levels of lactose in milk formula or breast milk 353

Using low-lactose infant milk formulas to reduce the levels of lactose in the diet 353
What resources can support parents of babies with infantile colic? 354

Complications and prognosis 352
Hypoallergenic infant milk formulas 354
Lactase 354
And infant milk formulas, managing treatments with 354
Low-lactose, lactose-free, and hypoallergenic infant milk formulas 354
Low-lactose and lactose-free infant milk formulas 354

Combined oral contraceptive

in Contraception 390, 402, 407, 411, 412
in Dysmenorrhoea 620, 625
in Menorrhagia 1223

Common cold 356

What is it? 358
How common is it? 358
How do I know my patient has it? 359
What else might it be? 359
Adults 359
Children 359
Infants 359

Complications 359
General issues 359
Pharmacological management, recommended 360
Prognosis 359
Supportive (non-pharmacological) management 360
Symptomatic treatments, common, not recommended by PRODIGY 360

Complementary therapies

in Allergic rhinitis 54
in Asthma 158
in Insomnia 1119
in Meniere's disease 1182
in Nausea and vomiting in pregnancy 1277
in Trichomoniasis 1778
in Warts and verrucae 1860

Congestive heart failure

see Heart failure

Conjunctivitis – allergic 362

What is it? 364
How common is it? 364
How do I know my patient has it? 364
What else might it be? 365
What topical treatments are available? 366
Should I prescribe a topical antihistamine or mast cell stabilizer? 366
What systemic treatments may be useful? 366
What general measures might be useful? 366

Allergic dermatitis with conjunctivitis 366
Antihistamines, topical 366
Assessment 365
Complications 365
Contact allergic dermatitis with conjunctivitis 365
Corticosteroids, topical (not recommended) 366
Examination 365
Giant papillary conjunctivitis 365, 367
Infective conjunctivitis 365
Irritant conjunctivitis 365
Mast cell stabilizers, topical 366
Rare types of 365
Red eye, three main serious causes of 365
Seasonal and perennial (atopic conjunctivitis) 364
Seasonal and perennial conjunctivitis 366
Signs 364
Symptoms 364, 365

Conjunctivitis – infective 368

What is it? 369
What are the infective causes of primary conjunctivitis? 369
How common is it? 369
How do I know my patient has infective conjunctivitis? 370
What are the clinical features of infective conjunctivitis? 370
How do I distinguish bacterial from viral conjunctivitis? 370
What else might it be? 370
Should I prescribe a topical antibiotic? 371
Which topical antibiotic should I prescribe? 371
Should I prescribe ointment or drops? 372
What should I do if infective conjunctivitis fails to respond to treatment? 372

Allergic conjunctivitis 370
Complications 370
Conjunctivitis of the newborn (ophthalmia neonatorum) 369, 372
Examination 370
General measures 371
Infective conjunctivitis, managing uncomplicated 371
Investigations 370
Irritant conjunctivitis 370
Prognosis 371
Red eye, excluding the serious causes of 370
Red eye, main three serious causes of 370
Symptoms 370

Constipation 374

What is it? 383
How common is it? 383
How do I know my patient has it? 383
What else might it be? 383

Bulk-forming agents (e.g. ispaghula) 384
Children 385
Complications and prognosis 383
Diabetics 386
Elderly 385
Examination 383
Faecal softeners / emollient laxatives (e.g. docusate) 385
General issues 384
History 383
Osmotic laxatives (e.g. lactulose, phosphate enemas) 385
Pregnancy 386
Specific situations 385
Stimulant laxatives (e.g. senna, bisacodyl) 385
Terminally-ill people 386
Treatments, drug 384
Treatments, non-drug 384

Contraception 388

Actinomyces-like organisms in cervical smears of IUD users 423
Amenorrhoea 411
Breakthrough bleeding 414
Breast cancer 409
Cerazette® 416
Cervical cancer 411
Colorectal cancer 408
Combined oral contraceptive pill 407
First choice of pill 412
Second choice/alternative pill 412

Compliance issues 421
Contraceptive methods, efficacy of 407
Copper intra-uterine devices 421
Current use of contraception 407
Diaphragms and caps 425
Diarrhoea and vomiting 413, 415
Disadvantages or adverse effects 422
Drug interactions 415, 419, 420, 421
Endometrial cancer 408
Female condom 426
Hormone replacement therapy (HRT) and contraception 428
Key drug interactions 413
Legal issues with young women 430
Liver cancer 411
Male condoms 426
Management of menstrual irregularities 415
Management of menstrual irregularities secondary to medroxyprogesterone acetate 418
Menstrual effects 425
Methods available 406
Missed pills 413, 415
Missing threads 422
Mortality 411
Myocardial infarction 409
Natural family planning 427
Ovarian Cancer 408
Pregnancy with an intra-uterine device in place 423
Progestogen-only contraceptive injection 417
  When to start 417
Progestogen-only intra-uterine system 423
Progestogen-only pills 414
Risk-benefit profile 408
Screening before starting a combined oral contraceptive 411
Specific contraceptive information 427
Spermicides 426
Starting the combined oral contraceptive pill 412
Starting the combined oral contraceptive pill in special circumstances 412
Starting the progestogen-only contraceptive injection in special circumstances 417
Starting the progestogen-only pill 415
Starting the progestogen-only pill in special circumstances 415
Starting the subdermal progestogen-only contraceptive implant in special circumstances 419
Starting the transdermal combination contraceptive patch 420
Starting the transdermal contraceptive patch in special circumstances 421
Stroke 409
Subdermal progestogen-only contraceptive implant 419
  Time of insertion 419
Suitability of methods 427
Surgery 414
Testing for sexually transmitted infection before IUD insertion 422
Transdermal combination contraceptive patch 420
  What to do if the patch either fully or partly detaches 421
Use of diaphragms and caps 425
Venous thromboembolism 409
Women over 35 years old 427
Women who are breastfeeding 428
Women who are overweight or obese 429
Women who smoke 429
Women with acne 429
Women with epilepsy 430
Women with migraine 430
Yasmin® 412

Contraception – emergency 435

What is it? 440
How does it work? 440
How often is it used? 440
When is emergency contraception indicated? 440

Adverse effects 442, 443
Contraindications 443
Emergency contraceptive products 440
Intra-uterine device 443
  Effectiveness 443
  Timing of post-coital IUD insertion 443
  Follow-up and IUD removal 443
Legal issues relating to providing emergency contraception to girls under 16 years 443
Post-coital copper-containing intra-uterine device (IUD), mode of action of 440
Progestogen-only emergency contraception, oral 440
  Recommended regimens 440
  Overall effectiveness 441
  Factors influencing effectiveness 441
  Timing of treatment 441
  Timing and frequency of unprotected sex 442
  Drug interactions 442
  Timing of next period 442
  Follow-up 442
  Subsequent contraception 442
Progestogen-only emergency contraception pills, mod of action of 440
Sexually transmitted infections, testing for 442, 443

Corneal superficial injury 446

What is it? 448
How common is it? 448
How do I know my patient has it? 448
How do I assess a corneal abrasion? 449
What else might it be? 448
How do I remove any conjunctival or corneal foreign bodies? 449
How should I manage superficial corneal abrasions that are not referred? 449
Which topical antibiotic should I use? 450
Should I prescribe antibiotic ointment or drops? 450
What treatments are not recommended for a superficial corneal injury? 450
When should I refer to a specialist? 449

Complications 448
Examination 448
History 448
Prognosis 449

Coronary heart disease risk – identification and management 452

What is coronary heart disease (CHD)? 459
How common is it? 459
How do I know my patient is at risk of CHD? 459
Who should be screened for risk of CHD? 459
Does hormone replacement therapy prevent CHD? 46

Alcohol consumption 464
Aspirin, low-dose 464
Aspirin, medicines management 464
Cardiovascular risk, recommended interventions to reduce 461
CHD risk, calculating 460
  Other risk calculators 461
Coexisting conditions, management of 465
  Additional measures for people with established occlusive arterial disease 466
Complications of CHD 459
Complications of other occlusive arterial disease 459
Diabetes 465

Dietary management 463
Exercise 462
Hyperlipidaemia 465
Hypertension 465
Lifestyle measures to prevent CHD 462
People with a 10-year CHD risk more than 30% but who do not have CHD 461
People with a 10-year CHD risk of 15–30% 461
People with a 10-year CHD risk of less than 15% 462
People with diagnosed CHD, stroke, TIAs, or PVD 461
Primary prevention of cardiovascular disease 464
Prognosis 459
Secondary prevention of cardiovascular disease 464
Smoking cessation 462
Weight control 463

Corticosteroids

in Allergic rhinitis 45, 51, 52, 53, 55
in Ankylosing spondylitis 116, 117, 123, 124
in Asthma 134, 135, 138, 140, 141, 145, 157, 158, 163
in Blepharitis 233
in Chest infections 291, 292
in Chronic obstructive pulmonary disease 330, 334, 343, 346
in Conjunctivitis – allergic 366
in Dermatitis – contact 507, 509, 518, 520, 521
in Eczema – atopic 730, 731, 732
in Gout 846, 850, 863, 864, 866
in Insect bites and stings 1107
in Osteoarthritis 1351, 1358, 1368, 1371, 1372, 1373
in Osteoporosis – treatment 1389
in Palliative care – dyspnoea 1438
in Polymyalgia rheumatica 1524, 1526, 1530
in Pruritus ani 1589
in Rheumatoid arthritis 1622, 1626, 1636, 1638, 1639
in Seborrhoeic dermatitis 1684, 1686, 1691
in Sinusitis 1722
in Urticaria and angio-oedema 1853

Coryza

see Common cold

D

Deep vein thrombosis 468

What is it? 471
How common is it? 471
How do I know my patient has it? 472
What else might it be? 472

Anticoagulant treatment, initial (following hospital discharge) 473
Anticoagulation (hospital-initiated) 473
Complications and prognosis 472
Compression stockings 473
Management, initial 472
Other treatments (given in hospital) 473
Pregnancy 474
Risk factors 471
Thrombophilia (increased tendency for blood clotting), screening for suspected 472
Travel-related deep vein thrombosis, risk of 474

Dental abscess 477

What is it? 479
How common is it? 479
How do I know my patient has it? 479
What else might it be? 479
What is the role of antibiotics? 480
Where, by whom, and what form of treatment should be given? 479
Which analgesia should be prescribed by medical practitioners? 479

Complications 479
Prognosis 479

Depression 481

What is it? 497
How common is it? 498
How do I know my patient has it? 498
What else might it be? 499
Should I use psychological treatments or antidepressants? 499

Antidepressants
Choice of 500
Adverse effects 501
Cost 502
Efficacy 501
Tolerability 501
Toxicity and suicide risk 501
Dosage of 502
Stopping 503
Switching 502
Bereavement 500
Complications 499
Driving 503
Dysthymia 498, 499, 500
Elderly people 500
Influence of other psychiatric disorders 500
Major depression 498, 499
Medicines management 500
Milder depression 499, 500
Postnatal depression 498, 499, 500
Pregnancy and breastfeeding 500
Prognosis 499
St John's wort (*Hypericum*) 503
Treatment, duration of 502
Treatment failure 502

Dermatitis – atopic

see Eczema – atopic

Dermatitis – contact 505

What is contact dermatitis? 514
How does contact dermatitis develop? 515
How common is it? 515
How do I know my patient has it? 515
What common allergens and irritants cause contact dermatitis? 516
What factors affect the response to allergens and irritants? 515
What are the likely causes of dermatitis in different skin areas? 516
What else might it be? 517
How much topical corticosteroid should be applied? 520
Should corticosteroids be applied once a day or twice a day? 520
Which topical corticosteroid should I prescribe? 518
What quantity of topical corticosteroid should I prescribe? 520
What are the adverse effects of topical corticosteroids? 521
When should systemic corticosteroids be used? 518
Which emollient should I prescribe? 518
How often should an emollient be applied? 521
What are the adverse effects of emollients and how are they managed? 521
How should emollients be applied with topical corticosteroids? 521
How should I manage acute dermatitis? 518
How should I manage infected dermatitis? 519
How should I manage persistent contact dermatitis? 520

How should I manage suspected occupational contact dermatitis? 520
What general advice should I give regarding avoidance? 519
What is the supporting evidence for emollients? 518
What is the supporting evidence for topical corticosteroids? 518
How can recurrence of contact dermatitis be prevented? 519

Barrier creams 519
Clinical features 516
Complications 517
Corticosteroids 518
Topical 520
Diagnosis and identifying the cause, confirming 516
Distinguishing features of irritant and allergic contact dermatitis 516
Emollients 518, 521
and 'after-work creams' 520
Management, overview of 517
Medicines management 520
Prognosis 517
Irritant contact dermatitis 517
Allergic contact dermatitis 517
Protective clothing, personal 519

Diabetes mellitus

see Diabetes Type 1 and 2 – foot disease
see Diabetes Type 1 and 2 – hypertension
see Diabetes Type 2 – blood glucose management
see Diabetes Type 2 – lipid management
see Diabetes Type 2 – renal disease
see Diabetes Type 2 – retinopathy
in Constipation 386
in Coronary heart disease risk – identification and management 454, 455, 457, 458, 465
in Eating disorders 709, 710
in Hypertension 991
in Preconceptual counselling 1544
in Prior myocardial infarction – prophylactic treatments 1567

Diabetes Type 1 and 2 – foot disease 523

What is it? 525
How common is it? 525
How do I know my patient has it? 525
What are the risk factors for developing diabetic foot ulcers? 526
What else might it be? 526

Care of people at high risk of foot ulcers 527
Care of people at increased risk of foot ulcers 527
Care of people at low current risk of foot ulcers 527
Care of people with foot emergencies or foot ulcers 527
Charcot's foot, management of 529
Complications 526
Foot care education 528
Footwear 528
Infected feet, management of 529
Infections, limb-threatening – hospital admission 529
Infections, non-limb-threatening – urgent referral to multidisciplinary foot care team 529
Management approach, general 527
Prognosis 527
Screening 528
Service arrangements for people with diabetes in respect of their foot care 527
Specialist referral 529
Ulcerated feet, management of 528
Ulcer development, prevention of 528
Management of other risk factors 528

Diabetes Type 1 and 2 – hypertension 531

What is it? 546
How common is it? 546
How do I confirm a raised blood pressure? 546
What else might it be? 547
Drug induced 547
Endocrine disorder 547
Miscellaneous 547
Renal disorder (considered to be the commonest secondary cause) 547
Vascular disorder 547
What are the benefits of blood pressure reduction? 548
When is drug treatment recommended and what is the target blood pressure goal? 549
When should aspirin be considered? 551
When should lipid-lowering therapy be considered? 551
What about hormone replacement therapy? 551

ACE and angiotensin II receptor antagonists (AIIRAs), combination of 550
ACE inhibitors 549, 551
Alpha-blockers 551, 552
Angiotensin II receptor antagonists (AIIRAs) 551
Antihypertensive medication, initial 549
If the person has microalbuminuria or proteinuria 549
If the person has no microalbuminuria or proteinuria 549
Antihypertensive treatment, add-on 549
Antiplatelet drugs 552
Beta-blockers 550, 552
Blood pressure, measures that lower 548
Blood pressure monitoring, ambulatory 546
Blood pressure monitoring, at home 547
Calcium-channel blockers (CCBs) 550, 552
Cardiovascular risk, additional measures that reduce 548
Complications 547
Drug selection, evidence to support 549
Angiotensin II receptor antagonists 550
General issues 548
Medicines management 551
Non-drug measures 548
Primary prevention 551
Prognosis 547
Secondary prevention 551
Thiazide diuretics 550, 552

Diabetes Type 2 – blood glucose management 555

What is it? 566
How common is it? 566
How do I know my patient has it? 566
What are the risk factors for developing Type 2 diabetes? 567

Acarbose 570
Supporting evidence for 570
Complications 567
General issues 568
Insulins 570
Supporting evidence for 571
Insulin secretagogues 569
Lifestyle interventions 568
Medicines management 571
Thiazolidinediones 571
Sulphonylureas 571
Supporting evidence for 569
Metabolic syndrome 572
Metformin 568, 571
Supporting evidence for metformin – glycaemic control 569

Supporting evidence for metformin – long-term outcomes 569
Monitoring 567
Self-monitoring 568
Patient education 568
Pharmacological management of Type 2 diabetes 568
Presentations 566
Prognosis 567
Supporting evidence for nateglinide and repaglinide 569
Supporting evidence for rosiglitazone and pioglitazone 570
Testing for diabetes 566
Thiazolidinediones (glitazones) 570

Diabetes Type 2 – lipid management 574

What is dyslipidaemia? 585
How common is dyslipidaemia in people with Type 2 diabetes? 585
How do I know my patient has abnormal lipid levels? 585
What else might it be? 585
How do I calculate cardiovascular risk? 586
What are the risk factors for cardiovascular disease in people with diabetes? 586
When should I treat and what should I use? 588
Should I use a 3-month trial of dietary management before starting drug treatment? 587
How long should people be treated for? 588, 591
What starting dose? 590
Which statin? 590
Can I offer treatment at lower lipid levels? 588
Can simvastatin be bought over-the-counter? 588
Is there an age limit for offering treatment? 588
What is the evidence for lipid-lowering therapy in people with Type 2 diabetes? 588

Anion-exchange resins 590
Aspirin, treatment with 587
Combination therapy 589
Complications 585
Dietary management 587
Ezetimibe 590
Fibrates 588, 589
Fish oils and omega-3 fatty acids 590
General issues 587
Interactions, significant 591
Lipid levels, measuring and monitoring toxicity 591
Medicines management 590
Nicotinic acid 590
Other tests 591
Primary prevention 588, 589
Prognosis 585
Risk, classification of 587
Secondary prevention 587, 588
Serum lipids, goals for lowering 588
Specialist referral, indications for 592
Statins 588, 589
Statins and fibrates, tolerability of 591

Diabetes Type 2 – renal disease 594

What is it? 596
How common is it? 596
How do I know my patient has it? 597
What else might it be? 597
Who should I screen? 597
Which test should I use? 597
What type of sample should I test? 598

ACE inhibitors and AIIRAs 599
Evidence for ACE inhibitors 599
Evidence for AIIRAs 599
Combination of ACE and AIIRAs 599
Blood glucose control 598
Blood pressure control 599
Cardiovascular risk factors, management of other 599
Complications 597
Dietary interventions 599
Disease progression, prevention of, and cardiovascular outcomes 598
Microalbuminuria and proteinuria, risk factors for the development of 598
Prognosis 597
Referral 598
Risk, classification of 598
Screening 597

Diabetes Type 2 – retinopathy 601

What is it? 602
How common is it? 602
How do I know my patient has it? 602
What are the risk factors for development and progression of retinopathy? 602
What else might it be? 602
How should screening be performed? 603

Blood glucose 604
Blood pressure 604
Complications 602
General issues 603
Ophthalmoscopy 604
Prognosis 602
Referral 604
Retinal photography 603
Risk factor modification 604
Surgical treatment 604
Visual acuity testing 603

Diet

in Anaemia – macrocytic 72
in Colic – infantile 353
in Coronary heart disease risk – identification and management 463
in Diabetes Type 2 – blood glucose management 555, 556
in Diabetes Type 2 – lipid management 587
in Diabetes Type 2 – renal disease 599
in Eczema – atopic 733
in Gout 867
in Hyperlipidaemia 955
in Irritable bowel syndrome 1127
in Obesity 1322
in Prior myocardial infarction – prophylactic treatments 1565
in Pruritus ani 1589

Diuretics

in Diabetes Type 1 and 2 – hypertension 550, 552
in Heart failure 910, 912
in Hypertension 970, 991, 993

Diverticular disease and diverticulitis 606

What is it? 610
What causes it? 610
How common is it? 610
How do I know my patient has it? 610
What investigations should I perform? 611
What else might it be? 611
How should I manage asymptomatic diverticula? 611
How should I manage diverticulitis? 612
How should I manage uncomplicated diverticular disease? 612
What advice should I give to prevent recurrence of diverticulitis? 612

Complications 611
Prognosis 611

Driving
in Alcohol – problem drinking 28
in Depression 503
in Epilepsy 779
in Opioid dependence 1346
in Parkinson's disease 1508
in Schizophrenia 1677

Dry eye syndrome 614
What is it? 616
What is the pathogenesis of dry eye syndrome? 616
How common is it? 617
How do I know my patient has it? 617
What else might it be? 617
How should I manage dry eye syndrome? 617
How should artificial tears and lubricants be prescribed? 617
What other treatment options are there for dry eye syndrome? 618
Causes of 616
Complications 617
Exacerbating factors and predisposing conditions 616
Examination 617
History 617
Investigations 617
Lubricants 617
Primary care, options available in 618
Secondary care interventions, options for 618
Tear physiology 616
Tears, artificial 617

DVT
see Deep vein thrombosis

Dysmenorrhoea 619
What is it? 623
How common is it? 624
How do I know my patient has it? 624
What may cause secondary dysmenorrhoea? 624
Combined oral contraceptive 625
Complications and prognosis 624
General issues 624
Nonsteroidal anti-inflammatory drugs 624
Primary 624
Secondary 624
Treatments
Drug, recommended 624
Other analgesics 625
Drug, other 625
Non-drug 625
Surgical 625
Not recommended 625

Dyspepsia – pregnancy-associated 628
What is dyspepsia? 629
What causes dyspepsia during pregnancy? 629
How common is it? 629
How do I know my patient has it? 630
What else might it be? 630
Pregnancy-related disorders 630
Disorders unrelated to pregnancy 630
What is first-line treatment? 630
What should I do if lifestyle measures fail? 630
When should I refer for specialist advice? 630
Complications and prognosis 630

Dyspepsia – proven DU, GU, or NSAID-associated ulcer 631
What is dyspepsia? 642
What is peptic ulcer disease? 642
What causes peptic ulcer disease? 642
How common is it? 642
How do I know my patient has peptic ulcer disease? 642
What else might it be? 643
What general measures are useful? 644
Which medication might be causing dyspeptic symptoms? 644
What lifestyle advice is recommended? 644
What is first-line treatment? 644
Which H pylori test should I use? 644
How do I use a carbon-13 urea breath test? 644
How do I use a stool antigen test? 644
What follow-up is needed? 644
What should I do if the H pylori re-test is positive? 645
What should I do if the H pylori re-test is negative? 645
What should I do if the person is H pylori *negative but symptoms persist?* 645
People with a duodenal ulcer 645
People with a gastric ulcer 645
People with a history of gastrointestinal bleeding or perforation 645
How should I manage people who still need NSAIDs? 645
When is repeat endoscopy indicated? 646
Which H pylori test? 646
Which H pylori eradication regimen should I use? 648
Which PPI? 648
Which dose of PPI? 648
How should I advise people to take on-demand PPIs? 648
Which agents are suitable for gastroprotection against NSAIDs? 649
Antibiotic resistance 648
Complications 643
Duodenal or gastric ulcer, people with a 644
Examination 643
History 642
H pylori eradication 646
H pylori eradication regimens, first-line 647
H pylori eradication regimens, second-line 647
Investigations 643
Management, overview of 643
Medicines management 648
NSAID-associated ulcer, people with an 644, 645
Peptic ulcer, preventing recurrence 647
Peptic ulcers, healing 647
Peptic ulcers due to NSAIDs 647
Healing 647
Preventing 647
Prognosis 643
Testing, initial (pretreatment) 646
Testing, post-eradication 646
Treatment strategies, supporting evidence for 646

Dyspepsia – proven gastro-oesophageal reflux disease 650
What is GORD? 657
How common is it? 657
How do I know my patient has GORD? 657
What else might it be? 658
Does H pylori play a role in GORD? 661
How should I advise people to take on-demand PPIs? 662
How should I follow up people whose symptoms respond to treatment? 660
How should I manage people whose symptoms persist despite treatment? 660
How should people with Barrett's oesophagus be managed? 660
How should people with other complications be managed? 660

What general measures are useful? 659
What is dyspepsia? 657
What is first-line treatment? 659
What lifestyle advice is recommended? 659
What should I do if symptoms recur? 659
What should I do if there is inadequate response to first-line treatment? 659
When is repeat endoscopy indicated? 660
Which dose of PPI? 662
Which medication might be causing dyspeptic symptoms? 659
Which PPI? 662

Antacids and alginates 662
Complications 658
History 657
H_2-receptor antagonists 662
H_2-receptor antagonists, prokinetics, antacids, and alginates 662
Investigations 658
Less common investigations 658
Management, overview of 659
Medicines management 662
Oesophagitis, acute healing of 661
PPI therapy, on-demand 661
Prognosis 658
Prokinetic agents 662
Reflux disease, endoscopy-negative 661
Surgery 661
Treatment, first-line 661
Treatment, inadequate response to first-line 661
Treatment, maintenance 661
Treatment, reviewing and stepping down 660
Treatment strategies, supporting evidence for 661

Dyspepsia – proven non-ulcer dyspepsia 664

What is dyspepsia? 671
How common is it? 672
How do I know my patient has non-ulcer dyspepsia? 672
What else might it be? 672
Which H pylori eradication regimen should I use? 675
Which H pylori test should I use? 673
How do I use a carbon-13 urea breath test? 673
How do I use a stool antigen test? 673
How should I advise people to take on-demand PPIs? 676
What general measures are useful? 673
What is first-line treatment? 673
What is non-ulcer dyspepsia? 671
What lifestyle advice is recommended? 673
What should I do if symptoms persist or return? 673
When is repeat endoscopy indicated? 674
Which dose of PPI? 676
Which eradication regimen should I use if my patient has had a recent course of antibiotics? 675
Which medication might be causing non-ulcer dyspepsia? 673
Which PPI? 676

Antacids and alginates 676
Antibiotic resistance 676
Complications 672
History 672
H_2-receptor antagonists 676
H_2-receptor antagonists, prokinetics, antacids, and alginates 676
Investigations 672
Management, overview of 673
Medicines management 675
Prognosis 672
Prokinetic agents 676
Psychological therapies 675
Treatment, reviewing and stepping-down 674
Treatment strategies, supporting evidence for 674
H pylori 'test and treat' 674
H pylori eradication regimens 675
Acid suppression 675
On-demand PPI therapy 675
Prokinetics 675

Dyspepsia – symptoms (uninvestigated by endoscopy) 678

What is dyspepsia? 691
How common is it? 691
What are the common underlying causes of dyspepsia? 691
How do I know what is causing dyspepsia? 692
What else might it be? 692
Who needs an initial referral for endoscopy? 693
Should I offer treatment while the person is awaiting endoscopy? 693
What general measures are useful? 693
Which medication might be causing dyspepsia? 693
What lifestyle advice is recommended? 694
What is first-line treatment? 694
Which H pylori test should I use? 694
How do I use a carbon-13 urea breath test? 694
How do I use a stool antigen test? 694
What should I do if symptoms persist or return? 694
Who needs to be referred for endoscopy if symptoms persist? 694
How should I follow up people whose symptoms respond to treatment? 695
How should I manage people whose symptoms persist despite treatment? 695
How do I manage dyspepsia associated with nonsteroidal anti-inflammatory drugs? 695
Which H pylori eradication regimen should I use? 698
Which eradication regimen should I use if my patient has had a recent course of antibiotics? 698
Which PPI? 698
Which dose of PPI? 698
How should I advise people to take on-demand therapy? 698
Which agents are suitable for gastroprotection against NSAIDs? 699

Antacids and alginates 699
Antibiotic resistance 698
Complications 692
Examination 692
History 692
H_2-receptor antagonists 699
H_2-receptor antagonists, antacids, alginates, and prokinetics 699
Investigations 692
Management, overview of 693
Medicines management 698
Prognosis 692
Prokinetic agents 699
Treatment, reviewing and stepping-down 695
Treatment strategies, supporting evidence for 696
Endoscopy referral criteria 696
H pylori 'test and treat' 696
Which *H pylori* test 696
Initial testing (pretreatment) 696
Post-eradication testing 697
Empirical PPI therapy 697
H pylori eradication regimens 697
On-demand PPI therapy 697
H_2-receptor antagonists and prokinetics 697
Preventing NSAID-induced complications 698

E

Earwax 701

What is it? 702
How common is it? 702
How do I know my patient has it? 702
What else might it be? 702

Complications 702
Ear drops to soften wax (cerumenolytics) 702
Ear irrigation 703
General issues 702
Removal techniques, mechanical, other (usually available only in secondary care) 703

Eating disorders 704

What is it? 704
How common is it? 705
How do I know my patient has it? 705
What else might it be? 706
How should anorexia nervosa be managed? 708
How should atypical eating disorders be managed? 710
How should binge eating disorder be managed? 710
How should bulimia nervosa be managed? 709
How should physical complications and coexisting disease be managed in anorexia nervosa? 709
How should physical complications and coexisting disease be managed in bulimia nervosa? 710
What is the role of pharmacological treatments in anorexia nervosa? 708
What is the role of psychological treatments in anorexia nervosa? 708
When should people with anorexia nervosa receive inpatient care? 709
What is the role of pharmacological treatments in bulimia nervosa? 709
What is the role of psychological treatments in bulimia nervosa? 709
When should people with bulimia nervosa receive inpatient care? 710
What is the role of primary care? 708

Anorexia nervosa 704, 705, 706, 707
Atypical 705, 707
Binge eating 705
Bulimia nervosa 705, 706, 707
Complications 706
Physical 706, 707
Social and emotional 707
Dental problems 710
Diabetes 709, 710
Diagnosing eating disorders, general points 705
Electrolyte disturbances 710
Osteoporosis and osteopenia 709
Overview 708
Pregnancy and the postnatal period 709, 710
Prognosis 707
Reproductive system 709
Weight gain 709

Eczema – atopic 712

What is atopic eczema? 727
What causes atopic eczema? 727
How common is it? 727
How do I know my patient has it? 728
What else might it be? 728
How do emollients work? 729
What types of emollient are there? 729
How do I choose a suitable emollient? 729
How much emollient should I prescribe? 730
How often should an emollient be applied? 730
Should I prescribe emollient soap substitute and/or bath emollients? 730
How should emollients be applied with topical corticosteroids? 730
What are the adverse effects of emollients, and how are they managed? 730
What is the evidence for the effectiveness of topical corticosteroids? 730
What potency of topical corticosteroid should I prescribe and for how long? 730
How much topical corticosteroid should be applied? 730
What quantity of corticosteroid should I prescribe? 731
Should corticosteroids be applied once a day or twice a day? 731
What are the adverse effects of topical corticosteroids? 732
How do I know when eczema is infected? 732
When should I prescribe an antibiotic? 732
How do I manage someone with eczema infected with herpes simplex? 732
What are the trigger factors for eczema and how do I manage them? 732
How do I know if diet is a significant trigger factor? 733
How do I know if house-dust mite is a significant trigger factor? 733
How is house-dust mite managed? 733
When should I refer to a specialist? 734
What treatments are available from specialists? 734
Which treatments have no proven value? 734
Can atopic eczema be prevented? 734

Appearance and distribution 728
Chronic eczema in adults, managing 729
Complications 728
Infection 728
Psychosocial impact 728
Dry skin, managing 729
Emollients 729
Endogenous factors 727
Environmental allergens 727
Environmental irritants 727
Flare-ups, managing 729
Flare-ups, managing frequent 729
Food hypersensitivity and eczema 733
General issues 728
Genetic factors 727
House-dust mite and other inhalant allergens 733
Infected eczema 732
Investigations 728
Irritants 732
Managing in primary care, overview of 728
Other inhalant allergens 733
Prognosis 728
Psychological stress and habitual scratching 733
Referral to a specialist 734
Topical corticosteroids 730
Acute flare up 730
Chronic lichenified eczema 730
Systemic adverse effects 732
Localized adverse effects 732
Widespread eczema, severe, managing 729

Eczema – contact

see Dermatitis – contact

Emphysema

see Chronic obstructive pulmonary disease

Endometriosis 736

What is it? 742
How common is it? 742
How do I know my patient has it? 742

What else might it be? 742

Analgesia 743
Complications 742
Drug treatments 743
Examination 742
General issues 743
History 742
Hormonal treatment 743
Types of hormonal treatment 743
Choice of hormonal treatment 744
Infertility 744
Investigations 742
Pre- and postoperative hormonal treatment 744
Prognosis 742
Surgical treatments 744

Enuresis – nocturnal 747

What is it? 749
How common is it? 750
How do I know my patient has it? 750
What else might it be? 750
At what age should treatment for nocturnal enuresis be initiated? 751
Which drug treatments are recommended for nocturnal enuresis? 752
How should drug treatment be prescribed? 753
What is the supporting evidence for drug treatment? 753
How safe is drug treatment? 754
Which non-drug treatments are recommended for nocturnal enuresis? 751
Where and by whom should a child with nocturnal enuresis be managed? 751
Which treatments are not recommended for nocturnal enuresis? 753

Advice for parents of a child with nocturnal enuresis 751
Causative factors and associations 750
Complications 751
Definitions 749
Desmopressin 752, 753, 754
Enuresis alarms 752
Examination 750
History 750
Investigations 750
Medicines management 753
Model of the cause of 749
Prognosis 751
Reward systems 751
Tricyclic antidepressants 752, 753, 754
Uncertain or controversial associations 750

Epilepsy 756

What is it? 771
How common is it? 772
How do I know my patient has it? 772
What else might it be? 773
How and when should antiepileptic drug withdrawal be managed? 776
How do epilepsy and antiepileptic drugs affect pregnancy? 777
How does hormone replacement therapy (HRT) affect epilepsy and antiepileptic drugs? 778
How is a person's driving licence affected by epilepsy? 779
How should provoked seizures be managed? 777
How should status epilepticus be managed? 779
In what way are drug formulations important in epilepsy? 776
To whom should a person with a seizure be referred? 774
What are the drug treatments for epilepsy? 775
What general drug issues are important in epilepsy? 775
What is the role of surgical treatment for epilepsy? 779
When should drug monitoring be undertaken in epilepsy? 776
Which drug interactions are important in epilepsy? 776
Which issues are important for a woman with epilepsy who is breastfeeding? 778
Which issues are important for a woman with epilepsy who is postpartum? 778
Which issues are important for a woman with epilepsy who requires contraception? 777
Which issues are particular to children with epilepsy? 778
Which issues are particular to elderly people with epilepsy? 779
Which issues are particular to people with learning difficulties who have epilepsy? 779
Which other treatments are recommended for epilepsy? 779

Carbamazepine 780
Clonazepam 781
Complications 773
Ethosuximide 781
Examination 773
General issues 774, 780
History 772
Investigation 773
Lamotrigine 780
Medicines management 780
Prognosis 774
Sodium valproate 780

Eye injury

see Corneal superficial injury

F

Febrile convulsion 784

What is it? 785
What causes febrile convulsions? 786
How common is it? 786
How do I know my patient has it? 786
What else might it be? 786
How do I manage the fever? 788
How should I counsel parents? 788
Does immunization increase the risk of febrile convulsions and other complications? 787
What conditions cause the fever in a child with febrile convulsions? 786
Bacterial meningitis 786
What is a febrile convulsion (or febrile seizure)? 785
What is the risk of epilepsy developing after a febrile convulsion? 787
What is the risk of recurrence after a febrile convulsion? 787
What measures should I consider to prevent febrile convulsions? 788
When should I admit or refer a child who has had a febrile convulsion? 787
When should I refer a child who has had a febrile convulsion? 788

Complications 787
Criteria for admission 787
Diagnose the cause of the fever 788
Examination 786
Fever, treat to ease symptoms 788
History 786
Investigations 786
Management, overview of 787
Prognosis 787

Flu

see Influenza

Fungal (dermatophyte) infections – skin and nails 791

What is it? 797
How common is it? 798
How do I know my patient has it? 798
What else might it be? 798

Athlete's foot, groin infection, or ringworm of the skin 799
Complications and prognosis 799
Fungal infection of the nails 800
General issues 800
History and examination 798
Hygiene measures 799, 800
Investigations 798
Scalp ringworm 800
Therapy, oral
With griseofulvin 801
With itraconazole 801
With terbinafine 801
Therapy, topical, with tioconazole or amorolfine 800
Treatment of athlete's foot, groin infection, or ringworm 799
Treatment of fungal infection of the nails 800
Treatment of scalp ringworm 800

Fungal infection

see Candida – skin and nails

G

Gastroenteritis 802

What is it? 821
How common is it? 821
Children 821
Adults 821
How do I know my patient has it? 822
How do I know my patient is dehydrated? 822
What else might it be? 823

Antibiotic treatment 825
Anti-emetics 825
Antimotility drugs 824
Campylobacter 825
Complications 823
Dehydration, prevention of 824
Dehydration, treatment of 824
Diarrhoea, chronic 826
Enterohaemorrhagic Escherichia coli infection (e.g. 0157 serotype) 825
Feeding during gastroenteritis 824
General issues 823
History 822
Investigations 822
Prognosis 823
Protozoa 826
Salmonella 825
Shigella 825
Symptoms and signs 822
Travellers' diarrhoea 822, 825

Genital Herpes

see Herpes simplex – genital

Gingivitis and periodontitis – plaque-associated 828

What is it? 831
What causes plaque-associated gingivitis and periodontitis? 831
What other important kinds of gingivitis are there? 831
How common is it? 832
How do I know my patient has plaque-associated gingivitis? 832
How do I know my patient has acute necrotizing ulcerative gingivitis? 832
What else might it be? 832
How can gingivitis and periodontitis be prevented? 833
What is the management of plaque-associated gingivitis and periodontitis? 833
What is the management of acute necrotizing ulcerative gingivitis (ANUG)? 834

Complications 832
Criteria for referral to maxillofacial department of the local hospital 833
Criteria for referral to a dentist 833
Medicines management 834
'Red flags' 832

Glaucoma 836

What is it? 837
How common is it? 837
How do I know my patient has it? 837
What else might it be? 837

Angle-closure, acute 837, 838
Treatment 838
Complications and prognosis 837
General 838
Open-angle, primary 837, 838
Treatment, drug 838
Surgical procedures 838
Trabeculectomy 838
Trabeculoplasty, laser 838

Glue ear 840

What is it? 841
How common is it? 841
How do I know my patient has it? 842
What else might it be? 842

Autoinflation 843
Complications 842
Examination, general 842
Hearing, assessment of 842
History 842
Management, initial, and indications for referral 843
Middle ear fluid, detection of 842
Prognosis 842
Treatments, medical (none recommended) 843
Treatment, surgical 843

Gout 845

What is it? 858
What causes gout? 858
How common is it? 859
How do I know my patient has it? 859
What else might it be? 860
How do I treat an acute attack of gout? 861
For how long should urate-lowering treatment be continued? 868
What treatment should I use? 861
How should I manage people with tophi? 863
What should I consider before initiating treatment? 861
What information is someone with gout likely to need? 861
What steps should I take to prevent future attacks of gout? 862
What are the indications for starting urate-lowering therapy? 862
What urate-lowering treatments should I use? 862
What is the evidence supporting the use of non-drug treatments during an acute attack of gout? 864

hat is the evidence supporting the use of NSAIDs for an acute attack of gout? 865
hat is the evidence supporting the use of colchicine for an acute attack of gout? 865
hat is the evidence supporting the use of corticosteroids for an acute attack of gout? 866
hat is the evidence supporting dietary measures to prevent recurrent attacks of gout? 867
hat is the evidence supporting the use of colchicine to prevent recurrent attacks of gout? 867
hat is the evidence supporting the use of urate-lowering therapy to prevent recurrent attacks of gout? 867
ow low should the target be for lowering plasma urate? 868
hy are sulfinpyrazone and probenecid not recommended? 868
hat is the role of systemic corticosteroids in treating gout? 863
hat systemic corticosteroids are available? 863
hat is the role of intra-articular corticosteroids in treating gout? 864
hich injectable corticosteroid should I use? 864
hen should I avoid injecting a joint? 864
hat regimen of allopurinol should I use? 864
hat are the adverse effects of allopurinol? 864
hat are the main adverse effects associated with colchicine? 863
hat dosing regimen of colchicine should I use? 863
ho should avoid taking colchicine? 863
hen is surgery required for tophi? 868
hich analgesic should I use? 864
hich NSAID should I use? 865

Adrenocorticotropic hormone 867
Alcohol ingestion, moderating 867
Allopurinol 864
Codeine 864
Colchicine 863
  Intravenous 866
  Oral 865
Complications 861
Corticosteroids, intra-articular 864, 866
Corticosteroids, intramuscular 866
Corticosteroids, oral 866
Corticosteroids, systemic 863
Criteria for the diagnosis of gout 860
Diagnosis, further information 860
Drug regimens for acute gout 864
Drug regimens for the prevention of gout 864
Drugs to prevent acute attacks of gout during treatment with allopurinol 864
Heat, application of 865
Ice pack, application of 864
Joints, resting affected 865
Management, overview of 861
Medicines management 863
Nonsteroidal anti-inflammatory drugs 863
  Effectiveness of 865
Paracetamol 864
Probenecid 868
Prognosis 861
Purines, moderating dietary ingestion of 867
Sulfinpyrazone 868
Urate-lowering therapy, effects of 867
Urate-lowering therapy, frequency of acute gout during the first months of 867
Urate, plasma, effect of aspirin on 865
Weight gain, avoiding, and losing weight 867

H

Haemorrhoids 871

What is it? 873
How common is it? 874
How do I know my patient has it? 874
What else might it be? 874
How should I manage someone with haemorrhoids? 875
How should I manage haemorrhoids in pregnant women? 876
What conservative measures should I recommend? 875
When should I refer someone with haemorrhoids? 876

Assessment 874
Behaviour modification 876
Complications 875
External 874, 875
Fibre intake, increased 875
Internal 874, 875
Phlebotonics 876
Prognosis 875
Signs 874
Symptomatic relief with topical therapies 875
Symptoms 874

Hay fever

see Allergic rhinitis
see Conjunctivitis – allergic

Headache 885

What is it? 890
How common is it? 890
How do I know my patient has it? 891
What else might it be? 892
How do I manage cluster headache? 893
How do I manage chronic tension-type headache? 892
How do I manage episodic tension-type headache? 892
How do I manage medication overuse headache? 892
What is the initial dose of amitriptyline and how should this be increased? 893
What monitoring is recommended for amitriptyline? 893
How should amitriptyline be withdrawn? 893
Which potentially hazardous interactions of amitriptyline should be avoided or monitored carefully? 893
Which formulation of sumatriptan should be used? 893
How should subcutaneous sumatriptan be administered? 893
What are the adverse effects of sumatriptan? 893

Amitriptyline 893
Cluster 891
Complications 892
Medication overuse headache 891
Medicines management 893
Migraine 891
Nonsteroidal anti-inflammatory drugs (NSAIDs) 893
Overview 891
Sumatriptan 893
Tension-type headache 891

Head lice 878

What is it? 882
How is it transmitted? 882
How common is it? 882
How do I know my patient has it? 882
What else might it be? 882
How should I treat head lice? 882
Can head lice infestation be prevented? 883
Do children with head lice need to be kept off school? 883
Who else should be checked? 882

Insecticides 884

Availability of 883
Resistance to 883
Medicines management 884
Products, other 883
Treatment failure 883
Treatments, supporting evidence for 883
Wet combing 884

Heartburn

see Dyspepsia – pregnancy-associated
see Dyspepsia – proven gastro-oesophageal reflux disease

Heart failure 895

What is it? 907
How common is it? 908
How do I know my patient has it? 908
What else might it be? 908

ACE and angiotensin-II receptor antagonists, combination of 911
ACE inhibitors 909
ACE inhibitors and angiotensin-II receptor antagonists 912
Acute heart failure 908
Angiotensin-II receptor antagonists 911
Beta-blockers 910, 912
Chronic heart failure 908
Complications 908
Diastolic heart failure 908, 912
Digoxin 910, 912
Diuretics 912
loop and thiazide 910
General issues in chronic heart failure 909
High-risk groups 909, 911
Medicines management 912
Prognosis 909
Revascularisation surgery 912
Spironolactone 910, 912
Surgical procedures, other 912
Treatment, initiation of 909, 910, 911
Treatments, other potentially useful drug 911
Treatments, surgical 912
Treatments of no proven benefit 911
Ventricular systolic dysfunction, left, recommended drug treatments for 909

Herpes labialis

see Herpes simplex – oral

Herpes simplex – genital 915

What is it? 920
How common is it? 920
How do I know my patient has it? 921
What else might it be? 921

Antiviral medication 922
Antiviral suppression therapy 923
Antiviral treatment of first episode 922
Antiviral treatment of recurrences 923
Complications 921
Immediate 921
Longer-term 921
Diagnostic procedures 921
General issues and patient education 922
Immunocompromised people, management in 923
Pregnancy, management in 923
Prognosis 921
Supportive measures 922
Symptoms and signs of first episode genital herpes 921
Symptoms and signs of recurrent genital herpes 921

Herpes simplex – ocular 925

What is it? 925
How common is it? 926
How do I know my patient has it? 926
What else might it be? 926
How is ocular herpes simplex managed in primary care? 927
How is ocular herpes simplex managed in secondary care? 927

Complications 926
Epithelial ocular herpes simplex, treatment of 927
General points 926
Prevention of 927
Primary 926
Prognosis 927
Recurrent 926
Signs 926
Stromal ocular herpes simplex, treatment of 927
Symptoms 926
Trigger factors 926

Herpes simplex – oral 929

What is it? 931
How is it transmitted? 932
How common is it? 932
How do I know my patient has it? 932
What else might it be? 932
Red flags 932
Can cold sores be prevented? 933
Do I need to use antiviral treatment? 933
How should I treat cold sores or gingivostomatitis? 93

Complications 932
Diagnostic tests 932
Differential diagnosis of cold sores 932
Differential diagnosis of herpes simplex gingivostomatitis 932
First attack (gingivostomatitis) 933
Immunocompromised people 933
Primary infection 932
Prognosis 933
Recurrent attacks (cold sores) 933
Recurrent disease 932
Possible triggers of 932
Treatments, other 933

Herpes zoster

see Shingles and postherpetic neuralgia

Hiccups 935

What is it? 936
How common is it? 936
What might the underlying cause of persistent or intractable hiccups be? 936

Complications and prognosis 936
Management 936

Hormone replacement therapy

in Angina 107
in Breast cancer – managing women with a family history 253
in Contraception 428
in Coronary heart disease risk – identification and management 466
in Diabetes Type 1 and 2 – hypertension 551
in Epilepsy 778
in Hyperlipidaemia 955
in Hypertension 993
in Menopause 1185, 1186, 1187, 1189, 1191, 1193, 1194, 1202, 1204, 1205, 1206, 1208, 1209, 121 1211

a Migraine 1247
a Osteoporosis – treatment 1389

ypercholesterolaemia

ee Hyperlipidaemia

yperemesis gravidarum

ee Nausea and vomiting in pregnancy

yperlipidaemia 938

What is it? 951
How common is it? 951
How do I know my patient has hyperlipidaemia? 951
Does my patient have a familial dyslipidaemia? 952
What else might it be? 952
How do I calculate coronary heart disease risk? 953
Who should be screened for hyperlipidaemia? 953
How should hyperlipidaemia be treated? 955
Is there an age limit for offering treatment? 955
Dietary management before starting drug treatment? 955
Who should be treated for hyperlipidaemia? 953
How long should people be treated for? 955
Does hormone replacement therapy prevent CHD? 955
What about people at lower risk of CHD? 953
Which statin? 957
What starting dose? 958
What is the place of over-the-counter simvastatin? 955

Complications and prognosis 952
- Decreased serum high-density lipoprotein 952
- Raised serum cholesterol 952
- Raised serum triglycerides 952

Dietary management of 955
Familial combined hyperlipidaemia 952
Familial hypercholesterolaemia 952
Goals for lowering serum lipids 954
Lipid-lowering agents, supporting evidence for other 957
Measuring lipid levels and monitoring toxicity 956
Referral, indications for specialist 954
Statins and fibrates 957
- Significant interactions 959
- Supporting evidence for statins 956
- Supporting evidence for fibrates 956
- Tolerability of statins and fibrates 958

Tests, other 956

Hypertension 962

What is hypertension? 982
How common is it? 982
How do I measure blood pressure? 982
What equipment and training do I need to measure blood pressure? 982
How should I measure BP in the consultation? 983
When is ambulatory blood pressure monitoring recommended? 983
How should ABPM be performed? 983
How should ABPM values be interpreted? 983
What are the advantages and disadvantages of ABPM? 983
When is blood pressure monitoring at home recommended? 984
How should home monitoring be performed? 984
How should the results of home monitoring be interpreted? 984
What are the advantages and disadvantages of home monitoring? 984
How do I confirm that the blood pressure is raised? 984
What are the causes of secondary hypertension? 984
What routine investigations should be done? 986
Why is cardiovascular risk assessed? 986
When should I assess cardiovascular risk? 986
How should I assess cardiovascular risk? 986
When do the cardiovascular risk charts incorrectly estimate risk and how should I manage this? 987
When should I recommend lifestyle interventions? 987
What lifestyle interventions are recommended? 987
What changes in BP can be expected from lifestyle interventions? 987
When should I recommend starting antihypertensive medication? 987
What drug should I start treatment with? 988
What does NICE currently recommend? 989
What does the BHS currently recommend? 989
What target blood pressure should I aim for? 989
What should I do if the target BP is not achieved with one drug? 989
What does NICE recommend for add-on treatment? 990
What does the BHS recommend for add-on treatment? 991
When can antihypertensive treatment be stopped or reduced? 991
Should beta-blockers or thiazide diuretics be prescribed for people at high risk of Type 2 diabetes? 991
Who is at high risk of developing Type 2 diabetes? 991
How should I manage older people? 992
Issues when treating people of Afro-Caribbean or South Asian ethnic origin? 992
When should I recommend low-dose aspirin? 992
How should I manage hyperlipidaemia? 992
When should I start a statin in people without cardiovascular disease? 992
When should I start a statin in people with cardiovascular disease? 992
What are target levels of total cholesterol, low-density lipoprotein cholesterol and total triglyceride should I aim for? 992
Should I prescribe hormone replacement therapy? 993
Which diuretics are indicated for the treatment of hypertension? 993
What dose of diuretic should I use? 993
What are the key adverse effects of thiazides? 993
Which key drug interactions are relevant for thiazides? 993
How should I monitor a person taking a thiazide? 993
Which beta-blockers are indicated for the treatment of hypertension? 993
What dose of beta-blocker should I use? 993
What are the key adverse effects of, and contraindications to, beta-blockers? 993
Which key drug interactions are common/potentially hazardous (with beta-blockers)? 994
How should I monitor a patient taking beta-blocker? 994
Which ACE inhibitors are indicated for the treatment of hypertension? 994
What dose of ACE inhibitor should I use? 994
Which AIIRAs are indicated for the treatment of hypertension? 994
What dose of AIIRA should I use? 994
What are the key adverse effects of, and contraindications to, ACE inhibitors and AIIRAs? 994
Which key drug interactions are relevant for ACE inhibitors and AIIRAs? 995
How should I monitor a patient taking an ACE inhibitor or AIIRA? 995
Which dihydropyridine calcium-channel blockers CCBs are indicated for the treatment of hypertension? 995
What dose of dihydropyridine CCB should I use? 995
What are the key adverse effects of, and contraindications to, dihydropyridine CCBs? 995
Which key drug interactions are relevant for dihydropyridine CCBs? 995

How should I monitor a patient taking a dihydropyridine CCB? 995
Which rate-limiting CCBs are indicated for the treatment of hypertension? 996
What dose of rate-limiting CCB should I use? 996
What are the key adverse effects of, and contraindications to, rate-limiting CCBs? 996
Which key drug interactions are relevant for rate-limiting CCBs? 996
How should I monitor a patient taking a rate-limiting CCB? 996
Which alpha-blockers are indicated for the treatment of hypertension? 996
What dose of alpha-blocker should I use? 996
What are the key adverse effects of, and contraindications to, alpha-blockers? 996
Which drug interactions are relevant for alpha-blockers? 997
How should I monitor a patient taking an alpha-blocker? 997

ACE inhibitors and angiotensin-II receptor antagonists (AIIRAs) 994
Alpha-blockers 996
Antiplatelet drugs 997
Beta-blockers 993
Blood pressure monitoring, ambulatory 983
Blood pressure monitoring, home 984
Calcium-channel blockers, dihydropyridine 995
Calcium-channel blockers, rate-limiting 996
Complications 985
Drug or toxin-induced 985
Drug treatment, general principles of 993
Endocrine disorder 985
Lifestyle interventions 987
Management, overview of 986
Medicines management 993
Prognosis 985
Renal disorder 985
Risk assessment, cardiovascular, in people with hypertension 986
Thiazide-type diuretics 993
Vascular disorder 985

Hypertension in pregnancy 1001

What is it? 1003
How common is it? 1003
How do I know my patient has it? 1003
What else might it be? 1003

Antihypertensive drugs to avoid 1005
Antihypertensive drugs used during pregnancy 1005
Chronic hypertension 1004
Complications and prognosis 1004
General issues 1004
Gestational hypertension 1004, 1005
Non-drug measures 1004
Pre-eclampsia 1004, 1005
Prevention of gestational hypertension and pre-eclampsia 1005
Severe hypertension and prevention of eclampsia, management of 1006

Hyperthyroidism 1007

What is it? 1008
How common is it? 1008
How do I know my patient has it? 1009
What else might it be? 1009
How do I treat subclinical hyperthyroidism? 1011
How do I treat Graves' ophthalmopathy? 1011
How do I treat hyperthyroidism during pregnancy and breastfeeding? 1010
What is the role of antithyroid drugs in hyperthyroidism? 1009
What is the role of beta-blockers in hyperthyroidism? 1010
What is the role of radioactive iodine in hyperthyroidism? 1010
What is the role of surgery in hyperthyroidism? 1010

Complications 1009
Medicines management 1011
Overview 1009
Prognosis 1009

Hypertriglyceridaemia

see Hyperlipidaemia

Hypnotic or anxiolytic dependence 1013

What is it? 1017
How common is it? 1017
How do I know my patient has it? 1017

Assessment, initial, of those dependent on high dosages 1018
Assessment, initial, of those dependent on therapeuti[c] dosages 1018
Benzodiazepines 1019, 1020
Buspirone 1019, 1020
Complications and prognosis 1017
Contacts, useful 1021
Examination 1018
General issues for those dependent on high dosages 1018
General issues for those dependent on therapeutic dosages 1017
History 1018
Hypnotics, newer (the 'z' drugs) 1019, 1020
Investigations 1018
Treatments, drug, for those dependent on high dosages 1020
Treatments, drug, for those dependent on therapeuti[c] dosages 1019
Treatments, non-drug, for those dependent on high dosages 1019
Treatments, non-drug, for those dependent on therapeutic dosages 1018
Withdrawal regimens for drug treatments 1019, 102[0]

Hypothyroidism 1022

What is it? 1024
How common is it? 1024
How do I know my patient has it? 1025
What else might it be? 1025
How do I treat hypothyroidism during pregnancy and breastfeeding? 1026
How do I treat overt hypothyroidism? 1025
How do I treat subclinical hypothyroidism? 1026
Which conditions are associated with hypothyroidism? 1024

Complications 1025
Medicines management 1026
Overview 1025
Prognosis 1025

I

Immunizations – childhood vaccination programme 1028

Can a child with a personal or close family history of febrile seizures be vaccinated? 1045
Can I give more than one vaccine at the same time? 104

an MMR vaccine be given to children with allergy to egg? 1045
an people with immunosuppression or HIV infection be vaccinated? 1045
ow common are these diseases? 1038
ow does vaccination lead to immunity? 1038
hat advice should I give about post-immunization pyrexia? 1042
hat are the diseases covered by the childhood vaccination programme? 1037
hat if a child has a tetanus-prone wound? 1043
hat if the vaccination history is unknown or incomplete? 1042
hat types of vaccines are available? 1039

Childhood immunization programme 1041
Complications of vaccination 1039
BCG vaccine 1040
Combined vaccines containing pertussis 1039
General information 1039
MMR vaccine 1040
Consent 1043
Contraindications to vaccination 1044
Delay vaccination, reasons to 1045
Diphtheria, tetanus, pertussis, poliomyelitis and Haemophilus influenzae type b 1041
Haemophilus influenzae (type b) 1043
Immunizations in schools 1044
Immunization of younger children 1044
Measles, Mumps, and Rubella 1041
Meningococcal C 1041
NOT contraindications to vaccination 1046
Suitability for vaccination 1044
Tuberculin testing 1042
Tuberculosis 1042
Vaccination procedures 1044
Administration of vaccines 1044
Record taking 1044
Storage and reconstitution of vaccines 1044

nmunizations – pneumococcal vaccine 1047

an a child with a personal or close family history of febrile seizures be vaccinated? 1051
an I give pneumococcal vaccine at the same time as other vaccines? 1049
ow common is invasive pneumococcal disease? 1048
ow does vaccination with pneumococcal vaccine lead to immunity? 1048
hould pneumococcal vaccine be re-administered? 1050
hat diseases does invasive pneumococcal infection cause? 1048
hat is the schedule for immunizing high-risk groups? 1049
Special groups 1049
hat types of pneumococcal vaccines are available? 1048
hich vaccine should I use? 1049
Supporting evidence 1049
ho should receive pneumococcal vaccine? 1049

Complications of 1049
Contraindications to 1051
NOT contraindications to 1051
Reasons to delay vaccination 1051
Suitability for vaccination 1051
Vaccination procedures 1050
Administration of vaccines 1050
Record taking 1050
Storage and reconstitution of vaccines 1050

nmunizations – travel vaccinations 1053

hy are travel vaccinations necessary? 1062
hich diseases commonly require vaccination? 1063
here are these diseases prevalent? 1064
What other diseases may require vaccination? 1063
Can I give more than one vaccine at the same time? 1069
Can people with immunosuppression or HIV infection be vaccinated? 1070

Cholera 1064, 1068
Conditions that are NOT contraindications 1071
Contraindications to 1070
Delay vaccination, reasons to 1070
Encephalitis, Japanese 1064, 1068
Encephalitis, tick-borne 1064, 1068
Hepatitis A 1063, 1066
Information sources 1065
Meningococcal meningitis 1063, 1067
Overseas, vaccinations that may be recommended for extended holidays or work 1067
Overseas travel, vaccinations commonly recommended for 1065
Overseas traveller, general advice for the 1064
Poliomyelitis 1063, 1067
Rabies 1064, 1067
Scheduling of 1068
Tetanus 1063, 1065
Typhoid fever 1063, 1065
Vaccination procedures 1069
Administration of vaccines 1069
Consent and record taking 1069
Payment and availability of travel vaccinations 1070
Storage and reconstitution of vaccines 1069
Yellow fever 1063, 1066

Impetigo 1072

What is it? 1073
How common is it? 1073
How do I know my patient has it? 1073
What else might it be? 1074

Antibiotics, oral 1074
Antibiotics, topical 1074
Antiseptic washes and cleansers 1074
Complications 1074
Drug treatment 1074
General issues 1074

Indigestion

see Dyspepsia – symptoms (uninvestigated by endoscopy)

Infertility 1076

What is it? 1078
How common is it? 1078
What causes it? 1078
When should I assess? 1080
How should I assess the woman? 1080
How should I assess the man? 1081
Which investigations are not generally recommended? 1081

Alcohol limitation 1081
Assessment in secondary care 1082
Assessment of the infertile couple in primary care 1080
Assisted conception 1083
Problems with 1084
Causes of infertility in men 1078
Causes of infertility in women 1078
Clothing 1082
Counselling and information on 1084
Donors, anonymity of 1084
Drugs 1078, 1079
Ectopic pregnancy 1084
Examination 1080, 1081
General issues 1079, 1082
Genital tract abnormalities 1079

History 1080, 1081
Investigations, initial 1080, 1081
Lifestyle advice 1081
Nutrition 1082
Outcomes of, likely 1079
    Without treatment 1079
    With treatment 1079
Ovulation, disorders of 1078
Ovulation hyperstimulation syndrome 1084
Referring the couple for specialist help 1082
Secondary and tertiary care management 1082
    National recommendations 1082
Smoking 1081
Spermatogenesis, defective 1078
Treatment, medical 1082
Treatment, surgical 1083
Treatment, types of 1082
Tubal, uterine and cervical factors 1078
Weight 1081

Influenza 1086

What is it? 1091
How common is it? 1092
How do I know my patient has it? 1092
What are the risk factors for contracting influenza? 1092
How and why is influenza monitored? 1093
What else might it be? 1093

Amantadine 1096, 1097
Antigenic drift and shift 1092
Antiviral drugs 1095
    Prophylaxis of influenza 1096
    Treatment of influenza 1095
Clinical features 1092
Complications 1093
Diagnostic tests 1092
Incubation period 1092
Infectivity, period of 1092
Oseltamivir 1096
Outbreaks of influenza in long-stay residential care, management of 1097
Prognosis 1093
Transmission 1092
Treatment of influenza in otherwise healthy individuals 1095
Vaccination 1094
    Adverse effects 1095
    Effectiveness 1094
    General 1094
    Influenza immunization for health and social care staff 1094
    National policy for 1094
    Suitability for 1095
Virus 1091
Zanamivir 1095, 1097

Inhaler devices

in Asthma 162, 164
in Chronic obstructive pulmonary disease 341, 347

Insect bites and stings 1099

What is it? 1103
How common is it? 1104
How do I know my patient has it? 1104
What else might it be? 1104

Adrenaline 1107
Anaphylaxis 1105
Antihistamines, oral 1107
Bites 1103, 1104, 1105
Complications 1104
Corticosteroids, topical 1107
Diseases transmitted by bites 1105
Infection 1104
Management, acute 1105, 1106
Management, future 1107
Medicines management 1107
Preventing bites 1106
Prognosis 1105
Reactions, local 1106
    large 1106
Reactions, systemic 1105, 1106
Reinfestation, preventing 1105
    Discovering the source of infestation 1105
    Confirming the source of infestation 1106
    Eliminating the infestation 1106
Stings 1104, 1106

Insomnia 1109

What is it? 1116
How common is it? 1116
How do I know my patient has it? 1116

Alternative remedies 1119
Benzodiazepines 1118
    Adverse effects of 1118
    Versus Z drugs 1118
Complications and prognosis 1116
Counselling and behavioural therapies 1117
Examination, physical 1116
General issues 1116
History 1116
Hypnotic usage, chronic 1120
Patient advice and self-management 1117
Treatments, drug, other 1119
Treatments, non-drug 1117
Treatments, standard drug 1118
    General issues in 1118
Zaleplon 1119
Zolpidem 1119
Zopiclone 1119

Irritable bowel syndrome 1122

What is it? 1125
How common is it? 1126
How do I know my patient has it? 1126
What else might it be? 1126

Antidepressants 1128
Antidiarrhoeal agents 1128
Antispasmodics 1128
Complications 1126
Diet and lifestyle 1127
Explanation and reassurance 1127
General issues 1127
Laxatives 1127
Onset 1126
Prognosis 1127
Referral 1129
Rome II criteria 1126
Treatments, drug 1127
Treatments, other 1128
Treatments, psychological 1128
Treatments, simple non-drug 1127

L

Lacerations 1130

What is it? 1139
How common is it? 1139

Antibiotic prophylaxis 1141
Antibiotic treatment 1141
Complications and prognosis 1139
Management, initial 1139

Skin-closure strips, sterile 1140
Suture material, choice of 1140
Suturing 1140
Tetanus prophylaxis 1140
Tissue adhesives 1140
Wound closure, timing of 1140

g cramps – unknown cause 1143

at are idiopathic leg cramps? 1144
at are the secondary causes of leg cramps? 1144
w common are idiopathic leg cramps? 1145
w do I know my patient has idiopathic leg cramps? 1145
at else might it be? 1145
w should I assess someone with leg cramps? 1145
w should an acute attack of leg cramp be managed? 1146
w should recurrent leg cramps be managed? 1146
at is the supporting evidence for stretching exercises? 1146
at is the supporting evidence for quinine? 1146
w should I manage leg cramps in pregnancy? 1146
at is the supporting evidence for drug therapy in pregnancy? 1146
at evidence is there for other drug treatments? 1147
w should quinine be prescribed? 1147
w safe is quinine? 1147
o should not be prescribed quinine for leg cramps? 1147
e there any significant drug interactions associated with quinine? 1147

Complications 1145
Investigations 1145
Medicines management 1147
Prognosis 1145
Secondary causes 1144
  Drugs 1145
  Medical conditions 1144
Signs 1145
Symptoms 1145
Trials, double-blind, randomised placebo-controlled crossover 1147
Trials, open-labelled 1147

g ulcer – venous 1150

at is it? 1161
at are the risk factors for venous leg ulcer? 1161
w common is it? 1161
w do I know my patient has a venous leg ulcer? 1161
at else might it be? 1161
w is a venous leg ulcer assessed? 1162
w is a venous leg ulcer managed? 1163
at treatments are available? 1163
w are complications managed? 1164
at follow-up is necessary? 1165
w can recurrence be prevented? 1165
o needs to be referred to a specialist clinic for further assessment? 1162
o should be involved in the management of venous leg ulcers? 1163

Allergens in dressings 1166
Ankle Brachial Pressure Index 1162
Care, organisation of 1163
Cleansing and debridement 1163
Complications 1162
  Dermatitis 1164
  Infection 1164
  Leg oedema 1164
  Pain 1165
Compression, multi-layer 1163
Compression bandaging 1166
Compression dressings 1163
  Other compression methods 1164
  Problems associated with compression 1164
Compression hosiery 1166
Dressings information 1165
Examination 1161
Investigations to consider, other 1161
Investigations to exclude an arterial component to the ulcer 1161
Medicines to improve ulcer healing 1164
Medicines to prevent recurrence 1165
Prognosis 1162
Treatments 1163
  Other treatment options 1164
Wound contact dressings 1163
Wound dressings 1165

M

Malaria prophylaxis 1168

What is it? 1171
What is the lifecycle of the malarial parasite? 1171
How common is it? 1172
What is the likelihood of a traveller contracting malaria? 1172
How do I know my patient has malaria? 1172
What else might it be? 1172
How should chemoprophylaxis be taken? 1175
What advice do travellers need about preventing mosquito bites? 1173
What advice do travellers need about the risk of malaria? 1173
Which chemoprophylaxis regimen is suitable? 1174
Who needs to carry emergency standby treatment? 1176

Antimalarial, factors affecting the final choice of 1174
Chemoprophylaxis, adverse effects of 1175
Complications and prognosis 1172
Foreign nationals returning to a malarious area, advice for 1176
Infants and children 1174
Mosquito repellants 1173
Sunscreens and DEET 1173
Symptoms, timing of 1172
Travellers, long-term 1174
Women 1174

Meniere's disease 1178

What is it? 1180
How common is it? 1180
How do I know my patient has it? 1180
What else might it be? 1180

Balance control, impaired 1182
Betahistine 1183
Cinnarizine 1182
Complications 1181
Hearing, loss of 1181
Lifestyle measures and alternative therapies 1182
Medicines management 1182
Prochlorperazine 1182
Prognosis 1181
Prophylaxis, drugs for 1181
Psychological distress 1182
Supportive measures 1181
Tinnitus 1182
Treatments available in secondary care 1181
Vertigo, drugs for acute attacks of 1181

Menopause 1184

What causes the menopause? 1199
What causes premature menopause? 1200
How common are menopausal symptoms? 1200
How do I know my patient has it? 1200
What are the options for managing menopausal symptoms? 1201
What are the options for managing the long-term health implications of the menopause? 1205
What are the long-term benefits and risks of HRT? 1202
Which hormones, which regimen, which route, which dose? 1207
Which hormones? 1207
Which regimen? 1208
Which route? 1208
Which dose? 1209
Is there a place for HRT in long-term disease prevention? 1204

Alzheimer's disease 1205
Breast cancer 1202, 1205
Cardiovascular disease 1204
Definitions 1199
Endometrial cancer 1203, 1206
Examination 1207
General points 1201
History taking and contraindication checking 1206
Hormones and the menstrual cycle at the menopause, changes to 1199
Hormones and the normal menstrual cycle 1199
Hot flushes and night sweats 1201
HRT
  Adverse effects, progestogen-related (other than bleeding) 1210
  Adverse effects of, managing the 1209
  Assessment of the woman prior to starting 1206
  Benefits, long-term 1202
  Benefits, unproven 1204
  Bleeding 1209
  Bleeding on monthly cyclical/sequential regimens, product-related 1209
  Bleeding on continuous combined HRT or during long-cycle HRT regimens 1210
  Changing 1210
  Comorbidity, use in women with 1205
  Contraception 1205
  Implants (oestrogen only) 1208
  Intranasal (oestrogen only) 1208
  Intra-uterine system (progestogen) 1208
  Monitoring and follow-up of women 1210
  Oestrogen dose 1209
  Oestrogen-related adverse effects 1210
  Oestrogens, vaginal 1208
  Oral (oestrogen with or without progestogen) 1208
  Premature menopause, for women with a 1204
  Progestogen dose 1209
  Risks 1202
  Risks, other 1204
  Starting 1206
  Stopping 1211
  Tibolone dose 1209
  Transdermal (oestrogen with or without progestogen) 1208
Investigations 1200, 1207
Libido and sexual dysfunction, decreased 1202
Long-term health implications of the menopause 1201
Mood or sleep disturbances 1201
Osteoporosis 1204
Other conditions 1206
Signs and symptoms of the menopause 1200
Stroke 1203
Thromboembolic disease (personal or family history) 1206
Thromboembolism, venous 1204
Urogenital symptoms 1202
Weight gain 1209

Menorrhagia 1214

What is it? 1220
How common is it? 1220
How do I assess a woman presenting with heavy periods? 1220
What else might it be? 1221
What medical treatments are available to manage menorrhagia? 1222
Should tranexamic acid be combined with an NSAID? 1223
What surgical treatments are available to manage menorrhagia? 1225
When should I refer? 1226
What points should be considered when choosing between hysterectomy and endometrial destruction? 1225

Complications and prognosis 1222
Contraceptives, combined oral 1223
Danazol 1224
Depot medroxyprogesterone acetate 1227
Endometrial ablation 1225
Etamsylate 1224
Examination 1221
Gonadotrophin-releasing hormone analogues 1224
History 1220
Hysterectomy 1225
  Endometrial destruction techniques 1225
Investigations in primary care 1221
Investigations in secondary care 1221
Medicines management 1226
  General information 1226
Nonsteroidal anti-inflammatory drugs 1223, 1226
Progestogen-only intra-uterine system 1223
Progestogens, oral 1224
  high-dose 1224
Progestogens long-acting – injection or implant 122
Tranexamic acid 1222, 1227
Treatment, overview of 1222

Migraine 1230

What is it? 1240
What are the predisposing and trigger factors? 1240
How common is it? 1240
How do I know my patient has it? 1240
What else might it be? 1242
How do I identify predisposing trigger factors? 1242
How do I manage trigger factors? 1242
How should I treat an attack of migraine first-line? 12
When should I use anti-emetics? 1243
When should I use rectal analgesia and anti-emetics? 1243
Why should I avoid codeine and other opioids? 1243
When should I prescribe a triptan? 1243
Which triptans are available? 1243
Which triptan should I use? 1243
Which formulation should I use? 1244
What should I do if my patient suffers a relapse immediately following triptan use? 1245
What should I do if triptans are ineffective or migrain are very frequent? 1245
When should I consider using drug prophylaxis? 124
Which drug should I use for prophylaxis? 1245
Which drug should I not use for prophylaxis? 1245
What advice can I give my patient during an attack? 1

What non-drug therapies are useful to prevent attacks of migraine? 1246
Which women should avoid using CHCs? 1246
What should I do if migraine with aura develops in a woman already taking CHCs? 1247
What alternative contraception should I prescribe? 1247
Should a woman with migraine be prescribed HRT? 1247
What should I do if a woman suffers a migraine attack for the first time while taking HRT? 1247
Who should avoid taking NSAIDs? 1248
Who should avoid taking an anti-emetic drug? 1248
When should my patient take a dose of triptan? 1248
Who should avoid taking triptans? 1248
What are the adverse effects associated with triptans? 1248
Are acute drugs still necessary? 1248
What dose should be taken? 1248
How long should prophylactic drugs be used for? 1248
Who should always avoid taking prophylactic drugs? 1248
When should I prescribe prophylactic drugs with extra caution? 1249
What are the adverse effects of prophylactic drugs? 1249
What evidence is there to support the use of first-line treatment in an acute attack? 1249
How effective are triptans? 1249
What evidence is there for adverse effects of triptans? 1250
How do triptans compare with each other? 1250
Is there evidence to support the combined use of anti-emetics or analgesics with triptans? 1250
How effective are beta-blockers in preventing migraine? 1250
How effective is amitriptyline in preventing migraine? 1250
How effective is sodium valproate in preventing migraine? 1250

Amitriptyline 1245
Analgesics and nonsteroidal anti-inflammatory drugs 1249
Analgesics and NSAIDs, standard 1248
Anti-emetic drugs 1248
Aura, migraine with (classical migraine) 1241
Aura, migraine without (common migraine) 1241
Beta-blockers 1245
Children 1241
Complications 1242
Contraceptives, management of women taking combined hormonal 1246
Evidence, supporting 1249
Anti-emetic drugs 1249
Hormone replacement therapy, management of women taking 1247
Management, overview of 1242
Medicines management 1248
Menstrual migraine 1241
Management of 1246
Non-drug therapies 1246
Pregnancy and breastfeeding, management during 1247
Prevention of, drugs for the 1248, 1250
Prevention of attacks, drug treatment for 1245
Prognosis 1242
Sodium valproate 1245
Treatment, first-line 1242
Trigger factors, managing 1242
Triptans 1248, 1249
Using 1243

Molluscum contagiosum 1253

What is it? 1253
How common is it? 1254
How do I know my patient has it? 1254
What else might it be? 1254

Anogenital lesions 1255
Complications 1254
Eczema 1255
HIV 1256
Inflamed 1255
Management, first-line 1255
Management, second-line 1255
Periocular 1255
Prognosis 1254
Treatments that are not generally recommended in primary care 1255

Monitoring people on disease-modifying drugs (DMARDs) 1258

What are the principles of monitoring people taking disease-modifying drugs (DMARDs)? 1258
How do I monitor for myelosuppression in someone treated with a DMARD? 1258
How do I monitor for renal and urinary tract toxicity in someone treated with a DMARD? 1260
How do I monitor for hepatotoxicity in someone treated with a DMARD? 1260
How do I manage someone exposed to the varicella-zoster virus (chickenpox or shingles)? 1260
How do I monitor someone treated with anakinra? 1260
How do I monitor someone treated with azathioprine? 1260
How do I monitor someone treated with ciclosporin? 1261
How do I monitor someone treated with cyclophosphamide? 1261
How do I monitor someone treated with intramuscular gold (sodium aurothiomalate)? 1262
How do I monitor someone treated with hydroxychloroquine? 1262
How do I monitor someone treated with leflunomide? 1263
How do I monitor someone treated with methotrexate? 1263
How do I monitor someone treated with penicillamine? 1264
How do I monitor someone treated with sulfasalazine? 1264
How do I monitor someone treated with TNF-alpha inhibitors: etanercept, infliximab, adalimumab? 1265

Morning-after pill

see Contraception – emergency

Morning sickness

see Nausea and vomiting in pregnancy

Mouth ulcer

see Aphthous ulcer

Myxoedema

see Hypothyroidism

N

Nappy rash 1267

What is it? 1269
What are the causative factors of nappy rash? 1269
How common is it? 1270

What else might it be? 1270

Complications 1270
Prevention of 1270
Treatment of 1270

Nausea and vomiting in pregnancy 1272

What is it? 1273
How common is it? 1274
How do I know my patient has it? 1274
What other causes of nausea and vomiting in pregnancy are there? 1275
What first-line measures should I recommend? 1275
What should I do if symptoms are severe despite first-line measures? 1276
Which drugs can be used to treat nausea and vomiting in pregnancy in primary care? 1276
When should I refer? 1276
Are vitamins an effective treatment? 1276
Are alternative and complementary therapies effective? 1277
How should drug treatment be prescribed? 1278
What are the adverse effects of drug treatment? 1278

Acupuncture, acupressure, and acustimulation 1277
Antihistamine anti-emetics – promethazine and cyclizine 1276
Clinical features 1274
Complications 1275
Cyclizine 1278
Domperidone 1276, 1278
Ginger 1277
Herbal remedies 1278
Homeopathic treatment 1278
Hypnosis, hypnotherapy, psychotherapy, and behaviour modification 1278
Investigations 1274
Management, overview of 1275
Medicines management 1278
Metoclopramide 1276, 1278
Multivitamins 1276
Prochlorperazine 1276, 1278
Prognosis 1275
Promethazine 1278
Pyridoxine 1276

Neck pain 1281

What is it? 1294
How common is neck pain? 1295
How do I know my patient has simple neck pain? 1295
What are the 'red flags' for simple neck pain? 1295
How do I know my patient has whiplash associated disorder? 1296
How do I know my patient has cervical radiculopathy? 1296
What else might it be? 1296
How do I manage simple neck pain? 1298
Which nonsteroidal anti-inflammatory drug should I use? 1299
What dose of diazepam should I use? 1299
What are the adverse effects of diazepam? 1300
What dose of amitriptyline should I use? 1300
What are the adverse effects of amitriptyline? 1300
Who should avoid taking amitriptyline? 1300
What dose of gabapentin should I use? 1300
What are the adverse effects of gabapentin? 1300
What is the evidence for treatments of simple neck pain? 1301
What is the evidence for treatments of acute whiplash-associated disorder? 1301
What is the evidence for treatments of chronic whiplash-associated disorder? 1301
What is the evidence for treatments of neck pain with radiculopathy? 1302
What is the evidence for acupuncture for chronic neck pain? 1302

Analgesia 1299
Assessment of neck pain and any disability due to neck pain 1298
Classification 1295
Codeine 1299
Comorbidity in chronic neck pain 1298
Complications 1297
Conditions which can cause neck pain, potentially dangerous 1298
Drug therapy 1298
Evidence, supporting 1300
Management of chronic pain, drugs for 1300
Management of simple neck pain, overview of 1298
Medicines management 1299
Muscle relaxants 1299
Nonsteroidal anti-inflammatory drugs 1299
Paracetamol 1299
Physical and manual treatment 1299
Prognosis 1297
Psychosocial factors that may indicate increased risk of chronicity and disability 1298
Radiculopathy, cervical 1295, 1297
Reassurance and information 1298
Risk factors for developing 1298
Simple 1294, 1297
  Differential diagnosis of 1296
  Incidence, prevalence, and health services usage 1295
Torticollis, acute 1295
  Incidence 1295
  Differential diagnosis of 1296
Treatments, invasive 1299
Treatments with evidence of benefit 1301
Treatments with evidence of lack of benefit 1301
Treatments with insufficient evidence to assess effectiveness 1301, 1302
Whiplash-associated disorder 1294, 1297
  Incidence and prevalence 1295

Nonsteroidal anti-inflammatory drugs (NSAIDs) 1305

What types of nonsteroidal anti-inflammatory drugs are there? 1305
What is the risk of a gastrointestinal adverse effect for someone taking an NSAID? 1305
How do the gastrointestinal adverse effects of NSAIDs compare? 1305
Who is at risk of developing serious NSAID-induced gastrointestinal adverse effects? 1306
How can I lower the chances of adverse gastrointestinal effects? 1306
What gastroprotective agents are available and are they effective? 1306
How should I manage someone taking an NSAID who experiences adverse gastrointestinal effects? 1307
Do COX-2 selective NSAIDs increase the risk of cardiovascular disease? 1307
Do standard NSAIDs affect the risk of cardiovascular disease? 1307
Does ibuprofen reduce the cardioprotective effect of low-dose aspirin? 1307
How should someone taking low-dose aspirin and an NSAID be managed? 1308
How should someone who has hypertension and who is taking an NSAID be managed? 1308
What led to the withdrawal of rofecoxib? 1308
What led to the suspension of valdecoxib? 1308

What should I be aware of when initiating an NSAID? 1309
Which NSAID is recommended in which clinical situation? 1309
When should NSAIDs be avoided? 1309
Can NSAIDs be used by pregnant or breastfeeding women? 1309
What monitoring is recommended? 1310
Which potentially hazardous interactions should be avoided or monitored carefully? 1310

Aspirin 1306
Cardiovascular disease 1307
COX-2 selective NSAIDs 1305
Etodolac and meloxicam 1306
Gastrointestinal adverse effects and NSAIDs 1305
Prescribing an NSAID 1309
Rofecoxib, withdrawal of 1308
Standard NSAIDs 1305
Valdecoxib, suspension of 1308

O

Obesity 1313

What is it? 1320
How common is it? 1320
How do I know my patient has it? 1321
What else might it be? 1321
Who do I treat? 1321

Complications and prognosis 1321
Dietary changes 1322
Drugs, anti-obesity 1323
General issues 1321
Physical activity 1322
Psychological and behavioural approaches 1323
Surgery 1323
Treatment, targets and timetables for weight loss, main components of 1322
Weight loss, benefits of 1321
Weight management programmes and national initiatives 1322

Opioid dependence 1325

What is it? 1337
How common is it? 1337
How do I know my patient has it? 1337
Which drug for initiation and stabilization? 1339, 1342
Which drug for detoxification? 1342

Assessment, initial 1338
Buprenorphine 1339, 1342
  Initiation and stabilization of 1340
Compliance with initiation and maintenance of treatment, improving 1341
  Assessment during treatment 1341
  Supervised consumption 1341
Complications 1337
Detoxification 1342
  Prescribing methadone for 1343
  Prescribing buprenorphine for 1343
Dihydrocodeine (not recommended) 1343
Driving ability, issues concerning 1346
Drug misuse, suspected 1337
Emergency situation, collapse due to opioid overdose, management of 1344
Examination 1337
General issues 1338
Harm reduction 1339
History 1337
History and examination 1338
Investigations 1337
Investigations to exclude complications 1338
Lofexidine 1342
Management plan 1339
Methadone 1339, 1342
  Initiation and stabilization of 1340
Naltrexone 1343
Opioid use, confirmation of 1338
Pain, management of 1346
Practice policy, deciding on 1347
  Useful contacts 1347
Pregnancy 1345
  Treatment issues 1345
Presentation 1337
Prognosis 1338
Relapse 1343
  Prevention of, after abstinence 1343
  Management of, after abstinence 1343
Reporting drug misuse 1346
Substitute therapy, writing prescriptions for 1343
Substitute treatment, changing 1341
  Buprenorphine to methadone 1341
  Methadone to buprenorphine 1341
Symptomatic treatments 1344
  Diarrhoea 1344
  Nausea and vomiting 1344
  General aches and pains (e.g. headache, muscular pains) or high temperature 1344
  Anxiety/agitation 1344
  Other symptoms 1344
Symptoms and signs of opioid withdrawal 1344
Tests, other 1339
Travelling abroad 1346
Treatment, initiation and stabilization of 1339
  General points 1339
Treatment, maintenance 1340
  Prescribing methadone 1341
  Prescribing buprenorphine 1341
Unknown patient, Management of 1345
  New patient or temporary resident 1345
  Unknown patient requesting a replacement prescription out of hours 1345
Urine drug screen 1338
Withdrawal syndrome, acute 1343

Osteoarthritis 1350

What is osteoarthritis? 1364
What are the risk factors for developing osteoarthritis? 1364
How common is osteoarthritis? 1365
How do I know my patient has osteoarthritis? 1365
What else might it be? 1365
How does paracetamol compare with NSAIDs in symptomatic pain relief for OA? 1366
When should I prescribe a COX-2 selective inhibitor? 1367
What evidence supports the use of topical NSAIDs? 1367
What is the role of intra-articular injections in OA? 1367
Which non-drug treatments are recommended for OA of the knee? 1367
What analgesia is recommended for OA of the knee? 1368
What evidence supports intra-articular corticosteroid injection use in knee OA? 1368
What evidence supports the use of intra-articular hyaluronic acid injections for knee OA? 1368
What evidence supports the use of glucosamine for knee OA? 1369
What is the role of chondroitin in knee OA? 1370
What is the role of magnetic bracelets in knee OA? 1370
When should I refer my patient with OA of the knee to an orthopaedic surgeon? 1370

Which surgical treatments are available for OA of the knee? 1370
Which non-drug treatments are recommended for osteoarthritis (OA) of the hip? 1371
What analgesia is recommended for OA of the hip? 1371
Is intra-articular corticosteroid injection recommended for hip OA? 1371
What is the role of chondroitin in hip OA? 1371
When should I refer my patient with OA of the hip to an orthopaedic surgeon? 1371
Which surgical treatments are available for OA of the hip? 1372
What is the role of magnetic bracelets in OA of the hip? 1372
Which non-drug treatments are recommended for OA of any other joint? 1372
What analgesia is recommended for OA of any other joint? 1372
Is intra-articular corticosteroid injection recommended for OA of any other joint? 1372
When should I refer my patient with OA of any other joint to an orthopaedic surgeon? 1372
Which surgical treatments are available for OA of any other joint? 1372
How should intra-articular corticosteroids be given? 1373
Which corticosteroid injection should I use? 1373
When should I avoid injecting a joint? 1373
What clinically important adverse effects should I be aware of? 1373

Analgesia recommendations summary 1366
Codeine 1372
Complications 1366
Corticosteroids, intra-articular 1373
Diagnostic criteria 1365
Hip, of the 1371
Differential diagnosis 1365
Investigations 1365
Joint, other, of 1372
Differential diagnosis 1365
Knee, of the 1367
Differential diagnosis 1365
Management, overview of 1366
Medicines management 1372
Nonsteroidal anti-inflammatory drugs 1372
Topical 1373
Paracetamol 1372
Prognosis 1366
Signs 1365
Surgery 1370, 1371, 1372
Symptoms 1365

Osteoporosis – treatment 1376

What is it? 1384
How common is it? 1384
What are the risk factors for osteoporosis? 1384
What are the risk factors for fracture? 1385
What are the secondary causes of osteoporosis? 1385
How do I know my patient has osteoporosis? 1385
What else might it be? 1385
Who should be offered treatment for osteoporosis? 1387
How should I treat osteoporosis? 1387
Which drug treatment should I use? 1387
What is the place of hormone replacement therapy? 1389
Does hormone replacement therapy prevent fractures in women with osteoporosis? 1389
What are the risks of using HRT? 1389
Who should be considered for HRT? 1389
Is bone mass maintained after drug treatment is stopped? 1389
Which treatment should I use to treat glucocorticoid-induced osteoporosis? 1389

Alendronate 1388
Alfaclacidol 1390
Antiresorptive treatments, other 1388
Bisphosphonates 1390
BMD, monitoring 1386
BMD scanning 1386
Methods that are not recommended 1386
Calcitonin, intranasal (salmon) 1390
Calcitriol 1390
Calcium + vitamin D, adjunctive treatment with 1388
Complications 1385
Corticosteroids, inhaled 1389
Elderly people 1388
Falls, assessing the risk of 1386
Falls, managing the risk of 1386
Fracture, osteoporotic, identifying people at risk of 1386
Fractures, risk of further 1385
Glucocorticoid-induced osteoporosis 1389
Supporting evidence 1390
Glucocorticoids, oral 1389
Glucocorticoids and bone mineral density 1389
Lifestyle interventions 1387
Measures to reduce the risk of falls and damage from falling 1387
Medicines management 1390
Men 1388
Postmenopausal women 1388
Pregnancy and breastfeeding 1391
Prognosis 1385
Raloxifene 1390
Risedronate 1388
Treatment, drug, supporting evidence for 1388
Treatment, first-line 1387
Treatment, second-line 1388
Treatments, other 1388

Otitis externa 1393

What is it? 1402
How common is it? 1402
How do I know my patient has it? 1402
What else might it be? 1403
What is the role of ear swabs in establishing the cause of otitis externa? 1403
When are oral antibiotics recommended? 1404
When are topical drug treatments recommended? 1404

Chronic 1403, 1404
Complications 1403
Considerations, special 1405
Diffuse, acute 1403, 1404
General measures 1404
Localized, acute(furunculosis) 1402, 1404

Otitis media – acute 1406

What is it? 1411
How common is it? 1411
How do I know my patient has it? 1412
What are the risk factors? 1412
Acute otitis media or otitis media with effusion? 1412
What else might it be? 1412
How effective are antibiotics? 1413
Should I prescribe an antibiotic? 1413
What is the preferred antibiotic? 1413
How long should I prescribe an antibiotic for? 1414
What dose of antibiotic should I use? 1414

Analgesia 1415
Complications and prognosis 1412
Preventative measures 1415
Referral advice 1415
Signs 1412

Symptoms 1412
Therapies, other 1415

Otitis media – chronic

see Glue ear

Pain

see Back pain – lower
see Neck pain
see Palliative care – pain
in Angina 103
in Back pain – lower 188, 194, 196, 198, 199, 203
in Leg ulcer – venous 1165
in Neck pain 1281, 1283, 1287, 1290, 1298, 1300, 1302
in Opioid dependence 1344, 1346
in Osteoarthritis 1361, 1366
in Palliative care – nausea/vomiting/malignant bowel obstruction 1462
in Palliative care – oral problems 1471, 1473, 1476
in Palliative care – pain 1479, 1489
in Prostatitis 1582, 1584
in Renal colic – acute 1615
in Rheumatoid arthritis 1628
in Shingles and postherpetic neuralgia 1705, 1708, 1710
in Sore throat – acute 1739
in Sprains and strains 1751

Palliative care – cough 1418

What is it? 1423
How common is it? 1423
How do I know the cause of my patient's cough? 1423
Is dyspnoea a feature of the cough? 1425
Should I treat the underlying cause of the cough? 1425
Should I suppress the cough? 1425
Should I use a cough suppressant? 1427
What dose of morphine should I use? 1426
What should I do if opioids do not suppress cough adequately? 1426

Bronchorrhoea 1427
Chest infection 1427
Cough suppressants 1426
Dexamethasone 1428
Dexamethasone, stopping 1428
Drug delivery, non-oral routes of 1428
Dry cough, treating the underlying malignant cause of 1426
Dry cough in palliative care, managing 1426
Simple measures 1426
Haemoptysis 1427
Help and advice in primary care, seeking 1425
Investigations of cough, primary-care 1423
Malignant causes of cough, managing the 1425
Medicines management 1427
Morphine 1427
Needs, social 1425
Needs, spiritual 1425
Palliative care, general issues in 1423
Productive cough, ineffective 1427
Productive cough, treating the underlying cause of 1427
Productive cough in palliative care (including haemoptysis), managing 1426
Psychological state, assessment of 1424
Symptoms, assessment and management of physical 1423
Syringe drivers, drugs commonly used in 1429
Syringe drivers, drugs for cough used in 1429
Terminal phase, adjustments in 1425
Terminal phase, recognising the 1425
Tranexamic acid 1428

Palliative care – dyspnoea 1431

What is dyspnoea? 1434
How common is dyspnoea in palliative care? 1434
How do I diagnose the cause of my patient's dyspnoea? 1434
Should I treat the underlying cause of dyspnoea? 1438
What dose of morphine should I use? 1440

Anxiety, acute, associated with dyspnoea, immediate management of 1439
Anxiety associated with dyspnoea, management of recurrent episodes 1439
Corticosteroids 1438
Dexamethasone 1441
Stopping 1441
Drug delivery, non-oral routes of 1441
Dyspnoea, acute, managing an episode of 1438
Dyspnoea, common non-malignant causes of 1435
Dyspnoea, general management of 1438
Dyspnoea, general points in diagnosing the cause of 1434
Dyspnoea, measures to reduce 1438
Exacerbations of chronic dyspnoea, managing recurrent 1438
Help and advice in primary care, seeking 1437
Help and advice in the management of dyspnoea, seeking 1440
Investigation of dyspnoea, Primary-care 1435
Lorazepam 1441
Malignant causes of dyspnoea, clinical features of 1435
Malignant causes of dyspnoea – further information 1435
Management of the physical causes of dyspnoea, Secondary care 1439
Medicines management 1440
Morphine 1440
Needs, social 1437
Needs, spiritual 1437
Oxygen therapy 1439, 1440
Palliative care, general issues in 1436
Perception of dyspnoea, treating 1440
Physical cause of dyspnoea, treating the underlying 1438
Psychological state, assessment of 1437
Psychological state, treating the underlying 1439
Symptoms, assessment and management of physical 1436
Syringe drivers, drugs commonly used in 1442
Syringe drivers, drugs for dyspnoea used in 1442
Terminal phase, adjustments in 1437
Terminal phase, recognising the 1437
Treatment of physical causes of malignant dyspnoea, Primary-care 1438
Treatment options 1438

Palliative care – malodorous malignant ulcer of the skin 1444

What is it? 1445
How common is it? 1445
Is discharge excessive? 1446
Is pain present? 1447
Is the ulcer bleeding? 1447
Is the ulcer dirty? 1446
Is the ulcer smelly? 1446

Activated charcoal dressings 1447
Complications 1446
General points 1446
Metronidazole, oral 1447

Metronidazole, topical 1447
Prognosis 1446

Palliative care – nausea/vomiting/malignant bowel obstruction 1449

What is palliative care? 1459
How common is it? 1459
What triggers nausea and vomiting? 1459
What are the causes of nausea and vomiting? 1459
How is nausea and vomiting assessed in palliative care patients? 1459
What else might it be? 1460

Antiemetic appropriate for the suspected cause, choosing a second-line 1463
Antiemetic drugs, starting treatment with first-line 1462
Antiemetic drugs for MBO 1462
Antiemetic therapy, summary of 1464
Antihistamines: cyclizine 1466
Antimuscarinics 1466
Antisecretory agents 1466
  For MBO 1463
Anxiety-related nausea and vomiting 1463
Chemically or metabolically induced nausea and vomiting 1463
Complications of prolonged nausea and vomiting, assessing the 1460
Dexamethasone 1465
  Stopping 1465
Diagnosing the cause of nausea and vomiting 1459
Drug delivery, non-oral routes of 1466
First-line therapy, persistent nausea and vomiting on 1463
Food and fluid, managing 1461
Gastric stasis 1463
Help and advice in primary care, seeking 1464
Intracranial pressure, raised 1462
Managing nausea and vomiting, steps in 1460
Medicines management 1464
Movement-related nausea and vomiting 1463
Nausea and vomiting of multiple or uncertain origin 1463
Obstruction, inoperable malignant bowel 1462
Obstruction, nausea and vomiting due to complete bowel 1462
Octreotide 1466
Pain in MBO, managing 1462
Phenothiazines/antipsychotics 1465
Prokinetics 1464
Reversible causes, other 1461
Reversible causes of nausea and vomiting, correcting 1461
Syringe drivers, drugs for nausea used in 1466
Terminal phase, adjustments in the 1464
Terminal phase, recognising the 1464
Tumour, abdominal and pelvic 1462, 1463
Tumour, nausea and vomiting caused directly by the 1461
Vestibular disturbance 1463
Vomiting due to functional or partial bowel obstruction 1462

Palliative care – oral problems 1468

How common are oral problems in palliative care? 1472
How do oral problems present? 1473
How do I diagnose the cause of oral problems in palliative care? 1473

Aphthous ulcers 1473, 1475
Candida infection, oral 1475
  As a cause of mouth pain 1473
Dry mouth 1474
  Causes of 1473
  Symptomatic management of 1474
  Treating the underlying cause of 1474
Examination, oral cavity 1473
Herpes simplex infection, oral 1475
Malodorous malignant ulcers 1473, 1476
Mouth care, routine 1474
Mouthwash, choice of 1474
Mucositis, chemotherapy- or radiotherapy-induced 1473, 1475
Oral problems, other 1473
Pain, diffuse oral 1476
Pain, localized 1476
Pain, mouth, causes of 1473
Pain, oral, systemic treatment of 1476
Pain, oral, topical treatment of 1476
Pain control for 1476
Preventing 1474
Salivation, excessive 1474, 1476
Terminal phase, adjustments in the 1477
Terminal phase, oral care in the 1476
Terminal phase, recognizing the 1477
Treating 1474
Ulcers, mouth 1475
Ulcers, neutropenic 1476

Palliative care – pain 1478

What is pain? 1486
How common is pain in people with cancer? 1487
What are the causes of pain in a person with cancer? 1487
How do I assess the causes of pain in a person with cancer? 1487
How do I assess the severity and impact of pain? 1488
How should I assess the severity of pain? 1488
How do I assess the impact of pain on a person's activities? 1488
Why is it important to assess mood? 1488
How do I distinguish between grief and depression? 148
How do I manage acute severe pain? 1489
Is treatment of the underlying cause of pain appropriate? 1489
Which types of pain may need a specific approach? 149
How should I manage neuropathic pain? 1490
How do I manage mixed pain? 1490
How do I manage predominantly neuropathic pain? 14
Which TCAs or AEDs are suitable for neuropathic pain? 1490
How should I manage bone pain? 1491
How should I manage myofascial pain? 1491
How should I manage muscle spasm? 1491
How should I manage bowel colic? 1491
How should I manage ureteric colic? 1491
How should I manage pain due to a skin ulcer? 1491
How should I manage the symptom of pain? 1491
Which standard analgesics are suitable for the WHO ladder steps? 1492
How should breakthrough pain be managed? 1492
What should I do if pain is still difficult to manage? 149

Adverse effects, minimizing 1495
Amitriptyline 1495
Analgesics, standard 1493
Analgesic ladder, WHO 1491
Analgesics for neuropathic pain, starting and titrating adjuvant 1495
Carbamazepine 1496
Causes of pain, malignant 1487, 1489
Causes of pain, non-malignant 1487, 1489
Codeine 1493
Conversion values 1495
Drug delivery, non-oral routes of 1496

Fentanyl patches, breakthrough analgesia options for patients taking 1495
Gabapentin 1495
Help and advice in primary care, seeking 1493
Imipramine 1495
Interventional techniques 1492
Investigations or treatment, pain due to 1487
Management, general principles of 1489
Morphine 1493
Adverse effects of, managing the 1494
Adverse effects of, minimizing common 1494
Alternative strong opioids to 1494
Modified-release, using 1494
Oral, starting and titrating 1493
Neuropathic pain, drugs for 1495
Nortriptyline 1495
Opioid, strong, switching 1492
Opioid toxicity 1494
Paracetamol and NSAIDs 1493
Syringe drivers, drugs commonly used in 1496
Syringe drivers, drugs for pain used in 1496
Terminal phase, adjustments in the 1493
Terminal phase, recognizing the 1493
Treatment of pain, immediate (while awaiting admission) 1489

Palliative care – respiratory secretions at the end of life 1499

What is it? 1500
How common is it? 1500
How do I know my patient has it? 1501
What else might it be? 1501
Is the sputum infected? 1502
Is the sputum loose and fluid? 1501
Is the sputum thick and tenacious? 1502
What dose of antimuscarinic should I use? 1502

Airway secretions with intact cough reflex, problematic 1501
Antimuscarinic drugs 1503
Drug delivery, non-oral routes of 1503
Medicines management 1503
Respiratory secretions, measures in all patients with problematic 1501
Respiratory secretions in the terminal phase, distress of 1501
Respiratory secretions in the terminal phase, managing 1501
Secretions from inside the respiratory tree 1501
Secretions from outside the respiratory tree 1501
Syringe drivers, drugs commonly used in 1503
Terminal phase, adjustments in 1501
Terminal phase, recognising the 1501

Parkinson's disease 1504

What is it? 1506
How common is it? 1506
How do I know my patient has it? 1506
What else might it be? 1507
Who should manage people with Parkinson's disease? 1508
What advice should people with Parkinson's disease be given about driving? 1508
Which drug treatments are used by specialists? 1508
Which drug treatments do specialists use as monotherapy for early Parkinson's disease? 1508
What strategies do specialists use to manage motor fluctuations? 1509
What is the role of surgical treatments? 1509
How do I treat depression in people with Parkinson's disease? 1509
How do I treat drug-induced Parkinsonism? 1509
How do drugs for Parkinson's disease work? 1510
Which drugs require monitoring? 1510

Adverse effects, minimizing common 1510
Antimuscarinics 1511
Complications 1507
Drug treatments, other 1509
Medicines management: drug-induced Parkinsonism 1511
Medicines management: Parkinson's disease 1510
Overview 1508
Prognosis 1507

Pelvic inflammatory disease 1513

see Chlamydia – genital
What is it? 1515
How common is it? 1515
How do I know my patient has it? 1515
What else might it be? 1516

Actinomyces and intra-uterine contraceptive devices 1518
Antibiotic treatment 1517
Complications 1516
General issues 1517
Intra-uterine contraceptive devices 1517
Investigations 1516
Referral to secondary care 1518
Risk factors for acquiring pelvic inflammatory disease 1515
Sexual partners, management of 1517
Signs 1516
Symptoms 1516

Periodontal disease

see Dental abscess

Periods, heavy

see Menorrhagia

Periods, painful

see Dysmenorrhoea

Piles

see Haemorrhoids

Pneumonia

see Chest infections

Poisoning 1520

What is it? 1520
How common is it? 1520

Assessment, general and admission to hospital 1521
Information, other sources of 1521
Information about poisoning, obtaining 1520
Intentional poisoning, people with 1521

Polymyalgia rheumatica 1522

What is it? 1529
How common is it? 1529
How do I know my patient has it? 1529
What else might it be? 1529

Complications 1529
Corticosteroid therapy 1530
Drug management 1530
General 1530
Erythrocyte sedimentation rate 1530
General issues 1530
Giant-cell (temporal) arteritis 1531
Osteoporosis prophylaxis 1531
Prognosis 1530

Referral 1530
Rheumatoid arthritis 1530

Preconceptual counselling 1533

What is it? 1540
How can a woman prepare for pregnancy? 1540
When is genetic screening advised? 1546

Advising women over 35 years old 1541
Advising women who have had pre-eclampsia or recurrent miscarriage 1546
Advising women who use illicit substances 1547
Advising women with chronic conditions 1542
Alcohol intake, reducing 1541
Asthma 1545
Bipolar affective disorder 1542
Cardiac disease 1545
Cervical smear, up-to-date 1541
Consanguineous couples 1546
Depression 1542
Diabetes 1544
Epilepsy 1542
Folic acid 1540
5 mg daily 1540
400 micrograms daily 1540
Genetic disorder, common types of 1546
Genetic screening and counselling, high-risk ethnic/minority groups who should also be offered 1546
Hypertension, chronic 1543
Immunization status to consider, other 1541
Medication, review of (including over-the-counter drugs) 1541
Miscarriage, recurrent 1546
Pre-eclampsia 1546
Renal disease 1544
Risks from the environment, assessing 1541
Rubella status, checking 1541
Schizophrenia 1542
Screening for haemoglobinopathies 1547
Sickle cell syndromes 1545
Stopping smoking 1540
Thalassaemias 1545
Thyroid disease 1544
Thromboembolism, venous 1545

Pre-eclampsia

see Hypertension in pregnancy

Pregancy-induced hypertension

see Hypertension in pregnancy

Pregnancy

in Alcohol – problem drinking 25
in Allergic rhinitis 45, 53, 55
in Anaemia – iron deficiency 66, 67, 69, 70
in Anaemia – macrocytic 76
in Asthma 160
in Bacterial vaginosis 210
in Candida – female genital 268, 275
in Chickenpox 311, 314, 315, 316
in Chlamydia – genital 320, 327
in Constipation 380, 386
in Contraception 423
in Deep vein thrombosis 474
in Depression 500
in Dyspepsia – pregnancy-associated 628, 629, 630
in Eating disorders 709, 710
in Epilepsy 777
in Haemorrhoids 876
in Herpes simplex – genital 919, 923
in Hypertension in pregnancy 1001, 1005
in Hyperthyroidism 1010
in Hypothyroidism 1026
in Infertility 1084
in Irritable bowel syndrome 1123
in Leg cramps – unknown cause 1146
in Migraine 1238, 1247
in Nausea and vomiting in pregnancy 1272, 1275, 1276
in Nonsteroidal anti-inflammatory drugs (NSAIDs) 1309
in Opioid dependence 1345
in Osteoporosis – treatment 1391
in Pelvic inflammatory disease 1513
in Preconceptual counselling 1540
in Pubic lice 1602
in Pyelonephritis – acute 1606
in Roundworm 1654, 1656
in Scabies 1664
in Smoking cessation 1728, 1733
in Threadworm 1758, 1761
in Thrombophlebitis 1762
in Trichomoniasis 1775, 1776, 1778
in Urinary tract infection (lower) – women 1810, 1814, 1816, 1827, 1828
in Urticaria and angio-oedema 1854

Prior myocardial infarction – prophylactic treatments 1551

What is it? 1564
How common is it? 1564
How do I know my patient has had an MI? 1564
How do I know my patient has heart failure? 1564
When do I start drug treatment? 1565, 1566
Which drugs? (in patients who do not have heart failure) 1565
Which drugs? (in patients who do have heart failure) 1566

Complications 1565
Diabetes, patient with prior MI who have 1567
Diet 1565
Evidence, supporting 1566, 1567
General issues 1565
Heart failure, patients with prior MI and 1566
Heart failure, Patients with prior MI who do not have 1565
Prognosis 1565
Rehabilitation 1565
Risk factors, other 1565
Treatment, continuation of 1566, 1567
Treatment, monitoring 1566, 1567

Prostate – benign hyperplasia 1569

What is it? 1571
How common is it? 1571
How do I know my patient has it? 1571
What else might it be? 1572
When do I perform a PSA test? 1572
When do I refer a raised PSA result? 1572

5-alpha reductase inhibitors (e.g. finasteride) 1573
Alpha-blockers 1573
Combination therapy: a 5-alpha reductase inhibitor with an alpha-blocker 1573
Complications 1572
Differential diagnosis
Herbal preparations 1573
Investigations for 1572
Prognosis 1572
Prostate specific antigen (PSA) 1572
Test limitations 1572
Test practicalities 1572
Referral, indications for 1574
Signs 1572
Symptoms 1571

Treatment choices 1573
Treatments, surgical 1574
Watchful waiting 1573

Prostatism

see Prostate – benign hyperplasia

Prostatitis 1576

What is it? 1581
How common is it? 1582
How do I know my patient has it? 1582
What else might it be? 1583

Abacterial, chronic, chronic pelvic pain syndrome (CPPS) 1584
Diagnosis 1582
Bacterial, acute 1581, 1582, 1583
Bacterial, chronic 1581, 1582, 1583
Chronic (bacterial and abacterial) 1583
Complications and prognosis 1583
Inflammatory, asymptomatic 1582
Pelvic pain syndrome, chronic (abacterial prostatitis) 1582

Pruritus ani 1586

What is it? 1588
How common is it? 1588
How do I know my patient has it? 1588
What are the secondary causes? 1588
How should I assess someone with perianal itching? 1588
How should I manage idiopathic pruritus ani? 1588
What is the role of local irritants? 1588
What advice should I give about perianal hygiene? 1589
Should dietary manipulation be recommended? 1589
What symptomatic treatments should I offer? 1589
What treatments are not recommended in primary care? 1589
When should I refer someone with pruritus ani? 1589
What is the evidence for good perianal hygiene? 1589
What is the evidence for dietary manipulation? 1589
What is the evidence for the use of systemic antihistamines? 1589
What is the evidence for soothing creams or ointments? 1589
What is the evidence for the use of corticosteroids? 1589

Complications 1588
Prognosis 1588

Pruritus vulvae 1591

What is it? 1595
How common is it? 1595

Complications and prognosis 1596
Dermatological conditions 1595
Diagnosis, confirming the 1596
Examination 1595
History and symptoms 1595
Infections 1595
Investigations 1595
Neoplasia 1596
Topical therapy for symptomatic treatment of vulval itch 1597
Treating the underlying cause 1596
Vulval conditions, general advice 1597
Vulval itching, history and examination of women with 1595
Vulval itching, underlying causes that may present with 1595
Other 1596

Psychological therapies

in Depression 499
in Dyspepsia – proven non-ulcer dyspepsia 675
in Eating disorders 708, 709
in Irritable bowel syndrome 1128
in Obesity 1323
in Schizophrenia 1677

Pubic lice 1599

What is it? 1601
How is it transmitted? 1601
How common is it? 1601
How do I know my patient has it? 1601
What else might it be? 1601
How should I treat pubic lice? 1601
How should treatment be applied? 1601

Antihistamines, sedating 1602
General 1601
Infestation, eyelash 1601
Insecticides 1602
Itch, treatment of 1601
Medicines management 1602
Pregnancy and breastfeeding 1602
Treatment failure 1601

Pyelonephritis – acute 1603

What is it? 1604
How common is it? 1605
How do I know my patient has it? 1605
What else might it be? 1605
Treatment – at home or in hospital? 1605

Antimicrobials for 1605
Complications 1605
Pregnancy, management in 1606
Prognosis 1605
Treatment, principles of 1605

R

Raynaud's phenomenon 1607

What is it? 1609
How common is it? 1609
How do I know my patient has it? 1609
What are the causes of secondary Raynaud's phenomenon? 1609

Arterial disorders, obstructive 1609
Blood disorders 1609
Causes of secondary, examples of 1609
Miscellaneous 1609
Occupational 1609
Complications 1610
Connective tissue disorders 1609
Drug-induced 1609
Examination 1609
General measures 1610
History 1609
Investigation 1609
Prognosis 1610
Treatment, drug 1610
Treatment, surgical 1610
Treatments, other drug 1610
Vasodilators 1610

Red eye

in Allergic rhinitis 42, 49
in Blepharitis 232, 233
in Chlamydia – genital 325
in Conjunctivitis – allergic 362, 364, 365, 366
in Conjunctivitis – infective 368, 370, 372

in Corneal superficial injury 448
in Glaucoma 837, 838
in Herpes simplex – ocular 925, 926, 927
in Shingles and postherpetic neuralgia 1695, 1706

Renal colic – acute 1612

What is it? 1614
How common is it? 1614
How do I know my patient has it? 1614
What else might it be? 1614

Admission 1615
Complications 1614
Diagnosis in secondary care 1614
General issues 1615
Home therapy with emergency outpatient referral 1615
Interventions, other 1615
Pain relief 1615
Prognosis 1615
Referral criteria 1615
Stones, preventing further 1615
Symptoms, classical 1614

Rheumatoid arthritis 1617

What is it? 1632
How common is it? 1632
How do I know my patient has rheumatoid arthritis? 1632
How do I know my patient has a flare of rheumatoid arthritis? 1632
What else might it be? 1633
What is the differential diagnosis of rheumatoid arthritis on first presentation? 1633
What is the differential diagnosis of a flare of rheumatoid arthritis? 1633
How are symptoms managed and function maintained? 1635
What is the role of nonsteroidal anti-inflammatory drugs? 1635
What is the role of corticosteroids? 1636
What is the role of disease-modifying antirheumatic drugs? 1636
What are disease-modifying antirheumatic drugs? 1636
When should disease-modifying antirheumatic drugs be used? 1637
Which disease-modifying antirheumatic drugs? 1637
What other treatments are used? 1637
How should complications be managed? 1637
How should infection be prevented and managed? 1637
What immunizations are recommended to prevent infection? 1637
How should people with RA be managed if they are exposed to the varicella-zoster virus (chickenpox or shingles)? 1638
How should people taking DMARDs or corticosteroids be managed if they have an infection? 1638
How do I recognise and manage septic arthritis? 1638
How is carpal tunnel syndrome managed? 1638
How do I recognise and manage cervical myelopathy? 1638
How do I manage cardiovascular risk factors? 1638
How do I manage anaemia? 1639
How do I prevent osteoporosis? 1639

Clinical features of a flare 1632
Clinical features on initial presentation 1632
Codeine 1639
Complications 1633
Corticosteroids 1639
  Intra-articular 1636
  Oral and intramuscular 1636
COX-2 selective inhibitors 1635
Disease-modifying antirheumatic drugs 1640
Investigations useful in the initial presentation 1632
Management, overview of 1634
Medicines management 1639
Nonsteroidal anti-inflammatory drugs 1639
  Topical 1635
Paracetamol 1639
Prognosis 1633
  Effects of comorbidity on the 1634

Rosacea 1644

What is rosacea? 1648
How common is it? 1649
How do I know my patient has it? 1649
What else might it be? 1649
What general advice should I give my patient? 1650
How should I manage facial flushing? 1650
How should I manage persistent erythema and telangiectasia? 1650
How should I manage papulopustular rosacea? 1651
Should I combine oral and topical treatments? 1651
How should I manage rosacea affecting the eye? 1651
When should I refer someone with rosacea? 1651
What is the supporting evidence for the treatment of rosacea? 1651
What is the evidence for topical treatments? 1651
What is the evidence for systemic antibiotics? 1651
How long should I treat for? 1652
What adverse effects are associated with topical treatments for rosacea? 1652
What adverse effects are associated with oral tetracyclines? 1652
What adverse effects are associated with oral erythromycin? 1652

Adverse effects 1652
Complications 1649
Management, overview of 1650
Medicines management 1652
Prognosis 1649

Roundworm 1654

What is it? 1655
How common is it? 1655
How do I know my patient has it? 1655
What else might it be? 1655

Complications and prognosis 1655
Drug treatment 1656
Drug treatment, prophylactic 1656
General issues 1656
Mebendazole 1656
Medicines management 1656
Piperazine 1656
Pregnancy and breastfeeding 1656

S

Scabies 1657

What is it? 1662
How is scabies transmitted? 1662
How common is it? 1662
How do I know my patient has scabies? 1662
Does my patient have crusted scabies? 1662
What else might it be? 1663
How should I treat scabies? 1663
How should treatment be applied? 1663
Do children with scabies need to be kept off school? 166

Acaricides 1664
Complications 1663
General points 1663
Itch, treatments for 1663, 1664

Medicines management 1664
Pregnancy and breastfeeding 1664
Prognosis 1663
Treatment failure 1664
Treatments, other 1663
Treatments, recommended 1663
Treatments (acaricides), supporting evidence for 1663

Schizophrenia 1666

What is schizophrenia? 1671
What is the course of schizophrenia? 1671
What are the risk factors for developing schizophrenia? 1671
How common is it? 1671
How do I know my patient has it? 1672
What are positive and negative symptoms? 1672
What else might it be? 1673
Who should start treatment for a first episode of schizophrenia? 1679
Should people on typical antipsychotics be changed to atypicals? 1681
When should depot injections be considered? 1681
When should re-referral be considered? 1677
What do the different mental health teams do? 1675

Adverse effects, minimizing common 1681
Antipsychotic drugs, types of 1678
Antipsychotic for a first episode, choice of oral atypical 1679
Antipsychotics, adverse effects of 1679
Antipsychotics, switching 1680
Carers, working in partnership with 1674
Complications 1673
Delusions 1672
Driving 1677
Drugs, differences between 1679
First episode 1675
Functional disorders, other 1673
Hallucinations 1672
Harm to self or others, people at high risk of 1676
Maintenance treatment 1678
Medicines management 1679
Mental Health Act, use of the 1676
Mortality, excess 1673
Organic disorders 1673
People with schizophrenia, working in partnership with 1674
Pharmacological interventions 1678
Physical health checks 1677
Primary Health Care Team, role of 1674
Prognosis 1674
    Factors associated with a poor 1674
Psychological interventions 1677
Rating scales, adverse effects 1680
Referral to specialist mental health services 1676
Risk factors, early environmental 1672
Risk factors, later environmental 1672
Social disability 1673
Specialist mental health services 1674
Stages of, managing the 1675
    Acute episode 1675
    Early post-acute period 1676
    Recovery phase 1676
Substance misuse 1673
Symptoms, negative 1673
Symptoms, positive 1672
Symptoms, secondary 1673
Thought disorders, other 1673
Thought possession, disorders of 1673
Treatments used by specialist mental health services 1677

Seborrhoeic dermatitis 1684

What is it? 1688
How common is it? 1688
How do I know my patient has it? 1688
What else might it be? 1689
How should I manage seborrhoeic dermatitis of the face and body? 1690
How should I manage seborrhoeic dermatitis of the scalp and beard? 1689
How should I manage widespread seborrhoeic dermatitis? 1691
How should I manage infantile seborrhoeic dermatitis? 1691

Acute phase, treating the 1689, 1690
Antifungal treatments 1691
Arachis (peanut) oil, products containing 1691
Classical 1688
Complications 1689
Corticosteroids, topical 1691
Cradle cap 1691
Education, patient 1689
HIV-positive, in people who are 1689
Infantile 1688
Management, principles of 1689
Medicines management 1691
Mild 1689
Moderate to severe 1690
Nappy rash 1691
Prognosis 1689
Remission, maintaining 1689, 1690, 1691

Shingles and postherpetic neuralgia 1693

What is it? 1703
How common is it? 1703
What are the risk factors for developing post herpetic neuralgia? 1703
How do I know my patient has it? 1704
What else might it be? 1704
What advice should I give about the rash? 1705
Are people with shingles infectious? 1705
How should I manage pain? 1705
Who should receive antiviral drugs? 1706
When should antivirals be started? 1706
How should I manage shingles of the ophthalmic nerve? 1706
How should I manage immunocompromised people? 1706
How should I treat shingles in an immunocompromised person? 1706
Who is regarded as clinically immunosuppressed? 1706
How should I manage non-immune contacts of someone with shingles? 1707
When should I investigate a child presenting with shingles to rule out immunodeficiency? 1707
What is the supporting evidence for oral antiviral drugs? 1707
What treatments are not recommended? 1708, 1709
What physical measures help to reduce pain? 1708
Which drugs are recommended for first-line treatment? 1708
What should I use for second-line treatment? 1708
How long should treatment for postherpetic neuralgia be continued? 1708
How should I manage postherpetic itch? 1708
What is the supporting evidence for the treatment of postherpetic neuralgia? 1709
Which antiviral drug should I use for acute shingles? 1709
What are the adverse effects of antiviral drugs? 1710
How should I use tricyclic antidepressants for neuropathic pain? 1710

How should I minimize adverse effects? 1710
How should I use antiepileptic drugs for neuropathic pain? 1710
How should I minimize adverse effects of gabapentin? 1710
How should I minimize adverse effects of carbamazepine? 1710
How should I advise people to use capsaicin cream? 1710
How should I use sedating antihistamines to manage itch? 1710

Acute shingles 1704
Adults 1704
Healthy 1707
Anaesthesia, topical 1709
Antidepressants, tricyclic 1709
Antiepileptic drugs 1709
Capsaicin, topical 1709
Children 1704
Complications 1704
Immunocompromised, in the 1705
Of postherpetic neuralgia 1705
Of shingles, common 1704
Of shingles, rare 1704
Immunocompromised 1704
Adults 1708
Medicines management 1709
Ophthalmic shingles 1704, 1707
Postherpetic neuralgia 1703, 1704, 1708
Prodromal phase of shingles 1704
Prognosis 1705
Of postherpetic neuralgia 1705
Of shingles 1705
Shingles (acute herpes zoster) 1705

Singultus

see Hiccups

Sinusitis 1713

What is it? 1719
How common is it? 1720
How do I know my patient has bacterial sinusitis? 1720
What else might it be? 1720
Which antibiotic should I prescribe?

Antimicrobial recommendation 1721
Antimicrobials 1721
Adults 1721
Children 1721
Bacteria 1720
Complications and prognosis 1721
Corticosteroids, intranasal 1722
Decongestants 1722
Definitions and pathology 1719
Investigations 1720
Pathophysiology 1720
Referral, following 1722
Steam inhalation 1722
Symptoms and signs 1720
Treatment, duration of 1722

Skin infections

see Boils, carbuncles, paronychia, & staphylococcal whitlow
see Impetigo

Smoking cessation 1724

What are the physiological effects of smoking? 1727
How common is smoking? 1728
What are the factors associated with smoking? 1728
What are the problems associated with smoking? 1728
What are the benefits of stopping smoking? 1728
How many people successfully stop smoking? 1729
Nicotine replacement therapy or bupropion? 1732

Advice, brief 1729
Essential features of 1729
Behavioural support 1729
Bupropion 1731
And seizures 1731
Use of 1731
Children and young people 1733
Consequences for the individual 1728
Effectiveness of interventions 1729, 1730, 1731
Environmental tobacco smoke (passive smoking) 1728
Interventions, self-help 1730
Interventions that are not recommended 1732
Interventions to help people stop smoking, ummary of effectiveness of 1732
NRT 1730
Use of 1731
NRT and bupropion, availability of 1731
NRT and bupropion, guidance on the use of (NICE) 1733
NRT and bupropion, use of a combination of 1732
Parental smoking 1728
Pregnancy 1733
Increased risk in 1728
Weight gain 1733

Sore throat – acute 1735

What is it? 1738
How common is it? 1738
How do I know my patient has it? 1738
What else might it be? 1738
What pain relief should be advised for a person with a sore throat? 1739
When should an antibiotic be prescribed for a person with a sore throat? 1739
When should tonsillectomy be considered for a person with recurrent sore throat? 1739
What are the indications for referral of a person with sore throat to a specialist? 1740

Complications 1738
General issues 1739
Prognosis 1739

Sprains and strains 1742

What is it? 1746
What is a sprain? 1746
What is a strain? 1746
How common is it? 1746
How do I assess someone with a sprain or strain? 1747
What else might it be? 1748
How do I manage an acute sprain or strain? 1748
Who needs referral? 1748
How do I initiate treatment for an acute sprain or strain? 1749
Which analgesic should I prescribe? 1749
What subsequent treatment is advised? 1749
Is there evidence to support the use of rubefacients, ultrasound, homeopathic arnica, and oral hydrolytic enzymes? 1749
What advice can I give about preventing sprains and strains? 1749
What is the supporting evidence? 1750
What is the evidence to support diagnostic strategies? 1752
What evidence supports treatments of sprains and strains? 1750
Is there a role for topical NSAIDs in treating pain due to acute sprains and strains? 1751
Does the use of NSAIDs speed recovery from sprains and strains? 1751

What evidence supports strategies to prevent sprains and strains? 1752

Abbreviations 1750
Ankle injuries in sport, evidence for prevention of 1753
Ankle sprains 1746
Assessment 1747
Complications 1748
Compression, evidence for 1751
Compression bandages 1750
Domestic violence 1747
Elevation, evidence for 1751
Homeopathic arnica, evidence for 1752
Hydrolytic enzymes, oral, evidence for 1752
Ice, cryotherapy, evidence for 1750
Injury in football, evidence for prevention of 1752
Investigation 1747
Knee injuries in sport, evidence for prevention of 1753
Management, overview of 1748
Medicines management 1749
Nonsteroidal anti-inflammatory drugs 1750
NSAIDs, evidence for 1751
Ottawa ankle rules, evidence for the 1752
Ottawa knee rules, evidence for the 1752
Paracetamol and codeine 1749
Prognosis 1748
For a sprained ankle 1748
Referral, criteria for 1748
Rest, immobilization, functional treatment, and surgery, evidence for 1750
RICE (Rest, Ice, Compression, Elevation), evidence for 1750
Rubefacients, evidence for 1751
Sport and recreation, evidence for risk factors for injury during 1752
Strains 1746
Stretching to prevent injury in sport, evidence for 1753
Trauma, major, or serious underlying condition, 'red flags' for 1748
Ultrasound, evidence for 1752

Statins

in Diabetes Type 2 – lipid management 575, 580, 588, 589, 590, 591
in Hyperlipidaemia 942, 945, 947, 948, 955, 956, 957, 958
in Hypertension 992
in Prior myocardial infarction – prophylactic treatments 1552, 1554, 1555

Stroke

in Atrial fibrillation 181, 185
in Contraception 409
in Coronary heart disease risk – identification and management 461
in Menopause 1203
in Transient ischaemic attack – not in atrial fibrillation 1770

Superficial thrombophlebitis

see Thrombophlebitis

Supraventricular tachycardia – paroxysmal 1755

What is it? 1756
How common is it? 1756
How do I know my patient has it? 1756
What else might it be? 1756
How do I manage someone with a history suggestive of paroxysmal SVT? 1757
How do I manage someone presenting with an episode of suspected SVT? 1757
What is recommended to treat an episode of SVT? 1757
Which treatments are recommended to prevent further episodes of SVT? 1757
Can my patient drive after an episode of SVT? 1757

Complications 1756
Examination 1756
History 1756
Investigations 1756

Surgery

in Allergic rhinitis 53
in Anal fissure 84
in Angina 107
in Ankylosing spondylitis 123
in Breast cancer – managing women with a family history 254
in Contraception 414
in Diabetes Type 2 – retinopathy 604
in Dysmenorrhoea 625
in Dyspepsia – proven gastro-oesophageal reflux disease 661
in Endometriosis 744
in Epilepsy 779
in Glaucoma 838
in Glue ear 843
in Gout 868
in Heart failure 912
in Hyperthyroidism 1010
in Infertility 1083
in Menorrhagia 1225
in Obesity 1323
in Osteoarthritis 1370, 1371, 1372
in Parkinson's disease 1509
in Prostate – benign hyperplasia 1574
in Raynaud's phenomenon 1610
in Sprains and strains 1750
in Transient ischaemic attack – not in atrial fibrillation 1771
in Trigeminal neuralgia 1783

T

Tetanus prophylaxis

in Bites – human and animal 216, 221
in Burns and scalds 261
in Immunizations – childhood vaccination programme 1033, 1035, 1036, 1041, 1043
in Immunizations – travel vaccinations 1054, 1063, 1065
in Lacerations 1140

Tetracyclines

in Acne vulgaris 13
in Blepharitis 228
in Rosacea 1644, 1647, 1652

Thiazide diuretics

in Diabetes Type 1 and 2 – hypertension 538, 550, 552
in Heart failure 910
in Hypertension 969, 970, 991, 993

Threadworm 1758

What is it? 1760
How common is it? 1760
How do I know my patient has it? 1760
What else might it be? 1760
Do children with threadworms need to be kept off school? 1761

Children less than 3 months 1761
Complications and prognosis 1760
Mebendazole 1761

Medicines management 1761
Piperazine 1761
Pregnancy and breastfeeding 1761
Treatments, drug 1761
Treatments, non-drug 1760

Thrombophlebitis 1762

What is it? 1764
How common is it? 1764
How do I know my patient has it? 1764
What else might it be? 1764

Complications 1764
Aseptic 1764
Managing 1765
Septic 1765
General issues 1765
Prognosis 1765
Aseptic 1765
Septic 1765
Treatments 1765

Thrush

see Candida – female genital
see Candida – oral

Thyrotoxicosis

see Hyperthyroidism

Tinnitus

see Meniere's disease

Torticollis

see Neck pain

Transient ischaemic attack – not in atrial fibrillation 1767

What is it? 1769
How common is it? 1769
How do I know my patient has it? 1770
What else might it be? 1770
What are the indications for switching from aspirin to clopidogrel? 1772
What common drug interactions should I look out for? 1772

Anticoagulation 1771
Antiplatelet treatment 1770
Aspirin 1771
Atheromatous event, other 1770
Clopidogrel 1771
Dipyridamole 1771
Drug treatments, other 1771
General issues 1770
Medicines management 1771
Prognosis 1770
Stroke, subsequent 1770
Surgery 1771

Trichomoniasis 1774

What is it? 1777
How common is it? 1777
How do I know my patient has it? 1777
What else might it be? 1777

Complications 1777
Drug treatment 1778
General issues 1777
Investigations 1777
Men 1777
Pregnancy and breastfeeding 1778
Prognosis 1777
Signs 1777
Symptoms 1777
Women 1777

Trigeminal neuralgia 1779

What is it? 1781
How common is it? 1781
How do I know my patient has it? 1781
What else might it be? 1781
What is first-line treatment? 1782
Which dose should I use? 1783
What is the supporting evidence for drug treatment? 178
How should I manage treatment failure? 1782
What are the adverse effects of carbamazepine, and can I avoid them? 1783
What are the adverse effects of gabapentin? 1784
What is the supporting evidence for neurosurgery? 1783

Carbamazepine 1782
Complications 1782
Examination 1781
History 1781
Investigations 1781
Medicines management 1783
Prognosis 1782
Second-line drug treatments, evidence for 1782

U

Upper respiratory tract infection

see Common cold

Urethritis – male 1785

What is it? 1789
How common is it? 1790
How do I know my patient has it? 1790
What else might it be? 1791

Antibiotic regimens for gonococcal urethritis 1792
Antibiotic regimens for NGU 1793
Antibiotic regimens for the empirical treatment of undiagnosed urethritis 1793
Chlamydial infection, investigations for diagnosis of 1791
Complications 1791
Empirical treatment of men who are unlikely or unabl to attend follow-up 1793
Gonococcal urethritis 1792
Gonorrhoea, investigations for diagnosis of 1791
Investigations 1790
Management of acute urethritis, general issues 1792
Non-gonococcal urethritis 1792
Persistent/recurrent 1793
Prognosis 1791
Signs 1790
Specimen collection 1791
Symptoms 1790
Trichomoniasis, investigations for diagnosis of 1791
Urethritis, investigations for diagnosis of 1791
Urinary tract infections and conditions, other, investigations for diagnosis of 1791

Uric acid arthropathy

see Gout

Urinary tract infection – children 1831

What is it? 1835
How common is it? 1836
How do I know my patient has it? 1836
What else might it be? 1838

Admission criteria 1840
Antibiotic treatment 1839

Length of 1840
Complications 1838
Follow-up 1840
General issues 1839
Imaging, aims of 1837
Imaging investigations following a first UTI, recommendations for 1838
Imaging investigations for children with urinary tract infection 1837
Imaging modalities 1837
Imaging policy issues 1838
Investigations 1836
Presentation 1836
Prognosis 1838
Recurrent 1838
Management of 1840
Referral criteria 1840
Risk factors 1836
Symptomatic treatment 1839
Tests, near-patient 1837
Treatments, other 1840
Urine culture 1836
Urine dipstick tests 1837
Urine microscopy 1837
Urine samples, collection, storage, and transport of 1836
Vesicoureteric reflux 1839

Urinary tract infection (lower) – men 1795

What is it? 1804
How common is it? 1804
How do I know my patient has it? 1804
What else might it be? 1805

Analgesia and antipyrexia 1807
Antibiotics 1806
Other 1807
Bacteriuria, asymptomatic 1807
Cefalexin 1806
Complications 1806
Conditions associated with or predisposing to lower urinary tract infection 1805
Conditions with presentations similar to lower urinary tract infection 1806
Cystitis, acute 1806
Elderly men, cystitis in 1807
Management 1807
Presentation 1807
Imaging and functional tests 1805
Investigations 1805, 1806, 1807
Management, overview of 1806
Nitrofurantoin 1806
Presentations of lower UTI, atypical 1805
Recurrent cystitis 1807
In men 1807
Treatment of 1807
Referral 1807
Relapse of infection (i.e. infection with the same strain of organism) 1807
Risk factors and associated conditions 1807
Risk factors for urinary tract infection 1804
Treatments, other 1807
Trimethoprim 1806
Typical presentation of lower urinary tract infection 1804
Urinary catheters, in men with chronic indwelling 1808
Prevention 1808
Treatment 1808
Urine culture 1805
Urine dipstick 1805
Urine microscopy 1805
Urine samples, collection, storage, and transport of 1805

Urinary tract infection (lower) – women 1810

What is it? 1822
What are the risk factors? 1823
How common is it? 1823
How do I know my patient has it? 1823
What else might it be? 1824

Antibiotics, other 1825
Antibiotics for cystitis/asymptomatic bacteriuria in pregnancy 1828
Antibiotic therapy for bacterial cystitis, blind 1826
Antibiotic treatment 1825
Length of 1825
Bacteriuria, asymptomatic 1828
In pregnancy 1827
Bacteriuria, symptomatic (cystitis) 1828
Cefalexin 1825
Clinical features 1823
Complications 1825
Cystitis/asymptomatic bacteriuria in elderly women 1828
Evidence base 1828
Presentation 1828
Cystitis/asymptomatic bacteriuria in pregnancy 1827
Treatment, duration of 1828
Cystitis, diagnosis 1823
Imaging and functional tests 1824
Infection occurring while taking prophylactic antibiotics 1827
Investigations 1823
Nitrofurantoin 1825
Prognosis 1825
Prophylaxis for recurrent cystitis NOT related to sexual intercourse 1827
Prophylaxis for recurrent cystitis related to sexual intercourse 1827
Recurrent cystitis 1826
Evidence from the UK General Practice Research Database 1826
Relapse and recurrence of cystitis in pregnancy 1828
Relapse of infection 1826
Treatment, principles of 1825
Treatment, symptomatic 1825
Treatments, other 1826
Trimethoprim 1825
Uncomplicated cystitis 1826
Urethral syndrome 1824, 1828
Urethral syndrome, acute 1823, 1828
Urethral syndrome, chronic (more than three episodes per year) 1829
Urinary catheters, in women with chronic indwelling 1828
Management 1828
Prevention 1828
Urinary tract infection, diagnosis 1822
Urine culture 1824
Urine dipstick 1823
Urine microscopy 1824

Urinary tract infection – upper

see Pyelonephritis – acute

Urticaria and angio-oedema 1844

What is it? 1850
What causes it? 1851
How common is it? 1851
How do I know my patient has it? 1851
How do I assess a person with urticaria and angio-oedema? 1852

Which investigations or prognostic tests are appropriate in urticaria and angio-oedema? 1852
What else might it be? 1852
When should I refer someone with urticaria? 1854

Acute Urticaria 1853
Cause 1851
Angio-oedema 1854
Without urticaria 1851
Antihistamines 1854
Pregnancy, use in 1854
Use of 1853
Antipruritics, topical 1853
Cardiotoxicity 1854
Chronic Urticaria 1853
Cause 1851
Complications 1852
Corticosteroids 1853
Oral 1853
General issues 1853
Interventions, other 1853
Medicines Management 1854
Prognosis 1852
Renal and hepatic disease, dosing in 1854
Sedation 1854
Signs and symptoms 1851

V

Vaccination

see Immunizations – childhood vaccination programme
see Immunizations – pneumococcal vaccine
see Immunizations – travel vaccinations

Varicella zoster

see Chickenpox

Vertigo

see Meniere's disease

W

Warts and verrucae 1856

What are they? 1857
How are warts caught and spread? 1858
How common are they? 1857
How do I know my patient has warts? 1858
What else might it be? 1858

Butchers' warts 1858
Common warts 1858
Differential diagnosis of 1858
Complications 1859
Cryotherapy 1859
Duct tape 1859
Epidermodysplasia verruciformis 1858
Ethylene glycol 1860
Filiform warts 1858
General issues 1859
Medicines management: topical salicylic acid 1860
Mosaic warts 1858
Treatment of 1860
Palmar warts 1858
Pharmacological and alternative treatments, other 1860
Plane/flat warts 1858
Differential diagnosis of 1859
Plantar warts 1858
Differential diagnosis of 1859
Prognosis 1859
Salicylic acid 1859
And cryotherapy, combination treatment with 1859
Treatments for use in primary care, recommended 1859